ENCYCLOPÆDIA
BRITANNICA

MACROPÆDIA

The Encyclopædia Britannica
is published with the editorial advice
of the faculties of the University of Chicago;
a committee of persons holding
academic appointments at the universities
of Oxford, Cambridge, London, and Edinburgh;
a committee at the University of Toronto;
and committees drawn from members of the faculties
of the University of Tokyo
and the Australian National University.

THE UNIVERSITY OF CHICAGO

"Let knowledge grow from more to more
and thus be human life enriched."

The New
Encyclopædia
Britannica

in 30 Volumes

MACROPÆDIA
Volume 7

Knowledge in Depth

FOUNDED 1768
15TH EDITION

Encyclopædia Britannica, Inc.
William Benton, Publisher, 1943–1973
Helen Hemingway Benton, Publisher, 1973–1974
Chicago/London/Toronto/Geneva/Sydney/Tokyo/Manila/Seoul

Evidence, Law of

To the end that court decisions are to be based on truth founded on evidence, a primary duty of courts is to conduct proper proceedings so as to hear and consider evidence. The so-called law of evidence is made up largely of procedural regulations concerning the proof and presentation of facts, whether involving the testimony of witnesses, the presentation of documents or physical objects, or the assertion of a foreign law. The many rules of evidence that have evolved under different legal systems have, in the main, been founded on experience and shaped by varying legal requirements of what constitutes admissible and sufficient proof. Although evidence, in this sense, has both legal and technical characteristics, judicial evidence has always been a human rather than a technical problem. During different periods and at different cultural stages, problems concerning evidence have been resolved by widely different methods. Since the means of acquiring evidence are clearly variable and delimited, they can result only in a degree of probability and not in an absolute truth in the philosophic sense. Only Soviet doctrine, under the influence of philosophical materialism, expresses a belief that absolute, objective truth can be attained through evidence. In common-law countries, civil cases require only preponderant probability and criminal cases, probability beyond reasonable doubt. In civil-law countries so much probability is required that reasonable doubts are excluded.

THE EARLY LAW OF EVIDENCE

Characteristic features of the law of evidence in earlier cultures were that no distinction was made between civil and criminal matters or between fact and law and that rational means of evidence were either unknown or little used. In general, the accused had to prove his innocence.

Nonrational sources of evidence. The appeal to supernatural powers was, of course, not evidence in the modern sense but an ordeal in which God was appealed to as the highest judge.

Trial by ordeal and battle

The judges of the community determined what different kinds of ordeals were to be suffered, and frequently the ordeals involved threatening the accused with fire, a hot iron, or drowning. It may be that a certain awe associated with the two great elements of fire and water made them appear pre-eminently suitable for dangerous tests by which God himself was to pass on guilt or innocence. Trial by battle had much the same origin. To be sure, the powerful man relied on his strength, but it was also assumed that God would be on the side of right.

Semirational sources of evidence. The accused free person could offer to exonerate himself by oath. Under these circumstances, in contrast to the ordeals, it was not expected that God would rule immediately but rather that he would punish the perjurer at a later time. Nevertheless, there was ordinarily enough realism so that the mere oath of the accused person alone was not allowed. Rather, he was ordered to swear with a number of compurgators, or witnesses, who confirmed, so to speak, the oath of the person swearing. They stood as guarantees for his oath but never gave any testimony about the facts.

The significance of these first witnesses is seen in the use of the German word *Zeuge*, which now means "witness" but originally meant "drawn in." The witnesses were, in fact, "drawn in" to perform a legal act as instrumental witnesses. But they gave only their opinions and consequently did not testify about facts with which they were acquainted. Nevertheless, together with community witnesses, they paved the way for the more rational use of evidence.

The influence of Roman-canonical law. By the 13th century, ordeals were no longer used, though the custom of trial by battle lasted until the 14th and 15th centuries. The judicial machinery destroyed by dropping these sources of evidence could not be replaced by the oath of purgation alone. With the decline of chivalry, the flourishing of the towns, the further development of Christian theology, and the formation of states, both social and cultural conditions had changed. The law of evidence, along with much of the rest of the law of Europe, was influenced strongly by Roman-canonical law elaborated by jurists in northern Italian universities. Roman law introduced elements of common procedure that became known throughout the continental European countries and became something of a uniting bond between them.

Under the new influence, evidence was, first of all, evaluated on a hierarchical basis. This accorded well with the assumption of scholastic philosophy that all the possibilities of life could be formally ordered through a system of a priori, abstract regulations. Since the law was based on the concept of the inequality of persons, not all persons were suitable as witnesses, and only the testimony of two or more suitable witnesses could supply proof.

The formal theory of evidence that grew out of this hierarchical evaluation left no option for the judge: in effect, he was required to be convinced after the designated number of witnesses had testified concordantly. A distinction was made between complete, half, and lesser portions of evidence, evading the problem posed by such a rigid system of evaluation. Since interrogation of witnesses was secret, abuses occurred on another level. These abuses were nourished by the notion that the confession was the best kind of evidence and that reliable confessions could be obtained by means of torture.

Despite these obvious drawbacks and limitations, through the ecclesiastical courts, Roman-canonical law gained influence. It contributed much to the elimination of nonrational evidence from the courts, even though, given the formality of its application, it could result only in formal truths often not corresponding to reality.

A COMPARATIVE SURVEY
OF THE PRINCIPLES OF LEGAL EVIDENCE

A comparison of the principles of evidence under different legal traditions can best be made by examining the rights and obligations of the plaintiff and the defendant in civil proceedings and of the prosecutor and the accused in criminal proceedings. The position of the judge is also crucial. Historically, two systems developed.

The inquisitorial system. The first, which may be called the inquisitorial system, had its origins in medieval Roman-canonical proceedings. It is distinguished by the active part played by the judge, who by virtue of his office, himself searches for the facts, listens to witnesses and experts, examines documents and orders the taking of evidence. In continental European countries, and those other countries that derive their law from them, this system has generally been retained for criminal proceedings. The prosecutor and the accused, of course, give their recital of the facts and indicate their evidence for specific assertions. But by virtue of his role in the case, the judge must make further investigations if he deems them necessary to obtain the truth. Under the Soviet code of civil procedure of 1964, this system is also applied to civil pro-

The judge's role in continental Europe

ceedings. Other Socialist countries have followed this example. In some western European countries, there is a definite inclination toward employing this inquisitional system in all legal proceedings that have, or could have, a substantial public legal impact; *e.g.*, matrimonial, status, administrative, social, labour, and financial matters.

The accusatorial (adversary) system. The second system, which employs what are usually called accusatorial or adversary principles, is used in the common-law countries for all civil and criminal cases. In this system, the parties and their attorneys are primarily responsible for finding and presenting evidence. The judge does not himself investigate the facts. Only if the efforts of the parties are incomplete must the judge make inquiries with regard to questions that have remained unanswered.

In civil matters, most continental European countries follow a mixed system of both principles. In some of these countries, the judge can, for example, hear witnesses who have not been designated by the parties, and in all countries he can, by virtue of his office, hear the parties and experts and order documentary evidence or the actual inspection of evidence. In contrast to criminal cases, the continental European judge is always bound by the motions and assertions of the parties—a situation that does not, however, obtain under Soviet law.

Oral proceedings. Under both systems of presenting and obtaining evidence, oral proceedings are generally accepted. The written proceedings favoured during the Middle Ages have been abolished, although the parties prepare their lawsuits through briefs, and parts of the preliminary proceedings can be handled in writing. The interrogation of witnesses, however, is oral. The Roman-based countries and Sweden, Austria, and the Soviet Union do not permit any exceptions, while other countries, such as Germany, permit written statements by witnesses in special cases and with the consent of the parties. In the common-law countries, an exception is made to the principle of oral proceedings for certain types of affidavits, and, particularly in civil cases, the practice has steadily gained in importance.

Direct interrogation of witnesses by the deciding court is an aspect of the law of evidence closely connected with oral proceedings. Generally, in continental European countries, witnesses are interrogated by the judges who decide the verdict, but a number of countries have an investigation procedure according to which another judge, or only one member of the judging body, interrogates the witnesses. Under both the inquisitorial and the accusatorial systems, the principle of direct interrogation is of special importance in the free consideration of evidence. In the common-law countries, the function performed by the judge in this regard is handled by attorneys for the prosecution or defense, with the judge's role restricted almost entirely to overseeing the questioning.

Another principle of substantial importance is the public trial, which was one of the aims of the French Revolution. The right to a public trial, long established under the common law, is now accepted by all continental European countries. There may be exceptions, however, if questions of morals or public order are involved, and public trials in the full sense need not be provided in circumstances in which the evidence, rather than being taken in open court, is heard before a *juge d'instruction* or examining magistrate.

Influence
of the jury

One major influence that has shaped the law of evidence has been the jury system. At least one writer has said that law of evidence is the child of the jury. Oral proceedings, direct interrogation and the public trial are much less problematic under the Anglo-American system than under the civil-law system to the extent that evidence is heard before the jury. But this system has spawned a large number of regulations for the admissibility of evidence in order to guarantee due process and fair procedure and to protect the jury from being misled. The initiative of the parties determines the handling of these regulations, for they must raise objections if, in their opinion, any of the numerous exclusionary rules is being violated. The judge then rules on the objection. By the complex working of this arrangement, the Anglo-

American system has become more formalistic in many respects than the continental European system.

The burden of proof. The burden of proof is a manifold and somewhat ambiguous concept in the law of evidence.

The burden of producing evidence means that in general the party that cites specific facts for the substantiation of its claim also has the burden of producing the evidence to prove these facts. This burden depends on the substantive law governing the claim. Permissible presumptions and legal rules can shift the burden in various situations.

The burden of conviction, on the other hand, comes into play at the end of the hearing of evidence, if doubts remain. This is simply to recognize that the evidence is not sufficient to convince the jury or the judge and that, in general, the party having the burden of pleading and producing facts favourable to itself and of giving evidence also carries the so-called burden of conviction.

Whereas, in civil proceedings, it is generally the plaintiff who has the burden of proof for facts supporting a claim, unless this burden has been shifted to the defendant through rules or presumptions, in criminal proceedings it is the prosecution that bears the burden of proof for all relevant facts. What this means is that the defendant cannot be found guilty as long as proof has not been supplied or as long as doubts still remain. In continental European law, no distinction is made between civil and criminal cases with regard to the standard of proof. In both, such a high degree of probability is required that, to the degree that this is possible in the ordinary experience of life itself, doubts are excluded and probability approaches certitude. In the common-law countries, the degree of probability required in civil cases is lower than that called for in criminal matters. Since, according to socialist rules of civil procedure, the judges themselves must search for the facts, it is dubious whether one can speak at all of a burden of proof under socialist law.

Difference
between
the burden
of proof in
civil and
criminal
proceedings

Relevance and admissibility. In civil proceedings that are determined by the adversary principle, evidence is both ascertained and simultaneously restricted by the assertions of the parties. If the allegations of one party are not disputed or contested by the other, or if the allegations are even admitted, then no proof is required. Proof would, in fact, be irrelevant. Evidence offered to prove assertions that are not in issue nor probative of the matter in issue would also be irrelevant. The only evidence that is, therefore, relevant, is evidence that to some degree advances the inquiry and has a probative value for the decision. While continental European judges, in ordering the hearing of evidence or in deciding on evidence, indicate the facts to be proved and thereby strictly eliminate irrelevant facts, Anglo-American judges first give the parties an opportunity to furnish any evidence that they deem suitable. If, during the hearing of witnesses, irrelevant questions are put, they are rejected after the adversary has objected to them.

It has been said that relevance depends on logical considerations and that admissibility depends on the law. In contrast to continental European law, the common law has developed a large number of rules governing the admissibility of evidence. Relevant evidence is not admissible, for example, if the witnesses are excluded from testifying because of incompetency, or if they are protected by privileges against self-incrimination, or in instances in which they would have to divulge confidential or professional communications that have a privileged status or government secrets, or, again, when the evidence is excluded by the rules against hearsay.

In criminal cases in which the adversary principle does not govern, relevance relates to such questions that are so far removed from the case that they have no evidence value at all. Admissions and confessions do not exclude further evidence. According to Anglo-American law, the accused may be a competent witness under the admissibility rules, but, in contrast to an ordinary witness, he has the privilege of not taking the witness stand. According to continental European law, the accused is neither a party nor a witness. He can be heard, but he cannot be forced to answer questions of fact. In general, Anglo-

American rules of admissibility apply to criminal proceedings much as they apply to civil cases.

The free evaluation of evidence. Freedom to evaluate all the evidence produced was established in Roman law but fell into disuse as a principle during the time of the formalistic Roman-canonical law of evidence that characterized the Middle Ages. Remnants of the medieval formal theory of evidence survive in various countries.

Conviction intime: the judge's opinion

In countries where remnants of the medieval formal theory of evidence are still preserved, the principle of free evaluation of the evidence by the judge generally dates from the French Revolution. The French introduced the concept of the judge's *conviction intime* (inner, deep-seated conviction) in contrast to rules of formal evidence that prescribed exactly when the evidence amounted to proof. The primacy this gave to the personal conviction of the judge meant that it was not even necessary to state the reasons for the inner conviction. This total dependence on the judge's discretion aroused a great deal of criticism, and, as a result, various judicial codes prescribed that in giving the grounds on which judgment was based, the judge had to specify in writing why he was convinced in each case. *Conviction intime* in its original sense is limited to the testimony of witnesses and experts and to the explanations of the parties. Both kinds of formal oaths made by parties to a case, the supplementary oath and the tendered oath, are still valid in Roman-law based countries, and both may lead to formal solutions, since the judge must follow the legal consequences of the oath. But these survivals of medieval formal evidence theory have been weakened. In France, for example, the judge's latitude under the principle of *conviction intime* has been extended to allow him to pass on the affirmation oath of the party, which formerly had to be given a certain value, regardless of his opinion of its worth. In other states, such as Austria, Germany, and the Scandinavian countries, the formal oath of the parties was abolished and replaced by the free depositions of the parties. Even if the parties take an oath on their testimonies during this process, the judge is not bound by it but may still make his own evaluation of the evidence. In addition, some remnants of the formal evidence theory have been preserved with regard to documentary proof where rules of procedure contain presumptions as to the conclusiveness of certain documents. Since reliance on documentary evidence prevails in some countries, these formal evidence rules are still of special importance.

In Anglo-American law the problem of free evaluation of evidence can be understood through the institution of the jury. Obviously, the evidence must be convincing to the common sense of the jury members, who form their judgment on the basis of free conviction. The function of the jury, however, is to decide questions of fact, rather than questions of law, which are left to the judge. The jury's verdict can be overturned by the judge if it is inconsistent with the evidence, or with his instructions as to the law governing the case. The judge's relationship to the jury therefore plays a role in the decisions, and there are difficult questions in which it is unclear whether the jury or the judge should consider the evidence. Some formal rules of evidence survive in Anglo-American law. In some cases evidence must be corroborated before it can constitute proof. In homicide cases, for example, a confession must be supported by additional evidence. In addition, evidence by witnesses is sometimes excluded by rules of admissibility.

Soviet and Swedish innovations

In recent years, some new principles for the evaluation of evidence have become evident in the law of Sweden and the U.S.S.R. Both countries have rejected all remnants of the formal theory of evidence, and both have tried to render the judges' conviction objective. Sweden demands that its judges undertake a discursive analysis of all the evidence. The Soviet procedure calls for judges to form their conviction on the strength of the evidence and according to their "socialist legal conscience."

THE CLASSIC MEANS OF PROOF

According to Anglo-American law, the classic means of proof are witnesses, documents, and real evidence (de-

rived from the actual inspection of objects). As a result of historical development, the status of witness was accorded to experts and to the parties in a civil lawsuit, and even to the accused in criminal proceedings. The development of continental European law has taken a different course. Parties cannot be witnesses, and evidence by experts is subject to special procedural rules. Consequently, there are essentially five separate sources of evidence: witnesses, parties, experts, documents, and real evidence.

Oral testimony. The oral testimony of witnesses competes in a sense with documentary evidence to the extent that one may exclude or supplement the other.

The importance of documentary evidence in some continental European countries goes back to the year 1566 and the French Ordinance of Moulins, which stated that contracts above a certain value could only be concluded in writing with the aid of a notary. This preference for documentary proof has persisted in articles of the French code of civil procedure and in other civil codes. According to the French practice, evidence by witnesses is excluded in the case of contracts above a certain value. But this strict regulation has been made more flexible by the growth of doctrine permitting evidence by witnesses once the origin of written proof is furnished and is not sufficient, or if the contracts in question are commercial in nature, or if it is impossible for one party to prove its claim through documents. Facts extrinsic to the document cannot be proved through witnesses. Even Soviet law prescribes that in special cases proof can be furnished only through documents.

Eligible witness. Under Anglo-American law, almost anyone can be a witness, including the parties and experts; even insane persons, children, and convicted felons may testify. Grounds once used for excluding such persons as witnesses are now used only to impeach their credibility. Continental European countries, as has been said, do not treat either the parties or experts as competent witnesses, and they are still suspicious of interested witnesses. Some of them, influenced by the Roman-based school, deny, on the whole, the capacity of those persons having a certain degree of relationship to the parties. Some consider insane persons incompetent to testify, others grant them the competency but exclude their testimony on the grounds of credibility. The capacity to be a witness does not depend on whether or not the person can testify about questions relevant to the specific case. In general, the tendency has been to utilize all persons who can testify about facts that will help to establish the truth. Competency as a witness has therefore been extended to as many persons as possible. On the other hand, many persons are protected by law from being forced to testify. This type of protection derives either from privilege, or from the right to refuse to give evidence, either case distinguishable from incapacity to testify. Whereas privilege or the right to refuse to give evidence may be either requested or waived, incapacity to testify takes effect automatically; *i.e.*, it must always be officially considered by the court.

Privileges. Privileges under Anglo-American law must be distinguished from the right to refuse to give evidence under particular circumstances as it exists in continental European practice. The latter is granted to witnesses for either personal or objective reasons. The personal reasons are the same as those that result in incapacity to testify under Roman-based law; *i.e.* relationship, affinity, and marriage. The objective reasons concern persons who, as a result of their profession (for example, clergymen, physicians, attorneys, journalists, etc.), have been put in possession of confidential facts. Such confidants have a limited right to refuse to give evidence so long as the person protected does not give his consent (the German solution). In some cases they are not admitted as witnesses without the consent of the protected person (the Swedish solution). Thus the Swedish judge officially decides whether the protected person has given his consent, whereas the German judge leaves the decision whether to testify up to the confidant. In addition, witnesses may refuse to testify if their testimony would cause direct financial damage to themselves or to their

Refusal to testify

families, or if it would publicly disgrace them or expose them to criminal prosecution. All persons may make their own decision as to whether or not they wish to testify, but judges are obliged to inform them about their specific rights in the matter. These procedural regulations have developed in order to avoid the situation in which the person protected becomes caught in a conflict between the truth and his personal interests. The interests of the protected person—perhaps partly out of realism—are thus given a higher value than the search for the facts. In this regard, Soviet law has adopted a different attitude, which places a higher value on objective truth than on the personal rights of third persons who, though not parties to a suit, may become involved as witnesses.

The Anglo-American privileges differ from the continental European right to refuse to testify insofar as privileged persons cannot decide whether or not they wish to testify. They may only cite their privileges, and the judge decides if they must testify. Under a system that stresses the free evaluation of evidence, the obligation to testify is subject to only a very few exceptions.

Self-incrimination. The privilege against self-incrimination has a twofold nature in Anglo-American law because, in civil proceedings, parties may appear as witnesses and, in criminal proceedings, the accused may appear as a witness. The privilege of an ordinary witness is considerably limited. He must submit to being designated and sworn in as a witness in all instances and must answer all questions except those which are self-incriminating. Consequently, either he or his attorney must sift out the incriminating questions that will evoke the privilege. This is not always easy, particularly since it is only the witness, and not the party or the party's attorney, who may cite the protecting privilege. Critics have called this privilege a sentimental institution, but it is worth noting, in this regard, that the privilege against self-incrimination was included in the U.S. Bill of Rights.

Personal and professional privilege. Privileges deriving from personal and professional relationships are generally not granted on principle, though historically a privilege for the protection of marital communications has developed. In England, an 1853 law decreed that a husband could not be forced to testify concerning information that his wife may have given him during the course of the marriage. This, naturally, also applies to the wife. In the United States, the courts contended that laws concerning testimony on matrimonial communications contained only a statement of the common law. Only the beneficiary of the privilege may cite it, and it is not applicable where criminal offenses by one spouse against the other or against the children are concerned, or in the case of a divorce proceeding.

Attorneys are considered to be under an obligation to refuse to testify about confidential communications with their clients. The privilege, however, protects the client, not the attorney, and, therefore, the client may waive it. This privilege is only properly explained in terms of the adversary system, which, so to speak, makes the attorney his client's champion.

Clergymen are likewise under obligation to refuse to answer questions concerning information given them in the secrecy of the confessional by believers. Again, the privilege protects the believer. This custom has been sanctioned by legislation in many U.S. states. In England, however, there is no common-law rule for this privilege.

Physicians, as a rule, must answer all questions since there is no common-law privilege regarding confidential information furnished by the patient. In some states an appropriate privilege has been created by legislation. In these states, it is again the patient who is protected and only he may waive the privilege.

Journalists, like physicians, occupy a position that is not entirely clear. In some jurisdictions they may refuse to testify about their sources of information, and in a number of U.S. states such a privilege has been specifically created by statute. In other U.S. states and in England the question does not yet seem to have been settled.

The journalist and his source

Privilege in civil and criminal cases. Differences between civil and criminal proceedings regarding the availability of privilege grow out of the protection from self-incrimination. It has already been pointed out that the accused no longer lacks competence as a witness but may exercise the privilege of refusing to be called or sworn as a witness. Unlike ordinary witnesses, the defendant may invoke this privilege with considerable latitude. But, if he does decide to step into the witness box, he renounces his privilege and may be interrogated as if he were an ordinary witness. The question arises, however, whether the waiving of the privilege against self-incrimination is limited to testimony concerning crimes of which he presently stands accused, or whether he must answer all questions regarding criminal acts. It appears to have become fairly well established that the prosecutor can, in fact, interrogate the defendant about previous criminal offenses. In civil cases, the parties have the same privilege for protection from self-incrimination as other witnesses; *i.e.*, they need not answer incriminating questions.

Methods of establishing the credibility of witnesses. Means for establishing the credibility of witnesses assumed a great deal of importance at the point when medieval formal evidence theory was replaced by the free judicial consideration of evidence.

The oath, perhaps the oldest means for encouraging truthful testimony, antedates this point, of course. The oath, in some sense, forms a link between court proceedings and religious belief since, in its usual form, witnesses swear by Almighty God that they are speaking the truth. Though the effectiveness of such an act has certainly diminished in secular societies, this appeal to God has for centuries been considered the surest means of obtaining truth. There are two kinds of oaths, the preliminary and the subsequent. In Anglo-American practice, the witness is sworn in before testimony. Under the German and other continental procedures, the swearing-in may occur after testimony as well. The latter method allows the judge to use his own discretion in individual cases as to whether or not the witness should be ordered to swear. In current German practice, very few witnesses are sworn in for testimony in civil proceedings, whereas in criminal proceedings all witnesses have to swear. Some continental European countries allow witnesses who object to oaths to substitute a solemn affirmation, and Denmark has abolished all oaths in legal procedures. Only Soviet law, intent on breaking with tradition, forbids any oath or solemn affirmation. The oath of a witness does not have the formal effect of binding the judge or the jury. They must evaluate it and testimony freely.

The swearing of witnesses

The cross-examination. Common-law judges and attorneys regard the opportunity to cross-examine as a guarantee of the reliability and completeness of testimony by a witness. Under the perfect operation of the adversary system it is not the judge but rather the parties or their attorneys who interrogate the witnesses. The plaintiff's attorney begins the "examination in chief," which is subject to a number of restrictions. Leading, misleading, and argumentative questions, for example, are not permitted. After the plaintiff's attorney concludes his interrogation, the defendant's attorney may cross-examine the same witness. This cross-examination generally consists of leading questions posed with the intent of weakening or invalidating the impression created by the direct testimony of the witness. The cross-examination must ordinarily be limited to subjects covered during direct interrogation. There is a recognizable tendency, however, for cross-examination to become as open-ended as possible. The plaintiff's attorney has the option, finally, to re-establish the credibility of his witness by re-examination. These interrogations are formally regulated and require a great deal of skill and experience on the part of the attorneys. Such formal questioning of the witness is unknown to the continental European rules of procedure, even though cross-examination is common. Continental rules of procedure require the judge to interrogate the witness first. Frequently, the witness begins with a free narration. Then, after the judge has finished his interrogation, the attorneys of both parties may question the witness. All this is done in an informal manner, and almost any question is permitted. In Roman-law countries the interrogation of witnesses is, however, rather formalistic because it is generally limited to questions concerning allegations specified in the evidence judgment. But here too, there is a tendency for the court to allow questions at its discretion.

The witness as "real evidence." Scientific examinations of witnesses are especially common in paternity and status proceedings with regard to blood-typing. These methods have now been so much improved that the suspicion of paternity may be definitely dismissed in many cases. In Germany and elsewhere, opinions based on biological and hereditary evidence are used for these same purposes. The use of fingerprint and ballistics evidence, among other types, has become quite customary in criminal cases. In the United States, there are varying opinions about the admissibility of lie-detector tests as evidence. The results of such tests are not yet admissible in the continental European countries.

The hearsay rule. The hearsay rule is perhaps the most characteristic feature of the Anglo-American law of evidence. It has also been said that, next to trial by jury, the hearsay rule constitutes the most important and original contribution of this system's practice.

Despite the obvious dangers involved in its use, free evaluation of the evidence furnished by hearsay testimony continues to be characteristic of continental European law. This somewhat surprising fact may be explained by reference to the historical development already traced here. Until the 19th century, the medieval formal evidence theory strictly prescribed when the judge had to be convinced by the testimony of a witness. Moreover, there was no jury in the continental countries to be protected by rules of evidence and therefore no need to introduce rules of hearsay. When the formal evidence theory was replaced by the requirement that the judge freely consider the evidence, his discretion naturally extended to hearsay testimony.

The creation of a body of rules for the exclusion of hearsay evidence was motivated by the arguments that such testimony could tend to mislead the jury, that the hearsay observer, unlike the legal witness, was not under solemn oath and was inaccessible to cross-examination, that such testimony furnished third-hand evidence, and that it violated the best evidence rule.

The
exceptions
to the rule
against
hearsay

Over the years, exceptions to the prohibition of hearsay testimony had to be permitted, however, and these have become so numerous that the opinion has sometimes been expressed that no exhaustive list of such exceptions could even be compiled. The judge must decide in each case whether testimony based upon hearsay is admissible under an exception to the rule—a further indication that regulations governing the admissibility of evidence are far more important in Anglo-American law than in continental law. The most commonly cited exceptions to the rule of hearsay relate to statements made by dead or absent persons, statements in public documents, and to confessions and admissions by parties.

Confessions. Confessions, as a source of evidence, are distinguished from admissions. Whereas a confession is a complete acknowledgment of guilt in criminal proceedings, an admission is a statement of fact in either a civil or a criminal case. In former times, the confession was considered the ultimate form of evidence. As soon as the accused confessed—often under duress—no further proof was required. In time, involuntary confession came to be rejected as evidence under English law, and the burden of proving that a confession was voluntary lay with the prosecutor. In the United States, the federal rule that confessions are inadmissible if obtained while the defendant was unlawfully detained has not gone quite so far, though the law is still in a state of considerable flux. Involuntary confessions, however, are not admissible for any purpose under Anglo-American law. In continental European law, on the other hand, confessions of the accused are always freely considered by the judge.

Differences between criminal and civil proceedings regarding admissions result mainly from the adversary principle governing civil proceedings. In Anglo-American procedure, if one party in a civil suit admits facts con-

trary to his interest, such an admission is conclusive and obviates the need for further evidence on the point. The same result follows in German or Swedish courts. Under the Roman-based laws of such countries as France, Italy, and Spain, an admission made before the court is a form of evidence that leads to conclusive proof binding upon the court. But admissions made out of court are subject to free evaluation by the judge and do not exclude further evidence. Only Soviet law gives no binding effect to admissions.

Party testimony in the continental European countries. Oral testimony by the parties in civil proceedings was introduced in Austria in 1895. Norway followed suit in 1915, Denmark in 1919, Germany in 1933, and Sweden in 1948. Party testimony is generally heard in the same way as the evidence of other witnesses, but there are some essential differences. For one thing, the interrogation of parties is a subsidiary source of evidence to be used only when all other means have been exhausted, but it may be also used together with other means of proof. In some countries, both parties must be heard; in others, only one party may be heard upon motion of the opponent. In most cases, the parties do not have to confirm their testimony by oath, but the court may decree that one of the parties must swear. In Swedish law, for example, the parties must solemnly declare that they have told the truth. In Soviet law, however, the interrogation of parties is completely informal.

In criminal proceedings under continental European law, the defendant may be heard, but his formal position is that of neither a witness nor a party. His depositions, nevertheless, do have value as evidence.

Expert evidence. Expert witnesses must have specialized knowledge, skill, or experience in the area of their testimony. For the most part, they do not testify concerning facts but draw inferences from them. With a few exceptions, they are treated in Anglo-American law as ordinary witnesses and are brought before the court by the parties in the same manner as other witnesses. Although ordinary witnesses are generally allowed to testify only concerning facts and not to express opinions, an exception to this rule is made for the expert, who must, of course, be allowed to give his opinion.

Qualifications of an expert witness

Generally speaking, anyone with special knowledge may be an expert in his respective field. In Anglo-American law, the expert is designated by the party, while in continental European law the court decides who may be an expert, generally selecting from a list on file in the court so as to guarantee that the experts designated are impartial. Experts may not, therefore, be cited by the parties.

The oral interrogation of experts is customary in Anglo-American law, and proceeds, with a few exceptions, under the same rules for the interrogation of ordinary witnesses.

Under continental rules of procedure, on the other hand, expert opinions are generally given in written form. Experts are allowed a rather wide scope of discretion, especially when the opinion involves scientific findings that often cannot be checked by the judge. But under some continental European rules, the parties or their attorneys may request that the experts testify before the court to defend their written opinion and tell how they arrived at it.

Documentary evidence. Documentary evidence is in many respects considered better than the evidence furnished by witnesses, about which there has always been a certain amount of suspicion. Documentary evidence differs considerably from the evidence of witnesses and is dealt with under special rules.

Criteria for establishing the authenticity of documents are only important if authenticity is contested. This is often impossible, however, if a presumption favouring the authenticity of a public document exists—which it frequently does under continental European law. Under Anglo-American law, a party may serve the adversary with a written request to corroborate the authenticity of any relevant document. Direct evidence of authenticity may be gotten through the testimony of persons who signed the original documents. This is often impossible, however, and in this case circumstantial evidence is permitted. Under Roman-based law, documents are proved genuine by special proceedings. In other continental European countries, a document may be proved genuine by any type of evidence.

The obligation to present documents in the Anglo-American system derives from what is known as the best evidence rule. If the original document is in the hands of a third person or the opponent, the party that must supply proof can ask the court for a writ of *sub poena duces tecum* compelling the third party to produce the document in court. If the original is not produced after this, second-hand evidence of its existence is then permitted. In continental law, there is no similar obligation to produce documents. The adversary or third persons can only be ordered to do so if there is a positive obligation under the substantive law. Among European countries, only Sweden has developed any extensive obligation for the parties to produce documents. Soviet law has gone farthest in this regard, extending the rule to all kinds of documents regardless of the interests of third parties.

Proof of documentary evidence

Extrinsic proof of the contents of documents in Anglo-American law is admitted only in special cases, since oral evidence is inadmissable to vary, contradict, or add to the terms of a written agreement—a rule that makes many documents conclusive as evidence. The method of Anglo-American law in this particular area is consequently negative, since evidence outside the content of the document is on principle not admissible. Continental law follows the medieval method, by attributing a certain value as evidence to particular documents, which is binding on the judge.

The consideration of documentary evidence by the judge therefore tends to be restricted, since the document itself furnishes conclusive proof if evidence by reference to facts outside the document is inadmissible. In most continental laws, judges are bound by presumptions in this respect, and only in Swedish and Socialist law are there no provisions restricting free judicial consideration of documentary evidence.

Real evidence. The remaining form of evidence that needs brief mention in this survey is so-called real evidence, also known as demonstrative or objective evidence. This is naturally the most direct evidence, since the objects in question are inspected by the judge or jury themselves. Problems arise in this area over who is obliged to present objects for inspection or to actually undergo inspection. The use of the jury system in Anglo-American law has made it necessary that any real evidence be shown to be both logically relevant and completely genuine before it may be admitted as proof. The exhibit of real evidence may sometimes be directly connected with the case (for example, when a weapon is shown to the court), or it may involve something used to illustrate testimony, as, for example, a model or skeleton to clarify testimony about an injury. In any case, real evidence may not be accepted as legal proof unless it is authenticated by the testimony of witnesses.

ADAPTATIONS OF THE BASIC SYSTEMS

Generally speaking, two different systems of the law of evidence are prevalent all over the world: the Anglo-American and the Continental European systems. The latter can be subdivided into three variants: the Germanic, the French or Roman, and the Socialist patterns. The Germanic variant tries to utilize all means of proof; it follows the principle of formlessness and balances between the accusatorial and the inquisitorial principles. The French or Roman variant favours evidence by documents and is dominated by a very formal procedure of "enquête" or investigation. The Socialist variant makes believe that objective truth might be ascertained by evidence. It therefore favours the inquisitorial principle and does not protect witnesses, parties, and experts by privileges or procedural rights.

Japan provides an interesting example of mixture of the Continental European system (Germanic and Roman variants) with the Anglo-American system with the con-

tinental model dominating, however. This can be seen historically. With the Meiji revolution in 1868 Japan began to adopt Western practices, including European law; so that eventually Japanese ideas of the law of evidence were replaced by European ones. The drafters of the first civil code of procedure in 1890 surveyed many legal systems, including the French, taking something from each. Their final product is, however, characterized as following the first draft of the German civil code. In its subsequent development, the Japanese legal system remained true to these sources, even in the development of a new code in 1929.

After the Second World War under American influence this code of civil procedure was changed in many respects; at the same time the Japanese code of penal procedure was changed.

In criminal procedure the Anglo-American influence can be found in several rules. The inquisitorial principle, for instance, lost its dominating place in favour of the accusatorial principle; it is not the judge but the defendant and his counsel who question witnesses. Evidence by hearsay is no longer allowed. Instead of the inquisitorial hearing of the defendant there is the hearing of the defendant as a witness. The fusion of the Continental European with the Anglo-American system of evidence leads to an unique combination of the interests of the defendant with the principle of impartiality of the court.

In Japanese civil procedure, however, the Continental European law of evidence still dominates. The Japanese adhere to the five classical means of proof: witnesses, experts, parties, documents, and real evidence. The hearing of witnesses is done by the parties and their counsels. The party that asked for the hearing of any person will start with the examination; thereafter the other party will cross-examine. But contrary to the Anglo-American law of evidence there are no strong admissibility rules regarding examination, cross-examination, and re-examination. Contrary to criminal procedure, the hearsay rule is allowed in civil cases. When the parties have finished their examinations, the judge can put questions to the witness or experts. As in the Continental European system, persons on the witness stand have no special privileges, though they have the right to refuse to give evidence that might lead to self-incrimination, the incrimination of relatives, or the revelation of state secrets.

There seem to be no current moves to change the law of evidence as it is now in force in Japan, perhaps because it was changed too often during the last hundred years.

BIBLIOGRAPHY

Historic development: T.F.T. PLUCKNETT, *A Concise History of the Common Law*, 5th ed. (1956); A. ENGELMANN, *Der Civilprozess Geschichte und System* (1889; Eng. trans., *A History of Continental Civil Procedure*, 1927); R.C. VAN CAENEGEM, "La Preuve dans le droit du moyen-âge occidental," *Recueil de la Société Jean Bodin*, vol. 17 (1965); H. NOTTARP, *Gottesurteilstudien* (1956), particularly for ordeals.

American law: C.T. MCCORMICK, *Law of Evidence* (1954); J.H. WIGMORE, *The Principles of Judicial Proof*, 2nd ed. (1931).

English law: G.D. NOKES, *An Introduction to Evidence*, 3rd ed. (1962); R. CROSS, *Evidence*, 4th ed. (1967); S.L. PHIPSON, *Manual of the Law on Evidence*, 10th ed. (1963).

German law: A. BLOMEYER, *Zivilprozessrecht* (1963).

Italian law: M. CAPPELLETTI and J.M. PERILLO, *Civil Procedure in Italy* (1965).

French law: *Répertoire de procédure civile et commerciale*, 2 vol., in the "Encyclopédie Juridique Series" (1955–56).

Spanish law: L. PRIETO-CASTRO, *Derecho procesal civil* (1964).

Swedish law: P.O. EKELOF, *Rättegång* (1963–66).

Soviet law: A.J. WYSHINSKII, *Theorie der gerichtlichen Beweise im sowjetischen Recht*, 3rd ed. (1955); H. ROGGEMANN, *Die Zivilprozessordnung der RSFSR* (1964).

For a comparative study of the laws of evidence in Germany, England, France, Italy, Spain, Sweden, and the Soviet Union see H. NAGEL, *Die Grundzüge des Beweisrechts im europäischen Zivilprozess* (1967).

(H.N.)

Evolution

Man's interest in his own origin, that of all living things, and that of the universe must be as old as man himself. It is reflected in literary form (which must itself be based on much older creeds) in legends of creation popular among the peoples of antiquity—Sumerians, Egyptians, Greeks, and Hebrews, whose sacred book, the Old Testament, contains two descriptions of the creation and traces of a third. The omnipotence that primitive peoples ascribed to their deities made it natural for them to believe that whatever is was created. This is the reason that problems surrounding the origins of the earth, heavens, seas, plants and animals, men and women were wrapped in unquestioned and unquestionable dogmas, some of which still hold sway. It is only comparatively recently, in societies and civilizations possessed of scientific knowledge and methods of investigation, that such dogmas have come under question. The Copernican system dethroned the geocentric view of the universe. Evolution, the changes that living beings are now known to have undergone since the origin of life on earth, has led to an even more profound revolution in the history of ideas because it has revealed the affinity of man to all other living beings and has shown that change, not stability, is the rule of life.

Evolution is the kernel of biology. It is significant that, before Charles Darwin established evolution as an inescapable fact and showed how it was brought about, biology was in a state of chaos. Organisms are found only as species, groups of individuals that resemble one another more than they resemble any others and that breed only among themselves, a concept that first became precise in the 17th century, when, however, each species was regarded as a product of the original creation, and no explanation was provided or even sought for the countless puzzles that presented themselves: why species differ from one another, what relation there was between living forms and the fossils found in the crust of the earth, why some organisms are found only in certain regions, why internal parasites such as the tapeworm infest man, and many other questions. Evolution provided the first unifying, general principle applicable to all living beings, which are as they now are because they have become what they are, having undergone modification during descent from other species.

Another aspect of the significance of evolution is that any fact discovered about one species may be applicable to other species, and, as the study of biology progressed and became diversified into many branches—including comparative anatomy, embryology, paleontology, genetics, physiology, etc.—each of these branches may have lessons for the others. The understanding of any biological phenomenon is helped by knowledge of evolutionary principles and mechanisms, and many phenomena are inexplicable without evolution.

Evolution also has practical significance for man. The art and practice of medicine are the outcome and integration of studies in many branches of biology and would make no progress without a realization of, for example, evolutionary changes in bacteria and viruses. Agriculture, including plant cultivation, animal domestication, and selective breeding, depends heavily on the application of evolutionary principles. Ethology, the study of behaviour, has yet to find the evolutionary basis for man's aberrant conduct that allows him to kill members of his own species wholesale, which other species do not do. The social importance of evolution in understanding human conduct in the past and in providing guidelines for the future is enormous.

This article is divided into the following sections:

I. History of evolutionary theory

An understanding of modern evolutionary theory requires examination of ideas that preceded those of Darwin. Some classical Greek philosophers held views that have been thought to have foreshadowed the concept of evolution; but they were abstract speculations not based on objective studies of facts in nature, and, until the 18th century, nobody dreamed of questioning that species had been created as they are.

The discovery in Java of flying lemurs (colugos, *Galeopithecus*), then regarded as bat-winged monkeys, led the French political philosopher Montesquieu to write in 1721:

Early ideas about evolution

> This would seem to corroborate my feeling that the differences between animal species can daily increase and similarly decrease; in the beginning there were very few species and they have multiplied since.

This acceptance of the possibility that species might change into other species was the kernel of the concept of *transformisme*, transmutation, or evolution.

Studies of abnormal or monstrous births and the transmission of striking hereditary traits (especially polydactyly, the possession of extra digits) led a French mathematician, Pierre-Louis de Maupertuis, in 1751 to envisage the multiplication of species as being due to fortuitous recombinations of elementary particles of organisms that lead to offspring deviating from their ancestral forms. This was not only an acceptance of evolution but also a crude attempt to explain it. The French philosopher Denis Diderot, in 1753, added the notion of community of descent:

> If we consider the animal kingdom, and we notice that among the quadrupeds there is none whose physical parts and functions, particularly the internal ones, are not quite similar, may we not readily believe that there was never more than one primeval animal, the prototype of all, while nature only lengthened, shortened, transformed, multiplied, or obliterated some of its organs?

In a monumental work on natural history, Georges Buffon, one of the leading naturalists of the 18th century, raised the question of the possibility that the ass is related to the horse, with which it can breed. He asked if these two species might not, perhaps, have been descended from a common ancestor; but the opposition of the theological faculty of the Sorbonne made him recoil:

> If we once agree that the ass belongs to the horse family, and differs from the horse only because it has degenerated, it could equally well be claimed that the ape belongs to man's family, that the ape is a degenerate man, and that ape and man had a common ancestry.

He went on to consider the possibility that all animals, including ape and man, could be regarded as related, and he answered himself, no doubt with tongue in cheek,

> No, it is certain from Revelation that all animals shared in the grace of Creation, and that each emerged from the hands of the Creator as it is today.

Linnaeus, the founder of modern biological nomenclature, expressed the same orthodox view in his early writings but by 1760 had been driven by his own observations to admit that species could vary. He thought, however, that genera were immutable.

Erasmus Darwin, the grandfather of Charles, by 1794

had concluded that evolution had occurred. He based his conclusion on changes undergone by animals during development (chrysalis into moth, tadpole into frog) and on changes by plants and animals under cultivation and domestication as well as on vestigial organs, crossing, monstrous births, and resemblances in comparative anatomy. He tried to explain evolutionary changes by imagining that desires and aversions, pleasures and pains, led to wants "due to lust, hunger, and danger" and that their satisfaction brought about modifications of species through "the power of acquiring new parts, attended with new propensities, directed by irritations, sensations, volitions, and associations."

Lamarck's inability to distinguish between species   A similar view was reached quite independently by the naturalist Lamarck, who experienced such difficulties in distinguishing between species and varieties that he concluded that there was no real difference between them and that, if enough closely related species were studied together, they merged into one another and differences between them could no longer be made out. In this he is known to have been wrong; however difficult the barrier between species may be to detect, it nevertheless exists. In 1809 Lamarck's views enabled him to propose a system of evolution and to draw up an evolutionary tree, from microanimals to man, with branches indicating community of ancestry between different groups. To explain evolution, Lamarck invoked two factors. The first was a supposed tendency to complexity and perfection (incompatible with the fact of evolution of degenerate forms), which meant that simple organisms alive in Lamarck's time must have arisen recently by spontaneous generation (which was disproved under the conditions of the time by the experiments of an Italian naturalist, Lazzaro Spallanzani, and the French microbiologist Louis Pasteur). His second factor was an imagined *sentiment intérieur*, which, he supposed, caused movements and introduced habits that produced new organs that satisfied the animals' needs. This was an unfounded speculation, and, since Lamarck provided no evidence in support of his views, they found no acceptance. It is perhaps regrettable that the term Lamarckism is not applied to evolution itself. However erroneous, his was the first systematic presentation of the subject. Instead, the term is now taken to describe a theory of the supposed heritable effects of use and disuse of organs ("the inheritance of acquired characters") and the direct action of environmental factors, which Lamarck was not the first to suggest and which are now known not to be inherited.

Georges Cuvier, another French naturalist, rejected evolution because he knew of no fossil forms intermediate between existing species and because 5,000-year-old mummified animals found by Napoleon's expedition in Egyptian pyramids were identical with existing forms. In rock strata of the Paris Basin, the lowest and earliest layers contained fossil faunas "ready-made," which Cuvier attributed to creation; their complete absence from later strata he attributed to catastrophe. He was, however, obliged to accept the fact that the fossils found in upper beds showed an advance in complexity over those in lower beds; this phenomenon, called progressionism, was left unexplained.

Etienne Geoffroy-Saint-Hilaire, who accepted the concept of evolution, was the first to use this word in the modern sense (it earlier had been used to denote embryonic development), in 1831, in a work on fossil reptiles found near Caen, France. In the following year, the British paleontologist Sir Charles Lyell used it in the same sense, although he rejected evolution, because his theory of uniformitarianism (long-continued action of existing geological causes) killed catastrophism, and he mistakenly regarded progressionism as associated with catastrophism.

The contribution of Charles Darwin   Lyell's uniformitarianism acted as an unexpected ferment in the mind of Charles Darwin, who, during the voyage of HMS "Beagle," was led to abandon the orthodox notion of the fixed nature of species and to accept a belief in evolution instead. This change of belief was based on four sets of observations that he had made: the presence in adjacent areas of a continent of related but different species; the similarity of structure between fossil and living forms in the same areas; the resemblance of species on isolated islands to those on the nearest continent; and differences between species on closely adjacent islands of the Galapagos Archipelago in relation to their modes of life and feeding. All these facts, Darwin felt, could be explained only if species were not specially created but had been descended with modification from common ancestral species.

Darwin realized that it would be useless to argue that evolution had occurred unless he could explain how the process itself and, in particular, the adaptations behind it had arisen. He solved this problem in 1838. The details are so closely involved in the process of natural selection that a description of the line of his thought is best deferred until the process itself is considered (see below *Natural selection*). In Darwin's day there was complete ignorance of mechanisms of heredity and of the origin and nature of heritable variation. After constructing his theory in 1838, Darwin remained silent about it for 20 years. During that interval, views favourable to evolution were expressed by others in Switzerland, Scotland, and Austria. Alfred Russel Wallace, working in the East Indies, formed a theory virtually identical to Darwin's in 1858, and papers by the two men were presented at the same meeting of the Linnean Society in 1858. Darwin's *Origin of Species* was published the following year.

It was not until the mid-20th century that a British statistician, Sir Ronald Fisher, and a number of others integrated information from many different areas of biology into a synthetic theory of evolution.

II. The evidence for evolution

The evolution of living organisms has gone on for 3,000,-000,000 years, and the 20 years during which Darwin studied the subject before publishing the *Origin of Species* was a ridiculously short space of time for modifications of species to be observed. It must be stressed that Darwin himself never claimed to provide proof of evolution or of the origin of species; what he did claim was that if evolution has occurred, a number of otherwise inexplicable facts are readily explained. The evidence for evolution was, therefore, indirect. Recently, however, direct evidence of evolution has been observed.

Evidence from structural similarities   The indirect evidence for evolution is based primarily on the significance of similarities found in different organisms, which are explicable only if they have derived the features in question, structures or functions, from a common ancestor during descent with modification, for the laws of probability insist that fundamental similarities can be traced only to one single origin.

Comparative anatomy provides the first set of witnesses. There are a quarter of a million different species of flowering plants, but all of them (except for a few parasitic forms) share the basic structures of roots, stem-bearing branches, leaves containing the green pigment chlorophyll, and flowers composed of modified leaves, sepals, petals, stamens, and pistils. They differ in detail between different species, but all are built on the same plan and live in the same way, absorbing salts in water through the roots and fixing carbon dioxide in the green plastids of the leaves in sunshine to synthesize more of their substance. The similarity of plan is easily explicable if all descended with modification from a common ancestor, by evolution, and the term homologous is used to denote corresponding structures formed in this way.

There are over three-quarters of a million species of insects. Despite broad variations in the details of their body plans, they all show a division of the body into head, trunk, and abdomen; they have three pairs of legs and two pairs of wings; and their mouthparts, whether used for sucking or for biting, are built on the same basic plan. In vertebrate animals, the skeleton of the forelimb is a splendid example of homology, in the bones of the upper arm, forearm, wrist, hand, and fingers, all of which can be matched, bone for bone, in rat, dog, horse, bat, mole, porpoise, or man. The example is all the more telling because the bones have become modified in adaptation to different modes of life but have retained the same fundamental plan of structure, inherited from a common ancestor.

Evidence from development

Embryology provides further examples. The German embryologist K.E. von Baer wrote:

In my possession are two little embryos in spirit, whose names I omitted to attach, and at the present I am quite unable to say to what class they belong. They may be lizards or small birds, or very young mammals, so complete is the similarity in the mode of formation of the head and trunk in these animals.

Darwin supplied the answer to the problem by showing that this embryonic similarity was due to the inheritance of the structure of these embryos from the embryo of a common ancestor.

Comparative anatomy and embryology present the phenomenon of transformed organs, structures that have changed their form and function with evolution. Among flying insects, the flies (Diptera) differ from most others in having one instead of two pairs of wings. The posterior pair have been modified into gyroscopic organs (halteres) that help in flight. Some fish have utilized the electrical potential of specialized muscles in organs whose electrical discharge is strong enough to serve as a sort of radar emission. The echo, perceived by certain sense organs, enables the fish to sense the proximity of objects in the water. Other fish have increased this function to such an extent that their electric organs are powerful enough to kill or paralyze predators and prey. Only descent with modification can explain the existence of such structures.

Some organs are called abortive or degenerate because they no longer serve a function. The possession of wings by ostriches, which cannot fly, is explicable if ostriches were descended from flying birds, in which the wings were functional. That this is, in fact, the case is evidenced by the structures of the cerebellum, the bones of the wing, and the tail, which show adaptations characteristic of flight. The appendix of man has no useful function, but it corresponds to the cecum of the alimentary canal of herbivorous mammals (and of man's ancestors) in which it is a sac in which bacteria digest the cellulose cell walls of vegetable food. Other examples are the vestiges of hind limb bones in snakes and of teeth in the jaws of young whalebone whales. Some marsupials, mammals that have been viviparous (live bearing) for 100,000,000 years, still show in their embryos vestiges of the egg tooth with which the embryo of the oviparous (egg-laying) ancestor cracked the eggshell.

Evidence from behaviour

Ethology (the study of behaviour) reveals similarities between different species that affirm their community of descent. This is the case, for example, in regard to the instincts in ants, bees, and wasps and to nest building among birds. Thrushes of separate species in Britain and in South America line their nests with mud in the same manner. Hornbills in Africa and in India both plaster up the female in a hole in a tree. In some cases it is possible to discern how instincts evolve. The three-spined stickleback has a complicated ritual of courtship behaviour, which resembles that of the ten-spined stickleback. The latter, however, utilizes simpler components of behaviour, demonstrating the evolutionary origins of the more complex acts performed by the three-spined stickleback.

The chemical characteristics of organisms are no less typical of their species than are their structures, embryonic development, or behaviour. Serology (the study of blood serum) provides evidence of the degree of divergence between the chemical composition of the blood of different animals. Human blood injected into a rabbit makes the latter produce antihuman serum, which, when mixed with human blood, causes clumping and settling (precipitation) of 100 percent of the blood protein. This antihuman serum precipitates blood of other species in the following percentages: gorilla, 64%; orangutan, 42%; baboon, 29%; ox, 10%; deer, 7%; horse, 2%; kangaroo, 0%. These figures serve as measures of chemical resemblance and affinity. It has been shown that seals resemble dogs, and whales resemble even-toed ungulates (*e.g.*, cattle)—results that, expressed as relative degrees of affinity, agree with the evidence from comparative anatomy, embryology, and paleontology.

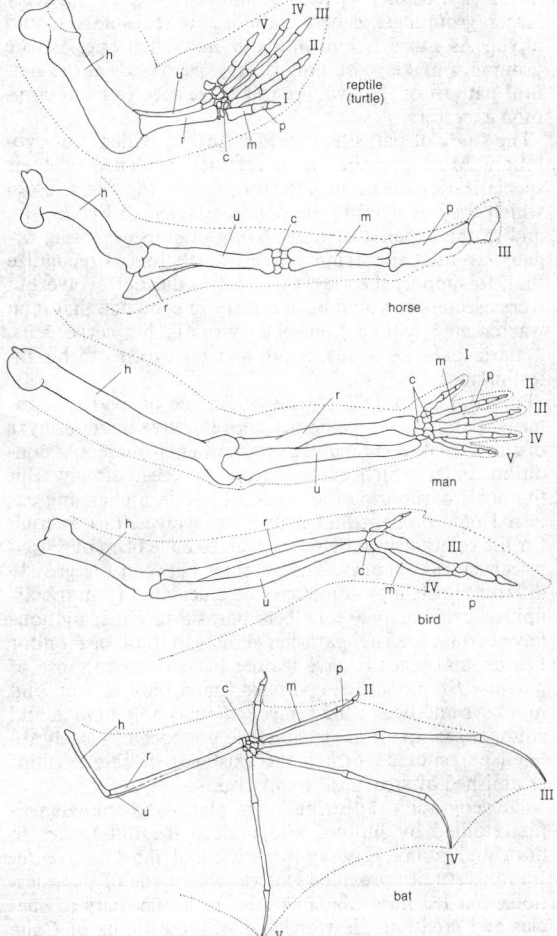

Figure 1: Homologies of the forelimb among vertebrates, giving evidence for evolution. Although the bones correspond, they are adapted to the specific mode of life of the animal. The abbreviations are: h, humerus; r, radius; u, ulna; c, carpals; m, metacarpal; p, phalanx. The Roman numerals indicate corresponding digits.

Biochemical evidence

Biochemistry provides countless further examples of similarities between species, of which one of the most instructive is the structure of the pancreatic enzyme insulin, which is made up of 51 amino acids, arranged in a particular order that varies in details in different related species. At the site where the insulin of cattle has serine, that of sheep has glycine; where insulins of both these species have alanine and valine, insulins of horse and pig have threonine and isoleucine, respectively, The general resemblance of the molecules of insulin in all these species is explicable as due to their descent from a common ancestor; the differences between them are due to adaptation evolved by each species.

An essential constituent of living cells is the protein enzyme cytochrome c, which carries out part of the process of respiration and has the same general chemical structure in bacteria, fungi, plants, and animals, but with differences in the arrangement of some of its constituents. The degrees of these differences make it possible to classify the organisms, in accordance with their evolutionary positions, into a phylogenetic tree (a diagramatic indication of evolutionary pathways). Assuming a fixed rate at which changes occur in evolution, it has been possible to calculate the time elapsed since the different forms of cytochrome c diverged from a common ancestor. In other words, the time lengths of the branches of the phylogenetic tree can be estimated.

The above results throw a new light on an old branch of biology: systematics, which is concerned with classification (see CLASSIFICATION, BIOLOGICAL). The basic biological unit in which organisms exist is the species; but species are not casually distributed as grains of sand on a beach or fancifully assorted as imaginary constellations

Evidence
from para-
sitology

in the sky. Rather, species fit naturally into successively larger groupings: genera, families, orders, classes, and phyla. As more is known about individual species, the groupings make sense only if they are based on the natural pattern of the evolution of these species from common ancestors.

The study of parasites provides further evidence of evolution. Most parasites have retained evidence of their specialization from an ancestral, free-living form, from which they evolved by becoming adapted to live on, in, and at the expense of other living organisms, losing organs essential for living a free life. Biologists recognize that, to support the view that species did not evolve but were created, it would be necessary to conclude that man was created with poliomyelitis virus in his nerve cells, malaria parasite in his blood, and tapeworms in his intestines.

Parasitology provides yet another line of evidence. Internal parasites (and external ones that live under a layer of fur or feathers) inhabit a constant environment, a condition under which evolution may proceed slowly. But the hosts harbouring the parasites live in a changing external environment and may have evolved fast enough for the relationships between them to have been obscured by structural changes. The affinities between the grossly different hosts may sometimes be elucidated from the affinities existing between their parasites. Thus, pythons have certain internal parasites similar to those of monitor lizards, and pigeons have feather lice similar to those of parrots. *Herpes simplex* virus is found only in man and monkeys and lice of the genus *Pediculus* only in man and chimpanzee. In all these cases, the presence of closely related parasites confirmed the existence of relationships established by structural comparisons.

Biogeo-
graphical
evidence

The geographical distribution of plants and animals was first studied by Buffon, who noticed the differences in flora and fauna between America and the Old World. Buffon's studies provided Darwin with some of the questions that led him to abandon belief in the fixity of species and creation. He wondered why the fauna of Cape Verde Islands has an African composition while that of the Galapagos Islands has South American characteristics. These similarities could be explained only by the evolution of Cape Verde species from African ones and Galapagos species from South American ones. The mechanism now understood for the origin of species makes it certain that each species originated only once and in only one area. There are many forms whose modern geographical distribution is discontinuous; for example, tapirs, now limited to South America and the East Indies. Lungfish are found only in South America, South Africa, and Australia. In each case, the distribution can be explained easily if the animals dispersed from the region where they originated and subsequently became extinct in intermediate regions. Extinct animals can often be found as fossils; fossil tapirs have turned up in North America, Asia, and Europe, and fossil lungfish have been found even more widely.

Evidence
from
paleon-
tology

Paleontology occupies a key position in evolutionary studies; the fossils in the earth's crust are objective evidence of the course taken by living organisms in their evolutionary history, or phylogeny (see PHYLOGENY). By themselves, fossils do not "prove" evolution, for it could be argued that they had all been specially created and then succumbed to catastrophes, as Cuvier believed. But such a view fails altogether to explain why the fossil forms in lineages studied on sufficient material fall in obvious series; nor does it explain why the feet, teeth, and body sizes of fossil horses are so closely correlated with the successive and different climatic conditions of their environment.

With the help of radioactive dating of the deposits in which they lie, it has been possible to determine the absolute ages of the fossils and to measure the rates at which different groups have evolved. The data are still approximate, but they provide an estimate of the dimensions of the fact and pageant of evolution and of its problems.

The earliest evidence of life in the crust of the earth

does not always consist of organisms themselves but may be found in chemical substances that are the result of the life of organisms, such as layers of oxidized iron and other chemical "fossils." In the atmosphere, the two stable isotopes of carbon, carbon-12 and carbon-13, are in a ratio of 99 to 1. Photosynthesis carried out by organisms, using sunlight energy, converts carbon dioxide into organic carbon compounds with a higher ratio of carbon-12 to carbon-13 than is found in ordinary rocks, thus indicating the former presence of living organisms, as in the Fig Tree deposits in Rhodesia, about 3,000,000,000 years old, in which traces of structure of bacteria and blue-green algae have been found, some surrounded by concentric layers of limestone secretion. Undoubted stalked bacteria and blue-green algae have been discovered in the Gunflint iron deposits of Ontario, nearly 2,000,000,000 years old. In the Bitter Springs Cherts of Australia, 1,000,000,000 years old, true green algae and fungi have been recognized. The oldest known fossil animal is an already well-developed wormlike form, *Xenusion*, 800,000,000 years old, from the Precambrian of Sweden. The first animals must have been soft and incapable of preservation as fossils. When the Cambrian Period began, 600,000,000 years ago, many forms of algal plants and invertebrate animals were already developed.

Genetic
evidence

It would require very special pleading to pretend that paleontology does not present objective evidence for evolution, but more direct evidence is now also available, first from cytogenetics. In long chromosomes of the fruit flies of the genus *Drosophila*, the genes in one species form a linear series that may be labelled ABCDEFGHI. In another species, the corresponding genes are in the order AEDCBFGHI; the section BCDE has been inverted. A third species has the order AEHGFBCDI; here the section DCBFGH of the second species has been inverted, which indicates that the third species was derived from the second, and it from the first.

III. The process of evolution

NATURAL SELECTION

Evolution is the product of improvement in adaptation, and it was adaptation that Darwin felt that he must explain before he could convince anyone of the fact of evolution. The logical approach to the principle of natural selection, therefore, begins with a consideration of adaptation.

Adaptation is a word with two meanings, one referring to a process and the other to its product. It is the biological process by which advantage is conferred on those organisms that have structures and functions enabling them to cope successfully with the conditions of their environment. The ecological position occupied by an organism, relative to the entire range of environmental variables, is called the niche. The word adaptation is also used to denote those structures and functions specialized for a particular role.

All living organisms are adapted to their modes of life in a general way, and each is adapted to the characteristics of its own niche. A plant depends on its roots, by which it absorbs water and inorganic salts in solution and by which it is anchored; it requires a stem, balanced by the geometrical distribution of its branches, as a result of which the plant is able to maintain a vertical position and support its leaves; and the leaves, in turn, are vital as sites of photosynthesis, the process whereby the energy from the sun is used to synthesize organic chemical compounds.

In addition to the general adaptations, which are common to all species in large groups of related organisms, there are also special adaptations that some species have and others lack, and it was for an explanation of the origin and cause of these adaptations that Darwin looked. A woodpecker, for example, possesses the gross adaptations common to flying birds: feathers, wings, beak, clawed, scaly feet, etc. As adaptations for subsistence on insect grubs hidden under the bark of trees, the typical woodpecker has four structures that make its search for food more efficient: two toes on each foot are turned backwards (instead of the usual one), enabling the bird to

toward smaller size

concealment from predators

heat dissipation in hot weather

structural problems relating to large size

capture of smaller prey

toward larger size

conservation of heat and water in cold weather

ability to see over vegetation to detect prey and predators

ability to go without food

mate selection

territorial defense

ability to subdue larger prey

Figure 2: Adaptive pressures that affect the size of a warm-blooded animal.

get a firm foothold on the bark of the tree; the tail feathers are stiff and serve to prop the bird in position while it bores; boring and flaking are done by a stout and strong beak, with which a hole is chiselled through the bark and into wood; finally, an exceptionally long tongue enables the bird to take the insects at the bottom of the holes. Among woodpeckers, each species has further specializations that adapt it to its own segment of the bark-foraging niche.

Another example is mistletoe, any of about 80 species of parasitic plants (the familiar species being in the genera *Phoradendron* and *Arceuthobium*) that live intimately spliced onto branches of trees, from which, not having true roots, the mistletoe obtains water and salts in solution while the chlorophyll in its green leaves enables it to carry on photosynthesis. In order to survive, mistletoe is dependent on three factors: an insect to pollinate its flowers; a bird to disseminate its seeds by eating the berries and depositing them with its droppings on the branches of suitable trees; and an appropriate tree on which the parasitic relationship can be established. These adaptations are held to have arisen from natural selection of heritable variations.

The change that can be achieved through selective breeding of parents possessing particular characters has been known since the Neolithic Period, when man began to cultivate plants and domesticate animals, increasing their size, yield, and other desired qualities. In Darwin's thinking, an important example of selection working on heritable variation was the comparison between wild bison (*Bison bison*) and Indian domestic cattle (*Bos indicus*) with humps, for the structural differences between them would certainly be recognized as of the value at least of separate species if they were found in nature, and one of them was not the result of artificial selection by man. Darwin was sure that the cause of change was selection and that those organisms that were better fitted to withstand the struggle for existence, which goes on everywhere, would prosper and perhaps oust those less well fitted. But how such a system of selection could operate in nature, long before any man was there to supervise it, baffled him until 1838, when he read English economist Thomas Malthus' *An Essay on the Principle of Population* and happened on the statement that, since human population, if unchecked, would increase in geometrical progression and double in 25 years while food supply increased only in arithmetical progression, famine, misery, and mortality constantly threatened the human race, and particularly its poorer classes.

Darwin saw that, since plants and animals are quite unable to increase their food supplies artificially, the principle of mortality automatically imposed by nature would apply to them in full force. Natural selection was entirely Darwin's idea, not derived from Malthus. The latter's theory of human population limitation did not take into account the great increases in per-acre food production made possible by modern agricultural tech-

niques and, therefore, requires modification in order to be entirely valid. It is, however, valid when applied to organisms in nature, and it explains how selection works in nature, in its most direct form, by killing the insufficiently adapted. Hence the term natural selection.

The basic principle of natural selection is fairly simple. Most organisms produce more offspring (eggs, seeds, or young individuals) than live to maturity. The number of individuals in most species remains more or less constant from year to year. There must be, therefore, a high rate of mortality (from starvation, predation, disease, malformation, and accidents of the physical environment), eliminating individuals at various stages of their lives: as eggs, embryos, larvae, juveniles, and adults. Within a population, individuals are not identical but show variation that may affect any character, structure, or function at random. Some variations have characters that allow their possessors to function more efficiently in the struggle for existence than those that lack these characters. In other words, they are better adapted, even by ever so little, to the conditions of their ecological niches. They live longer, leave more numerous and healthier offspring, and provide the majority of the parents of successive generations. Heredity ensures the resemblance between parents and offspring. By natural selection of heritable variation, successive generations will maintain and even improve on the degree of adaptation achieved by their parents.

Adaptations thus confer survival and reproductive value on their possessors, and the ecological conditions of the environment determine at every stage which variations are adaptive and which not. Natural selection therefore rams better adapted variants into their ecological niches under pressure and ejects other variants, thereby providing more available, unoccupied niches. The case of the woodpecker is explained by random variations in the foot, tail feathers, beak, and tongue, selected in the direction seen. It is relatively simple, but the same principle is involved in the complicated cases of parasites, such as malaria or tapeworm, both of which involve the interposition of an intermediate host (mosquito or fish) in the life history.

The mechanism of natural selection

VARIATION

Darwin never tired of repeating that without heritable variation natural selection could do nothing at all, and there would be no evolution. But neither Darwin nor anyone else at the time the *Origin of Species* was published had objective knowledge of variation, its nature and its origin, or of heredity. It was known that variation existed, and the only hypothesis then available was that of "blending inheritance," by which it was supposed that offspring struck an average between the characters of their parents. This meant that, at each generation, variance was halved and that after ten generations all variations would have been levelled off and obliterated. This meant, in turn, that the numerous observed variations would

Primitive views on variation

have to be recent. For instance, all the differences between two full brothers whose heredities were identical could only be explained as the result of variations that had arisen in their own early lifetimes.

It was known that "sports," now known as mutations (sudden changes in genetically controlled features), occurred and were inherited. It was also known that environmental factors and the effects of use and disuse could evoke bodily changes in individuals. It was then supposed that such effects also could be inherited, for one of the oldest folk beliefs (and fallacies) was the inheritance of acquired characters. (In Greek mythology, for example, when Phaethon drove the sun-chariot so close to the earth over Africa that it scorched the inhabitants black, they transmitted this character to their descendants, the Negro race.) It was found in the Old Testament, in the story of Jacob and Laban's sheep and goats, on which Jacob induced visual impressions to work at the time of conception. In some countries it was forbidden to show hares in shop windows in case pregnant women should see them and give birth to children with harelips.

In spite of faked results and the neglect of proper precautions in experiments, no case whatever is known of the inheritance of any modified character impressed on the body of a multicellular organism by the effect of the environment or use or disuse of organs. The proviso of multicellularity is necessary because in the reproduction of unicellular organisms, when the parent divides, part of its body (on which the environment may have induced a modification) passes straight into the bodies of the offspring, which may still show the environmental effect. This is not what is meant by inheritance, which results only from the transmission of genetic material in reproductive cells.

Mendelian genetics The Moravian monk Gregor Mendel filled the gap in Darwin's scheme in 1865, when he showed that characters are controlled by particles, now called genes, which exist in pairs (alleles), one member of each pair derived from each parent. He demonstrated that the particles do not become contaminated but remain pure and separate (segregate) at germ-cell formation, so that not more than one of each pair enters any one germ cell, and that they recombine at random at fertilization. At each cell division, genes copy themselves exactly but occasionally undergo sudden changes (mutations), after which they continue to copy themselves exactly in their changed state until they mutate again.

A further important fact discovered by Mendel was that some genes are stronger, more penetrant, than others and can make their effects visible in the offspring when such genes are inherited from one parent only—that is, are present in "single dose"; such genes control dominant characters. The weaker genes can manifest themselves in offspring only if inherited from both parents—that is, in "double dose"; such genes are called recessive, and when one is present in an organism paired with its dominant allele, its effects are hidden.

Mendel's work was ignored until 1900, when it was rediscovered. During the first 20 years of the present century, it was confirmed completely by a number of workers who showed that genes are carried in linear order in the chromosomes, which are visible in the nucleus at division. Genes carried on different chromosomes segregate at random exactly as required by Mendel's system, but genes carried on the same chromosome show "linkage" and are transmitted together unless the chromosome undergoes "crossing-over," when the linked genes become separated and segregate. The mechanism of the chromosomes provides exactly what is required to explain the distribution of Mendelian genes.

Genotype and phenotype To understand the role of inheritance in evolution, it is necessary to consider the relation between genetic transmission of factors (genes) and embryonic development of expressed characters, for it is only through embryonic development that characters arise at all. The genes of the organism, inherited from its parents, constitute its genotype, which determines and limits its capacity to respond to normal and abnormal environmental factors and to factors within the developing organism. Every event in embryonic development is a reaction and a response. No character is solely inherited and none solely acquired. Fish have had paired eyes in their heads since the Silurian Period, 400,000,000 years ago, yet today it is only necessary to add magnesium chloride to the water in which a fish is developing to obtain an abnormal fish with a median cyclopian eye. This means that 400,000,000 years of inheritance and the same period of the action of normal environmental factors have not fixed the development of paired eyes. Development is only normal in a normal environment. The product of development, the mature organism, is called the phenotype, and it is the result of interaction between the genotype and the environment. All that the genotype can do is to set the limits within which development takes place. Here attention must be turned to the problem of evaluating a variation that appears in a population, a problem that can only be solved by experiment. If the variation appears only when environmental conditions are changed (as when the organisms are moved from one climate to another or when the diet is changed) and disappears when the original environmental conditions are restored, the variation is nonheritable. It has not been incorporated into the genotype and is known as a modification or phenotypic variation. If the variation arises without any change in environmental conditions and continues to appear in the offspring, it is heritable and is known as a mutation or genotypic variation. Only genotypic variation provides heritable variation on which evolutionary change can be based; but the ability of an organism to undergo nonheritable modification in response to environmental factors may "cushion" it against some of the rigours of natural selection, and this ability itself may be genetically controlled.

Mutation is therefore the inception of heritable variation. It may affect only a single gene, as a result of imperfect replication of the molecule of deoxyribonucleic acid (DNA), of which the gene is composed, or it may affect whole chromosomes by duplicating one or more of them as extras, following imperfect cell division. In man the presence of one supernumerary chromosome is responsible for the serious disorder mongolism. When the complete set of chromosomes is increased two, three, four, or more times, the resulting condition, polyploidy, can play an important part in speciation in plants by producing genetic isolation between populations.

In addition to genotypic variation there is a category of "nongenetic" inheritance due to structures present in the extranuclear (cytoplasmic) part of the reproductive cell or fertilized egg. Such cytoplasmic transmission therefore does not involve Mendelian genes in chromosomes and is solely maternal, for the sperm has no cytoplasm. An example is the inheritance by plastids or plasmagenes (small bodies in the cytoplasm) that can be seen in some plants whose branches, normally green, change to white, and seeds from flowers born on such white branches give solely white plants. This type of inheritance does not have much potential for evolutionary change.

THE SYNTHETIC THEORY OF EVOLUTION

The evolution of dominance and recessiveness Even when Mendel's work was first rediscovered and was still imperfectly understood, it caused great controversy. On one side Mendelian geneticists maintained that their mutations were the only source of heritable variation and that their new characters appeared, ready-made, without any previous selection. The Darwinian selectionists objected that mutations were deleterious, if not pathological, that the sudden changes that they caused were incompatible with the slight gradual changes that Darwin's theory required, and that mutations, which bore no relation whatever to environmental conditions, were utterly incapable of explaining the origin and improvement of adaptation to those environmental conditions.

Such was the state of evolutionary studies when an English statistician, Sir Ronald Fisher, observed that the great majority of mutations controlled characters that were both recessive and deleterious and concluded that they were recessive because they were deleterious—in other words, that they had become recessive from a previous condition intermediate in character. That this view was correct was shown by experiments in which it was clear that the action of any one gene in controlling its character is itself under the control of the other genes, which form what is called the gene complex. The composition of the gene complex is constantly reshuffled at every fertilization when the segregated genes recombine at random. If a deleterious mutation appears, those gene complexes that reduce the effect of that mutation give survival value to their possessors; possessors of gene complexes that do not do this perish. This explains the remarkable situation of the dominant "eyeless" gene in the fruitfly (*Drosophila melanogaster*), a gene with obviously deleterious effects. Some individuals with "eyeless" genes can breed, but there is great mortality in the offspring. It is possible to establish a pure eyeless strain by careful maintenance of the breeding colony. If such breeding is continued for a few generations, flies are eventually produced that possess normal eyes. This does not mean that there has been any contamination of the eyeless gene, as is proved by crossing such genotypically eyeless (but phenotypically eyed) individuals with other individuals of the original wild type (the normal gene complex). The offspring of such crosses show the eyeless effect of the gene in all its original virulence. During the generations of breeding eyeless flies, there has been reshuffling of the gene complex at each generation with heavy mortality, but some gene complexes have obliterated the deleterious effects of the eyeless gene. This selection of gene complexes received experimental proof when the English geneticist E.B. Ford, studying the currant moth (*Abraxas grossulariata*), selected the same gene in opposite directions, making it dominant in one line and recessive in the other.

When one gene of a pair of alleles becomes recessive, the other necessarily becomes dominant, which is why the genotype of the "wild type" of organism found in nature contains so many dominant genes that mask recessives. These recessive genes are a contingency reserve for possible future use, any of which may be favoured by selection when conditions change, as they always do, unpredictably.

The relative importance of selection and mutation

The rates at which mutations of genes occur in nature have been estimated in organisms as diverse as bacteria, maize, flies, and man and found to be of the order of once in each gene pair, in each generation, in 500,000 individuals. This rate can be increased by physical and chemical mutagenic agents (X-rays, mustard gas, etc.), and in some cases the rate is itself subject to genetic control. In nature it is a slow rate, but it builds up into a stock of genetic diversity that supplies the heritable variation on which natural selection works.

The astronomical quantities of potential variation that can be produced by the Mendelian mechanism of segregation and recombination of genes is shown by Mendel's own example of the number of different genotypes produced in two generations when parents differing in only seven pairs of genes are mated; the number is 2,187. As the numbers of genes in higher organisms run into thousands, the number of genotypes resulting from their segregating and recombining at fertilization is three raised to the power of the number of differing genes. More heritable variation could be produced than ever is actually produced. This is the solution to the difficulty imposed on Darwin solely by the errors of the notion of "blending inheritance," the problem of accounting for a sufficient supply of heritable variation for natural selection to work on. Mutation maintains variation, while "blending inheritance" would annihilate it.

If mutations took place more frequently than they do, variants would be lost before natural selection had had time to derive from them what potential advantages they might present. Mutation not only need not but must not be too frequent.

Fisher's researches showed that the system of Mendelian genes that mutate occasionally, segregate, and recombine at random provides exactly the mechanism required to explain evolution by natural selection. They showed that

if the majority of mutant genes are recessive because they have become recessive, one may conclude that natural selection has acted against them (under the conditions that existed when they mutated). There is no "favourable breeze" of mutations, nor are mutations directed in any advantageous sense. When they first occur, mutations are not adaptive. This demonstration of the initial suppressive effect of natural selection on mutants means that all theories that include the concept directed variation (Lamarckism, program fulfillment, orthogenesis, providental guidance, and others) and that seek to explain evolution as a result of control of the direction in which mutation occurs, whether by supposed effects of use and disuse, satisfaction of needs, environmental factors, inherited "memory," or "inner urges," are contradicted flatly by the observed fact that natural selection acts against new mutants.

Mutation, at the rates at which it occurs, is quite incapable of establishing a character in a population if there is the slightest degree of selection exerted against it, and the forces of selection, or selective pressure, can be measured. The short-term effect of mutation on evolution is therefore minimal or nil. It has been calculated that previous mutations have already set up such a stock of potential heritable variation that if mutation were to stop altogether today, evolution would go on from now as far into the future as it has come in the past. It is selection, not mutation, that controls the direction, rate, and intensity of evolution. This conclusion, based on experiments in genetics, is confirmed from work in paleontology.

The way in which the character of organisms are affected by environmental changes is well illustrated by the evolution of the horse (Figure 3). At the start in Early Tertiary times (about 65,000,000 years ago), the habitat of the ancestral horses was swampy and the vegetation luxurious with leafy plants. To this environment the horse's ancestors (*Hyracotherium*) were adapted by feet with four splayed toes that did not sink in the mud and short teeth for browsing on and eating the soft leaves of trees and shrubs. Later, in the Miocene, the vegetation in many areas changed to grass, which contains silicon and would wear down short teeth. The horse's ancestors (*Merychippus*) then became adapted to this food by the evolution of long high-crowned teeth, capable of uninterrupted growth. At that time the ground was dry and hard, and the number of toes in the feet became reduced, finally to one, with a hoof and a spring joint. These animals were thus able to exploit the grassland niche, as it became more prevalent.

The evolution of the horse was never in a straight line. First many-toed, low-crown toothed browsers changed

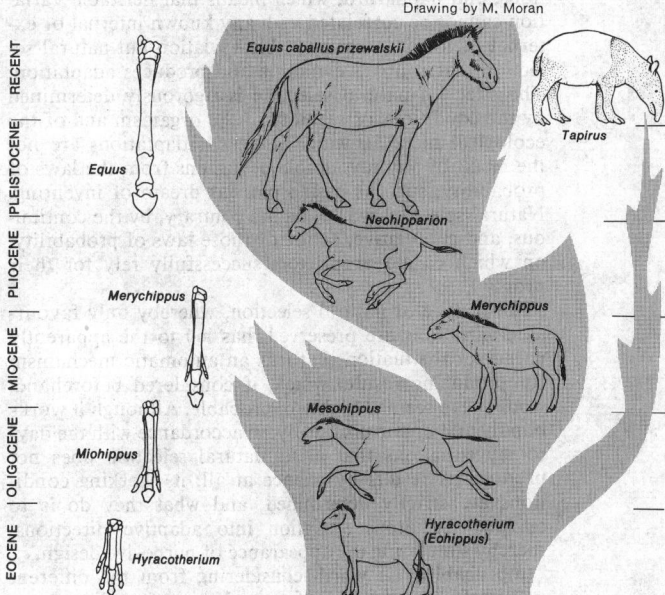

Drawing by M. Moran

Figure 3: Evolution of the horse.

into fewer-toed, high-crown toothed grazers; lastly, one-toed grazers were the surviving type. This evolution was correlated in each case with the changed conditions of the environment, both vegetable and physical, and as the various directions are different, the effect on the whole lineage is called "zig-zag" to stress the difference between this fact and the mistaken notion of "orthogenic" (straight line) evolution. In other words, it was adaptive, and in bringing it about natural selection acted opportunistically. Those forms that persisted in an old trend as the environment changed became extinct. Examination of a large number of specimens has shown that the direction and the speed of the various stages in the evolution of the horse were not correlated with the coefficients of variability of the organisms, nor with the length of life or generation time. At the start of the Tertiary, variability in *Hyracotherium* was great but tooth evolution slow; in the mid-Tertiary, teeth were evolving fast from the browsing to the grazing type, but variability was then small. As for generation time, it occupies only a few years in the opossums, which have evolved only little in the 60,000,000 years since the Eocene, during which time elephants, with a generation time of several decades, have evolved very rapidly.

Only natural selection, therefore, is left as the agent responsible for controlling the speed, direction, and intensity of evolution.

Attempts to invalidate natural selection On different grounds, attempts have been made to discredit natural selection, particularly by those who shy from its automatic mode of action. It has been alleged that structures of great complexity, such as the eye, would require an impossible degree of mathematical improbability if they were formed by "chance." But such a view betrays a misunderstanding of the problem. The eye was not produced out of nothing; ancestors of animals with eyes had simpler eyes, even single cells sensitive to light such as are found in the most primitive organisms. Improvement of function confers increased survival value from the start, and the same is true of all other cases subjected to rigorous analysis: electric organs, the origin of flight in birds, the parasitic habit of the cuckoo, the adaptation of whales to life in deep water, and the evolution of colour-vision. In each case, new functions and new organs were developed out of old ones. In colour-vision, the ability to distinguish colour is a by-product of two other improvements: accuracy of sight, and sight at low thresholds of light. Gradations can be made out, even in the evolution of such an organ as the eye. This is important because adaptations are not perfect and leave room for further improvement.

With regard to improbability and "chance," while mutation and recombination of genes are random, fortuitous, and haphazard, which means that heritable variation cannot be correlated with any known internal or external factor, it is not heritable variation but natural selection that controls evolution and produces adaptation. The effect of natural selection is rigorously determined by the conditions of viability of the organism and of the ecological niche in which it lives. Adaptations are not the result of any favourable deviations from the laws of probability, such as casino patrons dream of inventing. Natural selection works, on the contrary, by the continuous, and cumulative, action of those laws of probability, on which casino proprietors successfully rely for their profits.

The feature of natural selection, whereby only favourable variations are preserved, has led to the apparently paradoxical situation that it is an automatic mechanism for producing results which, if considered beforehand, would have seemed highly improbable. Although it works blindly and opportunistically, in accordance with the day-to-day situations that arise, natural selection does not produce its results by chance at all; its working conditions are strictly determined, and what they do is to channel fortuitous variation into adaptive directions, thereby simulating the appearance of purposive design.

Improbability is worth considering from the different points of view of time before and time after. The statistician Sir Ronald Fisher pointed out that the probability that a given man alive today should in the future have sons, grandsons, and successive descendants in the male line, uninterruptedly for 100 generations, is extremely small. By the very nature of sexual reproduction, however, every man alive today is living proof that such an uninterrupted line has in fact occurred, however improbable it might have been 100 generations ago.

The concept of purpose is another stumbling block for some in regard to natural selection, for adaptations are useful; they serve a purpose. In the eyes of those who, like the eighteenth century philosopher William Paley, believed that adaptations were evidence of the existence of a divine designer, an adaptation was the fulfillment of a design, and a proof of teleological purpose. Paley was uncomfortable in trying to reconcile the horrible cruelty and suffering in the animal kingdom with divine purpose. But the word purpose has two meanings. In the first, the concept of the end result to be achieved precedes the means used to achieve that end, as in theological teleology. In the second, the word purpose describes the use for which anything may serve, without implying that it came into existence in order to serve for that use. This is applicable to any structure or function that has arisen by natural selection of random and fortuitous variations. The opportunistic quality of natural selection rules out any teleological definition of purpose. The term teleonomic has been introduced to describe the purpose served by an adaptation.

It has been argued that natural selection cannot account for the evolution of beauty. Beauty is a subjective aesthetic impression, with which natural science is not competent to deal. Organisms which man calls beautiful can be explained on wholly functional grounds. Flowers are often cited to illustrate beauty. It may be noted that no plant that is pollinated solely by the wind has a coloured flower; coloured flowers were evolved as adaptations to attract insects, which serve for cross-pollination. In the same way, coloured fruits were evolved, attracting birds which eat them and disseminate the seeds. In each case, the selective advantage is obvious.

Several writers have suggested that, in addition to the "microevolution" that produces species, there is also a process of "macroevolution" that, through a sudden and major genetic change, may produce a whole new organism, assignable to a different major taxonomic category from that of its parents and founding a new line; but no evidence from nature has been offered to support such a theory, which appears to run counter to the wealth of information on natural selection. The evidence that all evolution has gone through the mill of speciation appears to be overwhelming.

NATURAL SELECTION IN ACTION

One of the most striking examples of observable evolution is the phenomenon known as industrial melanism, the prevalence in a normally light-coloured species of black or dark (melanic) individuals, due to environmental changes brought about by industry.

Industrial melanism Until the middle of the 19th century, the British peppered moth (*Biston betularia*) was known only in its grey form, admirably adapted by its coloration and habits to escape detection by birds when stationary in daylight on the lichens on the bark of trees. About 1850 an occasional black mutant (given the subspecific name *carbonaria*) appeared and was so conspicuous that black individuals were rapidly taken by bird predators on the bark of trees and the mutation was largely suppressed. Like most mutations, it was recurrent (further evidence of the non-adaptive nature of mutations) and the mutant moths suppressed. Meanwhile, the Industrial Revolution brought about a marked change in the environment in several parts of Britain, especially in manufacturing districts, where air pollution by carbon dust and soot killed the lichens on the trees and blackened the trunks and branches. Now it was the *carbonaria* mutant that was favoured, and the original pale *betularia* form penalized.

Direct observations of feeding birds by H.B.D. Kettlewell provided a measurement of the survival rates of the two forms in normal and in industrial areas. Some observations indicated that *carbonaria* survived 17% worse in unpolluted areas, and 10% better in polluted areas, where the populations of peppered moth were now completely dark by 1950. The dark moths are now blacker than those affected by the original mutation, due to reinforcing action of the gene-complex.

Here, then, is a mutation which conferred disadvantage on its possessors under the environmental conditions in which it arose, but which, as a result of an unpredictable change in those environmental conditions, now confers marked advantage in survival. It has resulted in the evolution of the moth from grey to black in a short space of time, under human observation. Similar changes have been observed in nearly 100 other species of insects and spiders, which reveal the opportunistic working of natural selection.

Sickle cell A gene called "Sickle" controls the synthesis of an abnormal hemoglobin in man's red blood cells and deforms them so that instead of disc-shaped they are elongated like sickles and liable to break down, resulting in anemia, thrombosis, or death. The gene is prevalent among inhabitants of West Africa, and is intermediate between dominance and recessiveness. When one sickle-gene is present, and the other gene is the normal allele, pathological effects are produced only in extreme conditions of oxygen deficiency: in shortness of breath, or at high altitudes. When two sickle-genes are present, pathological effects are manifest in normal conditions. The abnormal hemoglobin in the sickle red cells, however, has the unexpected property of preventing the malaria parasite *Plasmodium falciparum* from entering the cells and completing its life cycle in them. Sickle therefore confers immunity to malaria, and a balance is struck between the danger of death from malaria without sickle, and death from thrombosis with two sickle-genes. The condition of one normal and one sickle-gene is therefore favoured, and the equilibrium frequency of sickle in West Africa is about 20% of the population. Among Negroes in the United States, where there is no endemic malaria, the frequency has dropped to 9%. The change has taken place, under natural selection, in less than three centuries, and such a change in gene frequency in a population is itself evolution. Here again a deleterious mutation has come to confer survival value under the unpredictable environment factor of malaria.

Intensity of selection The mathematical implications of natural selection were worked out by Sir Ronald Fisher, geneticists J.B.S. Haldane and Sewall Wright and others. A coefficient of selective advantage is obtained by calculating the number of individuals of one form of variant that survive to breed, relative to the number of another. Selection coefficients are difficult to determine in natural populations, but in a few cases of strikingly evident variants, such as the melanic form of the peppered moth, figures have been gained by direct observations. Assuming a coefficient of 0.1% (1,001 of one type surviving for every 1,000 of the other) and assuming the mutant is dominant it would take 11,739 generations to increase the number of individuals in a population from one individual in one million to 500,000 in a million; if the mutant is recessive the number of generations required to achieve the same result is 321,444. Mutants, thus, have to become dominant if they are to spread through a population. These calculations are for a very weak coefficient of selection; but the peppered moth shows that the amount of change produced in the populations in the time observed, from 99% grey to 99% black in polluted areas, indicates a much higher selective advantage, which can reach 30%. This value can also fluctuate at different seasons. The peppered moth has evidently been subjected to intense selective pressure in polluted areas, to change the mean of the population from grey to black in only about 200 generations. This is an example of dynamic selection resulting, as always, from change in environmental conditions.

When an environment remains constant for an appreciable time, advantage accrues to the optimal phenotype already built up to that environment by natural selection, and variation from that phenotype is penalized. An ex-

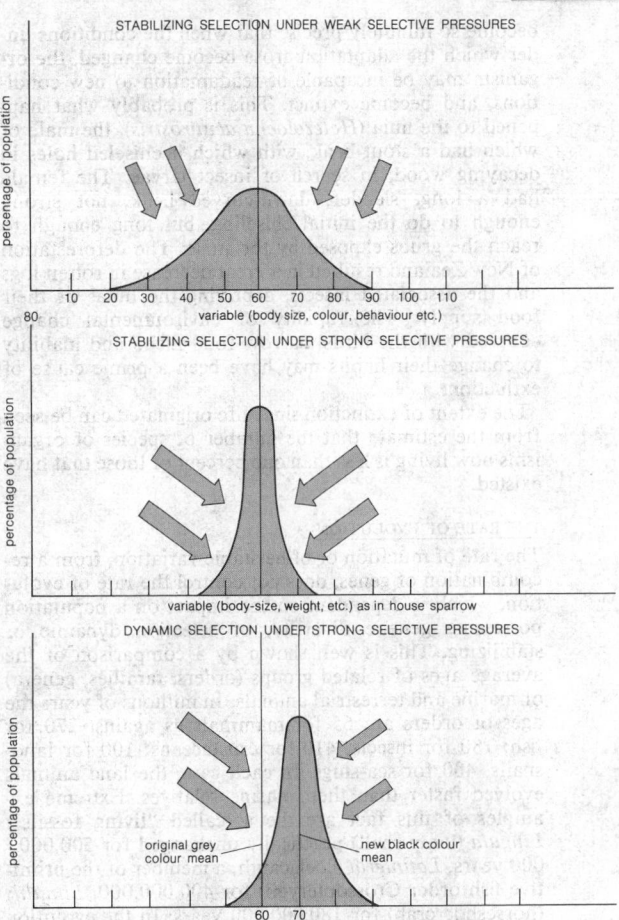

Figure 4: Effects of variation selective pressure of different strengths, under stabilizing and under changing conditions. Arrows indicate selective pressure.

ample is the observation of the viability of house sparrows picked up after very severe weather, and comparison of the characters of the survivors with those of the dead. The survivors were more uniform in size, weight, etc., and the dead more variable. Too big or too heavy was as bad as too small and too light. This is an example of stabilizing selection (also called centripetal), which can also vary in intensity and allow a population a wide or a narrow margin of tolerance in variation, according to the number and activity of predators or the rigour of physical conditions. At the same time it must be remembered that the many characters of an organism are exposed to selection in different directions; the phenotype is a compromise.

For theologians like Paley, adaptations were *ex hypothesi* perfect. This was not Darwin's experience, for in many of the places he visited on the voyage of the "Beagle," he found that recently introduced species had become more numerous than the old indigenous species, which meant that the latter were not perfectly adapted, and that others could do better. Adaptations may be imperfect in spite of the purpose which they generally serve. An example of a gene that is frequently maladaptive is the RH blood group (Rhesus factor) in man. An Rh+ fetus in the uterus of an Rh− mother produces antigens that cross the placental barrier into the mother's blood stream. The mother produces antibodies which pass back to the fetus and may cause fatal hemolytic disease. No positive adaptive value has yet been discovered for the Rh system. Mammals have been viviparous for a hundred and fifty million years, but the immunological mechanism has not yet become adapted to the Rh blood-group genes. The importance of the existence of imperfect adaptations is that it provides scope for further evolution; if adaptations were perfect, no improvement and no evolution would be possible.

Imperfect and excessive adaptation

On the other hand, adaptation may in other cases have

become so minutely precise that when the conditions under which the adaptation arose become changed, the organism may be incapable of readaptation to new conditions, and become extinct. This is probably what happened to the huia (*Heterolocha acutirostris*), the male of which had a stout beak, with which it chiseled holes in decaying wood, in search of insect larvae. The female had a long, slender, down-curved beak, not strong enough to do the initial chiseling, but long enough to reach the grubs exposed by the male. The deforestation of New Zealand resulted in a great decrease in rotten logs and the associated insects, depriving the huias of their food supply. The rapidity of environmental change coupled with the birds' narrow food niche and inability to change their habits may have been a prime cause of extinction.

The extent of extinction since life originated can be seen from the estimate that the number of species of organisms now living is less than one percent of those that have existed.

THE RATE OF EVOLUTION

The rate of mutation or of heritable variation, from a recombination of genes, does not control the rate of evolution, which is dependent on the impact on a population possessing genetic diversity, of selection dynamic or stabilizing. This is well shown by a comparison of the average ages of related groups (orders, families, genera) of marine and terrestrial animals. In millions of years the ages of orders are 65 for mammals as against 270 for fish; 180 for insects, 410 for crustaceans; 100 for land-snails, 400 for sea-slugs. In each case, the land animals evolved faster than their marine relatives. Extreme examples of this fact are the so-called "living fossils": *Lingula* (lamp-shell) practically unchanged for 500,000,-000 years, *Latimeria* (coelacanth, a member of the primitive fish order Crossopterygii) for 400,000,000, *Limulus* (horseshoe crab) for 180,000,000 years. In the evolution of horses during 60,000,000 years, the average rate per genus was 7,500,000 years.

Another method of estimating rates of evolution is to calculate the number of new genera known to have originated per million years. During approximately 60 million years of the Tertiary, the figure for mammals was 30, and for fishes only six. There are two reasons for this difference between marine and terrestrial animals in evolution rate. First, the marine environment has changed little and slowly; a form living in it is subjected more to stabilizing than to dynamic selection. On land, geological, physical, and biological (food-supply) factors have constantly changed, and unless a population could respond efficiently to the dynamic selection to which it was exposed, it became extinct. The second reason is that the waters in the oceans are continuous, resulting in less isolation of populations, an important factor in speciation.

It can be shown that the rate of evolution is also correlated with new possibilities of ecological advantage. The conquest of a new medium (freshwater, dry land, or air) by a successful group gives opportunities for rapid adaptive radiation (the attainment of diversity in an evolutionary line) such as was shown by early land plants, land animals, and by birds. In insects and flowering plants the ecological advantages are reciprocal; since the Jurassic, when both of these groups originated, adaptations of each group have been closely interrelated with those of the other. Insects get pollen and nectar from the flowers, and plants benefit from the cross-pollination that the visiting insects ensure. On the other hand, plants have had to contend with attacks by insects, and insects have had to adapt to the defense mechanisms of plants.

Adaptation to a new food supply is correlated with evolutionary acceleration, as shown by whales, which diversified rapidly at the start of the Tertiary. The large teeth of primitive whales, such as the Eocene *Protocetus*, enabled them to feed on large prey. Later, some whales took to feeding on small cuttlefish and evolved smaller dentition, as in modern beaked whales (Physeteridae). Finally, one line of toothed whales evolved baleen, al-

lowing them to take advantage of the enormous supply of tiny shrimplike crustaceans (krill) by turning their gaping mouths into shrimp nets. Each of these changes coincided with a bout of more rapid evolution.

The rate of evolution is also influenced by the place that an animal occupies in the food chain of its environment. Small organisms that drift about in the sea (plankton), algae, larvae, or krill have no chance against their predators, and their survival depends on high reproductive rate and acceleration of development to make up for losses. But in the case of animals that actively accomplish or resist capture by the use of efficient sense organs, nervous coordination, and muscular movement, as in mammals and birds, at the top of their food chains, evolution is rapid, and the reproductive rate usually is low.

These factors have played a part in the location of centres of evolution. Natural selection has most heritable variation to work on in species whose populations have large numbers of individuals, in which the incidence of recombination of genes and of mutation is greatest. Such populations cover wide areas, which is why the major centre of evolution of land animals was in the tropical regions of the Old World. There, with evolution occurring faster and natural selection more intense, the survivors became dominant groups while their predecessors, less efficient, were driven away to the ends of the landmasses, western Europe, South Africa, Australia, and South America. It is in these remote areas that discontinuous geographical distribution of relic faunas is principally found. Marsupials, which originally had a universal distribution, have become restricted to America and to Australasia, where they radiated, protected from the more efficient placental mammals by a water gap. There have been other centres of evolution for smaller groups. Elephants evidently originated in northeastern Africa and southern Asia, whence they spread all over the world. These far-flung elephant populations, despite adaptations for habitats other than that at the centre of origin, were mostly extinct by the end of the Pleistocene. It is possible that some may have been extirpated by Neolithic man. Horses and camels apparently originated in North America, then spread over the world, and later became extinct in North America. Man's centre of origin was East Africa.

It is evident, therefore, that selection has controlled the speed, intensity, and direction of evolution, in populations with genetic diversity. Selection has been able to do this because the Mendelian mechanism on which it works is able, as circumstances require, to produce either stability or change: stability because genes do not contaminate each other, are often "linked," and mutate only seldom; change because genes do mutate, can undergo "crossing-over," segregate at germ-cell formation, and are recombined at random at fertilization.

In view of the paramount part that natural selection has played in evolution, by acting on heritable variation in such a way as to originate and improve adaptation, it may be asked whether all characters of organisms are or were adaptive. The answer to the question is complex. For the majority of cases it is yes; for some special cases it may be no.

It cannot be doubted that, in general, characters were adaptive under the conditions in which they evolved. But conditions change, and characters that were advantageous can become neutral or even disadvantageous. An example of an adaptation that became a handicap is the antlers of the Irish elk (*Megaloceros*), which became extinct, possibly because the exaggerated size of their antlers impeded their movement in forests. Sir Julian Huxley has shown that the size of the antlers is a result of the mechanism of allometric growth—*i.e.*, that the growth of a part (the antlers) is an exponential function of the growth of the animal as a whole. Selection pressure in favour of the size of the animal (as in most ungulates) was then counterbalanced by selection against the excessive size of the antlers, and these are no longer adaptive but, instead, were harmful. This illustrates two principles: that characters that confer advantage in early adult life may become harmful in postreproductive stages

Nonadaptive and adaptively neutral mechanisms

and that characters controlled by an allometric growth mechanism may increase against selection pressure until it becomes too strong for the genotype as a whole.

Another method by which characters can arise without being selected for is by means of the fact that many genes have multiple effects (pleiotropy), and if they are selected favourably for some effects, others even if selectively neutral or slightly disadvantageous can arise and persist, provided that they do not become sufficiently harmful to outweigh the advantages of other effects, in which case natural selection would act against their possessors. Species can overcome this difficulty by rendering the advantageous effects of such pleiotropic genes dominant and their disadvantageous effects recessive or by the selection of other genes that mask the deleterious effects of the pleiotropic ones.

A method of short-term bypassing of natural selection and producing structures that appear to be nonadaptive is seen in those cases in which sheer reproductive ability of a member of a species results from characters that appear to be maladaptive. In birds of paradise, the fantastic ornamental feathers of the males may, through preferential sexual selection by females (see below), result in the greater reproductive success of the most extravagantly decorated males, to the detriment of the viability of the species, protected by lack of predators. In plants a comparable condition is found in which the greater speed of growth of the pollen tubes, from the stigma of the flower to the ovule, may result in reproductive advantage in spite of whatever disadvantageous genes the pollen tubes may carry. But natural selection eventually catches up with such bad characters when conditions harden. Great reproductive ability confers advantage only when it is the result of adaptation of the species as a whole to its environment.

Genetic drift

"Random genetic drift" has been proposed as a principle providing for the possibility that in isolated populations, so small that the laws of probability do not apply in the usual manner, random survival of characters may occur without selection, which would allow for the existence and survival of nonadaptive characters. But it would be possible only where the selective disadvantages of such survivals were extremely small and could not be effective against the most mild adverse pressure of selection in populations exceeding 500 individuals. So-called genetic drift cannot, therefore, be of more than negligible importance in evolution.

IV. Speciation

The origin of new species and evolution are not synonymous. A certain amount of evolution can take place, as in the peppered moth, without the end product ceasing to be of the same species. It therefore becomes necessary to define the species in modern terms: it is an interbreeding gene pool, such that a mutant that appears anywhere in its range is, in principle, capable of spreading to any other part of the range. This is why evolution can also be defined as a statistical change in the gene pool.

A new species arises when part of a population has undergone sufficient evolution (i.e., has accumulated enough genetic change) along the lines of adaptation to its own environment that interbreeding with other populations of the ancestral species is rendered at first unusual and later impossible (see SPECIES AND SPECIATION). The key criterion in determining whether or not speciation has occurred is whether the populations are reproductively isolated.

The usual first step toward speciation is the formation of different local races, a process that has been well studied in the spread of the house sparrow (Passer domesticus, also called English sparrow) in North America. First introduced about 1850 into the northeastern United States, this species spread to Mexico and the Pacific coast and became diversified into a number of distinguishable populations, differing mostly in accordance with certain ecological "rules." One of these, enunciated in 1847, states that body size in any species of warm-blooded animals is larger in populations inhabiting in colder climates than in those of warm climates. The adaptive significance of larger body size involves the reduction of heat loss by reduction of surface-volume ratio. It has also shown in 1833 that black pigment is reduced in hot, dry climates and brown pigment is reduced in cold damp climates. North American populations of the house sparrow have produced recognizable differences in fewer than 100 generations. It is doubtful that the differences are sufficient to affect interbreeding.

Populations actually in the process of speciation are seen in certain gulls of the genus Larus that occupy a U-shaped range around the North Pole, with the two ends of the loop overlapping in Great Britain, where the western end of the loop is occupied by the European lesser black-backed gull (L. fuscus), a medium-sized gull with a dark-gray mantle. Populations of the dark-mantled birds intergrade gradually eastward into those of the herring gull (L. argentatus), a light-mantled species of Siberia and North America. The herring gull extends across the Atlantic Ocean to England and Scandinavia, where it coexists with the lesser black-back. The British species also differs ecologically: the lesser black-backed gull breeds inland on moors and is migratory; the herring gull breeds on cliffs and is resident. The pitch and frequency of their calls are different. Here, then, are two gulls at opposite ends of their geographical range that still belong to the same gene pool if a mutant can be imagined as passing from gull to gull round the North Pole but that in Europe have become adapted to different ecological niches. The gulls are an example of both geographical and ecological isolation. Geographical and ecological isolation also is found in the ground finches of the Galapagos Islands, which drew Darwin's attention to the possibility of evolution.

Changes in chromosome number

Genetic isolation is produced when an organism multiplies the number of its chromosomes (polyploidy). This is particularly important in producing hybrids that cannot breed with either parental stock because of the incompatibility of their sets of chromosomes with each parental species. A hybrid primrose formed by crossing Primula floribunda with P. verticillata underwent a doubling of the number of chromosomes possessed by the parental species, which meant that each chromosome then had a compatible partner for the mechanism of cell division. This polyploid hybrid was then able to set fertile seed and develop into a plant with its own constant characters, whose offspring bred true. The new plant was intersterile with both its parent species. It therefore fulfilled all the requirements of a new species and is Primula kewensis, formed in the laboratory.

V. Major steps of evolution

THE ORIGIN OF LIFE

Whether the earth cooled from a molten mass or condensed out of cold dust, life could not have existed when the earth was formed some 5,000,000,000 years ago; it must have originated since. Several well-known scientists have shown that the primitive atmosphere must have been a reducing one (i.e., without free oxygen). When a sample atmosphere of hydrogen, water vapour, ammonia, and methane was subjected to electric discharges and ultraviolet light, large numbers of organic compounds—fatty acids and amino acids, the building blocks of proteins—were obtained by automatic synthesis. This proved that a prebiological synthesis of complex compounds was possible. It is now believed that phosphates, enzymes, and nucleic acids were formed in this way on the primeval earth under ultraviolet light energy. Enzymes accelerate the synthesis of complex compounds out of simple substances and nucleic acids replicate. As both processes are the characteristic of life, it is not unreasonable to suppose that life originated in a watery "soup" of prebiological organic compounds and that living organisms arose later by surrounding quantities of these compounds by membranes that made them into "cells." This is usually considered the starting point of organic ("Darwinian") evolution.

These organisms must have fed on compounds in the water in which they were bathed, as primary heterotrophs (food takers). But as the supply of compounds would become exhausted, the next stage must have been the development of mechanisms of synthesis, utilizing chemical energy (as in some bacteria) or light energy (as in other bacteria and blue-green algae), thus converting the organisms into autotrophs (food makers). In bacteria and blue-green algae the genetic material, deoxyribonucleic acid (DNA), was not organized into nuclei; such cells are called procaryotes.

SEX, PLANTS, AND ANIMALS

The fundamental basis of sex is not sexual differences but the interchange of genetic material (syngamy) between individuals, resulting in heritable variation through recombination. No such interchange has been observed in blue-green algae, which have remained virtually unchanged for 3,000,000,000 years. Bacteria show primitive and incomplete interchange.

Following the envelopment of living material in a membrane, the next step was the organization of DNA into nuclei in each cell, with chromosomes bearing the genes in linear order. Such organisms are called eucaryotes and include all organisms above bacteria. The mechanism of Mendelian genetics was then able to work and to increase enormously the scope of variation, on which natural selection acted. Another advance was the development of the green pigment chlorophyll, which enabled organisms to build up organic compounds from carbon dioxide in the air and salts in water in the soil, under the action of sunlight. Photosynthesis evolved in one-celled organisms (protists), which produced the higher plants (tracheophytes). Plants are complete autotrophs, the prime producers of proteins, carbohydrates, and fats.

Life involves not only synthesis but also the degradation of organic compounds, in which some bacteria play a part. Other organisms make use of decomposing matter as a source of supply and have lost the power of photosynthesis; these are fungi, which may be a separate evolutionary line. Other organisms obtain their food ready-made by eating living plants or other organisms that, like themselves, eat plants. These are animals that have completely lost the power of synthesizing their substance from simple compounds and, as secondary heterotrophs, are ultimately entirely dependent on plants for their existence.

VIRUSES

Viruses, very minute particles of nucleic acid surrounded by protein shells, present a problem. Their simplicity has led some to believe that they are relics of a precellular stage of organic evolution, but this is unlikely. Viruses are incapable of free existence and can persist only as parasites inside living cells. Their DNA behaves like genes and mutates (producing new strains of viral diseases) and their enzymes force the host-cells that they parasitize to synthesize more viruses out of the host cell's materials. Unlike living organisms that multiply only by some form of division of their own bodies, the "bodies" of viruses do not divide to produce the next "generation" of viruses. Instead, the new generation is the result of synthesis enforced on the parasitized organism. The prevailing view of virologists is that viruses were derived by degenerate evolution from portions of nuclei or even genes of parasitic bacteria or protozoa in living host-cells.

MULTICELLULAR ORGANIZATION, DEATH, AND EMBRYONIC DEVELOPMENT

Unicellular organisms, reproducing by division, are potentially immortal, barring accidents, and, being single cells, exchange genetic material by temporary fusion in pairs. In order to fuse, germ cells must be able to move and to meet, but in order that the fertilized egg about to embark on embryonic development can live, it must contain a supply of food to last until the developing organism can feed itself. This led to a differentiation between large germ cells containing food materials but incapable of movement (eggs) and small germ cells consisting of little more than a nucleus but capable of movement (sperms). Subsequent sexual differences follow from the

dimorphism between egg-producing females and sperm-producing males.

The multicellular stage of life arose, allowing greater size and differentiation of parts of the body, with different structures and functions, all of which conferred survival value. Syngamy, with its all-important production of variability for selection to work on, can take place only between single cells whose nuclei fuse and genes recombine. In multicellular organisms a division of labour has arisen, with single germ cells serving for reproduction of the organism and the whole of the rest of the body functioning to support and protect the germ cells. Syngamy, which is the fertilization of these germ cells (gametes, whose genetic material is potentially immortal), produces the next generation, by growth and differentiation to build up bodies similar to those of their parents. But the price to be paid for the advantages of multicellularity is that the multicellular body must die.

COLONIZATION OF LAND

After 2,500,000,000 years of life in water, organisms began to colonize land, about 500,000,000 years ago. At that time consequences of the different methods of feeding of plants and animals became conspicuous. Plants, needing nothing but ubiquitous carbon dioxide and salts in solution, remained stationary. Animals, requiring living food, had to move to obtain it and so evolved muscles and skeletal structures, sense organs to find the food, and nervous systems to coordinate the impulses from sense organs and transmit appropriate responses to muscles. Movement is most efficient along one axis in one permanent direction; the front end becomes a head and, in it, a brain. These features were already present in water, but in land animals they became accentuated.

The first plants and the first animals established on land were still in need of water for the sperm to swim in and find the eggs, as in the modern mosses, horsetails, ferns, and Amphibia. In the Amphibia, water remained necessary for the embryo to develop in. With the formation of pollen grains (containing the sperm) and ovules (containing the eggs), fertilization (pollination) in plants could take place in dry habitats. In animals, internal fertilization and the enclosure of the embryo in an eggshell likewise made life on dry land possible. Mammals improved on this system by retaining the fertilized egg within the mother's body.

When plants were established on dry land, ovule-producing and pollen-producing leaves, surrounded by coloured petals and protective sepals (also leaves), resulted in flowers that attracted insects that performed cross-pollination. Seeds are embryos packed up ready for dissemination.

VI. Patterns of evolution

Improvement and adaptive radiation. In the evolution of a lineage (a long continuous genetic line), it is possible to make out five stages. First comes divergence of parts of the species from the original stock. This splitting is the start of cladogenesis (the initiation of a new clade, or evolutionary line). Next comes improvement of the adaptation in relation to the environment. This can mean the degeneration associated with extreme parasitism, but in the vast majority of cases, improvement results in increased complexity and differentiation (anagenesis). If the improvement enables a lineage to break through and colonize a new environment (land, air), where there are usually very numerous and diverse ecological niches yet unfilled, there is a rapid increase in numbers and variation, and multiple divergence (adaptive radiation). Examples are seen in the succession of dominant forms in geological times: seed ferns, conifers, flowering plants; amphibia, reptiles, mammals, and birds. Next comes a phase of stability (stasigenesis) leading to persistent types (coelacanths) or "living fossils." Finally, extinction may overtake the lineage when conditions change, variability is insufficient to allow readaptation, and natural selection takes its toll.

Paedomorphosis and clandestine evolution. Embryos of related animals show great similarity, evidence of their

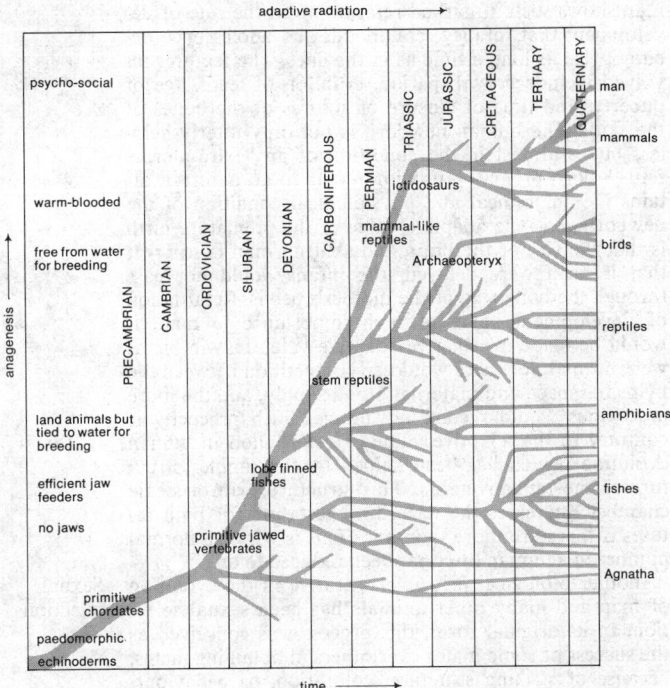

Figure 5: Anagenesis and adaptive radiation.

descent from a common ancestor whose embryonic development they repeat for early stages. The 19th-century German biologist Ernst Haeckel believed that in their embryonic development, the embryos of descendants recapitulated the evolutionary stages that their ancestors occupied as adults; the earlier the embryonic stage the more remote the adult ancestor. This theory, the reverse of the truth, would mean that evolutionary novelties were added only to the end stages of the development. Far from the young descendant representing the adult ancestor, it is much more important that in many cases the adult descendant resembles the young ancestor, by retardation of development, retention of the ancestral juvenile features, discarding the ancestor's adult stage, and evolving a new adult stage of its own. This process is known as paedomorphosis and is found in lineages that have led to markedly successful cases of evolution, with extensive adaptive radiation. It is a method of avoiding excessive specialization and has been suggested as a possible mode of origin of insects from young millipedes, of vertebrates from young (larval) echinoderms, and of man from juvenile apes.

Paedomorphosis has an important consequence for paleontology. It means that the evolutionary changes that will lead to the next step take place in the young stages, but these often lack hard skeletal structures and are not preserved as fossils. When the old adult stage is lost and a new adult stage takes its place, the new form arises without "paleontological warning," by clandestine evolution—one reason that the great successful groups appear more or less suddenly in the fossil record, with a gap between them and the ancestral form. The Carpoidea, fossils from the Lower Cambrian, hitherto classified with echinoderms, have been shown to have had gill slits and fishlike brains and to be related to ancestors of vertebrates. They are now called Calcichordata.

Mosaic evolution. In the evolution of each of the five classes of vertebrates, the fossil record has preserved forms that are roughly intermediate between two successive grades. The most important of these is *Archaeopteryx*, the remarkable feature of which is that some of its structures are purely reptilian (small brain, long tail, free fingers), others are purely avian (feathers, wing, furcula or wishbone, reversed fourth toe). In the transition from reptile to bird there was no general and gradual conversion of all the parts at the same time, but some remained reptilian while others became completely transformed to the bird type. This pattern is called mosaic evolution. It

can be recognized in the other intermediate forms, between fish and amphibia, amphibia and reptiles, reptiles and mammals, and also in the evolution of man.

Mosaic evolution can also be recognized in plants. In the seed ferns that formed the bulk of the coal forests, the stem and fronds were like those of true ferns from which they probably evolved, but the seeds were like those of cycads (flowering plants allied to conifers), into which they evolved.

Parallel and convergent evolution. Some groups of animals that have diverged can later evolve lineages that show resemblances. The simplest case of this is in parallel evolution. Marsupials were the dominant form of mammals in late Mesozoic times. In the Tertiary the greater efficiency of placental mammals resulted in the elimination of many marsupials, but in Australasia, protected from the placentals by a water gap, marsupials underwent adaptive radiation. A carnivorous marsupial, the Tasmanian wolf (*Thylacinus*), filled an ecological niche like that filled by the placental true wolf (*Canis*), and the two are similar in shape, teeth, and habits.

In some cases organisms from two or more unrelated or only distantly related lines show remarkable resemblances, a type of evolution called convergence. An excellent example is provided by marine reptiles and mammals that became fishlike. Reptiles as a group of land animals evolved from fish through amphibians. Several lines of reptiles have returned to the aquatic environment, and one group, the Mesozoic ichthyosaurs (literally, "fish-reptiles"), were fishlike in body shape and had dorsal and caudal (tail) fins. During the Triassic, when the ichthyosaur line was radiating in the marine environment, another line of reptiles, the terrestrial synapsids, produced the mammals. Several mammalian lines subsequently became adapted to the marine environment. Dolphins and porpoises especially, while preserving the basic mammalian characters, show close similarity to the fishes and ichthyosaurs in body shape and fins. Adaptation to a predacious life in a similar medium, through natural selection, resulted in this convergent evolution. In general, parallel evolution is the result of similar selection pressures on different but closely related forms. When not closely related, the result is convergent evolution.

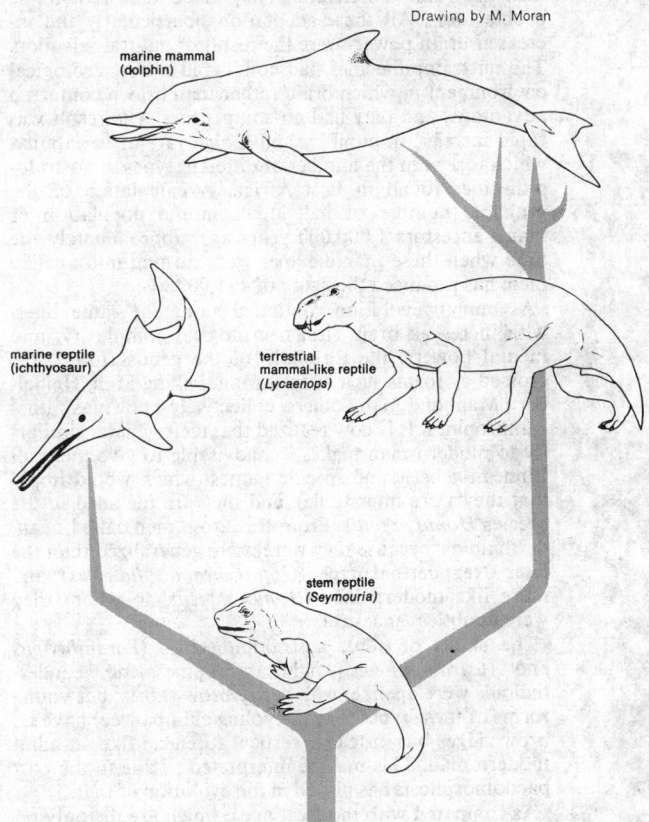

Drawing by M. Moran

marine mammal (dolphin)

marine reptile (ichthyosaur)

terrestrial mammal-like reptile (*Lycaenops*)

stem reptile (*Seymouria*)

Figure 6: Convergence of the stem reptile.

VII. The evolution of man
HOMINIZATION AND SEXUAL SELECTION
The evolution of man (hominization) shows some unique features, though traceable to processes found in other mammals (see MAN, EVOLUTION OF). Human ancestry began with small quadrupedal arboreal animals like the tree shrews (Tupaiidae) about 60,000,000 years ago. That man's ancestors had tails is shown by the vestige of a tail in the human embryo (representing the tail not of the adult ancestor but of the ancestor's embryo). Becoming larger, primates next resembled the tarsier, developing a vertical position of the trunk by clasping tree trunks with the fore and hind limbs. The next stage was the acquisition of the habit of brachiation, swinging from branches by the hands and moving in this way in forests, a habit that left its mark in the wide thorax, flat back, legs in line with the trunk, and almost universal joint of the arms at the shoulders, which are very wide apart, in man.

The brachiating stage persisted a long time in apes, as shown by the exaggerated lengths of their arms and the inefficiency of the legs in walking, but man's direct ancestors cannot have remained brachiators for long. They did not adopt the specializations of the apes but evolved a method of locomotion of their own, by taking to a terrestrial existence on the ground. These manlike primates, the australopithecines, of about 3,000,000 years ago, showed marked mosaic evolution. Some of their characters were purely apelike (small brain volume, massive projecting jaws, large molar teeth) and other features quite human (smooth, rounded forehead in juveniles, teeth arranged in a semicircular arch, molars worn in a way that showed the human method of chewing, arms delicately built, hip girdle and thigh bones showing vertical stance and gait). This upright posture supported solely by the legs, freed the hands from locomotor duties, and made possible their adaptation for manipulation.

These submen had a social structure (as have apes) that was of fundamental importance for their descendants. Although small, devoid of offensive structures like tusks or horns, and slow movers, they relied on their superior intelligence to enable them, in bands of 100 or 200 individuals, to outwit their enemies and to capture their prey and gather food. They made and used simple pebble tools. All these adaptations, particularly the increased brain power, were the result of natural selection. The australopithecines had conquered a new ecological environment in which brain rather than brawn conferred advantage, and they had no competitors. The result was rapid increase in numbers and a high rate of variability, which is seen in the number of different types of australopithecines found in East Africa. A calculation of the probable number of individuals in the population of man's ancestors 1,000,000 years ago, approximately the time when these manlike apes were turning into apelike men, has produced the figure of 125,000.

As human evolution continued along the same lines, with increased brain size, neurological complexity, and mental powers, the threshold of the genus *Homo* was crossed by forms such as Java Man, Peking Man, Heidelberg Man, and many others, collectively known as pithecanthropines. It is now realized that their general similarity to modern man makes it inadvisable to give them all Linnean generic and specific names (which would imply that they were intersterile), and they are included in the species *Homo erectus*. From this arose men called neanderthaloids, because they were more generalized than the later Neanderthal type (*Homo neanderthalensis*) and more like modern man (*Homo sapiens*) to whom they were doubtless ancestral.

The skulls of adult australopithecines (*Paranthropus* and *Australopithecus*), pithecanthropines, and neanderthaloids were apelike, with heavy brow ridges; but young forms of these types (like the young chimpanzee) have no brow ridges but instead a vertical forehead like an adult modern man. This may be interpreted as due to the part paedomorphosis has played in the evolution of man.

As compared with the great apes, which are the only related living forms with which he can be equated, modern man shows such a marked retardation in the rate of development that infancy, childhood, and adolescence occupy twice as long a time as in the apes. The features involved include growth period, eruption of teeth, age of puberty, and time of closure of sutures of the bones of the skull. The human newborn is not only utterly helpless but is almost in the condition of an "extra-uterine fetus," born prematurely with a year to go before it attains the anatomical and physiological condition of the newborn ape. The adaptive value of the premature birth is that the size of the brain and skull in man is so great that if birth were delayed, the infant would not pass through the bony ring of the mother's pelvis. Retardation of development being of such importance in man, it would be made of negative adaptive value if twin births were normal, for there would be competition between the twins for space and maternal blood supply, and the more precocious would receive advantage. Such precocity is contrary to the adaptive value of retardation in human evolution, which has been helped by the simpler structure of the human uterus. This structure, with a single chamber, increases the hazard of gestation for both fetuses if there are more than one. This is why the normal number in a human litter has been reduced to one.

Another biological principle operative in the evolution of man and many other animals has been sexual selection. In its original form, this process was conceived as the success of some males over others in obtaining mates, because of striking structure, coloration, or behaviour, and leaving more offspring than their less ornate rivals. This undoubtedly has taken place in some forms, such as the birds of paradise, and in man. It is a mistake to imagine that this process implies attributing to the females of non-human animals the power of aesthetic choice. The importance of sexual selection lies in the raising of the physiological state of sexual excitement in the female to the level at which she accepts to mate. In man, sexual selection has been mutual, intensified by the visual results of the adoption of the human mating position, consequent on the acquisition of upright stance, and it has affected the bodily distribution of fat, hair, and probably the development of a melodious voice. Darwin related how men of an African tribe choose their wives by lining them up and selecting the one who "projects most *a tergo*" (behind). It is easy to understand how a female could evolve features like those of the Paleolithic statuette "Venus of Brassempouy" (a small obese figurine), and later those of Venus de Milo.

There is a physiological function that has played a part in the biological process of hominization. In man, as in the great apes, the periodicity of ovulation and of female sexual excitement controlled by the hormonic mechanism of estrus has been succeeded by that of menstruation. Instead of being restricted by the periods of the estrous cycle without any sexual activity in intervening periods, mating can occur any time, a freedom of behaviour important for the social organization of man.

HUMANIZATION: PSYCHOSOCIAL EVOLUTION
The human newborn and child, utterly helpless for a considerable time, is entirely dependent for its survival on the care and skill of its parents. There is thus an overlap of many years between the generations, during which the development of the infant is not only protected but completed, and the parents are the most important factor in the survival of their offspring. They are able to play this role because the freedom of women from the sexual restrictions of the estrous cycle of lower mammals has made monogamy acceptable to men, and the family became a stable unit in society.

It is not only milk and, after weaning, other nourishment that the infant receives. In addition to affection and the psychological ties that bind mother and infant to each other, the latter, in its family, and surrounded by social stimuli, completes and perfects its own neurological mechanism, in a sort of cultural matrix that continues on a new and different plane the embryological development that the fetus underwent in the womb. Lack of this cultural matrix in early infancy leads to permanent mental

Sexual selection

The
evolution
of cultures

incompleteness, as shown by the occasional wild children brought up by female animals and children sequestered by inhuman parents.

The term inhuman in the last sentence is apt because it is by means of the cultural matrix of the family that man, hominized by natural selection, becomes humanized by what Sir Julian Huxley has called psychosocial evolution. In addition to the ordinary physiological aspects of child care, the infant becomes educated and slowly acquires a knowledge of the world into which it has been precipitated. At some stage in man's evolution, the superior mental powers of the brain, evolved through natural selection, gave him a wide range of abilities, all of which have a social bearing. Speech enabled him to communicate with his fellows, and reasoning enabled him to envisage deliberate aims; the patterns of flint implements found even in the earliest Paleolithic levels are evidence of the fact that a model was being followed for a purpose, and for the first time on earth, teleological purpose made its appearance. Reasoning produced experience, and memory converted this into tradition, the handing on of knowledge from person to person, most important, from parent to child.

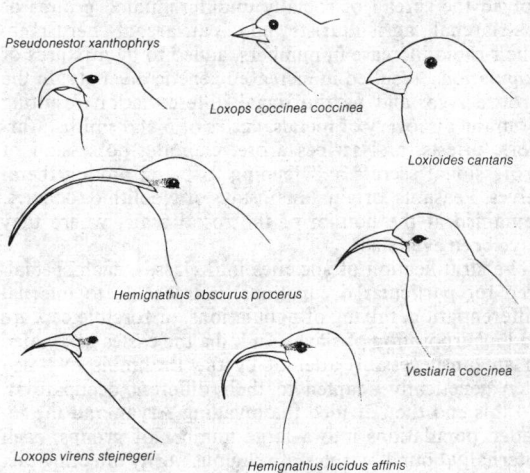

Pseudonestor xanthophrys

Loxops coccinea coccinea

Loxioides cantans

Hemignathus obscurus procerus

Vestiaria coccinea

Loxops virens stejnegeri

Hemignathus lucidus affinis

Figure 7: Radiation of beak shape in Hawaiian honeycreepers.

The fundamental difference between biological and psychosocial evolution is that, whereas biological information is transmitted automatically through the genes, whose variations are exposed to natural selection, psychosocial evolution does not involve biological heredity; it has to be imparted fresh at the start of each generation, from parents to child. The child, therefore, starts its effective behaviour and learns to recognize and react to wants, pains, satisfaction, and pleasure; it also begins to learn objective lessons from the outer world. Instincts are more or less sufficient to protect the young of animals with a very short infancy from hatching or birth to adulthood, but human childhood is so prolonged that no instincts could suffice to protect the child in the much more variegated condition of its environment. This is why a principle of authority acceptance by the child has conferred survival value by lowering accident rate.

Another difference between biological and psychosocial evolution is that, whereas the former is slow and has taken over 3,000,000,000 years to produce man, psychosocial evolution is alarmingly rapid and is accelerating. It has taken only 10,000 years for man to pass from bows and arrows to thermonuclear weapons, and the production of the latter has taken only 20 years.

Finally, psychosocial evolution is the producer of civilization. It has been selected in different directions in accordance with different ideologies, as may be seen by comparing the policies of ancient Sparta with those of a welfare state.

The most important difference between man and animals is his moral sense, and this presents difficult evolutionary problems. He claims to be the only species to have behaviour patterns aiming at the welfare and good order of society, in which he is less successful than lower vertebrates with their hierarchical organization, known as the "pecking order," which regulates priorities in access to females, food, and prestige, protected by natural selection simply because it conduces to good order and reduces casualties. This leads to the paradox that, despite his claimed moral sense, man is the only species in the animal kingdom that will perform wholesale massacres of its own members; animals are protected from doing this by innate behavioral control of aggression. Perhaps it is because man is a recent species, lately descended from australopithecines who owed their survival to aggressive behaviour in bands, with all that that implies in the way of mob psychology.

In view of this, it may seem premature to inquire how moral conduct originated when it fails so lamentably, but it nevertheless exists. Ethical behaviour develops in the child, and it has evolved in societies during their histories. Darwin believed that morals had also evolved from simple prototype components in the behaviour of lower organisms such as maternal affection and paternal self-sacrifice, through the advantage to the community of the social instincts of sympathy and the advantage that they would confer, leading to the well-known golden rule, ". . . whatever you wish that men would do to you, do so to them."

NATURAL SELECTION IN MAN

For all his professed civilization, natural selection continues to act in man, but with restrictions imposed by ethical standards. Medicine saves the lives of ill persons, surgery through Cesarian section enables birth to take place artificially, with the result that the genotypes whose phenotypes would not survive without these artificial aids are preserved and perpetuated.

It has been said that modern man is so far removed from "nature" that if he were plunged back into Paleolithic conditions he would perish quickly. On the other hand, Paleolithic man would not survive long in modern civilized conditions either, for he would succumb at once to epidemics to which modern man is fairly well adapted as part of his adaptation to living in highly populated towns. When, in Neolithic times, man started to live in crowded sedentary dwellings, with problems of sewage disposal, and closely associated with domestic animals, he became a prey to diseases caused by internal parasites, bacteria, and viruses, scourges from which the small roving bands of Paleolithic men must have been free, especially as concerns killer viruses that would have destroyed themselves as well as their victims, which were their only condition for continuance. These viruses originated in domestic animals, in which they (and their hosts) became adapted so as not to cause death.

There is another sanction that natural selection hangs over man's head. He is the only species that has broken out of ecological control of the birthrate, which in animals and Paleolithic man was kept down to the scale at which the territory occupied by each breeding unit limited the food supply available for young and adults.

VIII. Social evolution

SOCIOLOGY BEFORE DARWIN

The state of opinion on social questions in the 18th century was unpolarized. The Age of Enlightenment, largely the work of French speculative philosophers, envisaged the perfectibility of man, but the traditions of society and the precepts of theology prevented wide appreciation of the problems of sociology, which received a further deterrent from the excesses of the French Revolution. In 1795 appeared the French social thinker Marquis de Condorcet's *Sketch for a Historical Picture of the Progress of the Human Mind*, in which he distinguished nine epochs in the history of man, from the pastoral state to that of Liberty, Equality, and Fraternity that the Revolution had brought about. Each epoch passed to the next by jettisoning theological, social, and moral "prejudices" that had impeded progress. This was an optimistic example of conjectural history, and not the last.

Appalled at the ravages of the guillotine and terrified that the progress of the ungodly might establish a bridge-head in Britain, two clergymen set themselves the task of stemming it. Malthus endeavoured to show that man was unimprovable and that if the population increased too fast the poor would suffer famine and death and if too slowly the poor would have no incentive to work. It followed that medicine was antisocial and charity an "economic sin." Paley, in his *Natural Theology*, tried to show that adaptation implied a divine designer; his examples served Darwin as a catalogue of the products of natural selection. It is one of the great ironies in the history of ideas that Malthus and Paley, who did not believe in evolution, provided Darwin with exactly what he required to produce a successful theory, the reverse of their aims.

Meanwhile some Scottish philosophic historians had made conjectures on the economic stages in human history: hunting, pastoral, agricultural, and commercial, which are interesting to compare with the conjectural stages put forward by Marxists. The Scottish philosophers also used the method of comparison between existing savage tribes and hypothetical early stages of civilization to trace its conjectural development: an acceptance of the possibility of evolutionary change.

In 1797 John Frere found flint implements in Suffolk and concluded that they had been "used by a people who had not the use of metals." In 1819 a Danish archaeologist, Christian Thomsen, coined the terms Stone Age, Bronze Age, and Iron Age to denote successive stages in human prehistory. In 1846 a French antiquarian, Jacques Boucher de Perthes, founded prehistoric archaeology by his discoveries of flint implements.

Speech is a human attribute, and its study has revealed evolutionary possibilities. The English Orientalist Sir William Jones showed in 1786 that there were similarities between Sanskrit, Greek, and Latin that could only be explained if these languages had descended from an original language, perhaps dead. This hypothesis was confirmed and extended in 1816 by a German philologist, Franz Bopp, who introduced the term Indo-European to include the whole family of languages related to Sanskrit.

Auguste Comte, a follower of Condorcet and pioneer of philosophical positivism, gave an impulse to sociology conceived as a science or "social physics," excluding revealed religion and substituting humanism and ethics, based on history and aimed at improvement of human conditions. A great influence in social studies was Herbert Spencer, tireless exponent of evolutionary philosophy, who in 1852 published his belief in evolution, under the title of "The Development Hypothesis." This was based not on analysis of scientific evidence but on the *reductio ad absurdum* of alternative explanations.

All of these developments took place before 1859 and therefore without knowledge of Darwin's work. The study of sociology has frequently been concerned with what has been called "Social Darwinism," an attempt to consider human social interactions in terms of the struggle for existence. Sociology owes nothing to Darwin.

SOCIOLOGY AFTER DARWIN

The mechanism of natural selection, when taken out of its proper biological context by nonbiologists and made to apply to sociology, has had unfortunate results. Spencer, who coined for natural selection the unlucky phrase survival of the fittest (tautological and inaccurate), used it for his contention in favour of radical laissez-faire (uncontrolled) private enterprise, which should properly be called "social Spencerianism," applying the struggle for existence to individuals in society. Such views were widely held in the United States, where American clergyman Henry Ward Beecher wrote to Spencer, "The peculiar condition of American society has made your writings far more fruitful and quickening here than in Europe." Following his thesis to lengths of excess, Spencer extrapolated from the organic evolution of individuals to the "super-organic evolution" of societies of individuals, on the view that society was an organism.

Conversely, at the hands of Karl Marx, natural selection was made to serve as a "scientific" justification for the class war. In both cases the mistake was to imagine that a biological principle that works on organisms in nature can be made to apply to societies of men. In his naïve way, devoid of any historical sense, Darwin expressed this fact whimsically when he wrote to Baron von Scherzer, "What a foolish idea seems to prevail in Germany on the connection between Socialism and Evolution through natural selection."

EVOLUTIONARY GENETICS OF SOCIETY

It has been shown by English geneticist C.D. Darlington that studies in prehistory, history, and genetics make possible a sketch of the evolutionary origins of the genetic patterns of society. The important point is that without genetic diversity, resulting from crossbreeding, heritable variation is limited, adaptability to changed conditions is reduced, and survival of the population is precarious. Human societies have had to strike a balance between incestuous inbreeding, against which horror has generally prevailed because of its disastrous genetic results (accentuation of deleterious traits), and excessive outbreeding, which would impair the cohesion of the social unit.

In the Paleolithic expansion, groups were small, with a simple breeding pattern. The Neolithic expansion involved the spread of socially undifferentiated groups of matriarchal agriculturists and patriarchal herdsmen. Their rapid increase in numbers, added to by mixtures of populations, resulted in increased genetic diversity, in the Bronze Age; and by the social differentiation resulting from the discovery of metals, castes of metal smiths, warriors, priests, and scribes arose, claiming possession of professional secrets and tending to breed among themselves. Peasants, original mainstays of Neolithic societies, remained at the bottom of the social scale, where they have been ever since.

The stratification of societies into classes, each specialized for particular occupations, is traceable to internal differentiation, mixing of populations, or forcible capture and incorporation of slaves. In India the castes originated in an (unsuccessful) attempt by the Brahmins to breed men genetically adapted to their different occupations. To this end they divided the invading Aryan and the invaded populations into a large number of groups, each internally bound by rules of religious purity affecting diet and marriage, cooperating but never interbreeding with other groups. This class separation was combined with national unity, but at the genetic cost of reduction of the benefits of genetic diversity. The result has been that Hindu society has changed less than any other. Elsewhere, particularly in the China of Confucius, the possibilities of promotion and demotion to different levels in the social scale, favouring gene diffusion, has safeguarded those benefits, and new social structures arose.

EUGENICS

It was assumed by the English scientist Francis Galton, who believed in the hereditary nature of intelligence, that matings between parents possessed of especially favourable heredities would improve the genetic legacy of society, while the converse would deteriorate it. This notion, traceable to Plato, became the aim of a eugenics movement, launched in 1883. There are two approaches: positive eugenics, the enhancement of desirable characters through favourable matings, and negative eugenics, the suppression of deleterious genes by preventing their possessors from breeding. More recently some geneticists have stressed what American geneticist Hermann J. Muller called the "duty on the part of individuals to exercise their reproductive function with due regard to the benefit or injury thereby done to society." They have then gone on to suggest that sperm banks, supplied by outstanding men, and subsequent artificial insemination would not only allow of progeny testing but produce more men of genius. This program of positive eugenics suffers from the fact that the segregation and recombination of genes means that outstanding fathers may have inferior children and that the mother is as important as the father in transmitting genes. Sociologically, nobody is agreed on the qualities the ideal mass inseminator should have.

Negative eugenics suffered from ignorance of the action of the gene complex (see above) in suppressing the effects of disadvantageous genes, which invalidates the "scientific Calvinism" that supposed the impossibility of parents carrying unfavourable recessive genes producing any but socially undesirable progeny. Negative eugenics therefore has only limited acceptability. It would nonetheless be inadvisable for a person whose family contained a case of xenoderma pigmentosum (face cancer) to marry a freckled partner, especially a near relative, for fear of carcinoma in the offspring. The same prudence applies to families connected with hemophilia.

IX. The acceptance of evolution

Evolution is accepted by all biologists and natural selection is recognized as its cause by English-speaking biologists and others, though not widely in western continental Europe. Objections to evolution have come from theological and, for a time, from political standpoints.

Darwin did two things: he showed that evolution was a fact contradicting scriptural legends of creation and that its cause, natural selection, was automatic with no room for divine guidance or design. Furthermore, if there had been design, it must have been very maleficent to cause all the suffering and pain that befall animals and men. In 1860 T.H. Huxley demolished the arguments of Bishop Samuel Wilberforce. In the famous "monkey trial" conviction of schoolteacher John T. Scopes in 1925, a Tennessee law banning the teaching of evolution was upheld, but years later, in 1968, the United States Supreme Court ruled that anti-evolution laws were unconstitutional.

The Vatican leaves open the question of the evolution of man's body, provided it be believed that the body was derived from other living matter, that all mankind is descended from one pair (Adam and Eve), that man's soul was created by God, and that evolution took place under the dispensation of Divine Providence. Science cannot comment on the soul, but the other provisos are unacceptable to evolutionary biologists.

Political obstacles to scientific acceptance of evolution were for a time erected in Russia, where the ideological insistence that all characters are determined by the environment led to the stigmatizing of Mendelian genetics as bourgeois, metaphysical, reactionary, and leading to religion. The Soviet agronomist T.D. Lysenko attacked Darwin's theory as "metaphysical at base" and nothing but "flat evolutionism" because it worked so slowly. Lysenko contended that wheat plants produce seeds of rye and that cuckoos lay no eggs of their own but make foster parents' eggs grow into cuckoos. These views are now disregarded in the Soviet Union and elsewhere.

In more than a century since the appearance of Darwin's *Origin of Species*, the science of evolution has answered many questions and raised many more. Although new information frequently forces a re-examination of certain aspects, such as the rate of evolutionary change or the availability of genetic variation within populations, the main body of the synthetic theory of evolution remains firmly established.

BIBLIOGRAPHY. J.W. BURROW, *Evolution and Society* (1966), discusses social evolutionary theory before and after Darwin. SIR W.E. LE GROS CLARK, *History of the Primates*, 8th ed. (1962) and *Man-Apes or Ape Men?* (1967), present readable accounts of the ancestry of the primates and of man, respectively. C.D. DARLINGTON, *Evolution of Genetic Systems*, 2nd ed. rev. (1958), is a rather technical account of the relationship between genetics and evolution. CHARLES DARWIN, *On the Origin of Species* (1859), is the classic work on natural selection and well worth reading. A facsimile edition, with an introduction by E. MAYR, was published in 1964. A revision, *The Origin of Species*, 6th ed. (1872), was reprinted in 1963, with an introduction by SIR GAVIN DE BEER. See also Darwin's *The Descent of Man* (1871, 2nd ed. rev. 1930), an important discussion of human evolution. SIR GAVIN DE BEER, *Embryos and Ancestors*, 3rd ed. (1958), discusses the relation between embryological development and evolution; his *Atlas of Evolution* (1964), is a well-illustrated introduction to the subject, his *Handbook on Evolution*, 4th ed. (1970), a short popular manual. T.G. DOBZHANSKY, *Genetics and the Origin of Species*, 3rd ed. rev. (1951), is a standard work for the advanced student; *Mankind Evolving* (1962), an account of human evolution for the general reader. SIR RONALD A. FISHER, *The Genetical Theory of Natural Selection* (1930), provides the classic foundation of the synthetic theory of evolution. E.B. FORD, *Mendelism and Evolution*, 8th ed. (1965), is a short account of evolutionary genetics; his *Ecological Genetics* (1964) demonstrates the value of field genetic studies to evolutionary theory. J.B.S. HALDANE, *The Causes of Evolution* (1932), is a stimulating exposition on the subject of the title. D.L. LACK, *Evolutionary Theory and Christian Belief* (1957), provides a simple account of the conflict between biology and religion. E. MAYR, *Animal Species and Evolution* (1963), is a classic work on the mechanisms of speciation and the formation of higher categories; his *Populations, Species, and Evolution* (1970), is an abridged edition for the general reader. G. MENDEL, *Versuche über Pflanzenhybriden* (1866; trans. edited by J.H. BENNETT, *Experiments in Plant Hybridisation*, 1965), provides the groundwork for all subsequent studies in heredity. K.P. OAKLEY, *Frameworks for Dating Fossil Man*, 2nd ed. (1966), presents a chronology of man's evolution. B. RENSCH, *Neuere Probleme der Abstammungslehre*, 2nd ed. (1954; Eng. trans., *Evolution Above the Species Level*, 1959), is a classic work on the principles of evolution. G.G. SIMPSON, *The Major Features of Evolution* (1953), is a major work on paleontology, adaptation, and rates of evolution; G. LEDYARD STEBBINS, *Variation and Evolution in Plants* (1950), a standard reference work on plant speciation, and *Processes of Organic Evolution*, 2nd ed. (1971).

(G.de B.)

Exchange and Payments, International

Economic life does not stop at national boundaries but flows back and forth across them. The money of one country, however, cannot as a rule be used in another country; the flow of payments must be interrupted at national boundaries by exchange transactions in which one national money is converted into another. These transactions serve to cover payments so long as there is a balance between them: local money can be exchanged against foreign money only insofar as there is a counterbalancing offer of foreign money in exchange.

This article is organized as follows:

In the Soviet Union and other countries with the Soviet kind of economic planning, there are no legal markets for foreign exchange; in those countries the state has a monopoly of the business of foreign trade, which is generally conducted through formal agreements on a country-by-country basis. While the currencies of the Communist countries have official par values in terms of gold, these bear no particular relationship to their purchasing power or to the prices at which goods are exchanged. The international economic relationships of those countries therefore fall outside the scope of this article; they will be found elsewhere in discussions of international trade and economic planning.

I. Foreign exchange markets

The buying and selling of currencies

A foreign-exchange market is one in which those who want to buy a certain currency in exchange for another currency and those who want to move in the opposite direction are able to do business with each other. The motives of those desiring to make such exchanges are various. Some are concerned with the import or export of goods between one country or currency area and another, some with the purchase and sale of services. Some wish to move capital from one area to the other, and some wish to make gifts (the latter including governments, emigrants, and charitable foundations).

In any organized market there must be intermediaries who are prepared to "quote a price," in this case a rate of exchange between two currencies. These intermediaries must move the price quoted in such a way to permit them to make the supply of each currency equal to the demand for it and thus to balance their books. In an important foreign-exchange market the price quoted is constantly on the move.

A foreign-exchange market usually (but not always) differs from other organized markets—*e.g.*, those for commodities or securities, in that there is a standard, government-determined price at which one currency exchanges for another, called the "parity." There is usually no parity price for a commodity such as cotton unless some special arrangement has been made. The actual price quoted in a foreign-exchange market normally deviates from the parity price within moderate limits.

As between two countries (or currency areas, when several countries use the same currency), both on the gold standard, the parity is determined by the official gold content of the respective currencies. For many centuries there was also what almost amounted to a parity between gold-standard and silver-standard currencies, because of the fact that a number of countries operated what was called a bimetallic standard, under which the value of gold was fixed by law in terms of silver. The parity between a gold-standard currency and a silver-standard currency had a slightly blurred character because of the fact that not all the bimetallic countries had identical laws in regard to the silver value of gold. Though it may be paradoxical, these laws were effective for many centuries in fixing the silver value of gold in the free markets of the world. The bimetallic system was given up by those still adhering to it (the U.S., France, Italy, Switzerland, Holland, and Belgium) in 1873. Thereafter there was no parity of exchange between countries on the gold standard and countries on the silver standard.

EQUILIBRATING MOVEMENTS

If the demand by those holding a particular currency, say sterling, for another currency, say the dollar, exceeds the demand of dollar holders for sterling, the dollar will tend to rise in the foreign-exchange market. Under the gold-standard system there was a limit to the amount by which it could rise or fall. If a sterling holder wanted to make a payment in dollars, the most convenient way for him to procure the dollars would be in the foreign-exchange market. But under the gold standard he had another option; *i.e.*, he had a legal right to obtain gold from the authorities in exchange for paper currency at the established par value of that currency and remit the gold to the other country, where he would have a legal right to obtain its currency in exchange for bars of gold at the official valuation. Thus it would not be advantageous for a sterling holder to obtain dollars in the foreign-exchange market if the quotation for a dollar there exceeded parity by more than the cost of remitting gold. The foreign-exchange quotation at which it became cheaper to remit gold rather than use the foreign-exchange market was known as the "gold-export point." There was also a "gold-import point" determined on similar lines.

Arbitrage. Most of those seeking dollars did not undertake to remit gold even if the dollar quotation was at the gold-export point. The remission of gold was handled by arbitragers, who engaged in buying and selling currencies simultaneously on different exchanges in order to profit by small differences in the quoted rates. Their action would reduce the supply of sterling, since they would be selling sterling for gold to the British authorities, and increase the supply of dollars, since they would acquire dollars in exchange for gold from the U.S. authorities. The arbitragers would carry out these operations to the extent needed to prevent the scarcity of the dollar from raising its sterling price above the gold-export point for the U.K., and conversely. At the same time, the gold reserve of the British authorities would be diminished, and the gold reserve of the U.S. authorities increased.

Before 1931 the majority of countries were on the gold standard. In 1931 Great Britain departed from it, as did some other countries, including those of the British Commonwealth, the Scandinavian countries, and a number of others. These were countries maintaining a fixed parity of exchange with sterling.

After World War II most countries returned to what may be called a modified form of the gold standard. It resembles the gold standard in that each country establishes a legal gold valuation for its currency. This valuation is registered with the United Nations' International Monetary Fund (see below). The gold valuations serve to determine parities of exchange between the different currencies. It is also possible, as under the old gold standard, for the actual exchange quotation to deviate somewhat on either side of the official parity. There is agreement with the International Monetary Fund about the range, on either side of parity, within which a currency is to be allowed to fluctuate.

The modified gold standard

But there is a difference in the technical mode of operation. The service of the arbitragers in remitting physical gold from country to country as needed has been dispensed with. Instead the authorities are under an obligation to ensure that the actual exchange rates quoted within their own territories do not go outside the limits agreed upon with the International Monetary Fund. This they do by intervening in the markets of their own territories. If, for instance, the dollar is in short supply in London, the British authorities are bound to supply dollars to the market to whatever extent is needed to keep the sterling price of the dollar from rising above the agreed-upon limit. The same is true with the other currencies of the members of the International Monetary Fund who are discharging their obligations. Thus the obligation of the monetary authorities to supply the currency of any Fund member at a rate of exchange that is not above the agreed-upon limit has taken the place of the obligation under the old gold standard to give actual gold in exchange for notes.

It would be inconvenient for the monetary authorities of a country to be continually watching the exchange rates in its market of all the different currencies. Most authorities have confined themselves to watching the rate of their own currency against the dollar and supplying from time to time whatever quantity of dollars may be required. At this point the arbitragers come into service again. They can be relied upon to operate in such a way that the exchange rates between the various currencies in the various foreign-exchange markets are kept mutually consistent. This use of the dollar by many monetary authorities has caused it to be called the currency of "intervention."

The official fixing of exchange rates as limits on either side of parity, outside of which exchange-rate quotations are not allowed to fluctuate, bears a family resemblance to the gold points of the old gold-standard system. The question naturally arises why, in devising a somewhat different system, it was considered desirable to keep this range of fluctuation. In the old system it arose necessarily out of the cost of remitting gold. Since there is no corresponding cost in the new system, why did the authorities decide not to have a fixed parity of exchange from which no deviation would be allowed? The answer is that there is convenience in having a range within which fluctuation is allowed. Supply and demand between each pair of currencies will not be precisely equal every day. There will always be fluctuations, and if there were one rigidly fixed rate of exchange the authorities would have to supply from their reserves various currencies to meet them. In addition to being inconvenient, this would require each country to maintain much larger reserves than would otherwise be necessary.

Methods of currency dealing

Short-term movements. Commercial banks and other corporations involved in dealings across currency frontiers are usually able to see some (but not necessarily all) of their needs in advance. Their foreign-exchange experts will watch the course of the exchanges closely and, if a currency is weak (*i.e.*, below parity), will advise their firms to take the opportunity of buying it, even if somewhat in advance of need. Conversely, if the currency is above parity but not expected to remain so indefinitely, they may recommend postponing purchases until a more favourable opportunity offers. These adjustments under the influence of common sense and self-interest have an equilibrating influence in foreign-exchange markets. If a currency is temporarily weak, it is presumably because of seasonal, cyclical, or other factors. If on such an occasion private enterprise takes the opportunity to buy the currency while it is cheap, that tends to bring demand up to equality with supply and relieves the authorities from the need to intervene in order to prevent their currency from falling below the lower point whenever there is a temporary deficit in the balance of payments. The usefulness of such private movements of funds assumes complete confidence in the currency. (The question of deep-seated imbalances not due merely to temporary causes is deferred to a later section.)

Another equilibrating influence arises from the movements of short-term interest rates. When the authorities have to supply foreign currencies in exchange for the domestic currency, this causes a decline in the money supply in domestic circulation—unless the authorities deliberately take offsetting action. This decline in the money supply tends to raise short-term interest rates in the domestic money market. This will bring an inflow of money from abroad to take advantage of the higher rates or, what amounts to the same thing, discourage foreigners from borrowing in that country's money market since borrowing will have become more expensive. Thus, the interest-rate differential will cause a net movement of short-term funds in the direction required to offset the temporary deficit or, in the opposite case, to reduce a temporary surplus that is embarrassing to others. It must be stressed again that this interest-rate mechanism implies complete confidence that the parity will not be altered in the near future.

The helpful movement of interest rates may be reinforced by action of the monetary authorities, who by appropriate open-market operations may cause short-term interest rates to rise above the level that they would have attained under market forces and thus increase the equilibrating movement of short-term funds. The Bank of England provided the most notable example of the smooth and successful operation of this policy during many decades before World War I.

Forward exchange. The transactions in which one currency is exchanged directly for another are known as "spot" transactions. There can also be "forward" transactions, consisting of contracts to exchange one currency for another at a future date (*e.g.*, three months ahead)

but at a rate fixed on now. For instance, a German firm may have a commitment to pay a U.S. firm in dollars in three months' time. It may not want to take the risk that the dollar will rise relatively to the mark during the three months, so that it would have to surrender more marks in order to honour its commitment. It could of course buy the dollars right away and thus obviate this risk, but it may not have any spare cash and borrowing may be inconvenient. The firm has the alternative of buying dollars at a rate agreed upon now for which it does not have to surrender marks until three months have passed. Some firms have a regular routine procedure for covering all future commitments to be paid for in a foreign currency as soon as these are entered into. Of course, even a firm that does this may combine its routine procedure with a little judgment (*e.g.*, if there are good reasons for believing that the foreign currency will become cheaper during the relevant period). And firms with multinational commitments will vary the distribution of their assets among different currencies in accordance with changing conditions. The forward-exchange rate will, like the spot rate, be continually varying. It is not usually identical with the spot rate but in normal times has a regular relation to it. This relation is determined as follows.

Forward rates

Dealers in forward exchange usually balance their commitments; *e.g.*, a contract to deliver forward marks can be offset against one to deliver forward dollars, and nothing more has to be done about it. If a particular dealer cannot manage this he will be in communication with another who may be in the opposite position. It may not, however, always be possible to offset every transaction. If this is not done, the dealer must make a spot purchase of the currency—say marks—in excess demand in the forward market. If he did not do this he would risk an exchange loss on some of his forward transactions. For the purpose of evaluating the forward-exchange rate to be asked in a particular deal, it is always correct to suppose that the deal is one that cannot be offset. If the dealer has to purchase marks on the spot, he can earn the rate of interest prevailing in Frankfurt until the time comes when he has to deliver the marks. Whether this is advantageous or not depends on whether the rate of interest in Frankfurt is higher or lower than that in New York. If it is higher in Frankfurt the dealer will normally quote a rate per forward mark that is lower than the spot rate; but if the rate of interest in Frankfurt is lower, then the forward mark will normally stand above the spot mark to compensate the dealer for having to employ his liquid funds in a less remunerative market. When the relation of the forward rate to the spot rate is determined by a comparison of the short-term interest rates in the two centres in the manner just described, the forward rate is said to be at "interest parity."

The question arises as to what particular interest rates are used to calculate the interest parity. There is a variety of practice. In previous times the rate of interest on U.S. Treasury bills and the rate of interest on British Treasury bills were used to determine the interest parity of the sterling price for forward dollars. More recently the interest rates on Eurodollars and Eurosterling have been used—*i.e.*, the interest on dollar and sterling accounts held by European banks (see below).

In normal times arbitrage may be expected to hold forward rates to their interest parities. There have been times, and even rather prolonged periods, in which the forward rate for a currency has fallen below (or risen above) its interest parity. This may happen when there is a large one-way movement of funds (*e.g.*, when there is a lack of confidence in a particular currency). In some cases, such as a simultaneous multiple swapping of currencies, the arbitrager does not have to commit any funds, but in forward arbitrage funds have to be committed for a period of three months. It is true that an arbitrager who had bought three months' sterling could resell the sterling before the three months had elapsed, but if he did so he might have to accept a loss. If the one-way movement is very heavy there may be a shortage of funds available for forward arbitrage. Nonetheless the demand for forward sterling has to be kept equal to the supply of it, and if there is insufficient arbitrage for this purpose then a positive profit has to appear on the purchase of forward sterling—*i.e.*, its price has to fall below the interest parity.

If dealers in a forward currency cannot offset contracts for sale with contracts for purchase and find an excess of customers wishing to sell, the excess supply causes immediate pressure on the spot market, since arbitragers and others who supplement the forward demand for the weak currency must cover their positions by selling an equivalent amount spot. The only way in which the authorities can prevent an excess offer of their currency forward from causing an immediate drain on their reserves is by offering to buy it forward themselves, without simultaneously selling it spot. British authorities engaged in such operations during the period when sterling was weak, and similar operations have been conducted by other central banks in connection with the swap agreements for mutual accommodation to be described below.

The foregoing descriptions of the equilibrating movements of short-term funds do not apply when there is a serious lack of confidence that a given parity will be maintained. Occasions of lack of confidence have occurred much more frequently under the modified gold standard (International Monetary Fund) than they did under the old gold standard. The reason for this is simple. Under the old gold standard it was not expected that a country of good standing would alter the gold valuation of its currency (although in much earlier days "debasement" was common enough). A devaluation of the official gold content was regarded as not far removed from a declaration of bankruptcy, and it was assumed that a country would avoid it at all costs and in all times short of a major war or revolution. Under the International Monetary Fund this position has been altered quite deliberately. When a country's payments are in "fundamental disequilibrium," it may propose a change of parity. The reason why this remedy was proposed at the Bretton Woods Conference (1944), which set up the International Monetary Fund, was that it was thought to be better than alternative remedies, such as domestic deflation.

DISEQUILIBRATING MOVEMENTS

Whatever the merits from a long-term point of view, the idea that it is quite respectable for a country to alter the par value of its currency in certain circumstances has had disturbing effects on the movements of short-term funds —effects that may not have been clearly foreseen at the time of Bretton Woods. Such movements of funds have sometimes been very large indeed. These movements are not equilibrating, like those described in relation to a parity in which there is confidence; on the contrary, they are disequilibrating. If a currency becomes weak—*i.e.*, if the demand for it falls below the supply—this may give rise to the idea that the authorities having the weak currency may in due course decide to devalue it, as they are perfectly entitled, under International Monetary Fund principles, to do.

Covering. Foreign-exchange advisers to corporations have to watch for such possibilities and should propose a readjustment of assets entailing a movement out of the weak currency. It is not necessary that there should be, on an objective assessment, a probability that the currency in question will be devalued—*i.e.*, that there should be more than a 50 percent chance that it will be devalued. To provoke a disequilibrating movement of funds it is enough that there should be a small chance only—*i.e.*, much less than 50 percent—that it will be devalued. In strict theory, funds should be moved out of a given currency whenever the probability that it will be devalued outweighs the cost of moving the funds (*e.g.*, the cost of selling the suspect currency forward at a discount).

Four classes of covering

If a firm or its affiliate has foreseeable commitments to make payments in a currency other than that of the area in which it operates, it may think it wise to "cover" its position by buying the currency at once, in either the spot

or the forward market. Covering may take other forms also. If a contract to pay abroad is in the currency of the home country—*i.e.*, the paying country—then the prospective foreign receiver of these funds will have to consider whether he should not cover his own position by selling the currency of the paying country forward. Payments in the opposite direction have also to be considered. If these are in the currency of the home country, the foreigner due to make the payment will consider whether he should cover his position by buying the currency of the home country forward. If the payment is in the foreign currency, then the firm in the home country due to receive it will consider whether to cover itself by selling the foreign currency forward. Thus, there are four main classes of covering. In normal times it is probable that not all positions are covered in these four ways, although it is not impossible that they should be.

If a suspicion arises that a particular currency, say that of the "home" country, may be devalued, then the position is radically changed. The following arguments apply in reverse to the case when it is believed that a particular currency may be valued upward. It is necessary to go through the four classes of cases. Members of the home country who normally cover their commitments to make payments in a foreign currency would clearly continue to do so. And those, if any, who do not habitually do so would be strongly advised to do so when there is a possibility that the home currency may be devalued. To take the second case—that of outward payments to be made in the home currency—the same applies: foreigners who normally sell it forward should continue to do so, and those who do not normally sell it forward would be strongly advised to do so lest the currency be devalued before the payment is made. Coming to the payments due in to the home country, in the case of those to be made in the home currency, the foreigners who normally cover themselves by buying forward or spot should be advised to cease doing so immediately, since they may get the currency cheaper before the payment has to be made. Thus in this case the fear of devaluation causes those concerned to stop covering their positions. The same applies to inward payments to be made in foreign currencies; residents of the home country would be advised to cease from such covering, since in the interval their currency may be devalued, and therefore it would be foolish to sell the foreign currency due to come in advance of payment.

Effect of possible devaluation

Thus the prospect of devaluation may cause both additional covering and uncovering. Both types of change are adverse to the currency under suspicion. It is notable that the total value of the appropriate covering plus that of the uncovering when a currency becomes suspect is independent of the proportion of positions that are normally covered. If all positions are normally covered then the adverse effect will consist of an uncovering of about half of all positions. If all positions are not normally covered, then the adverse effect will be equal to the sum of the amount of extra covering and the amount of uncovering. The movement of funds under these heads can be very large in relation to a country's normal balance of incoming and outgoing payments. It makes no difference whether the changed action by the firms relates to the spot or to the forward markets. This is because, when there is a big one-way movement in the forward market, the whole of it is thrown, through the actions of the dealers, arbitragers, etc., onto the spot market.

Hedging. Whereas the word covering relates to payments foreseen or possible, the term hedging is used for operations related not to prospective payments but to existing assets. Thus, a non-British firm may need to have a sterling balance for an indefinite period ahead. It may think it desirable in this case to protect its position against the possibility of sterling being devalued in the near future by selling sterling forward at the existing quoted rate. If sterling is devalued before the forward contract matures, the operator will get a foreign currency —say the franc—at the old rate and can rebuy sterling at a cheaper rate. The profit that he makes recoups him for the loss in the franc value of his sterling due to the devaluation. If there is no devaluation he can renew his hedge at the date due, if sterling is still suspect, or he can terminate it without loss except for the actual cost of the hedging transaction.

An even more important use of hedging is to protect the international value of real assets such as securities, real estate, industrial buildings and plants, etc. If a non-British person conducts business and has assets in Britain, he may think it wise to protect the international value of these assets by selling a certain amount of sterling forward. A devaluation, if it occurs, will reduce the foreign-exchange value of the sterling assets; but the profit that the owner makes from selling sterling forward and buying it back at a cheaper rate will be an offset to this loss.

Speculation. The movements so far considered are of a precautionary nature. It is sometimes suggested, when there is a big movement of funds out of a currency, that those prompting it are actuated by some motive hostile to the suspect currency. This is usually quite wrong. Such large movements of funds are often referred to incorrectly as "speculative." This gives a false impression of what is happening. Speculation can, and often does, occur when a currency becomes suspect; but the word speculative should be confined to movements of funds made not to protect positions but purely in the hope of gain. A person may believe that the Deutsche Mark is likely to be valued upward and decide to buy Deutsche Marks, not because he has any commitments denominated in Deutsche Marks but because he wants to resell them afterward at a profit. He will probably buy the Deutsche Marks forward. Such speculation plays only a minor role in the big movements of funds in anticipation of a change of parity. It may, however, mount up very strongly in the last stages when an upward or downward revaluation has become almost certain.

A big outward movement of funds may precipitate a change of parity, desirable or undesirable in itself, simply because there are not enough reserves to finance the withdrawals. Even if the country in trouble is assisted by international credits (see below), in certain cases these may not be large enough to avert the need for devaluation. A great movement of funds from a particular country may occur because it is thought likely that it will have to devalue. There may also be a great movement into a country thought likely to value upward. The latter kind of movement will cause difficulties for other countries, since the funds must come from somewhere. This adverse effect may be concentrated on one other currency, as in the classic crisis centred on a possible upward valuation of the Deutsche Mark in November 1968, where the drain was mainly from the French franc; or it may be more widely diffused, as in the crisis of the mark in September 1969.

PROPOSALS FOR MORE FLEXIBLE RATES

Stability versus flexibility

When the inconveniences of the International Monetary Fund system, by which exchange rates can be adjusted from time to time, began to become evident, proposals were made to obtain the same result in a different way by having continuously flexible exchange rates.

If exchange rates were continually on the move, instead of being changed only on comparatively rare occasions, the movements would not provoke the large anticipatory shiftings of funds that have proved so inconvenient.

Freely floating rates. One proposal was to abolish any fixed parity, even a temporary one, and let rates move under the free-market influence of supply and demand, just as the prices of commodities do in an organized market. Such a system would relieve the authorities of all responsibility for interfering in the process of exchange-rate fixing and leave the whole business to market forces.

Critics argue that the system would have serious disadvantages. At any time there are likely to be discrepancies in the balance between supply and demand owing to seasonal, cyclical, and random causes. Under any system of (permanently or temporarily) fixed rates in which there is complete confidence, very small movements in a rate

cause helpful movements of funds of an equilibrating kind. On the other hand, when there is no fixed rate and no bottom limit, a small movement in the rate will not attract as large an equilibrating movement of funds. But, if there is a temporary deficit of a certain amount, as a result of the seasonal, cyclical, or random causes, some equilibrating movement is needed. To secure this under floating rates a larger downward movement will be required in order to attract the funds. Thus this system entails a larger oscillation in the actual market rate than would occur under the system in which there are fixed limits. Even if foreign-exchange advisers are able to form an objective and accurate judgment of what the long-run equilibrium rate is, an excessive oscillation will still be needed to induce the movement of funds. But such oscillations are detrimental to international trade and international investment.

Some carry the argument further. They hold that foreign-exchange advisers have shown themselves to be unduly influenced by irrelevant events and somewhat erratic in their judgment. To the extent that this might be so, still larger oscillations would be required in the actual rates to get the necessary movement of funds.

Flexible rates with official intervention. The idea of freely floating rates implies that the authorities will not meddle in the market. But most authorities will want to secure as much stability as possible. If there should be a downward movement that the authorities know to have been caused by some random event beyond the ken of the foreign-exchange advisers to corporations, the authorities will not want to let the foreign-exchange rate fall when they know quite well that the cause of weakness is temporary. They will naturally want to intervene to offset the special factor and to keep the exchange rate steady. If flexible rates are ever established as a regular system, it is almost certain that the authorities will insist on having the freedom to intervene when in their judgment intervention is expedient. Most experts hope that with better statistical analysis of the trends of the various magnitudes in the external balance, governments will be able to confine their interventions to offsetting temporary items and will not interfere with long-run trends as determined by underlying forces.

A notable experiment with such a system was made by the United Kingdom between 1931 and 1939. There was a high degree of official intervention. The rules of the game were that the authorities would intervene to offset imbalances due to temporary causes and also to offset movements of what came to be called "hot money," while allowing the rate to move toward its long-run natural level as determined by market forces. The experiment was too short-lived to yield many valuable lessons. The system was modified somewhat by the Tripartite Agreement in 1936 between the United States, the United Kingdom, and France, joined also by other countries, under which each authority was expected to do more to keep the rate stable than it might have been disposed to do if it had only its own interest to consider.

A flexible system on a wider international scale would require a consensus among the countries concerned as to the principles underlying the interventions and on how to diagnose an existing situation. For instance, if sterling were weak, British authorities might hold that the weakness was not due merely to temporary causes but to an underlying disequilibrium and that accordingly they should not intervene to prevent the exchange rate from going down. At the same time, Americans might take an opposite view, holding that sterling was not at present overvalued in relation to the dollar and that accordingly the British should support sterling and not let it drift downward. It would be still more difficult to get consensus among several powers; the change in the rate between two powers would affect the rates of all the others as well. While this may not be an objection in principle it would certainly be a very serious one in practice.

In the briefer period of the British experiment (1931–36), no consensus was required. The currencies of the world were then divided into two groups, those linked to sterling and those linked to gold. There were changes in the gold value of the dollar, but these amounted to changes in parity and not to a flexible rate system. Intervention in the exchange rate between the sterling area and the gold-attached currencies was executed by the Bank of England only; the Federal Reserve System did not intervene. This was a very special system with its consequent absence of a need for consensus and is not likely to occur again. So the problem of how to obtain consensus remains.

Crawling peg. Members of the International Monetary Fund have a right to adjust their rates of exchange (more strictly, to adjust the gold parity of their currencies) from time to time in the event of a "fundamental disequilibrium." This is often called the adjustable peg system. The expression crawling peg has been invented to describe another possible system. With the crawling peg there would still be a parity of exchange, but the parity itself would be allowed to move from day to day, the idea being that it should not move by a large amount, possibly not by more than 2 percent a year. There would have to be an initial consensus about this figure when the system was set up, but no further consensus would be required for any change of parity within the limit. The parity on each day (or for each week) would be fixed by reference to the average market rates of a preceding period, say a year. The authorities would cease to have power over the parity but would still have the duty to intervene in such a way as to prevent the actual market rates going outside the limits on either side of the changing parity. In connection with this proposal, it has also been suggested that the band on either side of parity between the upper and lower limits should be broadened so as to give the market forces a little more scope.

Two major advantages are suggested for the crawling-peg system. First, it is maintained that the prospect of a rate change of not more than, say, 2 percent in the course of a year would obviate those massive movements of precautionary funds that have been such an inconvenience under the adjustable-peg system. Second, the authorities would be relieved of deciding about the parity and could let market forces determine the direction and, within the prescribed limits, the amount of the exchange-rate movement.

There are difficulties in this. If reliance is placed on small exchange-rate movements to get adjustment from a position of fundamental disequilibrium, the remedy will be slow working. Accordingly, monetary authorities in every country will need larger reserves than under a system with a quicker adjustment mechanism. The question also arises whether 2 percent a year is enough. Another difficulty is that a country may suddenly encounter unusual disturbances in its domestic monetary system. Financial advisers will then raise the question whether this country will not be forced by the circumstances to abandon its loyalty to the crawling-peg system and have a larger devaluation. Then all the old troubles will begin again.

A modification of the strict scheme outlined above has also been suggested, whereby the authorities would agree to a maximum rate of change in parity of, say, 2 percent a year and would agree to space out that change so as not to provoke precautionary movements of funds; but the direction and the amount of that change, subject to the limits, would be determined by the authorities and not by market forces. This would entail losing what, in the opinion of some, is a valuable feature of the strict scheme.

Whatever changes may be made in the future, there is not likely to be a return to rigidly fixed and permanent exchange rates as under the old gold standard. There are some in central banking circles who would like rates under the existing system to be moved only very occasionally and as a measure of last resort. That is a rather different concept from the one that actuated the founders of the International Monetary Fund at Bretton Woods, who thought of exchange-rate change as a measure of adjustment to be used from time to time whenever circumstances seemed to require it. The reason for not going back to an absolutely rigid fixed-rate system is that a movement of the exchange rate, whether from time to time or continuously, is thought to be a valuable weapon of adjustment; in particular, it may prevent the need for a domestic deflation that would create a socially unacceptable level of unemployment in order to correct a deficit.

II. Balance of payments accounting

THE CURRENT ACCOUNT

When using balance of payments statistics it is important to understand their basic concepts. The balance of payments includes, among other things, payments for goods and services; these are often referred to as the balance of trade, but the expression has been used in a variety of ways. In order to be more specific, some authorities have taken to using the expression "merchandise balance," which unmistakably relates to trade in goods and excludes services and other occasions of international payment.

Figures for the merchandise balance often quote exports valued on a FOB basis (free on board) and imports valued on a CIF basis (including cost, insurance, and freight to point of destination). This swells the import figures relatively to the export figures by the amount of the insurance and freight included. The reason for this practice has been that in many countries the trade statistics have been based on customs house data, which naturally include insurance and freight costs for imports but not for exports. The authorities have more recently made a point of providing estimates of imports valued on an FOB basis.

Another expression, "balance of goods and services," is often used. The British, however, continue to use the term invisibles for current services entering into international transactions. For many years the "visible" balance was taken to be equivalent to exports quoted FOB and imports CIF as explained above. The British authorities have more recently instituted another linguistic usage by which the "visible" balance is equivalent to the true merchandise balance. The old usage still lingers on in the less expert literature.

And so the total current account is the balance of goods (merchandise) and services. The U.K. includes unilateral transfers among "invisibles" and in the current account. The U.S. statistics, more correctly, show them under a separate heading.

Services include such items as payments for shipping and civil aviation, travel, expenditures (including military) by the home government abroad and expenditures by foreign governments at home, interest and profits and dividends on investments, payments in respect of insurance, earnings of banking, merchanting, brokerage, telecommunications and postal services, films and television, royalties payable by branches, subsidiaries and associated companies, agency expenses in regard to advertising and other commercial services, expenditures by journalists and students, construction work abroad for which local payment is made and conversely, earnings of temporary workers such as entertainers and domestic workers, and professional consultants' fees. This list contains the more important items but is not comprehensive.

Among unilateral transfers the more important are outright aid by governments, subscriptions to international agencies, grants by charitable foundations, and remittances by immigrants to their former home countries.

THE CAPITAL ACCOUNT

There is also the capital account, which includes both long-term and short-term capital movements.

Long-term flows. Long-term capital movement divides into direct investments (in plant and equipment) and portfolio investments (in securities). In the 19th century direct investment in plant and equipment preponderated. The U.K. was much the most important contributor to direct investment overseas. In the early part of the century it even contributed to the industrial development of the U.S.; later its attention shifted to South

The various kinds of payments

America, Russia, other European countries, and India. Investment in what came to be called the "Commonwealth" and "Empire," not prominent at that time, became very important in the 20th century. The other countries of western Europe also made important contributions to direct investment overseas.

The most important items of direct investment were railways and other basic installations. In early stages direct investment may help developing countries to balance their payments, but in later stages there will have to be a flow of interest and profit in the opposite direction back to the investing country. The U.K. is frequently cited as the country whose overseas investments were most helpful for developing countries because her rapidly growing population and small cultivable land area permitted her to develop large net imports of food and to run corresponding deficits on her merchandise account. The complementary surplus this generated in the developing countries from which the imports came enabled them to pay the interest and profit on British capital without straining their balances of payments.

Between World War I and World War II the U.S. began to take a more active interest in overseas investment, but this was not always well advised. After the great world slump, which started in 1929, international investment almost ceased for lack of profit opportunities.

The international capital market

After World War II the U.S. began to build up a leading position as overseas investor. The process accelerated in 1956 and afterward, both on direct investment and on portfolio investment accounts. This may have been partly due to the desire of U.S. firms to have plants inside the European Common Market. Other countries also found more opportunities for capital export than there had been in the interwar period. The U.K. gave special attention to the British Commonwealth.

Short-term flows. In this context a very important distinction must be drawn between the short-term capital that flows in the normal course of industrial and commercial development and that which flows because of exchange-rate movements. The first class of short-term capital may be thought of as going in the train of direct long-term investment. A parent company may desire from time to time to supply its branch or affiliate with working capital. There may also be repayments from time to time. The second type of short-term capital flow was described in the section on foreign exchange. When there is confidence in a parity, these flows are normally equilibrating—*i.e.*, they tend to offset a surplus or deficit on other accounts. But when there is lack of confidence in the maintenance of a parity large disequilibrating flows occur, as has already been described.

Eurocurrency markets. An international capital market developed in the 1960s dealing in what are known as Eurocurrencies, of which much the most important is the Eurodollar. The prefix Euro is used because initially the market largely centred on the countries of Europe, but it has by no means been confined to them. Japan and the Middle Eastern oil states have been important dealers. While these short-term lendings normally move across national frontiers, they do not enter directly into balances of payments as they do not directly involve foreign exchange transactions. They may, however, indirectly cause such transactions to take place.

The nature of the market is as follows: In the ordinary course of affairs, an Italian, for example, acquiring dollars—say from exports or from a legacy—would sell these dollars for his own currency. But he may decide to deposit the dollars at his bank instead, with an instruction not to sell them for cash but to repay him in dollars at a later date. Thus the bank has dollars in hand and a commitment to pay them out in, say, three months. It may then proceed to lend these dollars to another bank, anywhere in the world. Since the lending and borrowing is done in dollars, no foreign exchange transaction is directly involved. The sum total of all operations of this sort is the Eurodollar market. It is not centred on any particular place and has no formal rules of procedure or constitution. It consists of a network of deals conducted by telephone and telex around the world. U.S. residents themselves lend to and borrow from this market.

One may ask why lenders and borrowers use this market in preference to more conventional methods of lending and borrowing. Ordinarily the answer is because they can get more favourable terms, since the market works on very narrow margins between lending and borrowing rates. This involves expertise; London has played the most important part in the creation of the market. The lender hopes to get a better rate of interest than he would on a time deposit in the U.S. (restrictions limiting interest payable on U.S. time deposits are said to have been a contributing cause of the growth of the market). At the same time, normally, the borrower will find that he has to pay a lower rate than he would on a loan from a commercial bank in the U.S.

This has not always been the case. In 1969 Eurodollar interest rates went to very high levels. One reason for this was the set of restrictions imposed by the U.S. on its commercial banks lending abroad. The second was that although the prime lending rates of the principal U.S. banks might be below Eurodollar rates, many individuals, including U.S. citizens, found that they could not get loans from their banks because of the "credit squeeze."

Because this form of international lending does not involve the sale of one currency for another, it does not enter into balances of payments accounts. Nonetheless it may have a causal effect on the course of the exchanges. For instance, the Italian cited above might have chosen to sell his dollars had he not been tempted by the more attractive Eurodollar rate of interest. In this case, the market causes dollars not to be sold that otherwise would have been. Others who have liquid cash at their disposal for a time may even *buy* dollars in order to invest them in the market at short term. That would be helpful to the dollar. There are countercases. An individual who has to make a payment in dollars but lacks cash may borrow the dollars in the Eurodollar market, when otherwise he would have got credit in his own country and used that to buy dollars; in this case the market is hurtful to the dollar because its existence prevents someone from buying dollars in the regular way.

ASSESSING THE BALANCE

To summarize, the overall balance of payments comprises the current account (merchandise and services), unilateral transfers (gifts, grants, remittances, etc.), and the capital account (long-term and short-term capital movements). If payments due in exceed those due out, a country is said to be in overall surplus; and when payments due out exceed payments due in, it is in overall deficit. The surplus or deficit must be balanced by a monetary movement in the opposite direction, and consequently the overall balance including monetary movements must always be equal.

Deficit or surplus

In practice, great difficulties have been found in assessing whether a country is in deficit or in surplus. It is often important to establish this with a view to possible corrective measures. The U.K. lays chief stress on the combined balance of current and long-term capital account—*i.e.*, excluding short-term capital. This may be the best plan. Such a balance, however, omits short-term movements that occur in the ordinary course of business, which may be called "normal" and which ought in principle to be included. On the other hand it is not desirable to include equilibrating or disequilibrating capital movements of the kind referred to above. These occur in consequence of a deficit (or surplus), actual or anticipated. But there may be great statistical difficulty in distinguishing between the normal short-term capital flows and those that are consequential on a surplus or deficit.

It has been noted that the overall balance, including monetary movements, must be equal, but it usually happens that the figures do not quite balance. United States statisticians call the residual figure that has to be inserted to square the account "errors and omissions." If the average value of this figure over a substantial period, such as ten years—an even longer period may have to be taken if a country is in persistent surplus or deficit—has a positive or negative value of substantial amount, then it may be taken to constitute genuine items that have escaped the statistical net. These may legitimately be included in assessing whether a country is in genuine surplus or deficit and whether corrective measures are needed.

The "errors and omissions" item is extremely volatile from year to year and often very large. Such movements up and down are probably caused by precautionary short-term capital movements. There have been periods when a minus item in the U.S. account was rather strikingly associated with a plus item in the U.K. account, and conversely. Accordingly, in the short term, the "errors and omissions" item should not be included in assessing whether a country is in surplus or deficit.

It has been noted that the U.K. lays chief stress on the balance of current and long-term capital accounts (which include unilateral transfers). The U.S. position is less clear. The official balance, published every quarter by the Department of Commerce, is called the "Commerce Balance" or the "Liquidity Balance." Recently stress has also been laid on what is called the "Official Settlements Balance."

In distinguishing between monetary and nonmonetary items, the Commerce Balance includes any increase in the holding of short-term dollar securities abroad as part of the U.S. deficit during the period; but it does not include as counterweight any increase in short-term foreign claims held by U.S. resident banks or others (apart from official holdings). Thus in this respect the treatment is asymmetrical. The rationale for this is precautionary. The argument is that short-term dollar assets held abroad outside the central banks may at any time be sold in the market or turned in to the central banks of the respective countries and thus constitute a drain, or the threat of a drain, on the U.S. reserves. On the other hand the corresponding foreign short-term assets held by U.S. resident banks or others are not readily mobilizable by the U.S. authorities for making payments. Thus by this reckoning, if during a period non-central-bank foreign holdings of short-term dollar securities and resident non-central-bank U.S. holdings of short-term foreign securities went up by an equal amount, the situation would be shown as having deteriorated, since the former class (liabilities) are a threat to the U.S. reserve, while the latter class (assets) cannot be mobilized by the U.S. authorities to meet such a threat. Thus, though the motive for this asymmetrical treatment may be understandable, it is statistically unsatisfactory and also unsatisfactory as a guide to corrective action.

The U.S. Official Settlements Balance reckons an increase in non-central-bank foreign holdings of short-term dollar assets as an inflow of short-term capital into the U.S.; similarly an increase in U.S. resident holdings of short-term foreign assets is an outflow of short-term capital. This is a logical treatment. But the balance thus defined proved in the 1960s to be extremely volatile. This was due to large movements of funds between foreign central banks and non-central-bank foreign holders, associated with the rise of the Eurodollar market. Oscillations of this kind do not represent changes in the fundamental balance that are needed in order to determine whether corrective measures are required. It may well be that the British method of omitting short-term capital movements altogether in the assessment of surplus or deficit is, although imperfect, the most practical available.

III. Adjusting for fundamental disequilibrium

Reference has been made to the Articles of Agreement of the International Monetary Fund, which permit a nation in "fundamental disequilibrium" to alter its exchange parity. A "fundamental disequilibrium" exists when outward payments have a continuing tendency not to balance inward payments. The sum total of payments going each way depends on such matters as the competitive-

ness of the country's prices for tradable goods, profit prospects abroad (encouraging capital to flow outward) and profit prospects at home (which may attract foreign capital), past events such as international investments on which interest and profit and perhaps repayments are continuing to accrue, the provision by the home country of services abroad and by foreign countries of services at home, the flow of gifts, etc.

Taking equilibrium as a starting point, a disequilibrium may occur for various reasons. Some may be grouped under the head of structural change (resulting from changes in tastes, habits, institutions, technology, etc.). Or a fundamental imbalance may occur if wages and other costs rise faster in relation to productivity in one country than they do in others. Imbalance may also result when aggregate demand runs above the supply potential of a country, forcing prices up or raising imports. A war may have a profoundly disturbing effect on a country's economy.

THE CLASSICAL VIEW

In the traditional "classical" view no intervention by the authorities was necessary to maintain external equilibrium, except for their readiness to convert currency into gold (or silver) upon demand. The system was supposed to work automatically. If a country had a deficit, gold would flow out, and the consequent reduction in the domestic money supply would cause prices to move downward. This would stimulate exports and tend to reduce imports. The process would continue until the deficit was eliminated. Classical doctrine did not embody a clear-cut theory about international capital movements. It was usually assumed that the trade balance (more strictly, balance on goods and services) would be tailored to accommodate any capital movement that occurred. Thus, if the country was exporting capital, gold flows would cause prices to move to such a level that exports minus imports would be equal to the capital flow; equilibrium in the overall balance was automatically secured.

In due course the classical scheme of thought came under criticism. Would an outflow or inflow of specie necessarily have a sufficient effect on the price level to ensure an equal balance of payments eventually? More important, might not a reduction in the money supply have a side effect on the level of economic activity? A critic might go further and argue that this side effect would be stronger than the effect on prices to such a degree as to cause unemployment to rise to an undesirable level. The criticism was carried still further by the argument that the whole system was undesirable if in its necessary working it caused bouts of severe unemployment from time to time. The last-mentioned point is especially associated with the name of Keynes, whose writings helped to shake the almost universal belief that an automatic gold standard was the ideal system.

CONTEMPORARY VIEWS

Monetary and fiscal measures. The belief grew that positive action by governments might be required as well. The doctrine was first related to monetary policy in particular. The idea was that interest-rate adjustments should be combined with open-market operations by a central bank to ensure that the domestic money supply and borrowing facilities were conducive to external long-period equilibrium. After World War II the idea came to be widely held that government budget policy (usually called fiscal policy) should be brought in to assist monetary policy. For instance, if aggregate domestic demand was running so high as to cause rising prices, this should be reduced both by having a tight monetary policy and by increasing taxation more than expenditure or reducing expenditure without reducing taxation. The correct apportionment of this task between the monetary and fiscal arms is still a subject of discussion.

Nor is there yet agreement about the scope of these policies or their ability to secure fundamental equilibrium in all cases. There is probably agreement that when overall demand is running in excess of the supply potential of

From laissez-faire to intervention

the economy, it should be reduced by monetary and fiscal policies. There is difference of opinion as to whether the reduction of aggregate demand will bring external payments into balance in all cases. For instance, a country may have a deficit owing to some underlying economic change (such as a shift in the pattern of world trade), even if domestic demand is not above the supply potential and prices are not rising. In this case, policies designed to reduce domestic demand (commonly called deflationary policies) would cause unemployment. Some hold that, if there is an external deficit, deflationary policies should be pursued to whatever extent may be needed to eliminate that deficit. Others hold that such a policy is socially unacceptable.

The varieties of governmental action

Opinions differ also about how deflationary measures work to improve the external balance. Some hold that they work mainly by reducing domestic activity and thereby the amount of imported materials that a country needs and the amount of income that people can afford to spend on imported goods. If this were the whole effect of a deflationary policy, it would improve the external balance only in proportion to the amount by which it increased unemployment. Those who hold that this is the only manner in which deflation affects the external balance are especially opposed to relying on deflationary policies alone to eliminate a deficit in conditions in which aggregate domestic demand is not running above the supply potential. Some hold that a reduction of home demand also helps because it makes producers look around more eagerly for export markets (and increase their selling efforts in the home market). This appears to be doubtful. There is further disagreement on the extent to which deflationary policies influence the course of prices. If aggregate demand is running above the supply potential of the economy, it is highly probable that deflationary policies will slow the increase of prices and thus make a country more competitive with foreign suppliers. There is not the same agreement about the effects when demand is initially running below the supply potential of the economy. Some hold that a deflationary policy, if pushed hard enough, will infallibly slow up price increases and so help the country's external balance. Others hold that it will not, and some even argue that higher interest rates and higher taxes (weapons of deflation) could cause prices to rise. Thus it is not absolutely clear that monetary and fiscal policies will in all cases suffice to cure an external deficit, at least without socially unacceptable results.

There is also the opposite case of countries with a trade surplus. It is clear that these countries will be unwilling to encourage policies that cause domestic prices to rise. Price inflation is a social evil and politically unpopular.

In the case of surplus countries, the same distinction must be made between the situation in which aggregate demand is fully up to or above the supply potential of the economy and that in which it is not. In the former case a further increase in demand would almost certainly have an inflationary effect; accordingly, surplus countries in this condition will be unwilling to use monetary and fiscal policies to eliminate their external surpluses. On the other hand, if aggregate demand is running below supply potential, then a surplus country might reasonably be asked to increase aggregate demand by monetary and fiscal policies on the view that the increase will not cause inflation but will tend to remove the external surplus by inducing more imports and possibly causing producers to be less active in their selling efforts abroad.

Incomes policy. Prices may be rising in a country even when aggregate demand is not in excess of the supply potential. This may be due to increases of wages and other factor incomes in excess of productivity increases. Some hold that this could be dealt with by monetary and fiscal policies designed to increase unemployment. Alternatively, efforts have been made to discourage excessive wage increases by a direct approach. This may consist of a campaign of education and propaganda on the evil effects of wage-price inflation, together with what are called "guideposts" or "guidelines" as to the maximum average rates of wage increases consistent with price stability. The matter can be carried further with legal sanctions against excessive wage increases. The attempt to deal with the problem directly in this way is generally known as "incomes policy." Efforts made in this direction so far have not had very marked results.

Devaluation and revaluation. Exchange-rate movements have already been discussed. For this purpose they might be effectuated either by a more frequent use of the "adjustable peg," as now allowed in the constitution of the International Monetary Fund, or by the adoption of flexible exchange rates. The weapon would work by making the products of a deficit country more price competitive or those of a surplus country less price competitive.

Any program (including an incomes policy) that seeks to rectify an imbalance by changing the level of prices will be effective only if demand is "price elastic." In other words, if the offer of an article at a lower price did not cause an increase in demand for it more than in proportion to the fall in price, the proceeds from its export would fall rather than increase. Economists believe that price elasticities are sufficiently great for most goods so that price reductions will increase revenues in the long run. The outcome is not quite so certain in the short run.

A much faster means of changing relative price levels is devaluation, which is likely to have a quick effect on the prices of imported goods. This will raise the cost of living and may thereby accelerate demands for higher wages. If granted, these would probably cause rises in the prices of domestically produced goods. A "wage-price spiral" might follow. If this went too quickly it might frustrate the intended effect of the devaluation, namely that of enabling the country to offer its goods at lower prices in terms of foreign currency. This means that if the beneficial effects of a devaluation are not gathered in quickly, there may be no beneficial effect at all.

The authorities of a country that has just devalued will therefore be especially active in preventing or moderating domestic price increases. They will need to use the other policy measures already discussed. Devaluation (or the downward movement of a flexible rate) is thus not a remedy that makes other forms of official policy unnecessary. Some have argued that if exchange rates were allowed to float, nothing further would have to be done officially to bring the external balance into equilibrium. This is a minority view.

One further point must be made regarding the exchange-rate weapon. It has been found in practice that governments resist upward valuation more than they do devaluation. Devaluations have in fact been larger and more frequent than upward valuations. This has an unfortunate consequence. It means that the aggregate amount of price inflation in deficit countries resorting to devaluation as a remedy will not be offset by equivalent price decreases in the surplus countries. Therefore this system, if more strongly resorted to, would have a bias toward worldwide inflation.

An exception to this must be made for the "crawling peg." Logically that system would produce in the world as much upward valuation as downward valuation and therefore as much tendency for prices to fall as for prices to rise, at least to the extent that price movements are affected by exchange-rate movements.

Trade restrictions. Since World War II the major industrial countries have attempted to reduce interferences with the free flow of international trade. This policy, by extending the international division of labour, should increase world economic welfare. An exception has had to be allowed in favour of the less developed countries. In the early stages of the development of a country, the effectiveness and feasibility of the three types of adjustment mechanism already discussed, particularly the all-important monetary and fiscal policies, may be much less than in the more advanced countries. The less developed countries may therefore be driven to protection or the control of imports, for lack of any other weapon, if they are to stay solvent. It has already been noted that, even in the case of a more advanced country, the effectiveness and appropriateness of the above-mentioned adjustment mechanisms are not always certain. Thus, there is no certainty that some limitation on foreign trade and on the international division of labour may not be a lesser evil than the consequences that might follow from a vigorous use of the other adjustment mechanisms, such as unemployment.

Restrictions on capital exports.   Interference with capital movements is generally considered a lesser evil than interference with the free flow of trade. Thus in 1964 the U.S. imposed an "Interest Equalization Tax" (on investment in foreign portfolio securities) and restraints on direct capital investment abroad. The theory of the optimum international movement of capital has not yet been thoroughly developed, but there may be a presumption in favour of absolutely free movement. The matter is not quite certain; for instance, it might be desirable from the point of view of the world optimum to channel the outflow of capital from a high-saving country into the less developed countries, although the level of profit obtainable in other high-saving countries might be greater. Or it might be expedient to restrain wealthy individuals in less-developed countries, where domestic saving was in notably short supply, from sending their funds to high-saving countries.

While there may be good reasons for interfering with the absolutely free international flow of capital in certain cases, it is not obvious that the outflow of capital from, or inflow of capital into, a country should be tailored to surpluses or deficits in current external accounts. It may be that in some cases the sound remedy for a deficit (or surplus) is to adopt adjustment measures such as those referred to above, bearing upon current items, rather than taking the easier way of adjusting capital movements to the de facto balance on current account.

IV. International cooperation

THE INTERNATIONAL MONETARY FUND

The
heritage of
Bretton
Woods

The International Monetary Fund, founded at the Bretton Woods Conference in 1944, is the official organization for securing international monetary cooperation. It has done most useful work in various fields, such as research and the publication of statistics and the tendering of monetary advice to less developed countries. It has also conducted valuable consultations with the more developed countries, and it has helped to introduce more order into currency movements and exchange relations than obtained, for instance, after World War I.

Drawing rights.   Of particular interest to this discussion is the Fund's system of Drawing Rights, which permits countries in temporary deficit to draw supplies of foreign currency according to predetermined quotas. These extra supplies of currency give a country more time in which to adjust its balance of payments and so avoid taking unsound or unneighbourly measures like import restrictions for lack of enough reserves to tide it over a difficulty. The mechanism is as follows. Members of the Fund—now numbering over 100—are required to make initial deposits according to their quotas, 25 percent in gold and 75 percent in their own currencies. The Fund makes its stock of members' currencies available to member countries that wish to draw upon their quotas. When creditor countries are presented with their own currencies previously deposited by them with the Fund, they are obliged to take them in final discharge of debts owed by other member countries. Since they previously deposited these currencies themselves they are in effect getting nothing from the debtor countries in respect of the debts owed to them, and their willingness to accept payment in this way is their contribution to the overall liquidity of the world system. Later the creditor countries may themselves become debtors and partake of the benefits. The debtors, who in a sense are getting something for nothing, have to repay the Fund usually in three to five years.

The exercise of Drawing Rights is subject to discussion and sometimes to conditions, except for drawings on what are called the gold tranches—i.e., sums equal to the members' original deposits of gold—which are given "the overwhelming benefit of the doubt." Countries are also

free to draw without discussion up to the net amount to which they have previously been drawn upon by other countries.

The International Monetary Fund as it finally emerged from the wartime discussions was a much more modest undertaking than had originally been conceived by the British. An early British proposal would have required creditor countries to receive payment in paper money up to the total amount of all the quotas of all the debtor countries. This seemed to many to be more than it was fair to ask creditors to do. The U.S. claimed that for a number of years after the war it was likely to be in credit against the whole of the rest of the world, and so it was. Under the British plan they would have had to give an unconscionably large amount of credit, with no certainty of repayment. At that time it did not seem at all likely that the U.S. would ever go into deficit at a later date, which, of course, it did.

The scarce currency problem.   The arrangement was bound to create difficulties should the debtor-creditor position among member countries be lopsided. The sum total of the quotas of the countries in debit might exceed the sum total of the quotas of the countries in credit. The debtor countries, having paid gold into the Fund and undertaken certain obligations, would naturally have the right, subject to discussions and to convincing the Fund that they would in due course put their houses in order, to draw the whole amount of their quotas as needed. But if the position was lopsided—e.g., if the sole creditor country was the U.S.—the Fund would not have enough dollars to satisfy the Drawing Rights of all the debtor countries. To meet this difficulty the "scarce currency" clause (article 7) was devised. If any country should become an overwhelming creditor, so that the supply of its currency available to the Fund became exhausted, this currency would be declared "scarce." The debtor countries would then have the right to discriminate in their monetary and commercial policies against the country in question. Thus the debtor countries would be able to maintain full trading relations with each other, while confining their restrictions to dealings with the creditor. This seemed a sensible arrangement.

But the scarce currency provision has not been applied. In the early postwar years the U.S. met the situation by giving "Marshall Plan Aid" on a generous scale and thereby relieving the world dollar shortage. Later, toward the close of the 1950s, the position was reversed and some countries of continental Europe became heavy creditors. But by this time the scarce currency clause had become ideologically unacceptable. Great efforts had been made to get rid of all forms of discrimination in international dealings, and it would have been thought objectionable to revive discrimination under this clause. Furthermore, many nations had in the meanwhile dismantled the administrative machinery needed for such discrimination. The difficulty would have to be met in another way.

OTHER EFFORTS AT FINANCIAL COOPERATION

The Group of Ten.   During 1961 there were signs of a crisis. The U.S. had been running a heavy deficit since 1958, and the U.K. plunged into one in 1960. It looked as if these two countries might need to draw upon continental European currencies in excess of the amounts available. Per Jacobssen, then managing director of the International Monetary Fund, persuaded a group of countries to provide standby credits amounting to $6,000,000,000 in all, so that supplementary supplies of their currencies would be available. The plan was not confined to the countries that happened to be in credit at that time but was extended to other important countries, the currencies of which might run short at some future time. This plan was known as the "General Arrangements to Borrow." The adhering countries were ten in number: the U.S., the U.K., Canada, France, Germany, Italy, The Netherlands, Belgium, Sweden, and Japan. They became known as the "Group of Ten."

The arrangement was subject to the agreement that

Problems
of the
1960s

countries actually supplying additional currency would have the right to take cognizance of how the Fund used it. This put them in a power position as against the International Monetary Fund itself. Since then the Group of Ten has worked together in deliberating on international monetary problems.

At the meeting of the International Monetary Fund in 1963 the idea was put forward that some reform would be needed in the international monetary system, especially by way of increasing liquidity, and the Group of Ten was asked to give this consideration. It was felt that before any new plan was proposed, prior agreement of the Group of Ten would be essential. After four years of discussion, the Group of Ten devised the "Special Drawing Rights" proposal adopted by the International Monetary Fund at the Rio de Janeiro meeting in 1967 (see below).

The dominant position gained by the Group of Ten has been due not only to their provision of standby credit but also to the manner in which they do their business. The ultimate authority of the Group resides in the finance ministers of the countries concerned, who meet from time to time. Their deputies meet more frequently for detailed work on particular problems. These deputies consist of high-ranking persons in their respective treasuries and central banks; they are resident in their own countries and have day-to-day knowledge of their problems and of what is politically feasible. In this respect they are in a much more advantageous position than the executive directors of the International Monetary Fund, who live in Washington, D.C., and have less contact with their home governments; they also tend to be persons of higher standing and authority.

The Basel Group. In 1930, a Bank for International Settlements was established at Basel; its main duty was to supervise and organize the transfer of German reparations to the recipient countries. This "transfer problem" had caused much trouble during the 1920s. There may also have been a hope in the minds of some that this institution might one day develop into something like a world central bank.

Not long after it was set up the Germans gained a moratorium on their reparations payments. By then, however, the Bank for International Settlements had become a convenient place for the heads of the European central banks to meet together and discuss current problems. This practice was resumed after the war, and the U.S., although not a member, was invited to join in the deliberations.

When Marshall Plan Aid was furnished by the U.S. to help European countries in their postwar reconstruction, a European Payments Union was established to facilitate multilateral trade and settlements in advance of the time when it might be possible to re-establish full multilateralism on a world scale. The war had left a jumble of trade restrictions that could not be quickly abolished. The European Payments Union also contained a plan for the provision of credit to European debtors. The U.K. was a member, and with it was associated the whole sterling area. Responsibility for working the machinery of the European Payments Union was assigned to the Bank for International Settlements. The European Payments Union was ultimately wound up after the countries of Europe were able to eliminate the last restrictions and make their currencies fully convertible in 1958.

In January and February 1961 there was a serious sterling crisis, due partly to the British deficit of 1960 and partly to a large movement of funds in anticipation of an upward valuation of the German mark, which happened, and thereafter in anticipation of a second upward valuation, which did not happen at that time. To help the British, the Basel Group of central banks provided substantial credits. These were liquidated when the U.K. transferred its indebtedness to the International Monetary Fund the following July. The Basel Group has provided further credits from time to time. The problems involved have continued to be discussed at the monthly meetings.

Special mention should be made of an arrangement for the support of the sterling area in 1968. After the devaluation of sterling in 1967 it was feared that the monetary authorities of the countries composing the sterling area might wish to reduce their holdings of sterling. As there was a continuing problem of world liquidity and sterling played an important part as a reserve currency, the international consensus was that any substantial reduction in the holding of sterling as a reserve currency would be damaging to the international monetary system. Under the arrangement made in 1968 the U.K. on its side agreed to give a dollar guarantee to the value of the greater part of the sterling-area reserves; there were slightly different arrangements with each monetary authority. On its side the Bank for International Settlement agreed to organize credits to finance payments deficits for some countries of the sterling area, should these occur at times when the U.K. might find it difficult to handle them.

The OECD. A body known as the Organization for European Economic Co-operation was set up in 1948 to make arrangements for the distribution of Marshall Aid among the countries of Europe. When its tasks in this connection were accomplished, it remained in existence, was broadened to include the U.S., Canada, and Japan, and was renamed the Organization for Economic Co-operation and Development. It has a permanent staff and headquarters in Paris. It undertakes research on a substantial scale and affords a forum for the discussion of international economic problems. Special mention should be made of Working Party No. 3 of its Economic Committee, which is concerned with problems of money and exchange; at times the personnel of the Working Party has been much the same as that of the deputies of the Group of Ten. It issued a very important report on balance of payments adjustment problems in 1966. The Organization for Economic Co-operation and Development has also set up an organization called the Development Assistance Committee, concerned with problems of assistance to the developing countries.

Working Party No. 3

Swap agreements. The informal system of swap agreements provides a mutual arrangement between central banks for standby credits designed to see countries through difficulties on the occasions of large movements of funds. These are intended only to offset private international flows of capital on precautionary or speculative account, not to finance even temporary deficits in countries' balance of payments. Arranged ad hoc and informally, they depend on the mutual goodwill and trust of the central banks involved. The system of credits, although informal, must be reckoned as important, since they are of large amount. For instance, in 1973 the U.S. had swap credits amounting to \$18,000,000,000.

Events may move in the future in one of two different ways. Some hold that the mutual swap system should be formalized and rendered permanent. In this form it would constitute an international arrangement of even greater importance than the International Monetary Fund itself. But it has to do only with large-scale precautionary and speculative movements of short-term private capital. And so the problem resolves itself into the question whether these large private movements must be expected to be a permanent feature of the international monetary world. If skillful craftsmanship (*e.g.,* the substitution of a more flexible official exchange-rate system for the "adjustable peg") can produce a state of affairs in which large flows cease to occur, then the provision of mutual standby swap credits will no longer be needed.

(R.F.H.)

V. International reserves

GOLD AND RESERVE CURRENCIES

Gold remained the most important medium available to the monetary authorities for international settlements in the 1960s, but the quantity of gold available declined as a proportion of international reserves. The founders of the International Monetary Fund had intended that the currencies of members should have a fixed value in gold to be altered only on occasions of official change of parity. The provisions of the International Monetary Fund, however, were not sufficient to secure this. It was necessary for governments with reserves of gold to intervene in the market to maintain the gold value of major

Intervention to maintain gold value

currencies at par. In the 1950s the British did this through the London gold bullion market. In the autumn of 1960, lack of confidence in the dollar developed, and financial advisers recommended the conversion of dollars into gold on a rather substantial scale. The result was a supernormal demand for gold in the London market, and the British had to turn to the U.S. for assurance that they would be reimbursed in gold for the dollars acquired in the process of holding down the gold price. The result of this was burdensome to the U.S., since dollars were by no means the only currency converted into gold. The British authorities acquired dollars because the dollar was the "currency of intervention." It seemed unfair that the U.S. should lose gold in respect of the total flight out of currencies, dollars or others. Accordingly, an arrangement was made for setting up what became known as the gold pool. It was agreed that when the British, to hold the price of gold down, had to sell it in the London market, the members of the gold pool would reimburse them for the gold lost. For several years this prevented a rise in the price.

In March 1968 there was a loss of confidence in the dollar of even larger dimensions. This was attributable partly to the continuing U.S. trade deficit and partly to doubts arising from the devaluation of sterling in the preceding November. The demand for gold became so great that the authorities decided to close the gold bullion market in London; when it reopened, no further attempt was made to hold down the price of gold. The gold pool arrangement came to an end. At the same time the former members of the gold pool agreed that their central banks would continue to exchange gold against currencies held by other central banks at the official rate. The result was the "two-tier system," in which gold circulated among central banks against currencies at the official valuation but usually circulated in free markets at a higher valuation. It lasted until November 1973, when the countries that had established it agreed to terminate it.

SPECIAL DRAWING RIGHTS

By the 1960s the limitations of the world's reserves of gold, sterling, and dollars had become painfully apparent. To resolve this difficulty, a new kind of reserve called Special Drawing Rights (SDR's) was devised by the International Monetary Fund. Members of the fund were to be allocated SDR's, year by year, in prearranged quantities, to be used for the discharge of international indebtedness. At the IMF meeting in 1969, agreement was reached for an issue extending over three years. These Special Drawing Rights differed from ordinary Drawing Rights in three important respects: (1) The use of Special Drawing Rights was not to be subject to negotiations or conditions. (2) There was to be only a very much modified form of repayment obligation. A member who used more than 70 percent of all the Special Drawing Rights allotted to him in a given period had to repay to the extent needed to reduce his average use of the rights during that period to 70 percent of the total. Thus 70 percent of all Special Drawing Rights issued could be thought of as reserves in the fullest sense, since a member who limited his use to this amount would have no repayment obligation. (3) In the case of Drawing Rights, the fund uses currencies as subscribed by members to provide the medium of payment. By contrast, the Special Drawing Rights were to be accepted in final discharge of debt without being translated into any particular currency. This should obviate the need for anything like the General Arrangements to Borrow. Though currencies would have to be subscribed by members receiving Special Drawing Rights, these would be in the background and would not be used, except in the case of a member in net credit on Special Drawing Rights account who wished to withdraw from the scheme.

SDR's versus Drawing Rights

VI. The system of floating rates

THE CRISIS OF THE DOLLAR

The international monetary system established at the Bretton Woods Conference in 1944 underwent profound changes in the 1970s. This system had assumed that the dollar was the strongest currency in the world because the United States was the strongest economic power. Other countries were expected to have difficulty from time to time in stabilizing their exchange rates and would need assistance in the form of credits from the International Monetary Fund, but the dollar was expected to remain stable enough to function as a substitute for gold in international transactions. In the second half of the 1960s these assumptions came into question. The war in Vietnam led to an inflation that produced enormous deficits in the U.S. balance of payments and ultimately forced devaluation of the dollar. In 1970 the U.S. balance of payments deficit was almost $10,000,000,000. The flood of dollars into other countries caused difficulty for the European central banks, which were forced to increase their dollar holdings in order to maintain their currencies at the established exchange rates. As the flood continued in 1971, the West German and Dutch governments decided to let their currencies float—that is, to let their exchange rates fluctuate beyond their assigned parities. Austria and Switzerland revalued their currencies upward in relation to the dollar. These measures helped for a time, but in August the outflow of dollars resumed, and on August 15 Pres. Richard M. Nixon formally suspended what remained of the U.S. commitment made in 1934 to convert dollars into gold. This ended the postwar monetary system established at the Bretton Woods Conference. Most of the major trading countries decided to abandon fixed exchange rates and let their currencies find their own values in relation to the dollar.

End of Bretton Woods system

THE SMITHSONIAN AGREEMENT AND AFTER

On December 17 and 18, 1971, representatives of the Group of Ten met at the Smithsonian Institution in Washington and agreed on a realignment of currencies. The dollar was devalued in terms of gold, while other currencies were appreciated in terms of the dollar. On the whole, the dollar was devalued by nearly 10 percent in relation to the other Group of Ten currencies (those of the U.K., Canada, France, West Germany, Italy, The Netherlands, Belgium, Sweden, and Japan).

Several months after the Smithsonian Agreement, the six members of the European Economic Community (EEC) agreed to maintain their exchange rates within a range of 2.25 percent of parity with each other, by means of purchases and sales of each other's currencies. This arrangement came to be known as "the snake in the tunnel"—the tunnel being the wider range of 4.5 percent permitted under the rules of the International Monetary Fund.

The Smithsonian Agreement proved to be only a temporary solution to the international currency crisis. A second devaluation of the dollar (by 10 percent) was announced in February 1973, and not long afterward Japan and the EEC countries decided to let their currencies float. At the time, these were thought of as temporary measures to cope with speculation and to prevent great shifts of capital from one currency to another. In fact, however, it was the end of the system of established par values. Throughout the rest of the decade the major currencies continued to float, their exchange rates being determined by the course of events from day to day or year to year. The quadrupling of the price of petroleum at the end of 1973, followed by the deepest recession since the 1930s together with a prolonged inflation, made a return to fixed par values impossible. Instead, the finance ministries and central banks began to seek ways of making the system of floating rates manageable.

Much of the work involved in learning to live with the system of floating rates was carried on by financial specialists meeting in various national capitals. The most important group was the Committee of Twenty, set up by the International Monetary Fund, which held its first meeting in September 1972 and concluded in June 1974 with an Outline of Reform. It proposed a system of "stable but adjustable par values," with occa-

Committee of Twenty

sional use of floating rates. The Special Drawing Rights would become the principal reserve asset, while gold and the dollar would play a reduced role.

In November 1975 the heads of government of France, West Germany, Italy, Japan, the U.K., and the U.S. met at the Château de Rambouillet near Paris to discuss monetary and economic questions. The meeting represented a compromise between French and American views on the exchange rate mechanism. The French had favoured an early return to stable par values, while the Americans had wanted to preserve the right of countries to let their currencies float. The two countries agreed to add to the Articles of Agreement of the IMF a provision that would permit currencies to float if the situation required it. The turbulent character of the exchange markets in ensuing years made a return to stable par values seem remote.

BIBLIOGRAPHY. E.M. BERNSTEIN (chairman), *Report of the Review Committee for Balance of Payments Statistics to the Bureau of the Budget* (1965), an authoritative analysis of the complex problems involved in the compilation and presentation of U.S. balance of payments statistics; R.N. COOPER, *Macroeconomic Policy Adjustment in Independent Countries* (1969); P. EINZIG, *The Euro-Dollar System: Practice and Theory of International Interest Rates* (1964), an analysis of the international market for short-term loans denominated in Eurocurrencies, with far-reaching implications for official balance of payments policies; O. EMMINGER, "Practical Aspects of the Problem of Balance-of-Payments Adjustments," *Journal of Political Economy*, 75:512–522 (Aug. 1967); J. MARCUS FLEMING, *Guidelines for Balance-of-Payments Adjustment under the Par-Value System* (1968); MILTON FRIEDMAN, "The Role of Monetary Policy," *American Economic Review*, 58:1–17 (March 1968), a discussion of the view that there should be a minimum of interference with the operation of market forces; GROUP OF TEN, *Report of a Study Group to the Deputies of the Group of Ten on the Creation of Reserve Assets* (1965), a detailed and systematic analysis of various viewpoints that constitutes an important landmark in the process leading to the adoption of Special Drawing Rights; GOTTFRIED HABERLER, *Der internationale Handel* (1936; Eng. trans., *Theory of International Trade*, 1959), a classic work; R. HARROD, *Money* (1969), a comprehensive treatise with a strong historical background; INTERNATIONAL MONETARY FUND, *The Role of Exchange Rates in the Adjustment of International Payments* (1970); H.G. JOHNSON, "Theoretical Problems of the International Monetary System," *Pakistan Development Review*, 7:1–28 (Spring 1967); JOHN MAYNARD KEYNES, *The Means to Prosperity* (1933), a brief booklet, published at the time of the World Economic Conference in London in 1933, containing the seminal ideas that led to his later proposals; F. MACHLUP, *International Payments, Debts and Gold* (1964); J.E. MEADE, *Theory of International Economic Policy* (1951), one of the most important systematic treatises on this subject; R.A. MUNDELL, *International Economics* (1968); ORGANIZATION FOR ECONOMIC CO-OPERATION AND DEVELOPMENT, ECONOMIC POLICY COMMITTEE, WORKING PARTY NO. 3, *The Balance of Payments Adjustment Process: A Report* (1966); W. SALANT *et al.*, *The U.S. Balance of Payments* (1963), an examination of the causes and nature of the U.S. payments deficit; B. TEW, *International Monetary Co-operation* (1967), a succinct volume dealing with principles and institutions; ROBERT TRIFFIN, *Gold and the Dollar Crisis: The Future of Convertibility* (1960); ROBERT SOLOMON, *The International Monetary System 1945–1976* (1977), a review of events since World War II by a financial economist who was closely involved with them.

(R.F.H./F.S.P.)

Excretion, Human

Excretion, the elimination of the waste products of metabolism and the removal of surplus substances from the tissues of the body, is performed by several organs. The lungs excrete carbon dioxide and water. The skin gives off water, salts, and a little urea. The intestines excrete some water along with the dietary residues and bacteria (see EXCRETION AND EXCRETORY SYSTEMS; SKIN, HUMAN; RESPIRATION, HUMAN). Most of the remaining excretion is through the urine, the product of the excretory system, consisting of the kidneys, the ureters, the bladder, and the urethra. The present article is concerned with the functioning of this system.

The ureters, urethra, bladder, and the collecting tubules and renal pelvis of the kidney function primarily as passageways or storage units for the urine that is produced by the nephrons, the 1,000,000–1,250,000 functioning units of each kidney. Each nephron consists of a glomerulus—a tuft or coil of the smallest of the blood vessels, the capillaries—and a long narrow tube, or tubule. The closed end of the tubule is widened and folded back to form a double-walled cup, called Bowman's capsule, which enfolds the glomerulus. The three main segments of the rest of the tubule, the proximal convoluted tubule, the loop of Henle, and the distal convoluted tubule, vary in diameter and structure and have specialized functions (see EXCRETORY SYSTEM, HUMAN).

The kidney has evolved so as to enable man as a complex organism to exist on dry land where water and salts must be conserved, wastes excreted in concentrated form, and the blood and the tissue fluids strictly regulated as to volume, chemical composition, and osmotic pressure. Under the drive of arterial pressure, water and salts are filtered from the blood through the capillaries of the glomerulus into the lumen, or passageway, of the nephron, and then most of the water and the substances it contains that are essential to the body are reabsorbed into the blood. The rest of the filtrate is drained off as urine. The kidneys, thus, help maintain a constant internal environment despite a wide range of changes in the external environment.

The kidneys regulate three essential and interrelated properties of the tissues—water content, acid-base balance, and osmotic pressure—in such a way as to maintain electrolyte and water equilibrium—that is, to maintain a balance between quantities of water and the quantities of such chemicals as calcium, potassium, sodium, phosphorus, and sulfate in solution. Unless the concentrations of mineral ions such as sodium, crystalloids such as glucose, and wastes such as urea are maintained within narrow limits, bodily malfunction rapidly develops leading to sickness or death.

The removal of both kidneys leads to an accumulation of urinary constituents in the blood (uremia) with death in 14–21 days. Whenever the blood contains an abnormal constituent in solution or an excess of normal constituents including water and salts, the kidneys excrete these until normal composition is restored. The kidneys are the only means for eliminating the wastes that are the end products of protein metabolism. They do not themselves modify the waste products that they excrete, but transfer them to the urine in the form in which they are produced in other parts of the body. The only exception to this is their ability to manufacture ammonia and hippuric acid. Both ammonia and hippuric acid are also products of metabolism, waste excreted in the urine. The kidneys also eliminate drugs and toxic agents. Thus the kidneys eliminate the unwanted end products of metabolism, such as urea, while limiting the loss of valuable substances such as glucose. In maintaining the acid-base equilibrium, the kidneys remove the excess of hydrogen ions produced from the normally acid-forming diet and manufacture ammonium radicals to remove these ions as ammonium salts.

To carry on its functions the kidney is endowed with a relatively huge blood supply. The blood processed in the kidneys amounts to some 1,250 millilitres a minute, or 1,800 litres (about 475 gallons) a day, which is 400 times the total blood volume and roughly one-fourth the volume pumped each day by the heart. Every 24 hours 170–180 litres (45–47.5 gallons) of water are filtered from the bloodstream into the renal tubules; and by far the greater part of this—some 168.5 litres of water together with salts dissolved in it—is reabsorbed by the cells lining the tubules and returned to the blood. The total glomerular filtrate in 24 hours is no less than 50–60 times the volume of blood plasma (the blood minus its cells) in the entire body. Only 1.5 litres of water, containing the waste products of metabolism, are passed out as urine in 24 hours, a fair daily average for an adult man on an ordinary mixed diet in temperate climates; but the actual volume varies with fluid intake and occupational and environmental factors. With vigorous sweating it may fall to 500 milli-

General function of kidney

Volumes of blood, water, and urine processed by kidneys

litres (about a pint) a day; with a large water intake it may rise to three litres, or six times as much. The kidney can vary its reabsorption of water to compensate for changes in plasma volume resulting from dehydration or overhydration.

The kidneys also perform certain nonexcretory functions. They secrete substances that enter the blood. These are of two kinds: renin, which is concerned indirectly with the control of electrolyte balance and blood pressure; and erythropoietin, which is important for the formation of hemoglobin and red blood cells, especially in response to anemia or deficiency of oxygen reaching the body tissues. Finally, the kidneys are subject to both nervous and humoral (hormonal) control; but they do possess a considerable degree of autonomy; i.e., function continues in the organ isolated from the nervous system but kept alive with circulating fluid. Indeed, if this were not so kidney transplantation would be impossible.

VASCULAR CONSIDERATIONS

The two kidneys are bean-shaped organs, more or less upright, with the convex side away from the centre of the body, and with the concave side toward it. Within each kidney are cone-shaped masses, called pyramids, each with its base toward the convex side of the kidney, and with the apex (papilla) protruding into the cavity, or pelvis, at the concave side of the kidney. A layer of tissue between the bases of the pyramids and the outside of the kidney is called the cortex; projections of the cortex extend down between the pyramids. The pyramids, collectively, are called the renal medulla. Each pyramid and its surrounding tissue is called a lobe. The point on the concave side of the kidney where blood vessels, nerves, and the ureter enter is called the renal hilum.

The main renal (kidney) artery divides in the renal hilum into five or six branches, which run outward through the medulla between the pyramids. At the junction of medulla and cortex, the branches give rise to the arcuate arteries, which turn at right angles to run over the bases of the pyramids between cortex and medulla parallel to the kidney surface. These arteries in turn give rise to the interlobular vessels, which branch off at right angles and enter the cortex. Each interlobular vessel is an end artery; that is, it does not join with its fellows. It gives off on all sides short wide branches, called afferent arterioles, thick muscular walled vessels that lead to the glomeruli. The afferent arterioles split up into the glomerular capillaries, forming a tuft or network enclosed in Bowman's capsule.

The glomerulus consists of this capillary bundle enfolded into the capsule of the nephron. The vessel, called an efferent arteriole, that carries blood from the capsule is half the diameter of the afferent vessel but of similar bore because its muscle coat is thinner; the efferent arteriole breaks up into a second set of capillaries that branch out around the proximal and distal convoluted tubules of the same and of neighbouring nephrons. From this capillary complex around the tubules the blood is collected into veins that drain via interlobular trunks to join the renal vein at the hilum. The afferent and efferent arterioles of the nephron can contract and dilate so as to condition the glomerular pressure over a wide range. The tubules receive only blood that has first passed through a glomerulus. They have little or no direct arterial supply.

The blood supply of the medulla is different from that of the cortex. The efferent arterioles from adjacent glomeruli send out straight branches, called vasa recta, that descend into the pyramids parallel to the Henle loops. They conform to the curve of the loops and return after branching as the ascending vasa recta to join the interlobular veins. The vasa recta form close functional units with the Henle loops and the collecting ducts in the medulla.

Intrarenal blood pressures

The renal arteries are short and spring directly from the abdominal aorta, so that arterial blood is delivered to the kidneys at maximum available pressure. The rate of flow in the cortex is many times greater than that in the medulla because of the rich network of vessels around the nephrons in the cortex. The blood pressure in the glomerular capillaries is higher than that in other parts of the body. Within the kidney there are no interconnections between the branches of the renal artery, but there are many between the intertubular capillaries and there are wide arteriovenous shunts (bypasses between arteries and veins) in the arcuate zone, the border area between cortex and medulla. These are unimportant under normal conditions, because they remain closed in order to direct all available blood to the cortex; but in certain circumstances, such as surgical shock, the shunts may divert blood rapidly from the arterial to the venous side of the circulation and bypass the cortex.

The shunt mechanism, together with arteriolar control of the afferent-efferent glomerular complex, affords a wide range of variability in blood supply to different parts of the kidney. The muscular coats of the arterioles are well supplied with sympathetic vasoconstrictor fibres (nerve fibres that induce narrowing of the blood vessels), and there is also a small parasympathetic supply from the vagus and splanchnic nerves that induces dilatation of the vessels. Sympathetic stimulation causes vasoconstriction and reduces urinary output, but severing of the nerves is without much effect. The vessel walls are also sensitive to circulating epinephrine and norepinephrine hormones, small amounts of which constrict the efferent arterioles, and large amounts of which constrict all the vessels; and to angiotensin, which is a constrictor agent closely related to renin.

Factors that affect renal flow

Because of these factors, the kidney has a remarkable capacity to regulate its internal circulation regardless of the systemic blood pressure, provided the latter is not extremely high or extremely low. The forces involved in circulation of the blood in the kidneys must remain constant if the monitoring of the water and electrolyte composition of the blood is to proceed undisturbed; and this autoregulation is preserved even in the kidney cut off from the nervous system and, to a lesser extent, in the isolated perfused organ (i.e., in an organ removed from the body and kept viable by having salt solutions of physiologically suitable concentrations circulated through it). The exact mechanism by which the kidney regulates its own circulation is not certainly known, but various theories have been proposed: (1) If systemic blood pressure rises, the renal blood flow remains constant because of the increased viscosity of the blood. Normally, the interlobular arteries have an axial (central) stream of red cells with an outer layer of plasma so that the afferent arterioles skim off more plasma than cells. If the blood pressure rises, the skimming effect increases, and the more densely packed axial flow of cells in the vessels offers increasing resistance to the pressure, which has to overcome this heightened viscosity. Thus the overall renal blood flow changes little. Up to a point, similar considerations in reverse apply to the effects of reduced systemic pressure. (2) Changes in the arterial pressure modify the pressure exerted by the interstitial (tissue) fluid of the kidney on capillaries and veins so that increased pressure raises, and decreased pressure lowers, resistance to blood flow. (3) If the renal blood flow tends to rise, there is a higher sodium content in the fluid in the distal tubules because of the increased filtration rate. This content stimulates the formation of renin, which causes constriction of the vessels and reduction of flow.

The effective renal flow of whole blood is about 1¼–1⅓ quarts (1,200–1,300 millilitres) per minute, equivalent to a quarter of the resting cardiac output, or 400 millilitres per 100 grams of kidney substance per minute. Women have smaller kidneys than men, and the corresponding flow figures are 15 percent less for the same standard body surface. The plasma flow per minute is some 600–700 millilitres, but only five-sixths of this, the effective plasma flow, is actually available for glomerular filtration, because some blood passes through inert connective tissue. The flow is greater when one is lying down than when standing; it is higher in fever; and it is reduced by prolonged vigorous exertion, pain, anxiety, and other emotions that constrict the arterioles and divert blood to other organs. It is also reduced by depletion of water and salts and, markedly, in shock, including operative shock, hemorrhage, and asphyxia. A profound fall in systemic blood pressure, as after severe hemorrhage, may so reduce renal blood flow that no urine at all is formed for a time. Death may occur from suppression of glomerular function if dehydration causes a fall in pressure. Simple fainting causes vasoconstriction and reduced urine output. Urinary secretion is also stopped by obstruction of the ureter when back pressure reaches a critical point.

Dependence of filtration rate on glomerular pressure

The importance of these vascular factors lies in the fact that the basic process occurring in the glomerulus is one of filtration, the energy for which is furnished by the blood pressure within the glomerular capillaries; and the higher this pressure, the greater the filtration rate. Indeed, the volume of urine formed depends more on the blood pressure than on the actual volume of blood flow. Glomerular pressure is a function of the systemic pressure as modified by the tonus (state of constriction or dilation) of the afferent and efferent arterioles, as these open or close spontaneously or in response to nervous or hormonal control. Constriction of the afferent vessels reduces blood flow, glomerular pressure, and filtration rate. Efferent constriction also causes reduced flow, but raises glomerular pressure and filtration. The arteriovenous shunt system comes into play only exceptionally, as after severe crushing injuries, when it may divert the blood flow massively from cortex to medulla and so cause a fatal destruction of cortical substance.

THE FORMATION OF URINE

The urine leaving the kidney shows great differences in composition from the plasma entering it (Table 1). The study of renal function must account for these differences; *e.g.*, the absence of protein and glucose from the urine and the very high levels of ammonia and creatinine in the urine, while sodium and calcium remain at similar low levels in both urine and plasma.

Table 1: Relative Composition of Plasma and Urine in Normal Men

	plasma g/100 ml	urine g/100 ml	concentration in urine
Water	90–93	95	—
Proteins and other colloids	7–8.5	—	—
Urea	0.03	2	× 60
Uric acid	0.002	0.03	× 15
Glucose	0.1	—	—
Creatinine	0.001	0.1	× 100
Sodium	0.32	0.6	× 2
Potassium	0.02	0.15	× 7
Calcium	0.01	0.015	× 1.5
Magnesium	0.0025	0.01	× 4
Chloride	0.37	0.6	× 2
Phosphate	0.003	0.12	× 40
Sulfate	0.003	0.18	× 60
Ammonia	0.0001	0.05	× 500

The modern view of the formation of urine is briefly as follows: a large volume of ultrafiltrate—a liquid from which the blood cells and the blood proteins have been filtered out—is produced by the glomerulus into the capsule. As this liquid traverses the proximal convoluted tubule, most of its water and salts are reabsorbed, some of the solutes completely and others partially; *i.e.*, there is a separation of substances that must be retained from those due for rejection. Subsequently the loop of Henle, distal convoluted tubule, and collecting ducts are mainly concerned with the fine control of water and electrolyte balance.

Glomerular filtration. Urine formation begins as a process of ultrafiltration of a large volume of blood plasma from the glomerular capillaries into the capsular space, colloids such as proteins being held back while crystalloids (substances in true solution) pass through. About 20 percent of the water in the plasma, together with its dissolved crystalloids, traverses the glomerular membrane, leaving the protein constituents behind. The actual filtration membrane consists of the wall of the capillaries, which is largely endothelium, or lining, and the wall of the capsule, the permeability of which is such as to suggest that it acts as a porous membrane and that the diameter of its pores determines the size of the molecules filtered. The pore size is just small enough to retain the plasma proteins. The smallest protein molecule— serum albumin, of molecular weight 72,000—is detained, whereas free hemoglobin (68,000) and gelatin (35,000) pass freely. An alternative theory is that plasma solutes diffuse across the basement membrane. But glomerular function accords with the known characteristics of artificial porous membranes in that larger particles pass as rapidly as smaller ones and all molecules smaller than the filter pores are transmitted. The only difference between plasma and filtrate is the absence from the latter of molecules above a certain borderline size. Since the capsular filtrate is a true ultrafiltrate, a rise in arterial pressure increases its volume and a rise in ureteric back pressure decreases it. Normally no protein passes the filter, but normal filtration depends on proper nutrition and oxygenation of glomeruli and capsules, and if these are damaged by lack of oxygen or by disease they become more permeable, and plasma proteins enter the urine. It should be added that certain quite healthy individuals, mostly young, have albuminuria (plasma protein albumin in the urine) when they are standing but not when they are recumbent, and that there is often temporary albuminuria during pregnancy, from pressure on the renal veins.

Thus the initial filtrate is produced by entirely physical means. It contains all the substances present in blood, and in the same concentration as in the blood, except the colloids and fats. It is virtually protein-free, it is isotonic (in balance) with plasma, and contains glucose, urea, creatinine, uric acid, and blood electrolytes. Animal experiments confirm that fluid collected directly from Bowman's capsule is identical in composition with plasma, minus only the protein of the latter.

Driving force in filtration

The driving force in filtration is the blood pressure in the glomerular capillaries, some 70 millimetres of mercury (mm Hg). (The average pressure in the arteries varies from about 80 to about 120 mm Hg.) But the effective filtration pressure is less than this because the osmotic pressure of the plasma proteins tends to retain water in the plasma and because of resistance within the capsule and from surrounding tissues. Pressure in the veins, in the ureters, and outside the kidneys also has to be overcome. Glomerular pressure must be greater than that in the capsule and capsular pressure must exceed the pressure in the ureter if urine is to flow normally. In practice, the effective glomerular pressure must always exceed at least 45 mm Hg, and probably 60 mm.

Tubule function. The role of the tubules may be assessed by comparing the amounts of various substances in the filtrate and in the final urine (Table 2).

Table 2: Effect of Tubular Reabsorption on Urine
(24-hour figures)

	glomerular filtrate	urine	tubular reabsorption (percent)
Water	170 l	1.5 l	99.1
Glucose	170 g	—	100
Sodium	560 g	5 g	99.1
Chloride	620 g	9 g	98.5
Phosphate	5.1 g	1.2 g	76.5
Calcium	17 g	0.2 g	98.8
Urea	51 g	30 g	41.4
Sulfate	3.4 g	2.7 g	20.6

General function of tubules

It is apparent that the filtrate must be modified in the tubules to account for the differing compositions of filtrate and final urine; *e.g.*, to allow for the total absence of glucose in the latter, the much smaller volume of urine than filtrate, and also for the acidity of urine compared with the neutrality of the filtrate. It is also clear that the composition of the fluid reabsorbed within the proximal tubule must be similar to filtrate, but not identical with it. It has less urea and sulfate and no creatinine, for these are wastes.

As the filtrate passes along the proximal tubule, most of its water and salts are reabsorbed into the blood of the network of capillaries around the tubules. Of other substances, some are reabsorbed completely, others in part, because this portion of the nephron separates substances that must be retained in the body from those destined for excretion in the urine. The function of the proximal tubule is essentially reabsorption of filtrate in accordance with the needs of homeostasis (equilibrium), whereas the distal part of the nephron and collecting duct are mainly concerned with the detailed regulation of water, electrolyte, and hydrogen-ion balance. All these tubular processes are both chemical and physical and are under hormonal control. Although the urine differs so markedly from filtrate, if tubule function is experimentally reduced by cooling or poisoning, the urine will come increasingly to resemble the filtrate. Also, the more rapidly filtration occurs, the less time there is for the urine to be modified during its passage through the tubules.

That tubular reabsorption occurs is established by animal experiments showing that filtrate withdrawn directly from the capsules contains substances, such as chlorides, that are much reduced or absent in fluid collected from the tubules. Absorption affects all the glucose of the filtrate, 80 percent of its water (the remainder is absorbed in the distal tubule), most of the sodium, potassium, and chloride ions, some of the uric acid, and little or none of the urea and sulfate. Of the total solids 75 percent are reabsorbed in the proximal tubule, leaving a fluid isotonic with the plasma of arterial blood. The first part of the tubule absorbs amino acids, glucose, and phosphate; the whole convolution absorbs sodium, potassium, calcium, chloride, and bicarbonate and acidifies the fluid slightly. Potassium is absorbed in the proximal tubule and secreted back into the urine in the distal tubule.

The tubule has only a certain capacity for reabsorption. Thus, normally all the glucose arriving in the filtrate is absorbed; but if plasma glucose is raised high enough, the glucose arrives at the tubule cells faster than they can absorb it—a condition that occurs in diabetes; in other words, there is a critical rate of delivery determined by plasma concentration and filtration rate, and a maximum reabsorptive capacity for each substance in the filtrate. The rate of tubular reabsorption has an upper maximum value that is constant for any given substance. Consequently, if the plasma level rises sufficiently, all surplus of the substance will pass out in the urine; this is true even for glucose, which is totally reabsorbed under normal conditions. On the other hand, the upper maximum value is much lower for phosphates, so there is normally always some phosphate in the urine. The amino acids also have their own maximum tubular reabsorption value, but this is high enough to ensure that they are entirely reabsorbed under normal conditions; in certain rare inherited disorders such as cystinuria, in which there is excessive excretion of cystine, their reabsorption is reduced.

Secretion in proximal tubules

Such little secretion as does occur in the kidney takes place in the proximal tubule, save for the secretion of potassium and some uric acid in the distal tubule. Secretion occurs both passively and also actively against the electrochemical gradient (passive secretion is movement of dissolved substances from a stronger to a weaker solution; active secretion, so called because it requires expenditure of energy, is from a weaker to a stronger solution). These actively secreted substances are mainly a few metabolic products, such as creatinine, histamine, and choline, as well as some drugs, such as penicillin. (The therapeutic level of penicillin in the plasma can be enhanced and prolonged by administering agents that block tubular secretion.) But any substance for which renal clearance exceeds filtration rate must be to some extent secreted.

Of the water in the filtrate 80–85 percent is reabsorbed as a passive accompaniment to the active reabsorption of 80–85 percent of the sodium ions in the filtrate. The energy required for absorption of this sodium uses 80 percent of the oxygen consumed by the kidney, and represents one-eighth of the oxygen consumption of a resting man. The water is absorbed because of the osmotic needs of the passage of sodium and chloride ions out of the tubular fluid, and water must accompany these ions as a vehicle to prevent a rising osmotic gradient (*i.e.*, to prevent a rising difference in the concentration of the sodium solution inside and outside the tubule). The sodium ions move passively from fluid to cells and are then actively expelled into the blood against a gradient at the cell membranes. The transfer of chloride ions is also a passive obligatory transfer to complement the sodium ions.

The overall effect is to keep the osmotic pressure of the fluid roughly identical with that of the filtrate throughout the proximal tubule, so that fluid entering the distal nephron, though much less in volume, is still in balance with plasma. The mechanism by which the degree of acidity or alkalinity of the fluid is stabilized in the tubule is the bicarbonate cycle.

The proximal tubule cell synthesizes carbonic acid from carbon dioxide and water under the influence of carbonic anhydrase. The carbonic acid then dissociates, and bicarbonate ions with reabsorbed sodium ions enter the tubular fluid and then enter the blood and the extracellular fluid. Hydrogen ions enter the tubular fluid and most combine with bicarbonate to form carbonic acid. The partial pressure of carbon dioxide in the tubule fluid rises and the gas diffuses back into the tubule cell. Thus the bicarbonate actually reabsorbed is not that of the filtrate, but the net effect is the same as if this were the case.

The proximal tubular reabsorption of phosphate is complex and is affected by the phosphate content of the filtrate and plasma, the diet, and the hormone of the parathyroid glands. Phosphate competes with glucose for reabsorption, and its reabsorption is reduced by parathyroid hormone and by vitamin D and increased by a high dietetic intake.

Function of the loops of Henle

The loop of Henle begins as a descending limb running towards the medulla from the proximal tubule; it then turns back in a hairpin bend to become the ascending limb running in a parallel course back to the distal convoluted tubule. Most of the loops originate from peripheral glomeruli in the cortex and are restricted to the cortex; but about a tenth arise from glomeruli near the medulla in the deeper layers of the cortex and extend well down in the pyramids toward their tips. These long loops and their accompanying vasa recta are important in concentrating the urine.

The fluid entering the loops from the glomeruli is in balance with plasma, and one function of the loops is to produce and maintain a state of increased concentration in the fluid occupying the bends of the loops; *i.e.*, in the deeper cortical and medullary parts of the kidney. It is now assumed that this increased concentration is achieved by what is known as countercurrent multiplication. The principle of this mechanism is analogous to the physical principle applied in the conduction of hot exhaust gases past cold incoming gas so as to warm it and conserve heat. That exchange is a passive one; but in the kidney the countercurrent multiplier system uses energy in transferring substances independent of concentration gradients to produce hypertonicity (high concentrations) at the bends of the loops and in the tissue fluid in the adjacent medulla.

The process may continue until the urine acquires an osmotic concentration many times that of plasma, and this tonicity is shared by the interstitial tissues and tissue fluid of the medulla, which is hypertonic compared with the cortex. The substances active in maintaining this high osmotic concentration are urea and sodium. There is more sodium at the bends of the loops, where the fluid is more concentrated. In the ascending limb sodium is absorbed more rapidly than water, so that the fluid leaving the system and arriving at the distal convoluted tubule is more dilute than that entering.

Functions of distal tubule

The functions of the distal tubule are: (1) urinary dilution, (2) final regulation of the amount of ammonium in the urine, (3) final regulation of the amounts of sodium, potassium, and hydrogen ions in the urine, (4) acidification of the urine, (5) transport of potassium and chloride ions, and (6) calcium excretion.

The fluid from the proximal tubule is isotonic with filtrate and plasma, but it is so altered in the loop of Henle that it arrives diluted at the distal tubule. The formation of a dilute urine is a function of the distal tubule, this part of the nephron being normally rather impermeable to water. The tubule also produces a fine and final adjustment of acid-base balance in the blood-urine system. There is a "sodium pump" in the tubule, activated by a hormone of the cortex of the adrenal gland, which pumps sodium out of the tubule into the tubule cells and extracellular fluid in exchange for potassium and hydrogen ions. The "pump" is very effective; and if the diet is salt-free the urine will contain little or no sodium.

Most of the urinary ammonia is formed in the distal tubules from glutamine (an amino acid). The more acid the urine is, the greater is its content of ammonium ions, which unite with obligatorily excreted surplus anions (negative ions) such as chloride, sulfate, and phosphate, thus sparing other cations (positive ions) such as sodium and potassium. The excretion of calcium and phosphate runs in parallel; most of the calcium is excreted as phosphate.

The collecting ducts receive dilute fluid, and concentrate it by means of reabsorption of water and salts as a fine adjustment to bodily needs under the ultimate control of a hormone, ADH, or vasopressin, that reduces urine output secreted by the posterior lobe of the pituitary gland. Basically, the final volume of urine excreted is determined, first, by the amount of osmotically active solutes filtered at the glomeruli and, second, by the amount of circulating ADH. The first amount is a function of the effective filtration pressure. Some 130 millilitres of filtrate are formed every minute, and of this perhaps 16 millilitres reaches the distal tubules. As the rate of urine formation is only one millilitre per minute, the reabsorption of fluid within the collecting ducts must be 15 millilitres per minute; *i.e.*, some 12 percent of all water reabsorption in the kidney occurs in the ducts, and this reabsorption results in progressive concentration of the urine. It is reconcentrated in the ducts to the osmotic pressure—the concentration—of the fluid in the bends of the loops of Henle. The concentrating power of the ducts has its limits, the limit being reached when the osmotic pressure of the urine (due mainly to its urea and salt content) becomes high enough to balance the resorptive power of the duct cells.

Influence of vasopressin on water reabsorption

The variable amount of water reabsorption in the duct is determined under the direct influence of vasopressin (ADH), which increases the permeability of the duct lining to water. The secretion of this hormone by the pituitary is part of a feedback mechanism responsive to the tonicity of plasma and extracellular fluid. This interrelation between plasma osmotic pressure and ADH output is mediated by specific and very sensitive receptors in the base of the brain. These receptors are particularly sensitive to sodium and chloride ions. At normal blood tonicity there is a steady receptor discharge and a steady stimulation of ADH output. If the plasma becomes hypertonic—has greater osmotic pressure than normal—from the ingestion of crystalloids such as sodium chloride, receptor discharge increases, ADH output goes up, and more water is absorbed from the ducts. If the osmotic pressure of the plasma becomes low, the reverse is the case. On the other hand, water ingestion dilutes the body fluids and reduces or abolishes ADH secretion, resulting in a water diuresis (excretion) so that larger amounts of tubular fluid enter the urine.

The situation is complex because there are also receptors in the atria of the heart and in the great blood vessels sensitive to changes in blood volume; and these receptors, too, can reflexly inhibit ADH output if there is any tendency to excessive blood volume. Exercise increases ADH output and reduces urinary flow. The same result may follow emotional disturbance, fainting, injury, or the use of certain drugs. Diuresis is an increased flow of urine produced as the result of fluid intake, hormone activity, or the taking of certain drugs. Urea and salts are diuretics because they have the power of retaining water within the tubules. If ADH secretion is inhibited by the drinking of excess water, or by disease or presence of a tumour affecting the base of the brain, water diuresis results; and the rate of urine formation will approach the figure of 16 millilitres per minute filtered at the glomeruli. In certain disorders of the pituitary—diabetes insipidus—there may be a fixed and irreversible output of a large quantity of dilute urine.

In general, the fluid entering the collecting ducts is either in balance with plasma or more dilute than plasma; the duct wall remains permeable under the influence of a steady output of ADH; more water than solute is reabsorbed, and the urine becomes concentrated, basically because of the osmotic gradient between the dilute fluid in the ducts and the highly concentrated interstitial fluid in the renal medulla produced by countercurrent processes in Henle's loops. In this final process of concentration, the collecting ducts and their accompanying vasa recta act as powerful exchange units in relation to the medulla.

TESTS OF RENAL FUNCTION

Quantitative tests. Tests of kidney function include renal (kidney) clearance, filtration fraction and glomerular filtration rate, excretion rate, and reabsorption of glucose. The results of each test are measured against standard or normal values to assess degree of abnormality.

The renal clearance of any substance is the volume of plasma containing that amount of the substance that is removed by the kidney in one minute. The basic formula is as follows: the clearance for the substance, in millilitres per minute, equals the concentration of the substance in the urine multiplied by the volume of urine excreted per minute and divided by the plasma concentration of the substance ($C = U \times V/P$). It is obvious that clearance is really an artificial concept, since no portion of the plasma is ever really cleared. Taking urea, for instance, if the plasma concentration is 30 milligrams (mg) per 100 millilitres and the amount of urea excreted by the kidneys in one minute is 20 milligrams, then 67 millilitres of plasma contains the amount of urea excreted in a minute. In fact, the plasma flow through both kidneys is some 700 ml per minute containing 210 milligrams urea; of this, 120 ml containing 36 mg urea is filtered through the glomeruli per minute, and of this urea 20 mg escapes in the urine, some being reabsorbed in the tubules. Thus the clearance value for urea is an abstraction, but is useful in assessing kidney function.

Filtration fraction and glomerular filtration rate

The filtration fraction (FF) represents the proportion of the plasma passing through the glomeruli that is actually filtered off. As can be seen from the example given, this fraction is some 15–20 percent (120 out of 700 ml). It is that percentage of the renal plasma flow that is actually turned into glomerular filtrate, since the fraction is equal to the glomerular filtrate divided by the renal plasma flow.

The glomerular filtration rate (GFR) is the volume of filtrate formed in unit time. It can be readily measured by injecting into the bloodstream some nontoxic agent that is soluble in plasma, not metabolized, freely filtered at the glomerulus, neither secreted nor reabsorbed by the tubules, and capable of accurate estimation in blood and urine. In these circumstances the filtrate will contain the substance in the same concentration as in the plasma, and all of it will be recoverable from the urine. In these conditions the clearance value and the glomerular filtration rate will be identical. Such a substance is the carbohydrate inulin. If this is given intravenously at such a rate as to maintain a constant plasma concentration of inulin, then the product of the concentrations of inulin in the urine and the volume of urine passed per minute, divided by the plasma concentration of inulin, is equal to the volume of filtrate per minute, and also equal to the volume of plasma completely freed of inulin per minute.

This procedure gives a simple measure of the actual glomerular filtration rate, which is independent of any actual constituent of blood or urine. In the normal adult the glomerular filtration rate is 125 ml per minute per 1.73 square metres of body surface. In the glomeruli of both kidneys together some 125 ml of fluid is filtered off each minute from the blood through the walls of the glomerular capillaries into the capsules of the nephrons, a filtrate, as has been seen, identical with plasma except that it contains no colloids. Female values are about 85 percent of these for the same standard area of body surface.

It follows from the above that for a substance partly reabsorbed from the filtrate when it reaches the tubules, the clearance value will be less than the glomerular filtration rate; while, for a substance that is additionally excreted into the tubules, the clearance value will exceed the glomerular filtration rate. Experimentally, the clearance values for inulin, creatinine, and sodium ferricyanide are identical, which suggests that all must be dealt with by physical filtration at the glomeruli and that the tubules exert no influence on their further excretion.

Excretion rate and renal blood flow (RBF)

Clearance value is not the same as excretion rate. For inulin and some other compounds, the clearance value is not altered by changing the amount of inulin in the plasma, because the amount of urine completely cleared of the agent remains the same. But the excretion rate equals total quantity excreted per millilitre of filtrate per minute, and this value increases in linear relation with the plasma concentration.

So far, clearance and other factors in terms of substances filtered at the glomerulus have been measured. But there are certain substances, such as p-aminohippuric acid (PAH) and iodopyracet, which are vigorously and totally excreted by the tubules after some glomerular filtration and are completely removed from the blood traversing the kidney if their plasma level is small. In such cases the clearance rate equals the renal blood flow. Thus, if plasma iodopyracet is one milligram per 100 millilitres, and the glomerular filtration rate (GFR) is 120 millilitres per minute, then this glomerular filtration rate is equivalent to a urinary content of 1.2 milligrams iodopyracet. Five hundred and eighty millilitres of plasma reach the tubules each minute. If the plasma contains one milligram of iodopyracet per 100 ml, it contains 580 mg iodopyracet, and the tubules actively secrete the whole of this from the blood so that all the original iodopyracet in the blood is excreted.

The maximum rate of reabsorption of glucose by the proximal tubule and the maximum rate of secretion of p-aminohippuric acid by the tubule are both indices of the maximum functioning ability of the proximal portion of the renal tubules. To arrive at this value for a particular substance, it is necessary first to assess the proportion of the substance excreted through the tubule rather than elsewhere (e.g., at the glomeruli).

The urea clearance, another effective test of renal function, is determined from the urea content of the urine and the urea content of the blood, measured at fixed intervals for two or three hours after drinking water to induce diuresis. The dilution test measures the kidney's response to a water load, as shown by the excretion of appropriately dilute urines. The level of blood urea is itself a useful index of renal function. But if protein intake is very low, the blood urea may be a less sensitive index of renal function than the blood creatinine, since the latter is much less affected by the nature of the diet.

Qualitative tests of renal function. It is often desirable to establish that a particular kidney is present and functioning—that there is a healthy kidney present on one side before an organ on the other side is removed or before the opposite kidney is transplanted. The simplest method is to give an intravenous injection of some dye such as methylene blue and to inspect the ureter openings through a cystoscope (an instrument for viewing the inside of the bladder) to note the jets of coloured urine. In intravenous pyelography (IVP) the kidneys are observed in X-rays by intravenous injection of a radio-opaque-iodine-containing contrast medium that they se-

lectively excrete. A series of X-rays then indicates when the contrast first appears and brings out the dense shadows of the renal structures; they also indicate the position of the organ; finally the dye collects in the bladder; it is then possible to see whether there is rupture or tumour in this structure. This test also gives a rough comparison of function in the two kidneys.

Intravenous pyelography

Retrograde pyelography is more an anatomical than a functional test. In the procedure, a fine catheter is passed into a ureter opening and up one ureter, and radio-opaque dye is injected to outline the ureter, renal pelvis, and calices. The test may be useful in showing that an organ that fails to perform in an IVP is nevertheless present. The radioactive renogram is obtained by injecting an agent tagged with a radioactive form of iodine. The radiation is detected with counters placed over the kidneys, and the counts can be transcribed on moving graph paper, yielding typical time curves for normal and disordered function. Finally, there is the scintillogram, obtained by injection of gamma-ray-emitting substances that are concentrated and persist in the kidneys. An agent such as an isotope of mercury can be used to render the kidney capable of producing exposure of an X-ray plate in the vicinity; that is, an autoradiogram to indicate the site, size, and shape of the organ and the presence of defects suggestive of cysts or tumours.

THE URINE

The volume and composition of normal urine vary widely from day to day even in health, as a result of food and fluid intake and of fluid loss through other channels as affected by environmental conditions and exercise. The daily volume averages 1.5 litres (about 1.6 quarts) with a range of 1–2.5 litres, but after copious sweating it may fall as low as 500 millilitres, and after excess fluid intake it may reach 3 litres or more. There is also a 24-hour variation. Excretion is minimal in the early hours, maximal during the first few hours after rising, with peaks after meals and during the early stages of exertion. The urine produced between morning and evening is two to four times the night volume. The excessive secretion of urine (polyuria) of chronic renal disease is typically nocturnal.

The volume of urine is regulated to keep plasma osmotic concentration constant, to control the total water content of the tissues, and to provide a vehicle for the transfer to the exterior of some 50 grams (g) of solids, mostly urea and sodium chloride, in a day. In a man who ingests 100 g of protein and 10 g of salt daily, the urine will contain 30 g of urea and 10 g of salt; there are many other possible constituents, but they amount to less than 10 g overall.

Volume and constituents of urine

Some urinary constituents (Table 3), the products of metabolism of nitrogenous substances obtained from food, vary widely in relation to the composition of the diet; thus the excretion of urea and sulfate is dependent on the diet-protein content. A high-protein diet may yield a 24-hour output of 17 g of nitrogen, a low-protein diet of the same calorific value only 3–4 g.

The urine is normally clear. It may be turbid from calcium phosphate, which clears if acetic acid is added.

Table 3: Urine Constituents (g/24 hours)	
Urea	25–30
Uric acid	.6–0.7
Creatinine	1.0–1.2
Hippuric acid	0.7
Ammonia	0.7
Amino acids	3.0
Sodium	1–5 (NaCl 15.0)
Potassium	2–4
Calcium	0.2–0.3
Magnesium	0.1
Chloride	7
Phosphate	1.7–2.5
Sulfate	1.8–2.5
Iron	0.003

Certain deposits may settle on standing: mucus from the lining of the urinary tract; a brick-red amorphous deposit of urates as the urine cools, redissolving on warming; crystals of calcium oxalate, triple phosphate, or calcium biphosphate in acid urine. Microscopic deposits include occasional casts, vaguely resembling in form the renal tubules from whose lining they have been shed.

The urine froths when shaken because of the presence of bile salts. Its colour depends on the concentration, but is normally a bright clear yellow from the pigment urochrome, an end product of protein metabolism. There are also traces of other pigments: urobilin and uroerythrin. The content of protein or amino acids is normally very small, less than 100 milligrams in a 24-hour period.

The specific gravity of urine may vary between 1.001 and 1.04, but is usually 1.01–1.025. Such variation is normal, and a fixed low specific gravity is an indication of chronic renal disease. If fluid intake is stopped for 24 hours, even a normal kidney will secrete urine with a specific gravity of at least 1.025. There is a limit to the concentrating powers of the kidney, so that the urine is rarely more than four times as concentrated as plasma. Since the protein and salt of the diet must be excreted, they need a minimum water output of 850 ml as a vehicle. If this is not available from intake it has to be withdrawn from the tissues, causing dehydration; but the usual intake is well above the minimum and the urine is rarely at its maximum possible concentration. Osmotic pressure runs roughly parallel to specific gravity.

The reaction of the urine is usually acid, with an overall range of pH 4 to 8 (lemon pie has a pH of 2.3; the value 8 is slightly alkaline, about equal to the pH of a 1 percent solution of sodium bicarbonate). The acidity is due to the excreted acid products of metabolism, the conversion of the sulfur and phosphorus of ingested proteins to sulfuric and phosphoric acid, buffered by potassium and ammonium. There is normally an excess of hydrogen over hydroxyl (OH) ions. This condition assumes a mixed diet containing some meat. If the diet is predominantly vegetarian or fruitarian, it contains sodium and potassium salts of organic acids, and the latter are metabolized leaving alkaline residues in the urine. Medicinal consumption of bicarbonate also gives an alkaline urine.

Components of urine

Of the anions, the chlorides are derived from the food and vary with intake; they may disappear on a salt-free diet or after major surgical operations. Sulfates result from oxidation of the sulfur in protein and are excreted as sulfates of calcium, potassium, sodium, magnesium, and ammonium. There is some sulfur passed as thiocyanate, cysteine, and mercaptan. Phosphate comes in part from the food, in part from oxidation of organic phosphates in food and tissue lecithins and nucleins. It can leave the body in either the feces or the urine; if there is much calcium or magnesium in the food, there will be more phosphate in the feces and less in the urine. Phosphates are present in the urine in forms which, if the urine is neutral or alkaline, may precipitate as a deposit. The phosphate formed by putrefaction of normal urine, ammonium phosphomagnesiate, yields crystalline deposits.

Of the cations, potassium varies with the diet, being increased by a high meat consumption; sodium also varies with intake. Calcium and magnesium are always present but in small amounts. There is always some ammonia, secreted in the distal tubules as a complement to acids derived from the food.

Organic components are nitrogenous or non-nitrogenous. As stated, the loss of nitrogen is dependent on diet. Urea accounts for up to 90 percent, ammonia 2 to 4 percent, creatinine 3 percent, uric acid 1 to 3 percent. There is also nitrogen in hippuric acid and in the various pigments. The urea content is an important index of the state of protein metabolism. There is an excess of urinary (and plasma) uric acid in gout. There are also traces of purine bases: xanthine, hypoxanthine, and adenine; tea and coffee drinking yield caffeine, theobromine, and derivatives. The hippuric acid is synthesized in the liver and increases on a vegetarian diet. The non-nitrogenous organic constituents include oxalic acid from the food (*e.g.*, rhubarb), lactic acid (increased by exertion), derivatives of the water-soluble vitamins and sex hormones, with many different intermediate metabolites at various times.

Foreign proteins of molecular weight less than 68,000 are excreted in the urine, while those of the plasma are retained in the body. If, however, the kidneys are damaged by disease or toxins, the glomeruli will transmit some of the normal serum albumin and globulin and the urine will coagulate on warming. Normally, the urine contains only very small amounts of protein: after exercise, in pregnancy, and in some persons when standing (orthostatic albuminuria). The protein loss may be greatly increased in certain chronic renal diseases; in nephrosis it may even reach 50 milligrams in a 24-hour period. Certain specific and easily identifiable proteins appear in the urine in diseases of the bone marrow.

Abnormal constituents of urine

Glucose is found in the urine in diabetes mellitus; but there may also be an abnormal amount of glucose in the urine because of a low threshold for tubular reabsorption, without any disturbance of glucose metabolism. Glucuronic acid is an oxidation product of glucose and is a detoxicating agent, combining with poisons in the liver to form glucuronides, which are excreted. Lactosuria (abnormal amount of lactose in the urine) may occur in nursing mothers. Ketone bodies (acetone, acetoacetic acid) are present in traces in normal urine but in quantity in severe untreated diabetes and in relative or actual carbohydrate starvation; *e.g.*, in a person on a high-fat diet.

The urine may contain hemoglobin or its derivatives after hemolysis (liberation of hemoglobin from red blood cells), after incompatible blood transfusion, and in malignant malaria (blackwater fever). Fresh blood may derive from bleeding in the urinary tract. Bile salts and pigments are increased in jaundice, particularly the obstructive variety; urobilin is greatly increased in certain diseases such as cirrhosis of the liver.

Porphyrins are normally present only in minute amounts but may be increased in congenital porphyria, marked by sensitivity to sunlight or by insanity, or after poisoning with the drug sulfonmethane, when there is purple urine.

Finally, the normally extremely small quantities of amino acids in the urine may be much increased in hepatitis, in failure of tubular reabsorption and in certain diseases due to inborn errors of protein metabolism. Phenylketonuria, a disease identified by the presence of phenylpyruvic acid in the urine, is due to lack of the enzyme phenylalanine hydroxylase, so that phenylalanine is converted not to tyrosine but to phenylpyruvic acid. This is excreted and its presence in blood and tissues causes mental retardation; if the urine of every newborn infant is tested, restriction of phenylalanine in the diet in such cases may be beneficial. Alkaptonuria, a disease identified by the presence of homogentisic acid in the urine, is due to lack of the enzyme that catalyzes the oxidation of homogentisic acid. Free homogentisic acid in the urine darkens on standing, and deposits of the acid in the tissues may cause chronic arthritis or spinal disease. Other such disorders are cystinuria, the presence of the amino acid cystine in the urine, when the bladder may contain cystine stones; and maple syrup disease, another disorder involving abnormal levels of amino acid in the urine and blood plasma.

URINE COLLECTION AND EMISSION

From the nephrons the urine enters the final 15 or 20 collecting tubules that open on to each papilla of the renal medulla, projecting into a minor calyx. There are some five to ten of these cuplike recesses, opening into two or three major calices, and these in turn open into the renal pelvis, the upper expanded portion of the ureter. The pelvis and calices together make up the renal sinus, which has been mentioned earlier. The ureter is a narrow thick-walled muscular tube that begins at its junction with the pelvis of the kidney, descends on the posterior abdominal wall behind the lining of the abdominal cavity (peritoneum), and opens into the base of

Passage of urine from nephron to bladder

the bladder. The ureters pass very obliquely through the thick musculature of the bladder wall, so that their orifices are virtually valvular, and this situation ensures that there is normally no reflux, or backflow, of urine when the bladder contracts during micturition (passage of urine).

Urine is passed down the channel of the renal pelvis and ureter by a succession of peristaltic waves of contraction that begin in the muscle fibres of the minor calices, travel out to the major calices and then along the ureter every 10–15 seconds. Each wave sends urine through the ureteric orifice into the bladder in discontinuous spurts; these can be seen through a cystoscope if a dye is injected into the bloodstream. Gravity aids this downward flow, which is faster when one is standing erect. Though the overall picture suggests that there is a pacemaker near the pelviureteric junction, this has never been satisfactorily demonstrated in the tissue. The pressure in the renal pelvis is normally low, but the smooth muscle coat of the ureter is a powerful one and the pressure above an obstructed ureter may rise as high as 50 millimetres of mercury. The ureters are doubly innervated from the splanchnic nerves above and the hypogastric network below.

The bladder. The bladder is a hollow three-layered organ of variable capacity, with a powerful intermediate muscle coat that empties the organ when it contracts, and two muscular sphincters that keep the exit closed at all other times. This smooth muscle coat constitutes the powerful detrusor muscle. At the base of the bladder the region of the bladder neck, or trigone, is demarcated by the two ureteric orifices and the internal opening of the urethra, the channel that runs from the bladder to external urinary meatus. Muscle fibres loop around the urethral opening to form the internal sphincter, which is under involuntary unconscious control. The external sphincter consists of two striated (striped) muscles under voluntary control: the compressor urethrae, which surrounds the membranous urethra, and the pair of bulbo-cavernosus muscles.

The mucous membrane lining the bladder is distensible; it is ridged in the empty organ and smoothed out in distension. In micturition the longitudinal muscle of the bladder shortens to widen the bladder neck and allow urine to enter the urethra. The urethra normally contains no urine except during the act of micturition, its walls remaining apposed by muscle tone. In the male, but not in the female, the external sphincter can maintain continence even if the internal sphincter is not functioning.

Innervation of bladder and urethra

The innervation of the bladder and urethra is complex and important. Essentially, there are three groups of nerves: (1) The parasympathetic nerves constitute the main motor supply to the detrusor; they make it contract, raise pressure within the bladder, relax the internal sphincter, and cause emptying. Afferent parasympathetic channels convey impulses from stretch receptors in the bladder wall to higher centres, permitting cognizance of the state of distension of the organ and stimulating the desire to micturate. (2) The sympathetic nerves stimulate closure of the ureteric and internal urethral orifices and contraction of the internal sphincter, and their action on the detrusor is inhibitory; i.e., the effect is to prevent bladder outflow. Thus the sympathetic serves to control the situation in the distending bladder up to the point when evacuation can be deferred no longer. Afferent paths in the sympathetic convey sensations of pain, overdistension, and temperature from the mucosa of the bladder and the urethra. (3) The somatic nerves cause contraction of the external sphincter; their sensory fibres relay information as to the state of distension of the posterior urethra.

Bladder function in micturition. Certain reflexes combine to ensure both maintenance of a steady holding state for urine and normal progressive micturition with complete emptying. When the internal pressure of the bladder rises, it contracts; and it also contracts when urine enters the urethra; the urethra relaxes when urine enters it; it also relaxes when the bladder contracts.

Both bladder sphincters are normally closed. As the

organ fills with urine, the contractile response of the muscle wall causes a rise in internal pressure. Relaxation then occurs as an active process of adjustment so that the organ may hold its contents at a lower pressure. As urine continues to enter the bladder, this rise and fall of pressure continues in steplike fashion, with the final pressure always gradually rising.

The repeated transient contraction waves at first are small and are not consciously felt; later, stimuli reach the brain and cause pain and a sharp rise of pressure. These later major contractions can be inhibited voluntarily. The desire to micturate begins at around a content of 400 millilitres, but it can be voluntarily overridden until the content reaches 600–800 ml, equivalent to a pressure of 100 ml water. Until this point the sphincters remain contracted to keep the urethral exit closed, but eventually the desire to micturate becomes urgent and irrepressible. Until this time, if it is socially inconvenient to urinate, voluntary inhibition of the detrusor and contraction of the perineal muscles keep the internal pressure as low as possible and prevent efflux. The threshold is dependent to some extent on the rate of filling and is higher when filling is slow; and training affects the amount the bladder can retain. In young children the situation is less controllable, and even small amounts of urine may excite reflex evacuation. Emotional influences are important. Anxiety inhibits the capacity of the bladder to relax on filling, so that under conditions of stress—e.g., on the battlefield—there may be frequent involuntary passage of small quantities of urine.

Normal micturition

Micturition. Micturition is a complex activity, partly reflex and unconscious and mediated by the lower spinal cord centres, partly under conscious control by the higher centres of the brain. Voluntary micturition begins with willed messages from the brain that reach the bladder via the motor fibres of the pelvic nerves to stimulate the detrusor, at the same time actively relaxing both urethral sphincters. But the reflexes already mentioned ensure that, once the process has begun and urine has entered the urethra, the contraction of the detrusor will continue and the sphincters will remain relaxed until evacuation is complete and the bladder empty. Evacuation is aided by voluntary contraction of a wide range of accessory muscles. The muscles of the abdominal wall contract to increase pressure on the bladder from without; the diaphragm descends and the breath is held; at the same time there is relaxation of the muscles of the perineal floor. Thus voluntary initiation and control of micturition is effected partly by an active process of stimulating parasympathetic sacral nerve outflow, partly by removing the normal inhibition exerted by the higher centres on the reflex centres in the spinal cord. Once begun, micturition is carried through to completion by lower and higher centres acting in concert; sensory messages from the urine-distended urethra also play a part. It follows that even if a bladder is not particularly distended and if reflex emptying is not urgent, the bladder can nevertheless be evacuated by voluntary contraction of the abdominal wall, so initiating the reflex process that, once begun, takes over.

Abnormal micturition

Because the bladder is a hollow organ with a powerful muscular coat, some function persists, however disordered, even if nervous control is damaged or abolished. Even the completely denervated organ retains some automatic emptying, if only from its own elasticity. Certain typical clinical situations may be differentiated, corresponding to different modes of disordered function:

1. Lack of conscious inhibition of micturition because of damage to the cerebral cortex or, more usually, from psychological causes results in a desire to micturate that cannot be suppressed although bladder volumes may be quite small; micturition is precipitate and continues till the bladder is empty.

2. Transverse lesions or other damage to the spinal cord above the reflex centres that also cause paralysis of the lower half of the body produce an "automatic" bladder. There is persistent unconscious control, but this is established only after an interval. At first the bladder is atonic (lacking in physiologic tone) and becomes greatly

distended; the detrusor relaxes and reflex micturition is abolished. Pressure finally rises sufficiently to overcome the spasm of the sphincters and urine is voided in small amounts. Further accumulation and partial voiding recur; that is, there is retention of urine with overflow incontinence. Under these conditions inflammation of the bladder readily develops, which may cause disability or death from chronic ascending urinary infection. If overdistension is prevented by regular catheterization, or by manual expression by firm pressure on the lower abdominal wall, an "automatic" bladder develops after some months. This is a small capacity organ with frequent emptying at a content of around 150 millilitres; there is reflex control mediated through the sacral segments of the spinal cord, the higher centres do not restrain the detrusor, and the internal sphincter relaxes more readily. Voluntary assistance from the abdominal muscles is a help in this situation, if these too have not been paralyzed; but there is always some residual urine from incomplete emptying and there is a risk of infection.

3. In contrast, there is the isolated, or "autonomous," bladder resulting from damage to the central nervous system below the sacral cord reflex centres. The bladder responds to distension like any hollow organ with a smooth muscle coat. It becomes tense but contracts only weakly so that, while small amounts of urine are voided, the residual urine may be as high as 200–300 millilitres. This condition is known as active incontinence as opposed to the overflow incontinence of the automatic bladder. Here again, active support from the abdominal muscles is helpful.

Finally, the effects of chronic obstruction to bladder outflow, as from narrowing of the urethra or compression of the urethra by an enlarged prostate, must be noted. There is chronic retention, the pressure within the bladder rises, but for a time hypertrophy of the muscle wall maintains normal micturition and overcomes the obstruction. Eventually severe chronic overdistension results with paralysis of the bladder wall and retention with passive overflow, dribbling of urine. In such circumstances, if surgical aid is not available, ascending infection of the urinary tract is inevitable.

HORMONES AND THE KIDNEY

Certain hormones are intimately related to renal function. The role of the antidiuretic hormone (ADH, or vasopressin) of the posterior lobe of the pituitary in controlling diuresis has already been discussed. Vasopressin regulates water excretion by increasing membrane permeability to water and by accelerating water and ion transfer in a direction determined by the osmotic gradient. The receptors of the base of the brain form part of the feedback mechanism that stimulates ADH output if the osmotic concentration of extracellular fluid (ECF) is high so as to concentrate the urine, and that reduces ADH output and so dilutes the urine if osmotic concentration of ECF and of plasma falls.

Hormones of the adrenal cortex

The hormones of the adrenal cortex are also important in influencing renal function, directly or indirectly. In stress situations, as after an injury or a surgical operation, the output of hydrocortisone and other corticosteroids is increased because the adrenals are stimulated by ACTH, the adrenocorticotropic secretion of the pituitary. Hydrocortisone increases protein breakdown, and consequently the output of nitrogen in the urine, and affects water metabolism; lack of hydrocortisone reduces the power of the kidney to deal with normal water loads. The hormone also promotes sodium retention and loss of potassium and hydrogen ions by the kidney. Aldosterone influences electrolyte metabolism by facilitating the reabsorption of sodium ions at the distal tubules, also at the expense of hydrogen and potassium excretion. The action of aldosterone has been described as priming the sodium reabsorption pump; it is probably the adrenal hormone most important to tubular function. Metabolites of corticosteroids devoid of activity are rapidly excreted in the urine, where they can be estimated to assess adrenocortical function.

The action of the parathyroid glands is to increase blood calcium by mobilizing calcium from the bones and other sources; if this hormone functions to excess, as in tumours of the glands, the urinary loss of calcium is much increased and calcium stones tend to form in the kidneys and the bladder. The pituitary growth hormone facilitates protein synthesis and decreases the urinary loss of nitrogen. The sex hormones estrogen and progesterone exert an ill-defined activity as regards salt and water metabolism.

Renin-angiotensin system

The juxtaglomerular apparatus (JGA), consisting of an asymmetrical cuff of large granular cells in the wall of the afferent arteriole near its entry into the capsule of the nephron, contains renin in the granules in the cells. Renin is a true internal secretion of the kidney. Entering the plasma, it acts as an enzyme that induces one of the plasma globulins to yield angiotensin I, which is inactive, and which gives rise in turn to angiotensin II, the most potent agent for constricting the blood vessels and raising the blood pressure. The formation of renin at the JGA is induced by a fall in blood pressure and inhibited by a rise. When the pressure falls, the output of angiotensin II raises the pressure and also excites the release of aldosterone from the adrenal cortex. This process is another example of a feedback mechanism analogous to that controlling the output of ADH.

BIOLOGICAL CONSIDERATIONS

During the greater part of pregnancy the glomerular filtration rate (GFR) is increased by as much as 50 percent, corresponding to an increase in renal blood flow of up to 25 percent in the middle three months of pregnancy. Glycosuria is frequent due to increased glucose loading of the filtrate, there is some sodium retention with a tendency to abnormal accumulation of serous fluid (edema), and some protein may appear in the urine.

The kidneys of the fetus begin to function well before birth, as indicated by a steady rise in the urea and uric acid content of the amniotic fluid in which the fetus exists; the fetus probably swallows fluid and voids it as urine. But even at birth, half the work of excretion is still being carried out via the placental circulation and the maternal kidneys, and this dependence is abruptly curtailed. Kidney function is far from fully developed in the newborn infant. The glomerular filtration rate is only some 30 millilitres per minute per square metre of body surface, compared to 75 in the adult, and tubular function does not attain adult performance until the end of the first year. The 24-hour output of urine is only some 20 millilitres; the output of water and the renal clearance of sodium, potassium, and phosphate is low; the urine is dilute and often contains protein. Because the kidney has such a poor capacity to excrete solids, the infant is exposed to the dehydrating effect of vomiting and diarrhea, which readily induce renal failure.

Rhythms in urine output

There is an increased urine output at the commencement of muscular exercise, due to the general stimulation of circulation, but a later falling off with the fatigue and sweating caused by severe prolonged exertion. The 24-hour rhythm in output has been mentioned. The small output in the early morning hours is a practical convenience to prevent disturbance of sleep. If the natural sleep rhythm is inverted, as by working on night shift, electrolyte and water output follow suit. The urine is acid at night and becomes less so, or alkaline, on rising. Output is maximal during the first waking hours and rises after meals. Because of all this variation in water and solute output, any analytic study of urine components must be conducted on 24-hour specimens.

Hydrogen-ion concentration in the urine may vary from pH 4 to 8; *i.e.*, from many hundred times that of the plasma to a fraction; hence the ability of the kidneys to regulate acid-base balance in body fluids. Essentially, they do so by controlling the rate of reabsorption of bicarbonate from the filtrate, and by excreting hydrogen ions with regeneration of bicarbonate. The mechanism is one of ion exchange, mediated through the reversible chemical reaction between water and carbon dioxide: water plus carbon dioxide yields carbonic acid, which yields hydrogen ions and carbonate ions ($H_2O + CO_2$

⇌ $H_2 CO_3$ ⇌ H^+ + HCO_3^-), so that hydrogen ion (H^+) in the tubule cells is exchanged for sodium ion (Na^+) in the filtrate. Only minor changes in pH occur in the proximal tubules, rather more in the distal tubules, where the fluid becomes slightly acid, but a major change toward acidity occurs in the distal collecting ducts. For every molecule of acid excreted in the urine, one molecule of sodium bicarbonate ($NaHCO_3$) is regenerated and returned to the blood in the vessels surrounding the tubules.

Regulation of body fluids

Constant composition of blood and body fluids is basically dependent on regulation of the volume, osmotic pressure, and constituents of the extracellular fluid (ECF). This fluid forms the internal environment of the tissues, and invariance is essential to life. It is an important part of homeostasis to keep the volume of ECF constant by adaptive changes in sodium and water output. Such maintenance is effected by the circulation, respiration, and ingestion, and also by selective renal excretion. Like the lungs, bowel, and skin, the kidney is an organ for exchanges between the ECF and the external environment; and these are large exchanges, the kidneys producing 170 litres of glomerular filtrate in 24 hours and reabsorbing all but 1.5 litres. The amount of water lost through the kidneys, however, corresponds closely to the body's current needs, whereas loss by skin and lungs is largely controlled by environmental factors such as humidity and temperature. Again, the bowel absorbs almost all ingested water as a load on the circulation, without relation to bodily needs. Thus it is the kidneys that are the fine regulators of water and solute content of the ECF. They adjust the volume and composition of blood and ECF within narrow bounds, but there are limits to this control. The kidneys cannot concentrate the urine to more than 1,400 milliosmoles per kilogram, equivalent to a specific gravity of 1.035. There is an obligatory excretion of excess electrolytes and end-products of protein metabolism such as urea, so that there is an obligatory output of urine as determined by solute and protein ingestion and rate of urea formation. If there is not enough water available for this vehicle, the blood urea rises; and if the protein intake is excessive more urine is needed to prevent such a rise. It is easier, in this context, for the kidney to produce a dilute rather than a concentrated urine; osmolarity may fall as low as 30 milliosmoles per kilogram; the function of ADH in part is to prevent such overdilution.

At least 90 percent of the osmotic pressure of ECF and of plasma is due to sodium chloride, the content of which is regulated by renal water excretion and reabsorption under the delicate control of the hypothalamic osmoreceptors and ADH. The volume of ECF depends largely on its sodium content, and so on the rate of renal excretion of sodium, which is very sensitive, adjusting even to minor changes of posture. Of the filtered sodium, 85 percent is reabsorbed obligatorily as sodium chloride in the proximal tubules without much regard for current needs. But in the distal tubules there is a fine facultative reabsorption in exchange for potassium and hydrogen ions, and this exchange is closely related to the body situation as regards mineral metabolism; it is effected under the control of the adrenal cortical hormones, particularly aldosterone, and also of the humoral renin-angiotensin system. Thus, if the body loses sodium, the concentration of sodium ions in the ECF falls, but normal osmolarity is restored by an increased water output; if the sodium content of the ECF rises, as in dehydration, water loss is reduced.

The control of potassium transfer is largely independent of the factors governing movements of sodium. A moderate potassium load is usually accurately excreted in the urine within an hour or two. What is important is not so much the preservation of a constant potassium level in plasma or ECF as its maintenance within individual cells. The kidney cannot conserve potassium as well as it does sodium, and potassium depletion may readily occur in severe vomiting or diarrhea. The rate of potassium excretion in the distal tubule is mainly determined by the amount of sodium ions available for exchange and by the influence of aldosterone on this exchange.

Water excess and deprivation

When water is drunk it is nearly all rapidly absorbed from the bowel into the bloodstream, slightly increasing the volume of the plasma and decreasing its osmotic pressure by dilution. There is an interchange with the ECF and the cells, with some excess water leaving the plasma and entering the ECF and then the cells, and with electrolytes leaving the cells and entering first the ECF and then the plasma.

The kidneys respond to the challenge after a latent period of about half an hour; urine output rises to a peak within 90 minutes and then declines slowly until the diuresis is all over, within a few hours. This response is selective to water intake, a great increase in water output in a dilute urine with little or no associated loss of solids. There is no accompanying increase in renal blood flow or glomerular filtration rate, but simply an inhibition of the ADH output so as to reduce water reabsorption in the distal part of the nephron.

Retention of excess water in the body, causing visible swelling of the subcutaneous tissues, or edema, may result from a number of factors: abnormal blood vessel permeability, a low level of plasma proteins, and failure of the right side of the heart, but a common cause is renal failure. Thus in acute nephritis there is a diminished urine output and much retention of fluid. Severe water intoxication, or "water poisoning," is the extreme condition, due to excessive intake, or to kidney disease or an abnormally large output of ADH; it produces headache, nausea, convulsions, coma, and even death.

Water deprivation leads to a fall in ECF volume and a consequent rise in its crystalloid osmotic pressure. Water enters the fluid from the cells, metabolism is disturbed, and there is a loss of potassium and protein. Urine output falls under the control of ADH and electrolyte excretion is increased. With continued deprivation of water even the plasma volume will eventually fall and urine concentration will lead to renal failure with gross nitrogen retention (uremia). Thirst is the biological response to such a situation, but it is emotionally as well as biologically conditioned; there may be thirst when the situation does not warrant it and an absence of thirst just when drinking is urgently required.

An excess of salt intake, as from drinking seawater, or a relative excess of salt content, as in dehydration, increases the crystalloid content and osmotic pressure throughout the body fluids and the volume of the ECF at the expense of cellular fluid. The kidneys cannot concentrate the urine to the osmotic pressure required; this failure leads to cellular dehydration and death.

Salt loss is usually due to sweating, as in stokers and miners, and forms part of the heat-exhaustion syndrome. It is only occasionally due to dietetic deficiency. It does not normally produce much thirst, though fluid and salt replenishment is urgent. The sodium content of the ECF and plasma falls, as does the volume of these fluids, leading to a reduced cardiac output, circulatory failure, impaired renal tubular function, and a rising level of urea in the blood. If water, but not salt, is supplied, the sodium deficiency will increase still further, causing cramps, collapse, rapid pulse, shock, and renal failure. There will be no chloride in the urine. The correct management consists of the administration of dilute saline solution by mouth or intravenously.

BIBLIOGRAPHY. The following works all provide detailed and well-written surveys of the whole field of kidney function in a form suitable for medical students and others with a good scientific grounding: E.J.M. CAMPBELL, C.J. DICKINSON, and J.D.H. SLATER (eds.), *Clinical Physiology*, 3rd ed., pp. 149–197 (1968); C.H. BEST and N.B. TAYLOR (eds.), *The Physiological Basis of Medical Practice*, pp. 1665–1720 (1966); G.H. BELL, J.N. DAVIDSON, and H. SCARBOROUGH, *Textbook of Physiology and Biochemistry*, 7th ed., pp. 698–733 (1968); and R. PASSMORE and J.S. ROBSON (eds.), *A Companion to Medical Studies*, sect. 33 (1968).

(D.Le V.)

Excretion and Excretory Systems

Every organism, from the smallest protist to the largest mammal, must rid itself of the potentially harmful by-products of its own vital activities. The physiological process by which the organism disposes of its nitrogenous by-products is called excretion. The mechanisms for that process constitute the excretory systems, particularly such organs of vertebrate animals as elaborate and complicated as the kidney and its associated urinary ducts.

GENERAL FEATURES

Definitions and distinctions. The meaning of excretion is most easily understood in the context of vertebrate physiology. The animal swallows food (ingestion). In the stomach and intestine some of the food is broken down into soluble products (digestion) that are absorbed into the body (assimilation). In the body these soluble products undergo further chemical change (metabolism); some are used by the body for growth, but most provide energy for the various activities of the body. Metabolism involves the uptake of oxygen and the elimination of carbon dioxide in the lungs (respiration). Besides carbon dioxide, compounds of nitrogen arise from metabolism and are eliminated, chiefly by the kidney, in the urine (excretion). Food not digested is eliminated through the anus (defecation).

These processes are characteristic of animals in general, but not of plants. A green plant takes in carbon dioxide from the atmosphere and nitrogen (as nitrate) from the soil. It uses the energy of sunlight to build these nutrients into the materials required for growth and in the process gives out oxygen (see PHOTOSYNTHESIS). The processes of ingestion, excretion, and defecation have no obvious parallels in plants, but see ELIMINATION.

In a broad sense animals live on plants, and the by-products of animals are the raw materials on which plants grow. These mutually supporting activities of plants and animals are kept precisely in balance by the activities of bacteria. Bacteria convert the urine and feces of animals (and also the dead bodies of both plants and animals) to carbon dioxide and nitrate. In the living world as a whole, carbon and nitrogen are in continuous circulation, driven by the energy of sunlight (see BIOSPHERE). Over most of the earth, for most of time, no by-products accumulate. Occasionally the cycles get out of balance, as they must have done during the prehistoric period when coal was being formed in the earth as a consequence of the failure of bacteria to decompose all the remains of plants (see COALS).

Products of excretion. Although every type of organism takes in some materials and eliminates others, excretion in the strict sense is a process found only in animals. For the purposes of this article excretion will be taken to mean the elimination of nitrogenous by-products and the regulation of the composition of the body fluids (see also HOMEOSTASIS).

Elimination and regulation

The primary excretory product arising naturally in the animal body is ammonia, derived almost entirely from the proteins of the ingested food. In the process of digestion proteins are broken down into their constituent amino acids. Some of the amino acid pool is then used by the animal to build up its own proteins, but a great deal is used as a source of energy to drive other vital processes. The first step in the mobilization of amino acids for energy production is deamination, the splitting off of ammonia from the amino acid molecule. The remainder is oxidized to carbon dioxide and water, with the concomitant production of the energy-rich molecules of adenosine triphosphate (ATP; see METABOLISM).

Since ammonia is highly toxic to most animals, it must be effectively eliminated. This is no problem in small aquatic animals because ammonia rapidly diffuses, is highly soluble in water, and escapes easily into the external medium before its concentration in the body fluids can reach a dangerous level. But in terrestrial animals, and in some of the larger aquatic animals, ammonia is converted into some less harmful compounds (detoxication). In mammals, including man, it is detoxified to urea, which may be considered as being formed by the condensation of one molecule of carbon dioxide with two molecules of ammonia (though the biochemistry of the process is more complex than that). Urea is highly soluble

in water but cannot be excreted in a highly concentrated solution because of the osmotic pressure (see below) it would exert. Conservation of water being a pressing need for most terrestrial animals, it is not surprising that many of them have evolved more economical methods for disposing of nitrogenous by-products. Birds, reptiles, and terrestrial insects excrete nitrogen in the form of uric acid, which is highly insoluble in water and can be removed from the body as a thick suspension or even as a dry powder.

EXCRETORY MECHANISMS

Osmotic pressure. In order to understand the advantages of the excretion of uric acid over urea it is necessary to know something about the behaviour of molecules in solution. Molecules of a solute (*e.g.* salt, sugar) in water tend to move by diffusion from a region where they are in high concentration to one where they are in low concentration, and molecules of water tend to move in the opposite direction. If a porous membrane is interposed between these regions, the movements of molecules may be variously restricted depending upon their size in relation to the size of the submicroscopic pores in the membrane. The passage of water molecules from pure water through such a membrane into a solution containing molecules that are too large to pass is called osmosis, a process that takes place spontaneously and does not require energy. This process can be reversed by applying hydrostatic pressure to the solution, a process that does require energy. The level of hydrostatic pressure at which there is no net movement of water in either direction across the membrane is called the osmotic pressure of that particular solution; the greater the concentration of dissolved molecules in the solution the greater is its osmotic pressure and the greater the force needed to remove water from it.

The osmotic process

Applying these principles to excretion, it can be seen why more energy is required to remove water from urine containing urea than from urine containing the same weight of uric acid. The molecule of urea is smaller than that of uric acid, so there are more molecules of urea to exert osmotic pressure. But an even more important difference is that whereas urea is highly soluble in water, uric acid is not. As water is progressively removed from a solution of urea, the osmotic pressure opposing further removal progressively increases. For the uric acid solution, however, as water is removed, the uric acid comes out of solution, or precipitates, when the solution is at a lower concentration, and, therefore, at a lower osmotic pressure, which does not increase further.

Regulation of water–salt balance. The mechanisms of detoxication that animals use are obviously related to their modes of life. This is true, with greater force, of the mechanisms of homeostasis, the ability of organisms to maintain internal stability. A desert-living mammal constantly faces the problem of water conservation; but a freshwater fish faces the problem of getting rid of the water that enters its body by osmosis through the skin. At the level of the individual cell, whether it be the cell of a unicellular organism or a cell in the body of a multicellular organism, the problems of homeostasis present themselves in similar ways.

For the continuation of its intracellular processes the cell must maintain an intracellular chemical environment in which the concentrations of various ions (see below) are kept constant in the face of changing concentrations in the medium surrounding the cell. This is the task of the cell membrane. In the higher animals the task is easier since cells in the interior of their bodies are bathed in an internal medium—the blood—whose composition is regulated so as to minimize the effects of changes in the external medium. This regulatory function is undertaken by specialized cells or organs such as the kidney, thereby lessening the regulatory burden of the other cells of the body.

The biological necessity for homeostatic mechanisms is particularly urgent for controlling the inorganic components of cells and body fluids. Inorganic salts can exert even greater osmotic pressure against membranes impermeable to them than urea. This is so because, under the conditions in the body, they are almost completely dissociated into their component ions. For example, a molecule of common salt (sodium chloride) is dissociated into a positively charged sodium ion and a negatively charged chloride ion, both of which can exert osmotic pressure.

Besides their osmotic effects, inorganic ions have profound effects upon metabolic processes, which in general will take place only in the presence of appropriate concentrations of these ions. The most important inorganic ions in organisms are the positively charged hydrogen, sodium, potassium, calcium, and magnesium ions, and the negatively charged chloride, phosphate, and bicarbonate ions. The membranes of cells are not completely impermeable to these ions and are in fact endowed with the ability to transport ions from one side to the other, whereby they control the concentrations of ions within the cells; when such transport is in the direction that requires a supply of energy, it is called active transport (see MEMBRANE, BIOLOGICAL).

Active transport of ions

Osmotic regulation is the maintenance of the normal concentration of the body fluids; *i.e.*, the total concentration of all dissolved substances (solutes) that would exert osmotic pressure against a membrane impermeable to them. Osmotic regulation controls the amount of water in the body fluids relative to the amount of osmotically active solutes. Ionic regulation is the maintenance of the concentrations of the various ions in the body fluids relative to one another. There is no hard and fast distinction between the two processes; organs that participate in one process at the same time participate in the other.

Principal excretory structures. Whereas the kidney is undoubtedly the principal organ subserving both nitrogenous excretion and osmotic and ionic regulation in the mammalian body, these functions are not always performed by a single organ in other animals. As indicated earlier, primitive aquatic animals do not require any special provision for nitrogenous excretion. But by reason of their permeable skins they may have serious problems of osmotic and ionic regulation, especially in freshwater, where cells covering the surface of the body have the ability actively to transport salts into or out of the animal. In some cases these nonkidney regulatory activities are performed by certain recognizably specialized cells; *e.g.*, in the gills of fishes (see below). In other cases, specialized cells are assembled into organs of salt uptake or salt elimination; *e.g.*, the salt glands of birds (see below).

This dispersal of the regulatory function may be the primitive condition, for it is only in the more highly evolved terrestrial animals that the regulatory function is restricted to an excretory system proper. This is readily understandable in view of the need of terrestrial animals to conserve water. This evolutionary development toward one system reaches its climax in the birds, reptiles, and terrestrial insects, in which all the processes of elimination that might involve loss of water—defecation, nitrogenous excretion, and ionic regulation—converge upon the same final channel.

For the excretory organs of a wide variety of vertebrate and invertebrate animals, there is evidence that the primary process of urine production is nonselective, in that in those animals all substances dissolved in their body fluids, with the possible exception of proteins, are found in the primary urine. In many animals the primary urine is produced by filtration from the blood. At a later stage, substances in the primary urine that are useful to the body are selectively reabsorbed. In addition, a few substances are known to be actively transported (secreted) into the urine.

The nonselective formation of primary urine serves another aspect of excretion: the elimination of foreign substances. Mechanisms of active transport are highly specific to the substances transported. All dissolved constituents of the body fluids pass freely into the primary urine and then specific reabsorptive mechanisms gather up the "wanted" substances. In this way a natural economy automatically eliminates "unwanted" substances simply by not providing mechanisms for their reabsorption.

INVERTEBRATE EXCRETORY SYSTEMS

In their detoxication mechanisms, so far as they have been investigated, the invertebrates in general conform to the principles applying to all animals, namely, that aquatic forms get rid of ammonia by diffusion through the surface of the body; terrestrial forms convert ammonia to uric acid. This implies that in aquatic forms the excretory organ is principally of importance for the composition of their body fluids. Normally, the body fluids of marine invertebrates have the same concentration as seawater; they usually differ, however, in the proportions of ions, with relatively more potassium and less magnesium than seawater. Furthermore, their urine normally has the same concentration as seawater, but correspondingly it contains less potassium and more magnesium. In freshwater invertebrates the urine is commonly, though not invariably, more dilute than the body fluids. By producing dilute urine a freshwater invertebrate conserves the salt content of its body while eliminating the water that enters its body by osmosis through its water-permeable surface.

Regulation of body fluids

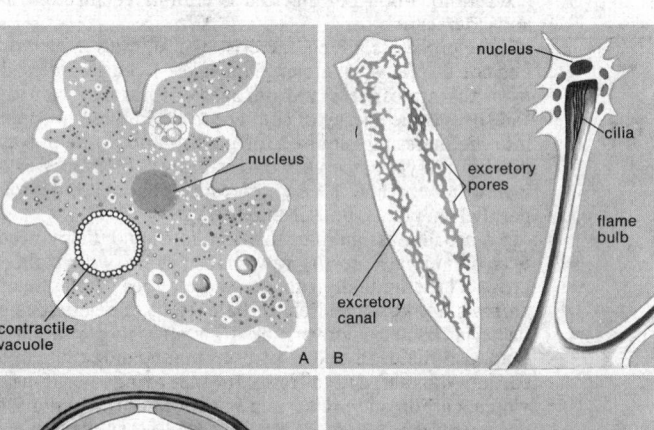
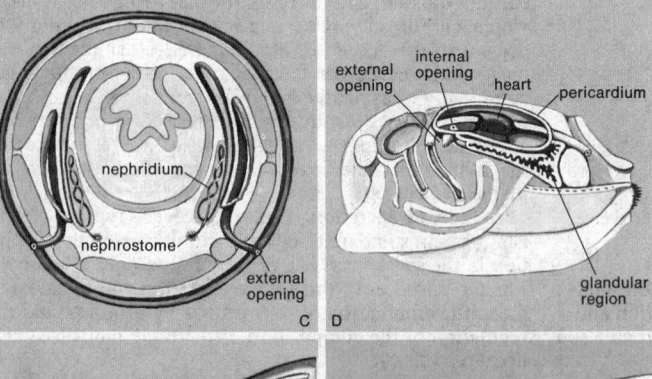
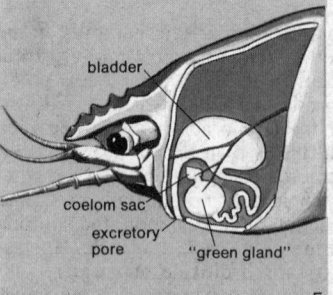
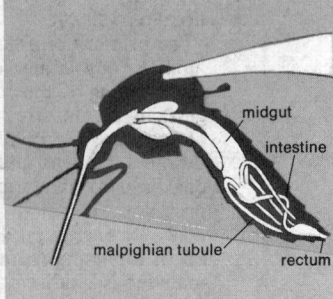

Figure 1: *Invertebrate excretory systems.*
(A) Contractile vacuole of an amoeboid protozoan.
(B) Protonephridial system of a flatworm, with enlargement of a single-celled flame bulb that terminates the tubules of excretory canals. (C) Metanephridial system of an earthworm, with paired nephridia in one segment. (D) Renal organ of a clam, cut away to show glandular region. (E) Renal system of a crayfish, exposed through cut-away shell. (F) Excretory system of a mosquito.

Some invertebrates, notably echinoderms, coelenterates, and sponges, have no organs to which an excretory function can be confidently ascribed. Since all of these animals are aquatic, it is reasonable to suppose that they excrete nitrogen (as ammonia) by simple diffusion. Their body fluids (where present) are closely similar to seawater in composition, and it may be presumed that regulation operates only at the cellular level.

The excretory organs of other invertebrates are of diverse evolutionary origin. This is not to say, however, that each invertebrate phylum has evolved its own particular type of excretory organ; rather, there appear to be five main types of invertebrate excretory organ: contractile vacuole, nephridium, renal gland, coxal gland, and malpighian tubule.

The contractile vacuoles of protozoans. Some protozoan animals possess an organelle having the form of an internal sac, or vacuole, which enlarges by the accumulation of a clear fluid and then discharges its contents to the exterior. The cycle of filling and emptying may be repeated as frequently as every half minute. The chief role of the contractile vacuole appears to be in osmotic regulation, not in nitrogen excretion.

Contractile vacuoles occur more frequently and are more active in freshwater species than in closely related marine species. In freshwater, the concentration of dissolved substances in the cell is greater than in the external medium, and the cell takes in water by osmosis. If the contractile vacuole is put out of action, the cell increases in volume. If the concentration of salts in the medium increases—which would have the effect of decreasing the rate of osmosis—the rate of output by the contractile vacuole diminishes. The fluid eliminated by the vacuole is more dilute than the cytoplasm.

The nephridia of annelids, nemertines, flatworms, and rotifers. The word nephridium applies in its strict sense only to the excretory organs of annelids, but it may usefully be extended to include the excretory organs of other phyla having similar characteristics. Annelids are segmented animals that typically contain a pair of nephridia on each segment. Each nephridium has the form of a very fine tubule, often of considerable length; one end usually opens into the body cavity and the other to the exterior. In some annelids, however, the tubule does not open into the body cavity but ends internally in a cluster of cells of a special type known as solenocytes, or flame cells. The possession of solenocytes by some annelids is one of the characters that allies them with other nonsegmented phyla that have no true body cavity. They also have a system of tubules opening at the surface and ending internally in flame cells embedded among the other cells of the body. In most cases, there is no regular arrangement of the various parts of the system.

Animals belonging to all of these phyla are primarily aquatic, and, in the few cases known, the main excretory product is ammonia. How much of it leaves the body by the nephridia and how much through the body surface is unknown.

Very few physiological studies have been made on nephridia other than those of the earthworm. Although the earthworm is considered a terrestrial animal, its relationships with its environment are characteristically those of a freshwater animal. The nephridium of the earthworm is longer and more complex than that of marine annelids, four regions being distinguishable. Body fluid enters the nephridium via an internal opening called the nephridiostome. As the fluid passes along the tubule, probably driven by cilia, its composition is modified. In the two lower regions of the tubule the fluid becomes progressively more dilute, presumably as a result of the reabsorption of salts. Finally, a very dilute urine passes into the bladder (an enlarged portion of the tubule) and then to the exterior through the external opening, or nephridiopore. The rate of urine flow for an earthworm may be as much as 60 percent of its body weight in a period of 24 hours.

The renal glands of mollusks. The anatomical form of the renal gland varies from one class of mollusks to another, but a common plan is clearly evident. The renal gland is a relatively wide tube opening from a sac (the pericardium) surrounding the heart, at one end and to the mantle cavity (effectively to the exterior) at the other. There is a single pair of renal glands; in some forms one member of the pair may be reduced or absent. Clams

The common plan of the renal gland

have the simplest arrangement; the region nearest to the pericardium has glandular walls and gives way to a nonglandular, wider tube that extends to the urinary opening.

The vast majority of mollusks are aquatic, and, as would be expected, excrete nitrogen in the form of ammonia. In octopuses, however, nitrogen is excreted as ammonium chloride, which is quite strongly concentrated in the urine. Terrestrial snails and slugs excrete uric acid but may also excrete ammonia when living in moist surroundings.

In all mollusks so far investigated the primary process in urine production appears to be filtration of the blood. This may take place through the wall of the heart into the pericardium, or from blood vessels that supply the glandular part of the renal gland. The composition of the primary urine may be altered by reabsorption or secretion, or both. In freshwater mollusks salts are reabsorbed in the glandular tube and in the wide tubule, and the final urine is more dilute than the blood. The rate of urine flow is high, up to 45 percent of the body weight per day in the freshwater mussel. In marine mollusks the urine has the same concentration as the blood, as would be expected, but (in the few cases examined) its ionic composition is different.

The coxal glands of aquatic arthropods. Coxal glands are tubular organs, each opening on the basal region (coxa) of a limb. Since arthropods are segmented animals, it is reasonable to suppose that the ancestral arthropod had a pair of such glands in every segment of the body. In crustaceans now living there is, as a rule, only a single pair of glands, and in higher crustaceans these open at the bases of the antennae. Each antennal gland is a compact organ formed of a single tubule folded upon itself. When unravelled the tubule is seen to comprise three or four easily recognizable regions. The tubule arises internally as a small sac, the coelomic sac, which opens into a wider region, the labyrinth, having complex infoldings of its walls. The labyrinth opens either directly into the bladder, as in marine lobsters and crabs, or into a narrow part of the tubule, the canal, which in turn opens into the bladder, as in freshwater crayfishes.

The coelomic sac, well-supplied with blood vessels, gives evidence that the primary process in urine production is filtration of the blood through the wall of the coelomosac in a manner analogous to filtration in the glomerulus and Bowman's capsule of the vertebrate kidney (see below). In lobsters and marine crabs the urine in all parts of the organ has the same ion concentration as the blood. In freshwater crayfishes the urine has the same concentration as far as the end of the labyrinth; from there on reabsorption takes place in the canal and the urine leaves the body as a very dilute solution. The addition of the canal to the system demonstrates one way crustaceans have adapted to life in freshwater. But this is not the only way in which the regulatory problem is solved in freshwater crustaceans. In freshwater crabs, for example, there is a great decrease in the water permeability of the surface (principally the gills) so that water enters by osmosis quite slowly. In contrast to the rate of urine flow in a freshwater crayfish (about 5 percent of the body weight per day), that of the freshwater crab is 100 times less (about 0.05 percent). In the crab the urine has the same concentration as the blood, but because the flow is so small the salt loss via the urine is negligible. A few semiterrestrial crabs are known to produce urine more concentrated than the blood.

In all crustaceans for which analyses are available the concentrations of ions in blood and urine differ. At a urine flow of 5 percent of the body weight per day the activities of the antennal glands are certainly capable of effecting changes in the composition of the blood. These activities are somehow coordinated with salt uptake by the cells of the body surface so as to subserve homeostasis. The role of the antennal glands in nitrogenous excretion seems to be unimportant.

The malpighian tubules of insects. Although some terrestrial arthropods (*e.g.*, land crabs, ticks) retain the coxal glands of their aquatic ancestors, others, the insects,

Ion concentration in urine

have evolved an entirely different type of excretory system. The malpighian tubules, which vary in number from two in some species to over 100 in others, end blindly in the body cavity (which is a blood space) and open not directly to the exterior but to the alimentary canal at the junction between midgut and hindgut. The primary urine issuing from the malpighian tubules has to pass through the rectum before it leaves the insect's body, and in the rectum its composition is profoundly changed. The insect excretory system therefore comprises the malpighian tubules and the rectum acting together.

The malpighian tubules are bathed in the insect's blood, but since they are not rigid it is impossible for any hydrostatic pressure to be developed across their walls, such as could bring about filtration. The primary urine is formed by a process of secretion in the following way: Potassium ions are actively transported from the blood into the cavity of the tubule and are necessarily followed by negatively charged ions so as to maintain electroneutrality. In turn, water follows the ions, probably by osmosis, and various other substances—sugars, amino acids, and urate ions—also enter the primary urine by diffusion from the blood.

The primary urine, together with soluble products of digestion and insoluble indigestible matter from the midgut, then passes to the rectum. Here (or in some insects at an earlier stage) the urine is acidified and the soluble urate is thereby converted to insoluble uric acid, which comes out of solution. Water is then reabsorbed together with the soluble products of digestion and other useful substances, including the bulk of the ions that entered the primary urine. In insects that live in dry surroundings the rectum has remarkable powers of reabsorption, its contents finally being voided as hard, dry pellets containing solid uric acid.

The activity of the excretory system in insects is under hormonal control. This has been most clearly demonstrated in the case of *Rhodnius*, a bloodsucking bug. Immediately after the ingestion of a blood meal there is a rapid flow of urine whereby most of the water taken in with the blood meal is eliminated. The distension of the body after ingestion is the stimulus that causes certain cells in the central nervous system to release a hormone that acts upon the malpighian tubules to promote a brisk flow of primary urine.

VERTEBRATE EXCRETORY SYSTEMS

The kidney and its associated ducts are the excretory system of the mammal, and, as already noted, most of the nitrogenous waste arising in the mammalian body is excreted as urea. Other nitrogenous compounds regularly present in the urine in smaller amounts are uric acid (or the closely related compound allantoin) and creatinine; both of these arise mainly as by-products of the renewal and repair of tissues.

In birds, reptiles and amphibians the kidneys are compact organs as they are in mammals, but in fishes they are narrow bands of tissue running the length of the body (see below under *Evolution*). In amphibians, as in mammals, the main excretory product is urea. In birds and reptiles it is uric acid. In most fishes the main excretory product is ammonia.

Structure and function. *In mammals.* The mammalian kidney (Figure 2) is a compact organ with two distinct regions: cortex and medulla. The functional unit of the kidney is the nephron, of which there are about 1,000,000 in each kidney of man, tightly packed together. Each nephron (Figure 2) is a tubular structure consisting of four regions. It arises in the cortex as (1) a small vesicle about one-fifth of a millimetre in diameter, known as Bowman's capsule, into which projects a tuft of capillary blood vessels, the glomerulus. Bowman's capsule is continuous with (2) the proximal convoluted tubule, which also lies in the cortex. Following the proximal convoluted tubule is (3) the loop of Henle, which descends into the medulla and then runs straight up again to the cortex where it continues as (4) the distal convoluted tubule. A collecting tubule, into which several nephrons open, courses through the medulla to open a wide cavity, the

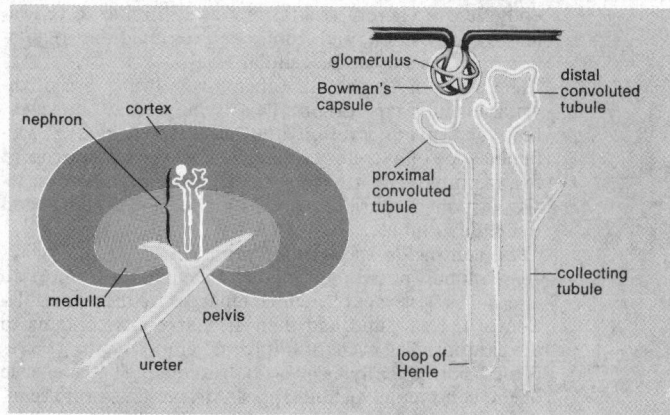

Figure 2: *The mammalian kidney.*
(Left) The kidney proper, with a single nephron (of thousands present) in white and somewhat larger proportionately.
(Right) Nephron enlarged to show component parts.

pelvis of the kidney. From the pelvis the ureter leads to the bladder, and from the bladder the urethra leads out of the body. (See also EXCRETORY SYSTEM, HUMAN.)

The mechanism of urine formation involves three processes: filtration, reabsorption, and secretion. Primary urine is formed by filtration from the blood. From this primary urine certain substances are reabsorbed into the blood and other substances are secreted into the primary urine from the blood. The word secretion is used by renal physiologists to imply transport, other than by filtration, from the blood to urine. Filtration implies that all molecules below a certain size are allowed to pass nonselectively into the primary urine; reabsorption and secretion imply the existence of specific mechanisms for the transport of specific substances.

The membrane covering the glomerulus is permeable to water and to all the constituents of the blood plasma except proteins. The glomerular capillaries are intercalated in the course of an artery, with the consequence that the pressure of the blood in these capillaries is higher than in the capillaries in other parts of the kidney. Opposed to the blood pressure are the pressure of the fluid within Bowman's capsule and the osmotic pressure exerted by the proteins of the blood plasma; but the blood pressure is sufficiently in excess of the sum of these to ensure a rapid flow of fluid, the glomerular filtrate or primary urine, into Bowman's capsule. The glomerular filtrate contains the nitrogenous compounds ultimately to be excreted in the urine. As the glomerular filtrate passes through the proximal tubule, 80 percent of the water, and many substances of value to the body (*e.g.*, glucose), are reabsorbed into the blood capillaries surrounding the tubule. This reabsorptive process is accomplished without any change in the concentration of the tubular fluid, which remains the same as that of the blood plasma.

After traversing the loop of Henle, the remaining 20 percent of the glomerular filtrate passes into the distal tubule, where further reabsorption, notably of salts, takes place. If this is accompanied by a proportionate reabsorption of water, the tubular fluid remains at the same concentration as the blood plasma, but if the reabsorption of water is restricted, as it may be in certain circumstances (see below), the tubular fluid becomes more dilute than the blood plasma. Under normal physiological conditions some 15 percent of the glomerular filtrate is reabsorbed in the distal tubule. Most of the remaining 5 percent is reabsorbed in the collecting tubule. The amount of fluid, at this point called urine, that reaches the pelvis of the kidney is only 1 percent of the volume originally filtered at the glomerulus; but it contains nearly all the nitrogenous waste of the filtrate in concentrated solution. A few substances are also secreted from the blood through the walls of the tubule into the tubular fluid.

The action of the loop of Henle is more difficult to describe. The descending and ascending limbs lie close together, and there is secretion of a small amount of salt from the ascending limb into the descending limb throughout the length of the loop. At any level the fluid in the descending limb is slightly more concentrated than the fluid in the ascending limb. As the fluid passes down the descending limb it becomes progressively more concentrated; as it passes up the ascending limb it becomes more dilute and leaves the loop more or less at the same concentration as the blood plasma. The net result of this activity on the part of all the loops in the kidney is to create at the inner margin of the medulla a region where all the fluids are more strongly concentrated than the normal blood plasma. The collecting tubules run through this region before opening into the pelvis; and since their walls are ordinarily permeable to water, water is removed from them by osmosis so that the final urine is more concentrated than the blood.

Desert-living mammals produce highly concentrated urine and their kidneys have a greater thickness of medulla because of the greater development of the loops of Henle. This mechanism is in full operation in an animal suffering from thirst; the water content of its body is conserved by the excretion of a small volume of concentrated urine. If the body has excess water, the mechanism becomes inoperative; instead, the reabsorption of salts (without a proportionate amount of water) in the distal tubule results in the production of a large volume of dilute urine (diuresis).

Although the kidney has a nerve supply, its activities are regulated by hormones in accordance with the body's needs. The pituitary gland at the base of the brain releases an antidiuretic hormone (ADH) into the blood. The ADH increases the permeability of the distal and collecting tubules to water, thereby facilitating the reabsorption of water. A slight increase in the concentration of the blood, such as would occur in the event of water deficiency, causes an increased secretion of ADH and the excretion of a small volume of concentrated urine. Conversely, dilution of the blood cuts off the release of ADH, decreasing the permeability of the tubules and causing diuresis. Another hormone, aldosterone, produced by the cortex of the adrenal gland, favours the excretion of potassium ions in preference to sodium ions.

In birds and reptiles. The main excretory product of birds and reptiles is uric acid. Since their glomeruli are relatively small, so also is their daily volume of urine. Not highly concentrated by mammalian standards—although it may be turbid with crystals of uric acid—the urine of birds and reptiles is conducted not to a urinary bladder but to the terminal portion of the alimentary canal, the cloaca; from the cloaca it is voided with the feces. Like mammals, and unlike the lower vertebrates, birds and reptiles have skins impermeable to water, and thus are well adapted to terrestrial life. The relative inability of the kidney to produce concentrated urine is compensated for in birds that possess salt glands, which remove excess salt from their bodies. These organs are modified tear glands that discharge a concentrated solution of sodium chloride through the nostrils. Salt glands enable marine birds to drink seawater with no ill effects.

In amphibians. The kidneys of amphibians have been much studied by renal physiologists, and the direct evidence for the occurrence of filtration at the glomerulus was first provided by experiments on the amphibian kidney.

Although amphibians are formally given the status of terrestrial animals, they are poorly adapted to life on land. They excrete nitrogen in the form of urea and cannot produce urine more concentrated than the blood. Their skins are permeable to water. On land amphibians are liable to lose water very rapidly by evaporation. In freshwater they suffer entry of water by osmosis, which is counteracted by the excretion of a large volume of dilute urine. The urine is stored in a large bladder before being voided, providing a reserve of water the animal can use when it comes on land.

When an amphibian leaves the water, a number of physiological adjustments are made that have the effect of conserving water. The rate of glomerular filtration is reduced by restriction of the blood supply, and this together with an increased release of antidiuretic hormone

results in the production of a small volume of urine of the same concentration as the blood. The antidiuretic hormone also increases the permeability of the bladder to water and allows the stored urine to be reabsorbed into the body.

Fishes. The homeostasis problem is the same for freshwater fishes as for other freshwater animals. Water enters the body by osmosis and salts leach out. To compensate, the kidney (which has large glomeruli) produces a relatively large amount (about 20 percent of the body weight per day) of dilute urine. This serves to remove the water but by itself is insufficient to prevent gradual loss of salts. Extremely diluted salts are taken up from the freshwater and transported directly into the blood by certain specialized cells in the gills. Nitrogenous excretion is no problem: some ammonia is carried away in the large volume of dilute urine, but most of it simply escapes to the external medium by diffusing through the gills.

By contrast, the homeostasis problem of marine fishes is unlike that of most marine animals. The salt content of the blood of marine fishes is less than half that of seawater (see below under *Evolution*), with the consequence that the marine fish tends to lose water and gain salt. This, it would seem, could be compensated most easily by the excretion of urine more concentrated than the blood, but the kidneys of fishes are not able to do this. In marine bony fishes the kidney has small glomeruli and produces only a small amount (about 4 percent of the body weight per day) of urine, which is of the same concentration as the blood. The fish replaces its lost water by continually swallowing seawater, and the special cells of the gills, working in reverse, reject salt to the external medium. Nitrogen is excreted mostly as ammonia but also as another detoxication product, trimethylamine oxide.

In sharks and rays ammonia is converted to urea, and urea plays an important role in homeostasis. Surprisingly, urea is retained in the blood to such an extent that the blood is slightly more concentrated than seawater. Thus loss of water by osmosis is prevented and these fish have no need to swallow seawater. Any excess of salt in their bodies is removed via the rectal gland, functionally analogous to the salt gland of birds.

Osmotic and ionic regulation in fishes is under hormonal control. This has been studied particularly in fishes such as eels and salmon, which are able to move between freshwater and seawater.

EVOLUTION OF THE VERTEBRATE EXCRETORY SYSTEM

Studies of the embryonic development of primitive vertebrates, such as the dogfish shark, clearly show that the excretory system arises from a series of tubules, one pair in every segment of the body between the heart and the tail. This continuous series of tubules constitutes the archinephros, the name implying that the kidney of the ancestral vertebrate had some such form as this. Each tubule opens internally to the body cavity and may, in the remote past, have opened separately to the exterior; but in all living vertebrates the tubules open on each side into a longitudinal duct, the archinephric duct. At the posterior end of the body cavity the two archinephric ducts unite before opening to the exterior. Later in development, Bowman's capsule arises as a diverticulum of each tubule, subsequently becoming indented by the glomerulus. Eventually, the tubules usually lose their internal openings to the body cavity. The most anterior tubules of the archinephros (pronephros) usually degenerate in the adult.

These ducts and tubules also subserve the reproductive function, and for this reason zoologists are accustomed to speak of them as the urinogenital system. The extent to which the ducts and tubules are shared is greater in the male than in the female. In the male the spermatic tubules of the testis connect with the kidney tubules in the middle region of the archinephros (mesonephros), and in some vertebrates (*e.g.*, the frog) where there is no development of the posterior region (metanephros), the tubules of the mesonephros serve to convey both urine

Characteristics of the uric acid of birds and reptiles

Excretion in marine fishes

Relationship between excretory and reproductive systems

and sperm. In the reptiles, birds, and mammals there is greater separation of function, the mesonephros being exclusively genital and the metanephros being exclusively urinary (see Figure 3).

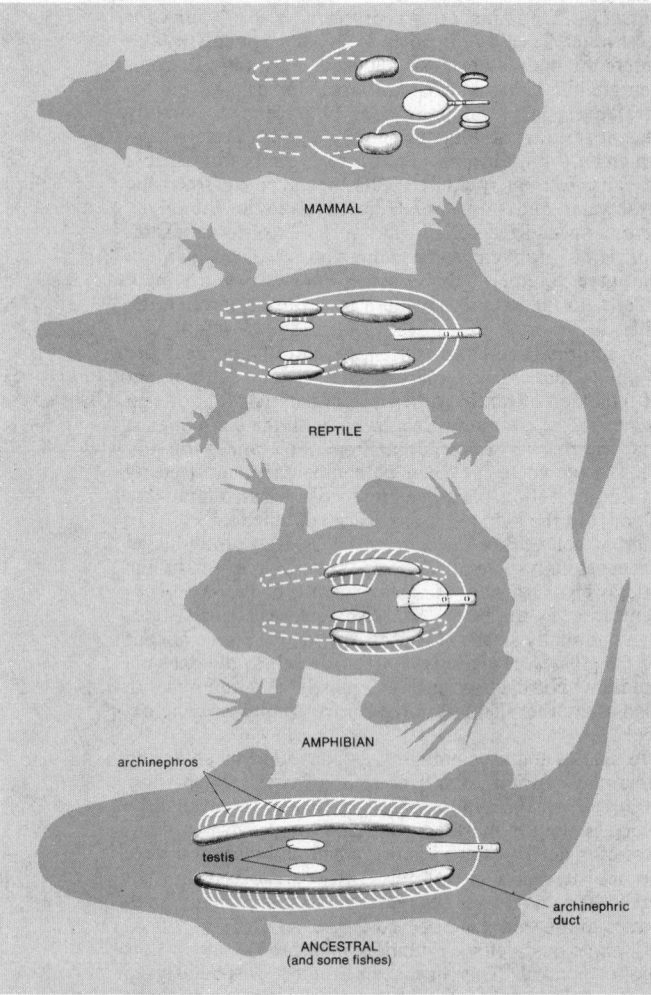

Figure 3: *Evolution of the urogenital system in male vertebrates.*
The ancestral archinephric condition has evolved in different patterns for the amphibians, reptiles, and mammals (birds have a pattern similar to reptiles). The broken lines indicate the change in ancestral plan in each of the major vertebrate classes.

In the female, even in the lower vertebrates, the two systems are confluent only at the posterior end. It has been held that the oviduct is a derivative of the archinephric duct, but the evidence for this is not compelling.

In primitive marine animals the blood is almost identical with seawater in composition; in typical freshwater animals the concentration of the blood is about half that of seawater. Many originally marine animals have evolved the ability to live in freshwater; relatively few animals, after having evolved into freshwater, have returned to the sea, and in none of them has the blood returned to its original "seawater" concentration. The earliest fossil vertebrates are found in marine deposits, but the fossil record shows clearly that the early evolution of fishes took place in freshwater. It is assumed that the blood of early freshwater fishes, like that of other freshwater animals, was osmotically equivalent to half-strength seawater. The sharks and rays returned to the sea during the Carboniferous Period, and no doubt at that time they evolved the device of urea retention. The bony fishes returned to the sea later, in the Mesozoic Era, and solved their problem by swallowing seawater and rejecting excess salt at the gills.

BIBLIOGRAPHY. H.W. SMITH, *From Fish to Philosopher* (1953), is a popular introduction to vertebrate evolution in terms of kidney evolution. Among the general sources of information on the comparative structure and function of excretory systems are: E. FLOREY, *An Introduction to General and Comparative Animal Physiology*, ch. 5, 13 (1966); E.S. GOODRICH, *Studies on the Structure and Development of Vertebrates* (1930), an older work of unchallenged authority on morphological and evolutionary aspects of all vertebrate systems, including the urinogenital; A.S. ROMER, *The Vertebrate Body*, 3rd ed., ch. 13 (1962), on excretory and reproductive systems; M.S. GORDON et al., *Animal Function: Principles and Adaptations*, ch. 7 (1968), on the regulation of water and salts in animals; W.S. HOAR, *General and Comparative Physiology*, ch. 8, 11 (1966); J. FIELD (ed.), *Handbook of Physiology*, sect. 4, *Adaptation to the Environment*, ch. 13–14 (1964), on the excretory function; presumes a greater background knowledge than do the works of Hoar, Florey, or Romer listed above.

More advanced books, covering parts of the subject, include: E.S. GOODRICH, "The Study of Nephridia and Genital Ducts since 1895," *Quart. J. Micro. Soc.*, 86:113–392 (1945), a review of research on the urinogenital systems up to the mid-1940s; W.T.W. POTTS and G. PARRY, *Osmotic and Ionic Regulation in Animals* (1963); and K. SCHMIDT- NIELSEN, *Desert Animals* (1964), with particular regard for the problems of water conservation in animals.

(J.A.R.)

Excretory System, Human

The excretory system, also called the urinary system, normally consists of two kidneys, which remove dissolved waste and excess substances from the blood and form urine; the bladder, where the urine is stored; the two ureters, which convey urine from the kidneys to the bladder; and the urethra, the passageway by which urine leaves the body (the development of this system is detailed in EMBRYOLOGY, HUMAN; its functioning, in EXCRETION, HUMAN). For a general treatment, see EXCRETION AND EXCRETORY SYSTEMS. This article is focussed on the structure of the system, including only such details of the functioning as are necessary to illuminate the structure.

THE KIDNEYS

General description and location.   Resembling kidney beans in shape and colour, the kidneys are reddish-brown, and are concave on one long side, convex on the opposite. They are normally high in the abdominal cavity and against its back wall, lying on either side of the vertebral column between the levels of the twelfth thoracic and third lumbar vertebrae, and outside the peritoneum, the membrane that lines the abdomen.

The location of the kidneys varies with changes in posture; they ascend somewhat when the body is recumbent and descend when it is erect. Their location is also influenced by movements of the diaphragm, the muscular partition between the chest and the abdomen that moves up and down as part of the processes of breathing. The right kidney is usually located about 1.5 centimetres (about 0.6 inch) lower than the left, as it is displaced downward by the greater bulk of the liver on the right side.

The long axis of the kidneys corresponds roughly with that of the body, except for a slight tilt that brings the upper ends closer to the backbone. Centred in the medial side of each kidney (the concave side toward the backbone) is a deep vertical cleft, the hilus, which leads into a cavity in the kidney known as the renal (kidney) sinus. The hilus is the point of entrance or emergence for the renal arteries, veins, lymphatic vessels, and nerves, and it includes the renal pelvis, the expanded upper end of the ureter.

The size of the kidneys varies. In adults their average length is 12 centimetres, their width seven centimetres, and their thickness 2.5 centimetres (in inches, about 4.7, 2.8, and one, respectively). Their average weight in men is about 145 grams (about five ounces); in women, about ten grams (0.4 ounce) less.

The kidneys are close to many other structures, separated from them only by the renal fascia (a sheet of connective tissue) or by fat. The relationships of the two kidneys differ.

In front, the right kidney is close to the liver, the right adrenal (suprarenal) gland, the descending part of the duodenum (the first portion of the small intestine), and

Size, colour, and shape of kidneys

the right colic flexure of the large intestine—the angle between the vertical section of the colon on the right (ascending colon) and the horizontal portion (transverse colon).

Almost the entire area near the liver, like the part near the small intestine, is covered by peritoneum, which the other areas lack. The upper front surface of the left kidney is near the left adrenal gland, the stomach, and the spleen; the narrow portion of the pancreas called its tail runs across the middle of the kidney, and coils of the small intestine cover its lower half.

Behind, both kidneys lie on a bed of fatty tissue. They are close to the diaphragm and two of its ligaments; to two muscles at the back of the abdominal cavity, the psoas major and the quadratus lumborum; and to the tendon of another muscle, the transversus abdominis.

Renal capsule and adipose renal capsule

Enclosing each kidney is the renal capsule, a smooth, tough covering. This covering is continuous with the lining of the renal sinus and with the connective tissue framework of the kidney.

The fat-laden retroperitoneal tissues, especially plentiful behind and to the outer side of each kidney, make up what is called the adipose renal capsule. Within the fatty tissue is a fibrous sheet, the renal fascia, that encloses—and forms a partial partition between—each kidney and its corresponding adrenal gland. The compartment formed by the renal fascia is relatively open below, so that any blood, urine, or pus that collects around a kidney as a result of injury or infection tends to spread downward along a ureter rather than to either side. In consequence, abscesses or collections of blood (hematomas) affecting either kidney rarely involve the opposite kidney or the space around it.

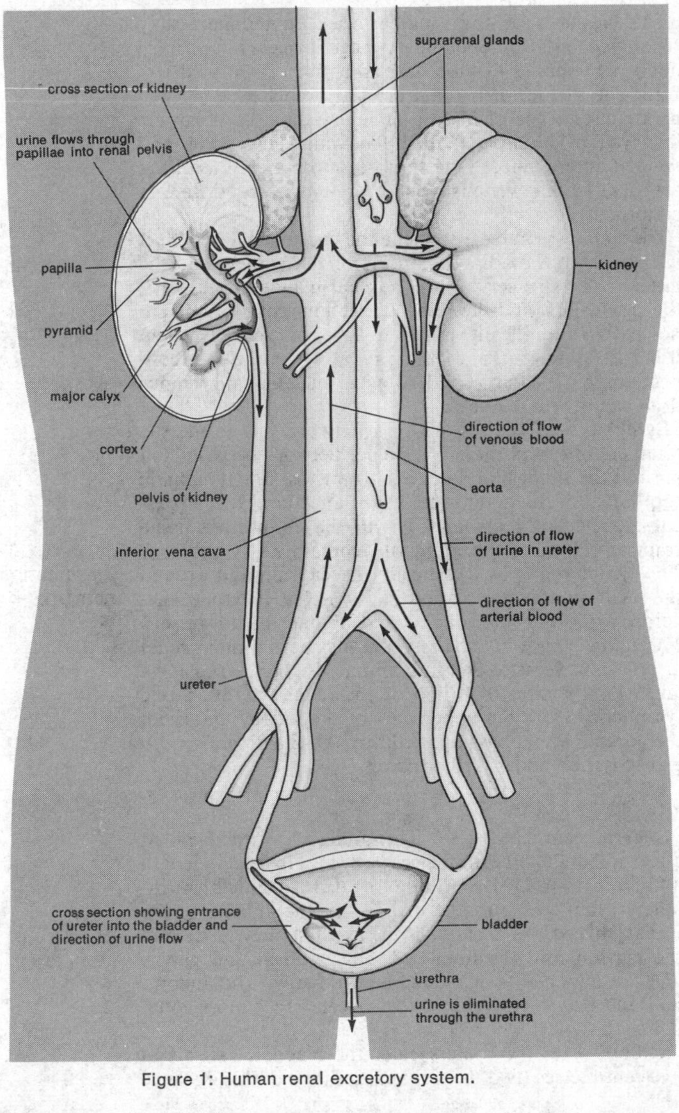

Renal vessels and nerves. The renal arteries are large and arise, one on each side, from the abdominal aorta, at a point opposite the upper border of the second lumbar vertebra (*i.e.*, a little above the small of the back). Because of the position of the aorta, ordinarily a little to the left of the midline, the right renal artery is longer than the left. Each artery, at places close to the renal hilus, gives off small branches to the adrenal gland and ureter and branches into anterior and posterior divisions. Each division then divides further to supply the various parts of the kidney.

The large veins carrying blood from the kidneys usually lie in front of the corresponding arteries and join the inferior vena cava almost at right angles. The left vein is about 7.5 centimetres (about three inches) long. The right vein is about 2.5 centimetres (about one inch) long, because the inferior vena cava lies closer to the right kidney.

The kidneys are supplied from both the sympathetic and the parasympathetic components of the autonomic nervous system, and the renal nerves contain both afferent and efferent fibres (afferent fibres carry nerve impulses to the central nervous system; efferent fibres, from it).

Internal configuration. A cross section of a kidney reveals the renal sinus—the large cavity that has already been mentioned—and areas of kidney tissue usually distinguishable by their colour. The paler tissue, called the renal medulla, is roughly in the form of cones, called renal pyramids, with bases outward and apexes projecting, either singly or in groups, into the renal sinus. The bases of the pyramids are irregular, with slender projections, called rays, extending toward the kidney surface. The darker tissue is the cortex. It arches over the bases of the pyramids and has extensions, called renal columns, that fill gaps between the pyramids.

Each projection of one or more pyramid apexes into the sinus is known as a renal papilla, and each group of pyramids that project into a papilla, together with the portion of cortex that arches over the group, is a renal lobe.

The renal sinus includes the renal pelvis, a funnel-shaped expansion of the upper end of the ureter, and, reaching into the kidney substance from the wide end of the funnel, two or three extensions of the cavity called the major calyces. The major calyces are divided in turn into six to twelve smaller cavities, the minor calyces, into which the renal papillae project. The renal pelvis serves as the initial reservoir for urine, which flows into the sinus through the urinary collecting tubules, small tubes that open into the sinus at the papillae.

Minute structure. The functioning units of the kidneys, the structures that actually produce urine in the process of removing waste and excess substances from the blood, are the nephrons, of which there are approximately 1,000,000 in each kidney. Each nephron is a long tubule, or extremely fine tube, at one end closed, expanded, and folded into a double-walled cuplike structure. This structure, called the renal corpuscular capsule or Bowman's capsule, encloses a cluster of microscopic blood vessels—capillaries—called the glomerulus. The capsule and glomerulus together constitute the renal corpuscle. Blood flows into and away from the glomerulus through tiny arteries called arterioles, which reach and leave the glomerulus through the open end of the capsule. This opening is called the vascular pole of the corpuscle.

In the renal corpuscle, fluid filters out of the blood in the glomerulus through the inner wall of the capsule and into the nephron tubule. As this filtrate passes through the tubule, its composition is altered by secretion of certain substances into it and by selective reabsorption of water and other constituents from it. The final product is urine, which is conveyed through the collecting tubules into the renal pelvis.

The tubules of the nephrons are 30–55 millimetres (1.2–2.2 inches) long. The corpuscle and the initial portion of each tubule, called the proximal convoluted tubule, lie in the renal cortex. The tubule then descends into a renal pyramid, makes a U-shaped turn, and comes back to the cortex at a point near its point of entry into the medulla. This section of the tubule, consisting of the two parallel lengths and the bend between them, is called Henle's loop

The nephrons

Figure 1: Human renal excretory system.

Labels in figure:
- suprarenal glands
- cross section of kidney
- urine flows through papillae into renal pelvis
- papilla
- pyramid
- major calyx
- cortex
- pelvis of kidney
- inferior vena cava
- ureter
- kidney
- direction of flow of venous blood
- aorta
- direction of flow of urine in ureter
- direction of flow of arterial blood
- cross section showing entrance of ureter into the bladder and direction of urine flow
- bladder
- urethra
- urine is eliminated through the urethra

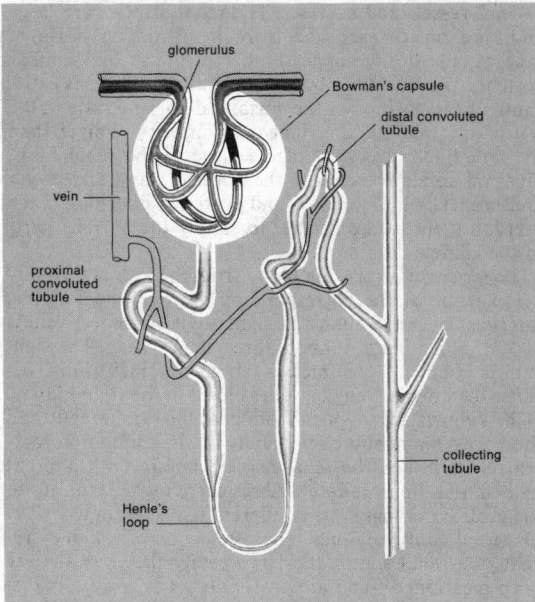

Figure 2: Stylized drawing of nephron, glomerulus, and collecting tubule.
From *Stedman's Medical Dictionary;* 21st ed. (1966); The Williams & Wilkins Co., Baltimore

or the nephronic loop. After its re-entrance into the cortex, the tubule returns to the vascular pole (the opening in the cuplike structure of the capsule) of its own nephron. The final portion of the tubule, the distal convoluted tubule, leads from the vascular pole of the corpuscle to a collecting tubule, by way of a short junctional tubule. Several of the collecting tubules join together to form a somewhat wider tubule, which carries the urine to a renal papilla and the renal pelvis.

The successive sections of the nephron tubule vary in shape and calibre (*e.g.*, one portion of Henle's loop is considerably narrower), and these differences, together with differences in the cells that line the sections, are associated with specific functions in the production of urine.

Intrarenal network of blood vessels. The intrarenal network of blood vessels merits particular attention, since it forms part of the blood-processing apparatus of the kidneys. The anterior and posterior divisions of each renal artery, mentioned earlier, divide into lobar arteries, each of which enters the kidney substance through or near a renal papilla. Each lobar artery gives off two or three branches, called interlobar arteries, which run outward between adjacent renal pyramids. When these reach the boundary between the cortex and the medulla they split almost at right angles into branches called arcuate arteries that curve along between the cortex and the medulla parallel to the surface of the kidney. Many arteries, called interlobular arteries, branch off from the arcuate arteries and radiate out through the cortex to end in networks of capillaries in the region just inside the capsule. En route they give off numerous branchlets, the arterioles that carry blood to the glomeruli and break up to form the capillaries of each glomerulus. They are then reconstituted to become the arterioles carrying blood away from the glomeruli. The arterioles bringing blood to the glomeruli are called afferent; those carrying blood away, efferent.

Throughout most of the cortex the efferent arterioles redivide into a second set of capillaries located between the nephron tubules; these capillaries participate with the nephron tubules in the complex process that begins with the glomerular filtrate and ends with urine.

The afferent arterioles are almost twice as thick as the efferent arterioles because they have thicker muscular coats, but their channels are almost equal.

Arterioles in juxta-medullary zone In the cortical region near the medulla, the area called the juxtamedullary zone, the efferent glomerular arterioles divide into vessels supplying the contiguous tubules and others that enter the bases of the renal pyramids.

Known as the arteriolae rectae spuriae, these vessels run toward the apexes of the pyramids. Ultimately uniting to form vessels called venae rectae, they drain into the arcuate veins that parallel the arcuate arteries. Some arterioles that arise in the cortex, in the juxtamedullary zone, run directly into the pyramids without breaking up into glomeruli. Since they become increasingly common with age, these arterioles are probably accounted for by the degeneration of glomeruli to which they were originally afferent.

Normally the blood circulating in the cortex is more abundant than that in the medulla, but in certain conditions such as those associated with severe trauma—*e.g.*, crushing of the limbs—most cortical vessels may become constricted and the juxtamedullary vessels dilated. In consequence much or even most of the renal blood flow may bypass the cortex and run through the relatively few but larger juxtamedullary glomeruli and arterioles. This is known as the renal shunt mechanism; because of the short-circuiting of most of the cortical glomeruli and tubules, the flow of urine is diminished, and in extreme cases may cease.

The renal venules (small veins) and veins accompany the arterioles and arteries closely and are referred to by similar names. The venules just beneath the renal capsule, called stellate venules because of their radial arrangement, drain into interlobular venules. In turn these combine to form the tributaries of the arcuate, interlobar, and lobar veins. Blood from the renal pyramids passes into vessels called venae rectae that join the arcuate veins. In the renal sinus the lobar veins unite to form veins corresponding to the main divisions of the renal arteries, and they normally fuse to constitute a single renal vein in or near the renal hilus.

The branches of the renal arteries interconnect only through capillaries. Such interconnections cannot provide adequate supplies of blood for an active organ; if, therefore, one of the main renal arterial branches is blocked as a consequence of disease or injury the area is largely deprived of blood and dies. The intrarenal veins and venules interconnect (anastomose) more freely than the arteries, so that venous disease or injuries produce less serious effects.

The stellate venules just inside the capsules interconnect with veins in the adipose capsule of the kidney, and the latter with veins serving the adrenal glands, the ureters, the sex glands, and the loins. These interconnections are normally insignificant, but in disease, particularly when it causes slow blockage of the renal veins, the interconnections may enlarge and provide an adequate venous drainage for the kidneys.

Lymphatic capillaries are in a network just inside the renal capsule, and there is a deeper network between and around the renal blood vessels. There are few lymphatic capillaries in the actual renal substance, and those present are evidently associated with the connective tissue framework, while the glomeruli contain no lymphatics. The lymphatic networks inside the capsule and around Lymphatic networks the renal blood vessels drain into lymphatic channels accompanying the interlobular and arcuate blood vessels. The main lymph channels run alongside the main renal arteries and veins to end in lymph nodes beside the aorta and near the sites of origin of the renal arteries. Some lymphatics from the upper part of the kidney and from the adrenal gland pass upward through the diaphragm to end in lymph nodes in the thorax.

THE URETERS

General characteristics. The ureters are thick-walled ducts, about 25–30 centimetres (9.8–11.8 inches) in length and from four to five millimetres (0.16–0.2 inch) in diameter, that transport the urine from the kidneys to the urinary bladder. Throughout their course they lie behind the peritoneum, the lining of the abdomen and pelvis, and are attached to it by connective tissue. The abdominal and pelvic portions of the ureters are almost equal in length.

In both sexes the ureters enter the bladder wall about five centimetres (two inches) apart, although this distance is increased when the bladder is distended with urine. The ureters run obliquely through the muscular wall of the bladder for nearly two centimetres (0.8 inch) before opening into the bladder cavity through narrow apertures. This oblique course provides a kind of valvular mechanism; when the bladder becomes distended it presses against the part of each ureter that is in the muscular wall of the bladder, and this helps to prevent the flow of urine back into the ureters from the bladder.

Structure of the ureteric wall. The wall has three layers, the adventitia, or outer layer; the intermediate, muscular layer; and the lining, made up of mucous membrane. The adventitia consists of fibroelastic connective tissue that merges with the connective tissue behind the peritoneum. The muscular coat is composed of smooth muscle fibres and, in the upper two-thirds of the ureter, has two strata—an inner layer of fibres arranged longitudinally and an outer layer disposed circularly. In the lower third of the ureter an additional longitudinal layer appears on the outside of the vessel. As each ureter extends into the bladder wall its circular fibres disappear, but its longitudinal fibres extend almost as far as the mucous membrane lining the bladder.

The effect of gravity on the passage of urine from the kidney to the bladder is minimal. The chief propelling force is produced by peristaltic (wavelike) movements in the ureter muscles. These movements may be initiated by pacemakers of specialized muscle cells located in the renal pelvis or its calices. The mucous membrane lining increases in thickness from the renal pelvis downward. Thus in the pelvis and the calices of the kidney the lining is two to three cells deep; in the ureter, four to five cells thick; and in the bladder, six to eight cells. The mucous membrane of the ureters is arranged in longitudinal folds, permitting considerable dilation of the channel. There are no true glands in the mucous membrane of the ureter or of the renal pelvis.

THE URINARY BLADDER

Shape and location of bladder

General description. The urinary bladder is a hollow muscular organ forming the main urinary reservoir. It rests on the anterior part of the pelvic floor (see below), behind the symphysis pubis and below the peritoneum. (The symphysis pubis is the joint in the hip bones in the front midline of the body and at its base.) The shape and size of the bladder vary according to the amount of urine that it contains. When empty it is tetrahedral in form and lies within the pelvis; when distended it becomes ovoid and expands into the lower abdomen. It is described as having a body, with a fundus, or base; a neck; an apex; and a superior (upper) and two inferolateral (below and to the side) surfaces, although these features are not clearly evident except when the bladder is empty or only slightly distended.

The fundus or base is triangular and faces backward and downward. In the male its lower part is close to the rectum. Its upper part is separated from the rectum by a pouch of peritoneum. In the female the bladder is close to the cervix and the anterior wall of the vagina and is connected to both by loose connective tissue. In both sexes the ureters enter the bladder through the superolateral angles (the angles above and to the side) of the base, while the urethra leaves it through the third or inferior angle.

The neck of the bladder is the area immediately surrounding the urethral opening; it is the lowest and most fixed part of the organ. In the male it is firmly attached to the base of the prostate, a gland which encircles the urethra. In the female there is no prostate, or only rudimentary glands representing it, and the bladder neck is continuous with the first part of the urethra.

The apex of the bladder points forward in both sexes toward the upper part of the symphysis pubis and the apex is attached to a ligament, the median umbilical ligament, that extends upward on the inside of the anterior abdominal wall to the umbilicus. When the bladder is distended the apex rises above the symphysis.

The superior surface of the bladder is triangular and is covered with peritoneum. The bladder is supported on the levator ani muscles, which constitute the major part of the floor of the pelvic cavity. The bladder is covered, and to a certain extent supported, by the visceral layer of the pelvic fascia. This fascial layer is a sheet of connective tissue that sheaths the organs, blood vessels, and nerves of the pelvic cavity. The fascia forms, in front and to the side, ligaments, called pubovesical ligaments, that act as a kind of hammock under the inferolateral surfaces and neck of the bladder.

Blood and nerve supplies. The blood supply of the bladder is derived from the superior, middle, and inferior vesical (bladder) arteries. The superior vesical artery supplies the dome of the bladder, and one of its branches (in some instances) gives off the artery to the ductus deferens, a part of the passageway for sperms. The middle vesical artery supplies the base of the bladder. The inferior vesical artery supplies the inferolateral surfaces of the bladder and assists in supplying the base of the bladder, the lower end of the ureter, and other adjacent structures. Small branches from other arteries often reach the bladder—in the female, branches from the uterine and vaginal arteries.

The nerves to the urinary bladder belong to the sympathetic and the parasympathetic divisions of the autonomic nervous system. The sympathetic nerve fibres carry to the central nervous system the sensations associated with distention of the bladder, are concerned with vasomotor functions (*i.e.*, with the constriction of the smooth muscle in the blood-vessel walls), and are believed by a majority of research workers to be involved in relaxation of the muscular layer of the vesical wall and with contraction of the sphincter mechanism that closes the opening into the urethra. The parasympathetic nerves are concerned with contraction of the muscular walls of the bladder and with relaxation of its sphincter. Consequently they are actively involved in urination (also called micturition) and are sometimes referred to as the emptying or detrusor nerves.

The nerves to the bladder

Structure of the bladder wall. The bladder wall has a serous coat over its upper surface. This covering is a continuation of the peritoneum that lines the abdominal cavity; it is called serous because it exudes a slight amount of lubricating fluid called serum. The other layers of the bladder wall are the fascial, muscular, submucous, and mucous coats.

The fascial coat is a layer of connective tissue, such as that which covers muscles. The muscular coat consists of coarse fascicles, or bundles, of smooth muscle fibres arranged in three strata, with fibres of the outer and inner layers running lengthwise, and with fibres of the intermediate layer running circularly; there is considerable intermingling of fibres between the layers.

In males the fibres of the outer layer pass into the prostate anterior and posterior to the urethra, while others blend with rectal muscular fibres to form the rectovesical muscle. (The prostate is a gland through which the urethra passes as it leaves the bladder. The rectovesical muscle is so called because it is shared by the rectum and the bladder.)

In females the outer layer is continuous with the musculature in the walls of the urethra and the vagina. Other fibre bundles in both sexes run into the pubovesical ligaments, mentioned previously as furnishing a support for the bladder.

The circular or intermediate muscular stratum of the vesical wall is thicker than the other layers. Its fibres, although running in a generally circular direction, do interlace.

The internal muscular stratum is an indefinite layer of fibres that are mostly directed longitudinally.

The submucous coat consists of loose connective tissue containing many elastic fibres. It is absent in the trigone, a triangular area whose angles are at the two openings for the ureters and the single internal urethral opening. Slim bands of muscle run between each ureteric opening and the internal urethral orifice; these are thought to maintain the oblique direction of the ureters during contraction of the bladder. Another bundle of muscle fibres connects the two ureteric openings and produces a slightly downwardly curved fold of mucous membrane between the openings. Behind the internal urethral orifice in males there is sometimes a slight bulge caused by the projection of the median lobe of the prostate. This bulge, called the uvula vesicae, may become much more prominent in older men with enlargement of the prostate.

The mucous coat of the bladderThe mucous coat, the innermost lining of the bladder, is an elastic layer impervious to urine. Over the trigone it is firmly adherent to the muscular coat and is always smooth and pink whether the bladder is contracted or distended. Elsewhere, if the bladder is contracted, the mucous coat shows multiple folds and has a red, velvety appearance. When the bladder is distended, the folds are obliterated, but the difference in colour between the paler trigonal area and the other areas of the mucous membrane persists. The mucous membrane lining the bladder is continuous with that lining the ureters and the urethra.

THE URETHRA

General description. The urethra is the channel that conveys the urine from the bladder to the exterior. In the male it is about 20 centimetres (about 7.9 inches) long and carries not only the urine, but also the semen and the secretions of the prostatic, bulbo-urethral, and urethral glands. During urination and orgasm it opens up, and its diameter then varies from 0.5 to 0.8 centimetre (0.2 to 0.3 inch) along its length, but at other times its walls touch and its lining is raised into longitudinal folds. The male urethra has three distinguishable parts, the prostatic, the membranous, and the spongy, each part being named from the structures through which it passes rather than from any inherent characteristics.

The prostatic section of the male urethra commences at the internal urethral orifice and descends almost vertically through the prostate, from the base of the gland to the apex, describing a slight curve with its concavity forward. It is about 2.5 to three centimetres (one to 1.2 inches) long and is spindle-shaped; its middle portion is the widest and most dilatable part of the urethra. The posterior wall of the prostatic section shows a longitudinal elevation, the urethral crest, and the shallow furrows on each side of the crest are the prostatic sinuses into which the numerous prostatic glands open through tiny pores. The crest becomes slightly more prominent at about its midpoint to form a further elevation called the seminal colliculus. The colliculus has three openings on its surfaces. On either side of the central opening, which leads to a short cul-de-sac, are the openings through which the right and left ejaculatory ducts discharge seminal fluid into the urethra.

The membranous part of the male urethra is so called because it is in the area between the two layers of a membrane, called the urogenital diaphragm. The urethra is narrower here than at any other point except at its external opening and is encircled by a muscle, the sphincter urethrae. The two small bulbo-urethral glands are on either side of it. The membranous urethra is not firmly attached to the layers of the urogenital diaphragm.

The spongy part of the male urethra is that part of the urethra that traverses the penis. It derives its name from the fact that it passes through the corpus spongiosum of the penis. The shape and calibre of this section of the urethra vary. As in other parts of the urethra, the walls are normally touching except during micturition and orgasm.

The ducts of the bulbo-urethral glands enter the spongy urethra about 2.5 centimetres (one inch) below the lower layer of the urogenital membrane; except near its outer end, many mucous glands also open into it.

The female urethraThe female urethra is much shorter (three to 4.5 centimetres, or 1.2 to 1.8 inches), and more distensible than the corresponding channel in men and carries only urine and the secretions of mucous glands. It begins at the internal opening of the urethra into the bladder and curves gently downward and forward through the urogenital diaphragm, where it is surrounded, as in the male, by the sphincter urethrae. It lies behind and below the symphysis pubis. Except for its uppermost part, the urethra is embedded in the anterior wall of the vagina. The external urethral orifice is immediately in front of the vaginal

opening, about 2.5 centimetres (about one inch) behind the clitoris, and between the labia minora, the inner folds at the outer opening of the vagina.

The lining is raised in longitudinal folds and, except during micturition, the walls of the urethra touch. Near the lower end of the urethra a number of mucous glands drain into the urethra through two short ducts opening on either side of the external urethral orifice.

Structure of urethral wall. The male urethra is a tube of mucous membrane supported on a submucous layer and an incomplete muscular coat. The membrane forms longitudinal folds when the tube is empty; these folds are more obvious in the membranous and spongy parts. There are many glands in the mucous membrane, more common in the posterior wall of the spongy part. The submucous layer is composed of fibroelastic connective tissue containing numerous small blood vessels, including more venules than arterioles.

The thin muscular coat consists of smooth muscle fibres. Around the prostatic and, to a lesser extent, around the membranous parts of the urethra, this coat can be differentiated into inner longitudinal and outer circular layers. Scanty bundles of smooth muscle fibres, disposed mainly in a circular or oblique fashion, surround the spongy part of the urethra.

The female urethra has mucous, submucous, and muscular coats. As in the male, the lining of the empty channel is raised into longitudinal folds. It also shows mucous glands, mentioned in the preceding paragraphs as existing in the male urethra.

The submucous coat resembles that in the male, except that the venules are even more prominent. In both sexes, but especially in females, this layer appears to be a variety of erectile tissue.

The muscular coat extends along the entire length of the female urethra and is continuous above with the musculature of the bladder. It consists of inner longitudinal and outer circular layers, and fibres from the latter intermix with those in the anterior wall of the vagina, in which the urethra is embedded.

BIBLIOGRAPHY. L.B. AREY, *Developmental Anatomy*, 7th ed. (1965), an excellent and well-balanced technical compendium on human development; D.A.K. BLACK (ed.), *Renal Disease* (1962), an authoritative account by various specialists on the kidney; W. BLOOM and D.W. FAWCETT, *A Textbook of Histology*, 9th ed. (1968), a finely illustrated and admirable text on histology and fine structure; D.J. CUNNINGHAM, *Textbook of Anatomy*, 10th ed. by G.J. ROMANES (1964), a traditional text on human anatomy; H. GRAY, *Anatomy*, 34th Eng. ed. by D.V. DAVIES (1967), a treatise frequently revised over the past century and still regarded as one of the greatest anatomical texts; A.W. HAM, *Histology*, 6th ed. (1969), a popular text paying particular attention to the correlation of structure and function; W.J. HAMILTON, J.D. BOYD, and H.W. MOSSMAN, *Human Embryology*, 3rd ed. (1962), one of the leading textbooks on human embryology; G.A.G. MITCHELL, "The Renal Fascia," *Br. J. Surg.*, 37:257–266 (1950), an article confirming earlier work, challenging former views on the renal fascia, and *Anatomy of the Autonomic Nervous System* (1953), a monograph including descriptions of the nerve supplies of viscera and vessels; H.W. SMITH, *The Kidney: Structure and Function in Health and Disease* (1951), a classical contribution to various renal problems.

(G.A.G.M.)

Excretory System Diseases

The term excretory system, a convenient label with which to cover the kidneys and the urinary tract in one system, describes with accuracy an important part of renal (kidney) function, that part which concerns the disposal of waste products; *i.e.*, compounds such as urea that are formed in the breakdown of food and tissue but that must be eliminated from the body because they cannot normally be used to supply either energy or structural material. Some such wastes are disposed of by the lungs, skin, and bowel; but the kidneys are the most specialized excretory organ.

The functioning unit of the kidney is the nephron, consisting of (1) a cluster of minute blood vessels or capillaries called the glomerulus; (2) a double-walled capsule, enclosing the glomerulus; and (3) continuous with the capsule a long, winding, narrow tube of varying diameter and wall thickness. Fluid filters from the blood through the walls of the glomerulus. The fluid normally differs from the blood in its lack of cells and proteins. The capsule and tubules reabsorb substances, including water, from the filtrate, and excrete into the filtrate substances that are waste products or in excessive supply.

If the task of excretion does not occur solely in the kidneys, neither does "excretion" fully describe everything that these organs do. Importantly, they also regulate the amount and composition of the body fluid, which accounts for well over half of the total mass of the body. This regulatory or homeostatic function of the kidneys has to be kept in mind if the mechanisms that underlie the varied manifestations of renal disorders are to be understood. The excretory and regulatory functions of the kidneys together constitute their most notable role in the body's economy; but the kidneys are also a source of important hormones, renin and erythropoietin. The impact of excretory system diseases on the two major aspects of renal performance—the elimination of wastes and the conservation of an appropriate amount and quality of body fluid—is the primary concern in this article. Many of the manifestations of renal disease can be accounted for in terms of disturbance of these two functions, and the alleviation of varieties of renal disease that cannot yet be cured is dependent on man's knowledge of these two functions.

The two major aspects of renal performance

The matter does not, of course, end with the formation of urine, a quite unconscious process; the urine has to pass down the ureters to the bladder, be stored there, and voided when convenient, under voluntary control. The whole mechanism can be deranged by structural changes in the lower urinary tract, by infection, or by neurological disorders that lead to abnormal emptying of the bladder. Disturbance of the lower urinary tract is an important cause of pain and distress, notably during pregnancy and in the elderly; and it can lead to serious and progressive damage to the kidneys, either by interfering with the drainage of urine or by allowing bacterial infection to have access to the kidney.

FUNCTIONAL ASPECTS OF EXCRETORY SYSTEM DISEASES
Diseases often manifest themselves as patterns of disordered function. In excretory system disease, the amount and composition of the urine may become grossly inappropriate to the needs of the body, with consequent distortions of body fluids as outlined in this section. Disturbances of urine flow are also considered, but abnormalities in the urine itself are dealt with in the article EXCRETION, HUMAN.

Effects of abnormal renal function on body fluid. The major constituents of body fluid are protein, water, and electrolytes—the dissociated salts of sodium and potassium. Renal disease in its diverse forms can lead to bodily deficits or excesses of water, sodium, and potassium, and also to protein deficits occasioned by great losses of protein in the urine. Inability of the kidney to function normally may lead to retention in the blood of the waste products of protein metabolism such as urea and uric acid, and of other nitrogenous compounds such as creatinine. There may be abnormally high levels of phosphates in the blood, which in turn can lead (for reasons about which there is still some disagreement) to low blood levels of calcium. The calcium deficiency can cause tetany, a condition marked by muscular spasms and pain, and calcium may be lost from the bones in the process of restoring normal calcium levels in the blood and tissue fluid. For descriptive purposes, changes in volume, changes in composition, and protein depletion of renal origin will be discussed separately, but these disturbances can and often do coexist.

Though body fluid is apparent only in the bloodstream, it is present, and in larger amounts, in the tissues, both between the cells (extracellular fluid) and within them (intracellular fluid). Extracellular fluids, including blood plasma, amount to 25 percent of body weight, and contain sodium as their predominant cation (positive ion; metals and hydrogen in solution are cations). Intracellu-

Edema and dehydration

lar fluids, amounting to 33 percent of body weight, have potassium as their predominant cation. These various "compartments" of body fluid are in osmotic equilibrium, so that if solute (*e.g.*, sodium chloride) is added to the extracellular compartment so as to increase the concentration of the extracellular solution, water will join it to reduce the concentration, and that compartment will increase. An increase in extracellular fluid, if it is considerable, may be clinically apparent as edema, a swelling of the tissues by fluid, which can usually be displaced by firm pressure. Edema is present in acute inflammation of the kidney (nephritis), in protein deficiency of renal origin, and in chronic nephritis complicated by heart failure associated with abnormally high blood pressure; a factor common to all these states is failure of the kidneys to excrete sodium in adequate amount. (If sodium were excreted, water would be also in order for the osmotic equilibrium to be maintained.) Importantly, the kidneys in such edematous states need not themselves be diseased; normal kidneys, in a patient with heart failure, may retain sodium when handicapped in their function by poor circulation and by abnormal amounts of sodium-retaining hormones, such as aldosterone. Increase in extracellular fluids is the only volume change that is both common and easily discernible in renal disease. The opposite condition, sodium depletion or clinical dehydration, occurs rarely, when the kidneys fail to conserve sodium properly; this can happen in intrinsic renal disease, but sodium depletion is more commonly the result of vomiting and diarrhea when they are complications of terminal renal disease. Dehydration can be recognized by a lack of elasticity in the superficial tissues, and by poor filling of the blood vessels, as well as by signs of impaired circulation, including a fall in blood pressure. Though changes in intracellular fluid volume occur in some diseases, especially when the potassium content of the body is affected, there is no easy way of detecting them.

Because of the importance of osmotic forces in determining fluid distribution within the body, an important attribute of body fluid is its overall osmotic concentration, or osmolality. This depends on the concentration of solutes; while all solutes contribute to it, small particles such as sodium or chloride ions are influential out of all proportion to their weight, and indeed account for over 90 percent of the osmolality of plasma. In the context of renal disease, changes in osmolality depend largely on how the kidney handles water. When the kidney either is incapable of conserving water or is not stimulated by the antidiuretic hormone of the pituitary to reabsorb water, water is lost from the body, and a state of water depletion develops, characterized by increasing osmolality of body fluid. At other times, the kidneys may retain too much water, especially when too much hormone is present; in this case, water excess results, giving a clinical state of water intoxication, with decreased osmolality of body fluids.

Besides osmolality, another very important general property of body fluid is its degree of acidity or alkalinity. This is largely regulated by the discharge of carbon dioxide in expired air, but the kidneys are involved in the excretion of nonvolatile acids, such as sulfate and phosphate. Imperfect function leads to retention of both organic and inorganic acid radicals, the state of so-called renal acidosis. (Acid radicals are the negative ions of acids, corresponding to hydrogen, the positive ion.) This may occur as part of generalized renal failure or as a specific disease of the renal tubules, one of whose functions is to convert the slightly alkaline glomerular filtrate into the (usually) acid urine. To do this, the tubules both secrete hydrogen ions and synthesize ammonia; both or either of these processes may be deficient.

Change in hydrogen-ion concentration

Apart from these general changes in body fluid, the pattern of individual constituents can be profoundly distorted in renal disease. For many substances, the problem is one of failure of excretion, with consequent increased concentration in body fluids. In so far as excretion is achieved by filtration, the rise in concentration may assist excretion, permitting prolonged states of balance, at the cost of increased, but often tolerable, levels of concentration. For example, a man in renal failure must put out as much urea as a healthy man taking the same diet; but he can only do so at a blood–urea concentration of 100 milligrams per 100 millilitres, instead of a normal blood–urea of 25 milligrams per 100 millilitres. Substances whose concentration increases in this way include urea, creatinine, uric acid, phosphate and sulfate, urochrome, and indeed all the usual constituents of urine apart from those that are "regulated" rather than simply "excreted." Potassium requires special mention because of the special danger associated with retention of this substance, which can lead to fatal irregularity of cardiac action. This is a recognized danger of acute renal failure, now commonly prevented by use of the artificial kidney and its semipermeable membranes, and sometimes by the use of resins that will take up potassium in the alimentary tract.

Normal urine contains traces of protein, and in many forms of renal disease there is an increased excretion of protein in the urine, usually representing an increased permeability of the tuft of capillaries forming the glomerulus. This increased proteinuria (often, but less correctly, known as albuminuria) generally amounts to 0.5 gram per day or more. When it exceeds five grams per day, and persists at this level, the loss of protein in the urine exceeds the capacity of the liver to produce new protein from the available materials; the concentration of protein in the blood decreases, and this leads to an increasing outflow of fluid from the bloodstream into the tissues (there is normally an equilibrium between the physical pressure in the capillaries, which tends to force fluids out, and the osmotic pressure of plasma proteins, the effect of which is to hold fluid in). This balance of forces is upset by a deficit of plasma proteins. The general loss of fluid into the tissues leads to massive edema, to which the kidneys contribute further by retaining salt and water. The combination of high levels of protein in the urine, low protein levels in the blood, and consequent edema is known as the nephrotic syndrome. This is a good example of a syndrome, defined as a recognizable pattern of manifestations that has not one but a number of possible causes. Other examples of syndromes in renal disease are acute renal failure and chronic renal failure.

Disorders of urine flow.   If little or no urine appears, it may be because the kidneys are forming little urine (oliguria) or none (anuria); or it may represent a holdup in the bladder or urethra affecting the outflow from both kidneys. About one person in 500 is born with only one kidney, and loss of a kidney from disease or accident is not rare. In such cases, patients with complete obstruction to the remaining ureter will experience the same effect as in obstruction of the entire lower urinary tract. Partial or complete failure to form urine is treated in the section on acute renal failure, obstructive conditions in the section on diseases of the urinary tract, below. Bladder emptying also depends on an intact nerve supply. The sensation of a full bladder is carried in the pelvic nerves to the sacral region of the spinal cord; this desire to micturate—urinate—may be inhibited by the higher centres in the nervous system. In the lack of inhibition, and indeed with voluntary initiation, micturition is effected by parasympathetic nerve impulses, again in the pelvic nerves. Spinal disease and injury, and general diseases of the central nervous system, can lead either to incontinence or to difficulty in emptying the bladder. The distended bladder may later overflow, when pressure within it builds up to overrule the failure of relaxation of the urethral sphincters—the phenomenon of overflow incontinence.

Pain associated with urination can arise from bladder distension, which is then relieved by effective micturition; from inflammation of the lower urinary tract, commonly due to infection but rarely caused by chemical irritants in the urine; and from mechanical irritation by tumour or during the passage of stones. The term dysuria is applied to pain that accompanies, or closely follows, the passage of urine. It is commonly, but not necessarily, associated with frequency of urination. This in turn may

represent either an irritable or contracted bladder; or the actual amount of urine formed may be unusually large (polyuria), in which case voiding is likely to be painless. Sometimes polyuria may not be noticed by day, but may manifest itself in the need to micturate on several occasions during the night (nocturia). The acute onset of dysuria and frequency suggests urinary infection; sustained polyuria is more likely to be due to renal failure (defective concentrating power) or to diabetes. In those who drink beverages into the night, nocturia is physiological.

Incontinence, the involuntary passage of urine (or feces), may be due to a faulty nerve supply, which either leaves the sphincters relaxed or allows them to be overcome by distension of the bladder. Comatose and disturbed patients, especially among the elderly, are commonly incontinent. Apart from nerve lesions, the sphincters that normally prevent the escape of urine may be damaged by repeated childbirth, by the growth of the prostate, or by other distortions of the bladder neck. Procedures have been devised to stimulate the sphincters electrically, when their nerve supply is damaged; or to stimulate the bladder to empty itself at set times. For the problem of chronic incontinence, however, devices to catch the urine and prevent soiling of clothing are the most practical.

DISEASES OF THE KIDNEY

In this section, attention is directed not only to specific diseases of the kidney but also to the syndromes of acute and chronic renal failure, which have multiple causes. Infective disorders of the kidney are dealt with later, as part of the general problem of infection of the urinary tract.

Acute renal failure.   Acute renal failure occurs when renal function suddenly declines to very low levels, so that little or no urine is formed, and the substances, including even water, that the kidney normally eliminates are retained in the body. There are two main mechanisms that can produce acute renal failure. When the cardiac output—the amount of blood pumped into the general circulation by the heart—is depressed by hemorrhage or by medical or surgical shock, the renal circulation is depressed to an even greater extent. This leads directly to inefficient excretion, but, more importantly still, the kidney tissue cannot withstand prolonged impairment of its blood supply and undergoes either patchy or massive necrosis (tissue death). Given time, the kidney tissue may regenerate, and it is on this hope that the treatment of acute renal failure is based. The form of acute renal failure that is due to a poor supply of blood (ischemia) has many causes, the commonest and most important being multiple injuries, abortion with abnormal or excessive bleeding from the female genital tract, internal hemorrhage, transfusion reactions, and severe heart attacks; an interesting special case is the transplanted kidney, which commonly goes through a phase of acute renal failure that is independent of possible rejection. The second common mechanism of acute renal failure is toxic. Many poisons are excreted by the kidney, and in the process just like other urinary constituents they become concentrated and, in this way, reach levels in the tubular fluid that damage the lining cells of the tubules. Though the tubular cells die, and are shed in the urine, regeneration can take place, and the patient survive, if he can be maintained during the period of depressed renal function and is not killed by other effects of the poison. Poisons that can affect the kidney in this way are numerous, but the main groups are heavy metals (mercury, arsenic, uranium); organic solvents (carbon tetrachloride, methanol); other organic substances (glycols, aniline, phenindione, insecticides); and antibacterial agents (sulfonamides, kanamycin, amphotericin). In addition to the ischemic and toxic causes of acute renal failure, mention must be made of fulminating varieties of acute renal illnesses that are generally mild (e.g., acute glomerulonephritis—see below), and of the acute form of immunologic rejection that can destroy a kidney irrevocably within minutes of transplantation.

The clinical course of acute renal failure can usefully

Stoppage
of urine
flow

Incontinence of
urine

Renal
failure due
to poisons

be divided into an onset phase, a phase of established acute renal failure, and a recovery phase. In general, but not invariably, the second of these phases is characterized by a low output of urine—oliguria—and the third by an increasing urine output (polyuria). The onset phase is dominated by general illness, in which the episode of acute renal failure arises; at this stage there may be evidence of threatened renal damage such as blood in the urine or pain in the loins. At this early stage, renal damage may be reversible by prompt treatment of circulatory failure or by infusion of diuretics, substances that increase urine flow. Once the onset phase has passed, and acute renal failure becomes established, diuretics are ineffective and may cause damage.

Renal failure: second phase of clinical course

In the second phase, small amounts of urine, often containing red blood cells, or hemoglobin, are passed; complete absence of urine is not common and suggests that an obstruction is preventing urine from being passed. In quantitative terms, a urine volume of less than 500 millilitres (about a pint) per day constitutes significant oliguria; this is the least amount in which the excretory demand imposed by an ordinary diet can be met. In the actual situation of acute renal failure, the excretory demands may in fact be much greater, since many of the causes of acute renal failure also are causes of increased breakdown of the tissues in general. The nonprotein nitrogen of the blood increases, the rate of increase being conditioned both by the degree of renal failure and by the amount of tissue breakdown. Besides nitrogen, the kidney can no longer excrete adequate amounts of water, sodium, and potassium. These various inadequacies point the way to the necessary management of acute renal failure—the elimination from intake of any dangerous substance that the kidney can no longer handle. The diet must either be free of protein or contain small amounts of high-quality protein to lessen tissue breakdown. It must also be free from sodium and potassium: many persons with renal failure have died from pulmonary edema, a correlate of sodium retention, and others from the acute toxic effects on the heart of a raised level of potassium in the blood. Water cannot be excluded from the intake but must be limited. The concentration of sodium in the blood is a good guide to the adequacy of water restriction, and a progressive fall in serum sodium implies that too much water is being taken in. Kidney function may recover, often in seven to ten days. The use of dialysis, the removal of waste products by straining the blood through semipermeable membranes, gives further time for renal recovery. Potassium can be removed from the body by resins, but this is less often required if dialysis is available.

Although by comparison with the oliguric phase the recovery phase presents fewer problems, the convalescent kidney takes time to recover its full regulatory function, and unusual losses of electrolytes may occur at this stage. Careful observation and measurements of nonprotein nitrogen and electrolytes are still required. Many make a complete recovery from acute renal failure, but in some persons residual renal damage persists. In a few, this is so severe as to bring them effectively into the category of chronic renal failure.

Chronic renal failure. The term uremia, though it is sometimes used as if it were interchangeable with chronic renal failure, really means an increase in the concentration of urea in the blood. This can arise in many acute illnesses in which the kidney is not primarily affected, and also in the condition of acute renal failure described above. Uremia ought to represent a purely chemical statement, but it is sometimes used to denote a clinical picture, that of severe renal insufficiency.

Chronic renal failure: four common causes

As with acute renal failure, there are many conditions that can lead to chronic renal failure. The two commonest causes are pyelonephritis and glomerulonephritis (kidney inflammation involving the structures around the renal pelvis or the glomeruli), and other common causes are renal damage from the effects of high blood pressure and renal damage from obstructive conditions of the lower urinary tract. All of these primary disorders are described below. What they have in common is a progressive destruction of nephrons (the functional units in the kidneys), of which there are normally some 2,000,-000, but which may be reduced to less than a twentieth of that number in disease. The quantitative loss of nephrons can account for the majority of the changes observed in chronic renal failure; the failure in excretion is due directly to loss of glomerular filters, and other features such as the large quantities of dilute urine represent a change in tubular function that could be accounted for by the increased load that each remaining nephron has to carry. There are many other causes of chronic renal failure besides the four common ones. They include congenital anomalies and hereditary disorders; diseases of collagen (the fibrous protein found in connective tissue); tuberculosis; the effects of diabetes and other metabolic disorders; and a number of primary disorders of the kidney tubules. Of the many causes, there are some that have importance out of proportion to their frequency, by virtue of their reversibility; these include renal amyloidosis (abnormal deposits in the kidney of a complex protein substance called amyloid), whose causes may be treatable; damage to the kidney from excessive calcium or deficiency of potassium; uric acid deposition in gout; the effects of analgesic agents—substances taken to alleviate pain—and other toxic substances.

The person suffering from renal failure may have no symptoms other than a feeling of thirst and a tendency (shared with many normal people) to pass urine at frequent intervals and through the night; or he may be in a coma, with occasional convulsions.

Effects of chronic renal failure

The general appearance of the sufferer may be sallow and "earthy," because of a combination of anemia and the retention of urinary pigment. Even if not in actual coma, the affected person may be withdrawn; muscle twitchings and more general convulsions may occur. The coma is thought to represent poisoning, and convulsions are often related to the severity of the high blood pressure that commonly complicates advanced renal failure. Blurred vision is also a manifestation associated with high blood pressure. Bruising and hemorrhages may be noticeable.

Although the toxin (or toxins) of uremia has yet to be identified, the rapid improvement that follows dialysis points strongly to a toxic component. Urea itself is not notably toxic. Not all the chemical alterations in uremia are simple retentions. There is acidosis—a fall in the alkalinity of the blood and tissue fluids—reflected clinically in deep respiration as the lungs strive to eliminate carbon dioxide. The capacity of the kidney to adjust to variation in intake of salt, potassium, and water becomes progressively impaired, so that electrolyte disturbances are common. Poor appetite, vomiting, and diarrhea are common in uremic patients, and these in turn add another component to the chemical disturbance. Phosphate is retained in the blood and is thus associated with low blood levels of calcium; the parathyroids are overactive in renal failure, and vitamin D is less than normally effective. (Parathyroid hormone causes release of calcium from the bones, and vitamin D promotes absorption of calcium from the intestines.) These changes can lead to severe bone disease in persons suffering from renal failure, because bone calcium is depleted and the calcium stores are not adequately replenished.

In chronic renal failure, excessive production of renin by the kidney can lead to severe high blood pressure, (hypertension); and the effects of this may even dominate the clinical picture. In addition to damage to the brain and the retina, the high blood pressure may lead directly to heart failure. Hypertension can also accelerate the progress of renal damage by its impact on the renal blood vessels themselves, setting up a cycle that can be hard to break.

The patient in advanced renal failure is vulnerable to infection and other complications, such as vomiting or diarrhea, which need special care. When symptoms of advanced renal failure appear, deterioration can be delayed by a strict low-protein diet, 18–20 grams of high-quality protein each day. In terminal renal failure, the affected person can be rescued only by some form of dialysis and then maintained by dialysis or transplantation.

Glomerulonephritis. Glomerulonephritis is the disorder commonly known as nephritis, or Bright's disease. The primary impact of the disease is on the vessels of the glomerular tuft, the cluster of capillaries in the nephron. The suffix "-itis" suggests an inflammatory lesion, and glomerulonephritis is indeed associated with infection, in the limited sense that it may begin soon after a streptococcal infection and may be aggravated in its later course by infections of various kinds. Nevertheless, there is convincing evidence that glomerulonephritis does not represent a direct attack on the kidney by an infective agent but is, rather, an "allergic" disorder, in the sense of the formation of antibodies that react against kidney tissue, or of antigen–antibody complexes that lodge in the glomerular tuft, with subsequent damage. This view of glomerulonephritis is based partly on analogy with the renal damage that can be induced in animals by allergic mechanisms, and partly on finding that a protein component of the allergic reaction is deposited in the diseased glomerulus. Within the general concept of an allergic disorder, there is ample room for a variety of primary stimuli and of later disease-causing mechanisms. Such a diversity is strongly suggested not only by the variations in the glomerular tissues observed both with the ordinary and with the electron microscope but also by the varying manifestations of the disease observed in the affected person.

Acute glomerulonephritis. Typically, acute glomerulonephritis appears one to two weeks after a sore throat, or—less commonly—after a streptococcal infection of the skin has been present for some time.

The affected person notices puffiness of the face and ankles, and at the same time the urine becomes scanty and noticeably blood-stained. On examination, loose tissues show edema, and the fluid is easily displaced by light pressure; both the blood pressure and the blood levels of urea are slightly or moderately increased. If fluids are not restricted at this stage, or if the blood pressure rises further, the person may experience severe breathlessness (due to accumulation of fluid in the lungs) or convulsions. A week or so later, there is often an increase in urine volume, there is no longer any blood in the urine, and the blood pressure is back to normal. Protein is still present in the urine, and this abnormality may persist for some weeks or months, even in persons who ultimately recover. The whole illness is an alarming one, but the fact is that the acute attack of glomerulonephritis needs no particular treatment other than some restriction of fluid and protein, and that nine out of ten affected persons recover completely. Exceptional outbreaks, with a higher mortality, have sometimes been observed.

As just indicated, the usual sequel is complete recovery. A very few patients may die in the acute attack, however, or in a few months' time, when the impact of the disease has been unusually severe. Another possibility is that the affected person may appear to have recovered completely, having lost all symptoms; but the disease process remains active, and there is progressive loss of nephrons, leading ultimately to chronic renal failure. This process may take 20 years, for many of which the person has no definite symptoms except that the urine contains protein and small numbers of red blood cells. This is the picture of latent nephritis, though it need not be assumed that the finding of protein in the urine (proteinuria) in the absence of symptoms means automatically that the patient has kidney disease; symptomless proteinuria has many causes and may indeed be found in young people who never develop any later evidence of renal disease. In summary, acute glomerulonephritis can lead to renal failure within a few months or even weeks, after many years of symptom-free proteinuria, or after a period of massive proteinuria, which causes the nephrotic syndrome. All of these manifestations may be seen although the affected person has never had, or cannot recall, an acute attack. Persons with acute glomerulonephritis who do badly are far outnumbered by persons who sustain an acute attack but thereafter do well.

Vascular disease. In the discussion of chronic renal failure, attention was drawn to the cycle in which high blood pressure secondary to renal disease can produce further damage to the kidneys. Clearly, primary vascular disease—disease affecting the blood vessels—could equally well be a cause of renal damage.

The most dramatic instance of this is the condition known as "malignant hypertension," or accelerated hypertension, which arises when the blood pressure attains really high levels, the diastolic figure (the blood pressure between heart contractions) being 140 millimetres of mercury or higher (the normal being around 80). Sustained levels of this magnitude cause serious damage to the arterioles, the smallest of the arteries; this damage is widespread, but as it affects the kidneys it produces rapid destruction of renal substance, with a scarred kidney. Unless the blood pressure is controlled, malignant hypertension can cause death in a few months; since treatment at an early stage is notably effective, the condition represents an important medical emergency. Since the retinas are damaged as rapidly as the kidneys, the affected person may first notice blurring or loss of vision.

More modest, but still elevated, levels of blood pressure can cause more gradual renal damage in elderly people or in those made prematurely aged by widespread arteriosclerosis ("hardening of the arteries"). Here, the damage is in the larger arteries rather than in the arterioles, and the condition is one of slowly progressive scarring. Renal damage can also arise, by various mechanisms, in a large number of diseases that impair the blood vessels, such as diabetes mellitus, the collagen disorders, bacterial inflammation of the heart lining, and many more.

Tumours. Tumours in general are covered in the article CANCER. Here those tumours peculiar to the excretory system, and their local effects, are briefly discussed. In the case of benign tumours, these effects include pressure on local structures and obstruction to hollow organs; with malignant tumours, one must add the possibilities of local invasion and of spread by the bloodstream or lymphatics to other organs (metastasis).

Carcinoma. The commonest tumour of the renal substance is a carcinoma (formerly called a hypernephroma), a malignant tumour, arising from epithelial cells (the cells of the bodily coverings and linings). One to two percent of all tumours are renal carcinomas, and most affected persons are aged from 40 to 60. The tumour may be symptomless or may first be apparent from the occurrence of metastases in the lungs, causing spitting up of blood; or in the bones, causing pathological fracture.

Much more commonly, the first evidence of the tumour is blood in the urine, which may be painless, or may cause colic of the ureter, if clots are being passed. There may also be a dull pain in the loins, from stretching of the kidney capsule. The tumour may be directly palpable, or it may be revealed by X-rays. The silhouette of the kidney, revealed by X-rays, may be distorted by a rounded swelling; or the renal pelvis, made visible by the injection of a contrast medium, may be displaced or distorted. Less common first indications of renal carcinoma are an obscure fever, or polycythemia (excess of red cells in the blood). Direct visual examination of the urinary tract with an instrument called a cystoscope may demonstrate the side that is affected, blood coming from one ureteric opening only. Since this could equally arise from a tumour of the renal pelvis, X-ray examination of the renal pelvis is usually called for. An exploratory operation may sometimes be needed; if carcinoma is found to be present, the kidney must be removed. There is some evidence that the results of surgery may be somewhat improved by radiation therapy. The overall outlook is poor, with a five-year survival rate no better than 50 percent. This is, however, one of the forms of malignant tumour in which arrest or even regression has been described.

Nephroblastoma (Wilms' tumour). Nephroblastoma is a less common, but nevertheless an important, tumour in childhood, in which other forms of cancer are less common. About half the cases occur at ages two to four, but

Glomerulonephritis: allergic disorder

Signs and symptoms of carcinoma

the tumour may be present even at birth. The tumour, a mixture of various tissues of embryonic origin, rapidly attains a large size, so that a mass in the child's abdomen is commonly the first abnormality noticed. Pain and blood in the urine are much less common than in renal carcinoma, affecting perhaps a fifth of patients. Spread of tumour to the renal veins, with subsequent spread to other structures, is common. The condition usually calls for removal of the kidney, and the outlook is poor; both kidneys may be affected, a situation that has on occasion been dealt with by removal of both, followed by transplant of a healthy kidney.

Other tumours. In addition to tumours of the renal substance, the renal pelvis may be affected by fernlike growths of the epithelium (papillomas).

Similar tumours affect the lower urinary tract, and the whole group is discussed later in this article. Benign tumours of the kidney substance occur, but rarely; on the other hand, cysts (abnormal sacs filled with liquid or semisolid substance) of the kidney are relatively common, but are not tumours in any strict sense, being rather malformations brought about by failure of the embryonic tubules to achieve a proper outlet. Several forms of renal cystic disease, most of them fatal, occur in infancy. In the "sponge kidney" (medullary cystic disease) the outlook is good. Various forms of solitary cyst occur, which may need local surgical treatment if they cause symptoms. The form of polycystic (multiple-cyst) renal disease that allows survival into adult life is a familial condition, in which several members of the family have little trouble until middle life but then are progressively affected by kidney malfunction. Episodes of blood in the urine and urinary infection are common, and the kidneys are large and irregular. Cysts of other organs—*e.g.*, the liver—may be present. X-rays show irregularity of the renal pelvis, through pressure from the cysts. Puncture of the cysts is possible, but the results are not encouraging; the general treatment is that of chronic renal failure, which may now include removal of the kidney and transplantation.

OBSTRUCTION TO THE FLOW OF URINE

Effect of urinary obstruction on kidney

The causes of obstruction to the flow of urine lie in the lower urinary tract and are dealt with in a later section; here it is appropriate to consider the effects of urinary obstruction on the kidney (obstructive nephropathy). It should first be noted, however, that obstructions may arise at the junction of the renal pelvis and the ureter, either from faulty action of smooth muscle or from the pressure of an abnormal blood vessel crossing the pelvis; such cases can benefit from a plastic operation on the renal pelvis or from division of the abnormal vessel. Whether the obstruction arises in this way, or lower down, it can lead to renal pain; to the passage of irregular amounts of urine when obstruction is intermittent; and to a mass in the kidney when obstruction persists. As the renal pelvis swells, the renal tissue shrinks, leading to the condition called hydronephrosis, in which a greatly swollen sac is surrounded by a mere rind of atrophied renal tissue. A massive hydronephrosis, with negligible renal substance remaining, may suggest removal of the kidney.

Trauma. The kidney may be wounded in military operations or in motor accidents, usually along with other viscera. It may be bruised or even ruptured in closed injuries, including those from explosions, on the football field, or by a foul blow in the boxing ring. Since the kidney receives about a fifth of the heart output, bleeding can be spectacular, both into the urine and into the tissues and the kidney, forming a large mass of blood, called a hematoma, and leading to surgical shock. Some bleeding may follow the procedure of renal biopsy—taking a specimen of kidney tissue for examination—but with proper precautions this is not severe. In the past, massive irradiation to the kidney region led to chronic renal damage (radiation nephritis); but with adequate precautions, this should now be of historical interest only.

The usual signs of traumatic injury to the kidney are blood in the urine and the development of a tender mass in the loin, with progressive signs of shock (pallor, sweating, fall in blood pressure). Such signs call for resuscitation, and for surgical exploration if the bleeding continues. The surgical treatment may be carried out to arrest the bleeding by closing the tear. Surgical removal of the kidney may be done if it cannot be saved. Abnormal solitary kidneys are not unknown, and such kidneys are more exposed to trauma by their size or position. Removal of such a kidney can lead only to death or emergency transplantation.

Dialysis and transplantation. The failure of a vital function normally, and by definition, leads to death; but in the case of the kidneys there are two methods of substituting for renal function. In principle the simpler of these two is to transplant a kidney from a donor, ideally an identical twin. The immunological and surgical problems of transplantation are dealt with in the article TRANSPLANTS, ORGAN AND TISSUE. Here only the part played by renal transplantation in the total care of renal disease is considered. The question of a transplant does not arise in most cases of acute renal failure when the loss of function is largely recoverable; and in chronic renal failure it arises only when the residual renal function is barely adequate to support life. Transplantation and dialysis are complementary rather than rival methods. Dialysis is used while a patient is awaiting transplant and during episodes of oliguria or of threatened rejection, while, on the other hand, patients who find dialysis a psychological burden can be offered a transplant. In addition to its complementary role in a transplant program, dialysis can be used independently in the maintenance of patients with chronic renal failure; and it can be used to preserve life in acute renal failure and in acute poisoning, to allow more time for recovery.

Occasions for use of transplants and dialysis

There are two main techniques of dialysis in current use. In peritoneal dialysis, the patient's own abdominal cavity is used as the container of fluid; the fluid is run in, allowed to reach equilibrium, and removed, taking with it urea and other wastes. The process is tedious and cannot be repeated over many occasions. But it has proved suitable for the short-term treatment of acute renal failure. Hemodialysis (filtration of the blood through semipermeable membranes) has also been used in the treatment of acute renal failure, since the method—the artificial kidney—was devised, in the 1940s; but, for chronic use, the problem was one of repeated access to the arterial bloodstream. This was largely solved by the introduction of a permanent shunt between an artery and a vein, which could be diverted through the "artificial kidney" when required. In the original artificial kidney, the patient's blood was pumped through cellophane tubing immersed in a large bath of physiological fluid (solution of the same osmotic pressure as blood); in some later models, streams of blood and of dialyzing fluid are made to flow in opposite directions, separated by plastic sheets. This introduction of the "countercurrent" principle has allowed the apparatus to be smaller, and disposable versions of both patterns are now available. Some patients on intermittent hemodialysis have been kept alive for nearly ten years now. Most continued hemodialysis is still done in hospitals or special centres; but some patients using automatic equipment have been successfully trained to carry out the procedure in their own home.

DISEASES OF URINARY TRACT

Obstruction. While it is possible for the urinary tract to be obstructed by a large mass (tumour, stone, or foreign body) lying in the bladder, the tubular portions of the tract (urethra and ureters) are much more vulnerable to obstruction. The urethra may be obstructed by the lodging therein of stones (calculi) formed in the bladder or kidneys; by fibrous contraction of the urethral wall (urethral stricture); and by congenital valve or diaphragm (membranous obstruction). Although not strictly a part of the excretory tract, the prostate lies inconveniently close to the bladder neck, and in older men it is an important cause of obstruction; fibrous disease of the bladder neck can also cause obstruction. The ureters can likewise be obstructed by calculi and stricture (narrow-

Situations leading to urinary infection

ing); by fibrosis—scarring—of surrounding tissue (retroperitoneal fibrosis); and by tumour, though this is more likely to cause blood in the urine.

Urinary calculi vary greatly in size and composition, but mostly they contain calcium, together with phosphate or oxalate. Stones of organic matter (uric acid, cystine) are also found. Predisposing factors include infection, a high rate of calcium excretion, a low rate of urine formation (*e.g.*, in tropical countries, because of fluid loss through sweating), and various metabolic disorders, notably gout. They may cause trouble by their size; or by entering the ureter or urethra, giving rise to colic, to hematuria—blood in the urine—and, in the event of impaction, to obstructive kidney disease. The direct treatment of calculi is surgical. The sufferer needs general investigation for any underlying cause; *e.g.*, a functioning parathyroid tumour that causes excessive excretion of calcium.

In the past at least, a common cause of urethral stricture was gonorrhea, in which inflammation of the urethra is followed by scarring and stricture. Bruising of the urethra by instruments during treatment can also occur. The affected person has increasing difficulty in passing urine, and the bladder becomes distended. Treatment may be either by repeated dilation of the stricture or by surgery.

Trauma. Apart from the urethra, the urinary tract is likely to be injured only in massive general injury or by accidental ligation (tying) of the ureters in a pelvic operation. The urethra can, however, be ruptured by a blow or fall on the perineum (crotch) if it is trapped between the external mass and the pelvic bone. If there is no external wound, the damage is indicated by the appearance of a swelling containing blood and urine, by the failure of any attempt to pass urine, and by bleeding from the urethra. The patient becomes shocked, and a surgical operation is urgently needed to repair the urethra and drain the potentially infected swelling.

Tumour. The occurrence of papillomatous tumours, initially benign but often becoming malignant, has already been mentioned in relation to the renal pelvis. Similar tumours can occur in the lower urinary tract, and these also give rise to painless hematuria. Workers with the chemicals naphthylamine and benzidine have been shown to have a high incidence of bladder tumours, often multiple and recurrent. Clinically, blood in the urine is the most frequent symptom, but irritation of the bladder with difficulty in urination appears later. Removal when practicable or destruction by diathermy are normal treatments.

Infection of urinary tract. Infection of the urinary tract is a common and important cause of both minor and major illness. At one extreme, an attack of cystitis—inflammation of the bladder—may cause only trivial discomfort; on the other hand, infection once established may cause lifelong discomfort, may be largely unresponsive to treatment, and may greatly shorten life itself. Infection may be with a great variety of organisms, but the commonest are those that inhabit the bowel, where they are relatively harmless, becoming a cause of disease only when they gain entrance to vulnerable tissue. Because of the short female urethra, urinary infections are more common in women than in men and occur especially during pregnancies, when there may be partial stagnation of the urine from pressure on the urinary tract. In later life, as prostatic disease enters the picture, urinary infection becomes more of a problem in men. Another vulnerable period is infancy, when the use of diapers probably facilitates entry of organisms into the urethra. The introduction of a catheter into the bladder may be necessary to relieve urethral obstruction, but since the procedure always carries a risk of introducing infection, it is not lightly undertaken.

In all forms of urinary infection the urine may be cloudy and may contain more ammonia than usual. Urination tends to be painful if the urethra is inflamed, and both painful and frequent if inflammation involves the bladder. Bladder infection may also cause fever, dull pain in the lower part of the abdomen, and vomiting. If the in-

fection reaches the kidneys, symptoms are even more severe, and there is pain in the loins, on one or both sides.

Urinary infection is diagnosed from the symptoms and from laboratory examination of the urine. Treatment is with sulfernamides or with broad-spectrum antibiotics.

Like other tissues, the excretory system can be involved in tuberculous infection. This is now relatively uncommon and, when it occurs, can often be managed by the general chemotherapy appropriate to tuberculous infection. Advanced renal tuberculosis requiring removal of the kidney rarely occurs.

BIBLIOGRAPHY. For further information, the following may be consulted in their latest available edition: H.E. DE WARDENER, *The Kidney*, 3rd ed. (1967), a clearly written short textbook; M.B. STRAUSS and L.G. WELT (eds.), *Diseases of the Kidney*, 2nd ed. (1971), a comprehensive textbook at an advanced level; D.A.K. BLACK (ed.), *Renal Disease*, 3rd ed. (1972), a multiple-author book, which concentrates on selected areas of current development.

(D.A.K.B.)

Exegesis and Hermeneutics, Biblical

Exegesis, or critical interpretation, and hermeneutics, or the science of interpretive principles, of the Bible have been used by both Jews and Christians throughout their histories for various purposes. The most common purpose has been that of discovering the truths and values of the Old and New Testaments by means of various techniques and principles, though very often, due to the exigencies of certain historical conditions, polemical or apologetical situations anticipate the truth or value to be discovered and thus dictate the type of exegesis or hermeneutic to be used. The primary goal, however, is to arrive at biblical truths and values by an unbiased use of exegesis and hermeneutics.

NATURE AND SIGNIFICANCE

Biblical exegesis and hermeneutics play a basic role in Jewish and Christian theology, since both Jews and Christians are traditionally "people of the book." The major part of that book, the Hebrew Bible in the original text or in one of its non-Hebrew versions, is common to Jews and Christians. To it Christians add the New Testament, and some Christians also include in their Bible the writings called the Apocrypha (from the Greek "hidden away"), most of which, while not forming part of the Hebrew Bible, were included in the Greek version of the Old Testament (the Septuagint), rendered by Hellenistic Jews *c*. 2nd century BC, which constituted the "authorized version" of the early church.

Biblical exegesis is the actual interpretation of the sacred book, the bringing out of its meaning; hermeneutics is the study and establishment of the principles by which it is to be interpreted. Where the biblical writings are interpreted on a historical perspective, just as with philological and other ancient documents, there is little call for a special discipline of biblical hermeneutics. But it has been widely held that the factors of divine revelation and inspiration in the Bible, which, according to Jewish and Christian belief, set it apart from other literature, impose their appropriate hermeneutical principles, although there has been divergence of opinion on what these principles are. Again, because of the place that the biblical writings have occupied in synagogue and church, their exploitation for apologetical or polemical ends, their employment as a source for dogma or as a means of grace, fostering individual and community devotion, and the use of certain parts (especially the psalms) in the congregational liturgy, the science of hermeneutics has been studiously cultivated as a theological discipline. To treat the Bible like any other book (even in order to discover that it is not like any other book) has been condemned by believers as an unworthy, not to say impious, attitude.

At times the languages in which the biblical texts were originally composed have for that reason been treated as sacred languages. Hebrew may be to the philologist a Canaanite dialect, not substantially different from Phoenician, or Moabite, or other Semitic languages, but for some people even today this language is invested with an aura of sacredness. As for the language of the New Testament, in the days before its place within the general development of Hellenistic Greek was properly appreciated, it could be called a "language of the Holy Ghost," as it was by the German Lutheran theologian Richard Rothe (1799–1867). And even scholars who know very well the true character of the biblical languages are tempted at times to make the Old and New Testament vocabularies, down to the very prepositions, bear a greater weight of theological significance than sound linguistic practice permits. Where in other Greek literature the context would be allowed to determine the precise force of this or that synonym, there is a tendency to approach the New Testament with definitions ready made and to impose them on the text: to give one example, of two common Greek words meaning "new," it is sometimes laid down in advance that *kainos* denotes new in character and *neos* new in time ("young"). Often such distinctions are valid, but their validity must be established by the context; where the context discourages such precise differentiations, they must not be forced upon it.

Again, it is a truism in linguistic study that the meaning of a word depends on its usage, not on its derivation. It may be of interest to know that the Hebrew word for "burnt offering" (*'ola*) etymologically means "ascending" (*cf.* the verb *'ala*, "ascend"), and to trace the stages by which it attained its biblical meaning, but this knowledge is almost wholly irrelevant to the understanding of the word in the Old Testament ritual vocabulary, and any attempt to link it, say, with the ascension of Jesus in the New Testament, as has been done, can lead only to confusion.

Similarly there has been a tendency to place the history contained in the biblical writings on a different level from "ordinary" history. Here the increasing knowledge of the historical setting of the biblical narrative, especially in the Old Testament, has helped to remove the impression that the persons and peoples portrayed in this narrative are not quite "real"; it has integrated them with contemporary life and promoted a better understanding of what they had in common with their neighbours and what their distinctive qualities were.

BIBLICAL CRITICISM

A prerequisite for the exegetical study of the biblical writings, and even for the establishment of hermeneutical principles, is their critical examination. Most forms of biblical criticism are relevant to many other bodies of literature.

Textual criticism. Textual criticism is concerned with the basic task of establishing, as far as possible, the original text of the documents on the basis of the available materials. For the Old Testament, until 1947, these materials consisted principally of: (1) Hebrew manuscripts dated from the 9th century AD onward, the Masoretic text, the traditional Jewish text with its vocalization and punctuation marks as recorded by the editors called Masoretes (Hebrew *masora*, "tradition") from the 6th century to the end of the 10th; (2) Hebrew manuscripts of medieval date preserving the Samaritan edition of the Pentateuch (first five books of the Bible); (3) Greek manuscripts, mainly from the 3rd and 4th centuries AD onward, preserving the text of the pre-Christian Greek version of the Hebrew Bible together with most of the apocryphal books (the Septuagint); (4) manuscripts of the Syriac (Peshitta) and Latin (Vulgate) versions, both of which were based directly on the Hebrew. Since 1947 the discovery of Hebrew biblical texts at Qumrān (then Jordan) and other places west of the Dead Sea has made it possible to trace the history of the Hebrew Bible back to the 2nd century BC and to recognize, among the manuscripts circulating in the closing generations of the Second Jewish Commonwealth (c. 450 BC–c. AD 135), at least three types of Hebrew text: (1) the ancestor of the Masoretic text, (2) the Hebrew basis of the Septuagint version, and (3) a popular text of the Pentateuch akin to the Samaritan edition. A comparative examination of these three indicates that the ancestor of the Masoretic text is

Biblical manuscript texts and editions

in the main the most reliable; the translators of the Revised Standard Version (1952) and New English Bible (1970) have continued to use the Masoretic text as their Old Testament basis.

For the New Testament the chief text-critical materials are (1) manuscripts of the Greek text, from the 2nd to the 15th centuries, of which some 5,000 are known, exhibiting the New Testament text in whole or in part; (2) ancient versions in Syriac, Coptic, Latin, Armenian, Georgian, Ethiopic, and other languages; and (3) citations in early Christian writers. A comparative study of this material enables scholars to get behind the Byzantine type of text, (the types that first diffused from Constantinople from the 4th century onward, gained currency throughout Greek-speaking Christendom and formed the basis of the earliest printed editions of the Greek testament) to a variety of types current in various localities in the generations immediately preceding; but the more recent discovery of manuscripts (mainly on papyrus) of the 3rd and even 2nd centuries, which cannot be neatly assigned to one or another of these types, makes the earlier history of the text more problematic, and the Revised Standard Version and New English Bible are both based on an eclectic text (in which, where the witnesses show variant readings, the reading preferred is that which best suits the context and the author's known style).

New Testament textual problems

Philological criticism. Philological criticism consists mainly in the study of the biblical languages in their widest scope, so that the vocabulary, grammar, and style of the biblical writings can be understood as accurately as possible with the aid not only of other biblical writings but of other writings in the same or cognate languages. New Testament Greek, for example, is a representative of Hellenistic Greek written in the 1st century AD, ranging from the literary Hellenistic of Hebrews, I Peter, and portions of Luke–Acts, to the colloquial or vernacular idiom of some other books (*e.g.*, the conversations in the Gospels). Some Aramaic influences have been discerned in parts of the New Testament that have a Palestinian setting, but not to a point where scholars are obliged to conclude that some books, or parts of books, were originally composed in Aramaic. Moreover, the Septuagint version exercised on some New Testament writers the kind of influence that the King James Version has exercised on many English writers, especially in the provision of a theological vocabulary in areas such as law, ethics, atonement, and sacrifice. The study of Old Testament Hebrew has been enriched by the study of other Semitic languages—Akkadian and Ugaritic among the ancient languages, and Arabic, which preserves many archaic features. Such comparative study has led to the suggestion of new meanings for a considerable number of biblical Hebrew words—a tendency that is amply illustrated by the New English Bible—but this department of philological criticism requires much more carefully defined guiding lines than have hitherto been laid down.

Literary criticism. Literary criticism endeavours to establish the literary genres (types or categories) of the various documents and to reach conclusions about their structure, date, and authorship. These conclusions are based as far as possible on internal evidence, but external evidence is also very helpful, especially where date is concerned. If the document under consideration is unmistakably quoted in another composition, for example, that quotation forms a *terminus ante quem* (later limiting point in time) for dating purposes. If, on the other hand, the document is clearly dependent on another document that can be dated on independent grounds, the date of the earlier document provides a *terminus post quem* (earlier limiting point in time).

Importance of literary genres

Proved dependence on such an earlier document may also throw light on the structure of the work being studied. But much of the evidence for the history of its structure is internal. The evaluation of such evidence is the province of what used to be called the higher criticism, a term first employed with a biblical reference by the German biblical scholar and orientalist Johann Gottfried Eichhorn (1752–1827):

I have been obliged to bestow the greatest amount of labour

on a hitherto entirely unworked field, the investigation of the inner constitution of the separate books of the Old Testament by the aid of the higher criticism (a new name to no humanist).

Eichhorn paid special attention to the Pentateuch; his work marks an important step forward in Pentateuchal criticism. The chronological arrangement of the successive law codes contained in the Pentateuch, or of the successive editions of one fundamental law code, has been related to the history of Israelite culture and religion recorded in the other Old Testament books—histories, prophecies, and psalms—with the mounting aid supplied by contemporary non-Israelite documents. The development of some Old Testament books is indicated expressly in their contents: one can note the composition of the first and second editions of the Book of Jeremiah in Jer. 36:4, 32; and scholars can reach some conclusions about later editions by a comparison of the longer edition in the Masoretic text with the shorter edition in the Septuagint (now also attested in a fragmentary Hebrew text from Qumrān). In the absence of such explicit evidence, conclusions about the structure of other prophetic books, such as Isaiah and Ezekiel, must be more tentative.

In the New Testament, literary criticism has centred principally on the Gospels. In the Synoptic Gospels (that is, those having a common source; *i.e.*, Matthew, Mark, and Luke) indicators as to source and composition are provided by the presence of so much material common to two or to all three of them. The majority opinion for well over a century has been that Mark served as a source for Matthew and Luke, and that the two latter had a further common source, generally labelled Q (for *Quelle*, the German term for "source"), comprising mainly sayings of Jesus. Aspects of the Gospel problem that literary criticism leaves unsolved are more likely to be illuminated by other critical approaches. The Fourth Gospel (John) having much less in common with the Synoptic Gospels than the latter three have among themselves, it presents an independent line of transmission, and a comparative study of those areas where the Johannine and Synoptic traditions touch each other yields valuable conclusions for the beginnings of the gospel story.

Tradition criticism. Tradition criticism takes up where literary criticism leaves off; it goes behind the written sources to trace the development of oral tradition, where there is reason to believe that this preceded the earliest documentary stages, and attempts to trace the development of the tradition, phase by phase, from its primary life setting to its literary presentation. The development of the tradition might cover a lengthy period, as in the Old Testament narratives of the patriarchs—Abraham, Isaac, and Jacob—and the judges, such as Deborah and Samuel, many of which were originally attached to particular sanctuaries. The recognition of the life setting of each successive phase is necessary to the interpretation of the material received and delivered by one generation after another.

In the New Testament, too, special attention has been paid to the oral stage of the Gospel tradition, though here the preliterary period is measured in decades, not (as in the Old Testament) in generations and centuries. Not only the record of the ministry of Jesus but the development of Christian theology in the short preliterary stage has formed the subject matter of this study.

Form criticism. Form criticism has become one of the most valuable tools for the reconstruction of the preliterary tradition. This discipline classifies the literary material according to the principal "forms"—such as legal, poetic, and other forms—represented in its contents, and examines these in order to discover how they were handed down and what their successive life settings were until they assumed their present shape and position. In their various ways laws, narratives, psalms, and prophecies are amenable to this approach. By this means some scholars have undertaken to recover the *ipsissima verba* ("very own words") of Jesus by removing the accretions attached to them in the course of transmission. The exegetical task assumes a threefold shape as scholars work back from (1) interpretation of the present Gospels

through (2) interpretation of the tradition lying behind them to (3) reconstruction of the proclamation of Jesus.

Scholars are not left completely to speculation as they attempt to reconstruct the stages by which the Gospel tradition attained its final form: here and there in the New Testament letters, and in some of the speeches included in Acts (which convey the general sense of what was said and should not be regarded as the author's free creations), there are fragments and outlines of the story of Jesus and of his teaching. Sometimes the characteristic terminology of tradition ("I received . . . I delivered") is used when such fragments are introduced, a decade or so before the composition of the earliest Gospel (*cf.* I Cor. 11:23; 15:3).

Other types of exegetical critical techniques. *Redaction criticism.* Redaction criticism concentrates on the end product, studying the way in which the final authors or editors used the traditional material that they received and the special purpose that each had in view in incorporating this material into his literary composition. It has led of late to important conclusions about the respective outlooks and aims of the four evangelists, Matthew, Mark, Luke, and John.

Historical criticism. Historical criticism places the documents in their historical setting and promotes their interpretation in the light of their contemporary environment. This is necessary for their understanding, whether they are historical in character or belong to another literary genre. If they are historical in character it is important to establish how faithfully they reflect their dramatic date—the date of the events they record (as distinct from the date of final composition). This test has been applied with singularly positive results to Luke–Acts, especially in relation to Roman law and institutions; and in general the biblical outline of events from the middle Bronze Age (*c.* 21st–*c.* mid-16th centuries BC) to the 1st century AD fits remarkably well into its Near Eastern context as recovered by archaeological research.

"History of religions" criticism. "History of religions" criticism, to use an ungainly expression, relates Old and New Testament religion to the religious situation of the contemporary world of the writings and tries to explain biblical religion as far as possible in terms of current religious attitudes and practices. This is helpful to a point, insofar as it throws into relief those features of Hebrew and Christian faith that are distinctive; it is carried to excess when it attempts to deprive those features of their unique qualities and to account completely for them in religious–historical terms. When the cult of Israel was practically indistinguishable from that of the Canaanites, the protests of the 8th-century BC Hebrew prophets Amos or Hosea stand out over against popular Yahweh worship (Hebrew) and Baal worship (Canaanite) alike. Another attempt has been made by historians of religion to recreate for the 1st century AD a pre-Christian Gnostic myth—referring to an esoteric dualism in which matter is viewed as evil and spirit good—of the primal or heavenly man who comes from the realm of light to liberate particles of a heavenly essence that are imprisoned on earth in material bodies and to impart the true knowledge. By men's acceptance of this secret salvatory knowledge (gnosis), the heavenly essence within man is released from its thraldom and reascends to its native abode. Fragments of this myth have been recognized in several books of the New Testament. But the attempt has not been successful: according to many recent (latter half of the 20th century) New Testament scholars and historians of the early church, it is probable that the concepts of primal man and redeemer-revealer were not brought together in Gnosticism *except* under the influence of the Christian apostolic teaching, in which Jesus fills the role of Son of man (or Second Adam) together with that of Saviour and Revealer.

On the other hand, the Iranian religious influence, primarily that of Zoroastrianism (see also ZOROASTRIANISM AND PARSIISM), on the angelology and eschatology (concepts of the last times) of Judaism in the last two centuries BC is unmistakable, especially among the Pharisees (a liberal Jewish sect emphasizing piety) and the Qumrān

Tracing the oral tradition

Biblical texts in relation to their historical milieu

community (presumably the Essenes) near the Dead Sea. In the latter, indeed, Zoroastrian dualism finds clear expression, such as in the concept of a war between the sons of light and the sons of darkness, although it is subordinated to the sovereignty of the one God of Israel.

The value of these critical methods of Bible study lies in their enabling the reader to interpret the writings as accurately as possible. By their aid he can ascertain better what the writers meant by the language they used at the time they wrote and how their first readers would have understood their language. If the understanding of readers today is to have any validity, it must bear a close relation to what the original readers were intended to understand.

TYPES OF BIBLICAL HERMENEUTICS

As has been said, the importance of biblical hermeneutics has lain in the Bible's status as a sacred book in Judaism and Christianity, recording a divine revelation or reproducing divine oracles. The "oracles" are primarily prophetic utterances, but often their narrative setting has also come to acquire oracular status. Quite different hermeneutical principles, however, have been inferred from this axiom of biblical inspiration: whereas some have argued that the interpretation must always be literal, or as literal as possible (since "God always means what he says"), others have treated it as self-evident that words of divine origin must always have some profounder "spiritual" meaning than that which lies on the surface, and this meaning will yield itself up only to those who apply the appropriate rules of figurative exegesis. Or again, it may be insisted that certain parts must be treated literally and others figuratively; thus some expositors who regard the allegorical (symbolic) interpretation of the Old Testament histories as the only interpretation that has any religious value maintain that in the apocalyptic writings that interpretation which is most literal is most reliable.

Interpretation of biblical inspiration

Literal interpretation. Literal interpretation is often, but not necessarily, associated with the belief in verbal or plenary inspiration, according to which not only the biblical message but also the individual words in which that message was delivered or written down were divinely chosen. In an extreme form this would imply that God dictated the message to the speakers or writers word by word, but most proponents of verbal inspiration repudiate such a view on the reasonable ground that this would leave no room for the evident individuality of style and vocabulary found in the various authors. Verbal inspiration received classic expression by the 19th-century English biblical scholar John William Burgon:

> The Bible is none other than *the voice of Him that sitteth upon the Throne!* Every Book of it, every Chapter of it, every Verse of it, every word of it, every syllable of it, (*where are we to stop?*) every letter of it, is the direct utterance of the Most High! (*From Inspiration and Interpretation,* 1861).

This explains Burgon's severe judgment that the revisers of the English New Testament (1881), in excluding what they believed to be scribal or editorial additions to the original text, "stand convicted of having deliberately rejected the words of Inspiration in every page" (*The Revision Revised,* p. vii, London, 1883). Such a high view of inspiration has commonly been based on the statement in II Tim. 3:16 that "all [Old Testament] scripture is God-breathed" (Greek *theopneustos,* which means "inspired by God") or Paul's claim in I Cor. 2:13 to impart the gospel "in words not taught by human wisdom but taught by the Spirit, interpreting spiritual truths in spiritual language." On this latter passage the English bishop and biblical scholar Joseph Barber Lightfoot (1828–89) remarked:

> The notion of a verbal inspiration in a certain sense is involved in the very conception of an inspiration at all, because words are at once the instruments of carrying on and the means of expressing ideas, so that the words must both lead and follow the thought. But the passage gives no countenance to the popular doctrine of verbal inspiration, whether right or wrong (From *Notes on Epistles of St. Paul from Unpublished Commentaries,* 1895).

The detailed attention that Lightfoot and his Cambridge University colleagues, Brooke Foss Westcott (1825–1901), successor of Lightfoot as bishop of Durham, and Fenton John Anthony Hort (1828–92), paid in their exegesis to the vocabulary and grammatical construction of the biblical documents, together with their concern for the historical context, sprang from no dogmatic attachment to any theory of inspiration but represented the literal method of interpretation at its best. Such grammatico-historical exegesis can be practiced by anyone with the necessary linguistic tools and accuracy of mind, irrespective of confessional commitment, and is likely to have more permanent value than exegesis that reflects passing fashions of philosophical thought. Biblical theology itself is more securely based when it rests upon such exegesis than when it forms a hermeneutical presupposition.

Moral interpretation. Moral interpretation is necessitated by the belief that the Bible is the rule not only of faith but also of conduct. The Jewish teachers of the late pre-Christian and early Christian Era, who found "in the law the embodiment of knowledge and truth" (Rom. 2: 20), were faced with the necessity of adapting the requirements of the Pentateuchal codes to the changed social conditions of the Hellenistic Age (3rd century BC–3rd century AD). This they did by means of a body of oral interpretation, which enabled the conscientious Jew to know his duty in the manifold circumstances of daily life. If, for example, he wished to know whether this or that activity constituted "work" that was forbidden on the sabbath, the influential school of legal interpretation headed by the rabbi Hillel (late 1st century BC to early 1st century AD) supplied a list of 39 categories of activity that fell under the ban.

The Bible as a guide to conduct

The Christian Church rejected the Jewish "tradition of the elders" but for the most part continued to regard the Ten Commandments as ethically binding and devised new codes of practice, largely forgetting Paul's appeal to the liberty of the Spirit, or viewing it as an invitation to indulge in allegory. In order to deduce moral lessons from the Bible, allegorization was resorted to, as when the *Letter of Barnabas* (*c.* AD 100) interprets the Levitical food laws prescribed in the book of Leviticus as forbidding not the flesh of certain animals but the vices imaginatively associated with the animals. To set up principles of exegesis by which ethical lessons may be drawn from all parts of the Bible is not easy, since many of the commandments enjoined upon the Israelites in the Pentateuch no longer have any obvious relevance, such as the ban on boiling a kid in its mother's milk (Ex. 23:19b, etc.), or on wearing a mixed woollen and linen garment (Deut. 22:11); and much of the teaching of Jesus in the Sermon on the Mount is widely regarded as a counsel of perfection, impracticable for the average man, even when he professes the Christian faith. Even summaries of the biblical ethic, such as the golden rule (Matt. 7:12; *cf.* Tob. 4:15) or the twofold law of love to God and love to one's neighbour (Deut. 6:5; Lev. 19:18), in which the Decalogue (Ten Commandments) is comprehended (Mark 12:29–31; *cf.* Rom. 13:8–10), involve casuistic interpretation (fitting general principles to particular cases) when they are applied to the complicated relations of present-day life. The difficulties of applying biblical ethics to modern situations do not mean that the task of application should be abandoned but that it should not be undertaken as though it provided an easy shortcut to moral solutions.

Allegorical interpretation. Allegorical interpretation places on biblical literature a meaning that, with rare exceptions, it was never intended to convey. Yet at times this interpretation seemed imperative. If the literal sense, on which heretics, such as the 2nd-century biblical critic Marcion, and anti-Christian polemicists, such as the 2nd-century philosopher Celsus, insisted, was unacceptable, then allegorization was the only procedure compatible with a belief in the Bible as a divine oracle. Law, history, prophecy, poetry, and even Jesus' parables yielded new meanings when allegorized. The surface sensuous meaning of the Canticles (the Song of Solomon) was gladly forgotten when its mutual endearments were understood to express the communion between God and the soul, or between Christ and the church. There are still readers who can reconcile themselves to the presence of a book such as Joshua in the canon only if its battles can be understood as pointing to the warfare of Christians "against the spiritual hosts of wickedness in the heavenly places" (Eph. 6:12). As for the Gospel parables, when in the story of the good Samaritan (Luke 10:30–37) an allegorical meaning is sought for the thieves, the Samaritan's beast, the inn, the innkeeper, and the two pence, the result too often is that the explicit point of the story, "Go and do likewise," is blunted.

Closely allied to allegorical interpretation, if not indeed a species of it, is typological interpretation, in which certain persons, objects, or events in the Old Testament are seen to set forth at a deeper level persons, objects, or events in the New. In such interpretations, Noah's ark (Gen. 6:14–22) is interpreted to typify the church, outside which there is no salvation; Isaac carrying the wood for the sacrifice (Gen. 22:6) typifies Jesus carrying the cross; Rahab's scarlet cord in the window (Jos. 2:18–21) prefigures the blood of Christ; and so on. These are not merely sermon illustrations but rather aspects of a hermeneutical theory that maintains that this further significance was designed (by God) from the beginning. Traces of typology appear in the New Testament, as when Paul in Rom. 5:14 calls Adam a "type" of the coming Christ (as the head of the old creation involved its members in the results of his disobedience, so the head of the new creation shares with its members the fruit of his obedience), or when in I Cor. 10:11 he says that the Israelites' experiences in the wilderness wanderings befell them "typically," so as to warn his own converts of the peril of rebelling against God. The fourth evangelist stresses the analogy between the sacrificial Passover lamb of the Hebrews and Christ in his death (John 19). The writer of the Hebrews treats the priest-king of Salem, Melchizedek, who was involved with Abraham as a type of Christ (Heb. 7)—without using the word "type"—and the Levitical ritual of the Day of Atonement as a model (though an imperfect one) of Christ's sacrificial ministry (Heb. 9).

Other hermeneutical principles. *Anagogical interpretation.* Anagogical (mystical or spiritual) interpretation seeks to explain biblical events or matters of this world so that they relate to the life to come. Jordan is thus interpreted as the river of death; by crossing it one enters into the heavenly Canaan, the better land, the "rest that remains for the people of God." "The Jerusalem that now is" points to the new Jerusalem that is above. In Judaism of the closing centuries BC, the Eden of Genesis, the earthly paradise, lent its name to the heavenly paradise mentioned occasionally in the New Testament (Luke 23:43; II Cor. 12:3; Rev. 2:7).

Another form of mystical interpretation is the Mariological (referring to Mary, the mother of Jesus) application of scriptures that have another contextual sense. Thus Mary is the second Eve, whose offspring bruises the serpent's head (Gen. 3:15); Mary is the star-crowned woman of Rev. 12, whose son is caught up to the throne of God, and in more popular piety the dark-faced Madonna of the monastery at Montserrat, near Barcelona, Spain, can be identified with the "black but comely" bride of the Song of Solomon.

Parallelism. Parallelism, the interpretation of Scripture by means of Scripture, is a corollary of the belief in the unity of Scripture. But as a hermeneutical principle it must be employed sparingly, since the unity of Scripture should be based on comprehensive exegetical study, rather than itself provide a basis. Where one or two biblical documents (*e.g.,* the letters to the Romans and to the Galatians) are treated as the norm of biblical doctrine, there is a danger that other parts of the volume (*e.g.,* the Letter to the Hebrews) will be forced to yield the same sense as the "normative" documents; the distinctiveness of certain biblical authors will then be blurred. One naive form of parallelism is the "concordant" method, in which it is axiomatic that a Hebrew or Greek word will always (or nearly always) have the same force wherever it occurs in the Bible, no matter who uses

it. There is, again, a harmonistic tradition that smooths out disparities in the biblical text (*e.g.,* as between the gospel narratives or the parallel records of Kings and Chronicles) in a manner that imposes a greater strain on faith than do the disparities themselves.

One exegetical device of the Jewish rabbis (teachers, biblical commentators, and religious leaders) was that of *gezera shawa,* "equal category," according to which an obscure passage might be illuminated by reference to another containing the same key term. There are several examples in Paul's Old Testament exegesis, one of the best known being in Gal. 3:10–14, where the mystery of Christ's dying the death that incurred the divine curse (Deut. 21:23) is explained by his bearing vicariously the curse incurred by the lawbreaker (Deut. 27:26). One may compare the explanation in Heb. 4:3–9 of God's "rest" mentioned in Ps. 95:11 by reference to his resting on the seventh day after creation's work (Gen. 2:3)—an explanation dependent on the Septuagint, not the Hebrew.

Analogical interpretation. Analogical interpretation traditionally includes not only interpretation according to the analogy of Scripture (parallelism, in other words) but also interpretation according to the "analogy of faith"—an expression that misapplies the language of Rom. 12:6 in the King James Version of 1611. It has at times been pressed to mean that no biblical interpretation is valid unless it conforms to the established teaching of a religious community, to the verdict of tradition, or to the "unanimous consensus of the fathers." Where the established teaching is based, in intention, on Scripture, then an interpretation of Scripture that conflicts with it naturally calls for further scrutiny, but such conflict does not rule out the interpretation beforehand; if the conflict is confirmed, it is the established teaching that requires revision.

Other types. There is an unconscious tendency to conform hermeneutical principles to the climate of opinion in and around the community concerned, and to change the hermeneutic pattern as the climate of opinion changes. It is not surprising that in the circles where Pseudo-Dionysius (early-6th-century writings attributed to Dionysius, a convert of St. Paul) was revered as a teacher, Scripture was interpreted in Neoplatonic (idealistic and mystical) categories, and if in the latter half of the 20th century there is an influential and persuasive school of existential hermeneutics, this may be as much due to a widespread contemporary outlook on life as was the liberal hermeneutic of the preceding generations.

At a far different level contemporary movements continue to influence biblical interpretation. The interpretation of prophecy and apocalyptic in terms of events of the interpreter's day, which has ancient precedent, is still avidly pursued. Just as in the 16th century the apocalyptic beast of Revelation was interpreted to be the papacy or Martin Luther (in accordance with the interpreter's viewpoint), so also today in some nonacademic circles the ten kings denoted by the beast's horns in Revelation are identified with the European Economic Community in its ultimate development, or the threat to "destroy the tongue of the sea of Egypt" (Isa. 11:15) is believed to be fulfilled in the condition of the Suez Canal in the years following 1967. Whatever critical exegetes think of such aberrations, historians of exegesis will take note of them and recognize the doctrine of Scripture that underlies them.

THE DEVELOPMENT OF BIBLICAL EXEGESIS AND HERMENEUTICS IN JUDAISM

Early stages. The beginnings of biblical exegesis are found in the Old Testament itself, where earlier documents are interpreted in later documents, as in the recasting of earlier laws in later codes, or the Chronicler's reworking of material in Samuel and Kings. In addition, even before the Babylonian Exile (586 BC) there is evidence of the kind of midrashic exposition (nonliteral interpretations) familiar in the rabbinical period (c. 300 BC–c. AD 500) and after.

In Isa. 40 and following, the restoration of Israel after the return from exile is portrayed as a new creation: the

characteristic verbs of the Genesis creation narrative—
"create" (*bara*), "make" ('*asa*) and "form" (*yatzar*)—are
used of this new act of God (*e.g.,* Isa. 43:7). Even more
clearly are the same events portrayed as a new Exodus:
on their journey back from Babylon, as earlier through
the wilderness, the God of Israel makes a way for his
people; he protects them before and behind; he champions them "with a mighty hand and an outstretched
arm," he brings water from the rock for their sustenance
(Isa. 43:2, 16, 19; 48:21; 52:12; Ezek. 20:33).

Later
events as
recapitula-
tions of
earlier
events

A pattern of divine action in mercy and judgment is discernible as one moves from the earlier prophets to the
later prophets and apocalyptists (those concerned with
the intervention of God in history). Yahweh's "strange
work" in bringing the Assyrians against Israel in the 8th
century BC (Isa. 28:21; 29:14) is repeated a century later
when he raises up the Chaldaeans (Babylonians) to execute his judgment (Hab. 1:5 fol.). Ezekiel's visionary
figure Gog is the invader whose aggression was foretold
in earlier days by Yahweh through his "servants the
prophets" (Ezek. 38:17), and one may recognize in him
a revival not only of Isaiah's Assyrian (Isa. 10:4 fol.) but
also of Jeremiah's destroyer from the north (Jer. 1:14
fol.; 4:6 fol.). The same figure reappears in the last "king
of the north" in Dan. 11:40 fol.; he too is diverted from
his path by "tidings from the east and the north" (*cf.* Isa.
37:7) and "shall come to his end, with none to help him"
(*cf.* Isa. 31:8).

In some degree these later predictions are interpretations, or reinterpretations, of the earlier ones, as when
the non-Israelite prophet Balaam's "ships . . . from Kit-
tim" (Num. 24:24) are interpreted in Dan. 11:30 as the
Roman vessels off Alexandria in 168 BC that frustrated
the Syrian king Antiochus IV Epiphanes (*c.* 215–164/163
BC) in his attempt to annex Egypt.

Ezra (*c.* 400 BC), whose role as the archetypal "scribe"
is magnified by tradition, is said in the canonical literature to have brought the law of God from Babylonia to
Jerusalem (Ezra 7:14), where it was read aloud to a large
assembly by relays of readers "with interpretation"—and
"they gave the sense, so that the people understood the
reading" (Neh. 8:8). This may be the first recorded use
of an Aramaic Targum—a paraphrase of the Hebrew
that included interpretation as well as translation.

In the scribal and rabbinic tradition, two forms of exposition were early distinguished—*peshaṭ*, "plain meaning" and *derash*, "interpretation," by which religious or
social morals were derived, often artificially, from the
text. There was, however, no sense of conflict between
the two.

The Hellenistic period. The translation of the Hebrew
Bible into Greek by Alexandrian Jews in the 2nd and 3rd
centuries BC provided opportunities for recording interpretations that were probably current in Hellenistic Judaism. Literal translations might be misleading to Greek

Metaphor-
ical and
philosoph-
ical inter-
pretations

readers; metaphors natural in Hebrew were rendered into
less figurative Greek. "Walking with God" or "walking
before God" was rendered as "pleasing God." Such renderings are scarcely to be called anti-anthropomorphisms
(that is, against depicting God in human terms or forms).
In certain books there are some renderings that might be
so described: in Ex. 24:10, for example, "they saw the
God of Israel" becomes "they saw the place where the
God of Israel stood"; but an examination of the Hebrew
context suggests that this is precisely what was seen.

There was a tendency to universalize certain particularist statements of the Hebrew: in Amos 9:11 fol. the
prophecy that David's dynasty will repossess the residue
of Edom becomes a promise that the residue of men (the
Gentiles) will seek the true God—a promise that is
quoted in the New Testament as a "testimony" to the
Christian Gentile mission.

The other main contribution to biblical exegesis in Alexandria was made by the Jewish philosopher Philo (*c.* 30/
c. 20 BC–after AD 40), whose interpretation of the Pentateuch in terms of Platonic idealism and Stoic ethics had
more influence on Christian than on Jewish hermeneutics.

In Palestinian Judaism the most distinctive exegetical

work in the Hellenistic period was that of the Qumrān
community (*c.* 130 BC–AD 70). The community, believing
itself raised up to prepare for the new age of everlasting
righteousness, interpreted Scripture so as to find there the
divine purpose about on the point of fulfillment, together
with its own duty in the impending crisis. Biblical prophecies in the Qumrān commentaries refer to persons and
events of the recent past, the present, or the imminent
future. The time of their fulfillment was concealed from
the prophets; only when this was revealed to the Teacher
of Righteousness, the organizer of the community, could
their intent be grasped.

Rabbinic exegesis was present in all the varieties of rabbinic literature but is found especially in the Targumim
and Midrashim (plural of Targum and Midrash). Among
the former, special interest attaches to the early Palestinian Pentateuch Targum; it preserves, for example,
messianic (referring to the expected anointed deliverer)
exegesis of certain passages to which later rabbis gave a
different interpretation because of the Christians' appeal
to them. The earlier Midrashim—those whose contents
are not later than AD 200—expound Exodus, Leviticus,
Numbers, and Deuteronomy and are almost entirely
Halakhic—*i.e.,* recording legal interpretations from
various schools. The later Midrashim are more homiletic
and include a considerable element of Haggada; *i.e.,* illustrative material drawn from all sources (see also TAL-
MUD AND MIDRASH).

Rabbinic exegesis was not haphazard; it observed certain rules, which were variously formulated in the
schools. The name of the famous interpreter Hillel is
linked with seven *middot* or norms: (1) inference from
less important to more important and vice versa, (2) inference by analogy, (3) the grouping of related passages
under an interpretative principle that primarily applies to
one of them, (4) similar grouping where the principle
primarily applies to two passages, (5) inference from particular to general and vice versa, (6) exposition by means
of a similar passage, (7) inference from the context. By
the time of Rabbi Ishmael (*c.* AD 100) these rules were expanded to 13, and Eliezer ben Yose the Galilaean (*c.* AD
150) formulated 32 rules, reflecting rational principles of
exegesis, which remained normative into the Middle
Ages.

Norms of
interpre-
tation

The medieval period. By the beginning of the Middle
Ages the Masoretes of Babylonia and Palestine (6th–10th
century) had fixed in writing, by points and annotation,
the traditional pronunciation, punctuation, and (to some
extent) interpretation of the biblical text. The rise of the
Karaites, who rejected rabbinic tradition and appealed to
Scripture alone (8th century onward) stimulated exegetical study in their own sect and in Judaism generally: in
reaction against them Sa'adia ben Joseph (882–942), *gaon*
(head) of the Sura academy in Babylonia, did some of his
most important work. He adopted as one basic principle
that biblical interpretation must not contradict reason.
He translated most of the Bible into Arabic and composed an Arabic commentary on the text.

The French Jewish biblical and talmudic scholar Rashi
(R. Solomon Yiṣḥaqi of Troyes, 1040–1105), the most
popular of all Jewish commentators, paid careful heed to
the language and rejected those midrashic traditions that
were inconsistent with the plain meaning of the text.
Abraham ibn Ezra, of Spanish birth (1092/93–1167), in
some respects anticipated the Pentateuchal literary criticism of later centuries. Other important names are Joseph Qimḥi of Narbonne and his sons Moses and David,
the last of whom (*c.* 1160–1235) commented on the
prophets and psalms; his psalms commentary took issue
especially with Christian exegesis.

The great philosopher and codifier Maimonides (Moses
ben Maimon, 1135–1204) composed, among many other
works, his *Guide For the Perplexed* to help readers who
were bewildered by apparent contradictions between the
biblical text and the findings of reason. Like his younger
contemporary David Qimḥi, he classified some biblical
narratives as visionary accounts.

Far removed from the rational exegesis of these scholars was the mystical tradition, or Kabbala, which com-

Mystical
interpreta-
tion

bined with an earlier mysticism—involving reflection on Ezekiel's inaugural chariot vision—the Neoplatonic doctrine of emanations. Adherents of this mystical exegesis of Scripture found some encouragement in the Pentateuch commentary of the Spanish Talmudist, Kabbalist, and biblical commentator Moses ben Naḥman (*c.* 1195–1270). The tracing of mystical significance in the numerical values of Hebrew letters and words (*gematria*) made a distinctive contribution to mystical exegesis. The chief monument of mystical exegesis is the *Zohar* ("brightness"), in form a midrashic commentary on the Pentateuch, produced in Spain in the 13th century. In the *Zohar* the *peshaṭ* (literal) and *derash* (nonliteral meanings) types of interpretation are accompanied by those called *remez* ("allusion"), including typology and allegory, and *sod* ("secret"), the mystical sense. The initials of the four were so arranged as to yield the word PaRDeS ("Paradise"), a designation for the fourfold meaning. The highest meaning led by knowledge through love to ecstasy and the beatific vision (see also JEWISH MYSTICISM).

The modern period.   Following a line marked out earlier by the Spanish philosopher and poet Moses ibn Ezra (1060–1139), Benedict de Spinoza (1632–77) put forward a thoroughgoing reappraisal of the traditional account of the origin of the Pentateuch in his *Tractatus Theologico-Politicus* (1679). In the following century the Jewish Enlightenment (Haskala) brought a fresh appreciation of the Bible as literature. The pioneer of the Enlightenment, Moses Mendelssohn (1729–86), prepared a German translation of the Pentateuch, which he furnished (along with Solomon Dubno and others) with a commentary; he also translated the psalms and the Song of Solomon.

The tradition of orthodox Jewish exegesis has been maintained to the present day. In the 19th century the Russian rabbi Meir ben Yehiel Michael, "Malbim," (1809–79) wrote commentaries on the prophets and the writings, making a special point of explaining differences between synonyms. In the 20th century the
traditional values of Judaism were popularly expounded in Joseph Herman Hertz's commentary on *The Pentateuch and Haftorahs* (1929–36) and in the Soncino *Books of the Bible* (1946–51). Martin Buber (1878–1965), the great modern Jewish philosopher, imparted to his many studies in biblical literature and religion—including his revolutionary German translation of the Bible (1926 and following), partly executed in association with the religious philosopher Franz Rosenzweig (1886–1926)—the qualities of his personal genius that was influenced by Ḥasidic (18th-century mystical) piety and an existential interpretation of life.

In recent decades the most valuable Jewish exegesis has been in association with the wider world of biblical scholarship. Journals such as the *Jewish Quarterly Review* and the *Hebrew Union College Annual* welcome contributions from non-Jewish scholars; in interconfessional projects such as the Anchor Bible, Jewish scholars cooperate in the Old and New Testament alike.

The whole field of biblical study, including exegesis, is cultivated most intensively in Israel. Yehezkel Kaufmann (1890–1963) produced the encyclopaedic *History of Israelite Religion from its Beginnings to the End of the Second Temple* (8 vols., 1937–56) in Hebrew that pursues a path involving a radical revision of current biblical criticism and interpretation. Mosheh Zevi Hirsh Segal (died 1968) dealt with a wide area of biblical and related literature, maintaining the essential Mosaic authorship of the Pentateuch (supplemented by later editors who worked in Moses' spirit). The most ambitious enterprise in this field is the "Bible Project" of the Hebrew University of Jerusalem, which aims to produce a critical edition of the Hebrew Bible but also fosters a number of ancillary studies in biblical text and interpretation, mostly published in its annual report *Textus*, in which non-Jewish as well as Jewish scholars participate.

THE DEVELOPMENT OF BIBLICAL EXEGESIS
AND HERMENEUTICS IN CHRISTIANITY

Early stages.   The earliest Christian exegesis of the Old Testament is found in the New Testament, not in the written texts only but in the oral tradition lying behind them. Some lines of exegesis are present in so many separate strands of primitive Christian teaching that they are most reasonably assigned to Jesus, who began his Galilaean ministry with the announcement that the time appointed for the fulfillment of prophecy, and the Kingdom of God that was its main theme, had arrived. If the accomplishment of his ministry involved his death, that was accepted in the same spirit; he submitted to his captors with the words: ". . . Let the scriptures be fulfilled" (Mark 14:49). The church began with the conviction that Jesus, crucified and risen, was the one of whom the prophets spoke. He was the prophet like Moses, prince of the house of David, priest of the order of Melchizedek, servant of the Lord, Son of man, and exalted Lord. If the prophets themselves were uncertain about the person or time indicated by their oracles, the early Christians were certain: the person was Jesus, the time was now. The New Testament writers shared a creative and flexible principle of exegesis that has regard for the literary and historical context and traces a consistent pattern of divine action in judgment and mercy, reproduced repeatedly in the history of Israel and manifested definitively in Christ. This exegesis is elaborated at times by means of typology and allegory, as when Paul illustrates the relationship between law and gospel by the story of Hagar and Sarah, the concubine and wife of Abraham, respectively (Gal. 4:21–31), or when Israel's tabernacle in the wilderness becomes the material counterpart to the heavenly sanctuary in which believers of the new age offer spiritual worship to God (Heb. 8:2 fol.). The writer to the Hebrews, indeed, occasionally relates the old order to the new order platonically in terms of the earthly copy of an eternal archetype.

At an early date Christians developed a line of Old Testament exegesis designed to show that they, not the Jews, stand in the true succession of the original people of God. This line is seen in the *Letter of Barnabas*, the apologist Justin's (*c.* 100–*c.* 165) *Dialogue with Trypho*, and the 3rd-century *Against the Jews* ascribed to the North African bishop Cyprian (*c.* 200–258).

The patristic period.   Alexandria had long boasted a
school of classical study that practiced the allegorical interpretation of the Homeric epics and the Greek myths. This method of exegesis was taken over by Philo and from him by Christian scholars of Alexandria in the 2nd and 3rd centuries. Clement of Alexandria (*c.* 150–*c.* 215) and Origen (*c.* 185–*c.* 254) did not completely rule out the literal sense of Scripture—Origen's *Hexapla*, a six column edition of various biblical versions, was a monument to his painstaking study of the text for its own sake —but claimed that the most meaningful aspects of divine revelation could be extracted only by allegorization. Clement stated that the Fourth Gospel was a "spiritual gospel" because it unfolds the deeper truth concealed in the matter-of-fact narratives of the other three. Origen treated literal statements of Scripture as "earthen vessels" preserving divine treasure; their literal sense is the body as compared with the moral sense (the soul) and the spiritual sense (the spirit). The true exegete, he claimed, pursues the threefold sense and recognizes the spiritual (allegorical) as the highest.

Later, the Antiochene fathers, represented especially by Theodore of Mopsuestia (*c.* 350–428/429) and John Chrysostom (*c.* 347–407), patriarch of Constantinople, developed an exegesis that took more account of literal meaning and historical context. But the allegorizers could claim that their method yielded lessons that (while arbitrary) were more relevant and interesting to ordinary Christians.

In the West, the Alexandrian methods were adopted by Ambrose (*c.* 339–397), bishop of Milan, and Augustine (354–430), bishop of Hippo, especially as formulated in the seven "rules" of Tyconius (*c.* 380), a Donatist heretic (one who denied the efficacy of sacraments administered by an allegedly unworthy priest), which classified allegorical interpretation in relation to: (1) the Lord and his church, (2) true and false believers, (3) promise and law, (4) genus and species, (5) numerical significance, (6) "recapitulation," and (7) the devil and his followers. There were other Latin exegetes, like Ambrosiaster (commentaries ascribed to Ambrose) and, supremely, Jerome (c. 347–419/420), the learned Latin Father, who paid close attention to the grammatical sense. In the Old Testament Jerome appealed from the Greek version to the "Hebraic verity" and in such a work as his commentary on Daniel provided some fine examples of historical exegesis. Augustine, though not primarily an exegete, composed both literal and allegorical commentaries and expository homilies on many parts of Scripture, and his grasp of divine love as the essential element in revelation supplied a unifying hermeneutical principle that compensates for technical deficiencies.

The medieval period. As the patristic age gave way to the scholastic age, the English monk Bede of Jarrow (died 735) wrote commentaries designed to perpetuate patristic exegesis, mainly allegorical: thus Elkanah with his two wives (1 Sam. 1:2) is interpreted as referring to Christ with the synagogue and the church.

The
fourfold
sense of
Scripture

In the early Middle Ages the fourfold sense of Scripture —developed from Origen's threefold sense by subdividing the spiritual sense into the allegorical (setting forth the doctrine) and the anagogical (relating to the coming world)—was increasingly expounded and received its final authority from Thomas Aquinas (1225/26–74). For Thomas, the literal sense, expressing the author's intention, was a fit object of scientific study; the figurative senses unfolded the divine intention.

Medieval exegesis was greatly influenced by the *Glossa Ordinaria*, a digest of the views of the leading fathers and early medieval doctors (teachers) on biblical interpretation. This compilation owed much in its initial stages to Anselm of Laon (died 1117); it had reached its definitive form by the middle of the 12th century and provided the exegetical norm of the *Summa theologiae* ("Summation of Theology") of Thomas Aquinas and others.

For all the interest in allegory, literal interpretation was cultivated in many centres in the West, often with the aid of Hebrew, knowledge of which was obtainable from Jewish rabbis. One such centre was the Abbey of Saint-Victor at Paris, where Hugh (died 1141) compiled biblical commentaries that fill three volumes of J.-P. Migne's (1800–75) *Patrologiae Cursus Completus* (Series Latina) and indicate the commentator's dependence on Rashi as well as on his Christian predecessors. Of Hugh's disciples, Andrew, abbot of Wigmore (died 1175), carried on his master's tradition of literal scholarship, and Richard, the Scottish-born prior of Saint-Victor (died 1173) pursued a line more congenial to his mystical temperament. Herbert of Bosham (c. 1180) produced a commentary on Jerome's Hebrew Psalter. Robert Grosseteste, bishop of Lincoln (died 1253), wrote commentaries on the days of creation and the Psalter that both drew on the Greek fathers and profited by his direct study of the Hebrew text. Nicholas of Lyra (c. 1265–c. 1349), the greatest Christian Hebraist and expositor of the later Middle Ages, compiled *postillae*, or commentaries, both literal and figurative, on the whole Bible; he insisted that only the literal sense could establish proof. Luther ranked him among the best exegetes: "a fine soul, a good Hebraist and a true Christian."

The Reformation period. The English theologian John Colet (c. 1466–1519) broke with medieval scholasticism when he returned from the Continent to Oxford in 1496 and lectured on the Pauline letters, expounding the text in terms of its plain meaning as seen in its historical context. The humanist Erasmus (c. 1466–1536) owed to him much of his insight into biblical exegesis. By the successive printed editions of his Greek New Testament (1516 and following), Erasmus made his principal, but not his only, contribution to biblical studies.

Reforma-
tion
principles

Martin Luther (1483–1546) was a voluminous expositor, insisting on the primacy of the literal sense and dismissing allegory as so much rubbish—although he indulged in it himself on occasion. The core of Scripture was to him its proclamation of Christ as the one in whom alone lay man's justification before God. John Calvin (1509–64), a more systematic expositor, served his apprentice-

ship by writing a youthful commentary on the Roman statesman and philosopher Seneca the Younger's (c. 4 BC–AD 65) *De clementia* ("Concerning Mercy"); systematic theologian though he was, he did not allow his theological system to distort the plain meaning of Scripture, and his philological–historical interpretation is consulted with profit even today.

Scientific exegesis was pursued on the Catholic side by scholars such as F. de Ribera (1591) and L. Alcasar (1614) who showed the way to a more satisfactory understanding of the Revelation. On the Reformed side, the *Annotationes in Libros Evangeliorum* (1641–50) by the jurist Hugo Grotius (1583–1645) were so objective that some criticized them for rationalism.

The modern period. The modern period is marked by advances in textual criticism and in the study of biblical languages and history, all of which contribute to the interpretation of the Bible. The German theologian J.A. Bengel's (1687–1752) edition of the Greek text of the New Testament with critical apparatus (1734), in which he framed the canon that "the more difficult reading is to be preferred," was followed by his exegetical *Gnomon Novi Testamenti* ("Introduction to the New Testament," 1742): "apply thyself wholly to the text," he directed; "apply the text wholly to thyself." The English bishop Robert Lowth's (1710–87) Oxford lectures on *The Sacred Poetry of the Hebrews*, published in Latin in 1753, greatly promoted the understanding of the poetry of the Old Testament by expounding the laws of its parallelistic structure. The German philologist Karl Lachmann (1793–1851) applied his expertise in classical criticism to editing the text of the New Testament; to him also belongs the credit of arguing that Mark was the earliest of the Gospels and a main source of Matthew and Luke (1835). The problem of the source analysis of the Pentateuch was given what for long appeared to be its final solution by Julius Wellhausen (1844–1918), who related the successive law codes to the development of the Israelite cultus. For the period preceding the 9th century BC, however, he operated in a historical vacuum that Near Eastern archaeology was in his day only beginning to fill; its subsequent findings have dictated radical modifications in his reconstruction of Israel's religious history. In the middle half of the 19th century, New Testament exegesis was overshadowed by the school of Ferdinand Christian Baur (1792–1860), which envisaged a sharply opposed Petrine (Peter) and Pauline (Paul) antithesis in the primitive church, followed in the 2nd century by a synthesis that is reflected in most of the New Testament writings. In France, Ernest Renan's (1823–92) works on early Christianity were helpful philological and historical studies; the most popular volume, his *Vie de Jésus* (1863), was the least valuable. In England, where the poet and educator Matthew Arnold (1822–88) endeavoured to find an impregnable moral foundation for biblical authority, New Testament exegesis received contributions of unsurpassed worth between 1865 and the end of the century from J.B. Lightfoot, B.F. Westcott, and F.J.A. Hort.

Source
analysis
and
historical
interpre-
tations

At the beginning of the 20th century a new direction was given to Gospel interpretation by the German scholar William Wrede (*Das Messiasgeheimnis in den Evangelien*, 1901) and the medical missionary theologian Albert Schweitzer (*The Quest of the Historical Jesus*, Eng. trans., 1910), who so emphasized the eschatological orientation of Jesus' mind and message that New Testament scholarship can never be the same again. The writings of the biblical scholar C.H. Dodd (*The Parables of the Kingdom*, 1935; *The Apostolic Preaching and its Developments*, 1936) stressed realized eschatology—that the standards of the last times were realized by Jesus and his disciples—in the preaching of Jesus and of the primitive church; he has been a leading pioneer of the "biblical theology" movement. Karl Barth's (1886–1968) commentary on Romans (1919) launched an existential interpretation of the New Testament, which has been pursued more radically by Rudolf Bultmann (1884–), under the influence of Wilhelm Dilthey (1833–1911), according to whom the interpreter must project

Existential
and form-
critical
exegesis

himself into the author's experience so as to relive it, and of Martin Heidegger (1889–), whose conception of the truly authentic man as capable of freedom because he has faced reality provides the "pre-understanding" for Bultmann's existential theology. Bultmann's disciple Ernst Fuchs (1903–) considers the hermeneutical task to be the creation of a "language event" in which the authentic language of Scripture encounters one now, challenging decision, awakening faith, and accomplishing salvation. The chief rival to existential exegesis is the "salvation-history" hermeneutic espoused by Oscar Cullmann (1902–).

Rudolf Bultmann and Martin Dibelius (1883–1947) pioneered the modern form-critical study of the Gospels. The form-critical method was fruitfully applied to the Old Testament by Hermann Gunkel (1862–1932) and Sigmund Mowinckel (1884–1965). Among Catholic scholars, exegetical studies are vigorously promoted by Jean Daniélou (with his researches into early Jewish Christianity), the Dominicans of the École Biblique et Archéologique (The School of the Bible and Archeology) in Jerusalem (to whom one must credit the Jerusalem Bible), and the Jesuits of the Pontifical Biblical Institute and others.

CONCLUSION

The encouragement given by the second Vatican Council (1962–65) of the Roman Catholic Church to biblical scholarship, to be cultivated in association with "separated brethren" and with consideration for the requirements of non-Christians, is one symptom of a new day in biblical exegesis, when this study is no longer pursued to vindicate sectional traditions but rather as a cooperative enterprise aiming at making widely available the permanent value of the Bible.

BIBLIOGRAPHY. *The Cambridge History of the Bible,* 3 vol. (1963–70), includes contributions by specialists on biblical interpretation from pre-Christian times to the present day. J. BARR, *Old and New in Interpretation* (1966), discusses the relation between the Old and New Testaments and examines critically some of the interpretative principles favoured by exegetes and theologians; another work on this subject is E.C. BLACKMAN, *Biblical Interpretation* (1957). C.E. BRAATEN, *History and Hermeneutics* (1966), discusses the relevance of the historical-critical method to theological study and the idea of revelation through history; F.F. BRUCE, *Biblical Exegesis in the Qumran Texts* (1959), examines the interpretative principles followed by biblical commentaries and other documents among the Dead Sea Scrolls. The major work on the theme of salvation-history in the Bible is O. CULLMANN, *Salvation in History* (1967). C.H. DODD, *According to the Scriptures* (1952), shows the various ways in which the Christian interpretation of important areas of the Old Testament provided the substructure of New Testament theology. F.W. FARRAR, *History of Interpretation* (1886, reprinted 1961), provides a classical survey of biblical exegesis from the early rabbinical period to the 19th century, although now outdated; R.M. GRANT, *A Short History of the Interpretation of the Bible,* rev. ed. (1963), is probably the best work of its kind. B. LINDARS, *New Testament Apologetic* (1962), studies the Old Testament quotations in the New Testament as evidence, in their text and interpretation, for the developing life and thought of the primitive church. J.M. ROBINSON and J.B. COBB (eds.), *The New Hermeneutic* (1964), expounds the modern hermeneutical concern to make the word of God existentially relevant to the present situation. B. SMALLEY, *The Study of the Bible in the Middle Ages,* 2nd rev. ed. (1952), remains the standard work on early medieval exegesis. G. VERMES, *Scripture and Tradition in Judaism* (1961), gives an account of the interaction of the written text and oral tradition in Jewish exegesis of the pre-Christian and early rabbinical age. An outline of the history of biblical interpretation and of the main exegetical trends of the mid-20th century is presented in J.D. WOOD, *The Interpretation of the Bible* (1958); A. RICHARDSON and W. SCHWEITZER (eds.), *Biblical Authority for Today* (1951), discusses the difficulties of applying biblical ethics to some of the most urgent concerns of the modern world.

(F.F.B.)

Exercise and Physical Conditioning

Exercise, within the context of this article, is the physical training of the body in order to improve its function. Active exercise is physical exertion as a voluntary effort; passive exercise is exercise involving a machine or the hands of another person. Physical conditioning is the enhancement of physical fitness through the proper employment of exercise.

After a consideration of other relevant terms, this article will discuss the contemporary need for exercise to compensate for sedentary or for physically specialized ways of living; the effect on the body of physical inactivity, and of physical inactivity coupled with a plentiful supply of food; the effect on obesity of exercise alone, and of exercise combined with a suitable diet; the physiological response to exercise of various degrees of intensity; the effects of physical conditioning; the development of physical behavioral patterns; and the types of exercise suited to specific needs.

GENERAL CONSIDERATIONS

Fatigue and exhaustion. Fatigue, defined with respect to the effect of exercise, is the diminution in subsequent performance following physical activity. Fatigue may be psychological (see FATIGUE) and be due to boredom, or ennui, or it may be physiological, and be due to exhaustion of the substances required for muscular contractions or to the accumulation of toxins that depress nervous system activity. Exhaustion is the extreme state of fatigue in which no further units of the physical activity can be performed—"I cannot climb another step."

Types of physical fitness. General physical fitness is the capacity of the body to perform work, to resist disease and infection, and to resist the physical stresses imposed by such things as heat, cold, atmospheric pressure changes at altitude or under water, and accelerative forces of jolts and vibrations. General physical fitness is, thus, the capability of the individual to dominate his usual environment, and the degree of fitness that one requires is related to the degree of stress that he must be able to overcome. The Samoan who lives peacefully in a warm climate with abundant food at arm's reach survives well with a low degree of general fitness. If the Samoan were to be transported suddenly to the frozen north, he would be unfit for the rigours of trapping. To become fit as a northern trapper, the Samoan would need to acquire specific physical fitness; that is, the special body structures and functions required to perform under the new set of unusually demanding conditions. Specific physical fitness, then, is a readiness of each system of the body to meet special demands. If unusually heavy loads must be moved, strength fitness must be acquired. Muscles must be strengthened and nerve–muscle coordination improved. If work is continuous, endurance fitness is needed. Short efforts of maximum intensity lasting less than ten seconds require anaerobic fitness, the ability of the body to work without oxygen. Exhaustive efforts of longer duration require aerobic fitness, the ability to consume oxygen efficiently. The ability to make sudden changes in posture requires orthostatic fitness. Orthostatic fitness is dependent on how well the blood circulation can adjust to a quick change of posture such as standing up after lying down.

Rapidity of movement, accuracy, and agility require speed fitness, an attribute of the brain and the sensory and motor nervous systems. Limiting rapidity of movement is relaxation fitness, the ability to elongate muscles quickly. Relaxation fitness includes ability voluntarily to reduce excess tension in the nerve–muscle system.

Types of physical conditioning. Physical conditioning commences the moment that physical effort exceeds the effort required by ordinary daily activity. The degree of physical conditioning that has occurred thereby is manifested by the improvement in performance that follows after recovery from the fatigue of the effort. Frequent and regular practice bouts of a new kind of activity induce lasting changes in body structure and function that help to make it fit for that activity. This adaptation to the new activity is termed general physical conditioning. After a few weeks, no further improvement occurs, and, in fact, a deterioration in fitness may be expected if the intensity of the activity is not continually increased. Continued improvement in fitness is achieved by specific physical conditioning, which consists of progressive overloads of the activity or its components to stimulate improvement in the structure and function of those body systems that support the new activity. This specific physical conditioning is accomplished by strength training, involving the daily lifting of progressively heavier weights; endurance training, both anaerobic (sprints) and aerobic (prolonged efforts); speed training (short bursts of activity at maximal rapidity); and relaxation training (letting go after deliberate overtensing of muscles) if these are components of fitness for the activity.

Health and fitness, and fitness and skill. In a discussion of the effects of exercise and physical conditioning, it is necessary to differentiate between health and fitness, and between fitness and skill. Health, in its narrowest definition, is the absence of disease; more broadly, it is the capacity of all body organs and systems for high-level function. Fitness relates to performance and survival. Usually, but not always, good fitness requires good health. Many exceptions are seen in sports competition. Sick athletes often win contests and sometimes break world records. Olympic contestants suffering from infections, dysentery, influenza, fever, and broken bones often turn in superior performances. Conversely, very healthy people who are not conditioned are unfit for strenuous occupations.

Again, skilled performance usually implies good fitness —and good health—but there are too many exceptions to make the generalization acceptable. The superbly skilled basketball player who has less strength and endurance than his opponents can sometimes handily outscore them. The drama of the sick, wounded, and nearly exhausted star football player who re-enters the game during the dying minutes and scores the winning points is played out regularly. This is not to say that the highly skilled player would not do better if he were more healthy and more fit; it is only to indicate that skill is a separate attribute.

THE MODERN NEED FOR EXERCISE

The sedentary person and exercise

It is easy to accept the fact that physical conditioning is necessary to achieve and maintain high levels of physical performance. The need for physical fitness among competitive athletes is clear. There is no question that explorers, soldiers, and firemen need to exercise regularly to be physically prepared for emergencies. Why a sedentary person in industrialized society needs exercise may not be so clear. What does physical fitness mean to the man or woman who needs only to push a button?

One who chooses ease and comfort and enjoys the soft life would be content to leave exercise to the athlete whom he watches on television or the fireman whom he can call in case of need. To some extent he can sit back, but if his exercise intensity falls below a certain level he will begin to suffer.

Each individual probably has a minimum level of physical activity below which serious deterioration occurs. The human body, like any living organism, must be used or it will lose its structure and function. The loss of structure and function that occurs when a broken arm is immobilized in a plaster cast clearly demonstrates the atrophy of disuse.

Fortunately for the person who is not predisposed to exert himself if he does not have to, only a small amount of exercise is necessary to preserve low-level, but normal, structure and function. This significant observation was made during studies to determine how much exercise man in space might need to counteract the state of weightlessness.

Bodily effect of physical inactivity. It appears that man in affluent cultures has progressed so rapidly from a hard, primitive life to a soft, modern one that he has retained the same energy mechanisms that enabled him to consume vast quantities of food and burn it all up in a day of vigorous physical activity. He has retained his potential capacity for hard physical work. All he needs to restore the potential capacity to actual capacity after long periods of physical idleness is a month or two of daily physical training. When his near-maximum physical capability is achieved, he can maintain it by exercising hard on alternate days. After he stops training, his physical capabilities drop to the pretraining level in a month or two. Thus, fitness for hard physical work can be seen to be a temporary condition. It can be gained and lost at will.

Coupled with a changing capability for work with increasing and decreasing exercise are changing utilization of energy and an accompanying change in requirement for food. The problem is that, as physical activity is decreased, there is no concomitant decrease in appetite. In fact, the opposite occurs; physical inactivity leads to increased food intake. Cattle raisers know this and pen their stock. The result of the inactivity and increased appetite can be predicted; a rapid gain in body fat and a softening of muscle tissue.

Although it seems an enviable situation when millions of people are supplied with an overabundance of food and at the same time have no hard physical work to do, for the majority the situation is disastrous because overfeeding and underexercise lead to death-dealing obesity and degenerative diseases of the heart and blood vessels.

Effect of exercise on obesity. Exercise requires energy, and energy is derived from foodstuffs stored in the body as fats, proteins, and carbohydrates. The nutritional unit of energy is the calorie, defined as the amount of heat required to raise the temperature of one kilogram of water $1°$ C. Exercise draws on the food reserves of the body for its energy requirements. If foodstuffs are not replaced in equal amount (*i.e.*, if one calorie is not supplied for every calorie consumed), the body becomes thinner. Fats, especially, are reduced, as these represent long-term stores of energy provided for just this kind of prolonged food shortage.

At the outset of physical training after a long period of idleness, the body becomes thinner and harder, but, because of increased muscle mass, there may be no loss of body weight. Muscle tissue is heavier than fat tissue, and muscles are enlarged when they are used repeatedly under moderately heavy loads.

Diet and exercise

After a few months of training, muscle enlargement tapers off, and the balance between food intake and energy output of physical activity is accurately revealed by changes in body weight. If food intake exceeds energy output, fat is stored and weight increases. A slight deficit in food intake results in fat and weight loss. It may seem easier to combat obesity by slight starvation rather than by forced exercise because of the large amount of exercise needed to consume an ounce of fat—about one mile of walking, jogging, or running (the speed makes little difference in the energy cost of traversing a mile in distance); weight control by diet alone, however, requires such severe restriction of food intake that it is difficult to obtain the required nutrients—proteins, vitamins, and minerals—and the sparse intake does not satisfy hunger. This is why reducing diets often fail.

With added exercise, one does not need to reduce food intake in order to lose fat, lose weight, and become thinner. Moreover, since exercise, especially before mealtime, lessens the appetite, it is easier to attain a lean body by a combination of increased physical activity and diet restriction.

Physiological responses to exercise. As was mentioned above, the cost of completing a mile, whether walking, jogging, or running, is about the same as far as energy is concerned. This says nothing, however, about the severity of exercise; the stress effect of exercise on the heart, lungs, and other structures of the body.

Light exercise. Walking is light exercise. It can be continued for hours. As is indicated in Table 1, the heart rate seldom exceeds 110 beats per minute and the rate of breathing is usually less than 17 per minute. The chemical changes brought about by muscular contractions proceed apace, and the blood constituents are undisturbed. Other light physical activities include bowling, archery, baseball, woodworking, auto repair, and housekeeping. Other exercise equivalents are shown in Table 2.

Moderate exercise. Jogging—easy running on level surfaces—is moderate exercise. A few minutes of con-

Table 1: Physiological Responses to Exercise*

intensity of exercise	heart rate beat /min)	blood pressure (mm Hg)		respiration (breaths/min)	ventilation volume (litres/min)	oxygen consumption (litres/min)	energy input (calories/hr)
		systolic	diastolic				
Maximum	200	200	85	50	120	5.0	1,440
Very heavy	150	180	80	30	70	3.5	1,008
Heavy	140	170	79	25	60	3.0	864
Fairly heavy	130	160	78	20	50	2.5	720
Moderate	120	150	77	18	40	2.0	576
Light	110	140	76	16	30	1.5	432
Very light	100	130	75	14	20	1.0	288
Resting	70	120	72	10	10	0.33	100

*These data are typical of college men and are variable according to age, body composition, physical condition, and environment.

Table 2: Exercise Equivalents to Other Activities*

intensity of exercise	equivalents					
	work output (calories /hr)	walk, jog, run (miles/hr)	climbing grades (%)	cycling (miles/hr)	sports	occupations
Maximum	300	13.0	12	20	running	digging
Very heavy	200	6.0	6	14	mountain-eering	chopping wood
Heavy	170	5.5	5	12	tennis	pick and shovel
Fairly heavy	140	5.0	4	10	volleyball	gardening
Moderate	110	4.5	3	9	golf	house painting
Light	80	4.0	2	8	table tennis	housekeeping
Very light	50	3.5	Level	7	bowling	shopping

*These values are representative only and subject to the variables mentioned in Table 1.

tinuous jogging is tiring unless the performer is well conditioned. During moderate exercise the heart rate is around 120 beats per minute and breathing rate is about 18 per minute. Blood changes are slight or nonexistent. Equivalent activities include golf (carrying clubs and walking 18 holes), basketball, football, downhill skiing, skating, and canoeing. (Some of these, such as basketball and football, include bursts of strenuous exercise.)

Strenuous exercise. Running at near-maximum speeds is strenuous exercise. It can be endured only for a few seconds. Heart rate exceeds 130 per minute; respirations are faster than 20 per minute. The chemical residues of muscle activity accumulate as acids in the blood. Within five minutes the nonathlete is exhausted. Similar strenuous activities are wrestling, fast rowing, speed swimming, sprint skating, gymnastics, and shovelling snow fast.

Static exercise. Gymnastics, weight lifting, and other strenuous activities involving static endurance (i.e., holding a stressful position, as when one links the fingers of the two hands and pulls outward) are in a separate category, since their fatigue is confined to the involved musculature. Nevertheless, when such static exercise is continued beyond one minute, the heart, lungs, and chemical processes are severely stressed.

Effects of physical conditioning. *Muscular development.* A bout of exercise leaves on almost every organ and system of the body an imprint that persists for several days. This is manifested by improvements shown in subsequent performances and by increased efficiency—need for less effort to produce the same work. The body quickly becomes "conditioned" to new physical work, mainly by improved skill, and by fewer wasted motions and less tenseness during the effort. There are other effects more important to general fitness.

Increase in muscular strength

The most obvious change in the body due to physical training is an increase in the strength, size, and hardness of the muscles used in exercise. Increase in muscular strength is derived in part from the increase in muscle mass—a bigger engine—but in greater part from the better organization of nerve impulses that reach the working muscles at a faster rate and draw them into a stronger contraction. There are nervous systems that inhibit the degree of contraction, probably as safety mechanisms. With training, inhibitions are lessened, allowing the mus-

cles to contract more nearly to their capacity. Weak muscles can be doubled in strength in two months or less by near-maximal loading every other day. It is not the number of times muscles are contracted but the degree of tension under which they are placed that dictates the strengthening effect of training. One strong contraction has far more effect toward development of strength than a thousand weak ones.

Increase in muscle size is, for some unknown reason, due to moderately heavy contractions repeated 15 to 20 times in a pumping motion. Single repetitions of near-maximal effort will increase the strength, but not the size of muscle. This fact is important to persons whose activities require speed and agility and to whom bulky, heavy muscle would be a disadvantage.

In situations in which mass is desired, as in shot putting or for the person who desires bulging muscles for vanity, the pumping form of weight training is effective.

Increased hardness of muscle is due to the greater degree of contraction that can be achieved by bringing more muscle fibres into action. In the relaxed state, the trained muscle is firm but supple, possibly because of its increased ratio of muscle fibres to fat.

Effects on circulatory and respiratory systems. The response of heart muscle to exercise training is similar to that of skeletal muscle. After such training the heart can contract more strongly and in a better coordinated way so as to wring out more blood with each contraction. In endurance training, the heart musculature becomes larger, adding to the potential power of each stroke. The heart rate becomes slower at rest; intensive endurance training can slow the resting rate ten beats per minute.

Benefit to coronary circulation

The heart muscles' private blood supply, the coronary circulation, increases as the result of exercise training. This increase in coronary vessels increases the endurance of the heart and may aid in surviving a heart attack.

In exercise training, new blood vessels appear in all active tissue, aiding in the delivery of supplies and the removal of waste. There is practically no increase in the volume of blood to fill these new vessels, but an improved control of pressures provides for a better diversion of blood to active muscles and away from tissues such as the kidneys, which tend to shut down during heavy exercise. Marathon runners who empty their bladders before the race have no need to urinate during the two and one-half hour run.

The lungs are little affected by exercise since their capacity to ventilate air is not taxed even during maximum effort. The muscles of breathing, the diaphragm and the rib musculature, however, are worked hard during strenuous exercise, and their fatigue can limit work.

The familiar "stitch-in-the-side" during continuous exercise is probably due to muscle cramp in a portion of the diaphragm. A phenomenon known as "second wind" appears when the respiratory system and other systems of the body adjust to the intensity of the effort.

Effects on the nervous system. It is the nervous system that is most affected by exercise training. In those untrained in exercise mere anticipation of exercise triggers an overwhelming response. As one becomes accustomed to exercise, however, the body seems to have the ability to size up the exact amount of effort the exercise would require and then to adjust all systems of the body to a proper setting to accommodate it.

Overanticipation of exercise

The nervous control of body systems from the perception of the task to the setting of the levels of response improves in accuracy with training. The improvement is due to a shift from volitional control, with all the imaginative inputs, to more of an involuntary control by conditioned reflexes. Overactive mental processes in the voluntary control of movement cause "paralysis by analysis." It is not until a task can be performed almost unconsciously that it can be accomplished with the greatest skill. This accounts for the apparent ease and casualness with which champions achieve record performances.

Learning new skills

Learning a new skill is accomplished most quickly and perfection is achieved most rapidly if the skill is practiced in the manner that most closely approximates the final performance. "Walking through" a movement is a good way to be introduced to a new skill, such as a dance step. As soon as possible, the tempo should be advanced to the proper rate. Every element—tempo, stride, force—should match in practice that of the hoped-for performance. This is because training is specific to the point that slow running does not improve sprinting; badminton play does not enhance tennis ability. Each pattern of movement has its own characteristic postures, interplays between opposing muscles, and sequences in which motion is started, stopped, speeded, and slowed. Through training these patterns are imprinted in the nervous system and are "replayed" automatically on signal, as when the music begins or the starting pistol is fired.

DEVELOPMENT OF MOVEMENT BEHAVIOUR

The baby. Habits of exercise probably start before birth. Later, this inherent behaviour is modified by the environment as the baby is encouraged either to move or to be still. The size of the baby's bed and playpen, and the kinetic nature of his toys influence his use of space.

The child. The child's movement behaviour is further modified by either rough-and-tumble or hands-off attitudes of parents and playmates. Constraint of physical activity may create emotional problems such as anxiety and fear of exploration.

Characteristic styles of movement. In preschool years the child develops characteristic styles of movement that tend to persist—characteristic ways of running, jumping, and climbing, for example.

When the child tries on a pair of roller skates for the first time, he does not learn the motions from scratch. He builds the new skills upon his old ones, starting with walking motions and converting them into gliding ones. Sometimes old habits of movement interfere with the acquisition of a skill and must be inhibited. The old habits may be modified, but they are never entirely broken. Early success in a new skill is achieved by permitting old habits of movement to be employed in the new pattern.

In teaching a new skill, such as striking a ball, one does not start with a model of a perfect stroke and expect every pupil to conform exactly to that model. Instead, the starting point is with each pupil's own way of stroking; one then gradually improves his technique.

Eye movement and hand movement patterns developed in active play are utilized when the child begins to read and write. A sense of direction, for example, comes from thinking about pushing a toy car from left to right along a "road." Stacking blocks and hammering pegs orient the child's cognitive and muscles sense to up and down, and top and bottom—all important in forming letters. Some reading and writing difficulties are corrected by constructive play in which such pattern clues are used.

A school program of physical education usually commences in the early grades with activities included to develop social behaviour, the ability to identify one's self as a functional member of a group, to discover one's own strengths and weaknesses, and to adjust behaviour accordingly. The child explores the whole spectrum of movement and learns what it means to lie perfectly still, to huddle, to stretch, to tense, to relax and let go, and to leap.

The youth. The youth in school is introduced to competitive sport and to the testing of his physical fitness. He learns the rules and the techniques of many sports and experiences the culture of each. He selects a team or a club and joins in its etiquette and its spirit.

The adult. After school years the adult is usually left to his own devices for exercise. The interests that he has developed in school may persist, and this is fortunate if the interests are sports such as golf or tennis, for places to play and partners are easily found.

Sports available to the adult

It is the player of varsity basketball, football, or other team sports who has difficulty when he graduates. Nonstrenuous team sports such as cricket can be played by older adults, but the more strenuous team sports are potentially dangerous for men in middle age.

Most people who remain active in sports throughout life reach an age when a less demanding type of sport is substituted for their previous activity. The handballer, for example, turns to bowling or golf as his vision declines and his reflexes slow.

EXERCISE NEEDS

Heart health regimen. Modern sedentary man past 30 begins to think of fitness for his survival as he sees his companions in their 40s die of heart attacks. This usually calls for exercise of a different nature from sport, unless he is a runner, an oarsman, a swimmer, or a cyclist and is continuing that activity.

It is estimated that maintenance of a physically active status decreases the chance of coronary heart disease by about a third. Exercise also aids in eliminating other conditions such as obesity and high blood pressure that are among the causes of heart disease.

In order to confer these benefits, exercise should require the expenditure of at least 300 Calories per day and should increase the heart rate above 120 beats per minute for at least three continuous minutes. Such exercise benefits metabolic and cardiovascular functions.

Exercises that require the expenditure of 300 Calories include walking, jogging, or running four miles; playing 18 holes of golf (walking); or an hour of bowling, canoeing, or ballroom dancing. The four miles need not be walked all at once; some busy housewives walk a total of six miles in an ordinary day.

None of the Calorie-burning activities mentioned except jogging, running, and possibly canoeing is vigorous enough to elevate the heart rate above 120 beats per minute. Hence the preventive program must include either these or other heart stimulators such as stair climbing—at least three floors, or 50 steps. To be sure the heart rate exceeds 120 beats per minute, the pulse can be counted. A six-second counting technique is easy; by simply adding a zero to the six-second total, the pulse for 60 seconds is obtained. Example: 12 beats in six seconds is a 120 heart rate.

Preliminaries to a program of exercise

The man who has been idle for years does not benefit from a "crash" attempt to make up for lost years of exercise by an exhaustive regimen. This can do more harm than good. After a long layoff, before exercise is undertaken a medical examination that includes an evaluation of response to exercise is prudent. According to specialists in sports medicine, it is more important for a person to seek medical advice before deciding to become inactive; the risks to health are greater than deciding to step up the level of exercise.

Unless exercise is contraindicated, a reconditioning regimen that commences at an easy level (walking) for brief periods (five minutes) will produce cardiovascular, neuromuscular, and metabolic benefits at any age and for persons in the poorest starting physical condition. In severely deconditioned individuals, the exercise heart rate during the first month of training should not exceed 100 per minute. During the month, the duration of daily exercise can be extended from five to ten minutes.

The second month, the exercise heart rate can be advanced to 110 per minute if no discomfort appears. Unusual responses such as pains of any kind call for medical review before exercise is resumed. Again, the duration of the exercise at the elevated heart rate progresses during the month from five to ten minutes. The third month, the exercise heart rate and duration are advanced as before, this time to a heart rate of 120. On days when the exercise does not feel comfortable, it should be stopped and the same program repeated the following day. It is not absolutely necessary to exercise every day, especially on days when ordinary life activities are moderately vigorous.

Exercise benefits do not persist more than a month following cessation of training. The beneficial effects of exercise, like those of food, cannot be stored but must be renewed almost daily.

As age advances, the capacity for strenuous exercise decreases. Maximum heart rate declines with age; an estimate for an adult can be calculated by subtracting his age in years from 220. Example: at age 48 the maximum heart rate is approximately 220 minus 48, or 172.

A safe level of unsupervised exercise in a healthy adult is about 20 beats per minute less than the maximum heart rate. The man aged 48, for example, has an estimated safe limit for unsupervised exercise of 152—172 less 20. Thus it can be seen that for this 48-year-old man the exercise heart rate should be not less than 120 per minute to constitute an effective training stimulus, and not more than 152 to remain within safe limits.

Fat reduction. Protection of the heart is the adult's main goal of exercise, but there are three other goals. The second, already mentioned, is the role 300 Calories' worth of exercise plays in the prevention of obesity. Three hundred Calories per day is approximately the expenditure level that allows a nutritious food intake without storage of fat.

Muscle strengthening. The third adult exercise need is for a loading of muscles above 50 percent of their maximum strength. Such muscle loading can be brief; as little as five seconds just once a day. Lifting an active child or carrying a heavy sack of groceries will prevent loss of muscle tissue and strength.

Circulatory adjustment. The fourth need is to stand up for a total of at least two hours every day. This meets a twofold objective, to maintain bone structure and to preserve orthostatic tone—the adjustment of blood pressure to postural changes that prevents fainting on sudden standing after reclining.

Avoidance of exercise injuries. Injuries that occur during physical activities are usually the result of forces from outside the body. It is doubtful that a muscle can tear itself by the force of its own contraction. When momentum or resistance is applied suddenly, however, the external force may be added to the internal force of contraction and cause damage. In running it is the swing of the leg against partially contracted hamstring muscles that causes the "pulled" muscle.

Most exercise injuries involve connective tissue. Muscle "pulls" usually include injury of the sheets of connective tissue, the fascial tissues, that enclose the muscles. Sore heels and "shin splints" are due to traumatic inflammation of the periosteum, the membrane that encloses each bone. Foot and knee pains are frequently ligamentous in origin. Many of the above listed problems can easily be avoided by progressing gradually from extremely light to heavy training and by using footwear or ground surfaces that absorb the shock of foot strike in jogging or running.

Although the heart muscle is no exception to the rule that a muscle cannot damage itself by exercise, vascular, metabolic, or other disease, if present, may be exacerbated by heavy activity. On the other hand, controlled exercise plays an important role in recovery following coronary heart disease, commencing with extremely light movement after healing of the injured tissue is complete. Through programs of exercise, postcoronary patients may regain full working capacity.

Enlargement of the heart muscle occurs as the result of prolonged periods of continuous heavy exercise. This normal hypertrophy characterizes "athlete's heart" and is a healthy enlargement of the heart muscle resulting from the increased work of the heart to meet the circulatory demands of heavy exercise.

Exhaustion. Exhaustion after many minutes of heavy exercise can be caused by excessive heat storage, "hyperthermia," leading to heat stroke.

When one is near exhaustion, hallucination may occur, leading to aberrant behaviour. Endurance athletes performing at high altitude or in hot weather frequently perceive sights and sounds that are not actually present.

The combined effects of extremely hot or cold baths and fatigue from exercise are potentially dangerous. After exercise the water temperature should be luke warm, 5° (F) or less above body temperature.

The phenomenon of "staleness" or overtraining in athletes is only imperfectly understood. The symptoms are lassitude and poor performance, the latter possibly due to a lessening of the training intensity. There are circulatory and respiratory overreactions to exercise, as in the untrained. A period of rest, a change of activity, or a win following a losing streak often acts to reverse the condition, suggesting that psychosomatic factors may be operating.

Assessment of exercise adequacy. If an adult is moderately active during the day, all of the needs for exercise may be met without the addition of formal exercise. Walking to work, or to shopping, doing manual chores while standing, and hurrying up a hill or up stairs while carrying a fairly heavy load once a day will meet all of an adult's needs for exercise.

There are two ways to see if exercise or other physical activity is adequate. One is by making a daily check of all four exercise needs. The other is to assess physical status along the following guidelines: ability to endure a busier than usual day without fatigue; ability to walk briskly for ten continuous minutes without discomfort; ability to climb three continuous flights of stairs without running out of breath; ability to lift and carry fairly heavy loads without strain; when the abdomen is held taut, the belly feels muscular, not fat; ability to get out of bed quickly without feeling dizzy or faint; bones are not easily broken; participation in an active hobby not less than twice a week; the daily activity level can be classified above the sedentary level, with some physical activity at least ten minutes of every hour all day, or with continuous, intensive exercise an average of not less than five minutes per day. If all of these conditions are met, the individual can be said to be well exercised and in good physical condition.

BIBLIOGRAPHY. P.O. ASTRAND and K. RODAHL, *Textbook of Work Physiology* (1970), a text emphasizing the regulatory mechanisms studied during physical activity; H.A. DE VRIES, *Physiology of Exercise for Physical Education and Athletics* (1966), a text discussing the reasons and methods for developing physical fitness and training for athletics; H.B. FALLS (ed.), *Exercise Physiology* (1968), an authoritative work on the effects of exercise and applications to competitive running, swimming, and diving; M.J. KARVONEN and A.J. BARRY (eds.), *Physical Activity and the Heart: Proceedings* (1967), research reports on the possible effects of exercise in retarding heart disease; L.E. MOREHOUSE and A.T. MILLER, JR., *Physiology of Exercise*, 6th ed. (1971), a frequently revised text written for students of physical education; B. RICCI, *Physiological Basis of Human Performance* (1967), a review of biochemical and physical alterations resulting from exercise.

(L.E.Mo.)

Existentialism

The various philosophies (dating from about 1930) that have been referred to by the term Existentialism have in common an interpretation of human existence in the world that stresses its concreteness and its problematic character.

NATURE OF EXISTENTIALIST THOUGHT AND MANNER

According to Existentialism: (1) Existence is always particular and individual—always *my* existence, *your* existence, *his* existence. (2) Existence is primarily the problem of existence (*i.e.*, of its mode of being); it is, therefore, also the investigation of the meaning of Being. (3) This investigation is continually faced with diverse possibilities, from among which the existent (*i.e.*, man) must make a selection, to which he must then commit himself. (4) Because these possibilities are constituted by man's relationships with things and with other men, existence is always a being-in-the-world—*i.e.*, in a concrete and historically determinate situation that limits or conditions choice. Man is therefore called *Dasein* ("there being") because he is defined by the fact that he exists, or is in the world and inhabits it.

Contrasts and directions of thought

With respect to the first point, that existence is particular, Existentialism is opposed to any doctrine that views man as the manifestation of an absolute or of an infinite substance. It is thus opposed to most forms of Idealism, such as those that stress Consciousness, Spirit, Reason, Idea, or Oversoul. Secondly, it is opposed to any doctrine that sees in man some given and complete reality that must be resolved into its elements in order to be known or contemplated. It is thus opposed to any form of objectivism or scientism since these stress the crass reality of external fact. Thirdly, Existentialism is opposed to any form of necessitarianism; for existence is constituted by possibilities from among which man may choose and through which he can project himself. And, finally, with respect to the fourth point, Existentialism is opposed to any solipsism (holding that I alone exist) or any epistemological Idealism (holding that the objects of knowledge are mental), because existence, which is the relationship with other beings, always extends beyond itself, toward the being of these entities; it is, so to speak, transcendence.

Starting from these bases, Existentialism can take diverse and contrasting directions. It can insist on the transcendence of Being with respect to existence, and, by holding this transcendence to be the origin or foundation of existence, it can thus assume a theistic form. On the other hand, it can hold that human existence, posing itself as a problem, projects itself with absolute freedom, creating itself by itself, thus assuming to itself the function of God. As such, Existentialism presents itself as a radical atheism. Or it may insist on the finitude of human existence—*i.e.*, on the limits inherent in its possibilities of projection and choice. As such, Existentialism presents itself as a humanism.

Diversity of interests and sources

From 1940 on, with the diffusion of Existentialism through continental Europe, its directions have developed in terms of the diversity of the interests to which they are subject: the religious interest, the metaphysical (or nature of Being) interest, the moral and political interest. This diversity of interests is rooted, at least in part, in the diversity of sources on which Existentialism has drawn. One such source has been the subjectivism of the 4th–5th-century theologian, St. Augustine, who exhorted man not to go outside himself in the quest for truth, for it is within him that truth abides. "If you find that you are by nature mutable," he wrote, "transcend yourself." Another source has been the Dionysian Romanticism of Nietzsche, who exalted life in its most irrational and cruel features and made this exaltation the proper task of the "higher man," who exists beyond good and evil. Still another source has been the nihilism of Dostoyevsky, who, in his novels, presented man as continually defeated as a result of his choices and as continually placed by them before the insoluble enigma of himself. As a consequence of the diversity of these sources, Existentialist doctrines have focussed on several aspects of existence.

They have focussed, first, on the problematic character of the human situation, through which man is continually confronted with diverse possibilities or alternatives, among which he may choose and on the basis of which he can project his life.

Second, the doctrines have focussed on the phenomena of this situation and especially on those that are negative or baffling, such as the concern or preoccupation that dominates man because of the dependence of all his possibilities upon his relationships with things and with other men; the dread of death or of the failure of his projects; the "shipwreck" upon insurmountable "limit situations" (death, the struggle and suffering inherent in every form of life, the situation in which everyone daily finds himself); the guilt inherent in the limitation of choices and in the responsibilities that derive from making them; the boredom from the repetition of situations; the absurdity of man's dangling between the infinity of his aspirations and the finitude of his possibilities.

Third, the doctrines have focussed on the intersubjectivity that is inherent in existence and is understood either as a personal relationship between two individuals, I and thou, such that the thou may be another man or God, or as an impersonal relationship between the anonymous mass and the individual self deprived of any authentic communication with others.

Fourth, Existentialism focusses on ontology, on some doctrine of the general meaning of Being, which can be approached in any of a number of ways: through the analysis of the temporal structure of existence; through the etymologies of the most common words—on the supposition that in ordinary language Being itself is disclosed, at least partly (and thus is also hidden); through the rational clarification of existence by which it is possible to catch a glimpse, through ciphers or symbols, of the Being of the world, of the soul, and of God; through existential psychoanalysis that makes conscious the fundamental "project" in which existence consists; or, finally, through the analysis of the fundamental modality to which all the aspects of existence conform—*i.e.*, through the analysis of possibility.

Approaches to the general meaning of Being

There is, in the fifth place, the therapeutic value of existential analysis that permits, on the one hand, the liberating of human existence from the beguilements or debasements to which it is subject in daily life and, on the other, the directing of human existence toward its authenticity; *i.e.*, toward a relationship that is well-grounded on itself, and with other men, with the world, and with God.

The various forms of Existentialism may also be distinguished on the basis of language, which is an indication of the cultural traditions to which they belong and which often explains the differences in terminology among the various authors. The principal representatives of German Existentialism are Martin Heidegger and Karl Jaspers; those of French personalistic Existentialism are Gabriel Marcel and Jean-Paul Sartre; that of French Phenomenology is Maurice Merleau-Ponty; that of Spanish Existentialism is José Ortega y Gasset; that of Russian Idealistic Existentialism is Nikolay Berdyayev (who, however, lived half of his adult life in France); and that of Italian Existentialism is Nicola Abbagnano. The linguistic differences, however, are not decisive for a determination of philosophical affinities. For example, Marcel and Sartre are farther apart than Heidegger and Sartre; and there is greater affinity between Abbagnano and Merleau-Ponty than between Merleau-Ponty and Marcel.

HISTORICAL SURVEY OF EXISTENTIALISM

Many of the theses that Existentialists defend or illustrate in their analyses are drawn from the wider philosophical tradition.

Precursors of Existentialism. The problem of what man is in himself can be discerned in the Socratic imperative "know thyself," as well as in the work of Montaigne and Pascal, a religious philosopher and mathema-

Socrates, Montaigne, and Pascal

tician. Montaigne had said: "If my mind could gain a foothold, I would not write essays, I would make decisions; but it is always in apprenticeship and on trial." And Pascal had insisted on the precarious position of man situated between Being and Nothingness: "We burn with the desire to find solid ground and an ultimate sure foundation whereon to build a tower reaching to the Infinite. But our whole groundwork cracks, and the earth opens to abysses."

The stance of the internal tribunal—of man's withdrawal into his own spiritual interior—which reappears in some Existentialists (in Marcel and Sartre, for example) already belonged, as earlier noted, to St. Augustine. In early-19th-century French philosophy, it was defended by a reformed *Idéologue*, Marie Maine de Biran, who wrote: "Even from infancy I remember that I marvelled at the sense of my existence. I was already led by instinct to look within myself in order to know how it was possible that I could be alive and be myself." From then on, this posture inspired a considerable part of French philosophy.

The theme of the irreducibility of existence to reason, common to many Existentialists, was also defended by a leading German Idealist, F.W.J. von Schelling, as he argued against Hegel in the last phase of his philosophy, and Schelling's polemic, in turn, inspired the scholar usually cited as the father of Existentialism, the religious Dane Søren Kierkegaard.

The requirement to know man in his particularity and, therefore, in terms of a procedure different from those used by science to obtain knowledge of natural objects was confronted by Wilhelm Dilthey, an expounder of historical reason, who viewed "understanding" as the procedure and thus as the proper method of the human sciences. Understanding, according to Dilthey, consists in the reliving and reproducing of the experience of others. Hence it is also a feeling together with others and a sympathetic participation in their emotions. Understanding, therefore, accomplishes a unity between the knowing object and the object known.

The immediate background and founding fathers. The theses of Existentialism found a particular relevance during World War II, when Europe found itself threatened alternately by material and spiritual destruction. Under those circumstances of uncertainty, the optimism of Romantic inspiration, by which the destiny of man is infallibly guaranteed by an infinite force (such as Reason, the Absolute, or Mind) and propelled by it toward an ineluctable progress, appeared to be untenable. Existentialism was moved to insist on the instability and the risk of all human reality, to acknowledge that man is "thrown into the world"—*i.e.*, abandoned to a determinism that could render his initiatives impossible—and to hold that his very freedom is conditioned and hampered by limitations that could at any moment render it empty. The negative aspects of existence, such as pain, frustration, sickness, and death—which 19th-century optimism refused to take seriously because they do not touch the infinite principle that these optimists believed to be manifest in man—become for Existentialism the essential features of human reality.

The thinkers who, by virtue of the negative character of their philosophy, constituted the exception to 19th-century Romanticism thus became the acknowledged masters of the Existentialists. Against Hegelian necessitarianism, Kierkegaard interpreted existence in terms of possibility: dread—which dominates existence through and through—is "the sentiment of the possible." It is the feeling of what can happen to a man even when he has made all of his calculations and taken every precaution. Despair, on the other hand, discovers in possibility its only remedy, for "If man remains without possibilities, it is as if he lacked air." Karl Marx, in holding that man is constituted essentially by the "relationships of work and production" that tie him to things and other men, had insisted on the alienating character that these relationships assume in capitalistic society, where private property transforms man from an end to a means, from a person to the instrument of an impersonal process that

subjugates him without regard for his needs and his desires. Nietzsche had viewed the *amor fati* ("love of fate") as the "formula for man's greatness." Freedom consists in desiring what is and what has been and in choosing it and loving it as if nothing better could be desired.

Emergence as a movement. Contemporary Existentialism reproduces these ideas and combines them in more or less coherent ways. Human existence is, for all the forms of Existentialism, the projection of the future on the basis of the possibilities that constitute it. For some Existentialists (the Germans Heidegger and Jaspers, for example), the existential possibilities, inasmuch as they are rooted in the past, merely lead every project for the future back to the past, so that only what has already been chosen can be chosen (Nietzsche's *amor fati*). For others (such as Sartre), the possibilities that are offered to existential choice are infinite and equivalent, such that the choice between them is indifferent; and for still others (Abbagnano and Merleau-Ponty), the existential possibilities are limited by the situation, but they neither determine the choice nor render it indifferent. The issue is one of individuating, in every concrete situation and by means of a specific inquiry, the real possibilities offered to man. For all the Existentialists, however, the choice among possibilities—*i.e.*, the projection of existence—implies risks, renunciation, and limitation. Among the risks, the most serious is man's descent into inauthenticity or into alienation, his degradation from a person into a thing. Against this risk, for the theological forms of Existentialism (as in Gabriel Marcel, a Socratic dramatist; Karl Barth, a Swiss Neo-orthodoxist; Rudolf Bultmann, a biblical interpreter), there is the guarantee of the transcendent help from God, which in its turn is guaranteed by faith.

Existentialism, consequently, by insisting on the individuality and nonrepeatability of existence (following Kierkegaard and Nietzsche), is sometimes led to regard one's coexistence with other people (held to be, however, an ineluctable fact of the human situation) as a condemnation or alienation of man. Marcel has said that all that exists in society beyond the individual is "expressible by a minus sign," and Sartre has affirmed in his major work *L'Être et le néant* (1943; Eng. trans., *Being and Nothingness*, 1956) that "the Other is the hidden death of my possibilities." For the other forms of Existentialism, however, a coexistence that is not anonymous (as that of a mob) but is grounded on personal communication conditions man's authentic existence.

Existentialism has had ramifications in various areas of contemporary culture. In literature, Franz Kafka, author of haunting novels, walking in Kierkegaard's footsteps, described human existence as the quest for a stable, secure, and radiant reality that continually eludes it (*Das Schloss* [1926; Eng. trans., *The Castle*, 1930]); or he described it as threatened by a guilty verdict about which it knows neither the reason nor the circumstances but against which it can do nothing—a verdict that ends with death (*Der Prozess* [1925; Eng. trans., *The Trial*, 1937]).

The theses of contemporary Existentialism were then diffused and popularized by the novels and plays of Sartre, by the writings of the French novelists and dramatists Simone de Beauvoir and Albert Camus. In *L'Homme révolté* (1951; Eng. trans., *The Rebel*, 1953), Camus described the "metaphysical rebellion" as "the movement by which a man protests against his condition and against the whole of creation." In art, the analogues of Existentialism may be considered to be Surrealism, Expressionism, and in general those schools that view the work of art not as the reflection of a reality external to man but as the free immediate expression of human reality.

Existentialism made its entrance into psychopathology through Karl Jaspers' *Allgemeine Psychopathologie* (1913; Eng. trans., *General Psychopathology*, 1965), which was inspired by the need to understand (in Dilthey's sense) the world in which the mental patient lives, by means of a sympathetic participation in his experience. Later, Ludwig Binswanger, a Swiss psychiatrist of the *Daseinsanalyse* school, in one of his celebrated works,

Kierke-gaard, Marx, and Nietzsche

Broader cultural ramifica-tions

Über Ideenflucht (1933; "On the Flight of Ideas"), inspired by Heidegger's thought, viewed the origin of mental illness as a failure in the existential possibilities that constitute human existence (*Dasein*). From Jaspers and Binswanger, the Existentialist current became diffused and variously stated in contemporary psychiatry.

In theology, Barth's *Römerbrief* (1919; Eng trans., *The Epistle to the Romans*, 1933) started the "Kierkegaard revival," the emblem of which was expressed by Barth himself; it is "the relation of this God with this man; the relation of this man with this God—this is the only theme of the Bible and of philosophy." Within the bounds of this current, on the one hand, there was an insistence upon the absolute transcendence of God with respect to man, who could place himself in relationship with God only by denying himself and by abandoning himself to a gratuitously granted faith. On the other hand, there was the requirement to demythologize the religious content of faith, particularly of the Christian faith, in order to allow the message of the eschatological event (of salvation) to emerge from among the existential possibilities of man.

METHODOLOGICAL ISSUES IN EXISTENTIALISM

The methods that the Existentialists employ in their interpretations have a presupposition in common: the immediacy of the relationship between the interpreter and the interpreted, between the interrogator and the interrogated, between the problem of being and Being itself. The two terms coincide in existence; for the man who poses the question "What is Being?" cannot but pose it to himself and cannot respond without starting from his own being.

Phenomenology, clarification, psychoanalysis

This common ground notwithstanding, each Existentialist thinker has defended and worked out his own method for the interpretation of existence. Heidegger, an Existentialist with ontological (nature of Being) concerns, availed himself of the philosophy of Edmund Husserl, founder of Phenomenology, which, as *logos* of the *phainomenon*, employs speech that manifests or discloses what it is that one is speaking about and that is true—in the etymological use of the Greek word *alētheia* (*i.e.*, the sense of uncovering or manifesting what was hidden). The phenomenon is, from Heidegger's point of view, not mere appearance, but the manifestation or disclosure of Being in itself. Phenomenology is thus capable of disclosing the structure of Being and hence is an ontology of which the point of departure is the being of the one who poses the question about Being, namely man.

Jaspers, an authority in psychopathology as well as in the philosophy of human existence, on the other hand, employed the method of the rational clarification of existence; he maintained that existence, as the quest for Being, is man's effort of rational self-understanding, or universalizing, of communicating—a method that presupposes that existence and reason are the two poles of man's being. Reason is possible existence; *i.e.*, existence that, as Jaspers writes in his *Vernunft und Existenz* (1935; Eng. trans., *Reason and Existenz*, 1955), becomes "manifest to itself and as such real, if, *with*, *through* and *by* another existence, it arrives at itself." This activity, however, is never consummated; thus, when the impossibility of its achievement is recognized, it is changed into faith, into the recognition of transcendence as providing the only possibility of its final achievement.

According to Sartre, the foremost philosopher of mid-20th-century France, the method of philosophy is existential psychoanalysis; *i.e.*, the analysis of the "fundamental project" in which man's existence consists. In contrast to Freudian psychoanalysis, which stops short at the irreducibility of the libido, or primitive psychic drive, existential psychoanalysis tries to determine the "original choice" through which man constructs his world and decides in a preliminary way upon particular choices (which, however, may place in crisis the primordial choice itself).

According to Marcel, a Christian Existentialist philosopher and dramatist, the method of philosophy depends upon a recognition of the mystery of Being (*Le Mystère de l'être* [1951; Eng. trans., *The Mystery of Being*, 1950–51]); *i.e.*, on the impossibility of discovering Being through objective or rational analyses or demonstrations. Philosophy should lead man up, however, to the point of making possible for him "the productive illumination of Revelation."

Finally, according to humanistic Existentialism, as represented by Abbagnano, the leading Italian Existentialist, and by Merleau-Ponty, a French Phenomenologist, the method of philosophy consists of the analysis and the determination—by employing all available techniques including those of science—of the structures that constitute existence; *i.e.*, of the relations that connect man with other beings and that figure, therefore, not only in the constitution of man but in the constitution of the other beings as well.

Mystery of Being and the structures of existence

SUBSTANTIVE ISSUES IN EXISTENTIALISM

Fundamental concepts and contrasts. Both the ontology and manner of human existence are of concern to Existentialism.

Ontic structure of human existence. The fundamental characteristic of Existentialist ontology is the primacy that that study of the nature of existence gives to the concept of possibility. This priority dominated the philosophy of Kierkegaard and also was amply utilized by Husserl, who had explicitly affirmed the ontological priority of possibility over reality. Possibility, however, is not understood by the Existentialists in the purely logical sense as absence of contradiction nor in the sense of traditional metaphysics as potentiality destined to become actuality but, rather, in the sense of ontic or objective possibility, which is the very structure of human existence; it is thus the specific modality of man's being.

Another way of expressing this thesis is the affirmation of Heidegger and Sartre that "existence precedes essence," which signifies that man does not have a nature that determines his modes of being and acting but that, rather, these modes are simply possibilities from which he may choose and on the basis of which he can project himself. In this sense, Heidegger has said that "*Dasein* is always its own possibility," and Sartre has written: "It is true that the possible is—so to speak—an option on being, and if it is true that the possible can come into the world only through a being which is its own possibility, this implies for human reality the necessity of being its being in the form of an option on its being."

As possibility, human existence is the anticipation, the expectation, the projection of the future. The future is its fundamental temporal dimension, to which the present and the past are subordinate and secondary; existence is always stretched out toward the future. As possibility, existence is also transcendence, being beyond, because all of its constitutive possibilities organize it beyond itself toward the other beings of the world and toward the world in its totality. To transcend thus means to move toward something that is not one's own existence; *i.e.*, toward things and toward other men, with which man is related in every situation in which he finds himself.

Yet for some Existentialists, the being of these other entities has a modality that differs from the being of man's existence: their existence is not possible being but real or factual being. To existence, Heidegger contrasts the presence of the things in the world—a presence that assumes, as man takes notice of these things for his needs, the aspect of utilizability. But utilizability is not a simple quality of things; it is their very being. Analogously, Sartre distinguishes the for-itself—the mode of being of man's existence that he identifies, following Descartes and Husserl, with consciousness—from the in-itself, the being or reality of things that he identifies with their utilizability. According to Jaspers, over against the existence of the possible (man, *Dasein*) stands the world as the infinite horizon that encompasses within itself each possible existence and, therefore, cannot itself be encompassed by any one of them. This is a world that is a reality of fact, at the origin of which there is a Being that is pure transcendence and that, therefore, never reveals itself.

Existence as the nothingness of Being

Similarly, the religious forms of Existentialism insist on transcendence, considering it to be the property of the Being that is beyond the existential possibilities and that can enter among them solely under the form of mystery (Marcel) and of the extratemporal revelation of faith (Barth, Jaspers). Marcel, in this regard, has contrasted Being, which is a mystery, with having, which is the condition of man in the world; that is to say, man has objects before him that are foreign to his subjectivity. He tries to organize them and discover the bond that ties them together so as to control and use them.

In all of these doctrines, there is the dominating theme of the contrast between the modality proper to existence, which is possibility, and the modality proper to Being, which is reality or facticity. As a result of this contrast, existence (as possibility) appears as the nothingness of Being, as the negation of every reality of fact. In a brief but famous essay, *Was ist Metaphysik?* (1929), Heidegger affirmed that "Human existence cannot have a relationship with being unless it remains in the midst of nothingness." Rudolf Carnap, a semanticist and leading Logical Positivist, in an equally famous essay, "Überwindung der Metaphysik durch die logische Analyse der Sprache" (1931; "The Elimination of Metaphysics Through Logical Analysis of Language"), criticized this hypostatization (or making real) of Nothingness as one of the grosser fallacies of metaphysics. In truth, Nothingness is, for the Existentialists, possible existence, as the negation of the reality of fact. Sartre has written: "The possible is the *something* which the For-itself lacks *in order* to be itself"; it is what the subject lacks in order to be an object; thus it does not exist except as a lacking.

This is also true of value, which is such insofar as it does not exist. For even when value occurs or is perceived in certain acts, it lies beyond them and constitutes the limit or the goal toward which they aim. Analogously, knowledge, in which the object (the in-itself) presents itself to consciousness (the for-itself), is a relationship of nullification, because the object cannot be offered to consciousness except as that which is not consciousness. Furthermore, another existence is such insofar as it is not mine; thus this negation is "the constitutive structure of the being-of-others."

But this reduction of existence to Nothingness can lead in two directions: it can lead to insisting on the lack of meaning—*i.e.*, on the absurdity of existence and of every possible project—as it does in Sartre, in Camus, and in atheistic Existentialism; or it can lead toward the quest for a more direct relationship of existence with Being, beyond the constitutive possibilities of existence, so that Being reveals itself, at least partly, in existence—through language or through faith or through some mystical form of religiousness, as happens in the later phase of Heidegger's thought, in Jaspers, and in all of the forms of theological Existentialism.

Manner and style of human existence. Existentialism is never a solipsism in the proper sense of the term (that I alone exist), because every existential possibility relates man to things and to other men. Sometimes it is presented as humanism in the sense that it places human destiny in the hands of men themselves. But this version is rejected by all of the currents of the movement that, starting with Heidegger, insist on the priority and the initiative of Being with regard to human existence. The opposition between these two points of view depends on how the different Existentialists solve the problem of freedom.

Destiny versus freedom of choice

Man always finds himself in a situation in which his constitutive possibilities are rooted. For Heidegger and Jaspers, this situation determines the choice that he makes among these possibilities; for Sartre, conversely, the situation is determined by the choice. Existentialism fluctuates in this way between the concept of a destiny in which, like Nietzsche's *amor fati*, man accepts what has already been chosen and the concept of a radical freedom whereby the choices are offered to man in an absolute indifference. From the first point of view, every project of life falls back on or is reduced to the situation from which it starts; thus the possibility of being, of acting, of

willing, of choosing is really, as Jaspers points out in his *Philosophie* (1932), the impossibility of being, acting, willing, and choosing in a manner different from the way things are; *i.e.*, from the factual conditions of the situation. From the second point of view, the fundamental project, which is the primordial choice, has no conditions; as Sartre says: "Since I am free, I project my total possible, but I thereby posit that I am free and that I can always nihilate this first project and make it past." From the first, or deterministic, point of view, the past determines the future and assimilates it to itself; from the second, or libertarian, point of view, the meaning of the past depends upon the present project. In the latter instance, freedom is a kind of damnation: as Sartre affirms: "We said that freedom is not free not to be free and that it is not free not to exist."

A choice, however, is offered to man even from the destinarian point of view: that between understanding and not understanding one's own nothingness. According to Heidegger, a man achieves what he calls "authentic existence" when he understands the impossibility of all of the possibilities of existence—the impossibility of which the sign or term is death. Jaspers affirms, in his turn, that the only choice offered to man is that between accepting or rejecting the situation with which he is identified. The rejection of it, however, is a betrayal that plunges him back into the situation itself.

Existentialist ontology thus fluctuates between Being and Nothingness and concludes by regarding Nothingness as the only possible revelation of Being. In the atheistic version, it is man, as Sartre affirms, who "strives to be God" and consumes himself vainly in the effort. In the cosmological or theological version, it is Being that intervenes, in a way that is more or less mysterious or hidden, to redeem man from Nothingness.

Problems of Existentialist philosophy. The key problems for Existentialism are those of man himself, of his situation in the world, and of his more ultimate significance.

Man and human relationships. Existentialist anthropology is strictly connected with its ontology. The traditional distinction between soul and body is completely eliminated; thus the body is a lived-through experience that is an integral part of man's existence in its relationship with the world. According to Sartre, "In each project of the For-itself, in each perception the body is there; it is the immediate Past in so far as it still touches on the Present which flees it." As such, however, the body is not reduced to a datum of consciousness, to subjective representation. Consciousness, according to Sartre, is constant openness toward the world, a transcendent relationship with other beings and thereby with the in-itself. Consciousness is existence itself, or, as Jaspers says, it is "the manifestation of being." In order to avoid any subjectivistic equivocation, Heidegger went so far as to renounce the use of the term consciousness, preferring the term *Dasein*, which is more appropriate for designating human reality in its totality. For the same reasons, the traditional opposition between subject and object, or between the self and the nonself, loses all sense. *Dasein* is always particular and individual. It is always a self; but it is also always a project of the world that includes the self, determining or conditioning its modes of being.

Self, body, and relationship with the world

All of these modes of being thus arise, as Heidegger shows in his masterpiece *Sein und Zeit* (1927; *Being and Time*, 1962), from the relationship between the self and the world. Heidegger has regarded concern (in the Latin sense of the term) to be the fundamental aspect of this relationship, insofar as it is man's concern to obtain the things that are necessary for him and even to transform them with his work as well as to exchange them so as to make them more suitable to his needs. Concern demonstrates that man is "thrown into the world," into the midst of other beings, so that in order to project himself he must exist among them and utilize them. Being thrown means, for man, being abandoned to the whirling flow of things in the world and to their determinism.

This happens inevitably, according to Heidegger, in inauthentic existence—day-to-day and anonymous existence in which all behaviour is reduced to the same level, made "official," conventional, and insignificant. Chatter, idle curiosity, and equivocation are the characteristics of this existence, in which "One says this" and "One does that" reign undisputed. Anonymous existence amounts to a simple "being together" with others, not a true coexistence, which is obtained only through the acceptance of a common destiny (see below).

Difficulty of intersubjective communication

All of the Existentialists are in agreement on the difficulty of communication; *i.e.*, of well-grounded intersubjective relationships. Jaspers has perhaps been the one to insist most on the relationship between truth and communication. Truths are and can be different from existence. But if fanaticism and dogmatism (which absolutize an historical truth) are avoided on the one hand while relativism and skepticism (which affirm the equivalence of all truths) are avoided on the other, then the only other way is a constant confrontation between the different truths through an always more extended and deepened intersubjective communication.

Sartre, however, denies that there is authentic communication. According to him, consciousness is not only the nullification of things but also the nullification of the other person as other. To look at another person is to make of him a thing. This is the profound meaning of the myth of Medusa. Sexuality itself, which Sartre holds to be an essential aspect of existence, fluctuates between sadism and masochism, in which either the other person or oneself is merely a thing. On this basis, the intersubjective relationship is obviously impossible.

The human situation in the world. Heidegger has pointed to the foundation of the intersubjective relationship in dread. When a man decides to escape from the banality of anonymous existence—which hides the nothingness of existence, or the nonreality of its possibilities, behind the mask of daily concerns—his understanding of this nothingness leads him to choose the only unconditioned and insurmountable possibility that belongs to him: death. The possibility of death, unlike the possibilities that relate him to other things and to other men, isolates him. It is a certain possibility, not through its apodictic evidence but because it continuously weighs upon existence. To understand this possibility means to decide for it, to acknowledge "the possibility of the impossibility of any existence at all" and to live for death. The emotive tonality that accompanies this understanding is dread, through which man feels himself to be "*face to face* with the 'nothing' of the possible impossibility of [his] existence."

But neither the understanding of death nor its emotive accompaniment opens up a specific task for man, a way to transform his own situation in the world. They enable him only to perceive the common destiny to which all men are subject; and they offer to him, therefore, the possibility of remaining faithful to this destiny and of freely accepting the necessity that all men share in common. In this fidelity consists the historicity of existence, which is the repetition of tradition, the return to the possibilities from which existence had earlier been constituted, the wanting for the future what has been in the past. And in this historicity participate not only man but all of the things of the world, in their utilizability and instrumentality, and even the totality of Nature as the locus of history.

Dread, therefore, is not fear in the face of a specific danger. It is rather the emotive understanding of the nullity of the possible, or, as Jaspers says, of the possibility of Nothingness. It has, therefore, a therapeutic function in that it leads human existence to its authenticity. From the fall into factuality into which every project plunges him, man can save himself only by projecting not to project; *i.e.*, either by abandoning himself decisively to the situation in which he finds himself or by being indifferent to any possible project—with regard to which Sartre says, "Thus it amounts to the same thing whether one gets drunk alone or is a leader of nations."

The pivotal point of that conclusion—the conclusion most widely held among the Existentialists and the one in fact often identified with Existentialism—is the antithesis

between possibility and reality. On the one hand, existence is interpreted in terms of possibilities that are not purely logical possibilities or manifestations of a man's ignorance of what exists but are, rather, effective, or ontic, possibilities that constitute man as such; on the other hand, contrasted to possibilities in this sense is a reality, a for-itself, a world, a transcendence that is a factual presence, insurmountable and oppressive, with respect to which possibility is a pure Nothingness. The contradiction to which this antithesis leads becomes clear when the same reality is interpreted in terms of possibility: when the being of things, for example, is reduced to their possibility of being utilized; when the being of other men is reduced to the possibility of anonymous or personal relationships that the individual can have with them; and when the being of transcendence, or of God, is reduced to the possibility of the relationship, although ineffable and mysterious, between transcendence, or God, and man.

The antithesis between possibility and reality

It has been said that a coherent Existentialism should avoid the constant mortal leap between Being and Nothingness; should not confuse the problematic character of existence with the fall into factuality; should not confuse the finitude of possibilities with resignation to the situation, choice with determinism; freedom conditioned by the limits of the situation with the acknowledgment of the omnipresent necessity of the Whole. In this inquiry, it is held, Existentialism could well benefit from a more attentive consideration of science, which it has viewed until now only as a preparatory, imperfect, and objectifying knowledge in comparison with the authentic understanding of Being, which it considers to be a more fundamental mode of the being of man in the world. Science, it is submitted, offers today the example of an extensive and coherent use of the concept of the possible in the key notions that it employs, especially in those branches that are interdisciplinary—among them such notions as indeterminacy, chance, probability, field, model, project, structure, and conditionality.

Some steps in this direction have been taken by Abbagnano and by Merleau-Ponty. According to the latter, considerations of probability are rooted in the being of man, inasmuch as he is situated in the world and invested with the ambiguity of his events. Merleau-Ponty has written in his *Phénoménologie de la perception* (1945):

> Our freedom does not destroy our situation, but is engaged with it. The situation in which we live is open. This implies both that it appeals to modes of privileged resolution and that it is of itself powerless to obtain one of them.

From this point of view, there is always a certain freedom in situations, although its degree varies from situation to situation.

Significance of Being and transcendence. Among the thinkers most frequently mentioned here, the concept of the necessity of Being prevails as the basis of their metaphysical or theological orientations. Heidegger has come more and more to insist on the massive presence of Being in the face of human existence, by attributing to Being all initiative and to man only the possibility of abandoning himself to Being and to the things that are the modes of the language of Being. For Heidegger, Being is interpreted better through the etymology of those words that designate the most common things of daily life than through the analysis of existential possibilities. Jaspers has seen the revelation of transcendence in ciphers—*i.e.*, in persons, doctrines, or poems—all of which can be interpreted as symbols of existential situations and above all of limit situations, the insurmountability of which, in provoking the total "shipwreck" of human possibilities, makes man feel the presence of absolute transcendence. In a less philosophically elaborate form, Being has been understood as mystery by Marcel; as the perfect actuality that guarantees the existential possibilities by Louis Lavelle, a leader of the French *philosophie de l'esprit;* and as the absolute value that man encounters in his own spiritual intimacy by René Le Senne, also of the *philosophie de l'esprit.*

Problems of Existentialist theology. Existentialism has a theological dimension. Though Heidegger rejects the label of atheist, he also denies to the Being of which he speaks the essential qualifications of divinity, inasmuch as it is not the ultimate cause and the Good. But Jaspers, in his last writings, emphasized more and more the religious character of faith in transcendence. Faith is the way to withdraw from the world and to resume contact with the Being that is beyond the world. Faith is life itself, in that it returns to the encompassing Whole and allows itself to be guided and fulfilled by it. Jaspers has even developed a theology of history. He speaks of an axial age, which he places between the 8th and 2nd centuries before Christ, the age in which the great religions and the great philosophers of the Orient arose—Confucius and Lao-tzu, the *Upaniṣads*, Buddha, Zoroaster, the great prophets of Israel—and in Greece the age of Homer and of classical philosophy as well as Thucydides and Archimedes. In this age, for the first time, man became aware of Being in general, of himself, and of his limits. The age in which man now lives, that of science and technology, is perhaps the beginning of a new axial age that is the authentic destiny of man but a destiny that is far off and unimaginable.

For Bultmann, the theologian of the demythologization of Christianity, inauthentic existence is tied to the past, to fact, to the world, while authentic existence is open to the future, to the nonfact, to the nonworld; *i.e.*, to the end of the world and to God. Thus, authentic existence is not the self-projection of man in the world but, rather, the self-projection of man in the love of and obedience to God. But this self-projection is no longer the work of human freedom; it is the saving event that enters miraculously through faith into the future possibilities of man.

In these theological speculations and in others that are comparable, the common presupposition of the Existentialists is recognized—*i.e.*, the gap between human existence and Being. There is either an acknowledgment of that gap, with existence assuming the role of the demonic (the alternative that Sartre and others have all illustrated above all in their literary works), or an acknowledgment of the hidden participation of human existence in Being through a gratuitous initiative on the part of Being.

Kierkegaard had earlier distinguished three stages of existence between which there is neither development nor continuity but gaps and jumps: the aesthetic stage is the one in which one lives for the pleasure of the moment; the ethical stage is the one based on the stability and continuity of life in work and in matrimony; and the religious stage is the one characterized by faith, which is always a "dreadful certainty"—*i.e.*, a dread that becomes certain of a hidden relationship with God.

The ethical and religious stages correspond roughly to what Heidegger and Jaspers call, respectively, the inauthenticity and the authenticity of existence. Art is not as a rule recognized by contemporary Existentialists as an autonomous stage; it is almost always for them an essential manifestation of existence itself. For Jaspers, it is a mode of reading in nature, in history, and in men the cipher of transcendence; *i.e.*, the negative symbol in which transcendence is revealed. According to Camus, it is an aspect of man's revolt against the world. The artist tries to remake the sketch of the world that is before him and to give it the style—that is to say, the coherence and unity—that it lacks. For this purpose, he selects the elements of the world and freely combines them in order to create a value that escapes man continuously but that the artist perceives and tries to salvage from the flux of history.

From this point of view, art would be a way of reshaping the world beyond its factual forms, in order that it might show their negative and troublesome characteristics. The directions of contemporary art that have deliberately forsaken the imitation of reality find their justification in this point of view.

SOCIAL AND HISTORICAL PROJECTIONS OF EXISTENTIALISM

The metaphysical or theological dimension of Existentialism does not leave man with nothing to do. Once the nullity of the existential possibilities is recognized, man cannot but resign himself to Being, which, in one of its new manifestations in the world or beyond it, conducts him to a new epoch. Even someone like José Ortega y Gasset, the leading Spanish Existentialist and writer, who, in examining the social aspects of existence, has characterized the present epoch by the advent of the masses and the socialization of man, has halted at the recognition of the crisis and the total uncertainty that dominates the future of man (*La Rebelión de las masas* [1929; Eng. trans., *The Revolt of the Masses*, 1932]).

On the other hand, humanistic Existentialism has recognized the positive and the to-some-degree determining function that man may have in history. It has insisted, as in Merleau-Ponty, on man's duty to assume the responsibility of an effective action for the transformation of society and, in general, of the world that he inhabits.

Along this line of assuming responsibility, Existentialism has moved toward Marxism, with which it shares the diagnoses of existence as the primordial and ineradicable relationship of man with nature and with society. In the *Critique de la raison dialectique* (1960; "Critique of Dialectical Reason"), Sartre attempted a synthesis between Existentialism and Marxism by modifying the notion of "project" that he defended in *L'Être et le néant* and by utilizing the notion of dialectic as understood by Marx. The project of which existence consists is not the result of an arbitrary choice (as Sartre had previously maintained); it is, instead, that of a conditioning by the objective possibilities that Sartre identifies (as does Marx) with "the material conditions of existence." The project remains, however, that of the particular individual of a unique consciousness—but of a consciousness that tries to become totalized; *i.e.*, to enter into relationship with others so as to constitute, with others, human groups that are more and more comprehensive. In this manner it tends toward a complete and definitive totalization without appeals. Dialectical reason would be precisely such a process of growing totalization; and it becomes, moreover, the true protagonist of history and becomes that with which the interior freedom of any individuals who participate in history is identified.

From the defense of the freedom of the individual, Sartre has thus moved to the defense of the absolute dialectical necessity of history despite its being interiorized and lived by individuals. An historical project of human life that tries to remove the characteristics of inauthenticity or of alienation from existence—a project that may bring Existentialism and Marxism close together—thus ends by losing, in this form, its risky and problematic character and the awareness of the conditions and the modalities of its realization. These features are also lost in the "transcendental project" of a new society elaborated by one of the leaders of the New Left, the German-born American Herbert Marcuse. While insisting on the requirement that the "transcendental project" be "in accord with the real possibilities open at the attained level of the material and intellectual culture," Marcuse entrusts its realization to an impersonal and contemplative Reason, which cannot but invite the "great refusal" of contemporary society.

Having developed in different and contrasting directions, Existentialism has furnished philosophy and the whole of contemporary culture with conceptual tools, of which the nature and techniques of employment have still not been clarified—as, for example, terms like "problematicity," "chance," "condition," "choice," "freedom," and "project." Although these tools can be employed usefully for the interpretation of existence—*i.e.*, to orient philosophical inquiry in the fields of epistemology, ethics, aesthetics, education, and politics—it is nonetheless indispensable that the pivot on which they turn, "possibility," be granted its own ontological status that does not reduce it either to Nothingness or to Being. It is indispensable, moreover, that a positive datum be perceived in possibility, a datum that is verifiable with appropriate techniques and that, while not offering infallible guarantees, allows man to project and to act in the world with calculated risks and with a prudent trust.

BIBLIOGRAPHY

Fundamental texts: SOREN KIERKEGAARD, *Philosophiske smuler* (1844; Eng. trans., *Philosophical Fragments*, 1936);

Marginal notes:

Aesthetic, ethical, and religious levels

Sartre's synthesis of Existentialism and Marxism

Afsluttende uvidenskabelig efterskrift til de philosophiske smuler (1846; Eng. trans., *Concluding Unscientific Postscript*, 1941). FRIEDRICH NIETZSCHE, *Also sprach Zarathustra* (1883–84; *Thus Spoke Zarathustra*, trans. by W. KAUFMANN in *The Portable Nietzsche*, 1954); *Zur Genealogie der Moral* (1877; *Toward a Genealogy of Morals*, trans. by W. KAUFMANN in *Basic Writings of Nietzsche*, 1966). KARL JASPERS, *Psychologie der Weltanschauungen* (1919), the first work of contemporary Existentialism, announcing all of the fundamental theses; *Philosophie*, 3 vol. (1932; Eng. trans., *Philosophy*, vol. 1–2, 1969–70; vol. 3, forthcoming); *Vernunft und Existenz* (1935; Eng. trans., *Reason and Existenz*, 1955). MARTIN HEIDEGGER, *Sein und Zeit* (1927; 10th ed., 1963; Eng. trans., *Being and Time*, 1962); *Was ist Metaphysik?* (1929; "What Is Metaphysics?" trans. by R.F.C. HULL and A. CRICK in *Existence and Being*, 1949); *Einführung in die Metaphysik* (1953; Eng. trans., *An Introduction to Metaphysics*, 1959). GABRIEL MARCEL, *Être et Avoir* (1935; Eng. trans., *Being and Having*, 1949); *Le Mystère de l'être*, 2 vol. (1950; Eng trans., *The Mystery of Being*, 1950–51); *The Philosophy of Existence*, (1949). NICOLA ABBAGNANO, *La struttura dell'esistenza* (1939); N. LANGIULLI (ed. and trans.), *Critical Existentialism* (1969). JEAN-PAUL SARTRE, *L'Être et le néant* (1943; Eng. trans., *Being and Nothingness*, 1956); *L'Existentialisme est un humanisme* (1946; Eng. trans., *Existentialism and Humanism*, 1948). MAURICE MERLEAU-PONTY, *La Structure du comportement* (1942; Eng. trans., *The Structure of Behavior*, 1963); *Phénoménologie de la perception* (1945; Eng. trans., *The Phenomenology of Perception*, 1962).

Special aspects: On Existential literature: HAZEL E. BARNES, *The Literature of Possibility* (1959). On the psychiatric directions of Existentialism: R. MAY, E. ANGEL, and H.F. ELLENBURGER (eds.), *Existence: A New Dimension in Psychiatry and Psychology* (1958). On the relationships of Existentialism with Marxism: WALTER ODAJNYK, *Marxism and Existentialism* (1965). On Existentialist aesthetics: ARTURO FALLICO, *Art and Existentialism* (1962). On Existentialism in pedagogy: G.F. KNELLER, *Existentialism and Education* (1966).

Other writings: MARJORIE GRENE, *Dreadful Freedom* (1948); HELMUT KUHN, *Encounter with Nothingness: An Essay on Existentialism* (1951); MAURICE NATANSON, *A Critique of Jean-Paul Sartre's Ontology* (1951); JAMES COLLINS, *The Existentialists: A Critical Study* (1952); WILLIAM BARRETT, *What Is Existentialism?* (1964); ADOLPH LICHTIGFELD, *Jaspers' Metaphysics* (1954); MARJORIE GRENE, *Martin Heidegger* (1957); THOMAS LANGAN, *The Meaning of Heidegger* (1959); "Studies on Existentialist Themes," *Buffalo Studies*, vol. 4 (1968); MARY WARNOCK, *Existentialism* (1970).

(N.Ab.)

Exploration, Surface and Underground

Exploration has played a historic role in human affairs, probably since before recorded times; the 20th century has witnessed the last stages of exploration on the surface of the earth and the first explorations of space. For an account of the history of early exploration of the earth's surface, see GEOGRAPHY. For a history of the exploration of space, see SPACE EXPLORATION. The present article focusses on modern earth exploration. Because of the facility of surface exploration by aircraft, the earth's surface has virtually lost its mystery; therefore scientific attention today is primarily directed beneath the surface of the earth.

The era of scientific exploration. Scientific interest in the earth increased considerably during the 19th century. Early efforts were characterized by a strong element of national competition and a lack of international coordination. After World War I a new era of international cooperation began. A dozen international scientific unions were coordinated by the International Council of Scientific Unions. Developments in communication and transportation during World War II improved the possibilities of international cooperation in scientific exploration. After World War II the United Nations Educational, Scientific, and Cultural Organization (UNESCO) provided a centre for coordination and a certain amount of financial assistance for the exchange of information.

One of the first major international scientific efforts was a systematic study of the earth and its environment undertaken by more than 70 nations during the International Geophysical Year, which began on July 1, 1957, and was ultimately extended to December 31, 1959. The exploration of Antarctica was greatly advanced by inter-ested nations, which on December 1, 1959, signed the Antarctic Treaty, suspending all territorial claims in Antarctica for a period of 30 years and promoting international cooperation in scientific research. At the end of the International Geophysical Year the work was continued under special committees for oceanographic, antarctic, and space research. Later, an Upper Mantle Committee was established by the International Council of Scientific Unions to coordinate the Upper Mantle Project, an international program of research on the solid earth that began in 1961.

PURPOSES OF EXPLORATION

Only about 30 percent of the earth's surface lies above sea level, and of this only about one-third, or 10 percent, is generally suitable for human occupation; the remainder is either too cold, too dry, too high, or too infertile. Modern exploration of the earth is directed largely beneath the surface in search of new mineral, fuel, and water resources or for the planning and construction of human facilities. The most interesting, however, is probably that carried out for scientific purposes.

Scientific exploration. Present knowledge of the earth's interior is based on indirect observations and is therefore subject to considerable uncertainty. The International Upper Mantle Committee has done much to encourage participating countries to extend scientific knowledge by a coordinated program of drilling into the crust. One of the most ambitious exploration projects of the last decade was the abortive U.S. Project Mohole, the primary objective of which was to obtain a core record through the layers of the earth's crust and the upper part of the underlying mantle. The ultimate objective was to drill to a total depth of 35,000 feet (10,500 metres), of which 15,000 feet (4,500 metres) was through water, from a ship stationed at a point in the ocean where the thickness of the earth's crust is minimum. Information from such boring would include heat flow measurements, thermal and electrical conductivity values, seismic velocities (that is, the speed at which earthquakes and tremors travel), radioactive and magnetic values, and other physical properties of the crust and upper mantle helpful in determining the origin and character of the earth.

Project Mohole

Drilling grows progressively more expensive; a 25,000-foot (7,600-metre) borehole may cost 10 times as much as a 10,000-foot (3,000-metre) borehole in the same material. Consequently, after an expenditure of some $20 million the National Science Foundation withdrew its support of the project in 1967 before the deep hole had been begun.

Another venture is the Deep Sea Drilling Project begun in 1966 and aimed at the recovery of cored samples from the sedimentary layer of the deep ocean basins. Scientific planning for the program was conducted under the auspices of the Joint Oceanographic Institutions for Deep Earth Sampling, a consortium of oceanographic institutes and universities.

In addition to deep-drilling activities, an extensive cooperative program of shallow and intermediate drilling is proceeding under the guidance of the Upper Mantle Committee. In this program scientists are profiting from a great deal of expertise acquired by the resource industries in subsurface exploration.

Resource exploration. Exploration for new resources is usually carried out in remote areas with indirect techniques which measure gravity or magnetic anomalies or the seismic response of the earth to artificially induced shock waves. Seismic methods are most commonly used for oil and gas exploration in areas where the geological structure shows promise. If the seismic survey is encouraging it is followed by drilling because the actual occurrence can be proved only when the drill penetrates the deposit. The cost of drilling depends on the depth, the type of material through which the drill must pass, and the remoteness of the area. The deepest hole ever drilled, just over 25,000 feet (7,600 metres), is located in Texas.

Economic mineral resources usually are found nearer

the surface than are oil and gas reservoirs. The largest mines in the world are open-pit mines, although the deepest mine was dug for gold (11,246 feet or 3,410 metres) in South Africa. Though many large mineral resources have been discovered by individual prospectors, airborne devices for detecting slight changes in the earth's magnetic field are much more important today.

Water supply. Water is one of the oldest motives for exploration. Almost all water comes to the earth as precipitation; some evaporates from the surface or is used by vegetation, while some runs off into lakes and streams, or sinks into the ground. Most urban supplies have always been obtained from lakes and rivers or from storage reservoirs designed to provide a continuous supply when rainfall is seasonal. Even when supplies are reasonably abundant, large amounts of water may be taken from the ground. The city of London, for example, obtains about one-sixth of its municipal water supply from wells.

Urban
water con-
sumption
Ancient villages required only about 3 to 5 gallons (11–20 litres) of water per person per day; modern cities consume more than 60 gallons (227 litres) per person per day. Once a city is established, its steadily increasing demand for water must be met and often groundwater is the only source. The little Middle Eastern nation of Kuwait, rich in oil but desperate for freshwater, which has to be either imported or distilled from the sea, persisted in exploration until the discovery, by drilling, of a significant source of groundwater in 1960.

Exploration for construction. Though the depth of exploration required for surface construction is seldom more than 100 feet (30 metres), for very heavy structures and for tunnels it is considerably deeper. The cost of the investigation is a small fraction of total construction cost, but for major structures, such as large dams, long-span bridge foundations, and deep or underwater tunnels, such exploration may be critically important. Exploration may seek information on earth materials relating to potential excavation difficulties, sand and gravel supplies for construction, groundwater characteristics, the stability of natural slopes, flooding hazards, and earthquake potential.

METHODS OF SUBSURFACE EXPLORATION

Exploration methods are of two general types: direct and indirect. Direct methods involve the collection and examination of samples; indirect methods are all those that do not. The methods selected for any particular purpose are necessarily based on economic considerations. Large programs are conducted in stages, with plans for each stage made on the basis of information derived from earlier stages.

Use of maps. Ordinary topographic maps show boundaries between water and land, contours of elevation, and the location of important features, but give no indication of subsurface conditions. Soil, or pedologic, maps describe the surface soils and their value for agricultural purposes. Geologic maps show the thicknesses and relative positions of bedrock materials and surface soils lying above them. All new subsurface investigations, whether for oil, minerals, construction materials, water supply, or civil-engineering construction, begin with the study of available maps. Map information is supplemented by studies of geological and engineering reports describing previous experiences in the area.

Remote sensing. The earliest form of remote sensing was visual observation from hills and treetops, often for military purposes. Balloons widened the horizon and aerial photography provided a permanent record of the view. Modern photographs from spacecraft and satellites show huge sections of the earth in minute detail. Even more remarkable than the ability to photograph is the development of photo interpretation into a reliable technique.

Photographs from aircraft, because they exaggerate the relief features of the earth when viewed stereoscopically, can be used to prepare extremely accurate contour maps at a fraction of the cost of ground surveys. Trained interpreters can identify landforms, interpret geology, locate sand and gravel deposits, predict landslide and flooding hazards, and conduct inventories of natural resources. In remote areas aerial photographs guide the selection of campsites and access routes; in built-up areas they assist land-use planning, expose traffic problems, and assist with man's studies and activities in many other ways.

Radar (*q.v.*), perfected during World War II, is an especially valued tool for remote sensing because it does not require clear weather conditions, is effective at night, and can penetrate dense vegetation. Radar operates near the long-wavelength end of the electromagnetic spectrum, well outside the visible light range, and provides an indirect image by scanning its target. Another recently developed method of imagery is the scanning infrared sensor that, operating at wavelengths between radar and visible light, provides relative surface temperature information and is useful in detecting moist areas, underground water, and other terrain features.

Sensors now being developed extend into the microwave region or beyond it into radio-frequency ranges and can penetrate the earth to a considerable depth. Their practical application is based on the premise that all materials have characteristic signatures at different wavelengths. Most of the early development took place in the military sphere and the results were not generally available in the early 1970s.

Geophysical methods. Geophysical exploration makes use of variations in the physical properties of earth materials to explore geologic structures. The most notable variations in earth materials are related to their density, magnetism, elasticity, and electrical conductivity; and the four related major geophysical methods are gravitational, magnetic, seismic, and electrical. Geophysical methods find practical application in the search for oil and minerals and, in engineering, in building-foundation investigations. Since geophysical methods are indirect and require careful interpretation, they are most effective when used in conjunction with other more direct observations.

Major geo-
physical
methods

The gravity method is based on the fact that the force of gravity varies from point to point on the surface because of variations in density of the underlying strata. A variation between a measured value and the computed normal value for any point will, therefore, reveal irregularities in the distribution of mass in the earth's crust. Gravity measurements are usually made with a pendulum, a torsion balance, or a gravimeter in which gravity is compared with an elastic spring force.

The law of magnetic attraction is similar to the law of gravitation and the method of searching for magnetic anomalies in the earth is similar to the gravitational method. Some remarkable mineral discoveries have been made with specially designed airborne magnetometers. Like gravity measurements, magnetic observations are subject to wide interpretation and require supplementary investigation for most uses.

The seismic method of exploration is based on the fact that shock waves travel through earth materials at speeds ranging from a few hundred to many thousands of feet per second, depending upon the elastic properties of the material, and that precise measurements can be made of the time required for an induced shock wave to travel between two or more points (see illustration). The shock wave is received at a series of detectors placed on the surface in such a way that a distinction can be made between reflected (directly returned) waves and refracted (bent) waves. Depths from the surface to changes in strata can be estimated from the arrival times of reflected and refracted waves if the wave velocity in the natural materials is known. In engineering, the method is particularly useful in estimating the depth of the soil over bedrock and in detecting the differences in the subsurface geology between two boreholes. In oil exploration it is most useful in searching large areas for promising geologic structures.

The variations in the electrical properties of soils, rocks, and minerals are used in a variety of ways to explore beneath the surface. Some ore bodies generate natural electrical currents by which they can be detected. The most

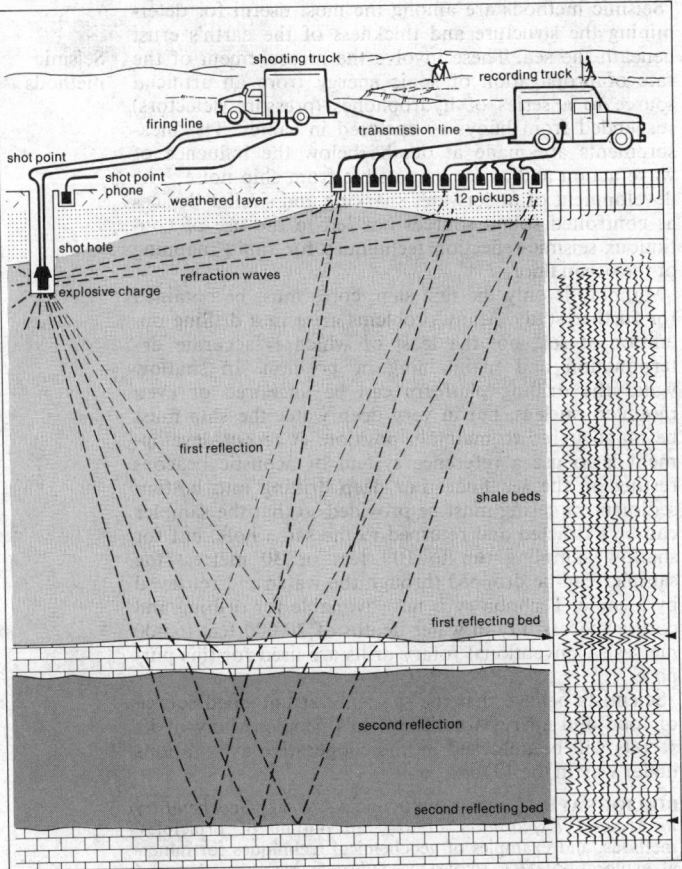

Seismic reflection method for geophysical prospecting. Field equipment is shown above, seismic wave paths below, and a seismogram at the right.

common method is to place electrodes in the ground and measure the resistance between them. The method is useful for detecting the depth of surface soil and rocks, subsurface anomalies, water-bearing strata, and other necessary information at large construction sites.

Geochemical prospecting. Geochemistry is concerned with the distribution and movement of chemical elements in the earth over long periods of time. Geochemical prospecting involves the systematic measurement of trace contents of certain elements in natural materials such as rock, surface materials, vegetation, and water that may indicate geochemical anomalies or patterns associated with the presence of ore in the vicinity. Early prospectors learned to associate various ore bodies with stains or the colour of the water or even with types of vegetation, but the large-scale systematic investigation of geochemistry as a method of prospecting was not begun until the early 1930s. The method has been facilitated by the development of rapid and reliable techniques of chemical analysis. It is still in an early stage of use and requires experienced judgment for planning, sampling, and interpretation of results.

Excavation, boring, and sampling. The indirect methods of exploration already described, however useful, cannot prove an oil or mineral deposit or ensure the adequacy of a construction site. They must be followed by more direct observation of the earth materials. This is usually achieved by boring, though for shallow observations it is often economical to excavate pits or trenches to the required depth. Construction excavations are watched carefully for confirmation of predicted ground conditions and, if necessary, designs may be changed at this stage.

Boring

The first questions to be settled, whether exploring for oil or evaluating a building site, are the number, type, and depth of borings. These decisions are largely dependent on the information gathered by indirect methods. In exploring for oil or minerals the first boring is aimed at the supposed deposit. Subsequent borings, if any, are

dictated by the geological information revealed by the first. In evaluating a specific construction site, the boring program depends on the size, value, and type of proposed construction, the anticipated properties and variability of the subsurface materials, and the amount of previous experience in the area. Variations in the program are usually required as the investigation proceeds.

The principal purpose of borings is to obtain samples of the ground for examination and testing. In resource exploration the soil above the bedrock is usually merely a barrier in the path of exploration. In civil engineering works, however, it is usually the main object of the investigation. Consequently, the tools for drilling and sampling are many and varied.

When the main objective is to penetrate the earth, a percussion or churn drill is often used. This consists of a heavy bit that is alternately raised and dropped to chop through the soil or rock. The various strata are evaluated both by the rate of drilling and by the sample cuttings that are periodically taken. This method is still widely used for finding water, but for oil it has been replaced by rotary drilling in which the hole is advanced by a rapidly rotating bit and the cuttings are removed by a pressure circulated drilling fluid. For shallow drilling in soils, a variety of hand- and power-operated augers are used.

It is important to know how well samples required for engineering evaluation represent the actual subsurface condition. It is impossible to obtain perfect samples of soil; the stresses on an element in the ground are changed by the insertion of the sampler and by the extraction of the sample, although these effects are minimized by keeping the borehole full of water or mud and by use of ingeniously designed samplers. The best samples of soft cohesive soils are obtained in thin-walled piston samplers. The sampler is inserted to the bottom of the borehole with the piston at the lower end; the piston is then held in place while the thin-walled tube is advanced into fresh soil. With the piston locked in position at the top of the tube, the assembly is withdrawn, carrying the sample with it; the tube is detached, sealed at both ends, and transported carefully to the laboratory.

Piston samplers

It is extremely difficult to obtain good samples of sands and gravels, because of their poor cohesion. In some cases the ground has been frozen artificially and cored, though this is very expensive. Various materials have been injected into sands and gravels to stabilize them for sampling, but this involves the complication of removing the injection material. Some recent experiments with chemical grouts (mortars) have been successful.

Strangely, rock is often the most difficult material to sample for engineering purposes, partly because of the difficulty of drilling. The first modern diamond core drill was built in 1862 by a Swiss engineer. It is standard equipment for mining and engineering exploration. Difficulties arise, not with the ability to obtain good cores from sound rock, but with the problem of identifying joints, fissures, and other defects in the rock. These are the features that control the engineering design, and not only may they be missed but the soundness of the core recovered may give a misleading impression of the mass.

On-site testing. The limitations of sampling and laboratory testing have led to the development of many tools for assessing the structural properties of soils on-site. The simplest test is to observe the effort required to drive or push a rod into the soil, but this reveals very little information. A widely used dynamic method, called the standard penetration test, measures the number of blows applied in a standard manner to a standard sampler to cause a penetration of a certain depth. The results of such tests have been correlated with the properties of many soils. This method has the advantage that a sample of the soil is obtained at the same time. A European method involves using a standard size cone on the end of a string of drill rods. Such dynamic penetration tests are useful only for evaluating coarse granular soils. Static penetration tests are used for fine-grained cohesive soils. Of these the "Dutch cone" is the best known. It is similar to the dynamic cone, but it is pushed slowly into the soil at a constant rate and the resistance to penetration is measured.

Another method of measuring soil strength employs a "vane borer." Though various designs are available, this device is essentially a four-bladed vane attached to the bottom of a rod. The assembly is pushed into the soil and then rotated slowly, causing the soil to shear along a cylindrical surface. The shearing resistance is computed from the measured torque (twist) required.

A fairly recent device, the pressure meter, is a flexible cylindrical bag that can be inserted into a borehole and expanded under increasing pressure. The degree of deformation of the material surrounding the borehole for a given amount of pressure is used to compute the structural properties of the material. Though used in all soils and rocks, it is especially useful for those that cannot be properly sampled.

Use of the borehole camera

Miniature geophysical tools have been developed to provide measurements of electrical and nuclear properties of earth materials. One of the most useful devices for evaluation in place is the borehole camera, a specially designed instrument that is lowered down small-diameter boreholes to take photographs through 360 degrees at any level. These devices can be hooked up to closed-circuit television for continuous viewing. They are especially useful in studying boreholes in defective rock.

Sampling of permafrost and ice. Exploration in permafrost regions is complicated by their remoteness and the frozen ground. Aerial photographs and other indirect exploration methods are significant in these regions because they are usually so far from easy transport. For many engineering purposes, however, because it is necessary to know how much ice is in the soil, samples must be obtained.

For shallow sampling, test pits are commonly dug, especially in stony soils or gravel. If these are excavated by hand during summer, natural thawing may aid the operation. The use of jackhammers to depths of 20 or 30 feet (6 to 9 metres) is now more common. Core drilling of stony material is extremely difficult, but it is quite successful for frozen fine-grained soils. Photographs record ice contents of fresh core samples because preservation in frozen condition is often difficult. Methods of diamond core drilling of rock are used for coring frozen soils; water, air, or oil is employed as the drilling fluid. Special precautions must be taken to prevent thawing of the core; drilling is usually continued without interruption to prevent "freezing-in" of the drill or caving of the hole.

Drilling for oil through permafrost introduces the problem of surface thawing and settlement due to melting ice. The warm drilling fluid from depth not only thaws the ground around the hole but, unless it is carefully controlled, can cause the whole area around the huge drill rig to deteriorate. In some cases the footings for the rigs have been underlain by refrigerated pipes to preserve the permafrost.

Special coring tools have been developed for taking ice samples. One of these consists of a perforated tube with saw teeth around the lower end. Samples to relatively shallow depths in glaciers have been easily obtained with this device. Samples to depths greater than 1,000 feet 300 metres) have been obtained in Antarctica, using a rotary well-drilling rig with compressed air as the drilling fluid. If samples are not required, a boring can be advanced by a thermal drill, an electrical resistance element on the end of a rod. Drilling of ice covers on lakes and rivers can be accomplished with a variety of hand- or machine-powered auger drills or core augers. Lightweight equipment is normally not as important as it is for the drilling of glaciers far from access routes.

Underwater exploration. Until recently, only very crude data about the depths of seawater and the character of the sea bottom were available (see also UNDERSEA EXPLORATION). Observations of the British "Challenger" expedition from 1872 to 1876 provided the first soundings and samples from the ocean bottom, but these were too infrequent to provide a serious picture. The development of echo-sounding devices in the early 1920s showed, for the first time, the actual irregularities of the seabed, and only since World War II has enough information been gathered to provide reliable ocean-floor maps.

Seismic methods

Seismic methods are among the most useful for determining the structure and thickness of the earth's crust beneath the sea. These involve the measurement of the rate of propagation of sonic energy from an artificial source to a series of hydrophones (pressure detectors) suspended from buoys or enclosed in cables. The measurements are made at depths below the influence of wave action and as far as possible from ship noise. The development of underwater sparking and similar devices as controlled sound sources has led to the use of continuous seismic-reflection techniques for rapid mapping of the ocean floor.

Mapping is only the first step; cores must be obtained for further study. Many problems arise in a drilling operation at sea, not the least of which is accurate determination and maintaining of position. In shallow water the drilling platform can be anchored or even mounted on legs, but in very deep water the ship must be manoeuvred to maintain position. A recent development is to use a reference system of acoustic beacons resting on the sea floor. For deep drilling into bottom sediments a casing must be provided so that the sampler can be extracted and returned to the same hole, but for shallow sampling (up to 100 feet or 30 metres) the sampler can be dropped through the water and retrieved by a cable. Technology is now available for drilling and coring successfully in water depths of 20,000 feet (6,000 metres). Conventional rotary drills are used for this purpose.

Scientists believe that the sea is a yet untapped source of food and energy for the world's people. Many of its secrets will be unlocked by the cooperative explorations under way in the 1970s.

BIBLIOGRAPHY. H.E. HAWKES and J.S. WEBB, *Geochemistry in Mineral Exploration* (1962), an outline of principles, methods, and examples of geochemical techniques for mineral exploration; M.J. HVORSLEV, *Subsurface Exploration and Sampling of Soils for Civil Engineering Purposes* (1949), a comprehensive general review of all methods used in subsurface exploration and sampling of subsurface materials; D.P. KRYNINE and W.R. JUDD, *Principles of Engineering Geology and Geotechnics* (1957), a reference book for practicing civil engineers and engineering geologists outlining the application of the earth sciences to the solution of civil engineering problems; R.F. LEGGET, *Geology and Engineering*, 2nd ed. (1962), a comprehensive review of the vital relationship between geology and civil engineering illustrated with hundreds of references to important case records from around the world; AMERICAN SOCIETY OF PHOTOGRAMMETRY, *Manual of Photographic Interpretation* (1960), a series of papers describing the development, technology, and use of aerial photography; *Permafrost International Conference: Proceedings* (1963), a collection of individual papers describing the occurrence, character, and properties of perennially frozen ground in the world; J.R. SCHULTZ and A.B. CLEAVES, *Geology in Engineering* (1955), an introduction to geology outlining the geologic principles and methods used in engineering with special emphasis on soils; F.P. SHEPARD, *The Earth beneath the Sea* (1959), a nontechnical outline of the geology of the ocean floor including discussions of some of its unusual characteristics and the factors affecting them; U.S. DEPARTMENT OF AGRICULTURE, *Water: The Year Book of Agriculture* (1955), a collection of papers containing much useful information on the nature, behaviour, and conservation of water; J.T. WILSON, *I.G.Y.: The Year of the New Moons* (1961), a description of the characteristics of the earth observed during the International Geophysical Year, written in terms understandable to the layman; KARL TERZAGHI and RALPH B. PECK, *Soil Mechanics in Engineering Practice*, 2nd ed. (1967), a comprehensive text including a review of the purpose, scope, and methods of soil exploration for civil engineering purposes; AMERICAN SOCIETY FOR TESTING AND MATERIALS, *Sampling of Soil and Rock* (1971), proceedings of a symposium dealing with the factors affecting the quality of soil and rock samples.

(C.B.C.)

Explosives

An explosive is any substance or device that can be made to produce a volume of rapidly expanding gas in an extremely brief period. There are three fundamental types: mechanical, nuclear, and chemical. A mechanical explosive is one that depends on a physical reaction, such as overloading a container with compressed air. Such a device has some application in mining, where the release of gas from chemical explosives may be undesirable, but otherwise is very little used. A nuclear explosive is one in which a sustained nuclear reaction can be made to take place with almost instant rapidity, releasing large amounts of energy. Experimentation has been carried on with nuclear explosives for possible petroleum extraction purposes; for a discussion of this field see PETROLEUM AND GAS EXTRACTION. Military applications of nuclear explosives are discussed under NUCLEAR WEAPONS. This article is concerned with chemical explosives, which account for virtually all explosive applications in engineering up to the 1970s.

TYPES OF CHEMICAL EXPLOSIVES

Basically, chemical explosives are of two types: (1) detonating, or high, explosives and (2) deflagrating, or low, explosives. Detonating explosives, such as TNT and dynamite, are characterized by extremely rapid decomposition and development of high pressure, whereas deflagrating explosives, such as black and smokeless powders, involve merely fast burning and produce relatively low pressures. Under certain conditions, such as the use of large quantities and a high degree of confinement, some normally deflagrating explosives can be caused to detonate.

Detonating explosives are usually subdivided into two categories, primary and secondary. Primary explosives detonate by ignition from some source such as flame, spark, impact, or other means that will produce heat of sufficient magnitude. Secondary explosives require a detonator and, in some cases, a supplementary booster. A few explosives can be both primary and secondary depending on the conditions of use.

BLACK POWDER

Chinese
fireworks

It may never be known with certainty who invented the first explosive, black powder, which is a mixture of saltpetre (potassium nitrate), sulfur, and charcoal (carbon). The consensus is that it originated in China in the 10th century, but that its use there was almost exclusively in fireworks and signals. It is possible that the Chinese also used black powder in bombs for military purposes and there is written record that, in mid-13th century, they put it in bamboo tubes to propel stone projectiles.

There is, however, some evidence that the Arabs invented black powder. By about 1300, certainly, they had developed the first real gun, a bamboo tube reinforced with iron, which used a charge of black powder to fire an arrow.

A strong case can also be made that black powder was discovered by the English medieval scholar Roger Bacon, who wrote explicit instructions for its preparation in 1242, in the strange form of a Latin anagram, difficult to decipher. But Bacon read Arabic, and it is possible that he got his knowledge from Arabic sources.

Some scholars attribute the invention of firearms to an early 14th-century German monk named Berthold Schwarz. In any case they are frequently mentioned in 14th-century manuscripts from many countries, and there is a record of the shipment of guns and powder from Ghent to England in 1314.

Not until the 17th century was black powder used for peaceful purposes. There is a doubtful claim that it was used in mining operations in Germany in 1613, and fairly authentic evidence that it was employed in the mines of Schemnitz, Hungary, in 1627. For various reasons, such as high cost, lack of suitable boring implements, and fear of roof collapse, the use of black powder in mining did not spread rapidly, though it was widely accepted by 1700. The first application in civil engineering was in the Malpas Tunnel of the Canal du Midi in France in 1679.

Composition of black powder

For 300 years the unvarying composition of black powder has been approximately 75 percent saltpetre (potassium nitrate), 15 percent charcoal, and 10 percent sulfur. The saltpetre was originally extracted from compost piles and animal wastes. Deposits found in India provided a source for many years. During the 1850s tremendous quantities of sodium nitrate were discovered in Chile, and saltpetre was formed by reaction with potassium chloride, of which there was a plentiful supply.

Chilean nitrate was not at first considered satisfactory for the manufacture of black powder because it too readily absorbed moisture. Lammot du Pont, an American industrialist, solved this problem and started making sodium nitrate powder in 1858. It became popular in a short time because, although it did not produce as high a quality explosive as potassium nitrate, it was suitable for most mining and construction applications and was much less expensive. To distinguish between them, the potassium nitrate and sodium nitrate versions came to be known as A and B blasting powder respectively. The A powder continued in use for special purposes that required its higher quality, principally for firearms, military devices, and safety fuses.

Manufacture of black powder. Manufacture of black powder was accomplished originally by hand methods. Ingredients were ground together with a mortar and pestle. The next step was to use crushing devices of wood (wooden stamps), also operated by hand, in wooden or stone bowls. The stamping process was gradually mechanized and, about 1435, the first powder mill driven by water power was erected near Nuremberg, Germany.

Metallic crushing devices, introduced in the early 1800s, slowly and steadily replaced the wooden stamp mills.

In the modern process, charcoal and sulfur are placed in a hollow drum along with heavy steel balls. As the drum rotates, the steel balls pulverize the contents; this device is called a ball mill. The saltpetre is crushed separately by heavy steel rollers. Next, a mixture of several hundred pounds of saltpetre, charcoal, and sulfur is placed in a heavy iron device shaped like a cooking pan. There it is continuously turned over by devices called plows, then ground and mixed by two rotating iron wheels, which weigh from 10 to 12 tons each. The process takes several hours; water is added periodically to keep the mixture moist.

The product of the mills is next put through wooden rolls to break up the larger lumps and is then formed into cakes under 3,000–4,000 pounds per square inch pressure. Coarse-toothed rolls crack the cakes into manageable pieces and the corning mill, which contains rolls of several different dimensions, reduces them to the sizes desired.

Glazing (the next operation) consists of tumbling the grains for several hours in large wooden cylinders, during which friction rounds off the corners, and, aided by forced air circulation, brings the powder to a specified moisture content. The term glazing derives from the fact that graphite is added during this process, forming a thin film over the individual powder grains. Glazed powder flows more readily than unglazed powder and is more moisture resistant.

After glazing the powder is graded by sieves into different sizes. Packaging is usually in 25-pound (11-kilogram) kegs.

Because the burning of black powder is a surface phenomenon, a fine granulation burns faster than a coarse one. Grain sizes are designated as F, 2F, etc., up to 7F, which is the finest, and from C up as the grains become larger. For the A powder the letter indicating the fineness becomes 3FA, etc., and if the powder is glazed, this is followed by the letter g; e.g., 3FAg. For many years the B blasting material was offered in pellet as well as granular form. Four pellets, each two inches (five centimetres) in length and from 1⅛ to 2½ inches (2.75 to 6.25 centimetres) in diameter, were packed in waxed paper cartridges. Each pellet had a hole through its centre to accommodate a safety fuse or an electric device used to ignite the powder. Pelleted powder was used almost entirely in underground coal mines, but federal regulations now prohibit both it and the granular type.

Ignition of black powder. Black powder is relatively insensitive to shock and friction and must be ignited by flame or heat. In the early days such devices as torches, glowing tinder, and heated iron rods were used to ignite the powder and, in most cases, a train of the powder was led to the main charge in order to give the firer time to get to a safe place.

In cannons a small touchhole was drilled into the breech and filled with fine powder. Ignition was usually by means of a slow-burning punk. The same principle was employed in flintlock muskets and rifles except that ignition resulted from sparks produced by contact between flint and steel.

Percussion methods of firing guns have long been in universal use. In the most common procedure, pulling the trigger releases a hammer, which strikes an impact-sensitive explosive mixture. This explosion then ignites the black powder or other powder charge.

Some black powder is still used as the propellant in guns in spite of the superiority of smokeless powder. Besides antique gun experts, who employ it mostly with hand-loaded shells and cartridges, hunters in South and Central America still use guns that require black powder.

In mining, a succession of crude means for ignition (fuses) included straws filled with pulverized black powder, reeds in which the pith was scooped out and replaced with a paste of powder and water (later bound with string and dried), or powder paste spread on wool threads. All of these fuses were ignited either by a piece of wool yarn impregnated with sulfur, called a sulfur mannikin, or some equivalent slow-burning device. A later, and extremely popular, type of fuse was formed of goose quills. The quills were cut so that they could be inserted one into the other and then filled with powder. Quill fuses could be ignited directly, that is, without any delaying element such as the sulfur mannikin. Unfortunately, their reliability was not high, and they often burned erratically.

Safety fuse. A major contributor to progress in the use of explosives was William Bickford, a leather merchant who lived in the tin-mining district of Cornwall, England. Familiar with the frequency of accidents in the mines and the fact that many of them were caused by deficiencies inherent in the quill fuse, Bickford sought to devise an improvement. In 1831 he conceived the safety fuse: a core of black powder tightly wrapped in textiles, one of the most important of which was jute yarn. The present-day version is not very different from the original model. The cord is coated with a waterproofing agent, such as asphalt, and is covered with either textile or plastic.

The safety fuse provided a dependable means for conveying flame to the charge. Its timing (the time required for a given length to burn) was amazingly accurate and consistent, compared to that of its predecessors, and it was much better from the standpoints of resistance to water and abuse.

Underground coal mining was formerly by far the largest consumer of black powder. From a performance standpoint, it is probably the best explosive for that purpose. Its relatively gentle, heaving action gives a high yield of lump and leaves the coal in good position for rapid loading. Before the advent of oil, gas, and electric heating and cooking, coal was produced in tremendous quantities for household use and lump demanded a premium price. But black powder has a dangerous tendency to ignite coal gas (mostly methane) and coal dust, and many mine explosions occurred. Around 1880 several European governments, seeking to develop safer substitutes for black powder, set up testing stations. Similar action was taken in the United States a few years later. The result was a series of special dynamites approved for use in gassy and dusty coal mines when used in the specified manner. Their blasting action was not as good as that of black powder, but they were very much safer. These dynamites are discussed below.

The use of black powder in underground coal mines is no longer allowed in most countries. As a result, black powder production has decreased tremendously. Further, black powder is now more expensive than dynamite and is used only for special purposes. There is, for example, no substitute for black powder in certain military applications and nothing equal to it has yet been found for the

manufacture of safety fuse. The fact that black powder is relatively nonshattering is of value in blasting certain types of stone.

NITROGLYCERIN

Nitroglycerin, another chemical explosive, was discovered by an Italian chemist, Ascanio Sobrero, in 1846. Though he first called it pyroglycerin, it soon came to be known generally as nitroglycerin, or blasting oil. Because of the risks inherent in its manufacture and the lack of dependable means for its detonation, nitroglycerin was largely a laboratory curiosity until Immanuel Nobel and his son Alfred made extensive studies of its commercial potential in the years 1859–61. In 1862 they built a crude plant at Heleneborg, Sweden; Alfred, a chemist, was basically responsible for the design of this factory that was efficient and relatively safe considering the state of knowledge of the times. Nevertheless, it exploded in 1864 and killed, among others, Alfred's youngest brother Emil Oskar. Though deeply affected by the accident, Alfred continued work, at first on a barge that he moored in the middle of a lake. In 1865 he erected a plant at Krümmel, Germany, and another in Sweden at Vinterviken near Stockholm. A third plant was built a year later in Norway. Nobel was granted a patent for the manufacture and use of nitroglycerin in the United States, in 1866, and since importation on a large scale was impractical, he visited the United States in an effort to interest local capital. The victim of a number of unscrupulous businessmen, he finally sold his American holdings in 1885 for only $20,000.

Even today most experts regard Nobel's invention of the blasting cap, a device for detonating explosives, in 1865, as the greatest advance in the science of explosives since the discovery of black powder. Combined with Bickford's safety fuse, the blasting cap provided a dependable means for detonating nitroglycerin and the many other high explosives that followed it. After a number of attempts that were only partially successful, Nobel settled on a charge of mercury fulminate, which had been known for many years, in a copper capsule. With one or two minor changes, this blasting cap remained in general use until the 1920s.

DYNAMITE

The second most important of Nobel's inventions was dynamite, in 1867. He coined the name from the Greek *dynamis*, "power." The basis for the invention was his discovery that kieselguhr, a porous siliceous earth, would absorb large quantities of nitroglycerin, giving a product that was much safer to handle and easier to use than nitroglycerin alone.

Dynamite No. 1, as Nobel called it, was 75 percent nitroglycerin and 25 percent guhr. Shortly after its invention, Nobel realized that guhr, an inert substance, not only contributed nothing to the power of the explosive but actually detracted from it because it absorbed heat that otherwise would have improved the blasting action. He turned, therefore, to active ingredients such as wood pulp for an absorbent, and sodium nitrate for an oxidizing agent. By varying the ratio of nitroglycerin to these "dopes," as they came to be called, Nobel not only improved the efficiency of dynamite but also was able to prepare it in varying strengths, termed straight dynamites. Thus 40 percent straight dynamite contained 40 percent nitroglycerin and 60 percent dope. Dynamites of this type are still in limited use.

Nobel patented the use of active ingredients in dynamite in 1869. Several others obtained similar patents at about the same time, however, and the result was that no one could establish a clear-cut claim to the invention.

Nobel's next outstanding contribution was his invention of gelatinous dynamites in 1875. There is a legend that he hurt a finger and used collodion, a solution of relatively low nitrogen content nitrocellulose in a mixture of ether and alcohol, to cover the wound. Later, unable to sleep because of the pain, Nobel went to the laboratory to find out what effect collodion would have on ni-

Invention of safety fuse by William Bickford

The blasting cap

Invention of gelatinous dynamites

troglycerin. To his great satisfaction, he found that after evaporation of the solvents, there remained a tough, plastic material. He discovered that he could duplicate this by the direct addition of 7 to 8 percent of collodion-type nitrocotton to nitroglycerin and that lesser quantities of nitrocotton decreased the viscosity and enabled him to add other active ingredients. He called the original material *blasting gelatin* and the dope mixtures *gelatin dynamites*. The principal advantages of these products were their high water resistance and greater blasting action power than the comparable dynamites. This added power resulted from a combination of higher density and a degree of plasticity that allowed complete filling of the borehole (the hole that was bored in the coal seam or elsewhere for implantation of the explosive).

The first large-scale manufacture of nitroglycerin in the United States is attributed to George Mowbray, a chemist of considerable ability who had followed the work of Sobrero and others in Europe with great interest. Mowbray published an advertisement offering to supply nitroglycerin. This led to an invitation to manufacture it for completion of the Hoosac Tunnel at North Adams, Massachusetts. Mowbray's plant was built near North Adams in the latter part of 1867. Most of its product went to the tunnel, but a substantial amount was shipped, frozen, throughout the eastern United States and Canada. Pure nitroglycerin, relatively insensitive in frozen form, freezes at about 52° F (11° C) and is, therefore, easy to keep frozen by packing it in ice. Before closing his plant down because of patent difficulties, Mowbray made about 1,000,000 pounds of nitroglycerin without accidents in either manufacture or shipment.

One of the earliest major uses of nitroglycerin in the United States was in blasting oil wells to increase the flow of oil. E.A.L. Roberts in that country obtained a patent covering this procedure and later acquired the right to manufacture and use nitroglycerin under the Nobel patents. Theoretically, this gave him a monopoly on shooting oil wells, and his company dominated the field, but many of his competitors ignored his patent rights.

After 1883 the use of nitroglycerin was, with a few unimportant exceptions, restricted to oil-well shooting. In recent years more efficient means have been developed for increasing oil flow. Nitroglycerin is still used occasionally because it is more economical in small wells.

Major tunnels blasted by explosives

Three tunnels stand out as benchmarks in the history of the use of explosives: first is Mont Cenis, a seven-mile railway tunnel driven through the Alps between France and Italy in 1857–71, much the largest construction job with black powder up to that time; second was the four-mile Hoosac, also a railway project, during the construction of which (1855–66) nitroglycerin first replaced black powder in large-scale construction; third was the Sutro mine development tunnel in Nevada (1864–74) where the switch from nitroglycerin to dynamite for this type of work started.

Ammonium nitrate. After the straight dynamites and gelatins, the next important advance in dynamite was the substitution of ammonium nitrate for part of the nitroglycerin to give a safer and less expensive product. The use of ammonium nitrate in explosives had been patented by others in Sweden in 1867, but it was Nobel who made the new "extra dynamites" successful by devising gelatins that contained from 20 to 60 percent ammonium nitrate.

During the period 1867–84, many people worked to develop nongelatinous ammonium nitrate mixtures, but nothing of value resulted, largely because ammonium nitrate is too hygroscopic; that is, it picks up moisture too readily. In 1885 R.S. Penniman, an American, found a solution to the problem by coating the ammonium nitrate with a small percentage of paraffin, or some similar substance, prior to use. With this development, a series of ammonia dynamites soon became popular. Coating was discontinued when other, safer means were developed to handle the moisture problem.

All major underground-coal-mining countries have similar explosives and regulations. In the United States explosives that have been approved by the U.S. Bureau of Mines for use in underground coal mines are called permissibles. Besides passing the Bureau's safety tests, these explosives must be used in a manner specified by the Bureau. In England the explosives are known as permitted; in France, *explosifs antigrisouteux;* in Belgium, *explosifs S. G. P. (sécurité, grisou, poussière),* and in Germany, *schlagwettersichere Sprengstoffe.* Almost without exception, the major ingredient in these explosives is ammonium nitrate, chosen because of its low explosion temperature, and nearly all of them contain a cooling agent such as sodium chloride (common salt) or ammonium chloride to prevent the heat of their explosion in a mine from igniting underground gases such as methane, or a combination of them and coal dust, and causing a fire or disastrous secondary explosion. The sensitizer is usually a small amount of nitroglycerin but in some cases it is TNT, trinitrotoluene (discussed later); for example, it is said that a typical Russian permissible would be 68 percent ammonium nitrate, 10 TNT, 20 sodium chloride, and 2 powdered bark.

Explosives used in underground mines

As synthetic ammonia became less expensive, because of improvements in manufacture and a raw material change from coal to natural gas, the explosives industry concentrated its efforts on substituting ammonium nitrate for nitroglycerin. Two important products were (1) low-density ammonia dynamites and (2) semigelatins. Prior to their development, the density of most dynamites was about the same and was quite high. Strength was changed in the different grades by varying the amount of explosives used. The new concept was to employ the strongest formula possible, with a minimum of nitroglycerin and a maximum of ammonium nitrate, and to dilute it systematically with suitable low-density ingredients such as bagasse (the pulp remaining after extraction of sugar from the cane) so that one stick of the new product would give the same blasting action as one of the old. This provided a substantial saving to the user because the cost per stick of the new product was much lower.

Synthetic ammonia and its products

The only difference between the low-density ammonia dynamites and the semigelatins is that the latter are partially gelatinized through the use of nitrocellulose and a higher nitroglycerin content. This gelatinization provides good water resistance and a degree of plasticity that is desirable in loading holes prior to blasting.

Means are available to obtain a moderate amount of water resistance in the ammonia dynamites without resorting to gelatinization of the nitroglycerin. The most common involve the use of water-repellents such as calcium stearate, and ingredients that form a water gel on the surface of the dynamite that slows down the further penetration of water. Examples of the latter are pregelatinized starch products and rye flour.

Low-freezing dynamite. Attempts to reduce the freezing point of nitroglycerin began shortly after the Nobels introduced it commercially. Frozen dynamite is very insensitive, sometimes so much so that it will not give dependable performance, and it is difficult to use, since it cannot be punched for the insertion of a blasting cap or slit and tamped into a borehole. Consequently, almost all of it had to be thawed for use and careless thawing methods caused many accidents. Not until 1907 was a reasonably successful procedure for producing low-freezing dynamite developed. This involved adding 20 to 25 percent of the liquid isomers (molecules with identical formulas but different structure) of TNT to the nitroglycerin. This was replaced for a short time by a nitrated solution of sugar in glycerin. In 1911 a practical way to manufacture diglycerin (a glycerin polymer) was discovered. Its nitration product, tetranitrodiglycerin, when mixed with nitroglycerin, reduced its freezing point materially.

The ultimate solution to the freezing problem was found in 1925, when synthetic ethylene glycol became available. The explosive properties of ethylene glycol dinitrate are practically identical with those of nitroglycerin and its low-freezing qualities are extremely good. Dynamite containing a mixture of it and nitroglycerin was stored in the open at Point Barrow, Alaska, for four years without freezing.

OTHER EXPLOSIVES

Chlorates and perchlorates. Interest in the chlorates and perchlorates (salts of chloric or perchloric acid) as a base for explosives dates back to 1788. They were mixed with various solid and liquid fuels. Many plants were built in Europe and the United States for the manufacture of this type of explosive, mostly using potassium chlorate, but so far as can be determined, all of them either blew up or burned up, and no chlorate explosives have been manufactured for many years.

Sprengel explosives. In England in 1871, Hermann Sprengel patented combinations of oxidizing agents such as chlorates, nitrates, and nitric acid with combustible substances such as nitronaphthalene, benzene, and nitrobenzene. These differed from previous explosives in that one of the ingredients was liquid and the mixture was made just prior to use. Sprengel explosives were quite popular in Europe but consumption in the United States was relatively small except for the spectacular Hell Gate blast in New York harbour in 1885, in which a combination of 75,000 pounds of No. 1 dynamite and 240,000 pounds of potassium chlorate–nitrobenzene were used to remove "Flood Rock," a menace to navigation. Cloth bags of the chlorate were soaked in the nitrobenzene and loaded directly from the soaking tank into the boreholes. The mixture was called Rack-a-rock.

Liquid oxygen explosives. In 1895 the German Carl von Linde (1842–1934) introduced carbon black packed in porous bags and dipped in liquid oxygen. This, which was a Sprengel-type explosive, came to be known as LOX. Because of the shortage of nitrates, LOX was widely used in Germany during World War I. Little if any was used in World War II, however, because ample supplies of nitrates could be obtained from synthetic ammonia.

Because the manufacture of liquid oxygen requires complicated and expensive equipment, the use of LOX was limited to areas that could consume very large quantities. In the United States several of the tremendous strip coal mines in the Midwest met this requirement. Maximum consumption of LOX explosive was 22,465,000 pounds in 1953, but it fell to zero in 1968. Cheap as LOX is, it cannot compete with ammonium nitrate–fuel oil mixtures.

Nitrostarch explosives. Nitrostarch, which is closely related to nitrocellulose, attracted early attention, but it was not until about 1905 that it proved possible to produce it in a stable form. In general nitrostarch explosives are similar to the straight and ammonia dynamites except that nitrostarch is used in place of nitroglycerin. Disadvantages are its relatively low strength, mediocre water resistance, and the fact that it cannot be transformed into gelatinous products. Nitrostarch explosives, however, do not produce the headaches from skin contact that are characteristic of mixtures containing nitroglycerin. For that reason they are still marketed.

Nitramon and Nitramex explosives. An important advance in explosives technology was the development by du Pont in 1934 of Nitramon, a canned product with a typical formula of 92 percent ammonium nitrate, 4 percent dinitrotoluene, and 4 percent paraffin wax. Some grades contain metallic ingredients such as aluminum and ferrosilicon. Nitramon is insensitive to the action of a line of detonating cord, a commercial blasting cap, shock and friction, or the impact of small-calibre ammunition. A large primer is required for its detonation and the one normally used is known as a Nitramon primer. This is also a canned product with Nitramon at each end but a centre section of amatol that can be detonated by either detonating cord or a blasting cap. The cans are provided in varying sizes. A minimum diameter of four inches for regular Nitramon is necessary to insure proper explosive effect if individual cans in a column become separated by some material such as a rock. Special grades are made for use in seismic exploration for gas and oil in 2- and 2½-inch diameters. In this case, however, the cans are threaded and intimate contact is assured because the column is screwed together.

Nitramex is similar to Nitramon but is much stronger because it contains TNT and a metallic ingredient such as

aluminum. Both it and Nitramon have been largely replaced by the water gels, which are described later.

Removal of a mountaintop

So far as is known, the largest commercial, non-nuclear blast was made on April 5, 1958, in Seymour Narrows, which lies between Vancouver Island and the mainland of British Columbia. The object of the blast was to remove the top of a submerged twin-peak mountain, known as Ripple Rock, which was only 9 feet below the surface at low tide. More than 120 vessels had been lost because of this obstacle. In preparing for the blast, a shaft was sunk on shore to the proper depth. From it a tunnel was driven to a point directly under the twin peaks, from which a vertical shaft finally was driven to the desired depth below the peaks. A series of small horizontal drifts and pockets was prepared for placement of the explosives, consisting of 2,756,000 pounds (1,253,000 kilograms) of Nitramex 2H and a special primer, fired by means of detonating cord.

After the blast the top of the rock was a minimum of 50 feet below the surface and no longer a menace to navigation.

MODERN HIGH EXPLOSIVES

The year 1955, marking the beginning of the most revolutionary change in the explosives industry since the invention of dynamite, saw the development of ammonium nitrate–fuel oil mixtures (ANFO) and ammonium nitrate-base water gels, which together now account for at least 70 percent of the high explosives consumption in the United States. The technology of these products is far more advanced in the U.S. than it is in other countries; so, at the present time, they have not replaced nearly as much of the older explosives in the rest of the world. In addition to a variety of packages, both ANFO and water gels are delivered in bulk by special trucks and loaded directly into boreholes.

Ammonium nitrate–fuel oil mixtures. In 1955 it was discovered that mixtures of ammonium nitrate and fine coal dust would give very satisfactory blasting results in the large (about 9-inch, 22.5-centimetre) holes used in open-pit coal mines to remove the rock and soil covering the coal. Polyethylene bags for this material both stretched to fill the holes and provided a moderate amount of water resistance.

Shortly thereafter, ANFO was extensively evaluated in the open-pit iron mines of Canada and the United States, with a high degree of success. From there ANFO spread to other open pits, such as copper, and to construction work such as road building and pipeline installation. It was then found that the mixture could be air blown into holes two inches (5 centimetres) in diameter, or even smaller, with excellent results. This led to its adoption in many underground mines.

Prills

ANFO applications were based on prilled rather than crystallized ammonium nitrate. Prills, or free-flowing pellets, were developed for the fertilizer market, which requires a coarse product that has little tendency to set and can be spread easily and smoothly. A small amount of kieselguhr is generally added to improve the flowing properties. Prills are made by allowing droplets of ammonium nitrate that is almost molten to fall freely from a high tower. When they reach the bottom, they are dry and solidified, and slightly porous, which allows them to absorb and hold a greater amount of oil and gives a more sensitive product. ANFO is almost universally prepared by mixing 94 percent of prills with 6 percent of No. 2 fuel oil. The latter imparts some water resistance and, if that is not enough, polyethylene bags can often be used to give the necessary protection.

Water gels. Water gels, or slurries, were introduced in 1958. These were, at first, mixtures of ammonium nitrate, TNT, water, and gelatinizing agents, usually guar gum and a cross-linking agent such as borax. (Cross-linking is a form of chemical bonding.) Later, aluminum and other metallic fuels were sometimes used and vastly better gelatinizers were discovered. In addition nonexplosive sensitizers were developed that could replace the TNT if desired. When the highest possible concentration of strength is needed, however, large quantities of TNT are still used.

Water gels have many advantages. Among them are a high concentration of strength, a high degree of water resistance, plasticity that permits them to displace air or water and completely fill the borehole, economy, ease of handling and loading, and good safety characteristics. These advantages were quickly recognized. In 1968 the consumption of water gels in the United States alone was 206,000,000 pounds, over 10 percent of all the industrial explosives used there.

NITROCELLULOSIC EXPLOSIVES

When Christian Schoenbein invented nitrocotton (guncotton) in 1845 by dipping cotton in a mixture of nitric and sulfuric acids and then removing the acids by washing with water, he hoped to obtain a propellant for military weapons. It proved, however, to be too fast and violent. About 1860 Maj. E. Schultze of the Prussian Army produced a useful nitrocellulosic propellant. He nitrated small pieces of wood by placing them in nitric acid and then, after removing the acid, impregnated the pieces with barium and potassium nitrates. The purpose of the latter was to provide oxygen to burn the incompletely nitrated wood. Schultze's powder was highly successful in shotguns but was too fast for cannon or even most rifles.

In 1884 a French chemist, Paul Vieille, made the first smokeless powder as it is now known. He partially dissolved nitrocellulose in a mixture of ether and alcohol until it became a gelatinous mass, which he rolled into sheets and then cut into flakes. When the solvent evaporated, it left a hard, dense material resembling horn. This product gave satisfactory results in all types of guns.

In 1887 Nobel introduced another of his revolutionary inventions, which he called Ballistite. He mixed 40 percent of a lower nitrogen content, more soluble nitrocellulose and 60 percent of nitroglycerin. Cut into flakes, this made an excellent propellant and it continued in use for over 75 years. The British refused to recognize Nobel's patent and developed a number of similar products under the generic name cordite.

The progress of smokeless powder in the United States was much slower than it was in Europe. Long-continued work, principally by E.I. du Pont de Nemours & Company, finally resulted in a material that was excellent for guns of all types and sizes. It was first marketed about 1909 and was the most important type of smokeless powder used by the Allies in World War I. It was made from a nitrocotton of relatively low nitrogen content, called pyrocellulose, because that type is quite soluble in ether–alcohol. A small amount of diphenylamine was used as a stabilizer and, after forming the grains and removing the liquid, a coating of graphite was added. The smokeless powder most widely used in the United States at the present time is much the same. Other popular types are mostly double-base and may contain from about 20 to 35 percent nitroglycerin. Cotton linters for nitration have been almost, if not entirely, replaced by purified wood cellulose.

BLASTING CAPS

Nobel's original fuse-type blasting cap remained virtually unchanged for many years, except for the substitution of 90–10 and 80–20 mixtures of mercury fulminate and potassium chlorate for the pure fulminate. This did not affect the performance materially and provided a substantial economy. Mercury fulminate is an example of an explosive that can be both primary and secondary. In its more compressed form it is a high density base charge; less compressed, a low density primer charge. Hexanitromannitol (nitromannite) functions in the same manner and is used that way in a very successful blasting cap.

Extensive work was carried out on replacements for the costly mercury fulminate; by 1930 very little of it remained in use, and by the 1970s it had disappeared from commercial use. Experience has shown that the cheaper replacements are actually superior.

Mercury fulminate

The dominant base-charge materials are now pentaerythritol tetranitrate (PETN) and cyclotrimethylenetrinitramine (RDX). These are as strong as nitroglycerin, quite safe to manufacture and handle, and relatively inexpensive. In addition to low density nitromannite, diazodinitrophenol, lead styphnate, and lead azide are widely used as ignition-primer charges. One other departure from Nobel's blasting cap is the fact that aluminum has now almost entirely replaced copper as the material used for the shell.

Electrical firing. The principal advantages of electric over fuse firing are exact control of the time when the blast is initiated, the simultaneous firing of a number of shots, if that is desired, and the ability to obtain a very high degree of water resistance. Attempts to make electric blasting caps date back to the 1700s, but nothing of a really practical nature was developed until late in the 19th century. There were two separate problems, the cap and the means to fire it.

Blasting machines. The first satisfactory electrical blasting machine was invented by H. Julius Smith, an American, in 1878. It comprised a gear-type arrangement of rack bar and pinion that operated an armature to generate electricity. When the rack bar was pushed down rapidly, it revolved the pinion and armature with sufficient speed to obtain the desired current. This current was released into the external, or cap, circuit when the rack bar struck a brass spring in the bottom of the machine. Smith's blasting machine was improved and made in a range of capacities; also, a small twist-type machine that employed basically the same principles was introduced. These machines are still in widespread use, although they have been replaced to a considerable extent by power firing, and capacitor-discharge blasting machines. The latter have a battery power source for energizing one or more capacitors and a safe, dependable means for discharging the stored energy. They have high capacity for their weight and size and are rapidly displacing the other firing systems.

Ignition systems. Except for the means of firing, there is little difference between electric and fuse-type blasting caps. With minor variations, the explosives used are the same.

It was in the 1880s that the forerunner of the modern electric blasting cap was first assembled. In contrast to the spark-type ignitions previously used, it employed a fine, high-resistance wire soldered between two insulated leg wires and embedded in, or coated with, an ignition mixture. The resistance wire was either platinum or one of its alloys, and the ignition mixture was based on mercury fulminate. The leg wires were insulated with two layers of cotton thread, wound in opposite directions. Except for coal-mine caps, the wire was then run through a bath of molten asphalt. Paraffin wax was used for the coal-mine caps because its white colour provided good contrast with the black coal. Sulfur, or a mixture of sulfur and mica or graphite, was used to hold the leg wires in place and seal the cap. Sulfur was well suited for this purpose because its melting point is very low and it is compatible with the explosive ingredients. Later, to obtain better water resistance, part of the sulfur was replaced by asphalt.

In 1939 the du Pont company introduced a revolutionary new type of ignition system. Nylon plastic was substituted for the cotton insulation, a rubber plug to hold the leg wires replaced the sulfur plug, and the bridge wire was welded to the leg wires instead of soldered. By that time alloys such as nichrome had largely replaced the platinum bridge wires. The shell was crimped tightly to the rubber plug, with the result that the cap would stand as much as 1,000 feet of water pressure. All electric blasting caps are now made substantially in this way. Polyvinyl chloride is widely used for the leg wire insulation and plastic is sometimes substituted for rubber in the plug.

Match-head ignition is very popular in Europe and is used by one manufacturer in this country. This consists of a piece of cardboard with a thin sheet of metal glued

Introduction of nylon insulation

to each side. A bridge wire is soldered to these sheets, around the end of the cardboard, and this part of the assembly is dipped in a slurry of ignition mixture, usually based on copper acetylide. After drying, the match head is given a protective coating and is then soldered to the leg wires.

Most countries require explosives in underground coal mines to be fired electrically but prohibit the use of aluminum-shell electric blasting caps. This is because aluminum burns with a very hot flame and is much more likely than copper to ignite coal gas. Otherwise, almost all electric blasting-cap shells are made of aluminum.

Delay systems. Delay, or rotational, shooting, has many advantages over instantaneous firing in almost all types of blasting. It generally gives better fragmentation, more efficient use of the explosive, reduced vibration and concussion, and better control of the rock. For these, and sometimes other reasons, most blasting operations are now conducted with a delay system.

It is probable that the first use of delay firing was in tunnels. The centre was shot out first and then successive rings around it until the desired tunnel dimensions were reached. The procedure was to cut all of the fuses to the same length and then trim them toward the centre; for example, the outside ring of fuses would be full length, the next ring a few inches shorter, and so on. Each cut was about ½ inch per foot of fuse (that is, a 3-inch cut for a 6-foot fuse, etc.). In addition, the fuses were lit from the centre out, causing a little more delay in the desired direction. This method of shooting could not be used until Bickford's safety fuse, which had a very uniform burning speed, became available.

Delay electric blasting caps are the most commonly used means for obtaining rotational firing. They are of two types: (1) the so-called regular delay, which has been in use since the early 1900s; and (2) the short-interval, or millisecond, delay, which was introduced about 1943. Except for a delay element placed between the ignition and primer charges, they are the same as instantaneous electric caps.

Types of delay caps

A typical series of regular delays would comprise 14 periods ranging from a few milliseconds to about 12 seconds. To avoid overlapping and because there is some variation in the burning speed of the delay element, the intervals are made longer in the higher periods; for example, the delay between periods 1 and 2 might be 0.8 seconds, whereas for 13 and 14 it might be 1.5 seconds. Ordinary delays have been largely replaced by short-interval delays but are still used to a considerable extent for such purposes as driving tunnels and sinking shafts.

The periods in short-interval delays are usually separated by 25 milliseconds up to 200 milliseconds, by 50 up to 500, and by 100 up to 1,000 (one second). This close spacing gives improved fragmentation, the ability to fire many holes with hardly any more vibration or concussion than would be obtained with one hole, less chance that the detonation of one hole will cut off an adjacent hole, and a reduction in the quantity and cost of explosives. Short-interval delays are used above ground in such work as excavating and quarrying, and for almost all types of underground mining. Their acceptance has been phenomenal and their development one of the major advances in explosives.

Delay elements for electric blasting caps function in about the same way as black powder in safety fuse, except that the chemical mixtures used are much faster. At times the delay mixture is simply pressed on top of the primer mix. Usually, however, it is put in the centre of a metallic tube in lengths that will give the desired delay interval.

DETONATING CORD

Detonating cord (detonating fuse) resembles safety fuse but contains a high explosive instead of black powder. The first successful one, patented in France in 1908, consisted of a lead tube, about the same diameter as safety fuse, filled with a core of TNT. It was made by filling a large tube with molten TNT that was allowed to solidify.

The tube was then passed through successively smaller rolls until it reached the specified diameter. In France the product was called *cordeau détonant*, elsewhere shortened to cordeau. Its velocity was about 16,000 feet per second.

Cordeaux

In 1936 the Ensign-Bickford Company, Simsbury, Connecticut, the American manufacturers of cordeau, developed Primacord, based on French patents and comprising a core of PETN covered with various combinations of textiles, waterproofing materials, and plastics. The velocity is approximately 21,000 feet per second. Many types of Primacord are available, for both military and commercial use, but the industrial varieties generally contain from 25 to 60 grains of PETN per foot. RDX is sometimes used in place of PETN for high temperatures, because the melting points are, respectively, 398.3° and 284° F (203.5° and 140° C).

Detonating cord has many applications in blasting. Any number of holes can be connected with it in just about any desired pattern. Attached to the blasting charge and knotted to a trunk line, it is fired by means of either a fuse-type or electric blasting cap. Sequential shooting may be obtained by cutting the trunk lines and inserting delay connectors, which have delay periods ranging from about 5 to 25 milliseconds.

MILITARY EXPLOSIVES

Military requirements for high explosives differ in many respects from those for commercial users. Military explosives must have insensitivity to shock and friction and must be unlikely to detonate from small-arms fire and yet have excellent shattering power. They must have the ability to withstand long periods of adverse storage without deterioration and must be able to be fired in projectiles or dropped in aerial time bombs without premature explosion. Some types are required to possess almost unlimited water resistance. Many types must have complex fuzes for detonation.

TNT. Trinitrotoluene (TNT) is the most useful military high explosive. Although it had been known for many years and was used extensively in the dye industry, it was not employed as an explosive until 1904. It is an excellent military explosive in itself, but its most valuable property is that it can be safely melted and cast either alone or as a slurry with other explosives. This is because there is a wide spread between its melting point and its decomposition temperature.

It has two shortcomings: first, it is extremely insensitive in the cast form, and second, it is difficult to cast without air holes. The first problem can be overcome by drilling a hole, about 1 inch (2.5 centimetres) in diameter, the length of the charge in the shell and filling it with trinitrophenylmethylnitramine (tetryl); the second, by using a mixture of 40 percent trinitroxylene (TNX) and 60 percent TNT. This mixture not only casts perfectly but can be detonated with a smaller tetryl booster. There is no indication that any TNX was used in World War II; it is believed to have been replaced by PETN and RDX.

Picric acid and ammonium picrate. Picric acid was used as a shell explosive in Europe during the 1880s and carried through World War I on a very large scale. Quantities of it were made in the United States but the Army and Navy used mainly TNT.

Ammonium picrate (Explosive D) has exceptional value as a charge for armour-piercing projectiles. Loaded in a shell with a suitably insensitive primer, it can be fired through 12 inches of armour plate and made to detonate on the far side. These armour-piercing shells were used in both World Wars.

Early in World War I it was found that mixtures of molten TNT and ammonium nitrate were almost as effective for shell loadings as pure TNT. The mixtures most commonly used were 80–20 and 50–50 AN and TNT, known as amatol. Their principal advantages were that they made the supply of TNT go further and were considerably cheaper. In World War II the amatols were used in aerial bombs as well as artillery shells.

Amatol

To conserve TNT in World War I, a nitrostarch-base

composition was also developed for loading hand grenades and trench-mortar shells.

Several explosives, although previously known, only came into use during World War II. The most important of these were RDX, PETN, and ethylenediaminedinitrate (EDNA), all of which were cast with varying amounts of TNT, usually 40 to 50 percent, and used where the highest possible shattering power was desired. For example, cast 60–40 RDX-TNT, called cyclotol, develops a detonation pressure of about 4,000,000 pounds per square inch. Corresponding mixtures of PETN and TNT have almost as much shattering effect. The EDNA mixtures, or ednatol, were used only to a limited extent and for special purposes. Probably the most powerful of all nonatomic military explosives are the cast mixtures containing aluminum. The torpedo warhead torpex, for example, is a cast mixture of RDX, TNT, and aluminum.

A series of plastic demolition explosives with great shattering power, designated Composition C-1 to Composition C-4, has had considerable publicity. These contain about 80 percent RDX combined with a mixture of various oils, waxes, and plasticizers. The only significant difference is in the temperature range through which they remain useful. C-3 stays plastic to $-20°$ F $(-29°$ C) and does not exude oil below $120°$ F $(49°$ C). In contrast, C-4 remains plastic to $-70°$ F $(-57°$ C) and does not leak below $170°$ F $(77°$ C).

Shaped charges. The shaped charge, principally the hand-fired rocket, is another highly publicized product introduced during World War II. A shaped charge normally consists of a cone made of metal or glass surrounded by a high strength, high density explosive and means to obtain the proper standoff, or distance to the target.

When the explosive is detonated, the cone is collapsed and vaporized, forming a small, high-temperature jet containing particles of liner material moving at 10,000 to 30,000 feet per second. This strikes the target with such heat and force that the target simply flows radially from the point of impact leaving a deep, nearly round hole. Spectacular as the results are, only about 15 percent of the explosive energy is focussed.

Only two commercial applications have been found for shaped charges. One is for drawing off molten iron or slag from open hearth and blast furnaces in the steel industry, and the other for perforating casings in the oil industry. In the first case, the principal advantage is safety as compared with oxygen lancing. In the second, shaped charges are almost always more efficient than the bullets they replace.

OTHER INDUSTRIAL APPLICATIONS

Explosive rivets. Blind rivets are needed when space limitations make conventional rivets impractical. One type of these is explosive; it has a hollow space in the shank containing a small charge of heat-sensitive chemicals. When a suitable amount of heat is applied to the head, an explosion takes place and expands the rivet shank tightly into the hole. The shank is normally open but can be sealed to eliminate noise and the ejection of metal fragments. Most explosive rivets are aluminum but they can be obtained in stainless steel and certain other metals. Their use is mainly in aircraft.

Explosive bonding. Explosives are sometimes used to bond various metals to each other. For example, when silver was removed from United States coinage, much of the so-called sandwich metal that replaced it was obtained by the explosive bonding of large slabs, which were then rolled down to the required thickness. These slabs are placed parallel to each other and approximately ¼ inch apart. An explosive developed especially for the purpose is placed on the top slab and its detonation slams the slabs together with such force that they become welded. Stainless steel is often joined to ordinary steel in this manner. One especially valuable feature of explosion cladding is that it can frequently be applied to metallurgically incompatible metals. Examples of this are aluminum to steel and titanium to steel.

Finally, the very fine industrial-type diamonds used for grinding and polishing are produced by the carefully controlled action of explosives on carbon.

BIBLIOGRAPHY. A.P. VAN GELDER and H. SCHLATTER, *History of the Explosives Industry in America* (1927), a highly detailed book covering the origin and development of all explosives of any importance throughout the world up to the date of its publication; M.A. COOK, *The Science of High Explosives* (1958), an advanced mathematical work devoted almost exclusively to theory, with a brief, interesting section on the history of explosives; C.H. JOHANSSON and P.A. PERSSON, *Detonics of High Explosives* (1970), an outstanding book describing the behaviour of high explosives, with emphasis on experimental data; E.I. DU PONT DE NEMOURS AND COMPANY, INC., *Blasters' Handbook*, 15th ed. (1969), a practical discussion of commercial blasting; INSTITUTE OF MAKERS OF EXPLOSIVES, "Safety in the Transportation, Storage, Handling and Use of Explosives" (1970), a pamphlet primarily designed for the guidance of the consumer; T.L. DAVIS, *The Chemistry of Powder and Explosives*, 2 vol. (1941–43), a general treatment of explosives with excellent coverage of pyrotechnics; T. URBANSKI, *Chemistry and Technology of Explosives*, 3 vol. (1967), an excellent treatment of these subjects, highly recommended; N.B. WILKINSON, *Explosives in History: The Story of Black Powder* (1966), a popular account, written primarily as a science supplement for high school students; U.S. BUREAU OF MINES, *Apparent Consumption of Industrial Explosives and Blasting Agents in the United States* (annual).

(N.G.J.)

Eyck, Jan and Hubert van

Two 15th-century painters surnamed van Eyck, presumably after their birthplace in the Belgian village of Maaseik, are, respectively, the most renowned and the most perplexing artists of their era. The life of Jan van Eyck is well documented, and more than 18 works securely attributed to him survive. For Hubert van Eyck, on the other hand, there are only a few ambiguous documents and no authenticated painting, and, were it not for his association with Jan, he certainly would have remained an obscure archive note.

Jan van Eyck must have been born before 1395, for in October 1422 he is recorded as the *varlet de chambre et peintre* ("honorary equerry and painter") of John of Bavaria, count of Holland. He continued to work in the palace of The Hague until the Count's death in 1425 and then settled briefly in Bruges before he was summoned, that summer, to Lille to serve Philip the Good, duke of Burgundy, the most powerful ruler and foremost patron of the arts in Flanders. Jan remained in the Duke's employ until his death, performing for him the duties of not only court painter but also diplomatic envoy. On behalf of his sponsor he undertook a number of secret missions during the next decade, of which the most notable were two journeys to the Iberian peninsula, the first in 1427 to try to contract a marriage for Philip with Isabella of Spain and a more successful trip between 1428 and 1429 to seek the hand of Isabella of Portugal. As a confidant of Philip the Good, Jan may have participated directly in these marriage negotiations, but he also was charged to present the Duke with a portrait of the intended. In 1431 Jan purchased a house in Bruges and about the same time he married a lady named Margaret, about whom little more is known than that she was born in 1406 and was to bear him at least two children. Jan's frank portrait of his wife is the most complete document of her life that remains. Residing now in Bruges, Jan continued to paint, and in 1436 he again made a secret voyage for Philip. He died shortly before July 9, 1441, and was buried in the church of Saint-Donatian, in Bruges.

Securely attributed paintings survive only from the last decade of Jan's career; therefore, his artistic origins and early development must be deduced from his mature work. Traditionally, Jan has been acclaimed the founder of Flemish painting, and scholars have sought his artistic roots in the last great phase of medieval manuscript illumination. It is clear that the naturalism and elegant compositions of Jan's later painting owe much to such early 15th-century illuminators as the anonymous Boucicaut Master and Pol, Herman, and Jehanequin de Limburg (the "Limburg Brothers"), who worked for the Bur-

Personal history of Jan van Eyck

Influences on Jan's artistic formation

gundian dukes, including the grandfather of Philip the Good and his illustrious granduncle, Jean, duc de Berry. A document of 1439 reports that Jan van Eyck paid an illuminator for preparing a book for the Duke; but central to the discussion of his ties to manuscript illustration has been the attribution to Jan of several miniatures, identified as Hand G, in a problematic prayer book known as the Turin-Milan Hours (Museo Civico, Turin). So long as these "Eyckian" miniatures were dated in the 1420s or even earlier, their authorship by Jan seemed indubitable; but recent investigations and manuscript discoveries strongly indicate that these miniatures were painted at least 20 years later and, hence, that they are by an imitator of the great master. With the elimination of the Turin-Milan Hours from Jan van Eyck's early *oeuvre*, his connections with International Gothic style illumination appear to have been less direct.

Certainly as important for Jan's artistic formation were the panel paintings of Robert Campin (*c.* 1378–1444), a Tournai painter whose important role in the history of Flemish art has only recently been re-established. Jan must have met Campin at least once—when he was feted by the Tournai painter's guild in 1427; and from Campin's art he seems to have learned the bold realism, the method of disguised symbolism, and perhaps the luminous oil technique that became so characteristic of his own style. In contrast to Campin, who was a Tournai burgher, Jan was a learned master at work in a busy court, and he signed his paintings, the first Flemish artist to do so. The majority of Jan's panels present the proud inscription: IOHANNES DE EYCK, and several bear his aristocratic motto, "*Als ich chan*" ("As best I can"). It is small wonder, therefore, that Campin's reputation faded and his influence on Jan was forgotten; nor is it surprising that many of Campin's artistic achievements were credited to the younger master whose fame remained undiminished.

Despite the fact that nine paintings by Jan van Eyck are signed and ten are dated, the establishment of his *oeuvre* and the reconstruction of its chronology present problems. The major difficulty is that Jan's masterpiece, the "Adoration of the Lamb" altarpiece in the Cathedral of Saint-Bavon in Ghent, has a wholly questionable inscription that introduces Hubert van Eyck as its principal master. This has caused art historians to turn to less ambitious but more secure works to plot Jan's development, including, most notably: the "Portrait of a Young Man" ("Leal Souvenir") of 1432, "The Marriage of Giovanni Arnolfini and Giovanna Cenami (?)" of 1434, the "Madonna With Canon van der Paele" of 1434–36, the triptych "Madonna and Child with Saints" of 1437, and the panels of "St. Barbara" and the "Madonna at the Fountain," dated, respectively, 1437 and 1439. Although they fall within a brief span of seven years, these paintings present a consistent development in which Jan moved from the heavy, sculptural realism associated with Robert Campin to a more delicate, rather precious pictorial style.

On stylistic grounds there seems little difficulty in placing the "Ghent Altarpiece" at the head of this development as indicated by the date 1432 in the inscription, but the question of Hubert's participation in this great work has yet to be resolved. The inscription itself is definite about this point: "The painter Hubert van Eyck, greater than whom no one was found, began [this work]; and Jan, his brother, second in art [carried] through the task . . . ." On the basis of this claim, art historians have attempted to distinguish Hubert's contribution to the "Ghent Altarpiece" and have even assigned to him certain of the more archaic "Eyckian" paintings, including "The Annunciation" (Metropolitan Museum of Art, New York) and "The Three Marys at the Tomb" (Museum Boymans-van Beuningen, Rotterdam). A problem arises, however, because the inscription itself is a 16th-century transcription and earlier references make no mention of Hubert's part in the "Ghent Altarpiece." The great 16th-century German artist Albrecht Dürer, for instance, praised only Jan van Eyck during his visit to Ghent in 1521; and as late as 1562 the Flemish historian Marcus

Hubert's participation in the Ghent altarpiece

van Vaernewyck referred to Jan alone as the author of the altarpiece. Furthermore, a recent philological study casts serious doubt on the dependability of the inscription, which scans more smoothly when the phrase naming Hubert is dropped. Thus, Hubert's participation in the Ghent polyptych is highly suspect, and any knowledge of his art must await new discoveries.

On the other hand, there is little doubt that Hubert did exist, the dubious reference to him on the "Ghent Altarpiece" aside. A "meester Hubrechte de scildere" (Master Hubert, the painter) is mentioned three times in the City Archives of Ghent; and a transcription of his epitaph reports that he died on September 18, 1426. Whether this Hubert van Eyck was related to Jan and why in the 16th century he was credited with the major share of the "Ghent Altarpiece" are questions that remain unanswered.

The confusion concerning his relationship to Hubert, the doubt about his activities as an illuminator, and the re-emergence of Robert Campin as a pre-eminent master do not diminish the achievement and significance of Jan van Eyck. He may not have invented painting with oils as early writers asserted; but he perfected the technique to mirror the textures, light, and spatial effects of nature. The realism of his paintings—admired as early as 1449 by the Italian humanist Cyriacus D'Ancona, who observed that the works seemed to have been produced "not by the artifice of human hands but by all-bearing nature herself"—has never been surpassed. For Jan, as for Campin, naturalism was not merely a technical tour de force, however. For him, nature embodied God, and so he filled his paintings with religious symbols disguised as everyday objects. Even the light that so naturally illuminates Jan van Eyck's landscapes and interiors is a metaphor of the Divine.

Because of the refinement of his technique and the abstruseness of his symbolic programs, the successors of Jan van Eyck borrowed only selectively from his art. Campin's foremost student, Rogier van der Weyden, tempered his master's homey realism with Eyckian grace and delicacy; in fact, at the end of his career, Campin himself succumbed somewhat to Jan's courtly style. Even Petrus Christus, who may have been apprenticed in Jan's atelier and who finished the "Virgin and Child, with Saints and Donor" (Frick Collection, New York) after Jan's death, quickly abandoned the intricacies of Jan's style under the influence of Rogier. During the last third of the century, the Netherlandish painters Hugo van der Goes and Justus van Gent revived the Eyckian heritage; but, when such early 16th-century Flemish masters as Quentin Massys and Jan Mabuse turned to Jan's work, they produced pious copies that had little impact on their original creations. In Germany and France the influence of Jan van Eyck was overshadowed by the more accessible styles of Campin and Rogier, and only in the Iberian peninsula—which Jan had visited twice—did his art dominate. In Italy his greatness was recognized by Cyriacus and by the humanist Bartolomeo Facio, who lists Jan, together with Rogier and the Italian artists Pisanello and Gentile da Fabriano, as one of the leading painters of the period. But Renaissance artists, as painters elsewhere, found him easier to admire than to imitate.

Interest in his painting and acknowledgment of his prodigious technical accomplishment have remained high. Jan's works have been copied frequently and have been avidly collected. He is referred to in the Treaty of Versailles, which specifies the return of the "Ghent Altarpiece" to Belgium before peace with Germany could be concluded after the end of World War I.

Influence of Jan's style

MAJOR WORKS

RELIGIOUS PAINTINGS: "The Adoration of the Lamb" ("Ghent Altarpiece," 1432; Cathedral of Saint-Bavon, Ghent); "The Annunciation" (*c.* 1434; National Gallery of Art, Washington, D.C.); "Madonna with Canon van der Paele" (1434–36; Groeninge Museum, Brugge); "The Lucca Madonna" (*c.* 1435–36; Städelsches Kunstinstitut, Frankfurt); "Madonna with Chancellor Rolin" (*c.* 1436; Louvre, Paris); "St. Barbara" (1437; Musée Royal des Beaux-Arts, Antwerp); "Triptych" (1437; Gemäldegalerie, Dresden); "Annunciation" (undated; Thyssen-Bornemisza Collection,

Castagnola, Switz.); "Madonna at the Fountain" (1439; Musée Royal des Beaux-Arts, Antwerp).

PORTRAITS: "Portrait of a Young Man" ("Leal Souvenir," 1432; National Gallery, London); "A Man in a Turban" (c. 1433; National Gallery, London); "The Marriage of Giovanni Arnolfini and Giovanna Cenami (?)" (1434; National Gallery, London); "Cardinal Albergati" (c. 1435; Kunsthistorisches Museum, Vienna); "The Goldsmith Jan de Leeuwe" (1436; Kunsthistorisches Museum, Vienna); "Portrait of Baulduyn de Lannoy" (c. 1436–37; Staatliche Museen Preussischer Kulturbesitz, Berlin); "Margaret van Eyck" (1439; Groeninge Museum, Brugge).

BIBLIOGRAPHY. Two monographs, the early study by W.H.J. WEALE, *Hubert and John van Eyck: Their Life and Work* (1908), indispensable for its documentary material; and the more recent volume by LUDWIG BALDASS, *Jan van Eyck* (1952), present basic surveys of the careers and art of the van Eyck brothers. A catalogue raisonné, which includes all attributed works and copies, is available in vol. 1 of M.J. FRIEDLANDER, *Early Netherlandish Painting* (1967), a translation from the German, updated in notes. The fundamental study of the entire period, ERWIN PANOFSKY, *Early Netherlandish Painting* (1953), considers Jan and Hubert van Eyck in great detail. Although Panofsky's attributions and chronology must be modified, his iconographic interpretations remain essential to an understanding of Eyckian painting. The technical examination of the Ghent Altarpiece inscription by A. AMPE, "De metamorfozen van het authentieke Jan-Van-Eyck-kwatrijn op het Lam Gods," *Jaarboek van het Museum voor Schone Kunsten-Antwerpen* (1969), with English summary, introduces serious questions about the role of Hubert van Eyck.

(H.L.Ke.)

Eye and Vision, Human

The eye is the organ through which man acquires knowledge of his environment by virtue of the light reflected from, or emitted by, the objects within the environment; it is the photoreceptor organ that, together with other types of receptors, allows the organism to react to, and to understand, the world around it. For man, the information provided by the eyes undoubtedly plays the dominant role in the interpretation of his environment; and one might, at first thought, expect to find man's visual apparatus more highly developed than that of lower animals. Thus, the dog seems to have poor vision compared with man, relying on his sense of smell to recognize objects rather than on his eyes. Examination of the respective eyes, however, fails to reveal differences of such magnitude as to suggest any fundamental inferiority on the part of the dog. Such an expectation of inferiority would, moreover, reveal a rather naïve approach to the study of vision, which does not merely consist in "seeing" but also in understanding; the dog's eye may well focus as accurate an image on its light-sensitive retina as does the human eye, but the power to integrate this image—to recognize its contours, its colours, and its relation to other objects, its probable feeling in response to touch, its motion, and so on—depends on the way the light-sensitive receptive cells are connected to the central nervous system; of this system the eye, as a whole, forms an integral part, being, in fact, an outgrowth of the forebrain. Similarly, the power to use visual information to govern bodily movements, so important to man in the execution of skilled tasks, and of vital importance to, for example, the swallow catching midges in flight, depends in great measure on the linking of the visual information with the motor centres of the brain. Thus the scope of this article, if it is to cover the true extent of the function of the human eye, must be wide; it must cover not only the manner in which the light from an external object is focussed as an image on the body's "photographic plate," the retina, but also the manner in which this light is converted into a message, and how this message is interpreted.

In general, sensory organs develop around a layer of nerve cells (neuroepithelium) that acquires a special sensitivity to one form of physical stimulus; with the eye, the light-sensitive layer must be accessible to light, and this means either having the layer on the surface of the body, as in lower forms of life, or having it deeper in the body and allowing light to reach it through a transparent cornea. The human eye, and that of all vertebrates, is built on this plan. The light-sensitive layer is in the retina, lining the rear wall of the globe, or eyeball.

This article is divided into the following sections:

Anatomy of the visual apparatus

STRUCTURES AUXILIARY TO THE EYE

The orbit. The eye is protected from mechanical injury by being enclosed in a socket, or orbit, which is made up of portions of several of the bones of the skull to form a four-sided pyramid the apex of which points back into the head. Thus, the floor of the orbit is made up of parts of the maxilla, zygomatic, and palatine bones, while the roof is made up of the orbital plate of the frontal bone and, behind this, by the lesser wing of the sphenoid. The optic foramen, the opening through which the optic nerve runs back into the brain and the large ophthalmic artery enters the orbit, is at the nasal side of the apex; the superior orbital fissure is a larger hole through which pass large veins and nerves. These nerves may carry nonvisual sensory messages—*e.g.*, pain—or they may be motor nerves controlling the muscles of the eye. There are other fissures and canals transmitting nerves and blood vessels. The eyeball and its functional muscles are surrounded by a layer of orbital fat that acts much like a cushion, permitting a smooth rotation of the eyeball about a virtually fixed point, the centre of rotation. The protrusion of the eyeballs—proptosis—in exophthalmic goitre is caused by the collection of fluid in the orbital fatty tissue.

The eyelids. It is vitally important that the front surface of the eyeball, the cornea, remain moist. This is achieved by the eyelids, which during waking hours sweep the secretions of the lacrimal apparatus and other glands over the surface at regular intervals and which during sleep cover the eyes and prevent evaporation. The lids have the additional function of preventing injuries from foreign bodies, through the operation of the blink reflex. The lids are essentially folds of flesh covering the front of the orbit and, when the eye is open, leaving an almond-shaped aperture. The points of the almond are

The layers
in the lids

called canthi; that nearest the nose is the inner canthus, and the other is the outer canthus (Figure 1). The lid may be divided into four layers: (1) the skin, containing glands that open onto the surface of the lid margin, and the eyelashes; (2) a muscular layer containing principally the orbicularis oculi muscle, responsible for lid closure; (3) a fibrous layer that gives the lid its mechanical stability, its principal portions being the tarsal plates, one in each lid, which border directly upon the opening between the lids, called the palpebral aperture; and (4) the innermost layer of the lid, a portion of the conjunctiva. The conjunctiva is a mucous membrane that serves to attach the eyeball to the orbit and lids but permits a considerable degree of rotation of the eyeball in the orbit.

The conjunctiva. The conjunctiva lines the lids and then bends back over the surface of the eyeball, constituting an outer covering to the forward part of this and terminating at the transparent region of the eye, the cornea. The portion that lines the lids is called the palpebral portion of the conjunctiva; the portion covering the white of the eyeball is called the bulbar conjunctiva. Between the bulbar and the palpebral conjunctiva there are two loose, redundant portions forming recesses that project back toward the equator of the globe. These recesses are called the upper and lower fornices, or conjunctival sacs; it is the looseness of the conjunctiva at these points that makes movements of lids and eyeball possible. (The ophthalmologist finds the lower conjunctival sac a useful cavity in which to place drops containing drugs by merely pulling the outer lid away from the globe. The drops are retained in the cavity long enough to act directly on the cornea and to diffuse through this into the internal structures of the eye.)

The fibrous layer. The fibrous layer, which gives the lid its mechanical stability, is made up of the thick, and relatively rigid, tarsal plates, bordering directly on the palpebral aperture, and the much thinner palpebral fascia, or sheet of connective tissue; the two together are called the septum orbitale. When the lids are closed, the whole opening of the orbit is covered by this septum. Two ligaments, the medial and lateral palpebral ligaments, attached to the orbit and to the septum orbitale, stabilize the position of the lids in relation to the globe. The medial ligament, by far the stronger, is well illustrated in Figure 1.

The muscles. Closure of the lids is achieved by contraction of the orbicularis muscle, a single oval sheet of muscle extending from the regions of the forehead and face and surrounding the orbit into the lids. It is divided into orbital and palpebral portions, and it is essentially the palpebral portion, within the lid, that causes lid closure. The palpebral portion passes across the lids from a ligament called the medial palpebral ligament and from the neighbouring bone of the orbit in a series of half ellipses that meet outside the outer corner of the eye, the

From P. Kronfeld, *The Eye*, vol. 1 (1962); Academic Press

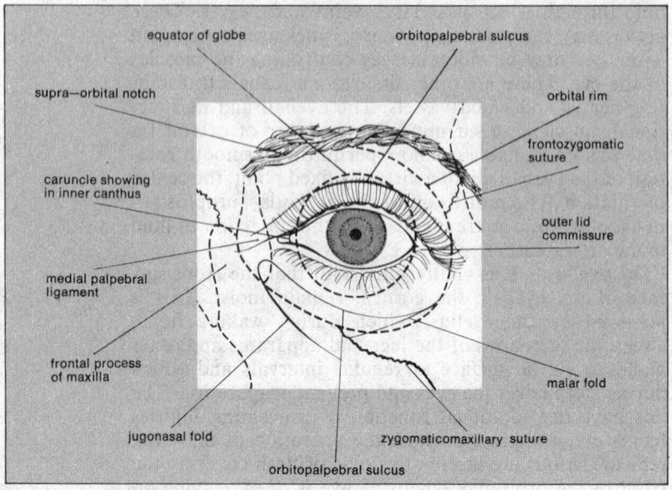

Figure 1: Frontal view of the eye and its related structures (see text).

lateral canthus, to form a band of fibres called the lateral palpebral raphe. Additional parts of the orbicularis have been given separate names—namely, Horner's muscle and the muscle of Riolan; they come into close relation with the lacrimal apparatus and assist in drainage of the tears. The muscle of Riolan, lying close to the lid margins, doubtless contributes to keeping the lids in close apposition, an important feature for maintaining the junction watertight. The orbital portion of the orbicularis is not normally concerned with blinking, which may be carried out entirely by the palpebral portion; however, it is concerned with closing the eyes tightly. The skin of the forehead, temple, and cheek is then drawn toward the medial (nose) side of the orbit, and the radiating furrows, formed by this action of the orbital portion, eventually lead to the so-called crow's feet of elderly persons. It must be appreciated that the two portions can be activated independently; thus, the orbital portion may contract, causing a furrowing of the brows that reduces the amount of light entering from above, while the palpebral portion remains relaxed and allows the eyes to remain open.

Horner's
muscle
and the
muscle of
Riolan

Opening of the eye is not just the result of passive relaxation of the orbicularis muscle but also is the effect of the contraction of the levator palpebrae superioris muscle of the upper lid. This muscle takes origin with the extraocular muscles at the apex of the orbit (the back of the eye socket) as a narrow tendon and runs forward into the upper lid as a broad tendon, the levator aponeurosis, which is attached to the forward surface of the tarsus and the skin covering the upper lid. Contraction of the muscle causes elevation of the upper eyelid. The nervous connections of this muscle are closely related to those of the extraocular muscle required to elevate the eye, so that when the eye looks upward the upper eyelid tends to move up in unison.

The orbicularis and levator are striped muscles under voluntary control. The lids contain, in addition, unstriped (involuntary) muscle fibres that are activated by the sympathetic division of the autonomic system and tend to widen the palpebral fissure (the eye opening) by elevation of the upper, and depression of the lower, lid.

In addition to the muscles already described, other facial muscles often cooperate in the act of lid closure or opening. Thus, the corrugator supercilii muscles pull the eyebrows toward the bridge of the nose, making a projecting "roof" over the medial angle of the eye and producing characteristic furrows in the forehead; the roof is used primarily to protect the eye from the glare of the sun. The pyramidalis, or procerus, muscles occupy the bridge of the nose; they arise from the lower portion of the nasal bones and are attached to the skin of the lower part of the forehead on either side of the midline; they pull the skin into transverse furrows. In lid opening, the frontalis muscle, arising high on the forehead, midway between the coronal suture, a seam across the top of the skull, and the orbital margin, is attached to the skin of the eyebrows. Contraction therefore causes the eyebrows to rise and opposes the action of the orbital portion of the orbicularis; the muscle is especially used when one gazes upward. It is also brought into action when vision is rendered difficult either by distance or the absence of sufficient light.

The skin. The outermost layer of the lid is the skin, with features not greatly different from skin on the rest of the body, with the possible exception of large pigment cells, which, although found elsewhere, are much more numerous in the skin of the lids. The cells may wander, and it is these movements of the pigment cells that determine the changes in coloration seen in some people with alterations in health. The skin has sweat glands and hairs. As the junction between skin and conjunctiva is approached, the hairs change their character to become eyelashes (Figure 2).

The glandular apparatus. The eye is kept moist by secretions of the lacrimal glands (tear glands). These almond-shaped glands under the upper lids extend inward from the outer corner of each eye. Each gland has two portions. One portion is in a shallow depression in the

Tear
glands

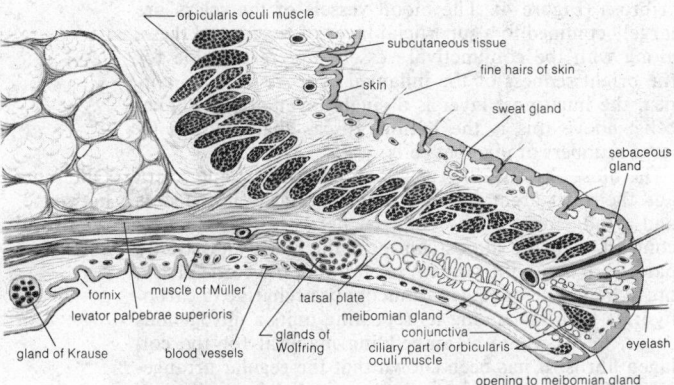

Figure 2: Vertical section through upper lid (see text).
By permission from Eugene Wolff, *Anatomy of the Eye and Orbit*. London:
H. K. Lewis & Co.

part of the eye socket formed by the frontal bone. The other portion projects into the back part of the upper lid. The ducts from each gland, three to 12 in number, open into the superior conjunctival fornix, or sac. From the fornix, the tears flow down across the eye and into the puncta lacrimalia, small openings at the margin of each eyelid near its inner corner. The puncta are openings into the lacrimal ducts; these carry the tears into the lacrimal sacs, the dilated upper ends of the nasolacrimal ducts, which carry the tears into the nose.

The evaporation of the tears as they flow across the eye is largely prevented by the secretion of oily and mucous material by other glands. Thus, the meibomian, or tarsal glands, consist of a row of elongated glands extending through the tarsal plates; they secrete an oil that emerges onto the surface of the lid margin and acts as a barrier for the tear fluid, which accumulates in the grooves between the eyeball and the lid barriers.

Extraocular muscles. Six muscles outside the eye govern its movements. These muscles are the four rectus muscles—the inferior, medial, lateral, and superior recti—and the superior and inferior oblique muscles. The rectus muscles arise from a fibrous ring that encircles the optic nerve at the optic foramen, the opening through which the nerve passes, and are attached to the sclera, the opaque portion of the eyeball, in front of the equator, or widest part, of the eye. The superior oblique muscle arises near the rim of the optic foramen and somewhat nearer the nose than the origin of the rectus medialis. It ends in a rounded tendon that passes through a fibrous ring, the trochlea, that is attached to the frontal bone. The trochlea acts as a pulley. The tendon is attached to the sclera back of the equator of the eye (Figure 3).

The inferior oblique muscle originates from the floor of the orbit, passes under the eyeball like a sling, and is attached to the sclera between the attachments of the su-

perior and lateral rectus muscles. The rectus muscles direct the gaze upward and downward and from side to side. The inferior oblique muscle tends to direct the eye upward, and the superior oblique to depress the eye; because of the obliqueness of the pull, each causes the eye to roll, and in an opposite direction.

The oblique muscles are strictly antagonistic to each other, but they work with the vertical rectus muscles in so far as the superior rectus and inferior oblique both tend to elevate the gaze and the inferior rectus and superior oblique both tend to depress the gaze. The superior and inferior recti do not produce a pure action of elevation or depression because their plane of action is not exactly vertical; in consequence, as with the obliques, they cause some degree of rolling, but by no means so great as that caused by the obliques; the direction of rolling caused by the rectus muscle is opposite to that of its synergistic oblique; the superior rectus causes the eye to roll inward, and the inferior oblique outward.

THE EYE

General description. The eyeball is not a simple sphere but can be viewed as the result of fusing a small portion of a small, strongly curved sphere with a large portion of a large, not so strongly curved sphere (Figure 4). The small piece, occupying about one-sixth of the whole, has a radius of eight millimetres (0.3 inch); it is transparent and is called the cornea; the remainder, the scleral segment, is opaque and has a radius of 12 millimetres (0.5 inch). The ring where the two areas join is called the limbus. Thus, on looking directly into the eye from in front one sees the white sclera surrounding the cornea; because the latter is transparent one sees, instead of the cornea, a ring of tissue lying within the eye, the iris. The iris is the structure that determines the colour of the eye. The centre of this ring is called the pupil. It appears dark because the light passing into the eye is not reflected back to any great extent. By use of an ophthalmoscope, an instrument that permits the observer to illuminate the interior of the eyeball while observing through the pupil, the appearance of the interior lining of the globe can be made out; this is called the fundus; it is characterized by the large blood vessels that supply blood to the retina; these are especially distinct as they cross over the pallid optic disk, or papilla, the region where the optic nerve fibres leave the globe.

The dimensions of the eye are reasonably constant, varying among individuals by only a millimetre or two; the sagittal (vertical) diameter is about 24 millimetres (about one inch) and is usually less than the transverse diameter. At birth the sagittal diameter is about 16 to 17 millimetres (about 0.65 inch); it increases rapidly to about 22.5 to 23 millimetres (about 0.89 inch) by the age of three years; between three and 13 the globe attains its full size. The weight is about 7.5 grams (.25 ounce), and its volume 6.5 millilitres (0.4 cubic inch).

The eye is made up of three coats, which enclose the

Visible parts of the eye

From P. Kronfeld, *The Eye*, vol. 1 (1962); Academic Press

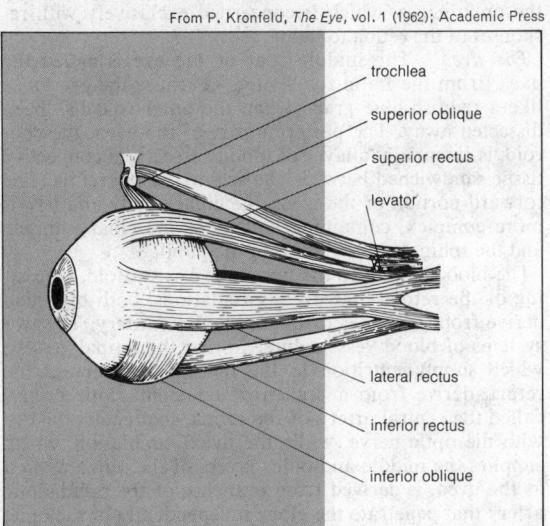

Figure 3: The extraocular muscles.

From H. Davson, M.D., *Physiology of the Eye*

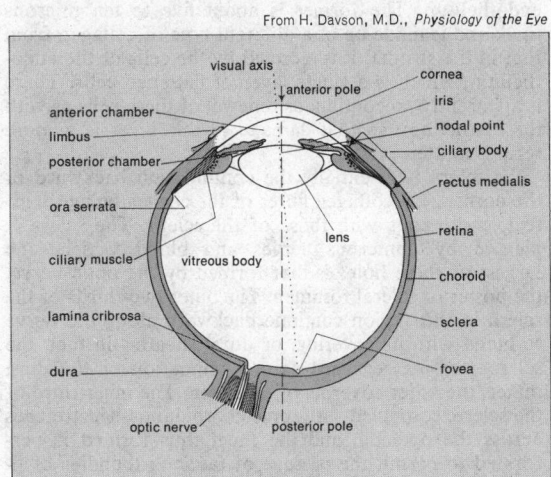

Figure 4: Horizontal section of the eye.

optically clear aqueous humour, lens, and vitreous body (Figure 4). The outermost coat consists of the cornea and the sclera; the middle coat contains the main blood supply to the eye and consists, from the back forward, of the choroid, the ciliary body, and the iris. The innermost layer is the retina, lying on the choroid and receiving most of its nourishment from the vessels within the choroid, the remainder of its nourishment being derived from the retinal vessels that lie on its surface and are visible in the ophthalmoscope. The ciliary body and iris have a very thin covering, the ciliary epithelium and posterior epithelium of the iris, which is continuous with the retina.

Within the cavities formed by this triple-layered coat there are the crystalline lens, suspended by fine transparent fibres—the suspensory ligament or zonule of Zinn—from the ciliary body; the aqueous humour, a clear fluid filling the spaces between the cornea and the lens and iris; and the vitreous body, a clear jelly filling the much larger cavity enclosed by the sclera, the ciliary body, and the lens. The anterior chamber of the eye is defined as the space between the cornea and the forward surfaces of the iris and lens, while the posterior chamber is the much smaller space between the rear surface of the iris and the ciliary body, zonule, and lens; the two chambers both contain aqueous humour and are in connection through the pupil.

Outer and middle tunics of the globe. *The outermost coat.* The outermost coat is made up of the cornea and the sclera. The cornea is the transparent window of the eye. It contains five distinguishable layers; the epithelium, or outer covering; Bowman's membrane; the stroma, or supporting structure; Descemet's membrane; and the endothelium, or inner lining. Up to 90 percent of the thickness of the cornea is made up of the stroma. The epithelium, which is a continuation of the epithelium of the conjunctiva, is itself made up of about six layers of cells. The superficial layer is continuously being shed, and the layers are renewed by multiplication of the cells in the innermost, or basal, layer.

The layers of the cornea

The stroma appears as a set of lamellae, or plates, running parallel with the surface and superimposed on each other like the leaves of a book; between the lamellae lie the corneal corpuscles, cells that synthesize new collagen (connective tissue protein) essential for the repair and maintenance of this layer. The lamellae are made up of microscopically visible fibres that run parallel to form sheets; in successive lamellae the fibres make a large angle with each other. The lamellae in man are about 1.5 to 2.5 microns (one micron = 0.001 millimetre) thick, so that there are about 200 lamellae in the human cornea. The fibrous basis of the stroma is collagen.

Immediately above the stroma, adjacent to the epithelium, is Bowman's membrane, about eight to 14 microns thick; in the electron microscope it is evident that it is really stroma, but with the collagen fibrils not arranged in the orderly fashion seen in the rest of the stroma.

Beneath the stroma are Descemet's membrane and the endothelium. The former is about five to ten microns thick and is made up of a different type of collagen from that in the stroma; it is secreted by the cells of the endothelium, which is a single layer of flattened cells. There is apparently no continuous renewal of these cells as with the epithelium, so that damage to this layer is a more serious matter.

The sclera is essentially the continuation backward of the cornea, the collagen fibres of the cornea being, in effect, continuous with those of the sclera. The sclera is pierced by numerous nerves and blood vessels; the largest of these holes is that formed by the optic nerve, the posterior scleral foramen. The outer two-thirds of the sclera in this region continue backward along the nerve to blend with its covering, or dural sheath—in fact, the sclera may be regarded as a continuation of the dura mater, the outer covering of the brain. The inner third of the sclera, combined with some choroidal tissue, stretches across the opening, and the sheet thus formed is perforated to permit the passage of fasciculi (bundles of fibres) of the optic nerve. This region is called the lamina

cribrosa (Figure 4). The blood vessels of the sclera are largely confined to a superficial layer of tissue, and these, along with the conjunctival vessels, are responsible for the bright redness of the inflamed eye. As with the cornea, the innermost layer is a single layer of endothelial cells; above this is the lamina fusca, characterized by large numbers of pigment cells.

The most obvious difference between the opaque sclera and the transparent cornea is the irregularity in the sizes and arrangement of the collagen fibrils in the sclera by contrast with the almost uniform thickness and strictly parallel array in the cornea; in addition, the cornea has a much higher percentage of mucopolysaccharide (a carbohydrate that has among its repeating units a nitrogenous sugar, hexosamine) as embedding material for the collagen fibrils. It has been shown that the regular arrangement of the fibrils is, in fact, the essential factor leading to the transparency of the cornea.

Differences between sclera and cornea

When the cornea is damaged—*e.g.*, by a virus infection—the collagen laid down in the repair processes is not regularly arranged, with the result that an opaque patch called a leukoma, may occur.

When an eye is removed, or a man dies, the cornea soon loses its transparency, becoming hazy; this is due to the taking in of fluid from the aqueous humour, the cornea becoming thicker as it becomes hazier. The cornea can be made to reassume its transparency by maintaining it in a warm, well-aerated chamber, at about 31° C or 88° F (its normal temperature); associated with this return of transparency is a loss of fluid.

Modern studies have shown that, under normal conditions, the cornea tends to take in fluid, mainly from the aqueous humour and from the small blood vessels at the limbus, but this is counteracted by a pump that expels the fluid as fast as it enters. This pumping action depends on an adequate supply of energy, and any situation that prejudices this supply causes the cornea to swell—the pump fails, or works so slowly that it cannot keep pace with the leak. Death is one cause of the failure of the pump, but this is primarily because of the loss of temperature; place the dead eye in a warm chamber and the reserves of metabolic energy it contains in the form of sugar and glycogen are adequate to keep the cornea transparent for 24 hours or more. When it is required to store corneas for grafting, as in an eye bank, it is best to remove the cornea from the globe to prevent it from absorbing fluid from the aqueous humour. The structure responsible for the pumping action is almost certainly the endothelium, so that damage to this lining can lead to a loss of transparency with swelling.

The cornea is exquisitely sensitive to pain. This is mediated by sensory nerve fibres, called ciliary nerves, that run just underneath the endothelium; they belong to the ophthalmic branch of the fifth cranial nerve, the large sensory nerve of the head. The ciliary nerves leave the globe through holes in the sclera, not in company with the optic nerve, which is concerned exclusively with responses of the retina to light.

The uvea. The middle coat of the eye is called the uvea (from the Latin for "grape") because the eye looks like a reddish-blue grape when the outer coat has been dissected away. The posterior part of the uvea, the choroid, is essentially a layer of blood vessels and connective tissue sandwiched between the sclera and the retina. The forward portion of the uvea, the ciliary body and iris, is more complex, containing as it does the ciliary muscle and the sphincter and dilator of the pupil.

Ciliary body and iris

The blood supply to the human eye is twofold, consisting of the retinal and uveal circulations, both of which derive from branches of the ophthalmic artery. The two systems of blood vessels differ in that the retinal vessels, which supply nutrition to the innermost layers of the retina, derive from a branch of the ophthalmic artery, called the central artery of the retina, that enters the eye with the optic nerve, while the uveal circulation, which supplies the middle and outer layers of the retina as well as the uvea, is derived from branches of the ophthalmic artery that penetrate the globe independently of the optic nerve.

The ciliary body is the forward continuation of the choroid. It is a muscular ring, triangular in horizontal section, beginning at the region called the ora serrata and ending, in front, as the root of the iris (Figure 5). The

From P. Kronfeld, *The Eye*, vol. 1 (1962); Academic Press

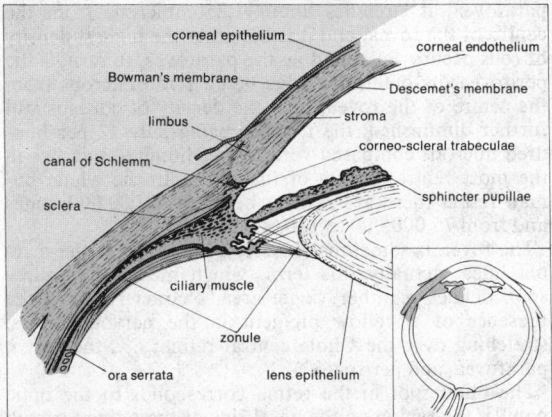

corneal epithelium
corneal endothelium
Bowman's membrane
Descemet's membrane
limbus
stroma
canal of Schlemm
corneo-scleral trabeculae
sclera
sphincter pupillae
ciliary muscle
zonule
ora serrata
lens epithelium

Figure 5: The anteronasal portion of a horizontal (meridional) section through a right eye. Shaded area of inset locates magnified portion. (See text).

surface is thrown into folds, called ciliary processes, the whole being covered by the ciliary epithelium, which is a double layer of cells; the layer next to the vitreous body (see below), called the inner layer, is transparent, while the outer layer, which is continuous with the pigment epithelium of the retina, is heavily pigmented. These two layers are to be regarded embryologically as the forward continuation of the retina, which terminates at the ora serrata. Their function is to secrete the aqueous humour.

The ciliary muscle is an unstriped, involuntary, muscle concerned with alterations in the adjustments of focus—accommodation—of the optical system; the fibres run both across the muscle ring and circularly, and the effect of their contraction is to cause the whole body to move forward and to become fatter, so that the suspensory ligament that holds the lens in place is loosened.

The most forward portion of the uvea is the iris. This is the only portion that is visible to superficial inspection, appearing as a perforated disc, the central perforation, or pupil, varying in size according to the surrounding illumination and other factors. A prominent feature is the collarette at the inner edge, representing the place of attachment of the embryonic pupillary membrane that, in embryonic life, covers the pupil. As with the ciliary body, with which it is anatomically continuous, the iris consists of several layers: namely, an anterior layer of endothelium, the stroma; and the posterior iris epithelium. The stroma contains the blood vessels and the sphincter and dilator muscles; in addition, the stroma contains pigment cells that determine the colour of the eye. Posteriorly, the stroma is covered by a double layer of epithelium, the continuation forward of the ciliary epithelium; here, however, both layers are heavily pigmented and serve to prevent light from passing through the iris tissue, confining the optical pathway to the pupil. The pink iris of the albino is the result of the absence of pigment in these layers. The cells of the anterior layer of the iris epithelium have projections that become the fibres of the dilator muscle; these projections run radially, so that when they contract they pull the iris into folds and widen the pupil; by contrast, the fibres of the sphincter pupillae muscle run in a circle around the pupil, so that when they contract the pupil becomes smaller.

Usually, a baby belonging to the white races is born with blue eyes because of the absence of pigment cells in the stroma; the light reflected back from the posterior epithelium, which is blue because of scattering and selective absorption, passes through the stroma to the eye of the observer. As time goes on, pigment is deposited, and the colour changes; if much pigment is laid down the eye becomes brown or black, if little, it remains blue or gray.

The inner tunic of the globe. The inner tunic of the rear portion of the globe, as far forward as the ciliary body, is the retina, including its epithelia or coverings. These epithelia continue forward to line the remainder of the globe.

The epithelia. Separating the choroid (the middle tunic of the globe) from the retina proper is a layer of pigmented cells, the pigment epithelium of the retina; this acts as a restraining barrier to the indiscriminate diffusion of material from the blood in the choroid to the retina. The retina ends at the ora serrata, where the ciliary body begins (Figure 4). The pigment epithelium continues forward as a pigmented layer of cells covering the ciliary body; farther forward still, the epithelium covers the posterior surface of the iris and provides the cells that constitute the dilator muscle of this diaphragm. Next to the pigment epithelium of the retina is the neuroepithelium, or rods and cones (see below). Their continuation forward is represented by a second layer of epithelial cells covering the ciliary body, so that by the ciliary epithelium is meant the two layers of cells that are the embryological equivalent of the retinal pigment epithelium and the receptor layer (rods and cones) of the retina. This unpigmented layer of the ciliary epithelium is continued forward over the back of the iris, where it acquires pigment and is called the posterior iris epithelium.

The retina. The retina is the part of the eye that receives the light and converts it into chemical energy. The chemical energy activates nerves that conduct the messages out of the eye into the higher regions of the brain. The retina is a complex nervous structure, being, in essence, an outgrowth of the forebrain.

Ten layers of cells in the retina can be seen microscopically. In general, there are four main layers: (1) Next to the choroid is the pigment epithelium, already mentioned. (2) Beneath the epithelium is the layer of rods and cones, the light-sensitive cells. The changes induced in the rods and cones by light are transmitted to (3) a layer of neurons (nerve cells) called the bipolar cells, which are analogous to the sensory neurons that carry messages from the touch and heat receptors of the skin and transmit them to the cells of the spinal cord or the medulla (the part of the brain that is a continuation of the spinal cord). These bipolar cells connect with (4) the innermost layer of neurons, the ganglion cells; and the transmitted messages are carried out of the eye along their projections, or axons, which constitute the optic nerve fibres. Thus, the optic nerve is really a central tract, rather than a nerve, connecting two regions of the nervous system, namely, the layer of bipolar cells, and the cells of the lateral geniculate body, the latter being a visual relay station in the diencephalon (the rear portion of the forebrain).

The arrangement of the retinal cells in an orderly manner gives rise to the outer nuclear layer (layer 4 in Figure 6), containing the nuclei of the rods and cones; the inner nuclear layer (layer 6), containing the nuclei and perikarya (main cell bodies outside the nucleus) of the bipolar cells, and the ganglion cell layer (layer 8), containing the corresponding structures of the ganglion cells. The plexiform layers are regions in which the neurons make their interconnections. Thus, the outer plexiform layer (layer 5) contains the rod and cone projections terminating as the rod spherule and cone pedicle; these make connections with the dendritic processes of the bipolar cells, so that changes produced by light in the rods and cones are transmitted by way of these connections to the bipolar cells. (The dendritic process of a nerve cell is the projection that receives nerve impulses to the cell; the axon is the projection that carries impulses from the cell.) In the inner plexiform layer (layer 7) are the axons of the bipolar cells and the dendritic processes of the ganglion and amacrine cells (see below). The association is such as to allow messages in the bipolar cells to be transmitted to the ganglion cells, the messages then passing out along the axons of the ganglion cells as optic nerve messages.

The photosensitive cells are, in the human and in most vertebrate retinas, of two kinds, called rods and cones,

The pigment epithelium

The rods and cones

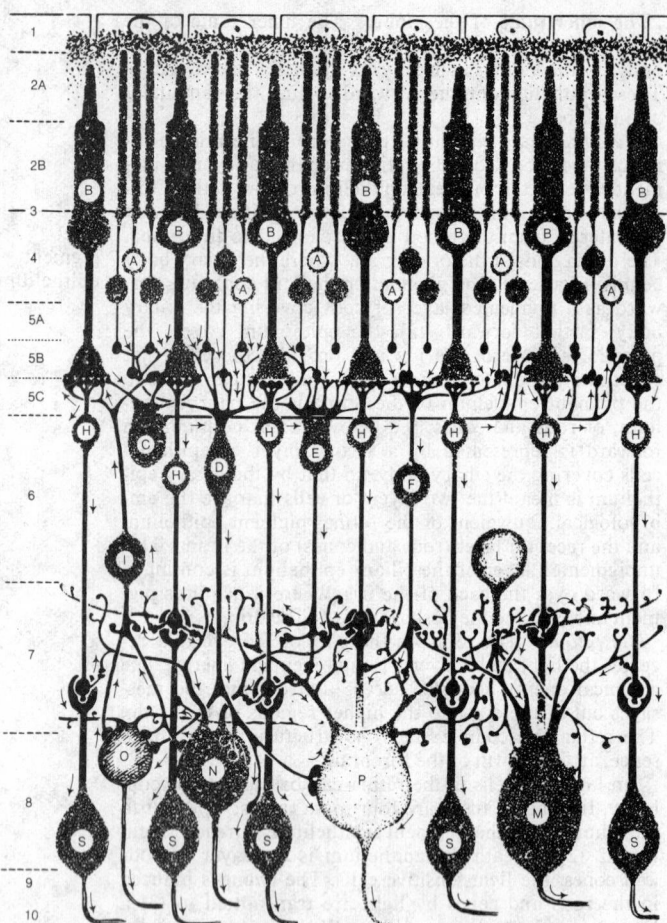

Figure 6: *The retinal cells directly involved in the visual process.*
(A) Rod and (B) cone cells, the photoreceptors. (C) Horizontal cells. (D) Mop, (E) brush, (F) flat-topped, (H) midget, and (I) centrifugal varieties of bipolar cells. (L) Several varieties of amacrine cells. (M) Parasol, (N) shrub, (O) small diffuse, (P) garland, and (S) midget ganglion varieties of ganglion cells.
By permission of Stephen L. Polyak

the rods being usually much thinner than the cones but both being built up on the same plan. The light-sensitive pigment is contained in the outer segment (layer 2), which rests on the pigment epithelium (layer 1). Through the other end, called the synaptic body, effects of light are transmitted to the bipolar and horizontal cells. When examined at high magnification in the electron microscope, the outer segments of the rods and cones are seen to be composed of stacks of disks, apparently made by the infolding of the limiting membrane surrounding the outer segment; the visual pigment, which is located on the surfaces of these disks, is thus spread over a very wide area, and this contributes to the efficiency with which light is absorbed by the visual cell.

The arrangement of the retina makes it necessary for light to pass through the layers not sensitive to light first before it reaches the light-sensitive rods and cones. The optical disadvantages of this arrangement are largely overcome by the development of the fovea centralis, a localized region of the retina, close to the optic axis of the eye, where the inner layers of the retina are absent. The result is a depression, the foveal pit, where light has an almost unrestricted passage to the light-sensitive cells. It is essentially this region of the retina that is employed for accurate vision, the eyes being directed toward the objects of regard so that their images fall in this restricted region. If the object of interest is large, so as to subtend a large angle, then the eye must move rapidly from region to region so as to bring their images successively onto the fovea; this is typically seen during reading. In the central region of the fovea there are cones exclusively; toward its edges, rods also occur, and as successive

zones are reached the proportion of rods increases while the absolute density of packing of the receptors tends to decrease. Thus, the central fovea is characterized by an exclusive population of very densely packed cones; here, also, the cones are very thin and in form very similar to rods. The region surrounding the fovea is called the parafovea; it stretches about 1,250 microns from the centre of the fovea, and it is here that the highest density of rods occurs. Surrounding the parafovea, in turn, is the perifovea, its outermost edge being 2,750 microns from the centre of the fovea; here the density of cones is still further diminished, the number being only 12 per hundred microns compared with 50 per hundred microns in the most central region of the fovea. In the whole human retina there are said to be about 7,000,000 cones and from 75,000,000 to 150,000,000 rods.

The fovea is sometimes loosely referred to as the macula lutea; actually this term, which means the yellow spot, defines a rather vague area, characterized by the presence of a yellow pigment in the nervous layers, stretching over the whole central retina; *i.e.*, the fovea, parafovea, and perifovea.

The blind spot in the retina corresponds to the optic papilla, the region on the nasal side of the retina through which the optic nerve fibres pass out of the eye.

Although the rods and cones may be said to form a mosaic, the retina is not organized in a simple mosaic fashion in the sense that each rod or cone is connected to a single bipolar cell that itself is connected to a single ganglion cell. There are only about 1,000,000 optic nerve fibres, while there are at least 150,000,000 receptors, so that there must be considerable convergence of receptors on the optic pathway. This means that there will be considerable mixing of messages. Furthermore, the retina contains additional nerve cells besides the bipolar and ganglion cells; these, the horizontal and amacrine cells, operate in the horizontal direction, allowing one area of the retina to influence the activity of another. In this way, for example, the messages from one part of the retina may be suppressed by a visual stimulus falling on another, an important element in the total of messages sent to the higher regions of the brain. Finally, it has been argued that some messages may be running the opposite way; they are called centrifugal and would allow one layer of the retina to affect another, or higher regions of the brain to control the responses of the retinal neurons. In primates the existence of these centrifugal fibres has been finally disproved, but in such lower vertebrates as the pigeon, their existence is quite certain.

The pathway of the retinal messages through the brain is described later in this article; it is sufficient to state here that most of the optic nerve fibres in primates carry their messages to the lateral geniculate body, a relay station specifically concerned with vision. Some of the fibres separate from the main stream and run to a midbrain centre called the pretectal nucleus, which is a relay centre for pupillary responses to light.

The transparent media. Within the cavities enclosed by the three layers of the globe described above there are the aqueous humour in the anterior and posterior chambers; the crystalline lens behind the iris; and the vitreous body, which fills the large cavity behind the lens and iris (Figure 4).

The aqueous humour. The aqueous humour is a clear colourless fluid with a chemical composition rather similar to that of blood plasma (the blood exclusive of its cells) but lacking the high protein content of the latter. Its main function is to keep the globe reasonably firm. It is secreted continuously by the ciliary body into the posterior chamber, and flows as a gentle stream through the pupil into the anterior chamber, from which it is drained by way of a channel at the limbus; that is, the juncture of the cornea and the sclera. This channel, the canal of Schlemm, encircles the cornea and connects by small connector channels to the blood vessels buried in the sclera and forming the intrascleral plexus or network. From this plexus the blood, containing the aqueous humour, passes into more superficial vessels; it finally leaves the eye in the anterior ciliary veins. The relation of the

Retinal organization

Secretion and course of aqueous humour

canal of Schlemm to the aqueous humour is clear from Figure 5. The wall of the canal that faces the aqueous humour is very delicate and allows the fluid to percolate through by virtue of the relatively high pressure of the fluid within the eye. Obstruction of this exit, for example, if the iris is pushed forward to cover the wall of the canal, causes a sharp rise in the pressure within the eye, a condition that is known as glaucoma. Often the obstruction is not obvious, but is caused perhaps by a hardening of the tissue just adjacent to the wall of the canal —the trabecular meshwork (Figure 5), in which case the rise of pressure is more gradual and insidious. Ultimately the abnormal pressure damages the retina and causes a variable degree of blindness. The normal intraocular pressure is about 15 millimetres of mercury above atmospheric pressure, so that if the anterior chamber is punctured by a hypodermic needle the aqueous humour flows out readily. Its function in maintaining the eye reasonably hard is seen by the collapse and wrinkling of the cornea when the fluid is allowed to escape. An additional function of the fluid is to provide nutrition for the crystalline lens and also for the cornea, both of which are devoid of blood vessels; the steady renewal and drainage serve to bring into the eye various nutrient substances, including glucose and amino acids, and to remove waste products of metabolism, such as lactic acid.

The vitreous body. The vitreous body is a jelly. It is remarkable for the small amount of solid matter required to give it this semisolid structure; the solid material is made up of a form of collagen, vitrosin, and a mucopolysaccharide, hyaluronic acid. Thus, its composition is rather similar to that of the cornea, but the proportion of water is much greater, about 98 percent or more, compared with about 75 percent for the cornea. The jelly is probably secreted by certain cells of the retina. In general, the vitreous body is devoid of cells, in contrast with the lens, which is packed tight with cells. Embedded in the surface of the vitreous body, however, there is a population of specialized cells, the hyalocytes of Balazs, which may contribute to the breakdown and renewal of the hyaluronic acid. The vitreous body serves to keep the underlying retina pressed against the choroid.

The crystalline lens. The lens is a transparent body, flatter on its anterior than on its posterior surface, and suspended within the eye by the zonular fibres of Zinn attached to its equator; its anterior surface is bathed by aqueous humour, and its posterior surface by the vitreous body. The lens is a mass of tightly packed transparent fibrous cells, the lens fibres, enclosed in an elastic collagenous capsule. The lens fibres are arranged in sheets that form successive layers; the fibres run from pole to pole of the lens, the middle of a given fibre being in the equatorial region. On meridional (horizontal) section, the fibres are cut longitudinally to give an onion-scale appearance, whereas a section at right-angles to this—an equatorial section—would cut all the fibres across, and the result would be to give a honeycomb appearance. The epithelium, covering the anterior surface of the lens under the capsule, serves as the origin of the lens fibres, both during embryonic and fetal development and during infant and adult life, the lens continuing to grow by the laying down of new fibres throughout life.

The visual process

THE WORK OF THE AUXILIARY STRUCTURES

The protective mechanisms. The first line of protection of the eyes is provided by the lids, which prevent access of foreign bodies and assist in the lubrication of the corneal surface. Lid closure and opening are accomplished by the orbicularis oculi and levator palpebri muscles; the orbicularis oculi operates on both lids, bringing their margins into close apposition in the act of lid closure. Opening results from relaxation of the orbicularis muscle and contraction of the levator palpebri of the upper lid; the smooth muscle of the upper lid, Müller's muscle, or the superior palpebral muscle, also assists in widening the lid aperture. The lower lid does not possess a muscle corresponding to the levator of the upper lid, and the only muscle available for causing an

Blinking

active lowering of the lid, required during the depression of the gaze, is the inferior palpebral muscle, which is analogous to the muscle of Müller of the upper lid (called the superior palpebral muscle). This inferior palpebral muscle is so directly fused with the sheaths of the ocular muscles that it provides cooperative action, opening of the lid on downward gaze being mediated, in effect, mainly by the inferior rectus.

Innervation. The seventh cranial nerve—the facial nerve—supplies the motor fibres for the orbicularis muscle. The levator is innervated by the third cranial nerve —the oculomotor nerve—that also innervates some of the extraocular muscles concerned with rotation of the eyeball, including the superior rectus. The smooth muscle of the eyelids and orbit is activated by the sympathetic division of the autonomic system. The secretion of adrenaline during such states of excitement as fear would also presumably cause contraction of the smooth muscle, but it seems unlikely that this would lead to the protrusion of the eyes traditionally associated with extreme fear. It is possible that the widening of the lid aperture occurring in this excited state, and dilation of the pupil, create the illusion of eye protrusion.

Blinking is normally an involuntary act, but may be carried out voluntarily. The more vigorous "full closure" of the lids involves the orbital portion of the orbicularis muscle and may be accompanied by contraction of the facial muscles that have been described as accessory muscles of blinking: namely, the corrugator supercilii, which on contraction pulls the eyebrows toward the bridge of the nose; and the procerus or pyramidalis, which pulls the skin of the forehead into horizontal folds, acting as a protection when the eyes are exposed to bright light. The more vigorous full closure may be evoked as a reflex response.

Voluntary full closure of lids

Blink reflexes. Reflex blinking may be caused by practically any peripheral stimulus, but the two functionally significant reflexes are (1) that resulting from stimulation of the endings of the fifth cranial nerve in the cornea, lid, or conjunctiva—the sensory blink reflex, or corneal reflex—and (2) that caused by bright light—the optical blink reflex. The corneal reflex is rapid (0.1 second reflex time) and is the last to disappear in deepening anesthesia, impulses being relayed from the nucleus of the fifth nerve to the seventh cranial nerve, which transmits the motor impulses. The reflex is said to be under the control of a medullary centre. The optical reflex is slower; in man, the nervous pathway includes the visual cortex (the outer substance of the brain; the visual centre is located in the occipital—rear—lobe). The reflex is absent in children of less than nine months.

Normal rhythm. In the waking hours the eyes blink fairly regularly at intervals of two to ten seconds, the actual rate being a characteristic of the individual. The function of this is to spread the lacrimal secretions over the cornea. It might be thought that each blink would be reflexly determined by a corneal stimulus—drying and irritation—but the results of extensive studies indicate that this view is wrong; the normal blinking rate is apparently determined by the activity of a "blinking centre" in the globus pallidus of the caudate nucleus, a mass of gray matter—nerve cells—between the base and the outer substance—of the brain. This is not to deny, however, that the blink rate is modified by external stimuli.

There is a strong association between blinking and the action of the extraocular muscles. Eye movement is generally accompanied by a blink, and it is thought that this aids the eyes in changing their fixation point.

Secretion of tears. The exposed surface of the globe (eyeball) is kept moist by the tears secreted by the lacrimal apparatus, together with the mucous and oily secretions of the other secretory organs and cells of the lids and conjunctiva; these have been described earlier. The secretion produces what has been called the precorneal film, which consists of an inner layer of mucus, a middle layer of lacrimal secretion, and an outer oily film that reduces the rate of evaporation of the underlying watery layer. The normal daily (24-hour) rate of secretion has been estimated at about 0.75 to 1.1

grams; secretion tends to decrease with age. Chemical analysis of the tears reveals a typical body fluid with a salt concentration similar to that of blood plasma. An interesting component is lysozyme, an enzyme that has bactericidal action by virtue of its power of dissolving away the outer coats of many bacteria.

Tear reflexes

Tears are secreted reflexly in response to a variety of stimuli—*e.g.*, irritative stimuli to the cornea, conjunctiva, nasal mucosa; hot or peppery stimuli applied to the mouth and tongue; or bright lights. In addition, tear flow occurs in association with vomiting, coughing, and yawning. The secretion associated with emotional upset is called psychical weeping. Severing of the sensory root of the trigeminal (fifth cranial) nerve prevents all reflex weeping, leaving psychical weeping unaffected; similarly, the application of cocaine to the surface of the eye, which paralyzes the sensory nerve endings, inhibits reflex weeping, even when the eye is exposed to potent tear gases. The afferent (sensory) pathway in the reflex is thus by way of the fifth cranial, or the trigeminal nerve. The motor innervation is by way of the autonomic (involuntary) division; the parasympathetic supply derived from the facial nerve (the seventh cranial nerve) seems to have the dominant motor influence. Thus, drugs the effect of which mimics the parasympathetic, such as acetylcholine, provoke secretion, and secretion may be blocked by such typical anticholinergic drugs (drugs the action of which counters that of acetylcholine) as atropine. Innervation of the lacrimal gland is not always complete at the time of birth, so that the newborn infant is generally said to cry without weeping. Because absence of reflex tearing fails to produce any serious drying of the cornea, and surgical destruction of the main lacrimal gland is often without serious consequences, it seems likely that the subsidiary secretion from the accessory lacrimal glands is adequate to keep the cornea moist. The reflex secretion that produces abundant tears may be regarded as an emergency response.

A drainage mechanism for tears is necessary only during copious secretion. The mechanism, described as the lacrimal pump, consists of alternately negative and positive pressure in the lacrimal sac caused by the contraction of the orbicularis muscle during blinking.

Movements of the eyes. Because only a small portion of the retina, the fovea, is actually employed for distinct vision, it is vitally important that the motor apparatus governing the direction of gaze be extremely precise in its operation, and rapid. Thus, the gaze must shift swiftly and accurately during the process of reading. Again, if the gaze must remain fixed on a single small object—*e.g.*, a golf ball—the eyes must keep adjusting their gaze to compensate for the continuous small movements of the head and to maintain the image exactly on the fovea. The extraocular muscles that carry out these movements are under voluntary control; thus, the direction of regard can be changed deliberately. Most of the actual movements of the eyes are carried out without awareness, however, in response to movements of the objects in the environment, or in response to movements of the head or the rest of the body, and so on. In examining the mechanisms of the eye movements, then, one must resolve them into a number of reflex responses to changes in the environment or the individual, remembering, of course, that there is an overriding voluntary control.

Centring images on the fovea

The axes of the eye. It is worthwhile at this point to define certain axes of the eyes employed during different types of study. The optic axis of the eye is a line drawn through the centre of the cornea and the nodal (central) point of the eye; it actually does not intersect with the retina at the centre of the fovea as might be expected, but toward the nose from this, so that there is an angle of about five degrees between (1) the visual axis—the line joining the point fixated (the point toward which the gaze is directed) and the nodal point—and (2) the optic axis.

Actions of muscles. The general modes of action of the six extraocular muscles have been described in connection with their anatomy: rotation of the eye toward the nose is carried out by the medial rectus; outward movement is by the lateral rectus. Upward movements are carried out by the combined actions of the superior rectus and the inferior oblique muscles, and downward movements by the inferior rectus and the superior oblique. Intermediate directions of gaze are achieved by combined actions of several muscles. When the two eyes act together, as they normally do, and change their direction of gaze to the left, for example, the left eye rotates away from the nose by means of its lateral rectus, while the right eye turns toward the nose by means of its medial rectus. These muscles may be considered as a linked pair; that is, when they are activated by the central nervous system this occurs conjointly and virtually automatically. This linking of the muscles of the two eyes is an important physiological feature and has still more important pathological interest in the analysis of squint, when the two eyes fail to be directed at the same point.

Binocular movements. The binocular movements (the movements of the two eyes) fall into two classes, the conjugate movements, when both eyes move in the same direction, as in a change in the direction of gaze, and disjunctive movements, when the eyes move in opposite directions. Thus, during convergence onto a near object both eyes move toward the nose; the movement is horizontal, but disjunctive, by contrast with the conjugate movement when both eyes move, say, to the right. The disjunctive movement of convergence can be carried out voluntarily, but the act is usually brought about reflexly in response to the changed optical situation—*i.e.*, the nearness of the object of gaze. A seesaw movement of the eyes, whereby one eye looks upward and the other downward, is possible, but not voluntarily; to achieve this a prism is placed in front on one eye so that the object seen through it appears displaced upward or downward; the other eye sees the object where it is. The result of such an arrangement is that, unless the eye with the prism in front makes an upward or downward movement, independent of the other, the images will not fall on corresponding parts of the retinas in the two eyes. Such a noncorrespondence of the retinal images causes double vision; to avoid this, there is an adjustment in the alignment of the eyes so that a seesaw movement is actually executed. In a similar way, the eyes may be made to undergo torsion, or rolling. A conjugate torsion, in which both eyes rotate about their anteroposterior (fore-and-aft) axes in the same sense, occurs naturally; for example, when the head tips toward one shoulder the eyes tend to roll in the opposite direction, with the result that the image of the visual field on the retina tends to remain vertical in spite of the rotation of the head.

Conjugate and disjunctive movements

Nervous control. The nerves controlling the actions of the muscles are the third, fourth, and sixth cranial nerves, with their bodies (nuclei) in the brainstem; the third, or oculomotor nerve, controls the superior and inferior recti, the medial rectus, and inferior oblique; the fourth cranial nerve, the trochlear nerve, controls the superior oblique; and the sixth, the abducens nerve, controls the lateral rectus. The nuclei of these nerves are closely associated; especially, there are connections between the nuclei of the sixth cranial nerve, controlling the lateral rectus, and the nucleus of the third, controlling the medial rectus; it is through this close relationship that the linking of the lateral rectus of one eye and the medial rectus of the other, indicated above, is achieved. Another type of linking is concerned with reciprocal inhibition; that is, when there are two antagonistic muscles, such as the medial and the lateral rectus, contraction of one is accompanied by a simultaneous inhibition of the other. Muscles show a continuous slight activity even when at rest; this keeps them taut; this action, called tonic activity, is brought about by discharges in the motor nerve to the muscle. Hence, when the agonist muscle contracts its antagonist must be inhibited.

Reflex pathways. In examining any reflex movement one must look for the sensory input—*i.e.*, the way in which messages in sensory nerves bring about discharges in the motor nerves to the muscles; this study involves

Fixation reflex

the connections of the motor nerves or nuclei with other centres of the brain.

When a subject is looking straight ahead and a bright light appears in the periphery of his field of vision, his eyes automatically turn to fix on the light; this is called the fixation reflex. The sensory pathway in the reflex arc leads as far as the cerebral cortex because removal of the occipital cortex (the outer brain substance at the back of the head) abolishes reflex eye movements in response to light stimuli. If the occipital cortex is stimulated electrically, movements of the eyes may be induced, and in fact one may draw a pattern of the visual field on the occipital cortex corresponding with the directions in which the gaze is turned when given points on the cortex are stimulated. This pattern corresponds with the pattern obtained by recording the visual responses to light stimuli from different parts of the visual field.

The remainder of the pathway—*i.e.*, from the occipital cortex to the motor neurons in the brainstem—has long been considered to involve the superior colliculi as relay stations, and they certainly have such a role in lower animals; but in human beings a pathway from the cortex to the eye-muscle nuclei independent of the superior colliculi is now generally assumed (the superior colliculi are areas in the midbrain).

Continual movements of the eyes occur even when an effort is made to maintain steady fixation of an object. Some of these movements may be regarded as manifestations of the fixation reflex; thus, the eyes tend to drift off their target, and, because of this, the fixation reflex comes into play, bringing the eyes back on target.

Nystagmus

Experimentally, the fixation reflex can be studied by observation of the regular to-and-fro movements of the eyes as they follow a rotating drum striped in black and white. (Such movements of the eyes directed at a moving object are called optokinetic nystagmus; nystagmus itself is the involuntary movement of the eye back and forth, up and down, or in a rotatory or a mixed fashion.) While the eyes watch the moving drum, they involuntarily make a slow movement as a result of fixing their gaze on a particular stripe. At a certain point, fixation is broken off, and the eyes spring back to fix on a new stripe. Thus, the nystagmus consists of a slow movement with angular velocity equal to that of the rotation of the drum, then a fast saccade, or jump from one point of fixation to another, in the opposite direction; the process is repeated indefinitely.

Another type of nystagmus reveals the play of another set of reflexes. These are mediated by the semicircular canals—*i.e.*, the organs of balance or the vestibular apparatus. Such a reflex may be evoked by rotating the subject in a chair at a steady speed; the eyes move slowly in the opposite direction to that of rotation and, at the end of their excursion, jump back with a fast saccade in the direction of rotation. If rotation suddenly ceases, the eyes go into a nystagmus in the opposite direction, the postrotatory nystagmus.

During rotation, certain semicircular canals are being stimulated, and the important point is that any acceleration of the head that stimulates these canals will cause reflex movements of the eyes; thus, acceleration of the head to the right causes a movement of the eyes to the left, the function of the reflex being to enable the eyes to maintain steady fixation of an object despite movements of the head. The reflex occurs even when the eyes are shut, and, when the eyes are open, it obviously co-operates with the fixation reflex in maintaining steady fixation. In many lower animals this connection between organs of balance and eyes is very rigid; thus, one may move the tail of a fish, and its eyes will move reflexly. In man, not only do the semicircular canals function in close relation to the eye muscles but so also do the gravity organ—the utricle—and the stretch receptors in the muscles of the neck. Thus, when the head is turned upward, there is a reflex tendency for the eyes to move downward, even if the eyes are shut. The actual movement is probably initiated by the reflex from the semicircular canals, which respond to acceleration, but the maintenance of the position is brought about by a reflex

through the stretch of the neck muscles and also through the pull of gravity on the utricle, or otolith organ, in the inner ear.

Voluntary centre. The eyes are under voluntary control, and it is thought that the cortical area subserving voluntary eye movements is in the frontal cortex. Stimulation of this in primates causes movements of the eyes that are well coordinated, and a movement induced by this region prevails over one induced by stimulation of the occipital cortex. The existence of a separate centre in man is revealed by certain neurological disorders in which the subject is unable to fixate voluntarily but can do so reflexly; *i.e.*, he can follow a moving light.

The nature of eye movements. So far, the relation of the movements of the eyes to the requirements of the visual apparatus and their control have been touched upon. To examine the character of the movements in some detail requires rapid, accurate measurement of the movements that the eyes undergo. Modern studies of this subject employ a contact lens fitting on to the globe; on the lens is a small plane mirror, and a parallel bundle of rays is reflected off this mirror onto a moving film.

By the use of refined methods of measuring the position of the eyes at any moment, it becomes immediately evident that the eyes are never stationary for more than a fraction of a second; the movements are of three types: (1) irregular movements of high frequency (30–70 per second) and small excursions of about 20 seconds of arc; (2) flicks, or saccades, of several minutes of arc occurring at regular intervals of about one second; and between these saccades there occur (3) slow irregular drifts extending up to six minutes of arc. The saccades are corrective, serving to bring the fixation axis on the point of regard after this has drifted away from it too far, and thus are a manifestation of the fixation reflex.

The significance of these small movements during fixation was revealed by studies on the stabilized retinal image: by a suitable optical device the image of an object could be held stationary on the retina in spite of the movements of the eye. It was found that under these conditions the image would disappear within a few seconds. Thus, the movements of the eye are apparently necessary to allow the contours of the image to fall on a new set of rods and cones at repeated intervals; if this does not occur, the retina adapts to their stimulus and ceases to send messages to the central nervous system. The small flicks mentioned above are essentially the same as the larger movement made when the two eyes fixate (fix on) a light when it suddenly appears in the peripheral field; this is given the general name of the saccade, to distinguish it from the slower movements occurring during convergence and smooth following. The dynamics of the saccade have been studied in some detail by several workers. There is a reaction time of about 120 to 180 milliseconds, after which both eyes move simultaneously; there is a definite overshoot and, with an excursion of 20°, the operation is completed in about 90 milliseconds. The maximum velocity increases with the extent of the movement, being 300° per second for 10° and 500° per second for 30°. A remarkable feature is the apparent absence of significant inertia in the eyeball, so that movement is halted, not by any checking action of antagonistic muscles but simply by cessation of contraction of the agonists; thus, the movement is not ballistic. Once under way, the saccade is determined in amount, so that the subject cannot voluntarily alter its direction and extent. The control mechanism for the saccadic type of movement can be described as a sampled data system, in the sense that the brain makes discontinuous samples of the position of the eyes in relation to the target and corrects the error. This is in contrast to a continuous feedback system that takes account of the error all the time.

The movements of the eyes when they converge onto a near object are in remarkable contrast to the saccade; the angular velocity is only about 25° per second, compared with values as high as 500° per second in the saccade. The great difference in speed suggested to two investigators that the two movements are executed by different muscle fibres. In fact, the extraocular muscles do

The saccade, disjunctive movements, and tracking

contain two types of muscle fibre with characteristically different nerve supplies, and some recent studies tend to support this view of a dual mechanism.

If a moving light suddenly appears in the field of view, and if its rate of movement is less than about 30° per second, the response of the eyes is remarkably efficient; a saccade brings the eyes on target, and they follow the motion at almost exactly the same angular velocity as that of the target; inaccuracies in following lead to corrective saccades. When the rate of movement of the target is greater than about 30° per second, these corrective saccades become more obvious because now smooth following is not possible; the eyes make constant-velocity movements, but the velocity rarely matches that of the moving target, so that there must be frequent corrective saccades. Studies have shown that the following movements are highly integrated and must involve a continuous feedback system whereby errors are used to modify the performance. Thus, the systems for control of saccades and tracking movements are fundamentally different.

Vision suppression during a saccade. If one looks into a mirror and fixates one of one's eyes and then fixates the other, one does not see the eyes moving; and it has been argued that, during an eye movement, vision is suppressed; if vision were not suppressed, moreover, it seems likely that the images of the external world would appear smeared during a movement. Experimental studies have shown that there is, indeed, a suppression of vision during a saccade.

THE WORK OF THE OPTICAL LENS SYSTEM

Refraction by cornea and lens. The optical system of the eye is such as to produce a reduced inverted image of the visual field on the retina; the system behaves as a convex lens but is, in fact, much more complex, refraction taking place not at two surfaces, as in a lens, but at four separate surfaces—at the anterior and the posterior surfaces of the cornea and of the crystalline lens. Each of these surfaces is approximately spherical, and at each optical interface—*e.g.*, between air and the anterior surface of the cornea—the bending of a ray of light is toward the axis, so that, in effect, there are four surfaces tending to make rays of light converge on each other. If the rays of light falling on the cornea are parallel—*i.e.*, if they come from a distant point—the net effect of this series of refractions at the four surfaces is to bring these rays to a point focus of the optical system, which in the normal, or emmetropic, eye corresponds with the retina. The greatest change of direction, or bending of the rays, occurs where the difference of refractive index is greatest, and this is when light passes from air into the cornea, the refractive index of the corneal substance being 1.3376; the refractive indices of the cornea and aqueous humour are not greatly different, that of the aqueous humour being 1.336 (as is that of the vitreous); thus, the bending, as the rays meet the concave posterior surface of the cornea and emerge into a medium of slightly less refractive index, is small. The lens has a greater refractive index than that of its surrounding aqueous humour and vitreous body, 1.386 to 1.406, so that its two surfaces contribute to convergence, the posterior surface normally more than the anterior surface because of its greater curvature (smaller radius).

Normal sightedness and near- and farsightedness. In contrast to the focussing of the normal (emmetropic) eye, in which the image of the visual field is focussed on the retina, the image may be focussed in front of the retina (nearsightedness, or myopia), or behind the retina (farsightedness or hyperopia). In myopia the vision of distant objects is not distinct because the image of a distant point falls within the vitreous and the rays spread out to form a blur circle on the retina instead of a point. In this condition the eye is said to have too great dioptric (refractive) power for its length. When the focus falls behind the retina, the image of the distant point is again a circle on the retina; and the farsighted eye is said to have too little dioptric power. The important point to appreciate is that emmetropia, or normal sight, requires

that the focal power of the dioptric system be matched to the axial length of the eye; it certainly is remarkable that emmetropia is indeed the most common condition when it is appreciated that just one millimetre of error in the matching of axial length with focal length would cause a person to require a spectacle correction. In general, however, the effects of variations in dimensions tend to compensate each other. Thus, for example, an unusually large eye might, at first thought, be expected to be myopic, but a large eye tends to be associated with a large radius of curvature of the cornea, and this would reduce the power—*i.e.*, increase the focal length—and so an unusually large eye is not necessarily a myopic one.

Accommodation. *Effects of accommodation.* The image of an object brought close to the eye would be formed behind the retina if there were no change in the focal length of the eye. This change to bring the image of an object upon the retina is called accommodation. The point nearer than which accommodation is no longer effective is called the near point of accommodation. In very young people, the near point of accommodation is quite close to the eye, namely about seven centimetres (about three inches) in front at ten years old; at forty years the distance has increased to about 16 centimetres (about 6 inches), and at 60 years it is 100 centimetres or one metre (39 inches). Thus, a 60-year-old would not be able to read a book held at the convenient distance of about 40 centimetres (16 inches), and the extra power required would have to be provided by convex lenses in front of the eye, an arrangement called the presbyopic correction.

Mechanism of accommodation. It is essentially an increase in curvature of the anterior surface of the lens that is responsible for the increase in power involved in the process of accommodation. A clue to the way in which this change in shape takes place is given by the observation that a lens that has been taken out of the eye is much rounder and fatter than one within the eye; thus, its attachments by the zonular fibres to the ciliary muscle within the eye preserve the unaccommodated or flattened state of the lens; and modern investigations leave little doubt that it is the pull of the zonular fibres on the elastic capsule of the lens that holds the anterior surface relatively flat. When these zonular fibres are loosened, the elastic tension in the capsule comes into play and remolds the lens, making it smaller and thicker. Thus, the physiological problem is to find what loosens the zonular fibres during accommodation. The ciliary muscle has been described earlier, and it has been shown that the effect of contracting its fibres is, in general, to pull the whole ciliary body forward and to move the anterior region toward the axis of the eye by virtue of the sphincter action of the circular fibres. Both of these actions will slacken the zonular fibres and therefore allow the change in shape. As to why it is the anterior surface that changes most is not absolutely clear, but it is probably a characteristic of the capsule rather than of the underlying lens tissue. Defective accommodation in presbyopia is not due to a failure of the ciliary muscle but rather to a hardening of the substance of the lens with age to the point that readjustments of its shape become ever more difficult.

Nerve action. Accommodation is an involuntary reflex act, and the ciliary muscle belongs to the smooth involuntary class. Appropriate to this, the innervation is through the autonomic system, the parasympathetic nerve cells belonging to the oculomotor nerve (the third cranial nerve) occupying a special region of the nucleus in the midbrain called the Edinger-Westphal nucleus; the fibres have a relay point in the ciliary ganglion in the eye socket, and the postganglionic fibres enter the eye as the short ciliary nerves. The stimulus for accommodation is the nearness of the object, but the manner in which this nearness is translated into a stimulus is not clear. Thus, the fact that the image is blurred is not sufficient to induce accommodation; the eye has some power of discriminating whether the blurredness is due to an object being too far away or too close, so that something more than mere blurredness is required.

The near point of accommodation

Four refractive surfaces

The pupil. The amount of light entering the eye is restricted by the aperture in the iris, the pupil.

When a person is in a dark room his pupil is large, perhaps eight millimetres (0.3 inch) in diameter, or more. When the room is lighted there is an immediate constriction of the pupil, the light reflex; this is bilateral, so that even if only one eye is exposed to the light both pupils contract to nearly the same extent. After a time the pupils expand even though the bright light is maintained, but the expansion is not large. The final state is determined by the actual degree of illumination; if this is high, then the final state may be a diameter of only about three to four millimetres; if it is not so high, then the initial constriction may be nearly the same, but the final state may be with a pupil of four to five millimetres. During this steady condition, the pupils do not remain at exactly constant size; there is a characteristic oscillation in size that, if exaggerated, is called hippus.

A pupillary constriction will also occur when a person looks at a near object—the near reflex. Thus, accommodation and pupillary constriction occur together reflexly and are excited by the same stimulus. The function of the pupil is clearly that of controlling the amount of light entering the eye, and hence the light reflex. The constriction occurring during near vision suggests other functions, too; thus, the aberrations of the eye (failure of some refracted rays to focus on the retina) are decreased by reducing the aperture of its optical system. In the dark, aberrations are of negligible significance, so that a person is concerned only with allowing as much light into the eye as possible; in bright light high visual acuity is usually required, and this means reducing the aberrations. The depth of focus of the optical system is increased when the aperture is reduced, and the near reflex is probably concerned with increasing depth of focus under these conditions.

Dilation of the pupil occurs as a result of strong psychical stimuli and also when any sensory nerve is stimulated; dilation thus occurs in extreme fear and in pain.

Neuromuscular mechanisms. The muscles of the iris have been described earlier. It is clear from their general features that constriction of the pupil is brought about by shortening of the circular ring of fibres—the sphincter; dilation is brought about by shortening of the radially oriented fibres. The sphincter is innervated by parasympathetic fibres of the oculomotor nerve, with their cell bodies in the Edinger-Westphal nucleus, as are the nerve cells controlling accommodation; thus, the close association between the accommodation and pupillary reflexes is reflected in a close anatomical contiguity of their motor nerve cells.

The sensory pathway in the light reflex involves the rods and cones, bipolar cells, and ganglion cells. As indicated earlier, a relay centre for pupillary responses to light is the pretectal nucleus in the midbrain. There is a partial crossing-over of the fibres of the pretectal nerve cells so that some may run to the motor nerve cells in the Edinger-Westphal nucleus of both sides of the brain, and it is by this means that illumination of one eye affects the other. The Edinger-Westphal motor neurons have a relay point in the ciliary ganglion, a group of nerve cells in the eye socket, so that its electrical stimulation causes both accommodation and pupillary constriction; similarly, application of a drug, such as pilocarpine, to the cornea will cause a constriction of the pupil and also a spasm of accommodation; atropine, by paralyzing the nerve supply, causes dilation of the pupil and paralysis of accommodation (cycloplegia).

The dilator muscle of the iris is activated by sympathetic nerve fibres. Stimulation of the sympathetic nerve in the neck causes a powerful dilation of the iris; again, the influx of adrenalin into the blood from the adrenal glands during extreme excitement results in pupillary dilation.

Many involuntary muscles receive a double innervation, being activated by one type of nerve supply and inhibited by the other; modern experimentation indicates that the iris muscles are no exception, so that the sphinc-ter has an inhibitory sympathetic nerve supply, while the dilator has a parasympathetic (cholinergic) inhibitor. Thus, a drug like pilocarpine not only activates the constrictor muscle but actively inhibits the dilator. A similar double innervation has been described for the ciliary muscle. In general, any change in pupillary size results from a reciprocal innervation of dilator and constrictor; thus, activation of the constrictor is associated with inhibition of the dilator and vice versa.

The near response. In general, as has been indicated, pupillary constriction and accommodation occur together, in response to the same stimulus; a third element in this near response is, of course, the convergence (turning in) of the eyes, mediated by voluntary muscles, the medial recti. Experimentally, it is often possible to separate these activities, in the sense that one may cause convergence without accommodation by placing appropriate prisms in front of the eyes; or one may cause accommodation without convergence by placing diverging lenses in front of the eyes. There are many experiments that show that accommodation and convergence are neurologically linked to some extent, however.

THE WORK OF THE RETINA

Some basic facts of vision. So far, attention has been directed to what are essentially the preliminaries to vision; it is now time to examine some of the elementary facts of vision and to relate them to the structure of the retina and, later, to chemically identifiable events.

Measurement of the threshold. An important means of measuring a sensation is to determine the threshold stimulus—*i.e.*, the minimum energy required to evoke the sensation. In the case of vision, this would be the minimum number of quanta of light entering the eye in unit time. If it is found that the threshold has altered because of a change of some sort, then this change can be said to have altered the subject's sensitivity to light, and a numerical value can be assigned to the sensitivity by use of the reciprocal of the threshold energy. Practically, a subject may be placed in the dark in front of a white screen, and the screen may be illuminated by flashes of light; for any given intensity of illumination of the screen, it is not difficult to calculate the flow of light energy entering the eye. One may begin with a low intensity of flash and increase this successively until the subject reports that he can see the flash. In fact, at this threshold level, he will not see every flash presented, even though the intensity of the light is kept constant; for this reason, a certain frequency of seeing—*e.g.*, four times out of six—must be selected as the arbitrary point at which to fix the threshold.

When measurements of this sort are carried out, it is found that the threshold falls progressively as the subject is maintained in the dark room. This is not due to dilation of the pupil because the same phenomenon occurs if the subject is made to look through an artificial pupil of fixed diameter. The eye, after about 30 minutes in the dark, may become about 10,000 times more sensitive to light. Vision under these conditions is, moreover, characteristically different from what it is under ordinary daylight conditions. Thus, in order to obtain best vision, the eye must look away from the screen so that the image of the screen does not fall on the fovea; if the screen is continuously illuminated at around this threshold level it will be found to disappear if its image is brought onto the fovea, and it will become immediately visible on looking away. The same phenomenon may be demonstrated on a moonless night if the gaze is fixed on a dim star; it disappears on fixation and reappears on looking away. This feature of vision under these near-threshold or scotopic conditions suggests that the cones are effectively blind to weak light stimuli, since they are the only receptors in the fovea. This is the basis of the duplicity theory of vision, which postulates that when the light stimulus is weak and the eye has been dark-adapted, it is the rods that are utilized because, under these conditions, their threshold is much lower than that of the cones. When the subject first enters the dark, the rods are the less sensitive type of receptor, and the threshold stimulus is the light energy required to stimulate the cones; during the first five or more minutes the threshold of the cones decreases; *i.e.*, they become more sensitive. The rods then increase their sensitivity to the point that they are the more sensitive, and it is they that now determine the sensitivity of the whole eye, the threshold stimuli obtained after ten minutes in the dark, for example, being too weak to activate the cones.

Scotopic sensitivity curve. When different wavelengths of light are employed for measuring the threshold, it is found, for example, that the eye is much more sensitive to blue-green light than to orange. The interesting feature of this kind of study is that the subject reports only that the light is light; he distinguishes no colour. If the intensity of a given wavelength of light is increased step by step above the threshold, a point comes when the subject states that it is coloured, and the difference between the threshold for light appreciation and this, the chromatic threshold, is called the photochromatic interval. This suggests that the rods give only achromatic, or colourless, vision, and that it is the cones that permit wavelength discrimination. The photochromatic interval for long wavelengths (red light) is about zero, which means that the intensity required to reach the sensation of light is the same as that to reach the sensation of colour. This is because the rods are so insensitive to red light; if the dark-adaptation curve is plotted for a red stimulus it is found that it follows the cone path, like that for foveal vision at all wavelengths.

Loss of dark adaptation. If, when the subject has become completely dark-adapted, one eye is held shut and the other exposed to a bright light for a little while, it is found that, whereas the dark-adapted eye retains its high sensitivity, that of the light-exposed eye has decreased greatly; it requires another period of dark adaptation for the two eyes to become equally sensitive.

These simple experiments pose several problems, the answers to which throw a great deal of light on the whole mechanism of vision. Why, for example, does it require time for both rods and cones to reach their maximum sensitivity in the dark? Again, why is visual acuity so low under scotopic conditions compared with that in daylight, although sensitivity to light is so high? Finally, why do the rods not serve to discriminate different wavelengths?

Bleaching of rhodopsin. It may be assumed that a receptor is sensitive to light because it contains a substance that absorbs light and converts this vibrational type of energy into some other form that is eventually transmuted into electrical changes, and that these may be transmitted from the receptor to the bipolar cell with which it is immediately connected. When the retina of a dark-adapted animal is removed and submitted to extraction procedures, a pigment, originally called visual purple but now called rhodopsin, may be obtained. If the eye is exposed to a bright light for some time before extraction, little or no rhodopsin is obtained. When retinas from animals that had been progressively dark-adapted were studied, a gradual increase in the amount of rhodopsin that could be extracted was observed. Thus, rhodopsin, on absorption of light energy, is changed to some other compound, but new rhodopsin is formed, or rhodopsin is regenerated, during dark adaptation. The obvious inference is that rhodopsin is the visual pigment of the rods, and that when it is exposed to relatively intense lights it becomes useless for vision. When the eye is allowed to remain in the dark the rhodopsin regenerates and thus becomes available for vision. There is now conclusive proof that rhodopsin is, indeed, the visual pigment for the rods; it is obtained from retinas that have only rods and no cones—*e.g.*, the retinas of the rat or guinea pig, and it is not obtained from the pure cone retina of the chicken.

Rhodopsin as the photo-pigment

When the absorption spectrum is measured, it is found that its maximum absorption occurs at the point of maximum sensitivity of the dark-adapted eye. Similar measurements may be carried out on animals, but the threshold sensitivity must be determined by some objective means—*e.g.*, the response of the pupil, or, better

still, the electrical changes occurring in the retina in response to light stimuli. Thus, the electroretinogram (ERG) is the record of changes in potential between an electrode placed on the surface of the cornea and an electrode placed on another part of the body, caused by illumination of the eye.

The high sensitivity of the rods by comparison with the cones may be a reflection of the greater concentration in them of pigment that would permit them to catch light more efficiently, or it may depend on other factors—*e.g.*, the efficiency of transformation of the light energy into electrical energy. The pigments responsible for cone vision are not easily extracted or identified, and the problem will be considered in the material on colour vision. An important factor, so far as sensitivity is concerned, is the actual organization of the receptors and neurons in the retina.

Synaptic organization of the retina. The basic structure of the retina has been indicated earlier. As in other parts of the nervous system, the messages initiated in one element are transmitted, or relayed, to others. The regions of transmission from one cell to another are areas of intimate contact known as synapses. An impulse conveyed from one cell to another travels from the first cell body along a projection called an axon, to a synapse, where the impulse is received by a projection, called a dendrite, of the second cell. The impulse is then conveyed to the second cell body, to be transmitted further, along the second cell's axon.

It will be recalled that the functioning cells of the retina are the receptor cells—the rods and cones; the ganglion cells, the axons of which form the optic nerve; and cells that act in a variety of ways as intermediaries between the receptors and the ganglion cells. These intermediaries are named bipolar cells, horizontal cells, and amacrine cells.

Plexiform layers. As was indicated earlier, the synapses occur in definite layers, the outer and inner plexiform layers. In the outer plexiform layer the bipolar cells make their contacts, by way of their dendrites, with the rods and cones, specifically the spherules of the rods and the pedicles of the cones. In this layer, too, the projections from horizontal cells make contacts with rods, cones, and bipolar cells, giving rise to a horizontal transmission and thereby allowing activity in one part of the retina to influence the behaviour of a neighbouring part. In the inner plexiform layer, the axons of the bipolar cells make connection with the dendrites of ganglion cells, once again at special synaptic regions. (The dendrites of a nerve cell carry impulses to the nerve cell; its axon, away from the cell.) Here, too, a horizontal interconnection between bipolar cells is brought about, in this case by way of the axons and dendrites of amacrine cells.

Inner plexiform layer

The bipolar cells are of two main types: namely, those that apparently make connection with only one receptor —a cone—and those that connect to several receptors. The type of bipolar cell that connects to a single cone is called the midget bipolar. The other type of bipolar cell is called diffuse; varieties of these include the rod bipolar, the dendritic projections of which spread over an area wide enough to allow contacts with as many as 50 rods; and the flat cone bipolar, which collects messages from up to seven cones.

Ganglion cells are of two main types: namely, the midget ganglion cell, which apparently makes a unique connection with a midget bipolar cell, which in turn is directly connected to a single cone; and a diffuse type, which collects messages from groups of bipolar cells.

Convergence of the messages. The presence of diffuse bipolar and ganglion cells collecting messages from groups of receptors and bipolar cells, and, what may be even more important, the presence of lateral connections of groups of receptors and bipolar cells through the horizontal and amacrine cells, means that messages from receptors over a rather large area of the retina may converge on a single ganglion cell. This convergence means that the effects of light falling on the receptive field may be cumulative, so that a weak light stimulus spread over about 1,000 rods is just as effective as a stronger stimulus spread over 100 or less; in other words, a large receptive field will have a lower threshold than a small one; and this is, in fact, the basis for the high sensitivity of the area immediately outside the fovea, where there is a high density of rods that converge on single bipolar cells. Thus, if it is postulated that the cones do not converge to anything like the same extent as the rods, the greater sensitivity of the latter may be explained; and the anatomical evidence favours this postulate.

It has been indicated above that the regeneration of visual pigment is a cause of the increased sensitivity of the rods that occurs during dark adaptation. This, apparently, is only part of the story. An important additional factor is the change in functional organization of the retina during adaptation. When the eye is light-adapted, functional convergence is small, and sensitivity of rods and cones is low; as dark adaptation proceeds, convergence of rods increases. The anatomical connections do not change, but the power of the bipolar cells and ganglion cells to collect impulses is increased, perhaps by the removal of an inhibition that prevents this during high illumination of the retina.

Absolute threshold and minimum stimulus for vision. As was indicated earlier, the threshold is best indicated in terms of frequency of seeing since, because of fluctuations in the threshold, there is no definite luminance of a test screen at which it is always seen by the observer, and there is no luminance just below this at which it is never seen. Experiments, in which 60 percent was arbitrarily taken as the frequency of seeing and in which the image of a patch of light covered an area of retina containing about 20,000,000 rods, led to the calculation that the mean threshold stimulus represents 2,500 quanta of light that is actually absorbed per square centimetre of retina. This calculation leads to two important conclusions: namely, that at the threshold only one rod out of thousands comes into operation, and that during the application of a short stimulus the chances are that no rod receives more than a single quantum.

A quantum, defined as the product of Planck's constant $(6.55 \times 10^{-27}$ erg seconds) times the frequency of light, is the minimum amount of light energy that can be employed. A rod excited by a single quantum cannot excite a bipolar cell without the simultaneous assistance of one or more other rods. Experiments carried out in the 1940s indicated that a stimulus of about 11 quanta is required; thus it may require 11 excited rods, each receiving one quantum of light, to produce the sensation of light.

Uncertainty principle

Quantum fluctuations. With such small amounts of energy as those involved in the threshold stimulus, the uncertainty principle becomes important; according to this, there is no certainty that a given flash will have the expected number of quanta in it, but only a probability. Thus, one may speak of a certain average number of quanta and the actual number in any given flash, and one may compute on statistical grounds the shape of curve that is obtained by plotting frequency with which a flash contains, say, four quanta or more against the average number in the flash. One may also plot the frequency with which a flash is seen against the average number of quanta in the flash, and this frequency-of-seeing curve turns out to be similar to the frequency-of-containing-quanta curve when the number of quanta chosen is five to seven, depending on the observer. This congruence strongly suggests that the fluctuations in response to a flash of the same average intensity are caused by fluctuations in the energy content of the stimulus, and not by fluctuations in the sensitivity of the retina.

Spatial summation. In spatial summation two stimuli falling on nearby areas of the retina add their effects so that either alone may be inadequate to evoke the sensation of light, but, when presented simultaneously, they may do so. Thus, the threshold luminance of a test patch required to be just visible depends, within limits, on its size, a larger patch requiring a lower luminance, and vice versa. Within a small range of limiting area, namely that

subtending about 10 to 15 minutes of arc, the relationship called Ricco's law holds; *i.e.*, threshold intensity multiplied by the area equals a constant. This means that over this area, which embraces several hundreds of rods, light falling on the individual rods summates, or accumulates, its effects completely so that 100 quanta falling on a single rod are as effective as one quantum falling simultaneously on 100 rods. The basis for this summation is clearly the convergence of receptors on ganglion cells, the chemical effects of the quanta of light falling on individual rods being converted into electrical changes that converge on a single bipolar cell through its branching dendritic processes. Again, the electrical effects induced in the bipolar cells may summate at the dendritic processes of a ganglion cell so that the receptive field of a ganglion cell may embrace many thousands of rods.

Temporal summation. In temporal summation, two stimuli, each being too weak to excite, cause a sensation of light if presented in rapid succession on the same spot of the retina; thus, over a certain range of times, up to 0.1 second, the Bunsen-Roscoe law holds: namely, that the intensity of light multiplied by the time of exposure equals a constant. Thus it was found that within this time interval (up to 0.1 second), the total number of quanta required to excite vision was 130, irrespective of the manner in which these were supplied. Beyond this time, summation was still evident, but it was not perfect, so that if the duration was increased to one second the total number of quanta required was 220. Temporal summation is consistent with quantum theory; it has been shown that fluctuations in the number of quanta actually in a light flash are responsible for the variable responsiveness of the eye; increasing the duration of a light stimulus increases the probability that it will contain a given number of quanta, and that it will excite.

Inhibition. In the central nervous system generally, the relay of impulses from one nerve cell or neuron to excite another is only one aspect of neuronal interaction. Just as important, if not more so, is the inhibition of one neuron by the discharge in another. So it is in the retina. Subjectively, the inhibitory activity is reflected in many of the phenomena associated with adaptation to light or its reverse. Thus, the decrease in sensitivity of the retina to light during exposure to light is only partially accounted for by bleaching of visual pigment, be it the pigment in rod or cone; an important factor is the onset of inhibitory processes that reduce the convergence of receptors on ganglion cells. Some of the rapidly occurring changes in sensitivity described as alpha adaptation are doubtless purely neural in origin.

Many so-called inductive phenomena indicate inhibitory processes; thus, the phenomenon of simultaneous contrast, whereby a patch of light appears much darker if surrounded by a bright background than by a black, is due to the inhibitory effect of the surrounding retina on the central region, induced by the bright surrounding. Many colour-contrast phenomena are similarly caused; thus, if a blue light is projected onto a large white screen, the white screen rapidly appears yellow; the blue stimulus falling on the central retina causes inhibition of blue sensitivity in the periphery; hence, the white background will appear to be missing its blue light—white minus blue is a mixture of red and green—*i.e.*, yellow. Particularly interesting from this viewpoint are the phenomena of metacontrast; by this is meant the inductive effect of a primary light stimulus on the sensitivity of the eye to a previously presented light stimulus on an adjoining area of retina. It is a combination of temporal and spatial induction. The effect is produced by illuminating the two halves of a circular patch consecutively for a brief duration. If the left half only, for example, is illuminated for 10 milliseconds it produces a definite sensation of brightness. If, now, both halves are illuminated for the same period, but the right half from 20 to 50 milliseconds later, the left half of the field appears much darker than before and, near the centre, may be completely extinguished. The left field has thus been inhibited by the succeeding, nearby, stimulus. The right field,

Meta- and para-contrast

moreover, appears darker than when illuminated alone —it has been inhibited by the earlier stimulus (paracontrast).

Flicker. Another visual phenomenon that brings out the importance of inhibition is the sensation evoked when a visual stimulus is repeated rapidly; for example, one may view a screen that is illuminated by a source of light the rays from which may be intercepted at regular intervals by rotating a sector of a circular screen in front of it. If the sector rotates slowly, a sensation of black followed by white is aroused; as the speed increases the sensation becomes one of flicker—*i.e.,* rapid fluctuations in brightness; finally, at a certain speed, called the critical fusion frequency, the sensation becomes continuous and the subject is unaware of the alterations in the illumination of the screen.

At high levels of luminance, when cone vision is employed, the fusion frequency is high, increasing with increasing luminance in a logarithmic fashion—the Ferry-Porter law—so that at high levels it may require 60 flashes per second to reach a continuous sensation. Under conditions of night, or scotopic, vision, the frequencies may be as low as four per second. The difference between rod and cone vision in this respect probably resides in the power of the eye to inhibit activity in cones rapidly, so that the sensation evoked by a single flash is cut off immediately, and this leaves the eye ready to respond to the next stimulus. By contrast, the response in the rod lasts so much longer that, when a new stimulus falls even a quarter of a second later, the difference in the state of the rods is insufficient to evoke a change in intensity of sensation; it merely prolongs it. One interesting feature of an intermittent stimulus is that the intensity of the sensation of brightness, when fusion is achieved, is dependent on the relative periods of light and darkness in the cycle, and this gives one a method of grading the effective luminance of a screen; one may keep the intensity of the illuminating source constant and merely vary the period of blackness in a cycle of black and white. The effective luminance will be the average luminance during a cycle; this is known as the Talbot-Plateau law.

Visual acuity. As has been stated, the ability to perceive detail is restricted in the dark-adapted retina when the illumination is such as to excite only the scotopic type of vision; this is in spite of the high sensitivity of the retina to light under the same conditions. The power of distinguishing detail is essentially the power to resolve two stimuli separated in space, so that, if a grating of black lines on a white background is moved farther and farther away from an observer, a point is reached when he will be unable to distinguish this stimulus pattern from a uniformly gray sheet of paper. The angle subtended at the eye by the spacing between the lines at the point where they are just resolvable is called the resolving power of the eye; the reciprocal of this angle, in minutes of arc, is called the visual acuity. Thus, a visual acuity of unity indicates a power of resolving detail subtending one minute of arc at the eye; a visual acuity of two indicates a resolution of one-half minute, or 30 seconds of arc. The visual acuity depends strongly on the illumination of the test target, and this is true of both daylight (photopic) and night (scotopic) vision; thus, with a brightly illuminated target, with the surroundings equally brightly illuminated (the ideal condition), the visual acuity may be as high as two. When the illumination is reduced, the acuity falls so that, under ordinary conditions of daylight viewing, visual acuity is not much better than unity. Under scotopic conditions, the visual acuity may be only 0.04 so that lines would have to subtend about 25 minutes at the eye to be resolvable; this corresponds to a thickness of 4.4 centimetres (1.7 inches) at a distance of six metres (20 feet).

Measurement. In the laboratory, visual acuity is measured by the Landolt C, which is a circle with a break in it. The subject is asked to state where the break is when the figure is rotated to successive random positions. The size of the *C,* and thus of its break, is reduced until the subject makes more than an arbitrarily chosen percentage of mistakes. The angle subtended at the eye by the

Resolving power and visual acuity [margin note]

break in the *C* at this limit is taken as the resolving power of the eye. The testing of the eyes by the optician is essentially a determination of visual acuity; here the subject is presented with the Snellen chart, rows of letters whose details subtend progressively smaller angles at the eye. The row in which, say, five out of six letters are seen correctly is chosen as that which measures the visual acuity. If the details subtended one minute of arc, the visual acuity would be unity. The notation employed is somewhat obscure; a visual acuity of unity would be expressed as 6/6; an acuity of a half as 6/12, and so on; here the numerator is the viewing distance in metres from the chart and the denominator the distance at which details on the letters of the limiting row subtend one minute of arc at the eye.

Anatomical basis; the retinal mosaic. From an anatomical point of view one may expect the limit to resolving power to be imposed by the "grain" of the retinal mosaic in the same way that the size of the grains in a photographic emulsion imposes a limit to the accuracy with which detail may be photographed. Two white lines on a black ground, for example, could not be appreciated as distinct if their images fell on the same or adjacent sets of receptors. If a set of receptors intervened between the stimulated ones, there would be a basis for discrimination because the message sent to the central nervous system could be that two rows of receptors, separated by an unstimulated row, were sending messages to their bipolar cells. Thus, the limit to resolution, on this basis, should be the diameter of a foveal cone, or rather the angle subtended by this at the nodal point of the eye; this is about 30 seconds of arc and, in fact, corresponds with the best visual acuity attainable. If this grain of the retinal mosaic is to be the basis of resolution, however, one must postulate, in addition, a nervous mechanism that will transmit accurately the events taking place in the individual receptors, in this case the foveal cones; *i.e.,* there must be a one-to-one relationship between cones, bipolar cells, ganglion cells, and lateral geniculate cells so that what is called the local sign of the impulses from a given foveal cone may be obtained. It must be appreciated that restriction on convergence (or its reverse, spread) of messages may be achieved by inhibition; the anatomical connections may be there, but they may be made functionally inoperative by inhibition exerted by other neurons; thus, the horizontal and amacrine cells might well exert a restraining influence on certain junctions, thereby reducing the spread, or convergence, of messages, and it seems likely that the improvement in foveal visual acuity from one to two, brought about by increased luminance of the target and its surroundings, is achieved by an increase in inhibition that tends to make transmission one-to-one in the fovea.

It must be appreciated that true one-to-one connections in the retina do not exist; a cone, although making an exclusive type of synapse with a midget bipolar, may also make a less exclusive contact with a flat bipolar cell; furthermore, midget bipolars and cones are connected laterally by amacrine and horizontal cells so that it is most unlikely that a given optic nerve fibre carries messages from only a single cone. The one-to-one relationship may in fact exist under certain conditions, but that is because pathways from other receptors have been blocked or occluded by inhibitory processes that keep the line clear for a given cone.

The low visual acuity obtained in night, or rod, vision is now understandable. It has been pointed out that a high sensitivity to light is achieved by the convergence of rods on the higher neurons to allow spatial summation, and it is this convergence that interferes with the resolution of detail. If hundreds of rods converge on a single bipolar cell and if many bipolar cells converge on a single ganglion cell, it is understandable that the unit responsible for resolution may be very large and thus that the visual acuity is very small.

The retinal image. It has been implied, in the comments on visual acuity, that the limiting factor is one of an anatomical arrangement of receptors and of their neural organization. A very important feature, however,

The Snellen chart [margin note]

Scotopic acuity [margin note]

must be the accuracy of the formation of an image of external objects by the optical system of the eye. It may be calculated, for example, that the image of a grating produces lines 0.5 micron wide on the retina, but this is on the basis of ideal geometrical optics; in fact, the optics of the eye are not perfect, while diffraction of light by its passage through the pupil further spoils the image. As a result of these defects, the image of a black and white grating on the retina is not sharp, the black lines being not completely black but gray because of spread of light from the white lines. (When the optical system of the eye is defective, moreover, as in nearsightedness, the imagery is worse, but this can be corrected by the use of appropriate lenses.) Physiologically, the eye effectively improves the retinal image by enhancing contrasts; thus, the image of a fine black line on a white background formed on the retina is not a sharply defined black line but a relatively wide band of varying degrees of grayness; yet to the observer the line appears sharply defined, and this is because of lateral inhibition, the receptors that receive most light tending to inhibit those that receive less; the result is a physiological "sharpening of the image," so that the eye often behaves as though the image were perfect. This applies to chromatic aberration, too, which should cause black and white objects to appear fringed with colour, yet, because of suppression of the chromatic responses, one is not aware of the coloured fringes that do in effect surround the images of objects in the external world.

The pupil
    The iris behaves as a diaphragm, modifying the amount of light entering the eye; probably of greater significance than control of the light entering the eye is the influence on aberrations of the optical system; the smaller the pupil the less serious, in general, are the aberrations. The smaller the pupil, however, the more serious become the effects of diffraction, so that a balance must be struck. Experimentally, it is found that at high luminances with pupils below three millimetres (0.12 inch) in diameter the visual acuity is not improved by further reduction of the diameter; increasing the pupil size beyond this reduces acuity, presumably because of the greater optical aberrations. It is interesting that when a subject is placed in a room that is darkened steadily, the size of the pupil increases, and the size attained for any given level of luminance is, in fact, optimal for visual acuity at this particular luminance. The reason that visual acuity increases with the larger pupils is that the extra light admitted into the eye compensates for the increased aberrations. When the gaze is fixed intently on an object for a long time, peripheral images that tend to disappear reappear immediately when the eyes are moved. This effect is called the Troxler phenomenon. To study it reproducibly it is necessary to use an optical device that ensures that the image of any object upon which the gaze is fixed will remain on the same part of the retina however the eyes move. Two investigators found, when they did this, that the stabilized retinal image tended to fade within a few seconds. It may be assumed that in normal vision the normal involuntary movements—the microsaccades and drifts mentioned earlier—keep the retinal image in sufficient movement to prevent the fading, which is essentially an example of sensory adaptation, the tendency for any receptive system to cease responding to a maintained stimulus.

Electrophysiology of the retina. *Neurological basis.* Subjective studies on human beings can traverse only a certain distance in the interpretation of visual phenomena; beyond this the standard electrophysiological techniques, which have been successful in unravelling the mechanisms of the central nervous system, must be applied to the eye; this, as repeatedly emphasized, is an outgrowth of the brain.

Receptive fields
    Records from single optic nerve fibres of the frog and from the ganglion cell of the mammalian retina indicated three types of response. In the frog there were fibres that gave a discharge when a light was switched on the "on-fibres." Another group, the "off-fibres," remained inactive during illumination of the retina but gave a powerful discharge when the light was switched off. A third group, the "on-off fibres," gave discharges at "on" and "off" but were inactive during the period of illumination. The responses in the mammal were similar, but more complex than in the frog. The mammalian retina shows a background of activity in the dark, so that on- and off-effects are manifest as accentuations or diminutions of this normal discharge. In general, on-elements gave an increased discharge when the light was switched on, and an inhibition of the background discharge when the light was switched off. An off-element showed inhibition of the background discharge during illumination and a powerful discharge at off; this off-discharge is thus a release of inhibition and reveals unmistakably the inhibitory character of the response to illumination that takes place in some ganglion cells. Each ganglion cell or optic nerve fibre tested had a receptive field; and the area of frog's retina from which a single fibre could be activated varied with the intensity of the light stimulus. The largest field was obtained with the strongest stimulus, so that, in order that a light stimulus, falling at some distance away from the centre of the field, might affect this particular fibre it had to be much more intense than a light stimulus falling on the centre of the field. This means that some synaptic pathways are more favoured than others.

    The mammalian receptive field is more complex, the more peripheral part of the field giving the opposite type of response to that given by the centre. Thus, if, at the centre of the field, the response was "on" (an on-centre field) the response to a stimulus farther away in the same fibre was at "off," and in an intermediate zone it was often mixed to give an on-off element. In order to characterize an' element, therefore, it must be called on-centre or off-centre, with the meaning thereby that at the centre of its receptive field its response was at "on" or at "off," respectively, while in the periphery it was opposite. By studying the effects of small spot stimuli on centre and periphery separately and together, one investigator demonstrated a mutual inhibition between the two. A striking feature was the effect of adaptation; after dark adaptation the surrounding area of opposite activity became ineffective. In this sense, therefore, the receptive field shrinks, but, as it is a reduction in inhibitory activity between centre and periphery, it means, in fact, that the effective field can actually increase during dark adaptation—*i.e.*, the regions over which summation can occur—and this is exactly what is found in psychophysical experiments on dark adaptation.

    Anatomical basis. The receptive field is essentially a measure of the number of receptors—rods or cones or a mixture of these—that make nervous connections with a single ganglion cell. The organization of centre and periphery implies that the receptors in the periphery of an on-centre cell tend to inhibit it, while those in the centre of the field tend to excite it, so that the effects of a uniform illumination covering the whole field tend to cancel out. This has an important physiological value, as it means, in effect, that the brain is not bombarded with an enormous number of unnecessary messages, as would be the case were every ganglion cell to send discharges along its optic nerve fibre as long as it was illuminated. Instead, the cell tends to respond to change—*i.e.*, the movement of a light or dark spot over the receptive field—and to give an especially prominent response, often when the spot passes from the periphery to the centre, or vice versa. Thus, the centre-periphery organization favours the detection of movement; in a similar way it favours the detection of contours because these give rise to differences in the illumination of the parts of the receptive fields. The anatomical basis of the arrangement presumably is given by the organization of the bipolar and amacrine cells in relation to the dendrites of the ganglion cell; it is interesting that the actual diameter of the centre of the receptive field of a ganglion cell is frequently equal to the area over which its dendrites spread; the periphery exerts its effects presumably by means of amacrine cells that are capable of connecting with bipolars over a wide area. These amacrine cells could exert an inhibitory action on the bipolar cells connected to the receptors of the central zone of the field, preventing them

Inhibitory effect of periphery receptors

from responding to these receptors; in this case, the ganglion cell related to these bipolars would be of an on-centre and off-periphery type.

Direction-sensitive ganglion cells. When examining the receptive fields of rabbit ganglion cells, investigators found some that gave a maximal response when a moving spot of light passed in a certain "preferred" direction, while they gave no response at all when the spot passed in the opposite direction; in fact, the spontaneous activity of the cell was usually inhibited by this movement in the "null" direction. It may be assumed that the receptors connected with this type of ganglion cell are organized in a linear fashion, so that the stimulation of one receptor causes inhibition of a receptor adjacent to it. This inhibition would prevent the excitatory effect of light on the adjacent receptor from having a response when the movement was in the null direction, but would arrive too late at the adjacent receptor if the light was moving in the preferred direction.

The electroretinogram. If an electrode is placed on the cornea and another, indifferent electrode, placed, for example, in the mouth, illumination of the retina is followed by a succession of electrical changes; the record of these is the electroretinogram or ERG. Modern analysis has shown that the electrode on the cornea picks up changes in potential occurring successively at different levels of the retina, so that it is now possible to recognize, for example, the electrical changes occurring in the rods and cones—the receptor potentials—those occurring in the horizontal cells, and so on. In general, the electrical changes caused by the different types of cell tend to overlap in time, so that the record in the electroretinogram is only a faint and attenuated index to the actual changes; nevertheless, it has, in the past, been a most valuable tool for the analysis of retinal mechanisms. Thus, the most prominent wave—called the *b*-wave—is closely associated with discharge in the optic nerve, so that in animals, or man, the height of the *b*-wave can be used as an objective measure of the response to light. Hence, the sensitivity of the dark-adapted frog's retina to different wavelengths, as indicated by the heights of the *b*-waves, can be plotted against wavelength to give a typical scotopic sensitivity curve with a maximum at 5000 angstroms corresponding to the maximum for absorption of rhodopsin.

Flicker. Electrophysiology has been used as a tool for the examination of the basic mechanism of flicker and fusion. The classical studies based on the electroretinogram indicated that the important feature that determines fusion in the cone-dominated retina is the inhibition of the retina caused by each successive light flash, inhibition being indicated by the *a*-wave of the electroretinogram. In the rod-dominated retina—*e.g.*, in man under scotopic conditions— the *a*-wave is not prominent, and fusion depends simply on the tendency for the excitatory response to a flash to persist, the inhibitory effects of a succeeding stimulus being small. More modern methods of analysis, in which the discharges in single ganglion cells in response to repeated flashes are measured, have defined fairly precisely the nature of fusion, which, so far as the retinal message is concerned, is a condition in which the record from the ganglion cell becomes identical with the record observed in the ganglion cell during spontaneous discharge during constant illumination.

The nature of fusion

Visual acuity. Although the resolving power of the retina depends, in the last analysis, on the size and density of packing of the receptors in the retina, it is the neural organization of the receptors that determines whether the brain will be able to make use of this theoretical resolving power. It is therefore of interest to examine the responses of retinal ganglion cells to gratings, either projected as stationary images on to the receptive field or moved slowly across it. One group of investigators showed that ganglion cells of the cat differed in sensitivity to a given grating when the sensitivity was measured by the degree of contrast between the black and white lines of the grating necessary to evoke a measurable response in the ganglion cell. When the lines were made very fine (*i.e.*, the "grating-frequency" was high), a point was reached at which the ganglion cell failed to respond, however great the contrast; this measured the resolving power of the particular cell being investigated. The interesting feature of this work is that individual ganglion cells had a special sensitivity to particular grating-frequencies, as if the ganglion cells were "tuned" to particular frequencies, the frequencies being measured by the number of black and white lines in a given area of retina. When the same technique was applied to human subjects, the electrical changes recorded from the scalp being taken as a measure of the response, the same results were obtained.

Colour vision. The spectrum, obtained by refracting light through a prism, shows a number of characteristic regions of colour—red, orange, yellow, green, blue, indigo, and violet. These regions represent large numbers of individual wavelengths; thus, the red extends roughly from 7600 angstrom units to 6500; the yellow from 6300 to 5600; green from 5400 to 5000; blue from 5000 to 4200; and violet from 4200 to 4000. Thus, the limits of the visual spectrum are commonly given as 7600 to 4000 angstroms. In fact, however, the retina is sensitive to ultraviolet light to 3500 angstroms, the failure of the short wavelengths to stimulate vision being due to absorption by the ocular media. Again, if the infrared radiation is strong enough, wavelengths as long as 10,000–10,500 angstroms evoke a sensation of light.

Within the bands of the spectrum, subtle distinctions in hue may be appreciated. The power of the eye to discriminate light on the basis of its wavelength can be measured by projecting onto the two halves of a screen lights of different wavelengths. When the difference is very small—*e.g.*, five angstroms—no difference can be appreciated. As the difference is increased, a point is reached when the two halves of the screen appear differently coloured. The hue discrimination (hue is the quality of colour that is determined by wavelength) measured in this way varies with the region of the spectrum examined; thus, in the blue-green and yellow it is as low as ten angstroms, but in the deep red and violet it may be 100 angstroms or more. Thus, the eye can discriminate several hundreds of different spectral bands, but the capacity is limited. If it is appreciated that there are a large number of nonspectral colours that may be made up by mixing the spectral wavelengths, and by diluting these with white light, the number of different colours that may be distinguished is high indeed.

Hue discriminations

Spectral sensitivity curve. At extremely low intensities of stimuli, when only rods are stimulated, the retina shows a variable sensitivity to light according to its wavelength, being most sensitive at about 5000 angstroms, the absorption maximum of the rod visual pigment, rhodopsin. In the light-adapted retina one may plot a similar type of curve, obtained by measuring the relative amounts of light energy of different wavelengths required to produce the same sensation of brightness; now the different stimuli appear coloured, but the subject is asked to ignore the colours and match them on the basis of their luminosity (brightness). This is carried out with a special instrument called the flicker-photometer. There is a characteristic shift in the maximum sensitivity from 5000 angstroms for scotopic (night) vision to 5550 angstroms for photopic (day) vision, the so-called Purkinje shift. It has been suggested that the cones have a pigment that shows a maximum of absorption at 5550 angstroms, but the phenomena of colour vision demand that there be three types of cone, with three separate pigments having maximum absorption in the red, green, and blue, so that it is more probable that the photopic luminosity curve is a reflection of the summated behaviour of the three types of cone rather than of one.

The Purkinje shift has an interesting psychophysical correlate; it may be observed, as evening draws on, that the luminosities of different colours of flowers in a garden change; the reds become much darker or black, while the blues become much brighter. What is happening is that, in this range of luminosities, called mesopic, both rods and cones are responding, and, as the rod responses become more pronounced—*i.e.*, as darkness increases—the rod luminosity scale prevails over that of the cones.

It may be assumed that the sensation of luminosity under any given condition is determined by certain ganglion cells that make connections to all three types of cone and also to rods; at extremely low levels of illumination their responses are determined by the activity aroused in the rods. As the luminance is increased, the ganglion cell is activated by both rods and cones, and so its luminosity curve is governed by both rod and cone activity. Finally, at extremely high luminances, when the rods are "saturated" and ceasing to respond, the luminosity curve is, in effect, compounded of the responses of all three types of cone.

Colour mixing. The fundamental principle of colour mixing was discovered by Isaac Newton when he found that white light separates spatially into its different component colours on passing through a prism. When the same light is passed through another prism, so that the individual bands of the spectrum are superimposed on each other, the sensation becomes one of white light. Thus, the retina, when white light falls on it, is really being exposed to all the wavelengths that make up the spectrum. Because these wavelengths fall simultaneously on the same receptors, the evoked sensation is one of white. If the wavelengths are spread out spatially, they evoke separate sensations, such as red or yellow, according to which receptors receive which bands of wavelengths. In fact, the sensation of white may be evoked by employing much fewer wavelengths than those in the spectrum: namely, by mixing three primary hues—red, green, and blue.

Three primary hues

Furthermore, any colour, be it a spectral hue or not, may be matched by a mixture of these three primaries, red, green, and blue, if their relative intensities are varied. Many of the colours of the spectrum can be matched by mixtures of only two of the primary colours, red and green; thus the sensations of red, orange, yellow, and green may be obtained by adding more and more green light to a red one.

To one accustomed to mixing pigments, and to mixing a blue pigment, for example, with yellow to obtain green, the statement that red plus green can give yellow or orange, or that blue plus yellow can give white, may sound strange. The mixing of pigments is essentially a subtractive process, however, as opposed to the additive process of throwing differently coloured lights on a white screen. Thus, a blue pigment is blue because it reflects mainly blue (and some green) light and absorbs red and yellow; and a yellow pigment reflects mainly yellow and some green and absorbs blue and red. When blue and yellow pigments are mixed, and white light falls on the mixture, all bands of colour are absorbed except for the green colour band.

Colour defectiveness. The colour-defective subject is one whose wavelength discrimination apparatus is not as good as that of the majority of people, so that he sees many colours as identical that normal people would see as different. About one percent of males are dichromats; they can mix all the colours of the spectrum, as they see them, with only two primaries instead of three. Thus, the protanope (red blind) requires only blue and green to make his matches; since, for the normal (trichromatic) subject the various reds, oranges, yellows, and many greens are the result of mixing red and green, the protanope matches all these with a green. In other words, he is unable to distinguish all these hues from each other on the basis of their colour; if he distinguishes them, it is because of their different luminosity (brightness). The protanope matches white with a mixture of blue and green and is, in fact, unable to distinguish between white and bluish-green. The deuteranope (green blind) matches all colours with a mixture of red and blue; thus, his white is a mixture of red and blue that appears purple to a person with normal vision. The deuteranope also is unable to discriminate reds, oranges, yellows, and many greens, so that both types of dichromat are classed as red-green-blind. For the protanope, however, the spectrum is more limited because he is unable to appreciate red. The trit-

anope (blue blind) is rare, constituting only one in 13,000 to 65,000 of the population; because he is blue blind, his colour discrimination is best in the region of red to green, where that of the protanope and deuteranope is worse.

Responses of uniform population of receptors. The scotopic (night) visual system, mediated by rods, is unable to discriminate between different wavelengths; thus, a threshold stimulus of light with a wavelength of 4800 angstroms gives a sensation of light that is indistinguishable from that evoked by a wavelength of 5300 angstroms. If the intensities are increased, however, the lights evoke sensations of blue and green, respectively. Rods are unable to mediate wavelength, or colour, discrimination while the cones can because the rods form a homogeneous population, all containing the same photopigment, rhodopsin. Thus, the response of a nerve cell connected with a rod or group of rods will vary with the wavelength of light, and probably in the manner indicated by Figure 7, in which the response, measured in

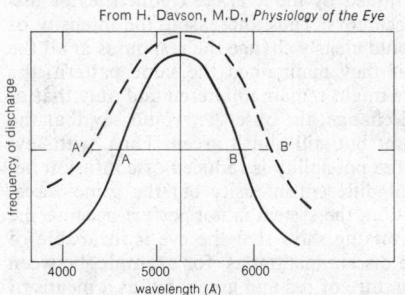

From H. Davson, M.D., *Physiology of the Eye*

Figure 7: Theoretical wavelength response curve for a single receptor of *Limulus* retina. The maximum response will occur at 5200 Å, the absorptional maximum of the retinal pigment. With wavelengths of light corresponding to the points A and B, the responses will be identical, so that no discrimination between these two wavelengths is possible. When the intensity of the light is changed and a new curve is obtained (the dotted line), the responses at A′ and B′ are also identical.

frequency of discharge in the bipolar or ganglion cell, is plotted against the wavelength of the stimulating light. The curve is essentially similar to the absorption spectrum of rhodopsin when the same amount of energy is in each stimulus; thus, blue-green of 5000 angstroms has the most powerful effect because it is absorbed most efficiently, while violet and red have the smallest effects. In this sense, the rods behave as wavelength discriminators, but it is to be noted that there are pairs of wavelengths on each side of the peak to which the same response is obtained; thus, a blue of 4800 angstroms and a yellow of 6000 angstroms give the same discharge. Moreover, if the intensity of the stimulus is varied, a new curve is obtained (as in the dotted line of Figure 7), and now the same response is obtained with a high intensity of violet at 4000 angstroms as with blue at the lower intensity. In general, it is easy to show that, by varying the intensity of the stimulus of a single wavelength, all types of response may be obtained, so that the brain would never receive a message indicating, in a unique fashion, that the retina was stimulated with, say, green light of 5300 angstroms; the same message could be given by blue light of 4800 angstroms, red light of 6500 angstroms, and so on.

Why rods fail to discriminate between colours

Ideally, colour discrimination would require a large number of receptors specifically sensitive to small bands of the spectrum, but the number would have to be extremely large because the capacity for hue discrimination is extremely great, as has been indicated. In fact, however, the phenomena of colour mixing suggest that the number of receptors may be limited.

Young-Helmholtz theory. It was the phenomena of colour mixing that led Thomas Young in 1802 to postulate that there are three receptors, each one especially sensitive to one part of the spectrum; these receptors were thought to convey messages to the brain, and, depending on how strongly they were stimulated by the coloured light, the combined message would be interpreted as that due to the actual colour. The theory was developed by Hermann Ludwig Ferdinand von Helmholtz, and is called the Young-Helmholtz trichromatic theory. As expressed in modern terms, it is postulated that there are three types of cone in the retina, characterized by the presence of one of three different pigments, one absorbing preferentially in the red part of the spectrum, another in the green, and another in the blue. A coloured stimulus—*e.g.*, a yellow light—would stimulate the red and green receptors, but would have little effect on the blue; the combined sensation would be that of yellow, which would be matched by stimulating the eye with red and green lights in correct proportions of relative intensity. A given coloured stimulus would, in general, evoke responses in all three receptors, and it would be the pattern of these responses—*e.g.*, blue strongly, green less strongly, and red weakest—that would determine the quality of the sensation. The intensity of the sensation would be determined by the average frequencies of discharge in the receptors. Thus, increasing the intensity of the stimulus would clearly change the responses in all the receptors, but if they maintained the same pattern, the sensation of hue might remain unaltered and only that of intensity would change; the observer would say that the light was brighter but still bluish green. Thus, with several receptors, the possibility is reduced of confusion between stimuli of different intensity but the same wavelength composition; the system is not perfect because the laws of colour mixing show that the eye is incapable of certain types of discrimination, as, for example, between yellow and a mixture of red and green, but as a means of discriminating subtle changes in the environment the eye is a very satisfactory instrument.

The direct proof that the eye does contain three types of cone has been secured, but only relatively recently. This was done by examining the light emerging from the eye after reflection off the retina; in the dark-adapted eye the light emerging was deficient in blue light because this had been preferentially absorbed by the rhodopsin. In the light-adapted eye, when only cone pigments are absorbing light, the emerging light can be shown to be deficient in red and green light because of the absorption by pigments called erythrolabe and chlorolabe. Again, the light passing through individual cones of the excised human retina can be examined by a microscope device, and it was shown by such examination that cones were of three different kinds according to their preference for red, green, and blue lights.

The nervous messages. If the three types of cones respond differently to light stimuli, one may expect to find evidence for this difference in type of response by examining the electrophysiological changes taking place in the retina; ideally, one should like to place a microelectrode in or on a cone, then in or on its associated bipolar cell, and so on up the visual pathway. In the earliest studies, the optic nerve fibres of the frog were examined—*i.e.*, the axons of ganglion cells. The light-adapted retina was stimulated with wavelengths of light stretching across the spectrum, and the responses in arbitrarily selected single fibres were examined. The responses to stimuli of the same energy but different wavelengths were plotted as frequency of discharge against wavelength, and the fibres fell into several categories, some giving what the investigator called a dominator response, the fibre responding to all wavelengths and giving a maximum response in the yellow-green at 5600 angstroms. Other fibres gave responses only over limited ranges of wavelengths, and their wavelengths of maximum response tended to be clustered in the red, green, and blue regions. The investigator called these modulators, and considered that the message in the dominator indicated to the brain the intensity of the stimulus—*i.e.*, it determined the sensation of brightness—while the modulators indicated the spectral composition of the stimulus, the combined messages in all the modulators resulting in a specific colour sensation. In the dark-adapted retina, when only rods were being stimulated, the response was of the dominator

Dominator impulse

type, but this time the maximum response occurred with a wavelength of 5000 angstroms, the absorption maximum of rhodopsin.

A more careful examination of the responses in single fibres, especially in the fish, which has good colour vision, showed that things were not quite as simple as the original investigator had thought because, as has been seen, the response of a ganglion cell, when light falls on its receptive field in the retina, is not just a discharge of action potentials that ceases when the light is switched off. This type of response is rare; the most usual ganglion cell or optic nerve fibre has a receptive field organized in a concentric manner, so that a spot of light falling in the central part of the field produces a discharge, while a ring of light falling on the surrounding area has the opposite effect, giving an off-response—*i.e.*, giving a discharge only when the light is switched off. Such a ganglion cell would be called an on-centre-off-periphery unit; others behaved in the opposite way, being off-centre-on-periphery.

When these units are examined with coloured lights, and when care is taken to stimulate the centres and surrounding areas separately, an interesting feature emerges; the centre and surrounding areas usually have opposite or opponent responses. Thus, some may be found giving an on-response to red in the centre of the field and an off-response to green in the surrounding area, so that simultaneous stimulation of centre with red and surrounding area with green gives no response, the inhibitory effect of the off-type of response cancelling the excitatory effect of the on-type. With many other units the effects were more complex, the centre giving an on-response to red and an off-response to green, while the surrounding area gave an off-response to red and an on-response to green, and vice versa. This opponent organization probably subserves several functions. First, it enables the retina to emphasize differences of colour in adjacent parts of the field, especially when the boundary between them moves, as indeed it is continually doing in normal vision because of the small involuntary movements of the eyes. Second, it is useful in "keeping the retina quiet"; there are about one million optic nerve fibres, and if all these were discharging at once the problem of sorting out their messages, and making meaning of them, would be enormous; by this "opponence," diffuse white light falling on many of these chromatic units would have no effect because the inhibitory surrounding area cancelled the excitatory centre, or vice versa. When the light became coloured, however, the previously inactive units could come into activity.

These responses show that by the time the effect of light has passed out of the eye in the optic nerve the message is well colour-coded. Thus all the evidence points to the correctness of the Young-Helmholtz hypothesis with respect to the three-colour basis. The three types of receptor, responding to different regions of the spectrum in specific manners, transmit their effects to bipolar and horizontal cells. The latter neurons have been studied from the point of view of their colour-coding. The potentials recorded from them were called *S*-potentials; these were of two types, which classified them as responding to colour (*C*-units) and luminosity (*L*-units).

S-potentials

The *C*-type of cell gave an opponent type of response, in the sense that the electrical sign varied with the wavelength band, red and green having opponent effects on some cells, and blue and yellow on others. These responses reflect the connections of the horizontal cells to groups of different cones, the blue-yellow type, for example, having connections with blue and red and green cones, while the red-green would have connections only with red and green cones.

Lateral geniculate cells. As indicated above, the cells at the next stage, the ganglion cells, give a fairly precisely coded set of messages indicating the chromatic (colour) quality and the luminosity (brightness) of the stimulus, organized in such a way, however, as to facilitate the discrimination of contrast. At higher stages—*e.g.*, in the cells of the lateral geniculate body—this emphasis on opponence, or contrast, is maintained and extended; thus, several types of cell have been described that differ in accordance with the organization of their receptive fields from the colour aspect; some were very similar to ganglion cells, while others differed in certain respects. Some showed no opponence between colours when centre and periphery were compared, so that if a red light on the periphery caused inhibition, green and blue light would also do so. Others had no centre-periphery organization, the receptive field consisting of only a central spot; different colours had different effects on this spot; and so on.

In the cerebral cortex there is the same type of opponence with many units, but because cortical cells require stimuli of definite shape and often are not activated by simple spot stimuli, early studies carried out before these requirements were known probably failed to elucidate the true chromatic requirements of these high-order neurons. In general, the responses are what might be predicted on the basis of connections made to lateral geniculate neurons having the chromatic responses already known. Thus the final awareness of colour probably depends on the bombardment of certain higher-order cortical neurons by groups of primary cortical neurons, each group sending a different message by virtue of the connections it makes to groups of cones, connections mediated, of course, through the neurons of the retina and lateral geniculate body.

The photochemical process. For the energy of light to exert its effect it must be absorbed; it has been stated above that the action-spectrum for vision (the sensitivity of the eye to light) in the completely dark-adapted eye has a maximum in the region of 5000 angstroms, and that this corresponds with the maximum of absorption of light by the pigment, rhodopsin, extracted from the dark-adapted retina of the same species. The chemical nature of rhodopsin must now be examined, as well as its localization in the rod and the changes it undergoes in response to the absorption of light. It must be appreciated at the outset that the amount of light energy absorbed by a single rod at the threshold for vision is extremely small—namely, one quantum—and this is quite insufficient to provide the energy required to cause an electrical change in the membrane of the rod that will be propagated from the point of absorption of the light to the rod spherule (which takes part in the synapse between rod and bipolar cell). There must, therefore, be a chemical amplification process taking place within the rod, and the absorption of a quantum must be viewed as the trigger that sets off other changes, which in turn provide the required amount of energy.

Rhodopsin. Visual purple, or rhodopsin, is a chromoprotein, a protein, opsin, with an attached chromatophore ("pigment-bearing") molecule that gives it its colour—*i.e.*, that allows it to absorb light in the visible part of the spectrum. In the absence of such a chromatophore, the protein would only absorb in the ultraviolet and so would appear colourless to the eye. The chromatophore group was identified as retinal, which is the substance formed by oxidation of vitamin A; on prolonged exposure of the eye to light, retinal can be found, free from the protein opsin, in the retina. When the eye is allowed to remain in the dark, the rhodopsin is regenerated by the joining up of retinal with opsin. Thus one may write:

Opsin and retinal (margin note)

$$\text{rhodopsin} \rightleftharpoons \text{retinal} + \text{opsin.}$$

The incidence of light on the retina causes the reaction to go to the right (that is, causes rhodopsin to form retinal plus opsin), and this photochemical change causes the sensation of light. The process is reversed by a thermal—*i.e.*, non-photochemical—reaction, so that for any given light intensity a steady state is reached with the regenerative process just keeping pace with the photochemical bleaching. Dark adaptation, or one element in it, is the regenerative process. The change in the rhodopsin molecule that leads to its bleaching—*i.e.*, the splitting off of the retinal molecule—takes place in a succession of steps; and there is reason to believe that the electrical change in the rod that eventually evokes the sensation of light occurs at a stage well before the splitting off of the

retinal. One may describe as a transduction process the chemical events that take place between the absorption of light and the electrical event, whatever that may be; the rod behaves as a transducer in that it converts light into electrical or neural energy.

The transduction process. Immediately after absorption of a quantum, the rhodopsin molecule is changed into a substance called prelumirhodopsin, recognized by its different colour from that of rhodopsin; this product is so highly unstable that at body temperature it is converted, without further absorption of light, into a series of products. These changes may be arrested by cooling the solution to $-195°$ C ($-319°$ F), at which temperature prelumirhodopsin remains stable; on warming to $-140°$ C ($-220°$ F) prelumirhodopsin becomes lumirhodopsin, with a slightly different colour; on warming further, successive changes are permitted until finally retinal is split off from the opsin to give a yellow solution. The important point to appreciate is that only at this stage is the chromatophore group split off; the earlier products have involved some change in the structure of the chromoprotein, but not so extreme as to break off the retinal. The precise nature of these changes is not yet completely elucidated, but the most fundamental one—namely, that occurring immediately after absorption of the quantum—has been shown to consist in a change in shape of the retinal molecule while it is still attached to opsin.

Prelumirhodopsin (margin note)

Thus retinal, like vitamin A, can exist in several forms because of the double bonds in its carbon chain—the so-called *cis-trans* isomerism. In other words, the same group of atoms constituting the retinal molecule can be twisted into a number of different shapes, although the sequence of the atoms is unaltered. While attached to the opsin molecule in the form of rhodopsin, the retinal has a shape called 11-*cis*, being somewhat folded, while on conversion to prelumirhodopsin the retinal has a straighter shape called all-*trans;* the process is called one of photoisomerization, the absorption of light energy causing the molecule to twist into a new shape. Having suffered this alteration in shape, the retinal presumably causes some instability in the opsin, making it, too, change its shape, and thereby exposing to the medium in which it is bathed chemical groupings that were previously shielded by being enveloped in the centre of the molecule. It may be assumed that these changes in shape induce alterations in the light-absorbing character of the molecule that permit the recognition of the new forms of molecule represented by lumirhodopsin, metarhodopsins I and II, and so on.

Photoisomerization (margin note)

The final change is more drastic because it involves the complete splitting off of the retinal; an earlier stage—namely, the conversion of metarhodopsin I to metarhodopsin II—has been shown recently to involve a bodily change in position of the retinal, which in rhodopsin is linked to the lipid (fatty) portion of the molecule, whereas in metarhodopsin II it is found to have become attached to an amino acid in the backbone-chain of the protein (amino acids are subunits of proteins). Thus, in its native unilluminated state, retinal is attached to a lipid, which is presumably linked to the protein, so that rhodopsin is more properly called a chromolipoprotein rather than a chromoprotein. The outer segments of the rods are, as has been stated, constituted by membranous disks, and it is well established that the material from which these membranes are constructed is predominantly lipid, so that one may envisage the rhodopsin molecules as being, in fact, part of the membrane structure. The techniques used for extraction presumably tear the molecules from the main body of the lipid, but some of the lipid remains with the protein and retinal to constitute the link holding these two parts together.

Within the retina these chemical changes are all reversible, so that when a steady light is maintained on the retina the latter will contain a mixture of several or all of the intermediate compounds. In the dark, all will be gradually reconverted to rhodopsin. Because lack of vitamin A, from which retinal is derived, causes night blindness, some of the retinal must get lost from the eye to the general circulation; and it is actually replaced by the cells of the pigment epithelium, which are closely associated with the rods.

As to which of these chemical changes acts as the trigger for vision, there is some doubt. The discovery that the transition from metarhodopsin I to metarhodopsin II involves an actual shift of the retinal part of the molecule from linkage to lipid to linkage to protein reinforces the belief that this particular shift is sufficient to lead ultimately to electrical discharges in the optic nerve.

Cone pigments. So far as colour vision is concerned, the changes that take place in the three cone pigments have not been analyzed, simply because, so far, they have defied isolation, presumably because their concentrations are so much less than that of the rod pigment.

THE HIGHER VISUAL CENTRES

The visual pathway. The axons of the ganglion cells converge on the region of the retina called the papilla or optic disk. They leave the globe as the optic nerve, in which they maintain an orderly arrangement in the sense that fibres from the macular zone of the retina occupy the central portion, the fibres from the temporal half of the retina take up a concentric position, and so on; when outside the orbit, there is a partial decussation (crossover). The fibres from the nasal halves of each retina cross to the opposite side of the brain, while those from the temporal halves remain uncrossed. This partial decussation is called the chiasma. The optic nerves after this point are called the optic tracts, containing nerve fibres from both retinas. The result of the partial decussation is that an object in, say, the right-hand visual field produces effects in the two eyes that are transmitted to the left-hand side of the brain only. With cutaneous (skin) sensation there is a complete crossing-over of the sensory pathway; thus, information from the right half of the body, and the right visual field, is all conveyed to the left-hand part of the brain by the time that it has reached the diencephalon (the posterior part of the forebrain, Figure 8).

Partial decussation

By permission from EugeneWolff, *Anatomy of the Eye and Orbit.* London: H. K. Lewis & Co. Ltd.

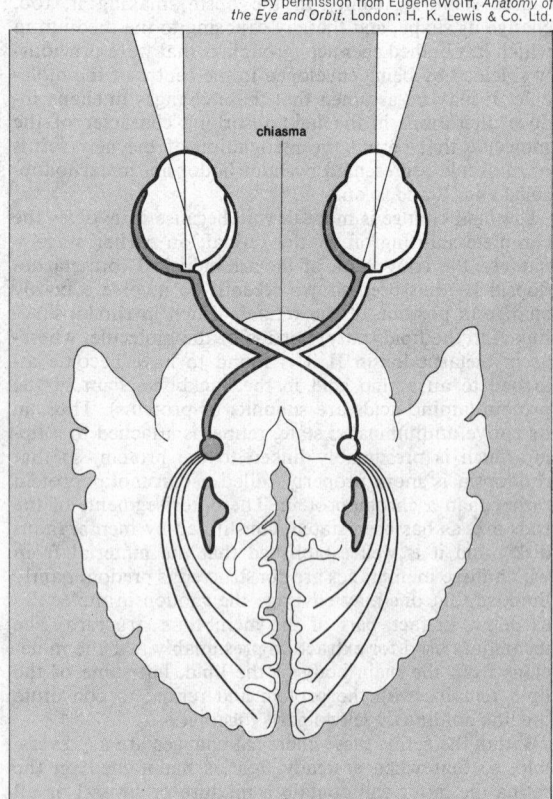

Figure 8: *Visual pathways.*
Fibres from the nasal side of the retina cross over in the chiasma to join the uncrossed fibres of the temporal half of the retina.

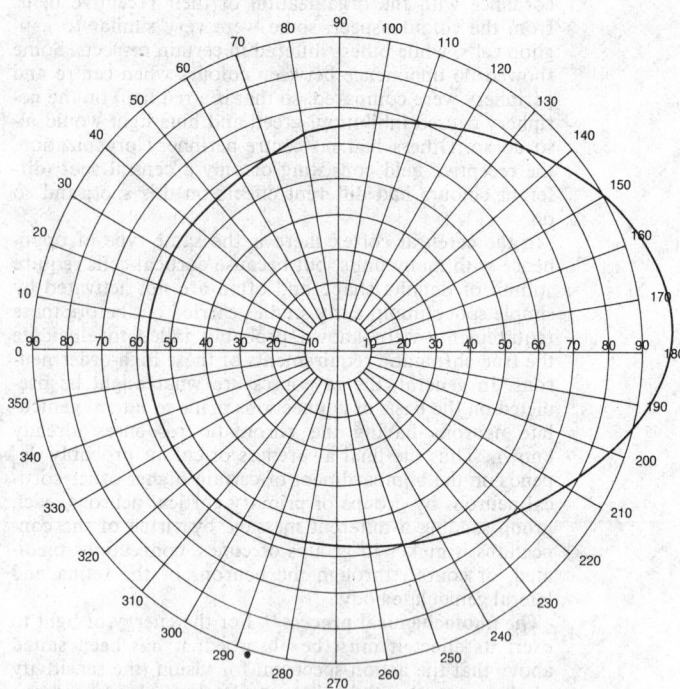

Figure 9: Perimeter chart showing normal visual field; figures on the perimeter indicate degrees of arc.
From H. Davson and M.G. Eggleton (eds.), *Principles of Human Physiology*

Fusion of retinal images. Partial decussation is an arrangement that serves the needs of frontally directed eyes and permits binocular vision, which consists in the fusion of the responses of both eyes to a single object—more loosely, one speaks of the fusion of the retinal images. In many lower mammals, with laterally directed eyes and therefore limited binocular vision, the degree of decussation is much greater, so that in the rat, for example, practically all of the optic nerve fibres pass to the opposite side of the brain.

The fibres of the optic tracts relay their messages to nerve cells in those parts of the diencephalon called the lateral geniculate bodies, and from the lateral geniculate bodies the messages are relayed to nerve cells in the occipital cortex of the same side. (The occipital cortex is the outer substance in the posterior portion of the brain.)

The visual field. If one eye is fixed on a point in space, the visual field for this eye may be thought of as the part of a surface of a sphere on to which all visible objects are projected. The limits to this field will be determined by the sensitivity and extent of the retina and the accessibility of light rays from the environment. Experimentally or clinically, the field is measured on a perimeter, a device for ascertaining the point on a given meridian where a white spot just appears or disappears from vision when moved along this meridian. (A meridian is a curve on the surface of a sphere that is formed by the intersection of the sphere surface and a plane passing through the centre of the sphere.) The field is recorded on a chart, illustrated by Figure 9. On the nasal side, the field is restricted to about 60° from the midline. This is due to the obstruction caused by the nose, since the retina extends nearly as far forward on the temporal side of the globe as on the nasal side. It is customary to refer to the binocular visual field as that common to the two eyes, the uniocular field being the extreme temporal (outside) region peculiar to each eye. It will be clear from the field of the single eye shown in Figure 9 that the binocular field is determined in the horizontal meridian by the nasal field of each eye, and so will amount to about 60° to either side of the vertical meridian.

Lateral geniculate body. The dorsal (posterior) nucleus of the lateral geniculate body, where the optic tract fibres relay, has six layers, and the crossed fibres relay in layers 1, 4, and 6, while the uncrossed relay in layers 2,

3, and 5; thus, at this level, the impulses from the two eyes are kept separate, and when the discharges in geniculate neurons are recorded electrically it is rare to find any responding to stimuli in both eyes.

Striate area. The optic tract fibres make synapses with nerve cells in the respective layers of the lateral geniculate body, and the axons of these third-order nerve cells pass upward to the calcarine fissure (a furrow) in each occipital lobe of the cerebral cortex. This area is called the striate area because of bands of white fibres—axons from nerve cells in the retina—that run through it. It is also identified as Brodmann's area 17. It is at this level that the impulses from the separate eyes meet at common cortical neurons, or nerve cells, so that when the discharges in single cortical neurons are recorded it is usual to find that they respond to light falling in one or the other eye. It is probable that it is when the retinal messages have reached this level of the central nervous

Point of
awareness
of visual
stimulus

system, and not before, that the human subject becomes aware of the visual stimulus, since destruction of the area causes absolute blindness in man. Because of the partial decussation, however, the removal of only one striate cortex will not cause complete blindness in either eye, since only messages from two halves of the retinas will have been blocked; the same will be true if one optic tract is severed or one lateral geniculate body is destroyed. The result of such lesions will be half-blindness, or hemianopia, the messages from one half of the visual field being obliterated.

Pupillary pathways. Some of the fibres in the optic tracts do not relay in the lateral geniculate bodies but pass instead to a midbrain region—the pretectal centre —where they mediate (transmit) reflex alterations in the size of the pupil. Thus, in bright light, the pupils are constricted; this happens by virtue of the pupillary light reflex mediated by these special nerve fibres. Removal of the occipital cortex, although it causes blindness in the opposite visual field, does not destroy the reaction of the pupils to light; if the optic nerve is cut, however, the eye will be both completely blind and also unreactive to light falling on this eye. The pupil of the blind eye will react to light falling on the other eye by virtue of a decussation in the pupillary reflex pathway.

Point-to-point representation. Because of the ordered manner in which the optic tract fibres relay in the lateral geniculate bodies and from there pass in an orderly fashion to the striate area, when a given point on the retina is stimulated, the response recorded electrically in either the lateral geniculate body or the striate area is localized to a small region characteristic for that particular retinal spot. When the whole retinal field is stimulated in this point-to-point way, and the positions on the geniculate or striate gray matter on which the responses occur are plotted, it is possible to plot on these regions of the brain maps of the retinal fields or, more usually, maps of the visual fields.

Visuopsychic or circumstriate areas. Area 17, the striate area, is the primary visual centre in the sense that, in primates at any rate, all of the geniculate fibres project onto it and none projects onto another region of the cortex. There are two other areas containing neurons that

Peristriate
and
parastriate
areas

have close connections with the eye; these are the parastriate and peristriate areas, or Brodmann's areas 18 and 19, respectively, in close anatomical relationship to one another and to area 17. They are secondary visual areas in the sense that messages are relayed from area 17 to area 18 and from area 18 to area 19, and, because area 17 does not relay to regions beyond area 18, these circumstriate areas are the means whereby visual information is brought into relation with more remote parts of the cortex. Thus in writing, the eyes direct the activities of the fingers, which are controlled by a region of the frontal cortex, so that one may presume that visual information is relayed to this frontal region. In the monkey, bilateral destruction of the areas causes irrecoverable loss of a learned visual discrimination, but this can be relearned after the operation. In man, lesions in this region are said to cause disturbances in spatial orientation and stereoscopic vision, but much more knowledge is required

before specific functions can be attributed to these circumstriate areas, if, indeed, this is possible.

Integration of the retinal halves. The two halves of the retina, and thus of the visual field, are represented on opposite cerebral hemispheres, but the visual field is perceived as a unity and hence one would expect an intimate connection between the two visual cortical areas.

Corpus callosum. The great bulk of the connections between the two sides of the cerebral mantle are made by the interhemispheric commissure (the point of union between the two hemispheres of the cerebrum) called the corpus callosum, which is made up of neurons and their axons and dendrites that make synapses with cortical neurons on symmetrically related points of the hemispheres. Thus, electrical stimulation of a point on one hemisphere usually gives rise to a response on a symmetrically related point on the other, by virtue of these callosal connections. The striate area is an exception, however, and it is by virtue of the connections of the striate neurons with the area 18 neurons that this integration occurs, the two areas 18 on opposite hemispheres being linked by the corpus callosum.

Stereopsis in the midline. Usually stereopsis, or perception of depth, is possible by the use of a single hemisphere because the images of the same object formed by right and left eyes are projected to the same hemisphere; however, if the gaze is fixed on a distant point and a pin is placed in line with this but closer to the observer, a stereoscopic perception of the distant point and the pin can be achieved by the fusion of disparate images of the pin, but the images of the pin actually fall on opposite retinal halves, so that this fusion must be brought about by way of the corpus callosum.

Callosal transfer. In experimental animals it is possible, by section of the chiasma, to ensure that visual impulses from one eye pass only to one hemisphere. If this is done, an animal trained to respond to a given pattern and permitted to use only one eye during the training is just as efficient, when fully trained, in making the discrimination with the other eye. There has thus been a callosal transfer of the learning so that the hemisphere that was not directly involved in the learning process can react as well as that directly involved. If the corpus callosum is also sectioned, this transfer is impossible, so that the animal, trained with one eye, must be trained again if it is to carry out the task with the other eye only.

Effect of
cutting the
corpus
callosum

Superior colliculi. The visual pathway so far described is called the geniculostriate pathway, and in man it may well be the exclusive one from a functional aspect because lesions in this pathway lead to blindness. Nevertheless, many of the optic tract fibres, even in man, relay in the superior colliculi, a paired formation on the roof of the midbrain. From the colliculi there is no relay to the cortex, so that any responses brought about by this pathway do not involve the cortex. In man, as has been said, lesions in the striate area, which would of course leave the collicular centres intact, cause blindness, so that the visual fibres in these centres serve no obvious function. In lower animals, including primates, removal of the striate areas does not cause complete blindness; in fact, it is often difficult to determine any visual impairment from a study of the behaviour of the animals. Thus, in reptiles and birds, vision is barely affected, so that a pigeon that has been subjected to the operation can fly and avoid obstacles as well as a normal one. In rodents, such as the rabbit, removal of the occipital lobes causes some impairment of vision, but the animal can perform such feats as avoiding obstacles when running and recognizing food by sight. In the monkey, the effects are more serious, but the animal can be trained to discriminate lights of different intensity and even the shapes of objects, provided that these are kept in continual motion. It seems likely, then, that it is the visual pathway through the colliculi that permits the use of the eyes in the absence of visual cortex, although the connections of the optic tract fibres with the pulvinar of the thalamus (an area in the diencephalon), established in some animals, may well permit the use of regions of the cortex other than those denoted as visual.

SOME PERCEPTUAL ASPECTS OF VISION

So far, the visual process has been considered from rather elementary aspects; the ability to detect light and changes in its intensity, and to discriminate colour and form. It is now time to deal with more complex features, particularly some phenomena of binocular vision. It will then be in order to return to the electrophysiology of the visual pathway to see how some of the phenomena can be interpreted.

Projection of the retina.   Objects are perceived in definite positions in space—positions definite in relation to each other and to the percipient. The first problem is to analyze the physiological basis for this spatial perception or, as it is expressed, the projection of the retina into space.

Relative positions of objects.   The perception of the positions of objects in relation to each other is essentially a geometrical problem. Take, for the present, the perception of these relationships by one eye, monocular perception: a group of objects, as in Figure 10, produces images

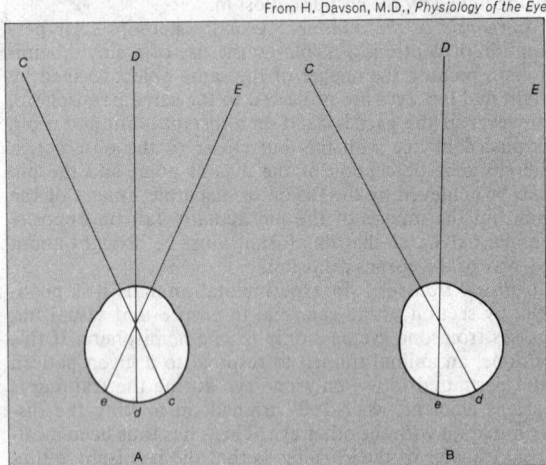

Figure 10: *Projection of retinal images into space.*
(A) A group of objects, C,D,E, produces images on the retina, c,d,e; the retinal images are projected outward in space toward the points evoking them. (B) The eye has moved to the left so that the image of c falls on d, previously projected to D but now projected to C; E no longer produces an image on the retina.

on the retina in a certain fixed geometrical relationship; for the perception of the fact that C is to the left of D, that D is to the left of E, and so on, it is necessary that the incidence of images at c, d, and e on the retina be interpreted in a similar, but, of course, inverted geometrical relationship. The neural requirements for this interpretation are (1) that the retina be built up of elements that behave as units throughout their conducting system to the visual cortex, and (2) that the retinal elements have "local signs." The local sign could represent an innate disposition or could result from experience—the association of the direction of objects in space, as determined by such evidence as that provided by touch, with the retinal pattern of stimulation. In neurophysiological terms, the retinal elements are said to be connected to cortical cells, each being specific for a given element, so that when a given cortical cell is excited the awareness is of a specific local sign. Studies of the projection of the retina on the cerebral cortex have confirmed this.

The retinal stimuli at c, d, and e in Figure 10 are appreciated as objects outside the eyes, the retina is said to be projected into space, and the field of vision is thus the projection of the retina through the nodal point. (In Figure 10 the nodal point is the point of intersection of Cc, Dd, and Ee.) It will be seen that the geometrical relationship between objects and retinal stimuli is reversed; in the retina c is to the right of d, and so on.

Position in relation to observer.   The recognition of the directions of objects in relation to the observer is more complex. If the eye (Figure 10B) is turned to the left, the image of C falls on the retinal point d, so that if d were always projected into the same direction in space, C would appear to be in D's place. In practice, one knows that C is perceived as fixed in space in spite of the movements of the eye; hence, the direction of projection of a retinal point is constantly modified to take into account movements of the eye; this may be called psychological compensation. It will be seen that correct projection is achieved by projecting the stimulated retinal point through the nodal point of the eye. Movements of the eye caused by movements of the head must be similarly compensated. As a result, any point in space remains fixed in spite of movements of the eye and head. Given this system of compensated projection, the recognition of direction in relation to the individual is now feasible. D may be said to be due north or, more vaguely, "over there"; when the head is turned, since D is perceived to be in the same place, it is still due north or "over there." In some circumstances, the human subject makes an error in projecting his retinal image, so that the object giving rise to the image appears to be in a different place from its true one; the image is said to be falsely projected. If the eye is moved passively, for example, by pulling on the conjunctiva with forceps, the subject has the impression that objects in the outside world are moving in a direction opposite to that of the eye.

The apparent movement of an afterimage, when the eye moves, is an excellent illustration of psychological compensation. A retinal stimulus, being normally projected through the nodal point, is projected into different points in space as the eye moves; an afterimage can be considered to be the manifestation of a continued retinal impulse, and its projection changes as the eye moves. The afterimage thus appears to move in the same direction as that of the movement of the eye. Whether the drift of an afterimage across the field of view is entirely due to eye movements is difficult to say. One certainly has the impression that the eye is chasing the afterimage.

Visual estimates.   *The directions of lines.* So far, consideration has been given to the problem of estimating the positions of points in relation to each other and to the percipient. The estimate of the directions of lines involves no really new principles, since, if two points, A and B, are exactly localized, the direction of the line AB can be appreciated. As will be seen, the organization of the neural connections of the retina and higher visual pathway is such as to favour the accurate recognition of direction; for the moment, the question of the maintenance of a frame of reference must be considered, in the sense that a map has vertical and horizontal lines with which to compare other directions. In fact, the vertical and horizontal meridians of the retina seem to be specialized as frames of reference; the accuracy with which a human subject can estimate whether a line is vertical or horizontal is very great.

An important point in this connection is that of the effects of eye movements on interpretation of the directions of lines because, when the eye moves to positions different from the primary straight-ahead position, the images of vertical lines will not necessarily fall on its vertical meridian. This can be due to an actual torsion of the eye about its anteroposterior (fore and aft) axis or to distortion of the retinal image. This means, then, that the line on the retina that corresponds to verticality in one position of the eye does not correspond to verticality in another, so that, once again, the space representation centre must take account not only of the retinal elements that have been stimulated but also of the corollary motor discharge.

Comparison of lengths.   The influence of the movements of the eyes in the estimation of length was emphasized by Helmholtz. An accurate comparison of the lengths of two parallel lines AB and CD can be made, whereas if an attempt is made to compare the nonparallel lines A'B' and C'D', quite large errors occur. According to Helmholtz, the eye fixates first the point A, and the line AB falls along a definite row of receptors, thereby indicating its length. The eye is now moved to fixate C, and if the image of CD falls along the same set of receptors the length of *CD* is said to be the same as that of *AB*. Such a movement of the eye is not feasible with lines that are not parallel. Similarly, the parallelism, or otherwise, of pairs of lines can be perceived accurately because on moving the eye over the lines the distance between them must remain the same.

Fairly accurate estimates of relative size may be made, nevertheless, without movements of the eyes. If two equal lines are observed simultaneously, the one with direct fixation and the other with peripheral vision, their images fall, of course, on different parts of the retina; if the images were equally long it could be stated that a certain length of stimulated retina was interpreted as a certain length of line in space. It is probable that this is roughly the basis on which rapid estimates of length depend, although there are such complications as the fact that the retina is curved so that lines of equal length in different parts of the retina do not produce images of equal length on the retina.

Optical illusions. Many instances have been cited of well-defined and consistent errors in visual estimates under special conditions. There is probably no single factor by which the errors can be explained, but the tendency for distinctly perceptible differences to appear larger than those more vaguely perceived is important.

The perception of depth. *Monocular cues.* The image of the external world on the retina is essentially flat or two-dimensional, and yet it is possible to appreciate its three-dimensional character with remarkable precision; to a great extent this is by virtue of the simultaneous presentation of different aspects of the world to the two eyes, but even when the subject views the world with a single eye it does not appear flat to him and he can, in fact, make reasonable estimates of the relative positions of objects in all three dimensions. Examples of monocular cues are the apparent movements of objects in relation to each other when the head is moved. Objects nearer the observer move in relation to more distant points in the opposite direction to the movement of the head. Perspective, by which is meant the changed appearance of an object when it is viewed from different angles, is another important clue to depth. Thus the projected retinal image of an object in space may be represented as a series of lines on a plane—*e.g.*, a box—these lines, however, are not a unique representation of the box because the same lines could be used to convey the impression of a perfectly flat object with the lines drawn on it, or of a rectangular, but not cubical, box viewed at a different angle. In order that a three-dimensional object be correctly represented to the subject on a two-dimensional surface, he must know what the object is; *i.e.*, it must be familiar to him. Thus a bicycle is a familiar object. If it is viewed at an angle from the observer the wheels seem elliptical and apparently differ in size. Because the observer knows that the wheels are circular and of the same size, he perceives depth in a two-dimensional pattern of lines. The perception of depth in a two-dimensional pattern thus depends greatly on experience —the knowledge of the true shape of things when viewed in a certain way. Other cues are light and shade, overlapping of contours, and relative sizes of familiar objects.

Binocular vision. The cues to depth mentioned above are essentially uniocular; they would permit the appreciation of three-dimensional space with a single eye. When two eyes are employed, two additional factors play a role, the one not very important—namely, the act of convergence or divergence of the eyes—and the other very important—namely, the stereoscopic perception of depth by virtue of the dissimilarity of the images presented by a three-dimensional object, or array of objects, to the separate eyes.

When a three-dimensional object or array is examined binocularly, the nearer points or objects require greater convergence for fixation than the more distant points or objects, so that this provides a cue to the three-dimensional character of the presentation. It is by no means a necessary cue, since presentation of the array for such a short time that movements of the eyes cannot occur still permits the three-dimensional perception, which is

achieved under these conditions by virtue of the dissimilar images received by the two retinas.

A stereogram contains two drawings of a three-dimensional object taken from different angles, chosen such that the pictures are right- and left-eyed views of the object. When the stereogram is placed in a stereoscope, an optical device for enabling the two separate pictures to be fused and seen single, the impression created is one of a three-dimensional object. The perception is immediate, and is not a matter if interpretation. Clearly, with the stereoscope the situation is simulated as it normally occurs. To appreciate the full implications of the stereoscopic perceptual process, one must examine some simpler aspects of binocular vision.

Figure 11 illustrates the situation in which a subject is fixating (fixing his gaze on) the point F so that the images of F fall on the foveal (retinal) points f_L and f_R, respectively. F is seen as a single point because the retinal points f_L and f_R are projected to the same point in space, and the projection is such that the subject says that the point F is straight in front of him, although it is to the right of his left eye and to the left of his right eye. The two eyes in this case are behaving as a single eye, "the cyclopean eye," situated in the centre of the forehead, and one may represent the projection of the two separate retinal points, f_L and f_R, as the single projection of the point f_C of the cyclopean eye. As will be seen, the cyclopean eye is a useful concept in consideration of certain aspects of stereoscopic vision.

The points f_L and f_R may be defined as corresponding points because they have the same retinal direction values. The images formed by the points A and B, in the same frontal plane as F, fall on a_L and a_R and b_L and b_R; once again the pairs of retinal points are projected to the same points, namely, to A and B, and they are treated as being on the left and right of F, respectively. On the cyclopean projection, they may be said to be localized by the outward projections of a_C and b_C, respectively.

In Figure 12, the subject is once again fixing the point F, but the point A is now no longer in the same frontal plane as the point F, but closer to the observer. The images of F fall on corresponding points and are projected to a single point in front. The images of A, on a_L and a_R, do not fall on corresponding points and are, in fact, projected into space in different directions, as in-

Perspective

Corre-
sponding
points

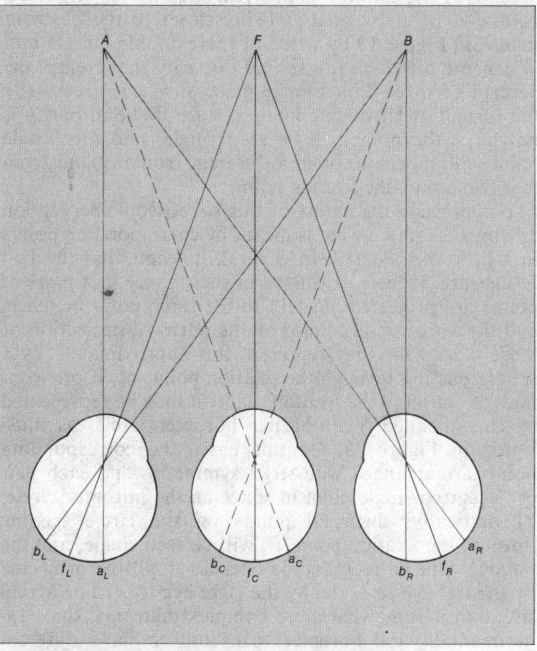

Figure 11: *The Cyclopean system of projection.*
The images of the points *F, A,* and *B* on the two retinas are transposed to the retina of a hypothetical eye midway between the two. The pairs of images, a_L and a_R, b_L and b_R, and so on, coincide on the cyclopean retina indicating that the stimulated retina points are projected to a common direction (see text).

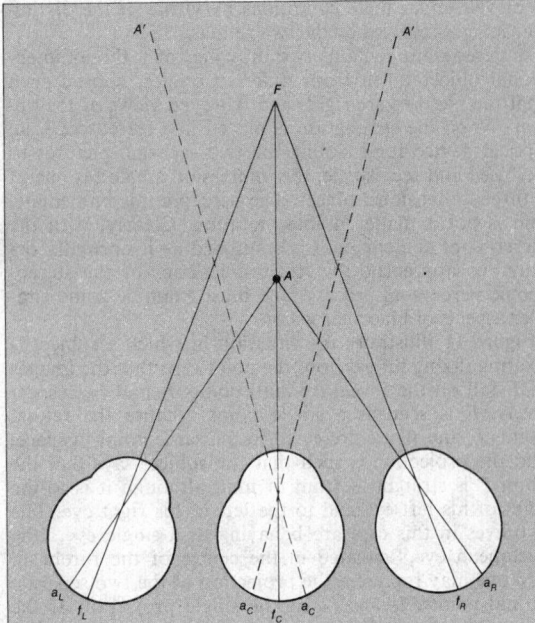

Figure 12: Physiological diplopia caused by an object, *A*, closer to the observer than the fixation point, *F*. The images of *A* fall on disparate or noncorresponding points on the two retinas, and these are projected to different points *A'* and *A'* (see text).

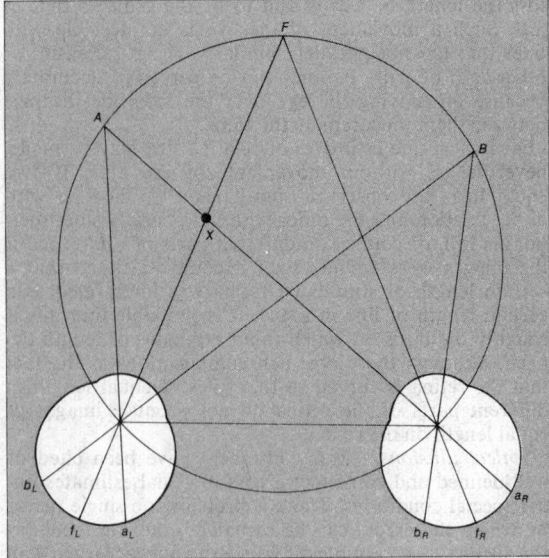

Figure 13: *The Vieth-Müller horopter circle.* *F* is the fixation point. If corresponding points are symmetrically distributed about the foveas, the points in space in the fixation plane, whose images fall on the corresponding points, lie on the circle. The images of the point *X* lie on disparate points (see text).

From H. Davson, M.D., *Physiology of the Eye*

dicated by the cyclopean projection. This means that *A* is seen simultaneously at two different places, a phenomenon called physiological diplopia, and this in fact does happen, as can be seen by fixing one's gaze on a distant point and holding a pencil fairly close to the face; with a little practice the two images of the pencil can be distinguished. Thus, when the eyes are directed into the distance the objects closer to the observer are seen double, although one of the double images of any pair is usually suppressed. To return to Figures 11 and 12, *F* and *A* in Figure 11 are seen single and in the same plane because their images each fall on corresponding points. *F* is seen single and *A* double in Figure 12 because the images of *A* fall on noncorresponding, or disparate, points. *A* is appreciated as being closer to the observer than *F* in Figure 12 by virtue of these double images but, in general, although it is retinal disparity that creates the percept of three-dimensional space, it is not necessarily the formation of double images, since if the disparity is not large the point will be seen single, and this single point will appear to be in a different frontal plane from that containing the fixation point.

To appreciate the nature of this stereoscopic perception one must examine what is meant by corresponding points in a little more detail. In general, it seems that the two retinas are, indeed, organized in such a way that pairs of points are projected innately to the same point in space, and the horopter is defined as the outward projection of these pairs. One may represent this approximately by a sphere passing through the fixation point, or, if one confines attention to the fixation plane, it may be represented by the so-called Vieth-Müller horopter circle, as illustrated in Figure 13. On this basis, the corresponding points are arranged with strict symmetry, and each pair projects to a single point in space on the horopter circle. Theoretically, then, all points on the circle passing through the fixation point, *F*, will be seen single, and the point *X* will be seen double because it will be projected by the left eye to *F* and by the right eye to *A*. The actual situation is somewhat more complex than this, since experimentally the horopter turns out to have different shapes according to how close the fixation point is to the observer. The point to appreciate, however, is that the experimentally determined line, be it circular or straight or elliptical, is such that when points are placed on it they all appear to be in the same frontal plane—*i.e.*, there is no stereoscopic perception of depth when one views

these points—and one may say that this is because the images of points on the horopter fall on corresponding points of the two retinas.

In Figure 14, to the left, are two eyes viewing an arrow lying in the frontal plane—*i.e.*, with no stereopsis—and to the right the arrow is inclined into the third dimension—*i.e.*, it tends to point toward the observer. All points on the arrow are, in fact, seen single under both conditions, and yet it is clear from the right-hand figure that, if the gaze is fixed on *A*, the images of *B'* will fall on noncorresponding points. *B'* is not seen double but, instead, the noncorresponding points, *b'_L* and *b'_R*, are projected to a common point *B'* and a stereoscopic percept is achieved. Thus the noncorresponding, or disparate, points on the retinas can be projected to a single point, and it is essentially this fusion of disparate images by the brain that creates the impression of depth. If the point *B'* were brought much closer to the eyes, its images would fall on such disparate points that fusion would no longer be possible, and *B'* would be seen double, or one double image would be suppressed. There is thus a certain zone of disparity that, if not exceeded, allows fusion of disparate points. This is called Panum's fusional area; it is the area on one retina such that any point in it will fuse with a single point on the other retina.

To return to the stereoscopic perception of three-dimensional space, one may recapitulate that it is because the two eyes receive different images of the same object that the stereoscopic percept happens; when the two images of the object are identical, then, except under very spe-

Fusion of disparate images

From H. Davson, M.D., *Physiology of the Eye*

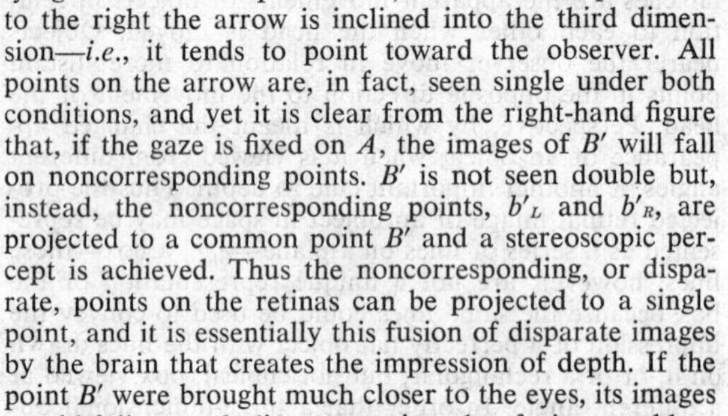

Figure 14: The distinction between corresponding points (*a_L* and *a_R*, *b_L* and *b_R*) and points that do not correspond (*b'_L* and *b'_R*; see text).

cial conditions, the object has no three-dimensionality. A special condition is given by a uniformly illuminated sphere; this is three-dimensional, but the observer would have to use special cues to discriminate this from a flat disk lying in the frontal plane. Such a cue might be the different degree of convergence of the eyes required to fixate the centre from that required to fixate the periphery, or the different degree of accomodation.

The difference in the two aspects of the same object (or group of objects), measured as the instantaneous parallax, is illustrated in Figure 15. *B* is closer to the observer

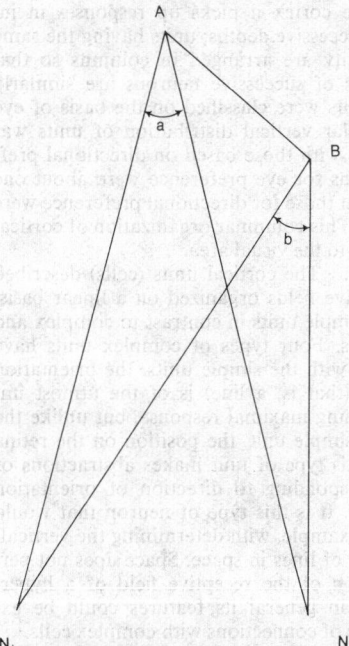

From Hugh Davson, M.D. *Physiology of the Eye*

Figure 15: *Binocular and instantaneous parallax.*
N_L and N_R are the nodal points of the left and right eyes, respectively (see text).

than *A;* the fact is perceived stereoscopically because the line *AB* subtends different angles at the two eyes, and the instantaneous parallax is measured by the difference between the angles *a* and *b*. The binocular parallax of any point in space is given by the angle subtended at it by the line joining the nodal points of the two eyes; hence, the binocular parallax of *A* is *a;* that of *B* is *b;* the instantaneous parallax is thus the difference of binocular parallax of the two points considered.

Accuracy of stereoscopic perception

If one places three vertical wires in front of an observer in the frontal plane, one may move the middle one in front of, or behind, the plane containing the other two and ask the subject to say when he perceives that it is out of the plane; under correct experimental conditions the only cue will be the difference of binocular parallax, and it is found that the minimum difference is remarkably small, of the order of five seconds of arc, corresponding to a disparity of retinal images far smaller than the diameter of a single cone. With two editions of the same book, it is not possible, by mere inspection, to detect that a given line of print was not printed from the same type as the same line in the other book. If the two lines in question are placed in the stereoscope, it is found that some letters appear to float in space, a stereoscopic impression created by the minute differences in size, shape, and relative position of the letters in the two lines. The stereoscope may thus be used to detect whether a bank note has been forged, whether two coins have been stamped by the same die, and so on.

The stereoscopic appearance obtained by regarding two differently coloured, but otherwise identical, plane pictures with the two eyes separately, is probably due to chromatic differences of magnification. If the left eye, for example, views a plane picture through a red glass

and the right eye views the same picture through a blue glass, an illusion of solidity results. Chromatic difference in magnification causes the images on the two retinas to be slightly different in size, so that the images of any point on the picture do not fall on corresponding points; the conditions for a stereoscopic illusion are thus present.

Retinal rivalry. Stereoscopic perception results from the presentation to the two eyes of different images of the same object; if two pictures that cannot possibly be related as two aspects of the same three-dimensional object are presented to the two eyes, single vision may, under some conditions, be obtained, but the phenomenon of retinal rivalry enters. Thus, if the letter *F* occupies one side of a stereogram, and *L* the other, the two letters can be fused by the eyes to give the letter *E;* the letters *F* and *L* cannot, however, by any stretch of the imagination be regarded as left and right aspects of a real object in space, so that the final percept is not three-dimensional, and, moreover, it is not a unitary percept in the sense used in this discussion; great difficulty is experienced in retaining the appearance of the letter *E,* the two separate images, *F* and *L,* tending to float apart. This is a mode of binocular vision that may be more appropriately called simultaneous perception; the two images are seen simultaneously, and it is by superimposition, rather than fusion, that the illusion of the letter *E* is created. More frequent than superimposition is the situation in which one or the other image is completely suppressed; thus, if the right eye views a vertical black bar and the left eye a horizontal one, the binocular percept is not that of a cross; usually the subject is aware of the vertical bar alone or the horizontal bar alone. Moreover, there is a fairly characteristic rhythm of suppression, or alternation of dominance, as it is called.

Ocular dominance. Retinal rivalry may be viewed as the competition of the retinal fields for attention; such a notion leads to the concept of ocular dominance—the condition when one retinal image habitually compels attention at the expense of the other. While there seems little doubt that a person may use one eye in preference to the other in acts requiring monocular vision—*e.g.,* in aiming a rifle—it seems doubtful whether, in the normal individual, ocular dominance is really an important factor in the final awareness of the two retinal images. Where the retinal images overlap, stereoscopic perception is possible and the two fields, in this region, are combined into a single three-dimensional percept. In the extreme temporal fields (*i.e.,* at the outside of the fields of vision), entirely different objects are seen by the two eyes, and the selection of what is to dominate the awareness at any moment depends largely on the interest it arouses; as a result, the complete field of view is filled in and one is not aware of what objects are seen by only one eye. Where the fields overlap, and different objects are seen by the two eyes—*e.g.,* on looking through a window the bars may obscure some objects as seen by one eye but not as seen by the other—the final percept is determined by the need to make something intelligible out of the combined fields. Thus, the left eye may see a chimney pot on a house, while the other eye sees the bar of a window in its place; the final perceptual pattern involves the simultaneous awareness of both the bar and the chimney pot because the retinal images have meaning only if both are present in consciousness. So long as the individual retinal images can be regarded as the visual tokens of an actual arrangement of objects, it is possible to obtain a single percept, and there seems no reason to suppose that the final percept will be greatly influenced by the dominance of one or other eye. When a single percept is impossible, retinal rivalry enters; this is essentially an alternation of awareness of the two fields— the subject apparently makes attempts to find something intelligible in the combined presentation by suppressing first one field and then the other—and certainly it would be incorrect to speak of ocular dominance as an absolute and invariable imposition of a single field on awareness, since this does not occur. Dominance, however, has a well-defined physiological meaning in so far as certain cells of the cerebral cortex may be activated exclusively

The choice of what is perceived

Ocular dominance

by one eye, either because the other eye makes no neural connections with it or because the influence of the other eye is dominant.

Binocular brightness sensation. When the two eyes are presented with differently illuminated objects or surfaces some interesting phenomena emerge. Thus fusion may give rise to a sensation of lustre. In other instances, rivalry takes place, the one or other picture being suppressed, while in still others the brightness sensation is intermediate between those of the two pictures. This gives rise to the paradox whereby a monocularly viewed white surface appears brighter than when it is viewed binocularly in such a way that one eye views it directly and the other through a dark glass. In this second case the eyes are receiving more light, but because the sensation is determined by both eyes, the result is one that would be obtained were one eye to look at a less luminous surface.

ELECTROPHYSIOLOGY OF THE VISUAL CENTRES

To elucidate the functions of the various stages in the visual pathway, one must examine the responses to a retinal light-stimulus of the individual neurons at the different stages.

Ganglion cells. The main features of the responses of ganglion cells have already been touched upon. These have receptive fields that indicate a dual type of connection with the rods and cones, as indicated by the centre-periphery organization. A spot of light falling on receptors in the centre of this field may provoke a discharge in the ganglion cell or its optic nerve fibre; it is called an on-response and consists usually in an increase in the background discharge occurring in darkness. If a spot of light falls on a ring of retina surrounding this central region, the effect is one of inhibition of the background while the light is on, and as soon as it is switched off there is a pronounced discharge, the off-response. Other ganglion cells have been shown to have a directional sensitivity, responding to a moving spot of light only if this moves in a preferred direction and showing inhibition of background discharge if movement is in the null direction.

Geniculate neurons. In general, the lateral geniculate neuron is characterized by an accentuation of the centre-periphery arrangement, so that the two parts of the receptive field tend to cancel each other out completely when stimulated together, by contrast with the ganglion cell in which one or another would predominate. Thus, when the retina is illuminated uniformly there is little response in the geniculate cells because of this cancellation. This represents a useful elaboration of the messages from the retina because, to the animal, uniformity is uninteresting; it is the nonuniformity created by a contour or a moving object that is of interest, and the brain is therefore spared from being bombarded by unnecessary information that would result if every receptor response were transmitted to the brain.

Cortical neurons. When investigators made records of responses from neurons in area 17 there was an interesting change in the nature of the receptive fields; there was still the organization into excitatory (on) and inhibitory (off) zones, but these were linearly arranged, so that the best stimulus for evoking a response was a line, either white on black or black on white. When this line fell on the retina in a definite direction, and on a definite part of the retina, there was, say, an on-response, while if it fell on adjacent areas there was an off-response. Changing the orientation of the line by as little as 15° could completely abolish the responses. The simplest interpretation of this type of receptive field is based on the connection of the cortical cell with a set of geniculate cells with their receptive fields arranged linearly.

Eye dominance. Most of these units (*i.e.*, cortical cells plus connections) could be excited by a light stimulus falling on either eye, although there was usually dominance of one eye, in the sense that its response was greater; when both eyes were stimulated together, the effects summated. In general, then, when a large number of units are studied, a certain proportion are fired by one

eye alone, others by the opposite eye alone, others by both eyes with dominance of one or other eye, while still others respond only when both eyes are stimulated. It is interesting that when kittens are deprived of the use of one eye from birth for several months, this deprived eye is virtually blind and the distribution of dominance in the cortical neurons is changed dramatically; if the left eye is deprived, the right hemispherical cortical neurons show a marked fall in dominance by the left eye, and an increase by the right eye. Thus, the ability of the eye to make use of cortical neurons is not fully developed at birth.

Cortical architecture. When an electrode is directed downward into the cortex it picks up responses in individual units at successive depths; units having the same directional sensitivity are arranged in columns so that the receptive fields of successive neurons are similarly oriented. When units were classified on the basis of eye dominance, a similar vertical distribution of units was found, overlapping with those based on directional preference. The columns for eye preference were about one millimetre wide, but those for directional preference were considerably finer. This columnar organization of cortical cells is not peculiar to the visual area.

Complex neurons. The cortical units (cells) described above, with receptive fields organized on a linear basis, have been called simple units in contrast to complex and hypercomplex units. Four types of complex units have been described; as with the simple units, the orientation of a slit stimulus (that is, a line) is of the utmost importance for obtaining maximal response, but unlike the situation with the simple unit, the position on the retina is unimportant. This type of unit makes abstractions of a higher order, responding to direction of orientation but not to position. It is this type of neuron that would be concerned, for example, with determining the verticality or horizontality of lines in space. Space does not permit of a description of the receptive field of a hypercomplex cell, but in general its features could be explained on the basis of connections with complex cells.

Stereoscopic vision. Of special interest is the behaviour of binocularly driven (stimulated) cortical cells, since their responses provide a clue to the fusion of retinal images. The cortical nerve cell receiving impulses emanating from both retinas must select those parts of the two retinal images that are the images of the same point on an object; second, for stereopsis, the nerve cell must assess the small displacements from exact symmetry that give the binocular parallax. In experiments, maximal response was often obtained only when the stimuli fell on disparate parts of the two retinas; these cortical cells were obviously disparity detectors, in contrast to others that gave maximal response when the stimuli fell on strictly symmetrically related parts of the two retinas—*i.e.*, on corresponding points. When successive units, during penetration of the electrode, were recorded, it was found that those requiring the same degree of disparity for maximal response were arranged in columns, as with direction sensitivity, so that, in effect, all these nerve cells were responding to stimuli in a strip of space at a definite distance from the fixation point.

BIBLIOGRAPHY. H. DAVSON (ed.), *The Eye*, 4 vol. (1962; 2nd ed., vol. 1, 1969), covers the whole field of eye physiology, written by a group of experts in their particular fields; W.S. DUKE-ELDER *et al.* (eds.), *System of Ophthalmology*, 15 vol. (1958–), authoritative accounts of the anatomy and physiology of the eye; E. WOLFF, *Anatomy of the Eye and Orbit*, 5th ed. (1961), the classic work on this aspect; H. DAVSON, *Physiology of the Eye*, 3rd ed. (1971), an up-to-date account of eye physiology covering all aspects; M.H. PIRENNE, *Vision and the Eye*, 2nd ed. (1967), a simple account of certain features of eye physiology; R.A. WEALE, *The Eye and Its Function* (1960), a short and elementary account; H. VON HELMHOLTZ, *Handbuch der physiologischen Optik*, 3rd ed. (1886–96; Eng. trans., *Physiological Optics*, 3 vol., 1924–25; reprinted in 2 vol., 1962), a classic account of the psychological aspects of vision—not at all out of date, although written nearly 100 years ago; H.H. EMSLEY, *Visual Optics*, 5th ed., 2 vol. (1952–53), a technical account of the detailed optics of the eye.

(H.Da.)

Variations
in response

Eye Diseases and Visual Disorders

The human visual apparatus includes the eyeball or globe, and its socket, or orbit, and auxiliary structures such as the lids and the muscles that control eye movement. These organs and their normal functioning are covered in the article EYE AND VISION, HUMAN. The visual apparatus of other organisms is discussed in PHOTORECEPTION. The present article briefly describes the more common diseases of the eye and its associated structures, and the methods used in examination and diagnosis; it also indicates the treatment and prognosis. The first section deals with conditions affecting the orbit, lids, and external eye, and the second with diseases of structures within the globe. Later sections deal with injuries, ocular conditions associated with general disease, disorders of vision, methods of examining the eye, and devices for correcting visual defects.

THE OUTER EYE AND AUXILIARY STRUCTURES

The orbit and lacrimal apparatus. The orbit is the bony cavity in the skull that contains the globe of the eye, the muscles that move the eye, the lacrimal gland, and the blood vessels and nerves required to supply these structures. The remaining space within the orbit is filled with a fatty pad that acts as a cushion for the eye and allows free movement of the globe. In old age this pad of fat tends to atrophy so that the globe recedes, causing the sunken appearance often seen in old people.

Inflammatory conditions of the orbit. As the bone that separates the orbit from the nose and the nasal sinuses is rather thin, infection sometimes spreads from the nasal sinuses into the orbit, causing the orbital tissue to swell and the eye to protrude. The condition is serious because of the possibility that the infection may spread into the cranial cavity along the pathways of the cranial nerves that enter the orbit to reach the eye. Infections can also spread to the cranial cavity by way of the blood vessels that lie in the upper part of the orbit, from lesions such as a boil on the skin of the lids or face in the neighbourhood of the eye. Large doses of an antibiotic such as penicillin, given immediately, in most cases eliminate such infections. The lacrimal glands, the small glands that secrete tears and are behind the outer part of each upper lid, are rarely inflamed but may become so as a complication of mumps. Inflammations of the lacrimal sac are much more common. The lacrimal or tear sac lies in a hollow at the corner of the eye in the front part of the nasal wall of the orbit; under normal conditions tears run along the edges of the lids toward the nose and are drained through two tiny holes connected by small tubes to the upper part of the lacrimal sac. The lower part of the sac is connected to the nose by a duct, the nasolacrimal duct, and infection may ascend this passage from the nose and cause an acute painful swelling at the inner corner of the eye. Blockage of the nasolacrimal duct prevents the passage of tears into the nose and results in a watering eye. Such a blockage, which is nearly always accompanied by chronic inflammation in the lacrimal sac, is usually best treated by an operation in which a new opening from the lacrimal sac to the nasal cavity is made.

Tumours of the orbit. Tumours in this area are comparatively rare, the most common being a tumour of the lacrimal gland. If the tumour is behind the globe in the optic nerve, it will cause a slow and gradual protrusion of the eye; such an abnormal position of the eye may prevent ocular movements from being coordinated with those of the normal eye, and the images of the two eyes, which are normally fused, may separate and give rise to double vision (or diplopia).

The lids. *Inflammatory conditions.* The chronic inflammation of the lid margins known as blepharitis is a common and distressing condition. The inflammation may be mild and consist simply of redness of the lid margin with scaling of the skin, or more severe, affecting the follicles of the eyelashes and leading to their destruction and distortion. Both types tend to be associated with greasiness of the skin and dandruff. The skin of the lids is particularly sensitive to allergic processes, and itching and scaling of the lids is a common reaction to drugs or cosmetics applied to the eye of a sensitized person.

Another common inflammatory condition of the lid is a sty; *i.e.*, an infection of a lash follicle—the sheath of the eyelash root—corresponding to a boil on the skin elsewhere. It starts as a painful swelling of the whole lid, so that at first it may be difficult to find a localized lesion; but soon one area becomes more swollen and, as pus forms, a yellow point associated with an eyelash can be seen near the lid margin. A rather similar appearance can be produced by an inflammation of the meibomian glands; *i.e.*, tiny glands in the thickness of the lid, opening on the lid margin. As the glands are embedded in tough fibrous tissue, the pain and reaction may be more severe than in an ordinary sty. Examination of the internal surface of the lid will show a red velvety area with a central yellow spot through which pus will later discharge. Sometimes the meibomian glands suffer from a chronic infection, and a painless firm lump appears in the lid and slowly increases in size. The skin can be moved freely over the surface of the lump, showing that the latter is in the deeper tissue of the lid. The inner surface of the lid will show a grayish area surrounded by a little inflammation. The lesion is treated by making an incision on the inner surface of the lid, and scraping out the contents.

Herpes zoster (shingles) may affect the skin of the eyelids and is of particular importance because the cornea (the transparent covering of the front of the eyeball) and the inner eye may also be affected. The condition starts with pain and redness of one part of the forehead and the eyelids of the same side. Vesicles, or small blisters, form later in the affected area. The pain may be severe, and some constitutional disturbance is usual.

Displacements of the lid. Malpositioning of the lid is common in elderly people, and although not serious in itself gives rise to considerable discomfort and irritation. The commonest condition is called ectropion, in which the lower lid falls away from the globe so that the tears overflow the lid. This constant wetting of the skin of the lower lid excoriates the skin and causes it to retract, which in turn increases the tendency of the lid to turn out. In the early stages, massage of the lid and the use of a bland ointment on the skin may help, but usually some plastic procedure is necessary to bring the lid back into its normal position.

The opposite condition is entropion, in which the lid turns inward and the lashes cause much irritation by rubbing on the eye. Unlike ectropion, it may affect either the upper or the lower lid. It may be caused by scarring of the deeper tissues of the lid following infection, or may be due to senile changes in muscle tone in which a band of fibres of the circular muscle surrounding the lids contracts more strongly than the peripheral fibres, thus tending to turn the lid inward. Surgical treatment is required to restore the lid to its normal position.

Tumours. Benign overgrowths of the blood vessels, called hemangiomas, may occur in the lids and give rise to soft bluish swellings that can be reduced by pressure over them. They are present at birth and tend to grow rapidly in the first few years of life. Often they disappear spontaneously, but they can be treated by surgical removal or the insertion of radioactive material. Simple overgrowths of skin, called papillomas, are common along the lid margin but require no special treatment except excision for cosmetic reasons.

The lids and the skin of the nose near the inner margins of the lids are common sites for the development of skin cancer in older people; the most usual type, called a rodent ulcer, starts as a small nodule in the skin that gradually enlarges and breaks down to form an ulcer with a hard base and rolled edges. Bleeding may occur from the base of the ulcer. Although rodent ulcers are malignant in the sense that they destroy tissue locally, they do not spread to distant areas of the body by means of the lymph system or the blood vessels. A more serious malignant tumour of the lids is a carcinoma, which develops as a more irregular ulcer of the lid and may spread to involve

Ectropion and entropion

the underlying bone. If left untreated the growth may spread to the lymph nodes in front of the ear or under the jaw.

Squint. In the lower vertebrates such as the fish the eyes are situated on either side of the head, to give the maximum view of the surroundings and an early warning of the presence of predators. The field of vision of each eye is separate except for a narrow sector immediately in front of the animal, where the two visual fields overlap. From the evolutionary point of view the improved judgment of distance obtained by viewing an object with both eyes conferred considerable biological advantage in the struggle for survival. In the higher animals, particularly the predatory species of birds and mammals, binocular vision became more and more important and structural changes in the placement of the eyes in the head permitted a larger overlap of the two visual fields, until the situation was reached in the higher mammals in which the visual axes—that is, the line of direct sight—became parallel. This desirable visual function has been fully attained in man. The structural changes necessary to bring this about have, however, lagged behind the function, and the geometrical axes of most eyes are still slightly divergent (*i.e.*, the two eyes at rest are directed slightly away from the nose). The bony structure of the orbit has lagged even further behind, so that the axes of the two orbits make an angle of about 45°.

It is in fact the function of using two eyes together that keeps the optic axes straight in a normal person. If, for example, one eye becomes blind, it tends to revert to an anatomical position of rest in line with the axis of the orbit. A blind eye will therefore appear to be diverging. The visual axes can remain straight only if each eye has reasonably good vision, the ocular muscles can move the eyes in the required direction of gaze, and the complex neuromuscular reflexes required to coordinate the movements of the two eyes are intact. Failure to maintain the visual axes parallel may therefore result from a visual defect in one or both eyes, a muscular defect resulting in loss of normal movement of the eye, or a defect in the central nervous system involving the coordinating nervous pathways. A true squint is a condition in which the visual axes are no longer parallel. An apparent squint may be seen in children as the result of prominent skin folds in the inner sides of the eyes, which make the eyes appear to be converging (*i.e.*, appear to cross). These skin folds usually disappear when the bony structure of the nose develops more fully.

Clinically, squints are divided into concomitant, in which the abnormal angle between the visual axes remains constant in all positions of gaze, and paralytic, in which the angle of squint varies with the direction of gaze. The commonest type of squint is the convergent concomitant type seen in small children (*i.e.*, the children are consistently or intermittently cross-eyed). It is usually first noticed between the ages of one and two and may be precipitated by a systemic disease such as measles. There is often a family history of squint. Children of this age are particularly interested in objects close to them, and in order to view an object clearly at close range two things are necessary: first, the visual axes must converge, so that both eyes can view the same object; and second, the focus of the eye must be adjusted for near vision. The link between convergence of the eyes and focussing, or accommodation, is very strong, and normally the two actions work in harmony. Most small children, however, are long-sighted, which means that, in order to see clearly close to, they have to exert an extra amount of accommodative effort. As accommodation and convergence are closely linked, the extra effort of accommodation tends to produce an overconvergence; but, provided that the visual acuity of each eye is normal and the motor control of the eyes is normal, this tendency is controlled. If the vision of one eye is reduced, for example by disease or an error of refraction, binocular vision breaks down and overconvergence occurs.

Once parallelism of the visual axes is lost, the image of objects no longer lies on a familiar area of retina, and instead of the images from the two eyes being fused into one, two images are perceived. This condition of double vision, or diplopia, is intolerable to the child, who reacts by "suppressing" the image from the squinting eye. If the suppression is allowed to continue, the central vision of the affected eye drops rapidly to a low level, so that even if the original disturbance that started the squint is corrected, this loss of vision, or amblyopia, of the squinting eye will prevent the restoration of normal binocular vision and thus perpetuate the squint. The longer the suppression is allowed to continue, the less likely is the child to regain normal vision in the squinting eye. Covering the good eye will usually encourage the recovery of the suppressed vision but must be started as soon as the squint is noticed. Any refractive error present—any defect that prevents light rays from focussing properly on the retina —must be corrected by glasses, and retraining of the binocular reflexes can be aided by special exercises. Early treatment on these lines may be all that is necessary, but if the visual axes are still abnormal surgery of the extraocular muscles will be required to correct the deviation.

Paralysis of one of the muscles that control the movement of the eyes results in limitation of movement of the globe in the direction of action of the muscle, with the result that double vision with separation of the images occurs on attempts to move the eye in this direction.

As earlier stated, accommodation and convergence are normally perfectly linked together so that the movements of the two eyes bring the visual axes to the point of focus. In many people this balance is not quite perfect and the eyes tend to converge or diverge too much for a given distance—a condition known as heterophoria.

The conjunctiva. The marine origin of the human species is betrayed by the need for the anterior surface of the eye to be bathed in salt water. A thin membrane lines the lids and covers the anterior surface of the globe, forming a sac, the conjunctival sac, the contents of which are lubricated by the tear glands. This warm, moist habitat provides a suitable environment for the growth of bacteria and other organisms, leading to conjunctivitis, inflammation of the conjunctiva. Bacterial conjunctivitis starts with a feeling of grittiness and discomfort, the eye is red and there is a discharge from it. The discharge is particularly noticeable after sleep, when the lids may be stuck together by the exudate on the lashes. Vision is not affected except by the strands of mucus, which can be blinked away from the cornea. Antibiotic drops usually clear the condition in a few days. Vernal conjunctivitis or spring catarrh is, as its name suggests, an allergic condition occurring in the early summer; it is more common in young people and probably results from sensitivity to external irritants such as dust and pollen. It usually responds well to treatment with drops of corticosteroid hormone.

Chronic conjunctivitis, causing a gritty feeling, with redness of the eyes and a slight mucoid discharge, is a common condition, the cause of which may be difficult to find. Often there is an infective element such as a chronic inflammation of the lid margin, and sometimes the condition is allergic and may result from sensitivity to cosmetics or to drugs applied to the eye. An unsuspected foreign body or a deficiency of tear secretion may cause similar symptoms.

Viral conjunctivitis. With the enormous increase in the use of antibiotics since the 1940s, bacterial infections in general are becoming less common. This is also true of infections of the eye, and in most western countries bacterial conjunctivitis is now less common than viral infection. Viruses tend to attack the cornea as well as the conjunctiva; the infection is contagious and may be responsible for outbreaks of epidemic keratoconjunctivitis (inflammation of the cornea and the conjunctiva). The onset is acute, with redness and swelling of the eye and lids and a tender swelling of the lymph node in front of the ear.

Trachoma can truly be described as one of the scourges of mankind. Although rare in England and North America, it is the largest single cause of blindness in the world as a whole. Almost universal in some Middle East countries such as Egypt, it has spread to Asia, India, Central and South America, and Africa. It occurs sporadically in southern and eastern Europe. The agent responsible has now been isolated and shown to belong to the group of organisms known as chlamydiae. They occupy a taxonomic position between bacteria and true viruses and unlike the latter are susceptible to treatment with sulphonamides and some antibiotics. The disease is contagious and thrives where populations are crowded together in poor hygienic surroundings. Shortage of water for washing, and the myriads of flies attracted to human waste, aid the dissemination of the disease. In some ways trachoma is more of a social than a medical problem; if living standards can be improved, overcrowding reduced, flies discouraged, and adequate water supplies ensured, the incidence of trachoma decreases rapidly.

The early symptoms of infection are pain, watering of the eye, and sensitivity to light. At this stage the conjunctival lining of the lids is red and velvety in appearance, and the cornea shows gray areas. Later, the conjunctiva appears to have grains of sand embedded in its tissue. Blood vessels grow into the cornea, which becomes thickened and hazy. Secondary bacterial infections are common, but the real dangers of trachoma lie in the scarring and contracture of tissue that occur when healing takes place. These changes affect the upper lid in particular, causing it to buckle inward so that the lashes rub across the already diseased cornea, and it is the corneal scarring thus produced that can cause blindness.

Degenerative conditions. Exposure to wind and dust frequently causes degenerative changes in the exposed part of the conjunctiva, particularly in older people. A yellow nodule forms, first on the nasal side of the cornea and later on the other side. It is without blood vessels and is frequently unnoticed until an incidental conjunctivitis causes it to stand out clearly against the red background of dilated conjunctival vessels. It causes no symptoms and requires no treatment.

A more serious degeneration is that known as a pterygium, found particularly in people who live in hot, dusty climates. It appears as a fleshy growth at the edge of the cornea, with a tendency to progress across its front surface, where it may interfere with vision. Treatment consists of surgical removal, but recurrences are common.

The cornea and sclera. The cornea is the clear window of the eye and its most important refractive surface. Any surface irregularity, any scar in the substance of the cornea, is likely to have a profound effect on vision. Almost the whole nerve supply of the cornea consists of nerve fibres sensitive to pain, so that corneal diseases are always painful and elicit a flow of tears by a reflex action that is part of the protective system of the eye.

Inflammation of the cornea. As with inflammations of the conjunctiva, bacterial infection of the cornea has become much less common and viral infections are increasingly important. Of these, the virus of herpes simplex, the virus that causes the common "cold sore" of the lips and skin, is the most frequent cause of corneal ulceration. Infection is spread by personal contact: a kiss from someone with an active cold sore on the lips may carry with it infection as well as affection. The herpes virus causes a typical ulcer of the cornea called, from the pattern of the lesion, dendritic ("branching"). The disease starts with an acutely painful eye, with tearing, and sensitivity to light. The ulcer may heal spontaneously or after medical treatment, but the virus often lies dormant in the tissues; recurrences are common, and with each recurrence there is more danger that the virus will extend deeper into the cornea and cause an intractable inflammation.

Application of the drug deoxyuridine (5-iodo-2-deoxyuridine) to the cornea causes the ulcer to heal more rapidly and reduces the recurrence rate. The action of the drug depends upon its limiting the multiplication of the virus by interfering with the formation of virus deoxyribonucleic acid (DNA) in the host cell.

Bacterial infections of the cornea still occur, usually after injury to the corneal surface, as few bacteria have the power to penetrate the intact surface layers of the cornea. Such ulcers may be extremely severe, and there is always a danger of perforation of the eye, particularly in debilitated patients.

Infection of cornea with herpes virus; bacteria; fungi

The spores of fungi are commonly present in the atmosphere. The normal cornea is resistant to infection by these organisms, but a fungal infection of the cornea can develop after a corneal injury or other lesion, particularly if corticosteroid drugs have been used in treatment. Intensive treatment with antifungal drugs is usually effective in killing the organisms, but a dense scar is usually left.

A corneal inflammation may start in the deeper layers, usually by spread of infection from the bloodstream. It is seen most commonly in adolescents who have congenital syphilis. Both eyes are usually attacked, although there may be an interval before the second eye is affected. The cornea rapidly becomes hazy, and blood vessels grow in from the surrounding tissues to form a red patch. With the decline in congenital syphilis in developed countries, the condition is now becoming a rarity.

Inflammation of the sclera. The sclera is the fibrous covering of the eye that shows up as a dense white layer beneath the transparent conjunctiva. A relatively mild nodular inflammation sometimes occurs in the superficial layers of the sclera; it is thought to be allergic in nature and usually responds well to anti-inflammatory treatment. Inflammation of the deeper sclera is more severe and often is painful. It occurs more frequently in older people and may be associated with tuberculosis or rheumatism; however, the cause of the condition is often not discovered.

Degenerative conditions. Keratoconus is the name of a curious condition in which the central part of the cornea, normally spherical in shape, begins to bulge and protrude forward as a cone. The only symptom is deterioration of vision due to the irregular astigmatism caused by the changing corneal curvature. Ordinary spectacles cannot correct the irregular refraction, but contact lenses are often of great value, and in more advanced cases corneal grafting is required.

There are numerous other rare types of corneal degeneration, some of which are familial; all produce a deterioration in vision that cannot be corrected with spectacles. Many of these conditions respond well to corneal grafting.

THE INNER EYE

The uveal tract. The uveal tract is a vascular layer of tissue—that is, a layer rich in blood vessels—lying next to the inner surface of the sclera. It is divided into three structures: the choroid, a highly vascular layer that supplies blood to the outer layers of the retina; the ciliary body, largely muscle tissue, which by its contraction and relaxation alters the focusing of the lens; and the iris, the coloured part of the eye, which forms the variable aperture of the eye, the pupil. The ciliary body, which lies at the base of the iris, also functions by forming the aqueous humour, the production and drainage of which regulate intraocular pressure; the aqueous humour also is the source of nutriment to the lens and cornea, which are avascular (without blood vessels).

Inflammation. Inflammations of the uveal tract are always potentially serious because of the secondary effects they may have on the retina and the lens. In most cases the disease affects either the anterior part of the uvea—that is, the iris and ciliary body—or the posterior part, the choroid. An attack of acute anterior uveitis starts with pain, redness, and mistiness of vision. The eye is sensitive to light, and, although there is no discharge as in conjunctivitis, the eye may water. The pupil tends to contract and the normally clear iris markings become less distinct. In chronic anterior uveitis the main symptom is blurring of vision. Acute choroiditis starts with sudden onset of blurring of vision with many black spots floating about in front of the sight.

Except for cases in which the uveitis follows a perforating injury or a corneal ulcer, it is believed that the inflammation is caused by an infective process within the body or by some other mechanism associated with systemic disease. Many infective conditions and parasitic diseases are known to cause uveitis. In a large proportion of cases, however, particularly when the inflammation is confined to the anterior segment, it proves impossible to be sure of the cause in any individual instance, and the investigation of a case of uveitis often poses one of the biggest problems in ophthalmology today. In men, a proportion of cases of anterior uveitis are associated with ankylosing spondylitis, a chronic disease of the joints of the spine, the cause of which is still obscure. Another association, again in men, is with Reiter's disease, a condition that starts as an infection of the urogenital tract with the later development of joint changes, particularly in the sacro-iliac joints of the lower back, and recurrent attacks of anterior uveitis. The organism that is responsible for this venereally contracted infection is still unknown, but may be a virus. Infections in the teeth and tonsils have long been held to be a cause of uveitis, and eradication of dental decay does occasionally have a favourable effect on the course of the disease.

Toxoplasmosis and its effect on fetus

Inflammations of the choroid—the posterior portion of the uveal tract—and the retina are more likely to be infective in origin. One of the organisms most commonly involved is *Toxoplasma gondii*, a protozoon of worldwide distribution among domestic animals, small mammals, and man. Although antibodies to the organism can be found in a high proportion of most populations, showing that infection is widespread, overt signs of disease are rarely seen; most people can acquire the infection without being aware of any systemic disturbance at all, and only in special circumstances does the organism cause disease. One of these special circumstances is pregnancy. If a woman becomes infected during pregnancy there is a short period in which invasion of the tissues takes place before circulating antibodies are formed by the mother. During this period it is possible for the organism to pass through the placenta and infect the unborn child. Fetuses appear to be particularly susceptible to the organism, nearly half of those exposed showing some evidence of infection with toxoplasmosis. In severe cases the child may be stillborn or may be born with congenital toxoplasmosis, a serious disease affecting many organs of the body and particularly the brain and eye. In less serious cases small foci of infection are left in the nervous system and the retina of the eye; these may not be apparent at birth and may remain quiescent, only to become active 15 or 20 years later in the form of an inflammation of the choroid and the retina. Children of subsequent pregnancies are unaffected.

The treatment of uveitis has been transformed by the advent of corticosteroid drugs. Even when a specific infection cannot be discovered and treated with the appropriate specific drug, therapy with corticosteroids is usually successful in controlling the worst ravages of the inflammation.

Tumours of the uveal tract. Pigmented tumours are the commonest tumours involving the uveal tract. They may be benign (the nevus or mole) or malignant. The choroid is the commonest site of these lesions, which push the retina forward and cause a retinal detachment. Disturbances of vision are the commonest symptom, but the tumour if neglected may enlarge and cause inflammation and raised pressure within the eye. Small portions of the tumour often enter the bloodstream and settle in distant organs, particularly the liver. The growth of these secondary deposits is often slow; they may not be apparent until many years after the diagnosis of the tumour in the eye.

The lens. The lens is a transparent, avascular organ surrounded by an elastic capsule. It lies behind the pupil and is suspended from the ciliary body by a series of fine ligaments. Its transparency is the result of the regular arrangement of the lens fibres; since these are being formed continuously, the lens continues to grow throughout life. Interference with this growth pattern will result in the formation of abnormal lens fibres that cannot transmit light as well as the normal lens fibres. A small opacity is thus seen in the lens. Minor irregularities are common in otherwise perfectly normal eyes. If the opacity is severe enough to affect vision it is called a cataract.

Congenital lens opacities of many varieties have been recognized and described since the early days of ophthalmology, but they remained curiosities until the work of an Australian ophthalmologist, Norman M. Gregg, threw new light on their cause, and, indeed, on that of many other congenital defects. In 1941 Gregg noticed that after an epidemic of German measles (rubella) many of the children whose mothers had contracted the disease in the first two months of pregnancy were born with cataract, sometimes associated with deafness and congenital heart disease. It is now known that the virus can be recovered from the lens for several months after birth.

Cataract in newborn child; in adult

Cataract in the adult may be the result of injury to the lens by a perforating wound, by exposure to radiation such as X-rays, or as the result of the ingestion of toxic substances or even of some drugs. The lens relies for its nutrition on the aqueous humour secreted by the ciliary body and, if the latter is severely damaged as the result of long-continued uveitis or a tumour, the metabolism of the lens suffers and a cataract develops. The commonest form of cataract is senile cataract, so called because it becomes progressively more common with advancing age. In spite of a large amount of work on the biological and biochemical changes that take place in the lens, the underlying cause of senile cataract is still unknown. Whatever the underlying biochemical changes may be, they result in an increasing clouding of the lens until the whole lens loses its normal transparency and becomes white and opaque. The only symptom is progressive diminution of vision. In the early stages of the condition some visual improvement can usually be obtained with spectacles, but, as the cataract progresses, the visual deterioration becomes sufficiently severe to warrant surgical treatment.

With modern techniques cataract extraction can be done as soon as the visual deterioration interferes with normal activities, and it is no longer necessary for patients to wait for many years in semiblindness to allow the cataract to become mature. Cataract extraction is one of the most successful and satisfying operations in ophthalmic surgery; if the eye is otherwise normal the visual results are excellent, although the refractive power of the lens has to be replaced by a rather thick spectacle lens or special contact lens.

The retina. Developmentally, the retina is part of the brain and as such has only a limited capacity for repair of its damaged tissue. In particular, the highly specialized rods and cones (the photoreceptors), which are the structures sensitive to light, and the nerve cells of the retina, like those of the brain, cannot be replaced if they are damaged. Death of these cells inevitably has a permanent effect on vision.

The retina is a thin transparent membrane that lines the inner eye. Its outermost layer, the pigment epithelium, is formed of pigmented cells that are closely adherent to the underlying blood vessels of the choroid. The layer of rods and cones is more loosely attached to the pigment epithelium and has complicated nervous networks that culminate in the innermost layer of nerve fibres. These fibres run back through the optic nerve to the brain. The inner two-thirds of the retina derives its blood supply from a special complex of vessels that enters the eye through the optic nerve.

Retinal detachment. A retinal detachment is a condition in which the main part of the retina becomes separated from the pigment epithelium. This may follow an injury to the eye or a tumour; or inflammation of the underlying choroid. The commonest type of detachment, however, has no such predisposing factors: the distinctive feature is the formation of a small hole or tear in the retina, usually at the periphery where the retina is thinner. In most cases the hole is caused by an adhesion forming between the retina and the jelly-like substance called the vitreous humour that fills the interior of the eye. Sudden movement of the eye, or an injury, causes the vitreous to pull on the retina, thus creating a tear or hole. When this has happened, fluid can pass through the hole and strip the retina off the pigment epithelium. Myopic (nearsighted) eyes are particularly prone to retinal detachment because they are larger than normal, and the coats of the eye are thinned and stretched. The periphery of the retina, in particular, often shows weak areas, and the vitreous is usually unduly thin and fluid.

Detachment of retina

The history is often quite typical. The pull of the vitreous on part of the retina creates a sensation of light noticed by the person affected as flashes that occur on movement of the eye. When an actual tear has developed, the retina starts to become detached and the person has the sensation of a shadow coming down over the vision.

The essential factor in treatment is to seal off the hole in the retina. The part of the retina containing the hole must be brought into close contact with the choroid and then by means of a gentle inflammatory reaction caused by using heat, cold, or intense light, the retina is made to stick to the underlying choroid and seal off the leak. The remaining fluid can then be drained away, allowing the retina to fall back into place. Provided that the detachment has not been of long standing, the retinal function recovers quite well once the retina is reattached. The small central area of retina, however, that subserves the most acute vision has only one source of blood supply, the underlying choroid; once it is separated from this some permanent damage ensues, even if the retina is subsequently replaced in its correct position. Thus, it is most important therefore that retinal detachments be treated early, before the central area of the retina becomes detached.

Retinal degeneration. Cases of retinal degeneration can be grouped in two broad classes: hereditary and genetic, and senile. A large number of genetically determined degenerations of the retina have been described. Although they are quite rare, the bizarre appearances of the retina and the inexorable advance of the disease have excited considerable interest among ophthalmologists. These conditions are typified by the disease known as retinitis pigmentosa, a hereditary condition. The earliest symptom is night blindness, which may first be noticed in childhood and is due to alteration in the function of the rods, which are the visual receptors used in dim light. The more peripheral parts of the retina are affected first, and while central vision may be good the field of vision progressively decreases until only a small "tubular field" remains. Cause of the disease is unknown. It is easily recognizable by the narrowing of retinal vessels and the scattering of clumps of pigment throughout the retina.

In senile degeneration, unlike the hereditary type, it is the central part of the vision that is first affected. The central part of the retina, known as the macula, derives its blood supply only from the choroid, and it is probably for this reason that it is likely to suffer first from the slowing of the metabolic changes and from the deficiency of circulation that occur in old age. While degeneration of the macula does not cause blindness, in the sense that the person affected is unable to see anything, it is extremely disturbing because it affects central visual acuity and makes reading or fine work difficult or impossible. There is as yet no satisfactory medical or surgical treatment, but considerable improvement can be obtained by the use of special magnifying spectacles.

The retinal changes that may occur in diabetes, arteriosclerosis, and vascular hypertension are described in a later section.

The optic nerve. The optic nerve, which carries about one million nerve fibres, leaves the globe from the back of the eye and passes through the apex of the orbit into the cranial cavity. It is surrounded by an extension of the membranes that surround the brain and this connection with the intracranial cavity is of some importance, because in some intracranial diseases the pressure within the skull rises and is transmitted along the sheaths of the optic nerve to cause swelling of the optic nerve head, which is visible inside the eye. This swelling of the nerve head, or papilledema, is one of the most important signs of increased intracranial pressure. If the swelling persists, damage to the fibres of the optic nerve takes place, with subsequent loss of vision.

Swelling of the optic nerve may also be caused by inflammatory changes in the nerve itself or in the surrounding sheath; this condition is known as optic neuritis. The symptoms are loss of vision in the central part of the visual field and pain on moving the eye. The condition is most common in young adults and may be due to the spread of infection from the adjacent nasal sinuses. The majority of cases, however, are manifestations of multiple sclerosis, a condition in which the sheath of the nerves becomes altered and interferes with the transference of nervous impulses. This may occur in any part of the nervous system, but the optic nerve is a common site, and the lesion is often the first to be noticed by the patient because of the visual symptoms that result from it. The disease is characterized by long periods of remission from symptoms, and after optic neuritis it may be ten years or more before other signs are apparent. Usually the function of the optic nerve recovers after an attack of optic neuritis, leaving little, if any, visual disturbance, but there is some atrophy of the fibres.

Optic atrophy may follow any serious disease of the retina involving a large amount of destruction of neural tissue. It may also follow damage to the optic nerve within the skull, or the optic chiasma—that is, the place where the optic nerves crisscross, close to the pituitary gland. Tumours of the pituitary gland nearly always compress the optic nerve fibres and cause some degree of atrophy with loss of vision in that part of the visual field subserved by the fibres concerned. Usually it is the fibres on the inner side of the optic nerve and those that cross at the chiasma that are most involved: these fibres supply the retina on the nasal half. This part of the retina receives visual images from the outer part of the visual field, and in pituitary lesions it is common to find that the outer parts of both visual fields are affected.

Certain chemicals and some drugs can also cause optic atrophy: among them are quinine and methyl alcohol. Optic atrophy is most unlikely to follow normal medical doses of quinine, and when it occurs it is usually from the large doses taken to cause abortion. Methyl alcohol (wood spirit or methylated spirits) is broken down in the body to acetyl aldehyde, which is toxic to neural tissue, and the risks of blindness from drinking methylated spirits are high.

Glaucoma. The thin coats of the eye are not sufficiently rigid in themselves to withstand distortion following the pull of the extraocular muscles when the eye is moved. The eyeball is kept rigid by the action of the ciliary body, which secretes sufficient amounts of the fluid called the aqueous humour to pump up the pressure of the eye to a level above the atmospheric pressure. This fluid is constantly being formed and drains away at the base of the iris through specialized drainage channels. Should these channels become blocked the pressure within the eye rises to abnormally high levels and impedes the entry of blood into the eye. The fibres of the optic nerve where it enters the eye are particularly susceptible to a reduction in blood supply, and if the intraocular pressure remains raised for long some of these nerve fibres will atrophy, causing loss of function of the retina from which they are derived. Glaucoma is the name given to a condition in which the intraocular pressure is raised to abnormal levels. In some persons this is due to other disease within the eye—such as inflammation or a tumour—but most have one of two distinct diseases, chronic simple glaucoma or closed-angle glaucoma.

Chronic simple glaucoma is a common disease that may affect one percent of people in the older age groups. Although the actual cause is not known it is almost certainly due to degenerative changes in the outflow channels for aqueous fluid. It is rare below the age of 40 but after this its incidence increases; in one recent survey it was found to affect 10 percent of those examined over the age of 80. Genetic influences are important and relatives of patients with glaucoma are five time more likely than others to develop the disease.

The symptoms are slight or absent in the early stages. The slow rise in pressure does not cause pain, and the early visual loss is in the peripheral parts of the visual field, affecting central vision only late in the disease. Both eyes are usually involved, although one may be more severely affected than the other. Since vision lost from glaucoma cannot be restored, successful treatment can only prevent further loss of vision. It is of great importance, therefore, that the disease be diagnosed as early as

Causes and effects of swelling of optic nerve head

Chronic simple glaucoma

possible. Measurement of the intraocular pressure is of great value in the diagnosis of glaucoma: this is a simple test that can be applied as a screening method for surveys of the normal population.

The medical treatment of chronic simple glaucoma consists of the use of drops that lower the intraocular pressure. Inhibitors of the enzyme carbonic anhydrase, when taken by mouth, reduce the formation of aqueous humour and are used as an additional measure when necessary. If the pressure remains raised in spite of all medical treatment, then surgical methods must be used to increase the drainage of fluid from the eye.

The other common type of glaucoma is called closed-angle glaucoma. This again has a familial incidence and occurs in people who have a rather small, long-sighted eye. Continued growth of the lens in these patients pushes the iris forward and narrows the gap at the root (the outer edge) of the iris where aqueous humour flows out of the eye. This fluid is formed in the ciliary body behind the

From H.G. Scheie, *Medical Ophthalmology: Ophthalmalogic Manifestations of Systemic Diseases*

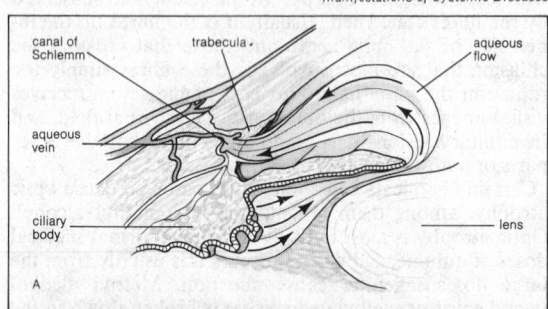

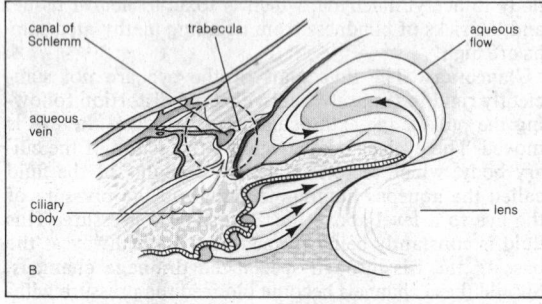

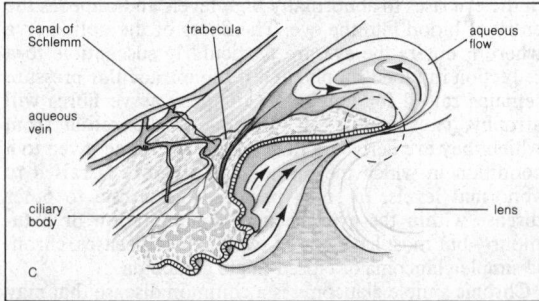

Normal flow of aqueous humour contrasted with two types of obstruction.
(A) Normal flow of aqueous humour. (B) Obstruction to flow of aqueous humour in chronic glaucoma. (C) Obstruction to flow of aqueous humour in closed-angle, or acute, glaucoma. Dotted circles indicate site of obstruction.

iris and flows forward through the pupil to the angle of the anterior chamber. The lens pushing against the iris acts as a valve and impedes the flow of aqueous through the pupil. The root of the iris, which is rather thin, is then pushed forward and may eventually completely close the exit for aqueous, so that the intraocular pressure rises rapidly. The eye becomes painful and the vision is lost; the pain may be so severe as to cause vomiting and prostration. The eye becomes red and stony hard to the touch. Urgent treatment is required to lower the pressure and prevent strangulation of the blood vessels entering the eye.

In some cases an acute attack such as this heralds the onset of the disease, but more frequently minor, sub-acute, attacks, which are relieved by rest and sleep, occur for months or years. Modern methods of medical treatment are usually effective in lowering the pressure in the acute attack; an operation is usually necessary to prevent further recurrences.

OCULAR INJURIES

The bony orbit provides excellent protection for the eye from blunt injuries. A blow from in front with a rounded instrument such as a fist or tennis ball, however, can cause a shock wave to travel through the eye and damage the retina at the back of the eye. Central vision may be reduced after such injuries without any very obvious changes in the appearance of the eye. In severe cases the bones of the orbit may be fractured. Perforating wounds from glass, sharp metal fragments, and so on, are always serious. Injuries to the lens will result in the formation of a cataract, and often after penetrating injuries the eye remains inflamed for a considerable time.

One type of inflammation following injury, sympathetic ophthalmitis, is of particular importance; fortunately it is now rarely seen. The sequence of events is that an injured eye remains irritable and after some weeks, months, or even years, the fellow—previously normal—eye may take part in the inflammation. This is the "sympathizing eye." The cause of sympathetic ophthalmitis is not known, but it is known that if an injured eye is removed within ten days sympathetic ophthalmitis never occurs in the other eye. In the past there was little effective treatment for the condition, but therapy with corticosteroid hormones has proved effective in controlling the inflammation in most cases, so that even if the disease becomes established the consequences are not as serious as they were previously.

Foreign bodies. Most foreign bodies that enter the eye remain near the surface. When they touch the cornea they cause intense pain and a flow of tears. The tears may be sufficient to wash the foreign body out of the eye, but if it becomes embedded in the cornea it may have to be removed surgically. Many small foreign bodies lodge in the under surface of the upper lid so that every time the eye blinks the foreign body rubs on the cornea, causing pain and irritation.

Small foreign bodies travelling at high speeds may penetrate the interior of the eye with remarkably few symptoms, and their presence may not be recognized until weeks or months later when inflammatory changes occur. The commonest foreign bodies to enter the eye in this way are fragments of metal from hammer-and-chisel accidents, or from moving parts of machinery. Whenever such injuries are suspected, it is important to locate the position of the fragment as carefully as possible, and to remove it by surgery. If the foreign body is magnetic, a large electro-magnet is invaluable in attracting the foreign body to the site of the incision in the eye, making extraction comparatively simple.

Chemical and radiation injuries. Strong acids and alkalis always cause severe injury if they enter the eye. Speed is the vital factor in first-aid treatment, and copious irrigation with water the first essential. Delay of first-aid treatment in the hope of finding a neutralizing substance is a serious error, as strong acids and alkalis quickly become bound to the ocular tissues and cause severe necrosis (death of tissue).

Except for extremely intense light such as that from a laser, the visible wavelengths of the electromagnetic spectrum—*i.e.*, visible light rays—rarely cause ocular injury. Ultraviolet light, however, is strongly absorbed by the cornea and is the cause of the not uncommon condition known as snow blindness. Symptoms, consisting of intense pain and copious flow of tears, may not occur until some time after exposure. Exposure to light is painful. The treatment consists of cold compresses to the eye and soothing lotions; usually the eyes recover without any permanent damage.

Long-continued exposure to infrared radiation, without adequate protection for the eyes, can cause cataract for-

Sympathetic ophthalmitis

Effects of ultraviolet and infrared rays

mation. The lens is also susceptible to X-rays, and the eyes must be shielded when therapeutic irradiation is used for growths around or near the eye. High-intensity microwaves such as those used in some military applications can also cause ocular damage. The widespread use of lasers in research departments and in industry has created a new ocular hazard, and a few cases of accidental exposure have already been reported.

MANIFESTATIONS OF SYSTEMIC DISEASE

The central nervous system.   Since the optic nerve and retina are, embryonically, an extension of the brain, it is not surprising that central nervous system diseases frequently affect the eye, and visual defects may be the earliest evidence of the general disease. The nerve supply to the ocular muscles, particularly the extraocular muscles, may also be involved early in some diseases of the central nervous system: this will result in defective movement of the eyes, causing lack of coordination between the two eyes and diplopia, or double vision.

The nerve fibres that connect the retina with the site of visual sensation in the occipital cortex—*i.e.*, the outer brain substance at the back of the head—are arranged throughout the brain in a regular pattern, and many lesions of the brain, such as tumours, impinge on part of this pathway. From a detailed examination of the sensitivity of the different parts of the retina, using tests of the visual field, it is often possible to localize the exact site of an intracranial lesion. An optic neuritis causing sudden onset of loss of central vision in one eye is a frequent first symptom of multiple sclerosis. Detailed ophthalmic examination is therefore essential in the case of any patient suspected of having disease of the central nervous system.

Arteriosclerosis and vascular hypertension.   The eye is the one structure in the body in which the blood vessels are easily visible to the examiner, and the changes that can be observed in the retinal vessels mirror those that are taking place in other parts of the body, particularly those in the brain. In arteriosclerosis degenerative changes occur in the walls of the arteries: this leads to thickening of the walls and narrowing of the bloodstream and may give rise to complete occlusion, or blockage of the vessel. If the central retinal artery is affected, loss of vision is complete and sudden and, unless the obstruction can be relieved within an hour or so, permanent. Occlusion of the retinal veins is more common than arterial occlusion and also has dramatic effects: the damming up of blood in the eye results in the bursting of small vessels, and multiple hemorrhages are scattered all over the fundus (that part of the inner eye which can be inspected through the pupil). Some degree of recovery of vision is usual but depends on whether a branch of the central vein or the vein itself is occluded.

Vascular hypertension, or raised blood pressure, usually occurs in association with arteriosclerosis. Typical changes can be recognized in the small vessels of the fundus, and in severe cases multiple hemorrhages and exudates, with swelling of the optic disk (the head of the optic nerve), may be present.

Diabetes.   The satisfactory control of diabetes with insulin has increased the incidence of eye complications, for it has become apparent that it is the duration of the disease rather than its severity that determines the onset of ocular changes. A special type of cataract may occur in young diabetics with severe untreated disease, but the most serious complication involves the blood vessels of the retina. The actual cause of the changes in the retinal vessels is still unknown, but the natural history of the disease is well recognized. The retinal capillaries dilate at weak points in the vessel wall—*i.e.*, form small aneurysms; these weak portions of the vessel wall may give way and cause hemorrhages into the retina. In the later stages the hemorrhages become more extensive and spread into the vitreous. New vessels grow into hemorrhagic areas and are followed by fibrous changes that may pull on the retina and cause detachment. Extensive changes of this nature lead invariably to blindness.

Destruction of the pituitary gland, either by direct surgery or by the implantation of a radioactive material, has given some hope of alleviating these severe retinal changes. The procedure is, however, a drastic one. Destruction of affected areas of the retina by the use of an intense beam of light, a process called photocoagulation, promises to be a useful form of treatment in selected cases. Degenerative changes in the retina remain the most serious complication of diabetes.

Thyroid disease.   The staring appearance of persons suffering from thyrotoxicosis, also called exophthalmic goitre or Graves' disease, is believed to be due to the stimulation of smooth muscle in the lids and orbit, causing the lid to retract a little from the globe and the globe itself to advance forward slightly. These changes normally regress if the thyrotoxicosis is treated. There is a more serious ocular complication of thyroid disease, which may follow excision of the thyroid for thyrotoxicosis or may, in some cases, arise in persons with normal or subnormal thyroid activity. It is characterized by swelling of the orbital tissues, including the extraocular muscles, so that the eyes cannot be moved properly and project forward between the lids to such an extent that the cornea becomes permanently exposed; the cornea may then ulcerate and even perforate and cause loss of the eye. Sewing the lids together may be sufficient to protect the cornea, but in many cases surgery to relieve the pressure in the orbit is necessary.

Rheumatism.   The ocular complications of rheumatoid arthritis mainly involve the sclera, patches of inflammation occurring under the conjunctiva in the scleral and episcleral tissues (the latter are connective tissues between the conjunctiva and the sclera). Although the condition may respond to treatment with corticosteroids, recurrences are common.

VISUAL DISORDERS

Subjective symptoms.   One of the commonest visual symptoms is the sensation of small, black objects floating in front of the eye. These move with the eye but lag slightly at the beginning of an eye movement and overshoot when the movement stops. They are due to cells and fragments of debris in the vitreous cavity of the eye. In certain conditions, as when looking at an empty sky, almost everybody can perceive them, and they are normal phenomena. A sudden increase in their number may indicate degenerative changes in the vitreous, which are particularly likely to occur in shortsighted eyes and in older people. These changes, although annoying, are of no serious import. The appearance of many "floaters," however, may be associated with inflammation or bleeding in the eye.

Blind areas in the field of vision occasionally force people to seek medical advice. Any condition that causes failure of function of part of the retina, the optic nerve, or the optic pathway to the brain, can cause such a blind spot, and the symptom requires careful investigation. There is a naturally occurring "blind spot" in each visual field that corresponds with the lack of retinal elements where the optic nerve enters the eye. The brain is so skillful in filling in the visual pattern that the normal blind spot can be detected only by special methods.

Flashing lights in the field of vision are caused by stimulation of the retina by mechanical means. Most commonly this occurs when the vitreous becomes degenerate and fluid and pulls slightly on its peripheral attachment to the retina. Similar symptoms also arise when the retina becomes detached, causing flashing lights to be seen.

Night blindness and defects of colour perception.   Defective vision under reduced illumination may be a rare congenital condition or may be acquired as a result of severe deficiency of vitamin A.

Defective colour vision affects about four percent of men and 0.4 percent of women. Total colour blindness is extremely rare and is nearly always associated with poor vision in ordinary light. The colour-defective person is rarely aware of his disability until special matching tests are used, when it is discovered that he is unable to distinguish between hues in one or other part of the visual

"Floaters"; blind areas; flashing lights

spectrum. Other visual functions are perfectly normal, and the only disadvantage is the restriction of certain types of occupation.

Eyestrain. Eyestrain, or asthenopia, is the term used to describe symptoms of fatigue and discomfort following the use of the eyes. Although such symptoms may result from intensive close work, particularly if this is unaccustomed, in people with perfectly normal eyes, they may indicate abnormalities of muscle balance or refractive errors. Eyestrain is more likely to be manifest during periods of fatigue or stress and is common among students working for examinations. Refractive errors require correction and muscle imbalance treatment. Psychological factors are often more important than physical factors.

Presby-
opia;
short sight;
long sight **Refractive errors.** In a normal eye rays of light from distant objects come to a focus on the retina. In near vision, the refractive power of the eye is increased by altering the shape of the lens to focus the image on the retina. A twelve-year-old can focus on an object four inches away from the eye but, with age, the ability of the lens to alter its shape decreases so that at the age of 40 the shortest distance at which an object can be kept in focus is about ten inches. The near point continues to recede with age until fine print, for example, cannot be read at a normal reading distance. This condition is known as presbyopia; it is corrected by the use of convex lenses for reading.

In some eyes rays of light from distant objects are not brought to a focus on the retina but are focused on a plane in front of the retina, as in myopia (short sight), or behind the retina, as in hypermetropia (long sight). In myopia, near objects are brought into focus on the retina but distant objects can only be seen clearly with the aid of concave lenses. In hypermetropia, distant objects can usually be brought into focus by using the accommodative power of the lens, and in young people there is usually sufficient accommodation to enable them to see reasonably near to them. The constant accommodative effort required, however, may produce symptoms, and the necessity for accommodating for distance can be overcome by wearing convex glasses.

Another type of refractive error is astigmatism. In this condition the refractive power of the eye varies in different axes because of variation in curvature so that vision at all distances is distorted and can only be corrected by the use of cylindrical lenses or contact lenses.

Minor degrees of refractive error are extremely common. The refractive state is genetically determined and there are marked racial differences. Myopia, for example, is common in the Far East and rare in the African Negro. Although most refractive errors are easily correctible by spectacles and such errors are rarely accompanied by any serious disease of the eyes, hypermetropia is a factor in the development of some kinds of squint and high degrees of myopia are often associated with serious degenerative changes within the eye.

OPHTHALMOLOGICAL EXAMINATION
AND CORRECTIVE DEVICES

Ophthalmological examination. An ophthalmological examination comprises a history of a patient's symptoms and signs, subjective tests to determine the visual function, and physical examination of the eyes by means of special devices. The most important subjective test is for visual acuity, and this is usually performed by presenting to the patient a series of letters of graded sizes at a set distance. He is required to read the lowest line legible to him; visual acuity can then be expressed in terms of the size of the letter and the distance at which it is read.

The visual field is assessed by moving an illuminated target inward from the periphery toward a central point viewed by the eye: the area in which the target is seen can then be drawn as a map of the visual field for that eye.

Other subjective examinations include colour-vision testing and tests of visual perception under reduced illumination. Examination of the external eye and part of the anterior segment is facilitated by the use of a binocu-lar microscope mounted horizontally, to which is attached a slit-lamp, a variable source of light that projects the image of a slit onto the eye. The ophthalmoscope has an illuminating system that lights up the interior of the eye and a viewing system through which the fundus can be observed. Photography of the anterior part of the eye and of the fundus is both possible and widely used.

Other specialized methods of examination include examination of the angle of the anterior chamber by means of a specially designed contact lens with the slit-lamp microscope. The electrical responses of the retina and brain to light entering the eye can also be recorded and are of great value in certain conditions.

Estimation of the intraocular pressure is an important part of an ophthalmological examination and is accomplished by an instrument called a tonometer. This instrument is rested lightly on the anesthetized eye and measures the amount by which the eye is deformed by a small known weight or force.

The refractive state of the eye can be measured objectively, or subjectively, or by a combination of both methods. The simplest method is subjective, using lenses of different powers to give a trial-and-error estimate of the best correcting lenses. More accurate results can be obtained by using an instrument known as a retinoscope, which gives an objective assessment of the refraction that can subsequently be modified by subjective methods to suit the individual requirements of the patient.

Optical aids. The most widely used optical aids are Types of
spectacles spectacles, and the technical design of spectacle lenses has advanced considerably in the last 50 years. A simple biconcave or biconvex lens causes considerable distortion of appearances if objects are viewed through the periphery of the lens, but if the back surface of the lens is made concave and the required power attained by altering the curvature of the front surface, improvement in peripheral definition results. All modern spectacle lenses are of this form.

Most older people require an additional lens for reading, and this can be incorporated with the distance correction in the form of a bifocal lens. In some occupations an intermediate distance is also required, and a third segment can be added, forming a trifocal lens. The complete range of correction from distance to near can only be achieved by means of a multifocal lens, and these are now available: the upper segment provides the correction for distance; as the eye moves lower down the lens its power increases, the lowest segment of the lens representing the reading correction. By slightly tilting the head it is possible to find the optimum correction for any intermediate distance.

The distortion of peripheral view when using conventional spectacles occurs because the correcting lens does not move when the eye moves. This problem can be completely overcome by the use of contact lenses, which are thin shells of plastic made to fit the anterior surface of the cornea and thus move with the eye. The earliest types of contact lens were larger than the cornea and were uncomfortable to wear, but the modern small "corneal" lenses have greatly increased the scope and usefulness of contact lenses and offer a practical alternative to the wearing of spectacles. Even so, there is a limit to the length of time for which they can be worn, and they should not be kept in at night. Their small size makes them easy to lose and difficult to manipulate, particularly for elderly persons. Further advances in design and in the use of new materials—for example, the flexible soft lenses—will doubtless extend the use of contact lenses even further.

For those persons who cannot obtain useful vision with ordinary spectacles or contact lenses, much can still be done by the use of compound lens systems known as low vision aids. These devices provide a magnified image but inevitably reduce the visual field. Their main value is to enable a person to read normal print who would otherwise be unable to read. They can be of use for distance, particularly when viewing conditions are relatively static, as with the cinema, theatre, or television.

Finally, for those who are completely blind from ocular

causes there is new hope in the development of implants into the visual cortex that can be connected to a small television camera in such a way that electrical signals can be applied to the visual cortex, completely bypassing the normal optic pathways. The miniaturization of electrical circuitry resulting from space research has made the design of such devices a practical possibility. Their application to human subjects is, however, still in the experimental stage.

BLINDNESS

It is difficult to obtain reliable statistical information on the incidence of blindness on a worldwide basis. Even in countries in which the registration of blind people is attempted, the definitions of "blindness" vary from one country to another; in large parts of the world there is no registration, and the only estimate that can be made depends on random surveys of small parts of the population. Figures collected by the World Health Organization vary from 39 per 100,000 of the population in Mauritius to 4,000 per 100,000 of the population in Yemen. An incidence of about 200 per 100,000 is fairly representative of countries in which the standard of medical care is high; it is probable that the incidence is ten times higher in countries in which medical care is rudimentary.

There is wide variation in the causes of blindness in different parts of the world. This is partly due to geographic and climatic conditions but, more important, it is also due to differences in standards of hygiene and the availability of medical care. Infections, particularly trachoma, spread most easily in warm countries where the population is often crowded into small villages with lack of adequate hygienic facilities. Cataract is still high on the list of causes of blindness in many countries in the world, and this is all the more tragic in that it is so easily curable by surgical means. As the standards of general medical care increase and the expectation of life increases, so the pattern of blindness changes and degenerative conditions, diabetic disorders of the retina, and genetically determined diseases become predominant. Advances in the prevention and the medical and surgical treatment of blindness can only be of benefit to a population that has access to medical care. Until the nutritional and hygienic standards of a large part of the world population can be improved, preventable blindness will remain at its present high level.

BIBLIOGRAPHY. SIR STEWART DUKE-ELDER (ed.), *Parsons' Diseases of the Eye*, 15th ed. (1970), a textbook for students concentrating on the more common eye conditions, and (ed.), *System of Ophthalmology*, vol. 1–5, 7–12 (1958–71; vol. 6, 13–15 in prep.) perhaps the most comprehensive textbook on any medical subject; F.W. NEWELL, *Ophthalmology*, 2nd ed. (1969), an up-to-date standard textbook; E.S. PERKINS and P. HANSELL, *Atlas of Diseases of the Eye*, 2nd ed. (1971), illustrations of common eye conditions with brief text; D.T. VAIL, *The Truth About Your Eyes*, 2nd ed. (1959), a description for the layman of the function of the eye and management of the more common eye diseases; F.B. WALSH and W.F. HOYT, *Clinical Neuro-Ophthalmology*, 3rd ed., 3 vol. (1969), a very detailed account of ophthalmic conditions associated with neurological diseases.

(E.S.P.)

Eyre, Lake

The great, normally dry Australian salt lake (salina) of Lake Eyre lies asymmetrically in the southwestern corner of a 500,000-square-mile (1,300,000-square-kilometre) closed basin of inland drainage in the heart of the continent. The annual rainfall in the lake is less than 5 inches (125 millimetres), making it the driest part of Australia, a factor worsened by a potential evaporation rate of 120 inches (3,050 millimetres) a year. The brutally harsh environment of the lake makes its value, in terms of settlement or exploitation of resources, limited in the extreme. The complex secrets of its origin, and the often bizarre plant and animal life associated with it, have, nevertheless, made Lake Eyre unique for its attraction for scientists, and its wildness offers a strange beauty.

The lake, whose lowest part lies 46 feet (14 metres) below sea level, consists of two sections. Lake Eyre North, 90 miles (144 kilometres) long and 40 miles (64 kilometres) wide, is joined by the narrow Goyder Channel to Lake Eyre South, which is 40 miles (64 kilometres) long and about 12 miles (20 kilometres) in width. The combined area of Lake Eyre North and Lake Eyre South is 3,600 square miles (9,300 square kilometres) so that it ranks about 16th in the list of the world's great lakes.

The lake is normally dry; filling is thought to occur twice in a century, but partial, minor fillings happen much more frequently. During 1949–50, following phenomenal rains in northern and eastern Australia, 25,000,000 acre-feet (31,000,000,000 cubic metres) of water flowed in, principally from such streams as the Cooper Creek and the Diamantina, forming a sheet of water filling Lake Eyre North and covering no less than 3,100 square miles (8,000 square kilometres). This volume of water was insufficient to rise above the highest point in Goyder Channel and thus did not flow into Lake Eyre South. The large deposits of salt on the bed of Lake Eyre North were completely dissolved, and the lake water became as saline as that of the sea. Fish lived and multiplied in it for a short time but soon died as the salinity rose with intense evaporation during the 1950–51 summer. By the end of 1951 the water was reduced to 8 percent of its former volume and had become a saturated salt solution from which crystalline sodium chloride began to separate. Within a year the lake was dry and its 400,000,000 tons of salt were again deposited as a crust in its large southern bays. The complete cycle of filling and drying up occupied 3½ years. The actual evaporation rate was of the order of 80–90 inches (2.0–2.3 metres) per annum. *The flood of 1949–50*

Exploration and scientific study. The lake was first sighted in 1840 by Edward John Eyre, one of the great 19th-century explorers, after whom it was named. Four years later Capt. Charles Sturt, whose expeditions were as important as those of Eyre, suffered terrible privations in the deserts to the east of the lake. Other explorers followed: in 1866, a party recorded the occurrence of salt three inches thick near the middle of the western shore, and established a fall of two and one-half feet in seven miles in the floor of the lake, reckoning from the northern shores; in 1872–73 a map was prepared showing the lake and the courses of the rivers to the east, thus opening the way to the establishment of cattle stations in the latter area.

Geological and physiographic background. The present landscapes of the Lake Eyre region can be understood only by tracing their geological evolution, a story of earth movements, erosion, laying down of sediments, and dramatic changes in climate going back hundreds of millions of years. Lake Eyre lies near the southwestern limit of the Great Artesian Basin, filled with sedimentary rock layers of the Mesozoic Era, less than 200,000,000 years ago, overlying a geologically ancient Precambrian basement or, in places, sediments of the Permian Period, about 260,000,000 years old. The earliest known deposits in the Lake Eyre region, however, are Jurassic terrestrial sandstones, laid down about 180,000,000 years ago. These indicate a depositional environment made up of rivers prone to episodic sheet floods, and a climate at first seasonally arid, but later moist and subtropical. The Great Artesian Basin was flooded by the sea some 50,000,000 years later, and its boundaries in South Australia widened as the transgression continued. The sea withdrew in Middle Cretaceous times, just over 100,000,000 years ago, and Lake Dieri, the ancestral Lake Eyre, came into being. From then until the end of the Mesozoic Era, around 70,000,000 years ago, up to 2,000 feet (600 metres) of lagoonal sediments were deposited in Lake Dieri as the region sagged; it is probable that Lake Dieri had an outflow to the sea. *Ancestral origins*

The details of Lake Eyre's evolution during the last 70,000,000 years (that is, during the Cenozoic Era) are still somewhat controversial, and the following account combines the results of geological and geomorphological studies. During the early part of this period, carbonaceous lake sediments some 120 feet (36 metres) thick were deposited in the region at present occupied by Lake Eyre, but outside this, thin spreads of gravel and sand were also deposited in places. Prolonged deep weathering and bleaching of rock layers near to the surface took place, forming a hard surface crust.

About 25,000,000 years ago the Lake Eyre Basin was affected by warping; positive movements along the marginal areas were compensated by negative movements near Lake Eyre, which thus accommodated further sediment down to 2,000,000 years ago, the time of early man.

A renewal of uplift then introduced a marked erosional phase ending in the development of broad, river-drained plains, separated by extremely low watersheds. Gypsite sediments, virtually the only resource of the region, were laid down at this time, and a higher rainfall and lower evaporation than at present permitted the existence of large, freshwater, brackish swamps, near which plant-eating marsupials flourished. An uplift of the eastern rim of the Great Artesian Basin resulted in the expulsion of artesian water in springs to the west and southwest of Lake Eyre, and in shallow pools surrounding these springs, the freshwater gastropod dolomitic limestones were formed and have been dated to 40,000 years ago.

Evidence from the western side of Lake Eyre strongly suggests that the present salina depression is a structural depression formed by a downfaulting in the earth's surface about 30,000 years ago, which blocked off the outlet to the sea. The western margin of the lake bed is a steep escarpment still seismically active, and springs occur along north–south lines in the lake bed of this region,

Formation of the present depression

presumably making fault zones. About 16 feet (five metres) of sediment have been deposited in the lake bed since this downfaulting, and as the climate became more arid, the finer sediments were blown off the lake surface to form the dunes of the Simpson Desert, to the north. Water reaching the lake now evaporates very rapidly, and the surface of the lake bed has a thin crust evaporated from the salt.

Water supply and chemical characteristics. Apart from the very low and intermittent local rainfall and small inflow of ground waters, the lake is fed in times of abnormal rainfall from a great, internal, continental drainage system. From the north, the Sandover, Georgina, and Mulligan rivers join the Diamantina, which enters Lake Eyre North via the Warburton and Kallakoopah Creek channels. The Thomson and Barcoo river systems converge to form the Cooper, and empty into the eastern side of Lake Eyre North as the Cooper, and into the southeastern sector as the Strzelecki Creek. Southern drainage from the Flinders Range enters by way of the Frome Channel. Other southern streams occasionally flood into Lake Eyre South; the biggest of these is the

Water supply

Margaret River. The main streams entering from the western side of Lake Eyre North include the Macumba and the Neales.

Beneath the surface, groundwater flow is centripetal to Lake Eyre, the main contributions coming from the Simpson Desert region to the north. The shallow groundwaters immediately north of Lake Eyre are composed of saturated brines.

The salt of Lake Eyre was once thought to be carried in atmospherically from the sea; but this is discounted by observations from Victoria that suggest that the influence of salts blown from the sea is limited to the immediate coastal zone. The current view is that the salt has been derived by solution from the rocks of the catchment area and carried, predominantly by shallow groundwater, to the hot, arid area of Lake Eyre, where it has been concentrated at various times during the last 2,000,000 years.

The thin salt crust of Lake Eyre North thickens southward, where it is up to nine inches (about 20 centimetres) thick; it is a coarsely crystalline aggregate, almost entirely of sodium chloride, hard and rigid, and capable of supporting heavy vehicles. It is invariably damp and satu-

Chemical content of the salt

rated with ground brine. The brines comprise essentially sodium chloride (90–95 percent), with lesser amounts of magnesium sulfate (5–7 percent), magnesium chloride (up to 4 percent), and calcium sulfate (up to 2½ percent).

The proportions of the various salts differ little with depth. The potassium content appears to be fairly constant throughout, being appreciably lower (0.11–0.34 percent) than that derived from solar evaporation of seawater and from the artesian waters of the area (0.6–7.7 percent). Fluorine, bromine, iodine, and boron contents are almost negligible.

Plant and animal life. The plant life of the area around Lake Eyre forms part of what is known as the desert complex; the dunes carry cane grass on the crest and spinifex in the sandy interdune corridors; small shrubs, such as needlebush, occur in sandy hollows. Shrub steppe occurs on clayey corridors between the dunes. A restricted, ephemeral plant life of crucifers (four-petalled flowers in the shape of a cross) and grasses is prominent seasonally. The insects of this region, of a type found widely across Central Australia, exhibit mechanisms and behaviour patterns that enable them to survive periods of high temperature and severe desiccation; periodic large-scale fluctuations in their numbers occur. The reptile life is dominated by desert-adapted lizards and numerous snakes. The remarkable and highly specialized white earless dragon, a variety of lizard, was found living on the salt-encrusted surface of Lake Eyre North; it lives in association with a species of harvest ant that feeds on seeds blown out over the surface of the lake; together they form a closed community remote from plant life. The thorny devil, a grotesquely armoured lizard, also feeds on small ants. True desert birds are the gibber bird and the cinnamon quail thrush. Mammals are rare, though subject to periodic local increase. The fossil record of the lake has given clues as to the evolution of marsupials: it includes the giant plant-eating marsupials, which abounded there until extinguished by the increasing aridity that has reached its peak today. The brines contain a number of micro-organisms, algal, protozoal, and bacterial.

Resources. The accumulation of chemical evaporites in the bed of Lake Eyre is thin. Being in such a climatically harsh area, and so far removed from centres of usage, the deposits of sodium chloride, calcium sulfate, and dolomite cannot compete with materials more easily obtained from the coastal regions of South Australia. The native sulfur, occurring as cores in shells of gypsum, in Madigan Gulf, is too limited in supply to be of present economic interest, and the main interest in Lake Eyre at present continues to be that of scientific inquiry.

BIBLIOGRAPHY. R.J. BEST (ed.), *Introducing South Australia* (1958), contains articles on Lake Eyre; R.K. JOHNS and N.H. LUDBROOK, "Investigation of Lake Eyre," *Rep. Invest. Dep. Mines S. Aust.*, 24:1–104 (1962), is a geological survey, including a good map of the drainage basin; L.W. PARKIN (ed.), *Handbook of South Australian Geology* (1969); H. WOPFNER and C.R. TWIDALE, "Geomorphological History of the Lake Eyre Basin," in J.N. JENNINGS and J.A. MABBUTT, *Landform Studies from Australia and New Guinea*, pp. 119–143 (1967).

(D.Hi.)

Ezekiel

Ezekiel was a prophet-priest of ancient Israel, the subject and, certainly in part, the author of a book of the Old Testament that bears his name. His ministry was conducted in Jerusalem and Babylon in the first three decades of the 6th century BC. In the history of Judaism (and Christianity) the faith of Ezekiel (shared especially by the prophet Jeremiah) in the ultimate establishment of a new covenant has been a sustaining factor of inestimable importance; and his insistence that God purposes to do this for his own sake and that of his holy name (an emphasis shared later by the Second Isaiah) has had profound influence on the theology of Judaism and Christianity.

For Ezekiel and his people, the years were bitter ones during which the remnant of the old Israelite domain, the little state of Judah, was subjugated and eliminated by the rising new Babylonian Empire under Nebuchadrezzar (reigned 605–562 BC). The capital city of Jerusalem surrendered to the Babylonians in 597 BC. Resistance was renewed, and in 587–586 the city was de-

Historical setting

stroyed after a lengthy siege by Nebuchadrezzar's forces. In both debacles, and indeed again in 582, large numbers from the best elements of the surviving population were forcibly deported to Babylonia.

Before the first surrender of Jerusalem, Ezekiel was a functioning priest probably attached to the Jerusalem Temple staff. He was among those deported to Babylonia in 597 where he was located at Tel-abib on the Kebar canal (near Nippur). He lived with his wife in his own house until, apparently very suddenly, she died. Quite apart from his professional status as prophet-priest, it is evident that he was, among his fellow exiles, a person of uncommon stature.

The Book of Ezekiel opens with what remains a standing puzzle:

On the fifth day of the fourth month in the thirtieth year, while I was among the exiles by the river Kebar, the heavens were opened and I saw a vision of God. (Alternative translation, The New English Bible.)

To what or to whom the reference to the thirtieth year applies is not known. But in the next verse, the vision that inaugurated Ezekiel's career as a prophet is unambiguously dated in "the fifth year of the exile of King Jehoiachin"; that is, about 592 BC. His latest datable utterance ("in the twenty-seventh year") would be, then, about 570 BC, 22 years later.

On several matters, interpreters of the Book of Ezekiel have been unable to come to agreement. Repeatedly the prophet addresses himself to those who remain in Judah and Jerusalem, a fact that has led some historians to conclude that the Babylonian setting must be a later fiction, and that Ezekiel in fact fulfilled his career in Jerusalem. This, however, remains a minority judgment. More striking is the conflict in assessment of the person of the prophet. By some he has been read in a strongly negative light—hard and insensitive to the point of being almost inhuman; a fanatic, and in the way of fanatics, arrogant and aggressively intolerant; and even (because in fact the prophet is more given to strange visions and extraordinary acts than any other biblical prophet) as a psychopath. On the other hand, he has been described as having a well-endowed, versatile mind, aware of the problems and doubts of the people he addresses and sensitive to the life about him. It is said that he devoted all his mental powers, his heart, and his imagination to his ministry, and there is wide agreement that he profoundly shaped the Judaism that was reformed in the centuries that followed, especially in the influence of chapters 40–48 upon the postexilic reconstruction and reorganization of Judaism.

With the possible exception of the closing section of the Book of Ezekiel, scholars are reasonably confident that it is the prophet himself who is revealed in the writing that bears his name. The first 24 chapters were written in the years immediately before Jerusalem's destruction and carry the message of violence and destruction. Chapters 33 to 35 bridge the chasm to the articulation of hope and the assurance of restoration in chapters 36 to 39, with a phenomenal vision in chapter 37 of the valley of dry bones—representing the moribund people of Israel—coming alive again.

Visions and symbolic acts

More than any of the classical biblical prophets—such as Isaiah and Amos and Jeremiah—Ezekiel is given to symbolic actions, strange visions, and even trances (although it is quite gratuitous to deduce from these, and from his words "I fell upon my face" (1:28) that Ezekiel was a cataleptic). He eats a scroll on which words of prophecy are written, to symbolize his appropriation of the message (3:1–3). He lies down for an extended time to symbolize the length of Israel's punishment (4:4ff). He is apparently struck dumb on one occasion for an unspecified length of time (3:26). As other prophets had done before him, he sees the God–People relationship as analogous to the relationship of husband to unfaithful wife, and therefore understands the collapse of the life of Judah as a judgment for essential infidelity. Ezekiel depicts the relationship in chapters 16 and 23 with consummate skill and passion.

There are other distinguished accounts of a prophet's calling (e.g., in the books of Isaiah and Jeremiah). But Ezekiel's vision, which constitutes his call in chapter 1, is the most sensitive and sophisticated. Ezekiel does not suppose that he has seen Yahweh (God) or even Yahweh's throne. He punctuates his account with repeated qualifying phrases and concludes the vision: such was the appearance of the likeness of the glory of Yahweh. These images of the divine glory were the basis of Merkava ("chariot") mysticism in later Judaism.

Finally, it is the majesty of Ezekiel's faith that is his most distinctive quality. Ezekiel is unshakably persuaded of Yahweh's purposeful impingement upon history, of the ultimate redemption of the life of his (the prophet's) people, and implicitly, of their fulfillment of destiny in the eventual blessing of all the peoples of the earth.

BIBLIOGRAPHY. OTTO EISSFELDT, "Ezekiel," in *The Old Testament: An Introduction* (1965), one of the great classic introductions; CARL GORDON HOWIE, "Ezekiel," in *The Interpreter's Dictionary of the Bible*, vol. 2 (1962); see also his *The Date and Composition of Ezekiel* (1950); J. LINDBLOM, *Prophecy in Ancient Israel* (1962); HERBERT G. MAY, "The Book of Ezekiel," in *The Interpreter's Bible*, vol. 6 (1956); B.D. NAPIER, *Prophets in Perspective* (1963), an assessment of the prophetic movement in ancient Israel, and "Insight and Resurrection: Ezekiel," in his *Song of the Vineyard* (1962), a theological introduction to the Old Testament; SAMUEL SANDMEL, "Ezekiel," in *The Hebrew Scriptures* (1963); ARTHUR WEISER, "Ezekiel," in *The Old Testament: Its Formation and Development* (1961), a volume presenting in compact form classical German biblical scholarship; JOHN W. WEVERS (ed.), *Ezekiel* (1969).

(B.D.N.)

Ezra

Ezra was a religious leader from among the Jewish exiles in Babylon, who, at some time in the 5th century BC or at the beginning of the 4th, went to Jerusalem, where he was instrumental in bringing about a great religious reform that resulted in the reconstitution of the Jewish community on the basis of Pentateuchal law—which was regarded as divinely revealed Torah, or Law; *i.e.*, religious and social regulations laid down in the first five books of the Old Testament (Pentateuch). Since his efforts did much to give Jewish religion the form that was to characterize it for centuries after, Ezra has with some justice been called the father of Judaism; *i.e.*, the specific form the Jewish religion took after the Babylonian Exile. So important was he in the eyes of his people that later tradition regarded him as no less than a second Moses.

Ezra showing the Law to the people, detail of an engraving by Gustave Doré (1832–83).

Knowledge of Ezra is derived from the biblical books of Ezra and Nehemiah, supplemented by the Apocryphal (not included in the Jewish and Protestant canons of the

Problem of dating of Ezra

Old Testament) book of I Esdras (Latin Vulgate form of the name Ezra), which preserves the Greek text of Ezra and a part of Nehemiah. It is said that Ezra came to Jerusalem in the seventh year of King Artaxerxes (which Artaxerxes is not stated) of the Persian dynasty then ruling the area. Since he is introduced before Nehemiah, who was governor of the province of Judah from 445 to 433 BC and again, after an interval, for a second term of unknown length, it is sometimes supposed that this was the seventh year of Artaxerxes I (458 BC), though serious difficulties are attached to such a view. Many scholars now believe that the biblical account is not in chronological order and that Ezra arrived in the seventh year of Artaxerxes II (397 BC), after Nehemiah had passed from the scene. Still others, agreeing that Nehemiah preceded Ezra but accepting that the two men were contemporaries, regard the seventh year as a scribal error and believe that perhaps Ezra arrived during Nehemiah's second term as governor. But the matter must be left open.

When Ezra arrived the situation in Judah was discouraging. Religious laxity was prevalent, the law was widely disregarded, and public and private morality was at a low level. Moreover, intermarriage with foreigners posed the threat that the community would mingle with the pagan environment and lose its identity. Although Nehemiah brought the community physical security and corrected various abuses, a sweeping religious reform was needed of the sort that he, a layman, could not manage—especially since laxity involved the high priestly family itself. It was this that Ezra came from Babylon to accomplish.

Ezra was a priest and "a scribe skilled in the law." He represented the position of stricter Babylonian Jews who had been upset by reports of laxity in Judah and desired to see matters corrected. Perhaps through the influence of highly placed Jews at the Persian court, the King (Artaxerxes) was persuaded to authorize Ezra to go to Jerusalem, together with such Jews as wished to accompany him, and to regulate religious affairs there in accordance with the law; he was also authorized to receive contributions for the Temple and to transmit them to the authorities in Jerusalem. Ezra set out in the spring at the head of a sizable caravan and, four months later, arrived at his destination. Ezra apparently had official status as a commissioner of the Persian government, and his title, "scribe of the law of the God of heaven," is best understood as "royal secretary for Jewish religious affairs," or the like. The Persians were tolerant of native cults but, in order to avert internal strife and to prevent religion from becoming a mask for rebellion, insisted that these be regulated under responsible authority. The delegated authority over the Jews of the satrapy (administrative area) "beyond the river" (Avar-nahara), or west of the Euphrates River, was entrusted to Ezra; for a Jew to disobey the law he brought was to disobey "the law of the king."

Ezra's reforms

The order in which Ezra took the various measures attributed to him is uncertain. He probably presented the law to the people during the Feast of Tabernacles in the autumn, most likely in the year of his arrival. He also took action against mixed marriages and succeeded in persuading the people to divorce their foreign wives voluntarily. His efforts reached their climax when the people engaged in solemn covenant before God to enter into no more mixed marriages, to refrain from work on the sabbath, to levy on themselves an annual tax for the support of the Temple, regularly to present their tithes and offerings, and otherwise to comply with the demands of the law. Ezra's work helped to give Judaism its essential character as a religion in which law was central. Through adherence to the law the Jews were enabled to survive as a definable religious community, even though without national identity and scattered all over the world.

Nothing further is known of Ezra after his reforms. The 1st-century Hellenistic Jewish historian Josephus states in his *Antiquities* that he died and was buried in Jerusalem. According to another tradition, he returned to Babylonia, where his supposed grave is a holy site.

BIBLIOGRAPHY. The books of Ezra, Nehemiah, and I Esdras, the biblical books which are our primary sources of knowledge; JOHN BRIGHT, *A History of Israel*, ch. 10 (1959); MARTIN NOTH, *The History of Israel*, 2nd ed., pp. 315–333 (1960), two recent treatments of Israel's history, both of which advocate the view that Ezra came to Jerusalem during Nehemiah's term as governor (*c.* 428 BC); H.H. ROWLEY, "The Chronological Order of Ezra and Nehemiah" pp. 135–168 in *The Servant of the Lord*, rev. ed. (1965), a comprehensive review of the history of the discussion, with a defense of the view that Ezra arrived in the seventh year of Artaxerxes II (397 BC); J.S. WRIGHT, *The Date of Ezra's Coming to Jerusalem*, 2nd ed. (1958), perhaps the best defense of the traditional view that Ezra arrived in the seventh year of Artaxerxes I (458 BC).

(Jo.Br.)

Fabales

Fabales is one of the three largest orders of flowering plants and is second only to the grass order (Poales) in economic importance. It includes a number of such familiar food products as beans, peanuts, and peas, as well as important sources of grazing food for animals, of which alfalfa and clover are the better known. In addition, most of the species are important elements of the natural ecosystem, in that they have the capacity, in conjunction with appropriate micro-organisms, to convert biologically inert atmospheric nitrogen into nitrates, in which form it is readily metabolized by plants. While a few other plant orders possess species with this capacity, the Fabales order is responsible for the great mass of such biological recycling. Because of this factor, together with the high nutritive value of its grazing plants, the species are commonly employed in crop rotation practices.

Latest estimates suggest that the order is composed of approximately 20,000 species distributed among 800 or so genera. Except for the family Krameriaceae, which has been removed from the order by most recent workers, the group is exceedingly natural—*i.e.,* all of its families are closely related. Thus, while nearly all treatments have recognized the order Fabales as being divisible into three families (or sometimes subfamilies), Caesalpiniaceae, Mimosaceae, and Fabaceae, none has suggested that these families might be related to other groups more closely than they are to each other.

GENERAL FEATURES

The order, while worldwide in distribution, shows the greatest diversity of morphological types in the tropical and subtropical regions of the world. This is particularly true for the predominantly woody families, Caesalpiniaceae and Mimosaceae. The former comprise the dominant tree members of the savanna lands of tropical Africa, South America, and Asia; the latter family is especially abundant as small trees and shrubs in the drier subtropical regions of Africa, America, and Australia.

Economic uses. In the more temperate regions of the world, the order is predominantly herbaceous, and most of the species belong to the large family Fabaceae. This family also contains the more important crop plants such as peanuts or groundnuts (*Arachis hypogaea*), chick pea (*Cicer arietinum*), soybean (*Glycine max*), common lentil (*Lens esculenta*), alfalfa or lucerne (*Medicago sativa*), sweet clover (*Melilotus* species), mung bean (*Phaseolus aureus*), kidney beans (*Phaseolus vulgaris*), peas (*Pisum sativum*), clovers (*Trifolium* species), vetches (*Vicia* species), and cowpeas (*Vigna* species).

Crop plants

The families Caesalpiniaceae and Mimosaceae do not contain many food crops and are perhaps best known for their shade and ornamental species, such as the Judas tree or redbud (*Cercis* species), orchid tree (*Bauhinia divaricata*), and huisache (*Acacia farnesiana*), although some of the more rapid growing weedy species, for example, the white popinac (*Leucaena glauca*) and *Albizia* species, are widely used as green manure and fodder crops. *Acacia* species are widely used in the production of gum exudates and wood, especially in South Africa and Australia, where the species are known as wattle trees.

Diversity of structure. The order Fabales is a predominately woody group and most workers believe that the more advanced herbaceous plant groups, characteristic of the temperate regions, evolved from such tropical, woody ancestors. Species of the order are abundant on all continents (except Antarctica), occurring as trees, shrubs, vines, delicate annuals, and sometimes, though rarely, as floating aquatics. An example of such an aquatic is *Neptunia oleracea*, a member of the family Mimosaceae, which is often tied to shallow lake bottoms in India so that it might be readily obtained for use as an edible vegetable. Bizarre species are especially abundant in the semidesert and savanna regions of western Australia; most of them belong to the tribe Podalyrieae of the family Fabaceae, and such oddities are presumably a reflection of the long isolation of that continent's flora from Asia.

Distinctive character of the fruit

The order Fabales is probably best known by its fruit. In fact, it is often referred to as the Leguminales order, because its fruit, a legume (often highly modified), is the most obvious single character by which the group is recognized. Technically speaking, a legume is typically a one-celled (chambered), two-valved, seed pod with marginal placentation (ovule attachment), such as occurs in the common pea (*Pisum sativum*). The legume assumes a variety of forms, however, such as samaras, which are single-seeded, winged, indehiscent (not splitting open along definite seams) pods and loments (many seeded, indehiscent pods, constricted between the seeds, which at maturity break off as separate reproductive units), and others. One of the more unusual legumes is that of the peanut (*Arachis hypogaea*), a fruit that matures underground. The peanut flower itself is produced above ground but as it ages it assumes a position close to the soil surface so the ovary can elongate and develop as a subterranean pod.

Seeds borne within the various legume types are also extremely variable, ranging from the size of a pinhead (in *Lotus* species) to that of a baseball (in *Mora excelsa*). Legume seeds are sometimes quite colourful; the *Abrus precatorius* and *Ormosia* species, for example, produce striking black and red seeds. These seeds have been used as currency by primitive people and because of their usually hard seed coats they are commonly used in the production of beads and handbags, which are sold as tourist merchandise, especially in the more tropical regions. They may be quite poisonous if eaten, however, and for this reason such merchandise is often refused entry by government inspectors.

NATURAL HISTORY

The worldwide distribution and large size of the order is undoubtedly a reflection of its early dispersion throughout the tropics and later adaptation to the numerous adjacent, more temperate, habitats. Effective

Seed dispersal

dispersal of the seeds is assured by the large variety of seed pods found in the order and by the largely self-pollinated flowers found in the more advanced tribes of the family Fabaceae. Seed coats are generally quite hard and impermeable to water, which permits the seed to endure long storage periods in nature. In fact, seeds of this order from the genus *Cassia* have been known to germinate after having been in dry storage at ordinary room temperatures for 200 years. Upon fracture of the seed coats, however, germination is readily effected, for dormancy periods, often necessary for seed germination in other plants, are generally not found in legumes. Other reproductive specializations include cross-pollination, cleistogamy (self-pollination resulting from floral modifications that prevent the entry of other pollen—such as non-opening flowers), and vegetative (asexual) reproduction.

An interesting adaptation in a few tropical and subtropical species belonging to the families Mimosaceae and Caesalpiniaceae is that of myrmecophilism, in which vegetative specializations have been developed to accommodate ants. Special secretory glands on the leaves that ants use for feeding purposes and unusually large thorns on the stem in which they live are two such features.

The adaptive significance of such mutualism is debatable, but many workers believe that in living off the

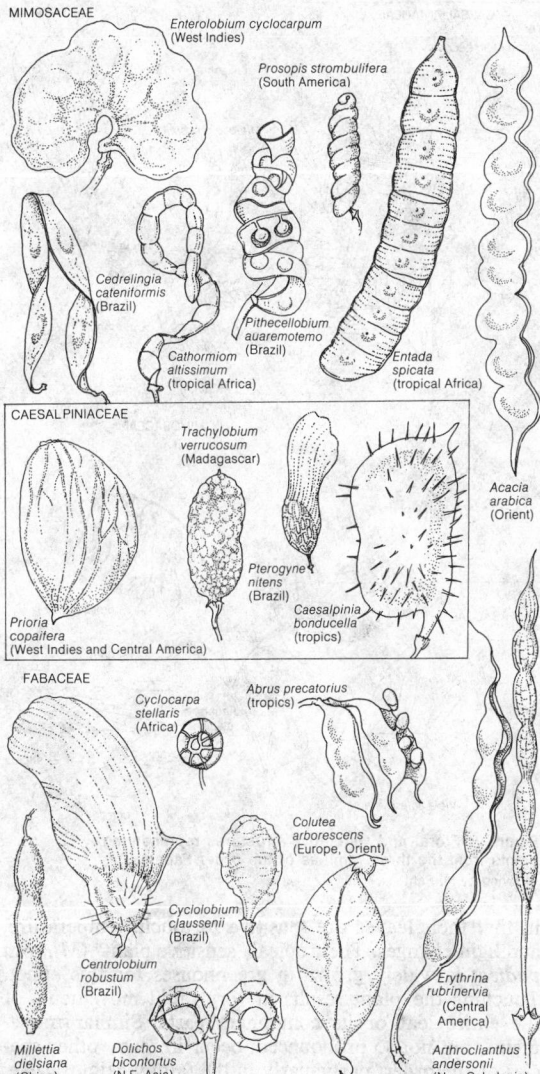

Figure 1: Representative fruits of the order Fabales. The characteristic fruit type, known as a legume, is the single character by which the order is best known and is the basis of the classical name of the order (Leguminales), still used by many authorities.

Drawing by M. Pahl based on (all except *Entada spicata, Millettia dielsiana, Erythrina rubrinervia*) J. Hutchinson, *Evolution and Phylogeny of Flowering Plants*

excretory products of the plant, the ants readily provide protective measures to the plant by warding off potential leaf eaters such as grasshoppers, aphids, and perhaps even some of the larger browsing animals.

Pollen dispersal in outbreeders is largely provided by insects, especially bees, which have relatively heavy abdomens and easily cause pollination through landings made on the keel of the flower, a special structure found in the Fabaceae that encloses most of the reproductive organs. Other pollinators exist, however, and in at least one genus of the family Mimosaceae (*Parkia*), tropical fruit bats are the principal means assuring pollination.

FORM AND FUNCTION

Vegetative characters. The three families that make up the order Fabales are readily distinguished by their vegetative features. The family Mimosaceae possesses mostly twice-compound leaves, which have several leaflets arranged along either side of a central axis, the leaflets themselves being subdivided into a number of smaller units in a similar arrangement. The family Caesalpiniaceae has mostly once-, or less often, twice-compound leaves, and the family Fabaceae has once-compound leaves, these often reduced to a trifoliolate (three leaflets) condition, as in the common clover, or modified with twining tendrils as in the sweet pea.

Certain members of the order are especially interesting

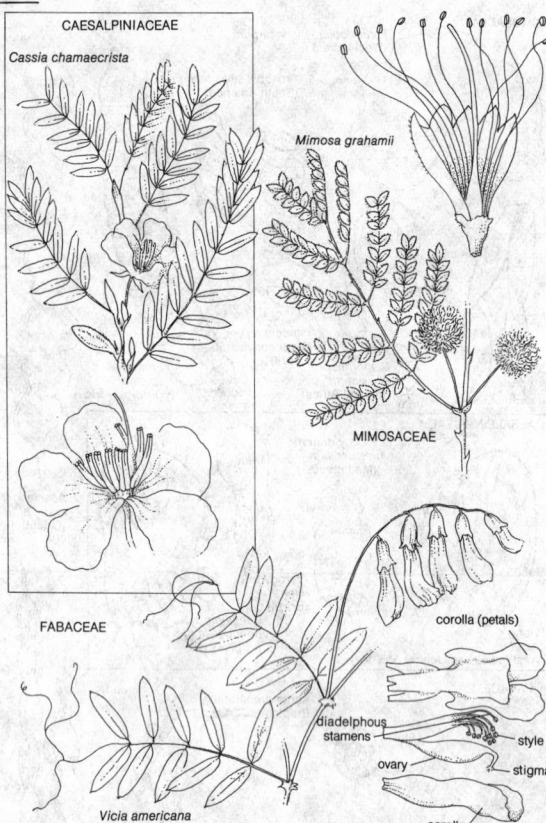

CAESALPINIACEAE

Cassia chamaecrista

Mimosa grahamii

MIMOSACEAE

FABACEAE

corolla (petals)

diadelphous
stamens

style

ovary

stigma

Vicia americana

corolla

Figure 2: Floral and vegetative structures representing
plants from the three families of the order Fabales.
Drawing by M. Pahl

**Leaves
sensitive
to touch**

in that their leaves are sensitive to touch, temperature, and light changes. The tropical "sensitive plant" (*Mimosa pudica*) is widely grown in greenhouses for this effect. Touching the plant results in very rapid movements of the entire leaf or its component parts. Similar movements, but not so pronounced, occur in many other species of the order, particularly in the family Mimosaceae. For example, the so-called "mimosa" tree (*Albizia julibrissin*) folds its leaflets together at dusk, decreasing at least by half the amount of leaf surface exposed to the atmosphere. The adaptive significance of such movements is unknown, but the movement itself is caused by water pressure changes in specialized structures at the base of both the leafstalks (petioles) and leaflets.

Flower and fruit characters. The single floral feature most characteristic of the entire order is the presence of an hypanthium, a structure formed by the fusion at the base of sepals, petals, and stamens (male reproductive structures) to form a cup (often very small) about the base of the ovary. With the exception of this characteristic, the floral types are quite variable, with flowers ranging from regular (*i.e.*, actinomorphic, radially symmetrical) in the family Mimosaceae to highly irregular (*i.e.*, zygomorphic, bilaterally symmetrical) in the family Fabaceae. Flowers of the family Caesalpiniaceae are somewhat intermediate between these extremes, as regards symmetry.

Especially noteworthy are the floral modifications found in the family Fabaceae. The petals, which are uniformly five in nearly all of the 15,000 or more species, are characteristically modified into a so-called papilionaceous (butterfly-like) flower in which the uppermost petal (the banner) is usually quite enlarged and colourful, the two lateral petals are wing-like structures (and are termed wings) and the two basal petals characteristically are united near their middle to form a boat-shaped structure called the keel.

Arrangement of stamens

The stamens, usually 10 in number, are also highly modified in this family. They are joined into a single, tubular structure (the stamens then being termed "monadelphous"), or more often into a set of nine united

stamens that reside in the keel, plus a separate stamen that stands above the nine and just below the banner itself. The latter state is termed "diadelphous." At least two of the more primitive tribes (Sophoreae and Podalyrieae) of the family Fabaceae, however, possess free stamens and separate keel petals, as do many species belonging to the family Caesalpiniaceae.

Pollen grains in the order are quite distinctive and have proven of value in defining many of the tribal groupings in the several families. The fruiting structures within the order, while uniformly derived from a single carpel (or simple ovary), are variable in size, shape, and texture, ranging from the herbaceous coiled, hispid (rough or bristly) fruits, characteristic of bur clover (*Medicago hispida*) to the elongate (two to three feet long), woody pods of the genera *Cassia* and *Caesalpinia*.

Physiological features. Species belonging to the order Fabales are perhaps best known agronomically for their capacity to "fix" atmospheric nitrogen; *i.e.*, to convert it into a form that plants can utilize, usually the nitrate form. This is accomplished by symbiotic fixation, in which root nodules (swellings) are formed on the plant in reaction to infections by soil bacteria belonging to the genus *Rhizobium*. Root nodulation, while occurring in all three families, presumably does not occur in all species, the phenomenon being more common in the family Fabaceae and relatively less so in the families Mimosaceae and Caesalpiniaceae.

Biochemical features. The Fabales order is noteworthy for the large range and variety of secondary compounds found in its member's leaves and fruiting parts, such as flavonoids, alkaloids, terpenoids, non-protein amino acids, and others. Some of these, for example the amino acid canavanine, may comprise up to 5 percent of the dry weight of seeds. The interesting chemical compound, rotenone, which is toxic to a number of organisms, is sufficiently abundant in the roots and stems of certain species belonging to the family Fabaceae that primitive peoples commonly used these plants to poison fish. More recently it has been shown that serious bone and neural diseases, afflicting both man (*e.g.*, lathyrism) and livestock may be caused by the ingestion of unusually large amounts of certain free amino acids. In sheep, ingestion of large quantities of the amino acid mimosine, found in *Leucaena glauca* and some other species of the Mimosaceae family, apparently causes the cessation of the growth of hair or wool, and in certain cases the fleece itself has been observed to shed. A wide variety of alkaloids are found in the order, most of them restricted to the family Fabaceae, however. Some alkaloids are found in sufficient concentration in range plants to be quite poisonous to livestock, especially in species belonging to the large genus *Astragalus*. Species of *Astragalus* are commonly referred to as "loco weeds" by cattlemen in North America because, following excessive consumption of these plants, cattle seem to become unmanageable and "go crazy" or "loco."

**Poisonous
plants**

In spite of the toxic nature of many of the species, most of the plants are highly palatable and are especially nutritious because of the high concentration of vitamins and proteins in their young growing parts (*e.g.*, in alfalfa) and in the storage components in seeds (*e.g.*, beans and peas). The American Indians very early appreciated this and, along with corn, adopted the common bean (*Phaseolus* species) as one of their staple foods.

Except for the soybean and peanut, species of the order are not noted for the oil content of their seeds; most seeds contain only about 10 percent oil content by weight. Indeed, the fat content of many of the legumes used for food by humans is only between 1 and 2 percent. In general, legume seeds are usually highest in nutritive content in carbohydrates, followed by protein and fat.

An interesting biochemical component of the legume seed is phytohemaglutinin, a large protein molecule that has proven specific in its capacity to agglutinate certain human blood types. Approximately 60 percent of the several thousand seeds belonging to this order tested to date contain the compound.

Phytohemaglutinin is particularly rich in the common bean (*Phaseolus* species) and has been extracted in a relatively pure state on a commercial scale from species belonging to this genus. In addition to its agglutination properties, the compound has been of interest because of its other biological effects. It is toxic to rats, it inactivates some human tumor cells, and has beneficial effects on aplastic anemia, the shortage of blood cells in man because of destruction of blood forming tissues.

Chromosomal features. Chromosomal data have been assembled for a wide range of species in the order, including representatives from all three families and most of the tribes and subtribes. The chromosomes for any given genus are usually quite uniform, in both number and morphology (form); most of the genera possess a single base number. The incidence of polyploidy (multiples of the basic chromosome number), as contrasted with most plant families, is also relatively low. The family Mimosaceae, in general, has small chromosomes (one to three microns, or about 1- to 3/25,000 inch in length), and most of the species possess haploid (*i.e.*, the base number, one-half the normal number of chromosomes in a typical body cell) numbers of 13 or 14. The family Caesalpiniaceae is quite variable as to chromosome size and structure, possessing genera with base numbers of seven through 12—with the exception of nine; species with this haploid number are strangely absent. The Fabaceae is the most variable family, chromosomally. Woody tropical groups usually have relatively small chromosomes with haploid numbers of 10 and 11; the more temperate, herbaceous derivatives (for example, the genera *Vicia*, *Lathyrus*, and *Lotus*), have mostly larger chromosomes at lower haploid levels such as six, seven, or eight. Although this purview is based upon only about 20 percent of the species in the family, surveys among genera are broad enough to suggest that additional sampling will not change the picture much.

Chromosome size and number

EVOLUTION

Fossil record. There are abundant fossils of the Fabales order dating back to the Early Tertiary Period (Eocene Epoch, beginning about 54,000,000 years ago), most of which are similar to present-day, woody genera such as *Gleditsia* (Caesalpiniaceae), *Prosopis* (Mimosaceae), and *Robinia* (Fabaceae). Thus, the order was presumably well developed on the several continents even earlier, probably in Cretaceous time (beginning 136,000,000 years ago). By then, the order's three families had already developed in essentially the same form as those represented today by living genera. Fossil materials do not exist that serve to link the order to other orders, consequently most phyletic treatments of the group are based almost entirely on comparative morphological and distributional data among living species.

Phylogeny. Most workers consider the Fabales order to be related to the order Rosales. The two groups are similar in possessing mostly alternate leaves with stipules, perigynous flowers (*i.e.*, flowers with a partly enclosed ovary) and fruits derived from one or more separate carpels (in the Rosales the latter often fuse at maturity, as in the apple). Nearly all workers also agree that the order has its origin in the tropical regions from woody ancestors, the herbaceous species being structurally reduced, but more highly evolved types, which arose independently in several phyletic lines, presumably in adapting to the more vigorous climatic conditions that developed in the temperate regions during Tertiary time. Within the order most workers reckon the family Caesalpiniaceae to be an ancestral group that gave rise to the more tropical and subtropical family Mimosaceae, on the one hand, and to the more temperate Fabaceae, on the other. The Mimosaceae and Fabaceae, while quite distinct, are inextricably linked through several genera belonging to the Caesalpiniaceae, such as *Swartzia*, *Amphimas*, and *Mora*.

CLASSIFICATION

Distinguishing taxonomic features. The Fabales order has been treated classically as consisting of but a single family (traditionally named Leguminosae) of the large order Rosales. As such, the family was subdivided into four subfamilies, Mimosoideae, Caesalpinioideae, Papilionoideae (sometimes called Faboideae), and Kramerioideae. More recently the trend has been to remove the latter subfamily, consisting of but a single genus (*Krameria*), to the order Polygalales; the three remaining subfamilies are then treated at the familial level as members of the order Fabales. So constructed, the order can be distinguished from the closely related order Rosales by its (usually) solitary carpel, compound leaves, often more numerous, united stamens, and above all by its fruit.

Classical treatment of taxonomic position

Annotated classification. There is no single character that serves to distinguish between the orders Fabales and Rosales, or among the families of the Rosales; but in combination, morphological characters can be found that readily distinguish both the order Fabales and its three families. Nearly all present-day workers accept the validity of the natural groupings indicated below, although many would recognize a larger number of subfamilies and tribes within the families themselves.

ORDER FABALES

Herbs, shrubs, trees, or vines; leaves mostly alternate, compound, or simple by suppression of leaflets, stipulate, or infrequently without stipules; flowers bisexual, actinomorphic (radially symmetrical) or zygomorphic (bilaterally symmetrical), perianth (sepals and petals) in two series, the calyx gamosepalous (with fused sepals) and 5-lobed, the corolla typically of 5 petals (rarely absent or reduced to a single petal) distinct or the 2 anterior ones basally fused; stamens mostly 10 (sometimes numerous in Mimosaceae), distinct, monadelphous (stamen-filaments fused), or diadelphous (stamens in 2 bundles of 9 plus 1); the anthers 2-celled, dehiscing (splitting open) by longitudinal slits or infrequently by pores; pistil 1; the ovary superior, 1-loculed, 1-carpelled, the placentation parietal (ovule attachment is to the ovary walls) or seemingly marginal along ventral suture; the ovules 2 to many in 2 alternating rows on a single placenta, amphitropous (half inverted and straight), anatropous (inverted and straight), or infrequently campylotropus (curved, bringing the apex and base nearly together), pendulous or ascending; fruit usually a legume, samara, or loment, sometimes a follicle, or indehiscent or tardily so, seed with a usually leathery testa (covering), funiculus (stalk) sometimes produced into a more or less fleshy aril (appendage) or callosity, the endosperm (starchy nutrient tissue in the seed for the developing embryo) none or very scant. Three families, about 800 genera, and perhaps 20,000 species. The order is cosmopolitan in distribution with the family Fabaceae being relatively more abundant in the temperate regions and the Mimosaceae and Caesalpiniaceae being more tropical.

Family Mimosaceae

Trees, shrubs, or rarely perennial herbs; leaves twice-pinnate (compound by branching from a central axis comb-fashion, in this case twice-compound) or rarely once-pinnate (reduced to a phyllode [flattened leafstalk] and appearing simple in certain species of *Acacia*), stipulate, the stipules often persisting as well-developed, paired thorns; flowers small, mostly perigynous but often appearing hypogynous (*i.e.*, with sepals and petals arising at the base of the ovary), bisexual (rarely male only or neuter), actinomorphic and valvate (edges of petals not overlapping) in bud (somewhat irregular and overlapped in tribes Mimozyantherae and Parkieae), usually sessile (without a stalk) in short spikes or globose heads, rarely in racemes (flower clusters having a central axis with flowers on short lateral stalks, maturing from the bottom upward) or in umbels (flower clusters with individual flowers on stalks radiating from a common point, umbrella fashion); sepals and petals 4 or 5; stamens few to numerous, monadelphous or attached to the floral tube and appearing free; anthers small, versatile (attached near their middles, turning freely), sometimes with a glandular body at the apex; ovary single (except in *Affonsea* and *Archidendron*, which have 2 to 6 free carpels), with slender style (upper part of the ovary), small terminal stigma (pollen-receiving surface at the top of the style) and numerous ovules; fruits dehiscent to indehiscent, the seeds ovate to orbicular, compressed, usually quite indurate (hard); aril rarely present; endosperm very thin or absent; cotyledons (seed-leaves) flat, the radicles (root end of the embryo) straight. A largely pantropical group consisting of about 3,000 species in 60 genera dispersed among 5 or 6 tribes. Two of the largest genera, *Acacia* (900 species) and *Mimosa* (600 species) are widely distributed in the drier subtropical regions, especially savanna and desert habitats of both the old and new worlds.

Family Caesalpiniaceae

Trees, shrubs, or rarely herbs; leaves once- or twice-pinnate, rarely simple; stipules present, but often small or soon deciduous (falling), only rarely transformed into thorns; flowers zygomorphic or rarely actinomorphic, perigynous, usually 5-merous (with basic parts in fives or multiples thereof), bisexual and showy; inflorescence (flower cluster) racemose or paniculate (much-branched); petals 4 or 5, or by fusion or reduction fewer, imbricate or (very rarely) valvate in bud; stamens 10 or fewer (rarely numerous), free to variously connate (fused); anthers of various shapes, dehiscing by slits or apical pores; ovary superior, 1-carpellate; fruit a pod, drupe, or samara; seeds often large, arillate or with endosperm; cotyledons fleshy or foliaceous (thin and leaflike), the radicle straight or only slightly oblique, never folded. Distribution largely pantropical. Forms highly variable, the group composed of approximately 3,000 species in 160 genera. The family has been classically treated as consisting of 7 tribes but some recent workers would perhaps double this number and treat these as belonging to two subfamilies, Caesalpinioideae and Brachystegioideae. *Cassia*, with 600 or more species, is the largest genus in the family, being especially abundant in the New World.

Family Fabaceae

Trees, shrubs, vines, or annual herbs; leaves once-pinnate and very often reduced to a trifoliolate (with 3 leaflets) or palmate (compound, the leaflets radiating from a common point) condition, rarely simple (single leaves) or reduced to scales, especially in the Australian tribe Podalyrieae; stipules mostly herbaceous, often adnate (joined) to the petiole (leafstalk); flowers zygomorphic (rarely actinomorphic or nearly so), perigynous; sepals and petals 5 or, by reduction, fewer; petals highly modified into banner, wings, and keel, the latter usually housing the reproductive structures; stamens 10 (rarely fewer), monadelphous, diadelphous, or rarely free; anthers uniform or dimorphic (of 2 forms), basifixed (attached near the base) or dorsifixed (attached along one side), often variable in the same androecium (male complex), opening by slits; ovary superior, of 1 carpel, 1-loculate (chambered), sometimes by intrusion of the marginal sutures appearing 2-loculate; fruit various, but typically a dehiscent pod or legume in the more temperate genera; tropical and subtropical groups often possessing indehiscent pods, samaras, drupes, loments, and burrs; seeds without endosperm or seemingly so; cotyledons small, the radicle inflexed (very rarely straight). Distribution worldwide, the group composed of approximately 500 genera and 15,000 species. Most of the woody species belong to tropical or subtropical genera while the herbaceous species are found primarily in temperate regions. The family has been treated classically, largely on grounds of convenience, as composed of 11 or 12 tribes but some recent workers have increased this to 50 or more. The largest genus is *Astragalus* with 1,500 or more species, ranking as one of the largest genera of flowering plants.

Critical appraisal. Nearly all workers recognize the order as an exceedingly natural one and most would relate it to the order Rosales. Other orders recognized as being phyletically close to the Fabales are the Saxifragales and Cunoniales. Some authorities, however, prefer to treat the three families of Fabales as subfamilies belonging to but a single family within the much larger order Rosales. In such a treatment the Saxifragales and Cunoniales orders are usually accorded familial status. There would be little opposition to the recognition of the Mimosaceae and Fabaceae as distinct families if it were not for the transitional nature of many genera belonging to the Caesalpiniaceae—*i.e.*, they have characteristics similar to both families. Because of the transitional genera, however, some workers believe the Caesalpiniaceae to be ancestral to these two groups. Most of the transitional genera, however, seem to link the Caesalpiniaceae to the Fabaceae, with the Mimosaceae standing somewhat more remote. It has been suggested that the Fabaceae, in part, has ancestors in more than one evolutionary line (*i.e.*, the family is polyphyletic) and that at least some of the tribes have arisen from different phyletic lines within the Caesalpiniaceae. Clearly there is much need of detailed morphological, cytological, and chemical study of the family Caesalpiniaceae for it is poorly known, and is represented in museums by relatively few collections and is generally neglected by cytologists and plant chemists. With more intensive study, especially in the area of chemosystematics (taxonomy systems based

(margin note) Need for further study

on chemical factors), it is likely that some of the tribes of the Caesalpiniaceae will be elevated to subfamily or family rank. In addition, considerable resorting of the genera among tribes of the Fabaceae seems likely, since at least some of them are believed to be classified on one or more technical characters of the fruit, which may or may not group together those genera with a common phyletic origin.

BIBLIOGRAPHY. E.G. HALLSWORTH (ed.), *Nutrition of the Legumes* (1958), a broad treatment of the soil factors affecting the growth of legumes including the rhizobial (bacteria in root nodules) component; J. HUTCHINSON, *The Genera of Flowering Plants* (1964), the most recent intensive taxonomic account of the families and tribes, with keys and descriptions provided for all genera recognized at the time, an indispensable reference; *Evolution and Phylogeny of Flowering Plants* (1969), a highly readable, authoritative account of the phyletic position of the order Fabales within the flowering plants, including an account of the wide morphological variation (nicely illustrated) found in the order; P. TAUBERT, "Leguminosae," in A. ENGLER and K. PRANTL (eds.), *Die Natürlichen Pflanzenfamilien* (1894), a classical text for the order, with keys and descriptions (in German) to the generic level, copiously documented as to the earlier work on the group and references to these; L. CAPITAINE, *Étude analytique et phytogéographique du groupe des légumieuses* (1912), a treatment of the order in which an attempt is made to show the phytogeographic relationships among the 30 or more tribes; R.O. WHYTE, G. NILSSON-LEISSNER, and H.C. TRUMBLE, *Legumes in Agriculture* (1953), an excellent account of the agronomic value of legumes and their role in agriculture with consideration of the regional value of both local and world-wide species in the order; J.B. HARBORNE, D. BOULTER, and B.L. TURNER (eds.), *Chemotaxonomy of the Leguminosae* (1971), a broad treatment of the chemical components (alkaloids, flavonoids, terpenoids, amino acids, proteins, enzymes, etc.) found in the three families, especially as they relate to the systematic treatment of taxa comprising the order.

(B.L.T.)

Fable, Parable, and Allegory

Fables, parables, and allegories are forms of imaginative literature or spoken utterance constructed in such a way that their readers or listeners are encouraged to look for meanings hidden beneath the literal surface of the fiction. A story is told or perhaps enacted whose details—when interpreted—are found to correspond to the details of some other system of relations (its hidden, allegorical sense). The poet, for example, may describe the ascent of a hill in such a way that each physical step corresponds to a new stage in the soul's progress toward a higher level of existence.

Many forms of literature elicit this kind of searching interpretation, and the generic term for the cluster is allegory; under it may be grouped fables, parables, and other symbolic shapings. Allegory may involve either a creative or an interpretive process: either the act of building up the allegorical structure and giving "body" to the surface narrative or the act of breaking down this structure to see what themes or ideas run parallel to it.

This article discusses the nature and objectives of fable parable, and allegory, goes on to cover allegory and cosmology, and the historical development of this imaginative literature in western culture, and, finally, discusses allegorical literature in the East.

NATURE AND OBJECTIVES OF FABLE, PARABLE, AND ALLEGORY

Allegory and myth. The fate of allegory, in all its many variations, is tied to the development of myth and mythology. Every culture embodies its basic assumptions in stories whose mythic structures reflect the society's prevailing attitudes toward life. If the attitudes are disengaged from the structure, then the allegorical meaning implicit in the structure is revealed. The systematic discipline of interpreting the real meaning of a text (called the hermeneutic process) plays a major role in the teaching and defense of sacred wisdom, since religions have traditionally preserved and handed down the old beliefs by telling exemplary stories; these sometimes appear to conflict with a system of morality that has in the meantime developed, and so their "correct" meaning can only be something other than the literal narration of events. Every culture puts pressure on its authors to assert its central beliefs, which are often reflected in literature without the author's necessarily being aware that he is an allegorist. Equally, determined critics may sometimes find allegorical meaning in texts with less than total justification—instances might include the Hebraic–Christian mystical interpretation of the Old Testament's Song of Solomon, an erotic marriage poem, or the frequent allegorizing of classical and modern literature in the light of Freud's psychoanalytic discoveries. Some awareness of the author's intention seems necessary in order to curb unduly fanciful commentary.

The allegorical mode. The range of allegorical literature is so wide that to consider allegory as a fixed literary genre is less useful than to regard it as a dimension, or mode, of controlled indirectness and double meaning (which, in fact, all literature possesses to some degree). Critics usually reserve the term allegory itself for works of considerable length, complexity, or unique shape. Thus, the following varied works might be called allegories: the biblical parable of the sower; *Everyman*; the medieval morality play; *The Pilgrim's Progress*, by John Bunyan; Jonathan Swift's *Gulliver's Travels; The Scarlet Letter*, by Nathaniel Hawthorne; William Wordsworth's "Ode: Intimations of Immortality"; Nikolay Gogol's *Dead Souls; The Picture of Dorian Gray*, by Oscar Wilde; and the plays *Six Characters in Search of an Author*, by Luigi Pirandello; *Waiting for Godot*, by Samuel Beckett; and *Who's Afraid of Virginia Woolf?*, by Edward Albee. No one genre can take in such modal range.

Fable. Fable and parable are short, simple forms of naïve allegory. The fable is usually a tale about animals who are personified and behave as though they were humans. The device of personification is also extended to trees, winds, streams, stones, and other natural objects. The earliest of these tales also included humans and gods as characters, but fable tends to concentrate on animating the inanimate. A feature that isolates fable from the ordinary folktale, which it resembles, is that a moral—a rule of behaviour—is woven into the story.

Parable. Like fable, the parable also tells a simple story. But, whereas fables tend to personify animal characters—often giving the same impression as does an animated cartoon—the typical parable uses human agents. Parables generally show less interest in the storytelling and more in the analogy they draw between a particular instance of human behaviour (the true neighbourly kindness shown by the good Samaritan in the Bible story, for example) and human behaviour at large. Parable and fable have their roots in preliterate oral cultures, and both are means of handing down traditional folk wisdom. Their styles differ, however. Fables tend toward detailed, sharply observed social realism (which eventually leads to satire), while the simpler narrative surface of parables gives them a mysterious tone and makes them especially useful for teaching spiritual values.

Derivation of the terms. The original meanings of these critical terms themselves suggest the direction of their development. Fable (from the Latin *fabula*, "a telling") puts the emphasis on narrative (and in the medieval and Renaissance periods was often used when speaking of "the plot" of a narrative). Parable (from Greek *parabolē*, a "setting beside") suggests a juxtaposition that compares and contrasts this story with that idea. Allegory (from Greek *allos* and *agoreuein*, an "other-speaking") suggests a more expanded use of deceptive and oblique language. (In early Greek, though, the term allegory itself was not used. Instead, the idea of a hidden, underlying meaning is indicated by the word *hyponoia*—literally, "underthought"—and this term is used of the allegorical interpretation of the Greek poet Homer.)

Diverse objectives. *Fable.* Fables teach a general principle of conduct by presenting a specific example of behaviour. Thus, to define the moral that "People who rush into things without using judgment run into strange and unexpected dangers," Aesop—the traditional "father" of the fable form—told the following story:

There was a dog who was fond of eating eggs. Mistaking a shell-fish for an egg one day, he opened his mouth wide and swallowed it down in one gulp. The weight of it in his stomach caused him intense pain. "Serve me right," he said, "for thinking that anything round must be an egg."

By a slight change of emphasis, the fabulist could have been able to draw a moral about the dangerous effects of gluttony.

Because the moral is embodied in the plot of the fable, an explicit statement of the moral need not be given, though it usually is. Many of these moral tag lines have taken on the status of proverb because they so clearly express commonly held social attitudes.

The Aesopian fables emphasize the social interactions of human beings, and the morals they draw tend to embody advice on the best way to deal with the competitive realities of life. With some irony, fables view the world in terms of its power structures. One of the shortest Aesopian fables says: "A vixen sneered at a lioness because she never bore more than one cub. 'Only one,' she replied, 'but a lion.'" Foxes and wolves, which the poet Samuel Taylor Coleridge called "Everyman's metaphor" for cunning and cruelty, appear often as characters in fables chiefly because, in the human world, such predatory cunning and cruelty are able to get around restraints of justice and authority. The mere fact that fables unmask the "beast in me," as James Thurber, the 20th-century American humorist and fabulist, put it, suggests their satirical force. Subversive topical satire in tsarist and Soviet Russia is often called "Aesopism"; all comic strips that project a message (such as the Charles Schulz creation "Peanuts" and Walt Kelly's "Pogo") have affinities with Aesop's method.

Parable. Parables do not analyze social systems so much as they remind the listener of his beliefs. The moral and spiritual stress of the form falls upon memory rather than on the critical faculty. The audience hearing the parable is assumed to share a communal truth but perhaps to have set it aside or forgotten it. The rhetorical appeal of a parable is directed primarily toward an elite, in that a final core of its truth is known only to an inner circle, however simple its narrative may appear on the surface (a number of the parables that Christ used for teaching, for example, conveyed figuratively the meaning of the elusive concept Kingdom of Heaven).

Allegory. Allegory, as the basic process of arousing in the reader or listener a response to levels of meaning, provides writers with the structure of fables, parables, and other related forms. By awakening the impulse to question appearances and by bringing order to mythological interpretation, allegory imparts cultural values. A measure of allegory is present in literature whenever it emphasizes thematic content, ideas rather than events. Generally, the allegorical mode flourishes under authoritarian conditions. Thus it found sustenance during the age of medieval Christendom, when Christian dogma sought universal sway over the mind of Western man. As such, allegory was a means of freedom under conditions of strong restraint. In general, realism, mimetic playfulness, and the resistance to authority tend to counteract the allegorical process, by loosening its stratified forms. This unbinding of symbolic hierarchies has forced allegory to seek new structures in the modern period. Nevertheless, through allegorical understanding, the great myths continue to be reread and reinterpreted, as the human significance of the new interpretations is passed down from one generation to the next. The abiding impression left by the allegorical mode is one of indirect, ambiguous, even enigmatic symbolism, which inevitably calls for interpretation.

Diversity of forms. Since an allegorical purpose can inform works of literature in a wide range of genres, it is not surprising to find that the largest allegories are epic in scope. A quest forms the narrative thread of both the Greek epic *Odyssey* and the Latin *Aeneid*, and it is an allegory of the quest for heroic perfection; thus, allegory is aligned with the epic form. Romances, both prose and verse, are inevitably allegorical, although their forms vary in detail with the prevailing cultural ideals of the

Personification of animals

The moral objective of fables

age. By comparison, the forms of fable and parable are relatively stable—yet even they may play down the moral idea or the mysterious element and emphasize instead the narrative interest, which then results in an elaboration of the form. (Such an elaboration may be seen in a given tale, as told by successive fabulists, such as a fable of the town mouse and the country mouse; with each retelling, the story is absorbed into a new matrix of interpretation.)

Shifts from naïve to sophisticated intent are accompanied by shifts in form. The early authors of fable, following Aesop, wrote in verse; but in the 10th century there appeared collected fables, entitled *Romulus*, written in prose (and books such as this brought down into the medieval and modern era a rich tradition of prose fables). This collection in turn was converted back into elegiac verse. Later masters of fable wrote in verse, but modern favourites—such as Joel Chandler Harris, author of "Uncle Remus" stories, Beatrix Potter, creator of Peter Rabbit, or James Thurber in *Fables for Our Time*—employ their own distinctive prose. Again, while for parables prose narrative may be the norm, they have also been told in verse (as in the emblematic poetry of the 17th-century English Metaphysical poets such as George Herbert, Francis Quarles, and Henry Vaughan).

Forms that mix prose and poetry Loosening the allegorical forms further, some authors have combined prose with verse. Boethius' *Consolation of Philosophy* (c. AD 524) and Dante's *The New Life* (c. 1293) interrupt the prose discourse with short poems. Verse and prose then interact to give a new thematic perspective. A related mixing of elements appears in Menippean satire (those writings deriving from the 3rd-century-BC Cynic philosopher Menippus of Gadara), as exemplified in Swift's *Tale of a Tub*. There a relatively simple allegory of Reformation history (the *Tale* proper) is interrupted by a series of digressions that comment allegorically on the story into which they break.

Even the lyric poem can be adapted to yield allegorical themes and was made to do so, for example, in the visionary and rhapsodic odes written during the high Romantic period after the late 18th century throughout Europe.

The lesson seems to be that every literary genre is adaptable to the allegorical search for multiplicity of meaning.

Diversity of media. In the broadest sense, allegorical procedures are linguistic. Allegory is a manipulation of the language of symbols. Verbally, this mode underwent a major shift in medium along with the shift from oral to written literature: allegories that had initially been delivered in oral form (Christ's parables, for example) were written down by scribes and then transcribed by subsequent generations. Much more remarkable transformations, however, take place when the verbal medium is replaced by nonverbal or partially verbal media.

The drama is the chief of such replacements. The enactment of myth in the beginning had close ties with religious ritual, and in the drama of classical Greece both comedy and tragedy, by preserving ritual forms, lean toward allegory. Old Comedy, as represented by the majority of plays by Aristophanes, contains a curious blending of elements—allusions to men of the day, stories suggesting ideas other than the obvious literal sense, religious ceremony, parodies of the graver mysteries, personified abstractions, and stock types of character. Aeschylus' *Prometheus Bound* uses allegory for tragic ends, while Euripides' tragedies make a continuous interpretive commentary on the hidden meaning of the basic myths. Allegory is simplified in Roman drama, submitting heroic deeds to the control of the fickle, often malignant goddess Fortuna. Christian symbolism is responsible for the structure of the medieval morality plays, in which human dilemmas are presented through the conflicts of personified abstractions such as the "Virtues" and their "Vice" opponents. The morality play The allegory in Renaissance drama is often more atmospheric than structural—though even Shakespeare writes allegorical romances, such as *Cymbeline*, *Pericles*, and *The Winter's Tale* (and allowed his tragedy of *Coriolanus* to grow out of the "fable of the belly,"

which embodies a commonplace of Renaissance political wisdom and is recounted by one of the characters in the play). In 1598 Ben Jonson introduced the comedy of humours, which was dependent on the biological theory that the humours of the body (blood, phlegm, black bile, yellow bile) affect personality: in Jonson's play *Epicoene, or The Silent Woman* (1609), the character Morose is possessed by the demon of ill humour. Comic allegory of this kind evolved into the Restoration comedy of manners, and through that channel entered modern drama, with Wilde, Shaw, and Pirandello. Ibsen, the master of realistic drama, himself used a free-style allegory in *Peer Gynt*, while the surrealism of modern dramatists such as Ionesco, Genet, and Beckett serves to reinforce the real meaning of their plays.

The degree to which the cinema has been allegorical in its methods has never been surveyed in detail. Any such survey would certainly reveal that a number of basic techniques in film montage builds up multiple layers of meaning. (Animated cartoons, too, continue the tradition of Aesopian fable.)

From time immemorial men have carved religious monuments and have drawn and painted sacred icons. Triumphal arches and chariots have symbolized glory and victory. Religious art makes wide use of allegory, both in its subject matter and in its imagery (such as the cross, the fish, the lamb). Even in poetry there can be an interaction of visual and verbal levels, sometimes achieved by patterning the stanza form. George Herbert's "Easter Wings," for instance, has two stanzas set out by the typographer to resemble the shape of a dove's wings. Such devices belong to the Renaissance tradition of the "emblem," which combines a motto with a simple symbolic picture (often a woodcut or engraving) and a concise explanation of the picture motto.

While allegory thrives on the visual, it has also been well able to embrace the empty form of pure mathematics. Number symbolism is very old: early Christian systems of cosmology were often based on the number three, referring to the doctrine of the Trinity (and in fact recalling earlier Hebraic and even Hellenic numerology). Musical symbolism has been discovered in the compositions of the 18th-century Baroque composers such as Johann Sebastian Bach. The most evanescent form of allegory, musical imagery and patterns, is also the closest to pure religious vision, since it merges the physical aspects of harmony (based on number) with the sublime and metaphysical effect on its hearers. The final extension of media occurs in the combination of spectacle, drama, dance, and music that is achieved by grand opera, which is at its most allegorical in the total artwork of Richard Wagner in the second half of the 19th century. His *Ring* cycle of operas is a complete mythography and allegory, with words and music making two levels of meaning and the whole unified by a type of musical emblem, which Wagner called the leitmotif. The use of musical symbolism

ALLEGORY AND COSMOLOGY

The allegorical mode has been of major importance in representing the cosmos: the earliest Greek philosophers, for example, speculated on the nature of the universe in allegorical terms; in the Old Testament's oblique interpretation of the universe, too, the world is seen as a symbolic system. The symbolic stories that explain the cosmos are ritualized to ensure that they encode a message. Held together by a system of magical causality, events in allegories are often surrounded by an occult atmosphere of charms, spells, talismans, genies, and magic rites. Science becomes science fiction or a fantastic setting blurs reality so that objects and events become metamorphically unstable. Allegorical fictions are often psychological dramas whose scene is the mind; then their protagonists are personified mental drives. Symbolic climate is most prominent in romance, whose heroic quests project an aura of erotic mysticism, perfect courtesy, and moral fervour that creates a sublime heightening of tone and a picturesque sense of good order.

The cosmic and demonic character of allegorical thinking is most fully reflected in the period of its greatest vogue, the High Middle Ages. During this period poets and priests alike were able to read with increasingly elaborate allegorical technique until their methods perhaps overgrew themselves. A belief had been inherited in the "great chain of being," the Platonic principle of cosmic unity and fullness, according to which the lowest forms of being were linked with the highest in an ascending order. On the basis of this ladderlike conception were built systems of rising transcendency, starting from a material basis and rising to a spiritual pinnacle. The early Church Fathers sometimes used a threefold method of interpreting texts, encompassing literal, moral, and spiritual meanings. This was refined and commonly believed to have achieved its final form in the medieval allegorist's

The "fourfold theory of interpretation"

"fourfold theory of interpretation." This method also began every reading with a search for the literal sense of the passage. It moved up to a level of ideal interpretation in general, which was the allegorical level proper. (This was an affirmation that the true Christian believer was right to go beyond literal truth.) Still higher above the literal and the allegorical levels, the reader came to the tropological level, which told him where his moral duty lay. Finally, since Christian thought was apocalyptic and visionary, the fourfold method reached its apogee at the anagogic level, at which the reader was led to meditate on the final cosmic destiny of all Christians and of himself as a Christian hoping for eternal salvation.

While modern scholars have shown that such thinking played its part in the poetry of the Middle Ages and while the Italian poet Dante himself discussed the theological relations between his poems and such a method of exegesis, the main arena for the extreme elaboration of this allegory was in the discussion and the teaching of sacred Scriptures. As such, the fourfold method is of highest import, and it should be observed that it did not need to be applied in a rigid four-stage way. It could be reduced, and commonly was reduced, to a two-stage method of interpretation. Then the reader sought simply a literal and a spiritual meaning. But it could also be expanded. The passion for numerology, combined with the inner drive of allegory toward infinite extension, led to a proliferation of levels. If four levels were good, then five or eight or nine might be better.

HISTORICAL DEVELOPMENT IN WESTERN CULTURE

Development of fable. The origins of fable are lost in the mists of time. Fables appear independently in ancient Indian and Mediterranean cultures. The Western tradition begins effectively with Aesop (6th century BC), of whom little or nothing is known for certain; but before him the Greek poet Hesiod (8th century BC) recounts the fable of the hawk and the nightingale, while fragments of similar tales survive in Archilochus, the 7th-century-BC warrior-poet. Within 100 years of the first Aesopian inventions the name of Aesop was firmly identified with the genre, as if he, not a collective folk, were its originator. Like the Greek philosopher Socrates, Aesop was reputed to have been ugly but wise. Legend connected him with the island of Samos; the historian Herodotus believed him to have been a slave.

Modern editions list approximately 200 "Aesop" fables, but there is no way of knowing who invented which tales or what their original occasions might have been. Aesop had already receded into legend when Demetrius of Phaleron, a rhetorician, compiled an edition of Aesop's fables in the 4th century BC. The poetic resources of the form developed slowly. A versified Latin collection made by Phaedrus, a freed slave in the house of the Roman emperor Augustus, included fables invented by the poet, along with the traditional favourites, which he retold with many elaborations and considerable grace. (Phaedrus may also have been the first to write topically allusive fables, satirizing Roman politics.) A similar extension of range marks the work of the Hellenized Roman Babrius, writing in the 2nd century AD. Among the classical authors who advanced upon Aesopian formulas may be named the Roman poet Horace, the Greek biographer Plutarch, and the great satirist Lucian of Samosata.

Beast epic. In the Middle Ages, along with every other type of allegory, fable flourished. Toward the end of the 12th century, Marie de France made a collection of over 100 tales, mingling beast fables with stories of Greek and Roman worthies. In another compilation, Christine de Pisan's Othéa manuscript illuminations provide keys to the interpretation of the stories and support the appended moral tag line. Expanded, the form of the fable could grow into what is called the beast epic, a lengthy, episodic animal story, replete with hero, villain, victim, and endless epic endeavour. (One motive for thus enlarging upon fable was the desire to parody epic grandeur: the beast epic mocks its own genre.) Most famous of these works is a 12th-century collection of related satirical tales called *Roman de Renart*, whose hero is a fox, symbolizing cunning man. The *Roman* includes the story of the fox and Chantecler (Chanticleer), a cock, a tale

Tales of the cunning fox

soon afterward told in German, Dutch, and English versions (in *The Canterbury Tales*, Geoffrey Chaucer took it as the basis for his "Nun's Priest's Tale"). Soon the *Roman* had achieved universal favour throughout Europe. The Renaissance poet Edmund Spenser also made use of this kind of material; in his "Mother Hubberd's Tale," published in 1591, a fox and an ape go off to visit the court, only to discover that life is no better there than in the provinces. More sage and serious, John Dryden's poem of *The Hind and Panther* (1687) revived the beast epic as a framework for theological debate. Bernard de Mandeville's *Fable of the Bees* (first published 1705 as *The Grumbling Hive, or Knaves Turn'd Honest*) illustrated the rapacious nature of humans in society through the age-old metaphor of the kingdom of the bees. In modern times, children's literature has made use of animal fable but often trivialized it. But the form has been taken seriously, as, for example, by the political satirist George Orwell, who, in his novel *Animal Farm* (1945), used it to attack Stalinist Communism.

Influence of Jean de La Fontaine. The fable has normally been of limited length, however, and the form reached its zenith in 17th-century France, at the court of Louis XIV, especially in the work of Jean de La Fontaine. He published his *Fables* in two segments: the first, his initial volume of 1668, and the second, an accretion of "Books" of fables appearing over the next 25 years. The 1668 *Fables* follow the Aesopian pattern, but the later ones branch out to satirize the court, the bureaucrats attending it, the church, the rising bourgeoisie—indeed the whole human scene. La Fontaine's great theme was the folly of human vanity. He was a skeptic, not unkind but full of the sense of human frailty and ambition. His satiric themes permitted him an enlargement of poetic diction; he could be eloquent in mocking eloquence or in contrast use a severely simple style. (His range of tone and style has been admirably reflected in a version of his works made by a 20th-century American poet, Marianne Moore.) La Fontaine's example gave new impetus to the genre throughout Europe, and during the Romantic period a vogue for Aesopian fable spread to Russia, where its great practitioner was Ivan Andreyevich Krylov. The 19th century saw the rise of literature written specifically for children, in whom fable found a new audience. Among the most celebrated authors who wrote for them are Lewis Carroll, Charles Kingsley, Rudyard Kipling, Kenneth Grahame, Hilaire Belloc, and Beatrix Potter. There is no clear division between such authors and the "adult" fabulist, such as Hans Christian Andersen, Lewis Carroll, Oscar Wilde, Saint-Exupéry, or J.R.R. Tolkien. In the 20th century there are the outstanding *Fables for Our Time*, written by James Thurber and apparently directed toward an adult audience (although a sardonic parent might well read the *Fables* to his children).

Development of parable. In the West, the conventions of parable were largely established by the teachings of Christ. The New Testament records a sufficient number of his parables, with their occasions, to show that to some extent his disciples were chosen as his initiates and followers because they "had ears to hear" the true meaning of his parables. (It has already been noted that the parable can be fully understood only by an elite, made up of those who can decipher its inner core of truth.) Despite a bias toward simplicity and away from rhetorical elaboration, the parable loses little in the way of allegorical richness: the speaker can exploit an enigmatic brevity that is akin to the style of presenting a complex riddle. Parable is thus an immensely useful preaching device: while theologians in the period of the early Christian Church were developing glosses on Christ's enigmatic stories, preachers were inventing their own to drive home straightforward lessons in good Christian conduct. For centuries, therefore, the model of parable that had been laid down by Christ flourished on Sundays in churches all over the Western world. Pious tales were collected in handbooks: the *Gesta Romanorum*, the *Alphabet of Thales*, the *Book of the Knight of La Tour Landry*, and many more. Infinitely varied in subject matter, these exemplary tales used a plain but lively style, presenting stories of magicians, necromancers, prophets, chivalrous knights and ladies, great emperors—a combination bound to appeal to congregations, if not to theologians. An important offshoot of the parable and exemplary tale was the saint's life. Here, too, massive compilations were possible; the most celebrated was *The Golden Legend* of the 15th century, which included approximately 200 stories of saintly virtue and martyrdom.

20th-century parables As long as preaching remained a major religious activity, the tradition of parable preserved its strong didactic strain. Its more paradoxical aspect gained renewed lustre in theological and literary spheres when the 19th-century Danish philosopher Søren Kierkegaard began to use parables in his treatises on Christian faith and action. In *Fear and Trembling* he retold the story of Abraham and Isaac; in *Repetition* he treated episodes in his own life in the manner of parable. Such usage led to strange new literary forms of discourse, and his writing influenced, among others, the German-Czech novelist Franz Kafka and the French "absurdist" philosopher, novelist, and playwright Albert Camus. Kafka's parables, full of doubt and anxiety, meditate on the infinite chasm between man and God and on the intermediate role played by the law. His vision, powerfully expressed in parables of novel length (*The Castle*, *The Trial*, *Amerika*), is one of the most enigmatic in modern literature.

Development of allegory. The early history of Western allegory is intricate and encompasses an interplay between the two prevailing world views—the Hellenic and the Hebraic–Christian—as theologians and philosophers attempted to extract a higher meaning from these two bodies of traditional myth.

In terms of allegory, the Greco-Roman and Hebraic–Christian cultures both have a common starting point: a creation myth. The Old Testament's book of Genesis roughly parallels the story of the creation as told by the Greek poet Hesiod in his *Theogony* (and the later Roman version of the same event given in Ovid's *Metamorphoses*). The two traditions thus start with an adequate source of cosmic imagery, and both envisage a universe full of mysterious signs and symbolic strata. But thereafter the two cultures diverge. This is most apparent in the way that the style of the body of poetry attributed to Homer—the ancient Greek "Bible"—differs from the Old Testament narrative. The Greek poet presented his heroes against an articulated narrative scene, a context full enough for the listener (and, later, the reader) to ignore secondary levels of significance. By contrast, the Jewish authors of the Old Testament generally emptied the narrative foreground, leaving the reader to fill the scenic vacuum with a deepening, thickening allegorical interpretation.

Old Testament. The Old Testament, including its prophetic books, has a core of historical record focussing on the trials of the tribes of Israel. In their own view an elect nation, the Israelites believe their history spells out a providential design. The prophets understand the earliest texts, Genesis and Exodus, in terms of this providential scheme. Hebraic texts are interpreted as typological: that is, they view serious myth as a theoretical history in which all events are types—portents, foreshadowing the

destiny of the chosen people. Christian exegesis (the critical interpretation of Scripture) inherits the same approach.

Typological allegory Typological allegory looks for hidden meaning in the lives of actual men who, as types or figures of later historical persons, serve a prophetic function by prefiguring those later persons. Adam, for example (regarded as a historical person), is thought to prefigure Christ in his human aspect, Joshua to prefigure the victorious militant Christ. This critical approach to Scripture is helped by the fact of monotheism, which makes it easier to detect the workings of a divine plan. The splendours of nature hymned in the Psalms provide a gloss upon the "glory of God." The Law (the Torah) structures the social aspect of sacred history and, as reformulated by Christ, provides the chief link between Old and New Testaments. Christ appeals to the authority of "the Law and the Prophets" but assumes the ultimate prophetic role himself, creating the New Law and the New Covenant—or Testament—with the same one God of old.

The Greeks. Hellenic tradition after Homer stands in sharp contrast to this concentration on the fulfilling of a divine plan. The analytic, essentially scientific histories of Herodotus and Thucydides precluded much confident belief in visionary providence. The Greeks rather believed history to be structured in cycles, as distinct from the more purposive linearity of Hebraic historicism.

Nevertheless, allegory did find a place in the Hellenic world. Its main arena was in philosophic speculation, centring on the interpretation of Homer. Some philosophers attacked and others defended the Homeric mythology. A pious defense argued that the stories—about the monstrous love affairs of the supreme god Zeus, quarrels of the other Olympian gods, scurrility of the heroes, and the like—implied something beyond their literal sense. The defense sometimes took a scientific, physical form; in this case, Homeric turmoil was seen as reflecting the conflict between the elements. Or Homer was moralized; the goddess Pallas Athene, for example, who in physical allegory stood for the ether, in moral allegory was taken to represent reflective wisdom because she was born out of the forehead of her father, Zeus. Moral and physical interpretation is often intermingled.

Plato, the Idealist philosopher, occupies a central position with regard to Greek allegory. His own myths imply that our world is a mere shadow of the ideal and eternal world of forms (the Platonic ideas), which has real, independent existence, and that the true philosopher must therefore be an allegorist in reverse. He must regard phenomena—things and events—as a text to be interpreted upward, giving them final value only insofar as they reveal, however obscurely, their ideal reality in the world of forms. Using this inverted allegorical mode, Plato attacked Homeric narrative, whose beauty beguiles men into looking away from the truly philosophic life. Plato went further. He attacked other fashionable philosophic allegorists because they did not lead up to the reality but limited speculation to the sphere of moral and physical necessity. Platonic allegory envisaged the system of the universe as an ascending ladder of forms, a "great chain of being," and was summed up in terms of myth in his *Timaeus*. Plato and Platonic thought became, through the influence of this and other texts on Plotinus (died 269/270) and through him on Porphyry (died *c.* 304), a pagan mainstay of later Christian allegory. Medieval translations of Dionysius the Areopagite (before 6th century AD) were equally influential descendants of Platonic vision.

Stoic allegory A second and equally influential Hellenic tradition of allegory was created by the Stoic philosophers, who held that the local gods of the Mediterranean peoples were signs of a divinely ordered natural destiny. Stoic allegory thus emphasized the role of fate, which, because all men were subject to it, could become a common bond between peoples of different nations. A later aspect of moral exegesis in the Stoic manner was the notion that myths of the gods really represent, in elevated form, the actions of great men. In the 2nd century BC, under Stoic influence, the Sicilian writer Euhemerus argued that theology had an earthly source. His allegory of history was the converse of Hebraic typology—which found the origin of the divine in the omnipotence of the One God—for Euhemerus found the origin of mythological gods in human kings and heroes, divinized by their peoples. His theories enjoyed at least an aesthetic revival during the Renaissance.

Blending of rival systems: the Middle Ages. At the time of the birth of Christ, ideological conditions within the Mediterranean world accelerated the mingling of Hellenic and Hebraic traditions. Philo Judaeus laid the groundwork; Clement of Alexandria and Origen followed him. The craft of allegorical syncretism—that is, making rival systems accommodate one another through the transformation of their disparate elements—was already a developed art by the time St. Paul and the author of the Gospel According to St. John wove the complex strands of the Hebraic–Christian synthesis. Over centuries of quarrelling, the timeless philosophy of the Greek allegorists was accommodated to the time-laden typology of the Hebrew prophets and their Christian successors and at length achieved a hybrid unity that permitted great allegories of Western Christendom to be written.

As a hybrid method, allegory could draw on two archetypal story lines: the war and the quest of Homer's *Iliad* and *Odyssey*, which was paralleled by the struggles and wanderings of the children of Israel. Throughout the Middle Ages the figure of the wandering Aeneas (who, in the second half of Virgil's Latin epic, *Aeneid*, fought bloody battles) was seen as a type in a system of hidden Christianity. Virgil's fourth *Eclogue*, a prophetic vision of the birth of a child who would usher in the "golden age," was read as a prophecy of the birth of Christ. Seen by many Christian commentators as the ideal allegorist, Virgil himself was hailed as a proto-Christian prophet. The blending of rival systems of allegory from widely assorted cultures became the rule for later allegory. Adapting the Latin writer Apuleius' fable of Cupid and Psyche, Edmund Spenser combined its elements with ancient Near Eastern lore, Egyptian wisdom, and dashes of Old Testament critical interpretation to convert the enclosed garden of the biblical Song of Solomon into the gardens of Adonis in *The Faerie Queene*, Book III. The pagan gods survived unharmed throughout the Middle Ages if wearing Christian costumes, because Christians were taught that pagan worthies could be read as figures of Christian rulers. The labours of Hercules, for instance, stood for the wanderings and trials of all Christian men; the Hellenic theme of heroic warfare took a Christianized form, available to allegory, when in the 4th century the poet and hymn writer Prudentius internalized war as the inner struggle of Christian man, suspended between virtue and vice. For complete triumph in explaining the significance of the world, Christianity needed one further element: a world-historical theory large enough to contain all other theories of meaning. This it found in the belief that God was the author of the world. His creation wrote the world. The world, read as a text, provided a platform for transforming the piecemeal, postclassical syncretism into some semblance of order. Firmly established in the West, Christianity, for all its strains of discord, slowly achieved a measure of coherence. St. Thomas Aquinas could write its *Summa*. Theocentric, authoritarian, spiritualist, and word oriented, the medieval model of allegory lent itself to the creation of the most wonderful of all allegorical poems, Dante's *Divine Comedy*, completed shortly before his death in 1321.

Before this could happen, however, the Christian world view had been subjected to an important pressure during the 12th century. It may be called the pressure to externalize. Alanus de Insulis (Alain de Lille), Bernard of Sylvestris, John of Salisbury, and other forerunners of the movement known as European Humanism "discovered" nature. Delighting in the wonders of God's cosmic text, they brought theological speculation down to earth. Romances of love and chivalry placed heroes and heroines against the freshness of spring. Everywhere nature shone, sparkling with the beauty of earthly life. The

externalization and naturalizing of Christian belief flowers most obviously in *The Romance of the Rose*, begun in the 13th century by Guillaume de Lorris and completed, in vastly complicated form, by Jean de Meung. The *Romance* personifies the experiences of courtly love, recounting the pursuit of an ideal lady by an ideal knight, set in an enclosed garden and castle, which permits Guillaume to dwell on the beauty of nature. With Jean de Meung the interest in nature is made explicit, and the poem ends in a series of lengthy digressive discourses, several of them spoken by Dame Nature herself. In medieval English poetry this same love of spring and seasonal pleasures is apparent everywhere—certainly in the poems of Geoffrey Chaucer, who, besides creating several allegories of his own, translated *The Romance of the Rose* into English.

Dante's *Divine Comedy* has physical immediacy and contains an immense amount of historical detail. He anchors his poem in a real world, accepting Christian typology as historical fact and adopting an ordered system of cosmology (based on the number three, proceeding from the Trinity). Dante's passion for numerology does not, however, block a closeness to nature that had perhaps not been equalled in poetry since Homer. He enfolds classical thought into his epic by making Virgil one of its main protagonists—again to prefigure Christian heroism. Perhaps only William Langland, the author of *The Vision of Piers Plowman*, could be said to rival Dante's cosmic range. *Piers Plowman* is a simpler apocalyptic vision than the *Comedy*, but it has an existential immediacy, arising from its concern for the poor, which gives it great natural power.

Renaissance. Romance and romantic forms provide the main vehicle for the entrance of allegory into the literature of the Renaissance period. The old Arthurian legends carry a new sophistication and polish in the epics of the Italians Boiardo, Ariosto, and Tasso and in the work of Edmund Spenser. By interlacing several simultaneous stories in one larger narrative, the literary technique known as *entrelacement* allowed digression—yet kept an ebbing, flowing kind of unity—while presenting opportunities for moral and ironic commentary. But although the forms and themes of romance were medieval in origin, the new age was forced to accommodate altered values. The Middle Ages had externalized the Christian model; the Renaissance now internalized it, largely by emphasizing the centrality of human understanding. This process of internalization had begun slowly. In rough outline it can be discerned in the belief that biological humours affected personality, in the adaptations of Platonic Idealism from which arose a new emphasis on imagination, in the rise of an introspective, soliloquizing drama in England. It can further be discerned in the gradual adoption of more self-conscious theories of being: Shakespeare's Hamlet, finding himself by thinking out his situation, prefigures the first modern philosopher, René Descartes, whose starting point for argument was "I think, therefore I am." Christopher Marlowe's characterization of Dr. Faustus epitomizes the new age. Pursuing power in the form of knowledge, he is led to discover the demons of allegory within himself. He is an essential figure for later European literature, archetypal in Germany for both Johann Wolfgang von Goethe and Thomas Mann and influential everywhere.

Modern period. With the Baroque and Neoclassical periods, allegory began to turn away from cosmology and toward rhetorical ambiguity. John Milton allegorized sin and death in his epic poem *Paradise Lost*, but allegory for him seems chiefly to lie in the ambiguous diction and syntax employed in the poem. Instead of flashing allegorical emblems before the reader, Milton generates a questioning attitude that searches out allegory more as a mysterious form than a visible content. His central allegorical theme is perhaps the analogy he draws between poetry, music, and ideas of cosmic order. This theme, which generates allegory at once, recurs in later English poetry right up to modern times with T.S. Eliot's *Four Quartets*.

The social and religious attitudes of the 18th-century

age of Enlightenment could be expressed coolly and without ambiguity—and thus there was little need for spiritual allegory in the period's literature. Oblique symbolism was used mainly for satirical purposes. John Dryden and Alexander Pope were masters of verse satire, Jonathan Swift of prose satire. Voltaire and the French writers of the Enlightenment similarly employed a wit whose aim was to cast doubt on inherited pieties and attitudes. A new vogue for the encyclopaedia allowed a close, critical commentary on the ancient myths, but the criticism was rationalist and opposed to demonology. Under such conditions the allegorical mode might have dried up entirely. Yet the new Romantic age of the late 18th and early 19th centuries revived the old cosmologies once more, and poetic forms quickly reflected the change, with the Romantic poets and their precursors (Blake, William Collins, Edward Young, Thomas Gray, and others) managing to reinstate the high destiny of the allegorical imagination. The Romantics went back to nature. Poets took note of exactly what they saw when they went out walking, and their awareness of nature and its manifestations found its way into their poetry. Appropriate poetic forms for expressing this sensibility tended to be open, rhapsodic, and autobiographical—qualities notably present in William Wordsworth and in Samuel Taylor Coleridge, for example. Percy Bysshe Shelley is the most strikingly allegorical of English Romantics; he not only followed the Platonic tradition of Spenser and the Renaissance—with ode, elegy, and brief romance—but he also invented forms of his own, such as *Epipsychidion*, a rhapsodic meditation, and he was working on a great Dantesque vision, *The Triumph of Life*, when he died. Visionary masterpieces came from Germany, where Novalis and Friedrich Hölderlin hymned the powers of nature in odes of mythic overtone and resonance. French Romanticism, merging gradually with the theory and practice of the Symbolist movement (dealing in impressions and intuitions rather than in descriptions), in turn followed the same path. The pantheist cosmology of Victor Hugo, the central writer of the somewhat delayed French Romantic movement, created an allegory of occult forces and demonic hero worship. It is fair to say that, in its most flexible and visionary forms, allegory flourished throughout the Romantic period.

There also developed a novelistic mode of allegory by which prose authors brought fate, necessity, the demonic, and the cosmological into their narratives. Émile Zola used a theory of genetics, Charles Dickens the idea of ecological doom, Leo Tolstoy the belief in historical destiny, and Fyodor Dostoyevsky the fatalism of madness and neurosis. Nikolay Gogol revived the art of the grotesque, picturing absurdities in the scene of tsarist Russia. Even the arch-naturalist playwright, Anton Chekov, made an emblem of the cherry orchard and the sea gull in his plays of those titles. However its dates are established, the modern period is exceedingly complex in its mythmaking. Psychoanalytic theory has been both a critical and a creative resource; modern allegory has remained internalized in the Renaissance tradition. But Marxist social realism has kept to the externals of dialectical materialism, though without notable aesthetic success. In the free play of American letters, where Nathaniel Hawthorne, Herman Melville, Edgar Allen Poe, and Henry James (particularly in his later novels) had essayed an allegorical mode, the future of its use is uncertain. T.S. Eliot's enigmatic style in a long poem, "Ash Wednesday," may be related to his search for a Dantesque dramatic style, for which he also tried in plays, most obviously *Murder in the Cathedral* (a morality) and *The Cocktail Party* (a philosophic farce). More clearly popular authors such as George Orwell and William Golding have used the most familiar allegorical conventions. D.H. Lawrence shaped novels such as *The Plumed Serpent* to project a thematic, cultural polemic. W.H. Auden's operatic librettos reflect once more the allegorical potential of this mixture of media.

Modern allegory has in fact no set pattern, or model, although Surrealism has provided a dominant style of discontinuous fragmentary expression. The only rule seems to be that there is no rule. Science fiction, an ancient field dating back at least to the earliest philosophers of Greece, has set no limits on the speculations it will entertain. The allegorical author now even questions the allegorical process itself, criticizing the very notions of cosmos, demon, and magic. It may be that modern allegory has completed a vast circle begun by the first conflict between ways of interpreting myth, as revealed in Homer and the Hebraic prophets.

(A.S.F.)

Complexity of mythmaking in the 20th century

ALLEGORICAL LITERATURE IN THE EAST

India. Fables appeared early in India, but it is impossible to determine whether they are older or later than the Greek. Undoubtedly there was mutual influence from very early times, for indirect contacts between Greece and India (by trade routes) had existed long before the time of Alexander the Great. In the form in which they are now known the Greek fables are the older, but this may be an accident of transmission.

The fable was apparently first used in India as a vehicle of Buddhist instruction. Some of the *Jātakas*, birth stories of the Buddha, which relate some of his experiences in previous animal incarnations, resemble Greek fables and are used to point a moral. They may date from as far back as the 5th century BC, though the written records are much later. The most important compilation is the *Pañcatantra*, a Sanskrit collection of beast fables. The original has not survived, but it has been transmitted (via a lost Pahlavi version) as the mid-8th-century Arabic *Kalīlah wa Dimnah*. Kalilah and Dimnah are two jackals, counselors to the lion king, and the work is a frame story containing numerous fables designed to teach political wisdom or cunning. From the Arabic this was translated into many languages, including Hebrew, which version John of Capua used to make a Latin version in the 13th century. This, the *Directorium humanae vitae* ("Guide for Human Life"), was the chief means by which oriental fables became current in Europe. In the fables of Bidpai, animals act as men in animal form, and little attention is paid to their supposed animal characteristics. It is in this respect that they differ most from the fables of Aesop, in which animals behave as animals.

(O.Ta.)

China. Chinese philosophers from the Ch'in dynasty (221–206 BC) onward often used extended metaphors (from which fable is the logical development) to make their points. This is believed to reflect the fact that, as "realistic" thinkers, the Chinese generally did not favour more abstract argument, Thus simple allegory helped to stimulate audience interest and to increase the force of an argument. A century earlier, Mencius, a Confucian philosopher, had used the following little allegory in illustrating his theory that an effort has to be made if man's natural goodness is to be recovered: "A man will begin searching when his dog or chicken is missing; but he does not go searching for the good character he was born with after it is lost. Is this not regrettable?" The same writer also used a parable to bring home his point that mental training could not be hurried, but was a gradual process: "A man in Sung sowed seeds in a field. The seedlings grew so slowly, however, that one day he took a walk through the field pulling at each one of the seedlings. On returning home he announced that he was exhausted, but that he had helped the seedlings' growth. His son, hurrying to the field, found the seedlings dead."

Tales such as this were often borrowed from folklore, but others were probably original creations, including a striking story that opens the *Chuang-tzu*, a summa of Taoist thought. It makes the point that ordinary people frequently deplore the actions of a man of genius because they are unable to understand his vision, which is not answerable to the laws of "common sense": "A giant fish, living at the northern end of the world, transformed itself into a bird so that it could make the arduous flight to the southernmost sea. Smaller birds, measuring his ambition against their own capabilities, laughed at the impossibility of it."

But the full development of fable, as it is understood in the West, was hindered by the fact that Chinese ways of thinking prohibited them from accepting the notion of animals that thought and behaved as humans. Actual events from the past were thought to be more instructive than fictitious stories, and this led to the development of a large body of legendary tales and supernatural stories. Between the 4th and 6th centuries, however, Chinese Buddhists adapted fables from Buddhist India in a work known as *Po-yü ching*, and they also began to make use of traditional Chinese stories that could further understanding of Buddhist doctrines. (Na.Mo.)

Japan. In Japan, the *Koji-ki* (712; "Records of Ancient Matters") and the *Nihon-shoki* (8th century, "Chronicles of Japan"), both of them official histories of Japan, were studded with fables, many of them on the theme of a small intelligent animal getting the better of a large stupid one. The same is true of the *fudoki* (local gazetteers dating from 713 and later). The form reached its height in the Kamakura period (1192–1333). Toward the end of the Muromachi period (1338–1573) Jesuit missionaries introduced the fables of Aesop to Japan, and the influence of these can be traced in stories written between then and the 19th century. (T.Io.)

BIBLIOGRAPHY

Fable: (Editions and translations): E. CHAMBRY, *Fables* (1927), in Greek and French; S.A. HANDFORD, *Fables of Aesop* (1956); B. PARES, *Krylov's Fables* (1926); MARIANNE MOORE, *Fables of La Fontaine* (1954). (Critical commentary): P. CLARAC, *La Fontaine, l'homme et l'oeuvre* (1947); B.E. PERRY, *Aesopica* (1952).

Parable: (Christian parables): A.M. HUNTER, *The Parables: Then and Now* (1971); ETA LINNEMANN, *Gleichnisse Jesu*, 3rd ed. (1964; Eng. trans., *The Parables of Jesus*, 1966); T.W. MANSON (ed.), *The Sayings of Jesus As Recorded in the Gospels According to St. Matthew and St. Luke* (1949). (Parables and literature): D.C. ALLEN, *The Legend of Noah: Renaissance Rationalism in Art, Science and Letters* (1963); HEINZ POLITZER, *Franz Kafka: Parable and Paradox* (1962).

Allegory: (General theory and history): D.C. ALLEN, *Mysteriously Meant: The Rediscovery of Pagan Symbolism and Allegorical Interpretation in the Renaissance* (1970); C.H. DODD, *The Authority of the Bible* (1958); WILLIAM EMPSON, *Seven Types of Ambiguity*, 3rd ed. (1953); A.S. FLETCHER, *Allegory: The Theory of a Symbolic Mode* (1964); NORTHROP FRYE, *Anatomy of Criticism: Four Essays* (1957); R.M. GRANT, *The Letter and the Spirit* (1958); EDWIN HONIG, *Dark Conceit: The Making of Allegory* (1959); C.S. LEWIS, *The Allegory of Love* (1936); JEAN PEPIN, *Mythe et allégorie* (1958); ROSEMOND TUVE, *Allegorical Imagery* (1966).

Pagan and Christian interpretation: KENNETH BURKE, *The Rhetoric of Religion* (1961); HENRY CHADWICK, *Early Christian Thought and the Classical Tradition* (1966); C.H. DODD, *The Interpretation of the Fourth Gospel* (1968); A.O. LOVEJOY, *The Great Chain of Being* (1936); H. DE LUBAC, *Exégèse médiévale: les quatre sens de l'Écriture* (1959–64); A. MOMIGLIANO (ed.), *The Conflict Between Paganism and Christianity in the Fourth Century* (1963); G. VON RAD, *Theologie des Alten Testaments*, 2nd ed. (1958; Eng. trans., *Old Testament Theology*, 2 vol., 1962–65); RENE ROQUES, *L'Univers dionysien* (1954); B. SMALLEY, *The Study of the Bible in the Middle Ages*, 2nd ed. (1952); H.A. WOLFSON, *The Philosophy of the Church Fathers*, vol. 1, *Faith, Trinity, Incarnation* (1956); *Philo: Foundations of Religious Philosophy in Judaism, Christianity, and Islam*, 2 vol. (1947).

Typology and typological symbolism: ERICH AUERBACH, "Figura," in *Scenes from the Drama of European Literature: Six Essays* (1959); A.C. CHARITY, *Events and Their Afterlife: The Dialectics of Christian Typology in the Bible and Dante* (1966); JEAN DANIELOU, *Sacramentum futuri: études sur les origines de la typologie biblique* (1950; Eng. trans., *From Shadows to Reality: Studies in the Biblical Typology of the Fathers*, 1960); AUSTIN FARRER, *A Rebirth of Images: The Making of St. John's Apocalypse* (1949); R.P.C. HANSON, *Allegory and Event* (1959); W.G. MADSEN, *From Shadowy Types to Truth: Studies in Milton's Symbolism* (1968).

Medieval allegory: ERICH AUERBACH, *Dante als Dichter der irdischen Welt* (1929; Eng. trans., *Dante: Poet of the Secular World*, 1961); M.W. BLOOMFIELD, "Symbolism in Medieval Literature," *Modern Philology*, 56:73–81 (1958), and *Piers Plowman As a Fourteenth–Century Apocalypse* (1962); EDGAR DE BRUYNE, *Études d'esthétique médiévale*, 3 vol. (1946); M.D. CHENU, *La Théologie au douzième siècle* (1957; Eng. trans. of 9 selected essays, *Nature, Man, and Society in the Twelfth Century*, 1968); E.R. CURTIUS, *Europäische Literatur und lateinisches Mittelalter* (1948; Eng. trans., *European Literature and the Latin Middle Ages*, 1953); RAYMOND KLIBANSKY, *The Continuity of the Platonic Tradition During the Middle Ages* (1939); C.S. LEWIS, *The Discarded Image: An Introduction to Medieval and Renaissance Literature* (1964); JOSEPH A. MAZZEO, *Medieval Cultural Tradition in Dante's Comedy* (1960); D.W. ROBERTSON and B.F. HUPPE, *Piers Plowman and Scriptural Tradition* (1951); CHARLES SINGLETON, *Dante Studies*, vol. 1, *Commedia* (1954).

Renaissance and modern allegory: DOUGLAS BUSH, *Mythology and the Renaissance Tradition in English Poetry*, rev. ed. (1963); WALTER BENJAMIN, *Ursprung des deutschen Trauerspiels* (1928); HAROLD BLOOM, *The Visionary Company* (1961); A.S. FLETCHER, *The Prophetic Moment: An Essay on Spenser* (1971); ALASTAIR FOWLER, *Triumphal Forms: Structural Patterns in Elizabethan Poetry* (1970); NORTHROP FRYE, *Fearful Symmetry: A Study of William Blake* (1947); U.M. KAUFMAN, *The Pilgrim's Progress and Traditions in Puritan Meditation* (1966); MICHAEL MURRIN, *The Veil of Allegory: Some Notes Toward a Theory of Allegorical Rhetoric in the English Renaissance* (1969); JEAN SEZNEC, *La Survivance des dieux antiques* (1939; Eng. trans., *The Survival of the Pagan Gods*, rev. ed., 1953); E.M.W. TILLYARD, *The Elizabethan World Picture* (1943); EDGAR WIND, *Pagan Mysteries in the Renaissance*, new ed. (1968).

Pictorial allegory: ROSEMARY FREEMAN, *English Emblem Books* (1948); ADOLF KATZENELLENBOGEN, *Allegories of the Virtues and Vices in Medieval Art from Early Christian Times to the Thirteenth Century* (1939); ERWIN PANOFSKY, *Studies in Iconology: Humanistic Themes in the Art of the Renaissance* (1939); MARIO PRAZ, *Studies in Seventeeth-Century Imagery*, 2nd ed. (1964).

Special topics: CHRISTOPHER BUTLER, *Number Symbolism* (1970); WILLIAM EMPSON, *The Structure of Complex Words* (1951); ALASTAIR FOWLER, *Silent Poetry: Essays in Numerological Analysis* (1970); JOHN HOLLANDER, *The Untuning of the Sky: Ideas of Music in English Poetry, 1500–1700* (1961); E.D. LEYBURN, *Satiric Allegory: Mirror of Man* (1956); W.K. WIMSATT, *The Verbal Icon* (1954).

(A.S.F.)

Fagales

The Fagales, or the beech order, consists of the family Fagaceae, 10 genera with about 1,000 species. The family, and hence the order, is made up exclusively of various shrubs and trees, often forest-forming trees that lend character and beauty to the landscape over great areas. By supplying timber and many other economically valuable products, the Fagales are of considerable importance to man.

GENERAL FEATURES

While some species are low shrubs, the majority are tree-like, often reaching mighty proportions. *Lithocarpus cyclophorus*, for example, attains a height of 45 metres (147 feet) and is held to be the largest tree of the Malay Peninsula. The stem girth of the English oak, *Quercus robur*, may reach 16 metres (52 feet), that of *Castanea sativa*, 28 metres (91 feet). The tropical-subtropical members of the order (*Lithocarpus, Castanopsis, Cyclobalanopsis*) are generally evergreen, with leathery-textured, usually smooth-margined leaves of uniform appearance. Outside the tropics the species as a rule are deciduous; that is, their leaves fall during unfavourable seasons. The leaves are usually lobed or toothed in different degrees around the margins. The species of *Nothofagus*, usually known as southern beeches, that grow in the Southern Temperate Zone often are found to have small, serrate or crenate (having rounded teeth) leaves that have some similarity to birch leaves, often causing the popular Australian name "birches" to be applied to these trees.

Distribution and abundance. The beech order is mainly distributed over the Northern Hemisphere. Four of the most important distribution centres may be distinguished. One of these is situated in southeastern Asia: the Indochinese peninsula and the East Indian archipelago (islands of Indonesia). Here there is a centre for the genera *Lithocarpus, Cyclobalanopsis,* and *Castanopsis,* while the small genus *Trigonobalanus* is restricted to this area and a few oak (*Quercus*) species occur in the northern part. A second important distribution area, which is in connection with the former, is the East Asian one. The genera

Size range

Cyclobalanopsis, Castanopsis, and *Lithocarpus* also occur here, though the species number decreases toward the north, while the oak species are here more numerous than in southeastern Asia and, moreover, some chestnut (*Castanea*) and beech (*Fagus*) species are added. A third distribution centre, though with a smaller species number, exists in the Mediterranean region together with Asia Minor and Caucasia. In this area there is especially a centre for section *Cerris* of the oak genus *Quercus*. A fourth and important centre is found in the eastern United States and Mexico, where the genus *Quercus* is richly represented.

In addition to these more important distribution centres, the order also occurs, though to a smaller extent, over other areas. In the western coast provinces of North America there is a distribution district where a number of oak species, one *Lithocarpus* species, and the endemic (restricted to that area) genus *Chrysolepis* are found. In middle and north Europe, the genera *Fagus, Quercus,* and *Castanea* are represented; only a few species occur, but they are important in the vegetation through their widespread occurrence. In the Southern Hemisphere there are isolated distribution areas for the genus *Nothofagus* (southern beeches) in western South America, Australia, and New Zealand; and in the tropical region, the distribution district of the genus *Trisyngyne* is located on New Guinea and New Caledonia.

Economic importance. Numerous species of Fagales are of importance to man through supplying timber for different purposes. The lumber of European and American oaks (*Quercus*) is used for construction and carpentry, including shipbuilding; in America especially, the "white oak lumber," obtained from *Quercus alba, Q. macrocarpa, Q. prinus,* and others, is much appreciated and used for building purposes. The beeches (*Fagus*) and chestnuts (*Castanea*) of both continents are used for carpentry, piles, railroad ties, etc., though the chestnut blight has reduced the importance of the American chestnut (*C. dentata*). In East Asia, the oaks *Quercus crispula* and *Q. glandulifera,* among others, are used for carpentry and construction, as are the beeches (*Fagus sieboldii* and *F. chinensis*), the chestnuts (*Castanea crenata* and *C. henryi*), and *Cyclobalanopsis glauca.* Among the numerous species used in Southeast Asia are *Lithocarpus spicatus, L. platycarpus, L. pachyphyllus, L. costatus, L. cyclophorus, Castanopsis argentea,* and *C. indica,* the two latter being used for building purposes. In the Southern Hemisphere, the *Nothofagus* species are much used for the same purposes as the beeches of the Northern Hemisphere.

Among other products obtained from members of the beech order is cork, especially supplied by *Quercus suber,* the cork oak, occurring naturally and cultivated in the western Mediterranean countries. Cork, however, is also obtained from other oak species, notably *Q. occidentalis, Q. pseudosuber, Q. fontanesii,* and in China from *Q. variabilis.* The bark of several *Quercus* species and of *Lithocarpus densiflorus,* the Californian "tanbark oak," is used for tanning, and the "gall nuts" and cupules of some species are also sources of tannin. The "aleppo galls" of *Quercus infectoria* and "valonia," the cupules of *Q. aegilops,* are well known as sources of tannin. In older times especially, other chemical products were obtained; for example, from *Fagus* species methyl alcohol, acetic acid, creosote, guaiacol, and tar were extracted, and from *Quercus robur* were obtained acetic acid, creosote, guaiacol, and tar. Several species in the order have been used for dyeing; *e.g., Quercus velutina* in N. America, *Q. incana* in India, and *Castanea crenata* in East Asia. The Mediterranean *Quercus coccifera* is host plant for a shieldlouse that supplies a pigment reminiscent of the red cochineal dye.

Edible fruits Many species of Fagales have edible fruits that have been used by man. The European chestnut, *Castanea sativa,* has been of special importance and has been cultivated in numerous varieties, as have some of the oak species, such as *Quercus ilex,* in the Mediterranean. In North America, the chestnut *Castanea dentata* and the chinquapin, *C. pumila,* have been used and also have

been offered for sale in the local markets. Acorns of *Quercus alba, Q. prinus, Q. lobata,* of *Fagus grandifolia* and *Chrysolepis sempervirens* and others have been used for food, especially by the American Indians. In East Asia, the chestnuts *Castanea crenata* and *C. mollissima* are under much cultivation and their nuts are consumed to a considerable extent in Japan and China; and the nuts of several *Lithocarpus* and *Castanopsis* species have found use in their home countries, for instance, *Lithocarpus edulis* and *Castanopsis delavayi* in China, *Lithocarpus garrettianus* and *Castanopsis boissi, C. poilanei, C. piriformis* in Indochina, *C. hystrix* and *C. ferox* in India, and *C. schlenckerae* in New Guinea.

Beech and oak acorns have also been of importance as food for domestic animals, and in South America even the wood of *Nothofagus* species is used as cattle food, after decomposition by bacteria and fungi. Some oak species of East Asia are of indirect importance for human nourishment, the logs being used for the cultivation of the edible "shiitake" mushroom, *Lentinus edodes,* which is much consumed, especially in Japan, and for other fungi. In Tierra del Fuego another edible fungus, *Cyttaria darwinii,* of great importance to the inhabitants, occurs on *Nothofagus* species.

Some species in the order are used for silkworm culture in Asia, for example, *Quercus aliena* and *Q. fabri* in China; *Cyclobalanopsis glauca, Quercus acutissima,* and *Castanea crenata* in Japan; and *Quercus incana* and *Q. semecarpifolia* in India.

NATURAL HISTORY

Life cycle. The time from seed germination to flowering in the mature trees of the beech order is usually long, about 50 to 60 years for the English oak, and 40 to 50 for the European beech, if the trees are free-growing. As in the gymnosperms, the time between pollination and fertilization is also long and, in some, the fruit requires two year's time to ripen, as in several species of *Lithocarpus* and *Quercus.* The flowers develop in the deciduous species after the leaves appear, male and female flowers as a rule on the same tree (the monoecious condition); occasionally entirely male or female trees occur (the dioecious condition). In the *Fagus* group especially, the flowering is often periodical, with intervals of up to 7 years between the "acorn years." In the evergreen species the leaves are, in some species, of several years' duration; in others they are one year old and fall when the new foliage develops. The age of the trees is sometimes very high. *Castanea sativa,* for example, may live more than 1,000 years, and *Quercus robur* may, under favourable conditions, attain a similar age. A tree of this species in Germany is reported to be about 1,500 years old. The common beech, however, will rarely be more than 300 years in age.

Ecology. In the wide distribution area of the Fagales order, the ecological conditions are, of course, quite varied. In the Southeast-Asiatic area, including the adjacent islands, favourable conditions are found especially on the mountain slopes with high humidity and frequent cloud formation, the temperature being tropical to subtropical. In the East-Asiatic centre and the northern part of the Indochinese peninsula, as well as in the Himalayas, the conditions are somewhat different. The temperature is not as high as in the Southeast-Asiatic area and the precipitation and air humidity are varying, very high on the southern slopes of the Himalayas, but low in some interior continental areas, where the conditions are more or less desert-like.

The special conditions in the Mediterranean area, summer dryness and winter rains, which also are found in part of western North America, give a dry-habitat character to members of the Fagales order occurring there, including such features as small leathery leaves that are spiny or hairy.

In the distribution areas of middle and north Europe and eastern North America, where temperate climate and rather great temperature variations are found to occur, the Fagales, as a rule, are deciduous. While in Europe large forests are formed by a sole species, in North Amer-

Structure and diversity of forms within the Fagales order.
Drawing by M. Pahl based on H. Hjelmqvist, "Studies on the floral morphology and phylogeny of the Amentiferea," *Botanical Notiser* supp. 2:1 (1948)

ica several species occur together mixed with other trees, and some species form low shrubberies on poor sand plains, (such as *Quercus ilicifolia* and *Q. prinoides*). In Mexico, the Fagales, especially the oak genus *Quercus*, find favourable conditions for growth on the eastern slopes of the Mexican highland. Humidity and warmth there are high, and some *Quercus* species develop gigantic leaves. In the interior the conditions are dry and warm, and the species acquire adaptations fitting them for existence where water supply is limited.

The distribution areas of the genus *Nothofagus* in the Southern Hemisphere are not only geographically but also ecologically widely separated from the others. The climatic character is oceanic, with small annual temperature change and great humidity. In parts of the South American district the mean annual temperature is very low and scarcely enough for cereal production; nevertheless, several *Nothofagus* species occur there and may reach up to the snow line.

FORM AND FUNCTION

Vegetative characters. Among the distinguishing characteristics of the Fagales order are the simple leaves, in the tropical species as a rule with entire unbroken margins and leathery texture, and in the temperate species often with lobed or toothed margins. Stipules, small leaf-like appendages at the bases of leaf stalks, occur but fall soon after development. The leaves are, as a rule, alternate, either evenly distributed around the stem in a spiral, or arranged in two rows. In the genera *Lithocarpus, Castanopsis,* and *Castanea* both possibilities occur in different species, but in *Quercus* and *Cyclobalanopsis* only the evenly distributed spiral form is apparent. In *Fagus,* on the other hand, the leaves are arranged exclusively in two rows along the branches, the rows being somewhat nearer to each other on the under side of the shoots. The same arrangement is found in most *Nothofagus* species, but the spiral distribution also occurs. An unusual arrangement is found in one species of *Trigonobalanus,* in which the leaves are in whorls in older shoots.

Flower and fruit characters. The flowers of the Fagales order are unisexual, though often with rudiments of the other sex present, and are usually arranged in dichasia (inflorescences with top flower and fork-like ramification) with 3 to 7 flowers, which in their turn are col-

lected in spikelike flower clusters, usually called catkins. With respect to the distribution of male and female flowers, three types of inflorescences (flower clusters) may be discerned: (1) all catkins are male in the upper, female in the lower part (some *Lithocarpus* species); (2) the upper catkins bear both male and female flowers, the lower being entirely male (*Castanea* and *Chrysolepis*); and (3) the upper catkins are wholly female, the lower male (*Quercus, Cyclobalanopsis, Castanopsis*). The genera *Fagus, Nothofagus,* and *Trisyngyne* differ from the usual condition in that the dichasia are not arranged in catkins but occur separately in the leaf axils, the points where leaf stalks join the stem.

An important distinguishing feature of the Fagaceae family (and hence the Fagales order) is the occurrence of a so-called cupule, a structure so characteristic that it provided the origin of the old family name Cupuliferae for the present Fagaceae family. This cupule is a structure that surrounds the fruit (acorn, nut, etc.) as a cup and on the outer side bears modified leaf structures developed as scales, spines, or thin plates. In the genus *Lithocarpus* each fruit is included in a cupule; the different cupules of a dichasium may, however, be more or less grown together. Similar cupules are found in the genera *Cyclobalanopsis* and *Quercus,* whose flowers, however, are solitary. In *Castanopsis* and *Castanea* the whole female dichasium is surrounded by a common cupule, which may burst at fruit-ripening. In *Chrysolepis* the cupule is a compound structure with separating walls between the fruits. In the *Fagus* group the cupule is divided into two to nine lobes; in some species of *Trisyngyne* it is much reduced.

The individual flowers of the Fagales order are simple and inconspicuous. In some genera, the perianth (the combined set of petals and sepals, or both, in a flower) is, in both the male and female flowers, made up of six perianth leaves, which are comparatively well-developed. In others, the perianth leaves of the male flowers are joined together, irregular in shape, and found to be of varying number, and the female flowers may also have a somewhat irregular perianth. Fusion of the flowers and reduction of the perianth is discernible in a few genera. In *Nothofagus* three diminutive perianth lobes may exist in the female flower, and in *Trisyngyne* the male perianth is often cup-like without discernible lobes.

The stamens (male flower parts) are in most genera about 12 in number, partly opposite the lobes of the perianth leaves, partly alternating with them. In *Quercus* the number is reduced, often to six, but in some *Nothofagus* species, on the other hand, it is increased and may be 30 to 40. The anthers (pollen bearing parts of the stamens) are in *Lithocarpus, Castanopsis, Castanea,* and *Chrysolepis* small, about as broad as high, attached at the middle, and are movable. In *Fagus, Nothofagus,* and *Trisyngyne* they are oblong, attached at the base, and immobile. They are also much bigger, especially in *Nothofagus.* The different development of the stamens is possibly connected with the pollination method. Those genera that have stamens of *Lithocarpus* type are—at least mainly—insect-pollinated, while the others are wind-pollinated.

As with the stamens, the pistil (female flower part) is also of different development in different genera and the pistil structure is probably connected with the pollination method. The wind-pollinated genera have a more or less enlarged stigma (sticky pollen-receiving area) surface, which, of course, provides a greater chance to catch the pollen suspended in the air.

Ovary (part of the female pistil) and fruit are rounded in shape in the *Quercus* and *Castanea* groups, except for *Chrysolepis.* Sometimes the nuts, however, are somewhat flattened through pressure of adjacent fruits, and in some *Lithocarpus* species, as *L. lindleyanus,* the fruits are weakly triangular. In *Chrysolepis* this triangular shape is more pronounced, especially in younger stages, and still more in *Trigonobalanus,* in which one of the species even has three-winged fruits. The nuts of *Fagus* and the fruits of *Nothofagus* are also decidedly triangular, while the dimerous (structure based on twos) top flower of *Nothofagus* and all female flowers of *Trisyngyne* develop flattened and more or less two-winged nuts, somewhat reminiscent of *Alnus* (alder) or *Betula* (birch) nuts. The ovules (developing seeds) are generally six in number, two in each of the chambers of the ovary; only one of them develops, however, into a seed.

EVOLUTION AND PALEONTOLOGY

Fossil record. Fossil Fagales show a high age of the order. *Quercus, Fagus,* and *Lithocarpus* are present in finds from Eurasia and North America, belonging to about the middle of the Cretaceous Period (about 100,-000,000 years ago), as is the fossil genus *Dryophyllum,* which was apparently related to *Castanea.* In the Southern Hemisphere the genus *Nothofagus* also appears in the Cretaceous. In the Tertiary Period (25,000,000 to 65,-000,000 years ago) *Castanopsis* and *Castanea* are reported from different countries and the order on the whole shows a rich development. Fossil pollen of *Nothofagus* from the Cretaceous of New Zealand is known, and in Europe pollen from younger Cretaceous deposits is known that shows great similarity to *Trigonobalanus.*

Phylogeny. Since several genera thus appear in the same early period, the fossil finds give scarcely any guidance for an estimate of the evolution in the order. The problems of evolution and relationships are thus better determined by morphology (structure), especially the organization of the cupule. The inflorescence (flower cluster) type, the different style, stigma, and anther types (female and male structures), and other considerations are also important features determining relationships.

CLASSIFICATION

Annotated classification.

ORDER FAGALES

Deciduous or evergreen monoecious trees or shrubs. Leaves alternate, rarely verticillate (whorled), simple, entire (smooth margins) or with shallow incisions, with deciduous stipules. Flowers unisexual, though often with rudiments of the other sex, with simple, inconspicuous perianth, arranged in catkin-like spikes, composed of dichasia or simple, or in dichasia in the leaf axils. Stamens 4 to about 40. Pistil 1, ovary inferior, usually with 3 or 6 loculi, and 3–12 styles; placentation axile, ovules 2 in each locule. Fruit a 1-seeded nut, the nuts or the female dichasium surrounded by a cupule of axial nature. Seed with a large embryo and no endosperm.

Family Fagaceae

The only family in the order, hence with the characters of the order.

Subfamily Castaneoideae

Catkins composed of dichasia, erect. Perianth well-developed, generally of 6 leaves. Anthers small, dorsifix, styles terete with apical pore. Germination hypogeous.

Tribe Pasanieae. Each female flower surrounded by cupule walls. Cupule indehiscent. Two genera, *Lithocarpus* with about 300 species, and *Chrysolepis* with 2 species.

Tribe Castaneae. The female dichasium surrounded by a common cupule, often bursting at fruit ripeness. Two genera, *Castanopsis* with about 150 evergreen species, and *Castanea* with about 12 deciduous species.

Subfamily Quercoideae

Catkins partly or completely simple, female catkins erect, male catkins pendulous. Perianth more or less irregular. Anthers basifix, stigma surface dilated. Each female flower with a cupule. Germination hypogeous. Two genera, *Cyclobalanopsis* with about 140 species, and *Quercus* with about 375 species.

Subfamily Fagoideae

Flowers in dichasia, sometimes reduced to one flower. Perianth sometimes 6-leaved, but often much reduced. Anthers basifix. Stigma surface dilated. Cupule enclosing a whole dichasium, divided into valves. Nut triangular or flat. Germination—as far as known—epigeous. Four genera, *Trigonobalanus* with 2 species, *Fagus* with about 10 species, *Nothofagus* with about 18 species, and *Trisyngyne* with about 20 species.

Critical appraisal. The family Fagaceae (hence, the order Fagales) has attracted the interest of many systematists (botanists who study classification of plants), and the opinions have been considerably divergent about the subdivision of the group. Sometimes a very great number of genera has been proposed, the sections of *Lithocarpus* and *Quercus* being given the rank of genera in these treatments. In other cases some of the genera have been united with each other, for example, *Cyclobalanopsis* has been joined with *Quercus,* and *Trisyngyne* with *Nothofagus.* The morphological differences between *Quercus* and *Cyclobalanopsis* are not very great, but the two groups are clearly distinct from each other and there are no transitional forms between them (as may be found between *Cyclobalanopsis* and *Lithocarpus*). They thus apparently belong to two different evolutionary lines, and on this account should be kept apart. Similar conditions are met with in the other case: *Nothofagus* and *Trisyngyne* apparently represent different evolutionary lines, which speaks in favour of the view that they are separate genera.

Among the groups related to the Fagales order, the order Betulales (birches) is the nearest. The 2 orders have, as a matter of fact, often been united into 1. New genera have been added to the family from time to time. The American species formerly placed in the genus *Castanopsis* were in 1948 recognized as a distinct genus, *Chrysolepis,* and, in the 1940s, a great number of species were discovered by an expedition to New Guinea. These, like some earlier known species from New Caledonia, are placed in the genus *Nothofagus* by some authorities but by others are regarded as a separate genus, *Trisyngyne.* In 1961 a new species was found in Borneo that, together with an earlier known but incompletely described species from Indochina, forms the new genus *Trigonobalanus.*

BIBLIOGRAPHY. AIMEE CAMUS, "Les châtaigniers," *Encyclopédie Économique de Sylviculture,* vol. 3 (1929), a monograph of the genera *Castanea* and *Castanopsis* with illustrations of all species, "Les chênes," *ibid.,* vol. 6–8 (1934–54), monographs of *Quercus, Cyclobalanopsis,* and *Lithocarpus,* with illustrations of all species; H. HJELMQVIST, "Studies on the Floral Morphology and Phylogeny of the Amentiferae," *Bot. Notiser,* suppl. vol. 2, no. 1, (1948), on floral morphology, relationships, and subdivision of the Fagales order.

(H.Hj.)

Fa-hsien

Fa-hsien (The Splendour of Religious Law; in Pin-yin romanization Fa-xian) was the spiritual name of a Chinese Buddhist monk, Sehi, who was born at Shansi during the 4th century AD and whose pilgrimage to India (AD 399–414) first began Sino-Indian relations. Living at the time of the emperor Yao Hsing, when Buddhism enjoyed an imperial favour seldom equalled in Chinese history, Fa-hsien was stirred by a profound faith to go to India, the "Holy Land" of Buddhism, in order to visit the sites of the Buddha's life and to bring back Buddhist texts that were still unknown in China.

The historical importance of Fa-hsien is twofold. On the one hand, a famous record of his journeys—*Fo Kuo Chi* ("Record of Buddhist Kingdoms")—contains valuable information not found elsewhere concerning the history of Indian Buddhism during the early centuries AD. Because of the fairly detailed descriptions of Fa-hsien, it is possible to envision Buddhist India before it was reconquered by the counterreforms of Hinduism and eclipsed by the Muslim invasion. On the other hand, he strengthened Chinese Buddhism by helping provide a better knowledge of Buddhist sacred texts. After studying them for ten years in India, he brought back to China a great number of copies of Buddhist texts and translated them from Sanskrit into Chinese. Among them, two of the most important were the *Mahāparinirvāṇa-sūtra*, a text glorifying the eternal, personal, and pure nature of Nirvāṇa (Enlightenment)—on which the Nirvāṇa school in China then based its doctrines—and the Vinaya (rules of discipline for the monks) of the Mahāsaṅghika school (see below), which thus became available for the regulation of the numerous monastic communities in China.

Overland journey to India

Fa-hsien first crossed the trackless wastes of Central Asia. His trip across the desert he recalled in a terrifying way:

> In the desert were numerous evil spirits and scorching winds, causing death to anyone who would meet them. Above there were no birds, while on the ground there were no animals. One looked as far as one could in all directions for a path to cross, but there was none to choose. Only the dried bones of the dead served as indications.

After arriving at Khotan, an oasis centre for caravans, he defied the terrors of snow during his crossing of the Pamirs; the mountain path was terribly narrow and steep:

> The path was difficult and rocky and ran along a cliff extremely steep. The mountain itself was just one sheer wall of rock 8,000 feet high, and as one approached it, one became dizzy. If one wished to advance, there was no place for him to place his feet. Below was the Indus River. In former times people had chiselled a path out of the rocks and distributed on the face of the cliff over 700 ladders for the descent (from Kenneth Ch'en, *Buddhism in China*, © Princeton University Press, 1964).

In northwestern India, which he entered in 402, he visited the most important seats of Buddhist learning: Udyāna, Gandhāra, Peshāwar, and Taxila. Above all, however, he was attracted by eastern India, where Buddha had spent his life and had taught his doctrines. His pilgrimage was completed by visits to the most holy spots: Kapilavastu, where Buddha was born; Bodh Gayā, where Buddha acquired the supreme Enlightenment; Banares (Vārānasi), where the Buddha preached his first sermon; and Kuśinagara, where the Buddha entered into the perfect Nirvāṇa. Everywhere Fa-hsien was amazed at the extraordinary flowering of the Buddhist faith.

Then he stayed a long time at Pāṭaliputra, conversing with Buddhist monks, studying Sanskrit texts with Buddhist scholars, and transcribing the Vinaya of the Mahāsaṅghika school—a dissident group of the Hīnayāna (Lesser Vehicle) born from the Council of Vesālī (*c.* 383 BC) that later became the Mahāyāna (Greater Vehicle). He also acquired another version of the Vinaya worked out by the Sarvāstivāda school—an early Buddhist group that taught the equal reality of all mental states (past, present, and future)—and the famous *Mahāparinirvāṇa-sūtra*. When he had deepened his knowledge of Buddhism and was in possession of sacred texts that were not yet translated into Chinese, he decided to go back to China. Instead of once more taking the overland route, however,

Return voyage

Fa-hsien took the sea route, first sailing to Ceylon, at that time one of the most flourishing centres of Buddhist studies. There, by securing the Mahīśāsakā Vinaya—a recension of the Hīnayāna Vinaya—and a selection of the Sarvāstivāda canon, he added to the number of Buddhist texts that he had collected.

After a two-year stay in Ceylon, he set sail for China, but the perils of the sea were as great as the hardships and dangers of desert and mountain he had faced in coming to India. A violent storm drove his ship onto an island that was probably Java. He took another boat bound for Canton. Instead of landing at the south China port, Fa-hsien's ship was driven astray by another storm and was finally blown to a port on the Shantung Peninsula. In all, Fa-hsien spent more than 200 days at sea. After returning to his homeland, Fa-hsien resumed his scholarly tasks and translated into Chinese the Buddhist texts he had taken so much trouble to bring back.

BIBLIOGRAPHY. The translations of Fa-hsien are part and parcel of the Chinese canon—edited for the first time under the Sung dynasty (960–1275)—which has not yet been translated into any European language. Several English translations of *A Record of Buddhist Kingdoms* of Fa-hsien are available. See also ABEL REMUSAT, *Foe Koue Ki* (1836); H.A. GILES, *The Travels of Fa-hsien* (1877); and J. LEGGE, *Travels of Fa-Hsien* (1886).

(H.A.)

Faidherbe, Louis

Louis-Léon-César Faidherbe, governor of French Senegal (1854–61, 1863–65), and a principal founder of France's colonial empire in Africa, was born in Lille on June 3, 1818. Graduating from the École Polytechnique, he joined the corps of military engineers in 1840. He showed little inclination for soldiering and fell into debt through gambling. He spent three undistinguished years, from 1843 to 1846, in Algeria. In 1847 he was posted to Guadeloupe, where his reserved and prickly temperament, his strong Republican sympathies, and his support for the campaign of the Republican politician Victor Schoelcher to abolish slavery alienated both the colonists and his fellow officers, and his superiors asked that he be recalled. Only when he returned to Algeria in 1849 and assumed his first independent command did he begin to demonstrate the resolution, administrative talent, and capacity for leadership that was to make his name famous and his progress rapid. His work now won commendation, and after further service in Kabylie he was made chevalier of the Légion d'Honneur.

In 1852 he was transferred to Senegal as deputy director of engineers and soon impressed the local merchant community as a capable and energetic administrator. Two years later, at the age of 36, he was promoted to the rank of major and appointed governor.

By courtesy of the Bibliotheque Nationale, Paris

Faidherbe, lithograph by A. Néraudau, 1873.

Faidherbe's years of service in Algeria were to exert a decisive influence on his conduct as governor of Senegal. Like most French officers with Algerian experience, he was impatient of metropolitan control and prepared to act on his own initiative whenever he considered it necessary. He was also preoccupied by the problems of military security and determined to impose French supremacy by military means. Having experienced the ferocity of Muslim resistance in Algeria, he was particularly alarmed by the growing power of the militant Islāmic leader al-Ḥājj 'Umar Tal on the frontiers of Senegal. In true Algerian fashion, therefore, he abandoned the cautious policies of his predecessors and took the offensive against all those who threatened French primacy. In a series of well-executed campaigns, some undertaken against the wishes of the Paris government, he subjugated the Moorish tribes in the north, drove the forces of al-Ḥājj 'Umar off the lower Sénégal River, and extended French control south toward the Gambia. By 1861 he had transformed his colony from a collection of scattered trading posts into the dominant political and military power in this region of West Africa.

Faidherbe's colonial policies

But Faidherbe was no mere conquistador; the glory of conquest appealed to him much less than did the challenges of government. Although not free from the racial prejudices characteristic of his age, he possessed a real sympathy for his African subjects and a genuine concern for their welfare. He remained an uncompromising enemy of slavery in all its forms; in 1858 he threatened to resign when the government attempted to recruit indentured Senegalese labour for the West Indian plantations. He sought to improve indigenous society without destroying it, and to this end he maintained the traditional authority of the chiefs while training their sons to become more efficient agents of French rule. Even his attitude toward Islām was far more sympathetic than his hostility to al-Ḥājj 'Umar might have suggested.

Faidherbe's other ambition was to make Senegal the cornerstone of a vast French African empire that he hoped might one day rival British India. He was convinced from the start of the West African interior's unlimited wealth and of his colony's potential for economic development. During his first period of office he encouraged experimental farming, founded Dakar, the future capital of French West Africa, and built Médina on the upper Sénégal as a base for further expansion inland. When he reassumed the governorship in 1863, after another tour of duty in Algeria, his principal objective was the extension of French power to the Niger and ultimately to Timbuktu and beyond. This time, however, he was less successful. Although the government allowed him to send an embassy to al-Ḥājj 'Umar's new empire on the upper Niger, it rejected his proposals for territorial expansion as too expensive. Nevertheless, his far-sighted policies laid the foundations for the West African federation that was finally created at the turn of the 20th century.

Later career

Faidherbe left Senegal in 1865 and returned again to Algeria, where he eventually was given command of the Constantine division. Recalled to France after the outbreak of the Franco-Prussian war, he was appointed commander in chief of the Army of the North in December 1870. Faidherbe realized the hopelessness of his task, but, as a good Republican, he remained loyal to the government of national defense and fought with skill and tenacity. In 1871 the three northern *départements* of Pas-de-Calais, Somme, and Nord all elected him to the National Assembly with overwhelming majorities, but he resigned almost immediately because of the assembly's anti-Republican proceedings. He was defeated in the senatorial elections of 1876 but was elected Republican senator for the Nord in 1879 and held the seat till 1888. As a final recognition of his services, he was made grand chancellor of the Légion d'Honneur in 1880.

By then, Faidherbe could no longer participate actively in political life, for years of service in Africa and the rigours of the northern campaign had left him paralyzed and half blind. He retained his interest in West African affairs, however, and continued to exert some influence

over them. In 1883, for example, he persuaded the Senate to vote funds for Senegalese railway construction even after the Chamber of Deputies had refused to do so. His best known book, published just before his death, was about his governorship of Senegal; significantly, it was dedicated to his old friend Victor Schoelcher.

Faidherbe died in Paris on September 29, 1889, revered as a war hero and respected as a great colonial governor. His reputation, particularly in the colonial sphere, has proved remarkably enduring. All historians of French expansion have paid tribute to his exceptional abilities. Even those who stress the authoritarian streak in his character and policies recognize the humanitarianism that set him apart from most of his contemporaries.

BIBLIOGRAPHY. There is no completely satisfactory biography of Faidherbe. The two standard works are A. DEMAISON, *Faidherbe* (1932); and G. HARDY, *Faidherbe* (1947), both in French. R. DELAVIGNETTE, "Faidherbe," in C.A. JULIEN (ed.), *Les Techniciens de la colonisation (XIXᵉ–XXᵉ siècles)*, 2nd ed. (1947), provides a brief but useful introduction. Faidherbe himself wrote several accounts of his governorship of Senegal, the fullest of which is *Le Sénégal, la France dans l'Afrique occidentale* (1889). He also discussed his role in the Franco-Prussian war in *Campagne de l'Armée du Nord en 1870–1871* (1871).

(A.S.K.-F.)

Fakhr ad-Dīn ar-Rāzī

Fakhr ad-Dīn ar-Rāzī, one of the foremost Muslim theologians and preachers, was a controversial figure whose intellectual brilliance was recognized even by his opponents.

He was born in 1149 at Rayy in Iran, the son of a preacher. After a broad education, in which he specialized in theology and philosophy, he travelled from country to country in an area comprising present-day northwestern Iran and Turkistan (U.S.S.R.) and finally settled in Herāt (now in Afghanistan). Wherever he went, he debated with famous scholars and was patronized and consulted by local rulers. He wrote about 100 books and gained fame and wealth. It was said that wherever he rode, 300 of his students accompanied him on foot; when he moved from one city to another, 1,000 mules carried his possessions, and there seemed no limit to his silver and gold.

Ar-Rāzī lived in an age of political and religious turmoil. The empire of the Baghdad caliphs was disintegrating; its numerous local rulers were virtually independent. The Mongols were shortly to invade the region and strike the final blow against the caliphate. Religious unity, too, had long crumbled: in addition to the division of Islām into two major groups—the Sunnī and the Shī'ah—countless small sects had developed, often with the support of local rulers. Ṣūfism (Islāmic mysticism), too, was gaining ground. Like the philosopher al-Ghazālī, a century earlier, ar-Rāzī was a "middle-roader" who attempted, in his own way, to reconcile a rationalistic theology and philosophy incorporating concepts taken from Aristotle and other Greek philosophers with the Qur'ān (Islāmic scripture). This attempt inspired *al-Mabāḥith al-mashriqīyah* ("Eastern Discourses"), a summation of his philosophical and theological positions, and several commentaries on Avicenna (Ibn Sīnā), as well as his extremely wide-ranging commentary on the Qur'ān (*Mafātīḥ al-ghayb* or *Kitāb at-tafsīr, al-kabīr* "The Keys to the Unknown" or "The Great Commentary"), which ranks among the greatest works of its kind in Islām. Equally famous is his *Muḥaṣṣal afkār al-mutaqaddimīn wa-al-muta'akhkhirīn* ("Collection of the Opinions of Ancients and Moderns"), which was accepted from the first as a classic of *kalām* (Muslim theology). His other books, in addition to a general encyclopaedia, dealt with subjects as varied as medicine, astrology, geometry, physiognomy, mineralogy, and grammar.

Ar-Rāzī's wide variety of works

Ar-Rāzī was not only a persuasive preacher, but a master of debate. His ability to refute the arguments of others, together with his aggressiveness, self-confidence, irritability, and bad temper, made many enemies for him. His worldly success made others jealous of him.

Moreover, on occasion he could show extreme malice. With his connivance, his elder brother, who openly resented his success, was imprisoned by the Khwārezm-Shāh (ruler of Turkistan), and died in prison. A famous preacher with whom he had quarrelled was drowned by royal command. It is reported, however, that one incident persuaded him to cease attacks against the Ismāʿīlīs—a Shīʿah sect of Islām also known as Seveners because they believe that Ismāʿīl, the seventh *imām* (spiritual leader), was the last of the *imām*s. After ar-Rāzī had taunted the Ismāʿīlīs as having no valid proofs for their beliefs, an Ismāʿīlī gained access to him by posing as a pupil and pointed a knife at his chest, saying: "This is our proof." It has been suggested further that ar-Rāzī's death was not from natural causes, but that he was poisoned by the Karrāmīyah (a Muslim anthropomorphist sect), in revenge for his attacks on them.

Ar-Rāzī loved disputation so much that he went out of his way to present unorthodox and heretical religious views as fully and as favourably as possible, before refuting them. This habit gave his opponents grounds for accusing him of heresy. It was said: "He states the views of the enemies of orthodoxy most persuasively, and those of the orthodoxy most unconvincingly." His thorough presentations of unorthodox views make his works a useful source of information about little-known Muslim sects. He himself admitted that, when unable to find a statement of arguments in favour of some position, he went to all lengths to present it as well as possible. He was thus a good "devil's advocate," though he maintained firmly that he championed only orthodoxy.

In his prime he was so keen on learning that he resented time spent eating. But toward the end of his life, he regretted his preoccupation with learning and disputation. In his testament, he stated:

I have examined the methods of theology and philosophy, and have not found in them the benefit I found in the Koran. For the Koran ascribes glory and majesty to God, and forbids meddling with obscurities and contradictions.

Before he died in 1209, he asked his pupils to conceal his body, lest his opponents dishonour it. So they buried him at dusk on a hill facing a village near Herāt. Ar-Rāzī was a many-sided genius and a colourful personality, regarded by some Muslims as a major "renewer of the faith." According to tradition, one such was due to appear each century, and al-Ghazālī had been the one immediately before ar-Rāzī. His aim, like al-Ghazālī's, was doubtless to be a revitalizer and reconciler in Islām, but he did not have al-Ghazālī's originality, nor was he often able to make readers aware of his personal religious experience, as al-Ghazālī could. His genius for analysis sometimes led him into long and tortuous arguments, yet he compensates for these shortcomings by his very wide knowledge, which incorporated most disciplines—even the sciences—into his religious writings. In the centuries after his death, Muslim philosophers and theologians were to turn to his works frequently for guidance.

BIBLIOGRAPHY. M.M. SHARIF (ed.), *A History of Muslim Philosophy*, vol. 1, pp. 642–655 (1963); YOUSSEF MOURAD, *La Physiognomie arabe, et le Kitab al-Firasa de Fakhr al-Din al-Razi* (1939); for information about ar-Rāzī's medical works, see C. ELGOOD, *A Medical History of Persia and the Eastern Caliphate* (1951); and FATHALLA KHOLEIF, *A Study on Fakhr al-Dīn al-Rāzī and His Controversies in Transoxiana* (1966), containing a useful introductory chapter; for information about Muslim sects, see A.S. TRITTON, *Muslim Theology* (1947); articles in the *Encyclopaedia of Islam;* and ar-Rāzī's great commentary, *Mafātīḥ al-ghayb* (various printings).

(J.A.H.)

Falconiformes

More than any other group of birds, the diurnal birds of prey, order Falconiformes, have long interested men, and for several reasons. They are often large, conspicuous birds of swift, graceful flight, attracting attention from the smaller birds. Falconiforms compete with man for food by occasionally preying on his domestic stock (though on a small scale). But more significantly, they feed upon pests of human food supplies. Because of their predatory, or raptorial, skill, a few falcons and hawks are used for falconry, mainly for sport, much less importantly to obtain food.

GENERAL FEATURES

Falconiforms are seldom abundant but may be common or widespread, occurring in varied habitats. All are diurnal, none truly nocturnal, though several are active at dawn and dusk. With few exceptions they feed on the flesh of other animals, taken alive or found dead. Although some, especially in high latitudes, migrate, most do not. Some, especially large eagles, are of economic importance, preying upon animals maintained by man (sheep, game birds, etc.), eating otherwise noxious carrion, or feeding upon pests of human crops (hares, rodents, game birds, locusts). The low population density of most species indicates that their economic importance is usually exaggerated. They do not feed upon man himself (except when he is dead, in the case of vultures), do not eat babies (as eagles have been accused of doing), and are not important disease vectors.

Falconiforms vary from tiny falconets (*Microhierax*), weighing 35 grams (1.2 ounces) or less, to huge vultures and eagles, with weights up to 14 kilograms (31 pounds), certainly the most formidable avian predators. Structure varies according to hunting methods, type of prey, and habitat. Carrion-eating vultures have broad, soaring wings and weak feet; speedy falcons have bullet-shaped bodies and long, pointed wings; manoeuvrable forest-living species, such as accipiters, some eagles, and forest falcons, have short, rounded wings and long, rounded or graduated tails. The beak is always hooked and is used to tear flesh from prey held in the feet; it may be further modified for special types of food, such as snails or bone marrow. The feet, which are the primary means of killing prey, are exceptionally strong, equipped with long, curved talons, except in the vultures, which feed on carrion. Sight and hearing are highly developed, but the sense of smell is usually poor or absent.

Falconiforms occur worldwide, on all continents except Antarctica, and on many oceanic islands. They are found from Arctic to equatorial latitudes, in almost stark desert and in tropical forest, but are commonest and most varied in warm, relatively open country; many, especially in South America, have adapted to forest life. They are never abundant, except locally, where gregarious species may roost or feed together, and are usually dispersed at the rate of a pair to 15 square kilometres (five square miles) or more. Their numbers are not always density dependent on those of food animals, but, where food is abundant, raptor numbers may be limited by territorial behaviour.

NATURAL HISTORY

Life history. Large falconiforms are among the longest lived birds, as shown both by records in captivity and by the slow breeding rates observed in the wild. Where not persecuted, populations of large falconiforms are remarkably stable; breeding rates are presumably adjusted to the mean life-span of individuals, taken from hatching. A species that averages two young annually per pair has a mean life-span of one year; and one that rears one young every two years, a life-span of four years.

The falconiform life cycle includes four stages, each of which varies mainly according to size—the larger the bird, the longer the stage. Latitude also affects these periods, with longer fledging periods in equatorial than in temperate latitudes for species of similar size.

The fledging period. The fledging period, from hatching to first flight, varies from 23 days in small accipiters to 120–130 days in large eagles and vultures and up to 150 in condors. In this stage the downy nestling develops to adult size (weight increases up to 40 times), grows feathers, and finally flies. It must be fed at first, but before its first flight it learns to tear up prey brought by the parents. Fledging periods are longer, in birds of a given size, in the tropics, probably associated with shorter summer day length.

Marginal notes: Assessment

Habits and appearance

Distribution

Four stages of life cycle

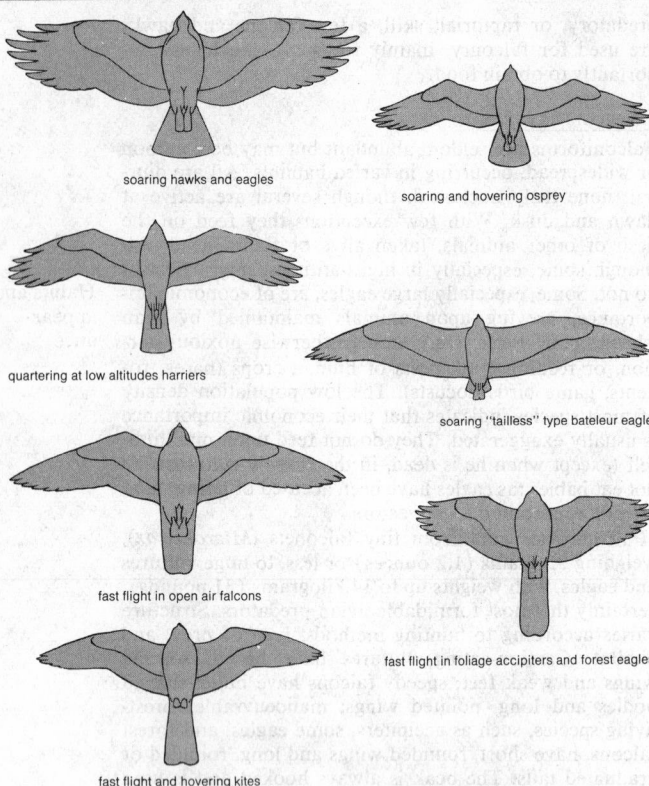

soaring hawks and eagles

soaring and hovering osprey

quartering at low altitudes harriers

soaring "tailless" type bateleur eagle

fast flight in open air falcons

fast flight in foliage accipiters and forest eagles

fast flight and hovering kites

Figure 1: Modifications for specialized types of flight among falconiforms.
Drawing by R. Keane

The post-fledging period. The post-fledging period, in which the young remain near the nest and food is brought by the parents, ends when the young become independent, apparently often of their own accord, not, as in some other birds, in response to increasing parental aggression. They grow no larger, but their flight quills harden. These immature birds are not strong on the wing for three to eight weeks after the first flight. This phase varies from one to 11 months or even more, again mainly according to size, but also showing specific variation. In the crowned eagle, the post-fledging period is nine to 11 months, but in the related martial eagle it is much shorter.

The period as a juvenile. The period as a juvenile, an independent, sexually immature form, is distinguished by various immature and subadult plumages, often very different from the adult. The young raptor flies about, migrates if necessary, kills its own prey, and behaves like an adult except that it cannot breed. This period varies from about nine months in small species, sexually mature in their first year (sparrow hawks, kestrels, and some kites), to four or more years in large eagles and up to seven years in condors. It is usually a period of heavy mortality, particularly in migrant species of temperate climates.

The breeding adult life. The breeding adult life is characterized by mating, nesting, and rearing young. Most adults pair. The duration of this phase has been rarely recorded for wild individuals, but a peregrine falcon (*Falco peregrinus*) bred on the Sun-Life Building in Montreal, Quebec, for 16 years. Two female crowned eagles bred for nine and eight years and one male for 13 years.

Life-spans of wild raptors may be calculated from banding (ringing) records, from observed changes of mate, and from the percentage of immatures in the population, especially if different ages are recognizable.

Life-span Recoveries of banded birds indicate that 50–75 percent of young raptors die before sexual maturity. The smaller falcons and accipiters apparently average less than three years total life-span, but some individuals may attain ten to 12 years. Larger species live longer. Ospreys and buteos may average eight to 10 years, but have higher mortality rates (75–80 percent in the first year). Life spans of

more than 20 years have been recorded from both groups, but the longest known life-span among wild falconiforms is that of a red kite of 26 years.

In certain large falconiforms, differences in plumage due to age and individual variation allow an observer to recognize individual birds. Since large eagles mate for life, it may be assumed that a change of mates indicates that one of the pair is dead. L.H. Brown has found that in crowned eagles (*Stephanoaetus coronatus*) such changes occur every six to seven years, giving a mean adult life of 12–14 years or 16–18 years when the four years prior to maturity are included.

In many species immature birds are easily distinguished from adults, and the percentage of immatures in the population can be related to assumed mortality before sexual maturity and to the number of years before adulthood, allowing an estimate of the average age of adults. Immatures comprise about 30 percent of the population in the bateleur (*Terathopius ecaudatus*), 18 percent in the lammergeier (*Gypaetus barbatus*), and 16–25 percent in the African fish eagle (*Haliaetus vocifer*). With about 75 percent loss during the period of immaturity and the acquisition of adult plumage at seven, five, and four years, respectively, the mean adult life-span in these species may be estimated at 23, 27, and 18–24 years.

Such methods provide, at best, an informed estimate and the potential life-span is rarely, if ever, attained in the wild state. In captivity many large raptors live for over 30 years, eagles and vultures for 40–50 years. A bateleur, at 55, is the oldest acceptable record; records of 60 or more years are poorly documented.

Behaviour. Falconiforms hunt by sight in daylight and normally roost on a perch, a tree branch, a rock ledge, or occasionally (harriers) on the ground in long grass. A few, including some falcons and sparrow hawks, are active at twilight; in fact, the bat hawk (*Machaerhamphus alcinus*) catches all its food in about half an hour at dusk. The only species actually recorded feeding at night are certain Indian vultures (in moonlight on tiger kills). Most raptors sleep all night, with head buried in the feathers of the back or hunched upon the shoulders.

Activity may begin soon after dawn with short "warming-up" flights, serious hunting beginning later. Some accipiters commence hunting at daybreak, when their avian prey is most active. Large, heavy species, however, do not usually start hunting or foraging until some time after dawn. Large vultures are unable to fly until updrafts are generated by thermal activity, but smaller species are able to fly soon after dawn. Certain specialized types with flapping flight, such as harriers, can fly equally easily at any time of the day. Bateleurs get on the wing early and fly most of the day, travelling perhaps 200–300 air miles on most days; however, very large species such as eagles and vultures probably fly for no more than four to six hours a day.

Before the day's flight, a raptor usually preens, casts, and defecates. Castings are regurgitated indigestible balls of fur, feathers, insect hard parts, etc. Preening is performed mainly with the bill, but falconiforms also scratch with their formidable talons. They frequently "rouse," fluffing out and shaking all their feathers.

Many falconiforms hunt daily, others every few days, feeding in the interim on the remains of their kills. Killing frequency depends on appetite and the size of the animal killed; a kestrel consumes many grasshoppers per day, a crowned eagle one suni antelope (about four kilograms; eight pounds) every three to four days. Appetite and crop capacity permit ingestion of several days' ration at a meal, and larger species can go without food for long periods without ill effect. With rare recorded exceptions, falconiforms will not hunt unless hungry and do not kill wantonly. Many species hunt from perches, flying from one to another. Others hunt on the wing, soaring or hovering at up to 100 metres above the ground or water. One species, the secretary bird (*Sagittarius serpentarius*), is mainly terrestrial, and several others (chanting goshawks, honey buzzards, and the spotted eagle) walk about on the ground. The honey buzzard digs out wasps' nests. One

General activity

Hunting and feeding

species, the Egyptian vulture (*Neophron percnopterus*), hurls stones at ostrich eggs with its beak to break them.

In warm climates, hunting time may be short, one to two hours in 24; in temperate winters, when prey is scarce, it occupies up to five to seven hours. When not hunting, falconiforms loaf on perches or soar, sometimes at great height. Vultures or eagles encountered soaring very high up are not hunting, especially when their crops are full.

Roosting Toward evening a falconiform may return to a regular roosting place or may settle for the night where it is. Vultures often return nightly up to 100 miles to regular roosting cliffs or trees. In many less active species, the roost is in the same general area as the nest. Members of a pair separated all day may rejoin at roosting time, and gregarious species (vultures, kites, and some others, such as the red-footed falcon) are most gregarious at roosts. Prior to settling to sleep, the bird usually preens again, but activity is reduced once the bird has settled on the perch for the night. Finally, when light fails, the raptor falls asleep on its perch and remains thus without moving until the following morning. If disturbed at night, however, it can fly well enough to save itself but will not travel any distance.

Locomotion. All falconiforms fly well, some excellently. Few hunt on the ground, but all can walk or hop. With one exception—the secretary bird—flight is the most important method of locomotion. Modes of flight include flapping, gliding, soaring, or diving (stooping) and are used to locate and kill prey, move from perch to perch, or migrate. Adaptations for swift or slow flight, mainly associated with habitat or type of prey, are varied.

All species can use flapping flight, but it is laboured in heavy species (vultures, condors). Most use it only to get under way or to move from perch to perch, thereafter gliding, hovering, or soaring. Harriers sustain flapping flight, interspersed with short glides, for long periods as they hunt small animals in open, grassy country. This also assists them to migrate across open water, usually avoided by soaring species because of the lack of thermal updrafts. Accipiters accelerate in pursuit by rapid flapping flight, and many other species travel short distances by flapping alternated with gliding, especially when air currents are lacking.

All of the large species are adapted for soaring flight and even accipiters, swift falcons, and the secretary bird can soar well. A typical soaring wing is rather long and moderately broad; *i.e.*, of low aspect ratio. High-aspect-ratio wings (long and extremely narrow), found in seabirds, would presumably be inconvenient to falconiforms, which often require manoeuvrability in tight spaces. The wing usually has the outer four to six primaries more or less emarginated on one or both webs, forming at the spread wing tip slots that reduce turbulence, and permitting each feather to bend as an individual airfoil under a differential load, thereby increasing lift. Such a wing is typical of eagles, buzzards, vultures, and kites. In a few species (Indian black eagle, African harrier hawk), the primaries are long, soft, slightly emarginated, and flexible, probably associated with slow flight.

Soaring on updrafts The ability to soar and circle in thermals is controlled by wing loading (the ratio of weight to wing area). The higher the wing loading, the larger the turning circle and the larger the thermal "bubble" required for soaring to gain height. Smaller species (*e.g.*, the black kite), with low wing loadings, can utilize smaller thermals than can heavy vultures. Wing loading increases proportionately with weight (as the cube of body size) while wing area increases as the square (see also FORM AND FUNCTION, BIO-LOGICAL). The general rule is varied by specific adaptations. Some species (lammergeier, harriers) have much lower wing loadings than others of similar weight and have more buoyant, easy flight. In soaring flight, forward velocity is attained by gliding, with the aid of gravity; the bird mounts on rising air. Increasing the angle of glide increases speed until, in a vertical dive (falcons), it is believed to attain 160–240 kilometres (100–150 miles) per hour. Some species (bateleur, lammergeier) are special-

ized for gliding, almost without wing flapping. Bateleurs glide at an airspeed of 55–85 kilometres per hour for much of the day; they have long wings and very short tails, steering by sideways tilting, or canting. Lammergeiers glide rather slowly, assisted by long, diamond-shaped tails.

Falcons, especially the large bird-killing species (peregrine, gyrfalcon, lanner, etc.), have heavy, bullet-shaped bodies and long, pointed wings; their high wing loading provides high diving speed. They often attack in the air and in a dive can overtake species that would easily evade them in straight flapping flight. Few eagles are as swift, but many combine distinguished soaring and gliding ability with swiftness and agility in attack upon prey.

Walking and hopping On the ground falconiforms progress by walking or hopping; in especially large vultures hopping is elaborated into bounding threat displays. On a branch they move sideways by sidling or by walking "hand over hand" (vulturine fish eagle, harrier hawk). On the ground eagles walk slowly and deliberately. African harrier hawks and South American crane hawks have long, slim legs that can bend somewhat backward at the tarsal joint, permitting the attainment of peculiar situations and enabling the birds to probe cavities.

The secretary bird is the only primarily terrestrial species. It flies only to move from place to place or in display but nevertheless has been seen soaring at 4,000 metres. It walks with a rapid, steady pace, head jerking to and fro, varying this regular progress with bouts of quick stamping steps, to flush possible prey. It has short toes (like the gruiform bustards) and long, crane like legs, suited for rapid walking over long distances. It roosts in trees but descends to the ground to hunt soon after daybreak.

Reproduction. Many falconiforms pair for life; others, notably migrant species, may pair anew each year. Occasionally, immatures pair with adults, but usually only sexually mature individuals attempt to breed. Immatures, however, often perform typical display movements and a pair bond may be formed between an adult and an immature, but the latter may be replaced by an adult if one should appear.

The breeding pattern follows the usual sequence of nuptial display, nest building, incubation, fledging period, and post-fledging period. The length of the breeding period varies from about three months in the smallest species to over 15 months in condors, crowned eagles, and probably harpy eagles. No species regularly produces two broods in a season, but second broods have been recorded, even in some large species. Some nomadic species, such as the elanine kites, may breed more often in response to, for instance, high local rodent populations.

Nuptial displays are often spectacular, sometimes inconspicuous. The common forms are: calling from a perch; calling from soaring flight; undulating flight, diving, and swooping up, often with loud calling; mutual displays, in which the male dives with lowered feet at the female, who turns over and raises her claws to his; rarely, cartwheeling, in which the pair lock feet and descend in whirling flight (*e.g.*, some eagles and kites). Most species perform several types of display, but species inhabiting woodland or forest display more often and more vociferously than related species of open country.

Nesting Most species build nests on trees, ledges of cliffs, or, rarely, on the ground. All Accipitridae, Pandionidae, Sagittariidae, and the caracaras construct nests, usually of sticks. The Cathartidae and the remaining Falconidae (forest falcons, falconets, and true falcons) do not make nests but use a hollow tree, another bird's nest, or a scrape on a ledge. Constructed nests vary from small structures of twigs and vines (*Aviceda*) to enormous, annually augmented piles of sticks (many eagles). Small species usually build a new nest annually; large species tend to return to, and repair, an old nest. Imminent occupation is usually indicated by fresh green material, which continues to be added until late in the fledging period but does not necessarily mean that eggs will be laid. The same site, but not always the same nest or ledge, may be occupied for several years, generations, or centuries. Some large eagles use the same nest for 50 years or more, others haphazardly use several alternates.

Many species lay only one egg; few lay more than four. The largest clutches are laid by small falcons and accipiters of temperate latitudes and by ground-nesting harriers. Clutches of related species are smaller in the tropics than in high latitudes. The eggs are laid at two- to four-day intervals, incubation beginning with the first egg. Falconiform eggs are rather large for the size of the birds and are usually rounded ovals, white or greenish, more or less heavily spotted, occasionally completely covered with brown or red-brown pigment. In Carthartae the colour of the inside of the shell is yellowish white; in Accipitridae, Sagittariidae, and Pandionidae it is green or blue green; and in Falconidae, buff or reddish. Incubation, usually by the female alone (the male sometimes takes a share), occupies from 28 days in small falcons to 50 days or more in large vultures. Buzzards (*Buteo*) incubate for 30–35 days, though some are larger than small eagles with incubation periods of 45 days.

The eggs hatch in the order in which they were laid. By the time the last egg has hatched, the first-hatched chick may have tripled its weight and may kill its sibling, either directly or through competition for food. Newly hatched chicks are covered in natal down, later replaced by a thicker, woollier coat; at this stage parental brooding is reduced by day. Feathers erupt during the fledging period and almost cover the nestling at midpoint. At this stage most young learn to tear up their own prey.

Parental attention is steadily reduced, from continuous brooding day and night to leaving the feathered young entirely alone except for brief feeding visits. The young make their first flights unaided by parental coaxing. The adult roles are usually clear-cut. In the early fledging period, the male kills for himself, his mate, and the brood, doubling or trebling his previous killing rate. When partly feathered young can tear up their prey, the female no longer stays near the nest but hunts and thereafter brings more prey than the male.

After their first flight, the young remain near the nest for several weeks or months. They are provided with food by the parents but may also learn to kill. The longest known post-fledging periods are in crowned eagles and condors; in the crowned eagle the young remains dependent for nine to 11 months, and this species normally breeds only every second year.

Especially in large species, breeding does not necessarily occur annually. The number of young reared per pair per year varies from 2.5 to three in small falcons and sparrow hawks of temperate climates to 0.4 or even less in some tropical eagles and vultures. Breeding success, like clutch size, tends to be lower in related species in the tropics than in temperate zones. Low breeding success may fluctuate with adverse winters, poor food supplies, or even territorial behaviour in crowded habitats.

Ecology. Falconiforms prey on small animals or eat carrion; the vulturine fish eagle, however, feeds mainly on oil palm fruits.

Food supplies exert a general influence over populations, but it also seems that when food is superabundant the population does not rise proportionately. In the Scottish golden eagle, the home range of a pair is about 4,400 hectares (11,000 acres), irrespective of food abundance. A breeding pair of raptors apparently maintains a territory containing much more food than it can possibly utilize. In some cases such home ranges are maintained by aggressive behaviour; in others the precise method is obscure. In colonial vultures no home range is maintained, and the only defended territory is the few yards round the nest.

Food requirements

From a combination of factors a reasonably accurate estimate of the minimum daily food need for a raptor can be made. The amount of kills wasted (varying from less than 5 to 20 percent by weight, according to type of prey taken) is added to the minimum daily food demand, to determine the amount that must be killed to maintain a pair and their young for one year. For example, if a falconiform weighs 1,200 grams, has a mean food requirement of 8 percent of bodyweight, eats 96 grams a day and 36 kilograms each year, and feeds on birds, involving waste of about 15 percent of all kills, it must kill 41 kilograms of prey each year to fulfill its needs.

Individuals of one species do not usually tolerate others of the same species in their home breeding range. The same area, however, may support several other species, preferring different types of prey and so not competing with one another. In an area of varied habitat, up to 20 different species may occur (even more with migrants), exerting a much greater and more complicated, but still broadly quantifiable, pressure on populations of available prey. Closely related groups may show ecological separation. For example, some African vultures feed in groups upon the soft flesh and intestines of preys, while others tear at sinews and hide or snatch meat from other species. Smaller vultures pick up scraps or use their slender beaks to reach cavities inaccessible to birds with heavier beaks. All these birds may feed together at the same carcass, but without competing for food, though individuals of each species maintain a dominance hierarchy by aggressive movements to each other.

In the Arctic only the gyrfalcon does not regularly migrate but subsists on wintering ptarmigan. In summer several other species arrive, but so do many species of prey, and lemmings multiply, greatly increasing food supplies. In African savannas and southern Indian rice fields, resident falconiform populations are greatly augmented in winter by migrant populations of buzzards, kites, harriers, and small falcons. This sharply increases the total predator pressure on prey populations, but it does not appear that this influx of migrants has any adverse effect on the resident populations, which may be breeding while the migrants are present.

In most cases it appears that falconiforms have a slight or negligible effect on prey populations. The annual needs of resident species may vary from $\frac{1}{20}$ to $\frac{1}{1,000}$ or even less of available prey. In migrant winter populations, the effect, locally, may be much greater than in resident breeding populations. The availability or visibility of the prey also plays a part. Among the food of the European sparrow hawk (*Accipiter nisus*), conspicuous or gregarious birds of open ground are more often killed than inconspicuous skulking species. Prey risk (the likelihood of an individual being killed) is increased by low prey numbers, reduced cover, and behaviour that exposes the animal. The total effect of falconiforms on their prey is compounded of their own behaviour and that of the animals they feed upon.

IMPORTANCE TO MAN

Beneficial effects

Most falconiforms are directly beneficial to man—feeding on pests or carrion—or neutral—feeding on animals and birds that do not directly affect man. A few species, usually large, spectacular, and uncommon (larger eagles, falcons, and accipiters), may prey on man's domestic stock or poultry or on game birds or fish. In East African grasslands about 86 percent of falconiforms are beneficial, 11 percent neutral, and only 3 percent potentially harmful. Such figures vary from one region to another, but potentially harmful species are always in the minority. It is the more regrettable that, because of ignorance and unreasoning prejudice (especially in the more advanced areas such as North America, Europe, and Australia), beneficial, neutral, and potentially harmless species are all indiscriminately destroyed, even rendered extinct locally.

Detailed quantitative studies invariably have shown that the harm done to man's interests by any falconiform has been grossly exaggerated; even the supposedly harmful species often kill other potentially harmful species (*e.g.*, crows, rats, mustelids). The predation effect of any species is relatively small in relation to the total number of potential prey in any home range. Moreover, even in potentially harmful species, few animals of potential or actual interest to man are taken. In the African fish eagle and Scottish golden eagle, the population may take a fraction of 1 percent of the human fish catch or of the lambs available in an average home range. In North America and Australia, where large eagles have been destroyed on a greater scale than elsewhere, persecution is not based on even rudimentary assessment of the eagles' diet and appetite. Damage to human interests is worst under poor management conditions; for instance, when unfed poultry are on free range or weak lambs live on overgrazed pasture. In rare cases, such as where hatchery trout or reared pheasants are unnaturally concentrated, individual hawks or eagles may have to be controlled when damage is proved; but this is no excuse for wholesale persecution of a species.

Entirely beneficial species include vultures, elanine kites, kestrels and other small insectivorous falcons, most buzzards (*Buteo* and related species), and many small eagles. Neutral species, such as snake eagles and chanting goshawks, can safely be ignored. Objective analysis of the predation situation indicates that diurnal raptors deserve protection except where extensive damage can be proved. Extensive damage is frequently claimed without proof; for instance, in the southwestern United States, where the golden eagle has been persecuted for alleged damage to sheep, improbable in any event and impossible on the scale claimed.

A few falconiform birds have been trained to secure game animals for man, either for sport or to provide food (see FALCONRY).

Need for protection Falconiforms need no protection except from man. Conservation problems, therefore, mean conserving raptors living in or passing through inhabited areas. Undoubtedly the main difficulty is ignorant prejudice against falconiforms by educated, civilized man, which is seldom found, much less effectively exercised, in more primitive human communities. A recent threat, since 1950, is the persistent effect of highly toxic agricultural chemicals (DDT, dieldrin, etc.)—again, the product of civilized man. Positive conservation of falconiforms must include the control of habitat destruction; of active persecution by shooting, trapping, poisoning, and collecting of eggs of threatened species; and of the widespread toxic effects of persistent agricultural chemicals.

Agricultural communities destroy some types of habitat, especially forests, but create others in the process. In Africa, for instance, some forest falconiforms may be eliminated, but much larger populations of adaptable species such as black kites, hooded vultures, and long-crested eagles may move in. The effect of agriculture is not always detrimental, especially when a mixed landscape of forest and open country results. Before the advent of chlorinated hydrocarbons, the peregrine was most numerous in Britain in habitats close to agricultural areas with high populations of avian prey. A sparse population of rural cultivators may have no appreciable effect on a mixed population of falconiforms over long periods of time.

Overcollecting for zoos and museums, and for falconry, has severely affected some species. The behaviour of the few individuals who collect the specimens or eggs of threatened species for commercial purposes must be controlled. In a few instances, chiefly of island species such as the Philippine monkey-eating eagle, this is urgent.

Effect of pesticides Toxic agricultural chemicals are the most difficult of conservation problems because of their subtle and widespread effects (affecting even migrant populations of some hawks that breed in uninhabited areas) and the benefits they confer on human food supplies. The best hope, other than new developments of less toxic substances, is realization of the probably serious overall effect of these long-lasting poisons in contamination of the whole environment. If, as appears likely, the chemicals eventually will adversely affect man himself, control of the use of these chemicals will follow; and the falconiforms will benefit indirectly. (See PEST CONTROL.)

FORM AND FUNCTION

The main distinguishing characters of falconiforms are: the hooked beak, used for tearing flesh; taloned feet, used for piercing, grasping, and killing prey; and large eyes, with very acute vision. The hooked beak and taloned feet are shared with the unrelated owls, which show similar or parallel evolution. In the falconiforms themselves, parallel evolution for scavenging is shown by the New World vultures (Cathartidae) and the Old World vultures (Accipitridae).

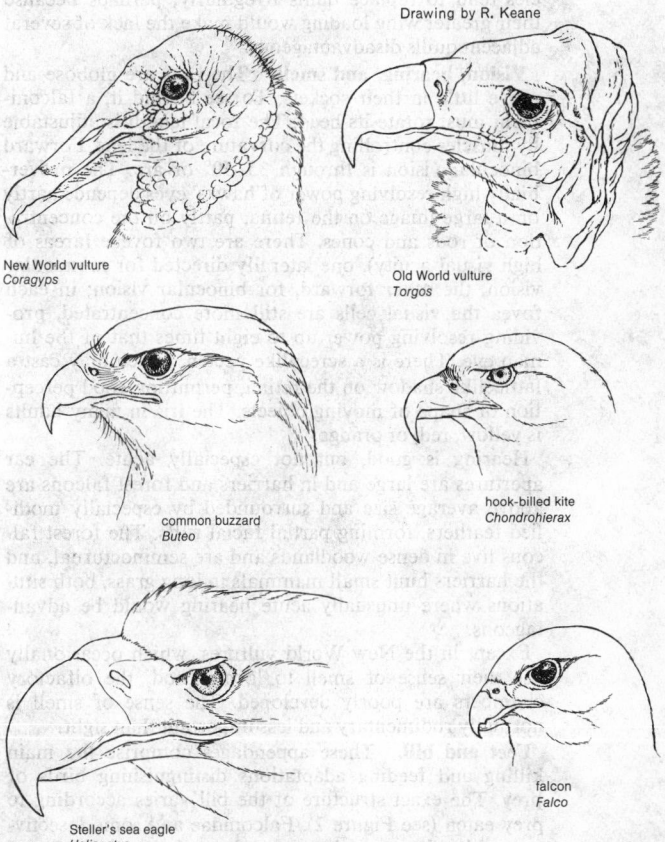

Drawing by R. Keane

New World vulture
Coragyps

Old World vulture
Torgos

common buzzard
Buteo

hook-billed kite
Chondrohierax

Steller's sea eagle
Haliaeetus

falcon
Falco

Figure 2: *Heads of some falconiforms.*
A New World vulture, *Coragyps*, with a weak beak for carrion eating; an Old World vulture, *Torgos*, with a stronger beak for tearing at larger animals; a buzzard, *Buteo*, with a simple raptorial beak for killing and eating small mammals; a hook-billed kite, *Chondrohierax*, with a strongly hooked beak for eating snails; a sea eagle, *Haliaeetus*, with a deep, narrow beak of uncertain adaptive value; a falcon, *Falco*, with a toothed beak for shearing and plucking feathers.

Size and weight. Most falconiforms are large. Extremes are the Andean condor (ten to 14 kilograms, wingspan three to 3.35 metres) and the tiny eastern falconets (*Microhierax* species; 35 grams or less). Many species range from 400–2,000 grams in weight. Females are normally 20–100 percent larger than males, especially in bird-killing falcons and accipiters. In vultures, however, the male is normally 10–15 percent larger.

Plumage and molt. Falconiforms are bulky, heavily feathered birds, lightweight in relation to their apparent size. The first plumage is usually white or gray down, the prepennae. The preplumulae, or second down, grows through the first after days or weeks and is itself superseded by feathers erupting from the prepennae follicles. The latest feathers to develop fully are wing and tail quills, which are large, strong, and often especially adapted.

The immature plumage, presumably representing a primitive type, usually differs markedly from the adult. Adult dress is acquired by a series of molts with, in large species, several intermediate or subadult stages. Immatures usually are brown and streaked or spotted; adults may be more brightly coloured. The sexes usually are alike in plumage. In some island species—*e.g.*, the Madagascar cuckoo falcon (*Aviceda*)—the plumage type found in the immature persists in adult life.

Plumage is replaced by a molt lasting four months to several years, slower and more irregular in larger species. Wing quills are molted in definite sequence. In many Accipitridae molt begins with primary feather number 1 (innermost) and proceeds in regular sequence to number 10 (outermost). In falcons it begins at primary feather 4 and proceeds both ways, outward and inward. Large species tend to replace quills irregularly, perhaps because their greater wing loading would make the lack of several adjacent quills disadvantageous.

Vision, hearing, and smell. The eyes are globose and move little in their sockets. To see behind it, a falconiform must rotate its head. The focal length is adjustable by muscles controlling the curvature of the lens. Forward binocular vision is through 35–50° of arc. The proverbially high resolving power of hawks' eyes depends partly on a large image on the retina, partly on the concentration of rods and cones. There are two foveae (areas of high visual acuity), one laterally directed for monocular vision, the other forward, for binocular vision; in each fovea the visual cells are still more concentrated, providing resolving power up to eight times that of the human eye. There is a screenlike pecten, which may cast a latticelike shadow on the retina, permitting good perception of shape of moving objects. The iris in many adults is yellow, red, or orange.

Hearing is good, but not especially acute. The ear apertures are large and in harriers and forest falcons are above average size and surrounded by especially modified feathers, forming partial facial ruffs. The forest falcons live in dense woodlands and are seminocturnal, and the harriers hunt small mammals in long grass, both situations where unusually acute hearing would be advantageous.

Except in the New World vultures, which occasionally use their sense of smell to locate food, the olfactory chambers are poorly developed. The sense of smell is normally rudimentary and less important than sight.

Feet and bill. These appendages comprise the main killing and feeding adaptations distinguishing birds of prey. The exact structure of the bill varies according to prey eaten (see Figure 2). Falconidae and some insectivorous kites have notches or teeth on the cutting edge of the beak. In falcons these assist in breaking the necks of prey, but their purpose in kites is obscure. In Old World vultures the bills vary, permitting ecological separation while at food.

Killing of prey

Prey is normally killed with the feet. Three toes are directed forward, one behind. The hind toe is usually heavier and longer taloned than the others. In the osprey the outer toe is reversible, for more effective handling of fish. Fish-eating falconiforms have sharp spicules on the soles of the toes to grasp slippery prey. The feet may vary from long, slim toed, needle taloned (bird killing, as in accipiters) to short, thick toed (snake grasping, *Circaetus*) or heavy toed, with thick, strong talons, capable of paralyzing medium-sized mammals. In Old and New World vultures, which seldom or never kill, the feet lack long sharp talons.

EVOLUTION AND PALEONTOLOGY

Falconiforms have no obvious evolutionary links with other birds. Currently they are placed between ducks, on the one hand, and game birds on the other; but they bear no clear resemblance to either, while fossil evidence does not indicate intermediate links. The most obvious physical specializations of falconiforms—the cutting, tearing bill and taloned feet—do not indicate close relationships with owls but are due to similar trends in evolution, though some recent anatomical work indicates that owls and the family Falconidae may be more closely related than was at one time thought.

Fossil falconiforms

Rather few fossils of falconiforms have been found, and those that have may repay re-investigation. A generalized type is known from the Eocene (50,000,000 years ago). The oldest known raptorial bird, *Lithornis*, of the upper Paleocene, may have been a cathartid vulture. The Cathartae may have evolved in the Old World, dying out

there and surviving only in the New World. Fossil New World vultures include a large terrestrial species, *Neocathartes grallator*, and a huge vulture, *Teratornis merriami*, from the La Brea tar pits in California. Because of their apparently ancient origin, cathartids may be regarded as primitive survivors.

The secretary bird is thought by some to be a descendant of formidable terrestrial predators, *Brontornis*, *Mesembryornis*, and *Diatryma*. These also may have evolved into the South American Cariamidae, which accordingly may be more closely related to the secretary bird than are the latter to other falconiforms.

Such evidence as there is indicates that the falconiforms diverged from their ancestral types 20,000,000 or more years ago, and that relationships with other groups have since become obscured. Certain evidence suggests that the order is polyphyletic in origin; however, their Mallophaga (feather lice) are similar throughout, and this question must remain unanswered until extensive additional information is available.

Among present-day falconiforms adaptive radiation has led to the development of certain climax types in apparently not very closely related birds. For instance, in Australia, buzzards (*Buteo*) are absent, but certain large kites have evolved to fit this niche. In South America the buzzard-like harpy eagle represents a climax of one line of evolution, filled in the Old World by large booted eagles such as *Stephanoaetus*. There has been much specialization for particular function in unrelated species; for instance, in the bullet-like shape of falcons, the spiculed feet of ospreys and certain eagles, and, perhaps most

Drawing by R. Keane

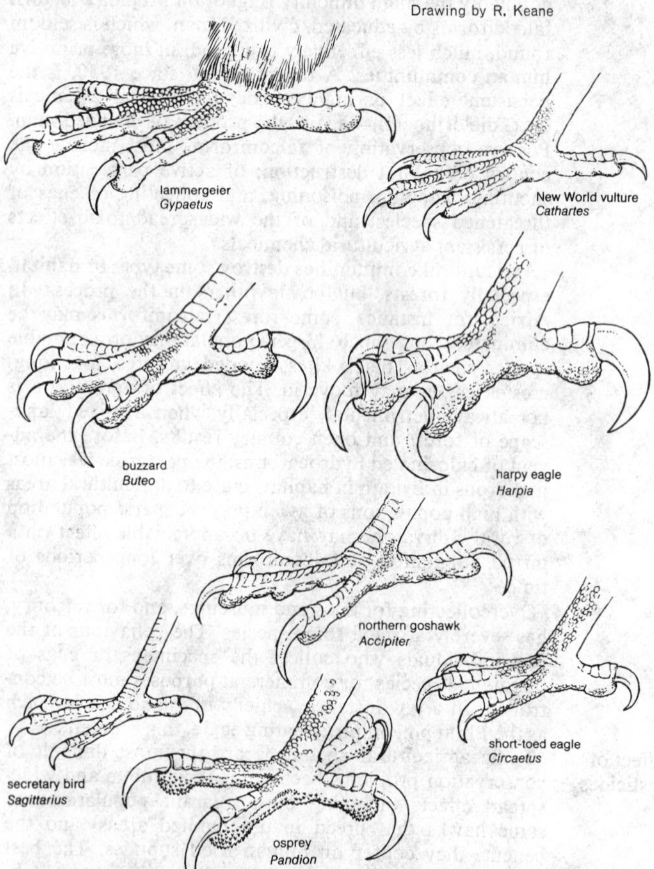

Figure 3: *Specialization of the feet of falconiforms.*
The moderately powerful foot of the lammergeier (*Gypaetus*); the weak foot of a New World vulture (*Cathartes*); the generalized raptorial foot of a buzzard (*Buteo*); the extremely powerful foot of the harpy eagle (*Harpia*); the foot of a bird-catching accipiter (*Accipiter*), with long toes and talons; the fish-gripping foot of the osprey (*Pandion*), with reversible outer toe and rough spicules on the soles; the foot of the short-toed eagle (*Circaetus*) for gripping snakes; the foot of the secretary bird (*Sagittarius*) adapted for walking.

striking, the auditory specialization of the harriers and the forest falcons.

CLASSIFICATION

No entirely satisfactory system of classification of the order Falconiformes has been agreed upon. Two rather different systems have been proposed, and much work is needed before some of the outstanding problems can be elucidated.

Distinguishing taxonomic features. The main features of falconiforms include the hooked "raptorial" bill; the basal cere, or bare skin, covering the nostrils; the powerful feet with hooked claws; sustained powers of flight and carnivorous habits; and difference in size between the sexes. Some suborders or families have additional characters; for instance, the Cathartae have pervious nostrils (*i.e.*, the partition between nostrils is incomplete) and a rudimentary hind toe; Pandionidae, a reversible outer toe; Sagittariidae, long legs with short, rather blunt toes; and Falconidae, toothed beak and long, sharply pointed wings, and a noncentrifugal wing molt. Some of these characters may indicate convergent evolution rather than true close relationships.

On the basis of inside eggshell colour, the order may be divided into three rather distinct groupings or suborders: the Cathartae, the Accipitres (with the secretary bird and osprey), and the Falcones. Biochemical analysis of egg-white protein tends to support these groupings and suggest that all are rather more closely allied to one another than to other groups of birds, even though there are some similarities with apparently unrelated orders, such as Procellariiformes. Egg-white proteins also indicate that cathartids are all closely interrelated and that they are related to Accipitridae. The Accipitridae are all rather closely related, though the egg-white patterns of Old World vultures and some kites indicate divergence. The egg-white patterns of Falconidae indicate close relationship within this family, but less close affinities with other falconiforms.

Annotated classification. The classification of L.H. Brown and D. Amadon, 1968, which is given below, was based upon that in J.L. Peters' *Check-List of Birds of the World,* modified as necessary in the light of modern knowledge. The main divergent view has been that of E. Stresemann, which was based largely on the sequence of wing molt and departed strongly from the order of Peters and from Brown and Amadon. Those groups indicated below by a dagger (†) are known only from fossils.

ORDER: FALCONIFORMES

Suborder Cathartae (New World vultures)
 Nearctic to Neotropical. Seven existing species; fossils dating back perhaps to Eocene.

†Superfamily Neocathartoidea
 One family, Neocathartidae. Fossil Nearctic, including *Neocathartes grallator,* differed from other Cathartae in having terrestrial habits.

Superfamily Cathartoidea
 Pleistocene fossil and present-day species, Nearctic and Neotropical, perhaps formerly Palearctic.

Family Cathartidae (New World vultures). Seven present-day Nearctic and Neotropical species and Pleistocene, Nearctic, and neotropical fossils. Pervious nostrils, rudimentary hind toe, large olfactory chambers. Large or medium sized (1.5–14 kg; 1.2–3 m wingspan); do not build nests; inside egg colour yellowish.

†Family Teratornithidae (teratorns). Very large-sized fossil Pleistocene species, including *Teratornis merriami* (estimated about 50 lb; 14 ft wingspan) and still larger species.

Suborder Accipitres

Superfamily Accipitroidea
 There are 207 worldwide existing species, small to large, and many fossils.

Family Pandionidae (osprey). One species, *Pandion haliaetus,* nearly worldwide, present-day; large, weight 900–1,500 g; wingspan 135–175 cm; resembles some kites in similar sternum and absence of bony eye shield; reversible outer toe, with talons rounded, not grooved; green inside eggshell; squirt droppings; littoral; builds own nest.

Family Accipitridae (kites, hawks, buzzards, harriers, eagles, Old World vultures). There are 206 species, worldwide, but some subgroups—*e.g.*, Old World vultures—confined to Europe, Asia, and Africa. Small to very large (100 g to about 10 kg); many adaptive radiations; forest or open country. In all, inside eggshell green; strong hooked talons in all but Old World vultures; squirt droppings; build own nests.

Superfamily Sagittaroidea
Family Sagittariidae (secretary bird). One species, *Sagittarius serpentarius,* central Africa; present-day, with some doubtful fossils. Large (weight 3.4–3.8 kg; wingspan 1.5–2 m); terrestrial, long legged, short toed; in nesting and display resembles Accipitridae. Inside eggshell green but certain other characters indicate affinity with South American Cariamidae. (See GRUIFORMES.) Usually accepted as falconiform but may not be.

Suborder Falcones
 There are 61 worldwide species, present-day and fossils. No superfamily designations; the order comprises only 1 family.

Family Falconidae (caracaras, milvagos, forest falcons, falconets, and true falcons). Some genera (*Polyborus, Daptrius, Herpetotheres, Milvago, Micrastur*) confined to New World, and others (*Microhierax*) only Oriental; very small to medium sized (35–1,800 g). Resemble Accipitridae in hooked beaks, talons, sexual dimorphism, etc.; differ in molt sequence, some anatomical characters, behaviour (droppings fall below perch; head bobbing in some; in all but caracaras no nest made); inside eggshell reddish.

Critical appraisal. Stresemann's classification of present-day falconiforms differed from the one given above in being based almost exclusively on the order of wing molt, classified in three ways: (1) beginning with primary number 4 and proceeding inward and outward from there; (2) "descendant," beginning with primary number 1 and working outward to the wing tip; (3) "irregular," with no clear sequence. The third category can again be subdivided into types that molt "descendant" (number 2 above) in juvenile molt and irregularly in adult plumage, and others that molt irregularly in all stages of plumage.

On this basis the order Accipitriformes of Stresemann (*cf.* Falconiformes of most authors) was divided into three suborders, Cathartae, Accipitres, and Sagittarii. The suborder Cathartae contained the New World vultures (*e.g.*, Cathartae of Brown and Amadon); the Accipitres included all those species included by Brown and Amadon in their suborders Accipitres and Falcones, with the exception of the secretary bird, Sagittariidae. Stresemann places the secretary bird alone in a separate suborder, Sagittarii. He thus included all but eight species of present-day falconiforms in the suborder Accipitres. Stresemann divided his Accipitres into two families: Accipitridae, molting "descendant" (number 2 above) or irregularly; and Falconidae, molting from primary 4 (as in number 1 above). Each of these families was divided into a number of subfamilies, and it was in the arrangement and order of these subfamilies that Stresemann's order of classification differed most strongly from the other current systems.

The relative merits of these two classifications are still open to discussion. That of Stresemann has been criticized on the ground that virtually all of the birds that molt irregularly are either large or very large. This applies to all his Cathartae; to all or most of his subfamilies Gypaetinae, Aegypiinae, Polyboroidinae, Circaetinae, Haliaeetinae, Machaerhamphinae, and Pandioninae of his family Accipitridae; to the larger and heavier members of his subfamily Accipitrinae; and to the secretary bird. No member of his Falconidae molts irregularly, but then none, except some caracaras and perhaps the gyrfalcon, can be called large and heavy. It appears at least as probable that the order of wing molt is as related to weight, size, and wing loading as to phyletic relationships. No one, however, questions the obvious differences between falcons and hawks, which are more strongly stressed by Brown and Amadon in their suborder Falcones than by Stresemann, who gives the falcons only family rank.

Modern birds usually are classified by the principle of placing the most primitive first and leading successively to the most highly evolved. Brown and Amadon suggested that Stresemann's ordering of subfamilies in his Accipitridae reversed that order by beginning with the rather specialized Old World vultures and ending with the sea eagles, kites, and osprey, which they regard as relatively primitive falconiforms. The position of the osprey remains controversial. Comparison of egg-white proteins indicates that the Old World vultures are closer to the typical eagles and buzzards than to the snake eagles and harriers. Stresemann concluded his large subfamily Accipitrinae with the buzzard-like harpy and monkey-eating eagles (*Harpia* and *Pithecophaga*), which Brown and Amadon considered less highly evolved than the booted eagles with feathered toes, such as *Spizaetus* and *Stephanoaetus*.

The whole subject of the classification of the Falconiformes is, in several respects, in need of thorough critical reappraisal and review. The best of the existing classifications is a compromise that still leaves many questions of precise relationships unanswered.

BIBLIOGRAPHY. R. AUSTING, *The World of the Red-Tailed Hawk* (1964), a photographic essay on the daily life of this common North American buteo; A.C. BENT, "Life Histories of North American Birds of Prey," *Bull. U.S. Natn. Mus.*, vol. 167, pt. 1 (1937), and vol. 170, pt. 2 (1938), a review by species of the natural history of all of the falconiforms and strigiforms (owls) found in North America; L.H. BROWN, *Eagles* (1955; shortened version, 1970), an account of the biology of these impressive birds, written for the layman, and with D. AMADON, *Hawks, Eagles and Falcons of the World* (1969), extensive information on the natural history of every species of the falconiforms; L.H. BROWN, *African Birds of Prey* (1971), an ecological study of falconiforms and strigiforms on the African continent; P.E. BROWN and G. WATERSTON, *The Return of the Osprey* (1962), a detailed account of the natural history of the osprey; J.J. and F.C. CRAIGHEAD, *Hawks, Owls and Wildlife* (1956), a detailed study of the food ecology of raptorial birds and their effect on prey populations; M.L. GROSSMAN and J. HAMLET, *Birds of Prey of the World* (1964), a heavily illustrated work dealing with both falconiforms and owls; J.J. HICKEY (ed.), *Peregrine Falcon Populations* (1969), a report of a symposium to determine the cause of the decline of the falconiform populations, especially that of the peregrine; H.K. SWANN, *Monograph of the Birds of Prey (Order Accipitres)*, vol. 1 (1930), vol. 2 (1945), a classic work on the biology of the falconiforms of the world, with many fine colour plates.

(L.H.B.)

Falconry

Falconry is the art of employing falcons, other hawks, and sometimes eagles in hunting game, often termed hawking. This article discusses the history and art of falconry, including the birds, falconry terms, and choosing and training the hawk. Representative works on falconry, including reprints of classic treatises, are listed in the bibliography.

History of falconry. Falconry is an ancient pastime practiced by man even before he learned to write. There is evidence of falconry in Assyria in the period of Sargon II (721–705 BC). Merchants, adventurers, and crusaders from Europe and England became familiar with falconry in the Orient and on their return home brought falcons and falconers with them. The sport flourished in western Europe and the British Isles in the Middle Ages as the pastime of the privileged classes. During the 17th century, after the advent of the shotgun and after the enclosure of the open lands and numerous social upheavals in the older countries, the noble sport of falconry died out, surviving in Europe largely through the enthusiasm of members of hawking clubs in various countries. In Great Britain the Falconers' Society of England was founded about 1770 but ceased in 1838 with the death of the then manager, Lord Berners. Because of the scarcity of herons (a main quarry of the club's peregrine falcons in East Anglia) and also partly because of the plowing up of the heath land over which the falconers rode, the centre of English falconry moved to The Netherlands, and in 1839 the Loo Hawking Club, an Anglo-Dutch society under the patronage of King William II of The Netherlands, was formed; in the first eight years of its existence, 1,500

herons were taken by its hawks. In 1853 the royal patronage was withdrawn and the Loo Club came to an end. For the next 10 years falconry was kept alive in England by a few amateurs and their professional falconers. Then, in 1864, the Old Hawking Club of England was founded, mainly to hawk rooks on the Wiltshire Downs. It was wound up in 1926 and the British Falconers' Club was founded in 1927. In the second half of the 20th century, the club had a membership of about 250. More than half the members were resident in the United Kingdom, but only about 30 kept and flew hawks. The reduction of the rabbit population by myxomatosis and the placing of many of the traditional quarries on the protected list both had a profound effect on the sport after World War II. All British birds of prey including owls came under the protection of the law, and a license was required from the Home Office before an intending falconer could take a young hawk for falconry.

Falconry clubs exist in other European countries. The French Club de Champagne went out of existence in 1870, but French falconers are organized in the Association Nationale des Fauconniers et Autoursiers Français. In Germany, the Deutscher Falkenorden was founded in 1923 and is a thriving club. Austria has its club, and Italy the Circolo dei Falconieri d'Italia. In the United States falconry is represented by the North American Falconers Association.

Falconry is still practiced in Libya, and sheikhs in Saudi Arabia and the Persian Gulf states still train their saker falcons to hunt bustard. In Indian and Pakistani Punjab and in the Northwest Frontier Province of Pakistan, falconers fly their falcons at duck and their goshawks at partridge. Much-prized hawk bells are made at Lahore and Amritsar. Japan has a few falconers, who fly their mountain hawk eagles at hare and their goshawks at pheasant.

A revival of interest in the sport occurred after World War II, and, with the reprinting of old treatises on the art, together with magazine articles and television programs on the subject, falconry attracted new adherents.

The birds and the art. Hawks, owls, and eagles are natural predators and kill in order to survive. With skill and patience, they may be trained by man to kill selected quarry, but none will retrieve game. Some, because of their temperament and flight habits, are more desirable than others. The most popular has long been the peregrine falcon, which possesses all the desirable traits. It can stand the climatic changes of any country, it is strong and swift, gentle and fierce as required, and when caught wild is readily trained by man. Only two groups of hawks (about a dozen species) possess such characteristics—the true falcons, or long-winged hawks, and the accipiters, or short-winged hawks. Among the latter are the goshawk and the European sparrow hawk. Because of the use of agricultural pesticides the hawks together with other birds of prey are on the decline.

Falconers have their own language. The male hawk, which is smaller than the female by one-third, is the tiercel. Only the larger female hawk is properly called the falcon. An eyas is a hawk taken from the nest when fully fledged but as yet flightless. Wild-caught immature birds are called passagers because they often are caught when migrating, and adults are haggards. After capture and until ready to be trained, eyases are "at hack." While being hacked the birds are fed regularly on fresh meat, tied to a board or block, always in the same spot. Eyases are seldom used in India and Africa but are commonly used in Europe and the U.S.

The would-be falconer's choice of hawk depends on the locality and cover conditions in which it will be used. The long-winged hawks are used in open country, while the short-winged accipiters are better equipped to work hedge-rows and woods. Another difference between the two groups of hawks being considered is their method of killing. Falcons usually kill their quarry in the air, cleanly and at the end of powerful dive, or stoop, but they do occasionally cling, or "bind to," their prey. The goshawk may perch in a tree watching intently while man and dogs

Falconry terms

beat the cover. When game is flushed, the goshawk dashes fiercely in pursuit, "binds to" its victim, carrying it to the ground, and then pierces the vital organs with its massive talons. Goshawks are used for hunting hares, rabbits, and pheasants. The smaller accipiters are best for starlings and small game such as partridges and quail.

Once the type of hawk is decided upon, the falconer must make another choice: whether to use an eyas or a wild-trapped hawk. The novice usually begins with an eyas—legally obtained. Trapping a wild hawk requires patience and skill. One method is to hide in a blind near a bow net set over a wild hawk's kill. As the hawk returns to its kill, the net is pulled with a cord, and if successful the falconer at once removes the bird, attaches leather thongs called jesses to its legs, and covers its eyes with a rufter (soft leather hood used on new-caught birds).

Training begins by carrying the hawk on the heavily gloved fist several hours each day while talking to it gently and stroking its plumage with a feather. When the hawk is able to feed from the fist without the rufter, it is ready to be broken to the hood and to people, dogs, and the like. Then it is trained to feed from the lure, a padded weight with wings of a pigeon or another bird attached and to which meat is tied. The lure is whirled on a cord and the hawk taught to fly aggressively to it over increasing distances. After this manoeuvre is mastered, the bird is trained to kill for itself. Now it is ready for hunting. Eyases are trained in much the same way as wild-caught birds.

BIBLIOGRAPHY. J.G. MAVROGORDATO has written two authoritative works: *A Hawk for the Bush* (1960), which specializes in the sparrow hawk as an accipiter, or short-winged hawk, and *A Falcon for the Field* (1966), on the flying of the longwinged hawk, or falcon, at every recognized quarry. M.H. WOODFORD, *A Manual of Falconry* (1960), is the best general work, suitable also for the beginner, with specialist's chapters on game hawking by S. Allen and rook and magpie hawking by J.G. Mavrogordato; a veterinary surgeon, Woodford has written a useful chapter on health and disease. Other useful works are GILBERT BLAINE, *Falconry* (1936, reprinted 1970); and E.B. MICHELL, *The Art and Practice of Hawking* (1900, reprinted 1960), accepted as the best treatise on the merlin. As many of the originals of the recommended books below have become collectors' items, for all practical purposes the works above relating to modern conditions and all the hawks used are to be especially recommended.

J.E. HARTING, *Hints on the Management of Hawk* (1898, reprinted 1970); F.H. SALVIN and W. BRODRICK, *Falconry in the British Isles* (1855, reprinted 1970). Important early works on falconry are the remarkable treatise by the Holy Roman emperor FREDERICK II (1194–1250), first printed in 1596 and translated into English by CASEY A. WOOD and F. MARJORIE FYFE as *The Art of Falconry* (1943); EDMUND BERT, *An Approved Treatise of Hawkes and Hawking* (1619, reprinted 1950).

(F.B.C./M.H.W./C.J.Mo.)

Falkland Islands and Dependencies

The Falkland Islands lie northeast of the southern tip of South America, 300 miles (480 kilometres) east of the mainland. Covering an area of 130 by 80 miles, the some 200 islands comprise a land area of approximately 4,700 square miles (15,800 square kilometres). The two main islands, East and West Falkland, account for about 4,300 square miles of the total. The Falklands are a self-governing colony under the British crown. British sovereignty over the group has been contested since the 1760s—first by Spain and then by Argentina, which in the early 1970s still maintained its claim. The capital is Stanley (Port Stanley), on East Falkland.

The Dependencies consist of groups of islands lying from 700 to 2,000 miles to the east and southeast of Port Stanley. They consist of South Georgia, the South Sandwich Islands, and the Shag and Clerke Rocks. British Antarctic Territory is administered from Port Stanley but since 1962 has formed a separate colony.

Capt. John Strong, an Englishman, made the first recorded landing in the Falklands, (1690), naming the

FALKLAND ISLANDS

sound between the two main islands after Viscount Falkland, then the treasurer of the British navy. The name later came to refer to the whole group. The term Las Islas Malvinas is in general use in South America. (See ANTARCTICA; for associated physical features, see ATLANTIC OCEAN; DRAKE PASSAGE.)

The natural environment. The main structural elements in the islands are two folds running east–west across the northern parts of the islands and parallel to Falkland Sound on the west. Ranges of hills follow the trend of these folds, occasionally rising to 2,300 feet. The coastal topography is typical of a drowned coastline, with long, winding creeks. The rivers are small and sluggish and occupy broad, peat-covered valleys.

The climate is dominated by the prevailing strong westerly winds; in Stanley the average wind speed is more than 16 miles per hour. Gales are recorded on an average of four times a month, but storm-force winds are almost unknown, though gusts have been recorded above 80 miles per hour. Rainfall, spread evenly throughout the year, reaches maximums in December and January and minimums in September and October. It averages 25 inches annually, falling from 16 to 21 days a month. Light falls of snow, soon melting, occur on about 50 days during the year. Temperature range is narrow, with seasonal uniformity but marked day-to-day variability: the mean average is about 42° F (5° C), with a maximum average of 64° F (18° C) and a minimum average of 25° F (−4° C). The air temperature has never been known to exceed 80° F (27° C) or to fall below 12° F (−11° C). Average daily sunshine is about four and a half hours.

Vegetation is similar to that of the Atlantic heath type, consisting of low, dense, shrubby vegetation in a barren landscape; white grass (*Cortaderia pilosa*) and diddle-dee (*Empetrum rubrum*) dominate the plant associations. There is little variety of species—only about 160, none of which is peculiar to the islands. The banks of peat, typical of the islands, are built up under a light-green carpet of *Astelia prunila* (a kind of lily) and reach 18 feet in depth. Around the coastline and on some small islands, an almost pure strain of tussock grass (*Poa flabellata*) is found; formerly, it was very extensively present. There is no natural tree growth.

There are no longer any land mammals indigenous to the Falklands, the indigenous wild fox being extinct. But unspoiled natural conditions and abundant food supply make the islands and the seas around them a unique area for wildlife. Sixty different species of birds, including the black-browed albatross, are known to breed there. Three main species of penguin breed in the thousands; more rarely, the king and macaroni penguins also breed. Inland are many geese and birds, including the military starling, the black-throated finch, the Falkland pipit, Cassin's falcon, and the red-backed buzzard. Marine mammals to be seen are Peale's porpoise and Commerson's dolphin. Of amphibious marine animals the southern sea lion is still the most abundant of the three major species breeding; fur seals are rare, but the elephant seal is common, and the leopard seal is seen, though it does not breed there.

The absence of trees and the abundance of clouds lend

Climate

Mammal life

an austere aspect to the landscape, which consists largely of moorland and hilly mountainside, scattered with outcrops of rocks and numerous clusters of large, quartzite boulders. But this austere aspect can quickly vanish when sunshine brings colour to the sea and to the lovely, indented coastline, with its graceful, sandy bays, fringed with surf, and countless islets.

History. It is not clear who discovered the Falklands. It seems likely that the English navigator John Davis in the "Desire" was the first to sight them, in 1592; Sebald van Weerdt, a Dutchman who was in the region in 1600, gave his name to them on maps of the 17th and 18th centuries. The French navigator, Louis-Antoine de Bougainville, in 1764, founded the first settlement on East Falkland. The British, in 1765, were the first to settle West Falkland. They were driven off in 1770, however, by Spanish troops, Spain having bought out the French. War between Britain and Spain was averted only when Spain agreed to return "the port and fort called Egmont" to the British. For economy the British naval garrison was withdrawn in 1774, leaving a plaque claiming full sovereignty over all the Falklands for the British crown. Spain maintained its settlement until 1806, when an uprising against Spanish authority broke out in Buenos Aires province, Argentina. Spain made no further claim to jurisdiction, but in 1816 the United Provinces of the Río de la Plata claimed to succeed Spain in sovereignty over the Falklands and took possession of Soledad in 1820. A local governor was installed in 1828. Four years later the British government reasserted its claims to the Falklands, and in 1833 a British force peacefully expelled the Argentine soldiers and their vessel from Soledad and raised the British flag. The British prime minister said in 1834 that the British were not prepared to permit "any other state to exercise a right as derived from Spain, which Britain had denied to Spain herself."

In 1842 the capital was moved to Stanley. Settlement continued, and by 1885 the community of nearly 1,800 persons was self-supporting. In 1892 the Falklands were granted the status of a colony. In World War I (on December 8, 1914) the Falklands were the scene of a naval battle between British and German fleets.

The colony. *The people.* The population—about 2,000 in 1970—is English speaking. Of these, 79 percent were born in the Falklands, and 98 percent have British nationality. Sixty-five percent of the population belong to the Church of England and 23 percent to other Protestant denominations, and 11 percent are Roman Catholic. The population first exceeded 2,000 in 1901, reached a peak of almost 2,400 in 1931, and declined slightly in the 1960s as emigrants sought more varied employment abroad, but this trend was offset by an increase of short-term, skilled contract personnel.

The pattern of living on the islands is sharply divided between that of small, isolated sheep-farming communities and the wide cross section of interests represented in Stanley. In the capital live government officials, professional groups, technicians, artisans, and the personnel of the British Antarctic Survey, the Radio and Space Research Station, and the telecommunications centre.

Falkland Islands and Dependencies, Area and Population

	area		population	
	sq mi	sq km	1962 census	1970 estimate
Islands				
East Falkland	2,550	6,605	1,700	...
Other islands	400	1,036	*	...
West Falkland	1,750	4,532	500	...
Total Falkland Islands and dependencies	4,700	12,173	2,200†	2,000

*Uninhabited. †Includes 50 persons on ships.
Source: Official government figures.

Economic life. The whole area of the islands, outside of Stanley, is devoted to sheep farming. Half the male population is thus employed. Farms vary in size from 3,600 acres to 161,000 acres. There are over 600,000 sheep, producing an average of 4,750,000 pounds of wool annually. This is sold in Great Britain and is the country's only resource. Public financial expenditure is some £450,000, the revenue being obtained from income tax. There is some revenue from customs duties levied on wines, spirits, malt liquids, and tobacco. The island's stamps, of notable philatelic interest, are a source of income from sales to collectors of current issues. While the colony is self-supporting, occasional help from Great Britain is received. The Falkland Islands Company, incorporated by Royal Charter in 1851, has played a notable part in the economic development of the islands.

More than 1,000 motor vehicles maintain land communications, using the 12 miles of concrete roads in Stanley or the unsurfaced tracks elsewhere when weather permits. A government-operated air service, using seaplanes, carries passengers, mail, and medical patients between farm settlements and Stanley on nonscheduled flights. There are no external air communications. A government launch and a ship, the "Darwin" of the Falkland Islands Company, sail around the islands to carry stores and collect the wool clip; the latter vessel goes to the mainland with passengers, mail, and freight, making about 12 trips a year to Montevideo. Four times a year a chartered vessel brings supplies directly from England, returning with the wool clip. External telecommunications are maintained by the government wireless station; internal communications are by landline and radio telephone.

Administration and social conditions. The government of the islands is democratic and independent. At its head the governor, appointed by the British crown, is advised by an executive council, the majority of the members of which are elected from and by the elected members of a legislative council. In Stanley there is a town council, empowered to levy property taxes to meet the cost of public services. General social conditions are good; there is no unemployment, and the one trade union negotiates wages and conditions for all employees. Housing is well built and adequate, the average number of rooms being more than seven, compared with an average of under five in the United States and Great Britain. There are systems for old-age pensions, children's and dependents' allowances, and workmen's compensation. Education is free and compulsory to the age of 15, with two schools in Stanley, a boarding school at Darwin, and schools at five other settlements. Children in outlying homes are taught by itinerant teachers, the whole program augmented by the use of radio. There is a free medical service with four doctors, a dental surgeon, and nursing staff and a 32-bed hospital in Stanley.

Cultural life is largely provided by radio, Stanley station relaying London's programs; but many people also directly receive the world's stations. Several social clubs provide a variety of indoor activities, and outdoor sports include football, cricket, golf, and trout fishing. Publications include the government's *Falkland Islands Gazette,* the *Falkland Island Monthly Review,* and the annual *Falkland Islands' Journal,* with items of historical, geographical, and general interest.

Prospects. Argentina continues to press its claim to sovereignty over the islands, but the British government rejects any transfer of sovereignty or change in the status quo. Economically, with the price of wool unsteady, the outlook is uncertain, but diversification of the economy is being pursued: commercial use may be made of the very large quantities of kelp around the islands, and tourism is being encouraged.

BIBLIOGRAPHY. SIR W.L. ALLARDYCE, *The Story of the Falkland Islands* (1909), provides an account of the discovery and early history. M.B.R. CAWKELL, D.H. MALING, and E.M. CAWKELL, *The Falkland Islands* (1960), presents a general picture of life in the islands. A.F. COBB, *Birds of the Falkland Islands* (1933), and *Wild Life of the Falkland Islands* (1910), are useful accounts of the islands' animal life. C.W. GUILLEBAUD, *Report on an Economic Survey of the Falkland Islands* (1967), is an expert and up-to-date account of the economy. See also the Falkland Islands Colonial Reports, published every two years by HMSO.

(C.J.T.)

Transport and communications

Cultural life

Family and Marriage

Almost all human beings have grown up in some kind of "family," but families have varied considerably in form, not only from one era to another and from one culture to another but also within eras, within cultures. In a culture the form of the family changes or disappears, giving way to others. All these many aspects of the family constitute an important part of social change. The first way to look at the family is as a group, a household.

The article is divided into the following sections:

I. Forms and functions of families and marital unions

HOUSEHOLD FORMS

There is no one accepted method of classifying households. The types discussed here are not mutually exclusive. (For a more extended treatment of familial and kinship terminology and of family and marriage in preliterate and agrarian societies, see KINSHIP.)

Corporate family. The corporate family is organized around a number of important activities, such as hunting in its territory, cultivating its land, trading its products, performing important rituals and rites, and rearing its children. Though common to preliterate societies, the pattern can also be applied to Western society, for members of Western households do share shelter, food, and resources, as well as activities arising from their use. Industrialization tends, however, to disperse the members of the household among different employers and occupations and to reduce the number and frequency of common rites or activities.

Extended family. The extended family includes not only the parents and unwed children but also married children and their wives or husbands and offspring. Among the wealthy, people generally live longer, and extended families of good economic standing may include as many as four generations, at least for a short period of time. Strictly speaking, a small extended family is no longer extended when one of the parents in the older generation dies. An extended family should thus be seen as a stage in the family cycle and as an ideal form that is difficult to attain in such poor countries as India or Iran.

Conjugal family. A husband and a wife almost always come from different families (the incest taboo), and therefore their bond, as a conjugal family, is not consanguine, or blood related. But the children in the conjugal family, of course, have consanguine bonds with their parents. This makes the concept of the conjugal family rather clumsy, and so it tends in modern literature to be replaced by the concept of the *nuclear family.*

Nuclear family. The nuclear family consists only of parents and their children. This type of family is universal; it forms the nucleus of the corporate as well as of the extended family and, of course, constitutes the first stage in both. The nuclear family is probably the oldest type of family, going back to the earliest ancestors of man, maybe half a million years ago or more. These beings lived in small bands, and their young were born at intervals of one or, at the most, two years, but it took several years before the young could manage for themselves. The mother must have had help from a husband in caring for them, and these parents and children must have formed rather stable nuclear families, although the best hunters may have taken an extra wife if, for example, a female had lost her husband.

As the cultural level of man rose and was adapted to climate and resources, the pattern of the nuclear family changed. Industrialism and geographical mobility seem to have had an unfavourable effect on the formation and maintenance of large families and even on the acceptance of the extended family as an ideal. Thus modern families now tend to remain nuclear families, and family activities and solidarity are reduced not only in the nuclear family but even more between the generations, particularly between young parents and their older kin.

The modern family as a nuclear family

Experimental family. Various other familial arrangements have sometimes been tried in new situations not suited for nuclear families. One of these is the *kibbutz* in Israel. There a large number of people from different countries, with different educations and backgrounds, were brought together in collectives, concentrating on the tasks of clearing land, irrigating it, and growing crops. Every member had to work for the collective; most of the women were engaged in making meals, washing and mending clothes, or caring for the children. The rather difficult circumstances in which most *kibbutzim* started allowed the couples only the evenings to see each other and their children in the privacy of their own room, and this evening family produced and consumed very little except emotional, sexual, and social contacts. This or a similar pattern persists in most *kibbutzim.* The younger members often enjoy considerable sexual freedom, but if they decide to form a family, they apply for a room of their own, and if they get it, this generally implies the official recognition of their union. Apparently the intense interaction within the *kibbutz* is able to compensate for the reduced interaction in the family.

Other experimental solutions are possible among modern young people who often try to form small groups, as isolated as possible from society. Mutual interaction among those involved may then be so dominant that a group family seems natural to them, at least for a time.

MARRIAGE FORMS

The nuclear family is monogamous by definition; that is, it has only one man with one wife. But in many cultures, the husband is allowed to take more wives in a marriage form called *polygyny;* and in some the wife is allowed to take more than one husband in a form called *polyandry. Polygamy* is a broader concept including polygyny as well as polyandry. Some anthropologists formerly believed that their data from a few preliterate cultures demonstrated the existence of *group families,* which included several husbands and wives, but few still believe that this type of family existed.

Monogamy. Monogamy is the commonest form of marriage in all cultures. A monogamous culture is simply one in which only monogamous marriages are legally accepted—polygamy being a crime. The ties between husband and wife in a monogamous marriage are strong in some cultures, weak in others. Strong ties may prevent divorce and even the remarriage of widows and widowers; weak ties generally lead to easy and numerous divorces.

Polygamy. In polygyny, the husbands are allowed and encouraged to take more than one wife. The famous anthropologist George P. Murdock classified 250 cultures according to the form of the family. Of these, 193 were classified as polygynous. It is doubtful, however, whether such Islāmic countries as Algeria, Tunisia, Egypt, and Pakistan should today be classified as polygynous; public opinion there seems now to favour monogamy.

If cultures with the usual proportions between the sexes are to practice polygyny, it is evident that they must either prevent some of the men from marrying at all or keep the marrying age low for women and high for men, especially for those marrying for the second or third time. Of course, from the economic point of view, polygyny is easier among the well-to-do.

Polyandry is rare; only two cases are cited in Murdock's sample. It seems to be associated with scarcity of women owing to the practice of infanticide of females. If a tribe is very poor and the wife herself can contribute very little, she will need several husbands to support her and the children—and may still be forced to reduce the number of children.

FUNCTIONS OF THE FAMILY

Personal or individual functions. *Psychological security.* An important function of the family—especially in Western societies where there is much tension—is emotional or psychic security. Independent nuclear families are especially associated with intimacy and emotional interdependence, either because they originally had this function or because they have taken it over from extended families or from other forms that have broken down. In Western culture, there is particular stress on the companionship between husband and wife, symbolizing the modern equality of sex roles and based on a division of labour that presumes to give the same value to male and female tasks. This companionship and parenthood seem to be the most important sources of psychological security because elsewhere, at work and in other groups, more value is placed on efficiency and matter-of-fact relations.

Sexual satisfaction. In all cultures an important marital reward, in addition to companionship and certain social privileges afforded married people, is the gratification of sexual relations. Western culture stresses the importance of sexual satisfaction, but it also keeps sexuality under comparatively strict control. Indeed, few societies have tried, as Western society has done, to restrict sexual intercourse exclusively to married couples. Although a married man in most cultures is forbidden intercourse with a woman married to another man, he may, nevertheless, have affairs with one or more of his female relatives. Premarital liaisons between an unrelated boy and girl are forbidden in only 54 cultures of a sample 250.

Within the family, the husband and wife are always allowed comparatively great sexual liberty with each other, although there may be a sexual etiquette to be followed, such as taboos on intercourse during menstruation, pregnancy, and lactation.

Physical security. An individual feels a sense of physical security because of the family's willingness or duty to protect one another, to care for the sick or injured, to provide one another with shelter, warmth, food, and clothes. With the usual distribution of tasks in the family, the husband might hunt game, tend cattle, or work in the fields or in a quarry, while the wife in most cultures remained in the vicinity of the home, carrying water, collecting roots and berries, making, mending, and washing clothes, tending the fire and bringing fuel for it, thus contributing her important share to the well-being and security of the family. Societies with a permanent place of residence as a rule pay more attention to their dwellings; families build houses or huts not only to obtain more comfort but also to realize more security and privacy than can be found in tents or temporary shelters. Physical security also depends heavily on the mores, codes, and legal system of the society.

Social functions. *Procreation and child socialization.* Societies that have paid too little attention to procreation have run the risk of extinction; and societies that are unable to educate or socialize their children in traditional fashion undergo change, lose some cultural traits, and probably invent or borrow other traits. In other words, a society cannot be stable unless it has made acceptable provision for procreation and child socialization.

The role of child socialization

Child socialization in most cultures is not considered a task but rather part of the daily labour—a labour in which children take their allotted part and, in the process, pick up necessary knowledge and lore. The socialization period generally ends in adolescence, but in most pre-literate cultures the adolescents are given the status and privileges of adults only after dramatic or painful passage rites, often interpreted as the killing of the boy and his rebirth as a young man. The girls generally receive less attention and ill-treatment, although their first menstruation is sometimes considered dangerous and is therefore associated with a period of isolation. Literate societies tend to change the passage rites into festivals.

Regulation of sexual behaviour. Because the sexual drive can be very strong and disrupt the regulated behaviour pattern in the family (because of jealousy or whatever), all cultures have found it necessary to control sexual relations between men and women, whether married or not. Murdock listed seven categories of sexual relations: *marital sexuality,* between a married couple; *adultery,* between two persons, at least one of whom is married to someone else; *incest,* between two persons whose bond of kinship, as defined by the culture, bars them from sexual relations; *mismating,* between members of different classes, castes, or ethnic, national, or religious groups that are not expected to have sexual relations; *status unchastity,* between two persons, at least one of whom has a social position demanding chastity; *incontinence,* between persons whose sexual relation contravenes taboos pertaining to menstruation, pregnancy, etc.; and finally *fornication,* between partners who adhere to all other rules and taboos but are themselves unmarried.

Categories of sexual relations in and out of marriage

All cultures prefer to prescribe marital sexuality and forbid incest, but the regulations concerning the remaining five classes of sex relations vary considerably. They are forbidden, allowed, or required according to circumstances. Western culture has prohibited even fornication, but only 3 societies in Murdock's example of 115 went as far as that, and so it must be recognized that the Western mode of strict sex regulation is atypical.

The sexual privileges within marriage need not exclude sexual freedom prior to marriage. Murdock found such freedom in about 70 percent of the societies about which he had information. The incest taboo is very rigorous, however—probably because it threatens the ties between husband and wife in the nuclear family and their ties to the children. Incest seems to have been allowed only among some ruling dynasties (Egypt, Hawaii, the Incas).

Contribution to social and economic life. The family is the most common economic unit, involving a relatively efficient division of labour between husband, wife, and children. Nowhere, however, do families, normally, live in isolation. They almost always form a part of a larger group, a community, in close contact with one another, probably because such a community makes it easier to produce food, to introduce a more advanced division of labour, to enjoy social intercourse, and to get help when injured, ill, or temporarily without means.

Contribution to order in society. The type of family, the social organization, and the sources of livelihood all depend on one another. Hunting, gathering, or herding creates or favours small migratory bands consisting of a few families. Agriculture tends to make the families adopt a more or less permanent place of residence and unite either in scattered neighbourhoods or concentrated villages, such as may also develop in a fishing economy. Bands of hunters or herders generally own their land collectively, whereas the farmers of neighbourhoods or villages with few exceptions own their fields privately, although pastures and woods may remain collective property. Similar communities, in communication with one another, tend to develop a culture together, to create a "we-feeling." Together they tend to develop a common kinship system, a common system of law, and eventually political unification. About half the societies in Murdock's sample had remained at the community level, and half consisted of several communities.

The smaller and the more isolated the community, the more important the family unit. Larger communities tend to organize collective action, to produce specialists, to invest authority in chieftains, and so forth, thus changing faster and often developing stronger social controls over facilities and individuals.

II. Historical background

The following are a few family systems from the past that are representative of Western patterns: the patriarchal pattern from the Bible, the old Roman family, Tacitus' picture of the Teuton family, the medieval family, the European peasant family pattern, and modern varieties.

PREMODERN WESTERN FAMILIES

The family pattern of the patriarchs, as described in the Bible, still influences present practices. Abraham, Isaac, and Jacob are described as nomad chieftains, owning great herds, married to several wives, allowed to take concubines and to get rid of them. The Old Testament accorded women a lower status than men and, in some respects, so did Christianity.

The Roman family The old Roman family gave extreme power to the father (*patria potestas*), who represented the community and had the right even to kill his own sons. He was his sons' guardian as long as he lived; and after marriage, they lived with their families in his household, forming a very extended family. The family was proud of its lineage and anxious to obtain for the sons brides of equally good family who would bring substantial dowries to increase the family fortune. But men were not allowed more than one wife and so officially remained monogamous. In practice the wife had considerable influence; and later, in imperial Rome, the power of the clan and of the father were reduced. Women, however, still had lower status and in fact were not permitted to manage their own affairs. Roman family law influenced all parts of the Roman Empire and lasted far longer than the empire itself, for it was taken over by many of the new nations and, up to a point, by the Roman Catholic Church as well.

The family in the Teuton tribes was described by Tacitus as a contrast to Roman decadence in the 1st century AD.

The marriage tie with them is strict: you will find nothing in their character to praise more highly. They are almost the only barbarians who are content with a wife apiece: the very few exceptions have nothing to do with passion, but consist of those with whom polygamous marriage is eagerly sought for the sake of their high birth. As for dower, it is not the wife who brings it to the husband, but the husband to the wife.

These tribes thus seem to have been monogamous and to have accorded women high regard, inheritance rights, and so forth; among the Heruli, brother and sister shared alike.

The medieval family in the Mediterranean countries tended to retain traits characteristic of Roman family law—representing the power of the father, a dowry, the lower status of women, and the extended family—but it was, of course, also influenced by the Roman Catholic Church and the feudal system. In the northern half of Europe, which was little urbanized and was dominated by the victorious Teuton tribes, the peasant families tended to follow their old family patterns but had to seek protection from the local lord, who was a member of the military aristocracy. Only the church could oppose the feudal lords, but the oath of celibacy prevented the clergy from forming a hereditary class. The concept of celibacy by implication painted women as sinful and unclean, a picture that was counteracted by the sublime idealization of the Holy Virgin and female saints and by the slightly less highly idealized concept of women in the romantic poetry of the minstrel, singing of the lady of his heart's desire.

European peasants up to modern times seem to have followed the same broad family pattern. The farm belonged to the family, but as H.J. Habakkuk has pointed out, the family had two conflicting aims: to keep its property intact and to provide for the younger children. In England the eldest son took over the family farm, but in France and the Rhineland the law stated that all children had the same right to inherit. All the same, there was a tendency to let the eldest son take over the farm, to represent it in the village, and to be the head of the immediate family to whom members could turn if they got into difficulties. It was his duty to look after them and to provide a bed and food for them. He had far-reaching powers over his children and his farmhands. The pattern was that of a patriarchal, monogamous family concentrating all resources in the hands of the father but also laying all the duties on him. His younger brothers could stay on the farm, but often they did not marry, unless they were able to establish themselves at least on a small scale. The housewife was responsible not only for the household but also for the cattle, sheep, goats, poultry, and kitchen gardens, which were the source of food, leather, cloth, and homemade utensils. This, however, did not give the housewife a strong economic position, because meat, milk, butter, cheese, and eggs in those days were not paid for in cash. Almost the only thing that brought in ready money was the sale of grain, and grain was produced by the men—farmhands working with oxen and horses. When the economy changed and the farms started to sell animal products, milk, and other items, the transports to and the contacts with the dairy-marketing organization were taken over by the men.

The members of the peasant families, it seems, had security but little freedom, and there may have been far more tyranny and restriction than might be imagined.

The families of the craftsmen and merchants in the towns had a similar division of labour, since they too produced crops and raised animals. As a rule, the households also included journeymen, apprentices, and servants.

THE ONSET OF INDUSTRIALIZATION AND URBANIZATION

The peasant family pattern in England, which stressed the need to keep the family farm in the hands of the eldest brother, seems to have stimulated the migration of the younger ones to the growing industrial centres; and, according to Habakkuk, the same tendency was evident in Germany, where the younger children of peasant families did inherit but got their share in cash and then tried to establish themselves elsewhere. If the children had equal rights, however (as in the regions under the Code Napoléon, they tended to marry and remain in the village, though they might work elsewhere for seasons or short periods to supplement the meagre family income or even to buy land to enlarge their holdings.

The family in the Industrial Revolution Industrialization often started as domestic industry or small workshops in areas where equal inheritance rights had divided the farms and forced the peasants to look for extra incomes. But large-scale industries had to be located in areas to which a reserve of farm hands could be induced to migrate permanently. Low-wage, large-scale industries would obviously have little chance against domestic industries in such countries as Russia, where the extended family was strong enough to keep its members together.

It is evident that industrial centres and towns mainly attracted unmarried and comparatively poor youngsters as permanent residents. These people did not necessarily break off communication with their families, but the family lost its grip on them; and if they managed to adapt themselves to working in town, they had little benefit from their family there. The family's claims and its lack of understanding of their new situation were a disadvantage no longer balanced by any advantages. Moreover, the new class of industrial workers felt freer to marry and have children, and their high rate of fertility soon made migration from the villages less vital for the process of industrialization.

Overpopulation and poor harvests could cause the mechanism to break down, however, and trigger great waves of migrating peasant families, from southern Germany at the beginning of the 19th century, from Ireland in the 1840s, and from Scandinavia later on, all moving to European cities or overseas to such lands as the United States.

The old family pattern in the United States was originally brought by the British colonists, but the transfer to the New World added new elements. Women, being fewer in number, achieved comparatively high status (though, as elsewhere, they were excluded from the right to vote). Religious social control was strict in Eastern areas, but on the frontier compromise became necessary.

MODERN SOCIETY AND FAMILY

Sociologists, comparing the preindustrial family pattern with the modern Western one, point out that men now work in factories or offices, not at home, that they receive their wages in cash, and that the family is no longer a producing but only a consuming unit. (There is even a trend toward letting industry take over much of the preparation of food.) Nor is it possible for the family to provide adequate care for the old and the sick; society has stepped in, providing hospitals, medical care, and special homes. The difficult task of socializing children is taken over by day nurseries, which are becoming more common as more mothers take work outside the home, and by the school system, which even provides school meals. Finally, recreation has been largely removed from the home by the entertainment industry.

The family has a number of functions left, however; it provides its members with a place where they are met with affection, where, in theory, they are protected from the stress to which they are subjected in their work and in the community, where the devotion between husband and wife can be expressed, and where they can have children and care for them. These functions are becoming more important as the family gives less attention to other things.

Sociological reasoning of this kind is based upon the fact that certain types of behaviour within the family are becoming less common, and others are becoming more common. In other words, there is a change in the functions of the family. But the emotional ties between husband and wife remain, as does their sexual behaviour. Children are still born within the framework of the family and receive within it care and security, something that seems to indicate the survival of the family and its emotional, sexual, and nurturing functions in the future.

This picture is simple only because all complicated data have been excluded. The Western rural family has been regarded as patriarchal and self-supporting, firmly anchored in its kin and its community, taking care of its members and representing the "good old times." Reality must have been considerably more varied and often difficult to stand, even if people did not have the schooling required to verbalize their sense of deprivation as far as consideration, comfort, and privacy were concerned.

III. Development and organization of the modern family

MECHANISMS OF MATE SELECTION

Customs of dating and courtship. Today's generation of young people seems to be evolving new patterns of developing contacts leading either to temporary liaisons or marriage. The patterns contrast with the one usually attributed to an earlier generation. In the former system (which is still widespread), *dating* was seen as an initial phase of marking available partners and testing them in standardized situations, which sometimes included sex relations. Once a boy and a girl started going steady and gave up dating others, they had advanced to the second phase, *courtship*, concentrating their attention and expectations on each other, trying to adjust to each other and to be accepted by each other's parents, to get a degree, a job, and so forth—goals often not easy to coordinate. Courtship might be officially recognized as *engagement*, meaning that the partners had given each other promises, exchanged rings, and the like; this ceremony was very important in northern Europe, for instance, because it gave more scope for sex, but its importance is now declining. In this "traditional" system, the success of a courtship is judged solely according to the outcome: did the partners marry? No consideration is given to whether the persons involved used this time really to seek emotional, social, sexual, educational, or economic adjustments or to find out on what points they differed irreconcilably.

These norms now seem less relevant to many of today's adolescents in their frantic search for emotional experience and contacts, for understanding, fun, and love. In the future, those who study the family may have to find a new design or pattern and study (1) the adolescent "contact pools," (2) the adolescents' peculiar evaluation of traits in dress, music, slogans, politics, and philosophy, and (3) their intellectual, emotional, and sexual partnerships, which are formed, broken, and reformed and in which intellectual factors seem to mean more and sexual contacts less than adults believe, since sexual contacts are often no longer considered the crowning experiences of togetherness. Partners needing security may choose to live together permanently, have children together, marry before or after doing so, leave the contact pool or stay in it notwithstanding. This pool of theirs, however, will soon become more or less segregated from younger pools, and all the time it will be shrinking in size as more hopeful couples or resigned individuals depart and only a small number of them return. In any event, the whole evolving pattern (or patterns) is unclear and difficult yet to systematize for examination.

Matrimonial agencies and marriage arrangements. Parents, having made many adjustments before or after their own marriage, are usually eager to hand on this wisdom to their children, who often doubt its relevance. Up to a point, parents are still able to arrange acceptable contacts by giving parties, taking their children with them to the right social gatherings, and so forth. They also use subtle techniques to encourage desirable contacts and discourage less desirable ones. This influence can still be effective, especially when the parents of the desirable partner willingly cooperate in the "matchmaking." In modern society, the choice of marriage partner is still considered one of the big decisions in life, and researchers have therefore studied selection and adjustment in courtship and marriage, pointing out the similarities and differences between partners that they maintain are important. These "prediction data" are then used in lessons on the problems of family life, in social work, and in counselling people seeking advice or contacts. On the basis of such data, official and private agencies give advice about the selection of a partner or about the process of adaptation and may even pair off suitable partners by registering clients and arranging for certain ones to meet.

Customary factors of selection. One's own selection of a marriage partner is usually restricted to the people one meets (one's own family excluded), and the more often one meets them the greater chance one has to discover and appreciate their merits, to demonstrate one's own merits, and to succeed in attracting the desirable partners. Casual acquaintances are thus weeded out from the selection process, and those who are left tend to live in the same neighbourhood, to have the same working hours, to work at the same place and in a similar type of job, to be about the same age, and to have the same interests, the same kind of education, and the same religion, ethnic background, friends, and social class; and all these tendencies must emerge according to the distribution pattern of social contacts.

There is, then, a general tendency to select a marriage partner of the same quality and social class, a tendency called homogamy (*homos*, "like"; *gamos*, "marriage"). The homogamous tendency, however, is often weak and sometimes even reversed: a man may compensate for his lack of youth by displaying a high income or compensate for a low income by displaying a good social background; girls use their looks for general compensatory purposes. But in some cases "opposites attract": dominating men, for instance, may prefer submissive women rather than willful ones.

In Western cultures the two partners are expected to be in "love" with one another. This is sometimes carried to the extent of believing that everyone has her Mr. Right or his Miss Right waiting somewhere. They are meant for each other, and the moment that they meet their hearts

Romantic love

can tell. It is disheartening if only one falls in love, not the other. Romantic love often gives rise to very strong expectations that generally have little to do with reality.

All partners ought to have something like the same opinions on procreation and parenthood. How many children? How shall they be spaced and how educated? These are points that the partners must agree on from the beginning or be able to compromise on—if they are going to be successful partners. If they marry despite differing opinions, they probably run a far larger risk of maladjustment and divorce.

Economic considerations are important and were even more important formerly, when the husband had to be able to bear the financial strain of a wife, home, and children, *before* he was ready for marriage. Now in developed societies the wife often has a job, too, and if necessary she can go on working. Should something serious happen to the family, modern society generally gives considerable assistance, and it is therefore no longer necessary to have financial reserves sufficient to meet all eventualities.

Another aspect to note is that strong social values are vested in the family: "socially valuable" people generally are expected to make a good marriage, and if they are either single or married to the wrong person, this often is taken to show that something is "wrong" with them. People eager to make a career therefore tend to marry with an eye to their partner in utility. The politician, for instance, usually must be a marital model in every respect; his wife, too. They must have the right kind of happy but in no way peculiar life, a nice comfortable home, a reasonable number of children who behave like other children, and so forth. The businessman needs a perfect hostess, either in the bright cocktail-party style or in some other useful area of service. Military officers often need a wife trained in the traditions and helpful as a channel for information and intrigues in the female side of the base. The ambitious female partners, as a matter of fact, sometimes seem to select men whom they can promote by their contacts and abilities, thus promoting themselves at the same time.

But partners may not be selected only because they seem to be good tools or investments; they may be the owners of power to be wielded, money to be used, or social contacts to be enjoyed. These direct advantages are usually evident to both partners, however, and the partner wanting them but lacking them has to compensate with other goods.

Uncustomary marital trends and patterns. The pattern of homogamy and marriage during young adulthood is strong, a fact reflecting the strength of the supporting social norms. Thus exceptions are few: young people under the age of 16, for instance, are rarely allowed by law to marry; couples who have passed their 50s are free to marry but are somehow considered overripe, if marrying for the first time. A partner far older than the other is often considered odd (especially if it is a woman), and there is suspicion that one is exploiting the other. Statistical data show that such marriages occur infrequently: in about 2 percent of the marriages in Sweden in 1969, for instance, both partners were under 20 years of age; in 2 percent both partners were over 50; in a little more than 3 percent the bridegroom was at least 10 years older than the bride; and only in rare cases were brides more than 10 years older than their husbands (that is, in only one-fourth of 1 percent of the marriages).

These social norms vary of course from one ethnic or cultural group to another. The Lapps in northern Scandinavia sometimes marry very early, and the law makes provision for them. European Gypsies follow a similar pattern but have to circumvent the law or get individual exemption. (In Europe the trend toward younger marriage partners is very pronounced, and family law has changed in this direction in some countries.)

In countries with several religious, ethnic, and other distinctive social groups, there is a tendency to avoid intermarriage between the different groups when one group

[margin: Early and late marriages]

[margin: Intergroup marriages]

enjoys more esteem in the society than the other. The members of the under-esteemed groups generally do not accept the low evaluation of themselves and are unwilling to compensate for a disadvantage based only on prejudice. They therefore prefer to marry within their own group, where they can get full value for their own marriage merits.

The general disapproval of illegitimate births and unmarried mothers tends to make such phenomena commoner among lower social classes, people in slum areas, underprivileged ethnic groups, younger age groups, and so forth, since all these groups are less restricted by sexual and social norms, feeling or believing that they have little to lose. Many very young brides, for instance, are pregnant, their pregnancy being just the reason why they break the convention about marrying early; among the brides about 20 years of age, the percentage who are pregnant is still comparatively high, but the percentage drops in higher age groups.

Disapproval of pregnancy out of wedlock is directed in the first place at the girl, in the second place at the boy, who has the chance of remedying the situation by marrying the girl. In some Western countries, in spite of the oral contraceptive "pill" and other contraceptive techniques, the number of illegitimate births increased during the 1960s—partly because so many young couples lived together, had children, and brought them up without bothering about wedding ceremonies. More recently, however, the trend has seemed to reverse: the number of births and especially illegitimate births among young girls has been decreasing, probably owing to more regular use of the pill.

PREPARATIONS FOR MARRIAGE AND THE MARRIAGE CEREMONY

Religious factors. The marriage ceremony and the vows given emphasize the bonds between husband and wife, their duty to share responsibility and to support their family according to their ability. These obligations are not always respected in practice and thus require strengthening by the formality of solemn promises given in front of witnesses.

The status of the marrying couple within the religious community depends to some degree on their ability to satisfy the norms of their church: they should belong to it, look happy, have the right clothes, the right attendants, and behave so as to revive sentimental memories in the married onlookers and strengthen the romantic wedding expectations of the unmarried. Even in a country like Sweden, where status in the congregation means very little, religious factors still strongly influence the image of the happy bridal couple: a very high proportion of marriages take place at Easter and Whitsuntide, important Christian festivals.

Civil factors. Traditionally, a wedding not only united the bride and groom, but also brought the two parent families and their kin together. They had to meet, to see one another, and to show that they accepted one another; and so the wedding became a feast, a demonstration of social background and resources in respect of food and drink, of clothes, looks, and *savoir vivre*, whereby the two kins formed two teams in a social game, to appreciate one another but not to be outshone by the other team. As a married couple, the bride and groom had more status than they had when unmarried; and they left their old peer groups, sometimes after send-off parties, to take their place as fully fledged members of society. In the upper classes, the initial difficulties in adjusting to each other were eased by a wedding trip, a honeymoon in a different environment, far from interfering busybodies.

All these civil factors are important only if the bride and groom are both marrying for the first time. There is a tendency to shorten the engagement and cut down on the ceremonies if the bridegroom has been married before, and this tendency is even more pronounced if the bride has been married before. This simplification of the civil ceremonies indicates that those not married before have a higher status on the marriage market.

MARITAL AND FAMILIAL DYNAMICS:
THE FAMILY LIFE CYCLE

Dating and engagement are said to facilitate adjustment between the prospective husband and wife and should at least allow them to verbalize their expectations vis-à-vis each other regarding house, home, and children and to form their patterns not only of persuasion and compromise but also of conflict and conflict resolution in everyday life. Some of these patterns they have learned at an early age from parents, sisters, and brothers, and such patterns often persist even when they are said to have been given up. Other expectations and patterns the couple take over from society in general: a husband should bring home an adequate portion of his pay, be faithful to his wife, and love his children; a wife must be a good mother, a pleasant and faithful companion, and so on, although such expectations are not easy to live up to in practice and seem old-fashioned when they collide with ingrained bachelor ways or some modern life patterns that, for instance, stress the married woman's duty to be gainfully employed, politically informed, as well as interested in literature or music. But then, most couples, once married, quite quickly fall into the traditional behaviour connected with the home, food habits, and so on—so quickly indeed that these tendencies seem to have been there all the time, although temporarily hidden. The transformation is probably bound up with a change in the forms of social intercourse. Once the couple have acquired a house of their own, they invite people in and expect them to admire it and to pay them back with the same kind of invitations. Because their unmarried friends tend to give them up (and vice versa), they are generally restricted to other young married couples who "share their interests"; adolescent patterns depart, and usually only the new patterns survive that have been adopted by most other couples. Lately, however, young couples seem to maintain better contact with their old friends and to take less interest in the "home"; and consequently there are now more new patterns among young married couples (one of these being, at present, the tendency to form families without getting married).

Psychologically the first period of adjustment in marriage seems to demand more of the wife than of the husband. He has to reduce his personal expenditures, to postpone decisions in order to let his wife take part in them, to bring his expectations regarding sexual satisfaction down to a realistic level, and so forth. His wife has not only to make the corresponding adjustments but also generally to cope with the household, buying and preparing food and using her taste in decorating the home—all behaviour that tends to put the wife in a subordinate position trying to serve, entertain, or influence her husband. Today these traditions are counteracted by strong tendencies toward equality in interaction, not only in the sexual sphere but also in those spheres that have always been considered female monopolies and therefore of little value—repairing clothes, dressing the children, and the like. These tendencies toward equality seem to be far stronger in the higher social classes than in the lower ones and seem to be associated with modern higher education.

Family planning Sexual intercourse may lead to pregnancy, but this chance can now be reduced or eliminated by using the pill or other contraceptives. Couples using them are thus able to postpone having a child, to determine the intervals between their having children, or intentionally to stay childless. At the other extreme, couples who desire pregnancy but have problems of sterility or infertility can resort to various drugs to improve or restore fertility. All such choices are influenced by social factors, because most people are eager to behave according to the social norms of their groups—or at least eager to say they do. Thus family planning is generally commoner in cities and among the upper classes. Significantly, though, in Sweden and parts of the United States, the upper classes have tended to plan and have *many* children, whereas the middle classes with their smaller resources have planned and had fewer children and the working classes still fewer—unless their resources have been so poor that they could not plan at all and had many children.

If a couple do have children, they then face the problem of raising them. Traditionally the father had the role of presumed expert in technical matters, sports, books, and so on, and this gave him an instrumental role as a leader, giving orders, making decisions, showing or telling people what to do and how to do it. The mother's role, on the other hand, was more "expressive," showing sympathy, giving support or consolation, releasing tension, joking. When married women also work outside the home, this gives them rather instrumental roles in their jobs and leaves them so little time at home that they have to adopt an instrumental role at home too, giving orders, making decisions, and having too little time to establish emotional contacts. It may then be that some husbands have more time to establish more expressive roles, reading stories, listening to the children, and so forth. The traditional allocation of roles is thus no longer always applicable.

The roles played by various members of a family change with the development of a child. The baby is closely related to its mother and to hardly anyone else until it needs less physical care, when the father and later its siblings are also able to give and receive affection. But the interaction changes all the time as the infant gets older, picks up new roles, finds its peer groups, goes to school, and then, as an adolescent, starts to take over the same adult role as the parents. At this time the parents should be able to accept the child as a responsible, mature person, although this means that they have to give up their roles of father and mother. Some parents are unable to make this adjustment; mothers, for instance, try sometimes to prevent their youngest sons from assuming this final adult role.

Because people now marry earlier and have children earlier, families tend to see their children leave earlier. Fathers seem able to stand this better than mothers, and mothers who have activities outside the home better than those who do not. But parents may have a married child return to the home, and they may have to look after their grandchildren if the mother in the younger family has a job or becomes ill.

The child-launching stage—when the child goes to college or takes his or her first job and finds a place to live —is not only the end of a role for the parents but also a trial: how should one behave in a new situation with new role expectations? The parents still exercise some control, use the telephone, write letters, expect letters and reports and so on; but this kind of control diminishes, and when the child marries it should disappear, unless an overambitious parent-in-law tries to take command in the new household as well.

By the time the children have left the home, the parents are generally middle-aged or old, their sexual activity and their energy reduced. They tend to give up goals exposing them to too much stress: a new business career, political engagements, and so forth. This pattern of retirement or near retirement is of course convenient for those who feel old and worn out, but it may be very disturbing for those who are—or consider themselves to be —fit for a long time yet. They often are very fit, but modern industrial society, which stresses social mobility, usually favours young, aspiring leadership rather than age and experience.

The retired husband (or wife) generally restricts his (or her) activity to the home and thus might upset the pattern of behaviour there, at least for a while. Old age affects the retired couple, of course, their interests and their health. The children sometimes let their parents live with them, especially when they have become seriously incapacitated. Grandparents seem to adjust more easily to life in the home of a daughter than in the home of a son, where the danger of tension arising between wife and mother-in-law seems to be greater. But grandparents living in a family seem on the whole to affect the family atmosphere favourably. Data seem to show that mothers are more stable when they have the help of grandparents and that children are treated more affectionately when a grandmother lives in the house. Grandparents and grandchildren seem to have some ground in common: both are centred in the home, away from the bustle of competitive society, which they regard with some fear and suspicion; both have time for and a need for contact.

ROLES AND ACTIVITIES THROUGHOUT THE FAMILY CYCLE

Sexual aspects. Sexual activity is in part a function of age. Alfred Kinsey, in his measure of male sexual activity, found a maximum number of orgasms at about age 17, after which the rate slowly decreases. The corresponding female curve had a later maximum and dropped more slowly. Kinsey was of the opinion that the drop was due more to the men's declining activity than to the women's.

Married men and women are sexually more active on the average than unmarried, partly because of selection (the active ones are usually more eager to get married), partly because of more frequent opportunity. Probably this difference is now smaller than it once was, because the pill and other contraceptive techniques have made coitus less risky and possibly commoner among unmarried, especially young, people. The average age at which young people make their sexual debut seems to be going down.

Economic aspects. Traditionally the husband has been the breadwinner and the wife has taken care of the home, the household, and the children. In the upper classes, a wife, home, and family are often adjuncts to the husband's career. Among those women with academic training in western Europe, however, there is a strong tendency in another direction: the wife considers her own career and salary just as important as her husband's. More women today retain their jobs after marriage and after childbirth. Working wives, moreover, tend to have fewer children, though cause and effect may be confused here, since wives with few or no children have less reason to stop working.

In the lower income classes it has generally been taken for granted that if the husband could not earn enough, his wife would have to take a job. But as living standards have risen, the better-paid workers have been able to afford to keep their wives at home—and have generally wanted them there. Sometimes, however, the trend seems to move in the opposite direction, at least in western Europe. During periods of labour shortage, married women are tempted by high wages to take jobs away from home. Nursery schools and similar social agencies have thus been organized on a large scale to take care of the infants; schools have often taken over the task of providing the pupils' lunch, thus absorbing another maternal task. Besides, the younger generation of wives have often accepted the idea of equality and have acquired an education that makes them almost as useful on the labour market as men. Such wives might feel frustrated if restricted to the home and so are inclined to take work outside the home in order to secure social contacts.

In poor families, children are frequently expected or forced to supplement the meagre income as soon as the law and compulsory school attendance permit. In such families, the youngest child is usually in the most favourable position and may even get an opportunity to acquire a higher education.

As the standard of living rises, a progressively smaller part of the income is spent on food. Recently married couples have to acquire a home with the usual capital goods. This takes time and money. The husbands have to give up their former expensive forms of recreation and adapt themselves to their family obligations, some changing into "experts" on household machinery, house repairs, and the like. If they become householders, they often remain in the "do-it-yourself" pattern for the rest of their lives. Otherwise, this object-oriented phase may pass with diminishing financial difficulties, and they can again turn to recreation, travelling, and fishing.

Many of the younger generation now seem to be ori-

Familial division of labour

ented toward experiences instead of toward objects. Emotions, new contacts, and ideas are important to them, not expensive clothes, cars, or gadgets.

Patterns of power distribution. Decisions in the family depend on the particular behaviour concerned, on the situation, on the traditional leadership in the family, and on other such factors. But the formal decisions made by the leader of the family have very often already been determined by the other members and by the situation. Probably the patterns of "patriarchy" or "matriarchy" are oversimplifications in most modern societies, since most family decisions are made as the result of interaction between members of the family, not as the result of argument; decision making proceeds unconsciously as members demonstrate their own needs and resources and find out one another's needs and resources and so come to a tacit understanding. Even in Japan, for instance, the traditional strict hegemony of the husband and father seems to be slowly eroding under modern pressures.

Traditionally the husband is granted more power or deference in the family, but there are limits to his power, and there are large areas that are closed to him. Should he go beyond them, he would not be obeyed. Similarly, the wife's decisions in the home may give her a dominant position but not for all activities and not contrary to the expectations of the family. In practice, modern society thus tends to reduce the distinction between husband-dominated and wife-dominated families because most families come fairly close to a decision-sharing pattern. On the surface, however, the upper and middle class families seem to have less husband dominance, working class and farmer families more. A large proportion of young families accept the idea of decision sharing.

Household tasks and their distribution. Interview data show that husbands are taking over more and more household tasks, especially in young middle class families in towns. Probably the husbands accept their fair share of the household tasks, and this share naturally grows considerably if the wife has a job. (In some countries, such as Sweden, however, wives with just as many working hours as their husbands still tend to do a much larger part of the household tasks.) What are the husbands' new tasks? To begin with, they have taken over such jobs as using household machines, polishing their shoes, making their beds. They also often try their hands at cooking and at buying the food. In modern families, the husband might cope with the baby, changing its diapers and preparing its bottles.

One would expect families with working wives to have more household machines and more rationalized tasks. This seems not to be the case. They spend less time on cooking and washing up, but this is due only to the fact that they seldom have lunch at home. They also spend less time on their children, mending clothes, sewing, sleeping, and so forth as their time is too short.

In large families, the older children are expected to take over some tasks, but evidently this is more an ideal than a reality, at least insofar as the boys are concerned.

Social activities. The neighbourhood is important to the pattern of the family's social activities, and families are therefore eager to find the right kind of neighbourhood with a school that suits their children, a church adapted to their need for new contacts, women's activities for municipal reforms, and so on.

Generally, young people moving into a new residential area stick to their old friends in other areas to begin with, although they tend to cultivate their old contacts in the new surroundings. Gradually day contacts may become evening contacts, new acquaintances are picked up in local group participation, and slowly the old contacts outside the area shrink, unless they are fortified by business dealings or strong interests in common. (Housewives, of course, often make contacts with one another during the day, take a cup of tea together, borrow small things, or take care of each other's children. These day contacts need not develop into evening contacts—ones, that is, that include the men in the families.)

The geographical mobility of modern families would

The role of the neighbourhood and geographical mobility

seem to influence their social activities considerably. Upper and middle class families tend to move more than working class families, who are consequently better able to keep their contacts intact, not only with their neighbours but also with relations living in the same area. Working class social life may therefore be seen as a last reminiscence of the former upper and middle class "society life," in which formal dinner parties were given, and relations, neighbours, and business acquaintances were brought together in a home organized for this type of entertainment, with a drawing room, a parlour, and a dining room—the family thus having to live their everyday life as best they could in this show place planned for guests and banquets. The old "society life" pattern disappeared in Europe during World War I.

Educational aspects. Education, as noted earlier, is an important factor in mate selection, and thus husband and wife tend to be on the same educational level. Couples on higher educational levels not only provide their children with a more intellectual milieu, more books and so on, but also expect them to get good marks at school and to go on to college or even to graduate studies. Parents seem to consider it a duty to push their children through the same school examinations that they took themselves —or, if possible, better ones. Although this might be taken as a hopeful identification—that one's children should succeed better in life than their parents—it could just as well be regarded as a means of safeguarding the social status of one's children, of making it possible for them to remain in the same social class or to climb a bit higher; for these purposes education is certainly a great help.

Upper class children on the average receive better marks in elementary school than working class children, and consequently a higher percentage of them enter higher schools. Even among children of the same intellectual achievement, judged by their school marks, the upper class children are far more likely than the working class children to enter higher education, partly because of economic factors, partly because of a more ambitious attitude among upper class parents.

Community aspects. The family is responsible not only for socializing the children but also for ensuring that all members conform to or share certain basic values. If the family is too divided, with the members openly quarrelling or even fighting, neighbours and friends reduce their interaction with it and avoid giving gifts and kindnesses, since these could be seen as siding with one party against another. Such a family, then, is excluded from the reciprocal exchange of services and obligations. On the other hand, families with so much loyalty among the members that they isolate themselves and withdraw from community activity are not appreciated either. Such families may be forgiven, at least for a time, if they can make an acceptable excuse—an excuse such as a very difficult task to be performed, prolonged illness, or serious family problems. And in the worst cases, the community may intervene and give social support or even therapy to families in need.

CONFLICT, CRISIS, DISSOLUTION

No family can escape conflicts, but each family has its own way of handling them. Generally a serious conflict makes the family leader eager to close the ranks of the family and try to persuade the member or members at the centre of conflict *not* to confide in others, especially not to outsiders. Usually only then can some compromise be reached. If outsiders—even counselling agencies, doctors, and so on—are brought in loyalty tends to die. The family leader may then get into difficulties and even lose the position of leader, which in turn may break up the family.

Consequently, social agencies that are trying to protect the rights of weak or very young members of the family sometimes find that instead of uniting a family in conflict, they cause it to break up. Even help in the form of money, however necessary, might dethrone the family leader from the position of breadwinner. Legal help may

do the same if it demonstrates the inability of the leader to cope with the circumstances in which the family finds itself. It seems that only the leader can bring in help from the outside to solve troubles without endangering the family unity.

Economic problems. Unemployment, if it hits the male breadwinner, not only threatens his leadership in the family and the family's standard of living but also forces other members of the family out onto the labour market, where they may have a better chance since women and young people are paid less and are more vulnerable to demands for extra service. If the wife has work but the husband has not, the rational solution would seem to be that the husband takes over the household tasks. Modern young couples sometimes adjust in this way, but in older generations it was too degrading to the husband. He left home "to look for a job" and if he could not find one, he might leave the family and not return. Very poor families in the cities often seem to break up this way, if the husband is unable to secure a job.

Even if the male breadwinner has a job, this is no guarantee that the family will be spared quarrels about money. He may keep too much for himself, or the wife may ask for more than he has to give. Most wives are not happy if their husbands have too strict a control of the expenses; thus if squeezed too hard between a tight-fisted husband and nagging children, wives sometimes take a job to obtain money that they may use as they wish. Quarrels about money, in any event, are not only frequent but also difficult to solve.

Child problems. One of the reasons why people want children is to have their expectations fulfilled. It is a hard blow, for instance, to get a mentally retarded child who is unable to live up to these expectations and yet is in need of love and care. Most parents react in a very primitive fashion in this situation and try to deny the problem: "If we only wait, everything will be all right!" They often do not dare ask the doctor or bring in experts, because they are unable to accept the truth, in spite of their suspicions. When they finally have to face it, they feel it is unfair. Why should this happen to them? Then comes the suspicion that after all they may have done something to cause this situation. They feel guilty. As few people are able to stand guilt of this kind, they tend to transfer it to others. Perhaps the physician made a mistake. Perhaps one's spouse may have been careless on some occasion. Part of their reaction is directed toward the retarded child, but generally such a reaction is transformed into overprotection. Marriages with retarded children are probably less stable than other marriages, because the strain is far greater. **Problems involving retarded or maladjusted children**

Maladjusted children also cause feelings of guilt in the parents, and indeed maladjustment in children in many cases is the result of maladjustment in the parents, who may expect unreasonably much from their children or behave asocially themselves at home. In trying to adjust to such pressures, the children may develop symptoms that protect them against violence and impossible demands and that are sometimes even useful in keeping the family together; but it is also possible that these symptoms may destroy the child's chances of adjusting at school, in the neighbourhood, and in society in general. Counselling agencies sometimes find that if the maladjusted child can be cured, or if he is taken away from his parents, the family is unable to survive losing its scapegoat and breaks up, or, alternatively, some other member goes to pieces. Delinquency among children is commoner in slum areas, cities, and lower social classes, but its occurrence in well-to-do families can often be diagnosed as a reaction against a lack of emotional warmth or a reaction to rigid discipline. But these factors are found at all levels of society.

Individual parent problems. The home and the family can be used as a repair shop by breadwinners who are subjected to stress at work, but the breadwinner with troubles at home seems to run greater risks of alienation and accidents in the job. Generally, however, work outside the home makes it easier for the breadwinner to **Problems of husband and wife**

survive family troubles, at least so long as they are of moderate proportions.

Housewives and family members who are at home all day tend to be more emotionally involved in the family and therefore more dependent on the interaction there, more vulnerable when members of the family meet with accidents, contract mental or physical illnesses, and so forth. It is then assumed that the housewife will take care of them. If she has a job herself, she will probably have to give it up temporarily or feign illness herself in order to nurse the victim and administer the traditional cures or the doctor's prescriptions. Should a family member die, the wife tends to feel more guilt and generally has less chance of having her attention distracted by other things.

Family members who are chronically ill are difficult to take care of in modern homes, and so the severe cases are placed in institutions. There again the housewife feels more responsibility for keeping contacts alive. This does not mean that the husband evades responsibility, only that he acts in a less emotional, more intellectual manner and that he has to give his support and understanding to his wife if she is to be able to stand her own feelings of guilt and sorrow.

Husband-wife problems. Generally, people marry because they have a good relationship and expect that marriage will make it still better, giving them more opportunity to meet, love, help each other, and have children, thus fulfilling their desire for recognition and success. They bring with them from their parental homes, however, a set of expectations and ideals that are scarcely known to themselves, although they are strongly influenced by them in their behaviour in the home, especially toward their children. These expectations can be so impossible to meet that the marriage proves to be a serious disappointment even in the first months. The husband may have a strong need to assert his will in all details, or the wife may want a perpetual courtship with compliments and overwhelming recognition on every occasion, sulking if she does not get it. The partners are seldom able to recognize their own individual patterns but prefer to rationalize, making the other partner responsible, pointing out his or her thoughtlessness, mistakes, or intentional rudeness. Generally at least one partner tries to adapt, but when his or her disappointment becomes sufficiently great, the scenes begin to have an effect and the weaker partner may be forced into desperate resistance, so that a kind of terror balance is achieved.

Most marriages have some tendencies in this direction, at least when one of the partners is depressed or worn out. Children often give rise to new sets of expectations. The unsuspecting father may be disappointed to find that instead of being a convenient plaything, the baby cries, takes a lot of time, and breaks up the former leisure pattern. The husband may even feel neglected and jealous if his wife is completely absorbed as a mother. Later, alliances between one of the parents and the child or children can alienate the other parent. This, of course, is a risk run to greater extent by the father since he has less time to invest in the children and is often forced to make up for this with gifts or money. If the alienation is great enough, the alienated partner may desert the family.

Extramarital relations

Newly married people often expect an unreasonable amount of sexual gratification. Unsatisfied with the limited amount available or unsatisfied with the personal relationship that they have found in their marriage, they may sometimes establish extramarital associations. Kinsey found in his studies of the U.S. population that about one-quarter of the married men (one-third of the younger married men) turned to other women. Ten percent of married teenagers' intercourse was with other women, a figure that dropped to five percent for those who were 45 years old or more. The corresponding figures for married women were low for wives under 25 but rose to more than 10 percent for wives over 40 years of age. Probably the figures for adultery are higher now in the United States, as elsewhere.

Separation. Separation means that husband and wife have agreed to live apart or that one of them has gone to court in order to have an agreement drawn up regarding the financial support of wife and children or the custody of the children. Separation does not allow the partners to remarry and is only a relief from a marriage that demands too much or gives too little.

In some countries, in Scandinavia for instance, separation is a first step toward divorce and is meant to give the partners at least a year to try out the economic and emotional consequences of living apart. If they move together again, the separation is nullified.

DIVORCE

Distribution. The frequency of divorces varies with the divorce laws of the country concerned and with the attitude toward divorce. Legislation not only affects behaviour but is itself affected by a number of circumstances that the lawmakers have consciously or unconsciously taken into consideration—such things as old customs and usage and, above all, public opinion. (For the legal aspects of divorce, see FAMILY LAW.) People who have been granted divorces must be able to go on living in their communities without being rejected or put in a position in which they cannot make a living for themselves. Industrialization has made it easier for women to support themselves, whether they are single, married, divorced, or widowed. In this connection, it is interesting to note that the Great Depression of the 1930s stopped the rise in the number of divorces in the United States for a time.

Changing mores regarding divorce

The frequency of divorce partly depends on the changing structure of the population. Because people tend to live longer and to marry earlier, marriages are exposed to danger for a longer period. The more people marry, the more marriages are exposed to danger, and a high marriage rate probably brings with it a higher frequency of risky marriages. Divorces are more frequent in cities than in rural areas, and the continuing immigration to cities may increase the frequency.

Public opinion may be more tolerant toward divorce now, but it is still considered a sign of maladjustment and consequently can be expected to be more common in slum areas and lower social classes. This, however, is counterbalanced to some extent by the fact that legal action demands a lawyer and some money, something a family with little economic latitude has difficulty in mobilizing.

Religious groups generally have a more uncompromising attitude toward divorce and thus a lower divorce rate. People in some occupations—clergymen and teachers, for instance—are expected to behave perfectly in their family lives; divorce might force them to change their profession. In the United States, politicians and high military officers have a similar disinclination for divorce, but in western Europe, such professionals deviate hardly at all from the common upper class pattern. Actors, authors, and other groups that have many contacts with the opposite sex and only slight control by colleagues or relatives tend to have a high divorce frequency. Data from Sweden indicates high frequencies for actors and artists (21%), authors and journalists (16%), athletes (14%), and officers (13%), and low frequencies for diplomats (7%), engineers (7%), clergymen's sons (6.5%), farmers' sons (6%), judges and magistrates (5%), teachers (4%), and clergymen (2%). These data, however, hold good only for prominent persons listed in *Vem är det?*, the Swedish equivalent of *Who's Who*, and only for the facts reported by the people concerned. The women in *Vem är det?* form a comparatively small group, dominated numerically by actresses, and this group therefore shows a divorce frequency far above the men's. Younger age groups, finally, tend to have a higher divorce frequency than older ones. Most youthful marriages, it should be remembered, were contracted because the girl or woman was pregnant.

The number of children in the marriage is also influential. Childless couples tend to have a higher divorce rate than couples with children. But couples who drift apart rapidly are probably careful not to have children. Childlessness can be a cause of divorce, but it can just as well be a consequence of the disharmony that eventually leads to divorce.

Social and psychological effects. Emotional ties are nearly always complicated in a marriage and may include such elements as intense aggression or serious masochism. Such elements deeply influence the interaction in the family, creating tension, feelings of guilt, or even open clashes, which, when acted out, bring some relief—at least temporarily—to the actor, but deeply disturb the other members of the family. This may result in threats of separation or divorce being made by both husband and wife, even though the aggressive or masochistic partner making or provoking such threats may be deeply attached to the other partner. If such a marriage breaks up, the more aggressive partner may find it exceedingly difficult to readjust and may feel very guilty, probably trying to put all the blame on the other partner. Most divorced persons exhibit weak but noticeable reactions of this kind and they are apt to act out their emotions, using their relations and friends as listeners or possibly as co-actors.

Socially a divorce generally disrupts the contacts between the former partners and the married couples with whom they formerly associated. Few former partners preserve respect and understanding for each other; generally they take a very negative view of their former partner and feel a need to have their friends share this view. People then feel forced to make a choice between the two and stick to it. Actually, the husband more easily retains the contacts resulting from professional interests; the wife the contacts dominated by domestic interests. (The children, too, are exposed to this competition for loyalty and tend of course to side with the parent who is given their custody, while at the same time they may try to preserve a tacit understanding with the other parent.)

Sexual adjustment after the divorce is likely to be difficult if the husband and wife have had a good sexual relationship that was suddenly broken by the separation. This, however, is unusual. Serious strife between the partners tends to destroy their sexual relations, so that the divorce seldom deprives them of a rewarding sex life. Before the divorce comes up in court, both partners have tended to avoid or hide sexual relationships outside the marriage, in order to improve their case in court. After the divorce, when they are free from such considerations, they often are unable to find acceptable partners whom they can trust and love and introduce to their children.

The divorce affects the children in many ways and may threaten their socialization if they are very young. This, however, may just as well be attributed to the strife leading to the divorce as to the divorce itself. Swedish data from a representative sample of Stockholm boys indicated that divorced families did not show a higher percentage of maladjusted boys than complete families. But, on the other hand, a group of seriously maladjusted boys contained a far higher percentage of boys from divorced families than the representative sample, 42 percent, compared with 13 percent. Probably very disturbed backgrounds were commoner among the seriously maladjusted boys, and divorce was just one of the elements in those backgrounds. It therefore seems that divorce need not increase the danger of maladjustment for the children, but it may be an indicator of serious trouble in the family, resulting in the maladjustment of the children as well.

Courts tend to entrust the mother with the custody of the children, unless there are serious reasons against this. Mothers, after all, are probably more ambitious as parents, but data suggest that boys who grow up with their mothers and without contact with their fathers or with other male behaviour patterns to follow may have difficulty in defining their own roles.

Most families readily accept divorce as a way out of serious conflict; they do not, however, like to think that their own conflicts are serious and they dislike divorce among their friends. Families react as if divorce were a disease or a threat to their own solidarity. The divorced friends may be shunned or treated as failures in order to neutralize their bad influence. Husbands and wives who behave in this way may be afraid of losing their partners, but there may also be a strong, unconscious desire to get rid of them.

REMARRIAGE

A divorce, on the one hand, may be a traumatic experience that makes the divorced person unwilling to risk another marriage; or, on the other hand, it may be the first step toward a new marriage. Generally more than half of those divorced are remarried, with new partners, within a couple of years. This is partly due to the pressure exerted by their married friends—and indirectly by their own children. Divorced people are often treated as undesirably free agents, and at least the members of their own sex seem anxious to neutralize them as quickly as possible in a new marriage, willingly helping to provide acceptable contacts but withholding status and friendship until the scheme has worked. Children may also increase their divorced parents' willingness to remarry because the parent with whom they live has generally less time for them and a lower standard of living than before the divorce; above all, children are accustomed to and need contact in the home with a father as well as a mother.

Widows and widowers are subject to similar pressures to remarry if they are still attractive, if they have children at home to care for, or if they feel a new attachment would help them get over their bereavement.

Distributional factors. Remarriage is somewhat more common among widowers and divorcés than among widows and divorcées. Age is obviously an important factor: young people remarry much more frequently than do the old. Clearly, countries or regions with a high divorce rate tend to have a high rate of remarriage, too, because their attitude toward marriage is likely to be less rigid and provide more opportunity for trial and error.

Considerations in selection. Statistics on remarriage are not plentiful, and they are difficult to interpret, but one trend can be pointed out. People who remarry choose new partners who themselves have been previously married to a far greater extent than can be explained by chance.

How stable are these new marriages? On the average they run a greater risk of ending in divorce. The reason may be that the people concerned know how to go about getting a divorce, but it may just as well be that people who have found it difficult to live with someone else the first time may find it just as difficult to do so the second time. These two reasons do not exclude each other, of course; on the contrary, they may easily appear in combination.

A third reason for the instability of remarriages is the difficulty involved in marrying a woman who has previous experience of marriage and may also have children. A new husband may be—or may feel as if he is being—compared to the former husband (who seems to come off best in most respects) or, still worse, to the deceased husband (who is often beyond all criticism). The wife and her children sometimes get together and make the new husband an outsider who is allowed to provide for them, although he is never accepted as a member of their family. If he is accepted by the wife but not by the children, the conflict may be harmful to the children's social adjustment. A woman who marries a man who has been married before and has children faces corresponding difficulties and the extra burden of being a stepmother. The role of stepfather seems to be less odious in some way.

Psychological adjustment. The rewards of remarriage seem in the first place to be social ones: a person who remarries has fulfilled the expectations of society, relations, and friends, has done his or her duty to the children, and so is given full status again. The emotional rewards may be just as satisfactory (a courtship, in some cases, may be the best way to forget the old ties and to cure psychological hurts); there is, however, considerable risk that the divorced person will still be emotionally tied to the former partner, not really caring about the new one, who was only accepted for social reasons. *Any* adjustments, however, may be easily disturbed, especially by children who jealously watch the stepparent, anxious to protect the rights that they have been given or have taken during a period when they tried hard to replace or compensate for the missing parent. In being forced to give up their heightened status, they may feel degraded, and they may put the blame for this partly on the intruder, partly on the parent whom they trusted but who they now feel let them down. The remarried parent in such a situation is caught between two loyalties. Conflicts of this kind are exceedingly difficult to resolve. The new parent is careful not to give open offense to the children but tends to exploit their indiscretions. The children in their turn try to avoid the stepparent and attempt to monopolize their own parent, who tries to play for time, hoping that the children will soon be out of the conflict.

IV. Transition of the form and structure of the modern family

SECURITY IN SOCIETY AND FAMILY

Reduced tasks or roles of the family

Modern societies try to protect their citizens against violence, distress, ignorance, and maladjustment. People are so anxious for this protection that they find it difficult to believe that exploitation, extermination, hunger, analphabetism, or vice on a grand scale need persist in their own society. But it can be argued that this unsafe world is safer than it has ever been before, thus making individuals in modern societies more independent of the protection and help of class, clan, family and peer groups. Evidently individuals should then be less dependent on the family and able to some extent to experiment with other forms of contact groups, not based on family ties. One possibility would seem to be the local work team, living in a collective, a *kibbutz*, or something similar; another possibility is the peer group forming a "group family," not winning their bread together but eating it together, having intellectual, emotional, and even sexual contacts with several other members. Intellectually such arrangements may have several advantages, but the difficulty seems to be that one's own individual process of growing up, in the overwhelming majority of cases, took place in a family and that one consciously or unconsciously tries to rebuild or recover the same constellation as that in which one advanced from the role of child to the role of adult. One thus finds it exceedingly difficult not to perform the tasks and not to demand the rights that one expects. This is above all the case in connection with the emotional and sexual monopoly of contacts with one's spouse and the role of pattern builder in relation to one's children.

THE EFFECTS OF TECHNOLOGY

Technology and society interact in a very complicated manner. Society eagerly accepts some technological innovations and completely disregards others, which often are just as useful. The technological innovations that are accepted may seriously affect or change industrial and agricultural production, consumption patterns, and ways of living.

Once the family was an important production unit; now industrialization and modern society have taken over most of its productive tasks. But efficient sales organizations have found the family a convenient target for their efforts, and mass media have found channels to the family's hearts and brains—or at least to the family's eyes and ears. Perhaps these tendencies can be interpreted as proofs of a new production era in the family; the technology of television, home freezers, washing machines, family cars, "do-it-yourself" kits, and so forth may give the family more tasks to perform together, more chances to survive.

On another level, however, technology often works in the opposite direction. New machinery and new factories generally are located in new areas, forcing employees to move from their families, creating long journeys to work or forcing them to leave the neighbourhood in which their family has lived. New products often replace old ones, causing changes of work or unemployment, and at the very least unemployment seriously affects family life. New technology, such as automation and atomic power, will probably have similar effects on a large scale, unless they are introduced slowly and under efficient social control. Even so, they may influence marriage, fertility, and education because there will be far less need for unskilled labour and far more need for technical knowhow or theoretical training. Adjustment to these new circumstances may be difficult for women in higher social classes, who will probably be pushed out by men, in spite of official acceptance of the pattern of equality; and adjustment also will be difficult for lower class men, whose labour will be in less demand, while working class women may find it far easier to find service jobs, which are less well paid.

THE DRIVE FOR FEMALE EQUALITY

The democratic ideology was once strong enough to convince the majority of people in Western cultures that all men should have equal civil and political rights. This, however, did not apply to women; and considerable political change was (and still is) necessary before women were (or will be) granted fundamental political and civil rights in the more advanced countries, though they now generally have educational opportunities as good as do the men and access to a number of professions. They generally receive, however, somewhat lower incomes and have smaller chances of promotion. Many married women, for instance, with jobs in workshops, offices, or in the professions, recognize that they will have a lot of housework to do when they get home and that they will have to stay at home on the days that their husband or one of the children is ill in bed. These duties of theirs, although extremely important to the family and society, will be little appreciated by their employers and will reduce their pay as well as their chances of promotion. If modern society has a serious need of married women in jobs outside the home, then the community probably will have to create better facilities for having young children and bedridden members of the family looked after and give women better positions and the same chances of promotion as men with the same formal merits. Shorter working hours, shorter workweeks, and longer holidays also will make it easier for married women to meet the double demands made on them by job and family.

The concept of equality of the sexes seems to irritate some women. This can be interpreted as showing that the pattern is now so established that it can easily stand some criticism. Modern sex technology also lends it support. The problem of having children of the sex desired is theoretically solved. In the future there could be little trouble about securing not only the number of children wanted but also the sex wanted. Then, peculiar ideas that sons are more valuable than daughters can be given free rein; and this may eventually result in sons and daughters being regarded as being of equal value. If people seriously do prefer sons, they will produce a surplus of them and so automatically create a greater demand for daughters. Too unequal a proportion between the sexes, however, will bring other difficulties in its train.

The pill has had a profound effect on sex mores, because it efficiently reduces the danger of unwanted pregnancy and therefore removes one reason for having one set of moral standards for men and another for women. If women can have coitus without risking pregnancy, it is hardly possible to demand that women remain chaste because of a possible child's future. Probably new types of relations between men and women will emerge, but in order to be described they will have to be studied in terms of contacts—sexual, emotional, intellectual, and otherwise—instead of in terms of contracts—households and families in the classical sense. These contacts should be easier to make and maintain if the partners share the same opinions and value the same things. Differences in background or age tend to raise barriers, and it takes energy, money or intellectual resources to break them down.

THE ROLE OF IDEOLOGY

Formerly, social classes or educational groups differed comparatively much from one another and so had little contact. The younger people took over the ideology of their parents very easily, changing it but little. Now most of them take over their more or less organized ideologies from other groups, generally their peer groups. This does not mean that all the members of the younger generation share the same ideology. They do not; there are still large differences between college students and those who have instead gone directly to the labour market. It does mean that there are now far greater differences between the old and the young within each social class or educational group than there were formerly. Even formerly, the ideological differences were large enough to make young people eager to leave their parents and marry, build homes, and have children; but now differences in ideology are even deeper, and they show not only in dress, taste, contacts, and political opinions but also in the forms of social life: some of the younger generation do not accept marriage and do not make homes, although they live with one another and have children together. These ideological differences and the clashes that they create, or are meant to create, can no longer be ignored. They have to be recognized and handled as seriously as class differences or ethnic differences.

BIBLIOGRAPHY. J. ALDOUS and R. HILL, *International Bibliography of Research in Marriage and the Family, 1900–1964* (1967), the most comprehensive bibliography available for the period up to 1964; N.W. BELL and E.F. VOGEL (eds.), *A Modern Introduction to the Family* (1968), a selection of excellent readings making use of structural-functional analysis; D.R. BLITSTEN, *The World of the Family* (1963), a good selection of material on the family from different cultures; GUNNAR H.R. BOALT, *Family and Marriage* (1965), a comparison of Scandinavian and Indian family systems with those in the U.S.; H.T. CHRISTENSEN (ed.), *Handbook of Marriage and the Family* (1964), a scholarly volume dealing with the total field of family sociology; N.N. FOOTE and L.S. COTTRELL, *Identity and Inter-Personal Competence: A New Direction in Family Research* (1955), one of the most significant books dealing with the role of the family in the development of its individual members; W.J. GOODE, "Horizons in Family Theory," in R.K. MERTON, L. BROOM, and L.S. COTTRELL (eds.), *Sociology Today* (1959), a good statement of the basic problems in developing theory in family sociology; W.J. GOODE, *World Revolution and Family Patterns* (1963), one of the best family texts on the fundamental theme of industrialization and the family; J. HEISS (ed.), *Family Roles and Interaction: An Anthology* (1968), a selection of readings concerned with the behaviour of persons in different family roles; C. KIRKPATRICK, *The Family: As Process and Institution*, 2nd ed. (1963), a basic text in family sociology; H.R. LANTZ and E.C. SNYDER, *Marriage: An Examination of the Man-Woman Relationship* (1962), a good illustration of social-psychological interpretation of dating, courtship, and marriage; G.R. LESLIE, *The Family in Social Context* (1967), a solid family text; OSCAR LEWIS, *Five Families: Mexican Case Studies in the Culture of Poverty* (1959), important for both the method and content; GEORGE MURDOCK, *Social Structure* (1949), a classic work presenting a social anthropological comparison of sample cultures; D.R. MILLER and G.E. SWANSON, *The Changing American Parent* (1958), a significant work attempting to relate child rearing to occupational structure.

(G.Bo.)

Family Law

Family law may in general be defined as the body of laws relating to the organization of the family. In the past such law has been closely connected with the law of property and succession, and from the records available, it must have had its principal origins in the economic and property questions created by the transfer of a woman from her father's family to the power and guardianship of her husband. Even in regard to parent and child, such legal concepts as guardianship, custody, and legitimacy were associated with family power structures and family economic interests. Family law also has to do with matters of personal status—for example, the question whether X is to be considered married or single or whether Y is to be classed as legitimate or as a bastard—although the incidents and importance of these distinctions often lead back to the law of property.

This article is not a treatise on the family laws of the world (which would require at least a volume) but a discussion of the application of law to family relations. It is a consideration of the role of law in regard to the family, an effort to identify the main problems on a comparative basis.

In recent decades, family law has been subject to re-examination in many parts of the world, and the greater legal status and independence acquired by married women has been a catalyst.

FAMILY GROUPS

A family group has a certain internal structure as well as relationships between itself and third parties. Family groups in some societies have tended to be complex, as, for example, the Roman paterfamilial group, the Chinese upperclass family, the Indian joint family, the Samurai family in Japan, and many customary family structures in Africa. The family may be a part of a larger group such as the tribe or clan.

The two-parent family. At present the dominant form of the family group consists of two spouses and the children they have produced or adopted. The law, therefore, is concerned mainly with the rights and duties of husband and wife and parent and child, particularly in questions of financial support. In a strictly monogamous society, the law will forbid a husband to marry again; while in other societies, it will regulate the number of wives (as does Islāmic law).

In various parts of the world some families are, in effect, matriarchal because the adult male is so frequently absent, as in fishing communities or among peoples with high concubinage rates. Where divorce and separation are common and where welfare programs are available to assist dependents, the one-parent family acquires an importance that is not adequately reflected in traditional law. Some European countries have had significant rates of illegitimacy, and the public services of these and other countries have been sympathetic to the one-parent family. It may be necessary to adapt the law to a greater extent to the needs of one-parent families in such areas as the organization of family and child welfare services and the legal and administrative machinery for family support, employment assistance, day nurseries, and the like. The head of a single-parent household may have difficulty affording the high cost of child care while working or training, especially on a modest or low income.

The one-parent family. Traditionally, family law has not concerned itself much with unions that are not commenced by legal marriage, though some systems of law permit the recognition of a "natural" child by a father for such purposes as inheritance or support. The family group based on concubinage has been largely neglected by the law because such unions are often transitory and difficult to define; are considered immoral; occur mainly among poorer or less educated classes (as in some parts of Latin America; or among serfs or slaves); or are associated with an inferior status of the female (particularly in Asian and African countries).

Even where the family is a two-parent group, it may encounter some of the problems of the one-parent family if the woman is employed outside the home. Some European countries, and the People's Republic of China, have probably gone further than most in proportions of women in employment, but many other countries also have changing patterns of female employment. In the poorer classes generally, women have traditionally worked outside the home at unskilled jobs; the new development in recent times is the growing number of middle class

The ways in which law has been applied to families

married women who are employed full-time or part-time for personal satisfaction, increased standard of living, or both.

Legal consequences of marriage. Marriage gives rise to certain automatic consequences. But two persons might, for example, produce the economic incidents of marriage by executing appropriate contracts or settlements. On this argument, a marriage provides a technically simple way of achieving what the parties could do for themselves in finance and property matters with greater expense and complexity. In some legal systems, in which agreement on property arrangements is central to the status of a legal wife, a contract in conventional form is the core of the constitution of marriage. The contract may be complex, with a variety of clauses, as in Muslim law or (more so formerly) as in major family unions under French or English law. In most countries today, however, the legal documentation of a marriage is mainly a registration of the event. So basically, in the legal sense, a marriage is the implied creation of certain rights or obligations such as maintenance, marital property and succession rights, and the custody of legitimate minor children.

In modern systems, the parties to a marriage can create the economic incidents of the marriage by a separate agreement. In some early legal systems and in present systems in which customary family law pertains, there is little choice as to the economic incidents of marriage because these are fixed by custom. In legal systems that allow substantial scope for personal independence, as in those of North America and western Europe, the spouses can take up a position of their own as to the economic basis of their family group by a marriage contract or a will.

Status and contract

According to the English legal scholar Sir Henry Maine legal history shows a movement from "status" to "contract"—meaning that modern private law is less concerned with a person's class (*e.g.*, slave, illegitimate son, serf, freeman, Roman citizen) than it is with voluntary agreements among persons. A maintenance obligation has a different practical significance in a country such as Sweden, where most married women are employed and there are extensive welfare programs, than, for example, in India. Rights of intestate succession will have a different social impact in a country where most people make wills than in one where most die intestate. In many countries there has been a tendency in the law to allow increasing freedom in setting up the family group and establishing its economic base. This is not true of some countries, and generally Communist legal systems impose at least a matrix of mandatory general principles designed to promote the political and social philosophy of the state. The extent of mandatory regulation, as compared with leaving decisions to the spouses voluntarily, is one of the important issues facing family law at the present time.

One feature that distinguishes marriage from a simple contract is that, in many countries, the parties cannot release themselves by mutual agreement. But some recent legislation in North America and western Europe comes close to permitting this; the grounds of divorce have been so widened that the marriage can be terminated, for example, after a period of separation.

The social environment. The family group is in some respects a microcosm of society, reflecting within it many facets of the whole social and legal environment. The great religions of the world have taken a special interest in family law, seeing in it opportunities for extending their moral and spiritual influence. Family law has at times been an element in promoting the interests of a particular class; in many countries there have been social hierarchies sustained by marriage and property laws. Practicing lawyers and the courts devoted much of their time to the interests of the dominant class. The family structures of the poor and the peasantry received much less attention in the law; the family law of these classes had more to do with workhouses, charitable institutions, unemployment relief, and welfare services. The 20th-century revolutions in Russia and China had as a main target the family structures of existing quasi-feudal regimes and consequently made large-scale changes in family law. The introduction of the Meiji code in Japan in 1898 similarly involved basic changes in the traditional family law, marking the emergence of a new society.

The institutions of the village and the commune have a long history in many countries. Such communities may contain a number of families who cooperate in various ways such as in the ownership or management of property; farming and handicrafts; communal help and welfare; religious observances. A significant proportion of the population of Asia, Africa, and Latin America lives in such communities. The administration of the community and the management of its property is usually governed by customary law.

The wide differences in social organization and custom indicate that there can be no universal "best" pattern for family law. The legal regulation of familial relationships should be approached with caution lest the prejudices of a majority be imposed unnecessarily on the private lives of individuals. As the English philosopher John Stuart Mill wrote in his "Essay on Liberty," "There is a limit to the legitimate interference of collective opinion with individual independence; and to find that limit, and maintain it against encroachment, is as indispensable to a good condition of human affairs, as protection against political despotism."

The range of problems falling within the general scope of family law may conceivably increase in the future, and there are legal scholars who predict that, within the next 50 or 100 years, family law may experience some of the most critical events in the history of human societies. First, rising population in some parts of the world may bring profound changes in laws relating to the family. Methods of limiting population and of controlling reproduction and heredity will, to the extent they are put into practice, have an important effect on family relationships and the principles of family law. Second, an increasing life expectancy is itself an important influence on marriage and family structure, because it lengthens the average cohabitation until dissolution of a marriage by death. Third, new dimensions in relations between the sexes could be introduced by a developed biotechnology in the control and management of genes, cells, etc., undoubtedly raising new legal problems. Fourth, the accelerating tendency for people to group in huge urban complexes is a social force bearing on the traditional structures of family law.

CHILDREN

Laws relating to the care of children

It is almost universally the rule that natural or adopting parents have a primary duty to maintain their minor children. In the great majority of cases, the care and upbringing of a child belongs to its biological parents automatically, without regard to their qualification or suitability. No doubt this arrangement was due originally to its convenience and to lack of alternatives, although examples may be found of groups rearing their children in common (usually in tribal societies). The parental system has been justified on religious grounds. Thus, in an Irish case the court declared: "The authority of a father to guide and govern the education of his child is a very sacred thing, bestowed by the Almighty, and to be sustained to the uttermost by human law." A criticism of this system is the inequality of opportunity and upbringing it can offer one child as compared with another. In many modern societies, public services and funds, in particular schools and educational systems, play an increasing part in the raising of children.

Legitimacy. By the common law of England, an illegitimate child was a *filius nullius* (without relatives). There may have been two main reasons for this former, discriminatory attitude. First, certain unions between the sexes were designated as lawful marriages, and a man of importance, agreeing to his daughter's marriage, would insist on her having the status of legal wife. Second, paternity, in the legal sense, was easier to establish in the case of a lawful marriage than in the absence of a marriage. The common law of England, for example, presumes in favour of legitimacy when the child is born in lawful wedlock, even if the biological facts may be otherwise. Civil-law systems—those derived from Roman law —have been less absolute than the common law; they provide ways of legitimating a child, such as through subsequent marriage of the parents or through an act of recognition by the father. Modern statute law has brought the positions in different systems closer together and removed some of the worst features of the doctrine of legitimacy. Legitimacy is a concept of diminishing importance in modern law, and even countries that still retain it have usually modified it. They have done so by basing support obligations on parentage rather than on a legally valid marriage and by giving rights of intestate succession (that is, the right to inherit property in the absence of a will) to children born out of wedlock. By the legal devices of legitimation and adoption, and by other means, the difference between the legal status of a legitimate and an illegitimate child has been narrowed. Family laws in all countries seem to be coming generally to the position that an illegitimate child is a member of a family group, albeit perhaps the group is a nonstandard one such as the one-parent family.

Illegitimacy is frequently associated with poverty; a contributing factor in this has been the tendency to exclude the child by law and social circumstances from what the community regarded as a customary and respectable family structure. The bastard has usually lacked the financial support available in the conventional family group. Sometimes the laws have been designed to prevent the cost of support from falling on those not biologically responsible for the birth. Thus, English legislation of 1576 provided that an order could be made on the putative father for the maintenance of a bastard by the parish (the local government). The distinction of legitimacy has been largely removed in some countries, and the thrust of modern law-reform proposals, in general, is that the welfare of all children should be a matter of honest and effective public concern, made mandatory by statutory provisions.

Adoption. In modern societies, adoption tends to be associated with illegitimacy because adoption of the children of unmarried mothers has become common in many countries, although in some jurisdictions there is also a nontrivial number of married parents who offer their children for adoption. The ordinary legal principle is that the consent of a natural parent (or guardian) is required for an adoption order by a court. This consent may be dispensed with if the correct person cannot be found or has proved to be an uninterested or cruel parent. Sometimes adoption without consent appears to go further, and an emerging problem for family law in some countries is whether courts or public agencies should be able to effect the transfer of a child away from the custody of its parents on the ground that that is best for the welfare of the child.

Adoption in the older legal systems (as in Roman law) was treated mainly in terms of succession law. It provided a way of introducing an outsider into a family group and so bringing him or her within the scope of the succession rules. In modern systems, succession rights as well as other legal obligations and rights in cases of adoption are usually treated by analogy with those of legitimate children; in some systems there is an explicit equation with legitimate children. Difficulties have been experienced with adoption in private international law because legal rules and procedures vary.

Education. The rapid development of education in the 19th and 20th centuries has had dramatic effects upon the family and upon the rights and obligations of family members. Until the latter part of the 19th century, even in highly developed countries, the organized education of children of the poorer classes tended to be casual or nil. Since then, the powers of a father to determine the upbringing of his child have declined before the advance of public education and the complex legislation and financing on which it rests. Today the pattern in some parts of the world is compulsory education up to the late teens, with extensive opportunities for higher educa-

tion into the early 20s and perhaps later. Present tendencies seem to be (in general) toward even longer and further involvement with the educational process. If this trend continues, the educational systems of many countries may become child-rearing systems providing services such as foster homes, boarding houses, children's villages, and various health and welfare facilities. The effect on family law may be to reduce the importance of the biological link between parent and child.

Decision making. The older law in many countries regarded decision making in regard to children as internal to the family, an area in which the courts should not intervene except in cases of serious child abuse or the like. In the English common law, for example, there are decisions of the latter part of the 19th century in which this doctrine of the "family veil" was carried to considerable lengths by giving an autocratic position to the father during his lifetime, and even longer, if a testamentary guardian was appointed upon his death. In most primitive societies, customary law gave similar authority to the father, although sometimes the custody and training of girls has been the special province of the mother. In modern law, the power of the father yielded to the principle that the welfare of the child is paramount; but this relaxation has raised important and difficult questions. The prevailing view is that the courts should take jurisdiction and intervene in family decision making in certain circumstances. Generally it may be said that they should intervene when injustice, oppression, or cruelty might result if exclusive private decision making were allowed to prevail—for example, in instances of significant danger to the welfare of the child and in cases of marriage breakdown between the parents. Prevailing theory seems to be that it would be an extreme and undesirable principle to make parent–child relations wholly private and exclude the jurisdiction of the courts, but that it would also be extreme and undesirable to have no private domain of decision making and to bring all family disputes to court. The practical rule lies between the extremes, and the application of such a rule is uncertain and there are bound to be differences of opinion.

A variant of this problem is that of determining the boundaries between private decision making in a family and decision making by public authorities and services, such as child welfare officials. Here the question is to what extent the public authorities ought to share in the bringing up of children. This is a policy issue of great difficulty; in modern times, the courts have tended to intervene more than formerly in cases in which children are neglected, abused, delinquent, and so on. In the Soviet Union and the People's Republic of China, state policy has had a strong influence on the general structure of the family codes and their interpretation by the courts, including the legal rights and duties of parents with respect to custody, guardianship, and child care.

Questions of custody. Cases can be cited to show the difficulty of reaching agreement among judges and others as to what constitutes the "best interests" and "welfare" of a child. The Supreme Court of Canada has supported the principle that a natural parent, such as an unmarried mother, should not be denied custody of her child merely because applicants wishing to adopt the child offer better material prospects or a two-parent instead of a one-parent household. Other views maintain that a young unmarried mother is, in general, not a suitable custodian of her newborn child and that therefore public intervention leading to adoption is usually in the child's best interests. Another disputed question is whether a difference of religion between a natural parent and an adoptive parent, or between two natural parents, is against the interests of the child. Various shades of opinion have been expressed: for example, that failure to raise a child in a particular religion may stunt its spiritual development; that a change of religious environment could be upsetting to a child already accustomed for some years to a certain religion.

Questions of custody cannot be determined solely by deduction from a rule of law. They require the exercise of judicial discretion that takes account of all the relevant circumstances, which may be very complex. Perhaps the child has been for some time previously in the same home; or there has been a long and acrimonious dispute between parents who are divorcing; or there have been conflicts between parents and child-welfare authorities. In divorce cases, the situation is often a de facto one: separation of the parents has taken place some time before the legal proceedings, and the child has already been given into the custody of one of them, so that the divorce decree may do no more than regularize in law what has already happened to the child in fact.

MARRIAGE

Marriage and its relation to property

The history of marriage is bound up with the legal and economic dependence of women upon men and the legal incapacities of women in owning and dealing with property. In Babylonian law, for example, one characteristic of a "legal wife" was that she brought property to the marriage (as a contribution to the support of the new family). Before there was a developed law of wills, there would be a distribution of property upon the death of a paterfamilias. The property taken by a daughter on marriage may have been to compensate for her not being in the family group at the next such distribution. It was also customary for the man to make gifts to his bride, either in property or by giving services to the bride's family, as a token of the seriousness of his intentions.

Marriage as a transfer of dependence. In systems in which the females are legally and economically dependent within a family hierarchy, the juridical essence of marriage is the transfer of the woman from control by her own family to control by her husband. Marriage customs of many times, countries, and religions exhibit this principle in a variety of forms: in certain kinds of Roman marriage; in marriages among the Japanese Samurai; in the traditional Chinese marriage; in the Hindu marriage based on the joint family; in Rabbinical law; in Muslim law; and in Germanic and Celtic customary law. The Germanic traditions were imported into England, where they combined with Norman concepts to become the basis of the English common law of marriage. The Germanic law provided, at least in higher class families with property, for a payment by the bridegroom for the transfer of the *mund* (responsibility for, and power over, the woman); for a settlement on the groom by the bride's family; and for a so-called *Morgengab*, which may have represented the completion of the settlement. The giving of a ring had a symbolic role in many kinds of wedding and betrothal ceremonies. The word wed derives from the Anglo-Saxon word for security given to bind a promise. The property used as security was not necessarily transferred but given symbolically (*i.e.*, the ring). In a modern Church of England wedding service, the giving of security is reflected in the words, "With this ring I thee wed," and the settlement of property in the words, "and with all my worldly goods I thee endow." The minister has previously asked, "Who giveth this woman to be married to this man?" and, on "receiving the woman at her father's or friend's hands," proceeds with the ceremony. This "giving away" of the woman by her family reflects the transfer of the *mund* to the bridegroom. In some systems the marriage forms may have a "bride purchase" origin, in the sense of compensation to her family (although there are differences of opinion as to the meaning of the customary forms): this was true in certain kinds of marriage in the earlier Roman republic, in Babylonian or Aramaic marriages, in early Arabic marriages, in certain Chinese unions (at least with regard to concubines, in which cases the transaction was more openly a purchase from the girl's parents), in customary marriage in some parts of Africa (*e.g.*, Nigeria, Ghana, Kenya), and in customary marriage among the nomadic tribes of Siberia (*e.g.*, the Kirgiz or Yakuts).

The ancient concept of marriage in many legal systems is that of a transaction between families (and this has sometimes persisted to the present day). Although the consent of the bride and bridegroom was almost always formally required, it may be questioned how real the consent was in the case of a child bride or in marriages between parties who did not see each other beforehand. Go-betweens and marriage brokers have been part of the marriage customs of many countries, especially in the East; in old Japan and China, for example, the go-between was considered an important person chosen to carry out a responsible task. The go-between and the professional marriage broker still have a substantial following in some countries. Some authorities have suggested that computer "matching" for marriage may become a modern development of the go-between concept.

Marriage as a voluntary relationship. The modern idea of marriage, which is becoming almost universal, is a voluntary exchange of promises between the man and the woman. Even though a marriage may involve substantial decisions as to property, these matters now tend either to be automatic (when there is no marriage contract) or to be formalized separately from the marriage ceremony. The ceremony itself is normally an exchange of consents accompanied by religious observances or a civil ceremony (or both). The purpose of the legal formalities is to differentiate the relationship from concubinage and to create certain recognized legal incidents such as maintenance, custody of children, rights under matrimonial regimes, intestate succession, claims under life-insurance policies and pension funds. The legal incidents could doubtless be provided by the execution of specific contracts, settlements, and wills, without a marriage contract.

Modern marriage law

In earlier legal systems, especially in Asia, the woman's consent was often unnecessary or of minor importance; the marriage negotiations took place between the woman's father and the man or his family. Voluntary consent of the parties became important in Roman times. Roman law during the period of the empire distinguished between an agreement for present marriage and an agreement for future marriage (*sponsalia per verba de praesenti* and *sponsalia per verba de futuro*). This distinction was taken over by Christianity, and a promise for marriage *per verba de futuro* was supported by a guarantee or "deposit" payment or by a penalty clause in a marriage contract.

Engagement. The view of the canon law of Christianity was that an engagement incapacitated a person from marriage to a different party and consequently provided ground for annulment of a marriage. This raised an issue that has troubled the civil lawyer but apparently not the common lawyer; *i.e.*, whether penalties, forfeiture provisions, damages, and the like for breach of engagement or betrothal are consistent with the exchange of voluntary consent at the marriage ceremony. Thus, French law has been led to reject an action of breach of promise (while permitting an action in delict—that is, on the charge that one party has been wronged). The common law, on the other hand, allows claims for breach of promise, although the modern tendency is to eliminate this form of action by statute.

The public interest. It has been difficult to delineate the boundaries between public and private interest in marriage law. The public interest is involved in the prevention of clandestine marriages; in requiring a license or the publication of banns as a condition precedent to marriage; in requiring parental consent for marriages between persons of certain ages; and in providing for the registration of marriages in a public manner. In practice, however, the marriage laws are often a mixture of functional administrative provisions (such as the requirement for registration, health certificates), old customs, religious ceremonies, and routine administrative precedents. Marriage statutes were introduced in modern times to combat the danger of clandestine marriages, which were possible under the old law in Europe and England by some form of mutual consent. Apart from direct establishment of this consent, it could be done indirectly by: engagement followed by intercourse (*matrimonium subsequente copula*); habit and repute marriage (evidence of acceptance in the community as being married persons). Clandestine marriage was of significance at a time when a man could acquire control over the property of a woman, including absolute ownership of much of it. The emancipation of women has put an end to the economic advantages of the clandestine marriage, but the legislation to which it gave rise has left an impress on the statute books.

Age. For a voluntary consent to a marriage, a party must have reached an age at which he or she is able to give a meaningful consent, and it is also implied that a person may be legally disqualified on mental grounds from having capacity to marry. Marriages of young children, negotiated by their parents, are prohibited in modern societies. Historically, the attitude of the English common law was that a person under seven years lacked the mental ability to consent to marriage, between seven years and puberty there could be consent but not a consummated marriage. At common law, therefore, the marriage of a person between the ages of seven and 12 or 14 was "inchoate" and would become "choate" on reaching puberty, if no objection was raised. Most modern legal systems provide for a legal minimum age of marriage ranging from 15 to 18 years. Many systems require parental consent to marriage when the parties are above the minimum age but below some other age, and failure to obtain this may be a ground for annulment. Parental consent has a long historical tradition, and there have been systems in which the girl's consent was virtually unnecessary. It is difficult to say, therefore, whether modern provisions have a valid social function or are the flotsam of older ideas on marriage.

Relationship. Other laws forbid marriage between persons having certain ties of relationship, either of blood or of marriage. "Forbidden degrees" of one sort or another exist in most social groups. The rules against marrying close relatives are sometimes said to be directed against the dangers of inbreeding, but this does not explain the prohibition against unions between persons who are related only by marriage. In classical Chinese society, marriage was regarded as a linking of different families, and the traditional pattern was exogamy (marriage outside the family). In ancient Egypt, on the other hand, where the pharaoh was deified, marriages within the blood were considered desirable in order to preserve its purity. Marriages between cousins are apparently encouraged in some Arab countries, perhaps to strengthen family ties and to keep the property together.

Religion. Religion has had a very strong influence on marriage law, often providing the main basis of authority. Hindu family law, which goes back at least 4,000 years (and may be the oldest known system), is a branch of Dharma—that is, the aggregate of religious, moral, social, and legal duties and obligations as developed by the Smritis or Institutes of the law. Islāmic and Jewish family law also rests on spiritual authority. Religious courts have had jurisdiction over family matters in various countries, and in some countries they still possess it. Some modern religious courts retain only their spiritual jurisdiction over marriage and divorce; their judgments have no standing in the secular law. In some Roman Catholic and Greek Orthodox Christian marriages and also in Muslim and Jewish marriages, the application of the religious law is regarded as binding upon persons belonging to the faith. Where religious texts provide the literal authority for legal principles, as in Islāmic law, it may be necessary to reinterpret the texts in order to reform the law. This raises complex issues in those Muslim countries where there are movements for greater equality of the sexes.

ECONOMIC ASPECTS OF FAMILY LAW

The variety of approaches to marital property

The comparative legal history of marital property, viewed in broad perspective, consists of a period stretching back for about 4,000 years, during which a husband was generally regarded as a quasi-guardian of his wife, who was dependent upon him economically and legally. The English common law removed the separate legal personality of a woman when she married and merged it in that of her husband, though she regained it if she became a widow. Her husband acquired extensive rights to the administration and ownership of her property, including full ownership (with no obligation even to give an ac-

counting) of any moneys she received from employment or business. Until quite recently, the only property of which a Hindu woman was the absolute owner was her *strīdhana*, consisting mainly of wedding gifts and gifts from relatives. Muslim women have traditionally owned and managed their own property. In Japan, before the Meiji Civil Code of 1898, all of the woman's property such as land or money passed to her husband except for personal clothing and a mirror stand. In early Vietnamese customary law, the property contributions of both spouses formed a common mass that was administered jointly and then divided, together with acquisitions made during their marriage, between the spouses and their heirs. In ancient Burmese law, all of the property of the spouses comprised a common mass that was their joint property but was administered by the husband with extensive powers. In 13th-century France, there was a concept of "community" on the lines of a partnership between the spouses; but by the 16th century, French husbands had secured the *puissance maritale* ("marital power") that gave them power over the disposal of property. In ancient Hungarian law, the bride usually brought property to the marriage, and a regime with a form of dowry persisted until World War II. The law of imperial Russia permitted a wife to own and deal with property independently of her husband—an attitude that differed from its treatment of women in other respects. A Roman wife, in some marriage forms, had a position of independence in regard to her property that was unusual for that era. In Celtic law, the man gave property to the woman's family; according to Brehon law (the ancient law of Ireland), the payment could be made by annual installments over 21 years (the woman's father kept the first installment, two-thirds of the second, half of the third, and so on, the remainder going to the wife).

The emancipation of women. The emancipation of women, which occurred in many countries during the latter part of the 19th century and the first part of the 20th, had a profound effect upon family law and marital property. The Scandinavian countries made radical reforms in their marital property laws in the 1920s; they introduced a new type of matrimonial regime in which the spouses retain independent control of their property except for some items for the disposal of which the consent of the other spouse is required, but the combined remaining matrimonial property is divided at the termination of the regime. This has been influential in the reforms of other countries. The Federal Republic of Germany introduced legal equality of the sexes as a constitutional principle in the 1950s, followed by substantial amendments to the civil code with respect to the financial and property relations of spouses; these included a new matrimonial regime on sharing the value of the economic gains of marriage, analogous in broad principle to the Scandinavian reforms, but containing new features. The French civil code received major revisions with respect to the matrimonial regimes in 1965. In 1969 the civil code of Quebec was revised to give full capacity to married women; it also created a new matrimonial regime, described as a partnership of acquests (that is, property acquired by the spouses after their marriage). In 1950 the People's Republic of China enacted a comprehensive marriage law including provisions giving the spouses equal rights with regard to ownership and management of marital property. The Soviet Union's Draft Principles on Marriage and the Family (1969) provide for community of acquests with equal rights of the spouses to possess, use, and dispose of property. The German Democratic Republic introduced a code of family law in 1965 based on principles of equality of the sexes in financial and property matters. Czechoslovakia's code of family law, enacted in 1964, introduced a concept of joint ownership with an equal share in management. Community sharing systems have been introduced by codes in Romania (1954) and Poland (1964). Substantial changes in the property capacity of Hindu women were made by the Hindu Succession Act of 1956. In the 1970s proposals for the reform of marital property were also under study in various other countries: for example,

England and Scotland; Belgium; Israel; and Ontario, Canada.

Maintenance. The law of maintenance and support has differed from that of marital property in most countries. A widow, for example, normally receives some share in her husband's estate upon his death. Some systems of law require that dependents receive a compulsory share in the estate or dependent's relief or family provision (that is, financial support out of the estate for a dependent in straitened circumstances). Most systems of law have traditionally regarded financial support as the responsibility of a husband and a father (to which any dowry or property from the wife was considered a contribution). But in a hierarchical structure, such as the Greek or Roman family, the responsibility might rest on the paterfamilias, if different from the husband. In Hindu law, the male members of a joint family, together with their wives, widows, and children, are entitled to support out of the joint property.

The influence of legislation. Social welfare legislation and the principle that a child's welfare is paramount have added a dimension and an inconsistency to the traditional principle of paternal responsibility. The new dimension is a public one and implies that society has an ultimate responsibility to see that children receive at least a minimum standard of maintenance. In some countries, including the United States, Canada, Great Britain, and various continental European countries, attempts have been made to combine both parental and public responsibility for the child's welfare.

The enforcement of the legal obligation of a parent to maintain a child runs into a number of difficulties in law and practice. The father may be too poor to support his child, or he may be impossible to locate, or he may already be in prison for refusal to pay. A wife may be reluctant to sue her husband (for personal reasons and perhaps in the hope of a reconciliation), and if she does not do so, the child will be deprived of financial aid and its welfare will suffer. Where there are social welfare programs supported by taxes, efforts may be made to protect the tax revenues by, for example, requiring a deserted wife to sue her husband as a condition of receiving welfare payments. Sometimes the authorities institute criminal or contempt proceedings against the husband. But in the North American and British experience, the payment record of obligants on maintenance orders is generally poor; the money recovered is usually inadequate to provide minimum support; and the cost of enforcement may approach the sums collected. Many people, moreover, wish to avoid getting involved with the law and the courts and will refuse to initiate action for maintenance. It is not difficult to see why a high proportion of one-parent families exist in poverty even in countries with highly developed economies.

Working wives. The introduction to the British Census of 1851 stated: "The duties of a wife, a mother, a mistress of a family, can only be efficiently performed by unremitting attention; accordingly it is found that in districts where the women are much employed from home, the children and parents perish in great numbers." Much has changed since then. Most modern countries provide that a husband and wife have mutual obligations of financial support according to their means, aiming at a common standard of living for them both. The older principle was that the husband supported the wife in return for obtaining most of her property or becoming *chef de la famille et de la communauté* in a community-property system. Some common-law systems are a curious mixture of old and new principles. In general it can be said that women tend increasingly to seek employment for other than economic reasons. Thus, in Canada in 1931, 10 percent of the women in the labour force were married; by 1961 the percentage had risen to 50. Two results of this trend are that (1) more married women now own some money and property and (2) on separation, divorce, or widowhood, a woman is more likely to be in employment and so not dependent for support.

Choice of regime. Recent reforms in marital-property laws have tended to reflect the wishes of spouses and their

families, rather than traditional customs, religious attitudes, and dogmatic formulas. The French civil code of 1804 began a European pattern of giving spouses a choice of matrimonial regime: the codifiers were confronted with a variety of customary laws in different parts of the country, and, not wishing to impose one of them, they included alternatives in the code, designating one, the Custom of Paris, as the legal regime that would apply if the parties did not select another in their marriage contract. In common-law countries, the tendency has been to favour separation of property—a tendency resulting more by accident than by intention. This has come about because most of these countries adopted married women's property legislation that removed the incapacity of a married woman to make contracts and deal with her property, thus destroying the existing system by which the wife's property passed into the control of the husband. No new matrimonial system was constructed, so that the spouses were placed in the position of separate individuals so far as property is concerned. They can, of course, draw up marriage contracts or settlements to express their own wishes, but such contracts are now rare. The laws of the Communist countries provide only one matrimonial regime, intended to promote the social and political policy of the government.

In countries where the spouses are given a choice of regime, many of them do not exercise their option. A survey made in France in 1963–64 indicated that 76 percent of the couples made no marriage contract and therefore were subject to the legal regime. The figures are probably similar in other countries. In Quebec, on the other hand, before the legislation in 1969 on marital property, more than 70 percent of marrying couples signed contracts for separation of property; part of the explanation for this may be that Quebec is surrounded by jurisdictions in which the common law prevails.

Separation of property. Even in modern times, in most cases husbands and wives differ in their potential for acquiring property. In separation of property, husbands and wives owning property and dealing with each other will be in the same position as unmarried adults. There are, however, grounds for distinguishing marital property questions from ordinary property questions because persons who cohabit on a domestic basis share a common standard of living and usually also the benefits of each other's property. A major element in many marriages is the raising of children, and the traditional female role places the married woman at a disadvantage so far as earning money and acquiring property are concerned. It is inconsistent of society to encourage a woman to take the domestic role of wife and mother, with its lower money and property potential, but in property matters to treat her as if she were a single person. It is also inconsistent to place upon the husband the sole responsibility for maintaining his wife and children, if his wife has regular employment outside the home. When the marriage is dissolved, if the wife has not been regularly employed and now enters the labour market on a full-time basis, she may be at a considerable disadvantage as far as salary and pension rights are concerned.

Community property. A marital-property system should try to balance two sets of interests: the interests of the spouses and the interests of third parties such as purchasers, creditors, and business partners. Community-property regimes emphasize the first but are less attractive in terms of the second, because the property is tied up in the community and is subject to the interests of both spouses, whereas the third party may be dealing with only one of them. Separation of property gives property independence to each spouse, but it does not provide for sharing unless the spouses place items of property under joint ownership. Consequently, there has been a trend in many countries toward new regimes giving the husband and wife independence in dealing with property but also providing rules for a division of net assets on liquidation of the marriage. The first country in Europe to initiate this type of system was Sweden, in 1920.

In some common-law countries, certain items of property have received special treatment. Examples are the matrimonial home in English law (under decisions of the courts beginning around 1950) where there has been concern about a wife's being evicted by a purchaser or mortgagee from her husband, and also about division of proceeds of the sale when both spouses have contributed something to the purchase, or where one has done improvements on the other's property, or where the husband's payments toward the purchase have been possible because the wife's money was used for the day-to-day domestic needs of the family, and so on. In parts of the United States and Canada, particularly the West and Midwest, there have been "homestead" laws providing that one spouse cannot dispose of or encumber the home without the consent of the other, that the use goes to the widow or family on the owner's death, and that the home cannot be sold in execution of a will.

Tort actions between spouses. In English common law, as amended by the property legislation of the 19th century, a husband could not sue his wife in tort (that is, for a wrongful civil act not arising from contract), and she could sue him only in respect of damage to her separate property. This has been variously explained as stemming from the doctrine of the unity of the legal personalities of husband and wife (so that the plaintiff and the defendant are the same legal person) or from the belief that it would be disruptive to the family to allow damage suits between spouses. The modern tendency is to permit any delict or tort action between spouses. This seems consistent with the fact that many damage suits, such as automobile accidents claims, are covered by insurance, and the litigation in such cases is therefore between two insurance companies with the spouses as nominal parties.

Movements exist in North America and Europe favouring a "no-fault" basis for delict or tort proceedings; this would transfer the emphasis in such actions to securing compensation for the person who suffered the damage, rather than determining whether the plaintiff can establish a cause of action (which usually means proving fault).

Co-ownership. Some marital-property systems that are basically separation of property have modifications for the situation in which, for example, an asset has been acquired by contributions from both spouses with the intention that both will benefit from its purchase—as with a home, furnishings, an automobile, a joint bank account, or joint investments. But the attitudes of husbands and wives as to their property after a marriage has broken down may be quite different from their intentions when an asset was acquired. There are decisions of the English courts that imply that in some of these circumstances, at least, the net value of the asset should be divided equally on the maxim that "equality is equity." The boundaries of this principle, however, are not at all certain.

Japanese marital-property law was revised in 1947, and the present legal regime is a modified form of separation of property. Under this regime, property to which only one spouse has title, but in the acquisition of which both have really cooperated during their marriage, is considered substantially co-owned. The civil code has been interpreted to the effect that substantially co-owned property is attributed to the title holder in a question involving third parties and to both spouses in a question between the spouses themselves.

DIVORCE

A marriage can terminate as a human relationship before it is dissolved by law. Quite often the court rulings as to property and the custody of children will merely confirm arrangements that have already been made by the parties concerned. In the United States and Canada, 80 to 90 percent of divorce proceedings are undefended; often the parties have made provisional arrangements about property, and one of them already has custody of the children. Before a union can be dissolved by divorce, there must have been a valid marriage. If a marriage has been imperfectly constituted in law, it may be annulled; grounds for annulment include lack of capacity, no real-

ity of consent by the parties, a vitiating defect in the marriage ceremony, or the subsequent discovery of a defect such as inability to consummate the marriage.

Repudiation. In old legal systems, marriage was conceived as the transfer of a woman from the power of her family to that of her husband under terms usually specified in the marriage contract. The standard method of dissolving a marriage if both parties were alive was repudiation, resulting usually in the return of the woman to the power of her family. Repudiation has had a considerable history; it has strongly influenced marriage law in Muslim, Jewish, Chinese, and Japanese law. In Muslim law, repudiation can occur without proof of legally designated fault or a breakdown of the marriage. In practice, of course, there are checks on the too facile use of this power by a husband, such as objection from the wife's family, the obligation to repay the value of a dowry, or religious disapproval. In Roman marriage law, unilateral repudiation at will was permitted, and this freedom existed for some time in the early Christian Era. The concern of the Roman law was for solemnity rather than grounds, and unilateral divorce was by a notification of repudiation before seven witnesses.

At the other extreme from repudiation at will is the sacramental view of marriage (as in the teaching of certain Christian churches) that a marriage may not be dissolved during the joint lives of the spouses. Formerly, a Hindu marriage was indissoluble (except by caste custom) and might be eternal.

Grounds for divorce. Between the extremes of repudiation at will and indissoluble marriage, there are various divorce formulas: divorce for fault, such as adultery, desertion, cruelty, addiction to alcohol or drugs, or imprisonment; divorce on grounds analogous to frustration of contract, such as incurable insanity subsequent to the marriage or disappearance of the spouse; divorce by mutual agreement; and divorce on the ground that the marriage has broken down. The variety of laws and attitudes with respect to divorce is bewildering. In comparing divorce laws, it should be remembered that the rates of divorce and of marriage breakdown are different; the latter are hard to ascertain, although the breakdown rate obviously exceeds the divorce rate. If the grounds for divorce are widened, then the divorce rate will rise; and if marriage is made indissoluble, the divorce rate will, of course, be zero.

A complicating factor in divorce law is the question of giving recognition to foreign divorces. The divorce laws of countries and states differ, and so do their rules for recognition of divorces elsewhere. A person living in a jurisdiction in which divorce is difficult to obtain may be able to go to another in which divorce laws are more liberal and obtain a dissolution of the marriage that will be recognized in the first jurisdiction. A feature of private international family law is the "limping" relationship—when a person is regarded as married by country X and as single by country Y, and a child as legitimate by country A and as illegitimate by country B. One reason why a country may restrict the recognition of divorces is that there are a number of jurisdictions in which divorce is granted on liberal grounds and with only nominal connections between the spouses and the divorce-granting jurisdiction (sometimes giving the impression of "divorce mills" that are operated for commercial reasons).

Some divorce laws provide for conciliation efforts (as in Sweden, Australia, and Canada), but these do not seem to have had any significant effect on divorce rates. In Chinese law, there is a long tradition of conciliation in many legal areas, including family law. But divorce stems from the desire to end an intimate human relationship that may have existed for some years. It is not an ordinary dispute at law; it has little in common with the interpretation of a business deal, a tax claim, a criminal charge, a wage dispute, or other legal questions that can be presented fairly precisely to a court or a mediator. In a divorce, only the spouses can really know the differences between them, and neglect of this distinction can produce reasoning by false analogy in relation to family law.

FAMILY COURTS

In some countries there are special courts for family matters, set up in pursuit of religious, political, or social objectives; these include the Christian, Muslim, and Jewish ecclesiastical courts. There are also people's courts and conciliation courts, particularly in Communist countries.

Another approach has been to establish social courts that have a functional relation to the legal problems affecting families. Such problems include marriage, divorce, annulment, matrimonial regime, maintenance (of spouses or of children), adoption, custody of children, legitimacy, filiation proceedings, juvenile delinquency, care and protection of children, assault on a spouse or a child, torts between spouses, marriage contracts, and judicial separation. Although these are the problems that produce the largest volume of private law litigation in most countries, family law has not, in many countries, been given a corresponding priority by the regular courts.

Those who favour special courts for family matters argue that family law is concerned with human relationships that require a judicial environment different from that of ordinary civil actions. The facts of the dispute in a family matter may not be as significant as the underlying problems (financial difficulties, health, addiction to drugs or alcohol) that have projected the issue. Another argument favouring family courts is that a high proportion of family proceedings are noncontentious or undefended; for example, proceedings concerning adoption and children in need of care are normally noncontentious and require not so much the application of law as an inquiry into what is in the best interests of the child. In family matters, moreover, the court has need of ancillary services—social workers, probation officers, liaison with various social agencies—and those connected with the court should have some interest and training in this area. Finally, since children and young persons are often involved, there is need of special legal officers to present inquiry material to the court or to represent the interests of the children (which may conflict with the positions taken by their parents).

A number of countries have special courts for cases relating to children and young people (sometimes with lay members), and special procedures for the disposition of such cases. Less progress has been made in the area of comprehensive family courts. One reason may be that family law is unrewarding and time-consuming as compared with more lucrative and prestigious fields of law.

It is sometimes argued that judges should be given a wide discretion in family cases. This seems to have been done in the family codes of eastern Europe and the People's Republic of China, which are loosely constructed with statements of politico-legal principles and leave much leeway in specific matters to the judges or conciliators. In England and the United States the proposal has been made that in a divorce case, for example, the court should have discretion not only as to the custody of children but also as to maintenance and property; the court should do what it thinks just, having regard to the history of the marriage and the behaviour of the spouses. Against this it is argued that such discretion tends to turn tribunals into courts of morals in which the prejudices of judges take precedence over legal consistency.

BIBLIOGRAPHY. Naturally the comparative family law of the world relates to an enormous literature. Further, the principal legal writings in each country are in the language of that country, and there has been little translation of law books or articles into other languages. The following are a few suggestions for further reading, the majority of the texts mentioned being in English or French, and a number relate to the complex subject of comparative marital property.

Comparative law: W. FRIEDMANN (ed.), *Matrimonial Property Law* (1955); A. ROUAST, J.B. HERZOG, and I. ZAJTAY (eds.), *Le Régime matrimonial légal dans les législations contemporains* (1957); and the journal *Revue international de droit comparé* (1949).

Western European and related systems: M.S. AMOS and F.P. WALTON, *Introduction to French Law*, 3rd ed. (1967); G. BEITZKE, *Familienrecht*, 14th ed. (1968); M. BRAZIER, *Le Nouveau droit des époux et des régimes matrimoniaux* (1965); J. CASTAN TOBEÑAS, *Derecho Civil Español Común y Foral*, 8th ed. (1951); A. COLOMER, *L'Instabilité monétaire et les régimes matrimoniaux* (1955); J. GERNHUBER, *Lehrbuch des Familienrechts* (1964); M. HAMIAUT, *Le Réforme des régimes matrimoniaux* (1965); V. DE SA PEREIRA, *Direitos de Familia*, 2nd ed. (1959).

Eastern European systems: K. GRZYBOWSKI, *Soviet Legal Institutions* (1962); E.L. JOHNSON, *Introduction to the Soviet Legal System* (1969); D. LASOK, *Polish Family Law* (1968); E. NIZSALOVSZKY, *Order of the Family* (Eng. trans., 1968); O. PLANKOVA, *Droit civil Tchécoslovaque* (1969).

Common law systems: P.M. BROMLEY, *Family Law*, 3rd ed. (1966); H.H. CLARK, *Law of Domestic Relations in the United States* (1968); H.H. FOSTER and D.J. FREED, *Law and the Family* (1966–69); R.H. GRAVESON (ed.), *A Century of Family Law, 1857–1957* (1957); M. PLOSCOWE and D.J. FREED, *Family Law* (1963).

Muslim law: A.A. FYZEE, *Outlines of Muhammadan Law* (1964); Y. LINANT DE BELLEFONDS, *Traité de droit Musulman comparé* (1965); J. SCHACHT, *Introduction to Islamic Law* (1964).

Hindu law: J.D. DERRETT, *Introduction to Modern Hindu Law* (1963); D.H. MULLA, *Principles of Hindu Law*, 13th ed. (1966).

Asian and African systems: J.N. ANDERSON (ed.), *Family Law in Asia and Africa* (1968); D.C. BUXBAUM, *Family Law and Customary Law in Asia* (1968); *Conference on Chinese Family Law and Social Change* (1968); R. LINGAT, *Les Régimes matrimoniaux du sud-est de l'Asie* (1952); DUC NGUYEN PHU, *La Veuve en droit Viêtnamien* (1964); A.T. VON MEHREN (ed.), *Law in Japan* (1963).

(I.F.G.B.)

Faraday, Michael

Michael Faraday, English physicist, chemist, and physical chemist or, as he himself would have said, natural philosopher, was the discoverer of electromagnetic induction, of the laws of electrolysis and of fundamental relations between light and magnetism, as well as being the originator of the conceptions that underlie the modern theory of the electromagnetic field. Faraday was born on September 22, 1791, at Newington, Surrey, which later became part of the borough of Southwark in south London but was then in the country. His father was a blacksmith who had migrated from Yorkshire. The family having moved to north London, Michael, at the age of 14, was apprenticed to a bookseller and bookbinder, in whose shop he read with keen interest books on science that came into his hands. Having heard Humphry Davy lecture at the Royal Institution of Great Britain and conceiving an eager desire to "enter into the service of science," to use his own words, he applied to Davy for employment, sending him as evidence of his interest the notes that he had made of the lectures. As a result he was, at the age of 21, appointed assistant to Davy to help with both lecture experiments and research. He accompanied Davy on a tour in Europe where he had many menial duties to perform but also saw much of the active scientific research and, in general, expanded his view. As the English chemist J.H. Gladstone, who knew him well, wrote:

Dedication

> His University was Europe; his professors the master whom he served and those illustrious men to whom the renown of Davy introduced the travellers.

Early work. His first published paper, which appeared in 1816, was of no importance. In 1820 he was devoting much attention to steel, the preparation of a rustless steel being one of his objects, and this work continued for some years, but, beyond finding that small quantities of added metals had a pronounced effect on the properties of steel, no result of importance was obtained. In 1820 Faraday discovered two unknown chlorides of carbon and a new compound of carbon, iodine, and hydrogen. It was in this year that the Danish physicist H.C. Ørsted announced his discovery that a wire conveying an electric current deflected a pivoted magnetic needle brought up close to the wire, a discovery that aroused great interest but was imperfectly understood. Faraday grasped that the force was a circular one surrounding the wire and on this basis made in 1821 the first of his great electrical discoveries, that of electromagnetic rotation. He set up a simple experiment in which a wire carrying an electric current rotated in the field of a horseshoe magnet. This discovery brought Faraday widespread fame but also some trouble with W.H. Wollaston, who had been unsuccessfully attempting something similar. In the same year Faraday married Sarah Barnard, a union that was happy though childless.

In 1823 Faraday liquefied chlorine, arousing the jealousy of Davy, who considered that he had initiated the work and was entitled to the credit. In consequence, he opposed Faraday's election to the Royal Society, which nevertheless took place in 1824. The next year Faraday made a chemical discovery of the first importance by isolating benzene or, as he called it, bicarburet of hydrogen, from a liquid obtained in the production of oil gas. About the same time he was pursuing research on optical glass, to which he devoted prolonged labour with little result. The "heavy glass" that was one of the products of the research, however, played an essential part in his great discovery of the rotation of the plane of polarization of light in a magnetic field. It was in 1825 that Faraday's position at the Royal Institution was improved by his promotion to the post of director of the laboratory. The next year he began to give formal lectures for the members of the Institution on Friday evenings, a custom that has continued as Friday evening discourses ever since. He also initiated the Christmas lectures for young people, known formally as Christmas Courses of Lectures Adapted to a Juvenile Auditory, of which he himself gave 19 courses. Faraday was supreme as a lecturer and deviser of effective lecture experiments, and there are many contemporary accounts of the interest and enthusiasm that his discourses aroused.

Major work. The second period of Faraday's researches may be said to have begun in 1831. He was convinced that the various forces of nature with which physics—always termed by him natural philosophy—was concerned were intimately interconnected. Electric current produced magnetic force, and, conversely, magnets had an effect, as he had shown, on electric currents. He was certain that magnetism could produce electricity: in fact, as early as 1822 his notebook contains the words "Convert magnetism into electricity." From time to time he had tried to produce currents by placing magnets near wires or coils of wire but had no success. In ten days in 1831 he carried out a series of experiments convincingly demonstrating the discovery of electromagnetic induction—the production of electric current by a change in magnetic intensity. These experiments were of such importance that in 1931 their centenary was celebrated at an international conference organized by the Institution of Electrical Engineers in London. The most famous experiment was that of the induction ring, a ring of soft

Faraday, oil painting by T. Phillips, 1842. In the National Portrait Gallery, London.

iron bearing two separate windings of insulated wire, the ends of one of which were connected to a galvanometer (an instrument for measuring electric current). When the ends of the second wire were connected to a battery there was no effect, but when that circuit was made or broken, by closing or opening a switch, the galvanometer indicated that a current was flowing in the first wire. A similar effect was obtained with an iron cylinder that had a wire wound around it in a helix: when, by means of magnets, the magnetic flux in the cylinder was changed, there was a momentary current in the helix. A variation of this experiment was to introduce a magnet into a helical coil of wire or to withdraw it. These experiments all have in common a change of magnetic flux through a circuit that produced a current in the circuit.

Faraday produced what was, in effect, the first dynamo: he placed a rotating copper disk between the poles of a large permanent magnet and showed that a current could be obtained in a wire extending from the axis of the rotating disk to its edge. He soon followed these experiments with others demonstrating that a current in one circuit could induce a current in another without the necessity of an iron core. In discussing these fundamental discoveries Faraday employed the conception of magnetic lines of force to make his ideas clear, for he was no mathematician. Somewhat later, in the course of his researches on static electricity, he developed the analogous conception of lines of electric force whose course and concentration expressed the various effects of electric current. It is in acknowledgment of his fundamental discoveries concerning the functions of dielectrics, or nonconducting materials, that the unit of capacity is named the farad. In this work he discovered the significance of what he termed specific inductive capacity, later called dielectric constant.

Faraday's conceptions of electric and magnetic force and their interrelations, expressed in terms of his lines of force, were fundamental. From them James Clerk Maxwell (*q.v.*) developed the equations that underlie all modern theories of electromagnetic phenomena.

It was shortly after his work on electromagnetic induction that Faraday, once more in search of unity, showed that the five kinds of electricity then distinguished—frictional, galvanic, voltaic, magnetic (induced current), and thermal—were fundamentally the same. "Electricity, whatever may be its source, is identical in its nature." In the same period of his researches he arrived at the basic laws of electrolysis that bear his name and introduced the terms now universally used: anode, cathode, anion, cation, and electrode.

After this succession of epoch-making discoveries ensued a period of exhaustion from which Faraday recovered only gradually. The third, and last, period of his researches began about 1844 and included as the main discovery that of the rotation of the plane of polarization of light in a magnetic field, in which his heavy glass played an essential part. This, again, resulted from his fixed idea that light and magnetism must be connected. In 1850 he tried to show experimentally a relation between gravity and electricity, concluding his paper with:

Here end my trials for the present. The results are negative. They do not shake my strong feeling of the existence of a relation between gravity and electricity, though they give no proof that such a relation exists.

In 1858 he retired to live near Hampton Court, Surrey. At that time he still retained a lively interest in science, but his health and his powers gradually waned and there he died peacefully on August 25, 1867.

Faraday was possibly the greatest experimental genius the world has known. Incessantly he was prompted to believe that certain fundamental relations were waiting to be found, and he was not dismayed by dozens of fruitless experiments from persisting until basic discoveries were finally established. In theoretical physics he provided the fundamental concept—expressed by his lines of force—that the medium was the site of electromagnetic action; at the hands of Maxwell this led to the conception of electromagnetic waves. To all his other gifts he added the ability to describe his ideas in clear and simple language.

BIBLIOGRAPHY. MICHAEL FARADAY, *Experimental Researches in Chemistry and Physics* (1859) and *Experimental Researches in Electricity*, 3 vol. (1839–55); H. BENCE JONES, *The Life and Letters of Faraday*, 2 vol. (1870); THOMAS MARTIN (ed.), *Faraday's Diary*, 8 vol. (1932–36); SYLVANUS P. THOMPSON, *Michael Faraday: His Life and Work* (1898); JOHN TYNDALL, *Faraday as a Discoverer* (1868, reprinted 1961), a first and charming biography; L. PEARCE WILLIAMS, *Michael Faraday* (1965), a definitive modern study.

(E.N. da C.A.)

Farm Buildings

The buildings on a farm generally consist of the farm family's house, the dwellings of hired workers, and the various structures and facilities for farming operations. Because farming systems differ widely, there are important variations in the nature and arrangements of farm buildings. This article deals with farmhouses and service buildings that can be classified as follows: livestock barns and shelters; machinery- and supply-storage buildings; buildings and facilities for crop storage, including fodder; and special-purpose structures. (For facilities used in livestock production, see LIVESTOCK AND POULTRY FARMING.)

History. Historical knowledge of farm buildings is scant; it is rare for farm buildings more than three centuries old to remain standing. The farmhouses in Europe of centuries ago were simple, with only one floor and, often, a single room. Later, the common room, where the meals were cooked and eaten, was separated from one or several sleeping rooms.

At first a hole in the roof served as chimney for a fireplace in the centre of the house. Then, in countries using masonry construction, large chimneys began to appear; they are still frequently seen in old European farmhouses. Their huge fireplaces were used for heating, cooking, and smoking and curing. In some underdeveloped areas, for example in Africa, single-room huts are still the rule. Shapes differ, and materials employed are found on the spot. In tropical Africa, "banco," a mixture of straw, clay, and animal hair, is used for walls, with the same material laid on boughs or thatch for the roof. Elsewhere, the huts are wood structures that are covered with palm leaves.

Early housing for livestock

The first sedentary breeders kept their animals near their living places, inside natural or handmade fences. At a certain stage, however, it became necessary to have roofs, mainly to facilitate operations such as milking and feeding. Cattle were tied up in the barn and remained so until the 20th century, when the loose-housing system reappeared. In the underdeveloped areas of the world, livestock enclosures still range from simple fences to roofed buildings.

The storage of crops became a preoccupation in the first stage of agriculture. Cereals often were stocked in a loft inside the house. In the 20th century, private and co-operative cereal producers developed grain elevators, and the problem of cereal storage in the farm lost its importance as far as the cash-grain farms were concerned. This soon became true for the other agricultural cash products, such as fruits and potatoes.

General layout. The location of the farmstead and the relative position of its different buildings are influenced by several factors, external and internal. Among the external factors, mainly natural, are soil conditions, climatic conditions, and access facilities to the main road and to the fields.

Internal factors depend on the type of business enterprise the farm is suited for. Among general principles that must be taken into account are the necessity of some partition between the farmhouse and service buildings, minimizing of transportation between buildings, the possibility of enlarging buildings, and security against fire. Four general layouts may be defined: large crop farms, large stock farms, farms in underdeveloped areas, and small to medium mixed farms.

Large crop farms. Independently owned farms of this type, mainly cash-grain farms, are numerous in North America. The layout is simple, for there are generally two types of service buildings, one for storage and the other for machinery. The layout is similar in the Communist collective farms mainly harvesting cereals (*kolkhoz* and *sovkhoz* in the Soviet Union; cooperative and state farms in eastern Europe). Large farms specializing in fruit production have a shed for the conditioning and storing of products, the other main building being a machinery and supply shelter. Some large farms specializing in viticulture include buildings that are equipped with wine cellars.

Large stock farms. Two types of large stock farms, extensive and intensive, may be distinguished. The extensive type is exemplified by the cattle ranchers of the United States. At the extreme, there are no buildings, only equipment. In Australia and New Zealand, dairy cows are kept without housing. The only building houses the milking parlour and the milk room, in the centre of the pasture. In the western United States, the most important beef ranches have several thousand head, entirely free on the range. The only building is the elevator with the milling and mixing machinery. For the animals there are only troughs and fences. Among intensive stock farms are the big dairy units—with several hundred cows—in the United States, in western Europe (France, north Italy), and in eastern Europe and the Soviet Union. There are three major layouts: parallel buildings; monobloc buildings (Hungary, East Germany); and circular layout, with the milking parlour in the centre (United States, north Italy). The covered feedlots for fattening beef, in the United States Middle West and elsewhere, feed from several hundred to several thousand head and are generally built with a shelter for the animals and with tower or bunker silos. Large units for hog production often have many buildings, partly to reduce disease risks and partly to separate the various animals—*e.g.*, the suckling sows, in-pig sows, fattening pigs, and boars. Some systems, however, use only one or two types of buildings. Large poultry units, specialized either for egg or for broiler production, use large identical buildings, the number depending on the unit size.

Extensive and intensive stock farm types

Farms in underdeveloped areas. In the underdeveloped areas, two types of buildings are found: those of the latifundia, or large plantation-type farms, and those of the small-owner or tenant farms. In these, buildings are generally small and scattered, the construction of a single large building being too expensive.

Mixed farms. The small and medium farms, which characterize European agriculture and which exist in many other parts of the world, are managed on the traditional mixed-farming and animal-husbandry system. Consequently, this type of farm normally has several service buildings: one for machinery, one for hay and cattle, another for hogs, another for sheep. In mountain areas, however, there often is a single building, including the house. With the increase of the farms' average size in these areas, there is relative specialization, and the number of buildings in the newly built farms is decreasing.

Building and enclosure materials and construction. These include homes (farmhouses), livestock barns and shelters, buildings for machinery and supplies, and crop-storage and special-purpose structures.

Farmhouses. The basic requirements for the farmer's family are about the same as those of the urban family, but certain features of the farmhouse depend on the farm-life pattern. Because the farmer generally comes directly from the fields or the service buildings, with soiled clothes and boots, it is necessary to provide a rear entrance with a washroom or lavatory and clothes-storage space. For the same reason, many farmers prefer a dining place close to the kitchen or included in it. The house must include an office and a large food-storage place with ample refrigeration, including a freezer in many countries, as most farm families are large. There are usually three or four bedrooms.

Satisfactory modernization of old farmhouses is difficult in some cases, but if the available surface is important and the main walls strong, renovation can give good results. The cost of a new house must be proportionate to the farmer's income; for this reason, farmhouses in underdeveloped regions have a smaller surface with a main room (kitchen and dining room), two or three bedrooms, a large washroom, and a storage place.

Livestock barns and shelters. These tend to become the most important elements of the farm layout. Two general types of animal shelters may be distinguished: the multipurpose type, a single-story building with clear-span roof construction, useful for feed storage and machinery, as well as for livestock; and the specific type, designed for a particular type of animal.

There are two major cattle-housing methods, the stall barn (or stanchion barn) and the loose-housing system. In the stall barn, each animal is tied up in a stall, for resting, feeding, milking, and watering. The typical plan has two rows of stalls. In older buildings, hay and straw are stored in an overhead loft, but in modern layouts adjacent buildings are generally used.

In cold and moderate climates the barns need insulated walls and ceilings, as well as ventilation systems, either natural or power-operated. In mild and hot areas the barns are open on one or two sides. The loose-housing system, developed in the United States after World War II, is now employed throughout the world. Basically, it includes a wood- or metal-framed shelter, arranged so that the animals can move freely inside and sometimes also between the shelter and an outside yard. Depending on the bedded areas, four types can be distinguished: loose housing on permanent litter—*i.e.*, straw, corncob, sawdust; loose housing in free stalls or cubicles; loose housing on slatted floors; and loose housing on sloped concrete.

In some countries, in old as well as in new buildings, dairy cows are housed in stall barns that include milk rooms. Milking takes place in stalls, and the milk is carried either in cans or directly by pipeline to a refrigerated tank in the milk room. Modern layouts with loose housing always include a milking parlour, either stationary or rotary. Two types of loose housing are used: loose housing on permanent litter and loose housing in free stalls, either under a clear-span roof or under a narrow lean-to roof. Beef-breeding cows often live on pastures, with only open-front sheds, during the calving period. In France and Scotland, however, they are kept in barns all winter. For fattening steers there are two major housing systems. The first of these is the American system, with very large groups of animals and a wide surface per animal. In the western United States, the open feedlots include only fences, troughs, and alleys for feed distribution. In the Midwest Corn Belt, a shelter is often included. The second, the European system, is characterized by very small groups (10 to 20 animals each) and a very small surface, generally covered. Any of the four loose-housing systems can be used.

For horses and ponies it is customary to use individual stalls, where the animal can move freely, even though this requires more space. Mules may be kept together in large pens. In mild climates, sheep and goats live on pastures without any shelter. The facilities include fences, waterers, corrals, dipping vats, and lambing and shearing sheds. In moderate and cold climates, the flock is wintered in sheds. The trend is toward clear-span buildings, with large alleys so that trailers can distribute feed into racks and troughs. Ewes are housed by groups (50 to 100 each) and special pens are kept for lambs. Feed racks and fence partitions are generally movable. For the dairy ewes there are special milking parlours. Goats are housed either in tie stalls, for small flocks under 50 head, with milking on the spot, or in pens, for larger flocks housed by groups, with milking in a special milking parlour. Pig housing varies for sows and fattening pigs. The sow lives with its litter for four to eight weeks according to the weaning age chosen. During this period there are two types of housing: movable, individual houses (generally of wood) located on or close to pastures and fixed in place, and central farrowing houses. A sow may farrow and live with its piglets in a single pen or farrow in a special stall, to avoid possibly crushing the piglets, or may farrow tied up by a chain or a harness. The pregnant sows live either free in groups of six to 12

or tied up or blocked up inside individual stalls. In cold climates the house is heated; in all modern practice infrared lamps or tubes are used to keep the piglets warm.

Fattening pigs, like fattening beef cattle, may be kept either in a simple feedlot, in large groups with a wide surface per head and a simple open shelter, a system widely used in the United States Corn Belt, or penned in a closed building, isolated and ventilated, each pen holding seven to 15 pigs. This is the most common system in Europe. Size of the pig units varies all the way from five sows or 20 pigs to large farms of up to 100,000 pigs. Poultry is the most industrialized type of animal production. Some of the breeding phases no longer take place in farms but in specialized plants; the farmer buys either chicks for broiler production or young layers for egg production. The typical modern broiler house holds from 10 to 100,000 birds, with automated feeding. Two types of facilities can be used. The broilers can be put on the ground on a deep litter of wood shavings, on wire mesh above a pit, or on a combination of these two floors. Alternatively, the broilers can be housed in metal cages, on three stories, each cage holding three to ten animals. In this case, feeding and cleaning are mechanized and the density is higher. The typical laying house holds several thousand hens. The same facilities as for broilers are used, but use of the cage is more common for layers. There are several types of cages, some of which are mechanized to facilitate feeding, cleaning, and egg collecting. Each cage can hold one to five hens. The density can reach about 23 hens per square metre (0.5 square feet per hen). The main types are cages in two- or three-story batteries (California cages), which are not superposed but rise in tiers; and flat-deck cages, which allow maximum mechanization. The buildings are generally one story, fully enclosed; they have insulated structures with sophisticated ventilation systems. Turkeys and other fowl are housed like poultry but generally on the ground. Rabbit production involves housing by groups in cages, on one, two, or three stories.

Buildings for machinery and supplies. This type of building is designed solely to afford protection from the weather, mainly rain. Machinery storage should have as much surface as possible between the interior posts, without being too deep, so that each machine can be taken out easily. The best solution is a clear-span shed, wood- or metal-framed, eight to ten metres wide (26 to 33 feet), open on one side and 4.5 metres (15 feet) high under the gutter. At the end of the shed, one bay is reserved for repair and maintenance and another for tools. This part is equipped with sliding or overhead doors. The same shed, or another, can be used for storing the fertilizers, seeds, and pesticides.

Crop storage. Wheat, barley, shelled corn (maize), and other cereals can be stored in farm bins if the moisture is below a certain limit (from 10 to 15 percent). In some cases artificial drying is necessary before storage, though it is possible to store wet grain, especially shelled corn, in airtight silos for animal fodder. The most common methods of storage of dry grain are (1) in piles of 1.5 to three metres (five to ten feet) on a waterproof floor in a building with reinforced walls; (2) in square or round bins erected within a building, usually of timber, plywood, corrugated steel, or wire mesh lined with waterproof paper; and (3) in watertight bins, often of corrugated metal, with their own roofs, for outside erection. Ear corn is dried by natural ventilation through a crib of limited width, located in a building or outside. Loose or baled hay is stored and sometimes dried by ventilation with fresh or heated air, either under sheds or in special installations called hay towers. Silage is made to conserve moist fodders, such as corn, sorghum, and grass. There are two types of silos. The horizontal silo is a parallelepiped, either cut into the ground (trench silo) or built above ground (bunker silo). The floor is natural earth or concrete. The walls can be concrete, timber or plywood, or sheet steel. The capacity varies but can be large. The tower silo is an above ground cylinder, with a six- to nine-metre (20- to 30-foot) diameter and a 15- to 20-metre (50- to 65-foot) height.

Ordinary silos, which are only watertight, are of wood, concrete, masonry staves or blocks, or steel. Special airtight silos with steel walls and a fused-glass surface are used for storage of high dry-matter silage, called "haylage." Fruit and vegetable storage for family consumption is usually in caves or cellars. For crops to be marketed, conditioning and storage generally are handled by commercial enterprises, but some large, specialized farms have their own storage. The buildings are insulated, and temperature control is assured either by ventilation with outside air (*i.e.*, for potatoes and onions) or by refrigeration (*i.e.*, for apples).

Special-purpose structures. Many secondary farm structures, such as smokehouses and well houses, are a leftover of the past, but some are necessary in specialized farms. A typical example is the tobacco barn, built for static air circulation.

Table 1: Farm-Building Expenditures in Developed Countries

	year	expenditure ($000,000)
France	1960–62*	130
West Germany	1960–62*	300
United Kingdom	1968	240
United States	1960	1,500

*Average for years given.

Economic impact. There are no complete statistics on farm-building expenditures. It is only possible to quote figures for some developed countries. These are given in Table 1. The trend is toward a rapid increase, except in the United States. The statistics given in Table 2 show farm-building values in some developed countries.

Table 2: Farm-Building Values in Some Developed Countries

	average farm surface		building value per hectare (in dollars)
	hectares	acres	
United States	157	388	117
Norway	13	32	344
Finland	19	47	261
Denmark	20	49	1,016
Austria	16	40	568
Switzerland	16	40	1,049
Greece	3.1	7.7	128
Japan	1.1	2.7	974

BIBLIOGRAPHY. ORGANIZATION FOR EUROPEAN ECONOMIC COOPERATION, *Farm Buildings, Including Their Remodelling and Adaptation*, 2 vol. (1958–60), is a survey of farm building practice in the United States and western Europe, including farmhouses. JOHN B. WELLER, *Farm Buildings* (1965), is the most comprehensive technical book on the subject; BIRGER NYSTROM and BERTIL LILLIEHOOK, *Jordbrukets Driftsbyggnader* (1960), also deals with the whole subject, excluding farmhouses, and includes many photographs and legends of figures written in English. Some works on animal housing are: DAVID SAINSBURY, *Animal Health and Housing* (1967), emphasizing physiologic and sanitary aspects; *Pig Housing*, 2nd ed. (1970), with good explanations on the numerous facilities described; and ALBERT MEHLER and WERNER HEINIG, *Bauten für die Rinderhaltung* (1968), the most recent and comprehensive work on cattle housing, including many figures. The ELECTRICITY COUNCIL, LONDON, *Grain Drying and Storage* (1968), provides a short but exhaustive guide on the subject. See also the ORGANIZATION FOR ECONOMIC COOPERATION AND DEVELOPMENT, *Capital and Finance in Agriculture* (1970), one of the very few documents about the national economic impact of farm buildings; and the AGRICULTURAL RESEARCH COUNCIL, LONDON, *A Bibliography of Farm Buildings Research* (1969), including publications on a wide range of subjects related to farm buildings from many countries.

(R.Ma.)

Farm Management

Farm management normally consists of making and implementing the decisions involved in organizing and operating a farm for maximum production and profit. Farm management draws on agricultural economics (*q.v.*) for information on prices, markets, agricultural policy, and economic institutions such as leasing and credit. It also draws on plant and animal sciences for information on soils, seed, and fertilizer, on control of weeds, insects, and disease, and on rations and breeding; on agricultural engineering for information on farm buildings, machinery, irrigation, crop drying, drainage, and erosion control systems; and on psychology and sociology for information on human behaviour. In making his decisions, a farm manager thus integrates information from the biological, physical, and social sciences.

Because farms differ widely, the significant concern in farm management is the specific individual farm; the plan most satisfactory for one farm may be most unsatisfactory for another. Farm management problems range from those of the small, near-subsistence and family-operated farms to those of large-scale commercial farms where trained managers use the latest technological advances, and from farms administered by single proprietors to farms managed by the state.

The individual farm

In Southeast Asia the manager of the typical small farm with ample labour, limited capital, and only four to eight acres (1.6–3.2 hectares) of land, often fragmented and dispersed, faces an acute capital–land management problem. Use of early maturing crop varieties; efficient scheduling of the sequence of land preparation, planting, and harvesting; use of seedbeds and transplanting operations for intensive land use through multiple cropping; efficient use of irrigation and commercial fertilizer; and selection of chemicals to control insects, diseases, and weeds—all of these are possible measures for increasing production and income from each unit of land.

In western Europe the typical family farmer has less land than is economic with modern machinery, equipment, and levels of education and training, and so must select from the products of an emerging stream of technology the elements that promise improved crop and livestock yields at low cost; adjust his choice of products as relative prices and costs change; and acquire more land as farm labour is attracted by nonfarm employment opportunities and farm numbers decline.

On a typical 400-acre (160-hectare) corn-belt farm in the United States with a labour force equivalent to two full-time men, physical conditions and available technologies allow a wide range of options in farming systems. To reach a satisfactory income requires operating on an increasing scale of output and increasing specialization. Corn and soybean cash-crop farming systems have increased in number along with corn-hog-fattening farms and corn-beef-fattening farms. Thus, the choice of a farming system, the degree of specialization to be chosen, the size of operation, and the method of financing are top concerns of management.

For a typical crop–livestock farm in São Paulo's Paraíba Valley, Brazil, large-scale use of hired labour creates a substantial management problem. With 30 to 40 workers per establishment, procuring and managing the labour—keeping abreast of demand and supply conditions for hired labour, working out contractual arrangements (wage rates and other incentives), deciding how to combine labour with other inputs, and supervising the work force—are of critical importance.

A rancher with thousands of acres, whether in the pampas of Argentina, the plains of Australia, or the prairies of the United States, is concerned about the rate of increase of the herd through births and purchases and herd composition—cows, calves, yearlings, steers, heifers. Risks from drought, winter storms, and price changes can be high. Weather, prospective yields, and the price outlook are the constant concern of competent and alert farm managers.

On a collective farm in the Soviet Union with 30,000 acres (12,000 hectares) and 400 workers, major management decisions are made by party–state representatives; the collective-farm chairman responds largely to their directives, though in the 1960s signs appeared to point to greater autonomy for the farm manager. Major manage-

The collective farm

ment concerns are determining optimal size of the collective, improving labour incentives, increasing crop and livestock yields, and reducing unit costs—with emphasis on levels of fertilizer, on pesticide and herbicide use, and on conservation of soil and water in crop production.

Thus, the character of the world's agriculture is shaped as millions of farmers manage the resources under their control in ways to obtain as much satisfaction as possible from their decisions and actions, which are made in a large variety of settings in regard to human, capital, and land resource combinations; technological possibilities; and social and political arrangements. Future agricultural progress depends on improving the quality of management and the environment in which farmers make decisions and on helping them adjust their decisions to the changing environment. In the low-income agricultures of the world in the 1970s, expanded research, improved input supplies and transport facilities, enlarged market opportunities, and an otherwise encouraging environment promise to open up a much wider area for managerial choice and decision making.

BASIC FARM MANAGEMENT PROBLEMS

Land, livestock, and labour. A good farm manager is familiar with the legal description of the farm property for which he is responsible, location relative to other property, roads, markets, and sources of supply, the details of the field arrangement and farmstead layout, the farm's capital position or relation of debts to assets, and the resources of the farm, such as the capabilities of its soils. Such facts enable the manager to analyze and evaluate his resources and plan their use. To calculate profit potential, the farm manager estimates the yield expected from each acre or hectare of land and from each head of livestock. He then applies money prices to these quantities.

Calculating farm size

The size of a farm business, an indication of its profit-making potential, is measured by the total number of acres or hectares in the farm, acres or hectares planted to cash crops, productive man-work units (the number of workdays of labour required under average efficiency to care for crops and livestock), livestock units kept, capital invested, and total cash receipts. While total acreage is often used to describe farm size, it is not a very satisfactory measure since it does not specify how much land is hilly, stony, swampy, or otherwise unproductive. Total cropped land, total receipts, invested capital, or productive work units are better measures. Though livestock are counted by the head for the sake of comparison, for management purposes one cow is roughly equal in value to two calves, five hogs, ten young pigs, seven sheep, 14 lambs, or 100 laying hens.

While the amount of land in a farm is more or less fixed, many farmers buy or rent additional acreage to increase their volume of output as a means of reducing unit costs. If such acreage is available within a reasonable distance, then land can often be profitably exploited. Other ways of increasing volume include bringing unimproved pasture and woodland into the cropping plan and shifting either to more intensive methods of cultivation or to more valuable crops. Before making major changes, the farm manager attempts to assure himself that the new crops will grow well and will find a market in his area. Almost all the governments of the world today have departments or ministries of agriculture which have been established for the purpose of advancing agricultural welfare by spreading technological information. Often these agencies perform extensive experimentation with new crop varieties, new cultivation techniques, and improved breeds of livestock, thus reducing the burden of risk upon the individual farm manager contemplating such changes. Considerable experimentation and research are also carried out by private agricultural supply firms that hope to improve their competitive position in the marketplace by developing a valuable new product.

In some of the developing countries, traditional patterns of land tenure and laws of inheritance may result in one farmer holding many quite small plots at some distance from each other. To reduce the resulting labour inefficiency and low productivity and to spur development of large-scale agriculture, governments in these countries have frequently legislated to permit or compel consolidation of such holdings (see LAND REFORM AND TENURE).

Some kinds of farm work are directly productive, some are indirectly productive, and some are not productive at all. Work such as plowing, planting, cultivating, harvesting, feeding, and milking is directly productive. Maintenance of fences, buildings, and machinery, though often necessary, is not directly productive. Such work as trimming shrubbery and mowing lawns, unless it adds to the market value of the farm, is not considered productive. Similarly, capital can be highly productive, as in the case of livestock; indirectly productive (*e.g.*, tractors, buildings, and supplies); or unproductive, as a large, showy barn or house. Land, too, can be highly productive, moderately so, or waste. Analysis of farm records has shown that farmers often overequip their property, thus using buildings and machinery to less than full capacity. Generally speaking, small farmers have been shown to have a higher proportion of their total investment in buildings than in machinery. In the developing countries, where relatively large quantities of human labour and relatively small amounts of capital are employed, a rather different problem exists. In these areas, farm managers need large numbers of people to work the fields during planting and harvest and far smaller numbers to perform routine cultivation tasks. In consequence, these countries face a problem of underemployment of agricultural labour during much of the year.

Productive and non-productive farm labour

Financial management and large-scale operation. Among the financial tools a farmer can use to analyze, plan, and control his business are financial statements, profit and loss statements, and cash-flow statements. A financial statement tells the amount of money invested in farm assets, outstanding debts, the owner's equity in the business, and the degree to which the farm is liquid and solvent. Liquidity is the ability to meet financial obligations on time, whereas solvency is the ability to pay all debts if the business is forced to discontinue. A profit and loss statement shows sources and amounts of income and operating expenses. Comparison of profit and loss statements over a period of years tells which resources have been most profitable and whether there has been an advance or decline in net income. A cash-flow statement shows the sources and uses of funds at given periods during the year. Such a statement provides a useful check on the accuracy of the farm's other business records.

For the traditional farmer, land and labour (his own and that of his family) are the major resources. Under favourable conditions, the farmer has changed his role from labourer to operator-manager; much larger farm units with high capital investments have resulted. Such conditions include the existence of a considerable body of applicable scientific knowledge, an opportunity for greater efficiency from large-scale operations, the existence of good markets and transportation, the opportunity to routinize and centrally direct farm work, and an absence of community antagonism to large-scale agriculture.

Conditions favourable to large-scale operations

The trend to the substitution of capital for labour is especially noticeable in the United States, for example, where capital accounts for a steadily increasing proportion of farm inputs. In the United States in 1940, capital comprised 30 percent of farm inputs, labour 55 percent, and land 15 percent; by 1970 capital accounted for 65 percent of farm inputs. By 1980, it is estimated that capital will probably comprise 75 percent of inputs, labour 10 percent, and land 15 percent. Capital typically replaces labour when large machines do the work of several men using smaller implements; when chemicals replace the scythe and hoe for weed control; when milking parlours, pipelines, and bulk tanks replace hand-milking operations; when a mechanized installation replaces the fork and bushel basket in dairy, beef, or hog feeding; when automated sprinklers bring irrigation water to crops; when cisterns and lagoons handle animal waste; when combines and forced-air crop drying speed the harvesting of small grain; and in similar substitutions.

The technical knowledge that a modern large-scale farm manager must possess is frequently held to be far greater than that required of most businessmen with equal investment; the capital required to operate such a farm is beyond the reach of many. In consequence, financial-management techniques resembling those of industry are often employed. Capital is imported from the outside; production is scheduled to meet quantity, grade, and timing requirements; and labour is given specific tasks, as in a factory.

Recognizing the economic benefits of large-scale agriculture, many underdeveloped countries have attempted to create conditions for its existence. National governments, often with outside help, have financed large-scale development programs, involving irrigation or improvement of huge acreages by means of dams, drainage facilities, and canals, and these have revolutionized the lives of many traditional farm managers within the space of a few years. Improvements in crops and livestock, marketing techniques and organization, and transport and power have in some cases increased agricultural productivity and income several times over. Since capital and management have been in the hands of government, the traditional farm manager has, however, often lost some of his independence, and not all such programs have succeeded. Poor planning and management by government authorities and resistance from the farmers themselves have led to some expensive failures.

Reducing market risks. The marketplace for agricultural commodities is exceptionally risky for three important reasons. First, no single farm producer can place or withhold enough of a single item on the market to affect the market price; second, the quantity of a commodity taken off the market does not increase in proportion to price declines; third, the farm manager cannot respond to falling prices by quickly switching production from an unprofitable item to a profitable one. To reduce his risks and safeguard profits, the farm manager may specialize or diversify depending on conditions; he may also use the futures market (see below).

A specialized farm manager concentrates his effort on the production of one item such as wheat, cotton, milk, eggs, or fruit. By such specialization he can realize the benefits of large-scale production and can make the most money from an enterprise in which he is highly skilled. On the other hand, the specialist is vulnerable to sudden changes in the market, to plant and animal diseases, and to soil exhaustion resulting from cultivation of a single crop.

Diversification—the spreading of one's talents over more than one farming enterprise—may be accomplished horizontally or vertically. Horizontal diversification means the production of more than one item for sale. In vertical diversification, the farm manager handles raw products after harvest by processing, packaging, transporting, or even selling at retail. A poultry farmer who produces eggs and washes, candles, grades, packages, and markets them at retail is said to be vertically diversified. He has taken on some of the jobs that could have been performed elsewhere, and as a result he generally receives a better return for his efforts.

Programs of agricultural diversification have been carried out by some developing countries, with the government acting as a kind of national farm manager. Upon achieving independence, nations such as Ghana and Nigeria, in West Africa, found their economies highly dependent upon a single raw agricultural export (cocoa for Ghana; palm oil for Nigeria). Sharply falling prices for these commodities or epidemics of plant disease were seen to have disastrous effect on national prosperity. Erosion problems also caused concern. The governments responded by horizontally diversifying into other profitable crops and vertically diversifying in establishment of industries to process these commodities or turn them into manufactured goods before export.

A capable farm manager may use the futures market to try to minimize his risks. In the futures market, the farm manager contracts with some buyer to deliver a given quantity of some commodity at a specified date in

the future for an agreed price. The buyer is often a speculator who hopes that prices will rise, enabling him to sell the commodity or the contract at a profit. Futures markets enable the farm manager to establish in advance a price for a crop or earn payment for holding a crop in storage. Futures markets also permit some farmers to speculate on a price increase without storing a crop, establish in advance the price of livestock feed intended for later use, and establish an advance price for livestock.

MANAGING LARGE, SMALL, AND MIDDLE-SIZED FARMS

Farm management specifics vary all over the world; it is possible here to cite only some of the most typical practices in several leading agricultural countries.

Large-farm management. Research has shown that large farms produce more efficiently than small farms. In sugarcane production, for example, the most efficient farm may include many thousands of acres or hectares. Yet, a well-managed dairy farm might achieve greatest efficiency with two men and fewer than 100 cows. In the future, as technology advances, the farms that are managed most efficiently will probably be larger than the most efficient farms at present.

Large farms can reduce costs by claiming volume discounts on their purchases. They can negotiate prices on fertilizer, seed, crop chemicals, petroleum products, machinery, and repair services. Large operators also have an advantage in selling their products. Managers of large corn farms, for example, can contract directly with a large processor for an entire year's production of given quantity and quality for a specific date in the future, thus commanding a higher price. The middleman is eliminated, and production, handling, and processing can be prescheduled for greater efficiency. Large farms also have a smaller investment in machinery and buildings per crop acre.

United States. The increase in the capital requirements of United States farms has already been described above. These changes in American agriculture are, to a large degree, the result of a revolution in financial management. Up to about 1930, little outside capital was needed to finance farming operations. Today, capital investment has vastly increased; farmers obtain their production goods and services—land, machines, breeding stock, seed, fertilizer, and other necessities—in a variety of ways.

Renting land is one way. In contrast to earlier days when land ownership was considered the ideal, renting land is now a widely accepted management practice. Large acreages of corn land in the Corn Belt, wheat land in the Great Plains, and cotton land in California and Arizona are operated by renters. Renting land enables farmers to operate on a much larger scale than would be possible under ownership. Specialized rice growers in the Sacramento Valley of California, who own tractors, tillage tools, and harvesters, receive rice-acreage allotments from the federal government. Such growers own no land, renting it instead from owners who have no rice allotment. Growers prepare the ground, irrigate it with water supplied by the landowner, and contract for application of seed and fertilizer. When the crop is ripe, the growers harvest the rice with their own combines and haul it to a warehouse for drying and storage. In upland areas of the valley, other growers raise tomatoes under contract from a canner, renting their land from a general crop farmer.

Farmers who do not wish to tie up capital in high-priced farm machinery can contract for harvesting of such crops as wheat, corn, grain sorghum, and barley. An airplane operator may seed, fertilize, and apply weed spray for a rice grower. Vegetables, fruit, and nuts may be picked under contract by shipper-packers whose crews move from farm to farm. Similar operations in livestock include sheepshearing, dehorning, branding, and artificial insemination.

Rental of machinery is another management device farmers use to obtain the services of equipment too expensive to be owned individually. Rental of livestock is also receiving attention. In the northeastern United States, dairy farmers lease cows. The owner of the cows

The commodity market

Meeting capital requirements

may be a contracting firm, a local bank, or an individual investor for whom the bank serves as agent. The scheme is useful both to older farmers who wish to retire but want to retain their interest in dairying and to young dairymen who want to expand but have limited capital.

Soviet Union. Following the Bolshevik Revolution of 1917, large landholdings were expropriated by the state and the land was distributed among the peasants. In 1928, collectivization of Soviet agriculture was initiated on a large scale; a three-part structure composed of state farms (*sovkhoz*), collective farms (*kolkhoz*), and private plots emerged. The state farms, or *sovkhoz*, are owned, managed, and operated by the state. Workers on state farms are salaried employees of the state; farm managers are state appointees. During the 1960s state farms increased sharply in numbers and declined in size. Much of the increase in numbers is the result of new state farms being established in the virgin land areas and the consolidation of smaller collective farms into state farms.

The collective farm leases land from the state and is worked by members of the collective under an elected committee that, as the management unit, has the responsibility of organizing land, labour, and capital in accordance with production requirements. Until recently, payment to collective members consisted of their share of the collective's produce or income from its sale. Each individual's share was determined by a workday unit that took into account the time spent performing a job and the level of skill required for the job. Although the system is still used, most collective farms have shifted to a monthly wage similar to that used by state farms.

Private plots up to two acres (0.8 hectares) in size and operated by individual workers occupy only 3.2 percent of the planted area in the Soviet Union but produce nearly half the potatoes, 40 percent of the eggs, 20 percent of the meat, and 13 percent of the vegetables.

The Soviet farm manager

Though the Soviet farm manager's role has in the past not included primary decision making, which has been done for him, there has been a trend since the 1960s toward more management autonomy in farm production. The Soviet government is promoting greater efficiency in agriculture by increasing the level of inputs and by improving incentives to farm labourers. These measures include financial concessions to farmers and expanded use of fertilizers, pesticides, irrigation, and drainage. The Soviet farm manager has additional functions that in other countries are performed by government and welfare officials, such as providing roads, recreation, education, health, and welfare to members of the collective.

Israel. A unique feature of the management of agriculture in Israel is its cooperative settlements, which evolved as a result of the needs encountered by immigrants who were new both to their surroundings and to farming as a profession.

The two basic types of cooperative settlement are the moshav and kibbutz. A moshav is a village containing up to 150 farm family units and supported by a strong multipurpose cooperative organization. Each family is an economic and social unit, living in its own house and managing and working its own fields. Although each farmer is independent, his social and economic security is ensured by the cooperative structure of the village, whose organization markets his produce, purchases his farm and household equipment, and provides him with credit and other services.

A kibbutz, numbering from 60 to 2,000 members, is a true collective based on common ownership of resources and on pooling of labour and income; it functions as a single democratic unit. Under the supervision of a manager, each member performs an assigned task but receives no salary or wages because all his needs are provided by the kibbutz.

Israel's agriculture is highly organized into farm societies. One society, the Farmer's Federation, has a membership of 7,000 citrus growers. There are plantation development companies and associations of wine, fruit, milk, and cotton producers.

Production for export

Australia. A significant characteristic of farm management in Australia is the emphasis on production for

export markets. Since the production of fine wool is the most important rural industry, grazing of sheep is a leading enterprise. Production of wheat, meat, dairy products, and fruit for export also figures large in the nation's agricultural economy. Australian export production is highly organized through statutory marketing authorities. Ten such authorities supervise the marketing of wheat, dairy products, meat, eggs, canned fruits, dried fruits, apples and pears, wine, honey, and wool.

Getting started in almost any farming venture in Australia requires substantial amounts of capital.

Management of small and middle-sized farms. *Canada.* Canadian agriculture consists largely of family farms, managed and operated by the owners. Less than one farm in 100 has hired management. A Canadian farm may vary in size from a factory-type broiler chicken plant of an acre or two (up to one hectare) to a cattle ranch that includes several townships. On a mechanized grain farm a farmer may operate 1,000 acres (400 hectares) or more with very little hired help. While most farmers in Canada own the farms they operate, there is a growing tendency to rent additional land. Current management trends also include increased use of commercial fertilizer and chemicals for pest control.

Farm management practices vary widely. Some farmers who rent land pay cash rent. In other cases the landlord takes a share of the crop or a share of the income from the sale of livestock or milk. On farms where most of the income is derived from the sale of grain, it is common for the tenant to give the landlord one-third of all grain produced. The landlord supplies the land, pays the taxes and fire insurance on the buildings, and provides materials for maintaining buildings and fences. Integration, the management of two or more stages of production and marketing, is spreading, with the trend most noticeable with sugar beets and canning crops.

United Kingdom. British farmers are well known for their efficient management and use of mechanical aids. Milking machines are employed on all but the smallest farms; electricity is widespread; grain combines are common; and there is one tractor for every 35 acres (14 hectares) of arable land. British farmers also use great quantities of commercial fertilizer per acre, the cost of which is subsidized by the government. The government also subsidizes the cost of lime, eradication of tuberculosis, construction of silos and other capital equipment, and pays part of the cost of voluntary consolidation of small farms into more efficient commercial units.

Several agricultural commodities are subject to the authority of government marketing boards: some buy produce, others control producer–buyer contracts, and still others maintain broad control over marketing conditions. Cereals, potatoes, eggs, sugar beets, and wool are the principal products governed by marketing bodies.

Cooperatives in Denmark

Denmark. In Denmark, successful farmer cooperatives play a major management role, extending credit and controlling production, marketing, import, export, purchasing, and sales. Through these cooperatives, Danish farmers enjoy the benefits of large-scale production and distribution despite the small size of individual farms. About 90 percent of Denmark's output of pork and milk and about 50 percent of egg output is marketed cooperatively. The number of farms in Denmark has been declining in recent years, but those remaining are becoming larger. Average size in 1967 was 40 acres or 16 hectares. The family farm predominates.

Farm management in developing countries. Many of the problems of the farm manager in developing countries have been described above. For further information, see AGRICULTURAL ECONOMICS; ECONOMIC DEVELOPMENT; and LAND REFORM AND TENURE.

India. Farm management practices in India range from the modern and sophisticated to some that have been in use for centuries. Illiteracy, inadequate water, unreliable power supplies, poor transportation and communications, making the timely acquisition of supplies and marketing of produce difficult—all hamper the development of modern farm management practices. For example, many farmers are unable to read the directions on a sack of fertilizer, to write an application for a production loan, or to calculate their profit and loss. Where progress has been made in introducing improved farm management techniques, visual and oral methods of instruction and training are being used successfully. Training techniques include on-farm demonstrations, farmer exchange programs, tours, short courses, literacy classes, exhibits, and audio-visual vans.

Republic of Zaire. Shifting cultivation is the typical method of farming in the Republic of Zaire, formerly known as the Democratic Republic of Congo. The native farmer clears two or three acres (about one hectare) in the forest or savanna, crops it until the fertility of the land declines, then moves on to another area. Fertilizer, insecticides, and fungicides are not generally available.

A land-settlement plan, called the paysannat system, in which strips of cultivated land were alternated with bush and grassland, was introduced in the 1930s to increase production. This system, however, has disintegrated since independence due to the lack of management personnel, government extension services, and disruption of marketing channels. Often side by side with traditional farms are large modern plantations owned, managed, and operated by individual Europeans and corporations. Plantation crop yields are two to ten times those of indigenous farms, probably pointing the direction of future development.

BIBLIOGRAPHY. In *Principles of Farm Management*, 2nd ed. (1960), H.C.M. CASE and PAUL E. JOHNSTON describe the scope and principles of farm management, the technique for achieving a coordinated farm plan, and the procedures to follow to achieve success. In *Profitable Farm Management*, 2nd ed. (1963), JAMES E. HAMILTON and W.R. BRYANT set forth the principles of efficient farm management and explain the ways to apply these principles to gain more profit and a better living from farming. DON PAARLBERG, *Future of the Family Farm* (1971), discusses the changes taking place in farming in the United States and current trends that indicate future developments in the management of American farms. D. HOWARD DOANE, *Vertical Farm Diversification* (1950), discusses the financial advantages of performing services beyond production of raw farm products, such as storing, processing, packaging, transporting, and retailing. TRIMBLE R. HEDGES, *Farm Management Decisions* (1963), outlines the principles and procedures for making intelligent farm management decisions and improving the skills used in the decision-making process. I.F. HALL and W.P. MORTENSON, *The Farm Management Handbook*, 4th ed. (1963), explains the principles of farm organization, planning, management, and operation used by successful farmers. ELTON B. HILL and MARSHALL HARRIS, *Family Farm-Operating Agreements*, rev. ed. (1963), explains a sequence of agreements through which young farmers can acquire equity in the family's farming enterprises. *Economic Principles in Financial Management* by WEIGLE and RIECK (1971), points out the role of good farm business management in profitable farming. TRIMBLE R. HEDGES and GORDON R. SITTON, *Farm Management Manual* (1956), shows how to inventory farm resources, plan for their best use, and analyze farm operations to achieve maximum efficiency. G.W. FORSTER, *Farm Organization and Management*, 3rd ed. (1953), treats farm management in both theory and practice with emphasis on the use of approved management techniques. FRANK P. KING and L.S. HARDIN, *Better Farm Management* (1956), is designed to help young men prepare for a career in farming as a business and provide guidance in making wise management decisions. The UNITED STATES DEPARTMENT OF AGRICULTURE, *Yearbook of Agriculture* (1970), includes a summary of developments in new farm management practices. *Managing Our Financial Future* by extension economists at the University of Minnesota, the University of Wisconsin, and the United States Department of Agriculture (1971), cites the adjustments that are taking place in the resource mix in modern farming, especially the rapid increase in inputs of capital and management relative to land and labour and the greater skill needed to manage farm finances successfully. The *Use of Future Markets* by DOBSON and WEIGLE (1971), describes the use of future markets as a tool that can be used to help reduce the risk from unexpected price changes. J.H. SITTERLEY, *Opportunities in Commercial Farm Management* (undated, Ohio State University), presents a background for those who are considering farm management as a career. L.L. JONES, *Soviet Union Agriculture with Emphasis on Cotton Production and Distribution* (1970), describes the organizational structure of present-day Soviet agriculture and the developments that led to the present management system. *Farming in Canada*, published by the CANADA DEPARTMENT OF AGRICULTURE (1970),

outlines the physical and social conditions under which farming is carried on in Canada. Current worldwide agricultural developments that reflect the farm management practices being followed are reported in *Foreign Agriculture* (weekly) and in various publications of the United States Department of Agriculture.

(M.E.Bl.)

Farnese, Alessandro, Duke of Parma

Alessandro Farnese, duke of Parma and regent for the Netherlands under King Philip II of Spain, played a crucial role in the maintenance of Spanish possessions there. First as a general and brilliant strategist and later as an equally gifted diplomat and political administrator, he succeeded in winning back the Catholic southern Netherlands from the control of the rebellious United Provinces and defending them against the Union's Protestant leader, William the Silent, prince of Orange.

By courtesy of the Soprintendenza alle Gallerie de Parma, Italy

Alessandro Farnese, duke of Parma, oil painting by Frans Pourbus the Elder (1545–81). In the Galleria Nazionale, Parma, Italy.

The family of condottieri (chiefs of bands of mercenaries) into which Alessandro Farnese was born obtained its high position in the 15th century in the service of the popes, as well as through a custom of contracting politically useful marriages. A Farnese even became pope in 1534, assuming the name of Paul III; he set up the papal states of Parma and Piacenza as a duchy in order to award them to his illegitimate son Pier Luigi. A son of Pier Luigi, Ottavio (duke of Parma from 1547 to 1586), married Margaret of Austria, the illegitimate daughter of the Habsburg emperor Charles V; and from this union twins were born on August 27, 1545, only one of whom, Alessandro, survived.

The lineage of his mother and the quarrels of his father with the Emperor determined Alessandro's destiny. When still a child, he was sent to the court of Philip II of Spain, another member of the Habsburg family, as a guarantee of Duke Ottavio's loyalty to the Habsburgs. Philip was then in Brussels, in the Netherlands, and Alessandro stayed there from 1556 to 1559, becoming acquainted with men who would be the principal actors in the dramatic religious and political conflict soon to tear the Netherlands asunder. In 1559 he went to Madrid, where he became a friend of the royal family. He next returned to the Netherlands, in 1565, where his mother, Margaret of Parma, had been regent for six years. In the same year, at the age of 20, he married the Portuguese infanta Maria after protracted matrimonial negotiations. He did not meet his betrothed until two days before his marriage, and the household that established itself at Parma in 1566 was not particularly happy, since the chief interests of the young husband remained hunting, riding,

Early career

and warfare. Alessandro's correspondence of this period is filled with complaints of his enforced idleness.

The opportunity for action that he had so long awaited arrived unexpectedly in 1571, when, appointed as a lieutenant to Don John of Austria, he fought brilliantly against the Turks in the Battle of Lepanto. The following year, however, Alessandro returned, not without resentment, to Parma. Religious disturbances in the Netherlands soon freed him from inactivity when, in 1577, Don John, by then the Spanish governor general, charged with suppressing the revolt, appealed for his support. In 1578 Alessandro fought energetically in the Battle of Gembloux, in which the rebellious Dutch forces were routed, and punished a number of towns with a harshness that contrasts with his subsequent attitude.

Governor general of the Netherlands

Don John died October 1, 1578, and a few days later Philip II appointed Alessandro as governor general of the Netherlands. For the first time the sovereign had made a fortunate choice. Farnese, Italian on his father's side, had all the intellectual flexibility of that nation, which in the Netherlands contrasted favourably with the Castilian severity and sectarianism. He was a great soldier, with a fundamental knowledge of his profession. A sociable man, gifted with considerable natural attraction, he rejected all fanaticism. In many ways he resembled his foe William of Orange, who had also, for the first time, encountered an adversary of his own stature.

Thus, Alessandro began, at the age of 34, a brilliant career, which ended only with his death. He immediately showed the full measure of his astuteness by undertaking a diplomatic reconciliation with the Dutch states that had Catholic majorities, while continuing military operations against the Union of Utrecht, the alliance of rebellious provinces, mostly Protestant, led by William of Orange. Although seriously ill, Alessandro conducted the difficult siege of Maastricht and captured the town on June 29, 1579, thus delivering a heavy blow to the prestige of his adversary. His negotiations with the southern, largely Catholic, provinces, in the meantime, were concluded by the Treaty of Arras in May 1579. One of the main achievements of his administration was accomplished in this treaty, which restored peace in the southern provinces. The agreement was reached at the cost of certain Spanish concessions, which included the removal of foreign troops and Farnese's own departure within six months. An expert politician, Farnese succeeded, however, in keeping himself in the Netherlands as commander and regent, going so far as to enter into conflict with his mother, whom the King had initially appointed to the position in order to attain his purpose.

The removal of foreign troops and the organization of a "national" force left Farnese with only 15,000 poorly trained soldiers, the majority of whom were of the same nationality as their opponents. It was a pitiful band that he led to the sieges of the next two years. Unable to attempt long sieges, Farnese negotiated as quickly as possible and granted honourable surrenders. He captured the city of Tournai in November 1581 and permanently established his government there. He succeeded in forcing another surrender the following year, but his army was at the end of its strength and could no longer undertake extensive operations against the Union of Utrecht, which continued under the leadership of William.

Farnese, using all of his talents of persuasion, then succeeded in obtaining from the King, and from the Spanish-controlled provinces, the recall of Spanish troops and the dispatch of Italian units into the Netherlands. Finally, with sufficient reinforcements, he switched to the offensive at the end of 1582. Heading an army of 60,000 men, with full powers to act, he devised and carried out an excellent strategy.

Toward the middle of 1583, by conquering the towns of Diest and Westerlo, he endangered communications between Antwerp and Brussels. He subdued several coastal towns and tentatively planned to encircle the United Provinces by capturing the county of Zutphen. In the first half of 1584 he conquered three more strategic positions, thus cutting off Antwerp from the sea. Ypres and Bruges surrendered in turn.

Without further delay, Farnese launched the siege of Antwerp. In order to isolate the city, Farnese built fortlets and a pontoon bridge across the lower Scheldt River and succeeded in frustrating all attempts of the beleaguered forces to leave the city. The city surrendered at the end of 13 months, on August 17, 1585, concluding one of the most celebrated sieges of military history. The capture of Antwerp

The capture of Antwerp was the climax of Farnese's career: the construction of a solid line of defense against the United Provinces consolidated the union of the Catholic Netherlands, which later became Belgium. The assassination of William of Orange at Delft on July 10, 1584, moreover, relieved Farnese of a redoubtable adversary. On the death of his father in 1586, Alessandro became duke of Parma.

Farnese undoubtedly would have pressed the war northward if Philip II had not compelled him to participate in his scheme for the conquest of England. He was instructed to concentrate his forces on the Channel coast preparatory to invading England, but the defeat of the Invincible Armada in 1588 ended that dream. In Spain part of the responsibility for the disaster was laid on Farnese, and his popularity underwent a serious decline. Last years

At this point Alessandro fell ill and was tended at Spa, while his lieutenants were left to face the Dutch army, reconstituted by Maurice of Nassau, as well as they could. Exhausted by illness, he died at Arras on December 3, 1592, at the age of 47, just in time to avoid learning of his intended disgrace at the hands of Philip II.

Of all the regents for the Netherlands during the reign of Charles V, none could rival Alessandro Farnese, either as strategist or as diplomat. His great achievement was the restoration of Spanish rule in the southern provinces and the secure perpetuation of Catholicism there.

BIBLIOGRAPHY. L. VAN DER ESSEN, *Alexandre Farnèse, prince de Parme, gouverneur général des Pays-Bas, 1545–1592*, 5 vol. (1933–37), a basic work with an impressive bibliographic and documentary listing; *Alexandre Farnèse et les origines de la Belgique moderne (1545–1592)*, 2nd ed. (1943), a summary of the preceding work; J. LEFEVRE, "Farnese," in *National Biography*, published by the Belgian Royal Academy of Sciences, Letters and Fine Arts, vol. 35, suppl. to vol. 7, pt. 1, col. 229–260 (1969), a recent biographical article.

(J.-L.Ch.)

Fascism

Fascism comprises a political attitude and a mass movement that tended to dominate political life in central, southern, and eastern-central Europe between 1919 and 1944. Common to all fascist movements was an emphasis on the nation (race or state) as the centre and regulator of all history and life, and on the indisputable authority of the leader behind whom the people were expected to form an unbreakable unity. The word fascism itself was first used in 1919 by Benito Mussolini in Italy; in the following years the influence of Fascism made itself felt in countries as far away as Japan, Argentina, Brazil, and the Union of South Africa, its specific aspects varying according to the country's political traditions, its social structure, and the personality of the leader. The Italian word *fascio* (derived from the Latin *fasces*, a bundle of rods with an ax in it) symbolized both aspects: the power of many united and obeying one will and the authority of the state, which was the supreme source of law and order and all national life.

THE PHILOSOPHICAL BASES OF FASCISM

Fascism rejected the main philosophical trends of the 18th and 19th centuries, the "spirit" of the American and French revolutions with their emphasis on individual liberty and on the equality of men and races. The message of the Enlightenment had served to enhance the dignity of the individual and had emphasized openness in a secularized society. In contrast, fascism extolled the supreme sovereignty of the nation as an absolute. It demanded the revival of the spirit of the ancient *polis* (city-state), above all of Sparta with its discipline and total devotion to duty, and of the complete coordination of all intellectual and political thought and activities against modern individualism and scientific skepticism. The Italian slogan "to believe, to obey, to combat" was fascism's antithesis to "liberty, equality, fraternity," and to the prophetic and Christian messages of peace. The combination of an unquestioning faith and of a virile combativeness was to transform the nation into a permanently mobilized armed force to conquer, maintain, and expand power.

In its beginnings fascism was not a doctrine and had no clearly elaborated program. It was a technique for gaining and retaining power by violence, and with astonishing flexibility it subordinated all questions of program to this one aim. From the beginning it was dominated by a definite attitude of mind that exalted the fighting spirit, military discipline, ruthlessness, and action and rejected all ethical motives as weakening the resoluteness of will. Stressing the irrational and instincts and activism, fascism insisted that the strong will always prevail over the weak, the more resolute over the irresolute. Ultimately everything depended upon the decisions of the leader, decisions to be blindly obeyed and immediately executed. Fascism returned to an authoritarian order, based upon the subordination of the individual and the inequality of caste and rank.

The reliance on power. Power is, of course, an element present in all political life. The first major writer to abandon the moral and normative approach to politics in favour of pure power was the Florentine man of letters Niccolò Machiavelli (1469–1527). A man of the Renaissance, he looked to the people of pre-Christian antiquity as the original possessors of *virtú*, the civic virtue necessary to the modern ruler; he believed that Christianity was, unfortunately, "true," but that its stress on meekness and humility would damage political man, weakening and at the same time fanaticizing him. Machiavelli's methodology involved the empirical observation of human nature and behaviour, which he believed to be changeless. His deep feelings about the degradation and corruption of Italy at his time led him to put his hope into the daring and the violence of a great man who would exercise power ruthlessly but with prudence. Power, Machiavelli apparently believed, legitimized the state, if rationally applied, as *raison d'état*, by a man able to manipulate the people and use the army for his own purposes. In his quest for a "new prince" and a new principle of policy he knew that he was opening "a road as yet untrodden by man." The road led to the absolute sovereign state.

The emphasis on sovereign-state power. In the bitter and protracted religious conflict of 16th-century France, the French jurist Jean Bodin (1530–96) stressed the importance of the sovereign, but by no means unlimited, power of the state in effective government. During the constitutional crisis of 17th-century England philosopher Thomas Hobbes (1588–1679), saw sovereign power as more absolute, unlimited by the subjects who have authorized it and responsible only to God. For Machiavelli the state was a work of art, created by the skill of the prince whom Machiavelli wished to teach the rules of conduct; for Bodin and Hobbes the state was a rational contrivance to lift central authority above religious and civil disputes. The peace treaty of Westphalia in 1648, in an attempt to end over a century of religious warfare, gave the secular sovereign, generally a hereditary absolutist monarch, the right to determine the religious beliefs of his subjects. The maintenance of law and order became the highest guiding principle, but even at this stage the state had not yet become the object of awe or emotional veneration.

The state in German Romanticism

The state became such only after the French Revolution, and above all in the emotional teaching of German Romantic philosophers, such as Johann Gottlieb Fichte (1762–1814) and Georg Wilhelm Friedrich Hegel (1770–1831). For these men the national collectivity assumed, morally and politically, an absolute rank. Fichte's utopian "closed state" was authoritarian, anti-individualistic, and economically self-sufficient.

But Fichte did not endow the state with the sacral aura that Hegel gave it. For a century, German historiography was to accept the Hegelian concept of the absolute-power state that acts in its own self-interest without consideration for humanitarian principle or for the rights of individuals or of other states. Hegel's followers, like those of Fichte, overlooked the complexity and ambiguity of his philosophy and concentrated on his exaltation of the state as an end in itself, as the "actuality of the ethical idea," as "absolutely rational," and as the source of all "concrete freedom." Only as a subject of the state (specifically, for Hegel, the Prussian monarchy) does the individual gain objective reality and an ethical life. The state's unconditional sovereignty reveals its nature above all in war.

The integrally autarkic state: the Dreyfus Affair. In the first part of the 19th century Hegel was, then, the philosopher of a militaristic monarchy opposed to the growing strength of 19th-century middle class liberalism. At the end of the century another antiliberal, anti-individualistic, and authoritarian movement made its influence felt, this time in the middle class democracy of the French Republic. Its leader was Charles Maurras (1868–1952), who repudiated the disunity and verbosity of parliamentarianism. He admired the Roman Catholic Church (but not Christianity, which in his opinion glorified universalism, social unrest, and pacifism), but for the virtues of hierarchic discipline and traditionalist order. The supreme norm of political life was to Maurras the absolute primacy of France and this meant action in France's interest instead of hesitation, parliamentary discussion, and consideration of world opinion.

Maurras and Barrès: the state can do no wrong

In 1894, a military tribunal convicted Capt. Alfred Dreyfus, the only Jewish officer in the French general staff, of pro-German espionage. Dreyfus insisted on his innocence, and his case became the centre of a bitter dispute involving questions of the precedence of national interest over objective justice. If Dreyfus were innocent, then the French army command on which France depended was dishonoured and stood accused of intrigue and worse. Antiliberal forces saw in the dispute an opportunity to overthrow the parliamentary republic, in which many high army officers and the church saw something fundamentally un-French, the work of Freemasons and Protestants, Anglo-Saxons and Jews. Whereas Maurras, in his struggle against democracy, pleaded for a return to the ancient monarchy, his compatriot, Maurice Barrès (1862–1923), saw the remedy in a leader who, being in close touch with the masses, would be the embodiment and the effective will of their thought and feeling. Against the rational cosmopolitanism of the "uprooted" intellectuals (a term that he made the title of his most famous novel in 1897), Barrès extolled the close community of a nation with its deep roots in past generations and in the ancestral soil (the "blood" and "soil"—*Blut* and *Boden* of Hitler). To Barrès the individual was merely a link in the chain of generations, inevitably determined by the blood of common forefathers.

Vitalism and elitism. The beginning of the 20th century felt the influence of Friedrich Nietzsche's (1844–1900) contradictory and often misunderstood work. Not a forerunner of fascism, Nietzsche despised German nationalism, anti-Semitism, and the authority of the state. He was, in fact, an extreme individualist, in revolt against all uncritical obedience by believers or followers and against the traditional values of church and fatherland. But he also despised the common man and democracy; he believed in great personalities and their exclusive rights. He found his time lacking in greatness and heroism, and he glorified the courage of warriors, though he meant first of all warriors of the mind, strong enough to overcome their own pettiness and their acceptance of faith or belief that came to them from second or third hand.

Oswald Spengler (1880–1936) shared Nietzsche's feeling of the decadence of Western civilization, brought about by Christianity and democracy, and his faith in the need for an aristocratic elite. Writing during World War I, Spengler insisted that all history is struggle among nations and that each nation's future will be decided by

Spengler and Sorel: the struggle of peoples

its power relationships to other peoples. Each people must be "in condition" for inevitable struggle and must trust its leaders; what is significant is not the victory of truth but the triumph of the will-to-power.

The French radical antiliberal Socialist Georges Sorel (1847–1922) in his revolutionary syndicalism emphasized the dynamism and new vitality of a heroic proletariat against an effete bourgeoisie. In his *Reflections on Violence* (1908) Sorel claimed that the working-class movement needed irrational myths to carry out its role in history. This idea influenced many Socialists in Latin countries, especially in north-central Italy, at the time Benito Mussolini was growing up. Violence, Sorel declared, was "sublime" when it was exercised by a movement with a historical mission. In Sorel, radical socialist theory of the left fused with a radical conservatism of the right in common rejection of bourgeois "mediocrity."

Among Italian pre-1914 social philosophers, other more conservative forerunners preached an elitist doctrine of vitality and the competitive power struggle. They turned from Count Cavour's liberal faith in parliamentarianism, which had established the unified Italian kingdom of 1861, to a quest for new elites and new rationales. Among them was Gaetano Mosca (1858–1941). Mosca's *Elimenti di scienza politica* (1896; Eng. trans. *The Ruling Class*, 1939) owed much to the Austrian professor of public law Ludwig Gumplowicz (1838–1909), whose fundamental work *Der Rassenkampf* ("Racial Struggle") in 1883 established the "group" as the fundamental unit of sociology, which he interpreted as the science of the interaction of groups. Material need was to Mosca the prime motive of human conduct; conquest and the satisfaction of the conqueror's need by the labour of the conquered, the fundamental essence of history.

Mosca and Vilfredo Pareto (1848–1923) argued that there had always been a ruling class of a few men who held power over the majority; that society is, thus, hierarchically organized, though the elites may change and, in fact, the change of elites is as much the essence of history as are wars between ethnic groups. The new elites carry with them their own values, expressed in social myths that can neither be proved nor disproved and that serve as a call and inspiration to action. The collective psychology of Scipio Sighele (1868–1913) and Gustave Le Bon (1841–1931) hypothesized that crowds obey collective subconscious emotions rather than the rational individuality of their single members, and, therefore, that crowds are highly susceptible to manipulation by leadership that can arouse in them heroism or savagery of which the individual alone would be incapable. Endlessly reiterated statements rather than rational thought influence public morality.

THE CONDITIONS FOR THE EMERGENCE OF FASCISM: POLITICAL PREREQUISITES

The troubled state of Europe in the years before 1914 was greatly intensified by the pressures that World War I put on societies that were not yet socially and politically modernized. This was true in varying degrees of Germany, Italy, and Japan, all of whom had entered the war in the expectation of great gains in territory and status, and of acquiring full equality with the older societies of the West. The deep moral depression and confusion which the defeat of 1918 produced in Germany was due to the apparently inexplicable difference between expectations and final failure.

National frustration

The discrepancy between Germany's advanced industry and her semifeudal-state structure, with its traditional authoritarian basis, had weakened her war effort. The failure on the battlefield led to a deeply emotional nationalism which ascribed the shortcomings not to Germany's backward political structure but to enemy plots and domestic "enemies." Thus, the authoritarian militarist elite was not discredited by the defeat of 1918; on the contrary, the fear of Bolshevism brought support for the defense of the traditional structure.

Though Italy was to be among the victors in World War I, the relative backwardness of its political, social, and economic structure in 1914 put an immense strain on all aspects of Italian society and life. The failure of expected gains from the war to materialize led to a weakening of the country's insecure liberal foundations. Those who, like Benito Mussolini, had agitated for Italy's entrance into the war in 1915, tried to direct the discontent and fear of the population against the victorious democracies who, unlike Italy, had emerged strengthened from the war. Social unrest frightened the propertied classes, the major landowners, and the church. Instead of carrying through long overdue reforms, they sought for a strong man who could sway part of the masses, war veterans, and lower middle class and turn them against the threat of Bolshevism. Fascism was, thus, regarded as a bulwark against the modernization of Italy. Though this was an underestimation of the syndicalist and radical aspects of Mussolini's original position, he was able to achieve, more than Hitler did later, an accommodation with the old ruling class, the monarchy, the army, and the church.

Fascist movements, wherever they have arisen, have frequently been inspired by national feelings of disappointment, and by the assumed need to close ranks in order to reach often fantastic goals (*e.g.*, the revival of Roman glory). Japan's fascist movement was linked to its attempt in World War I to establish a protectorate over China, which was frustrated, largely, as Japan felt, by the United States. Similarly, the strength of the fascists in Hungary owed much to the bitter national resentment at the loss of its non-Magyar subjects to new or enlarged nation-states created at the end of the war. These new states were not politically strong, and, as in Spain or Latin America, traditional right-wing conservatism, backed by the church and the pre-1914 oligarchy, found itself in conflict with the dynamism of fascism and its contempt for traditional ideas. Later, both were to enter into uneasy alliances in their fear of Bolshevism.

SOCIAL AND ECONOMIC CONDITIONS THAT ENCOURAGE THE DEVELOPMENT OF FASCISM

Politically and socially the modern, industrial middle class societies that developed in Britain, Scandinavia, Switzerland, the Low Countries, and France in the 19th century showed a great power of resistance to fascism, which was, on the whole, confined to fringe movements. Even in Germany, with her bitter resentments accumulated from her failure in World War I, which Hitler masterfully manipulated and fused with older resentments, fascism would probably not have come to power had it not been for the inflation crisis of 1923 and the widespread unemployment of the early 1930s. Finally, the rise of fascism in Germany owed much to the weakness of civilian democracy in that country. Germany had originated as a nation-state in 1871, thanks almost entirely to the military-authoritarian tradition of Prussia and the victories achieved by its army without the aid of any other power. The new *Reich* was proclaimed at the gates of Paris, the capital of the defeated enemy, and the German middle classes and German scholarship all willingly accepted the traditional values of the efficient ruling class, though by 1900 these values were insufficient to support an expanding modern industrial society.

Neither a capable semimilitary bureaucracy nor a scientific technology existed in Italy, Spain, Portugal, Greece, or Romania, where low urban and rural productivity during the early 20th century constantly widened the gap between these countries and the modern West and provided a basis for the growth of fascism.

In Italy, the farthest advanced of these countries, it was estimated in 1900 that half the population could neither write nor read. Though the north of Italy made great progress in the first 15 years of the present century, the fact is that even in 1914 the per capita income of the country, measured in standard gold units, was only 105 compared with 237 for Britain and 182 for France. Southern Italy's peasant population lived, according to one account, "in conditions of utmost destitution, illiteracy was the rule. Afflicted with gross dietary deficiency, accustomed to deprivation, and mulled by ceaseless toil, whole regions were innocent of the most elementary education and were consequently not equipped to participate in the challenge" offered by modern civilization. Archaic traditions and authoritarian religion preserved in Italy and Spain, in Romania, Greece, and Hungary a social system that was outside the modern world.

Fascism was an effort to employ anti-individualism and authoritarianism in modernizing economically backward societies. Arturo Labriola (1873–1959), an early syndicalist, spoke of Italy as a colony of "plutocratic Europe." The leader of an aggressive Italian nationalism, Enrico Corradini (1865–1931), influenced by Nietzsche and Maurras, saw the future as a conflict not between workers and capitalists but between proletarian and plutocratic nations. It was in that sense that fascism may have influenced the new African nations as they tried to organize themselves in the 1950s and 1960s. Despite its reactionary view of man, fascism regarded itself as representing youth against senility, the wave of the future against the effete heritage of the 19th century, biological vitality against the craving for peace and comfort.

THE ITALIAN EXPERIENCE

It has been shown that fascist movements arose where traditions and social structures favoured them. Unlike democracy, fascism demands a charismatic leader, a "new prince" as Machiavelli called him, who can gather all the prefascist emotional and social strains into one persuasive philosophy and will appeal to the masses. In Italy Benito Mussolini (1883–1945) was such a leader. From 1902 to 1914 Mussolini wrote many articles in the spirit of a radical Marxist. In this Marxist period of his life he became in 1912 editor of Italy's leading socialist daily, *Avanti!*, in Milan, a position of great influence for such a young man. He was then an extremist in his Marxist views, stressing revolutionary idealism and militant antimilitarism but deprecating dogmatism.

Dynamics of Italian Fascism

Whereas Marx's conception of history was based on 19th-century humanism and rationalism, Mussolini's was influenced by an early 20th-century emphasis on vitality and biological vital force, on a synthesis of Nietzsche and Sorel with Marx. This inclination to a heroic and active life-force made him, together with Gabriele D'Annunzio (1862–1938), the poet and glorifier of action, the chief propagandist of Italy's entrance into the war on the side of the Allies. It was over this issue that he broke with the Socialist Party, resigned from his editorship, and founded his own paper, *Il Popolo d'Italia*.

Mussolini's philosophy. Mussolini's philosophy, which developed slowly as his struggle for power and for a powerful state progressed, was officially presented in his article on the *Dottrina del fascismo* ("Doctrine of Fascism") in the *Enciclopedia Italiana* (1932). It reveals the pragmatic beginnings of the movement with complete frankness: "Our program is simple. We wish to govern Italy. They ask us for programs, but there are already too many. It is not programs that are wanting for the salvation of Italy but men and will power." By 1932 he had found a traditional philosophical garb for his vitalistic doctrine in the neo-Hegelian idealism of Giovanni Gentile (1875–1944), which saw the state as the source of all ethics and all individual life.

For Mussolini, all theoretical considerations were subservient to the "inexorable dynamics" of the factual situation. It is, he insisted, the role of the leader to master this dynamic process: he knows that the "iron logic of nature" will make the strong prevail over the weak. In contrast to Marxism, which asserts a rational logic of history that it claims will bring about the final triumph of the weak in an act of universal salvation, there is no fulfillment of history in Fascism. Instead, all history is incessant struggle, and the struggle itself is welcomed for its own ethical value. For

> war alone brings up to their highest tension all human energies and puts the stamp of nobility upon the peoples who have the courage to meet it. Fascism carries this antipacifist struggle into the lives of individuals. It is education for combat . . . . War is to the man what maternity is to the woman. I do not believe in perpetual peace; not only do I not believe in it but I find it depressing and a negation of all the fundamental virtues of man.

Triumph and decline of Italian Fascism. From 1922, when he first seized control of the Italian government in Rome, until 1927, Mussolini progressively consolidated his dictatorship, and the Fascist state took form (see ITALY, HISTORY OF). State and party became monolithic instruments in the hands of Mussolini, the *capo di governo* (head of the government) of the state, the *duce* (leader) of the party. The *legge fascistissime* (most Fascist laws), drafted by the leading Fascist jurist Alfredo Rocco, turned Parliament into a party congress, practically fused legislative and executive power, and made the Grand Council of Fascism an instrument of the duce, who alone could summon it and determine its agenda.

With this success Mussolini began to look farther into the future. Until 1930 he had emphasized the long overdue modernization of a backward country by a strong and efficient government and a new dedicated elite that could communicate a sense of vitality, virility, and energy to the whole people. But on Oct. 25, 1932, Mussolini assured a Milan audience of the world leadership of fascist Italy. "Today, with a fully tranquil conscience, I say to you, that the twentieth century will be a century of fascism, the century of Italian power, the century during which Italy will become for the third time the leader of mankind." In 1934 Mussolini claimed that Fascism, an Italian movement in 1922, had "since 1929 become not merely an Italian phenomenon but a world phenomenon." To achieve his ends, Mussolini demanded the transformation of Italy into a *nazione militarista* and *guerriera*. In this goal he succeeded even less than in that of Italy's modernization.

In his earlier stages Mussolini regarded Fascism as a development within Western civilization and looked with distrust generally upon Germany and specifically upon Hitler's National Socialism, which he recognized as "one hundred percent racism: Against everything and everyone: Yesterday against Christian civilization, today against Latin civilization, tomorrow, who knows, against the civilization of the whole world." But his imperialism and his overestimation of the power of Fascism drove him into the arms of National-Socialist Germany.

The ambition of Italian Fascism

The conquest of Ethiopia (1935) opposed Italy to the West and the League of Nations. In the following year, dazzled by German success, Mussolini began to speak of a Rome-Berlin Axis and celebrated it during his visit in Berlin in 1936 and Hitler's return visit in May 1938. Hitler's sincere admiration for him as "the leading statesman in the world, to whom none may even remotely compare himself" increased Mussolini's self-delusion. The intervention for Fascism in Spain's Civil War and the Munich accord with England in September 1938 seemed a crowning success in Mussolini's policy; in reality they masked, with Italy's acceptance of German anti-Semitic laws, the fall of Italy to the position of Germany's satellite. As such, but also out of desire for glory and booty, Italy in June 1940 entered the war started by Germany in September 1939. The war revealed Italy's backwardness and inefficiency, until three years of warfare brought the fall of Mussolini and his party.

THE GERMAN EXPERIENCE

Hitler found a much better prepared soil in the antidemocratic traditions of the German *Reich* than Mussolini did in the tradition of the Italian Risorgimento, the 19th-century movement for Italian unity. Like Maurras and unlike Mussolini, Hitler had never been a Socialist or a man of the left. He was entirely unknown even in 1919 when as an agitator for the *Reichswehr* (army) he attacked the Western and German democrats, moderate Socialism, and Russian Bolshevism. He was, unlike Mussolini, the man of the one idea, which in him assumed demonic or maniac dimensions, but he was in tune with older currents of German thought and emotionalism.

Hitler's "Mein Kampf" and German anti-Semitism. Hitler grew up as a subject of the multi-ethnic Catholic Habsburg monarchy. He shared with the Austrian Georg von Schönerer (1842–1921) a virulent hatred for the

Hitler's racial myths

Habsburgs, the "inferior" Slavs, for Catholicism as un-German, and above all for Jews and Judaism as non-Aryan. Hitler's propaganda methods were influenced by another Austrian, Karl Lueger (1844–1910) who, though a supporter of the dynasty and church, became a popular mayor of Vienna by opposing capitalistic liberalism and Marxian Socialism and appealing to the emotions of a lower middle class that felt threatened by both. In the restless years after 1918 Hitler took up this appeal. His anti-Semitism went far beyond Lueger's, becoming an obsession with him; the Jewish problem was no longer political, religious, or economic but the all-explaining theme of history. Hitler regarded the Nordic Aryans as the only creative race on earth, the only source of human greatness and progress. He believed that its end would mean the end of all civilization. Since he saw the German *Reich* as the highest expression of Aryanism, he proclaimed that it was necessary, not only for Germany but for the salvation of mankind, to secure the victorious survival of Germany by maintaining the purity of German "blood" against contamination by inferior races.

The total rejection of all miscegenation was one of the two fundamental pillars in Hitler's two-volume *Mein Kampf,* which he wrote in 1924 and 1926, and which became the bible of the new faith. The other was the absolute necessity of conquering a vast land base in eastern Europe, which was to become German by the ejection and enslavement of the "inferior" though white Slavic peoples. Germans would settle the immense and fertile plains and thus create a geopolitically unassailable *Reich.* The existing (and any future) Slav leadership class was to be exterminated to secure German domination. To these two fundamental ideas Hitler remained faithful from the very beginning of his agitation until his death. They had no parallel in Mussolini's writings, which glorified war and its spirit but presented no plan of a great aggressive war or any racial fanaticism. When Hitler dictated his last will shortly before his suicide, he repeated once more his fundamental interpretation of history: "Above all, I demand of the nation's leaders and followers scrupulous adherence to the race laws and to ruthless resistance against the world poisoners of all peoples, international Jewry," which he identified with the despised liberalism of Western capitalism and the socialism of Russian Marxism. His last words in 1945 expressed the same ideas that had guided him in 1919.

Hitler's persuasion of the Germans. From the beginning, Hitler served the fascist movement by his understanding of the potential of the spoken word and the psychology of the masses. His appeal to the Germans as the most exalted race in the world counteracted the disillusionment and inferiority complex of a people believing itself surrounded by a hostile world. Hitler wrote in *Mein Kampf* that all propaganda must hold its intellectual level at the capacity of the least intelligent of those at whom it is directed and that its truth is less important than its success. "The slighter its scientific ballast, and the more exclusively it considers mass emotions, the more complete will be its success." In 1937, moreover, at the ninth party congress in Nürnberg, Hitler declared that "Germany has experienced the greatest revolution in the national and racial hygiene which was undertaken for the first time on an organized basis in the country. The consequences of this German race policy will be more decisive for the future of our people than the effects of any other laws. For they are creating the new man."

Many Germans believed in the reality and the superiority of this new man. Thus the racial interpretation of history and the fascist contempt for democracy lured Germany into war against communism and democracy at the same time. By 1942 Germany had challenged the whole world and seemed at that point to have a good chance of emerging victorious from this total ideological war. Three years later it collapsed.

OTHER FASCIST MOVEMENTS IN EUROPE

The defeat of German fascism sealed the future of many other fascist movements that had come to power or grown in importance in many European countries partly with Germany's help or protection. In some of them, radical revolutionary fascism, eager for the modernization of the country, found itself in conflict with the authoritarian, semifeudal structure with which it often made common cause against Western liberalism, represented by a generally weak domestic middle class, and against an often exaggerated threat of Bolshevism from the outside. Yet reactionary authoritarianism and fascism fused in different ways in different countries, and with Italy's and Germany's defeat, the merely authoritarian reactionary regimes survived more easily than did the outright fascist ones.

In most European countries there were a number of competing small fascist parties with no strong leader. Some of these came to power by National Socialist military success. In other cases (Britain, Switzerland, Sweden, or Denmark) the liberal parliamentary forces proved to be strong enough to keep the fascist movements within narrow bounds, and in others reactionary elements were able to use fascist movements as their support. The only one of these movements that could claim world attention on the international scene was the originally very radical Falange Española under the leadership of José Antonio Primo de Rivera (1903–36). The Spanish republican regime was established in April 1931, and Rivera was elected a deputy of the right in 1933. But in the next year he broke with it and united the Falange with the Juntas de Ofensiva Nacional Sindicalistas (Committees of Nationalist Syndicalist Offensive), "a movement steeped in true Spanish frenzy, launched by the young and dedicated to combatting . . . the irresponsible hypocrisy of the bourgeoisie" (Eugen Weber, *Varieties of Fascism,* D. Van Nostrand Co., Inc., Princeton, New Jersey, 1964, p. 117). The Falange was ultranationalist and eager for a thorough reform of Spain's antiquated social order. But in the election of 1936, won by the popular front of leftist moderate and radical parties, the Falange was unable to elect even a single deputy.

When civil war broke out in Spain in 1936, the republican government outlawed the Falange, which sided with General Francisco Franco; and in 1937 Franco united it with the military formations of the deeply reactionary Catholic Carlists, the Requetés, and made it an instrument of his personal leadership. But whereas in Italy and Germany fascism had absorbed the state, in Spain the victorious conservative oligarchy absorbed fascism.

In a similar way the authoritarian and traditionalist oligarchy in António de Oliveira Salazar's Portugal kept fascist movements within very narrow limits, while using some of Mussolini's conservative slogans, as did the clerical semi-fascism in Austria under the two chancellors Engelbert Dollfuss (assassinated by the National Socialists in 1934) and Kurt von Schuschnigg and the Slovakian independence movement under Father Josef Tiso.

Radical fascist movements developed in some Balkan countries—most prominently in Croatia, Hungary, and Romania. They shared with the conservatives the bitter hostility to Marxism and the Soviet Union, but they were obsessed by an extremist spirit of terroristic violence in a strange union with religious fanaticism. As a result of German victory the Croatian Ustaše, a party under the leadership of Ante Pavelić (1889–1959), turned Croatia into a state on the model of the most extremist National Socialist Party formation, the SS, or Schutzstaffel, into which only the most dedicated and racially pure Germans were admitted. The Ustaše persecuted and killed many thousands of Orthodox Serbs, Jews, and Muslims. Catholic monks and other priests are alleged to have taken an active part in this struggle for the "purity" of the Croatian land and faith, and the Ustaše envisaged the revival of the Great Croatian kingdom as it had existed under Peter Krešimir (1058–74) and Dimitrije Zvonimir (1076–89). The dream was destroyed first by Fascist Italy's occupation of Croatian Dalmatia and of Slovenia and finally by the collapse of Italy and Germany. Pavelić escaped to Argentina, where he died.

Fascism ruled in Croatia only four years; an even more

The Spanish Falange

Fascism in the Balkans

violent fascism disturbed the political life of Romania for almost 25 years. Independent of the rise of Italian or German fascism, the fascism of Corneliu Zelea Codreanu was rooted in older traditions of the Romanian Orthodox Church and the Romanian peasantry. As a student at the University of Iasi, Codreanu organized fellow students, sons of poor priests and peasants, into a National Christian Anti-Semitic League, which indulged in murder and a strange fanatical morality. In 1927 the movement was reorganized as a Legion of the Archangel Michael, characterized not by a flag but by an icon and by its members' dedication to a frugal ascetic life. The Iron Guard, as the Legion called its armed branch, represented an attempt at a fundamental reform of Romanian life. But the attempt to build a new life was made on the basis of wild blood sacrifices, one of whose victims in 1938 was Codreanu himself. In 1940, after the abdication of the King, a civil war within a coalition of the conservative Army under Gen. Ion Antonescu and the Legion under Horia Sima, Codreanu's successor, ended with the Army crushing the Legion in January 1941. Antonescu's Romania actively participated in Germany's war against Russia, but the Romanian fascist movement remained, after orgies of death, crushed, and its surviving leaders found refuge in National Socialist Germany.

In a similar way the fate of fascism and of reactionary circles was intertwined in Hungary. The Hungarian government under the regency of Miklós Horthy (1868–1957), the last commanding admiral of the Austro-Hungarian Navy, dreamed of the restoration of the former nine-centuries-old Great Hungarian realm. The suppression of the short-lived communist regime in Budapest in 1919 combined with the fascist hatred of Bolshevism to produce, what was for that time, an unprecedented "white" terror. But Horthy himself was a moderate conservative and even when Hungarian extreme nationalism led him to form a profascist government under Gyula Gömbös in October 1932, Horthy followed a moderate course. Gömbös died suddenly in October 1936. Meanwhile a Hungarian National Socialist Workers Party had been formed with an arrow cross as its symbol. In 1935 it found its leader in Ferenc Szálasi, who had been a capable general staff officer in the army but now developed a fanatical racial faith in Hungarism, which in some ways recalled Hitler and Codreanu. After Hungary's entry into the war, the Germans in 1944 occupied Hungary and interned Horthy. Szálasi was finally the head of a state, which he planned as the "Corporatist Order of the Working Nation." But the war was soon lost after a bloody winter of massacres of Jews and political opponents. Szálasi was executed; Horthy found refuge in Portugal.

Fascism elsewhere in Europe

Fascism outside Italy and Germany suffered from the lack of charismatic leaders who could embody a nationalist myth and yet be adroit political tacticians. In Nordic Germanic Europe, which, according to racial doctrine, should have shown a strong penchant for National Socialism, except for Norway few sympathized with German fascism—much fewer than among the eastern and southern Europeans. In Norway the great writer Knut Hamsun (1859–1952) and Vidkun Abraham Quisling (1887–1945), former minister of war in the farmers' party administration and son of a rural clergyman, took a pro-Nazi stand based on their opposition to Western "plutocracy" and their fascination with peasant rootedness, the opposition of the "natural" countryside to the "corruption" of urban civilization. Quisling founded, in 1933, the Nasjonal Samling, with the cross of St. Olaf as a symbol and the restoration of the greatness of Viking Norway as a goal. Under the German occupation Quisling became prime minister, but his following remained insignificant in his native land.

Stronger than in northern Europe was the fascist movement in Belgium. This was partly due to the fact that the Belgian nation was divided into a dominant French-speaking minority and a Flemish-speaking majority that struggled for complete equality. In 1931 Flemish extremists formed the Verbond van Dietsche Nationalsolidaristen, the Union of Dutch National Solidarists, who dreamed first of a Great Netherlands, later of a Great Burgundy, both times avoiding a close cooperation with German National Socialism. A more important fascist group originated in French-speaking Belgium and found in Léon Degrelle an energetic demagogue and leader who strove for an agreement with the Flemish and showed understanding for modern social developments. Degrelle had grown up as a Catholic and in his young years had been influenced by Charles Maurras. He called his organization Rex and virulently attacked the parliamentary system. After a rapid growth his party lost its influence and Degrelle himself was defeated in a by-election in 1937 by a typical representative of the Belgian upper middle class with the approval of the Catholic primate. Degrelle's Flemish adherents joined the radical wing of the Flemish nationalists, the Vlaamsche National Verbond, and Degrelle formed a Walloon legion for the German SS and fought in the war against Russia. The confused character of the Rexists was symbolized by its red flag with a crown and a cross on it. In Belgium, as in Switzerland and The Netherlands, the parliamentary system of the conservative middle class was too strong to allow the success of a fascist party, and any threat of communism was too remote and improbable. In these countries terroristic violence so characteristic for the regimes of Mussolini, Hitler, Codreanu, or Szálasi remained unknown.

Of a very different nature was the short-lived fascist movement in England, where Sir Oswald Mosley, a member of the aristocracy, formerly a member of the Conservative Party, and later a member of the Labour government, founded in 1932 under the impact of the economic crisis the British Union of Fascists. The Union's plan was to replace the "old gang" of politicians by a new young elite, in tune with the new time. The paramilitary form of his party meetings and its "defence force" ran so deeply counter to Britain's centuries-old civilian tradition, that in spite of Mosley's undeniable rhetorical and intellectual gifts the English masses resisted him, and the strong British Conservative government of the period offered little foundation for arousing fear of a domestic "Bolshevik" threat. The Conservative government was intelligent enough to forbid, after some street fighting in 1936, all paramilitary uniforms. By 1938 Mosley, perhaps the most intelligent and rational of all fascist leaders, ceased to be a figure of public importance.

The picture offered by France in the critical years was more complex. But there, too, fascist movements were diffuse and short lived. One of the followers of Charles Maurras, George Valois, disappointed with Maurras's lack of active interest in social reforms, founded in 1925 the Faisceau, composed largely of war veterans; but only the crisis of the 1930s produced a number of groups, all nationalist, anticapitalist, and anti-Marxist. The largest of them, the Croix de Feu (Fiery Cross) of Col. François de La Rocque, rejected dictatorship and most of the fascist rhetoric. Characteristic for French fascism were the "proletarian" anti-Communists, led by former Socialists and Communists like Marcel Déat, the founder of the Rassemblement National Populaire, and Jacques Doriot, the former Communist mayor of Saint-Denis, a Parisian "red" suburb, who founded the Parti Populaire Français. More than in other countries, these French fascist groups were joined by some intellectuals who were disenchanted with the apathy of French life and yearned for revolution and action. The most prominent of them, Pierre Drieu La Rochelle (1893–1945), summed up the nihilism, which is fundamental to all fascism, when he wrote in 1934: "Liberty is exhausted. Man must seek new strength in his black basic nature. I say it, an intellectual, the eternal libertarian." (From *Socialisme Fasciste*, Gallimard, Paris, 1934, p. 102.)

FASCIST MOVEMENTS OUTSIDE EUROPE

Reaction and fascism in Japan

Like nationalism, socialism, and communism, fascism was a European movement. But in the 1930s, when economic crisis seemed to reveal weaknesses of the liberal tradition, in general, Fascism spread to Asia and Latin America, adapting itself to the social conditions of the countries there. Only in two cases did it become significant and assume an official role. The first instance was Japan, where fascism resembled German National Socialism in its reassertion of ancient models of life. On Feb. 26, 1936, the army took control of Japan and supported a national or tribal mysticism that bore a close resemblance to that of Germany's. Young "patriotic" officers tried to assassinate a number of leading Japanese statesmen, aristocrats, and high officers who seemed to them to represent the influence of foreign "dangerous thought," of the West, of liberalism, and of individualism, which threatened the traditional military spirit and absolute dedication to the cult of the emperor. In a number of cases the young officers were able to kill their victims. "The massacre was immensely popular in the army. The army acted as though the revolt was the work of the whole body and had succeeded. In its new orders the army said that it could not tolerate liberalism, that internationalism and individualism must be banished, and nationalism and the Japanese principle be promoted." (A. Morgan Young, *Imperial Japan 1926–1938*, William Morrow and Co., Inc., New York, 1941, p. 34.)

Different from other fascist countries, Japan saw the embodiment of its national ideal, not in a popular leader but in the emperor. The national destiny was to be fulfilled by observing the duty to the throne and thus attaining the highest pinnacle of morality. The imperial will was to fix standards of justice and injustice, of right and wrong. Philosophy was regarded as good only when it was in conformity with the imperial will. Except for Germany, Japan was then the only nation that thought itself strong enough to extend its national ideal over the five continents. In the late 1930s Japanese professors and writers, similar to their German colleagues, demanded the rejection of rational and universal ethics and the return to the ancient tribal gods in order to make the nation the most perfect instrument for its mission of conquest. The war in China was "not presented as one of conquest and exploitation but rather as a holy crusade to rid the land of unjust rulers [Chiang Kai-shek, red communists] and inaugurate there a regime of peace, righteousness and prosperity." (Harley F. MacNair, *The Real Conflict Between China and Japan*, The University of Chicago Press, Chicago, 1938, p. 193.) Later Japan spoke of a coprosperity sphere of a new Japan-led Asia.

Perón's fascistic populism Less ambitious were the aspirations of fascism in Argentina, where the movement resembled that of Italy rather than of Germany. The initiative in Argentina came, however, not from former socialists and syndicalists but from officers, the Grupo de Oficiales Unidos (Group of United Officers), who seized power in 1943. The initials of the group's name stood for *gobierno* (authoritarian government), *orden* (order), and *unidad* (national unity). The officers believed that as a result of its relative wealth and its ethnically purely Caucasian population, Argentina was to assume the leadership in the struggle against "Yankee imperialism" and in the modernization of the continent. Among the officers, Juan Perón assumed a leading role and turned the movement into one of national socialism. With the help of his wife, Eva María (1919–52), he sought the support of the poorer masses, the *descamisados,* or shirtless ones. His attack on the traditionally ruling oligarchy brought him wide popular support, so that he was twice elected president of Argentina, 1946 and 1951. Perón organized the workers into a Confederación General del Trabajo, which was devoted to him, and claimed to have replaced "plutodemocracy." He created a mass party standing for "justicialism," a middle way between communism and capitalism. But his own inconsistent policies and the accusation of widespread graft provoked a revolt of the armed forces in September 1955, as a result of which Perón left the country and settled in Spain.

By 1970 fascism seemed to have lost the attractions it had exercised in the 1920s and 1930s. Communist Russia and China seemed in 1970 less conquerable than in 1940. After the fall of fascism in Germany and Japan both nations experienced a wave of great prosperity, which weakened, especially in the young generation, the formerly strong appeal of a militant nationalism. The conquest of a "living space," which Germany, Japan and Italy before World War II thought indispensable for the growth of their national economy, not only revealed itself as unachievable even to a broad anticommunist coalition, such as the three leading fascist powers established in 1937, but as a superfluous fancy, for the loss of empire brought misery neither to Britain nor Germany, the Netherlands or Italy, France or Japan. An unexpected industrial and agrarian productivity raised the living standards of the masses in the democracies, which could now concentrate upon the necessary domestic reforms and abandon the lure of military glory. By 1970 fascism seemed a trend characteristic of the recent and yet faraway past. Except for small marginal movements, most elements were seeking to secure what fascism had denied, the cooperation of peoples of various civilizations and ideologies and the condemnation of war.

BIBLIOGRAPHY. H. ROGGER and E.J. WEBER (eds.), *The European Right: A Historical Profile* (1965); S.J. WOOLF (ed.), *European Fascism* (1969); H. KOHN, *Political Ideologies of the Twentieth Century*, 3rd rev. ed. (1966), a discussion of fascism and other ideologies in their historical setting; E. NOLTE, *Der Faschismus in seiner Epoche* (1963; Eng. trans., *Three Faces of Fascism*, 1965), the best theoretical analysis of fascism, and *Die Krise des liberalen Systems und die faschistischen Bewegungen* (1968), a continuation of his earlier work, with an extensive bibliog.; G.A. BORGESE, *Goliath, Der marsch des fascismus* (1938), on the historical and intellectual roots of Italian Fascism; D.L. GERMINO, *The Italian Fascist Party in Power: A Study in Totalitarian Rule* (1959); E. WISKEMANN, *Fascism in Italy: Its Development and Influence* (1969); R. DE FELICE, *Mussolini*, vol. 1, *Il rivoluzionario, 1883–1920* (1965); A.J. GREGOR, *The Ideology of Fascism* (1969), an analysis based upon the philosophy of Giovanni Gentile, with an extensive bibliog.; F.W. DEAKIN, *The Brutal Friendship: Mussolini, Hitler and the Fall of Italian Fascism* (1962); M. BAUMONT et al. (eds.), *The Third Reich* (1955), an authoritative symposium by European and American scholars; W. EBENSTEIN, *The Nazi State* (1943); H. RAUSCHNING, *Die revolution des nihilismus* (1938; Eng. trans., *The Revolution of Nihilism: Warning to the West*, 1940); H. MOHNE, *Der Orden unter dem Totenkopf*, 2 vol. (1969), a detailed study of the most militant Nazi organization, the SS; A. BULLOCK, *Hitler: A Study in Tyranny* (1952); R. HILBERG, *The Destruction of the European Jews* (1961); G. BRENAN, *The Spanish Labyrinth: An Account of the Social and Political Background of the Civil War* (1943); S.G. PAYNE, *Falange: A History of Spanish Fascism* (1961); H. THOMAS, *The Spanish Civil War* (1961); C.A. MACARTNEY, *A History of Hungary, 1929–1945*, 2 vol. (1956–57); J. PLUMYENE and R. LASIERRA, *Les Fascismes Français, 1923–1963* (1963); E.J. WEBER, *Varieties of Fascism: Doctrines of Revolution in the 20th Century* (1964); H.F. MacNAIR, *The Real Conflict between China and Japan: An Analysis of Opposing Ideologies* (1938); A. DEL BOCA and M. GIOVANA, *I "figli del sole": mezzo seculo di nazifascismo nel mondo* (1965; Eng. trans., *Fascism Today: A World Survey*, 1969), a well-documented comprehensive survey of the resurgence of fascism after 1945.

(H.K.)

Fatigue

Fatigue, like anxiety, relatively permanent impairment, and illness or disease, is a form of human inadequacy. All of these everyday terms lack precision and distinction, and definition is, therefore, a fundamental problem.

Fatigue was once used as the name for an ostensibly identifiable complex of inner feelings thought to be descriptive only of people and taken to be the result of some kind of taxing activity (such as work). The not particularly rigid concept was applied to specific parts of the body as well as to the person as a whole. If major discomfort was felt in a leg, it was said that the limb was fatigued or tired, just as at other times the person might say that he was tired. Such usage eventually became generalized so that even inorganic materials were said to be "tired": structural steel broke down under "fatigue"; *i.e.*, became brittle through crystallization. Such broadening of the meaning of the word fatigue added many connotations. Seriously accepting all the meanings that the word fatigue has would make it a meaningless synonym for inadequacy in general.

Fatigue and work

The once-held belief that work was the cause of fatigue led to efforts to use the work output of factory workers, for example, as direct measures of fatigue. Early studies by industrial psychologists and engineers failed to show a close connection between how an individual worker said he felt and the amount of work he accomplished; production-oriented investigators were even led to attribute no significance at all to inner feelings of fatigue, and their attention shifted from the inner condition of the worker to external phenomena not related to the worker at all. In the process it was forgotten that work output is a product of, rather than a description of, the worker. For other researchers who retained an interest in the worker himself, study was typically directed to specific, observable body processes rather than to the overall internal state of the worker as manifested in how he said he felt. Studies of body processes disclosed, among other things, that oxygen and glucose (sugar in the blood) were consumed during work and that waste products such as carbon dioxide (excreted from the lungs) and uric acid (in the urine) were produced. Hence, for some investigators fatigue came to mean a bodily state in which waste products were present in high concentration. All such studies clearly revealed specific results of exertion and disclosed evidence for the burning of food materials (metabolites); taken by themselves, the data provided a picture of the human organism as an energy-converting system and showed a definite relation of this process to energetic (work) performance. Such studies are a part of basic physiological research and apply most closely to what may be expected of people under heavy exertion in the workaday world (*e.g.*, strenuous labour) and in sports and athletics. Feelings and other signs of fatigue can arise suddenly and disappear equally suddenly, and the onset, duration, and termination of fatigue symptoms may appear to bear little relation to exertional (work) activity. When fatigue arises in nonexertional situations, there is a temptation simply to say that the fatigue is "psychological" or "motivational" (see MOTIVATION). Relatively little research has been devoted to fatigue as descriptive of the person himself and of the full range of demands he has to meet, although many of these demands lie outside the simple energy requirements of more-or-less arduous work. Accordingly, understanding fatigue involves determining the ways that the human organism is related both to his internal states and to his external environment; potentially fatiguing demands on the individual may arise from both within and without.

Man is able to—and may—respond to any situation in more than one way and at more than one level of behavioral complexity. The most readily observable ways are grossly physical and chemical; but these, in turn, underlie other levels of response such as primitive sensory activity (becoming aware of stimuli) and still higher levels such as perceiving (*e.g.*, evaluating the nature and objectives of work activity). At the highest level of activity the relationship often is spoken of as existing between the whole person and the environment. Since most investigative attention in industrial or other production situations has been directed toward what man can do in terms of his being only a machine that converts food energy into useful work, an understanding of the fine details of the relation between fatigue and physiological body processes has preceded experimental efforts to specify the role of personal attitudes (such as the individual's own evaluation of his abilities). Such self-evaluations (*e.g.*, a worker's judgment that he cannot continue activity) rather than any exhaustion of the energy available within the body result in the termination of activity. Often when such changes in performance are attributed to motivation, or to any of a number of factors called psychological, one's allegiance to ancient views of the nature of man may tempt him to think of mental factors disjoined and unrelated to any physical, energistic description of the organism. Yet, a fully useful definition of fatigue would require that all relevant factors be considered. Indeed, modern efforts to achieve a unified, integrated definition of fatigue rest on studies in which higher-order mental processes (such as thinking, perceiv-

ing, and emoting) are investigated to find whether they seem to stem from physical body processes (*e.g.*, see EMOTION).

Fatigue as it is applied to the whole person involves an individual's feelings of discomfort and aversion, his inner awareness of making mistakes, and any changes in observable signs of effort required to carry on the performance involved. These aspects are found to be related in various ways to measurable variations in work output. Investigators who typically focus primarily on work output are apt to be concerned with the applied, practical view of the person as a productive worker; interest is more likely to be concentrated upon the worker himself by those scientists who wish to study fatigue even if their findings are not directly productive of work output. The worker himself is interested in how he feels and what makes him feel as he does.

At any rate, in accounting for fatigue, it is useful to make distinctions between what pertains to the man as a whole and what pertains only to some part or organ of the man. That the total man's behaviour is spoken of as personalistic, or psychological, is not simply because self-awareness (inner feeling of fatigue) is involved but because at this level, resources are directed toward ends that go beyond the limited function of any one body part. This situation is illustrated by a simple example in muscular activity. When muscle activity is described in itself (at a given subpersonalistic level), it is simply called muscle contraction. Muscle contraction occurring as an integrated part of more complex personalistic behaviour may be called reaching; this action is an integral part of grasping a pencil, which is part of the more personalistic act of writing to one's friends.

While fatigue is one consequence of grossly observable activity, it can occur in the absence of manifest muscular exertion. It can develop, for example, as a rather immediate response to a socially exercised demand (such as that of a nagging supervisor), of which the person suddenly becomes aware but may not like. The feeling of fatigue produced in the absence of productive work seems to be essentially the same as that produced by goal-directed labour. Some components nevertheless are different, such as aching muscles in the one case and not in the other, but the factors that give fatigue its identity and differentiate it from other states of inadequacy are present in both. In each case conditions exist that can even result in one's total inability to carry on, whether his muscles contain high concentrations of waste products or not.

Muscular exertion does, however, produce biochemical changes in the body that are quite complex and that differ in various tissues and organs such as the heart or the brain. The consequence almost invariably is to produce secondary effects, perhaps muscular stiffness, and these in turn give rise to higher level effects such as one's sensory awareness of pain and discomfort. At a more personalistic level, the individual may develop a change in attitude with regard to the task or activity in progress; *e.g.*, he may begin to feel aversion for the work. The whole process, in effect, yields the individual's self-generated assessment of his own ability to carry on. If he continues his exertions under his personal assessment that such activity will produce more pain or will become more nearly intolerable or even impossible, the anticipated consequences include less efficient work performance. As the worker becomes preoccupied with his discomfort and with his waning production, the effect typically is to produce still more inefficient work. Thus fatigue defined as muscular inability to carry on and fatigue defined as a kind of felt aversion for exertion and as feelings of inability to carry on are all produced.

Performance may be observed to deteriorate (among factory workers, for example) even when there are no signs of the feeling state and of the aversive, pessimistic self-assessment defined here as personalistic fatigue. Indeed, often enough one may be "fatigued" without knowing it, indicating the predominance of relatively subpersonalistic factors at work. Such factors can be lumped under the term impairment, mentioned originally as one

Fatigue without physical exhaustion

Pain and fatigue

of the major forms of human inadequacy. While transient impairment and personalistic fatigue generally have not been distinguished from each other by many psychologists, in numerous studies impairment, rather than the feeling of fatigue, has been the point of interest.

Impairment of this sort reflects alterations in the chemical processes that occur within the cells of the body. That the alterations are reversible is illustrated in alcohol intoxication and oxygen lack (hypoxia). When such transient impairment incapacitates the individual for energetic activities without greatly affecting his brain processes, he is likely to feel tired and weak. Thus, it can be said that transient physiological impairment and personalistic fatigue are closely related, one being a basis for the other. When brain processes are so sharply affected as to reduce perceptual or attitudinal awareness, impairment may produce marked behavioral consequences without associated feelings of fatigue. In such cases, feelings of weakness and tiredness may not be reported by the individual since his abilities for self-evaluation have been dulled. The failure of people to have feelings of fatigue as a consequence of physiological impairment is characteristic of some forms of hypoxia, which can be brought on in several ways. One of these is by a fairly abrupt reduction in atmospheric oxygen pressure, as would occur in one's being deposited atop a mountain by helicopter. Feelings of fatigue are much more likely to set in when oxygen reduction is gradual and associated with exertion (as in mountain climbing). Along with lack of oxygen, other factors of the climber's task play their roles, and the climber's own awareness of the negative factors that are developing produces the full syndrome of fatigue, including both the inability to carry on and the aversive attitude.

In contrast to this, oxygen lack can be produced much more quickly in a decompression chamber in a laboratory, without any associated muscular exertion. It is possible to reach levels of hypoxia that abruptly reduce the subject's efficiency in exercising self-assessment, and personalistic fatigue in such cases fails to develop.

ENVIRONMENTAL FACTORS IN FATIGUE

Limiting conditions. In considering what it is in the environment that promotes fatigue, those conditions, such as lack of oxygen, that limit physiological function act directly at subpersonalistic levels. Other examples of limiting conditions are temperature extremes and lack of salt, water, or sugar. Regardless of one's personalistic attitudes, these factors limit physiological function and eventually can make the person unable to carry on.

High environmental temperatures put excessive demands upon the heat-regulating mechanisms of the body and soon can become seriously incapacitating. This incapacitation stems, in part, from the kind of immediate sensory feeling of being overheated that the person does not like and, in part, from physiological derangement and failure of the body regulating processes involved adequately to reduce the rising temperatures within the person. Man is not passive to thermal (heat) conditions, some of which make excessive demands upon the internal processes that generate, release, and dissipate body heat. There are special temperature-regulation centres in the human brain. Depending upon whether heat needs to be generated to keep the body from becoming chilled or to be dissipated to forestall overheating, various patterns of activity (*e.g.*, shivering) are initiated (see HOMEOSTASIS). When the load on any of the body mechanisms involved becomes great, various symptoms of distress begin to emerge. Fatigue is one of the earliest symptoms, appearing even when physiological distress is not extreme, long before prostration occurs.

Salt depletion (hyponatremia), water lack (dehydration), and sugar loss (hypoglycemia) and other limiting conditions bring on complex bodily imbalances that produce changes in sensory function (such as distortions in perceptual processes), in thinking, and in emotional behaviour. Sugar lack not only impairs the individual for exertion but results in feelings of fatigue. Muscular exertion requires blood sugar as its chief fuel. The symptoms of

low blood-sugar level (hypoglycemia) are signs of bodily weakness, headache, and other distress. In a study of industrial workers in which diet was investigated in relation to physical efficiency, it was noted that at particular times of the day, work output dropped and complaints of fatigue and irritability arose. It was hypothesized that there might be a direct relation between these vocal complaints, worker blood-sugar level, and the daily pattern of food intake among these employees. When the number of meals was varied over a range of two to five per day and the effects of fasting on blood-sugar level were studied, it was found that by spacing meals closer together, thus permitting workers to eat more often, blood-sugar levels remained desirably high for greater periods of the work day even when the total food intake was held practically constant. With widely spaced meals, the amount of blood sugar fluctuated between feedings, reaching lower levels than those observed when meals were eaten closer together. Other measures of bodily function were found to be similarly related to differences in the daily distribution of food intake; that is, respiratory (breathing) and muscular efficiency remained higher when meals were closely spaced. Although the apparent impetus for carrying on the investigation derived from personalistic complaints of tiredness and weakness, the research centred on physiological factors in the situation. Apparently, it was taken for granted that when blood-sugar level, respiratory activity, and muscular efficiency were well maintained, feelings of fatigue would be minimized.

Occupational demands. Aside from the general, physiologically pervasive limiting factors, there are conditions specifically imposed by occupational situations; *e.g.*, poor ventilation, presence of toxic fumes, poor design of working equipment, conditions inherent in keeping up the rate of worker performance (*e.g.*, in keeping pace with machines). Rest periods, coffee breaks, and background music are often introduced in work situations in efforts to reduce fatigue.

Beyond the limiting conditions noted above, there are, from the standpoint of occupational demand, several other classes of fatigue-producing situations. These include conditions of work calling for the expenditure of considerable energy; work assignments that require paced performance; those demanding prolonged uninterrupted activity; emotionally frustrating situations; and work demands that exceed the competence of the individual. Although fatigue most directly stems from a specific set of bodily conditions, the classes of occupational factors just given can be distinguished as environmental precursors of fatigue that can be altered in seeking to mitigate internal sources of distress.

While energy expenditure produces bodily waste products, the fatiguing effects are not limited to such clearly biochemical changes. Subtler, less grossly physiological factors such as familiarity with the task are also found to be related to one's fatigability. Thus, performing different tasks supposedly with the same parts of the body still can produce differing fatigue responses. An unfamiliar task that involves new patterns of movement may be experienced as unusually taxing even though it seems to require no more exertion than does a better learned, habitual performance. This situation seems to occur because the new task typically involves a unique set of muscle fibres, and because learning to perform efficiently involves a reorganization of activity among the active fibres. Older, habitual muscle patterns of activity that serve to accomplish a task tend to be more streamlined than do newly formed or temporary modes of behaviour. The overall result of coping with an unfamiliar set of work movements may include soreness and aching of muscles, as well as general discomfort (malaise).

While the greatest transformation of bodily energy occurs in the muscles themselves, slowdown in production (work decrement) is not all accounted for on an exertional, muscular basis; not all activity is muscular—there is, for example, neural activity in the brain. Many studies of fatigue thus face the problem of specifically accounting for how fatigue, exhaustion, or whatever it is

Temperature extremes

called, occurs while one is waiting for a bus but may not occur while he is busily engaged in an absorbing conversation; or how it is that people get tired from lying in bed. Obviously the pattern of fatigue symptoms is somewhat different from case to case or from situation to situation.

Paced performance is typified by the kind of worker activity involved in keeping up to a factory machine. This situation occurs when one is feeding pieces of metal into a continuously operating stamping machine, the action demanding the repetitious performance of some pattern of movements. The tendency of people ordinarily is to vary their activity even when maintaining their performance to repeatedly achieve the same end. Hence, the requirement of going through the same motions over and over again is often difficult to meet and brings on bodily discomfort. This discomfort is one of the bases for feelings of fatigue.

Prolonged activity involves some of the same factors as does paced performance. Various negative conditions, such as improper posture, though inconsequential in short tasks, build up to levels of considerable importance when performance is prolonged. Frustrating situations, those in which intended activity is blocked, are exemplified among sprinters or swimmers plagued by a series of false starts in a race. This blockage is reflected in muscle tensions and other internalized activities such as feelings of impatience and of being thwarted. Under prolonged frustration, the experiential (attitudinal) result often is fatigue, enhanced by considerable alterations in underlying bodily processes.

Visual fatigue

Demands too extreme for specific bodily mechanisms to meet are well illustrated in challenges placed on the activity of the sense modalities (*e.g.*, vision and hearing). Seeing, for example, is a muscular function as far as the initial processes in the eye are concerned. Some visual tasks require tiny sets of muscles within the eye to contract in changing the shape of the lens to accommodate shifts in looking at near and far objects. Other muscles rotate the eyeballs within the skull. These demands often can be met comfortably for short periods, but feelings of fatigue that develop after a few minutes disclose the task inadequacy of the visual mechanisms involved. With proper eyeglasses, the occupational demands may be met more effectively, so that performance (seeing) can continue for much longer periods without discomfort or work decrement. The fatigue that arises in visual tasks is not the decrement; it is the discomfort and task aversion that accrues, sometimes to the point of becoming intolerable.

Visual "fatigue" is a common complaint made to physicians or optometrists. This complaint may simply mean that after a short period of reading the print appears to blur. In such cases, the "fatigue" is a self-diagnosis that suggests sensory impairment rather than a direct description of a feeling of being visually "tired" or fatigued. When, however, the person means that for some reason or other he develops discomfort and task aversion after reading for a short time, he indeed might be said to suffer visual fatigue. The same principle applies to what is called "mental" fatigue, feelings of aversion or malaise that arise in an intellectual task, such as creative writing. The adjective (*e.g.*, visual or mental) that modifies the word fatigue refers to the task situation and does not imply that fatigue is essentially different from one situation to another.

While the class of unfavourable circumstances called limiting conditions (*e.g.*, extreme temperature) contribute to fatigue by directly affecting vital processes, some potentially limiting conditions also act upon man in subtler ways, for example, in sound stimulation (*e.g.*, noise). Auditory stimuli can be so violent (*e.g.*, a jackhammer for breaking pavement) as to damage sensory mechanisms, and such stimuli would belong in the class of limiting conditions. The role of less intense noise in producing fatigue, however, is highly variable from person to person. Some people seem to be habituated to high-intensity auditory stimulation in the form of rock and roll music. A teenager may be able to perceive the

sounds as music in apparent comfort for hours; his father may develop severe auditory fatigue after hearing it as gross noise for a minute or so.

Social factors that can affect fatigability and output in work situations include competition, prestige, and even the feeling of being watched. Various environmental factors that mean much to some may have little effect on others; social aspects of the environment are among those that vary this way. A notable series of studies in industry demonstrated the effect of allowing employees engaged in telephone manufacture to participate in planning their daily activity. The study showed that worker involvement in planning was more effective in raising work output than was the introduction of improvements in lighting and other ostensibly beneficial conditions of work.

PERSONAL ASPECTS OF FATIGUE

State of health. Fatigue is a condition of the organism as a whole, and to understand it the underlying bodily conditions of the individual must be taken into account. These include infectious diseases and other acute afflictions as well as more chronic, general conditions such as nutritional deficiencies and the lowered energy states characteristic of old people. Acute disease often generates fatigue that may persist throughout and after convalescence; many people remain especially fatigable for months after recovering from the active (acute) phase of influenza, for example. Other disturbances notable for producing fatigue include disorders of the thyroid gland, diabetes, emphysema, arthritis, rheumatism, and anemia.

Effects of an underactive thyroid gland

Symptoms of an underactive thyroid gland (hypothyroidism) are seen in the sufferer's inability to keep awake, his intolerance for low environmental temperatures, his muscle weakness and various discomforts, all of which make the person prone to task aversion and feelings of fatigue. Emphysema makes it difficult to breathe easily and obviously hampers the victim during even minor exertion. Myasthenia gravis, a chronic disease in which muscles become pathetically weak, can readily be seen as a potent basis for fatigue. Arthritis and rheumatism with their pervasive aches and pains can deter the individual from energetic activity, making everyday activities miserably fatiguing. All of these disorders involve definite tissue and organ abnormalities that are directly treated in the attempt to relieve fatigue.

Metabolic difficulties become increasingly frequent fatigue factors in old age, and efforts to relieve the tendency toward quick and easy exhaustion include the administration of substances that stimulate body metabolism (*e.g.*, so-called anabolic agents such as compounds derived from a chemical called aspartic acid). When fatigue arises from nutritional deficiencies appropriate dietary changes are indicated. Sometimes nutrients such as calcium and vitamin B_{12} are injected to hasten recovery; injections of substances containing iron often have spectacular effects in dissipating fatigue associated with some forms of anemia.

Indeed, some substances can benefit almost anyone who complains of undue fatigue. These may help by alleviating bodily discomfort; by improving muscle activity; and by elevating the sufferer's mood.

A common drug helpful in the alleviation of fatigue is aspirin, which is genuinely effective in dispelling a substantial range of general bodily discomforts. Much indisposition among people at any age stems from relatively minor, but general, aches and pains; and aspirin tends to relieve this common aspect of fatigue. While it might be supposed that aspirin's analgesic (pain-relieving) power might also dull one's sensory activity, alertness tends to be enhanced rather than impaired.

Caffeine, known for centuries in tea, coffee, and cocoa (it is also added to many cola beverages), is popularly used for its favourable effects on mood and feelings of tiredness. Among these influences is an effect on muscle activity that forestalls fatigue. When used to excess, caffeine may also contribute to fatigue by producing restlessness, sleeplessness, and irritability. Many other drugs for elevating mood also tend to relieve fatigue, but a number of them are addictive and easily overused. These include such psychic energizers or antidepressants as the class of chemical compounds called amphetamines (in slang sometimes called "speed" or "uppers" or "bennies"), which, used without careful medical supervision, represent a genuine hazard.

Some factors that predispose people to fatigue represent the interacting effects of bodily afflictions and difficulties that seem to be psychiatric or emotional. One of these is a transient form of low blood pressure called orthostatic hypotension (or postural hypotension). A relatively normal, extremely brief episode of postural hypotension may develop when one in suddenly standing after a train ride experiences such momentary symptoms as dizziness and blurred vision. Some people are abnormally susceptible to the problem. Others, possibly men more often than women, exhibit signs of orthostatic hypotension in very specific, apparently emotionally unpleasant situations. The person may begin to have the feeling, after being called upon to stand for awhile, that he is going to collapse; he feels weak and unsteady. Some men report that such symptoms specifically arise when they have to wait while their wives shop. In such cases, there is little for the husband to do that interests him, and he frequently may feel upset about being in the way of the other customers. As blood pressure sharply drops, these men begin to feel so exhausted, weak, and unable to stand that some are driven to call for help. Under less distressing circumstances, the symptoms fail to appear. Some of the same individuals who find themselves experiencing fatigue while with their shopping wives do not reach this state under other conditions in which erect posture also is maintained for considerable periods.

Psychiatric factors. Fatigue can be a most persistent accompaniment of a number of psychiatric disorders, including depressions of all kinds, a neurotic disturbance once popularly called neurasthenia, and what is known variously as the effort syndrome, Da Costa's syndrome, irritable heart, soldier's heart, anxiety neurosis, and neurocirculatory asthenia. (There is some controversy whether all of the latter terms actually refer to exactly the same cluster of symptoms.) At any rate, the term soldier's heart or irritable heart seems first to have been used to describe soldiers serving in the Crimean War while Da Costa's syndrome was a popular diagnostic label during the U.S. Civil War. In both cases, one of the first symptoms to appear was diarrhea followed by rapid pulse (which typically outlasted the digestive upset), headaches, and disturbed sleep. About the same kinds of cases began to show up quite frequently in World War I, during which time the cluster of symptoms was labeled the effort syndrome, or shell shock. Fatigue was a prominent complaint in all these cases, which by World War II came to be called combat fatigue or flight (pilot) fatigue. Similar cases arise in civilian life; one curious difference reported is that difficult, rapid breathing in the civilian cases fails to subside during sleep, whereas among soldiers the respiratory signs abate with the onset of slumber. In all of these fatigue-ridden disorders (no matter what they are called), exertion appears to be the essential precipitating feature. Exertion seems to manifest its results in a cluster of consequences, some digestive, some circulatory, and on top of this, a set of personalistic manifestations not to be expected from mere exertion. In military combat, some individuals show signs of personalistic upset (*e.g.*, terror and hate). The effort syndrome may be said to be one expression of personalistic inadequacy. The cause is ordinarily not as obvious in civilian life; nevertheless, there seems to be a class of individuals who express the results of exertion (*e.g.*, the tensions even of sedentary work) in the curious diffuse fatigue pattern just described rather than primarily in some kind of muscular tiredness.

The syndrome nowadays is seen as a psychogenic one, and various causes for it have been suggested. Be all this as it may, this is one pattern of context and response in which fatigue and work insufficiency show up.

Hypochondriasis, a neurotic tendency to be preoccupied

with and to exaggerate the significance of even the slightest signs of bodily ailment, is another very fertile basis for fatigue. Hypochondriacs are expected to be among the first to become tired. Hypochondriacs are so focussed on how they feel that they tend to tolerate much less discomfort than do people generally. Thus what ordinarily are perceived as minor discomforts by most people are readily taken as deterrents to effort in hypochondriasis, and the experience of fatigue arises sooner than in other persons. In this connection, it appears that people vary over a wide range with reference to the degree of discomfort they will tolerate before giving up a task; hypochondriacs tend to fall at the low end of this range.

Almost all individuals suffer from what is commonly called depression, sometimes only rarely and briefly. Among others the depression may persist or may come and go; many of these people seem almost always inclined to be pessimistic. Whatever the origins of depression (and there are many), it is a state in which fatigue is likely to be prominent. According to some authorities, about 85 percent of the patients seen in general medical practice suffer mild, chronic (prolonged) depression of some sort; important complaints among these people include easy fatigability and frequent headaches. Depressed individuals often display enough malfunction of body process (*e.g.*, some have mild thyroid deficiencies) to make them appropriate candidates for medicines used in treating physical disorders. Favourable response to the medication, however, need not be taken to indicate that the patient's trouble is solely a matter of gross physiological disturbance. A number of components that underlie the complaints must be recognized; malfunction in terms of treatable disease combines with personalistic difficulty involving the person's attitudes, interpretations, and motivations.

Chronic fatigue. Some people are puzzled and disturbed to find themselves almost always fatigued. Physicians are most likely to be called upon to treat this form, called chronic fatigue. Various drugs have been administered, such as mood elevators, sedatives, and tranquillizers, often enough with unsatisfactory results. Insufficiency of the adrenal glands and vitamin deficiency sometimes have been identified as factors in the trouble, but neither adrenal hormones (corticosteroids) nor vitamin therapy have proved invariably satisfactory.

It has been suggested that chronic fatigue patients are of two sorts—the physically depleted person (*e.g.*, someone with chronic anemia) who is exhausted by very slight effort, and the psychogenically (mentally) tired person who begins to feel fatigue from the mere anticipation of effort. The latter person, however, is sometimes benefitted from the very activity he anticipates with aversion and may actually brighten up nicely after some mild stair climbing, for example. Other chronically fatigued individuals are those persons who start out well in the morning only to tire and quit easily; by contrast, there are others who take considerable time during the early part of the day to get started but by evening are feeling very good and perform at their best. Careful study of such groups remains to be carried out.

Chronic fatigue also is to be considered from the standpoint of the environment of the sufferer. There have been brutally simple circumstances (such as leaking gas pipes in the home) that, when corrected, have led to "miraculous" cures. Alternatively, chronic fatigue sometimes seems to be the result of one's having learned an unfortunate, gloomy way of looking at life, perhaps from childhood disappointments and frustrations. If this is a sizable factor, medicines may be of less avail than are efforts to retrain the individual emotionally (*e.g.*, by widening his opportunities for social success and gratification).

In general, it may be said that fatigue is one of the overall responses people make to demands placed upon them. Sometimes the demand is an industrial or other occupational situation; sometimes it is any one of the countless tasks one imposes on himself (*e.g.*, his efforts to "win friends and influence people"). At other times,

Military fatigue

Hypochondriacs

Types of chronic fatigue patients

the demand arises from one's chronic attitude of pessimism or hopelessness that may extend to mere routine activities in which none of the usual exertional demands exist.

Various conditions can be manipulated in formal work situations to minimize the need for effort and to allow for rest and relief from monotony (*e.g.*, pleasant music in a factory). Certain aids for the relief of fatigue involving bodily discomfort or disease can be supplied in drugs and other treatment. In all cases, fatigue seems best regarded as a personalistic outcome arising from any combination of physical, biochemical, social, or personal causes.

BIBLIOGRAPHY. S. HOWARD BARTLEY, "Some Things to Realize About Fatigue," *Journal of Sports Medicine and Physical Fitness*, 4:153–157 (1964), a description showing what some may erroneously expect to hear from psychologists about fatigue, *Fatigue: Mechanism and Management* (1965), a short monograph for the physician and athletic coach, indicating the role of drugs in alleviating feelings of fatigue and inadequate performance, "What Do You Mean 'Tired'?" *Today's Education*, 58:40–41 (1969), a description of fatigue in a form adapted for teachers and others in education, and with E. CHUTE, *Fatigue and Impairment in Man* (1947, reprinted 1969), a technical description of fatigue and syndromes confused with it, with many references; D.A. and E.C. LAIRD, *Tired Feelings and How to Master Them* (1961), a nontechnical treatment of various forms of inadequacy, loosely labelled fatigue, with some practical advice.

(S.H.Ba.)

Fāṭimids

The Fāṭimid dynasty, which ruled an empire in North Africa and then in the Middle East from AD 909 to 1171, tried unsuccessfully to oust the 'Abbāsid caliphs as leaders of the Islāmic world. It took its name from Fāṭima, the daughter of the Prophet Muḥammad, from whom it claimed descent (see also NORTH AFRICA, HISTORY OF; CALIPHATE, EMPIRE OF THE; ISLAM, HISTORY OF).

Before the Fāṭimids, there had been other rulers in North Africa and Egypt who had succeeded in making themselves virtually independent of the 'Abbāsid caliphs in Baghdad; but they had been loyal Sunnī Muslims, willing to recognize the token suzerainty of the caliph as head of the Islāmic community and to content themselves with lesser claims and titles. The Fāṭimids, however, were moved by more than personal or dynastic ambition; they were the heads of a great religious movement —the Ismā'īlī branch of the Shī'ah sect—and as such **Aims of** aimed at nothing less than the overthrow of the existing **the** religious and political order in all Islām. Unlike their **Ismā'īlīs** predecessors, they refused to offer even nominal recognition to the 'Abbāsid caliphs, whom they rejected as usurpers. They themselves—as Ismā'īlī *imām*s (spiritual leaders), descendants of the Prophet through his daughter Fāṭima and his kinsman 'Alī—were, in the eyes of their followers, the rightful caliphs, both by descent and by divine choice the custodians of the true faith and the legitimate heads of the universal Islāmic state and community. Their purpose was not to establish another regional sovereignty but to supersede the 'Abbāsids as the 'Abbāsids had superseded the Umayyads and to found a new caliphate in their place.

A regional sovereignty was, in fact, all that they succeeded in creating, despite an immense effort—at once political, religious, military, and economic—to overthrow their 'Abbāsid rivals. The effort began during the 9th century, when Ismā'īlī missionaries in many parts of the Islāmic empire preached a doctrine of revolution against the Sunnī order and the 'Abbāsid state. Their cause was symbolized in the person of the hidden *imām*—a descendant of 'Alī and Fāṭima and thus of the Prophet—in whose advent they believed with messianic fervour. Several generations of *imām*s remained hidden as a precaution against persecution. After a number of unsuccessful risings, the Ismā'īlīs were able to establish a firm base in the Yemen; from there they sent emissaries to North Africa, where they achieved their greatest success. By 909 they were strong enough for their hidden *imām* to emerge from hiding and proclaim himself caliph, with the

significantly messianic title of al-Mahdī (the divinely guided one). This marked the beginning of a new state and dynasty.

The Fāṭimid dynasty. For the first half-century the Fāṭimid caliphs ruled only in North Africa and Sicily, where they had to deal with many problems. Most of their subjects were Sunnīs of the Mālikī school; others—

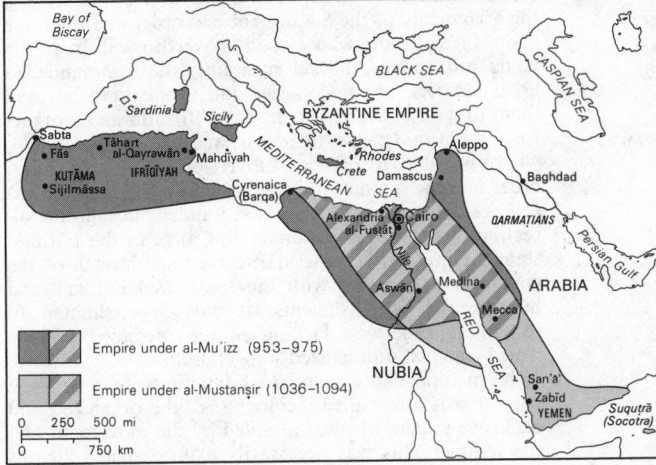

Adapted from Abbas Hamdani, *The Fatimids* (1962); Pakistan Publishing House

The Fāṭimid Empire.

a substantial minority—were Khārijites. Neither group was well disposed toward the Ismā'īlī doctrines of the new rulers, and they offered stubborn resistance to them. Even among the Ismā'īlīs themselves, a conflict soon arose between the state and the revolution—that is, between the caliph al-Mahdī (reigned 909–934) and the missionaries who had brought him to power. The necessary adaptation of the Ismā'īlī doctrine and mission to the needs of the Fāṭimid state and empire was carried out at the cost of bitter struggle and much bloodshed. There also were political problems with fractious Berber tribes and neighbouring Muslim rulers, as well as a war against the Byzantines in Sicily and Italy that the Fāṭimid rulers had inherited from their North African predecessors.

While coping with these difficulties, the Fāṭimids never lost sight of their ultimate aim, expansion to the East, where the centre of 'Abbāsid strength lay. The first step **The** was the conquest of Egypt, and for this the Fāṭimids pre- **conquest** pared for half a century. The first caliph, al-Mahdī, estab- **of Egypt** lished his capital at Mahdīyah (founded 920) on the east coast of Tunisia. His successors al-Qā'im (reigned 934–946), al-Manṣūr (reigned 946–953), and al-Mu'izz (reigned 953–975) ruled from there. In 913–915, 919–921, and 925 unsuccessful expeditions were sent against Egypt. Finally, in 969, under the caliph al-Mu'izz, the first stage in the advance to the East was completed. Fāṭimid troops conquered the Nile Valley and advanced across Sinai into Palestine and southern Syria. Near al-Fusṭāṭ, the old administrative centre of Muslim Egypt, the Fāṭimids built Cairo, which became the capital of their empire, and in it a new cathedral mosque and seminary, called al-Azhar, after Fāṭima az-Zahrā (the resplendent), the ancestress of the dynasty (see also EGYPT, HISTORY OF).

The Fāṭimid challenge to the Sunnī caliphate was now closer and stronger and was maintained by a great power —for a while the greatest in the Islāmic world. For more than a century the Fāṭimid rulers in Cairo pursued their aim of establishing the universal Ismā'īlī imamate. At times they were compelled by other problems—war on the frontiers, trouble in the Mediterranean, unrest at home or in the provinces—to reach some agreement with their Sunnī rivals; but such arrangements were always temporary, and subordinate to the grand objective.

The Fāṭimid caliphate was a regime at once imperial and revolutionary. At home, the caliph was a sovereign, governing a vast empire and seeking to expand it by normal military and political means. Its heart was Egypt; its provinces at its peak included North Africa, Sicily, the

Red Sea coast of Africa, Syria, Palestine, the Yemen, and the Hejaz, with the two holy cities of Mecca and Medina. Control of these was of immense value to a Muslim ruler, conferring great religious prestige and enabling him to exploit the annual pilgrimage to his advantage.

The caliph was not only an emperor; he was also an *imām*—the spiritual head of the Ismāʿīlīs wherever they were and, according to Ismāʿīlī doctrine, the embodiment of God's infallible guidance to mankind. As such he was the archenemy of the Sunnī ʿAbbāsid order and the hope and refuge of those who wished to overthrow it. In all the lands still under ʿAbbāsid suzerainty, he commanded a great network of missionaries and agents, and he used them to gain converts for the Ismāʿīlī faith and workers for the Fāṭimid cause; their task was also to preach and, where possible, to practice subversion against the Sunnī order and the regimes that supported it. The mission was elaborately and secretly organized under the supreme direction of the chief missionary in Cairo. In the Fāṭimid state the mission became in effect a third branch of the government, together with the traditional military and bureaucratic establishments; it thus approximated to something otherwise lacking in the medieval Islāmic world—an institutionalized state church.

The mission had a number of functions. One of these was what is now called ideology; *i.e.*, the organized and exclusive system of ideas adopted by the movement and the regime. This was necessarily expressed in religious terms. Ismāʿīlī theology supplied the arguments by which the Fāṭimids denied the ʿAbbāsid claim to the caliphate and asserted their own, and was thus a powerful weapon in their armoury. First in Tunisia and then in Egypt, a series of distinguished theologians wrote what became the classical formulations of Ismāʿīlī doctrine. Most of these authors had served in the mission; some had been its chiefs. Their task was not without difficulty. From the beginning of the Fāṭimid caliphate in North Africa, the conflicting needs of government and of revolution led to disputes between radicals and conservatives. Sometimes these were no more than arguments between colleagues; sometimes they led to defections, schism, and even armed conflict.

The primary tasks of the mission were thus the formulation and dissemination of Ismāʿīlī doctrine. These included much that in modern terms might be considered education and propaganda. The Fāṭimids founded great libraries and colleges, whose functions were to train missionaries to go out into the field, and to provide further instruction for the converts sent to Cairo for this purpose.

Extension of Fāṭimid rule

The work of the mission was only a part—albeit an important one—of the Fāṭimid grand strategy against the Sunnī Empire; in this strategy, the universal aims of the Ismāʿīlī faith and the imperial purposes of the Fāṭimid state met and merged. Linked with these actions was a great commercial expansion and an economic policy aimed at developing the Red Sea trade between Asia and the Near East, to the detriment of the alternative route through the Persian Gulf, which was controlled by the Sunnī powers. In the course of this effort, the Fāṭimids extended their rule down both shores of the Red Sea, established their supremacy in Yemen, and sent missionaries to eastern Arabia, to Central Asia, and to India.

Beginning of Fāṭimid decline. The high-water mark of Fāṭimid expansion to the East was reached in 1057–59, when a dissident general in Iraq changed sides and proclaimed the Fāṭimid caliph in Mosul and then, for a year, in Baghdad itself. The Fāṭimids were unable to provide support, however, and the general was driven out of Baghdad by the Seljuq Turks. This proved to be a turning point and the beginning of the decline of both Fāṭimid power and Ismāʿīlī influence.

Several reasons may be adduced for the failure of the Fāṭimid bid for Islāmic leadership. One was their adoption and retention of a religious doctrine that was ultimately unacceptable to the Sunnī majority. Fāṭimid Ismāʿīlism, as a theology, represented a great spiritual and intellectual achievement; but it was remote from the central consensus of Islām, and with the Sunnī revival of the 11th and 12th centuries its rejection became certain. The

coming of the crusaders indirectly sealed its fate, for in the great 12th-century contest between Islām and Christendom there was no room for a schismatic caliphate on the Muslim side.

In their ventures abroad, the Fāṭimids achieved many successes, the most notable being the conquest of Egypt itself. They suffered repeated setbacks, however, in Palestine and Syria; these difficulties, on the Fāṭimids' very doorstep, contributed in no small measure to their ultimate failure. Despite the sympathies of important elements in the population, they were never really able to control Syria, where, in addition to local opponents, they also had to face major attacks from outside—by the Byzantines, the Turks, and then the European crusaders. It was in Syria that the great Fāṭimid advance to the East was delayed and halted; and it was in Syria that a new power arose that in time destroyed them.

These troubles abroad no doubt fed, and were fed by, the growing discontents in Egypt. At first the caliphs retained full personal control of affairs, presiding over an essentially civilian government. The army's importance increased, however, and it was there that the first signs of trouble appeared. At first the army was largely Berber. Berber troops conquered Egypt, and for a while the Berber garrisons in Cairo, Damascus, and other cities—as well as the Tunisian merchants and officials who followed the caliphs to Egypt—maintained the character of the Fāṭimid caliphate as a North African ascendancy in the Middle East. But this did not last; during the reign of al-ʿAzīz (reigned 975–996), the second caliph in Egypt, Turkish and other Mamlūks were recruited and quarrels broke out between them and the North Africans. Later, a third force was added to the racial conflict, with the formation of regiments of black slaves from Nubia and the Sudan. Fights between the different groups first became a factor during the reign of al-Ḥakim (reigned 996–1021), in whose time, partly because of his own highly eccentric behaviour, the personal authority and religious prestige of the caliph began to decline. His successors became little more than puppets in the hands of their viziers and their generals. During the long reign of al-Mustanṣir (reigned 1036–94) factional strife brought Egypt into a vicious circle of anarchy and tyranny, made worse by recurring famine and plague. The provinces, in east and west, were lost to local dynasts or invaders; even the Hejaz, vital to the religious claims of the caliphate, refused to share the Egyptian famine and turned instead to Baghdad. Finally, in 1073, an able soldier, Badr al-Jamālī, went to Cairo at the invitation of the caliph and seized power; in one night his officers rounded up the leading generals and officials and put them to death. He assumed the titles of commander of the armies, director of the missionaries, and vizier, symbolizing his control of the military, religious, and bureaucratic establishments; it is by the military title that he is usually known.

Badr al-Jamālī and his successors

Badr al-Jamālī restored order and, for a while, even brought some measure of prosperity. Egypt was now ruled by a military regime, headed by the commander of armies and maintained by his troops. The office became permanent; Badr was succeeded by his son and then by a series of military autocrats who kept the Fāṭimid caliphs in tutelage. The later commanders were not even Ismāʿīlīs.

The end of the Fāṭimid state. Badr and his successors saved the Fāṭimid state from collapse and postponed its end for nearly a century. At first Badr retained and even tried to revive the aims and claims of the Fāṭimids to universal dominion, but it was too late. Responding to the Seljuq challenge from the East, he pursued an active policy in Syria, Arabia, and elsewhere, using both religious and worldly weapons. In Syria, however, the armies of the Fāṭimids suffered repeated defeats; in Arabia their following was reduced to insignificance. Badr's son and successor al-Afḍal in effect renounced the claims of the Egyptian Fāṭimid dynasty to the universal caliphate. On the death of al-Mustanṣir in 1094 it was al-Afḍal who chose the new caliph. Al-Mustanṣir had nominated his elder son, Nizār, who had been accepted by the Ismāʿīlī leaders; the younger son, Aḥmad, was a youth without allies, who would be entirely dependent on his sponsor. It was no doubt with this in mind that al-Afḍal married his sister to Aḥmad and, on al-Mustanṣir's death, proclaimed his brother-in-law as caliph with the regnal name al-Musta'lī (reigned 1094–1101); in doing so, al-Afḍal split the sect from top to bottom. Even in Egypt there was some opposition; in Persia, Iraq, and Central Asia the Ismā'īlī mission, now led by the redoubtable Ḥasan-e Ṣabbāḥ, refused to recognize the new caliph and broke off relations with the Fāṭimid authorities in Cairo. Ḥasan-e Ṣabbāḥ's new Ismā'īlī movement, known after its Syrian branch as the Assassins, proclaimed Nizār and his descendants as rightful *imām*s and condemned the caliphs in Cairo as usurpers. Even those Ismā'īlīs, chiefly in the Yemen, who had accepted al-Musta'lī broke away in 1130 when al-Musta'lī's son al-Āmir (reigned 1101–30) was murdered by the Assassins and was succeeded by his cousin al-Ḥāfiz (reigned 1130–49). Claiming that al-Āmir had left an infant son who was now the hidden *imām*, the Yemenites refused to recognize al-Ḥāfiz or his successors in Cairo. The divergence between empire and revolution, discernible from the accession of the first Fāṭimid caliph, was now complete.

The end of the dynasty came in 1171. The last four caliphs were no more than a local Egyptian dynasty, without power, influence, or hope. In 1171, as the last caliph lay dying in his palace, Saladin, who as nominal vizier had become the real master of Egypt, allowed a preacher to recite the bidding prayer in the name of the 'Abbāsid caliph of Baghdad. The Fāṭimid caliphate, already dead as a religious and political force, was now formally abolished. After more than two centuries, Egypt had returned to the Sunnī fold.

BIBLIOGRAPHY. A useful account of the Fāṭimid caliphate, with full bibliographical guidance, is given by M. CANARD in the article "Fatimids," in the *Encyclopaedia of Islam,* 2nd ed., vol. 2 (1965); see also the article on Fāṭimid art by G. MARCAIS. The Fāṭimid period may be studied within the larger context of Islāmic history in the *Cambridge History of Islam,* vol. 1 (1971); and in general works on medieval Egypt. S. LANE-POOLE, *A History of Egypt in the Middle Ages,* 2nd rev. ed. (1914), is in many ways out of date, but still useful. The contributions of GASTON WIET to two general histories of Egypt present a more modern view; they are the anonymously edited *Précis de l'histoire de l'Égypte,* vol 2 (1932); and GABRIEL HANOTAUX (ed.), *Histoire de la nation égyptienne,* vol. 4 (1937). There are only two monographs on the Fāṭimid caliphate in Western languages: F. WUESTENFELD, *Geschichte der Fatimiden-Chalifen* (1881); and DE LACY E. O'LEARY, *A Short History of the Fatimid Khalifate* (1923). Both are superseded, but the former retains some value. Particular aspects of Fāṭimid religion and history are discussed in P.J. VATIKIOTIS, *The Fatimid Theory of State* (1957); and B. LEWIS, *The Assassins* (1967). Articles on Fāṭimid history are listed in J.D. PEARSON, *Index Islamicus 1906–1955,* pp. 479–480 (1958, and supplements).

(B.Le.)

Faulkner, William

Imagination is the simple quality that assures Faulkner's place among the major novelists of his time. Never at home in the literary world, he projected a little world of his own: Yoknapatawpha County, "William Faulkner, sole owner and proprietor," as he lettered on a map drawn for one of his books. He peopled the county with extraordinary characters, white, black, and red, all living intensely, almost convulsively; then, as their story developed from novel to novel, he made it a fable of the real American South in history and, beyond that, of human destinies everywhere.

Youth and first writings. The oldest of four brothers, he was born September 25, 1897, in New Albany, a county seat in northern Mississippi. His parents were Murry C. and Maud Butler Falkner; it was the novelist himself who later added a "u" to the name. Soon the Falkners moved to Ripley, in the adjoining county, and then 50 miles southwestward to Oxford, where the novelist was to spend most of his life. In Oxford his father owned and lost a livery stable and a hardware store before he became business manager of the state university. The family was proud of its Southern heritage and re-

Faulkner.
Robe Capa—Magnum

vered the memory of the boys' hot-tempered great-grandfather, Col. William C. Falkner, who had served with distinction during the Civil War. Later, besides building a railroad from Ripley into Tennessee, he had written a romantic novel, *The White Rose of Memphis,* popular enough to be reprinted 36 times. When Billy Falkner was in the third grade, his teacher asked what he wanted to do when he grew up. He rose from his seat and answered, "I want to be a writer like my great-granddaddy."

Billy, or "Memmie"—as he was called by the family and also by a devoted servant, Caroline Barr, who told him stories remembered from slavery days—was an imaginative boy, always leading his brothers into scrapes. His imagination was fed by haphazard reading. There was no public library in Oxford then, but the house was stocked with books, including Dickens and many other English classics. He was not interested in formal studies and dropped out of the local high school after his second year. At the time, he was in love with a girl in the same block, Estelle Oldham. Dreaming of marriage, he went to work in his grandfather's bank. Meanwhile, another neighbour, Philip Stone, soon to enter the family law office, took charge of his reading and provided him with books unknown in Oxford, many of which were in the Symbolist or Modernist tradition: Charles Baudelaire, Paul Verlaine, and Stéphane Mallarmé (Faulkner taught himself to read French). These men and others in the same tradition, such as Oscar Wilde, James Joyce, T.S. Eliot, and Conrad Aiken, appeared a little later in lists of his favourite authors.

Early literary influences

Estelle married another man and went to live in the Orient. Faulkner enlisted in the Royal Air Force Canada and was sent to Toronto as a cadet pilot. That was in the summer of 1918, and the war ended before he had finished his basic training. Home again in Oxford, he was admitted to the University of Mississippi—"by special dispensation for returned troops," he said in a letter—but he stayed there only long enough to join a fraternity and contribute poems to the literary magazine. During the years that followed, he engaged in a series of occupations to earn enough for "paper, tobacco, food, and a little whiskey" while he was learning to write. Thus, in the fall of 1921, he worked as a clerk in a New York City bookstore. For the next three years he was postmaster of the university station, just outside of Oxford—"the damndest postmaster the World has ever seen," Phil Stone wrote of him. It was Stone who put up most of the money for the publication of his first book, a cycle of pastoral poems, *The Marble Faun* (1924).

The first half of 1925 he spent in New Orleans; perhaps it was the only time when Faulkner moved in a talkative literary circle, though he did little of the talking. It was

First novel

also the time when he wrote his first novel, *Soldiers' Pay*, about the return to Georgia of a fatally wounded aviator. The novelist and short-story writer Sherwood Anderson was then the great man of the New Orleans circle, and he recommended the novel to his own publisher. In July Faulkner sailed for Italy on a slow freighter; soon he made his way to Paris, partly on foot. He was living there alone, on the Left Bank, when he heard that the novel had been accepted for publication the following spring. The advance against royalties of $200 paid for most of his passage to New York and his railroad ticket to Oxford, where he arrived before Christmas. In Oxford (and, during the summers, in Pascagoula, on the Gulf coast of Mississippi) he continued for some years to support himself by odd jobs: by working as house painter, carpenter, golf professional, deckhand on a shrimp trawler, and, by his own account, rum smuggler on a speedboat that dodged through the Louisiana bayous. Meanwhile he was writing furiously, mostly at night.

His second novel, *Mosquitoes* (1927), was a heavily satirical picture of the New Orleans literary circle. It was also, in effect, a rejection of the circle and of others resembling it. He was to do his future work in something close to isolation. Besides novels and poems, he was producing a great number of stories, each of which was handed over to Phil Stone, typed by his secretary, and sent off to several magazines. The stories always came back, and, at one time, Stone reported that a drawer of his filing case was nearly full of rejected manuscripts. A third novel, *Flags in the Dust*, finished in the autumn of 1927, was refused by the publisher of the other two. Faulkner became persuaded that his work would never again appear between hard covers. "Now I can write," he said to himself before starting *The Sound and the Fury*. A translation of the remark might be, "Now I can forget the public and live in my imagination."

Flags in the Dust was given a new title, *Sartoris*, and was finally accepted by another publisher, after changes in the manuscript by an unknown hand; it appeared in January 1929. Disproportioned and sometimes emotionally overwrought, it is the last of his apprentice works, but also the first to deal with his imagined community and to state many of the themes he would later develop at length. *The Sound and the Fury*, accepted by still another publisher, appeared in October of the same year. Describing as it does the decay and fall of the aristocratic Compson family—and, implicitly, of a social order—from four different points of view, it is extraordinary for its technical and psychological range and is the first of his masterworks.

Estelle Oldham came back from China after the failure of her first marriage, and she and Faulkner were married in June 1929. During the spring of that eventful year he had written a draft of *Sanctuary*—"the most horrific tale I could imagine"—and had sent it to his new publisher, Harrison Smith. "Good God, I can't publish this. We'd both be in jail," Smith reported, but without returning the typescript. During the late autumn, Faulkner wrote *As I Lay Dying* while he worked as night fireman at the university power station. Reviews of *The Sound and the Fury*, more impressive than its sale, were persuading editors to take a second look at his short stories. "A Rose for Emily" was the first to appear in a national magazine (April 1930), and it was soon followed by others. Faulkner took the risk of buying a big, dilapidated house—which he called Rowanoak—built shortly before the Civil War.

Mature works. He was now well along in what later came to be known as his major phase. The sheer number of his books was becoming impressive. In the years from 1930 to 1942 he published two collections of stories, a second and last book of poems (*A Green Bough*, 1933) and nine novels—all this besides working on movies in Hollywood and making repairs on Rowanoak with his own hammer and saw. The novels are *As I Lay Dying* (1930), about a poor-white family and its journey through fire and flood to bury the mother in Jefferson, the county seat of Faulkner's Yoknapatawpha County; *Sanctuary* (1931), his one popular success—the publisher had

changed his mind about it and Faulkner had rewritten it in proof, without softening the horror; *Light in August* (1932), with its portrait of Joe Christmas, who may or may not be a mulatto and can live in neither the white world nor the black world; *Pylon* (1935), about barnstorming aviators, published in the same year that his youngest brother, Dean, was killed while piloting the plane that Faulkner had bought two years earlier, when he had been working for the movies; *Absalom, Absalom!* (1936), a fable of the old South that is one of his best books but was the most scathingly reviewed, so that his readers began to drop away; *The Unvanquished* (1938), about the Sartoris clan in and after the Civil War; *The Wild Palms* (1939), two separate stories counterpointed in alternate chapters; *The Hamlet* (1940), first volume of a projected trilogy about the rise of the unscrupulous Snopes family; and *Go Down, Moses* (1942), about the Mississippi wilderness and the white and the black descendants of a planter who lived on the edge of it. Except for *Pylon*, all these novels contribute to the Yoknapatawpha cycle.

That cycle was not something planned in advance, as Emile Zola's *Les Rougon-Macquart* series had been. Faulkner started with his own countryside, his own kinfolk, his own memory of stories told him by Caroline Barr—Mammy Callie—or overheard on Saturday afternoons in the Oxford town square; but the stories grew in his imagination, where he sublimated, as he liked to say, "the actual into the apocryphal." Sometimes his version of an incident or his judgment of a character changed from novel to novel, but he was not disturbed by such inconsistencies: "I know these people better now," he used to explain. In the end the novels are even more remarkable for their unity than for their diversity. They all have in common three qualities that, before their time, were somewhat exceptional in American fiction: a sense of place, with events partly determined by their background in nature; a sense of history—that is, of the living past; and a sense of community. Often, Faulkner's narrator is the imagined voice of the community.

Unified as they are in their essential subject, the novels are extremely diverse in their approach to it. Each of them adopts a new method or a number of methods to solve a particular problem that the author had set himself. Sometimes the novel had started with a mental picture—Faulkner says, for instance, that *Light in August* started with the picture of a pregnant woman walking barefoot on a dusty road, and the problem was to explain how she got there and what happened next; the author himself didn't know when he was writing the first chapter. The case was different with *As I Lay Dying*, where the whole story existed in Faulkner's mind before he set the first word of it on paper (writing very rapidly, he says, on the back of an upturned wheelbarrow). Three other books —*The Unvanquished*, *The Hamlet*, and *Go Down, Moses* —first existed as magazine stories, and the problem was to bring the stories together into a novel. Each of the three provides a completely different solution. Among the methods that Faulkner adopted were some he had learned from his reading of Symbolist or Modernist authors—for example, the interior monologue as developed by Joyce and others—but he also acquired and applied the principle that every author should invent his own methods and, if possible, push them further in each new book. Thus, his interior monologues were sometimes those of idiots or of persons on the edge of insanity. A technique he made peculiarly his own was that of delayed meaning, so that he circled round the subject of a novel as if it were a hidden city in the jungle. In matters of style, he set the modern against the traditional, the simple against the involuted or sometimes the needlessly obscure, and mingled Shakespearean grandiloquence with Southwestern humour. "Take chances!" was the motto he chose for himself. Some of his experiments were monumental failures, but others succeeded so well that in later years they were to change the tone and scope of American fiction.

His widespread influence, however, was still in the future. During the early 1940s, Faulkner seemed close to

Faulkner's methods of writing

being forgotten—not in France, where his novels had been ably translated; not by his fellow American novelists, some of whom admired his work intensely; but by the American public at large. Although *The Hamlet* and *Go Down, Moses* contain some of his best writing—including a superb story, "The Bear"—they had gone almost unnoticed. In 1945 his novels were effectively out of print, except for a few copies of *Mosquitoes* in his first publisher's warehouse. Faulkner himself, unable to live by writing fiction, had accepted a long-term contract to write movie scripts in Hollywood at a modest salary.

Rediscovery as a writer. His second rise to fame, steeper than the first, began with the publication in 1946 of *The Portable Faulkner*. It presented his Yoknapatawpha legend as a whole, with extracts from most of his books arranged in historical order. Some of the novelists who admired his work—notably Robert Penn Warren—seized the opportunity to write illuminating essays about it. The public began to take notice, and Random House, his final publisher, put the books back into print, one after another. In 1948 Faulkner published a new novel, *Intruder in the Dust*, about a white boy who saves a proud Negro from being lynched. It was the first of his books since *Sanctuary* to have even a modest popular success. *Collected Stories*, published early in 1950, won the National Book Award. At the end of the same year Faulkner was awarded the Nobel Prize (for 1949) and accepted it in an address famous for his prediction that man would survive in a world on the brink of self-destruction. Academic critics had gone to work on his books, which were providing the raw material, sometimes transformed beyond recognition, of a thriving industry.

Work for U.S. State Department Much against his private inclination, Faulkner had become a public figure. He travelled abroad for the State Department: to Peru and Brazil in 1954; to Japan (where he had enthusiastic readers), the Philippines, and western Europe in 1955; to Greece in 1957; and to Venezuela in 1961. He was happier as writer in residence at the University of Virginia (1957 and 1958), because his only daughter and his grandchildren were living nearby. Meanwhile, he had taken a stand on at least one public question, that of the Negroes in Mississippi. Faulkner profoundly sympathized with the Negroes, but he had a strong residue of Southern nationalism and believed that the South should integrate for itself, without Northern interference. His opinions irritated the extremists and even the liberals of both races.

It was known that Faulkner drank heavily at intervals, but most of the time he kept hard at work, as is shown by the record of his publications. In 1951 his book was a three-act play, *Requiem for a Nun*, with a narrative prologue to each act that gave it the effect of a novel. (Although staged in several European countries, its production in New York was not a success.) In 1954 Faulkner published his longest novel, *A Fable*, on which he had been working for nearly ten years; its hero is Christ reincarnated in a French corporal during World War I. Turgid and apocalyptic, the book leaves its readers uncertain of what the author is trying to say. In other novels of his last period, Faulkner was rounding out the Yoknapatawpha story, which continued to grow in his imagination; the county became a kindlier place as he looked back on it. Some of the demonic fire had gone out of his writing, which now expressed a more tolerant view of human nature. *The Town* (1957) and *The Mansion* (1959) are the concluding volumes of the Snopes trilogy. There is much high-flown talk in both of them, but *The Mansion* is redeemed by the story of Mink Snopes and how he returns from prison to kill the head of his clan. *The Reivers*, Faulkner's last book, is a nostalgic comedy of boyhood that appeared, to great acclaim, only a month before he died in a hospital near Oxford (July 6, 1962). His death followed that of Hemingway by a year and marked the passing of a generation that had invented new shapes for American fiction.

MAJOR WORKS

NOVELS: *Soldier's Pay* (1926); *Mosquitoes* (1927); *Sartoris* (1929); *The Sound and the Fury* (1929); *As I Lay Dying*

(1930); *Sanctuary* (1931); *Light in August* (1932); *Pylon* (1935); *Absalom, Absalom!* (1936); *The Unvanquished* (1938); *The Wild Palms* (1939); *The Hamlet* (1940); *Go Down, Moses* (1942); *Intruder in the Dust* (1948); *Requiem for a Nun* (1951), part novel, part play; *A Fable* (1954); *The Town* (1957); *The Mansion* (1959); *The Reivers* (1962).

SHORT STORIES: *These 13* (1931); *Dr. Martino and Other Stories* (1934); *Knight's Gambit* (1949); *Collected Stories* (1950); *Big Woods* (1955).

POEMS: *The Marble Faun* (1924); *A Green Bough* (1933).

BIBLIOGRAPHY. More books and scholarly articles have been written about Faulkner than about any other American writer of the 20th century. As yet there is no bibliography that includes all the biographical and critical studies. JAMES B. MERIWETHER, *William Faulkner: A Check List* (1957), is complete for Faulkner's published writing to that time.

By far the largest collection of Faulkner manuscripts, including many preliminary drafts, is on deposit at the Alderman Library of the University of Virginia. After most of the collection was displayed at Princeton, Meriwether described it in an admirable book-length catalog, *The Literary Career of William Faulkner* (1961).

There is no collected edition of Faulkner in English (there is one in Spanish), but his books are faithfully kept in print. MALCOLM COWLEY (ed.), *The Portable Faulkner* (1946, rev. 1967), is a selection based on the Yoknapatawpha County cycle.

The authorized record of his life, abundantly detailed, is by JOSEPH L. BLOTNER, *William Faulkner: A Biography*, 2 vol. (1972). There is firsthand information about the man and his background in JOHN FAULKNER, *My Brother Bill* (1963); in a book by another brother, MURRY C. FALKNER, *The Falkners of Mississippi* (1967); and in JOHN B. CULLEN and FLOYD C. WATKINS, *Old Times in the Faulkner Country* (1961). ROBERT COUGHLAN, *The Private World of William Faulkner* (1954), is largely anecdotal. Almost all the interviews with Faulkner, including those in Japan, are collected in JAMES B. MERIWETHER and MICHAEL MILLGATE (eds.), *Lion in the Garden* (1968). MALCOLM COWLEY, *The Faulkner-Cowley File* (1966), contains 26 of Faulkner's letters.

Many critical studies of Faulkner's work have elaborated the symbolic elements to the neglect of the sense and the structure. A better balanced treatment of all the novels is MICHAEL MILLGATE, *The Achievement of William Faulkner* (1966); an earlier one is IRVING HOWE, *William Faulkner: A Critical Study*, rev. ed. (1962). CLEANTH BROOKS, *William Faulkner: The Yoknapatawpha Country* (1963), is unsurpassed for the novels and stories in the Yoknapatawpha cycle. Other critical books that contribute to a full picture are WILLIAM VAN O'CONNOR, *The Tangled Fire of William Faulkner* (1954); OLGA W. VICKERY, *The Novels of William Faulkner: A Critical Interpretation* (1959); H.H. WAGGONER, *William Faulkner: From Jefferson to the World* (1959); WARREN BECK, *Man in Motion: Faulkner's Trilogy* (1961), about the Snopes novels; and JOHN LONGLEY, JR., *The Tragic Mask: A Study of Faulkner's Heroes* (1963). Shorter critical essays are collected in FREDERIC J. HOFFMAN and OLGA W. VICKERY (eds.), *William Faulkner: Three Decades of Criticism* (1960), which also contains a selective bibliography by Vickery; and in ROBERT PENN WARREN (ed.), *Faulkner: A Collection of Critical Essays* (1966), which is notable for Warren's introduction.

(Ma.C.)

Feast and Festival

Throughout the history of human culture, certain days or periods of time have been set aside to commemorate, ritually celebrate or re-enact, or anticipate events or seasons—agricultural, religious, or socio-cultural—that give meaning and cohesiveness to an individual and to his religious, political, or socio-economic community. Because such days or periods generally originated in religious celebrations or ritual commemorations that usually included sacred community meals, they are called feasts or festivals.

The terms feast and festival usually—though not always in modern times—involve eating or drinking or both in connection with a specific kind of rite: passage rites, death rites, sacrificial rites, seasonal observances, commemorative observances, and rites celebrating the ending of fasts or fast periods. Fasting, the opposite of feasting, has often been associated with purification rites or as a preparatory discipline for the celebration of feasts and associated rites. Festivals often include not only feasting but also dramatic dancing and athletic events, as well as revelries and carnivals that at times border on the licentious. Depending upon the central purpose of a feast or festival, the celebration may be solemn or joyful, merry, festive, and ferial.

Another term associated with the events and activities of days of sacred significance is "holy day," from which is derived the word holiday. This term has come to mean a day or period of special significance not only in religious calendars (e.g., the Christian Christmas and the Jewish Ḥanukka) but also in the secular (e.g., May Day in the Soviet Union and Labor Day in the United States and Canada, both of which holidays celebrate especially the accomplishments of the working class).

This article, though it will concentrate on feasts and festivals in the history of religions, will also give attention to the holidays of what has been termed the secular (or profane) sphere. Most secular holidays, however, have some relationship—in terms of origin—with religious feasts and festivals. The modern practice of vacations—i.e., periods in which persons are "renewed" or participate in activities of "recreation"—is derived from the ancient Roman religious calendar in a reverse fashion. More than 100 days of the year were feast days dedicated to various Roman gods and goddesses. On the days that were sacred festivals, and thus holy days, persons rested from their routine daily activities. Days that were not considered sacred were called *dies vacantes*, vacant days, during which people worked. In modern times, however, vacations (derived from the term *dies vacantes*) are periods of rest, renewal, or recreation that may be sacred or secular holidays—or simply periods of time away from everyday work allowed by modern business or labour practices.

The value of studies of feasts and festivals

Feasts and festivals, originating in the dim past of man's social, religious, and psychic history, are rich in symbols that have only begun to be investigated in the 19th and 20th centuries by anthropologists, comparative folklorists, psychoanalysts, sociologists, historians of religion, and theologians. Such investigations will not only elucidate mythological, ritualistic, doctrinal, aesthetic, and psychic motifs and themes but will also provide educative insights to modern man, who has been caught up in social and religious forces that he has found difficult to understand. Feasts and festivals in the past have been significant informational and cohesive devices for the continuity of societies and religious institutions. Even when the feasts or festivals have lost their original meanings in doctrinal or mythological explanations, the symbols preserved in the rites, ceremonies, and arts (e.g., pictorial, dramatic, or choreographic) have enabled persons in periods of crisis or transition to preserve an equanimity despite apparent evidences of disintegration within their cultures or societies. Thus, the scholarly investigations of the many and various facets of feasts and festivals will provide different forms of information that will be of help to modern man in achieving an understanding of his origin, identity, and destiny.

NATURE AND SIGNIFICANCE

Concepts of sacred times. By their very nature, feasts and festivals are special times, not just in the sense that they are extraordinary occasions but more so in the sense that they are separate from ordinary times. According to Mircea Eliade, a Romanian-American historian of religion, festival time is sacred; i.e., it participates in the transcendent (or supernatural) realm in which the patterns of man's religious, social, or cultural institutions and activities were or are established. Through ritualistic re-enactment of the events that inform man about his origin, identity, and destiny, a participant in a festival identifies himself with the sacred time:

Religious man feels the need to plunge periodically into this sacred and indestructible time. For him it is sacred time that makes possible the other time, ordinary time, the profane duration in which every human life takes its course. It is the *eternal present* of the mythical event that makes possible the profane duration of historical events.

In religions and cultures that view time as cyclical—and this applies to most non-monotheistic religions and the cultures influenced by them—man understands his

status in the cosmos, in part, through special times (e.g., New Year's festivals) celebrating the victory of order in nature over chaos. New Year's festivals have been celebrated in recorded history for more than five millennia. In ancient Mesopotamia, for example, Sumerians and Babylonians celebrated the renewal of the life-sustaining spring rains in the month of Nisan—although some cities of Mesopotamia retained an ancient custom of celebrating a second similar festival when the rains returned in the month of Tishri (autumn). Sacrifices of grain and other foods were dedicated to the gods Dumuzi (or Tammuz) or Marduk, major fertility deities, at a ziggurat (tower temple), after which the people participated in feasting, dancing, and other appropriate ritualistic activities.

Man's view of himself in cultures that see time as cyclical

In the 20th century, the view that New Year's Day is a time significant in the victory of order over disorder has been celebrated, for example, in areas influenced by Chinese religions. In order to frighten the *kuei* (evil or unpredictable spirits), which are believed to be dispersed by light and noise, participants in the New Year's festival light torches, lanterns, bonfires, and candles and explode firecrackers. In 1953, when the first day of the lunar New Year coincided with a solar eclipse, the government of the People's Republic of China (which has been anti-religious in its propaganda and official activities) expressed an anxiety that the repressed "religious popular superstitions" might encourage some form of anti-government activity. According to the views of Confucius (6th–5th centuries BC) and Mencius (4th–3rd centuries BC), two of China's great religious teachers, whose social and ethical influences have extended into the 20th century, a solar eclipse during the New Year's festival is a sign of a coming disaster and of a lack of favour by Shang Ti, the Heavenly Lord, who sends omens to indicate his disapproval of man's evil activities.

In religions and cultures that conceive of time as linear, progressing from a beginning toward an end time, when the whole cosmos will be renewed or changed, man understands his status (i.e., his origin, identity, and destiny) in relationship to particular events in history that have a significance similar to those expressed in the myths of people who view time as cyclical. The Jew understands his status as a member of the "people of God," who were "chosen" during the Exodus of the Hebrews from Egypt in the 13th century BC to be witnesses to the liberating love of Yahweh (their God). His being one of the chosen "people of God" is celebrated especially during the Passover festival—in which the Exodus is ritually re-enacted and commemorated—in the month of Nisan (spring). Similarly, the Christian understands his status as a member of the "new people of God." He believes that he has been chosen by Christ, who was crucified and resurrected by God in the 1st century AD, to work for the Kingdom of God that was inaugurated in the first advent of Christ and will be consummated at the Parousia, the Second Coming of Christ as king and judge. The festival of the Resurrection, or Easter, is ritually re-enacted every year in order that the believer might participate in the present and future kingdom of peace. The eucharistic feast (the Holy Communion), though celebrated at many and various times during the year, originated in the event (namely, the Lord's Supper on Holy Thursday preceding Christ's Passion) that has been interpreted as a commemoration of the crucifixion and Resurrection. Just as the New Year's festivals of the religions that interpreted sacred time as cyclical incorporated both remorse and joy in their celebrations, so also the feasts of the Passover and the Resurrection include sorrow for the sins of the individual and of mankind and joy and hope for the salvation of man and the world (see also CALENDAR; JEWISH RELIGIOUS YEAR; and CHURCH YEAR).

Man's view of himself in cultures that see time as linear

Times of seasonal changes. *The significance of seasonal renewal in prehistoric times.* Before the development of agriculture, with its associations with solar and lunar calendars, ritual feasts were probably celebrated by hunters and gatherers of tubers and fruits. Paleolithic (Old Stone Age) peoples from about 30,000–10,000 BC and those living in what are called "Stone Age" cultures in the 20th century, such as the Aborigines in Australia and New Guinea, have celebrated various rites in which feasts have assumed positions of significance. Seasonal variations—important in the maintainance of the food supply—were associated with the migrations and fertility of animals and the growth and decay of tubers and fruits upon which the clan or tribe depended for its very existence. Thus, out of an acknowledgment of seasonal change, rituals—often including ceremonial feasts—most likely developed in relationship to beliefs that the continuance of the food supply depended on the sacred or holy powers that controlled various aspects and facets of nature: e.g., animals, vegetation, the change in climatic conditions, weather phenomena, mountains, and rivers.

Access to the sacred or holy powers was obtained and maintained by certain religious personages (e.g., shamans, or persons having healing and psychic transformation powers, priests, clan or tribal leaders, and other persons having special learned or inherited powers). Though interpretations by scholars vary and the evidence is still subject to much speculating, Paleolithic cave paintings—such as that of the "sorcerer" (a bearded figure wearing a mask on the top of which were antlers of a deer) at Les Trois Frères in France—and rock paintings of the Aruntas of central Australia—such as totemic animals (symbolizing clan and animal relationships) or mythological nature heroes (e.g., Katuru, the "lightning man")—may indicate that fertility of animals and vegetation has been a primary concern (though not the only concern) in the ritual control of the food supply. Rituals connected with controlling the food supply generally centre on a feast in which eating, drinking, dancing, and the chanting of efficacious formulas play important symbolic roles.

At some point in human history (about 8,000–6,000 BC in the ancient Near East), when calendrical seasons were associated with planting and harvesting, special days or periods most likely were set aside for fasting (because of a paucity in the food supply) or for feasting (because of an increase in the food supply). Thus some calendrical periods inspired feelings of discouragement and remorse (when the food supply was low) or feelings of encouragement or joy (when the food supply was sufficient to meet immediate and future needs). Certain days were set aside during these periods for special rituals (often including feasts) that celebrated seasonal renewal, later interpreted in terms of individual spiritual or social renewal. In Zoroastrianism and Parsiism, for example, the annual seasonal renewal festival of Nōrūz (New Year) in the spring, dedicated to Rapithwin (the time of the midday meal), is at the same time a solemn and joyful celebration of new life in nature and the anticipated resurrection of the body when the world will be restored to its original and intended goodness—after the defeat of Ahriman (the spirit of evil and chaos) and his demons.

The significance of seasonal renewal in ancient Egypt. Seasonal-renewal motifs in ancient Egypt were often incorporated into other aspects of sacred times—such as times of passage rites (e.g., ascension of the pharaoh to the throne), of death rites (e.g., the transformation of the dead person into a glorified person, a *ȝḥu*), and of commemorating certain historical events (e.g., military victories in which the pharaoh preserved *maʿat*—i.e., order, truth, and justice—which was active in the realms of nature and society).

In Egypt during the 5th millennium BC, astronomers in the Nile Delta region associated the annual inundation of the river—which covered wide areas with fertile soil—with celestial movements, especially that of the star Sirius (i.e., Sothis) and the sun. From such observations the Egyptians developed a solar calendar of 365 days, with 12 months of 30 days each and five festival days at the end of the year. Though priests assumed important functions at the festivals centred about the fertility of the soil irrigated by the Nile and the life-giving warmth of the sun, the pharaoh, the sacred king, embodied the continuity between the realm of the sacred (i.e., the transcendent sphere) and the realm of the profane (i.e., the sphere of time, space, and cause and effect). The pharaoh

was believed to be the son of the sun god Horus of the Horizon (Harakhte), symbolized by the falcon; the sun god was also known as Re, among other names. The eastern horizon (*ȝḫt*) was viewed as the meeting point of the underworld of the dead and the world of the living. The sun god also was known as Atum, which means "to be at the end," or the west. Osiris, the god of the afterlife (the world of the dead) was believed to be embodied in the recently deceased pharaoh, who passed on his sacred powers and position to the new pharaoh, his son. At the *śd* festival, the new pharaoh, as the son of Horus and of Re, as well as of Osiris, was invested with both kingly and priestly powers. At his coronation festival the pharaoh was believed to gain the power to restore *maʿat* after the death of the previous pharaoh, and also to restore economic prosperity.

During the royal festivals—i.e., ascension to the throne, the coronation, and the *śd* festival—feasting presumably occurred. Festivals associated with seasonal renewal, however, involved sacrifices, eating, drinking, and sometimes dramatic or carnival-like events. Some scholars hold that the Egyptian terms for festival, however, contain concepts that became extremely significant in later Hellenistic (Greco-Roman) religions—e.g., the mystery, or salvatory, religions, such as those of Mithra, Isis, and the Eleusinian mysteries—and Semitic–based religions—e.g., Judaism, Christianity, and Islām. According to this view Egyptian terms for festival, such as *ḥb*, *ḫʿ*, and *pr.t*, all contain concepts of resurrection and epiphany (i.e., the manifestation of a god). In Eastern Orthodox Christianity, for example, the festival of the Epiphany (January 6) celebrates Christ's manifestation to the Magi of the East (presumably followers of Zoroaster, a 6th-century BC Iranian prophet) and his Baptism in the Jordan River. The usual Greek designation for Epiphany is "the day of the light" (*hē hēmera tou phōtou*), in reference to the words in the Bible, in John 1:4, that Jesus is the "light of men." Under the influence of the Christian Catechetical school at Alexandria (led by Clement and Origen in the 2nd and 3rd centuries AD), the earlier religious speculations of the Egyptians concerning their festivals were enhanced by further mystical and spiritual interpretations that affected Christian worship, piety, doctrine, and iconography, especially in Eastern Christianity.

The Egyptians celebrated many festivals that were connected with seasonal renewal, some of which became elaborated into sacred times of cosmic significance. Among their more popular festivals were those dedicated to Osiris, Amon-Re (the sun god), Horus, and Hathor (the sky goddess, represented by a cow).

Of special interest is the festival dedicated to Min, celebrated during the harvest month of Shemou (April). A statue of Min, represented as an ithyphallic god of fertility in iconography, was placed on an inclined pedestal, which was the symbol of *maʿat*. This pedestal represented the primordial mountain, a symbol of resurrection, renewal, and rebirth. During the processional honoring Min, hymns were sung and ritual dances and perhaps other types of dances were performed. The pharaoh and his queen entered the shrine and presumably enacted a sacred marriage rite. After the pharaoh's enthronement at the harvest Festival of Min, four arrows were shot toward the north, east, south, and west; and birds also were released in the directions of the four cardinal points of the compass. The releasing of the birds and arrows announced the harmonious union of man—both as an individual and as a corporate being—with the divine powers of nature inherent in the pharaoh as "Horus son of Min and Osiris." Though the pharaoh was symbolically significant in the feasts and festivals of ancient Egypt, the priests of the various cults officiated in the rituals and sacrifices to the many gods and announced the proper times for the differing forms of celebrations (see also SACRED KINGSHIP).

The significance of seasonal renewal in ancient Mesopotamia. In ancient Mesopotamia, in Babylon, where the king was viewed not as the son of a god but as a god's agent, or representative, on earth, the New Year's festival (Akitu), in the spring month of Nisan, contained not

Probable reasons for feast and fast days

The pharaoh in Egyptian feasts and festivals

Egyptian terms for and concepts of festivals in later religions

The Festival of Min

only seasonal renewal motifs but also themes centring on the renewal of man and his community. The *Enuma elish*, the epic of creation, was read at the festival in order to remind the participants that cosmos (order) arose out of chaos by means of a struggle between Marduk, the god of heaven, and Tiamat, the goddess of the deep and the powers of chaos. The New Year's festival was sometimes celebrated over a period of 10 to 12 days in Babylon. On the fifth day, a sheep was beheaded; the body of the sheep was thrown into the river, and the head was taken into the wilderness. This ritual act, in which an exorcist (*mashmashu*)—one who casts out demonic powers—participated, symbolized the ridding of the community of the powers of chaos. (It was similar to the scapegoat ritual of the ancient Hebrews, in which the sins of the community were ceremonially transferred to a goat, which was later led to a wilderness area to wander about far from the community.)

Before sunrise of the third day following the scapegoat ceremony, the Babylonian king, as the representative of a sinful people as well as the agent of the god, had to submit to ritual acts of humiliation: his symbols of power were removed, and the priest (*urigallu*) hit him in the face and enjoined him to pray for the forgiveness of his sins and the sins of his people. After a profession of innocence, the priest absolved the king, restored his regal insignia, and performed ceremonies with the king to ensure the continuous support of the powers of order in nature. During the three days between the sacrifice of the sheep and the reinvestiture of the king, the populace of the city engaged in chaotic activities, perhaps of a carnival-like nature, to symbolize the presence of chaos in nature and society during this period of the apparent absence of the king and the god. When the king reappeared to his people, with his royal symbols of office and in the presence of the statue of Marduk, a procession of statues of the various gods together with their adoring devotees then took place, leading to a sanctuary (*bītakītu*) outside the city. On the 10th day, a banquet involving the king, priests, temple functionaries, and the gods was held to celebrate the renewal of nature, man, and society.

The significance of seasonal renewal in areas of other religions. Among the pre-Columbian Maya, the first month (*uinal*), Pop, of the New Year—which would be July in the presently used calendar—became a time for several renewal ceremonies. Old pottery and fibre mats were destroyed, and new clothes were put on. The temple was renovated to meet the needs of the god that was especially venerated during a particular year (the annual god changed from year to year). New wooden and clay idols were made, and the portals and implements of the temple were reconsecrated with blue paint, the sacred colour. The god of the year entered the sacred precincts according to the cardinal point of the compass that he represented (and thus there were only four New Year's gods). The purpose of the processional rite was to ward off the forces of evil that might prevail against the people of the area. Dances by old women and sacrifices of live dogs (by throwing them down from the temple pyramid) were some of the activities that occurred during the Maya New Year's festival.

In Japan, among those engaged in agriculture, the *ta-asobi* ("rice-field ritual") festival is celebrated at the beginning of the year to ensure a plentiful harvest. Dances, songs sung with a *sasara* (musical instrument), sowing of seeds, and feasting play important roles in securing the aid of the *kami* (gods or spirits). Divination by means of archery, in which the angle of the arrow on the target is significant, has been used in shrines to help determine the methods that should be used in securing a good crop. In Hinduism, the Makara-Saṃkrānti, a New Year's festival in the month of Māgha (January–February), is celebrated with a fair that continues for a month's duration, with much rejoicing. The Śrī Pañcamī, a festival (*utsava*) of seasonal renewal on the fifth day of Māgha, symbolizes the ripening of crops. Feasts and festivals centring on seasonal renewal can be found among all peoples of the world, both past and present. Rogation festivities (Days of Asking), originally held by the ancient Romans to

counteract the effectiveness of the deity (Robigus) of red mildew on wheat, were reinterpreted by early medieval Christians of the West from the 5th century on as litanies for the blessing of the seed. Rogation Day, the fifth Sunday after Easter, is still practiced in the 20th century in rural Roman Catholic, Anglican, and Lutheran churches.

Other sacred times. *Crucial stages of life.* Birth, puberty, marriage, and death have been times of sacred significance for peoples of all races from time immemorial. They signify changes in the status of a person's being in terms of a person's relationship with fellow members of his or her society and the realm of the sacred or holy that informs the person of the practical and symbolic ramifications of the new status. These times of change, therefore, have become occasions for feasts and festivals. Some are very elaborate and of long duration; others, especially under the influence of modern secularization, have been abruptly shortened or eliminated.

Birth, a most sacred time in the religions of the world, is celebrated by rites and festivities that appear to be incongruous or inconsistent in many religions. Mothers of newborn children are considered both as participants of the sacred by having brought forth a new being into the world and as persons who are ritually unclean (*e.g.*, among the Israelites and Zoroastrians), probably because of the presence of blood at birth, the loss of which may symbolize the loss of some of the life-sustaining force. Among Brazilian Indians, however, both the father and the mother participate in a ceremony of seclusion for five days (eating only certain foods) in order to protect the sacredness and health of the new mother and child. Seclusion, thus, need not be interpreted negatively. Among the Kikuyu of eastern Africa, seclusion is a symbol of death and resurrection. The mother and child symbolically die and rise again during and after a ceremony of seclusion, after which a feast is held in which a goat is sacrificed and prayers are said. The whole community rejoices that a new child has become a part of the family of man.

The Christian celebration of birth culminates in the sacrament of Baptism, a symbol of the death of the old person and the rebirth of the new person in Christ. As such, it is a rite of purification, using water and the words of institution by Christ. After the sacrament has been solemnized, Christians in many areas have engaged in much feasting to emphasize the joy inherent in the "new birth."

Among the ancient pre-Christian Norsemen, baptism by means of water was believed to impart divine and eternal life to men and even to preserve men from death—so that they "will not perish in war" nor "fall before any sword." Thus, when St. Boniface baptized members of Germanic tribes in the 8th century, he was ordered by Pope Gregory III to do so only according to the formula "in the name of the Father, and of the Son, and of the Holy Spirit." Because whole tribes became Christian en masse during this period, the feasts celebrating the incorporation of the tribe into the church often lasted for several days and included folk customs of which the church did not especially approve, such as those connected with merrymaking (*e.g.*, the drinking of mead).

Puberty, the transition into adulthood, has been celebrated since ancient times by various rituals and festivals. In the secular sphere, it is celebrated in democratic countries by the granting of the right to vote to persons upon the attainment of a certain age. In ancient Greece, young men of the ages of 16 or 17 were admitted as full members of the city-state; but before they were granted voting privileges, they had to swear allegiance to the religion of the city; this made them religious citizens and subsequently adults. After he had attained adulthood, a young Greek could participate in military service and could marry. In the United States in the early 1970s, citizens having attained the age of 18 were granted the right to vote; but the ceremony commemorating this right has been a secularized de-emphasis of this important rite of passage: the mere signing of one's name on a registration certificate.

Puberty rites are celebrated in various ways according

to the prevailing religious and social customs. Among the Masai of eastern Africa, youths pass from childhood to adulthood by the rite of circumcision. After various preliminary activities, the boys (12 to 16 years of age) are circumcised and the blood released from the operation is later placed on their heads. After four days of seclusion and a period during which they are dressed in female attire, their heads are shaved and they attain the status of adults and thus can become warriors. Girls attain adulthood by means of similar practices: the cutting or piercing of sexual organs. Among the Akambas of eastern Africa, who perform similar puberty rites of passage, those initiated into adulthood are given presents, and offerings are made to the ancestors. A significant aspect of the festival celebrating the rite of passing from childhood to adulthood is the return from seclusion; this return to their communities symbolizes a type of resurrection and renewal as new persons—adults.

Among the churches of the 16th-century Reformation, the rite of confirmation in the Anglican and Lutheran churches has been a type of puberty rite. The child, who had been a baptized member of the church, became, in effect, an adult, assuming personal responsibility and the privilege of participating in the Eucharist. In the early 1970s, however, the instructional aspect of confirmation—important in almost all pre-puberty practices—has been diminished, especially in some Lutheran churches in the United States, thus de-emphasizing the importance of confirmation as a rite of passage. As the church has become increasingly influenced by secularization processes in the 20th century, the customary feasting to celebrate the rite of confirmation has decreased in practice.

Rites and feasts connected with marriage

Marriage, the rite of passage from the single to the united state, has been celebrated with many forms of feasts and festivals. Connected with the *hieros gamos* ("sacred marriage") of the Mesopotamian Akitu (New Year's festival), and of the Israelite Sukkot (Feast of Tabernacles)—during the month of Tishri (the first month of the year)—which had both sexual and covenantal overtones, the rite of marriage developed into a legal and religious act in Judaism and into a sacrament in Roman Catholic and Eastern Christianity. In most religions the married state is considered superior to the single, though tensions between these two states of existence exist in most religions. Monks and nuns who vow to live in a celibate state often celebrate a symbolic marriage to the founder of their religion (*e.g.*, to Christ) or to a religious institution (*e.g.*, the church). In the Talmud, a compendium of Jewish law, lore, and commentary, the statement is made that "He who does not marry is like a murderer and he mutilates (violates) the image of God." In the Avesta, the sacred book of Zoroastrianism, a similar statement is made: "The man who is married stands above him who is not married." Thus, the wedding has become the most significant domestic festival in both the secular and religious realms, in spite of the ascetic tendencies that exist in certain sectors of Christianity, Buddhism, and other religions. The wedding ceremony has often been accompanied by feasting and gift-giving to express the concern of the community for a successful participation within the community and an extension of the community through the procreation of children. Among African religions, marriage as a rite of passage is incomplete if procreation is avoided or not accomplished. After a wedding among the Batoro of Uganda in Africa, dancing and feasting last until the following morning. Later on, gifts are given to the bride's family in order to show gratitude, to compensate for her absence, and to legalize the marriage agreement.

Rites and feasts connected with death

The final rite of passage, death, has brought about numerous festival customs, all the way from the ritual sacrifice of the widow in Hinduism (until the 19th century) to the commercialization of death rites in Western societies. Just as the early Hebrews believed that life passes on to death when the breath (*ruaḥ*) leaves the body, so also do Eskimos in the 20th century believe that death occurs when breath (soul) leaves the body and that death may be a moment when one is translated into another form of life. Among the ancient Greeks, Thanatos (death) is the twin brother of Hypnos (sleep), and from this conceptional relationship may come the view that death is merely a sleeping state in the passage from this life to an afterlife. Festivities surrounding rites include the customs of playing mournful (and, sometimes, joyful) music, speaking eulogies, performing sacramental acts (*e.g.*, extreme unction in the Roman Catholic Church), performing elaborate or simple embalming practices (*e.g.*, the lengthy procedural techniques of the ancient Egyptians and the rapid techniques of modern morticians), utilizing appropriate and expected bodily gestures and vocal expressions, and feasts of varied elaborateness, depending on the economic or social circumstances of the deceased or his next of kin. Flowers often play important roles in the festivities connected with death rites. In the 20th century, a change from mourning to joyful expectation has occurred in the funeral rites of some Christian churches. Among some African tribes, such as the Ndebele of Rhodesia, funeral processions, sacrifices, ceremonial washings, and protective medicine are included in the festivities that symbolically celebrate man's conquest over death (see also PASSAGE RITES; DEATH RITES AND CUSTOMS).

Times of commemoration and remembrance. Festivals of commemoration are among the most important of the sacred times. Some festivals commemorate important events in mythology or the birth, inauguration, or victory of a founder of a religion, a god, or a hero. In Hinduism, for example, the Vaikuṇṭha-ekādaśī festival in December–January commemorates the victory of the goddess Ekādaśī Devī in her killing of a demon; and the Gaṇeśacturthī commemorates the birthday of Gaṇeśa, the elephant-headed god of fortune. Another major Hindu festival, Navarātri, commemorates the victory of the goddess Durgā over the buffalo-headed demon Mahiṣa; and Rāma-navamī commemorates the birth of Rāma, the hero of the *Rāmāyana*, one of India's great epics. In Chinese Buddhism, the birthdays of Kuan-yin (or Avalokiteśvara), Amitābha, and Śākyamuni (the first two being *bodhisattva*s, or buddhas-to-be, and the last being the Buddha himself) were celebrated before the 1950s with much ceremony. The nativity of Christ (or Christmas) is the most widely celebrated "birthday" of a divine being, though in the 20th century it has been subjected to a wide variety of secular influences.

TYPES AND KINDS OF FEASTS AND FESTIVALS

National and local festivals. Feasts and festivals vary greatly in types and kinds. Though most are religious in background and character, other types have flourished for various lengths of time in cultures and civilizations of the world, both ancient and modern. Included among such types are social and cultural festivals: *e.g.*, New Year's Day in the 20th century, sword-dance festivals in Scotland, the Olympic festivals in ancient Greece and the modern world, the Great Dionysia of ancient Greece during which dramatic contests took place, and May Day celebrations. National festivals in the United States include Thanksgiving Day (in November), which commemorates the survival of the Pilgrim colony in New England in the early 17th century; Independence Day (July 4), which commemorates the Declaration of Independence of the American colonies from the British crown; St. Patrick's Day (March 17), celebrated mainly in Chicago and New York City as a secular–religious feast; Mother's Day (in May); Memorial Day (in May), commemorating those who have died, especially in war; Flag Day (June 14); and others. National or local festivals in other countries include: Bastille Day (July 14), commemorating the beginning of the French Revolution in 1789; Dominion Day (July 1) in Canada; and independence days in many countries. Birthdays of national founders or heroes are also types of commemorative festivals. In some Protestant countries, Reformation Day has assumed the position of a holiday either nationally or locally. In Israel, Holocaust Day—commemorating the systematic destruction of European Jews by Nazi Germany in the 1930s and 1940s—has been placed on the national calendar of events to be remembered.

The relationship of secular holidays and festival activities to religious festivals

Secular modernist festivals. Secular modernist festivals are often mixed with previous religious festivals. May Day, once mainly a springtime fertility festival that can be traced back to the Magna Mater (Great Mother) festivals of Hellenistic (Greco-Roman) times, has become a festival of the labouring class in Socialist countries. Saturday and Sunday football games in the U.S. have all the external trappings of religious festivals. A person from a preliterate culture would see a large congregation gathered together to witness a ritual combat, conducted according to precise ritualistic rules. The participants are dressed in appropriate identifiable garb, or costumes, as they engage in their ritual combat—one side representing evil and the other good, depending upon the viewpoint of the members of the audience. Leading the congregation are priestesses (cheerleaders) dressed in appropriate garb, participating in ritualistic dances, and chanting various formulas that are supposedly efficacious. Operating on the principle of sympathetic magic, the priestesses attempt to transfer the enthusiasm of the crowd to the appropriate combatants. The fact that lay participation in congregational worship in the United States and other Western countries has—for a long time—been little more than a spectator sport, according to some critics, may well have contributed to the festival character of weekend sports activities.

Carnivals and saturnalias. Some feasts and festivals provide psychological, cathartic, and therapeutic outlets for persons during periods of seasonal depression. The Holī festival of Hinduism during February–March was once a fertility festival. Of early origin, the Holī festival incorporates a pole, similar to the maypole of Europe, that may be a phallic symbol. Bonfires are lit; street dancing accompanied by loud drums and horns, obscene gestures, and vocalized obscenities are allowed; and various objects, such as coloured powders, are thrown at people. Various interpretations have been given for such activities.

One of the most well-known festivals of ancient Rome was the Saturnalia, a winter festival celebrated from December 17–24. Because it was a time of wild merrymaking and domestic celebrations, businesses, schools, and law courts were closed so that the public could feast, dance, gamble, and generally enjoy itself to the fullest. December 25, the birthday of Mithra, the Iranian god of light and the contract and the day devoted to the invincible sun, as well as the day after the Saturnalia, was adopted by the church as Christmas, the nativity of Christ, to counteract the effects of these festivals.

Carnival-like celebrations were held on Shrove Tuesday, the day before the Lenten fast began, in England until the 19th century. Originating as a seasonal renewal festival incorporating fertility motifs, contests involving ball games were held that often turned into riots between opposing villages, feasts of pancakes and much drinking following the contest. The tradition of merrymaking continues in the United States in the Mardi Gras festival on Shrove Tuesday in Louisiana.

CONCLUSION

Feasts and festivals, whether religious or secular, national or local, have served to meet specific social and psychological needs. They serve a function of providing cohesiveness to institutions of society: *e.g.*, church, state, and esoteric or socially nonaccepted groups. The cohesiveness engendered in the celebration of feasts and festivals of minority groups (*e.g.*, Christians in the early Roman Empire) often provides a position of strength to the minority group in influencing the institutions of the society and culture of the majority. When a particular religion becomes triumphant in its contest with other religions, it often incorporates elements from the feasts and festivals of the previously predominant religions into its own religious calendar. This has been an important practice of all the world religions, both ancient and modern, in their attempts to bring about social solidarity, order, and tranquility. Similarly, individuals can find cohesiveness psychologically by their participation in feasts and festivals.

During periods of crisis in society, feasts and festivals may lose some of the impact of their interpretive and cohesive functions. Just as the sacraments of the medieval Western Church lost some of their earlier interpretive values during the 16th century under the impact of the Reformation and as the month of fasting before the Feast of Bēma ("judge's seat")—a Manichaean festival commemorating the death of Mani, a 3rd-century AD Iranian prophet who founded the syncretistic Manichaean religion—probably became the prototype of the Muslim fast month of Ramaḍān under the impact of the Islāmic invasions of the 7th century AD, so also can persons living in the 20th century expect reinterpretations of the feasts and festivals to which they have become accustomed. Reinterpretations of feasts and festivals may thus provide impulses for institutional changes, which generally occur in times of crisis and transition.

BIBLIOGRAPHY. E.O. JAMES, *Seasonal Feasts and Festivals* (1961), is a classic work on feasts and festivals of seasonal renewal and on folk festivals and customs of the Western world from prehistoric times to the early 20th century. MIRCEA ELIADE, *The Sacred and the Profane* (1959), is a classic treatment of the concept of sacred time. W. BREDE KRISTENSEN, *The Meaning of Religion* (1960), treats feasts and festivals from the point of view of the phenomenology of religion in various sections of his book. C. JOUCO BLEEKER and GEO WIDENGREN (eds.), *Historia Religionum: Handbook for the History of Religions*, vol. 1, *Religions of the Past* (1969), and vol. 2, *Religions of the Present* (1971), incorporates feasts and festivals into the general framework of the particular religions. WALTER KRICKEBERG et al., *Die Religionen des alten Amerika* (1961; Eng. trans., *Pre-Columbian American Religions*, 1968), treats the various feasts, festivals, and associated rites in the general coverage of the religions of the particular Indian peoples. JOHN S. MBITI, *African Religions and Philosophy*, pp. 110–165 (1969), provides an excellent coverage of the feasts and festivals associated with African passage rites. JEAN HERBERT, *Aux Sources du Japon: le Shintô* (1964; Eng. trans., *Shinto*, 1967), covers the feasts and festivals of Shintō in detail (pp. 147–224). JOHN B. NOSS, *Man's Religions*, 4th ed. (1969), is the best one-volume work that covers the feasts and festivals of the various religions of the world within the general framework of the history, teachings, and practices of the religions.

(L.F.)

Federalism

Federalism is today one of the most widespread principles of political organization. Federal systems were at least nominally operative in 17 counties in 1971, and at least 18 others utilize federal principles to incorporate a measure of decentralization into their systems of government. Federalism is, in every case, a means of organizing power and the relationships that flow from it. Most particularly, it is a means for sharing power in political and social systems. Conceived in the broadest sense, federalism looks to the linkage of people and institutions in lasting yet limited union by mutual consent, without the sacrifice of their respective integrities, as the ideal form of social or political organization.

As a basis of political association, federalism may be defined as the mode of political organization that unites separate polities within an overarching political system in such a way as to allow each to maintain its own fundamental political integrity. Federal systems do this by requiring that basic policies be made and implemented through negotiation in some form, so that all the members can share in making and executing decisions. The political principles that animate federal systems emphasize the primacy of bargaining and negotiated coordination among several power centres; they stress the virtues of dispersed power centres as a means for safeguarding individual and local liberties.

The very terminology of federalism is characterized by a revealing ambiguity. The verb federalize is used to describe the unification of separate states into a federal polity and also the permanent diffusion of authority and power within a nation among general and subnational governments. In this ambiguity lies the essence of the federal principle: the perpetuation of both union and noncentralization.

Union and noncentralization

Federalism is more than simply a structural arrangement; it is a special mode of political and social behaviour as well, involving a commitment to partnership and to active cooperation on the part of individuals and institutions that at the same time take pride in preserving their own respective integrities.

HISTORY OF FEDERALISM AND THE FEDERAL IDEA

Federal institutions have developed in response to two different situations. On the one hand, federalism has been used as a means to unite a people already linked by bonds of perceived nationality or by common laws; in such cases, the polities that constitute the federal system are unalterably parts of the national whole, and federalism invariably leads to the development of a strong national government operating in direct contact with the people, just as the constituent governments do. The United States is a good example of this form.

On the other hand, federalism has been used as a means to unify separate peoples for important but limited purposes, leaving the individual polities a considerable degree of autonomy. Yugoslavia is one example of this form.

Precursors and prototypes. The principles of strong national federalism were first applied by the ancient Israelites, beginning in the 13th century BC, to maintain their national unity by linking their several tribes. The record of and rationale for their effort is presented in the Bible, particularly in the Books of Joshua, Judges, Samuel, and Ezekiel. It was to have a profound influence on the political principles of later generations, particularly at the time of the revival of federal ideas in the 16th and 17th centuries.

The Greek cities experimented with federal-style institutions as means for the promotion of intercity harmony and cooperation, primarily for defensive purposes, through such associations as the Achaean League (280–146 BC). These came close to what are today defined as confederations. But the Greek political philosophers ignored federalism as a political principle, because the very idea contradicted their conception of the small, unified polis as the basis of the good society. A modified form of the Greek view was developed by the 16th-century theorists of international law, who held that a federation could be no more than a permanent league of states that delegated limited powers to a common governing council while retaining full internal sovereignty.

When the American federal system was created in the late 18th century, its architects developed a conception of federalism much like that of ancient Israel, a conception already rooted in American soil as a result of earlier experiments. American federalism was adapted to serve a people with a single national identity who desired a strong national government. In advocating ratification of the Constitution, the authors of *The Federalist* felt it necessary to describe the system as "partly national and partly federal" in deference to the accepted view. But in their usage the term federalist soon came to mean the older conception of federalism as a noncentralized national union having a general government superior to the governments of the constituent states.

As the American system became the prototype for other modern federal systems, the American conception of federalism became the generally accepted one in the modern world. The other conception deriving from the Greek experience came to be called confederation. These different terms correspond roughly to the German terms developed in the mid-19th century: *Staatenbund* ("confederation") and *Bundesstaat* ("federation"). In French and Spanish, however, the meaning of the terms is often reversed.

Though the American conception of federalism as a strong national union has become the conventional meaning of the term, the idea of confederation remains a living and legitimate aspect of the federal idea in its largest political sense. Confederation is advocated by certain proponents of European political union (the European Economic Community, or Common Market, is confederally organized) and by many "world federalists."

Cultural home rule and feudalism. Two major forms of government, both of ancient origin, utilize what seem to be federal principles but actually are not.

Several great empires, notably the Persian and Roman, structured their political systems around a principle that may be described as cultural home rule, a pattern followed today by the Soviet Union and China. Political life was closely involved with religion and culture in the ancient world, and imperial recognition of local ways implied a measure of contractual devolution of political power. Such home rule was not a matter of local right but represented a conditional grant subject to revocation.

The political system of feudalism is often seen as a manifestation of certain federal principles because of its emphasis on contractual relationships. The Holy Roman Empire came to be the exemplary embodiment of quasi-federal feudalism. The hierarchical character of those relationships, however, and the lack of practical mechanisms to maintain the terms of the contract prevented them from being truly federal. The federalism of some Latin American states is a contemporary manifestation of feudal arrangements because the constituent states are often governed by local military leaders (caudillos) who resemble feudal barons.

The Middle Ages. More genuinely federal were the leagues of medieval commercial towns in central Europe, formed for mutual defense and assistance. In their corporate form of internal organization, these cities paralleled the Jewish communities of Europe and the Mediterranean world that had always organized themselves on federal principles. All Jewish communities were considered partnerships in Jewish law, created by *askamot* (articles of agreement). Beginning in the 12th century, these Jewish communities frequently joined in leagues similar to those of the new non-Jewish cities.

In 1291 the Swiss cantons formed a confederation for mutual aid in defense of their independence. While it has since undergone several reconstitutions, the Swiss Confederation remains essentially intact, the oldest continuing federal system in the world. It succeeded partly because it was rooted in popular government from the first.

The Christian states on the Spanish peninsula created a political system that ultimately came very close to authentic federalism. During the reconquest of Spain from the Moors, most of the peninsula was reorganized under the *fuero* system, which established local governments with relatively liberal political institutions to encourage resettlement. Three new states arose that joined in a quasi-federal arrangement under the crown of Aragon, each of them (plus several in Italy added later) retaining its own constitution and governing institutions as well as acquiring representation in the overall Aragonese government. The union of Aragon and Castille (a unitary state) under Ferdinand and Isabella undermined the evolution toward federalism in Spain.

In the 16th century, the ideas of the Protestant Reformation (particularly its Calvinist and Zwinglian elements) and the example of the Spanish system of political organization led to new applications of federal principles. The Habsburg heirs to the Spanish crown had applied Spanish principles to organize their other European possessions. In the Netherlands they laid an organizational basis for the subsequent federation of the United Provinces in the late 16th century, influenced in part by Calvinist ideas. When the country gained its independence it established a political system that, while failing to solve the technical problems of federalism, maintained itself in federal style for 200 years. Even after Napoleon put an end to the republic, a residue of noncentralization remained; The Netherlands is now a constitutionally decentralized unitary state.

The Reformation gave impetus to the development of federalism as a social principle in Switzerland, Scotland, The Netherlands, England, and parts of France and Germany. The assumptions of the Puritan, Presbyterian, and Reformed churches were manifested in the formation of communities of the saved; these covenanted together to create congregations (and, in some cases, states) that they could govern as partnerships. The Swiss and the Dutch

The ancient Israelites and Greeks (margin note)

Pseudo-federal systems (margin note)

Antecedents of modern federalism (margin note)

Early
modern
theorists

American
federalists

Jacobin
hostility to
federalism

19th-
century
federalists

created federal states; the Scots re-established their national identity through the Scottish national covenant; and the Puritans organized their New England colonies and churches on federal principles. The French term for the Protestants, Huguenot, was a corruption of the German *Eidgenossen*, which meant confederates bound together by oath.

Modern approaches. The Dutch and Swiss precedents stimulated the first serious efforts to formulate federal theories based on modern political principles. The French political philosopher Jean Bodin analyzed the possibilities of federation in the light of the problem of sovereignty, concluding that the necessity of maintaining sovereignty indivisible within states rendered federalism in the modern sense impossible, though Greek-style leagues for defensive purposes were not incompatible with national sovereignty. The Dutch jurist Hugo Grotius and the German writer Samuel Pufendorf examined federal arrangements as aspects of international law. Grotius, with the Dutch experience before him, concluded that closely knit leagues could prove viable, but Pufendorf held that federalism and sovereignty were so incompatible as to make leagues of any kind infringements upon sovereignty.

The German jurist Johannus Althusius, analyzing the Dutch and Swiss constitutions, perceived that federalism was really concerned with problems of national unity. The first systematic theorist of federalism, he was also the first to connect federalism with popular sovereignty and to distinguish among leagues, multiple monarchies, and confederations. His retention of hierarchical principles and his emphasis on the corporate organization of society reflected the realities of his time.

The application of federalism to the problems of unifying the new nation-states of the 16th and 17th centuries encountered three problems: (1) the difficulty of reconciling a traditionally hierarchical society with the need for fundamental social equality in the sharing of power; (2) the conflict between local autonomy and the need for a strong central government; and (3) the problem of executive leadership and succession, which was not solved until the American federalists invented the elected presidency.

It was the British who created the requisite popular institutions in their colonization of North America and the biblically influenced colonists who established the social basis and the theoretical justification for those institutions. The Americans assumed that their relationship to the British government was federal, even though London entertained no such notion. The Americans' response to the imperial system led them to develop the federal ideas they were later to use so creatively.

In transforming the principles of federalism into a practical system of government, the Americans had the advantage of working with an entirely modern, postfeudal society that was not weighted down with traditional social hierarchies having differential political rights. Being a relatively isolated nation, they escaped the foreign entanglements that create a demand for the centralization of power. Even so, the internal problems of applying the federal principle eventually led to a major civil war.

Almost every other nation attempting the federal solution to the problems of popular government in pluralistic civil societies has attempted to imitate either the forms or the principles of federal organization worked out in the United States. The theoretical framework for those principles was developed in the debate over ratification of the Constitution. At its core was the classic formulation of the principles of modern federalism in *The Federalist* by Alexander Hamilton, John Jay, and, principally, James Madison. Equally important were the arguments of the "antifederalists," those who wished to preserve even greater state autonomy; many of their arguments remained alive and worked to promote extraconstitutional decentralization in the United States during the 19th century.

The French Revolution, for all of its democratic ethos, was essentially hostile to the spirit and institutions of federalism. Jacobin democracy drew its inspiration from Rousseau's concept of the general will as interpreted by the revolutionary leadership. Unlike federal democracy, which views the constitutional sharing of power among multiple centres (noncentralization) as the keystone of popular government, Jacobin democracy is committed to centralized majority rule whereby a single elite guides the state by interpreting the general will of its citizens as seen in "public opinion"—whether expressed or manipulated. The immediate heirs of the French Revolution endeavoured to destroy federal institutions in western Europe in the name of democracy, and subsequent generations have proved equally hostile to federal ideas—except insofar as some of them have equated federalism with decentralized government. The minority tradition among the French that endorsed federalism was later to emerge as an intellectual force in the works of Alexis de Tocqueville and as a political movement in the moderate Socialism of Pierre-Joseph Proudhon and Claude-Henri Saint-Simon.

In the 19th century, several of the new Latin American nations experimented more or less successfully with federalism. The three largest Latin American nations, Argentina, Brazil, and Mexico, retain federal systems of varying political significance, as does Venezuela; federal principles are also included in the political systems of Colombia and the Central American Common Market (established in 1958). Latin American federalism, however, has remained primarily a modern manifestation of feudalistic federalism, with *jefes* and caudillos replacing counts and dukes.

In the mid-19th century, some Europeans turned to federalism as a form of democratic political organization. They were stimulated by necessity, the American example, and the very influential studies of Tocqueville. Numerous works were written, primarily in the German-speaking countries, where federal or quasi-federal solutions to the problems of political integration were highly regarded and widely used. The most important of these works were the theoretical formulations of the Swiss jurist J.K. Bluntschli, based on his observations of federal reorganization in Switzerland, and the historical studies of the German jurist Otto von Gierke. Federal principles were used in the unification of Germany (1866–71); and Switzerland adopted a modern federal constitution. The Netherlands, Sweden, Belgium, and the Austro-Hungarian Empire adopted quasi-federal institutions to meet particular problems of unification and decentralization.

Later in the century, a school of British theorists and men of affairs emerged advocating the transformation of the British Empire into an imperial federation. Canada and Australia were given federal constitutions and dominion status in 1867 and 1901, respectively; the foundations were laid for the federal unification of India; and an attempt to give New Zealand a federal form of government was abandoned only at the request of the New Zealanders. Theorists such as James Bryce and E.A. Freeman, interested in imperial unity and internal devolution, made their own contribution to federal theory.

Federalism was also taken up in the 19th century by ethnic groups seeking national unity and political autonomy but not in a position to achieve them in any other way. This was the case in Austria-Hungary and in the Balkan countries. In the 20th century, federalism has been used as a means to unify multi-ethnic nations. Several of the ethnically heterogeneous nations created or reconstructed after World War I, including the Soviet Union and Yugoslavia, have formally embraced federalism as a solution to their nationality problems. The British added a federal dimension to accommodate the Ulster Irish. The emergence of new independent countries in Asia and Africa, where ethnic diversity is even greater than in Europe, has led to a further application of federal principles—in India and Malaysia, federalism has been used to secure political and cultural rights for large ethnolinguistic groups; in Africa, federalism has been applied in several nations, including Nigeria and Cameroon, as a device primarily for sharing political power.

Mention should be made of certain experiments in confederation since World War II that have sought to link independent countries for mainly economic purposes: the European Economic Community, or Common Market; the East African Community, linking Kenya, Tanzania, and Uganda; the Central American Common Market, established by Costa Rica, El Salvador, Guatemala, Honduras, and Nicaragua; and the Confederation of Arab Republics comprised of Egypt, Libya, and Syria.

FEDERAL PRINCIPLES

The use of federal principles in non-federal systems

In addition to full-fledged federal systems, there are other forms of political order that make use of certain principles: multiple monarchies, legislative unions, empires, decentralized unitary systems, and unions of nonterritorial units.

The multiple monarchy is a union that exists only in the person of the sovereign and is maintained only through the exercise of executive power in his name. There is no common legislature, no common legal system, nor much of any common political substructure. Each constituent polity maintains its own political system, which the monarch guarantees to support.

Multiple monarchies have historically been somewhat incompatible with democratic government, and this has been a source of their instability. Attempts to transfer sovereignty away from the monarch are likely to destroy the union. Thus, the Austro-Hungarian Empire disintegrated when the Habsburgs ceased to rule. The dual monarchy of Sweden and Norway ceased to function when democratic government was introduced. In Spain, on the other hand, where circumstances required some form of peninsular union, the multiple monarchy was replaced by something approximating a unitary state.

One method of better integrating multiple monarchies while preserving decentralized government is by legislative union. This was used in the United Kingdom, uniting England, Wales, Scotland, and Northern Ireland. The 17th-century dual monarchy linking England and Scotland was stabilized through a legislative union of the two nations in 1707. Legislative union resembles federal union at several crucial points. It is created by a perpetual covenant that guarantees the constituent parties their boundaries, representation in the national legislature, and certain local autonomies in such matters as municipal law. In the United Kingdom, the Cabinet has acquired a supremacy not foreseen in 1707; but, within the framework of cabinet government, Northern Ireland has been granted its own Parliament with substantial local autonomy, Scotland has acquired a national ministry of its own with a separate administrative structure for most of its governmental programs, and Wales has gained a Welsh Office with growing administrative powers.

Federal principles in empires and unitary states

Some empires make limited use of federal principles through grants of cultural home rule. The Persian and Roman empires did so in the ancient world, and the U.S.S.R. may well be the modern counterpart. In both cases, highly centralized political authorities possessing a virtual monopoly of power decide, for reasons of policy, to allow local populations with different ethnic or cultural backgrounds to maintain a degree of home rule provided that they remain politically loyal to the imperial regime. Efforts to transform such home rule into serious political power are invariably suppressed by the central government.

The use of federal principles is also found in decentralized unitary states. These guarantee their local governments considerable autonomy in some areas, limited to matters determined by the central authorities to be local. Such local powers are subject to national supervision, restriction, and even withdrawal. The central government may hesitate to take such action in areas where local privileges are well established, but, as the English experience has shown, even powerful traditions supporting local autonomy have been overridden by democratically elected parliaments with the support of a national majority.

Some apparently centralized states are actually quasi-federal unions of ethnic, religious, or ideological groups that, while not organized territorially, have acquired corporate characteristics of their own and have been able to secure constitutional arrangements designed to preserve their respective integrities within a common polity. Belgium, with its linguistic communities, Lebanon, with its religious communities, Cyprus, with its ethnic communities, and Israel, with its ideological parties, exemplify this arrangement. In most of these cases, domestic services and responsibilities are shared by the subcommunities, which are responsible for serving their adherents under the general aegis of the state.

Federative and confederative arrangements are widely used outside the governmental realm to unify or integrate religious, labour, commercial, and cultural organizations. Federative organization is particularly common in the Calvinist and Reformed churches, ranging from the fully federal Presbyterians to the loosely confederated Baptists. Labour unions and business groups are frequently functional federations. Liberal democracy, with its emphasis on pluralism, is highly conducive to such arrangements.

CHARACTERISTICS OF FEDERAL SYSTEMS

The various political systems that call themselves federal differ in many ways. Certain characteristics and principles, however, are common to all truly federal systems.

Diffusion of power

Basic elements.   *Written constitution.* First, the federal relationship must be established or confirmed through a perpetual covenant of union, usually embodied in a written constitution that outlines the terms by which power is divided or shared in the political system; the constitution can be altered only by extraordinary procedures. Every existing federal polity possesses a written constitution, as do most of the other systems incorporating elements of the federal principle. These constitutions are distinctive in being not simply compacts between rulers and ruled but involving the people, the general government, and the polities constituting the federal union. The constituent polities, moreover, often retain constitution-making rights of their own.

Noncentralization.   Second, the political system itself must reflect the constitution by actually diffusing power among a number of substantially self-sustaining centres. Such a diffusion of power may be termed noncentralization. Noncentralization is quite different from decentralization, which is the conditional diffusion of specific powers by a central government to local governments subject to recall by unilateral decision. It is also more than devolution—the unilateral grant of powers to subnational units by a central government, not normally rescindable. Noncentralization is a way of insuring in practice that the authority to participate in exercising political power cannot be taken away from the general or the constituent governments without common consent.

Areal division of power.   A third element of any federal system is what has been called in the United States territorial democracy. This has two faces: the use of areal divisions to ensure neutrality and equality in the representation of the various groups and interests in the polity and the use of such divisions to secure local autonomy and representation for diverse groups within the same civil society. While seemingly contradictory, both faces are closely related to the purposes of federalism, and manifestations of both are frequently found side by side within the same federal system. Territorial neutrality has proved highly useful in societies that are changing, allowing for the representation of new interests in proportion to their strength simply by allowing their supporters to vote in relatively equal territorial units. At the same time, the accommodation of very diverse groups whose differences are fundamental rather than transient by giving them territorial power bases of their own has enhanced the ability of federal systems to function as vehicles of political integration while preserving democratic government. Examples are Yugoslavia, where each constituent republic is organized around a different nationality group, and Canada, where the province of Quebec contains a population of French descent.

Territorial democracy

Historically, constitutionally fixed areal divisions of

power have been necessary to maintain noncentralization. In modern democratic theory, the argument between federalists and pluralists has frequently revolved around the respective values of areal and functional diffusions of power. Those who have argued the obsolescence of federalism while endorsing its values have generally based their case on the argument that the areal division of powers is unnecessary to preserve liberty and, indeed, may interfere with its protection. Proponents of the federal-areal division argue that the deficiencies of territorial democracy are greatly outweighed by the advantages of a guaranteed power base for each group in the political system, arguing further that any other system devised for giving them power has proved unable to cope with the complexities and changes of a dynamic age.

Other elements of federalism. Other supportive elements supplement the three basic ones. They can be grouped according to their primary impact on the systems they serve.

Elements maintaining union. Modern federal systems generally provide direct lines of communication between the citizenry and all the governments that serve them. The people may and usually do elect representatives to all the governments, and all of them may and usually do administer programs that directly serve the individual citizen.

The existence of those direct lines of communication is one of the features distinguishing federations from leagues or confederations. It is usually based on a sense of common nationality binding the constituent polities and people together. In some countries this sense of nationality has been inherited, as in Germany, while in the United States, Argentina, and Australia it had to be at least partly invented. Canada, Switzerland, and Yugoslavia have had to evolve this sense in order to hold together strongly divergent nationality groups. In the newly formed federal systems of India, Malaysia, and Nigeria, the future of federalism is endangered by the absence of such a common national sense.

Geographic necessity has played a part in promoting the maintenance of union within federal systems. The Mississippi Valley in the United States, the Alps in Switzerland, the island character of the Australian continent, the mountains and jungles surrounding Brazil have all been influences promoting unity; so have the pressures for Canadian union arising from that country's situation on the border of the United States and the pressures upon the German states generated by their neighbours to the east and west. In this connection, the necessity for a common defense against common enemies has stimulated federal union in the first place and acted to maintain it.

Elements maintaining noncentralization. The constituent polities in a federal system must be fairly equal in population and wealth or else balanced geographically or numerically in their inequalities. In the United States, each geographic section has included both great and small states. In Canada, the ethnic differences between the two largest and richest provinces have prevented them from combining against the others. Swiss federalism has been supported by the existence of groups of cantons of different size categories and religiolinguistic backgrounds. Similar distributions exist in every other successful federal system.

Equality and balanced inequalities

A major reason for the failure of federal systems has often been a lack of balance among the constituent polities. In the German federal empire of the late 19th century, Prussia was so dominant that the other states had little opportunity to provide national leadership or even a reasonably strong alternative to the policy of the king and government. In the Soviet Union, the existence of the Russian Soviet Federated Socialist Republic occupying three-fourths of the area and containing three-fifths of the population would severely limit the possibility of authentic federal relationships in that country even if the Communist system did not.

Successful federal systems have also been characterized by the permanence of their internal boundaries. Boundary changes may occur, but such changes are made only with the consent of the polities involved and are avoided except in extreme situations. The United States divided Virginia during its civil war, Canada enlarged the boundaries of its provinces, and Switzerland has divided cantons—but these have been exceptions rather than the rule, and in every case the formal consent of the constituent polities was given. Even in Latin America, state boundaries have tended to remain relatively secure; one of the major bulwarks of Latin American federalism has been the coincidence of state boundaries with major social and economic interests or ethnic–cultural groups.

In a few very important cases, noncentralization is given support through the constitutionally guaranteed existence of different systems of law in the constituent polities. In the United States, each state's legal system stems directly and to a certain extent uniquely from English (and, in one case, French) law, while federal law occupies only an interstitial position binding the systems of the 50 states together. The resulting mixture of laws keeps the administration of justice substantially noncentralized, even in federal courts. In Canada, the existence of common-law and civil-law systems side by side has contributed to French-Canadian cultural survival. Noncentralized legal systems are a particularly Anglo-American device, based as they are on traditional common law. Federal systems more often provide for modification of national legal codes by the subnational governments to meet special local needs, as in Switzerland.

The point has often been made that in a truly federal system the constituent polities must have substantial influence over the formal or informal constitutional-amending process. Since constitutional changes are often made without formal constitutional amendment, the position of the constituent polities must be such that serious changes in the political order can be made only by the decision of dispersed majorities that reflect the areal division of powers. Federal theorists have argued that this is important for popular government as well as for federalism.

Constitutional changes

Noncentralization is also strengthened by giving the constituent polities guaranteed representation in the national legislature and often by giving them a guaranteed role in the national political process. The latter is guaranteed in the written constitutions of the United States and Switzerland. In other systems, such as those of Canada and Latin America, the constituent polities have acquired certain powers of participation, and these have become part of the unwritten constitution.

Perhaps the most important single element in the maintenance of federal noncentralization is the existence of a noncentralized party system. Noncentralized parties initially develop out of the constitutional arrangements of the federal compact, but once they have come into existence they tend to be self-perpetuating and to function as decentralizing forces in their own right. The United States and Canada provide examples of the forms that a noncentralized party system may take. In the two-party system of the United States, the parties are actually coalitions of the state parties (which may in turn be dominated by specific local party organizations) and function as national units only for the quadrennial presidential elections or for purposes of organizing the national congress. Party financing and decision making are dispersed either among the state organizations or among widely divergent nationwide factions.

In Canada, on the other hand, the parliamentary form of government, with its requirements of party responsibility, means that on the national plane considerably more party cohesiveness must be maintained simply in order to gain and hold power. There has been a fragmentation of the parties along regional or provincial lines. The one or two parties that function on a nationwide basis are subject to great shifts in popular support from one election to another. They are also divided internally along provincial lines, each provincial organization being more or less autonomous; at the same time, individual provinces are frequently dominated by parties that send only a few representatives to the national legislature. The party victorious in national elections is likely to be the one able to expand its provincial electoral bases temporarily to national proportions.

Federal nations with less developed party systems frequently gain some of the same decentralizing effects through what the Latin Americans call *caudillismo*—in which power is diffused among strong local leaders operating in the constituent polities. Caudillistic noncentralization apparently exists also in Nigeria and Malaysia.

Respect for the federal principle

Ultimately, however, noncentralization is maintained through respect for the federal principle. Such respect requires recognition by the decision-making publics that the preservation of the constituent polities is as important as the preservation of the nation as a whole. As the American chief justice Salmon P. Chase said, federalism looks to "an indestructible Union, composed of indestructible States" (*Texas* v. *White* [1869]). This recognition may spring from loyalty to particular polities or from an understanding of the way federalism functions. Those who value a politics of conciliation and local autonomy are most likely to have respect for the federal principle.

The historical record indicates that federal systems have arisen out of the dual purpose implied in Chase's dictum at least as often as from a desire for political unification. The Canadian confederation was formed not only to unite the British North American colonies but also to give Ontario and Quebec autonomous political systems. Similarly, a guiding purpose in the evolution of the Swiss confederation has been to preserve the independence of the cantons both from outside encroachment and from revolutionary centralism. A good case can be made that similar motivations also played a part in the creation of most other federal systems.

Elements maintaining the federal principle. Several of the devices commonly found in federal systems serve to maintain the federal principle itself. Two of these are of particular importance.

The sharing of power and responsibility

The maintenance of federalism requires that the nation and its constituent polities each have substantially complete governing institutions of their own, with the right to modify those institutions unilaterally within limits set by the compact. Both separate legislative and separate administrative institutions are necessary. This does not require that all governmental activities be carried out by separate institutions on each plane. The agencies of one government may serve as agents of the other by mutual agreement. But each government must have enough of its own institutions to function in the areas of its authority without depending upon the other and the structural wherewithal to cooperate freely with the other's counterpart agencies.

The contractual sharing of public responsibilities by all governments in the system appears to be a central characteristic of federalism. Sharing, broadly conceived, includes common involvement in policy making, financing, and administration. Sharing may be formal or informal; in federal systems, it is usually contractual. The contract is used as a legal device to enable governments to engage in joint action while remaining independent entities. Even where there is no formal arrangement, the spirit of federalism tends to infuse a sense of contractual obligation.

There is likely to be continued tension in any federal system between the federal government and the constituent polities over the years, with different balances between them at different times. The existence of this tension is an integral part of the federal relationship. The questions of intergovernmental relations that it produces are perennially a matter of public concern, because they are reflected in virtually every political issue that arises. This is particularly true of those issues that affect the very fabric of society. The race question in the United States, for example, is a problem of federal–state relations, as is the cultural question in Canada and the linguistic question in India.

Federal systems or systems strongly influenced by federal principles have been among the most stable and long lasting of polities. But the successful operation of federal systems requires a particular kind of political environ-

ment, one that is conducive to popular government and has the requisite traditions of political cooperation and self-restraint. Beyond this, federal systems operate best in societies with sufficient homogeneity of fundamental interests to allow a great deal of latitude to local government and to permit reliance upon voluntary collaboration. The use of force to maintain domestic order is even more inimical to the successful maintenance of federal patterns of government than to other forms of popular government. Federal systems are most successful in societies that have the human resources to fill many public offices competently and the material resources to afford a measure of economic waste as part of the price of liberty.

BIBLIOGRAPHY. Comparative discussions of federalism in various countries include: KARL W. DEUTSCH *et al.*, *Political Community and the North Atlantic Area* (1957); IVO D. DUCHACEK, *Comparative Federalism* (1970); CARL J. FRIEDRICH, *Trends of Federalism in Theory and Practice* (1968); URSULA K. HICKS *et al.*, *Federalism and Economic Growth in Underdeveloped Countries* (1961); ARTHUR W. MACMAHON (ed.), *Federalism, Mature and Emergent* (1955); WILLIAM H. RIKER, *Federalism: Origin, Operation, Significance* (1964); B.M. SHARMA, *Federalism in Theory and Practice*, 2 vol. (1951); and K.C. WHEARE, *Federal Government*, 4th ed. (1963).

Theoretical works on federalism are: JOHANNES ALTHUSIUS, *Politica methodice digesta*, ed. by CARL J. FRIEDRICH (1932), reprinted from the Latin text of 1614, including the preface of the 1603 edition and an English introduction; MARTIN DIAMOND, "The Federalist," in LEO STRAUSS and JOSEPH CROPSEY (eds.), *History of Political Philosophy* (1963); OTTO FRIEDRICH VON GIERKE, *Das deutsche Genossenschraftsrecht*, vol. 4 (1913; Eng. trans., of 5 subsections, *Natural Law and the Theory of Society, 1500 to 1800*, 2 vol. 1934); ALEXANDER HAMILTON, JAMES MADISON, and JOHN JAY, *The Federalist* (1788); YEHEZKEL KAUFMANN, *The Religion of Israel, from its Beginnings to the Babylonian Exile* (1960), an abridged translation of an 8-vol. Hebrew work; ARTHUR MAASS (ed.), *Area and Power: A Theory of Local Government* (1959); PERRY MILLER, *The New England Mind: The Seventeenth Century* (1939); and SOBEI MOGI, *The Problem of Federalism*, 2 vol. (1931).

Numerous books and articles treat federalism in specific countries, including: WILLIAM ANDERSON, *The Nation and the States: Rivals or Partners?* (1955), a description of the U.S. federal system; VERNON V. ASPATURIAN, "The Theory and Practice of Soviet Federalism," *Journal of Politics*, 12:20–51 (1950); A.H. BIRCH, *Federalism, Finance, and Social Legislation in Canada, Australia, and the United States* (1955); JOAN BONDURANT, *Regionalism Versus Provincialism: A Study in Problems of Indian National Unity* (1958); GEORGE ARTHUR CODDING, *The Federal Government of Switzerland* (1961); ZELMAN COWEN, *Federal Jurisdiction in Australia* (1959); DANIEL J. ELAZAR, *The American Partnership: Intergovernmental Co-operation in the Nineteenth-Century United States* (1962) and *American Federalism: A View from the States* (1971); J.H. ELLIOTT, *Imperial Spain, 1469–1716* (1964); EDWARD A. FREEMAN, *History of Federal Government in Greece and Italy*, 2nd ed. (1893); W. BROOKE GRAVES, *American Intergovernmental Relations: Their Origins, Historical Development, and Current Status* (1964); MORTON GRODZINS, *The American System* (1966); RICHARD H. LEACH, *American Federalism* (1970); AMERICAN ACADEMY OF POLITICAL AND SOCIAL SCIENCE, *Intergovernmental Relations in the United States*, ed. by HARRY W. REYNOLDS (1965); R.L. WATTS, *New Federations: Experiments in the Commonwealth* (1966); R.H. WELLS, *The States in West German Federalism: A Study of Federal-State Relations, 1949–1960* (1961); and AARON WILDAVSKY (ed.), *American Federalism in Perspective* (1967).

(D.J.E.)

Feeding Behaviour

The living cell depends on a virtually uninterrupted supply of materials for its metabolism. In multicellular animals—single-celled members of the Protista are discussed in the article PROTOZOA—the body fluids surrounding each cell are the immediate source of nutrients. The contents of these fluids are kept at a relatively constant level in spite of tolls taken by the cells, primarily by mobilization of nutrients stored in the body; in vertebrates, for example, glucose is stored in the liver, fats in the fat tissues, calcium in the bones. These stores, however, will become exhausted sooner or later, unless the animal takes up nutrients from outside. Movements performed for this purpose are termed feeding behaviour.

NUTRITIONAL REQUIREMENTS OF HIGHER ANIMALS

Cells use nutrients as fuel for energy production (catabolism) and as material for processes of maintenance and growth (anabolism). Multicellular animals derive energy solely from the breakdown of complex organic molecules, mainly carbohydrates and fats. Because the fuel for the maintenance of animal life comes only from other living organisms or their remains, animals are known as heterotrophic organisms. All animal life depends ultimately on the existence of organisms (largely green plants) that can use inorganic sources of energy, of which solar radiation is by far the most important; some microorganisms, however, obtain energy from oxidation of simple inorganic compounds.

For anabolic purposes, food must provide adequate amounts of all chemical elements needed by the cells. Of the approximately 35 elements now known to occur in animal cells, four (oxygen, carbon, hydrogen, and nitrogen) make up about 95 percent of the cell weight; another nine (calcium, phosphorus, chlorine, sulfur, potassium, sodium, magnesium, iodine, and iron) contribute about 4 percent. All of these elements have indispensable functions. The remaining 20-odd, together constituting less than 1 percent of cell weight, are called trace elements, because they occur in minute quantities. Although some of them may become incorporated into cells by accident, many fulfill vital functions (see NUTRITION).

It is important to note that animal cells cannot synthesize from simple compounds certain necessary complex molecules. Instead, certain large organic molecules must serve as building blocks; such so-called essential dietary components include the vitamins, some amino acids, and certain fatty substances. In general, higher animals appear to have more restricted synthetic powers than lower ones and to require a correspondingly greater number of essential foodstuffs. Micro-organisms in the intestines of vertebrates may synthesize materials essential for the host, so that the food of the latter need not contain these substances.

TYPES OF FOOD PROCUREMENT

Because much of animal evolution, as regards behaviour, as well as anatomy and physiology, involves adaptation for the procurement of food, the extent of the meaning of the term feeding behaviour is not clear. Migratory habits of birds, for instance, no doubt evolved in part as a result of seasonal food shortages; individual birds now, however, start migration before food becomes scarce. Migration, therefore, important though it may be in the feeding ecology of a species, is not considered in this article (see MIGRATION, ANIMAL), which concentrates on food-directed activities that are enhanced by a need for nutrients in the body of an individual. For similar reasons, host finding and acceptance by internal parasites for themselves or their offspring also are excluded.

Even with these restrictions, the diversity of feeding patterns is bewildering. A useful classification has been put forward by British zoologists C.M. Yonge and J.A.C. Nicol, based on the structural mechanisms utilized, although, as Nicol observed, "many animals make use of a variety of feeding mechanisms, conjointly, or separately as occasion demands":

A classification of mechanisms of food procurement

I. Mechanisms for dealing with small particles.
   A. Pseudopodial (*e.g.*, many protozoans). Pseudopods consist of fingerlike projections of the cell membrane and its contents (cytoplasm) that surround and engulf food.
   B. Ciliary (*e.g.*, sponges, bivalve mollusks). Cilia are minute hairlike projections of cell membranes that, by concerted beating in wave rhythm, set up water currents or physically move food particles.
   C. Tentacular (*e.g.*, certain sea cucumbers). Tentacles are slender, flexible organs on the head. They may function in sensory perception and in actually securing food.
   D. Mucoid (*e.g.*, many snails, such as *Vermetus*). In this case, the food particles become attached to a sticky

mucous sheet secreted by special cells.
   E. Muscular (*e.g.*, certain coelenterates). In the jellyfish *Rhizostoma*, pulsations of the bell-shaped body draw water and food in through perforations in the arms, then expel the water after the food is removed.
   F. Setous (*e.g.*, many small crustaceans, such as copepods). Setae are bristlelike projections of the cuticle and are found on the appendages of many invertebrates.

II. Mechanisms for dealing with large particles or masses.
   A. For swallowing inactive food, such as bottom deposits (*e.g.*, many polychaete worms, some fishes).
   B. For scraping and boring (*e.g.*, some gastropod and bivalve mollusks).
   C. For seizing prey.
      1. For seizing and swallowing only (*e.g.*, *Hydra*, many polychaete worms, many lower vertebrates).
      2. For seizing and masticating (*e.g.*, Crustacea, mammals).
      3. For seizing followed by external digestion (*e.g.*, some starfishes, spiders).
      In such cases, the secretory and absorptive surfaces of the digestive system may be applied to the food by everting (*i.e.*, turning inside out) the stomach, a method employed by starfish. Alternatively, digestive enzymes may be injected into the prey, liquefying the tissues, which may then be ingested by the predator. This mechanism is found in spiders.

III. Mechanisms for taking in fluid or soft tissues.
   A. For piercing and sucking (*e.g.*, leeches, mosquitoes).
   B. For sucking only (*e.g.*, many flies, butterflies).
   C. For absorption through surface of body (*e.g.*, various invertebrates feeding on decaying organic matter, internal parasites such as tapeworms, which lack a digestive tract).

A different classification, often used, rests on the nature of the behaviour for procuring food:
   A. Filter feeders strain food from the surrounding medium more or less indiscriminately.
   B. Selective feeders analyze the environment with their sense organs before aiming feeding responses at chosen items.

Some feeding patterns, however, cannot be easily fitted into either of these classes alone; spiders, for example, sieve prey from the air with webs but perform directed responses to the insects trapped. Class I of the Yonge-Nicol system comprises mainly filter feeders; most members of classes II, IIIA, and IIIB are selective feeders. Selective feeding requires good sensory and nervous equipment and, in most cases, considerable mobility. It is therefore found mainly among higher animals. Yet the primitive sea anemones are selective feeders in that, capable of paralyzing relatively large prey with their stinging cells, they do not discharge them until informed by chemical and tactile senses that prey is present. At the other extreme, whalebone whales are filter feeders, even though they are highly evolved mammals. Swimming at the surface with mouth open, they filter off large plankton (krill) using several hundred horny plates with hairlike fringes hanging down from the roof of the mouth; availability of a rich food source has caused the evolution of their feeding patterns to diverge widely from that of most other mammals.

In all cases, the feeding patterns adopted by species are the result of evolutionary interplay between (1) structural properties inherent in their phylogenetic line and (2) the ecological situations to which they have been exposed. These interactions are too complex to make generalizations profitable. The best approach is to study each species as a separate case in the light of its entire biology. A few examples are given below.

Evolutionary forces and limits on feeding pattern

Filter feeders occur among sponges, coelenterates, polychaete worms, echinoderms, brachiopods, mollusks, arthropods, protochordates, fish, birds, and several other groups. As might be expected, filtering devices are diverse.

In the oyster, constantly lashing cilia drive a water current—up to 34 litres (about 36 quarts) per hour—through the openings of perforated gill plates. Particles only two microns (0.002 millimetres) in size are wrapped in mucus and transported by other cilia to special food grooves, along which they pass to the mouth by the action of yet further cilia; particles that are too large, too heavy, or capable of producing irritation are sorted out and rejected by various mechanical means.

The polychaete worm *Chaetopterus* uses a bag of mucus, secreted by special body appendages, to strain the water it pumps through its burrow. The mesh openings of the bag, about 40 angstroms (4×10^{-7} millimetres) wide, can even trap single molecules of large proteins. Every 20 minutes the food-laden bag is taken to the mouth, consumed, and replaced by a new one.

The sessile marine snail *Vermetus gigas* secretes mucus strings up to 30 centimetres (12 inches) long that extend away from the shell and entangle fine plankton. At intervals the strings are drawn back toward the mouth and swallowed.

Selective feeders, found among major animal groups, including coelenterates, annelids, echinoderms, mollusks, arthropods, and vertebrates, show even greater diversity of feeding patterns than do filter feeders. One striking point is that different groups deal in different ways with the same food in accordance with special capacities. Animals feeding on bivalve mollusks provide one example. The starfish *Asterias* forces the valves apart by the relentless pull of its sucker tube feet and then everts its stomach through its mouth to digest the soft tissues inside the shell. The snail *Sycotypus* attacks an oyster by stealth: waiting until the valves open, it thrusts its shell between the valves and pushes its tubular feeding organ, or proboscis, into the soft parts. Another snail, *Natica*, supports the scraping action of a filelike structure called a radula with chemical dissolution by sulfuric acid, which is secreted by a gland on the proboscis, and drills a neat hole in a clam. Another snail, *Fulgur*, cracks a clam shell against its own shell by contracting its columellar muscle. Among birds, the oyster catcher (*Haematopus ostralegus*) adroitly cuts the closing muscles of a cockle with its chisel-shaped bill; herring gulls (*Larus argentatus*) break a shell by dropping it onto a rock. A sea otter (*Enhydra lutris*) cracks a clam on its chest, while floating on its back, by pounding it on a stone held between the forepaws.

A few additional examples further illustrate the wealth of adaptations in selective feeding. The sluggish praying mantis (orthopteran insects of the family Mantidae) stalk insect prey until within reach, then carefully orient themselves and accurately and rapidly extend forelegs adapted for grasping. For detecting prey in murky habitats, bats use an ultrasonic echolocation system; some fish use electric pulses in a somewhat comparable manner. Anglerfish dangle a baitlike appendage of the first dorsal spine (luminous in deep-sea species) to lure the fish on which they feed toward their enormous mouths. Certain labroid fishes, which eat parasites off the bodies of other fish, induce their hosts to submit to treatment by a dancing approach; certain blennies treacherously mimic this behaviour and then rapidly bite the fin of the unsuspecting victim. Shrikes perform special wiping movements to remove the sting from certain prey, even without previous experience of stinging insects. The peregrine falcon (*Falco peregrinus*) dives at birds at speeds above 160 kilometres (100 miles) per hour; and the cheetah, or hunting leopard (*Acinonyx jubatus*), pursues antelope at more than 95 kilometres (60 miles) per hour. More than a thousand cormorants may join in a single fish drive. Instead of hunting, some species rob food collected by members of other species; among these robbers are the marauding skuas and jaegers (*Stercorariidae*) and man-of-war birds (*Fregata*), which force weaker cousins to disgorge already swallowed prey, and various tropical flies that take up positions along the line of march of army ants and rob the passing workers.

The driving force for the evolution of each of these adaptations is the survival value to the species of selecting the food sources for which it can successfully compete. For the same reason, closely related species living in the same area may tend to exploit separate parts of the environment; *e.g.*, woodland titmice (*Parus*) forage in different parts of the trees, and the larvae of different species of the moth genus *Eupithecia* prefer different food plants. The result of such evolution may be that a species becomes specialized to one kind of food, as have many internal parasites and phytophagous (plant-eating) insects. Such food may be exotic, as is that of the larva of a moth (*Galleria*) that feeds on beeswax. In other species, such as the herring gull, on the other hand, each individual exploits a broad range of foods, thereby lessening the risk of starvation, as it is unlikely that all types of food will become exhausted at the same time.

REGULATION OF FOOD INTAKE

Metabolic expenditure cannot exceed food intake for very long if an animal is to survive. One way to equalize the two processes is to decrease metabolism to a level sustainable by maximum intake, which may be limited by the ability to extract food from a meagre habitat. Data for filter feeders suggest that, in certain cases, continuous filtration at maximal rates may be barely sufficient to support normal growth and maintenance. Selective feeders have been found to undergo a more or less drastic reduction of metabolism during temporary starvation. Secondly, the capacity of the digestive system may set a limit on nutrient supply to the body. There is evidence that this is so in the minute filter-feeding crustacean *Daphnia magna*. Such limitations are known to play a role in human feeding behaviour.

In man and many other selective feeders, nevertheless, the capacities of food-gathering and digestive systems exceed all but the most extreme demands of metabolism. To maintain nutritional balance, feeding must then be geared to metabolic rate. Information on the mechanisms and even on the existence of such regulation of intake is scanty, except for mammals and some insects.

Vertebrates. Most information on the control of feeding behaviour in vertebrates has come from studies of mammals, but the general patterns found in mammals appear to be present in fish, amphibians, reptiles, and birds. Food intake requires a well-ordered sequence of searching, food getting, and ingestive activities. Sometimes the behaviour is elaborate. The following elements are distinguished in the various cats: stalking, spying, pouncing, thrusting down with the head, biting the neck, carrying into cover, plucking, and devouring. In grazing animals, the pattern is much simpler. In any case, the movement a feeding animal performs at a given moment depends largely on external stimuli; search and pursuit, for example, are unnecessary when prey is within reach. In this sense, any feeding act is a response to the environment, but it is not a simple "reflex." On repeated presentation of the same food situation, the individual sometimes shows the appropriate response but at other times will fail to do so. These fluctuations in responsiveness are roughly parallel in all elements of feeding behaviour. Responsiveness tends to be higher with increasing lack of food in the body. It appears that responsiveness of the brain mechanisms for feeding is governed by messages reporting the nutritional state of the body. The contents of these messages, in other words, are primary determinants of the level of feeding motivation (for other influences see below *Relation of feeding to other functions*). High and low levels of feeding motivation are the objective counterparts of the everyday concepts of hunger and satiety. Regulation of food intake, then, must hinge on the physiological mechanisms of the feeding motivation.

Specific hungers. Lack of any nutrient with a specific anabolic function, such as vitamins or minerals, must be redressed by increased uptake of the particular substance. Little is known thus far of the specific hunger mechanisms that ensure increased uptake, but good evidence exists that a nutrient deficiency causes a specific rise in responsiveness to food containing the substance needed. In the case of thiamine (vitamin B_1), a learning process is involved. The deficient animal tries various kinds of food and concentrates on those that remove the deficiency. Specific appetite for salt in a sodium deficient subject, on the other hand, appears to rest on a genetically determined increase in reaction to the taste of sodium chloride and does not require any learning.

Various methods of feeding on bivalve mollusks

Elements of feline feeding behaviour

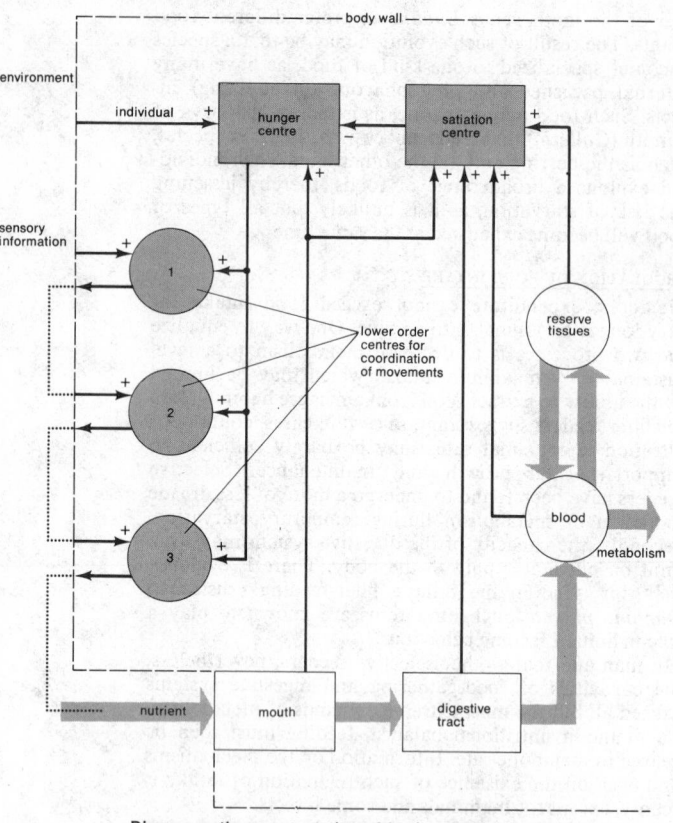

Diagrammatic representation of feeding control in a generalized mammal. Thin black arrows represent information flow; shaded arrows the flow of nutrients. The hunger centre is stimulated by general sensory information (e.g., environment suitable for feeding behaviour). It, in turn, activates lower order brain mechanisms for food searching (1), food getting (2), and eating (3); performance of each of which prepares the animal for the next. Ingested food passes through the various compartments of the body, each of which sends messages to the satiation, or satiety, centre, which inhibits the hunger centre correspondingly. In addition, taste messages from the mouth stimulate the hunger centre.

Caloric regulation. Lack of fuel in the body can be corrected by intake of any of a variety of possible substances that provide energy. Most natural food contains a mixture of such substances. Energy deficiencies can be alleviated by increased responsiveness to food in general. Ingested food (*i.e.*, calories) passes from (1) the mouth to (2) the digestive tract to (3) the bloodstream; if not needed at once for catabolic processes, the digested food passes to (4) storage sites, of which the fat tissues are the most important. These four regions are continuously monitored. A considerable amount is known about the monitoring roles of the organs for taste, smell, and touch in the mouth region; in addition, distension receptors in the digestive tract monitor the volume there, and chemoreceptors monitor the nature of the contents. Information concerning the availability of glucose (the most commonly utilized sugar) and possibly other fuels in the blood is recorded by cells located probably both in the brain itself and elsewhere (*e.g.*, in the liver). Finally, circumstantial evidence suggests that the contents of fat tissues are also monitored. All food that passes through the body contributes to each of these four messages in succession, until it is eventually catabolized.

The signals converge on the brain mechanisms for the feeding motivation over nervous and, possibly, humoural (chemical) pathways. Here they have effects of two kinds: (1) if signals from the four regions report increased fuel contents, the feeding motivation is lowered (satiety is raised), and (2) if taste (and perhaps other, *e.g.*, visual) receptors are stimulated by palatable food, the feeding motivation is increased. Intake stops when accumulation of signals of the first kind, overriding those of the second kind, causes hunger to drop below a

critical level. Feeding is resumed when hunger surpasses this level as a result of fuel depletion by catabolism and emptying of the digestive tract by digestion and absorption. Once started, intake is enhanced by the positive effects of the food stimulus. The net result of this interplay of positive and negative feedbacks from food responses is that caloric intake, observed over a sufficiently long period (at least several days), is equal to energy output over that period, so that body fuel content (body weight in fully grown individuals) remains constant.

The brain mechanisms involved in vertebrate feeding motivation consist of a complex network, not yet well understood, encompassing, among other areas of the brain, the limbic system (the marginal zone of the forebrain) and the hypothalamus. The lateral hypothalamus ("hunger centre") facilitates feeding responses. Electrical or chemical stimulation of this area elicits voracious feeding in satiated subjects, and its destruction causes more or less prolonged noneating (aphagia). If the subject is kept alive by artificial feeding, however, other brain areas may take over and reinstate more or less normal feeding. In contrast, the ventromedial (lower central) nucleus of the hypothalamus appears to be a clearinghouse for satiety signals. Subjects with lesions in this area stop feeding only at an abnormally high level of energy content (obesity) and grossly overeat (hyperphagia) until this level is reached.

Invertebrates. One of the few invertebrates in which the physiology of feeding behaviour has been extensively studied is the blowfly *Phormia regina*. Sucking is elicited by food stimuli on taste organs of the tarsi (the terminal sections of the legs) and proboscis. The meal continues until adaptation of these receptors causes their signals to decrease below the threshold of the sucking-response mechanism. This threshold is modulated, in the following manner, by food present in the digestive tract and in body fluids. As long as food is present in the foregut, the threshold is raised by signals from distension receptors in that area. The foregut is kept filled after a meal by release of food from the crop, where food taken up at the meal in excess of the capacity of the gut is temporarily stored. The threshold will remain high, therefore, until the crop is completely voided. The rate of crop emptying is directly related to the nutrient concentration of body fluids. The latter depends on the balance between absorption from the gut and uptake by the metabolizing tissues. The harder the fly works, therefore, the sooner sucking will be resumed, with the result that food intake is kept equal to caloric expenditure through appropriate spacing of meals.

SELECTION OF FOOD ITEMS

Most natural habitats offer a diversity of food objects, and most selective feeders are more or less euryphagic—*i.e.*, they ingest a variety of different foods; strict monophagy is less common. On the other hand, no euryphagic species includes in its diet all potential food objects present in the habitat, nor are those that it does eat taken in proportion to the amounts in which they are available. On what grounds, then, are diets selected?

Vertebrates. A plant species constituting only a fraction of 1 percent of a pasture may make up the greater proportion of the diet of a sheep. Insectivorous birds also take a highly biased selection from the insect menu offered by the habitat. Although the relative abundance of different kinds of food is reflected in diets to some extent, this does not usually go so far that a single kind of food, however attractive and abundant, will become the sole constituent. Most vertebrates appear to take a varied diet whenever possible.

Responses to encountered food. Diet selection in adult vertebrates proves to be largely the result of individual learning processes that guide the genetically determined response potentialities of the newborn individual into certain definite channels.

Innate responsiveness appears to be broad in species that forage for themselves from birth and thus must deal with many different food situations. The pecking of newly hatched chicks of domestic fowl at all kinds of small ob-

Control of feeding behaviour in the blowfly

Instinctive feeding in young animals

jects, edible or not, is an example. Yet these chicks have certain innate preferences for colour and other features. Such preferences may foreshadow the composition of adult diets. In newly hatched snakes, for instance, feeding responses are more easily elicited with extracts of the natural food of adults of the same species than with preparations of food of closely related species. In contrast, colour preferences of ducklings of different species are similar, although the adult diets differ.

Innate responsiveness may be narrow, however, in young vertebrates for whom the parent is the only source of food. Herring-gull chicks beg for food in response to a few "sign stimuli" provided only by the parent's head among all objects in the natural habitat. Sucking behaviour of newborn mammals is a somewhat comparable example. In such cases, responsiveness must be profoundly reorganized when the individual forages on its own.

Responsiveness is channelled into the adult pattern through experience of taste, nutritional value, and possible noxious properties of various objects. In this way the individual is able to attach a definite palatability rating to each type of food regularly encountered and to associate this with visual or other characters by which it recognizes objects from a distance. As demonstrated in experiments, insectivorous birds may discriminate precisely among as many as 40 different prey species in this manner.

In addition to palatability, detectability of food objects is a factor in diet selection. This has been studied in detail in visually foraging vertebrates. Detectability of an object depends on its degree of contrast with the background as to colour, shape, and movement. The individual predator can learn to detect prey that it finds only with difficulty at first; such "searching image formation" occurs only if the prey is palatable and encountered often.

Finally, responses to encountered prey also depend on (1) the hunger level of the individual and (2) its experience regarding the general food situation. Hungrier predators have lower palatability requirements and may take greater risks to secure prey. At one and the same hunger level, a prey of slight palatability may be rejected if the predator "knows" that further search will probably bring better food but accepted if it "knows" that nothing tastier is available. As a result of these two influences, animals concentrate during scarcity on food scorned in times of plenty.

Food searching and diet. The general type of food taken is often determined by the innate search method of the animal and the section of the whole habitat being exploited. A fish-eating bird, such as the osprey (*Pandion haliaetus*), which secures prey by diving into water (but not swimming), is limited in its diet to fish species that are active near the surface. The much discussed question of whether food searching is random is relevant here, for certain kinds of nonrandomness can influence diets. No simple answer can be given. Search must be random in the sense that oriented reactions to food objects can be made only after detection; at the same time, however, the search may be systematic in that (1) places not recently traversed are favoured over those just unsuccessfully explored, and (2) the locality where a prey has just been caught or seen may be searched with special attention. Further, (3) it is most common for individuals to restrict their foraging to parts of the home range where ample food has been previously found, although exploration of other parts is interspersed and may change the destination of further trips if successful. In all, food searching appears to have sufficient nonrandomness to influence diets provided that different kinds of food concentrate in different parts of the home range, as is often the case.

To sum up, vertebrate diet selection is largely molded by learning processes. Insofar as their course depends on chance experiences of individuals, differences in diet may develop even among members of one population of a species. On the whole, however, patterns of food selection are typical of the species, as all its members have similar genetic makeup and live in broadly similar ecological situations.

Invertebrates. Learning processes appear to play a relatively small role in food selection by invertebrates. Diets are largely, though not entirely, determined by genetically fixed preferences. Intensive studies have been made of host-plant selection by phytophagous insects. Here, as in host selection by animal parasites, the question is one of the choice of a place to live rather than of food alone, and the selection criteria may be largely a matter of compromise between nutritional requirements and other ecological functions. Leaving aside these complications, the factors leading to selection of a particular plant as food are predominantly chemical, although other properties, such as structure, also play a role. The chemicals involved in part are the nutrients themselves, but often the feeding responses are largely elicited by token substances that are not nutritionally essential but are characteristic of the species or family of plants that provide the natural hosts for the insect concerned.

SPECIALIZED ASPECTS OF FEEDING BEHAVIOUR

Relation of feeding to other functions. In principle, feeding must proceed throughout life at a pace equal to that of metabolism, but in many cases intake does not closely follow expenditure. It is permissible for intake to lag when there are reserves in the body. In some cases it is clear that large reserves are present in anticipation of increased metabolic demands or predictable food shortage—*e.g.*, hibernating mammals store large amounts of tissue fat before the onset of dormancy; migrating birds do the same before departure. Insect larvae store nutrients to last them through the pupal stage. Adults of many insects, such as mayflies, do not eat at all and have reduced mouthparts. Other species, such as the hamster, solve similar problems by laying in extracorporeal hoards of food.

Discrepancies between intake and expenditure, whether large or small, amount to distortion of the basic pattern of caloric regulation for the benefit of other functions.

Like most biological processes, feeding has a diurnal periodicity; *i.e.*, depending on the species, the active period may fall in daylight or during the night. Only in filter feeders is the activity often continuous.

Priority claims of other functions may lead to suppression of feeding even in hungry animals. Thirsty mammals or birds eat much less than normal because food intake would aggravate water shortage in the body in various ways. The same is true of mammals in a hot environment —*i.e.*, food intake increases heat production in the body and would thus intensify the heat stress—and of female mammals during estrus (periods of fertility). In all these cases, more or less marked loss of body weight results.

Social facilitation is a further cause of discrepancies as here considered. Individuals often start feeding when they observe other members of the same (or other) species doing so. Both timing of feeding and choice of food are affected in this way. Unfamiliar food is accepted more readily by individuals observing others eating it. Such phenomena have been noted in mammals, birds, and fish.

Food-directed activities in social situations. A further complication is that food-directed activities may be performed for the benefit of other individuals. This may serve their nutrition or some other function. Marked weight loss may occur in songbirds as they feed most of the prey to their nestling young. Courtship feeding in many birds (and insects), in which the male gives food to the female, strengthens the pair bond rather than having a role in nutrition.

Remarkably intricate is the behaviour by which individuals of social-insect species—honeybees, for example— ensure nutrition of the colony. Tropical honey ants store nectar collected by the workers of the colony in the crops (stomachs) of certain workers that remain inside the nest and become so gorged that they are hardly more than storage bins. They disgorge droplets upon solicitation by other ants in the nest. "Dairying" ants keep aphids as suppliers of honeydew, a sugar- and protein-rich secretion. They milk the aphids by gently stroking them and, in return, protect them against enemies. The aphids may

Determination of search area by a predator

even be carried to the nest at the approach of winter and returned to a plant the following spring.

A number of ants and termites cultivate fungi for food. Workers of tropical leaf-cutting ants carry pieces cut off the green leaves of trees to the nest, where other workers use them for making a bed on which the fungi grow. When a queen sets out to start a new nest, she carries a pellet of mycelium (the "root" system of the fungus) in a special pocket on her head during her nuptial flight and subsequent burrowing. After depositing it in the new nest, she manures it with a special secretion until the first workers start bringing in leaf fragments.

The motivational background of behaviour as discussed above has not yet been sufficiently analyzed. Much remains to be done in the more intricate—and even in the more straightforward—cases before satisfactory insight into the functions and causes of the behaviour of animals toward their food is achieved.

BIBLIOGRAPHY. R.A. HINDE, *Animal Behaviour: A Synthesis of Ethnology and Comparative Psychology*, 2nd ed. (1970), is an excellent survey of the modern approach to the analysis of behaviour in general, and contains valuable material on several aspects of feeding behaviour. J.A.C. NICOL, *The Biology of Marine Animals* (1960), gives a good introduction to the classification of feeding patterns with typical examples. W.C. ALLEE *et al.*, *Principles of Animal Ecology* (1949), a classical survey of the entire field, is still useful as an introduction to the relations of animals to their food environment and gives many examples. The best review available of the physiology of feeding behaviour is C.F. CODE (sect. ed.), "Control of Food and Water Intake," in *Handbook of Physiology*, sect. 6, vol. 1 (1967), which is largely though not entirely restricted to vertebrates. A more recent, but much more specialized, volume on the same subject is P.J. MORGANE (ed.), "Neural Regulation of Food and Water Intake," *Ann. N.Y. Acad. Sci.*, 157:531–1216 (1969), which is completely restricted to vertebrates. A methodologically important systems analysis of the behaviour of vertebrate and invertebrate selective feeders may be found in C.S. HOLLING, "The Functional Response of Predators to Prey Density and Its Role in Mimicry and Population Regulation," *Mem. Ent. Soc. Can. 45* (1965), and "The Functional Response of Invertebrate Predators to Prey Density," *ibid. 48* (1966). C.B. JORGENSEN, "Quantitative Aspects of Filter Feeding in Invertebrates," *Biol. Rev.*, 30:391–454 (1955), discusses the effectiveness of filter feeding mechanisms in relation to the food particle content of natural waters. An introductory survey of the relations of insects to their food plants (and feeding behaviour of insects in general) is presented by V.G. DETHIER in P.T. HASKELL (ed.), *Insect Behaviour* (1966). More detailed and specialized material on this point is contained in J. DE WILDE and L.M. SCHOONHOVEN (eds.), *Insect and Host Plant* (1969). Selective food responsiveness in newly hatched snakes is described in G.M. BURGHARDT, "Comparative Prey-Attack Studies in Newborn Snakes of the Genus Thamnophis," *Behaviour*, 23:77–114 (1969). A recent study of the role of searching images in avian feeding behaviour is H.J. CROZE, "Searching Image in Carrion Crows: Hunting Strategy in a Predator and Some Anti-Predator Devices in Camouflaged Prey," *Z. Tierpsychol.*, suppl. 5 (1970).

(L.deR.)

Feldspars

The feldspars comprise an important group of aluminum silicate minerals of widespread occurrence in nature. It has been estimated that feldspars constitute nearly 50 percent of all rocks exposed at the Earth's surface. Upon weathering they yield clay minerals and therefore can be considered to make up an appreciable fraction of all soils, marine clays, and other unconsolidated sediments as well. The feldspars are principal elements in systems of rock classification, are widely used in the glass and ceramics industry, and certain of them provide ornamental stone and semiprecious gems.

General identification of the feldspar minerals

Characteristic of the feldspar group of minerals are solid solution series—*i.e.*, a single crystalline phase whose chemical composition can vary between finite limits that are called end-members. There are three such end-members in the feldspar group, namely, orthoclase, a potassium aluminum silicate ($KAlSi_3O_8$); albite, a sodium aluminum silicate ($NaAlSi_3O_8$); and anorthite, a calcium aluminum silicate ($CaAl_2Si_2O_8$). At temperatures above 700° C (1,300° F) there is complete solid solution between orthoclase and albite. The minerals involved have compositions that vary between pure potassium feldspar and pure sodium feldspar; these constitute the alkali feldspar series. There is also complete solid solution at high temperature between the end-members albite and anorthite. These minerals theoretically vary between pure sodium feldspar and pure calcium feldspar and are called the plagioclase feldspar series. There is commonly a certain amount of potassium in the plagioclase feldspars and some calcium in the alkali feldspars. This is, however, generally not greater than 10 percent of the feldspar molecule. Other elements that enter the feldspars in appreciable amounts are barium, rubidium, and strontium. The barium feldspar ($BaAl_2Si_2O_8$), known as celsian, is very rare, and minerals with compositions intermediate to celsian and potassium feldspar are known collectively as hyalophane.

The importance of the feldspars in the classification of igneous rocks (those rocks that have crystallized upon the cooling of silicate melts known as magma) is such that the alkali and plagioclase series of minerals are further subdivided. The plagioclase series is designated in terms of the fraction of the albite (Ab) component and anorthite (An) component in each intermediate mineral. Because Ab plus An must total 100 percent in each mineral, the content of only one of the end-members need be specified. That is: albite (Ab = 100–90), oligoclase (Ab = 90–70), andesine (Ab = 70–50), labradorite (Ab = 50–30), bytownite (Ab = 30–10), and anorthite (Ab = 10–0).

In the alkali series the feldspar names are related to the structural state as well as to chemical composition. At temperatures above 700° C (1,300° F) there is complete solid solution from albite through anorthoclase to high sanidine. At lower temperatures intermediate members of the series consist of intimate intergrowths of a sodium-rich and a potassium-rich feldspar; these intergrowths have the general name perthite. Perthites are subdivided according to their size: those called perthites are visible to the naked eye; microperthites are visible only under the microscope; and cryptoperthites are invisible under the microscope. It may seem from this that the name cryptoperthite would be of little use; an optical effect observed in moonstone, however, is sufficient to indicate that the mineral is a cryptoperthite. In addition, X-ray-diffraction analysis will indicate the occurrence of a sodium–potassium feldspar consisting of two phases intergrown on a submicroscopic scale.

Economic use and importance

Feldspars find wide application in the glass and ceramics industry mainly because of the lack of colour of some varieties and relatively low melting temperatures. Because they make up the large bulk of many pegmatites (very coarse-grained igneous rocks), relatively pure feldspar can be obtained in large amounts. Cheap glass for bottles is made from granite without removal of the impurities, and, in consequence, the glass is green or brown in colour.

In recent years feldspar has replaced varieties of silica in scouring powders because of the health hazard caused by some varieties of silica in the manufacturing process.

China clay, which is used for making good quality china, is mainly composed of the clay mineral kaolin [$Al_2Si_2O_5(OH)_4$]—a decomposition product of feldspar.

Feldspar-bearing rocks have been used as decorative stones, the most spectacular being the larvikite (from Norway) and anorthosites containing labradorite, which show pronounced iridescence. Many building stones depend on pink feldspars for their beauty, and some feldspars are used as semiprecious gemstones. The chief varieties are moonstone, a cryptoperthite showing pronounced pale-blue iridescence; and aventurine feldspar, or sunstone, plagioclase or orthoclase containing oriented flakes of hematite that produce a copper-coloured lustre called schiller. Orthoclase and labradorite that exhibit a pale-yellow colour because of the presence of small amounts of iron are also used in jewelry.

This article treats the crystal structure, chemical composition, and physical properties of the feldspars, as well as some aspects of equilibrium relations that have been discovered by experimental studies. For further information on the basic properties of crystal structures and the method of X-ray-diffraction analysis, see CRYSTALLOGRAPHY; for an overview of rock-forming minerals and a closely related mineral group, see, respectively, SILICATE MINERALS and FELDSPATHOIDS. The relation of the feldspars to clay and soils is given in the articles CLAY MINERALS and SOILS; gem and ornamental varieties are covered in the article GEMSTONES. See also GEOCHEMICAL EQUILIBRIA AT HIGH TEMPERATURES AND PRESSURES for more information on phase equilibrium relations and mineral synthesis; and IGNEOUS ROCKS for an explanation of the use of feldspars to classify rocks.

CRYSTAL STRUCTURE

General considerations. Feldspars crystallize in the monoclinic or triclinic system. Crystals in the monoclinic system are referable to three unequal crystallographic axes; one axis is perpendicular to the other two, which are not at right angles to each other. In the triclinic system there are three unequal axes, each of which is inclined with respect to the other two. Crystals in this system show the lowest order of symmetry of all minerals, but the feldspars show strong pseudo-symmetry.

Silicon–
aluminum
ratios

All the feldspars are made up of SiO_4 and AlO_4 tetrahedra (*i.e.*, there are four oxygen atoms at the vertexes surrounding and bonded to a central silicon or aluminum atom) that are linked together in a three-dimensional framework by the sharing of oxygen atoms between adjacent tetrahedra. Potassium, sodium, calcium, or barium occupy the cavities in the framework. When two tetrahedra are linked by an oxygen atom, the centres of both cannot be occupied by aluminum atoms, and therefore substitution of silicon by aluminum in tetrahedral (4-fold) coordination cannot exceed 50 percent. In $KAlSi_3O_8$ and $NaAlSi_3O_8$ the replacement is 25 percent, whereas in $CaAl_2Si_2O_8$ it is 50 percent, and thus, in the plagioclase series, the replacement of silicon by aluminum is between 25 and 50 percent.

In the structure of $CaAl_2Si_2O_8$, the silicon and aluminum tetrahedra must be very systematically arranged; every silicon tetrahedron is surrounded by four aluminum tetrahedra and vice versa; this means that the structure is ordered with respect to silicon and aluminum. In all other feldspars, the aluminum content is lower than the 1:1 ratio of aluminum to silicon in anorthite, and this permits the existence of aluminum and silicon disorder. It is this factor that chiefly is responsible for the differences between feldspars that crystallize after being quickly cooled from a high temperature, such as those in lavas, and those that may have formed at high temperatures but only after cooling slowly over a long period of time, so that they can equilibrate at a low temperature.

Although the feldspars have framework structures, these structures can be considered as being made up of linked chains that are parallel to the a axis, formed of linked rings of four tetrahedra that, when viewed along the b axis, present a zigzag appearance (see Figure 1).

The two prominent cleavages (*i.e.*, the tendency to split along preferred crystallographic directions) of the feldspars are (010) and (001) and these break only the bonds linking the chains. The only monoclinic feldspars are the potassium-rich alkali feldspars sanidine and orthoclase. Sanidine microperthites and sanidine cryptoperthites frequently appear to be monoclinic; because they consist of an intimate intergrowth of a monoclinic potassium phase and a triclinic sodium phase, however, they cannot be described as monoclinic in the strict sense. High albite and solid solutions with a small amount of potassium acquire monoclinic symmetry at elevated temperature but automatically revert to triclinic symmetry on cooling.

The sanidine structure. The structure of sanidine (Figure 2) can be used to illustrate the crystal structure of all the feldspars. Because sanidine has monoclinic symmetry, only one-half of the cell need be shown; the other half is its mirror image. The chains parallel to the a axis can be seen in this projection, and the positions of the potassium atoms are also indicated at heights 0 and 50.

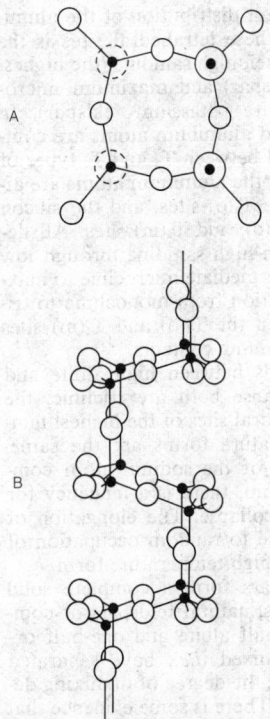

Figure 1: (A) Idealized rings formed from Si–O or Al–O tetrahedrons in feldspar structures. (B) Chains formed by linking the tetrahedral rings. These chains lie parallel to the "a" crystallographic axis.
From W. Taylor, "The Structure of Sanidine and other Feldspars," *Zeitschrift fur Kristallographie*, vol. 85 (1933)

The oxygens at the corners at height 15 and halfway along the "a" cell edge at height 35 are those that link this chain to adjacent chains.

There are a total of 16 (aluminum + silicon) atoms in the cell; these occupy two 8-fold sites, which are usually designated T_1 and T_2. In the triclinic potassium feldspar microcline, however, the eight T_1 sites are replaced by four $T_1(o)$ sites and four $T_1(m)$ sites, and, likewise, the eight T_2 sites are replaced by four $T_2(o)$ sites and four $T_2(m)$ sites. This nomenclature has been incorporated in Figure 2 to indicate the different tetrahedral sites in triclinic potassium feldspar, but it should be understood that, in sanidine, $T_1(o)$ is equivalent to $T_1(m)$ because these are related by a diad axis—*i.e.*, one of twofold symmetry in which the same crystal relations obtain after rotation of 180°.

Silicon
and
aluminum
sites

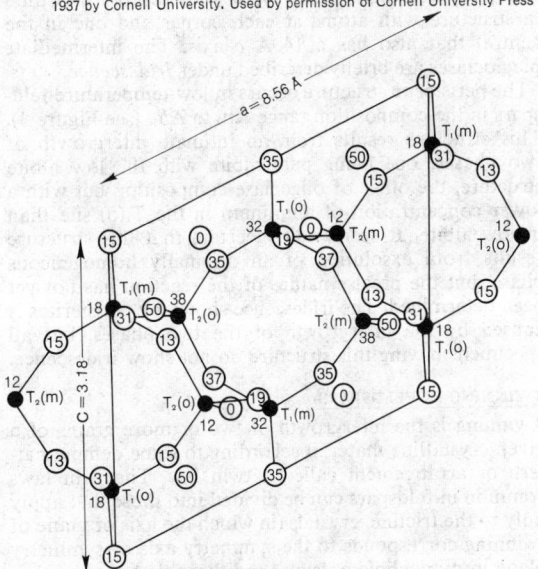

Figure 2: The structure of sanidine, showing one half of the unit cell. The projection is parallel to (010).

As noted above, the different distribution of the aluminum and silicon atoms in these tetrahedral sites is the cause of the difference between high sanidine (the highest temperature potassium feldspar) and maximum microcline (the lowest temperature potassium feldspar). In high sanidine, the silicon and aluminum atoms are completely randomly distributed between T_1 and T_2 types of sites, whereas, in microcline, the aluminum atoms are almost all concentrated in the $T_1(o)$ sites, and the silicon atoms occupy the $T_1(m)$, $T_2(o)$, and $T_2(m)$ sites. All degrees of ordering exist, from high sanidine through low sanidine, orthoclase, and intermediate microcline to maximum microcline. The transition from monoclinic to triclinic symmetry occurs when the $T_1(o)$ and $T_1(m)$ sites have different statistical aluminum contents.

A similar relationship holds between high albite and low albite except that, because both are triclinic, the nomenclature for the tetrahedral sites of the highest temperature and lowest temperature forms are the same. Because of the smaller size of the sodium atom compared with the potassium atom, there is a tendency for the framework partially to collapse. The elongation of the sodium atom may be due to random occupation of two sites and is greater in the high-temperature form.

Although the alkali feldspars form a complete solid solution at high temperatures, natural feldspars of composition near $Ab_{50}Or_{50}$ (one-half albite and one-half orthoclase) are invariably unmixed (*i.e.*, have separated upon cooling) to some extent; the degree of unmixing depends on the rate of cooling. There is some evidence that feldspars that have cooled rapidly are initially homogeneous but will unmix gradually even at temperatures as low as 150° C (300° F). Feldspars that have cooled slowly to low temperatures consist of almost pure low albite and pure potassium feldspar in an intimate intergrowth. Between these two extremes there are all intermediate stages in degrees of unmixing. It should be noted that, whereas the sodium-rich phase is highly disordered in the case of high-temperature perthites and highly ordered in the case of low-temperature perthites, the same is not true of the potassium-rich phase, wherein there are all possible gradations in the degree of order.

Plagioclase structures. Structural variation with composition of the plagioclase feldspars is shown in Figure 3. Although the phase diagram of the plagioclase feldspars usually shows complete solid solution between albite and anorthite at high temperature, pure anorthite has a 14 Å *c* axis even at the highest temperature, whereas albite has a 7 Å *c* axis. In the case of pure anorthite, the aluminum and silicon distribution is completely ordered; this is primitive anorthite. With the substitution of sodium for calcium and the accompanying replacement of some of the aluminum by silicon, the primitive anorthite structure gives way to body-centred anorthite (a structure with atoms at each corner and one in the centre) that also has a 14 Å *c* axis. The intermediate plagioclases are briefly described under *Iridescence*.

Peristerite structure

The peristerite structure occurs in low-temperature feldspars in the composition range An_2 to An_{16} (see Figure 3). This structure results from an intimate intergrowth of two phases, one being pure albite with the low albite structure, the other of oligoclase composition but with a lower concentration of aluminum in the $T_1(o)$ site than in low albite. It seems fairly certain that this structure results from exsolution of an originally homogeneous phase, but the precise nature of the reaction has not yet been determined. The iridescence shown by peristerites is caused by the intergrowth of the two phases, but all specimens having this structure do not show iridescence.

TWINNING IN FELDSPARS

Twinning is the intergrowth of two or more grains of a given crystalline material according to some definite pattern or arrangement called a twin law. The twin laws common in feldspars can be divided into those that apply only to the triclinic crystals (in which the axis or plane of twinning corresponds to the symmetry axis or symmetry plane in monoclinic crystals) and those that apply either to the monoclinic or triclinic crystals.

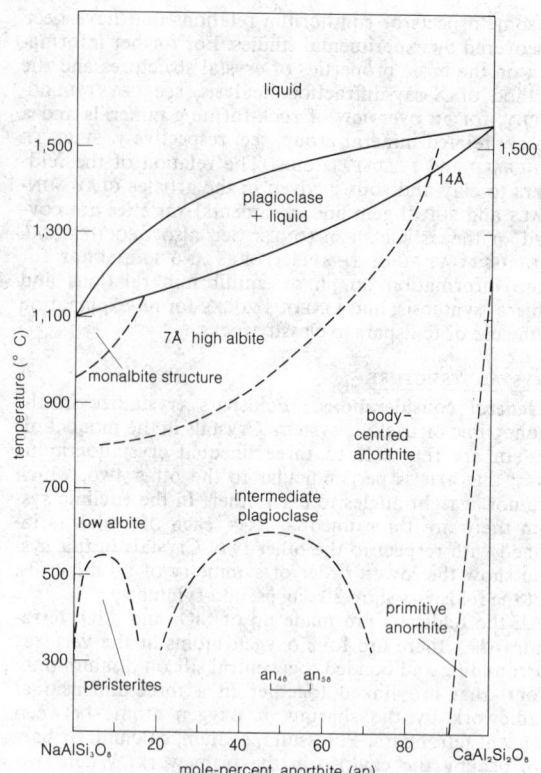

Figure 3: Plagioclase system, showing structural variations with compositional change within the system.
From J.V. Smith and P.H. Ribbe, "Atomic Movements in Plagioclase Feldspars: Kinetic Interpretation," in *Contr. Mineral. and Petrol.*, Bd. 21, S. 157–202 (1969); Berlin–Heidelberg–New York: Springer

Twinning in monoclinic and triclinic crystals. The twin laws that commonly are found in both monoclinic and triclinic crystals are called Carlsbad, Manebach, and Baveno (see Figure 4). The twins result from the zigzag

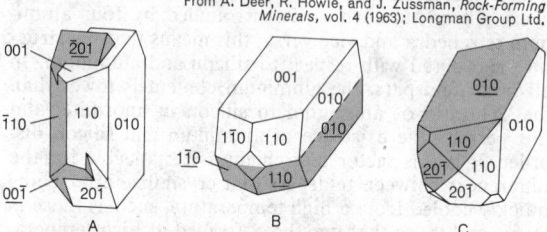

From A. Deer, R. Howie, and J. Zussman, *Rock-Forming Minerals*, vol. 4 (1963); Longman Group Ltd.

Figure 4: Common feldspar twins. (A) Interpenetrant Carlsbad twin. (B) Manebach twin. (C) Baveno twin.

chains of one part being joined to those of the other part by the oxygen atoms, which provide the linkages between the chains of a single untwinned crystal. In the case of Carlsbad twinning, the twin-axis lies in the plane perpendicular to the *b* axis and is described as a parallel twin. The Manebach and Baveno twins, in which the twin-axis is perpendicular to the twin plane are normal twins.

Carlsbad, Manebach, and Baveno twins

Twinning restricted to triclinic crystals. Twin laws that occur only in triclinic crystals are very numerous, but many of the laws are of rare occurrence. The two most common types are according to the so-called albite and pericline laws, and these are frequently found in the same crystal. The albite twin is a normal twin, whereas the pericline is a parallel twin that occurs in an irrational plane containing the *b* axis. Albite twinning represents an attempt on the part of the crystal to retain the plane of symmetry, and pericline twinning is an attempt to retain the axis of twofold symmetry of the monoclinic crystals. In two varieties of alkali feldspar, namely, microcline and anorthoclase, there is no doubt that the symmetry of the crystals was originally monoclinic; but the crystals subsequently inverted to triclinic symmetry, and, in doing so, twinning occurred according to both twin laws. This condition has been described as

Albite and pericline twins

M-type twinning to indicate the origin in a monoclinic crystal; this type of twinning is readily detected by single crystal X-ray studies. It also is recognized optically because of the crosshatched, or tartan, appearance of the crystals when viewed in thin section.

In plagioclase feldspars the original symmetry of the crystals was triclinic, and the twinning may be primary (formed during crystallization), or it may be secondary (formed subsequent to crystallization, perhaps by deformation). The appearance of the twinning is different from that shown by M-type twinning in that lamellae (thin layers, seen as lines in thin sections) of one twin are frequently cut off by twin lamellae approximately at right angles, and so the tartan effect is not produced.

In the plagioclases the position of the pericline twin lamellae depends both on the chemical composition and on the structural state. It may indicate a relict structural state in certain instances.

PHYSICAL PROPERTIES

Hardness. In general, feldspars are quoted as having hardness 6 to 6.5 on the Mohs scale of hardness (on the Mohs scale talc is 1, orthoclase is 6, and diamond is 10). Thus, feldspars are just softer than most minerals that are used as gemstones. Albite is just slightly harder than orthoclase, and, in the plagioclase series, there is a very slight decrease in hardness from albite to anorthite. Detailed study of indentation hardness of the plagioclase feldspars reveals two inflections in the curve of hardness plotted against composition; these inflections occur at An_{25-30} and An_{45-55}. It has been tentatively suggested that these may be correlated with structural breaks in the plagioclase series. Hardness is a property that is not easy to measure accurately and consequently has very limited value as a means of identification of individual feldspars.

Specific gravity. The densities of the feldspars are dependent on both chemical composition and structural state, but, toward the anorthite end of the plagioclase series, the differences in structural state gradually disappear, and so also do density differences.

Table 1: Densities of Feldspar Group End Members

	high form	low form
$KAlSi_3O_8$	high sanidine 2.558–2.560	microcline 2.560–2.564
$NaAlSi_3O_8$	high albite 2.606	low albite 2.624
$CaAl_2Si_2O_8$		anorthite 2.760

Accurate measurements of density are difficult to make because inclusions and flaws in crystals are common. Consequently, densities usually are calculated from the unit cell volume and molecular weight. Unfortunately, small errors in the cell volume may result in noticeable errors in density. The densities of the two forms of potassium feldspar are roughly the same because the cell volumes appear to be nearly identical, whereas, in the case of sodium feldspar, there is a significant difference in cell volume. The relation between density and composition for the two series of feldspars is, as far as can be determined, linear.

Cleavage. Feldspars have two perfect cleavages along the crystallographic planes (001) and (010); the (001) cleavage is the most pronounced. Parting (*i.e.*, the tendency to separate) parallel to a number of faces is reported, and lamellae of sodium feldspar in a perthite may produce an apparent direction of parting.

Colour. The feldspars are commonly milky white in colour; indeed, the name albite is derived from the Latin word *albus*, meaning "white." Many of the feldspars are

By courtesy of The American Museum of Natural History, New York; photographs, E. Javorsky—EB Inc.

(Left) Microcline, Pikes Peak, Colorado. (Right) Albite, Amelia Court House, Virginia.

transparent with a yellowish or green colour, and sometimes they are translucent. Feldspars frequently are reddish brown in colour due to staining by iron, more commonly in potassium-rich feldspars. Some have a small amount of iron in their structure and occur as transparent yellowish crystals. The latter are either iron-bearing orthoclases or iron-bearing labradorites, both of which are used as semiprecious gemstones. Their perfect cleavage is a disadvantage in this connection. Feldspars that are green in colour are called amazonite. When transparent they are used as gemstones and when cloudy as decorative stones.

Iridescence. The property of iridescence is shown by different types of feldspars. Moonstones, which are alkali feldspars that are made up of a submicroscopic intergrowth of potassium-rich and sodium-rich feldspar, usually have a very attractive pale-blue iridescence and are used as semiprecious gemstones. Plagioclases in the albite–oligoclase composition range (peristerites) that

Play of colours

By courtesy of the Department of Geology, The University of Manchester, England; photographs, Susan Maher

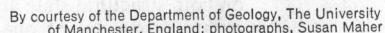

(Left) Moonstone showing pale-blue iridescence, origin unknown. (Top right) Polished slab of labradorite showing iridescence colors and polysynthetic twinning, from Labrador. (Bottom right) Aventurine feldspar showing schiller produced by flakes of hematite, from Bjordammen, Norway.

consist of submicroscopic lamellae of two phases, one of which is almost pure albite, also show iridescence. The name is derived from the Greek word *peristera* in allusion to the resemblance of the iridescence colour to that of a pigeon or dove.

Some feldspars in the labradorite composition range show a play of colours that varies through red, gold brown, yellow, blue, and green. Although there is some overlap, the colours are related to the bulk composition of the sample: blue may be shown by samples of composition $An_{48.5}$–An_{52}; green to yellow, by An_{52}–$An_{55.5}$; and orange to red, by An_{55}–$An_{58.5}$ (Figure 3). The potassium content apparently is critical as to whether iridescence is produced or not, because all specimens that lack iridescence have less than 2.1 mole (gram-molecular weight) percent of orthoclase. Although many workers have tried to explain this effect, there is no consensus of opinion as to its cause. If it is caused by an intergrowth of two phases, then these are extremely similar in structure. Recent work on this topic suggests that unmixing into two phases appears to be the most likely explanation of this phenomenon.

The property of schiller is shown by a type of feldspar known as aventurine, sometimes known as sunstone. The feldspar is usually of oligoclase composition but is sometimes potassium feldspar. The appearance is that of a copper-coloured schiller due to oriented hematite lamellae. When the specimen is heated above 1,200° C (2,200° F), these lamellae disappear, presumably due to solid solution in the feldspar, and they may reappear on annealing at 1,000° C (1,800° F).

Crystal form and habit. The feldspars have fairly strong pseudosymmetry, and in the triclinic feldspars this is the cause of polysynthetic (multiple) twinning. This is in some instances hexagonal pseudosymmetry, with the *c* axis serving as the sixfold axis (*i.e.*, one that reveals the same crystal relations with each 60° rotation).

Orthoclase and microcline commonly have prismatic habit, whereas sanidine is frequently tabular (see Figure 5). Albite in pegmatites forms very thin tabular crystals parallel to (010)—a plane parallel to *a* and *c;* this is

From A. Deer, R. Howie, and J. Zussman, *Rock-Forming Minerals*, vol. 4 (1963); Longman Group Ltd.

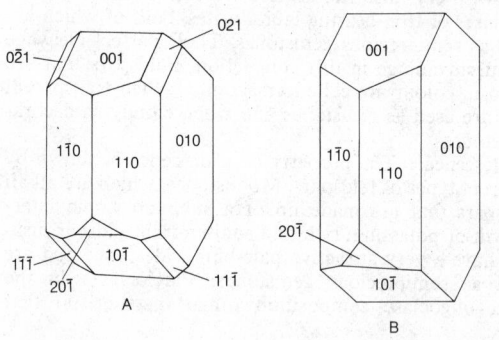

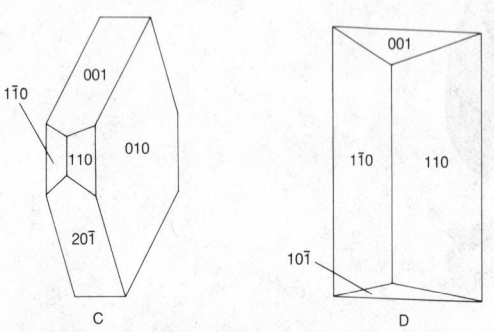

Figure 5: Common feldspar habits. (A) and (B) prismatic habit of orthoclase, microcline, and plagioclase; (C) tabular habit of sanidine; (D) adularia habit.

called cleavelandite. Pericline is a variety of albite found in low-temperature veins. Pericline is characteristically elongated along the *b* axis and has simple pericline twinning. The pericline twin law is named from this variety of feldspar.

The feldspars of some volcanic rocks in Norway are rather unusual in that, like adularia, they have a rhomb-shaped outline.

Optical properties. Optical properties of minerals require specialized knowledge both for determination and understanding. Although there are other optical properties of significance with regard to the feldspars, only refractive index—the ratio of the velocity of light in a vacuum (in air, as commonly measured) to that in the mineral—will be discussed here.

Table 2: Optical Properties of Feldspar Group End Members

	refractive indexes			optic axial angles	extinction angles	
	α	β	γ		(001) section	(010) section
High sanidine	1.518	1.522	1.522	(−) 64°	0	(+) 2°
Orthoclase	1.519	1.524	1.526	(−) 32°	0	(+) 5°
Microcline	1.522	1.526	1.529	(−) 70°–80°	(+) 5°–15°	(+) 5°
High albite	1.527	1.532	1.534	(−) 45°–55°	(+) 0°–2°	+ 9°
Low albite	1.529	1.533	1.539	(+) 78°	(+) 3°	+ 20
Anorthite	1.575	1.584	1.589	(−) 77°	(−) 43°	(−) 39°

Refractive indices of feldspars depend on chemical composition and, to a lesser extent, on the structural state. A graph of refractive indices and composition of alkali feldspars clearly indicates that the substitution of potassium for sodium has a small effect on the refractive index. Measurements must be very accurate to have any value for determining chemical composition. Minor elements such as calcium, strontium, and barium also affect the plot, so that little useful information on alkali feldspars can be obtained by measuring approximate refractive indices except to indicate whether they are potassium- or sodium-rich compositions. In the plagioclase series, on the other hand, measurements of refractive indices have long been recognized as having useful determinative value, but, unless the structural state is known, the accuracy is not as great as might be desired, particularly for sodium-rich compositions.

An alternative method, very useful for relatively unzoned crystals, consists of fusing the crystals to a glass and then measuring the refractive index of the glass. A curve relating chemical composition to the refractive index of the glass for synthetic feldspar glasses may then be used for analysis. Because feldspars are frequently chemically zoned, sometimes in a very complex manner, it may be desirable to determine the composition of the separate zones, a distinction usually made by optical determinations; but, because this measurement depends on both structural state and chemical composition, an accurate knowledge of one of these must be obtained by some other method. A large number of optical techniques for determining the compositions of feldspars are available. These methods were becoming largely outdated in the 1970s, however, with the increasing availability of the electron microprobe.

Refractive indices

PHASE EQUILIBRIA OF FELDSPAR SYSTEMS

Alkali feldspars. At atmospheric pressure pure potassium feldspars and compositions from pure orthoclase (Or) to about $Or_{50}Ab_{50}$ melt incongruently (*i.e.*, they react with the liquid to produce a new solid phase) and yield leucite plus liquid (see Figure 6). The

$$NaAlSi_3O_8–KAlSi_3O_8$$

system is not binary for those compositions above the beginning of melting. For all temperatures below the beginning of melting, however, the relations can be represented in a temperature–composition diagram. There is a minimum melting relationship, and the minimum is near $Or_{35}Ab_{65}$, as shown in Figure 6.

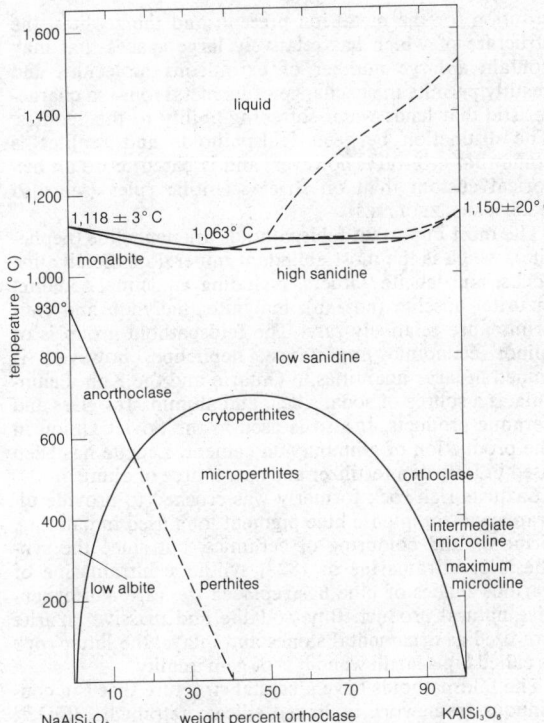

Figure 6: The alkali feldspar system, showing the liquidus, solidus, and subsolidus relations (see text).

From N. Bowen and O. Tuttle, "The System NaAlSi₃O₈–KAlSi₃O₈–H₂O," *Journal of Geology*, vol. 58 ©1950; the University of Chicago Press

degree of aluminum–silicon order in the specimens used to define the solvus. Thus, the solvus shown is drawn only approximately, on the assumption that its crest is above 700° C and near $Or_{50}Ab_{50}$, and in the knowledge that low albite and maximum microcline show a limited solid solution of potassium and sodium, respectively.

The dashed line sloping from 930° C at albite composition and intersecting the solvus represents the non-quenchable monoclinic–triclinic inversion in sodium-rich alkali feldspars; below the solvus this is denoted by a dotted line to indicate that it is metastable in this region.

Temperature ranges for the stabilities of the various forms of sodium and potassium feldspars cannot be shown because the various forms are not accurately defined, there being a gradual transition from the highest to the lowest temperature form (see Figure 6). The boundary between anorthoclase and sanidine is at $Or_{40}Ab_{60}$ because single-phase crystals of a composition more sodium rich than this are triclinic when observed at room temperature, and compositions more potassium rich are monoclinic at room temperature.

At a water pressure of five kilobars, the melting curves on this system are lowered considerably because of the incorporation of water in the silicate melt, and the minimum is replaced by what appears in projection to be a eutectic (*i.e.*, the lowest melting point possible in mixtures of components that do not form solid solutions). The degree of aluminum–silicon disorder in the two feldspars in equilibrium with the liquid at the temperature of this pseudo-eutectic is likely to be very high; hence the stable solvus close to the melting curves might be expected to be that determined experimentally. The effect of pressure on the solvus is to raise it slightly. (See Figure 8.)

Plagioclase feldspars. At high temperature the plagioclase feldspars form a solid solution series with no maximum or minimum. At lower temperatures the phase diagram is extremely complex and not yet fully understood, but the latest ideas are incorporated in Figure 3. The form of sodium feldspar stable at the melting point is monoclinic albite, but, with increasing calcium this quickly gives way to a triclinic form with a 7 Å c axis, which extends across the diagram to near anorthite, where the body-centred form with a 14 Å c axis is the stable form. The relations at the anorthite end of the series are extremely complex, and recent studies suggest a possible solvus for bytownite compositions. At the albite end of the series, where the peristerites are found in the composition range An_2–An_{16}, it is likely that these represent a solvus, although it has not been proved experimentally, nor has the temperature of the crest of this possible solvus been determined. At high water pressures the solidus and liquidus are lowered, but the shape of the plagioclase loop is not greatly changed.

The melting relations also have been determined in the absence of water at pressures of one bar and 10 and 20 kilobars (Figure 7). At ten kilobars anorthite melts incongruently to corundum + liquid, and at higher pressures the corundum + liquid field extends to more sodium-rich compositions. At 26 kilobars congruent melting occurs only between pure albite and $Ab_{85}An_{15}$. At pressures above 32 kilobars albite melts to jadeite + liquid, so that above this pressure no plagioclase of any kind can crystallize from a melt.

Ternary system. Phase relations in the ternary feldspar system (*i.e.*, the sodium–potassium–calcium feldspar system) have not been completely determined experimentally, mainly because of the viscosity of the melts and the difficulty of attaining equilibrium. At atmospheric pressure only the liquidus surface has been determined, and, because of the incongruent melting of potassium-rich compositions, the system is quaternary.

Crystallization in this system is exceedingly complex because the two solid phases are ternary solid solutions, and with falling temperature these solid solutions approach each other in composition. For certain bulk compositions it can be shown that, at some stage during equilibrium crystallization, one of the feldspars present may be dissolving while the other is precipitating. Different bulk

Importance of the solvus

The most important feature of the diagram is that it is dominated by a solvus (a boundary between a homogeneous field of solid solution and a field of two or more solid phases derived from the homogeneous one), whose crest lies at some temperature above 700° C. The experimentally determined solvus has a crest at about 690° C at a water pressure of two kilobars, but this was determined using completely disordered feldspars: it is likely that some aluminum–silicon order is present in the crystals stable at this temperature, and the effect is to raise the crest of the solvus. The exact location of the solvus cannot be determined precisely because there will be an infinite number of metastable solvi, depending on the

Plagioclase solid solution series

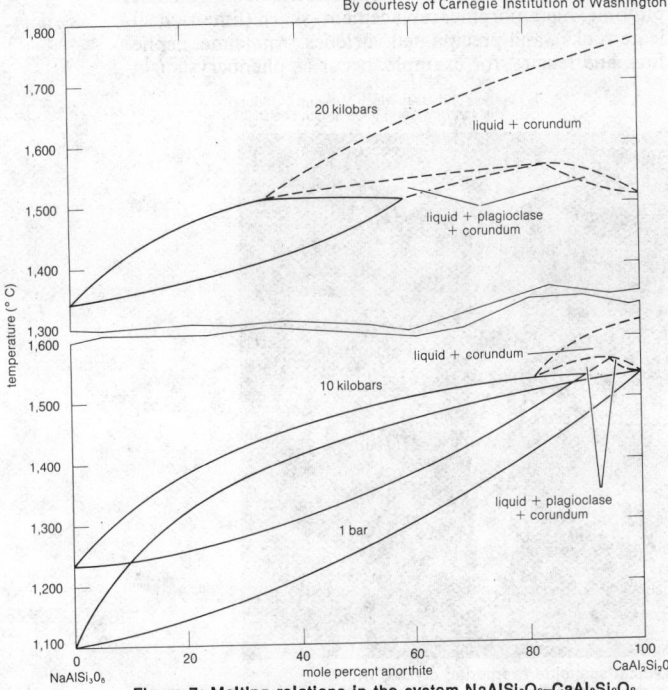

By courtesy of Carnegie Institution of Washington

Figure 7: Melting relations in the system NaAlSi₂O₈–CaAl₂Si₂O₈ at one bar, 10 kilobars, and 20 kilobars (see text).

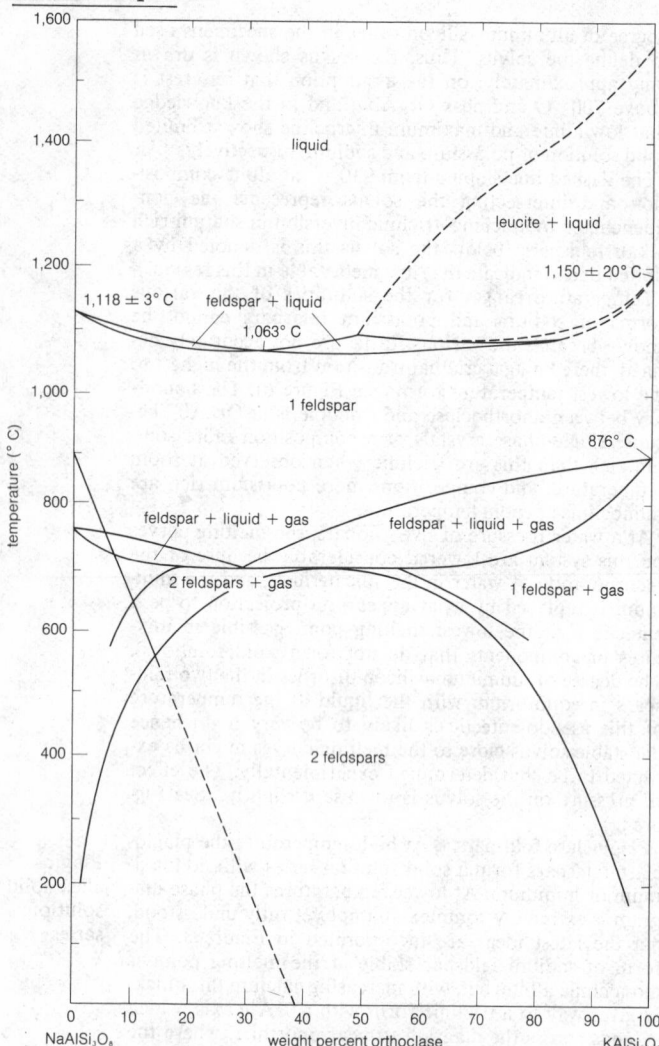

Figure 8: Phase relations in the system NaAlSi₃O₈–KAlSi₃O₈ at atmospheric pressure and at P_{H_2O} = 5 kb, showing the effect of P_{H_2O} on the melting point (see Figure 6) and the solvus.

compositions behave differently, and a detailed discussion of the variations in crystallization paths is beyond the scope of this article.

BIBLIOGRAPHY. W.A. DEER, R.A. HOWIE, and J. ZUSSMAN, *Rock-Forming Minerals*, vol. 4, *Framework Silicates* (1963), a standard work on the common rock-forming minerals, giving chemical analyses of representative samples, crystal structures, optical properties, and paragenesis—includes an extensive, well-illustrated section on the feldspars; T.F.W. BARTH, *Feldspars* (1969), a good modern text on the mineral group; H.V. BAMBAUER, "Feldspat-Familie," in *Optische Bestimmungen der gesteinbildenden Minerale*, vol. 2 (1966), a useful text on the optical properties of feldspars; *Thema Feldspäte*, vol. 47, no. 1 of *Schweizerische Mineralogische und Petrographische Mitteilungen* (1967), consists of 34 papers on all aspects of feldspars by a variety of authors; A.S. MARFUNIN, *The Feldspars: Phase Relations, Optical Properties and Geological Distribution* (1966; orig. pub. in Russian, 1962).

(W.S.MacK.)

Feldspathoids

The feldspathoids are a group of aluminosilicate minerals that contain the alkali metal sodium and, in some varieties, potassium and calcium. Because extensive chemical substitution occurs in natural feldspathoids, their compositions and crystal structure vary widely and, hence, their physical properties show great variation. Nevertheless, they are often identifiable in the field on the basis of colour, crystal form, and geological environment. Chemically, the feldspathoids lie between the feldspars, the structure of which contains no extraneous molecules (*i.e.*, water, sulfate, or carbonate) and permits slow chemical sub-

stitution for the metal ion present, and the zeolites, the structure of which has relatively large spaces that may contain a large number of extraneous molecules and readily permits the exchange of its metal ions—a characteristic that lends water-softening ability to the zeolites. The distinction between feldspathoids and zeolites is somewhat arbitrary, however, and is based more on historical custom than on strict scientific rules (see also FELDSPARS; ZEOLITES).

The most important feldspathoids are nepheline (nephelite), which is the most abundant mineral of the alkaline rocks, and leucite. Others, including analcime, sodalite, lazurite, noselite (nosean), haüynite (haüyne), and cancrinite, are relatively rare. The feldspathoid group is of minor economic importance; nepheline, however, is mined in large quantities in Ontario and the Kola Peninsula as a source of soda, silica, and alumina for glass and ceramic products. It also is used in the Soviet Union in the production of alumina and cement. Leucite has been used in Italy as a fertilizer and as a source of alum.

Lazurite-rich rock formerly was crushed to provide ultramarine, an intense blue pigment long used in painting, printing, and colouring of ceramics, but since the synthesis of ultramarine in 1828, synthetic ultramarine of various shades of blue has replaced the rare and expensive natural product. Blue sodalite and massive lazurite are used as ornamental stones and inlays; the latter rock is called lapis lazuli when it is of gem quality.

The feldspathoids have a crystal structure that is a continuous framework of linked silicate tetrahedra (SiO_4^{2-}, the basic building block of silicate structure), in which a silicon atom is surrounded by and bonded to four oxygen atoms arranged at the corners of a tetrahedron; aluminum replaces silicon in some of the tetrahedrons. Each oxygen atom is part of two tetrahedrons and provides the linking necessary for a continuous structure. Alkali metals and other large atoms and molecules occupy the holes (spaces) between the oxygen atoms. It is the open framework that permits extensive chemical substitutions in the feldspathoids.

The feldspathoids are characteristic of rocks that are relatively poor in silica and rich in alkalies and aluminum. In these rocks they form as a substitute for the more common feldspars (the German name for the group, *Feldspat Vertreter*, "feldspar substitute," reflects this), which require a higher silicate to alkali ratio. Thus, the feldspathoids can never occur in rocks that contain free silica (quartz; SiO_2) as an original constituent. They occur in a variety of alkali-rich rocks, including volcanic, plutonic, metamorphic, replacement, skarn (lime-rich silicate rocks), and precipitated varieties. Analcime, nepheline, and leucite, for example, occur as phenocrysts (sin-

Economic importance

Typical scapolite (wernerite) crystal, with a tetragonal prism capped by a pyramid, Pierrepont, New York.

(Left) Typical trapezohedral analcime crystals, the Alps, northern Italy. (Centre) Sodalite (blue), cancrinite (yellow), nepheline (greasy luster), feldspar (white), and ferromagnesine minerals (black) in a syenite, Litchfield, Maine. (Right) Leucite crystals, with typical trapezohedral shape, weathered out of volcanic rock, Vesuvius, Italy.

By courtesy of (right) Northwestern University Geology Department, Evanston, Illinois; photographs, (left, centre) Katherine H. Jensen—EB Inc., (right) Mary Root—EB Inc.

gle crystals in a finer matrix), and analcime is also precipitated in saline lakes and occurs on the sea floor.

This article treats the crystal structure and physical and chemical properties of the feldspathoids, as well as their occurrence in nature and laboratory synthesis. For further information on crystal structure, see CRYSTALLOGRAPHY, and for associated minerals and mineral groups, see MINERALS and SILICATE MINERALS. Ornamental varieties are treated in the article GEMSTONES.

CHEMICAL COMPOSITION AND CRYSTAL STRUCTURE

Classification of the feldspathoids

Because extensive chemical substitution occurs in natural feldspathoids, a wide range of compositions and associated crystal structures is represented by members of this mineral group. Classification of the feldspathoids, therefore, is best accomplished by grouping members on the basis of chemical composition and structure. Such a classification is presented in the Table, which lists mineral composition, crystal system, and unit cell dimensions. It should be noted that the compositions of most feldspathoids range widely about the ideal formulae that are listed.

The reasons for this classification of feldspathoids will be apparent from consideration of the several feldspathoid groups, the first of which is the nepheline group.

The nepheline group. Nepheline, kalsilite, and kaliophilite have structures similar to that of the high-temperature form of silica called tridymite, and the structure of carnegieite is similar to another form of silica called cristobalite (see SILICA MINERALS).

The idealized structure of kalsilite has potassium atoms occupying the centres of the large voids in a framework that contains sheets of tetrahedra. The vertices of these tetrahedra are oxygen atoms, and at their centres are silicon and aluminum atoms. Alternate tetrahedra point up (U) like an Egyptian pyramid and share one oxygen (at the tetrahedron's base) with each of three tetrahedra pointing down (D), as shown in Figure 1. The next higher

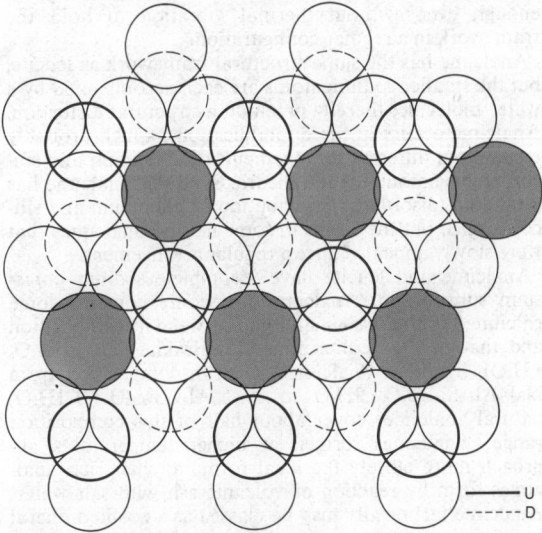

Figure 1: Crystal structure of kalsilite (see text).

sheet is joined to the first sheet by sharing of oxygen atoms at the top of U tetrahedra so that, in projection, U of the first sheet is under D of the next higher sheet. D of the first sheet comes over U of the next lower sheet. In this structure the oxygen atoms are arranged in the stacking pattern called hexagonal close packing. When smaller sodium atoms substitute for the potassium atoms, the framework buckles to reduce the size of the cavities. For ideal nepheline, there are three small holes for sodium and one large hole for potassium. The expanded kalsilite is able to accommodate only a few sodium atoms before it buckles to the nepheline structure, which can accommodate an extremely large range of compositions. The cell dimensions (see the Table) change with the chemical substitution, and the chemical composition can be estimated from X-ray diffraction data (see CRYSTALLOGRAPHY). Not only does nepheline permit sodium–potassium substitution but it also permits substitution of silicon for aluminum with corresponding absence of alkali atoms to adjust the charges. Kaliophilite and other rare minerals have different degrees of distortion. The relation between tridymite and cristobalite frameworks is analogous to hexagonal and cubic close packing of equal spheres; in

Classification of Feldspathoids According to Composition and Structure

	idealized composition	crystal system*	unit cell dimensions†
Nepheline	$Na_3KAl_4Si_4O_{16}$	hexagonal	a 10.0, c 8.4
Kalsilite	$KAlSiO_4$	hexagonal	a 5.1, c 8.7
Kaliophilite	$KAlSiO_4$	hexagonal	a 26.9, c 8.5
Carnegieite (high)	$NaAlSiO_4$	isometric	a 7.3
Carnegieite (low)	$NaAlSiO_4$	triclinic?	?
Leucite (high)	$KAlSi_2O_6$	isometric	a 13.4
Leucite (low)	$KAlSi_2O_6$	tetragonal	a 13.7
Analcime	$NaAlSi_2O_6 \cdot H_2O$	isometric	a 13.7
Sodalite	$Na_4Al_3Si_3O_{12}Cl$	isometric	a 8.9
Hydroxysodalite	$Na_4Al_3Si_3O_{12}OH$	isometric	a 8.9
Noselite (nosean)	$Na_8Al_6Si_6O_{24}(SO_4)H_2O$	isometric	a 9.1
Haüynite (haüyne)	$Na_6Ca_2Al_6Si_6O_{24}(SO_4)_2$	isometric	a 9.1
Cancrinite	$Na_6Ca_2Al_6Si_6O_{24}(CO_3)_23H_2O$	hexagonal	a 12.7, c 5.1
Natrodavyne	$Na_{10}Al_6Si_6O_{24}(CO_3)_2 \cdot xH_2O$	hexagonal	a 12.7, c 5.1
Vishnevite	$Na_8Al_6Si_6O_{24}(SO_4)3H_2O$	hexagonal	a 12.7, c 5.1
Scapolite	(family name)		
Marialite	$Na_4Al_3Si_9O_{24}Cl$	tetragonal	a 12.1, c 7.6
Meionite	$Ca_4Al_6Si_6O_{24}CO_3$	tetragonal	a 12.2, c 7.6

*In the isometric system crystals are referable to three mutually perpendicular crystallographic axes of equal length. Tetragonal crystals also are referable to three mutually perpendicular axes, two of which are of equal length and the third longer or shorter. In the hexagonal system three axes of equal length intersect at angles of 120° and are perpendicular to a fourth axis that may be longer or shorter. The three axes of triclinic crystals are inclined relative to each other and are of differing lengths. †The unit cell is the smallest volume that contains a complete sample of the atomic or molecular groups that comprise a particular mineral. Dimensions are given in angstrom units (one angstrom equals 10^{-8} centimetres), and the letters a and c refer to directions along the crystallographic axes. In the isometric system all axes are of equal length and only one value (a) is given. Similarly, in the tetragonal system a refers to the two axes that are of equal length and c to the third, and in the hexagonal system a represents the cell dimensions along each of the three axes of equal length and c represents the fourth.

hexagonal close packing, every second layer is oriented the same as the original layer, whereas in cubic close packing every third layer has that orientation. At high temperatures, nepheline of composition $NaAlSiO_4$ changes to carnegieite, the cristobalite-like framework of which consists of identical sheets of U and D tetrahedra, but every third sheet is rotated by 60° with respect to the ideal tridymite structure. Upon cooling, the high-order, isometric (cubic) symmetry of carnegieite changes discontinuously at 690° C (1,275° F) to low-order symmetry as a result of framework collapse. The crystal system of this carnegieite may be triclinic, as indicated in the Table.

Nepheline that has been annealed in metamorphic (altered) rocks shows complex X-ray patterns that indicate a special arrangement of atoms. Nepheline from volcanic rocks typically deviates considerably from the composition $Na_3KAl_4Si_4O_{16}$, whereas nepheline from low-temperature environments is much closer to this ideal formula. Calcium commonly substitutes for sodium and iron for aluminum.

Leucite and analcime. Leucite has an aluminosilicate framework that is too complex to describe here: four-, six-, and 12-membered rings of tetrahedra occur in the framework. Above 625° C (1,150° F) leucite has isometric symmetry, with potassium atoms vibrating at the centre of the large cavities; below 625° C the framework buckles sharply, producing a one-sided distortion and reduction of size of the cavities occupied by the potassium atoms. The mineral pollucite, a cesium-bearing hydrated aluminosilicate ($CsAlSi_2O_6 \cdot H_2O$), remains isometric at all temperatures because the cesium atoms are large enough even without thermal vibration to hold the framework in a regular configuration.

Analcime has the same structural framework as leucite, but the smaller sodium atoms are each accompanied by a water molecule, thereby precluding structural distortion. Analcime occurs in three modifications, which probably result from different arrangements of aluminum and silicon atoms among the tetrahedra. Synthetic analcime has a random (disordered) distribution of aluminum and silicon atoms, but the atoms in some natural analcimes that were slowly annealed have a regular arrangement.

Analcime and leucite have incomplete sodium–potassium substitution. Analcime commonly contains some calcium, but there is a major gap between its composition and that of the zeolite mineral wairakite ($Ca_{0.5}AlSi_2O_6 \cdot H_2O$). Synthetic analcimes range in composition from $Na_{1.2}Al_{1.2}Si_{1.8}O_6O \cdot 9H_2O$ to $Na_{0.75}Al_{0.75}Si_{2.25}O_6 \cdot 1.1H_2O$; natural analcimes cover about half of this composition range. Analcimes formed at higher temperatures approach more closely the ideal formula; silica-rich analcimes form by reaction of volcanic ash with salt water. Analcime technically may be classed as a zeolite mineral because the water is removed reversibly by heating up to 150° C (300° F) and because the alkali atoms can be ion exchanged reversibly (for these properties of analcime see ZEOLITES).

The sodalite and cancrinite groups. The sodalite and cancrinite groups have aluminosilicate groups related in an elegant way (see Figure 2). In sodalite the aluminum and silicon atoms lie at the corners of imaginary truncated octahedra (the Archimedean semiregular polyhedron, which has eight hexagonal faces formed by truncating the six corners) close packed on the hexagonal faces to fill the space completely. Although the symmetry is isometric, it appears to be hexagonal when viewed perpendicular to one set of imaginary faces; there are three sets of parallel hexagonal faces that are so stacked one behind the other that in projection they appear to have a hexagonal orientation around a central hexagonal face. The centres of the hexagonal faces in sodalite have positions that are analogous to the cubic close packing of spheres.

In cancrinite, two sets of hexagonal faces are stacked one behind the other so that in projection they form a hexagonal pattern around a rather large 12-sided void. The centres of the hexagons in this case have positions analogous to hexagonal close packing of spheres.

Modifications of analcime

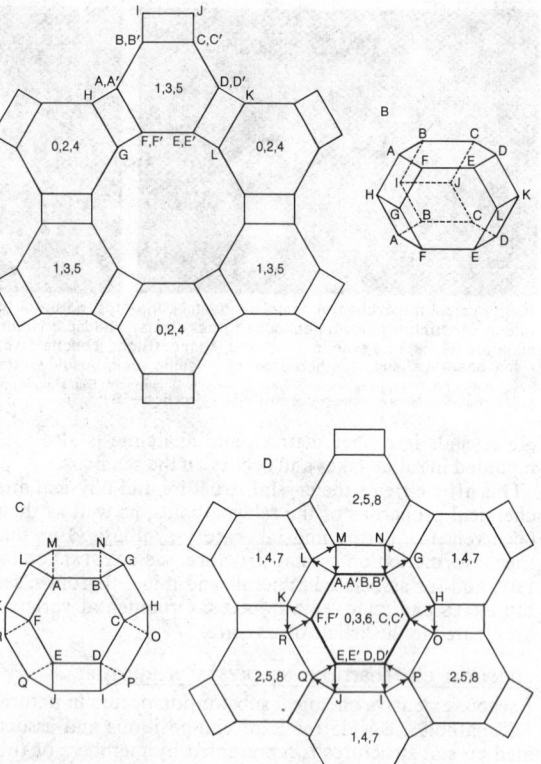

Figure 2: *Two-dimensional projections of three-dimensional aluminosilicate frameworks of cancrinite and sodalite.*
The Si and Al atoms occur at the line Intersections and oxygen atoms at the middle of the line segments. In cancrinite (A), there are hexagonal rings superimposed so that they lie either at heights 0,2,4, etc., or at 1,3,5, etc. The edges of the rings form tilted squares. In (B) a perspective diagram shows the unit formed from the labelled intersections of (A). In sodalite (C), the hexagonal rings superimposed at 0,3,6, etc., 1,4,7, etc., and 2,5,8, etc., forming truncated octahedra as shown by the perspective drawings of (D). Corresponding intersections are labelled. The upper hexagonal face of a truncated octahedron is emphasized in (C), and descending lines are shown by the arrows.

In sodalite all of the cavities between the oxygen atoms (which lie nearly at the centres of the edges of the truncated octahedron) are near spherical and are connected by apertures in the six-membered rings. In cancrinite there are much larger cavities connected by 12-membered rings, and, in addition, there are smaller cavities. The large cavities and channels permit easy movement of atoms. In the sodalite group, the large chlorine, sulfate, or sulfide units fit nicely in the truncated octahedra, while the sodium atoms lie close to the six-membered rings of oxygen atoms. In cancrinite the carbonate group lies at the centre of the large cavities, while the sodium atoms and water molecules occupy other convenient positions.

The scapolite group. The aluminosilicate framework of scapolite, sometimes also called wernerite, is composed of two types of four-membered rings of tetrahedra. One type has alternate tetrahedra pointing upward (U) and downward (D), and the other type has tilted tetrahedra (T_1, T_2), each of which has an innermost edge that is horizontal and an outermost edge that is vertical; the rings of T_1 and of T_2 tetrahedra are at different levels (see Figure 3). These four-membered rings are so linked that each U tetrahedron has a D tetrahedron above it and a T_2 tetrahedron below it and to the side, whereas each D tetrahedron has a U tetrahedron below it and a T_1 tetrahedron above it and to the side. This arrangement forms vertical five-membered rings composed of two U, two D, and one T tetrahedra.

Chlorine atoms or carbonate groups lie in the large cavities between the T rings. Calcium atoms occur in the elongated cavities bonded to oxygen atoms and to chlorine atoms or carbonate groups.

The distribution of aluminum and silicon atoms in

Structures of the scapolite group

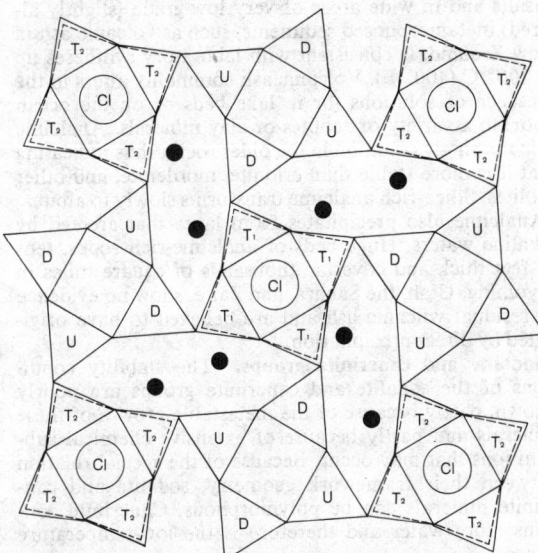

Figure 3: Scapolite structure shown as two-dimensional projection. (See text for explanation of U, D, and T.) Chlorine atoms lie in cavities marked Cl, while Ca atoms occupy in projection the places marked by heavy dots.

scapolite is complex. In all framework structures, the best electrostatic stability results when not more than one aluminum atom is attached to each oxygen. In marialite, each aluminum atom alternates with three silicon atoms in conformity with this rule. In pure meionite with one aluminum atom for each silicon atom, this rule would be violated because no more than two aluminum atoms would be placed in the five-membered rings. Indeed, few if any scapolites closely approach the meionite composition. The relatively low-order symmetry of at least some scapolites is probably caused by special ordering patterns of the aluminum and silicon atoms and perhaps by special orientations of carbonate molecules.

PHYSICAL PROPERTIES OF FELDSPATHOIDS

Identification of feldspathoids

The physical properties of feldspathoids are rather variable because of the extensive chemical substitutions. Visual examination of hand-sized specimens or microscopic study of thin sections often permits qualitative identification of feldspathoids, but X-ray diffraction and chemical analysis, especially with the electron microprobe, are desirable for quantitative identification. Simple chemical tests also are useful. Feldspathoids decompose in weak mineral acid because of the high aluminum content, and this serves to distinguish them from feldspar. The hardness of all feldspathoids is 5–6 on the Mohs scale (in which talc, the softest, is 1 and diamond, the hardest, is 10).

Nepheline has a specific gravity of 2.56–2.66, is usually white or gray, has a greasy lustre, and is shapeless in plutonic rocks; simple hexagonal prisms are the predominant form in volcanic rocks. Basal and prismatic cleavages (mineral surfaces that parallel crystallographic planes, along which the mineral tends to split) are poor, and the mineral rarely exhibits twinning—*i.e.*, intergrowths of two or more grains in accord with some preferred crystallographic surface or orientation.

Kalsilite is similar to nepheline, but the specific gravity is 2.59–2.62 and its optical properties differ. The most distinctive property for diagnostic purposes is the potassium/sodium ratio, which can be determined by X-ray diffraction.

Leucite and analcime are white, gray, or pink and usually have trapezohedral forms. Leucite shows intimately twinned crystals on the dodecahedron faces when viewed in thin section, and analcime exhibits very poor cleavage. Specific gravity ranges from 2.45–2.50 for leucite and from 2.24–2.29 for analcime. The minerals are best distinguished optically.

Sodalite, noselite, and haüynite can occur in almost any colour when in hand-specimen size, but they are colourless or pale blue in thin section. Specific gravities range from 2.3–2.5, and dodecahedral or shapeless forms are characteristic. Members of the sodalite group are best differentiated chemically because all are isometric with similar optical properties.

Cancrinite and vishnevite also exhibit almost any colour. In thin section these minerals are usually colourless, and perfect prismatic cleavage is characteristic. Specific gravities range from 2.3–2.5, and their perfect cleavage and different optical properties serve to distinguish these minerals from those of the scapolite group.

Scapolite is usually white but, again, colour can be variable. Tetragonal prisms capped with pyramids are typical forms. Major property changes are associated with the structural–compositional change from marialite to meionite. Specific gravity varies from 2.5–2.6 in marialite to 2.6–2.8 in meionite. The optical properties of scapolite, marialite, and meionite vary with the sodium/calcium ratio and thus provide a good estimate of composition. In addition to their optical properties, the scapolite minerals are distinguished from feldspar minerals by their cleavage angle and absence of twinned crystals and from cancrinite by their lesser solubility in hydrochloric acid.

SYNTHESIS AND NATURAL OCCURRENCE

The natural occurrence of minerals can be treated from a geographic viewpoint, but knowledge of the reasons for such occurrences or the interpretation of the conditions of formation stems largely from experimental data on mineral synthesis. In this sense, the synthesis and natural occurrence of the feldspathoids are best considered jointly, particularly because they commonly grow and develop under metastable conditions; that is, conditions that may permit further change before final stability.

Nepheline and kalsilite. At low temperatures, the stability fields (as a function of temperature for varying compositions between $NaAlSiO_4$ and $KAlSiO_4$) of nepheline and kalsilite are separated by an area in which the two phases do not mix and thus coexist. At temperatures of less than 400° C (750° F) the boundary (solvus) of this area approaches the compositions $KAlSiO_4$ and $KNa_3Al_4Si_4O_{16}$. Nepheline inverts to carnegieite at 1,250° C (2,280° F), and kalsilite inverts to an orthorhombic form (one referable to three mutually perpendicular but unequal crystallographic axes) at 900° C (1,650° F).

Kalsilite occurs in volcanic rocks rich in potassium from Uganda, Zaire, and Italy as phenocrysts (isolated crystals) and in the groundmass (fine-grained matrix). Some phenocrysts consist of an intergrowth of kalsilite with nepheline resulting from breakup of a high-temperature, potassium-rich nepheline. Kalsilite also occurs in the linings of blast furnaces.

Kaliophilite occurs only in ejected blocks from Italian volcanoes, where it probably grew metastably at a temperature of about 1,000° C (1,800° F).

Nepheline–leucite–analcime. The occurrence of these minerals is intimately related to that of feldspar in the three-component system SiO_2–$NaAlSiO_4$–$KAlSiO_4$. To delineate the stability fields of these minerals it is necessary to consider temperature, hydrostatic pressure, and the pressure of water vapour. In laboratory synthesis, pressure commonly is applied in the form of water vapour. When the crystal products are anhydrous (*i.e.*, waterless), the addition of water acts merely as a catalyst promoting the growth rate. When analcime or melt is involved, however, the water actually enters the silicate material.

Mineral stability fields

Figure 4 shows the composition ranges for the crystallization of the first mineral from a silicate melt containing excess water at a pressure of 1,000 atmospheres (one atmosphere is the barometric pressure at sea level—1.03 kilograms per square centimetre, or 14.7 pounds per square inch). The contours show the temperatures for the beginning of crystallization: these are generally 200°–400° C (350°–700° F) lower than for the dry system. In agreement with these data, kalsilite, leucite, nepheline, and alkali feldspar occur as phenocrysts in volcanic rocks of appropriate chemical composition.

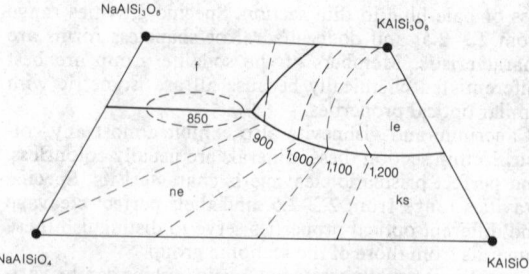

Figure 4: Composition regions at which nepheline (ne), kalsilite (ks), leucite (le), and sanidine feldspar (f) are the first to crystallize from the melt at 1,000 atmospheres H_2O pressure. Temperatures in °C (some estimated) are shown by contours. The boundary between the nepheline kalsilite fields is probably near the 1,200° C contour.

When the liquid has been consumed by crystallizing minerals, the minerals that coexist over temperatures ranging down to 700° C (1,300° F) are as shown in Figure 5. Nepheline coexists with either sanidine feldspar,

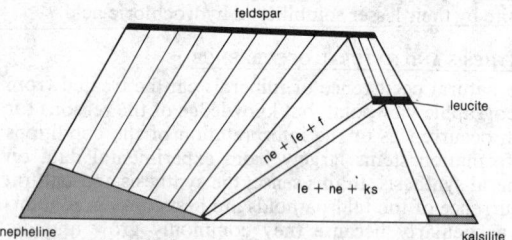

Figure 5: Composition regions in which feldspathoids coexist at temperatures from 700° C to the beginning of melting. In the triangles, three minerals coexist. In the shaded areas one mineral exists. In the striped area two minerals coexist with compositions represented by the ends of the line.

feldspar + leucite, or leucite + kalsilite. At temperatures below 500° C (930° F), leucite is no longer stable, and sanidine feldspar is replaced by microcline and albite.

The natural occurrence of leucite is compatible with the laboratory syntheses because leucite occurs only in potassium-rich volcanic rocks. Important localities are Leucite Hills, Wyoming; central Montana; Rome; Uganda; and Zaire. Pseudo-leucite is the name for trapezohedral crystals of a mixture of nepheline and feldspar plus alteration products. Their origin is controversial, but the most probable explanation is that phenocrysts of leucite, containing considerable sodium, are reconstituted as nepheline and feldspar.

Origin and distribution of nepheline and analcime

Nepheline is the most abundant mineral of the alkaline rocks, such as nepheline-syenites and gneisses, in which it is typically associated with feldspars. Whether these rocks form by igneous processes or by the chemical alteration of sediments by sodium-rich fluids is controversial. Famous localities are the Haliburton-Bancroft area of Ontario; Oslo, Norway; and Alnö, Sweden; Norra Kärr, Finland; and Kola Peninsula, Russian Soviet Federated Socialist Republic. Local reaction of silica-poor magma with carbonate-rich sediments produces other nepheline-bearing rocks in the British Isles at Camas Mor, Muck, and Scawt Hill. Nepheline commonly is accompanied by sodalite, cancrinite, or scapolite. Nepheline in volcanic rocks is glassy, but in deep-seated rocks it has a greasy lustre that is caused by alteration to cancrinite and other minerals. Nepheline occurs in walls of furnaces. In the chemical industry, the $NaAlSiO_4$ composition at temperatures near 100° C (212° F) in aqueous solution yields an important zeolite known as Type A.

Analcime has a tremendous range of environmental occurrences. Under high water pressure, analcime replaces nepheline and feldspar as the mineral first crystallizing from a melt of potassium-poor material. This explains its occurrence as phenocrysts in extrusive rocks, such as phonolites and trachybasalts. At lower pressures, analcime is not stable with a liquid, but it occurs at lower temperatures for a composition range overlapping that of $NaAlSi_3O_8$. The occurrence of analcime in vesicles of basalts and in wide areas of very low-grade (slightly altered) metamorphosed sediments, such as volcanic ash in New Zealand, is consistent with laboratory syntheses up to 200° C (400° F). Volcanic ash commonly alters in the presence of solutions (or in lake beds or on the ocean floor) to a variety of zeolites or clay minerals. Analcime is increasingly common in the older rocks, thus indicating that it is more stable than erionite, mordenite, and other zeolites. Silica-rich analcime transforms slowly to albite.

Analcime also precipitates from lakes that are fed by alkaline waters. Huge beds of analcime-rich rocks, tens of feet thick and covering thousands of square miles in Wyoming, Utah, the Sahara, and Zaire, show no evidence of residual volcanic ash and are believed to have originated by direct precipitation.

Sodalite and cancrinite groups. The stability conditions of the sodalite and cancrinite groups are poorly known, partly because of the metastable growth of these minerals and partly because of extensive chemical substitutions that may occur. Because of the special relation between their framework geometry, sodalite and cancrinite minerals can be polymorphous. Cancrinite contains more water and therefore is the low-temperature phase.

Cancrinite grows from 200° to 1,250° C (400° to 2,300° F), at which temperature it melts to nepheline plus liquid. Hydroxycancrinite grows up to 800° C (1,500° F). Natrodavyne breaks down above 600° C (1,100° F) to a sodium carbonate form of noselite. Continuous chemical substitution exists between noselite and haüynite but not with sodalite. Hydroxysodalite has been synthesized extensively during growth of zeolite molecular sieves. Noselite and haüynite typically occur in volcanic rocks, which is consistent with the data for breakdown of natrodavyne. Noselite occurs in phonolites of the Cape Verde Islands and Wolf Rock, Cornwall, and in ejected blocks of Laacher See, Rhine district. Haüynite occurs in Italian and Laacher See volcanoes and in alnöite rocks at Oka, Quebec, and Winnett, Montana.

Chlorine-rich sodalites occur in both volcanic and plutonic rocks and in metasomatic rocks, indicating a very wide temperature range of formation. Famous localities include the nepheline–syenites of Litchfield, Maine; Rhodesia; Korea; nepheline–syenite pegmatites of Burma, the Republic of Guinea, and Bearpaw Mountains, Montana; phonolites of Scotland and the Sahara; trachytes of Naples and Laacher See. In Angola, sky-blue crystals as long as 20 centimetres occur. The hackmannite variety, characterized by a pink colour that fades on exposure to light, occurs in Bancroft, Ontario; Magnet Cove, Arkansas; Kola Peninsula; and Korea. Famous feldspathoid localities

Cancrinite minerals typically occur as alteration products of nepheline and feldspar or by contact metamorphism of a limestone by an igneous intrusion. Famous localities are at Alnö, Sweden; Fen district, Norway; Iivaara, Finland; and Iron Hill, Colorado.

The scapolite group. Very little is known about the stability of scapolite minerals: indeed, the first proven syntheses were accomplished only in 1962. Scapolite does not occur as phenocrysts in volcanic rocks and, typically, is a metamorphic and metasomatic (completely replaced by chemical substitution) mineral requiring the availability of carbonate and sulfate. The principal occurrences are in regionally metamorphosed rocks of all metamorphic grades in Quebec and Ontario; hydrothermally altered igneous rocks associated with iron ores at Kiruna, Sweden, and Bucks County, Pennsylvania; contact skarns between limestone and igneous rocks in Queensland, Australia; and metamorphosed volcanic blocks of Laacher See.

BIBLIOGRAPHY. W.A. DEER, R.A. HOWIE, and J. ZUSSMAN, *Rock-Forming Minerals*, vol. 4, *Framework Silicates* (1963), is the standard reference with coverage of primary scientific literature up to 1961. LAWRENCE BRAGG and G.F. CLARINGBULL, *Crystal Structures of Minerals* (1965), is the standard reference for crystal structures of minerals covering primary references up to 1964. Primary scientific papers can be located in *Mineralogical Abstracts* (quarterly) and *Chemical Abstracts* (weekly).

(J.V.S.)

Fellini, Federico

With films such as *La strada*, *La dolce vita*, and *8½*, the Italian director Federico Fellini assured for himself a place of prime importance in the history of film making. His best films, all of which were in part written by him, are freely structured tales in which dream and reality, autobiography and fantasy, mingle in a world of symbols. Breaking with traditional techniques of motion-picture production, he succeeded in making the film such a personal medium that his own creative and personal problems became a legend. At the same time he revitalized the medium by emphasizing the dramatic solitude of man in the modern world.

Fellini, 1965.

Family and childhood influences

Federico Fellini was born on January 20, 1920, in Rimini, Italy, a summer-resort area on the Adriatic. Throughout his films there are allusions to persons, scenes, and incidents associated with his childhood and youth in Rimini. Fellini's father, a simple, middle-class food-products salesman who died in 1956, was recalled nostalgically both in *La dolce vita* and in *8½*. His mother, his grandmother, and his aunts also play important roles in the world of childhood that his films evoke. The Catholic boarding school that he attended in Fano is recreated imaginatively as a combination of meanness and liturgical pomp in *8½*. Other salient childhood influences were the theatre and especially the circus, the dazzling impact of which may be seen in his 1970 film for television, *Clowns*. And Fellini's adolescence, during which he often was the ringleader in the escapades of his schoolmates, is reproduced in his film *I vitelloni*.

Bored with his aimless existence in Rimini, Fellini, who was gifted with a talent for drawing, went in 1938 to Florence, where he worked on a humorous weekly and on science fiction serials. In 1939 he went to Rome in the hope of becoming a journalist, and sold caricatures in restaurants. At this time he met the actor Aldo Fabrizi, whose tales of the rough life of the small-time comic actor were to be used by Fellini in some of his films. In 1940, during World War II, Fellini became an editor of *Marc'Aurelio*, a popular satirical weekly magazine. In 1943 he wrote a radio serial in which the actress Giulietta Masina appeared; she became Fellini's wife in that year. When Allied forces took Rome in 1944, Fellini opened a "funny face shop," in which he drew caricatures and made voice recordings of soldiers passing through.

Associations with Rossellini and Lattuada

Fellini became a friend and associate of the director Roberto Rossellini, who was then making *Roma città aperta* (1945; *Open City*), in which Fabrizi played the lead. The film became the best known example of Italian neorealism. Fellini made an even more significant contribution to Rossellini's next film, *Paisà* (1946; *Paisan*). By then, Fellini had fallen in love with cinema, and he went on to contribute to the writing of some of the most important neorealist films, including *Il miracolo* (1948; *The Miracle*), the highly controversial second part of

Rossellini's *Amore;* the U.S. Supreme Court ruled that it could not be banned for being "sacrilegious."

A decisive step in Fellini's career came in 1950, when he codirected and coproduced *Luci del varietà* with Alberto Lattuada, a prominent Italian director for whom Fellini had worked as a writer. Fellini's wife appeared in it and played a very small part in the next film he directed, this time on his own, *Lo Sceicco bianco*, the story of a bride on her honeymoon who is infatuated with the hero of a photographic comic strip. Though neither film was successful financially, he went on the following year to make *I vitelloni*, which struck deep and with bitter sarcasm at the idle mamma's boys of the provinces. It won an award at the Venice Film Festival, and some critics still consider it to be Fellini's masterpiece.

In 1954 Fellini resumed work on an old project, the story of two wandering, scruffy mountebanks, *La strada*. Starring Giulietta Masina, the film was shot on location in the desolate countryside between Viterbo and Abruzzo; the great empty spaces reflect the virtual inhumanity of the relationship between the principal characters. Although it was criticized by the left-wing press in Italy, the film was highly praised abroad, winning the Academy Award and the New York Film Critics award as the best foreign-language film of 1956.

Fellini's next film, *Il bidone* (*bidone* is Roman slang for "gyp"), dealt with petty swindlers. More successful was *Le notti di Cabiria*, again starring Giulietta Masina, this time as a simple Roman prostitute whose confidence in the future never flags. It again won an Academy Award for Fellini. He had a difficult time in getting his next film underway, however, because of its allegedly chaotic script and nearly unknown star (Marcello Mastroianni), but he found an understanding producer in the publisher Angelo Rizzoli, with whom he worked for the next seven years. In the course of making the film, *La dolce vita*, Fellini had Rome's main thoroughfare, the Via Veneto, rebuilt as a set. When the film was finished, it proved to be a panorama of the times, a compelling indictment of the ruthless journalists and *paparazzi* (unscrupulous yellow-press photographers), of television, of the movie-star craze, of decadent intellectuals and aristocrats. Immediately hailed as one of the most important films ever made, it won first prize at the Cannes Film Festival.

The making of *La dolce vita*

Like *La dolce vita*, Fellini's next film has no conclusion but is a tale freed from conventional limitations. Entitled *8½*, after the number of films Fellini had made to that time, it shows the plight of a famous director who is in a creative paralysis, unable to make a film. It achieves a perfect balance between symbolism and realism. It met with violent controversy but also with widespread applause.

A world of fantasy was again explored in *Giulietta degli spiriti*, his first full-length colour film, again starring Giulietta Masina. Its scant success and a series of misunderstandings led to an end to the relationship between Rizzoli and Fellini, who spent the next few years looking for new ideas, and a new financial patron. His next major venture was the *Fellini Satyricon*, inspired by the ancient Roman writer Petronius but also drawing on the works of another ancient Roman author, Apuleius, and others. The film tells of the wanderings of a group of aimless young men in the world of antiquity. Without concern for historical accuracy, Fellini attempted to explore the human condition in an age before men knew Christianity and the concept of original sin. Fascinating in its flamboyant, colourful images, *Fellini Satyricon* is often bizarre. Perhaps as a reaction, Fellini's next film, *Clowns*, sponsored by Italian, French, and German television, returned to autobiography. A moving tribute to the world of the circus, it recalls, because of its simplicity and coherence, the poetic spell of *La strada*.

MAJOR WORKS
Luci del varietà (1950; *Variety Lights*); *Lo Sceicco bianco* (1952; *The White Sheik*); *I vitelloni* (1953; "Spivs"); *La strada* (1954; "The Street"); *Il bidone* (1955; *The Swindle*); *Le notti di Cabiria* (1956; *The Nights of Cabiria*); *La dolce vita* (1960; "The Sweet Life"); *Otto e mezzo* (1963; *8½*); *Giulietta degli spiriti* (1965; *Juliet of the Spirits*); *Fellini Satyricon* (1969); *The Clowns* (1970).

BIBLIOGRAPHY. ANGELO SOLMI, *Storia di Federico Fellini* (1962; Eng. trans., *Fellini*, 1967), contains critical analyses of the production and contents of Fellini's films and includes biographical notes.

(A.So.)

Fencing

Fencing (French *escrime;* Italian *scherma*) is a sport involving the skillful use of swords for attack or defense according to set rules and movements. It has a long and fascinating history, and its roots can be traced to the traditions of chivalry. The sport has been included in the program of every Olympic Games since their revival in Athens in 1896, and today it is increasingly practiced throughout the world. The sport is divided into three major branches, depending on the weapons employed: foils, sabres, and épées.

This article covers the origins and early history of swords and swordsmanship and the development and organization of fencing as a sport of national and world competition and championships. Fencing weapons and equipment, the conduct of matches, and principles and techniques are described in the context of understanding the action and strategy of the sport.

HISTORY

Origins and early history. Swords in many different forms have been used by man since before the dawn of recorded history. There are many examples of well-made swords dating from the Bronze Age. Swordsmanship was practiced widely by all the ancient civilizations—Persian, Babylonian, Egyptian, Greek, and Roman—both as a pastime and in single combat and war.

The earliest record of a fencing match is to be found in a relief carving in the temple of Madīnat Habu near Luxor in Upper Egypt built by Rameses III about 1190 BC. This certainly depicts a practice bout or a tournament and not a battle or duel, because the points of the swords are covered, and the fencers, who are parrying with narrow shields strapped to the left arm, are wearing masks, tied to their wigs and fitted with large bibs and padded over the ears. The relief includes a group of spectators from Syria, the Sudan, and Egypt, and the judges and other officials can be recognized by their feathered wands. A hieroglyphic inscription records one fencer as saying "On guard and admire what my valiant hand shall do."

In the Middle Ages swords were heavy and clumsy, and an astonishing amount of strength was required to wield the long two-handed swords, the battle axes, and the maces and other lethal weapons that have survived. The general use of armour made it impossible to apply skill and finesse in the use of the weapons required to bludgeon the well-protected adversary into submission.

The introduction of gunpowder in the 14th century led gradually to the disuse of complete armour in war, and this caused a transformation of weapons to lighter and more manageable forms. Without the protection afforded by armour, skillful swordplay became of paramount importance. By the 15th century, guilds of fencing masters were formed throughout Europe to develop the art of swordsmanship. One of the first, and perhaps the most famous, of these guilds was the Marxbrüder or the Association of St. Marcus of Löwenberg, with headquarters at Frankfort and branches in many other towns. The Marxbrüder were granted letters patent by the Emperor Frederick at Nürnberg in 1480.

The guilds, or fencing schools, became very powerful and jealously guarded their monopoly of teaching fencing. The early fencing methods were somewhat rough and ready and included almost as many wrestling tricks as fencing strokes. Various strokes were "discovered" by different guilds and were sold for large sums to their pupils as being guaranteed to bring success in combat. These "secret" strokes were, of course, more or less orthodox fencing movements, some of which are still in use. But when they were first devised and assiduously practiced in great secrecy, they no doubt proved most effective when suddenly produced in combat.

An example of this occurred during a duel which took place at Saint-Germain-en-Laye on July 10, 1547, between Guy Chabot, baron de Jarnac, and François de Vivonne, seigneur de La Châtaigneraie, the finest swordsman and wrestler in France, in the presence of King Henry II and his court. La Châtaigneraie was so certain of success that he had had a banquet prepared to celebrate his victory. But suddenly Jarnac produced a hitherto unknown stroke, a drawing cut inside the knee that severed the hamstrings of his opponent, who was so mortified that he refused all aid and died from loss of blood. This stroke is known as the *coup de Jarnac.* Another secret stroke called *botte de Nevers*, reportedly invented by a Parisian fencing master and first used in a duel by the Duc de Nevers was in fact a stop hit between the eyes.

Emergence of swordsmanship. The Italians are said to have been the first to discover the effectiveness of the dextrous use of the point rather than the edge of the sword. By the end of the 16th century, their lighter weapons and simple, nimble, and controlled fencing style had spread throughout Europe as rapier fencing. The Italians may therefore be credited with being the originators of true swordsmanship that emphasizes skill and speed rather than force. Most of the wrestling tricks were abandoned, the lunge was discovered, and fencing may be said to have been established as an art.

The long rapier then used was a beautifully balanced sword, excellent in attack and for keeping the opponent at a distance but too heavy to carry out all the offensive and defensive movements required in combat. Defense was effected by parrying with the left hand, which was armed with a dagger or protected by a gauntlet or cloak. The opponent's thrusts were often avoided by ducking (*passata sotto*) or by the side step (*in quartata*). Rapier fencing was thus a two-handed contest in which the fencers stood almost square to each other as they circled around seeking advantage of light or terrain.

In the early 17th century, the Spaniards developed a specialized school of rapier fencing based on a complex series of movements related to various lines drawn within a circle on the ground about which the fencers moved with mathematical precision. This method was never adopted as widely as the Italian school.

In the last half of the 17th century, the evolution of swords and swordsmanship changed dramatically with a general change of style in dress. At the court of Louis XIV in France, fashion decreed the wearing of silks and satins—panniered dresses and elaborate coiffures for the ladies, silk stockings, breeches, and brocaded coats for the men. The long trailing rapier had been appropriate for the doublet and hose, the top boots, and cloaks of an earlier age but was no longer suitable for the elegance of the court of the Sun King. Every gentleman had, however, always to carry a sword, ready to defend his honour, so fashion decreed the wearing of a light, short court sword. The French court set the tone in Europe as surely as the Italians had done in earlier times. Proficiency with the small sword soon became an indispensable accomplishment for every gentleman.

Development as a sport. Although at first regarded with derision as mere "toys," it was soon recognized that the short court sword was an ideal light weapon with which all attacking and defensive movements could be performed using one weapon wielded with one hand. The use of the left hand or of the dagger was no longer required. Hits were made with the point only, and defense was effected mostly by the blade alone. Swift and subtle swordplay became a reality, and true fencing, as it is understood today, emerged as the light sword of the French school rapidly displaced rapier fencing. The speed with which light swords could be used at close quarters, even when practicing with blunted weapons, involved the risk of injury to the eyes: indeed it was said that no good fencing master could hope to end his days with two eyes. It is a curious fact that although the mask was used by the ancient Egyptians, it was quite unknown in Europe until the second half of the 18th century.

To minimize the risk of injury to the participants, it became necessary to impose rules and conventions to regulate fencing with the court sword or its practice counter-

Earliest recorded match

Early schools

Styles in dress and swords

Introduction of rules and conventions: foils

part, the foil. Thus, valid hits were restricted to those that arrived on the right breast, and the fencer who initiated an attack had the "right of way"—*i.e.*, the right to complete his movement, unless it was effectively parried, before his opponent could in turn attack or riposte (offensive action after a successful parry). The "invention" of the mask by the celebrated French master La Boëssière about 1750 made it possible to engage in more complex swordplay. Once the mask was established in general use, longer phrases (sequences of movements), including the remise or redoublement (renewed attacks after the original attack is parried), the counter-riposte (riposte following the parry of the opponent's riposte), and compound movements (attack or riposte involving one or more feints), became possible without undue risk of injury.

The rules and traditional conventions already mentioned had to be maintained and indeed amplified because otherwise swift and complex blade movements made at close quarters, instead of building up a fencing phrase, or conversation with the foils, would have degenerated into a brawl of simultaneous actions that would have been inconclusive and of little interest. These rules and conventions have endured as the basis of the modern rules that govern foil and sabre fencing.

Fencing with the foil became increasingly stylized, but meanwhile duelling continued. The complexities of foil fencing as practiced under the ideal conditions of the schools, with reverence for the set rules and conventions, produced a game that became an art of absorbing interest. But this orthodox, controlled swordplay was of little account on a cold gray morning on greensward or gravel path, when facing a determined opponent with a sharp and heavier weapon who disregarded all conventions. The *épée de combat* was therefore evolved in the mid-19th century. The épée was a regulation, though blunted, duelling sword, and it was used without limitation of target or other conventions. Indeed, when training for a duel, it was customary for those concerned to fence without mask or jacket and with sharp triple points attached to their weapons.

The épée became an established competition weapon fenced without limitation of target or conventions under rules approximating as closely to the conditions of a duel as the use of protective clothing allowed. At first, competitions usually took place out of doors with bouts for a single hit. With the introduction of an electrical judging apparatus, épée competitions were fenced indoors, and the number of hits in a bout were increased to five.

The heavy cutting weapons of the Middle Ages continued as the backsword (single-edged) or the broadsword (double-edged) until the 18th century. Indeed, backswording with "wasters," or wooden swords, or with basket hilted cudgels or singlesticks (one-handed wooden swords or sticks) continued far longer as popular amusements, especially in the English countryside.

In the late 18th century the Hungarians introduced a curved sabre adapted from the Eastern scimitar for the use of their cavalry, and this was soon adopted by other European armies. The heavy military sabre (and its counterpart, the naval cutlass) with its hanging guard and wide circular cuts was used in the fencing schools until the end of the 19th century. During the last quarter of that century, the Italians introduced a light sabre that was soon adopted universally both as a fencing and as a duelling weapon.

The technique of fencing with light sabres was developed by the famous Milanese master Giuseppe Radaelli. This method was later considerably modified by the Hungarian school, which was developed by Italo Santelli (1866–1944) and proved far superior in competitions. Sabre fencing in schools and competitions has become a formal sport with a limited target and is governed by conventions and rules similar to those in force at foil.

Organization and governing bodies. The earliest organizations were the European guilds of fencing masters, mentioned above. In Britain, swordsmanship was practiced from the earliest times. But a statute of Edward I enacted in 1285 forbade the teaching of fencing or the holding of tournaments within the precincts of the city of London because the city fathers regarded fencing schools as places that encouraged duelling, brawling, and all manner of ruffianism. Indeed, swordsmen continued to be regarded with disfavour until Henry VIII, a great lover of all manly sports, granted letters patent to a Corporation of Masters of Defence some years before 1540, thus banding together the more reputable British and foreign masters attached to schools in the first governing body for fencing in Great Britain. The Corporation was given a coat of arms and privileges that included the lucrative monopoly of teaching the art of fencing in the King's realms.

The first governing bodies for fencing in European countries were corporations of fencing masters generally called academies that regulated the training of young masters attached to schools and held regular tests of skill before granting diplomas.

Although fencing had been practiced in schools and clubs for centuries, both as an academic pursuit and as a preparation for duelling, it was only toward the last quarter of the 19th century that it became a competitive sport. The necessity of establishing rules for competitions led to the formation of amateur governing bodies. In Great Britain, a fencing branch of the Amateur Gymnastic Association was formed in 1895, and the Amateur Fencing Association was founded as a separate governing body in 1902. The Fédération des Salles d'Armes et Sociétés d'Escrime was formed in France in 1906.

After the Olympic Games of 1912 at Stockholm, when France refused to take part and Italy withdrew from the épée events because they disagreed with the rules, it was decided to form an international federation to codify the rules for all three weapons. On Nov. 29, 1913, the Fédération Internationale d'Escrime was founded at a meeting in Paris attended by the representatives of nine countries. It has become the amateur governing body for world fencing to which all national governing bodies recognized by their national Olympic committees are affiliated.

Fédération Internationale d'Escrime

Professional fencers have their own governing bodies, or academies, in many countries, and there is a professional world governing body, the Académie d'Armes Internationale.

Competition. Europe has always been the centre of world fencing; but, especially since World War II, the sport has spread to all five continents; and in the 1970s there were over 70 nations affiliated to the International Federation. Besides the Olympic Games, a World Championship and a World Youth (under 20) Championship are organized annually for fencing with all weapons, and these have been staged in such distant places as Moscow, Montreal, Cuba, Ankara, Chicago, and Teheran. Fencing is also included in many regional games such as the British Commonwealth Games; the Pan-American Games; the Caribbean Games; the Oceanic Games; and the Universiade, or World University Games.

The earliest forms of competitive fencing were matches fought for stakes, or prizes, popularly known as prize fights, which consisted of displays and trials of swordsmanship and, from the 16th century, were exceedingly popular with all ranks of the population and were frequently patronized by royalty. In Great Britain these prize fights were held on a stage erected in a hall or a public garden, and the champions would challenge each other to bouts with a variety of weapons. These bouts were often fought with "sharps" (as opposed to blunted blades) and were most sanguinary encounters.

During the early 18th century, James Figg, known as the Atlas of the Sword and the first British boxing champion, introduced fisticuff fights into prize fights. Eventually these bare-knuckle fights became so popular that they ousted the bouts with swords so that prize fights came to be associated with boxing rather than with fencing.

From the end of the 19th century, the major international competitions at foil and épée were dominated by France and Italy and at sabre by Hungary and Italy, although, of course, individual champions emerged from time to time from other countries such as Cuba, Denmark, Sweden, Belgium, The Netherlands, and Poland. In the mid-1950s, however, what has come to be known as the eastern European school was established. This was based on a simplified technique with emphasis on speed, mobility, and physical attributes and the virtual abandoning of the concept of fencing as a complex and highly technical art.

This development was enhanced, especially at foil, by the introduction of the electrical judging apparatus in 1955 that removed much of the uncertainty of human judgement and led to the objective of scoring hits by the simplest methods, secure in the knowledge that the apparatus would record them. This reinforced the emphasis on youth and speed in international fencing, and many world and Olympic champions now may be in their teens or early 20s, a situation that would have been unthinkable only two decades earlier. During that period especially, interest in fencing spread throughout the world. The Japanese, for example, for centuries devoted to their highly stylized sport of fencing with staves (*kendō*), have taken up modern fencing and developed impressive proficiency, especially at foil. The long domination of international fencing by France and Italy has virtually been replaced at all weapons by the U.S.S.R., Poland, Romania, Hungary, and other eastern European countries, and the U.S.S.R. now produces the dominant teams and individual champions at all weapons.

THE SPORT OF FENCING

Challenges and attractions. Fencing provides concentrated physical exercise in a short space of time, independent of the weather, without excessive cost, without the need for a large number of players (any multiple of two persons can fence), or without expensive venues or apparatus. It develops coordination of mind and body. Indeed, it is so concentrated, swift, and absorbing that it is impossible to fence and to think of anything else at the same time. The hard physical exercise combined with total concentration of the mind makes an evening in the *salle d'armes* a complete relaxation from other cares that brings a sense of freshness and well-being.

Those concerned with sport, especially for young people, have long recognized the value of fencing for developing quick thinking, poise, balance, and muscular control and for strengthening the limbs and back. As an individual combat sport, it suits many young people who have no aptitude for ball or other games. It can be started at an early age, say 9 to 12 years old, and can be continued into maturity. Despite the recent emphasis on youth in international competition, there are many fencers who have still been in championship class at the age of 50 or more, and fencers well beyond that age can often hold their own in the *salle* with far younger and faster opponents who lack their experience and technique.

Fencing is a game of skill, speed, and finesse in which there is little advantage in mere brute strength. Control of movement and quick thinking can overcome to a great extent lack of height, reach, or strength that would be a severe handicap in many other sports.

Foil fencing is as suitable for women as for men, and, for the reasons given in the preceding paragraph, members of both sexes can fence together on far more equal terms than is possible at most active sports.

Fencing for women

Fencing is a complex and difficult art to master. The stance, lunge, and footwork do not come naturally to most people, and much practice is needed before the necessary discipline of mind and muscles can be acquired to enable a beginner to use light weapons accurately at close quarters and with considerable speed.

Much of the interest in fencing derives from the need of the fencer not only to induce the opponent to misjudge his real intentions, but to correctly anticipate the opponent's reactions so that he can avoid them. When a thrust is made, for example, the opponent's natural reaction is to deflect the threatening blade by moving his own blade laterally to meet it; this is a simple parry. When making such a parry the sword hand has to move only a few inches across the defender's body whereas the attacker's point must travel several feet to reach the target. Obviously, to land an attack successfully this handicap of time and distance must be overcome.

The simplest way to make an opening for an attack is to straighten the sword arm and make a direct thrust with the point threatening some unprotected part of the opponent's target; this is called a feint. When the opponent moves his hand across to parry the feint, this parry is deceived, or avoided, by moving the attacker's point to the part of the defender's target that is perforce left exposed by the parry.

If the parry is made as described above by moving the sword hand laterally from one side of the body to the other, it can be deceived by passing the attacker's blade under the defender's blade to the opposite and now exposed side of the target, a manoeuvre called a disengagement.

But a parry may also be made by keeping the sword hand in the original on guard position while making a circular movement with the blade to gather the attacker's blade and bring it back to the original position. If the opponent performs this circular form of parry, it obviously cannot be deceived by a disengagement because the circular movement of the defender's blade will collect the attacker's blade. In this case the correct stroke after making a feint is to perform a circle with the point just ahead of the defender's circular parry so that the attacker's blade ends up on the "open" side of the target toward which the original feint was made; this is called a doublé.

Therefore it is obvious that when launching this simple form of attack—a feint followed by a deception of the parry—it is necessary for the attacker correctly to anticipate the defender's reaction to the feint; that is, which form of parry he will favour if the attack is to have any chance of being concluded successfully.

Anticipating the defense

When facing a new opponent, the fencer tries by various feints and movements to ascertain the opponent's likely reaction in order to choose the stroke likely to outwit him. But fencing is a game of subtlety, bluff, and counter-bluff, and an astute opponent may realize what is happening and may appear to favour some form of reaction to induce a certain stroke or strategy from which he, in turn, can profit.

The quicker and more complex the actions that experienced fencers attempt during a bout, the greater the speed of anticipation and execution of the counter movements that will be required. As a result, fencing has been likened to a game of chess played at lightning speed.

Equipment and weapons. Fencing equipment is relatively inexpensive. It consists of a fencing jacket, a mask, a glove, a foil, or other weapon, with trousers or fencing breeches, white stockings and rubber-soled gym shoes or flat-soled fencing shoes.

There is no danger in fencing—even when a blade breaks—provided regulation equipment and a mask in good condition are used at all times. In particular, the material from which fencing clothing is made must be of adequate strength for the weapon used. Thus a stronger canvas is required to resist the stiffer épée blade than is necessary at foil or sabre, and the sleeve, armpit, and breast on the swordarm side must be double lined and an undergarment, or plastron, must be worn. Ladies' jackets must include rigid breast protectors.

Weapons. The fencer's weapon consists of a blade and mounting. The stronger half of the blade, which is nearer to the guard, is called the forte and the remainder is called the foible (see Figure 1). The mounting consists of

From C. de Beaumont, *Fencing: An Ancient Art and Modern Sport* (1970); A.S. Barnes & Co., Copyright © 1970 Kaye & Ward Ltd.

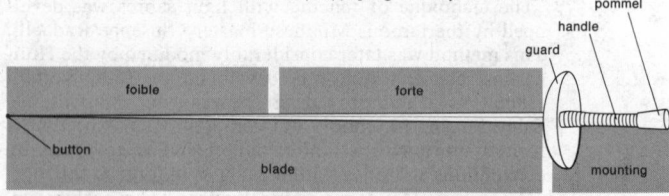

Figure 1: Parts of the sword.

the guard, the form of which varies according to the weapon and within which there is often a small cushion to protect the fingers. There is a handle or grip with which the weapon is held and manipulated and through which passes the shank, or tang, of the blade, to the end of which a pommel or locking nut is screwed. The pommel not only serves to hold the whole sword together but also balances the weapon.

Modern fencing is practiced with three weapons: the foil, the épée, and the sabre. The foil is just over one metre long (1.1 metre or 43.3 inches) and it weighs up to 500 grams (about 17.5 ounces). The blade is rectangular, tapering, flexible, and has a blunt point called the button. The épée is the same length as the foil but is heavier, up to 770 grams (about 27 ounces), and the blade is triangular in section and is rigid. When electrical apparatus is not used, the épée is tipped with three small prongs. When the electrical apparatus is used at foil or épée, a flattened, spring-loaded point is attached to the blade from which wires running down the blade connect to the apparatus. To score a hit by depressing the point requires a force of 500 grams (17⅝ ounces) at foil and 750 grams (26¾ ounces) at épée. The sabre is the same weight as the foil but is a little shorter (1.05 metres or 41.3 inches); the blade is V-shaped and narrow, rigid on the cutting edges but flexible on the flat. The sabre guard sweeps around the back of the hand to the pommel to protect the knuckles against cuts. Because of the emphasis on speed, weapons used are often lighter than the maximum weights stated above.

The piste. The fencing mat, or piste, on which bouts are held consists of a linoleum, cork, rubber, or composition mat or strip about 2 metres (6 feet 6¾ inches) wide and 14 metres (46 feet) long, with an extension or run back at either end of 2 metres (6 feet 6¾ inches). It is marked with a centre line, on-guard lines, warning lines, and rear-limit lines. If a retreating fencer crosses the rear-limit line after having been warned at the warning line he is penalized one hit; if he steps off the side of the strip, he incurs penalties which vary according to the weapon used. When an electric judging apparatus is used at foil or épée the whole of the piste and its extensions are covered with an insulated mat of metal mesh.

Foil fencing. The foil is the basic weapon with which the technique of fencing is learned, even though later on the fencer may prefer the épée or sabre. This is because the foil is the most easily manipulated of the three, and all fencing movements can be carried out with it. Also, the rules and conventions enforced at foil teach appreciation of fencing time, distance, and phrasing. A sound basic technique acquired at foil is easily adapted to the requirements of épée and sabre.

There have long been two main methods of fencing both at foil and at épée, the French and the Italian schools, and practically all variations of technique approximate to one or the other. The fundamental difference between them is the form of the mounting, which determines the method of manipulating the weapon. The French foil or épée has a bell-shaped guard and a plain, slightly curved handle. The sword is held lightly in the hand and is manipulated by the fingers. The first finger and thumb, called the manipulators, direct the sword and impart movements to the blade either by "pulling" or "pushing" with these fingers or by rolling the handle between them. The remaining fingers are wrapped round the handle and are known as the aids. The Italian foil or épée has a crossbar fixed to the inner edge of the guard and sometimes has two metal rings within. The first fingers of the sword hand are slipped through the crossbar, while the pommel of the shorter handle is bound to the wrist by a strap or a long leash. This gives great strength when holding the weapon, but there is a corresponding limitation of finger play. Neither school is superior to the other, but one or the other may prove best suited to the individual fencer's temperament and physique.

Besides these two types, a variety of specialized handles, known as orthopaedic handles, are designed to fit the hand and give greater strength of grip. They often have a flattened extension strapped to the wrist and their use approximates to the Italian style, although they are usually fitted to a French type of guard. Many fencers favour them for the heavier electrical weapons.

The on-guard position. The basic position adopted by a fencer is known as the on-guard position. It is designed to be the position of perfect balance from which the fencer can perform all fencing movements swiftly and smoothly. The distance maintained between two fencers when facing each other on guard is called the fencing measure, normally one at which a fencer cannot hit the nearest part of his opponent's target merely by extending his sword arm but must make a full lunge to do so.

Obviously, the fencing measure will vary according to the height and reach of the fencers, but it also varies at the different weapons. Thus at foil, the nearest part of the opponent's target is the body, and so the fencing measure is shorter than at épée or sabre where the nearest part of the target is the opponent's wrist or forearm.

A fencer adjusts the fencing measure by advancing or retiring on the piste, which is known as gaining or breaking ground. Normally this is done by taking short steps in rapid succession by advancing the leading foot a short pace and immediately bringing up the rear foot the same distance. This enables the fencer to move up and down the piste swiftly and smoothly while preserving the position of perfect balance. Other methods of adjusting the fencing measure are by a short jump forward, known as a balestra, usually followed by a lunge or by a running attack at great speed, known as a flèche.

The most effective way of landing a hit on the opponent's target from the on-guard position is by a swift extension of the sword arm, body, and legs, known as the lunge. The lunge and the recovery to the on-guard position are called the development and the return to guard.

The target. The target area on which a hit is valid varies with the weapon. At foil it is restricted to the opponent's trunk, back, and front and excluding the head, arms, and legs. The collar of the jacket is included in the target, but the bib of the mask, which covers part of the collar, is not. Hits must be made with the point of the foil only and are valid only if they land on the target.

For convenience, the target is divided by imaginary lines into parts that are related to the positions in which a fencer places his sword hand when on guard. When a fencer comes on guard, the parts of his target that his opponent can see above the swordhand are called the high lines and those below, the low lines. The target is divided also by a vertical line; the parts farthest from the

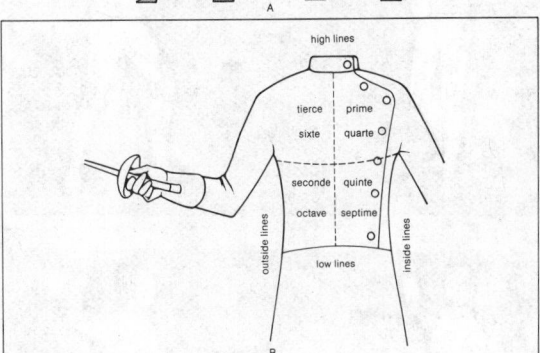

From C. de Beaumont, *Fencing: An Ancient Art and Modern Sport* (1970); A.S. Barnes & Co., Copyright © 1970 Kaye & Ward Ltd.

Figure 2: (A) Foil target. (B) Parts of the target.

sword arm are known as the inside lines, and those on the same side as the sword arm are the outside lines.

There are, in theory, eight lines that are named after the parries that are designed to protect them. Two cover each quarter of the target area. When a fencer is on guard, his sword hand will be so placed that his blade is "covering," or protecting, one of the lines of his target. This is called his fencing position, and he is said to be "on guard in quarte" or some other line.

Basic guard and parry positions. The four positions that are most commonly used are quarte and sixte, septime and octave. The first two protect the high lines on either side of the target, while the last two similarly protect the low lines. In these positions the sword hand is either in supination—that is, with the fingernails upward —or in half supination, with the fingernails to the side. The four remaining positions, prime and tierce (high lines) and seconde and quinte (low lines), are less usually used at French foil. In all four the sword hand is in pronation; that is, with the fingernails downward.

When a fencer threatens with his blade some part of the opponent's target, the latter will move his sword across his body to deflect the attacking blade, which is known as the parry. The parry is named according to the line it is covering. Thus a fencer may "parry quarte" or "parry sixte" and so on.

When two fencers are on guard and cross swords, this is known as the engagement. In this position one fencer is said to be covered when he protects a line with his opponent's blade outside his own so that a direct thrust cannot reach his target. Obviously this covered position is one of

Engagement and disengagement

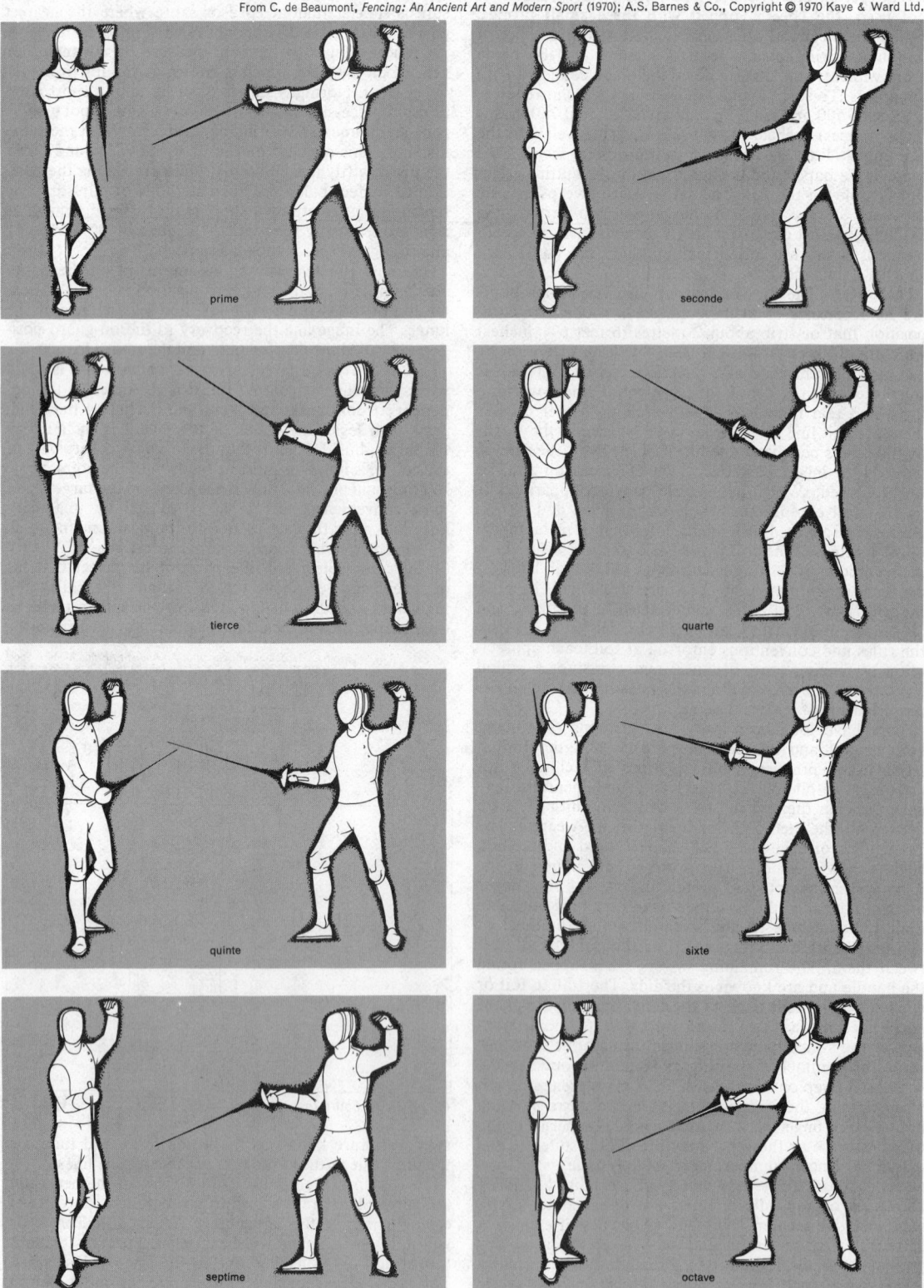

Figure 3: Eight foil parries forming the eight fencing positions.

advantage and security because, in order to attack successfully, the opponent must move his blade into another line either by passing his blade under his opponent's blade by a disengagement or over it by a cutover, or coupé. Fencers frequently endeavour to gain a covered position when on guard by a change of engagement; that is, by moving the blade swiftly by finger play to another line with the opponent's blade outside. This movement can be circumvented by a counterdisengagement.

If two fencers come on guard without crossing blades, they are said to be fencing with absence of blade.

Attacks and parries. The object of fencing with any weapon is to land a hit on the opponent's target. There are two main types of attack. A simple attack is made by a thrust either in the line of engagement (direct) or in an opposite line by a disengagement, cutover, or counterdisengagement (indirect). A compound or composed attack is one in which the final thrust is preceded by one or more false attacks or feints designed to draw the opponent's premature parry, thus leaving some part of his target open for a hit to land.

In defense, a parry is not made by striking the threatening blade aside, which would lead to wide, easily deceived movements, but seeks to place the defender's blade in such a position that it covers the line into which the attack is launched in such a way that if the attack is pressed home it will be deflected clear of the target.

Parries and ripostes

There are three basic types of parries. The simple, or direct, parry is made by the natural reaction that moves the sword laterally across the body to cover the line that is being attacked. The semicircular, or indirect, parry is made from an engagement in the high line to meet an attack directed into a low line, or vice versa. In a semicircular parry, the defender's blade describes a half circle while the sword hand is maintained in its original position. The circular or counterparry is made by a circular movement of the blade without altering the position of the sword arm, so that the threatening blade is gathered and brought back to the original line of engagement.

The riposte. After a fencer has successfully parried an attack, he can, in his turn, take up the offensive by making a reply, or riposte. Ripostes are similar to attacks in that they may be simple, either direct or indirect, or compound.

If an attack is parried and the riposte is parried, the next offensive movement made by the original attacker is called the counterriposte. Counterripostes may be simple or compound, and there may be a whole series of counterripostes in a fencing phrase before a hit is scored.

Counterattacks. In certain circumstances, when an attack is launched, the defender may be able to seize the initiative and score with a counterattack either by making a direct thrust or stop hit or by making a stop hit with opposition that deflects the attacker's blade at the same time. If an opponent can be induced to attempt a stop hit, either by an invitation or a false attack, this can be turned to advantage by parrying the stop hit and scoring with a riposte. This is called countertime, or second intention, and is used especially at épée and sabre.

Preparations of attack. Against an experienced opponent, it is often necessary to create an opening for an attack. This may consist merely of a change of distance by a step forward or backward or some movement designed to deflect the opponent's blade or obtain a reaction from it. Preparations of attack may consist of attacks on the blade such as a beat, pressure, or graze along the opponent's blade or of *prises de fer* (taking the blade) by an envelopment, bind, or *croisé.* These various forms of preparation may be used singly or combined in various ways. They may be used strongly—for example, a strong beat that strikes the defender's blade aside—or with subtlety—for example, a slight pressure that induces the opponent to respond in the same line. These preparations may precede a simple or compound attack and they can be used equally well to make an opening for a riposte.

Competition foil fencing is subject to rather complex rules designed to encourage a sequence of movements that will build up a fencing phrase and discourage a mere series of simultaneous jabs. The judging of a bout at foil is based on the convention referred to above; namely, that an attack, which may be defined as an offensive movement that continuously threatens some part of the opponent's target, has the right-of-way until it is deflected or parried, after which the right-of-way passes to the defender for his riposte. If the riposte is parried, the right-of-way reverts to the original attacker for his counterriposte, and so on until a hit is scored.

Right of way and fencing time

An exception to the foregoing is the stop hit, which is a counterattack made on the opponent's offensive movement. It is usually attempted if the attack is made slowly or with a bent arm or with too many feints or while the attacker is advancing. Under the rules, a stop hit is only valid if it arrives at least one period of "fencing time" before the attack. Fencing time is defined as the time taken to perform one single fencing movement, which may be a blade movement, an arm movement, or a foot movement such as a step forward. As different fencers will perform such movements at different speeds, the period of fencing time will vary according to the fencer.

Épée fencing. The épée is held and manipulated with the fingers in the same way as the foil. The on-guard position, however, is somewhat different because the forearm, being part of the target, has to be protected at all times by the guard of the weapon. Moreover, as already mentioned, the fencing measure is taken from the opponent's wrist. Mobility and lightness of footwork are essential to overcome this wider measure or prevent the opponent from doing so, and for the same reason the flèche attack is much used. Accuracy in placing the point on the small and usually moving target provided by the wrist or forearm, at speed and from any angle, is an essential attribute for an épéeist. The stop hit, countertime, and renewals of attack are much used in bouts with this weapon. Indeed, the everpresent threat of a stop hit brings a special caution to épée fencing. To minimize this risk, preparations of attack, especially *prises de fer*, are much used, and the épéeist tries to ensure that his movements are made covered.

The rules governing épée fencing are designed to make this weapon conform as closely as possible to the conditions of a duel. Hits made with the point are valid wherever they arrive on the opponent or his equipment. There are no conventions about rights of attack and so on. If both fencers are hit, priority between the hits is established entirely according to the relative time of the arrival of the hits. If no practical difference of time between the hit exists, a hit is scored against each competitor, called a double hit. Similarly, if a bout ends with an even score of hits against each, a double defeat is recorded.

A modern duel

Sabre fencing. The sabre is the cut and thrust weapon. Hits at sabre may be made with the whole of the front edge or the third of the back edge nearest the point (cuts) as well as with the point. The valid target includes the arms, head, and trunk down to a line just below the waist.

The sabre is held somewhat differently than the other two weapons, but it is similarly manipulated by finger play. The blade is directed by the thumb and first finger, but these movements are assisted by the little finger. To make a cut, the sword arm is extended and the edge of the sabre is presented at the target.

Great mobility of footwork and exact judgement of distance are essential to deal with the wide fencing measure usually maintained, and the balestra and flèche are much used. The wide target necessitates constant vigilance against a stop hit on the forearm, and attacks on the blade and countertime are much used.

The use of cuts as well as thrusts introduces a special variety into sabre play and gives an advantage at this weapon to the attack over defense. Parries often have to withstand cuts made with considerable force. It is therefore essential that parries be taken firmly by opposing the edge of the sabre to the attacker's blade and ensuring that the principle of defence—namely, opposing the forte of the defender's blade to the foible of the attacker's (which indeed applies at all weapons)—is strictly observed.

There are six parries at sabre covering every part of the target and corresponding, of course, to the lines of engagement. While sixte is rarely used, the normal third position with the hand breast high is differentiated from the low third with the hand held level with the hip and the blade almost vertical.

Sabre fencing, which is conducted according to rules and conventions similar to those that govern foil fencing, combines the conventional orthodoxy of the foil with the tactics and opportunism of the épée. It requires more athletic qualities than either of the other weapons. The use of the edge as well as the point, combined with the comparatively wide target, increases the variety of strokes available. Variations of cadence and rhythm are much used.

Judging of bouts. A bout between men at foil, épée, or sabre is fenced for five hits (best of nine hits). At ladies' foil a bout is four hits. The time limit for a bout is six minutes of actual fencing time for men and five minutes for ladies.

Judging a fencing competition requires great experience because of the complexity and speed of movements and the constant mobility of the competitors. A good judge must be able to "read the phrase"; that is, to follow and

From C. de Beaumont, *Fencing: An Ancient Art and Modern Sport* (1970); A.S. Barnes & Co., Copyright © 1970 Kaye & Ward Ltd.

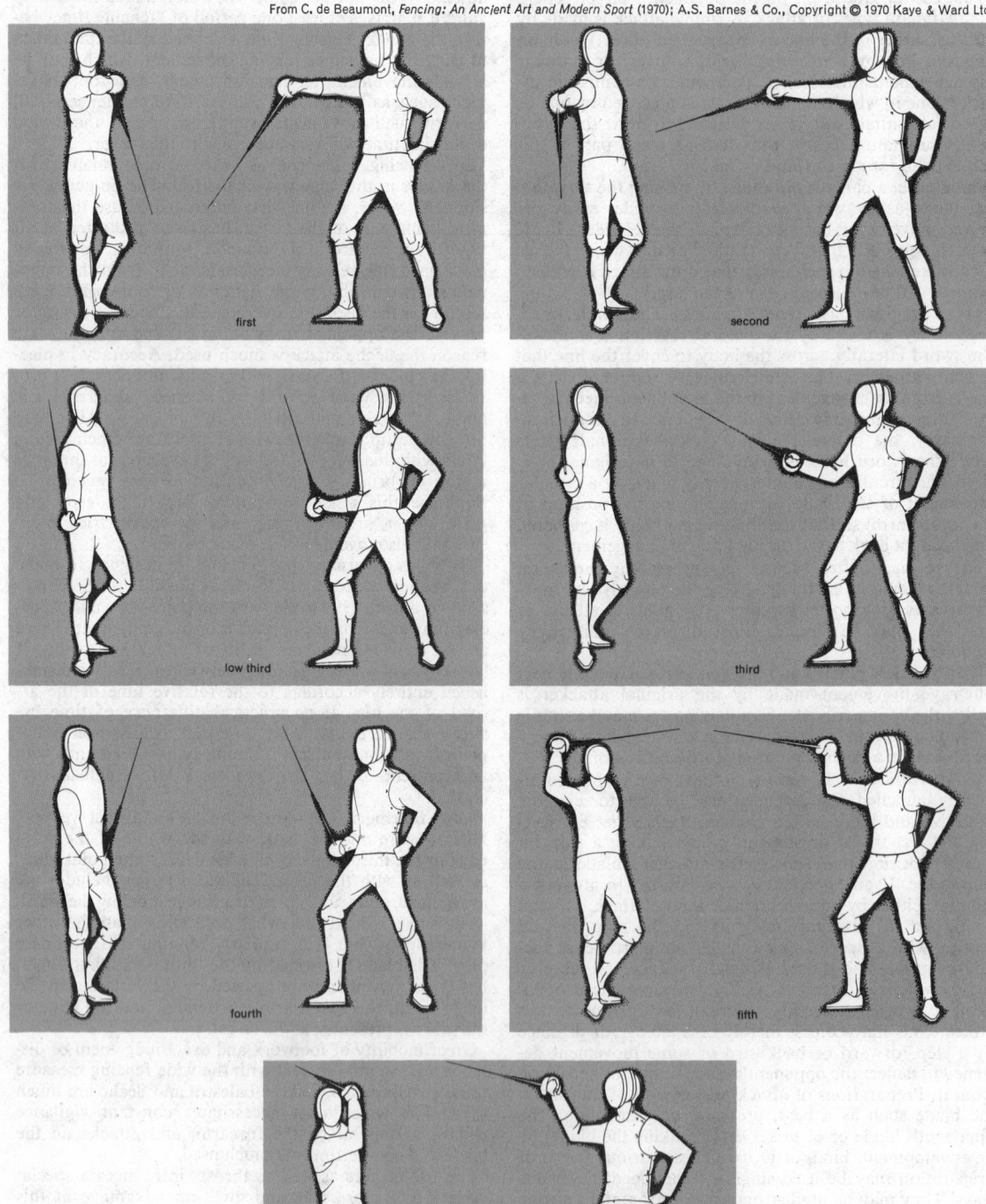

Figure 4: The sabre parries.

be able to reconstruct all the fencing movements exchanged that led up to the scoring of a hit.

Foil and épée competitions are judged with an electrical judging apparatus that registers the arrival of hits. The weapon is fitted with a spring-loaded point connected by fine wires that run down a groove in the blade to a plug inside the guard; this is connected through wires running inside the sleeve of the fencer's jacket to a spring-loaded spool at the end of the piste that takes up the slack as the fencers move up and down, which in turn is connected to the central judging apparatus that registers hits on either fencer by light and sound signals.

At foil it is necessary for the apparatus to differentiate between hits made on the target (the trunk) and hits that arrive off the target. The fencers, therefore, wear metallic overjackets that entirely cover the valid target. A hit on the target is registered by a coloured light, while a hit off the target is registered by a white light. A white and a coloured light on the same side of the apparatus shows that a hit off the target has preceded a valid hit. Otherwise the foil apparatus does not indicate any priority between the arrival of hits on either fencer. It is therefore necessary to have a president (also called a referee or director) to "read the phrase" and award hits according to rules and conventions applicable to foil fencing.

At épée, the apparatus judges completely and automatically because it can time exactly the arrival of hits. If a hit on one fencer arrives more than $\frac{1}{25}$ of a second before he makes a hit on his opponent, only the first hit will be recorded. If both fencers are hit within $\frac{1}{25}$ of a second the apparatus registers a double hit. At épée, therefore, the president directs the bouts and sees that the rules are observed, but the arrival and judgement of hits is completely registered by the apparatus without his intervention.

No electrical apparatus is used for judging sabre. It is necessary, therefore, to have two pairs of judges, one pair at either end of the piste, to observe the arrival of hits and decide whether such hits are on or off the target. The president controls the bout and awards hits according to the rules and conventions applicable to sabre fencing.

BIBLIOGRAPHY. C.L. DE BEAUMONT, *Fencing: Ancient Art and Modern Sport*, new ed. (1970), a standard textbook on all aspects of fencing; E. MANGIAROTTI and A. CERCHIARI, *La Vera Scherma* (1966), a profusely illustrated textbook in Italian on weapon technique; R. CLERY, *L'escrime aux trois armes: fleuret—épée—sabre* (1948, reprinted 1965), a textbook in French by a well known master; ROGER CROSNIER, *Fencing with the Foil* (1951, reprinted 1967), *Fencing with the Épée* (1958), *Fencing with the Sabre*, 2nd ed. (1965), and *Fencing with the Electric Foil* (1961), textbooks dealing with teaching methods, written by a former British national coach; Z. BEKE and J. POLGAR, *The Methodology of Sabre Fencing* (Eng. trans. 1963), a textbook on sabre technique; M.A. EGERTON CASTLE, *Schools and Masters of Fence: From the Middle Ages to the Eighteenth Century*, 3rd ed. (1969), the classic work on the history of swordsmanship.

Classic bibliographic works include: C.A. THIMM, *A Bibliography of Fencing and Duelling* (1886); of French books, A. VIGEANT, *Bibliographie de l'escrime ancienne et moderne* (1882); of Italian works, J. GELLI, *Bibliografia generale della scherma* (1890); of Spanish and Portuguese books, E. LEGUINA, *Libros de esgrima españoles y portugueses* (1891). Standard histories in English are ALFRED HUTTON, *Old Sword Play* (1892), *Cold Steel* (1889); L. BARBASETTI, *L'escrime à travers des siècles* (1928; trans. in *The Art of the Foil*, 1932); and C.E. NEWTON-ROBINSON, *The Revival of the Small-Sword in the 19th Century and After* (1905).

The bi-monthly organ of the Amateur Fencers League of America, *American Fencing*, contains technical articles as well as current reports of competitions.

(C.-L.de B.)

Ferdinand II, Emperor

Ferdinand II, Holy Roman emperor, archduke of Austria, king of Bohemia and Hungary, is known principally as the emperor of the Counter-Reformation—the reassertion and reform of Catholicism—and for his attempted eradication of Protestantism in his lands, which led to the Thirty Years' War. He was born in Graz on July 9, 1578, the eldest son of the archduke Charles, the ruler of Inner Austria (Styria, Carinthia, and Carniola),

and Maria, a daughter of Albrecht V, duke of Bavaria. From 1590 to 1595 Ferdinand was educated by Jesuits at the University of Ingolstadt whose aim was to make him a strict, rigidly Catholic ruler. In 1596 he took over his hereditary lands and, after a pilgrimage to Loreto and Rome, set about suppressing Protestantism by forcing the great majority of his subjects to adopt the Catholic faith. In 1600 he married Maria Anna of Bavaria, who bore him four children. He avoided committing himself in a quarrel between his cousins, the emperor Rudolf II and his brother Matthias, who eventually succeeded Rudolf as emperor. Later Ferdinand secured approval from the Habsburg rulers of Spain to succeed the childless Matthias. In return he promised in a secret treaty (1617), to cede to them the Alsace and the imperial fiefs in Italy. In the same year Ferdinand was recognized by the Bohemian Diet as king of Bohemia and in 1618 was elected king of Hungary. In 1619, however, the largely Protestant diet of Bohemia deposed him, electing Frederick V, elector of the Palatinate, as their king. This was, in effect, the beginning of the Thirty Years' War. Though elected emperor on August 28, 1619, Ferdinand was able to maintain himself only with support from Spain, Poland, and various German princes. Aided by Maximilian I, duke of Bavaria, his troops annihilated the rebel army on the White Mountain, near Prague, on November 8, 1620. He confiscated the estates of the rebel magnates, reduced the diet to impotence by a new constituent ordinance (1627), and forcibly catholicized Bohemia. Protestants of Upper and Lower Austria were subjected to compulsory conversion.

Ferdinand II, engraving by an unknown artist.
By courtesy of the Bild-Archiv, Osterreichische Nationalbibliothek, Vienna

During the first decade of the Thirty Years' War, Ferdinand strengthened his position by transferring the Palatinate's electoral office to Maximilian of Bavaria and, with the help of Spain and the league of Catholic princes of Germany, but chiefly through the victories of his generalissimo Albrecht von Wallenstein, gained important successes over his opponents in Germany and the King of Denmark. Until then the war largely had been confined to Germany, but Swedish and, later on, French intervention turned it into a European conflict. Ferdinand's Edict of Restitution (1629), which forced Protestants to return to the Roman Catholic Church all property seized since 1552, revealed to the German princes the threat of imperial absolutism. Their opposition forced Ferdinand in 1630 to dismiss Wallenstein, the mainstay of his power. The victorious advance of the Swedish army, however, made the Emperor recall Wallenstein. Eventually, for reasons of state, Ferdinand reluctantly gave his consent to a second dismissal and the assassination of Wallenstein, who had treacherously entered into

(margin left column) Electrical judging apparatus

(margin) Early years

(margin right) Ferdinand and Wallenstein

negotiations with the enemy (1634). After his victory over the Swedes (September 1634) at Nördlingen, Ferdinand reached a compromise with the Protestant princes in the Peace of Prague (1635) and, in 1636, succeeded in having his son Ferdinand elected king of the Romans (successor-designate to the emperor). Ferdinand II, who had been married to his second wife, Eleonora Gonzaga of Mantua, since 1622, died in Vienna on February 15, 1637.

Assessment

In the prime of his life Ferdinand was described as a blue-eyed, somewhat corpulent, middle-sized man who wore Spanish court dress. A good-natured, benevolent, affable monarch, he was imbued with the belief in the splendour of the imperial crown and the greatness of his dynasty. Besides German he spoke Italian, French, and Spanish, was fond of music, and liked reading religious books, but his passion was hunting. Although he kept a frugal court, he was a bad financier who too generously gave away the greatest part of confiscated estates to his faithful followers. A very pious Catholic, he especially favoured the Jesuits. Yet, basing his policies chiefly on religious principles, he suffered from discrepancies between his religious goals and the maxims of a modern raison d'état. An indecisive man, he depended much on the influence of his councillors and his Jesuit confessors. Yet in the face of the shifting fortunes of war he showed much steadfastness, although he often lacked political agility. A person of moderate talents and willpower, he nevertheless exerted a strong influence on the events of his time by his strict and uncompromising religious policy.

By promoting the Counter-Reformation, Ferdinand II set the course of Austrian Habsburg policy for the next century. By creating an independent Austrian court chancellery and by establishing in his will the principles of Austria's indivisibility and of primogeniture in his family, he made an essential contribution to the country's national integration. Yet by maintaining the country's historical provinces and estates, after their subjugation, he preserved the principle of federalism in Austria. Ferdinand's Catholic contemporaries considered him a saint-like monarch; his Protestant opponents feared him as a tyrant. Catholic historiography of the 19th century assigned him too high a place, while liberal historians were likely to underestimate his importance. Modern historians tend to view Ferdinand's religious policy as determined by his time, to acknowledge his importance in molding Austria's provinces into an integral whole, and to see in his imperial policy an attempt at creating a Catholic German state, however, inconsistently carried out.

BIBLIOGRAPHY. F. HURTER, *Geschichte Kaiser Ferdinands II. und seiner Eltern*, 11 vol. (1850–64), still has to be referred to above all, in spite of its biassed glorification of Ferdinand. F. STIEVE, "Kaiser Ferdinand II.," in *Allgemeine Deutsche Biographie*, vol. 6 (1877), is the first critical biographical valuation of the Emperor, with a strong liberal colouring. H. HANTSCH, "Kaiser Ferdinand II.," in *Gestalten der Geschichte Oesterreichs* (1962), evaluates the deeds of Ferdinand very positively from a strictly Catholic point of view; H. VON SRBIK, *Wallensteins Ende* (1952), is very critical of Ferdinand. An English-language account is C.V. WEDGWOOD, *The Thirty Years War* (1944).

(H.St.)

Ferdinand II, the Catholic, of Aragon

Known by different names in Sicily, Aragon, Castile, Naples, Navarre, and other kingdoms under his unified government, Ferdinand II of Aragon (Ferdinand V of Castile), called the Catholic, was a monarch who formed a bridge between the Middle Ages and the modern period. He established important bases for national unity in Spain, created the framework for the modern sovereign state, and initiated an international policy of imperial expansion. He has been controversial because of some of his personal qualities and methods of government, but historians have regarded him as a political king, a master of statecraft.

Early life

Ferdinand was born in Sos on March 10, 1452, the son of John II of Aragon and Juana Enríquez, both of Cas-

Ferdinand II (right), detail of an oil painting by an unknown Hispano-Flemish Master. In the Prado, Madrid.
By courtesy of the Museo del Prado, Madrid

tilian origin. In 1461, in the midst of a bitterly contested succession, John II named him heir apparent and governor of all his kingdoms and lands. Ferdinand's future was assured when he came of age, in 1466, and when he was named king of Sicily, in 1468, in order to impress the court of Castile, where his father ultimately wished to place him. In addition to participating in court life, the young prince saw battle during the Catalonian wars. In the summer of 1468, beginning to sow his wild oats, he went courting; the first fruits of these adventures were Alfonso of Aragon, future archbishop of Saragossa and his father's favourite, and Juana of Aragon.

John II was careful about Ferdinand's education and took personal charge of it, making sure that Ferdinand learned as much as possible from experience. He also provided him with teachers who taught him humanistic attitudes and wrote him treatises on the art of government. Ferdinand had no apparent bent for formal studies, but he was a patron of the arts and a devotee of vocal and instrumental music.

Ferdinand had an imposing personality but was never very genial. From his father he acquired sagacity, integrity, courage, and a calculated reserve; from his mother, an impulsive emotionality, which he generally repressed. Under the responsibility of kingship he had to conceal his stronger passions and adopt a cold, impenetrable mask.

He married the princess Isabella of Castile in Valladolid in October 1469. This was a marriage of political opportunism not romance. The court of Aragon dreamed of a return to Castile, and Isabella needed help to gain succession to the throne. The marriage initiated a dark and troubled life, in which Ferdinand fought on the Castilian and Aragonese fronts in order to impose his authority over the noble oligarchies, shifting his basis of support from one kingdom to the other according to the intensity of the danger. Despite the political nature of the union, he loved Isabella sincerely. She quickly bore him children: the infanta Isabella was born in 1470; the heir apparent, John, in 1478; and the infantas Juana (later Joan the Mad), Catalina (later Catharine of Aragon), and María followed. The marriage began, however, with almost continual separation. Ferdinand, often away in the Castilian towns or on journeys to Aragon, reproached his wife for the comfort of her life. At the same time, the restlessness of his 20 years drove him into other women's arms, by whom he sired at least two female children, whose birth dates are not recorded.

Early reign

Between the ages of 20 and 30, Ferdinand performed a series of heroic deeds. These began when Henry IV of Castile died on December 11, 1474, leaving his succession in dispute. Ferdinand rushed from Saragossa to Segovia, where Isabella had herself proclaimed queen of Castile on December 13. Ferdinand remained there as king consort, an uneasy, marginal figure, until Isabella's war of succession against Afonso V of Portugal gained his acceptance in 1479 as king in every sense of the word. That same year John II died, and Ferdinand succeeded to the Aragonese throne. This initiated a confederation of kingdoms, which was the institutional basis for modern Spain.

The events of this period bring out the young king's character more clearly. In portraits he appears with soft, well-proportioned features, a small, sensual mouth, and pensive eyes. His literary descriptions are more complicated, although they agree in presenting him as good-looking, of medium height, and a good rider, devoted to games and to the hunt. He had a clear, strong voice. He was something of a ladies' man, which caused Isabella jealously for several years.

From 1475 to 1479 Ferdinand struggled to take a firm seat in Castile with his young wife and to transform the kingdom politically, using new institutional molds partly inspired by those of Aragon. This policy of modernization included a ban against all religions other than Catholicism. The establishment of the Spanish Inquisition (1478) to enforce religious uniformity and the expulsion of the Jews (1492) were both part of a deliberate policy designed to strengthen the church, which would in turn support the crown.

Conquest of Granada

The years 1482–92 were frantic for Ferdinand. In the spring months he directed the campaign against the Kingdom of Granada, showing his military talent to good effect, and he conquered the kingdom inch by inch, winning its final capitulation on January 2, 1492. During the months of rest from war he visited his kingdoms, learning their geography and problems firsthand.

The conquest of Granada made it possible to support Christopher Columbus' voyages of exploration across the Atlantic. It is not known what Ferdinand thought of Columbus or how he judged his plans, nor can it be stated that the first trip was financed from Aragon; the sum of 1,157,000 maravedis came from the funds of the Santa Hermandad (Holy Brotherhood). Nevertheless, Ferdinand was present in the development of plans for the enterprise, in the negotiations to obtain the pope's backing for it, and in the organization of the resulting American colonies.

At the age of 50 Ferdinand was an incarnation of royalty, and fortune smiled on him. For various reasons, particularly for his intervention in Italy, Pope Alexander VI gave him the honorary title of "the Catholic" on December 2, 1496. But he also suffered a succession of tragedies: the heir apparent and his eldest daughter both died, and the first symptoms of insanity appeared in his daughter Joan. He was wounded in Barcelona in 1493, but this was unimportant compared with the family injuries he suffered, which culminated in the death of Isabella in 1504, "the best and most excellent wife king ever had."

To secure his position in Castile, Ferdinand married Germaine de Foix, niece of the King of France, on October 19, 1505; this was a political marriage, although he always showed her the highest regard. A stay in Italy (1506–07) demonstrated how badly he was needed by the peninsular kingdoms. Once more in Castile, he managed his European policy so as to obtain a hegemony that would serve his expansionary ends in the Mediterranean and in Africa. In 1512, immediately after the schism in the church in which the kings of Navarre participated, he occupied their kingdom and incorporated it into Castile—one of the most controversial acts of his reign.

In 1513 his health began to decay, though he was still able to direct his international policy and to prepare the succession of his grandson Charles. In early 1516 he began a trip to Granada; he stopped in Madrigalejo, the little site of the sanctuary of Guadalupe, where he died on January 23, 1516. The previous day he had signed his last will and testament, an excellent picture of the monarch and of the political situation at his death.

Assessments of Ferdinand

Many considered Ferdinand the saviour of his kingdoms, a bringer of unity. Others despised him for having oppressed them. Machiavelli attributed to him the objectionable qualities of the Renaissance prince. The German traveller Thomas Müntzer and the Italian diplomat Francesco Guicciardini, who knew him personally, compared him with Charlemagne. His will indicates that he died with a clear conscience, ordering that his body should be moved to Granada and buried next to that of his wife Isabella, so that they might be reunited for eternity. He died convinced that the crown of Spain had not been so powerful for 700 years, "and all, after God, because of my work and my labour."

BIBLIOGRAPHY. *V Congreso de Historia de la Corona de Aragón*, 5 vol. (1956–62), the most important study of Ferdinand's life and work, with a full critical bibliography; J. VINCENS VIVES, *Fernando el Católico, príncipe de Aragón, rey de Sicilia (1452–78)* (1951), a well-documented account of the period to 1479; R. DEL ARCO, *Fernando el Católico, artifice de la España imperial* (1939), a fairly recent and complete biography; W.H. PRESCOTT, *History of the Reign of Ferdinand and Isabella, the Catholic of Spain*, 4th ed., 3 vol. (1846), an outstanding seminal work, now somewhat dated; H. KAMEN, *The Spanish Inquisition* (1965), an important contribution to the understanding of this institution; B. NETANYAHU, *Don Isaac Abravanel, Statesman and Philosopher* (1953), an indispensable study for understanding Ferdinand's role in the expulsion of the Jews; T. DE AZCONA, *Isabel la Católica: estudio crítico de su vida y su reinado* (1964), a study of many aspects of Ferdinand's life and work, particularly his religious and ecclesiastical policy.

(T.d.A.)

Ferdowsī

The Persians regard Ferdowsī (Firdawsī, Firdusi, Firdousi) as the greatest of their poets. For nearly a thousand years they have continued to read and to listen to recitations from his masterwork, the *Shāh-nāmeh* ("Book of Kings"), in which the Persian national epic found its final and enduring form. Though written before the Norman conquest, it is as intelligible to the average, modern Persian as is the Authorized (King James) Version of the Bible to a modern Englishman. The language, based as the poem is on a Pahlavi original, is pure Persian with only the slightest admixture of Arabic. European scholars have criticized what they have regarded as the monotonous metre, the constant repetitions, and the stereotyped similes of this enormous poem; but to the Persian it is the history of his country's glorious past, preserved for all time in sonorous and majestic verse.

Legends of his life. The real name of the creator of the *Shāh-nāmeh* was Abū ol-Qāsem Manṣūr (or Ḥasan or Aḥmad), Ferdowsī being a nom de plume. He was born *c.* 935 in a village on the outskirts of the ancient city of Ṭūs (near the city of Meshed in northeast Iran). In the course of the centuries many legends have been woven around the poet's name but very little is known about the real facts of his life. Something can be gathered from the personal references scattered here and there throughout his poem, but otherwise the only reliable source is the account given by Neẓāmī-ye ʿArūẓī, a 12th-century poet who visited Ferdowsī's tomb in 1116 or 1117 and collected the traditions that were current in his birthplace less than a century after his death. According to Neẓāmī, Ferdowsī was a *dehqān* or landowner, deriving a comfortable income from his estates. He had only one child, a daughter, and it was to provide her with a dowry that he set his hand to the task that was to occupy him for 35 years. The *Shāh-nāmeh* of Ferdowsī, a poem of nearly 60,000 couplets, is based mainly on a prose work of the same name compiled in the poet's early manhood in his native Ṭūs. This prose *Shāh-nāmeh* was for the most part the translation of a Pahlavi (Middle Persian) work, the

Composing the *Shāh-nāmeh*

Ferdowsī (lower left corner) with three poets in a garden, miniature from a Persian manuscript, 17th century. In the British Museum.

Khvatāy-nāmak, a history of the kings of Persia from mythical times down to the reign of Khosrow II (590–628), but it also contained additional material continuing the story to the overthrow of the Sāsānians by the Arabs in the middle of the 7th century. The first to undertake the versification of this chronicle of pre-Islāmic and legendary Persia was Daqīqī, a poet at the court of the Sāmānids, who came to a violent end after completing only 1,000 verses. These verses, which deal with the rise of the prophet Zoroaster, were afterward incorporated by Ferdowsī, with due acknowledgements, in his own poem.

The *Shāh-nāmeh*, finally completed in 1010, was presented to the celebrated sultan Maḥmūd of Ghazna, who by that time had made himself master of Ferdowsī's homeland, Khūrāsān. Information on the relations between poet and patron is largely legendary. According to Neẓāmī-ye 'Arūẓī, Ferdowsī came to Ghazna in person, and through the good offices of the minister Aḥmad ebn Ḥasan Meymandī was able to secure the sultan's acceptance of the poem. Unfortunately, Maḥmūd then consulted certain enemies of the minister as to the poet's reward. They suggested that Ferdowsī should be given 50,000 dirhams, and even this, they said, was too much, in view of his heretical Shī'ite tenets. Maḥmūd, a bigoted Sunnite, was influenced by their words, and in the end Ferdowsī received only 20,000 dirhams. Bitterly disappointed, he went to the bath and, on coming out, bought a draft of *foqā'* (a kind of beer) and divided the whole of the money between the bath attendant and the seller of *foqā'*.

Fearing the sultan's wrath, he fled first to Herāt, where he remained in hiding for six months, and then, by way of his native Ṭūs, to Mazanderan, where he found refuge at the court of the Sepahbād Shahreyār, whose family claimed descent from the last of the Sāsānians. There Ferdowsī composed a satire of 100 verses on Sultan Maḥmūd that he inserted in the preface of the *Shāh-nāmeh* and read out to Shahreyār, at the same time offering to dedicate the poem to him, as a descendant of the ancient kings of Persia, instead of to Maḥmūd. Shahreyār, however, persuaded him to leave the dedication to Maḥmūd's name, bought the satire from him for 1,000 dirhams a verse and caused it to be expunged from the

Flight from the sultan

poem. Neẓāmī adds that Ferdowsī also destroyed his rough copy of the satire and that in his day only six verses remained extant. This is, of course, inconsistent with the fact that the whole text, bearing every mark of authenticity, has survived to the present day.

Last days. It was long supposed that in his old age the poet had spent some time in western Persia or even in Baghdad under the protection of the Būyids, but this assumption was based upon his presumed authorship of *Yūsof o-Zalīkhā*, an epic poem on the subject of Joseph and Potiphar's wife, which, it later became known, was composed more than 100 years after Ferdowsī's death. For an account of his last days it is necessary to fall back upon the narrative of Neẓāmī-ye 'Arūẓī. Sultan Maḥmūd was returning from one of his campaigns in India when the minister Aḥmad ebn Ḥasan Meymandī, by means of an apposite quotation from the *Shāh-nāmeh*, reminded him of his shabby treatment of Ferdowsī. The sultan determined to make amends and, upon returning to Ghazna, gave orders that 60,000 dinars' worth of indigo should be given to Ferdowsī and that it should be transported to Ṭūs on the royal camels. The indigo reached Ṭūs in safety; but as the camels were entering the town by one gate, Ferdowsī's bier was being carried out through another. A fanatical preacher had denied the poet burial in the Muslim cemetery, and his body was being taken to its final resting place in a garden that belonged to the poet outside the walls of the town. Ferdowsī was survived by his daughter, who proudly refused the sultan's gift; in the end the money was spent on repairing a resthouse on the boundaries of Ṭūs. Neẓāmī does not mention the date of Ferdowsī's death. The earliest date given by later authorities is 1020 and the latest 1026; it is certain that he lived to be more than 80.

BIBLIOGRAPHY. The only complete translation of the *Shāh-nāmeh* ("The Book of Kings") is still the French version by J. MOHL, facing the text of his edition of the original (1838–78) and also published separately (1876–78). The best and most recent English translation is *The Epic of the Kings* by REUBEN LEVY (1967), which embraces the whole work but summarizes many of the linking passages. T. NOELDEKE's splendid monograph, *Das iranische Nationalepos*, 2nd ed. (1920), remains unsupersoded; and E.G. BROWNE, *A Literary History of Persia*, 2 vol. (1902–06), may still be consulted with profit; but for a digest of research of the past 50 years, see J. RYPKA et al., *History of Iranian Literature* (1968), which also contains a very full bibliography.

(J.A.Bo.)

Fermat, Pierre de

Together with René Descartes, Pierre de Fermat was one of the two leading mathematicians of the first half of the 17th century. In the modern theory of numbers he was without a peer until the time of Leonhard Euler, a century later. Independently of Descartes, Fermat discovered the fundamental principle of analytic geometry. For his methods for finding tangents to curves and their maximum and minimum points, he has been regarded as the inventor of the differential calculus. Through his correspondence with Blaise Pascal he was a co-founder of the theory of probability. For Fermat, a punctilious counselor of the parliament of Toulouse and a lover of classical learning, mathematics was only an avocation. Since he made his living as a jurist, he became known as the "Prince of Amateurs."

Fermat is reported to have been born on August 17, 1601, at Beaumont-de-Lomagne (on his tombstone his age at death is given as 57). Little is known of his early life and education; of Basque origin, he received his primary education in a local Franciscan school. He studied law, probably at Toulouse and perhaps also at Bordeaux. Having developed tastes for foreign languages, classical literature, and ancient science and mathematics, Fermat followed the custom of his day in composing conjectural "restorations" of lost works of antiquity. By 1629 he had begun a reconstruction of the long-lost *Plane Loci* of Apollonius, the Greek geometer of the 3rd century BC. He soon found that the study of loci, or sets of points with certain characteristics, could be facilitated by the application of algebra to geometry through a coordinate

Early work in geometry

system. Meanwhile, Descartes had observed the same basic principle of analytic geometry, that equations in two variable quantities define plane curves. Because Fermat's *Introduction to Loci* was published posthumously in 1679, the exploitation of their discovery, initiated in Descartes' *Géométrie* of 1637, has since been known as Cartesian geometry.

Fermat, portrait by Roland Lefèvre (1608–77). In the Musées de la Ville de Narbonne, France.

In 1631 Fermat received the baccalaureate in law from the University of Orléans. He served in the local parliament at Toulouse, becoming councillor in 1634. Sometime before 1638 he became known as Pierre de Fermat; there is uncertainty as to the authority for this designation. In 1638 he was named to the Criminal Court.

Fermat's study of curves and equations prompted him to generalize the equation for the ordinary parabola $ay = x^2$, and that for the rectangular hyperbola $xy = a^2$, to the form $a^{n-1}y = x^n$. The curves determined by this equation are known as the parabolas and hyperbolas of Fermat according as n is positive or negative. He similarly generalized the Archimedean spiral $r = a\theta$. These curves in turn directed him in the middle 1630s to an algorithm, or rule of mathematical procedure, that was equivalent to differentiation. This procedure enabled him to find equations of tangents to curves and to locate maximum, minimum, and inflection points of polynomial curves, which are graphs of linear combinations of powers of the independent variable. During the same years he found formulas for areas bounded by these curves through a summation process that is equivalent to the formula now used for the same purpose in the integral calculus. Such a formula is:

$$A = \int_0^a x^n dx = a^{n+1}/(n + 1).$$

It is not known whether or not Fermat noticed that differentiation of x^n, leading to na^{n-1}, is the inverse of integrating x^n. Through ingenious transformations he handled problems involving more general algebraic curves, and he applied his analysis of infinitesimal quantities to a variety of other problems, including the calculation of centres of gravity and finding the lengths of curves. Descartes in the *Géométrie* had reiterated the widely held view, stemming from Aristotle, that the precise rectification or determination of the length of algebraic curves was impossible; but Fermat was one of several mathematicians who, in the years 1657–59, disproved the dogma. In a paper entitled "De Linearum Curvarum cum Lineis Rectis Comparatione" ("Concerning the Comparison of Curved Lines with Straight Lines") he showed that the semicubical parabola and certain other algebraic curves were strictly rectifiable. He solved also the related problem of finding the surface area of a segment of a paraboloid of revolution. This paper appeared in a supplement to the *Veterum Geometria Pro-*

Analyses of curves

mota, issued by the mathematician Antoine de La Loubère in 1660. It was Fermat's only mathematical work published in his lifetime.

Fermat differed also with Cartesian views concerning the law of refraction (the sines of the angles of incidence and refraction of light passing through media of different densities are in a constant ratio), published by Descartes in 1637 in *La Dioptrique;* like *La Géométrie*, it was an appendix to his celebrated *Discours de la méthode*. Descartes had sought to justify the sine law through a premise that light travels more rapidly in the denser of the two media involved in the refraction. Twenty years later Fermat noted that this appeared to be in conflict with the view espoused by Aristotelians that nature always chooses the shortest path. Applying his method of maxima and minima and making the assumption that light travels less rapidly in the denser medium, Fermat showed that the law of refraction is consonant with his "principle of least time." His argument concerning the speed of light was found later to be in agreement with the wave theory of the 17th-century Dutch scientist Christiaan Huygens, and in 1849 it was verified experimentally by a French physicist, A.-H.-L. Fizeau.

Through the mathematician and theologian Marin Mersenne, who, as a friend of Descartes, often acted as an intermediary with other scholars, Fermat in 1638 maintained a controversy with Descartes on the validity of their respective methods for tangents to curves. Fermat's views were fully justified some 30 years later in the calculus of Sir Isaac Newton. Recognition of the significance of Fermat's work in analysis was tardy, in part because he adhered to the system of mathematical symbols devised by François Viète, notations that Descartes' *Géométrie* had rendered largely obsolete. The handicap imposed by the awkward notations operated less severely in Fermat's favourite field of study, the theory of numbers; but here, unfortunately, he found no correspondent to share his enthusiasm. In 1654 he had enjoyed an exchange of letters with his fellow mathematician Blaise Pascal on problems in probability concerning games of chance, the results of which were extended and published by Huygens in his *De Ratiociniis in Ludo Aleae* (1657). Fermat vainly sought to persuade Pascal to join him in research in number theory. Inspired by an edition in 1621 of the *Arithmetic* of Diophantus, the Greek mathematician of the 3rd century AD, Fermat had discovered new results in the so-called higher arithmetic, many of which concerned properties of prime numbers (those positive integers that have no factors other than 1 and themselves). One of the most elegant of these had been the theorem that every prime of the form $4n + 1$ is uniquely expressible as the sum of two squares. A more important result, now known as Fermat's lesser theorem, asserts that if p is a prime number and if a is any positive integer, then $a^p - a$ is divisible by p. Fermat seldom gave demonstrations of his results, and in this case proofs were provided by Gottfried Leibniz, the 17th-century German mathematician and philosopher, and Leonhard Euler, the 18th-century Swiss mathematician. For occasional demonstrations of his theorems Fermat used a device that he called his method of "infinite descent," an inverted form of reasoning by recurrence or mathematical induction. One unproved conjecture by Fermat turned out to be false. In 1640, in letters to mathematicians and to other knowledgeable thinkers of the day, including Blaise Pascal, the French writer and scientist, he announced his belief that numbers of the form $2^{2n} + 1$, known since as "numbers of Fermat," are necessarily prime; but a century later Euler showed that $2^{25} + 1$ has 641 as a factor. It is not known if there are any primes among the Fermat numbers for $n > 5$. Carl Friedrich Gauss in 1796 in Germany found an unexpected application for Fermat numbers when he showed that a regular polygon of N sides is constructible in a Euclidean sense if N is a prime Fermat number or a product of distinct Fermat primes. By far the best known of Fermat's many theorems is an unsolved problem known as his "great," or "last," theorem. This appeared in the margin of his copy of Diophantus' *Arithmetic* and states that the equation

Fermat numbers

$x^n + y^n = z^n$, where x, y, z, and n are positive integers, has no solution if n is greater than 2.

Fermat was the most productive mathematician of his day. But his influence was circumscribed by his reluctance to publish. During the three centuries following his death at Castres on January 12, 1665, no substantial biography appeared.

BIBLIOGRAPHY. Much of Fermat's work, edited by his son, was published in *Opera mathematica*, 2 vol. (1679). The definitive edition, in Latin and French, is the *Oeuvres de Fermat*, ed. by PAUL TANNERY and CHARLES HENRY, 5 pt. (1891–1922). A substantial and authoritative summary of Fermat's achievements is provided in J.E. HOFMANN, "Pierre Fermat—ein Pionier der neuen Mathematik," *Praxis der Mathematik*, 7:113–119, 171–180, 197–203 (1965); and MICHAEL S. MAHONEY, *The Mathematical Career of Pierre de Fermat, 1601–1665* (1973). For more specialized aspects of Fermat's work see L.E. DICKSON, *History of the Theory of Numbers*, 3 vol. (1919–27); C.B. BOYER, *History of Analytic Geometry* (1956) and *History of the Calculus and Its Conceptual Development* (1959); ISAAC TODHUNTER, *A History of the Mathematical Theory of Probability from the Time of Pascal to That of Laplace* (1865, reprinted 1949); and PER STROMHOLM, "Fermat's Methods of Maxima and Minima and of Tangents: A Reconstruction," *Arch. Hist. Exact Sci.*, 5:47–69 (1968).

(C.B.B.)

Fermi, Enrico

Enrico Fermi, Italian–U.S. theoretical physicist, was one of the chief architects of the nuclear age. He discovered the effectiveness of the "slow" neutron in producing artificial disintegration of the atom and was also the first to achieve a controlled nuclear chain reaction. In theoretical physics he is well-known for the so-called Fermi–Dirac statistics, a mathematical method for predicting atomic structure and behaviour.

By courtesy of the University of Chicago

Fermi.

Fermi was born in Rome on September 29, 1901, the youngest of the three children of Alberto Fermi, a railroad employee, and Ida de Gattis. Enrico, an energetic and imaginative student prodigy in high school, decided to become a physicist. At the age of 17 he entered the Reale Scuola Normale Superior, which is associated with the University of Pisa. There he earned his doctorate at the age of 21 with a thesis on research with X-rays.

After a short visit in Rome, Fermi left for Germany with a fellowship from the Italian Ministry of Public Instruction to study at the University of Göttingen under the physicist Max Born, whose contributions to quantum mechanics were part of the knowledge prerequisite to Fermi's later work. He then returned to teach mathematics at the University of Florence.

Contributions to theoretical physics
In 1926 his paper on the behaviour of a perfect, hypothetical gas impressed the physics department of the University of Rome, which invited him to become a full professor of theoretical physics. Within a short time, Fermi brought together a new group of physicists, all of them

in their early 20s. In 1926 he developed a statistical method for predicting the characteristics of electrons according to Pauli's exclusion principle, which suggests that there cannot be more than one subatomic particle that can be described in the same way. In 1928 he married Laura Capon, by whom he had two children, Nella in 1931 and Giulio in 1936. The Royal Academy of Italy recognized his work in 1929 by electing him to membership, as the youngest member in its distinguished ranks.

This theoretical work at the University of Rome was of first-rate importance, but new discoveries soon prompted Fermi to turn his attention to experimental physics. In 1932 the existence of an electrically neutral particle, called the neutron, was discovered by Sir James Chadwick at Cambridge University. In 1934 Frédéric and Irène Joliot-Curie in France were the first to produce artificial radioactivity by bombarding elements with alpha particles, which are emitted as positively charged helium nuclei from polonium. Impressed by this work, Fermi conceived the idea of inducing artificial radioactivity by another method: using neutrons obtained from radioactive beryllium but reducing their speed by passing them through paraffin, he found the slow neutrons were especially effective in producing emission of radioactive particles. He successfully used this method on a series of elements. When he used uranium of atomic weight 92 as the target of slow-neutron bombardment, however, he obtained puzzling radioactive substances that could not be identified.

Fermi's colleagues were inclined to believe that he had actually made a new, "transuranic" element of atomic number 93; that is, during bombardment, the nucleus of uranium had captured a neutron, thus increasing its atomic weight. Fermi did not make this claim, for he was not certain what had occurred; indeed, he was unaware that he was on the edge of a world-shaking discovery. As he modestly observed years later, "We did not have enough imagination to think that a different process of disintegration might occur in uranium than in any other element. Moreover, we did not know enough chemistry to separate the products from one another." One of his assistants commented that "God, for His own inscrutable ends, made everyone blind to the phenomenon of *atomic fission*."

Late in 1938 Fermi was named a Nobel laureate in physics "for his identification of new radioactive elements produced by neutron bombardment and for his discovery of nuclear reaction effected by slow neutrons." He was given permission by the Fascist government of Mussolini to travel to Sweden to receive the award. As they had already secretly planned, Fermi and his wife and family left Italy, never to return, for they had no respect for Fascism.

Meanwhile, in 1938, three German scientists had repeated some of Fermi's early experiments. After bombarding uranium with slow neutrons, Otto Hahn, Lise Meitner, and Fritz Strassmann made a careful chemical analysis of the products formed. On January 6, 1939, they reported that the uranium atom had been split into several parts. Meitner, a mathematical physicist, slipped secretly out of Germany to Stockholm, where, together with her nephew, Otto Frisch, she explained this new phenomenon as a splitting of the nucleus of the uranium atom into barium, krypton, and smaller amounts of other disintegration products. They sent a letter to the science journal *Nature*, which printed their report on January 16, 1939.

Meitner realized that this nuclear fission was accompanied by the release of stupendous amounts of energy by the conversion of some of the mass of uranium into energy in accordance with Einstein's mass–energy equation, that energy (E) is equal to the product of mass (m) times the speed of light squared (c^2), commonly written $E = mc^2$.

Fermi, apprised of this development soon after arriving in New York, saw its implications and rushed to greet Niels Bohr on his arrival in New York City. The Hahn–Meitner–Strassmann experiment was repeated at Columbia University, where, with further reflection, Bohr suggested the possibility of a nuclear chain reaction. It was agreed that the uranium-235 isotope, differing in atomic weight from other forms of uranium, would be the most effective atom for such a chain reaction.

Fermi, Leo Szilard, and Eugene Wigner saw the perils to world peace if Hitler's scientists should apply the principle of the nuclear chain reaction to the production of an atom bomb. They composed a letter, which was signed by Einstein, who, on October 11, 1939, delivered it to Pres. Franklin D. Roosevelt, alerting him to this danger. Roosevelt acted at once, and ultimately the Manhattan Project for the production of the first atom bomb was organized in 1942. Fermi was assigned the task of producing a controlled, self-sustaining nuclear chain reaction. He designed the necessary apparatus, which he called an atomic pile, and on December 2, 1942, led the team of scientists who, in a laboratory established in the squash court in the basement of Stagg Field at the University of Chicago, achieved the first self-sustaining chain reaction. The testing of the first nuclear device, at Alamogordo Air Base in New Mexico on July 16, 1945, was followed by the dropping of atom bombs on Hiroshima and Nagasaki a few weeks later.

Having satisfied the residence requirements, the Fermis had become American citizens in 1944. In 1946 he became Distinguished-Service Professor for Nuclear Studies at the University of Chicago and also received the congressional Medal of Merit. At the Metallurgical Laboratory of the University of Chicago, Fermi continued his studies of the basic properties of nuclear particles, with particular emphasis on mesons, which are the quantized form of the force that holds the nucleus together. He also was a consultant in the construction of the synchrocyclotron, a large particle accelerator at the University of Chicago. In 1950 he was elected a foreign member of the Royal Society of London.

Fermi made highly original contributions to theoretical physics, particularly to the mathematics of subatomic particles. Moreover, his experimental work in neutron-induced radioactivity led to the first successful demonstration of atomic fission, which is the basic principle of both nuclear power and the atom bomb. The atomic pile in 1942 at the University of Chicago released for the first time a controlled flow of energy from a source other than the sun; it was the forerunner of the modern nuclear reactor, which releases the basic binding energy of matter for peaceful purposes. Element number 100 was named fermium in his honour, and the Fermi Award was established by the U.S. Atomic Energy Commission. He was named the first recipient of this award of $25,000 in 1954. Fermi died of cancer on November 28, 1954, in Chicago.

BIBLIOGRAPHY. LAURA FERMI, *Atoms in the Family* (1954), a biography written by Enrico's wife; BERNARD JAFFE, *Men of Science in America*, ch. 20 (1958), covers the life and work of Enrico Fermi; EMILIO SEGRE, *Enrico Fermi: Physicist* (1970), written by his earliest and closest collaborator; HENRY D. SMYTH, *Atomic Energy for Military Purposes* (1945), a detailed description of Fermi's work on the first atomic pile, released immediately after the dropping of the first atomic bomb.

(Be.J.)

Fern

Ferns are plants belonging to the vascular plant class Polypodiopsida (Filicopsida of some classifications). Estimates of the number of fern species range from as low as 9,000 to as high as 15,000, the numbers varying because certain groups are still poorly studied and new species are still found in unexplored tropical areas. The ferns are extremely diverse in habitat, form, and reproductive methods. In size alone they range from minute filmy ferns only two to three millimetres (0.08 to 0.12 inch) tall to huge tree ferns ten to 15 metres (30 to 50 feet) in height. Some ferns are twining vines; others float on the surface of ponds. The majority of ferns grow in warm, damp areas of the Earth, their numbers diminishing with increasing latitude and decreasing moisture. Dry, cold areas have few or no ferns.

Some ferns play a role in ecological succession, growing from the crevices of bare rock exposures and in open bogs and marshes prior to the advent of forest vegetation. The best known fern genus over much of the world, *Pteridium*, the bracken, is characteristically found in old fields, where in most places it is ultimately succeeded by woody vegetation. The finest display of fern diversity is seen in the tropical rain forests, where in only a few acres over 100 species may be encountered, some of which may comprise a prominent element of the vegetation. Also, many of the species grow as epiphytes (upon the trunks and branches of trees).

As a class of plants, ferns are not of much use to man. A few, however, are used for decoration, some are popular in horticulture, and edible fern crosiers (young leaves with rolled, hook-shaped tips) are popular in some parts of the world. The major significance of ferns is probably in biological research, for they have retained a primitive life cycle, involving two separate and more or less independent generations or growth phases, the plants of which are wholly different in many respects. The familiar plant is the sporophyte generation, a moderately large leafy plant that produces spores in special structures usually located on the lower surfaces of the leaves. Much less conspicuous and usually overlooked is the gametophyte generation, a tiny plant resembling in some respects a tiny moss and often living only for a short time. The ferns constitute an ancient class of vascular plants, some of them as old as the Coal Age (Carboniferous Period, beginning about 345,000,000 years ago) and perhaps older. Their type of life cycle, dependent upon spores for dispersal, long preceded the seed-plant life cycle.

NATURAL HISTORY

Life cycle. The typical fern, a sporophyte, consists of stem, leaf, and root; it produces spores, and its cells each have two sets of chromosomes, one set from the egg and one from the sperm. The sporophyte of most ferns is perennial—it lives for several years—and reproduces by vegetative propagation from offshoots of the underground stem, or rhizome, often forming large, genetically uniform colonies or clones. A few ferns propagate by root proliferations, and some reproduce by leaf proliferations. The fern sporophyte, in contrast to that of mosses and liverworts, is obviously the dominant generation. In the ferns, however, unlike seed plants, which also have dominant sporophytes, reproduction is accomplished by production of spores—minute single cells covered by a protective wall and readily carried by wind—rather than by seeds. In this respect, the ferns are similar to club mosses (*Lycopodium*), spike mosses (*Selaginella*), quillworts (*Isoetes*), and the scouring rushes and horsetails (*Equisetum*). The life cycles of all of these plants are referred to as pteridophytic, or fernlike, in contrast to spermatophytic (seed plant-like).

The spores are haploid—*i.e.*, they have one set of chromosomes—and are produced in specialized organs, the spore cases, or sporangia. Once released, the spores are carried by wind currents, and a small percentage of them fall in appropriate germination sites to form the sexual plants, or gametophytes. In ferns the gametophytes are commonly referred to as prothallia, and they are best known to biologists as laboratory objects in artificial culture. They are rarely observed in nature without arduous searching, and the gametophyte stage of the majority of fern species has never been seen in the wild.

The prothallia are tiny—usually less than five millimetres (0.2 inch) long—and kidney-shaped in the majority of species. They grow only until the new sporophyte is formed by fertilization; then they dry up and die. The process of fertilization is accomplished by sperms and eggs produced upon the same or different gametophytes, and both the fertilized egg (zygote) and the resultant embryo are held within the tissues of the prothallium until the embryo grows out as an independent plant.

Ecology. Ecologically, the ferns are mostly plants of shaded, damp forests of both temperate and tropical zones. Some fern species grow equally well on soil and upon rocks; others are confined strictly to rocky habitats,

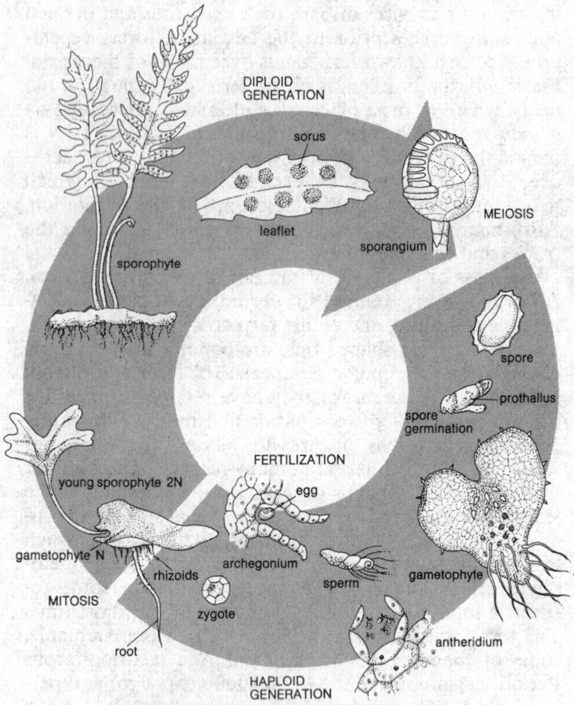

Figure 1: Fern life cycle.
Drawing by M. Pahl

where they occur in fissures and crevices of cliff faces, boulders, and talus. Acidic rocks such as granites, sandstones, and quartzites have characteristic associations of species in contrast to those of alkaline rocks such as calcites and dolomites. A few appear to be confined to serpentine and related rocks. In the tropics as many as one-third of the ferns of an area may grow as epiphytes, or air plants, on the shaded lower trunks or in the crowns of trees, often on exposed boughs. A number of so-called epiphytic ferns are actually climbers that originate upon the ground and grow up tree trunks. In these, the lower fronds (bathyphylls) are usually sterile and often differ in form from those at the higher levels (acrophylls), which are entirely or partly fertile in that they bear sporangia over their surfaces.

Both epipetric (upon rocks) and epiphytic ferns may show structural adaptations to dry habitats similar to those of desert plants. These adaptive features include such specializations as hard tissues and thick texture; in addition, the surface cells, or epidermis, may be provided with a very thick cuticle (a waxy layer), and abundant hairs or scales may be found on the leaf and stem surfaces. Terrestrial ferns growing on the ground may also possess such modifications, especially those that grow in salt marshes (*e.g.*, leather ferns, *Acrostichum*) and open, fully exposed prairies and savannas (*e.g.*, bracken, *Pteridium*; lip ferns, *Cheilanthes*; brakes, *Pteris*).

Ferns that grow in the open are often referred to as sun ferns and do not (at least as mature plants) require shade, as do most ferns. Water ferns—waterclovers (*Marsilea*), water spangles (*Salvinia*), and mosquito ferns (*Azolla*)—surprisingly, are very commonly inhabitants of dry regions. They appear only after rains, however, and their growth and life cycles are accomplished very rapidly, probably as an adaptation to the need for quick utilization of water. These ferns have two types of spores that essentially lack the vegetative phase of other ferns; they simply produce sex organs and sperms and eggs rapidly, utilizing food in the spores. Many inhabitants of dry rock cliffs, especially in the maidenhair family, Adiantaceae, have developed a modified type of life cycle, known as "apogamous," in which fertilization is bypassed. This type of life cycle is also believed to foster quick reproduction in connection with brief damp periods; the gametophytes grow fast, and the sperms do not require free water for fertilization.

Apogamous reproduction

Parasites and animal grazers upon ferns do not seem to be numerous, although the information available is not very complete. Fungi infect ferns, some of them producing sorus-like (*i.e.*, resembling the sorus, or sporangium cluster of ferns) dark bodies, or sclerotia. Snails commonly attack young, uncurling fronds of some species, and various beetles have been observed to graze upon ferns. Damaged fronds are not commonly observed in most fern species, however, which suggests that they may possibly contain repulsive substances that ward off grazers.

The sporophytes of certain ferns (*e.g.*, wood ferns, *Dryopteris*; holly ferns, *Polystichum*) evidently require a resting or dormant period, especially in the temperate zones; others, however, are capable of growing continuously, whenever conditions are suitable, even in warm winter periods (*e.g.*, spleenworts, *Asplenium*). Although the sporophyte is long-lived, the fern gametophyte is usually ephemeral. It develops in a microenvironment characterized by: little competition from other plants (including even mosses and algae); exposed humus, rotten plant materials, or fresh mineral surfaces; deep to moderate shade; and a humid atmosphere. Even ferns whose sporophytes tolerate sun and drought tend to have these requirements for their gametophytes. On rocks, for example, the gametophytes form in protected crevices in which light is minimal and moisture maximal. Because of their requirements for exposed soil, development of fern gametophytes is promoted by damage to mature vegetation, such as wind blowdowns in the forest, flooding, and deep erosion. Prothallia are observed in nature most commonly upon shaded soil banks in forests and along streams and upon rotting, mossy logs. As the bulk of reproduction of ferns is probably vegetative in the sporophytic stage, the presence of a large "stand" of a particular kind of fern results not necessarily from sexual reproduction by gametophytes but rather from clone formation by rhizomes (horizontal, rootlike stems) and in some cases by root or leaf proliferations.

Distribution and abundance. Geographically, most ferns are confined to the tropics. Arctic and Antarctic regions have few species. On the other hand, a small, tropical country such as Costa Rica in Central America may have more than 900 species of ferns—approximately three times as many as are found in all of North America north of Mexico. Ferns are conspicuous in the moist tropics not only for their diversity but for sheer numbers as well, and indeed certain forest communities may be dominated by them. A number of families and subfamilies are almost exclusively tropical—*e.g.*, Marattiaceae, Gleicheniaceae, Grammitidoideae, Schizaeaceae, Vittarioideae, Cyatheoideae, and Davallioideae. Most of the other families and subfamilies occur in both the tropics and the temperate zones. Only certain genera are primarily temperate and Arctic, and they tend to extend

Tropical ferns

Drawing by M. Pahl

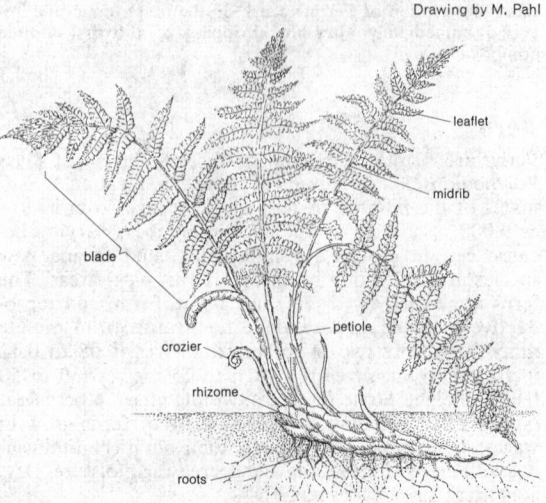

Figure 2: Generalized fern sporophyte.

into the tropics at high altitudes on the peaks of mountain ranges and volcanoes.

Ferns as weeds are uncommon, although a few occur in greenhouses, conservatories, and in tropical gardens. Fern species have been introduced into tropical or subtropical areas (*e.g.*, southern Florida and Hawaii); in some cases the species have become naturalized and have spread into the native forest. Examples include some of the most familiar ferns in the world: the giant polypody (*Phymatodes scolopendrium*), Japanese climbing fern (*Lygodium japonicum*), green cliff brake (*Pellaea viridis*), silver fern (*Pityrogramma calomelanos*), Japanese holly fern (*Cyrtomium falcatum*), "garden" maidenhair (*Adiantum hispidulum*), Cretan brake (*Pteris cretica*), and ladder brake (*P. vittata*).

Because of their ability to disperse by spores and their capacity to produce both sex organs on the same gametophyte and to self-fertilize, it would seem logical to assume that the ferns possess higher powers of long-distance dispersal and establishment than do seed plants. This conclusion tends to be supported by facts that indicate that remote disjunctions—separated growing regions—in range are frequent among ferns. Some of the patterns of distribution include interisland and intercontinental disjunctions east and west, as well as wide north–south disjunctions; included are examples of species found in the Northern and Southern hemispheres that skip the tropics. Some disjunctions seem to follow the pattern of prevailing winds; the main centre of distribution of a species often may have downwind groups consisting of one or a few small populations sometimes hundreds or thousands of miles away. Examples of west-to-east transcontinental North American disjunctions are Wright's cliff brake (*Pellaea × wrightiana*), mountain holly fern (*Polystichum × scopulinum*), and forked spleenwort (*Asplenium septentrionale*)—all of these ferns are well known in the Western United States, and they exist as tiny populations in the mountains of the East as well.

FORM AND FUNCTION

The spore. The fern spore—a single living cell, usually protected by a thick wall—is the main source of population dispersal, being readily carried by wind. Ferns display a wide diversity of spore types in terms of shape, wall structure, and sexuality, and these types have proved to have great value in determining taxonomic relationships. The full functional significance of the different types, except on the grossest scale, is not yet fully understood; for example, the minute differences in sculpturing of the outer wall surface do not, in the present state of knowledge, appear to have functional significance.

Spore shape. The basic spore shape among ferns is tetrahedral; the proximal face (the one facing inward during the tetrad, or four-cell, stage following reduction division, or meiosis) is made up of three sloping planes, and the distal, or outer, face consists of a single, rounded surface. The tetrahedral structure is commonly obscured in so-called globose spores, the walls of which are thin and soft. Typically, the wall is composed of exospore (outer spore layer) only, there being no additional jacket, or perispore. The wall may be either unsculptured and smooth or provided with a variety of sculpture patterns. The tetrahedral spore is formed by simultaneous division of the products of the spore mother cell.

In contrast, the bilateral spore type of many fern species is formed by successive cell divisions of the spore mother cell. Where the tetrahedral spore possesses a triradiate scar on the proximal face—corresponding to the contact with three other spores in the tetrad—the bilateral spore has only a narrow, linear scar running parallel to the long axis. Most bilateral spores in ferns are bean shaped and jacketed by a perisporial layer, a distinctive covering of the outer wall.

Spore size. A few fern families have dimorphic spores, small ones (the microspores) and large ones (the megaspores). The gametophytes of ferns with dimorphic spores are endosporous; that is, they do not emerge in germination and fail to grow beyond the confines of the spore walls. Photosynthesis is essentially lacking, the food being stored in the spore. The microspores produce sperms in antheridia, and the megaspores produce eggs in archegonia. The vegetative phase of the gametophyte in these forms has been practically eliminated, and the developing embryo in the megaspore lives on stored food materials. The differentiation between male and female gametophytes ensures cross-fertilization. This set of conditions, known only in the families Marsileaceae, Azollaceae, and Salviniaceae, is called "heterospory." All other living ferns are homosporous (*i.e.*, they produce uniformly sized spores), although some do show slight spore differentiation, suggesting incipient heterospory.

Thick-walled spores are capable of survival for a number of years, in some cases up to several decades. Some spores have walls so thick that they fail to germinate at all under normal culture conditions in the laboratory, and some have never been germinated. Most natural germination of fern spores (except for water ferns) occurs on exposed damp surfaces of rock, soil, or dead plant materials.

A number of fern genera (*e.g.*, *Osmunda*, *Grammitis*, and *Hymenophyllum*) possess thin-walled spores. In practically all known examples, such thin-walled spores are also green pigmented, being provided with chloroplasts. Such spores are common among rain forest genera; they are short-lived and require a very short time for germination.

The gametophyte. When the spore wall cracks under appropriate moist conditions, the fern gametophyte is formed. Emerging from the spore at the time of germination are a nongreen rhizoid (rootlike organ), which attaches the plant to the growing surface, and a green, single cell—the mother cell that gives rise to the rest of the gametophyte. At first, in most homosporous ferns, growth is in the form of a single filament, which may continue in this fashion if lighting conditions are weak. If lighting is optimum, however, the gametophyte becomes a two-dimensional sheet of cells and later a layered, three-dimensional structure. The apical cell soon is replaced by an embryonic zone, or meristem, which, as a result of the directions of cell division and enlargement, comes to lie in an apical notch in the gametophyte, surrounded on either side by the prothallial wings—flat, platelike protrusions one cell thick. The average size of the gametophyte at the time of fertilization is approximately one to four millimetres (0.04 to 0.16 inch) long and up to three millimetres wide.

Specialized gametophyte forms. From a basic type of gametophyte, probably somewhat like that just described, a number of highly specialized forms have evolved that are characteristic of certain genera. Ribbonlike gametophytes are known especially among tropical rain forest ferns, such as the subfamilies Vittarioideae, Grammitidoideae, and Hymenophylloideae, and are characterized by attenuate, flat thalli that are usually irregularly and extensively branched, forming large masses of intertwining ribbons. Some of these are actually more abundant than their corresponding sporophytes in certain localities (*e.g.*, the Appalachian Mountains, where "pure cultures" of gametophytes totally lacking sporophytes have commonly been found). Filamentous gametophytes are known in the genera *Trichomanes* (Hymenophylloideae) and *Schizaea* (Schizaeaoideae).

Tuber-like gametophytes occur in several groups—the family Ophioglossaceae (all members), subfamily Schizaeaoideae (*Actinostachys*), and the family Gleicheniaceae (*Stromatopteris*). All are nongreen, underground plants that have close associations with fungi and are therefore assumed to be saprophytic; *i.e.*, dependent for nutrition upon rotting organic material in the soil. They commonly occur five to ten centimetres deep.

In heterosporous ferns, the endosporous gametophytes are much reduced. The male gametophyte in the microspore is made up of the equivalent of one antheridium and its complement of sperms. The female gametophyte, although considerably larger in size, is equally reduced in a morphological sense, the greater space within the

The tetrahedral spore

Growth of the gametophyte

megaspore being filled by stored nutritive materials and tissues formed around the base of the female sex organs.

Vegetative reproduction. Vegetative propagation of some photosynthetic fern gametophytes is accomplished by continued growth and fragmentation, but this does not spread the gametophyte very far. Some subfamilies (Vittarioideae, Grammitidoideae, Hymenophylloideae) produce specialized filaments, or gemmae, that break off and are carried away by water droplets or wind to initiate new colonies. Some gemmae are formed upon specialized cells (sterigmata) and are spindle shaped or more or less ovoid. Others occur as chains of cells.

Sexual reproduction. The sex organs of ferns are differentiated. The sperm-producing organs, antheridia, are composed of a sterile jacket of cells and sperm-producing cells within. The antheridia may be sunken (as in the families Ophioglossaceae and Marattiaceae) or protruding. Antheridia vary in size from those with hundreds of sperms to those with only 12 or so. The egg-producing organ, the archegonium, contains one gamete (sex cell), which is always located in the lower, more or less dilated portion of the archegonium, the venter. The upper part of the archegonium, the neck, consists of four rows of cells containing central neck cells. The uppermost of the neck cells are the neck canal cells; the lowest cell is the ventral canal cell, which is situated just above the egg.

Fertilization is attained by the ejection of sperms from antheridia; the sperm swim through free water toward simple organic acids released at the opening of the archegonium, the neck of which spreads apart at the apex, permitting the neck cells to be extruded and the sperm to swim in and penetrate the egg. The sperms are made up almost entirely of nuclear material, but their surface is provided with spiral bands of cilia, hairlike organs of locomotion. When the egg is fertilized, the base of the

neck closes, and the embryo develops in the expanding venter.

The embryo. Within the archegonial venter the zygote undergoes characteristic cell divisions to form the embryo, which remains encapsulated in the gametophyte until it breaks out and becomes an independent plant. The pattern of development in most ferns is a distinctive one, and indeed only in the orders Ophioglossales and Marattiales are found conditions of embryonic development resembling those of seed plants. In *Botrychium* subgenus *Sceptridium* and in all species of the family Marattiaceae thus far studied, the first division of the zygote is transverse, and the inner cell grows inward, producing the stem and first leaf. The outer cell divides to form a foot, a mass of tissue that exists as part of the embryo and disappears when its function, presumably absorption, is over. The root appears later within the stem and grows outward. In all other known ferns, the zygote divides neatly into four quadrants, the first division approximately parallel to the long axis of the archegonium and the following division at right angles. This results in initial cells that give rise to four organs: the outer forward cell (*i.e.*, toward the growing apex of the gametophyte and the neck of the archegonium) becomes the first leaf, the inner forward cell the stem apex, the outer back cell the first root, and the inner back cell the foot. Thus, the majority of ferns tend to have a precise arrangement of the organs and the divisions that produce them in the embryo.

The young sporophytes of ferns remain attached to the gametophytes for varying lengths of time, absorbing nutrients from the gametophyte through the foot. The gametophyte soon shrivels away, once the sporophyte has developed independent existence and the root has penetrated the soil. The first few leaves are generally sharply different from the mature leaves, not only in their size but in their architecture as well. A common, overall pattern is a falsely dichotomous condition, in which the central part of the leaf blade is aborted (undeveloped) and midribless, and the main veins are forked. Certain ferns, however (*e.g.*, grape ferns, *Botrychium*; and sword ferns, *Nephrolepis*), have first leaves that are organized ternately (three parted) or pinnately (with a central axis from both sides of which veins or leaflets branch).

The stem. Fern stems vary from the tall, narrow trunks of certain tree ferns that reach over 20 metres (70 feet) tall down to creeping rootstocks, or rhizomes. Rhizomes are the most common stem form; the majority of them grow horizontally upon or just beneath the surface of the soil. Some fern stems are so narrow as to be threadlike, as in many tropical epiphytic ferns. A few ferns in different parts of the world have evolved radically specialized stems containing ant-filled chambers. The role of the ants in the lives of these ferns is unknown. Vinelike ferns are common, but shrubby ferns are extremely rare. The nearest to shrubby ferns are members of the genus *Oleandra*, which have stiffly branched, woody-textured stems.

Stem growth is initiated by one to several large apical cells. These are usually well protected by various types of hairs or scales and by the over-arching embryonic leaves. Leaves and leaf bases play a major role in protection of fern stems, and many stems are said to have a leaf armour. Such stems are densely covered with old, sclerified (hardened) leaf bases, which increase the apparent size of the stem many times. In most species the stems are indeterminate in growth, and thus can theoretically continue to grow indefinitely. Annuals—short-lived species that complete development, shed spores, and die in a single growing season—are exceptional; only one or two examples are known.

Whether covered with leaf armour or not, the surface of the fern stem is protected by an epidermis, or "skin," a single layer of epidermal cells, which are more or less flat cells with thick outer walls. There are usually also protective epidermal hairs or scales in most ferns; these are so distinctive that they are valuable in identification and classification. The trichomes (*i.e.*, epidermal emergences, or "plant hairs") embrace such diverse types as

Structure of the archegonium (margin note)

Ant chambers in fern stems (margin note)

Drawing by M. Pahl

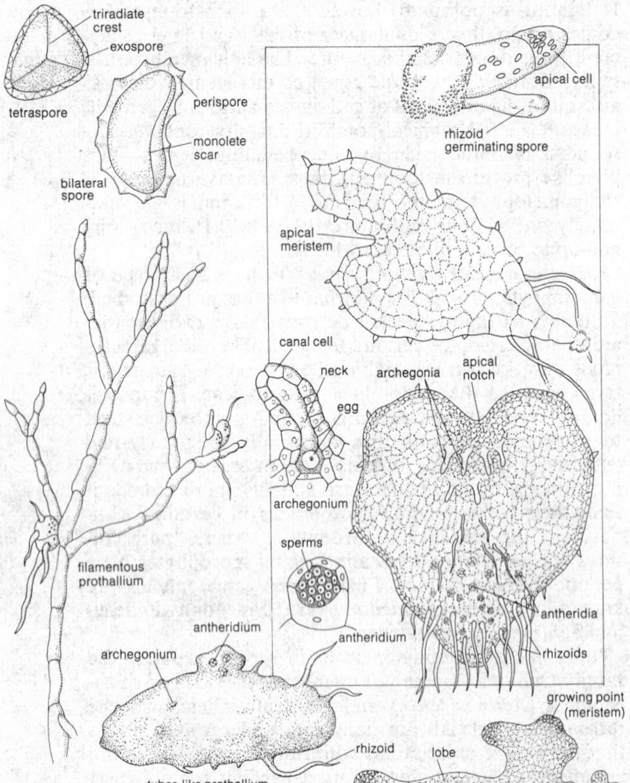

Figure 3: Fern gametophytes and associated structures.

simple glands (unbranched, one- to several-celled hairs with a headlike cluster of secretory terminal cells); simple (unbranched), nonglandular hairs; dendroid hairs (branching filaments); and scales (flat cell plates) of many patterns. Scales (known as paleae, or ramenta) are defined as trichomes with a cell plate of two or more cell rows, at least at the base. Most scales are attached broadly at the base and become narrowed toward the usually pointed apex; but a number of species, especially among epiphytes, possess peltate (shieldlike) scales, the attachment of which is central with the scale cells radiating out in all directions. Scales are generally brownish or tannish in colour; the walls are evenly pigmented except when they are very young, when they are white or hyaline (clear or transparent). In some scales, however, the top and bottom walls are transparent and unpigmented, but the lateral walls are thickly coated with dark-maroon or black secondary walls. Such scales are called clathrate (*i.e.*, latticework) scales and when present are valuable for recognizing certain genera.

Drawing by M. Pahl

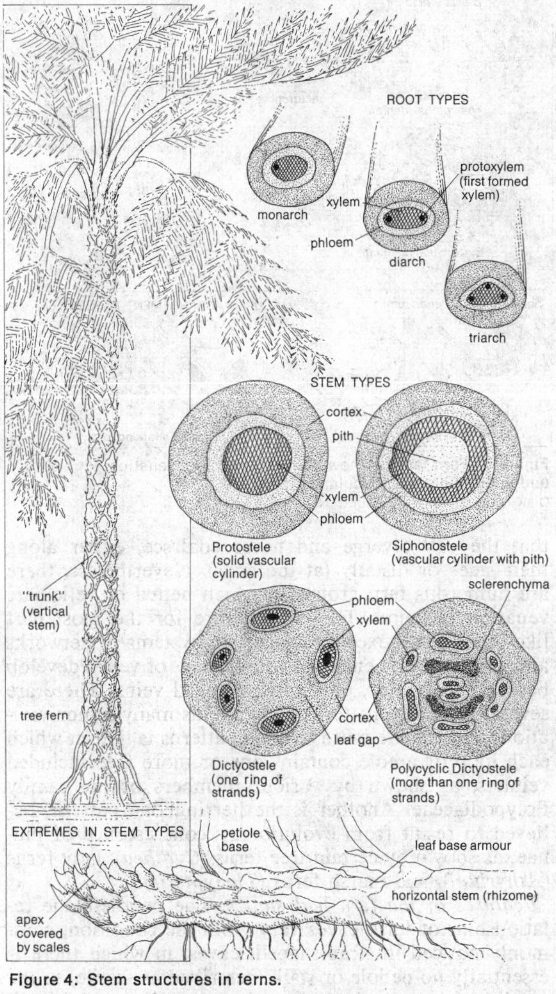

Figure 4: Stem structures in ferns.

The cortex—the region outside the vascular cylinder but below the surface of the stem—is composed of ground tissue consisting of storage parenchyma cells (a relatively generalized cell type) with more or less thick walls. Rooting animals, such as pigs, occasionally dig up fern rhizomes for the starchy materials contained in them. There is a strong tendency for the outermost cortical cells to become darkly pigmented and thick walled.

Vascular tissues. The patterns of vascular tissue, or steles—cylinders of vascular tissues in stem centres—in ferns are so various that a brief description is not possible. Basically, most common ferns possess "dictyosteles," steles consisting of interconnected vascular strands so that, in any given cross section of a fern stem, several distinct bundles can be observed. These are separated by

regions filled with parenchyma cells known as leaf gaps. There are, however, solenostelic ferns, in which the gaps do not overlap and a given section shows only one gap; and numerous protostelic ferns, in which there are no gaps formed at all. Very complex stelar patterns are known in some species, as in the common bracken fern (*Pteridium*), which has a dorsiventral, polycyclic dictyostele, one in which one stele occurs within another stele. Strands of fibre-like cells running between them form mechanically specialized hard tissue, or sclerenchyma. In certain genera and subgenera of the order Ophioglossales are found steles that somewhat resemble those of seed plants in a number of ways. That is, they exhibit secondary growth (growth rings), radial alignment of cells, development of endodermis (a special layer of cells surrounding the stele), and the same relative position of xylem and phloem tissues (water- and food-conducting vascular tissue).

Usually fern stems can be distinguished from those of seed plants because the former lack secondary growth. No rhizomes of ferns have yet been discovered that show stelar patterns, such as those of monocotyledonous flowering plants (*i.e.*, grasses, palms, orchids, lilies, and others) with scattered vascular bundles. Like monocots, however, fern bundles are usually closed and incapable of undergoing secondary thickening.

Cells of the vascular system. The cells of the vascular strands in ferns are mainly tracheids, sieve cells, parenchyma, and endodermal cells. The tracheids, which comprise the xylem, or water-conducting tissue, are normally long, very narrow, and attenuated at the tips. Their secondary walls display ladder-like (scalariform) pitting. The largest fern tracheids are several centimetres long, but most are much smaller. Vessel cells, which have evolved in several lines of fern evolution, are modified tracheids in which the end walls have lost their primary membranes, thus enabling direct, unimpeded connections for water transport between the cells. Vessels, the longitudinal channels composed of linear series of such perforated cells, have been reported from such diverse ferns as waterclover (*Marsilea*) and bracken (*Pteridium*). The phloem cells of ferns are composed mainly of sieve cells —narrow, elongated units that differ from the tracheids in having persistent protoplasts and nuclei (*i.e.*, they are still alive at functional maturity) and in lacking secondary walls with elaborate pitting. Sieve cells usually display more or less distinguishable sievelike areas, through which, presumably, organic foods pass in their travels through the stem and other plant organs. There are various arrangements of xylem and phloem, but usually a single strand composed of both is surrounded by parenchyma cells, the pericycle (a thin zone of living cells just within the endodermis), and by an outer layer of cells with specialized walls, the endodermis. Endodermal cells in young stems are provided with special strips of secondary wall material known as Casparian strips on their radial walls (*i.e.*, on all the cell walls except the two that face toward the stem axis and the stem surface). As the stems age, however, there is a tendency for the endodermal cells to become thick walled all around.

Other cell types. The pith is made up of parenchyma cells as a rule, but in many fern genera scattered tracheidlike cells are found as well. True stone cells, such as the brachysclereids or astrosclereids ("bone-shaped" or dumbbell-shaped and "star-shaped," thick-walled structural cells, respectively), so common in many seed plants, are absent. Likewise, the cells of fern stems differ from those of many seed plants in lacking collenchyma, modified parenchyma cells with expanded primary walls. Latex-producing cells are rare in ferns.

Most common ferns produce leaves alternately along the rhizome, and the leaf traces (strands of vascular tissue) run from either side of each leaf gap in the stele out through the cortex into the leaf base, or petiole. The basic leaf trace departure from the stele is therefore double, two strands arising from the stele for each leaf. There are, however, many variations on this theme. The vascular strands that arise from the stele to serve the

Types of vascular cylinders

Cellular construction of ferns contrasted to other plants

roots also arise in the leaf gap, usually at its base. Thus, each leaf as a rule has its own associated root system.

The root. Taproots are unknown in ferns. All fern roots are referred to as adventitious, in the sense that they arise at points along the stem. Observed superficially, their association with leaves is more or less obvious, depending on the genus and species. In internal structure, fern roots are generally regarded as being much less diverse than stems. They are protostelic, lacking pith and gaps, and they grow from one or more apical initials (cells that divide to produce all the cells and tissues of an organ), producing a root cap outwardly and the permanent tissues of the root inwardly. They lack secondary growth—continued growth in thickness—entirely. The surface cells of the epidermis produce root hairs near the root apex. These are generally thin walled, in contrast to the cells of the inner cortex, which ultimately may become very thick walled. The root hairs have fundamental importance in absorption of water and nutrients and in attachment to the soil or other growing surface. The endodermis of the root is well marked, and Casparian strips are present, as in the stem. There is also a tendency for the endodermis in older parts of the roots to become thick walled and sclerified. The production and development of xylem tissue in the steles of most fern roots is diarch or triarch; *i.e.*, the first matured xylem is along two or three lines at the outer periphery of the xylem strand. The xylem is surrounded by phloem, and the branch roots arise from the endodermis, unlike the main roots produced by the stem, which arise from the pericycle.

The appearance of roots in relation to the stems is a valuable identification tool. For example, in certain tree ferns (*e.g.*, *Cibotium*), the entire surface is covered by masses of roots, as it is also in the royal ferns (*Osmunda*). Pieces of such root masses have proved to be useful in horticulture for purposes of cultivating orchids and bromeliads; if large enough, the dead tangles of roots can be cut with a saw into various shapes suitable for attaching epiphytic greenhouse plants. Certain tropical ferns have elaborately hairy roots; their surfaces are covered with locks of silky golden or brown trichomes.

The leaf. *Leaf shapes.* The basic plan of leaf construction is pinnate (*i.e.*, "feather-like"—with a central axis and smaller side branches) in practically all ferns, and this is considered to be the primitive condition because of its widespread occurrence. Although the ultimate ancestors of the ferns may well have had repeatedly forking, or dichotomous, leaves, the immediate ancestor, at least of ferns living today, is thought to have had pinnately constructed leaves. From this basic type there has evolved a very broad diversity of forms. Some ferns have palmate leaves (with veins or leaflets radiating from one point), and some have secondarily evolved falsely dichotomous leaves.

Whether a given leaf is divided into segments (compound) or not (simple) is of considerable value in identification. The difference between divided and undivided leaves is not a profound one, however, and closely related species will commonly differ from one another in whether their leaves are divided or not. In some situations, in fact, simple-leaved species are known to cross with compound-leaved species to form viable hybrids.

The extent of division in fern leaves ranges from the conditions in which the leaf margins are merely so deeply lobed as to have narrow-based segments to the ultimate condition of having obviously stalked leaflets or pinnae. The pinnae themselves may also be lobed or truly divided with stalked segments as well, and the resulting segments, the pinnules, may also be lobed or divided. Depending on the degree of cutting, fronds are described as simple, once divided, twice divided, thrice divided, and so on. Some ferns are known in which the blades are exceedingly divided and delicate, with blades five times compound that result in segments so small as to be almost hairlike.

Leaf venation. Basically, the vein patterns (which can be seen readily by holding the specimen up to a strong light) are pinnate and the veins are free, in the sense

The primitive fern leaf plan

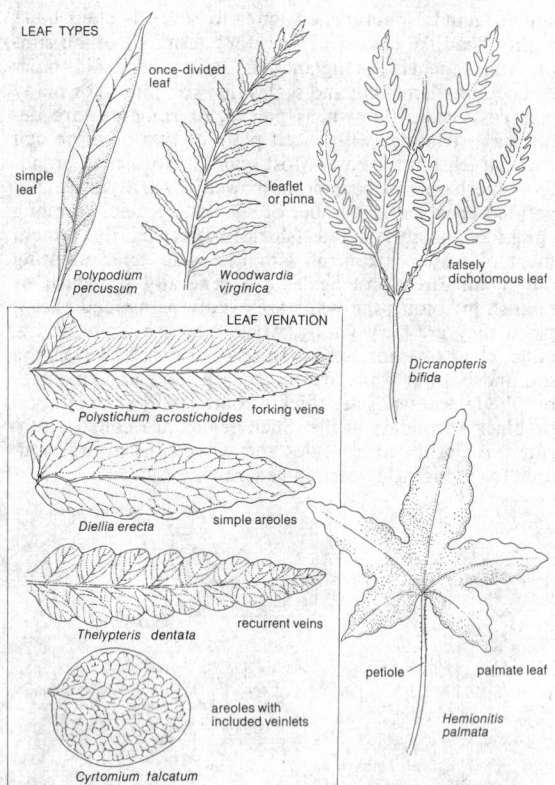

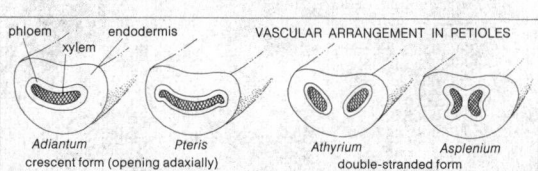

Figure 5: Fern leaves, showing leaf types, leaf venation, and internal petiole vascularization.
Drawing by M. Pahl

that they all diverge and never coalesce, either along their sides or distally (at the ends). Nevertheless, there are numerous fern groups in which netted or reticulate venation is found. The patterns are for the most part like other ferns, except that various systems of networks and areoles (areas enclosed within loops of veins) develop between the major, pinnately arranged veins. There are several reticulate patterns known, plus many minor variations. One of the more striking patterns is that in which each loop or areole contains one or more free included veinlets, as shown by various members of the family Polypodiaceae. Another is the herringbone pattern, believed to result from evolutionary concrescence of pinnae, as shown by certain tree ferns (*Cyathea*), lady ferns (*Athyrium*), and marsh ferns (*Thelypteris*).

Features of the fern leaf stalk. The petiole-blade relationships of fern leaves vary from the condition, commonly noticed in strap-shaped leaves, in which there is essentially no petiole or stalk (described as sessile) to the condition, commonly observed in broadly oval or triangular leaves, in which there is a pronounced leaf stalk, or stipe (the petiolate, or stipitate condition). Narrowly elongated leaves in ferns are usually erect, spreading, or, in certain epiphytes, pendent. Leaves that are broadly ovate or triangular tend to be borne at right angles to the incident light. Broad-leaved ferns thus become more or less bent at the blade base, an arch occurring at the top of the petiole.

Anatomically, the petioles or stipes of pteridophylls (fern leaves) show nearly as much diversity in cross-sectional pattern as do the stems. The simplest vascular strands of fern petioles are round or (more commonly) crescent shaped, single bundles. In more and more elaborate petiolar patterns, the crescent takes on the form of the Greek letter *ōmega*, opening adaxially (*i.e.*, up-

Leaf position

ward or toward the central axis of the plant). The latter shape, with many variations, occurs very widely among ferns, especially those considered on other grounds to be primitive. Double-stranded ferns (the ōmega now divided into two parts and unconnected below) are usually associated with more specialized genera. Any of the generalized patterns may exist as broken-up strands; the separation is commonly associated with size—small leaves have only one or two strands; large leaves have many. Just as in stems, this size factor plays a role in the number of strands observed. Petiolar vascular bundle shapes have been found to be so definitive as to have a certain value in separating fern genera and families.

Tissues of the fern leaf. At the tissue level, the leaf blades have certain differences from those of other plants, but the same general picture prevails: there is an upper epidermis without stomates (microscopic pores) or with only a few and a mesophyll, or inner layer of spongy cells, with more or less large, intercellular spaces except for the adaxial side, which is composed of palisade cells, elongate cells arranged parallel and oriented with the long axis vertical to the leaf surface. The veins range from the massive trunks of the major midribs, or rachises, which have well-defined xylem, phloem, pericycle, and endodermis, to the delicate capillaries (fine veinlets) represented by little more than a single file of tracheids and that sometimes end in a cluster of terminal, somewhat modified tracheids. Underneath a sporangium, or sorus, the veins may become dilated and multilayered (the so-called fertile veins). In some ferns the palisade layer of the mesophyll is substituted for by parallel, inward projections of the epidermal cells that contain chloroplasts (small bodies that contain the photosynthetic pigment, chlorophyll) and presumably function as do the typical palisade cells. In many ferns all or nearly all of photosynthesis is accomplished by the epidermis, either one layer or two, the mesophyll having been eliminated in evolution. An example is the common maidenhair fern (*Adiantum pedatum*), the blade of which, between veins, is made up of mainly two layers, the upper and lower epidermis, in which most of photosynthesis occurs.

The trichomes—hairs and scales—of fern leaves are like those of the stem but usually fewer, more widely separated, and smaller in dimensions. Many ferns are described as having glabrous leaf blades (*i.e.*, bald), but in many instances this is misleading because there are actually at least a few microscopic hairs, which are usually glandular and appressed to the blade surface.

Comparisons with leaves of other plant groups. The fern leaf or pteridophyll is most similar to that of the cycads when compared to other living vascular plant groups. The pteridophyll differs from the leaf (euphyll, or "true leaf") of the flowering plants in its vernation, or manner of expanding from the bud, which is circinate—it unrolls from the tip and has the appearance of a fiddle-

head rather than expanding from a conduplicate, or folded, condition. It also differs in its venation, which is usually free or simply reticulate, rather than being highly complex and made up of areoles containing numerous branched free-ending veinlets. Fern leaves differ from the leaves (sphenophylls) of conifers and articulates or horsetails (*Equisetum* species) in their usually well-developed central midrib with lateral vein branches rather than a dichotomous, midribless pattern or a mere simple vein in a narrow needlelike or straplike leaf. Although a few ferns that have narrow leaves also have only a single central vascular strand (*e.g.*, certain species of *Schizaea*), these may usually be distinguished readily from the merely scalelike or awllike leaves (microphylls) of lycopsids (club mosses) on the basis of other characteristics, such as the position of the sporangia and the mode of leaf development. A few genera of ferns (*e.g.*, sword ferns, *Nephrolepis; Jamesonia; Blechnum* subgenus *Salpichlaena;* climbing ferns, *Lygodium;* and staghorn ferns, *Dicranopteris*) have members with more or less indeterminate—continuous—leaf growth accomplished by periodically quiescent buds, but fern leaves are mostly determinate; *i.e.*, they stop growing at a certain stage of development. They grow from apical cells in most ferns, and these delicate embryonic cells are protected by the curled over spiral of the crozier (unrolling tip of a young fern leaf) and by trichomes. When the blade formation is complete, there is no longer an embryonic tip.

In overall length, mature leaves vary from one or two millimetres (0.04 or 0.08 inch) in certain filmy ferns (subfamily Hymenophylloideae) to 30 or more metres (100 feet; family Gleicheniaceae). The term frond, which presumably derives from the concept of a large, compound leaf, such as that of a wood fern, cycad, or palm, has been traditionally applied to the leaves of ferns, even when they are only small, simple leaves resembling superficially the euphylls—true leaves—of flowering plants. Approximately one-third of all living ferns have simple, nonfrondose leaf blades.

The sporangium and sorus. *The sporangium.* The sporangia, or spore-producing structures, in ferns range from globose, sessile (nonstalked) organs over one millimetre in diameter down to microscopic stalked structures, the capsules of which are only 0.3 millimetre (0.01 inch) in diameter. The former are known as eusporangia, the latter as leptosporangia. Eusporangia occur in the orders Ophioglossales and Marattiales, and leptosporangia occur in the majority of the species in the order Polypodiales, as well as in the Marsileales and Salviniales. There are, however, many intermediate forms between the two types of sporangia, and these are known in various primitive species of the Polypodiales, such as members of the family Osmundaceae.

The capsule wall in eusporangia tends to be relatively massive and made up of two layers or more. In leptosporangia, in contrast, the wall is thin and, at least at maturity, composed of one layer of cells. Opening of the capsule in eusporangia, such as those of the genus *Botrychium* and intermediate types such as *Osmunda*, is accomplished by separation along a well-differentiated line of dehiscence (opening); but in most typical leptosporangia, except for a few stomial—"mouth"—cells that separate along one side, the process of dehiscence tears the cells apart more or less irregularly. The opening process in eusporangia is the result of a generalized stress on drying walls, the cells of which are differentially thickened. There is no mechanism to throw the spores, and they are simply carried away by the wind. In contrast, leptosporangia display more or less specialized bows, or annuli, consisting of usually a single row of differentially thickened cells. The mechanical force for opening and for throwing the spores derives, apparently, entirely from these bow cells—all the other capsule cells are thin walled and unmodified. The drying of the bow cells imposes stresses that result in the collapse of the outer sides of the cells, thus straightening out the bow and ripping the soft lateral cells of the capsule apart. As the bow cells continue to be deformed by the cohesive forces of the increasingly tense water molecules within, the spore case

Plant hairs on fern leaves

Types of spore-producing structures

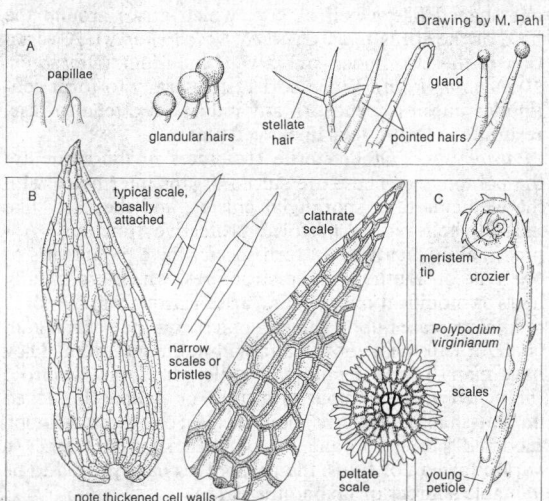

Drawing by M. Pahl

A
papillae
glandular hairs
stellate hair
gland
pointed hairs

B
typical scale, basally attached
clathrate scale
narrow scales or bristles
note thickened cell walls
peltate scale

C
meristem tip
crozier
Polypodium virginianum
scales
young petiole

Figure 6: *Representative surface structures.*
(A) Types of hairs. (B) Scale types. (C) Uncurling leaf, or crozier, showing circinate vernation and surface scales.

becomes completely open. Finally, the cohesive capacity of the water molecules is exceeded, the water film between the outer walls of the bow cells breaks, and the entire bow snaps back to its original position, tossing the spores into the air.

Most primitive sporangial types are stalkless, or sessile. If a stalk is present at all, it is merely a slightly raised multicellular area at the base of the sporangial capsule. In typical leptosporangia, however, there are commonly well-developed stalks, and these are often extremely long and narrow (*e.g.*, as in *Davallia* and *Loxoscaphe*), made up of only one or two rows of cells and up to 1.7 to two millimetres (0.07 to 0.08 inch) in length.

The trend in sporangial evolution is evidently from solitary large capsules to more and more elaborate groupings of smaller sporangia. These changes are accompanied by the appearance of such refinements as paraphyses and indusia. Paraphyses are sterile structures that grow among the sporangia. Indusia are papery tentlike structures that cover clusters of sporangia.

Drawing by M. Pahl from (top) F.C. Steward, *About Plants: Topics in Plant Biology* (1966); Addison-Wesley, Reading, Mass. and (bottom right) P. Martens & N. Pirard, "The Glandular Organs of *Polypodium virginianum*," *La Cellule*, 49(3): 383–406 (1943)

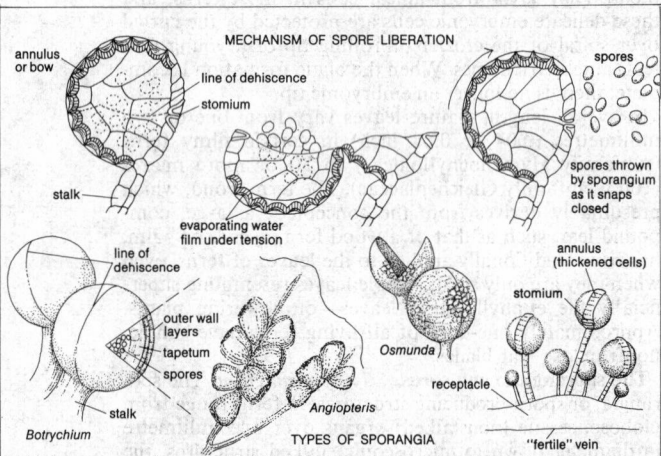

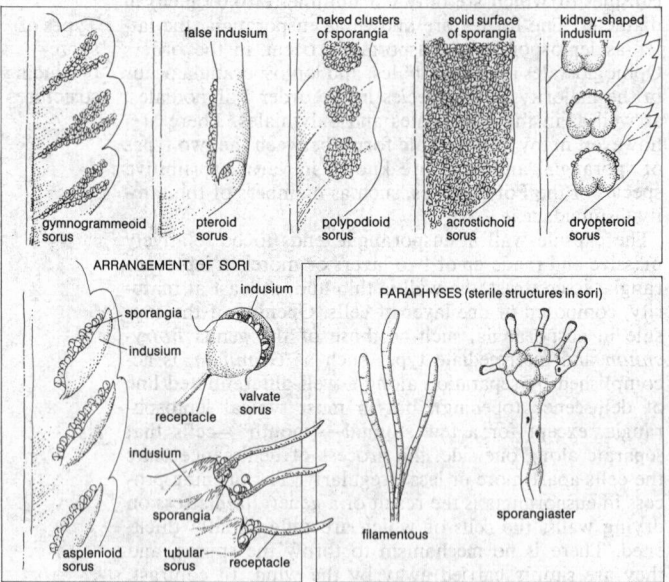

Figure 7: Fern sporangia, their arrangement into sori, and other structures found in the sorus.

The sorus. Hand in hand with the reduction in size of single sporangia are seen more and more complex aggregations of sporangia known as sori. The meristematic area—the region of new cell growth—that produces them may continue its activities over a number of weeks, producing sporangia of all ages, the older ones becoming pushed aside as the new ones mature in their turn. Persons seeing sori developing upon the leaves of their house

ferns for the first time have often interpreted the young stages as tiny insects or older stages as fungus diseases, not realizing that such organs are necessary for the normal reproduction of the plant.

The stages in progressive evolution of sori can be visualized as follows: (1) simple clusters of sporangia, these more or less coalesced (family Marattiaceae) or separate (Gleicheniaceae), all of them maturing at the same time; (2) gradate clusters of sporangia, the outermost ones maturing first, the innermost last; and (3) mixed clusters of sporangia, all ages present, the younger ones arising from the same meristematic zones as the older ones. The adaptive significance of this change is probably related to the duration of spore production, the mixed condition of specialized sori extending the period beyond that of solitary sporangia or of simple, simultaneously maturing sori.

Sorus types. Sporangia and especially sori have traditionally been the most important characters for fern classification. Indeed, many unrelated ferns were once classified together because of what are now believed to have been coincidental convergences in soral structure. Adjectives derived from the classical generic names of ferns, which were based upon superficial resemblances, are still used to describe the prominent types. Between one-half and two-thirds of the species of ferns have one or another of the following six soral types: (1) The gymnogrammeoid type (from the genus *Gymnogramme*, meaning "naked line") is a linear arrangement of sporangia along veins, avoiding the leaf area between the veins. It is found in many fern genera, especially in the family Adiantaceae. (2) The pteroid sorus (from *Pteris*, a classical fern genus) is a line of sporangia along the leaf edge, protected usually by a rolled-over and modified laminar margin. (3) Polypodioid sori (from *Polypodium*) are round and naked. (4) Acrostichoid sori (from *Acrostichum*) are so large that they are usually expanded over the entire undersurface of the blade or pinna. Acrostichoid sori probably arose by fusion or smaller clusters. Of the many types of indusiate sori (*i.e.*, sori that are protected by indusia, special scalelike structures), two of the most widespread types are (5) the asplenioid (from *Asplenium*), a linear or oblong sorus covered from one side by a narrow indusium, and (6) the aspidioid (from *Aspidium*), in which the sorus is round but covered with a kidney-shaped or shieldlike indusium.

The indusium. The protection of the sporangial cluster from exposure, drying, and other factors is accomplished in various ways—by the formation of the sori in grooves or pockets or by the production of various forms of covers. The false indusium is the rolled-over leaf margin, under which the sporangia form and mature. The indusium is a separate and unique structure, the structural origins of which are not clear, which develops a more or less papery covering over the sorus. A widespread type of indusium among members of the family Cyatheaceae is one shaped like a bell or cup, which arises around the base of the sorus (*e.g.*, *Cyathea*, *Trichomanes*). A variation is the two-lipped or valvate indusium (*Dicksonia*, *Hymenophyllum*). When sori fuse laterally to form continuous lines or coenosori, any indusia also tend to fuse, resulting in continuous linear cell plates.

Paraphyses. Other sterile structures in the sorus are the paraphyses. These are sterile organs intermixed with the elements of a sporangial cluster, and they are, like indusia, believed to perform protective functions. Approximately one-third of fern species have paraphyses of one type or another. These structures, which are usually hairs or modifications of hairs, arise variously in the sorus —in some cases upon the receptacle, on the sporangium (stalk or capsule or both), and within the indusium. They have many forms, including simple, glandular, dendroid (branched in the manner of a tree), or stellate (branched in "star-shaped" patterns) hairs; scales; or obviously much modified sterile sporangia—so-called sporangiasters. In various genera of ferns, the paraphyses have proved to be valuable sources of taxonomic data.

Cytogenetics in fern biology. The study of chromosomes, hybrids, and breeding systems has revealed much of value in understanding ferns. The chromosomes of

Marginal notes:

Stages in the evolution of the sorus

Sterile structures in the fern sorus

ferns tend to have high base or x numbers, ranging from approximately 20 to 70, with the majority between 25 and 45. The familiar genus *Osmunda*, for example, has $x = 22$, *Pteris* has 29, *Asplenium* 36, *Dryopteris* 41, *Botrychium* 45, and *Pteridium* 52. Among homosporous ferns, exceptions to the rule of high chromosome numbers are rare; in one species of filmy fern (*Hymenophyllum peltatum*) $x = 11$, the lowest number reported. Among heterosporous ferns, however, the situation is conspicuously different, and all have low base numbers (Marsileaceae, $x = 10$, 13, or 19; Salviniaceae, $x = 9$; *Azolla*, $x = 22$). The explanation traditionally adopted by cytologists is that the high numbers in homosporous ferns arose from polyploidy, the repeated reduplication of whole sets of chromosomes. Indeed, some workers regard homosporous ferns as nearly 100 percent polyploid. An alternative hypothesis should also be considered, however, namely that homosporous ferns were primitively high numbered and that heterosporous ferns derived their low numbers through reduction.

The base chromosome numbers (indicated by the symbol x) have been used for systematic (classification) purposes. Commonly, the base number is uniform for a genus or family, or it fluctuates around a given number. More rarely, the number varies drastically, as in the genus *Thelypteris*, which has x numbers ranging from 27 to 36, or *Lindsaea*, with x numbers from 34 to about 50. In groups in which the chromosome base number does vary so much, it suggests that the "genus" concerned may be unnatural. Simple polyploid series—multiples of the base number—are very common among ferns, and a few species have been reported to have diploid (with two times the base number of chromosomes), tetraploid (four times), and hexaploid (six times) races or forms (*e.g.*, the fragile fern, *Cystopteris fragilis*, has races with the number of chromosomes per nucleus in the sporophyte generation—represented by $2n$—equal to two, four, and six times the base number of $x = 42$, or $2n = 84$, 168, and 252). Species with both diploid and tetraploid forms are common, especially among widespread, abundant ferns. In most cases the cytological races are differentiated on quantitative characters, especially the sizes of such cells as spores, epidermis guard cells (cells next to stomates), and hair cells. The genetics of polyploidy in ferns is not understood, but good hypotheses exist that eventually are expected to provide an explanation.

Genetically, homosporous ferns differ from heterosporous pteridophytes and from seed plants in their ability for intragametophytic selfing—fertilization of an egg by a sperm produced in the same gametophyte. One gametophyte may have both antheridia (sperm-producing structures) and archegonia (egg producers) present on the thallus simultaneously, enabling the formation of an embryo and sporophyte that is homozygous for all alleles (*i.e.*, the homologous—matching—chromosomes contributed by the egg and sperm are identical). This not only bears upon the evolutionary potential of invading (into new areas) fern individuals derived from single spores but also may have significance in interpreting the high chromosome numbers. This may also explain why a number of ferns have wide ranges with large disjunctions (interruptions in distribution).

In certain temperate fern genera, such as spleenworts (*Asplenium*), wood ferns (*Dryopteris*), and holly ferns (*Polystichum*), hybridization between species may be so frequent as to cause serious taxonomic problems. Hybridization between genera is rare but has been reported. Fern hybrids are conspicuously intermediate in their characteristics between their parents, and simple dominance of single characters is unusual. Occasionally, when the interspecific crosses involve strongly different characteristics, the hybrid displays an irregularity in expression of these characteristics, often involving marked asymmetry. The majority of hybrids are sterile and reproduce, if at all, only by vegetative propagation.

Reproduction in sterile fern hybrids is also accomplished by the process of apogamy, in which spores possessing the same chromosome complement as the sporophyte are produced—normal spores have only half the

chromosome number as the parent plant cells. These unreduced spores (diplospores, which have the $2n$ number of chromosomes) are viable and germinate into normal-appearing gametophytes, which may or may not form sex organs. The hybrid gametophytes do not, however, undergo normal sexual fusion. Instead, the meristematic (cell-producing) region of the prothallium simply buds off a new sporophyte, and there is a direct conversion in growth from gametophyte to sporophyte generations. In the ameiotic form of apogamy the spore mother cells simply undergo mitosis (simple cell division) to form unreduced diplospores. In another and much more common form, meiotic apogamy, the spore mother cells are unable to form bivalents (chromosome pairs) at meiosis, and reduction division merely results in irregular, deformed, and inviable spores. In some or most of the sporangia, however, automatic doubling of chromosomes occurs by endomitosis (duplication of chromosomes without formation of two nuclei), and each of the spore mother cells has a restitution nucleus—one with doubled chromosomes. In these doubled sporangia there are, therefore, only eight spore mother cells rather than the usual 16, and they undergo meiosis, producing viable diploid spores. The rest of the process of sporogenesis is like that in ameiotic apogamy. Apogamous ferns are known in a number of genera of higher ferns in various families, including *Adiantum*, *Asplenium*, *Cheilanthes*, *Dryopteris*, *Pellaea*, *Polypodium*, and *Pteris*.

Besides apogamous hybrids, there are numerous demonstrated or suspected "allopolyploid hybrids" that are believed to have originated by doubling of the chromosomes of sterile crosses through faulty mitotic or meiotic divisions. Although intermediate in their characteristics between well-known parental species, these crosses tend to behave like normal, divergent species, alternating sporophytes with gametophytes and undergoing normal meiosis and fertilization. Both apogamous and allopolyploid hybrids may enjoy wide geographical ranges and occur in as great abundance as do normal species. Both types of hybrids are also capable of creating additional hybrids by backcrossing (to the parent species) or by crossing with other species. In apogamous ferns it is assumed that the sperms are generally viable and capable of fusing with eggs of other, normal species. In total, hybrids—sterile, apogamous, and allopolyploid—may make up as many as 20 percent of the "kinds" of ferns in a given flora.

ORIGIN AND EVOLUTION OF FERNS

Fossil record. Fernlike characteristics are known to be combined in numerous fossils coming from geological strata as old as the Devonian (beginning about 395,000,000 years ago). Modern ferns, however, are relatively uniform in basic structure, and they share a large number of characteristics, combined in a very distinctive way. All of the living families, with the exception of the heterosporous ones, possess a ground plan of correlated characteristics that seems clearly to bind them together as being a monophyletic (*i.e.*, one evolutionary line) assemblage. In spite of this, as shown in the enumeration of character trends given below, there is still wide variation present. The norm of modern ferns is so distinctive that the vast majority of them can be immediately recognized as members of this class of plants. Nevertheless, various workers, especially among paleobotanists, have singled out fossil fragments and speculated that they represent fern ancestors, sometimes giving them such names as *Archaeopteris* (primitive fern) or *Protopteridium* (first fern). No convincing fern ancestors are known, however, and the first relatives of modern ferns in the fossil record are usually classifiable into living groups.

The earliest true ferns arose during Carboniferous times (about 280,000,000 to 345,000,000 years ago) and have been classified in four families—Marattiaceae, Osmundaceae, Gleicheniaceae, and Schizaeaceae. So-called Coenopteridales (members of an extinct order of fernlike plants) may represent related lines of evolution, but, since so many Carboniferous plants showed fernlike properties, they are no better candidates for fern ancestors than certain other groups. The immediate ancestors of the seed

Fern hybrids

Age of fossil fernlike vegetation

ferns (pteridosperms) may also have been the immediate ancestors of modern ferns, judging from numerous data on sporangial arrangements and shapes and on leaf anatomy. What used to be considered impressions of fern leaves from the Coal Age (Carboniferous Period) have been shown in many cases to have borne seeds or to have been associated with seed-bearing plants. By the time of the Mesozoic Era (beginning about 225,000,000 years ago), the modern fern families were well established, and there are fossil records of the families Osmundaceae, Marattiaceae, Schizaeaceae, Matoniaceae, Dipteridaceae, Adiantaceae, Cyatheaceae, Aspleniaceae, Marsileaceae, Azollaceae, and Salviniaceae.

Evolutionary development. Despite a relatively large number of theories, the actual origins of the vegetative organs of the ferns are still unknown. It is usually suggested that the original fern stem was protostelic, but this is not necessarily true of the immediate ancestor of modern ferns. In fact, it is conceivable that eustelar stems with secondary growth (*i.e.*, in thickness like those of modern conifers and woody flowering plants) gave rise to modern fern stems through reduction and disappearance of cambial—secondary—growth and replacement of the cauline (stem) stele by its elimination and by the substitution of overlapping leaf traces. The leaf is equally—if not more—problematical from the standpoint of its ultimate origin. Various hypotheses have been made to account for its origin, of which the telome theory (viz., that the leaf arose from fusions and rearrangements of branching stem systems) and the "enation theory" (that the leaf arose from the elaboration of original, simple enations, or outgrowths, such as modern leaf primordia) are the two most popular. The true story seems to be lost in antiquity and perhaps will never be known. Modern fern leaves or pteridophylls, with their characteristic fiddleheads, acropetal growth (*i.e.*, "seeking the apex"—the leaf tissues mature from the base toward the tip, where the youngest tissues are produced), and pinnate structure, are, nevertheless, very distinctive and differ in various respects from sphenophylls such as those of coniferophytes, and from euphylls such as those of flowering plants. It is possible that these leaf types had different origins and even that different examples of each had different origins.

(margin note:) Theories of fern-leaf evolution

CLASSIFICATION

Annotated classification. The classification presented here is derived mainly from Copeland (1947), Alston (1956), Holttum and Sen (1961), and Pichi-Sermolli (1958). It attempts to harmonize differences among these systems by ultilizing, in addition to family, the category of subfamily. Numbers given for the species are only rough approximations of living groups.

CLASS POLYPODIOPSIDA (true ferns)
Spore-dispersed vascular plants with free-living sporophyte and gametophyte generations, the sporophyte dominant. Leaves frondose, circinate (expanding by unrolling), possessing petiole (stalk), midrib, and blade, the latter or its subdivisions with free or netted venation patterns. Sporangia solitary or variously soriate (in clusters) and borne upon the leaf blades or their modified parts, marginally or abaxially (on the under surface, or surface facing away from the central axis of the plant). Stems upright or creeping, mostly lacking secondary thickening, and bearing roots associated with leaf bases. Meristems (growing points) protected by hairs or scales. Gametophytes monomorphic (all with similar structure) and developing outside of the spores (exosporic), hermaphroditic, surficial (growing on the surface) and photosynthetic, or subterranean and saprophytic and symbiotic with fungi; or gametophytes dimorphic (with two forms), endosporic, antheridial (male) or archegonial (female).

Order Ophioglossales
Leaf divided into sterile and fertile segments, leaf base more or less clasping; eusporangiate (with unstalked, globose sporangia); ferns mostly small and fleshy, occurring in early ecological succession. Not known as fossils. Three living genera with about 55 species.

Family Ophioglossaceae. Characters of the order.

Subfamily Botrychioideae (grape ferns, moonworts). Leaf blade pinnately lobed or divided; veins free; sporangia not sunken, borne upon branches of many-branched fertile struc-

ture. Two genera (*Botrychium, Helminthostachys*) and 25 species.

Subfamily Ophioglossoideae (adder's-tongue ferns). Leaf blade simple or furcately (forked) lobed, midrib obscure or absent; veins reticulate; sporangia sunken in unbranched silique-like (elongate capsule-like) "spike." One genus (*Ophioglossum*) with 30 species.

Order Marattiales (giant ferns)
Leaves pinnately divided, pulvinate (enlarged or swollen at leaf base or stem region just below attachment point of leaf stalk) in living genera, and with well-developed fleshy stipules (appendages at leaf base); sporangia eusporangiate, in sori, or more or less coalescent in "synangia" (clusters). Mostly massive, fleshy ferns of tropical forest. About 100 species.

Family Marattiaceae. Characters of the order. Six genera, including *Angiopteris, Marattia, Danaea.* (The extinct Carboniferous and Permian *Psaronius* may belong here or in separate family.)

Order Polypodiales
Leaves nonpulvinate and mostly nonstipulate; sporangia intermediate or leptosporangiate (stalked), solitary or in sori; if soriate, then with or without indusia (protective coverings) and paraphyses (sterile structures). Mostly medium-sized sclerenchymatous (with hardened tissues) plants with cosmopolitan distribution; the order includes most common ferns.

Suborder Osmundineae (royal ferns)
Sporangia on axes of much-reduced segments or along veins on unmodified blade, maturing nearly simultaneously, intermediate between eusporangia and leptosporangia, lacking a definite annulus; petioles with distinct stipule-like dilations. About 20 species.

Family Osmundaceae. Characters of the suborder. Three genera (*Osmunda, Todea, Leptopteris*) and 20 species, plus 5 to 10 extinct genera from the Carboniferous and Permian periods.

Suborder Polypodineae
Sporangia with clearly differentiated annuli or bows; petioles lacking distinct stipular organs or at most dilated at base. Genera number 170 to 250 with about 7,000 to 9,000 species, many tropical ones still undescribed.

Family Plagiogyriaceae. Leaves 1-pinnate, dimorphic (two forms), with trophophylls (sterile fronds) and sporophylls (fertile fronds), the latter contracted and containing scattered sporangia with strongly oblique annuli (rings of special cells); petiole bases swollen; stem apex and young leaves covered with mucilage from secretive hairs. One genus (*Plagiogyria*) and about 30 species distributed in tropical regions.

Family Gleicheniaceae (staghorn ferns). Leaves mostly sprawling over other vegetation, falsely dichotomous, the segments mostly narrowly lobed; sporangia with oblique annuli and organized in simple sori; stems creeping, protostelic. *Gleichenia, Hicriopteris,* and 3 other genera with about 150 species distributed in the tropics.

Family Matoniaceae. Leaves either fanlike, with lobed, narrow segments, or climbing with long midribs; sporangia with oblique annuli, the simple sori covered by a thick peltate indusium-like structure. Two genera (*Matonia* and *Phanerosorus*) and about 4 species distributed in the Old World tropics.

Family Dipteridaceae (umbrella ferns). Leaves fan-shaped, venation free or finely reticulate with free, included veinlets; sporangia with oblique annuli; sori small, with paraphyses; stem with solenostele, covered with narrow bristle-like trichomes. One genus (*Dipteris*) with about 8 species.

Family Cheiropleuriaceae. Leaves dimorphic, with complex reticulate veins, the sterile leaves midribless, once or twice forked; sporangia with oblique annuli and 4-rowed stalks; sorus acrostichoid and with paraphyses; stem protostelic or solenostelic. One genus and species (*Cheiropleuria bicuspis*) distributed in the Old World tropics.

Family Polypodiaceae. Plants mostly epiphytic; leaves usually lobed or simple; sporangia with typical erect bows, numerous, borne in round sori. Genera 42 to 64, with about 1,050 species, mainly tropical in distribution.

Subfamily Polypodioideae (true polypodies). Exposed epiphytes, often in fairly dry habitats; leaves with articulate petioles and reticulate veins; stem creeping, dictyostelic; scales commonly clathrate (latticed); spores bilateral nongreen; gametophyte cordate (heart-shaped), nongemmiferous (not producing gemmae, tiny clusters of cells that break off and grow new gametophytes). Genera include *Polypodium, Pyrrosia, Platycerium,* and 30 to 50 others depending upon the authority consulted, with 550 species.

Subfamily Grammitidoideae (dwarf polypodies). Shaded rain forest epiphytes; leaves nonarticulate, veins free; stem upright, solenostelic or dictyostelic; stem scales with uniform walls; spores tetrahedral-globose, green; gametophyte narrowly cordate to ribbon shaped, gemmiferous. *Grammitis* and 8 to 10 additional genera and 500 species. This subfamily has long been confused with true polypodies.

Family Schizaeaceae. Vegetative organs various; sporangium with its annulus composed of a subapical uniseriate or multiseriate ring of thickened cells. Six genera and about 160 species, mostly tropical.

Subfamily Anemioideae. Leaves typically frond-like; sporangia with apical plate within annules composed of several cells, borne upon margins of unmodified pinnae or upon erect, strongly dimorphic pinnae; spores tetrahedral. Two genera (*Anemia, Mohria*) and 90 species.

Subfamily Lygodioideae (climbing ferns). Leaves climbing by their twisting rachises (central axes); sporangial apical plate of a single cell ordinarily; sporangia attached laterally in two rows, produced on specialized lobes of the blade; spores tetrahedral. One genera (*Lygodium*) with 40 species.

Subfamily Schizaeoideae. Leaves long-petioled, often rather grasslike, simple or forked; sporangial apical plate of a single cell; sporangia borne within extremely contracted and folded blades; spores bilateral; gametophytes filamentous or tuber-like and subterranean. Three genera: *Schizaea, Lophidium, Actinostachys* (these genera are commonly merged into one as subgenera) and 30 species.

Family Adiantaceae. Sporangia in lines along the veins or on or at the vein tips, either unprotected, in grooves, or covered by more or less rolled leaf margin—the "false indusium" —or rarely acrostichoid; sporangia with typical erect bows; spores mainly tetrahedral, nonperisporial. About 16 to 23 genera and 850 species, cosmopolitan in distribution.

Subfamily Adiantoideae (cliff brakes, maidenhair ferns, lip ferns). Mainly small, xerophytic (with adaptations to dry habitats) ferns, the plants epipetric (growing upon rocks) or terrestrial and rigid; leaves 1- to multipinnate; veins mostly free. *Adiantum, Cheilanthes, Notholaena, Pellaea, Pteris,* and 5 to 10 other genera with a total of 750 species.

Subfamily Ceratopteridoideae (aquarium ferns). Plants soft, rooted in mud or floating; leaves 2- to 3-divided, upright or spreading; veins anastomosing. One genus (*Ceratopteris*) and 3 species.

Subfamily Vittarioideae (shoestring ferns). Plants leathery, epiphytic; leaves simple, pendent; veins anastomosing. *Vittaria, Antrophyum,* and 3 to 5 other genera with 100 species.

Family Cyatheaceae. Habit extremely diverse, ranging from mosslike plants to tree ferns; trichomes mainly simple hairs or very narrow scales (except in certain members of the subfamily Cyatheoideae); sori indusiate, the indusia basically tubular or 2 lipped; spores mostly tetrahedral, nonperisporial. Genera number 24 to 57 with about 1,500 species, mainly tropical in distribution.

Subfamily Cyatheoideae (tree ferns, brackens). Terrestrial, medium to very large ferns, the rhizomes ranging from ropelike and creeping to trunklike and upright. Genera number 22 including *Thyrsopteris, Loxsoma, Dicksonia, Cibotium, Lophosoria, Cyathea, Dennstaedtia, Microlepia, Pteridium,* with 850 species.

Subfamily Hymenophylloideae (filmy ferns). Rain forest epiphytes; mostly tiny ferns with lamina of only 2 or 1 cell thickness between veins; spores globose, green, commonly with triradiate germination; gametophyte ribbon shaped or filamentous, gemmiferous. Principal genera are *Hymenophyllum* and *Trichomanes.* Numerous subgenera or segregate genera are maintained by some authorities resulting in number of genera from 2 to 35; there are 500 species.

Subfamily Lindsaeoideae. Mainly terrestrial, medium-sized ferns with protostelic or solenostelic creeping stems covered with hairs or narrow scales; leaves appearing for the most part to be glabrous (smooth), the divisions or segments having cuneate (wedge-shaped) bases; sori marginal, either terminal on single veins or fused on a submarginal connecting vein. Genera include *Lindsaea, Sphenomeris, Odontosoria,* and 8 others, with a total of 250 species.

Family Aspleniaceae. Rhizomes mainly scaly; sori abaxial with peltate (shieldlike), reniform (kidney-shaped), oblong, or linear indusia; sporangia with typical leptosporangiate bows; spores mostly bilateral, provided with perispore (an outer coat). The most common and largest family of ferns, cosmopolitan in distribution, and containing 67 to 82 genera and approximately 3,000 species.

Subfamily Dryopteridoideae (wood ferns, lady ferns, halberd ferns, and others). Rhizome scales nonclathrate; sori various, but basically round—connected by intermediates to a wide variety of derived forms, including asplenioid and acrostichoid. Fifty to 60 genera and 1,900 species.

Subfamily Blechnoideae (chain ferns). Rhizome scales non-clathrate; sori in "loops" along the major veins, following the costal areoles, the indusia opening inward; young foliage commonly red, turning to green. Genera 5 to 10 including *Blechnum* and *Woodwardia,* with 250 species.

Subfamily Asplenioideae (spleenworts). Rhizome clathrate; petiole strand x-shaped; sori lunate (crescent-shaped) to linear, indusiate; sporangia with single-rowed stalks. Genera 12 including *Asplenium* and *Phyllitis,* with 800 species.

Order Marsileales

Aquatics with long, usually rooted rhizomes; leaves long-petioled with 2 or 4 terminal leaflets or none; sporangia contained in sporocarps along petiole; heterosporous. Three genera and about 70 species.

Family Marsileaceae. Characters of the order. *Marsilea* (waterclover), *Pilularia, Regnellidium.*

Order Salviniales

Floating aquatics with small, rounded sporangia contained in saclike indusia; leaves sessile; heterosporous. Two genera and 15 species.

Family Salviniaceae (water spangles). Leaves in whorls of 3, 2 oval in outline and floating, with complex hairs on the top surface, the third finely divided and hanging rootlike in the water; true roots absent. One genus (*Salvinia*) with 10 species.

Family Azollaceae (mosquito fern). Leaves alternate, overlapping, vertically divided into two lobes, the upper floating, the lower submersed; true roots present. One genus (*Azolla*) with 5 species.

Critical appraisal. The classification of ferns has been in a state of flux over the past several decades, but there is increasing agreement over relationships between genera. The differences in classification have more and more to do with the level of categories deemed appropriate, and the system that is presented above is a compromise between extremes. It has the advantage of serving the purposes of workers dealing with small fern floras, who would want to use the families only, and those dealing with large, complex fern floras, who would find the subfamilies of value as well.

Many fern groups show their relationships more by connecting links rather than by single character clusters shared by all members. In this sense, then, the ferns are polythetic, and many of the groups, such as the family Cyatheaceae of the present classification, are difficult to define with a single description.

Some authorities still regard the ferns as being related to club mosses (class Lycopodiopsida), horsetails (Equisetopsida), and whiskferns (Psilotopsida) and refer to all of the latter as "fern allies." In many respects, pertaining especially to the life cycle, the ferns do indeed resemble the so-called fern allies, but in other respects, especially those having to do with the vegetative body of the plant, the ferns are quite distinct.

Comparisons with other fernlike plants

BIBLIOGRAPHY. F.O. BOWER, *The Ferns (Filicales) Treated Comparatively with a View to Their Natural Classification,* vol. 1, *Analytical Examination of the Criteria of Comparison,* vol. 2, *The Eusporangiatae and Other Relatively Primitive Ferns,* vol. 3, *The Leptosporangiate Ferns* (1923–28), a classic work of comparative morphology and systematics that emphasized the need, now being realized, for a broad spectrum of comparative data; H. CHRIST, *Die Geographie der Farne* (1910), still the only broad treatment of fern distribution; CARL F.A. CHRISTENSEN, *Index Filicum* (1906), nomenclature for the taxonomy of ferns, since followed by other supplements by Christensen and by Pichi-Sermolli; *Index Filicum: Supplementum Quartum, Pro Annis 1934–1960* (1965), a quarter-century of publication in fern taxonomy summarized in bibliographies and new taxa described during the period; EDWIN BINGHAM COPELAND, *Genera Filicum: The Genera of Ferns* (1947), a valuable treatment of the classification and characteristics of ferns, containing many of the author's original correlations; *Fern Flora of the Philippines,* 3 vol. (1958–60), one of the major recent tropical fern floras; T. DELEVORYAS (ed.), "Origin and Evolution of Ferns: A Symposium," *Mem. Torrey Bot. Club,* 21:1–95 (1964), a series of short essays summarizing available knowledge and emphasizing the paleobotanical data on fern evolution; L. DIELS, "Polypodiaceae," in A. ENGLER and K. PRANTL (eds.), *Die natürlichen Pflanzenfamilien,* vol. 1, pt. 4, pp. 139–339 (1902), source work for many later studies, a complete statement of diversity for its time; A. MURRAY EVANS, "Interspecific Relationships in the *Polypodium pectinatum-plumula* Complex,"

Ann. Mo. Bot. Gdn., 55:193–293 (1968), a modern monographic study that contains much information about the family Polypodiaceae in its strict sense; FERNANDO FABBRI, "Secondo Supplemento alle *Tavole Cromosomiche delle Pteridophyta* di Alberta Chiarugi," *Caryologia*, 18:675–731 (1965), the chromosome numbers of ferns and other pteridophytes, with bibliographies and previous listings tabulated; F. GORDON FOSTER, *Ferns to Know and Grow* (1971), a popular book on horticulture of ferns for the amateur with many helpful tips on cultivation; R.E. HOLTTUM, *A Revised Flora of Malaya*, vol. 2, *Ferns of Malaya* (1954), a well-illustrated enumeration and description of the ferns of Malaya, giving many of the author's ideas of systematic relationships; IRENE MANTON, *Problems of Cytology and Evolution in the Pteridophyta* (1950), a milestone in the biology of ferns containing, for the first time, accurate data on chromosomes in relation to evolution and systematics; WILLIAM R. MAXON, "Pteridophyta of Porto Rico and the Virgin Islands," *Scient. Surv. P. Rico*, 6:373–521 (1926), a model of careful floristic reportage, still a major reference on Latin American ferns; JOHN T. MICKEL, "A Monographic Study of the Fern Genus *Anemia*, Subgenus *Coptophyllum*," *Iowa St. J. Sci.*, 36:349–482 (1962), not only illustrative of modern approaches to the comparative study of ferns, but contains much useful information on the relationships of Schizaeaceae; B.K. NAYAR and S. KAUR, "Gametophytes of Homosporous Ferns," *Bot. Rev.*, 37:295–396 (1971), a thorough summation of the knowledge of the haploid generation of ferns, including extensive bibliography; Y. OGURA, "Anatomie der Vegetationsorgane der Pteridophyten," in K. LINSBAUER (ed.), *Handbuch der Pflanzenanatomie*, sect. 2, pt. 2, vol. 7 (1938), brings together data on fern anatomy up to the 1930s, but is written in German and needs much updating; R.E.G. PICHI-SERMOLLI, "The Higher Taxa of the Pteridophyta and Their Classification," in OLOV HEDBERG (ed.), *Systematics of Today*, pp. 70–90 (1958), an essay on classification, of special interest for its viewpoint on the relationships of ferns with other pteridophytes; K.R. SPORNE, *The Morphology of Pteridophytes: The Structure of Ferns and Allied Plants*, 2nd ed. (1966), a brief book summarizing ideas of fern structure; FRANS VERDOORN (ed.), *Manual of Pteridology* (1938); EDGAR T. WHERRY, *The Fern Guide: Northeastern and Midland United States and Canada* (1961), an excellent example of a useful field guide, scientifically accurate but useful to amateurs.

(W.H.Wa.)

Ferrites

Ferrites are hard, brittle, ceramic-like materials with magnetic properties that make them useful in portable radios, television receivers, computers, and other types of electronic equipment. They are polycrystalline (made up of a large number of small crystals) and are generally gray or black in appearance. They can be formed into permanent magnets and can be used as core material for electrical transformers, used to change voltages, and coils, used to produce electromagnetic effects; they have a very high electrical resistance and can be operated at high frequencies without excessive losses.

A ferrite material is basically an iron oxide (iron is represented by the symbol Fe and oxygen by O) with which another metal has been chemically combined. Many variations of its chemical composition and crystal structure are possible, leading to an almost infinite variety of characteristics and permitting ferrites to be tailor-made for specific applications.

History. Although the classical ferrite, the ferric oxide called magnetite (Fe_3O_4), was known to man long before biblical times, the peculiar properties of natural and man-made ferrites were not recognized until late in the 19th century, and synthetic ferrites were first prepared in 1909. Important theoretical studies, leading to microwave applications of ferrites, were formulated by two Soviet scientists in 1935, and the new materials and their properties were studied by a number of researchers, culminating in the work of the Dutch physicist Jacob Louis Snoek and his co-workers, whose experiments created a solid foundation for ferrite physics and technology. The announcement of their results in 1946 marked the beginning of industrial use and of intense research effort by hundreds of scientists and engineers in Europe, the United States, and Japan. A French physicist, Louis Néel, formulated an extensive theory of ferrites on the atomic scale, coining the term ferrimagnetism

to distinguish ferrite properties from those of ferromagnetic metals.

Properties. The crystal structure, chemical composition, and heat treatment of ferrites determine their magnetic and electric losses. In general, the ferrite material behaves in most respects like a ferromagnet, exhibiting domains (regions in which all elementary north–south magnetic poles [dipoles] are aligned in a common direction), a hysteresis loop (a curve showing how the material reacts to magnetizing and demagnetizing forces), and saturation of the magnetization M at relatively low applied magnetic fields (see the Table). Practical values for Curie temperature (the temperature at which the magnetic properties disappear) range from 100° to 600° C (200° to 1,100° F). Resistivity, or opposition to the flow of electrical current, comparable to that of good insulators has been obtained.

Each type of crystal structure (spinel, garnet, and hexagonal) permits adjustment of ferrite properties over a wide range as needed for particular applications. A typical spinel ferrite is nickel (Ni) ferrite, $NiFe_2O_4$. Other ferrites may be obtained by substituting magnetic ions (cobalt, nickel, manganese) or nonmagnetic ions (aluminum, zinc, copper) for some of the nickel or iron ions, to produce the desired characteristics. Yttrium–iron garnet (YIG), $Y_3Fe_5O_{12}$, a classical ferrimagnetic garnet, combines very low magnetic loss with high resistivity at very high radio (microwave) frequencies. Substitution of magnetic rare-earth ions (gadolinium, ytterbium, holmium, europium) for yttrium and of nonmagnetic ions (gallium, aluminum) for some of the iron ions leads to many different ferrite compositions with a wide range of properties, including exceptional temperature stability.

Manufacture. Ferrite manufacture is similar to that of other ceramic materials in its use of the sintering process (heating a powdered mixture to a high temperature) for the formation of crystallites (small crystals) of prescribed chemical composition. The need for simultaneous control of mechanical, electrical, and magnetic properties, however, imposes stringent requirements on a complex series of operations, starting with the precise weighing of raw materials. Normally, extremely pure powdered metal oxides are mixed to a high level of uniformity and presintered at about 1,000° C (1,800° F). The material is then broken up into granules of uniform size and mixed with a binder or lubricant to prepare it for the formation of the desired piece parts by pressing or extrusion. The final step is a sintering process in a controlled atmosphere within an electric furnace. Preformed piece parts are heated to a temperature between 1,200° and 1,500° C for several hours and then cooled at a controlled rate to room temperature.

Any shaping of the ferrite pieces after sintering can be done by normal ceramic machining techniques such as grinding, diamond-saw cutting, and ultrasonic drilling.

Applications. Many types of ferrite materials formed into hundreds of shapes are being used to perform a multitude of tasks. To distinguish among major fields of applications, it is convenient to separate ferrites into five groups: soft, square-loop, hard, microwave, and single-crystal (see the Table).

Soft ferrites. These have a slender, S-shaped hysteresis loop and tend to lose their magnetism very easily after the magnetizing field is removed. Manganese–zinc and nickel–zinc ferrites with spinel structure exhibit these properties and permit their adjustment over a wide range of values through variations in composition. These ferrites are uniquely suited as cores for radio, television, and carrier telephony coils and transformers and permit miniaturization of such components. Movable ferrite cores can be used for easy adjustment of inductance (opposition to the flow of alternating current) in coils. Small and effective antennas for portable radios can be built by taking advantage of electromagnetic-field concentration in a ferrite core.

Square-loop ferrites. These materials exhibit an almost rectangular hysteresis loop and return to one of two distinct states of magnetization when the magnetizing field is removed. All practical square-loop ferrites

Ferrimagnetic structures

Summary of Ferrite Applications

type	crystal structure	typical composition	typical properties	typical frequency	applications
Soft	spinel	$Ni_{1-x}Zn_xFe_2O_4$ $Mn_{1-x}Zn_xFe_2O_4$	high permeability μ_i = 15 to 10,000, low loss, remanence, and coercive force, temperature stability	15 kHz to 100 MHz	carrier telephony inductors, television inductors and transformers; radio antennas
Square-loop	spinel	Mg–Mn–Zn ferrites, Li–Ni ferrites	rectangular hysteresis loop, low coercive force, temperature stability	pulsed operation 1 MHz	large two- and three-dimensional computer memory systems, logic devices for computers
Hard	hexagonal	$BaFe_{12}O_{19}$ $SrFe_{12}O_{19}$	high coercive force 2,000 to 10,000 oersteds	. . .	permanent magnets in loudspeakers, small motors and generators, measuring instruments, novelties, toys
Microwave	garnet	$Y_3Fe_5O_{12}$ (YIG) Gd, Yb, Ho and Ga, Al substitutions	M = 200 to 800Gs, low dielectric and magnetic losses	1–5 GHz	reciprocal and nonreciprocal phase shifters, on-off and transfer switches, isolators, 3-port and 4-port circulators, tunable devices, latching devices
	spinel	$MeFe_2O_4$ Me = Ni, Co, Mn, Al, Cu, Zn	M = 1,000 to 5,000 gauss, low dielectric and magnetic losses	2–30 GHz	
	hexagonal	$BaFe_{12}O_{19}$ Sr, Ni, Co, Al substitutions	high anisotropy fields which act as biasing fields	30–100 GHz	
Single-crystal	spinel, garnet	$Y_3Fe_5O_{12}$ with rare-earth substitutions	optically transparent (garnets), extremely narrow line width, high anisotropy, nonlinear response to signal strength	. . .	recording heads for high-fidelity tape recorders, magnetic bubble devices for computer memory and logic functions, microwave filters, microwave power limiters, magneto-optical devices

have a spinel structure. The magnesium–manganese–zinc system has retained its pre-eminent position in computer-memory applications for more than two decades since its discovery in 1951. Recently, lithium–nickel ferrites and more complex systems containing lithium, manganese, and aluminum have become competitive in applications requiring stability and fast switching over a wide range of temperatures.

Ferrite toroids for computer memories   Billions of tiny ferrite toroids (doughnut-shaped cores) with diameters as small as 0.014 inch (0.36 millimetre) are manufactured annually for use in the core memories of large electronic computers. Because such a core retains its magnetization in either one of two directions, it permits storage of bits of information; typically, magnetization in one direction would indicate a 0 and in the other direction a 1 in a binary system. A change in the state of magnetization resulting from a current pulse through a wire threading the core produces a signal on a second threaded wire for recovering the stored information. Only current pulses above a threshold value will permit a signal to be stored or recovered. Pulses below threshold will leave the ferrite core unchanged.

This feature of the ferrite core has been exploited in the design of circuitry for selectively recovering information from large computer memories with thousands, even millions of individual cores. Typically, each core is threaded by three wires, two crossed wires (x and y, Figure 1) for write-in, and one for read-out. Two equal

and simultaneous (coincident) current pulses on one of the x- and y-wires produce a combined magnetic-field strength sufficient to change the state of the core threaded by both wires. All other cores on the same x- and y-wires receive only half of the required pulse and thus remain unchanged. A reversal of magnetization on any one core produces a signal on the read-out wire. This coincidence method permits individual addressing of, for example, 10,000 cores with 100 x- and 100 y- circuits whereas 10,000 circuits would be needed otherwise.

Hard ferrites.   These are characterized by a hysteresis loop enclosing a large area and by the ability to function as a permanent magnet.

Typical hard ferrites have a hexagonal crystal structure with barium (Ba) serving as the metal combining with the iron oxide, leading to the chemical formula $BaFe_{12}O_{19}$. The barium may also be replaced by strontium. Many hard ferrites are highly anisotropic; *i.e.*, their magnetization occurs along a specific direction. This anisotropy is built-in during manufacture by orienting the tiny individual crystals with a strong magnetic field. An important application of hard ferrites is as permanent magnet cores in high-fidelity loudspeakers. Permanent ferrite magnets are also found in small motors, generators, measuring instruments, novelties, toys, and many other products for home and industry.

Microwave ferrites.   These have garnet, spinel, and hexagonal crystal structure, with low electric- and magnetic-loss factors. Substituted and pure garnets, magnesium–manganese–aluminum ferrites, and magnesium–manganese ferrites are used at the lower part of the microwave spectrum. In the millimetre-wave region at frequencies of 30 to 100 gigahertz (one gigahertz equals 1,000,000,000 hertz, or cycles per second), nickel–zinc ferrites and hexagonal ferrites of various compositions are employed.

Principles of microwave applications   Whereas applications of soft and hard ferrites exploit the properties of the hysteresis loop, the fundamental mechanism in microwave applications is interaction of electromagnetic waves with properly aligned, precessing (a motion at right angles to the direction of spin) electron spins in the crystal lattice. An applied adjustable magnetic field supplies the alignment; and the microwave energy, impinging on the ferrite at right angles to the magnetic field, causes the precession of spinning electrons, producing an effect similar to that of an array of spinning tops. The electron spins go through a gyromagnetic resonance phenomenon the frequency range of which increases as the strength of the magnetic field increases and lies somewhere in the microwave region. If

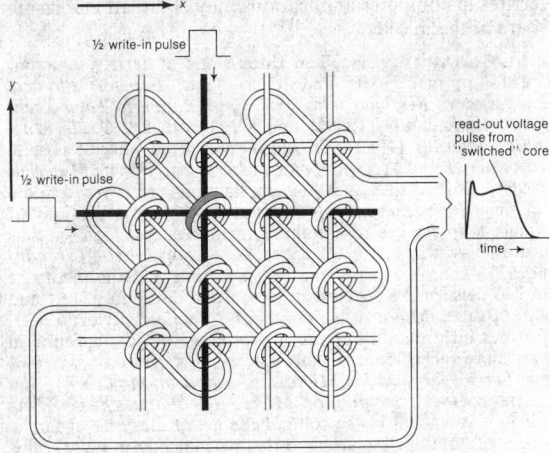

Figure 1: Array of ferrite cores wired for coincident memory use.

microwave energy of the proper sense of circular polarization interacts with a ferrite at its resonance frequency, much of the microwave energy will be absorbed. The frequency range over which this absorption takes place is very narrow, leading to the designation of low-loss ferrites as narrow line-width materials.

This highly selective absorption permits the ferrite to distinguish between forward and reverse propagation of microwave energy and to act as an isolator by absorbing energy flow in one direction while letting energy flowing in the other direction pass through essentially unattenuated, much as traffic on a one-way street.

If electric fields in a microwave signal are oriented in a specific direction (linearly polarized), this direction can be changed by transmission through a ferrite rod in a steady magnetic field, through an effect called Faraday rotation. The effect is nonreciprocal; *i.e.*, it can be used to distinguish between opposite directions of propagation. Because variation of the superimposed magnetic field changes the angle of rotation, electrically controlled microwave circuit elements such as switches and attenuators can be designed.

The ability to rotate electromagnetic field configurations and to distinguish between two directions of propagation have led to the invention of perhaps the most important and versatile microwave ferrite device, the junction circulator. Equally suitable for several different types of microwave transmission lines, this device functions somewhat like a traffic circle in which every traveller must leave by the first available exit. As shown in Figure 2, energy entering at port 1 emerges at port 2, energy en-

Faraday rotation

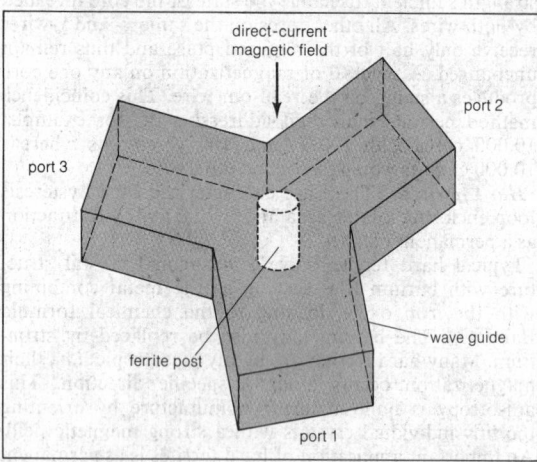

direct-current magnetic field

port 2

port 3

wave guide

ferrite post

port 1

Figure 2: Three-port junction circulator wave guide.

tering at port 2 leaves from port 3, and so on. Both three- and four-port circulators for radar and carrier telephony applications have been built in large numbers.

The effective permeability of the ferrite material for circularly polarized microwave signals can be varied by varying an external biassing (superimposed) magnetic field. This feature can be used to control the flow of microwave energy in switches and phase shifters. Both reciprocal and nonreciprocal control is possible. A relatively new class of ferrite devices takes advantage of the square-loop properties of certain ferrites similar to those discussed earlier. In these devices, the external biassing field is replaced by a current pulse on a wire threading a ferrite shaped like a rectangular toroid and placed in a wave guide. Pulsed into saturation, the ferrite retains its magnetization as if it had been inserted into a biassing field until a current pulse of opposite direction reverses the magnetization. Devices of this type can insert a phase shift of fixed magnitude into a microwave circuit. They have been used for electronic steering of a radar beam.

A variable biassing field can be used to change the microwave permeability in a ferrite that is part of a tuned circuit. Thus, remote electronic tuning becomes possible. In applications of this type, however, ferrites must compete with other elements such as semiconductor diodes.

The most important microwave applications of ferrites

continue to be in isolators and circulators in which their unique nonreciprocal properties are exploited.

Single-crystal ferrites. Grown by conventional crystal-growing techniques, from liquid melt or by a flame fusion process, these ferrites have a spinel or garnet structure and various compositions. Of greatest practical importance are single-crystal rare-earth garnets grown in a flux of molten lead oxide. Because some of these crystals are transparent, their magnetic domains can be observed under a microscope. Other important properties are extremely narrow line width, as described above, and a highly nonlinear response to a microwave signal of increasing power. The narrow line width is used to build microwave filter circuits with tiny yttrium–iron garnet spheres. The nonlinear behaviour permits design of microwave power limiters that protect sensitive microwave circuits from prohibitively strong signals.

Rare-earth garnets

Other single-crystal rare-earth garnets have been grown on a substrate as thin plates with a preferred direction of magnetization perpendicular to the plate. In these plates, tiny round magnetic domains called bubbles can be formed by an applied magnetic field. These bubbles can be propagated, erased, manipulated, and detected. Thus, very compact devices can be built that perform binary (two-state) functions in computers including logic, memory, counting, and switching. Because the bubbles are extremely small in diameter, memory densities of one million bits (individual units of information) per square inch are possible. Manipulation of the bubbles proceeds at high speeds and requires little energy. A typical data rate is 3,000,000 bits per second.

The interaction of infrared and visible light with the electron spins in single-crystal ferrites is called the magneto-optic effect. This effect permits electronic modulation of a beam of light that propagates through a single-crystal garnet. Devices of this type are of great potential interest as possible modulators for laser beams.

Production. Ferrite materials are produced mainly in the United States, the Soviet Union, Great Britain, Japan, France, West Germany, and The Netherlands. Worldwide figures on ferrite production and consumption are not available because much of the material is produced and used in the same company, never reaching the open market.

In the United States, the estimated dollar volume for ferrite production rose from $125,000,000 in 1966 to $160,000,000 in 1970. An annual increase of 9 percent in production was forecast for the early 1970s. Manufacture of ferrite cores for computer memories accounted for 32 percent of the total in 1966. Hard ferrites for permanent magnets followed with 26 percent, soft ferrites for telephone applications with 13 percent, and microwave ferrites with 3 percent. The balance of 26 percent goes to soft ferrites for miscellaneous applications. Because research in materials and development of ferrite applications is continuing, production of ferrite materials is expected to increase for some time to come. Hard ferrites in small motors and generators for automobiles and single-crystal ferrites in computer applications may claim an increasing share of the market.

BIBLIOGRAPHY. Excellent discussions of ferrite materials are found in J. SMIT and H.P.J. WIJN, *Ferrites: Physical Properties of Ferrimagnetic Oxides in Relation to Their Technical Applications* (1959); and K.J. STANDLEY, *Oxide Magnetic Materials* (1962). Of more specialized interest is W.H. VON AULOCK (ed.), *Handbook of Microwave Ferrite Materials* (1965). Soft ferrites and their applications are covered in detail in E.C. SNELLING, *Soft Ferrites* (1969). Applications of square-loop ferrites to computer memories and logic circuits are discussed in C.J. QUARTLY, *Square-Loop Ferrite Circuitry* (1962). The physics of microwave ferrites and the theory of ferrite devices are covered in exhaustive detail in B. LAX and K.J. BUTTON, *Microwave Ferrites and Ferrimagnetics* (1962). Further information on microwave ferrite devices is found in two more recent books: W.H. VON AULOCK and C.E. FAY, *Linear Ferrite Devices for Microwave Applications* (1968); and J. HELSZAJN, *Principles of Microwave Ferrite Engineering* (1969). Advances in the state of the art of all types of ferrite materials and devices are recorded periodically in IEEE *Transactions on Magnetics.*

(W.H.v.A.)

Ferromagnetism

Ferromagnetism is the phenomenon in which certain electrically uncharged materials strongly attract others. Two materials found in nature, lodestone or magnetite (an oxide of iron, Fe_3O_4) and iron, possess or have the ability to acquire such attractive powers, and they are often called natural ferromagnets. They were discovered over 2,000 years ago, and all early scientific studies of magnetism were conducted on these materials.

Ample evidence exists that some atoms or ions, depending on their electronic structure, have a permanent magnetic moment, μ. This moment may be pictured as a dipole consisting of a positive, or north pole, of strength m separated from a negative, or south, pole $-m$ by a distance d and with $\mu = md$. In ferromagnets, which need not contain iron, the large coupling between the atomic magnetic moments leads to some degree of dipole alignment and hence to a net magnetization, m, the magnetic moment per unit volume. Presence of a spontaneous magnetization, from which the attractive property originates, has sometimes been used as the definition of a ferromagnet. Mainly since 1950, however, research on ferromagnetic metals, alloys, semiconductors, and insulators has shown that a variety of arrangements of the atomic moments occurs and, therefore, further classifications have been made to distinguish the different kinds of ferromagnets.

Magnetic order. The principal types of magnetic ordering found in solids are illustrated in Figure 1. In the clas-

netic, many with a parallel moment structure. Some of these compounds are electrical insulators; others have a conductivity of magnitude typical of semiconductors. The compounds investigated to date include oxides, chalcogenides (sulfur [S], selenium [Se], tellurium [Te]), halides (fluorine [F], chlorine [Cl], bromine [Br], iodine [I]), and their combinations. (Examples are $La_{0.7}Pb_{0.3}$, MnO_3, $CuCr_2Se_4$, $CdCr_2S_4$, $CrBr_3$, EuO, EuS, and $EuSe$, of which only $CrBr_3$ is an insulator.) The ions with permanent dipole moments in these materials are manganese (Mn), chromium (Cr), and europium (Eu); the others are diamagnetic.

At low temperatures, the rare-earth metals holmium (Ho) and erbium (Er) have a nonparallel moment arrangement that gives rise to a substantial spontaneous magnetization. These solids have a hexagonal crystal structure in which the atoms are packed in layers called the basal plane; the direction perpendicular to this plane is known as the c-axis. The atomic moments have a conical or spiral structure about the axis, which corresponds to the vertical direction in the diagrams of Figure 1B. Clearly there is a net moment in the c-direction, whereas in the basal plane the components of the moments average to zero. Some ionic compounds with the spinel crystal structure (for example, $HgCr_2S_4$ and possibly $CdCr_2S_4$) also possess a spiral ferromagnetic ordering.

A different structure leads to a spontaneous magnetization in thulium (Tm) below $32°$ K, which can be represented by a longitudinal wave, or antiphase structure, in which three atomic moments point "up" along the c-axis for each four that point "down" (Figure 1C).

In some solids, the strong coupling between the atomic dipoles favours an antiparallel arrangement. As originally conceived by L. Néel, these materials would consist of two sublattices, one with atomic moments aligned antiparallel to those of the other. If the magnetic moments of the two sublattices are equal (Figure 1D), the net moment of the material will be zero. Such materials are called antiferromagnets. It has been established that many solids have this simple antiparallel ordering, including manganese oxide (MnO), cobalt oxide (CoO), nickel oxide (NiO), manganese fluoride (MnF_2), chromium oxide (Cr_2O_3), iron sulfide (FeS), iron chloride ($FeCl_2$), and copper chloride hydrate ($CuCl_2 \cdot 2H_2O$) (see MAGNETISM).

If the two sublattices have differing magnetizations, however, a spontaneous magnetization results (Figure 1E); this phenomenon is known as ferrimagnetism. Lodestone is actually a ferrimagnet. (Other examples are $NiFe_2O_4$, $MnFe_2O_4$, $CoFe_2O_4$, and $Y_3Fe_5O_{12}$, which are often referred to as ferrites.) Because most ferrimagnetic materials have low electrical conductivity and sizeable magnetizations, they have numerous applications in high-frequency devices (see FERRITES). The concept of ferrimagnetism has been broadened to include materials with more than two sub-lattices (the rare-earth iron garnets) and with the triangular moment arrangement shown in Figure 1F (note that the net magnetization is nonzero).

In some simple two sublattice antiferromagnets there exists an additional interaction that tilts the atomic moments towards each other, as depicted in Figure 1G. As a result, there is a small spontaneous magnetization. Materials with this structure are often said to possess parasitic or weak ferromagnetism and are a type of antiferromagnet. Examples include rust or hematite, rhodochrosite, and the rare-earth orthoferrites. Weak ferromagnetism can also be produced in some antiferromagnets by the application of an external stress; this effect, called piezomagnetism, has been detected in the fluorides of manganese and cobalt.

More complex antiferromagnetic structures, for which the spontaneous magnetization is zero, have been observed. The helical arrangement of Figure 1H is found for terbium (Tb), dysprosium (Dy), and holmium (Ho) metals in a temperature range above that required for ferromagnetic ordering, the oblique helix of Figure 1I for erbium between $20°$ and $54°$ K, and the oscillatory longitudinal wave of Figure 1J for erbium between $54°$ and

Fe	Ni	Co	Ho_L	Tm_L	MnO	Fe_3O_4	Mn_3O_4	α-Fe_2O_3	Tb_H	Er_I	Er_H
Gd	Tb_L	Dy_L	Er_L		CoO	$NiFe_2O_4$	$MnFe_2O_4$	NiF_2	Dy_H		Tm_H
$CuAlMn_3$	MnAs				MnF_2	$Y_3Fe_5O_{12}$	?	$LaFeO_3$	Ho_H		
$La_{0.7}Pb_{0.3}MnO_3$					FeF_2	(YIG)					
A			B		C	D	E	F	G	H	I	J

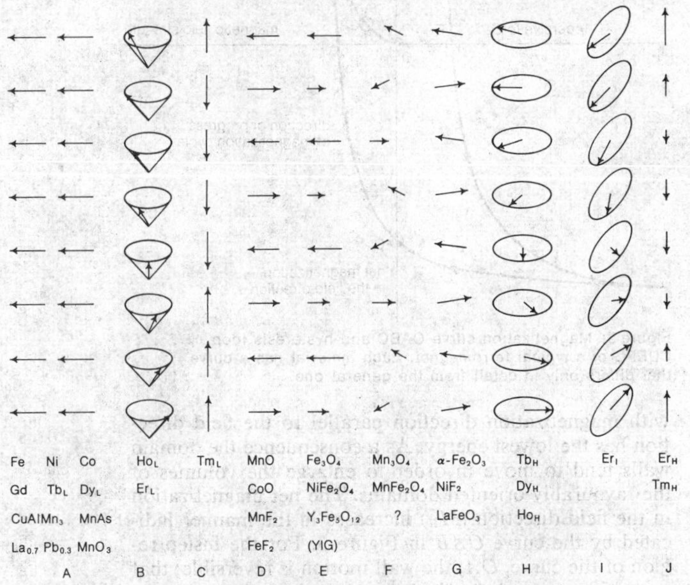

Figure 1: Principal types of magnetic ordering in various solids identified by their chemical formulas. Subscripts H and L refer to temperatures higher and lower than that required for ferromagnetic ordering; I indicates intermediate temperature (see text).

sical concept of a ferromagnet, the dipole moments were envisaged to be aligned parallel by the strong coupling (Figure 1A). This is indeed the magnetic arrangement found for the elemental metals iron (Fe), nickel (Ni), and cobalt (Co) and for their alloys with one another and with some other elements. These materials still constitute the largest group of ferromagnets used in applications (see MAGNETS AND ELECTROMAGNETS). The other elements that possess a colinear ordering are the rare-earth metals gadolinium (Gd), terbium (Tb), and dysprosium (Dy), but the last two become ferromagnets only well below room temperature. Some alloys, although not composed of any of the elements just mentioned, nevertheless have a parallel moment arrangement. Examples are the Heusler alloy $CuAlMn_3$ and MnAs, where the manganese (Mn) atoms have magnetic moments; manganese metal itself is not ferromagnetic.

Since 1950, and particularly since 1960, several ionically bound compounds have been discovered to be ferromag-

Ferromagnetic substances

85° K and for thulium between 40° and 56° K. (This list does not exhaust all the possibilities.)

Sources of ferromagnetism. The permanent magnetic moment of atoms or ions has two possible sources: the motion of the electrons about their atomic nucleus (orbital angular momentum) and the rotation of the electron about its own axis (spin angular momentum). The plane of an electron's orbit can have only certain orientations, and as a consequence the magnetic moment along a specified direction, usually the direction of an applied magnetic field, is some integral multiple of a basic atomic unit, the Bohr magneton, that is equal to one-half the product of the electronic charge and h-bar (Planck's constant divided by 2 pi) divided by the product of the electron mass and the velocity of light, or $\mu_B = e\hbar/2mc$ (-9.274×10^{-21} erg/gauss), in which μ_B is the Bohr magneton, e is the electronic charge, $\hbar$ is Planck's constant/2π, m is the electron mass, and c is the velocity of light. The component of magnetic moment along the field direction associated with an electron's spin is almost equal to one Bohr magneton. Only atoms or ions with an unfilled shell have a nonzero total angular momentum and therefore a magnetic moment. Elements in the periodic table important in ferromagnetism are some of the iron group with unfilled 3rd shells and the rare-earth group with unfilled 4f shells. With iron group atoms or ions, the internal electrostatic fields in solids reduce or eliminate the orbital contribution to the moment, whereas for the rare-earth elements both the orbital and spin angular momentum contribute.

A magnetic structure that is not collinear can be inferred if the measured magnetization is less than that expected for complete alignment of the atomic dipoles. The most information on structure, however, has been obtained from neutron diffraction studies. A neutron, although electrically neutral, has a nuclear spin and hence a magnetic dipole moment. The interaction of the dipole moment of a neutron with the electronic dipole moment of an atom will produce magnetic scattering. In a magnetically ordered material, the scattering is coherent, and lines characteristic of the magnetic structure appear in the diffraction pattern. Other techniques useful for the determination of spin ordering are nuclear magnetic resonance (*q.v.*) and the Mössbauer effect (*q.v.*); both these methods depend on the hyperfine interaction between the electronic and nuclear magnetic moments.

Domain structure. Ferromagnets have another type of magnetic order of a more macroscopic nature, postulated by Pierre-Ernest Weiss, and called domain structure. For simplicity, consider a ferromagnet with collinear order and suppose that the configuration of Figure 2A occurs.

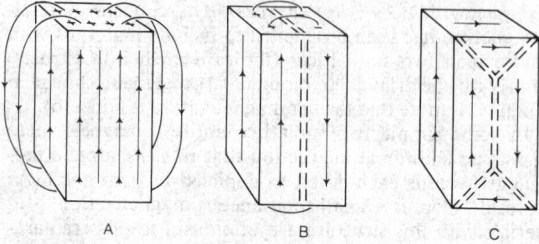

From A. Morrish, *The Physical Principles of Magnetism* (1965); John Wiley & Sons, Inc.

Figure 2: Domain structure in ferromagnetic material (see text).

Magnetic poles appear on the specimen's ends, and a magnetic field is established in the surrounding space, as indicated by the flux lines. The magnetostatic energy associated with the field can be reduced if two antiparallel regions, called domains, appear (Figure 2B). The transition region between the domains is called a domain wall, and its introduction requires energy. The preferred, or stable, configuration will be the one with minimum total free energy. Some domain configurations reduce the magnetostatic energy to zero; an example is given in Figure 2C. The net magnetization is also zero. Basically this is the way some ferromagnets, such as soft iron, may be in an unmagnetized state.

Domain structure can be observed directly. In one technique, a colloidal solution of small magnetic particles, usually magnetite, is placed on the surface of a ferromagnet. When surface poles are present, the particles tend to concentrate in certain regions to form a pattern, which is readily observed with an optical microscope. Patterns with some regularity are only observed on well-polished surfaces of single crystals. Iron whiskers contain relatively few imperfections, and indeed are the nearest things to perfect crystals known. Even weak ferromagnets that have a small magnetostatic energy, such as hematite (Fe_2O_3), have a domain structure. Domain patterns have also been observed with polarized light, polarized neutrons, electron beams, and X-rays.

Ferromagnets in an external magnetic field. To consider the effect of applying an external magnetic field, first suppose the domain structure is such that the net magnetization of the ferromagnet averages to zero (the origin [O] of Figure 3). When a field is present, a domain

From A. Morrish, *The Physical Principles of Magnetism* (1965); John Wiley & Sons, Inc.

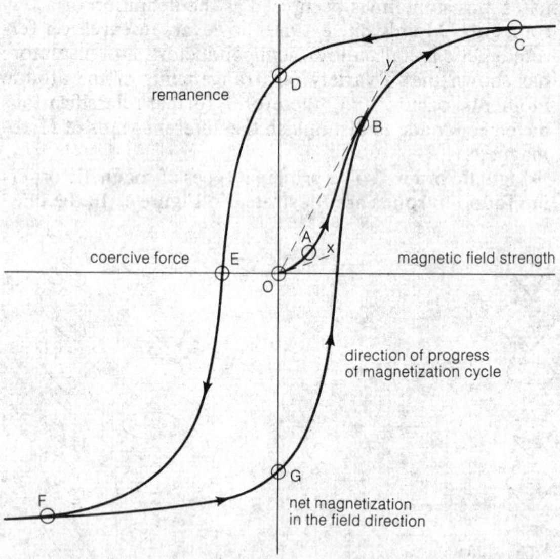

Figure 3: Magnetization curve OABC and hysteresis loop CDEFG of a typical ferromagnet. Each material has a curve that differs only in detail from the general one.

with magnetization direction parallel to the field direction has the lowest energy. As a consequence the domain walls tend to move in order to enlarge the volumes of the favourably oriented domains. The net magnetization in the field direction (M_H) increases in the manner indicated by the curve OAB in Figure 3. For the instep region of the curve, OA, the wall motion is reversible; that is, on removal of the field the domain walls return to their initial positions. At higher fields, between A and the knee of the curve at B, the domain walls are displaced beyond internal energy barriers that arise from nonmagnetic inclusions or inhomogeneous strains. Then, on decreasing the field, the walls do not return to their previous location—that is, the motion is irreversible, and energy is required. At still higher fields (region BC), the domain walls may be almost or entirely removed; further increase in M_H may then occur by rotation of the domain's magnetization toward the field direction. At C the specimen is a single-domain with magnetization direction parallel to the field H. The magnetization then has its saturation value and is essentially equal to the spontaneous magnetization within a domain. By performing the sequence of operations of reducing the field to zero, increasing it in the reverse direction, decreasing it to zero, and then increasing it to the initial value, the curve $CDEFGC$, known as a hysteresis curve or loop, is obtained. The work performed on taking the ferromagnet through one cycle is equal to the area enclosed by the loop.

Ferromagnetic materials are often described by quantities associated with the curves of Figure 3. The magnetization at point D is called the remanence, M_r, and the field at point E the coercive force, H_c. The susceptibility, χ (chi), defined as the ratio of the net magnetization in the field direction to the magnetic field, or M_H/H, has an initial value given by the slope of $\bar{O}x$ and a maximum value given by the slope of $\bar{O}y$.

No domain structure may be possible in a ferromagnet that is a very small particle; instead it will be a single domain even in a zero applied field. The only way the magnetization can be changed is by rotations. These rotations will be difficult and require a large applied field if, for example, the particle is needlelike in shape.

A material composed of aligned particles makes an excellent permanent magnet. Alnico, an alloy, is believed to owe its good permanent magnet properties to aligned rodlike ferromagnetic precipitates. Recently developed materials with superior permanent magnet characteristics are combinations of cobalt with platinum and with samarium, PtCo and SmCo₅.

It is sometimes possible to change the moment arrangement with applied fields, depending, of course, on whether or not a state of lower free energy will be achieved. For bromides and chlorides of iron, cobalt, and nickel (FeBr₂, CoCl₂, NiCl₂) and others in which adjacent ferromagnetic layers are arranged antiferromagnetically via a weak coupling, a sufficiently large magnetic field produces a transition from the antiferromagnetic to the ferromagnetic state. This phenomenon is often called metamagnetism. When a field is applied parallel to the axis of a simple antiferromagnet (collinear with the moments of Figure 1D), at a certain critical value the moments will rotate through 90°. This change from parallel to perpendicular orientation is called spin flopping. A type of spin flop or metamagnetic behaviour may also be observed in a helical spin system; examples are manganese gold (MnAu₂), dysprosium (Dy), holmium (Ho), and erbium (Er).

The temperature dependence of ferromagnetism. Above a critical temperature, called the Curie temperature, T_f, the spontaneous magnetization vanishes. At the Curie point the thermal energy, or Boltzmann constant times the Curie temperature—i.e., kT—is sufficient to overcome the internal aligning forces. The Curie temperatures for some important ferromagnets are: iron (Fe), 1,043° K; cobalt (Co), 1,388° K; nickel (Ni), 631° K; gadolinium (Gd), 289° K; and dysprosium (Dy), 85° K.

Above the Curie point, the ferromagnetic material becomes a paramagnet. For temperatures a few degrees above the Curie temperature, the inverse susceptibility $(1/\chi)$ of many materials including iron (Fe), nickel (Ni), cobalt (Co), and gadolinium (Gd), is a linear function of the temperature described excellently by the Curie-Weiss law: the inverse susceptibility is equal to the difference of the absolute temperature and the paramagnetic Curie point, divided by the Curie constant.

$$\frac{1}{\chi} = \frac{T - \Theta}{C}$$

in which $1/\chi$ is the inverse susceptibility, I is the absolute temperature, Θ is the paramagnetic Curie point, and C is the Curie constant. The intercept with the T-axis, when the susceptibility is plotted versus the absolute temperature, is the paramagnetic Curie point, and has the values 1,093° K, 1,428° K, and 650° K for iron (Fe), cobalt (Co), and nickel (Ni), respectively. Just above the Curie point, a small curvature, concave upward, appears in the plot of $1/\chi$ versus T. This effect is believed to be the result of order persisting within small atomic groups. Data from other measurements, including that of specific heat, support this short-range order theory.

Although below the ordering temperature (T_f) the spontaneous magnetization is nonzero, only at absolute zero are all the atomic moments or spins aligned parallel in a collinearly ordered ferromagnet. Just above $T = 0°$ K, the thermal energy (kT) may reverse the direction of an atomic spin. If so, this reversed spin will not remain localized at one atom, but instead will travel from one atom to another to form a spin wave, or magnon. As the temperature is raised further, more spin waves are created and the spontaneous magnetization decreases, slowly at first but then rapidly as the Curie temperature is approached. Experimentally, the saturation magnetization is measured and the spontaneous magnetization obtained by extrapolation to zero applied field. The difference between the spontaneous and saturation magnetization is negligible except near the Curie point, where the difference is about 1 percent. The variation of the spontaneous magnetization with increasing temperature observed for iron, cobalt, and nickel is shown in Figure 4 below.

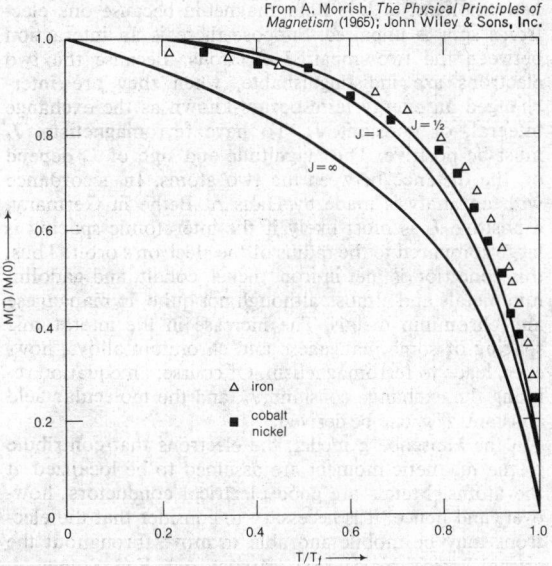

From A. Morrish, *The Physical Principles of Magnetism* (1965); John Wiley & Sons, Inc.

Figure 4: *The change of spontaneous magnetization with temperature.*
The theoretical curves correspond to different values of spin momenta ($J = \frac{1}{2}$, 1, and ∞, $J = \frac{1}{2}$ being the best fit to experimental data). Magnetization at temperature T [i.e., $M(T)$] is expressed as a fraction of magnetization at absolute zero [$M(T)/M(0)$]; temperature is expressed as a fractional value of the Curie temperature (t_f).

Theories of ferromagnetism. One of the primary objectives in a theory of ferromagnetism is to understand the strong interactions that produce the magnetic ordering. The idea that each atom or molecule has a permanent magnetic moment was first proposed by W.E. Weber in 1852. Then, in 1890, J.A. Ewing assumed that atomic magnets interacted via the same magnetic forces (now often called the dipole–dipole interaction) that enter in the attraction and repulsion of laboratory or household-sized bar magnets. Ewing showed from calculations and from models composed of many small bar magnets that magnetization curves and hysteresis loops with the shape of those shown in Figure 3 were obtained.

The magnetic forces considered by Ewing, however, are not large enough to create ferromagnetic alignment; this fact was recognized by P. Weiss who, in 1907, postulated the existence of a large internal magnetic field, which he called the molecular field (H_m). Although Weiss did not concern himself with the origin of the molecular field, he assumed it was proportional to the (spontaneous) magnetization (M) and was equal to a constant due to the molecular field (called the Weiss constant) times the magnetization, or $H_m = N_W M$, in which H_m is the molecular field, N_W is the Weiss constant, and M is the magnetization. Earlier, in 1905, P. Langevin had derived an expression for the magnetization of a paramagnet when an external magnetic field is applied (see MAGNETISM). In addition to the external field, Weiss substituted the molecular field into Langevin's expression and obtained the curve marked $J = \infty$ in Figure 4 for the magnetization as a function of the temperature. With the advent of quantum mechanics, it became clear that the angular momenta, and hence the magnetic moment,

Ewing's contribution

of the atomic electrons could not take any possible orientation but instead were spatially quantized. As a consequence, Langevin's expression required modification to one derived by L. Brillouin in 1927 in which J is a quantum number that characterizes the angular momentum. The temperature dependence of the magnetization for $J = \frac{1}{2}$ and $J = 1$ is shown in Figure 4. The best fit to the experimental data is obtained for $J = \frac{1}{2}$, which corresponds to the spin angular momentum of one electron.

Origin of the molecular field

The origin of the molecular field remained obscure until a German physicist, Werner Heisenberg, in 1928, showed that it was the result of the quantum-mechanical exchange interaction. This exchange interaction has no classical analog. Consider two atoms, each with a magnetic moment of one Bohr magneton because one electron's spin is unpaired. Suppose there is an interaction between the two unpaired electrons. Because the two electrons are indistinguishable, when they are interchanged an energy term occurs known as the exchange integral, or constant, J_e. To have ferromagnetism, J_e must be positive. The magnitude and sign of J_e depend on the distance between the two atoms. In accordance with an analysis made by Hans A. Bethe in Germany, a positive J_e is most likely if the interatomic spacing is large compared to the radius of the electron's orbit. Thus, this condition is met in iron, nickel, cobalt, and gadolinium metals and almost, although not quite, in manganese and chromium metals. The increase in the interatomic spacing of some manganese and chromium alloys, however, leads to ferromagnetism. Of course, an equation relating the exchange constant, J_e, and the molecular field constant, N_w, can be derived.

In the Heisenberg model, the electrons that contribute to the magnetic moment are assumed to be localized at the atoms. Metals are good electrical conductors, however, and hence, it is necessary to consider that the electrons may be mobile and able to move throughout the crystal lattice (see METALS, THEORY OF). E.C. Stoner, in 1938, developed the collective electron theory of ferromagnetism for itinerant electrons in the 3d band; he assumed that the exchange interaction between the electrons could be represented by a molecular field. Good agreement with the experimental data for iron and nickel was achieved. Current opinion appears to favour the view that the magnetic electrons for both iron and nickel are itinerant. On the other hand, the 4f electrons of the rare-earth metals are believed to be localized. Even here, however, the interaction between the 4f electrons on adjacent atoms is believed to proceed via the conduction electrons (the outer 6s–5d electrons), which become polarized; that is, more conduction electrons have their spins parallel than antiparallel.

In many calculations of the exchange interaction, only adjacent atoms are considered. It is now clear that in some materials, for example, those with spiral ordering, atoms farther away must be considered. In compounds such as the oxides and the chalcogenides, the atoms with a magnetic moment are separated by a nonmagnetic atom or anion (for example, oxygen $[O^{2-}]$ and sulfur $[S^{2-}]$). It is believed that the coupling proceeds via the intermediate anion, and it is known as the superexchange interaction. Even with a better knowledge of the functions that describe the state of an atom and the employment of modern digital computers, calculations of the exchange energy still leave much to be desired and continue to be an active area of investigation.

Crystal structure and magnetism

Thus far the magnetization has been treated as though it has no preferred orientation with respect to the crystal axes. The electron orbits, however, reflect the symmetry of the lattice because of the crystalline electric field and the overlap of the orbits of adjacent atoms. Therefore, the atomic moments tend to lie only along certain directions; for example, the preferred or easy direction for a single crystal of iron is along the cube edge, whereas for nickel it is along the cube diagonal. Within a domain, the magnetization will lie along the easy direction, provided that other factors, such as strain, are absent. In some materials, the crystalline anisotropy (physical characteristics differing greatly from different directions) may be very large; in some rare-earth metals it is larger than the exchange energy and must be included in an analysis of the magnetic ordering. The magnetic or dipole–dipole interaction is also anisotropic, though usually smaller than the crystalline anistropy. In recent years, more complex magnetic systems have been discovered and studied; an interpretation of their properties has required the extension of existing theories and the inclusion of all pertinent, and some new, interactions.

BIBLIOGRAPHY. Classical treatments of the subject include: J.H. VAN VLECK, *Theory of Electric and Magnetic Susceptibilities* (1932); R. BECKER and W. DORING, *Ferromagnetismus* (1939), in German; E. KNELLER, *Ferromagnetismus* (1962), an updating and revision of the work by Becker and Döring, also in German; and E.C. STONER, *Magnetism and Matter* (1934), on a more elementary level than those previously cited. A.H. MORRISH, *The Physical Principles of Magnetism* (1965); D.H. MARTIN, *Magnetism in Solids* (1967); and S. CHIKAZUMI and S.H. CHARAP, *Physics of Magnetism* (1964), are general texts, the last more technologically oriented. Experiments and apparatus have been described by L.F. BATES, in *Modern Magnetism*, 4th ed. (1961); extensive experimental data in R.M. BOZORTH, *Ferromagnetism* (1951). For an elementary and pictorial treatment of domains, see D.J. CRAIK and R.S. TEBBLE, *Ferromagnetism and Ferromagnetic Domains* (1965). Advanced theoretical work may be found in D.C. MATTIS, *The Theory of Magnetism: An Introduction to the Study of Coop. Phenomena* (1965); and in the multivolume reference work by G.T. RADO and H. SUHL (eds.), *Magnetism: A Treatise on Modern Theory and Materials* (1963–67).

(A.H.M.)

Fertilization

Fertilization, the completion of the cycle of sexual reproduction, may be formally defined as the union of a spermatozoal nucleus, of paternal origin, with an egg nucleus, of maternal origin, to form the primary nucleus of an embryo. In all organisms the essence of fertilization is, in fact, the fusion of the hereditary material of two different sex cells, or gametes, each of which carries half the number of chromosomes typical of the species. The most primitive form of fertilization, found in micro-organisms and protozoans, consists of an exchange of genetic material between two cells.

Summary of events. The first significant event in fertilization is the fusion of the membranes of the two gametes resulting in the formation of a channel that allows the passage of material from one cell to the other. Fertilization in advanced plants is preceded by pollination, during which pollen is transferred to, and establishes contact with, the female gamete or macrospore. Fusion in advanced animals is usually followed by penetration of the egg by a single spermatozoon. The result of fertilization is a cell (zygote) capable of undergoing cell division to form a new individual.

Formation of the zygote

The fusion of two gametes initiates several reactions in the egg. One of these causes a change in the egg membrane(s), so that the attachment of and penetration by more than one spermatozoon cannot occur. In species in which more than one spermatozoon normally enters an egg (polyspermy), only one spermatozoal nucleus actually merges with the egg nucleus. The most important result of fertilization is egg activation, which allows the egg to undergo cell division. Activation, however, does not necessarily require the intervention of a spermatozoon; during parthenogenesis, in which fertilization does not occur, activation of an egg may be accomplished through the intervention of physical and chemical agents. Invertebrates such as aphids, bees, and rotifers normally reproduce by parthenogenesis.

In plants certain chemicals produced by the egg may attract spermatozoa. In animals, with the possible exception of some coelenterates, it appears likely that contact between eggs and spermatozoa depends on random collisions. On the other hand, the gelatinous coats that surround the eggs of many animals exert a trapping action on spermatozoa, thus increasing the chances for successful sperm-egg interaction (see also REPRODUCTION).

The eggs of marine invertebrates, especially echino-

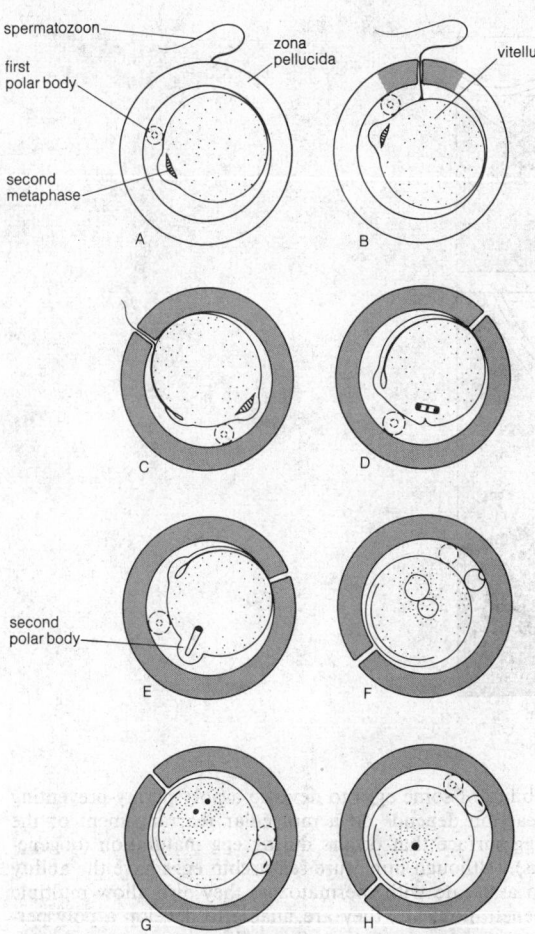

Figure 1: *Steps in fertilization in the rat egg.*
(A–C) Entrance of spermatozoon; shading denotes zona reaction. (D, E) Completion of meiotic division. (F) Pronuclear development. (G) Reappearance of chromosome group. (H) First cleavage metaphase.

Adapted from *Biological Review Cambridge Philosophical Society* (1957); reprinted by permission

derms, are classical objects for the study of fertilization. These transparent eggs are valuable for studies observing living cells and for biochemical and molecular investigations because the time of fertilization can be accurately fixed, the development of many eggs occurs at about the same rate under suitable conditions, and large quantities of the eggs are obtainable. The eggs of some teleosts and amphibians also have been used with favourable results, and techniques for fertilization of mammalian eggs in the laboratory may allow their use even though only small numbers are available.

Characteristics of the mature egg. Maturation is the final step in the production of functional eggs (oogenesis) that can associate with a spermatozoon and develop a reaction that prevents the entry of more than one spermatozoon; in addition, the cytoplasm of a mature egg can support the changes that lead to fusion of spermatozoal and egg nuclei and initiate embryonic development.

Egg surface. Certain components of an egg's surface, especially the cortical granules, are associated with a mature condition. Cortical granules of sea urchin eggs, aligned beneath the plasma membrane (thin, soft, pliable layer) of mature eggs, have a diameter of 0.8–1.0 micron (0.0008–0.001 millimetre) and are surrounded by a membrane similar in structure to the plasma membrane surrounding the egg. Cortical granules are formed in a cell component known as a Golgi complex, from which they migrate to the surface of the maturing egg.

The surface of a sea urchin egg has the ability to affect the passage of light unequally in different directions; this property, called birefringence, is an indication that the molecules comprising the surface layers are arranged in a definite way. Since birefringence appears as an egg matures, it is likely that the properties of a mature egg mem-

(Cortical granules — margin note left)

brane are associated with specific molecular arrangements. A mature egg is able to support the formation of a zygote nucleus; *i.e.*, the result of fusion of spermatozoal and egg nuclei. In most eggs the process of reduction of chromosomal number (meiosis) is not completed prior to fertilization. In such cases the fertilizing spermatozoon remains beneath the egg surface until meiosis in the egg has been completed, after which changes and movements that lead to fusion and the formation of a zygote occur.

Egg coats. The surfaces of most animal eggs are surrounded by envelopes, which may be soft, gelatinous coats (as in echinoderms and some amphibians) or thick membranes (as in fishes, insects, and mammals). In order to reach the egg surface, therefore, spermatozoa must penetrate these envelopes; indeed, spermatozoa contain enzymes (organic catalysts) that break them down. In some cases (*e.g.*, fishes and insects) there is a channel, or micropyle, in the envelope, through which a spermatozoon can reach the egg.

The jelly coats of echinoderm and amphibian eggs consist of complex carbohydrates called sulfated mucopolysaccharides; it is not yet known if they have a species-specific composition. The envelope of a mammalian egg is more complex. The egg is surrounded by a thick coat composed of a carbohydrate protein complex called zona pellucida. The zona is surrounded by an outer envelope, the corona radiata, which is many cell layers thick and formed by follicle cells adhering to the oocyte before it leaves the ovarian follicle.

Although it once was postulated that the jelly coat of an echinoderm egg contains a substance (fertilizin) thought to have an important role not only in the establishment of sperm-egg interaction but also in egg activation, fertilizin now has been shown identical with jelly-coat material, rather than a substance continuously secreted from it. Yet there is evidence that the egg envelopes do play a role in fertilization; *i.e.*, contact with the egg coat elicits the acrosome reaction (described below) in spermatozoa.

Events of fertilization. *Sperm-egg association.* The acrosome reaction of spermatozoa is a prerequisite for the association between a spermatozoon and an egg (Figure 2), which occurs through fusion of their plasma membranes. After a spermatozoon comes in contact with an egg (2A), the acrosome, which is a prominence at the anterior tip of the spermatozoa, undergoes a series of well-defined structural changes. A structure within the acrosome, called the acrosomal vesicle (labeled a), bursts, and the plasma membrane (labeled s) surrounding the spermatozoon fuses at the acrosomal tip with the membrane surrounding the acrosomal vesicle to form an opening (2B). As the opening is formed, the acrosomal granule (labeled g), which is enclosed within the acrosomal vesicle, disappears. It is thought that dissolution of the granule releases a substance called a lysin, which breaks down the egg envelopes, allowing passage of the spermatozoon to the egg. The acrosomal membrane region opposite the opening adheres to the nuclear envelope of the spermatozoon and forms a shallow outpocketing, which rapidly elongates into a thin tube, the acrosomal tubule (labeled t) that extends to the egg surface and fuses with the egg plasma membrane (2C, 2D). The tubule thus formed establishes continuity between the egg and the spermatozoon and provides a way for the spermatozoal nucleus to reach the interior of the egg. Other spermatozoal structures that may be carried within the egg include the midpiece and part of the tail; the spermatozoal plasma membrane and the acrosomal membrane, however, do not reach the interior of the egg. In fact, whole spermatozoa injected into unfertilized eggs cannot elicit the activation reaction or merge with the egg nucleus. As the spermatozoal nucleus is drawn within the egg, the spermatozoal plasma membrane breaks down; at the end of the process, the continuity of the egg plasma membrane is re-established. This description of the process of sperm-egg association, first documented for the acorn worm *Saccoglossus* (phylum Enteropneusta), generally applies to most eggs studied thus far.

During their passage through the female genital tract of mammals, spermatozoa undergo physiological change,

(Acrosome reaction — margin note right)

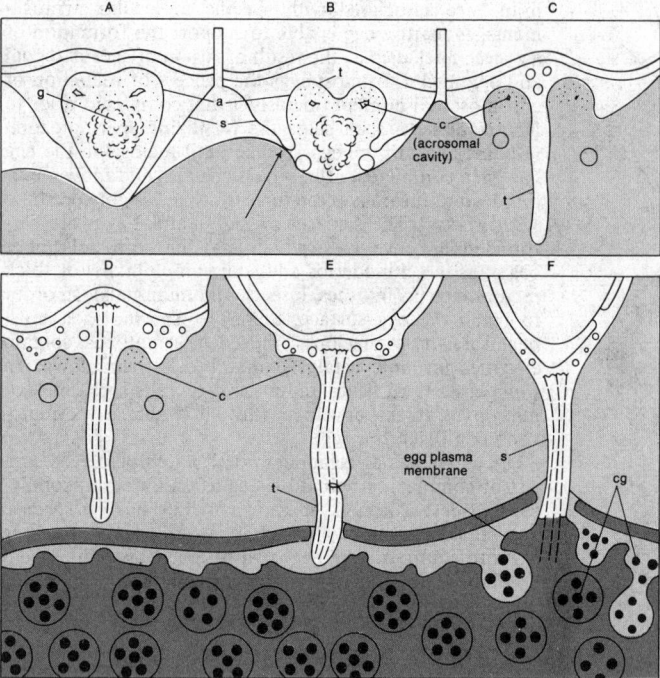

Figure 2: A diagrammatic representation of successive stages of the sperm penetration in the egg of *Saccoglossus*.
From Colwin and Colwin, *Journal of Cell Biology*, vol. 19 (December 1963)

called capacitation, which is a prerequisite for their participation in fertilization; they are able to undergo the acrosome reaction, traverse the egg envelopes, and reach the interior of the egg. Dispersal of cells in the outer egg envelope (corona radiata) is caused by the action of an enzyme (hyaluronidase) that breaks down a substance (hyaluronic acid) binding corona radiata cells together. The enzyme may be contained in the acrosome and released as a result of the acrosome reaction, during passage of the spermatozoon through the corona radiata. The reaction is well advanced by the time a spermatozoon contacts the thick coat surrounding the egg itself (zona pellucida). The pathway of a spermatozoon through the zona pellucida appears to be an oblique slit.

Association of a mammalian spermatozoon with the egg surface occurs along the lateral surface of the spermatozoon, rather than at the tip as in other animals, so that the spermatozoon lies flat on the egg surface; several points of fusion occur between the plasma membranes of the two gametes (*i.e.*, the breakdown of membranes occurs by formation of numerous small vesicles).

Specificity of sperm-egg interaction. Although fertilization is strictly species-specific, very little is known about the molecular basis of such specificity. The egg coats may have a role. Among the echinoderms solutions of the jelly coat clump, or agglutinate, only spermatozoa of their own species. In both echinoderms and amphibians, however, slight damage to an egg surface makes fertilization possible with spermatozoa of different species (heterologous fertilization); this procedure has been used to obtain certain hybrid larvae.

The eggs of ascidians, or sea squirts, members of the chordate subphylum Tunicata, are covered with a thick membrane called a chorion; the space between the chorion and the egg is filled with cells called test cells. The gametes of ascidians, which have both male and female reproductive organs in one animal, mature at the same time; yet self-fertilization does not occur. If the chorion and the test cells are removed, however, not only is fertilization with spermatozoa of different species possible, but self-fertilization also can occur.

Prevention of polyspermy. Most animal eggs are monospermic; *i.e.*, only one spermatozoon is admitted into an egg. In some eggs, protection against the penetration of the egg by more than one spermatozoon (polyspermy) is due to some property of the egg surface; in others, however, the egg envelopes are responsible. The

ability of some eggs to develop a polyspermy-preventing reaction depends on a molecular rearrangement of the egg surface that occurs during egg maturation (oogenesis). Although immature sea urchin eggs have the ability to associate with spermatozoa, they also allow multiple penetration; *i.e.*, they are unable to develop a polyspermy-preventing reaction. Since the mature eggs of most animals are fertilized before completion of meiosis and are able to develop a polyspermy-preventing reaction, specific properties of the egg surface must have differentiated by the time meiosis stops, which is when the egg is ready to be fertilized.

In some mammalian eggs defense against polyspermy depends on properties of the zona pellucida; *i.e.*, when a spermatozoon has started to move through the zona, it does not allow the penetration of additional spermatozoa (zona reaction). In other mammals, however, the zona reaction either does not take place or is weak, as indicated by the presence of numerous spermatozoa in the space between the zona and egg surface. In such cases the polyspermy-preventing reaction resides in the egg surface. Although the eggs of some animals (*e.g.*, some amphibians, birds, reptiles, and sharks) are naturally polyspermic, only one spermatozoal nucleus fuses with an egg nucleus to form a zygote nucleus; the other spermatozoa degenerate.

Formation of the fertilization membrane. The most spectacular changes that follow fertilization occur at the egg surface. The best known example, that of the sea urchin egg, is described below. An immediate response to fertilization is the raising of a membrane, called a vitelline membrane, from the egg surface. In the beginning the membrane is very thin; soon, however, it thickens, develops a well-organized molecular structure, and is called the fertilization membrane. At the same time an extensive rearrangement of the molecular structure of the egg surface occurs. The events leading to formation of the fertilization membrane require about one minute.

At the point on the outer surface of the sea urchin egg at which a spermatozoan attaches, the thin vitelline membrane becomes detached. As a result the membranes of the cortical granules (cg, see Figure 2F) come into contact with the inner aspect of the egg's plasma membrane and fuse with it, the granules open, and their contents are extruded into the perivitelline space; *i.e.*, the space between the egg surface and the raised vitelline membrane. Part of the contents of the granules merge with the

Roles of the egg surface and coats

vitelline membrane to form the fertilization membrane; if fusion of the contents of the cortical granules with the vitelline membrane is prevented, the membrane remains thin and soft. Another material that also derives from the cortical granules covers the surface of the egg to form a transparent layer, called the hyaline layer, which plays an important role in holding together the cells (blastomeres) formed during division, or cleavage, of the egg. The plasma membrane surrounding a fertilized egg, therefore, is a mosaic structure containing patches of the original plasma membrane of the unfertilized egg and areas de-

Effects on membrane properties

rived from membranes of the cortical granules. The events leading to the formation of the fertilization membrane are accompanied by a change of the electric charge across the plasma membrane, referred to as the fertilization potential, and a concurrent outflow of potassium ions (charged particles); both phenomena are similar to those that occur in a stimulated nerve fibre. Another effect of fertilization on the plasma membrane of the egg is a several-fold increase in its permeability to various molecules; this may be the result of activation of some surface-located membrane transport mechanism.

Formation of the zygote nucleus. After its entry into the egg cytoplasm, the spermatozoal nucleus, now called the male pronucleus, begins to swell, and its chromosomal material disperses and becomes similar in appearance to that of the female pronucleus. Although the membranous envelope surrounding the male pronucleus rapidly disintegrates in the egg, a new envelope promptly forms around it. The male pronucleus, which rotates 180° and moves towards the egg nucleus, initially is accompanied by two structures (centrioles) that function in cell division. After the male and female pronuclei have come into contact, the spermatozoal centrioles give rise to the first cleavage spindle, which precedes division of the fertilized egg. In some cases fusion of the two pronuclei may occur by a process of membrane fusion; two adjoining membranes fuse at the point of contact to give rise to the continuous nuclear envelope that surrounds the zygote nucleus.

Biochemical analysis of the events of fertilization. Many of the early studies on biochemical changes occurring during fertilization were concerned with the respiratory metabolism of the egg. The results, however, were deceiving; the sea urchin egg, for example, showed an increased rate of oxygen consumption as an immediate response to either fertilization or parthenogenetic activation, in apparent support of the idea that the essence of fertilization is the removal of a respiratory or metabolic block in the unfertilized egg. Extensive comparative studies have shown that the increased rate of oxygen consumption in fertilized sea urchin eggs is not a general rule; indeed, the rate of oxygen consumption of most animal eggs does not change at the time of fertilization and may even temporarily decrease.

At the time of fertilization the egg contains the components required to carry out protein synthesis, and hence development, through an early embryonic stage called the blastula. Most immediate post-fertilization protein synthesis is directed by molecules of ribonucleic acid, known as messenger RNA, that were formed during oogenesis and stored in the egg. In addition, protein synthesis up to the blastula stage (up to a much earlier stage in the mammalian embryo) is directed by the cell components called ribosomes, which are present in the unfertilized egg; new ribosomes, as well as molecules of another type of RNA involved in protein synthesis, and called transfer RNA, are synthesized at a later stage in embryonic development (gastrulation). Eggs fertilized and allowed to develop in the presence of the antibiotic actinomycin, which suppresses RNA synthesis, not only reach the blastula stage but their rate of protein synthesis is the same as that in untreated embryos.

Unfertilized sea urchin eggs, as well as those of other marine animals studied thus far, have a very low rate of protein synthesis, suggesting that something in the unfertilized egg inhibits its protein synthesizing machinery.

Protein synthesis

Since the rate of protein synthesis increases immediately following fertilization, it may depend on some change in,

or removal of, an inhibitor. In the sea urchin egg, for example, the low efficiency of the protein synthesizing apparatus apparently depends on certain properties of the ribosomes. Most of the ribosomes found in an unfertilized sea urchin egg are single ribosomes (so-called monosomes); soon after fertilization, however, the single ribosomes interact with messenger RNA molecules thus giving rise to the polyribosomes, which are the active units in protein synthesis. This process also occurs in eggs of a few other marine animals that have been studied. The protein-synthesizing inefficiency of unfertilized sea-urchin-egg ribosomes is caused by an inhibitor that is associated with them and interferes with the binding of messenger RNA molecules to the ribosomes; the inhibitor is removed almost immediately following fertilization, perhaps by enzymatic breakdown.

It thus appears that at least in the sea urchin egg the overall rate of protein synthesis is controlled at the ribosome level and that the first step in the activation of protein synthesis following fertilization is the "turning on" of the ribosomes.

In vertebrates such as amphibians, activation of protein synthesis takes place at the onset of egg maturation, apparently initiated by the action of a hormone, progesterone. The effect of progesterone is not mediated by the nucleus but is a direct effect on the cytoplasm.

BIBLIOGRAPHY. C.B. METZ and A. MONROY (eds.), *Fertilization*, 2 vol. (1967–69), a major source of current information; A. MONROY, "Biochemical Aspects of Fertilization," in R. WEBER (ed.), *The Biochemistry of Animal Development*, vol. 1, pp. 73–135 (1965), *Chemistry and Physiology of Fertilization* (1965), a brief, understandable text; E.B. WILSON, *The Cell in Development and Inheritance* (1906; 3rd rev. ed., *The Cell in Development and Heredity*, 1925), a classic work.

(A.Mo.)

Fibres, Man-Made

Man-made fibres consist of two broad groups, based upon the origin of the fibre-forming substance. The first group, of which rayon and acetate are examples, are produced by modifying natural fibre-forming materials such as cellulose. The second group, frequently called synthetics and including such fibres as nylon and polyester, are produced from synthetic chemicals. Like other textile fibres, man-made types are long and narrow; they are composed of long, threadlike molecules, which are made up of hundreds or thousands of atoms strung together in a chain.

HISTORY AND DEVELOPMENT

The English physicist Robert Hooke suggested in the 17th century the possibility of extruding artificial silk by a mechanical imitation of the silkworm. In the 19th century, an English weaver named Louis Schwabe successfully produced filaments from molten glass by forcing the liquid through nozzles ending in fine holes; on contact with air the glass hardened into a fibre.

Cellulose as a raw material

This first man-made fibre was not suitable for textiles. The natural cellulose of wood was subsequently considered as a potential raw material for the production of textile fibres. Wood cellulose is associated with various gummy substances, however, making it unsuitable for textile use. Experiments were undertaken with the object of dissolving the cellulose, separating the resulting liquid from its impurities, and then extruding and hardening the liquid to form a fibre. In 1846 a German chemist discovered that cellulose could be converted into another substance, nitrocellulose, by treatment with nitric acid. Unlike its parent material, nitrocellulose dissolves readily in solvent substances such as a mixture of ether and alcohol. The molecules retain their long, threadlike shape, and small groups of atoms become attached to their sides, making the new substance more soluble. A patent was issued in 1855 for the manufacture of nitrocellulose fibres, but despite their strength and flexibility, their extreme flammability made these fibres unacceptable for textile manufacture.

In 1883 Sir Joseph Wilson Swan, a British scientist working on the problem of producing a filament for an

Development of rayon

electric light, patented a process for squeezing a nitrocellulose solution through holes to form filaments, then treating the filaments with chemicals to change the flammable nitrocellulose back into harmless cellulose. Swan exhibited articles made from his filament, but he did not attempt to develop its potential for textile manufacture. In France, Count Hilaire de Chardonnet produced a fibre that he called artificial silk. Like Swan, he employed a nitrocellulose solution squeezed through tiny holes, hardened in warm air, and then converted back into cellulose by chemical treatment. Chardonnet exhibited materials woven from this artificial fibre at the Paris Exposition in 1889 and secured financial backing to build a factory at Besançon, in the east of France. Manufacture of Chardonnet silk, later known as rayon, the first commercially produced man-made fibre, began in 1891.

Although Chardonnet's process was simple and involved a minimum of waste, it was slow, expensive, and potentially dangerous. In 1890 another French chemist had patented a process that made use of the earlier discovery that cellulose could be dissolved in cuprammonium liquor, a solution of copper salts and ammonia, and after extrusion be regenerated in a coagulating bath, forming continuous filaments. The cuprammonium process replaced the Chardonnet process, but was expensive and fell into disuse for some time until development of an improved spinning method, permitting manufacture of very fine filaments, revived the popularity of cuprammonium rayon. In 1892 another method of producing a regenerated cellulose fibre was devised, involving the chemical treatment of cellulose to form a crumblike material called cellulose xanthate, which could be dissolved to form a viscous liquid known as viscose. Extrusion of the fine jets of viscose into an acid coagulating bath resulted in the regeneration of the cellulose in the form of filaments. Commercial production began in 1905, and the industry developed rapidly, with viscose becoming a major man-made fibre.

A second artificial fibre made from cellulose was developed after World War I. Two Swiss brothers, Henry and Camille Dreyfus, established factories in Great Britain and the United States to produce a cellulose acetate solution used as varnish for the fabric wings of aircraft. At the end of the war, with no further demand for aircraft varnish, the Dreyfus brothers turned to fibre production, and in 1921 they began commercial manufacture of the product called Celanese. This process involves conversion of the cellulose to a derivative, cellulose acetate, which is then dissolved in a solvent such as acetone, forming a solution that is extruded to form a filament.

Although cellulose remains the most important source of man-made fibres derived from natural substances, other natural materials capable of forming fibres are also used commercially. Proteins, for example, existing in such natural fibres as wool, hair, and silk, also exist in nonfibrous forms that can be manipulated to make fibres. Fibres produced from protein materials include casein, from milk; zein, from maize (corn); and arachin, from peanuts.

The protein is dissolved and the solution is extruded in the form of fine jets that can be hardened into filaments. None of these has achieved the success for textile applications of fibres derived from cellulose.

Alginic acid, extracted from seaweed, is a chemical relative of cellulose that is also used as a raw material to produce fibres. Because they are easily dissolved, alginate fibres have specialized applications in the manufacture of very sheer wools and laces, but are of minor importance as textiles fibres.

Development of synthetic polymers

In the period following World War I, chemists carried out extensive research on methods of forming the chainlike molecular structures called polymers by linking up atoms or groups of atoms to create long molecules. Various synthetic polymers were made, including plastic and rubber types. Finding that many of these polymers could be dissolved in solvents, researchers extruded the polymer solutions through spinneret holes to determine whether filaments could be formed in the same way as rayon.

An experimental fibre had been produced by German chemists from the organic chemical compound polyvinyl chloride as early as 1913, but it had little potential for textile use. In 1928 fibres were spun in Germany from a copolymer, a chainlike molecular structure formed of two or more simple chemical compounds, in this case vinyl chloride and vinyl acetate. Possibly the first synthetic textile fibre was commercially produced in 1936 from chlorinated polyvinyl chloride but was of limited value for textile applications.

The real beginning of the synthetic fibre industry began with research on polyesters and polyamides, both chemically produced substances having their atoms assembled in long molecular chains, under the direction of Wallace H. Carothers at E.I. du Pont de Nemours & Company, in the United States. This work led to the development of nylon fibre in 1935.

Increasing research in polymer chemistry after World War II resulted in the development of many new classes of commercially important synthetic polymers for use as textile fibres, including polyamides, polyesters, polyacrylonitriles, polyvinyl chloride, polyvinyl alcohol, polyolefins, and polyurethanes.

Industrial uses of new fibres

Outside the textile field, new fibres have been produced to fill the technological needs of modern industry. The space industry employs carbon, boron, and metallic fibres in the construction of composite materials having high strength and heat resistance. Glass, aluminum silicate, and other inorganic fibres have varied applications in industry, ranging from the filtration of corrosive materials to insulation of equipment against heat and sound.

Fundamentals of production

The manufacture of a synthetic or semisynthetic fibre requires a raw material having the requisite long threadlike molecules. Although the raw material for semisynthetic fibres already exists in nature, in synthetic fibres the substance is built up from simpler chemicals.

SPINNING

A substance that is to be converted into fibre must first be converted to a liquid or semiliquid state either by being dissolved in a solvent, or by being heated until it melts. This process frees the long molecules from close entanglement with each other, allowing them to move independently.

The resulting liquid is extruded through small holes, or spinnerets, emerging as fine jets of liquid that are hardened, forming solid rods having all the superficial characteristics of a very long fibre, or filament, such as silk.

The extrusion of liquid fibre-forming material, followed by hardening to form filaments, is called spinning, and is similar to the spinning process of silkworms and spiders, producing continuous filaments.

Several spinning techniques are used in practice, including wet spinning, dry spinning, or melt spinning.

Wet spinning. In wet spinning the solution of fibre-forming material is extruded into a coagulating bath that causes the jets to harden as a result of chemical or physical change.

Viscose, for example, is wet spun. The solution of cellulose xanthate is extruded into an aqueous solution of acids and salts, in which the cellulose, being insoluble in water, is regenerated to form solid filaments.

Dry spinning. In dry spinning the fibre-forming substance is dissolved in a solvent before the solution is extruded. As the jets of solution emerge from the spinneret, a stream of hot air causes the solvent to evaporate from the spinning solution, leaving solid filaments. Acetate is dry spun by extruding acetone solutions of cellulose acetate into hot air.

Melt spinning. In melt spinning the fibre-forming material is melted and extruded through spinnerets, and the jets harden into solid filaments as they cool on emerging from the spinneret. Nyon is a melt-spun fibre.

STRETCHING AND ORIENTATION

The extrusion process produces some orientation of the long molecules forming the filament. Orientation is especially pronounced on the outer surface of the filament, where the molecules have been influenced by the edges of the spinneret hole, and the surface of an extruded filament is usually more highly oriented than the inner portion. This surface alignment, known as the skin effect, influences the dyeing properties of the fibre.

Skin effect

Orientation of the long molecules is completed by stretching the filament, pulling the long molecules into alignment along the longitudinal axis of the fibre, and causing them to lie alongside one another and develop cohesion. The degree of orientation depends upon the amount of stretch to which the filament is subjected, and by controlling the stretching, or drawing, it is possible to control the tensile strength to a high degree.

The production of a synthetic fibre allows control over the chemical nature of the fibre-forming substance, producing a fibre with well-defined chemical properties and characteristic behaviour. Control of the chemical structure also allows control of the shape and physical behaviour of the long threadlike molecules produced.

Slender, uniform molecules may be packed alongside one another more efficiently than irregular molecules having awkward knobs and angles that destroy their uniformity, just as a bundle of bamboo canes will pack together more tightly than a bundle of twigs.

In producing a synthetic fibre, it is usual to design the long-chain molecules in a form allowing them to pack together with reasonable efficiency. Large groups of atoms attached to the sides of long molecules prevent the close packing that contributes to fibre strength.

Crystalline and amorphous regions. Wherever the threadlike molecules are able to pack closely together in a fibre, there is a tendency toward an ordered arrangement of the atoms with respect to one another. These tight-packed bundles of thread molecules are regions of crystallinity, possessing the regular and precise arrangement of atoms characteristic of all crystals.

Between these regions of crystallinity are regions in which the molecules have not been able to align themselves so precisely. These are the amorphous, or noncrystalline, regions of the fibre. In considering fibre structure the long threadlike molecules may be regarded as passing through regions of ordered crystalline arrangement that are embedded in amorphous material.

During the stretching operation the long molecules slide over one another as they are pulled into alignment in the direction of the fibre's longitudinal axis. As drawing continues, more and more of the molecules are brought to a state where they can pack alongside one another into crystalline regions; in these regions, the molecules are able to hold tightly together as a result of their cohesive forces and will resist further movement with respect to one another.

When nylon is drawn after spinning, the filament may stretch to as much as five times its original length, and will then resist further stretching. At this point the molecules are aligned as effectively as possible into crystalline regions and are holding tightly together. The filament is then able to withstand great force without further stretching; if the load becomes too great the filament will rupture.

Resistance of nylon to stretching

Effects of stretching and orientation. The degree of alignment of fibre molecules affects the properties of a fibre in several ways. The more closely the molecules pack together, the greater is the tenacity, or breaking strength, of the fibre. This increase in tenacity is accompanied by a decrease in the amount of elongation the fibre can sustain before reaching its breaking point; the molecules are not able to slide over one another as they could before alignment took place. Because the closely packed molecules no longer have great freedom of movement, a high degree of orientation also tends to increase fibre stiffness or rigidity.

Water is unable to penetrate between the molecules in a crystalline region of the fibre as readily as it penetrates the amorphous regions; therefore, increased alignment tends to lower the moisture absorption of the fibre. Increased resistance to water penetration affects the dyeing properties in highly oriented fibres; the molecules of dyestuff cannot migrate from the dyebath into the spaces between the fibre molecules. Increased resistance to penetration by foreign molecules improves the general chemical stability of a fibre; highly oriented fibres are more resistant to chemical attack.

Fibres change in appearance as they are drawn. In the undrawn state, nylon is usually dull and opaque; as the filaments are drawn and orientation increases, the filaments acquire the transparency and lustre characteristic of drawn nylon.

FILAMENT MODIFICATION

Manipulation and modification of the spinning process can produce various changes in the physical structure and form of a filament, which in turn affect the behaviour in use and the "hand" of fabrics made from them. Hand, or handle, is a general term for the characteristics perceived by the sense of touch when a fabric is held in the hand, such as drapability, softness, elasticity, coolness or warmth, stiffness, roughness, and resilience.

Cross section. The cross-sectional view of a filament may be varied by the shape of the spinneret holes through which the material is extruded. Such modification is increasingly important because of the many changes it can produce in the characteristics of both yarns and fabrics. Because circular cross-section filaments have poorer covering power, or ability to occupy space, than the lobed cross sections typical of the normal viscose filament, many synthetic fibres are now produced with dog-bone and trilobal cross sections, providing greater density when made up into fabric.

Straw-shaped filaments are sometimes produced; flat filaments are formed by extrusion through slit orifices instead of circular openings. Although these filaments have improved covering power, they tend to have a harsh feel.

Special effects may be produced in fabrics by the use of filaments in which the diameter is varied continuously between thick and thin.

Bubble-filled filaments. Yarn that has relatively high bulk for its weight produces fabrics having good covering power. The covering power of the filaments used to make up a yarn may be increased by spinning methods that cause bubbles of air or other gas to be trapped inside the filament. This effect may be achieved by spinning a solution that has been previously agitated to entrap air bubbles. A disadvantage of this technique is the tendency for the air bubbles to cause breaks in the filament during the spinning process. Breakage may be overcome by generating the gas bubbles after spinning. This effect may be achieved by adding a small proportion of sodium carbonate to viscose, so that bubbles of carbon dioxide are formed inside the filament by reaction with the acid of the coagulating bath.

Bubble-filled viscose filament was produced in the United States during World War II for use as a kapok substitute in life jackets, pontoons, insulated clothing, and similar items. In the production process, air injected in the filament during extrusion produced a continuous filament containing discrete bubbles about $\frac{1}{8}$ to $\frac{1}{4}$ inch (three to six millimetres) long.

Spun-dyed filament and staple. Control of the spinning process enables the manufacturer to mix finely dispersed pigments with the solution or melted substance before extrusion. When spinning is completed, the pigments are locked inside the filaments, thus providing spun-dyed fibres that have good colour retention when exposed to light and laundering conditions. White titanium dioxide is sometimes added by this method to dull the natural sheen of man-made fibres.

Crimp. Man-made fibres cut to predetermined lengths in preparation for spinning into yarn are called staple, or staple fibre. The spinning qualities of staple are usually enhanced if the fibre has a waviness, or crimp, similar to that of wool. This crimp may be introduced mechanically by passing the filament between gear-like rollers, or chemically by controlling the coagulation of the filament to create a fibre having an asymmetrical cross section.

Chemical crimp has mainly developed from experimental work carried out in Japan, where much of the viscose

Chemical crimp

staple produced is now crimped. The crimp is introduced by spinning viscose into a coagulating bath containing less acid and more salt than usual, followed by carefully controlled stretching. The resulting crimped filament is cut into staple and dried.

Filaments produced in this way have an asymmetrical cross section, with one side thick-skinned and almost smooth, and the other side thin-skinned and highly serrated. When wet, such fibres swell to a greater extent on the thin-skinned side than on the thick-skinned side, causing a tendency to curl.

A similar effect may be introduced into rayon by using the bicomponent technique originally developed for use in the production of certain synthetic fibres. This process involves the extrusion of twin filaments through orifices set side by side in such a way that the two filaments join as they coagulate. The composite filament is composed of two viscose solutions, each having different swelling properties. Moisture encourages the filament to curl as one side swells more than the other.

The amount of crimp given to a fibre depends greatly upon the denier, or fibre size (the denier is the weight in grams of 9,000 metres of fibre). Fibres of 1½ denier may have 12 crimps per inch (1 inch is 2.5 centimetres); 3-denier fibres may have 8 crimps per inch. Too much crimp may cause neps, or tangles, during processing; too little crimp may cause low cohesion during processing.

Surface-modified fibre. The nature of the fibre surface influences the processing properties of the fibre and affects its behaviour in use. The striated surface of a regular viscose fibre, with its typical lobed cross section, influences the spinnability of viscose staple and affects the appearance and feel of viscose yarns. Because particles of dirt tend to cling to such indentations, fibres of this type are often more difficult to clean than similar fibres having nonserrated surfaces.

The scaly surface of wool contributes to the ability of this fibre to resist soil and wear, and attempts have been made to create similar surfaces on man-made fibres. One use for such fibres would be to provide improved blends with wool. Surface modified fibres have been produced by means of finishing treatments, and also by extruding the fibre through vibrating spinnerets.

PHYSICAL FORMS OF MAN-MADE FIBRES

Man-made fibres may be produced in almost any desired length. When a number of filaments produced from a spinneret are twisted together, they form continuous filament yarns. Continuous filaments may be combined to form a thick rope, called a tow, containing thousands of individual filaments. A tow may be cut or broken into short lengths of staple fibre, similar in length to such natural fibres as wool or cotton. Staple fibre may be combed and spun into yarns by techniques similar to those used in spinning natural fibres. The yarns produced in this way are called staple, or spun, yarns.

Continuous filament yarns. Continuous filament yarns, consisting of unbroken filaments, tend to be smooth and compact and are used for satins, taffetas, failles, and similar fabrics.

For many applications, continuous filament yarns are less satisfactory than the looser, fuller staple yarns. Techniques have been developed to modify the texture of continuous filament yarns, however, to give them some of the characteristics of spun yarns. Yarns modified in this way are known as textured yarns. Various texturizing processes may be employed to introduce crimps, loops, or curls, giving these yarns a fuller, more open form; to introduce a high degree of elasticity, forming stretch yarns; or to increase the bulk of a yarn without necessarily introducing stretch characteristics.

Spun, or staple, yarns. Spun, or staple, yarns consist of short fibres held together by the twist given to an attenuated (reduced in size) strand of fibres. The short fibres lie at various angles with respect to the long axis of the yarn, with the degree of uniformity depending on the combing and other treatments given to the fibre strands before they are twisted together. The surface of a spun yarn is rougher to the touch because of the protruding

fibre ends, and spun yarns generally have a fuller hand and are warmer than continuous filament yarns. Spun, or staple, yarns are popular for sports shirts, suitings, sheets, blankets, upholstery materials, and other fabrics.

Monofilaments. Monofilaments, used for fishing lines and nets, consist of fibre-forming polymers spun into filaments sufficiently thick to be used singly.

Natural polymer fibres

Polymers are large molecules made by linking together many smaller, unattached molecules, or monomers. Natural polymer fibres are produced by altering substances of natural origin to raw materials that can be made into fibres suitable for textiles. Such products include rayon and acetate, made from cellulose; casein and zein fibres, from protein materials; and alginate fibre, from a seaweed substance.

RAYONS

The production of rayon requires the conversion of cellulose to a soluble compound. The original Chardonnet process converted the cellulose to the highly flammable nitrocellulose. The development of safer methods led to the growth of the rayon industry.

Viscose rayon. One of the new methods, developed in 1892 by three British chemists, dissolved the cellulose to form a viscous liquid called viscose. A method of producing textile filaments from viscose was developed, as well as an aging process to improve spinning qualities, a multiple hole spinning jet, and a spinning box that coils the newly formed filaments by centrifugal force.

The raw materials for viscose rayon may be cotton linters, the short fibres adhering to the cotton seed, or wood pulp derived from such timber as northern spruce, western hemlock, eucalyptus, or southern slash pine. The pulps of these soft woods, containing about 94 percent cellulose, are especially suited to fibre manufacture.

The cellulose is purified and formed into thin sheets that are steeped in caustic soda and then shredded, forming powdery crumbs. During the aging period that follows, the caustic soda reacts with the cellulose, forming alkali cellulose. The aged crumbs of alkali cellulose are mixed with carbon disulfide in a revolving drum, forming cellulose xanthate, and are then treated with a dilute solution of caustic soda, forming sodium cellulose xanthate, a thick orange-brown solution.

The result is the viscose spinning solution, which is allowed to ripen for several days at carefully controlled temperatures, during which time it undergoes repeated filterings and increases in viscosity. After a final filtering stage, the solution is forced through the tiny holes bored in the metal cap forming the spinneret. Emerging from the spinneret hole, the jet of viscose enters a coagulating bath of acids and salts, in which it is reconverted to cellulose, which coagulates to form a solid filament (see lower left of illustration). The filament may be manipulated and modified during the spinning process to produce variations of the cross-sectional shape, to increase covering power, to allow solution dyeing, or to introduce crimp or is cut into short fibres (see lower right of illustration).

The use of high-strength rayon in tires, conveyor belting, transmission belting, hosepipes, and similar products developed rapidly during World War II. The high-tenacity yarns employed for such uses are produced by application of a high degree of stretch during manufacture, when the individual filaments are in a pseudoplastic state. The stretching is influenced by selection and control of the chemicals used in both the spinning solution and spinning bath.

Increased understanding and control of spinning and processing techniques have led to the development of new types of viscose. The high-wet-strength, or polynosic, fibres are high-tenacity viscose rayons in which modification of the molecular structure has resulted in a fibre having high strength, especially when wet, and good dimensional stability and firmness.

In man-made fibres, the importance of rayon is similar to that of cotton among the natural fibres. Viscose rayon,

Textured yarns

Raw materials for viscose rayon

RAW MATERIAL consists of bundles of cellulose in the form of wood pulp sheets.

CELLULOSE XANTHATE is produced by churning shredded cellulose with carbon disulfide.

VISCOSE is formed by adding caustic soda to cellulose xanthate.

CONTINUOUS FILAMENT SPINNING

SPINNING filament yarn by centrifugal or "box" method.

SPUN YARN is wound into cakes.

WASHING removes impurities from cakes of yarn.

HYDROEXTRACTING removes most of moisture from yarn cakes.

DRYING yarn cakes by storing in a heated room.

DISPATCHING of finished yarn to processors, weavers, knitters.

SOAKING. Wood pulp sheets are steeped in caustic soda.

SHREDDING. Alkali cellulose is shredded into crumbs.

RIPENING.

VISCOSE SPINNING SOLUTION is ripened and filtered.

STAPLE SPINNING AND CUTTING

SPINNING AND CUTTING. Filaments are cut into short fibres.

CLEANING. Loose fibres are washed and dried.

BALING. Dried rayon fibres are bundled.

DISPATCH to spinners.

Basic steps in the manufacturing processes of viscose rayons.
Drawing by Don Meighan based on J.G. Cook, *Handbook of Textile Fibres* (1968); Courtaulds, Limited

produced in greater quantity than any other man-made fibre, is cheap and has a wide range of applications. It is a cellulose fibre, similar to cotton in its cellulosic structure, but it provides a range of yarns and fabrics with their own characteristic properties.

Viscose rayon conducts heat more readily than silk, has a cooler feel against the skin, and is highly absorbent, enhancing its value as a clothing material. The loss of strength occurring in most rayons when wet is a serious shortcoming, but modern resin finishes are overcoming this problem, and properly finished rayon garments have high-dimensional stability when wet.

Rayon staple

The introduction of rayon staple has allowed the blending of rayon with other natural and synthetic staple fibres, contributing moisture absorption and other cellulosic characteristics to blends of stronger and less absorbent fibres, among them most of the synthetics. Staple lengths suit particular blends and systems; a two-inch staple can be handled on cotton machinery and a four- to six-inch staple may be used with wool.

Rayon in its many forms is highly versatile, and is used in every branch of the textile industry, including men's, women's, and children's outerwear and underwear; furnishings and carpets; household textiles; and medical fabrics. Crimped rayons are widely used in the manufacture of tufted carpets and rugs, tufted chenilles, curtains, upholstery, and nonwoven fabrics for surgical use. Spun-dyed rayon provides exceptional stability in textiles subjected to light, as in curtains and car upholstery.

Rayon and acrylic fibre blends are popular for knitted goods. Jersey knit fabrics, plain knits without a distinct rib, have long been made of cotton, characterized by low shrinkage; good hand, or feel; and good cover, or density. The introduction of foam-backed fabrics and laminates, in which two layers of fabric are joined together, has allowed other textiles to offer the advantages of cotton, and the use of spun-dyed rayon has increased in this field.

Flat filament viscose is used in materials for which increased lustre and a firmer hand are required. A potentially important use of flat filament staple is in blending with wood pulp in paper production.

Cuprammonium rayon. Cuprammonium rayon, also known by the trademark name Bemberg, was developed in 1890, six years after the introduction of Chardonnet's process, but was not commercially successful until 1919. In the cuprammonium process, cellulose is dissolved in a solution of copper salts and ammonia, called cuprammonium liquor, and regenerated cellulose fibres are produced by extrusion of this solution into a coagulating bath.

Cotton linters or wood pulp are the raw material for cuprammonium rayon. Cotton linters, yielding very pure cellulose, are preferred for high-quality products, although the use of the less costly wood pulp has increased.

After purifying, the cellulose material is mixed into the cuprammonium liquor at low temperature, and stabilizing agents and caustic soda are added. The resulting solution is filtered by passing through a succession of nickel filter screens, and then is deaerated.

The filtered spinning solution is pumped to a nickel spinneret and extruded through the very fine holes. The jets of solution emerging from the spinneret holes flow into a glass funnel, meeting a stream of pure water that flows down through the funnel, and are coagulated to form plastic filaments. As the filaments are carried along by the stream of water, they are stretched continuously.

Manufacturers of cuprammonium yarns, or cupro, have been particularly successful in producing novelty yarns, such as slub yarn, having alternating thick and thin sections, and nub yarns in which lumps are intentionally introduced. These yarns may be made by extruding the spinning solution through spinnerets having two sets of orifices. The filaments from one set of orifices collect on a flat surface, forming bundles that adhere together, and are carried away at intervals to join the filaments extruded from the other sets of orifices, forming a composite yarn with the bundles creating slubs at intervals.

Cuprammonium rayon is generally more expensive than other man-made cellulosic yarns, but its extra fineness and strength, attractive hand, subdued lustre, and good draping properties justify the extra cost for the manufacture of high-quality goods. This rayon, similar to other cellulosics in behaviour during laundering and dry cleaning, should be treated in the same way as viscose.

Desirable characteristics of cuprammonium rayon

Cuprammonium rayon is made into satins and such sheer fabrics as chiffons, nets, and ninons, and is popular for underwear, dress fabrics, and linings. Fine denier slub yarns are used in dresswear, sportswear, curtains, and fine drapery fabrics; heavier denier slub yarns are used in suitings, upholstery fabrics, bedspreads, draperies, and other fabrics.

Yarn-dyed fabrics are popular for high-quality silklike linings, and for dress and upholstery fabrics. Reel-spun yarns produced in skeins ready for yarn-dyeing in the untwisted state are especially suited for such applications. The dyed yarn remains untwisted to form the crosswise weft of the fabric, and is twisted for the lengthwise warp.

Saponified cellulose ester. In the early manufacture of cellulose acetate, the fibre was often treated with alkali as a prelude to dyeing, partially converting the material back to cellulose. This treatment, called saponification, was eliminated from the dyeing process with the development of new methods for dyeing cellulose acetate. The process was revived, however, for application in the stretching operation. Saponification with a caustic soda solution during stretching deacetylizes the substance, producing a strong fibre, extremely fine in diameter, that is no longer cellulose acetate but has been converted to a highly oriented filament of regenerated cellulose.

Saponified rayon yarns are used for applications in which a high ratio of strength to volume and excellent dimensional stability are advantageous; *e.g.*, in parachute ropes and fabrics, tire cords, belting, hoses, and balloon fabrics. The high degree of fineness possible in filaments made by this technique has enabled the yarns made from them to replace natural silk in such applications as electrical insulation materials; *e.g.*, in hearing-aid equipment. Coated fabrics provide light, strong tarpaulins and other protective fabrics.

CELLULOSE ESTER FIBRES

Viscose and cuprammonium are regenerated cellulose, resembling cotton or flax in their chemical structure. There is another important form of cellulosic man-made fibre in which treatment with acetic acid changes the wood or cotton cellulose to an entirely different substance, rendering it soluble and spinnable, and the filament remains in its changed chemical form after spinning. This fibre is made from a chemical derivative of cellulose, cellulose acetate.

Secondary cellulose acetate

Fibres spun from secondary cellulose acetate, in which the cellulose is not completely acetylized, or converted by acetic acid to cellulose acetate, were formerly described as acetate rayon. In modern terminology, rayon is used only in describing fibres consisting of regenerated cellulose, such as viscose and cuprammonium rayons. The secondary cellulose acetate fibres are now known simply as acetate, and fibres spun from primary cellulose acetate, or completely acetylized cellulose, are called triacetate.

Acetate fibres. In the production of acetate fibres, the spinning solution consists of secondary acetate blended from a large number of batches to assure a high degree of uniformity. The blended acetate is dissolved in a solution of the solvent acetone and a small proportion of water, up to 5 percent of the weight of the acetone, and pigments may be added at this stage. Finely divided carbon black may be added in making black fibre; titanium dioxide is added to produce a dull fibre when a high degree of lustre is not desired.

The treated spinning solution, containing 20–30 percent cellulose acetate, known as dope, is filtered and deaerated. After a final filtering the dope is pumped through very fine holes in the spinneret, then emerges into a spinning tube, an enclosed vessel through which hot air flows at a temperature of about 100° C (212° F). As the jets of spinning solution meet the hot air stream, the acetone is evaporated, leaving solid filaments of cellulose acetate. More than 90 percent of the acetone in the jets is evaporated during the fraction of a second that the jet is moving downward through the spinning tube.

The newly formed filament of cellulose acetate is stretched slightly while still plastic, aligning the long molecules and developing the strength of the filament. Acetate filament yarns produced in this way are ready for immediate textile use without any of the washing or purification treatment necessary for wet-spun fibres.

The natural attractiveness of cellulose acetate, combined with its useful practical properties, has created a demand for acetate fibre that has continuously increased since the 1920s. Modern acetate fabrics can be treated in much the same way as natural fibres and rayons. They can be dyed and finished, washed and dry-cleaned, and will withstand all the conditions met in ordinary commercial and domestic use.

Because acetate is fundamentally different in its chemical structure from the rayons and natural fibres, certain differences in behaviour must be considered in the handling of acetate materials. Acetate is thermoplastic, softening at high temperatures, and will deform under pressure at about 205° C (400° F).

The tendency for acetate fibres to soften with heating is useful in the processing of acetate goods, so that fabrics can be embossed with patterns that are impressed on the warmed material.

The relatively low-moisture absorption of acetate fi-

bres makes acetate less subject to damage by staining from many substances. Fruit juices, ink, food, and other water-soluble stains are easily sponged or washed out. Acetate fabrics dry rapidly, and are thus particularly suitable for bathing suits, rainwear, and umbrellas. Because cellulose acetate does not conduct heat readily, acetate garments are cool in summer and warm in winter.

Desirable characteristics of acetate

Acetate has little natural colour, so that the dyer can produce acetate fabrics in a range of shades varying from delicate tints to deep, heavy colours. The richness and variety of the possible shades, allied with the softness and pliability of the acetate fibre, have helped to make acetate into a beauty fibre. Acetate garments drape well and have an attractive hand. They are soft and never harsh, retain their shape if treated with reasonable care, and do not easily wrinkle.

Triacetate fibres. Complete acetylation of cellulose yields primary cellulose acetate, or cellulose triacetate. This product is soluble in chloroform and methylene chloride, but unlike the secondary cellulose acetate, is insoluble in acetone.

In 1950 Courtaulds Ltd., London, began the commercial development of cellulose triacetate fibres. Later, Courtaulds and British Celanese Ltd., Coventry, Warwickshire, linked their efforts to produce a triacetate fibre, under the trademark Tricel, with British Celanese Ltd. as the producer. In 1954 Celanese Corporation, U.S., began production of a triacetate fibre under the trade name Arnel, and triacetate fibres are now produced in several countries.

Experience gained in the production of secondary cellulose acetate was applied in the commercial development of cellulose triacetate.

Cellulose triacetate from many batches is blended and dissolved in a 20 percent solution of alcohol and methylene chloride. The solution is then filtered, deaerated, and pumped to the spinneret, emerging into a vertical spinning tube where it meets a stream of hot air. The methylene chloride evaporates to leave solid filaments of cellulose triacetate. An antistatic and lubricating substance is applied; the fibres are collected in the same way as secondary acetate filaments.

The chemical relationship between triacetate and acetate is a close one, but it is only in their tensile properties that the two fibres bear any real resemblance to each other. Triacetate has greater heat resistance than acetate. In many respects, triacetate behaves more like a true synthetic fibre than a semisynthetic fibre, possessing the thermoplastic properties and low moisture absorption associated with synthetic fibres.

Triacetate fibres retain some 70 percent of their strength when wet, and thus fabrics made from triacetate are easily washed and quickly dried. The heat-setting characteristics of triacetate are of great practical value, because heat setting renders fabrics free from shrinkage, imparts excellent dimensional stability, and permanently sets the fabric in the desired shape. Heat treatment applied after dyeing increases the fastness of the dyestuffs to washing and light.

Desirable characteristics of triacetate

Permanent effects may be produced in triacetate fabrics by heat treatment. Permanent pleats may be set in woven fabrics, and permanent embossing may be set in both knitted and woven materials. The permanency of pleats in blended fabrics depends upon the amount of triacetate in the blend, and two-component blends with cellulosic fibres require a minimum of 67 percent triacetate for permanent pleating to take effect.

The high melting point of triacetate provides a wide margin of safety in high-temperature treatment used in clothing manufacture and laundering.

Because triacetate fabrics have little tendency to shrink even before heat treatment, tighter constructions are required in triacetate and triacetate-blended fabrics than in equivalent fabrics of acetate; therefore, these fabrics do not tighten up during dyeing and finishing.

PROTEIN FIBRES

Fibres manufactured from the regenerated protein substances obtained from plant and animal sources are sometimes known by the generic name of azlon. Sources for these materials include milk, peanuts, corn (maize), soybeans, egg albumen, chicken feathers, and gelatin.

Casein fibres. About 1935 Antonio Ferretti, an Italian chemist, produced pliable casein fibres having many of the properties associated with wool. Casein fibres have since been made under various names in a number of countries—*e.g.,* Lanital in Belgium and France; Fibrolane in Great Britain; and Merinova, an improved form of the original Lanital, in Italy.

Casein is obtained by treating skimmed milk with acid, causing it to coagulate and form a curd that is washed, dried, and ground to a fine powder. It is then dissolved in caustic soda. After the solution has ripened to suitable viscosity, it is filtered and deaerated.

The spinning solution is wet-spun by extrusion through spinnerets into a coagulating bath containing such chemical ingredients as sulfuric acid, formaldehyde, and glucose with water. The jets of solution coagulate into filaments in a manner similar to the coagulation of viscose filaments, and are stretched to some degree during coagulation.

Bunches of filaments are collected together into a tow as they leave the coagulating bath and are then steeped in a formaldehyde solution to harden. Further stretching may be applied at this stage. After treatment, the tow is washed and dried, crimped mechanically, and cut into staple.

Uses of casein fibre

The low strength of casein fibre, and its sensitivity to water, have restricted its use, but it has found a number of applications in certain textile fields, especially as blend fibres for mixture with wool, cotton, rayon, acetate, nylon, and other synthetic staple fibres. In blends with cotton and rayon staple, casein brings warmth, resilience, and a full, soft hand. It allows production of good whites, and prolonged wear trials have shown that the whiteness of fabrics made from these yarns is preserved throughout the life of the garment, irrespective of the number of launderings.

Blends containing one part casein to two parts of either rayon staple or cotton are particularly satisfactory. Twill and float weaves bring out maximum suppleness in the fabric. Crease resistance is good and may be strengthened where required (*e.g.,* in suitings) by application of a crease-resistant finish. Shrink-resistant finishes are also used where necessary to improve the shape, stability, and resistance to shrinkage on washing.

Because casein filaments can be spun to very fine diameter, they may be blended with the finest qualities of wool. The proportion of casein used in blends with wool depends upon the effect required; one-third casein is generally satisfactory. Because casein may increase the shrinkage in finishing in some constructions, allowance for shrinkage in the setting of the cloth is necessary.

Alginate fibres. In 1883 an English chemist discovered alginic acid, a substance in common brown seaweed that serves a purpose similar to that of cellulose in land plants. During World War II, coarse monofilaments of chromium alginate were first produced at the University of Leeds. They were green in colour and were originally manufactured for use in camouflage netting.

In the production of alginate fibres seaweed is dried and milled to a fine powder. The alginic acid in the seaweed is converted to sodium alginate, and a sodium alginate solution is wet spun into a coagulating bath containing dilute sulfuric acid and sodium sulfate, to produce alginic acid fibre, or a bath containing calcium chloride and dilute hydrochloric acid to produce calcium alginate fibre. The jets emerging from the spinneret are coagulated into filaments of calcium alginate that are brought together, washed, oiled, dried, and wound.

The nonflammability of the alginate fibres has made them valuable for several applications in which fire hazards might exist, as in theatre curtains. Although nonflammability is desirable for certain types of clothing, the low wet strength of the fibres is a disadvantage, and a satisfactory fibre that can survive washing and also provide wearing comfort has been difficult to devise.

The solubility of calcium alginate fibres in alkali (*e.g.,*

sodium carbonate solution), while a drawback to most applications, has been an advantage in some. In the production of loosely spun wool yarns the alginate fibres are dissolved away after knitting, leaving a fluffy lightweight fabric that could not have been made by normal methods.

Special applications of alginate fibres

Calcium alginate yarn is useful in hosiery manufacture. Socks are linked together by a few courses of alginate yarn, allowing continuous production, and are separated by cutting the yarn and dissolving away the remains. This technique enables perfect welts to be obtained in socks of all types.

Calcium–sodium alginate yarn has medical application, providing styptic elastic dressings and dressings that are hemostatic, nontoxic, and absorbable in the bloodstream. It is also used in dental surgery to plug cavities.

Other protein fibres. Other fibres have been made from protein regenerated from such natural sources as peanuts (groundnuts), corn (maize), soybeans, and collagen (insoluble fibrous animal protein). These fibres have been excessively soft and tended to lose strength when wet, and few have been successful.

Research into new uses for products of developing countries resulted in a fibre made from the protein of peanuts, a staple crop in many hot, humid regions. Experimental production of the fibre, called Ardil for the town of Ardeer in Scotland where it was first produced, began in 1946 and was suspended in 1957.

A fibre called Vicara, made from zein, the protein material of maize, was manufactured in the United States between 1948 and 1957. The woollike fibres were low in strength and were mainly used in blends.

The Ford Motor company of the U.S. pioneered in attempts to make a useful fibre from the protein of soybeans, manufacturing a fibre for use in automobile upholstery between 1939 and 1942. Production cost was high and fibre strength was poor, and the process was taken over by another company, which discontinued production after a short time.

Marena, a protein fibre manufactured in Germany from the collagen obtained from leather and hide waste, was used mainly for the bristles of brushes, and was not produced after 1959.

Continued research is aimed toward finding a cheap, waste-protein source having textile-fibre potential.

NATURAL RUBBER FIBRES

A technique for production of rubber filaments was perfected in the 1930s. Rubber latex, a suspension of rubber globules in water, is mixed with vulcanizing agents and other materials and extruded in the usual way. The jets of latex emerge from the spinneret into a coagulating bath, forming filaments of rubber that are subsequently vulcanized. This new technique made possible the production of very slender round filaments, in virtually unlimited lengths.

In the 1950s, rubber filaments achieved prominence because of improvements in thread quality that allowed production of white filaments that will not discolour unduly in use and are resistant to degradation by oxygen, light, and other agents. At the same time the introduction of high-speed warp knitting allowed a rapid expansion in the production of elastic fabrics with two-way stretch, thus increasing the demand for lightweight body-support garments.

Applications of natural rubber fibres

Rubber threads are used in knitted and woven fabrics, either in the bare form or covered with spirally wound textile yarns. A wide variety of fabrics has been designed employing rubber threads to improve garment fit or provide support. Use of the appropriate type of rubber yarn and associated textiles allows a wide range of fabric hand, from relatively stiff batistes and nets to soft and supple swimwear and underwear fabrics, all providing exceptional comfort.

Synthetic fibres

The synthetic fibres are made entirely from complex organic chemicals such as polyamides, polyesters, polyvinyls, polyolefins, and polyurethanes.

POLYAMIDE FIBRES

Polyamides are polymers, or chainlike structures of linked molecular units, containing recurring amide groups as integral parts of the main polymer chains. Synthetic polyamide fibres form nylon, a major textile fibre. Synthetic polyamides are produced by a condensation reaction between small molecules, in which the linkage of the molecules occurs through the formation of amide groups. They may be produced by the interaction of a diamine, a compound containing two amino groups, and a dibasic acid—e.g., hexamethylenediamine and adipic acid—or by the self-condensation of an amino acid, or a derivative.

Fibres have been spun experimentally from thousands of polyamides produced by one of these condensation reactions, but only a very few have attained commercial importance in textile manufacture. Nylon was the first commercially successful synthetic textile fibre.

The term nylon, coined by du Pont, was defined as a generic term for any long-chain synthetic polyamide, which has recurring amide groups as an integral part of the main polymer chain, and which is capable of being formed into a filament in which the structural elements are oriented in the direction of the axis.

Nylon nomenclature

A method of nomenclature has been devised that retains the term nylon, but distinguishes between the different forms of polyamide. The number of carbon atoms in the constituents of the nylon are indicated by appropriate figures, with the diamine being considered first in polyamides made by condensing diamine and dibasic acid. The original nylon, made from hexamethylenediamine and adipic acid, is nylon-6,6, with the diamine and dibasic acid both containing six carbon atoms. The nylon made from hexamethylenediamine and sebacic acid is nylon-6,10.

When the polyamide is made by self-condensation of a single constituent (e.g., an amino acid), the nature of the polyamide is indicated by a single figure representing the number of carbon atoms in the molecule of the original constituent. Nylon-6 is the fibre made by self-condensation of the amide caprolactam.

Nylon-6,6. Nylon-6,6 fibre is spun from polyhexamethylene adipamide, a polyamide made by condensation of hexamethylenediamine and adipic acid.

Unlike rayon and acetate, nylons are melt spun. The polymer is heated until it melts, and the molten material is forced through holes in spinnerets. As the jets of molten nylon emerge, they are cooled and solidified by contact with a stream of cold air, forming solid filaments. The filaments are drawn to produce a lustrous and strong fibre. Nylon-6,6 fibres offer a range of properties that make it one of the most successful of all synthetic textile fibres.

Desirable mechanical properties of nylon

The outstanding mechanical properties of nylon include high strength-to-weight ratio, high breaking elongation, excellent recovery from deformation, high abrasion resistance, and high flex resistance. These properties are affected only slightly by moisture, and fabrics remain strong and stable when wet.

The nylon fibre, yarn, or fabric may be heat-set readily in dry heat or steam. Nylon fabric that has been heat-set holds its shape during processing in boiling water and has wrinkle recovery characteristics commensurate with the severity of the setting operation. The thermoplastic nature of nylon-6,6 has allowed successful development of a wide variety of permanent bulking and textured effects on continuous filament yarn.

These nylons are widely used in home furnishing manufacture for carpets and upholstery. Useful characteristics of nylon for carpet manufacture include appearance retention, because of abrasion resistance; texture retention; recovery from crushing; durability; and dye fastness. In upholstery, the combination of strength, dyeability, abrasion resistance, high light-fastness, and lustre provided by nylon fabrics is valued for beauty, performance, and practicality. In wearing apparel fabrics nylon-6,6 offers protection, aesthetic appeal, ease of care, durability, appearance retention, and comfort.

Nylon lends itself to most types of fabric construction, including such apparel fabrics as surah, plain and brushed tricot, simplex (reversible knit), various linings, circular and fully fashioned hoisery, taffeta, crepe, satin, reinforced twill, ski-wear fabric, velvet fleece, brocade, matelassé, circular and full-fashioned knits, tape and ribbon, lace, sheer, organza, and seersucker. These nylon fabrics are used for lingerie, swimwear, women's outerwear, men's outerwear, stretch sportswear, hunting apparel, uniforms, hoisery, sweaters, dresses, socks, and gloves.

Industrial applications of nylon-6,6

The high strength, elasticity, abrasion resistance, and other characteristics of nylon-6,6 contribute to its suitability for a wide variety of industrial fabrics, including air springs, belting, filter fabrics, fish net, twine, hose, wash nets, press covers, ironer covers, paddings, parachutes, webbing, sewing thread, cordage coated fabrics, body armour or ballistic cloth, screening, felts, reinforced plastics, ropes, blend paper, papermakers' felts, tires, and the gray fabric used to back cloth to be roller printed.

The high strength and abrasion resistance of nylon-6,6, coupled with such properties as resistance to moisture and heat, and good resistance to fatigue and rupture, have made this nylon popular for tire cords.

Nylon-6. Nylon-6 fibre is spun from polycaproamide, a polyamide made by the polymerization, or linking together, of 6-aminocaproic acid molecules.

It is melt-spun by a process similar to that used for nylon-6,6. Nylon-6 polymer melts at 215°–217° C (419°–423° F); i.e., about 35° C (95° F) lower than polyhexamethylene adipamide, or nylon-6,6 polymer. Molten polycaproamide is comparatively stable and may be held under an inert atmosphere at 250° C (482° F) for 16–24 hours without deterioration. Polycaproamide is much less sensitive to spinning conditions than nylon-6,6, and the spinning of polycaproamide directly from the polymerization vessel may be carried out more readily.

Nylon-6 filaments are drawn by passing over two sets of rollers, the second set moving with about four times the surface speed of the first set.

Nylon-6 offers a range of properties generally similar to those of nylon-6,6, except for certain differences, such as those resulting from the lower melting point of nylon-6.

Nylon-11. Nylon-11 fibre is spun from polyundecanamide, made by the self-condensation of 11-aminoundecanoic acid. This fibre was developed in France, with the cooperation of an Italian firm, and is now produced in France, Brazil, India, and the U.S.S.R.

The compound used to produce nylon-11 may be made from castor oil, from ethylene and carbon tetrachloride, or from dodecane. Polymerization is carried out in three stages, with the monomer, the material in the form of small, unattached molecules, fed as an aqueous suspension into the reaction vessel.

Molten nylon-11 polymer is highly stable at the temperature used during melt spinning (about 215° C, or 419° F), and may be stored for long periods without deterioration. Oxidation is prevented by maintaining the molten polymer under an inert atmosphere.

The spinning process is similar to that used for nylon-6, and the filaments are drawn to a degree depending on the type of fibre required.

Nylon-11 resembles nylon-6 and 6,6 in many important properties, but has certain features affecting its potential applications. The melting point of nylon-11 (189° C, or 372° F) is on the low side for general textile use, and care must be taken in such elevated-temperature treatments as ironing.

The initial modulus, or stiffness, of nylon-11 is higher than those of the other nylons, making it useful in applications such as brush bristles; it also makes for easier processing. Nylon-11 yarns do not stretch as easily as nylon-6 or 6,6 yarns when subjected to such physical processing as winding.

The high initial modulus of nylon-11 makes it useful for the automobile tire cord market, because tires reinforced with nylon-11 are not subject to formation of flat spots when the car is parked in cold weather to the extent that nylon-6 and nylon-6,6 reinforced tires are.

The low moisture absorption of nylon-11, enabling it to retain its excellent insulation properties at high humidities, is a useful characteristic in electrical applications.

Having a specific gravity of only 1.04, nylon-11 is a light fibre, with greater covering power than other polyamides. It is used in a variety of textile applications, such as tricot knitted lingerie and underwear, hosiery, and woven fabrics, and serves in the same areas as nylon-6,6 and nylon-6, combining their ease-of-care characteristics with durability and comfort.

Heat-setting processes are used in the same way as with other thermoplastic fibres, and permanent pleats and creases may be obtained effectively.

Nylon-6,10. Nylon-6,10 fibre is spun from polyhexamethylene sebacate, made by the condensation of hexamethylenediamine and sebacic acid.

Nylon-6,10 fibres are similar to those of nylon-6 and 6,6 in many respects, but moisture absorption is lower than that of either, and the fibres are unusually resilient.

Other polyamide fibres. During the 1960s a number of new types of polyamide fibre came on the market. Some were designed to serve in comparatively narrow specialized fields, and others extended the range of textile applications and brought improvements in the characteristics of nylon fabric generally.

Adjustment of the segment of the polymer chain separating the amide groups in a polyamide allows significant modification of the properties of the polyamide. This technique has been used in the production of polyamides now serving in specialized fields for which the normal nylon fibres are unsuitable. High-temperature resisting polyamides (*e.g.*, Nomex [HT-1 nylon]) and polyamides suitable for use as electric insulation (*e.g.*, nylon-11) are examples.

POLYESTER FIBRES

Polyesters are polymers made by a condensation reaction taking place between small molecules, in which the linkage of the molecules occurs through the formation of ester groups. They are usually made from esters of ethylene glycol and terephthalic acid.

In 1941 British researchers developed a synthetic fibre from polyethylene terephthalate by condensing ethylene glycol with terephthalic acid. These fibres are manufactured in many countries, in both their original and in modified forms. Other polyesters have been produced and spun into fibres, some achieving commercial importance.

Polyethylene terephthalate fibres. Polyethylene terephthalate (PET) fibres are made by the condensation of terephthalic acid, or a derivative such as dimethyl terephthalate, with ethylene glycol. The spinning procedure is like that used for polyamide fibres.

The molten polymer, pumped through holes in a spinneret, emerges in the form of filaments that solidify and are wound into packages of undrawn yarn. This yarn is stretched to about five times its original length on draw-twist machines, at elevated temperature. In the production of high tenacity yarns, the filaments are drawn to a higher degree than in the manufacture of regular tenacity yarn.

The desirable properties of PET polyester fibres, both filament and staple, include low moisture retention, high dry and wet strengths, high initial modulus, high resistance to and recovery from bending, low creep, ability to be heat-set, high abrasion resistance, good electrical insulation properties, good resistance to exposure to elevated temperatures, good resistance to most common chemicals, and good resistance to common solvents. The end uses for PET polyester fibres have developed largely around these useful characteristics, making PET one of the most versatile of all modern synthetic fibres.

Poly-1,4-cyclohexylenedimethylene terephthalate (PCDT) *fibres.* In 1958 the United States firm Eastman Chemical Products Inc., introduced a new type of polyester fibre under the trademark Kodel. This fibre is spun from the polymer made by condensing terephthalic acid with 1,4-cyclohexanedimethanol and is therefore of funda-

mentally different constitution from the polyethylene terephthalate polyesters that form the bulk of commercial polyester fibres. The polymer (PCDT) from which Kodel-211 is spun is made by condensing terephthalic acid with 1,4-cyclohexanedimethanol.

As the polymer is melt-spun, the filaments solidify as they meet cold air. They are then drawn to 4½ to 5 times their original length at a temperature of about 120° C (250° F).

Fibres of PCDT generally resemble PET fibres, but certain differences exert a significant effect on their uses. Fibres of PCDT have lower tenacity and elongation than the PET fibres but have superior recovery from stretch. They serve in applications where resilience and bounce are of greater importance than high tenacity, as in carpets, rugs, and knitwear.

The lower tenacity of these fibres contributes to their improved resistance to pilling, and the fabrics will shed pills (the small tangles of fibres resulting from friction) more readily than fabrics made from the stronger polyester fibres.

The moisture absorption of PCDT fibres is similar to that of PET fibre, producing similar behaviour. Mechanical properties are not affected by moisture and electrical properties are excellent, but the accumulation of electrostatic charges may cause difficulties.

Fibres of PCDT have a lower specific gravity than PET fibres, thus giving increased covering power and providing lightweight fabrics of great warmth and comfort. The high melting point of PCDT fibre allows a high safe-ironing temperature (about 218° C, or 424° F).

Fabrics containing PCDT fibre may be heat-set at a relatively low temperature—*e.g.*, about 160° C (320° F) —an especially useful quality in the finishing of blended fabrics containing wool.

POLYVINYL DERIVATIVES

Polyacrylonitrile fibres. During the period 1955–60, polyacrylonitrile fibre factories were established in Germany, Japan, Italy, Belgium, Canada, France, and The Netherlands, and later in many other countries.

These polyacrylonitrile fibres, known by the generic name of acrylic, are spun from polymers consisting of at least 85 percent by weight of acrylonitrile units, produced from ethylene oxide and hydrocyanic acid. The polymerization of acrylonitrile and its comonomer is commonly carried out by stirring the monomers with water in the presence of a catalyst and surfactants (detergents or other surface-active agents that reduce surface tension).

In dry spinning, the polymer is dissolved in an organic solvent such as dimethylformamide to form a solution containing 25–40 percent of polymer. This is degassed, filtered, and heated almost to the boiling point, then extruded through spinnerets.

The fine jets of solution emerge into a vertical tube or spinning cell, through which flows air or other gas at high temperature. As the jets fall through the tube, the solvent evaporates, leaving solid filaments of polymer. These filaments are brought together at the base of the spinning cell and stretched while hot to several times their original length.

In wet spinning, the polymer is dissolved in a suitable solvent and the solution degassed and filtered. It is then pumped through spinnerets into a coagulating bath containing a liquid in which the solvent is soluble, but the polymer is insoluble, and the jets of polymer solution coagulate into fine filaments. These fibres may be produced in a variety of cross-sectional shapes, each affecting the nature of the fabrics produced from them.

The stress–strain relationships of different acrylic fibres vary over a wide range, depending upon the chemical and physical structures of the specific fibre. The tenacities of acrylic fibres are generally between those of standard rayon and nylon. Acrylics are sufficiently strong for all the normal apparel applications but are rarely considered for those high-strength applications in which nylon and polyester fibres serve. Acrylic fibres are usually made into staple, although some producers market continuous filament yarns, and high tenacity acrylics are also in production.

Good tenacity and extension are combined with excellent elastic recovery and high initial modulus, mechanical properties contributing to the production of fabrics of good dimensional stability, which are unaffected in conditions that would tend to bring about deterioration in many other fibres. Acrylics are not significantly affected by exposure to sunlight, moisture, micro-organisms, chemicals, or solvents. Fabrics constructed from these fibres have an attractive hand characteristic. Acrylic fibres have low specific gravity, slightly higher than that of nylon, and provide lightweight fabrics that bulk well. The water absorbency of acrylic fibres is generally low, but is higher than that of polyester fibres. Acrylics rarely accumulate static electricity to the extent that polyester fibres do, and successful static elimination can be achieved with suitable antistatic finishes. The small water absorption contributes significantly to their dyeability.

Acrylic fibres tend to be heat-sensitive, and heat-setting is necessary for good stability. At very high temperatures, the fibres decompose rather than melt, but such temperatures are unlikely to be encountered in normal textile applications. Fabrics made from 100 percent acrylic fibre or from blends with 50 percent or more acrylic fibre may be durably pleated.

Acrylic goods are only moderately flammable; they have outstanding resistance to the effects of sunlight, micro-organisms, insects, and aging; and show excellent outdoor weathering resistance. They also display good resistance to all the chemicals likely to be encountered in normal textile use, including bleaches, dilute acids and alkalies, and dry-cleaning solvents.

The modacrylic polyacrylonitrile fibres include modacrylic fibres spun from polymers consisting of less than 85 percent by weight of acrylonitrile units, but do not include those copolymers in which acrylonitrile is not the major component. Fibres in this category are spun from an extensive range of copolymers of acrylonitrile, in which the nature and proportion of the second, and possibly additional components, may vary within wide limits. The modacrylic fibres that can be produced within this broad category provide wide variations in properties, depending on their composition and method of manufacture.

Details of the chemical structure of individual modacrylic fibres are not always available. The second component of the polymer, however, is commonly chosen from vinyl chloride, vinylidene chloride, or vinylidene dicyanide.

Polyvinyl chloride (PVC) *fibres.* Fibres of PVC, spun from polymers or copolymers of vinyl chloride, are manufactured in a variety of forms and modifications. They have achieved a limited success in textile manufacture, but their low softening point, often as low as 70° C (160° F), restricts their possible applications. Fibres of PVC, however, have characteristics that are highly suited to certain applications: they do not burn, and they have resistance to many chemicals. Their tendency to shrink at relatively low temperatures is useful in the production of high bulk yarns.

Vinyl chloride is produced in large quantity for the production of polyvinyl chloride plastics, and fibre manufacture uses only a small part of the output. It is polymerized typically as an aqueous emulsion in autoclaves (pressure vessels), under pressure of 45–50 atmospheres and a temperature of about 65° C (150° F). The polymer forms a suspension in the water and is recovered by spray drying. The fibres may be spun by dry-, wet-, or melt-spinning processes.

Polyvinylidene chloride (saran) fibres. In 1940 the Dow Chemical Company, of the U.S., introduced a new synthetic fibre consisting of a copolymer of vinylidene chloride and vinyl chloride that was given the generic name saran. Production of saran fibres spread to other countries, and it is now established as a specialty textile fibre.

In its production vinylidene chloride and the vinyl chloride or other comonomer are polymerized in an aqueous emulsion in the presence of a catalyst. The copolymer is melt spun through spinnerets at about 180° C (360° F), and the filaments are immediately cooled with water before being drawn to develop satisfactory tenacity. Pigments may be incorporated in the molten polymer before spinning, and titanium dioxide is used to dull the filament.

Saran is a flexible fibre, with a soft warm hand, its smooth rounded surface contributing to soiling resistance and easy dirt removal. It is unusually tough and durable, with excellent flex resistance, and fabrics woven from this fibre have excellent resistance to abrasion and hard wear.

The moisture absorption of saran is very low, and its mechanical properties are unaffected by moisture. Saran fabrics are dimensionally stable, washing and drying easily and quickly, and their low moisture absorption contributes to stain resistance; ink, food, drink, and many other stains may be removed with soap and water.

Because of saran's low resistance to heat, coupled with its negligible moisture absorption, its use in garment fabrics has been restricted. The fibre's nonflammability is an asset, and saran fabrics are popular for draperies and other application, where fire hazards are present. Saran has excellent resistance to sunlight, aging, and general weathering conditions, and is completely resistant to attack by insects and micro-organisms.

Polyvinyl alcohol fibres. Polyvinyl alcohol fibres have been commercially produced in Japan since 1950, and later in South Korea, North Korea, China, France, Germany, Poland, and the U.S.S.R.

Polyvinyl alcohol is made by the hydrolysis of polyvinyl acetate, and fibres are commonly produced by wet spinning, or by a process combining features of dry and melt spinning. The fibres produced by the regular wet-spinning process are heat treated at about 240° C (450° F), followed by acetalization, usually with an aldehyde such as formaldehyde. Benzaldehyde may be used instead of formaldehyde to provide a fibre of high resilience. Aldehydes containing active groupings, such as amino groups, may be used to confer special dye affinity on the fibre.

Polyvinyl alcohol fibres have the flexibility associated with a flattened-tube type of cross section, and fabrics made from these fibres are soft and warm, with excellent hand, so that they feel comfortable when worn next to the skin. The fabrics are durable and hard wearing, with high tensile and bursting strength, and excellent impact and abrasion resistance.

The elastic recovery of polyvinyl alcohol fibres is on the low side, suggesting that dimensional stability and wrinkle resistance may not be high. Mechanical properties are not unduly affected by water, and the ability to absorb moisture contributes to the comfort of garments worn next to the skin. Fabrics made from these fibres will burn only with difficulty. The fibres are resistant to insects, micro-organisms, and other influences encountered in outdoor applications. Their high resistance to acids, alkalies, and many other chemicals is an important factor in the industrial applications of polyvinyl alcohol fibres. Polyvinyl alcohol fibres are potentially very cheap, and their future is apparently in the field of hard-wearing, low-cost fabrics and garments.

Polytetrafluoroethylene (PTFE) fibres. In 1954 PTFE fibre was introduced by du Pont under the trademark Teflon, and such fibres are now produced by other manufacturers and in countries other than the United States, including the U.S.S.R., where it is called Ftorlon and Polifen.

Tetrafluoroethylene is purified and polymerized under heat and pressure in stainless steel autoclaves in the presence of a peroxide catalyst. After polymerization is completed, the dispersion is extruded through a spinneret, the jets emerging into an aqueous coagulating bath of a dilute solution of hydrochloric acid. The dispersion is coagulated, and the particles of PTFE hold together as weak filaments in which the particles remain entirely separate. The filaments are then heated rapidly to about 385° C (725° F) and maintained at that temperature for several seconds, fusing the polymer particles into a coherent filament. This product is cooled quickly and drawn at room temperature to three or four times its original length.

PTFE fibres are unique in that they combine the resistance to chemicals, solvents, and elevated temperatures associated with inorganic fibres derived from mineral sources, with the flexibility and toughness typical of many organic fibres derived from animal and vegetable sources.

Because PTFE fibres are extremely costly, they are not suitable for general textile use. In addition, they have an unpleasant, greasy hand, no moisture absorption, high density, and low modulus. The outlet for these fibres is in end-uses where performance is of greater significance than initial high cost, such as filter fabrics and felts, gaskets, electrical tapes, and low friction backings.

Fluorinated ethylene-propylene copolymer (FEP) fibres. Fibres spun from FEP are similar to PTFE fibres, except that they are thermoplastic, melting at about 290° C (550° F).

Polyvinylidene dinitrile fibres. Vinylidene dinitrile was synthesized in the United States in 1947 by the B.F. Goodrich Company. Polymers and copolymers were made that led to the development of a new type of synthetic fibre produced under the trade name Darlan, later changed to Darvan. The manufacture of Darvan was discontinued in the United States in mid-1961.

POLYOLEFIN FIBRES

Polyolefin fibres are spun from polymers or copolymers of such olefin hydrocarbons as ethylene and propylene. Two types of fibre, polethylene and polypropylene, dominate the field. Polyethylene fibres are limited to certain specialized applications; polypropylene fibres are of increasing importance, showing prospects of becoming major textile fibres in the late 20th century.

Polyethylene fibres. In the high-pressure–high-temperature process, ethylene is polymerized by heating at temperatures in the region of 150°–200° C (300°–400° F), with pressures of 1,000–2,000 atmospheres. The reaction is promoted by traces of oxygen or other catalysts. In the low-pressure–low-temperature process polymerization takes place at much lower pressures and at temperatures below 100° C (212° F). A variety of catalyst systems is used.

Polyethylene is extruded into monofilaments of round, flat, or other cross sections by extrusion techniques similar to those used with such other thermoplastic polymers as nylon and saran.

The commercial development of polyethylene fibres in the general textile field has been hampered by low softening point, high shrinkage, low stiffness, poor creep characteristics, and inability to take dyes. Such shortcomings restrict its use to specialized nonapparel applications.

Industrial uses of poly-ethelene fibres Low-density polyethylene fibres are used for various industrial applications, including ropes and cordage, filtration fabrics, and protective clothing. They are used in the form of resilient shrinkable yarns for the production of three-dimensional fabrics. High-density polyethylene fibres are used in aerial tow targets, high-altitude balloons, and in equipment designed for Arctic conditions, in which the retention of strength and flexibility at low temperatures are invaluable. The strength, lightness, and water- and rot-resistance of polyethylene fibres have established them in the marine cordage field for the production of ropes and nets that float, do not rot, and do not absorb water. Furniture fabrics, car upholstery fabrics, curtains, protective clothing, tarpaulins, and filter fabrics are other applications making use of the special properties of polyethylene fibres.

Polypropylene fibres. The specific conditions under which polymerization of propylene is carried out are proprietary. Catalysts are used, such as an organometallic compound of aluminum in the presence of titanium tetrachloride, and the reaction is carried out under pressure at about 100° C (212° F).

Polypropylene fibres are made by extrusion of molten polymer, followed by drawing to orient the molecules and crystals in the filaments. Polymer of high viscosity is spun to obtain optimum fibre properties. The filaments are cooled in air as they emerge from the spinneret and are then collected on bobbins.

Polypropylene monofilaments have applications similar to those of polyethylene, but offer higher strength, increased toughness, resilience, abrasion resistance, and creep resistance, and a higher melting point. These properties are allied to their water-resistance and chemical inertness. Polypropylene monofilaments have become established in a number of fields where they compete successfully with other fibres for such uses as ropes and cordage, fishing nets and twines, filter fabrics, and protective clothing.

The introduction of fine-denier multifilament yarns and staple fibre extended the range of potential applications for polypropylene fibre to the textile and apparel fields, bringing them into competition with established natural and synthetic fibres in applications where the shortcomings of polypropylene fibres often place them at a disadvantage. Despite the attractive characteristics of polypropylene fibres, less desirable properties, such as dyeing difficulties and relatively low melting points, have tended to limit progress.

POLYURETHANE FIBRES

Polyurethane fibres are spun from polymers made by a reaction taking place between small molecules, in which the linkage of the molecules occurs through the formation of urethane groups. Linear polyurethanes may be made by reaction of a glycol with a diisocyanate. The reaction of butanediol with toluene diisocyanate results in the formation of a polyurethane.

In recent years, polyurethanes have achieved increasing importance in textiles, becoming the basis of a novel type of elastomeric fibre known generically as spandex. **Spandex** Spandex fibres are spun from segmented polyurethanes made by a series of chemical stages, beginning with production of a low-molecular-weight polymer, or prepolymer, followed by a reaction of the prepolymer with diisocyanate and the coupling of isocyanate-terminated prepolymer to form segmented polyurethane.

The technique used in spinning spandex fibres depends upon the type of polymer spun. Some segmented polyurethanes are essentially linear molecules, soluble in solvents. Other segmented polyurethanes may be insoluble branched or cross-linked structures.

Soluble polyurethanes are dissolved in an appropriate solvent, and the solutions may be extruded through spinnerets into a coagulating bath (wet spinning), or into an atmosphere that removes the solvent (dry spinning). The techniques are essentially the same as those used for spinning hard synthetic fibres, with allowance being made for the elasticity of spandex fibres.

When the molecule of polyurethane is allowed to grow into a three-dimensional structure, it is insoluble and cannot be spun by either wet or dry processes. Instead, a chemical spinning process may be used. The isocyanate-terminated prepolymer is spun at a stage when it forms a viscous melt, the jets emerging into an environment containing a chain extender that diffuses into the fibre and reacts to link the prepolymer molecules into their final form, thus producing the branched or cross-linked polyurethane in fibrous form.

Because of their segmented structure, spandex fibres may be made stronger than rubber fibres. To achieve a given stretch, spandex fibres require a force twice as high, over the entire range of elongation, as the force required by rubber. In contrast to hard fibres, such as nylon, spandex fibres have a very low modulus of elasticity. Spandex fibre has about twice the effective power of rubber at the important elongations at which additional stretch of 50 to 100 percent is available.

The durability of spandex fibre in garments, in which resistance to flexure, abrasion, and needle-cutting are necessary, is high. Spandex-fibre fabrics show high resistance to flex and low growth compared to their rubber-fibre counterparts. The durability of spandex fibres allows production of very fine, or high denier, yarns that have opened up new applications for elastic fibres. In addition, spandex fibres were the first elastomeric fibres that could be readily dyed.

Inorganic synthetic fibres

Fibres produced from inorganic substances include glass, aluminum silicates, metallics, and various other types having special industrial applications.

GLASS FIBRES

Glass fibres are spun from glasses of many different compositions depending on end use. Silica sand (silica) and limestone (calcium carbonate) are the basic ingredients to which are added varying amounts of other materials such as soda ash (sodium carbonate), potash (potassium carbonate), aluminum hydroxide or alumina (aluminum oxide), magnesia (magnesium oxide), or boric oxide.

The ingredients are charged into a furnace, where they are fused at high temperature to form molten glass. Filaments may be spun directly from this melt, or the glass may be formed into marbles of about ⅝-inch (16-millimetre) diameter that are passed to the spinning machines, also called fiberizing units.

Continuous filament strands are produced by allowing molten glass to flow through perforated tips on the baseplate of a platinum melter, or bushing, drawing away a stream of glass from each tip to form a fibre, and attaching the fibres to a high-speed winding device. The bushings may be mounted on glass-melting tanks, or may form the basis of independent fiberizing units, being fed with glass by the remelting of glass marbles.

As the 50 or more filaments are drawn from the orifices, they are brought together into a strand, and a lubricating size, or finish, is applied to facilitate subsequent processing. Strands intended for use in textile weaving may be converted through conventional textile processes into suitable yarns. There are various methods of producing glass staple fibre; the most important include the centrifugal, jet, and rod-drawing processes.

In the centrifugal process, molten glass is thrown out of holes in the base of a metal spinner rotating at high speed. The resulting fibres are bonded into a web for use in heat and sound insulation. This technique is not generally used for production of textile-grade glass fibres.

Centrifugal process for glass fibres

In the jet process, staple fibre is produced from molten glass that flows under gravity through holes in the base of platinum bushings, as in the production of continuous filament. The streams of glass are drawn into fibres by the action of high-speed streams of turbulent gas or steam, and the turbulence breaks the solidified fibres into staples of 8 to 15 inches (200 to 380 millimetres) that are collected into a web on a revolving vacuum drum. The web may then be guided from the drum and formed into a glass staple sliver, a continuous strand of loosely assembled fibres that is processed on conventional textile machines for weaving into glass-fibre staple fabrics.

The rod-drawing process is a modern development of the traditional process for making glass filaments. In a typical modern machine, 125 glass rods, usually about four millimetres (0.2 inch) in diameter, are mounted vertically and adjacent to one another in a kind of spinning frame. The rods are kept moving slowly downward, and are simultaneously melted at a temperature of about 1,200° C (2,200° F), either by individual movable and adjustable gas burners or by electric heating coils in a fireclay chamber. Drops of glass fall away from the ends of the rods, drawing glass filaments after them.

Glass is a heavy fibre, with a specific gravity of the order of aluminum, and has good transparency. Its moisture absorbency is negligible, and the fibre shows no swelling or shrinkage. This latter characteristic is useful in applications in which dimensional stability in the presence of water is desirable, and in electrical applications, but it is detrimental in apparel, where absorption of moisture is useful.

Water affects the tensile properties of glass fibre, bringing about a reduction in tenacity after a very short time,

caused by the leaching out of some of the soluble materials from the glass, including alkali silicates; glass with a low alkali-content is most satisfactory in this respect.

The high coefficient of friction of glass against glass, taken in conjunction with the high flexibility of fine glass filaments, results in poor abrasion resistance. The movement of filament against filament during use brings about fracture of the filaments, creating a hairy fabric. Suitable lubricants and finishes can minimize such effects, and metal coatings may be applied to glass fibres to reduce surface friction.

Glass fibre has the highest strength-to-weight ratio of any fibre, and one of the lowest elongations. These characteristics are useful in applications requiring high dimensional stability, as in the reinforcement of plastics. The low elongation is not useful in apparel fabrics, in which resiliency is an important factor. Glass fibres exhibit almost perfect elasticity, returning instantly and completely to their original dimensions upon release from strain. This characteristic, however, is exhibited over only a very small range.

Glass fibre has excellent resistance to the effects of heat over a wide temperature range, with fabrics showing an increase in strength up to about 205° C (401° F), after which strength and flexibility begin to fall. At 370° C (700° F), glass filaments retain 50 percent of their original strength; at 538° C (1,000° F) they retain about 25 percent. The effect of temperature depends greatly upon the composition of the glass.

Resistance of glass fibre to heat

Glass is completely nonflammable and is used where resistance to the spread of flame is of overriding importance. The high heat conductivity of glass is a useful attribute in electrical-insulation applications, where closewoven glass fabrics dissipate heat rapidly. Despite this quality, glass fibre is useful as a heat insulation material and is employed in the form of mats and waddings in which entrapped air provides the insulation.

Glass has high resistance to most chemicals but is disintegrated by alkalies. Glass fibres may be attacked by certain strong mineral acids and by phosphoric acid, but show complete resistance to biological degradation.

ALUMINUM SILICATE FIBRES

Fibres are spun from aluminum silicate, with or without the addition of minor amounts of other materials. Aluminum-silicate fibres were developed originally for use in jet engines to provide high-temperature-resistant, lightweight, strong, fibrous material of low thermal conductivity. These fibres are also used for such products as high-temperature filters, packings, gaskets, and for thermal, electrical, and acoustical insulation.

In the production of aluminum silicate a mixture of equal parts of alumina and silica with a small proportion of sodium borate added to produce short staple, or zirconia to produce long staple, is fused in an electric furnace. The molten aluminum silicate is poured from the furnace in a small stream. As it falls, the stream disintegrates into tiny droplets or particles that are attenuated into fine fibres as they are blown through the air and collect on a mesh screen, forming a mat of fibre.

Aluminum-silicate fibres are used largely for insulation purposes, filling a gap that exists from about 400° C (about 750° F), where glass, mineral wool, and asbestos are often inadequate, to about 1,260° C (2,300° F). Aluminum silicate fibres can be used for short exposures at higher temperatures, with a slight loss of resilience and some shrinkage. The devitrification taking place at these temperatures does not affect the insulating properties of the fibres. Extremely low thermal conductivity is an outstanding feature of aluminum-silicate fibres.

Aluminum silicate provides a lightweight, high-temperature heat barrier with excellent thermal shock resistance, flame resistance, resilience, chemical stability, and electrical properties. Because the fibres of aluminum silicate interlock, there is no brittle structure to develop stresses during sudden heating or chilling.

Aluminum-silicate fibres are used for a variety of high-temperature applications, including thermal, acoustical, and electrical insulation; and filters, packings, and gaskets; and containment and conveyance of molten nonferrous metals.

METALLIC FIBRES

Fibres produced from metals may be used alone or in conjunction with other substances. Those used in modern textile manufacture are of two main types: (1) metallic single-component, or SC, fibres and (2) metallic multicomponent, or MC, fibres.

Metallic single-component fibres. Late in the 1950s, the development of high-speed flight and space travel created demands for flexible materials capable of withstanding unique environmental conditions for use in the manufacture of protective garments, antenna membranes, parachutes, and other space-program structures. It was determined that the requirements for such applications could be met by the production of fibres of adequate flexibility, made from high-temperature metals or alloys; *e.g.*, of the stainless steel type.

Applications of SC fibres in space technology

Methods of producing metal filaments of the required fineness were developed in the 1960s, and metal fibres have since become available in quantities and at a cost entitling them to consideration as genuine textile fibres.

Metallic SC filaments are produced by drawing either single filaments or multifilament strands. Single filament drawing produces excellent quality metallic fibres, but multifilament drawing offers the best possibility of reducing cost and increasing availability. One method of drawing multifilament yarns involves enclosing a bundle of two-mil (0.002-inch, or 0.05-millimetre) wires in a sheath of a dissimilar alloy. The sheathed bundle is drawn to the required extent, and the sheath is removed with nitric acid, leaving the multifilament yarn ready for sizing, warping, and weaving.

Metals possess a number of general characteristics that can be of practical use in textile applications. The potential high yield and fracture strengths of most metals allow production of fabrics exceeding in strength those that can be produced from existing organic or glass fibres. The absence of a significant viscous behaviour characteristic in metal fibres ensures dimensional stability in certain structures that would be difficult to achieve with conventional textile materials.

The most significant difference between organic fibres and metal fibres is in the rigidity or stiffness of the material. Most organic textiles have a stiffness less than one-twentieth that of most metals.

This high stiffness previously excluded metals from use as textile materials because it placed severe limitations on the processability and end uses of the fibres. Adequate flexibility has been achieved, however, with the advent of modern ultrafine metal fibres.

The higher weight of most metals, in comparison with organic materials, can be a serious disadvantage in the use of metal fibres for many applications. On the other hand, the resistance of metals to chemicals at room and elevated temperatures covers ranges generally exceeding those of organic fibres, thus allowing metal fibres to be employed in many military and industrial end uses in which specific chemical resistance is a requirement. In some applications, however, metals may suffer corrosion by chemical action.

Many metals can tolerate and endure temperatures higher than those that organic fibres will generally withstand. Most metals are good conductors of heat, and metal fibres may function as heat-sinks when used in adequate proportion in blends. The high electrical conductivity of most metal fibres provides an effective method of eliminating static electric charges.

Metallic multicomponent fibres. Multicomponent fibres are made from metal in association with other materials, commonly plastics. Modern metallic fibres of the multicomponent type are based largely on aluminum, which provides sparkle and glitter at a fraction of the cost of the early types of decorative fibre based on such substances as gold.

The aluminum in these fibres is in the form of a narrow ribbon-filament of either metal foil, or a plastic film that has been vacuum-plated with vaporized aluminum and coated with a plastic film. In these composite structures, the metal is protected from corrosive influences of its environment and from mechanical damage. Multicomponent metallic fibres have achieved popularity as decorative fibres and are an important part of the modern textile industry.

Modern metallic filaments are made by sandwiching a thin layer of metal, usually aluminum, between thin sheets of the appropriate types of plastic film. The lamination may be carried out in several ways. In the production of the acetate butyrate aluminum-foil metallic fibre, for example, a thermoplastic adhesive, either coloured or clear, is applied to both sides of a sheet of aluminum 0.00045-inch (0.01-millimetre) in thickness. The coated foil is then heated to about 90° C (200° F) and passed through a set of rollers, together with two sheets of cellulose acetate butyrate, in such a way that the aluminum foil becomes the centre of the "sandwich." The laminated material is then slit into narrow ribbonlike filaments of the desired width; *e.g.*, ⅛ to ¹⁄₁₂₈ inch (3.2 to 0.20 millimetres).

Metallic filament "sandwiches"

In some types of metallic filament, the centre of the sandwich consists of a plastic (*e.g.*, polyester) film that has been vacuum-coated with aluminum, and this may then be protected by the application of layers of lacquer or plastic film as above.

Many types of coloured metallic filament are produced, including those with the metallic glitter of the aluminum shining through the coloured adhesive and those having coloured outer plastic films. Gold-coloured filaments are made by using an orange-yellow dyestuff or pigment in the adhesive; a silver colour requires only the natural glitter of the aluminum.

Metallic MC yarns are used almost entirely as decorative materials for the textile industry. The aluminum foil that provides the glitter in a modern metallic yarn is protected from any ambient corrosive materials by the plastic film in which it is enclosed. Polyester types will withstand repeated launderings without losing sparkle. Because metallic yarns are not affected by seawater or the chlorinated water of swimming pools, they are widely used in swimwear. The dyestuffs used in colouring metallic fibres are usually fast to light, thus retaining bright colour.

Because metallic MC yarns are used primarily for decorative purposes, they do not usually contribute significantly to the strength of fabrics or garments. They may, however, be used as weft or warp yarns, and are sufficiently strong to withstand weaving and knitting operations. When necessary, metallic yarns are combined with such supporting yarns as nylon. The plastic film of the metallic yarn is flexible, and the yarns are extensible to a degree depending upon the type.

Aluminum corrodes and tarnishes in air and in contact with seawater, but in metallic fibres it is protected so effectively that it retains its glitter for long periods. The chemical resistance of a metallic filament is generally equal to the chemical resistance of its coating of plastic film. In the case of polyester films, this is outstanding.

If metallic fibres remain in contact with strong alkaline solutions for prolonged periods, the aluminum may be attacked at the unprotected edges of the ribbon. Such fibres should not, therefore, be subjected to alkaline reagents of significant strength. Organic solvents also may attack the laminate adhesive or lacquer coating, and care is required in dry cleaning to ensure the use of an appropriate type of solvent. The plastic films in metallic fibres are thermoplastic, softening at elevated temperatures, and delamination may occur if the fibres are heated. Acetate types in particular should be processed only at low temperatures.

The plastic films may be permanently embossed by heat and pressure, thus allowing the introduction of special effects.

MISCELLANEOUS INORGANIC SYNTHETIC FIBRES

Fibres play an increasingly important role in engineering, where they are used as constituents of composite

Com-
posites

materials. Embedded in a matrix, which may be plastic, metal, or ceramic, fibres contribute their unique properties to the composite to function in a manner similar to the steel rods embedded in reinforced concrete.

Composite materials containing fibres are used in applications in which high strength and low weight are needed, as in aeronautics and astronautics. Fibres retaining high strength at elevated temperatures are valuable in high temperature applications. Since World War II, many types of fibre have been used in composite materials, and the demand for new materials to meet the demands of modern engineering applications has stimulated development of new types.

Composites are heterogeneous structures consisting of a continuous matrix in which the fibrous material is dispersed and embedded. Efficient performance of the composite requires a strong bond between the fibre and the matrix. Techniques used in producing composites from fibres and matrices depend upon the nature of the materials and the purposes for which the composite is required.

Fibres may be in the form of continuous filaments, masses of staple fibre, yarns formed from continuous filaments or spun from staple fibre, or fabrics produced from yarns.

Continuous filaments may be used to build structures by a winding technique. The structure is built up by winding the filament around some kind of form, the structure being held together by a matrix as it is created. This technique is used in constructing pressure vessels and rocket bodies.

Staple fibre is commonly mixed with the matrix; e.g., in the production of reinforced plastic materials. Yarns and fabrics may be used in layering processes, and glass-fibre-reinforced plastics are used in building boat hulls and car bodies.

Carbon and graphite fibres. Because the element carbon has the ability to form strong bonds between its atoms, carbon atoms hold together in strong three-dimensional structures, such as that of diamonds, and in two-dimensional structures, as in graphite, and they also hold together in strings, forming long, single-dimension polymer structures in the same way that molecules form the basic structural units of fibres.

The fibres used in textiles are based almost entirely on organic polymers; the molecules consist of long chains of carbon atoms, with other atoms or groups of atoms attached as appendages to the carbon backbone. By removing the appendages from an organic fibre molecule it is possible to produce long molecules consisting entirely of carbon atoms. When a chemical operation of this sort is carried out on a highly oriented organic fibre, carbon fibres can be obtained in which the molecules retain a high degree of orientation.

Such carbon fibres may be produced by treatment of organic fibres under carefully controlled conditions. Cellulosic fibres, such as viscose rayon, or acrylic fibres are the favoured starting materials, and acrylic fibres are widely used in the commercial production of carbon fibres.

The nature of the carbon fibre produced depends upon the conditions under which pyrolysis, the subjection to the action of heat, is carried out. At lower temperatures, carbon fibres are formed; at higher temperatures, the carbon atoms in the fibre are arranged in the crystalline form of graphite.

Carbon fibres have a high strength-to-weight ratio, as well as high modulus and stiffness. They are thermally stable, retaining high strength at temperatures where other engineering materials suffer significant loss of strength. Graphite fibres are softer and have high electrical conductivity.

Composite materials containing carbon fibres are used in making the compressor turbine blades in jet engines, and in the construction of aircraft and spacecraft. They are used in deep-sea submersibles, in heavy-duty bearings, and in pressure vessels. In spacecraft re-entry shields, carbon fibre composites are able to retain their structural form at the high temperatures developed.

Boron and boron-derivative fibres. The development of boron fibres has provided the engineering industry with high-modulus continuous filaments used in high-performance composites. Boron filaments may be made by depositing the element boron on a fine core filament of a conducting material such as tungsten or carbon. Boron trichloride is passed over such a filament, which is then heated electrically, thus causing the boron trichloride to decompose and deposit boron on the core filament.

Boron-nitride fibers are commercially useful because they have properties similar to those of graphite fibres, including high strength, low weight, and high elastic modulus. They conduct heat readily, and are thermally stable, but differ from graphite fibres in being good electrical insulators.

Refractory oxide fibres. In modern engineering, the demands made upon materials are of increasing stringency; materials are required to retain such properties as high strength when used at high temperatures and under corrosive conditions. These requirements have stimulated great interest in production of fibres from refractory oxides and similar materials. Alumina or silica, for example, may be used at high temperature and in an oxidizing environment. Many such materials are difficult to spin, however, because of their comparatively sharp melting temperatures and narrow viscosity ranges.

Special techniques have been devised to meet particular problems. Alumina may be spun by packing it into a tube of fused silica. The end of the tube is melted, and the fibres drawn from the molten material consist of crystalline alumina filaments enclosed in silica sheaths.

Silica-carbon fibres may be made by drawing continuous filaments from a solution of viscose rayon and sodium silicate. The filaments are pyrolyzed (heated to a high temperature) in nitrogen, to form a silica-carbon fibre that may be converted to a silicon carbide fibre by heating at temperatures above 1,500° C (2,700° F).

Whiskers. Single crystals of extremely high strength, called whiskers, have been the subject of scientific investigation for many years. They are a form of fibre, and have potential importance in the fibre composite field.

Whiskers produced from alumina and silicon have very high elastic moduli and do not exhibit plastic deformation. Used in composites (e.g., with resins, metals, or ceramics), whiskers provide engineering materials having unique and valuable characteristics. Titanium compressor blades reinforced with silicon-carbide whiskers, for example, retain high strength at elevated operating temperatures. The future of such materials depends mainly upon the development of commercially viable techniques of producing whiskers.

Economic aspects

From the original production of Chardonnet silk in the 19th century, synthetic fibres have had a large and growing economic impact throughout the world. Before World War II, the production of man-made fibres consisted almost entirely of cellulose-derived fibres, mainly viscose and acetate. During the 1930s, as a result of intensive fibre research, several new synthetic fibres were produced experimentally. In the late 1930s these tentative steps led to the production of nylon, the first commercially successful synthetic-textile fibre.

Since that time, the development of synthetic-fibre production has continued. The years following World War II were marked by the introduction of new types of synthetic fibre; nylon was joined by the polyesters, acrylics, polyolefins, and others as fibre producers worked to establish themselves in the new technically based industry. Some of the new types of fibre have achieved high acceptance; others have not lived up to their early promise and have disappeared.

Because the commercial development of a synthetic fibre requires substantial expenditure on research, technology, and plant construction, a commitment to produce a particular type cannot be easily changed to produce another of marginally better properties. Manufacturers, who must recoup their original investments, work

History of
fibre
development

to improve the chosen fibre. A stage is commonly reached in the development of a new technologically-based industry where consolidation becomes necessary, and the synthetic industry reached this stage, to a large degree, in the 1960s. Producers who had committed themselves to the production of polyamides, polyesters, acrylics, and other commercially accepted fibres concentrated much of their attention on the improvement of basic products. There was rapid commercial development of techniques increasing the versatility of established fibre types. The development of texturizing, chemical crimping, multicomponent fibres, and film fibres extended applications of synthetic fibres, and the production of polynosic, or high wet modulus, and other modified rayons stimulated interest in the natural polymer fibres field.

Several new fibres were introduced, however, during this consolidation period. Polyurethanes and polypropylenes made a powerful impact on the textile market and other new fibres were in the experimental stage.

In the early 1950s, man-made-fibre production accounted for about 13 percent of the world fibre total. The proportion increased steadily, reaching over 29 percent in 1968–69. During this same period, the total fibre production increased from 35,212,000,000 pounds in the early 1950s to 55,281,000,000 pounds in 1968–69.

Expansion of man-made fibre production

The man-made-fibre industry thus increased its output from 4,630,000,000 pounds in the early 1950s to 16,164,-000,000 pounds in 1968–69, achieving expansion of almost 400 percent in less than two decades. This rapid development has exerted a powerful influence on many aspects of the industrial world. New fibres have required new production techniques, new processing machinery, and new developments in textile, clothing, and other industries, and in retail merchandising.

Man-made fibres are produced almost entirely from organic polymers, constructed from various carbon derivatives. In the natural polymer fibres, cellulose is the basic material from which the most commercially important fibres are made, and, although ample supplies of cellulose are available, conversion to a form suitable for fibre production presents certain problems. The raw materials of synthetic fibres, however, are simple organic chemicals that come from stores of available carbon compounds. Initially, the industry relied heavily upon coal for such materials, but petroleum has largely superseded it. The rapid development of synthetic-fibre production has made heavy demands on the resourcefulness of the petrochemicals industry.

As world population expands, the demand for textiles may be expected to increase. In addition, a need for greater versatility in textile materials is likely. The man-made-fibre industry is expected to supply an increasingly large share of the total world fibre output, and because man-made fibres can be tailor-made to meet particular needs, a portion of the increased production will consist of specialized types. The greatest production, however, will be in "bread-and-butter" fibres, such as polypropylene, that can be produced cheaply to provide the kind of textiles that have long been produced from cotton.

BIBLIOGRAPHY. H.F. MARK, N.G. GAYLORD, and N.M. BIKALES (eds.), *Encyclopedia of Polymer Science and Technology: Plastics, Resins, Rubbers, Fibers*, 9 vol. (1964–68), provides a comprehensive survey of fibre science and technology. J.G. COOK, *Handbook of Textile Fibres*, 4th ed., 2 vol. (1968), treats the production, properties, processing, and applications of natural and man-made textile fibres. *Industrial Fibres* (Commonwealth Secretariat 1968), is a survey of production, trade, and consumption relating to both natural and man-made fibres. Works primarily of interest to textile technologists include: W.E. MORTON and J.W.S. HEARLE, *Physical Properties of Textile Fibres* (1962); and J.W.S. HEARLE and R.H. PETERS (eds.), *Fibre Structure* (1963). Useful works for the general reader include: I.B. WINGATE, *Textile Fabrics and Their Selection*, 6th ed. (1970), and (ed.), *Fairchild's Dictionary of Textiles* (1967).

(J.G.Co.)

Fibres, Natural

A natural fibre may be defined as an agglomeration of cells in which the diameter is negligible in comparison with the length. Although nature abounds in fibrous materials, especially cellulosic types such as cotton, wood, grains, and straw, only a small number can be used for textile products or other industrial purposes. Apart from economic considerations, the usefulness of a fibre for commercial purposes is determined by such properties as length, strength, pliability, elasticity, abrasion resistance, absorbency, and various surface properties. Although no fibre combines the optimum of all desirable properties, most have some unique property particularly adapted to the special requirements of certain textile products.

This article is divided into the following sections:

I. General considerations

HISTORY OF FIBRE PRODUCTION

The use of natural fibres for textile materials began before recorded history. The oldest indication of fibre use is probably the discovery of flax and wool fabrics at excavation sites of the Swiss lake dwellers (7th and 6th centuries BC). Several vegetable fibres were also used by prehistoric man. Hemp, presumably the oldest cultivated fibre plant, originated in Southeast Asia, then spread to China where reports of cultivation date to 4500 BC. The art of weaving and spinning linen was already well developed in Egypt by 3400 BC, indicating that flax was cultivated sometime before that date. Reports of the spinning of cotton in India date back to 3000 BC. The use of natural fibres for spinning and weaving textiles considerably predates the establishment of these ancient civilizations. The manufacture of silk and silk products originated in the highly developed Chinese culture; the invention and development of sericulture (cultivation of silkworms for raw-silk production), and methods to spin silk date from 2640 BC. With improved transportation and communication, highly localized skills and arts connected with textile manufacture spread to other countries and were adapted to local needs and capabilities. New fibre plants were also discovered and their use explored. In the 18th and 19th centuries, the Industrial Revolution encouraged the further invention of machines for use in processing various natural fibres, resulting in a tremendous upsurge in fibre production. The introduction of regenerated cellulosic fibres (fibres formed of cellulose material that has been dissolved, purified, and extruded), such as rayon, followed by the invention of completely synthetic fibres, such as nylon, challenged the monopoly of natural fibres for textile and industrial use. A variety of man-made fibres having specific desirable properties began to penetrate and dominate markets previously monopolized by natural fibres. Between 1950 and 1970 total world fibre production increased from 35,000,000,000 pounds to 55,000,000,000 pounds (16,000,000,000 to 25,000,000,000 kilograms). About one-third of this increase was in natural fibres and two-thirds, or about 12,000,000,000 pounds, resulted from increases in the production of man-made fibres. Man-made-fibre production increased fourfold in this period, and its percentage of the total fibre production increased from 13 percent in 1951 to 29 percent in 1969. Recognition of the threat from man-made fibres resulted in intensive research directed toward the breeding of new and better strains of natural-fibre sources with higher yields, improved production and processing methods, and modification of fibre yarn or fabric properties. The considerable improvements achieved have permitted increased total production, although the actual share of the market has decreased with the influx of the cheaper, man-made fibres requiring fewer man-hours for production.

In 1968–69, natural fibres accounted for over 70 percent of the world's total fibre production, with cotton remaining the most important. Estimated total annual world production of natural fibres in this period amounted to about 40,000,000,000 pounds. Table 1 provides figures on world production for the major natural and man-made fibres.

Table 1: Estimated Total World Fibre Production, 1968–69

(000,000 lb)

	total production	percentage
Natural fibres		
Wool	3,537	6.4
Cotton	25,566	46.2
Silk	83	0.15
Flax	1,487	2.7
Hard fibres and hemp*	2,421	4.4
Jute and allied fibres*	6,023	10.9
Man-made fibres		
Rayon filaments	3,125	5.6
Rayon staple	4,747	8.5
Noncellulosic man-made	8,292	15.0
Total	55,281	

*Excluding China and the U.S.S.R.
Source: *Textile Organon* 1970.

CLASSIFICATION AND PROPERTIES OF NATURAL FIBRES

The vegetable fibres

Natural fibres can be broadly classified according to their origin. The vegetable, or cellulose-base, class includes such important fibres as cotton, flax, and jute; the animal, or protein-base, fibres include wool, mohair, and silk; the most important fibre in the mineral class is asbestos.

The vegetable fibres can be divided into smaller groups, based on their origin within the plant. Cotton, kapok, and coir are examples of fibres originating as hairs borne on the seeds or inner walls of the fruit, where each fibre consists of a single, long, narrow cell; flax, hemp, jute, and ramie are bast fibres, occurring in the inner bast tissue of certain plant stems and made up of overlapping cells; abaca, henequen, and sisal are fibres occurring as part of the fibrovascular system of the leaves. Chemically, all vegetable fibres consist mainly of cellulose, although the various fibre types are associated with varying amounts of such substances as hemicellulose, lignin, pectins, and waxes that must be removed or reduced by processing.

The animal fibres consist exclusively of proteins, and, with the exception of silk, constitute the fur or hair that serves as the protective epidermal covering of animals. Silk filaments are extruded by the larvae of moths and are used to spin their cocoons.

Asbestos, the only naturally occurring mineral fibre currently used commercially for textile purposes, is found as asbestos rock, formed of tightly packed crystallized fibres that can be readily separated.

Value of moisture-absorbing quality

With the exception of mineral fibres, all natural fibres have an affinity for water in both liquid and vapour form. Under standard conditions, the moisture content of vegetable fibres is from 6 to 10 percent; while animal fibres, including silk, have a moisture content of 10 to 15 percent. This ability to absorb moisture makes natural fibres particularly suitable for clothing. The transfer of moisture from the body through the fibres to the surrounding atmosphere provides considerable comfort to the wearer. The presence of moisture also serves to inhibit the build-up of static electricity that, especially in dry weather, can cause considerable discomfort in garments made of synthetic fibres. The strong affinity of natural fibres for water, producing the swelling of the fibres connected with the uptake of water, facilitates dyeing in watery solutions. The considerable increase of diameter in water, and the very limited swelling in the longitudinal direction, are characteristic of natural fibres.

Most natural fibres consist of extended chains of polymers (large molecules formed from smaller molecules)

that can be packed together in a regular arrangement, resulting in high density. Wool and other keratin (insoluble protein, forming such horny epidermal tissue as hair, horn, and feathers) fibres are exceptions, consisting of irregular, overlapping, scalelike cells, elongated spindle-shaped cells, and either air-filled cells or a hollow tube, resulting in close packing or interlocking. The mechanical properties of the natural fibres are a direct reflection of their structure and the orientation of their molecules. The cellulosic fibres have a fairly high modulus, or resistance to stress, and are low in extensibility, or ability to stretch; but the animal fibres have a low modulus and high extensibility resulting from the unfolding of the helical structure during extension. Breaking strength, or tenacity, is measured in grams per denier (1 denier equals the weight in grams of 9,000 metres of the fibre), permitting comparison of the amount of stress that can be resisted without breakage by fibres having a specific number of units of weight for a specific unit length. The breaking strength per denier of the common fibres is: cotton, three to six grams; jute, three to six; hemp, six to seven; flax, three to eight; ramie, five to eight; abaca, six to seven and a half; wool, one to two; and silk, three to six grams.

Unlike most synthetic fibres, all natural fibres are nonthermoplastic, that is, they do not soften when heat is applied. At temperatures below the point at which they will decompose, they show little sensitivity to dry heat, and there is no shrinkage or high extensibility upon heating, nor do they become brittle if cooled to below freezing. Decomposition resulting in discoloration starts at about 225° C (437° F) for cotton at a heating rate of 5° C (40° F) per minute; wool begins to decompose at approximately the same temperature. Cellulosic fibres ignite and burn readily and present a fire hazard unless properly treated. Protein fibres are somewhat less flammable. Natural fibres tend to yellow upon exposure to sunlight and moisture and extended exposure results in loss of strength. Jute, because of its high woody tissue (lignin) content, is particularly sensitive to sunlight.

Microbial decomposition

All natural fibres are particularly susceptible to microbial decomposition, including mildew and rot. Cellulosic fibres are decomposed by attack from aerobic bacteria (those that live only in oxygen) and fungi. Cellulose mildews and decomposes rapidly at high humidity and high temperatures, especially in the absence of light. Wool and silk are also subject to microbial decomposition by bacteria and molds, and wool that has been damaged chemically appears to be even more susceptible to subsequent microbial action. Animal fibres are also subject to damage by moths and carpet beetles; termites and silverfish attack cellulose fibres. Protection against both microbial damage and insect attacks can be obtained by chemical modification of the fibre substrate; modern developments allow treatment of natural fibres to make them essentially immune to such damage.

Reactive chemical groups present in the polymer molecules making up the various natural fibres make them particularly susceptible to chemical modification and therefore to alteration of characteristics that may be undesirable for a specific application. Cellulosic fibres have good resistance to alkalies but are severely degraded or even dissolved by mineral acids. Wool and other hair fibres have excellent resistance to dilute acids but are degraded or dissolved by hot alkali. Silk, attacked and dissolved by both alkalies and strong acids, has fair resistance to weak acids. The extent of fibre damage is dependent upon the type and concentration of the chemical used as well as the length and temperature of exposure.

II. Vegetable fibres

Fibres of vegetable origin are composed chiefly of cellulose, a carbohydrate substance manufactured by the plant from water and carbon dioxide gas. Although cellulose fibres are available from numerous plant sources, only a limited number of them are suitable for textile use because of the difficulties involved in separating them from other substances. The three main groups of useful vegetable fibres, based upon the portion of the plant in which they originate, are the seed and fruit group, the bast group, and the leaf group.

SEED- AND FRUIT-HAIR FIBRES

The group of vegetable fibres originating as single-celled seed or fruit hairs includes the commercially most important textile fibre, cotton, together with such less important fibres as coir and kapok.

Cotton. *History.* Cotton, the world's most important nonfood agricultural commodity, was one of the first vegetable fibres used for textile purposes. Cotton materials have been found in tombs in India dating as far back as 3000 BC, and a Hindu hymn of 1400 BC describes the manufacture of cotton yarns and the weaving of cotton cloth. Cotton was probably cultivated in Egypt by about AD 600–700; it was also produced by early Chinese civilizations. It was produced in the Mediterranean basin during the time of the Roman Empire (first half of 1st millennium AD) and was grown on the Greek mainland from the 8th century AD. Arab traders introduced cotton to the rest of the African continent.

In the 12th century Venice became a major cotton-manufacturing city, processing cotton from the Mediterranean area into cloth for sale in central Europe, and in the Middle Ages Germany became a cotton-manufacturing centre. The cotton trade was of great importance in the development of the British East India Company and other great trading companies of the 17th and 18th centuries. In the New World, cotton grave cloth has been found in pre-Incan Peru (before 2000 BC) and cotton yarns in the prehistoric Pueblo settlements of Arizona. Columbus, landing in the West Indies, was met by Indians offering cotton yarn for barter. Cotton cultivation in the United States began early in the 17th century and was closely connected with the introduction of slavery. After the invention of the cotton gin, which separates the fibre from the seeds, in 1793, the United States became a major cotton producer, with production concentrated in the southern and southeastern states. In the post-Civil-War period the large plantations were subdivided into small plots worked by tenant farmers, but with mechanization of cotton production and other farming operations, allowing cultivation by relatively few labourers, small farms were consolidated into larger operations. By the mid-20th century, cotton cultivation was well-established on irrigated land in the Western states of California, Arizona, and New Mexico, which led the traditional cotton states in production, and the trend throughout the United States was toward even greater mechanization.

Production. Cotton, belonging to the botanical family Malvaceae, genus *Gossypium*, is normally cultivated as a shrubby annual in temperate climates but can be found as a perennial in treelike plants in tropical climates. The cultivated shrub grows from four to six feet tall (about one to two metres) over a growing period of six to seven months.

Warm and humid climates with sandy soil are the most suitable. Although cotton can be grown between latitudes 30° N and 30° S, yield and fibre quality are considerably influenced by climatic conditions, and best qualities are obtained with high moisture levels resulting from rainfall or irrigation during the growing season and a dry, warm season during the picking period. Rain or strong wind may cause damage to the opened bolls.

Within 80–100 days after planting, the plant develops white blossoms, which change to a reddish colour. The blossoms fall off after a few days and are replaced by small green triangular pods, called bolls, that mature after a period of 55–80 days. During this period the seeds and their attached hairs develop within the boll, which increases considerably in size. The seed hair, or cotton fibre, reaching a maximum length of about two and a half inches (approximately six centimetres) in long fibre varieties, is known as lint. Linters, fibres considerably shorter than the seed hair and more closely connected to the seed, come from a second growth beginning about ten days after the first seed hairs begin to develop. When ripe, the boll bursts into a white, fluffy ball containing

Factors influencing cotton crops

three to five cells, each having seven to ten seeds embedded in a mass of seed fibres. Two-thirds of the weight of the seed cotton (*i.e.*, the seed with the adhering seed hair) consists of the seeds. To avoid damage by wind or rain the cotton is picked as soon as the bolls open, but since the bolls do not all reach maturity simultaneously, an optimum time is chosen for harvesting by mechanical means. Handpicking, carried out over a period of several days, allows selection of the mature and opened bolls, so that a higher yield is possible. Handpicking also produces considerably cleaner cotton; mechanical harvesters pick the bolls by suction, accumulating loose material, dust, and dirt, and cannot distinguish between good and discoloured cotton. A chemical defoliant is usually applied before mechanical picking to cause the plants to shed their leaves, thus encouraging more uniform ripening of the bolls.

Cotton is attacked by several hundred species of insects, including such harmful species as the boll weevil, pink bollworm, cotton leafworm, cotton fleahopper, cotton aphid, rapid plant bug, conchuela, southern green stinkbug, spider mites (red spiders), grasshoppers, thrips, and tarnished plant bugs. Limited insect control can be achieved by proper timing of planting and other cultural practices, or by selective breeding of varieties having some resistance to insect damage. Chemical insecticides, which were first introduced in the early 1900s, require careful and selective use because of ecological considerations but appear to be the most effective and efficient means of control.

Damage by insects and microorganisms

The boll weevil (*Anthonomus grandis*), the most serious cotton pest in the United States in the early 1900s, was finally controlled by appropriate cultivation methods and by the application of such organic insecticides as chlorinated hydrocarbons and organic phosphates. A species of boll weevil resistant to chlorinated hydrocarbons was recorded in the late 1950s; this species is combated effectively with a mixture of toxaphene and DDT (dichlorodiphenyltrichloroethane). The pink bollworm (*Pectinophora gossypiella*), originally reported in India in 1842, has spread throughout the cotton-producing countries, causing average annual crop losses of up to 25 percent in India, Egypt, China, the Soviet Union, and Brazil. Controls and quarantines of affected areas have helped limit the spread of the insect, and eradication has been possible in a few relatively small areas with sufficiently strict controls. The bollworm (*Heliothis zea*, also known as the corn earworm) feeds on cotton and many other wild and cultivated plants. Properly timed insecticide application provides fairly effective control.

Cotton plants are subject to diseases caused by various pathogenic fungi, bacteria, and viruses, and to damage by nematodes (parasitic worms) and physiological disturbances also classified as diseases. Losses have been estimated as high as 50 percent in some African countries and in Brazil. Because young seedlings are especially sensitive to attack by a complex of disease organisms, treatment of seeds before planting is common. Some varieties have been bred that are resistant to a bacterial disease called angular leaf spot. Soil fumigation moderately succeeded in combatting such fungus diseases as fusarium wilt, verticillium wilt, and Texas root rot, which are restricted to certain conditions of soil, rainfall, and general climate. The breeding of resistant varieties, however, has been more effective.

Processing. Before it is spun into yarn and woven into cloth, cotton must pass through a number of processes including ginning, baling, grading, marketing, opening, picking, carding, combing, drawing, and roving.

Ginning is the process of separating the cotton lint from the seeds. Separation was originally accomplished entirely by hand. The earliest mechanical device employed was probably the churcka gin, developed many centuries ago in India, which has the longest history of use. In this device, seed cotton is fed manually between a pair of rollers, and the lint caught between the rollers is drawn out and pulled from the seed, which is too large to pass through the compression point of the rollers. This method, best suited for Indian varieties with clean, naked, and

The ginning process

hardy seeds having slight fuzz, results in a very small production rate. Cotton ginning was revolutionized when hand methods were replaced by the saw gin, invented by Eli Whitney of the United States in 1793, and by an improved model, invented by Hogden Holmes, also of the United States, in 1796, which became the ancestor of the modern gin.

In modern ginning plants the gin stand is one unit in a series of machines. The modern roller gin, incorporating the basic principles of earlier versions, consists of a series of toothed circular saws projecting between the slits in a series of metal ribs. The revolving saws catch the fibres in their teeth, and the limited clearance between the saw blade and the rib plate allows only the plucked fibres to pass through the slits, leaving the seeds behind. The lint is then removed from the gin by air blast or by a large cylinder brush. Some gins are equipped with lint cleaners that further clean the cotton after it has been removed from the seed.

Because mechanical harvesting may pick up considerable leaf, twigs, boll, burrs, and plant trash, improved machines have been developed to perform extensive drying and cleaning before ginning, and to clean the lint after the seed is separated from the fibres. The separated lint is conveyed to pressing boxes, where it is pressed into bales of approximately 500 pounds (225 kilograms) each. The seeds are shipped to crushing mills where they are processed to obtain various by-products.

Cotton is sold in local markets generally held around the gin. The buyer may be the ginner, an agent for the spinning mill, or a merchant or banker to whom the grower is indebted. In the United States much cotton has gone into the cotton-loan program promulgated in 1933 and is not purchased by an independent buyer but is transferred from the gin to approved warehouses, on the basis of which the seller obtains a loan on the negotiable receipt.

Quality variations in cotton result from differences in such factors as the varieties planted, soils, irrigation methods, rainfall, fertilizers used, climatic conditions, insect damage, length of growing season, exposure of open cotton before harvesting, and ginning methods.

Classification of cotton

Classing, the classification of cotton, is a method of describing quality by grade and staple, or fibre length. Although classing systems vary throughout the cotton-producing and consuming countries of the world, they are essentially based on fibre length and grade. Grade is determined by colour, leaf (foreign matter), and preparation (ginning).

There is a strong correlation between cotton-fibre length and strength. Generally, longer staple (fibre) varieties are much finer and stronger than the shorter staple cottons and, consequently, they can be spun into finer and stronger yarns.

The three major groupings are based on length, fineness, and lustre.

1. Long-staple fibres, 1–2½ inches (2½–6 centimetres) long, fine, and of good lustre, include Sea Island varieties, grown mainly in the West Indies and in the southwestern United States; Egyptian (cultivated mainly in the Nile River valley); and Egyptian-American, or Pima, a variety developed in the United States from Egyptian cotton (*Gossypium barbadense*).

2. Intermediate fibres, or medium staple, the most important type, have a length of about two inches (five centimetres) and are somewhat coarser. An example is Upland cotton (*Gossypium hirsutum*) probably originating in Central America, grown in the southern United States, and also bred into other varieties grown throughout the world. Deltapine and Acala are currently the main medium-staple cotton varieties. Medium-staple cotton has considerably higher yields than the long-staple cotton but brings lower prices.

3. Short-staple fibres, ⅜ to ½ inch (about 1.2 centimetres) long, coarse, and without lustre, include Indian and Asiatic cotton (*Gossypium herbaceum* and *G. arboreum*), grown in India, Pakistan, and China.

Only the species of the genus *Gossypium* mentioned above are commercially cultivated.

To produce cotton yarn of good quality and to achieve high performance during processing, several bales of similar fibre length and fineness are intimately blended. Blending is achieved either by feeding small amounts of cotton from several bales stacked behind blending hoppers or by sandwiching quantitatively proportioned opened cotton in bins. In Egypt and the United States blending may be carried out before baling the cotton for shipment.

Picking machines

The blended and opened cotton is processed through the picking operation, which opens, blends, cleans, reduces the lump size, removes waste and dust, and prepares the cotton for carding. Handling, cleaning, and metering (assuring uniformity of feed) is facilitated by reducing the cotton particles or lumps to the smallest possible size. This reduction is accomplished on the picking machines, where the cotton mass is plucked by steel spikes or blades, rotating at high speed and striking the fibres against the undercasing of the beater. Three to four such machines, or beaters, are arranged in series, depending upon the cleanliness of the raw material. The cotton is moved through these machines by air currents. At the last picking machine, the cotton is condensed in a sheet form called lap.

The opened cotton, still containing small unopened tufts of fibres, is further fractionated into individual fibres on the carding machine. This process also removes trash, vegetable matter, and short fibres detrimental to processing performance and yarn quality. Carding is accomplished by the action of suitably arranged inclined wires mounted on cylinders rotating at different speeds. The fibres are teased apart, then transferred to the wire points of another large cylinder, or doffer, and eventually stripped by a high-frequency vibrating comb into a thin sheet of web. This is collected into a rope form, called sliver, about ¾ to one inch (about 2–2.5 centimetres) in diameter, and deposited in cans. Cottons may be combed to remove short fibres (about 5 to 20 percent in weight), thus achieving improved uniformity of staple length and greater lustre and strength in yarns.

Drawing and roving

Drawing, or drafting, is the process of straightening and parallelizing the fibres in the direction of the strand. It also performs the function of blending by combining several slivers, called doubling, and reducing the mass of fibres in the strand without breaking the continuity. This reduction is achieved by processing slivers through several pairs of rollers running at different surface speeds. It is customary to employ two drawing operations after carding and two after combing.

The sliver is reduced in size by roller drafting and slightly twisted to form what is called roving, which is wound on a special bobbin for feeding to the spinning frame. Carded- or combed-drawn sliver is reduced by stretching on the roving frame to a size suitable for spinning.

Spinning, the final process in the conversion of fibres into yarns, involves reduction of the size of the strand by drafting rollers; twisting the drawn material; and winding the yarn into a suitable package.

A single cotton yarn is a continuous twisted strand of fibres that has received its final attenuation. The first operation is carried out by drafting rollers; twisting and winding is accomplished by the spindle and traveller (a small metallic wire piece bent into C or D shape) on a ring spinning frame. In other modern systems twisting may be performed by a high-speed rotor disk, as in open-end spinning.

In the metric system, the size of a cotton yarn is designated as tex; *i.e.*, the weight in grams of 1,000 metres (3,300 feet) of yarn. If 1,000 metres of a yarn weigh 20 grams, its tex is 20. Count is a numerical designation indicating yarn size and based on the number of unit lengths per pound of a particular yarn.

Cotton yarns are produced in a variety of types. The three main classifications are warp yarns, used as the longitudinal thread in the fabric; filling or weft yarns, used for crosswise interlacing and generally containing less twist; and knitted yarns, used to make knit fabrics. Knitted yarns have less twist than weft yarns and are made with considerable care to achieve good uniformity.

Other classifications are carded and combed yarns, named for the process used.

Even after the harsh mechanical action of the gin, cotton fibres retain a certain amount of seed-coat fragments, assorted seeds, and sometimes fragments of the cotton plant. These impurities are known as motes. In addition to motes, such impurities as pectins, proteinic substances, ash, wax, and natural pigments must be removed before dyeing and finishing. The process that removes all undesirable materials is known as scouring. Most cotton is scoured (treated at the boil with caustic-soda solution), bleached, and mercerized (see below) in the form of cloth, but a small quantity is also boiled out in the loose or in yarn form. The first stage in the removal of these impurities is scouring in hot alkaline solutions. Loose cotton or yarn in skein form is boiled in pressure vats at a temperature of 240° F (116° C) for eight hours in a 4 to 6 percent sodium hydroxide solution. During this treatment, the natural impurities either become soluble in hot alkali or are rendered removable by decomposition, saponification (for fats and oils: separation into salts of fatty acids and glycerol), or emulsification (suspension of minute particles in liquid). A weight loss of 6 to 9 percent is normally experienced after scouring. Scouring tends to make cotton considerably whiter and smoother in feel.

Cotton is generally bleached by three distinct systems, which employ, in the order of their development, hypochlorite, hydrogen peroxide, and chlorite. These oxidative treatments are highly selective, attacking the impurities rather than the cellulose. Nearly 80 percent of cotton bleached in fabric form is bleached with hydrogen peroxide because of its adaptability to continuous processing. Sodium chlorite is a popular bleaching agent in Europe, where 25 percent of the cotton bleaching is done with it. When raw stock or yarn is bleached in packages with sodium hypochlorite it is piled into a kier (vat) and the bleach liquor is circulated continuously through the goods at a temperature ranging from 55° to 70° F (13° to 21° C). After bleaching, cotton is washed and treated to remove residual hypochlorite by absorbing it in sulfur dioxide or sodium bisulfite. Hydrogen peroxide bleaching is generally performed at temperatures around the boiling point of water, and the higher the temperature, the shorter the bleaching time. Sodium chlorite bleaching offers advantages in bleaching cotton because it reduces requirements for desizing and scouring, produces little or no cellulose degradation, involves low weight loss, and gives better hand (feel) to the fabric.

Cotton is mercerized to impart permanent, increased lustre. In addition, the process contributes to improvement of dye affinity, chemical reactivity, dimensional stability, strength, and smoothness and makes immature fibres readily dyeable. In mercerization, cotton is treated while under tension with caustic soda of mercerizing strength (between 16 and 24 percent), and the excess caustic soda is rinsed away before tension is released. Mercerizing may be carried out on gray cotton or after scouring and bleaching. Long-staple cottons generally respond best to mercerization.

By-products of cotton processing include linters used for stuffing material in mattresses and upholstery, and to form the base for cellulose acetate and rayon fibres and for other cellulose derivatives used as explosives, films, lacquers, and plastics. Hulls, constituting almost half the weight of the cottonseed, are crushed and used mainly to feed cattle. Cotton cake, left after the oil has been removed from the seed, is ground into cottonseed meal, rich in nitrogen, which is used for fertilizer and cattle feed.

Fibre properties. Cotton fibres are single plant cells consisting of an outer, or primary, cell wall and an inner core of growth layers comprising the secondary wall. The fibre grows daily and growth layers are deposited around a central canal, or lumen, carrying liquid to the living cell. These growth layers can be observed microscopically when the fibre is fully swollen. When a ripened boll opens under the pressure of the fibres, the liquid dries rapidly and the lumen collapses. After drying, the fibre has the appearance of a twisted ribbon. The twists or convolutions result from changes occurring in the fibre as it matures. The number of twists per inch ranges from 150 to 300, depending on the different varieties. The cross sections of dry cotton fibres are normally oval or kidney-bean shaped.

The cell walls are composed of many layers of very small fibrils arranged in a spiral pattern, with a distinct angle to the fibre axis, and with numerous reversals.

Chemical analysis of the major constituents of the cotton reveals that it is close to 95 percent cellulose. The secondary wall, or secondary layers, are nearly pure cellulose. Other substances such as waxes, are confined almost entirely to the primary wall; the protoplasmic residue, pigment, ash, and sugars, are found in the residue of the lumen.

Cotton is never truly white. All cotton samples have a soft, creamy tint with some of the long-staple strains more creamy by several shades than the Upland cotton and Sea Island types. Some of the shorter staple cottons are highly coloured, ranging from deep caramel, to khaki, to beige. In the 1970s it was reported that Soviet scientists were breeding coloured strains to produce marketable cotton with built-in colour. Most of the pigments, however, are unstable to sunlight.

The breaking strength of cotton fibres is related to the molecular-chain length and the orientation of the cellulose. Strengths ranging from 70,000 to 116,000 pounds per square inch have been determined on fibre-bundle tests. Breaking strength decreases considerably if longer test specimens are used, because the probability of finding a weak spot in the fibre increases. The elongation of cotton fibres before breaking averages 7 percent, considerably higher than that of the other natural cellulosic fibres.

The effect of moisture on cotton-fibre properties is significant. Bone-dry cotton fibres cannot be spun because of their lack of electric conductivity; the correct moisture content for spinning is essential. The considerable affinity of cotton for moisture contributes to comfort, making cotton superior to most synthetic fabrics used in apparel. Moisture content has a considerable effect on the strength of the cotton fibre, which increases with relative humidity. An oven-dried yarn may be as much as 30 percent weaker than a conditioned yarn, which increases in strength upon immersion in water. This surprising effect of moisture on strength is caused by the water in the fibre structure permitting a more uniform distribution of stresses. The cross-sectional area of cotton fibres increases by about 44 percent at saturation with water, and the average increase in length is about 1.1 percent.

Cotton cellulose is a carbohydrate composed of the elements carbon, hydrogen, and oxygen. Complete hydrolysis (decomposition in water) of the cellulose with strong mineral acids yields the sugar glucose. The basic unit of the cellulose chain is the organic molecule cellobiose, and cellulose consists of long chains of this unit. Estimates of the molecular weight, or degree of polymerization (large molecule formation), of native cotton cellulose is controversial; some workers believe that the chain molecules of native cellulose are so long that they are insoluble in all solvents in the native state. Presumably, solubilization can result only if some of the interconnecting glucosidic (consisting of compound substances derived from glucose) links are broken. It is generally agreed that cotton cellulose has a higher molecular weight than wood cellulose; ramie, nettle fibre, and flax cellulose are higher in molecular weight than the native cotton cellulose. Cotton cellulose apparently consists of a large number of cellulose chains of different degrees of polymerization, and the distribution of chain length has a maximum at a degree of polymerization of about 2,000. Cotton cellulose crystallizes in several forms. The native form, having a monoclinic unit cell (with one oblique intersection of the axes of the crystal), cellulose I, can be transformed into cellulose II by a mercerization treatment with alkali; cellulose II occurs in general in regenerated cellulose fibres. Reports on the degree of crystallinity of cotton cellulose vary over a wide range, depending on the testing method used. X-ray diffraction methods give an approximate value of 72–80 percent crystallinity. The degree of orientation of the crystals is considerably poorer than in a number of other textile fibres because of the spiral arrangement of the fibrils in cotton. A comparison of the average angle of the spirals for several cellulosic fibres is interesting; hemp, 0 degrees; ramie, 3.5 degrees; flax, 5.5 degrees; cotton, up to 50 degrees.

The basic building blocks of cotton fibres are chemically reactive, making cotton susceptible to chemical modifications. Research has led to an understanding of the effects of chemical modification on various cotton-fibre properties, thus helping cotton to maintain its position as a competitive textile raw material against the increasing number of synthetic fibres. One example of an industrially used chemical modification is the introduction of durable-press treatments for cotton garments. Such finishes compete in performances with garments made from synthetic fibres, although losses in strength and abrasion resistance frequently result. Durable-press cotton is obtained, at least in part, by the introduction of cross links between the cellulose chains in the fibre structure.

Cotton is resistant to the chemicals encountered in normal use, such as dyestuffs, mild bleaching agents, and many organic solvents. It is attacked, however, by strong oxidizing agents, leading to losses of tensile strength, a hazard of the bleaching process. Control of the oxidation process during bleaching is necessary. Colouring matter must be destroyed, while leaving the cellulose with a minimum of damage. Hot, dilute acids hydrolyze cellulose, leading to the disintegration of the polymer chains. Cellulose is resistant to alkali, which swells the fibres without degrading them chemically, leading to the mercerization process that changes the crystalline structure of cotton cellulose from cellulose I to cellulose II, when applied in sufficient strength. The cellulose chains are held together by hydrogen bonds, and breaking of these bonds by sufficiently strong hydrogen-bond-breaking agents leads to solubilization of the cotton cellulose without major degradation.

Esterification (chemical modification to produce desired properties) of cotton cellulose can be achieved by reaction with various acids or acid derivatives under suitable conditions. Cellulose nitrate and cellulose acetate are cellulose esters that have achieved commercial importance. Cotton linters are still used as a raw material for the production of cellulose acetate.

Cotton fibre loses strength upon exposure to moisture at elevated temperature, and this degradation is increased under the influence of sunlight. With proper storage, cotton can remain in a warehouse for extended periods without deterioration. Cotton cloth samples taken from tombs centuries old show very little deterioration in strength. Cotton is, however, affected by fungi and bacteria. Mildews cause considerable damage under warm moisture conditions, leading to rotting or weakening. Chemical modification, however, prevents such attacks, and cotton fabrics so treated become essentially rot-resistant.

World production and consumption. Annual world production of cotton in the late 1960s was 53,712,000 bales, each bale weighing 500 pounds (225 kilograms) gross. In the early 1970s, annual production figures in bales for the major cotton-producing countries included the United States, about 10,000,000; U.S.S.R., 9,000,000; China, 7,000,000; India, 4,850,000; Brazil, 3,100,000; Pakistan, 2,500,000; Egypt, 2,500,000; Turkey, 1,850,000; Mexico, 1,750,000; and The Sudan, 1,000,000. The first four countries accounted for nearly 60 percent of total production.

Production has nearly doubled since the early 1930s. The United States is still the world's largest producer, but its share has decreased drastically from 60 percent of the total for the season 1929–30, to 29 percent for the season 1964–65, and only 19.2 percent in the 1969–70 season.

In the late 1960s, 25,216,000 pounds of cotton were consumed annually. The world's major consuming countries were the United States, China, the U.S.S.R., India,

and Japan. The chief exporting countries were the United States, Brazil, Egypt, Mexico, The Sudan, Syria, Pakistan, and Turkey, and the major importers were Japan, the countries of the European Common Market, and India (mainly of longer staple cottons).

Coir. *Production.* The fruit of the coconut plant (*Cocos nucifera*) is surrounded by a husk consisting of a fibrous material yielding coir fibre. The coconut palm takes about seven to ten years to reach maturity and yields as many as 150 nuts per year. The fruits must be collected before ripening, because the fibres become increasingly coarse and darker in colour as the fruit ripens. In Sri Lanka (Ceylon), where most of the coir fibre originates, the fruits are plucked every alternate month throughout the year.

Processing. After removal of the fruit, the husk is quartered and subjected to retting (a soaking process accomplished by submerging in retting ponds, tanks, or saltwater lagoons, so that fermentation takes place, freeing the fibre from other materials). Depending on retting conditions, this process can require up to several months. The husks are next crushed, thus removing the woody portion, and the fibres are hackled (combed) and dried. In some factories, retting time is drastically reduced by presoaking with hot water and then crushing the husks between fluted rollers. Approximately 70 to 80 pounds (30 to 36 kilograms) of bristle fibre can be derived from 1,000 coconut husks. In the late 1960s the combined annual production of Sri Lanka and the western coast of India, the world's major coir producers, was estimated at 260,000 tons of bristle, of which 150,000 were exported, and total world output was about 280,000 tons. Other producers, on a smaller scale and limited to local production, included the Philippines, Kenya, Nigeria, and the West Indies.

Fibre properties. The coir-fibre cell walls are thick and rather irregular, resulting in an irregular outline of the lumen, the cavity running longitudinally through the fibre. The fibres are light, naturally resilient, durable, and resistant to dampness, and although they are less durable and rougher-surfaced than those made of other fibre, their low production cost makes them competitive despite their limitations.

Uses. The finest and longest variety fibre is the mat or yarn type, used for matting, ropes, and twines. The coarser and thicker bristle fibre is used for brushes and brooms, and the shorter fibres as mattress and upholstery stuffing.

Coir (coconut) by-products. By-products of coir production, derived from the husk or inner shell of the coconut surrounding the fruit, include coconut-oil cake, used to feed cattle; and coconut oil, a colourless, odourless oil, with the consistency of butter, that is used in foods, soap, and various industrial products.

Kapok. Kapok is obtained from the seeds of the silk-cotton or kapok tree (*Ceiba pentandra*) of the family Bombacaceae. It is produced mainly in Java, but also in other parts of Southeast Asia and Indonesia. Capsules containing the seeds are picked and broken open with mallets. After drying in the sun, the seeds and fibres are separated by hand, yielding a short fibre with a silky lustre and of exceedingly light weight.

Fibre properties. The fibre, thin-walled and of circular cross section with a wide lumen, or longitudinal central cavity, consists of a single cell, containing about 64 percent cellulose, 13 percent lignin, and 23 percent pentosans. Kapok is moisture resistant, resilient, and buoyant, but because it is soft, brittle, and inelastic it does not lend itself to spinning.

Uses. Kapok is used as upholstery and sleeping-bag stuffing, for insulation, and in the manufacture of life jackets.

Other seed fibres. Other seed fibres used commercially, usually as a wadding or upholstery material, are also obtained by breaking open seed capsules and separating the seeds and fibres. Fibres obtained from several varieties of plants of the Bombacaceae family, mainly found in Brazil and other parts of tropical America, are known as bombax cotton. Indian kapok, the floss secured from the seeds of *Bombax malabaricum*, has been used as stuffing material for pillows. It is similar to Java kapok in its extremely low weight and is used for the same purposes. The floss of the milkweeds, especially that obtained from two of the more than 80 species of the genus *Asclepias*, is also used as a substitute for kapok. The plants are distributed throughout the United States and are perennials when cultivated. Attempts to use the extremely brittle fibres for spinning have failed.

A considerable number of other seed fibres, such as calitropis floss (akund or mudar), cattail fibres (*Typhaceae*), and fibres growing on certain cacti belonging to the genus *Cereus*, have been used for the manufacture of buoyant materials, for heat insulation, and in acoustic materials.

BAST FIBRES

Bast fibres, obtained from the inner bast tissue of the bark of the stem of dicotyledonous plants (those having two seed leaves), include some of the most commercially important fibres, such as jute, flax, hemp, ramie, sunn, kenaf, urena, and nettle. These fibres, often several feet long, are composed of individual long cells. The designation "soft fibres" distinguishes them from leaf fibres, frequently referred to as "hard fibres."

The bast fibres lie beneath the bark and are held together by gummy materials. These tissues must be softened, dissolved, and washed away to allow extraction of the fibres from the stem, a process accomplished by steeping the stems in water, or retting. The bundles of bark, weighted down with stones or earth, are steeped in running waters or ponds for varying periods of time, depending on such factors as temperature and type of water. The process generally requires five to 30 days, and the optimum temperature for retting is 80° F (27° C). Decomposition of the gums and softening of the tissues is caused by micro-organisms. After retting is complete, the fibres are freed from the stalk and then are washed and dried.

Jute. *History.* Jute has been cultivated in India as a fibre-producing plant since ancient times, and records of its spinning and weaving for apparel and cordage date back several centuries. Successful modification of flax-spinning machinery for use with jute resulted in the development in the 19th century of a growing export market and considerable expansion of the area cultivated for jute in India. Jute mills were set up in the United States and France, as well as in India.

Production. Jute fibres are obtained from the bark of two herbaceous annuals, *Corchorus capsularis* and *Corchorus olitorius*, belonging to the family of Tiliaceae. The former is grown on about 60 percent of the jute-growing land in India; from it, white jute is obtained, while tossa or daisee jutes are obtained from the latter. Jute is the most important of all bast fibres and is cultivated in China and Bangladesh as well as India. It makes considerable demands on the soil and must compete with rice and other food plants; similar fibres, such as kenaf, roselle, and urena, are less demanding and can be grown in rotation with other crops.

Jute is usually grown as a cash crop in fairly small holdings; the grower's family cultivates, harvests, and extracts the crop. Grown during the rainy season, jute thrives best in damp heat, in humidity of about 70 to 90 percent. The sowing time must be adjusted so that the crop reaches a height of three to four feet (about a metre) before the heavy monsoon rain starts. *C. capsularis* is generally sown early in February–March, and *C. olitorius* in April–May. Depending on the time of sowing, soil, and climatic conditions, the vegetative period for both is three to five months. Plants are harvested at the flowering or pod-formation stage, when about 50 percent of the plants are in pod and both the yield and the quality of the fibre are good. Plants are cut with a sickle, close to the ground; in flooded areas the cutters often have to dive underwater to cut the stems. A trained cutter cuts as many as six to eight plants at one dive. On highlands the plants are left for two to three days after cutting to allow shedding of the leaves. The average yield, depend-

ing on soil, rainfall, and farming practices, is approximately 1,240 pounds (560 kilograms) per acre in India. Fibre content is 4.5 to 7.5 percent of the weight of the green stem.

Processing. Jute fibres are loosened from the bark by retting, induced by chemical or bacterial methods, so that the fibres in the stem are separated from the adjacent tissues and woody core by removal of pectins, gums, and other mucilaginous materials. In India and Bangladesh, retting is usually done in water, the steep-retting process, in which the action is bacterial. Bundles of stalks are soaked in running streams or stagnant pools, fully submerged and weighted down. This process usually takes from ten days to a month, depending upon temperature, type of water, depth of immersion, and plant maturity. During retting, the bacterial organisms decompose gums, pectins, and other substances that bind the fibres together.

The colour, lustre, and strength of jute fibres are greatly influenced by the retting process. Early stem removal can cause difficulty in fibre separation, while overretting renders the fibres weak and inferior in quality. Retting in slow-moving streams is favourable to fibre quality because of the prolonged aerobic (oxygen present) phase of retting and gradual removal of decomposition products. Rapidly moving water sweeps away the retting bacteria, adversely affecting the retting process. After retting is completed, the stalks are placed in water two to three feet deep, and the fibres are stripped from the bark by one of several methods. In the most common a few stems are treated at a time. The root end of the bundle of stems is beaten with a paddle, loosening the fibres; the stems are broken near the root end, the short broken ends are jerked away, and the loose fibres are then stripped from the remaining stems. The fibre bundle is washed to get rid of the decomposed foreign matter, wrung out, and hung to dry.

The cleaned and dried jute fibre moves from the growers to the village market and through a series of middlemen to the baling centres where a baler grades it. The graded jute is packed into bales weighing about 250 pounds (110 kilograms) for use in the home market. Next, the remaining jute moves to larger terminal markets where it is regraded for export or shipment to spinning mills in India or Pakistan. Export jute is graded for further classification according to the system used in the importing country.

Commercial grading of jute is not presently based on laboratory tests, although methods have been developed in India and the United Kingdom to relate such measurable fibre characteristics as length, fineness, and strength to the properties of the yarns spun from each grade. Fibres that can be spun into fine yarns are the most valuable. Such characteristics as colour, length, fineness, strength, lustre, cleanliness, softness, uniformity, and low percentage of root are considered in the grading process. White jute, the most common, varies from whitish yellow to gray or yellowish tan; the best grades have high lustre. Daisee jute ranges from gray to black; tossa jute has a russet tinge, varying from golden brown to reddish brown.

In the conversion of jute fibres into yarns, the jute is selected by type, mark, and grade based on quality, colour, cleanliness, strength, texture, and price. The objective is to blend fibres to achieve uniform colour, strength, and fibre-length distribution; to parallelize and orient the fibres in the long direction of the yarn; and to twist them into continuous strands.

Bales of fibre having compatible physical properties are opened and blended together. The bale opener, a massively built machine with intermeshing heavy flute rollers, makes the dried jute soft and pliable. The heads are split into smaller bundles, called stricks, that are fed to the spreader board, the root end of one strick overlapping the crop end of the previous one. The stricks move through a pair of fluted rollers and onto the pins mounted on a lattice. Oil, water, and emulsifiers are added to soften the jute to improve process performance. The spreader converts jute into sliver, which can be pre-

Retting of jute

Competition with food plants

Conversion to yarn

sented to carding machines. The remaining processes of carding, drawing, roving, and spinning are similar to flax and hemp spinning.

The unit for describing the size or count of jute yarn and roving (a strand in an intermediate state between sliver and yarn) is the weight in pounds of a spyndle, the equivalent of 14,400 yards. It is also described in the same way as cotton by the tex system.

Fibre properties. Jute fibre is a multicellular structure made up of a number of ultimate cells of regular polygonal cross section cemented together with noncellulosic substances such as lignin and hemicellulose. Chemical treatments that remove these cementing substances affect the structure and lead to the deterioration of the physical properties of the fibre. Dry tensile strength is hardly affected by removal of either lignin or hemicellulose, but wet tensile strength drops drastically because only ultimate cells remain.

Jute fibre is fairly weak, with low longation (stretchability) and elasticity, and is characterized by coarseness, stiffness, and brittleness. Jute consists of 58 to 63 percent α-cellulose, 21 to 24 percent hemicellulose, 12 to 14 percent lignin and such minor components as wax, pectin, and organic salts, nitrogenous substances, and colouring matter. The α-cellulose isolated from jute plant material is intimately associated with other carbohydrate constituents. Lignin is mainly responsible for the yellowing of jute when it is exposed to light.

Jute is susceptible to the action of acids and alkalies. Dilute acids have a brightening effect, but extended acid treatment at high temperatures, or use of stronger acids, leads to extensive hydrolysis (decomposition) and strength losses. Concentrated alkali causes swelling, and the fibres are also sensitive to oxidizing agents.

Uses. About 75 percent of the jute produced annually is manufactured into sacks and bags. It is also widely used for twine, carpet yarns, and cloth backings for linoleum and carpet. The Calcutta jute industry uses about 60 percent of the total world supply of raw jute and the European industry about another 30 percent. In the early 1970s the Indian jute industry sought to extend the use of jute to decorative fabrics.

The use of jute as a packaging material is increasingly threatened by other bast fibres, by synthetic fibres, and by new methods and techniques of packaging and transportation. The mechanization of jute production has made little progress, and manufacture is still dependent on the availability of cheap labour. Because jute is grown on soil that can also be used for growing rice and because high-yield rice varieties result in larger profits, it is likely that jute will be at least partially replaced by rice, especially in such countries as India and Bangladesh. The survival of jute as a major fibre seems to depend on the development of new jute varieties with high response to fertilizers and on further mechanization and improvement of manufacturing processes.

World production and consumption. Annual world production of raw jute for 1969–70 was about 2,870,000 tons, of which about 90 percent came from India and Bangladesh, then East Pakistan (India, 1,300,000 tons; Bangladesh, 1,350,000 tons), most of the rest from China, Burma, and Thailand. Production in China was estimated at about 150,000 tons. India and China retain their production for use in their own jute mills, so that Bangladesh dominates the world market. The chief importing country is the United Kingdom.

Flax. *History.* The fibre obtained from the flax plant, from which linen cloth is manufactured, is one of the most ancient textile fibres. The manufacture of linen was already an established art in Egypt by 3400 BC, where both fine and coarse canvas-like linen cloth has been found in burial chambers. Some mummies have been wrapped in as much as 1,000 yards (900 metres) of very fine linen. The use of linen spread from Egypt throughout the Mediterranean and was carried to northwest Europe by the Romans. France and the Low Countries became famous for their linen. Ireland, which has an ideal climate for linen spinning and weaving because of its dampness, became an important producer. Linsey-

woolsey, a fabric made from linen warp and wool filling, was popular for outer wear up to the mid-19th century, when the availability of cheap cotton fabrics largely eliminated it.

Production. The flax plant (*Linum usitatissimum*) is grown both for the linen fibre and for its seed, which is important for linseed oil; flax is the second most important bast fibre.

Flax requires a temperate climate free from heavy rains and frosts. Frequent moist winds during the growing season are advantageous. Hot, dry summers produce a short and harsh but strong fibre; moderately moist summers produce plants yielding fine, strong, silky linen. Flax is difficult to grow because of the soil preparation required before sowing and the heavy applications of artificial fertilizers needed.

After slow initial growth, the plants grow as rapidly as one inch per day for 30 to 40 days. Blossoms then begin to develop and stem growth ceases. Flax is normally a three-month crop, although this growing time varies with climatic and other growing conditions.

Flax is attacked by several fungus and virus diseases, usually kept under fair control by chemical treatments of the seed or by cultivation of resistant varieties. Harvesting is carried out when the lower two-thirds of the stem has become yellow and the leaves have fallen off, about a month after the appearance of the first flowers. The choice of harvest time is important because lignification (conversion to woody tissue) takes place if the plants are left too long before harvesting, and yield will be lower if harvesting is too early. Harvesting is normally carried out by pulling the plant from the ground by hand or machine. Pulling is considered superior to cutting; flax tends to deteriorate at the cut, and the cut straw is shorter than pulled straw, with a consequent loss of fibre. Yields of fibre per acre vary from 450 pounds to about 800 pounds (200 to 360 kilograms).

Processing. Like the other bast fibres, jute, hemp, and ramie, linen must be separated from the stalks by retting. Water retting, which is essentially bacterial, is practiced in areas such as the Philippines, Taiwan, and China; most of the crop grown in the Soviet Union and the United States is dew retted, which is predominantly fungal. In this method the harvested flax straw is left in the field and allowed to remain until the combined action of the moisture from dew and micro-organisms makes separation of the fibres possible. The process depends very much on the temperature and chemical nature of the water but takes only six to eight days under controlled temperature conditions. After removal of the stalks from the retting medium, thorough drying is necessary to prevent further fermentation.

The retted and dried fibres are removed from the woody remainder of the stem by the process of scutching, in which the stems are first broken by a passage through a series of fluted metal rollers, and the fine pieces of the woody portion of the straw, called shives, are beaten out. About a tenth of the original flax stem is fibre.

Fibre properties. Under the microscope, linen fibres show the transverse lines characteristic for most bast fibres. In cross section, they are round to polygonal with a small central lumen (horizontal cavity). The boiled-off and bleached linen fibre is almost 100 percent cellulose and shows the same reactions with alkalies and acids as does cotton. Linen is the strongest of the vegetable fibres, showing greater strength in the wet state. Colour varies, depending on the retting conditions, from cream to brown; the fibre is usually bleached to white or near white. Linen fibres range from 12 to 30 inches (30 to 75 centimetres) in length and from five to 28 microns in diameter.

Uses. Linen has a variety of uses. The first grades are used for such fabrics as damask, and in sheeting, lace, and apparel; the coarser grades are used for twines, canvases, bags, fishnets, sewing threads, and fire hoses.

World production and consumption. Flax is grown chiefly in the Soviet Union, which produced about 450,-000 tons annually in the late 1960s, and eastern Europe. Together they accounted for more than 80 percent of

Marginal notes:

Problems of jute manufacture

Clothing of linsey-woolsey

Water retting of flax

total world production, which was estimated at 664,000 tons. The bulk of Soviet production is for domestic use, and only in the late 1960s did export trade achieve any importance. The Common Market countries of western Europe are substantial exporters. Belgium is the most important exporter of high-quality flax, followed by France and The Netherlands. In the late 1960s Belgium, with its exceptional retting facilities, was also the largest buyer, followed by the United Kingdom, France, and Italy.

Ramie. *Production.* Ramie fibre is obtained from the stem of the many-stemmed shrub *Boehmeria nivea* of the nettle family (Urticaceae). The plant, a native of China, is also called China grass, and has been cultivated for its fibre for hundreds of years, reaching Europe early in the 18th century. Several other plants of the nettle family yield fibres from their stems but have only local commercial importance. The plant producing ramie fibre is a perennial with stems three to eight feet (one to two and a half metres) high, originating from a rootstock, and having few branches. When the stems are cut during the growing season, the rootstocks send up new shoots, producing two to four crops from the plant each year, depending on climate and soil conditions.

Ramie cultivation

Successful cultivation requires rich, well-drained, sandy, loam soil, which retains sufficient moisture throughout the growing season; high temperature and humidity, with an annual rainfall of not less than 45 inches (104 centimetres). Rainfall should be spread throughout the year; prolonged flooding kills the rootstocks. The necessity for heavy fertilization increases with each growing year. One crop of ramie is considered 16 times more exhausting to the soil than cotton, unless the waste material is returned to the soil.

Because raising plants from seeds takes one to two years, vegetative propagation is frequently practiced. Cuttings from reproductive underground shoots, or rhizomes, are planted in prepared holes. Weeding is important only in the early stages of growth because the plants are planted densely enough to shade the ground and smother weeds.

The time for harvesting is judged by the discoloration of the stems, which turn brown upon maturing. The plants are usually cut by hand with a sickle, close to the ground to prevent new stalks from arising from the old stump. Mechanization of harvesting is difficult because of possible damage to the new stalks. The cut stems, about five to six feet long, are dried, frequently after the leaves have been stripped from the plant. Defoliation by chemical means may be practiced. Yields, varying widely according to soil, climate, and the use of fertilizer, are usually reported as pounds of crude un-degummed ramie per acre per year and range from 800 to 2,000 pounds (360 to 900 kilograms) per acre.

A pest of ramie in Japan is the black caterpillar, which attacks plants in June or July; spraying with lead arsenate or DDT has been effective. White fungus disease occurs occasionally, attacking the root system and sometimes infecting whole areas, which then become unsuitable for ramie planting for several years.

Processing. Decortication, removing the bark and woody parts of the stalk and part of the gummy material, frees the fibres as strands. Decorticated fibre strands are usually known as crude ramie fibres. Decortication machines such as the raspador, invented in France in 1896, are used almost exclusively. Their efficiency varies, but yields of crude fibre in the range of 2.5 to 3.5 percent, based on the weight of the green stalks, can usually be achieved.

The crude fibres are next dried and baled in bundles ranging from 100 to 500 pounds (45 to 225 kilograms). No general grading standards are used; quality is usually based on length and cleanliness of the fibre, pliability, and colour.

The fibres are degummed before spinning to remove the gums, waxes, and pectins that remain on the crude fibre. This process, usually performed by the mills that spin the fibre, is carried out by bacteriological or chemical means. The most commonly used chemical process consists of treating the fibres in caustic soda solutions containing wetting and reducing agents. After a 24-hour soaking period, the fibres are boiled for one to four hours, then rinsed, neutralized, washed, centrifuged, oiled, and dried.

The fibres have to be cut or sorted to the appropriate length before spinning. The spinning process employs machinery adapted from wool or cotton spinning, depending on fibre length.

Fibre properties. Ramie fibre is white, with high lustre, and is highly resistant to bacteria and fungi, including mildew. High moisture absorption and rapid drying are characteristic of ramie yarns and fabrics. The fibre cells are about 15 centimetres (six inches) in length, considerably longer than flax or hemp fibres. Diameters of individual bast cells range from 25 to 75 microns (.00098 to .00295 inch). The mature cell has an almost cylindrical cross section, thick cell walls, and a well-defined lumen. A longitudinal view reveals small nodelike ridges and striations without twist. The degummed fibre consists of 96 to 98 percent α-cellulose with little lignin.

Uses. Ramie has the same uses as flax and hemp. It has considerable strength, lack of stretch, and high wet strength. It dries quickly, making it useful for fishing nets, although the use of synthetic fibres for such purposes has increased. The short tow is used for the manufacture of specialty papers, such as for cigarettes and banknotes. In the Far East, ramie is used for clothing, tablecloths, handkerchiefs, canvas, and mosquito nets. It is also used for the packing of ship propeller shafts, for hats, upholstery, and in various fabrics. It is, however, too expensive for mass-produced articles and cannot be spun into fine yarns.

World production and consumption. China is the world's largest producer of ramie; Japan is also a major producer. The chief importers are Germany, France, and the United Kingdom.

Hemp. Hemp (*Cannabis sativa*) is the common name for the only species in the genus *Cannabis*, an annual of the Cannabaceae family. Although it has many varieties, strains, types, or lines, it should not be confused with the very different Mauritius hemp, Manila hemp, sisal hemp, or New Zealand hemp, all of which are fibre-producing plants, but none of which has any botanical relationship to true hemp.

Probably the oldest cultivated fibre plant, it originated in Central Asia and spread to China, where it has apparently been cultivated for more than 6,000 years.

Production. Hemp grows in nearly all countries of the temperate zone and is cultivated in most of central Europe and the Balkan countries, the Soviet Union, China, Turkey, Japan, Chile, and the United States.

The form of the plant and its yield of fibre vary with climatic conditions and the variety. Those varieties cultivated for fibre production have long stalks with little branching, and only small quantities of seed, which are used mainly for propagation. Where large quantities of seed are desired, varieties are short in height and mature early. The variety *Cannabis sativa*, cultivated for the production of the drug hashish, or marihuana, is short and many-branched, with small, dark-green leaves, and is grown mainly in tropical regions.

Hemp growing

Hemp thrives in a mild, temperate climate with humid atmosphere but can endure considerable changes in temperature. Hemp seed is sown early in the spring and requires little cultivation. The fast-growing hemp seedlings soon cover the ground, choking out the weeds. The plants are ready for harvesting when the male plants change from a deep green to a light brown. An optimum yield of high-quality fibres is obtained if harvesting is carried out when the flowers begin to open and shed pollen. Harvesting before maturity results in lower yields and weaker, but finer and softer, fibres. Harvesting considerably after maturity yields more seeds and results in harsh and brittle fibres. The normal time from planting to harvesting is about four to five months in temperate climates. The plants are normally cut off by hand with a hemp knife about one inch (2.5 centimetres) from the ground, and the stems are spread on the ground to dry.

Processing. After retting, drying, and scutching to isolate the bast fibres from the bark or stem, the hemp is dressed and softened (beetled) and is ready for the market. No generally recognized grading standards exist. For shipment to the spinning mills, the hemp is pressed into bales weighing up to 790 pounds (360 kilograms).

Fibres are sorted in the spinning mill and grouped into batches of different grades. The bundles are then passed through a machine fitted with sets of fluted rollers, which make them soft and flexible. The remaining woody matter is crushed to powder. The fibres, measuring about two to three metres (seven to ten feet) in length, are reduced to about 80 centimetres (30 inches) to facilitate handling in the rest of the processing. Bundles are generally divided into base, middle, and top portions by stretching, allowing them to snap at the right places. The middle portion contains the highest quality fibres. The fibres are combed and parallelized on the hackling machine, and the hackled tow is converted into sliver on the spreadboard machine. The sliver is doubled and attenuated on draw frames and further reduced in size on the roving frame. The roving is processed into yarns by either dry or wet spinning. Wet spinning produces the finest yarns; the fibres are separated with the aid of boiling water to ensure proper drafting.

Fibre properties. Hemp fibres are longer and generally coarser than flax fibres but have less flexibility. Bleaching is difficult, and the fibre is not used for fine textiles. The finest quality, originating in Italy, is a white and pale-gray colour with silky lustre and softness similar to that of flax. Strands are over six feet (two metres) long. The less valuable hemp produced in the Soviet Union and the United States is coarser, with greater strength and durability. Hemp has a cellulose content of 67 percent and contains about 16 percent hemicellulose, with a Z twist in contrast to the S twist of flax.

Uses. Hemp is used for ropes, twines, cables, nets, sailcloth, canvas, and tarpaulins, but its main use is as a substitute for flax in the manufacture of yarn and twine. It has been replaced as a material for rope by such stronger fibres as sisal, abaca, and synthetics.

Hemp yields several by-products, and varieties are grown either for their fibre content; for the seeds, which are used as a food additive; or for the resinous juice obtained from the stalks, leaves, or flowers of a variety called Indian hemp, grown in tropical regions and yielding narcotics. Depending on the preparation or the part of the plant used, the narcotic, a composition of various compounds, is known in India as *charas* (the resinous juice), *ganja* (obtained from the dried flowering top of the female plant), bhang (dried leaves and flowering shoots from either the male or female), or hashish (Turkish preparation of the leaves). As a narcotic hemp is usually known as marihuana in the Western Hemisphere and as kef in North Africa. Its use is unlawful in many countries, and in the early 1970s, many studies were under way on its controversial effects.

World production and consumption. The world's hemp output is about 206,000 tons (excluding China for which figures are unavailable). The Soviet Union is the largest producer of hemp in the world, with annual production of about 100,000 tons in the late 1960s, with most of this production used domestically; the major exporting countries are Italy and Yugoslavia. Romania, Hungary, Poland, and Bulgaria are other major producers of hemp. West Germany and France are among the major importers.

Sunn, or sann, hemp (Crotalaria juncea). *Production.* Sunn hemp, a member of the pea family (Leguminosae), is grown for fibres or as a green manure. The plants thrive in poor soils and relatively arid areas because of their strong tap-root system that penetrates deeply into the soil to reach low-ground water levels. Sunn hemp is cultivated on a commercial scale mainly in India, where it has been used since prehistoric times, and to a lesser extent in Sri Lanka. Three distinct types of sunn-hemp fibre are grown in India, including white, having a grayish colour, shiny lustre, and fine texture; green, coloured greenish to grayish, stronger than white fibre, and

therefore more valuable; and one called *dewghuddy*, creamy in colour, with good length and fine texture. Considerable differences in fibre quality depend on cultivation and growing conditions. Most of India's production consists of the white fibre, closely followed by the green. About 1 percent consists of the *dewghuddy* type, considered to be best in quality.

Processing. Retting and extraction is accomplished by the same hand methods as are applied to the cleaning of jute. In modern practice the breaking operation, in which the woody portion of the stalk is crushed to set the fibres free, is done mechanically.

After scutching, the fully extended, straightened, and smooth fibres are twisted into hemp stricks, and 140 to 200 are assembled into bales weighing about 120 pounds (50 kilograms). The quality of hemp is assessed from the fibre material obtained after the process of packing. Grades include heavy, strong, clear, long, and hemp of good colour. These characteristics are essentially dependent upon proper fertilization, maturity, and retting conditions. Hemp of poor grades may result from premature or delayed harvesting, from excessive application of nitrogen fertilizers, and from insufficient drying and retting of the fibres.

Use. Sunn hemp is used locally to make fishing twines, thick canvas, ropes, and cordage.

World production and consumption. In the late 1960s, about 65,000 tons were produced annually by India, which used most of its production domestically.

Kenaf, roselle, and urena. Kenaf, roselle, and urena are bast fibres used as jute substitutes. These fibres closely resemble jute, although they are somewhat shorter and coarser and are usually combined with jute. All three belong to the mallow family (Malvaceae), one of the most important of all fibre-plant families.

Production. Kenaf is obtained from the stems of *Hibiscus cannabinus*, an herbaceous annual with a straight, slender, prickly stem that may reach heights up to 12 feet (four metres). Roselle is the fibre obtained from the stem of *Hibiscus sabdariffa*, a native of tropical Africa. *Urena lobata*, another member of the Malvaceae family, produces fibres in its stem. Both the fibre and the plant of urena are known under different names in various countries.

While jute makes considerable demands on the soil and must compete with rice and other staple food plants where it is commonly grown, kenaf is more adaptable to various kinds of soil and climatic conditions, although sensitive to frost and limited to tropical and subtropical regions. It can be grown in rotation with other crops on well-drained sandy loams. During the four-to-five-month growth period of the plant, rainfall of about 22 inches (56 centimetres) is necessary. The tap root penetrates deep into the soil, and proper development and aeration of the root systems require seedbeds prepared to an appropriate depth. Sowing usually occurs at the beginning of the rainy season, and weeding is essential in the first few weeks of growth. The stems reach 12 to 15 feet (four to five metres) under favourable conditions, and harvesting begins when the plant has a few flowers. Where seed production is required, the plants are allowed to mature fully, but at that stage the fibres are considerably coarser and of less value. Yields of fibre per acre range from 1,000 to 3,000 pounds (450 to 1,350 kilograms), depending on harvesting time and climatic and soil conditions. Most of the fibre in the kenaf stem is in the lower portion; the top part of the stem is removed before retting or ribboning, with a loss of only about 3 percent of the total fibre. The plants are cut by hand with a machete similar to the implement used in jute harvesting.

Processing. Removal of the fibres from the stalk is usually performed mechanically, although in some areas retting and hand stripping are still practiced. Ribboning machines remove the fibre-containing bark, which is then retted. After retting, the fibres are obtained by beating the ribbons on the surface of the water. Further processing of the fibres to the yarn stage is similar to that of jute.

Fibre properties. Fibre strands are three feet or more in length, and light and creamy in colour, with the same lustre as jute. Strength is also comparable to that of jute. Individual cells are more or less cylindrical, with thick cell walls surrounded by a layer of lignin, and an irregular and broad lumen. Fibre composition is similar to that of jute.

World production and consumption. Large quantities of kenaf are grown in India, where the fibre is called *mesta*. In the late 1960s India annually produced 161,-000 tons, of which 18,000 tons were exported. Thailand was a large producer with 140,000 tons, and the major portion was exported. The plant was introduced into China in 1936, where it is known as *taschkentii*. Together with abutilon (see below), the kenaf production of China amounts to approximately 325,000 tons. The future importance of kenaf, still fairly new on the world market, is difficult to estimate.

The roselle fibre plant is a native of tropical Africa, where it is almost exclusively grown. *Urena lobata* has been cultivated in several countries in warmer regions, including West Africa, the Congo, Madagascar, some areas in India and Indochina, and the coastal areas of Queensland and Brazil. The fibre production is almost exclusively used in the countries of origin.

Abutilon. Abutilon, belonging to the Malvaceae family, has been a fibre crop in China for many years and is used there for ropes and twines and in admixtures with jute. Some of the abutilon fibre exported from China reaches the world's market as China jute. The plant, also cultivated in the Soviet Union, is known there as *kanatnik* and is better suited than jute for cultivation because it is more hardy and resistant to disease. It can be grown as far north as the 56th parallel of latitude in western Siberia.

Several other members of the Malvaceae family have fibres in their stems and are being used for fibre production. They usually grow wild and are used locally for purposes similar to jute or the other bast fibres. These plants include the *Sida* species, the *Pavonia* species, the *Thespesia* species, and several others.

LEAF FIBRES

Leaf fibres are structural elements in the fibrovascular system of the leaves of certain plants. Too stiff for most fabric uses, this group contains two of the most important cordage fibres: abaca, or Manila hemp, and sisal. Other leaf-fibre plants of commercial value are henequen, Mauritius hemp, and New Zealand flax or hemp (*Phormium tenax*).

Plants yielding leaf fibres are usually perennials propagated by root cuttings or rhizomes (horizontal subterranean plant stems). The most important group of plants, the agaves, store water and grow in both arid and humid climates. Their rate of plant growth and the formation of fibre-containing leaves depend on the amount of moisture available. Although the rate of growth is faster in East Africa, Indonesia, and the Philippines, the total leaf and fibre production during the life of a plant is approximately the same as that of much slower growing plants in Mexico. In harvesting, the leaves are cut at their base with sickle-like knives, then tied into bundles.

Other important leaf fibres include abaca, obtained from the banana family; and Mauritius hemp and phormium both from the agave family. These perennials, propagated by root cuttings, require considerable rain. Approximately 10 to 25 leaf stalks form one pseudostem, which is cut at the base upon maturity; then new pseudostems are formed from spreading rhizomes.

In the late 1960s annual world production of the principal hard fibres, sisal, abaca, and henequen, decreased by 5 percent to some 850,000 tons. Sisal is by far the most important of these fibres, contributing nearly 70 percent of the total output. Sisal fibre is grown mostly in Kenya, Tanzania, Brazil, Angola, and Mozambique. Other hard fibres are grown mainly in the Philippines (abaca) and Mexico (henequen). Abaca represents only 7–9 percent of the principal hard fibres.

Abaca, or Manila hemp. *Production.* Abaca fibre is obtained from the plant *Musa textilis*, belonging to the banana family (Musaceae), and is also known as Manila hemp, named for the port from which it was first shipped. It is not related to true hemp, a soft fibre that is the product of *Cannabis sativa*. Fibres from a number of other species of the Musaceae family are used locally in various countries but have little or no commercial value.

Musa textilis is of the same family as the banana plant, but its stalks are usually more slender, with smaller and narrower leaves and smaller, inedible fruit. Like other *Musa* species, *Musa textilis* has a rhizome, or branching underground stem, bearing numerous small roots, which develops 10 to 25 pseudostems growing in a cluster. Each is composed of up to 25 broad leafstalks with their broad bases overlapping one another and growing into a kind of trunk 12 to 16 inches (30 to 40 centimetres) in diameter. The leaf blade, tightly rolled until it leaves the pseudostem, unfolds into a leaf from three to eight feet (one to 2.5 metres) long and about a foot wide, which forms a crown at the top of the pseudostem. The true stem rises through the middle of this structure, forming an aerial shoot that eventually becomes a spike with many flower clusters.

Abaca requires loose soil, rich in humus and with good drainage, and humidity both in the atmosphere and in the soil. It is grown under tropical conditions with heavy rainfalls more or less evenly distributed throughout the year.

Abaca, a perennial, is usually propagated by root cuttings or from the suckers (rapidly developing shoots) rising at the base of the parent plant. Plants grown from seed take about one or two years longer to mature than those from shoots or root cuttings. The stalks mature in two to three years, but the plant will not yield a full crop of mature stalks until it is four to five years old. The fibre reaches maximum tensile strength just before the shoot flowers, at which point harvesting is carried out.

In the Philippines the minimum stem height for harvesting is eight feet. The entire stalk is cut close to the ground, and the parent root stalk then sends out rhizomes from which further stalks shoot up. Two to four stalks may be harvested every four to six months from each mat or parent root stalk. The various leaf sheaths are stripped from the stem of the parent stalk. The fibre in the sheath varies in colour and quality (depending on the position of the sheath in the stalk), becoming softer, whiter, and weaker from the outside sheath to the innermost sheath.

The most serious disease of abaca, called bunchy top disease, is caused by a virus transmitted by the brown banana aphid. Once attacked, the whole plant becomes infected and cannot recover. Destruction of infected plants or even whole plantations is the only known remedy. Another serious affliction of abaca in the Philippines is the mosaic disease, also caused by a virus and transmitted by a number of aphids. Again, the only known remedy is destruction of all infected plants. Mosaic disease has threatened the entire abaca industry in southern Mindanao.

The introduction of the abaca plant into other tropical regions such as Indonesia, India, and Central America was successful when World War II cut off abaca supplies from the Philippines. At that time, production of the abaca fibres increased considerably in Costa Rica, Guatemala, Panama, and several of the other Central American countries.

Processing. Operations to remove the fibres from the leaf sheaf include the tuxying process, separating the fibrous outer layer from each leaf sheaf, and the stripping process, in which the pulpy material is removed, freeing the fibre strands. Both operations must be carried out soon after the stalk has been cut. Tuxying is usually done in the field with a knife; stripping is done either by hand or with a machine, the *hagotan*. After stripping, the fibre is hung in the sun to dry.

Abaca fibres are also cleaned with decorticator ma-

Margin notes:

Types of leaf fibres

Abaca cultivation

chines, which remove the outer layers, usually operating in conjunction with a mechanical drier.

Fibres are graded and baled for export at a warehouse and sold at regularly scheduled public auctions. Official Philippine grading standards include: (1) Hand or spindle stripped fibres specially prepared for tagal braid (a straw braid mostly used for hats), and other fine textile uses; (2) hand or spindle stripped fibres prepared for cordage; and (3) decorticated fibre. Grades are based on fineness, lustre, cleanliness, colour, and strength. After grading, the fibres are pressed into export bales, weighing 278.3 pounds (126.2 kilograms) each.

Fibre properties. The commercial fibre consists of fibre strands made up of bundles of individual fibres held together by natural gums. Length varies from three to nine feet (one to three metres). The fibre has a natural high lustre with colour ranging from pure white to ivory and dark brown. Abaca fibres have excellent strength, reasonable elongations of 2 to 4 percent, and high resistance toward micro-organisms found in saltwater. Individual fibres can be isolated from the fibre strands by boiling in alkaline solution. Abaca has been found to consist of 63–64 percent cellulose, 19.6 percent hemicellulose, and 5.1 percent lignin, and to have a 10 to 12 percent moisture content.

Uses. In the Philippines, abaca is used for making slippers, ropes, twines, and hammocks. In other countries, it is also used for the manufacture of marine ropes, in which use it is sometimes preferred to sisal. Abaca's exceptional strength and resistance to water make it particularly suitable for these purposes. It is the strongest
of all hard fibres, followed by sisal, phormium, and henequen. Abaca ropes can also be used for mining and well drilling, and the fibre is also used to a large extent in the paper industries for teabags, mimeograph mats, and for other specialty materials.

World production and consumption. The Philippines is the only important producer of abaca. Most of the 67,-000-ton annual harvest in the late 1960s was exported to the United States, Japan, and the United Kingdom.

Sisal. Sisal (*Agave sisalana*) is one of about 300 species of plants belonging to the agave family (Agavaceae), all originating in the tropical and subtropical parts of the Western Hemisphere; they have been introduced to other places, including East Africa, the West Indies, Indonesia, and the Philippines. The name sisal comes from the name of the port in the state of Yucatán in Mexico, from which the fibre was first exported.

Production. The plant produces leaves two to six feet (0.6 to 2 metres) in length, tapering off to a sharp thornlike point. The growth rate depends on the availability of water, for sisal is a water-storing plant, growing when water supplies are available but stopping to conserve water in times of drought. It may produce six to eight leaves per month during the wet season, and none in the dry season. Sisal grows in areas where the rainfall and soil conditions are unsuitable for other species of agave, and under a much wider range of growth conditions than henequen. The life processes and activity of the plant depend on soil conditions and climate. There are two growing seasons per year in East Africa, as against one in Mexico, but the plants live through approximately the same number of growing seasons in both areas, producing fibres at a considerably higher rate in East Africa, but with the total yield per lifetime approximately the same. Sisal prefers dry, permeable soils, with some lime, but also grows on well-drained, black, cotton land. Suckers (rapidly developing shoots) were formerly used for propagation because they can be planted immediately after their removal from the parent plant, but the modern practice is to use buds, or bulbils, for propagation, placing them in nurseries for about 12 to 18 months before they are planted in the field. Planting of the bulbils is usually done during the rainy season. Toward the end of its life, the plant starts to pole, and the pole can reach a height of 20 or more feet (six metres or more), being branched at the last five feet. After the pole stops growing, the branches throw out stems on which the yellow sisal flowers develop, eventually dying and falling off. The bulbils formed when the flowers die grow to a length of about four inches, at which size they are easily removed. The plant dies after the pole has developed bulbils, each pole yielding about 2,000.

The time needed before a new sisal plant is ready for
cutting depends on the conditions under which it is grown. From two and a half to four years may be needed. Leaves that are ready for cutting are severed at their base with a sickle-like knife. Yields of 17 tons per hectare (seven tons per acre) can be obtained from properly cut plants. The leaves weigh between one and one and a half pounds each, and are tied into bundles of 30 leaves, with 70 bundles making up a task. Each leaf contains about 1,000 individual fibres, which constitute about 2 to 5 percent of the weight of the leaves. Yields of 1,800 to 2,500 pounds of fibre per acre (2,000 to 2,800 kilograms per hectare) per year are obtained on the best plantations in East Africa and Indonesia.

Processing. Decortication of the leaves is carried out in large stationary machines that crush the leaf, scrape the fibre clean, and wash it to remove the remaining pulp pieces. Fibre intended for export is graded and baled. Grade designation and bale weight differ widely, depending on the country of origin.

Fibre properties. In world trade sisal appears as a white to yellowish fibre, three to five feet in length. One of the coarser hard fibres, it is strong but not as flexible as abaca. Like abaca, commercial sisal fibres consist of strands containing a large number of small individual fibres held together by natural gums. The average length of sisal fibres varies from three to four feet (about a metre) or longer. The strands are usually white and of high lustre. Sisal fibres have good breaking elongation, and high resistance to seawater.

Use. Most sisal is used for the manufacture of binder twine and bailer twine, although efforts are being made to find new uses, such as for matting. A weakness of sisal rope is a tendency to break suddenly without warning, in contrast to abaca ropes, which show threatening signs before breaking.

World production and consumption. Total annual world production of sisal was over 600,000 tons in the late 1960s. Tanzania was the largest producer with nearly 33 percent, followed by Brazil with nearly 30 percent, and then by Angola, Kenya, and Uganda. The largest importers of sisal were the Common Market countries, which imported 195,000 tons.

Henequen (Agave fourcroydes). Another fibre of commercial value derived from the agave family is also sometimes called sisal; to avoid confusion, the local Mexican name henequen is extensively used. The plant has been used and cultivated for hundreds of years in Yucatán by the Mayan Indians. As in other agaves, the young plant consists of a rosette of leaves rising from the ground, but a trunk is developed up to five feet high as the plant grows, because the lower leaves die off or are cut. The leaves grow up to six feet (two metres) long and four to six inches (10 to 15 centimetres) wide and are grayish in colour in contrast to those of the sisal-producing *Agave sisalana*, which are green. At the end of their life, the plants form a pole similar to that of the sisal plant. In Mexico, the life of the henequen plant is about 20 to 30 years while in East Africa it lives only about seven or eight years. Both varieties produce roughly the same number of leaves during their lifetime. A smaller number of leaves are taken each year from the henequen plant. The first harvest is made after about five or six years, and cutting with a machete is usually done twice a year. Fibre content is about 3 to 4 percent by weight. The fibre is yellow in colour, with cylindrical form, length 30–60 inches (75–150 centimetres), firm texture, and high moisture absorbency. Henequen is used for twines and small ropes and is also woven into sacking and coarse rugs. Mexico is the only country producing henequen on a large scale, with annual production of nearly 150,000 tons in the late 1960s.

Cantala. Cantala (*Agave cantala*) is another fibre from the agave family that probably originated in Mexico and was transported to the Philippines and Indonesia during the early years of the Spanish settlements in Central America. The plant is one of the few species growing well in moist and humus-rich soil. The cantala leaves can easily be distinguished from the other two commercial agave species by the black marginal spines curving upward like a cat's claw on the leaves, and also by the long, black, terminal spines, which must be removed by the cutters. The chief producers of cantala are the Philippines and Indonesia. In Indonesia the fibre is generally extracted from the leaves with machines (raspadors). Fibre production in the Philippines is carried out by retting in saltwater or freshwater. Cantala is pure white, in contrast to the other agave fibres, and can be used for binder twine, sacks, and hammocks. It it not as strong as sisal or abaca. Production has decreased considerably in the second half of the 20th century. Fibres are produced on a commercial scale from various other members of the agave family, such as *Agave letona*, *Agave lecheguilla*, and *Agave funkiana*, the last two of which are used in the manufacture of brushes.

Production and uses of cantala

Mauritius hemp. Fibre-producing plants of some commercial importance occur in the *Furcraea* species of the agave family. They resemble other agaves in form and habit, have short stems, and produce rosettes of large and fleshy leaves. The leaves are much longer than sisal; they continue to elongate for about five months after leaving the central spindle of the plant. Like other agaves, the *Furcraea* plant flowers once and dies.

Mauritius hemp is obtained from the leaves of *Furcraea gigantea*. The leaves are four to seven feet (one to two metres) in length, less rigid, wider, and longer than sisal leaves. The leaves, ending in a sharp spine, have a smaller fibre content than sisal leaves. At flowering time, the plant puts out a flowering pole up to 40 feet (12 metres) long, bearing white flowers. The plant normally has a life of seven to 10 years and is mature and ready for cutting after three to four years. Most of the fibres produced in Mauritius are obtained from plants found growing wild, although 2,000 acres (800 hectares) were under cultivation in the late 1960s. Cultivated plants give considerably higher yields than wild plants. Cutting is done every two years and yields are as high as two tons of fibre per acre. The local sugar-sack factory in Mauritius absorbs almost all the fibre production. Mauritius hemp is whiter, finer, and longer than sisal, but less strong. It is sometimes used mixed with abaca or sisal for cordage manufacture to give the ropes a better colour.

Several others of the *Furcraea* species of the agave family produce fibres from their leaves that are used commercially. The most important is *F. gigantea*, growing wild in several countries in South America, and in South Africa, India, and the West Indies. Local production, especially in Brazil, reaches considerable levels, although little is exported. Other fibres used locally are produced from such species as *F. macrophylla*, *F. andina*, *F. humboldtiana*, and *F. cubensis*.

Phormium. *Phormium tenax*, also of the agave family, is known in New Zealand as New Zealand flax or New Zealand hemp, and in South America as formio. The plant does not have a central trunk but a short, branched rootstock about two inches in diameter. It puts up a collection of tough, sword-shaped leaves growing in a fanlike manner. The leaves vary in length from three to 14 feet (one to four metres) and are one to five inches (2.5 to 12.5 centimetres) wide, depending on the growing conditions of the plant. One phormium plant yields about 20 to 30 rhizomes, which are used for propagation. Although almost any soil seems able to support the growth of *Phormium tenax*, the plant requires good soil for best results. The fibre produced from wild stands of phormium in New Zealand still plays a considerable part in the phormium industry, but cultivation of the plant has also been carried out. Harvesting time is judged by the texture and firmness of the leaves and varies with the geographical location. The leaves are cut about six to eight inches (15 to 20 centimetres) above the ground and tied into bundles of about 70 pounds (30 kilograms) each. They have a considerably higher percentage of fibre (10 to 14 percent) than sisal leaves, and are also longer, pro-

ducing a longer fibre. The white to pale-red fibre is soft, with considerable lustre and flexibility. The fibre has a cellulose content of 45.1 percent and contains 30.1 percent hemicellulose and 11.2 percent lignin.

Other plants that are members of the agave family containing fibres in their leaves and that are used locally for such purposes as making twines, ropes, and mats and packs for matting, are *Sansevieria*, mainly grown in Mexico, and the *Yucca* species, of which the common yucca is most suitable for fibre production. The latter was called silk grass by the early Virginia settlers and is abundant in the sandy soils of Virginia, Georgia, and Alabama.

III. Animal fibres
Fibres of animal origin are based on proteins and include wool and other hairlike fibres and cocoon materials.

WOOL
History. Wool was probably the first fibre that man successfully made into a fabric, as far back as the earliest Stone Age, 1,750,000 years ago. Serviceable fabrics of wool have been found in the ruins of the Swiss lake dwellers. In Tall al-Asmar, Iraq, archaeologists have found seals indicating trade in wool as early as 4200 BC. It was evidently from Central Asia that sheep and wool were introduced into other areas of the world. Because sheep adapt easily to their environment, many variations of shape, fleece, or other characteristics have developed. The ancestor of the finest wool-bearing sheep is the Spanish Merino, bred from a number of different types, including that introduced into Spain by the Phoenicians long before the Christian era. Merinos contributed to the foundation of a wool-raising industry that became worldwide.

Early wool trading

Production. The term wool is generally understood to refer to the fleece obtained from sheep; the fleece of other mammals used in the production of textiles is referred to as hair, such as mohair (from the Angora goat) or camel's hair. Because of the many environmental adaptations, it is impossible to determine the many original breeds of sheep contributing to modern types. Most fleece wools can be classified on the basis of fineness and length into one of five types: fine wool, medium wool, long wool, crossbred wool, and carpet, or mixed, wool. Such properties as length, fineness, strength, colour, lustre, waviness, shrinkage potential, and felting properties (ability of fibres to interlock with each other, forming a compact material) vary according to breed. Numerous breeds of sheep are covered by these five general types, but all vary slightly in certain properties.

Only the Merino families can be classified as fine-wool breeds. Many medium-wool breeds originating in Great Britain, such as Hampshire, Suffolk, Shropshire, and Oxford Down, were bred primarily for meat production. The long-wool breeds, Lincoln, Romney, Cotswold, and Leicester, famous for their fleece in the Middle Ages, are among the largest purebred sheep. Wool breeds were crossbred to obtain an optimum in both meat and wool production. Crossbreds, among the most famous being the Corriedale and Columbia breeds, produce medium-fine wool and are sometimes classified with the medium-wool breeds. Such breeds are usually developed by crossing a Merino with a long-wool type. Carpet or mixed wools are usually obtained from broadtail sheep living under primitive conditions in Asian countries.

Most of the world supply of wool is shorn. The finer qualities of wool, from the Merino sheep, are generally found in such warm and dry regions as Australia, South Africa, and northern Argentina. Richer pastures are required for crossbreds, found in the United States, the Soviet Union, and in areas of the Southern Hemisphere with more plentiful rainfall.

Shearing is seasonal and may be done whenever the fleece has grown sufficiently to warrant shearing, although it is generally unwise to shear in the cold winter months because of the need of the fleece to protect the sheep from respiratory diseases. Sheep are usually shorn with machine shears, following a definite method developed in Australia. The sheep is shorn in such a way that

Sheep shearing

the fleece is unbroken and all the parts remain in their natural position. The fleece is then rolled with the inside out, tied with paper twine, and packed in sacks or pressed into bales at the shearing shed.

Sheared wool is classed, baled, and branded on the sheep stations. The classed wool is packed in hessian (burlap) bales before export or sale. Size and average bale weight differ in various countries of origin. Wool originating in South American countries is heavily compressed; bales generally weigh 1,000 pounds (450 kilograms), except those from the United States and Commonwealth countries, which are usually smaller.

The wool auction In the British Commonwealth of Nations, wool is marketed by public auction, but in South America and the United States it is sold by private treaty or direct negotiations between the individual grower and a buyer. In the auction system, representative sample bales, or sometimes whole lots, are displayed in buildings where they are exposed to the best natural light for inspection by buyers.

Processing. The basic steps in wool processing have remained unchanged for centuries. Wool obtained from different parts of the sheep varies in fibre fineness, length, and crimp (succession of waves). There are variations between locks, or cohering bunches of wool, and between fleece from different areas of the sheep. The quality of wool obtained from the belly is short and burry; the shoulders yield the finest wool. Sorting is the separation of the different qualities of wool from the fleece. The most important property is usually fibre fineness, closely related to softness of handle, the tactile properties that can be observed when textiles are held in the hand. In sorting, variations between locks and between fleece from different areas are taken into consideration, as well as brightness, crimp, fibre purity, fineness, softness, and length. The sorter unrolls the fleece on the sorter's board, usually waist-high, and cuts away any wool carrying tar or paint marks. He next removes the coarsest wool, placing it in a separate basket, and finally reaches the fine wool on the shoulders. A sorter can generally sort up to 10,000 pounds (4,500 kilograms) of Australian fleece in a normal working week.

Wool is scoured (washed) to remove such impurities as wax, suint (dried perspiration), dung, earth and sand, ointments, and brands. Suint is water soluble; wool wax, a mixture of compounds, is insoluble in water but soluble in organic solvents. The wool is scoured either by emulsion or by solvent extraction. In the emulsion method, wool is passed gently through a series of bowls containing scouring liquors generally composed of soap and sodium carbonate. The wool is first steeped in lukewarm water to dissolve some of the suint. The liquor is then clarified and used in the second bowl, where the hot suint liquor (130° F, or 54° C) emulsifies the wool grease. Higher temperatures may cause higher fibre breakage in carding and combing. The wool is rinsed in the third bowl; soap is added to the fourth rinse and the final rinse is completed in the fifth bowl. Wax is often recovered from the suint liquor by centrifuging while clarifying the liquor. These waxes in purified form are the source of the lanolin used in cosmetics. Wax and grease can also be recovered by the solvent extraction of greasy wool.

Vegetable matter collected in the wool must be removed, because any remaining small fragments of burr may cause end breakage in spinning and thus affect yarn regularity. Vegetable matter is removed either mechanically or by chemical (carbonizing) methods. Most of the burr remaining in the scoured wool is removed mechanically in the early stages of carding. In the chemical method, burrs are carbonized by sulfuric acid treatments. The scoured wool is steeped in a 6 percent sulfuric acid bath for 15 to 20 minutes, and the liquor is removed either by centrifuging or by squeezing the wool through a set of rollers. The squeezed wool is placed in a drier and subjected to temperatures increasing from 180° to 220° F (82° to 104° C), remaining at high temperature for only a short time. The acid and heat treatment reduces most of the burrs to carbon. The fibre mass is then passed through heavy rollers, disintegrating the carbonized

burrs, and is later shaken to remove the dust. It is then neutralized to remove acid by passing through warm water, then into a neutralizing bath containing sodium carbonate, rinsed in a weak soap solution, and dried as after scouring.

Main factors in wool grading The most important factors taken into consideration in wool grading are fibre fineness, length, crimp, yield or clean-wool content, vegetable matter (burr content), and fibre strength. Wool quality is determined at the raw stage. Classers in various producing countries have their own standards. For example, the assessment of quality by Australian wool classers and wool experts is closely related to the number of crimps per inch; in the United States it is based on fibre fineness (diameter). The English quality scale was originally based on spinnability, the finest worsted count that could be spun from the tops. In the blood system, the blood designation is based on the divergence from the pure blood standard of the Merino sheep, considered the best strain for breeding and crossbreeding.

Finer wools generally contain higher numbers of crimps per inch. There is a strong correlation between fibre fineness and the finest yarn that can be spun. Staple length is of great significance in processing because it governs the spinning performance when spinning at the limiting count or size. Fibre crimp, in the range in which it is encountered in Merino and fine crossbred wools, does not play an important role in spinning, but classers do not emphasize staple length when assessing quality. Other criteria include colour, soft handling, and suitability for weaving.

Carding and spinning Blended wool fibres are carded to disentangle the locks, mix the fibres, remove remaining foreign matter, and convert the fibre into a sliver for further processing. The carding action is accomplished by teasing the fibres between sets of wire points moving at different surface speeds. In woolen carding the top set of wires is held in a series of rotating rolls. The card web is fed to a condenser and divided into continuous strips along its length, then rubbed to impart some cohesion, and wound onto a bobbin. The resulting material, called slubbing, is taken to the spinning frame for conversion into yarn.

Wools may be classified as woollen or worsted types, according to the spinning method employed. Woollen yarns are made up of fairly short fibres, loosely spun and with little twist. Fabrics woven from woollen yarns have a soft, fuzzy surface and are somewhat loosely woven. Worsted yarns are smooth and even, with high twist, and fabrics made from them are usually closely woven with a smooth surface.

In worsted spinning, the wool card sliver of Merino and fine crossbred wool is first cleaned, or backwashed, by scouring, and the fibres made parallel by gilling, or pin-controlled drafting. In this process movement of the fibres in the space between two pairs of rollers is controlled by rows of pins moving forward with the sliver. The gilled, parallelized slivers are combed to remove short fibres and burr from the bulk. In combing, fibres are drawn through a bed of pins while one end of the fibre beard is held and the combed short fibres are collected. Two types of combing machines are used in worsted processing—the Noble, or circular comb, and the French, or rectilinear comb. The combed sliver, or the top, is finished by gilling and wound into a ball. It is then blended and attenuated by a series of drawing processes and finally spun into yarn.

Bleaching processes Wool that is to be dyed to bright or light shades, or made into white yarns and fabrics, is bleached to achieve whitening, usually in yarn or fabric form, by either the storing method or by hydrogen peroxide bleaching. In storing, the wool is placed in a closed chamber and exposed to sulfur dioxide. Coloured impurities are converted to colourless substances by gas produced by burning sulfur. This process may not produce permanent whitening, as oxygen in the air may cause the changed substances to take on colour again. The hydrogen peroxide bleaching process is more permanent, as the wool is immersed in a dilute solution of hydrogen peroxide, which destroys the coloured impurities.

Fibre properties. Wool is the fibre constituting the protective covering of the sheep and is similar to the fibres of similar function occurring in many of the mammals. Its origin is related to that of various other mammalian skin tissues such as nails, horns, and hoofs, and it consists mainly of keratin, an insoluble protein. The wool fibre is an organized structure consisting of cells growing from a root, or follicle, situated in the dermis, or the middle layer of the skin. The fibre is extruded from the shaft of the follicle by the pressure of newly formed cells. During this process, just before emergence of the fibre from the skin, a partial alignment of the protein chains occurs and is stabilized by the process of keratinization. Mature keratinized fibre seen above the skin surface is dead tissue, consisting of three structural components. The cuticle forms a skin consisting of various cuticular layers and scale cells. The scales are laid down in an overlapping fashion with their scale edges pointing toward the fibre tip, much like the arrangement of seeds in a pinecone. The cortex constituting the bulk of the fibre consists of elongated spindle-shaped cells arranged parallel to the fibre axis. The core of the fibre is formed by the medulla, consisting of a number of air-filled cells or a completely hollow tube. The medulla is absent in fine wool, and some coarse wools are also only partially medullated. The cortex can be separated into the *ortho*-cortex and the *para*-cortex, slightly differing in amino-acid composition and physical properties. The distribution of these two cortical segments, either bilateral or radial, determines the crimp or lack of crimp of the wool fibre. In the radial distribution the *ortho*-cortex is in the centre of the fibre; in the bilateral distribution the *ortho*-cortex is on the inside of the crimp.

Fleece density varies among breeds, ranging from about 100,000,000 fibres per sheep for the fine Merinos to 15,000,000 to 20,000,000 in the coarse-wool breeds. The distribution of density within the fleece of a sheep varies considerably, with density greatest along the spine region and decreasing toward the belly. Before selective breeding, the body covering of sheep consisted of two distinctly different fibres, an outer coat of long, coarse, medullated, and brittle hairs, and an inner one of fine, short, and wavy wool.

As a result of selective breeding, most sheep used mainly as a source of wool have a high proportion of the inner coat, or wool, and a very small amount of the outer coat, or coarse hair. Although annual shedding of any remnant of the outer coat occurs, the wool can attain a length of several times its annual growth if not shorn. Kemp fibres, particularly coarse hairs, relatively flattened, with long tapering tip and heavy medulla, are shed periodically, with considerable differences existing between breeds in this respect.

Technologically, the diameter, or fineness, of the wool fibre is one of its most important properties, determining to a large extent the grade assigned to a lot of wool. Diameters range from 16 microns (millionths of a metre) in the finest Merinos to over 40 microns in the coarsest long-wool types. Changes in nutrition result in considerable variation in both diameter and cross-sectional shape between fibres within a lot of wool, as well as along the length of the individual fibre. The staple length of the wool fibre is determined both by breed and by the environmental conditions during the growth of the wool. Staple length generally increases with increasing fibre diameter, ranging from 1½ to three inches (four to eight centimetres) for fine Merino up to 10 to 14 inches (25 to 35 centimetres) for coarse Cotswold wool. Staple length is lower than mean fibre length because of the crimp that results in a helical configuration in an individual fibre and a uniplanar wave in the staple. Crimp frequency per inch is related to fibre fineness.

Wool fibres are hygroscopic, absorbing water vapour from a moist atmosphere in a reversible way. Because most fibre properties are dependent on moisture content, this characteristic is extremely important, especially in numerous processing steps, including carding, combing, spinning, and weaving. Relative humidity in the processing plants must be controlled for optimum processing conditions. Upon uptake of water, the fibre swells anisotropically (nonuniformly), increasing up to 16 percent in diameter while the change in length is only about 1.2 to 1.5 percent. The ability of wool fibres to absorb and release moisture contributes to wearing comfort in garments made of wool.

The mechanical properties of wool are a reflection of the complex structure of the fibre, and mechanical properties depend strongly on the moisture content of the wool as well as the rate of extension. The outstanding properties of wool are its high extensibility and its unusual elastic properties, permitting recovery from very high deformations.

The molecules of wool fibres have a curled structure, and the fibre has a natural crimp, or waviness, both factors contributing to the high resiliency of wool fibres. At an extension of 2 percent wool has 99 percent recovery, so that upon release the fibre returns almost completely to its original length. The fibre breaks at extensions of about 40 to 50 percent.

Wool has unique frictional properties because of the arrangement of the cuticular scales. Friction is greater when the fibre is rubbed against the scales, from the tip to the root end, than when it is rubbed with the scales. Mobility of the fibre is therefore preferential in the direction of the root end. This phenomenon, called the directional frictional effect, forms the basis of felting. When a mass of fibres is subjected to mechanical action, especially in the wet state, the fibres preferentially move in one direction relative to other fibres, forming irreversible entanglements. The property of felting, unique for wool, is used industrially to produce fabrics or large continuous felted structures such as the papermaking felts. The felting tendency in loosely structured wool goods, such as sweaters, is a disadvantage because laundering causes matted structures that shrink. Considerable research has resulted in improved control of the felting process. Various chemical processes have been devised to reduce shrinkage and avoid felting, leading to the manufacture of machine-washable woollen garments. Tensions in fabrics may be used by preshrinking, in which the cloth is wetted and allowed to relax. Antifelting treatments involve chemical modification of the fibre surface, greatly reducing the friction produced when the fibre is rubbed against the scales.

Wool has the most complex molecular structure of all textile fibres, reflecting the fact that wool is composed of about 20 different α-amino acids (organic acids forming the chief constituent of proteins) with side chains containing various functional groups and that these amino acids are grouped in unique spatial arrangements.

Amino-acid composition varies considerably with the breed of the sheep and can be substantially influenced by changes in the diet. Typical figures for the average amino-acid composition of Merino wool are given in Table 2. The table figures are averages, not reflecting the differ-

The medulla

Moisture content

Directional frictional effect

Chemical composition of wool

Table 2: The Amino-Acid Composition of Wool

type of side chain	amino acid	mole (percent)
Hydrocarbon (or hydrogen)	glycine	8.8
	alanine	5.5
	valine	5.6
	leucine	7.6
	isoleucine	3.1
	phenylalanine	2.8
Hydroxy	serine	11.5
	threonine	7.0
	tyrosine	4.0
Acidic (free and as amide)	aspartic acid	6.2
	glutamicacid	12.2
Basic	lysine	2.6
	arginine	7.1
	histidine	0.8
Sulfur-containing	cysteine	0.2
	cystine	6.3
	methionine	0.5
Heterocyclic	proline	7.5
	tryptophan	0.9

ences among the various components of the wool structure. For example, considerable differences exist between the cortex and the cuticle, and differences in amino-acid composition have also been reported between the *ortho*-cortex and the *para*-cortex. The amino-acid composition of the whole wool fibre, as well as that of the various components, is known with a considerable degree of accuracy, but very little is known about the sequence in which the amino acids are arranged to form the protein molecules. As the Table shows, wool consists of amino acids containing functional groups. Because of the presence of acidic and basic groups, wool is amphoteric, combining reversibly with acids as well as with bases. The existence of positively (amino) and negatively (carboxyl) charged groups is of considerable importance in the dyeing process.

The disulfide bond of the amino acid cystine, which is colourless crystalline, is one of the most important reactive centres in wool. The reactivity of combined cystine in wool has been extensively studied and its importance in many industrial processes is acknowledged. The breaking of the disulfide bond by chemical reduction is essential for various setting treatments of wool used to introduce irreversible deformations. Reductive treatments lead to the formation of free thiols that can act as catalysts for a disulfide interchange mechanism. This mechanism, in which disulfide bonds can exchange position, forms the basis of all irreversible deformations of the wool fibre. Under basic conditions disulfide bonds can be converted into the amino acids lanthionine and lysinoalanine, which are incapable of participating in interchange reactions and therefore help stabilize the keratin structure. Oxidative treatments are of considerable importance in bleaching and shrink-proofing treatments. In these processes the treatment is intentionally restricted to the surface layers having considerably higher cystine content than the cortex. Oxidation usually leads to a breaking of the disulfide bonds and the formation of cysteic acid. This oxidative degradation of the proteins in the cuticular region is essential for improved felt resistance.

Complete breaking (scission) of the disulfide bonds and subsequent solubilization of the keratin chains has led to isolation of two major fractions of modified proteins. One fraction has a high sulfur content and has been associated with the highly disulfide-crosslinked matrix; the other fraction is low in sulfur and probably originates from the protein chains forming the microfibrils. The molecular weights of these two major fractions and various subfractions that have been isolated vary over a considerable range, indicating that wool must be considered as made up of a complex mixture of polypeptides. There is still little evidence that polypeptides with identical sequences of amino acids exist, or that certain amino-acid sequences are repeated over an extended chain length of the protein chain.

World production and consumption. Annual world wool production in 1970 reached an all-time record of 1,590,000 tons of raw wool. The major finer quality wool-producing countries are Australia, the Soviet Union, New Zealand, Argentina, and South Africa. India, Pakistan, China, the Middle East, and North Africa are the major producers of carpet-type wool. Leading consuming countries are the United Kingdom, United States, Japan, France, and the Soviet Union.

The major wool producers

SPECIALTY HAIR FIBRES

Many animal fibres not taken from the fleece of sheep are used industrially, mostly in the manufacture of clothing. Frequently used in blends with sheep's-wool fibres, they add softness, lustre, or colour. The largest group, called specialty hair fibres, is taken from the fleece of goats and camels and is often classified as wool. Other such fibres are obtained from cows, horses, and fur-bearing animals.

Mohair. Mohair, the most important specialty fibre, is taken from the fleece of the Angora goat, named for the province of Angora (historic name for Ankara), in Turkey, where it has been raised for many centuries. The United States, Turkey, and South Africa are the only

countries in which this goat is currently bred and raised commercially.

Three principal fleece types exist. The finest, called tight lock, is produced by a variety bred in late fall; the kids are born five months later. The first shearing takes place when the kid is six to seven months old, producing fall kid, the finest type of mohair. The next shearing, carried out the following spring, results in spring kid. A shearing at the age of a year and a half produces yearling mohair; from then on the mohair is classified as adult. Shearing is performed with hand shears or machine clippers, and the fleeces are packed separately.

Types of mohair fleece

The hair of the Angora goat grows in long, uniform locks with little crimp and no felting properties. The microscopic structure is much like wool, although the scale structure is less developed and there is little overlapping of the scales. A problem in processing mohair is the existence of kemp fibres, much coarser and stiffer than the normal mohair fibre, that adversely affect spinnability and dyeability. Moisture content and physical properties of mohair fibres are similar to those of wool. Because mohair consists almost exclusively of orthocortical cells, it is more sensitive to various chemicals than wool, a consideration in such manufacturing processes as scouring, dyeing, carbonizing, and bleaching. Mohair fibres are used mainly in apparel.

Cashmere. Cashmere, a very fine and soft animal fibre, is obtained from the undercoat of several types of goats designated as Kashmir or down goats, found in the mountainous regions of Asia. The Kashmir goat has two coats, the fine down, or undercoat, and the coarse outer coat. The undercoat is particularly well developed. The annual production of the three major cashmere producing countries, China, Mongolia, and Iran, is about 8,000,000 to 12,000,000 pounds (4,000,000 to 5,000,000 kilograms). The average goat yields about one-half pound; thus the total number of Kashmir goats can be estimated as from 16,000,000 to 24,000,000. Grading and pricing of cashmere fibre depends upon the country of origin, and is usually based on the amount of down fibres, or true cashmere, present; in commercial samples it varies between 15 percent and 90 percent. The finest down fibres originate in China and Mongolia.

The strength of cashmere fibres is about 10 percent below that of the finest wool, and moisture content and chemical properties are very similar to fine wool. Sensitivity to chemical treatment is even more pronounced than that of mohair, essentially because of the extreme fineness of cashmere fibres. This characteristic particularly applies in the bleaching process, a common practice because of the higher price brought by white cashmere fibres. The heavy pigmentation of dark cashmere fibres requires special bleaching processes, sometimes leading to considerable fibre damage and reductions in tensile strength. Dehairing processes, separation of the hair and the down fibres, are necessary for the production of high quality cashmere. Considerable losses occur in these processes and the resulting dehaired product commands high, though fluctuating, prices. It is used mainly in apparel, either alone or combined with sheep's wool, which increases durability.

Common goat hair. Common goat hair, produced in countries producing cashmere and in Greece and Argentina, is used mainly for the production of cheap felts and automobile carpets. The down and beard hairs, occurring in a ratio of 1 to 9, are not separated, and the fineness varies over a wide range.

Camel's hair. Camels used as camel's-hair sources include both the Arabian or Syrian camel having one hump, also known as the dromedary, and the Eastern Asiatic, or Bactrian, camel with two humps. The camel's hair, gathered in the molting season in late spring or early summer, is usually collected after it has fallen off. Frequently a man at the end of a camel caravan collects the hair tufts and strands that fall off during the journey, and the total yield is sold at the first town the caravan reaches. Each animal yields about five pounds of hair per year.

Gathering camel's hair

Camel fleece is similar to that of the Kashmir goat,

with a soft down of great fineness underneath a coarse outer coat reaching up to 15 inches (38 centimetres) in length. A dehairing process, usually accomplished by combing, is necessary for a high-grade camel's-hair wool. Considerable differences exist between the hair of the Bactrian and that of the Arabian camel, so that the origin of the hair may be established easily, even in the finished fabric.

Camel's hair is used in the apparel industry for high-grade overcoating and knit wear; in addition it is used for rugs and in industrial fabrics in which high strength is desired.

Llamas. The higher grasslands of the Andes, in South America, form the exclusive habitat of animals of the genus *Lama*, close relatives to the camels. Species belonging to the camel family include the llama, alpaca, vicuña, and guanaco.

The llama, the largest of the Andean Camelidae, is chiefly a burden carrier, although it is also used for its meat, milk, and fleece. There are about 3,000,000 llamas in the Andean Highlands. The heavy, thick coat is a mixture of fine and coarse hairs and kemp and is frequently of a brown colour, although pure whites and blacks have also been found. The other domesticated species is the alpaca, occurring in two varieties, the *huacayo* (or *huacaya*) and the *suri*. The alpaca, smaller than the llama, has been used for its fleece since pre-Inca days. Hybrids of llama and alpaca frequently occur, and are called *huarizo* with a llama sire, and *misti* when sired by an alpaca. Fleeces of these hybrids are not as fine in quality as that of the alpaca.

Llama fleece, similar to that of the camel, consists of an outer coat of coarse, straight hairs and an undercoat of woollike, crimped fibres. Coarse-fibre content in commercial lots usually amounts to about 20 percent.

Fleece production is dominated by the alpaca, providing up to 90 percent of the export. The alpaca is usually kept in flocks ranging from 200 to 300 up to several thousands. The flocks are shorn during the rainy season, from November to March. The fleece, generally allowed to grow for two years, averages about seven to eight pounds per animal. Shearing with conventional machines is difficult. The fleeces, separately rolled and tied, are sold to the exporters in the city of Arequipa, Peru. Fleeces are classed and sorted according to colour and quality, then pressed into bales of 220 pounds (100 kilograms).

The main difference between the fleece of the two alpaca varieties, *huacayo* and *suri*, is that the *huacayo* fibres are crimped and *suri* fibres are straight or occasionally widely waved. Considerable variation of fineness occurs along the length of the two years' growth of the fibres. This difference is caused by the seasonal conditions connected with the lack of rainfall and availability of food.

The mechanical properties of the two fibre varieties show considerable differences; the *huacayo* fibres are more extensible and show greater tensile strength. The *suri* fibres have a high elastic modulus, resulting in stiffer fibre. This rigidity and the lower scale profile probably contribute to the lower felting rates and less dense entanglements formed during felting, compared with wool fibres of the same diameter. *Huacayo* fibres have a silver lustre; *suri* has a silky lustre close to that of kid mohair. The similarities between *huacayo* fibres and coarse wool and the *suri* fibre and mohair also extend to the amino-acid composition, considerable differences between the two alpaca varieties being found.

Bleaching of dark alpaca fibres is frequent because of the price difference between white and coloured alpacas. Bleaching frequently produces considerable fibre damage and reduction of wet tensile strength.

Vicuña. The vicuña, the smallest of the *Lama* species, is less than three feet (one metre) in height and weighs 100 pounds (45 kilograms) or less. Its fibre is the rarest and finest, much sought after since pre-Inca times. Before the Spanish Conquest, hunting was strictly regulated and only persons of high rank were permitted to use its skin and wool. During the colonial period hunting with firearms threatened the species with extinction. In 1825 the killing of vicuñas was prohibited. Domestication was encouraged but has met with limited success.

Shearing occurs in early summer. Most of the annual vicuña exports, however, estimated at up to 50,000 pounds (23,000 kilograms), are obtained from killed animals, mainly from Bolivia.

Vicuña fleece contains about 10 percent beard hair mixed with fine wool-type hair. Vicuña fibres closely resemble the *huacayo* alpaca variety but are finer. Because of their extreme fineness, vicuña fibres are very sensitive to chemical treatment. Vicuña is used in rugs, blankets, and apparel of the highest quality.

Guanaco. Another luxury fibre, the down of the guanaco, was introduced into the woollen industry about the middle of the 20th century. The swiftest of the four llama species, guanacos are shy and travel in small herds ranging as far south as the Straits of Magellan. Argentina is the principal source of guanaco furs and peltries (undressed skins). The fibres are very fine, much softer and of higher lustre than wool fibres of comparably small diameter.

Cow hair. Cow hair, usually pulled from the skin after slaughter, is extensively used for coarse carpet yarns, blankets, felts, and mattress stuffings. The body hair is graded into long, medium, and short and also according to colour. Cow-tail fibres are much coarser.

Horsehair. Horsehair is used in textile manufacture to make haircloth interlinings for tailored garments. The best quality tail hair from Argentina is packed in bales in the form of bundles and graded according to length. Horsehair is also usually dressed in the United Kingdom and then sold to brush makers. Mane and tail horsehair undergoes a series of treatments including sorting and washing, hackling (combing out of short fibres), bundling (sorting according to length), dressing (trimming of the ends), and flagging (splitting of tip ends for paintbrushes). Horsehair is also used for violin bows, upholstery, and mattress filling.

Fur fibres. *Angora-rabbit fibres.* The fibre of the Angora rabbit has been used in the textile industry since the mid-19th century. The animal is usually raised on a very small scale. The rabbits generally molt four times a year, when the hair is approximately three to 3½ inches (eight to nine centimetres) long, and it is collected, shorn, clipped or plucked. The fibres are silky, light in weight, and warm. Because of their high cost, Angora-rabbit fibres are used only in luxury fabrics, sometimes in blends with other fibres.

Common rabbit fibres. The felt-hat industry uses a considerable number of other rabbit-fur fibres, and a certain amount is also used in the textile industry. The pelts are graded according to size, length of fibre, and yield, and the production of fur fibres involves softening, stretching, plucking, clipping (removal of undesirable guard hair), carroting (improvement of felting properties by chemical treatment), cutting (removal of fibres from the skin), and blending and blowing (elimination of guard hairs and dirt particles). A bleaching process usually follows.

SILK

History. Silk is said to have originated in 2640 BC, when the Chinese empress Hsi-ling Shih discovered the method of raising silkworms and unwinding the silk filaments of the cocoons. This knowledge was jealously guarded in China for 3,000 years, but eventually sericulture, the art of raising silkworms, spread to Japan, India, and Iran. It may have been brought back from India by Alexander III (the Great), but if so the knowledge was subsequently lost to Europe. A silk industry was finally established in Byzantium under the emperor Justinian (AD 527–565), after two Persian monks returned from China with silkworm eggs and seeds of the mulberry tree concealed in hollow staves. The Arabs acquired the knowledge of sericulture by the 8th century, and in the 12th century the Italians introduced it to Europe, where for centuries silk remained the premier luxury fabric.

Production. Silk fibre is a continuous protein filament secreted by various insects, especially the larvae of a certain caterpillar, in forming cocoons. This caterpillar, the silkworm, belongs to the order of Lepidoptera, or scale-winged insects, genus Bombyx. The principal species, the *Bombyx mori*, or mulberry silkworm, produces most of the raw silk used commercially. Various strains of Japanese, Chinese, and European worms have been crossbred in Japan, where silk from their cocoons is used in the raw-silk reeling industry. These cocoons yield filaments with a reelable length of 600 to 900 metres (2,000 to 3,000 feet).

Eggs laid by the moth are kept in cold storage for six to ten months, and germination is started in an incubator at the appropriate season of the mulberry tree, the leaves of which serve as food for the larvae. After ten days in an incubator, one ounce of eggs produces 40,000 to 60,000 worms. During their growth and development the caterpillars shed their skins four times, drastically increasing in size and weight until they are about five to nine centimetres (two to 3½ inches) long. After about 30 days the worm begins to develop two large silk-producing glands in which the silk secretion is formed. The liquid fibroin flows through channels to one common exit tube in the head of the insect. The two fibroin filaments are connected together by the silk glue, or sericin. The worm builds an oval cocoon by adding layer after layer, moving its head in arcs of circles crossing in figure eights, and the cocoon is completed in 24 to 72 hours. The silkworm then undergoes the transformation from a caterpillar to the inert pupa, and then rapidly develops into a moth that cuts an opening through the cocoon with the aid of a secretion. The whitish-gray moth, with rudimentary wings, has no mouth and is unable to eat. After mating the female lays about 500 eggs and dies after a life of one to four days.

Only enough moths to supply eggs for the next crop are allowed to emerge from the cocoon. For the rest, growth of the pupa is usually interrupted by refrigeration. The cocoons are sorted and transferred to the filature, or silk-reeling, establishment. Before they are reeled, they are boiled in water to soften the gum, causing the original figure eights of the cocoon filament to straighten out. After the boiling, the loose ends are picked up through brushing and the number of necessary filaments to form the size of the raw-silk thread desired is passed through porcelain guides. Two general systems are used, the Chambon, or French system, and the Tavelle, or Italian system. In the Chambon system, two groups of cocoon filaments are twisted around each other to yield a thread; in the Tavelle system, the thread is twisted around itself. From four to nine cocoon filaments are required to produce a 14-denier silk thread (14 grams per 9,000 metres).

The tussah silkworm, *Antheraea pernyi*, a native of China, feeds exclusively on one type of oak tree, *Quercus serrata*, and only out of doors on trees of shrub height. Although it can produce both a spring and an autumn crop, only the autumn crop is usually used for silk production. Tussah cocoons contain more gum and calcium compounds than mulberry worm cocoons, and must be boiled in sodium carbonate solution for one and a half hours, followed by the normal boiling procedure before reeling.

Processing. Silk throwing requires a special skill. The raw silk thread, after soaking in an oil or soap emulsion, is wound onto bobbins, and the threads are doubled together and twisted. This process converts the raw silk thread into a yarn of the proper size by regulating the twist, producing the various silk yarns for the manufacturing process.

Waste silk originating from processing or from the original production is degummed in soap solutions, dried, processed for the removal of short fibres and foreign matter, and spun into a silk yarn used for the production of fabrics with soft, pliable finish, known for its spreading qualities in pile.

Silk by-products

Fibre properties. The silk filament consists of two fibroins, or brins, of triangular cross section. Slight surface striations parallel to the fibre axis indicate that the fibre is structurally composed of minute filaments, or fibrils. The moisture content of silk varies between 9 percent and 12 percent at 65 percent relative humidity, depending upon whether it is raw silk or degummed. Silk has a tensile strength of about four grams per denier and a breaking elongation of about 20 percent. The truly elastic region is only about 1 to 2 percent, followed by a yield region in which slippage of the extended chains past one another occurs. The silk protein consists of extended chains, in contrast to the helical configuration found in wool proteins. The packing of these extended chains into what is called a β (beta)-pattern results in the formation of sheets that are packed into crystallites. The density of degummed silk is somewhat lower than that of cotton, wool, and hair fibres. Silk has been used as an electrical insulator because of its poor electric conductivity. Static electricity is easily accumulated on silk, and processing must be carried out at high humidity.

Silk fibroin and sericin are the two major components of raw silk. Silk fibroin is the predominant component, comprising 70–76 percent; sericin constitutes about 15–25 percent. Minor components are about 2 percent wax, which presumably acts as a water repellent for the cocoons, and about 1 percent salt.

Major components of raw silk

Sericin, an albuminoid protein mixture consisting of about 15 amino acids, is a gummy coating on raw-silk filaments. It is an excellent buffer for dye solutions, making the silk fibres stiff and harsh and forming a protective layer for the various manufacturing processes. Soap or oil is applied in soaking solutions, softening the sericin and permitting the introduction of twist during the throwing operation.

Sericin is removed by a treatment called degumming, or stripping, to make silk fabric soft and glossy. Degumming, essentially an alkaline scouring operation, is carried out at a temperature of 205° F (96° C). The degumming process probably involves a chemical reaction leading to a progressive degradation and solubilization of the sericin molecules. The boil-off solution, heavily charged with sericin, is used as a buffer agent in the dye bath.

Silk fibroin consists of extended protein chains of various molecular weights formed by amino acids, with glycine (44 percent) and alanine (30 percent) predominant. Strong alkaline solutions and various mineral acids may cause it to dissolve. Silk fibres treated with concentrated sulfuric acid for several minutes, then rinsed and neutralized, contract up to 50 percent in length without significant damage. This action of concentrated acid has been used to introduce crepon effects (crepe effects produced by variations in the twist of the yarns) by printing the silk fabric with wax and then immersing it in concentrated acids.

Silk, valued for its lustrous appearance, resiliency, elasticity, and strength, has a wide variety of textile uses and can be woven or knitted into fabrics ranging from light chiffons to heavy velvet piles.

World production and consumption. The Far East, India, and the Mediterranean countries are the main silk-producing areas. Annual production of raw silk during the late 1960s amounted to nearly 83,000,000 pounds, of which slightly more than half was produced in Japan. The other major producing countries were China, the Soviet Union, India, South Korea, and Italy. Japan, China, and South Korea were the three major silk exporters. The five largest importers of raw silk were Italy, Japan, the United States, France, and Switzerland.

IV. Mineral fibres

The only mineral fibres of commercial importance are a group of magnesium silicates comprising the asbestiform group.

History. The use of asbestos was recorded in the 1st century AD by Pliny the Elder, a Roman naturalist. It was apparently used by the Greeks considerably before that date; the Romans used it for lampwicks and cremation cloths, but it was apparently forgotten in medieval Europe. In the 13th century Marco Polo brought back from China news of cloths that did not burn when thrown into a fire. The commercial importance of asbestos began with its use in steam engines in the 19th century.

Production. The name asbestos is given to a group of 30 or more minerals of fibrous crystalline structure of which only six have economic significance. These are, in order of their importance: chrysotile (which accounts for about 95 percent of the world production of natural mineral fibres), crocidolite, amosite, anthophyllite, tremolite, and actinolite. Chrysotile is a fibrous form of serpentine; the other five are amphiboles (rock-forming minerals composed mainly of silica).

The yield of fibres from the ore is relatively small, ranging in Canadian mines from 3–12 percent. Of the total asbestos fibres extracted from the rock, only about 3–4 percent consist of grades suitable for spinning or processing into textiles. The fibres are separated from the mother rock by several stages of crushing, each followed by screening and air separation. The fibres are then further opened, cleaned, graded according to length, and bagged for shipment. The longer fibres, separated by hand, are the most expensive grade and are used in textiles. Crude, or unmilled, fibres and the longest milled grades are suitable for spinning into yarn.

Asbestos ore

Processing. The processing steps necessary to make the milled or crude fibres into an asbestos yarn involve blending and mixing to arrive at the desired characteristics of tensile strength in the finished product. Carriers, or supporting materials, are usually such organic fibres as cotton or rayon. In the carding operation, opening and cleaning of the fibres is completed, leading to a relatively parallel arrangement and a continuous web. This web, or sliver, is turned into roving and the finer yarn is produced from these untwisted strands. The roving is twisted to provide tensile strength and the resulting single yarn is twisted with other single yarns.

Chrysotile fibre properties. Chrysotile is a hydrated magnesium silicate. Other elements such as iron, calcium, and aluminum appear as impurities in the crystal structure. Chrysotile fibres are particularly useful for the manufacture of asbestos textiles because of their length, strength, toughness, and flexibility or pliability. Their tensile strength is high, values of up to 800,000 pounds per square inch having been recorded. The heat resistance of chrysotile is high among asbestos fibres. Loss of water occurs upon long exposures at $1,110°$ F $(600°$ C$)$ and fusion eventually at $2,770°$ F $(1,520°$ C$)$. Under short-time exposure, however, the fibres have been shown to withstand temperatures as high as $6,000°$ F $(3,300°$ C$)$. Chrysotile fibres are extremely fine. Canadian chrysotile has a dark-green lustre, but the fibres appear white when fully opened and are known as white asbestos.

Uses. Asbestos textiles are used for numerous purposes usually connected with their incombustibility or ability to endure extremely high temperatures. Safety clothing, fire blankets, fireproof curtains and draperies, and insulation material for wires and cables in home and industrial appliances and for rocket nose cones and combustion chambers are some of the applications.

World production and consumption. World production in the late 1960s reached over 3,000,000 short tons, with Canadian output amounting to over 1,500,000 tons a year. Rhodesia (formerly Southern Rhodesia), Swaziland, and the U.S.S.R. are also important suppliers.

BIBLIOGRAPHY. D.S. HAMBY (ed.), *The American Cotton Handbook*, 3rd ed., 2 vol. (1965–66), a collection of authoritative contributions on subjects ranging from cotton growing to the final finished fabric; KYLE WARD, JR. (ed.), *Chemistry and Chemical Technology of Cotton* (1955), a reliable, detailed reference source dealing with such topics as the chemical properties of cotton cellulose and the chemistry and chemical technology of various preparatory and finishing processes; EVELYN E. STOUT, *Introduction to Textiles*, 3rd ed. (1970), a general introduction to textile fibres and yarn and fabric technology, with natural fibres receiving comparatively brief, but well-written coverage; MARJORY L. JOSEPH, *Introductory Textile Science* (1966), a college-level introduction to textile science intended for students with some background in chemistry; W. VON BERGEN (ed.), *Wool Handbook*, 3rd enl. ed., 2 vol. (1963–70), a standard reference and textbook for the wool industry covering all phases from wool growing to cloth manufacture, with contributing authors who are experts in their specific fields; M.L. RYDER and S.K. STEPHENSON, *Wool Growth* (1968), a series of college lectures in which the authors attempt to link physiology with the genetics of wool growth and fleece structure; R.H. PETERS, *Textile Chemistry*, vol. 1, *The Chemistry of Fibres* (1963), an introduction to the field of the chemistry of fibre-forming polymers, with a number of chapters treating the structure in chemistry of natural fibres, for students with a knowledge of chemistry and physics; R.H. KIRBY, *Vegetable Fibres* (1963), a study of the botany, cultivation, and utilization of vegetable fibres with the exception of cotton, with emphasis on the production of fibres; R.R. ATKINSON, *Jute: Fibre to Yarn* (1965), a detailed treatise on jute covering the botanical background, cultivation, and marketing up to the spinning and winding of jute yarns; M.S. SARMA, "Jute," *Fld. Crop Abstr.*, 22:323–336 (1969), a brief review article on the botany and cultivation of jute, as well as retting, disease, and pest control; W.J. ONIONS, *Wool* (1962), a comprehensive survey of the entire field of wool technology covering the rearing of sheep as well as all the processes to the finished wool fabric; LUIGI CASTELLINI, "Hemp," *Ciba Rev.*, no. 5, pp. 2–31 (1962), a short review article on the botany, cultivation, and processing of the hemp fibre, with excellent illustrations; ASBESTOS TEXTILE INSTITUTE, *Handbook of Asbestos Textiles*, 2nd ed. (1961), a comprehensive treatise on the manufacture of asbestos fibres with emphasis on the various textile products made from asbestos; LONDON, COMMONWEALTH ECONOMIC COMMITTEE, *Industrial Fibres* (annual), a review of the production, trade, and consumption statistics relating to industrial fibres, with considerable emphasis on natural fibres; E.V. TRUTER, *Wool Wax: Chemistry and Technology* (1956), a discussion of the chemical characteristics of wool wax and the technology used for its isolation and purification; P. ALEXANDER and R.F. HUDSON, *Wool: Its Chemistry and Physics*, 2nd ed. by C. EARLAND (1963), the classic textbook on wool fibre science.

(H.-D.H.W.)

Fichte, Johann Gottlieb

Johann Gottlieb Fichte was the first major representative of the movement called transcendental Idealism that developed out of the work of the German philosopher Immanuel Kant and dominated German philosophy during the first third of the 19th century. His thought, which is termed ethical Idealism, and his personal life were characterized by a moral rigorism. Fichte constructed a systematic deduction of the entire body of knowledge, based on the unconditioned absolute principle of the ego, or self-affirmation.

Fichte was born at Rammenau in Upper Lusatia on May 19, 1762, the son of a ribbon weaver. Educated at the Pforta school (1774–80) and at the universities of Jena (1780) and of Leipzig (1781–84), he started work as a tutor. In this capacity he went to Zürich in 1788 and to Warsaw in 1791 but left after two weeks' probation.

Early life and career

The major influence on his thought at this time was that of Kant, whose doctrine of the inherent moral worth of man harmonized with Fichte's character; and he resolved to devote himself to perfecting a true philosophy, the principles of which should be practical maxims. He went from Warsaw to see Kant himself at Königsberg, but this first interview was disappointing. Later, when Fichte submitted his *Versuch einer Kritik aller Offenbarung* ("An Attempt at a Critique of All Revelation") to Kant, the latter was favourably impressed by it and helped to find a publisher (1792). Fichte's name and preface were accidentally omitted from the first edition, and the work was ascribed by its earliest readers to Kant himself; when Kant corrected the mistake while commending the essay, Fichte's reputation was made.

In the *Versuch*, Fichte sought to explain the conditions under which revealed religion is possible; his exposition turns upon the absolute requirements of the moral law. Religion itself is the belief in this moral law as divine, and such belief is a practical postulate, necessary in order to add force to the law. The revelation of this divine character of morality is possible only to someone in whom the lower impulses have been, or are, successful in overcoming reverence for the law. In such a case it is conceivable that a revelation might be given in order to add strength to the moral law. Religion ultimately then rests upon the practical reason and satisfies the needs of man, insofar as he stands under the moral law. In this

Fichte, lithograph by F.A. Zimmermann after a painting by H.A. Daehling (1773–1850).
Deutsche Fotothek, Dresden, Ger.

conclusion are evident the prominence assigned by Fichte to the practical element and the tendency to make the moral requirements of the ego the ground for all judgment on reality.

In 1793 Fichte married Johanna Maria Rahn, whom he had met during his stay in Zürich. In the same year he published anonymously two remarkable political works, of which *Beitrag zur Berichtigung der Urteile des Publikums über die französische Revolution* ("Contribution to the Correction of the Public's Judgments Regarding the French Revolution") was the more important. It was intended to explain the true nature of the French Revolution, to demonstrate how inextricably the right of liberty is interwoven with the very existence of man as an intelligent agent, and to point out the inherent progressiveness of the state and the consequent necessity of reform or amendment. As in the *Versuch*, the rational nature of man and the conditions necessary for its realization are made the standard for political philosophy.

The philosophy of Fichte falls chronologically into a period of residence in Jena (1793–1798) and a period in Berlin (1799–1806), which are also different in their fundamental philosophic conceptions. The former period is marked by its ethical emphasis, the latter by the emergence of a mystical and theological theory of Being. Fichte was prompted to change his original position because he came to appreciate that religious faith surpasses moral reason. He was also influenced by the general trend that the development of thought took toward Romanticism.

Years at the University of Jena In 1793 there was a vacant chair of philosophy at the University of Jena, and Fichte was called to fill it. To the ensuing period belongs his most important philosophical work. In this period he published, among other works: *Einige Vorlesungen über die Bestimmung des Gelehrten* (1794; Eng. trans., *The Vocation of the Scholar*, 1847), lectures on the importance of the highest intellectual culture and on the duties that it imposed; several works on the science of knowledge (*Wissenschaftslehre*), which were revised and developed continually throughout his life; the practical *Grundlage des Naturrechts nach Principien der Wissenschaftslehre* (1796; Eng. trans., *The Science of Rights*, 1869 and 1889); and *Das System der Sittenlehre nach den Principien der Wissenschaftslehre* (1798; Eng. trans., *The Science of Ethics as Based on the Science of Knowledge*, 1897), in which his moral philosophy, grounded in the notion of duty, is most notably expressed.

The system of 1794 was historically the most original and also the most characteristic work that Fichte produced. It was incited by Kant's critical philosophy and especially by his *Kritik der praktischen Vernunft* (1788; Eng. trans., *Critique of Practical Reason . . .*, 1949). From the outset it was less critical, precisely be-

cause it was more systematic, aiming at a self-sufficient, well-rounded doctrine in which the science of knowledge and ethics were intimately united. Fichte's ambition was to demonstrate that practical (moral) reason is really (as Kant had only intimated) the root of reason in its entirety, the absolute ground of all knowledge as well as of humanity altogether. To prove this, he started from a supreme principle, the ego, which was supposed to be independent and sovereign, so that all other knowledge was deduced from it. Fichte did not assert that this supreme principle was self-evident but rather that it had to be postulated by pure thought. He followed, thereby, Kant's doctrine that pure, practical reason postulates the existence of God, but he tried to transform Kant's rational faith into a speculative knowledge on which he based both his theory of science and his ethics.

In 1795 Fichte became one of the editors of the *Philosophisches Journal*; and in 1798 his friend F.K. Forberg, a young, unknown philosopher, sent him an essay on the development of the idea of religion. Before printing this, Fichte, to prevent misunderstanding, composed a short preface, "On the Grounds of Our Belief in a Divine Government of the Universe," in which God is defined as the moral order of the universe, the eternal law of right that is the foundation of all man's being. The cry of atheism was raised, and the electoral government of Saxony, followed by all of the German states except Prussia, suppressed the *Journal* and demanded Fichte's expulsion from Jena. After publishing two defenses, Fichte threatened to resign in case of reprimand. Much to his discomfort, his threat was taken as an offer to resign and was duly accepted.

Years in Berlin Except for the summer of 1805 (which he spent at Erlangen, delivering a longer version of his Jena lectures of 1794), Fichte resided in Berlin from 1799 to 1806. Among his friends were the leaders of German Romanticism, A.W. and F. Schlegel and Friedrich Schleiermacher. His works of this period include *Die Bestimmung des Menschen* (1800; Eng. trans., *The Vocation of Man*, 1848), in which he defines God as the infinite moral will of the universe who becomes conscious of himself in individuals; *Der geschlossene Handelsstaat* (also 1800), an intensely socialistic treatise in favour of tariff protection; two new versions of the *Wissenschaftslehre* (composed in 1801 and in 1804; published posthumously), marking a great change in the character of the doctrine; *Die Grundzüge des gegenwärtigen Zeitalters* (1806; lectures delivered 1804–05; Eng. trans., *The Characteristics of the Present Age*, 1844), analyzing the Enlightenment and defining its place in the historical evolution of the general human consciousness but also indicating its defects and looking forward to belief in the divine order of the universe as the highest aspect of the life of reason; and *Die Anweisung zum seligen Leben, oder auch die Religionslehre* (1806; Eng. trans., *The Way Towards the Blessed Life*, 1844). In this last-named work the union between the finite self-consciousness and the infinite ego, or God, is handled in a deeply religious fashion reminiscent of the Gospel According to John. The knowledge and love of God is declared to be the end of life. God is the All; the world of independent objects is the result of reflection or self-consciousness, by which the infinite unity is broken up. God is thus over and above the distinction of subject and object; man's knowledge is but a reflex or picture of the infinite essence.

Last years The French victories over the Prussians in 1806 drove Fichte from Berlin to Königsberg (where he lectured for a time), then to Copenhagen. He returned to Berlin in August 1807. From this time his published writings were practical in character; not until after the appearance of the *Nachgelassene Werke* ("Posthumous Works") and of the *Sämmtliche Werke* ("Complete Works") was the shape of his final speculations known. In 1807 he drew up a plan for the proposed new university of Berlin. In 1807–08 he delivered at Berlin his *Reden an die deutsche Nation* (Eng. trans., *Addresses to the German Nation*, 1922), full of practical views on the only true foundation for national recovery and glory. From 1810 to 1812 he was rector of the new Berlin University. During the great effort of Germany for national independence in 1813, he lectured "Über den Begriff des wahrhaften Krieges" ("On the Idea of a True War").

At the beginning of 1814, Fichte caught a virulent hospital fever from his wife, who had volunteered for work as a hospital nurse. He died on January 27, 1814.

BIBLIOGRAPHY.

Collected works: Neither I.H. FICHTE's edition of his father's collected works, 8 vol. (1845–46, reprinted 1965), nor the reliable selected works edition of FRITZ MEDICUS, 6 vol. (1908–11, reprinted 1962), can compare with the scholarly definitive edition issued by der Bayerischen Akademie der Wissenschaften (Bavarian Academy of the Sciences), *J.G. Fichte—Gesamtausgabe,* ed. by REINHARD LAUTH and HANS JACOB (1962). As to translations, WILLIAM SMITH published *The Popular Works of Johann Gottlieb Fichte,* 2 vol. (1848–49; 4th ed., 1889).

Life: For analytical evidence about Fichte's life, see FRITZ MEDICUS, *Fichtes Leben* (1914; 2nd rev. ed., 1922); XAVIER LEON, *Fichte et son temps,* 3 vol. (1922–27, reprinted 1959); and HANS SCHULZ, *Fichte in vertraulichen Briefen seiner Zeitgenossen* (1923), which builds up a picture of Fichte as his contemporaries saw him. How subjective this image has become today emerges from a comparison of the Festschrift of the Free University of Berlin, in West Berlin, *Idee und Wirklichkeit einer Universität,* published in 1960 on the sesquicentennial anniversary of its foundation with the Festschrift that resulted from a colloquium held at the Humboldt-Universität zu Berlin, in East Berlin, *Johann Gottlieb Fichte: Ein deutscher Patriot* (1962).

Thought: For a balanced evaluation of Fichte the thinker, see ROBERT ADAMSON, *Fichte* (1881; 1903 ed. reprinted 1969) and his article in the *Encyclopædia Britannica,* 11th ed. (1910); XAVIER LEON, *La Philosophie de Fichte: ses rapports avec la conscience contemporaine* (1902); and ELLEN B. TALBOT, *The Fundamental Principle of Fichte's Philosophy* (1906). For an overall view of Fichte's philosophy within the framework of European thought and with specific reference to German Idealism and Romanticism, see RICHARD KRONER, *Von Kant bis Hegel,* 2 vol. (1921–24; 2nd ed., 1 vol., 1961); RENE WELLEK, *Confrontations: Studies in the Intellectual and Literary Relations Between Germany, England and the United States During the Nineteenth Century* (1965); and the Festschrift *Wissen und Gewissen,* ed. by MANFRED BUHR (1962).

Bibliography: For citations of books and articles on specific aspects of Fichte's work, see *J.G. Fichte: Bibliographie,* ed. by H.M. BAUMGARTNER and W.G. JACOBS (1968).

(R.Kr.)

Fielding, Henry

The 19th-century novelist Sir Walter Scott called Henry Fielding the "father of the English novel," and the phrase still indicates Fielding's place in the history of literature. Though not actually the first English novelist, he was the first to approach the genre with a fully worked-out theory of the novel; and in *Joseph Andrews* (1742), *Tom Jones* (1749), and *Amelia* (1751), which a modern critic has called comic epic, epic comedy, and domestic epic, respectively, he had established the tradition of a realism presented in panoramic surveys of contemporary society that dominated English fiction until the end of the 19th century. In his lifetime a controversial figure, Fielding was often seen by the Victorians as a writer who was "offensive to delicacy": what is impressive today, apart from his uninhibited comedy, is the breadth of his sympathies, his concern for morality, and his compassion for human weaknesses. His other activities, too, are important for his work as a novelist. As a playwright he learned how to handle dialogue and how to compose the scenes he incorporated in his fiction, while both his novels and his zeal as a police magistrate reflect his aim of reforming the manners of his age. He was at once its historian and its critic, and in his works, particularly *Tom Jones* and *Amelia,* a relatively new literary form achieves a degree of perfection that, despite changes in literary fashion, is still unsurpassed.

Early life. Fielding was born at Sharpham Park, near Glastonbury in Somerset, on April 22, 1707, of a family that by tradition traced its descent to a branch of the Habsburgs; hence the 18th-century English historian Edward Gibbon's remark in his memoirs (1796):

Fielding, engraving by James Basire, after a drawing by William Hogarth; frontispiece to Fielding's *Works* (1st ed., 1762). In the British Museum.
By courtesy of the trustees of the British Museum; photograph, J.R.Freeman & Co., Ltd.

The successors of Charles the Fifth may disdain their brethren of England; but the romance of *Tom Jones,* that exquisite picture of human manners, will outlive the palace of the Escurial, and the imperial eagle of the house of Austria.

The 1st earl of Denbigh, William Fielding, was a direct ancestor, while Henry's father, Colonel Edmund Fielding, had served under John Churchill, duke of Marlborough, an early-18th-century general, "with much bravery and reputation," and his mother was a daughter of Sir Henry Gould, a judge of the Queen's Bench, from whom she inherited property at East Stour, in Dorset, where the family moved when Fielding was three years old. His mother died just before his 11th birthday. His father having married again, Fielding was sent to Eton College, where he laid the foundations of his love of literature and his considerable knowledge of the classics.

Leaving school at 17, a strikingly handsome youth, he settled down to the life of a young gentleman of leisure; but four years later, after an abortive elopement with an heiress and the production of a play at the Drury Lane Theatre in London, he resumed his classical studies at the University of Leiden in Holland. After 18 months he had to return home because his father was no longer able to pay him an allowance. "Having," as he said, "no choice but to be a hackney-writer or a hackney-coachman," he chose the former and set up as playwright. In all, he wrote some 25 plays. Although his dramatic works have not held the stage, their wit cannot be denied. He was essentially a satirist, and his target was the political corruption of the times. In 1737 he produced at the Little Theatre in the Hay (later the Haymarket Theatre), London, his *Historical Register, For the Year 1736,* in which the prime minister, Sir Robert Walpole, was represented practically undisguised and mercilessly ridiculed. It was not the first time Walpole had suffered from Fielding's pen, and his answer was to push through Parliament the Licensing Act, by which all new plays had to be approved and licensed by the lord chamberlain before production.

The passing of this act marked the end of Fielding as a playwright. The 30-year-old writer had a wife and two children to support but no source of income. He had married Charlotte Cradock in 1734, this time after a successful elopement, the culmination of a four-year courtship. How much he adored her can be seen from the two characters based on her, Sophia Western in *Tom Jones* and Amelia in the novel of that name: one

Distinguished antecedents and relatives

Portraits of his wife in novels

the likeness of her as a beautiful, high-spirited, generous-minded girl, the other of her as a faithful, much-troubled, hard-working wife and mother. To restore his fortunes, Fielding began to read for the bar, completing in less than three years a course normally taking six or seven. Even while studying, however, he was editing, and very largely writing, a thrice-weekly newspaper, the *Champion; or, British Mercury*, which ran from November, 1739 to June, 1741.

Maturity. As a barrister, Fielding, who rode the Western Circuit (a judicial subdivision of England) twice a year, had little success. In 1740, however, Samuel Richardson published his novel *Pamela: or, Virtue Rewarded*, which tells how a servant girl so impressed her master by resistance to his every effort at seduction that in the end "he thought fit to make her his wife." Something new in literature, its success was unparalleled. A crop of imitations followed. In April 1741, there appeared a parody entitled *An Apology for the Life of Mrs. Shamela Andrews*, satirizing Richardson's sentimentality and prudential morality. It was published anonymously, and, though Fielding never claimed it, *Shamela* was generally accepted as his work in his lifetime, and stylistic evidence supports the attribution. Moreover, there is a similarity to his *Joseph Andrews*.

Described on the title page as "Written in Imitation of the Manner of Cervantes, author of *Don Quixote*," *Joseph Andrews* begins as a burlesque of *Pamela*, with Joseph, Pamela's virtuous footman brother, resisting the attempts of a highborn lady to seduce him. The parodic intention soon becomes secondary, and the novel develops into a masterpiece of sustained irony and social criticism, with, at its centre, Parson Adams, one of the great comic figures of literature and a striking confirmation of the contention of the 19th-century Russian novelist Fyodor Dostoyevsky that the positively good man can be made convincing in fiction only if rendered to some extent ridiculous. Fielding explains in his preface that he is writing "a comic Epic-Poem in Prose." He was certainly inaugurating a new genre in fiction.

Joseph Andrews was written in the most unpropitious circumstances; Fielding was crippled with gout, his six-year-old daughter was dying, and his wife was "in a condition very little better." He was also in financial trouble, from which he was at least temporarily rescued by the generosity of his friend the philanthropist Ralph Allen, who appears in *Tom Jones* as Mr. Allworthy.

In 1743 Fielding published three volumes of *Miscellanies*, works old and new, of which by far the most important is *The Life of Mr. Jonathan Wild the Great*. Here, narrating the life of a notorious criminal of the day, Fielding satirizes human greatness, or rather human greatness confused with power over others. Permanently topical, *Jonathan Wild*, with the exception of some passages by his older contemporary the Anglo-Irish satirist Jonathan Swift, is perhaps the grimmest satire in English and an exercise in unremitting irony.

After the *Miscellanies* Fielding gave up writing for more than two years, partly, perhaps, out of disappointment with the rewards of authorship, partly in order to devote himself to law. His health was bad; his practice at the bar did not flourish; worst of all, his wife was still ill. In the autumn of 1744 he took her to Bath for the medicinal waters; she "caught a fever, and died in his arms." According to Lady Mary Wortley Montagu, the 18th-century letter writer and Fielding's cousin, his grief "approached to frenzy," and it was almost a year before he recovered his fortitude. By then he had taken a house in London in the Strand (on the site of the present law courts), and there he lived with his daughter, his sister Sarah, also a novelist, and Mary Daniel, who had been his wife's maid. In 1747, to the derision of London, he married Mary, who was pregnant by him. According to Fielding himself, writing shortly before his death, she discharged "excellently well her own, and all the tender offices becoming the female character . . . besides being a faithful friend, an amiable companion, and a tender nurse."

In 1745 came the Jacobite Rebellion (an attempt to re-store the descendants of the deposed Stuart king James II), which led Fielding to write the pamphlet "A Serious Address to the People of Great Britain. In Which the Certain Consequences of the Present Rebellion, Are Fully Demonstrated. Necessary To Be Perused by Every Lover of his Country at This Juncture." As a strong Church of England man, he warned his readers of the implications of this rising led by the Roman Catholic pretender to the throne, Prince Charles Edward. A month later, he became editor of a new weekly paper, *The True Patriot: And the History of Our Own Times*, which he wrote almost single-handedly until it ceased publication on the defeat of the Pretender at the Battle of Culloden (April 16, 1746). A year later, Fielding edited another one-man weekly called *The Jacobite's Journal*, the title of which indicates its ironical approach to current affairs. Its propaganda value was deemed so great that the government purchased 2,000 copies of each issue for free distribution among the inns and ale-houses of the kingdom.

Fielding was now a government man. His reward came in 1748, when he was appointed justice of the peace (or magistrate) for Westminster and Middlesex, with his own courthouse, which was also his residence, in Bow Street in central London. The office carried no salary; former Bow Street magistrates had made what they could out of the fees paid by persons brought before them and, often, out of bribes. Fielding was a magistrate of a different order; as he wrote in *The Journal of a Voyage to Lisbon*:

> . . . by composing, instead of inflaming, the quarrels of porters and beggars (which I blush when I say hath not been universally practised), and by refusing to take a shilling from a man who undoubtedly would not have had another left, I had reduced an income of about £500 a year of the dirtiest money upon earth, to little more than £300; a considerable portion of which remained with my clerk.

According to a 20th-century British historian, G.M. Trevelyan, Fielding was one of the two best magistrates in 18th-century London, the other being his blind half brother Sir John Fielding, who succeeded him at Bow Street. Together, they turned an office without honour into one of great dignity and importance and established a new tradition of justice and the suppression of crime in London. Among other things, Fielding strengthened the police force at his disposal by recruiting a small body of able and energetic "thieftakers"—the Bow Street Runners. To improve relations between the law and the public, he started a newspaper, *The Covent Garden Journal*, in which the following appeared regularly:

> All persons who shall for the future suffer by robbers, burglars, etc., are desired immediately to bring or send the best description they can of such robbers, etc., with the time, and place, and circumstances of the fact, to Henry Fielding, Esq., at his house in Bow Street.

Last years. *The History of Tom Jones, a Foundling* was published on February 28, 1749. With its great comic gusto, vast gallery of characters, and contrasted scenes of high and low life in London and the provinces, it has always been the most popular of his works. The reading of this work is essential both for an understanding of 18th-century England and for its revelation of the generosity and charity of Fielding's view of humanity.

Two years later *Amelia* was published. Being a much more sombre work, it has always been less popular than *Tom Jones* and *Joseph Andrews*. Fielding's mind must have been darkened by his experiences as a magistrate, as it certainly had been by his wife's death, and *Amelia* is no attempt at the comic epic poem in prose. Rather, it anticipates the Victorian domestic novel, being a study of the relationship between a man and his wife and, in the character of Amelia, a celebration of womanly virtues. It is also Fielding's most intransigent representation of the evils of the society in which he lived, and he clearly finds the spectacle no longer comic.

His health was deteriorating. By 1752 his gout was so bad that his legs were swathed in bandages and he often had to use crutches or a wheelchair. In August of 1753 he decided to go to Bath for rest and the waters. That

Career in government

year was a particularly bad one for crime in London, however, and, on the eve of his leaving, he was invited by Thomas Pelham-Holles, duke of Newcastle (then secretary of war) to prepare a plan for the Privy Council for the suppression of "those murders and robberies which were every day committed in the streets." His plan, undertaking "to demolish the then reigning gangs" and to establish means of preventing their recurrence, was accepted, and despite the state of his health—to gout had been added asthma and dropsy—he stayed in London for the rest of the year, waging war against criminal gangs with such success that "there was, in the remaining month of November, and in all December, not only no such thing as a murder, but not even a street-robbery committed."

In the following June, Fielding set out for Portugal to seek the sun, writing an account of his journey, *The Journal of a Voyage to Lisbon*. This work presents an extraordinarily vivid picture of the tortuous slowness of 18th-century sea travel, the horrors of contemporary medicine, the caprices of arbitrary power as seen in the conduct of customs officers and other petty officials, and, above all, his indomitable courage and cheerfulness when almost completely helpless, for he could scarcely walk and had to be carried on and off ship. Fielding landed at Lisbon on August 7, 1754. At first it seemed that the Portuguese climate was therapeutic, but he died on October 8 and was buried in the British cemetery at Lisbon.

MAJOR WORKS

NOVELS: *The History of the Adventures of Joseph Andrews and His friend Mr. Adams, Written in Imitation of the Manner of Cervantes* (1742); *The History of Tom Jones, a Foundling* (1749); *Amelia* (1751, dated 1752).

PLAYS: *Love in Several Masques* (1728); *Tom Thumb* (1730); *The Temple Beau* (1730); *The Modern Husband* (1732); *The Mock Doctor; or, the Dumb Lady Cur'd* (1732); *The Miser* (1733); *An Old Man Taught Wisdom; or, the Virgin Unmasked* (1735); *Pasquin: A Dramatick Satire on the Times* (1736); *Historical Register, For the Year 1736* (1737).

NEWSPAPERS: *The Champion; or, British Mercury* (1739–41); *The True Patriot: And the History of Our Own Times* (1745–46); *The Jacobite's Journal* (1747–48); *The Covent Garden Journal* (1752).

OTHER WORKS: *Miscellanies*, 3 vol. (1743, including *The Life of Mr. Jonathan Wild the Great*); *A Serious Address to the People of Great Britain* (1745); *The Journal of a Voyage to Lisbon* (1755).

BIBLIOGRAPHY. *The Complete Works of Henry Fielding, Esq.*, ed. by W.E. HENLEY, 16 vol. (1903), is at present the standard edition, but it is expected to be displaced by the more scholarly and comprehensive *Complete Works*, ed. by FREDSON BOWERS and MARTIN C. BATTESTIN, now in process of publication. Standard biographies are WILBER L. CROSS, *The History of Henry Fielding*, 3 vol. (1918, reprinted 1963); and F. HOMES DUDDEN, *Henry Fielding: His Life, Works and Times*, 2 vol. (1952); many scholars prefer the earlier book. MARTIN C. BATTESTIN, *The Moral Basis of Fielding's Art: A Study of Joseph Andrews* (1959); and ANDREW H. WRIGHT, *Henry Fielding, Mask and Feast* (1965), are valuable critical studies; RONALD PAULSON (ed.), *Fielding: A Collection of Critical Essays* (1962), gathers together important critical statements. ERNEST A. BAKER, *The History of the English Novel*, 10 vol. (1924–39); and IAN P. WATT, *The Rise of the Novel* (1957), place Fielding in the context of the history of fiction.

(W.E.A.)

Fields, Theory of, in Physics

A field in physics may be defined as a continuous distribution of some observable quantity in space and time. The observable quantity, which must be measurable, may be any of a variety of phenomena, including (but not limited to) such things as the colour in a liquid, the density of dust in the atmosphere, temperature distribution in a body, the flow pattern of a stream, or the magnetic field surrounding the earth. But under all circumstances, whatever is described as a field must be measurable by some technique.

If the observed quantity varies in space but does not change with time, the field is said to be static. Otherwise it is called a time-varying field. In the examples above, the field was considered in three-dimensional space; *i.e.*, in terms of length, breadth, and depth. The field concept is capable of generalization, however, to spaces of more than three dimensions, as will be indicated later in this article, just as the idea of space can be expanded to any number of dimensions. Though a time-varying field is, strictly speaking, a field in four dimensions, it is customary to describe such a field as a variable three-dimensional field.

Mathematical treatment of fields. The mathematical description of the field is in terms of the measurable dimensions of the space under consideration. This means that the field is considered to be a function of the space; *i.e.*, in order to discuss the properties of the field mathematically, it is necessary that points in the field must be discussed. Any point in the field is identified in terms of its position in space relative to other points. To locate any point in the field, several types of three-coordinate systems may be used; for example, x, y, and z represent three spatial directions and distances of the points from a common point. When the measured property has magnitude but no direction it is called a scalar. When a measured property has direction it is called a vector and the spatial coordinates are, therefore, vectors. In mathematical language, then, a field is a function, signified by f, of the three space coordinates, signified by r, and the time coordinate, signified by t. This is written $f(r, t)$. Ordinarily r is a vector designating a point in three-dimensional space with coordinates x, y, z, but it may also symbolize a space of any number of dimensions. A field is said to be known when: (1) the function $f(r, t)$ is known, and (2) the observable property to which f refers is given. Vectors and scalars

While the preceding statements formally define a field, they do not fully characterize the kinds of fields that are useful in physical science. Such fields must satisfy one additional requirement: they must be defined by a known law that permits their calculation and prediction. The law is usually expressed as a differential equation (an equation that contains rate of change of variable quantities).

This article is devoted to a description of various fields useful in science and the laws that apply to them. The physical disciplines in which the fields occur are treated elsewhere; *e.g.*, under ELECTRICITY; MAGNETISM; ELECTROMAGNETIC RADIATION; NUCLEUS, ATOMIC; GRAVITATION; THERMODYNAMICS, PRINCIPLES OF; ENERGY; and MECHANICS, QUANTUM.

Classification of fields. *Material and nonmaterial.* There are various ways of classifying fields. One important distinction, that between material and nonmaterial fields, must be made at the outset but need not be pursued further in its manifold philosophical implications. In a material field, the observable property signified by f describes some property of matter, such as the density, pressure, or the temperature of a gas, or the velocity of a portion of liquid. A nonmaterial field is not descriptive of any material property (although it is usually caused by matter) but describes some latent effect that would take place at a point of space under certain circumstances. The electric field is of this kind. Its "observable" is the electrostatic field indicated by E and its value at a point defined by the coordinates x, y, z is given by the field function. Nothing, however, may actually exist or be evident at that point. What matters is that *if* a charge were placed at the point defined by x, y, z it *would* experience a force proportional to the function of the field; *i.e.*, as explained above, $E(x, y, z)$. Other nonmaterial fields are the magnetic field, the field of general relativity, and a variety of what are called probability fields, which are discernible as a statistical probability of occurrences, such as the state of an electron in an atom, treated as a function of quantum mechanics.

Material fields are introduced into physics because the variables to which they refer are of direct physical interest. Nonmaterial fields are usually introduced to simplify the theoretical description of phenomena by replacing the notion of action at a distance with that of local interactions. By saying that a charge located at r Nonmaterial fields (*r* is the resultant vector at a point identified by *x*, *y*, *z* coordinates) sets up an electric field designated as *E* (*r*), throughout space, one can more simply describe how a second charge at *r*₂ is affected by the first: the second charge interacts locally with the electric field at *r*₂.

Scalars. Fields can be classified according to whether the observable function *f* (*i.e.*, the field quantity) is a scalar, a vector, or a tensor. A scalar is ordinarily defined as a quantity having magnitude but no direction. Examples include mass, density, and temperature.

Vectors. A vector is said to be a quantity endowed with direction in space, like a force, or the strength of an electric or magnetic field. A vector field is symbolized by **V** (*r*) and has three space components, as has been explained, and these are symbolized by V_x (*r*), V_y (*r*) and V_z (*r*).

Tensors. When the measurable function of a field cannot be expressed as a simple scalar or vector quantity, but many such quantities must be considered together, and their dependency must also be taken into account, a tensor may be set up. The nature of a tensor can be illustrated by the example of the stress tensor, denoted by **S**. It has nine components, signified as S_{ij}, both *i* and *j* ranging from 1 to 3. This means that *i* and *j* together have three times three, or nine different quantities. Each subscript corresponds to a direction in space; S_{ij} is the component of force along the *j*-direction of a cube of matter due to a deformation along *i*. Thus **S**, when fully written, amounts to an assemblage of nine quantities, as follows:

$$\mathbf{S} = \begin{matrix} S_{11} & S_{12} & S_{13} \\ S_{21} & S_{22} & S_{23} \\ S_{31} & S_{32} & S_{33} \end{matrix} .$$

The idea of a tensor can be generalized in two ways. First, the number of dimensions in space can be increased from three to *n*, as was suggested in the introduction, and the tensor then takes on *n* times *n*, or n^2 components. Second, the rank of the tensor can be raised; *i.e.*, the number of suffixes may be changed from two to *m*. For example, in *n* dimensions, S_{yk}, a tensor of rank 3, has n^3 components.

Given a field of a certain type (*e.g.*, a vector field), it is possible to generate for purposes of study and calculation other vector fields, scalar fields, tensor fields, and so on. Certain transformations between scalar and vector fields are also useful and have their own symbols.

Examples of fields in ordinary space. Some examples of different kinds of fields are here given in very general terms. It should be noted that the same differential equation may control the behaviour of quite different fields, and it should be stressed that differential equations have many solutions and, therefore, the field is not specified simply by the equation. Boundary conditions must also be imposed; that is, the field must be specified in certain regions. The differential equation then allows computation of the field at certain points in space and time if the value at some other point has already been specified.

Scalar fields. A simple example is provided by the pressure at different heights in the atmosphere. It is known that pressure exists everywhere in the atmosphere and that it is actually the result of gravitational attraction between the earth and gas molecules. In other words, pressure is the result of air molecules accelerating toward the earth in the gravitational field. This movement, however, is then offset by the motion of the molecules due to their heat energy, which makes them bombard one another continuously, with the result that there is a constant tendency in the atmosphere to expand, and the expansion can only be upward. A steady state is achieved between the two tendencies: the gas does not all collect on the surface of the earth, as a liquid does, nor does it expand and vanish into space against the gravitational attraction (as it does on the moon, where the gravitational field is not strong enough to counteract the expansion). The atmosphere is most dense closest to the earth, where the gravitational field is strongest and the tendency of the gas to expand is most effectively balanced by its tendency to move toward the earth. Thus, the pressure is a function of the height, decreasing with height.

The differential equation, then, states that the change in pressure over a specific, small difference in height equals the acceleration of gravity times the change in density at that height. With this equation, therefore, the whole field —which is pressure of the atmosphere—can be mapped to its outer limits.

The density of matter in a moving fluid forms a scalar field, which can be said to obey a general law, the factors to be considered being: change in density at a point in the flow over a small period of time, the rate of diffusion, and the variation in density between two points.

An equation of the same form holds for the temperature field (also a scalar field) in a medium that, because its temperature is not uniform, is involved in a temperature readjustment; *i.e.*, heat is being transmitted from one area to another. The differential equation then relates the change in temperature over a small period of time, the coefficient of heat conductivity, the specific heat, the density, and the temperature at the point of observation.

The gravitational potential (*i.e.*, the work done on a unit mass in bringing it from infinity to the point defined by the space coordinates) obeys an equation (known by the name of its originator, Siméon-Denis Poisson) that is also applicable to other fields. It relates the gravitational potential (a scalar quantity), the gravitational constant, and the density of matter there.

Electrostatic potential, the repulsion between like charges or the attraction between unlike charges, is given as a differential equation of the scalar field; it relates the potential to the charge density (the number of charges per unit volume of space). A similar equation is used for the magnetostatic field potential, the magnetostatic field being taken to be the attraction or repulsion between unlike or like magnetic poles.

Any medium pervaded by a wave becomes the site of a wave field that satisfies the wave equation. As an example, with sound, the pressure in an acoustic field is controlled by the wave equation.

Vector fields. In a moving fluid the velocity vector forms a field each of whose components is a function of the *x*, *y*, *z* coordinates. They must satisfy the equations of continuity, which include the fluid density, which may vary from place to place. If it is constant (*i.e.*, if the fluid is incompressible) then the full equation asserts that the amount of fluid flowing from a point is equal to the amount flowing into it.

Perhaps the most important vector field of mathematical physics is the electromagnetic field, characterized by vectors for the electric field and for the magnetic field. When these two fields are nonstatic, they interact in characteristic ways, and the law governing them cannot be written for either one alone. It takes the form of equations that, in free space, include the velocity of light in vacuum.

The field quantity in many types of waves (*e.g.*, light waves, elastic disturbances in solids, seismic waves in the earth's crust) is a vector. It obeys the same form of wave equation but with the proper vector quantity.

Tensor fields. One important example will be considered, namely the pressure field in a hydrodynamic system; *i.e.*, a fluid in complicated motion with different temperatures at different points inside the fluid. In this case the vectors are: the average velocity of particles at a point in the fluid, the heat flow vector (calories changing per second), and the force per unit area in the direction resulting from the motion in the *i*-direction. The tensor appears in numerous important hydrodynamic equations, notably that of energy flow. Its knowledge, together with velocity and heat flow vectors, provides a complete understanding of the behaviour of the hydrodynamic system. The law controlling it consists of five differential equations, known as the Navier-Stokes equations. They contain the coefficient of viscosity and the thermal conductivity.

This example illustrates the interaction of several fields: the pressure, temperature, and flow fields.

Fields with distributions in more than three dimensions. *Thermodynamic phenomena.* In connection with the laws of thermodynamics, a space can be constructed of 6*n* di-

Phase
space

mensions to account for the behaviour of a system of n particles. It is called phase space, and certain rules of correspondence relate ρ, the field quantity representing density in this space, to such thermodynamic observables as temperature, entropy (a measure of disorder in a system), free energy, and others. To aid visual intuition, ρ is thought of as a cloud of dust of varying density in phase space, and the movement of the cloud (*i.e.*, the field under consideration) determines the values of the quantities measured in thermodynamics.

Relativity. Perhaps the most interesting example of a field in more than three dimensions occurs in the theory of general relativity, where the behaviour of all matter is described in what is called the metric field. It operates in a space of four dimensions, x, y, z, t (see above *Mathematical treatment of fields*). A metric field tensor defines empty space as Euclidean (or flat). The presence of matter causes curvature of the space. Once the tensor is known, the motion of any particle can be calculated. The components of the tensor obey Einstein's law of gravitation, which relates them to the distribution of matter in the universe.

Quantum mechanics. The fundamental constructs (or quantities) of quantum mechanics, the state functions, are also fields. In classical mechanics, the motion of a particle is described by specifying its position as a function of time. In quantum theory, one deals no longer with the particle's position but with the probability of finding it at that position, and that probability forms a field.

BIBLIOGRAPHY. Popular accounts concerning the nature of fields and their uses in physical theories may be found in A. EINSTEIN and L. INFELD, *The Evolution of Physics*, ch. 3 (1938); and in R.E. PEIERLS, *The Laws of Nature*, ch. 2 (1956). For a general account of the types of fields used in physics, the equations they satisfy, and techniques for solution of the equations, see H. MARGENAU and G.M. MURPHY, *The Mathematics of Physics and Chemistry*, 2nd ed., ch. 4, 7, and 12 (1956); and P.M. MORSE and H. FESHBACH, *Methods of Theoretical Physics*, ch. 1–2, 10–11 (1953).

(H.Ma.)

Fiji

Fiji (Viti in the Fijian language), an independent dominion in the Commonwealth of Nations, is an archipelago surrounding the Koro Sea in the South Pacific Ocean, about 1,300 miles (2,100 kilometres) north of Auckland, New Zealand. It forms part of the Melanesian island group.

The archipelago consists of about 840 islands and islets scattered over about 1,000,000 square miles. The Fiji group includes more than 300 islands, of which about 100 are inhabited. The total land area is 7,055 square miles (18,274 square kilometres), and the population numbers almost 531,000. The capital, Suva, which has a population of about 63,000, is on the southeast coast of the largest island, Viti Levu ("Great Fiji"). About 400 miles north of Suva, the island of Rotuma has an area of about 18 square miles (47 square kilometres) and a population of about 6,000.

Fiji, for 96 years a British colony, gained independence on October 10, 1970. The population of Fijian descent (which is of mixed Melanesian and Polynesian origin) is outnumbered by the Indian population, which is descended from 19th-century immigrants. There are also European, Chinese, and Rotuman minorities. The economy of Fiji, which has a humid tropical climate, is primarily agricultural; sugar is the principal export. It is expected that the various racial groups on the islands will cooperate in upholding a tradition of interracial harmony. (For coverage of the region as a whole, see PACIFIC ISLANDS; PACIFIC OCEAN; for coverage of historical aspects, see OCEANIA, HISTORY OF.)

The natural environment. *Relief.* The islands forming the Fijian archipelago present varied relief types. The larger islands are of volcanic origin; the smaller ones are mostly formed of low coral reefs. To the east are the low-lying coral islands of the Lau group; the two main islands, Viti Levu to the west and Vanua Levu to the north, are volcanic masses of complex shape; the islands of Ovalau and Taveuni consist of volcanic craters. Encircling the islands is a series of intricate coral reefs that are a constant menace to shipping. The islands are all situated on a submerged platform, created by the uplift that raised the volcanic areas above sea level. The coral deposits were formed after the main uplift.

Viti Levu, with an area of 4,011 square miles (10,388 square kilometres), and Vanua Levu, with an area of 2,137 square miles (5,535 square kilometres), both have a complex geological structure, having been formed of volcanic and sedimentary rocks jumbled together. Neither has much level country. In Viti Levu, the main level areas occur in the Sigatoka River Valley and in the deltas of the other principal rivers—the Rewa, the Ba, and the Navua. The Dreketi is the chief river of Vanua Levu; it breaks through the island's mountainous backbone to form a particularly fine valley.

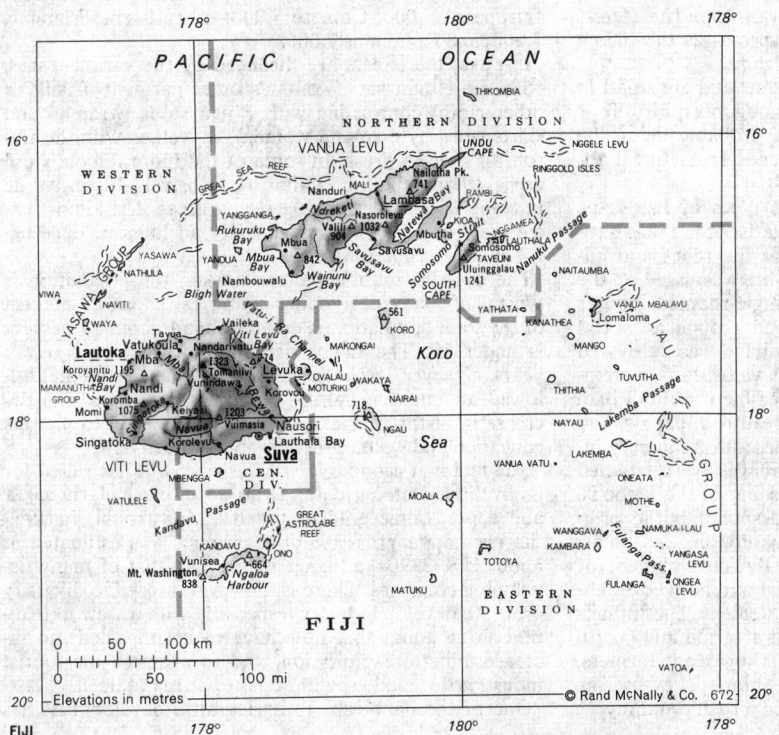

FIJI

Mountains and coastal features

Mt. Tomaniivi (4,341 feet [1,323 metres]) is the highest point on Viti Levu, and Mt. Nasorolevu (3,386 feet [1,032 metres]) the highest on Vanua Levu. More spectacular scenery, however, often occurs near the coasts, which are marked by ravined hills that often reach down to the sea to form headlands. The coastal landscape is also occasionally dominated by an old volcanic plug (a dead volcano with its vent filled with solidified material), the best known of which is Joskes Thumb (1,570 feet), a landmark among the hills that flank Suva's harbour to the west.

Climate. Fiji is generally hot and wet, but many annual and seasonal variations occur, as well as differences due to local topography. The islands lie in the path of the southeast trade winds, which blow fairly steadily throughout the year, creating moist air conditions. The weather is warmest from about December to April and coolest from June to September, although "warm" and "cool" are relative terms. The temperature, which rarely falls below 65° to 70° F (18° to 21° C), for much of the year ranges during a day from about 75° to 85° F (24° to 29 °C) with the daily maximum usually rising to over 90° F (32° C) in the hot season. The main characteristics are high and uniform temperatures, high humidity, and winds from the east and southeast. Rainfall is heavy but uncertain on slopes to windward and is light and uncertain on the leeward slopes. The mean annual rainfall on the western or dry sides of Vanua Levu and Viti Levu is less than 70 inches (1,780 millimetres), but at Suva, on the eastern or wet side of Viti Levu, it is over 120 inches (300 centimetres). Considerable variations in rainfall may occur from year to year. Bright skies and long hours of sunshine occur in the west and southwest, but Suva and the eastern areas frequently experience rainy or cloudy weather. Hurricanes develop occasionally between December and April, often causing severe damage.

Vegetation. In the centre of the two main islands the annual rainfall is often over 300 inches; the mountains are consequently covered with thick forest. To the west, a somewhat dry savanna (grassland) type of vegetation occurs; it is often parched brown and is locally known as *talasiga*, meaning sunburned country. It contrasts vividly with the forest and luxuriant bush country that occurs to the east.

Mangrove swamps are found around the coasts, particularly in the east. Behind many of the beaches in the west and in land under cultivation in general, coconut palms provide a graceful backdrop; the pandanus, or screw-pine tree, with its curiously rooted trunk, adds a bizarre touch, as also does the multi-trunked banyan tree. The forests contain such valuable timber tree species as the dakua and dilo, which are related to mahogany.

Animal life. Animals, which are few and are small in size, include bats, dogs, pigs, and mongooses; birdlife is limited, the most numerous species probably being the minah and the bulbul, both introduced from India. Pigeons and parrots are also found.

Human settlement. The different types of landscape under human settlement and the patterns of life that have developed them are as diversified as the relief and climate. The original Fijian pattern of life was based on the village, a settlement of large, single-roomed houses (bures), with thatched roofs arranged around a central open space. The land around the village was cultivated mainly for such subsistence crops as yams, taro (a stemless plant with a tuberous, starchy, edible root; its Fijian name is *dalo*), bananas, coconuts, breadfruit, papaw, and mangoes. Because of the mountainous and frequently inaccessible interior, many of the villages were situated close to the sea, thus facilitating fishing in the lagoons. This pattern of settlement is still widespread, but its original simplicity has been considerably modified by the arrival of Europeans, who initiated the development of towns, and by an influx of Indian labourers, who established a different pattern of rural settlement. The Indians usually live in scattered houses built of wood and corrugated iron. They form the bulk of the sugarcane farmers, often working farms of ten acres or more. They use the plow extensively, and have developed a cash economy.

Fijian and Indian settlement patterns

Suva, the capital, has a deep-water harbour much used by tourist ships; many goods are obtainable free of tax. Large shops are European-owned while many smaller shops are Indian-owned. There are several modern hotels. The University of the South Pacific is located nearby, at Laucala Bay. Suva's total population is about 63,000, and includes over 28,000 Indians, 16,000 Fijians, 3,000 Europeans, and 2,000 Chinese. Lautoka, the second town of Viti Levu, has a population of about 12,000 and a similar racial pattern.

The average density of population for the whole country is about 75 persons per square mile; this figure, however, conceals wide variations, from the uninhabited mountain areas and waterless islands at one extreme, to the high population density of Suva at the other.

People and population. Indigenous Fijians, mostly of Melanesian stock, show strong resemblances to the Solomon Islanders and to the inhabitants of Papua New Guinea, although they are generally of larger physique. There has been some intermarriage with Polynesians, especially Tongans, particularly in the eastern islands. The majority of the Fijians are Christian, with Methodists forming almost 40 percent of the total. Roman Catholics form the next largest group, followed by Anglicans. The Fijian language belongs to the Malayo-Polynesian group, but there are several dialects; the most widely used is that from Bau, the old Fijian centre, built on a tiny island off the east coast of Viti Levu.

The Indians, who now outnumber the Fijians, are mainly descendants of indentured labourers who first went to Fiji in 1879 to work on the sugar estates. The indenture system continued until after World War I. More recently, Indians with professional, technical, and commercial skills have also emigrated to Fiji. Most of the Indians are Hindus, who form over 40 percent of the total population. There is also a significant Muslim group. Those who are part European form another group, but with a less easily defined identity. Most of them use English as their first language and are Christian.

The Europeans are mainly of British origin, often from Australia and New Zealand, as well as from Great Britain itself.

The three other main ethnic groups are formed by the Chinese, by other Pacific islanders, and by the Rotumans. (Rotuma was annexed by Great Britain in 1881; its population is mainly Polynesian.)

The total estimated population at the end of 1970 was about 524,000; of these, Fijians were estimated to number 225,000; Indians 266,000; part-Europeans 10,000; Europeans 5,000; Chinese 5,000; other Pacific islanders 7,000; and Rotumans 7,000.

In Suva, the streets are thronged by the various races, with the Hindu sari (woman's outer garment of silk or other cloth) contrasting with Fijian sulus (wrap-around skirts worn by men and women), as well as with the European style of dress. In some of the more remote rural areas, the population is almost exclusively Fijian, while in some of the sugarcane-growing areas it is almost exclusively Indian. There is virtually no intermarriage between Fijians and Indians.

The age distribution pattern among the population is typical of many developing countries: about 45 percent of the total population is under 15, and about 55 percent is under 19. The major demographic factor of recent years, however, has been the fall in the birth rate that followed an intensive family planning campaign. The decrease in births, it is expected, will allow Fiji to plan its education and welfare services more effectively.

Age distribution

The national economy. In the past, Fiji has relied for its livelihood on agricultural produce, particularly sugar and copra. Some gold is mined at Vatukoula. In 1969 the per capita gross national product was estimated at about U.S. $390—a higher figure than that of many developing countries. There is, however, a need to diversify crops, to develop industry (especially with a view to manufacturing goods that now have to be imported), to increase mineral exploitation, and to promote the tourist industry, if a good growth rate is to be maintained.

One of the handicaps to agricultural development has

Fiji, Area and Population

	area		population	
	sq mi	sq km	1966 census	1971 estimate
Divisions				
Central				
Provinces*				
Naitasiri	643	1,666	39,000	...
Namosi	220	570	3,000	...
Rewa	105	272	70,000	...
Serua	321	830	8,000	...
Tailevu	369	955	34,000	...
Eastern				
Provinces				
Kandavu	185	478	9,000	...
Lau	188	487	16,000	...
Lomaiviti	159	411	13,000	...
Northern				
Provinces				
Mathuata	774	2,004	44,000	...
Mbua	532	1,379	10,000	...
Thakaundrove	1,087	2,816	30,000	...
Western				
Provinces				
Mba	1,017	2,634	136,000	...
Nandronga-Navosa	921	2,385	37,000	...
Ra	518	1,341	22,000	...
Total Fiji	7,055†‡	18,274†	477,000‡§	531,000

*The provinces are autonomous only with respect to local affairs. They
are subdivided or amalgamated or both for various administrative
purposes.   †Includes the land area of Rotuma (18 sq mi, or 46 sq km),
which is a dependency of Fiji.   ‡Figures do not add to total because of
rounding.   §Includes the population of Rotuma (3,000) and 1,000
people on board ships at the time of the census.
Source: Official government figures.

been the system of land tenure. Over 80 percent of the
land belongs, by communal right, to the Fijians; although
Indians are able to rent land, few of them have been
able to buy it in order to develop it intensively.

In 1970 exports increased to about $54,000,000 and
imports to about $79,000,000. The visible trade deficit
was more than covered by the "invisible" earnings of the
tourist industry and by a considerable investment of
foreign capital.

Apart from sugar and copra, other exports are coconut
oil, gold, bananas, molasses, biscuits, and manganese.
The United Kingdom is the biggest importer of Fiji's
produce, followed by the United States, Canada, Australia, and New Zealand. Imports are mainly from Australia, Great Britain, Japan, New Zealand, and the United
States.

Fiji's sixth development plan, covering the period from
1971 to 1975, envisages an annual increase in the gross
domestic product of more than 6 percent, providing that
world conditions continue to be favourable. Great
Britain's entry into the European Common Market, however, could affect the marketing of sugar. It is anticipated
that gross receipts from tourism, which amounted to an
estimated $21,000,000 in 1970, will triple by 1975.

Apart from the general intensification of agriculture, it
is hoped that other new developments in forestry and
fishing will strengthen the economy. The government intends to pursue a monetary policy designed to encourage
new projects considered desirable by granting tax concessions. Industrial expansion is now limited by lack of a
cheap source of power. About 80 percent of governmental revenue is obtained from customs and excise
duties, income taxes, and other forms of direct taxation.

Transport. Fiji's two main ports of entry are Nandi
(or Nadi) International Airport and the port of Suva.
Nandi accommodates the largest aircraft used on world
routes and is used regularly by seven major airlines as
well as the locally based Air Pacific (formerly Fiji Airways). Almost 3,200 miles (5,100 kilometres) from
Honolulu, almost 2,000 miles (3,200 kilometres) from
Sydney, and about 1,300 miles (2,000 kilometres) from
Auckland, Nandi provides a convenient refuelling and
servicing stop as well as a tourist disembarkation point.
Suva's own airport, at Nausori, 135 miles (217 kilometres) by road from Nandi, is served by Air Pacific,
with air routes linking it to Tonga, Western Samoa, Cook

(margin) Air
services

Islands, Gilbert and Ellice Islands, Nauru, New Hebrides, the Solomons, and Papua New Guinea.

Suva is the major port of Fiji; the second port is
Lautoka on the west coast of Viti Levu. Both are served
by interisland ships, cargo and passenger, some of which
run to a scheduled timetable.

The roads are usually unpaved, except in the towns,
although there are plans to tar the road from Suva to
Nandi. Although there are more than 1,500 miles (2,500
kilometres) of all-weather motor roads, there is a need
for feeder roads to move agricultural produce to the
towns. Some of the rivers are used to float bananas and
other crops down to the coast by raft. A narrow-gauge
railway is operated by the sugar-refining industry; free
passenger service is available on part of the railway twice
a week.

Administration and social conditions.   Fiji is a dominion, with the British sovereign as head of state, represented by a governor general. The legislature is bi-
cameral, consisting of a House of Representatives and a
Senate. Under a constitution introduced at the time of
independence, a general election was held in May 1972,
when 52 members of a new House of Representatives
were elected; 12 Fijians, 12 Indians, and 3 general members (i.e., members elected by voters, mainly European
and Chinese, who are ineligible for inclusion on the Fijian and Indian voting rolls) were elected on communal
rolls; and ten Fijians, ten Indians, and five general members were elected on national rolls in which electors of all
races voted together. The upper house, the Senate, was
inaugurated in November 1970; it consists of 22 members, eight nominated by the Great Council of Chiefs,
seven by the prime minister, six by the leader of the opposition, and one by the Rotuman Council.

Apart from Suva and Lautoka, seven other urban areas
constitute townships. These are Ba, Nandi, Sigatoka,
and Nausori (all on the island of Viti Levu); Levuka (on
the island of Ovalau); and Labasa and Savusavu (on the
island of Vanua Levu). Members of the city council of
Suva and Lautoka and the boards of the seven townships
are elected; the elections are frequently keenly contested.

The most interesting feature of the rural local administration is the Fijian Administration, which was first
established in 1876 and deals exclusively with Fijians.
The Great Council of Chiefs, the supreme body of the
Fijian Administration, advises the government on the
general welfare of Fijians. The Fijian Affairs Board is responsible for the administration of the 14 provinces and
for imposing land taxes. Fifteen locally chosen non-Fijian
advisory councils work in conjunction with 14 elected
Fijian provincial councils.

Fiji, a multiracial country, clearly faces potential racial
tension, and every effort is made to create a harmonious
atmosphere. The dominant social problems are likely to
become the increasing drift from the rural areas to the
towns, the wide variations in personal incomes, and the
scarcity of land. Although there are no shantytowns, an
increasing number of both Indians and Fijians live in
overcrowded and insanitary conditions in urban shacks.
Social services, although relatively well developed, are increasingly faced with the problem of overcrowding in the
towns.

Fiji is a healthy country. Malaria is unknown, and many
tropical diseases have been practically eradicated. Education is relatively widespread. About 86 percent of
children of primary school age attend school; unfortunately, however, school enrollment has outstripped the
present capacity of the country to train enough teachers.
Vigorous steps to train more teachers are now being
taken both in teacher-training colleges and at the University of the South Pacific.

Cultural life.   The Fijian way of life is based on a form
of society headed by chiefs, and ceremony still plays an
important part in it; long and intricate welcome ceremonies are particularly noteworthy. Yaqona (kava), a
drink prepared from the root of the pepper plant, is the
basis of a friendly welcome and is presented with due
ceremony. Traditional stories are kept alive by songs and
dances; the dancers often wear clothes partly made from

(margin) Ceremo-
nies of
welcome

masi (tapa), a cloth prepared from the bark of the mulberry tree.

Fijian traditional arts include the making of pandanus palm mats, wood carving, and pottery, as well as the preparation of *masi*. A remarkable spectacle is the firewalking ceremony performed by the people of the island of Beqa, who heat small boulders in a large fire in a pit and then walk barefoot on the white-hot stones.

The Indian population has preserved much of Indian culture from India, including the celebration of Dīwālī, the Hindu festival of lights; other Indian traditions also include fire walking. Muslims observe the fast of Ramadān. Indian temples and Christian churches are common sights in the towns, and it is rare to find a Fijian village without a church.

Modern sports and a Western form of dancing are often interracial activities. Rugby is the leading Fijian game and football (soccer) the Indian game. The Hibiscus Festival of Suva is interracial in character; it is a week of carnival held in September. Newspapers and magazines are published in Fijian and Hindi; the only daily newspaper, the *Fiji Times*, is published in English. The Fiji Broadcasting Commission broadcasts its national program in English and other programs in Fijian and Hindi.

Prospects for the future. Economically Fiji is in a stronger position than many other newly independent countries. The government is pursuing a policy of attracting foreign capital in order to diversify its economy and to develop its mineral and biological resources more fully. Important as these aims are, the attainment of a stable and harmonious future for Fiji ultimately depends on the removal of potential causes of racial tension. This necessitates improving the living conditions of Fijians with lower incomes, permitting Indians to gain easier access to land for farming, and the avoiding by the Chinese and European minorities of any appearance of exploiting the Fijians and Indians. If these aims can be achieved, Fiji can look forward to a bright social and economic future.

BIBLIOGRAPHY. R.G. WARD, *Land Use and Population in Fiji* (1965), a comprehensive geographical survey well illustrated with a variety of maps; E.K. FISK, *The Political Economy of Independent Fiji* (1970), a modern economic survey, realistically written on the eve of independence; *Fiji's Sixth Development Plan 1971–1975*, Fiji Parliamentary Paper No. 25 (1970), a policy document outlining the economic policy for the first five years of independence; A.C. MAYER, *Indians in Fiji* (1963), an account of the coming of the Indians to Fiji and the problems resulting from this; C.S. BELSHAW, *Under the Ivi Tree: Society and Economic Growth in Rural Fiji* (1964), a series of socio-economic case studies in southwest Viti Levu; P. FRANCE, *The Charter of the Land: Custom and Colonization in Fiji* (1969), an account of Fijian customary land rights.

(R.C.H.)

Finance, Business

Business finance is concerned with the raising and managing of funds by business firms. The scope of business finance may also include the making of policies that affect a firm's financial status—that is, its ability to raise funds through the sale of its securities.

Because of the importance of the planning, analysis, and control operations for which he is responsible, the financial manager is usually close to the top of the organizational structure of a firm. Typically, he is a member of the first level of the corporate staff in a large organization. In very large firms major financial decisions are often made by a finance committee. In small firms, the owner-manager himself usually conducts the financial operations. Much of the day-to-day work of business finance is conducted by lower level staff; their work includes handling cash receipts and disbursements, borrowing from commercial banks on a regular and continuing basis, and formulating cash budgets.

Financial decisions affect both the profitability and the riskiness of a firm's operations. An increase in the cash position, for instance, reduces risk; but, since cash is not an earning asset, converting other types of assets to cash reduces the firm's profitability. Similarly, the use of additional debt raises the profitability of the firm, but more debt means more risk. The task of finance is to strike a balance between risk and profitability that will maintain the long-term value of the firm's securities.

SHORT-TERM FINANCIAL OPERATIONS

Financial planning and control. Short-term financial operations are closely involved with the financial planning and control activities of the firm. These include financial ratio analysis, profit planning, financial forecasting, and budgeting.

Financial ratio analysis. A firm's balance sheet contains many items that taken by themselves have no clear meaning. Financial ratio analysis is a way of appraising their relative importance. The ratio of current assets to current liabilities, for example, gives the analyst an idea of the extent to which the firm can meet its current obligations. This is known as a liquidity ratio. Financial leverage ratios (such as the debt–asset ratio and debt as a percentage of total capitalization) are used to make judgments about the advantages to be gained from raising funds by the issuance of bonds (debt) rather than stock. Activity ratios, relating to the turnover of such asset categories as inventories, accounts receivable, and fixed assets, show how intensively the firm is employing its assets. The firm's primary operating objective is to earn a good return on its invested capital, and various profit ratios (profits as a percentage of sales, of assets, or of net worth) show how successfully it is meeting this objective. *(margin note: Analysis of the balance sheet)*

Ratio analysis is used to compare a firm's performance with that of other firms in the same industry or with the performance of industry in general. It is also used to study trends in the firm's performance over time and thus anticipate problems before they develop.

Profit planning. Ratio analysis applies to the firm's current operating posture. But the firm must also plan for future growth. This requires decisions as to the expansion of existing operations and, in manufacturing, to the development of new product lines. The firm must choose between productive processes requiring various degrees of mechanization or automation—that is, various amounts of fixed capital in the form of machinery and equipment. This will increase fixed costs—that is, costs that are relatively constant and do not decrease when the firm is operating at levels below full capacity. The higher the proportion of fixed costs to total costs, the higher must be the level of operation before profits begin, and the more sensitive will profits be to changes in the level of operation.

Financial forecasting. The financial manager must also make overall forecasts of future capital requirements to assure that funds will be available to finance new investment programs. The first step in making such a forecast is to obtain an estimate of sales during each year of the planning period. This estimate is worked out jointly by the marketing, production, and finance departments: the marketing manager estimates demand; the production manager estimates capacity; and the financial manager estimates availability of funds to finance new accounts receivable, inventories, and fixed assets.

For the predicted level of sales, the financial manager estimates the funds that will be available from the company's operations and compares this amount with what will be needed to pay for the new fixed assets (machinery, equipment, etc.). If the growth rate exceeds 10 percent a year, asset requirements are likely to exceed internal sources of funds, so plans must be made to finance them by issuing securities. If, on the other hand, growth is slow, more funds will be generated than are required to support the estimated growth in sales. In this case, the financial manager will consider a number of alternatives, including increasing dividends to stockholders, retiring debt, using excess funds to acquire other firms, or, perhaps, increasing expenditures on research and development.

Control through budgeting. Once the firm's general goals for the planning period have been established, the next step is to set up a detailed plan of operation—the budget. A complete budget system encompasses all aspects of the firm's operations over the planning period. It may even allow for changes in plans as required by factors outside the firm's control.

Budgeting is a part of the total planning activity in the firm, so it must begin with a statement of the firm's long-range plan. The long-range plan includes a long-range sales forecast. This forecast requires a determination of the number and types of products that will be manufactured in the years encompassed by the long-range plan. Short-term budgets are formulated within the framework of the long-range plan. Normally, there is a budget for every individual product and for every significant activity of the firm.

Establishing budgetary controls requires a realistic understanding of the firm's activities. For example, a small firm purchases more parts and uses more labour and less machinery; a larger firm will buy raw materials and use machinery to manufacture end items. In consequence, the smaller firm should budget higher parts and labour cost ratios, while the larger firm should budget higher overhead cost ratios and larger investments in fixed assets. If standards are unrealistically high, frustrations and resentment will develop. If standards are unduly lax, costs will be out of control, profits will suffer, and morale will drop.

The cash budget and management of cash. One of the principal methods of forecasting the financial needs of a business is the cash budget. The cash budget forecasts the combined effects of planned operations on the firm's cash flow. A positive net cash flow means that the firm will have surplus funds to invest. But if the cash budget indicates that an increase in the volume of operations will lead to a negative cash flow, additional financing will be required. The cash budget thus indicates the amount of funds that will be needed or available month by month, or even week by week.

A firm may have excess cash for a number of reasons. There are likely to be seasonal or cyclical fluctuations in business. Resources may be deliberately accumulated as a protection against a number of contingencies. Since it is wasteful to allow large amounts of cash to remain idle, the financial manager will try to find short-term investments for sums that he will need later. Short-term government or business securities can be selected and balanced in such a way that he obtains the maturities and risks appropriate to the financial situation of his firm.

Managing accounts receivable. Accounts receivable are the credit a firm gives its customers. The volume and terms of such credit vary among businesses and among nations; for manufacturing firms in the United States, the ratio of receivables to sales ranges between 8 and 12 percent, representing an average collection period of approximately one month. The basis of a firm's credit policy is the practice in its industry; generally, a firm must meet the terms offered by competitors. Much depends, of course, on the individual customer's credit standing.

To evaluate a customer as a credit risk, the credit manager considers what may be called the five C's of credit: character, capacity, capital, collateral, and conditions. Information on these items is obtained from the firm's previous experience with the customer, supplemented by information from various credit associations and credit-reporting agencies. In reviewing his firm's credit program, the financial manager should regard losses from bad debts as part of the cost of doing business. Accounts receivable represent an investment in the expansion of sales. The return of this investment can be calculated as in any capital budgeting problem.

Managing inventories. Every company must carry stocks of goods and materials in inventory. The size of the investment in inventory depends on various factors, including the level of sales, the nature of the productive processes, and the speed with which goods perish or become obsolescent.

The problems involved in managing inventories are basically the same as those in managing other assets, including cash. A basic stock must be on hand at all times. Because the unexpected may occur, it is also wise to have

safety stocks; these represent the little extra needed to avoid the costs of not having enough. Additional amounts—anticipation stocks—may be required to meet future growth needs. Finally, some inventory accumulation results from the economies of purchasing in large quantities: it is always cheaper to buy more than is immediately needed, whether of raw materials, money, or plant and equipment. There is a standard procedure for determining the most economical amounts to order, one that relates purchasing requirements to costs and carrying charges. While carrying charges rise as average inventory holdings increase, certain other costs (ordering costs and stock-out costs) fall as average inventory holdings rise. These two sets of costs comprise the total cost of ordering and carrying inventories, and it is fairly easy to calculate an optimal order size that will minimize total inventory costs.

Short-term financing. The main sources of short-term financing are (1) trade credit, (2) loans from commercial banks, and (3) commercial paper.

Trade credit. A firm customarily buys its supplies and materials on credit from other firms, recording the debt as an account payable. This trade credit, as it is commonly called, is the largest single category of short-term credit. Credit terms are usually expressed with a discount for prompt payment. Thus the seller may state that if payment is made within ten days of the invoice date, a 2 percent cash discount will be allowed. If the cash discount is not taken, payment is due 30 days after the date of invoice. The cost of not taking cash discounts is the price of the credit. (The effective rate of interest in this case is 36.7 percent annually.)

Commercial banks. Commercial bank lending appears on the balance sheet as notes payable and is second in importance to trade credit as a source of short-term financing. Banks occupy a pivotal position in the short-term and intermediate-term money markets. As a firm's financing needs grow, banks are called upon to provide additional funds. A single loan obtained from a bank by a business firm is not different in principle from a loan obtained by an individual. The firm signs a conventional promissory note. Repayment is made in a lump sum at maturity (when the note is due) or in installments throughout the life of the loan. A line of credit, as distinguished from a single loan, is a formal or informal understanding between the bank and the borrower as to the maximum loan balance the bank will allow at any one time.

In the United States, the role of commercial banks in the financing of business is somewhat unusual. The Banking Act of 1933 required the separation of investment banking and commercial banking functions, whereas in most other countries commercial banks are a source of long-term as well as of short-term financing.

Commercial paper. Commercial paper, a third source of short-term credit, consists of promissory notes of well-established firms sold primarily to other business firms, insurance companies, pension funds, and banks. Commercial paper is issued for periods varying from two to six months. The rates on prime commercial paper vary, but they are generally slightly below those on prime business loans.

A basic limitation of the commercial paper market is that its resources are limited to the excess liquidity that corporations, the main suppliers of funds, may have at any particular time. Another disadvantage is the impersonality of the dealings; a bank is much more likely to help a good customer weather a storm than is a commercial paper dealer.

Use of security in short-term financing. Most short-term business loans are unsecured. It is ordinarily better to borrow on an unsecured basis, but frequently a borrower's credit rating is not strong enough to justify an unsecured loan. The most common types of collateral used for short-term credit are inventories and accounts receivable.

Financing through accounts receivable can be done either by pledging the receivables or by selling them outright (called factoring in the U.S.). When the receivables

Cash and credit management

Working capital

Financing
equipment

are pledged, the borrower retains the risk that the person or firm who owes the receivable will not pay; this risk is typically passed on to the lender when factoring is involved.

When loans are secured by inventory, the lender takes title to them. He may or may not take physical possession of them. Under a field warehousing arrangement, the inventory is under the physical control of a warehouse company, which releases the inventory only on order from the lending institution. Canned goods, lumber, steel, coal, and other standardized products are the types of goods usually covered in field warehouse arrangements.

Intermediate-term financing. Whereas short-term loans are repaid in a period of weeks or months, intermediate-term loans are scheduled for repayment in one to 15 years. Obligations due in 15 or more years are thought of as long-term debt. The major forms of intermediate-term financing include (1) term loans, (2) conditional sales contracts, and (3) lease financing.

Term loans. A term loan is a business credit with a maturity of more than one year but less than 15 years. Usually the term loan is retired by systematic repayments (amortization payments) over its life. It may be secured by a chattel mortgage on equipment, but the larger, stronger companies are able to borrow on an unsecured basis. Commercial banks and life insurance companies are the principal suppliers of term loans. The interest cost of term loans varies with the size of the loan and the strength of the borrower.

Term loans involve more risk to the lender than do short-term loans. The lender's funds are tied up for a long period, and during this time the borrower's situation can change markedly. To protect themselves, lenders often include in the loan agreement stipulations that the borrower will maintain his current liquidity ratio at a specified level, limit his acquisitions of fixed assets, keep his debt ratio below a stated amount, and in general follow policies that are acceptable to the lender.

Conditional sales contracts. Conditional sales contracts are a common method of obtaining equipment by agreeing to pay for it in installments over a period of up to five years. Until payment is completed, the seller of the equipment continues to hold title to the equipment.

Leasing. It is not necessary to purchase assets in order to use them. Railroad companies in the United States, for instance, have acquired much of their equipment by leasing it. Whether or not leasing is advantageous depends—aside from tax advantages—on the firm's access to funds; leasing provides an alternative method of financing. A lease contract, however, being a fixed obligation, is similar to debt and uses some of the firm's debt-carrying ability. It will generally be advantageous to a firm to own its land and buildings, because their value is likely to increase, but this consideration does not apply to equipment.

The statement is frequently made that leasing involves higher interest rates than other forms of financing, but this need not always be true. Much depends on the firm's standing as a credit risk. Moreover, it is difficult to separate the money costs of leasing from the other services that may be embodied in a leasing contract. If the leasing company can perform nonfinancial services, such as maintenance of the equipment, at a lower cost than the lessee or someone else could perform them, the effective cost of leasing may be lower than for funds obtained from borrowing or other sources.

Although leasing involves fixed charges, it enables a firm to present lower debt-to-asset ratios in its financial statements. Many lenders, in examining financial statements, give less weight to a lease obligation than to a loan obligation.

LONG-TERM FINANCIAL OPERATIONS

Managing
the capital
structure

Use of bonds. Long-term capital may be raised either through borrowing or by the issuance of stock. Long-term borrowing is done by selling bonds, which are promissory notes that obligate the firm to pay interest at specific times. Secured bondholders have prior claim on the firm's assets. If the company goes out of business, the bondholders are entitled to be paid the face value of their holdings plus interest. Stockholders, on the other hand, have no more than a residual claim on the company: they are entitled to a share of the profits, if there are any, but it is the prerogative of the board of directors to decide whether a dividend will be paid and how large it will be.

Long-term financing involves the choice between debt (bonds) and equity (stocks). Each firm will choose its own capital structure, seeking the combination of debt and equity that will minimize the costs of raising capital. As conditions in the capital market vary (*e.g.*, changes in interest rates, the availability of funds, and the relative costs of alternative methods of financing), the firm's desired capital structure will change correspondingly.

Long-term debt. The larger the proportion of debt in the capital structure (leverage), the higher will be the returns to equity. This is because bondholders do not share in the profits. The difficulty with this, of course, is that a high proportion of debt increases the firm's fixed costs and increases the degree of fluctuation in the returns to equity for any given degree of fluctuation in the level of sales. Leverage increases the returns to owners if used successfully but decreases the returns to owners if used unsuccessfully. Indeed, if leverage is unsuccessful, the result may be the bankruptcy of the firm.

Forms of long-term debt. There are various forms of long-term debt. A mortgage bond is one secured by a lien on fixed assets such as plant and equipment. A debenture is a bond not secured by specific assets but accepted by investors because the firm has a high credit standing or obligates itself to follow policies that assure a high rate of earnings. A still more junior lien is the subordinated debenture, which is secondary to all other debentures and specifically to short-term bank loans.

The use of long-term debt will be encouraged when: sales and earnings are relatively stable; profit margins are large enough to make more leverage advantageous to the stockholders; an increase is expected in profits or the general price level; the existing debt ratio is relatively low; the price–earnings ratios on common stock are low in relation to the levels of interest rates; management is concerned with maintaining voting control over the company; cash-flow requirements under the bond agreement are not burdensome; and the restrictions on management written into the bond indenture are not onerous.

Stock. Equity financing is done with common and preferred stock. Preferred stock usually has priority over common stock with respect to earnings and claims on assets in liquidation. Preferred stock is usually cumulative—that is, the omission of dividends in one or more years creates an accumulated claim. The dividends on preferred stock are usually fixed at a specific percentage of face value. A company issuing preferred stock gains the advantages of limited dividends and no maturity—that is, the advantages of selling bonds but without the restrictions of bonds. Companies sell preferred stock when they seek more leverage but wish to avoid the fixed charges of debt. The advantages of preferred stock will be reinforced if a company's debt ratio is already high and if common stock financing is relatively expensive.

If a bond or preferred stock issue was sold when interest rates were higher than they are at present, it may be profitable to call the old issue and refund it with a new, lower cost issue. This depends on how the immediate costs and premiums that must be paid compare with the annual savings that can be obtained.

Earnings and dividend policies. The size and frequency of dividend payments are critical issues in company policy. Dividend policy affects the financial structure, the flow of funds, corporate liquidity, stock prices, and the morale of stockholders. If earnings are paid out as dividends, they cannot be used for company expansion. Some stockholders are interested in receiving maximum current returns on their investment, while others prefer reinvestment of earnings so that the company's capital will increase.

Companies tend to reinvest their earnings to a higher

degree when there are chances for profitable expansion. Thus, at times when profits are high, the amounts reinvested are greater and dividends are smaller. For similar reasons, reinvestment is likely to decrease when profits decline, and dividends are likely to increase.

Companies having relatively stable earnings over a period of years tend to pay high dividends. Well-established large firms are likely to pay higher than average dividends because they have better access to capital markets and are not as dependent as other firms on internal financing. In the same way, if a firm has a strong cash or liquidity position, it is likely to pay higher dividends than if it has not. A firm with heavy indebtedness has implicitly committed itself to paying relatively low dividends and retaining earnings to service the debt. It may decide, however, to continue with high dividends in order to facilitate a stock issue or a refunding of its debt. If the directors of a company are concerned with maintaining control of it, they may retain earnings so that they can finance expansion without having to issue stock. Some companies favour a stable dividend policy rather than allowing dividends to fluctuate with earnings; the dividend rate will then be lower when profits are high and higher when profits are temporarily in decline. Companies whose stock is closely held by a few high-income stockholders are likely to pay lower dividends in order to permit the stockholders to avoid personal income taxes.

In Europe, until recently, company financing tended to rely heavily on internal sources. This was because many companies were owned by families and, also, because a highly developed capital market was lacking. In the less developed countries today, firms rely heavily on internal financing; they also tend to make more use of short-term bank loans and other forms of short-term financing than is typical in other countries.

Convertible bonds and stock warrants. Companies sometimes issue bonds or preferred stock that give holders the option of converting them into common stock or of purchasing stock at favourable prices. Convertible bonds carry the option of conversion into common stock at a specified price during a particular period. Stock purchase warrants are given with bonds or preferred stock as an inducement to the investor; they permit him to buy common stock in the company at a stated price whenever he chooses. Such option privileges make it easier for small companies to sell bonds or preferred stock. They help large companies to float new issues on more favourable terms than they could otherwise obtain. When bondholders exercise conversion rights, the company's debt ratio is reduced because bonds are replaced by stock. The exercise of stock warrants, on the other hand, brings additional funds into the company but leaves the existing debt or preferred stock on the books. Option privileges also permit a company to sell new stock at more favourable prices than those prevailing at the time of issue, since the prices stated on the options are higher. They will be most popular, therefore, at times when stock prices are expected to have an upward trend.

GROWTH AND DECLINE

Mergers and consolidations. Companies often grow by combining with other companies. One company may purchase all or part of another; two companies may merge by exchanging shares; or a wholly new company may be formed through consolidation of the old companies. From the financial manager's viewpoint, this kind of expansion is like any other investment decision: the acquisition should be made if it increases the acquiring firm's net present value as reflected in the price of its stock.

The most important term that must be negotiated in a combination is the price the acquiring firm will pay for the assets it takes over. Present earnings, expected future earnings, and the effects of the merger on the rate of earnings growth of the surviving firm are perhaps the most important determinants of the price that will be paid. Current market prices are the second most important determinant of prices in mergers: depending on whether or not asset values are indicative of the earning power of the acquired firm, book values may exert an important influence on the terms of the merger. Other, nonmeasurable, factors are sometimes the overriding determinant in bringing companies together: synergistic, or "two-plus-two-equals-five," effects may be present to a sufficient extent to warrant paying more for the acquired firm than earnings and asset values would indicate.

A merger may be treated as either a purchase or a pooling of interests. In a purchase, a larger firm generally takes over a smaller one and assumes all management control. The amount actually paid for the smaller firm is reflected in the acquiring firm's balance sheet; if more was paid for the acquired firm than the book value of its assets, the difference is reflected in the acquiring firm's financial statements as goodwill. In a pooling of interests, the merged firms are usually about the same size; both managements carry on important functions after the merger; and common stock, rather than cash or bonds, is used in payment. The total assets of the surviving firm in a pooling are equal to the sum of the assets of the two independent companies, and no surplus remains to be written off as a charge against earnings.

The basic requirements for the success of a merger are that it fit into a soundly conceived long-range plan and that the resulting firm have performance characteristics superior to those attainable by the previous companies independently. In the heady environment of a rising stock market, mergers have often been motivated by superficial financial aims. Companies with stock selling at a high price relative to earnings have found it advantageous to merge with companies having a lower price–earnings ratio; this enables them to increase their earnings per share, thus appealing to investors who purchase stock on the basis of earnings.

Some mergers, particularly those of the "conglomerate" kind, which bring together firms in unrelated fields, owe their success to economies of management. In the 1950s certain large-scale changes in managerial technology occurred. The role of the general management functions (planning, control, organizing, information) and other functions centralized at top management levels (research, finance, legal services) increased in importance. The costs of managing large, diversified firms were substantially reduced. This explains generally the spread of conglomerate mergers in the United States in the 1960s.

In mergers, one firm disappears. An alternative is for one firm to buy all or a majority of the voting stock of another and to run it as an operating subsidiary. The acquiring firm is then called a holding company. There are several advantages in the holding company: it can control the acquired firm with a smaller investment than would be required in a merger; each firm remains a separate legal entity, and the obligations of one are separate from those of the other; and stockholder approval is not necessary, as it is in the case of a merger. There are also disadvantages to holding companies, including the possibility of multiple taxation and the danger that the high rate of leverage will amplify the earnings fluctuations of the operating companies.

An important source of financing in developing countries is through "financial groups." These are groups of enterprises centred around a nucleus of a commercial bank or an industrial finance company. They are not conglomerates or holding companies; they are held together primarily by personal and financial ties between the principals involved.

Reorganization. When a firm cannot operate profitably the owners may seek to reorganize it. The first question to be answered is whether the firm might not be better off by ceasing to do business. If the decision is made that the firm is to survive, it must be put through the process of reorganization. Legal procedures are always costly, especially in the case of business failure; both the debtor and the creditors are better off if matters can be handled on an informal basis rather than through the courts. The informal procedures used in reorganization are (1) extension, which postpones the settlement of outstanding debt, and (2) composition, which reduces the amount owed.

Growth
by combi-
nation

If voluntary settlement through extension or composition is not possible, the matter must be taken to court. If the court decides on reorganization rather than liquidation, it appoints a trustee to control the firm and to prepare a formal plan of reorganization. The plan must meet standards of fairness and feasibility: the concept of fairness involves the appropriate distribution of proceeds to each claimant; the test of feasibility relates to the ability of the new enterprise to carry the fixed charges resulting from the reorganization plan.

BIBLIOGRAPHY. Comprehensive introductions to business finance include J. FRED WESTON and EUGENE F. BRIGHAM, *Essentials of Managerial Finance*, 2nd ed. (1971), and *Managerial Finance*, 3rd ed. (1969); JAMES C. VAN HORNE, *Financial Management and Policy*, 2nd ed. (1971); and ROBERT WILLARD JOHNSON, *Financial Management*, 3rd ed. (1966). Examples of the case approach are EUGENE F. BRIGHAM *et al.*, *Cases in Managerial Finance* (1970); J. KEITH BUTTERS (ed.), *Case Problems in Finance*, 5th ed. (1969); and PEARSON HUNT and VICTOR L. ANDREWS, *Financial Management* (1968). Collections of basic readings include EUGENE F. BRIGHAM (ed.), *Readings in Managerial Finance* (1971); J. FRED WESTON and DONALD H. WOODS (comps.), *Basic Financial Management: Selected Readings* (1967); and EDWARD J. MOCK (ed.), *Financial Decision-Making* (1967).

(J.F.W.)

Finland

Now an independent republic in northern Europe, Finland (Finnish Suomi; in full, Suomen Tasavalta) was a part of Sweden from the 12th century until 1809. It was a Russian grand duchy until, following the Russian Revolution, the Finns declared their independence, on December 6, 1917; independence was formally recognized by the Soviet Union on October 14, 1920. Ahvenanmaa (Åland Islands), an archipelago at the entrance to the Gulf of Bothnia, forms an integral, although autonomous, part of Finland.

Finland is bordered on the north by Norway, on the northwest by Sweden, on the west by the Gulf of Bothnia, on the south by the Gulf of Finland, and on the east by the Soviet Union. Its area is just over 130,000 square miles (337,000 square kilometres), of which Ahvenanmaa comprises just over 581 square miles. Finland's area was reduced by about one-tenth in 1944, when it ceded to the Soviet Union a large part of southeastern Karelia (an autonomous region within the Russian S.F.S.R.) and the Petsamo (Pechenga) area, which had provided a corridor to the ice-free Arctic coast. About one-third of Finland lies north of the Arctic Circle.

The character of the country

The most remote of the Scandinavian countries, Finland seems little known outside that area. But its trading and cultural relations with other countries have steadily increased in the last decades. It has close ties with the Scandinavian bloc, sharing a free labour market and participating in various economic and scientific projects. Finland shares with these countries a common law and since 1955 has sent representatives to the Nordic Council, which makes suggestions to member countries on coordination of policies. Finland is a member of the Organization for Economic Co-operation and Development (OECD) and an associate member of the European Free Trade Association (EFTA). In July 1972 Finland initialled a free trade agreement with the Common Market (EEC). Finland's trade with the Soviet Union represents less than 15 percent of the total. Politically, Finland is carefully neutral; although its 1948 treaty of friendship with the Soviet Union requires Finland to repel any attack on the Soviet Union through its own territory, Finland has no other military obligations to the Soviet bloc. (For related information, see SCANDINAVIA, HISTORY OF; RUSSIA AND THE SOVIET UNION, HISTORY OF; HELSINKI; and BALTIC SEA.)

THE LAND

The natural environment. *Topography.* Finland, heavily afforested, mainly with conifers, and containing about 55,000 lakes, numerous rivers, and an extensive area of marshland, looks from the air like an intricate blue and green jigsaw puzzle. Except in the northwest, relief features do not vary greatly, and a traveller on the ground or on the water will rarely see beyond the trees in his immediate vicinity. The landscape, nevertheless, possesses a striking—if sometimes bleak—beauty.

Ancient underlying rocks

Finland's underlying structure is a huge worn-down shield composed of extremely ancient rock, mainly granite, dating from the Precambrian Era (4,600,000,000 to 570,000,000 years ago). The land is low-lying in the southern part of the country and higher in the centre and the northeast, while the few mountainous regions are in the northwest, adjacent to Finland's borders with Sweden and Norway. In this area there are several high peaks, including Haltiatunturi, at 4,357 feet (1,324 metres), Finland's highest mountain.

The islands comprising Ahvenanmaa are mainly low-lying, especially around the central Bay of Lumparen, but toward the northern coastline rise to upland heights such as Orrdalsklint (423 feet). The islands, like mainland Finland, are heavily wooded.

Drainage and soils. Finland's inland waters occupy nearly 10 percent of the country's total area; there are about 150 lakes of about eight square miles (2,000 hectares) in area and innumerable smaller ones. The largest lake, Saimaa, in the southeast, covers 1,699 square miles. There are many other large lakes near it, including Päijänne and Pielinen, while Oulujärvi is near Kajaani in central Finland, and Inari is in the extreme north. Away from coastal regions, many of Finland's rivers flow into the lakes, which are generally shallow: only three lakes are deeper than about 300 feet. Saimaa itself drains into the much larger Lake Ladoga in Soviet territory, via the Vuoksi River. Drainage from Finland's eastern uplands is through the lake system of Soviet Karelia to the White Sea. In the extreme north the Paatsjoki and its tributaries drain considerable areas into the Arctic. On Finland's western coast a series of rivers flow into the Gulf of Bothnia. These include the Torniojoki, which forms part of Finland's border with Sweden, and the great Kemijoki (343 miles), Finland's longest river. In the southwest the Kokemäenjoki, one of Finland's greatest rivers, flows out past the city of Pori. Other rivers flow southward into the Gulf of Finland.

Glacial influences in soil formation

Soils include those found in eskers, remarkable winding ridges of stratified gravel and sand laid down subglacially. There are extensive marine and lake postglacial deposits in the form of clays and silts; these provide the country's most fertile soils. The northern third of Finland has thick layers of peat, the humus soil of which is being steadily reclaimed. Such marshland still covers as much as 30 percent of the countryside. In Ahvenanmaa the soils are mainly clay and sand.

Climate. Approximately one-third of Finland lies north of the Arctic Circle and suffers extremely severe and prolonged winters. Temperatures can fall to $-22°$ F ($-30°$ C). In these latitudes the snow never melts from the north-facing mountain slopes; but in the short summer (Lapland has 73 days of the midnight sun) from May to July, temperatures can reach as high as 80° F (27° C). Further south the extremes are slightly less marked. Annual precipitation, about one-third of which falls as sleet or snow, is about 24 inches in the south and a little less in the north. All Finnish waters are subject to some surface freezing during the winter.

Vegetation and animal life. Much of Finland is dominated by conifers, but in the extreme south there is a zone of deciduous trees, comprising mainly hazel, aspen, maple, elm, lime, and alder. The conifers are mainly pine and spruce. Pine extends to the extreme far north, where it can be found among the dwarf Arctic birch and pygmy willow. Lichens become increasingly common and varied in kind toward the north. In autumn the woods are rich in edible fungi. More than 1,000 species of flowering plants are recorded. The sphagnum swamps, which are widespread in the northern tundra or bogland area, yield harvests of cloudberries and, less happily, plagues of mosquitoes.

Finland is relatively rich in wildlife. Seabirds, such as the black-backed gull and the Arctic tern, nest in great numbers on the coastal islands; waterfowl, such as the black and white velvet scoter duck, nest on the internal lakes. Other birds include the Siberian jay, pied wagtail, and, in the north, the eagle. Many birds migrate southward in winter. Native woodland animals include bear, wolf, wolverine, lynx, and Finnish elk. Wild reindeer have almost disappeared, and those remaining in the north are domesticated. A noticeable feature, attributed by some to climatic change, is the recent northward advance of flora and fauna.

Salmon, trout, and the much esteemed *siika* (whitefish) are relatively abundant in the northern rivers. Baltic herring is the most common sea fish, while the crayfish is caught during a brief summer season. Pike, char, and perch are also found.

The vegetation and wildlife of Ahvenanmaa is much as that of southern Finland.

The three principal regions

The human imprint. *Traditional regions.* Three principal regions may be distinguished in Finland: a coastal plain, an interior lake district, and an interior tract of higher land that rises to the fells (*tunturi*) of Lapland. The coastal plain comprises a narrow tract in the south, sloping from Salpausselkä to the Gulf of Finland, the southwest plain lands of Turun ja Porin Lääni (province), and the broad west coastal lowlands of the region of Pohjanmaa facing the Gulf of Bothnia. The coastal region has the most extensive stretches of farmland, the most continuous settlement, and the largest number of urban centres. Associated with it are the offshore islands, which are most numerous in the archipelago off Turku on the southwest coast. Further north in the Gulf of Bothnia another group of islands lies off Vaasa.

The "lake district," with its inland archipelagoes, is the heart of Finland. It has been less subject to external influences than the coastal region, but recently its population has increased, and it has become considerably industrialized. The northeast and north comprise what may still be called "colonial" Finland, areas of expansion and development, where many economic and social interests conflict. This area includes, in the far north, the area of *saamelaisalue*, or Lapp territory, the upland fells.

Ahvenanmaa is naturally a region entirely distinct from Finland, not only because of its geographical separateness but because of its seagirt situation. The islands—whose inhabitants are almost entirely Swedish speaking—are autonomous and fly their own flag.

Settlement patterns. Although increased industrialization in Finland, as elsewhere, has steadily raised the proportion of the population living in towns, about 25 percent of the population are still engaged in farming and forestry, and rural settlement therefore remains intensive. Most farms are small holdings, usually owner occupied. Farms are more frequent in the meadowland regions of the southwest, where land is most fertile and where the 9 percent of agricultural land that is used for crop rearing is mostly found. In these areas mixed farming is practiced, whereas in the north farmers usually concentrate on small dairy herds and forestry. In Finnish Lapland there is some nomad life, based mainly on reindeer husbandry.

Urban settlement in the south

Major urban settlement is all in the southern third of the country, with a large number of cities and towns on the coast, either on the Gulf of Finland, as is Helsinki, the capital, or on the Gulf of Bothnia, as are Vaasa and Oulu. The only fair-sized town in the north is Rovaniemi, capital of the *lääni*, or province, of Lappi. Helsinki is by far its largest city, with a population in the early 1970s of more than 500,000, as against the 150,000 plus of Tampere, its nearest rival in size. The other largest cities or towns are Turku, the country's capital until 1812, with a population rivalling that of Tampere; Espoo, Lahti, Oulu, and Pori, with populations in the 70,000 to 90,000 range; and Jyväskylä, Kuopio, Lappeenranta, and Vaasa, with populations varying between 30,000 and 60,000.

On Ahvenanmaa farming is a more usual occupation than fishing; there are mixed farms, as in the southwest of Finland, but fruit is also grown. The population of Mariehamn, Ahvenanmaa's capital and only large town, is about 10,000.

THE PEOPLE

Racial, linguistic, and religious groups. There is evidence of settlement in Finland for fully 5,000 years. Archaeological remains suggest that early people came from or had contact with what was to become Russia and also Scandinavia and central Europe. Peoples of Finno-Ugric stock dominated two settlement areas. Those who entered southwest Finland across the Gulf of Finland were the ancestors of the Tavastlanders, the people of Hämeen Lääni; those who entered from the southeast were the Karelians. The proto-Lapps probably retreated northward before these colonists. Scandinavian peoples occupied the western coast and archipelagoes and also Ahvenanmaa. Present-day Finns, therefore, belong to the Scandinavian and Baltic races.

The two official languages

Finland has two official languages, Finnish and Swedish. The Swedish-speaking population, found mainly in the southwest, in the islands, and especially in Ahvenanmaa, is gradually declining and comprises somewhat more than 7 percent of the total. More than 90 percent of the population speaks Finnish, and the language is an important nationalist feature, although it is spoken in strong regional dialects. The Lappish-speaking minority in the extreme north numbers about 3,800.

Christianity entered Finland from both the west and the east as early as the 12th century. About 93 percent of the population belong to the Evangelical Lutheran Church, a national church the bishops of which are nominated by the head of state. There are one archbishop, whose see is at Turku, and seven bishops; the country is divided into nearly 600 parishes. Just over one percent of the population belong to the Greek Orthodox Church of Finland. The Finnish Orthodox Church was granted autonomy from Moscow in 1920, and in 1923 it was transferred to the jurisdiction of the patriarch of Constantinople. It has one archbishop, with his see at Kuopio, one other bishop, and 25 parishes.

No other Christian denomination in Finland claims more than about 7,000 members. In 1970 just over 5 percent of the population regarded themselves as having no church affiliation.

Finland, Area and Population				
	area*		population†	
	sq mi	sq km	1960 census	1970 census‡
Provinces (*Läänit*)				
Ahvenanmaa	572	1,481	21,000	21,000
	581	1,505		
Häme	6,844	17,725*	581,000	639,000
	7,978	20,662		
Keski-Suomi	6,087	15,764	245,000	239,000
	7,080	18,337		
Kuopio	6,461	16,733	271,000	257,000
	7,727	20,014		
Kymi	4,145	10,736	338,000	345,000
	4,960	12,846		
Lappi	36,267	93,932	205,000	198,000
	38,301	99,198		
Mikkeli	6,342	16,425	235,000	220,000
	8,363	21,659		
Oulu	21,895	56,707	407,000	403,000
	23,609	61,147		
Pohjois-Karjala	6,942	17,980	208,000	186,000
	8,278	21,441		
Turku ja Pori	8,500	22,014	660,000	678,000
	8,886	23,015		
Uusimaa	3,807	9,859	833,000	1,012,000
	3,997	10,351		
Vaasa	10,085	26,119	444,000	423,000
	10,370	26,859		
Total Finland	117,945§	305,475	4,446,000§	4,622,000§
	130,129§	337,032§		

*Where two figures are given, the first is the land area, the second the total area. †De jure. ‡Preliminary. §Figures do not add to total given because of rounding.
Source: Official government figures.

Demographic trends. The population, numbering about 421,500 in 1750, 1,636,900 in 1850, and 2,655,900 in 1900, had risen to 4,029,800 in 1950 and to over 4,600,000 in the early 1970s. This figure includes the approximate 21,000 of Ahvenamaa. In the early 20th century the decline in the birth rate exceeded that in the number of deaths, but in the 1930s the birth rate increased and did spectacularly so during the years immediately following the war. Although the birth rate is now less high again, the death rate rose slightly over the 1960s. In 1971 there was 13 births per 1,000 of the population, as against 10 deaths.

Emigration from Finland was heavy in the first decade of the 20th century, when an estimated 159,000 people left the country. In the 1960s an increasing number of Finnish workers were employed in Sweden. The figure rose from 42,000 in 1960 to 107,000 10 years later. This movement was in part simply a reflection of mobility of labour, but, with unemployment problems continuing in Finland, the majority of these workers were expected to remain in Sweden. Immigration rates are much lower; between 1961 and 1970 just over 3,600 foreigners became naturalized Finns. Internal movements of population have been steadily toward the towns; in 1800 more than

Emigration and labour mobility

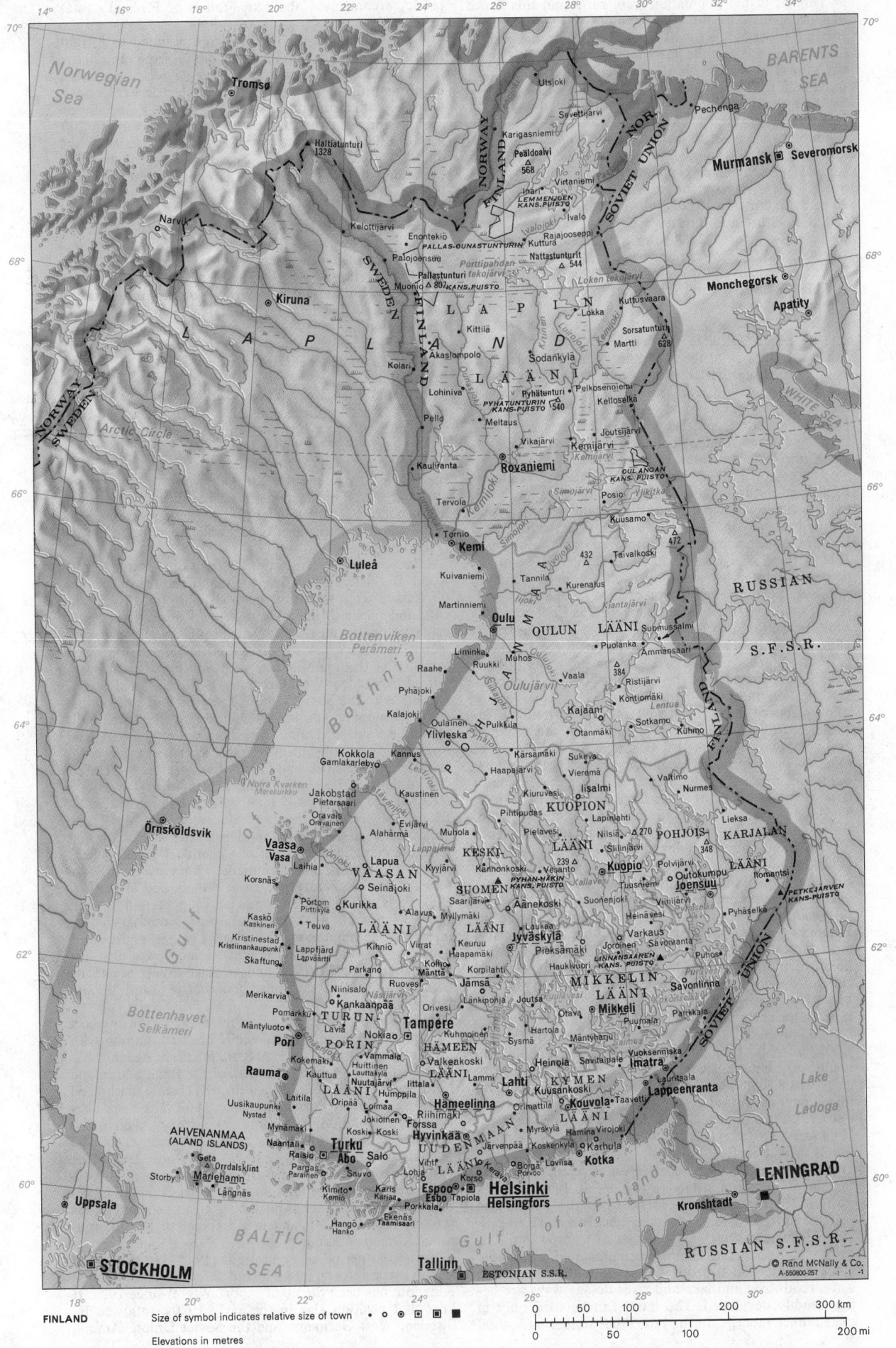

Norwegian Sea

BARENTS SEA

Tromsø

Haltiatunturi 1328 ▲

NORWAY
FINLAND

Utsjoki

Karigasniemi
Peäldoaivi 568 ▲

Kuttura

Severomorsk
Murmansk

Narvik

SOVIET UNION

Inari
Virtaniemi

Pechenga

Kelottijärvi

Enontekiö
Palojoensuu

Kuttura

Ivalo
Rajajooseppi
Nattastunturit 544 ▲

Monchegorsk

Apatity

SWEDEN
FINLAND

PALLAS-OUNASTUNTURIN
Pallastunturi 807 ▲
KANS. PUISTO

Muonio
Kittilä
Akaslompolo

Lokka

WHITE SEA

NORWAY
SWEDEN

Kiruna

LEMMENJOEN KANS. PUISTO
Porttipahdan tekojärvi
Loken tekojärvi

Kutusvaara

L A P L A N D

Koiari

Sodankylä

Sorsatunturi 628 ▲
Martti

L A P I N

L Ä Ä N I

Lohiniva

Pelkosenniemi
Kelloselkä

Joutsijärvi

Arctic Circle

Pello

PYHÄTUNTURIN KANS-PUISTO
Pyhätunturi 540 ▲
Meltaus

Kemijärvi

OULANGAN KANS. PUISTO

Kauliranta

Rovaniemi

Posio
Yli-Kitka

Tervola

Simojärvi

Kuusamo

Luleå

Tornio
Kemi

Kuivaniemi
Tannila
Martinniemi

Kurenalus

Klantajärvi

432 ▲
Taivalkoski

472 ▲

RUSSIAN

S. F. S. R.

Oulu
OULUN LÄÄNI

Suomussalmi

Liminka
Muhos
Raahe
Ruukki

Vaala
Ristijärvi
384 ▲

Puolanka
Ämmänsaari

Bottenviken
Perämeri

Pyhäjoki

Kajaani
Kontiomäki

Kalajoki
Oulainen
Pulkkila

Otanmäki
Lentua

Sotkamo
Kuhmo

F I N L A N D

Ylivieska

Kärsämäki

Sukeva

Kokkola
Gamlakarlebyo
Kannus

Haapajärvi

Kiuruvesi
Iisalmi

Valtimo
Nurmes

Örnsköldsvik

Jakobstad
Pietarsaari
Oravais
Oravainen
Kaustinen

Pihtipudas

Vieremä

Nilsiä
270 ▲

Lieksa

Norra Kvarken
Merekurkku

Evijärvi
Alahärmä
Muhola

Pielavesi

KUOPION
LÄÄNI

Siilinjärvi

POHJOIS-

348 ▲

KARJALAN

Vaasa
Vasa
Laihia
Lapua

KESKI-

239 ▲
Kannonkoski
Vesanto

Kuopio
Polvijärvi

Outokumpu
Iitomantsi

LÄÄNI

Korsnäs

VAASAN

Seinäjoki
Saarijärvi

PYHÄN-HÄKIN KANS. PUISTO

Tuusniemi

Joensuu

Pörtom
Pirttikylä

Alavus
Myllymäki

Äänekoski

Heinävesi

Pyhäselkä

PETKEJÄRVEN KANS-PUISTO

Kaskö
Kaskinen
Teuva

Kuortane
Kihniö
Virrat

LÄÄNI
Keuruu
Kolho

LÄÄNI
Haapamäki

Jyväskylä
Laukaa

Varkaus

Savonranta

Kristinestad
Kristiinankaupunki

Lappfjärd
Lapväärtti
Skaftung

Parkano

Mänttä

Korpilahti
Hankasalmi

Pieksämäki
Joroinen

LINNANSAAREN KANS. PUISTO

Puhos

Ruovesi

Jämsä

Haukivuori

Puumala

Merikarvia

Niinisalo

Länkipohja
Joutsa

MIKKELIN

Savonlinna

Pomarkku
Kankaanpää
Lavia

Orivesi
Otava

LÄÄNI

Parikkala

Mäntyluoto

TURUN-

Tampere
Nokia

Kuhmoinen

Mikkeli

Pori
PORIN
Vammala

HÄMEEN

Sysmä

Hartola
Mäntyharju

Vuoksenniska

Rauma
Kokemäki
Huittinen
Lauttakylä

Valkeakoski

LÄÄNI

Heinola
Savitaipale

Imatra

Kauttua
Nuutajärvi
Iittala

Lammi

KYMEN

Taavetti

Lappeenranta

Lauritsala

Laitila
Oripää
Loimaa
Humppila

Hämeenlinna
Riihimäki

Lahti
Kuusankoski

LÄÄNI

Uusikaupunki
Nystad
Mynämäki

Jokioinen
Forssa

Orimattila

Kouvola

Karhula

Lake Ladoga

LÄÄNI
Koski
Koski

Hyvinkää

Myrskylä
Hamina
Virojoki

AHVENANMAA
(ÅLAND ISLANDS)

Naantali
Raisio

UUDENMAAN
Järvenpää
Koskenkylä

Kotka

Geta
Ørrdalsklint

Turku
Åbo
Salo
Sauvo

Lohja
Kerava
Borgå
Lovisa
Porvoo

Storby
Mariehamn
Långnäs

Pargas
Parainen

LÄÄNI
Vihti

Kimito
Kemiö

Karis
Karjaa

Korso

Espoo
Esbo
Tapiola

Helsinki
Helsingfors

Uppsala

Porkkala

LENINGRAD

Hangö
Hanko
Ekenäs
Taamisaari

Kronshtadt

Gulf of Finland

STOCKHOLM

BALTIC SEA

Tallinn
ESTONIAN S.S.R.

Gulf of Finland

RUSSIAN S.F.S.R.

© Rand McNally & Co.
A-550800-257

FINLAND   Size of symbol indicates relative size of town   • ◦ ⊙ ▫ ◻ ◼

Elevations in metres

0   50   100   200   300 km
0   50   100   200 mi

94 percent of the population were rural, but this figure had dropped to about 49 percent in the 1970 census. Because most of the towns are in the south, the drift is in that direction, but the development of Finland's "frontier" areas always keeps a small trickle of population moving in the opposite direction.

With a slightly falling birth rate and a changing death rate, the proportion of elderly people in the population is bound to increase. In fact, while in 1930 some 30 percent were under 15, more than 63 percent between 15 and 65, and more than 6 percent elderly, it was estimated that in 1975 the respective proportions would be 26, 64, and 10 percent. Out of a 1972 employed population of 2,100,-000, agriculture and forestry accounted for 408,000 persons; industry for 572,000; the construction branch for 165,000; and the service branches for 911,000. The number of unemployed was almost 75,000. In all demographic fields it seems likely that present trends will continue.

THE NATIONAL ECONOMY

International economic standing

Finland is not one of the world's (or Scandinavia's) richest countries; its productivity is relatively low, but, because its population is low also, the share per head of the country's gross national product is above that of the United Kingdom, Austria, and Italy. Wages are lower than in adjacent Sweden (which, as has been noted, draws Finns into its labour market) but higher than in Eastern bloc countries. Finland was for many years a predominantly agricultural country, and some of its low productivity is attributable to the infertility of the terrain. By the 1970s, however, industry had surpassed agriculture and forestry in terms of numbers employed. Reparations payable to the Soviet Union after World War II, at first a desperate burden, eventually proved a boon to Finland, necessitating the development of heavy industry, which later found markets in western as well as in eastern Europe. Subscribing to the General Agreement on Tariffs and Trade since 1949, Finland is the one associate member of the European Free Trade Association, and in 1969 it became a member of the Organization for Economic Cooperation and Development.

The resource background and sources of national income. *Mining and quarrying.* Finland is not rich in mineral resources; it has neither coal nor oil. A diversity of minerals occurs in the Precambrian bedrock, but mining output is modest. Outokumpu, in the east, Finland's largest copper mine, produces large quantities of copper, zinc, and iron sulfides annually. Limited amounts of iron, vanadium, and titanium are produced at Otanmäki, near Kajaani, and there are new iron-ore developments at Äkäslompolo in the northwest. Some granite is quarried, and cement output is increasing at Pargas and Lohja in the southwest and at Lappinranta in the southeast.

Agriculture, forestry, and fishing. About 20 percent of Finland's population work in agriculture and forestry; most farms include some forest land. Of about 300,000 holdings, more than one-third have less than 12 acres of cultivated land. The main crops are sown grasses and clovers, oats, barley, potatoes, wheat, rye, sugar beet, and rape. In the early 1970s Finland had about 85,000 horses, 889,000 milch cows, 984,000 other cattle, 189,000 sheep, 1,002,000 pigs, 145,000 reindeer, and about 8,000,000 poultry. Animal husbandry has been concentrated on dairy cattle, but there has been serious overproduction, involving a subsidized export of dairy goods and, in 1970, a severe culling of dairy herds. At the same time (between 1968 and 1970) about 200,000 acres of land were taken out of production.

Finland is nearly 65 percent forest covered, and wood remains its most important raw material. But forest resources are running out, especially in the north, and marshland is not being reclaimed quickly enough to provide adequate restocking. The costs of transporting timber from remote areas can often eliminate all profit; adequate exploitation depends on accessibility, and sleigh ways, roadways, and lake and river flotage ways are being steadily developed. The latter can be used only in the summer months. In the late 1960s timber and wood products comprised about two-thirds of Finland's total exports.

In 1970 Finland's total fish catch amounted to 87,000 metric tons. Fish caught include salmon, sea and rainbow trout, whitefish, pike, and char. Some degree of river pollution and also dams built for hydroelectric works have adversely affected natural spawning habits, especially of salmon and sea trout, and there are now more than 200 fish-breeding stations at which artificial spawning is induced. Dry fodder is used. There is some trawling for Baltic herring, which are also taken in the winter by seine fishing (dragging nets under the ice) around the offshore islands.

Hydroelectric and nuclear power stations. Most of Finland's power comes from hydroelectric plants, but the low fall of water makes dam building necessary. In 1971, total production was 23,500,000,000 KWh. The loss in 1944 of Karelian hydroelectric resources turned attention to the north, where seven plants were due to be built on the Oulujoki by 1975, and nine were also in progress on the Kemijoki. Finland's electricity grids are linked with those of Sweden, from where electricity is also imported.

The role of nuclear energy

Two nuclear power stations with a capacity of 440 megawatts each will be erected at Loviisa, east of Helsinki, and will be ready for commercial cooperation in 1976 and 1978. The Soviet Union will deliver the reactors, equipment for the turboalternator plant, and nuclear fuel for a 20-year period. Large deliveries of equipment are made by Finnish industries, notably in the case of ice condensers made under a license agreement with Westinghouse Electric Corporation, the international conglomerate.

Manufacturing. The dominant basis of industry is softwood. In the course of time the manufactures of tar and pitch have given way to sawn goods, pulp (mostly chemical), and paper. Mills are situated on lakes, rivers, and estuaries, while integrated plants produce wallboard, plywood, and veneer. A further sophistication of the wood industry is the manufacture of furniture, which is exported to Sweden, West Germany, and the United States, as well as to the Soviet Union. The iron and steel industry is developing, and in the 1960s a new plant was built at Raahe, south of Oulu. The number of engineering and shipbuilding establishments greatly increased after 1944. Railway rolling stock and locomotives are manufactured at Tampere, while shipbuilding is centred at Turku and Helsinki, icebreakers and luxury liners being a specialty. Electrical goods are mainly produced at Helsinki. There are oil refineries, of which the largest are at Porvoo and Naantali, and there are various chemical works where nitrogen and phosphates are made. There are textile factories at Turku, Tampere, Vaasa, Forssa, and Hyvinkää. Helsinki is said to have Europe's largest porcelain factory, while Riihimäki, Karhula, Iittala, and Nuutajärvi have international reputations for glass. Leather and pewter goods are also made. Beer is brewed and vodka distilled, and liqueurs, soft drinks, and various sweets are made from cloudberries, currants, gooseberries, and lingonberries.

Finance and foreign trade. Finland is seriously short of capital and since World War II has, in common with most other countries, suffered from inflation. Responsibility for financial stability is a task of the Bank of Finland (Suomen Pankki), established in 1811 and guaranteed and supervised by Parliament since 1868. The bank controls the circulation of the national currency, which Finland has had since 1860. The markkaa (made up of 100 pennia) was devalued in 1949, 1957, and 1967. The bank fixes interest rates, which are usually high. It provides a clearinghouse for commercial banks and in fact is one itself, although it has no private customers and grants few private loans. Finland is a member of the International Monetary Fund.

During the period of reparations (1944–52), the Soviet Union made inroads into Finland's trade, but the United Kingdom has been the main export market since 1921. It kept that position also in the early 1970s, followed by Sweden, West Germany, and the Soviet Union. Among other export markets are the United States, The Netherlands, and France. The main imports are from Sweden, followed by West Germany, the United Kingdom, the Soviet Union, and the United States. Trade relations with the Soviet Union are maintained by a series of five-year agreements, the fifth of which covered the period 1971 to 1975. In 1969 a total of 65 percent of Finland's trade was with countries of the European Economic Community (EEC) and of EFTA. The most valuable exports are wood and wood products, but heavy machinery and transport equipment were growing in importance in the early 1970s.

Economic policies and taxation. Beside maintaining internal financial stability, the government needs to achieve a healthy external balance of payments position. Attempts to counter inflation included the introduction of wage and price controls from 1968. Fluctuations in external trade (Finland had deficits in 1967, 1969, and 1970 but a surplus in 1968) have led to the imposition of some import controls. Increasing investment is made, especially in the public services, industry, and agriculture, but much more is required.

Finland derives its highest revenue from sales duties, followed by income tax and taxes on property, inheritance, and gifts. Of current expenditure, about one-third goes to education and social services. State business enterprises include an alcohol monopoly and softwood processing plants, and the state holds substantial share capital in commercial organizations.

Transportation. Until comparatively recently, the problems posed to internal communications and transport by Finland's difficult terrain and weather conditions had hardly been tackled, and communities were very isolated. External communications were mainly by sea and, especially as a result of the period of Swedish rule, account for the series of well-developed ports on the Gulf of Bothnia and the Gulf of Finland.

In 1971 there were just over 45,000 miles (about 73,600 kilometres) of roads in Finland, of which about 66 miles were major motorways. There is a quite good network of major and minor roads, but the lakes tend to make routes indirect in the southeast, while north of the Arctic Circle the roads are still few. One-third of the public roads are paved. Bridges and car ferries are beginning to assist road travel in the lakeland areas and in the island archipelagoes, as, for instance, off Turku.

With only about 5,500 miles (about 8,800 kilometres) of track, the railway system is much less adequate than that of the roads: the southwest of the country is the best served area. The railways are state owned, and diesels are replacing steam engines.

Finland has more than 4,000 miles of navigable waterways, comprising lakes, rivers, and canals. A further approximate 26,000 miles of waterways are suitable for the floating down of felled timber. More than 120,000 ships and about 19,000 timber rafts navigate the canals annually. In 1963 the Soviet Union leased to Finland the Soviet end of the canal linking Lake Saimaa with the Gulf of Finland; it was opened in 1968 for ships with a draft of 13 feet or less and not more than 255 feet long and 36 feet wide. Most of Finland's overseas cargoes are carried in its own merchant marine, which in 1970 amounted to nearly 1,400,000 gross tons. There are passenger liners, and car ferries operate to Denmark, Sweden, and East Germany.

Beside Helsinki, where a new air terminal was built in the late 1960s, Finland has about 16 airports, the most northerly of which is at Ivalo, at Lake Inari. In addition to providing for internal flights, Finnair, the national airline offers international service to various places in the Soviet Union and western Europe and also to New York City.

ADMINISTRATION AND SOCIAL CONDITIONS

The central government. Finland adopted a republican constitution in 1919. Legislative power rests in the unicameral Parliament (Eduskunta) of 200 members elected for a four-year term and in the president of the republic, whose term of office is six years. Executive power is shared by the president and the Council of State, or Cabinet, at the meetings of which he takes the chair. A clause in the constitution specifically stresses that government ministers are responsible to Parliament.

The president's six-year term of office and the possibility of his re-election enhance his powers and provide the country with an important source of stability, in view of the frequent changes of government caused by the multiparty system. In cases of complete deadlock, the president can appoint a nonpolitical caretaker government. Government bills are introduced into Parliament in the president's name; he can refuse to sign a bill, but, if it is passed in a subsequent Parliament, he must then endorse it. The president can dissolve Parliament at any time. He has certain decree-making powers and is the head of the armed forces. The president conducts his country's foreign policy, but decisions on major treaties and questions of war and peace must be validated by Parliament.

Regional and local government. Finland is divided into 12 *läänit* (provinces), each under a governor (*maaherra*) appointed by the president. The provinces are, in the order of density of population, Uusimaa, Häme, Kymi, Turku ja Pori, Vaasa, Kuopio, Keski–Suomi, Ahvenanmaa (which is autonomous), Mikkeli, Pohjois-Karjala, Oulu, and Lappi.

The provincial governor is in charge of the provincial office (*lääninhallitus*) and of the local sheriffs (*nimismies*); in the early 1970s there were almost 240 sheriff districts. Ahvenanmaa, in addition to having a provincial governor, has its own local council, elected by universal suffrage, and a county executive board. The provinces are divided into communes, which may be rural or urban in character. The commune councils, elected for a four-year term, each choose their executive board. Communes, of which there were over 520 in the early 1970s, are responsible for local health, education, and social services and for such amenities as roads in their particular areas.

Elections, political parties, and trade unions. At the start of the present decade, every citizen of Finland who had reached the age of 20 was enfranchised and was regarded as eligible for election to any position. A bill to reduce the voting age to 18 was passed by Parliament in 1972. Presidential elections are indirect; they are arranged by means of the general electorate choosing a college of electors of 300 members, who then conduct the election proper. In Finland there are always more

Inflation and trade fluctuations

The importance of navigable waterways

The role of the president

By courtesy of the Finnish Tourist Association

Barge moving logs along the Lempäälä canal in Finland.

than two candidates for the presidency and sometimes as many as six. Parliamentary elections are conducted by a system of proportional representation. There are 15 electoral districts. The same system is used for the election of the communal councils.

The use of proportional representation in elections invariably leads to a proliferation of political parties, and this is the case in Finland. In the election held in 1970, for example, eight parties won representation in Parliament. Governments are mostly coalition ministries. In 1970, in the first election of the decade, the Sosialidemokraatinen Puolue (Social Democrats) won nearly 24 percent of votes cast; the conservative Kansallinen Kokoomus Puolue, the Centre, formerly Agrarian Party, the Keskusta Puolue, and the Communist People's Democratic League (SKDL) won between 16 and 18 percent; the Rural Party won more than 10 percent, while the liberal Kansan Puolue and the particularist Swedish party, Svenska Folkpartiet, won just over 5 percent each. The Christian League won considerably less than 1.0 percent of votes cast. The Centre and Social Democratic parties have always played an important role in Finland's political life, and have been included in almost every government. The Communist People's Democratic League is also influential.

Finland has both a Finnish Employers' Confederation and a Federation of Finnish Trade Unions, the latter having a membership of more than 700,000. There are also a Confederation of Salaried Employees (with more than 200,000 members) and a smaller Confederation of Academic Professional Associations. Monetary and inflationary troubles have caused periodical unrest and have resulted in disruptions of industry through major strikes. A few of the important unions show strong Communist influence.

Justice and the armed forces. The Finnish judiciary is independent of the legislature and executive; judges are removable only by judicial sentence. There are district courts, held in towns by the burgomaster and his assessors and in the country by a judge and 12 jurors. Appeal from these courts lies to courts of appeal in Helsinki, Turku, Vaasa, and Kuopio. The Supreme Court, in Helsinki, appoints the district judges and those of the appeal courts. The chancellor of justice (*oikeuskansleri*) is the supreme judicial authority and also acts as public prosecutor.

By the Treaty of Paris (1947), made with the Allied Powers after World War II, Finland may maintain an army of 34,000 men, an air force of 3,000 men and 60 aircraft (bombers being forbidden), and a navy of 4,500 men with ships to a total tonnage of 10,000. All male citizens between the ages of 19 and 60 are liable for military service. Most undergo training lasting from 240 to 330 days, and the total trained reserve is about 650,-000. In the early 1970s the army consisted of one armoured brigade, six infantry brigades, and four artillery regiments, the total manpower amounting to just over 34,000. The navy possessed two frigates, a training ship, two corvettes, two minelayers, and more than 50 diverse smaller vessels. Its total manpower was about 2,500. The air force had three operational groups, a transport squadron, and various training establishments. The combat units possessed 38 Soviet MiG-21 fighters, as well as various training and transport aircraft. Its personnel numbered about 3,000.

Education. In Finland it is compulsory for children to attend school for seven years from the age of seven. A child may move to a secondary school between the ages of 10 to 13. The state meets a large part of primary school costs, but fees are charged in both state-controlled and private secondary schools. There are a large number of schools or institutions providing vocational training for many professions or trades, including navigation, all branches of agriculture, domestic science, and social science. Additional adult education is provided in worker's institutes.

The only higher education institutions in Finland that were founded before the country achieved independence are the University of Helsinki, founded at Turku in 1640

and transferred to Helsinki in 1828, and the Helsinki Institute of Technology, founded in 1849. The latter was always subject to considerable state control, but the university played an important part, historically, in fostering Finnish nationalism, and the Finnish constitution specifically guarantees its traditions of self-government. There are also universities at Jyväskylä, Oulu, and Tampere and two (one Finnish- and one Swedish-speaking) at Turku. Of these universities and other institutes, including five schools of economics, the majority are privately run, although receiving some state aid.

Health and welfare services and housing. Social security in Finland comprises a system of pensions and care for the aged, unemployment benefits, and family welfare schemes. The state pays disability pensions and old age pensions to those persons 65 years of age and older. The cost of these pensions is met from premiums originally paid by the beneficiaries, payments by employers, and by the central and local government. The Central Pensions Security Institute administers a further, earnings-related old age pension, available also to farmers and other self-employed people.

The Health Welfare Department provides care and attention for the elderly and in 1971 opened recreational centres to provide social amenities for them. Unemployment benefits and compensation for industrial accidents are paid. Maternity benefits were first introduced in 1937 and family allowances for all children under 16 in 1948.

The state does not supply free medical services but reimburses the patient to an average of 60 percent of his medical costs. From 1946 students have had a comprehensive medical care and insurance scheme.

The National Board of Housing supervises problems of supply and development in its area. There is a general housing shortage, acute in the towns and especially so in Helsinki. Property values and rents are high. Low-income families are eligible to obtain state-subsidized flats, and government loans for mortgages are also obtainable. Houses, whether of traditional Nordic style or of imaginative new architectural form, are still usually timber built, although such material as concrete is used for apartment blocks.

The police authorities are subordinated by the Ministry for Internal Affairs. The cities pay to the state a part of the expenses for the local police force.

Social conditions. Finland shares many of the economic problems of the developed countries, notably balance of payment deficits and steady inflation. Between 1960 and 1966, for example, the cost of living rose by an average of nearly 5 percent each year; during 1967 it was nearly 6 percent and in 1968 nearly 9 percent. A slowing down of the process to something under 3 percent was achieved in 1969 and 1970, largely by means of imposing wage and price controls, and has been more or less maintained. But, despite strikes, real wages have not kept up with price rises, and in 1971 the President proposed a general wage increase of 10 percent during the 15 months ending in March 1972.

Class distinctions, based on economic status, are clearly discernible in Finland. Statistics show that the majority of the working population are manual workers, although the trend since World War II has been toward a slight increase in the upper classes (landowners, industrial entrepreneurs, professional men) and the middle classes (government employees, business personnel, white-collar workers generally).

CULTURAL LIFE AND INSTITUTIONS

Finland's national epic, the *Kalevala*, compiled in the 19th century by the scholar Elias Lönnrot from old Finnish ballads, lyrics, and incantations, played a vital part in fostering Finnish national consciousness and pride. Indeed, the development of almost all Finland's cultural institutions and activities has been involved with and forced on by nationalist enthusiasm. This theme can be demonstrated in the growth and development of Finnish theatre and opera, in writing and music, in art and architecture, and also in sport. The festivals of various arts, held annually at places such as Helsinki, Kuopio, Vaasa.

The prevalence of coalition governments

University of Helsinki

The Kalevala, Finland's national epic

and Kaustinen, and the recent proliferation of museums in Finland show an awareness of the individuality and importance of Finland's contribution to world culture. Savonlinna, in particular, is celebrated for its annual opera festivals.

Theatre, opera, and music. Drama in Finland is truly popular in the sense that vast numbers act in, as well as watch, theatrical productions. Beside the 40 or so theatre companies in which all the actors are professionals, there are some in which a few professionals or even the producer alone are supplemented by amateur performers. There are amateur theatrical companies in almost every commune.

The most important theatre is the National Theatre of Finland, established in 1872 with the dynamic enthusiast Kaarlo Bergbom as producer and manager; its granite building in Helsinki was put up in 1902. There are also seven municipal theatres. One of the most exciting in the country is the Pyynikki Summer Theatre of Tampere, the auditorium of which revolves in a complete circle. There are innumerable institutions connected with the theatre, including the Central Federation of Finnish Theatrical Organizations, which runs a drama school. There is a wide repertory of Finnish as well as of international plays. The theatre receives some degree of state assistance.

The Finnish National Opera, housed in the empire-style opera house built in Helsinki in 1879 as a Russian theatre, opened in 1919 with a performance of Verdi's *Aida*. There are about 250 members of the company. Finnish as well as foreign opera is performed, often on modern themes, as in Tauno Pylkkänen's *Opri and Oleksi*, set at the time of the war of 1939 to 1940.

Finland's most famous composer, Jean Sibelius (1865–1957), brought Finnish music into the repertoire of international concert halls; in the other direction, the work of foreign composers has influenced those in Finland. For instance, among 20th-century composers, Uuno Kalervo Klami has been influenced by Ravel and Einojuhani Rautavaara by Shostakovich and Bartók. Yrjö Kilpinen perpetuated traditional folk themes in his *kanteletar* songs, and Tauno Martinen's *Kokko, Bird of the Air* takes themes from the *Kalevala*. The centre for higher musical studies is the Sibelius Academy at Helsinki. An international Sibelius violin competition is held every five years.

Writing, art, and architecture. Literature has contributed particularly to Finnish nationalism. The first novel written in Finnish was *Seitsemän veljestä* (1870; *Seven Brothers*), by Aleksis Kivi. In the 1880s an important group of liberal writers developed. Calling themselves Young Finland (Nuori Suomi), they included Arvid Järnefelt, Eino Leino, and Teuvo Pakkala. The works of Johannes Linnankoski and Aino Kallas were translated into various other languages, including English, in the 1930s.

Gradually writing became more self-critical, and modern techniques were practiced, such as the use of monologue and flashbacks in *Alastalon Salissa* (1933; "In the Parlour at Alastalo"), by Volter Kilpi, who died in 1939. In poetry, free verse and exotic themes became usual. Among its exponents were Katri Vala and Lauri Viljanen. Later followers are Paavo Haavikko, poet and playwright, the humorist Veikko Huovinen, and novelists Antti Hyry, Veijo Meri, and Hannu Salama, whose novel *Juhannustanssit* (1964; "Midsummer Dance") aroused much critical interest.

Literature in Swedish also has a long tradition in Finland. Among 19th-century writers, J.L. Runeberg and Zacharias Topelius are nationally known and loved. A later group of authors having a strong influence on modern poetry both in Finland and Scandinavia included Edith Södergran, Gunnar Björling, and Rabbe Enckell. Representing a still younger generation are the poet and playwright Bo Carpelan and the novelists Christer Kilhman and Jörn Donner.

From the time that the *Kalevala* inspired the paintings of Akseli Gallén-Kallela, there has been a distinctive school of Finnish painters, but the Finnish artistic genius seems more drawn to three-dimensional work. Sculpture is important, highly abstract, and experimental; Eila Hiltanen's monument to Sibelius in Helsinki is composed of chrome, metal, and steel tubes.

Modern Finnish architecture is among the most imaginative and exciting in the world. Its development was closely allied to the nationalist movement, and among its pioneers were Eliel Saarinen, whose work is exemplified by the National Museum and Helsinki's railway station, and Lars Sonck, whose churches in Helsinki and Tampere are particularly notable. Both these men used huge granite blocks.

In the 20th century, functionalism was developed by Gustaf Strengell. In the 1920s Alvar Aalto and Eric Bryggman were partly inspired by the work of the Swiss-born Le Corbusier. Among the most striking of Aalto's work are the Paimio Sanatorium, the library at Viipuri, and Finlandia House, a concert and congress hall in Helsinki. There is general experimentation, using concrete and metals, in industrial buildings and flats and in environmental design, as at the garden town of Tapiola outside Helsinki.

Finnish imaginative design is also shown in furniture, glass, porcelain, and jewelry.

Sport. In Finland the basic national sport, originally a necessity for getting about, is skiing. Nationalism again encouraged the development of special proficiency, which was fostered by ski fairs and competitions held at Oulu from the late 1890s. Finns soon began to compete successfully in Scandinavian competitions.

Nationalism also encouraged an interest in athletics, developed from the time that the Finns took part in the interim Olympic Games held in Athens in 1906. At Stockholm in 1912 Hannes Kolehmainen won three gold medals, and in 1920, 1924, and 1928, Paavo Nurmi, a Finnish national hero, won six gold medals for his middle- and long-distance running. At the 1972 Olympics Lasse Viren won two gold medals. The Finns, and especially Timo Makinen, have kept Finland's name well to the fore in international automobile rallying. Popular sports also include water-skiing, riding, fishing, and shooting.

Newspapers, radio, and television. Newspapers in Finland, immediately after independence, were mainly organs of the various political parties, but an increasing number are now independent. There are more than 200 newspapers published in Finnish, of varying sizes, and about 20 published in Swedish. Of periodicals, appearing once a week or monthly, there are about 400 in Finnish, about 50 of mixed language, and fewer than 20 in Swedish.

The state has a monopoly in radio broadcasting. The Finnish Broadcasting Corporation, which broadcasts in Finnish and Swedish, receives its income from the revenue derived from license fees. There has been television service since 1958 and colour television since 1969. There is one commercial television company, operating from Helsinki.

THE OUTLOOK

Finland shares with most other developed countries numerous economic problems—inflation, unemployment, shortage of investment capital, and trade deficits. But the diligence and enterprise of the Finns, coupled with their sense of national purpose, equip them to deal with their difficulties. Finland's cultural impact on the world, especially through its arts and architecture, is meanwhile steadily increasing; the actual country, too, is becoming better known, tourism growing by about 10 percent each year.

Poised delicately between East and West, Finland has had a difficult political position to maintain. But the establishment, in 1969, of Helsinki as the initial venue of the strategic arms limitations talks (SALT) between the United States and the Soviet Union suggests that Finland is gaining acceptance of its status as a neutral state; and in the foreseeable future the role of mediator and conciliator is clearly one of the most valuable that any nation can perform.

Modern architecture

BIBLIOGRAPHY. Good general books on Finland are WALTER BACON, *Finland* (1970); HILLARD KALLAS and SYLVIE NICKELS, *Finland: Creation and Reconstruction* (1968); and WILLIAM R. MEAD, *The Delineation of Finland* (1968). *The American-Scandinavian Review* (quarterly) regularly contains articles on Finland. For the geography of Finland and general traveller's impressions, HENRY M. BELL, *Land of Lakes* (1950), is an outstanding personal account, by the first British representative in independent Finland. B. PIHL-STROM, *Finland* (1970), is an efficient travel guide; while R.R. PLATT, *Finland and Its Geography* (1955), is a serious geographer's account of the country. Books on special aspects include WILLIAM R. MEAD, *Farming in Finland* (1953); and NILS E. WICKBERG, *Architecture in Finland* (1959). The standard English translation of the *Kalevala* is by W.F. KIRBY (1907), but A.K. JOHNSON produced a new prose version in 1950. See also URHO KEKKONEN, *Neutrality: The Finnish Position* (1970); MAX JAKOBSON, *Diplomacy of the Winter War: An Account of the Russo-Finnish War, 1939–40* (1961) and *Finnish Neutrality* (1968). The Ministry for Foreign Affairs has also published a number of useful publications on Finnish affairs.

(Ed./C.F.S.)

Finno-Ugric Religion

The religion of the Finno-Ugric peoples, who inhabit regions of northern Scandinavia, Siberia, the Baltic area, and central Europe, is an admixture of agrarian and nomadic primitive religion and of Christianity and Islām. This article is concerned primarily with the pre-Christian and pre-Islāmic elements of Finno-Ugric religion.

Geographical and cultural background. *The Finno-Ugric peoples.* The area inhabited by the Finno-Ugric peoples is extensive: from Norway to the region of the Ob River in Siberia and southward into the Carpathian Basin in central Europe and the Ukraine. The history of their geographical dispersion is based almost entirely on linguistic criteria, since historical knowledge is recent and archaeological finds are scanty and interpreted variously.

The Finno-Ugric languages and the Samoyed languages together form the Uralic family of languages, which began to split up about 4000 BC. The original Uralic people are thought to have lived in the region between the Ural Mountains and the middle reaches of the Volga River. Their descendants in the north are the Samoyeds (four tribes of about 25,000 people, living on the shores of the Arctic Ocean between the Taymyr and the Kanin peninsulas). In the south, the original speakers of the parent Finno-Ugric language probably began to disperse between 3000 and 2500 BC, when the Ugrians formed their own group. One branch moved northeast, behind the Ural Mountains: the Ostyaks (who in their own language call themselves Hanti), numbering about 19,000 and living east of the Ob River, and the Voguls (who call themselves Mansi), numbering about 6,000 and living west of the Ob River. The other branch spread southward and made contact with the Bulgar Turks and the Khazars; in the year 895 this branch (the Magyars), together with certain Turkish tribes, conquered what is now Hungary. In this way, the largest (numbering over 10,000,000), but at the same time linguistically the most isolated, Finno-Ugric nation came into existence. Other Magyars (over 2,000,000) live in the countries of Romania and Czechoslovakia.

The Permyak branch of the Finno-Ugric populations living in central Russia split from the other groups between 2000 and 1500 BC; the linguistic differentiation is not very great between the present-day Permyaks, who are divided into Votyaks (called Udmurt, now numbering about 400,000 and living between the Kama and Vyatka rivers) and Zyryans (called Komi, now numbering about 600,000 and living in the region between the upper reaches of the Western Dvina River, Kama, and Pechora) —the differentiation only occurred a little over 1,000 years ago.

Further to the south, the differentiation of the Volga Finns probably began about 1000 BC. The Volga Finns consist today of 1,500,000 Mordvins (including the Mokšas [Mokshas] in the southeast and the Erzas in the northwest) living in a rather large region near the middle reaches of the Volga River and 500,000 Cheremis

(the Mari) living in the vicinity of the confluence of the Volga and the Kama.

When the Baltic Finns came to the regions bordering on the Baltic Sea is not certain. The latest possible date would be *c.* 500 BC (the evidence being the Baltic loan words in proto-Finnic), when the "proto-Finns" still maintained contact with the Mordvins and the Lapps. A much earlier date is possible, however, as there must have been many and repeated migrations by the Finno-Ugric populations westward from the Ural Mountains toward the Baltic regions. Initially, settlement was sparse, as is always the case with hunting cultures, but language differentiation sped up with the change to stable agriculture. The Lapps (called the Sābme, numbering about 31,500) have been the slowest of the Finno-Ugric peoples to relinquish the hunting culture—which has withdrawn slowly towards the north, and they themselves have moved from the direction of Lakes Ladoga and Onega (northeast of Leningrad, U.S.S.R.) to the northern parts of Fennoscandia and the Kola Peninsula (northeast Soviet Union).

After separating from early proto-Finnic about 2,500 years ago, the Lappish language became divided into a number of very different dialects. The oldest population settlements of the Baltic Finns were to the south of the Gulf of Finland and to the south of Lake Ladoga. The most westerly group, the Livonians (now numbering 700, in the north of Courland), is disappearing. In Estonia there are approximately 900,000 Estonians, and they are one of the three most advanced of the Finno-Ugric peoples, the others being the Finns and the Hungarians. Small but interesting cultures are represented by the Votes and the Ingrians (today these are nearly extinct Greek Orthodox groups) in Ingria (near the head of the Gulf of Finland), the Veps (numbering about 16,000 and living between Lake Onega and Belozero), and the Karelians (numbering about 200,000 in Karelia and Finland), as well as the Ludes in Olonets, who speak a transition dialect. The population moved into Finland from the south and southeast; there are at present 4,500,000 Finns.

Ecological and intercultural factors. To attain a proper understanding of the history and phenomenology of the religion of the Finno-Ugric peoples, two basic influences must be borne in mind: the ecological factors and the pressure of alien cultures on the original religious tradition. The result of both factors has been a very great variation in the religious atmosphere in different places.

The Lapps, Samoyeds, Voguls, and Ostyaks—who all have been associated with a nomadic and hunting culture in Arctic regions—retain a religious life that has many primitive elements. The Finns, Karelians, and Zyryans have practiced hunting up to the present, but they have been familiar with agriculture for thousands of years. The peoples on the south side of the Gulf of Finland, such as the Estonians, have long practiced agriculture and cattle breeding as well as fishing, but hunting has not been as important to them. The Finno-Ugric peoples of the southeast, like the Votyaks and the Cheremis, have practiced agriculture and cattle breeding only. The agrarian economy of the Hungarians, with its seminomadic features, is the outcome of a complicated history.

Habitat, climate, and other ecological factors have had an important influence on economy and social organization and on traditional religion. Some of the differences between the various Finno-Ugric peoples, however, can be traced to outside cultural influences. The eastern Finno-Ugric peoples have been marked by Turko-Tatar influence. In the 8th century the Votyaks and the Cheremis came under Bulgar domination; the conversion of the Bulgars to Islām in 922 and the subsequent Tatar domination in eastern Russia (1236–1552) gave added significance to the Arab–Islāmic tradition. In the 16th and 17th centuries, the Volga Finns, the Permyaks, the Ob Ugrians, and the Samoyeds finally came under the domination of Moscow; before this, Orthodox missionaries had worked, for example, among the

Zyryans (St. Stephen, 14th century) and the Baltic Finns.

The influence of Slavic tradition on the Finno-Ugric peoples has been considerable—from the point of view of both folk religion and the more institutionalized Orthodox faith, though some of this influence in many places is late and superficial. Pre-Christian practices were still alive in the early 20th century, and among the Votyaks, the Ob Ugrians, and the Samoyeds there were still people who were unbaptized. Roman (Catholic) and Byzantine (Orthodox) traditions met one another in Finland and Estonia, but the Orthodox groups remain established only in the eastern regions. Most of Finland was converted to Christianity by way of Sweden, beginning in the 12th century, and the country remained Catholic until Lutheranism was established in the 16th century. The position of the Hungarians, who formed a pocket surrounded by alien cultures, resulted in an extremely mixed array of contacts at different levels.

Thus, each of the Finno-Ugric peoples has its own cultural history, habitat, and level of civilization. In considering their religion, all this must be borne in mind. The Hungarians, Finns, and Estonians have the longest literary traditions, while a number of the other peoples are only now becoming literate. Ancient popular belief, preserved in oral tradition, has for the most part developed more freely on the periphery, but near centres of culture it has become a minor growth alongside institutional religions.

The problem of the concept of a Finno-Ugric religion. Since it is not possible to find a single formula to cover Finno-Ugric cultures and religions and since the relationship between the peoples is often distant both geographically and historically, it may well be asked whether there is any utility in attempting, by means of comparative methods, to discover some common or basic substratum in Finno-Ugric religion. Many earlier scholars attempted this enthusiastically, but today there is general agreement that a hypothetical reconstruction representing the "original religion" of a single language family is virtually impossible. That ancient tradition may have been preserved in different regions, although fragmented and adapted to new conditions, is, of course, possible, and indeed seemingly trustworthy discoveries have been made that substantiate this view. One must, however, be extremely circumspect in projecting hypotheses applying to the entire linguistic group. Genetic–historical considerations are of great importance when dealing with those areas of the language family where a cultural connection has subsisted long and late.

The search for a common historical tradition is not, however, the most rewarding aspect of the study of Finno-Ugric religions. The religio-phenomenological approach is equally interesting and significant. In the course of conducting nonhistorical studies of similarities and differences in Finno-Ugric religious material, scholars have uncovered a spectrum running all the way from Arctic hunting and fishing cultures to southern cattle breeding and agriculture.

Mythology. *Creation, cosmography, and cosmology.* The most widely spread account of the creation among the Finno-Ugric peoples is the earth-diver myth. In the north it is known in an area extending from eastern Finland to the Ob River, and in the south it is found, for example, among the Mordvins. This myth, which is well-known in North America and Siberia, is fairly constant in form among the Finno-Ugric peoples; in the Mordvin variant, God sits on a rock in the middle of the primeval sea and spits into the water; the saliva begins to grow and God strikes it with a staff, whereupon the devil comes out of it (sometimes in the form of a goose). God orders the devil to dive into the sea for earth from the bottom; at the third attempt, he succeeds but tries to hide some of the earth in his mouth. While God scatters sand, the earth begins to grow and the devil's deceit is unmasked, and the earth found in his cheek becomes mountains and hills. The eastern Finnish myth contains an interesting detail; God stands on the top of a golden statue and orders his reflection on the water to rise, and this becomes the devil.

Etiological (causal) continuations are common; the devil demands for himself a piece of earth the size of the end of a stick, and from the hole that results vermin emerge— mice, fleas, mosquitoes, flies, and other such living things. Indo-Iranian influence has been seen in the dualism of the myth—setting God against the devil—since religious dualism is most significant in Indo-Iranian religion. A water bird may be older than the devil; it also occurs, however, without the dualistic emphasis. Thus, in an account by the Yenisey Ostyaks, the great shaman (a medicine man with psychic abilities) Doh glides above the primeval sea among the water birds, asks the red-throated loon to dive for earth from the bottom of the sea, and with the earth makes an island. A rarer, but apparently ancient, myth is found among the Voguls; the god of the skies lets earth come down from heaven and places it on the surface of the great primeval sea.

The world made from an egg is a myth best known in equatorial regions, though the most northerly points of its distribution are in Finland and Estonia. A water bird or an eagle makes its nest on the knee of the creator (Väinämöinen), who is floating in the water; it lays an egg, which rolls into the water, and pieces of it become the earth, the sky, the moon, and the stars. Myths concerning the creation of man are found in the north among the Voguls and in the south among the Volga Finns. The common element among all such myths is that man, on the brink of achieving perfection, had his hairy covering transferred to the dog by the devil, whose spit blighted man and made him subject to disease and death. In Finland the variant of yet another anthropogonic (origin of man) myth has been found; a hummock rises from the sea, a tree stump thereon splits open, and the first human couple steps forth.

Finno-Ugric cosmographic (world description) concepts include the following well-known mythological themes: a stream or sea encircling the round world; a canopy of the heavens, the central point of which is the North Star (a kind of nail on which the sky rotates); a world pole supporting the sky; a world mountain and a world tree rising in the middle of the earth; animals carrying the earth; and the nub of the earth and the nub of the sea (an abyss that swallows ships). From these and from other materials more or less coherent cosmographies have been formed in different places; the central components are the sky, the earth, and the underworld. Among the Ob Ugrians and the Samoyeds is found a myth of the seven- or nine-storied heaven.

The cosmogonic (origin of the world) and cosmographic myths have had important ritual functions and have provided the basis for cosmology (the order of the world). When, in incantations and prayers, numerous natural, cultural, and social phenomena derive from these basic myths, it is not a matter of giving an explanation but of finding the connection with the decisive primeval events that gave the world its lasting order. A pillar representing the world pole has been worshipped by the Lapps and the Ob Ugrians, especially as a symbol of the world order.

High gods. The semantic elements "sky" and "god of the sky" are found to be so close in the terminology of certain of the Finno-Ugric peoples (for example, Cheremis Jumo, Finnish Jumala, Votyak Inmar, Zyryan Jen, Samoyed Num) that the association cannot be a recent phenomenon. The tradition of the god of the sky is many layered, and the influence of monotheism, especially of Christianity and Islām, is widely exhibited. This influence was evidently preceded by that of ancient southern high cultures. Thus the Cheremis Jumo has a real court with servants in his heaven, and these servants act as intermediaries between men and the god of the sky. This indicates a Turko-Tatar influence, which can also be seen in the Votyak Inmar; Christian elements, however, are also found (Inmar's mother is related to the Virgin Mary). "Great," the most common epithet for Inmar and Jumo, reminds one of Allāh. The Mordvin god of the sky (Škaj, "creator, birth giver," among the Mokša people, and also Ńiśké-pas, "the great inseminating god") is the chief of the gods, all knowing and all seeing, who is not approached for trivial things. He appears, however, very

---

Difficulties involved in the study of Finno-Ugric religion

Cosmic egg myth

concretely in a festival connected with the beginning of the spring ploughing. In this festival an old man represents the god of the sky and from an attic or a tree answers questions put to him by people who pray about health, the grain harvest, the weather, and other matters.

Sky gods The gods of the sky of the Arctic Finno-Ugric peoples (Samoyed Num; Ostyak Num-Turom, Sängke; Vogul Num-Tarom; Lappish Tiermes, Horagalles, and Radien) are the high gods of hunting and nomadic cultures, which sometimes appear in myths as creator gods and culture heroes (often as *dei otiosi,* or "inactive gods," without a cult) and sometimes as venerated gods of the economy (as the promoters of fishing, hunting, and reindeer herding), especially as weather gods. Originally the Finno-Ugric peoples probably had no concept of a hierarchic family of gods with its supreme god acting as chief man; the attribute found in many places, "lofty" or "high" merely means "being above"—that is to say, a god appearing in the sky.

The concept of a begetting sky is stressed in southern agricultural cultures, in which an increasing importance of the "earth mother" may be observed; it is no longer a mere local field spirit but rather has the role of a great birth giver. "The god of the sky is our father, and the earth mother is our mother," say the Mordvins. The earth mother's function is not limited to field sacrifices, but also includes child giving; she is the begetter *par excellence.*

System of spirits. The high gods are usually encountered in connection with a rite; they are distant, invisible, and do not make surprise visits. With the guardian spirits, however, matters are different. They are first and foremost supranormal beings that appear in definite visions, auditory experiences, and other such occurrences. They appear especially when a social norm involving a guardian-spirit sanction is broken. The guardian spirits—along with the spirits of the dead—are significant as important regulating factors in daily behaviour and normally are solitary local spirits, believed to "govern" and "own" a particular area: a cultural locality (*e.g.,* household spirits), a natural region (*e.g.,* guardian spirits of forest or water), and a natural element or phenomenon (*e.g.,* fire spirits or wind spirits). There are also special guardians (of man or of treasure) and various demonic beings that—though similar to the guardian spirits—are not worshipped.

The names of guardian spirits are normally compounds of words, the first element of which indicates the sphere of action, the second being a name such as "man" or "master" (Votyak Korka-murt, "house-man," Vu-murt, "water-man"), "old man" or "old woman" (Cheremis Pört-kuguza, "the old man of the house," or Pört-kuwa, "the old woman of the house"), or "father" or "mother" (Mordvin Jurt-at'a, Jurt-ava). The system of social values is revealed by the system of guardian spirits; the home spirit protects the luck of the home; the cattle spirit watches over the cattle during the winter (in the summer the cattle come under the forest spirit); the barn spirit looks after threshing luck. In representing these values the spirit may appear in a number of roles. Thus, the Ingrian house spirit appears as "owner," the original owner of the plot on which a house is built; "moralist," punisher of crimes against norms that may endanger the luck of the house; and "sympathizer," one who warns in advance of catastrophes threatening house or family. With some peoples—the Mordvins, for example—the guardian-spirit system is very specific and there is a very large number of spirits; with others, such as the Arctic Lapps, the Samoyeds, and the Ob Ugrians, there are fewer of them, and Herr der Tiere (Master of Animals) game spirits predominate.

Sacred ancestors. The oldest form of Finno-Ugric religion is thought to be ancestor worship. Some of the main terms (*e.g.,* "grave," "hades," and "soul") go back several millennia. The cult concerned only dead members of the family; other dead beings were experienced as restless haunters, and aggressive expelling rites were used to dispel them. The worship of ancestors must be understood as a family institution in which intercourse between the living and the dead is the internal activity of a social primary group. The dead belong to the family, and they have both rights and duties; they protect the happiness of the family, assist it in its means of livelihood, and receive their share of the produce; they are also considered to be counsellors, moralists, and judges. The cult of the dead can be divided in the following manner: (1) rites at the moment of death; (2) funeral preparations (washing the corpse, attiring it, and watching by it; making the coffin); (3) the committal; (4) celebrations in memory of a single dead person; (5) annual memorial ceremonies for the dead; (6) offerings and prayers to the dead in connection with earning the means of subsistence; and (7) occasional rites (*e.g.,* when moving to a new place or during illness).

Ancestor-cult rites

The most important of the ritual ceremonies for a dead person are those that take place during the transition period, which may last for six weeks and may include addressing the departed euphemistically and in dirges. The departed person remains in the dwelling place, separated from his body; agreements are made with him about the distribution of property; he is given advice about how to live on the other side; he is invited to return for the celebration of his anniversary; and so on. The most important matter is the ensurance of harmony between the newly departed and his relations in the graveyard. Of central importance in the collective worship of the dead is the visit of the departed members to their old home; among the Eastern Finno-Ugric peoples this approximates with the Christian feast of Easter, and among the Western it is in late autumn (*e.g.,* the Finnish *kekri,* November 1, an ancient festival to celebrate the seasonal change). Living members of the family also visit the graves on the anniversary days of the departed. Customs among the Arctic Lapps, the Samoyeds, and the northern Ostyaks differ somewhat from the above; among the Lapps, the departed person is represented by a clothed log and among the Ostyaks and the Samoyeds by a doll-effigy that is kept for as long as three years.

The other world is viewed as two-storied and consists of (1) a graveyard hades, or underground village of the dead in a holy forest near the village; and (2) a distant hades, far in the north behind the burning stream (with an admixture of paradise concepts). Name-giving rites suggest continuity and reincarnation; a child is given the name of a dead relative, and the child thereby is believed to receive the personality of the deceased relation. If the result is unsuccessful, a name-changing rite can be performed.

Divine heroes. Hero worship in Finno-Ugric religion does not point to culture heroes who are described in myth and whose actions are located in cosmogonic contexts. In general, culture heroes are not worshipped. The matter is otherwise when dealing with divinized historical figures, the cults of which are found among several of the Finno-Ugric peoples. Mardan of the Yelabuga Votyaks is viewed as the progenitor of 11 villages and the one who led the dwellers therein from the north to their present habitations. There is a sacrificial ceremony in his honour every year. Also, there are signs of the worship of tribal chiefs, for example in the forest sanctuary worship of the Votyaks (*lud*) and the Volga Finns (*keremet*). The best known of the Cheremis princes, called "the old man of the Nemda mountain," is a great ancient warrior under whose rule the people were strong and united. According to this myth, he promised to return when war threatened; once he was called for unnecessarily and after discovering the betrayal, he ordered an annual propitiation sacrifice, a foal. The Ob Ugrians have a large number of "local gods" of whom pictures have been made and who are sometimes associated with ancient mighty men or Christian heroes and saints. A death doll made from a shaman may also have been the origin of a hero cult; the Samoyeds have been known to cherish and feed such a doll for as long as 50 years.

Sacred animals. In the "hunters' religion" preserved among the northern Finno-Ugric peoples, bear ceremonies are central. The Ostyaks, Voguls, Samoyeds, Lapps, Finns, and Karelians have all been acquainted with myths and rites connected with the bear. The myths recount that the bear is of heavenly origin and is the son of the god of

Bear ceremonies

the sky; it descends from heaven and, when it dies, returns there. There is also a story about a marriage between a bear and a woman from which a tribe of the Skolt Lapps (in Finland) is said to be descended. The bear-killing ceremony is divided into two acts—the killing itself and the feast afterward. Killing a bear that was protected by a forest guardian spirit involved a complicated ritual, which ended with bringing the bear home. Women believed that they had to keep at a distance so that the bear would not make them pregnant. The feast to celebrate the killing of the bear lasted two days and was full of marriage symbolism. The bear was addressed euphemistically, and a young man or woman was chosen to be its mate. A large meal made of the meat of the bear was consumed. Finally, the skull of the bear was carried in procession to the branch of a pine tree on the top of a mountain. This was the custom in Karelia. A number of miniature dramas were connected with Ob Ugrian bear rites. Masked participants tell the bear that members of a strange tribe have killed it.

The exogamic patrilineal clans (involving marriage outside a particular group) of the Ob Ugrians are often known by animal names—"bear," "falcon," "frog," or "dog." The animal is regarded as the manifestation (*epiphania*) of the family guardian spirit and is not allowed to be killed or eaten. Evidence of totemistic systems, in which animals are associated with blood-related groups, has been found among the Lapps and the Samoyeds. Some scholars consider the names of relations (animal names) found among other Finno-Ugric peoples, such as the Hungarians and Karelians, as evidence of a lost totemism.

Institutions and practices. *Cult authorities.* The male head of the family has long had a central role in leading different home and family cults. In the *lud* sanctuaries of the Votyaks, for example, worship was performed by members of the family; the head of the family had the responsibility of organizing the cult and the task was hereditary. Women also were able to supervise certain minor home rituals—such as those performed in connection with cattle breeding (offerings to the guardian spirit of the cattle shed and the forest). In hunting and nomadic cultures, the head man (*e.g.*, the oldest of the hunting party or the reindeer chief) supervised the rites. The official authorities of the rites (*i.e.*, the religious specialists) among the Finno-Ugric peoples were of the following types: shamans (among the Samoyeds and the Lapps); seers (the counterparts of the shaman among southern peoples); sacrificing priests (the leaders of the annual rites, especially in cattle-breeding cultures and agricultural communities); guardians of the sanctuary (the protectors of holy groves, buildings, and other places and the controller of the rites); professional weeping women (the "vocalists," especially of the cult of the dead but also of weddings, who were the verbal expressers of the content of the ritual); the masters of ceremonies at weddings; and many more. The shaman had many and various tasks in Arctic regions, but further south particular tasks were undertaken by various cult authorities: the seer (healing and counselling) and the weeping woman, or psychopomp (*i.e.*, "conductor of souls"), guiding the soul to the other world. The two last-mentioned are verbal ecstatics; the task of the seer, especially in solving critical problems, was of the utmost importance. The task of the sacrificing priest was more of a routine affair, but among the Volga Finns and the Permyaks, for example, the long and skillful prayers as well as the complex ceremonies performed by the priests required great professional competence.

Home and forest sanctuaries

Cult centres. The home sanctuary of the Votyaks is a *kuala*, a primitive log cabin near the dwelling house. In a corner at one end of the *kuala* is a shelf, at the height of a man, on which there are branches of deciduous trees and conifers, and on top of them a *voršud* (a box with a lid). A weekly offering is made here. Another Votyak sanctuary is the *lud*—a fenced-off area in an isolated place in the forest. In the middle is a primitive table for sacrificial gifts. In the *lud* regular animal sacrifices are offered and occasional crisis rites performed (sacrifices to dispel accidents or disease). The cult group in both *kuala*

and *lud* is the family; the office of the sacrificing priest of the *lud* is hereditary, and in the principal house of the family there is a great *kuala*, which is visited three times a year in addition to the offerings made in the small *kuala* at home. The small *kuala* is built on a foundation of earth and ashes brought from the big *kuala*. The system is exogamous—the woman visiting the *kuala* of her own father and not that of her husband's father. The Votyaks also have large groves near a spring or a brook in the vicinity of a village, where common sacrifices for the whole village are made. There are, in addition, larger sacrificing groups, which may include dozens of villages and which meet every third year for a festival lasting many weeks. The Volga Finns also have fenced-in *keremet* groves for the family cult and places of worship common to the whole village. Evidence also exists concerning sacrificial groves among the Baltic Finns and from group villages in Karelia and Ingria. In the thinly populated parts of Finland, the family cult took place either at cup stones (sacrifice stones with shallow cuplike depressions) or at holy trees. Among the nomadic Lapps (those involved in reindeer herding and fishing) *seita* (sacrificial stone) places for worship arose near a reindeer migration route or a good fishing place, and for such a place an outstanding stone generally was chosen. The Ob Ugrians had a kind of "mobile temple" for the wooden idols (normally kept in the corner of the house) that were placed on special sledges.

Cult practices. All the main categories of rites are found among the Finno-Ugric peoples: cyclic rites (concerning the means of livelihood), rites of passage (the transition of the individual from one status to another), and crisis rites (concerning threats of disaster). The character of these rites varies considerably, depending on ecological factors and cultural contacts. Generally, an agrarian culture produces a cult system that is more stable and formal than that produced by a mobile hunting culture or a nomadic way of life. In the latter, sacrifice rites tend to be more improvised and the cult group smaller. An example of a formal system is the distinction "upward" and "downward" in worship found among the Votyaks and the Cheremis; sacrifices of white animals are made in deciduous groves to the god of the sky and to certain nature gods, the direction of prayer being to the south; sacrifices of black animals are made to the departed and to the guardian spirits of the earth near conifers, the direction of prayer being to the north.

Conclusion. Two phenomena may be consistently observed with regard to the religious customs of the Finno-Ugric peoples. These are the ecological adaptation of religion and the stratification of tradition in connection with acculturation. A number of examples of the former have already been given. As far as acculturation is concerned, it may be said that the "syncretism" it produces does not result in any conflict in the religious field, except perhaps for short periods of adjustment. Old and new elements of different origins are moulded into an active system, and choice and adaptation take place according to practical religious need. Christianity and Islām have in many places provided a religious superstructure, but they have not been accepted as such; certain elements from them have been adapted to the depth structure of a primitive religion. The best example of this is the preservation of folk religion in Hungary, Finland, and Estonia, where Christianity, supported by a literate culture, is ancient. Popular belief has become intertwined with the religious tradition because it has always had a function that no Christian practice has replaced. Only mass media and urbanization have jeopardized the ancient belief tradition.

BIBLIOGRAPHY. A comprehensive presentation of "Finno-Ugric Mythology" by UNO HOLMBERG-HARVA is published in the *Mythology of All Races*, vol. 4 (1927, reprinted 1964). More recent surveys with extensive bibliographies are "Die Religionen Nordeurasiens" by IVAR PAULSON in *Die Religionen der Menschheit 3* (1962); and "Religion der finnisch-ugrischen Völker" by LAURI HONKO in *Handbuch der Religionsgeschichte*, vol. 1 (1971). References to standard monographs on the religion of various Finno-Ugric peoples are available in these sources.

(L.O.H.)

Fire Prevention and Control

Fire protection, undertaken in order to safeguard human life and property, includes preventing, detecting, and extinguishing fires. It is also concerned with: improving the methods of prevention and suppression by research into the causes of fire; the study of engineering data leading to establishment of standards in building design and construction that will limit fire hazards; the education of the public as well as professional fire-fighting personnel to take prompt and correct emergency action; the maintenance and improvement of fire-fighting equipment; and the inspection of buildings for compliance with established fire-preventive practices.

Modern fire-safe designs

Until after World War I little official attention was given to fire prevention, for most departments were thinking of fire extinguishment only; today nearly all large cities have at least a small staff exclusively concerned with it. Modern engineers and architects have discarded the fictitious notion of fireproof construction; their fire-safe designs seek to limit interior combustibles so that fires will be slower, to build cutoffs and compartmentalize structures so that fires will be smaller, to minimize the probability of a source of ignition coming in contact with combustible material, to include facilities for rapidly detecting and extinguishing fires, and to provide space around buildings, thus giving easy access to fire fighters. Once a building is built, periodic inspection helps to insure compliance with fire codes.

Table 1: Fire Statistics for Selected Countries*

	population (000)	number of fire deaths	number of fires	loss in U.S. dollars
Australia (1969)	12,372	196	86,000	102,273,000
Austria (1969)†	7,371	88	9,329	22,279,000
Belgium (1969)‡	9,630	76	11,641	...
Canada (1969)	21,089	624	64,667	180,511,000
Denmark§ ||	4,870	77	12,949	43,924,000
Finland (1969)§ ¶	4,688	110	11,900	12,600,000
France (1968)	49,795	219	62,206	190,036,000
Italy (1969)‡	54,280	...	48,180	...
Japan (1969)‡	101,321	1,334	56,304	189,221,000
The Netherlands (1969)‡	12,944	73	17,779	49,815,000
New Zealand (1969)♀	2,786	33	15,657	9,036,000
Norway (1969)¶	3,851	85	10,000	45,080,000
Sweden (1969)§	7,969	110	20,000	48,275,000
Switzerland (1968)§	6,115	...	7,418	12,344,000
U.K. (1969)	55,534	987♂	253,225‡	288,960,000
U.S. (1969)♀	204,180	12,200	2,425,350	2,447,600,000
West Germany (1969)	58,774	...	366,000♂	289,170,000¶

*All figures estimates. †Excludes losses of under 500 shillings each ($19.30). ‡Fire brigade or department calls only. §Buildings chiefly. ||April 1, 1968-March 31, 1969. ¶Paid by insurance companies. ♀Includes chimney, rubbish, and brush fires. ♂1968.

FIRE PREVENTION

A specific fire-prevention program of a company, institution, or government has as its goals the creation of employee and public interest; the planning of safe buildings, equipment, and processes; the elimination of the causes of fire and explosion; the provision and maintenance of protective equipment such as automatic sprinklers and portable fire extinguishers; and the organization of professionals, volunteers, or employees for emergency action.

Policy formulation. A company-policy statement typically stresses the importance of safety, prevention of loss, and the responsibilities of supervisory employees. A city or other governmental ordinance details the duties of fire-prevention personnel, methods of storage and use of explosives and flammables, installation and maintenance of alarm and protection systems, maintenance and regulation of fire escapes and exits, investigation of causes and circumstances of fires, and conducting of fire-prevention campaigns.

Public awareness. Public-awareness campaigns in many cities have had notable results in the removal of fire hazards in homes, places of business, and institutions; the better maintenance of equipment; the better preparations for fire emergencies; and the better public support for the needs of the professional fire-fighting force. In the United States many such efforts are related to National Fire Prevention Week, held during the week in which October 8–9 falls—these being the dates on which, in 1871, both the Chicago Fire and the Peshtigo, Wisconsin, forest fire raged.

Building design. City building codes usually contain strict building-design requirements aimed toward fire prevention and safety. Every area of a building will have at least two separate exits, for example, arranged to minimize the possibility of a fire blocking both. Often an exterior stairway of open iron or an interior stairway enclosed in fire-resistant construction will be provided from roof to street.

Planning to avert panic

Any fire, especially one involving explosions or structural collapse, may cause panic, a major cause of loss of life; intelligent construction plans consider all such potential circumstances. Exit stairs, for example, are separated from floors by heavy, metal, self-closing and self-latching fire doors rated by established fire-testing laboratories to resist fire of a specified intensity for a specified number of hours. Plans also include alarm systems, signs indicating exits, safeguarding of unusual hazard areas such as rooms in which highly flammable or explosive materials are stored, and design of interior finish and contents to inhibit rapid spread of flame. Glass with wire embedded in it may be used in exterior windows to prevent fires from spreading to or from adjoining structures and in fire doors to allow users to see through the door.

Fire-retardant coatings, paints with good heat-insulating qualities, have been developed for application over combustible surfaces and have shown excellent results in reducing surface combustibility. Such coatings, often applied in older structures, help to smother small fires and slow the progress of large blazes long enough for the building to be evacuated and for fire fighters to confront the fire. Another development is fire-retardant lumber, produced by impregnating wood with fire-retardant chemicals—water-soluble inorganic salts including ammonium bromide, borax, boric acid, phosphates, and sodium salts—under high pressure. The treatment of fabrics used for curtains and draperies to reduce their combustibility, while frequently referred to as fireproofing, actually only retards the development and spread of flame. Regulations in practically all countries require that fabrics used in theatres and other buildings where large numbers of people congregate must be either incombustible (as fibreglass) or treated to reduce combustibility. A problem common to such treatments is that many impregnating chemicals are water soluble; thus, each time the fabric is washed, the treatment must be renewed. To minimize holiday-season fires in the homes, Christmas trees are often sprayed with fire-retarding chemicals, a process called flocking. Trees may also be dipped into fire-retardant solution or the trunk may be immersed in chemicals that act to preserve the tree and keep it moist.

Preventing holiday-season fires

Fire-safe construction. A broad range of structures are capable of withstanding fires of specified intensity and duration without failure. Although the structures are relatively safe, combustible materials used in interior furnishings, ceilings, or trim, can contribute fuel to a fire. For this reason, sprinkler systems (described below) are indispensable, particularly in such buildings as factories and warehouses in which large amounts of combustible materials are handled or stored.

Several types of construction are basically fire-resistive. Heavy-timber construction, with masonry walls, timber columns and beams, and heavy plank floors, is not immune to fire, but the mass of wooden members slows the burning; the char that forms on wooden surfaces serves to insulate the wood within. Exposed steel-beam construction with masonry, metal, or asbestos panel walls is commonly termed noncombustible. Under moderate fire exposure, the steel may warp, buckle, and collapse; therefore sprinkler systems are required except where occupancy is low hazard. Ordinary construction, consisting of noncombustible masonry bearing (supporting) walls and combustible interior framing, floors, and roofs—the bulk of which is less than that of heavy-timber construction, is less fire-resistant. Protected ordinary construction has floor and roof construction of one-hour fire-resistance rating (*i.e.*, it will resist fire, as defined by standard test procedures, for one hour), and all openings through floors, including stairways, are enclosed by partitions with one-hour ratings, the minimum permitted or recommended in most places. This type of building predominates in congested areas of many of the world's largest cities. In wood-frame construction, exterior walls, as well as partitions, floors, and roofs are wood, but exterior walls may be sheathed with brick or other fire-resistant siding. This construction can be made reasonably safe for light-hazard, low-density occupancy if enough exits are provided, and combustible interiors are minimized. Sprinkler protection, however, greatly improves safety.

Protection of hazardous equipment. Electrical equipment, internal-combustion engines, storage tanks, pipelines carrying liquids or gases at high temperature, and debris are potential hazards in all buildings. The best protection against most of these hazards is sound basic design, but frequent inspection and good housekeeping practices are always necessary. Flammable-liquid storage requires approved pumps and containers. Where hazards are unavoidable, extinguishers must be provided.

High-hazard processes such as chemical production must be isolated and protected in building design, and personnel facilities planned to minimize danger.

Study of causes of fire and explosion. It is important to ascertain likely causes of fire so that they can be eliminated. A study of more than 25,000 fires of all kinds in the United States over a ten-year period showed the following principal causes: electrical, 23 percent; smoking, 18 percent; friction (from such industrial sources as hot bearings and misaligned machines), 10 percent; overheated materials, 8 percent; hot surfaces (resulting from defects or heat from boilers, furnaces, flues, lamps, and other appliances or processes), 7 percent; burner flames, 7 percent; combustion sparks (released from incinerators and other equipment), 5 percent; spontaneous ignition (sometimes called spontaneous combustion), 4 percent; and cutting and welding, 4 percent. Other causes include exposure to neighbouring fires, incendiarism, mechanical sparks, molten substances, chemical action, and static electrical sparks, including lightning.

Spontaneous ignition

Spontaneous ignition sometimes occurs when combustible solids or liquids are stored loosely enough so that large areas of surface are exposed to oxidation but with inadequate air circulation to dissipate heat. As the combustible material slowly oxidizes (unites chemically with atmospheric oxygen), it releases enough heat to raise the temperature of the stored material perceptibly. As additional air seeps in, the temperature is gradually raised until the ignition temperature is reached. Soft coal tends to spontaneous ignition. Spontaneous ignition can also occur in hay, which should be stored in a cool, dry, well-ventilated barn. In the home, this phenomenon most often occurs among oily rags. Prevention of spontaneous ignition is accomplished either by total exclusion of air or by good ventilation.

CLASSES OF FIRES

The system or classification described below, based on types of combustible, is very widely used throughout the world.

Class A fires involve paper, wood, cloth, trash, and other ordinary combustibles and are by far the most common class of fire. They are most effectively extinguished by cooling until combustion can no longer be supported. Extinguishers for such fires, called Class A extinguishers, may use water, soda–acid, loaded stream (*i.e.*, solution of fire-extinguishing chemicals), foam, or multipurpose dry chemical. (Operation of these extinguishers is explained below under *Fire-extinguishing materials.*)

Class B fires involve flammable liquids such as gasoline, oil, paint, and tar. Because the flames are on the surface, the extinguishing agent must not cause the liquid to flow and spread; this condition explains why water is not suitable for such fires. The best Class B extinguishing agent smothers the fire by cutting off its oxygen supply or interrupting the combustion process; if a suitable cover is available a Class B fire can be smothered.

Class C fires involve electrical equipment and pose the special hazard of electrocution. The oxygen-exclusion principle is used against them. Nonconductive agents in Class C extinguishers include carbon dioxide, dry chemicals, or certain compounds containing halogen elements (fluorine, chlorine, etc.), called Halons (described below).

Class D fires involve such burning metals as magnesium, aluminum, zinc, potassium, and sodium and newer metals of the nuclear age. Class D fire extinguishers employ special extinguishing agents such as the dry powder (described below, under *Fire-extinguishing agents*), and require special training for their use.

Large fires usually involve more than one class of combustibles, and very large fires involve all four. The term conflagration is usually reserved for very large fires that involve many buildings and which cross natural or prepared barriers, such as streets or fire walls. Fires that are extensive in damage but not in area, as in a single industrial complex or group of warehouses, are generally called group fires.

The conditions described as fire storms in cities attacked with incendiary bombs in World War II were conflagrations in the sense of fires burning over large areas, but they differed from peacetime conflagrations because multiple fires were started in such numbers that the flame from the individual fires merged into a single convective column producing so much heat that all the buildings beneath were set on fire. Whereas a conflagration spreads along a defined path, and population can retreat, the fire storm is an area phenomenon and the population is trapped. Life loss in fire storms is likely to be far greater than in conflagrations.

FIRE CONTROL EQUIPMENT

Alarm and signalling systems. A protective-signalling system is designed to accomplish several objectives. First, it must alert building occupants to permit prompt evacuation of the premises; to do this it must be distinctive and take precedence over all other signals, such as paging or music, and it must be appropriate—*i.e.*, visual signals for deaf people or signals limited to custodial personnel only in an institution where a general signal might create panic. Drills are of critical importance in practicing orderly evacuation; the alarm for a drill must be the same as that for an emergency. Second, an alarm system must notify the fire-fighting agency and signal the location of the fire. The system must be designed to minimize accidental or malicious interference. A third function of a comprehensive alarm system is to monitor automatic extinguishing facilities and signal failures. A fourth function is to monitor building functions and industrial processes and signal any dangerous phase, such as a boiler or furnace failure, or breakdown of electrical or air-conditioning equipment.

Special signalling systems

Signal systems may be classified as manual or automatic and with respect to the scope of their function. Local systems simply warn occupants of the protected area; these often have separate auxiliary systems to notify the public fire-fighting force. The familiar fire-alarm box seen in many cities all over the world notifies the local fire station by means of signals carried over wire lines. Remote-station systems may register alarms in an office or fire department located away from the premises. Proprietary systems may transmit signals to a central location, usually in a large complex, such as a major industrial facility. Central-station systems serve a number of unrelated communities or industrial plants.

Heat-sensitive devices. Automatic fire-detecting systems employ a variety of detecting devices, of which the most common are simple thermostats set to a certain fixed temperature. Bimetallic-strip types operate against a fixed contact; the distance the strip must travel to close against the contact determines the temperature rating. A difficulty is that as the strip approaches the contact, a slight jar may cause a false alarm. In the United States and some other countries, thermostats are nonadjustable (that is, they are responsive to heat only at the rated temperature). In the United Kingdom and some European countries, however, the unit is fitted with movable stops and can be adjusted to lower or higher temperatures.

The snap-action disk, also of bimetallic construction, flexes from concave to convex when its rated temperature is reached. The greater mechanical force required to make the electrical contact greatly reduces the possibility of a false alarm.

The fusible link and quartzoid bulb use the same principle; they restrain the operation of an electrical switch until a certain temperature is reached. The solder-type link melts at this temperature; the quartzoid bulb breaks. Both are replaced after operation. In the thermostatic cable system, two steel cables are held apart by heat-sensitive insulating material. At the rated temperature, the covering melts and the two wires come into contact to initiate the alarm.

Rate-of-rise detectors usually combine two functioning elements, one to trigger the alarm on a rapid rise in temperature, the other on a slow rise. These detectors combine a number of advantages: they usually operate faster than fixed-point devices; they can be used in high- and low-temperature areas; they recycle rapidly and, thus, are more quickly available for continued service than fixed-point devices; and they can tolerate a slow increase in room temperature without triggering an alarm. They have two disadvantages: they may sound a false alarm if the room temperature rises rapidly and they may fail to signal a fire that propagates very slowly.

Rate-of-rise detectors are of two types. (1) Pneumatic-tube detectors use a tubing circuit filled with air. Pressure is built up in the detector diaphragm (bellows-like chamber) when heat reaches the tubing and causes the air inside to expand. When the temperature reaches the set point, the pressure expands the diaphragm to close the alarm circuit. The system contains breathing vents to compensate for small temperature changes. (2) Thermoelectric detectors have two sets of thermocouples (devices for measuring temperature that depend upon the electrical current produced when two different conducting metals are joined) mounted in a single housing. One set points outward to sense heat transferred by convection or radiation; the other set is shielded to sense only ambient (surrounding) heat. When one set of thermocouples gets hotter than the other, an electrical voltage difference is produced. When this difference becomes great enough, a detector circuit signals the alarm.

Combined rate-of-rise and fixed-temperature detectors are being used increasingly because they have the advantages of both types.

Rate-compensation devices operate on the rate-of-rise principle but also compensate for intermediate changes in this rate. Their construction is based on a cylinder containing thin struts held in compression, on which electrical contacts are mounted. Because of the difference in rates of expansion between the cylinder and the struts, a signal is given for both low- and high-temperature rise. They also actuate the alarm signal at a predetermined maximum temperature.

The following two devices are used to actuate fire extinguishing equipment; however, any other detecting device can be used to actuate extinguishing equipment.

Pneumatic rate-of-rise actuating devices consist of one or more thin-walled, bulb-shaped chambers or tubing connected to a releasing mechanism. Heat expands air in the system, and this expanded air actuates a mechanical or electrical release. Small air vents prevent tripping caused by slow, normal temperature changes.

Metal-expansion rate-of-rise actuating devices use two metal rods of different size to trigger a small valve at each detector; this valve action, in turn, trips a release that controls a sprinkler system.

Smoke detectors. Smoke detectors are used where the materials stored are likely to create much smoke before generating enough heat to activate a heat-detection system. Some are designed to be placed in heating and cool-

ing ducts. Some are backed up by a heat-sensing unit set at a fixed temperature. Smoke detectors are best located after an engineering survey determines the effects of air velocity, ventilating and air-conditioning facilities, and existing dust or vapours that could affect their operation. All detectors must be kept clean.

The photoelectric type of smoke detector measures the change in current caused by smoke as it partially obscures the transmission of a beam of light. An alarm is tripped when the density reaches a critical value. Lamps usually run on six volts of current and last 5,000 hours. The ionization smoke detector employs a chamber that is bombarded by particles from a minute amount of radioactive material. Oxygen and nitrogen molecules in the air are ionized by the radioactive particles and carry a very small electric current across the chamber. Combustion particles in the air attach themselves to the oxygen or nitrogen ions and slow them down to reduce current flow and increase the voltage applied across the chamber. A sensing element triggers the alarm when the current flow drops below (or voltage increases above) a predetermined level. The amount of nuclear radiation emitted by the radioactive material in some units is large enough to require licensing by the appropriate government agency.

The refraction smoke detector uses the principle that particles of smoke can reflect and scatter light. A small chamber, open to the atmosphere, contains a light source set at an angle to a photoelectric cell. When smoke particles enter the chamber, some of the light reaches into the cell. This light changes the electrical resistance of the photoelectric cell and a signal is given.

Other types include a flame detector that is responsive to the changes of light intensity caused by the flickering of flames; a unit that measures variations in wire tension as a result of heat expansion; and a balanced (Wheatstone bridge) circuit in which products of combustion bring about fast impedance (electrical resistance) changes that upset the balance of the circuit to trigger an alarm.

Single-station alarms. Single-station alarm units composed of a self-contained sensing element, power supply, and sounding mechanisms are of three types. In the gas-powered-horn type, a metal softens from heat and releases gas to sound the horn. Several heat-sensitive mechanisms can be connected to one gas-operated horn. The mechanical type is powered by a spring. When triggered by a heat-sensitive mechanism, the spring is released to sound a bell. The photoelectric (or optical) smoke detector type is powered by house circuit. Several ionization type home alarm units now marketed are powered by flashlight cells. Not having been tested by recognized fire-testing laboratories, these have no established proof of reliability.

Spacing of sensing devices. In most countries, established fire-testing laboratories and safety organizations recommend spacing for fire detection devices. Where there are smooth ceilings and large open areas in the structure, sensing devices are spaced about 10 to 15 feet (3 to 4.5 metres) apart. Devices are installed in all parts of a building, including unused and service areas. Because it takes time for heat to be transferred to reach the heat-sensitive device and its signal-actuating part, the temperature of the surrounding air in case of fire is higher than the operating temperature of the device itself. This is called thermal lag.

Fusible links. In addition to triggering alarms, fusible links, consisting of two metal parts held together by a solder that melts at low temperature, are used as a release element for fire doors, tank and hatch covers, and extinguishers. Once the fusible link melts, electro-mechanical elements take over to close doors or perform other work. Power for operation is usually an electric solenoid or a weight tripped by the system.

Extinguishing systems as detectors. Automatic sprinklers also can be used for fire detection, signalling through a water-flow alarm switch. To overcome the possibility of a false alarm as a result of water-system pressure fluctuations, a retarding device delays transmission of the alarm signal until the flow has persisted for some specified time.

Sprinkler-system effectiveness

Automatic sprinkler installations. Automatic sprinkler systems can be designed to extinguish or control virtually every type of fire. Sprinkler protection involves the automatic discharge of water in density sufficient to control or extinguish a fire before it can build up. Four factors are involved in the effectiveness of a sprinkler system: the system design itself, the building construction, special hazards of occupancy, and the water supply.

Records from cities throughout the world show that from 1925 to 1969 automatic sprinklers proved 96 percent effective, with 65 percent of alarms resulting in complete extinguishing and 32 percent in control until other equipment could be mobilized. The few failures were generally attributable to insufficient water supply or an inadvertently shut-off water valve.

Water damage has been cited as an objection to installing automatic sprinklers. In the great majority of recorded cases, however, fire damage would have been more severe. Precautions must be taken to prevent unnecessary discharge of water as a result of mechanical injury, freezing, overheating, or corrosion.

There are five major types of sprinkler systems in wide use: wet pipe, dry pipe, preaction, deluge, and on-off. In the wet-pipe system, water stands in the pipes at all times ready for discharge. Where the possibility of freezing exists, a dry-pipe system, in which the pipes are filled with air under pressure, with the water held back by a valve, is preferred. Water is released to the sprinkler pipes when the actuated sprinklers cause a loss of air pressure. The preaction system is a dry-pipe system with a smaller time lag between the tripping of the dry-pipe valve and the release of water from the sprinklers. A separate detector sends a preliminary warning signal to the valve, which opens to let the line fill with water. An alarm may be sounded, permitting an attempt to suppress the fire with hand extinguishers. If the fire increases in intensity, the individual sprinklers open to release water. These systems are used primarily to protect properties such as computer areas where there is danger of serious water damage as a result of defective pipes or sprinkler operation. Deluge systems have open sprinklers with the water held back by a central valve. When fire is sensed by the detector system, a signal is sent to the central valve and water is released to all the sprinklers at once. Wetting down an entire floor is an advantage in extra-hazard occupancies, such as where flammable liquids or rocket propellants are handled or stored and where there is a possibility that a flash fire may spread ahead of the operation of ordinary sprinklers, or in an area such as an aircraft hangar, with a very high ceiling where air drafts may deflect the heat of a fire and confuse an individually activated sprinkler system. On-off multicycle sprinkler systems are heat-actuated in both directions—turning on water to the sprinklers when fire strikes and off when the fire is under control. If fire redevelops, the control again turns the water on. Detectors actuate the individual sprinklers as in a conventional system. The on-off cycle can be repeated any number of times. The valves can also be operated manually.

Extra-hazard areas

Variations in building contents and materials determine proper sprinkler spacing. Minimum spacing is normally six feet (two metres); closer spacing is sometimes used with baffles to keep an operating sprinkler from wetting (and thus cooling) an adjacent sprinkler. Sprinklers are positioned close to the ceiling if they are designed to operate fast, because hot gases rise quickly to the ceiling.

Where occupancy hazards are classed as light, effective protection can be anticipated from water supplies and sprinklers; most apartments, churches, hotels, public buildings, offices, and schools are in this class. Occupancy hazards classed as ordinary (kitchens, stores, or manufacturing plants) or extra (oil, chemical, or explosive plants) may require increased protection.

Water supply. Sprinkler systems can be supplied with water from one or more sources: street mains, gravity tanks, reservoirs, fire pumps, pressure tanks, rivers and lakes, and wells. Both a primary and one or two secondary supplies must be considered, because a single supply may be temporarily low or disabled.

Major sources of sprinkler-water supply include direct connections to municipal mains; connections to mains through private water-supply systems; gravity tanks; fire pumps (usually automatic); pressure tanks; and fire-department connections, designed to match fire department hose fittings.

The minimum water flow for adequate sprinkler supply is about 250 gallons (1,000 litres) per minute for light-hazard occupancy and up to six times as much for ordinary-hazard occupancy. Water pressure must suffice to overcome system-pressure losses. The discharge rate of a sprinkler is proportional to the pressure of the water at the sprinkler. As the discharge rate rises, however, the pressure required rises faster. A typical relationship for a sprinkler head of one-half inch (12.7 millimetres) orifice diameter is 10 pounds (4.5 kilograms) per square inch at a discharge rate of 18 gallons (72 litres) per minute, rising to 25 pounds (11.4 kilograms) for 28 gallons (102 litres), 50 pounds (23.5 kilograms) for 41 gallons (164 litres), 75 pounds (34 kilograms) for 50 gallons (200 litres), and 100 pounds (45 kilograms) for 58 gallons (232 litres). Other orifice sizes are available where different flow rates are needed.

Sprinkler mechanism. The discharge of water from an automatic sprinkler is restrained by a cap or valve held tightly against the orifice by a system of levers and links anchored by struts (see Figure 1). The linkage is de-

From *Fire Protection Handbook;* 13th ed.

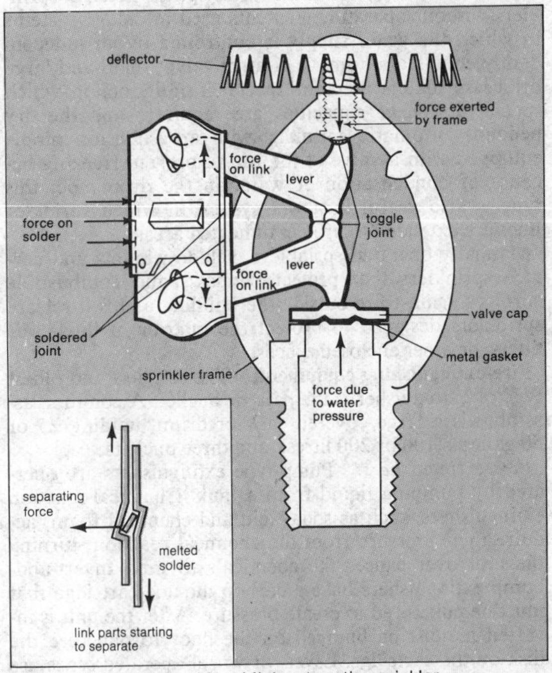

Figure 1: Parts of a soldered-link automatic sprinkler.

signed to give way at a certain temperature. There are three types of automatic sprinklers: (1) The common soldered-link automatic sprinkler is held closed by the smallest safe amount of metal and solder possible, so that operation will be rapid. It usually takes a minute or two before a sprinkler begins to operate over an ordinary fire. This interval allows time for use of a hand extinguisher or early smothering of the fire. (2) Frangible-bulb sprinklers use a brittle glass bulb containing a liquid and a small air bubble. As the liquid is expanded by heat the bubble is compressed and, finally, absorbed by the liquid. At this point, the pressure in the bulb rises rapidly and shatters the bulb to release the valve cap. (3) Frangible-pellet sprinklers use a fusible pellet in a cylinder containing a sliding plunger. When heated, the plug melts and the plunger moves to release the valve cap. Because solder (used in the first type) starts to lose its strength somewhat below its actual melting point, the maximum safe room temperature can be closer to the sprinkler's operating temperature in these last two types.

Temperature ratings of all soldered-link sprinklers are stamped on the link; for other types, temperature rating is on one of the releasing parts. Ordinary temperature-rating heads are used where room temperatures do not exceed 100° F (38° C), as in schools, hospitals, offices, hotels, and apartments, and if they are not exposed to direct rays of the sun. Intermediate ratings are used for ordinary occupancy in industrial and commercial properties. Higher ratings are specified in hotter areas, such as foundries, and in areas in which a fast-developing high-heat-release fire can be anticipated. This difference reduces the number of sprinklers that would otherwise operate outside the fire area.

Water distribution. The most widely used sprinkler (Figure 1) has a deflector that directs the water horizontally and downward in a uniform umbrella pattern. At a distance of four feet (1.2 metres) below the deflector, the spray covers a 16-foot- (4.8-metre-) diameter area when discharging at a rate of 15 gallons (57 litres) per minute. Other sprinklers for specialized uses include ceiling or flush-type sprinklers, whose minimum projection of working parts makes them suitable for installations in ceilings where appearance is important; sprinklers for corrosive conditions with protective wax coatings; picker

trunk sprinklers with smooth deflectors that reduce collection of lint and fibre in such locations as air ducts; side-wall sprinklers used near the junction of walls and ceilings, equipped with a deflector that distributes the water toward one side in a quarter-sphere pattern; sprinklers without operating elements used in deluge systems in which the water supply is controlled by an independently actuated automatic-control valve; small and large orifice sprinklers used for special installations in which special discharge capacities are required; and the dry pendant automatic sprinkler with an extension nipple equipped with a valve at the top to prevent freezing because of condensation of water in the drop pipe; this type is also useful in a wet system in which sprinkler lines are extended to protect unheated areas.

Manually operated sprinklers include window and cornice sprinklers that protect windows and combustible cornices against fire outside the building and full-release sprinklers designed to protect the interior of ducts, air filters, or other enclosed spaces.

Fire-extinguishing equipment. The simplest and oldest type of extinguisher is the pail, or bucket. A common assembly is a large covered cask or drum, holding 25 or 50 gallons (100 or 200 litres), and three buckets.

Fire extinguishers. Pump-type extinguishers are operated by pumping liquid from a tank. Chemical-reaction extinguishers, such as soda–acid and chemical foam, acquire their pressure from the chemical reaction; turning the unit over causes the chemicals to mix. Invert-and-bump extinguishers have a carbon dioxide cartridge that must be punctured to create pressure. After the unit is inverted it must be bumped on the floor to puncture the disk on the cartridge. Lever- or wheel-operated types use stored pressure from compressed air, carbon dioxide, nitrogen, or other gas. They are activated by a trigger, lever, or wheel that opens a valve or punctures a disk.

The type, size, number, and location of extinguishers is a matter of engineering judgment, involving the type of fire anticipated, including heat and smoke. Most modern buildings require more than one type of protection. A hospital, for example, needs Class A extinguishers for patients' rooms, corridors, and offices; Class B extinguishers in laboratories, kitchens, and in places where flammable anesthetics are used and stored; and Class C extinguishers to protect electrical switchgear or emergency-generator rooms. Class A and B extinguishers are normally located on walls (that are marked with a red square or other indication) in places that limit travel distance to reach them to about 75 feet (23 metres). In general, the area protected by each extinguisher does not exceed 3,000 square feet (about 300 square metres). For Class B exposures, the maximum travel distance is usually limited to 50 feet (15 metres).

Fire engines and other motorized equipment. In practically all modern communities, the basic fire-fighting vehicle is the fire engine, a gasoline- or diesel-engine truck that carries hose, water tanks, pumps, ladders, and portable tools and other appliances. Normal life of motorized equipment is about 15 to 20 years, depending on use and maintenance. Normally a third or a fifth of the fire-fighting manpower is on duty at one time. Most cities keep extra equipment available for emergencies and as a reserve when first-line equipment is undergoing repairs or service. The four major standards to which fire apparatus throughout the world conform are National Fire Protection Association Standard No. 19 (North America), DIN-14530 Standard in West Germany, the British National Standards, and the National Fire Service Bureau in Japan. German and British fire-equipment manufacturers supply a large proportion of the world's equipment outside North America.

Apparatus-carrying pump trucks have pump capacities of up to 2,000 gallons (8,000 litres) per minute for high-hazard and industrial service. Most trucks carry a water tank for supplying water before hydrants or suction sources can be brought into use. Much hose is carried. (See discussion under *Hose* and *Transportable Equipment,* below.)

Ladder and rescue trucks are equipped with ladders, forcible-entry tools, generators, lights, and rescue equipment. Pumpers are positioned at the fire for best use of available water; rescue equipment is placed for most expedient use. About one-third of the labour at a fire is in truck and rescue work. Aerial-ladder units and elevating-platform trucks usually are employed for this service; their power-operated equipment reaches higher than manual ladders and can provide effective water-tower service. Besides aerial ladders, manually raised ladders, often aluminum, are also carried. A common arrangement is a booster pump, water tank, and small hose on an aerial-ladder truck. Less common is a pumper–ladder combination. Because pumpers of 1,000 gallons (4,000 litres) per minute capacity or larger seldom carry enough hose to use their capacity fully, some fire departments provide a hose truck or a second pumper with additional hose, called a hose-carrier wagon. Other fire departments have trucks carrying 5,000 feet (1,500 metres) or more of extra hose and heavy, water-stream equipment. Multiple lines often are required to bring enough water across a long distance. Two 2½-inch-diameter (64 millimetre) hoses will move 500 gallons (2,000 litres) per minute over 1,000 feet (300 metres).

Staff and command officers usually are provided with separate transportation in fire-chiefs' vehicles, equipped with warning lights and sirens, radio-communications equipment, protective clothing, water-distributions system, and with fire extinguishers and self-contained breathing apparatus.

In outlying areas, water-tank units, mobile water-supply apparatus, are commonly provided. Units have a pump for filling tanks, suitable discharge hose, manpower space, and a minimum of fire-fighting tools, in addition to their 1,000 to 1,500 gallon (4,000 to 6,000 litre) tank.

Fire trucks with hydraulically operated elevating-platform apparatus, sometimes called snorkels, have become standard equipment (see Figure 2). These vary from 50 to 90 feet (15 to 27 metres) maximum elevation. Equipped with a standpipe, they can throw an 800-gallon- (3,200-litre-) per-minute stream through one or more turret nozzles on the basket at the maximum elevation. Because they can lift a 700-pound (315-kilogram) load in addition to equipment normally carried on the boom or basket (such as emergency lights, short ladders, axes, and communications equipment), the units can be used to hoist men and equipment or for removing endangered persons. Controls are located in both the basket and at the turntable base. Most large fire departments use elevating platforms and aerial ladders as complementary equipment.

Hydraulically operated water towers, capable of elevating a nozzle at least 50 feet (15 metres) above ground level, can provide a stream of water up to 1,000 gallons (4,000 litres) per minute. Towers may be installed on pumpers or on squad (ladder and rescue) trucks.

Figure 2: Elevated-platform fire apparatus, known as a snorkel, consisting of a hydraulically operated boom attached to a truck-mounted turntable and equipped with a turret nozzle.
By courtesy of the Seattle Fire Department

Figure 3: Fireboat in action.
By courtesy of the U.S. Coast Guard

Specialized squad-truck units carry emergency equipment to supplement pump and ladder trucks. Crews are trained in emergency work as well as in general fire fighting. Units carry respiratory-protective equipment, resuscitation equipment, and first-aid and rescue equipment. Sometimes a pumping engine is used as the basic squad truck. Rescue trucks, usually completely enclosed, provide shelter for first-aid and emergency work during inclement weather and are manned by especially trained personnel. Trucks for forest, grass, and brush-fire control carry a water tank, water-type extinguishers, and much light-weight, small-diameter hose. Light plant or floodlight trucks carry a large-capacity electric generator, cables, flood and spot lights, and various power-operated tools. Such trucks usually are found only in the largest cities, because auxiliary lights are also carried on standard ladder trucks and on squad and rescue trucks. Salvage trucks are used in large cities to reduce water damage. Salvage equipment includes covers and runners (large pieces of canvas used to cover furnishings in a building to protect against water damage), sprinkler stoppers, brooms, shovels, squeegees, buckets, dewatering pumps, and sometimes smoke ejectors.

Fireboats. Fireboats (see Figure 3) vary from large seagoing tugs to fast, jet-propelled fire-rescue craft. Their principal services include protecting vessels in harbour; protecting piers and cargoes on the waterfront; protecting yacht basins and marinas; serving in marine rescue operations; acting as pumping stations for fires within reach of hose (often in combination with fireboat-tender trucks); and breaking ice in harbours and rivers.

Fireboats carry much the same equipment as motorized land equipment: pumps, ladders, and rescue equipment. In addition, they have considerable foam-making capacity and special extinguishing agents, such as carbon dioxide systems. Speed is a minimum of ten knots (ten nautical miles per hour); pumping capacity ranges from 500 gallons (2,000 litres) per minute for a very small craft, to over 10,000 gallons (40,000 litres) per minute.

Airport trucks. Airport crash trucks, used for aircraft rescue and fire-fighting service, are equipped with foam or other extinguishing agents. They are usually capable of providing continuous protection, for about five minutes, before backup apparatus arrives. These lightweight vehicles (up to about 8,000 pounds or 3,600 kilograms) are designed to reach the crash site quickly and get rescue operations started in a few seconds; the backup equipment, weighing up to 30 tons (27,000 kilograms) per vehicle, is designed and positioned to arrive before the crash trucks have exhausted their foam.

Hose. Fire hose is designed to be rugged and dependable, capable of carrying water under substantial pres-

sure, yet flexible and easy to manage. Properly maintained hose lasts a minimum of ten years. After use, hose is dried thoroughly. Hose is usually tested annually, for three to five minutes at working pressures. The nozzle is closed so that the hose must take the full pressure.

Suction hose is used on the supply side of the pump. It is of larger diameter (two-and-one-half inches, or 63 millimetres, and up), furnished in ten-foot (three-metre) lengths, and reinforced to prevent collapse from atmospheric pressure. The cover is woven of mildew-resistant cotton, cotton polyester, or all polyester.

If infrequent use is anticipated, unlined linen hose may be provided on pin-racks inside buildings, and connected to wet standpipe systems. Unlined hose leaks water, which makes it useful in fighting forest fires. It has twice the pressure loss of rubber-lined hose. Lightweight rubber-lined hose is favoured for use inside buildings and in connection with sprinkler systems.

Uses of unlined hose

Transportable equipment. Other apparatus is carried on motorized equipment. Pumper trucks carry suction and fire hose of various size, such as 1,200 to 2,000 feet (360 to 600 metres) of double-jacket 2½-inch (63-millimetre) to four-inch (100-millimetre) large-diameter suction hose, 400 to 1,000 feet (120 to 300 metres) of 1½-inch (38-millimetre) hose, and 200 to 300 feet (60 to 90 metres) of three-quarter-inch (18 millimetre) or one-inch (25-millimetre) hose, if reels are provided. The 1½-inch and smaller hoses are for use inside buildings. Solid-stream, spray, or combination nozzles are also carried. A monitor nozzle can be attached to two or three hoses to combine their output in situations where additional "throw" is required; and a distributor nozzle, which produces a powerful stream of water for use in cellars or roof spaces, and a bayonet nozzle for directing a thin stream of water behind a plaster wall may be included. Various tools and fittings for connecting to hydrants and nozzles and for handling hose are carried.

Rescue equipment includes a first-aid kit, wool blankets, and self-contained breathing units. Lighting and power equipment and portable extinguishers also are carried. In rural areas, back-pack manual pumps, rakes, and long-handled pointed shovels may be carried. Salvage equipment described above, may also be carried.

Ladder trucks, so-called because ladders are their most prominent feature, carry a large inventory of equipment, including axes, shovels, picks, rope, pitchforks, six- to sixteen-foot (two- to five-metre) pike poles, sledges, battering rams, bolt and wire cutters, hydraulic spreaders, power saws and blades, blocks and tackles, hooks, gas

Ladder-rescue equipment

and water shut-off wrenches, and a complete assortment of hand tools. Considerable rescue equipment is also carried, including stretchers; a resuscitator; a life gun (for firing lifelines 100 to 650 feet, or 30 to 195 metres, for water rescue); a life net; and pompier, or scaling, ladders that can be hooked over window sills. The crew is especially trained for search and rescue service and the use of self-contained breathing apparatus and gas masks.

All trucks carry portable Class A, B, and C extinguishers. A small pump and hose is often carried. Emergency electric power (at least 2,000 watts), floodlights, and cables are standard equipment.

Ladders are available in many types: folding; pompier; roof; wall; and extension ladders from 16 to 45 feet (5 to 15 metres) in length and from two- to six-man capacity. Ladder steps are designed for placement of the ladder at a distance from the building of one-fourth the distance from the base to the top support.

Nozzles are available for spray or straight stream for one-inch (25-millimetre), 1½-inch (37-millimetre), and 2½-inch (63-millimetre) hose and in a variety of other special types with various flow characteristics. Adjustable, combination, and high-pressure spray nozzles are used, in addition to monitor and other nozzles already described, depending on the specific type needed and the amount and pressure of the water supply. Hose couplings have been standardized by national or other authorities. Where fittings require it, adapters are added to the couplings.

Smoke ejectors are used to move smoke and blow in fresh air in order to reduce smoke damage from minor fires. Heat and flames from large fires can sometimes be channelled through a smoke ejector if this seems advisable. Smoke ejectors are of at least 5000 cubic feet (140 cubic metres) per minute capacity.

Fire-extinguishing agents. These include foaming agents, wetting agents, fog, carbon dioxide, dry chemical systems, Halons, and steam and inert-gas systems.

Foaming agents. Foam apparatus may be fixed or portable and may be automatically or manually operated. Discharge rates vary from low to high volume; the larger systems are employed to protect areas in which paint, oil, or asphalt is used. Foam systems can extinguish oil-tank fires by subsurface injection of foam that rises both to cool and smother the fire. Shutting off the fuel supply as quickly as possible is important.

There are two types of foam: chemical and mechanical. Chemical foam is formed by a chemical reaction in which masses of bubbles of carbon dioxide gas and a foaming agent produce an expanded froth. There are four general types of equipment: self-contained units; closed generators; hopper generators; and stored-solution systems. The self-contained unit has two solutions, both stored separately and mixed before use. Closed generators have chemical-foam powder stored in large hoppers. When the hopper is opened, the powder is added to a generator that mixes it with water to make foam, which is forced through outlets. It is used mainly on flammable-liquid storage-tank farms, where a single foam-making unit can service a number of tanks. Hopper generators, either permanent or portable, permit continous refilling if needed. Lines or towers permit foam application to burning oil-storage tanks. Stored-solution systems have large, permanently installed tanks that contain two foam-producing solutions stored separately. To make foam, pumps force the solution to outlets where they mix and discharge as foam.

Mechanical foam is made by adding a liquid concentrate to water in a 2 to 6 percent (by volume) ratio and by then mixing air into the solution. These concentrates are of two types: protein and nonprotein, or synthetic. Protein types (especially the fluoroproteins) are used to put out fires of hydrocarbon compounds such as oil or gasoline. They can be used with a special stabilizer on substances such as alcohol and ether, which mix with water. Nonprotein compounds, similar to synthetic detergents, are proportionately fed to water flowing through a hose. The proportion can be varied to create foam or foamless liquid as needed. Nonprotein compounds are

used to extinguish certain types of alcohol fires against which unstabilized protein foam is ineffective. Low in viscosity, these compounds spread quickly over the surfaces of burning liquids. They are not effective against burning liquefied petroleum gas and are not recommended for class A (ordinary) combustibles or class C (electrical) fires.

High-expansion foam uses wetting agents in ratios from 100 to 1 to as high as 1,000 to 1, with a very low water content. This foam is mechanical; *i.e.*, it is formed by passing air or other gas through a screen wetted by an aqueous solution or surface-active (acting to reduce the surface tension of a liquid) foaming agent. Principally a smothering agent, it is used to fight fires in inaccessible places such as coal mines and on ships, as well as in ordinary combustibles. It causes minimum water damage. It is not recommended for petroleum fires.

Wetting agents. Wet water contains a chemical that reduces its surface tension, thereby increasing its penetrating, spreading, and emulsifying properties and, thus, its cooling ability. It can be applied as a liquid or as a foam. As a clinging foam it is often used to protect structures from exposure fires (which might spread from a structure that is already burning), the foam acting as an insulating blanket. As heat breaks down the foam, hot water flows away from the protected surface. If a fluorochemical wetting agent (*i.e.*, one containing the element fluorine) is used to make the foam, the foam can be used on certain flammable liquids. Known as light water, this substance was developed by the U.S. Navy.

Slippery water is formed when a polyethylene oxide polymer is added to water in a proportion of 30 pounds per 120,000 gallons (13.5 kilograms per 480,000 litres). It flows more smoothly than ordinary water at high velocity; by reducing friction, slippery water increases the capacity of small-diameter hose.

Tests in Great Britain indicate that the time required for sprayed-on foam to extinguish a fire is reduced by polyolefin plastic balls floating on the surface of a flammable liquid in a tank. In addition to inhibiting evaporation of the flammable liquid, these plastic balls permit the foam layer to form more easily once it is applied to the burning tank.

Ablative water is formed by mixing water with additives, usually high-molecular-weight polymers, which convert it into a thick film that flows like honey, egg white, or even wet sand. Much thicker than foam, these films provide more insulation and act in a manner similar to the ablators (heat shields) on spacecraft that char, consuming thermal energy as they decompose.

Fog. Conventional sprinklers deliver a rather coarse spray, but with a special head a fog pattern can be developed. Flame is a burning vapour or gas about one-three thousandth the weight of water and sometimes only a fraction of an inch or a few millimetres thick. The amount of heat that water will absorb depends on the amount of water surface in contact with the fire. The more droplets that the water divides into, the more surface produced for a given amount of liquid water. Water fog is quickly evaporated by flame or superheated air. Because a small amount of water can be made to vapourize into a large volume of steam, a fire can be extinguished both by cooling and by smothering, with very little water damage to premises.

Fog nozzles have been tested and found suitable for use on electrical-equipment fires. At a minimum distance of ten feet (three metres), equipment up to 25,000 volts can be protected. Fog is also effective in controlling oil fires, which a conventional stream might stir into a fiercer blaze. Fog nozzles protect fire-fighting personnel who might be entering a gas fire to shut off a valve, by providing a curtain of water, and they neither kick under high pressure nor whip if dropped.

Carbon dioxide. Carbon dioxide systems are used to protect areas in which water must not be used, areas in which fire can be extinguished by diluting the oxygen, and areas containing electrical equipment, flammable materials, or hazardous processes. The compressed gas is stored in high-pressure cylinders at normal temperature,

Marginal notes:
Foam-powder hoppers

Use of slippery water

or in an insulated pressure vessel kept at 0° F (−18° C) so that pressure can be reduced. Low-pressure systems permit storage of large quantities more economically than high-pressure systems. Liquid carbon dioxide is delivered through pipelines to nozzles that can deliver up to 2,500 pounds (1,125 kilograms) per minute. Release may be manual or automatic but is delayed until integral warning alarms alert persons working in the area. After a fire is extinguished, the area must be ventilated thoroughly because there may not be sufficient oxygen present to sustain life. Fixed tanks of carbon dioxide with hose reels permit a limited range of fire fighting. Some units may be transported by hand trucks. Hand units are available for small electrical and laboratory fires. Care must be taken not to spray a hot steam line with carbon dioxide, because the sudden chilling could rupture the line.

Dry-chemical systems. Dry-chemical piped systems quickly extinguish flammable liquid or electrical fires; they are operated either automatically or manually. Extinguishing action results mainly from the chemical agent's interruption of the flame chain reaction. (See COMBUSTION AND FLAME.) This chemical agent usually is a powdered mixture of sodium or potassium bicarbonate or ammonium phosphate base chemical. Potassium chloride (KCl) and KCl/urea are also used against flammable liquid and electrical fires, except where delicate electrical contacts are present. Ammonium phosphate also is suitable for fires of ordinary combustible materials. Dry chemicals are designed to be stored in a tank that is pressurized by an inert-gas cylinder or in a pressurized container. Dry-chemical systems can also be mounted on vehicles or in portable extinguishers. The dense stream of a dry chemical has a range of six to 15 feet (two to 4½ metres). The portable extinguisher takes ten to 17 seconds to discharge. Wheeled and stationary units require from 30 to 90 seconds.

Dry powder. Designed to extinguish burning metal, such as magnesium, alkali metals, or nuclear-reactor fuel metals, dry powder is usually dispensed by a special extinguisher or can be simply applied with a shovel. No single powder is successful on all metal fires. G-1 powder, graded granular graphite with organic phosphate added to improve effectiveness, one of the oldest approved powders, is used against magnesium and magnesium-alloy fires and is applied with a scoop. Met-L-X, sodium chloride (common salt) with tricalcium phosphate added to improve flow characteristics and metal stearates for water repellency, is used in pressurized extinguishers from 30- to 2,000-pound (12.5- to 900-kilogram) capacity on sodium, potassium, sodium–potassium alloy, and magnesium fires. X-8, a dry granulated shale-like material mixed with pitch or tar and crystalline ammonium chloride, is effective on almost all combustible metals. Other materials include dry sand, talc, asbestos powder, powdered limestone, graphite powder, and sodium carbonate (soda ash).

Halons. Halons, or halogenated hydrocarbons, are created when methane or ethane have some or all of their hydrogen atoms replaced with atoms of halogen elements such as bromine, chlorine, or fluorine, which change them from flammable substances to fire-extinguishing agents. Chemically they resemble the higher-molecular-weight fluorocarbons used for refrigerants and plastics (*e.g.*, Teflon). The presence of fluorine in a molecule usually increases its inertness and stability; other halogen elements, particularly bromine, increase its fire extinguishing effectiveness. These compounds extinguish a fire by inhibiting the flame chain reaction and ion formation. The U.S. Army Corps of Engineers devised a system for numbering the Halon compounds, which is used worldwide. The first digit of each identifying number represents the number of carbon atoms in the molecule; the second digit, the number of fluorine atoms; the third, the number of chlorine atoms; the fourth, the number of bromine atoms; and the fifth, the number of iodine atoms. Terminal zeros are dropped. Any atoms unaccounted for are hydrogen.

All the Halons are either vaporizing liquids or liquefied gases at room temperature. A very large number exist, but only seven are of importance:

Halon 104 (carbon tetrachloride) appeared in fire extinguishers in the U.S. and Europe early in the 20th century. Unfortunately, the vapours are highly toxic; also, when exposed to flame or hot metal, it can form phosgene, a poisonous gas. Halon 104 is no longer approved as a fire-extinguishing agent for general use.

Halon 1001 was used during World War II by both the United Kingdom and the United States in fixed systems protecting engine nacelles (enclosed shelters for the engine of an aircraft), and aircraft wheel wells. It is extremely toxic, and is not approved for general use.

Halon 1011 is seldom used because it endangers life in places from which people can not evacuate quickly, or in which operators of extinguishing equipment can not avoid the vapours. Developed in Germany during World War II, its present major use is for extinguishing ground and aircraft-engine fires under well-ventilated conditions.

Halon 1211 has been used in Europe and Australia since 1955. It is approved for use in both fixed and portable equipment by governmental authorities in the United Kingdom, The Netherlands, Germany, Switzerland, Australia, and some other countries.

Halon 1202 has been used in only a few types of applications, including fixed systems on aircraft.

Halon 1301, a promising agent to eliminate the smoke and heat damage of a fire, has been used as the agent in explosion-suppression systems, in full-flooding systems where both Class A and Class B fire hazards are present, in museums and libraries, as well as in some passenger aircraft.

It is a liquefied gas, extinguishing in extremely low concentration; only 3.3 percent by volume in air is required to put out a butane fire. Properly used, it has no harmful effects, and if detection is early enough, it acts rapidly. Halon 1301 is quite expensive, but is about 10 times more efficient than carbon dioxide.

Halon 2402, used in Italy and other countries, has proved effective in combination with foam or dry-chemical agents. A vaporizing liquid, it can be expelled as a liquid stream. The higher density of its vapours generates an inhibiting atmosphere that renders flashbacks or reignition unlikely.'

Steam and inert gas. Automatic or manually controlled steam-jet systems are used to smother fires in small rooms or in closed containers such as heaters, drying kilns, smokehouses, asphalt-mixing tanks, and dry-cleaning tumbler dryers. These systems require a large supply of steam and pose a personal-injury hazard from burns.

Inert gas is used to replace a specified percentage of the oxygen in air; carbon dioxide, nitrogen, helium, argon, or flue gas (gases resulting from combustion in a furnace, mostly nitrogen, carbon dioxide, and water vapour) may be used. Depending on the type of combustible material involved and the type of inerting gas used, the amount of oxygen is reduced from about 21 percent to between 2 and 16 percent. The system is used to prevent gas, vapour, or dust fires and explosions, because when the oxygen content of the atmosphere is less than 16 percent, many common materials will not burn.

FIRE DEPARTMENT ORGANIZATION AROUND THE WORLD

In Paris, the Brigade des Sapeurs-Pompiers, founded in 1811 by Napoleon I, looks after the fire protection needs of the entire metropolitan area of about 6,000,000 persons. Marseilles has 640 marine fire fighters, administered by the navy. The rest of France is divided into sectors, each having a maximum radius of about 7½ miles or about 11 kilometres, covered by about 3,600 paid firemen and 236,000 volunteers. West Germany has 59 professional fire brigades with a total of more than 12,000 men; these cover the central areas of cities greater than 100,000 population. There are also 23,500 voluntary fire brigades with about 775,000 men and 500 work brigades with about 15,000 men. A major activity of city fire departments in West Germany is ambulance service. Every fire fighter is trained in first aid, and most fire sta-

[margin notes:]
Liquid carbon dioxide

Powders for metal fires

tions have at least one ambulance. Italy has a single national fire service (Corpo Nazionale-Vigili del Fuoco) of 8,500 paid and 17,000 to 20,000 part-time and volunteer fire fighters. These are organized into 92 provincial commands, coordinated by inspectors from 12 regional centres. These centres have mobile units that can cope with large-scale disasters. In the United Kingdom, the fire service is placed under the authority of 146 counties, boroughs, and special districts—all under the supervision of the Chief Inspector of Fire Services. There are about 23,500 fully paid personnel, helped by about 17,000 part-time fire fighters. Eighteen of Switzerland's 22 cantons have fire-police forces and official fire-insurance establishments. Professional fire brigades exist in six cities. There are about 220,000 fire fighters, paid, volunteer, and industrial. In Denmark, local authorities responsible for municipal fire protection can contract with private firms for fire fighting service; the firms are supervised by the national Ministry of Justice. Forty-four towns and 800 rural communities have contracts; 60 towns have municipal fire brigades.

In the Russian Soviet Federated Socialist Republic, one of 15 republics that make up the Soviet Union, which contains a little more than half of the entire country's population and covers about 17,000,000 square kilometres, there are 72 administrative regions, each with a council controlling a fire-protection department, which administers both paid and volunteer fire brigades.

The Soviets stress fire prevention. As a result, the number of fires per thousand population is a small fraction of the number in the United Kingdom and the United States. The Soviet people are deluged with fire-protection propaganda. The reasoning is that with state ownership, it is only good citizenship to protect communal property. Schools often have their own fire brigades, and children are encouraged to join junior brigades outside of school in which they are provided with helmets, uniforms, belts, and badges—even a fire engine with hose (and an adult driver).

The Melbourne, Australia, Metropolitan Fire Brigade has 45 fire stations and more than 1240 officers and men to protect 353 square miles of land and a population of 2,350,000. The remainder of the state of Victoria is protected by the Country Fire Authority, headquartered at Malvern. One of the greatest problems in Australia is grass and forest fires, especially in midsummer (January through March). Great efforts are made to combat this menace.

Japan has 43 regional and three metropolitan fire departments under national supervision, staffed with about 35,000 paid fire fighters; 9,200 part-time, industrial fire fighters; and 1,600,000 volunteers. Fire Prevention Week is in November, at the start of the dry season. Hong Kong has a severe fresh water shortage, aggravated by hilly terrains that cause water-pressure problems even where sufficient water is present. Hence, fire departments must often pump seawater onto fires.

Fire protection of life and property in Canada is a provincial or territorial government responsibility. Fire marshals or commissioners are appointed by these governments and are responsible for all property within their respective areas of jurisdiction, with the exception of properties under the administration and control of the federal government, which are the responsibility of the Dominion Fire Commissioner (except for national defense and aircraft-crash fire fighting). The Canada Emergency Measures Organization has developed a proposed fire defense plan for use in the event of a nuclear emergency.

In the United States, fire protection is under local jurisdiction. It is estimated that there are 25,000 fire departments, operating approximately 110,000 pumpers and 10,000 aerial ladder and elevating platform trucks. There are approximately 250,000 full-time professional fire fighters and about 1,250,000 volunteers and paid-on-call men. In 1971, there were 147 colleges and universities offering 200 programs in fire service education. Approximately 13,700 students were enrolled.

All industrial countries have extensive facilities for training professional fire fighters. Several weeks or months of indoctrination for recruits are followed by continued in-service study by all fire fighters, practical fire training of units on special grounds or on condemned structures, or courses for command personnel working toward promotion. Germany provides full college engineering training for ranking officers. The Soviet Union has fire technical schools at Moscow and Leningrad in which full-time students receive about 4,000 hours of instruction, about half of which is practical work. Sweden has a Fire Service College; Denmark, a school in Charlottenlund; and London has a fire-brigade training centre in which 16-year-old boys are given a two-year course covering all phases of fire-brigade activity. Yugoslavia's Workers' University offers a two-year work–school course in safety engineering, which includes fire protection.

Training facilities

FIRE-FIGHTING TECHNIQUES

Alarms received by the devices described earlier, and direct calls for help are quickly transmitted. Mobile teleprinters and computers are now being used for dispatching. Volunteer or off-duty personnel are called when needed. The location and nature of the fire must be determined quickly, and the proper agencies and manpower mobilized; many fire-fighting forces have regional mobilization and mutual-aid plans worked out in advance. Once a fire starts, the key factor is time.

In cities, a full-time, professional fire-fighting force is available. In rural and sparsely populated areas, however, volunteer fire departments, composed of local residents who serve when needed, are formed. When a fire alarm is received, these volunteers assemble at the scene. To contact them, radio is generally used. If possible, each volunteer fire fighter carries a small, portable radio receiver, tuned to pick up fire calls. When an alarm is received, the radio sounds a loud alerting tone followed by a voice message stating the location of the fire. Telephone hookups have also been developed in which a single telephone call alerts all volunteers.

Alerting volunteer firemen

Urban fires. Though operational plans vary, in most cities of the world the safe response to a fire in a low-hazard (well-spaced) residential area is at least three pieces of equipment: two pumpers and either a ladder, squad, or rescue unit. For fires in larger structures, including schools, at least double this minimum response is needed. In high-hazard business or industrial districts, an additional task force is required to attack the rear of the structure and to reduce the possibility of exposure fires in adjoining structures. Additional pumpers and tanks may also be called.

After a fire situation is surveyed, rescue operations commence. Prompt placement of hose streams and ladders is essential. The next steps are to reduce exposure, confine and extinguish the fire, and to assure that the fire does not rekindle. Ventilation and salvage may be required at any time. The first areas attacked are those that threaten adjoining structures. A coordinated attack from front and rear is usually made.

Communications at the scene of a fire are effected by means of hand signals, loudspeakers, rope signals, and two-way radio. When the noise level is high, hand signals may be preferred to loudspeakers. Rope signals are employed when two or more men (often rescue workers) are connected together by means of a life line. Two-way portable radio is used also; some firms offer such devices fitted into the face masks of life-support equipment. Mobile repeater units are used to relay messages from men inside a building or in a "dead spot." Fire departments also install two-way radios in their trucks for communications with headquarters.

Fires generally are controlled by applying cooling agents to absorb heat or reduce fuel temperatures and by using insulating agents to separate the fuel from the oxygen, smothering the fire. Because heated gases expand and are lighter than air, fires set up thermal columns that can move with drafts or air currents. As combustion products rise, air (oxygen) is drawn to the base of the fire. The unburned vapours rise with the heat and smoke and spread or mushroom at the highest level. If fire continues without ventilation, heat and smoke may bank down and fill the entire structure to a point where introduction of oxygen in large amounts can cause a smoke (particulate and vapour) explosion and an intense fire. For this reason, most structural fires are fought by the over-and-under method that involves both ventilation to prevent smoke buildup and hoses placed at the top level of the fire to prevent further upward or horizontal expansion. The main attack comes from below the fire; the front entrance and the main stairway are usually the first attack positions for hose lines. Control of the stairs provides access to the building and a means for rescuing occupants. If the fire is on the lower floor, the aim is to prevent it from moving upstairs; on the upper floors, advantage is taken of the cooler air beneath it.

It usually is bad practice to attack a fire from the outside if interior positions are tenable; such action hinders the advance of crews working inside and may drive the fires into other areas and endanger occupants.

When a fire is in a basement or on a lower floor, the over-and-under operation is important, because lines are needed above the fire to prevent upward extension while other lines move in to extinguish it.

Fires in sparsely populated areas. Rural properties usually are quite combustible; they are seldom subject to adequate building and fire-prevention regulations. The fires can be devastating; distance and limited water supplies compound the problem. In addition to the customary fire-company apparatus, response equipment often includes water-tank trucks and portable pumps for placement at ponds, cisterns, and other static water sources. Normally, at least two fire companies will respond, if possible.

Grass, bush, and forest fires involve two types of response. When protected by an organized fire department, such fires usually are handled by the same units that do structural fire fighting. In prolonged dry, windy weather, additional personnel may be mobilized. Special apparatus may include patrol cars with small water tanks and pumps, tankers, bulldozers, reserve water tanks, and small hose. Some communities use aircraft. Backpack units for personnel often are carried on pumpers and trucks for use on grass and brush fires.

Outdoor fires are seasonal, influenced by weather conditions. They present one of the chief hazards in thousands of communities, where dwellings are located in areas with extremely combustible ground cover; combustible roofs often add to the problem.

Woodland-area fires usually are the responsibility of national, state or provincial, and private forest-fire protection agencies. Some districts have mutual-assistance pacts with nearby municipal fire departments. Forestry agencies commonly use labour crews directed by skilled foresters. Crews use lightweight, small-capacity hose and portable pumps, hand tools for cutting and trenching fire lines, and back fires (fires started to check an advancing fire by clearing the area) as controls. Fire-retardant materials, such as bentonite clay and chemical solutions, are used for maintaining fire lines. Fire-retardant slurries (water mixtures) can be dumped from aircraft.

Modern forest-fire-fighting techniques include a carefully organized chain of command, preplanned supply services, aerial reconnaissance, frequent issuance of fire-line maps, and coordinated communications.

Patrols and lookout towers are used during fire seasons to spot incipient fires. Aerial reconnaissance and air drops of fire fighters and equipment are used in rural areas. Evacuation plans are made for residents of woodland areas. Fire trails are maintained along ridges, in valleys, and at other places requiring special access. Fires spread very rapidly up slopes, however, and unpredictably in shifting winds, limiting the value of trails as firebreaks.

Extinguishing fires in space vehicles and pressure chambers. Until the Apollo tragedy of January 1967 in which three United States astronauts lost their lives, pressure chambers and chambers with oxygen-rich atmospheres did not include special fire-protection systems or

strict control of combustibles within the chamber. High-pressure chambers have become common in medical, space, and underwater research. Two problems complicate fire-fighting in such environments. First, rapid escape is impossible; a person brought rapidly from high pressure to normal atmospheric pressure is in serious danger from decompression sickness. Second, the combustion rate of materials increases as air pressure increases; materials only slightly combustible under normal atmospheric pressure ignite and burn under high pressure. As in ordinary fire situations, the best protection is prevention. Construction specifications call for sealed electrical circuits, water-turbine motors, minimum electrical wiring in the chamber, and fire-retardant finishes and plastics. Electric motors and combustible materials are kept out of the chamber. Spark-inducing clothing, instruments, or other sources of static electricity are not permitted in the chamber. Workers in the units are trained for emergencies.

Sprinkler systems for such chambers are pressurized to 65 pounds per square inch (29 kilograms per square centimetre) above the pressure in the chamber, and the system is designed to activate within one second. Under pressure, the spray pattern from sprinkler heads is smaller than under atmospheric pressure, even though flow is about the same; usually at least twice as many sprinklers are needed. When sprinklers are actuated, electricity is shut off in the chamber and emergency battery-powered lights go on. The water storage tank has a capacity about double that required to extinguish a fire in any one chamber. For oxygen-enriched atmospheres, water-spray is also effective.

Tests of fires in zero-gravity conditions have demonstrated that ordinary convection (rise) of hot combustion products ceases completely. Ignition of combustibles occurs in a manner similar to that at normal gravity, but the products of combustion refuse to vacate the site of burning, and no new oxygen can displace the combustion gases. Further combustion is starved to a point of self-extinction of the fuel.

BIBLIOGRAPHY

General, municipal, and industrial fire protection: NATIONAL FIRE PROTECTION ASSOCIATION, *Fire Protection Handbook* (quintennial), a standard reference on structural and municipal fire protection; FACTORY MUTUAL ENGINEERING CORP., *Handbook of Industrial Loss Prevention,* 2nd ed. (1967), recommended practices for the protection of property and processes against damage by fire, explosion, lightning, wind, and earthquake; CHARLES V. WALSH, *Firefighting Strategy and Leadership* (1963), problems and objectives of fire fighting, fire fighting strategy, management and leadership; JAMES F. CASEY (ed.), *Fire Service Hydraulics,* 2nd ed. (1970), an excellent, well-illustrated treatise about extinguishing fluids, physics of water, distribution systems, pumps, engine and nozzle pressures and streams, automatic sprinklers and standpipes, foams, and foam systems; NORMAN J. THOMPSON, *Fire Behavior and Sprinklers* (1964), an explanation of how fire behaves when extinguished by sprinklers; HORATIO BOND and WARREN Y. KIMBALL, *Industrial Fire Brigades Training Manual,* 4th ed. (1968), instructions on how to fight a fire, use extinguishing equipment, salvage and rescue, care and inspect equipment; HORATIO BOND (ed.), *N.F.P.A. Inspection Manual,* 3rd ed. (1970), text for property owners, fire departments, and insurance and government inspectors for making and keeping buildings fire safe.

Specialized fire protection subjects: JOHN T. O'HAGAN, *Fire Fighting During Civil Disorders* (1968), methods of coping with disorder emergencies; WILLIAM D. CLAUDY, *Respiratory Hazards of the Fire Service* (1957), suffocation and toxicity hazards and procedures and equipment for overcoming them; HORATIO BOND, *A First Book on Fire Safety in the Atomic Age* (1952), discussion of industrial and municipal fire protection required as a result of threat of A-bombing and saturation (incendiary) bombing; CLAUDE C. STUBBE (ed.), *Fire Prevention for the Farm* (1966), the why and how of farm fire prevention.

Directories and standards: ALFRED M. BEST CO., *Environmental Control and Safety Directory* (biennial), manual on many types of protection equipment; UNDERWRITERS' LABORATORIES, INC., *Fire Protection Equipment List, Building Materials List, Electrical Construction Materials List, Electrical Appliance and Utilization Equipment List, Hazardous Locations Equipment List, Gas and Oil Equipment List, Index of*

Over-and-under operation

Combatting forest fires

Combustion under high pressure

Classified Products (annual), lists of approved equipment, materials, models, and manufacturers; UNDERWRITERS' LABORATORIES OF CANADA, annual approval listings; NATIONAL FIRE PROTECTION ASSOCIATION, *National Fire Codes; Flammable Liquids, Boiler-Furnaces, Ovens; Gases; Combustible Solids, Dusts, and Explosives; Building Construction and Facilities; Electrical; Sprinklers, Fire Pumps, and Water Tanks; Alarm and Special Extinguishing Systems; Portable and Manual Fire Control Equipment; Occupancy Standards and Process Hazards; Transportation,* (annual), lists of the NFPA standards, codes, recommended practices, and manuals.

See also *Fire Journal* (bimonthly); *Fire Technology* (quarterly); *Fire Research Abstracts and Reviews* (3/yr); *Fire Command!* (monthly); and *Fire Engineering* (monthly).

(F.E.McE.)

Fiscal and Monetary Policy

Government measures to stabilize the economy

The term fiscal and monetary policy refers to the various measures that governments may take to stabilize their economies at high levels of employment and output. Fiscal policy relates to taxes and expenditures; monetary policy has to do with the financial markets and with the supply of credit, money, and other financial assets. The essential idea is that in a capitalistic economy the public authorities may take action to increase or decrease the level of employment and output and to influence the trend of prices.

Tools of fiscal policy. In discussing fiscal policy it is useful to distinguish between actions that affect government spending and those that bear upon revenues. The government may, for example, increase its expenditure on equipment, buildings, public services, or social security. This will tend to have an expansionary effect on the economy through higher investment and consumption. The government may also achieve an expansionary effect through action on the revenue side of the budget; *i.e.,* by reducing taxes. It may reduce personal income taxes or indirect taxes such as sales taxes; alternatively, it may seek to stimulate investment by giving tax abatements to firms that invest—by reducing indirect taxes on capital goods such as machinery and building or by liberalizing depreciation allowances in corporation income taxation.

Correspondingly, when economic activity is at a high level, with a rapid rate of price increase, the government may slow it down by reversing the above measures: by reducing government spending, by increasing taxes, or by stiffening the rules for depreciation allowances.

Tools of monetary policy. Another way to manage the aggregate level of demand is to influence conditions in financial markets. In time of unemployment the central bank may stimulate private investment expenditure, and possibly also household spending on consumer goods, by reducing interest rates and taking measures to increase the supply of credit, liquid assets, and money. The customary tools for doing this are: (1) open market operations, (2) the discount rate of the central bank, and (3) reserve requirements for the commercial banks.

In open market operations the central bank buys government securities—bonds and treasury bills—from the private sector. The effect is to reduce interest rates by bidding up bond prices. The sellers of the government securities obtain cash which they deposit in the banks, thus increasing the cash reserves of the banks and enabling them to expand credit to private borrowers; this in turn causes interest rates in the private sector to fall and the terms of credit to become easier. In response, firms are likely to increase their investment expenditures, and households are likely to spend more on consumer goods.

The second tool of monetary policy, often used together with open market operations, is the discount rate of the central bank. This is the interest rate at which commercial banks can borrow funds from the central bank. If the discount rate is reduced, banks become more willing to extend credit to private borrowers because they can obtain funds themselves on easier terms. In many countries, changes in the discount rate tend to be followed by similar changes in the interest rates charged by banks to their borrowers.

The third tool of monetary policy is that of the cash reserve requirements, or liquid asset ratios, under which the banks must maintain money balances (in the form of deposits in the central bank) at a certain proportion of their liabilities. This means that the banks cannot expand their earning assets, such as government securities and private loans, beyond that point. If the government reduces the reserve requirements, the banks can expand their loans further, thus increasing the total volume of credit outstanding. In some countries the required reserves consist of money deposits plus certain types of government securities.

Monetary policy, like fiscal policy, may also be used to combat inflationary tendencies by reversing the above measures: the central bank will then sell government securities (thereby increasing interest rates and reducing the supply of private credit and money), raise the discount rate, or increase reserve requirements.

Conflicts in fiscal and monetary policy. The problems of stabilizing an economy are much more complex than the foregoing discussion would suggest. The reason for this is that stabilization involves the pursuit of more than one goal—including not only full employment but reasonably stable prices and an equilibrium in the balance of foreign payments. Measures that help to achieve one may sometimes hinder the achievement of another. Conflicts may also arise between the overall aim of stabilization and other economic aims such as improved income distribution, better allocation of resources, or special political considerations.

The complexity of the problems

The two most obvious conflicts in stabilization policy in recent decades have been the conflict between full employment and price stability and the conflict between domestic policy objectives (the "internal balance") and the balance of payments (the "external balance"). Some of the efforts made to reduce these conflicts are discussed below.

THE ORIGIN OF COMPENSATORY FISCAL AND MONETARY POLICY

The use of fiscal and monetary policy as a means of stabilizing the economy is relatively recent, for the most part a development of the period after World War II. During the 19th century the only stabilization policy was that associated with the international gold standard. Under the gold standard, if a deficit occurred in a country's balance of payments, gold tended to flow out of the country. To counteract this process, the monetary authorities would raise interest rates and stiffen credit requirements, causing a fall in prices, income, and employment; this in turn led to a reduction in imports and an expansion of exports, thus improving the balance of payments. If a country had a surplus in its balance of payments, gold tended to flow in; this meant that the interest rate fell and the supply of money and credit was increased. As a consequence, imports were stimulated and exports discouraged so that the surplus in the balance of payments tended to disappear. The adjustment mechanism also included another important element: capital movements between countries. When interest rates fell in surplus countries and rose in deficit countries, mobile international financial capital tended to flow from the former to the latter, contributing to the elimination of deficits and surpluses in the balance of payments. The working of this mechanism was partly automatic and partly the result of deliberate actions by the monetary authorities in each country.

The gold standard as a means of economic stabilization

In this form of stabilization policy, external stability was achieved at the cost of stability in the domestic economy: fluctuations in domestic prices, incomes, and employment functioned as the levers for bringing about equilibrium in the balance of payments. Occasionally governments attempted to reduce the impact of this mechanism on the domestic economy, particularly on the price level. In particular, governments in some surplus countries took "sterilization actions" to prevent the gold inflow from increasing the supply of money and credit to the maximum extent. This could be done if the central bank offset its purchases of foreign exchange and gold with sales of government securities on the domestic credit market.

Developments of the 1920s and 1930s

A somewhat more ambitious type of stabilization policy emerged in the period after World War I. During the late 1920s and early 1930s the need to reduce unemployment acquired more urgency. Previously, the exchange rate, the balance of payments, and occasionally the price level had been considered more important than the situation in the labour market. During the 1920s unemployment in Great Britain rose to very high levels (between 20 and 30 percent of the labour force). Consequently, there was much discussion of whether employment could be increased by actions of the public authorities. At first, the discussion in Great Britain centred on the feasibility of public works programs as a means of putting men to work, but there was a growing belief that public works programs might also be a good means of raising the general level of economic activity through their effect on purchasing power. Some also maintained that budget deficits (*i.e.*, a policy of expanding government expenditure without raising taxes to cover it) would also raise the level of economic activity. An active part in this discussion was taken by the economist J.M. Keynes, and also by the Liberal Party, which in 1928 published its proposals for government intervention under the title *Britain's Industrial Future.*

The first countries to adopt the new policies were Sweden and Germany. When the Nazi Party took power in Germany in 1933, its rearmament policies helped to reduce unemployment and to stimulate the economy. In Sweden, the new Social Democratic government attempted in more modest ways to expand the economy and ease unemployment through increased government expenditures in 1932–33. In the United States, some very limited attempts were made by the administrations of Presidents Herbert Hoover and Franklin D. Roosevelt; they were too slight, however, to have any significant effect on unemployment, which persisted at a high level until World War II.

THE THEORETICAL BASIS OF FISCAL AND MONETARY POLICY

The work of J.M. Keynes

The new stabilization policy needed a theoretical rationale if it was ever to win general acceptance from the leaders of public opinion. The main credit for providing this belongs to J.M. Keynes. In his *General Theory of Employment, Interest and Money* (1936) he endeavoured to show that a capitalist economy with its decentralized market system does not automatically generate full employment and stable prices and that governments should pursue deliberate stabilization policies. There has been much controversy among economists over the substance and meaning of Keynes's theoretical contribution. Essentially, he argued that high levels of unemployment might persist indefinitely unless governments took monetary and fiscal action. At that time he believed that fiscal action was likely to be more effective than monetary measures. In the deep depression of the 1930s, interest rates had ceased to exert much influence on the ways in which wealth owners disposed of their funds; they might choose to hold larger cash balances instead of spending more money as the traditional theory had suggested. Nor were investors inclined to take advantage of low interest rates if they could not find profitable uses for borrowed funds, particularly if their firms were already suffering from excess capacity. Keynes's pessimistic view of monetary policy had a strong influence on economists and governments during and immediately after World War II, with the result that monetary policy was not tried very much during the 1940s. It was often forgotten during the policy discussions of the time that Keynes's views on the efficacy of monetary policy were related to the particular situation of the 1930s.

Another influential idea embodied in Keynes's writing was that of economic stagnation. He suggested that in the advanced industrial countries people tended to save more as their incomes grew larger and that private consumption tended to be a smaller and smaller part of the national income. This implied that investment would have to take a continually larger share of the national income in order to maintain full employment. Since he doubted that investment would rise sufficiently to do this, Keynes was rather pessimistic about the possibility of achieving full employment in the long run. He thus suggested that there might be some permanent tendency to high levels of unemployment. This also had considerable influence on economic policy during the early postwar period; it was some time before those in decision-making positions realized that inflation, rather than stagnation and unemployment, was to be the main problem confronting them.

The acceptance of full employment as an aim of government

The desirability of government policies to maintain high levels of employment was generally accepted in most industrial countries after the war. In 1944 the British government stated in its White Paper on Employment Policy that "the government accept as one of their primary aims and responsibilities the maintenance of a high and stable level of employment after the war." One of the most influential British economists at this time was Sir William Beveridge, whose book *Full Employment in a Free Society* had a strong impact on general thinking. Similar ideas were expressed in the United States in the Employment Act of 1946, which stated: "The Congress hereby declares that it is the continuing policy and responsibility of the Federal Government to . . . promote maximum employment, production and purchasing power." The Employment Act was less specific as to policy than the British government's White Paper, but it established a council of economic advisers to assist the president and called upon him to present to every regular session of congress a report on the state of the economy. The president was also required to present a program showing "ways and means of promoting a high level of employment and production." Similar programs were adopted in other countries. In Sweden in 1944 the Social Democrats published a document somewhat similar to the British White Paper, and other such declarations were made in Canada and Australia.

EXPERIENCE IN VARIOUS COUNTRIES

The conflict between prewar ideas and postwar reality

The application of full-employment policies after World War II was made more difficult by the fact that the postwar situation was radically different from that of the 1930s, when much of the policy thinking had been done. Most governments and their advisers expected a depression after the war, but it never materialized. One explanation is that the reallocation of resources from military to civilian uses proceeded much more smoothly than had been expected. Another explanation is that the consumers spent a considerably larger part of their disposable income than they had been observed to do in the 1930s; this upset some of the sophisticated statistical projections based on empirical data from those years. A third explanation, which applies perhaps to the years after 1948, was the Cold War between the United States and the Soviet Union, which raised defense spending in many countries.

The period of the late 1940s and early 1950s proved to be characterized by tendencies to inflation rather than to unemployment. Governments were slow to realize this and to shift their emphasis from employment-creating policies to anti-inflationary policies. The fact that governments had accepted to a large extent the belief that monetary policy was not very important made it difficult for them to combat the tendencies to inflation. In most countries a very passive, even expansionary, monetary policy was in effect; interest rates were kept down and the supply of money was allowed to grow faster than would have been consistent with stable prices. Inflationary tendencies were further stimulated by the Korean War and the great increases in raw material prices that accompanied it.

During the 1950s several important developments influenced the attitudes of governments toward stabilization policy. Most of the economic controls engendered by the war were removed, particularly in international trade and finance. The western European countries found themselves in a period of rapid economic growth. With the removal of direct controls on prices, imports, and building investment, governments began to develop and refine the tools of monetary and fiscal policy. In most countries the passive attitude toward monetary policy disappeared during the early 1950s; there was increased interest in more flexible monetary management. Interest also grew in developing a systematic fiscal policy that would offset the cyclical swings in production and employment. The most energetic attempts to devise a countercyclical fiscal policy were made in Britain and Sweden. The United States and continental European countries placed more reliance on monetary policy.

The
revival of
monetary
policy

In the United States, a contributing factor in the revival of monetary policy was a theoretical reformulation that took place among monetary and banking experts. This was the so-called availability theory of credit: that monetary policy had its effect on spending not only directly through interest rates but also by restricting the general availability of credit and liquid funds. It was argued that even rather small changes in the rate of interest for government securities could have a considerable impact on the supply of private credit; if the supply diminished, this would induce banks and other financial institutions to stiffen their credit standards and ration credit to their customers; this in turn, it was argued, would tend to curb investment and thus have a braking effect on the economy. Similar ideas were at work in other countries, but with more emphasis on limiting the availability of credit through credit rationing, loan ceilings, control of private bond issues, regulation of installment credit for the purchase of durable consumer goods, and so on.

Serious attempts have been made to put a countercyclical monetary policy into practice in most advanced industrialized countries since the middle of the 1950s. In some, such as the United States, the emphasis has been, as suggested above, on changes in the interest rate and in the supply of money and credit; in others, such as France, Italy, and Japan, the emphasis has been on the rationing of credit by the central bank.

Fiscal policy has found less use than monetary policy in efforts to control cyclical fluctuations in the economy. It has been most favoured in Britain, the Scandinavian countries, and the Netherlands. One can point to specific situations in which fiscal measures have been used to stimulate the economy in other countries, as in Belgium and Germany during the recessions of 1958 and 1962. Another example is the postponement of certain military expenditures in the United States as an anti-inflationary measure during the boom of the mid-1950s, and most notably of all, the tax cut passed by Congress in 1964 on the recommendation of the Council of Economic Advisers as a stimulus to economic expansion. Several countries have taken restrictive fiscal actions to overcome balance-of-payments crises, including France and Finland on various occasions. During the 1960s there was an increasing tendency to employ fiscal policies in the short run, partly in order to assist monetary policy in the solving of cyclical problems.

PROBLEMS AND CONTROVERSIES

Discretion-
ary and
automatic
policies

One may make a broad distinction between two types of stabilization policies: discretionary and automatic. Discretionary policies involve deliberate actions taken by the authorities, such as open market operations, changes in discount rates and reserve requirements, and changes in tax rates or government expenditures. Automatic policies put reliance on built in stabilizers that function without any deliberate intervention by the authorities. In the monetary field, for example, an increase in commodity prices tends to reduce the real value of financial assets, and if the government does nothing to offset this by increasing the volume of financial assets in the system, private spending will tend to decline. On the fiscal side, the main automatic stabilizer is the relation between tax revenues and cyclical changes in the economy: during booms, tax revenues will rise and the need for expenditures on unemployment compensation will decrease, channelling a larger proportion of the national income into government coffers; these effects are accentuated if the tax system is progressive (*i.e.*, if tax rates are pro-

portionately higher on higher incomes), because tax revenues will rise more rapidly than money incomes. Provided that the government does not raise its expenditures along with the increased revenues, the budget will tend to have a braking effect on private expenditure in boom times; correspondingly, it will have an expansionary effect in times of recession.

The problem of time lags. There has been much discussion over the merits of discretionary policies as against automatic stabilizers. One advantage ascribed to automatic stabilizers is that the effects occur without the necessity of any deliberate policy action by the government, which means that there will be no delay because of political controversies, administrative problems, or difficulties in determining whether the time has come to act. The problem of delay, or lag, requires further elaboration. It is usual to distinguish three types of lag in economic policy: the recognition lag, the decision lag, and the effect lag.

The recognition lag is the time it takes for the authorities to discover the need to make a change in economic policy. The reasons for this type of lag are that statistical information is often somewhat behind the event, and that it is sometimes difficult to distinguish between random fluctuations and fundamental shifts in economic trends. Governments prefer to wait until there is certainty that, say, an increase in unemployment is not a passing thing.

Difficulties
of imple-
menting
policy

The decision lag is the period between the time when the need for action is recognized and the time when action is taken. Although the recognition lag is presumably of about the same duration for both monetary and fiscal policies, the decision lag is usually considerably shorter for monetary policy than for fiscal policy. The central bank can change monetary policy almost overnight, whereas a change in fiscal policy is more complex, both politically and administratively. In many countries changes in income taxes, for example, can be made only at the beginning of a calendar year; such changes are often complicated by political discussions in the nation's legislative body. The recognition lag and the decision lag are sometimes called together the inside lag of economic policy; that is, the lag resulting from delays within the political and administrative machinery.

The third lag, the effect lag, may be called the outside lag because it results from factors outside the policy-making machinery. The duration of this lag will vary. Monetary policy is thought to involve longer delays than fiscal policy; the length of time between a change in monetary policy and its ultimate effect on private investment may be between one and two years.

Some economists argue that the sum of all the lags is so long that the best strategy is not to take any action at all, since by the time the effects occur the economic situation may be radically different from that which the action was designed to correct. Attempts have been made in various countries to shorten the lags in fiscal and monetary policy. One obvious way of reducing the recognition lag is to improve the techniques of forecasting. This has been achieved to some extent by more sophisticated methods of collecting and interpreting economic information; an example is the development of questionnaires for finding out what businesses plan to invest in buildings, machinery, and inventories, and how much consumers intend to spend on durable goods. Another example is the construction of elaborate econometric models consisting of mathematical equations that describe the relationships among different parts of the economy. These have become more practical with the development of electronic computers, and in some countries they are in common use to forecast business conditions in the immediate future.

In order to reduce the decision lag in fiscal policy, attempts have been made in some countries to give the authorities power to take limited action without the prior consent of the legislature. In Britain, the government has the power to change tax rates on durable consumer goods within certain limits. In Belgium and West Germany, the governments also have some discretionary powers to change tax rates without first asking the legislature. In most countries, however, the legislative bodies have been reluctant to give up their control of the budget.

Attempts to shorten the effect lag of fiscal policy have produced some new policy tools. Some countries now use systems of taxes or subsidies to influence business investment within a relatively short time. Sweden has reduced the effect lag in this sphere to less than a year. Attempts have also been made to reduce the effect lag in monetary policy. Some countries have tried to speed things up by using various tools of credit rationing rather than relying on traditional measures such as open market operations. But the effect lag still constitutes a serious problem for monetary policy.

The multiplicity of goals

Conflicts among goals. Perhaps the most serious unsolved problem of stabilization policy is the multiplicity of goals that policy makers must consider. Every government has aims other than stabilizing the economy. First, it must stay in power—a need that is likely to limit the alternatives open to stabilization policy, particularly in periods of prosperity immediately before elections, when it is very difficult to take restrictive measures, such as raising taxes. Second, some monetary and fiscal actions impinge heavily on particular groups in society, and governments may wish to avoid what appear to be discriminatory policies. Third, the goal of stabilization comprises in itself several different goals, such as full employment, price stability, and equilibrium in the balance of payments. A policy designed to achieve one of these goals may prevent the achievement of another.

Full employment and price stability. The conflict between full employment and price stability seems to arise in two different sets of circumstances. Sometimes wage increases that are made in the normal collective bargaining process are greater than the increases in labour productivity (or output per man-hour); such wage increases tend to increase the cost of production and to force prices upward. The government is then confronted with a choice between two unpleasant alternatives. One is to allow the general price level to rise approximately in proportion to the increase in production costs; the other alternative is to try to hold prices down by taking measures to restrict aggregate demand, thus making it difficult for firms to shift their increased costs to the consumer through higher prices. The latter alternative means increased unemployment. Many governments have been confronted with exactly this choice of alternatives. Wage gains made in collective bargaining have forced them to choose between allowing prices to move upward or attempting to hold prices stable at the cost of greater unemployment.

Another reason for the conflict between full employment and price stability is the tendency of wage increases to accelerate when the level of unemployment falls and the number of job vacancies increases. In other words, as the economy approaches full employment wages tend to rise at an increasing speed. (This is the so-called Phillips' curve problem, named after the British economist A.W. Phillips, who was the first to demonstrate statistically the correlation between the level of unemployment and the rate of wage change.) As prices begin to rise, the conflict between full employment and price stability may be further exacerbated by the expectation that they will rise still further; this may, for example, induce employees and their organizations to press for greater wage increases than they otherwise would in order to compensate for the expected price increases.

The balance of payments and price stability. Another conflict in policy may arise with respect to the balance of payments. When the economy is in a period of boom, there is a tendency for imports to increase, and sometimes for exports to decrease as well, with obvious difficulties for the balance of payments. The crisis may be heightened by short-term capital movements if buyers and sellers of foreign exchange expect that there may be a devaluation of the country's currency. This has caused much difficulty for many countries in the period since World War II. In Britain and Denmark, notably, periods of boom have usually been accompanied by balance-of-payments problems. When that occurs, the government must sooner or later take restrictive actions that slow the economy down and increase unemployment; if speculation in the currency is already under way, it may be necessary to pursue the restrictive policy far into the next recession. The problem is accentuated if there have been substantial price increases during the boom that have reduced the country's ability to compete with other countries. It is ironic that a temporary improvement in the employment situation may, if it leads to an accelerated increase in the price level, serve to create greater unemployment in the future, when restrictive actions become necessary for balance-of-payments reasons.

Efforts to control inflation

Incomes policy. Attempts have been made to eliminate these conflicts of policy. One remedy that has been widely discussed is "incomes policy," meaning direct efforts by the government to prevent employers and unions from raising prices and wages. Various methods have been tried. The most moderate is the so-called guideposts system, under which the government announces the need for restraints on wage increases and perhaps also sets targets to guide unions and management; this was attempted in the United States in the early 1960s. In some countries, responsibility for limiting wage increases has been assigned to labour-management organizations, as in Sweden, where bargaining takes place in a very centralized fashion. A more interventionist approach is for the government to enter the bargaining process and try to persuade unions to limit their wage demands. The government may go still further and announce a wage freeze, or even a system of wage and price control. In The Netherlands and Australia, the courts have occasionally been empowered to set wages; but the resulting decisions have often been rather uncoordinated with the rest of stabilization policy.

Incomes policies have sometimes succeeded for short periods. Generally, however, public refusal to accept the restraints has eventually led to their collapse. In the United States, the guideposts broke down during the boom of the mid-1960s, and attempts at incomes policy in Sweden and Britain have not been notable. Even in The Netherlands and Australia the system has failed in recent years to limit the rate of wage increase.

The question of governmental competence. Governments have displayed serious deficiencies in their ability to handle stabilization policy. Political leaders often lack economic information and understanding, and their economic advisers find it difficult to explain the economic situation to them and to apprise them of the relevant tools. There are also, as pointed out above, a variety of political inhibitions against taking action. One consequence is that what is designed to be a countercyclical policy becomes a procyclical one; instead of stabilizing the economy it tends to destabilize it. The postwar experience in Britain is held by some to demonstrate the deficiencies of government in handling monetary and fiscal policy. In time of boom the government often followed an expansionary course; when a balance-of-payments crisis developed it then took restrictive action—too late—and pushed the economy into deeper recession than would otherwise have occurred. On the basis of this experience, some economists have argued that a policy that did not attempt to counter the short-run swings in the economy would have been more successful in achieving stabilization. They maintain that the authorities should concentrate on the goal of letting the volume of money and credit increase steadily at a rate dictated by the long-term growth trend of the economy. Those who hold this view believe that capitalist economies are inherently stable, that crises are usually the result of bad policies on the part of the public authorities. Most economists do not share their optimism as to the stability of the economy if left alone; they continue to believe that governments must seek better tools for the purpose of short-run stabilization.

RECENT DEVELOPMENTS

The study of fiscal and monetary policy has become increasingly subtle. It has been established, for example,

The various effects of budget deficits

that the size of the budget surplus or deficit is not a good criterion of its effects on the economy. Quite different types of fiscal action may produce the same surplus or deficit, but they will not have the same effects on the economy. Thus a tax increase for poor households will have a different effect than a tax increase for high income groups; and an expenditure on government purchases of goods and services will have a different effect than a tax reduction of the same amount for corporations, even though both may produce the same budget deficit. In short, one cannot cite changes in the size of the budget surplus or deficit as an indication of whether its effects are expansionary or not.

Attempts have been made to appraise budgets in terms of what their effect on the economy would be at high levels of employment. Thus a "full-employment surplus" means that a particular budget would show a surplus if the economy were at full employment, although in fact the budget may be in deficit. The importance of this is that it enables the authorities to distinguish between a budget deficit that will have an expansionary effect in the present state of the economy and one that simply reflects a low level of economic activity.

Selective fiscal policy

Fiscal policy in recent years has tended to become more selective than formerly, largely because most Western economies have been operating much of the time at levels close to full employment. It is not unusual to have full employment, or even labour shortages, in some sectors of the economy at the same time that there is unemployment in other sectors. The fiscal approach to this problem is to stimulate the economy in areas where there is unused capacity, perhaps through subsidies or tax reductions, and to constrain it in other areas.

Another problem for stabilization policy is the discovery that immediately following a boom there may be a continuing tendency for prices to rise, despite the fact that unemployment is increasing. This has been manifest in a number of countries, most notably perhaps in Britain and the United States at the end of the 1960s. The rate of increase in the price level seems to reach its maximum about 12 to 18 months after the peak of the business cycle. This complicates stabilization policy considerably. It emphasizes the need to check the boom at an early stage in order to avoid price increases in the forthcoming recession.

There has been considerable discussion as to whether the conflict between full employment and the balance of payments might not be reduced by a system of freely fluctuating exchange rates. It is argued that allowing exchange rates to move freely would automatically bring about equilibrium in the balance of payments, whatever the internal situation. On the other hand, such flexibility might make it more difficult to maintain stable prices; a deficit in the balance of payments during a boom would immediately be reflected in a depreciated currency, and this might tend to push prices up because of the higher costs of imported goods. At the same time, fixed exchange rates may also be incompatible with price stability. At fixed exchange rates, international price changes are automatically transmitted to the domestic economy. There is a problem, then, whether the exchange rate should be used mainly to equilibrate the balance of payments, in which case freely fluctuating rates would be appropriate, or to shield the domestic economy from international price changes and to stabilize the domestic price level. In the latter case a flexible exchange-rate policy that would allow for discretionary changes in the exchange rate would be appropriate.

BIBLIOGRAPHY. Surveys of the principles of fiscal and monetary policy may be found in standard textbooks on economics. The works listed below are more specialized.

Theory of fiscal policy: BENT HANSEN, *Finanspolitikens ekonomiska teori* (1955; Eng. trans., *The Economic Theory of Fiscal Policy*, 1958, reissued 1967); R.A. MUSGRAVE, *The Theory of Public Finance* (1959).

Theory of monetary policy: J.G. GURLEY and E.S. SHAW, *Money in a Theory of Finance* (1960); A. LINDBECK, *A Study in Monetary Analysis* (1963); DON PATINKIN, *Money, Interest and Prices*, 2nd ed. (1965); W.L. SMITH and R.L. TEIGEN

(eds.), *Readings in Money, National Income, and Stabilization Policy* (1970); A.D. ENTINE (ed.), *Monetary Economics: Readings* (1968).

Empirical studies: E.S. KIRSCHEN (ed.), *Economic Policy in Our Time*, 3 vol. (1964), a broad survey of economic policy in a large number of countries; ERIK LUNDBERG, *Instability and Economic Growth* (1968), a study of stabilization policy during the postwar period; BENT HANSEN, *Fiscal Policy in Seven Countries, 1955–1965: Belgium, France, Germany, Italy, Sweden, United Kingdom, United States* (1969), a study of the application of fiscal policy.

(A.Li.)

Fischer von Erlach, Johann Bernhard

Johann Bernhard Fischer von Erlach, architect, sculptor, and architectural historian, inaugurated the style that came to be known as Austrian Baroque, leaving a legacy of significant buildings, notably in Vienna and Salzburg, and in the Habsburg dominions. The development of this artistic style coincided with the rise of the Habsburg Empire after its victories over the Turks at the end of the 17th century. Taking his elements from the architecture of ancient Rome, from that of the Renaissance, as well as from Italian, French, and English Baroque architecture, Fischer created a new style by a lofty intellectual and formal synthesis. His buildings can be considered "total works of art" in which architecture and the figurative arts are united to express a predominant idea—the glorification of God or the patron saint in ecclesiastical architecture; or the allegorical glorification of the ruler or of the noble patron in secular buildings. Not only were they a source of inspiration for later Austrian and south German architects but they also provided the setting in which Austrian Baroque painting and sculpture could unfold.

Early career in Italy. Son of a provincial sculptor and turner, Fischer was baptized July 20, 1656, at Graz, Austria. After a craftsman's training in his father's workshop, he went to Rome when he was about 16 years old. He had the good fortune to enter the studio of the great Baroque sculptor and architect Gian Lorenzo Bernini, where he learned the art of designing and making medals as well. In 1679 and 1682 he received his first known commissions as a medallist. In Rome he came into close contact with the circle of archaeologists and antiquarians around Queen Christina of Sweden, who had converted to Roman Catholicism, abdicated, and then settled in Rome. From that association he acquired considerable knowledge of ancient art and of the scientific methods then beginning to be used in archaeology—methods that formed the basis for his own later archaeological reconstructions. He also studied ancient Roman, Renaissance, and Baroque art and architecture and the architectural theory of those periods. About 1684 he went to Naples, then under Spanish rule, probably in the service of the Spanish viceroy. He is reported to have been very active there and even to have acquired considerable wealth, although exactly what work he did is not known.

Training in Bernini's studio

Return to Austria. After some 16 successful years in Italy, Fischer returned to his homeland at an opportune time; after the imperial victories over the Turks, the Habsburg Empire was emerging as a great European power, and the emperor Leopold I wished to emulate King Louis XIV of France by representing his power as an absolute monarch visibly in magnificent buildings. The aristocracy followed his example by erecting splendid palaces, and the Catholic clergy, too, wanted to glorify the victory over the infidel as well as that over the Reformation in ecclesiastical architecture. Moreover, the Turks had destroyed many country seats of the aristocracy and had severely damaged the suburbs of Vienna during the siege of 1683. The need for new buildings as well as the quick economic recovery following the victories brought about a great increase in building and a resultant flowering of art and architecture. In 1687 Fischer embarked on a brilliant career as court architect to three successive emperors, Leopold I, Joseph I, and Charles VI, and also designed buildings for the aristocracy and the Archbishop of Salzburg. In 1689 Leopold I appointed him to teach his elder son, Joseph, perspective and the

Court architect to three emperors

theory and history of architecture. In 1690 Fischer won public recognition with two temporary triumphal arches erected in Vienna to celebrate Joseph's entry into the city after his coronation as king and future ruler of the Holy Roman Empire in Frankfurt am Main. During the next ten years, Fischer was much sought after·as an architect in Vienna and Salzburg and in the Habsburg lands. In 1693 alone he had 14 important buildings in hand; at the same time he was also producing sculpture and designing for the decorative arts—notably goldsmiths' work.

Fischer's early innovations in secular architecture. During these years he created a new type of country house, combining the most important achievements in suburban architecture since the 16th century. He united the ideas of the French Baroque country palace made up of many joined pavilions with that of the classically inspired Renaissance villa, typical of Andrea Palladio, surrounded by low detached wings. By using the powerful curving forms of the Roman Baroque architects, especially Bernini, he gave his villas a more dynamic form. One of their outstanding features is the spacious oval hall in the centre of the plan, as in Schloss Neuwaldegg, near Vienna, and in Schloss Engelhartstetten, in Lower Austria. Fischer's country house designs had a decisive influence on the architects of his time. In a similar synthesis of Roman and French Baroque seasoned with Palladian elements, he also created a new type of town palace characterized by impressive form, structural clarity, and the dynamic tension of its decoration. The Winter Palace of Prince Eugene of Savoy, begun in 1695, and the palace of the ban of Croatia, Count Batthyány, begun in 1699, both in Vienna, are notable examples of this type.

The most important of Fischer's palace designs, however, remained unexecuted: his first project for Schönbrunn Palace on a hill near Vienna. His plan was for an enormous residence befitting the ruler of the Holy Roman Empire; it would have surpassed all previous palaces, even Versailles, by combining and harmonizing features from all of them. Fischer deeply regretted the fact that he was allowed to build only a much smaller palace in the valley below, the Schönbrunn Palace of today, begun in 1696 and later radically altered under Maria Theresa.

Ecclesiastical architecture for the Archbishop of Salzburg. As architect to Johann Ernst, Graf von Thun, the Archbishop of Salzburg, Fischer displayed his talent in church architecture and town planning. The domes and towers of his churches changed the whole appearance of Salzburg. In their exquisitely proportioned, lofty interiors he tried to achieve a balance between the longitudinal and central schemes, a problem all great church architects had been faced with since Michelangelo's projects for St. Peter's in Rome. All of Fischer's churches have two-towered facades accented by dynamic curves and elegant decoration, but each has its own special quality, determined by its location and by its particular function, as attached to a seminary, a university, or a nunnery. The elegant concave facade of Holy Trinity Church, for example, contrasts to and heightens the effect of the sober front of the adjoining seminary buildings. The almost geometric forms of the University Church surmounted by the undulating forms of its towers crown the university complex, providing a new architectural and symbolic accent to a city dominated by its massive cathedral, as Salzburg had been. Fischer also designed a new facade for the Archbishop's stables and laid out a square in front of it. He changed an old quarry into a summer riding school and built the Archbishop's summer residence, Schloss Klesheim, outside Salzburg.

Foreign travels and change of style. At the turn of the 18th century Fischer was at the height of his career. In a visible sign of his success as a court architect, he was raised to the nobility in 1696. The imperial alliance with Prussia, Holland, and England during the War of the Spanish Succession enabled Fischer, in 1704, to visit those countries and to study their architecture, particularly in relation to Palladio. The result was a remarkable change in his architectural style. In 1707 he went to Venice to study Palladian architecture at its source. The

result was his development of a new type of "Palladian" palace facade, classical in its proportions but enlivened with richly sculptured decoration. It consists of a central projection accentuated by a giant order and surmounted by a triangular pediment, and of relatively unarticulated lateral sections. Its models were English and North German Baroque interpretations of Palladian architecture as well as the works of Palladio himself and of his Italian followers. Fischer's most important achievements in this field are the facades of the Bohemian Chancellery and Trautson Palace, both in Vienna, and of the Clam-Gallas Palace, in Prague, which were imitated by architects all over the Habsburg Empire.

During the first ten years of the 18th century, however, Fischer designed fewer buildings than in the years before. His time was taken up by his administrative duties as chief inspector of court buildings and his work on a great history of architecture, *Entwurf einer historischen Architektur.* His book, which reveals the wide range of his learning, was the first comparative history of the architecture of all times and all nations; it included significant specimens of Egyptian, Persian, Greek, Roman, Muslim, Indian, and Chinese architecture, illustrated by engravings with explanatory notes. Some of the archaeological reconstructions that appeared in the book were among the best of Fischer's time. At the end of the historical survey he placed his own achievements, which he saw as a logical continuation of the Roman tradition of architecture. The book was published in 1721.

Final projects. When his second imperial patron, Joseph I, died in 1711, Fischer's position as the principal architect at the Viennese court was no longer uncontested. Many preferred the more pleasing and less demanding architecture of his rival Johann Lucas von Hildebrandt to Fischer's lofty conceptions. Yet he was also able to gain the favour of Charles VI, to whom he dedicated his history of architecture in manuscript in 1712, and to obtain commissions for the greatest architectural undertakings in Vienna—the rebuilding of the imperial palace and the building of the Karlskirche (Church of St. Charles Borromeo).

Charles had vowed to build the Karlskirche as an offering to his patron saint for the city's deliverance from an epidemic of the plague. In its imperial grandeur the building Fischer conceived not only glorified St. Charles but was also a monument to the Emperor himself. In this church he attempted to incorporate and harmonize the main ideas contained in the most important sacred buildings of past and present, beginning with the Temple of Jerusalem and including the Pantheon and St. Peter's in Rome, the Hagia Sophia in Istanbul, and also the Dôme des Invalides in Paris and St. Paul's in London. The relatively independent parts of the building—a pair of Roman triumphal columns, low towers, a high oval dome, a central portico modelled after a Roman temple facade, a transept and presbytery—are harmonized to form a visual unity from whatever point they are seen. The complex formal and symbolic structure of the building is the result of its twofold function. For example, the most striking feature of the church, the pair of giant triumphal columns on either side of the portico, is decorated with spiral reliefs glorifying the life of St. Charles. The pair of columns, however, also alludes to the Emperor's emblem, the "pillars of Hercules." As the last Habsburg king of Spain, Charles had in vain dreamed of establishing a worldwide monarchy by uniting the crowns of Spain and the Empire. Yet the columns of the Karlskirche bear the crown of Spain at their summits, flanked by eagles, the heraldic bird of the Holy Roman Empire.

Fischer did not live to see his masterpiece completed. He died in Vienna, on April 5, 1723. His son Joseph Emanuel Fischer von Erlach completed the church with some alterations. He also completed the Imperial Stables and built, according to his father's designs, the Imperial Library, the interior of which was the most imposing library hall of its time.

Fischer's significance. The form of Fischer's architecture is determined by its function. Each single form conveys not only aesthetic value but also a symbolic

Fischer's imprint on Salzburg

The Karlskirche of Vienna

meaning. Fischer looked to the already existing great works of similar function to find a new, even unique, solution for each task, the best of all possible solutions. All of his works are composed of several different elements or contrasting features that are harmonized in a unified whole and in reference to their natural and artistic environment.

Fischer's contemporaries admired his genius in inaugurating a new artistic period. His strongly individual architectural solutions, however, could neither be taught nor imitated. Only those works which introduced new general types, such as the country houses and palace facades, had a direct influence on the architecture of the period. The universality of his architectural conceptions has been recognized only recently.

MAJOR WORKS

ARCHITECTURE: Hall of the Ancestors, Frain Castle (1688–95; Vranov nad Dyji, Czechoslovakia); Stratmann Palace (1692–93; Vienna); Schloss Neuwaldegg (1692–97; Vienna); high altar of Pilgrimage Church (1692–1704; Mariazell, Austria); summer riding school, north facade, and horse pond of the Archbishop's stables (1690–94; Salzburg); Schloss Engelhartstetten (Niederweiden; *c.* 1693; Austria); Dreifaltigkeitskirche (Church of the Holy Trinity and Priests' House; 1694–1702; Salzburg); Johannesspital and Johanneskirche (Hospital and Church of St. John the Baptist; before 1695–1704; Salzburg); Winter Palace of Prince Eugene of Savoy (1695–1700; Vienna); Kollegienkirche (University Church; 1696–1707; Salzburg); Schönbrunn Palace (1696–1711; Vienna); Ursulinenkirche (Ursuline Church; 1699–1705; Salzburg); Batthyány Palace (1699–1706; Vienna); Schloss Klesheim (1700–09; near Salzburg); high altar of Franziskanerkirche (Franciscan Church; 1708–09; Salzburg); Bohemian Chancellery (1708–14; Vienna); Trautson Palace (1710–16; Vienna); Clam-Gallas Palace (begun 1713; Prague); Karlskirche (Church of St. Charles Borromeo; begun 1715; Vienna); Elector's Chapel in Cathedral (1715–21; Wrocław, Poland); Nationalbibliothek (Imperial Library; designed in 1716, built 1723–37 by Fischer's son in Vienna); Hofstallungen (Imperial Stables; 1719–23; Vienna).

WRITINGS: *Entwurf einer historischen Architektur* (1721; *A Plan of Civil and Historical Architecture*, 1730).

BIBLIOGRAPHY. The most comprehensive account of Fischer and his work is H. SEDLMAYR, *Johann Bernhard Fischer von Erlach* (1956), a German monograph with catalogue raisonné and bibliography. H. AURENHAMMER, *J.B. Fischer von Erlach* (in prep.), a briefer English monograph with a complete list of works and a bibliography, also includes the material and literature published during and after the commemorative exhibition of 1956. G. KUNOTH, *Die historische Architektur Fischers von Erlach* (1956), is a study devoted to Fischer's history of art and its sources.

(Ha.A.)

Fish

The term fish is applied to a variety of cold-blooded aquatic vertebrates of several evolutionary lines. It describes a life form, rather than a taxonomic group. Modern fishes represent about five classes, as distinct from each other as the four classes of familiar air breathing animals, amphibians, reptiles, birds, and mammals.

The study of fishes, the science of ichthyology, affects everyone although most are not directly aware of it. There are many reasons why fishes are of interest to man, but the most important, his relationship with and dependence on the environment, is not always immediately apparent. A more obvious reason for interest in fishes is their role as a moderate but important part of man's food supply. This resource, once thought unlimited, is now realized to be quite finite, and in delicate balance with the biological, chemical, and physical factors of the aquatic environment. Overfishing, pollution, and alteration of the environment are the chief enemies of proper fisheries management, both in fresh waters and in the ocean. For a detailed discussion of the technology and economics of fisheries, see FISHING, COMMERCIAL. Another practical reason for studying fishes is their use in disease control. As predators on mosquito larvae, they help curb malaria and other mosquito-borne diseases.

Fishes are valuable laboratory animals in many aspects of medical and biological research. The readiness of many fishes to acclimate to captivity has allowed biologists to study behaviour, physiology, and even ecology under relatively natural conditions. In the study of animal behaviour, especially, fishes have provided a broad base for the understanding of the more flexible behaviour of the higher vertebrates.

There are aesthetic and recreational reasons for an interest in fishes. At least 5,000,000 people in the United States alone keep live fishes in their homes for the simple pleasure of observing the beauty and behaviour of animals not otherwise familiar to them. To many, aquarium fishes provide a personal challenge, allowing them to test their ability to keep a small, beautiful section of the natural environment in their often extremely artificial homes. Sport fishing is another way of enjoying the natural environment, also indulged in by millions of people every year. Interest in aquarium fishes and sport fishing support multimillion-dollar industries throughout the world.

This article is divided into the following sections:

General features
   Structural diversity
   Distribution and abundance
Natural history
   Life history
   Behaviour
   Locomotion
   Reproduction
Form and function
   Body plan
   The skin
   The muscle system
   The digestive system
   The respiratory system
   The circulatory system
   Excretory organs
   Endocrine glands
   The nervous system and sensory organs
Evolution and paleontology
Classification
   Distinguishing taxonomic features
   Annotated classification

GENERAL FEATURES

Structural diversity. Fishes have been in existence for over 450,000,000 years, during which time they have evolved repeatedly to fit into almost every conceivable type of aquatic habitat. In a sense, land vertebrates are simply highly modified fishes, for when fishes colonized the land habitat they became tetrapod (four-legged) land vertebrates. The popular conception of a fish as a slippery, streamlined aquatic animal that possesses fins and breathes by gills applies to many fishes, but far more fishes deviate from that conception than conform to it. The body is elongate in many forms, greatly shortened in others; it is flattened in some (principally in bottom-dwelling fishes) and laterally compressed in many others; the fins may be elaborately extended, forming intricate shapes, or they may be reduced or even lost; the positions of the mouth, eyes, nostrils, and gill openings vary widely. Air breathers have appeared in several evolutionary lines.

Many fishes are cryptically coloured and shaped, closely matching their respective environments; others are among the most brilliantly coloured of all organisms, with a wide range of hues, often of striking intensity, on a single individual. The brilliance of pigments may be enhanced by the surface structure of the fish, so that it almost seems to glow. A number of unrelated fishes have actual light-producing organs. Many fishes are able to alter their coloration, some for the purpose of camouflage, others for the enhancement of behavioral signals.

Fishes range in adult length from less than 10 millimetres (2/5 inches) to more than 20 metres (60 feet) and in weight from about 1.5 grams (0.05 ounces) to about 4,000 kilograms (8,000 pounds). Some live in shallow thermal springs at temperatures slightly above 42° C (100° F), others in cold Arctic seas a few degrees below 0° C (32° F) or in cold deep waters more than 10,000 metres (3,500 feet) beneath the ocean surface. The structural and, especially, the physiological adaptations for life at such extremes are relatively poorly known and provide the scientifically curious with great incentive for study.

Distribution and abundance. Almost all bodies of natural water on the earth bear fish life, exceptions being very hot thermal ponds and extremely salt-alkaline lakes such as the Dead Sea and Great Salt Lake in Utah. The present distribution of fishes is a result of the geological history and development of the earth as well as the ability of fishes to undergo evolutionary change and to adapt to the available habitats. Fishes may be seen to be distributed according to habitat and according to geographical area. Major habitat differences are marine and fresh waters. For the most part the fishes in them, even in adjacent areas, are different, but some, such as the salmon, migrate from one to the other. The freshwater habitat may be seen to be of many kinds. Fishes found in mountain torrents, Arctic lakes, tropical lakes, temperate streams, and tropical rivers will all differ from each other both in obvious gross structure and in physiological attributes. Even in closely adjacent habitats where, for example, a tropical mountain torrent enters a lowland stream, the fish fauna will differ. Marine habitats can be divided into deep ocean floors (benthic), midwater oceanic (bathypelagic), surface oceanic (pelagic), rocky coast, sandy coast, muddy shores, bays, estuaries, and others. Also, for example, rocky coastal shores in tropical and temperate regions will have a different fish fauna, even when such habitats occur along the same coastline.

Although much is known about the present geographical distribution of fishes, far less is known how that distribution came about. Many parts of the fish fauna of the fresh waters of North America and Eurasia are related and undoubtedly have a common origin. The faunas of Africa and South America are related, extremely old, and probably an expression of the drifting apart of the two continents. The fauna of southern Asia is related to that of central Asia and some of it appears to have entered Africa. The extremely large shore fish faunas of the Indian and tropical Pacific oceans comprise a related complex, but the tropical shore fauna of the Atlantic, although containing Indo-Pacific components, is relatively limited and probably younger. The Arctic and Antarctic marine faunas are quite different from each other. The shore fauna of the North Pacific is quite distinct, and that of the North Atlantic more limited and probably younger. Pelagic oceanic fishes, especially those in deep waters, are similar the world over, showing little geographical isolation in terms of family groups. The deep oceanic habitat is very much the same throughout the world, but species differences do exist, showing geographical areas determined by oceanic currents.

NATURAL HISTORY

Life history. All aspects of the life of a fish are closely correlated with adaptation to the total environment, physical, chemical, and biological. In studies of fish life, all the interdependent aspects of their life such as behaviour, locomotion, reproduction, and physical and physiological characteristics must be taken into account.

Correlated with their adaptation to an extremely wide variety of habitats is the extremely wide variety of life cycles that fishes display. The great majority hatch from relatively small eggs a few days to several weeks or more after the eggs are scattered in the water. Newly hatched young are still partially undeveloped and are called larvae until body structures such as fins, skeleton, and some organs are fully formed. Larval life is often very short, usually less than a few weeks, but it can be very long, some lampreys continuing as larvae for at least five years. Young and larval fishes, before reaching sexual maturity, must grow considerably, and their small size and other factors often dictate that they live in a habitat different than that of the adults. For example, some tropical marine shore fishes have pelagic larvae. Larval food also is different and they often live in shallow, more protected waters.

After the fish reaches adult size, the length of its life is subject to many factors, such as innate rates of aging, predation pressure, and the nature of the local climate. The longevity of a species in the protected environment of an aquarium may have nothing to do with how long members of that species live in the wild. Many small fishes live only one to three years at the most. In a few large species some individuals may live as long as 10 or 20 years or even longer.

Behaviour. Fish behaviour is a complicated and varied subject. As in almost all animals with a central nervous system, the nature of a response of an individual fish to stimuli from its environment depends upon the inherited characteristics of its nervous system, on what it has learned from past experience, and on the nature of the stimuli. Compared with the variety of human responses, however, that of a fish is stereotyped, not subject to much modification by "thought" or learning, and investigators must guard against anthropomorphic interpretations of fish behaviour.

Fishes perceive the world around them by the usual senses of sight, smell, hearing, touch, and taste, and by special lateral-line water-current detectors. In the few fishes that generate electric fields, a process that might best be called electrolocation aids in perception. One or another of these senses often is emphasized at the expense of others depending upon the fish's other adaptations. In fishes with large eyes the sense of smell may be reduced; others, with small eyes, hunt and feed primarily by smell (e.g., some eels).

Specialized behaviour is primarily concerned with the three most important activities in the fish's life: feeding, reproduction, and escape from enemies. Schooling behaviour of sardines on the high seas, for instance, is largely a protective device to avoid enemies, but it is also associated with and modified by their breeding and feeding requirements. Predatory fishes are most often solitary, lying in wait to dart suddenly after their prey, a kind of locomotion impossible for beaked parrot fishes, which feed on coral, swimming in small groups from one coral head to the next.

Sleep in fishes, all of which lack true eyelids, consists of a seemingly listless state in which the fish maintains its balance but moves slowly. If attacked or disturbed most can dart away. A few kinds of fishes lie on the bottom to sleep. Most catfishes, some loaches, some eels and electric fishes are strictly nocturnal, being active and hunting for food during the night and retiring during the day to holes, thick vegetation, or other protective parts of the environment.

Communication between members of a species or between members of two or more species often is extremely important, especially in breeding behaviour (see below *Reproduction*). The mode of communication may be visual, as between the small so-called cleaner fish and a large fish of a very different species. The larger fish often allows the cleaner to enter its mouth to remove gill parasites. The cleaner is recognized by its distinctive colour and actions and therefore is not eaten, even if the larger fish is normally a predator.

Locomotion. Many fishes have a streamlined body and swim freely in the open water. Fish locomotion is closely correlated with habitat and ecological niche (the general position of the animal to its environment).

Many fishes in both marine and fresh waters swim at the surface and have mouths adapted to feed best (and sometimes only) at the surface. Often such fishes are long and slender, able to dart at surface insects or at other surface fishes and in turn to dart away from predators; needlefishes, halfbeaks, and topminnows are good examples. Oceanic flying fishes escape their predators by gathering speed above the water surface, with the lower lobe of the tail providing thrust in the water. They then glide hundreds of yards on enlarged, winglike pectoral and pelvic fins. South American freshwater flying fishes escape their enemies by jumping and propelling their strongly keeled bodies out of the water with their pectoral fins, which function as flapping wings.

Habitats

Longevity

Sleep

So-called midwater swimmers, the most common type of fish, are of many kinds and live in many habitats. The powerful fusiform tunas and the trouts, for example, are adapted for strong, fast swimming, the first to capture prey speedily in the open ocean, the second to cope with the swift currents of streams and rivers. The trout body form is well adapted to many habitats. Fishes that live in relatively quiet waters such as bays or lake shores or slow rivers usually are not strong, fast swimmers but are capable of short, quick bursts of speed to escape a predator. Many of these fishes have their sides flattened, examples being the sunfish and the freshwater angelfish of aquarists. Fish associated with the bottom or substrate usually are slow swimmers. Open-water plankton-feeding fishes almost always remain fusiform and capable of rapid, strong movement (for example, sardines and herrings of the open ocean and also many small minnows of streams and lakes).

Special adaptations of bottom dwellers
Bottom-living fishes are of many kinds and have undergone many types of modification of their body shape and swimming habits. Rays, which evolved from strong swimming, midwater sharks, usually stay close to the bottom and move by undulating their large pectoral fins. Flounders live in a similar habitat and move over the bottom by undulating the entire body. Many bottom fishes dart from place to place, resting on the bottom between movements, a motion common in gobies. One goby relative, the mudskipper, has taken to living at the edge of pools along the shore of muddy mangrove swamps. It escapes its enemies by flipping rapidly over the mud, out of the water. Some catfishes, synbranchid eels, the so-called climbing perch, and a few other fishes venture out over damp ground to find more promising waters than those that they left. They move by wriggling their bodies, sometimes using strong pectoral fins; most have accessory air-breathing organs. Many bottom-dwelling fishes live in mud holes or rocky crevices. Marine eels and gobies commonly are found in such habitats and usually seldom venture far beyond their cavelike homes. Some bottom dwellers, such as the clingfishes (Gobiesocidae), have developed powerful adhesive disks that enable them to remain in place on the substrate in areas such as rocky coasts where the action of the waves is great.

Reproduction. The methods of reproduction in fishes are varied but most fishes lay a large number of small eggs, fertilized and scattered outside of the body. The eggs usually remain suspended in the open water in pelagic fishes. Many shore and freshwater fishes lay eggs on the bottom or among plants. Some have adhesive eggs. The mortality of the young and especially of the eggs is very high, and often only a few individuals grow to maturity out of hundreds, thousands, and in some cases, millions of eggs laid.

Males produce sperm, usually as a milky white substance called milt, in two (sometimes one) testes within the body cavity. In bony fishes a sperm duct leads from each testis to a urogenital opening behind the vent or anus. In sharks and rays and in cyclostomes the duct leads to a cloaca. Sometimes the pelvic fins are modified to help transmit the milt to the eggs at the female's vent or on the substrate where the female has placed them. Sometimes accessory organs are used to fertilize females internally; for example, the claspers of many sharks and rays.

In the females the eggs are formed in two ovaries (sometimes only one) and pass through the ovaries to the urogenital opening and to the outside. In some fishes the eggs are fertilized internally but shed before development takes place. Members of about a dozen families each of bony fishes (teleosts) and sharks bear live young. Many skates and rays bear live young. In some bony fishes the eggs simply develop within the female, the young emerging when the eggs hatch (ovoviviparus). Others develop within the ovary and are nourished by ovarian tissues after hatching (viviparous). There are also other methods utilized by fishes to nourish young within the female. In all live-bearers young are born at a relatively large size and are few in number. In one family

of primarily marine fishes, the surfperches from the Pacific coast of North America, the U.S.S.R., and Japan, the males of at least one species appear to be born sexually mature, although not fully grown.

Some fishes are hermaphroditic, an individual producing both sperm and eggs, usually at different stages of its life. Self-fertilization, however, is probably rare.

Successful reproduction and in many cases defense of the eggs and young is assured by rather stereotyped but often elaborate courtship and parental behaviour, either by the male, the female, or both. Some fishes prepare nests by hollowing out depressions in the sand bottom (cichlids, for example), build nests with plant materials and sticky threads excreted by the kidneys (sticklebacks), or blow a cluster of mucus-covered bubbles at the water surface (gouramis). The eggs are laid in these structures. Some cichlids and catfishes incubate eggs in their mouths.

Some fishes, such as salmon, undergo long migrations from the ocean and up large rivers to spawn in gravel beds where they themselves hatched (anadromous fishes). Others undertake shorter migrations from lakes into streams, or in other ways enter for spawning habitats that they do not ordinarily occupy.

FORM AND FUNCTION

Body plan. The basic structure and function of the fish body is similar to those of all other vertebrates. The usual four types of tissues are present: surface or epithelial, connective (bone, cartilage, and fibrous tissues, as well as their derivative, blood), nerve, and muscle tissues. The organs and organ systems parallel those of other vertebrates: for a more detailed discussion, see ORGANS AND ORGAN SYSTEMS, ANIMAL.

The typical fish body is streamlined and spindle shaped, with an anterior head, gill apparatus, and heart, the latter lying in the midline just below the gill chamber (see Figure 1). The body cavity, containing the vital organs,

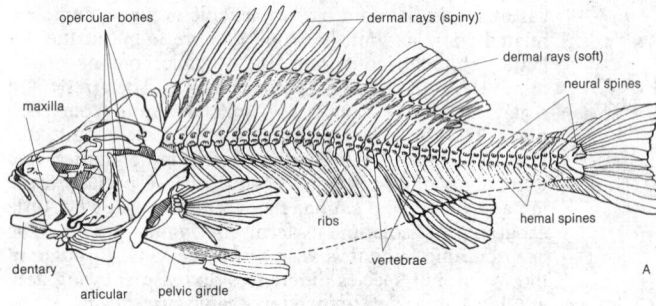

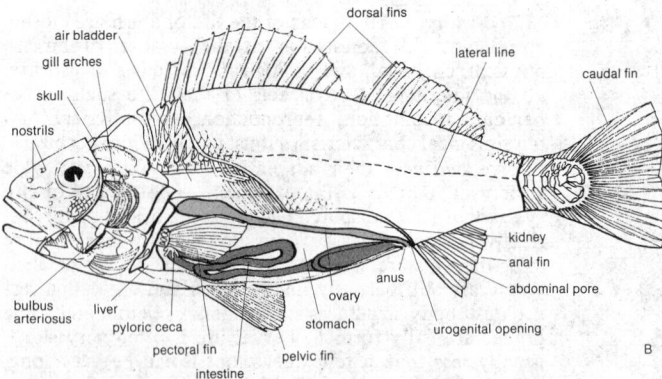

Figure 1: *Internal structure of fishes.*
(A) Skeleton of a perch. (B) Dissection of perch.

is situated behind the head in the lower anterior part of the body. The anus usually marks the posterior termination of the body cavity and most often occurs just in front of the base of the anal fin. The spinal cord and vertebral column continue from the posterior part of the

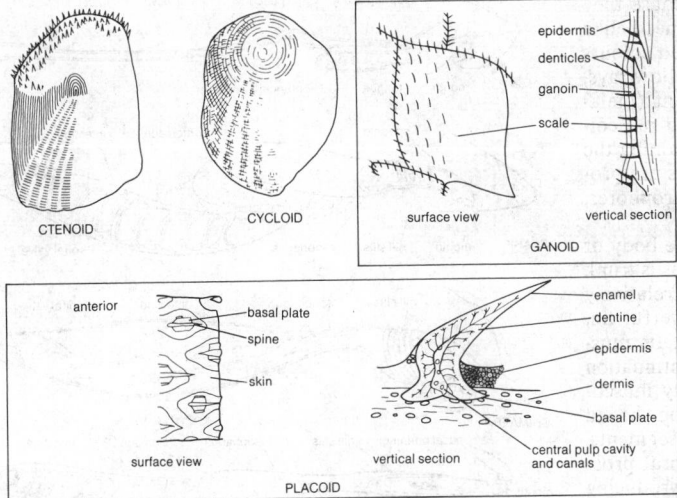

CTENOID   CYCLOID

surface view   vertical section

epidermis
denticles
ganoin
scale

GANOID

anterior
basal plate
spine
skin

surface view   vertical section

enamel
dentine
epidermis
dermis
basal plate
central pulp cavity
and canals

PLACOID

Figure 2: Scales of bony fishes.
From T. Storer and R. Usinger, *General Zoology* (1957); McGraw-Hill Book Company

head to the base of the tail fin, passing dorsal to the body cavity and through the caudal (tail) region behind the body cavity. Most of the body is of muscular tissue, a high proportion of which is necessitated by swimming. In the course of evolution this basic body plan has been modified repeatedly into the many varieties of fish shapes that exist today.

The skeleton forms an integral part of the fish's locomotion system, as well as serving to protect vital parts. The internal skeleton consists of the skull bones (except for the roofing bones of the head, which are really part of the external skeleton), vertebral column, and the fin supports (fin rays). The fin supports are derived from the external skeleton but will be treated here because of their close functional relationship to the internal skeleton. The internal skeleton of cyclostomes, sharks, and rays is of cartilage; that of many fossil groups and some primitive living fishes is mostly of cartilage but may include some bone. In place of the vertebral column, the earliest vertebrates had a fully developed notochord, a flexible stiff rod of viscous cells surrounded by a strong fibrous sheath. During the evolution of modern fishes the rod was replaced in part by cartilage and then by ossified cartilage. Sharks and rays retain a cartilaginous vertebral column; bony fishes have spool-shaped vertebrae that in the more primitive living forms only partially replace the notochord. The skull, including the gill arches and jaws of bony fishes, is fully, or at least partially, ossified. That of sharks and rays remains cartilaginous, at times partially replaced by calcium deposits but never by true bone.

The supportive elements of the fins (basal or radial bones or both) have changed greatly during fish evolution. Some of these changes are described in the sections below (*Paleontology and evolution; Classification*). Most fishes possess a single dorsal fin on the midline of the back. Many have two and a few have three dorsal fins. The other fins are the single tail and anal fins and paired pelvic and pectoral fins. A small fin, the adipose fin, almost always without fin rays, occurs in many of the relatively primitive teleosts (such as trout) on the back near the base of the caudal fin.

The skin. The skin of a fish must serve many functions. It aids in maintaining the osmotic balance, provides physical protection for the body, is the site of coloration, contains sensory receptors, and, in some fishes, functions in respiration. Mucous glands, which aid in maintaining the water balance and offer protection from bacteria, are extremely numerous in fish skin, especially in cyclostomes and teleosts. Since mucous glands are present in the modern lampreys it is reasonable to assume that they were present in primitive fishes, such as the ancient Silurian and Devonian agnaths. Protection from abrasion and predation is another function of the fish

skin, and dermal (skin) bone arose early in fish evolution in response to this need. It is thought that bone first evolved in skin and only later invaded the cartilaginous areas of the fish's body, to provide additional support and protection. There is some argument as to which came first, cartilage or bone, and fossil evidence does not settle the question. In any event, dermal bone has played an important part in fish evolution and has different characteristics in different groups of fishes. Several groups are characterized at least in part by the kind of bony scales they possess.

Scales have played an important part in the evolution of fishes. Primitive fishes usually had thick bony plates or thick scales in several layers of bone, enamel, and related substances. Modern teleost fishes have scales of bone, which, while still protective, allow much more freedom of motion in the body. A few modern teleosts (some catfishes, sticklebacks, and others) have secondarily acquired bony plates in the skin. Modern and early sharks possessed placoid scales, a relatively primitive type of scale with a toothlike structure, consisting of an outside layer of enamel-like substance (vitrodentine), an inner layer of dentine, and a pulp cavity containing nerves and blood vessels. Primitive bony fishes had thick scales of either the ganoid or the cosmoid type. Cosmoid scales have a hard, enamel-like outer layer, an inner layer of cosmine (a form of dentine), and then a layer of vascular bone (isopedine). In ganoid scales the hard outer layer is different chemically and is called ganoin. Under this is a cosmine-like layer and then a vascular bony layer. The thin, translucent bony scales of modern fishes, called cycloid and ctenoid scales (the latter distinguished by serrations at the edges), lack enameloid and dentine layers.

Skin has several other functions in fishes. It is well supplied with nerve endings and presumably receives tactile, thermal, and pain stimuli. Skin is well supplied with blood vessels. Some fishes breathe in part through the skin, by the exchange of oxygen and carbon dioxide between the surrounding water and numerous small blood vessels near the skin surface.

Skin serves as protection through the control of coloration. Fishes exhibit an almost limitless range of colours. The colours often blend closely with the surroundings, effectively hiding the animal. Many fishes use bright colours for territorial advertisement or as recognition marks for other members of their own species, or sometimes for members of other species. Many fishes can change their colour to a greater or lesser degree, by expansion and contraction of the pigment cells (chromatophores). Black pigment cells (melanophores), of almost universal occurrence in fishes, are often juxtaposed with other pigment cells. When placed near iridocytes or leucophores (bearing the silvery or white pigment guanine) melanophores produce structural colours of blue and green.

These colours are often extremely intense, because they are formed by refraction of light through the needlelike crystals of guanine. The blue and green refracted colours are often relatively pure, lacking the red and yellow rays, which have been absorbed by the black pigment (melanin) of the melanophores. Yellow, orange, and red colours are produced by erythrophores, cells containing the appropriate carotenoid pigments. Other colours are produced by combinations of melanophores, erythrophores, and iridocytes.

The muscle system.   The major portion of the body of most fishes consists of muscles. Most of the mass is trunk musculature, the fin muscles usually being relatively small. The caudal fin is usually the most powerful fin, with the largest amount of direct musculature. Its musculature is really a structural and functional continuation of the main musculature of the body. The body musculature is usually arranged in two rows of chevron-shaped segments on each side. Contractions of these segments, each attached to adjacent vertebrae and vertebral processes, bends the body on the vertebral joint, producing successive undulations of the body, passing from the head to the tail, and producing driving strokes of the tail. It is the latter that provides the strong forward movement for most fishes.

The digestive system.   The digestive system, in a functional sense, starts at the mouth, with the teeth used to capture prey or collect plant foods. Mouth shape and tooth structure vary greatly in fishes, depending on the kind of food normally eaten. Most fishes are predacious, feeding on small invertebrates or other fishes and have simple conical teeth on the jaws, on at least some of the bones of the roof of the mouth, and on special gill arch structures just in front of the esophagus. The latter are throat teeth. Most predacious fishes swallow their prey whole, and the teeth are used for grasping and holding prey, for orienting prey to be swallowed (head first) and for working the prey toward the esophagus. There are a variety of tooth types in fishes. Some, such as sharks and the piranhas, have cutting teeth for biting chunks out of their victims. A shark's tooth, although superficially like that of a piranha, appears in many respects to be a modified scale, while that of the piranha is like that of other bony fishes, consisting of dentine and enamel. Parrotfishes have beaklike mouths with short incisor-like teeth for breaking off coral and have heavy pavement-like throat teeth for crushing the coral. Some catfishes have small brushlike teeth, arranged in rows on the jaws, for scraping plant and animal growth from rocks. Many fishes (*e.g.*, the Cyprinidae or minnows) have no jaw teeth at all but have very strong throat teeth.

Types of teeth

Some fishes gather planktonic food by straining it from their gill cavities with numerous elongate stiff rods (gill rakers), anchored by one end to the gill bars. The food collected on these rods is passed to the throat where it is swallowed. Most fishes have only short gill rakers that help keep food particles from escaping out the mouth cavity into the gill chamber.

Once reaching the throat, food enters a short, often greatly distensible esophagus, a simple tube with a muscular wall leading into a stomach. The stomach varies greatly in fishes, depending upon the diet. In most predacious fishes it is a simple straight or curved tube or pouch with a muscular wall and a glandular lining. Food is largely digested here and leaves the stomach in liquid form.

Between the stomach and the intestine, ducts enter the digestive tube from the liver and pancreas. The liver is a large, clearly defined organ. The pancreas may be imbedded in it, diffused through it, or broken into small parts spread along some of the intestine. The junction between the stomach and the intestine is marked by a muscular valve. Pyloric ceca (blind sacs) occur in some fishes at this junction and have a digestive or an absorptive function, or both.

The intestine itself is quite variable in length depending upon the diet. It is short in predacious forms, sometimes no longer than the body cavity, but long in herbivorous

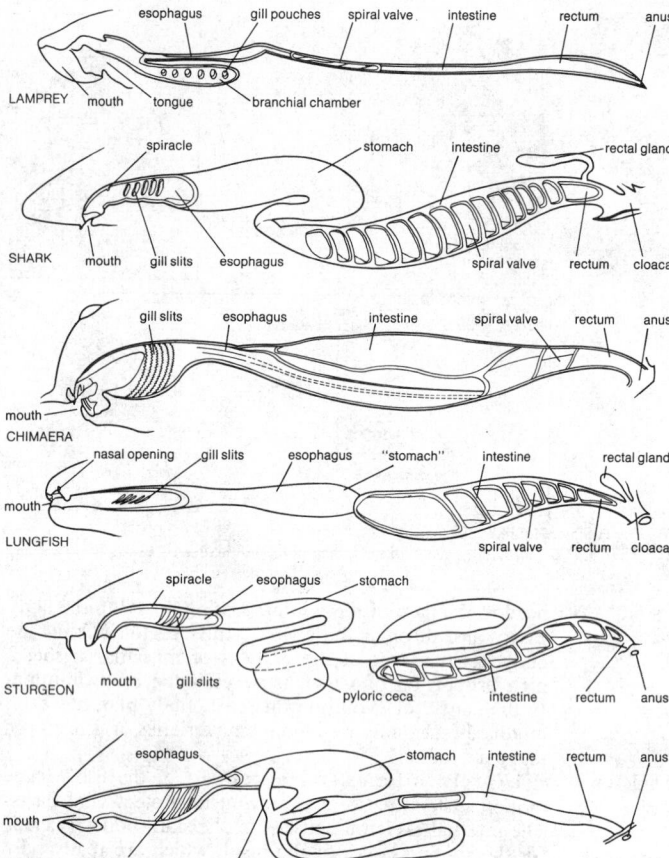

Figure 3: *Digestive tracts of various kinds of fishes.* Lampreys and chimaeras have no stomachs; the stomach of a lungfish is merely an enlargement of the esophagus. From B. Dean, *Fishes Living and Fossil*, in A.S. Romer, *The Vertebrate Body*, 4th ed. (1970); W.B. Saunders Company

forms, being coiled and several times longer than the entire length of the fish in some species of South American catfishes. The intestine is primarily an organ for absorbing nutrients into the bloodstream. The larger its internal surface, the greater its absorptive efficiency, and a spiral valve is one method of increasing its absorption surface.

Sharks, rays, chimaeras, lungfishes, surviving chondrosteans, holosteans, and even a few of the more primitive teleosts have a spiral valve or at least traces of it in the intestine. Most modern teleosts have increased the area of the intestinal walls by having numerous folds and villi (fingerlike projections) somewhat like those in man. Undigested substances are passed to the exterior through the anus in most teleost fishes. In lungfishes, sharks, and rays it is first passed through the cloaca, a common cavity receiving the intestinal opening and the ducts from the uro-genital system.

The respiratory system.   Oxygen and carbon dioxide dissolve in water and most fishes exchange dissolved oxygen and carbon dioxide in water by means of the gills. The gills lie behind and to the side of the mouth cavity and consist of fleshy filaments supported by the gill arches and filled with blood vessels, which give gills a bright red colour. Water taken in continuously through the mouth passes backward between the gill bars and over the gill filaments, where the exchange of gases takes place. The gills are protected by a gill cover in teleosts and many other fishes, but by flaps of skin in sharks, rays, and some of the older fossil fish groups. The blood capillaries in the gill filaments are close to the gill surface to take up oxygen from the water and to give up excess carbon dioxide to the water.

Most modern fishes have a hydrostatic (ballast) organ, called the swim bladder, that lies in the body cavity just below the kidney and above the stomach and intestine. It originated as a diverticulum of the digestive canal. In advanced teleosts, especially the acanthopterygians, the

Swim bladder

bladder has lost its connection with the digestive tract, a condition called physoclistic. The connection has been retained (physostomous) by most relatively primitive teleosts. In several unrelated lines of fishes the bladder has become specialized as a lung or, at least, as a highly vascularized accessory breathing organ. Some fishes with such accessory organs are obligate air breathers and will drown if denied access to the surface, even in well-oxygenated water. Fishes with a hydrostatic form of swim bladder can control their depth by regulating the amount of gas in the bladder. The gas, mostly oxygen, is secreted into the bladder by special glands, rendering the fish more buoyant; it is absorbed into the bloodstream by another special organ, reducing the overall buoyancy and allowing the fish to sink. Some deep-sea fishes may have oil in the bladder, rather than gas. Other deep-sea and some bottom-living forms have much reduced swim bladders or have lost the organ entirely.

The swim bladder of fishes follows the same developmental pattern as the lungs of land vertebrates. There is no doubt that the two structures have the same historical origin in primitive fishes. More or less intermediate forms still survive among the more primitive types of fishes such as the lungfishes *Lepidosiren* and *Protopterus.*

The circulatory system. The circulatory, or blood vascular, system consists of the heart, the arteries, the capillaries, and the veins: it is in the capillaries that the interchange of oxygen, carbon dioxide, nutrients and other substances such as hormones and waste products takes place. The capillaries in turn lead to the veins, which return the venous blood with its waste products to the heart, kidneys, and gills. There are two kinds of capillary beds, those in the gills and those in the rest of the body. The heart, a folded continuous muscular tube with three or four sacklike enlargements, undergoes rhythmic contractions, and receives venous blood in a sinus venosus. It then passes the blood to an auricle and then into a thick, muscular pump, the ventricle. From the ventricle the blood goes to a bulbous structure at the base of a ventral aorta just below the gills. The blood then passes to the afferent (receiving) arteries of the gill arches and then to the gill capillaries. There waste gases are given off to the environment and oxygen is absorbed. From there the oxygenated blood enters efferent (exuant) arteries of the gill arches and then into the dorsal aorta. From there blood is distributed to the tissues and organs of the body. One-way valves prevent backflow. The circulation of fishes thus differs from that of the reptiles, birds, and mammals, in that oxygenated blood is not returned to the heart prior to distribution to the other parts of the body.

Excretory organs. The primary excretory organ in fishes, as in other vertebrates, is the kidney. In fishes some excretion also takes place in the digestive tract, skin, and especially the gills (where ammonia is given off). Compared with land vertebrates, fishes have a special problem in maintaining their internal environment at a constant concentration of water and dissolved substances, such as salts. Proper balance of the internal environment (homeostasis) of a fish is in a great part maintained by the excretory system, especially the kidney.

Water balance The kidney, gills, and skin play an important role in maintaining a fish's internal environment and checking the effects of osmosis. Marine fishes live in an environment in which the water around them has a greater concentration of salts than they can have inside their body and still maintain life. Freshwater fishes, on the other hand, live in water with a much lower concentration of salts than they require inside their bodies. Osmosis tends to promote the loss of water from the body of a marine fish and absorption of water by that of a freshwater fish. Mucus in the skin tends to slow the process but is not a sufficient barrier to prevent the movement of fluids through the permeable skin. When solutions on two sides of a permeable membrane have different concentrations of dissolved substances, water will pass through the membrane into the more concentrated solution, while the dissolved chemicals move into the area of lower concentration (diffusion).

The kidney of freshwater fishes is often larger in relation to body weight than that of marine fishes. In both groups the kidney excretes wastes from the body, but that of freshwater fishes also excretes large amounts of water, counteracting the water absorbed through the skin. Freshwater fishes tend to lose salt to the environment and must replace it. They get some salt from their food, but the gills and skin inside the mouth actively absorb salt from water passed through the mouth. This absorption is performed by special cells capable (like those of the kidney) of moving salts against the diffusion gradient. Freshwater fishes drink very little water and take in little water in their food.

Marine fishes must conserve water, therefore their kidneys excrete little water. To maintain their water balance marine fishes drink large quantities of seawater, retaining most of the water and excreting the salt. By reabsorption of needed water in the kidney tubules, they discharge a more concentrated urine than do freshwater fishes. Most nitrogenous waste in marine fishes appears to be secreted by the gills as ammonia. Some marine fishes, at least, can excrete salt by clusters of special cells in the gills and intestine.

There are several teleosts—for example, the salmon—that travel between fresh water and seawater and must adjust to the reversal of osmotic gradients. They adjust their physiological processes by spending time (often surprisingly little time) in the intermediate brackish environment.

Marine lampreys, hagfishes, sharks, and rays have osmotic concentrations in their blood about equal to that of seawater so do not have to drink water nor perform much physiological work to maintain their osmotic balance. In sharks and rays the osmotic concentration is kept high by retention of urea in the blood. Freshwater sharks have a lowered concentration of urea in the blood.

Endocrine glands. Endocrine glands secrete their products into the bloodstream and body tissues and, along with the central nervous system, control and regulate many kinds of body functions. Cyclostomes have a well-developed endocrine system, and presumably it was well developed in the early Agnatha, ancestral to modern fishes. Although the endocrine system in fishes is similar to that of higher vertebrates, there are numerous differences in detail. The endocrine glands of fishes are the pituitary, thyroid, suprarenals, adrenals, pancreatic islets, sex glands (ovaries and testes), the inner wall of the intestine, and the ultimobranchial bodies. There are some others whose function is not well understood. These organs regulate sexual activity and reproduction, growth, osmoregulation, general metabolic activities such as the storage of fat and the utilization of foodstuffs, blood pressure, and certain aspects of skin colour. Many of these activities also are controlled in part by the central nervous system, which works with the endocrine system in maintaining the life of a fish. Some parts of the endocrine system are developmentally, and undoubtedly evolutionarily, derived from the nervous system.

The nervous system and sensory organs. As in all vertebrates, the nervous system of fishes is the primary mechanism coordinating body activities, as well as integrating these activities in the appropriate manner with stimuli from the environment. The central nervous system, the brain, and spinal cord, are the primary integrating mechanisms. The peripheral nervous system, consisting of nerves that connect the brain and spinal cord to various body organs, carries sensory information from special receptor organs such as the eyes, internal ears, nares (sense of smell), taste glands, and others to the integrating centres of the brain and spinal cord. The peripheral nervous system also carries information via different nerve cells from the integrating centres of the brain and spinal cord. This coded information is carried to the various organs and body systems, such as the skeletal muscular system, for appropriate action in response to the original external or internal stimulus. Another branch of the nervous system, the autonomic system, helps to coordinate the activities of many glands and organs and is itself closely connected to the integrating centres of the brain.

The brain

The brain of the fish is divided into several anatomical and functional parts, all closely interconnected but each serving as the primary centre of integrating particular kinds of responses and activities. Several of these centres or parts are primarily associated with one type of sensory perception such as sight, hearing, or smell (olfaction).

Olfaction. The sense of smell is important in almost all fishes. Certain eels with tiny eyes depend mostly on smell for location of food. The olfactory, or nasal, organ of fishes is located on the dorsal surface of the snout. The lining of the nasal organ has special sensory cells that perceive chemicals dissolved in the water such as substances from food material and send sensory information to the brain by way of the first cranial nerve. Odour also serves as an alarm system. Many fishes, especially various species of freshwater minnows, react with alarm to the body fluids produced by an injured member of their own species.

Taste. Many fishes have a well-developed sense of taste, and tiny pitlike taste buds or organs are located not only within their mouth cavities but also over their heads and parts of their body. The barbels ("whiskers") of catfishes, which often have poor vision, serve as supplementary taste organs, those around the mouth being actively used to search out food on the bottom. Some species of naturally blind cave fishes are especially well supplied with taste buds, these being often over most of their body's surface.

Sight. Sight is extremely important in most fishes. The eye of a fish is basically like that of all other vertebrates, but the eyes of fishes are extremely varied in structure and adaptation. In general, fishes living in dark and dim water habitats have large eyes, unless they have specialized in some compensatory way with another sense such as smell being dominant, in which case the eyes will often be reduced. Fishes living in brightly lighted shallow waters will often have relatively small but efficient eyes. Cyclostomes have somewhat less elaborate eyes than other fishes, with skin stretched over the eyeball perhaps making their vision somewhat less effective. Most fishes have a spherical lens and accommodate their vision to far or near subjects by moving the lens within the eyeball. A few sharks accommodate by changing the shape of the lens, as in land vertebrates. Those fishes that are heavily dependent upon the eyes have especially strong muscles for accommodation. Most fishes see well, despite the restrictions imposed by frequent turbidity of the water and by light refraction. Experimental evidence indicates that many shallow-water fishes, if not all, have colour vision and see some colours especially well, but some bottom-dwelling shore fishes live in areas where the water is sufficiently deep to filter out most if not all colours, and these fishes apparently never see colours. When tested in shallow water, they apparently are unable to respond to colour differences.

Colour vision

Hearing. Sound perception and balance are intimately associated senses in a fish. The organs of hearing are entirely internal, located within the skull, on each side of the brain and somewhat behind the eyes. Sound waves, especially those of low frequencies, travel readily through water and impinge directly upon the bones and fluids of the head and body, to be transmitted to the hearing organs. Fishes readily respond to sound; for example, a trout conditioned to escape by the appoach of fishermen will take flight upon perceiving footsteps on a stream bank even if it cannot see the fisherman. Compared with humans, however, the range of sound frequencies heard by fishes is greatly restricted. It is thought that many fishes communicate with each other in a crude way by producing sounds in their swim bladders, in their throats by rasping their teeth, and in other ways.

Other senses (touch, pain, and special senses). A fish or other vertebrate seldom has to rely on a single type of

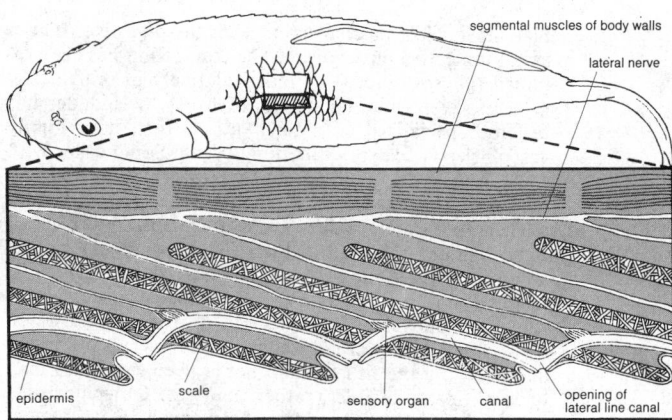

Figure 4: Magnified longitudinal section through a carp's body wall showing lateral line sensory system.
From T. Storer and R. Usinger, *General Zoology* (1957); McGraw-Hill Book Co.

sensory information to determine the nature of the environment around it. A catfish uses taste and touch when examining a food object with its oral barbels. Like most other animals, fishes have many touch receptors over their body surface. Pain and temperature receptors also are present in fishes and presumably produce the same kind of information to a fish as to humans. Fishes react in a negative fashion to stimuli that would be painful to human beings, suggesting that they feel a sensation of pain.

An important sensory system in fishes that is absent in other vertebrates (except some amphibians) is the lateral line system. This consists of a series of heavily innervated small canals located in the skin and bone around the eyes, along the lower jaw, over the head and down the midside of the body where it is associated with the scales. Intermittently along these canals are located tiny sensory organs (pit organs) that apparently detect changes in pressure. The system allows a fish to sense changes in water currents and pressure, thereby helping the fish to orient itself to the various changes that occur in the physical environment.

Lateral line system

EVOLUTION AND PALEONTOLOGY

Although a great many fossil fishes have been found and described, they represent a tiny portion of the long and complex evolution of fishes and knowledge of fish evolution remains relatively fragmentary. In the classification presented in this article fishlike vertebrates are divided into seven classes, the members of each having a different basic structural organization and different physical and physiological adaptations for the problems presented by the environment. The broad basic pattern has been one of successive replacement of older groups by newer, better adapted groups. One or a few members of a group evolved a basically more efficient means of feeding, breathing, swimming, or several better ways of living. These better adapted groups then forced the extinction of members of the older group with which they competed for available food, breeding places, or other necessities of life. As the new fishes became well established, some of them evolved further and adapted to other habitats, where they continued to replace members of the old group already there. The process was repeated until all or almost all members of the old group in a variety of habitats had been replaced by members of the newer evolutionary line.

The earliest vertebrate fossils of certain relationships are fragments of dermal armour of jawless fishes (class Agnatha, order Heterostraci) from the Middle Ordovician Period in North America, about 450,000,000 years in age. Early Ordovician toothlike fragments from the U.S.S.R. are less certainly remains of the class Agnatha. It is uncertain whether the North American jawless fishes inhabited shallow coastal marine waters, where their remains became fossilized, or were freshwater vertebrates washed into coastal deposits by stream action.

Early jawless fishes

Jawless fishes probably arose from ancient small, soft-bodied filter-feeding organisms much like and probably also ancestral to the modern sand-dwelling filter feeders, the Cephalochordata (*Amphioxus* and its relatives). The body in the ancestral animals was probably stiffened by a notochord. Although a vertebrate origin in fresh water is much debated by paleontologists, it is possible that mobility of the body and protection provided by dermal armour arose in response to streamflow in the freshwater environment and to the need to escape from and resist the clawed invertebrate eurypterids that lived in the same waters. Because of the marine distribution of the surviving primitive chordates, many paleontologists doubt that the vertebrates arose in fresh water.

Heterostracan remains are next found in what appear to be delta deposits in two North American localities of Silurian age. By the close of the Silurian, about 400,000,-000 years ago, European heterostracan remains are found in what appear to be delta or coastal deposits. In the Late Silurian of the Baltic area, lagoon or freshwater deposits yield jawless fishes of the order Osteostraci. Somewhat later in the Silurian from the same region, layers contain fragments of jawed acanthodians, the earliest group of jawed vertebrates, and of jawless fishes. These layers lie between marine beds but appear to be washed out from fresh waters of a coastal region.

It is evident, therefore, that by the end of the Silurian both jawed and jawless vertebrates were well established and already must have had a long history of development. Yet paleontologists have remains only of specialized forms that cannot have been the ancestors of the placoderms and bony fishes that appear in the next period, the Devonian. No fossils are known of the more primitive ancestors of the agnaths and acanthodians. The extensive marine beds of the Silurian and those of the Ordovician are essentially void of vertebrate history. It is believed that the ancestors of fishlike vertebrates evolved in upland fresh waters, where whatever few and relatively small fossil beds were made probably have been long since eroded away. Remains of the earliest vertebrates may never be found.

By the close of the Silurian, all five known orders of jawless vertebrates had evolved, except perhaps the modern cyclostomes, which are without the hard parts that ordinarily are preserved as fossils. Cyclostomes were unknown as fossils until 1968, when a lamprey of modern body structure was reported from the Middle Pennsylvanian of Illinois, in deposits almost 300,000,000 years old. Fossil evidence of the four orders of armoured jawless vertebrates is absent from deposits later than the Devonian. Presumably they became extinct at that time, being replaced by the more efficient and probably more aggressive placoderms, acanthodians, selachians (sharks and relatives), and by early bony fishes. Cyclostomes survived probably because they early evolved from anaspid agnaths and developed a rasping tonguelike structure and a sucking mouth, enabling them to prey on other fishes. With this way of life they apparently had no competition from other fish groups.

Early jawless vertebrates probably fed on tiny organisms by filter feeding, as do the larvae of their descendants, the modern lampreys. The gill cavity of the early agnaths was large. It is thought that small organisms taken from the bottom by a nibbling action of the mouth, or more certainly by a sucking action through the mouth, were passed into the gill cavity along with water for breathing. Small organisms then were strained out by the gill apparatus and directed to the food canal. The gill apparatus thus evolved as a feeding, as well as a breathing, structure. The head and gills in the agnaths were protected by a heavy dermal armour; the tail region was free, allowing motion for swimming.

Appearance of bone

Most important for the evolution of fishes and vertebrates in general was the early appearance of bone, cartilage, and enamel-like substance. These materials became modified in later fishes, enabling them to adapt to many aquatic environments and finally even to land. Other basic organs and tissues of the vertebrates such as the central nervous system, heart, liver, digestive tract, kidney, and circulatory system undoubtedly were present in the ancestors of the Agnatha. In many ways, bone, both external and internal, was the key to vertebrate evolution.

The next class of fishes to appear was the Acanthodii, containing the earliest known jawed vertebrates, which arose in the Upper Silurian, over 400,000,000 years ago. The acanthodians declined after the Devonian but lasted into the Lower Permian, a little less than 280,000,000 years ago. The first complete specimens appear in Lower Devonian freshwater deposits, but later in the Devonian and Permian some members appear to have been marine. Most were small fishes, not over 75 centimetres in length.

We know nothing of the ancestors of the acanthodians. They must have arisen from some jawless vertebrate, probably in fresh water. They appear to have been active swimmers with almost no head armour but with large eyes, indicating that they depended heavily on vision. Perhaps they preyed on invertebrates. The rows of spines and spinelike fins between the pectoral and pelvic fins give some credence to the idea that paired fins arose from "fin folds" along the body sides.

The relationships of the acanthodians to other jawed vertebrates are obscure. They possess features found in both sharks and bony fishes. They are like early bony fishes in possessing ganoid-like scales and a partially ossified internal skeleton. Certain aspects of the jaw appear to be more like those of bony fishes than sharks, but the bony fin spines and certain aspects of the gill apparatus would seem to favour relationships with early sharks. Acanthodians do not seem particularly close to the Placodermi although, like the placoderms, they apparently possessed less efficient tooth replacement and tooth structure than the sharks and the bony fishes, possibly one reason for their subsequent extinction.

The first record of the jawed Placodermi is from the Early Devonian, about 390,000,000 years ago. The placoderms flourished for about 60,000,000 years and were almost gone at the end of the Devonian. Nothing is known of their ancestors, who must have existed in the Silurian. The evolution of several other, better adapted, fish groups soon followed the appearance of the placoderms and this apparently led to their early extinction. Their greatest period of success was approximately during the middle of the Devonian, when some of them became marine. As their name indicates (placoderm means "plate skin"), most of these fishes had heavy coats of bony armour, especially about the head and anterior part of the body. The tail remained free and heterocercal (*i.e.*, the upper lobe long, the lower one small or lacking). Most placoderms remained small, 30 centimetres or less in length, but one group, the arthrodires, had a few marine members that reached 10 metres in length. Important evolutionary advances of the placoderms were in the jaws (which usually were amphystylic—*i.e.*, involving the hyoid and quadrate bones) and development of fins, especially the paired fins with well-formed basal or radial elements. The jaws tended to be of single elements with strongly attached toothlike structures. These were too specialized to be considered ancestral to the more adaptable jaws of subsequent bony fish groups. It has been proposed that sharks arose from some group of placoderms near the Stensioelliformes and that the chimaera line (class Holocephali) arose from certain arthrodires; this suggestion, however, is uncertain.

A peculiar, five-centimetre fish, *Palaeospondylus*, from Middle Devonian rocks in Scotland, is probably not a placoderm, although classed with them here. Various suggestions that its relationships are with the agnaths, placoderms, acanthodians, sharks, and even lungfishes and amphibians are unconvincing and its relationships remain completely unknown.

Origin of sharks

Sharks (class Selachii) first appear in the Middle Devonian about 375,000,000 years ago, became quite prominent by the end of the Devonian, and are still successful today. Two Early Devonian orders of primitive sharklike fishes, the Cladoselachiformes and the Cladodontiformes, became extinct by the end of the Permian, about 230,-

000,000 years ago, while the freshwater order Xenacanthiformes lasted until the Middle Triassic, about 200,-000,000 years ago. The final Devonian order, Heterodontiformes, still has surviving members.

Modern sharks and rays arose during the Jurassic Period, about 135,000,000 to 190,000,000 years ago, probably from an older group, the hybodont sharks. Presumably marine cladoselachians gave rise to the hybodont Heterodontiformes during the close of the Devonian. These had the placoderm amphystylic jaws but had paired fins of a more efficient type. In turn the hybodonts are thought to have given rise to the living but archaic mollusk-eating Port Jackson sharks (heterodonts). The relationships of the surviving (but archaic) hexanchiform sharks are unknown. The two main orders of modern Selachii, the Lamniformes (sharks) and Rajiformes (skates and rays), appeared between 140,000,000 and 180,-000 years ago during the Jurassic Period. They are characterized by a hyostylic jaw (in which articulation involves only the hyoid bone), an improvement allowing greater mobility of the jaws and an important feature in the methods of predation used by modern selachians.

Skates and rays evolved from some bottom-living shark-like ancestor during the Jurassic. The primary evolution and diversification of modern sharks, skates, and rays

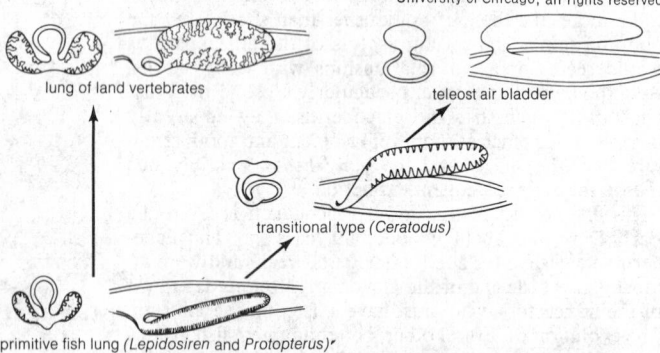

lung of land vertebrates

teleost air bladder

transitional type *(Ceratodus)*

primitive fish lung *(Lepidosiren* and *Protopterus)*

Figure 5: *Evolution of lungs and swim bladder.*
Each example consists of (left) a cross section through the gut and saclike growth and (right) a longitudinal section.

took place in the Cretaceous Period and Cenozoic Era. Thus, along with the teleost fishes (discussed below) most surviving sharks, skates, and rays are essentially of relatively recent origin, their main evolutionary radiation having taken place within the last 140,000,000 years.

The class Holocephali, the chimaeras or ratfishes as their modern survivors are called, first appeared in the Upper Devonian but were most common and diversified during the Mesozoic Era. Only one of the seven known orders survived beyond the close of the Cretaceous Period about 65,000,000 years ago. Although not many modern species of chimaeras are known, they are sometimes relatively abundant in their deep-sea habitat. The relationships of these fishes are in question. It has been proposed that they are related to the Devonian ptyctodont arthrodires, which had a chimaera-like shape and pelvic claspers. It has also been suggested that they are closely related to the Selachii because both selachians and holocephalians have many characters in common, such as placoid scales, pelvic claspers, and absence of true bone. It has been suggested recently that both holocephalians and selachians are related to the acanthodians on the basis of the gill arch structures. Further evidence is needed to solve the problem.

The class Sarcopterygii are extremely ancient in origin, their first remains appearing in Lower Devonian strata of Germany, about 390,000,000 years old. The most important group, the rhipidistians, which gave rise to the amphibians by the end of the Devonian, became extinct about 120,000,000 years later, near the beginning of the Permian. Two lesser groups, the coelacanths and the dipnoans (lungfishes), have barely survived. Recognition of the class Sarcopterygii is controversial in that some ich-

thyologists believe that the two major groups, the Crossopterygii (including the rhipidistians and coelacanths) and the Dipnoi, have independent origins, their present structure being widely divergent. The primitive members, however, show several similarities, supporting the view that they had a common ancestor. The nature of the ancestor or ancestors remains a mystery. The Sarcopterygii probably evolved from unknown Silurian jawed freshwater fishes that may also have been ancestral to the actinopterygians.

The rhipidistian crossopterygians apparently flourished in the fresh waters of the Middle Devonian where, in adapting to a habitat subject to seasonal droughts, some evolved pectoral and pelvic appendages strong enough and flexible enough to enable them to leave drying pools to seek out those ponds that retained water. Paradoxically, terrestrial vertebrate amphibians first rose through the need to survive in water.

The early coelacanths of the Upper Devonian were small freshwater and inshore fishes, and it was not until the Late Permian and Triassic that they became marine and grew larger and more diverse. They are not known as fossils later than the Cretaceous, and it was therefore a great surprise when in 1938 a live, 160-centimetre specimen was taken at 120 metres off the coast of eastern South Africa.

The dipnoans first appeared in the Lower Devonian and were fully differentiated at that time. They flourished until the close of the Triassic, when their numbers became greatly reduced. The modern Australian lungfish differs little from one of the Triassic forms. The living South American and especially African lungfishes are elongated, specialized fishes adapted to live and survive in more or less annual ponds.

The Actinopterygii, or "ray-finned" fishes, is the largest class of fishes. In existence for about 390,000,000 years, since the Lower Devonian, it consists of some 52 orders containing more than 480 families, at least 80 of which are known only from fossils. The class contains the great majority of known living and fossil fishes, with about 20,-000 living species. The history of actinopterygians can be divided into three basic stages or evolutionary radiations, each representing a different level of structural organization and efficiency.

The Chondrostei have a 300,000,000-year history. They arose first in the Lower Devonian, increased in numbers and complexity until about the Permian, and thereafter declined, becoming almost extinct by the middle of the Cretaceous, 100,000,000 years ago. The chondrostean order Palaeonisciformes is the basal actinopterygian stock from which all other chondrosteans and the holosteans evolved. They were the most common fishes of their time, relatively small and typically like later fishes in appearance. In comparison with today's fishes they had peculiar looking jaws and tails. Their tails were heterocercal. On their bodies were thick ganoid scales that abutted each other, rather than overlapping, as in most modern fishes. Palaeonisciformes often had large eyes placed far forward, long mouths with the upper jaw firmly bound to the fully armoured cheek, and a relatively weak lower jaw muscle. They gave rise to a great variety of types, with elongate bodies and jaws (vaguely like the modern pike), bottom-living types that fed on micro-organisms, deep-bodied marine reef fishes and coral-eating reef fishes. Almost all of these were replaced by modern teleosts. Surviving Chondrostei are the bottom-feeding marine and freshwater sturgeons, the strange plankton-feeding paddlefishes of the Mississippi of North America and the Yangtze River of China, and the freshwater bichirs and reed fishes (family Polypteridae) of Africa. The relationship of the polypterids are in some doubt and the group is sometimes placed in the Sarcopterygii.

Several of the chondrostean orders developed characters that approached the holostean level of anatomical organization, sometimes called subholosteans. One of these orders, the Parasemionotiformes, evolved from the Palaeonisciformes in the Lower Triassic and may have given rise to at least some of the holosteans. This evolutionary

Chondrosts

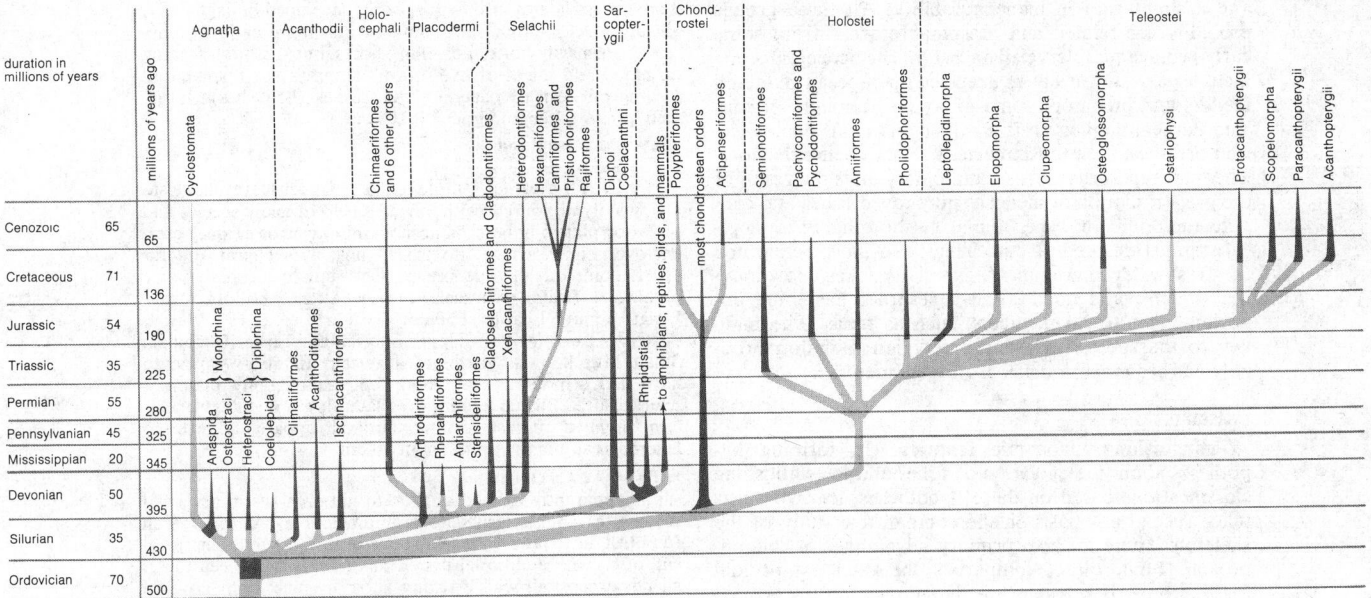

Figure 6: Phyletic family tree for fishes.

line leads to the Pholidophoriformes, which gave rise to modern bony fishes, or teleosts.

The holosteans are thought to be of mixed origin and to represent a stage in the evolution of a group of chondrostean orders. If so, the infraclass Holostei does not represent a single lineage. Important holostean characters are the approach of the tail toward the homocercal condition and the equal number of fin rays and basal elements of the fin rays. Both of these conditions make the holostean a more efficient swimmer than the chondrostean, as does thinning of the holostean body scales. Another important advance of holosts was the freeing of the upper jaw from the preopercular bone of the cheek, allowing greater movement of the gill chamber and jaws, with more powerful development of the lower jaw muscle.

Five orders of holosteans are known, with their greatest evolutionary radiation occurring during the Triassic, Jurassic, and Cretaceous periods, when the chondrosteans were declining and the teleosts just beginning to expand. Two holostean groups survive today, the bowfin, *Amia calva,* and the several species of gars, *Lepisosteus,* all found in North America.

The modern bony fishes, infraclass Teleostei, include the great majority of living fishes. They first appear in the fossil record about 190,000,000 years ago (as the family Leptolepididae) with their homocercal caudal fin and caudal skeleton already fully developed. They arose from an order of holosteans now extinct, the Pholidophoriformes. This group was intermediate in character between the chondrosteans and the teleosts. Teleosts have reached their fullest extent within the last 50,000,000 years and represent a distinct functional advance over their holostean ancestors. They have greater swimming ability, due to the improvement in the tail structure, and have a still more efficient feeding and gill ventilating apparatus.

The bony fishes represent the culmination of a long evolution toward a body plan with maximum swimming efficiency. Particularly important in this evolution have been changes in fins and in the tail. Some authorities believe that the paired fins arose from a single continuous tail and anal fin that was divided at the vent and extended forward along each side to the head. Later, the sections between the pectoral, pelvic, anal, and caudal fins were lost. The fin rays of sharks and rays are of a horny material, but those of many primitive fossil fishes are of bone. The bony fin rays of sarcopterygians and actinopterygians probably arose from scales lying in the fin folds. Modern teleost fishes have flexible fin rays (called soft rays) of jointed segments of bone, or spiny rays, each of solid continuous bone. The first dorsal fin of acanthopterygian fishes is of the spiny type. The original tail fin of primitive

fishes was not an effective swimming organ, due to its asymmetry. The steady improvement in tail shape over 400,000,000 years is one of the prominent features of fish evolution. In primitive fishes the tail (vertebral) axis turned upward (heterocercal) or downward (hypocercal) and a lobe of flesh projected from it. This form of tail cannot provide a powerful driving mechanism because the driving force is unevenly distributed, relative to the body axis. With an asymmetrical tail, the fish swims by an undulating motion of the body and tail. In some fishes with a diphycercal tail (with the axis of the vertebrae extending down the middle of the fin lobe), developed in both modern and ancient fishes, the tail remains relatively ineffective because it has remained too rigid for proper propulsive action. The development of a true homocercal tail fin, in which powerful muscles move strong fin rays with a very flexible basal joint and in which the upper and lower lobes are about equal, is a development exclusive to teleost fishes.

As suggested by the existence of more than 400 families, teleosts are extremely varied in anatomical form and in the habitat occupied. They can be divided into about nine superorders, each with distinct evolutionary significance. The Leptolepidimorpha, an extinct, relatively primitive group, has uncertain relationships with other teleosts and is as yet poorly understood. The second group, the Elopomorpha, retains some relatively primitive living members, such as the tarpons, but is mostly represented by the large variety of specialized true eels. The Clupeomorpha includes the herrings and anchovies, relatively primitive fishes, mostly specialized for existence near the surface of the open ocean. A few species are anadromous, breeding in fresh water, but spending most of their lives in the sea. The fourth superorder, the Osteoglossomorpha, consists of a group of relatively primitive teleosts, most of which are now extinct. The few surviving members are tropical and worldwide in distribution, but adapted for restricted habitats. The Protacanthopterygii is a varied collection of relatively primitive orders, marine, deepsea, and freshwater in distribution; trouts, smelts, and argentines are examples. The sixth superorder, the Ostariophysi, is an important group of primarily freshwater fishes, including the characins, carps, minnows, loaches, suckers, and catfishes.

The remaining three superorders have a complex fossil history and are not yet fully understood, but all seem to possess similar evolutionary trends. Each group shows a tendency to develop spiny fin rays in the dorsal and anal fins (reduced in some) and a shelf of bone under the eye. There is a tendency for the pelvic fins to move forward on the body, with a reorganization of swimming methods

Advent of advanced bony fishes

and a slight gain in manoeuvrability. All three groups probably are related and presumably arose from some early protacanthopterygian ancestor. The Scopelomorpha includes a wide variety of deep-sea open-ocean plankton feeders and predators, some of which bear light organs. The Paracanthopterygii is a rather miscellaneous collection of fishes, the most important to man being the cods. The final superorder, the Acanthopterygii, is the result of the great radiation of modern spiny-rayed fishes and contains the dominant fishes in marine shore habitats, tropical, temperate, and Arctic. They also have penetrated the freshwater environment, especially lakes, slow-moving streams, and ponds. The superorder has some important open-ocean members, such as tunas. The main key to the successful acanthopterygian radiation probably has been their mobile, protractile mouth.

CLASSIFICATION

Distinguishing taxonomic features. In forming hypotheses about the evolution of fishes and in establishing classifications based on these hypotheses, ichthyologists place special emphasis on the comparative study of the skeleton. There are two primary advantages of this approach. First, direct comparison between extant and fossil groups is possible, the latter usually represented only by bony remains. The second advantage is that the bones of living fishes are relatively easy to observe and to study, compared with other body structures. Proper preservation and special preparation of the nervous system, for example, is difficult and expensive when the fishes compared are from the far ends of the earth. In the study of the relationships of species within a group major use has been made of similarities and differences in the dimensions of external features such as head and body length, and of counts of external characters, such as teeth, fin rays, and scales. Colour pattern is also important. In recent years valuable data on classification of fishes has been obtained from studies of comparative behaviour, physiology, genetics and functional anatomy.

Annotated classification. The following classification has been derived primarily from the works of C. Patterson, Miles, P.H. Greenwood and co-workers, D.E. Rosen and C. Patterson, and K.S. Thomson. Fish classification has undergone major revisions in recent years and further modifications can be expected in the future. Ichthyologists frequently disagree on major as well as minor concepts of phyletic relationships. There remains much to learn about both living and fossil fishes. The geographical distribution given for a poorly known fossil group usually represents only the location of fossil finds not necessarily the true distribution of the group. In the classification presented here groups indicated by a dagger (†) are known only from fossils.

CLASS AGNATHA

Vertebrates with a suctorial or filter-feeding mouth; no true jaws; 2 (possibly 1 sometimes) semicircular canals; pelvic fins lacking, pectoral finlike structures, when present, lacking fin rays; persistent notochord, without bone or cartilage; bony skeleton, when present, formed in skin; true gill arches absent, gill basket present. Habitat of fossil groups uncertain; earliest probably in fresh water (see AGNATHA).

Subclass Monorhina
With 1 nostril.

†*Order Osteostraci.* Late Silurian to close of Devonian. Heavily armoured with bony plates and scales; bony head shield present; bone cells tend to be absent; pectoral appendages present in some; eyes dorsal, close together; no common gill opening; bottom-dwelling with heterocercal tails. Length about 8–75 cm.

†*Order Anaspida.* Late Silurian to Late Devonian. Heavily armoured with bony plates and scales; head protected by small bonelike plates; bone cells present; pectoral appendages various, spine or fleshy fold; eyes not close together but facing laterally; no common gill opening; probably swam above bottom with tail lobe extending downward (hypocercal). Length about 10–25 cm.

Order Cyclostomata (Lampreys and hagfishes). Pennsylvanian and Recent. Freshwater and marine, breeding in fresh water (lampreys); or marine only (hagfishes). Without dermal ossification of any sort; pectoral appendages absent; eyes more or less lateral or dorsal (poorly developed in hagfishes); gill openings multiple, not common; tail more or less diphycercal. Primarily bottom-dwelling fishes, but suctorial, feeding on blood and juices of live fishes (lampreys) or rasping and feeding on flesh of dead or dying fishes (hagfishes); horny teeth present. Length about 15–100 cm.

†**Subclass Diplorhina**
With 2 nostrils.

†*Order Heterostraci.* Ordovician to Upper Devonian. Usually heavily armoured, with a head shield in many species and scales or plates; bone cells absent; thin layer of enamel present over bone surface; no paired fins; eyes lateral and far apart; common gill opening present; tail hypocercal. Some perhaps midwater swimmers, others flattened bottom forms. Length about 5 to at least 30 cm.

†*Order Coelolepida.* Upper Silurian and Lower Devonian. Small, little known agnaths of uncertain affinities. Appear to have had armoured head; body with small bony plates or scales; paired fins uncertain; eyes lateral; gill openings uncertain; number of nostrils uncertain; tail apparently reversed heterocercal. Length up to about 10 cm.

†CLASS ACANTHODII

Jaws apparently formed of the 3rd gill arch (as in all jawed vertebrates) but attached to cranium and hyoid (4th) arch (amphistylic); jaws with teeth; pectoral and pelvic fins present, often with additional paired fins or spines between these; all fins except tail with a strong anterior spine; body covered with bony scales of the ganoid type, with bone cells tending to be lost in some members; no head shields but small dermal plates over head; some known with partially ossified vertebral column; cranium partially ossified; gill opening between jaws and hyoid arch apparently reduced to a spiracle; 3 semicircular canals (as in all higher fishes); an opercle (gill cover) present, attached to hyoid arch, followed by a series of smaller opercles, 1 over each remaining gill opening; caudal fin heterocercal. Active, free-swimming fishes with large eyes placed laterally. Small species probably freshwater, some larger species may have gone to sea.

†*Order Climatiiformes.* Upper Silurian to Lower Carboniferous. With 2 dorsal fins; 2 or more free spines present between pectoral and pelvic fins; operculum not covering entire gill chamber; supplementary operculae present or in some cases operculum covering entire gill chamber; no extramandibular bone. Mostly small, about 10 cm long.

†*Order Ischnacanthiformes.* Upper Silurian to Middle Carboniferous. With 2 dorsal fins; no free spines between pectoral and pelvic fins; operculum complete; no extramandibular bone.

†*Order Acanthodiformes.* Upper Silurian to Lower Permian. With 1 dorsal fin; no intermediate spines (or with a single pair) between pectoral and pelvic fins; operculum covering all or nearly all of opercular chamber; extramandibular bone present. Length to about 30 cm.

†CLASS PLACODERMI (placoderms)

Jaws amphystylic (supported by both the cranium and hyoid arch); pelvic fins present or absent; pectoral fins or finlike structures often present; often with ossified or partially ossified vertebral column and internal cranium; gill arches present; skeletal ossification reduced in some groups; caudal fin most often heterocercal or some modification of this form. Habitat in many cases uncertain, but apparently most later groups were marine (for further information, see PLACODERMI).

†*Order Arthrodiriformes* (arthrodires). Throughout the Devonian, especially common in last half of the period. Head and gill and trunk (thoracic) shields present (the two hinged upon each other in later Devonian forms); entire body more or less fusiform, sometimes flattened; pectoral and pelvic fins usually present and not encased in armour; jaws (when well preserved) of tusklike dermal bony elements. Some early groups freshwater; later groups with giant species (up to 10 m), marine.

†*Order Rhenanidiformes.* Found throughout the Devonian, but more common in first half of the period. Covered with small bony plates, head shield present in some; body flattened, raylike with eyes on top of head; gill chambers typically placoderm in occupying a large area below head; pectoral fins greatly enlarged; transverse jaws armed with teeth; apparently primarily marine. Average length about 24 cm.

†*Order Antiarchiformes* (antiarchs). First known from Middle Devonian, extinct by end of the period. Head and thorax shield present; internal skeleton partially ossified in some; body fusiform but flattened ventrally for bottom living; pectoral fins movable but encased in armour; jaws of small transversely placed bony plates; eyes close together on top of head; well-preserved specimens show intestine with a spiral

valve and lunglike structures; apparently mostly small bottom-dwelling freshwater fishes. Length about 10–40 cm.

†*Order Stensioelliformes.* Lower Devonian. Not well-known but appearing to have a general lack of bone development, isolated tubercles covering skin in some; gill bars and jaws well developed in reasonably well-preserved specimens; marine. Small; length about 25 cm.

†*Order Palaeospondyliformes.* Middle Devonian. Relationships uncertain, not a typical placoderm. Dermal armour lacking; ring-shaped vertebral centra and neural arches present; jaws apparently present. One genus, *Palaeospondylus,* many specimens, probably of a single species. Length about 4 cm.

CLASS SELACHII (sharks, skates, rays, and relatives)

Vertebrates with jaws; dermal and endochondral bone absent, cartilage often calcified but no true bone except possibly at base of teeth and denticles (controversial); scales placoid, of dentine and enamel, present over entire body and enlarged to form teeth on jaws; scales and teeth do not grow once fully formed but are replaced when worn out; notochord often reduced, partially replaced by cartilage, which joins the connective tissue covering of the notochord; labial cartilages present in some; spiracle present (sometimes lost); claspers (pterygopodia) often present in pelvic fins of males, used in mating; intestinal spiral valve present in modern forms (condition in fossils unknown); lungs or swimbladder-like structures absent in modern forms (see SELACHII).

†*Order Cladoselachiformes.* Middle Devonian to close of Permian. Notochord persistent in adult; 2 dorsal fins; each with a spine; no anal fin; basal cartilages or cartilages of pectoral fin remain along base of fin, radial cartilages unjointed; pelvic fins without claspers; tail fin externally almost symmetrical but internally heterocercal; jaws amphistylic (upper jaw articulates with cranium and hyoid bone); rostral region of cranium small; postorbital process of cranium large; teeth with 1 large median cusp and smaller lateral cusps; 5 gill openings; marine predators.

†*Order Cladodontiformes.* Middle Devonian to about end of Permian. Notochord persistent in adult; 2 dorsal fins each with or without dorsal spine; anal fin absent; basal cartilage or cartilages of pectoral fin remain along base of fin; radial cartilages unjointed; pelvic fins with claspers; tail fin externally equilobate but internally heterocercal; jaws amphistylic; rostal region of cranium small; postorbital process of cranium large; teeth with 1 large median cusp and smaller lateral cusps; 5 gill openings; marine predators.

†*Order Xenacanthiformes.* Upper Devonian to Middle Triassic. Notochord persistent, but reduced, in adult; some cartilage present; 1 long-based dorsal fin, no spines; postoccipital head spine present; 2 anal finlike structures present; basal cartilages of pectoral fins in series and enter fin as axial element, radial cartilages unjointed; pelvic fins with claspers; tail fin diphycercal; rostral region of cranium small; postorbital process of cranium large; teeth with a small central cusp and a large lateral cusp on each side; 5 gill openings; freshwater predators.

Order Heterodontiformes. Upper Devonian to Recent. Notochord persistent in primitive forms, replaced partially in advanced ones; 2 dorsal fins, each with a spine; anal fin present; 3 basal cartilages in pectoral fin or a modification of this condition; fin more mobile than 3 preceding orders, radial cartilages of pectoral fins jointed; pelvics with claspers; tail heterocercal or modified from this; jaws remain amphistylic but trend toward hyostylic (supported by movable hyomandibular cartilage); postorbital process of cranium large to reduced; rostral region of cranium usually small; teeth cladodont-like to very modified and rounded; 5 gill openings; marine, several modern forms mollusk eating in habit (heterodonts). Includes the more primitive fossil hybodonts and more specialized, living, heterodonts or hornsharks (Heterodontidae).

Order Hexanchiformes. Jurassic to Recent. Notochord persistent but in some constricted anteriorly; 1 posterior spineless dorsal fin present; anal fin present; basal cartilages of pectoral fin reduced in number; radial cartilages of pectoral fins jointed; pelvic fins with claspers; tail heterocercal to nearly diphycercal; jaws essentially amphystylic but contact with hyoid arch absent in Hexanchidae; postorbital process of cranium reduced; teeth trifid in Chlamydoselachidae, many-pointed in Hexanchidae; 6 to 7 gill openings; marine predators; 2 living families, Chlamydoselachidae (frilled shark) and Hexanchidae (cowsharks).

Order Lamniformes (typical sharks). Lower Jurassic to Recent. Notochord in adults replaced by calcified cartilaginous centra; 2 dorsal fins present, opened or not; anal fin present or absent; 2 basal cartilages of pectoral fin reduced (except Orectolobidae, which has 2); pelvics with claspers,

and with basal cartilage; tail heterocercal; jaws hyostylic, mobile, shortened and protrusible; postorbital process of cranium reduced; teeth with varied cusps; 5 gill openings; rostral area elongate; about 15 living families, typical sharks, mostly marine predators, free-swimming and bottom-dwelling, few in freshwater. Length to about 20 m.

Order Pristiophoriformes (sawsharks). Cretaceous to Recent. Like Lamniforms, but with 6 gill openings. Elongated, flattened snout with sawlike teeth along sides in Recent members; body somewhat flattened but elongated; marine shore fishes and in fresh water, tropics. Length (in modern species) to about 1.2 m.

Order Rajiformes (rays, banjofishes, and sawfishes). Upper Jurassic to Recent. Notochord replaced with calcified cartilage; 2, 1 or no dorsal fins; spines absent or present; anal fin absent; pelvic fins with claspers; tail heterocercal to modified, whiplike; jaws modified, supported by pseudohyoid cartilage, very mobile; 5 gill openings; rostral area elongate; marine bottom-dwelling sharklike fishes, flattened; spiracle (lateral opening) used for intake of water to gill chamber; eyes on top of head; gills ventral; greatly enlarged pectoral fins extend forward along gill opening, attached to sides of head and even meet in front of head in some; swim by wavelike motions of pectoral fins; 8 extant families, including Torpedinidae (electric rays). Medium to large fishes; maximum width (in manta ray) to 7 m, weight to 1,700 kg; length (in sawfish) to 11 m with weight to at least 2,500 kg.

CLASS HOLOCEPHALI

Jaws holostylic (the palatoquadrate) supporting the upper jaw completely fused to cranium; hyoid arch complete, unmodified; branchial arches below cranium; internal skeleton of cartilage, often calcified but never of bone; dermal skeleton of dentine or dentine-like tissue (placoid scales), never with true bone; scales do not continue to grow once fully formed; pelvic and cephalic claspers in males of some groups.

Order Chimaeriformes (chimaeras). Upper Devonian to Recent. Teeth in a single series of a few tooth plates along each jaw ramus (half); pectoral with 2, and pelvic fins with 1 basal element; pelvic fin claspers present; dermal armour frequently present on head; primitive forms with placoid scales covering body, lost in certain advanced forms; scales specialized in some; dorsal fin spine present or absent; cephalic clasper present in some; marine.

†*Order Copodontiformes.* Devonian to Carboniferous. Known from teeth only; relationship uncertain. Marine.

†*Order Psammodontiformes.* Lower to Upper Carboniferous. Teeth only; little known. Marine.

†*Order Helodontiformes.* Lower Carboniferous to Upper Permian. Teeth numerous, about 10 series on each jaw ramus, some fused into tooth plates; no specialized symphyseal teeth; no cephalic clasper; pelvic claspers unknown; placoid scales cover body; marine.

†*Order Petalodontiformes.* Fossil only; Lower Carboniferous to Upper Permian. Known from teeth only, relationships uncertain; marine; Europe, Asia, North America.

†*Order Edestiformes.* Fossil only; Lower Carboniferous. Known only from specialized symphyseal (fused) teeth; marine; Europe, North America.

†*Order Chondrenchelyiformes.* Lower Carboniferous. Upper jaw with 4 pairs of tooth plates; lower jaw with 3 pairs of tooth plates; dermal plates on skull, cephalic clasper and dorsal fin spine absent, dorsal fin long, continuous along back; marine; known only from Scotland.

CLASS SARCOPTERYGII (fleshy-finned fishes)

Primitive members of the following 2 orders show certain similarities and so are placed together in this class. Some of these similarities are: Heterocercal tail fin with a small amount of fin development above the vertebral column at the posterior end of the tail fin; 2 dorsal fins present; pectoral fins an archipterygium of variable form (an axial median support with side branches); cosmoid scales present, similar to that in acanthodians; modern freshwater forms have lungs; presumably lungs were present in fossil freshwater forms also. Scales grow throughout life of the individual. The internal nares of the Crossopterygii and the Dipnoi may or may not have the same origin.

Order Crossopterygii (coelacanths and fossil relatives). Lower Devonian to Recent. Cranium divided into 2 parts (anterior and posterior) at region for exit of the 5th cranial nerve, these parts movable on each other; choanae (internal nares) present (lost in coelacanths); teeth labyrinthodont (*i.e.,* with complicated unfoldings of the enamel surface); 2 important groups, suborder Rhipidistia, Lower Devonian to Early Permian, mostly shallow freshwater and thought to have given rise to terrestrial vertebrates during the Devonian, and the suborder Coelacanthini, Upper Devonian to Recent, mostly marine, includes the so-called living fossil, *Latimeria chalumnae*, from South Africa, which lacks lungs. Length of rhipidistians to about 3 m; of coelacanths to about 2 m (see CROSSOPTERYGII).

Order Dipnoi (lungfishes). Lower Devonian to Recent. Cranium not divided into movable parts; teeth on upper jaw early reduced and lost in later members; pterygoid bones with fused teeth in plates modified for eating mollusks; 3 surviving types of lungfishes, 1 each in Australia, Africa, and South America (see DIPNOI). Length 60–200 cm.

CLASS ACTINOPTERYGII (ray-finned fishes)

Fins supported by rays of dermal bone rather than by cartilage or cartilage bones. A group of jawed fishes so diverse that no single definition for them can be derived; better understood by determining the distinctive characters of the primitive members and then tracing their various lines of evolution. Primitive actinopterygians can be separated from the sarcopterygians by the following characteristics. Scales ganoid; single dorsal fin; pectoral fins with a series of thin radial bones, rather than basal plates and fleshy lobes; no internal nares. Other important characters: skeleton usually well ossified; scales grow throughout life; swim bladder present (occasionally modified to a lunglike structure).

Infraclass Chondrostei

A mixed group that has undergone many evolutionary diversifications. The remaining orders of the Chondrostei are specialized, often for special habitats and ways of life, but many of the groups show trends toward the holostean level of organization, especially in median fin structure and the development of hemiheterocercal tail in which externally at least the tail appears nearly homocercal (see CHONDROSTEI).

†*Order Palaeonisciformes.* Lower Devonian to Middle Cretaceous. Mostly fusiform fishes with heterocercal tail; maxillary bone of the upper jaw bound to the preopercle bone space for the muscle restricted to lower jaw, limiting its power and function; many more fin rays than basal elements in the median fins; 37 families of wide distribution, early members freshwater, later marine.

†*Order Tarrasiiformes.* Carboniferous. Palaeoniscid-like, but with elongate body, a diphycercal tail and dorsal and anal fins continuous with it. One family, Tarrasiidae, Scotland and Illinois.

†*Order Haplolepiformes.* Upper Carboniferous. Peculiar fishes with stout unbranched fin rays; large gular plates; small opercular apparatus. One family, Teleopterinidae; Europe and North America.

†*Order Perleidiformes.* Lower to Upper Triassic. With ganoid scales; fin rays equal number of basal supports rather than exceed them as in Palaeonisciformes and other Chondrostei; tail hemiheterocercal. Three families; worldwide.

†*Order Redfieldiiformes.* Lower and Middle Triassic. Like Perleidiformes but fin rays more numerous than basal elements in dorsal and anal fins. One family, Dictyopygidae, fresh water of South Africa, Australia, and North America.

†*Order Dorypteriformes.* Upper Permian. Similar to Bobasatraniiformes but with very modified skull; scales confined to anterior part of trunk. One family, Dorypteridae; Europe, China.

†*Order Bobasatraniiformes.* Lower Triassic. Body deep, laterally compressed; fin rays slightly more numerous than basal supports; opercular apparatus with small opercle, large preopercle; crushing dentition; pelvics absent. Thought to perhaps have been a coral feeder. One family, Bobasatraniidae; marine; widely distributed.

†*Order Pholidopleuriformes.* Lower to Upper Triassic. Some relatively long and slender; dorsal and anal fins far back on body, origin of anal fin anterior to dorsal fin; fin rays more numerous than basal elements; tail hemiheterocercal; jaw support almost vertical or moderately oblique, rather than extremely oblique as in most Chondrostei. One family, Pholidopleuridae; marine and freshwater; wide distribution.

†*Order Peltopleuriformes.* Upper Triassic. Large eyes; hemiheterocercal tail almost symmetrical externally; dentition weak. Two families, Peltopleuridae and Habroichthyidae; marine, perhaps some plankton feeding; Italy, China.

†*Order Platysiagiformes.* Lower Triassic to Lower Jurassic. Elongate, fusiform body, tail hemiheterocercal; median fins holostean, in that rays probably equalled basal elements; teeth large, conical. One family, Platysiagidae; marine; probably predacious; Italy and England.

†*Order Cephaloxeniformes.* Middle to Upper Triassic. Body deep, fusiform; thick head bones and crushing dentition; tail hemiheterocercal. One family, Cephaloxenidae; marine; probably bottom-dwelling mollusk eaters; Italy.

†*Order Luganoiiformes.* Middle and Upper Triassic. Almost holostean in character; body fusiform; head somewhat

flattened in the horizontal plane; some head bones fused; jaw suspension inclined forward; fin rays apparently equal to basal elements in number; tail hemiheterocercal. One family, Luganoiidae; marine; probably predacious midwater fishes; Italy.

†*Order Ptycholepiformes.* Middle Triassic to Upper Jurassic. Structure near that of holosteans; fusiform body; fin rays of median fins nearly equalling basal elements in number; jaw support almost vertical; teeth small. One family, Ptycholepididae; marine; presumably plankton feeders; Europe.

†*Order Saurichthyiformes.* Lower Triassic to Upper Jurassic. Elongate, slender; snout elongate; single dorsal fin far back on body, opposite anal fin; tail diphycercal in appearance; number of scale rows reduced, 1 dorsal, 1 ventral, and 1 along each side; jaw suspension almost vertical; teeth large, conical, jaws long. One family, Saurichthyidae; marine and freshwater; predacious; worldwide. Length about 7–150 cm.

†*Order Chondrosteiformes.* Lower Triassic to Upper Jurassic. Body scales and skull bones reduced; snout moderately developed, maxillary and opercular bones reduced; jaw support somewhat inclined backward; median fins paleoniscid-like, rays more numerous than basal supports. Probably gave rise to sturgeons. One family, Chondrosteidae; marine; some were suctorial feeders like sturgeons; England.

†*Order Parasemionotiformes.* Lower Triassic. Very near holosteans in structure but preopercle large and true suborbital bones still present, as in chondrosteans. Two families; marine; Siberia, Greenland, and Madagascar.

Order Acipenseriformes (sturgeons and paddlefishes). Upper Cretaceous to Recent. Almost no internal ossification; scales as large scutes in isolated rows (Acipenseridae); snout enlarged and tactile (Polyodontidae); median fins chondrostean in having more fin rays than basal elements; tail heterocercal. Marine and freshwater, bottom suctorial feeders (sturgeons, Acipenseridae; Europe, Asia, North America) and plankton feeders (paddlefishes, Polyodontidae; China and North America). Length (sturgeons) up to 9 m, weight to 1,400 kg.

Order Polypteriformes (bichirs and reedfish). Pleistocene to Recent. Relationships controversial, placed in own subclass by some and thought related to crossopterygians by others. Typical chondrostean characters, such as ganoid scales and a paleoniscoid type of preopercle. Fins modified into long continuous dorsal, tail diphycercal; freshwater; Africa.

Infraclass Holostei

Tail hemiheterocercal; maxillary scale free of preopercle; rays of median fins about equal basal elements in number; spiracle lost; vertebral column tended to increasing ossification; trend toward thinning scales and loss of ganoid layer (see HOLOSTEI).

Division Holosteans

Preoperculum intimately bound to and supporting the posterior border of the palate.

Order Amiiformes (bowfin and fossil relatives). Upper Triassic to Recent. Relatively conservative holosteans with typical holostean characters as given above; some specialized in body shape (elongate); most typical fusiform holosteans. One living member of the family Amiidae, with 1 species, *Amia calva* (bowfin), of North America; marine and freshwater, almost worldwide; 6 families.

†*Order Pachycormiformes.* Lower Jurassic to Upper Cretaceous. Long snout, suggesting the teleost swordfishes, Xiphiidae. Two families; Europe and North America.

Order Semionotiformes (gar pikes and fossil relatives). Upper Permian to Recent. Two families of widely divergent fishes; probably independent of the Amiiformes but with typical holostean characters; the fossil Lepidotidae with normal holostean fusiform bodies, which become relatively deep and slab-sided in some members; marine and freshwater, widely distributed. Gar pikes (Lepisosteidae) are elongated, sharp snouted, primarily freshwater predators, still extant in North America; length to about 3.5 m.

†*Order Pycnodontiformes.* Lower Jurassic to at least Eocene. Very deep bodied, with jaws and teeth modified for nibbling; perhaps fed on coral; marine and widespread.

†Division Halecostomes

Holosteans but with a preoperculum not buttressing the bones of the palate.

†*Order Pholidophoriformes.* Upper Triassic to Upper Cretaceous. Difficult to separate from the more primitive of the teleost orders (below). Holosteans with some trends toward teleosts, notably: loss of ganoine from fin rays, scales, and dermal bones; loss of peg and socket joints between scales; loss of bone cells in scales retained in some teleosts; development of intermuscular bones; loss of scalelike bones (fulcra) on leading edges of fins (retained in caudal fin of

some teleosts); loss of some skull bones; a "sinking" of skull bones beneath the skin. The caudal skeleton is the major difference between the pholidophoroids and teleosts. Pholidophoroids have the caudal centra incompletely ossified and lack "splint" bones called uroneurals (modified neural arches) that give ridged support to the terminal 4 or 5 vertebrae in teleosts. About 7 families, of which the Jurassic Pholidophoridae are the most likely ancestors of the teleosts; marine and freshwater, of wide distribution.

Infraclass Teleostei (bony fishes)

Tail homocercal; caudal skeleton with perichordally (around the spinal chord) ossified centra; neural arches modified into elongate uroneurals extending forward onto the preural centra, "stiffening" the joints between the terminal 4 or 5 vertebrae. Two hypural bones supporting the lower caudal fin lobe. (Note: Although the above statement can be used to define and separate early teleosts from holosteans, many later groups of teleosts have modified the tail structure greatly, so the definition will not "fit" at first sight. It can be readily shown, however, that all teleosts have a caudal structure derived from that described above.) Teleosts never have ganoid scales; typically, their scales when present are thin, overlapping plates of bone that continue to grow throughout life; their lower jaws lack certain bones found in many chondrosteans or at least have some of these bones fused to single elements (see TELEOSTEI).

†*Superorder Leptolepidimorpha.* The recognition of this superorder is highly tentative pending determination of the relationships of these fishes with other teleosts. Sometimes classified with the Halecostomi, these fishes were clearly teleosts in their caudal fin structure. Preopercle supported the palate (as in some holosteans) but with several shifts in this region to a teleost-like preopercular-jaw arrangement and with the adductor muscle of the mandible attached to preopercle; no bone cells in scales; more than 1 supraorbital; gular plate present; apparently no adipose fin; rostral elements with a bone enclosed commissure.

†*Order Leptolepidiformes.* Triassic to Middle or Upper Cretaceous. The characters of the order are those listed above for the superorder. Four families; widely distributed.

Superorder Elopomorpha. A diverse group including very primitive fishes and specialized fishes such as eels and therefore difficult to define. Some primitive members with a gular plate (absent in eels), ethmoid commissure present in some forms in a dermal rostral bone (lost in many eels); a leptocephalus larva; no bone cells in scales of primitive members; pelvic fins abdominal when present.

Order Elopiformes (tarpons, tenpounders, and bonefishes). Upper Jurassic to Recent. Body fusiform, typical fishlike shape; bone-enclosed ethmoid commissure present; roofed post-temporal fossae; primary bite a tongue-parasphenoid type; marine; worldwide in temperate and tropical zones (see ELOPIFORMES).

Order Anguilliformes (eels). Cretaceous to Recent. Body elongate; fins reduced and gill chamber modified; displaced posterior to much of head; opercular apparatus reduced; pectoral girdle free of skull; caudal and other fins often greatly reduced; bony ethmoid commissure sometimes present; marine and freshwater, worldwide in temperate and tropical regions. Length about 15–300 cm (see ANGUILLIFORMES).

Order Notacanthiformes (deep-sea spiny eels). Middle Cretaceous to Recent. Ethmoid commissure present, like that of elopomorphs; body relatively elongate and tail skeleton reduced; opercular apparatus complete. Three marine, deep-sea families, Halosauridae, Lipogenyidae, and the Notacanthidae (deep-sea spiny eels). Average length about 50 cm.

Superorder Clupeomorpha. Special type of ear–swim-bladder connection present, consisting of a diverticulum of the swim bladder, forming bulla (cavity) within the ear capsule; head lateral line canals on operculum. A diverse group of mostly oceanic, silvery, compressed fishes, many of great commercial importance.

Order Clupeiformes (herrings, anchovies, and allies). Lower Cretaceous to Recent. Characters of the superorder; marine and freshwater, some anadromous; worldwide (see CLUPEIFORMES).

Superorder Osteoglossomorpha. A diverse group of freshwater fishes with a relatively primitive jaw suspension and shoulder girdle. The primary bite of the mouth between parasphenoid and tongue (basihyal and glossohyal); paired rods present, usually bony, at the base of the second gill arch; no bony ethmoid commissure; no leptocephalus larvae (see OSTEOGLOSSOMORPHA).

Order Osteoglossiformes (bony tongues, freshwater butterfly fishes, mooneyes, knife fishes). Middle Cretaceous to Recent. Circumorbital bones well-developed; scales with an irregular reticulated pattern (except Pantodontidae); fresh water, almost worldwide except extremely cold regions. Four families.

Order Mormyriformes (mormyrs). Pleistocene to Recent. With electricity-producing organs; orbital bones reduced; the cerebellum greatly enlarged; swim-bladder–ear connection reduced in adult; sometimes with long snouts for feeding in mud; 2 families, the elephant fishes, Mormyridae, and the Gymnarchidae; fresh water, Africa.

Superorder Protacanthopterygii. A diverse group of relatively primitive teleosts, mostly related by their lack of the specializations (or, in some cases, primitive features) found in the other teleost superorders. Vertebrae usually more than 24; adipose fin present in many members; mesocoracoid bone usually present; glossohyal teeth usually prominent (lost in some); upper jaw usually not protrusible; proethmoid and a series of several perichondral ethmoid commissure; 1 supraorbital bone; no gular plate.

Order Salmoniformes (salmons, trouts, whitefishes, smelts, pikes, and allies). Cretaceous to Recent. Characters are those given for superorder; endochondral ossification often somewhat reduced; marine and freshwater, worldwide. A large and important order, comprising about 35–40 extant and about 6 fossil families. Length about 4–115 cm; weight to about 50 kg (see SALMONIFORMES).

Order Ctenothrissiformes. Mostly Upper Cretaceous, marine fishes of uncertain affinities; possibly close to the basal stock from which the acanthopterygians are derived. The living marine family Macristiidae may belong here.

Order Gonorhynchiformes (milkfish and certain deep-sea fishes). Cretaceous to Recent. Toothless; with epibranchial organs and a characteristic caudal skeleton; marine of Indo-Pacific and freshwater of Africa. The anterior ribs and vertebrae show affinities with the superorder Ostariophysi and the group may belong with the ostariophysans rather than with the Protacanthopterygii. Length about 10–150 cm.

Superorder Ostariophysi. A group of 5,000–6,000 species, including the majority of known freshwater fishes. Characterized by possession of a Weberian apparatus, (a swim-bladder–internal-ear connection with three movable bones; see OSTARIOPHYSI).

Order Cypriniformes (characins, tetras, some knifefishes, carps, and minnows). Lower Eocene to Recent. Parietal, symplectic, and subopercular bones present; worldwide in fresh water except Antarctica and Australia. A few North Asian forms enter the sea.

Order Siluriformes (catfishes). Paleocene to Recent. Parietal, symplectic, subopercular, and true scales absent; often with dermal plates or little bony spines in the skin. Fusion of the supportive parts of the Weberian apparatus extensive. About 30 families; distribution of the superorder, primarily freshwater but some families marine, with the majority of the 2,000 species in Africa and South America.

Superorder Scopelomorpha. This superorder, like the Paracanthopterygii and Acanthopterygii (below), is characterized by a tendency toward fin spines, subocular shelves, and separated exoccipital condyles. Scopelomorphs frequently retain such primitive structures as an adipose fin and an asymmetrical caudal fin skeleton.

Order Myctophiformes. Cretaceous to Recent. Characters of the superorder. Distinctive jaw musculature, like that of Paracanthopterygii (below). Two subgroups of this order differ in ecology and structure. One contains several families of deep-sea fishes, often elongated predators with large teeth. The second contains benthic or bottom-dwellers (*e.g.*, Aulopidae), tropical inshore fishes (Synodontidae, or lizardfishes), midwater deep-sea fishes with light organs (the large family Myctophidae, or lantern fishes), and bottom-dwelling deep-sea fishes (*e.g.*, Bathypteroidae, or spiderfishes). Order contains about 15 families, worldwide; marine. Mostly small fishes 10–15 cm; maximum length about 95 cm.

Superorder Paracanthopterygii. Most with a distinctive type of jaw musculature (involving levitor maxillae superioris muscle and associated structures); caudal vertebrae with the 2nd ural centrum fused with the upper hypural, 2 or fewer epurals and a full neural spine on the 2nd preural centrum; pelvic fins usually placed anteriorly, thoracic (midbody) or even further forward. In general these fishes have tended to lose primitive acanthopterygian characters. For a more detailed discussion of this suborder see PARACANTHOPTERYGII.

Order Polymixiiformes (barbudos). Middle Cretaceous to Recent. Barbels suspended from the hypohyal bones (anterior part of the gill arches); spines on the dorsal and anal fins; pelvic fins subthoracic. Retain some primitive paracanthopterygian characters, such as an antorbital bone, a free second ural centrum, 6 autogenous hypurals, 2 uroneurals, and Baudelot's ligament to the 1st vertebra. Adipose fin lacking. Deepwater marine fishes; 1 family, probably only 2 species. Adult length about 30 cm.

Order Percopsiformes (trout perches, pirate perches, and cave fishes). Eocene to Recent. Mouth gape and bucal dentition reduced; median fin spines reduced or lost; head with spine ornamentation of the head; scale covering of the adipose fin lost. All living species freshwater, North America; length 8–13 cm. Three extant families, 1 fossil family.

Order Gadiformes. Lower Eocene to Recent. Early gadiforms were similar in structure to early percopsiforms but almost all remained marine and subsequently specialized into a variety of environments. Reduced caudal skeleton; elongate body; altered head and jaw structure. Primitive gadiforms have 7 branchiostegal rays, primitive percopsiforms 6. All with very reduced fin spines; marine, worldwide. Order includes cods, hakes, cusk eels, pearlfishes, eel pouts, grenadiers, and rattails. Length 7 to about 200 cm.

Order Batrachoidiformes (toadfishes). Miocene to Recent. Bottom fishes with short, small, spinous dorsal fins; long soft-rayed dorsal fins; flat heads; 1 family, Batrachoididae; marine, occasionally freshwater, shore fishes of tropics. Length to about 40 cm.

Order Lophiiformes (goosefishes, anglerfishes, frogfishes and batfishes). Eocene to Recent. Spinous dorsal fin modified as a movable lure. Some deep-sea forms with light organs and males parasitic on females. Marine, widespread; in shallow-water and deep-sea habitats. About 15 families. Length to about 130 cm.

Order Gobiesociformes (clingfishes). Recent questionable fossil from Miocene of California. Flattened, depressed fishes with a ventral sucker formed of the pelvic fin and surrounding tissue; no spiny dorsal fin; 1 family, Gobiesocidae; marine and occasionally freshwater in tropics and along many temperate seacoasts.

Superorder Acanthopterygii (spiny-rayed fishes). Spiny fins usually emphasized, rather than reduced (as in paracanthopterygians). Mobile, protractile mouth due to the almost universal lack of the levator mandibula superioris muscle; pectoral fin relatively higher on side of body; Baudelot's ligament almost always attached to basicranium. The 13 orders of the superorder Actinopterygii may be divided into 2 categories (sometimes called series), on the basis of the number of vertebrae, the condition of the fin spines, the position of the pelvic fins, and the presence or absence of ctenoid scales. The series Atherinomopha contains only the order Atheriniformes, the series Percomorpha the remaining actinopterygian orders.

Order Atheriniformes. Eocene to Recent. Fin spines present or absent, but frequently weak when present; vertebral number higher than 24; ctenoid scales rare; pelvic fins abdominal, subabdominal, or thoracic in position. Marine shore fishes, also freshwater, tropical and temperate, worldwide. About 16 families, including the oceanic flying fishes (Exocoetidae), killifishes (Cyprinodontidae), live-bearing topminnows (Poeciliidae), and silversides (Atherinidae). Mostly small fishes (2–10 cm) but some needlefishes (Belonidae) to about 130 cm (see ATHERINIFORMES).

Order Lampridiformes. Paleocene to Recent. Intermediate in some ways between polymixioids and acanthopterygians, but all living members very specialized. All lack a subocular shelf and pelvic spine; some have a peculiar condition (hypurostegy) in which caudal rays are expanded. Marine, oceanic, tropic, and temperate regions. About 9 families. Medium to large size; to about 2 m and 300 kg in the opah (Lampridae) and about 10 m, but far less weight, in the more slender oarfishes, Regalecidae (see ATHERINIFORMES).

Order Beryciformes.—Squirrelfishes and certain deep-sea fishes. Cretaceous to Recent. Spines present in fins; pelvic fins subthoracic; retained primitive number of caudal branched fin rays (17); primitive number of epurals (3); exoccipital condyles poorly developed; orbitosphenoid present. About 15 families of small to medium-sized fishes. Length 5–60 cm. Marine, worldwide in tropical and temperate regions (see ATHERINIFORMES).

Order Zeiformes (dories, boarfishes, and relatives). Lower Eocene to Recent. Anal fin with 1–4 spines; pelvic fin with 1 spine and 5–9 branched rays; caudal fin with less than 15 principal rays; about 6 families, of which the dories, Zeidae, are best known; marine, deep-sea, widespread. Length to about 1 m (see ATHERINIFORMES).

Order Gasterosteiformes (sticklebacks, tubenoses, and seahorses). Eocene to Recent. Frequently with strong spines in dorsal fin and pelvic fins, spines absent in some; snout often elongate; body often with dermal plates; 9 families, marine and freshwater, widely distributed. Length about 3–200 cm (see GASTEROSTEIFORMES).

Order Channiformes (snakeheads). Pliocene to Recent. Elongate bodies; dorsal and anal fins present; depressed head with an accessory air-breathing apparatus in the gill chamber. Snakeheads, Channidae; fresh water, tropical Old World. Length 15–95 cm.

Order Synbranchiformes (swamp eels). No fossil record. Fins reduced, fin spines absent, pharynx modified for breathing air. Three families, restricted to fresh water, in tropics. Length 20 to about 50 cm.

Order Scorpaeniformes (scorpionfishes, sculpins, and relatives). Eocene to Recent. A complex group of widely divergent fishes that may be polyphyletic and is difficult to characterize. Three separate groups may be recognized here: scorpaenoid, hexagramoid-cottoid, and anoplopomatoid. United as an order because of a distinctive caudal skeleton and a bony process connecting the 3rd orbital with the preoperculum in most members. Some members with external bony plates. About 21 families; primarily marine, some freshwater, tropical and temperate regions (see SCORPAENIFORMES).

Order Dactylopteriformes (flying gurnards). Pliocene to Recent. Bottom-dwelling shore fishes with dermal armoured plates, movable modified pectoral fin rays. Marine. One family, Dactylopteridae (see SCORPAENIFORMES).

Order Pegasiformes (dragonfishes). No fossil record. Bottom-dwelling marine fishes with dermal armour and large pectoral fins. One family, Pegasidae (see SCORPAENIFORMES).

Order Perciformes. Upper Cretaceous to Recent. Fins usually with spines; pelvic fin with 1 spine and not more than 5 rays, usually below pectoral fins; caudal fin with 15 rays; no orbitosphenoid, mesocoracoid, or intermuscular bones. An extremely varied assemblage of fishes, with a variety of body plans and other adaptations. About 140 families, divided among about 20 suborders. Mostly marine, worldwide. Adult length from about 1 cm (certain gobies) to about 4.8 m (swordfish); weight to about 900 kg (see PERCIFORMES).

Order Pleuronectiformes (flatfishes). Eocene to Recent. Both eyes on same side of head, skull twisted and asymmetrical, fins usually without spines. Seven families include flounders, soles, and halibuts; mostly marine; bottom fishes; worldwide in tropical and temperate regions (see PLEURONECTIFORMES).

Order Tetraodontiformes. Eocene to Recent. With a beaklike snout, gill opening restricted to a small opening; probably related to acanthuroids. Eleven families; marine, occasionally freshwater, worldwide in tropics and subtropics (see TETRAODONTIFORMES).

BIBLIOGRAPHY. Titles listed below pertain to the biology of fishes generally. Works on individual fish classes, subclasses, or orders are cited in the bibliographies accompanying the articles on the appropriate groups.

General works: E.S. HERALD, *Living Fishes of the World* (1961), a clearly written and extensively illustrated introduction to fishes; G. STERBA, *Freshwater Fishes of the World* (1962; orig. pub. in German, 1959), a general account of freshwater aquarium fishes; P.P. GRASSÉ (ed.), *Traité de zoologie*, vol. 13, *Agnathas et Poissons*, 3 pt. (1958), a classic and authoritative review in French of the classification, anatomy, and biology of fishes; J.R. NORMAN, *A History of Fishes*, 2nd ed. by P.H. GREENWOOD (1963), N.B. MARSHALL, *The Life of Fishes* (1965), and K.F. LAGLER, J.E. BARDACH, and R.R. MILLER, *Ichthyology* (1962), college-level introductory texts of general ichthyology.

Regional works: A.H. LEIM and W.B. SCOTT, "Fishes of the Atlantic Coast of Canada," *Bull. Fish. Res. Bd. Can.*, no. 155 (1966), a good general account, completely illustrated; H.B. BIGELOW et al., *Fishes of the Western North Atlantic*, 5 vol. (1948–66), a comprehensive treatment of the biology of western North Atlantic fishes; J.E. BÖHLKE and C.C.G. CHAPLIN, *Fishes of the Bahamas and Adjacent Tropical Waters* (1968); W.B. SCOTT, *Freshwater Fishes of Eastern Canada*, 2nd ed. (1967); W.A. CLEMENS and G.V. WILBY, "Fishes of the Pacific Coast of Canada," *Bull. Fish. Res. Bd. Can.*, no. 68, 2nd ed. (1961); W.A. GOSLINE and V.E. BROCK, *Handbook of Hawaiian Fishes* (1960), an excellent handbook of fishes from the central Pacific ocean; T.C. MARSHALL, *Fishes of the Great Barrier Reef and Coastal Waters of Queensland* (1964); T. KAMOHARA, *Fishes of Japan in Color* (1967); J.T. NICHOLAS, *The Fresh-Water Fishes of China* (1943), somewhat old, but still the most complete coverage on fishes of eastern Asia; I.S.R. MUNRO, *The Marine and Freshwater Fishes of Ceylon* (1955), the only inclusive illustrated recent account of fishes from the Indian Ocean area; J.L.B. SMITH, *The Sea Fishes of Southern Africa*, 4th ed. (1961); H. COPLEY, *The Game Fishes of Africa* (1952), strictly on sport fishes but with information about other books on fishes of Africa; R.M. BAILEY et al., "A List of Common and Scientific Names of Fishes from the U.S. and Canada," *Spec. Publs. Am. Fish. Soc.*, no. 6, 3rd ed. (1970). Somewhat more local, but applicable to much of North America, are the following: M.B. TRAUTMAN, *The Fishes of Ohio with Illustrated Keys* (1957); F.B. CROSS, *Handbook of Fishes of Kansas* (1967); and W.F. SMITH-VANIZ, *Freshwater Fishes of Alabama* (1968); C.L. HUBBS and C. LAGLER, *Fishes of the Great Lakes Region*, rev. ed. (1958).

Natural history: C.M. BREDER and D.E. ROSEN, *Modes of Reproduction in Fishes* (1966), a summary of reproductive behaviour of fishes; N.B. MARSHALL, *Aspects of Deep Sea Biology* (1954), a college-level introduction to deep-sea biology; B.W. HALSTEAD, *Poisonous and Venomous Marine Animals of the World*, vol. 2 and 3 (1967, 1970), an extensive treatment of poisonous and venemous marine fishes, beautifully illustrated in colour; H.S. DAVIS, *Culture and Diseases of Game Fishes* (1953), a general aid to the culture of North American game fishes.

Form and function: R.M. ALEXANDER, *Functional Design in Fishes* (1967), a short college-level book on functional anatomy of fishes; M.E. BROWN (ed.), *The Physiology of Fishes*, 2 vol. (1957), and W.S. HOAR and D.J. RANDALL (eds.), *Fish Physiology*, 3 vol. (1969–   ), advanced general texts.

Paleontology and classification: L.S. BERG, *System der rezenten und fossilen Fischartigen und Fische* (1958), a German translation from the 2nd Russian edition, a revised edition of Berg's 1940 classification of recent and fossil fishes; A.S. ROMER, *Vertebrate Paleontology*, 3rd ed. (1966), a college-level text with a good review of fish evolution; P.H. GREENWOOD et al., "Phyletic Studies of Teleostean Fishes with a Provisional Classification of Living Forms," *Bull. Am. Mus. Nat. Hist*, vol. 131, art. 4, pp. 341–455 (1966), scholarly recent review of teleost fish classification.

Bibliographic reference: B. DEAN et al. (eds.), *A Bibliography of Fishes*, 3 vol. (1916–23), an almost complete bibliography of works on recent and fossil fishes up to about 1923.

(S.H.W.)

Fish and Marine Products

Fish and marine products include freshwater and ocean fish, shellfish, ocean mammals, and seaweed as well as plankton. They are a major food source, especially valuable for the protein they provide, and also a source of industrial products.

Ancient heaps of discarded mollusk shells, some from prehistoric times, have been found in coastal areas throughout the world, including those of China, Japan, Peru, Brazil, Portugal, and Denmark. These shell mounds indicate that marine mollusks were among the early foods of man. The predominance of the shells of bivalves shows that consumption of this group, including clams, mussels, and oysters, exceeded that of the gastropods, the group including snails and abalone, in both quantity and variety. As suggested by references in ancient Chinese and Japanese documents, the culture of clams, and the development of farms devoted exclusively to this industry, probably originated in the Far East.

Evidence from shell mounds

Archaeological evidence shows that man next learned to catch fishes in traps and nets. Limited at first to the lakes and rivers, as he improved his boats and fishing devices he ventured into sheltered coastal areas and river mouths and eventually farther out on to the continental shelves, the relatively shallow ocean plains between the land and the deeper ocean areas. In some shelf areas where seaweed was abundant, this was also incorporated in his diet.

Fishing technology continued to develop throughout history, employing improved and larger ships, more sophisticated fishing equipment, and various food preservation methods. In the middle of the 20th century, man became concerned with greater utilization of the resources of the world's waters to feed an expanding population and especially in filling the need for high protein foods. At the same time, he became aware of the effects of overfishing and the importance of conservation measures (see FISHING, COMMERCIAL).

ROLE IN THE HUMAN DIET

Aquatic organisms are consumed in almost every area of the world. They may be eaten raw or cooked and may be

Table 1: Comparison of Protein and Protein Calories Provided by the Foods Commonly Consumed in Various Areas of the World

	% protein weight	% protein calories
Yams	2.1	8.2
Sweet potato	1.8	6.5
Plantains	1.4	6.2
Taro	1.8	6.1
Cassava	0.9	2.3
Tapioca (cassava product)	1.5	1.8
Rice (polished)	5–8	5.7–8.8
White potato	2	9.4
Chinese cabbage	1.8	19
Beans (dry)	19	23
Fish (flesh)	18–25	48–85
Oysters	10	50
Shrimp	21	87
Pork	16	29
Beef	17	39
Veal	19	45
Poultry	21	56

preserved by salting, smoking, freezing, or other methods. Certain species are undesirable as human food because their flesh is either watery or too dry, contains too many bones, is lacking in flavour, or is extremely oily. However, the flesh of many other species is agreeable in flavour, appearance, and texture.

The muscular tissue of fishes consists of 13–20 percent protein; varying amounts of fat, ranging from under one to over 20 percent; and 60–82 percent water, varying inversely with fat content. Exact proportions vary among different species, and seasonal and feeding variations result in differences among individuals of the same species. The proteins and fats of both fishes and shellfishes are readily digested and compare favourably in food value with other meats.

Vitamins, minerals, and fats. The composition of the diet affects nutritive content, as well as flavour, of the flesh of fish. For example, only eels and related species deposit vitamin A in their flesh; it is not adequately synthesized by other species. However, fish liver contains vitamin A as a result of the passing of this nutrient along the food chain, the sequence in which each organism uses the next lower member as food. The halibut, for example, yields rich quantities of this vitamin, because it feeds mainly on *Sebastes*, a redfish found in the deep waters of the North Atlantic that has great quantities of vitamin A in its liver oil. The nutrient originates earlier in the food chain, starting with the drifting plant life called phytoplankton.

In many developing countries, the diet is low in fats, minerals, and vitamins. When fish is among the staple foods in these areas, the fatty species are preferred. In addition to supplying needed fat, such fish also provide the fat-soluble A, D, and E vitamins. The flesh of marine fish also supplies such essential minerals as iodine, fluorine, and calcium, providing two to three times the amount of flourine obtained from the meat of land animals.

In the 1960s and 1970s medical scientists were exploring the relationship between consumption of polyunsaturated fatty acids and reduction of vascular disturbances in man. These acids, more readily broken down than other fatty acids, are characterized by a chemical composition in which the chains of carbon atoms, low in hydrogen, are connected by double bonds that are susceptible to the addition of oxygen. Because the fats in fish are high in polyunsaturated fatty acids, fish are recommended for the human diet.

Polyunsaturates

Proteins. In an adequate human diet at least 12 percent of the caloric intake needs to be proteins, essential constituents of living cells. Table 1 compares the proteins provided by the major foods consumed in various areas of the world with those of seafoods and of meat from land animals. Seafood, usually more readily available and less costly than other meat foods, stands out as an efficient protein source, requiring fewer calories for the amount of protein intake than most other foods.

Foods from aquatic sources have great potential in helping to alleviate shortages of food, and especially of high value protein, in many of the world's undeveloped areas. In the humid tropics, where diets are dominated by sugars or such low-protein tubers as cassava, taro, and plantain, the addition of aquatic protein can eliminate the common protein deficiency diseases. Kwashiorkor and other protein deficiency diseases do not occur in the coastal areas of Central America, tropical West Africa, or northeast Brazil when adequate supplies of fish are available. Aquatic protein is also valuable in diets dominated by corn (maize) or rice, and together with soybeans, seafood is a major ingredient of the daily diet in Japan and Southeast Asia.

Protein deficiency diseases

In the period of 1967–68 protein from aquatic sources accounted for 18 percent of total animal protein consumed. Fish and shellfish consumed directly provided 14.5 percent, and fishmeal included in the diets of food animals accounted for another 3.5 percent. Table 2

Table 2: Direct Intake of Animal Protein by Man (1967–68)
(in 000,000 metric tons)

land animal meats		land animal products		fish and shellfish	
Beef and veal	5.5	Milk	8.5	Commercial	3.4
Pork	5.1	Eggs	1.8	Subsistence	0.5
Others	1.7				
Total	12.3	Total	10.3	Total	3.9
Total direct animal protein intake: 26.5					

shows world consumption of animal protein foods in terms of millions of metric tons. In addition to the above figures for direct consumption, 2,200,000 metric tons of fishmeal protein were used as animal feed, rendering about 1,100,000 metric tons of the directly animal protein consumed by humans.

In many countries, especially in Asia, per capita consumption greatly exceeds the overall world average, accounting for as much as one-half to two-thirds of total animal protein consumed. The percentage of total animal protein consumption supplied by aquatic protein is 74 percent in Korea. Portugal, the largest seafood consumer in Europe, averages 44 percent. The Caribbean countries also consume large relative quantities of seafood, with aquatic protein supplying 30–50 percent of total animal protein intake.

Table 3 shows per capita consumption of fish in several countries that are traditionally large consumers of

Table 3: Per Capita Intake of Fish Protein as a Portion of Total Protein Consumed
(1966–69 average)

	fish flesh (kg/year)	fish protein (g/day)	animal protein (g/day)	fish protein as percent of animal protein
Japan	64.1	15.8	28.2	56
Portugal	56.5	13.9	31.7	44
Denmark	44.5	11.0	60.2	18
Norway	38.6	9.5	50.4	19
Korea	34.4	8.5	11.5	74
Jamaica	25.2	6.2	18.7	33

seafood. It can be seen that the actual amount of fish consumed does not indicate its importance in the individual diet. For example, Denmark consumes more fish per capita than Korea, but Korea relies on the protein provided by seafood for a greater percentage of total animal protein.

The significance of fish in the world's food balance and in that of individual countries may be evaluated by computing the acreage required to produce equivalent amounts of animal protein employing agricultural technology in its present state. This calculation reveals that to produce land-animal protein equivalent to the fish protein now harvested, Europe would require 60,000,000 hectares (150,000,000 acres), equivalent to 40 percent of the land area presently under cultivation. The U.S.S.R.

would require 16 percent of its presently cultivated land, China would require 23 percent, and, most dramatic of all, Japan would require 380 percent.

Similar expansion would be required in the dairy industry of each country to equal the value of aquatic protein now consumed. Table 4 shows both sets of figures.

Table 4: Expansion of Milk Production Required to Equal Fish as a Source of Animal Protein (1966–67)

	fish acreage*	expansion percent of milk production
Japan	380	675
Netherlands	249	59
West Germany	148	58
Israel	80	78
South Africa	31	83
Spain	25	133
Mexico	17	51
U.S.S.R.	16	34
U.S.	6	38

*Percentage of present tilled land required for equivalent protein production.

DISTRIBUTION AND HABITAT

The total registered world aquatic catch in the year 1969 was 63,100,000 metric tons (excluding whales). Of this amount, 7,400,000 metric tons, approximately one-seventh of the total, was made up of fishes originating in the fresh waters of lakes, rivers, and ponds and mainly consumed directly as human food (see Tables 5 and 6).

The greater portion of the catch, 55,700,000 metric tons, was obtained from marine waters, the oceans of the world. Shellfish accounted for about one-tenth of this amount, with the remaining 50,800,000 metric tons made up of ocean fish. Almost two-thirds of the ocean fishes were obtained from the Northern Hemisphere. The Pacific Ocean yielded 55 percent; the Atlantic Ocean accounted for 39 percent; the Indian Ocean, with the adjacent Arabian and Red Seas, supplied 4 percent; and 2 percent came from the Mediterranean and Black seas.

Oceans. The oceans constitute the largest factories of living organic matter on earth, both in magnitude and total productive biomass. Average organic production per acre is identical to that on land, although productivity varies greatly from one area to another, ranging from luxuriance to almost barren deserts. Production in any specific area varies with the seasons and is subject to large and sporadic fluctuations.

The primary production area of the oceans is the photic zone, the relatively thin surface layer, 25 fathoms deep (50 metres), that can be penetrated by light, allowing the process of photosynthesis, the use of energy derived from sunlight in the manufacture of food, to take place. All marine life is directly or indirectly tied to this zone, on which both recycling and decomposition, also in other spheres of the ocean, depend. Those few micro-organisms deriving their energy from sources other than light have little significance in the overall productive balance of the oceans.

Photic zone

In the photic zone, growth rate depends on light intensity and available nutrients. Nutrients are constantly depleted by the slow sinking toward the bottom of dead plankton, the floating and mainly miniature plant and animal life, which forms the primary link in the ocean food chain. Simultaneously, fertility is constantly restored as the nutrient-rich deeper waters are brought to the surface. The ocean is ploughed by the action of winds drifting surface waters away from coastal areas, by nutrient-rich waters welling up from the depths, and during the winter season of the temperate regions by cooled surface waters becoming heavier and sinking downwards, forcing nutrient-rich waters to rise.

As a rule tropical surface waters do not interchange with the mineral-supplying waters below as much as those of colder regions and are therefore less productive. However, under certain conditions in some regions of the tropics and subtropics, currents and winds induce a sus-

Table 5: Fish Catch in Top Ten Countries
(000,000 metric tons)

country	1938	1948	53–55	56–58	59–61	62–64	65–67	1968	1969
Peru	0.02	0.08	0.20	0.60	3.7	7.66	8.79	10.52	9.22
Japan	3.7	2.5	4.7	5.2	6.3	6.64	7.27	8.67	8.62
China	...	...	2.2	3.3	...	5.80	...	...	...
U.S.S.R.	1.5	1.5	2.2	2.6	3.0	4.02	5.41	6.08	6.50
Norway	1.1	1.4	1.8	1.8	1.5	1.44	2.81	2.80	2.48
U.S.	2.3	2.4	2.7	2.8	2.9	2.80	2.55	2.44	2.50
Canada	0.8	1.1	0.97	1.0	1.0	1.18	1.30	1.49	1.41
India	...	...	0.83	1.1	0.98	1.11	1.37	1.53	1.61
Spain	0.41	0.55	0.69	0.80	0.94	1.15	1.32	1.50	1.49
South Africa*	0.06	0.18	0.62	0.59	0.88	1.16	1.43	2.20	2.13
World total	21.0	19.6	27.5	31.7	40.3	49.30	57.10	64.30	63.10

*Includes S.W. Africa.
Source: *FAO Yearbook of Fishery Statistics* (1967; 1968; 1969).

Table 6: Food Fish and Feed Fish, 1954–68
(000,000 metric tons)

	1954	1968	increase	percentage increase
Food fish	24.1	33.1	9.1	37.4
Freshwater	3.8	8.3	4.5	118
Marine	20.3	24.8	4.5	18.5
Feed fish	4.3	23.8	19.5	454
Shellfish	3.2	5.4	2.2	69
Total	27.3	62.3	35.0	128

Food chains

tained upwelling of mineral nutrition from lower strata, producing spectacular results. Such regions include the waters around the west coasts of South and Southwest Africa and South America. Consideration of such conditions demonstrates that the production of fish-supporting plankton is not related to latitude but depends upon the presence of "new water" high in nutrient salts.

The marine food chains, ranging from minute floating phytoplankton, sometimes called the "grass" of the sea, to the large predatory species, have many more links than terrestrial equivalents. Each transfer of food value from a lower to a higher level involves a considerable loss in the amount of recoverable organic matter, and consequently of food, so that the amount of organic matter is much greater at the plankton level than it is in fishes. The daily production in kilograms per square metre of dry organic matter beneath a hectare (2.5 acres) of sea surface in the English Channel is as follows: phytoplankton (plant life) 4–5; zooplankton (animal life) 1.5; pelagic fish (living near the surface) 0.0016; bottom fish 0.0010.

The plankton eaters, although they tend generally to be small in size, include the basking shark, the largest of all fishes. Typical consumers of marine plankton include such species as the herrings, menhaden, sardines, and pilchards. Because of this plentiful food source, these fish exist in tremendous numbers, forming the basis of important fisheries.

Demersal fishes, including such species as haddock and halibut, live primarily near the ocean floor, where they feed on various invertebrate marine animals. Most of the large fish, such as tuna, swordfish, and salmon, feed on smaller fishes.

Fishery biologists generally agree that, with proper control and management, the world's marine fisheries could yield approximately twice the amount of the present harvests, providing a sustained yield of upwards of 100,000,000–120,000,000 metric tons, as against the present marine catch (1969) of around 55,700,000 metric tons. This can only be achieved if nations agree to long-term plans for conserving, developing, and working marine resources. Without such agreement, and with continued uncontrolled exploitation of these resources, the most accessible stock may become overfished, or exhausted, followed by overfishing of the remaining stocks.

Inland waters. Fresh water does not support the abundance of fishes to be found in saltwater. Some fishes are most abundant in the transition zone of brackish water

between salt and fresh, as at the mouths of streams, and most of these can also live in either fresh water or salt water. Fishes in the Arctic regions cross the line between fresh water and salt water more freely than fishes in warmer areas, but tropical saltwater fishes freely enter local fresh water that is heavily impregnated with lime.

Because there are various natural barriers to the dispersal of freshwater fishes, and these fishes do not cross salt water, those of one part of the world differ from those of another. Fishery science has devised various methods for improving the quality and yield of inland water fish catches. Fish populations may be increased by stocking with fishes from hatcheries, or reduced to increase poundage in the remaining fishes, and some species can be transplanted to entirely new areas that they did not formerly inhabit. Habitats have been improved by removal of obstructions to migration and by control of predators. The use of artificial farm ponds allows control of production conditions, and such ponds may yield as much as a ton of fish per acre annually.

MARINE TYPES

Table 7 includes some of the more important kinds of bony fishes that are commercially fished and used as food. Major species of ocean, or saltwater, fishes consumed as human food include salmon, herring, codfish, flatfish, redfish, jack mackerel, tuna, and mackerel.

Fishes. Salmon are anadromous, migrating to ocean waters for growth and returning to fresh water for spawning. Pacific salmon return to the freshwater rivers once, to spawn and die; the Atlantic salmon make several returns. Industrial pollution, silting, and damming of rivers for hydroelectric power have seriously threatened the salmon. Only through such large-scale management measures as bypass streams and hatcheries has it been possible to save the Pacific salmon; similar measures in respect to the Atlantic salmon have been less successful.

The herring is probably the most abundant fish in the near surface waters of the seas. The Atlantic species (*Clupea harengus*) and its Pacific counterpart (*C. pallasi*) travel in immense schools several miles long and wide, containing thousands of millions of individuals. Herring feed on small marine animals and other plankton; in turn, such predators as cod, mackerel, tuna, and sharks, as well as some whales and birds, eat freely from the vast herring schools.

One species of anchovy (*Engraulis ringens*) from the Peru Current constitutes the largest single catch of any marine species, exceeding 11,000,000 tons annually. Together with another fish, the South African pilchard (*Sardinops ocellata*) from the Benguela Current off southwest Africa, it is almost exclusively diverted to the manufacture of fishmeal and fish oil. Menhaden, also important as a source of fishmeal and fish oil, constitutes a large portion of the annual world catch. The abundant herring family accounts for two-fifths of the marine catch.

The codfishes, including cod, hake, haddock, whiting, pollack, and saithe, share with herring the leading place among edible marine fish. The U.S.S.R., with its modern long-distance fishing fleets, emulated by most other Eu-

Table 7: Important Food Fishes

fish	habits	description
Herring (*Clupea* species)	northern; inshore; pelagic; schooling; plankton feeders	8 to 17 in.; silvery, rather deep-bodied; compressed; sawlike scales on belly
Pilchard and sardine (*Sardinops* and *Sardinella* species)	temperate; inshore; pelagic; schooling; plankton feeders	6 to 8 in.; silvery, with row of dark spots on side behind head; cylindrical
Menhaden (*Brevoortia* species)	temperate to subtropical; inshore; pelagic; schooling; plankton feeders	12 to 15 in.; silvery, with row of dark spots on side behind head; compressed; sawlike scales on belly
Anchovies (family Engraulidae)	tropical; inshore; pelagic; schooling; plankton feeders	to 6 in.; usually cylindrical; piglike overhanging snout
Shad (*Alosa* species)	temperate; anadromous; schooling; plankton feeders	12 to 30 in.; silvery, with row of spots on sides; sawlike scales on belly
Atlantic salmon (*Salmo salar*)	north temperate; anadromous; loose schooling; fish eaters	24 in. or more; silvery or brown, with many spots on sides; slightly compressed; adipose fin on back
Pacific salmon (*Onchorhynchus* species)	north temperate; anadromous; loose schooling; fish eaters	18 in. or more; silvery or dark, with spots on sides; slightly compressed; adipose fin on back
Tuna (*Thunnus* species)	tropical; offshore; pelagic; schooling; fish eaters	2 to 10 ft; darkish above; compressed; row of finlets on back and belly
Mackerel (*Scomber* species)	temperate; offshore; pelagic; schooling; fish eaters	10 to 30 in.; gray above, silvery below; cylindrical; row of finlets on back and belly
Cod (*Gadus* species)	northern; bottom; mollusk eaters	2 to 5 ft; greenish or reddish; cylindrical; three dorsal and two anal fins
Haddock (*Melanogrammus aeglefinus*)	northern; bottom; mollusk eaters	10 to 30 in.; grayish, with dark spot on shoulder; cylindrical; three dorsal and two anal fins
Whiting or hake (*Merluccius* species)	temperate; inshore; loose schooling; fish eaters	10 to 30 in.; grayish; cylindrical; two dorsal and one anal fin
Drums or croakers (family Sciaenidae)	warm temperate; inshore; on sand bottom	to 2 ft; usually deep-bodied; two dorsal and one anal fin; all make noises
Redfish or ocean perch (*Sebastes* species)	temperate; bottom; shrimp eaters	10 to 24 in.; reddish; deep-bodied; with spines on head
Flounders and halibut (families Pleuronectidae and Bothidae)	bottom; most food types northern or temperate	to 3 ft; very compressed; both eyes on one side of the head

ropean countries, has raised the annual catch of Atlantic cod to almost 1,000,000 tons; the total by all nations close to 4,000,000 tons (1968). Japan and the U.S.S.R. have expanded their catch of Alaska pollack, used mainly for fishmeal and fish oil, to 2,552,000 tons (1969).

Flatfish include a great many species, such as plaice, halibut, and sole, living largely at the bottom of the coastal shelves. The stock of each species is quite limited, however, and halibut was one of the first species for which catch quotas were established. In the North Pacific, the U.S.S.R. and Japan have expanded their catch of several kinds of flatfish.

A major change in ocean fishery since World War II is the intense exploitation of redfish (*Sebastes species*), also called ocean perch. The catch reached 500,000 metric tons in 1958 but has since receded to around 350,000 tons. Correspondingly the U.S.S.R. raised the catch of rockfishes in the Pacific to 423,000 tons (1965) since dropped to 79,000 (1969). The related seabream shows significant gains in Spain and the U.S.S.R.

Jack mackerel (*Trachurus trachurus*), one of the earliest fishes used for human food, continues as an important food source. Although it lives in midocean, the catch has increased one-third in the last decade, principally because of the fishing efforts of the U.S.S.R. and the Philippines.

The true tuna fishes include albacore, bluefin, bigeye, yellowfin tuna, bonito, and skipjack. These species represent a significant marine source of human food, hunted

since ancient days. Both Atlantic and Pacific stocks have been heavily fished in recent decades, and signs of excessive harvest have appeared. More than half the global catch is canned or frozen for the U.S. market. Spanish mackerels and swordfish belong in this group but, despite efforts toward bigger catches, remain minor items.

Both the Pacific and Atlantic mackerel have almost trebled in catch during the 1960s to reach 2,500,000 tons (1969) due to special efforts by Japan and Norway respectively. A similar relative gain is shown by the Indian or striped mackerel (376,000 tons in 1969) in Thailand, India, and the Philippines.

There are some 250 species of shark. Like the whale, sharks have a broad range of feeding habits. Although many are predators, some, including two of the largest fishes in the oceans, the basking shark of the northern temperate zone and the whale shark of tropical waters, are plankton feeders. Shark meat is commonly eaten in warm latitudes but elsewhere is little esteemed, except for the fins, high in protein and considered a delicacy, that are frequently used in squid soups.

Since World War II, many new fish species have been exploited. The clearest indication of this is the doubling of the catches of nonidentified fishes, a category that equals the volume of codfishes.

Shellfish. The term shellfish is generally applied to all invertebrate marine organisms having visible shells. They may be broadly categorized as crustaceans and mollusks.

The crustaceans include lobsters, crabs, crayfish, and both shrimp and the closely related but larger prawns. The shells consist mainly of a hard, inedible substance called chitin. Crustaceans molt frequently during growth. Blue crabs (*Callinectes sapidus*) are eaten when molting and soft-shelled. Marine lobsters (*Homarus americanus*) are eaten when about five years old and have by then molted about 25 times.

With the development of satisfactory freezing techniques in the 1940s, shrimping expanded considerably, becoming a global operation. The U.S. is a major consumer, importing shrimp, mainly frozen, from more than 60 countries. South Africa and Australia have developed a worldwide market for rock lobster (*Palinuris*), and Japan and the U.S.S.R. dominate the world market for king crab (*Paralithodes camtschatica*).

The major mollusks consumed as food are oysters, mussels, clams, scallops, whelks, and snails. The best known marine snail is the abalone, encountered in many warm waters.

This group also includes the octopus, squid, and cuttlefish, popular seafoods in both Mediterranean countries and the Far East. The annual world catch of cephalopods now exceeds 1,000,000 metric tons, with Japan accounting for about 75 percent.

Sea cucumbers (holothurians), or sea slugs, are usually marketed under the name of trepang or bêche-de-mer. Rich in protein, they are eaten in China, Southeast Asia, Australia, and Italy.

Reptiles. Marine reptiles include several species of snakes and turtles. Marine snakes, found mainly in Pacific and Indian Ocean waters from the Persian Gulf to Japan, and especially numerous in the Gulf of Siam, are generally regarded as a nuisance; yet they are a source of food in some regions. The scales and skin are removed and the flesh around the ribs and back is eaten.

Green turtles are the best known of the several marine-turtle species, comprising about a fifth of all the turtles found in the warm seas of the world. In their early years they weigh from 10–90 lbs (4.5 to 40.8 kg) and feed on small invertebrates. Later, they graze on submarine pastures of turtle and eel grass. Although plentiful when Europeans first came to the Caribbean, they have been intensively hunted through the years and have gradually disappeared from the shores of most islands. Since 1959 efforts have been undertaken to save the green turtle from eradication and to redistribute it to the beaches where it formerly thrived in order to increase the food supply of undernourished Latin American countries. Eggs have been protected, and hatchlings airlifted to create new nesting grounds, with limited success. Turtles in African and Asian waters are equally threatened.

Mammals. Ocean mammals include such cetaceans as whales, porpoises, and dolphins, as well as seals and walruses. Whales are a source of meat, fats, and oils, hormones such as insulin, and chemicals. They exist at all levels of ocean food chains. The blue whale mainly devours small reddish shrimp called krill, while the formidable killer whale feeds on salmon, seals, and sharks. The number of species, although still large, has declined considerably. Early hunting of these animals was concentrated on a few numerous and large species, including the blue whale, the sperm whale, and the humpback.

As whale stocks of the North Atlantic and Pacific began to decline, whalers turned to the abundant herds of the Antarctic, which today in turn are showing signs of depletion. Only Japan and the U.S.S.R. are engaged in large-scale whaling operations today.

The hunting of porpoises and dolphins preceded whaling in history. Dolphins were eaten in ancient times around the Mediterranean, and Xenophon and his Greek army found sizeable stores of salted dolphin meat in earthenware vessels on the Black Sea coast. Their use as food there continued until banned recently by the U.S.S.R. in the interest of preserving the animals for biological research. Many tropical islanders still hunt dolphin on a large scale. Freshwater dolphins are caught in many of the world's great rivers, including the Ganges, Indus, and Brahmaputra, the Amazon, the La Plata. The dolphins of Chinese rivers have been eradicated, but a number survive in the lake regions of the upper Yangtze.

Seals and walruses of the Arctic region provide sustenance for many Eskimo tribes. They are also encountered along the northern coasts of the United Kingdom, the southern coasts of South America, and the Antarctic. In Labrador and Newfoundland there are 1,200,000 adult Greenland seals and 500,000 baby seals. Hunted principally for their furs, seals were in danger of extinction in the 1960s and 1970s; many measures were being enforced to protect them.

Seaweeds and plankton. Marine plants may be divided into two groups: grasses and algae. There is only one subaquatic grass of any significance, namely eelgrass. Algae that grow in a fixed location, generally called seaweeds, may be categorized according to colour, into green, brown, red, or blue-green. Brown algae, sometimes called kelp, may grow to exceptional sizes; some specimens attain a length of 165 feet (50 m) or more.

Seaweeds are heavily exploited in many parts of the globe for human as well as animal food. Several species are extensively cultivated on the coastal shelves of China, Japan, the Philippines, and elsewhere. Brown species in particular are harvested in Japan and made into a number of food products. Several are used as new material for various thickening agents; see below.

Cultivated red seaweeds belong to the genus *Porphyra*. Their sun-dried, blackish fronds are shaped into sheets and used in the Orient as a wrapping for rice. Harvested along the coasts of Ireland and Scotland, red seaweed is made into a powder and used as the main ingredient of a kind of bread called laver. Seaweeds contribute to the diet accessory nutrients such as vitamins B_6 and B_{12}.

Phytoplankton does not offer man a suitable food and can hardly be used even as feed for animals. Many species are toxic; the rest are scarcely digestible. In addition, most plankton finish their life cycle within a few days or weeks and are usually devoured by predators. Consequently, the amount of plankton in the water at any given moment is small, even though total plankton production over a year may, in a particular water, well exceed that of fish. Plankton harvesting is therefore very difficult, because of the volume of water that must be sieved.

To date, no technical devices have been contrived to harvest plankton in adequate quantities, even in waters where they abound. The Japanese, Burmese, and East Indians have managed to develop profitable fisheries for certain tiny shrimp that feed on plankton. The shrimp are dried or fermented into pastes. Elsewhere similar plankton-fed shrimp are sun dried and sold as a snack.

Unicellular green algae, such as *Chlorella* and *Scenedesmus*, have been artificially cultivated, yielding 30 tons per acre per year, compared to the standard wheat yield of 1.0 to 1.5 tons. However, the process is costly, since algae, in addition to harvesting, require decolorization and special processing to remove or break down the cell walls through drying and enzyme action in order to become digestible. It is far more efficient to use such plankton directly as fish feed in cultivation ponds or in the raising of cattle and poultry. Blue-green algae easily create waterblooms, slimy accumulations that may be dried in the sun and molded into small loaves with a nutlike flavour and high in protein. This food is extracted from Lake Chad in tropical Africa, and the Aztecs made a similar product. In China a scum called *lan*, collected from ponds and freshwater lakes, provides sustenance for large numbers of people. A related scum, *keklap*, found in Java, is used chiefly as fish feed. Another species is made into dried sheets in Japan and prepared for food by heating in water. Successful cultivation of some blue-green species has been carried through on a semicommercial scale.

A healthy, adult blue whale needs about 1,000,000 calories a day, corresponding to man's requirement for a year. In terms of the shrimp called krill, this amounts to 3,000 to 5,000 lbs (1350–2250 kg) daily. The lactating female blue whale produces 200 to 500 gallons (800–2000 litres) of milk a day to sustain a daily weight gain in her baby of 60 to 150 lbs (27–68 kg), depending on age. The baby grows to be 65 feet (20 m) long when weaned at the age of two. Krill is obviously quite nourishing.

On the average, there are about 1,000 lbs (450 kg) of krill per acre of Antarctic Ocean, comparing favourably with rich pasture lands yielding about 700 lbs (320 kg) of cattle and sheep per acre each year. As blue whales are threatened with extinction, krill trawling has been suggested. Soviet experimentation in krill processing, however, has encountered considerable difficulties in the removal of the indigestible chitin shells and in making attractive products other than pastes.

FRESHWATER TYPES

The freshwater fishes that inhabit ponds, lakes, rivers, and swamps include such major food species as carp, eel, whitefish, pike, pike perch, and catfish. Species differ in characteristics according to the type of water they inhabit. Freshwater fishes currently constitute 13.5 per cent of the global catch, with an annual harvest that has more than doubled since World War II.

Fish culture can be broadly considered as a branch of animal husbandry, as it is concerned with both the cultivation of fish and the harvesting and management of wild fish. Most cultivated fish are freshwater species, such as carp and eel. The common carp, the oldest of the domesticated fishes, has been raised in China since about 2000 BC. Another Chinese species, the grass carp (*Ctenopharyngodon*), with the unique quality among fishes of grazing from higher plants, has been transferred to various countries for the purpose of controlling waterweed infestation. Carp also are grown in lakes, reservoirs, and artificial ponds of temperate regions; several species of tilapia are raised in warm regions; and eels, once raised in ponds of medieval European monasteries, are cultivated widely. Carp and eel also have traditionally been raised in rice fields, a practice called wetland cultivation. This method is increasingly jeopardized by sprays used to control pests and diseases and by toxic agents resulting from industrial development.

Pollution produced by chemical preparations applied for agricultural purposes has also created serious problems for the world's freshwater fisheries; fish cultivation is increasingly restricted to man-made waters. Traditional freshwater fisheries still supply basic protein to China, Southeast Asia, and tropical Africa but have been seriously affected in the U.K., continental Europe, Japan, the U.S.S.R., and the U.S.

QUALITY CONTROL

In marketing fishery products, grading and quality standards are essential, and most governments establish ap-

Phytoplankton as food

Fish culture

propriate legislation and inspection systems. Requirements regarding species, form, size or unit per package, and distribution are primary considerations. Compliance with product identity standards, fill of container or net weight provisions, assurance of wholesomeness, and proper labelling are normally required. Sanitation requirements are concerned with exclusion or limitation of harmful or toxic micro-organisms and of objectionable material.

Quality of fish is usually assessed by taste and odour. Bacteriological and chemical analysis, although useful, does not always give a true picture of quality and requires special equipment and trained personnel. Objective taste and odour observation tests therefore retain their importance.

Spoilage factors. Marine fishes are unfit for human consumption when affected by disease, when carrying parasites, or when showing signs of decomposition. Initially biochemical decomposition is later controlled by micro-organisms originating in slime, viscera, water, or through contamination.

Decomposition induces characteristic changes. The odour becomes sour, rancid, or rotten; the gills turn greyish or brownish, becoming slimy or coated; and the entrails decompose. The belly and cut surfaces turn slimy, often showing yellowish or brownish discolorations and the flesh becomes soft and inelastic. Rancidity begins in fatty fish, particularly mackerel and salmon, even prior to spoilage of the flesh, in particular when the fish are kept cool but insufficiently protected from the air.

Handling procedures influence the rate of natural spoilage of fish and fish products. Rough handling, which breaks the skin, facilitates penetration into the flesh by micro-organisms. Dirty or reused ice, or ice stored for long periods, harbours large numbers of fish spoilage bacteria. Any laxity in temperature control results in accelerated bacterial growth. The exposed flesh of fillets provides a favourable medium for bacterial growth; filleting knives, tables, boards, filleter's gloves, and wash water must be kept clean.

Preservation methods. The primary aim of all fish processing is to retard or eliminate the activities of spoilage agents. Partial inhibition is achieved by maintaining the temperature close to 32° F by the use of ice or refrigerated brine.

Chemical preservatives operate in a similar way. Antibiotics of the tetracycline group also produce a temporary remission of bacterial growth, yielding considerable extension of storage life. Smoking may ensure such partial inhibition of bacterial growth but is generally combined with chilling, brining, and drying. By removing water, freezing, salting, and drying create conditions that make bacterial growth impossible. In modern salting the inhibition is only partial and supplemented by refrigeration. Some salt-loving bacteria (halophiles) carry red pigments and cause discoloration by surface growth. Sorbic acid may be used in dips to avert mold growth on smoked fish such as chubs, herring, and others. Microbial growth is checked in most fermented and marinated fish products through acids produced in the fermentation and in pickling by direct addition.

In heat processing, micro-organisms are eliminated by destructive high temperatures in closed containers to achieve practical sterility. Poor sanitation in the handling of the products prior to filling may jeopardize the processing efficiency. Very high standards of plant sanitation and operator personal hygiene are necessary in plants producing ready-made seafood, such as fish sticks or fish dinners, because the extremely heat-sensitive natural flora is largely wiped out and may, under poor sanitary conditions, be replaced by contaminants from human sources.

OTHER INDUSTRIAL PRODUCTS

Fishmeal and oil. Overwhelmingly important among fish products are oils, manufactured largely by pressing and refining, and meal, manufactured through drying or solvent extraction. Both of these products have attained major significance on the world market. Fish oils are used in the manufacture of margarine and paints. Meal is employed in making concentrate feeds for livestock, competing in this area with soybean meal.

Fishmeal and oil, as well as condensed solubles, are made from the fish less suited for food. The most important source in the U.S. is the menhaden, today used entirely for such manufactured products. The catch of Alaskan herring, small in volume, is used largely for meal and oil. Wastes from fish industries also are utilized. The meal and oil industries of Iceland, the U.K., and Norway are based mainly on Atlantic herring. Sand eel is used in Denmark. Pilchard, anchovy, Pacific mackerel, and jack mackerel also are used in various countries. Alaska pollack has become an important source for fishmeal manufacture in the North Pacific, both in the U.S.S.R. and Japan. Since 1958 anchoveta from the Peruvian and Chilean coasts has become the major source, currently with an annual catch exceeding 12,000,000 tons.

Fish protein concentrate (FPC). Fish meal has repeatedly been upgraded for use as human food and given the designation fish flour. This is accomplished by careful choice of raw material, special sanitary precautions, and carefully controlled manufacturing. A stable, odourless, and colourless final product is made from white-fleshed fish species such as hake. Various extraction procedures remove fat or dissolve the protein for subsequent precipitation, rendering fish protein concentrate, a product that has shown considerable promise as a flexible protein supplement to the diets of underdeveloped countries. FPC may not adapt well to regional diets, however, and serious distribution problems exist. Also, fish catches of adequate volume and concentration may not be available.

Glue and isinglass. The large salt-cod industry is the basis for a substantial by-product industry for the manufacturing of fish glue and isinglass, important in Japan. Glue is manufactured from bottom fish skins, and sometimes from heads and bones, in a manner quite similar to that employed in the preparation of other animal gelatin glue. When made carefully from the best skins, it can be used for photoengraving. Glues of lower quality are prepared from bones and other waste. Isinglass may be manufactured from other fish, such as hake.

The word isinglass comes from the German word *Hausenblase,* meaning sturgeon's bladder, the original raw material from which this product was made. It is the purest form of fish gelatin and is employed as a clarifying aid, primarily in the manufacture of wine. One ounce of isinglass will clarify 200 to 300 gallons of wine.

Leather. Sharks have been a principal source for fish leather skins. Skin leather is available as a by-product in countries still extracting vitamin A from shark liver. Suitability of such skins for leather depends upon the size of the pieces and the absence of defects. The skins are carefully removed from the shark either aboard the fishing vessel at sea or as soon as the vessel lands its catch. They are then coated with salt, cured in piles, and shipped in bundles to the tannery.

Pharmaceuticals and additives. A significant new development is the extraction of drugs from various ocean sources. Marine medicine and pharmacology are emerging as new disciplines. Some marine fungi make potent antibiotics. Virus-killing agents have been extracted from ocean gastropods; other molluscans have rendered anti-cancer substances. Potent antimicrobial agents originate with sea cucumbers, sponges, and similar sources. Special significance has been attached to the wealth of toxins, appearing in almost all categories of marine animals, several of which are under intensive study.

Valuable new animal compounds extracted from the internal organs and glands of whales include steroids, pituitary hormones, insulins, and enzymes.

Insulin is more easily extracted from fish than from cattle. The insulin-producing Langerhans' islets are separate in some fishes and attached to gall bladder, bile duct, mesentery, etc. Fish insulin is more stable, not being subject to decomposition by protein-splitting enzymes from the pancreas. Viscera of tuna, bonito, and cod, as well as whale, are sources generally used in the U.S.S.R. and Japan. Depending on species, whale pancreases weigh 15–500 kg, as compared with 0.3 kg for that of a cow.

Insulin

A principal constituent of seaweeds is cellulose, usually together with other polymer carbohydrates such as mannitol, laminarin, alginic acid, and fucoidin. Many of these are isolated and used as thickeners for pharmaceutical or microbial laboratory work. Phycocolloids of commercial importance are chiefly agar, algin, and carrageenin. Algin is produced from brown seaweeds, agar and carrageenin from red varieties. These compounds are used as thickeners, humectants maintaining water content, coagulants, bulking agents, flocculation agents, and antibiotic carriers. In a number of countries, including the U.S., Canada, France, India, Japan, Norway, New Zealand, the U.K., South Africa, Spain, and the U.S.S.R., these items are manufactured from such seaweeds as Irish moss, dulse, and purple laver. Seaweed meal has successfully been used in feeding cattle.

FISH AND MARINE PRODUCTS AS A SOURCE OF MATERIALS FOR OTHER INDUSTRIES

Scale and shell products. A number of products are made from the scales and shells of fishes. Herring scales are a source of pearl essence, a suspension of guanine crystals sprayed on beads, textiles, and other articles to impart an iridescent sheen. Marine and freshwater shells, harvested mostly in Australia and the Far East, are used to manufacture buttons, buckles, and similar items. Freshwater mussel shells are taken for the same purpose from the Mississippi River and its tributaries. Many are exported to Japan to be used as spherical core matrices for the artificial cultivation of pearls.

Oyster and clam shells are commonly ground for use in poultry feed. In some locations such as southern California, huge deposits of clam shells in tide flat areas are "mined" by dredging at low tide.

Tortoise shells were first employed for ornamental purposes more than 300 years ago in Japan. The marine hawksbill tortoise (*Eretmochelys imbricata*) has been the favoured source. Other ocean varieties employed are other *Eretmochelys* and *Caretta* species and the river tortoise in South America (*Podocnemis*). The plates of the shell are used in inlaid products, toilet articles, knife handles, cuff links, combs, hairpins, and earrings.

Pearls. Natural pearls are formed when some foreign matter accidentally becomes inserted between the shell and the soft body tissues of mollusks. The prevalence of natural pearls has been sharply declining due to the deterioration of harvesting grounds and the expansion of pearl culturing. Natural pearls have been produced up to the present in the Persian Gulf, around the northwest coast of Sri Lanka (formerly Ceylon), in the Bay of Aden in the Red Sea, on the northwest coast of Australia, and in the South Pacific.

Cultured pearls were pioneered by the Japanese and others in the 19th century. Several species of marine and freshwater mussels, oysters, and clams are employed. Pearl farms have most recently been developed in the Kuri Bay area of Australia and in India.

Corals. Corals, largely of the genus *Corallium,* have been harvested since ancient days in the Mediterranean and were at one time an article of commerce with the Far East, whose own coral fisheries date only from the 19th century, starting in Malaya Peninsula and moving to waters off Japan.

Coral is divided into three categories according to its colours. Pink and red corals are the most valuable. Black corals, of the genus *Antipathes,* are harvested and worked into various ornamental items in the West Indies, Malaysia, the Red Sea region, southeast India, and Indonesia.

Sponges. The skeletons of sponges consist of resilient spongin, making them well suited for cleaning purposes. But sponge fishing, once flourishing in the Mediterranean and the West Indies, where sponge farms were established, is another of the many marine industries threatened with depleted stocks and possible extinction of species due to excessive harvesting.

BIBLIOGRAPHY. J.E. BARDACH, *Harvest of the Sea* (1968), a survey of the harvests of the oceans and research related to this aspect, contains ample references; G.A. BORGSTROM (ed.), *Fish as Food,* 4 vol. (1961–65), a comprehensive treatise on the biochemistry and microbiology of fish and shellfish; F.T. CHRISTY, JR. and A.D. SCOTT, *The Common Wealth in Ocean Fisheries* (1965), a critical analysis of man's handling of the ocean resources; W.J. CROMIE, *The Living World of the Sea* (1966), a semipopular review of all major categories of marine life, with good references to scientific books for each group; F.E. FIRTH (ed.), *The Encyclopedia of Marine Resources* (1969) a comprehensive treatment of ocean resources and their utilization, with emphasis on economic activities; M. GRAHAM (ed.), *Sea Fisheries: Their Investigation in the United Kingdom* (1956), the standard reference book on the biology of the oceans despite its age and geographical restriction; SIR ALLISTER HARDY, *The Open Sea: Its Nature and History* (1965), a profound study of the living world of the oceans; C.F. HICKLING, *Fish Culture* (1962), a key study on traditional fish cultivation; A. MCKEE, *Farming the Sea* (1969), a discussion of recent developments in the raising of ocean fish; R.S. WIMPENNY, *The Plankton of the Sea* (1966), a recent survey of the planktonic world and its utilization; M.E. STANSBY (ed.), *Industrial Fishery Technology* (1963), a survey of methods for harvesting, preserving, and processing fish and shellfish.

(G.A.B.)

Fishing, Commercial

Fishing, which involves the recovery of food and other valuable resources from bodies of water, is one of the oldest employments of mankind. The commercial fisherman works for profit and to satisfy his own needs, in contrast to sport fishing, which has a recreational purpose. Commercial fishing is carried on in all types of waters, in all parts of the world, except where impeded by depth or dangerous currents or prohibited by law. In seawaters, fishing is the oldest form of marine exploitation, having begun long before man extracted oil or minerals from these areas.

Commercial fishing can be done in a simple manner with small vessels, little technical equipment and little or no mechanization as in small local, traditional or artisanal fisheries. It can also be done on a large scale with powerful deep sea vessels, and sophisticated mechanical equipment similar to that of modern industrial enterprises.

Man takes both plants and animals from the sea. Two types of fish are caught: demersal, living at or near the bottom, although sometimes in midwater; and pelagic, living in the open sea near the surface. Cod, haddock, hake, pollock, and all forms of flatfish are common demersal fish. Herring and related species and tuna and their relatives are examples of pelagic fish. Both demersal and pelagic fish can sometimes be found far from coastal regions. Other aquatic animals that may be the object of commercial fishery include, most notably, crustaceans (lobster, spiny lobster, crabs, prawns, shrimps, crayfish) and mollusks (oysters, scallops, mussels, snails, squid, octopuses). Certain mammals (whale, porpoises, seals), reptiles (serpents, crocodiles), amphibians (frogs), many types of worms, coelenterates (coral, jellyfish), and sponges are also sought by commercial fishermen. Most of these animals are legally regarded as fish in many countries.

The most important water plants commercially obtained in seawater and freshwater are algae. Seaweed is harvested in the water or collected on the seashore. Algae play an important role in many countries, not only as human food but also as fodder for cattle, as fertilizer, and as a raw material for certain industries. Other water plants such as rush, reed, and even edible herbs, fruits and roots, are also harvested. Some of the above animals and plants are cultivated in natural waters or in artificial ponds and lakes.

Fisheries are classified in part by type of water: in freshwater—lake, river, and pond—and in the ocean—inshore, midwater, and deep sea. Another classification is based on the object—as in whaling, salmon fishing, and sponge fishing. Sometimes the fishing method is used as the classifying characteristic: diving, fish poisoning, harpooning, and trawling. (For detailed statistics on the world's fish catch and for information on processing and marketing of fish, see FISH AND MARINE PRODUCTS. See also FOOD PRESERVATION.)

Commercial water plants

HISTORY

Fishing, like farming, is a form of primary production. Food-gathering people first obtained fish and other aquatic products in the shallow water of lakes and along the seashore, in small ponds remaining in inundation areas, in areas with ebb tides, and in small streams. Some authorities believe that in the earliest times fish were rarely caught because of the inadequacy of fishing gear. Shellfish, however, can be gathered easily by hand and large prehistoric shell mounds indicate their importance as food. Such hills, known by the Danish term kitchen middens, are found in many parts of the world, sometimes also on inland lakes.

In earliest times most foodstuffs were used at once and not stored, but as expanding populations increased food needs, techniques were developed for preserving fish by drying, smoking, salting, and fermentation. It became desirable to catch large quantities, and specialized equipment was devised. Individual fishing was replaced by collective efforts involving larger, more effective gear.

Fishing equipment and methods improved through the centuries, until bulk fisheries were established in Europe. Herring were caught in huge numbers in northern Europe in the Middle Ages. Cod fishery began on the Grand Banks of Newfoundland even before the Italian explorer John Cabot made his voyage there in 1497. Whaling with large fleets began in the 17th century, both in the Atlantic and in the South Pacific.

Mechanization came to fishing in the 19th century. The steamer replaced sailing boats in sea fisheries during the final quarter of that century, and was supplanted in turn by motor vessels. Small fishing boats became motorized at the beginning of the 20th century. In the 1940s, instrumentation—such as the echo sounder (for vertical searching) and, later, sonar (for horizontal searching)—was introduced in sea fisheries and in some freshwaters. The total catch of fish and other living aquatic products tripled from 1948 to 1968. Today, some industrial countries lack sufficient manpower for their fisheries and are attempting to automate, with the help of seaborne computers.

Develop-
ment
of fishing
technique

The development of commercial fishery is linked to the development of fishing techniques that grew in response to various pressures, especially the growth of the market. Larger catches could be obtained by increasing the number or the size of the fishing gear or both. Simple lines armed with one or a few hooks were replaced by longlines with thousands of hooks. Single small traps were combined into systems of hundreds, and pots were set in large quantities. Nets were greatly enlarged; net-making machines were invented that produced netting in large sheets. Mechanical netmaking brought replacement of the old local netting fibres (linen and hemp), with cotton and hard fibres. But all natural fibres, especially those of cellulose, begin to rot in time; thus, the introduction after World War II of rotproof nets made of synthetic fibres represented a major advance. Mechanical netmaking remained unchanged for the most part, though for certain fishing gear the usual knotted netting was replaced by knotless netting.

The development of fishing gear in another direction stemmed from the desire to fish in deep water, where larger fish are more common. Fishing in deeper waters required not only gear adapted to the depth but also suitable vessels, although today properly equipped fishermen in small boats can fish at considerable depths. The fisherman of Madeira, for example, catch espada preto (*Aphanopus carbo*) at depths up to 1,000 metres (3,300 feet) with lines up to 1,000 fathoms (6,000 feet, or 1,800 metres) long. The famous coelacanth of the Mozambique Channel is caught with lines in depths up to 400 metres (1,300 feet). To set and haul lines from such depths by hand, however, is hard work. Labour costs increase significantly with depth, especially for heavy gear. A modern fishing vessel, such as a stern trawler or purse seiner, is a specialized, sophisticated equipage in which vessel, gear, and crew act as a unit. Originally, bottom trawling was done out to the edge of the continental shelf, where the depth is about 200 metres, or 650 feet; today it is done at depths up to 600 and even 1,000 metres. The time required for shooting and hauling gear, however, is an economic barrier to fishing in great depth.

With the extension of fisheries in noncoastal waters and the development of efficient refrigeration methods, long-distance fishery developed. Trawlers from northern Europe made their first expeditions in the Mediterranean and off the west coast of Africa before World War I. Today some nations, such as Japan and the Soviet Union, fish around the world.

Earliest
mechani-
zation

As fishing gear increased in size and weight, more people were needed to handle it. Yet it was not until the end of the last century that mechanization of fishing techniques began with winches and pulley blocks. Power-driven winches were introduced for fishing gear at the end of the 19th century, but it was many years before specialized hauling devices, such as rope-coiling machines and power-driven rollers, facilitated easier hauling of netting. In the beginning of the 1950s, mechanization took a great stride forward in purse seining (see below), when the power block was invented for hauling the gear. Another important hauling device was a power-driven drum to haul and store seine nets, gill nets, purse seines, and even the large trawl nets. The Japanese introduced drums in longline fishing for tuna. Another important innovation was the stern chute for stern trawlers, a development made possible by cooperation between naval architects and fishing-gear experts, which permitted large-scale mechanization of gear handling. A trend in the early 1970s was toward full automation, with the help of shipborne computers that will supply information to the engine room and the on-board fish-processing plant and will influence navigation, fish searching, and gear handling.

Statistical treatment of fishermen varies. According to international law all personnel working on a fishing vessel are considered fishermen, including processors, radio operators, kitchen help, stewards, medical personnel and others. Less official statistical sources often include in the fishing population women who repair nets and other members of a fisherman's family. Not all fishermen work full time the year round; there are many part-time fishermen engaged in seasonal businesses, such as farming. In Iceland a person is statistically a fisherman if he earns more than 50 percent of his income from fishing. The Japanese have a nearly identical definition, adding that, in sea fisheries, he must stay at sea at least 30 days a year. Because of these varying definitions of the term fisherman it is impossible to give a reliable number for the world's fishing population. There are more than 100,000 in the countries of the European Common Market and more than 500,000 in all of Europe. In North America there may be more than 200,000 and more than 500,000 in Central and South America. About 4,000,000 fishermen live in Asia, much smaller numbers in Africa and Australia. The total number of fishermen in all parts of the world may be estimated at 5,500,000. Most of these are men, with the number of women actually engaged in fishing no more than 1 percent. World numbers of fishermen are decreasing because of mechanization, especially in the industrial countries.

FISHING METHODS AND FISHING GEAR

An international classification of fishing methods recently adopted includes 16 types: (1) Fishing without gear; (2) Grappling and wounding gear; (3) Stunning; (4) Line fishing; (5) Trapping; (6) Trapping in the air; (7) Fishing with bag nets; (8) Dredging and trawling; (9) Seining; (10) Fishing with surrounding nets; (11) Driving fish into nets; (12) Fishing with lift nets; (13) Fishing with falling gear; (14) Gillnetting; (15) Fishing with entangling nets; and (16) Harvesting machines.

The simplest and oldest form of fishing, collecting by hand, is still done today by both professionals and non-professionals along the shore during ebb tide in shallow water and in deeper water by divers with or without diving suits. Even when small tools such as knives or hoes are used, such collecting is classified as without gear. Diving to collect sponges, pearl oysters, or corals belongs under this classification, as does fishing with hunting animals. The Chinese still use trained otters, and the Japanese sometimes employ cormorants.

To extend the reach of the human arm, long-handled tools were invented, such as spears, which can be thrust, thrown, or discharged, and clamps, tongs, and raking devices for shellfish harvesting. A special form is the harpoon, composed of a point and a stick joined together by a rope. Such gear also includes spears, blowpipes, bows and arrows, and rifles and guns, which are used in fish shooting.

The method called stunning may involve poisoning with toxic plants and special chemicals or mechanical stunning by explosions under water. The most modern practice in this field is to stun the fish by means of an electrical shock.

In line fishing the fish can be attracted by a natural or artificial bait or lure devised to catch and hold the fish. Generally, the bait is combined with a hook or with a gorge, as is used in France in line fishing for eels. There are handlines, as in pole-and-line fishing for tuna; setlines, such as bottom longlines with hundreds of hooks, used for cod or halibut; drift lines with a single hook and drifting longlines for tuna, shark, and salmon; and troll lines for mackerel and some game fish. Another method of fishing with hooks is done without bait, by raising and lowering arrays of hooks to gig (hook in the body) such large species as cod and sturgeon.

Genuine mechanical traps, which close by a mechanism released by the prey, are seldom employed for fishing. Most commercial fishing traps are chambers entered easily by the prey but from which escape is prevented by labyrinths or retarding devices, such as gorges or funnels. Fish traps can be simple hiding places, such as bushes or tubes, into which fish or shrimps swim for shelter but cannot escape later when the device is hauled in. The octopus pot used on the Italian coast and by the fishermen of South and East Asia is an example. Other types include small basket-like or cagelike traps made of wood, netting, wire, or plastic pots and fyke nets (long bag-shaped nets kept open by a series of hoops; Figure 1, bottom); and large pound nets (Figure 1, top) used in the Mediterranean for tuna, off the western Baltic coast

From R. Graumont and E. Wenstrom, *Fisherman's Knots and Nets*,
© 1948; Cornell Maritime Press, Inc.

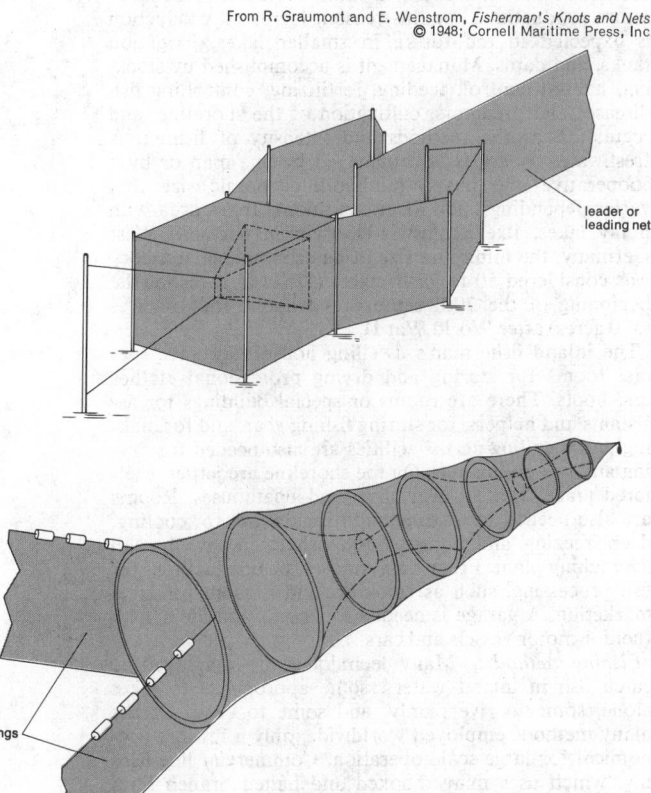

Figure 1: (Top) Pound net and (bottom) fyke net.

leader or
leading net

wings

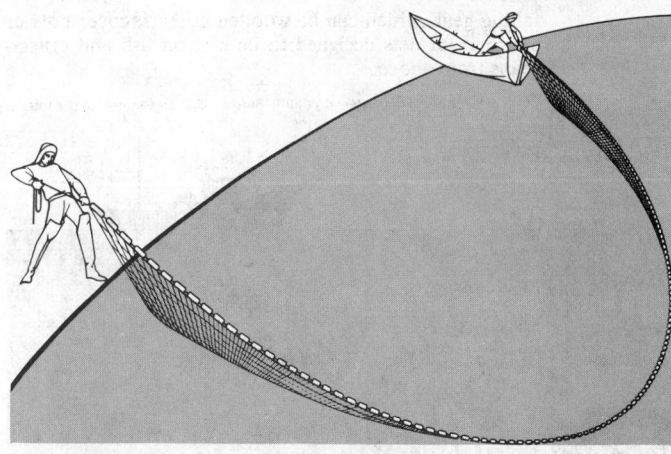

Figure 2: Seine net.
From R. Graumont, *Fisherman's Knots and Nets*

for eels, herring, and other species, and off both coasts of the northern Pacific for salmon. A special class are aerial traps for catching flying fish and shrimps. The fish are stirred up, then caught in the air with the help of special gear called veranda nets. South Sea islanders catch flying fish at night by attracting them with torches.

(The uses of specific nets in seawater and freshwater fishing are covered in those sections of the article.) Bag nets are kept vertically open by a frame and held horizontally stretched by the water current. There are small scoop nets that can be pushed and dragged and big stownets, with and without wings, held on stakes or on anchors with or without a vessel. There is also a special winged type with boards or metal plates (otter boards) that keep it spread open. Stownets, larger than scoop nets and held in place against a current, are used in many rivers and by the Koreans for sea fishing in the strong current off the southwest coast of their country. In this case the stownet is anchored with a vessel.

Nets

Dragged gear includes dredges, used mostly for shellfish and operated by hand in shallow waters, and trawls. Bottom trawling is done with different types of gear that vary in design according to the way in which the bottom of the trawl is horizontally stretched. A modern development is the midwater trawl that drags the fishing gear through the water midway between the bottom and the surface. Trawls are the most important fishing gear of the commercial fisheries of northwest Europe and are second only to purse seines in total catch of the world.

The seine net (Figure 2) has very long wings and towing warps (tow lines), with or without bags for the catch.

Purse seines (Figure 3), also lampara, and other types of surrounding nets, capture the highest percentage of the total annual yield of the world. Pelagic fish are surrounded not only from the side but also from underneath, preventing them from escaping by diving downward. Purse seines can be operated by a single boat, with or without auxiliary skiff, or by two vessels. Many sardine-like fishes—herring, tuna, mackerel, cod, and salmon—are commercially fished in this manner.

Another class of fishing methods involves driving the fish into a net or gear. A drive-in net may be one of those already mentioned or may be specially made, such as the dustpan-shaped stationary gear used in some fisheries in south Asia.

Driving fish into a net

A further fishing method employs lift nets, which are submerged, then raised or hauled upward out of the water to catch the fish or crustaceans above them, often attracted by light or natural bait. This group includes small hand-operated lift nets, such as hoop and blanket nets, as well as large, mechanically and pneumatically operated lift nets. Some of these employ levers, or gallows, and are installed on the beach or on a vessel. The fish wheels used on the Tiber, Rhône, and Columbia rivers can be considered as mechanized lift nets. The most important examples of this fishing method are the stick-held dip nets of the Japanese. In contrast to the lift nets are falling gear, which can be wooden baskets, cover pots or a variety of nets designed to be cast on fish and crustaceans from above.

By courtesy of the Fish and Wildlife Service, U.S. Department of the Interior

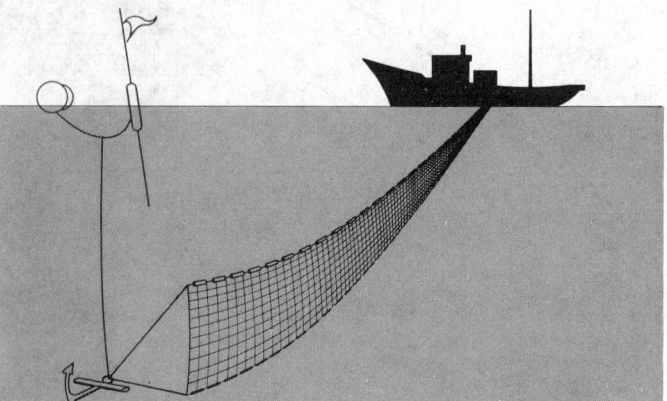

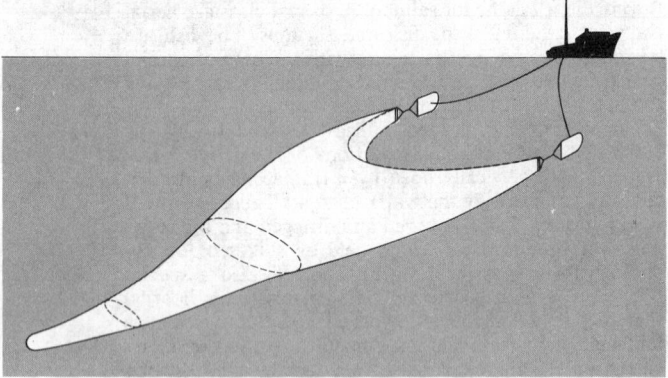

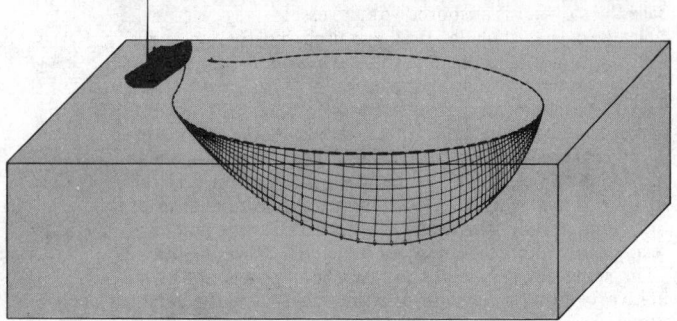

Figure 3: (Top) Gill net, (centre) otter trawl, (bottom) purse seine.

Gill nets (Figure 3), which catch the fish in their meshes, are mostly used in long rows. As setnets they are anchored or fixed by stakes; as drift nets they are allowed to drift freely or with a fishing craft. Before the invention of midwater trawls, drift nets, with surrounding nets, were the principal gear for fishing pelagic fishes.

Sometimes gill nets do not catch by meshing but by entangling the fish, especially those too large for the mesh size or provided with spines or hard fins. Single-walled tangle nets are widely used to catch sturgeon, salmon, and shellfish, such as the king crab. Some tangle nets are double walled; most are triple walled, such as the trammel nets used especially for flatfish.

Harvesting machines include comparatively new types of gear that may separate the fish or shellfish from the water by pumps (pump fishing) or by mechanized dredges, as well as floating machines that dig out mollusks by means of underwater jets and transport them out of the water with the help of conveyor belts.

FRESHWATER FISHERIES

Freshwater fishing is carried out in lakes and rivers and to some extent in natural and artificial ponds. In tropical

areas, swamps with shallow water, sometimes overgrown with vegetation, are important inland fisheries. Before transportation and distribution of ocean fish was organized, freshwaters were the only resource for fish and other aquatic products for the inland population. Their importance decreased with the growing bulk fisheries of the seas. Today, freshwater fish comprise only 11 percent of the total catch of water products of the world. Nevertheless, in some countries the production of freshwater fish is still very high, more than 300,000 tons in Indonesia, more than 200,000 tons in Bangladesh and the Soviet Union, and more than 100,000 tons in Uganda, Egypt, Burma, and Chad. Widely different species—feeding on bacteria or detritus, plants or plankton, or living as predators—are used for human consumption. Well-known species include trout and whitefish, carp and other cyprinids, catfish, murrals, and tilapias. The desirability of some anadromous fishes—those, such as salmon and sturgeon, that spawn in freshwater but live in the sea—and catadromous fishes—those, most notably the eel, that spawn in the sea but live in freshwater—has led to specialized fisheries in inland waters.

Freshwater fish production

The kind and quantity of fish found in lakes and rivers vary greatly with the physical and chemical condition of the water. Limnologists, scientists who study conditions in freshwater, classify freshwaters by the quantity of oxygen and essential nutrient salts (nitrates, phosphates, and potash) they contain. Fishermen classify waters by the principal fish to be caught therein. Rivers, for example, are divided into different zones beginning with the source, which is often good trout water, and ending in the estuary, where many coastal varieties of ocean fish can be caught. In like manner, fishermen classify lakes by expected catch (e.g., eels, tilapias, or crayfish).

The great variations in the productivity of inland waters are explained by differences in their physical and chemical properties. Though some rivers may produce as much as 200 kilograms per hectare (180 pounds per acre) each year and some lakes may yield 160 kilograms per hectare (140 pounds per acre), the world average is about eight kilograms per hectare or seven pounds per acre.

Management of freshwater fisheries in small bodies of water is easier than management in large bodies or in the oceans, because it is easier to control fish stocks for maximum production. For this reason, increased production is expected in the future in smaller lakes, irrigation tanks, and dams. Management is accomplished by stocking, habitat control, feeding, fertilizing, controlling fish diseases and predators, cultivation of the shoreline, and regulation of the methods and intensity of fishing. A freshwater fishery is best managed by one man or by a cooperative and has a minimum economic size that varies depending upon local conditions. In an area with many lakes, like Schleswig-Holstein in northern West Germany, the minimum size of an economic lake fishery was considered 50 to 75 hectares (125–185 acres) at the beginning of the 20th century and about 150 hectares (370 acres) after World War II.

The inland fisherman's dwelling house may have special rooms for storing and drying professional clothes and boots. There are rooms or special buildings for assistants and helpers, for storing fishing gear, and for making and mending nets. Facilities are also needed for drying and preserving nets. On the shoreline are jetties, sheltered places to keep fish alive, and boathouses. Rooms are also needed for sorting and packing fish, for cooling, deep-freezing, and storage. Some fishermen have a small ice-making plant. Frequently, houses include facilities for fish processing, such as smoking, and a room for local marketing. A garage is needed for trucks and tanks with fuel for motor vessels and cars.

Fishing methods. Many techniques are employed to catch fish in inland waters, some appropriate to lakes alone, some to rivers only, and some to both. Of the many methods employed worldwide, only a few are economical for large-scale operation. Commercial line fishing, which uses many hooked and baited branch lines tied to a single main line, is widely practiced. A simpler technique is handlining, in which single lines with baited hooks are tied to small sticks or trees along the shore or to special devices set along the side of a hole in ice. Handlining is used for deep fishing or for catching in rocky areas. Drifting lines with one or more hooks can also be used on lakes, though seldom in rivers. Lines may also be trolled (trailed) behind a moving boat. On some rivers in tropical and temperate areas, fish are caught by fouling with sharp-pointed hooks. The main difficulty in line fishing is to keep the lines clear and to obtain baits in needed quantity.

Passive and stationary fishing gear

Passive and stationary fishing gear is so important in many lakes and rivers that some fishermen specialize entirely in trapping. Since deep and rocky shores, however, do not favour the use of traps, these devices cannot be used in all areas. Fish seeking shelter may be caught in simple brushwood devices when the brushwood is lifted quickly. More important are traps, such as wooden baskets made of wickerwork or of split bamboo, with retarding devices such as funnels or valves at the entrance. Wooden baskets, generally used in rivers with strong currents, can be set according to the longline system in which the baskets are tied with branch lines on a main line lying across the bottom of the river. Such baskets are usually baited, with the bait sometimes held in small bags or boxes. Today, in river fisheries as in coastal sea fisheries, traps, especially those used for eels, are made of plastic.

A more modern type of trap is the bag-shaped fyke net, held open by hoops; linked together in long chains, these are used to catch eels in rivers. When equipped with wings and leaders, fyke nets are employed in lakes where there are sheltered places with abundant plant life. Hundreds of such nets can be combined into systems where it is not economical to build large traps. (Wings are short leading netwalls at both sides of the opening of a fyke net, see Figure 1 bottom; leaders are long leading walls of netting guiding the fish to the trap, Figure 1, top.)

Another fishing method important in freshwater fisheries employs small scoop nets or large net bags (stow nets). Such gear is known on many European and Asian rivers. The net bag is fixed to the river bottom to catch migrating or drifting fish. Some human control may be necessary; sometimes a watchman lives on a vessel or raft next to the stownet or on a special platform. Though stownets are especially popular in European rivers for eel fishing, their importance is lessening due to increased boat traffic and to pollution. Moreover, the gear can be too large to be moved easily. In Indonesia stownets up to 100 metres (330 feet) long and up to 40 metres (130 feet) across the mouth are used. Small scoop nets can be operated by hand, pushed or towed over the bottoms in shallow waters. Sometimes this is done by fishnetting parties, in which all the men of a village form a line across the river, with a scoop net in each hand. Sometimes the fisherman stands on a platform built on the side of the stream and simply scoops up fish as they pass; this is done by some African fishermen in Malawi and was done by American Indians on the Columbia River in Oregon.

Seining

One of the most common fishing methods in freshwater lakes and rivers is seining, which is done in temperate zones especially in autumn and winter when fish are concentrated in deeper parts of the lakes. Because part of the seine must be dragged over the lake bottom while it surrounds the fish, seining is practicable only where the lake bottom is smooth and where favourable areas (*i.e.*, with fish concentrated near the bottom) are known. In some lakes such areas have been known for a long time and may be named and marked on fishing maps. Seine nets in lake fisheries can be very large with wings of 1,000 metres (3,300 feet) each. Since traditional seining required considerable labour, mechanization became desirable. A modern mechanized seine-net fishery requires only a small number of men. In northern countries seine nets are used under ice. For this purpose a number of ice holes are needed for guiding the towing warps with the net on the underside of the ice sheet. Here also manpower is saved by motorized towing and coiling lines and by drilling the holes in the ice with power drills.

Some success has been achieved in increasing the efficiency of seine nets by electric light. Fish trying to evade the net can be caught by stunning or eels lying in the mud during the cold season (generally a time when eel fishing is poor) can be attracted out of the mud by an electrical current. The disadvantage of all seine nets is that they are not selective; many undersized fish which should be preserved cannot escape.

Trawls and purse seines are used in large lakes only and are discussed below with sea fisheries. But lift nets are often used in freshwater, not only to catch bait fish for line fishing but also to catch crayfish or other freshwater crabs. There are small hand-operated lift nets tightened by frames and larger ones lifted from a gallows or with one or two vessels. Unframed blanket nets are used in rivers in Italy, each corner held by a gallows placed on the banks. Cover pots and cast nets also have some importance in commercial freshwater fisheries. Cover pots are especially used in rice fields or shallow waters with rich vegetation. Cast nets are more used in clear waters in lakes and in rivers; considerable skill is required to cast these. In the Soviet Union shooting mechanisms are employed to cast larger nets. Much more important in freshwater fisheries, however, are gill nets. The mesh size of the net can be used to regulate the size of the fish caught; thus smaller, undesired species escape. Lake fishermen use mostly stationary gill nets, anchored near the bottom or floating. River fishermen use gill nets that drift with the current, with one side tied to the boat and the other to a drifting buoy. With entangling two-walled nets and trammel nets, yield can be increased by frightening the fish into the netting; this is accomplished by beating the water or throwing stones.

Sources of extra income. Freshwater fisheries often must double as other types of enterprise in order to be economically successful. Many harvest water plants, collect shellfish or frogs, sell gravel, or, in areas with cold seasons, sell natural ice. Some freshwater fishermen have tried to combine fishing with the breeding of mink or other fish-eating animals.

SALTWATER FISHERIES

Fishing in salt water ranges from small traditional operations involving one man and a rowboat to huge private or governmental enterprises with large fleets for deep-sea and distant fisheries. Because industrial fishery grew from traditional beginnings, many similarities exist between the two.

Demarcation of coastal waters

Coastal waters and freshwater are demarcated by law in most countries. Inshore and coastal fisheries are separated from sea fisheries by the frontier limit, traditionally three miles or about five kilometres in most countries. This area is reserved for fishing vessels with small gear; trawling is often forbidden. Some traditional fishing vessels also fish in the deep sea, however. Small traditional vessels from the French Atlantic coast operate seasonally off the Irish coast and off the west coast of Africa. Small Portuguese vessels fish in the northwest Atlantic from Newfoundland to Greenland, and small Canadian and American vessels operate along the Pacific coast of North America. The best example of far distant sea fishery by artisans on a small scale is the fishermen of Ghana, who pilot their open, often unpowered canoes along the West coast of Africa from Senegal to Gabon.

Objects of sea fishery. Generally speaking, shellfishes (mollusks and crustaceans), seaweed, sponges, corals, and small coastal fish are objects of traditional fishery. Most other commercial fish are caught both by traditional and industrial vessels. In the United States, sports fishing also has an important effect on the stocks of commercial fish. Nevertheless, some species may be considered typical prey of industrial fishermen. Among these are all larger species of tuna.

The most important sea fish are herring-like fishes—such as anchovies, herring (in the North Atlantic), and pilchard (off the coasts of South Africa). In second place are representatives of the cod family, such as the Atlantic cod, the Alaska pollack, and the haddock. The third group includes such fish as the horse mackerel and the mackerel. In estimating the importance of species, both quantities and market values of landings are considered. From this point of view, different species of tuna (especially yellowfin tuna and skipjack); salmon and capelins; milkfish; flatfishes (especially plaice and halibut); hake; croakers and redfish; mullets and sauries; menhaden and the North Pacific herring; many mollusks (especially squid, clams, scallops, and abalones); a large number of crustaceans—such as king crabs, lobster and spiny lobster, prawns, and shrimps—are important. Sea mammals, such as whale and seals, also have or had substantial economic value.

Sea-fishing methods. As noted above, purse seining for pelagic fish and trawling for demersal fish are the most important methods in the sea fisheries of the world. Other methods, widely in use, include diving for oysters and sponges; using spears and harpoons to catch tuna, whale, and seals; and using suction methods to remove clams from the bottom of the sea.

Whaling. Grappling and wounding gear used to catch sea fish includes spears and harpoons employed for whaling and sealing and for catching big fish, such as swordfish and sharks. The symbol of fishery, the trident of Neptune, is the old Mediterranean spear for fishing tuna. Harpooning is still important for whaling in the Arctic and Antarctic. Originally small whale were hunted from the shore in open sailboats and rowboats (a practice still current in the Azores) or by driving the animals toward shallow water as is done today in the Faroe Islands. (The whale are then killed with hand harpoons and lances.) Fishermen of the Basque country (southern France and northern Spain) hunted whale from the 14th century off Newfoundland and from the 16th century off Iceland and Greenland. In the year 1660 the Dutch introduced blunderbusses for whale shooting. For flensing (stripping the blubber), the whale was towed ashore, where oil cooking was also done, if the salted blubber was not transported home. Later on, flensing was done at sea outside the vessel, a practice continued up to the beginning of this century. Large whalers were used to transport hunting boats and to carry the blubber home. Old-style whaling reached its peak between 1650 and 1750. In 1731 the whale gun was invented. The Americans organized prosperous whaling in the South Seas between 1820 and 1850. They fished in other seas also; the last sailing vessels from New Bedford, Massachusetts, visited the Azores in 1913. The old whaling industry was destroyed by the introduction of petroleum for illumination, but new industrial uses for whale were found, and the modern era began with important innovations. In 1903 the Norwegians sent the first floating oil cookery to Spitsbergen and in 1924 the first mother ship or factory vessel with a chute on the stern was built. In this vessel the whale could be processed on board with nothing lost. Such a mother ship is accompanied by eight to 12 high-powered catching vessels, characterized by a long gangway connecting the bridge with a harpoon gun on the bow. This gangway enables the operator of the gun to assume his position very quickly. Catching vessels have a crow's nest for observation or are accompanied by airplanes or helicopters. The harpoon is connected with a line more than 1,000 metres (3,300 feet) long. This line is wound on a special winch and, to avoid its being broken by the struggles of the whale, it is run over a block hung on strong springs. The head of the harpoon contains a high-explosive shell that kills the whale instantly. Some species of whales sink rapidly when killed; to keep them afloat until they can be taken by the factory vessel, they are inflated with air. The peak of modern whaling was reached in the season of 1930–31, when more than 30 mother ships caught more than 40,000 whales. Since this time the catch has diminished; in 1946 a maritime convention protected whale stocks by limiting catches (see WHALING).

Pole fishing and line fishing. Line fishing at sea is very popular, not only in traditional fisheries with small boats employing a limited number of hooks but also in industrial operations with large vessels or fleets using thousands of hooks. For centuries, line fishing was carried on in coastal waters and far at sea in the dory fishery famous today. A sailing mother ship carried the dories from Portugal, France, Canada, and the United States to the Grand Banks for cod. The one-man dory operated near the carrier setting longlines and sometimes fishing with handlines. In the evening the catch was carried back to the mother ship where each man prepared his catch for salting. The Portuguese still use dory carriers today, in the Davis Strait between Newfoundland and Greenland. Some large-scale modern enterprises also fish with hooks and lines, sometimes in far distant waters, as for tuna and halibut.

Pole-and-line methods are used in tropical Pacific and Atlantic waters to catch young bluefin and yellowfin tuna, and smaller tuna species—such as albacore, skipjack, bonito, and little tunny. The pole, generally bamboo, ranges in length from two to ten metres (seven to 33 feet), with a line of roughly the same length. Hooks of various sizes are barbless to facilitate baiting and removing the captured fish. To hold onto the pole a "rod rest" is generally used, which is made of canvas, leather, or old rubber tires. Depending on the size of the vessel, the crew may number 30 or more. A large crew is needed, since fishing time may be limited and the maximum possible number of rods must be worked. If larger and heavier fishes are sought, two, three or even four poles may be linked to a single hook. In this case the fishermen must cooperate closely. The tuna is attracted and kept near the vessel by chumming, throwing live bait overboard. The bait is kept alive on board in special tanks in which seawater circulates constantly. Bait can be an expensive problem for tuna fishermen; to catch one metric ton of tuna, roughly 100 kilograms (220 pounds) of live bait fish are needed. Sometimes the hooks are baited, sometimes artificial lures are used with hooks hidden in feathers. When the tuna is "hot" (very eager to take the bait), a naked hook is sufficient. Pole-and-line fishing for tuna is done in daytime from slow-moving vessels. Since considerable space is needed for the angling crew to stand side by side on the lee side of the vessel, Japanese vessels for pole-and-line fishing have a long extended bow. To simplify hauling in the catch these boats also have a low freeboard (*i.e.*, their sides ride low above the water). American tuna vessels hang special racks outside the ship over the water; water spraying helps to attract the tuna; it also serves to camouflage the shadows of boat and crew.

Drifting longlines. Used for tuna—especially in Japan, Taiwan, and Korea and to a limited extent in South Africa, Cuba, and French Oceania—drifting longlines are particularly successful in the tropical Atlantic for big fish in depths from 60 to 250 metres (about 200 to 800 feet). More than half the fish caught in this manner are yellowfin tuna, one third are albacores, and the remainder bigeye and bluefin tuna. Sharks, marlins, swordfish, and sailfish, also caught with drifting longlines, are sometimes included in the tuna statistics. Sharks can cause serious losses by damaging hooked tuna. Originally longlining for tuna was a Japanese inshore fishery. At the end of the 19th century, the Japanese were fishing 30 to 40 miles (50–65 kilometres) off their coasts. This fishery was extended when sailing boats were replaced by motorized craft, and by 1926 the Japanese began longlining for tuna off Taiwan, by 1929 in the Indian Ocean, by 1930 in the South Pacific, by 1938 in the eastern Pacific, by 1952 off the southeastern coast of Australia, and since 1955 in the Atlantic. Longlining for tuna is the most important Japanese fishing method by value. A longlining crew must be willing to do a hard, though lucrative, job and remain far from home for long periods. The gear is a line composed of 400 to 450 sections, each section with a length of 150 to 400 metres (500 to 1,300 feet) stored in a basket. The total line can have a stretched length of up to 180 kilometres (about 110 miles). Each section is composed of subsections of different length. The branch lines with the hooks are composed of three sections that vary in number and length. From one to 12 (generally five) branch lines with hooks form one section; 2,000 hooks are considered the greatest

Flensing whales *(margin note)*

Attracting the tuna *(margin note)*

number that can be operated in one set by a vessel. With decreasing catches, attempts have been made to increase the number of hooks; Korean fishermen are said to operate as many as 3,000. The shooting of the line from the stern of the vessel begins early in the morning before sunrise, when the vessel is moving at a speed of about five knots (five nautical miles per hour) or more. During shooting the lines have been tied together and the hooks are baited with frozen Japanese sauries. Each section is tied with a float line and a buoy. Depth of the gear can be regulated by the length of the float lines and the distance of the floats. Ten to 14 men require four hours to perform the task. Hauling from the forepart of the vessel begins in the early afternoon with the help of a line hauler. Depending on the quantity of the catch, hauling can take more than ten hours with a crew of eight to ten. With preparing and sorting the catch, the usual working day of a crew member totals some 18 hours. Because of this and the fact that vessels stay at sea more than 200 days per year, the Japanese and Taiwanese have experienced difficulty in procuring crews; this problem has led to the

Labour-saving technology

development of new technology to simplify the work and reduce manpower. One such improvement is the reel system, made especially for larger vessels. The total line is set, hauled, and stored on a drum. Though the floats and branch lines must still be tied by hand, research is being done on a coupling apparatus to do this automatically. Another invention is a line-winder system practicable for small vessels. In this a single line is used, hauled and coiled by a line winder in special tanks in the aft part of the vessel. Though such ideas can be considered first steps in the modernization of longlining, catches have been decreasing since their peak in 1963, so the future is uncertain.

Bottom longlines. More popular in commercial sea fisheries are bottom longlines mentioned above with the dory fishery. These catch many species of the cod family, including cod, haddock, coral fish, hake, and pollack, as well as rays, and many flatfish, such as halibut. There are also longline fisheries for groupers, hairtails, croakers, and sea breams. Bottom lines are not as long as the more easily controlled drift lines. The hooks do not always lie on the bottom but may hang above it to protect the bait against unwanted bottom predators, such as starfish, snails, or crabs. Typically, bottom lines are used for halibut in the northern Pacific. A relatively heavy main line is divided in sections of approximately 50 fathoms (300 feet or 90 metres). The branch lines, each about five feet (1.5 metres) long, are tied at intervals of 13 to 18 feet (four to 5.5 metres). Modern synthetics, with their greater strength and lighter weight, have replaced natural fibres for main lines. Fishing depth usually ranges between 45 and 150 fathoms (270 feet or 80 metres and 900 feet or 275 metres), depending on the grounds and season. The setline is anchored on both ends, marked by a floating keg and a lighted flag buoy at night. Originally only two-man dories fished this way, but today special mechanized boats with small crews and high yield per man do longline fishing. In Norway, for example, machines cut fish for bait, and, in the Faroe Islands special machines are used to bait the hooks.

Traps. There are only a few areas in the world where water or weather conditions prohibit the use of traps. A single small vessel can operate hundreds of traps, though lack of storage space may cause difficulties. Thus collapsible traps of netting on a wire framework are preferred not only for fish but also for crustaceans. Many plastic traps are made today, especially for lobster. Some can be dismantled for easy transportation. Water snails, such as whelk in England and other species in Korea, are also trapped, as are cuttlefish and octopuses. As in freshwater, fyke nets can be set in long rows or in connected systems. Commercial sea fisheries set long rows of

Setting traps

pots or framework traps by the longline system; *i.e.,* single pots are tied with a branch line to a main line. Hauling is accomplished with small hand-operated or motor-driven winches. More important for catching fish in commercial sea fisheries are the big wooden corrals, or weirs, and the large pound nets. The oldest type may be the

Italian tonnara, used in the Mediterranean for tuna from the Bosporus to the Atlantic. Very large pound nets are also used by the Japanese on the Pacific coast, by the Danes and their neighbours off the eastern coasts of the Baltic, and for salmon fishing off the Pacific and Atlantic coasts of North America. The difficulty in setting large traps lies in placing them on the bottom. If the water is not deep and the bottom is not hard, the weirs can be held by sticks or piles. Where the water is deeper and the ground is hard or rocky, the weirs must be anchored.

Dragged gear. Dredges and trawls are of great importance in commercial sea fisheries. Dredges are generally used in shallow water by small vessels, although a deep-sea dredge is operated by research vessels at depths of up to 1,000 metres (3,300 feet). The simplest dredges in sea fishery are hand operated. Fitted with a stick up to five metres (16 feet) long, they resemble rakes combined with a bag for collecting the catch—usually mollusks or crustaceans. Heavier dredges with a triangular or quadrangular iron frame may be towed along the sea floor by small vessels or pulled some distance from the shore or from an anchored vessel and then towed back with a winch. For digging out mollusks, some dredges have iron teeth on the lower edge of the frame. They may also have a pressure plate on the upper part and chains on the lower part, depending on the catch sought. The bag of the dredge is made of wire rings that have good resistance to friction and of hard fibre netting. Usually more than one dredge is operated by a vessel, and they are towed with the help of outriggers. The great disadvantage of dredging is that much of the catch is damaged, wasting effort and needlessly killing fish.

Trawling in sea fishery can be done by small vessels or even rowboats (as in the estuary of the river Tejo near Lisbon, Portugal). More important, however, are fleets of highly mechanized trawlers whose gross registered tonnage may reach 5,000 and whose horsepower approaches 6,000. The trawl is a towed net bag with a wide opening at the mouth and an end closed by a special knot. The mesh size of the opening can be large—600 millimetres (two feet) from knot to knot—to diminish water resistance during towing. The closed end can have meshes of six millimetres (one-quarter inch) according to the species of fish or shrimp sought. The trawl is designed in a smooth funnel-like shape to guide the fish into the closed end. To keep the mouth of the trawl open, a large horizontal beam may be used. Up to 12 metres or 39 feet long, the beam is based on two guides that glide over the bottom. The Dutch catch flatfish with beam trawls that have heavy chains, called tickler chains, dragging on the sea floor in front of the net opening between the two gliders to frighten the fish from the bottom into the trawl. Though beam trawls were the original gear of deep-sea steam trawlers, today they are used by smaller vessels only. Beam trawls are usually towed in pairs, one on each side of the vessel. Such an arrangement can considerably decrease the stability of the vessel and is dangerous except in craft specially designed for the purpose. Another method involves two vessels stretching the horizontal opening of the trawl between them. Two vessels have more power to tow a bigger trawl at greater speed. Spanish pareja fishing is an example of this method, called bull trawling in some countries. The skippers of the two vessels must cooperate very closely. The most recent and presently the most important method for spreading a trawl opening employs two large boards or metal plates (otter boards), rectangular or oval in shape, which are attached to each side of the net and caused to flare apart by the pressure of the water.

Trawling

Midwater trawling involves dragging the trawl with one or two vessels in the area between the ocean bottom and its surface to catch pelagic fish and crabs. Depth of the trawl is regulated by the length of the towing warps and speed of the towing vessel. With longer warps and lower speed, the trawl sinks; it rises with shorter warps and higher speed. The fisherman attempts to trawl at the depth where fish are observed. A special type of midwater trawl is the semipelagic trawl, originally invented in Iceland and now operated primarily by French fishermen. In this technique the otter boards remain in touch with the bottom but the trawl floats at some distance above it. Semipelagic trawls were constructed because fish often are concentrated at a short distance from the bottom outside the range of the usual bottom trawl with a low vertical opening. To overcome this difficulty, a higher opening of the trawl is needed. Though the opening of a bottom trawl can be stretched vertically by various means, such stretching decreases the horizontal width of opening. Some modern bottom trawls are constructed with a high vertical and horizontal opening, and many consider them the best available gear for bottom trawling.

Seine nets. Mentioned above as important large-scale gear in freshwater fisheries, seine nets are similarly employed in beach seining, where fish shoals are near to beaches. Large beach-seining operations for sardine-like fishes and other species are carried on in the Indian Ocean. The importance of this method has decreased as pollution has cut the available stocks of fish in this region and as manpower costs have risen: not all fishing methods lend themselves to mechanization. More successful are boat seines, better known (because of their origin in Denmark in 1849) as Danish seines. The gear consists of a typical seine net with a large bag and long wings connected with long towing ropes. The ropes act both to keep the net open and to herd the fish toward the net bag. One of the ropes (about 100 metres or 330 feet long) is tied to an anchored buoy. The other rope is tied to the vessel, which steams in a wide circle, returning to the buoy and capturing fish in the wings and bag of the net. Next, the vessel drops anchor and hauls both ropes together until the net bag is taken on board. Special winches and coilers for the long ropes are situated in fore-and-aft position on the deck. These coilers, together with large quantities of coiled rope, typify vessels used for Danish seining. This method is used in northern Europe for flatfish and cod and in Japan has become the most important method of inshore fishery for bottom fish, after two-boat trawling.

Surrounding nets. The most important sea-fishing gear is the surrounding net, represented by the older lampara nets and the more modern purse seines. Both are typical gear for pelagic fish schooling in large and dense shoals. When these nets are used, a shoal of fish is first surrounded with a curtain or wall of netting that is buoyed at the surface and weighted at the bottom. The lampara net has a large central bunt, or bagging portion, and short wings; the school of fish is worked into the bunt and captured. With the purse seine, once the school is surrounded, the bottom of the net is closed by drawing a line through purse rings attached to the lead line; the fish are then concentrated and removed by a brail (dip net) or are pumped aboard the fishing vessel.

Surrounding nets are used for tuna, herring, sardines and related species, salmon, mackerels, and even cod (when they come to spawn in the pelagic zone). For these nets to be successful, the fish must be in large and dense shoals; light and bait are sometimes used as lures to produce such shoaling.

Lift nets. Fish can also be caught, in limited quantities, by lift nets: stationary types operated along the shoreline, movable ones from rafts and boats, and large blanket nets held on each corner by a small boat. The Soviets operate a large commercial lift-net fishery on the Caspian Sea to catch sardine-like fish attracted by light. Each vessel operates two conical nets, setting one while the other is being lifted. Another effective lift net is the large, boxlike *basnig* of the Philippines, operated with a luring light during the night beneath a single outrigged vessel; sardines, mackerels, hairtails, squid and other pelagic prey are caught. The Japanese have a special kind of lift net for sauries; the fish, attracted by light, swim over the netting lowered into the water and are caught when the netting is hauled.

Gill nets and drift nets. Quite important in commercial sea fisheries, gill nets are sometimes operated in large sets thousands of metres long. These generally drift

with the vessel or are set as anchored nets in long rows at or near the bottom of the sea. Gill nets are used for many pelagic fishes, such as herring, pilchards, sardines and related species, mackerels, croakers, salmon, and tuna. They also are used for many bottom fishes—cod, Alaska pollack, and others. For cod, Icelandic fishermen set up to 90 nets, each about 50 metres (160 feet) in length, in depths up to 180 metres (600 feet). About 15 nets are generally set in combination, anchored on each end and marked by floating buoys. Though these nets are checked daily some have been lost in storms, leading to complaints of damage to cod in the area.

Drift nets are widely used to catch pelagic sea fishes. In northern Europe, before the introduction of trawling, drift nets were the most important method of deep-sea fishery. In the old herring fishery of northwestern Europe, drifters commonly set more than 100 nets, each about 30 metres (100 feet) in length. Thus a fleet of drift nets might measure three or even four kilometres (10,000–13,000 feet). The nets are set in the late afternoon to catch the herring as they ascend in the evening from ocean bottom to higher water levels. During the night the vessel drifts with the nets like a buoy. Hauling, done by hand or with mechanical aids, begins at midnight and, when big catches are taken, can continue until late morning. The fish are shaken out of the meshes by hand or with shaking machines.

Historic importance of drift nets

Entangling nets. Similarly operated are entangling nets, single or double walled, and three-walled trammel nets. These are used in sea fisheries for hake, shark, rays, salmon, sturgeons, halibut, plaice, shrimps, prawns, lobster, spiny lobster, king crabs, and turtles. Single-walled nets are used in the southern part of the Caspian Sea and in the Black Sea to catch sturgeons by entangling. Iranian fishermen set about 150 sturgeon nets in one row perpendicular to the shoreline. Setting requires much labour; between each two nets a line is tied, which is connected to a short wooden peg driven into the bottom. The Turkish Black Sea fishermen sometimes set sturgeon nets in another form. Two nets always form an angle open to the sea. The nets are held by sticks rammed into the bottom. Sturgeon nets are checked once or even twice each day, depending on weather. For this purpose an Iranian fisherman lies on the bow of his sailboat, towing the vessel along the float line of the net. The sturgeons are taken from the water by hand or with a gaff. In the Soviet portion of the Caspian Sea sturgeon fishery is forbidden, because the sturgeons are caught for caviar when descending the rivers. The Iranian fishery is a government-operated large-scale fishery, in contrast to the traditional private sturgeon fishery in Turkey.

The most important sea fishery for crustaceans is the king-crab fishery in the northern Pacific. For the Japanese, who use entangling nets, this is a very important distant fishery ranking with whaling and tuna and salmon fishing. Originally carried on close to shore, king-crab fishing was extended in the northern Pacific after its beginnings in the 1870s. The old land stations for processing were replaced by floating factories that accompanied the fishing vessels. The entangling nets are set on the bottom, sometimes 200 nets with a total length of ten kilometres (about six miles) in one row. Larger catching vessels set 1,200 to 1,300 nets a day, usually in parallel rows about 500 metres, or 1,600 feet, apart. Nets stay in the water from five to seven days and are hauled by small open vessels with motor-driven reels, which can take from 2,500 to 3,000 nets per day out of the water. When hauling, the floats and sinkers are untied and the entangled king crabs are taken from the netting. The catch and nets are then transported to the mother ship, where the catch is processed and the nets cleaned, an operation that may require 30 minutes per net. Large racks for drying and cleaning the entangling nets are characteristic of this type of vessel. A single fishing unit may own a permanent set of 15,000 to 30,000 nets.

Harvesting machines. A relatively new type of fishing gear is the harvesting machine combined with a pump, used by the Soviets in the northern part of the Caspian for sardine-like fish and by the Americans for squid off

Squid fishing

Decline of beach seining

the California coast. In both cases the prey is attracted by light. Squid fishing can be done near the surface, but in the Caspian the fish are sucked on board with pumps from depths up to 110 metres (360 feet). In pumping, the suction nozzle is moved up and down with attracting lamps. Once on board the fish or squid are strained from the water. The difficulty in fish pumping is to avoid damage to the catch. Only small objects can be pumped without injury.

Another type of harvesting machine is the hydraulic dredge, with pumps and conveyors. These dredges wash out deeply buried mussels with jets of water under high pressure. The Americans operate such hydraulic dredges to harvest soft clams, and the British use similar machines for cockles. Harvesting machines also are used to cut kelp off California. Giant kelp is harvested by cutting to a maximum depth of 1.2 metres (four feet) below the surface of the water and is transferred by conveyor belt into the open hold of the vessel.

Fish finding. Traditionally, sea fishermen have known the time and place to find their catch, but the history of fishing has demonstrated more than once that even old and rich fishing places can become exhausted quite suddenly. This is especially true with pelagic fish like herring, pilchards, or sardines. The herring yields of the Schonen fishery and later on of the Bohuslaine fishery (1744–1809) in the Baltic fell so severely that the very existence of the Hanseatic League was compromised. This sudden change did not result from overfishing but was caused instead by natural fluctuations in the development of stocks. Recently, the herring fishery in the North Sea and off the Norwegian coast has decreased very quickly. Sardine fishing collapsed off the California coast in 1952. Similar disasters have occurred in other parts of the world not only because of overfishing but also for natural reasons. When this happens new fishing places must be found. It is difficult to explain how good fishing places in great depths were found in ancient times, but fish in shallow waters, fjords, or small bays can easily be seen. Even on the high seas, fish can be located when they surface temporarily. Fish searching by direct observation from a vessel is important even today. But in modern times fish, whale, or seal searching is done in many areas by airplanes or helicopters. Both commend a wider range of vision than a boat, and an experienced air-spotting pilot can detect fish under the surface. Identification by species is accomplished by observing the shoal's form or colour or behaviour and sometimes by the presence of accompanying birds. During the night, fishes can be located through the phenomenon of bioluminescence; *i.e.*, when their passage through the water causes tiny marine organisms to luminesce. Accompanying birds have played an important part in fish searching for centuries, because a concentration of birds can be seen from a distance. Very often the birds are not attracted by the fish sought but by smaller fishes and squid, which may have taken refuge from large species by swimming to the surface. Other animals may also indicate fish concentrations by their presence. Porpoises, for example, are known companions of tuna. With the help of porpoises, fish in deeper water can be detected. According to the Inter-American Tropical Tuna Commission, 62 percent of the yellowfin catches with purse seines were accompanied by porpoises in 1962. To find

Identifying fish in deep waters

fish in deeper waters by other means was difficult if not impossible in the past. Herring fishermen used signal lines to find their prey in deep waters. These were long wires dropped from a boat; the fisherman holding the line in his hand could feel the vibration caused by the fish touching the line, which was named the herring's telephone. Other fish were also found by signal lines, often tied with fishing gear. In modern industrial fisheries, experiments have been made with direct listening for fish, but this method has been found impractical. Sea fishermen have also learned to judge where fish can be expected by observing environmental conditions. The colour of the water and the presence of current or of a borderline between different water bodies are some common fish indicators. One of the most important physical

properties for fish finding is the temperature of the water. The use of thermometers was one of the first practices fishermen learned from oceanographers, not only for fish finding but also for forecasting availability of the desired species.

All these direct and indirect observations can be made by vessels or airplanes. Today, some research is being carried on to find how and to what extent such observations can be made by satellites.

It is possible to judge the vertical distance between the bottom of the ocean and the hull of a vessel by transmitting sound waves and measuring the time required for the reflected wave to return. A shoal of fish registers on such equipment (echo sounder) as an obstacle. An experienced operator can locate fish with such equipment and can even judge their quantity. Some fish give typical signals, so that even the species can be identified. Horizontal sounders (sonar) are also employed: indeed, echo sounding has become decisive for success in fishery, especially in purse seining and midwater trawling. A sonar transducer can be tied on the headline of a trawl in midwater and bottom trawling. This implement, called a netsonde, signals the distance of the trawl from the bottom or from the water surface, registers the size of the trawl mouth, and signals if fish are entering the trawl. A multi-netsonde has been constructed that alternatively measures and records the water under or over and in front of the gear. New types of netsonde have been combined with a device for temperature measuring, enabling the captain to choose the most favourable environmental temperature during trawling. Effective operation of fish-finding devices requires considerable experience. Fish behaviour can change unpredictably, and fishing captains study each new situation in order to interpret correctly the signals of their equipment.

Fishing vessels and fleets. In the past, fishing vessels constituted a much neglected sector of the fishing industry. Naval architects, boat designers, builders, and engineers took little account of fishing methods and the industry's special requirements at sea. Today conditions have changed. The fishing vessel has become the largest single item of investment in the industrial fishery of developed countries, greater than harbours, cannery plants, and retail stores. There exists, therefore, a strong incentive to produce highly efficient fishing vessels.

For a long time fishery followed the general lines of vessel development. Even today, rafts of bamboo or light wood are important in coastal areas of Southeast Asia. Simple wooden boats, such as canoes, are still important for fishing in many parts of the world, including the African coast. Raftlike boats are employed in Guinea and in South America. Wooden boats such as pirogues, with or without outriggers, are used off the Malagasy Republic, Indonesia, and the Philippines. There are also small vessels made of a skin-covered framework—the kayaks of the Eskimos, British coracles and Irish curraghs (both the latter now canvas covered), and the bitumen-coated guffa of Iraq. These small vessels are easy to carry and to navigate during fishing. In the traditional coastal and inshore fisheries of industrial countries, most of the smaller boats are made of wood, which means they can be repaired by the fishermen. Many smaller vessels today are made of aluminum, plastic, or reinforced concrete. Modern cutters and all bigger vessels are now made of steel.

Fishing rafts

It has been found in sea fisheries that the size of a vessel, its horsepower, and its age are decisive for efficiency. The size of a fishing vessel can be characterized by the number of the crew; the overall length; vessel capacity in terms of fresh, frozen, or filleted fish; the capacity of the fishhold in cubic feet or metres; and the gross registered tonnage of the vessel. Judged on this basis, the size of vessels in sea fisheries has increased considerably in the recent past. There are active fishing vessels today of more than 5,000 gross registered tons; the number of vessels at sea is decreasing but the total tonnage is rising. For statistical purposes, fishing vessels are very often classified according to tonnage, and then broken down into subcategories.

Its means of propulsion also determines a fishing vessel's efficiency. Rowboats and sailboats are still common in small inshore fisheries. Some fishermen, like those of Ghana, can be seen in open sailboats 30 kilometres (20 miles) or more off the coast of West Africa. Most of the old sailing vessels of the whaler and bank fishermen were replaced by steamships in the last quarter of the 19th century, but the latter were supplanted in turn by motor-driven vessels, the lighter engines of which take less space, require less maintenance, and run longer between refuelings. Though motorization of fishing vessels began in the first decade of the 20th century, progress was slow until after World War I. Horsepower has increased steadily since that time. The first experiments with atomic propulsion were made in the fisheries of Japan after World War II.

Vessel efficiency decreases, of course, with age. Statistics generally show the average age of the total fleet. In West Germany, for example, average age of the deep-sea fleet in 1961 and 1962 was 7.4 years, a marked improvement from 1949 when it was 18.4 years.

There are also many large differences among fleets according to the type of vessel engaged in fishery. There are true fishing vessels and auxiliary craft. Fishing vessels, strictly speaking, are only those that use their own gear to catch fish or other marine products. Moreover, the statistics for fishing vessels include craft such as mother ships and carriers, which permanently accompany a fleet or which visit the fleet to carry catches away and to bring supplies. There are also factory vessels that process catches on board. Included also in the statistics for fishing vessels are the protection or inspection vessels, which are mostly government owned. Originally, these vessels were naval craft.

Fishing vessels employing a particular method often ⟨margin: **The whaler's catching boat**⟩ have characteristic shapes and deck arrangements. A typical example is the whaler's catching boat with a gangway, or catwalk between the bridge and the whale gun, allowing the harpoon gunner to reach his place quickly even while high seas sweep the main deck. Another conspicuous feature is the high crow's nest for spotting whales. Vessels for harpooning swordfish or sharks, such as used by the swordfisherman of New England, have a pulpit for the harpooner built forward on the bow of the vessel. The Chinese have harpooning boats with a lengthened bow allowing one or two harpooners to stand high over the water surface. American tuna clippers from which linefishing is practiced have a low stern with fishing platforms or racks hanging outside the vessel and a high bow for increasing the seaworthiness of the vessel in rough weather. For line fishing, Portuguese dorymen ride a ship that may carry 50 to 100 one-man dories piled up on deck like plates. Another typical line-fishing vessel is the troller, which tows a lure or baited hook from its stern. Typical for these vessels are the long outriggers for the lines and a high bridge where the captain can watch for strikes on the trolled gear.

One of the most significant advances in ship design was the development of the stern trawler from the once universal side trawler. Gear is much easier to handle on the stern trawler, account need not be taken of the wind in setting out (shooting) the trawl, and catches of up to 100 tons can be handled without difficulty.

Fishing harbours and port markets. For small vessels, landing places are not difficult to find, when the seacoast is neither too unsheltered nor too rocky. But even coasts with high-breaking waves have been no barrier to fishermen with small beach-landing vessels. The boats are towed ashore manually or with winches. Small boats, with or without motors, can land without special facilities in many areas, allowing easy distribution of marine products to the consumer. Groups of fishermen called water nomads operate in Tierra del Fuego, south of the Malagasy Republic, in Ghana, and along the African coast, travelling from one coastal town to another to sell their catch. For fishermen with heavier vessels, such as motorized cutters, safe water is needed which must be sought in natural or artificial harbours. Such fishing harbours are often commercial ports as well. A fishing harbour provides safety for boats, vessel maintenance, and facilities for storage, processing, and marketing of fish.

Small harbours are often built by governmental authorities in the hope that such places will become fishing centres. Such installations may be small landing places, as in Ireland, or a system of jetties built on unsheltered coasts. The main objective of a fishing harbour is to transfer the fish as quickly as possible to the market or consumer and to speed the vessel's landing, departure, and maintenance. Thus, not only landing quays are needed but also facilities for unloading, sorting, and weighing, as well as auction halls, merchants' buildings, ice plants, and cold-storage warehouses. For vessel repair a shipyard is needed or at least a slipway. Service should be available for fishing gear, engines, and electronic equipment. Fuel is supplied by floating or stationary stations. Freshwater is needed both for drinking and for cleaning, and electric power is required. Finally, waste disposal arrangements must be made to prevent harbour pollution.

Planning for the special facilities required for a fishing harbour must be careful to avoid loss of money and time. Fishing ports and the incorporated port markets ⟨margin: **Port-market organization**⟩ are often planned, constructed, and administered by governments. The government may lease the harbour and market to special organizations, often private companies. Or sometimes a special authority is set up, consisting of a partnership between the government, which has built the harbour, and the local community, which owns the land. The authority is responsible for the facilities of the fishing harbour and of the market. Customers of the harbour pay dues for moving a vessel, for mooring it at a quay, and for unloading. These dues are often set quite low in order to attract vessels to the harbour and to supply the market with sea products. A greater profit is made from auction sale commissions, rents for land and buildings, and from various service charges. Often such facilities are operated by port or market authorities themselves. These arrangements differ widely from one place to another, according to the political and economic situation.

FISH-FARMING AND AQUACULTURE

A very ancient method for catching fish involves driving the prey toward a beach and closing off the area with a wall of mud or stone or with a wicker fence. Netting was later employed for this purpose, and today fishermen are experimenting with air-bubble screens and electric fences for restraining fish in bays or fjords. By this method, the catch can be kept alive if not needed immediately. There are definite limits however, to the length of time a captured fish can survive; lack of oxygen, unfavourable temperature, and disease are the main hazards. In freshwater, fish may be stored in mesh boxes that float or hang near the landing place in a lake or river. When large quantities of fish must be kept alive, they may be confined in temporary cages of netting or wire. Small quantities are stored in baskets or keep nets similar to those used by sportsmen.

Fish may be stored in order to comply with market regulations, or to stabilize supply. In some cases, fish caught in polluted waters may be transported to clean water to allow them to rid their bodies of readily excretable pollutants. If the fish are stored for some time, they usually lose weight, although some success has been achieved in feeding stored catches. If the fish do eat and are kept under good conditions, they often gain weight faster than under natural conditions. This, of course, amounts to a primitive form of fish-farming.

Farming and rearing in hatcheries. Fish-farming as originally practiced involved capturing immature specimens and then raising them under optimal conditions in which they were well fed and protected from predators and competitors for light and space. Carp have been raised in ponds for several thousand years in China and India. Other species were cultivated before 1400 BC, as ⟨margin: **First artificial fertilization**⟩ Egyptian drawings attest. It was not until 1733, however, that a German farmer successfully raised fish from eggs that he had artificially obtained and fertilized. Male and female trout were collected when ready for spawning. Eggs and sperm were pressed from their bodies and mixed together under favourable conditions. After the eggs hatched, the fish fry were taken to tanks or ponds for further cultivation. Recently, methods have been developed for artificial breeding of saltwater fish, and it now appears possible not only to rear sea animals but to have the complete life cycle under hatchery control. Some authorities claim that the time is coming when farming the edges of the sea could solve the protein and hunger problems of the world's growing population. Currently, however, saltwater fish-farming emphasizes the higher priced and luxury varieties such as lobster, shrimps, and oysters.

Carp. Carp raising, practiced worldwide, is a good example of advanced techniques. For the whole life cycle at least three different types of ponds are used in Europe. Special shallow and warm ponds with rich vegetation provide a good environment for spawning, a process which today is often aided by hormone injections. After spawning, the parent fish are separated from the eggs and taken to a second pond. The fry, which hatch after a few days, are transported to shallow, plankton-rich nursing ponds, where they remain until the fall of the year or the next spring. In tropical areas, such as India, carp spawned from wild fish can be collected by experts in natural waters. To collect eggs or fry from wild fish is disadvantageous, however, because the breeder cannot influence the breeding stocks in a desired direction. In Asia, therefore, the fry of common or golden carp are generally bred under culture conditions in hatcheries. Bigger ponds are needed for rearing the fish in the second year of life. There are large carp ponds in Czechoslovakia, while in Asia common carp are often cultivated in rice fields. For feeding carp in ponds, soybean meal, rice bran, and similar agricultural products are used. Concentrated food in the form of pellets has also been successfully introduced. During the winter season in the temperate zone, the carp are kept in deeper winter ponds with a dependable flow of water to protect them against freezing. In Central Europe, carp are ready for the market after the third summer. In southern Europe, Hungary, and Yugoslavia, carp may be sold after the second summer. In tropical areas the fish grow even faster. To accelerate growth, warm-water ponds now exist in the temperate zone. The first experiments of this sort showed that carp could be kept in small aquariums with a permanent circulation of warm water of 23° C (73° F). Under these conditions they grew rapidly, attaining a marketable size and weight after two years. Similar results were obtained in warm-water ponds fed by heated industrial waters. In the temperate zone an average harvest of 400 to 500 kilograms per hectare (about 360 to 400 pounds per acre) is normal in intensive cultivation of carp. By scientific management and careful selection it is now possible to obtain yields as high as 3,500 kilograms per hectare (3,100 pounds per acre) for carp in warm-water ponds. Other fish, such as Chinese carp or grasse carp, may be similarly raised in ponds, as are decorative species, such as golden and silver carp.

Trout. Although trout was the first fish to be artificially fertilized, trout cultivation in Europe and North America is much younger than carp cultivation. Trout are cold-water fish and must have a constant supply of sufficient oxygen, making cultivation more difficult. Though trout ponds can be smaller than carp ponds, good year-round water circulation is essential. Trout farms are therefore often located in mountainous areas where plentiful pure water is available. The young fish are obtained exclusively by artificial fertilization; thus, hatchery buildings with low-temperature fountain water and good filters are the centre of this type of pond fishery. Here the eggs are kept under control during breeding in special small tanks. As soon as the hatched fry can swim and eat on their own, they are transplanted to rearing ponds for feeding.

Trout are carnivores; meat-packing by-products are used for feed. Formerly, these and similar products were also used to feed more mature trout. A special refrigerated feed house for keeping and cooking the food was the second main building typical in trout farms. Dry fodder is now preferred, however, and synthetic pellet-type feeds have been developed that require no refrigeration. Such food may be released into the ponds at predetermined intervals by automatic compressed-air dispensers. Though many authorities claim that trout should have as much natural foodstuff as possible and therefore should be raised in natural ponds only, in many countries rearing is done in concrete-lined ponds or concrete tanks, which are easy to keep clean and permit disinfectant application. The length of time necessary to rear fish and the yield per hectare depend on feeding. Some trout farms not only sell their fish fresh and frozen but also smoked and filleted.

With trout, a new system of fish cultivation has been introduced in recent years. Instead of ponds, enclosures of netting or other materials are placed in natural waters, such as lakes, and also in brackish waters. By this means, areas formerly of low value can be farmed intensively. Farming trout in brackish water or seawater was of especial interest. Since the period preceding World War II, trout farming in seawater has grown tremendously. Keeping trout and other fish in such cages is much easier, construction costs are far lower, and surprisingly dense populations can be raised.

Many other fish are raised artificially by various methods. Among these are salmon, sturgeon, eels, milkfish, mullet, and tilapias.

Other types of aquaculture. *Mollusks.* Other important objects of cultivation in many parts of the world are mollusks. Though few water snails are cultivated, bivalves, especially oysters, are quite important in Asia, Europe, and North America. For centuries French fishermen cultivated oysters by placing twigs in the water to which free-swimming oyster larvae could attach. In northern Europe, oysters have been cultivated on the ocean bottom, but low winter temperatures limit the extent of this activity. In the Mediterranean, the Romans are said to have been the first to farm oysters. Today, oysters are cultivated on the Pacific coast of North America, as well as on the southern Atlantic coast and the Gulf of Mexico. Australia, the Philippines, and South Africa also possess farms, and the Japanese grow edible oysters from Hokkaido in the north to Kyushu in the south. Japanese farms are divided into two classes: some cultivate seed oysters only, while others raise them for food, especially for export. The Japanese cultivate oysters on the sea bottom (horizontally) and on sticks (vertically). To collect the larvae, which affix themselves to any firm object, such as an old shell or a stone, fishermen place various devices in the water. These may be bamboo sticks with shells attached or a rope with shells hanging from it; limed tiles and wooden plates have been used for the same purpose in Europe. Production is greatest in places with good shelter against rough seas, a tidal current to carry food to the larvae, adequate salinity, and optimum temperature.

After some growing time, the larvae are loosened and transported to other areas for maturation under the best conditions. While growing to marketable size, the oysters must be protected against predators, such as starfish and oyster drillers. Starfish are removed from growing areas by lowering a device that resembles a mop, in which the predators entangle themselves. As starfish damage cannot be completely avoided when growing oysters on the bottom, a vertical system of culture is preferred in many areas; the oysters hang in clusters or in baskets, or are fixed on poles in sheltered bays. In an alternative system, the oysters remain in horizontal trays kept at some distance from the bottom. Though such tray-raised oysters are expensive, they generally survive better than those reared directly on the bottom.

Blue mussels are cultivated in Italy, Spain, France, the Netherlands, and near West Germany in the North Sea and the Baltic. Here, too, horizontal bottom methods have been replaced by vertical culture. Originally, the young mussels, collected from wild stocks, were spread

Warm-water ponds

on controlled banks leased by a fisherman from the government. Their capacity to grow in very extensive and dense beds is highly advantageous. Before full-grown mussels are sent in sacks to the market, special purification methods are employed to wash out sand. Today vertical culture is practiced with sticks pushed into the ocean bottom or with lines hanging from rafts. Unfortunately, line cultures may be damaged in winter; thus, experiments have been made with polyethylene net bags and endless tubes of polypropylene netting. These bags must be strong enough to carry the mussels until harvesting.

Many other mollusks are cultivated, including soft clams and scallops. The Japanese even raise octopuses and squid. For bivalves, the problems are roughly the same as mentioned above: collecting the larvae; raising the young mussels under good conditions; protecting them against predators; harvesting the adults without injury; and sometimes cleaning for the market.

Pearl oyster culture

Among inedible bivalves, pearl oysters deserve mention. Pearl farming is one of the most famous industries of Japan, dating to 1893, when a Japanese first succeeded in cultivating pearls. Under the skin of an oyster, the pearl farmer inserts a pearl nucleus (a small spherical shell fragment wrapped in a piece of living oyster tissue). The treated oyster is placed in a culture cage on a floating raft, and after a period of some months or years, the cultured oyster produces a pearl. Japan's pearl producing centres, once scattered along the coast, are today concentrated in the Inland Sea.

Crustaceans. Crustaceans, mainly shrimps, are also cultivated. In traditional Japanese practice, immature shrimps are caught in coastal waters and transferred to ponds. Today, mostly in the United States and Japan, shrimps are cultivated by catching adult egg-bearing females. The presence of eggs can be detected by examining the ovaries, usually visible through the shell. The female shrimps are transferred to large seawater ponds adjacent to the sea or to tanks. After hatching, the shrimps are fed in indoor tanks with cultivated plankton. After ten days they are brought to shallow ponds for further cultivation or for distribution to other farms.

Americans and Europeans have shown interest in commercial lobster culture. Current methods are not yet economical, however, because the animals grow slowly and have a high mortality rate, often dying during molting of the shell. Lobsters must molt in order to grow and are quite vulnerable during this period.

Seaweed. A final important item in aquaculture is seaweed. Laver, a red alga, is a traditional part of the Japanese diet. The Japanese first cultivated this plant in the late 17th century in the brackish water of Tokyo Bay. Originally, a vertical method was used, with bushes placed in the water. A horizontal method is now employed: large meshed netting made of rough materials is hung horizontally between poles at the proper depth. The algae grow there by themselves and the owners harvest them from the nets by hand. Harvesting begins early in November and continues until about March. After the season is over, the gear is removed and stored. Part-time fishermen or land farmers often engage in such algae culture. Though other algae are used for food and in industry today, commercial farming has yet to begin.

PRODUCTION

According to the statistics of the Food and Agriculture Organization of the United Nations (FAO) most fish are caught in the sea, with only about one tenth coming from freshwater. Since the late 1930s, the total world catch has been increasing at a rate of some 7 percent per year and recently seems to double each decade. During this time, the world total catch in tons has been as follows:

1938 23,000,000
1948 21,600,000 (a decrease of 7% because of the war)
1958 36,600,000 (an increase of 69%)
1968 71,000,000 (an increase of 93%)

The next year, 1969, showed a decrease of 2 percent, but the world catch in 1970 of approximately 74,000,000 tons represented an increase of 6 percent. Nevertheless, there have been doubts that fishery alone can solve the world's food problem. It has been found that the natural fluctuations in fish stocks caused by climatic changes are not always predictable events. Fish with short lives and pelagic fish in general are especially affected. It has also been found that the fishing industry can damage stocks, sometimes permanently, if it takes large catches when fish stocks are low due to these natural fluctuations. Some authorities estimate that the total world catch should not exceed 61,000,000 tons per year. Others calculate, however, that annual yield of all edible products of the water all over the world could range up to 4,000,-000,000 tons. Many scientists think that 100,000,000 to 200,000,000 tons is realistic for the 1970s. Yet the increasing pollution of the world's freshwaters and oceans causes uncertainty, not only because entire stocks of fish and other products can be destroyed, but also because an increasing number of living organisms are contaminated at harvest with poisons, such as DDT and mercury.

BIBLIOGRAPHY. Most literature about commercial fisheries deals only with local or small areas. Reports are regularly published by the United Nations Food and Agriculture Organization (FAO) or edited by members of its Department of Fisheries, such as the annual *Yearbook of Fisheries Statistics;* and J.A. GULLAND (ed.), *The Fish Resources of the World,* FAO Tech. Pap., no. 97 (1970). A worldwide study of commercial fisheries (in German) is F. BARTZ, *Die grossen Fischereiräume der Welt,* 2 vol. (1964–65). Summary reports about fishing gear, methods, and tactics may be found in the reports of two FAO congresses: H. KRISTJONSSON (ed.), *Modern Fishing Gear of the World,* 2 vol. (1959–64, vol. 3 in prep.); and A. VON BRANDT, *Fish Catching Methods of the World* (1964), on all types of fishing gear. Integration of commercial fisheries in modern exploitation of the sea is considered in J.F. BRAHTZ, *Ocean Engineering* (1968). Fishing vessels are discussed in J.O. TRAUNG (ed.), *Fishing Boats of the World,* 3 vol. (1955–69); fish farming in freshwater in M. HUET, *Traité de pisciculture* (1970); and aquaculture in seawater in the *Proceedings of the FAO World Symposium of Warm-Water Pond Fish Culture,* no. 44 (1967–). A new summary was given by E.S. IVERSEN in *Farming the Edge of the Sea* (1968).

(A.v.B.)

Fishing, Sport

Fishing is one of man's oldest activities; in earliest times in all parts of the world he fished, as he hunted, to obtain food. Even when his existence depended on success in catching fish or hunting animals, he found pleasure in both pursuits, and the desire to hunt and fish is still strong today in men of all nations and races.

Evidence of the excitement man has found in pitting his wits against fish and animals is found in his artistic expressions. Paleolithic man drew on cave walls the animals he hunted and the fish he caught. Two thousand years before the birth of Christ an Egyptian angling scene depicted figures fishing with rod and line and with nets. About the 4th century BC there is reference in Chinese writings to fishing with a silk line, a hook made from a needle, and a bamboo rod, with cooked rice as a bait. There is reference, too, to fishing in ancient Greek, Roman, Assyrian, and Jewish writings. In modern times man's infatuation with rod and line is shown by angling's vast literature, which is the finest and fullest of any sport.

Today, fishing, often called angling or sport fishing to distinguish it from commercial fishing, is, despite the growth of towns and the increase of pollution from many sources, one of man's principal relaxations and in very many countries is the largest participant sport. Despite—and probably because of—the stresses of modern life, modern man, like his ancestors, still finds excitement in "tempting the unknown with a fishing line."

This article is divided into the following sections:

I. History

One of man's earliest tools was the fishhook. To begin with this was a gorge—a piece of wood, bone, or stone an inch or so in length, pointed at both ends, and secured off-centre to the line. The gorge was covered with some *Early* form of bait. When a fish swallowed the bait, a pull on *fishhooks* the line wedged the gorge across the gullet of the fish. *and rods*

When skill in the use of metals was achieved, a hook was one of the first tools made. This was attached to a line of animal or vegetable material. Such a combination is efficient only when used from a boat, and early man all over the world must soon have seen the advantage of a rod, a stick or tree branch, which allowed him to fish from the bank and over vegetation.

For thousands of years, for reasons unknown, the fishing rod remained short, only a few feet in length. It was not until Roman times that reference is made to a longer rod and one that was jointed, that is, made in several parts that could be fitted together for use and taken apart for easy transport. Historians have long argued whether this was a fishing rod or a fowler's rod: the likely answer is that it would be both, for a nation so advanced and with many forms of hollow bamboo in its empire would surely have seen how simple and convenient it would be to fit different-bore sections together. In Roman times, too, Aelian (*c.* AD 170–235) wrote of how the Macedonians caught trout on artificial flies and even gave the "dressing" of the fly; that is, the materials and methods of making it. The rod used was only six feet (two metres) long and the line the same length, so the method used must have been dapping (see below *Dapping*).

The history of fishing as a sport can be said to have really started with the printing at Westminster by Wynkyn de Worde in 1496 of the *Treatyse of Fysshynge With an Angle*, part of the second edition of *The Boke of St. Albans*. This was the first fishing manual and is thought to have been written by Dame Juliana Berners.

BASIC METHODS

The four basic methods of angling that were then practiced, some of which already had been practiced for thousands of years and all of which are still practiced today, are as follows.

Bait fishing. In bait fishing, a bait of meat, a small fish, an insect, worm, grub, piece of bread—anything, in fact, edible by fish—is placed on the hook and cast onto the bottom of the water or suspended at a required depth.

Fly-fishing. In fly-fishing either a natural fly—or more frequently an artificial fly, insect, or other natural food— is used to lure the fish.

Bait casting, or spinning. Bait casting, or spinning, is fishing with a live or dead fish or a lure that, when drawn through the water, looks like a small fish. This method is used for predatory fish.

Trolling. In trolling a mounted dead fish or an artificial lure imitating a small fish is trailed behind a boat. Again, this method is used to catch fish that feed on other fish.

FISHING TACKLE

At the time of the publication of the *Treatyse* the tackle used had altered little in many hundreds of years. The artificial flies described were surprisingly modern (six of the dozen mentioned are still in use), but the rest of the equipment was crude, comprising a very long (18 to 22 feet [five to seven metres]) rod with a line of plaited horsehair tied to the end. The development of angling as a popular sport has depended to a great extent on the development of fishing tackle, and the history of improved fishing methods is broadly the history of the equipment that made these methods possible.

The first great improvement came in the middle of the 17th century, the period when Izaak Walton was writing his immortal *The Compleat Angler* and Col. Robert Venables and Thomas Barker were making considerable contributions to early fishing literature. Until that time the line was tied to the rod end, limiting the distance that could be cast and allowing a hooked fish to be controlled only within the limits of the joint length of rod and line. Some unknown angler attached a wire loop, or ring, to the end of his rod. This simple invention permitted a running line to be used, giving much greater casting distance and allowing the playing of a fish with much greater efficiency.

This invention meant that fishing lines became much longer (Barker in 1667 mentions a salmon-fishing line of 26 yards [24 metres]), and there was in consequence a need for some form of winder on which to hold the line when fishing and prevent it becoming tangled, and thus the fishing reel was born. To begin with it was simply a wooden spool with a metal ring that fitted over the angler's thumb. The line was wound and unwound by hand.

There are many other mentions of improvements in tackle in the mid-1600s. Although horsehair remained the most common material for lines and for the hardly visible link between line and hook, experiments with other materials were being made. In 1667 Samuel Pepys mentioned in his *Diary* the use of a gut string, and nine years later Robert Venables wrote of using a lute string. The use of a "landing hook"—now termed a gaff—a large hook on a shaft used for lifting large fish from the water, was mentioned by Barker in 1667.

Very important was the perfecting of improved methods of fishhook making by Charles Kirby in 1655. Kirby, *Improved* a London hook maker, also invented the Kirby bend, a *fishhooks* distinctive shape of hook with offset point, and hooks of this type are still in common use all over the world. Kirby, like many other hook, fishing-tackle, and needle makers, lived and worked near Old London Bridge. This cottage industry was dispersed by the plague and the Great Fire of London in 1666 and eventually resettled in the small Worcestershire town of Redditch about 70 years later.

Anglers, it would appear, were slow to see the advantages of the end ring and running line. In 1726 there is reference in the *Gentleman Angler* to rods with rings or guides all along their length and to the use of "Winch or wheel." The reference suggests, however, that such rods and reels were not in common use.

Around 1730, as previously mentioned, British needle makers resettled themselves in Redditch and set about changing the nature of the industry from a cottage type to a factory type, powered by water mills. From needles they extended their interests to a kindred product, the fishhook, and from hooks moved on to other articles of tackle. By 1780 John Mills was exporting his hooks to America and Jamaica, and 30 years later most of the world's fishhook trade was based on Redditch. The availability of efficiently made, factory-produced tackle was, over the next hundred years, to have a profound effect on angling all over the world.

Development of bait-casting and centre pin reels

By 1770 the rod with guides along its length and fitted with a reel came into common use. The first reel to find favour was a multiplying reel, geared for fast line retrieve and in appearance remarkably similar to the modern American bait-casting reel. These reels, which were used under the rod, never won favour in Great Britain. They were, however, to act as models for American craftsmen, notably the Kentucky watchmakers George Snyder and Jonathan Meek, who in the early 1800s pioneered the bait-casting reel. Indeed, from this period, the development of tackle, which heretofore had been entirely confined to Britain, was now shared by the United States.

While the bait-casting reel was being developed in Kentucky, another type of reel, the centre pin, was being developed in the ancient English lacemaking town of Nottingham. Based on the wooden lace bobbin, it was a wide-drum, ungeared, very free-running reel, ideal for allowing float tackle to float downstream with the current in the style known as long trotting (see below, *Long*

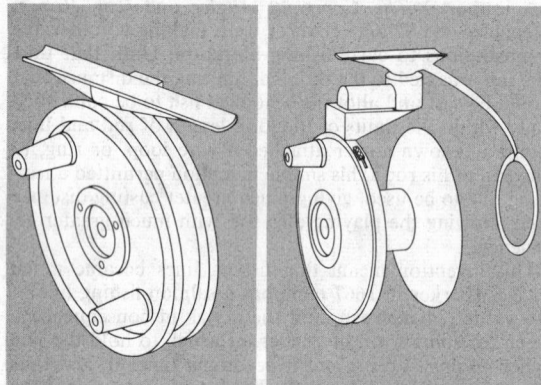

Figure 1: Early centre-pin fishing reels. (Left) Nottingham centre-pin reel (1840–50); (Right) Malloch turntable reel (1884).

trotting and stretting). The Nottingham reel was also suitable for the casting of dead fish and lures for predatory fish, for various forms of sea fishing, and it had no small influence on the design of reels for fly-fishing.

While great improvements were being made in fishing reels, progress was likewise being made in rods. Heavy native woods were superseded by straight-grained, tough, elastic woods, imported from South America and the West Indies and known as lancewood and greenheart, and by various sorts of bamboo. By the end of the 18th century experiments were in hand to glue several strips of bamboo together, retaining the strength and pliancy of the cane but greatly reducing the thickness. By 1847 rod tops were available in this form, and between 1865 and 1870 complete hexagonal rods, made by laminating six triangular strips of bamboo, variously known as split bamboo, split cane, and built cane, were produced on both sides of the Atlantic, with the Americans winning the race by a short head.

From 1880 on progress in tackle design was rapid. The fly-fishing line, made for centuries of horsehair, was replaced by lines made from silk and covered with coats of oxidized linseed oil. Such lines were heavy, easy to cast, sank deeply if ungreased or floated if greased. They trebled the distance the average angler could cover and made possible many new methods of fly-fishing, notably dry-fly fishing and sunk-line fishing (see below *Wet and dry fly-fishing*). Fly reels became lighter and the Nottingham reel, originally made in wood, became available in ebonite (vulcanite, a hard rubber) or metal. These reels also became easier to use. They were very free spinning and, unless controlled during a cast, revolved faster than the line runoff, resulting in a considerable tangle. Various types of governor were fitted to Nottingham reels to make them easier for average anglers to use.

During the same period the American bait-casting reel was being improved and made more free running, so that

light lures could be cast. As with the Nottingham reel, control of the drum speed during the cast was a problem and various mechanical aids were added to prevent what Americans call a backlash and the British an overrun. In 1896 William Shakespeare of Kalamazoo, Michigan, invented the level-wind, which automatically spread the line evenly on the spool and made using these reels much easier.

The difficulty in using the Nottingham reel led in 1880 to the invention of the first turntable reel by the firm of Malloch in Perth, Scotland. In this reel one side of the spool was open, and, to cast, this was turned 90°, so that it was in line with the rod guides. During the cast the line slipped off the end of the spool with a minimum of inertia, making casting extremely simple. To recover line the spool was turned back 90°.

The Malloch reel was principally used for casting relatively heavy lures for salmon fishing, but it must have had some influence on the thinking of Holden Illingworth, a Bradford, Yorkshire, textile magnate who in 1905 invented what the British call a fixed-spool reel and the Americans a spinning reel. In this type of reel the open spool is permanently facing up the rod and the line peels off in the cast as on the Malloch. Retrieve, however, was operated first by a hook in a revolving flyer and then, as the reel was improved, by various pickup mechanisms.

Fixed-spool reels and mono-filament lines

The improvements in the various casting reels led to great improvements in artificial lures in metal and wood, which, when drawn through the water, spun or wobbled, represented the struggles of a wounded fish and thus attracted the attention of predators.

Throughout the 20th century tackle has improved at a rapid rate. Rods have become shorter and lighter without losing any power. Split-bamboo rods, which superseded those in greenheart and lancewood, have been almost superseded in their turn by rods in fibre glass, and these in turn may well be replaced by rods in carbon fibre. Reels have become lighter and stronger with more parts being made from reinforced plastics. The fixed-spool reel, which was little used outside Great Britain until the 1930s, spread first to Europe, then, after World War II, to North America, causing the spinning boom, and thence to all parts of the world. The stationary-drum principle also has been adopted in America for spin casting, or closed-face, reels in which the spool is enclosed in a cone-shaped hood. The fixed-spool principle was greatly aided by the development of nylon monofilament line in the late 1930s. Although this material did not become freely available in continuous length until after World War II, it coincided with the boom in spinning and gave the fixed-spool reel the lively, smooth line it needed for ultimate performance. It also superseded silkworm gut, which from 1722 on had been the best nonvisible link between line and hook. Braided lines in other synthetic materials—nylon, Terylene, Dacron—have given the angler many advantages, especially when used with revolving drum reels. Fly lines now have plastic coverings and either float without the use of grease, or sink slowly or quickly as desired. Plastic also is being greatly used for artificial lures and for various tackle containers.

The modern angler has excellent tackle and it will, as always, continue to improve. Despite its excellence, his problems are still those of his ancestors. He must know where to find his fish and how to approach them without being seen. He must know what they are feeding on or what they can be tempted with. He must understand wind and weather. Fishing remains what it has always been, a problem in applied natural history.

II. Freshwater fishing

BAIT FISHING

Bait fishing is commonly called still-fishing in North America and bottom fishing in England. Fishing with different types of bait is certainly the oldest form of angling and is practiced in most countries of the world. This style of fishing has been brought to a high degree of efficiency in England, where, in particular, it is used to catch the species classed as "coarse fish." The methods used in England, therefore, will be described, and other types used elsewhere will be discussed as variations.

General method. As previously explained, the method broadly is to impale a bait on a hook, which the fish swallows; it is then hooked and eventually landed. Common baits are worms, the maggots of various flies, small fish, bread paste, and cheese. Less common baits are slugs, caddis flies, stewed wheat, hempseed, and fruit. The bait is either fished on the bottom, weighted down by some form of lead weight called a ledger (in America, a sinker), and fished on the bottom, or close to it, or at any depth, suspended by a buoyant object called in England a float and in America a bobber. The float, which is usually made of bird or animal quill, cork, wood or a combination of all three, or of plastic, suspends the bait at a required depth, acts as an indicator that a fish is taking or has taken the bait, can be used to allow the bait to follow the current of river or stream and thus to "search" the water, and is sometimes used as a casting weight to allow a long cast to be made.

Ledgering. When a ledger but no float or bobber is used, the general method is known as ledgering. Selection of the right sort of water is important in all types of angling and, when fishing with a ledger, selection will depend greatly on the species sought. If bream (*Abramis brama*) were the quarry, slow, deep water would be chosen; if barbel (*Barbus barbus*), faster, streamy stretches would be fished. On a lake the shallow or deep areas would be chosen according to the time of year and the type of fish sought.

It is always important in fishing to avoid unnatural movement of the bait or lure and also to ensure that the fish has the minimum indication that the bait or lure contains a hook and is attached to a line. With a ledger this latter provision is sometimes difficult to achieve, because, as the fish takes the bait, it may feel the weight of the ledger. For this reason ledgers are made either with a hole drilled through them, or with a metal ring. The line is passed through either hole or ring, and the ledger is prevented from running right down the line to the hook by attaching a split shot to the line. Split shot is commonly used in bottom fishing. It is, as its name indicates, lead shot as used with a shotgun, which has been partially split. The "V" of the split is placed over the line and clamped tight. With the line running free through the ledger the fish will not feel an unnatural weight as it takes the bait.

Ground bait or chum. The ledger angler then selects the type of water where he expects fish of a certain species to be, selects what he considers will be the right bait, and casts his bait to the part of the water he believes will contain fish. In order both to concentrate the fish around his bait and to encourage them to take his bait, he throws in what the British call ground bait, and the Americans, chum, in the area close to his hook bait.

Ground bait consists mainly of soaked bread or meal to which various constituents may be added, including frequently a certain amount of the bait used on the hook. The constituency of the ground bait will depend on the water fished—light for still or slow water, heavy for deep or fast water, in which, in order to take full advantage of the current, it obviously needs to be introduced well above the area fished.

Feeling the bite. Once the ledger and bait have been cast to the correct area, the main problem in this style is knowing that a fish has taken the bait. Some anglers hold the line between their fingers, feeling the bite in this way. Others watch the line or the rod top. Various bite indicators are used. A piece of silver paper can be placed on the slack line between reel and first ring. If it moves the angler strikes; that is, he raises his rod sharply, tightening the line and setting or driving home the hook.

In recent years bite indicators called swing tips and quiver tips have been developed. These are short lengths (six to eight inches [15 to 20 centimetres]) of pliable plastic attached to the rod's end, the line passing through guides on the tip. Any movement indicates a bite.

Ledgering tackle. Tackle for ledgering varies considerably. The rod may be any length from seven feet up

to 14 feet (two to four metres). Nine-foot (three-metre) rods are popular for one style of swing tipping and those around 12 feet (four metres) for another. All are made of hollow fibre glass. The reel used is invariably of the fixed-spool type, loaded with line from 1½- to 6-pound (680- to 2,700-gram) breaking strain (test). Hook size varies according to the size of the species sought; the length of "trail"—the line between ledger and hook—is a matter of personal preference.

Although the main purpose of the ledger is to hold the bait on or near the bottom, particularly in moving water, another style has been developed, known as the rolling ledger. The weight selected is too light to anchor the bait on the bottom. It is cast across the current and allowed to roll along the bottom until it comes to rest under the bank and below the angler. In this way much water can be searched.

Float ledgering. A float is sometimes used in conjunction with a ledger, so that the bite can be clearly seen. This method is called float ledgering.

Float fishing. For float fishing in the English style no ledger is used. The rod is of fibre glass and long, somewhere between ten and 15 feet (three and six metres). The length is needed because deep water is often fished, and if the distance between float and hook is longer than the rod, casting and landing a fish become most difficult. A long rod also gives good line control and allows hooking fish at a distance.

The reel used is usually a fixed-spool model, although some types of closed-face (spin-casting) reels are becoming more popular. The Nottingham reel is now little used. The line is of nylon monofilament, from about one-pound to six-pound (450- to 2,700-gram) breaking strain. Floats vary greatly in size and design, from small (two-inch [five-centimetre]) models in quill, to large ones (13-inch [33-centimetre]) in wood (called zoomers or darts) that are designed for long casting. Below the float there is a length of nylon monofilament to which the hook is tied or whipped, and it is to this that one or more split shot are fixed. The purpose of this "shotting" is to give casting weight, to "cock" the float—that is, to cause it to float upright in the water with the right amount of tip showing —and, most importantly, to control the speed at which the bait sinks in the water. In fast, heavy water, for example, where the bait needs forcing down to reach the required depth quickly, the tackle is heavily shotted. Alternatively, in fishing slow water, the bait is often required to sink very slowly and one tiny shot is used.

Selecting the swim. The depth at which the bait is fished is crucial in all types of float fishing. Some species such as bream and tench (*Tinca tinca*) feed mainly on the bottom and the bait should be placed there. Others, like the dace (*Leuciscus leuciscus*) and the grayling (*Thymallus thymallus*), will take the bait in midwater. The angler establishes the depth and varying depths of his "swim"— the area he is fishing—by the use of a plummet, a lead weight that he attaches to his hook. With this aid he takes soundings and adjusts his float accordingly to give him the depth he requires.

In still water, or very slow-flowing water, the successful angler selects his swim, fishes in the right place at the right depth, and attracts and conditions the fish to take his hook bait by skillful groundbaiting. Indication of a taking fish is given by movement of his float, which may be pulled under the water, or, because bottom-feeding fish often lift the bait off the bottom, by an upward movement.

Long trotting and stretting. In faster water different and more active methods are necessary, for the current can be used to carry the float a long way, thereby searching the water and taking the bait to far-off fish. This style of fishing is known as long trotting or swimming the stream. The art in this style is to present the bait in the most natural way, so that it moves with the current. Control of the line, so that the float is not pulled across the current, causing the bait likewise to be pulled, is essential. Another successful manoeuvre is to hold the float back for a few seconds, so that the bait is raised in the water, a movement that has long proved attractive to

Marginal notes:

Use of ledgers or sinkers

Use of floats or bobbers

fish. Conversely, in one method of float ledgering that is sometimes used, called stretting or stret-pegging, the distance between float and bait is considerably in excess of the depth of water. The cast is made across the current and the bait is allowed to rest on the bottom for perhaps 30 seconds. Then it is allowed to move a little further downstream and again is allowed to remain on the bottom. In this way the swim is thoroughly searched.

Bait-fishing contests

Match fishing. All the methods described are used for what is called match fishing in England. Competitions between a few dozen up to several thousand anglers are held, both on a club and an individual basis. There are large cash prizes, sweepstakes, and a great deal of betting. Several thousand pounds can be won in a match of four or five hours' duration by the angler or team catching the greatest weight of fish. Unlike most other countries, in particular those in Europe, the coarse fish in England are not eaten. As they are caught they are put in a large sac-like net, called a keep net, which is lowered into the water. At the end of the match or at the end of the day's fishing, the fish are returned to the water.

The basic methods described are used in Europe for similar fish, but the tackle there is different from that used in England. Rods are often much longer, sometimes being well over 20 feet (six metres) in length and made usually from hollow fibre glass. Frequently no reel is used and the line is tied to the rod end. Fishing with this tackle is known as *le moyen classique*—the classic method, and it is quite often used for matches, even the "World Championship," which is fished between certain European countries. On the Continent matches are not won on weight alone but on a combined weight and number-of-fish basis, which puts the emphasis on catching small fish.

Still-fishing in North America. In North America, where most fish are predatory rather than insectivorous and herbivorous, the emphasis has always been on types of fishing best suited for fish of this nature. Bait fishing, commonly called still-fishing, is practiced on basically the same lines with much less specialized tackle: when bait fishing, Americans generally use the type of tackle used for bait casting, spinning, or fly-fishing. The traditional gear, however, is a long—ten or 12 feet (three or four metres) or more—one-piece, bamboo-cane pole (now often of fibre glass and in sections) with a line tied to the tip. Such gear is still commonly used in fishing off piers, breakwaters, and bridges, from rowboats on small inland lakes, and from the banks of small streams. The most popular quarry are perch, crappies, bluegills, and other pan fish, which also are caught on small flies and lures. In some places the object of still-fishing is catfish, carp, sucker, or other species.

Ice fishing. This winter sport is especially popular in the northeastern United States and the Upper Mississippi-Great Lakes-St. Lawrence Valley region of the United States and Canada. Holes are cut through the ice to fish; one fisherman often tends several holes. Minnows, grubs, and nymphs are favoured baits, usually used with a very small jig or ice spoon. Equipment commonly includes a short (three feet [one metre]) whippy, fibre glass rod with a simple centre-pin reel or a cleat-like device to hold a nonfreezing monofilament line and a tip-up or tilt that signals when a fish has taken the bait; it is allowed to run before the hook is set. For larger fish the tip-up may hold the reel, in some models below water to prevent freezing. Many pan fish (mostly crappies, bluegills, and perch) are caught, but also caught are northern pike (especially in the Great Lakes region), walleye, pickerel, bass, and lake trout, with occasional catches of other species.

Ice fishing is little practiced elsewhere, but is becoming more popular in Scandinavia and in some European countries (not Great Britain, where it is rarely cold enough). Methods are as in the United States.

TROLLING

Trolling is the style of fishing in which a live or dead fish or other bait, mounted on a tackle that allows it to spin or wobble as it is drawn through the water (or an artificial lure that moves similarly) is trailed behind a slow-moving boat. In theory it is a simple form of fishing that permits covering a large area, but in practice there is a great deal of skill involved in it.

Locating the fish. Used mostly on very large lakes and reservoirs, where fish are difficult to locate and where they may be at a considerable depth, it has been brought to a high degree of efficiency in North America. Much of the skill lies in locating the fish and presenting the bait or lure at the right depth and the right speed. Originally much depended on the water sense of the angler, who, by studying the topography of the lake and by taking soundings, would know where shallows, shoals, deep water, and very deep water occurred. Allying this with his knowledge of the habits of the fish sought, he would be fishing in the right place, with the right bait, at the right time. Electronic aids that show the depth of the lake and its contours as well as in some cases actually locating the fish have greatly simplified the problem, but even with such aids, there is still much skill in taking fullest advantage of them, and the experienced fisherman will still outfish the less experienced.

Tackle. In trolling for fish that are feeding near the surface, the type of tackle used for spinning, bait casting, and even fly-fishing can be used perfectly effectively, but when greater depth is needed, specialized equipment is essential. Sometimes heavy sinkers are used, but nowadays the weight is mostly contained in the lines, which may be metal (*e.g.*, Monel Metal) or braided lines (*e.g.*, of Dacron) with a lead core. Such lines allow the lure to fish in a more lifelike way besides giving the hooked fish a more sporting chance. The amount of line out controls the depth at which the lure is worked. Rods in North America are usually short, five to seven feet (about two metres) and are used with a multiplying trolling reel for fast retrieve. The rod is held at right angles to the direction of the boat to take advantage of its resilience when and if a fish strikes.

Trolling at depth

Trolling is little practiced in Great Britain, on the Continent, or in Scandinavia. Salmon (*Salmo salar*) and big trout (*Salmo trutta*) are sought in this way on the Scottish lochs, the Irish loughs, and on big lakes in Norway, as are pike (*Esox lucius*). Trout and pike are also trolled for on big waters in other European countries.

Harling. A form of trolling called harling is also used to catch salmon in big rivers in Scotland and Norway. The lure is fished from the stern of the boat while the boatman holds the boat in the current, allowing the bait or lure to hang over the areas known to hold fish, and the flow of the stream causes the bait or lure to behave like a small fish.

Apart from mounted live or dead fish most of the lures described for spinning and bait casting are suitable for both trolling and harling.

BAIT CASTING, SPINNING, SPIN CASTING

The terms bait casting, spinning, and spin casting describe the same method of fishing carried out with different outfits and in particular with different types of reel. In Great Britain all three are termed spinning, although the spin-casting reel is hardly known. In the United States, bait casting usually denotes the use of a bait-casting reel mounted on top of a short (five to six feet [about two metres]) bait-casting rod, spinning means fishing with a fixed-spool reel, and spin casting means using a spin-casting (*i.e.*, fixed-spool, closed-face) reel with a spin-casting rod. Monofilament line is generally used, although on the bait caster braided nylon or Dacron is often preferred. When fishing for certain predatory fish with sharp teeth, a wire "leader" (called a trace in Great Britain) is used between line and lure.

The purpose with all three outfits is to cast out a bait or one of a vast number of artificial lures, so that when retrieved in still water or when it is subject to the current in running water, the bait or lure behaves like a small, wounded, or sickly fish. In nature the desire to kill infirm creatures is strong among predators, be they bird, fish, or mammal, and the erratic movement of a natural or artificial lure has long been known as an effective means of catching many species of fish.

Casting artificial lures

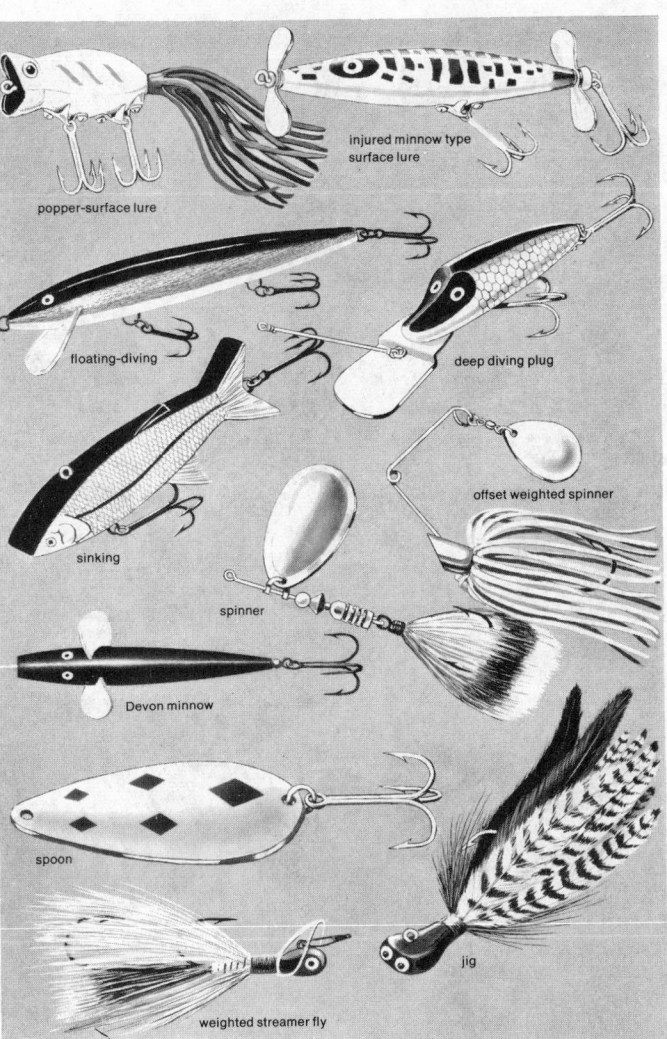

popper-surface lure

injured minnow type surface lure

floating-diving

deep diving plug

sinking

offset weighted spinner

spinner

Devon minnow

spoon

jig

weighted streamer fly

Figure 2: Types of bait-casting, or spinning, lures.

The number of artificial lures available to the angler is enormous. Popular all over the world is the metal spoon, so called because many somewhat resemble the broad, dished end of the domestic spoon. Also popular are lures in a vast variety of shapes and colours that spin, wobble, and flicker in the water. Most popular in Great Britain is the Devon minnow, which is a cylinder-shaped lure with two fins near the head to make it spin. In North America the plug—in wood and even more now in plastics—in a bewildering number of shapes, imitates the behaviour of almost everything that swims in or on water. These lures can be fished at all levels, from close to the bottom to right on the surface, representing deep-swimming fish or swimming mice or frogs.

In still or very slow running water the method of fishing is to cast the lure where fish are thought to be and to impart movement to it by retrieving line by winding the reel. Speed of retrieve sometimes cannot be too slow; again, the angler can hardly wind too fast.

On running water the current imparts movement to the lure and frequently the angler does not wind in until it has moved across the stream and is under his own bank. An effective method of fishing is to cast upstream and wind the lure down as fast as possible.

Spinning rods in Great Britain are rather longer than those in North America. Single-handed rods, used with the fixed-spool reel, are usually about seven feet (two metres), and double-handed ones, used for salmon or pike with a fixed-spool or bait-casting reel, run between eight and ten feet (two and three metres) in length.

FLY-FISHING

Trout fishing. The methods used to catch trout (*Salmo* species) all over the world are also used to catch other freshwater species such as char (*Salvelinus* species), grayling (*Thymallus* species), whitefish (*Corregonus* species), and many others. In some cases a natural fly is used, but much more frequently an artificial lure, made usually from silk, fur, or feathers, is at the end of the angler's line.

Dapping. With the natural fly a style of angling known as dapping is the most common method. Two different techniques are employed. The first is used along the well-bushed sections of river, brook, or lake. A natural fly, usually a bluebottle fly or a daddy longlegs spider, is impaled on the hook. The angler approaches the water with great caution and, keeping well out of sight, lowers the insect into the water surface, where its struggles attract a fish. Sometimes an artificial lure is used, being lowered to and raised from the surface, creating a slight disturbance that attracts the fish.

Much more common is the method used on Scottish lochs and Irish loughs, in particular during a hatch of mayflies or when crane flies (daddy longlegs) are blown onto the water. A very long rod, 14 to 16 feet (four to five metres), is used from a boat. The line is very light, with silk or nylon floss (embroidery floss) tied near the end. A breeze is essential for this method, and the natural insect is carried out well away from the boat by the action of wind on floss. Sometimes a large, fuzzy artificial fly is used. This is an effective method of catching large trout and sea trout, the latter of which is a migratory form of brown trout that spends part of its life in the sea and returns to fresh water to spawn.

Midge fishing. In the Maritime Provinces of Canada a style known as midge fishing is used in the spring. One or two natural up-winged flies (*Ephemeridae*) are hooked on and cast like an artificial fly.

The use of natural flies is very limited, and fishing with artificial flies is practiced on a much wider scale. The artificial fly represents anything that the fish sought may feed on—aquatic or terrestrial insects, small fish, freshwater shrimps, and snails. In many cases a "fancy" fly is used that imitates nothing, but that over the years has proved attractive to trout and other fish.

Fly casting. The first problem in any form of fishing with an artificial fly is presenting it to the fish, for unlike so many other baits and lures the fly has virtually no weight. A flexible rod usually of hollow fibre glass is used, its length somewhere between seven and ten feet (two to three metres), with around seven to eight feet (two to two and one half metres) most popular in North America and eight to nine feet (two and one half to three metres) in Europe. A thick, heavy line is used to give casting weight; it is usually made with a nylon or Dacron core with a plastic covering. The thickest part of these lines will be usually between 50 and 60 thousandths of an inch (0.13 to 0.15 centimetre), but normally they are made in tapered form and the end nearest to the fly will be much finer to allow for delicate presentation. The reel is of simple single-action construction, its sole purpose being to contain the line and, as will be explained, to assist in tiring the hooked fish.

Attached to the line is a length of nylon monofilament called in North America a leader and in Britain a cast. Normally this will be some three yards in length and either tapered to a fine end or level throughout its length. The fly or flies are attached to this link.

The fly is cast by a combination of the springlike action of the rod and the weight of the line. A proficient caster will be able to lay down his fly 60 feet (18 metres) away, and distances of 120 feet (37 metres) are attainable with slightly specialized tackle when necessary.

Wet and dry fly-fishing. There are a number of different methods of fly-fishing, but broadly they are based on the behaviour of certain insects that spend their lives mostly in the water but have a short life in the air close to lake or river. The varying styles will be described in relation to these flies.

The three most important species of flies to the fly fisherman are the up-winged or mayflies (*Ephemeroptera*), the caddis or sedge flies (*Trichoptera*), and the midges (Diptera; in particular the genus *Chironomus*). All these

Fishing with natural flies

Casting artificial flies

Life cycles of flies

flies spend most of their life in water as nymphs, caddis grubs, bloodworms, and pupae and form a substantial part of the diet of trout and other insectivorous fish. At the appropriate time of year they swim to the surface, where they shed their underwater skins and emerge as winged insects. As soon as their wings are strong enough, they make for dry land. Mating takes place in the air, generally overland, and the females later return to the water to lay their eggs either in or on it. Trout feed on these insects during all these stages when the insect is available to them, and the angler seeks to imitate their appearance and behaviour in order to deceive his quarry. He is therefore either fishing his fly in the water at various levels, known as wet-fly fishing, or on the surface, in the style known as dry-fly fishing.

The wet-fly fisherman uses a line that is designed either to sink rapidly, to sink slowly, or to float. With the first named he will be fishing close to the bottom of river or lake and on a river will make his cast across the stream and allow the current to make it swing round. On a lake he will move the fly by pulling in line by hand. His fly will imitate some insect, aquatic creature, or small fish that spends most of its time on the bottom. The speed at which the fly is allowed to move is important. Frequently more than one fly is attached to the leader by means of short (two-inch [five-centimetre]) links called droppers.

With the slow sinker the angler will be exploring mid-water and his fly will probably imitate an ascending nymph or pupa. On running water the cast will be made across and the flies allowed to swing around with the stream. With the floating line he will be fishing high in the water and his fly or flies will most likely be representing the nymph or pupa just prior to its emergence as a winged insect or during its emergence. On such occasions the cast may be made across, or may be made upstream.

There are many different sorts of wet fly, but always they are made so that they sink quickly through the surface film. Most have feather hackles, which move in the water and thus give a semblance of life.

Indication of a trout taking a fly fished on sinking lines is a firm pull on the line, causing the angler to "strike" or "set his hook" by raising his rod. With the floating line the fish may be felt, but more often than not the fish disturbs the water as it takes and at this sign the angler pulls home the hook. This water disturbance to either a natural or artificial fly is called a rise.

The dry fly is designed to float on the surface and in consequence is fuzzy. It is always used with a floating line and between casts requires whisking through the air, frequently several times, called false casting, to shake the water off it.

The most effective time to fish the dry fly is when trout are rising to flies as they emerge and as they float on the surface before becoming airborne, although "fishing the water"—casting to likely places even though the fish are not rising—can at times produce good sport. During a hatch of fly the angler will select a fly that imitates the fly on the water and on such occasions correct imitation can be important, as fish become very selective. On running water the cast is generally made upstream and the fly allowed to float down with the current, although at times a cast across and down, in which the fish sees the fly before the leader, can be very successful. On still waters the fly is cast out and allowed to remain still for some time.

Another effective time to fish the floater is when the female flies return to the water, usually in the evening, to lay their eggs. After doing so, they die and float on the surface, offering the fish an easy meal.

As with all types of fishing, it is vital that the fly behave in a perfectly natural manner, and one of the problems with the dry fly on running water is to prevent the push or pull of current on line or leader from pulling the artificial so that it moves unnaturally—a circumstance called drag. The angler prevents drag by casting a slack or curved line that delays the pull of the current.

Of all types of fishing, the dry fly is probably the most interesting, for the fish can be seen feeding, the natural fly identified, the correct artificial mounted, cast delicate-

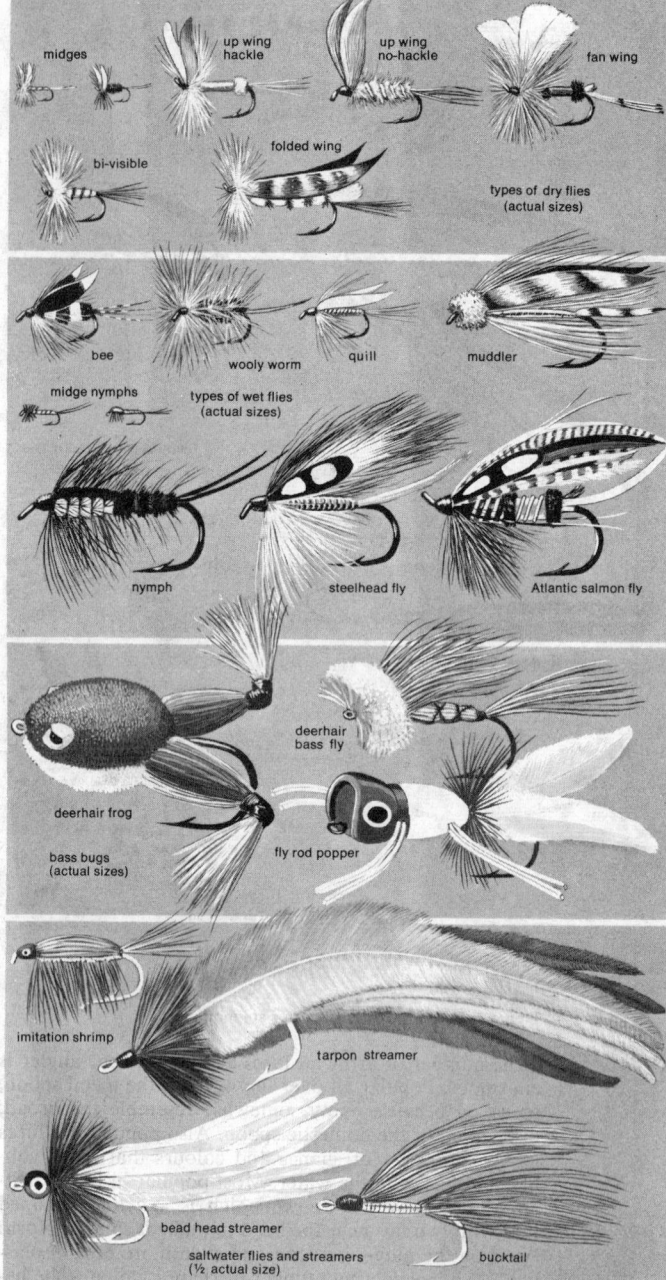

Figure 3: Types of flies.

ly and accurately to the rising fish with the likelihood either of an exciting rise or the fish clearly seen taking the angler's offer into its mouth.

Salmon fly fishing. The difference between fly-fishing for Atlantic salmon (*Salmo salar*) and other fish is that the former, which hatches from an egg in a river, where it spends usually two years, thereafter migrating to the sea, again usually for two years before returning to freshwater to spawn, does not feed at all after it enters the river. The angler therefore is not seeking to offer an imitation of any particular insect but rather some lure in fur or feather that appeals to the salmon's latent predatory nature.

Atlantic salmon are caught in eastern Canada (and Maine), in Iceland, Scandinavia, Great Britain, France, and Spain. The methods are broadly similar, but the North American angler uses a short rod, single-handed, of eight to ten feet (two to three metres), whereas the others use a double-handed rod from 12 to 15 feet.

There are three basic methods of catching salmon on artificial flies. In cold water conditions at the start of the season—that is, February and March in Great Britain;

April, May, and early June in North America; and June and July in Norway—a sinking line is used with a big (sometimes three-inch [eight-centimetre]) fly. This is cast across the current and allowed to swing around as slowly and deeply as possible. The indication of a "take" is a firm pull on the line. This method is also used in the autumn, often, however, with a small (¾-inch to 1-inch [2- 2½-centimetre]) fly.

When the water temperature rises to 45° F (7° C) a much smaller (½-inch to 1¼-inch [one- to three-centimetre]), slimmer fly is used, with a floating line. The cast is made across the stream and the fly allowed to swing fairly quickly with the current. Unnatural movement is prevented (as in dry-fly fishing) by line control. This is a particularly exciting form of fishing as the salmon frequently rises, as does the trout to the dry fly.

In Canada, the salmon take a dry fly larger than that used for trout but fished in basically the same way. It is rare for salmon to be taken on the floating fly elsewhere because, it is believed, the temperature does not rise high enough.

The two sporting varieties of Pacific salmon, the coho or silver (*Oncorhynchus kisutch*) and to a lesser degree the chinook, tyee, king, or spring (*Oncorhynchus tshawytscha*), can be taken on flies. The flies are either cast or trolled in saltwater, or cast in rivers. The methods used are those broadly described for trout wet-fly fishing. Transplanted coho and other salmon in Lake Michigan are taken mainly on spoons and other bait-casting or trolling lures.

CASTING TOURNAMENTS

World casting championships are held annually by the International Casting Federation, which also recognizes world records in ten official accuracy and distance events.

Both single- and two-handed distance events are held for fly casting and for bait casting with revolving spool reels using ⅝-ounce (18-gram) plugs and fixed spool reels using ⅜-ounce (11-gram) and (two-handed) 30-gram (one-ounce) plugs. Highly specialized rods and reels are used and few restrictions are imposed on techniques for attaining distance or hitting the target, a floating ring of 30 inches (76 centimetres) or less.

Accuracy events include skish, a refined version of tournament casting that limits the bait-casting line to not less than nine pounds (4,100 grams) and the reel to standard design, although not the rod and not the fly rod, reel, or line. All casting in the skish events, however, must be performed as in fishing and without exaggerated windup.

Casting competitions are especially popular in North America, and annual tournaments are held by member clubs of the American Casting Association. In addition to fly and bait-casting events, American tournaments include a bass-bug accuracy event. (For world records and world champions see SPORTING RECORD in the *Ready Reference and Index*.)

FRESHWATER FISH SOUGHT BY ANGLERS

A great variety of freshwater fish furnish sport to anglers around the world. Some of these fish are common to more than one area, while others are limited to particular waters in North America, Africa, and Europe, and a few are limited to one particular region in a single country. A number of the more desirable sporting species have been successfully transplanted outside their native habitats to other areas and countries. Table 1 lists the principal freshwater fish sought by anglers and includes the species for which official records are kept for specimens caught by rod and reel.

III. Saltwater fishing

The basic methods of fishing in freshwater described above are likewise used in saltwater. Bait fishing and trolling are widely used; casting and spinning are used much less but are rapidly growing in popularity, especially in U.S. waters. Fly-fishing, although also growing in popularity, is practiced only in a few areas and for only a few species of fish. Whereas the methods are basically the same as those used in freshwater, the tackle used is often very different because of the size of the quarry and the conditions of greater depths, wider areas, rocks, and tides and currents.

BAIT FISHING

The various methods of fishing with natural bait are commonly used for sea fish, irrespective of whether the angler is fishing from a beach, off rocks, from a pier, or from a boat. The baits used are those that form a normal part of the diet of sea fish—worms that live in sand or mud, marine shellfish, and small sea fish, either whole or cut up.

The most commonly used methods are those similar to the freshwater methods of bait fishing. A lead sinker, or ledger, sometimes one pound in weight, though more normally four to eight ounces, is used. Shapes and weights vary greatly according to the type of bottom, the depth of the water, and the number of hooks, which may be held away from the line and leader by wire or plastic booms, a rig known to British fishermen as paternoster.

Such tackle can be cast out from beach or rocks, cast or lowered into the water from a pier or jetty, or lowered from a boat to where the fish are known or suspected to be.

Handline fishing. Bait fishing, or still-fishing, in its basic form includes the primitive handline or throw line. Closely related to this method is the use of a cane pole. The methods are usually, but not always, associated with fishing from bank or pier. The throw line, clumsy by rod-and-reel standards, is stored on a spindle or frame. It is fitted with one or two hooks and a lead weight of several ounces. In throwing, line is stripped from its frame and coiled at the feet of the thrower, who whirls weight and baited hooks over his head, releasing them when they have gained sufficient momentum. Once the bait has been deposited in the water, the free end of the line is held by the angler, or it may be clipped to a bell or rattle that has been secured to a piling or plank. When the bell sounds to the movements of a biting fish, it is time for the angler to go to work. Warning bells enable an angler to fish three or four lines. | Throwing the handline

Whereas the rudimentary handline is normally the instrument of the shore caster seeking small species, it is successfully used against such giants of the sea as marlin and sharks by commercial fishermen of several countries. Resistance to the fish is applied by quick and momentary hand pressure on the sliding line. Despite the obvious threat of friction burns, an experienced handline fisherman suffers little but callouses from his role.

Pole fishing. In many situations it is necessary to use a pole, sometimes a very long one, to clear rocks, pilings, or other obstacles beyond the reach of the handliner. This may be a version of the old-fashioned bamboo-cane pole, with the line tied to the tip. But in most situations casting or spinning the weighted line and bait out with rod and reel permits the fisherman to fish a larger area, provides more sport when a fish is hooked, and enables him to play and land a larger fish with lighter tackle than is possible without a reel.

Float fishing. Fishing with a float or bobber is practiced all over the world for fish that can be caught close to the surface, and because very light tackle can be employed it is a particularly sporting way of catching saltwater fish. Freshwater tackle is often used; a very popular outfit is a seven-foot, light spinning rod and a fixed spool reel. Many species of fish are caught by such means, and members of the bass, mullet, and mackerel families are taken on float tackle all over the world.

Chumming. The use of ground bait, called chum in the United States and rubby-dubby in Great Britain, whereas not so frequently and extensively practiced as by the British freshwater bait fisherman, is still used in many parts of the world. Chum consists of bits of fish, fish chunks, even whole live fish or shrimp; pulped-up oily fish such as the North American menhaden or the Cornish pilchard are widely used. Bags containing the crushed fish are either trailed behind a boat or placed so that the current or tide carries out a slick to draw fish to the bait on the angler's hook. Sometimes minced fish or

Table 1: Fresh-Water Fish Sought by Anglers

species	where caught*	weight of good catch		comments
		lb	kg	
Barbel (Barbus barbus)	most European countries except Norway, Sweden, Finland, Ireland	8–10	4–5	mostly caught bait fishing but will take spinner, particularly in June after spawning
Bass, black, largemouth (Micropterus salmoides)	all North America, South Africa, and Kenya (both very successful), Cuba, France, Spain	2–5	1–2	one of the most popular North American game fish; caught by all methods but especially on surface lures
Bass, black, small-mouth (Micropterus dolomieui)	North America, in colder waters, transplanted from northern United States and northeastern Canada; South Africa, Kenya, Sweden	1.5–3	0.7–1.4	one of the world's great sporting fish, excellent eating; caught on fly, spinner, plug, and bait
Bass, redeye (Micropterus coosae)	central and southern United States	2	1	popular pan fish in its range; good eating; caught on bait, small flies, and lures
Bass, spotted (Micropterus punctulatus)	southern two-thirds of eastern United States	2–5	1–2	much like largemouth black bass
Bass, white (Roccus chrysops)	southeastern United States			see spotted bass
Bluegill (Lepomis macrochirus)	all North America, South Africa	1	0.5	very popular pan fish; caught on bait, also very small surface lures and flies
Bream, common (Abramis brama)	most European countries except Scandinavia	2	1	caught on float and ledger tackle
Bream, silver (Blicca bjoernka)	as common bream	6–8	3–4	caught on float and ledger tackle; name sometimes given to several pan fish in North America
Bullhead, black (Ictalurus melas)	Mississippi Valley and watershed	1–1.5	0.5–0.75	caught on bait and spinning, spin-casting lures
Carp (Cyprinius carpio)	all European countries except Norway, North America, southern Africa	20	9	caught on a variety of baits including boiled potato and bread; highly valued on the Continent as a food fish; in parts of North America considered a pest
Carp, crucian (Carassius carassius)	all Europe except Switzerland, Spain, southern Italy, northern Finland	2	1	caught by bait fishing
Catfish, blue (Ictalurus furcatus)	Mississippi Valley	10	5	mostly caught bait fishing
Catfish, channel (Ictalurus punctatus)	Mississippi Valley	5	2	mostly caught bait fishing
Char, arctic (Salvelinus alpinus)	northern Canada, northern Europe, Scandinavia, Iceland, Greenland	15	7	ranks with other Salvelinus (trout) as great game fish; occur in Great Britain, but are too small to be of sporting value
Chub (Squalius cephalus)	central Europe except Denmark, Sicily, northern Scotland, Ireland	5	2	caught on bait, fly, or spinner
Crappie, black (Pomoxis nigromaculatus)	North America	1	0.5	popular pan fish; caught on bait, small lures, flies
Crappie, white (Pomoxis annularis)	North America			much like black crappie
Dace (Leuciscus leuciscus)	all Europe except Ireland, northern Scotland, and Norway	1	0.5	caught on fly or float tackle
Dorado (Salminus maxillosus)	northern half of South America	20	9	the outstanding freshwater game fish native to South America; takes flies, spinning lures
Eel (Anguilla anguilla)	worldwide	3	1	caught by bait fishing
Gar, alligator (Lepisosteus spatula)	North America, Mississippi Valley, and southern waters	50	25	heavy tackle, bait; edible, but almost never eaten
Gar, longnose (Lepisosteus osseus)	St. Lawrence River, Great Lakes, southern U.S. waters	6–8	3–4	same as alligator gar
Grayling (Thymallus thymallus)	all Europe except southern France, southern Italy, Portugal, Spain, Ireland	2	1	generally caught on fly or bait tackle but will take spinning lures
Grayling, arctic (Thymallus arcticus)	native to Alaska, northern Canada, Montana (subspecies tricolor)	2–4	1–2	a splendid sporting fish, takes fly, spinner, and bait
Huchen (Salmo hucho)	Danube and tributaries	20	9	a salmon peculiar to the Danube; caught generally in winter and by spinning
Mahseer (Barbus tor)	India, Pakistan, Burma, Malaya	varies greatly; over 100	45	caught on bait by spinning in cold rivers
Muskellunge (Esox masquinongy)	northeastern and north central United States	15–20	7–9	a very large member of the pike family; caught on fish or large lures
Perch, common (Perca fluviatilis)	all Europe except Spain and southern Italy	2	1	caught by all methods
Perch, nile (Lates niloticus)	tropical rivers and lakes of Africa	200	90	generally caught trolling
Perch, white (Roccus americanus)	Atlantic seaboard	2	1	caught on bait and casting lures
Perch, yellow (Perca flavescens)	eastern North America	1	0.5	very popular pan fish, especially the Great Lakes region; mostly caught bait fishing and on flies
Pickerel, eastern chain (Esox niger)	eastern and southern United States	5	2	a small pike
Pike, northern (Esox lucius)	all countries; the pike is the only freshwater fish native to Europe including the U.S.S.R., and to North America	15	7	caught mostly by spinning and trolling but will take bait and large fish imitating flies

*Italics indicate species has been transplanted.

crushed clams, mussels, fragments of crabs, crawfish, or other shellfish is dropped into the water sparingly to sink to the bottom or drift with the current or tide, releasing oil or juices and creating a visible slick on the surface. Predacious fish crossing the stream of chum will turn and follow it to its source, or to the baits that are released into the current with the chum.

Bottom feeders and reef fishing. Flounders and similar bottom feeders are also responsive to chum. At times they may be lured with such odd fare as canned corn kernels and boiled rice, even canned cat and dog food. The simple process of stirring the bottom to create a mud slick will often pull fish to an anchored boat. Reef fishermen the world over are well acquainted with the efficacy of chum balls fashioned out of wet sand and minced fish. As the ball sinks and disintegrates, fish are at first visually attracted by the display of broken chum balls. Then their appetites are sparked by the fragments, and soon the aroused fish find the baited hooks.

Live-bait chumming. Live-bait chumming is practiced wherever the essential baitfish is plentiful and easily caught. In southern California, party boats load their bait wells with thousands of anchovies as they head offshore for the deep-water grounds plied by such favourite sport fishes as the Pacific yellowtail and the long-finned albacore. Once the quarry has been searched out, the live bait is dipped overboard. The fun begins as the predacious game fish charge into the helpless chum and seize the baited hooks lowered into it.

Shark fishing. Releasing chum from a drifting boat is standard procedure for shark fishing. Sometimes blood and offal are added to the slick to further entice the shark. Once the chumming has established a long, tide-borne slick in the water, baits are introduced. Live fish caught from the bottom may be used on the hook. More times than not the angler will simply fasten on pieces or whole members of the baitfish used as chum. When sharks of great size are known to be present, exotic baits

Chumming

Table 1: Fresh-Water Fish Sought by Anglers (continued)

species	where caught*	weight of good catch		comments
		lb	kg	
Roach (Rutilus rutilus)	all Europe north of the Alps and Pyrenees	2	1	caught mostly on float or ledger tackle but will take flies and tiny spoons; Europe's most popular fish
Rudd (Scardinius erythrophthalmus)	most European countries	2	1	caught mostly by float fishing but takes the fly well
Salmon, atlantic (Salmo salar)	Iceland, Norway, Sweden, Finland, U.S.S.R., Britain, Ireland, France, Portugal, Spain; also in Greenland, eastern Canada, Maine	15–20	7–9	all methods, but spinning and/or bait fishing is banned on some waters; fly only permitted in North America
Salmon, chinook (Oncorhynchus tshawytscha)	Pacific coast of North America, California to Alaska, Great Lakes; South Island, New Zealand	40–60	18–27	largest of the Pacific salmon; also known as king, tyee, spring, quinnat (N.Z.); caught by trolling (mooching), fly-fishing, and bait or plug casting
Salmon, coho (Oncorhynchus kitsutch)	North America as chinook; Lake Michigan very successful	9–10	4–5	very game fish; also known as silver salmon caught by trolling, bait casting, and on a fly
Salmon, landlocked (salmo salar sebago and s. salar ouananiche)	Maine (sebago) and Lake St. John area, Quebec (ouananiche), New Brunswick, Nova Scotia	8	4	Atlantic salmon that do not migrate to sea; fine sporting fish; takes fly and spinner very well
Sturgeon, white (Acipenser transmontanus)	Pacific coast of North America, California to Alaska	100	50	caught by bottom fishing with crustaceans, larva, and other bottom life
Sunfish, redear (Lepomis microlphus)	southern and eastern United States	1	0.5	resembles bluegill; back of gill-cover bright orange-red; plucky pan fish; caught on bait, small lures, and flies
Tench (Tinca tinca)	all European countries except Scandinavia and Scotland	4–5	2	float and ledger fishing are exclusively used
Trout, brook (Salvelinus fortinalis)	originally northeastern United States, eastern Canada, all North America, northern Europe, South Africa, Sweden, South America	1–10	0.5–5	a char, it requires cold water; voracious, will take most baits and lures, sunken flies; excellent eating
Trout, brown (Salmo trutta)	all European countries; brown trout have also been introduced into North America, India, South America, Africa, Australia, and New Zealand	2 (river) 4 (lake)	1 2	all methods; although many waters permit only fly fishing
Trout, cutthroat (Salmo clarki)	Pacific drainage, California to Alaska	4	2	a true trout, voracious, will take fly, bait, or lure
Trout, dolly varden (Salvelinus malma)	British Columbia, western United States	6–8	3–4	a voracious, bottom-feeding char; will take any bait or lure
Trout, golden (Salmo aguabonita)	southern Sierra Nevada of western United States	2	1	a true trout, caught mostly on flies
Trout, lake (Salvelinus [cristivomer] namaycush)	northern North America	10–12	5–6	largest north American char; also known as Great Lakes trout; fly and bait casting, spinning, deep trolling, bait fishing; excellent table fish
Trout, rainbow (Salmo gairdneri)	Pacific drainage, other areas of North America, Europe, other countries where temperature permits	1	0.5	a true trout; wonderful sporting fish; takes fly, lure, and bait; at Lake Pend, Oreille, Idaho, called Kamloops or Kootenay
Trout, sea (Salmo trutta)	all sea-board countries of Europe except Holland and Belgium; in many countries—New Zealand, North America, South America, where brown trout have been introduced some have become migratory in habit and "runs" of sea-trout occur	8	4	all methods are used, but fly fishing and spinning are considered the most sporting; sea trout are shy fish and can often be caught only at night
Trout, steelhead (Salmo gairdneri)	California to Alaska, Great Lakes	10–12	5–6	migratory sea-run rainbow; caught on bait, flies, and spinners
Trout, sunapee (Salvelinus aureolus)	Lake Sunapee and other lakes, New Hampshire and Maine	2–3	1–1.5	a char
Tigerfish (Hydrocyon lineatus)	central Africa	10–15	5–7	a very game fish that takes fly or spinner and leaps repeatedly after being hooked; has large, sharp teeth and a high percentage of hooked fish escape
Walleye (Stizostedion vitreum vitreum)	originally Canada west to Alberta and south to Great Lakes-Mississippi; now all United States and Canada	2–5	1–2	also known as walleye, pike perch, and (Canada) doré; prized game fish, excellent eating
Warmouth (Chaenobryttus gulosus)	southeastern to midwest United States	1	0.5	a popular pan fish of its range; sometimes known as warmouth bass, warmouth perch; caught on bait, small lures, and flies
Whitefish, mountain (Prosopium williamsoni)	northern North America	1–1.5	0.5–0.75	caught on bait, flies, and spinners
Zander (Lucioperca lucioperca)	northern Europe	6–8	3–4	closely related to the North American walleye; caught by spinning and bait fishing; recently introduced into Great Britain

*Italics indicate species has been transplanted.

such as chunks of porpoise or seal meat may be used. A giant white shark will swallow a small harbour seal in a single gulp. It should be reported that the use of animal matter as chum or bait disqualifies the catch for possible record recognition under International Game Fish Association rules.

Ground fish and fish baits are quite sufficient for most shark-fishing operations, however. With such attractants, members of the Shark Angling Club of Great Britain catch as many as 5,000 sharks annually from all parts of Britain and Ireland struck by the Gulf Stream. Most of the sharks caught there are blues and porbeagles, although the spectacular, leaping makos are most eagerly sought. Individual Cornwall fishermen sometimes land several dozen sharks in a day.

In the western Atlantic, shark fishing finds new adherents each year, as more and more private boatmen become better equipped for big-game fishing. In many United States fishing ports, charter captains specialize in

catching sharks. The availability of the quarry, the simplicity of the chumming method, and the promise of energetic action (not without some danger) recruit anglers from all walks.

The shark has been recognized as a worthy angling adversary by the International Game Fish Association since the organization began its record-keeping. Six species invite competition. They are the mako, the great white shark, the blue shark, the porbeagle, the thresher, and the tiger shark.

While giant members of each species undoubtedly roam the oceans of the world, the largest specimens have been fairly caught on rod and reel only in Australian waters. Several great white sharks (also identified as white pointer sharks and man-eaters) of more than a ton in weight have been landed by anglers in the Great Australian Bight, a huge, crescent-shaped curve along the southern coast of the continent. Of the many fishermen who have pitted themselves against such monstrous fish, one man stands unsurpassed. Alfred Dean of Mildura, Australia, has set and broken his own white shark records several times. His best specimen weighed 2,664 pounds (1,208 kilograms). But Dean also hooked and fought sharks up to 20 feet (six metres) in length, one of which he thought exceeded 4,000 pounds. This angler chums with whale oil and uses whole seal carcasses for bait.

Party-boat fishing. Still-fishing is perhaps carried to the ultimate on open party or "head" boats that sail on daily schedules to the fishing grounds off many ports, carrying anglers to the nearby grounds for a stipulated head fee. When the boat has reached the grounds, the anchor is set. Anglers drop lead-weighted lines to the bottom carrying down baits of clams, crabs, sea worms, cut fish, or squid. A sudden strike or pull on the line is the signal for the fisherman to tighten his grip on the rod and reel up his catch. Fishes vary according to the countries and the seasons. Fish as large as the giant sea bass, which may weigh several hundred pounds, have been caught by head-boat anglers. Such large and valiant fighters as the amberjack, bluefish, grouper, and cobia, among the many, are taken regularly. Most of the species that fill out the party-boat fisherman's bag, however, are bottom feeders of modest size—tautogs, eels, members of the weakfish family, porgies, and lesser sea basses are examples.

Fish sought by party boats

In larger ports, news of party-boat catches is carried in the outdoor columns of the daily newspapers. The sport has thousands of enthusiasts who descend on coastal ports, winter and summer, intent on a good catch and the camaraderie of fellow anglers. Competition is the essence of such group fishing. Not only does every man strive to prove his mettle as an angler but, as a show of confidence, he invariably invests in the boat pool with a chance of winning a substantial sum should he catch the largest fish of the day.

Significantly, the pollution that is rampant in the inner and outer harbours of almost all large cities does not deter the party-boat angler—nor the private boat fisherman, nor the commercial netter, for that matter. Often the day's fishing is done within a few minutes' run of the grounds used as sludge repositories by the city's sewage treatment plants. Industrial wastes of noxious liquids sometimes flow with the tidal currents through vast areas of the outer harbour, turning the water a sickening green or yellow, even staining the fishermen's lines. If the poisonous liquids are quickly diluted and sufficient oxygen remains in the water, fish usually adjust to the unnatural habitat and remain as long as food is available—and the fishermen with them. Neither fish nor fishermen, however, may make compromise with the sludge dumping areas. Studies have shown that the descending sludge covers the bottom in a thickening blanket until all marine life but the most elemental worms is extinguished. In some outer harbours the sludge blanket may bury a dozen square miles of sea floor.

While catch records demonstrate a gradual decline in many of the species that seasonally visit heavily fished seaport grounds, factors aside from waste disposal contribute to the reduction. Increased pressures both from commercial and sport fisheries often tax the resource. Attrition of fish spawning and nursery grounds in the bays and estuaries as the result of run-off from the land, as well as the destruction of salt marshes or wetlands through industrial and residential encroachment, play major roles in the decline of many popular species.

CASTING

Surf casting. Casting, in Great Britain called spinning, is adaptable either to shore or boat fishing. Most often associated with the surf and the fishes of the littoral, the techniques of surf and shore, or beach, casting have made great strides through innovations in tackle—the strong, supple fibre glass rod, synthetic lines, and the worldwide ascendancy of the fixed-spool, or spinning, reel over the centrepin or revolving spool reel. While longer casts are sometimes possible with the revolving spool reel, the spinning reel's freedom from troublesome snarls and backlashes as well as its ease of operation are responsible for its popularity among surf casters, particularly neophytes. In competitive casting using standard surf spinning tackle, casts up to 480 feet (150 metres) have been made. This is about 15 or 20 feet (five or six metres) short of the best casts made with standard revolving spool reels, however.

Casting in shallow waters

Most surf casters are content to place their lures or baits beyond the curling breakers, distances of 100 to 200 feet (30 to 60 metres). This is readily accomplished with a rod nine to 12 feet (three to four metres). Rods vary in weight and strength in keeping with the demands made upon them. In the British Isles, where swift currents wash many shorelines and heavy bottom-grabbing sinkers are required, stout rods up to 15 feet (five metres) in length are often used. In contrast, slender eight- or ten-foot (two- or three-metre) rods may suffice on beaches where the water rolls placidly. The well-travelled surf angler may own rods for varying situations. Other special surf-casting equipment includes armpit waders, spray parka, and a webbed belt for holding a lure case, fish chain, and gaff. On rocky coasts, the experienced caster wades deep into the surge, where he hooks, fights, gaffs, and chains his catch without abandoning his strategic fishing location. A battery lamp worn on the head or chest completes the ensemble for night fishing, often the best time in the surf.

Shore casting. *Light tackle.* Shore casting, casting while wading in the shallow waters of bays and inlets, may be accomplished with the equivalent of light freshwater tackle. Even the fly rod is brought into play by an increasing number of ardent anglers. Tarpon and bonefish are frequently taken by wading light-tackle casters, more with spinning tackle than with the fly. Tarpon well over 100 pounds (45 kilograms) are frequently subdued in such narrow field of combat. Along the Gulf of Mexico, wading fishermen sometimes catch weakfish, or sea trout, tempting the tender-mouthed species with shrimp bait drifted from floats that sound noisily when drawn through the water. Fishermen long ago discovered that the popping or gurgling sounds made by an activated float are irresistible to a hungry weakfish.

Fly casting. The flies used in saltwater fly casting are lures imitating small fish, shrimps, etc. Generally, a strong, nine-foot (three-metre) rod is used, for long casts have to be made and many of the fish caught are relatively big and powerful. Europe and the British Isles have few places suitable for fly-fishing in the sea, but Florida and some of the other southern states of the U.S. offer splendid fly-fishing for bonefish, small tarpon, and other species including bluefish and sea trout. Farther north, the striped bass takes a fly well in places on both the Atlantic and Pacific coasts, whereas on the latter fly-fishing for coho salmon offers splendid sport.

A group of anglers who identify themselves as the Salt Water Fly Rodders of America, Int., have caught enough prize fish to establish a category of world records for fish caught on the fly rod.

Casting from boats. The increased mobility made possible by casting from a boat offers a marked advantage over shore fishing. Because lengthy casts are not vital for the boat-borne caster, a shorter rod serves him well. Boat casting pays dividends when game fish actively feed on surface baitfish, a situation that is often pinpointed by hovering seabirds. Then, the boat is cautiously directed to the turmoil of slashing fish and diving birds. Anglers eagerly whip plastic plugs, artificial squids, weighted bucktails, or jigs into the melee, retrieving them rapidly to simulate crippled baitfish. Often the action is frantic and continues until the boat drifts out of range of the school, or the fish sound.

Much boat casting takes a leaf from freshwater fishing. Fishermen direct their lures at sunken boulders in a rocky surf or cast them into pot holes and pockets where fish may be expected to lurk. Of the larger species, sailfish and marlin, school tuna and tuna-like fishes are occasionally caught by boat casters who relish the advantage they give to these large fish with their frail tackle. Even the fly rod has been successfully used in such deep-sea casting, although only a handful of experts press their luck in this direction. One fly-rod angler of supreme skill landed a 148-pound (67-kilogram) striped marlin off Ecuador on an inexpensive fly rod and reel to prove it could be done. The ensuing fight lasted four-and-a-half hours.

Many high-powered small craft have been devised for the specialized skills of the caster. Most of them are outboard powered or served with an inboard engine and stern drive (sometimes called an inboard-outboard) that permits them to operate in waters too shallow for standard inboard craft. Such versatile vehicles are used by Florida Keys guides to transport fishermen over vast distances in extremely shallow water at great speed.

TROLLING

Trolling, trailing a natural bait or artificial lure behind a moving boat, is greatly practiced for sea fish, for it is the best way of locating fish in great expanses of water, often of considerable depth. With the exception of trolling for what are known as big-game fish, a specialized technique that will be dealt with separately, the methods of fishing are very similar to those used for freshwater fish.

Typical of saltwater trolling is the method used on the west coast of North America to catch the large Pacific salmon. All types of craft are used, from rowboats to special power-driven ships designed for this sport. Behind such crafts are trailed spoons, plugs, and dead fish, either whole or cut up. A very popular method is known as mooching (here meaning to skulk or sneak—the bait is sneaked among a school of feeding salmon). A preferred bait is a dead herring preceded by a large spoon called a herring dodger. The dodger acts both as an attractor and as a way of causing the herring to move in a lifelike manner. Basing itself on this sport of trolling for Pacific salmon is the famed Tyee Club of Campbell River, British Columbia. This club lays down rules as to tackle that may be used, and presents buttons to anglers who catch large specimens of these salmon—bronze for 30-pound (14-kilogram) fish, silver for 40-pound (18-kilogram) fish, gold for 50-pound (23-kilogram) fish, and diamond for those of 60 pounds (27 kilograms) or more.

BIG-GAME FISHING

The quarry sought in big-game or deep-sea fishing are principally the members of the tuna, shark, and swordfish, or billfish, families; individual specimens may run from 100 pounds (45 kilograms) to well over 2,000 pounds (900 kilograms).

Beginnings of the sport

The beginning of big-game fishing inevitably is traced to the day in 1898 off Santa Catalina Island, California, when C.F. Holder tried a stout rod and reel against an up-to-that-time untouchable giant bluefin tuna and succeeded in taking a fish of 183 pounds (83 kilograms), the first of such size to fall victim to an angler. It has been said that the most formidable part of Holder's equipment was his great courage and a burn-proof thumb. In the infancy of big-game fishing, slip-clutch reels were unknown. Whatever drag that might be applied to the spool was done so with thumb pressure as the line whirled away into the water. Friction pads or thumb stalls were used to lessen the threat to the angler's fingers. But even when the fisherman mastered the scorching reel, he was additionally threatened by the revolving handles that flew around double or triple the rate of the whirling spool.

Despite the odds drawn against him, Holder proved equal to the fish that day off Santa Catalina Island. News of the conquest quickly spread and fired the imaginations of fishermen everywhere. Soon enough Holder's feat was accomplished by others and with other species of giant fish, including marlin and broadbill swordfish.

Holder's historic catch, made with a 16-ounce (450-gram) rod, not including the butt, led to the formation of the Catalina Tuna Club, which soon set the early ground rules for big-game fishing. Rod tips were limited to 16 ounces, lines to 24-thread, which, with three pounds (1½ kilograms) to the thread, meant a breaking strength of 72 pounds (33 kilograms). The catch, and the others that followed in rapid order as growing numbers of saltwater fishermen elevated their sights to include the heretofore untouchable species, served to emphasize the inadequacy of the available tackle, particularly the reels. Not until 1913, however, when reel maker Julius vom Hofe of Brooklyn, New York, responding to the suggestions of thwarted big-game fishermen, produced a reel with an internal drag, were the problems of a scorching spool and knuckle-cracking handles solved.

Big-game fishing is considered the ultimate in sport fishing. Most serious participants are guided by the strict rules of competition set down by the International Game Fish Association, whose members act as referees and judges for record-contending fish in many countries of the world. The same rules are also applicable to saltwater fishermen of every level. Many of the records kept by the organization were made by fishermen who aspired for anything but record-breaking fish. Every angler who abides by the rules is eligible to have his name inscribed in the books if his particular catch improves on the species listed in one of several line-strength categories.

Deep-sea trolling. The most popular, effective, and sporting method of big-game fishing is trolling. Deep-sea trolling is a highly specialized form of fishing requiring a boat designed for the purpose and tackle designed for handling very heavy fish. The craft for big-game fishing must be capable of withstanding heavy seas and is equipped with a "fighting seat," a turntable chair from which the angler can exert the maximum pressure on a fish many times his own weight. The rod, a massive one of fibre glass or laminated wood, has a butt that fits into a socket in the chair. The reel is usually a very large multiplying reel, although some British big-game fishermen prefer a centre-pin reel; it is usually designed so that a harness that fits over the angler's shoulders or around the small of his back can be connected to it, thus allowing the fisherman to use all his strength against the fish. The reels have a throwout lever or other device to release the spool and allow it to run free, and a braking device or drag to regulate line tension. The line is made of Dacron or Terylene and the leader of wire.

Equipment required for big-game trolling

Craft designed for such fishing generally have outriggers—long poles to which the lines are attached by what Americans call clothespins and the British clothes pegs, which hold the lines well clear of the boat, thus allowing more than one line to be used. The age-old problem of locating fish and determining the depth at which they are feeding has been solved in part by the use of echo sounders and other electronic aids.

All sport-fishing cruisers are not of the optimum design. This does not necessarily alter their ability to cope with huge fish. The almost primitive dory-like cruisers of the Canadian Maritime fishermen are regularly used to set new records for giant tuna. Fish of over 1,000 pounds (450 kilograms) have been caught on rod and reel from such minimal angling vessels, with the catch towed to port when it could not be lifted aboard.

Big-game fishing is not the exclusive domain of the wealthy. Its realm includes sea anglers of all ranks, and International Game Fish Association records amply attest to the truth of the statement. The majority of the listings are the product of fishing craft of modest size and structure and of fishermen whose principal asset was zest. As a matter of fact, most big-game fishermen usually go to sea to take the measure of whatever species are at hand, most of which require little muscle for landing, although hooking may be something else again.

Techniques. In trolling, the angler-boatman tows his lures or natural baits, as the case may be, at varying distances from the boat and at varying depths according to the habits of the species sought. Speed is the third factor the fisherman takes into consideration. Boat speed will influence the trolling depth and action of the lure. The churn of a rapidly spinning propeller will create a wake that many species, particularly the tunas, find attractive. When trolling for such species, the lures are usually brought into the white water close behind the vessel. For species that shy from a passing boat only to converge after its passing, long trolling lines may be called for. Deep-swimming species may be reached through the ad-

Table 2: Saltwater Game Fish

species	where caught	weight of good catch		comments
		lb	kg	
Albacore (*Thunnus alalunga*)	New Zealand, Hawaii, Peru, Ecuador, California, Mediterranean, Azores, Caribbean, Gulf Stream from Bahamas to offshore New York	30	14	distinguished by long pectorals, valued commercially as the white-meat tuna; trolled and chummed with live bait
Amberjack (*Seriola*)	Bermuda, Bahamas, Hawaii, Puerto Rico, Brazil, Mediterranean	50–60	23–27	likes live baitfish but will take cut baits, strong tackle is needed to dislodge it from reef hideouts
Barracuda (*Sphyraena*)	Florida, Bahamas, Gulf of Mexico, West Indies, East Indies, Japan, Australia	30–35	14–16	voracious predator, sporty on light tackle, not nearly as bad as reputation, older specimens sometimes toxic
Bass, black sea (*Centropristes striata*)	southern New England to North Carolina	5	2	often called simply sea bass, a staple fish of party boats, often associated with porgies
Bass, channel (*Sciaenops ocellata*)	Delaware Bay to Gulf of Mexico	50	23	heaviest fish are caught off North Carolina's Outer Banks; called redfish, identified by black spot on tail
Bass, European (*Morone labrax*)	northern European waters	8–10	4–5	caught by all means of angling including sometimes fly fishing; very sporting fish
Bass, giant sea (*Stereolepis gigas*)	central California to Baja California, Costa Rica	300	140	also known as California black sea bass; reaches 600 lbs; not a great fighter despite its size, large baits
Bass, striped (*Roccus saxatilis*)	Atlantic waters from Maine to South Carolina, strays to Canada and Florida, Pacific waters of California and Oregon	45–50	20–23	also called striper, rockfish, greenhead, or linesides; bait fishing and plug casting are best methods; most popular quarry among inshore surf casters
Blackfish (*Tautoga onitis*)	New England to the Carolinas	12	5	a rough-and-tumble fighter of rough bottom, tricky to hook; also known as tautog
Bluefish (*Pomatomus saltatrix*)	east coast of North America, North Africa, South Africa, eastern South America, Australia, Japan	12–15	5–7	takes almost any lure trolled or cast, is readily chummed; called tailor, shad, fatback, elf (South Africa); snapper when young
Bonefish (*Albula vulpes*)	Florida Keys, Bahamas, Bermuda, Puerto Rico, Cuba, Hawaii, Japan, Australia	10	5	a wary bottom feeder that often forages in water only inches deep; known for its long, fleeting runs; caught on bait or lures, may be chummed
Bonito, oceanic (*Euthynnus pelamis*)	western Atlantic, Cuba, Bermuda, Puerto Rico, Barbados, Madeira, Morocco, Dakar, Chile, California, Hawaii, New Zealand	15–18	7–8	often feeds on surface in splashing schools, readily trolled; commercially described as skipjack; other names, striped bonito, leaping bonito, arctic bonito, and aku
Bream, black (*Spondyliosoma cantharus*)	northern Europe	3	1	caught by float and bottom fishing in late spring and early summer in English Channel
Cobia (*Rachycentron canadum*)	Gulf of Mexico, Bermuda, Jamaica, Brazil, Senegal, Guinea, Australia, Japan, Persian Gulf, Florida	40	18	also called cabio, crabeater, ling, lemonfish, sergeant fish; strong fighter that loiters around wrecks and sea buoys
Cod (*Gadus morhua*)	western Atlantic from Greenland to the Virginia capes, Iceland, Scandinavia, British Isles	45–50	20–23	staple food fish of many nations; favourite of the winter sport fishery
Conger (*Conger conger*)	British Isles, northern Europe	30	14	usually taken by bottom fishing close to rocks or wrecks; a very strong eel running 70–80 lbs and bigger
Dab (*Limanda limanda*)	northern European waters	1.5	0.7	a small flatfish caught over mud or sand
Dolphin (*Coryphaena hippurus*)	almost worldwide where water temperatures reach 70° F (21° C), Cape Cod to Brazil, Caribbean, Gulf of Mexico, Mediterranean, Hawaii, Southern California to the Bay of Panama, Ecuador, Japan Sea, Philippines, Australia, Kenya, West Africa	35–40	16–18	not to be confused with mammal dolphin; this brilliant fish often lurks under floating flotsam
Drum, black (*Pogonias cromis*)	eastern North America	6	3	also called sea drum
Flounder (*Platichthys flesus*)	northern Europe	3	1	an estuarial flatfish frequently caught on baited spoon
Halibut (*Hippoglossus hippoglossus*)	northern British waters	100	45	a very large flatfish now being caught on rod and line in far northern British waters
Jewfish (*Epinephelus itajara*)	Florida, Gulf of Mexico, West Indies to Brazil, eastern Pacific, Baja California to Panama	300	140	largest of the giant bass, also known as giant sea bass and warsaw grouper; sometimes caught by shore and bridge fishermen on heavy handlines
Ling (*Molva molva*)	Greenland to Bay of Biscay	30	14	a highly predatory fish caught in deep water often in the vicinity of wrecks

dition of heavy trolling weights or through the use of a metal planer, a device that reacts to water pressure and dives deep into the wake carrying the attached lure with it. Wire lines created from extruded Monel Metal or stainless steel assist in the sinking of a moving lure. Nylon fibre braided around a lead core is the structure of another line used to troll lures below the surface. (But fish caught on metal or metal core lines are not eligible for International Game Fish Association records.) No matter what form the trolling takes, the purpose is the same—to attract a game fish to an apparently injured baitfish, which is the lure. Sometimes an angler finds it expedient to keep his baits aboard the boat until the quarry is sighted. This approach is often used in fishing for broadbill swordfish which, normally, are not baited until they have revealed themselves finning on the surface. As soon as the boat closes on the lolling fish, the large bait of whole squid or fish is launched and manoeuvred 100 feet (30 metres) behind the boat, then sunk in front of the fish. If the swordfish follows the bait down, a strike may result. This method is also used for large sharks discovered swimming on the surface.

Live baits appeal to many game fishes. Small baitfishes are netted or taken with hook and line to be stored in live-bait wells or aerated containers aboard the fishing craft. Such bait is generally fished from a high-rising outrigger at extremely slow speed. Kite fishing is a phase of this live-baiting method. The kite replaces the outrigger

Kite fishing

Table 2: Saltwater Game Fish (continued)

species	where caught	weight of good catch		comments
		lb	kg	
Mackerel (Scomber scombrus)	north Atlantic, Europe and America	2	1	if caught on light tackle is a magnificent sporting fish; caught by all means
Mackerel, king (Scomber-morus cavalla)	Florida Straits to Cape Hatteras and south to the Caribbean	35–40	16–18	a spectacular leaper, it will sometimes arc a dozen feet into the air to land precisely on a trolled bait
Marlin, black (Makaira indica)	throughout warm water of Pacific, also present in the Indian Ocean, East Africa, Japan to New Zealand and Australia, greatest concentrations of 1,000-lb fish in Humbolt Current off Peru and Ecuador	400–500	180–230	largest of the finfish, a giant of 2,250 lbs was once harpooned off Cabo Blanco, Peru; rigid pectoral fin distinguishes it from other marlins; trolling best method
Marlin, blue Atlantic (Makaira nigricans)	western Atlantic from New England to Florida and Bahamas, Cuba, Jamaica, Puerto Rico, Venezuela, Brazil, west Africa	200–250	90–110	takes trolled baits, often runs with white marlin, a smaller and more plentiful relative; cobalt blue colour fades after capture
Marlin, blue Pacific (Makaira ampla)	throughout tropical and subtropical Pacific, East African coast	200–250	90–110	prize catch of Hawaii; pectoral fin folds back to distinguish blue from black marlin; long confused with Atlantic blue marlin, it is now proclaimed a separate species
Marlin, striped (Makaira audax)	coastal waters of Ecuador, Chile, Peru, Hawaii, Southern California, Mexico, Panama, Australia, Bay of Islands, New Zealand	200–225	90–100	readily identified by its vivid vertical bars, a spectacular jumper, caught on trolled, whole-fish baits or squid
Marlin, white (Makaira albida)	western Atlantic from Cape Cod to the Caribbean, Bahamas, Cuba, Bermuda	80–90	35–40	smallest of the marlins; ranks second to the sailfish in popularity among anglers; trolled bait and artificial lures
Mullet, gray (Mugil cephalus)	northern Europe	3	1	excellent sporting fish frequently caught on light float tackle
Permit (Trachinotus falcatus)	Bahamas, Florida Keys, Gulf of California, Panama	25–30	11–14	a round, compressed member of the pompano family, it is often found in the shallowest water; a fine light-tackle fighter
Plaice (Pleuronectes platessa)	northern Europe	3	1	caught over mud or sand often by drifting with baited spoon; excellent table fish
Pollock (Pollachius)	northeast Atlantic waters of the United States, British Isles, Norway	25–30	11–14	a handsome hard-fighting relative of the cod; also called codfish and Boston bluefish
Sailfish, Atlantic (Istiophorus albicans)	Florida (Atlantic and Gulf coasts), Bahamas, Cuba, Puerto Rico, Jamaica, Venezuela, British Honduras	70	30	most fish are caught trolling; one of the most sought after trophy fish
Sailfish, Pacific (Istiophorus greyi)	Hawaii, Japan, Guam, Philippines, Tahiti, Solomon Islands, Indian Ocean, Southern California to Salinas, Ecuador	125	55	caught with trolled baits, more than double the average size of Atlantic sailfish
Snook (Centropomus)	coastal waters of Gulf of Mexico, Florida, Bahamas, Puerto Rico and south to Venezuela, Southern California to Peru, West Africa	25	11	some of the heaviest are caught by shore and bridge fishermen who use either lures or bait; also called robalo
Swordfish (Xiphias gladius)	widely distributed in both hemispheres, Newfoundland to New York, Cuba, Iceland, Scandinavia to Portugal, Cape of Good Hope, Mediterranean, Bosporus, Sea of Marmara, Black Sea, Cape Province, Durban, Madagascar, from Southern California to Chile, northern Japan to Australia and New Zealand	350	160	a highly prized game fish, difficult to hook and hard to hold because of soft mouth; except for man principal enemy is the mako shark; called broadbill, albacora, espadon
Tarpon (Megalops)	waters of tropical rivers, inlets, and back bays, especially Florida, Río Pánuco, and West African coasts	100–125	45–55	best methods are bait and plug casting and fly-fishing; sharp hooks are essential; a ferocious fighter
Tuna, allison (or yellowfin) (Thunnus albacares)	tropical and subtropical waters around the world, Japan, Philippines, Somalia, Australia, Hawaii, Northwest Africa, Caribbean to Brazil	80	35	most abundant in Pacific waters, older specimens develop lengthening of dorsal and anal fins; known as allison tuna and ahi in Hawaii
Tuna, big-eyed (Thunnus obesus)	tropical waters of Pacific, eastern Atlantic to Azores, northwest coast of South America, Indonesia, Hawaii, Indian Ocean	150	70	second largest after bluefin tuna, deep-swimming tuna, does not often rise to surface lures
Tuna, bluefin (Thunnus tynnus)	most warm and temperate waters, United States, Bahamas, waters between Sweden and Denmark, Bay of Biscay, Mediterranean, East and South African coasts, Australia	80 (school tuna); 600–700 (giants)	35 270–320	another much-sought-after trophy; fish over 1,000 lbs have been caught on rod and reel
Wahoo (Acanthocybium solanderi)	Bermuda, Bahamas, northern Brazil, Ecuador, Baja California, Panama, Japan, Philippines, Australia	50	23	also called peto, queenfish, ono; the cigar-shaped wahoo is among the swifter fish of the ocean; distinguishing it from other mackerel-like fish, the wahoo has a moveable upper jaw
Weakfish (Cynoscion regalis)	Cape Cod to Gulf of Mexico, Gulf of California to Peru	4–5	2	favourite of bay and shore anglers, the tender-mouthed weakfish or squeteague is also called sea trout because of its looks and dash; some Pacific members grow to 20 lbs
Yellowtail (Seriola dorsalis)	Southern California to Baja, Mexico, New Zealand, Australia	35	16	an amberjack that fights as hard as the rest of the family; most are caught with live chum and bait, some are trolled

transporting the struggling baitfish well away from the boat. Fishing kites are fashioned from silk cloth mounted on an X-shaped frame. Their size is dictated by the weight of the bait used and the velocity of the wind.

When a fish has been hooked it is brought to the boat by "pumping." In pumping a large fish, the angler places both hands on the rod grip, arms straight before him, body bent forward. Legs push against the footrest, shoulder muscles against the harness. The rod is slowly forced to the perpendicular. Switching the right hand to the reel handle, the angler starts forward again, winding up the short length of line, which slackens as the rod descends. Pumping a fish has been compared to a slow rocking chair motion and is accomplished without changing the tension on the line. The backward stroke pulls the fish a little closer. The forward motion stores the line gained. When properly performed, pumping results in minimum fatigue even with the largest fish, which is evidenced by the number of women and children who land fish many times their own weight.

Tackle. The choice of rods and reels for a day's fishing depends on the type and size of the fish sought, or the humour of the fisherman. In the main, light or medium outfits are used in trolling for small or medium-sized pelagic species such as school tuna, bluefish, kingfish, mackerel, and dolphin. Often, however, fishermen find it sporting to take on large fish with light equipment. "Three-six tackle" was the name applied by the Catalina

Tuna Club to the rod less than six feet long, with a tip weighing less than six ounces and using a standard six-thread linen line.

With the introduction of the lightweight but strong rod made of glass fibres and resin the whole concept of the balanced rod and reel changed. Glass rod tips are several ounces lighter than rods of split bamboo or solid or laminated woods and immeasurably stronger. Fine-gauged monofilament lines or braided synthetics increase the capabilities of the extremely light outfit.

Working tools of a serious big-game angler might include a rod with six-ounce tip, fitted with a reel filled with 30-pound (14-kilogram) test line. This outfit is suitable for smaller species but capable of fish up to 50 or 60 pounds (23 or 27 kilograms). An intermediate outfit would include an eight-ounce (230-gram) tip and 50-pound (23-kilogram) test line. The heavy-duty outfit, with strength for all but the largest fish, would comprise a 14-ounce (400-gram) tip with 80-pound (36-kilogram) test line. For giant bluefin tuna, broadbill swordfish, black marlin, blue marlin, and exceptionally heavy sharks a 22-ounce (620-gram) tip may be required. Required line will test at 130 pounds (59 kilograms).

If weight records of the various game fishes continue to inch upwards—and they do—the reason must surely bear a relationship to the mounting numbers of anglers. More sports-oriented people with more leisure time discover that fishing is at once a means of relaxation while offering enough complexities to arouse their interest. Manufacturers of tackle, motors, and boats have kept pace with the surging demand for equipment, providing fishermen and boatmen with the benefit of the technical advances of modern industry.

Contributions to science. Big-game fishermen have been the beneficiaries of many scientific advances in tackle and boat equipment. In turn, some fishermen have made important contributions to the study of several larger pelagic species. Largely through the cooperative help of anglers, the Woods Hole Oceanographic Institution in the United States has been able to partially map the migrations of several fishes of worldwide importance. This has been done through tagging—the insertion of an imprinted plastic marker in the dorsal muscle of an angled fish, which is then released unharmed. The tags, developed by the institution, are distributed to interested fishermen. Best of the devices is in the form of a dart, which is thrust into a tiring fish as it is brought alongside the boat. The dart is driven home as with a harpoon, the leader is snipped and the weary fish is free to swim off and rejoin the school. Fish caught on rod and reel and promptly released have a much higher survival rate than those netted, hence the recruitment of big-game anglers to the study.

Migrations of large fishes, notably the bluefin tuna, have excited the curiosity of naturalists and fishermen since the time of Aristotle, but it is only since the introduction of the tag that such fishes have been tracked, often with astonishing results. Favourite tagging grounds for the giants is the eastern edge of the Gulf Stream in the Straits of Florida. Of the many fish tagged there during the several years of the study, six bluefins were recaptured in Norwegian waters, establishing beyond doubt that the bluefin is a trans-Atlantic traveller. Four of the fish were recaptured after only 50 to 119 days at large, during which time they must have travelled at least 4,200 nautical miles.

Further confirmation of the tuna's capacity for ranging over great distances resulted from extensive tagging of small fish along the east coast of the United States. From this operation, 36 school tuna of 50 pounds (23 kilograms) or less were recaptured in the Bay of Biscay on the French-Spanish coasts. While evidence is wanting to prove that the roving tuna swims a circuit of the Atlantic, many scientists believe such is the case. The French Institut Scientifique et Techniques des Pêches Maritimes hopes to give substance to the theory with tagging in the European realm of the tuna. European fishermen already have made important progress in tracing movements of bluefin tuna between various fishing grounds off the con-

Mapping migrations of fish

tinent. Four large tuna released near Bergen, Norway, were recaptured near Cadiz, Spain. Several smaller tuna caught and released off Cadiz supplied clinching evidence that Atlantic tuna mingle with those of the Mediterranean. Two of these tagged fish were recaptured off Ceuta, Morocco, and La Línea, Spain. Another was retaken in the Gulf of Lion off southern France.

From bluefin tuna taggings undertaken by American and Japanese agencies it is now believed there is an interchange of the species from both sides of the Pacific Ocean. Taggings have also shown migrations from West Australia to New Zealand. In other taggings participated in by sportsmen, the Pacific striped marlin has been revealed as a long-distance traveller, as has the Atlantic white marlin, whose migratory circuit has been shown to extend from New England waters to the Caribbean.

INTERNATIONAL GAME FISH ASSOCIATION

Sitting in judgment on all big-game fishing in the role of umpire and record-keeper is the International Game Fish Association. While its headquarters is located in Fort Lauderdale, Florida, it functions through member clubs or designated representatives in over 60 regions around the globe, excluding only the Soviet Union and the nations in the Soviet orbit. Established in 1939, largely through the organizational efforts of American big-game fishermen, the IGFA attained international stature in the years of burgeoning ocean sport fishing after World War II. Serious marine fishermen everywhere subscribe to its rules and accept its decisions on record-contending fish. In seeking recognition for a catch the angler will contact either the association headquarters or a regional representative. He will be required to fill out a form provided him. This affidavit will be returned along with ten yards (nine metres) of the line used, as well as a photograph of the catch.

While records seek to spotlight the largest of each of the 49 species in contention, subdivisional records are also kept for all 49 species in several line strength categories. In addition to the all-inclusive All-Tackle class are record categories for 12-pound (five-kilogram) test, 20-pound (nine-kilogram) test, 30-pound (14-kilogram) test, 50-pound (23-kilogram) test, 80-pound (36-kilogram) test and 130-pound (59-kilogram) test lines. Only fish caught according to the rules of the International Game Fish Association are accepted by the association for record purposes.

Big-game fishing records

SALTWATER FISH SOUGHT BY ANGLERS

A great variety of saltwater fish furnish sport to surf, shore, and deep-sea anglers. Table 2 lists the most popular saltwater game fishes, their scientific names, areas where caught, weights for a good catch, and descriptive comments. The list includes the species for which world records are kept by the International Game Fish Association. For list of world records see in SPORTING RECORD in the *Ready Reference and Index*.

BIBLIOGRAPHY. A.J. MCCLANE (ed.), *McClane's Standard Fishing Encyclopedia and International Angling Guide* (1965), covers most types of fishing in many parts of the world.

Freshwater fishing: (*On British coarse fishing*): BILLY LANE and COLIN GRAHAM, *Billy Lane's Encyclopaedia of Float Fishing* (1971); ALAN WRANGLES (ed.), *Newnes Complete Guide to Coarse Fishing* (1967); R.S. WALKER, *Still-Water Angling*, 2nd ed. (1955). (*On salmon fishing*): W.J.M. MENZIES, *Salmon Fishing* (1935); ARTHUR OGLESBY, *Salmon* (1971); J. HUGHES-PARRY, *Fishing Fantasy* (1949); R.V. RIGHYNI, *Salmon Taking Times* (1969). (*On trout fishing*): E. DURAND, *Wanderings with a Fly-Rod* (1938); VISCOUNT EDWARD GREY OF FALLODON, *Fly-Fishing* (1899; rev. and enl., 1930); F.M. HALFORD, *Dry Fly Fishing in Theory and Practice* (1889); J.W. MILLS, *Summer on the Test*, 4th ed. (1946); T.C. IVENS, *Still Water Fly-Fishing*, 3rd ed. (1970); CHARLES RITZ, *Pris sur le Vif* (1953; Eng. trans., *A Fly Fisher's Life*, 1959); FRANK SAWYER, *Nymphs and the Trout* (1958); G.E.M. SKUES, *The Way of a Trout with a Fly* (1921); W.C. STEWART, *The Practical Angler* (1857; new ed., 1942); DERMOT WILSON, *Fishing the Dry Fly* (1970). (*On British and European sea fishing*): HUGH STOKER, *The Modern Sea Angler*, rev. ed. (1964); ALAN WRANGLES (ed.), *Newnes Complete Guide to Sea*

Angling (1965). (*On natural and artificial flies*): JOHN GODDARD, *Trout Fly Recognition* (1966) and *Trout Flies of Stillwater* (1969); JOHN RICHARD HARRIS, *An Angler's Entomology* (1956); A. COURTNEY WILLIAMS, *A Dictionary of Trout Flies*, 2nd ed. (1951). (*On casting*); T.L. EDWARDS and E. HORSFALL TURNER, *The Angler's Cast* (1960); TERRY THOMAS, *Casting* (1960). (*History*): WILLIAM RADCLIFFE, *Fishing from the Earliest Times*, 2nd ed. (1926); A. COURTNEY WILLIAMS, *Angling Diversions* (1946). (*On fishing in different countries*): D.W. BEAMISH, *Trout and Other Fishing in New Zealand* (1953); E. CRETIN and G.H. LACY, *The Angler's Handbook for India* (1915); DAVID G. STEEL, *Fish of Australia* (1902); A.C. HARRISON et al., *Fresh-Water Fish and Fishing in Africa* (1963); F.H. WOODING, *The Angler's Book of Canadian Fishes* (1959). (*On British waters*): H.F. WALLIS (ed.), *Where To Fish* (biannual). (*Classics*): DAME JULIANA BERNERS, *The Treatyse of Fysshynge wyth an Angle* (1496, reprinted 1885); IZAAK WALTON, *The Compleat Angler* (1653, reprinted 1966).

Saltwater fishing: EDWARD C. MIGDALSKI, *Angler's Guide to Salt Water Game Fishes* (1958), an angling guide to the various saltwater species written by a trained fishery scientist; JERRY JANSEN, *Successful Surf Fishing* (1968), a how-to-do-it book by an expert in this specialized phase of the sport; ARTHUR L. CONE, *Fishing Made Easy* (1968), the practical aspects of catching everything from panfish to giant tuna told by a veteran angler; VLAD EVANOFF, *How to Fish in Salt Water* (1962), one of the acknowledged masters of saltwater fishing draws on his long experience to aid the novice; MILT ROSKO, *Fishing from Boats* (1968), an authoritative and well-illustrated textbook on the many saltwater fishing methods; JIM BOB TINSLEY, *The Sailfish: Swashbuckler of the Open Seas* (1964), an exhaustive study on one of the ocean's trophy fishes; HARLAN MAJOR, *Salt Water Fishing Tackle*, 3rd ed. (1955), often considered the standard authority on methods and tackle for catching marine species; HENRY LYMAN and FRANK WOOLNER, *Complete Book of Striped Bass Fishing* (1954), a favourite fish of the littoral is expertly treated by two skilled anglers; JOSEPH W. BROOKS, *A World of Fishing* (1964), an eminent angler and author describes his fishing experiences around the world; ROBERT SCHARFF, *Standard Handbook of Salt-Water Fishing*, rev. ed. (1966), the tackle, boats, and varied techniques of saltwater fishing are described by the author and contributing experts.

(F.E.K./T.B.T.)

Fitzgerald, F. Scott

Francis Scott Key Fitzgerald was the most representative novelist of the American twenties, the decade that saw the emergence of such writers as Faulkner and Hemingway, Sinclair Lewis and John Dos Passos, Ezra Pound and T.S. Eliot. It was a decade so rich in talent that it constituted a kind of American renaissance. Though the fashionable posture in the 1920s was a pose of disillusionment, it was in fact a decade of hope and enthusiasm, of what Fitzgerald was later to call "a romantic readiness" for life, one of those times when people are eager to believe they can wipe out the past and rebuild the world into something far better. In a more representative way than did any other writer of the age, Fitzgerald expressed these feelings for them.

He was born in St. Paul, Minnesota, September 24, 1896, the only son of an unsuccessful, aristocratic father and an energetic, provincial mother. Half the time he thought of himself as the heir of his father's tradition, which included the author of "The Star-Spangled Banner," Francis Scott Key, after whom he was named, and half the time as "straight 1850 potato-famine Irish." As a result he had typically ambivalent American feelings about American life, which seemed to him at once vulgar and dazzlingly promising.

He also had an intensely romantic imagination, what he once called "a heightened sensitivity to the promises of life," and he charged into experience determined to realize those promises. At both St. Paul Academy (1908–10) and Newman School (1911–13) he tried too hard and made himself unpopular, but at Princeton he came close to realizing his dream of a brilliant success. He became a prominent figure in the literary life of the university and made lifelong friendships with Edmund Wilson and John Peale Bishop; he became a leading figure in the socially important Triangle Club and was elected to one of the leading clubs of the university; he fell in love with Ginevra King, one of the beauties of

F. Scott Fitzgerald with his wife, Zelda, and daughter Scottie, c. 1927.
Culver Pictures

her generation. Then he lost Ginevra and flunked out of Princeton.

He returned to Princeton the next fall, but he had now lost all the positions he coveted, and, in November 1917, he left to join the army. In July 1918, while he was stationed near Montgomery, Alabama, he met Zelda Sayre, the daughter of an Alabama Supreme Court judge. They fell deeply in love, and, as soon as he could, Fitzgerald headed for New York determined to achieve instant success and to marry Zelda. What he achieved was an advertising job at $90 a month. Zelda broke their engagement, and after an epic drunk, Fitzgerald retired to St. Paul to rewrite for the second time a novel he had begun at Princeton. In the spring of 1920 it was published, he married Zelda, and

Marriage to Zelda

riding in a taxi one afternoon between very tall buildings under a mauve and rosy sky, I began to bawl because I had everything I wanted and knew I would never be so happy again.

Immature though it seems today, *This Side of Paradise* was, in 1920, a revelation of the new morality of the young; it made Fitzgerald famous. This fame opened to him magazines of literary prestige, such as *Scribner's*, and high paying popular ones, such as *The Saturday Evening Post*. This sudden prosperity made it possible for him and Zelda to play the roles they were so beautifully equipped for and they became what one of their friends, Ring Lardner, called them, the prince and princess of their generation. Though they loved these roles, they were frightened by them, too, as the ending of Fitzgerald's second novel, *The Beautiful and Damned* (1922), shows. *The Beautiful and Damned* describes a handsome young man and his beautiful wife, who gradually degenerate into a shopworn middle age while they wait for the young man to inherit a large fortune. Ironically, they finally get it, when there is nothing of them left worth preserving.

To escape the life that they feared might bring them to this end, the Fitzgeralds moved in 1924 to the Riviera, where they found themselves a part of a group of American expatriates whose style was largely set by Gerald and Sara Murphy; Fitzgerald described this society in his last completed novel, *Tender Is the Night*, and modelled its hero on Gerald Murphy. Shortly after their arrival in France, Fitzgerald completed his most brilliant novel, *The Great Gatsby* (1925). All of his divided nature is in this novel, the naïve Midwesterner afire with the possibilities of the "American Dream" in its hero, Jay Gatsby, and the compassionate Princeton gentleman in its narrator, Nick Carraway. *The Great Gatsby* is the most profoundly American novel of its time; at its conclusion, Fitzgerald connects Gatsby's dream, his "Platonic conception of himself," with the dream of the discoverers of America.

The next decade of the Fitzgeralds' lives was disorderly and unhappy. Fitzgerald began to drink too much, and Zelda suddenly, ominously, began to practice ballet dancing night and day. In 1930 she had a mental breakdown and in 1932 another, from which she never fully recovered. Through the 1930s they fought to save their life together, and, when the battle was lost, Fitzgerald said, "I left my capacity for hoping on the little roads that led to Zelda's sanitarium." He did not finish his next novel, *Tender Is the Night*, until 1934. It is the story of a psychiatrist who marries one of his patients, who, as she slowly recovers, exhausts his vitality until he is, in Fitzgerald's words, *un homme épuisé* ("a man used up"). Though technically faulty and commercially unsuccessful, this is Fitzgerald's most moving book.

Last years in Hollywood

With its failure and his despair over Zelda, Fitzgerald was close to becoming an incurable alcoholic. By 1937, however, he had come back far enough to become a scriptwriter in Hollywood, and there he met and fell in love with Sheilah Graham, a famous Hollywood gossip columnist. For the rest of his life—except for occasional drunken spells when he became bitter and violent—Fitzgerald lived quietly with Miss Graham. In October 1939 he began a novel about Hollywood, *The Last Tycoon*. The career of its hero, Monroe Stahr, is based on that of producer Irving Thalberg. This is Fitzgerald's final attempt to create his dream of the promises of American life and of the kind of man who could realize them. In the intensity with which it is imagined and in the brilliance of its expression, it is the equal of anything Fitzgerald ever wrote, and it is typical of his luck that, on December 21, 1940, he died of a heart attack with his novel only half-finished. He was 44 years old.

MAJOR WORKS

NOVELS: *This Side of Paradise* (1920); *The Beautiful and Damned* (1922); *The Great Gatsby* (1925); *Tender Is the Night* (1934); *The Last Tycoon*, unfinished (1941).

SHORT STORIES: *Flappers and Philosophers* (1920); *Tales of the Jazz Age* (1922); *All the Sad Young Men* (1926), includes "The Rich Boy" and "Absolution"; *Taps at Reveille* (1935).

NOTEBOOKS AND LETTERS: *The Crack-up*, ed. by Edmund Wilson (1945); *Letters*, ed. by Andrew Turnbull (1963).

BIBLIOGRAPHY. JACKSON R. BRYER, *The Critical Reputation of F. Scott Fitzgerald* (1967), contains bibliographies of Fitzgerald's work and of books and articles about him. Fitzgerald's manuscripts and papers are in the Princeton Library, and his novels are all in print. A selection of his short stories was edited by MALCOLM COWLEY in 1951, and *The Fitzgerald Reader*, ed. by ARTHUR MIZENER (1963), contains a selection of novels, short stories, and essays. Other work is collected in *Afternoon of an Author*, ed. by ARTHUR MIZENER (1957); *The Pat Hobby Stories*, ed. by ARNOLD GINGRICH (1962); and *The Apprentice Fiction of F. Scott Fitzgerald*, ed. by JOHN KUEHL (1965). Fitzgerald's letters have been edited by ANDREW TURNBULL (1963). There are two biographies: ARTHUR MIZENER, *The Far Side of Paradise* (1965); and ANDREW TURNBULL, *F. Scott Fitzgerald* (1962). Major critical studies are: H.D. PIPER, *F. Scott Fitzgerald* (1965); ROBERT SKLAR, *F. Scott Fitzgerald* (1967); AARON LATHAM, *Crazy Sundays* (1971); and *F. Scott Fitzgerald: A Collection of Critical Essays*, ed. by ARTHUR MIZENER (1963).

(A.Mi.)

Flaubert, Gustave

A romantic by temperament, Gustave Flaubert is regarded as the great master of the Realist school of French literature. Whether he chose a romantic subject (*La Tentation de Saint Antoine*) or one that seemed better suited to the doctrines of Realism (*Madame Bovary*), his work was always based on scrupulous research and observation. He was an indefatigable stylist who strove for complete objectivity and precise expression of the underlying emotions of his characters. His profound compassion for the characters in his novels and his relentless contempt for the bourgeoisie are particularly evident in *Madame Bovary*.

Flaubert, drawing by E.F. von Liphart, 1880. In the Bibliothèque Municipale, Rouen, France.

Early life and works. Flaubert was born in Rouen on December 12, 1821. His father, Achille Cléophas Flaubert, who was from Champagne, was chief surgeon and clinical professor at the Hôtel-Dieu hospital in Rouen. His mother, a doctor's daughter from Pont-l'Évêque, belonged to a family of distinguished magistrates typical of the great provincial bourgeoisie.

Gustave Flaubert began his literary career at school, his first published work appearing in a little review, *Le Colibri*, in 1837. He early formed a close friendship with the young philosopher Alfred Le Poittevin, whose pessimistic outlook had a strong influence on him. No less strong was the impression made by the company of great surgeons and the environment of hospitals, operating theatres, and anatomy classes, with which his father's profession brought him into contact. It was, for instance, with Jules Cloquet, the most learned anatomist of his time, that Flaubert, on receiving his *baccalauréat* in 1840, was sent by his father to visit the Pyrenees and Corsica. Later, on reading *Graziella*, Flaubert was to remark that Alphonse de Lamartine would have written a more powerful novel if he had had a doctor's eye.

Early influences and friendships

Flaubert's intelligence, moreover, was sharpened in a general sense. He conceived a strong dislike of accepted ideas (*idées reçues*), of which he was to compile a "dictionary" for his amusement. He and Le Poittevin invented a grotesque imaginary character, called "le Garçon," to whom they attributed whatever sort of remark seemed to them most degrading. Flaubert came to detest the "bourgeois," by which he meant anyone who "has a low way of thinking."

In November 1841 Flaubert was enrolled as a student at the Faculty of Law in Paris. At the age of 22, however, he was recognized to be suffering from a nervous disease that was taken to be epilepsy, although the essential symptoms were absent. This made him give up the study of law, with the result that henceforth he could devote all his time to literature. His father died in January 1846, and his beloved sister Caroline died in the following March after giving birth to a daughter. Flaubert then retired with his mother and his infant niece to his estate at Croisset, near Rouen, on the Seine. He was to spend nearly all the rest of his life there.

On a visit to Paris in July 1846, at the sculptor James

Pradier's studio, Flaubert met the poet Louise Colet. She became his mistress, but their relationship did not run smoothly. His self-protecting independence and her jealousy made separation inevitable, and they parted in 1855.

In 1847 Flaubert went on a walking tour along the Loire and the coast of Brittany with the writer Maxime du Camp, whose acquaintance he had made as a law student. The pages written by Flaubert in their journal of this tour "over fields and shores" were published after his death under that title, *Par les champs et par les grèves*. This book contains some of his best writing—*e.g.*, his description of a visit to Chateaubriand's family estate, Combourg.

Mature career. Some of the works of Flaubert's maturity dealt with subjects on which he had tried to write earlier. At the age of 16, for instance, he completed the manuscript of *Mémoires d'un fou*, which recounted his devastating passion for Elisa Schlésinger, 11 years his senior and the wife of a music publisher, whom he had met in 1836. This passion was only revealed to her 35 years later when she was a widow. Elisa provided the model for the character Marie Arnoux in the novel *L'Education sentimentale*. Before receiving its definitive form, however, this work was to be rewritten in two distinct intermediate versions in manuscript: *Novembre* (1842) and a preliminary draft entitled *L'Éducation sentimentale* (1843–45). Stage by stage it was expanded into a vast panorama of France under the July Monarchy—indispensable reading, according to Georges Sorel, for any historian studying the period that preceded the coup d'etat of 1851.

The composition of *La Tentation de Saint Antoine* provides another example of that tenacity in the pursuit of perfection that made Flaubert go back constantly to work on subjects without ever being satisfied with the results. In 1839 he was writing *Smarh*, the first product of his bold ambition to give French literature its *Faust*. He resumed the task in 1846–49, in 1856, and in 1870 and finally published the book as *La Tentation de Saint Antoine* in 1874. The four versions show how the author's ideas changed in the course of time. The version of 1849, influenced by Spinoza's philosophy, is nihilistic in its conclusion. In the second version the writing is less diffuse, but the substance remains the same. The third version shows a respect for religious feeling that was not present in the earlier ones, since in the interval Flaubert had read Herbert Spencer and reconciled the Spencerian notion of the Unknown with his Spinozism. He had come to believe that science and religion, instead of conflicting, are rather the two poles of thought. The published version incorporated a catalog of errors in the field of the Unknown (just as *Bouvard et Pécuchet* was to contain a list of errors in the field of science).

From November 1849 to April 1851 Flaubert was travelling in Egypt, Palestine, Syria, Turkey, Greece, and Italy with Maxime du Camp. Before leaving, however, he wanted to finish *La Tentation* and to submit it to his friend the poet Louis Bouilhet and to du Camp for their sincere opinion. For three days in September 1849 he read his manuscript to them, and they then condemned it mercilessly. "Throw it all into the fire, and let's never mention it again." Bouilhet gave further advice: "Your Muse must be kept on bread and water or lyricism will kill her. Write a down-to-earth novel like Balzac's *Parents pauvres*. The story of Delamare, for instance. . . ."

Eugéne Delamare was a country doctor in Normandy who died of grief after being deceived and ruined by his wife, Delphine (*née* Couturier). The story, in fact that of *Madame Bovary*, is not the only source of that novel. Another was the manuscript *Mémoires de Mme Ludovica*, discovered by Gabrielle Leleu in the library of Rouen in 1946. This is an account of the adventures and misfortunes of Louise Pradier (*née* d'Arcet), the wife of the sculptor James Pradier, as dictated by herself; and, apart from the suicide, it bears a strong resemblance to the story of Emma Bovary. Flaubert, out of kindness as well as out of professional curiosity, had continued to see Louise Pradier when the "bourgeois" were ostracizing her

as a fallen woman, and she must have given him her strange document. Even so, when inquisitive people asked him who served as model for his heroine, Flaubert replied, "Madame Bovary is myself." As early as 1837 he had written *Passion et vertu*, a short and pointed story with a heroine, Mazza, resembling Emma Bovary. For *Madame Bovary* he took a commonplace story of adultery and made of it a book that will always be read because of its profound humanity. While working on his novel Flaubert wrote: "My poor Bovary suffers and cries in more than a score of villages in France at this very moment." *Madame Bovary*, with its unrelenting objectivity—by which Flaubert meant the dispassionate recording of every trait or incident that could illuminate the psychology of his characters and their role in the logical development of his story—marks the beginning of a new age in literature.

Madame Bovary cost the author five years of hard work. Du Camp, who had founded the periodical *Revue de Paris*, urged him to make haste, but he would not. The novel, with the subtitle *Moeurs de province* ("Provincial Customs"), eventually appeared in installments in the *Revue* from October 1 to December 15, 1856. The French government then brought the author to trial on the ground of his novel's alleged immorality, and he narrowly escaped conviction (January–February 1857). The same tribunal found the poet Charles Baudelaire guilty on the same charge six months later.

To refresh himself after his long application to the dull world of the bourgeoisie in *Madame Bovary*, Flaubert immediately began work on *Salammbô*, a novel about ancient Carthage, in which he set his sombre story of Hamilcar's daughter Salammbô, an entirely fictitious character, against the authentic historical background of the revolt of the mercenaries against Carthage in 240–237 BC. His transformation of the dry record of Polybius into richly poetic prose is comparable to Shakespeare's treatment of Plutarch's narrative in the lyrical descriptions in *Antony and Cleopatra*. A play, *Le Château des coeurs*, written in 1863, was not printed until 1880.

Later years. The merits of *L'Éducation sentimentale*, which appeared a few months before the outbreak of the Franco-German War of 1870, were not appreciated, and Flaubert was much disappointed. Two plays, *Le Sexe faible* and *Le Candidat*, likewise had no success, though the latter was staged for four performances in March 1874. The last years of his life, moreover, were saddened by financial troubles. In 1875 his niece Caroline's husband, Ernest Commanville, a timber importer, found himself heavily in debt. Flaubert sacrificed his own fortune to save him from bankruptcy. Flaubert sought consolation in his work and in the friendship of George Sand, Ivan Turgenev, and younger novelists—Émile Zola, Alphonse Daudet, and, especially, Guy de Maupassant, who was the son of his friend Alfred Le Poittevin's sister Laure and who regarded himself as Flaubert's disciple.

Flaubert temporarily abandoned work on a long novel, *Bouvard et Pécuchet*, in order to write *Trois Contes*, containing the three short stories "Un Coeur simple," a tale about the drab and simple life of a faithful servant; "La Légende de Saint Julien l'Hospitalier"; and "Hérodias." This book, through the diversity of the stories' themes, shows Flaubert's talent in all its aspects and has often been held to be his masterpiece.

The heroes of *Bouvard et Pécuchet* are two clerks who receive a legacy and retire to the country together. Not knowing how to use their leisure, they busy themselves with one abortive experiment after another and plunge successively into scientific farming, archaeology, chemistry, and historiography, as well as taking an abandoned child into their care. Everything goes wrong because their futile book learning cannot compensate for their lack of judgment.

The profound meaning of *Bouvard et Pécuchet*, which was left unfinished by Flaubert and which was not published till after his death, has been seriously misunderstood by those critics who have regarded it as a denial of

Liaison with Louise Colet

Composition of La Tentation de Saint Antoine

Sources of Madame Bovary

Theme and characteristics of Bouvard et Pécuchet

the value of science. In fact it is "scientism" (and by analogy the confusion of doctrines) that Flaubert is arraigning—*i.e.*, the practice of taking science out of its own domain, of confusing efficient and final causes, and of convincing oneself that one understands fundamentals when one has not even grasped the superficial phenomena. Intoxicated with empty words, Bouvard and Pécuchet awake from their dream only when catastrophe overtakes all of their efforts.

Flaubert has been accused of presenting them as imbeciles, but in fact he expresses his compassion for them: "They acquire a faculty deserving of pity, they recognize stupidity and can no longer tolerate it. Through their inquisitiveness their understanding grows; having had more ideas, they suffered more." Flaubert's satire is thus to some extent the history of his own experience told with a sad humour.

Flaubert died suddenly of an apoplectic stroke on May 8, 1880. He left on his table an unfinished page and notes for the second volume of his novel. Bouvard and Pécuchet, tired of experimenting, were to go back to the work of transcribing and copying that they had done as clerks. The matter that they chose to transcribe was the subject of the notes: it was to be a selection of quotations, a *sottisier*, or anthology of foolish remarks. There has been much controversy about this bitter conclusion, as the form that it was to take was left undetermined in the notes Flaubert left, though the materials were gathered and have been published.

Method of composition. Flaubert's aim in art was to create beauty, and this consideration often overrode moral and social issues in his depiction of truth. He worked slowly and carefully, and, as he worked, his idea of his art became gradually more exact. His letters to Louise Colet, written while he was working on *Madame Bovary*, show how his attitude changed. His ambition was to achieve a style "as rhythmical as verse and as precise as the language of science" (letter of April 24, 1852). In his view "the faster the word sticks to the thought, the more beautiful is the effect." He often repeated that there was no such thing as a synonym and that a writer had to track down *le seul mot juste*, "the unique right word," to convey his thought precisely. But at the same time he always wanted a cadence and a harmony of sounding syllables in his prose, so that it would appeal not only to the reader's intelligence but also to his subconscious mind in the same way as music does and thus have a more penetrating effect than the mere sense of the words at their face value. Composition for him was a real anguish.

Flaubert sought objectivity above all else in his writing: "The author, in his work, must be like God in the Universe, present everywhere and visible nowhere." It is paradoxical, therefore, that his personality should be so clearly discernible in all his work and that his letters, written casually to his intimates and full of disarming sincerity, delicate sensibility, and even exquisite tenderness—side by side with jovial coarseness of expression—should be considered by some critics as his masterpiece.

(R.Dum./J.Ba.)

Importance of the "right" word

MAJOR WORKS

NOVELS: *Madame Bovary, Moeurs de province*, 2 vol. (1857), notable translations are those by Gerard Hopkins (1949) and F. Steegmuller (1957); *Salammbô* (1862; *Salambo*, trans. by E. Powys Mathers, new ed., 1950); *L'Education sentimentale: Histoire d'un jeune homme*, 2 vol. (1870; *Sentimental Education*, trans. by Robert Baldick, 1964); *La Tentation de Saint Antoine* (1874; *The First Temptation of Saint Anthony*, trans. from the version of 1856 by René Francis, new ed., 1924; *The Temptation of Saint Anthony*, trans. by Lafcadio Hearn, new ed., 1932); *Trois Contes* ("Un Coeur simple," "La Légende de Saint Julien l'Hospitalier," and "Hérodias," 1877; *Three Tales*, trans. by Robert Baldick, 1961); *Bouvard et Pécuchet: Oeuvre posthume* (1881; *Bouvard and Pécuchet*, trans. by T.W. Earp and G.W. Stonier, 1936); *Novembre* (1928; Eng. trans., 1932).

PLAYS: *Le Candidat* (1874); *Le Château des coeurs* (1885).

OTHER WORKS: *Par les champs et par les grèves* (1886); *Le Dictionnaire des idées reçues* (1913; *Flaubert's Dictionary of Accepted Ideas*, trans. by Jacques Barzun, 1954); *Bibliomanie* (1926; Eng. trans., 1929).

BIBLIOGRAPHY. The definitive text of Flaubert's novels, short stories, and travel notes is the critical edition, 12 vol. (1938–46), by RENE DUMESNIL, which gives variant readings and an introduction and annotations. For Flaubert's juvenilia and for his plays, reference may be made to the Conard edition, 9 vol. (1926–33), and to the *Supplément à la correspondance générale*, 4 vol. (1954), ed. by RENE DUMESNIL, JEAN POMMIER, and CLAUDE DIGEON.

The standard biography is RENE DUMESNIL, *Gustave Flaubert: l'homme et l'oeuvre* (1932); for a record in English of his life, see P. SPENCER, *Flaubert: A Biography* (1952). Flaubert's passion for Elisa Schlésinger is the subject of E. GERARD-GAILLY, *L'Unique passion de Flaubert* (1932) and *Le Grand amour de Flaubert* (1944). A.A. BERTRAND, *Gustave Flaubert et ses amis* (1927), gives an account of Flaubert's significant relationships with contemporary writers and thinkers.

Of the many critical works on Flaubert, the following 19th-century studies are especially recommended: G. SAINTSBURY, "Gustave Flaubert," *Fortnightly Review*, 29:575–595 (1878); P. BOURGET, *Essais de psychologie contemporaine* (1883, also 1920); and F. BRUNETIERE, *Le Roman naturaliste* (1896). The novelist's work is put into historical perspective in L. DEGOUMOIS, *Flaubert à l'école de Goethe* (1925); F. MAURIAC, *Trois grands hommes devant Dieu* (1930), compares Flaubert to Molière and Rousseau. A. THIBAUDET, *Gustave Flaubert* (1935), and E. MAYNIAL, *Flaubert* (1943), combine biography with critical chapters on the major works and on style and aesthetics.

There have been a great number of studies that deal with the individual works by Flaubert, but among the more modern general criticism are: V.H. BROMBERT, *The Novels of Flaubert* (1966); STRATTON BUCK, *Gustave Flaubert* (1966); and B.F. BART, *Flaubert* (1967). ENID STARKIE, *Flaubert: The Making of the Master* (1967), is a penetrating analysis. Flaubert's influence on, and links with, modern literary developments are discussed by H. KENNER, *The Stoic Comedians* (1964), a comparative study of Flaubert, Joyce, and Beckett; and by J.L. DOUCHIN, *Le Sentiment de l'absurde chez Gustave Flaubert* (1970). JEAN-PAUL SARTRE, *L'Idiot de la famille: Gustave Flaubert*, 2 vol. (1971), is a study of the novelist, whom the writer uses as a tool for his own dissection of France's bourgeoisie.

Flight, History of

It is a curious fact, but true, that man's age-long observation of birds in flight impeded, rather than accelerated, the development of man flight. All human attempts to fly on flapping wings led only to frustration or disaster, for what comes naturally to birds is almost certainly impossible for man to duplicate with his clumsy mechanisms. The only valid bird flight/man flight analogue appears to be in gliding and soaring. Wing flappers (ornithopters) have contributed little to man-flight history, and, although some research is still in progress, they seem likely to be of little significance.

In this article, the generic term man flight is used to describe any human navigation above the surface of the earth in any form of vehicle—balloon, airship, glider, powered aircraft, rocket, etc. "Aviation" refers generally to flight in heavier-than-air craft. "Aeronautics" is the science of aviation; "aerostatics" is the science of lighter-than-air flight; and "astronautics" the science of space flight. A fuller treatment of certain specialized areas of this subject will be found in AIRCRAFT; AIRCRAFT, MILITARY; ROCKETS AND MISSILE SYSTEMS; and TRANSPORTATION, AIR.

From a historian's point of view, exploring the development of man flight is a rewarding exercise. A substantial percentage of the significant events to be dealt with have occurred within the memory of persons still living in the 1970s, and many of the early experimenters were themselves articulate. Their notebooks and other records have been preserved, and a considerable amount of the actual hardware with which they worked still exists. Of greater importance, the invention and development of flight vehicles coincided historically with the development of photographic processes. Excellent visual records of many of the men, machines, and events that made flight history are available.

The subject has always attracted widespread coverage by the press, sometimes with dubious accuracy. Fortunately, it also engaged the serious attention of scholars concerned with separating fact from fancy. James Means of Boston, an early collector and compiler of aeronautical literature, made a notable contribution in this area with the publication of his *Aeronautical Annual*s—in 1895, '96, and '97. More recently, Charles Dollfus and Henri Bouché in France, J.E. Hodgson and Charles Gibbs-Smith in England, and Paul Garber of the Smithsonian Institution in the U.S. have established a firm and factual base for future air historians to build on. Other important contributors include V.M. Sokolsky in the Soviet Union, Ernst Klee in Germany, and Hidemasa Kimura in Japan. Their published works have provided prime sources of information for this condensed survey of flight history.

This article is divided into the following sections:

I. Flights of fancy

Had the early philosophers not been obsessed with the wing-flapping flight of birds, something resembling the gliders of the late 19th century might have evolved earlier. All the necessary materials—woods, fabrics, and cordage—were readily at hand, and skilled craftsmen were plentiful. What was lacking was the concept of air as a fluid and of its behaviour as it flows around three-dimensional bodies (see AIRCRAFT).

Practically all religions clothed their celestial beings in birdlike forms. Egyptian, Minoan, and Syrian deities were equipped with magnificent wings. The Greek and Roman gods and goddesses seemed to fly without visible means of support (except for Mercury with his winged heels), but the seraphim and cherubim of the Hebrews and the heavenly hosts of later persuasions were all provided with wings.

As time went on, earthly kings often assumed the role and perquisites of deities. Accordingly, magicians and court historians were called upon to create, if not the fact, at least the legend that their masters had been airborne. Thus, during the Han dynasty in China (206 BC to AD 220), the emperor was reputed to have travelled far in his flying chariot, while the throne of the Persian king Keykāvūs was supposed to have been airborne by four eagles.

In Europe serious speculation about man flight occupied such thinkers as Roger Bacon (*c.* 1214–1294) and Leonardo da Vinci (1452–1519). John Wilkins (1614–1672), lord bishop of Chester and one of the founders of the Royal Society, summarized four possible ways in which man might fly: (1) with the spirits of angels, (2) with the help of fowls, (3) with wings fastened to his body, and (4) in a flying chariot. He questioned the practicability of the first three but forecast the evolution of the fixed-wing airplane thus:

> If fowl can so easily move itself up and down in the air without so much as stirring the wings . . . it is not improbable that when all due proportions of [a suitable apparatus] are found out, and when men by long practice have arrived to any skill and experience, they will . . . come very near unto the imitation of Nature.

Flight in early science fiction

During the next 100 years, science-fiction writers popularized the idea of flight—including space flight. Francis Godwin (1562–1633), Samuel Brunt (*c.* 1727), Cyrano de Bergerac (1619–1655), and others described flights to the moon and elsewhere. Restif de la Bretonne (1734–1806) pictured explorers cruising over wilderness areas of Australia on a combination of batwings and umbrellalike devices.

The invention of the balloon in 1783 brought the imaginative writers back to earth. Once a means had been found for man to leave the ground, fancy became somewhat related to fact; and for a time, fantastic adventures by balloon and airship were popular subjects.

Toward the end of the 19th century, the greatest of aviation fiction writers, Jules Verne (1828–1905), emerged in France. He himself was not an inventor and made only one balloon ascension in his life (with Godard at Amiens in 1873), but in imagination he developed an extraordinarily prophetic feeling for the future of the in-

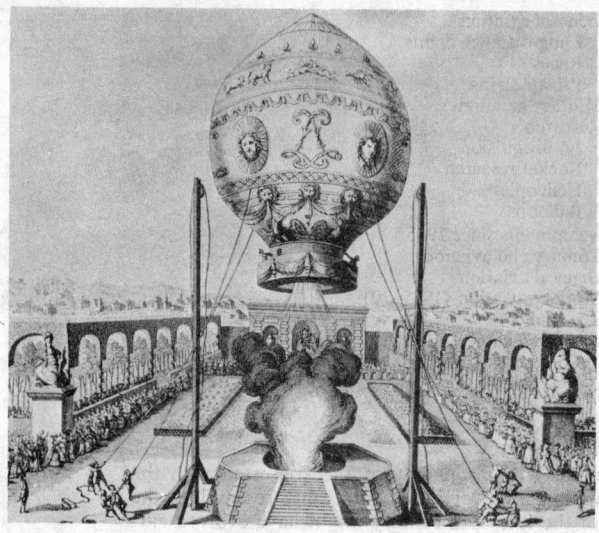 

Figure 1: *Early lighter-than-air craft*.
(Left) Montgolfier balloon carrying Pilâtre and d'Arlandes on the first manned free balloon
flight, November 21, 1783. (Right) Santos-Dumont airship, about 1900.
By courtesy of (right) the National Air and Space Museum, Smithsonian Institution, Washington, D.C.;
photograph, (left) Brown Brothers

ventions of his day. He wrote of exploratory voyages
around the world by airship and by helicopter and forecast a rocket trip to the moon from a launching site in
Florida. He even described in detail the weightlessness
that space travellers were to experience in flight.

II. Developments to 1900

LIGHTER-THAN-AIR—EARLY SPECULATIONS

It took many years for man to realize that the air around
him was a thing, not impalpable nothingness extending
to the outer limits of the sky. The invention of the mercury barometer in 1643 provided the first proof that air
was, in fact, a gas that not only had weight but that also
responded (as do all gases) to changes in temperature
and pressure. Once that was recognized, the way was
opened for speculation as to why smoke rose through air.
Eventually, as advancing scientific sophistication permitted the isolation of lighter-than-air gases, it was logical to think of a bubble of such gas floating like a cork
in a sea of denser air. The first hint of the application of
this concept occurs in the notes of the medieval philosopher Roger Bacon, after which, for many years, nothing
further was recorded on the subject.

About 1670 a Jesuit monk, Francesco de Lana, hit upon
the same idea, but in reverse. He concluded that no air
should be lighter than some air and, therefore, that a
bubble of vacuum should rise through, and at some
point of equilibrium, float about in the denser atmospheric air. He published a design for a man-carrying airship
supported by four such vacuum balloons. The theory
was good, but its realization was difficult. The thin copper
spheres he proposed to evacuate would have collapsed
under the external air pressure long before any measurable lifting force was developed. Impractical as it was,
the concept was a notable philosophical achievement for
the time. De Lana abandoned any effort to develop it,
however, on the ground that any attempt to fly would be
regarded by the Creator as impious.

Later (c. 1755), after the structure of the Earth's atmosphere was better understood, another priest, Galien, in
France, reasoned that a bagful of low-density air collected from the higher altitudes should float about at
lower levels and could support a considerable load. In
1766 the isolation of hydrogen by the British chemist
Henry Cavendish had a profound effect on lighter-than-
air activity. Although the special properties of hydrogen
had been known to scientists since 1766, its application to
aeronautics (or, more properly, to aerostatics) did not occur to anyone for well over a decade. The honour of the
first lighter-than-air demonstration and subsequently the
first man flight went to a much more common gas—hot
air.

BALLOONS AND BALLOONISTS (1783–1900)

The work of the Montgolfiers and J.-A.-C. Charles.
The inventors of the balloon were Joseph and Étienne
Montgolfier, sons of a paper manufacturer of Annonay,
in southeastern France. Watching smoke rise in the chimney, they had concluded that it possessed some mysterious property, which they called "levity." They made up a
small silk bag, which they held over a fire. It filled with
smoke and, when released, rose to the ceiling. After several other private experiments, they issued invitations to
all the citizens of Annonay (including members of the
Departmental Council, who happened to be meeting at
the time) to assemble in the town square on June 5, 1783,
to witness an ascension of their "Globe Aérostatique."
This was a spherical bag about 30 feet in diameter (about
23,000 cubic feet), made up of light fabric backed by
paper. Early prints show it as fastened together by rows
of buttons and buttonholes. Held over a smoky fire
fuelled by chopped wool and straw (it was assumed that
"levity" was a special property of smoke), it rapidly inflated to its full spherical form and, to the great astonishment of the audience, rose rapidly (allegedly over a mile
in the air) and drifted more than a mile and a half from
its starting point before touching down.

The excitement was great, and reports of the event
spread rapidly throughout France. The Academy of Sciences asked for full information, and Étienne journeyed
to Paris to report to that distinguished body.

Use of hydrogen. Even before Étienne arrived in Paris, the physicist J.-A.-C. Charles, with the assistance of
two Robert brothers, Anne-Jean and Nicolas-Louis,
sought to duplicate the Montgolfier performance. Not
knowing then of the simple means used to inflate the balloon at Annonay, they adopted the newly isolated gas,
hydrogen. (For some years thereafter, any hydrogen balloon in France was called a "Charlière.") They fabricated a balloon of varnished silk, some 15 feet in diameter, and produced hydrogen to fill it on a scale never before attempted. Released from the Champ de Mars, Paris,
before an enthusiastic crowd, on the afternoon of August
27, 1783, it rose through a heavy rainstorm and descended some 15 miles away near the small village of
Gonesse. The local peasants, alarmed by the apparition
descending from the clouds, attacked the "monster" with
scythes and pitchforks and tore it to pieces.

On September 12 Joseph Montgolfier appeared by invitation before the Academy (Benjamin Franklin was in the
audience) to describe the work at Annonay. Montgolfier
was invited to repeat his experiment before Louis XVI
and his court at Versailles. A large aerostat was built but
was destroyed in a storm four days before the scheduled
event. A new one was hastily put together, and at about

The Mont-
golfiers'
"Globe
Aéro-
statique"

1:00 PM on September 19, 1783, it was released from the Great Court at Versailles carrying a sheep, a rooster, and a duck as passengers. The objective was to determine whether or not high-altitude travel had any deleterious effects on living creatures. They survived the ordeal, and the stage was set for man's first venture into the air.

A new and enlarged aerostat—some 70 feet in height —was prepared. It differed from its predecessors in having a circular gallery slung beneath it for the accommodation of the aeronauts, with arrangements for maintaining a smoky fire of straw and wool during flight. At first it was proposed that a pair of condemned criminals be used for the experiment. One Jean-François Pilâtre de Rozier, who had volunteered for the flight, however, protested that such were not worthy of the honour of being first to take to the air. In this he was joined by François Laurent, marquis d'Arlandes, who wished to share the adventure.

Man's first flight

Louis XVI finally gave his consent, and after a number of tethered test flights (the longest of which lasted nine minutes at an altitude of 320 feet), Pilâtre and d'Arlandes took off in free flight from the Jardin de la Muette in the Bois de Boulogne. The date was November 21, 1783. Some 23 minutes later, after reaching an altitude of over 3,000 feet and an estimated distance of something short of ten miles, they landed safely near Gentilly, to complete man's first aerial voyage (see Figure 1, left).

Shortly thereafter (December 1, 1783), J.-A.-C. Charles, accompanied by Nicolas-Louis Robert, took off from the Tuileries Gardens in a large "Charlière." About two hours and 27 miles later, the balloon descended gently near the small town of Nesle, northeast of Paris. Robert climbed out of the car. The lightened balloon with Charles aboard promptly rose and continued the flight to land finally some miles away near Tour-de-Laye.

A comparison of notes by the aeronauts at once established the supremacy of the hydrogen balloon. Whereas Pilâtre de Rozier and d'Arlandes had remained airborne only by continuous labour to keep their smoky fire alive, Charles and Robert had drifted comfortably over the landscape without effort. The pattern for future development was thus set. The explosive nature of hydrogen gas was only learned later, over subsequent decades and at a cost of a number of lives. It was not until the loss of the German airship "Hindenburg" at Lakehurst, New Jersey, in 1937, that hydrogen was abandoned as a lifting gas.

Broadening interest. Meanwhile, the Paris flights stirred a worldwide interest in ballooning that carried into the 20th century. In the first 50 years following 1783, over 800 ascensions were made in England alone, and over 470 aeronauts (persons known to have made one or more flights) were recorded. Forty-nine of these were women.

Jean-Pierre Blanchard

Many names crowd the early records. Notable among them was Jean-Pierre Blanchard, who between 1784 and 1809 made flights in most European capitals. He crossed the English Channel by air on January 7, 1785, accompanied by a Boston physician, John Jeffries. He made the first balloon flight in America at Philadelphia on January 9, 1793, in the presence of George Washington and indoctrinated John Wise, the first American balloonist. Blanchard performed the earliest experiments in parachuting, using animals as subjects. He died in Paris in March 1809 after a fall from a balloon.

Among other experimenters of the period were the Sadlers, father and son, of Ireland; Lunardi and Zambeccari of Italy; Gay-Lussac and Biot in France; and Green and Coxwell in England. The latter four are credited with making the first scientific observations of meteorological phenomena and of human behaviour in the upper atmosphere.

Félix Nadar of France must be mentioned on two counts: (1) he made the first aerial photographs from a captive balloon in 1858 and many successful aerial photographs (1863) from a huge balloon, "Le Gèant," fitted with a complete photographic laboratory; and (2) he was instrumental in organizing the *Ballon Poste,* which carried mail and passengers out of Paris during the siege in 1870.

Military balloons. The potential of the balloon in military situations had long been recognized. Francesco de Lana, who had proposed the use of vacuum globes (1670) as noted, had foreseen the advantages of balloons in war but concluded that "God would not suffer such an invention to take effect, by reason of the disturbance it would cause to the civil government of men." In spite of such forebodings, the first balloon corps in history was formed in France in 1793. Captive observation balloons were used at the siege of Mainz in 1794, and free balloons took part in the Battle of Fleurus in June 1794.

During the American Civil War, observation balloons were in use by both sides. T.S. Lowe, a Connecticut Yankee and a pupil of John Wise, provided four balloons and their portable gas generators to the Federal Army's Aeronautics Corps. These were used during the campaigns of 1862–63 for observation, and the westward movement of Lee's army from its Rappahannock camp to start the Gettysburg campaign was first detected by balloon observation. At one time, direct telegraphic communication was established between a balloon and the White House. The Confederacy made only two known attempts to launch observation balloons—one of the hot air variety and one filled with illuminating gas at Richmond—but neither was particularly successful.

Ill-fated North Pole attempt. The last great ballooning adventure of the 19th century began when August Andrée and two companions, Strindberg and Fraenkel, set out July 11, 1897, from the island of Spitsbergen, in a free balloon, to attempt to drift across the North Pole. They vanished into the Arctic wastes. Some 33 years later (1930), a Norwegian exploring party discovered their frozen bodies, together with Andrée's journal and even photographic plates, which were developed and printed. The balloon had drifted eastward, off course, and gone down; Andrée and his crew had been able to survive the crash but had perished in their attempt to walk back to civilization.

AIRSHIPS PRIOR TO 1900

From earliest ballooning days, man sought to free himself from his dependence upon the uncertain winds. Truly to navigate the skies, propulsion was needed. Sails, oars, and paddle wheels for balloons were tried repeatedly. All failed. Not until the principle of the Archimedean screw was revived and applied to propulsion was any degree of success attainable.

The transformation of the spherical free balloon into a navigable airship required two things: adoption of the cigar shape, and invention of an adequate power plant.

Gen. J.-B.-M. Meusnier of the Engineer Corps of the French Army came close to many of the right answers— on paper—as early as 1783, but he was well ahead of the state of the mechanical arts and died before anything practical could be accomplished.

A century passed before the first airship capable of steady flight under control, able to return to its starting point at will, could be demonstrated. Meanwhile, many inventors tried, and some nearly made it. Sir George Cayley, the "father of British aeronautics" (see below *Heavier-than-air—the experimenters*), like Meusnier, committed his ideas on airship design to paper (1816– 34) but never reduced them to practice.

Early power plants. The greatest drawback of the time was lack of a lightweight, self-contained power plant. A model airship driven by clockwork was demonstrated in London in 1843. Later (1850), a Parisian clockmaker, Pierre Jullien, built a model, "Le Précurseur" (also fitted with clockwork power), that incorporated all the elements of a modern, nonrigid airship.

In 1852, making use of the sketches of Meusnier and Cayley and inspired by Jullien's model, Henri Giffard built a steam-driven airship with a cigar-shaped gasbag some 144 feet in length with a capacity of 88,000 cubic feet. He took off from the Hippodrome in Paris on September 24, 1852, and flew under control to Elancourt, near Trappes. He did not attempt to fly against the wind nor to return to his point of departure, but the date establishes the beginning of man's practical conquest of the

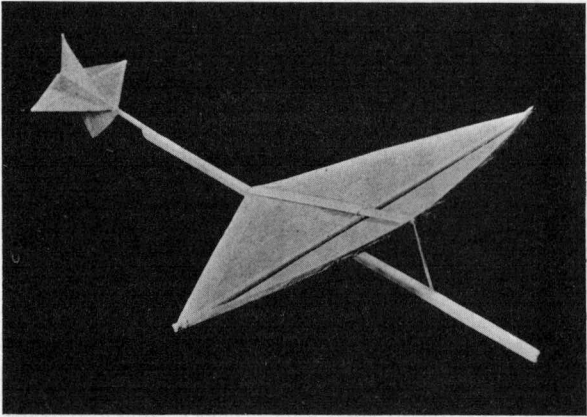 

Figure 2: *Early gliders.*
(Left) Model of a glider by Sir George Cayley, of Yorkshire, England, about 1804. (Right)
Biplane glider built by Otto Lilienthal of Germany, 1895.
By courtesy of (left) the National Air and Space Museum, Smithsonian Institution, Washington, D.C.;
photograph, (right) Authenticated News International

The first
dirigibles

air. It also marked the introduction of the term dirigible, meaning steerable, as applied to airships. The terms airship and dirigible since then have remained almost synonymous.

Several attempts at airship design were reported from America between 1866 and 1870; *e.g.*, the Marriott steam-driven dirigible in San Francisco and a pedal-powered, elongated balloon of Solomon Andrews from Perth Amboy, New Jersey. Neither was a success.

In 1865 a German inventor, Paul Haenlein, filed a patent for a semirigid airship to be driven by an internal-combustion gas engine. The machine, 164 feet long, was actually built in 1872 but lacked sufficient power for effective propulsion and control.

An interesting but abortive attempt to apply electric power to airships occurred in 1883. Gaston and Albert Tissandier, inspired by the Exposition d'Électricité in Paris in 1881, built a small, elongated dirigible powered by an electric motor and a large bank of lead storage batteries. The ship made a trial flight on October 8, 1883, but its heavy batteries and feeble power made it helpless in even the mildest breeze, and the Tissandiers shortly abandoned their effort.

Success finally came on August 9, 1884, when two French army captains, Charles Renard and A.-C. Krebs, flew the airship "La France" from Chalais-Meudon to Villacoublay and back in 23 minutes. "La France" was also electrically powered, but its large lifting capacity, coupled with redesigned and more efficient electrical motor and batteries, made the difference. A number of other successful flights were made in the months following. Although only little further work was done with electrical power, the day of controlled mechanical flight had finally arrived.

The closing years of the 19th century were marked by the appearance in Paris of one of the most colourful figures in flight history—the Brazilian-born sportsman-scientist Alberto Santos-Dumont. He built and flew his first small airship in 1898 and continued his experiments first in lighter-than-air and subsequently in heavier-than-air craft well into the first decade of the 20th century (see below *Aviation in adolescence; Balloons and airships*).

Beginning in 1896, Germany took an active interest in airships. Even before Graf von Zeppelin launched his first large, rigid airship in 1900 (see below *Balloons and airships*), two interesting developments appeared: the Wölfert dirigible, "Deutschland" (June 1897), and the Schwarz all-metal airship (November 1897). Neither was successful; both crashed during test flights. But Wölfert was the first to install a gasoline engine in any flight vehicle, and Schwarz pioneered the use of thin sheet aluminum (a relatively rare metal at the time) as a covering material for aircraft.

HEAVIER-THAN-AIR—THE EXPERIMENTERS

George Cayley. Throughout the years, the conflicting claims of inventors to priority have plagued aviation historians. On one point, however, there is clear consensus. The title of "father of British aeronautics" and, in fact, of all aeronautics rests with Sir George Cayley.

It is true that Leonardo had sketched wing-flapping devices and even a form of helicopter (*c.* 1500), and kites in many forms were commonplace prior to the 17th century. Also, the records of the 18th century contain accounts of many weird and wonderful machines for mechanical man flight. But at that time, as always, men's dreams far exceeded their scientific and technical capabilities.

It was in the early 1800s that George Cayley came upon the scene. Charles Dollfus characterizes Cayley as "the outstanding technical mind [in the field of flight] of the first third of the nineteenth century . . . the true inventor of the airplane . . . one of the most powerful geniuses in the history of aviation."

Cayley's active interest in man flight spanned the years from 1792 to his death in 1857. A perceptive theorist and an active experimenter with models (see Figure 2, left) and with full-scale gliders, he eventually had at his disposal all the aerodynamic theory required for the design of a man-carrying airplane. The problem, as he saw it, was "to make a surface support a given weight by the application of sufficient power to overcome the resistance of the air." Unfortunately, no light-weight, self-contained power plant was then available. That vital component was still half a century away.

This was the problem that plagued all inventors who considered the flight of heavier-than-air craft up to the end of the 19th century. Until earthbound automobiles generated a requirement for a compact power plant that could operate on available liquid fuels, would-be aircraft designers saw no choice but to turn to the crude steam engines of the day. The best of engines, with the necessary boilers, fireboxes, condensers, fuel, and water, ran up the ratio of total weight to available power to an impossibly high figure for aeronautical use. Even now, with the advantages of light metals, high-energy fuels, and the most modern design techniques, no serious attempt is being made to apply steam power to aircraft, though in the 1800s some came remarkably close to configurations resembling successful 20th-century aircraft.

The search
for a
suitable
power
plant

Gliders, models, and kites. On the record, it is apparent that those who concentrated on experiments with gliding flight made the most substantial contributions toward the final man-flight solution. They did not waste effort in attempts to solve the extremely difficult and costly task of combining crude and undeveloped mechanisms with light and fragile structures. Flights by Cayley and many others in the second half of the 19th century contributed much to basic knowledge of flight in machines without power.

Model makers and kite flyers also made important contributions, notably the mid-century collaboration of William Samuel Henson and John Stringfellow, which resulted in some far-reaching predictions on the format of a modern airplane and on future intercontinental airline operations—but only on paper. The invention of the box kite (1893) by Lawrence Hargrave in Australia had a positive influence on airplane design in the early 1900s.

Premature attempts at powered flight. The most conspicuous (and expensive) failures of the period were experienced by those courageous optimists who made premature attempts to take the giant leap to full-scale powered flight without intermediate steps. In 1857 Félix du Temple, a French naval officer, constructed a monoplane design fitted with a locomotive-like boiler and smokestack, but succeeded only in puffing his way down a long ramp without leaving the ground. In 1875 Thomas Moy, a British engineer, in a tethered conglomeration of wires and fabric steamed his way around a circular track, rose briefly for a few inches, but never actually took off.

A more ambitious project took shape in Russia in 1884, when Aleksandr Mozhaysky designed and built a steam-driven monoplane. Launched down the ramp of a ski jump, and airborne for a few seconds before hitting the ground, it provided the basis for a subsequent Russian claim of the world's first airplane flight.

In France, also in 1884, M.-A. Goupil, encouraged by results obtained with a kite-glider prototype, built a bird-like monoplane and a steam power plant to install in it. He never put the two together, and no attempt to fly it ever took place. The construction, however, is of interest on two counts: (1) his design was the first to incorporate opposite-acting ailerons for lateral control, and (2) many years later (1917) Glenn Curtiss, in America, built and flew a reproduction of Goupil's airplane (powered, however, with a gasoline aircraft engine) as a part of his attempt to set aside certain Wright patents covering lateral control devices.

One near miss of the period must be noted. A French self-made engineer and mechanical genius, Clément Ader, built a batlike steam-propelled monoplane that he christened "Eole." On October 9, 1890, on a friend's estate near Paris, he succeeded in leaving the ground under power. He was airborne for some 160 feet (50 metres). This was substantiated by witnesses, but despite Ader's subsequent claims of "flight" the most that can be said is that he made a short-duration hop. It was in no sense a sustained, controlled, powered flight such as was made by the Wrights in 1903, and all subsequent investigations have established that "Eole" was totally incapable of such flight.

Moy's concept of testing tethered aircraft on a circular track appealed to other experimenters. His former associate, Horatio Phillips (who, in 1884 and the years following, patented the first designs for the thick wing sections, with curved upper and lower surfaces, now used on all airplanes), so tested (1893) a curious multiplane model whose wing system resembled a Venetian blind. Except to confirm his own wing theories, no other use was made of the device.

The most spectacular and certainly the most expensive test rig of this character was put together at Baldwyn's Park in Kent by Sir Hiram Maxim, inventor of the Maxim machine gun. Over many years his experiments in aviation, which were said to have cost him some £20,000, culminated finally in the design and construction of a huge steam-driven biplane with two propellers. It was tested in rails on a circular track, fitted with a restraining rail designed to prevent lifting off more than a few inches. During one of its trials, a guard rail broke; the machine swerved off the track and was extensively damaged. Discouraged, Maxim terminated the project.

Otto Lilienthal. Though the steamers held centre stage for a decade, they all huffed and puffed without results, and it fell to the gliders to cross the final gap—to provide the flight experience needed to take advantage of internal-combustion power when it became available. The greatest of them, and the man whose work provided the initial impetus to the Wright brothers, was Otto Lilienthal (1848–96) of Germany.

Lilienthal's early studies of bird flight had led him to experiment (1868) with wing-flapping devices (ornithopters), but shortly he turned to gliding and in this area made his greatest contribution. He built a number of batlike monoplane and biplane gliders (see Figure 2, right) and between 1893 and August 9, 1896 (the day of his fatal crash), made over 2,000 gliding flights from hilltops. On one occasion he covered over 1,000 feet in gliding flight. Eventually, he was able to fly in winds up to 15 miles per hour.

Lilienthal was primarily concerned with the stability and control of his machines. Originally, he did not use any movable aerodynamic control surfaces in flight but sought for an inherently stable machine that could be controlled by shifting his body weight. This proved to be unsatisfactory, and it was in the course of an experiment to test a movable elevator that his glider spun out of control and he sustained fatal injuries. He was convinced that it was essential to get the feel of flight in gliders before attempting powered flight—a lesson that was scrupulously followed by the Wrights five years later and that unquestionably contributed to their success.

Octave Chanute. Lilienthal's work was widely reported and came to the attention of a French-born, American-educated engineer, Octave Chanute, who was himself deeply interested in the problem of man flight. In 1896, when he was well over sixty years old, he and a group of assistants began gliding experiments on the sand dunes of Lake Michigan near Chicago. He wanted a better system of control than the Lilienthal body-shifting technique. He sought "an apparatus with automatic stability in the wind." During 1896–97 his group built and made over 1,000 flights in five different glider types. They kept careful records and were the first to use a series of single photographs (motion-picture cameras were not then available) showing consecutive phases of a single flight.

Chanute became a close friend and frequent correspondent of the Wright brothers as they began their gliding experiments in 1900. They adopted his bridge-truss biplane configuration and drew heavily on his gliding experience. On at least one occasion (1901) Chanute visited their camp at Kill Devil Hills near Kitty Hawk and made photographs of some of their glider flights.

III. Developments from 1900 to 1914

INTRODUCTION OF THE GASOLINE ENGINE

By 1899 a number of lines of experimentation were converging. Vast sources of petroleum had been discovered and tapped, and chemists had found the means of unlocking its ancient sun-generated energy. Metallurgists could produce high-strength steels and had already isolated lightweight aluminum. Toolmakers had evolved methods and machines to fabricate intricate mechanical devices, and scientists had harnessed electrical energy. All these in combination were essential to the development of the lightweight internal-combustion engine, the indispensable missing ingredient for man flight.

A requirement for such a source of power had already been established by the horseless carriage. In Europe and in America curious vehicles without harness and shafts (but usually with whip sockets still in place) were already churning up road dust to the gibes and guffaws of a skeptical public. So, by 1900, for the first time in history, the necessary power plant in a crude but usable form was waiting in the wings—for its wings.

During the first two years of the new century, while the Wrights were testing their gliders at Kitty Hawk, an Austrian piano maker turned engineer, Wilhelm Kress (1846–1913), was putting together a flying boat with three monoplane wings in tandem. The machine had two large propellers amidships, belt-driven by a Mercedes engine designed to produce 40 horsepower at a weight of 440 pounds. Actually, however, the engine delivered only 30 horsepower with a total weight of 836 pounds—a combination that militated against successful flight. Kress, himself, then 68 years of age, made the first attempted takeoff (1901) from Lake Tullnerbach. The machine showed some signs of leaving the water but was

Attempts to use steam power *(margin)*

Glider stability and control *(margin)*

Kress's flying boat *(margin)*

wrecked when it ran aground. It was, however, notable for two innovations: (1) it marked the first attempted use of a gasoline engine in an airplane; and (2) it employed thin-walled steel tubing for its body structure. (Steel tubing for fuselage construction became commonplace only in the early 1920s.)

SAMUEL PIERPONT LANGLEY (1834–1906)

The distinguished third secretary of the Smithsonian Institution, astronomer, mathematician, and inventor, spent the last twenty years of his life in active research in aeronautics. Few men before him pursued the subject more painstakingly or more scientifically, and none left as complete a record of experimental results. The *Langley Memoir on Mechanical Flight* (Smithsonian, 1911) is required reading for all serious students of man-flight history. But, in the end, Langley failed to fly. His only reward was ridicule and accusation of wasting public funds.

Aerodynamic research. He began his work (c. 1886) when he was professor of astronomy at the Western University of Pennsylvania (now the University of Pittsburgh). The wind tunnel as a tool for aerodynamic research had not appeared in America. Langley adopted a whirling arm device as his original test rig. This was a counterweighted 30-foot beam, pivoted at one end, and arranged to rotate horizontally, sweeping a 60-foot-diameter circle. With a steam engine driving the central shaft, top speeds up to 70 miles per hour could be attained. Models of wings and other shapes (including several stuffed birds) were mounted at the free end of the arm, and measurements made of their air resistance and other characteristics as the arm rotated. This was the first serious effort at systematic aerodynamic research in America. Appropriately, one of the principal U.S. government flying fields and its associated research laboratories bear Langley's name.

After his appointment to the Smithsonian (1887), Langley continued his aeronautical work. While still in Pittsburgh he had begun experiments with small models powered by twisted or stretched rubber bands. By 1891, in Washington, he had built and tested over 30 different configurations, keeping accurately detailed records of their characteristics and performance. Late in 1891 he realized that rubber-powered models had little practical future and began work to develop small steam power plants. At this time he coined the term aerodrome (Greek, "air runner") to describe his flying vehicles. By 1896 he had designed, redesigned, built, rebuilt, and tested Aerodromes numbers 0 to 6. This work involved literally thousands of changes and modifications to the hundreds of mechanical components involved. These are all carefully documented in his *Memoir*.

Between 1894 and early 1896 a number of launchings were attempted from a catapult device mounted on top of a small barge anchored in the Potomac River below Washington, D.C. Results were uniformly disappointing until May 6, 1896, when Aerodrome Number 5 went off successfully and flew some 3,200 feet in a series of wide circles. Recovered from the water, Number 5 made a second flight on the same day, this time covering some 2,300 feet. On November 28, in the same year, a modified machine of the same general design (Number 6) made a stable flight of some 4,200 feet in one minute, 45 seconds. These flights were observed and photographed by the inventor of the telephone, Alexander Graham Bell, himself an active student and experimenter in aeronautics (see below *Glenn Curtiss and the Aerial Experiment Association*).

Charles Manly, later to become Langley's principal assistant, introduced Part II of the *Memoir* (1897–1903) as follows:

> Although in 1896 Mr. Langley had made a firm resolution not to undertake the construction of a large man-carrying machine . . . yet the longing to take the final great step of actually transporting a human being through the air, which the successful flights of the models had now for the first time in the history of the world actually proved to be possible, soon became irresistible.

At this point history took a hand. The United States was then involved in a war with Spain over Cuba. With unusual prescience, Pres. William McKinley and the War Department, intrigued by the possibilities of a flying machine as an instrument of warfare, granted Langley an allotment of $50,000 with which to build a man-carrying Aerodrome (December 1898).

Power-plant problems. Langley had no doubts of his ability to build the airframe, but he was gravely concerned, as were all experimenters before him, over the power plant. Steam was out of the question. Some form of internal-combustion engine was clearly indicated, but none of the automobile manufacturers of the time would undertake to build an engine to meet his specifications; *i.e.*, to develop 12 horsepower continuously at a total weight not to exceed 100 pounds.

Finally, after communicating with all known sources in America and in Europe, he signed a contract (December 12, 1898) with one S.M. Balzer, an engine builder in New York City, to deliver an engine to the Langley specification by February 28, 1899. The engine proved to be a disappointment, and Langley went to Europe to search for a suitable power plant. Before his departure he turned the design problem over to his young engineering assistant, Charles M. Manly, recently graduated from Cornell. Langley returned empty-handed, but Manly's reworking of the Balzer engine was beginning to bear fruit. Actually, Manly abandoned most of the original design and built his own engine.

It was a remarkable accomplishment. By the spring of 1903 the engine, with a weight of 187 pounds, was developing over 50 horsepower. On a later occasion (August 1904, after the ill-fated flight tests), the Manly engine ran for ten consecutive hours at a rating of 52.4 horsepower. No other engine was to equal that record for many years.

Final attempts. While work was progressing on the large engine, a one-quarter scale Aerodrome was built, powered by a small, air-cooled, five-cylinder gasoline engine that developed just over three horsepower at 1800 rpm. Although work on the model was completed by October 1901, because of work priority given to the large machine it was not test-flown until August 8, 1903. Only one flight was made—1,000 feet in 27 seconds—but it demonstrated to Langley's satisfaction that the design of the large Aerodrome was fundamentally correct. This, incidentally, was the first flight of a heavier-than-air vehicle powered by a gasoline engine.

Shortly after the model flight, the full-scale machine was ready for test. By early October the necessary modifications had been made on the launching mechanism to accommodate the Aerodrome. On October 7, Charles Manly took his place at the controls, the engine roared, and the machine was released. Result: total failure. The Aerodrome plunged nose down into the river only a few yards from the boat. As a skeptical and disgruntled reporter described the incident in the next morning's *Washington Post*, "It simply slid into the water like a handful of mortar." Manly was unhurt and the wreckage salvaged. Two months later, December 8, the test was repeated. Immediately after launching, the rear wing structure collapsed and the machine went into the river, tail first. To the end of his life, Langley ascribed the accident to a failure of the launching mechanism. Again, Manly survived unhurt.

This was the end for Langley. He was subjected to a flood of ridicule and abuse in the press. Government funds were cut off, and a congressional investigation was threatened over wastage of public money "because, some man, perchance a professor wandering in his dreams, was able to impress [the War Department] that his aerial scheme had some utility." Langley never recovered, and he died two years later.

Only nine days after the Aerodrome's final crash, Orville Wright rose from the sands of Kitty Hawk on man's first successful airplane flight.

Curtiss and the Langley machine. There is a historical footnote to the Langley machine: in connection with a long and bitter legal controversy over claims of Glenn

Langley's aerodromes

Manly's engine

Curtiss and the Wright patents, the original Langley Aerodrome was lent to Curtiss by the Smithsonian Institution in 1914 and sent to his factory at Hammondsport, New York. There it was reconditioned, allegedly in accordance with the original plans, though significant structural modifications were made to enable the craft to operate off the water as a seaplane. It made one or two brief off-the-water hops (five seconds) with the original Manly engine, and later, after further structural changes, and with the substitution of a Curtiss aircraft engine and a propeller, it made several straightaway flights at low altitude over Lake Keuka, in New York. Returned to the Smithsonian, it was then labelled as "the first airplane capable of sustained free flight with a man," to the great annoyance of Orville Wright (Wilbur Wright had died in 1912).

The entrance of the United States into World War I, and the subsequent pooling of all aeronautical patents, ended the legal controversy, but the personal bitterness between Wright and the Smithsonian persisted for many years. In view of the institution's claims, Orville refused to deposit the original "Flyer" in the Smithsonian. In 1928 he sent the historic aircraft to the Science Museum in London, where it remained on display (except for the war years 1939–45, when it was placed underground for safety) until 1948. At that time, after due apologies by the then Smithsonian secretary, C.G. Abbot, the machine was returned to the United States aboard a U.S. aircraft carrier and, on December 17, 1948, formally installed in the Arts and Industries Building in Washington, D.C., where it is now displayed.

WILBUR AND ORVILLE WRIGHT

That the Wright brothers of Dayton, Ohio, were the actual inventors of the world's first practical powered airplane is unequivocally accepted by all serious aeronautical historians.

The notion that the Wrights were semi-literate bicycle mechanics who happened to stumble upon the secret of flight is fanciful. The fact is that, with limited formal education, they became research scientists in the most literal sense. Says Dollfus, "Brought up in austere simplicity, they shared the same character, combining the soul of the apostle with the spirit of practicality. . . . These qualities permitted them to triumph where all their forerunners had been halted." The Wrights first tried printing and publishing a newspaper, then built up a bicycle manufacturing and repair business in Dayton. This provided them with the tools, the mechanical knowledge, and the income on which their subsequent experiments in aviation were based. In 1899, after becoming interested in bird flight and reading of Lilienthal's experiments, they determined to make a serious study of aviation. A request to the Smithsonian in Washington, D.C., for a list of books and articles on flying was the starting point. Chanute's *Progress in Flying Machines*, published in 1894, became their basic text, but they absorbed everything else that was available. In a relatively short time their intensive studies transformed them into scientists. Their own contributions to the literature of flight are contained in over a thousand pages of the two-volume edition of *The Papers of Wilbur and Orville Wright*, edited by M.W. McFarland of the U.S. Library of Congress.

The Wrights did not make the mistake common to many of their predecessors; *i.e.*, to attempt powered flight without first learning to fly. They made their first tests on kites (1899–1900). From this they progressed first to tethered gliders (1900) and finally to gliders in free flight (1901–02). Only after becoming airmen in the true sense of the word were they ready in 1903 to attempt powered, man-carrying, controlled flight.

Between 1900 and 1903, they embarked on a remarkable program of research and development. The prior art had produced little but speculation and a record of unsuccessful experiments. Wilbur summarized the difficulties that then obstructed success as "(1) those which relate to the construction of sustaining wings; (2) those which relate to the generation and application of the power required to drive the machine through the air; (3) those relating to the balancing and steering of the machine after it is actually in flight." He conceded that some progress on items (1) and (2) had already been made, but considered that until item (3) could be resolved, "all other difficulties are of minor importance."

Methodically and persistently they set about finding solutions to all three, but in the end it was their work on the interrelated problems of flight stability and control that brought success.

Considering today's vast accumulation of aerodynamic, structural, and power-plant data in thousands of textbooks and hundreds of millions of informational bits stored in computers, the Wright's technical resources were thin indeed. Step by step they had to test every wing and propeller shape, first by mounting crude measuring devices on the handlebars of a moving bicycle, later in a small wind tunnel of their own construction. Painstakingly, they recorded, tabulated, and applied these data. But it was on stability and control research that they concentrated their greatest effort.

Kites and gliders. They began with kites. They built the first in August 1899, a biplane of five-foot span of the Chanute type, fitted with control wires by which the wing cellule could be twisted—or warped—in flight. Wing-warping to achieve lateral control became the core of the subsequent Wright patents. The success of the kite led them to undertake a larger (17-foot span) man-carrying glider. It was completed in September 1900, and they moved their experiments to a site near Kitty Hawk, North Carolina, where the U.S. Weather Bureau had reported the existence of steady and reasonably constant winds and where the sand dunes offered cushioning for hard landings. (Secrecy was never a factor in the selection of Kitty Hawk, as has sometimes been asserted.)

The new machine was first flown as an unmanned kite, and after some skill had been acquired, it was flown with a man aboard but with ground control. The few attempts at free flight were disappointing (based on Lilienthal's data, the wing area appeared to be too small), and the brothers returned to Dayton to reconsider.

During that winter they built a larger (22-foot span) glider with an innovation—a front horizontal rudder (*i.e.*, elevator). Returning to Kitty Hawk in July 1901, the Wrights found that their revised calculations were still uncertain. At one point they almost duplicated Lilienthal's fatal crash. They did succeed, however, in overcoming some of the machine's erratic behaviour, and they eventually made a successful glide of some 300 feet. Octave Chanute spent some time at the Kitty Hawk camp and made a number of photographs of the Number 2 machine in flight.

At this point, discouraged by the scarcity of reliable aerodynamic information ("Truth and error were everywhere so intimately mixed as to be indistinguishable," Wilbur wrote in the *Century* magazine in September 1908), they almost gave up. But building their own wind tunnel, they began systematic compilation of their own data. (The original wind tunnel and some of the experimental wing and propeller sections tested are now in the Franklin Institute in Philadelphia.) Here they became scientists. When they interpreted and applied their results to the construction of a practical flying machine, they became engineers.

In 1902 they turned the corner. In August and September 1902, they built Glider Number 3 (see Figure 3, top) which incorporated all their experimental findings. It retained the forward elevator but added a double fixed fin, which later was to become the rudder. Returning to North Carolina in September, they made over 1,000 glides on this machine. The early flights were unsatisfactory, but when the fixed tail fins were made steerable, so that banking and yawing (turning) could be coordinated (a characteristic common to all successful airplanes), the stability and control problem was solved. Gibbs-Smith writes, "After this vital step, the Wrights had a fully practical glider—the first in history—and with it made some hundreds of perfectly controlled glides." They applied for a patent in March 1903.

Flights with Curtiss engine

Early research of the Wrights

Figure 3: *The Wright brothers' aircraft.*
(Top) Modified Glider Number 3 in flight at Kill Devil Hills, near Kitty Hawk, North Carolina, 1902. (Bottom) Orville Wright piloting the "Flyer" at Kill Devil Hills, December 17, 1903.
By courtesy of (top) Air Force Central Museum, Wright-Patterson Air Force Base, Ohio, (bottom) National Air and Space Museum, Smithsonian Institution, Washington, D.C.

Powered flight. Back in Dayton, with this achievement behind them, they finally turned their attention to powered flight but like Langley, they could find no manufacturer to make an engine of the power and weight they could use. Like Langley, they designed and built their own in their bicycle shop, with the expert help of their assistant, Charles Taylor.

Wright "Flyer I" (later known as the "Kitty Hawk") was not a reconstruction of Glider Number 3, with engine attached. It was an entirely new machine. A biplane with a wing span of 40 feet four inches and a wing area of 510 square feet, it retained the front elevator and rear rudder configuration of 1902. The Taylor engine was a horizontal four-cylinder type mounted in the centre of the lower wing, turning two chain-driven, counter-rotating, pusher propellers. The pilot, as in the gliders, lay prone on the lower wing beside the engine. It was designed to land on a pair of sledlike skids, and takeoff was accomplished from a simple droppable dolly running along a 60-foot monorail track.

The inevitable constructional and mechanical delays put off the trials until late in 1903. With winter almost upon them, the machine was finally ready for test by mid-December. On December 14, 1903, they tossed a coin for the first-flight honour. Wilbur won and made the attempt. Due to overcontrol of the elevator, the "Flyer" plowed into the sand at the end of the launching rail. Three days later, after repairs and a weather delay, Orville had his turn. At 10:35 AM, on December 17, into a 20–22-mph wind, he made a successful takeoff, flew for 12 seconds, and landed without damage—the first controlled man-carrying mechanical flight in history (see Figure 3, bottom).

That morning, three more flights were accomplished, with alternating pilots. On the fourth, Wilbur flying, the machine was airborne for 59 seconds, covering 852 feet on the ground, the equivalent of a flight of one-half mile in still air. After the fourth flight, while the aircraft was being returned to the starting rail, a strong gust of wind overturned and damaged it beyond immediate repair.

Before breaking camp and starting back to Dayton, Orville sent a wire to his father: "Success four flights

History-making flight at Kitty Hawk

Thursday morning all against twenty-one mile wind started from level with engine power alone average speed through air thirty-one miles longest 57 seconds inform press home Christmas." The "57 seconds" was a telegrapher's error—59 seconds was correct.

Aftermath. Ten years later, Orville Wright, looking back on that day, said,

With all the knowledge and skill acquired in thousands of flights in the last ten years, I would hardly think today of making my first flight on a strange machine in a twenty-seven mile wind, even if I knew that the machine had already been flown and was safe . . . Yet faith in our calculations and the design of the first machine, based upon our tables of air pressures, secured by months of careful laboratory work, and confidence in our system of control developed by three years of actual experiences in balancing gliders in the air, had convinced us that the machine was capable of lifting and maintaining itself in the air, and that, with a little practice, it could be safely flown.

Few editors paid any attention to the story, and those who used it embroidered it with facetious embellishments à la Jules Verne. Incredibly, almost five years went by before the citizens of the United States really accepted the fact that the Wrights had flown in 1903. Even their friends and neighbours in Dayton took the news very calmly. Wilbur and Orville were a pair of nice fellows, but who were they to make such claims when the most learned professors of the day had already proved mathematically that mechanical man flight was impossible!

Later flights. Wilbur and Orville also took the situation very calmly; in fact, it was exactly to their liking. They called no press conferences; they could not spare the time. During the winter of 1903–04 they built a new and larger "Flyer," with a much improved engine. In the spring of 1904 they rented a 90-acre cow pasture, "Huffman Prairie," near Dayton. There they set up shop, assembled the new machine, and began to fly.

The Wrights were not secretive about their work. It was there in the open for anyone to see. When first ready to test the Number 2 "Flyer," they sent invitations to the press, but after one or two postponements of the promised flight due to weather, and unforeseen mechanical difficulties, the already skeptical reporters went off on more promising leads.

The summer of 1904 was employed in perfecting their flight techniques and eventually in learning to make turns in the air. On September 20, Wilbur made the first full circle in flight and returned to land at his starting point. This feat generated the first published eyewitness account in history of the flight of any airplane. It appeared, strangely enough, in the January 1905 issue of a small magazine called *Gleanings in Bee Culture*, published in Medina, Ohio. The editor, A.I. Root, had travelled to Dayton to see the Wrights fly and had observed the first circular flight. On November 9, Wilbur stayed in the air for over five minutes, making almost four complete circles of the pasture.

First full-circle flight

"Flyer" Number 3, incorporating all the improvements gained from the experience with Number 2, was first flown at Huffman Prairie on June 23, 1905. By October 16 some 49 flights had been completed, including several ranging in length from 11 to 24½ miles, at average speeds of 38 mph. Most flights were terminated only because of exhaustion of fuel. It could be said, and with confidence, that for all practical purposes the conquest of the air had been accomplished.

The Wrights' attitude toward publicity had also changed. The word had got around, and others, particularly abroad, were beginning to show interest in their work as possible competitors. Their basic patent had not yet been granted (it was not to be issued until 1906), and the Wrights were concerned about legal protection of, and financial reward for, their work. To avoid possibilities of military or commercial surveillance, they stopped all flights and prohibited any public inspection of their airplanes from October 16, 1905 until May 6, 1908. They then went back to Kitty Hawk with the greatly improved Number 3 machine to refresh their skill as pilots.

The changes in detail were many, but the most obvious

were the upright positions of both pilot and engine. The prone pilot position was abandoned in favour of a seated configuration on the lower wing, facing forward. The flat engines of the No. 1 and No. 2 Flyers were replaced by a more powerful and more efficient vertical, in-line type.

Signal Corps project and European activities. Between 1907 and 1908 the Wrights entered into negotiations with the U.S. War Department for an experimental airplane for military use. Their original proposal was received with a notable lack of enthusiasm. The Signal Corps could see little value in a flying machine but finally drafted a specification that was designed to discourage, if not to eliminate, all bidders. Required was a machine capable of flying for one hour carrying a pilot and a passenger (combined weights not less than 350 pounds); top speed at least 40 mph, and enough fuel on board for 125 miles of flight. In addition, the aircraft had to be readily demountable to be transferred from place to place in a standard horse-drawn army wagon. All this for a price of $25,000.

Although understandably discouraged by their own government's attitude, the Wrights went to work on the project. At the same time, however, they began to look for markets overseas.

A few experimental short-duration, straightaway hops had already been made in France by Santos-Dumont, Ferber, Blériot, and others, but nothing had been seen in Europe comparable to the by now routine performances at Dayton. When reports finally did filter through, the reaction abroad was total skepticism. A technical paper on the Wrights' work, read before the French Aéro-Club early in 1906, was covered by the *New York Herald* (Paris edition) under the headline "Flyers or Liars?"

In 1907 the brothers divided the field: Orville remained at home to develop the machine to meet the Signal Corps specification; Wilbur packed up a new and much improved "Flyer" and shipped it to France for demonstration.

Orville was the first to get his machine into the air. (Wilbur's "Flyer" was unaccountably impounded by French Customs and was not released for many months after its arrival.) The army demonstrator was shipped to Ft. Myer, Virginia, and, beginning September 3, was put through public trials on the parade ground. With Orville Wright at the controls, it passed or exceeded all specifications. Suddenly the American press awoke to the realization of its mistake, and press reports became ecstatic and numerous.

But the triumph was short-lived. On September 17, with Lieut. Thomas E. Selfridge as passenger, a guy wire snapped, fouled a propeller, and the machine dove into the ground out of control. Selfridge was killed instantly, to become the first fatality in a powered airplane. Orville was seriously injured.

Wilbur
Wright
at Le Mans

In France, after many delays, Wilbur made his first flight at Le Mans on August 8, 1908. In the following months he proved to the world that both his piloting and his "Flyer" were far superior to anything that Europe could offer. On December 31 he established a world endurance record of two hours 20 minutes, covering a distance of 77½ miles to win the Michelin Prize. The European press and the technical community went wild. The Wrights were indeed flyers—not liars.

Orville, still suffering the effects of the Ft. Myer accident, joined Wilbur in France in mid-January 1909. After making demonstration flights in several European countries, they returned to the United States in May to prepare for renewed Signal Corps trials with a new machine. Orville again began test flights at Ft. Myer on June 28. By July 30 the army was satisfied that the specifications had been met (or exceeded), and the Signal Corps acquired its first airplane. This machine is now on display in the National Air and Space Museum in Washington, D.C. That fall, Wilbur set up the army's first flying school at College Park, Maryland.

Later years. Wilbur Wright contracted typhoid fever and died on May 30, 1912. For a few years Orville Wright carried on alone, manufacturing and testing his own aircraft and becoming involved in a bitter controversy with Glenn Curtiss over basic patents.

GLENN CURTISS AND THE AERIAL EXPERIMENT ASSOCIATION

Between 1908 and 1914 Curtiss had become the Wrights' greatest competitor. It was no friendly rivalry. Not only fame but potential fortunes were at stake, and the bitterness ran deep on both sides.

Curtiss was a natural competitor. Basically a mechanic and a showman, he was never a scientist nor even an engineer. He emerged first as a racer of motorcycles. His growing reputation as a designer and manufacturer of light-weight, high-speed gasoline engines brought him to the attention of Thomas Baldwin, then (1904–09) building and flying nonrigid airships (see below *Balloons and airships*). In 1907 his work with Baldwin attracted the notice of Alexander Graham Bell, experimenter with large tetrahedral kites and aspirant to the solution of the man-flight problem.

Aerial Experiment Association. Bell was the key figure and financial backer of the Aerial Experiment Association (AEA) with headquarters at Hammondsport, New York, and a test site at Bell's estate in Nova Scotia. He gathered around him a group of young, enthusiastic, and capable men, including Lieut. Thomas E. Selfridge (later killed in the crash of the Wright "Flyer" at Ft. Myer), F.W. Baldwin, J.A.D. McCurdy, and Glenn Curtiss. The association's objective was to conduct scientific research in heavier-than-air flight.

The AEA adopted the pusher-biplane configuration of Chanute and the Wrights, with the added advantage of more powerful and lighter engines, and a decided improvement in takeoff and landing gear, a three-wheeled undercarriage. The latter permitted operation from reasonably smooth fields without the somewhat clumsy launching rail and landing skid required by the Wright machines. (Gibbs-Smith considers the use by the Wrights of skids, after everyone else had shifted to wheeled landing gear, to have been one of their few serious mistakes.)

Wheeled
landing
gear

In turn, each of the association's members tried airplane design. Baldwin was first off, with Selfridge's "Red Wing." On March 12, 1908, he flew 319 feet from ice-covered Lake Keuka. A few months later (May 22, 1908), Baldwin's "White Wing," piloted by Curtiss, flew more than 1,000 feet in 19 seconds. Curtiss' own design, "June Bug," covered some 2,000 yards in one minute 43 seconds on July 4, 1908, to win a prize posted by *Scientific American* magazine. Later (November 1908), he mounted the aircraft on a pair of canoe-like floats, renamed it the "Loon," and attempted unsuccessfully to take off from the surface of the lake.

McCurdy's contribution, "Silver Dart," was tested at Bell's Nova Scotia estate. On February 23, 1909, he took off from the frozen surface of a nearby lake to record the first heavier-than-air flight in Canada.

During the next few years Glenn Curtiss became one of the leading figures in aviation both in the United States and abroad. In an improved machine, the "Gold Bug" (four-cylinder, 30-horsepower engine), he made the first public flights in New York City and won the second *Scientific American* prize at Mineola, Long Island, New York, on July 17, 1909, with a flight of 24.7 miles at 35 mph. This also won for him official representation for the Aero Club of America at the Gordon Bennett Cup race at Reims, France, in August of that year. With a more powerful engine (eight-cylinder, 50-horsepower) and some structural modification, his "Golden Flyer" won the race at 47 mph.

Back in the United States, Curtiss in 1910 won a $10,-000 prize posted by the New York *World* for a flight from Albany to New York City. These successes established him as the principal competitor of the Wrights and led to the battle over patents that dragged through the courts for several years. Principal issue was the method of lateral control: wing warping (Wright), or opposite-acting ailerons (Curtiss). Finally, on January 13, 1914, the courts ruled in favour of the Wrights, by which time wing warping was a dead issue. Practicality and aerodynamic superiority had long since decided in favour of the aileron.

Seaplanes. While the Wright litigation was in full swing, Glenn Curtiss established a reputation in another vital area—he gave wings to the United States Navy by the development of successful hydro-airplanes and flying boats. Although the "Loon" of 1908 had not got off the water, the concept had been pursued.

Curtiss first cooperated with the navy in proving that an airplane could be launched from and landed upon a ship. The initial demonstration was a takeoff by Eugene Ely, a U.S. civilian pilot, from a platform erected on the bow of the cruiser USS "Birmingham" at Hampton Roads, Virginia, November 14, 1910. A little over two months later (January 18, 1911) Ely, in a similar machine, landed aboard the battleship USS "Pennsylvania" in San Francisco harbour, was turned around, and took off safely for a return flight ashore.

Shortly after Ely's flights Curtiss' research on properly shaped floats for seaplanes paid off. In the A-1 (a modification of the standard land plane) he made successful water takeoffs and landings. On February 17, 1911, he flew from the naval base at San Diego out to the USS "Pennsylvania" at anchor in the harbour, landed alongside, and was hoisted aboard by one of the ship's cranes. After paying his respects to the commanding officer, he and his plane were lowered into the water for a successful flight back to the base. For this, Curtiss was awarded the Collier Trophy for 1912 "for the greatest achievement in aviation in America . . . during the preceding year," and the navy became airborne.

With the navy's interest assured, Curtiss turned his attention to developing a truly integrated water aircraft. So far, his hydro-airplanes had been simply standard land types mounted on floats instead of wheels. In 1912 he built the "Flying Fish," the prototype for all true flying boats—a boatlike hull to accommodate pilot and passengers, to which wings, engines, and propellers were attached.

AVIATION IN ADOLESCENCE

Activities in Europe. While the Wrights were successfully flying circles and figure eights in America, aviation in Europe was only slowly coming to life. The hopes raised by Lilienthal and Pilcher in 1890 had faded. The dream of man flight had once more seemed out of reach. Gibbs-Smith summed up the situation between 1902 and 1905 as follows:

No systematic, persistent and progressive study of the problems of glider control was made, hence no one came near to any kind of proficiency in gliding, let alone mastery . . . Europeans had available all the necessary facts and clues in Chanute's articles, and . . . in the two excellent Wright papers of 1901 and 1902, which were easily accessible. Yet, during the three years (1902–04) the total product of European endeavors amounted to only some four ineffectual gliders.

Ferber, Archdeacon, and Esnault-Pelterie tried so-called exact copies of Wright gliders with little success. Léon Levavasseur learned little from a full-sized bird-form machine (1903). They all failed to solve the basic stability and control problems.

Only little progress was made through 1905. A few tentative trials of float-mounted gliders towed behind motor boats were made in France by Archdeacon, Blériot, and Voisin. All followed Wright designs, or showed strong relationship to Hargrave's box kites, and the results were not promising.

The turning point in Europe came late in 1906. After two unrelated failures (one in France and one in Denmark), Alberto Santos-Dumont coaxed his awkward canard (tail first) 14-bis biplane off the ground at Bagatelle for six flights, the longest covering some 720 feet in 21⅕ seconds, at a maximum altitude of six feet. It was a modest achievement compared with the Wrights' performances, but it earned him an Aéro-Club de France prize of 1,500 francs and the honour of having made the first powered airplane flight in Europe. His reputation as an airplane designer, however, rests more solidly on a subsequent machine, the fly-weight single-place "Demoiselle" of 1909.

During 1907 things began to move, but slowly. Of some 14 aircraft tested, only six showed any ability to get off the ground. Of these, only one, built by Gabriel and

Charles Voisin for the French sportsman Henri Farman, remained airborne over a minute. Its nearest competitors were up only 55 and 45 seconds. Farman, in the course of his one minute-plus record, achieved the first full circular flight in Europe. Less spectacular, but possibly of greater importance, was the appearance (late in 1907) of Léon Levavasseur's eight-cylinder, 50-horsepower Antoinette engine, which was to power many of Europe's successful aircraft.

Finally, in 1908, European aviation got off the ground. Greatest impetus came from the performance of the imported Wright "Flyer" at Le Mans in August 1908. Wilbur Wright's mastery of the air astonished the European experimenters after their years of disbelief.

Even before the Wright demonstration, however, some progress had been made. Henri Farman and Léon Delagrange were rated the best of the European pilots. The former flew 12 miles in 20 minutes in July after having made a short hop with a passenger in May. By year's end Farman had doubled his July performance. Louis Blériot, in a monoplane of his own design, came close to Farman's records. Each made true cross-country flights of 11 and 20 minutes, respectively, in October. Elsewhere in Europe, England, Denmark, Germany, and Italy, dozens of curiously designed aircraft were making tentative hops.

Two major events marked the year 1909: (1) the crossing of the English Channel on July 25; and (2) the first

Figure 4: *Historic flights.*
(Top) Louis Blériot's Blériot XI plane, which flew the English Channel from Les Boraques, near Calais, to Dover, July 25, 1909. (Centre) The Curtiss NC-4, which flew from the U.S. to England via Newfoundland, the Azores, and Portugal, May 1919. (Bottom) The Ryan "Spirit of St. Louis," flown by Charles A. Lindbergh nonstop from Long Island, New York, to Paris, May 20–21, 1927.

Figure 5: *Early autogiro and helicopter designs.*
(Left) Autogiro Number 4, designed by Juan de la Cierva of Spain, about 1923. (Right)
Helicopter attempt by the Russian Igor Sikorsky, 1909.

By courtesy of (left) National Aeronautics and Space Administration, (right) the National Air and Space Museum,
Smithsonian Institution, Washington, D.C.

great aviation meet at Reims in August. The Channel
crossing ended the concept of political isolation by
oceans, and the second established beyond all doubt that
aviation was here to stay.

English
Channel
crossing

The English Channel posed a challenge to aviation that
could not be resisted. At midsummer three of Europe's
best pilots, Hubert Latham, Louis Blériot, and the Count
de Lambert, were encamped along the Pas-de-Calais preparing for the attempt. De Lambert was delayed by aircraft damage. Latham, in an Antoinette monoplane, got
away first in early morning July 19. Halfway across his
engine quit, and he landed in the water, to be rescued
shortly by a French torpedo boat. Six days later, Blériot,
in his Blériot XI monoplane, took off from Les Boraques
near Calais and after a flight of 37 minutes landed on a
hillside near Dover (see Figure 4, top).

The Blériot flight touched off a flurry of excitement all
over Europe and focussed attention on the first of the
great aerial circuses that marked the years 1910–12.
The Grande Semaine d'Aviation, at Reims, sponsored by
the local champagne industry, attracted not only the best
airplanes and pilots of the world but also tens of
thousands of people from all walks of life anxious to see
for themselves the miracle of man flight. Prizes totalled
over 200,000 francs.

Meets and prizes. For the next few years prize money
for record flights became plentiful, many of the donors
being newspapers eager to profit from the attendant
publicity. Race meets and aerial circuses brought keen
competition among itinerant pilots.

From 1910 to the advent of war in 1914, the aviation
carnival in America as in Europe became a "movable
feast." The first important meet was held in Los Angeles
in January 1910 with Curtiss and Louis Paulhan setting
world speed and altitude records. In September, the Harvard–Boston Meet at Squantum, Massachusetts, attracted
United States and European competitors, with thousands
of spectators, including Pres. William Howard Taft. The
biggest show was staged in Belmont Park, Long Island,
New York, October 22–31. Some 40 aircraft, mostly of
American or French design, participated. Thousands of
New Yorkers turned out to witness speed runs (up to 61
mph), altitude records (over 9,700 feet), and a race
around the Statue of Liberty. The newspapers of the
country posted substantial prizes ($15,000–$30,000) for
record flights to or from their respective cities. A manufacturer of a popular soft drink subsidized the first transcontinental flight. C.P. Rodgers, in a well-marked ("Vin
Fizz") Wright biplane, accompanied all the way by a
special train carrying first-aid equipment, a mechanic,
spare parts, and his wife, flew from New York to Los
Angeles in a series of 68 hops (and almost as many
crashes) between September 7 and November 5, 1911.
His plane is now in the Smithsonian Institution. In Europe the London *Daily Mail* put up £10,000 for a flight
to be completed in less than 24 hours covering 183 miles

between London and Manchester. Two pilots, Claude
Grahame-White and Louis Paulhan, both in Farman
biplanes, made a race for it on April 23–28, 1910, with
Paulhan the winner in four hours two minutes.

The Italian Aviation Society offered 70,000 francs for
the first pilot to cross the Alps. Jorge (or George) Chávez
flew from Switzerland to Italy via the Simplon Pass on
September 23, 1910, in a Blériot monoplane, but on landing his machine crashed, and he was killed.

By 1911–12, racing from town to town, called "circuit racing," became popular in Europe, over courses
up to 1,000 miles. The temptation to fly in all kinds of
weather in such contests left a long trail of wrecked machines and dead pilots. But stimulated by such competition, airplane and engine performance improved tremendously. Altitudes leaped to thousands of feet, speeds
approached 100 mph, and endurance flights were measured in hours rather than minutes.

Circuit
racing

France was still the aviation leader of Europe, but other
countries were joining the sport: in January 1911 France
had 353 certified pilots, England 57, Germany 46, Italy
32, Belgium 27. Rather amazingly, the United States,
where heavier-than-air flight had begun, had only 26.

HELICOPTERS

During the decade when the first airplanes were attracting wide public attention, the concept of vertical flight by
direct action of Archimedean-screw propellers (envisioned by Leonardo and postulated by Cayley) was not
entirely forgotten. A number of helicopter models had
appeared at the London Aeronautical Exhibit of 1868,
and flying models with steam and electric drives were
demonstrated during the late 1870s. Also, Jules Verne's
fictional hero, Robur le Conquérant (1886), cruised
around the world in a remarkable craft airborne by 37
pairs of vertical propellers mounted atop 37 masts.

In 1904 Col. Charles Renard (who had piloted the first
controlled airship) used an unmanned, twin-rotor, gasoline-powered helicopter as a part of his continuing researches in aerodynamics. About the same time, Paul
Cornu tried a model of somewhat similar configuration.
Encouraged by its performance, he tried a full-scale machine powered by a 24-horsepower Antoinette engine.
On November 13, 1907, Cornu made several lift-offs of
a few seconds' duration, the first by any helicopter. Once
airborne, however, the machine proved uncontrollable
and was shortly abandoned.

In America in 1908, Thomas Edison, after experimenting with vertical air screws driven by electric motors
mounted on platform scales to measure lift, commented,
"Whatever progress the airplane might make, the helicopter will come to be taken up by the advanced students
of aeronautics." But over 30 years were to pass before
his prediction came true. A young Russian, Igor Sikorsky,
at that time was making his first serious studies of the
helicopter. During 1909 and 1910 he built two machines

powered by a 25-horsepower Anzani engine (see Figure 5, right). The most that either helicopter could do was to lift its own weight off the ground without a pilot. Many years later (November 1964) in a lecture before the New York Wings Club, Sikorsky said of his experiences in 1910,

> ... by that time I had learned enough to recognize that with the existing general state of the art, engines, materials and ... lack of experience.... I would not be able to produce a successful helicopter at that time.

Nevertheless, several others tried. After Cornu gave up, a large and ungainly combination of airplane and helicopter (the Broquet–Richet No. II) managed to rise a few feet, only to crash on landing. Also, a persistent Danish experimenter, J.C.H. Ellehammer, in his twin-rotor helicopter attained a maximum altitude of about two feet (1912) but did not achieve flight. The real difficulty, then and for many years thereafter, was control. Until Juan de la Cierva (see below *Rotary wing aircraft*) designed independently articulated roto blades for his first autogiro, that problem remained unsolved.

BALLOONS AND AIRSHIPS

With the advent of the steerable airship (dirigible), little interest remained in free ballooning until it became an important tool for upper-atmospheric research in the 1930s. Actually, scientific research of this sort had its beginnings very early. Blanchard and Jeffries made scientific observations on their cross-Channel flight in January 1785, and the French Academy of Sciences sponsored several upper-air research flights by Gay-Lussac and Biot in 1804. Coxwell and Glaisher in England (September 1862) recorded atmospheric data up to an altitude of approximately five miles. On July 31, 1901, two German physics professors, A. Berson and A.J. Sürring, made an atmospheric survey flight to an altitude of some 35,000 feet, a record that stood for 30 years, when it was exceeded by Auguste Piccard.

Ballooning. During the first decade of the 20th century ballooning was looked upon largely as a form of sport. The Aéro-Club de France encouraged competition by establishing rules for racing and by promulgation of records for distance, altitude, etc. Its Balloon Park at Saint-Cloud near Paris became a centre for amateur and professional aeronauts. During 1913 some 479 ascensions were recorded from this site alone.

Balloon racing became an international sport. Every year new records were made and broken, both in Europe and in America. But apart from such popular activities, limited use was made of free balloons as preliminary training for airship crews.

Airships. With the increasing availability of suitable engines (*c.* 1900), airship experimentation proliferated. New and improved designs emerged, and it became necessary to differentiate among three distinct categories: nonrigid, semirigid, and rigid airships.

Nonrigid airships consist simply of an elongated fabric gasbag (envelope), below which a car for the accommodation of crew and power plant is suspended by ropes or cables. The bag holds its shape solely because of the gas pressure inside. If the gas escapes, the whole apparatus collapses into a shapeless mass of fabric. All airships prior to 1900 were of this class.

Semirigid airships have a structural keel (or truss) fore and aft to which the envelope is directly attached. The keel provides housing for crew and power plant. If the gas escapes, only the envelope collapses. This type became popular in the 1900–20 period.

Rigid airships are characterized by an external structural skeleton covered by light fabric to preserve the overall shape surrounding a series of internal lifting-gas cells. Power plants, control surfaces, and passenger and crew accommodations are integrated into the main structure of the airship. The external appearance of the ship remains the same whether or not the gas cells are inflated. These make up the Zeppelin class of airship, which reached its developmental peak during World War I and persisted in both military and commercial form into the 1930s.

Nonrigid airships. Prior to 1904 when he turned his attention to heavier-than-air flight, Alberto Santos-Dumont was the world's greatest builder of nonrigid airships. A wealthy sportsman, Santos-Dumont flew largely for fun but created great public interest in aviation and contributed much to the technology of airship flight. Success came largely from his adoption for aeronautical purposes of the light gasoline engine then in popular use in small tricycle automobiles. His ships numbers 1–3 (1898–99) were not successful. None was able to return to the point of departure under its own limited power. Number 4, with a nine-horsepower engine (1900), did little better, but it established the configuration for Number 5, which, with installation of a 16-horsepower engine weighing only 215.6 pounds, began to show positive results. The car was an elongated, open, triangular wooden framework with a single propeller at the rear and with engine and pilot located near the centre (see Figure 1, right). The engine was in the open, but the aeronaut rode in a small wicker balloon basket mounted some 20 feet forward of the engine. The whole apparatus was suspended beneath an elongated fabric envelope by means of steel piano wire, the first use of metal instead of rope in nonrigid airship construction.

In this machine Santos-Dumont made his first attempts at the Deutsch de la Meurthe Prize established in 1900 for the first flight from the Aero Park at Saint-Cloud, around the Eiffel Tower, and return. His first several tries were unsuccessful and included one crash in the courtyard of the Trocadéro. That same evening he started construction of a new airship, Number 6, in which, after several more abortive efforts, he completed the flight to win the prize. During the following five years a series of 11 more of his airships appeared at Saint-Cloud, including one, Number 9, a small ship of only three horsepower, in which he landed and took off on the Champs-Élysées and in the Bois de Boulogne.

After Santos-Dumont turned to airplanes, interest in nonrigids tapered off in Europe. The French Société Zodiac built a series of small ships that were sold in limited numbers to the military services of France, The Netherlands, Russia, and Belgium, prior to World War I.

In America, exhibition flights in nonrigid airships (along with parachute jumps from hot-air balloons) became stock features at county fairs and expositions. A dozen or more pilots and their ships toured the racing circuits around the country from 1900 to 1910. Thomas Scott Baldwin, one of the prominent figures in this activity, in search of a suitable light-weight engine for his airship, discovered Glenn Curtiss, then building motorcycle engines, and started him on his career as an airplane designer and pilot. The Baldwin-Curtiss team produced the first U.S. military aircraft, the SC-1 airship, test flown at Ft. Myer, Virginia, in 1905 and subsequently purchased by the U.S. Army. Little further interest was shown in nonrigid ships by the military services of any country until the latter part of World War I, when both France and Britain built large numbers for offshore antisubmarine patrol work.

Semirigid airships. The success of a series of large semirigid airships built for the French government by Paul and Pierre Lebaudy (1903–07) focussed attention on this class of airship. "La Jaune" was the first (1902), followed in sequence by "La Patrie," "La République," and "La Liberté" (1908), each larger and more powerful than its predecessor. The latter two were 200 feet long, 33 feet in diameter, and powered by 70-horsepower engines. Each carried a crew of four. Ships numbers 2 and 3 were destroyed in accidents, but the performance of the fleet was so impressive that foreign governments became interested. Russia purchased two French airships, and England followed suit, taking delivery of one in September 1910 and another later in the year. The latter covered the 230 miles from the factory at Moisson, France, to Farnborough, England, in 5½ hours.

By 1902 Germany was committed to the development of rigid airships under Graf von Zeppelin but was also keeping a watchful eye on the French semirigids. Under the supervision of Maj. August von Parseval, several

Santos-Dumont's airships

Upper-air research

Lebaudy airships

semirigid ships were built between 1906 and 1911. The largest and most successful was 224 feet long, 47 feet in diameter, and was driven by two 120-horsepower engines. It was demonstrated as a passenger carrier at the Frankfurt Aeronautical Exhibition in 1909 and later participated in military and naval exercises. But the performance of the Zeppelins was so far superior that by 1911 all other lighter-than-air programs were abandoned.

Only two American attempts at semirigids are recorded. In 1906 Walter Wellman, a journalist living in Paris, began construction of the "America"—185 feet long and powered by an 80-horsepower engine. His objective was to fly to the North Pole. Two attempts were made, in September 1907 and October 1909. Both failed. He then enlarged "America" (228 feet long, with two engines) for a transatlantic attempt. Wellman and his crew took off from Atlantic City, New Jersey, on October 15, 1910. Motor trouble developed almost immediately, and after drifting as a free balloon for two days to a point some 400 miles east of Hampton Roads, the ship descended. The crew was rescued by a passing steamer, and the ship was abandoned.

One of Wellman's crew, Melville Vaniman, decided to try again in the "Akron," a semirigid of his own design. While on a test flight off Atlantic City on July 2, 1912, it caught fire and crashed, killing Vaniman and his four companions. This was the end of semirigid development in the United States until a brief but abortive program was undertaken in 1923.

Rigid airships. Among all classes of lighter-than-air craft, the large rigid dirigible had the longest and most spectacular history. It began when Ferdinand, Graf von Zeppelin, launched his first ship from Lake Constance in 1900. It terminated when the "Hindenburg" exploded and burned on the naval air station at Lakehurst, New Jersey, in early May 1937.

Zeppelin, as a military observer, had witnessed U.S. Army balloons in service during the American Civil War, and he made his own first ascent at St. Paul, Minnesota, in 1863. Around 1873 he became convinced that the future of lighter-than-air development lay in very large rigid ships. This concept was not wholly original. David Schwarz, a German, had built a ship with an external aluminum framework in Russia in 1897. It proved unsuccessful and was abandoned. Zeppelin was the first, however, to reduce the idea to practice. He patented his first design in 1898 and built LZ-1 (Luftschiff Zeppelin Nummer 1) during the next two years.

Assembled in a floating hangar on Lake Constance and launched from the water on July 2, 1900, the ship was 420 feet long with 38-foot maximum diameter. Its structure consisted of 24 longitudinal girders and 16 transverse rings, all of aluminum, tied together with a forest of diagonal bracing wires. The outside covering was smooth cotton cloth. Its 16 internal cells of rubberized fabric held a total of 338,410 cubic feet of lifting gas. Two 16-horsepower gasoline engines were mounted in separate cars rigidly attached to the keel girder. Although all subsequent Zeppelins (up to and including LZ-129, the "Hindenburg") varied widely in size, shape, and mechanical detail, the basic pattern was established with LZ-1.

The first trials of LZ-1 were reasonably encouraging, but the following years (1900–10), in which LZ-1 to LZ-6 appeared, were marked by disasters and discouragement. The ships were continuously improved and enlarged, but natural forces, mechanical failures, and financial difficulties almost brought the program to a standstill. But Zeppelin, foreseeing a commercial potential for his airships, organized Delag (Deutsche Luftschiffahrts-Aktien-Gesellschaft) in 1910 and began to carry passengers for hire. In the years remaining before the outbreak of World War I, Delag's five airships ("Deutschland," "Schwaben," "Viktoria Luise," "Hansa," and "Sachsen") spent over 3,000 hours in the air and carried 34,228 passengers a distance equivalent to four times around the Earth, without injury to passengers or crew. In late 1913, this remarkable record was marred when LZ-14 and LZ-18, both on military missions, were destroyed with a loss of 50 lives.

The onset of war changed the character of Zeppelin development. By 1918 some 100 airships had been built, primarily for the bombardment of London.

Britain was the only other country that, before the war, took any interest in rigid airships. One ship, at the time the largest in the world (510 feet long, 40 feet diameter, with two 200-horsepower engines), was constructed by Vickers Ltd., under Admiralty orders.

Christened "Mayfly," the aircraft was destined never to leave the ground. While being towed out of her hangar, she was caught in a severe crosswind and broken in two.

PARACHUTES (LEONARDO TO WORLD WAR I)

Though parachutes are not flight vehicles within the meaning of this article, their operation depends upon aerodynamic principles, and their association with man flight is intimate and of long standing. Even before any human being left the ground, Leonardo had sketched a fall-breaker in the form of a cloth pyramid and had discussed the aerodynamic factors involved (1514). Fausto Veranzio (1595) published a book containing a drawing of a man ("Homo Volans") descending from the top of a tower supported by a fabric panel stretched over a rectangular wooden framework. In 1632 Desmarets de Saint-Sorlin published a novel in Paris (*Ariane*) in which the hero escapes from a prison tower by jumping with a parachute made from a bed sheet.

Blanchard, the early balloonist, claimed to have experimented with parachutes as early as 1777. Prior to the invention of the hot-air balloon, Joseph Montgolfier is reported to have dropped a sheep, without damage, in a basket tied below a seven-foot parasol from a tower in Avignon. Several similar attempts were reported between 1785 and 1797, when the first manned parachute drop was accomplished.

On October 22, 1797, André-Jacques Garnerin took off from the Parc Monceau in Paris in a basket attached to an umbrella-like parachute suspended beneath a balloon. At an altitude of about 3,000 feet, he cut the suspension cord and descended without injury. Wilbur Wright later characterized this as one of the most courageous acts in aviation history.

Garnerin's original canopy-type set the pattern for virtually all subsequent parachutes. A conical parachute studied by Cayley and tested (July 1837), with fatal results, by Robert Cocking, attracted early attention but was shortly abandoned.

During the greatest period of free ballooning, hundreds of parachute drops were made, mostly to provide thrills for the public at county fairs. It was not until the latter part of World War I that the device began to be important as a means of saving the lives of pilots in disabled planes.

IV. Developments of the World War I era

The circus-and-carnival era of man flight ended abruptly with the outbreak of World War I in 1914. The millions that belligerent governments were willing to pay aircraft designers suddenly made aviation big business on a scale no one had yet contemplated. Aircraft had found work to do, and the frantic competition of wartime brought, in a few years, performance improvements that might otherwise have required decades.

In the first weeks of the war, aircraft played a considerable role in reconnaissance; French aircraft spotting the movements of the German 1st Army led to the Battle of the Marne. But few thought that airplanes could be effectively armed.

In 1914 France mobilized some 150 military planes and several airships, Germany about 260 planes plus a fleet of 14 Zeppelins, and Britain fewer than 100 aircraft. The planes of course were flimsy kitelike structures powered by engines of uncertain power and longevity. At best, they could climb 2,000–3,000 feet and fly at 60–70 mph, sometimes for as much as 200 miles. At worst, they could barely get off the ground. But four years later, 150–200-horsepower single-seat fighters, armed with two synchronized machine guns, were fighting each other at 15,000

Zeppelin's dirigibles

Garnerin's parachuting

feet or higher. Two-place reconnaissance machines were supplying hundreds of photographs of the ground action daily, and heavy bombers were penetrating deep into enemy territory both by day and by night. Airplanes had not only found jobs to do but had evolved into highly diversified forms to meet specialized requirements.

The production of aircraft, engines, and related material expanded tremendously to keep pace with combat needs. For the first time the need to manufacture large numbers of aircraft of identical types put builders on a production line rather than a jobbing basis. Also, mass training of pilots became a prime necessity. Flying had, indeed, ceased to be a game.

The following sections emphasize the status of aviation in the various belligerent nations. A more detailed description of the leading military aircraft and their armament appears in AIRCRAFT, MILITARY.

GERMANY

In the immediate prewar period, German planes and pilots held world endurance (24 hours 12 minutes) and distance (1,178 miles) records. German aircraft appeared over Paris within weeks of the declaration of war. Germany produced military planes of standardized design for ease of maintenance and replacement, fitted with excellent engines by Benz and Mercedes. In a rapidly changing technology, however, too much standardization can be a liability. The air war rapidly became a seesaw affair with the better aircraft on one side soon outperformed by newer machines of the enemy.

Probably the greatest contributor to German aircraft development was a Dutch designer, Anthony H.G. Fokker, whose synchronized forward-firing machine guns restored combat superiority to the Germans in 1915 and whose excellent triplane fighter D·VII, used by Baron von Richthofen, could compete with anything put up by the Allies in 1917–18.

Fokker's fighter planes (margin note)

By 1918 the imperial government's inventory included many well-known single-seat fighters—Albatros, Roland, Halberstadt, Pfalz—and a series of efficient two-place observation types—Aviatik, A.E.G., Rumpler, Albatros, etc. A number of seaplanes, largely twin-float, single-engined biplanes, were produced for fleet cooperation.

Airships. Germany's initial long-range heavy bombardment effort centred about its fleet of rigid Zeppelin-type airships. During the war over 100 were built by Zeppelin and some 20 more by the Schütte-Lanz Company. Many raids were launched against London and other cities, but by 1916 the Allied defenses had improved to the extent that airship missions became too costly in men and machines. During the latter phases of the war the big airships were used only for naval patrols at sea and for general over-land observation.

Performance, however, had improved tremendously. In the summer of 1917, LZ-120 made a 100-hour observation flight over the Baltic Sea. In November 1917, LZ-59 attempted a relief mission deep into German East Africa. Although the mission failed to reach its destination, the airship stayed in the air for more than 95 hours and covered over 4,000 miles.

Large bombardment aircraft. With the blunting of the Zeppelin attacks against London and a need to provide an operational capability for night attack against other distant cities, German interest toward the end of the war centred on bombardment airplanes of very large size. Some 60 such aircraft were built in 1916–18. Most familiar were the Gotha biplanes of 1916, with a wingspan of nearly 90 feet, powered by two Mercedes engines of 260 horsepower each. With a 2,000-pound bomb load they had an operating range of some 300 miles. The largest of these giants, however, was the Siemens-Schückert R-VIII, with a wingspread of over 150 feet and powered by six 300-horsepower engines.

FRANCE

France entered World War I with the largest inventory of military aircraft and probably the largest cadre of aviators. Most of the machines were the immediate descendants of the 1910–12 racers (Blériot, Deperdussin,

Nieuport, Morane, etc.), but production was under way on improved and specialized military types, including the R.E.P. monoplanes and the Farman, Voisin, and Caudron biplanes. Bréguet and Durand designs with fabric-covered fuselages were already in evidence.

French military aircraft improved tremendously under the pressures of war. The early birdcage Voisin and Caudron bombers and observation planes gave way to the more efficient long-range Bréguet and Letord day bombers. In the single-seat fighter category, France made great progress. In the end, French, British, and American fighter pilots flying single-seat Nieuports and Spads proved a match for the German Fokker, Pfalz, and Albatros squadrons. Of great importance was the mass production of reliable engines, particularly the eight-cylinder Hispano-Suiza, which was used in the Spads and in the British S.E. 5 fighters.

Ground-support aviation (margin note)

Apart from combat operations, the French developed ground-support aviation to a high degree. Photographic missions over the lines provided ground commanders with needed battlefield information. Radio telegraphy and visual signals were also widely employed. For naval support, for scouting, and for bombing attack against submarines, a number of float-type seaplanes were in service.

In the early stages of the war the small fleet of non-rigid airships was used by the Army for reconnaissance and for bombardment, but these slow, low-flying machines were so vulnerable to ground and air attack that surviving specimens were turned over to the navy in 1917 for antisubmarine patrol use. Captive balloons were used in large numbers on all fronts for observation purposes.

The growth of the French aviation effort in the course of the war was enormous. As of November 1918, some 180,000 people were employed in the aircraft-manufacturing industry.

GREAT BRITAIN

Of the three major western European powers, Britain went into World War I in the weakest position in the air. The Royal Flying Corps (RFC), organized in 1912, mustered only 1,800 officers and men and fewer than 150 flyable aircraft when war was declared in 1914. By November 1918, however, the corps consisted of some 300,000 officers and men, with 22,000 aircraft organized in over 200 squadrons.

Coincident with the formation of the RFC, a Royal Aircraft Factory had been established at Farnborough. Between 1912 and 1914 several experimental military machines were turned out from designs by De Havilland (first of the D.H. series); the British Experimental 2c; and the Sopwith Tabloid. The Tabloid was the ancestor of later high-performance fighters used by both American and British pilots—the Camels, Snipes, Kittens, Bullets, and Hawks—but the 70-horsepower, 75-mph B.E. 2c was the backbone of the RFC in 1912. By 1918, however, the Hispano-Suiza-powered British S.E. 5 performed with the best that Germany could put up.

The earlier British airplanes made use of French engines, Gnome and Clerget radial, and Renault in-line types. Later, the Hispano-Suizas were widely used. As the war progressed, however, excellent British-built engines—Rolls-Royce, Sunbeam, and Beardmore—became available in quantities. Such engines powered the D.H. 4 day bombers and the long-range Handley Page night bombardment types. Night operations began in 1916. By 1918 Handley Page bombers were being turned out in quantity in England and in America.

Naval aviation (margin note)

Naval aviation developed rapidly in Britain. Squadrons of seaplanes and flying boats were used for the protection of principal naval bases and for antisubmarine patrol offshore. Eventually, some 350 airplanes were assigned to the British Grand Fleet. During the last two years of the war, over 100 bombing attacks were made against German submarines at sea.

The modern aircraft carrier had its genesis during this period. Experiments were conducted in launching small fighter planes from platforms built over battleship gun turrets, or from barges towed behind high-speed destroyers. At least one former passenger liner was fitted experimentally with a large landing platform above its superstructure.

Interest in nonrigid airships revived early in the war for antisubmarine convoy and coastal patrol work. Hundreds of blimps (from "British Class B airship" plus "limp"—*i.e.*, nonrigid) were built during the four-year period. In the last year of the war over 9,000 sorties against floating mines and submarines are recorded. Also, in spite of the disastrous experience with the rigid airship "Mayfly" in 1911, and based on designs of several Zeppelins shot down in England, construction was begun on several rigid ships. These had little significance during the war but did touch off a brief (and disastrous) postwar airship program (see below, *Developments from 1918 to 1930: Significant technical developments*).

OTHER COUNTRIES

Only three other countries—Italy, Russia, and the U.S.—made significant contributions to aviation during World War I.

Italy. Italy was among the first to recognize the importance of aircraft in warfare. Beginning in 1911, its bombardment squadrons were active in Libya. Out of this experience emerged the multi-engined Caproni bombers. Italian manufacturers in 1914–18 produced a considerable number of trainers, observation planes, and single-seat fighters, but the most spectacular were the large two-, three-, and four-engined Capronis. Day bombing started in 1916. Night operations with larger types were begun early in 1917. Built originally as two-engined biplanes, the later Capronis (some of which were produced under contract in the United States, with Liberty engines) were three- and four-engined triplanes.

Caproni bombers

Russia. Russia's contribution to aviation development of the period was a giant four-engined bomber (1915) by Sikorsky. It was derived from the "Ilya Mourometz" of 1912. After Sikorsky had abandoned (temporarily) his work with helicopters, he designed and built the first successful multi-engined plane—a large biplane carrying 16 passengers in a closed cabin, powered by four 100-horsepower Mercedes engines. A bomber version of this machine with four 120-horsepower engines was used on the Russian front in 1915.

United States. When the U.S. entered the European war in April 1917, army aviation was still a section of the Signal Corps. It mustered 65 officers and 1,087 men and possessed not a single aircraft capable of combat. The naval air arm consisted of 38 naval aviators, some 160 enlisted men, and possibly a dozen hydro-airplanes and embryonic flying boats, all based at a single air station at Pensacola, Florida. None of the flyable airplanes carried any armament.

An Aircraft Production Board was appointed by Pres. Woodrow Wilson, and the decision was made to manufacture British, French, and Italian planes and engines in quantity. The only fighting plane that came out of the program in time to see action was the American-built British D.H. 4. Some 1,370 were in Europe at the Armistice, but only 740 ever saw service at the front.

A major United States accomplishment, however, was the rapid design and production of the famous Liberty engines. By October 21, 1917, the first 12-cylinder Liberty was test-flown. At the Armistice, orders on the books totalled 52,000. Some 13,000 had already been delivered, and production was 150 engines a day.

V. Developments from 1918 to 1930

From 1914 to 1918 all aviation activities focussed on a single objective, the winning of a war. When that task ended, most of the machines and the thousands of people involved suddenly found themselves unemployed. Thousands of aircraft were simply piled up and burned. Manufacture of aviation equipment of all kinds halted. Former military pilots, trying to make a living by their war-acquired flying skill, revived the circus-and-carnival atmosphere of the prewar period. With a surplus "Jenny" or "Avro" or "Cannuck," the barnstormers provided

The barn-stormers

thrills wherever they could get a crowd; they sustained popular interest in aviation, and, even more important, they sold rides to the public—the thin wedge that, a decade later, cracked open the air-transport market.

A few found employment in flying the mail. In the spring of 1918 the U.S. Post Office Department had sought bids for special mail-carrying airplanes to operate between Washington and New York. With nonmilitary aircraft in short supply, the U.S. Army was requested to undertake the assignment. Flights were inaugurated in May, but by midsummer the army had found that with the heavy demands of the war in Europe it could not spare either planes or pilots for the mail service. On August 12, 1918, the Post Office took over the New York–Washington airmail run as a civil operation. On September 8, 1920, transcontinental airmail was inaugurated. At first, operations were restricted to daylight hours, but on February 22, 1921, day and night flights were started, marking the real beginning of commercial air transport in America and creating a new demand for more pilots and better airplanes.

One of the factors that limited technical development well into the mid-1920s was the great surplus of wartime engines that were in production at the time of the Armistice. The result was that for the first five or six years, in spite of far superior power plants on drawing boards, or actually running on test stands, economic necessity dictated that new airplane designs be laid out around wartime engines.

Toward the latter half of the 1920s substantial advances in design and construction of aircraft came into being. Concurrently, organized research laboratories, both governmental and private, were established to meet the needs of the scientifically oriented designers and engineers entering the industry.

Guggenheim Fund. In January 1926 an event occurred in America that had a profound effect on all subsequent development everywhere—announcement of the establishment of the Daniel Guggenheim Fund for the Promotion of Aeronautics. Daniel Guggenheim (1856–1930), who never in his life owned an airplane, nor derived any profit from participation in aviation, made grants totalling $3,000,000 (beginning January 16, 1926) for the following purposes: (1) To promote aeronautical education both in institutions of learning and among the general public. (2) To assist in the extension of fundamental aeronautical science. (3) To assist in the development of commercial aircraft and aircraft equipment. (4) To further the application of aircraft in business, industry, and other economic and social activities of the nation. By February 1, 1930, when the fund was completely liquidated, each of its objectives had been fulfilled many times over. Its greatest importance was in the fields of education and research. Beginning in 1926, several Guggenheim schools of aeronautics and Guggenheim aeronautical laboratories were established. These centres attracted such outstanding scholars and teachers as Alexander Klemin, Theodore von Kármán, Robert and Clark Millikan, and William F. Durand. Many of the most significant advances in aviation—and in space exploration since the 1940s—were the result of work by graduates of Guggenheim schools or by recipients of Guggenheim research grants.

GOVERNMENT-SPONSORED RESEARCH

Government-sponsored aeronautical research in the United States lagged far behind that of other major powers in 1914. Since 1866 the Aeronautical Society of Great Britain had been stimulating research and experimentation and fostering the exchange of information in the aeronautical sciences. The Royal Aircraft Factory was actively engaged in development projects by 1912. France had several major experiment stations: Eiffel's two wind tunnels, one at the tower and one at Auteuil; an army laboratory at Chalais-Meudon; and the Institut Aérotechnique at Saint-Cyr. Germany supported research laboratories in universities and technical schools at Göttingen, Aachen, and Berlin and operated a national installation at Adlershof. Italy and Russia had

Table 1: Principal Record Flights (1919–30)

1919	
February 21	U.S. Army, using Thomas Morse "Scout" with 300-hp Hispano-Suiza engine, sets American speed record of 164 mph.
May 6–31	A squadron of U.S. Navy Curtiss flying boats attempts first Atlantic crossing. NC-1 and NC-3 lost at sea off Azores, crews rescued. NC-4 completes crossing, (see Figure 4, center) via Azores, arriving at Plymouth, England.
June 14–15	Capt. John Alcock and Lt. Arthur Brown (ex-RFC) fly from Newfoundland to Ireland in Vickers "Vimy" 2-engined biplane.
July 2–13	British dirigible R-34 makes round-trip flight from England to New York with 6 officers and 21 men.
September 18	Roland Rohlfs in Curtiss "Wasp" sets 34,910-ft altitude record.
1922	
March 30–June 5	Two Portuguese officers, Capt. S. Cabral and Vice Admiral G. Coutinho, fly by stages from Lisbon to Rio de Janeiro in British-built Fairey seaplane to record first crossing of South Atlantic.
October 18	World speed record set by General William Mitchell in Curtiss racer at 222.96 mph.
1923	
May 2–3	U.S. Army pilots Kelly and Macready make first nonstop transcontinental flight (New York to San Diego) in Liberty-powered T-2 monoplane.
August–December	Former German Zeppelin L-72 acquired by France after war, renamed "Dixmude," makes series of five flights across Mediterranean into North Africa.
November 4	Lieut. A.J. Williams raises world speed record to 266.6 mph in Navy-Curtiss Racer.
1924	
April–September	Four U.S. Army Douglas "World Cruisers" attempt round-the-world flight. Two lost en route; two, "New Orleans" and "Chicago," complete 26,345-mi. trip.
May 21	Lieut. J.A. Macready, USAS, sets altitude record at 35,239 ft.
October 12–15	Zeppelin LZ1-1126 (ZR1-13) renamed "Los Angeles," crossed from Friedrichshafen (Ger.) to Lakehurst for delivery to U.S. Navy.
1925	
April–November	Italian Commander de Pinedo and mechanic in single-engined Savoia flying boat, fly from Italy to Australia, returning via Japan—30,000 miles.
November	Alan Cobham flies from London to Cape Town via Cairo—8,500 miles in 94 hours.
1926	
May 9	Commander Byrd and copilot Floyd Bennett fly from Spitsbergen over North Pole and return in 3-engined monoplane "Josephine Ford."
May 11–14	Amundsen and crew fly over North Pole from Spitsbergen to Pt. Barrow, Alaska, in Italian-built semirigid dirigible "Norge."

1927	
May 20–21	Charles A. Lindbergh, after a one-stop flight from San Diego to New York, in the Ryan-built monoplane "Spirit of St. Louis," makes first nonstop flight from New York to Paris (33 hours, 30 minutes) to win the Orteig Prize (see Figure 4, bottom).
June 4–5	Clarence Chamberlin and Charles Levine in a single-engine Bellanca monoplane, fly from New York City to Eisleben, Germany.
June 28	Lieuts. Maitland and Hegenberger (U.S. Army) in 3-engined Fokker fly from Oakland, Calif. to Honolulu, 2400 miles over open ocean.
June 29–30	Cmdr. Richard Byrd and crew of three fly from New York to France in 3-engined Fokker "America."
July 4	Lieut. C.C. Champion, USN, pushes world's altitude record to 37,995 ft over Washington, D.C., in a Wright "Apache."
July 14–15	Bronte and Smith fly 2340 miles from Oakland, Calif. to Molokai, Hawaii in 25 hours, 36 minutes.
October 14–15	Costes and Le Brix in Breguet biplane cross from Senegal, Africa, to Rio de Janeiro in 21 hours, 18 minutes.
November 6	Lieut. A.J. Williams in Schneider Cup Racer establishes an unofficial speed record of 322.6 mph.
1928	
February	Bert Hinkler makes solo flight London to Australia. Lady Mary Heath flies solo from Cape Town to London.
April 12–13	German Junkers monoplane "Bremen" makes first east-west Atlantic crossing.
May–June	Charles Kingsford-Smith and crew of three in Fokker "Southern Cross" fly from Oakland, Calif. to Sydney, Australia via Honolulu and the Fiji Islands.
June 17–18	Amelia Earhart with pilots Stultz and Gordon fly Atlantic in monoplane "Friendship."
October 11–15	Airship "Graf Zeppelin" flies from Friedrichshafen, Germany to Lakehurst, N.J. with 23 passengers.
1929	
January 1–7	U.S. Army Fokker C-2 "Question Mark" flies for 150 hours, 40 minutes over Los Angeles in first major air-to-air refueling test.
August 15–20	Mamer and Walker in single-engined Buhl monoplane "Spokane Sun God" make nonstop transcontinental round-trip from Spokane, Washington, in 115 hours, 45 minutes with 11 air-to-air refuelings en route.
August	"Graf Zeppelin" makes first round-the-world airship flight including nonstop distance record from Friedrichshafen to Tokyo of 6,980 miles.
November 28–29	Commander Byrd and crew of three fly over South Pole in Ford 3-engined monoplane "Floyd Bennett."
1930	
May–July	Kingsford-Smith in "Southern Cross" makes round-the-world flight.
July 4	Lieut. Apollo Soucek, USN, raises world altitude mark to 43,166 ft.
July 29–August 1	British airship R-100 flies from England to Canada in 78 hours, 51 minutes.
September 1–2	Costes and Bellonte make first Paris-New York City flight—4100 miles in 37 hours, 18 minutes.

National Advisory Committee for Aeronautics

well-organized laboratories before the United States took its first official steps in that direction.

Following a study of the United States position with respect to wartime aviation in Europe, the Smithsonian Institution in 1915 recommended to Congress the establishment of a National Advisory Committee for Aeronautics (NACA). In addition to other activities the committee was authorized to own laboratories and to conduct research. The enabling legislation was approved on March 3, 1915, and the first full committee meeting was held on April 23.

During the next decade the record of aeronautical research progress at Langley Field, Virginia, the site of the committee's first research laboratory, was phenomenal. From a standing start in 1917, with a handful of technical personnel and three or four test airplanes, it was recognized by 1930 as the greatest research centre in the world, with a large and growing scientific staff and a capability of testing virtually all forms of aircraft in all regimes of flight under controlled conditions in the laboratory.

GOVERNMENT COORDINATION OF AVIATION ACTIVITIES

Slowly but surely a market for new aircraft began to grow. Aircraft manufacture revived to meet the demand for new military types and to serve the needs of a growing airmail service. Intercompany competition for new customers benefited airplane and engine performance. Airplanes became more reliable, more comfortable, easier to fly. There was some preliminary activity in building larger planes to carry passengers and cargo for profit on regular schedules.

By 1925, however, it was apparent everywhere that the expanding manufacture and use of aircraft must be subject to some overall coordination and regulation if chaos was to be avoided. In the United States, a board was appointed by Pres. Calvin Coolidge to establish a national policy for the development of all aspects of aviation. The board's recommendations resulted in passage of the Air Commerce Act of 1926, the Navy Five Year Aircraft Program (1926), and the Army Five Year Aircraft Program (1926). These acts provided a relatively stable base for American aviation development for the next decade.

The same problems were attacked by governments everywhere. Britain, France, Italy, and other countries established air ministries at Cabinet level to coordinate their civil and military aviation requirements. When international commercial flights became possible, international commissions were established to control traffic and to promulgate rules and regulations covering flight operations and passenger safety.

RECORD FLIGHTS

With the growing improvement in performance and reliability, public interest focussed on long-range flights, both cross-country and intercontinental. Just as the English Channel had posed a challenge to Latham and Blériot in 1909, so ocean crossings and transpolar flights became the targets of many ambitions in the middle

1920s. Again, for their publicity value, newspapers and wealthy private citizens posted substantial prizes for such flights. The London *Daily Mail* offered £10,000 for a nonstop Atlantic crossing, and in 1919 Raymond Orteig established a $25,000 prize for a nonstop flight between New York and Paris. Later (1927) first and second prizes of $25,000 and $10,000 were posted by James Dole for a race from California to Hawaii.

Although the military services of most countries were ineligible to compete for monetary prizes, many special long-range flights were organized for their value as military exercises. To illustrate the expanding capabilities of aircraft during the 1920s, a selection of successful transcontinent and transocean flights (both by airplane and by airship) is given in Table 1. Between 1927 and 1930, of 31 transatlantic attempts, only 10 succeeded, and 16 men and three women died in the failures. The Dole Race across the Pacific (August 1927) cost six planes and ten lives. A few milestones in speed and altitude performance have been included in the table.

SIGNIFICANT TECHNICAL DEVELOPMENTS

While the public imagination was captured by the headline flights, sound technical progress behind the scenes was contributing powerfully to the great forward steps of the 1930s and 1940s. A number of postwar ideas tested and found wanting eventually disappeared, notably airships and autogiros.

Airships. Development of nonrigid airships (blimps) in Europe halted at the end of the war. In the U.S., however, both the army and the navy carried on limited programs during the 1920s. Most interesting design innovation was the navy's all-metal ZMC-2, first tested in 1929. Only one was built.

The U.S. Army purchased the 400-foot semirigid airship "Roma" from Italy in 1921. It crashed and burned at Langley Field in 1922 with a loss of 34 lives. This not only ended the use of hydrogen as a lifting gas in the U.S. airships but terminated U.S. interest in this class of airship.

As noted above, Britain had become actively involved in a rigid-airship construction program toward the end of the war. The successful transatlantic round trip of the R-34 induced the U.S. Navy to order a British-built ship (R-38), which was completed in mid-1921. During a test flight on August 21, however, she broke up in the air and crashed with a loss of 45 men. This terminated U.S. interest in British airships.

Britain's construction program continued, however, and culminated in 1930 with the launching of two super-airships of the Zeppelin type, the R-100 and R-101, designed for the transatlantic and the Far East trade. The R-100 made one round trip to Canada in July, but the R-101 crashed and burned on a French hillside on her maiden voyage to India, killing a number of high-ranking RAF and civil officials and terminating British interest in airships.

Meanwhile, the United States had some disastrous home-grown experiences. Parallel with the construction of the ill-fated British R-38, the U.S. Navy built an airship at the Philadelphia Naval Aircraft Factory and assembled it at the Naval Air Station, Lakehurst, New Jersey. The 680-foot "Shenandoah" was the first rigid dirigible to be filled with helium rather than with hydrogen. She was commissioned in October 1923 and for two years participated in naval exercises over land and with the fleet at sea. In September 1925 she ran into a storm over southern Ohio and broke up in the air with a loss of 14 officers and men. Twenty-seven of her complement were saved by riding sections of the ship to the ground as free balloons.

A month later the German-built LZ-126 (ZR1-13), acquired by the United States under reparations agreements, arrived at Lakehurst. Commissioned as the "Los Angeles," she was operated for nine years on missions of many kinds, in all weather conditions, without accident or serious incident, an all-time record for airships. Decommissioned in June 1932, she was kept intact for test purposes and finally broken up in 1939.

On the strength of the experience with the "Los Angeles," the navy ordered construction of two much larger ships, the "Akron" and the "Macon," from the U.S. Goodyear-Zeppelin Corporation. The "Akron" went into service on October 27, 1931. After a year and a half of active service, including successful experimentation as a carrier for fighter aircraft, she went down in a storm at sea, losing 73 officers and men.

The "Macon" was well along when the "Akron" was lost. She went into service on June 23, 1933, and operated successfully until February 12, 1935, when, after what appeared to be a minor structural failure, she collapsed and was lost off Point Sur, California. Most of her crew were rescued, but this terminated U.S. interest in airships.

Graf von Zeppelin had died in March 1917, and Germany's defeat had stopped all airship construction except for those due for delivery to the Allies under the reparations program. Restrictions on commercial airship construction were relaxed in 1926, and work was started on LZ-127, best known as the "Graf Zeppelin." She was launched in September 1928. Under the command of Hugo Eckener, Zeppelin's successor, she explored many areas of the world as a passenger carrier. Her successful performance encouraged the construction of a much larger ship, the "Hindenburg," in the early 1930s.

During the summer of 1936 the "Hindenburg" made 10 routine round trips between Friedrichshafen and Lakehurst, New Jersey. On her first trip the following year (May 5–6) as she was approaching the mooring mast at Lakehurst, for reasons that have never been fully explained, the ship exploded and burned. She, like all her European predecessors, was hydrogen-filled. This terminated interest in rigid airships everywhere in the world.

Rotary-wing aircraft. Interest in vertical mechanical flight lapsed during World War I except for an abortive effort by a young Hungarian scientist, Theodore von Kármán, to substitute a tethered helicopter for the conventional gas-filled military observation balloon. During the 1920s, however, an amazing variety of experimental vertical risers appeared in Europe and in America, all conspicuously awkward and complicated in configuration, all conspicuously unsuccessful as flying machines. Most of these machines, with a great deal of thrashing about, managed to rise a few feet off the ground but once airborne proved to be virtually uncontrollable.

It remained for a Spanish engineer, Juan de la Cierva, in a search for an airplane that could be slowed down in flight and landed vertically, to provide the key to practical rotary-wing flight. Between 1920 and 1923 he built a series of machines with conventional airplane fuselages (including engine and propeller) above which was mounted in a horizontal position a large multibladed windmill. The unpowered windmill was free to rotate under aerodynamic forces as the machine was driven forward by the action of its normal propeller. This autorotation of the wing system produced the required lift and gave the device its name—the autogiro.

Cierva's work was uniformly unsuccessful until in 1923 he hit upon the idea of articulating (or hinging) the rotor blades at the hub and allowing them to respond individually to the aerodynamic and centrifugal forces involved (see Figure 5, left). This arrangement not only solved the immediate problems of the autogiro but provided the experience that paved the way for helicopter development of 1930 and later.

During the early 1930s the autogiro created a great wave of popular interest everywhere, particularly in Britain and in America. Ninety autogiros were in service by 1932 in the United States alone, some in the hands of private owners, some for advertising and publicity purposes, a few under experimentation by the military services and the Post Office Department, which considered them for transferring mail from post office rooftops to airfields.

Although design improvements were continuous during the 1930s, and many new applications for autogiros were found, the type had virtually disappeared by 1940 and is unlikely to be revived in any appreciable numbers, sim-

[margin notes:]
Prizes for record flights

The "Shenandoah" disaster

The autogiro

ply because there is nothing that autogiros could do that helicopters cannot do better and more economically.

Aircraft-carrier operations. Carrier operations were forecast as early as 1911 when Eugene Ely made the first landings and takeoffs from a U.S. Navy ship in a Curtiss biplane. During World War I the Royal Navy of Great Britain developed the first true aircraft carrier, the HMS "Argus," converted from a commercial vessel. In the early 1920s both the United States and Japan took active interest. The USS "Langley" (converted from the collier "Jupiter") and the Japanese "Hosho" both went into operation in 1922. The Washington Arms Limitation Treaty of 1922 put a size limitation on conversions and new construction. During the late 1920s a number of such vessels were under construction, including the USS "Saratoga" and USS "Lexington." These were the experimental ships on which were tested the carrier-based aircraft and operating techniques that were to play such dramatic and determining roles in World War II, a dozen years later.

Blind-landing research. By the mid-1920s it became obvious that all aircraft operations, both military and commercial, had to be made independent of weather. By that time, long-range flights over land areas were feasible, using rudimentary radio direction finders and lighted beacons at night, but the problem of landing and take-off when the pilot could not see where he was or where he was heading was still unsolved. Instrument displays in cockpits had vastly improved over the improvised arrangements of wartime, but the pilots of rapidly moving airplanes required a reliable fix in three-dimensional space for landing and takeoff in conditions of limited visibility.

To deal with this problem, the Daniel Guggenheim Fund established a Full Flight Laboratory at Mitchel Field, Long Island, in cooperation with the Army Air Corps and the several manufacturers of aircraft instruments. Lieut. (later Lieut. Gen.) James H. Doolittle was selected to head the operation. On September 24, 1929, in a fully hooded cockpit, he made the first completely blind flight in history, taking off, flying over a predetermined course, and landing at the point of departure, all by instruments alone.

Rocket research. The idea of flying by rocket power goes far back into history. By 1920 it had captured the imagination of Robert H. Goddard, a young professor of physics at Clark University in Worcester, Massachusetts, who had made his first theoretical studies of a liquid-fuel rocket in February 1909. His basic patent for a rocket apparatus was granted in July 1914, and in 1918 he developed and patented a rocket missile, the forerunner of the shoulder-type rocket launcher of World War II known as the bazooka.

In September 1916 he applied to the Smithsonian Institution for a research grant to continue his work on rockets. He received $5,000, and in September 1919 the Smithsonian published his classic paper, "A Method of Reaching Extreme Altitudes." The first experimental liquid-rocket flight was made on March 16, 1926, from a farm near Auburn, Massachusetts. Three years later and after a number of spectacular and noisy rocket firings, the local fire and police authorities suggested that he move to some more remote place. By 1930, supported by a grant of $50,000 from the Guggenheim Foundation, Goddard's entire operation was moved to a desert site near Roswell, New Mexico.

Meanwhile, rocket research was going forward independently elsewhere in the world. Unknown in the '20s (but amply documented in later years), active rocket research was under way in the Soviet Union under the direction of Konstantin Tsiolkovsky. Germany's official interest in rockets as weapons stemmed from the limitations imposed by the Treaty of Versailles on development of conventional artillery. As a by-product of the military-research program, an active society for space travel by rocket was formed in 1927. The first flight of a rocket-powered aircraft was made on September 30, 1929, by Fritz von Opel in a glider with a gunpowder rocket attached to the rear.

The first aircraft carrier

Robert H. Goddard

Gliders and sailplanes. Between 1910 and 1920 interest in gliders almost disappeared. The airplane had taken over. Beginning in 1919, however, and again as a direct result of the limitations in the building and use of powered aircraft imposed on Germany by the Treaty of Versailles, a renaissance of gliding and soaring occurred. It is still actively going on.

At first ostensibly a sport, gliding in Germany became a means of training fighter and bomber pilots to man future Luftwaffe squadrons. Furthermore, the design and construction of light and efficient sailplanes gave German scientists and engineers an opportunity for sophisticated research in aerodynamics and in the efficient use of light materials, which proved useful in the early 1930s when Hitler abrogated treaty limitations and began to rearm Germany in the air.

The first motorless aircraft competition was held in the Rhön Mountains in 1920. Some two dozen machines participated. Best performance was a flight of 6,000 feet in about 2½ minutes. Two years later, a permanent soaring centre had been established at the Wasserkuppe in Germany, and competitions were being staged frequently in France, Switzerland, and England. Thousands of young glider pilots were in training. By that time, as a result of improvements in design and in piloting techniques, the soaring record had been raised to over three hours.

By 1930 development was well under way in America. A number of soaring and gliding sites had been established, notably at Elmira, New York, and on the West Coast near San Diego, where wind and terrain conditions were favourable.

Periodic competitions at such centres attracted machines and pilots from all over the world. Using highly efficient sailplanes and taking advantage of mechanical updrafts (along mountain ridges) and thermal updrafts (in the vicinity of thunderstorms), by 1930 altitudes of over 17,000 feet had been reached, and flight ranges extended to nearly 300 miles.

Amphibians. In the early 1920s interest developed in amphibious airplanes that could operate equally well from land or from water. Chief proponent of the idea was an American engineer, Grover Loening. As a successor to an experimental air yacht, his first amphibian was test-flown in June 1924. In appearance it was unique —a biplane powered with an inverted Liberty engine on a deep fuselage-hull combination with a long, slipper-like forebody to protect the propeller. A number of these machines were built for the military services and Coast Guard and were eventually sold to a number of airlines and to a few private owners.

A number of smaller amphibious types appeared in Europe in the late 1920s (Schrek, Savoia, etc.). By 1929 Pan American Airways Corporation had begun service to South America using Sikorsky S-38 and S-40 amphibians, but these were shortly replaced by large flying boats.

In the next ten years, however, interest in amphibious aircraft declined. High first cost and maintenance expense limited their acceptance by both military and civilian users. In addition, the greatly increased availability of suitable landing fields all over the world reduced the advantage of their dual operational capability.

The first glider competition

THE RISE OF COMMERCIAL AIR TRANSPORT

Commercial air transport, the carrying of paying passengers from point to point on preannounced schedules, began with the inauguration of Graf von Zeppelin's airship service, Delag, in 1912, and revived briefly in 1919. Since that time, however, the only commercial lighter-than-air operation (apart from sight-seeing flights by blimps at such places as Miami and Los Angeles) was that offered by the "Hindenburg" in 1936. All other commercial development has been based on the use of airplanes and (more recently) on helicopters.

Shortly after the close of World War I, international air transport services in Europe began to proliferate. By 1920 passenger flights on regular schedules were offered between many major cities. The equipment was war surplus, ranging from converted small craft with one or two

The first regular passenger flights

seats up to modified Handley Page and Farman bombers. Seating accommodations were Spartan at best, usually a row of wicker chairs replacing the former military gear in the uninsulated, unheated fuselages. Such ships were noisy and uncomfortable, and, passengers, for the most part, once embarked, got along without any attention from the crews. Operating procedures were sketchy. Air-to-ground communications were uncertain or lacking. There was little available in the way of ground equipment, either for servicing the aircraft or for flight information for pilots. Originally all such services were far from reliable, and accidents were not uncommon.

Major European governments early recognized the economic and political advantages of airline development under their own flags and gave official encouragement in the form of substantial subsidies to their nationals to extend their air services on the Continent and out to their colonial possessions. In the course of 10 years, Europe was crisscrossed with a regular air transport network. During this period the great airlines of Europe had their origins—Imperial Airways Ltd. (later BOAC and BEA), Air France, KLM (Royal Dutch Airlines), Lufthansa, Swissair, Alla Littoria. Also, with increasing competition for passengers, the earlier converted bombers disappeared, and especially designed passenger aircraft with more comfortable accommodations and better services for the customers (both on the ground and in the air) became standard equipment.

While the European countries were underwriting their passenger-carrying systems, the United States was expanding its airways and airway communications for the benefit of its rapidly growing airmail system, operated by the Post Office Department. It was not until 1925 that private companies were encouraged to handle U.S. airmail under contract, actually as a form of subsidy to encourage the development of passenger traffic. The present U.S. airline system can trace its origins to legislation passed in 1925 and designed to connect a large number of American cities and towns to the transcontinental mail routes operated by the Post Office. Passenger service supported by the system began on April 4, 1927, with a flight from Boston to New York City. Passenger demand was light until Lindbergh's flight in May of 1927. From 1927 to 1930, business began to boom, encouraged by Lindbergh's survey flights around the United States and his pioneering of new routes to South and Central America. Pan American Airways was already reaching out into the international market. Internally, new transcontinental and interurban lines were being formed by merger. New equipment, including the famous Ford and Fokker trimotors and the Sikorsky Clippers, was becoming available.

VI. Developments from 1930 to 1945

To pinpoint the exact time when aviation turned a corner and won recognition as an important contributing factor to the world's economy would be difficult, but a definite breakthrough in this realm did occur in the early 1930s. Aeronautical research programs that had been developing in university- and government-supported laboratories both in Europe and in America in the late 1920s began to produce results. A rapidly accumulating body of experimental data became available to aircraft and engine designers. It became possible to make accurate mathematical forecasts of performance and flight behaviour and to check out calculations in wind tunnels (up to full-scale) before subjecting machines to the hazards of free flight. Much of this information was circulated in the form of scientific reports or technical publications.

Simultaneously a growing cadre of young, optimistic, and enthusiastic aeronautical engineers and scientists was coming out of the schools and universities in Europe and the United States, all eager to apply these data to new designs that would fly higher, farther, faster. Apart from purely military objectives, there now emerged a new and eventually more important idea: that aircraft could be designed to produce profit for their owners in commercial operations.

As a result, the external configurations and the inboard arrangements of virtually all categories of airplane underwent radical changes in the 1929–32 period. There were occasional exceptions, but the average pre-1930 airplane was only slightly distinguishable from its World War I prototype—a wood, fabric-covered, "stick and wire" braced biplane with fixed-pitch propellers and an open or only partially enclosed, pilot's cockpit. Passenger accommodations (if any) were primitive.

By 1932 the impact of research was clearly in evidence. Streamlining had become the order of the day. Again, there were exceptions, but the average airplane in all categories became an externally smooth, internally braced, low-wing, all-metal monoplane with air-cooled engine (or engines) and with controllable-pitch propellers (*i.e.*, the blade angle could be adjusted); landing gear retracted completely in flight, and pilots and passengers were housed in insulated and sound-proofed compartments. Except that jet engines have replaced the 1930–40 air-cooled engine-and-propeller combination, the same general description applies to most military and commercial configurations of the 1970s. Stream-
lining

COMMERCIAL AVIATION

Europe. In Europe, commercial air transportation was well developed by the early 1930s. By then the converted bombers from World War I had largely been replaced by aircraft designed primarily for the handling of passengers and cargo. For the western European services, because city-to-city distances were short, comfort and convenience for the passengers were more important than high speed. On long colonial routes, however, conditions were reversed. Passenger comfort was compromised in favour of higher speeds and longer range.

Most of the aircraft in use were multi-engined (usually three-engined) monoplanes, such as the German Junkers G 24 (prtoype of the Ju 52), the French Wibaut 210, the Italian Savoia Marchetti SM.73, etc. Britain, however, for many years retained the huge, four-engined Handley Page biplanes that lumbered between London and Paris at about 100 mph. In the late 1930s Imperial Airways introduced the fast and efficient four-engined "Ensign"-class monoplanes on many of its services. This machine was useful as a troop carrier in World War II.

United States. In the United States commercial air transport got off to a slow start. Until 1927 developmental emphasis was focussed on the airmail service rather than on passenger carrying. This in the end proved advantageous, for when the commercial demand developed, the country was already laced together by a network of established airways, beacon-lighted for night operations and equipped with relatively reliable radio navigation and communication facilities. U.S.
emphasis
on airmail
service

The United States airways system was operated by the Post Office Department until September 1, 1927, when the mail routes were turned over to a group of private corporations under contract. Under the impetus of U.S. government subsidy for carrying the mail, many small companies combined into larger units, extended their range of operations to more distant cities, and began to think in terms of improving and standardizing both ground and airborne equipment. About this time (1928) Henry Ford's interest in aviation led to the production of the Ford trimotor all-aluminum plane as a competitor to the all-wood Fokker trimotor, which was a civil version of the U.S. Army's Fokker bombers.

During the first few years of the 1930s, airline passengers in Europe and the U.S. totalled only a few thousand annually. Accidents were common, the fatality rate being about one for every 8,000,000 passenger-miles. But a decade later several million passengers a year were riding the world's airlines, and the average fatal accident rate had dropped to less than three for every 100,000,000 passenger-miles.

The most apparent change (from the standpoint of the travelling public) was in the aircraft themselves. Almost overnight (1933–34) old planes vanished, and in their places came the streamlined, all-metal, efficient, and comfortable Boeing 247D's, the Douglas DC-2's and 3's, and the Lockheed 10's. These were to become the nucleus of most air-transport fleets in America and in Europe for many years. They and their direct descendants established performance standards that served the travelling public well for more than a decade; *i.e.*, until the introduction of jet aircraft in the 1950s.

Intercontinental service. For intercontinental commercial transport it first appeared that the flying boat was the logical vehicle. During the 1930s these reached the peak of their development, both in Europe and in America. A German-built Dornier WAL flying boat successfully explored the North Atlantic routes in 1930, and in the same year the world's largest flying boat, the 12-motored Dornier Do X, built for Lufthansa, left Friedrichshafen in November and, after a series of accidents and mechanical delays, finally reached New York nine months later (August 1931). It was shortly abandoned to end its days in a German museum. Meanwhile, France had established a service across the South Atlantic using Latecoeur-300 flying boats.

By the summer of 1939 French, German, and Italian air services were operating regularly between Africa and South America. Germany, in particular, was penetrating deep into South America with passenger and cargo operations. It had also piled up three years' experience with mail-carrying seaplanes catapulted from ocean liners in both the North and South Atlantic. All such activity terminated with the outbreak of World War II.

Britain's Imperial Airways and Pan American Airways of the U.S. cooperated in opening up passenger services between North America and Europe. Both were operating experimental services between New York and Bermuda in 1937. Shortly thereafter, flights were extended across the North Atlantic via Newfoundland and Ireland or the Azores.

Pan American World Airways. The history of America's intercontinental airlines was, for many years, largely the history of Pan American World Airways. Founded in 1928, the company originally operated between Florida and Cuba; by 1938 routes circled South America and reached across the Pacific to Manila and across the Atlantic to England. Large amphibians, then two- and four-engined flying boats were used.

In opening its Pacific routes in 1935, the company put into service the Martin M-130 four-engined flying boat (see Figure 6). It was replaced in 1938 by the still larger

By courtesy of Pan American World Airways, Inc.

Figure 6: The China Clipper, flying over the partially completed Golden Gate Bridge in San Francisco, on the first day of its service to the Orient, November 22, 1935.

Boeing 314 Clipper, which performed service in both the Atlantic and Pacific through World War II.

But the flying boat had outlived its usefulness as a commercial vehicle, and by 1950 virtually all overseas schedules by major airlines were being flown by the more economical and more flexible land-type aircraft.

U.S. government regulation. The development of air transportation in the United States was not without problems. Assignment of routes and regulation of rates, certification and licensing of airplanes and pilots, and the establishment of safety standards came under the general purview of the Aeronautics Branch of the Department of Commerce. In 1934 a scandal over allegedly illegal contract awards led to the sudden cancellation of all existing domestic mail contracts. Concurrently, the President ordered the Army Air Corps to take over the airmail services. Many problems ensued, and a temporary airmail law was rushed through Congress to enable the mail services to be returned to private contractors. The bill carried with it provision for the appointment of a Federal Aviation Commission to make a study of the overall aviation situation and to make recommendations for its future reorganization. This resulted in the Civil Aeronautics Act of 1938 and the creation of a Civil Aeronautics Authority. Later, in July 1940, the Civil Aeronautics Authority became a licensing and regulatory agency within the Department of Commerce, and a Civil Aeronautics Board (directly under the secretary of commerce) was established to control airline economic and safety functions. In 1968 these agencies were transferred to the newly created Department of Transportation.

GENERAL AVIATION

All nonmilitary and non-airline airplanes and helicopters are considered to be engaged in general aviation activities.

Long-distance flights. Popular interest in spectacular long-distance flights was strong up until the outbreak of World War II. Whereas successful ocean crossings had been the prime objectives of pilots in the late 1920s, around-the-world attempts provided headlines for the 1930s. Since no nonstop, around-the-world capability then existed, such flights of necessity required numerous refuellings en route. Refuelling in the air had previously been tested by Sir Alan Cobham in England and by the Air Corps in America, but the logistics of an around-the-world refuelling system were beyond then-current capabilities.

Notable around-the-world attempts. Wiley Post and Harold Gatty left Roosevelt Field, New York, on June 23, 1931, in the single-engined Lockheed monoplane "Winnie Mae" and returned to their starting point on July 1 after covering 15,474 miles around the Northern Hemisphere in eight days 16 hours flying time. Wiley Post took off alone in the "Winnie Mae" from Floyd Bennett Field, New York, on July 15, 1933, and returned on July 22, after covering 15,596 miles on the same course.

Amelia Earhart (after her successful solo transatlantic and transpacific flights) made two attempts at a world flight in a twin-engined Lockheed Electra with Fred Noonan as navigator. In March 1937 they took off on a westbound course from San Francisco, but sustained takeoff damage in leaving Honolulu, which necessitated shipping the airplane back to the United States for repair. On a second attempt they departed from Florida, eastbound, on May 21, crossed the South Atlantic, traversed Europe and southern Asia, and started across the Pacific from Australia. Somewhere in the vicinity of Howland Island they disappeared. In spite of an extensive sea and air search no traces were found.

Howard Hughes, a motion-picture producer and sportsman pilot, took off from Floyd Bennett Field on July 10, 1938, in a twin-engined Lockheed 14 with a crew of four. Three days and 19 hours later they returned, having flown some 15,500 miles.

Other notable long-range flights. In 1933 and again in 1939 Commander Richard E. Byrd and the Arctic explorer Lincoln Ellsworth led separate expeditions into Antarctica, exploring huge unknown areas by air.

In the summer of 1931 Col. and Mrs. Charles A. Lindbergh flew a single-engined Lockheed Sirius monoplane on floats to Shanghai, China, via Canada, Alaska, and Japan. In 1933, in the same aircraft, they made a survey flight on behalf of Pan American Airways over

Flying boats (margin note)

Origin of Civil Aeronautics Authority (margin note)

the North Atlantic to England, across Europe, down the West Coast of Africa, over the South Atlantic to Brazil, thence to New York City, a cruise of over 30,000 miles.

In July 1933 the Italian air minister, Italo Balbo, led a flight of 24 twin-engined Savoia Marchetti flying boats from Italy to Chicago via Iceland, Labrador, and Canada. The squadron returned to Italy via New York.

In 1937 the Soviet Union established an air-supplied navigation and communications base on the ice less than 15 miles from the North Pole. In June, two Soviet single-engined monoplanes (using this facility for navigation purposes) made nonstop flights from Moscow to the United States, the first landing in Oregon and the second in central California.

Races. A notable sporting event of the period was the MacRobertson International Race from England to Australia staged in 1934. The winners were the British pilots C.W.A. Scott and T. Campbell Black flying a specially built twin-engined de Havilland Comet racer. Second and third places were won by standard American transport planes: a Douglas DC-3 flown by a KLM (Royal Dutch Airlines) crew, and a Boeing 247D flown by an American pilot, Roscoe Turner. The result had some influence on the subsequent decisions by a number of European airlines to adopt American flying equipment.

Closed-course racing, popular in the 1910–14 period, was revived both in Europe and in America. In theory, at least, the point of the competition was to improve the equipment. The most spectacular and probably the most costly show of this sort was the international competi-
The Schneider Cup
tion for the Schneider Cup. Established in 1916, it was awarded for top speed in a free-for-all class. In the early 1930s, annual races were run in highly specialized, high-powered seaplanes developed and flown under government sponsorship. In 1931 Britain won the cup with a Supermarine S.6B at 340 mph. Several years later an Italian Macchi raised the record to 440 mph. Many of the competing machines were direct ancestors of single-seat fighters of World War II. By 1939 a stripped-down, super-powered German Messerschmitt fighter (not in a race) was officially clocked at 469 mph.

In Europe during the prewar period a number of less spectacular race meets were established under civilian auspices, designed for amateur participation. Every year, British pilots raced for the King's Cup over a course around the British Isles. Germany not only encouraged competition among glider pilots but fostered interest in amateur powered flying in annual round-Germany races. In the United States the National Air Races at Cleveland became annual September events. The practical value of such events is open to question. Though they were originally thought to be good publicity for aviation, the fact is that participation by amateur pilots in home-built racers sometimes left a trail of wreckage and fatalities that had the opposite effect.

Private flying. Far more important for the development of aviation was the great upsurge in private ownership of aircraft for business and personal use that followed the Depression years. This trend was visible both in Europe and in the United States. Flying clubs and both private and municipal flying fields became centres of popular interest. By 1939 there were over 33,000 certified civilian pilots in the United States, and the records show that private owners were logging over 50,000,000 miles of flying annually for business and pleasure.

In spite of these impressive totals, however, private flying was not yet firmly established. Wartime demands of the early 1940s channelled development in other directions.

MILITARY AVIATION

During the 1920s economic conditions and arms-limitation agreements reduced most military budgets to a minimum and left relatively little for new aircraft. Behind the scenes, some aeronautical research and development went on in government and university circles, but until Italy, Japan, and Germany began rebuilding their military establishments in the early 1930s, little that was radically new came into aviation inventories.

Two new strategic concepts put into practice during the period had far-reaching effects on developments throughout the 1930s and well beyond World War II. The first was typified in U.S. Gen. William ("Billy") Mitchell's publicly expressed conviction, which cost him his job and his rank by court-martial, in favour of an air force completely independent of ground and naval forces. The other was the Italian Gen. Giulio Douhet's doctrine that wars of the future would be won in the air by huge formations of bombers striking deep into enemy territory against industrial targets and centres of civilian population to disrupt production and to destroy national morale.

Two innovative tactical concepts were fully developed and widely employed in World War II. The first was the massive assault by paratroops with air-dropped supplies, developed first by the Soviet Union as early as 1932. The second was the intensive development of carrier-based aviation by the navies of the major powers. This greatly increased range and striking power of waterborne fleets and eventually all but eliminated the heavy battleship as a major element of naval power.

Active aerial warfare was resumed with Japan's invasion of Manchuria (1931) and Italy's war against Ethiopia (1935). Most of the aircraft used were derived from World War I types, but by the mid-'30s the effects of research and development programs began to be in evidence. The Spanish Civil War (1936) and the Russian attack against Finland (1939) offered testing opportunities for German, Italian, and Soviet planes and pilots that subsequently participated in World War II.

Germany's rearmament program began in 1933 when Adolf Hitler came to power. Consistent with the beliefs of General Mitchell, Hitler established an independent Luftwaffe (air arm). Between 1934 and 1939 German factories produced 15,927 combat aircraft and 13,889 train-
The Luftwaffe
ers and other types.

After 1936 Hitler took few pains to conceal his program. A number of qualified observers from the United States were permitted to visit certain factories and research centres and reported what they saw. But Britain, France, and the United States were slow to react. It was only after the Munich crisis of 1938 that Britain inaugurated an emergency air-force expansion, and it was not until after more than a year of active warfare that British factories began to approach the German output of aircraft. The French situation was even worse, and the defeat of 1940 prevented its being remedied.

In the U.S., though the fiasco of the army's attempt to carry the mails in 1934 attracted public and congressional attention, air corps appropriations, only $25,-000,000 in 1933, rose only to $74,000,000 in 1938. Under the impetus of the outbreak of war in Europe they jumped to $320,000,000 in 1939. Finally, the German blitzkrieg of May 1940 led Pres. Franklin D. Roosevelt to propose a combined active strength for the air corps and the navy of 50,000 airplanes, backed by a production capacity of 50,000 new planes per year. The cost of such a program was estimated at over $7,000,000,000. Though the proposal seemed fantastic at the time, the actual accomplishments of the next five years went far beyond it. The magnitude of the efforts of the United States, Germany, and Japan are shown in Table 2.

RESEARCH

In periods of international tension and of actual warfare, research is seldom pure; *i.e.*, it is seldom a search for new knowledge with which to augment the general welfare. It inevitably becomes developmental research; *i.e.*, research for the improvement of weaponry. This was the principal characteristic of aeronautical research of the period. In Germany, the theoretical work of scientists at Aachen and Göttingen was put to practical application at the laboratories of the Deutsche Versuchsanstalt für Luftfahrt (DVL) at Adlershof, and at the rocket research station at Peenemünde. Although it was not realized at the time, extensive research in supersonic aerodynamics, essential for the development of the V-2s and other rockets, was assigned to Gudonia, Italy's great research centre near Rome.

Table 2: Military Aircraft Production			
year	U. S.*	Germany†	Japan‡
1939	2,141	8,000	...
1940	6,019	10,000	...
1941	19,433	11,500	5,090
1942	47,838	14,500	8,861
1943	85,898	23,500	16,693
1944	96,318	38,500	28,180
1945	47,714	...	11,066

*Aviation Facts and Figures, Aircraft Industries Association of America (1953). †Overall Report—European War, U.S. Strategic Bombing Survey (1945) (rounded numbers). ‡Effects of Strategic Bombing on Japan's War Economy, USSBS (1946).

In the U.S. during the early 1930s, the research programs of the National Advisory Committee for Aeronautics Laboratories at Langley Field were directed toward the general improvement of commercial aviation, but beginning in 1937 the emphasis shifted to research directly connected with improving military aircraft.

The paragraphs following outline only a few of the more important areas of research covered by this period, particularly those that have had a major influence on present-day aircraft.

Jet propulsion. The most radical developments of the period occurred in jet propulsion. In 1928 an Englishman, Frank Whittle, published his fundamental thesis on the use of gas turbines for aircraft, and by 1930 he took out his first patents on a jet engine. Hans von Ohain, in Germany, doing research in the same area, applied for a patent in 1935. The first flight of a jet-powered aircraft was made by a Heinkel He 178 at Rostock, Germany, on August 27, 1939. The first Whittle engine (W-1) was flown in a Gloster E.28/39 at Cranwell, England, on May 15, 1941 (see Figure 7). In June 1941 a prototype W-1X

The first jet flight

By courtesy of the Royal Aeronautical Society

Figure 7: A Gloster E.28/39, a pioneer jet-propelled plane.

Whittle engine was flown to the United States, where copies were quickly made by General Electric, and an experimental aircraft was designed by Bell Aircraft of Buffalo. On October 1, 1942, the Bell XP-59A, powered by two GE I-16 engines, made the first U.S. jet flight at Muroc Lake, California.

The idea spread quickly. By the end of the war the Junkers Jumo 004 engine was in full production for the Messerschmitt Me 262 fighters, of which some 1,400 were produced. The Gloster Meteor twin-jet fighter was in limited production by the end of the war, but only a few reached service status, and no combat is on record. The U.S. Lockheed XP-80 fighter prototype was test-flown on Jan. 9, 1944, with a British-built engine.

These events marked a major breakthrough in aviation. From this point there was almost no limitation to the power that could be applied for man flight. Horizons, in fact, became unlimited.

Rocket research. The flight of the first rocket-powered Opel glider in Germany (1929) has been noted (see above Developments from 1918 to 1930: Rocket research). That

same year (though it was not known abroad until some time later) the Soviet Union published the first section of a nine-volume encyclopaedia on interplanetary flight. The first demonstration of a rocket-assisted takeoff took place in Germany. In 1930 the Deutsche Verein für Raumschiffahrt set up a test site near Berlin, and the German Army Ordnance Corps established a rocket weapon experimental station at Kummersdorf. Later (1937) the Rocket Test Center at Peenemünde was opened. The Soviet Union had already established rocket research centres at Moscow, Leningrad, and Kazan.

During 1942 initial test flights were conducted at Peenemünde on the A-4 rocket, later widely known as the V-2. After several disastrous failures, the first successful launching occurred in October of that year. Two years later, after the usefulness of the V-1 pulse-jet-powered flying bomb had been neutralized by the British defenses, the first V-2 rockets began to fall on London. Between November 1944 and March 1945 over 1,200 of these weapons landed in the London area. Another 800 were used against Antwerp.

The V-2 rockets

Meanwhile, in the U.S., Robert Goddard continued his rocket research. Early in 1930 he had moved his operations to a desert site near Roswell, New Mexico. There, for the next ten years (with occasional interruptions when funds ran out) he continued to work on liquid-fuelled rockets. The results of his work were carefully studied by the German rocket experts at the time, and similarities between Goddard's designs and the later V-2s are unmistakable.

Helicopters. For almost a decade interest in the helicopter seemed to have disappeared. In Germany, however, designers had been quietly at work. In 1937, without prior notice, the Focke-Achgelis Company announced that it had built a helicopter that had all the desired qualifications; i.e., vertical ascent and descent, the ability to hover, and a capability of flying forward, backward, or sidewise at the will of the pilot. Skepticism, particularly in the United States, was dispelled by repeated cross-country flights (including one from Bremen to Berlin at an average speed of 68 mph) and by spectacular public demonstrations by Hanna Rasche inside the great Deutschlandhalle in Berlin (1938). In the following year Ewald Rohlfs set an altitude record of 11,700 feet, but there was little evidence of further helicopter development. No available records indicate the use of helicopters by Germany during the war.

About that same time a spark of interest came alive in the United States. Igor Sikorsky, who had tried and failed to fly helicopters in Russia in 1910–11 (see above Developments from 1900 to 1914: Helicopters) and had then focussed his interest on airplanes, designed and built an experimental machine under the aegis of United Aircraft Corporation. The first flight of the VS-300, with Sikorsky at the controls, occurred on September 14, 1939. During 1940 he was able to stay in the air for 15 minutes at a time and in 1941 set an official world's endurance record of one hour 32½ minutes. Although the machine was demonstrated successfully for the NACA, the Air Corps, and the U.S. Navy, the increasingly heavy pressures of wartime put off further development of the helicopter until after 1945.

Balloons. Despite the use of barrage balloons to protect cities against aerial bombardment, and an abortive attempt by Japan to bomb the United States mainland by drifting explosives in free balloons across the Pacific (1944–45), the most significant employment of balloons during the period was in the area of upper-atmosphere research.

Until 1931 the highest human penetration of the Earth's atmosphere had been at about 35,000 feet by A. Berson and A.J. Süring (1901). The limiting factor had been the inability of the aeronauts to survive low temperatures and pressures in an open balloon basket.

Early in 1930 Auguste Piccard, a Swiss physicist, conceived the idea of enclosing crew and scientific instruments in an airtight, pressurized, and air-conditioned spherical gondola suspended from a balloon. With such equipment he reached an altitude of 51,775 feet in May

Auguste Piccard's ascensions

1931, and 53,152 feet in August 1932. In 1933 three Soviet scientists (G. Profkoviet, F.N. Birnbaum, and K.D. Godunow) were reported to have reached 60,680 feet in a similar balloon.

In the United States, under the auspices of the air corps, the navy, and the National Geographic Society, a number of upper-atmosphere research flights were made between 1933 and 1935, the most successful of which took place on November 11, 1935, when Capt. A.W. Stevens and Capt. O.A. Anderson of the air corps set an altitude record at 72,395 feet.

VII. Developments since 1945
Early in 1944, when jet propulsion was familiar chiefly to readers of science fiction, the following prescient comment appeared (*Wings After War*, page 11, Duell, Sloan & Pearce Inc., N.Y. 1944):

There is little reason to expect that the jet principle will have any appreciable effect on post-war commercial aviation of the next five years. Ten years from now the picture may be different.

By 1955 the picture had indeed changed. All major powers had adopted jet propulsion for combat aircraft. All major airlines were deeply involved in the design and procurement of jet-powered passenger and cargo planes and were watching with intense interest the performance of a four-jet De Havilland Comet (1952), a turbine propeller-driven Vickers Viscount (1953), first placed in service on Britain's airlines in 1953–54, and the French Caravelle with twin jets mounted at the rear of the fuselage.

Fifteen years later the revolution was complete. Research and development had solved the problem of speed with economy, and the conventional engine-plus-propeller combination that dominated the scene until the end of World War II virtually disappeared from both military and commercial aircraft. By 1970 this configuration was limited almost entirely to general aviation types (see also JET ENGINE).

COMMERCIAL AVIATION
Postwar expansion Commercial air transport revived and expanded rapidly after the war. In 1939 U.S. air carriers had carried fewer than 2,000,000 passengers with a combined fleet of some 340 aircraft. A decade later, they handled over 16,700,000 passengers with an inventory of some 1,080 aircraft. In 1949, however, all these machines were direct descendants of prewar configurations, including DC-3s, DC-4s, DC-6s, Convair 240s, Martin 202s, and Lockheed Constellations. All were powered by two or four radial air-cooled engines with conventional propellers.

Between 1949 and 1959 the revolution came. The first jet airplane to appear on commercial routes was the British De Havilland Comet, which began service in 1952. Two serious accidents, later shown to have been caused by metal fatigue, led to the grounding of the aircraft. It was reintroduced into commercial service in 1958. In spite of this discouraging experience, the swing toward all-jet operation began.

America's first jet transport, the prototype four-engined Boeing 707, was first test-flown on July 15, 1954. It went into airline service in 1958. Other jet types soon began to appear, Boeing 720, Convair 880, McDonnell Douglas DC-8, Vickers VC10, the three-jet Boeing 727, the British Aircraft Trident, and the Sud-Aviation Caravelle, the twin-jet Boeing 737, BAC One-Eleven, McDonnell Douglas DC-9, and Dassault SE-20. By 1969 U.S. airlines were flying some 2,200 turbine-powered aircraft with fewer than 300 piston-powered machines remaining in their inventories. By 1971 most of these had also disappeared.

During the 1950s and 1960s the Soviets, also starting from scratch, made great strides in their development of jet-powered and turboprop commercial air-transport equipment. Beginning with the post-World War II development of twin-engined propeller-driven machines (similar in size and performance to the U.S. DC-3s), they produced in a little over a decade a large fleet of pure jet and turboprop transports of a size and capability equal to any in the world. Typical are the Tu-104 pure jet and the large multiple turboprop transport the Tu-114.

Originally, jet-powered transports were accepted reluctantly by operators, who were dubious as to their technical and economic feasibility. Experience soon indicated, however, that maintenance and operating problems were not as formidable as had been anticipated, and the availability of fast, safe, comfortable transportation to virtually any point on the globe created a new travel demand that very quickly made airlines the dominant form of transportation. There was a comparable growth in cargo transportation (see TRANSPORTATION, AIR).

In 1970 the second phase of the civil jet age began. Beyond the stretched versions of DC-8s and 727s (stretched to increase their passenger capacity), a number of wide-bodied jets came into service. An example of these is the Boeing 747, a 720,000-pound, four-jet aircraft 185 feet long, carrying, depending upon seating arrangement, between 365 and 490 passengers at 625 mph. Several European designs for "Airbus" configurations were in prospect. All of these aircraft were subsonic.

Supersonic flying The third phase of the civil jet age opened in the spring of 1970, when the British-French Concorde (see Figure 8) and the Soviet Tu-144 first flew at supersonic speeds. Both are Mach 2 aircraft, with approximately 1,200 mph maximum speed. Commercial transatlantic services were forecast for 1975, but the future of the Concorde was clouded by economic problems and that of the Tu-144 by a fatal crash at an exhibition in Paris in 1973.

The possibility of adverse environmental effects was cited by opponents of supersonic aircraft in the United States. A government contract was awarded to the Boeing Company for a Mach 3 supersonic transport (SST), expected to fly in 1972, but in the spring of 1971 the U.S. Congress cut off all government funding for this purpose.

GENERAL AVIATION
Favourable economic conditions in the United States fostered an enormous postwar growth in non-airline flying. This category includes more than 50 times as many machines as are in the combined U.S. airline fleets, and they carry more passengers annually. Great interest in non-airline flying exists in many countries, but on a much smaller scale. Detailed statistics are generally not available.

The use of single- and twin-engined types carrying four to ten passengers for business purposes is rapidly increasing. The decentralization of many large corporations has increased the need for rapid transportation of personnel and critical materials between widely separated points. Commercial airlines, however, serve less than 10 percent of American cities, and it is this situation that has encouraged the growth of third-level air carriers (other than trunk or feeder airlines) to provide air taxi services on a charter or nonscheduled basis. At the same time many business concerns have found increasing use for their own planes, to connect with airline stops, to fly directly from point to point, utilizing the thousands of available smaller airports, or to land at flight strips at their own plants.

Although their numbers are still relatively small, helicopters and STOL (short takeoff and landing) machines are increasingly popular. In the latter category, more interest has been evidenced in Europe, where distances are generally shorter and local airports smaller. An increasing number of STOL transports for 10 to 20 passengers are now available, including Canada's De Havilland, Britain's Britten-Norman, and the Short Brothers Skyvan, Germany's Dornier, and Switzerland's Pilatus Porter. In the U.S., Fairchild Hiller, Robertson, Helio, and Wren are developing similar machines designed to operate from runways less than 500 feet long.

Crop dusting Substantial numbers of general-use aircraft are employed in agriculture, mainly for the spreading of insecticides over large farm areas. Crop dusting began in the late 1920s with surplus World War I airplanes fitted with powder-storage bins and crude distribution devices. These proved effective but hazardous because of the low-

Figure 8: The Concorde, a British-French supersonic jetliner, taking off from Heathrow Airport, London, September 14, 1970.
The Press Association Ltd.

altitude flight requirement, including the need for frequent tight turns near the ground. Machines specially designed for low-level, highly controllable slow flight have become available that are effective in spreading large loads of powder or liquids, or both, accurately and evenly over large areas.

On the strictly private, flying-for-fun side, less than 20 percent of the more than 500,000 licensed private pilots in the U.S. own aircraft. The majority rent planes on an hourly basis, or participate in flying clubs that own and service the planes to be rented to members at relatively low rates.

With increased interest in personal and private flying there has come a revival of sporting aspects of all kinds, including high-speed, closed-circuit racing, gliding and soaring competitions, parachute jumping, sky diving, model flying contests, and even hot-air balloon racing.

MILITARY AVIATION (1945–70)

By early 1960 most military and naval combat aircraft had shifted to jet power. In the U.S. the rocket-powered Bell X-1 had demonstrated (October 1947) that the so-called sonic barrier was not impregnable. Soon the new fighter aircraft of all major powers were supersonic.

As flying speeds increased, the performance capabilities of the aircraft began to exceed the physical limitations of human pilots. More and more automatic electronic equipment was necessary for the detection, pursuit, and destruction of enemy aircraft. Some single-seat fighters began to approach the size and weight of some bombers of World War II.

External configurations also changed. Swept-back wings and delta plan forms replaced the straight or tapered wings of World War II types. The U.S. McDonnell Douglas F-4 Phantom series, the Anglo-French Jaguar swept-wing interceptor, and the Swedish Saab AJ 37 delta-wing tailless canard are good examples. Soviet fighters exhibited similar characteristics.

In the late 1960s several variable-geometry arrangements (with sweep or wing camber variable at will to achieve maximum efficiencies in slow-speed or high-speed flight regimes) were tested in the U.K. and U.S. The most novel fighter of the period was the Hawker Siddeley Harrier with both direct-lift capability at zero forward speed and Mach 2 capability in normal flight.

Bomber types have also undergone radical changes. Jet engines and aerodynamic improvements (*e.g.,* swept wings) have made higher speeds possible. In-flight refuelling from aircraft tankers has extended flight ranges.

In the early 1950s the prototypes of Britain's V series bombers were flying (Avro Vulcan, H.P. Victor, and Vickers Valiant) and the six-jet swept-wing Boeing B-47 was replacing the B-29s in the U.S. Strategic Air Command (SAC). In 1957 the B-47s were replaced by eight-jet Boeing B-52s. Also in 1957 SAC acquired the first Mach 2 bomber, a four-jet delta-winged B-58 Hustler. More than 100 were built. Some were still in service in 1970, though production had been terminated in the early 1960s. In 1957 a contract was let for three experimental Mach 3 bombers. A prototype was built and flown in the fall of 1964, but the project was eventually abandoned (1968) in view of increasing intercontinental missile capability.

The military requirement for intelligence, both strategic and tactical, has forced the development of reconnaissance aircraft carrying extensive electronic and photographic gear. In the early 1950s surplus bombers and transport types were modified for the purpose, but as the Cold War progressed the need for sophisticated equipment for the collection of data over large areas of the world was recognized. Highly specialized aircraft were developed for such purposes; *e.g.,* naval, land, and carrier-based antisubmarine tracking and patrol machines; the much-publicized U-2 high-altitude reconnaissance and meteorological research plane of the late 1950s; and the long-range Mach 3 Lockheed SR-71 strategic reconnaissance aircraft in use by the USAF. In the 1960s much of this activity shifted to reconnaissance satellites.

Worldwide military and diplomatic operations require a capability to move officials, troops, and supplies rapidly over long distances on short notice. All major powers maintain transport fleets, ranging from luxurious high-speed jets and helicopters for official use to huge personnel and cargo carriers capable of delivering men, heavy equipment, and supplies to remote areas, sometimes by parachute. In 1969 the largest machine for such purposes, the Lockheed C-5 Galaxy, went into service with the USAF. This aircraft, with a gross weight of 728,000 pounds, cruises above 400 mph over ranges up to 5,500 nautical miles.

The most unusual items in the transport category are the large helicopter "Skycranes" designed to lift large and bulky loads over relatively short distances. Such machines have been under development in the Soviet Union and in the United States and are in active military service in a number of areas.

With the end of World War II, the aircraft-carrier fleets of the combatants were largely decommissioned or destroyed. The surviving naval powers, however, continued

Modern bomber types

The Skycrane

operational development with a limited number of aircraft carriers. Aircraft in service include carrier-based strike fighters, antisubmarine search and destroy aircraft, carrier- and land-based transports, helicopters, and a few amphibians. The strike and attack types are high-performance, catapult-launched jets with supersonic capability. The others, except for the helicopters, are generally propeller-turbine- or propeller-engine-powered.

For landing on carriers, naval aircraft (except helicopters) are provided with reinforced fuselage structures and retractable tail hooks to engage arresting gear on landing decks. The most unusual feature of ASW (antisubmarine warfare) types for tracking and early warning is a housing for a radar antenna resembling a large pie plate mounted over the midsection of the fuselage.

An outstanding development of the military actions in Korea and in Indochina was the use of helicopters in large numbers for transport of troops and supplies, for evacuation of wounded, and as gun ships firing both rockets and normal ordnance.

RESEARCH

During the course of World War II the emphasis in all countries was on aeronautical development; *i.e.*, accepting the best scientific data available and applying them to the improvement of existing aircraft to outperform those of the enemy. In the first postwar decade, as immediate pressures were removed and as general economic conditions improved, funds again became available for long-range scientific research in aeronautics. Although such work made considerable progress in the U.K. and Canada and revived in other countries, the most extensive and most widely reported research was performed by the then National Advisory Committee for Aeronautics (now the National Aeronautics and Space Administration, or NASA) at its laboratories at Langley Field, Virginia; Moffett Field, California; and at Cleveland, Ohio; and its Test Flight Centers at Edwards Air Force Base, California, and at Wallops Island, Virginia.

Some of the aircraft-oriented projects undertaken since World War II, indicating the scope and extent of the work, are trans-sonic wind-tunnel research that resulted in the so-called Coke-bottle shape for fuselages and swept- or delta-wing configurations for supersonic aircraft; flight tests on supersonic aircraft to determine stability and control characteristics; studies on variable-geometry wing configurations; analysis of structural flutter and vibration problems at high speeds; studies of helicopter stability and control; research in wind tunnels and in towing basins on high-speed submarines and on jet-powered flying boats; studies of arrested landing problems on carrier decks and on short runways; analyses of flexible-wing aircraft; studies of aerodynamic heating and the behaviour of aircraft materials at high temperatures; vertical takeoff and landing research; and research, development, and flight-testing the X-15 high-altitude Mach 6 airplane.

The X-15 airplane

Of these, the last is of particular significance, for the X-15 may represent the ultimate in airplane performance and bridge the gap between man flight in the Earth's atmosphere and man flight in space. Three of these special-purpose research machines were built under joint auspices of the U.S. Air Force, Navy, and NACA and flown by their pilots. First flight occurred on June 8, 1959, and in the following ten years (to September 28, 1968) a total of 197 flights were made. Speeds over 4,500 mph and altitudes of over 350,000 feet were attained.

THE FORESEEABLE FUTURE

Early man-flight prophets gazed into crystal balls and forecast wonderful things to come for centuries ahead. Accomplishment has almost always exceeded their anticipation. The temptation, therefore, is to follow their example and take off into the wild blue future, but caution, plus a considerable respect for physical facts and economic uncertainties, suggests but a limited look ahead—approximately a decade.

Commercial aviation. The pattern for the 1970s seems reasonably well established. Short of political or eco-

nomic catastrophe, the passenger demand on world airlines should about double, with a possible fourfold increase in cargo tonnage carried. By 1980 most of the present large jet transports will still be in service, supplemented by possibly 150 new subsonic wide-bodied and 50 to 60 supersonic machines in intercontinental services. Hypersonic transports and space shuttle craft will still be in the future.

Airport operations. Not much improvement over the current high level of passenger comfort in the air can be anticipated, although much must be done to improve the handling of passengers and their luggage at airports, particularly at international terminals. The problems involved in getting passengers to and from airports might be eliminated if vertical landing and takeoff by high-speed aircraft can be effected economically, but this seems unlikely by 1980.

Environmental problems. In the early 1970s, the sonic boom was still a major concern for prospective SST operators. A short-term solution is to prohibit supersonic flight over populated areas. It now seems possible, however, that research may uncover means of controlling the propagation of shock waves to dissipate their energy before they reach the ground. Landings and takeoffs over cities are no problem, as none of these aircraft achieve supersonic speeds until they reach high altitudes. In addition, long-range environmental effects of the SST on the Earth's atmosphere call for continuing study.

Flight safety. Flight safety is of continuing concern, for the prospect of a mid-air collision between two fully loaded large jets, or of an SST crashing in a populated area, cannot be tolerated. By 1980, however, fully automated flight patterns, including takeoffs and landings, and in-flight collision avoidance will be possible. Each flight will be pre-programmed from takeoff to touchdown to follow automatically the safest, fastest, and most comfortable flight profile with only minimum attention by flight crews. In the spring of 1971 a system of fully automated landings was successfully demonstrated using a Boeing 747 aircraft.

Automated flight patterns

General aviation. The future use of small aircraft and helicopters for business or pleasure will depend on the general economic conditions of the 1970s. It is certain that the costs of such flying will continue to rise, particularly since all aircraft flying beyond the vicinity of home airports in any but clear weather will be required to carry enough radio and navigational equipment to enable them to use established air routes subject to air-traffic control.

Military aviation. The immediate prospects for military aviation depend both on the economic and the political situation. If economic conditions are favourable, and no immediate hostilities are in prospect, long-range research and development will continue, and year by year bigger and better fighters, bombers, and missiles will be added to the inventories of all countries that can afford to stay in the competition. If active warfare threatens, research funds will dry up, and maximum effort will be focussed on producing what is then available in the greatest possible number.

BIBLIOGRAPHY. C. DOLLFUS and H. BOUCHE, *L'Histoire de l'aéronautique* (1932), the classic and definitive history of flight to the early 1930s; C.H. GIBBS-SMITH, *The Aeroplane: An Historical Survey* (1968), a comprehensive and detailed compilation by a noted British historian; *Jane's All the World's Aircraft* (annual), specifications and photographs of all known aircraft and missiles; G. LOENING, *Our Wings Grow Faster* (1935), and *Takeoff into Greatness* (1968), a review of the development of the U.S. aeronautical industry by a pioneer and long-time participant; NATIONAL AERONAUTICS AND SPACE ADMINISTRATION, *Fifty Years of Aeronautical Research* (1968), a well-illustrated survey of aeronautical research progress; J.L. PRITCHARD, *Sir George Cayley* (1961), an in-depth biography of the father of British aeronautics; SMITHSONIAN INSTITUTION, *Langley Memoir on Mechanical Flight* (1902), a detailed and fully illustrated account of the aeronautical research of Samuel Pierpont Langley; H.S. VILLARD, *Contact: The Story of the Early Birds* (1968), personal reminiscences of planes and pilots of the pre-World War I era; WILBUR and ORVILLE WRIGHT, *Miracle at Kitty Hawk*, ed. by F.C. KELLY (1951), a compilation of the Wrights' research data; T. VON KARMAN, *The Wind and Beyond* (1967), a report on technical flight progress by an outstanding scientist.

(S.P.J.)

Floor Coverings

Included in this article is a treatment of both handmade and machine-made rugs and carpets and of smooth-surfaced floor coverings. The history of floor coverings is sketched from early primitive types through the development of the modern carpet and rug industry and the smooth-surfaced flooring industry. Modern manufacturing techniques, including both processing steps and the various end products, are examined and economic aspects of the industry set forth. Aesthetic and decorative aspects are treated in the article RUGS AND CARPETS.

Although the words carpet and rug are frequently used interchangeably in referring to textile floor coverings, in modern usage carpets are fastened to the floor and usually cover an entire floor area, and rugs are not fastened and rarely cover the entire floor. Carpets and rugs may be classified as handmade or machine-made.

Handmade carpets and rugs are usually made by knotting a number of pile tufts to a backing structure so that the loose knot ends form the pile. Mainly produced in Asia and the East, knotted types are often given the general name of Oriental carpets and may be classified according to the country of manufacture, such as Persian (originating in Iran) or Chinese. Well-known districts or towns may give their names to the carpets they produce; the Persian Kirman is an example. Other hand-knotted rugs include the Savonnerie rugs of France and the modern rya rugs of the Scandinavian countries. Handmade rugs woven by the tapestry method, often described as the Aubusson type, for the French town in which the method was perfected, have a flat or slightly ribbed surface instead of pile. Hooked rugs are made by drawing yarn or fabric strands through a basic material so as to form a pile of loops that may be clipped or remain uncut.

Machine-made carpets include such woven types as Axminster and Wilton, and also tufted, knitted, and flocked types. Axminsters resemble hand-knotted carpets, but their pile yarn is mechanically inserted and bound and not knotted. Wilton types may have looped (uncut) or cut pile, with designs formed by bringing yarns of the desired colour to the surface and burying the others beneath the surface. Velvet carpeting is made by looping strands that form the pile over wire strips that are removed as each row of loops is completed. Chenille rugs have soft, deep pile formed by long, furry strips. The pile of tufted carpets is formed by tufts inserted into a backing with needles. In knitted carpets, the backing, locking, and pile yarns are all looped together. Flocked types are produced by systems in which adhesives are used to bind fibres or yarns to the backing fabric.

Smooth-surfaced floor coverings include linoleum, rubber floor coverings, cork tile, asphalt tile, printed felt base, and the vinyl types. Most are available in varying degrees of thickness, usually from $\frac{1}{16}$ to $\frac{3}{16}$ inch, and may have some form of backing. Although flexible types are available in rolls at least six feet wide, square tiles are increasingly popular in all types. The various materials differ in their ability to take colour or pattern, and mottled or spatter effects are often achieved by blending in one or more mixes of the same general composition as the basic material.

HISTORY OF FLOOR COVERINGS

Early floor coverings. Prehistoric man may have happened upon a method of forming thread from twisted grass or hair. Evidence obtained from recent excavations near the Caspian Sea indicates that the shearing of sheep and goats, and the spinning and weaving of the fibres obtained, was practiced as early as 6000 BC. Before the development of weaving, fibres were probably interlaced to produce a simple form of plaited basket-work matting, replacing still earlier crude mats made of strands of dry stalks and tendrils.

Findings in burial mounds at Pazyryk in southern Siberia, 2,400 years old, indicate that furs, leather, woven textiles, and felts were used, not as floor coverings, but as wall hangings. The first true carpets, characterized by pile surfaces, were probably rough cured skins that early hunters laid on the floors of their crude dwellings. Most carpets still retain the same tough flexible backings and upright pile, affording protection from cold and hard floors, agreeable to the touch, and serving a decorative function.

Smooth floorings also have ancient origins. In the Late Bronze Age (1600–1000 BC) water-worn pebbles were laid as flooring in Crete and also on the Greek mainland. The Greeks refined the technique between the 6th and the 4th centuries BC, and ancient decorative pebble mosaics have been found in Greece, Asia Minor, and Sicily. Such mosaics were also made of marble, serpentine alabaster, some forms of granite, and other stones suitable for polishing. Timber flooring, originally used in rough form for a strictly functional purpose, was eventually made into smooth boards, and was later used decoratively in parquetry designs.

Carpet and rug weaving. Although the exact origins of carpet weaving have not been determined, it is known that the Egyptians of the 3rd millennium BC wove carpets for the most part of linen ornamented by sewn on brightly coloured pieces of woollen cloth. Egyptian influence apparently spread throughout the Middle East and then to Mongolia and China. Some investigators credit Central Asia, Turkestan, and China with the origination of carpets, and in the early 1950s a rug dating back 2,400 years, made with Turkish knots, was found in Siberia.

Early Chinese carpets were made of knotted silk pile with backings of wool or cotton, but the pile of later carpets was made of wool. Wool pile was also used in Central Asia by early nomadic tribes who acquired it easily in their wanderings. Nomadic rugs were woven on simple horizontal frames that could be rolled up for travelling.

Early looms consisted of two forked branches joined by a crosspiece holding the suspended warp, or lengthwise threads, through which the weft, or crosswise threads, were woven. A wooden bar was used to flatten the binding weft threads, allowing the loose warp ends to stand out to form the luxurious pile. The early weavers used wools in their natural gray, white, cream, fawn, brown, or black colours, but eventually learned to produce fast colours with dyes made from vegetable, flower, and insect materials.

During the Middle Ages, Italian merchants imported Oriental rugs to Europe, where they were usually hung on the walls; Europeans continued to cover their floors with rushes and straw. Moorish weavers were probably taken from Spain in the 13th century to set up the looms at Aubusson in France. Eleanor of Castile introduced Spanish rugs to England in 1255, and carpets imported from Turkey in the 15th century encouraged the development of an English rug-weaving industry.

By 1600 French carpet weavers had formed a strong guild, and in 1608 Henry IV set up looms in the Louvre. During the reign of Louis XIV, carpet manufacture was revived at Aubusson, where it had suffered from the religious wars of the 16th century, and was established at Beauvais, in Normandy. The revocation of the Edict of Nantes, that had guaranteed religious and civil freedom to French Protestants, drove French and Walloon Protestant artisans into England and Germany, where they contributed to the development of spinning and weaving techniques.

English carpet weavers were chartered at Wilton and Axminster in 1701, and in 1740 the Earl of Pembroke brought weavers from France to perform Brussels and Wilton weaving. At about the same time, carpet weaving was also established at Kidderminster, and the trade extended to northern England and Scotland. In 1830 a Parliamentary paper noted that carpet wool comprised one-twenty-eighth of the wool produced in the United Kingdom.

In the 18th century Richard Arkwright and others invented machinery that radically improved textile manufacture and together with the steam engine led to the development of the power loom, first applied to carpet

Early matting

Early looms

making in 1839. The so-called Jacquard mechanism, which employed punched cards to control the warp yarns, gradually began to replace the complicated harness of the hand loom for the production of designs. The tapestry process of printing patterned carpets was evolved in Edinburgh in the 1830s, and in 1839 a chenille Axminster process, which was patented by James Templeton of Glasgow, gave increased colour range to carpet designs.

The U.S. carpet industry began by adapting the British system on a modest scale. Largely a cottage industry, it was organized by agents who marketed the small amount produced, until the first half of the 19th century. By 1830, the use of carpets had become popular throughout the eastern U.S., and factories were being established in New England, New York, and Pennsylvania. The continued dominance of the U.S. market by British carpets led U.S. manufacturers to encourage the development of power equipment, and a power loom first appeared in 1841. In 1876 an Axminster loom was invented. This development stimulated the carpet industry by permitting an unlimited range of colour and design with an economy of pile.

Loom widths increased from the formerly conventional 18, 27, or 36 inches (46, 69, or 91 centimetres), to the broadloom, usually 12, 15, or 18 feet (4, 5, or 6 metres) wide, resulting in large economies in weaving costs and producing larger and more convenient unseamed areas for laying. After World War II, needle tufting developed, employing a prewoven backing for the basic construction, and the major portion of carpeting manufactured in the U.S. was produced by this system. Some tufted carpet manufacturers even began to produce outdoor carpets and imitation lawns.

Smooth-surfaced floor coverings. In 1860 Frederick Walton of Great Britain patented a process for making linoleum, the first widely used smooth-surfaced floor covering. Plain linoleum, without design, was popular until the mid-1930s, when decorative linoleum was developed. In the 1920s, dark-coloured asphalt sheet and tile materials were developed in the U.S., made from mixtures of asbestos fibre, mineral fillers, and asphalt, and although light-coloured resins, not containing asphalt, became available within the next ten years, the name asphalt tile persists in the U.S. for this type of flooring. In the U.K. the term asphalt tile was used for a different product, and the somewhat misleading term thermo-plastic tile was applied to a similar British product. Vinyl asbestos tiles, containing asbestos fibres, were developed next and introduced at the Chicago World's Fair in 1933, but resin shortages prevented quantity production until 1948. Vinyl, a newer composition material with a high content of polyvinyl chloride resins, was eventually perfected. The number and variety of smooth-surfaced floor coverings multiplied after World War II, and plastics had considerable impact. Although traditional linoleum was still in use, such materials as asphalt, cork, rubber, vinyl asbestos, and the various types of vinyl were achieving greater popularity. A new development in the 1960s was a type of flooring applied directly to the area to be covered and allowed to harden; epoxy resins have generally been used.

HANDMADE CARPETS AND RUGS

Orientals. Major classifications of Orientals, based on place of origin, include Persians, the largest and most important group; Turkomans, popular red carpets including Turkoman, Afghan, and Baluchistan rugs made in Central Asia; Caucasian carpets, from Caucasia and Transcaucasia; the Turkish Anatolian group, less intricately designed than other Orientals; and the Indian, Pakistani, and Chinese group, frequently less durable than the other types.

Materials. The availability of excellent materials is probably the factor most responsible for the origin of carpets in the East. The nomads had access to fibres from their camels, goats, and sheep; cotton was cultivated in Persia and China, and silk in China. Nomadic carpet makers often used wool for the warp and weft of a rug

foundation fabric, as well as for the pile. Although a variety of materials may be used in making Oriental rugs, wool is the most important pile fibre, and cotton is most often used as the base and binder material.

Knots. The pile surface of knotted rugs is formed entirely by the ends of knotted tufts. The Ghiordes, or Turkish, knot brings both tuft ends to the surface together between two warp yarns. It is common in the Near East, especially in Turkey and the Caucasus. The Sehna, or Persian, knot brings each end of the tuft to the surface separately. It predominates in Central Asia and the Far East, mainly in Afghanistan, India, Pakistan, Turkestan, and China. In Iran either knot is used, depending upon the origin or site of the tribe or town producing the rug.

Ghiordes and Sehna knots

From I. Wingate, *Textile Fibers and Their Selection* 5th ed. Prentice–Hall Inc. © 1964

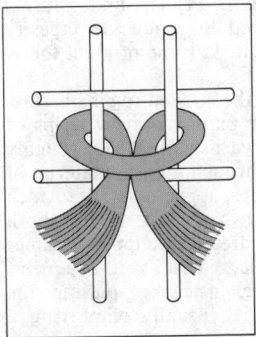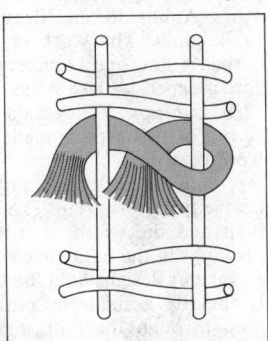

Figure 1: (Left) Ghiordes knot. (Right) Sehna knot.

Looms. The loom employed is upright, consisting of two strong beams connected by two vertical posts to make a steady frame. It is often adjustable for the weaving of different sized carpets and rugs. The weaver is positioned conveniently in relation to the row of knots being worked either by means of a seat that can be raised, moving him upwards, or by winding each completed row of knots onto a separate cloth beam. The warp, or lengthwise, threads stretched between the two beams are evenly spaced and regularly spun, assuring that the pile forming beneath the surface will also be even.

Weaving. The weaver ties his rows of knots forming the pattern, and when an entire row of pile is knotted, the two, three, or four weft, or crosswise, threads are forced down by a comb or knife, causing the pile to stand out. Density of pile is about 300 knots to the square inch and a weaver completes about 8,000 per day; several weeks' work is needed to produce an ordinary carpet, and possibly months for a more complex one. The weaving instructions required to produce the desired pattern may be chanted by a Salim or may be provided on a coloured chart of squared paper.

Dyestuffs. In olden days, craftsmen used natural dyestuffs, obtaining reds from the roots of the madder plant; carmine red from cochineal, the bodies of the female *Coccus cacti;* reddish-browns from ox blood; yellow from the reseda plant or from saffron crocus, vine leaves, and pomegranate skins; and blue from the indigo plant. Mixtures of certain blues and yellows produced greens; and natural wool shades produced greys and brown, although nutshells and bark were also used. Oak apples were often used to produce black, but if their iron oxide content was high the wool was likely to be damaged; some old carpets today show the most wear in the black portions. Modern synthetic dyestuffs allow greater flexibility than these traditional dyes.

Characteristics. Persian rugs have intricate all-over patterns, mainly floral, but sometimes including animal or human figures, often with a central medallion. Colours include soft pastels and muted reds, browns, and blues. The rugs are fringed at both ends.

Turkoman rugs are woven in geometric designs, employing vivid reds, browns, and greens, and usually have webbed fringes at the ends. Caucasian rugs have sharply outlined, bold, geometric patterns. Brilliant and strongly contrasting colours are employed, frequently including reds, yellows, and blues. Turkish rug patterns have precise, stylized geometric or floral designs, with bright, sharp, contrasting colours. Indian rugs are made with botanical designs in a naturalistic style and are brilliant in colour. Chinese rug designs include religious symbols. Designs are usually in blue, and background colours include dulled yellows, browns, and roses.

Other handmade carpets and rugs. *Tapestry weave.* Another kind of hand weaving is the tapestry method, wherein the coloured weft threads, wound upon wooden needles, are threaded around and between the warp ends, leaving a flat or slightly ribbed surface. Since a tapestry carpet lacks a tufted pile, it does not have a luxurious texture, even though a fine pitch, the number of warps per inch, can be employed, and the richest and most delicate effects of design and colour obtained. Carpets of this type have long been made at Les Gobelins, Paris, Aubusson, and Beauvais in France, and Tournai in Belgium. The work involved in producing tapestry carpet is slow and requires great skill; the product therefore is expensive (see TAPESTRY).

Hooked rugs. The origin of the hooked rug is obscure. A rug of this type is made by pulling narrow strips of wool or cotton cloth or wool yarn, with a tool roughly resembling a buttonhook, up through a basic material of coarse linen or burlap. The loops, approximately ½ inch high and the width of from two to four of the mesh openings in the basic material, are often clipped. Frames of various designs hold the basic material taut. Frequently the rug is made by pushing, instead of pulling, the loop through the basic material, usually employing a large threaded needle.

Modern handweaving. It is possible to weave rugs, with or without a pile surface, on hand looms. Almost any material can be used for hand-weaving, including plastic strips and some forms of rope. Weaving speed can be increased by the use of a chain-and-pedal drive similar to that used on bicycles. In modern times, handweaving is mainly limited to design development and study in educational institutions and to the most costly floor coverings, frequently made to order and considered fine works of art.

MACHINE-MADE CARPETS AND RUGS

Early machine processes employed hand or water power to duplicate processes originally performed completely by hand. The invention of the power loom greatly reduced the amount of time and labour, and therefore the cost, of carpet manufacture.

Nomenclature and types. Machine-made rugs and carpets take their names from the looms employed, such as Wilton or Axminster, or the construction method, such as ingrain or Brussels.

Ingrain. After 200 years of use, the ingrain became almost obsolete during the 1930s because of its relatively poor wearing qualities. Also called Kidderminster or Scotch, it is flat ribbed, reversible, and completely without pile, and usually could be made with two- or three-ply warp and weft yarns, dyed before weaving.

Design on the surface of the carpet was easily produced by bringing to the surface, at the chosen area, the desired colour of the weft; the latter almost completely formed the surface colouring. Although the warp intruded into the design, its colour was carefully chosen to blend satisfactorily. The term Venetian has been applied to lesser grades of ingrain carpet.

Wire-formed piles. Brussels carpet, with uncut looped pile formed by round wires, was first introduced about the mid-18th century. Shortly after, Wilton followed with the development of bladed wires producing a cut pile. Both were capable of producing elaborate pile designs, and the Jacquard device was used with them from about the 1820s, when it replaced hand selection of coloured pile threads. Bigelow's power principles were applied to the loom from about 1849. Pile not used for surface design is woven longitudinally into the body of the backing fabric. Brussels carpets, woven on the Wilton loom, but with their pile remaining uncut, are no longer sold in large quantities.

Velvet carpet is basically a Wilton type with the design printed on the yarn before weaving. Normally, up to five or six different coloured pile threads per dent, the space between two wires, are used for Jacquard Wilton (*i.e.*, five or six frames of pile yarn). Velvet carpet with only one frame is sometimes termed plain (coloured) Wilton.

Tapestry carpet, although constructed as velvet, remained uncut. A full set of threads produced the desired design in the outer loop pile carpet. Basically a two-process carpet, it was more economical than Wilton or Brussels because of its single-frame design, and was woven more quickly because no jacquard was required. Invented about 1830 in Scotland, tapestry carpets are now virtually obsolete, with few of them produced in the main carpet centres (Kidderminster, West Riding of Yorkshire, and Scotland) after World War II.

Typical high quality Wilton and Brussels carpets contain about 120 tufts per square inch with up to 13 rows per inch. Tapestry, generally up to about 80 tufts per square inch, but as low as 50, is possible. Velvet may be similar in density to tapestry, but not necessarily so; it can be made with pile as dense as Wilton if desired.

Wilton carpet can be produced on the "face-to-face" principle. Two carpets are simultaneously woven sandwiched one above the other, and the two are then cut apart by a reciprocating blade traversing the loom width. The linear rate of production is thus almost doubled; Jacquard designs can be produced by this method.

Loom-formed pile. Axminster carpets, in which all of the pile yarn is effectively used for design (unlike Wilton and Brussels that waste some "dead" pile yarn by hiding it in the body of the carpet) include spool, gripper, and chenille.

Spool looms were invented in the U.S. in 1876, and the gripper Axminster loom was developed about 1890. The chenille two-stage process was invented in Glasgow about 1830.

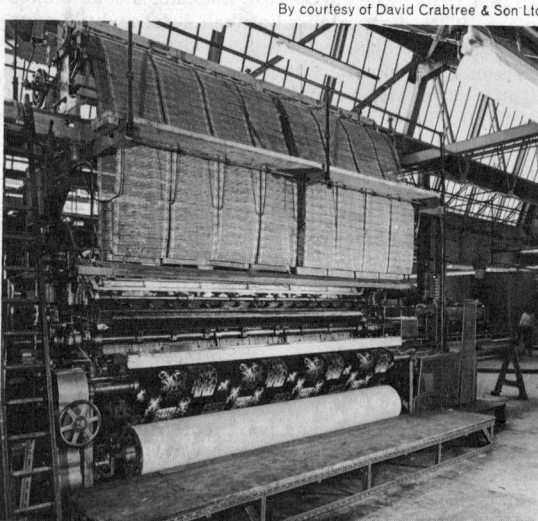

By courtesy of David Crabtree & Son Ltd.

Figure 2: Gripper-Jacquard carpet loom, producing patterned and coloured Axminster pile carpet. The carpet is woven entirely in the loom, which is supplied with weft, warp, selvage threads, and pile yarn. The pile yarn is contained in creels at the rear of the machine.

With the first loom, each row of pile is drawn from an individual spool, and two blades cut away the tufts when woven. On the gripper loom, each tuft is held by its beak-like gripper and taken from its yarn carrier to the fell of the carpet, the point at which the warp and weft intersect, after being precisely cut away by a traversing knife blade. One type of spool-gripper Axminster loom employs spools instead of a jacquard; the tufts are taken from them and woven on the gripper principle. Chenille pile (from the French word for caterpillar) is formed on the carpet loom by weaving the "fur," or pile yarn, as a weft. The tufts are usually bound by cotton threads forming a long strand. The fur is woven in the first weav-

Kidder-minster

Axminster carpets

ing process on normal cloth looms and cut longitudinally into the requisite patterned strips; pile yarn is woven as weft, and the warp is the cotton binding threads. A simple gauze or the lacelike leno weave is used to bind the weft pile yarn so that the pile does not fall away when the strips are cut, before they can be woven into the carpet.

Jute weft and cotton warp are common materials for Axminster carpets. All-wool pile is popular, although nylon–wool mixtures and various combinations of natural and man-made fibres are becoming common. Carpets made of 100 percent man-made fibres are increasing in popularity. Spool and gripper qualities average about 40 to 50 tufts per square inch, the two extremes being about 30 and 60.

Unconventional carpets: tufted, knitted, and bonded. In tufted carpets, the tufts are inserted by means of vertically reciprocating needles pushing through prewoven backing and are held below the carpet backing by loopers. The loop pile slips off the loopers, or is severed when cut pile is desired, as the formed carpet moves away from the looping elements. The rate of pile yarn feed from the creel, the bar holding the bobbins, governs pile height. The variation of this rate for groups of pile threads is the basis for certain patterned effects resulting from the inclusion of both high and low pile areas or achieved by alternating two different coloured threads across the full width, emphasizing the pattern in one colour by hiding the other low-pile colour with higher adjacent loops. Different rates of feed can be obtained by electrical or mechanical means. In the former, the pattern, in small scale, is placed on a pattern drum, and feelers touching the pattern areas change the delivery rate of the pile feed roller. Photoelectric means of influencing the delivery rate have also been devised. The mechanical device pushes down the required pile lengths by means of a castellated metal plate cut to the required pattern. Other effects can be obtained from fancy or printed yarns, and some tufting machines reciprocate the carpet widthwise to obtain a longitudinal zigzag effect. Designs including up to eight colours are possible, with quality almost as satisfactory as in traditional carpets having an equal number of colours.

Quality ranges now vary as much as for traditional carpets, since needle spacings may be as high as 12 to the inch, giving the same number of tufts per square inch as in Wilton. Traditional pile materials are employed, but polypropylene, a synthetic fibre, is commonly used on prewoven backing. There has also been some development of nonwoven backings.

Production rates can be many times greater than that of Axminster looms; one machinery manufacturer has developed a yarn looping technique whereby the backing is pierced by a needle and the pile is then blown through the resulting opening. This method increases the rate of production up to about 1,200 rows of pile per minute. Patterned carpets have been produced mainly in the United States with either cut or loop pile, or a combination of both. In warp knitting, beams are used to feed in the yarn supply; in weft knitting, the yarns are fed from smaller packages.

A Czechoslovakian Arachne stitch-bonding machine achieves high production rates with low pile costs, employing a fibrous web stitched on the knitting principle with yarns drawn from beams. An East German Malipol machine uses knitting principles to bind pile to a backing fabric, although a later model uses unknitted weft threads instead of backing. Production rates for knitting are higher than for traditional looms, but do not reach the high speeds of modern tufting. The quality of the materials used and the finished carpet are much like that of the middle range of traditional carpets. No spectacular growth, however, in the sales of such carpets has occurred, since there are currently limitations in design, although development work is progressing. Several methods use the principle of bonding fibres, fibrous webs, or yarns with various adhesives. The technique imposes design limitations, but the less complicated pile forming method results in high production rates. The needle loom

principle involves a fibrous lap attached to a base fabric and another method forms a lap into a loop pile sheet and sticks it to a base fabric. A special finishing operation can convert the loops into cut pile.

A German device projects positively charged fibres toward a negative pole; the fibres are then stuck to an adhesive-coated backing fabric. A Czechoslovakian technique makes double, or face-to-face, carpet by looping and bonding a fibrous web to two backing fabrics; the full layer is then cut into two separate carpets. A French machine cuts fibres from a sheet and then binds them to a fabric backing, with electrostatic means used to keep the fibres vertical.

Manufacturing methods. *Raw material preparation.* The warp and weft backing structures of carpets, and the pile yarn superimposed upon it, made originally from natural fibres, are now mostly synthetic. Backing yarns are frequently made from the lower priced cut-staple normal or high-tenacity viscose rayons. Selvages of synthetic filaments and pile yarns are produced from mixtures of cut-staple man-made and natural fibres, the latter primarily wool. Pile yarns composed of the more expensive synthetic materials are increasingly used, and viscose rayon has been used extensively for less costly carpets. As the use of man-made filament pile yarns has increased, traditional processing of natural and staple man-made fibres has decreased in importance.

The preparation of natural fibres for backing and pile yarns involved many labour-consuming operations. Fibres had to be cleansed, often by mechanical means and a wet treatment. Pile-yarn wools had to be thoroughly scoured, and cotton fibres also needed special cleaning treatment. Straightening of fibres prior to spinning was a long-drawn-out process, with spinning often followed by additional single twisting operations to form ply or cable yarns. In contrast, man-made filament yarns are extruded in clean, continuous, and parallel form, and the twisting operation is uncomplicated. Backing fabrics are currently made from fibrilated yarns, consisting of small fibres twisted together, and sliced narrow tapes are made from sheets of synthetic film.

Selection and preparation of design. Design creation or selection involves consideration of the range or limitations of the various methods of carpet manufacture. The number of colours that can be used for Jacquard Wilton and gripper Axminster are limited; spool and chenille Axminster allow unlimited colour range. Density tends to be greatest for Wilton carpet, sometimes reaching as high as 130 per square inch.

Spool Axminster designs are made from a chain of spools, with one spool to each row of pile. There are usually seven threads to the inch across the width, with a pile yarn length per thread of about 35 feet (11 metres). Spool width varies according to the loom, the smallest is usually 18 inches (46 centimetres) wide. The person operating the machine creels all necessary colours for the tufts in a row and winds the full spool, repeating the process until the full set for the design is made.

Gripper Axminster and Wilton Jacquard looms utilize a perforated card system to select the required combination of different coloured threads per row of pile. There is one card per row, punched according to the predetermined design, and the possible colour choice for each tuft is usually one in five for Wilton and one in eight for gripper Axminster. "Planting" of several additional colours in the pile-yarn creel may increase the number of different colours possible in a design. High- and low-cut and uncut effects are also possible in Wilton carpets. Normally employed on tufted carpets, the process can be applied to all types. Different pile height effects are produced in tufted carpets by using different rates of yarn feed, and are sometimes emphasized by alternating the colours and hiding the colour of low pile under adjacent high pile. Mechanical and photoelectric devices are used to regulate the rate of yarn feed to the tufting needles.

Construction. The basic structure of traditionally manufactured carpets consists of the backing fabric and the pile, which is bound under and between the weft. Pile

---

Polypropylene backing

Preparation of natural fibres

is formed on Axminster looms by inserting weft, with reciprocating needles, across the warp chain yarns. A central stuffer warp usually separates top from bottom weft. In Jacquard Wilton and Brussels carpet, the pile not used for surface design effect is concealed between top and bottom weft; Axminster carpet uses all pile yarn for surface effect. Wilton pile is formed by looping the yarn over wires that project it mechanically across the width of the loom and beneath the decorative pile yarns. When the wires are withdrawn, they either cut the pile, forming Wilton, or leave it uncut to form Brussels carpet.

In spool Axminster carpets each row of tufts is inserted and cut away from the spools. On gripper Axminster looms each tuft is inserted by its individual beaklike gripper, after being cut away from the carrier. Backing fabrics have warps held on flanged beams; in Wilton weaving, weft threads wound on cones are shuttled across the loom. Axminster weft is drawn from large stationary cones at the side of the loom.

Tufted carpets

Tufted carpets differ basically from traditional types because they have a prewoven backing into which the tufts are inserted. One unconventional method of making carpet involves the forming of pile on knitted structures. Another method involves the application of pile yarns or even undulating webs of fibres to backing fabric by means of adhesives. These methods often lack the means for controlling design.

Finishing. After weaving, carpeting may require machine brushing to remove loose fibre or yarn, before any correction of processing faults. Traditional carpets have a separate reparation process, but on tufted carpets, missing pile, the most common fault, is stitched in by a portable "gun" operating a reciprocating needle. The carpet pile is then sheared to uniform level with cutting blades similar to those of a wide lawn mower. Steaming of the pile causes it to expand or "burst" into an aesthetically enhanced state. Natural back-sizings were formerly applied to Axminster carpets, and Wilton and Brussels weft threads on their cones were soaked in sizing. Increasing use of such synthetic backing compounds as polyvinylacetate, and different kinds of lattice backings now produce excellent tuft bind and stiffness.

Other modern finishing processes include mothproofing of wool, often performed in the dyeing sequence, and application of soil-resistant finishes to man-made pile, rot-proofing, and antistatic treatment.

Reinforcement or screening, particularly used for tufted backing, may employ adhesives on open structure woven materials, and the use of such cushioning materials as synthetic rubber foam is increasing.

SMOOTH-SURFACED FLOOR COVERINGS

Linoleum. Linoleum is produced by pressing a sheet containing oxidized linseed oil, gums and resins, ground cork or wood flour, and pigments on to a backing, and it is hung in huge "curing" stoves to toughen.

Two general types, plain and printed, or inlaid, linoleum, are produced; the latter has a constant pattern throughout its thickness. Different methods are employed to create various design effects. Thickness ranges from about 1.6 to 4.5 millimetres, depending upon the traffic expected; a standard width is six feet (two metres), and the weight in 3.2 millimetres gauge is about 7.6 pounds per square yard (3.5 kilograms per square metre). Recently developed products are specially hardened to resist indentation. Certain alkalies and organic solvents, however, will attack linoleum if left in prolonged contact; staining and discoloration can arise from certain anti-oxidants in tires, rubber castors, or rubber heels. Linoleum is resilient, warm, unaffected by reasonable floor temperatures, and does not readily support combustion.

Printed felt base. Printed felt base is formed by applying a heavy film of paint to felt saturated with asphalt; the felt is sealed at both the top and bottom with one or more layers of coating before application of paint, preventing discoloration from the paint and leveling the surface. The paint used has low volatility and little flow, dries quickly in thick layers, and gives high gloss with good wearing properties. Wooden blocks are used to apply the paint on the base, with several colours being printed separately. The material is next dried in an oven, with the product hanging from racks or festooned, and this maturing process requires several days. Rugs or rolls are available in several thicknesses and sizes.

Asphalt tile. The tiles are made from asphalts (25 percent) or synthetic resins, asbestos fibres (25 percent), pigments, and mineral fillers (50 percent). If asphaltic binder is used, colour is restricted to black, brown, and dark reds. The plasticised resin-based tiles are much lighter in colour, including blues, reds, yellows, and greens, and some recently developed tiles have a small amount of vinyl binder, giving brighter, clearer colours and improved grease resistance. The ingredients are mixed at relatively high controlled temperatures to form a dough, that is then forced through successive calenders until the required thickness and finish is obtained. The sheet is die cut when cool, ensuring dimensional stability. Common sizes are nine inches (22 centimetres) by nine inches by 1/8 inch or 1/10 inch (three or two millimetres). The tiles are resistant to fungal attack, mild acids and alkalies, and oils and grease; and they are suitable for use where floor heat is less than 80° F (27° C). Sweeping and washing with warm water and soap or detergent keeps them clean; wax or resin emulsion polishes improve their appearance and prolong life.

Vinyl floor coverings. Vinyl asbestos tiles were developed from asphalt tiles. Asbestos fibres, mineral fillers, and pigments are all bonded together with copolymers of vinyl chloride, or with vinyl acetate. Vinyl resin binders have greater flexibility without requiring heat treatment prior to installation.

Asbestos tiles

Vinyl sheet coverings are made by calendering from various combinations of vinyl chloride resins, pigments, stabilizers, and fillers. Tiles 9 inches, 12 inches, or 18 inches (23, 30, or 46 centimetres) square can be cut from these sheets; widths vary from 3 to 6 feet (1 to 2 metres). Sheets can be unbacked or backed with felt, hessian, plastic foam, cork, or fabric. One method adds a coat of vinyl to a backing, and the surface appearance is influenced by the nature of the backing. Jointless seam welding can usually be applied to vinyl sheeting. A blowing agent can be added to vinyl paste, producing a foamed back and fully bonded vinyl floor covering. A thin layer of the paste and agent is spread on the back of a premanufactured vinyl sheet; these are passed through a heated tunnel causing the release of a gas from the agent, forming the foam.

An "all through" flushing in the mix can be used for secondary colour effects. Some laminated sheets have rotogravure pattern printed with vinyl inks and covered by a protective layer of transparent vinyl. Backed vinyl sheets can have added coloured chips, with a final clear coating producing a three-dimensional effect. Embossing allows the addition of a second colour into the resultant depressions, producing an inlaid effect.

Rubber floorings. Production figures for this material are comparatively small. Previously made with natural rubber, it is now produced with synthetic rubber mixed with pigments, fillers, resins and curing materials, and when sheeted is heat cured. Mottled effects are available, and thicknesses around two- and three-sixteenths of an inch (three to four millimetres) are available in tiles up to one foot square or in rolls. It is a comparatively expensive, excellent wearing flooring, although somewhat susceptible to grease damage, and is appropriate for use in public buildings where traffic is heavy.

Cork tiles and carpet. When ground cork is heated, either for long periods or by rapid high-frequency heating, the granules adhere, creating a resilient mixture that can be formed into tiles, usually two- to five-sixteenths of an inch thick, and six or nine inches square. This tile has a comfortable resilient feel and absorbs sound, but appearance and wear properties are only fair.

Cork carpet, although limited in use, can be produced from graded cork granules and polymerized linseed oil, homogeneously pigmented and calendered on a jute canvas backing.

Epoxy resins. Flooring compositions based on epoxy resins have developed steadily, giving a hard, chemical-resistant, seamless, and firmly adherent floor covering. The resin and curing agent must be blended immediately before use; colours and fillers can be added. The comparatively high cost of epoxy-resin systems restricts them principally to repairing or surfacing existing flooring substrates; *e.g.,* concrete. They frequently employ composition based on a cement aggregate and natural rubber latex. Polyvinyl acetate may be substituted for rubber latex, and such resins as acrylic, polystyrene, and styrene-butadiene have also been employed.

ECONOMIC ASPECTS

Modern research and development have resulted in improved equipment, processes, and materials contributing both to increased production and greater product durability. Although per capita use has increased, greater competition exists. Larger companies usually have larger facilities for development and expansion than smaller companies and are more likely to survive any large decrease in profit margins. The heavy capital expenditure required for increasingly sophisticated processes, and the equipment they require, may accelerate the trend in the developed countries toward larger groups of floor-covering manufacturers and their suppliers.

BIBLIOGRAPHY. R.S. BRINTON, *Carpets,* 2nd ed. (1932), traditional carpet structures and processes described at a basic technical level, including some that are obsolete or obsolescent; A. CROSSLAND, *Modern Carpet Manufacture* (1958), a description of carpet processes and structures, including nonwoven types, with helpful diagrams; B. JACOBS, *The Story of British Carpets* (1968), a history of the British carpet industry; P. LIEBETRAU, *Orientalske Taepper i farver* (1962; Eng. trans., *Oriental Rugs in Colour,* 1963), an illustrated treatment of the making and nature of Oriental rugs; G. ROBINSON, *Carpets* (1966), a textbook on carpet manufacture with short sections on nonwoven carpets; F. WALTON, *The Infancy and Development of Linoleum Floorcloth* (1925), a history of linoleum by its inventor; D.T. WARD, *Tufting: An Introduction* (1969), on the development of the tufting process; TEXTILE INSTITUTE and SOCIETY OF DYERS AND COLOURISTS, *Review of Textile Progress,* vol. 14, 16, and 17 (1962, 1964, 1965–66), brief treatments of important international developments; E.W. ALLEN, "Adhesives for Flooring," R.F. BRIGGS, "Contract Flooring: Its Use, Misuse, and Abuse," W.J. WARLOW, "Plastics for Flooring, Their Use and Assessment," and J.G. BRAMLEY and W.V. WILKINSON, "Epoxy Floor Coatings," in *Floorcovering Symposium* (1965), papers on major developments and problems in hard floorcovering industry; R. BEAUMONT, *Carpets and Rugs* (1924), on the design and manufacture of carpets and rugs, not new but has some relevancy; S.R. COCKETT, *An Introduction to Man-Made Fibres* (1966), a general treatment of man-made fibres and their production; R.B. HOLT, *Rugs, Oriental and Occidental, Antique and Modern* (1901), rug making outlined in a brief and straightforward manner; E. KORNREICH, *Introduction to Fibres and Fabrics,* 2nd ed. (1966), a quick introduction to several important basic ideas in textiles; F.J. MAYERS, *Carpet Design and Designing* (1934), on various aspects of carpet designing; HENRI MUCHERIE, *Du Tapis de Roi au Tapis pour Tous* (1966), an illustrated descriptive outline of carpet structures (in French); H. OSSWALD, *Die Teppichindustrie,* 3rd ed. (1965), detailed technical coverage of main fields of carpet manufacture (in German).

(P.E.)

Floral Decoration

Since the earliest days of civilization, man has used floral decorations, composed of living or dried cut-plant materials or artificial facsimiles, to embellish his environment and his person. They have played an important part in folk festivals, religious ceremonials, public celebrations of all kinds, and, of course, courtships. Sophisticated cultures have generally expressed a love for decorating with flowers by carefully arranging them in especially chosen containers, while less sophisticated societies have used them more informally: strewn, made into garlands and wreaths, or casually placed in water-holding vessels without thought of arrangement.

This article will cover the elements and principles, the materials, the techniques and forms, and, finally, the historical and stylistic developments of floral design.

ELEMENTS AND PRINCIPLES OF DESIGN

The term flower arrangement presupposes the word design. When flowers are placed in containers without thought of design, they remain a bunch of flowers, beautiful in themselves but not making up an arrangement. Line, form, colour, and texture are the basic design elements that are selected, then composed into a harmonious unit based on the principles of design—balance, contrast, rhythm, scale, proportion, harmony, and dominance. Line is provided by branches or slender, steeple-like flowers such as snapdragon, delphinium, and stock. Form and colour are as varied as the plant world itself. Moreover, forms not natural to the plant world can be created for contemporary abstract compositions by bending and manipulating branches, vines, or reeds to enclose space and create new shapes. Texture describes surface quality and can be coarse, as in many-petaled surfaces such as chrysanthemums, or smooth, as in anthuriums, calla lilies, and gladioli. There are many variations between these extremes. Leaves and woody stems also have varied textural qualities.

A flower arrangement includes not only the flowers themselves but the container that holds them and the base on which the container may rest. If an accessory, such as a figurine, is included, that too becomes a part of the total design. The whole composition should relate in textural quality to its frame of reference, which might be a wood or glass table top or a linen cloth, and should be in close harmony with the style of the room for which it was planned, be it Louis XV or Danish modern.

As the components of a design are selected and combined, a silhouette, or arrangement outline, is created. This outline is generally considered most interesting when the spaces in the composition vary in size and shape. Third dimension, or sculptural quality, is accomplished by allowing some of the plant materials in a grouping to extend forward and others to recede. Flower heads turned sideways, or toward the back, for example, break up contour uniformity and draw the eye into and around the composition. When a formal, static quality is sought, the contour is restricted or evenly shaped, often into such graduated forms as a pyramid or mound.

Line and mass

Balance is psychologically important, for an arrangement that appears to be leaning, top-heavy, or lopsided creates tension in the viewer. (Occasionally, however, as in some modern arrangements, this is the very effect desired.) Colour as well as the actual size of the plant material influences design stability. Dark colour values look heavier than light values; a deep red rose, for example, appears heavier in an arrangement than a pale pink carnation, even though they are the same size. An arrangement in which dark colours are massed at the top and light colours at the bottom can therefore appear top-heavy. Similar flowers placed in identical positions on either side of an imaginary vertical axis create symmetrical balance. If there is an unequal distribution of varying flowers and leaves on either side of the axis but their apparent visual weight is counterbalanced, asymmetrical balance is achieved. This compositional device is more subtle and often more pleasing aesthetically than symmetrical balance, for its effect is less apparently contrived and more varied. Contrasts of light and dark, rough and smooth, large and small, also give variety to the composition. An arrangement generally has a dominant area or centre of visual interest to which the eye returns after examining all aspects of the arrangement. An area of strong colour intensity or very light values, or a rather solid grouping of plant material along the imaginary axis and just above the container's rim, are devices commonly used as compositional centres. The rhythm of a dynamic, flowing line can be achieved by the graduated repetition of a particular shape, or by the combination of related colour values. Scale indicates relationships: the sizes of plant materials must be suitably related to the size of the container and to each other. Proportion has to do with the organization of amounts and areas; the traditional Japanese rule that an arrangement should be at least one and a half times the height of the container is a generally accepted use of this principle.

Rhythm, scale, proportion, and harmony

Proportion also relates to the placement of the arrangement in a setting. A composition is either overpowering or dwarfed if placed on too small or too large a surface or in too small or too large a spatial setting. Harmony is a sense of unity and belonging, one thing with another, that comes with the proper selection of all the components of an arrangement—colour, shape, size, and texture of both plant materials and container.

MATERIALS

Living plant materials

Many different kinds of plant materials are used in floral decorations, among them flowers, foliage, grasses, grains, branches, berries, seeds, nuts, cones, fruits, and vegetables. The materials may be living, dried, or artificial. Initially, man was restricted to using native wildings, or uncultivated plants, but as civilization developed over a period of thousands of years, man became less dependent on the seasons and on the resources of the particular region in which he lived. As means of transportation improved and trading grew, plants were introduced from foreign countries and many have since been hybridized to improve or vary shape, size, and colour. In the 20th century the floral decorator has an enormously varied medium in which to create because plant materials can be flown from one part of the world to another. Since the 19th century, when extensive greenhouse cultivation first made it possible to purchase fresh flowers at any time of the year, there have been commercial growers of plant materials who supply the world's floral wholesale markets. The Netherlands, for example, is famous for the ten-mile stretch of greenhouses at Aalsmeer near Amsterdam. In the United States, California and Florida, particularly, have vast areas under cultivation for commercial flowers.

Dried plant materials are generally used for what is traditionally called a winter bouquet. The cultivated flowers that are often dried are those with a naturally dry, stiff surface quality—such as strawflowers (*Helichrysum bracteatum*), globe amaranth (*Gomphrena*), and statice. North temperate zone wildings picked and preserved for dried arrangements include pearly everlasting, heather, and the sea lavender of salt marshes, as well as goldenrod, orange bittersweet berries, cattails, dock, teasel, and sumac. Many kinds of grasses—pampas, sea oats, millet, and sorghum, for example—are also dried, as are seed-bearing capsules such as the flat paper disks of honesty (*Lunaria*), orange Chinese lanterns (*Physalis*), and the wood roses from the Hawaiian morning glory (*Ipomoea tuberosa*). Other dried materials sometimes used in floral decorations are cones and nuts, long used for making wreaths and festoons for such winter festivals as Christmas; straw, used for Christmas decorations in Sweden and Lithuania; and grains, especially wheat and oats, often arranged in bunches for harvest decorations in Europe and America. Because of their fleshy substance, most fruits and vegetables do not dry well; the main exceptions are gourds, pomegranates, and artichokes.

There are various ways of drying plant materials. Certain garden flowers (among them celosia, blue salvia, globe thistle, alliums, and hydrangeas) can be gathered at their peak of bloom and dried by hanging them upside down in a dark, dry place for several weeks. Flowers may also be individually dried using one of several techniques. A 17th-century Italian writer on horticulture, P. Giovanni Battista Ferrari, described a process of gently burying the flower heads in clean, sun-dried sand and allowing them to remain in a sun-heated place for several months. The same method was used in the 19th century. Later, borax was used, and in the 20th century silica gel, because of its ability to absorb moisture. This solution is gently brushed between and over every petal. Since this method of drying does not preserve the stems, the flower heads must be wired before they are arranged.

Leaves and ferns are dried by pressing. The most delicate pressed flowers and foliage have been composed, mounted, and framed as pictures—a practice especially popular with 19th-century Romantics, who preserved floral souvenirs as sentimental personal memorabilia.

Throughout history and in almost every conceivable

medium man has created artificial plant materials. The Chinese fashioned peony blossoms and fruits from semiprecious stones and carved jade leaves, which they assembled into small trees. Gold lotus blossoms were highly treasured in eastern Asia. For European royalty in the late 19th century, the Russian-born jeweller Peter Carl Fabergé (1846–1920) designed exquisite single-stemmed flowers of gold, enamel, gems, and semiprecious stones set in small rock-crystal pots. During the 18th and 19th centuries, the Sèvres porcelain factory in France produced porcelain flowers with stems and leaves of ormolu (a metallic alloy resembling gold). At the same time, the Royal Worcester, Crown Staffordshire, and Royal Doulton factories in England became world-famous for their highly realistic porcelain floral arrangements, which are still made. The Victorians developed a home craft of making and arranging flowers and fruits. Wax, cloth, yarn, feathers, shells, and seeds were used

Artificial plant materials

Shell-flower arrangement, English, early 19th century. Shells, fastened to the surface of a superstructure, have been used to form an intricate artificial bouquet. In the Victoria and Albert Museum, London.

to make the flowers and fruits, which were then either framed or placed under glass domes. Perhaps the most curious of these 19-century decorations were the wreaths and floral displays made by twisting, knotting, and weaving the hair of one's family and friends around wire supports. Beaded flowers for cemetery and funerary bouquets have been popular in France since the 19th century; and paper flowers for festivals and home decoration have become a major folk art medium in Mexico and Japan. Because of their relatively low cost, durability, and easy maintenance (an occasional washing or dusting), plastic flowers and plants are in such great demand that their production has become an important 20th-century industry. Though still primarily used in public places, plastic plant materials are increasingly found in private homes, especially in the United States.

TECHNIQUES

Cut plant materials, especially flowers, need special care and treatment before they are placed in vases. Ideally, flowers are picked some hours before they are arranged and never in the heat of the day. Generally, the bottoms of the stems are cut on a slant, placed in deep tepid water, and kept in a cool place, preferably overnight. Different materials have different conditioning needs. Woody stems are split several inches with pruning shears, then soaked in hot water. Stem ends may be crushed with a mallet instead, but clean cuts make it easier to impale branches on a needle holder. Milky stems, such as those of poppies, poinsettias, and large dahlias, are sealed by placing the tips in boiling water or over a flame for a few seconds. Foliage and flowers are protected from steam and flame by inserting the stems through a hole punched in newspaper, which is then drawn up over them. When arranging flowers, all foliage below the water line must be removed in order to prevent bacterial decay and the resulting unpleasant odour. Since the stems of flowers often seal over while being held in a florist shop or market, they must be recut by the purchaser. Packaged formulas do not aid in revival but are meant to be used during the preliminary soaking period. Roses and woody-stemmed flowers such as chrysanthemums can frequently be revived by recutting and placing them in hot water.

Arranging techniques
Many tall containers can easily display flowers without holding mechanics, but if necessary they can be stuffed with upright pieces of privet or fine evergreens, such as juniper, which are sheared flat across the vase opening. The Japanese *kenzan*, or metal pin holder, usually called a needlepoint holder, is the most generally used mechanical aid. It is held in place with floral clay. In silver vases, melted paraffin is used as a fastener, for, unlike clay, it will not tarnish the container and can be removed easily with hot water. Crumpled chicken wire, or wire netting, is frequently stuffed into vases as an aid to support, and a water-absorbing plastic foam, sold in bricklike blocks, has also become very popular.

The selection of a suitable container is an individual problem in every arrangement. It is considered a part of the overall design of the arrangement and is related to it in scale, colour, and texture. Its colour must enhance, not compete with, the arrangement. For the same reason many floral decorators prefer to use simply shaped, unadorned vases. The texture of the container is also chosen for compatibility with the floral arrangement. Coarse, heavy plant materials are usually arranged in a substantial container of pottery, pewter, copper, or wood. Delicate flowers and foliage are usually displayed in porcelain, glass, or silver. Fruits and vegetables are often arrayed in wooden or pottery bowls and baskets. The size of the container is also important. If it is too small, the plant materials will overpower it and the arrangement will appear top-heavy. If it is too large, it will not only dwarf the arrangement but will frequently destroy the unity of the composition, dividing the viewer's attention between the floral arrangement and the container. Containers are not used for all arrangements of plant materials. Compositions of driftwood, flowers, fruits, and vegetables are often arranged on a flat base of wood or bamboo, a tray, or slab of wood. To keep them fresh, flowers or foliage used in such an arrangement often are placed in solid-walled pin holders that hold water.

A wooden base frequently completes a composition, since it can add visual weight at the bottom, which assists in balance. The Japanese traditionally use wood or lacquer bases and stands with all arrangements, and a porcelain vase in China was not considered complete without a carved teakwood stand. The stand has both aesthetic and practical advantages: it adds height to a display and prevents moisture stains on furniture or textiles.

FORMS OF FLORAL DECORATION

Plant materials are customarily arranged in containers, woven into garlands, and worn or carried for personal adornment. Flower bouquets that are carried include the nosegay and corsage. In the mid-19th century, the nosegay, or posy (a small bunch of mixed flowers), was much in fashion. No well-dressed Victorian lady appeared at a social gathering without carrying one, edged with a paper frill or delicate greens and sometimes inserted into a silver filigree holder. Messages of love were often spelled out in the flowers of the nosegay, for the "language of flowers" was carefully studied at the time, and courtships progressed through the sending of such floral symbols.

Nosegays and corsages

Elegant 19th-century use of flowers for personal adornment: "Empress Eugénie," oil on canvas by Édouard Dubufe, 1854. In the Musée National de Versailles et des Trianons, Versailles, France.

Worn since the 18th century, the corsage has become especially popular in the 20th century. Instead of a nosegay, an admirer frequently sends a lady an orchid, a gardenia, or a small bunch of wired flowers to be worn at the waist, shoulder, or on the wrist, or attached to a handbag and carried. Only the flower heads are used in a corsage. Wires are inserted through the calyx (the usually green or leafy external portion of a flower) and bent to thrust the flowers forward or to the side; then the ends are bound together with tape or ribbon. Leaves or foliage threaded crosswise with wire are usually added. A ribbon bow often completes the corsage.

Sprays are large, flat bouquets of long-stem plant material. They are either carried or placed on caskets or at tombs as commemorative offerings. If the plant material used is short-stemmed, wire is used to add length. The ends of the stems or wire extensions are frequently thrust into a block of moss or stiff plastic foam to secure the arrangement. A blanket of flowers is often laid over a casket at a funeral or over a racehorse in the winner's circle. Blankets are made by stretching burlap over a frame, covering it with a layer of flat fern, and then adding delicate asparagus fern (*Sprengeri*). The fern surface is then covered with flower heads, which are threaded with wire and fastened on the underside of the blanket.

Garlands are bands of plant materials that have been woven or in some other way attached together; they are not arranged in a container. A circular garland is called a wreath, or if it is worn around the head, a chaplet. Garlands draped in loops are called festoons or swags. The origin of these forms is unknown, but evidence of

Garlands and wreaths

their use dates from ancient times and is not restricted to any particular culture.

Garlands have been used for many purposes. Ancient Egyptians placed them on mummies. The Greeks used them to decorate their homes, civic places, and temples. For festive occasions the ancient Romans wore garlands of strung rose petals. When these garlands of roses were suspended from ceilings, the conversation that took place beneath them was sub rosa. On European festival days such as Corpus Christi, cattle are bedecked with neck garlands. On Indian holy days, the Hindus take garlands to the temple to be blessed before wearing them; they also hang garlands on the statues of their deities.

In the ancient world it was probably the Romans who most fully developed the ornamental form and use of the festoon. Fine examples are carved in marble on the Ara Pacis or Altar of Peace (13–9 BC) near the Mausoleum of Augustus in Rome. Roman festoons were usually made of fruit, grain, leaves, and flowers. In the late 17th and early 18th centuries it was fashionable, particularly in England, to create artificial festoons over fireplace mantels. Called swags, they were usually carved of wood. Among the most famous are those executed by the English sculptor Grinling Gibbons.

Wreaths have been both worn and displayed. In antiquity the wreath was bestowed upon public officials, athletes, poets, and returning warriors. The ancient Greco-Roman custom of bestowing a laurel crown, or wreath, upon a poet was revived during the Renaissance, especially in Italy. Napoleon chose a laurel wreath of gold for his crown, emulating the emperors of the Roman Empire. At Christmas time since the 19th century, wreaths of evergreens, holly, or pinecones and nuts have been traditionally hung as decorations in northern Europe, the United States, and Canada. In medieval and Tudor England the boar served for Christmas dinner had a wreath of rosemary and bay. During Advent, a period including the four Sundays before Christmas, a wreath with four candles (each symbolizing one of the Advent Sundays) is traditionally hung in Christian homes and churches.

Plant materials have been used for personal adornment in forms other than corsages, nosegays, garlands, and wreaths. Ancient Egyptian wall paintings show women with lotus blossoms in their hair, and today the hibiscus adorns the hair of women of the South Seas. Necklaces of flowers are commonly worn in South and Southeast Asia. In Hawaii, Vanda orchids or velvety frangipani blossoms are strung into long necklaces called leis, the customary gifts of both welcome and farewell.

Many types of dress accessories are decorated with flowers. Staffs ornamented with plant material are seen in ancient art and mentioned in ancient literature. Egyptian servants or standard bearers were often depicted holding staffs of papyrus and lotus blossoms. An attribute of Dionysus and his satyrs was the thyrsus, a staff topped by a pinecone and sometimes further decorated with vine or ivy leaves and grapes. Well-known flowering staffs or rods include those of Aaron, the brother of Moses, and St. Joseph, the earthly father of Jesus.

Pictorial effects have been achieved by using cut flower heads or petals to create masses of colour that are then worked into patterns. The traditional carpet of flowers laid down on the Via Livia in Genzano, Italy, for the feast of Corpus Christi is incredibly intricate and colourful. Figures of angels, madonnas, and saints, geometric designs, and coats of arms are worked out with flower petals to form a carpet over which the religious procession passes. Mexicans frequently carpet their churches with mosaics of wild flowers, and in The Netherlands during tulip time flower pictures are made for competition. About 12 feet square, made for the most part of tulip and hyacinth blossoms, they are designed on inclined backgrounds for better visibility. Some of these pictures are three-dimensional.

For centuries flower-covered floats have been used in parades. The Italian painter and architect Giorgio Vasari (1511–74), for example, described 21 garland-decorated floats he designed for a pageant in Florence. The most famous of modern floral parades is the Tournament of Roses parade held on New Year's Day at Pasadena, California. Floats up to 50 feet (15 metres) in length are constructed over the chassis of motor vehicles. Rough framework is covered with chicken wire shaped and sprayed with a polyvinyl coating. Flower heads are attached with either glue or wire.

Flower pictures and floats

HISTORICAL AND STYLISTIC DEVELOPMENTS

Western. *Ancient world.* There is evidence through painting and sculpture that during the Old Kingdom (c. 2686–c. 2160 BC) the Egyptians placed flowers in vases. In the tomb of Perneb bas-relief carvings show lotus blossoms and buds alternately arranged in flared bowls that were set upon banquet tables or carried in processions. Paintings of functional vases with spouts designed to support the heavy-headed lotus flower are found in the tombs of Beni Hasan (c. 2500 BC). Formal bouquets of lotus and berries offered to the dead are represented in the paintings from the tomb of Apuy at Thebes. Garlands and wreaths, floral headdresses, and collars were woven. Because of the formalized rules of Egyptian art, the lotus (*Nymphaea*), sacred to the goddess Isis, and papyrus, both of which were easily conventionalized, were the plant materials depicted almost exclusively for 2,000 years. During the Ptolemaic era (305–30 BC) perfume recipes, flower garlands found on mummies, and Greek and Roman writings reveal a more varied native plant life and show that foreign plants had been introduced, most notably the rose.

The ancient Greeks' love of flowers was expressed mainly in the making and wearing of wreaths and garlands. Vase paintings, temple friezes, and architectural ornamentation all illustrate their widespread use. They were also frequently mentioned in Greek literature. The techniques of making garlands and wreaths, the most appropriate plant materials, and the proper time and way to wear or display them, were the subjects of several treatises. Fruits and vegetables mounded in baskets or spilling in profusion out of a cornucopia were types of arrangements used for religious offerings.

The earliest depiction of mixed cut flowers, artfully arranged in a container, is a mosaic dating from the early 2nd century AD of a basket of flowers from the emperor

Figures wearing wreaths of leaves and flowers, "Heracles and Telephos Before the Personification of Arcadia," Roman wall painting from Herculaneum (c. 1st century AD), after a Hellenistic original, early 2nd century BC. In the Museo Archeologico Nazionale, Naples.

(Top) Stylized bouquets of lotus and buds bound with rows of petals and berries, "Apuy and His Wife Receiving Offerings," tempera copy of an Egyptian wall painting from the tomb of Apuy at Thebes. In the Metropolitan Museum of Art, New York. (Bottom) Earliest representation of mixed flowers artfully arranged in a container, "Basket of Flowers," Roman mosaic, 2nd century. The basket holds Roman hyacinths, roses, tulips, red carnations, a double anemone, and a blue morning glory. In the Vatican Museum, Rome.

By courtesy of (top) the Metropolitan Museum of Art, New York; photograph, (bottom) SCALA, New York

Hadrian's villa at Tivoli near Rome. Garlands and wreaths continued to be popular among the Romans, as did displays of fruits and vegetables in cornucopias and baskets.

Middle Ages. Little evidence remains of floral decoration in early medieval Europe. In the mosaics of Ravenna, the Byzantines depicted highly contrived formal compositions. Symmetrical, with an emphasis on height, these arrangements were usually spires of foliage with regularly placed clusters of flowers or fruit.

Illuminated manuscripts of the Gothic period (from the 13th century to the 15th) occasionally include simple floral bouquets holding symbolic flowers. This was a time of intense religious fervour, and plant symbolism assumed great importance. There was both a liturgical and a secular language of flowers. In the church, for example, the rose symbolized the Virgin; in the chivalric courts, passionate love. Usually plant materials were casually placed in utilitarian containers such as earthenware jugs, bottles, glass tumblers, and in majolica, or glazed and enamelled pottery, drug jars called albarelli. The still life in the foreground of the open centre panel of the "Portinari Altarpiece" by the Flemish painter Hugo van der Goes is an illustration of this type of arrangement. Metal ewers often held Madonna lilies (*Lilium candidum*), as in the 15th-century painting "The Annunciation" by Rogier van der Weyden (Metropolitan Museum of Art, New York).

15th and 16th centuries. Floral decorations became more studied and elaborate during the Renaissance period of the 15th and 16th centuries. The revival of interest in antiquity influenced the widespread use of garlands and wreaths in Renaissance Europe, especially in Italy.

Medieval plant symbolism

They were popular for pageants and feasts as well as for decorating houses and churches, and were commonly depicted in the art of the time. Among the most notable examples are the terra-cotta wreaths that framed the decorative ceramic plaques and reliefs made by the della Robbia family in the late 15th century, and the garlands of flowers, fruits, and vegetables in the paintings of such northern Italian masters as Andrea Mantegna and Carlo Crivelli. Cut-plant materials were generally arranged in either high sparse bouquets or tight low bunches. There were also pyramidal compositions in pedestal vases, such as those in the background of the painting "Virgin and Child and St. John" (Borghese Gallery, Rome) by the Florentine artist Sandro Botticelli. Arrangements of fruits and vegetables on salvers or in baskets also were popular.

17th century. The arrangement of plant materials truly became an art and an important decorative device in the 17th century. During this period of worldwide exploration, colonization, and commerce, new plants were introduced into Europe, where an avid interest in horticulture developed. Still-life paintings of the late 16th, 17th, and early 18th centuries reveal what a great variety of plants there was in the gardens of Europe. Beginning with Jan Brueghel (called "Velvet Brueghel"; 1568–1625), a tradition of flower painting developed in Flanders and Holland, which culminated with the works of Jan van Huysum (1682–1749). The canvases of the many hundreds of still-life painters of the period are valuable source material for the student of the history of floral decorations and gardens. They must, however, be considered as idealized compositions and not as literal translations onto canvas of actual bouquets. Early 17th-century pictures, particularly those of Jan Brueghel, who painted one-of-a-kind arrangements, seemed most interested in displaying the content of the garden itself. Depictions of later 17th-century bouquets show profuse arrangements that reflect the sensuality and exuberance of the Baroque style. Curvilinear elements such as sinuous S curves are other Baroque devices of design used to cre-

SCALA, New York

Symbolic use of flowers, "Portinari Altarpiece" (detail from the central panel) by Hugo van der Goes, c. 1476. The scattered violets indicate Christ's humility; the columbine flowers represent the seven gifts of the Holy Spirit with which Christ was endowed at birth. The fleur-de-lis indicates royalty, and the flowers in the albarello are in royal colours, for Christ was of the royal line of David. In the Uffizi, Florence.

Formal and elaborate arrangement of fruits, vegetables, and flowers characteristic of Renaissance floral decoration, "Madonna of Victory," altarpiece by Andrea Mantegna, 1495. In the Louvre, Paris.
Giraudon

coco bouquet and its variations remained popular into the 20th century. English bouquets of the corresponding Georgian period were often more profuse than the Rococo. Many books written to catalog the wide variety of plant materials available in 18th-century England gave incidental information on how to care for and display them. One of the best known of these works is the two-volume *Gardeners Dictionary* by the horticulturist Philip Miller. In it he mentions dried bouquets and chimney flowers. It was customary in English homes to arrange flowers and branches in the hearth during the summer months when the fireplace was not in use. These arrangements were referred to as "bough pots." The best known English illustrations of Georgian flower arrangements are those designed by the Flemish artist Peter Casteels for a nursery catalog called *The Twelve Months of Flowers* (1730). Since the flowers in each bouquet are numbered and keyed to a list at the bottom of the plate, and are one-of-a-kind collections, they are not truly representative of live arrangements. Jacob van Huysum's monthly paintings display flowers more naturally. Both series are invaluable as source material for garden flowers.

The Neoclassical period of the late 18th and early 19th centuries brought about a revival of wreaths and garlands in the style of Greco-Roman antiquity. Floral bouquets were arranged in vases of classical severity.

19th century. The interest of the 19th-century Romantics in nature made floral arrangements an important part of a decorative scheme. With the advent of the clipper ship more exotic plant materials were introduced into Europe and the United States. From China came new varieties of chrysanthemums, bleeding heart, rhododendrons, and azaleas; from South Africa, the gladiolus, freesia, and pelargoniums; and from Mexico, the dahlia, gloxinia, and fuchsia. Many old garden favourites were greatly improved as a result of widespread scientific interest in horticulture and botany. The Industrial Revolution made it possible to manufacture a great variety of economically priced ceramic and glass containers. Artificial flowers were extremely popular and were made in many different materials in both home and factory.

The books and magazines of the Victorian age agreed that the art of arranging flowers was an accomplishment all young ladies should acquire. Except for the single flower in the small bud vase, the most popular style of Victorian arrangement was a tightly compact mass of flowers, greens, grasses, and ferns. The two-level epergne, with a flared top for flowers and lower tier for fruit, frequently was used for the centre of the dining table. Since the flowers selected were usually of a brilliant hue, strong colour contrast was a characteristic of Victorian arrangements. These gay floral groupings, however, were usually softened by ferns and other kinds of foliage. {.sidenote} Victorian arrangements

20th century. The book *Flower Decoration in the House* (1907) greatly influenced the development of 20th-century floral decoration as an art. The author was Gertrude Jekyll, already notable in the gardening world. For a long time, floral decoration in big houses had been the charge of the head gardeners or the local florists; in smaller houses, the charge of the mistress of the house. In any case, arrangement was done with varying degrees of skill and little guidance. With Gertrude Jekyll's book, the idea that flower decorations actually could be planned and designed in such a way as to heighten the quality of a room came to be widely accepted. Interior decorators added their specialized knowledge to the practical expression of this view.

The rise of the women's Garden Club movement in the 1930s and the growth of flower shows led to establishing definite rules for arrangement, especially in the United States. The classic Japanese rules of design (see below) were adopted, and others were formulated. Three main types of arrangement were recognized—the mass, the line, and the combination line-mass. Emphasis was placed on design shapes such as the crescent, or Hogarth curve, and colour studies in related or contrasting harmonies. In exhibitions thematic compositions were popular, and often arrangements interpreted abstract ideas, emotions, places, and natural phenomena. Naturalistic

ate grandiloquent, dramatic compositions. The massed bouquets of the Baroque period are studies in dominance, contrast, rhythm, and sculptural effect. The eye is drawn around and into the bouquets by the turning of flower heads, the reversing of leaves, and the curving of graceful flower stems.

{.sidenote} National styles of arrangement

The French style of the Louis XIV period (1643–1715) is best exemplified in the flower engravings of Jean-Baptiste Monnoyer. The plates for his famous portfolio *Le Livre de toutes sortes de fleurs d'après nature* (*Book of All Kinds of Flowers from Nature*) accurately portray flowers from a horticultural standpoint and at the same time show prototypes of display. These floral arrangements are freer and more airy than those of the Low Countries and yet suggest Baroque opulence. *Flora ouero cultura di fiori* ("*Flora:* The Cultivation of Flowers"), a renowned garden book published in Rome in 1633 by the horticulturist P. Giovanni Battista Ferrari, illustrates the styles of floral displays preferred by the Italians and also describes arranging techniques and devices. Among the ingenious devices illustrated is a vase with holes in its removable top that made it easy to arrange flowers and change water.

18th century. The floral arrangements of the early 18th century were dominated by French and English taste. In France, cultural and social life centred in the intimate rooms of Parisian town houses rather than in the vast rooms and halls of Louis XIV's Versailles palace. Bouquets, therefore, were comparatively small, to be in scale with their setting. The more delicate colouring and lighter visual weight of these arrangements can be attributed in part to feminine taste, which decidedly influenced the Rococo style. Personal and charming, the Ro-

(Left) An exuberant and dramatic Baroque flower arrangement, "Flowers in a Vase," oil on panel by Jan van Huysum, 1726. In the Wallace Collection, London. (Right) An intimate and delicate bouquet of the 18th century, "A Vase of Flowers," oil on canvas by J.-B.-S. Chardin (1699–1779). In the National Gallery of Scotland, Edinburgh.

compositions with just a few flowers made use of stones, moss, and branches or driftwood with striking line interest. In the mid-20th century flower arranging tended to follow contemporary art trends. A Japanese revolt against traditional aesthetic canons also had great influence on Western development of free-style arrangements that reject naturalism and are often unconventional in their placement and use of treated material. Traditional principles of visual design are often rejected in such modern arrangements.

Assemblages and abstract arrangements   Assemblages of diverse elements outside the plant world, such as scrap metal, rope, and plastic, are composed with a minimum of plant material. Transition and rhythm yield to heightened contrast. Space is important, and new forms are created by bending plant material to create new shapes. Psychological tension is created by upsetting balance and symmetry.

Naturalistic 20th-century composition of spring flowers: daffodils, daisies, primroses, and pasqueflowers arranged with moss and heath in a frame of bracket fungus.

Eastern. *China and Korea.* The ancient Chinese could enjoy and feel themselves at one with the growth, maturity, and decline of a few flowers or a branch. The floral expressions of the Chinese have traditionally been based on the Confucian art of contemplation, the Buddhist principle of preservation, and Taoist symbolism. For the Confucian, a floral arrangement was philosophically contemplated both as a symbol of organic existence and for its aesthetic aspects. Buddhists used flowers sparingly because of their religious doctrine prohibiting the taking of life. At least since the T'ang dynasty (AD 618–907), flowers have been placed on temple altars in a *ku*, an ancient bronze ceremonial wine beaker dating from the Shang dynasty (*c.* 1766–*c.* 1122 BC) whose shape was translated into porcelain in later dynasties. Hua Hsien, the flower goddesses of the Taoists, have traditionally been represented carrying flower-filled baskets. In Taoist symbolism, the four seasons were denoted by the white plum blossom of winter, the peony of spring, the lotus of summer, and the chrysanthemum of autumn. Each month also had its own flower. Longevity in plant arrangements was symbolized by pine, bamboo, and the long-lasting *ling chih* fungus. New Year floral displays featured the paper-white narcissus, and the tree peony (*Paeonia moutan*), designated the "king of flowers," was used to symbolize good fortune.

Usually the floral arrangements of the Chinese, like those of the Koreans, appear to be more casual, less obviously contrived than those of the Japanese. A composition frequently will be made of two or more floral arrangements placed in containers of different heights and shapes and often grouped with rocks or decorative objects. Chinese bouquets in baskets have a bouquet-like quality reminiscent of Western floral arrangements.

Japan.   The arrangement of flowers in Japan is an elaborate and unique art form, with highly developed conventions and complex symbolism. The oldest studied form of this art, developed from the custom of offering flowers to the Buddha, was introduced into Japan early in the 7th century by Ono Imoko, Japanese ambassador to China and, in Japan, founder of the first and oldest school of floral art, called the Ikenobō. All the

"Western Queen Mother" (detail of flower border), silk and metal thread embroidered on silk, Chinese, 19th century. The plant material includes (left to right) plum, pine, citron, lotus, orchid, magnolia, peony, peach, chrysanthemum, *Osmanthus*, and *Narcissus tazetta*. In the Metropolitan Museum of Art, New York.
By courtesy of the Metropolitan Museum of Art, New York, bequest of William Crawford, 1929

Early Japanese styles

later masters of the Ikenobō school are descendants of the founder. Most important among the earliest styles was the *mitsu-gusoku*, an arrangement of three or five articles often consisting of an incense burner, a candlestick in the form of a stork, and a vase of flowers. These were usually displayed before pictures of the Buddha or of founders of Buddhist sects.

Early styles were known as *tatebana*, standing flowers; from these developed a more massive and elaborate style, *rikka* (which also means standing flowers), introduced by the Ikenobō master Senkei around 1460. The early *rikka* style symbolized the mythical Mt. Meru of Buddhist cosmology. *Rikka* represented seven elements: peak, waterfall, hill, foot of the mountain, and the town, and the division of the whole into *in* (shade) and *yō* (sun). (In Chinese the characters for *in* and *yō* are read *yin* and *yang*, the passive or female and the active or male principles of oriental philosophy.) Formal *rikka* is arranged out of nine main branches and some accessory ones. Three branches are placed so that their tips form a triangle with unequal sides. From this pattern all later styles of Japanese floral art developed.

By courtesy of the Tokyo National Museum

Traditional *rikka* flower arrangement of nine different plant materials. In the Tokyo National Museum.

In the early 18th century a three-branch, asymmetrical style, *shōka*, evolved from the *rikka* and was cultivated by the Ikenobō school. *Shōka* is written with Japanese characters meaning living flowers. These characters can also be read *seika* and *ikebana*; *seika* is the preferred reading by some schools, while *ikebana* today is the general term applied to any style of Japanese floral art. Up to the advent of *shōka* all styles of arrangements other

than *rikka* had been known as *nageire*, meaning to throw, or fling into. This term was confined to arrangements in tall vases, and *heika*, vase flowers, is preferred to *nageire* by some schools. *Shōka* utilized three main branches, and emulated the natural growth of plant life. This illusion of growth was achieved by using buds, foliage, and blossoms; by superimposing stems as they emerged from the container; by turning up the tip ends of branches unless of a naturally drooping kind; and by placing tree branches above flowers and mountain material above that of the lowland. All combinations were seasonally correct. Uneven numbers of materials were always used, and rules of proportion dictated that plant material be at least one and one half times the height of the container. By the late 18th and early 19th centuries the *shōka* style had supplanted the *rikka* in popularity and many new schools flourished, including Enshūryū, Koryū, Kōdōryu, and Mishōryū. All these new schools utilized the three-branch form but adopted different nomenclatures for them.

Western flowers were introduced into Japan following the Meiji restoration (1868). The flower master Unshin Ohara, who established the Ohara school (early 20th century), devised for them a new container, based on the low bowls used for dwarfed plants. This new style, known as *moribana* (heaped-up flowers), permitted greater freedom in the choice and placement of materials. A variation was the creation of small realistic landscapes called *shakei*, sometimes referred to as memory sketches. In these, exposed water surface was a part of the design. In 1930 a group of art critics and flower masters proclaimed a new style of floral art called *zenei-bana* (avant-garde flowers), free of all ties with the past. Foremost in this group was the Ikenobō master Sofu Teshigahara (b. 1907), who had founded the Sōgetsu school in 1926. The new style emphasized free expression. *Zenei-bana* utilized all forms of plant life, living and dead, and elements that had been previously avoided, such as bits of iron, brass, vinyl, stone, scrap metal, plastic, and feathers. Vines and branches were bleached and painted and even used upside down. Stems were crossed, even numbers of materials were used, and containers were often crude and exotic in shape.

Until 1868 Japanese flower arrangement was generally a man's avocation, engaged in primarily by Buddhist priests, warriors, and the nobility. Following the Meiji restoration and particularly after the beginning of the 20th century, it was taken up by large numbers of women. Men, however, still head most of the principal schools.

The total number of schools throughout Japan in the 20th century is believed to number from 2,000 to 3,000, varying in size from several thousand to millions of adherents. Each school has its own rules of arrangement, though styles may differ only slightly from one another. All arrangements are asymmetrical and achieve a three-dimensional effect. The traditional styles are still taught, many with modern variations, but the bolder, less restrained, and unconventional free-style forms of arrange-

Modern Japanese styles

ment now seem to be the most popular. The material used in Japanese floral arrangements is held in position by various artifices, the most popular of which are the *kubari*, forked twig, and the *kenzan*, needlepoint holder.

Japanese flower arranging has influenced that of the West considerably, particularly in the mid-20th century. Many popularizations of the art have flourished in the United States.

Other cultures. Outside the West and the Far East, the arranging of plant materials was more a casual part of everyday life than a formally recognized medium of artistic expression. The elaborate stylistic traditions evolved and formulated in the West and Far East through centuries of sophisticated creative activity are rarely found, therefore, in other cultures. In the Islāmic world, for example, simple, modestly scaled arrangements predominated: sparse, symmetrically arranged bouquets; casually grouped bunches of flowers; or blossoms floating on liquid surfaces. The garlands made in India for adorning home, temple, statuary, and man himself were simpler than the bouquet or arranged floral materials found in the more aesthetically complex traditions of the West and Far East. Also in contrast to these artistically self-conscious arrangements are the stiff, mounded groupings of plant materials made for festivals in Southeast Asia.

BIBLIOGRAPHY. LIBERTY HYDE BAILEY and ETHEL ZOE BAILEY (comps.), *Hortus Second: A Concise Dictionary of Gardening, General Horticulture and Cultivated Plants in North America* (1941), basic for nomenclature; VICTOR LORET, *La Flore pharaonique d'après les documents, hiéroglyphiques et les spécimens découverts dans les tombes*, 2nd ed. (1892), includes information concerning wreaths and garlands; CHARLES VICTOR DAREMBERG and E. SAGLIO, *Dictionnaire des antiquités Grecques et Romaines d'après les textes et les monuments*, vol. 1, pt. 2 (1877), lists flowers grown and ornamental uses (under "Corona" and "Coronarius et Coronaria"); JOHN GERARD, *The Herball* (1597), descriptions and contemporary wood engravings of English garden flowers; JOHN PARKINSON, *Paradisi in Sole Paradisus Terrestris* (1629), descriptions and usage of flowers in 17th-century England; P. GIOVANNI BATTISTA FERRARI, *Flora ouero cultura di fiori* (1633), on the culture and care of cut flowers, including how to preserve, arrange, and ship them, with interesting illustrations; PHILIP MILLER, *The Gardeners Dictionary*, 2 vol. (1735), an important and popular 18th-century work, with full descriptions of garden flowers and illustrations; HELEN GERE CRUICKSHANK (ed.), *John and William Bartram's America* (1957), contains information about new plant discoveries and exchanges of garden material between America and England in the 18th century; *Godey's Lady's Book* (1830–98), almost monthly advice in the editorial pages about gardening or arranging flowers; J. RAMSBOTTOM, *A Book of Roses* (1939), information about old-fashioned roses; RALPH G. WARNER, *Dutch and Flemish Flower and Fruit Painters of the 17th and 18th Centuries* (1928), profusely illustrated; JULIA S. BERRALL, *A History of Flower Arrangement*, rev. ed. (1968), on all styles and periods, including original source lists of plant materials and many illustrations; MARGARET FAIRBANKS MARCUS, *Period Flower Arrangement* (1952), emphasis on art; JOSIAH CONDER, *The Theory of Japanese Flower Arrangements* (1935), reprint of an original paper read by the author in 1889 to the Asiatic Society of Japan, to which have been added 36 colour plates of Ikenobō and *moribana* arrangements; ALFRED KOEHN, *The Art of Japanese Flower Arrangement (Ikebana): A Handbook for Beginners* (1934), with actual photographs instead of paintings; DONALD RICHIE and MEREDITH WEATHERBY (eds.), *The Masters' Book of Japanese Flower Arrangement: With Lessons by the Masters of Japan's Three Foremost Schools: Sen'ei Ikenobo, Houn Ohara, Sofu Teshigahara* (1966), contains an excellent historic section illustrated from the arts and photographs in colour and black and white of contemporary expressions; SHOZO SOTO, *The Art of Arranging Flowers* (1966), on all aspects of Japanese flower arranging, with excellent colour and black-and-white illustrations.

(Ju.S.B.)

Florence

A former republic, a former seat of the duchy of Tuscany, and a former capital of Italy, Florence (Italian, Firenze; Latin, Florentia) lies almost at the centre of the Italian peninsula, some 145 miles northwest of Rome. The rolling Tuscan hills that rise around the city are stitched with villas and farms, vineyards and orchards, very much the varied domestic tapestry of the early Florentine artists. The city was founded to control the only practicable north–south crossing of the Fiume Arno (Arno River) to and from the three passes through the Appenines, one to Faenza, two to Bologna. Two thin streams, the Mugnone and the Affrico, come down through town to meet the Arno. The latter, not long out of its source in the Appenines, is most of the time a grudging gurgle amid wide gravel beds far below the quays, but sometimes it rises and ravages the city, as it did with appalling consequences to Florence in 1966.

The present glory of Florence is its past. Its buildings are works of art abounding in yet more works of art. The splendours of the city are stamped with the personalities of the men who made them. The geniuses of Florence were backed by men of towering talent, and the city is made of the bones of their personal passions for religion, for art, for power, or for money. Among the most famous of the city's giants are Leonardo da Vinci, Michelangelo, Dante, Machiavelli, Galileo, and its most renowned rulers, the generations of the Medici family.

Character of the city

It is still a matter of fascination for scholars that this small city of money lenders and cloth-makers without much political or military power produced what Bernard Berenson called a "diluvial influence upon the entire white man's world, and beyond it." The Florentine vernacular became the Italian language; and the local coin, the florin, became a world monetary standard. Florentine artists formulated the laws of perspective; Florentine men of letters, painters, architects, and craftsmen began the Renaissance; and a Florentine navigator, Amerigo Vespucci, gave his name to two continents.

For information on related topics, see the articles ITALY; ITALY AND SICILY, HISTORY OF; and RENAISSANCE. See also biographies of the major Florentines mentioned in the article.

THE HISTORY OF FLORENCE

Founding and growth. Founded around the 1st century BC as a colony for soldiers of the armies of Rome, Florentia (the flourishing town) was laid out as a rectangular garrison town (*castrum*) below the hilltop Etruscan town of Faesulae. Its streets formed a pattern of rectangular blocks, with a central forum and temple. By the 3rd century AD it was a provincial capital of the Roman Empire, a major crossroads of the Italian peninsula, and a prosperous commercial centre.

Monasteries preserved the older culture during centuries of domination by Goths, Byzantines, and Lombards, but during the Carolingian period, from the late 8th century, the town began to revive and rebuild. Ruling margraves of Tuscany and the growing authority of bishops gave the town increasing autonomy from the Holy Roman Empire in the late 11th century, the beginning of the period that witnessed, in Romanesque church architecture, the first flowerings of the Florentine arts. By 1197 the Tuscan League solidified the strength that the commune of Florence had achieved through many decades of expansion at the expense of feudal lords and the empire itself; and a new and large system of walls symbolized the physical growth of the city.

Turmoil and artistic fertility. The 13th and 14th centuries saw Florence awash with the battles of the Guelfs and the Ghibellines, factions that alternately ruled the city in uncomfortable union or engaged in open warfare with one another. Alliances with popes or foreign powers, warfare with other Italian cities (notably Ghibelline Pisa), and the temporary ascendancy of one or the other party (with or without intrigue, popular support, or bloodshed) made of the centuries a confusion of rulers and transfers of power, of changing forms of civic and regional rule, of shifting allegiances and balances of power among groups of nobles and the several major and minor merchant and craft guilds.

The Guelfs and the Ghibellines

During this period, however, Florence continued its climb to eminence among the Italian cities. Its florin was first minted in the 13th century, and Florentine bankers became the most powerful in Europe. Churches rose in the new Gothic style; Florentine historians and poets, chief among them Dante, Petrarch, and Boccaccio, raised the Tuscan dialect to a place of dignity above others of Italy; and such painters as Cimabue and Giotto brought the visual arts to the aesthetic boundaries of the Renaissance, which were shortly to be crossed by the architects Brunelleschi and Alberti, the sculptors Donatello and Ghiberti and the Della Robbias, and the painters Masaccio and Uccello—among a host of others.

Rule of the Medici. The Medici family came from a background of banking prestige and solidity. After Giovanni di Bicci de' Medici had been elected chief arbiter in 1421 and his son Cosimo 13 years later returned from exile to popular acclaim, the history of this family and that of Florence and Tuscany were intertwined for three centuries.

For over a century the Medici ruled Florence without benefit of public title, combining their financial resources with diplomacy, frequent magnanimity, personal flourish, and artistic taste to fashion the Florence of the Renaissance, the city that by and large has impressed itself upon the present. The dynasty perhaps reached its height under Cosimo's grandson Lorenzo (1449–92). A brief intermission occurred during the theocratic republic of the fanatical friar Girolamo Savonarola, from 1494 to his execution in 1498, after which the Medicis returned and, in 1527, proclaimed the republic.

The reign of Cosimo I (1519–74), created grand duke in 1569, brought a long period of peace and Medici alliances across Europe by marriage and diplomacy. With the extinction of the line in 1737, title to Florence passed to the duke of Lorraine, husband of Maria Theresa of Austria.

Evolution of the modern city. The 18th century, under the dukes of Lorraine, saw great changes toward more modern theories of government, economics, and church–state relations, but in the 19th, Florence suffered politically and economically from the chaos engendered by the Napoleonic Wars. While it was beginning to feel the coming of modern industry and technology, it was becoming a centre of international fame for its past and a haunt of exiles, writers, and artists. It united with the new kingdom of Italy in 1861 and from 1865 to 1871 was the provisional capital.

Yet during these and succeeding years much of Florence's past was seriously jeopardized: many of its finest structures were altered or defaced, its medieval walls pulled down, its ancient centre laid waste. City boundaries and population continued to grow chaotically into the 20th century, when order and sense were slowly restored to the renovations.

Even graver problems, however, were impending. In addition to the human despoliation, nature had been an occasional adversary of Florentine life, mainly in the form of floods of the Arno. The bridges were destroyed in the 12th century, again in 1333. In 1557 the Ponte Vecchio (Old Bridge) held fast, but the others were destroyed. In 1944 their replacements were blown up by the retreating German Army, which spared the Ponte Vecchio but destroyed antique quarters at either end of it. Of the latter, the oldest were rebuilt with the fragments according to the original 16th-century plans.

The most devastating occurrence was the flood of November 1966: the city's cultural heritage was grievously damaged by waters coursing through the streets and swirling into buildings, depositing debris, mud, and oil. In some places the water rose as high as 20 feet, submerging sculpture, paintings, mosaics, and manuscripts in the city's libraries. An armada of international experts, financed by contributions from around the world, arrived to try to save the water-and-muck-damaged treasures. To an astonishingly large degree they succeeded, although the work of restoration was still underway in the early 1970s.

The salvage operations revealed to the world what officials of Florence had known for a century: the city had never recovered from the costly honour of being Italy's provisional capital. The municipal treasury was depleted. The museums, palaces, and convents had been turned into offices, schools, barracks, and hospitals; and money

Human and natural despoliation

for their reconversion was not forthcoming. There was not enough money for the simplest safeguards or maintenance. In the libraries and archives, uncataloged volumes piled up in cupboards and on floors for lack of shelf space and personnel. The few scientific and cultural experts who gnawed at the mountain of work—preservation, restoration, classification, examination—accepted their posts at financial sacrifice and laboured without proper space or equipment. As for protection against future floods, the city has had plans as far back as the 15th century, but it has done little more than replace the riverbanks with high walls. Administrators hoped that the city's position in the 1970s as a seat of one of Italy's provinces would allow Florence the autonomy to carry out its plans for self-preservation.

THE CONTEMPORARY CITY

Present-day Florence, the capital of Firenze province, covers an area of 39.54 square miles (102.41 square kilometres) and holds a population of some 480,000. Nearly 1,700,000 tourists visited the city annually in the early 1970s, deluging the 20,000 beds of the 350 hotels and pensions and the facilities of youth hostels and religious hospices.

Viewed from the hills, the riverbank city has not changed beyond recognition since the time of its temporal greatness. The highest tower is still the one built for the people's government at the end of the 13th century, and it shares the skyline with the early-15th-century cathedral dome. The inner city is still structured somewhat on the lines of the Roman *municipium*. The forum of Roman times, a centre of commerce and socializing, is now the Piazza della Repubblica, still the city centre. The main avenues of the city trace the pathways of antiquity through and out of the city.

Layout and ambiance

Thousands of Florentines work in industrial suburbs, but the city lives primarily from tourism and from the traditional handicrafts—glassware and ceramics, wrought iron, leatherwork, wares of precious metals, art reproductions, and the like—with some high-fashion clothing and shoe production. Festivals of music, opera, and the visual arts continue through much of the year, many of them resplendent with the trappings of medieval pageantry and procession.

Craft work is sold throughout the city, but several traditional marketplaces still exist. The vendors of straw objects—from tiny figurines to full-sized dresses—raise the awnings of their stalls almost to the lofty roof beams of the Loggia di Mercato Nuovo (New Market. 1547–51). Goldsmiths, silversmiths, and jewellers are concentrated on the Ponte Vecchio, one of the world's most famous bridges. They opened for business there in the 16th century, when Grand Duke Ferdinand I deemed it inelegant for butcher shops to line the bridge as they had for the previous 200 years. He ordered practitioners of the "vile arts" to give way to workers in precious metals. The new occupants eventually enlarged their shops by building outward over the water, propping their three-story additions on brackets from the bridge. The back elevations of these extensions give the bridge its picturesque higgledy-piggledy air. Above the shops a covered passage was constructed in 1564–65 to connect Cosimo's palace (the Pitti Palace) on the left bank with the newly erected government offices (the Uffizi) on the right bank.

Artisans who fashion the gold, silver, jewelry, straw, intarsia (Florentine mosaic), leather goods, glass, pottery, and embroidery complain that they are being squeezed out of existence by the pressures of modern economic life. They can be seen today through the open doors of their workrooms engaged in the tasks and poised in the attitudes shown in the carvings on the 15th-century facade of the guildsmen's church, Or San Michele.

The passersby in these same narrow streets—they display the agility of fish in passing one another and the cars and delivery vans—have the strong-boned Tuscan faces of the Renaissance sculptures and paintings. Although the days of Florentine power long ago evaporated, the men of this city retain much of the swagger of swordsmen of the bygone age, and their dandyism psychically clothes them in hose and doublet. Their vanity, patently masculine, is made visible at the early evening hour, when they troop to the cafés while performing the rites of hair smoothing, lapel patting, and trouser adjusting.

FLORENTINE TREASURES OF THE PAST

This rich, materialist, worldly capital expelled its prince in an hour of peril in 1528 and formally elected Jesus Christ to be king of Florence, his mother Mary to be queen. At the same time, it asked the genius of the age, Michelangelo, to redesign the defenses of the city. Part of his work can be explored today along the south bank of the Arno. The rest of the city wall was razed at the end of the 19th century; and outer avenues, the Viali di Circonvallazione, were laid along their course. Eight of the city gates remain, most of them dating from the 13th century.

Centres of government and commerce. Much of Florence's political history was made in the Piazza della Signoria. Named for the 13th-century fortified castle that occupies one side of the square, the piazza was created when the Guelfs razed the townhouse of a Ghibelline family. Ironically, the head of that family earlier had prevented the Ghibellines from razing all Florence.

Work on the castle, built as the seat of government (which it still is), was begun in 1299. At first the building was called the Palazzo del Popolo e del Commune, then dei Priori (Dante Alighieri was one of the first *priori* "superiors" installed there), and finally della Signoria. After the first grand duke of Tuscany, Cosimo I, installed himself in the recently completed Pitti Palace, the old palace was called the Palazzo Vecchio. It is a stern stone square, five stories high, topped by a crenellated, machicolated gallery. The 308-foot-high tower, square and slender, rises first to a battlemented gallery of the same design; from the latter rises an open belfry roofed by a miniature reproduction of the same martial gallery.

In 1537, Cosimo de' Medici installed himself in this traditional seat of the commune's political power. He had most of the interior redecorated in the sumptuous style it displays today. The lower house of the Italian legislature sat here in 1865–71, where the City Council holds forth today. The mayor's chambers are also in the palazzo.

An equestrian statue of Cosimo I (by Giambologna, 1594), stands to the left below the palazzo, part of the open-air sculpture gallery that the piazza has become. The central Neptune Fountain, with bronze and marble figures, dates from *c.* 1565. Before it is a marble disk to mark the spot where, as it says, "the iniquitous sentence" of hanging and burning was carried out on Savonarola and his two companions in 1498.

The ubiquity of sculpture

A copy of Michelangelo's "David"—the original was moved to the Accademia in 1873—stands naked at the top of the steps, and behind him the doorway is flanked by fig-leaved Philemon and Baucis. Down below are a copy of Donatello's Florentine lion, the "Marzocco" (original in the Bargello, also known as the Museo Nazionale), supporting the city's lily-emblazoned shield, and his "Judith and Holofernes."

To the right of the palace is the Loggia dei Lanzi (1376–82), so called because Cosimo I stationed his lancers there. Among the dozen statues in the loggia is the "Perseus" (1553) of Benvenuto Cellini, another Florentine master. The loggia, a sort of carved stone canopy, or an arched, unwalled building, is one of 12 that survive of the 26 that decorated Florence in the 16th century. Many palaces had *loggie* serving as grandstands for their martial tilts and holiday dances, as well as for the family's outdoor drawing room at weddings, betrothals, and obsequies—during which the townspeople gathered in the street received gifts and refreshment.

From behind the loggia and from the flank of the palazzo, the tall, colonnaded, twin wings of the Uffizi stretch down to the Arno. An elegant exercise in Mannerist architecture by Giorgio Vasari, it was begun in 1560 to house the grand ducal offices. In 1574, Grand Duke Francesco I ordered the top story converted to display the Medici art treasures. The Uffizi's collection, one of the most precious in the world, offers examples of painting from the 13th century through the 18th and includes most of the significant names in Florentine art.

A little further inland is another high-towered civic palace-fortress, the Bargello. Completed in 1255, some 43 years before the Palazzo della Signoria, it was the seat of the Capitano del Popolo, then became the seat of the mayor (*podestà*), and finally that of the chief of police (*bargello*), whose prison cells were removed along with other impedimenta in the restoration of 1857. A state museum since 1865, it has whole vaulted rooms devoted to the sculptures of Michelangelo, Donatello, Cellini, and Della Robbia.

Between the civic centre and the religious centre lies the old mercantile centre, currently the Piazza della Repubblica and the core of animation of the inner city. From medieval times, it was the Old Market, from which the Loggia del Pesce (Fish Market) was taken down and re-erected among the open-air food vendors on the Via Pietrapiana. Scores of antique buildings were ripped out of the district in clearing the square in 1880, in order to "revive it from its ancient squalor," as the inscription says on the 19th-century arch. The square is now bordered by cafés; and one side is arcaded, giving shelter to booksellers, newspaper dealers, expensive shops, a cinema, and the central post office. From under the arcades issues

Centre of the old and modern city

Bazzechi—Grimold

The skyline of Florence from the Piazza Michelangelo. At far left is the Ponte Vecchio over the Fiume Arno. Rising above the city are the slender tower of the Palazzo Vecchio (left), the Duomo (centre) and the church of Sta. Croce (right).

a happy uproar, a continually excited, echoing hubbub pierced by shrill cries.

Religious structures and their holdings. Further inland is the historic religious centre of the city, site of the Battistero S. Giovanni (baptismal church of St. Giovanni) and the Duomo (the cathedral "house"—*i.e.*, House of God). The baptistery is probably the oldest surviving building in Florence, although its date of construction is uncertain. Florentines generally accept the year 1000, some other scholars opting for a century or more later. It is an octagonal, three-storied structure with a tentlike roof. The exterior, like that of the cathedral and many local churches, is polychromatic. Cunningly worked bands of green marble accent the structural lines and lend movement and perspective to the exterior of the white marble-clad building. Like its near contemporary, S. Miniato al Monte (1062), this Tuscan Romanesque church includes classical elements, the graceful use of which contributed to the Florentine development of Renaissance architecture in the 15th century.

Since Baptism was administered only twice a year, the baptistery is large, with three huge sculptured bronze doors, two sets of which are the masterpieces of Lorenzo Ghiberti, who spent from 1403 to *c.* 1453 carving the 20 gilded panels. The east door, containing Old Testament scenes, was the last to be done; it was said by Michelangelo to be "worthy of paradise."

The cathedral of Sta. Maria del Fiore was begun in 1294 and consecrated in 1436. It is Gothic, but a Tuscan Gothic that mutes or transmutes the international conventions. Rather than soaring paeans in stone, it offers broad harmonies in marble, an airy flow rather than a fevered thrust. The first architect was Arnolfo di Cambio (often called the greatest architect of the Middle Ages, to whom the Palazzo della Signoria is attributed), succeeded (1334–37) by the painter Giotto, who designed the Campanile, then (1337–48) by Andrea Pisano, then (1349–59) Francesco Talenti, and (1360–69) Giovanni di Lapo Ghini. Talenti continued Arnolfo's unfinished facade but never completed it, and it was removed in 1588. In 1875 a facade was finally erected in correct but cold imitation Gothic. The marvellous dome was designed by Filippo Brunelleschi *c.* 1420.

The first Renaissance building

While Brunelleschi was constructing the Gothic dome, he was also designing the facade of the Ospedale degli Innocenti (Foundling Hospital), which has been called the first Renaissance building. It stands on the Piazza Santissima Annunziata, a lovely Renaissance square decorated with 17th-century bronze fountains.

The hospital has a ground floor colonnade of delicate Corinthian columns supporting wide, airy arches, the spandrels of which are decorated with Della Robbia's blue-and-white terra-cotta medallions of a swaddled babe —reproductions of which are the stock in trade of souvenir-vending Florence. The Roman motifs in the building seem to refer more to Florentine Romanesque than to empire originals. Later, Brunelleschi went to Rome (*c.* 1433) to study and sketch the antique ruins, after which his work became more purely Roman revival, as in his centrally planned Sta. Maria degli Angeli, begun in 1434 but left unfinished (restored and roofed in 1937).

The facade of the church of SS. Annunziata adjoining the hospital echoes the Foundling facade. A medieval church, rebuilt from 1444 to 1477, its round east end is a direct copy by Michelozzo of the Temple of Minerva Medica in Rome. The miraculous portrait of the Virgin, whose face was said to have been painted by angels while the 13th-century artist slept, became the centre of veneration by the whole city. The Florentine calendar was adjusted to begin the year on March 25, Annunciation Day, and remained righteously unchanged until 1750.

Among the medieval religious practices still in force is the Exploding of the Cart on Easter Sunday. The "cart," a wheeled pagoda four stories high and gilded, panelled, tassled, and topped with a crown, stops before the Duomo. From the High Altar a dove (aided by a wire) swoops through the open door and strikes the cart, which thereupon bursts into flames before the appreciative crowd and the alert fire brigade.

Behind the cathedral is the museum (Opera del Duomo) of works that once decorated the baptistery and the cathedral. Most notable are the sculptured marble choir lofts: the Donatello (1435–38) decorated with chubby, cavorting children; and the Luca della Robbia (1431–38) vibrant with youthful choristers, musicians, and dancers. Among the works in the cathedral itself is Michelangelo's "Deposition," carved in his last year.

On a corner of the cathedral square (Piazza del Duomo) and the Via Calzaioli stands another Florentine–Gothic structure, the Loggia del Bigallo (1352–58), in which orphans were shown to prospective foster parents. The L'Arciconfraternita della Misericordia, formed in the 16th century and one of the city's most esteemed institutions, is across the street. Its members are prepared to answer emergency calls clad in their black hoods and robes. On the far side of the baptistery is the 16th-century archepiscopal palace.

From the Piazza del Duomo the Via Borgo S. Lorenzo leads to the Medici parish church of S. Lorenzo, for which Brunelleschi began the Old Sacristy in 1423 before rebuilding the 11th-century church entirely. Michelangelo was later commissioned to add a facade, a project cancelled because transport of the marble from the quarry was too cumbersome and costly, and as of the early 1970s the church remained faced with bare brick. Michelangelo was asked instead to construct the New Sacristy, a family chapel (1521–34) of which the architecture is obscured by the power of the sculptures he made for the tombs of Julius II and Lorenzo II. He also designed the Laurentian Library (starting 1524) to the left of the church. In the severely disciplined, artificial architecture that Michelangelo devised, some experts profess to see the beginnings of the Baroque, and others, with more justice, the seeds of Mannerism. The library's treasures include da Vinci notebooks, a Horace annotated by Petrarch, a 1384 *Decameron*, a 5th-century Virgil, and the Pandects of Justinian of 533.

Further north toward the edge of the city is the Convento di S. Marco (Monastery of St. Mark), rebuilt for Cosimo de' Medici by Michelozzo in 1437. Each of the cells in the top story is painted with a mystery of the Christian faith by Fra Angelico. The cell of Savonarola is preserved with furnishings from the period of his passionate evangelism, when S. Marco was the centre of Florentine religious fervour.

Across the river the church of S. Spirito, built—not entirely faithfully—to the designs of Brunelleschi, marks another advance toward the Renaissance. The feeling of order and harmony sought by the architect in his search for the mastery of space is revealed in the proportions he imposed: the height of the nave is the double of its width; the ground floor and the clerestory are of exactly equal height; the height-to-width proportions of the nave are repeated in the aisle bays. Nearby, the church of Sta. Maria del Carmine contains frescoes by one of the painter-founders of the Renaissance, Masaccio.

S. Spirito of Brunelleschi

The churches of the two rival orders, Dominican and Franciscan, are on opposite sides of the central section of the city. To the west is the Dominican Sta. Maria Novella (1278–1350), behind a 15th-century polychrome facade by Leon Battista Alberti, a brilliant Florentine noble, architect, writer, and aesthetic theorist, most of whose major buildings were constructed outside his native city. It has frescoes by Masaccio and Orcagna, its Green Cloister decorated by Uccello and, off the cloister, the Spanish Chapel.

The chapel, built *c.* 1350 as the chapter house, is covered from floor to ceiling in vivid Gothic frescoes from the ardent hand of Andrea da Firenze. In it, the Dominicans are shown as the Hounds of God—Domini Canes—rending the wolves of heresy.

Santa Croce, built by the Franciscans on the east end of town, is larger, its facade an afterthought (*c.* 1860), its interior regrettably modernized by Vasari in 1560. Among its jewels are Giotto frescoes, a Cimabue crucifix almost destroyed by the 1966 flood, Donatello carvings, a splendid classical chapel (1430–45) by Brunelleschi for the Pazzi family, whose forebears tried to assassinate

Lorenzo the Magnificent in this church, and a Medici chapel by Michelozzo (1434). Michelangelo, Galileo, Machiavelli, and the composer Gioacchino Rossini are buried there.

The Countess of Albany, wife of Bonnie Prince Charlie of Scotland, also is entombed in the church; and there is a memorial plaque to Florence Nightingale, born in the city in 1823. From the late 18th to the mid-20th century a large Anglo-American colony was an integral part of the Florentine scene. The poet Elizabeth Barrett Browning, who is buried in the small English cemetery, noted that the city was "cheap, tranquil, cheerful and beautiful." The Horne Museum, near Sta. Croce, and the Stibbert Museum in the north are examples of houses and collections left by foreigners to their adopted city.

Palaces and parks. Of the 57 palaces built as private residences, the biggest and historically the most imposing is the Palazzo Pitti. It is another of the world's great museums, stuffed with the works of Raphael (11), Titian (14), Tintoretto (eight), Veronese (five), and Rubens (12), among the principal works. The central block of the palace was started in 1440 for Luca Pitti, a merchant banker who wanted to outshine the rest of Florence but lost his fortune trying to break the rival Medicis and left the building unfinished. In 1549, Elenora of Toledo, wealthy daughter of the viceroy of Naples and wife of Grand Duke Cosimo I, bought the property. Cosimo's enlargements were continued by successors until 1852. The palace was the official residence of King Victor Emmanuel II while Florence was Italy's capital. The facade, huge blocks of partly smoothed stone virtually bare of decoration, is 627 feet long, spanning 23 grand windows. The interior of this enormous and forbidding hulk is light and, depending on the periods and purposes of the rooms, gay or stately and always implacably rich.

Delights
of outdoor
Florence

The hill behind the house, from which much of the building stone had been quarried, was transformed into the Boboli, among the most admired gardens of the Renaissance world. Grotto-dotted, statue-strewn, planted with orchards, pools, fountains, knolls, glades, arbors, and alleys, it is still a place of surprises and pleasures. The amphitheatre, hewn from the hill, is still used for summer entertainments. Above the gardens is the restored Palazzetto di Belvedere, built in the late 16th century, which served for several centuries as the Forte di San Giorgio.

The Boboli is only one of the splendid public parks with which Florence is graced. Although the city centre is all pavements, towers, and pressing people, the area immediately surrounding it is handsomely endowed with green spaces, including 22 sports grounds and four large outdoor swimming pools. The largest park is the Cascine (cowshed), along the right bank of the Arno, which Cosimo I bought as a cow pasture and which eventually became a park with promenade for aristocrats' carriages. Today, among other attractions, it offers tracks for various kinds of horse racing, riding paths, tennis courts, and a modern outdoor velodrome. At the Campo di Marte sports centre, architect Luigi Nervi built a stadium (1930–32) of curved concrete slabs in tension. It became a landmark of modern architecture, with curved cantilevered roof arcing out some 50 feet and a meshed pair of cantilevered spiral staircases in back.

Although the other Renaissance palaces of Florence are not so immense and glowering as the Pitti, they are all massive, with heavy cornices and heavily rusticated blocks of stone. Renaissance feelings of delicacy and movement are apparent only in their courtyards. The first was the Medici Palace, begun by Michelozzo in 1444. Once the seat of Lorenzo the Magnificent's court of philosophers, artists, and poets, it is now the seat of the provincial prefecture.

The Palazzo Rucellai was designed by Alberti in 1458 and exemplified his theories of achieving harmony and "all-pervading order" through mathematical rules of proportion. With this building, Alberti was the first to replace medieval eaves with Renaissance cornices and to employ the three superimposed architectural orders in the pilasters. The Palazzo Strozzi was begun in 1489, but because of the political vicissitudes of the Strozzi family, the palace was not completed even after it had been restored to their ownership in 1568. In 1937 an insurance association bought the long-neglected, money-gobbling palace from Prince Rodolfo Strozzi and restored it. The low stone bench across the front has become the traditional display stand for flower sellers. The iron rings for tethering horses, the torch holders, flag and bunting brackets, and the spike-crowned lanterns, all designed by the original architects and wrought by Niccolo Grosso, a 16th-century ironmaster, are Florentine masterpieces.

Cultural institutions. Florence has a total of 40 museums, mostly devoted to painting and sculpture. The Biblioteca Nazionale Centrale (National Central Library) has been the Italian library of deposit since 1870, receiving a copy of every book published in the nation. It houses more than 3,000,000 autographs, manuscripts, letters, incunabula, and books, including many rare editions. The Ricardiana and Moreniana libraries adjoining the Palazzo Medici-Riccardi have the most complete collection, including valuable manuscripts, of works on Tuscan history. The Biblioteca del Gabinetto Scientifico Letterario G.P. Viesseux is a library founded in 1821 by Jean-Baptiste Viesseux, who was the central figure of a group that included the leading literary figures of Italy at that time.

After Lorenzo de' Medici transferred the "Studio Fiorentino" (founded 1349) to Pisa in 1472, the medical school remained behind, leading the scientific movement in Italy and forming the nucleus for the university that was legally constituted only in 1923. The Academy of the Crusca was established in 1582 to prepare an Italian dictionary; its name means "bran," its symbol is a sieve, and its object remains to winnow impurities from the language. The new edition of the dictionary is due in the year 2000. Other specialized learned institutions include an observatory; academies of fine arts, science, letters, and agrarian economics; institutes of Etruscan and Italian studies, of the history of art, and of the history of optics. The Italian Dante Society, the Italian Botanical Society, and the Society for Geographical Studies are in Florence.

An increasing number of foreign nations and universities conduct study institutes in Florence. The Harvard University Center for Italian Renaissance Studies is located at the exquisite Villa I Tatti, in the hills at Settignano, bequeathed by art historian Bernard Berenson. The universities of Grenoble, Paris, Syracuse, and Stanford, the universities of The Netherlands, and the state colleges of California are represented.

BIBLIOGRAPHY

General works: MARY MCCARTHY, *The Stones of Florence* (1959), an analytic examination of the city past and present with an emphasis on works of art, rich in historical background; EDWARD HUTTON, *Florence*, new ed. (1966), a comprehensive presentation of the city's districts and places of interest; EVE BORSOOK, *The Companion Guide to Florence* (1966), a historical introduction followed by an area-by-area survey, with summaries of the chief monuments in each; EDMOND RENE LABANDE, *Florence* (1949; Eng. trans., 1951), an examination of the monuments in the centre of the city and the principal museums, with descriptive tours of both sides of the Arno and a few excursions into the countryside.

History: FERDINAND SCHEVILL, *Medieval and Renaissance Florence*, 2 vol. (1963; a reduced reprint of the 1936 edition entitled *History of Florence*), a scholarly summation of the city's past; GIUSEPPE MARTINELLI (ed.), *Tutto su Firenze Rinascimentale* (1968; Eng. trans., *The World of Renaissance Florence*, 1968), exceptionally well illustrated with 300 colour pictures accompanied by text by various scholars on many aspects of public and private life; VINCENT CRONIN, *The Florentine Renaissance* (1967), a description of Florentine civilization as a whole during the 15th century based on primary sources, including a list of the whereabouts of works of art mentioned in the text or reproduced as illustrations.

Art: MARCO ROSCI, *The Uffizi and Pitti Galleries* (Eng. trans. 1964), a well-documented survey with illustrations in black and white and colour; FILIPPO ROSSI, *Art Treasures of the Uffizi and Pitti* (1957), many reproductions, with explanatory text; ROBERT SALVINI, *The Uffizi Gallery: Visitors' Guide and Catalogue of Paintings* (1965), a serviceable, popular guide with brief comments on the works; EVELYN SANDBERG VAVALA, *Uffizi Studies: The Development of the Florentine School of Painting* (1948), for the intelligent visitor who wishes to become better informed about the history and character of Florentine painting.

Chiefly photographic: MARTIN HURLIMANN and HAROLD ACTON, *Florence* (1961), historical notes accompanying 138 pictures in photogravure and 12 colour plates; LAZZARO DONATI, *Florence* (1959), views of landmarks, daily life, churches, art, and other aspects of the environment; BENNO PREMSELS, *This Is Florence* (1954), smaller paperback, but with excellent photographs and informative text.

Special topics: JOSEPH MACLEOD, *People of Florence* (1969), the character and way of life of the inhabitants as they are shaped by their locality, told in a personal, essayist style; FRANCO NENCINI, *Firenze, i giorni del diluvio*, 5th ed. (1966; Eng. trans., *Florence: The Days of the Flood*, 1967), a journalistic account of the November 1966 flood, with 107 photographs of its ravages.

(B.E.)

Florida

The geographical situation of Florida has been the key factor in a long and colourful development that is without parallel in the United States and goes a long way to explaining the striking contemporary character of the state. The greater part of Florida lies on a peninsula protruding southeastward from the North American continent, separating the waters of the Atlantic Ocean from those of the Gulf of Mexico and leading toward the island of Cuba and the Caribbean Sea beyond. The nearest foreign territory is the Bahamian island of Bimini, some 50 miles to the east of the state's tip. With the exception of Hawaii, Florida is the most southern state of the United States, with its northernmost point lying 100 miles farther south than California's southern border. The Florida Keys, an island crescent forming the state's southernmost portion, lie within 1,700 miles of the Equator. Florida lies in the same latitude as Egypt. Its size, 58,560 square miles (151,670 square kilometres), is comparable to that of England and Wales.

The state lies close to the geographical centre and the median population point of the New World land mass and its position commands not only the entrance to the Gulf of Mexico but also the strategic crossroads between North and South America and historic routes to the European and Mediterranean worlds. Florida played a prominent role in the struggles of the European powers to control the New World, and it is fitting that St. Augustine, on its northeastern coast, founded in 1565, should be the oldest European settlement within the boundaries of what became the continental U.S.

After a long and turbulent early history, Florida became a U.S. possession in 1821, entering the Union in 1845. Even then, the full development of the state by peoples of European descent had to await the final elimination of the indigenous population, and the opening of the territory by an injection of northern capital into the transportation system. Only in the late 19th century did the rich potential of Florida's beautiful tropical and subtropical environment—another endowment of its geographical position—undergo full development. The population soared: the total shown by the 1850 census, the first taken after the state entered the Union, was 87,445, ranking last among the states; by 1900 it had expanded to 528,542 (33rd among 45 states), and a spectacular 20th-century expansion carried its total over the 7,000,000 mark by 1971, when it ranked among the top 10 states, as well as being among the top three fastest growing states. Although agriculture and the manufacturing industry of Florida continue to be important, the climate and scenery of the "Sunshine State" have attracted enormous numbers of visitors, and tourism is now the mainstay of a well-diversified local economy. Some 3,400 persons a week were taking up permanent residence in the state by the early 1970s, and a good proportion of these were making their retirement homes in Florida, making a distinctive contribution to the character of the state. During the same period, Florida has become a global centre for the most modern of explorations, that of space, with the vast launching complex at Cape Kennedy. (For related information see UNITED STATES, HISTORY OF THE; UNITED STATES; NORTH AMERICA; and EVERGLADES.)

HISTORY

Exploration and settlement. The early history of Florida reflected the conflicts of the Spanish, French, and English crowns for empire and wealth. Juan Ponce de León's quest for the Fountain of Youth brought him to the mainland in 1513, and 1521. An abortive settlement in 1528 led to eight years of Indian captivity and wandering through the South and Southwest by Alvar Núñez Cabeza de Vaca and three companions. A colony of Protestant Huguenots established on the St. Johns River was wiped out in 1565 by Spaniards, who boasted of slaughtering the Frenchmen not for their nationality but for their religion. This Spanish expedition, under Pedro Menéndez de Avilés, proceeded to found St. Augustine near the decimated settlement. *(margin: Spanish dominion)*

Shifting alliances and allegiances. The following centuries saw frequent raids by English seafarers, including Sir Francis Drake in 1586, and clashes with French colonizers along the northern coasts of the Gulf of Mexico and English settlers in the Carolina and Georgia colonies. Shifting alliances among the three powers reflected the vicissitudes of European politics, and St. Augustine and the English ports of Savannah and Charleston were besieged at various times through the first half of the 18th century.

England received Florida in return for Havana in 1763 and instituted civil for military government. Expenditures for economic development brought prosperity as well as loyalty from most Floridians during the Revolution, when the colony was used as a base for attacks on American coastal cities. Three decades of political and social instability followed Florida's return to Spain after the Revolution, with American expansionist interests in constant conflict with the Spanish presence. Pensacola was a base for the British during the War of 1812, when Indians and runaway Negroes were employed to harass American settlements. General Andrew Jackson's capture of Pensacola led finally to cession of Florida to the United States in a treaty signed in 1819 and ratified in 1821.

Statehood. The Seminole War of 1835–42, the result of attempts to remove the indigenous people to Oklahoma after their centuries of relative peace with the Spanish, became the darkest chapter in Florida's history. By 1845, when Florida was admitted to the Union as the 27th state, all but a few hundred Seminoles had been transported from their ancestral home.

Florida was a part of the Confederacy during the Civil War, but action in the state was limited to the capture of coastal cities by Union troops. In the 1880s an era of railroad building began that opened the state to permanent settlers and a new tourist trade and brought it into the heart of the nation's economic life as the winter vegetable and citrus centre of the East. *(margin: Evolution of the contemporary state)*

The 20th century. The growth of Florida in the 20th century was frantic to the point of chaos. Land booms and the building of high-rise resort and convention cities paralleled economic diversification and military installations such as the missile site at Cape Kennedy.

THE LANDSCAPE

Natural landscape. *Physiography.* Florida is a geologically young, low-lying plain, mostly under 100 feet, with its highest point, in Walton County, a mere 345 feet. Sedimentary deposits of sand and limestone cover most of the state, with areas of peat and muck marking where freshwater bodies once stood. The contemporary topography has been largely molded by running water, waves, ocean currents, winds, changes in sea level, and the wearing away of limestone rocks by solution. These forces have produced enough variation in the state's surface to permit classification into seven basic physiographic regions: the coastal lowlands, the Lake Okeechobee–Everglades Basin, the Kissimmee lowlands, the Marianna lowlands, the central highlands, the Tallahassee hills, and the western highlands, although these scientific divisions are scarcely apparent to the naked eye.

Soils and vegetation. Soils and vegetation are closely related to the basic physiographic provinces. In general, Florida's soils consist of sands, sandy loams, clayey marls, peat, and mucks, and over 300 soil types have been mapped. The variety of trees is great, with more than 300 species being described: more than 60 percent of the state is covered by trees. Dominant trees include pines, oaks, cypresses, palms, and mangroves. Most tropical plants will thrive in south Florida, while beech, red maple, sweet gum, tulip, magnolia, and hickory are common in the north. Almost half of the tree species of the United States grow in the state, and more than 3,500 non-tree plants have been identified. Included in this number are many imports.

Six broad soil–vegetation regions may be described. The Flatwood lowland soils form the largest soil region in Florida, which corresponds roughly to the coastal lowlands. The terrain here is level and underlain by a hardpan that impedes drainage and encourages flooding; slash and longleaf pine, oaks, sabal palm, and grass typify the region. Organic soils are found in many parts of Florida, but the type locality is the Lake Okeechobee–Everglades Basin—probably the largest area of neutral organic soils in the tropics—where saw grasses, cypress, sabal palm, myrtle, willow, elderberry, and gum are important. In this soggy environment, submergence often prevents the oxidation, decay, and shrinkage of peat and muck, but, when the soils are drained, they deteriorate rapidly. Southern limestone soils occur in the Kissimmee Valley, the Big Cypress Swamp, and the Miami-Homestead area. Pines and oaks grow in some areas, but grasses, along with saw palmetto and sabal palms, predominate in the Kissimmee Valley. Cypress, bays, and gumbo-limbo, a tall tree with a brown, bright lacquered trunk, are typical of the extreme southern areas of this type. Northern upland soils occur in the region stretching across the north of the state and support hardwoods, loblolly pine, and longleaf pine, while northern slope soils lie immediately to the south, producing slash and longleaf pine, oak, and saw palmetto. Central upland soils—with a vegetation similar to that found in northern slope soils—are located in the higher ridge area of central Florida and westward to the Apalachicola River. A number of other distinctive zones of soils and vegetation exist: dune types fringe the magnificent beaches of the state, while the lush, dank mangrove swamps, along with tropical hardwoods and sand pine and oak, are found in the Ocala National Forest.

Water. The flat Florida landscape is covered by a latticework of 1,711 named streams (mostly in the north and northwest) and no fewer than 30,000 named lakes (mostly in the central region). The state also contains 17 of the 75 first-magnitude artesian springs in the nation, most of them located in the central region. Some 39 drainage basins are recognized, with the Lake Okeechobee–Everglades Basin (17,000 square miles) being the largest. Lake Okeechobee (700 square miles) is the third largest freshwater lake entirely in the United States (after Lake Michigan and Lake Iliamna, Alaska). This vast water network is fed by the state's porous limestone substructure, which stores large quantities of water.

Wildlife. Florida's rich and distinctive tropical and subtropical environment is inhabited by a huge and varied wildlife population, the rarer forms of which are fully protected. Approximately 100 species of mammals are represented, and the range includes deer, puma, bobcat, boar, black bear, armadillo, otter, mink, and gray fox, while bats and other smaller animals are numerous. Manatees (sea cows) still inhabit streams and canals in the south, and several species of porpoises and dolphins lend their own distinctive charm to the clear coastal waters.

Over 400 species and subspecies of birds have been cataloged: land birds include the turkey, quail, dove, eagle, hawk, owl, and most smaller birds common to the southeastern states, while coastal birds—gulls, brown pelican, sandpiper, osprey, and cormorant—are also numerous.

The organic-soil complex

Huge and varied wildlife population

Freshwater and marsh birds include the gallinule (marsh hen), duck, goose, coot, egret, heron, ibis (stork), and flamingo. Vast natural rookeries exist in the Everglades, and numerous wildlife refuges are maintained for the protection of migratory birds.

The less attractive alligator is the king of Florida reptiles, his role as a builder of water holes being vital to south Florida's ecology, while the crocodile still inhabits part of the Everglades National Park. The 40 species of snakes in the state include the nation's four poisonous types: coral, rattlesnake, moccasin, and copperhead (the latter restricted to limited areas of north Florida); turtles, tortoises, lizards, and frogs are also abundant.

Florida's 4,000,000 acres of water (of which 2,750,000 acres are inland) contain more than 700 species of fish and shellfish. Common saltwater varieties are bluefish, pompano, flounder, mackerel, mullet, trout, redfish, snapper, grouper, snook, sailfish, tarpon, shad, weakfish, bonefish, marlin, and shark, and others. Crawfish, oysters, stone and blue crabs, clams, and shrimp may be added to the list. The largemouth black bass is the state's foremost freshwater species, while others include bream (bluegill), sunfish, speckled perch, and catfish.

Climate. Climatically, Florida is divided into two regions. The tropical zone lies generally south of a west–east line drawn from Bradenton, via the south shore of Lake Okeechobee, to Vero Beach, while to the north of this line the state is subtropical. Summers are uniform throughout Florida, and, while freezing weather, of short duration (but often crippling to agriculture), can occur as far south as Miami, the Keys—a crescent of islands strung out at the southern tip of the state—have never experienced frost.

Rainfall is heaviest in summer, with drier weather prevailing in the winter months. The average annual rainfall ranges from 39.8 inches (1,011 millimetres) in Key West to 61.7 inches (1,567 millimetres) in West Palm Beach. Snow falls occasionally in the northern areas and has been reported as far south as Fort Myers. Hurricanes, occurring about once a year on the average, bring much needed rain to the state near the end of the rainy season. These storms may cause great damage, although Florida is no more vulnerable than the other Gulf states or, indeed, the Atlantic coast up to Boston. The hurricane season is from June to November, although September is the month they are most likely to occur.

Average annual temperatures show little variation, ranging from 68° F (20° C) in Tallahassee in the north to 77° F at Key West in the south. Corresponding monthly averages range from the middle 40's F (in the north) to the middle 50's F (in the south) in January, and are in the lower 80's F in August.

Hurricanes

Regions. North and south Florida are often distinguished as separate regions. North Florida is often thought of as colder, historically older, oriented toward field agriculture and timber, rural, and hilly; and south Florida is regarded as warmer, more recently settled, citrus–livestock–vegetable oriented, tourist centred, urban, and flat. A refinement would add central Florida, with its lake region and citrus belt. A more scientific regionalization might identify the east coast, the west coast, central Florida, the Keys, the Everglades, and the panhandle. More popular regional names are: the Gold Coast (the Miami–West Palm Beach metropolitan sprawl), the Sun Coast (the Tampa Bay area), and the Big Bend (centring on Tallahassee). Lesser known designations include the Silver or Platinum Coast (a term applied to the lower southwest), the Island or Mangrove Coast (the extreme southwest), Suwanneeland (the Suwannee River basin), Miracle Strip (the upper northwestern coast), Florida's Crown (the northernmost part of the peninsula), the Surf Coast (mideast coast), and the Tropi-Coast (Miami–West Palm Beach).

Cultural landscape. *Rural life.* To a stranger entering the state from the north, the Florida landscape may appear quite empty and devoid of human imprint. It is, in fact, in use, but the use is of a type unfamiliar to many eastern Americans. About 55 percent of Florida is covered by commercial, national, and state forests, state and federal parks, lakes, cities, highways, military reservations, and beaches. Of the remaining 45 percent, only one-fifth is in farmland, and half of this is in either pasture or timber: the net result is that only about 5 percent of Florida's total land is in harvested crops, with field crops accounting for half the harvested total, citrus fruit for one-quarter, and vegetables for one-quarter.

The effect on the landscape is striking: farmsteads are generally common in north Florida, where field crops are important, but even here timber covers thousands of acres. Citrus groves occupy much of central Florida and the east coast, while along the west coast and north and south of the citrus belt spread vast expanses of cattle land. Around Lake Okeechobee, the cultivation of sugarcane and vegetables has produced the modern equivalent of plantation agriculture. The small, private farm has little place in these systems, the settled farmer having been superceded as a result of mechanization and the use of migratory labor. The social conditions of the latter, which have, on occasion, given rise to national concern, remain one of the less happy aspects of a generally affluent state. The rise of what has been termed corporate agriculture has thus led to an inevitable increase in farm size and a corresponding reduction in farm numbers. Since 1940, the number of Florida farms has almost halved, while, by the early 1970s, one-half the total farm acreage was owned by fewer than 1,000 farmers.

Urban settlement. Even the small town seems to be disappearing, as more and more people find it relatively easy to commute from urban and suburban centres: at the 1970 census, 80.5 percent of the people were urban, and, of the remainder, only 2 percent lived on farms. Seventy percent of the total state population lived, in fact, in 10 of the 67 counties, with 30 percent occupying the extensive Miami–West Palm Beach urban complex in the southeast of the state. This area appeared to many observers to be duplicating the less desirable aspects of the great urban belts burgeoning in other areas of the nation. On the west coast, the Tampa Bay metropolitan area contained another 15 percent of the population. Further north, the Orlando–Cape Kennedy–Daytona Beach triangle is central Florida's dominant urban area; Jacksonville is the major centre of the upper east coast and southeast Georgia; and Pensacola dominates the western panhandle and part of Alabama. Lesser metropolitan areas—notably, Tallahassee, Gainesville, and Fort Myers—are hubs of local influence.

THE PEOPLE OF FLORIDA

Cultural and racial groups. *The legacy of the Indians.* Ancient Indian groups drifted into Florida from the north as early as 10,000 years ago, but farming did not appear much before 500 BC, and some southern indigenous groups remained hunters, fishers, and gatherers until their extinction. Indians continued to arrive in small numbers after 500 BC, and contacts with Cuba, the Bahamas, and, possibly, Yucatán reflected Florida's unique situation. By 1750 virtually all of these peoples had been destroyed by disease, slavers, and wars, responsibility largely resting with English and Creek raiders from Georgia. The latter, accompanied by a few runaway Negro slaves and renegade whites, were collectively called Cimarrónes (Spanish: "wild, unruly, runaway"). The name Seminole evolved from *cimarrón*, and there were approximately 5,000 Seminoles in Florida when it came under formal United States jurisdiction in 1821. Within 25 years, this population declined to about 150, at which juncture most Seminoles were removed to Oklahoma; by the 1970s some 2,000 of the descendants of those who remained lived in three south Florida reservations.

Early European contributions. The first Spanish settlement, of 1559, was abandoned in 1561, but San Augustín (St. Augustine), founded in 1565 after the destruction of the French settlement there, became the first permanent European settlement in the United States. For the next 250 years, Florida was little more than a wilderness in terms of any permanent European settlement, although its importance as a historical pawn was considerable. A population of European origin was not to grow until the

United States established effective civil control in 1822, and the great increases of the late 19th and 20th centuries owed much to economic factors (see below *The state's economy*).

The Black contribution. It is not known when the first Negroes arrived in Florida, but it is known that some accompanied the first Spanish expeditions. A few runaway slaves came in with the Seminoles, but it was only with American rule that the Negro population began to increase. By 1830 there were as many Negroes as whites (about 11,000 each). The subsequent increase of Negro population coincided with the development and spread of the Southern plantation system, based on slavery. The U.S. Civil War overthrew the slave system, but the agricultural patterns remained, and not until the end of the 19th century did an influx of whites cause their component of the population to increase faster than that of the Negroes. The Negro percentage of the total population continued to decline in the 20th century, and by the 1970s the proportion of black Americans amounted to about 17 percent, although larger percentages were still found in the old plantation belt (north central Florida) and in the Everglades truck-farming region.

Other distinctive groups. Cubans came to Key West after 1868, when, as a result of revolutionary turmoil in Cuba, Vicente Martínez Ybor moved his cigar factories there from Havana. Labour troubles and disastrous fire encouraged Ybor to move again in 1886, this time to Tampa, and again many Cubans followed the factories. A similar Cuban influx occurred after the revolution of the early 1960s, with over 350,000 Cubans fleeing their homeland. A third of these settled in Florida (mostly in the Miami area) during the decade.

Immigrants from northern Spain came to Tampa about the time of World War I, drawn largely by the expanding cigar industry and the prospect of living in a Spanish-speaking community. Italians also came in large numbers. By the 1970s, approximately 20 percent of Tampa's population remained Spanish speaking.

Tarpon Springs was settled around 1880, and by 1905 Greek immigrants, drawing on the traditions of their homeland, had established the nation's major sponge industry. Greek is still widely spoken, and the city is a centre for the Greek Orthodox religion. Other ethnic contributions lending character to the overall population of the state range in size from the distinctive Jewish community at Miami–Miami Beach (over 100,000) to the Slovak settlement at Masaryktown (about 1,000).

Demography. Florida's 1970 resident population of 6,789,443 marked a 37.1 percent increase over that in 1960. The population passed the 7,000,000 mark in 1971 and was confidently projected to exceed 8,000,000 by the close of the decade. While the birthrate (17.0) was close to the national rate of 17.7 per 1,000 in 1969, the death rate was 11.6 per 1,000, as compared with a national rate of 9.6 per 1,000 in 1968. Florida's death rate has climbed steadily since 1960, when it was 9.7 per 1,000, while the birthrate has dropped from 23.3 per 1,000; in part, this trend undoubtedly reflects the immigration of older people. During the late 1960s, excess of births over deaths added approximately 30,000 persons a year to the state total, while immigration, on the other hand, brought in some 180,000 persons annually. By the early 1970s, Florida was the third fastest growing state, with a 2.7-percent annual increase, exceeded only by Arizona (2.8 percent) and Nevada (5.0 percent). This still represented a slowing of Florida's hectic growth in the 1950s, when the total population registered a remarkable 79-percent increase.

In terms of intrastate trends, it appears that the state's northwestern counties will continue to lose population to the large urban areas, while those areas heavily dependent on military and space programs may well be affected by the budgetary vicissitudes affecting those activities. Key West, for example, a Navy-oriented city, suffered a 19-percent population loss over 1960, while Brevard County (in which Cape Kennedy is located) registered a gain of no less than 106 percent. On the other hand, cutbacks in the space program created Florida's

Margin notes:

Corporate agriculture

Contacts with Central America

highest unemployment rate in the latter area during the first years of the 1970s, and further rapid growth appeared unlikely. Instead, developing southwest Florida seemed destined to be the next boom region of the state, for Charlotte and Collier counties each gained more than 100 percent in population over the 1960s, while Lee County increased by 93 percent. Overall, the accelerating urbanism of the early 1970s led to predictions that, within a decade or so, Florida's population would be less than 10 percent rural, while some 11 counties, containing approximately 90 percent of the population, would be totally urban.

THE STATE'S ECONOMY

Overall factors. Florida experienced virtually no economic development before 1821, when the United States took formal possession, and the 60 years to follow were dominated by small-farm and plantation agriculture; the supplying of naval stores and the production of beef and hides, pork, salt, tobacco, and cotton were the main activities. The 1880s, by contrast, marked the beginning of a new era in Florida, for, in 1881, phosphate—the state's most important mineral—was discovered in the Peace River Valley, while in that same year Hamilton Disston, a Philadelphia industrialist, bought 4,000,000 acres in the Everglades for 25 cents an acre. This key action freed the state from its post-Civil War debt and opened the way for the development of much of the peninsula. In the west, a railroad reached Pensacola in 1883, and in the following year another thrust as far as Tampa; this, too, was financed by a northern capitalist—in this case, Henry B. Plant—while on the east coast his counterpart, Henry M. Flagler, was building a rail and hotel empire that would soon extend past Miami to Key West. Agricultural development, settlement, industry, and tourism all followed the rails: the 1890 population of the state was double that of 1870, while the total passed the half-million mark by the turn of the century and continued its spectacular growth thereafter.

Role of Northern capital

Distribution of resources. Directly or indirectly, Florida's tropical and subtropical climate affects almost every aspect of the local economy, and it can be quite justifiably considered as the state's chief resource. Together with land and water—both of which have possessed a rich potential for economic development—it forms the basis of the state's wealth. The water resources, important to fisherman and tourist alike, include not only 4,424 square miles of fresh inland water but also an even larger area of adjacent saltwater. In the United States, only Alaska has a tidal shoreline whose length exceeds that of Florida, which totals no less than 8,426 miles (Gulf coast, 5,095 miles; Atlantic coast, 3,331 miles). On land, forestry activities and livestock rearing are supported by the fact that about 60 percent of the state (mostly in the north) is wooded, while grasslands spread over another 20 percent (mostly in the central and southern areas). Florida also yields several important minerals, with phosphate—used in fertilizer and livestock feed and by chemical industries—being the principal one. It is found in the west central portion of the state, whose production accounts for 75 percent of the national total. Titanium (used in paint and jet engines), zircon (used in foundries, gas engines, and atomic reactors), and such other important heavy minerals as thorium and cerium are mined near Jacksonville, Starke, Vero Beach, and in west central Florida. Petroleum is produced at Jay, (north of Pensacola), and averages 180,000 barrels a month. A small field in Collier County produces 25,000–40,000 barrels monthly. Kaolin is mined in Putnam County; Fuller's earth comes from the Tallahassee region; while clay, sand, and gravel are mined in numerous locations, with pure silica sand being extracted mostly in areas around the 100-foot contour line. Limestone, from the northern portion of the peninsula, is used as cut building stone and road-surfacing material and in cement, concrete, and fertilizer; peat, used as a soil conditioner, is dug in many areas. The versatility of the marine resources of Florida is indicated by a plant at Port St. Joe on the Gulf coast for the recovery of magnesium from seawater.

Sources of income. *Tourism.* Approximately 23,000,000 tourists visited Florida annually in the early 1970s, spending a total, each year, in excess of $6,000,000,000. Tourism is by far the predominant industry and has developed into a year-round activity, with July and August being the leading months.

Manufacturing. Manufacturing contributes, on a value-added basis, in excess of $4,000,000,000 annually, second only to tourism. Production is well diversified, with food processing leading in value.

Agriculture. Cash farm income amounted to some $1,500,000,000 annually by the 1970s. Florida produces about 75 percent of the nation's total citrus fruit, and the state is second only to California in vegetable production. Although Florida has almost 2,000,000 head of cattle, it is perhaps better known as one of the leading North American regions for the rearing of thoroughbred horses.

Agricultural specialties

Completing the major sources of income for the local economy, the state's annual manufactured value of forest products exceeds $600,000,000, and of minerals, $320,000,000; and commercial fishing brings in almost $40,000,000. This overall diversification of a developing economy, utilizing the richly varied natural endowment, has been a key factor in the remarkable population growth of the state in the 20th century.

Management of the economy. Labour-management relationships in Florida tend to follow the national pattern. Manufacturing, mining, communication, and transportation tend to be unionized; services, less so; while the professions and agriculture are generally nonunion. The cooperative movement is especially strong in citrus and commercial fishing. The Florida Citrus Mutual works closely with growers and the state in research, production, processing, marketing, and regulation, while about eight fishing cooperatives exist, primarily to help market the catch.

The state government cooperates closely with the private sector of the economy; it is instrumental in inspection, licensing, regulation, and research and education, but the state rarely competes with private business.

Transportation. *Overall patterns.* Florida's transportation system is a comprehensive one, covering the entire state except for certain isolated areas in the Everglades. In general, highway arteries run across the north of the state, from Jacksonville to Pensacola; down the east coast, from Jacksonville to Miami; diagonally across the state, from Jacksonville to Tampa–St. Petersburg on the west coast, bisecting the state from Tampa–St. Petersburg to Daytona Beach; and through the southwestern portion, linking Tampa–St. Petersburg to Miami. Rail and air traffic follow these patterns, with one exception: although there is no direct Miami–Tampa railroad, air traffic on this route is extremely heavy.

Component systems. Florida has approximately 87,000 miles (47,000 paved miles) of state, county, and municipal roads. The most heavily travelled through routes are the interstate and state turnpike systems that connect all major cities. There are 20 airports with regularly scheduled flights, augmented by numerous private airfields, and the international terminals at Tampa and Miami are among the most modern in the world. An extensive rail network, some 4,348 miles long, provides an adequate passenger and freight service to most areas. An integrated system for domestic and foreign shipping is provided by 13 deepwater ports and several lesser ports and harbours, while more than 1,000 miles of navigable channel are maintained by the federal government. Construction of the Cross-Florida Barge Canal was halted by President Richard Nixon in 1971, pending further ecological studies.

Florida has the world's only moonport, the John F. Kennedy Space Center at Cape Kennedy, which occupies 88,000 acres. Not only is this a major Florida industry (employing as many as 35,000) but it has also become a prime tourist attraction.

Cape Kennedy

ADMINISTRATION AND SOCIAL CONDITIONS

Governmental structure. *The constitution.* The government of Florida operates under the revised constitution of 1968, with the executive department—headed by the governor and six Cabinet officers (secretaries of agriculture, state, and education; comptroller; attorney general; and treasurer)—the law-administering and law-enforcing branch. Essentially, the Cabinet officers control their departments, divisions, and assorted boards directly, while the governor controls nine departments of quasi-Cabinet status that report to him. The legislature is composed of a Senate of 48 members and a House of Representatives of 119 members. Senators serve four-year terms, and half that body is elected every two years, while House members are elected for two-year terms.

The legal system. The judicial department is the law-interpreting branch, and its powers are exercised primarily through courts established by the constitution: the Supreme Court, 4 district courts of appeal, 20 circuit courts, and a variety of county and municipal courts are found, with most judges elected for four-year terms. Florida is also part of the 5th judicial circuit of the federal court system and has three lower level district courts.

Though the Florida of the early 1970s was becoming a two-party state in many respects, Democrats typically outnumbered Republicans in both houses by about two to one, a preponderance traditionally reflected in national representation. The growing population of the state has occasioned constant reapportionment of representation at both the federal and national levels and was partially responsible for the adoption of the new constitution of 1968.

Taxation. Florida has no state income tax on individuals or corporations, and approximately 50 percent of the state's tax revenue comes from sales and use taxes and the gasoline tax. The remainder is derived from a wide range of other taxes, including those on pari-mutuel betting, principally at horse- and dog-racing tracks.

The social framework. Socially, Florida regards itself as a progressive state, and a major proportion of the state's financial resources certainly go into those areas that serve the public, with education, welfare, health, and hospitals receiving 64 percent of the total appropriations. The state supports the public school system to the extent that no child is deprived of a minimum standard of education, while the counties are expected to supplement this minimum. Virtually the entire population of the state is within commuting distance of a state-supported college or university, part of an extensive system of higher education.

Florida has about 200 hospitals, with approximately 30,000 beds; in general, there has been a steady improvement in health and health-care facilities during the recent decade, not unconnected with the growing proportion of elderly residents.

At the start of the 1970s, Florida's per capita income was close to $3,600 per year, the highest in the southeast of the nation and 54 percent higher than a decade earlier, while, in total personal income, Florida ranks tenth in the nation. There are no serious labour shortages in Florida except in a few highly skilled and professional occupations and, at certain times, in service occupations. Unemployment in Florida usually runs below the national average, and the diversified economy of the state has not been as subject to labour fluctuations as in many other areas where one industry dominates the economy. Cost of living is generally below the national urban average, and in some areas, such as clothing, it is considerably below the average—another small but significant benefit accruing from the favourable climate.

CULTURAL LIFE AND INSTITUTIONS

Florida is well endowed with a variety of cultural activities and supporting institutions, a situation stemming partly from the importance of tourism and partly from the increasing leisure time available to the growing number of retired residents. The state itself maintains over 800 parks and recreation areas, many of historic or natural-historic interest; counties and municipalities support another 1,300 parks, as well as almost 600 indoor centres; and the Everglades National Park contains 1,400,-

Political trends

Employment and living costs

500 acres in the heart of a unique natural region. Florida's rich history is preserved in such places as St. Augustine, the nation's oldest town, portions of which have been restored, while its famous fort, Castillo de San Marcos, has been made a national monument.

Sarasota is a centre for both art and theatre. The John and Mable Ringling Museum of Art possesses an internationally famous collection, and the city—once the winter quarters of the famous Ringling Circus—also contains a circus, museum, and hall of fame. The Florida State Museum, located in Gainesville, is but one among the numerous noncommercial cultural attractions in Florida, while the Florida State Fair is held every February in Tampa, in combination with Gasparilla, a festival whose proportions are comparable to those of the great Mardi Gras celebrations of New Orleans.

Sports are well represented in the state, with the Orange Bowl in Miami, the Gator Bowl in Jacksonville, and Tampa Stadium attracting major university and professional events. The climate of Florida enables it to host a number of outdoor events, including five major golf tournaments and three internationally known auto races. Horse racing is also important.

Commercial attractions seem almost countless; many are educational and contribute not only to the cultural well-being of the state but also their share of taxes. Walt Disney World (near Orlando), which opened in late 1971, appeared to have a good chance of becoming the largest tourist attraction in the country, affecting the entire economy of central Florida. Before the opening of this project, Busch Gardens, in Tampa, was Florida's leading attraction, with over 30,000 visitors a day during the winter months.

In addition to other cultural offerings, Florida's universities and educational-television stations offer broad programs in continuing and adult education and similar ventures, on a scale larger than that of most other American states.

PROSPECTS

Florida is one of the fastest growing states in the nation and seems to have a good chance of meeting the projected annual increase of approximately 140,000 people a year during the 1970s. Employment is increasing in certain categories of professional and skilled occupations, but prospective residents have found it to their advantage to investigate the job market very carefully before moving into the state. Whereas a few years ago a newcomer could, for example, enter business by purchasing or building a small motel, the motel industry of the early 1970s was fast becoming a chain or franchise operation, with costs averaging $10,000 per rental unit. The same pattern was to be noted in agriculture, where farm and grove units are larger than in the past, and mechanization requires a heavy investment. Even migratory agricultural labour—hitherto an important, if decidedly unattractive, source of employment for the unskilled—is on its way out, while heavy industry, with its large labour demands, seems highly unlikely to become a part of the Florida scene, primarily because of the lack of power resources. Manufacturing, already the number two income producer in the state, appears likely to continue to expand, especially in the more sophisticated areas of modern technology. As the state's urban character continues to intensify, it appears that many of the new housing units will be condominium, cooperative, or modular form: sprawling suburban developments have already begun to be less evident, and this trend will continue as the cost of land continues to mount. Tourism shows no signs of losing its pre-eminent position, but new areas—particularly central, west central, and southwestern Florida—are beginning to feel its impact and are already showing indications of becoming future growth regions. Air- and water-pollution controls are well established in Florida and play an important role in any activity that affects the quality of the environment. The dredge-and-fill era of Florida bays has come to an end, and some communities have ordinances prohibiting the cutting of trees. Wanton and irresponsible exploitation of

Conservation measures

the state's resources is being halted, and the earlier concept of short-term gain is being replaced with one of beneficial, long-range development. As a result, it is to be hoped that Florida, one of the last states of the United States to be developed, will be able to preserve its beautiful environment and avoid a repetition of some of the more obvious defects that have afflicted the longer established regions of the country lying further to the north.

BIBLIOGRAPHY

General works: A.C. MORRIS, *The Florida Handbook* (biennial), the most valuable book for general information, containing statistics, personality sketches, history, geography, and detailed material on the state government; *Florida Trend* (monthly), Florida's foremost magazine of business and finance with information on many other subjects, providing one of the most reliable sources of current information about Florida; F. COWLES *et al.*, *What to Look For in Florida, and What to Look Out For*, 2nd ed. (1969), an up-to-date book about living in Florida, with information on prices, housing, real estate, employment, business, taxes, and government; E. RAISZ and J.R. DUNKLE, *Atlas of Florida* (1964), an excellent, comprehensive atlas of the state in full colour with hundreds of maps, graphs, and charts; H.F. BECKER and D.E. CHRISTENSEN, *Florida Reference Atlas* (1960), a valuable reference work with maps of all aspects of the state's geography, history, economy, and government; R.B. MARCUS, *A Geography of Florida* (1964), the only geography of Florida, containing information on history, geology, water resources, vegetation, soils, agriculture, minerals, industry, tourism, and climate; O.C. BRYAN, *Soils of Florida and Their Crop Adaptation* (1960); K. BUTSON, *Climates of the States: Florida*, U.S. Weather Bureau, rev. ed. (1962).

Standard histories: C.W. TEBEAU, *A History of Florida* (1971), the best history available; M.S. DOUGLAS, *Florida: The Long Frontier* (1967); J.E. DOVELL, *Florida: Historic, Dramatic, Contemporary*, 4 vol. (1952); FEDERAL WRITERS' PROJECT, *Florida: A Guide to the Southernmost State* (1939); S.J. FLYNN, *Florida: Land of Fortune* (1962); D.B. MCKAY (ed.), *Pioneer Florida*, 3 vol. (1959).

For statistical data on Florida, see the publications of various state agencies and the *Florida Statistical Abstract* (annual).

(R.H.Fu.)

Fluid and Electrolyte Disorders

The chemical events by which the bodily tissues are built and maintained and by which energy is provided for bodily activity can take place only in a watery solution in which the hydrogen ions and electrolytes (discussed below) are kept within relatively narrow limits (see HOMEOSTASIS). Disturbances of water, electrolyte, and acid–base balance occur as a consequence of a large number of pathological conditions; these impair the functioning of many organs, especially those concerned with contractility and nerve conduction.

THE NORMAL FUNCTION OF WATER AND ELECTROLYTES IN THE BODY

The fluids and electrolytes of the body are the water that pervades it and the ions formed from the acids, alkalis, and salts that are dissolved in it. Ions are atoms or groups of atoms bearing positive or negative electrical charges. Those bearing positive charges are called cations; those bearing negative charges are anions. The ions are called electrolytes because the solution that contains them is able to transmit an electrical current.

The fluids in the body may be classified into two main divisions: the fluid in the cells and that outside (the extracellular fluid). The extracellular fluid can be further divided into the fluid within blood vessels (the intravascular fluid), and the fluid around the tissues.

Electrolytes. The electrolytes and their concentrations are shown in the Table. They are not dispersed evenly throughout the fluids of the body. Sodium and chloride are confined mainly to the extracellular fluids; potassium, magnesium, phosphate, and organic acids are present in highest concentration inside the cells. Bicarbonate is found in the extracellular fluid at a little more than twice its concentration in the tissue cells, while the concentration of free hydrogen ions is twice as great within the cells as outside them. This difference with respect to hy-

Normal Distribution of Ions in Intracellular (Muscle) and Extracellular Fluids in Man		
	intracellular (mEq/kg) H_2O	extracellular (mEq/kg) H_2O
Cations		
Sodium (Na^+)	10	145
Potassium (K^+)	150	5
Calcium (Ca^{++})	2	3
Magnesium (Mg^{++})	15	2
Total	177	155
Anions		
Chloride (Cl^-)	5	105
Bicarbonate (HCO_3^-)	10	25
Organic acids	120	6
Phosphate ($PO_4^{\equiv}$)		2
Proteins	42	17
Total	177	155

Source: J.R. Robinson, "Water and Life," *World Review of Nutrition and Dietetics.*

drogen means that most tissue cells are slightly more acid than the fluid that bathes them.

Because of the permeability of the walls of the capillaries, the smallest of the blood vessels, the concentrations of electrolytes in the plasma (the blood apart from its cells) and in the extracellular fluid outside the blood vessels is similar. Interchange between these two extracellular compartments is limited, however, in respect to protein molecules, the concentrations of which, except in the fluid bathing the cells in the liver, is much greater in the plasma.

Thus, the plasma volume is largely the result of two opposing forces—the hydrostatic pressure, which tends to force water outward, and the osmotic pressure of the plasma proteins, which attracts water into the network of vessels. In spite of the differences in the pattern of ions in the cells and in the extracellular fluid, their osmotic pressure under normal conditions is identical. By hydrostatic pressure, in this context, is meant the pressures in the bodily fluids as a result of the mechanical forces exerted upon them. These forces include that resulting from the contractions of the heart. Osmotic pressure comes into play when two solutions of differing concentrations are separated by a semipermeable membrane. The solvent—*e.g.,* water—tends to move through the membrane into the more concentrated solution.

Hydrostatic and osmotic pressures

Hydrogen-ion concentration. Life is possible only if the blood is kept within a narrow range of alkalinity. The normal range, in terms of hydrogen-ion concentration (pH), is from 7.35 to 7.45. This range is close to neutrality, represented by a pH of 7; a pH of less than 7 represents acidity.

The blood contains the bases bicarbonate, proteins, and phosphate, and the weak acid, carbonic acid. The degree of alkalinity of the blood depends principally upon the ratio of the concentration of carbonic acid (H_2CO_3) and the base bicarbonate (HCO_3^-).

In the pulmonary alveoli, the small air-filled spaces in the lungs from which oxygen is removed and into which carbon dioxide from the blood is added, the partial pressure of carbon dioxide is about 40 millimetres of mercury; in a mixture of gases the partial pressure of each gas is the proportion of the total gaseous pressure contributed by that particular gas. This alveolar carbon dioxide pressure gives rise to a concentration of carbonic acid in the blood plasma of about one milliequivalent per litre. (A milliequivalent [mEq] is the number of grams of a substance dissolved in one millilitre of normal solution.) The alveolar pressure of carbon dioxide is kept steady by the equal rate at which carbon dioxide is produced by the tissues and eliminated by the respiratory system.

Bicarbonate concentration, on the other hand, is regulated in the kidneys by the tubules. These are the long, fine tubes of the kidney's functional units, the nephrons. In health the bicarbonate concentration is kept at about 22–24 milliequivalents per litre of plasma. When the plasma bicarbonate falls below 24 milliequivalents, the amount filtered out of the blood in the kidneys is entirely reabsorbed by the tubules until the concentration is raised to this level; when the concentration rises above 24 mEq per litre, all the bicarbonate filtered out is excreted in the urine.

Water. The body of a normal man weighing 65 kilograms (about 145 pounds) contains approximately 40 litres (about 42 quarts) of water; of this about 28 litres are inside the cells of the body and 12 litres are outside. Of the 12 extracellular litres, about 2–3 litres are in the blood plasma—and the rest are around the tissues outside the blood vessels.

Water passes rapidly through almost all cell membranes and readily enters and leaves almost all the bodily spaces normally containing fluid. Its final distribution is determined by osmotic and hydrostatic pressures.

The volume of bodily water normally remains constant because the amounts ingested and eliminated are equal. Physiologically, thirst and satiety are influenced by a group of nerve cells in the hypothalamus, at the base of the brain.

Imperceptible loss of water At rest, and in temperate climates, there is an imperceptible loss of water from the surface of the body and in the air breathed out. This loss amounts to about 800 millilitres (about 0.85 quart) in 24 hours. It is increased when the surrounding temperature is elevated or when atmospheric humidity is low. Losses in this range become perceptible in other circumstances and form the cloud of moisture in one's breath on a winter day or the moisture that condenses on the inner side of a waterproof garment. Greater losses of water occur, of course, during vigorous exercise in the heat, and the losses from the bodily surfaces are then perceptible as sweat. The amount of water lost in the urine amounts to from one to two litres in 24 hours.

THE DEPLETION OF WATER AND SALTS IN THE BODY

Sodium depletion. In health the equality between the amount of sodium excreted and the amount ingested depends largely on normal kidney function. In temperate climates negligible amounts of sodium are lost in the stools and from the skin, and the power of the normal kidneys to conserve sodium in the face of reduced intake is virtually absolute. Salt depletion is usually the result of excessive loss of salt through faulty kidney function, rather than of inadequate intake.

Loss of sodium is usually accompanied by a reduction in body water. Pure sodium depletion unaccompanied by water loss, although uncommon, may arise when the response to abnormal losses of salt and water is unrestricted water intake, as, for example, when excessive sweating occurs in unfavourable environments and when the fluid loss is replenished by salt-free liquids. In these circumstances, the change in total body water may be negligible, in spite of considerable salt deficiency.

Causes. Failure of the kidney to conserve salt may occur because of kidney disease or because of inadequate hormonal control. Thus, a chronic infection of the urinary tract, acute ischemic renal failure (failure of the kidney to function normally because of inadequate blood supply), or insufficient adrenocortical hormones—hormones from the outer substance of the adrenal gland— Sodium loss during diabetes may be responsible. Excessive loss of salt and water in the urine also occurs during the excessive secretion of urine that is induced by high levels of blood sugar in the disease diabetes mellitus. If the diabetes causes acidosis, which is a decreased alkalinity of the blood and tissue fluids, the process by which sodium is returned to the blood from the tubular filtrate in return for hydrogen ions is upset. Salt depletion may also be induced by the excessive or prolonged use of diuretics, substances that induce increased excretion of urine. Salt depletion also results from diarrhea, vomiting, and other situations involving external loss of salt-containing fluids.

Consequences. Because sodium is predominantly extracellular, salt depletion leads quickly to a fall in the volume of extracellular fluid. Water tends to be excreted to balance intracellular and extracellular osmotic pressures. This volume decrease is responsible for such effects as loss of elasticity of the skin, diminution of the pressure within the eyeballs, and dryness of the tongue.

Thirst may be prominent, but tends to be less severe when the sodium levels in the blood are low. The fall in blood volume causes fainting, low blood pressure, a reduced rate of glomerular filtration in the kidney, and a reduced volume of urine. (The glomeruli are clusters of minute blood vessels, capillaries, through the walls of which fluid is filtered from the blood into the nephrons, in the first stage of the production of urine.) The capacity of the body to rid itself of wastes decreases, and kidney failure develops. The pulse rate rises. Constriction of blood vessels diminishes the circulation through the skin so that the skin and the hands and feet become cold.

Treatment. Persons with mild cases of sodium depletion, whose blood pressure is normal, usually need merely to drink salted water to recover a normal sodium level. In more severe cases, or when there is vomiting, the physician injects isotonic salt solution into a vein. (An isotonic salt solution is of the same osmotic pressure as the plasma; it contains about 0.9 percent sodium chloride.) When there is severe sodium depletion there often are losses of other electrolytes, which must also be restored.

Water depletion. The reduced water intake that is most often responsible for water depletion may result either from difficulties in drinking, as when there are sores in the mouth and throat, or from circumstances that cut off access to fresh water—for example, shipwreck, or becoming lost in the desert.

Excessive loss of water in the urine because of disease that interferes with the kidney's ability to concentrate the urine is a less common cause of water depletion.

As water is lost from the blood, the plasma concentration of sodium rises. Water is drawn from the cells, and intracellular dehydration occurs. The body loss of water is thus shared both by the extracellular and the intracellular fluids. For this reason, the clinical features of dehydration are not as obvious as those of salt depletion. Thirst, the result of stimulation of a thirst centre in the hypothalamus, is usual unless the person is senile, confused, or unconscious. The migration of water from the intracellular fluid to the extracellular helps to maintain the volume of the latter for a time, so that the blood pressure remains unaltered until considerable water depletion has occurred. The affected person then often shows mental confusion or complains of dizziness and difficulty in swallowing. Ultimately, flow of blood to the kidneys is reduced, and blood levels of urea and other wastes become abnormally high. The water depletion is treated by giving liquids; these should be salt-free unless salt loss is also present.

Potassium depletion. Potassium depletion occurs in a wide variety of disorders. The healthy person eliminates about one-quarter of his daily intake of potassium in the stools and three-quarters in the urine. The bulk of urinary potassium is delivered into the channel of the nephron tubule by the cells lining the far end of the tubule (the distal tubule); these cells excrete potassium or sodium ions and, in exchange, take sodium ions from the liquid filtered out of the blood and into the tubule from the glomerulus.

Causes. Potassium depletion results from excessive Two types of potassium loss loss of potassium from the intestinal tract or in the urine. Gastrointestinal losses are caused by severe acute or chronic diarrhea and by loss of intestinal fluid from vomiting, drainage through a gap in the intestinal wall (a fistula), or by aspiration—withdrawal of intestinal contents by suction in the course of medical treatment.

Loss of potassium in the urine is more subtle in its development. It occurs when the excretion of potassium ions in exchange for sodium ions is increased in the renal tubules. This increased excretion may result from administration of large amounts of sodium-containing fluids or from the use of diuretics, or it may occur as one feature of disorders such as Cushing's syndrome (a symptom complex resulting from overproduction of adrenocorticotropic hormone by the pituitary) or aldosteronism (the overproduction of the hormone aldosterone by the adrenals).

Excessive loss of potassium also results from diseases or drugs that suppress tubular secretion of hydrogen ions;

with fewer hydrogen ions to exchange for sodium, more potassium will be lost in the exchange process.

Conditions that interfere with the activity of the cells in the maintenance of their concentration of potassium and in excluding or eliminating sodium (the process called the sodium pump) also lead to potassium depletion and increased loss in the urine. These conditions include a deficiency of oxygen; impaired carbohydrate metabolism, as in starvation or diabetes; dehydration; and acidosis.

Consequences and treatment. Because most of the body's potassium is inside the cells, severe depletion of potassium may occur without alteration in the potassium level of the plasma, and identification of the disorder is made difficult by the inaccessibility of the intracellular fluid to analysis.

Symptoms of potassium depletion

A person whose potassium is depleted tends to be apathetic and physically weak; he is mentally confused, and his abdomen is distended. Potassium deficiency, sufficiently severe to cause a fall in plasma-potassium levels, is characterized by generalized muscular weakness with some degree of paralysis. Sensations of pins and needles in the skin are common. The electrocardiogram—tracings reflecting heart activity—shows characteristic changes. Severe potassium depletion may lead to death if uncorrected.

The condition is treated by administration of potassium salts orally or by injection into a vein. Oral administration is more commonly used and is less dangerous.

THE ABNORMAL ACCUMULATION OF WATER AND SALTS IN THE BODY

Potassium intoxication. A rise in plasma-potassium levels above normal usually occurs only when the kidney fails to function normally and there is a resultant reduction in the amount of urine excreted.

Persons with this disorder are dull, lethargic, and confused. The condition of weakness and paralysis of muscles is indistinguishable from that seen in persons with low blood levels of potassium. The pulse becomes irregular, and some degree of heart block develops. (In heart block, the upper and lower chambers of the heart tend to beat independently, which interferes with the heart's efficiency as a pump.) If the plasma-potassium level rises above eight milliequivalents per litre, there is danger that the heart will stop beating.

Measures taken to correct the high plasma levels of potassium include avoidance of fruits and fruit juices that are rich in potassium, avoidance of protein, and taking of substances such as sodium- or calcium-ion-exchange resins, which tend to absorb potassium from the blood and from the intestinal secretions.

Magnesium deficiency and intoxication. The adult body contains about 25 grams (0.9 ounce) of magnesium, 60 percent of which is in the bones. The most frequent cause of deficiency of magnesium is replacement of fluids lost during prolonged diarrhea or vomiting with fluids containing electrolytes, but without magnesium supplements. Depletion also may result from prolonged use of diuretics, chronic diarrhea, severe malnutrition, and alcoholism. In addition, excessive secretion of the hormone aldosterone or of parathyroid hormone may lead to magnesium deficiency. Magnesium chloride and magnesium hydroxide are given to correct the condition.

Magnesium intoxication occurs in kidney failure and causes symptoms related to the central nervous system. When the kidney recovers normal function, the abnormal levels of magnesium disappear without special treatment.

Water intoxication. When healthy persons drink large volumes of water, they can respond to this with corresponding increases in the amounts of urine excreted. The capacity of the body to excrete water depends upon many factors, which include the rate of glomerular filtration and the power of the distal tubules of the kidneys to produce a dilute urine; this condition in turn depends upon the presence of sodium in the distal renal tubules and the ability of the nephron to reabsorb the sodium without reabsorbing water. (Each distal tubule is that portion of the nephron tubule that is furthest from the portion of the nephron that encloses the glomerulus.)

Many persons who are ill have a restricted ability to dilute the urine when given large amounts of water, including persons suffering from acute and chronic kidney disease, severe heart failure, disease of the adrenal glands, and cirrhosis of the liver (a disease involving destruction of liver cells and formation of scar tissue). Occasionally, tumours of the ovaries or bronchus secrete a substance with antidiuretic properties that lead to water intoxication. After surgery some people may be incapable of diluting the urine because of the liberation of vasopressin by the stress of the operation. Vasopressin is a hormone released by the hypothalamus; its many functions include contraction of small blood vessels and suppression of urine excretion.

Effects of vasopressin

In all the circumstances mentioned, even a modest water intake reduces the level of sodium ions in the plasma and may produce disordered cerebral function, dizziness, headache, nausea, mental confusion, convulsions, coma, and death.

Treatment consists of restricting water intake. In severe cases salt solution is injected into a vein.

Water and salt retention (edema). Abnormal accumulation of water and salt in the body has fascinated physiologists and clinicians for several centuries, and before the discovery of modern diuretic drugs gross edema was a common complication of a variety of diseases, the victim being drowned, as it were, in the high tide of his own body fluids. Death from edema was well known to the ancients, who often made a series of superficial cuts in the limbs in an attempt to release the fluid from the distended tissues as a remedy of the last resort.

Causes. The fundamental cause of edema is a fault in the physiological mechanisms that control the volume of the extracellular fluids. Figure 1 illustrates how a healthy individual undergoes slight fluctuations in the water and salt content even when consuming a diet fixed in calories, nitrogen, water, and salt. These natural ripples on the

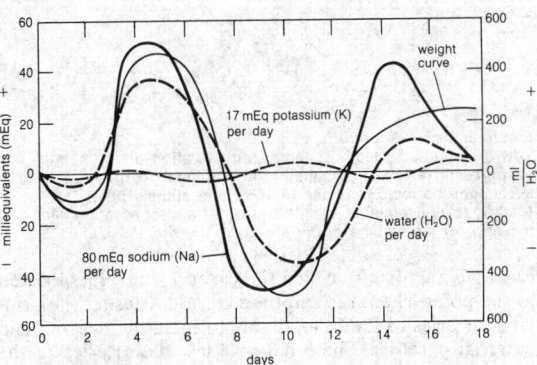

Figure 1: Cumulative sodium (Na⁺), potassium (K⁺), and water (H₂O) balance in subject on a constant diet at rest.

surface of the body fluids, which ebb and flow over periods of several days, are due to the operation of a hunting, or servo-feedback, mechanism for the control of body fluid volume. Such a mechanism must involve (1) a detector that identifies lack of stability in the system, (2) an integrator that analyzes the information, and (3) an effector organ that adjusts the rate of excretion of water and salt according to need. Whatever its clinical cause, edema represents a vast tidal wave upon the extracellular sea and arises from a breakdown in the system responsible for volume control. Little is known about the first two components of the volume-control system, but the kidney is certainly the effector organ, and edema arises when the kidney fails to meet its biological commitment.

The common primary event responsible for all types of generalized edema is an inadequate blood volume induced either by loss of plasma proteins or by inadequate cardiac output. The first condition may arise because of excessive loss in the urine or from the gastrointestinal tract, failure of protein synthesis by the liver, or as a result of gastrointestinal malabsorption or of malnutrition; inadequate filling of the arterial circulation also occurs in heart failure.

From R. Passmore and J.S. Robson (eds.), *Companion to Medical Studies*

A fall in the concentration of plasma proteins disturbs the balance of factors that influences the exchange of fluid between the vascular and extravascular compartments. As a result, fluid moves from the blood into the tissues, where it accumulates. The resulting fall in blood volume activates the volume-control system and stimulates the kidney to conserve water and salt in an attempt to repair the deficit; as a result, the accumulation of edema fluid is merely aggravated. The physiological link between low blood volume and reduced arterial-filling pressure, on the one hand, and renal water and salt retention by the kidney, on the other, is far from clear, but probably includes the operation of pressure-sensitive areas in the thyrocarotid and renal arteries, the atria (upper chambers) of the heart, the juxtaglomerular apparatus in the kidney, and the adrenal cortex (Figure 2). The thyrocarotid pressure-

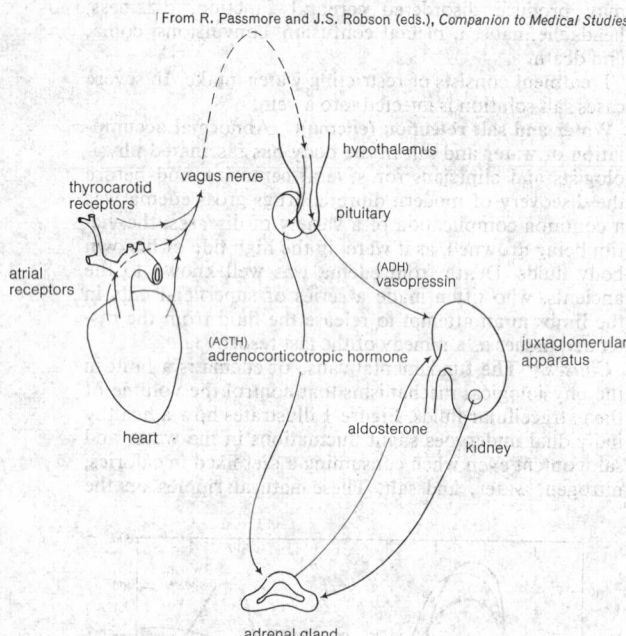

Figure 2: *Volume-control system.*
Low blood volume leads to increased secretion of vasopressin (also called antidiuretic hormone, ADH), adrenocorticotropic hormone (ACTH), and aldosterone, leading to conservation of salt and water and consequent increase in the volume of the blood.

sensitive area is also called the carotid sinus; it is located at the point where the common carotid arteries, the principal arteries to the head, divide to form the internal and external carotids. The renal arteries, the arteries to the kidneys, are branches of the abdominal portion of the aorta. The juxtaglomerular apparatus is made up of specialized cells in the middle coat of the arterioles (small arteries) that bring blood to the glomeruli. As a consequence, both the rate of secretion of aldosterone and vasopressin (ADH) is increased, and water and salt conservation is promoted. In addition, hemodynamic effects on the renal circulation and the influence of other hormonal agents (as yet inadequately defined), which may act principally on the reabsorption of sodium in the proximal convoluted tubule of the kidney, may contribute.

Consequences.   The effects of generalized edema vary with its severity and with the part of the body predominantly affected. All tissues are involved to some extent, but swelling of the legs is almost universal and is partly the result of the hydrostatic effect of the upright posture. In the nephrotic syndrome, in which the urinary loss of protein is caused by glomerular disease, the edema is generalized; in heart failure it tends to accumulate either in the pulmonary circulation (pulmonary edema) or in the systemic circulation—*i.e.*, in the legs and the abdominal cavity; in liver disease caused by local factors within the liver and disturbance in the portal circulation, the peritoneal cavity (the space that in disease develops between the membrane lining the abdomen and the membrane covering the abdominal organs) is the most com-

monly involved. Edema in this region is called ascites. Localized edema may arise in a limb or other single part from venous or lymphatic obstruction; even localized edema activates the volume-control system, since the edema fluid is derived from the body fluids as a whole. The detector mechanism is stimulated, and water and salt retention encouraged. When the water and salt content of the rest of the body then remains within normal limits, the swelling of the affected part continues.

Treatment.   The treatment of edema is the correction of the underlying cause of the disturbance; this correction involves appropriate therapy for kidney, heart, and liver disease, and measures aimed at ameliorating absolute and conditional undernutrition. If, as is often the case, this is not possible, the kidneys may be induced to excrete water and salt by the administration of diuretics that specifically inhibit sodium transport somewhere in the nephron; a large number of these agents are available and are remarkably successful.

DISTURBANCES IN ACID–BASE BALANCE AND MINERAL METABOLISM

Disturbances in acid–base balance.   Fluctuations in hydrogen-ion concentration arise in many circumstances in health and disease. Four primary types of disorder are recognized: metabolic acidosis and alkalosis, and respiratory acidosis and alkalosis. The first two of these involve increased or decreased alkalinity of the blood plasma because of some change in the metabolic process; the second two arise from disorders in the carbon dioxide exchange in the lungs.

Metabolic acidosis.   Metabolic acidosis arises from three main causes: (1) there may be an increased formation of acids during the metabolic process, as occurs, for example, in diabetes or starvation, during exercise, or as a result of reduced levels of oxygen in the tissues (acetoacetic and lactic acids are especially important in these contexts); (2) there may be diminished excretion of hydrogen ions, as occurs in several situations, including kidney failure; (3) there may be increased loss of base such as bicarbonate ions, as occurs in diarrhea and as a result of fistulas (openings) in the walls of the intestines.

The increased concentration of hydrogen ions in the plasma interferes with the reversible process by which carbon dioxide combines with water to form carbonic acid, and by which carbonic acid in turn becomes ionized into hydrogen ions and bicarbonate ions. Because of the high hydrogen-ion concentration, the production of bicarbonate falls and carbonic-acid levels rise.

The increase in hydrogen ions also stimulates the respiratory centres in the brain to increase the rate and depth of breathing. Increased amounts of carbon dioxide are, thus, eliminated by the lungs, and the carbon dioxide pressure in the blood plasma falls below normal levels. This decrease reduces the formation of carbonic acid and lessens the tendency of the blood to become less alkaline.

Recovery of the normal alkalinity depends on the regeneration of bicarbonate by the cells of the kidney tubules during the process of hydrogen-ion excretion in exchange for sodium ions. In severe cases, this process is assisted by administration of sodium bicarbonate.

Respiratory acidosis.   If the ability of the lungs to expel carbon dioxide is impaired—for example, by depression of the respiratory centre, as occurs in barbiturate or morphine poisoning, or because of paralysis of respiratory muscles, as in poliomyelitis—carbon dioxide is retained in the body and the plasma-carbon dioxide pressure rises above its normal value of 40 millimetres of mercury. As a result, levels of carbonic acid and of hydrogen ions rise in the tissues and blood. This situation is mitigated by the acceptance of hydrogen ions by substances such as proteins, with the resultant generation of bicarbonate ions. The kidneys also respond to the elevated carbon dioxide pressure by reabsorbing bicarbonate ions and forming new bicarbonate ions.

Respiratory acidosis is dealt with by treatment of the underlying disease. Occasionally assisted or artificial respiration is needed.

Pressure-sensitive areas

Causes of respiratory acidosis

Metabolic alkalosis. During digestion of a large meal the secretion of hydrochloric acid (HCl) by the stomach involves the withdrawal of hydrogen ions from the blood. If vomiting occurs, the hydrogen ions are lost from the body along with chloride ions, and the blood-hydrogen-ion concentration falls, increasing the alkalinity of the blood plasma. At the same time, the plasma levels of bicarbonate ions rise.

The fall in hydrogen-ion concentration reduces the stimulus to respiration. Carbon dioxide elimination by the lungs is reduced, and the pressure of carbon dioxide in the plasma rises, causing increased formation of carbonic acid and reducing the excess alkalinity.

Chronic metabolic alkalosis, induced by the taking of large amounts of sodium bicarbonate over long periods, especially when there is a high intake of calcium in the diet, may lead to deposition of calcium in the kidneys.

Severe potassium depletion also causes metabolic alkalosis, and depletion of chloride ions sometimes contributes to the condition. In the maintenance of sodium balance, sodium cations filtered into the nephron tubules from the glomeruli are reabsorbed in conjunction with chloride anions and also by the exchange process involving hydrogen or potassium cations. When the body is deficient in chloride, as may occur as a result of prolonged vomiting, the conservation of sodium by the nephron tubules is achieved by employment of hydrogen and potassium exchange for sodium ions to a greater extent than normal. This conservation leads to excessive loss of hydrogen and potassium ions and, thus, to metabolic alkalosis.

The electrolyte disorders may be corrected by intravenous administration of an isotonic solution containing sodium, ammonium, and potassium chloride.

Causes of respiratory alkalosis

Respiratory alkalosis. When one climbs a mountain of about 12,000 feet (about 3,650 metres), oxygen lack becomes a significant stimulus to respiration, and carbon dioxide is eliminated in larger amounts than occurs at sea level. As the carbon dioxide pressure falls, the plasma-hydrogen-ion concentration is reduced; but the extent of the reduction is lessened by the release of hydrogen ions by nonbicarbonate buffers such as proteins and by a compensatory kidney excretion of bicarbonate ions. A similar response occurs in hysterical overbreathing, in salicylate poisoning, after head injury, and in severe liver failure.

When respiratory alkalosis is the result of hysterical overbreathing, breathing into and out of a paper bag is often helpful.

Disturbance in calcium metabolism. Calcium is an essential component of bone, being present in the hydroxyapatite crystals of the intercellular substance (hydroxyapatite is a calcium phosphate). The adult human skeleton contains about 1.2 kilograms (about 2.6 pounds) of calcium. Because the skeleton takes about 20 years to be formed, the growing child must retain from his diet an average of 160 milligrams of calcium a day. There is a continuing turnover of skeletal calcium, about 500 milligrams being reabsorbed from the bone and replaced daily. The surfaces of the hydroxyapatite crystals have a layer of ions and water, and it is around this layer that exchange of calcium and other ions takes place.

Among the many factors that affect calcium-plasma levels are the two hormones thyrocalcitonin and parathyroid hormone, vitamin D levels, and the hydrogen-ion concentration of the plasma.

High levels of parathyroid hormone tend to raise plasma levels of calcium, and vitamin D causes absorption of calcium from the intestine. Thyrocalcitonin depresses the plasma-calcium levels.

Common causes of calcium disorders

Disorders of calcium metabolism are most commonly the result of endocrine abnormalities or of nutritional deficiency. Thus oversecretion and undersecretion of parathyroid hormone cause elevated and depressed levels of calcium in the plasma, respectively. Increased secretion of thyrocalcitonin is extremely rare, but may result from a tumour of the thyroid cells that secrete the hormone.

In kidney failure, high levels of urea in the blood appear to increase resistance to the action of parathyroid hormone and of vitamin D; this increased resistance causes a depressed level of calcium in the plasma, which, in turn, leads to secondary enlargement of the parathyroid glands.

Low levels of plasma calcium are also found in rickets and osteomalacia. These two related diseases, occurring in children and adults, respectively, involve inadequate deposition of calcium and phosphorus in the bones; a principal cause is insufficient intake of vitamin D. In another disease, osteoporosis, characterized by light, brittle bones, the plasma levels of calcium are normal or only slightly reduced, and no benefit is derived from taking increased amounts of vitamin D.

Disturbances in phosphorus metabolism. The human body contains about 700 grams (about one and one-half pounds) of phosphorus; of this about 80 percent is in the bones. Phosphorus deficiency is known to occur in cattle that graze on poor land and has been held responsible for stunting of growth and weakness. The existence of a primary phosphate deficiency in man is not yet established. It may occur in persons who take large doses of nonabsorbable antacids such as aluminum and magnesium hydroxide, which interfere with the intestinal absorption of phosphate.

BIBLIOGRAPHY. D.A.K. BLACK, *Essentials of Fluid Balance,* 4th ed. (1967), a good introductory account of fluid and electrolyte disorders; C.L. COMAR and F. BRONNER (eds.), *Mineral Metabolism,* 3 vol. (1960–69), a modern comprehensive review of mineral metabolism with an extensive bibliography; E.B. FLINK, "Therapy of Magnesium Deficiency," *Ann. N.Y. Acad. Sci.,* 162:901–905 (1969), a useful summary of modern research in all aspects of magnesium metabolism; J.L. GAMBLE, *Chemical Anatomy, Physiology and Pathology of Extracellular Fluid,* 3rd ed. (1954), a classic, historically valuable work on fluid and electrolyte balance; L.J. HENDERSON, *Blood* (1928), a classic work on acid–base balance in the blood; H.L. MARRIOTT, *Water and Salt Depletion* (1950), a classic, simple account of problems of water and salt balance; G.G. NAHAS, "Current Concepts of Acid-Base Measurement," *Ann. N.Y. Acad. Sci.,* 133:3–4 (1966), a good summary of modern research and thought on problems of acid–base balance; P.B. OLIVA, "Lactic Acidosis," *Amer. J. Med.,* 48:209–225 (1970), a good, well-documented review of lactic-acid acidosis; J.P. PETERS and D.D. VAN SLYKE, *Quantitative Clinical Chemistry,* 2 vol., 2nd ed. (1946), a classic introduction to problems of acid–base control in man; J.R. ROBINSON, *Fundamentals of Acid-Base Regulation,* 3rd ed. (1967), a modern, simple introduction to problems of acid–base control in man; J.S. ROBSON, J.M. BONE, and A.T. LAMBIE, "Intracellular pH," vol. 11:213–277, *Advances in Clinical Chemistry* (1968), a modern, well-documented review of the concepts and measurement of intracellular pH; O. SIGGAARD-ANDERSEN, *The Acid-Base Status of the Blood,* 3rd ed. (Eng. trans. 1965), a modern account of acid–base control in the blood and in man; J.M. VAUGHAN, *The Physiology of Bone* (1970), a modern, short, well-documented review of calcium and bone metabolism.

(J.S.Ro.)

Fluidics

Fluidics is the technology of using the flow characteristics of liquid or gas to operate a control system. The name is a combination of two words, fluid and logic. The newest of the control technologies, fluidics has in recent years come to compete with mechanical and electrical systems. (For a description of control systems in general, see CONTROL SYSTEMS.)

Although fluidic principles are fairly old, it was not until about 1960 that researchers attempted to use fluidics commercially. The demand for reliable controls in space research stimulated progress. In the 1930s Henri Coanda, a Romanian scientist, described what is now known as the Coanda effect, a major contribution to fluidic technology. He observed that as a free jet emerges from a jet nozzle the steam will tend to follow a nearby curved or inclined surface. It also "attaches" itself to and flows along this surface if the curvature or angle of inclination is not too sharp. Coanda explained this tendency as being caused by the jet stream's entraining (picking up) nearby fluid molecules. When the supply of these molecules is limited by an adjacent surface, a partial vacuum develops between the jet and the surface. If the pressure on the

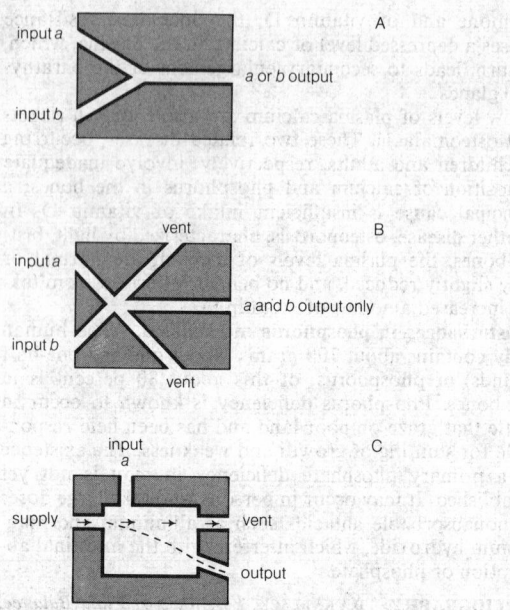

Figure 1: (A) OR circuit, (B) AND circuit, and (C) proportional circuit (see text).

other side of the jet remains constant, the partial vacuum, which is a lower pressure region, will force the jet to bend and attach itself to the wall.

Because fluidics is not as rapid as electronics, it is unlikely to compete in fields with ultrahigh-speed requirements. On the other hand, in many applications, fluidics is advantageous. It is now possible to detect, interlock, and power complex operations by using air throughout a system. Controls can be installed by a competent fitter who might not be capable of dealing with electronic or electrical systems. The elimination of electrical contacts eliminates a possible fire hazard.

Pneumatic circuits require controls with simple interlocking, performed by air-piloted and mechanically operated control valves. Because it employs the same medium, fluidics is useful for sensitive detection and complex control as part of a pneumatic system.

Combining hydraulics and fluidics is more complicated, however, because the same medium is not used. Yet since both systems require plumbing expertise, labour problems can be reduced. Power-output devices handling hydraulic pressures that respond to fluidic signals are available commercially.

The basically simple and robust character of fluidics, its resistance to contamination and damage, and its high degree of reliability give it an important place in the rapidly expanding field of control.

Fluidic devices operate on either the digital principle (they are either "on" or "off") or the analogue principle (the output of the device is continuously proportional to the input). Figure 1 illustrates the distinction.

In Figure 1A input a or b can produce an output signal, because each has a path through which the signal can flow to the output. This system is called logical (and digital) because no output is possible without an input. Either condition will satisfy the required output (the OR function, as an output is produced whenever one OR the other input is energized).

In Figure 1B both inputs are required for an output because the flow from a or b alone, without a counterbalancing force, will go out one of the vents. If both are applied, they will collide, producing flow out of the centre port marked a and b. This again is logical (and digital) because no output is possible unless both signals are applied. All conditions must be satisfied before an output is obtained (the AND function) as an output signal will be produced only if an input is applied to both inputs a and b simultaneously.

In Figure 1C fluid flowing from the supply will go out of the vent unless input a is applied. This is an analogue effect because the output can be altered proportionally

from minimum to maximum by varying the power of input a.

Fluidic devices can thus produce both logic (digital) and analogue (proportional) effects or functions. The OR and the AND are the most common logic functions.

In most fluidic devices, low-value input pressures or flows can control higher output pressures or flows. This is what is meant by the term fluid amplifier. A supply of fluid entering a device becomes a stream forced to follow a chosen path through carefully designed internal shapes before giving an output. Input jets of far lower power are positioned to give the greatest possible effect on the stream, thereby controlling the output. Fluid amplifiers respond to very small fluid signals provided by such devices as temperature or velocity detectors, generally by input sensors attached to existing mechanical movements. The number of devices controlled by one similar device is called the fan-out ratio. For example, if the output of one device is so strong that it can switch four others at the same time, the fan-out ratio is four. The following terms are important to an understanding of fluidics.

Logic function or "gate." This is an element or combination of elements that can satisfy a logic function. That is, if the correct inputs are applied, the correct output is obtained, as shown by the illustrative OR and AND devices (Figure 1A, B). A gate is a circuit that has one output and several inputs. The output is not energized until certain predetermined conditions are met.

An element. This is an indivisible part of a logic function or circuit, like a component.

Active element. An element requiring a constant supply of power to remain operative is called an active element. Figure 1C illustrates such a device.

Passive element. An element not requiring a constant supply of power and operated solely by input signals is a passive element. Figure 1A, B illustrate passive devices.

Pure fluid amplifier. This is an amplifier in which fluid flows give required outputs solely by changing the characteristics or direction of flow.

Moving-part amplifier. This is an amplifier that changes the direction of flow or even shuts off the flow entirely by means of moving parts such as spool valves or balls inside the device. Control inputs move the mechanical parts into the position that produces the desired output.

Digital amplifier. For all practical purposes, this amplifier works on the all or nothing principle. The output and input signals are either on or off (see Figure 1A, B).

Analogue amplifier. An analogue amplifier produces variable output values corresponding to progressively increasing or decreasing input signals as shown by the device in Figure 1C.

Wall attachment. Fluid flow attaches to a surface and continues to flow over it unless an opposing or interrupting fluid signal is applied.

Momentum exchange. Fluid flows interact with each other and change direction in accordance with the relative forces used.

Laminar turbulence. A smooth (laminar) fluid jet flows across a gap to give an output, unless prevented from doing so by a signal that makes it turbulent.

Vortex effect. Fluid is made to move in a circular path by a signal or shape. The constant change in direction reduces velocity to give control over flow.

PRINCIPLES OF COMMERCIAL DEVICES

Since most fluidic devices use air as their operating medium, air is assumed to be the fluid in all of the devices described.

Wall attachment. When fluid flow touches a surface, friction slows it down. The fluid nearest the surface is overtaken by the remainder and space is created at the surface (Figure 2A). This attracts faster fluid flowing above which "bends down" to fill the space. A low-pressure vortex bubble is formed, maintaining attraction.

The flow can be attracted to preferred surfaces. The fluid jet (Figure 2B) causes surrounding fluid (air) to move with it, drawing air into the device (entrainment)

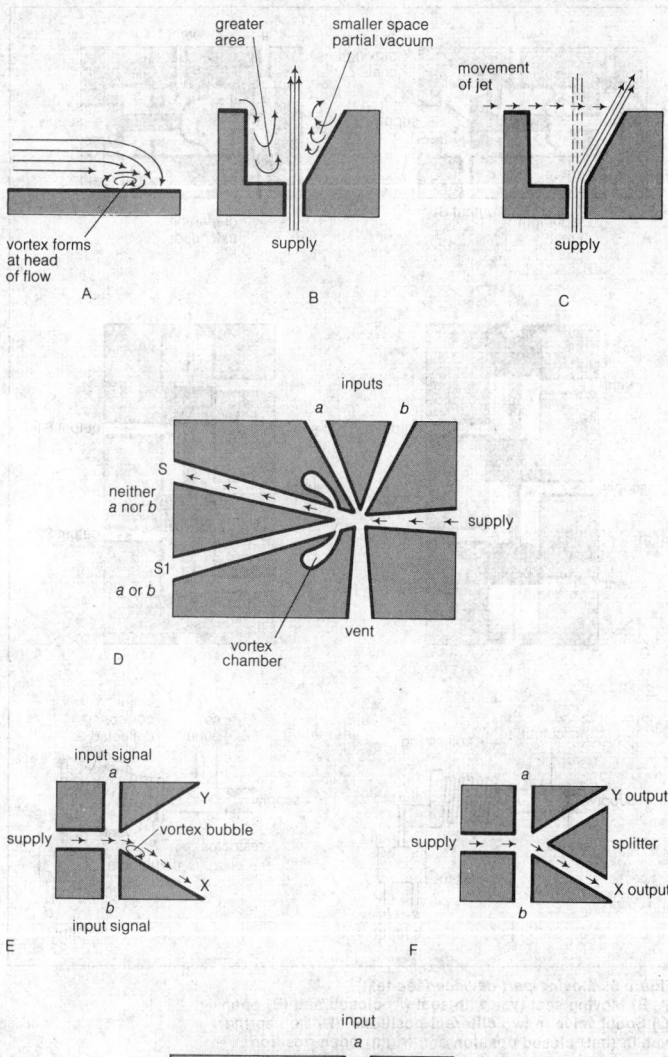

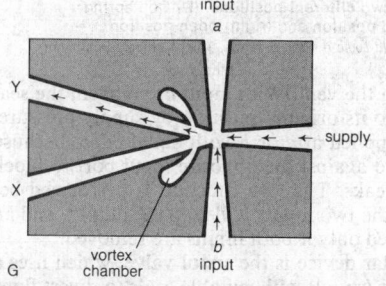

Figure 2: Operating principles of several types of commercial fluidic devices (see text).
By courtesy of I-T-E Imperial Corporation

stable states (bistable), with the fluid maintaining flow over one wall or the other until switched. A brief pulse at *a* will give a maintained output at X, and a brief pulse at *b* will give a maintained output at Y. In Figure 2F, the wedge shape, called a splitter, separates the two flow paths so that X or Y can provide pressure outputs. In Figure 2G, a commercial flip-flop outline is shown. The flow indicated by arrows in the upper channel is the stable condition obtained by input *b*.

The above devices are digital: there is present either a full signal or no signal at all. They are active devices requiring a constant power supply. Vents ensure stable operation when the outputs are fully loaded.

Commercial wall-attachment devices are made of injection-molded plastic; connections are made by mounting them flat on manifolds that contain suitable ports for supplies, etc. Most wall-attachment devices require supply pressures of approximately two to 15 pounds per square inch (psi).

Momentum exchange. If two passages are in line and sufficient power is applied, fluid will flow from one to the other across a gap, producing an output at the other side.

In Figure 3A the supply will normally flow across the gap to output S, but, as shown in Figure 3B, with an input signal at *a*, the jet stream will deflect and go out

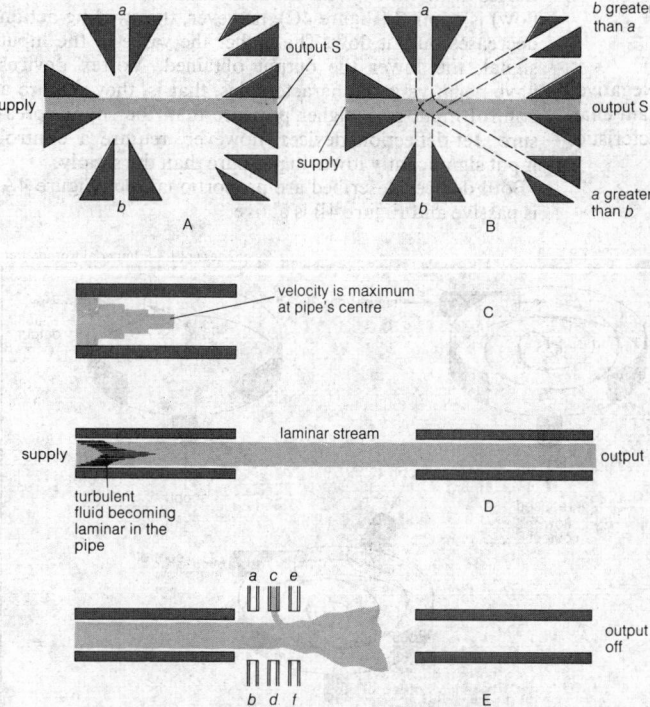

Figure 3: *Momentum-exchange and laminar–turbulence effects.* A momentum-exchange device is shown (A) with no input and (B) with inputs at *a* and *b*. Application of laminar flow and turbulence to an amplifier is indicated in C, D, and E (see text).

to replace that "pulled out" by the jet (shown by arrows). Because there is less space for replacement air to enter, a greater shortage of air exists at the wall nearest the jet, which moves toward this wall to make up the loss. The closer it gets to the wall, the less air can enter and the greater the attraction will be. Finally, the jet will stay against the wall because of the low-pressure region previously explained (Figure 2C). All of this will have happened very quickly, with a total switch-over time of about one millisecond.

In one device (Figure 2D), the supply is attracted to the upper wall and flows out of port S. An input at *a* or *b* will detach the flow from the upper to the lower wall, giving output S1. This device is said to be monostable because a constant input at *a* or *b* is required to obtain output S1. It is called an OR/NOR because either input *a* or *b* gives output S1, and neither *a* nor *b* can be present if output S is required.

In Figure 2E fluid is attracted to either wall equally spaced around a jet. The supply will flow to either X or Y depending entirely on chance. This device has two

from the lower output. An input at *b* can deflect the jet stream out from the upper output. With both inputs applied it is possible to get an output from the upper port if *b* is greater than *a*. The opposite also applies. This device is proportional: its output values vary according to the value of the inputs. It is also active: a constant power supply is required.

Many proportional devices have only two outputs. With no signals applied, the supply divides about a splitter to provide equal flow from both outputs. Maximum to minimum flow can be obtained from either output depending on the value of inputs applied. Supply pressures vary but are normally between one to 15 pounds per square inch.

Laminar and turbulent flow. In the turbulence amplifier, flow can be prevented from reaching an output by a change in condition. If air at certain pressures is applied

**Mono-
stable
devices**

**Pro-
portional
devices**

to channels or tubes of correct size, natural turbulence is reduced to such an extent that air will emerge from the output in a smooth (laminar) condition (Figure 3C). The air is flowing in layers, with the centre at a higher velocity than the outside, due to friction of the passageway. Thus, there is little loss across a gap. Figure 3D shows the stream crossing a gap to provide an output.

With an input applied, Figure 3E, the laminar stream immediately becomes turbulent. It cannot cross the gap with sufficient power to provide an output (input c is used in the diagram). Several inputs can be positioned around the laminar stream, each being equally effective in preventing an output. Typical switching times are one to two milliseconds. The turbulence amplifier provides the NOR function because any one input will stop an output and all inputs must be removed before an output is obtained. It is digital, providing full or no output. It is active because a constant supply is necessary, and monostable because maintained input signals are required.

Vortex. In Figure 4A a supply applied to a cylindrical chamber forces fluid to move in a circular path to reach the output. This reduces its velocity and output flow. Figure 4B shows that if fluid is applied in the opposite direction, a full flow is obtained because a circular path is no longer followed.

In Figure 4B the supply can flow straight out of the device with little or no hindrance. If an input (control flow) is applied (Figure 4C), however, the swirling action decreases output flow. The higher the value of the input signal, the lower the output obtained. Vortex devices have negative gain characteristics, that is, they require a control input at a higher pressure than the supply pressure. Jet-deflection devices, however, require a control input significantly lower in pressure than the supply.

Negative gain characteristics

Both devices described are proportional, but Figure 4A is passive and Figure 4B is active.

By courtesy of I-T-E Imperial Corporation

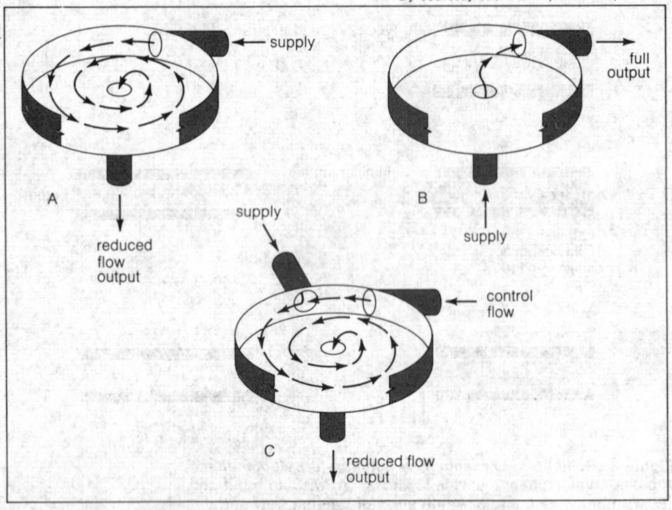

Figure 4: Principles of vortex action (see text).

A typical commercial device based on the principles of Figure 4C can handle flows up to 56 cubic feet per minute at 50 psi, depending on the size used. The controlling pressure has to be about 1½ to 3 times as large as the supply pressure for maximum effect. This varies with the model and medium used. The output is a large central port, the supply being another large port. The control flow is applied to the smaller ports that are arranged to oppose each other if differential values are required.

Moving-part devices. In recent years many moving-part types have appeared. Some common principles are illustrated.

In Figure 5A a supply (30–90 psi) enters from the right-hand side and provides output S by forcing the moving seal against its seat. An input applied at a acts upon the diaphragm that moves to the right, forcing the seal to shut off the supply, Figure 5B. Output S is then ex-

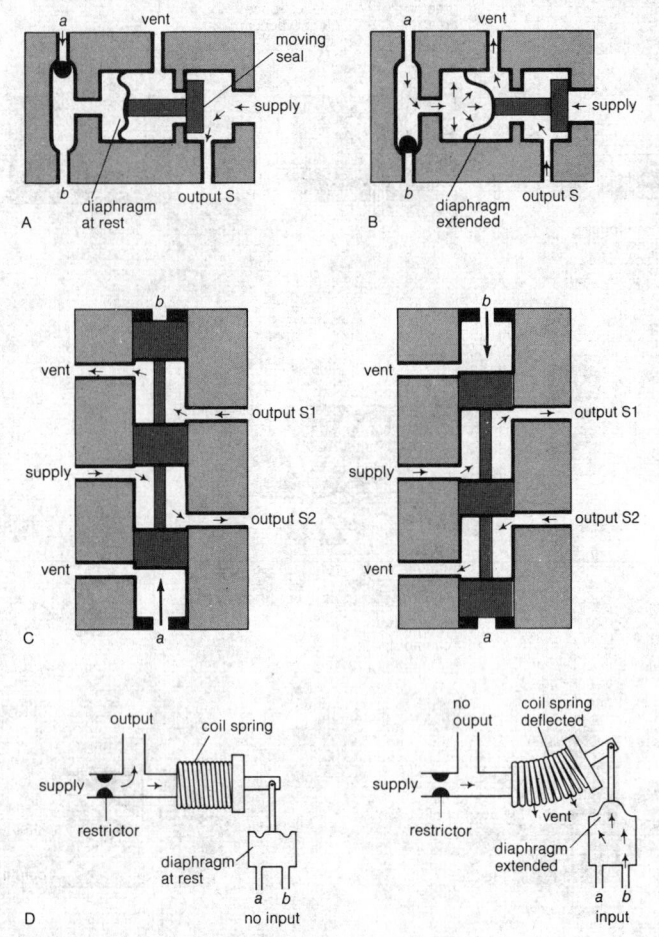

Figure 5: *Moving-part devices* (see text).
(A, B) Moving seal type with seal (A) closed and (B) open.
(C) Spool valve in two different positions. (D) Coil spring type in (left) closed position and (right) open position.
From M.J. Moylan, *Fluid Logic in Simple Terms*, The Machinery Publishing Company Ltd,

hausted through the vent. With input a removed, the seal is forced back to its original position by supply pressure. Inputs can be applied at a or b with equal effect because the ball is forced against the opposite input port to block it and prevent leaks. The NOR function is performed because either of the two inputs will stop the output, and an output is obtained only if both inputs are removed.

Another popular device is the spool valve, which uses a moving member (spool) with suitable seals to divert flow. In Figure 5C, the supply (30–150 psi) provides output S2. If an input were applied at b, the spool would move downward and supply would be directed to output S1. Output S2 would be vented. Because the inputs that position the spool need only be pulses, this device can be bistable. If input a were a maintained pressure or a spring, however, an input at b of a greater value could act against this force to provide a monostable effect.

Figure 5D shows an element using a close-coiled spring as its moving part. With no input applied, an output is obtained. When an input operates the diaphragm, it bends the spring and pressure leaks from the coils. Since air escapes from the coils faster than it can be replaced by the restrictor, no output is possible. The NOR function is performed and the device can handle pressures up to 15 psi.

In all of these digital devices, spool valves have an advantage, because bistable operating positions are maintained even if the supply is removed and reapplied. This is not usually the case with other devices.

FLUIDICS IN INDUSTRY

Fluidics has been applied to industrial problems on a wide scale, with no particular industry emerging as an obvious choice. Fluidics can operate in hazardous environments and sense objects by methods not available previously.

Input and output devices. Fluidic input devices generally employ two principles—back-pressure sensing and interruptible-jet sensing.

Back-pressure and interruptible-jet sensing

When the back-pressure sensor vent (Figure 6A) is not blocked, there is no output because the air supply escapes from the vent faster than it can be replaced through the restrictor. With the vent in close proximity to an object, air cannot leak away fast enough and an output is obtained.

From Turbulence Amplifier Engineering Data Sheet no. 104; Howie Corporation

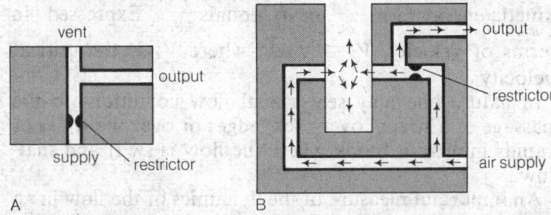

Figure 6: Two types of sensing devices: (A) back-pressure and (B) interruptible-jet (see text).

Simple devices like this have to be very close to an object (about 0.005 inch) before an output is obtained. Latest developments include proximity sensors that provide signals from distances of approximately 0.25 inches.

A typical interruptible jet is shown in Figure 6B. The supply provides two opposing jets. This impact prevents all the restricted supply from being vented and an output is obtained. When the jets are interrupted by an object, the restricted supply can flow from the right-hand jet without opposition, and, (as in the back pressure sensor) the output ceases. This device is also non-clogging (continuous air bleed).

Power outputs are provided in various forms to suit fluidic elements. A step-up relay is provided for low pressure elements that will directly control 100 psi power supplies from signals as low as $\frac{1}{10}$ psi.

Elements that operate at higher pressures can generally use conventional diaphragm or cylinder-operated valves. These respond to signals of about 5 psi and can control 150 psi power supplies.

Typical applications. Applications of fluidics are numerous, but on a relatively small scale. Some such applications include a weighing system that selects ten different weights of raw material before machining; air-jet detection of delicate material (the roof lining of an automobile) that would be damaged by mechanical methods; and sonic detectors operating in the highly inflammable, contaminated area of a paint-spray booth. These detectors sense sound waves without disturbing the freshly painted surface.

Modular construction of fluidic circuits is evident as the technology advances. Among the latest advances in fluidics is modular construction of circuits, that is, construction of combinations of components that can be readily fitted together to form whole systems.

A motor governor system converts pulsating frequencies of air motor exhausts into pressure levels, which are then compared to preset values. The difference in pressure is amplified to provide speed regulation of the motor. Converting the frequency of ON/OFF pulses into progressively increasing or decreasing values is called digital proportional. Fluidic devices are stacked in layers to provide a common supply and interconnections.

NEWER DEVELOPMENTS

Advances in the technology are continuous. A new development is the edge tone amplifier, which works very much like a musical instrument; air blown at a sharp wedge oscillates at very high frequencies (about 5,000 cycles per second) to produce an output that is virtually continuous. Frequency of oscillation (sound) is controlled mechanically or by varying the force of the air directed at the wedge. Since the flow responds rapidly to

signals, the amplifier shows considerable promise in high-speed switching for the future.

Sound detection is possible with laminar streams that can be made sensitive to certain sound frequencies (as in the paint booth example cited). A beam of sound can span distances for detection without even the slight force exerted by an air jet.

BIBLIOGRAPHY. M.J. MOYLAN, *Fluid Logic in Simple Terms* (1968), a description of logic circuitry, basic principles, and binary written for the layman; F.T. BROWN (ed.), *Fluid Jet Control Devices*, a symposium paper of the American Society of Mechanical Engineers (1962); and *Fluid Amplication Symposium*, 2 vol. (1962–64), many valuable historic references and early descriptions; COLLEGE OF AERONAUTICS, BEDFORD, ENGLAND, *Fluid Logic Devices: A Review* (1963), a very broad survey but interesting historically as it attempted to point the way at an early stage; C.J. CHARNLEY and H.S. STEPHENS (eds.), *International Conference on Fluid Logic and Amplification*, proceedings of the 1st Cranfield Conference, Paper B1 (1965), an intensive study of the internal geometry of devices; H.S. STEPHENS (ed.), *Cranfield Fluidics Conference*, proceedings of the 2nd Cranfield Conference, Paper D3 (1967), a good description of spool valves in logic circuitry; U.S. TRADE CENTRE, LONDON, *Fluidics and Advanced Switching Mechanisms Symposium* (1969), a straightforward description of acoustic fluidic sensors with further useful references.

(M.J.M.)

Fluvial Processes

Over much of the world the reduction of mountains, the building of plains, and the sculpture of the landscape is brought about by the flow of water. As the rain falls and collects in watercourses, the process of erosion not only degrades the land but the products of erosion become themselves the tools with which the rivers carve the valleys in which they flow. The process varies over time and from place to place. Materials eroded from one location are transported and deposited in another, only to be eroded and redeposited time and again before reaching the ocean. At successive locations the riverine plain and the river channel itself are products of the interaction of the mechanics of transport by the flow and the characteristics of the sediments brought down from the drainage basin above.

The fluid in a river is not pure water. Not always visible, the load of the river may be carried in solution, in suspension, or dragged along the bed. Solutes and particulate matter are both organic and inorganic. Neither the discharge of the water nor the related rates of erosion and deposition are constant in time or in space. Steep, narrow, rock-walled canyons may be excavated by corrasion of flowing water armed with abrasive particles aided by corrosion through chemical action. Elsewhere, sediments may be deposited to form broad alluvial fans (*q.v.*), floodplains, or river deltas (*q.v.*) in lakes along the river course.

Man manipulates the river environment to suit his needs and desires. Dams create lakes for the storage of water and the production of hydroelectric power, thereby regulating the flow of rivers; the natural river channel may be deepened or walled in to provide for navigation; water may be diverted for cities, industries, and agriculture; harbours may be constructed both at the edge of the continent or along the rivers themselves to facilitate commerce. To the extent that these activities modify an existing system involving the motion of the water of the river and the sediments it carries, such modifications may markedly alter the system. A reservoir constructed on a river that is transporting sediment will become the locus of deposition of a delta where the river joins the newly created lake. Below the dam creating the impoundment the river can be expected to erode the channel and transport newly acquired sediment to replace that left behind in the delta. Changes in the physical environment will in turn induce changes in the biota. In the absence of floods, for example, trees may grow up in the channel. Both upstream and downstream effects of the reservoir may extend for many miles above and below the reservoir itself. If a navigation channel is to operate properly, it must be so designed that the movement of sediment, its deposi-

Man's manipulation of the river environment

tion, and redeposition will not interfere with navigation by creating shoals within the channel. Harbours constructed in estuaries (q.v.) at the margin of the continents must contend with the results of deposition of sediments brought down from the land to the sea by rivers that flow into the estuary. In every instance, while the pattern of "nature" may be altered, the river processes will continue to operate either to the benefit or to the detriment of the intended purpose.

Both the form of a river channel and the deposits associated with it at any given place and time represent the interaction of basic processes of fluid flow and sediment transport. While myriad combinations of hydrology and geology occur in nature, a few basic principles underlie the complex interactions that constitute the behaviour of rivers. These provide a basis for understanding river channels themselves, a means of analyzing the ways in which the alterations of the river environment will ramify, and in turn, a guide for planning and design of man-made works. See also RIVERS AND RIVER SYSTEMS for additional information on channel form and hydraulic geometry and for a discussion of fluvial landforms.

FLOW OF WATER IN A NATURAL CHANNEL

Basic principles of flow

The flow of water in a natural channel may be described in terms of the geometry of the channel and the dynamics of the flow itself. The rate of flow can be written in the form $Q = A V$, where Q is the volume rate of flow per unit time, A is the area of the cross section, and V the mean velocity. For a roughly rectangular natural channel, the area A may be expressed as the product of the width, w, and the depth, d.

A difference in elevation at successive points along a river channel provides the source of energy for the flow. If both the velocity and depth of flow remain constant, then the energy provided by the difference in elevation is equal to the heat produced by viscous resistance, a term often referred to as the energy loss due to friction. The energy transformation between successive sections is expressed by an equation of the following form. When h_f, the loss term, is omitted, the equation is referred to as Bernoulli's equation:

$$d_1 + \frac{V_1^2}{2g} + Z_1 = d_2 + \frac{V_2^2}{2g} + Z_2 + h_f$$

where g is the acceleration due to gravity, h_f is the loss in energy, and d, V, and Z are as shown in Figure 1. Both the depth d and the elevation Z represent measures of potential energy, whereas $\frac{V^2}{2g}$ represents the kinetic energy of the flow.

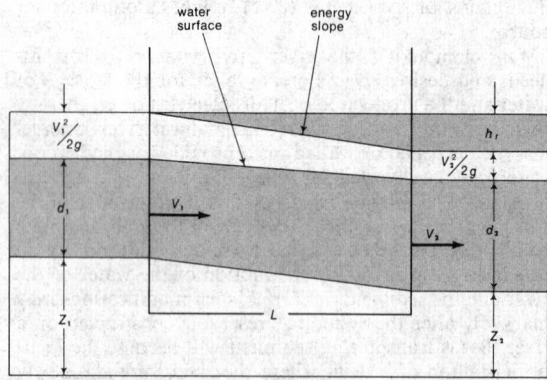

Figure 1: Steady flow in an open channel showing the relationship between elevation, velocity, depth, and energy loss as well as the relationship between the water surface and the energy slope (see text).

Because neither the cross section nor the bottom elevations of a natural channel are uniform, the velocity and depth vary from section to section. For any flow in a given length of channel there is only one depth at which the mean velocity will remain constant throughout

the reach and the slope of the bottom will be the same as the energy slope (the sum of the energy terms is shown in Figure 1). If the slope of the bed increases, velocity will increase at the expense of depth and vice versa. Similarly, if the cross section contracts, velocity will increase at the expense of depth.

These variations in depth and velocity characterize an interaction or exchange of kinetic and potential energy. In a rectangular channel, if the depth is made smaller and smaller, a value is reached at which the sum (referred to as the specific energy) $d + \frac{V^2}{2g}$ becomes a minimum. This depth, known as the critical depth, is equal to twice the kinetic energy term $\frac{V^2}{2g}$, or d_c, equals $\frac{V^2}{g}$. Expressed in terms of velocity, $V_c = \sqrt{gd_c}$, where V_c is the critical velocity.

In nature one may see critical flow conditions in the passage of a stream over rock ledges or over the riffles or rapids in a trout brook where the flow is swift and shallow.

Froude and Reynolds numbers

An important measure of the dynamics of the flow in an open channel can be derived by considering further the expression for the critical velocity. The ratio $V/\sqrt{gd}$, called a Froude number after its discoverer, William Froude, the English engineer, is a dimensionless number and in fact represents the ratio of an inertial force to a gravitational force. In addition, the expression $\sqrt{gd}$ is equal to the celerity of a shallow-water gravity wave of small amplitude in water of depth d. Thus, when the Froude number, $V/\sqrt{gd}$, equals 1, the velocity of flow equals the wave velocity (celerity) and waves formed on the surface appear as "standing" waves. A Froude number of 1 then represents a transition. Below this value, that is when the depth is greater than the critical depth, the flow is termed tranquil. Above it (high velocity and shallow depth) the flow is called shooting. These conditions are important in describing the dynamics of flow as well as the relationship of the flow to the movement of sediment.

A second parameter characterizing the dynamics of the flow is the Reynolds number, after Osbourne Reynolds, the English hydrodynamicist, which is the ratio of inertial to viscous forces. The Reynolds number for open channel flow is $\frac{Vd}{v}$ where v is the kinematic viscosity $\frac{\mu}{\zeta}$ in which μ is the dynamic viscosity and ζ the density of the fluid. At a constant kinematic viscosity as velocity and depth increase, the Reynolds number increases. Or, as velocity and depth increase, the significance of the viscous forces relative to the inertial forces declines.

The parameters that describe the dynamics of the flow in a river channel can be summarized in a simple diagram defined by the two dimensionless numbers. Figure 2 shows four possible regions of flow defined by the relative importance or relative effectiveness of the several forces, as well as some typical examples of flow in each region. These regions simply represent high or low values of the Reynolds and Froude numbers in different combinations. Comparable to the transition at a Froude number of 1, a Reynolds number of about 500 represents a transition from laminar to turbulent flow in an open channel. Because the behaviour of the river channel—including both the flow and the transport of materials—is governed by these conditions, such dynamic parameters are fundamental to the description of river processes.

Flow resistance and bed roughness

If the flow in a given section of a natural channel does not accelerate in the downstream direction, then the component of the force of gravity tending to move the water down the channel must be precisely balanced by the resisting forces or "drag" forces along the boundaries of the channel. The component of the weight (gravitational force) tending to move the water down the slope is given by γALS, where γ is the weight of a unit quantity of water (the weight equals the product of mass density ρ and g, or ρg), A is the area of the cross section, L is the length of the channel, and S the gradient. When

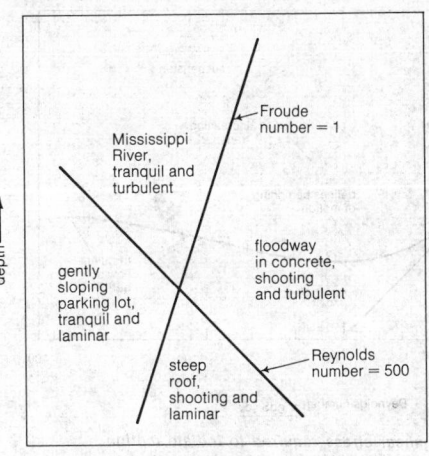

Figure 2: *Regions of flow defined in terms of the Reynolds number and the Froude number.*
For Reynolds numbers above 500, flow is turbulent; below 500, it is laminar. Above a Froude number of 1, flow is shooting; below it is tranquil. Examples are of common conditions of flow found in the real world.

the slope is very small, the tangent S can be substituted for the sine of the angle of slope (Figure 3). If the average shear stress or drag on the boundary is given by τ_0, the total drag or resisting force over a unit distance is $pL\,\tau_0$, where p is the wetted perimeter of the channel. Equating the two forces and solving for the drag gives $\tau_0 = \gamma\,\dfrac{A}{p}\,S$. Because many rivers are wide and shallow, the width very nearly equals the wetted perimeter and A/p nearly equals the depth, d; thus, $\tau_0 = \gamma dS$. When the flow is turbulent, it has been shown experimentally that the drag is nearly proportional to the square of the velocity, or $\tau_0 = V^2$. By equating these two relationships for the shear stress and rearranging the terms, one obtains the expression $V^2 = \dfrac{1}{ff}\,\dfrac{\tau_0}{\rho}$ in which the coefficient ff is referred to as a coefficient of resistance. Because $\tau_0 = \gamma ds$, the equation states that velocity is directly proportional to the depth and slope and inversely proportional to the resistance coefficient.

Physically the coefficient ff expresses a measure of the "roughness" of the channel. It reflects those features of the channel including the boundary itself that tend to retard or to increase the resistance to flow. Considering for example an open channel with a bed comprised of uniform, well-packed gravel, one might assume that a significant characteristic influencing the resistance to flow

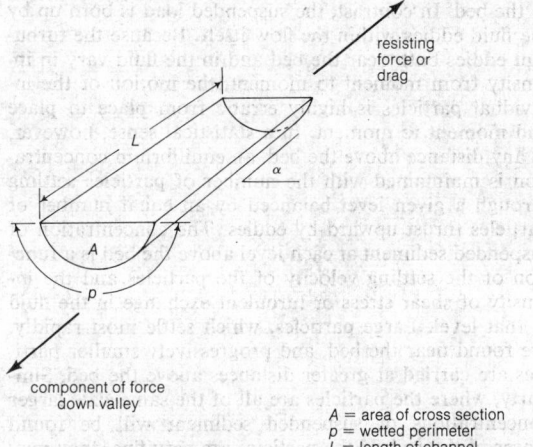

Figure 3: *Resistance to flow in an open channel, $\gamma\,ALS$,* in which γ is the weight of a unit quantity of water, A is the cross-sectional area, L is the channel length, and S is the slope. For small angles of slope, sine α approximately equals tangent α, which equals S.

A = area of cross section
p = wetted perimeter
L = length of channel
α = slope

might be the size, distribution, and packing of the particles of gravel themselves. This is indeed true. Where the flow is turbulent, the smaller the particles on the bed for a given depth of flow, the higher the velocity. This is shown on the right hand side of the schematic diagram in Figure 4 for the region of fully developed turbulent flow. At low Reynolds numbers in the laminar flow range, where viscous effects predominate, resistance is a function of viscosity and the conditions of flow. A transition exists in the range of Reynolds numbers between laminar and fully turbulent flow. The Reynolds number for the flow of most natural rivers falls within the turbulent range (Figure 2) where, for a given size of particle on the bed, as the depth becomes greater, the relative effect of the particle is lessened and, hence, velocity increases and resistance decreases.

In a natural river many additional factors contribute to the resistance or retardance of flow. Few rivers have uniform particles on the bed, nor are they perfectly straight and without obstructions. Thus such factors as the range of particle sizes from fine silts and clays to cobbles and boulders, their spatial distribution in the channel, the configuration of the bed, irregularities and curvature of the boundary, as well as the effects of vegetation and other obstructions all tend to influence the velocity and depth of flow that will occur in the channel for a given gradient and quantity of flow. The greater the number of boulders, vegetation, and bends, the greater the depth will be at the expense of velocity.

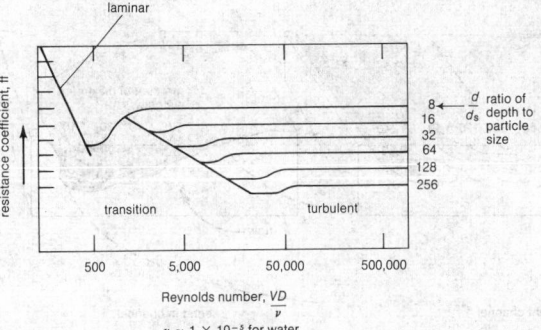

Figure 4: *Resistance coefficient as a function of Reynolds number.*
Three regions of flow are shown: laminar, a transition range, and fully developed turbulent flow. In fully developed turbulent flow, as the horizon lines indicate, the resistance coefficient is a function of the ratio of the depth of flow to the size of particle on the bed of the stream. Resistance declines as depth increases for a constant particle size.

Although the average flow velocity is the quotient of discharge divided by the area of the cross section, $V = Q/A$, the distribution is not uniform throughout the section. At the boundary the velocity is zero and increases rapidly to higher values in the moving fluid nearby. The slower moving fluid near the boundary retards the flow of the more rapidly moving fluid farther away that in turn tends to speed up the slower flow. This momentum exchange is ultimately transmitted to the boundaries and constitutes the drag or the force resulting from the shear stresses acting over the boundary surface. These effects are reflected in the nature of the velocity gradient or rate of change of velocity away from the boundary. For laminar flow molecular exchange of momentum dominates. When the flow is turbulent, the primary exchange of momentum takes place by the random movement of eddies from one region of the flow to another. In both cases, velocity increases with distance from the boundary; however, the exchange of momentum or mixing through the motion of eddies results in a more even distribution of velocity at some distance from the boundary. Theory confirmed by experiment indicates that velocity increases with the logarithm of the depth.

A natural river channel of roughly rectangular form has two boundaries, one with the solid earth and one with

Velocity distribution and boundary velocities

the air at the water surface. Assuming the drag of air to be small relative to that at the solid boundary, because velocity increases with distance from both the bed and banks of the channel, one would expect the highest velocity at or near the free water surface in the centre of the channel at the maximum distance from the boundary. In a wide straight channel, and in many natural rivers, the velocity is at a maximum in the centre near the water surface (Figure 5). Because width is often very much greater than the depth, in a straight channel the velocity distribution may be quite uniform over a considerable part of the channel. Where the flow is curved, however, and the depth small relative to the width, the velocity distribution is asymmetrical and the highest velocity occurs near the outside of the bend and below the surface. Asymmetry results from the higher elevation of the water surface on the outside of the bend and from the fact that the velocity of flow at the surface is higher than the velocity of the flow near the bed. As the water turns in the bend, water moving more rapidly at the surface turns less sharply than the slower moving water near the bed. This difference and the greater depth on the outside of the bend as a result of centrifugal acceleration create a component of flow across the section perpendicular to the direction of flow. Circulation or secondary spirals are created, with components of flow near the bed moving from the outside of the bend toward the inside and a component at the surface moving in the opposite direction. A single circulation spiral usually dominates in the bend. The complete circulation includes then a downward

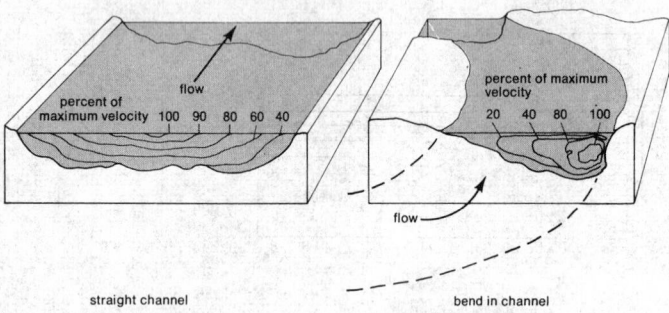

Figure 5: Velocity distribution in channels (see text).

component at the outer margin and an upward component at the inner section (Figure 5). Very wide channels in nature may exhibit a number of circulation "cells" within a given cross section.

ENTRAINMENT AND TRANSPORT
OF SEDIMENTARY PARTICLES

Erosion and transport of sedimentary particles is initiated when the drag exerted on the boundaries of a natural channel by the flowing water is sufficient to detach a particle from the boundary. As noted above, the drag or shear stress exerted on the bed and banks is defined by the velocity distribution (Figure 5). From the derivation given earlier, the average shear stress, τ_0, is equal to γdS and in turbulent flow is proportional to the square of the velocity, V^2.

Initiation of motion of noncohesive particles from the bed of a natural channel occurs when the shear stress, τ_0, exerted by the fluid exceeds the forces holding the particles in place. A particle of a given size and weight will begin to move when the shear stress exceeds a component fraction of the weight of the particle under water. The critical shear stress then is defined by the relation $\tau_0 = kd_s$, where d_s is the particle diameter and k a coefficient that includes the effects of particle shape, distribution, and packing within the bed. The relationship between particle size and increasing critical shear stress is shown in Figure 6. The ability of a stream to move a particle of a given size is sometimes referred to as the competence of the stream.

Because, as the discussion of flow resistance demonstrated, shear stress varies with the Reynolds number of

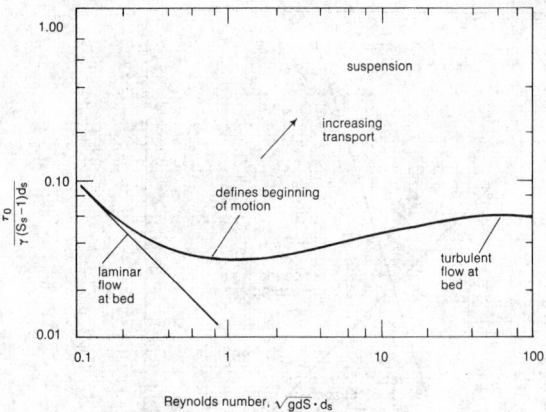

Figure 6: *Critical shear stress required to initiate motion of particles on the bed of a stream channel.*
The curve shows some variation of critical shear stress with the condition of flow as defined by the Reynolds number. At high Reynolds numbers, for larger particles, critical shear stress required to initiate movement is directly proportional to article size. For higher values of τ, the rate of transport increases.

the flow, the relationship between particle size and critical shear stress is not linear over the entire range of flow conditions found in nature. In addition, for smaller particles the force or velocity required to dislodge a particle from a matrix of other particles is greater than that required to maintain movement of the particle once entrained within the flow, and thus the velocity at which deposition takes place is less than the velocity required to initiate movement.

Beyond the point of incipient motion, the rate of transport of sediment is primarily a function of the total shear stress available within the fluid. Work must be done by the fluid to initiate and maintain the movement of the particles. A wide variety of theoretical and empirical expressions have been derived to relate the rate of sediment transport to flow parameters such as discharge, velocity, shear stress, or power (the rate of doing work). All depend upon the basic flow laws, which relate the distribution of velocity to a measure of the characteristics of the flow whether laminar or turbulent, to the geometry of the boundary, and to the shear stress. In general, increasing flow accompanied by increasing velocity and shear stress results in progressive entrainment of particles from the bed and higher rates of transport.

There are essentially two distinct physical modes of transport of sediment. Bed load is that portion of the material in transport that is in continuous or partial contact with other particles on the bed; thus the weight of the moving particles is supported by contact with grains in the bed. In contrast, the suspended load is born up by the fluid eddies within the flow itself. Because the turbulent eddies both near the bed and in the fluid vary in intensity from moment to moment, the motion of the individual particles is highly erratic from place to place and moment to moment. In a statistical sense, however, at any distance above the bed, an equilibrium concentration is maintained with the number of particles settling through a given level balanced by an equal number of particles thrust upward by eddies. The concentration of suspended sediment at each level above the bed is a function of the settling velocity of the particles and the intensity of shear stress or turbulent exchange in the fluid at that level. Large particles, which settle most rapidly, are found near the bed, and progressively smaller particles are carried at greater distances above the bed. Similarly, where the particles are all of the same size, larger concentrations of suspended sediment will be found closer to the bed. If the particles are very fine, they may be nearly uniformly distributed with depth. The curves in Figure 7 show the way in which sediment concentration varies with depth for particles of different sizes or settling velocities at a constant condition of flow. Settling velocity is primarily a function of the size of the particle.

Modes of
sediment
transport

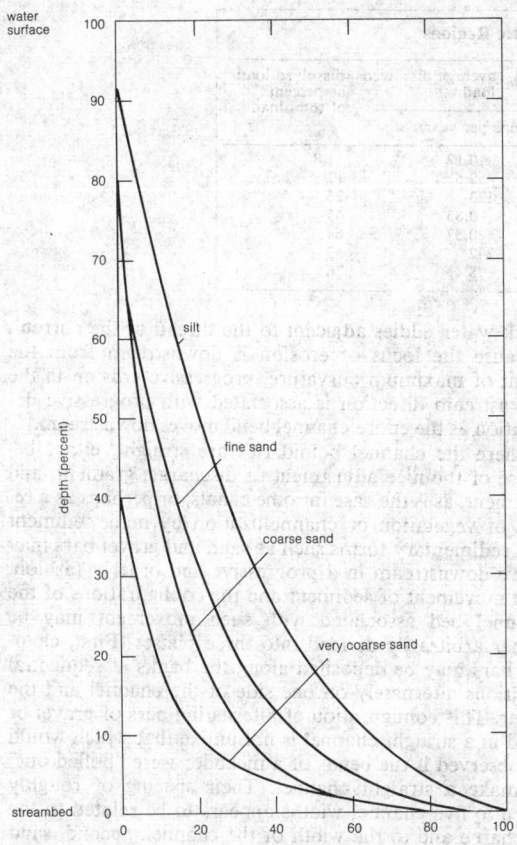

Figure 7: *Distribution of suspended load with depth for particles of different sizes.*
Coarse particles are concentrated closer to the bed, while finer particles, such as silt, are more uniformly distributed with depth.

Assuming the availability of a range of particle sizes in a river, as the flow fluctuates and velocity or shear stress changes, particles transported near the bed at one time may be entrained and move in suspension at a higher flow. With diminution of the flow larger particles cannot be maintained in suspension and will settle to the bed.

Where the bed of a natural channel is comprised of noncohesive particles such as sand, as velocity and depth increase with increasing flow the particles in motion no longer behave solely as discrete individuals but instead the bed itself is deformed, resulting in the formation of sand ripples, dunes, and waves. As the rate of transport increases, these bed forms change progressively with changes in depth and velocity. The sand near the bed moves in a zone close to the dune or ripple surfaces. Particles are carried up the backslope of the dune and deposited usually after sliding down on the steeply dipping face producing the downstream movement of the dune. Under some circumstances the bed form may move upstream. Because deformation of the mobile boundary influences the flow distribution itself, the interaction between the flow, the boundary form, and sediment transport is complex. These interactions, and the progressive changes in bed forms observed in natural channels during passage of a flood, are discussed below, under *Erosion and deposition in natural channels.*

MATERIALS TRANSPORTED BY NATURAL RIVERS

The materials actually transported as a clastic or particulate load as well as those in solution in natural rivers are a reflection not only of physical laws governing the competence and capacity of the flow to transport material but also of the availability of materials themselves. For example, pure limestone terrain containing no insoluble materials would supply no sediment to streams draining the region. With the exception of occasional blocks broken off from limestone canyon walls, the rivers would carry only dissolved materials, and the stream

beds would be devoid of sand, silt, and gravel bars. Such extremes, of course, are rare and, in general, rivers transport a mixture with coarser sediment in the bed load, finer particles in suspension, and ions in solution. Although these distinctions represent mechanisms of transport rather than sources of material, the sources are reflected in both the composition and relative abundance of each fraction.

The relative abundance of different portions of the load of materials carried by natural rivers can be obtained by measurement and in part by computations based on formulas developed from theoretical and laboratory studies. Because of the variety and complexity of the conditions found in natural rivers, however, neither measurement nor computation provides wholly satisfactory results. The accuracy of each varies with the local conditions found in different rivers. A few of the methods of measurement and computation are noted here.

Measurements of bed load in rivers are made in three ways: (1) by means of traps set on the bottom of the river with openings that are designed to catch material moving along the bed, (2) by means of trenches dug perpendicular to the flow across the entire channel width, such that the material moving near the bed falls into the trench and is conveyed laterally to a collecting system and there weighted, and (3) by hydrographic surveys of the total load accumulating in ponds, lakes, or deltas. To obtain the bed load, computations may sometimes be made based upon the coarser fraction of the accumulated sediments or a measured suspended load may be subtracted from the total accumulation.

Measurements of the suspended load are made with a streamlined sampling device resembling a fish that is lowered and raised through the flow. Streamlining minimizes interference with the flow. The resulting "depth integrated" sample represents a range of the concentrations weighted by the velocity of flow at each of the points in the vertical. Alternatively, samplers can be lowered in a vertical array and instantaneous samples obtained at specific points in the flow. To obtain a representative sample, sampling is done at a number of verticals across the river section. Because of the design of the samplers, they cannot be placed at precisely the interface between the moving bed and the fluid itself. As a result, the region immediately adjacent to the bed is difficult to sample properly. The significance of this omission varies with the concentrations of flow, particle size, and turbulence near the bed. The resulting observations are referred to as the "sampled" load, which is nearly equivalent to the theoretical suspended load in many cases but is not always so.

Computation of the transport of sedimentary materials in rivers is based on a separation of the mechanisms of transport, as noted above, into bed and suspended load. Because of the complexities of these relationships in natural rivers, the accuracy with which such computations can be made is often quite low. In some instances, however, estimates may be made within an accuracy of ± 20 percent, depending on the uniformity of the bed material, the variability of the shape and pattern of the natural channel, and the variability of the flow itself. (Roughly speaking the transport of bed material as bed load is proportional to the velocity raised to a power of 2 or 3.) If the concentration of suspended load is known at any point, an equation describing the relationship between suspended load and the shear stress in the fluid can be used to compute the total suspended load in the vertical at a number of sections. The accuracy of this computation under laboratory conditions is quite high, but some of the parameters are difficult to define for natural conditions, and the variability of the results remains large.

Unlike both the bed material and suspended load, which respond to the hydraulic conditions prevailing in the flow, the "wash load" of fine materials such as clays and fine silts derived from the watershed may settle so slowly that the quantity transported depends essentially upon the quantity supplied and not upon the dynamics of the flow. Thus the wash load need not be closely correlated with the velocity and shear stress but may vary over a large range, depending upon such factors as weathering, land

Bed load and suspended load

Wash load and the dissolved load

Dissolved and Suspended Load in Selected Rivers in Different Climatic Regions

river and location	drainage area (square miles)	average suspended load	average dissolved load	dissolved load as percent of total load
		(000,000 tons per year)		
Canadian River near Amarillo, Texas	29,700	6.41	0.12	1.8
Green River at Green River, Utah	40,500	19	2.5	12
Mississippi River, at the mouth	1,245,000	344	123	26
Delaware River, at Trenton, N.J.	12,300	1.0	0.83	45
Juniata River, near New Port, Pa.	3,354	0.32	0.57	64
Amazon River, at mouth, Brazil	2,722,000	499	242	33
Congo River, at mouth, Congo	1,425,000	31	98	76

use, and climatic conditions over the drainage basin. So far as measurement is concerned, wash load is a part of the suspended load, but the wash load cannot be computed from the suspended load equations using particle sizes found in the channel bed.

The relative proportions of dissolved and particulate or clastic load as well as the distribution of the clastic fraction between bed load and suspended load are highly variable in nature (Table). In general, the percentage of clastic load increases as the climate becomes more arid. Less effective solution and weathering in arid regions apparently reduce the supply of dissolved solids to the stream channel system, whereas in more humid regions larger quantities of dissolved material are made available to streams. Topography, and particularly the composition of the bedrock, also can markedly influence the composition and quantity of the load. The Saline River in Kansas, for example, has a salinity of 1,000 parts per million by weight, a function of the saline deposits found in the watershed. Similarly, extreme concentrations of sediment have been measured in some rivers such as the Yellow River in China, where sediment comprised 40 percent of the total fluid, or tributaries of the Colorado River, in which 60 percent of the flow was sediment. In general, concentrations of suspended load in natural rivers vary from several hundred to 10,000 parts per million (1 percent) by weight. Some sand channels, such as the Loup River in western Nebraska, may transport 50 percent or more of the total load as bed load, but values of about 10 to 20 percent are probably more common.

EROSION AND DEPOSITION IN NATURAL CHANNELS

Equilibrium conditions and the migration of meanders

The supply and movement of sediment is intimately involved in the determination of the form and pattern of the river channel. A natural river flowing in sediments of its own making can maintain a stable configuration in two ways: first, by a balance of forces in which the drag of the fluid tending to erode the perimeter of the channel at any point is equalled or exceeded by the frictional or cohesive forces tending to resist the eroding force, and second, by maintenance of a rate of deposition equal to the rate of erosion. In contrast, a channel incised in rock is less free to adjust its form and pattern through deposition and erosion, but the bed of the channel will rise and fall with changes in the rate of transport of debris. The first case, in which a precise balance is maintained between the erosive force and the resistance of the boundary materials without any erosion, is relatively rare in nature. The banks of such a channel in noncohesive material are roughly parabolic and, if the flow is large, the channel cross section will consist of a wide central portion with a flat bottom and banks at each side roughly parabolic in form. Ideally, the maintenance of such an erosional equilibrium requires a delicate balance between the opposing forces, a relatively uniform material, and a constant flow, conditions reproducible in the laboratory but only approximated in nature.

A natural river channel in which the rate of erosion is balanced by the rate of deposition and the outflow of sediment to the reach equals the inflow can maintain a stable form while moving laterally across the alluvial plain. A meandering river is the most common illustration of this process. Erosion takes place on the outside of each bend near the point of maximum shear stress as a result of the curvature of the flow. Deposition on the opposite bank is associated with transverse flow near the bed and with slack water eddies adjacent to the thread of the current. Because the locus of erosion is downstream from the point of maximum curvature, progressive erosion in the downstream direction is associated with progressive deposition as the entire channel bend moves downstream.

Sand and gravel bars and kinematic wave theory

Where the channel boundaries are straight, either because of the nice adjustment of discharge, gradient, and sediment, as is the case in some canals, or perhaps as a result of vegetation or channellization by man, sediment and sedimentary forms such as sand and gravel bars may move downstream in a progressive and orderly fashion. The movement of sediment and the configurations of the channel bed associated with such movement may be rather arbitrarily divided into three phases. First, channel bars may be deposited along the banks at sequential positions alternately on one side of the channel and the other. This configuration of alternating bars of gravel or sand in a straight channel is not unlike that which would be observed if the bends of a meander were "pulled out" to make a straight channel. Their spacing of roughly three to five channel widths appears to be related to the discharge and to the width of the channel. Second, sand and silt may move as dunes or ripples, a mode of transport determined by particle characteristics and the interaction of boundary form and the flow. A third mode of sedimentary deposit involves successive movement and deposition of discrete particles. Larger particles may move different distances depending upon their size, shape, and specific gravity. Boulders will move less frequently and, on the average, more slowly than smaller particles, producing a differential rate of downstream migration of particles of different sizes.

Accumulation and movement of gravel and sand in bars appear to resemble the movement of what is called a kinematic wave. Discrete particles do not move independently of one another but interact or interfere with each other in much the same way as automobiles on a highway. As a result of this interaction, the particles accumulate in groups or agglomerations that move downstream as "waves." The average downstream rate of movement is then represented not by the movement of the individual particles but rather by the average rate of movement of the group of particles constituting the wave. This wave phenomenon is similar to that observed on a highway crowded with automobiles, where, when the number of automobiles is low, the automobiles interact very little and each moves at its own rate. With an increase in the number of automobiles, however, interaction takes place and groups begin to form such that there are agglomerations and openings in successive positions along the highway. The celerity or rate of movement of these waves is determined then by the density of particles (or automobiles) in a given length of stream channel (or road), by the characteristics of the particles, and by the conditions of flow.

Flow and transport variation with time

Because the flow of water in natural channels is not constant, each mode of transport in a river also varies with time. The alternation of high and low flow in most of the rivers of the world not only influences the rate of transport but also the attendant forms of the channels themselves and the deposits associated with them. In the natural world the time scale of variations in flow may be matters of minutes, days, years, decades, or millennia. Peak flows from thunderstorm rainfall may occur in a matter of minutes after the start of heavy rain in streams or in urban rivers. Storms of longer duration may produce high water lasting for days or weeks. At another time scale are the seasonal or annual variations such as the cyclical rise and fall of the Nile each spring as a result of snow melt and rains in the headwaters, a variation common to many major river systems such as the Colorado, the Rio Grande, the Ganges, and the Yukon. Lastly, successions of dry years may be followed by wet ones. Such climatic variations are less periodic in occurrence and may encompass periods from decades to thousands of years in duration.

Variations in flow rate are associated with variations in transport. The dissolved load, responding to the characteristics of the source rocks as well as the flow, often decreases in concentration as a result of dilution of the salt concentration by the direct runoff from streams. In contrast, suspended load generally increases with increasing flow. Wash load may be readily removed from the watershed, for example, when spring rains follow the melting of snow and particles of soil are detached by cycles of freezing and thawing in early spring and late winter. The first spring rains readily remove the prepared materials to the streams. The transport of bed load also increases in response to increase in velocity and shear stress accompanying the passage of higher flows or floods. As in the theoretical or laboratory condition, the change in flow in the river channel is accompanied by a change not only in the concentrations of dissolved, suspended, and bed materials but by changes in the form of the bed itself as the flow increases in depth and velocity. Changes in the form of the bed associated with the passage of a high flow in a river are shown in Figure 8, whereas Figure 9 shows concurrent changes in flow, velocity, and depth.

From *Bulletin of the U.S. Geological Survey* (1960)

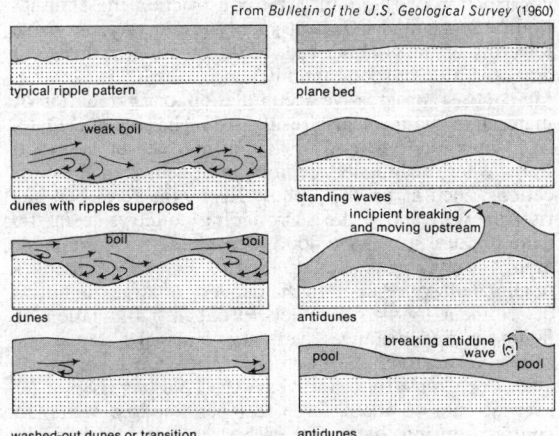

typical ripple pattern

plane bed

weak boil

dunes with ripples superposed

standing waves

incipient breaking and moving upstream

boil · boil

dunes

antidunes

breaking antidune wave

pool · pool

washed-out dunes or transition

antidunes

Figure 8: *Forms of bed roughness in alluvial channels.* This sequence of forms is related to the depth and velocity of flow and to the rate of sediment transport.

Bed forms: ripples, dunes, plane bed, and antidunes

As noted earlier, after the initiation of movement, ripples and dunes develop on the bed. With increasing depth and velocity of flow in the channel, the dunes grow in size. Experimental and field observations indicate that the amplitude or height of the dune increases until the velocity of flow over the dune prevents further accumulation on the crest. At equilibrium, dunes may cover the bed in the same way that they do the windblown surface of a sandy desert. If velocity increases more rapidly than depth, as the Froude number approaches 1, a transition occurs, dunes begin to be erased, and all or part of the bed will be planar, with dunes covering the remainder. Beyond this transition, continuing increase in velocity leads to the formation of antidunes. Dune forms on the bed move upstream as a result of the displacement of material by scour at the upstream position while net transport continues in the downstream direction. The formation of antidunes is associated with the formation of standing waves on the water surface. Unlike dunes, the crests and troughs of antidunes are in phase with the crests and troughs of the surface waves.

With declining flow in the channel and reduction in velocity and depth, the sequence is reversed. At succes-

sively lower Froude numbers, the bed is transformed from the antidunes to the mixed and planar bed, to dunes, and thence to an irregular bed of sand if the flow declines to zero. A smooth bed is rarely if ever attained inasmuch as declining flow both erodes the dunes and deposits finer sediments on the channel bed. Thus the forms remaining in a sand channel are usually dissected dunes and ripples.

Each of the successive configurations of the bed is associated with a particular set of flow conditions, and with changing discharge a complex interrelationship exists between the geometry of the boundary as defined by the configuration of the channel bed, the concentration of sediment, and the flow parameters such as velocity and depth. In some cases the same discharge on the rising stage of a flood may be associated with a high velocity and a relatively low depth, while on the declining stage the depth may be higher and the velocity lower (Figure 9). From the earlier discussion of resistance it will be seen that the resistance to flow then is greater on the falling than on the rising stage. This difference is presumed to be due primarily to decline in flow so rapid that there is insufficient time for the transition of the bed forms. Dunes of larger amplitude associated with the higher flow remain at the lower stage and these larger forms provide a greater resistance.

The scale of dune forms may be exceedingly large. In a large river such as the Mississippi, at depths of flow from 70 to 90 feet (21 to 27 metres), dunes or dunelike forms of major proportions have been observed, with amplitudes from 15 to 40 feet (5 to 12 metres) and longitudinal spacing from crest to crest of 50 to 500 feet (15 to 152 metres). Dunes can be seen in the beds of many rivers and creeks carrying sand, and dunes of cobbles and gravel occasionally have been observed after the passage of great floods where large depths and high velocity permitted transport of the coarse material.

Variations in flow produce variations not only in the rate of movement of particles of different sizes but also in the distances that these move in successive intervals of time. A large boulder in a small trout stream may be moved only by rare and very large floods. In contrast, material in solution is transported continuously as long as there is flow in the stream. Between these extremes lies a continuous range. Small particles are carried more often and for greater distances during each rise in the flow than are successively larger ones. Huge boulders may be moved a matter of feet or perhaps hundreds of feet by a flood that occurs on the average perhaps once in a hundred years. Sand may be transported continuously in a stream where the flow never declines below the point of incipient motion of the sand particles. Thus individual particles move in steps of varying lengths that depend upon the duration of the flow in which they are transported and their size, shape, and distribution.

Flood events of large magnitude but infrequent occurrence may move very large particles as well as large quantities of material but only for short periods of time. In contrast, more frequent events will move smaller sizes but over longer periods of time. In sand bed channels of ephemeral streams, such as those in the southwestern United States, most of the movement of both suspended and bed materials may occur during relatively infrequent events, which recur perhaps four or five times per year. These few floods not only mold the channel form, but they may transport 80 to 90 percent of the total annual load carried by the river. In contrast, where flow is perennial and of relatively large magnitude, more of the dissolved and suspended load may be transported by flows of modest magnitude throughout a large part of the year. Under such circumstances, the relative contribution of the large and infrequent flood event is thus of lesser significance. To the extent that generalization is possible, existing evidence suggests that the greater the variability of stream flow and the larger the particles to be carried, the more significant are the floods of large magnitude and infrequent occurrence. Similarly, where flow is less variable, dissolved load a significant proportion of the total load, and the suspended load composed of fine particles, more frequent events assume greater importance.

Magnitude and frequency of flow events

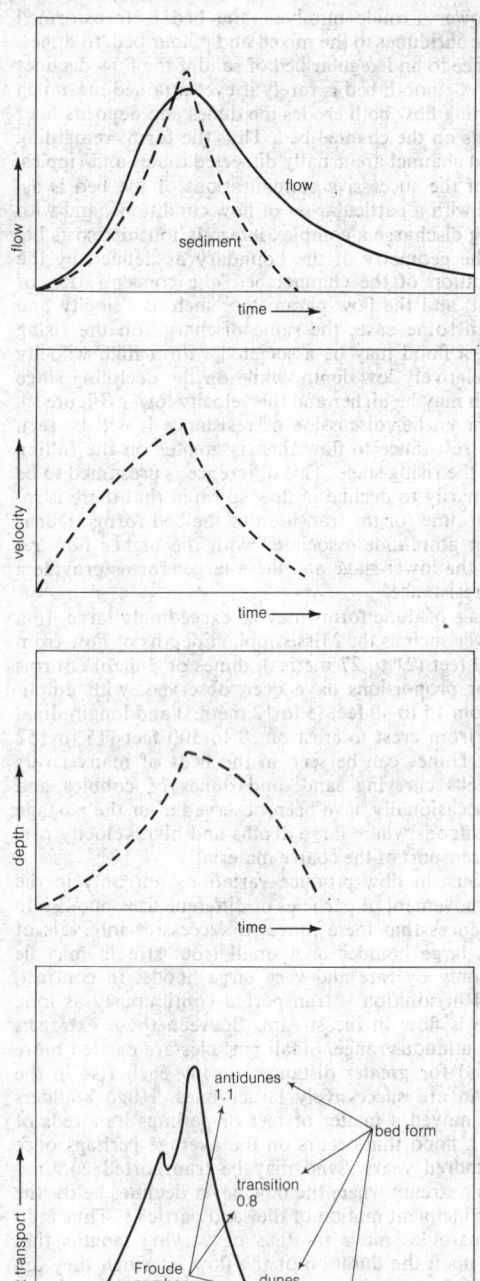

Figure 9: Sequential changes in flow (discharge), velocity, depth, and sediment transport associated with the passage of a flood in a natural channel with a sand bed. Changes in bed form and the approximate Froude number at which such changes might be observed are shown in association with changes in the rate of sediment transport.

Scour and fill and environmental conditions

In a given reach of channel, fluctuations in flow, accompanied by changes in the rate of transport of both suspended and bed material, produce a scouring or filling of the channel bed. In a straight channel this may amount to a few inches. In bends or narrow reaches, scour may be to depths of several feet and in rock-walled canyons as much as 20 to 30 feet (6 to 9 metres). The cumulative effect in any given year may result in the temporary lowering of the stream bed. The bed may be lowered in some years and raised in the next or succeeding years. Over a period of time the average elevation will remain constant. A similar process of erosion and deposition characterizes the lateral or down-valley movement of the channel. In

any one year erosion may exceed deposition, but over a period of years the pattern and form of the channel remain the same. Thus, the equilibrium referred to earlier constitutes an adjustment to the quantity of water and sediment delivered to the channel, an adjustment maintained within the natural variations in flow and sediment load normally experienced in a given climate or hydrologic environment. Equilibrium of the river channel then is associated with a constancy of climate viewed as an average over a period of years.

A progressive increase in the amount of rainfall on the watershed, a change in the vegetative cover, or a combination of such factors, however, may produce a progressive change in the hydrologic conditions governing the river channel at any point. Such changes might be climatic, they might result from changes in land use or, for example, they might be brought about by construction of a dam and major reservoir. These long term or progressive changes are referred to as degradation or aggradation in contrast to the processes of scour and fill that encompass fluctuations of short duration. Changes associated with man-made works, in fact, provide a good illustration of the nature of the river response to changes in climate. A reservoir, by impounding flood flows for release during periods of low natural flows, alters the frequency distribution or pattern of river flows. In addition, the reservoir becomes a sediment trap, which reduces the quantity of sediment delivered to a channel below. A river previously in equilibrium with the natural flow and sediment supply is thus subjected to a new set of controls that, in turn, result in a succession of changes in the river channel itself. Thus, where scour took place in one year to be followed by deposition in succeeding years prior to construction of the dam, after construction the elimination of floods and sediment supply produces progressive lowering of the channel bed, or degradation, rather than an alternation of scour and fill.

In contrast, progressive accumulation, or aggradation of material in channels, also results from changes in climate, from man-made works, or at the interface of land and water where sediments accumulate in deltas. In some locations, such as on the Yellow River, the river bed has risen to well above the surrounding countryside in the delta because successive floods deposited coarse sediment along the river banks and on the bed. Elsewhere, changes in climate have resulted in the delivery of large quantities of sediment to river channels, producing alluviation or filling for great distances over entire channel systems.

Rates of erosion and deposition

Rates of accumulation or degradation are highly variable. For over a thousand years the Nile has risen at an average rate of about three feet per hundred years. In contrast, during the period of hydraulic gold mining in the Sierra Nevada the Sacramento River rose as much as ten feet in 35 years. Valley fills or terraces along major rivers in the great plains of the western United States indicate that some rivers may have cut through the alluvial materials in their valleys at rates on the order of ten feet (3 metres) or more in 100 years, although these estimates are crude at best. Below Hoover Dam on the Colorado River, the bed of the channel was lowered ten feet in five years after closure of the dam.

RIVER FORMS AND FLUVIAL PROCESSES
IN DIFFERENT ENVIRONMENTS

The characteristics of a river and the processes associated with it are determined by a combination of the geology of a region and the climatic conditions responsible for providing the flow in the river. The term geology includes the underlying structure of the region, such as the presence or absence of mountains, as well as the composition and distribution of the bedrock. The latter, in turn, determine the quantity and often the size fractions of the materials delivered to the stream system. In contrast, although the climate may be influenced by the elevation of the region, major aspects of the atmospheric circulation will determine the amount of precipitation and seasonal variations in temperature. Indirectly these will affect the vegetation, characteristics of the soils, and the distribution of runoff or flow to the river system.

Clearly, innumerable combinations of geologic and climatic controls must exist in nature. Each segment or reach of a river will be dominated by a set of conditions of local origin as well as by a set determined from the larger area of the drainage basin upstream. Despite these obvious variations, however, some combinations of controls are sufficiently common to allow rather rough characterization of rivers in different regions. It must be emphasized, however, that the key to understanding why rivers look and behave as they do lies in a knowledge of the mutual interaction of the controlling factors such as discharge, sediment, and rock type. What might be called characteristic regional types simply represent particular combinations of these factors as well as the existence of a control in some regions or environment. Many complex factors are involved in developing a certain type of river or stream; each stream is classified according to the factors affecting it.

Grant Heilman

A boulder-bed high mountain stream, Crandall Creek, Wyoming.

The trout stream and the arroyo

The so-called trout stream, or brook, for example, is indeed a recognizable type of river. It is usually characterized by a vigorous flow (of cool water), high gradient, and a bed of cobbles and boulders bordered by mossy banks and trees. Climate and elevation determine the availability of the flow, whereas the coarse bed material is a function of the steep gradient determined by the geologic structure. A high gradient permits the flow periodically to move some of the larger cobbles producing in time a series of pools and riffles. In some brooks, particularly those in coarse sand or cobbles, the spacing of the riffles or shallows appears to be proportional to channel width.

A second rather distinctive river in an opposing climatic regime is the arroyo of the Spanish-speaking world, the wadi of the Middle East and Mediterranean region. These dry washes, which experience periodic torrential flows, are otherwise dry sand channels comprised primarily of sands, perhaps dissected dune forms, some gravel, and occasional cobbles, depending on the local geology and topography. Because of the aridity and high temperature of the bed, vegetation is usually sparse. The combination of dry bed, absence of vegetation, and rapid changes in flow permit large variations in the configuration of the sand bed and in the amount of scour and fill. In addition, because such channels are often on relatively steep slopes and in noncohesive materials, they tend to be wide and shallow and subject to high velocities at shallow depths, a condition promoting the formation not only of dunes but of antidunes along with rapid rates of sand transport.

Channels in humid-temperate regions

In contrast to these rivers in semi-arid regions, the well-defined channels of the humid region are a response not only to the regularity of the flow but to the presence of fine sediments and vegetation that stabilize the river banks, emerging point bars, and other deposits laid down by the river. These channels, composed of silt banks stabilized with vegetation, are narrower and less mobile.

Not infrequently floods that overtop the banks deposit on the adjacent plain varying amounts of silt, sand, and mud, thus creating a floodplain composed of channel and bar deposits overlain by finer "overbank" deposits. Where the channel is confined or maintains itself within a relatively narrow belt within which it meanders, the fine-grained deposits of floods may predominate in the floodplain.

The preceding descriptions suggest that in alluvial river channels flowing in sediments of their own making, there is a range of channel or river types, from the wandering channel that deposits bars over a vast shallow plain to the well-fixed, stabilized, narrow channel bordered by vegetation. In the former the ability of the channel to alter its course at will by erosion and deposition, a condition common to large rivers flowing on an apron of debris deposited at the front of a glacier, creates a broad flat plain composed of sand and gravel bars deposited within the channel and in rapidly migrating bends, coupled with the overbank materials that are deposited from rapid rises in stage.

At the opposite extreme, the established channel in cohesive material bordered by vegetation will move laterally at a modest rate accompanied by deposition of sediments upon which vegetation will become established. With each flood above the normal bank height (a level attained on the order of once each year or two) sediments may be deposited over nearly the entire width of the valley. Where the river channel traverses the valley with rapidity, the bottomland is virtually all in channel deposits, while in the less mobile environment overbank or nonchannel deposits predominate.

Between the extremes, the wandering and stabilized channels, lies a spectrum of processes and resultant alluvial landforms, each dependent upon the relative rates of lateral migration of the river and of overbank deposition; that is, upon relative rates of erosion and sediment transport, and upon the frequency distribution of river flow. A given channel then may fall anywhere within this spectrum. The channel of the Missouri River along the boundary between northern Iowa and Nebraska, for example, contains many bars that may shift with each flood. At the same time, the river moves laterally in a broad meandering pattern experiencing progressive erosion as well as deposition over broad areas.

Rivers in canyons

Rivers in canyons such as the Colorado in the Grand Canyon, the Yangtze Gorge, or the limestone valleys on a smaller scale in Kentucky and Tennessee in the United States are confined by bedrock walls and valley floors. No longer free to alter either form or pattern save over long periods of time, the characteristics of the river are determined primarily by the rock itself and by slow erosional processes of abrasion and scour of rock material. Falls may occur where resistant beds are in con-

Josef Muench

Arroyo trenching an alluvial valley in the Carrizo Mountains, Arizona.

tact with less resistant ones such as at Niagara, or long smooth stretches may be encountered where, unbroken by changes in lithology or by joints or faults, abrasion by the river has produced smooth polished surfaces. Elsewhere, as in the bottom of the Colorado River, deep pools scoured by the flow may be separated by rocky rapids. In some places lateral abrasion excavates sheltered coves where rockwalls overhang the river itself. Rock canyon sections may occur in any climatic region where water has been or is currently available to scour the bedrock.

In extreme climates, such as in Arctic, Antarctic, or periglacial (cold, frozen ground) regions, the river may be frozen throughout much of the year. Here the river processes will be determined by the configuration of the bedrock geology and by the annual climatic regime, which determines both the way in which the river freezes with the onset of winter and the way in which the ice breaks up in the spring. Some rivers, such as the Yukon, break up throughout the length of the river in a relatively short period of time. The resultant breakup and the rising spring flood with which it is associated produce enormous forces that not only shatter the ice but cause it to accumulate in ice jams, to override the river banks, and to erode the channel banks as the high flow moves down the river.

This type of river presents quite a different pattern from that observed on other kinds of cold region rivers such as the Nelson River in Canada, which flows from Lake Winnipeg to Hudson Bay. The Nelson consists of a series of lakes and open water sections linked by bedrock falls or rapids. Freeze-up and breakup are discontinuous, beginning in the lakelike sections and controlled by the backing up of water above the controls at the rapids. The breakup of the ice is sequential and does not occur over the entire river, but instead the ice melts in the lakes and intervening backwater sections and, as the water rises, it begins to flow through and over the ice covering the falls. The flow scours areas adjacent to the falls themselves and gradually erodes through the ice capping the falls. The presence of ice and the movement of large ice blocks from the bedrock falls provide additional force to scour and to move boulders along the bed of the river.

The "typical" river

If these represent distinctive types of rivers, is there a "typical" river resulting from a set of "typical" river processes? The answer is yes and no. Although there is no typical river, there are a set of processes of common occurrence that can be used to define a model case. The discharge in such a river would probably include a seasonal peak and a skewed distribution of daily flows with low flows exceeding the number of high flows. The largest volume of sediment would be transported as suspended load and the dominant mode of movement along the channel bed would be in the form of dunes. As a rule, the sediments comprising the banks would be finer and more cohesive than those in the bed. Whereas the channel would appear roughly rectangular, the ratio of width to depth is large and in many instances the cross section, when drawn to scale, would be nearly saucer shaped. With the passage of a flood, such a river would scour on the order of a foot or two. Some lateral movement of the channel would be accompanied by deposition of bars, and at bends sediments would be deposited opposite loci of erosion on the outside of the bend. Occasional floods would deposit successively finer materials on these channel sediments. Thus, a floodplain would be progressively eroded and recreated by the river that flows within it.

Although these generalizations can be made about the characteristic behaviour of rivers and associated processes in different environments, in reality, of course, a single factor may dominate the scene at a particular point and essentially determine the characteristics of the river at that point. Thus the presence of canyon walls may dictate that the river be narrow and deep. Elsewhere the variability of flow, as for example on the Great Plains of the United States, coupled with sediment sources providing much silt and sand, may ensure that the natural river channel is shallow, characterized by high variability and by broad areas of bare sand. Even in such terrain, a succession of relatively wet years may see the development of a dense cover of vegetation that gradually inhibits or confines the channel system. A major flood may destroy the vegetation, widen the channel, and once again expose an area of bare sand. This alternation in place and in time can be repeated again and again in the history of the river and reflects the dynamism inherent in the processes that mold the riverine landscape.

BIBLIOGRAPHY. B.R. COLBY, "Fluvial Sediments: A Summary of Source, Transportation, Deposition, and Measurement of Sediment Discharge," *Bull. U.S. Geol. Surv.* 181-A (Nov. 1963), a brief review of the range of river sediment relationships; F.M. HENDERSON, *Open Channel Flow* (1966), a modern text in the hydraulics of flow in all kinds of open channels, includes several excellent chapters on sediment transport and the behaviour of natural rivers not found in any other text, for the advanced student; S. LELIAVSKY, *An Introduction to Fluvial Hydraulics* (1955), contains varied treatment of specific topics related to natural channels and canals, includes information from river control works in Europe; L.B. LEOPOLD, M.G. WOLMAN, and J.P. MILLER, *Fluvial Processes in Geomorphology* (1964), a textbook in analysis of landforms with primary emphasis upon rivers, contains much empirical information on rivers, as well as brief treatment of related hydraulic phenomena; H. ROUSE (ed.), *Engineering Hydraulics* (1950), a treatise containing separate chapters on a variety of topics in hydraulics ranging from hydraulic machinery to sediment transport, for the advanced student.

(M.G.W.)

Foch, Ferdinand

Ferdinand Foch, marshal of France and commander of the Allied forces in the closing months of World War I, is generally considered to be the man most responsible for the Allied victory. Marshal Joseph Joffre, one of the French military leaders in World War I, once said, "Intelligence is plentiful, but strength of character is not." Foch had both.

He was born at Tarbes (Hautes-Pyrénées) on October 2, 1851, the son of a civil servant. His family had originally lived in Valentine, a village in the Comminges area to which he used to return every year.

Early years

As a very young child he had been inspired by the Napoleonic epic through the stories of the campaigns of his maternal grandfather, who was an officer during the Revolution and then under the emperor, and at the age of six he began to devour the descriptions of military battles he found in historical works. Thus, at an early age, he indicated the direction his career was to take.

After attending several schools, in 1869 he entered the well-known Jesuit school of Saint-Clément in Metz, in order to prepare for the entrance examination for the École Polytechnique (Polytechnic School). At Saint-Clément he also worked out the solid religious training he had received from his family. His religious faith was later to be one of the essential elements of his moral strength; yet, it was to make him the object of petty hostility, even though he remained aloof from politics.

EB Inc.

Foch.

In Metz, the experience of France's defeat in the Franco-Prussian War left an indelible impression on him. When he passed his examinations in July of 1870, the war had already broken out, and cannons were thundering nearby. Once back home, he enlisted in the army but did not take part in the fighting. In 1871, after the armistice, when he returned to Saint-Clément, he was forced to live alongside the German soldiers who were there. Metz had become a German city. His pain and anger dictated the decision that was to give meaning to his life: he would become a soldier in order to return Lorraine and Metz to France.

Rise in the military hierarchy

After two years at the École Polytechnique, he entered the École d'Application de l'Artillerie (the artillery training school) in 1873. As an artillery officer, he proved himself to be both an ardent cavalryman and an experienced technician. After appointment to the Artillery Committee in Paris, he was married in Brittany in 1883 and acquired the château of Trofeunteuniou, which then became his second family home.

In contrast to many officers who sought action in colonial campaigns, Foch chose study and meditation. But his studies were meant to do more than just enrich his knowledge; they were a constant education of his own will. He studied the lives of the great men of history and sought out the duties expected of a leader. Consequently, when difficult times befell him, he was steeled for them.

In 1885 he entered the École Supérieure de Guerre (War College), which for the next 25 years was to be his "laboratory" to prepare for war. He returned there as a major in 1895 to become an assistant professor—and soon a full professor—teaching general tactics. Finally in 1908, when he was a brigadier general, the prime minister, Georges Clemenceau, appointed him head of the school, even though he had to overcome bitter opposition. In the meantime Foch had exercised commands and served on various staffs, thus adding to his experience and judgment. He formulated his doctrine of action in two works: *Les Principes de la guerre* (1903) and *De la conduite de la guerre* (1904).

"Thought" and "will" were the key words of the teachings that his harsh and abrupt, but inspired voice—his disciples called it a prophet's voice—imprinted on the minds and hearts of generations of officers.

After commanding a division in 1911 and briefly commanding an army corps, he was in August 1913 put in command of the XX Army Corps in Nancy, which protected the Lorraine frontier. It seemed to be the crowning point of Foch's career because he would reach retirement age in three years.

Under Joffre in World War I

When war broke out on August 2, 1914, Foch first fought on the right flank, in Lorraine. On August 28 a dangerous gap appeared in the centre, and the commander in chief, Joseph Joffre, called Foch to command the army detachment—which later became the IX Army—that was being formed there. The enemy tried to break through, but Foch held on. He had taught that "Where there is a will, there is victory." His tenacity made it possible for Joffre to win at the first of the battles of the Marne. The same was true at the battles of the Yser and of Ypres, where he had been sent by Joffre to coordinate the efforts of the English, the French, and the Belgians, who were being severely attacked. King Albert I of Belgium later said of Foch, "That man could make the dead fight."

For two thankless years—1915 and 1916—Foch, commanding the Northern Army Group, vainly tried to break through the German line in Artois and at the Somme. This time his will could not make up for the lack of equipment and supplies.

On May 15, 1917, he was appointed chief of the war minister's general staff, a position that made him adviser to the Allied armies. But advising was not commanding.

Russia was about to collapse, thus allowing Germany to bring all its forces back to the Western Front, where the Belgians, the English, and the French were lined up under separate commands. Foch predicted that, when the battering ram struck this poorly consolidated front, each force would think only of its own fate and that the front would be broken up. That was why he advocated the establishment of a single command. But the British prime minister David Lloyd George and Clemenceau, who had in November 1917 once again been appointed premier, refused to listen to Foch, believing that an agreement of cooperation between the English and French commanders in chief, Field Marshal Douglas Haig and Gen. Philippe Pétain, would suffice.

Events, however, were to prove Foch right. On March 21, 1918, the British front in Picardy collapsed under the impact of the German attack. On March 23, the Anglo-French agreements were outstripped by events. On March 24, it was already "every man for himself." Douglas Haig was thinking about his embarkation ports, and Pétain was thinking about Paris. The severance of the two armies had begun. The Germans, who saw that the enemy had become nothing more than a body without a head, were already crying victory.

Lloyd George and Clemenceau shared that feeling. They realized that there was only one possible head to fill that void, and that was Foch, the very personification of determination. And so on March 26, on the very brink of disaster, they gave Foch the responsibility of "coordinating the action of the Allied Armies on the western front." These powers were enlarged at the inter-Allied conference in Beauvais on April 3 and were extended to the Italian front on May 2.

Generalissimo of the Allied Armies

The battle of two wills began: Erich Ludendorff, who was in virtual command of the German forces, versus Foch. Ludendorff, who had the initiative and superiority in numbers, redoubled his attacks. Foch had to resign himself to parrying, in order to hold out until the mass arrival of the American armies. Deaf to the calls of distress, he husbanded his meagre reserves, urging his men on to the limits of their endurance. His shrewd tenacity succeeded in stopping Ludendorff in Picardy and then in Flanders. On May 8, Foch received the official title of commander in chief of the Allied Armies.

But, in order to give full support to the English, who were being pushed back to the sea by Ludendorff, Foch did not hesitate to withdraw troops from the French front. Ludendorff took advantage of this. On May 27, he broke through that front, and his troops spread as far as the Marne. On June 9 a new gap appeared at the Oise: Foch stopped it up again. Ludendorff then decided to gamble everything he had, for the Americans were about to join the battle. On July 15 he made a massive attack in Champagne. Two days later he was stopped; he had lost.

Foch's will had gained the upper hand; now it was his turn to strike. In two offensives on July 18 and on August 8—Ludendorff was to call the latter a "black day"—Foch drove him back to a defensive position.

The honour of marshal of France was conferred on Foch on August 6, just as he was intensifying his offensive and unrelentingly striking the German front, giving no respite to the enemy nor to his own troops. Finally, the German Army, already bled white, was threatened by disintegration by the revolution in Germany. It had moreover, been abandoned by its allies and now found itself forced to ask for an armistice the conditions of which were dictated by Marshal Foch in the name of the Allies on November 11, 1918, at Rethondes. On November 26 Foch returned to Metz. He had given Alsace and Lorraine back to France: the lifelong goal that he had set for himself had been reached.

Foch, who had been made a marshal of Great Britain and of Poland and who had been elected a member of the Académie Français and of the Supreme War Council, died in Paris on March 20, 1929. He is buried near Napoleon under the dome of the Church of Saint-Louis-des-Invalides.

BIBLIOGRAPHY. FERDINAND FOCH, *Des Principes de la guerre* (1903; Eng. trans., *The Principles of War*, 1918), and *De La Conduite de la guerre* (1904), are works essential for understanding the formation of the Marshal's military thought and of his character. See also his *Mémoires pour servir à l'histoire de la guerre de 1914–1918*, 2 vol. (1931; Eng. trans., *The Memoirs of Marshal Foch*, 1931), a well-balanced review of Foch's thought and action; MAXIME WEYGAND, *Foch* (1947), a major study (in French) by the chief of the general staff from August 1914 to April 1923, who as Foch's faithful friend, brings alive the personality of the Marshal from his birth to his death; and *Mémoires*, vol. 1, *Idéal vécu* (1953), an excellent account of Foch's wartime activities, particularly those of 1918; and ANDRE LAFFARGUE, *Foch et la bataille de 1918* (1967), presently the most complete work on Foch's conduct of operations in 1918, written by a participant in the battles of 1918, who was in personal correspondence with the Marshal. A fine study in English is that of B.H. LIDDELL HART —*Foch: The Man of Orleans* (1931).

(C.A.La.)

Fokine, Michel

No other single artist had as much influence over classical ballet repertoire in the 20th century as Michel Fokine. His fame rests in large part on his manifesto of 1914, setting out his choreographic principles, and the great variety of choreographic styles that he either developed or initiated. He was the pioneer of the one-act ballet and introduced many of its forms: dance drama (*Petrushka*); pure dance (*Les Sylphides*); lyrical pas de deux (*Le Spectre de la rose*); ballet-divertissement (*Carnaval*); expressive solo (*The Dying Swan*); and ensemble (the *Polovtsian Dances from Prince Igor*).

Mikhail Mikhaylovich Fokine was born of a prosperous middle class family in St. Petersburg (Leningrad), Russia, on April 26, 1880. In 1889 he entered the Imperial Ballet School at the Mariinsky Theatre, where he distinguished himself for the breadth of his interests and studies. Fokine was not only talented as a dancer but also as a student of music and painting. He had a fresh and inquiring attitude toward everything connected with the ballet and began quite early to plan choreography, to seek appropriate music in the school library, and to sketch designs. His development as a dancer—he made his debut with the Imperial Russian Ballet on his 18th birthday—was paralleled by his development as a choreographer and designer.

In 1904 he wrote the scenario for his first ballet, which was based on the ancient Greco-Roman legend of Daphnis and Chloe. He sent it to the director of the Imperial Theatre with a note about reforms he wanted to see adopted by choreographers and producers. His crusade for artistic unity in ballet had already begun, but at this stage it made little impact. He was not encouraged to produce *Daphnis et Chloé* (he created it later, in 1912, for the Diaghilev ballet).

All the same, although at St. Petersburg he had no power to implement his beliefs, he began to work as a choreographer. His first ballet, created 1905 for performance by his pupils, was *Acis et Galatée*, based on an ancient Sicilian legend. Fokine's enthusiasm for antiquity owed nothing in origin to the "free dance" ideas of the American dancer Isadora Duncan, although her appearance in Russia in 1905 greatly consolidated his own views. In 1905 he also composed the brief solo *The Dying Swan* for the Russian ballerina Anna Pavlova. He continued to create ballets and three of his Mariinsky works were included in revised versions in the momentous season of the Ballets Russes that the impresario Sergey Diaghilev arranged in Paris in 1909: *Le Pavillon d'Armide*, *Une Nuit d'Égypte* (*Cléopâtre*) and *Chopiniana* (*Les Sylphides*).

Association with Diaghilev's Ballets Russes

Fokine was an integral part of the Ballets Russes's Paris triumph. Diaghilev's genius for bringing artists together in successful collaboration made Fokine, as his chief choreographer, the link between the dancers Tamara Karsavina, Vaslav Nijinsky, and Adolph Bolm; the designers Alexandre Benois and Léon Bakst; and the composer Igor Stravinsky, in such superbly unified creations as *L'Oiseau de feu* (1910; *The Firebird*) and *Petrushka*.

Fokine's relationship with the Diaghilev ballet deteriorated when Diaghilev launched Nijinsky as choreographer; but he remained with the company until 1914, when he returned to Russia. Also in that year, he set down his manifesto on ballet in a letter to *The Times* (London), advocating the creation in each ballet of a new form of movement corresponding to the subject, period, and character of the music; that dancing and mime have no meaning unless they express dramatic action; that conventional

Fokine as Perseus in *Medusa*.
By courtesy of the Dance Collection, the New York Public Library at Lincoln Center, Astor, Lenox and Tilden Foundations

mime should be used only when the style of the ballet requires it; otherwise, meaning should be expressed by the movement of the whole body; that this expressiveness should extend from the individual to the group, to ensembles as much as to solos; and that there should be complete equality in the alliance of the component arts that make up a ballet—dance, music, and scenic and costume design.

Leaving Russia in 1918, Fokine made his home in New York from 1923. He worked with various companies in the U.S. and Europe, creating new ballets, such as *L'Épreuve d'amour* (1936) and *Don Juan* (1936). None of these later ballets, however, had the impact of his earlier work. He created his last ballet, a comedy, *Helen of Troy*, for the American Ballet Theatre. It was premiered at Mexico City on September 10, 1942, after he had died from pneumonia in New York City on August 22. His wife, the dancer Vera Fokina, who had performed in many of his ballets, survived him until 1958.

Appraisal

One of the few choreographers to come to a first rehearsal with very clear and complete ideas for a ballet, Fokine had great facility and speed in choreographic invention, intense musicality, and the ability to memorize an orchestral score. He was by no means equable at work. Tamara Karsavina wrote in her autobiography *Theatre Street* that "he was extremely irritable and had no control of his temper," but she emphasized that dancers became devoted to him.

The vocabulary of classical ballet has been enormously extended since Fokine's day, and subsequent audiences sometimes feel that his choreography is dated. Those of his ballets remaining in production have inevitably suffered distortion. He himself was conscious that this would happen. "The longer a ballet exists in the repertoire," he wrote in his *Memoirs*, "the further it departs from its original version. . . . After my death the public, watching my ballets, will think 'What nonsense Fokine staged!' "

BIBLIOGRAPHY. *Memoirs of a Ballet Master*, ed. by ANATOLE CHUJOY, trans. by VITALE FOKINE (1961), is a valuable but unfortunately heavily cut version of Fokine's own memoirs. CYRIL W. BEAUMONT, *Michel Fokine and His Ballets* (1935), is a thorough account to its publication date of the man and his work by an English ballet historian and critic.

(K.S.W.)

Folk Dance

Folk dance, like "folk" and "folklore," is a controversial term. Though it is most commonly applied to the gay, recreational dances of various nationalities, its precise meaning is the subject of much debate among scholars and has not been fully resolved.

NATURE AND FUNCTIONS

Attempts at definition. Folk dance should be the dance of the folk. Who are the folk? In dictionaries "folk" is synonymous with people. The term is defined succinctly in *Webster's New Collegiate Dictionary* (8th edition):

The great proportion of the members of a people that determines the group character and that tends to preserve its characteristic form of civilization and its customs, arts and crafts, legends, traditions, and superstitions from generation to generation.

The adjective "folk" relates folk products to the common people. In dictionaries there are many definitions of "folklore," including those of rites, dances, and music. Terms such as tradition, anonymity, and peasantry recur in these diverse explanations.

Scholars and dancers differ in what they admit under the label of "folk dance." One may see folk dance as the traditional dances of a country that evolve spontaneously from the everyday activities and experiences of its people. Another may define it as embracing only dances with magical and economic functions, or as comprising all nonprofessional dances.

The discussions dwell upon the confusion between such terms and concepts as "folk dance," "primitive dance," "ethnic dance," and "stage dance" and on the distinction between folk dance and modern recreational forms of ballroom dancing.

Remnants of primitive dance persist in Africa, Oceania, and South America, among peoples who have retained some degree of their aboriginal religion and ways of life. Such dance throws light on the origins of dance of the Western world. In its retention of its original functions, primitive dance is distinct from the dances of more sophisticated people, which may fluctuate between ritual and recreation.

The term "ethnic dance" seems flexible. Some authorities see no difference between the terms ethnic dance and folk dance. The eminent American dancer Ted Shawn, however, would have ethnic dance subsume folk dance as a subspecies. He considers pure, authentic and traditional racial, national, and folk dance to be "ethnic"; he calls the theatrical handling of them "ethnologic," and he refers to the free use of these sources of creative raw material as "ethnological." Although these distinctions are not hard and fast, they reflect the trend of much ethnic dance toward professionalization. In still another view, folk dance is the dance from which the art dance of a nation inevitably grows, both in technique and in spirit. This concept is particularly applicable to such nations and regions as Japan, India, and Andalusia, where art forms of the dance were a natural outgrowth of the traditional dances.

Purists are disturbed by a trend toward the deliberate "staging" of folk dances, and especially by their increasing professionalization: they might call the adaptations folkloric. Professional dance and secular folk dance have been distinguished as one might separate art from craft, even when the scenarios and choreography of modern dance and ballet adopt materials from folk dance or the larger field of folk culture. Most scholars, however, exclude from folk dance the dances of the commercial theatre, television, and film. Though they generally consider jazz dancing an American folk style, they would exclude formal choreographies in jazz style.

These selected points of view indicate the fluctuating boundaries of folk dance, especially in reference to its functions. Although patterns and movement styles are significant, the function and locale of folk dances have greatest weight in distinguishing them from primitive and theatrical manifestations. Frequently the dances of

Varieties of folk dance

rural peoples reveal their ritual origins on certain occasions, though they also serve recreational purposes. The origins may be very ancient. Generally, but not always, dances favoured in urban centres have secular purposes and may be of recent, perhaps consciously creative, origin. As in the case of folk song, the origin need not be anonymous, though usually it has been lost in the passage of time. Folk dances have grown out of creative inspiration, and they continue to sprout from the imaginations of individuals and groups, people of all classes who sense the traditions and the aspirations of their environment.

Functions. Many folk dances best reveal their ancient functions when performed in their native habitat. Outside this context, in a school gymnasium or on a stage, they lose their aura, but on the village green the British Morris dances and the Abbots Bromley Horn dance speak of renewed May Day vegetation and of Paleolithic elk worship. Again, some dances serve various functions. The Spanish Aragonese jota is best known as a rural entertainment for men and women, but it may enliven funerals or appear on American stages.

The above British examples reflect the transition from pagan to Christian religions and, in more recent times, the change from the attitudes of village and agriculture to those of town and industry and the consequent changes in social relations. As the English scholar Douglas Kennedy pointed out, when primitive religion weakens, some of the mystery and the magic departs from the dances that express it. The dancer becomes less a medicine maker than a performing artist as ritual changes imperceptibly into art. In short, man's social adjustment to the environment, for purposes of survival, created both the original dance rituals and their subsequent functional or formal changes. Vestigial animal dances echo ancient animistic rites. The Ainu tribes of northern Japan still mime bear and fox hunts, portraying the animals very realistically. In West Africa, an antelope hunt in dance has ritualistic overtones, while monkey mimes are for entertainment alone.

A far-reaching example of adjustment and change applies to the Balkans and to Central America. These far-removed parts of the world share ecological circumstances, notably a basically agricultural civilization. Geographically, both narrow into bottlenecks connecting two continents; both combine high and rocky mountain ranges with agricultural lowlands and uplands; both bulge into peninsulas seething with culture. Both have submerged their ancient religious customs to innovations, those of Catholicism and, in the Balkans, of Islām as well. Yet both have maintained their ancient native customs with such compromises as those to the events of the Christian calendar, Christian names, or Islāmic styles. Recently both areas have been receptive to the influx of 19th-century secular European dance forms and have transmuted these importations to suit the native styles.

Dance as ritual and entertainment

Combat and agricultural dances. In both areas three dance types show varying degrees of modernization. One type, which takes the form of combat, remains highly ritualistic, albeit with a mixture of pagan and Christian elements. A second, agricultural in function, involves more of the community than the combative type and fluctuates between celebrations of sowing and harvest and of social festivities. The third type, derived from central and western Europe, is completely secular and social.

Male combat dances of the Balkans echo ancient pre-Christian rites for initiation into brotherhoods, the heralding of spring and of animal fecundity, and healing. Fierce battles ensue at the seasonal rituals of the Macedonians, of the Slovenes, and of the Romanians. Animal maskers and buffoons enact resurrection dramas. Along the coasts of Croatia and Dalmatia the battling factions have, under Christian influence, been renamed Moors and Christians or Moors and Turks. These battle dances have relatives in other European countries, from Spain to Great Britain. They also have relatives in Central

America, where early Spanish missionaries introduced Moors and Christians to replace the earlier ritual combats of the Indian populations.

Rural celebrations of planting and of harvests feature communal round dances, such as the kolo of Yugoslavia, the *horo* of Bulgaria, the hora of Romania, and a variety of Greek chain dances. The celebrations include vestiges of ancient vegetation festivals, impersonations of fertility deities, and "rain magic." The same rounds, however, appeared also at weddings and other secular or semisecular gatherings. Such rounds survive in the mountains of Mexico as *mitotes*. Although they concluded most Aztec and Mayan ceremonies, they have become scarce since the Spanish Conquest. They are still performed to procure rain and an abundant harvest.

Secular forms. Rural and urban gatherings include the social square dances and couple dances for men and women. Within the last century the Bohemian polka, the Austrian waltz, the Polish mazurka, and the Hungarian czardas have appeared in the northern Balkans. In Central America similar social and courtship dances have become increasingly popular. Each region has a version of the dances known as *jarabe* or huapango. The *jarabe tapatío* of Jalisco, better known as the Mexican hat dance, combines steps from many European nations. All regional dances use polka or waltz steps and European music. With their lively and showy styles, these couple dances are suited to stage performances and occur as such.

In other parts of the world, folk dancers are shifting from a man-deity and man-nature purpose to a man-man or male-female attitude. This is noticeable not only in adaptations of former dances of supplication but also in dances miming agricultural and other occupations, as the Polish sowing of rye and oats, the Hungarian haymaking, the Swedish flax reaping, the clothes washing of Denmark, and the spinning mime of Spain. Some of these occupational dances derive from enactments by medieval guilds or from the mime in medieval branles. They survive as entertainment in adult couple dances and in children's games, often in settings remote from their origin.

In the course of centuries, changes in the beliefs and in the methods of producing the essentials of life have produced numerous adjustments such as the adaptation of the calendar from a basis in agricultural ecology to a basis in Christian festivals and the resultant shifts in the organization of dance groups.

Occasions for dancing. Notwithstanding the trend toward sociable and theatrical objectives, many folk dances celebrate original festivals. In Europe and Europeanized America, however, they show many adjustments to the Christian feasts. In the Balkans, Austria, and other countries the long series of dances for renewed vegetation and life now celebrate Epiphany (Twelfth Night), Carnival, Easter, Pentecost, Corpus Christi, and St. John's Day (June 24). As noted previously, the midwinter dances emphasize male combat and animal impersonations, whereas the springtime dances dwell on new vegetation, in southerly climates on first fruits. Two festivals are particularly spectacular—Carnival and Pentecost.

Carnival festivals of Europe and the Americas precede Lent, filling the three days before Ash Wednesday. In Austria they perpetuate many pagan dances, particularly in Innsbruck and Imst, with the masked and ghostly phantoms and witches and noisy processions with songs, bull-roarers, drums, and whips. In Spanish and Latin American villages the unruly characters enact a more orderly "combat of winter and summer," in the guise of the ancient Moors and Christians, with the obvious victory of summer. Devils and deaths (*diablos y muertes*) are also on the loose in the role of buffoons. Morality plays are relics of medieval ideology, with speeches in the local vernacular and decorous steppings of Sin, Death, the Devil, Pastorcitas (shepherdesses in white communion dress), and masked animals from the Garden of Eden or bears or tigers.

Urban carnivals bring out animal maskers, deaths, and

devils, without ritual connotations in, for instance, Munich. The famous carnivals of Rio de Janeiro and New Orleans draw huge crowds of tourists to observe the masking, competitive parades of floats, and street and ballroom dancing. In the Brazilian medley the street and ballroom dances show interesting contrasts: the samba in the streets is ecstatic, improvisatory, and disorderly, whereas the samba of the ballrooms is more sedate and has set steps. Such urban carnivals have lost sight of the original ritual purpose.

On the other hand the observances of Pentecost, the springtime feast that falls 50 days after the Christian Easter, fit the dances into a framework that meaningfully combines Christian and pre-Christian, New and Old Testament, forms. The Jewish Shavuot festival follows by the same period the Passover, which often coincides with Easter. The Pentecost, known also as Whitsunday, has since AD 200 commemorated the descent of the Holy Spirit on the Apostles, and the Shavuot, originally a feast of thanksgiving for first fruits, has been associated by rabbis with the giving of the Law at Sinai. Both express the joyous resurgence of animal and spiritual powers and of new vegetation.

In the southerly climates the festival may already celebrate the first fruits. Everywhere Jewish celebrants bring offerings of fruits and flowers to the temple, with chanting and prayers. In Haifa, Israel, white-clad youths and maidens dance and sing. In Yugoslavia and Slovenia girls dance for Pentecost, and the community winds in snakelike kolos. In England the community circles around a tree, then around the church, or it holds a maypole dance. In some villages, such as Bampton-on-the-Bush and those of the Cotswolds region, "Morris men" dressed in clean white caper and leap in a procession or in double files, waving white kerchiefs or green branches. The dancers may have the company of clowns, a Jack-in-the-Green clad in greenery. In some English villages and in British-inspired American locations, such dances take place on May Day rather than Pentecost.

Agricultural festivals, especially harvests, may adjust their dates not only to the local climate but to the particular year's weather. The Iroquois Indians of New York State and Ontario adjust their calendar to the ripening of the crops of berries, beans, and corn. They may hold their thanksgiving rounds for green corn between the third week of August and the middle of September. The square dances of the American farmers were held on the occasion of husking bees—before combines took over the work—whenever the corn was ready. Farmers continue their square dances, or "country dances," in barns or in grange halls at odd times or even weekly. Their urban imitators perpetuate these dances assiduously when square-dance and folk-dance societies, often mingling the traditional American dances with those of immigrant peoples, meet in national halls or centres, school or college gymnasiums, or other locations. The gatherings of these enthusiasts and analogous groups on both sides of the Atlantic are legion.

Certain secular or semisecular celebrations adhere to a definite date. Such political holidays as the French Independence Day (July 14) and the Mexican national holiday (May 5) and Independence Day (September 16) feature regional dances outdoors and at indoor balls. The Guelaguetza at Cerro Fortín, Oaxaca, formerly a ritual festival, now combines religious and regional dances for the general public on July 16. Such festivals attract vast numbers of dance teams, native visitors, and tourists.

FORMS AND TECHNIQUES

Organization of participants. Although attendance at such public fiestas is haphazard, the participants in many dance gatherings observe closely knit organization and definite rules for the individual's place in the community and in the communal dances. The men in European combat dances belong to a sworn brotherhood of ancient origin. The male and female members of a Mexican votive society, the Concheros, have an intertribal hierarchy paralleling that of the forces of the conquistador Cortés.

Margin labels:

Polka-and waltz-based forms

Festival dancing

Harvest dancing

headed by a *capitán general*. In second rank are the officials of each local group, first and second captains, sergeants, standard bearers, each with specific duties, followed by the common rank of *soldados* and, finally, such attendant characters as Cortés' interpreter-mistress Malinche, the devil, sorcerers, and mythological figures. At present they do not regulate their rituals according to the calendar, though their ancestors probably did.

Although such societies cut across family ties, other organizations are based on descent, especially among American Indians. Iroquois and Pueblo Indians group their clans into two moieties, or halves, of the entire social scheme, matriarchal and patriarchal respectively. In their ceremonies and social events the Iroquois stress the interaction of moieties, with the alternation of moieties in the dance file. However, the New Mexican Pueblos usually feature separate dances for the two moieties and even assign festivals of the two seasons to the summer and winter moieties.

Sex and age roles. These same tribal groups also observe strict regulations according to sex. Iroquois women manage the summer rites for agriculture; the men manage fall and winter ceremonies for animals and cures. Among the Iroquois as well as the Pueblo, men and women hold esoteric dances separately, or men occupy one-half of the dance line and women follow in the second half. In less sacred dances and always in social rounds men and women alternate. Observers report similar customs not only among the natives of the New World but also in the Old, as in Serbia and Great Britain. Men perform the traditional Morris and sword dances, but the sexes mingle in country dances, reels, and quadrilles. The solos in Scottish sword dances are traditionally male performances, but, as a nonauthentic deviation, girls may now execute the tricky steps of the dances.

The traditions of age grades are also becoming diluted. From Greece to New Mexico, almost universally, the older, experienced men and women are the leaders, while the children bring up the rear of dance lines as apprentices. Warrior societies of Great Plains tribes of the United States once observed strict gradations of dance rituals according to age. But these societies are all but extinct, and public war dances admit all ages of males, with females in the background. With the dissemination of folk dances into the schools, children are learning adult routines. However, in remote villages of Europe youngsters have their special dances, and adolescents may enter the adult circles modestly.

Individual and ensemble dances. Generally the individual is submerged in the larger society and must fit into the dance group harmoniously. Some peoples, the Pueblo Indians for example, uphold strict standards of restraint, and within the natural variations of greater or less energy, a member of a dance group should not show off. However, other peoples such as the Iroquois appreciate improvisatory clownery or virtuoso display by talented males. In the Balkans the male leader of a dance line may engage in acrobatics—crouches, leaps, or pivots —while the rest of the group adheres to the traditional steps. In the Basque provinces of Spain, in the Ukraine, and in Poland male experts have the opportunity to display high kicks or spectacular leaps. The improvisations of these privileged experts have often led to the introduction of permanent new elements into the dances.

Styles of movement. Function, sex, and age all have an effect on a dancer's style of movement. Other psychological factors of group and individual temperament and mood have, for untold centuries, determined the quality and the type of steps and gestures. The climate and topography may have had an effect on the development of regional styles.

National and regional style. According to Douglas Kennedy, the ideal of English folk dancers is to hold the body in a straight line from head to toes, creating a vertical equilibrium that makes the dancer light on his feet. This uplifted carriage allows him to reach out and form the contact essential for a unified dance ensemble. This ideal would apply to many folk dance types of

Europe, the United States, and Canada, and to some Asiatic round dances, but it does not fit the more dramatic dances of the British Isles nor myriad dances in other parts of the world. Even within England, Kennedy points out the frequently bent-up position and the power of male sword dancers.

In Spain the erect ease of Aragonese line dances contrasts with the swaybacked incisiveness of Andalusian flamenco dances. In Yugoslavia the eastern villages have acquired the vibrations of Turkish dancers, and gypsies use more undulating movements than the Serbs about them. In Asia such hill tribes as India's Todas circle with simple steps and an erect posture, whereas demon dancers of the Pariah caste stamp and leap, and the practitioners of the ancient *Nātya* style combine elaborate, symbolic hand gestures with body sways and stamps.

Although India's caste system has produced extreme contrasts, differences in occupation and social class have everywhere affected the spirit and quality of movement. During the late Middle Ages and Renaissance the courtiers who borrowed such rural dances as the branle and the bourrée watered down their rustic vigour. In 19th-century colonial California the descendants of upper class Spaniards performed the polkas, mazurkas, and waltzes with an elegance that contrasted with the rowdy renderings by the gold miners.

Variations by sex. In modern square dancing the difference between male and female styles is negligible, but in most folk dances the women move more gently than the men, with smaller steps, lower leaps, and less raising of the knees or feet. The women dancers have a more sinuous, alluring style in southern Spain; they spin gently in the Austrian and Bavarian *Schuhplattler* and the Caucasian *lezghinka*, while the men jump, clap, and shout. Among American Indian tribes the women have a more subdued style and often special, tiny steps except in couple dances that have been adapted from the mainstream of Western social dancing.

Ecological influences. The setting affects the movement style. Joan Lawson suggests differences due to the natural environment—a theory that will need more investigation. She maintains that in rich agricultural plains or river valleys, such as the Danubian Plains and parts of France, and Denmark, movements are accented downward as if the body were being drawn toward the soil. Dancers perform in large groups, using the same step, closely linked together by fingers, hands, elbows, or shoulders. By contrast, in mountainous areas there is a good deal of leaping and individual display, especially among the males.

Mimetic and abstract movements. Regional variations include preferences for mime or for abstract movements. India's folk dancers and, half a world away, those of Scandinavia favour mimetic gestures, respectively graceful and comic. Serbia's peasants are interested in purely decorative steps and Ireland's experts are fond of tricky solo steps or complex group patterns that are in no way imitative of outside phenomena. In general, the mime of folk dancers is stylized, having lost the realism of the primitive animal impersonators and of actors in folk dramas.

Opportunities for mimetic dancing are drastically reduced when the hands are required for other formal patterns of the dances. Most folk dancers use their hands and arms for contact in circles, lines, or couples; they wave kerchiefs, as along South America's Pacific coast; they swing soft balls in complex patterns, as in the *poi* dance of the New Zealand Maoris; the women swirl full skirts, as in Spain and Mexico; or everyone lets the arms hang loose or places hands on hips, thus emphasizing foot and ground patterns.

In India, dance-dramas based on the life of the god Kṛṣṇa (Krishna) are enacted in Manipur by young women who use simplified gestures descended from the large, complex system of hand gestures known as mudras. The basic gestural symbols derive from the wrist position, the position of the palm, and the poses of the fingers. Each gesture has its prescribed musical accompaniment. A trembling leaf, for example, is symbolized by the *alapal-lava*, a rotation of the wrist accompanied by a folding and unfolding of the fingers. In Hawaii, a few older women can execute hula gestures clearly descended from the mudras, but younger dancers have diluted the tradition by introducing purely decorative gesture.

In Scandinavian countries male and female imitators of occupations likewise stylize their harvest motions. The youths who portray rough-and-tumble fights, as in the Swedish oxen dance, duel good-naturedly, pull each other's hair, and pretend to box one another's ears. In this last gesture, as in the German *Watschenplattler*, the aggressor merely pretends to touch his opponent, who claps his hands to simulate the blow.

Slavic men and some other skilled performers use steps recalling former animal mime, as the goatlike caper or cabriole, the pawing horse-step or pas-de-cheval, the side-kicking, cowlike rue-de-vache, and the feline pas-de-chat leap. But folk dancers of many nationalities exploit the imageless mazurka or variants of the polka, waltz, and twostep, all in appropriate rhythms. The walking, running, sliding, skipping, or jumping movements are so universal in folk dance that they cannot, by themselves, be considered mimetic.

On the one hand, line dancers of a single region may develop intricate variations of a basic step. Lawson identifies 15 ways of performing the basic kolo step, a step-to-the-side and close. The variants include gliding, swinging of the free leg, crossing, jumping. On the other hand, a widely disseminated step may appear in many forms in different regions. The triple-time waltz is step-together-step in Austria, with pivots at specific times. As the Mexican *atole* step it is forward-back-forward; in the Venezuelan joropo every first beat is heavily accented. As a ballroom dance it reveals diverse patterns: as a propelling step in Spanish and New Mexican quadrilles, a light-footed waltz may balance from side to side, progress forward or backward, or go round and round.

The type of step depends also on the purpose of the dance, whether a solemn processional or an exhibition of skill in leaps or crouches; on the sex or age of the various participants; and on the type of ground plan.

Ground plans. Simple circling leaves the dancer's attention free for elaborate steps, whereas complex ground plans take the mind away from stepping and necessitate the simplest kind of progression by walking or running. Throughout the world the erstwhile ritual dances may involve a simple run, as in the Iroquois corn and bean dances and the serpentine stomp that spread from the ancient Aztecs to Indian agriculturalists of the U.S. Choreographies may combine complexities of step, of rhythm, and of ground plan, like the "game animal dances" along the Rio Grande, but as a rule they emphasize one or another factor.

The Balkan chain dances feature intricate steps and rhythms, but simple formation of closed or open circles. During closed rounds the men and women remain within the same spot as they inch along counterclockwise. Likewise, participants in French branles circle on location, usually clockwise—the typical direction of northwest Europe. In chain dances the circle is not closed. A leader guides the line, linked by hands or a prop, in meanders and spirals perhaps across open fields. On reversal a tail man will guide the meanders. Such serpentines, of ancient origin, are favourites in the Near East; throughout Europe, especially as the French farandole and the Catalan sardana; in North America, in both native and Europeanized dances; and in such parts of Asia as Manipur. They predominate among agricultural peoples, for they originated in chthonic symbolism.

A specialized form of meander is called the hey in England. Two lines of dancers weave past each other in opposite directions. In a circular formation this is known as the square dance "Paul Jones" or, if the participants are attached by ribbons to a central pole, as a maypole dance. Here the two opposing groups are or should be male and female. The most elaborate form akin to the hey is the *kolattam*, a stick dance of South India. In the *pinnal*

Serpentine and meander dance formations

kolattam the dancers weave in and out, at the same time striking short sticks in precise patterns. (The intricacies were diagrammed by Hildegard L. Spreen: see Bibliography.)

Dances in two parallel lines have a more limited distribution. As in the case of rounds, the performers may start shoulder-to-shoulder or aligned in the same direction. The lines may cross over or circulate in opposite directions, or pairs of dancers can cross directly or diagonally. Morris dancers use a large vocabulary of interlacings, which resemble those of the American "Virginia Reel"; respectively, the participants are men only and men-and-women. Multiple parallel lines of men and women are customary in Southeast Asia and the South Pacific; Cambodian girls display elegant poses; Balinese men carrying spears mass together in the *baris* dance; and while executing the warlike gestures of the *peruperu*, Maori men remain in one spot.

Linear dance formations

As noted previously, ritual principles often dictate that in more sacred dances the sexes be separated, whereas in more secular dances they usually alternate or are aligned face-to-face. In modern folk dances, couples circulate within circular formations, as in Moravian rounds and American square dances, or in the extremely elaborate Irish reels of eight couples. In ballroom dances couples generally ignore any geometric designs, and individuals ignore the rest of the group.

In the "possession rite" of Ghana's Akhan society, circle dances by devotees, frenzy dances, and circling by everyone alternate with prayers, chants, offerings, and speeches. A similar structure is evident in the possession dances of Brazil and Trinidad and of the Christian Holiness services in the U.S.

Couples and solos. In the course of history the general trend, during secularization, has been toward increasing complexity, from round or double file to quadrilles, and then from cohesion to a breakup into couples and solos. This disintegration is distinct from the individualism that may be present in primitive dances, for there the soloist had a mimetically compulsive, even priestly, function and was the focus of group activity. Concurrent with the elaboration of patterns, the symbolism has been disintegrating. The vegetation symbols of meanders and arches have been lost, but the designs remain. Face-to-face formations and couple arrangements retain meaning as courtship actions, and despite the loss of the modern folk dancer's relation to, or attempt to act upon, the physical environment, the social contacts between dancers remain.

The type of ground plan affects the contacts between not only the dancers but also the dancers and the spectators. Square dances offer the maximum possibilities of intermingling within a formation, but they exclude spectators. Chain dances lack the give-and-take, but they may wind about or through the spectators, who may enter at any time. Contact, whatever form it may take, is essential to folk dance.

Accompaniment to the dance. The evolutionary process in the relations between the dance and other arts is very similar to the development of the dance itself. From the nearly total integration of dance and life in primitive ritual to modern rock-and-roll, many factors—the passage of centuries, the change from animism to Christianity, the shift from hunting, agriculture, and handicraft to industrialization, the trend from country to city, from sanctuary to village green to stage—have exerted a profound influence on the totality of dance experience.

In the esoteric dance rituals of Australia, in the mythological dance enactments of India and Indonesia, in Nigeria and such of its distant New World derivatives as the vodun, dance is immersed in the larger drama of the rite. The symbolism of the movement patterns is locked into the symbolism of song texts, the traditional music, and the meaning of masks and costumes, not to speak of the setting in a sacred grove. Here and there the decorative invocations to animistic spirits have survived, mysteriously, in the masked animal ghosts of the Austrian Alps, in the "game animal dances" of New Mexico's Tewa Indians. Perhaps these vestiges are not really folk dances. Perhaps folk dances—that is, dances of the people—do not require the integration of all of the arts for gatherings or programs.

Music. In general, the musical accompaniment to folk dances has persevered fairly well. In village and urban hall the devotees use the tunes intended for particular routines, though these tunes may be played on modern instruments. Morris dancers usually preserve the traditional order of a suite—Laudnum Bunches, Bean Setting, Rigs o'Marlow, Shepherd's Hey, Constant Billy. In the execution of isolated kolos, ländler, or country dances, natives and imitators fit the steps to traditional tunes, to live music, piano, or recordings, which may feature old-time clarinets, tabours, drums, and even band arrangements or accordions.

The coordination of tempo and rhythm between dance and music is rarely problematic. It is easy to follow the slow and the fast tempo of a set like the Norwegian *gangar* and *springar*, or the acceleration of an Israeli hora. It is easy to follow the metres of the polka, of the waltz with its accent on the first beat, or of the mazurka with its accent on the second, although the melody may have independent rhythms. It takes more skill to follow some of the Bavarian tunes that shift their metres, and it takes an expert to follow the unusual metres of Greek and Serbian dances, especially when the phrases of the tunes overlap the phrases of steps.

Self-accompaniment. It takes practice also to provide self-accompaniment in rhythm or melody. Rarely do folk dancers provide their entire self-accompaniment, as do the Mexican *viejitos* who play small stringed jaranas, or Hawaiian hula dancers who chant and shake rattles. Frequently, the dancers add percussive effects to the accompaniment by special musicians. They stamp on the ground, on the floor, or on a resonant platform with bare feet, boots, or high-heeled shoes, sometimes in complex counter-rhythms. Hungarian men click spurs; Russians click the heels of their boots as they leap. Austrian and Bavarian *Schuhplattler* males swat various parts of the anatomy in set rhythms. Sword dancers click swords; stick dancers click sticks in Spain, Portugal, England, Mexico, Brazil, and India. Andalusians punctuate their incisive foot rhythms with crisp sounds of finger castanets; Greek males click spoons in their *zabakelos;* and American Indians sometimes shake rattles. In such secular dances as the Cuban rhumba or Argentinian *carnavalito,* accompanists use rattles. Sound makers may be attached to the costume, as the bell pads of Morris dancers or the ankle bells of India's nautch dancers. In many parts of the world exuberant dancers dispense with instruments and clap or shout at specified times or whenever the spirit moves them. They may also sing to various instruments or without instrumental accompaniment.

Song. Self-accompaniment by song is significant for several reasons. First, it is probably one of the most ancient forms of accompaniment because of the independence from any instruments. Second, it is aesthetically pleasing. Finally, the songs have texts of historical, sociological, or ecological importance. Such singing may be in unison, with women's voices an octave higher than the men's; it may employ harmonies characteristic of the region, with intervals of a third or a fourth, and it may involve antiphony between a leader and the dance group or two groups of dancers. Such antiphony occurs in widely separated parts of the world, frequently in connection with serpentine chain dances as in Manipur and in America's Southeastern woodlands. Frequently the responses use nonsense syllables, and they may involve gestural responses, as in the Cherokee "stomp dance" and its predecessor, the ancient Aztec serpent dance.

The song texts are varied. The most frequent topics are courtship, as in the "Llorona" of Mexico's Tehuantepec, or sheer joy, as in the German "Freut euch des Lebens." In the Faeroe Islands the topics are narratives from legends, which are mimed by the round dancers. Sometimes the topic refers to agriculture, as in the French Canadian children's round, "Avoine" ("good grain").

The previous remarks mentioned the sound-producing

items of costumes, as boots and bells. Visually effective items include kerchiefs and female full skirts, which permit numerous manipulations. Other visual effects are the designs of regional dress in the various countries, from the flouncy flamenco skirts to the white trousers of sword dancers. In the United States square dancers sometimes affect full skirts for women and plaid shirts for men.

CONTEMPORARY TRENDS

Two contrasting modern trends are the development of American jazz dance and a revival of interest in traditional folk dances of various nations.

Jazz dance. The many forms of jazz dance represent virtually the opposite end of the scale from primitive ritual, with only ballroom dancing at a further remove. Jazz dancing owes much of its inspiration to African sources, to various tap dances of the vaudeville and minstrel stage, and to one- and two-steps of early 20th-century ballroom dancing. Decade by decade fashions in ballroom and jazz dancing changed, as the paths diverged.

In an outburst of "danceomania" after World War I, the "shimmy" and "grizzly bear" involved couples in a tight clinch. But soon the leg-flinging Charleston and Lindy demanded solo or couple acrobatics, at their best in Harlem's Savoy Ballroom. In the "swing era," the 1930s, the Big Apple integrated solo and couple improvisations with a group circle. Within a form of refrain and variations, men and women in a circle executed grotesque steps and gestures, cries of "Praise Allah," and the like; then, on a leader's call, an individual or a couple improvised on boogie-woogie steps. The steps had such names as mooch, sand, duck-walk, camel-walk, Rochester, fish-tail, truckin', and Suzy Q. Despite some of the names, the steps were only vaguely mimetic, and not at all derived from the natural environment. They returned to deepest Africa in the insistent, flat-footed emphasis, the sway-back posture, the bent or overstretched leg, the full use of the entire body in motions at one moment barely perceptible, in the next daringly acrobatic.

This quality persevered into the 1950s, sometimes in orderly patterns of face-to-face lines, as "the stroll"; sometimes in ludicrous pantomime, as the "cowboy chicken" stylizing horseback riding, and "drivin' home," with its imitation of automobile driving.

Gradually the beat changed as rock-and-roll combos usurped television and radio. Couple contact loosened up during the craze of the "twist," about 1962, a craze that spread to all parts of the world including Africa. Then television brought two kinds of rock dancing: trained groups in stylized routines, and jam sessions with increasing isolation of the individual. Subsequently teenagers milled around, squirmed with masklike expressions, and bounced vertically, because crowding prohibited any horizontal formation.

These developments of America's unique folk dance and its worldwide contagion appeared to be on the last lap of dissociation between man and nature, even between person and person. The only possible evolutionary direction might be a return to group cohesion and geometric pattern, a turn back toward a dance more closely allied to nature.

Revivals. The other trend, the revived interest in national folk dances, is equally dissociated from ecology, unless a folk dance group has a leader with folkloric knowledge. Folk dancing inspires the weekly gatherings of groups in civic centers, colleges, and other centres, even the entire schedules of summer folk-dance camps. Congresses sponsored by the Folk Dance Federation of California produced a uniform repertoire for groups throughout North America. In addition, new immigrants introduced occasional new dances. Most of these groups dance for the sheer pleasure of dance, and more expert ensembles stage programs and enter contests, both in the New and Old World. But although such revivals and the consequent preservation of traditions were heartening and brought about good fellowship, healthful exercise, and, avowedly, international understanding, such danc-

Margin notes:

Percussive effects produced by dancers

Dances of the 1920s, '30s, and '40s

Rock dances

ing had no connection with the aboriginal purposes of folk dancing, which continued only in villages or on Indian reservations.

Role of costuming

The modern style of costuming was a far cry from the masks for spirit impersonators and the symbolic designs painted or woven on all costumes of the ritual dances. Such paraphernalia survived in some dances that straddle ritualism and folk dance, as the animal and corn dances of the Pueblo Indians. But the trend was increasingly toward contemporary dress. Even the Iroquois ritualists usually wore ordinary clothes. Members of folk dance clubs rarely wore traditional costumes at their informal gatherings, although these clothes were customary for staged programs. And the jazz dancers wore the current dress, formerly full skirts, later tight, short skirts for girls and Levi's for boys.

As a contrasting trend, professional folkloric troupes exaggerated costume effects, doubled the volume of skirts, added spangles, and increased the instrumental volume and the tempo. Frequently the directors composed scenarios, as in the reconstructions of Aztec rituals by the Ballet Folklórico de México. Their spectacles had a great audience appeal, compensating in part for the nonkinetic and the prosaic in modern folk dancing.

Continuity and change. The folk arts are by and large expressive of traditions deeply rooted in the life styles and in the social organizations of peoples and cultures throughout the world. But as those styles and organizations change over time, in response to environmental, economic, technological, and other factors, so do the concomitant artistic expressions evolve in terms of function, form, and mode of existence. But change has been brought about, too, by the creativity of individuals and of cohesive groups.

Influence on other forms of the dance

Professional dancers found folk materials a rich source of inspiration that they used in several ways. Authentic dances were intensified for the stage by such companies as the Philippine Bayanihan troupe and the Ceylon National Dancers. The sophisticated dance-dramas of India's Uday Shankar, who performed widely in the West, often contained folk dances. His work with the Russian ballerina Anna Pavlova in *Radha and Krishna* showed, too, the rich potentialities for East-West collaboration. A folk atmosphere can be evoked without using folk materials, notable in *La Malinche* by José Limón. Finally, seemingly incompatible styles were fused: Mary Wigman was among the first to blend the rather stark idiom of modern dance with the ornate and exotic styles of the Orient.

Although the origins of many traditional dances are lost in a nebulous past, the observed emergence of new forms may give clues to the age-old processes of change. Inspired individuals may have molded the patterns of the ancient round-dance figures much as numerous leaders of dance in the 20th century have invented variations on the steps or devised steps and patterns to fit new rhythms, passing on their innovations by teaching or imitation. Again, creators have developed entire new dance structures from traditional materials, as the choreographers of modern Israeli dances have done most skillfully.

Another inevitable process is that of crystallization. For various reasons—sanctity, nostalgia, or whatever—groups tend to maintain routines through time. But not forever. If a dance does not die of old age, of having totally outworn its function and of having a form or spirit out of tune with a new age, it will continue to gain new life from improvised variations on basic steps or ground plans or from conscious elaborations of its forms by professional directors of ethnic dance groups and programs. Such kinds of creativity, individual and group, contribute to that constant cycle of orderly change within traditional parameters which accounts for the rich variety of the dances of the people.

BIBLIOGRAPHY. V. ALFORD and R. GALLOP, *The Traditional Dance* (1935), authoritative, popular account of Europe's ancient ritual dances; C.M. BARBEAU (comp.), *Roundelays: Folk Dances and Games Collected in Canada and New Zealand* (1958), children's mimed rounds from French Canada, with descriptions, music, and bilingual texts; E. BURCHENAL, *Folk-Dances from Old Homelands* (1922), descriptions of European folk dances, for use in schools; N. CHILKOVSKY, *American Bandstand Dances in Labanotation* (1959), notations of jazz dances, for reconstruction by experts in the Laban system of notation; L.K. CZARNOWSKI, *Dances of Early California Days* (1950), splendid historical account, with descriptions and music, for use in schools; A.S. DUGGAN et al., *The Folk Dance Library*, 5 vol. (1948), descriptions of dances from European and North American nations, with diagrams, music, and historical background, for school use; D.N. KENNEDY, *England's Dances* (1949), survey and interpretation of British ritual and folk dances; G.P. KURATH, *Iroquois Music and Dance*, U.S. Bureau of American Ethnology Bull. 187 (1964), and *Music and Dance of the Tewa Pueblos* (1970), analysis of dances and music, with many notation scores, interpretations, and background notes, not for reconstruction; LA MERI, *Spanish Dancing* (1948), skilled presentation of Spanish folk dances, with regional distinctions and some analysis of movement routines; J. LAWSON, *European Folk Dance* (1953), analysis of regional European steps and rhythms, with examples, useful facts, and questionable hypotheses; L. LEKIS, *Folk Dances of Latin America* (1958), exhaustive, annotated bibliography, with reliable comments on meanings and forms; M. MAYO, *American Square Dance*, rev. ed. (1948), a practical book for folk dance groups, with careful instructions and some music; C.J. SHARP (ed.), *The Country Dance Book*, 6 pt. (1909–22), exhaustive treatise on British folk dances by a scholarly pioneer, with diagrams and music; H.L. SPREEN, *Folk-Dances of South India* (1945), unusual, exotic material for schools, with movement descriptions, music, and bilingual texts; MARIA LEACH (ed.), *Dictionary of Folklore, Mythology and Legend*, vol. 1 (1949), definitions and scholarly interpretations.

(G.P.K.)

Folk Literature

Folk literature is the lore chiefly of unlettered peoples transmitted by word of mouth. It consists, as does written literature, of both prose and verse narratives, poems and songs, myths, dramas, rituals, proverbs, riddles, and the like. Nearly all known peoples, now or in the past, have produced it.

Until about 4000 BC all literature was folk literature, but beginning in the years between 4000 and 3000 BC writing developed both in Egypt and in the Mesopotamian civilization at Sumer. From that time on there are records not only of practical matters such as law and business but increasingly of written literature. As the area in which the habitual use of writing extended over Asia, North Africa, and the Mediterranean lands and eventually over much of the whole world, a rapid growth in the composition of written literature occurred, so that in certain parts of the world, literature in writing has to a large extent become the normal form of expression for storytellers and poets.

Nevertheless, during all the centuries in which the world has learned to use writing, there has existed, side by side with the growing written record, a large and important activity carried on by those actually unlettered, and those not much used to reading and writing. And when the earth as a whole is considered, and all those people included to whom the use of writing has not yet come, even now the majority of men and women on the earth are still using folk literature, since it is the only kind they know.

ORIGINS AND DEVELOPMENT

Of the origins of folk literature, as of the origins of human language, there is no way of knowing. None of the literature available today is primitive in any sense, and only the present-day results can be observed of practices extending over many thousands of years. Speculations therefore can only concern such human needs as may give rise to oral literature, not to its ultimate origin.

Nor can any evolution in folk literature or any overall developments be spoken of explicitly. Each group of people, no matter how small or large, has handled its folk literature in its own way. Depending as it does upon the transmission from person to person and being subject to the skill or the lack of skill of those who pass it on and to the many influences, physical or social, that consciously or unconsciously affect a tradition, what may be observed is not evolution but only continual change. An item of folk literature sometimes shows relative stability and sometimes undergoes drastic transformations. If these changes are looked at from a modern man's point of view, judgments can be made as to whether they are on the whole favourable or unfavourable. But it must be remembered that the folk listening to or participating in its oral literature may have completely different standards from those of their interpreters.

Nevertheless, two directions in this continually changing human movement may be observed. Occasionally a talented singer or taleteller, or perhaps a group of them, may develop techniques that result in an improvement over the course of time from any point of view and in the actual development of a new literary form. On the other hand, many items of folk literature, because of historic movements or overwhelming foreign influences or the mere lack of skillful practitioners of the tradition, become less and less important, and occasionally die out from the oral repertory. The details of such changes have been of great interest to all students of folk literature.

Early development

The beginnings of written literature in Sumer and Egypt 5,000 or 6,000 years ago took place in a world that knew only folk literature. During the millennia since then written literature has been surrounded and sometimes all but overwhelmed by the humbler activity of the unlettered. The emergence of the author and his carefully preserved manuscript came about slowly and uncertainly, and only in a few places initially—the literary authorship that flourished in the Athens of Pericles or the Jerusalem of the Old Testament represented only a very small part of the world of their time. Nearly everywhere else the oral storyteller or epic singer was dominant, and all of what is called literary expression was carried in the memory of the folk, and especially of gifted narrators.

All societies have produced some men and women of great natural endowments—shamans, priests, rulers, and warriors—and from these has come the greatest stimulus everywhere toward producing and listening to myths, tales, and songs. To these the common man has listened to such effect that sometimes he himself has become a bard. And kings and councillors, still without benefit of writing, have sat enthralled as he entertained them at their banquets.

This folk literature has affected the later written word profoundly. The Homeric poems, undoubtedly oral in origin and retaining many of the usual characteristics of folk literature, such as long repetitions and formulistic expressions, have come so far in their development that they move with ease within a uniform and difficult poetic form, have constructed elaborate and fairly consistent plots and successfully carried them through, and have preserved in definitive form a conception of the Olympic pantheon with its gods and heroes, which became a part of ancient Greek thinking.

Not everywhere has the oral literature impinged so directly on the written as in Homer, which almost presents a transition from the preliterate to the literate world. But many folktales have found their place in literature, from the "Cupid and Psyche" of Apuleius down to the present. The medieval romances, especially the Breton lays, drew freely on these folk sources, sometimes directly. It is often hard to decide whether a tale has been learned from the folk or whether a literary story has gone the other way and, having been heard from priest or teacher or doctor, has entered oral tradition and has been treated like any other folktale or folk song. The unlettered make no distinctions as to origins.

Influence on modern literature

As the European Middle Ages lead into the Renaissance the influence of folk literature on the work of writers increases in importance, so that it is sometimes difficult to draw a sharp line of distinction between them. In literary forms such as the *fabliaux* there are many anecdotes that may have come ultimately from tales current among unlettered storytellers, but these have usually been reworked by writers, some of them belonging in the main stream of literature, like Boccaccio or Chaucer.

Only later, in the 16th and 17th centuries, in such works as those of Straparola and Giambattista Basile, did writers go directly to folk literature itself for much of their material.

Since classical times composers of written literature have borrowed tales and motifs from oral narratives, and their folk origin has been forgotten. Examples abound in Homer and *Beowulf*. In their literary form these stories have often lived on side by side with tellings and retellings by oral storytellers. Modern examples of traditions so used are found in Ibsen's *Peer Gynt* and Gerhart Hauptmann's *The Sunken Bell*. Particularly frequent in all literature are proverbs, many of them certainly of folk origin.

In Finland a good example of the direct use of folk literature in the construction of a literary epic is seen in the *Kalevala*, composed by Elias Lönnrot in the 1830s, primarily by fusing epic songs that he had recorded from Finnish singers. The *Kalevala* itself is a national literary monument, but the songs Lönnrot heard are a part of folk literature.

Writers and songmakers have always used themes taken from oral legends and folk songs and in their turn have affected the traditions themselves. In recent years the cinema has presented old folktales to an appreciative public, and interest in folk songs especially has been stimulated by the radio and television. Inevitably this oral literature has become less truly oral, and much pseudofolk literature has been presented to the public, habituated as it is to the usual literary conventions.

Within urbanized Western culture it is clear that folk literature has been gradually displaced by books and newspapers, radio, and television. Persons interested in hearing authentic oral tales, traditions, or songs must make special efforts to discover them. There still exist isolated groups that carry on such traditions—old people, recent immigrant enclaves in cities, and other minority populations, rural or urban. Children are also important for the carrying on of certain kinds of oral traditions such as singing games, riddles, and dance songs. These go on from generation to generation and are added to continually, always within an oral tradition.

During the past few generations folk festivals have flourished. These have become almost worldwide and of the greatest variety. They are likely to revive older dances or bring in new ones from other countries, but they also have some singing and occasionally taletelling. Usually a real attempt is made to keep them within the authentic local tradition, and they have been a stimulus to the preservation of a disappearing phase of modern life.

If folk literature is actually dying out, the process is very slow. It is now, as it has always been, the normal literary expression for the unlettered of all continents.

CHARACTERISTICS OF FOLK LITERATURE

The most obvious characteristic of folk literature is the fact that it is oral. In spite of certain borderline cases it normally stands in direct contrast with written literature. The latter exists in manuscripts and books and may be preserved exactly as the author or authors left it, even though this may have happened centuries or even millennia ago. Through these manuscripts and books the thoughts and emotions and observations and even the fine nuances of style can be experienced without regard to time or distance. With oral literature this is not possible. It is concerned only with speaking and singing or listening, and this depends upon the existence of living people to carry on a tradition. If any item of folk literature ceases to exist within the memory of man it is completely lost.

Effects of oral transmission

The oral speaker or singer is carrying on a tradition that he has learned from other speakers and he delivers it to a living audience. It may well be that his listeners have heard this material many times before and that it has a vigorous life in the community, and they will see to it that he does not depart too far from the tradition as they know it. If acceptable to his listeners, the story or song or proverb or riddle will be repeated over and over again as long as it appeals to men and women, even through the ages and over long stretches of land.

In some cultures nearly everyone can carry on these traditions, but some men and women are much more skillful than others and are listened to with greater pleasure. Whatever the nature of these tradition bearers, the continued existence of an item of oral literature depends upon memory. As it is passed on from one person to another it suffers changes from forgetting or from conscious additions or substitutions. These may improve a tale or song or damage it through the bungling of unskillful singers or tellers, but in any case the item changes continually.

The more skillful tradition bearers take pride in the exactness with which they transmit a tale or song just as they have heard it many years before, but they only deceive themselves, for every performance differs from every other one. The whole material is fluid and refuses to be stabilized in a definite form. If really skillful, the teller is likely to see places where he can make great improvements and he may well begin a new tradition that will live as long as it appeals to other tellers. It thus happens that in nearly all cultures certain people specialize in remembering and repeating what they have heard. There are semiprofessional storytellers around whom large groups of people assemble in bazaars or before cottage fires or in leisure hours after labour. Some of these storytellers have prodigious memories and with only slight variations from time to time may carry on to a new generation hundreds of tales and traditions that they heard long ago.

Forms and functions   Certain bards and minstrels and songmakers develop special techniques of singing or of telling epic or heroic tales to the accompaniment of a harp or other musical instrument. In the course of time in various places special poetic forms have been perfected and passed on from bard to bard. Such must have been the way in which the remarkably skillful heroic meters of the Greek epics were developed. And so, whether before the princely or kingly audience that we learn about in the *Odyssey* or in *Beowulf* or the more humble groups of modern listeners in eastern Europe, a heroic tradition gradually rises out of the oral stream of narrative and may eventually, after suffering many and strange changes, cease to be oral literature at all and live on in manuscripts or books.

Another special kind of craftsman is found in many parts of the world. He often performs the offices of a priest or religious leader. It is through him and those he has trained that elaborate religious rituals are carried on through the generations. Frequently these rituals must be remembered word for word and are not believed to be effective unless they are correctly preserved. The ideal of such priestly transmitters of oral tradition is complete faithfulness to that which has been passed down to them.

Not least important of the many reasons for the existence and perpetuation of folk literature is the need for release from the boredom that comes on long sea voyages or in army camps or everywhere on long winter evenings. Some folk literature is primarily didactic and tries to convey to simple men the information they need to carry on their lives properly. Among some peoples the relation of man and the higher powers is of especial concern and gives rise to myths that try to clarify this relationship. Cooperative labour or marching is helped by rhythmic songs, and many aspects of social life give rise to various kinds of dance.

A great many of the special forms of literature now in manuscripts and books are paralleled in traditional oral literature, where history, drama, law, sermons, and exhortations of all kinds are found, as well as analogues of novels, stories, and lyric poems.

Relation to folklore and mythology   Folk literature is but a part of what is generally known as folklore: customs and beliefs, ritualistic behaviour, dances, folk music, and other nonliterary manifestations. These are often considered a part of the larger study of ethnology, but they are also the business of the folklorist.

Of special importance is the relation of all kinds of folk literature to mythology. The stories of Maui and his confreres in the Pacific and of gods and heroes of African or American Indian groups have behind them a long and perhaps complicated history. This is especially true of the highly developed mythologies of India, and the Greek, Irish, and Germanic pantheons. All are the results of an indefinitely long past, of growth and outside influences, of religious cults and practices, and of the glorification of heroes. But whatever the historical, psychological, or religious motivations, the mythologies are a part of folk literature and have been subject to continual changes at the hands of the taletellers, singers of stories, or priestly conductors of cults. Eventually singers or storytellers of philosophical tendencies have systematized their mythologies and have created with fine imagination the figures of Zeus and his Olympic family and his semidivine heroic descendants. Though the details of these changes are beyond the scope of this article, stories of the gods and heroes and of supernatural origins and changes on the earth have played an important role in all folk literature.

TECHNIQUES OF FOLK LITERATURE

Since the tales, legends, and epic and lyric songs discussed here are a part of the experience of a preliterate group or at least of the essentially unlettered, they differ in many ways from literary works addressed to a reading public. Long forgotten are the person or persons originally responsible for the tradition that has resulted in examples of folk literature. Only the tale or song remains to be repeated and often changed by subsequent storytellers, singers, or bards. In the course of its history it is listened to by generations of the unlettered and the unsophisticated, and its success and its very survival depend on how well it satisfies their emotional needs and intellectual interests.

Since in essence all folk literature is oral and subject to its survival in the minds of men, it is full of devices to aid memory. Perhaps most common of all is mere repetition. Especially in folktales and epics it is common to hear the same episode repeated with little or no verbal change. As the hero encounters his successive adversaries the description changes only enough to indicate the increasing terror of the enemy, always leading to a climax and usually to the hero's success. These long repeated passages often enable the teller of tales or the singer of an epic to extend his performance as much as he desires.

Technique of repetition in folk tales

Aside from repetition of entire episodes, folk literature of all kinds is filled with formulistic expressions. It may be the beginning or the ending of a folktale—the "once upon a time" or the "married and lived happily ever after" or sometimes quite meaningless expressions—or standard epithets attached to certain persons or places. These formulas are so characteristic of oral literature that an abundance of such commonplaces seems to be a guarantee of authentic oral origins even of a great epic.

These formulas are matters not only of words but of structure. The storyteller or singer has at his disposal a large variety of conventional motifs and episodes and may use them freely. How appropriately they are made a part of his composition depends on his skill, but his listeners are not likely to be very critical so long as he keeps them interested. Indeed it is remarkable that in spite of this apparent freedom of improvisation so many rather well-articulated plots have lived for centuries retaining all their essential features. It is this combination of a basic narrative type with a freedom of treatment within traditional limits that makes it possible to identify hundreds of versions of the same tale or song as they appear over long stretches of time and space.

Though much of narrative folk literature is frankly fictional and filled with unrealistic events, the successful storyteller or epic singer gives his story credibility by the use of realistic details. Often these are merely homely touches linking the never-never land of the tale or song to everyday life or emotions. For the unlettered listeners such realistic details may allow a stretching of the imagination to embrace a larger world. Heaven or hell it may be or kingly palaces where the peasant hero rules with a splendour only known to those who have never seen a court. Often these details are given only to ensure that willing suspension of disbelief characteristic of all fiction, but sometimes a realistic touch, even in the midst of weak motivation and violence, may give nobility to a mediocre tale or song.

Repetition, formulas both in words and in structure, realism enough to support the marvelous in tale or song, violent actions and simple strong emotions—these are generally found in all folk literature. The demands of the listeners are all-important. In some cultures this implies that actions should be well motivated so that listeners may identify themselves with certain characters. But in others, such as in many parts of India and in many preliterate cultures, motivation is often weak or entirely lacking.

For lyric songs, proverbs, riddles, and charms (and often legends), the relation of artist and audience is of little importance.

REGIONAL AND ETHNIC MANIFESTATIONS

In many particulars of form and substance there will be found great variations in the ways folk literature is manifested. The interests of people in one culture may differ profoundly from those of people in another. One group may enjoy singing folk songs, another listening to romantic folktales, and a neighbouring group may even be concerned only with legends and traditions. This difference is often geographical, so that the student of folk literature in the Pacific islands who may later investigate a central African tribe will find a completely different emphasis in the two areas. These differences may well depend upon the varieties of religious concepts held by the group or its natural environment, whether islands or jungle or cultivated farm lands, or its stability or mobility. These characteristics are likely to become especially deep seated in groups that have been settled in one place over a long period of history. Frequently they may correspond to national frontiers, but more often they are aspects of the general culture of an area and may well be quite independent of political or linguistic boundaries.

The Russian epic songs are found only in Russia, but the wonder story such as Cinderella or Snow White is a part of the folk literature of a good portion of the world. The Navaho Indians of the southwestern United States place great emphasis on their remarkable chants and lengthy folktales. Their neighbours throughout the Great Plains tell many well-constructed unified stories but confine their rituals largely to the dance. In Europe the Irish excel in storytelling, both of legends and fictional tales, so that even today it has been possible to record a prodigious number for their national archive. But in England and Wales the folktale is little cultivated, preference having been given to legends and ballads. As expected, there is a contrast between the abundance of oral saints' legends in Spain and Italy and their rarity in Scandinavia. Finland, meeting place of Eastern and Western tradition, shows an abundance of nearly every kind of folklore. From eastern Europe to Central Asia the folk epic flourishes.

Tales and origin legends have been collected in great numbers from various parts of Oceania, where there is a common mythological background extending over enormous distances. Except for probable early contact by way of Indonesia, these folktales seem to show little Eurasian influence. In many parts of South America the merging of Iberian, Indian, and Negro materials seems almost complete.

The folk literature of the North American Negroes is in a state of continual change, reflecting their history. Much certainly goes back to Africa, usually by way of the West Indies, and much was borrowed long ago. But the Negroes have themselves in a truly oral fashion developed songs and stories, and particular music styles. Of very special character is the folklore of modern Israel. Jews coming from various lands to the East and the West have brought together folk literature from all these countries. Assimilation of this is a long task, and since divergent language backgrounds are unimportant for

folktales, the problem is to absorb the great variety of forms.

Taken the world over, folk literature is found everywhere, though the emphasis differs from place to place.

MAJOR FORMS OF FOLK LITERATURE

Folk song. Some kind of singing is almost universal and it is probable that where there are no reports of it information is simply missing. Folk song implies the use of music, and the musical tradition varies greatly from one area to another. In some places the words of songs are of little importance and seem to be used primarily as support for the music. Frequently there are senseless monosyllables and much repetition to accompany the voice or the musical instrument. In much of the world drums and rattles, beating time by hands or feet or the stroking of a harp give a strong rhythmic effect to all folksinging. In others, flutelike wind instruments or bowed fiddles of one kind or another affect the nature of the folk-song texts. In many places these apparently meaningless folk songs are of great importance, serving as excitement to war or love or as a part of religious or secular ritual. Through them the group expresses its common emotions or lightens the burden of communal labour. In certain preliterate groups, and sometimes elsewhere, folk songs are used for magic effects, to defeat enemies, to attract lovers, to invoke the favour of the supernatural powers. Sometimes the magic effect of these songs is so greatly valued that actual ownership of songs is maintained and their use carefully guarded. They may come to the owner in a dream or as the result of fasting or other austerities.

Even when folk songs are not used for such practical purposes but only for the pleasure of singing or listening, the greater part of the world uses them for the expression of ideas or emotions held in common by the group. Only in societies used to the songs of composers or poets does purely personal expression enter into the folk song. This is not frequent, and songs of this type are hardly to be distinguished from some of the simple lyrics of poets such as Robert Burns. Folk songs, essentially expressions of commonly shared ideas or feelings, are often trivial but sometimes they may be profoundly moving.

The lyric folk song in one form or another is found almost everywhere, but this is not true of narrative singing. Unless the reporting of the activities of preliterate cultures has been very faulty, it would seem that the combination of song and story among these peoples has been rare, in spite of a wealth of prose narrative. On the other hand, in major Western and Asian civilizations the narrative song has been important for a long time and has been cultivated by the most skillful singers. In the course of time these songs of warfare, of adventure, or of domestic life have formed local cycles, such as the *byliny* of Russia or the heroic songs of Yugoslavia and Finland or the ballad tradition of western Europe and elsewhere. Each of these cycles has its own characteristics, with its distinctive metrical forms, and its formulas both of events and expression. Any reader of the Homeric poems will be aware of their essentially oral and musical nature, and all the early literary narratives of Sumer and the Near East suggest a long previous development of narrative singing.

Ballad. A special tradition of tales told in song has arisen in Europe since the Middle Ages and has been carried to wherever Europeans have settled. These ballads, in characteristic local metrical forms and frequently with archaic musical modes, are usually concerned with domestic or warlike conflict, with disasters by land or sea, with crime and punishment, with heroes and outlaws, and sometimes, though rarely, with humour. Despite a folk culture fast being overwhelmed by the modern world, these ballads are still being sung and enjoyed (see BALLAD).

Folk drama. Belonging only remotely to oral literature is folk drama. Dances, many of them elaborate, with masks portraying animal or human characters, and

Ethnic variations in relating folktales

Function of the folk song

Narrative singing

sometimes containing speeches or songs, are to be found in many parts of the preliterate world. Though the action and the dramatic imitation is always the most prominent part of such performances, these may be part of a ritual and involve speaking or chanting of sacred texts learned and passed on by word of mouth.

The ancient Greek mysteries, as well as secret societies even down to the present, have retained this method of transmitting dramatically their traditions and their teachings and commentary. Some dramatic rituals indeed were not secret but part of a public cult. Thus in ancient Greece the feast of Dionysus led eventually to classical Greek drama, and in the Middle Ages the dramatic celebrations of the Christian Church developed into the medieval folk dramas and at long last into the literary drama of the Renaissance and later.

The medieval mummers' plays and their modern survivals, the Passion plays, the Mexican re-enactment of historic scenes such as "The Moors and the Christians," and the modern pageants—all these are based on written texts, however crude, and are beyond the scope of this treatment (see RITUAL and DRAMATIC LITERATURE).

Fable. Fables, whether of the well-known Aesop cycle, with animals acting according to their real natures, or those from India, where animals simply act as men and women, are literary in origin. But they have had an important influence on folk literature. In addition to appearing in written collections, a number of these are told by storytellers in many parts of the world. Such fables as "The Ant and the Grasshopper," with appropriate morals, have been frequently recorded along with oral tales and have undoubtedly served as models for new animal stories. Sometimes these new tales have eventually received literary treatment, as in the medieval "Reynard the Fox," and then been carried back around the world by storytellers. In such narratives the borderline between folk literature and other literary expression is impossible to draw.

Folktale. The oral fictional tale, from whatever ultimate origin, is practically universal both in time and place. Certain peoples tell very simple stories and others tales of great complexity, but the basic pattern of tale-teller and his audience is found everywhere and as far back as can be learned. Differing from legend or tradition, which is usually believed, the oral fictional tale gives the storyteller absolute freedom as to credibility so long as he stays within the limits of local tabus and tells tales that please.

A folktale travels with great ease from one storyteller to another. Since a particular story is characterized by its basic pattern and by narrative motifs rather than by its verbal form, it passes language boundaries without difficulty. The spread of a folktale is determined rather by large culture areas, such as North American Indian, Eurasian, Central and South African, Oceanic, or South American. And with recent increasing human mobility many tales, especially of Eurasian origin, have disregarded even these culture boundaries and have gone with new settlers to other continents.

In many preliterate cultures folktales are hardly to be distinguished from myths, since, especially in tales of tricksters and heroes, they presuppose a background of belief about tribal origins and the relation of men and gods. Conscious fictions, however, enter even into such stories. Animals abound here whether in their natural form or anthropomorphized so that they seem sometimes men and sometimes beasts. Adventure stories, exaggerations, marvels of all kinds such as other world journeys, and narratives of marriage or sexual adventure, usually between human beings and animals, are common. Much rarer, contrary to the views of earlier students, are explanatory stories. Tales of this description are especially characteristic of Africa, Oceania, and the South American Indians.

In much of the world, especially Europe and Asia, the folktale deals with a greater variety of incidents than just described. In the course of time folktale scholars have given most attention to this area and have classified these

Variety of types

stories so that the vast collections of them in manuscripts or books can be referred to with exactness.

All readers of such collections as those of Grimm will easily recall examples of tales of speaking animals. These may be old Aesop fables or parts of the medieval Reynard epic, but most of them are based on some ancient oral tradition. Such animal stories are especially numerous in eastern Europe. But better known perhaps are the ordinary folktales that deal with human beings and their adventures. For these tales, usually laid in a highly imaginative time and place—a never-never land—and filled with unrealistic and often supernatural creatures, there exists no good English word, so that usually scholars use the German term *Märchen*. Here belong "The Dragon Slayer," "The Danced-Out Shoes," the "Swan-Maiden" tales, "Cupid and Psyche," "Snow White," "Cinderella," "Faithful John," "Hansel and Gretel," and their like. Here also belong certain stories with religious or romantic motivation and tales of robbers and thieves—"Peter at the Gate of Heaven," "The Clever Peasant Daughter," "Rhampsinitus."

A major division of this classification of tales deals with jests and anecdotes. Examples are the many stories of numskulls, of clever rascals, and tall tales filled with exaggerations or lies. Finally come formula tales like "The House that Jack Built."

Jests and anecdotes

Among jokes and anecdotes a number are risqué or actually obscene. The indexes of the classification have included only those occurring in the published regional surveys. These surveys, and the books and manuscripts on which they have been based, have been subject to severe editing in order to avoid social or even legal offense. Some of the older anthropologists thought to avoid the eyes of the nonscholar by writing such tales in Latin, but a newer generation is much less squeamish. Folk stories now appear in print covering the gamut of the erotic—tales of seduction, realistic descriptions of normal or abnormal sexual activity, and scatological stories of great indecency.

This index of tale types fits the region for which it was planned and is constantly being improved and expanded, but it was never designed to cover the world. The Eurasian types are usually recognizable in any part of the globe and for them this type index is valuable. But for use with stories on a worldwide basis something less formal is needed, a classification of the possible or likely narrative motifs, minute or extended, and wherever found. Such a motif index has in fact proved useful outside of the Eurasian area, wherever comparative studies are undertaken, for parallels or analogues in simple motifs occur even in far distant places, often presenting extremely puzzling problems.

By use of such indexes and from the labours of many scholars, much material for examination of the folktale is available. These studies have been pursued since the 18th century, though until about 1900 most of them were premature attempts to answer the general question of where folktales come from. Eventually it became clear that no satisfactory solution is available, but that every tale has its own history and can be studied only with laborious attention to detail.

In contrast to a literary story, with its standard text and author living in a definite time and place, the folktale is anonymous. Its originators have long been forgotten and it exists in many versions, all equally valid. Instead of being fixed like a literary document, it is in continual flux. But with hundreds of versions of a particular tale available for study it is possible to establish certain norms of plot structure and to point with some assurance to the varieties of subtypes that give clues to its life history. Such an analytical study of these hundreds of versions usually results in some hypothesis about the original form of the plot and the passage the tale has taken through time and space. In this way some 30 or 40 of the more complicated stories have been studied.

Folktale scholarship

These geographical and historical investigations depend on the fact that the plot of the tale is complex enough to admit of really analytical study. For simpler stories and anecdotes scholars have had to be content with less exact methods, usually resulting in nothing more than accounts of their distribution and the known facts of their history.

Most of the attention of students of folktales during the 20th century has been given to historical questions and to preparing the apparatus for studying them—collecting, with ever improved techniques, arranging and archiving materials from manuscripts or books, and indexing types and motifs, so as to make collections even in remote or difficult idioms available to the serious investigator. But the folktale also has given rise to studies that are not strictly historical.

The attempts during the 19th century to find hidden meanings in tales were generally based upon the theory that they were broken-down myths and had lost their original meanings through linguistic misunderstanding. The result was that this "original meaning" was always found to be some conflict between weather or seasonal phenomena (winter: summer; clouds: sunshine; etc.). This type of interprétation has now generally gone out of fashion and has given place sometimes to explanations based upon ancient rituals or to some variety of psychoanalytic treatment. Though both of these possible sources of folk literature merit examination, the resultant interpretations have usually been merely astonishing to those acquainted with the actual history of the tales studied.

A much more fruitful approach to an investigation of folktales has been the studies of the tellers of stories and their audiences. From these has come an appreciation of the way in which folk literature is carried on in a tradition. A great deal more may be expected from such investigations, usually based on an intimate knowledge of the living lore of a single people.

Structural studies, especially of the folktale, have been engaging the attention of more and more scholars. Though particular plots may occur over large parts of the world, the form and literary style of the narrative is likely to be traditional within certain historical or geographic limits. The direction and strategy of these studies of structure are still unclear, but progress is being made.

Legend and tradition. Generally folktales are considered both by tellers and listeners as purely fictional. The line, however, between belief and unbelief is vague and varies from culture to culture and even from person to person, and even in the most sophisticated societies legends of strange things from the past or present continue being told and are usually believed.

Credibility of the legends Stories about marvelous creatures are worldwide. Often these are merely mentioned or described and the belief in their existence is taken for granted. Frequently, however, there are circumstantial accounts of meetings with them, which result in adventures pleasant or distressing. With such creatures it is sometimes hard to tell whether we are dealing with a fictional story such as that of the dragon slayer of the typical European fairy tale or with a legend actually believed, such as that of St. George and the dragon. Though the folk in all parts of the world handle these stories with varying degrees of belief, there exists everywhere a remarkable resemblance among these supernatural creatures. The dragon, for example, in something of its characteristic serpent or crocodile form, is of great importance in China as well as in Europe and is represented in both places as a guardian of great treasure. Hardly less well known is the unicorn, and various combinations of man and beast such as the centaur and the minotaur, or the combinations of man and dog, have been a part of the legends of the Old World and occasionally of the New. Giant birds carrying men off in the claws, the phoenix reviving from its own ashes, flying horses carrying men through the air, sirens, mermaids and mermen, and unbelievable creatures resembling these appear in traditions all over the world. There are treasure animals of all kinds, not only the goose that lays the golden egg but the cow that furnishes treasure from its ear. The horse may warn the hero of danger or may determine which of two roads he should

take. Important building sites are said to have been determined by the actions of a wise animal. Speaking animals, of course, figure prominently in all folk literature and even in such literary forms as the fable. Animals may speak to each other on Christmas Eve, or they may have governments and elect kings or celebrate weddings. These are only a few of the traditions current with a large part of mankind.

The relation between the animal and the human is very close in all folk literature. In the preliterate cultures of the American Indians, the Pacific Islanders, or the Central Africans, the culture heroes who are responsible for the good and the bad in the life of the tribe may upon one occasion appear as animals and upon another as men. Such was true of the ancient gods of Egypt or Greece. The question whether Coyote of the American Indian tribes is an animal or a man apparently makes no difference to those who tell stories about him.

Super-natural creatures in legends Aside from these semidivine creatures, now animal or bird or man as they wish, stories are found everywhere about supernatural and ill-defined creatures much more difficult to visualize. Fairies or their counterparts appear in the legends of a good part of the world. It is hard to define them, for in one place they will appear in full human size, in another as little creatures inhabiting mounds or caves or living under the roots of trees. In some countries they are benevolent creatures, helpful to men and women. They reward human services but punish misdeeds. They marry or consort with human beings. In some traditions they are malevolent creatures, and meetings with them always bring disaster or bad luck. Almost every country has produced its own variety of helpful and harmful creatures. Stories of the activity of witches and devils, or water spirits and the supernatural guardians of mountains or trees vary in details from land to land, but many of the incidents related about them are easily transferred from one to another. Stories of visits to quite other supernatural realms, fairyland, for example, may be told in all their details in Russia or Greece. Giants are usually considered to be ogres of one kind or another but they may also be considered the most stupid of all beings and may be the subjects of hundreds of numskull anecdotes. Underground creatures like the dwarfs in "Snow White" are usually helpful and kindly, but other underground creatures bring only disaster.

The widespread belief in the return of the dead has resulted in many stories of encounters with ghosts or of actual resurrection. These stories differ greatly in various parts of the world and are much influenced by the current religious ideas. It is likely that in the whole world of traditional literature the belief in ghosts has survived longest.

Historicity of some legends Traditions of historic characters have a tendency to repeat themselves from land to land and although they are told as facts may form as definite patterns as any fictional folktale. Such stories as Joseph and Potiphar's wife or the exposure and ultimate return of the hero appear in many places. The expected return of King Arthur from Avalon or of Barbarossa from his cavern are only two examples of a widespread motif of this kind.

It is difficult and perhaps impossible to distinguish the explanatory legend from the myth. Tales explaining the origins of customs or of the shape or nature of various animals and plants, of such distant objects as the stars, or even of the world itself often ascribe such origins to the action of some ancient animal or to some magic transformation. These are often connected with stories of the gods or demigods and may even be a part of the religious beliefs of those who tell them.

Generally, legends and traditions of this kind are simple in their form and contain only a single motif or at most two or three. The problem of proper classification for the purpose of studying these has proved very difficult, for while the materials of these legends and traditions show many interesting parallels and resemblances, they vary greatly from place to place. The relation of these stories to actual history, to mythology, and to the fictional folktale is of much interest to students of folk literature.

Proverbs, riddles, and charms. Three of the shorter forms of folk literature—proverbs, riddles, and charms—are not confined to oral expression but have appeared in written literature for a very long time. The proverb that expresses in terse form a statement embodying observations about the nature of life or about wise or unwise conduct may be so much an oral tradition as to serve in some preliterate societies as a sanction for decisions and may even be employed as lawyers employ court precedents. In literature it dominates certain books of the Old Testament and is found even earlier in the writings from Sumer. There has been a continual give and take between oral and written proverbs so that the history of each item demands a special investigation.

Proverbs and riddles in preliterate societies

While the proverb makes a clear and distinct statement, the purpose of the riddle is usually to deceive the listener about its meaning. A description is given and then the answer is demanded as to what has been meant. Among examples in literature are the riddle of the sphinx in Sophocles and the Anglo-Saxon riddles, based on earlier Latin forms. In oral literature the riddle may be part of a contest of wits. But even if the answer is known, the listeners enjoy hearing them over and over. In our own culture the riddle is especially cultivated by children.

Charms, whether for producing magic effects or for divining the future, also exist in folk literature as well as in the well-known Anglo-Saxon written form. The study of these extends over all parts of the world and back to the earliest records.

Children's use of folk literature. As a part of their play activities children not only play old games but repeat counting-out rhymes and retain play-party songs that have long ceased to be a part of adult activity in Western culture. Although the knowledge of those matters is available to children in their books, in actual practice it is passed on by word of mouth or by imitation, and the tradition may spread from school to school over a continent with great rapidity (see CHILDREN'S LITERATURE).

STUDY AND COLLECTION

As abundant as folk literature is and has been everywhere and always, its investigation has been seriously undertaken only within the last two or three centuries. The principal difficulty has been the assembling of material on which to base such studies. Its very oral nature makes it impossible for one man to be acquainted at first hand with more than an extremely small part of this activity. It is only when some sort of written record has been made of the oral material that any general studies are possible.

For the still unlettered peoples, the reports of ethnologists and anthropologists, as a part of their general studies of the cultures of widely distributed groups, have often given good accounts of folk literature and have frequently furnished texts of material they heard. Though these reports are extremely uneven and often fragmentary, they do give a sampling of the literary expression of many and diverse parts of the earth.

When attention is shifted to the ancient world before the use of writing, scholars are almost entirely dependent on analogies from the unlettered groups just mentioned. It will never be known what tales were told or what songs were sung by the builders of the Egyptian Pyramids or the temples in Sumer, but it seems fair to assume that even then these peoples were not silent. Of course it must be remembered that they did eventually develop a written literature, so that the analogy with modern unlettered peoples may not be completely valid.

For folk literature since the development of writing, scholars are dependent on several things. There may be specific references in literary documents to the existence of particular tales or songs and often to their manner of production. The Old Testament is a good source for these, and both the *Odyssey* and *Beowulf* contain good pictures of the performances of folk minstrels and bards.

Many collections of folktales and legends, of lyric and heroic songs, and of riddles and proverbs have been recovered directly from popular tradition within the past three or four centuries. When the collection of this material began it was nearly always rewritten in the prevailing literary fashion. Excellent examples of such rewritten tales will be found in the collections of Giambattista Basile (1634–36), Charles Perrault (1697), and various German writers such as Johann Karl August Musäus and Clemens Brentano in the 18th and early 19th centuries. The Brothers Grimm with their *Kinder und Hausmärchen* (1812–15) has as their ideal the exact recording of tales as heard from oral tellers, though it is clear that many stories in their famous work are not folk literature at all. In the same way, collections of folk songs and ballads were severely edited well into the 19th century.

Partly as a result of the Romantic movement in literature and partly of the interest in primitivism and the common folk, the recording of all sorts of songs and oral tales since about 1800 has been phenomenal. More and more the attempt has grown to recover material as it actually exists. Many thousands of volumes are to be found in great libraries that give a good sampling of folk literature in all parts of the world. The last century has also seen the development of large regional or national archives, many of them containing hundreds of thousands of items available for study. All of these books and manuscripts have become increasingly valuable as the techniques of collecting have progressed from casual longhand notes and rewritings through various stages to mechanical recording on discs and tapes.

Preservation of folk material

With mechanical recording it has been possible to assemble properly attested folk literary material from all parts of the world. This improved collecting has proceeded at an impressive pace and makes possible comparative studies of all kinds, based on the oral record.

As for the folk literature of peoples predominantly unlettered, these greatly expanded bases for study have brought out not only the characteristics found everywhere but have pointed up the differences found from place to place. Generalizations formerly accepted have to be reviewed in the light of these differences. With increased collecting, for example, do the likenesses or unlikenesses of American Indian tales and legends become more manifest? Does folk literature in a certain part of the world follow culture areas or language boundaries or some other principle? Such problems can now be investigated with the assurance that modern collectors have made every effort to record the oral tradition as it actually exists.

Much the same may be said of the 20th-century folk literature that exists among literate people side by side with written works. The collecting has improved both in quantity and quality. And not only have libraries been receiving new books of folk literature collections from interested persons everywhere but these collectors are better trained and equipped. The greatest improvement, however, in the study of folk literature transcribed in writing has been the development of folklore archives, of which a large part are concerned with various kinds of oral literature. These are growing rapidly, are scattered over much of the world, and are becoming well indexed and accessible.

BIBLIOGRAPHY. The best general treatment of the borderline between folk literature and sophisticated literature is H.M. and N. CHADWICK, *The Growth of Literature*, 3 vol. (1932–40). S. THOMPSON, *The Folktale* (1946), gives an introduction and extensive bibliography for the field of oral narrative literature. For myths of all parts of the world, see *Mythology of all Races*, 13 vol. (1916–32), valuable information, though some of the bibliographies are out of date. *The Journal of Folktale Studies* (3/yr.), and *FF Communications* (irreg.), are of primary importance. They include articles in English, French, and German. *FF Communications* is undoubtedly the leading series for all aspects of folklore. A good recent series of folktale collections in English is "Folktales of the World" ed. by R.M. DORSON. Important also is the much larger series in German, "Märchen der Weltliteratur." For the folktales of the ancient world good introductions are W.M.F. PETRIE (ed.), *Egyptian Tales Translated from the Papyri*, 2 vol. (1899);

and s.n. KRAMER, *Sumerian Mythology: A Study of Spiritual and Literary Achievement in the 3d Millennium B.C.*, rev. ed. (1961). The standard Renaissance collection is *The Pentamerone of Giambattista Basile*, ed. and trans. from the Italian of BENEDETTO CROCE by N.M. PENZER, 2 vol. (1932). The commentaries on these tales are especially valuable. The new translation of Grimm's folktales, *German Folk Tales* by F.P. MAGOUN and A.H. KRAPPE (1960), is convenient for English readers. For folktales of the North American Indians, the American Negroes, and the peoples of Oceania and Israel, the following works are standard: W. MATTHEWS, *Navaho Legends* (1897); S. THOMPSON (ed.), *Tales of the North American Indians* (1929, reprinted 1966), an anthology with exhaustive comparative notes, valid until about 1926; M. JACOBS, *The Content and Style of an Oral Literature: Clackamas Chinook Myths and Tales* (1959), tales of a vanishing North Pacific tribe; W.A. LESSA, *Tales from Ulithi Atoll: A Comparative Study in Oceanic Folklore* (1961); K. LUOMALA, *Voices on the Wind: Polynesian Myths and Chants* (1955); R.M. DORSON, *American Negro Folktales* (1967); and D. NOY and D. BEN-AMOS (eds.), *Folktales of Israel* (1963). Types and classifications of folktales and legends are: A.A. AARNE, *The Types of the Folktale*, 2nd rev., trans. and enl. by S. THOMPSON (1961), a standard list of tales of old world provenance; S. THOMPSON, *Motif-Index of Folk Literature*, rev. ed., 6 vol. (1955–58); and R.T. CHRISTIANSEN, *The Migratory Legends* (1958), a classification of European legends. A good example of a survey of tales of a particular country is S. O'SUILLEABHAIN and R.T. CHRISTIANSEN, *Types of the Irish Folktale* (1963). A general introduction to folk song is G. HERZOG, "Song: Folksong, and the Music of Folksong," in *Funk and Wagnall's Standard Dictionary of Folklore*, vol. 2, pp. 1032–1050 (1949–50). A comprehensive introduction and listing of all the classical fables is in B.E. PERRY, *Babrius; and Phaedrus* (1965). The proverb, the riddle, and the charm are treated in A. TAYLOR, *The Proverb* (1962), *English Riddles from Oral Tradition* (1951), and W.R. BASCOM, *Ifa Divination: Communication Between Gods and Men in W. Africa* (1969). Important also is the work of L. DEGH, *Folktales and Society* (1969), a study of a Hungarian storyteller; A. DUNDES, *The Study of Folklore* (1965); V.A. PROPP, *Morphology of the Folktale* (1958); and T.A. SEBEOK, *Myth: A Symposium* (1965), a collection of theoretical treatments of mythology. An outstanding discussion of narrative folk song is A.B. LORD, *The Singer of Tales* (1960). A model historical and geographical study is W.E. ROBERTS, *The Tale of the Kind and the Unkind Girls* (1958).

(S.T.)

Folklore

No field of learning is perhaps more misunderstood than folklore. The public at large, and many academic persons as well, do not know that folklore is an intellectual subject with its own substantial, worldwide body of scholarship. Part of the confusion lies in the double use of the word folklore to signify both the content and the study of traditional materials. Further misunderstanding results from the varying senses of folklore in different countries. In much of South America and in some European nations, folklore in popular usage generally applies to public performances of song, dance, and festival, and in scholarly usage the term refers to the study of peasant culture. In the United States, the word folklore often conjures up an image of long-haired folksingers or grizzled old-timers spinning yarns of Paul Bunyan and Johnny Appleseed, who are largely contrived heroes. The German term *Folklorismus* and the English term *fakelore* have been coined to distinguish between genuine folk traditions and the synthetic revival or imitation of those traditions.

THREE APPROACHES TO FOLKLORE

Serious students of folklore by no means agree on the boundaries of their discipline but they tend to follow one of three prevailing perspectives.

Humanistic perspective. The humanistic folklorist sees the materials of folklore in large part as "oral literature" and the folk as artistic performers of tale or song. Accordingly, he emphasizes the creative role of the narrator or bard, seeks information on his biography and personality, closely observes his interaction with the audience, and analyzes his total repertoire much as a literary critic assesses the achievement of the novelist, poet, or

Emphasis on narrator

dramatist. Usually the exponents of this approach, among the older generation, have entered folklore from departments of modern language and literature or music or classics. A case in point is Albert Lord, professor of Slavic literature at Harvard University, whose folklore interests developed from a concern with the south Slavic oral epic, still sung by bards in Yugoslavia. After collecting and studying these epics, Lord came to the conclusion that each epic singer constructed his narrative song by improvising and elaborating around a stock of fixed images, epithets, and conventional expressions, which he alone kept firmly in mind. This "oral-formulaic" theory Lord then applied to the Homeric epics, which are now known only in their written forms but which he conjectured had been orally composed in the same manner as the contemporary Slavic epic songs. Since the appearance of Lord's work, *The Singer of Tales* (1960), other humanistic folklorists have applied his theory to various traditional texts, from Norwegian ballads to the Anglo-Saxon epic *Beowulf* to medieval romances. The interest in the human carrier of tradition, in his world-view and belief system, his cultural inheritance and acculturative experiences, distinguishes this species of folklorist.

Anthropological perspective. The anthropological folklorist examines the materials of folklore using the hypotheses of the social sciences. He looks for cultural norms and values and predictable laws of behaviour that form a consistent pattern in the nonliterate society he has closely observed. Folklore to him is an aesthetic product of this society, mirroring its values and offering a projective screen that illuminates its fantasies. Hence the folkloristic anthropologist frequently reports a one-to-one correlation between the value system and the tale repertoire of a given culture, whereas the humanistic folklorist promptly points out that the same tales are found in many parts of the globe and so can scarcely be said to reflect the ethos of a particular people, even when they have been strongly localized.

Emphasis on cultural norms and values

At different periods folklore and anthropology have enjoyed an intimate relation in England and America. The father of anthropology in England, E.B. Tylor (1832–1917), drew heavily upon the materials of folklore in his two great works, *Primitive Culture* (1871) and *Researches into the Early History of Mankind* (1865), which in turn contributed to the growth of a school of so-called anthropological folklorists. The leader of this school, Andrew Lang (1844–1912), a versatile man of letters, in many clever essays and books elaborated a theory of "survivals" based on Tylor's hypothesis that from the beliefs and customs held by peasants and contemporary savages the folklorist could reconstruct the ideas of prehistoric man. In the United States, Franz Boas (1858–1942), the father of American anthropology, influenced many doctoral students, later eminent in their own right, to pay attention to folklore in their fieldwork. Boas himself considered that tribal traditions preserved an ethnological record of older culture traits and should be consulted in lieu of written documents. His disciple and successor as editor of the *Journal of American Folklore*, Ruth Benedict (1887–1948), pointed out that the tribal mythology depicted violations of taboos, such as the hero-trickster sleeping with his mother-in-law, which would never be tolerated in real life. Another student of Boas, Melville J. Herskovits (1895–1963), broke with the Boasian concentration on North American tribes to explore African cultures but retained the same emphasis on folklore and inculcated this emphasis in his own students.

American folklore-minded anthropologists all experienced difficulty in employing the term folklore within a culture almost wholly oral and traditional and resorted to various substitutes. William Bascom, a student of Herskovits, suggested the term verbal art to denote the oral aesthetic traditions of tale, proverb, song, and riddle in the culture, leaving out the supernatural-belief system and the plastic arts, which a humanistic folklorist includes in his concept. Bascom also clarified the functional uses of folklore in nonliterate societies, in accord with the anthropologists' stress on the social mechanisms that enable a society to perform its business. His book, *Ifa Divination* (1969), demonstrates how Yoruba diviners have recourse to the tribal repertoire of traditional narratives in arriving at their analyses of individual problems. The beans they throw on the Ifa board fall in a series of complex patterns that the diviners key to folktales, whose contents are then applied to the particular situation in hand. English and American anthropologists of the 1960s have in the main moved away from the soft, foloric parts of culture to the hard, sociological data of kinship organization and political structures.

Emphasis on behaviour

Psychological-psychoanalytic perspective. The psychological-psychoanalytic folklorist views the materials of folklore neither aesthetically nor functionally but behaviouristically. Myths, dreams, jokes, and fairy tales express hidden layers of unconscious wishes and fears. Sigmund Freud drew extensively upon folk sources in such works as *The Interpretation of Dreams* (1899), *Jokes and Their Relation to the Unconscious* (1905), and *Totem and Taboo* (1913). In his view, and that of many writers on folklore influenced by him, folklore texts are to be interpreted symbolically in terms of sexual imagery and the Oedipus complex. In "Jack and the Beanstalk," the stalk is construed as a phallic symbol and Jack's chopping it down signifies a masturbation fantasy. "Little Red Riding Hood" tells a tale of a young virgin, identified by the red cap, a menstrual symbol, who wanders from the straight and narrow path, to be devoured (seduced) by the wolf in disguise of the grandmother, an Oedipal figure. In the modern college legend of "The Hook," a coed narrowly averts assault from an escaped lunatic, one of whose arms has been replaced with a metal hook; the psychological interpretation explains the hook as the phallus and the episode as the coed's fear of the sexual act. When C. G. Jung broke with his mentor Freud and substituted the symbolism of social unconsciousness for the symbolism of sexual drives, he still retained his deep interest in myths, dreams, and tales as psychoanalytic media, and the Jung Institute in Zürich continues to offer courses on the uses of folklore in psychology.

Such a work as *The Trickster*, edited by the American anthropologist Paul Radin, with commentaries by the mythologist Karl Kerényi and by Jung, offers within one volume three psychoanalytical interpretations of the Winnebago cycle of trickster tales. Kerényi, although a collaborator of Jung, takes a Freudian position and sees the trickster as a phallic figure, the spirit of disorder. Jung finds unconsciousness as the chief and alarming characteristic of the trickster, whom he considers the forerunner of the Saviour. Radin synthesizes both Freudian and Jungian analyses in his conception of the trickster as evolving from a psychically unaware to a socially developed being, reinterpreted by each new generation as god, hero, or buffoon. The most committed Freudian folklorist of the 1960s is Gershon Legman, Hungarian by birth, who resides in the United States and France. In *The Rationale of the Dirty Joke* (1968), Legman properly gives attention to the most current folktale genre of modern society but looks beneath the seemingly obvious motivations of dirty jokes to violate sexual and anal taboos and imputes to them such latent impulses as castration fears, female revulsion at the sexual act, and homosexual drives.

The three perspectives of folklore are not mutually exclusive. Anthropologists may at times employ an essentially humanistic approach, as Daniel J. Crowley has done in his detailed ethnography of the styles and repertoires of Bahamian narrators, *I Could Talk Old-Story Good* (1966). They also have shown sympathy for the psychological-psychoanalytical node. A case in point is the study of *Water-Witching, U.S.A.* (1959), by anthropologist Evon Vogt in collaboration with the psychologist Ray Hyman, who explained the widespread phenomenon whereby diviners located underground water with a forked branch as an anxiety-releasing mechanism for depressed farmers. Younger folklorists of the 1960s trained

as humanists have shown an increasing orientation toward social-science methods of model building and statistical techniques.

THE ORIGINS OF FOLKLORE

Grimms' Fairy Tales and the collection of folklore

When scholars and other intellectuals began to recognize early in the 19th century the presence in their midst of a vast floating body of folk traditions and practices, they promptly began to speculate on its origins. When in 1812–14 the German philologist Jacob Grimm (1785–1863), together with his brother Wilhelm (1786–1859), published the first volume of the *Kinder und Hausmärchen* (customarily translated as *Grimms' Fairy Tales*), thus initiating the science of folklore, he connected his collecting of village tales to an elaborate mythological system of origins, outlined in his *Deutsche Mythologie*. This influential work was first issued in 1835, and its fourth edition was translated into English (3 volumes, 1883–88) under the title *Teutonic Mythology*. A German nationalist, Grimm postulated a highly developed religious pantheon of pre-Roman times suppressed by the medieval church and surviving only in broken fragments of peasant beliefs and stories. The *Märchen*, or tales, were the detritus of the old myths.

In the mid-19th century, following the discovery of Sanskrit as the ancient classical language of India and the parent of European tongues, a pan-Aryan theory of origins developed. In 1856 Max Müller, a German-born scholar who went to London to translate from the Sanskrit the *Sacred Books of the East* and stayed on at Oxford University, published a long essay on "Comparative Mythology," introducing the new theory. Through a process he called "disease of language," Müller conjectured that myths arose from forgetfulness of the original names of deities, transferring to them metaphorical qualities suggested by the names. Thus Dyâus, the sky deity of old India, would be thought of and narrated about as the sky, or by association, heavens, clouds, storms, and winds. The Greek myths sprang from the Indic—Zeus was the linguistic counterpart of Dyâus—and could be explained on the same grounds. Although Müller applied his theory only to the advanced Indo-European Aryan civilizations, he did point to similar myth-making among primitive peoples. Some of his followers, notably George W. Cox, carried the school of solar mythology to extreme limits and explained all folk narratives, epics, and ballads as originating in early man's poetic rendering of the conflict between the sun and the night.

"Evolutionary" and "devolutionary" theories of folklore

Tylor added a new conception of the origins of folklore without challenging Müller's solar mythology but by pushing the starting point back beyond the Aryans to prehistoric man. Looking at the universe animistically, primitive man endowed the elements, the animals, the plants, and the rocks with personalities and souls. Such beliefs survived into modern civilization among the unlettered lower classes and formed a crust of folklore. The strongest challenge to Tylor's evolutionary theory of culture and "devolutionary" theory of folklore (in the phrase of Alan Dundes) first emerged in a hypothesis advanced by the German scholar Theodor Benfey in his introduction to the Indian story collection *Panchatantra* (1859). Benfey claimed that India, the seat of an ancient high civilization that had spread to Europe, was the home of the master tales subsequently found in the Grimms' collection. Along with language and mythology, these wonder tales had diffused from India to Europe in ancient times and again in historic times along well-travelled trade routes. Benfey's arguments persuaded other folklorists, notably Emmanuel Cosquin in France and William Alexander Clouston in Scotland, who added to his evidence of story migration from India eastward. In the past century, the primacy of ancient India as the fountain of world folklore has gradually been whittled away by the claims of other dispersal points, such as Egypt and Greece, and by the growing realization that no sweeping generalization could account for folklore origins. According to the Finnish folklorists, whose historical-geographical method attracted most scholars in the first half of the 20th century, the life history of each complex tale and ballad requires separate investigation. After exhaustively comparing the traits of all the assembled variants of a given tale type, the Finns (specifically Kaarle and Julius Krohn and Antti Aarne) believed they could establish its original form and approximate place and period of genesis. The subscribers to this theory accepted the premise that an anonymous composer had created every substantial folklore item at one point in time, much as a novelist produces a novel.

Various other origin theories have gained attention. The school of Cambridge University anthropologists, theorizing on the great comparative study by Sir James George Frazer, *The Golden Bough* (1st ed., 1890), converged on a central idea of myth-ritual origins of all folklore. In their view, a mythic narrative accompanied and explained a sacrificial fertility ritual among the heathens. In the course of time the myth becomes separated from the rite and floats independently in oral tradition, to splinter in turn into magic tales, popular ballads, nursery rhymes, and other folklore genres. Psychological folklorists ascribe the source of many folk narratives to dreams; the Hungarian Geza Roheim considers that dreams, precipitated by full bladders, engendered the widespread flood myth. Ballad scholars, such as Francis Gummere in *Old English Ballads* (1894) and other works, attributed the composition of ballads not to any single bard but to the joint efforts of a singing, dancing throng.

Origins by social classes have also formed the basis for widely held theories. One thesis, particularly identified with the German Hans Naumann and his term *gesunkenes Kulturgut* (literally, "downsinking cultural value"), contends that folklore originates with the aristocratic upper class, whose court poetry, mimes, bardic recitals, and pageants filter down in debased form to the peasantry. Soviet and east European folklorists have sharply challenged this idea since the 1930s and substituted their own concept that folklore arises from the people, the folk, in expression of protest and outrage against the exploiting nobles and landowners. Hence in the Soviet Union folk bards and storytellers are honoured along with novelists and poets. In "A Theory for American Folklore" (1959), Richard M. Dorson has argued for a distinction between Old World and New World folklore origins. The folk traditions of North and South America combine the imported lore of the conquerors, the aboriginal lore of Indian tribes, and the lore arising since the colonizing period as a result of New World history and geography.

THE FORMS OF FOLKLORE

The elusive materials of folklore can best be defined through the formal genres into which they fall. Genre definition has its own pitfalls, since attempts at neat categories invariably slice off related forms, but folklorists agree on certain broad kinds of traditions. These may be divided into oral literature, custom and festival, and material culture.

Oral literature. The genres of oral literature cover spoken and sung expression. They may be further divided into the two large groupings of folk narrative and folk song, and such other smaller genres as proverbs, riddles, and beliefs or superstitions. *Folk narrative* is an umbrella for a wide range of oral prose traditions. Among them can be mentioned the *myth*, a semisacred adventure of a god or demigod set in the remote past; the *Märchen* or *fairy tale* (also *wonder tale* or *magic tale* and sometimes just *folktale* or *tale*), a pan-European popular fiction with aristocratic characters, magical episodes, and a symmetrical structure; the *legend*, a believed report often told conversationally and allusively; the *saga*, a personal, family, or local chronicle of marvellous oral history; the *romance*, a lengthy, adventure-filled narration with realistic characters; the *noodle* or *numskull tale*, relating the comical stupidities of a foolish person or a village of fools; the *jest* or *joke*, a short humorous fiction, often obscene and usually climaxed with a punch line; the *anecdote*, a brief traditional incident concerning a laughable action or saying of a historical personality; the *ani-*

mal tale, characterized by talking animals with human traits; the *cante-fable*, a story containing songs or rhymes; and still other forms. Folk song too embraces myriad species. An important aspect of all folk songs is their association of text with tune, requiring the folklorist to trace the melodic as well as the textual history. A major division separates the *ballad*, which embodies a narrative, and the *lyric*, which expresses emotion, although, like *Märchen* and legend, the two basic forms often coalesce. The ballad can be further subdivided into the *Child ballad*, named for Francis James Child, who assembled 305 basic types of the English and Scottish traditional ballad (1882–98); the *broadside ballad*, a later development of the 16th and 17th centuries when balladmongers wrote up sensational events on broadsheets or broadsides and hawked them in the streets; and *European* and *American ballads*, which have evolved from local events. Other folk song genres range from the Russian *bylina*, or epic songs of a medieval hero, to the *lullaby*, used to sing a child to sleep.

Still another category of oral literature comprises *folk speech*, as distinct from formal or standard speech, and various traditional kinds of expressive utterances. Prominent among them are the *proverb* or folk saying, embodying wisdom in pithy phrases; the *riddle*, an enigmatic question paired with a deceptive answer; the *tongue twister*, a nonsense sentence difficult to pronounce because of its string of assonances; the *toast*, a convivial expression voiced as a drinking salutation; along with other forms involving a special use of language. *Beliefs* or *superstitions* are sometimes expressed as wise sayings, although they may also appear in tales and in customs.

Material culture. At the opposite pole from oral literature in the spectrum of folklore lies material culture or folk life, terms used to denote the physical objects produced in traditional ways. Material culture thus embraces folk architecture, folk arts, and folk crafts. Under these headings can be placed the construction of houses, the design and decoration of buildings and utensils, and the performance of home industries, according to traditional styles and methods. The shape of fences, the making of sorghum molasses, and the sewing of quilts all fall under material culture.

Custom and festival. Between oral and physical folklore there is a large middle ground filled by custom, ritual, festival, children's games (believed to be versions of adult rituals), folk drama, play parties, rites of passage, folk dances, and equivalent genres involving action, performance, and paraphernalia. To the verbal and tangible elements are added group behavioral traits.

The functions of these three genres vary for individuals and societies, but generally it may be said that material culture fills economic and aesthetic functions, that oral literature fills didactic, recreational, and educational functions, and that custom and festival function to provide psychic reassurance against external dangers. Rites placate gods and demons, tales and songs entertain and instruct, and home-baked bread on a hand-carved table fills the stomach while pleasing the eye.

THE GENERAL FUNCTIONS OF FOLKLORE

A behavioral classification of functions. Oral literature, like written literature but even more pronouncedly, satisfies the desires of mortals to transcend their mundane world. In the myths the heroes visit the otherworld; in the legends ordinary folk are taken to fairyland; and in the *Märchen* the youngest son or daughter of a peasant family makes a royal marriage. Gold, treasure, and wealth are prominent in narrative folklore. Jason and the Argonauts in Greek myth set out for the Golden Fleece; in fairy tales a magic goose lays golden eggs; and in real life, treasure seekers dig for the buried booty of pirates and outlaws. The Irish tradition of "Seán Palmer's Voyage to America with the Fairies" (in *Folktales of Ireland* by Sean O'Sullivan), told as an actual experience befalling Seán Palmer of County Kerry, combines the traditional theme of fairies transporting mortals to distant cities with a wish fulfillment fantasy. Seán believes the

Folklore and fertility ritual

Genres of oral literature

The escapist function

fairies take him by boat overnight to the United States, where he visits relatives in New York and Boston and is given money, new clothes, and tobacco. Many Irishmen have relatives in the U.S. whom they consider rich and long to visit.

Another way in which folklore lifts man above his narrow confines is in the breaking of powerful social taboos. What man can never do in actuality without incurring severe punishment the trickster in American Negro narratives, for example, does with impunity, such as John the slave slapping the face of his white mistress. Modern jokes with their heavy emphasis on genital-anal humour similarly arouse merriment by flaunting taboos.

The etiological function

Mythic narratives and explanatory episodes in other kinds of folktales answer man's perennial questions: How did the world begin? Who created man, the animals, and the plants? The book of Genesis in the Bible gives two versions of a creation myth with worldwide analogies. Myths of origin are always ethnocentric; they explain the creation, by supernatural powers, of the people possessing the myth, a chosen people. The hostile, formidable, mysterious universe assumes a familiar outline through the personification of a creator and his adversary and of associated deities and demons with their own spheres of influence. Tribal peoples need their myths to safeguard their identity. An Ojibwa Indian in northern Michigan asked a researcher on their first meeting, "Do they have thunder storms in South America?" On receiving an affirmative answer the Ojibwa turned morose and taciturn and refused to speak further. He had wished reassurance that thunderstorms existed only in the neighbourhood of Lake Michigan, since the Ojibwa protective deities were thunder spirits. Later, when mollified, he related a version of the creation myth, synthesized with the flood myth. The culture hero-trickster figure, Winabijou, flees from the underneath serpents, who send flood waters after him. He takes refuge atop a pine tree and barely keeps his head above the water that covers the earth. Water animals swim to him, and he sends them down to the bottom; the muskrat comes up with mud in its paws, with which Winabijou makes a little island. Each day the island gets bigger, and Winabijou sends the fox along the shore to circle it and report back. Eventually the island grows to the size of the present earth. "And you can see a fox trotting along the shore today," the narrator concluded. "The shore gets bigger too. Sand multiplies. When I first came here the beach on the cove was only half as big as it is now." The myth satisfactorily accounts for his universe.

The justifying function

Just as myths are generated to explain the physical world and its inhabitants, so does folklore at large provide support for the institutions and behaviour patterns of a culture. In nonliterate societies the central events of human life—birth, attainment of manhood, marriage, and death—are invested with elaborate ceremonials by which the social organism marks the mortal's progress and final exit to the afterlife. In modern society the quasi-religious character of these passage rites, as Arnold van Gennep has termed them, can be observed in the rituals of baptism, confirmation or graduation, weddings, and funerals, which are sometimes secular, sometimes ecclesiastical, and sometimes a mixture of both. In contrast to supernatural beings, who acquire anthropomorphic personalities and walk the earth (like Winabijou, or Christ and St. Peter), historical heroes acquire supernatural attributes and move heavenward. The illustrious secular heroes and heroines—like Joan of Arc, Confucius, Peter the Great, Julius Caesar, King Alfred, and George Washington—become national symbols, consecrated with monuments, holidays, hagiographic literature, and folk legends. They function in the national culture as standard-bearers of the values and goals of the nation. The legend of young George Washington saying to his father, "I cannot tell a lie, it was I who chopped down the cherry tree," drives home the moral of the proverb ascribed to Benjamin Franklin (but actually common in Europe in the 17th century and earlier), another culture hero: "Honesty is the best policy."

A good deal of folklore, especially the proverbs, fables, cautionary tales, and confessional ballads, serves to instruct and remind members of society of wise codes of conduct. The proverb and the fable may teach the same lesson; "Pride goes before a fall" is illustrated in Aesop's fable of the cat who praised the crow's singing voice, so that the crow up in the tree started to sing and dropped the cheese from her mouth to the ground. Proverbs may sometimes appear contradictory. "Look before you leap" is challenged by "He who hesitates is lost," but each saying contains its truth to be applied to a given situation. A whole ethic may be summarized in a proverb, as is the Protestant ethic of hard work in the saying, "Early to bed, early to rise, makes a man healthy, wealthy, and wise."

The pedagogic function

Although proverbial expressions are still frequently uttered in industrialized societies, they are used as mild commentary and poetic cliché rather than, as in African societies, for firm codes with the force of judicial precedent. The African novelist Chinua Achebe writes in *Things Fall Apart*, "Among the Ibo the art of conversation is regarded very highly, and proverbs are the palm-oil with which words are eaten." And his novels are sprinkled with proverbs. Actual court cases among the Anang Ibibio of Nigeria in which judges were swayed by proverbs have been recorded by the anthropologist John Messenger. On one occasion the chief judge advised the plaintiff and his witnesses, "If you visit the home of the toads, stoop," when they refused to make their statements under oath and thereby forfeited their case. The equivalent precept, still forceful in modern life, is "When in Rome do as the Romans do." Among the Bambara-speaking people of Mali in Africa, the *griots*, the celebrated epic bards, customarily "warm up" before their recitations and during breaks in their lengthy performances by singing proverbs in rapid sequence. This practice serves the function of gaining the attention and respect of the audience, who think of proverb sayers as wise men knowing how the society works; hence the listeners will be ready to credit the historical tradition that follows.

The controlling function

Besides suggesting rules for conduct, folklore also drives home the need for proper social behaviour by holding up to scorn those who depart from socially accepted norms and by eulogizing those who follow them. Jokes, the most popular form of oral literature in modern society, ridicule stereotyped characters who display traits disparaged by the Establishment. The stingy Scotsman, the miserly Jew, the ignorant Irishman, and the stupid Polack are all caricatured in joke cycles whose implicit values laud the qualities of liberality, generosity, intelligence, and cleanliness. Anecdotes of local characters similarly excoriate the slovenly, shiftless, degenerate, gullible, and naïve. One favourite theme of anecdotes is the lazy man, often identified with some local ne'er-do-well. Starving to death, the lazy man is offered popcorn: "Is it shelled?" he asks, and prefers to starve rather than do the labour of the shelling. Just as proverbs teach the gospel of work, so do such anecdotal legends mock the idle and improvident. Conversely, folklore also exalts individuals who exemplify the virtues considered admirable in the culture. Saints' legends recount the miraculous cures and rescues that the saint revered by the folk (who is not necessarily canonized by the church) has effected for the faithful. Devout members of the Mormon Church continue to relate experiences of succour given them in distress by one of the three Nephites, who appears as a stranger in white garments to render assistance and vanishes as mysteriously as he materializes. Heroes in ballad, legend, and *Märchen* reflect the dominant values of their societies and are rewarded by success. The champion of heroic epics is an invincible warrior. The hero of Negro ballads is a big-talking badman. The modern hero in the anecdotal legends of youthful dissenters is the antihero who sells LSD pills or marijuana and outwits narcotic agents, the police, and draft boards. All these heroes symbolize ideal types for their social groups. Deviation from the ideal brands the nonconformist a coward, an Uncle Tom, or an Establishment toady. In the form of folklore known to 17th-century American Puritans as the "remarkable providence," God punished sinners, blasphemers, heretics, witches, marauding Indians, and critics of the state with acts of supernatural vengeance, while rewarding his elect with supernatural assistance during their wilderness trials. Puritan clergy collected and published these providences as lessons and guideposts for their people. In Socialist countries of the 20th century, the governments have taken a hand in the process of regulating conformity by awarding prizes to folk poets and folk narrators who attack bourgeois and capitalist villains and extol peasant and Socialist heroes.

A cultural-geographical classification of functions. Generalizations about the functions of folklore need to be qualified by considerations of culture area and social milieu. One kind of distinction should be made between Old World and New World folk traditions, since North and South America were colonized by Europeans, who then transported African slaves to their overseas empires. Consequently, a given country of the New World possesses several coexisting and interacting traditions; the indigenous Indian; the colonizing Spanish, Portuguese, French, or English; the African Negro; the 19th- and 20th-century European and Asian immigrant; and the national and regional, shaped by new historical and environmental factors. The continent of Australia also belongs with the New World in this regard, its folklore being divided between the Aborigines and the English settlers. In the colonized nations, each folk tradition serves to reinforce the group identity of its members in a pluralistic culture. Syncretism, or the fusion of different traditions, is a process especially characteristic of New World folklore. The miraculous appearance of the Virgin of Guadalupe to the Aztec Indian Juan Diego in 1531, who received from her a painting of herself on his cape, brought together Spanish-Catholic and pre-Conquest Indian strains. Mexican Indians and mestizos identified the Virgin with an Aztec goddess Tonantzin, pictured her as dark in hue, and celebrated her with costumed dances of pagan origin but within the framework of Roman Catholic worship and beatification. The ballad of "John Henry," relating the contest between a brawny Negro labourer and a new steam drill on a railroad tunnel in West Virginia in the 1860s, is widely sung by both American blacks and whites. John Henry dies "with his hammer in his hand," and interpreters see him as a symbol of the unequal struggle of the black man against the white, and of man against the machine. Immigration has brought large numbers of Slavs to western Canada, Japanese to Brazil, Italians to Argentina, Germans to Chile, and many peoples to the United States, whose folkways partially survive the transoceanic crossing. The traditional lore physically connected with the original homeland seems to vanish the most quickly; thus the Irish belief in fairies does not survive, since the grassy circular "fairy rings" inhabited by the fairies of the Old Country are not found in America.

Literate and nonliterate functions Another large distinction in the functioning of folklore separates the so-called nonliterate societies lacking written languages from the advanced civilizations engulfed in print. Reliance on the oral tradition is obviously far greater in the nonliterate cultures. The matter of recording history provides one example: instead of referring to printed books containing a great many facts that no one person could or would wish to keep in his head, the tribal groups depend upon reciters of historical traditions, some of whom, like the *whare wananga* of the New Zealand Maori, the sagamen of 11th-century Iceland, and the *griots* of Mali, have a professional status. These annals and genealogies bear little resemblance to documented written histories and belong properly to the products of oral literature, since they include magical and marvellous episodes of folktales and legends. They do correspond in function to national histories in celebrating the achievements and culture heroes of a chosen people. An ingenious study by two teams of American anthropologists who collected traditions from two rival Indian tribes in northern California revealed a similar patterning but contrasting roles for the same characters and events. The enemy tribe was always guilty of the provocative incident, fought dishonourably, and suffered defeat.

Even in literate civilizations large enclaves of largely oral, tradition-directed cultures persist. Narrators with enormous repertoires have been located in the 20th century in the Gaelic-speaking highlands and islands of western Scotland and western Ireland. Peig Sayers of the Great Blasket Island related 375 tales to the collectors of the Irish Folklore Commission, many of them long wonder tales taking all evening or several evenings to complete. In modern urban, technological society, such reciters find no audiences. Life has too many distractions and diversions and sources of information. Nevertheless, story-telling continues among the highly literate, in the form of joke-telling sessions, which may last an hour or two; but the jocular narratives are relatively brief, snappy, and quickly climactic. They serve as icebreakers to establish camaraderie in a group, although they may also give offense to some members of a social gathering with differing political or moral views. Ballad making originally made possible the dissemination of sensational news in attractive form and receded with the advent of newspapers, which emulated many of the same techniques of ballad makers in their handling of lurid news items.

Correspondence between oral and literary cultures Oral and literary cultures are no longer sharply divided. On the lower levels of society cheap printed sources—such as chapbooks, broadsides, jestbooks, mass magazines, almanacs, and newspapers—feed materials into and draw from oral streams of lore. In the electronic age, according to Marshall McLuhan, the literate world is reverting to an oral-aural community.

Folklorists at first identified their subject with the rural peasantry. Seasonal festivals, old wives' remedies, supernatural beliefs in demonic figures, and magic makers flourished in the countryside. Cities were the centres of learning, industry, and wealth, and the spoilers of tradition and folklife. This easy contrast is being revised as folklore scholars turn their attention to the cities where ethnic neighbourhoods and occupational workers form closely knit, tradition-bound societies. A team project of Hungarian folklorists investigating Budapest reported many vigorous manifestations of traditional behaviour, such as May Day celebrations, dancing parties held by tradesmen, housewarming ceremonies, and occupational jokes. In a detailed study of a Tokyo district, R.P. Dore reported on households that maintain traditional festival practices and the ancient Shintō beliefs in *kami* (deities) and *fuda* (shrine amulets). But city life does of course affect traditional ways brought in from the country. The ubiquitous Japanese-peasant conception of the *Kappa*, a dangerous boy-goblin with an inverted saucer on his head containing magical water, is found in Tokyo in newspaper comic strips, on decorative designs, or as a character in a novel by Akutagawa Ryūnosuke. In a series of ethnographic studies in Yucatán, the American anthropologist Robert Redfield compared four communities, ranging from the simple village to the complex town, and found that living rituals in the village become desiccated superstitions in the town.

Field research in the steel-manufacturing cities of Gary and East Chicago, Indiana, by Indiana University folklorists has shown not only a decrease in the folklore genres of the many ethnic groups living there but also an emergence of a new city lore. The chief elements of this lore derive from the human side of the all-encompassing steel industry, from fears and rumours about crime and the Mafia, and from anecdotes and stereotypes about other racial and ethnic groups. This emerging lore provides a sense of solidarity and rootedness in the impersonal, unlovely city.

THE DIFFUSION AND ACCULTURATION OF FOLKLORE

Folklore is at once remarkably stable and remarkably shifting. These phenomena have intrigued folklorists.

who explain the apparent paradox through the mechanism of diffusion. A complex item of folk tradition, whether an epic song, a house style, a folk drama, or a wonder tale, once it has attained coherent form, may travel across continents and oceans and endure through the centuries. The basic type retains its outline but external features are continuously modified and adapted to new surroundings. Barriers of language, religion, and culture offer no obstacles to the movements of folk products. The most bitter of enemies share the same traditions. Supporters of diffusion challenged the upholders of independent invention in the latter decades of the 19th century and eventually won the day as depth field studies proved clearly the wanderings and migrations of individual texts. The first comparative study of a folktale, Marian Cox's *Cinderella* (1893), brought together 345 variants of the same recognizable story plot. Even legends, seemingly so anchored in time and place to specific historical events and personalities, were shown to migrate and become attached to different localities and heroes. The legend of the Returning Hero, sleeping in the fastnesses of the mountain with his warriors until his people would summon him to their rescue, fastened on to Frederick Barbarossa, King Arthur, and Thomas the Rhymer and is still told of modern figures. How did folklore diffuse? Proponents of diffusion offered various explanations: sailors, merchants, and travellers transported folk matter along the great historic trade routes; Gypsies acted as peddlers of folklore; borders between peoples served as bilingual zones through which songs, tales, and styles easily moved; imperial powers planted the traditions of the mother country in distant places. All these hypotheses have some merit; European tales found among North American Indians, for instance, undoubtedly date back to the period of their first culture contact with French and Spanish missionaries, soldiers, and traders. Yet Indian tales did not lodge in the narrative repertoires of the European settlers. The flow appears to go from literate to nonliterate cultures.

Acculturation represents a somewhat different phenomenon of folklore movement. Here not the lore but the folk move, bearing with them their ancestral heritage. What happens to this heritage when peasants of India resettle in Africa, when Chinese move to Malaysia, when European communities pour into the New World? The resulting process of adjustment, adaptation, compromise, and assimilation is called acculturation. But what takes place in this process is not so easily understood. Parts of the Old Country tradition recede into "memory culture," to be recalled on direct stimuli but otherwise lying dormant in the recollections of the first generation. Other parts remain in vigorous use. Still other parts take on New World coloration. Among Greek immigrants in the United States, for instance, the telling of paramythia (or *Märchen*) and the sighting of creatures like the *vrykólakas,* a vampire demon, have virtually ended, but the belief in the power of the evil eye and of the protective power of saints remains as strong as ever. As a general principle, the beings of lower mythology do not transplant into an alien environment, whereas the daily and seasonal rituals and associated beliefs can be maintained within compactly settled groups. The rate of acculturation will vary greatly between immigrant societies, depending upon what conservative forces are at work. Such groups as the Pennsylvania German Amish and the Hasidim in Brooklyn, N.Y., retain a high degree of their magical belief system, folk arts, and ritual observances, because they have made strenuous efforts to wall themselves in from the mainstream of American culture, an effort strengthened by their independent churches. By contrast, Irish-Americans after a century in their new homeland have lost most of their distinctive folklore and blended in with the rest of the general Catholic and middle class population.

The mobility and technology of modern man have noticeably affected the diffusion and acculturation of folklore. People emigrate by airplane, communicate by telephone, and soak information from the mass media. Yet old ways of thinking and believing show remarkable tenacity. Many folk today discredit the landing of men on the moon as a publicity hoax contrived by the United States government and the television networks. These are the people who have seen flying saucers, been cured by faith healers, and conversed with revenants. Folklore is as old, and as young, as man.

Movement of folklore by acculturation

BIBLIOGRAPHY. A. AARNE, *The Types of the Folktale,* 2nd rev., trans. and enl. by S. THOMPSON (1961), the standard index and reference work for the most widely distributed European folk narratives; F.J. CHILD (ed.), *The English and Scottish Popular Ballads,* 5 vol. (1882–98), the classic assemblage of 305 ballad types, with variant texts and learned headnotes; W.A. CLOUSTON, *Popular Tales and Fictions,* 2 vol. (1887), an early discussion of the wandering and migrations of folktales between India and Europe; M.R. COX, *Cinderella* (1893), the first comparative study of an international folktale, bringing together 345 variants, and contributing to the thesis of diffusion rather than independent invention of complex tales; L. DEGH, *Folktales and Society* (1969), a depth field study of storytelling behaviour in a Hungarian peasant community, with biographical portraits of leading folk narrators; R.M. DORSON, *American Folklore* (1959), an historical presentation of various folk traditions in the U.S., *The British Folklorists: A History,* and (ed.), *Peasant Customs and Savage Myths: Selections from the British Folklorists,* 2 vol. (both 1968), a history of the concept of folklore as it emerged in England with the 16th-century interest in antiquities and came to fruition among Victorian private scholars in the late 19th century—the volumes of selections present illustrative writings of the folklorists discussed in the history, and "Folktales of the World" (1963–), a series of authoritative volumes each of which is prepared by an eminent folktale scholar from the country represented; A.B. FRIEDMAN, *The Ballad Revival* (1961), interest in the ballad in England by antiquaries, poets, and the public treated in terms of literary history; JACOB GRIMM, *Teutonic Mythology,* trans. by J.S. STALLYBRASS, 4 vol. (1883–88), the encyclopaedic and influential work in which Grimm expounded his theory of the degeneration of an ancient high pantheon of Germanic deities into the extant fairy tales and witch beliefs of the contemporary peasantry; F.R.S. RAGLAN, *The Hero: A Study in Tradition, Myth, and Drama* (1956), a highly controversial explanation of all mythic narratives as following a uniform pattern derived from ancient sacrificial fertility rituals; Y.M. SOKOLOV, *Russian Folklore,* trans. by C.R. SMITH, (1950), a history of Russian folklore research given from the Soviet viewpoint regarding folklore as an expression of the class struggle; S. THOMPSON, *Motif-Index of Folk-Literature,* rev. ed., 6 vol. (1955–58), the major reference work in comparative folklore; J. VANSINA, *Oral Tradition* (1961), presentation of an historical methodology for the African historian enabling him to use oral historical chronicles and genealogies as legitimate source materials; D.K. WILGUS, *Anglo-American Folksong Scholarship Since 1898* (1959), a judicious appraisal of the recent schools of interpretation in ballad and folk-song studies.

(R.M.D.)

Folk Music

Differences between folk music and other types of music, such as popular music and cultivated, art, or classical music, are by no means precise. Typically, folk music lives in oral tradition; it is learned through hearing rather than reading. It is functional in the sense that it is associated with other activities. Primarily rural in origin, it exists in cultures in which there is also an urban, technically more sophisticated musical tradition. Folk music is understood by broad segments of the population, while cultivated or classical music is essentially the art of a small social, economic, or intellectual elite. On the other hand, that widely accepted type of music usually called "popular" depends mainly on the mass media—records, radio, and television—for dissemination, while folk music typically is disseminated within families and restricted social networks. But the introduction of songs from folklore into the mass media blurs the distinction, and folk music in earlier times may be discussed separately from that of the period after World War II. Moreover, while folk music as defined above exists in all cultures in which there is also a cultivated musical tradition, such as Japan, China, Indonesia, India, and the

Middle East, the usefulness of the concept varies from culture to culture. It is most convenient as a designation of a type of music of Europe and the Americas.

GENERAL CHARACTERISTICS

Perhaps the most important characteristic of a folk song is its dependence on acceptance by a community—that is, by a village, nation, or family—and its tendency to change as it is passed from one individual to another and performed. This process is known as "communal recreation."

Origins and functions

A piece of folk music is the property of the entire community. But contrary to beliefs promulgated in the 19th century, folk songs are normally created not by groups of people but by individuals. When it is first composed, each song is the work of one composer, though it is re-created constantly by the performers who learn and sing it. The composer may create new songs by drawing together lines, phrases, and musical motifs from extant songs, possibly combined with entirely new ones and with standard opening or closing formulas. In European folk music, a small number of tune types account for most of the repertoire. English folk music, for example, is believed to consist largely of about 40 "tune families," each of which descends from a single song. And the majority of English folk songs are members of only seven such tune families.

There is frequent interchange of tunes between neighbouring countries. A few tune types are found throughout the European culture area. Each country, however, tends to have a repertory of its own, with stylistic features as well as tunes that are not shared with neighbours. Textual types (such as ballad stories) are more widely distributed than tune types.

The 20th century has seen the decline of folk tradition in many areas, particularly those that became heavily urbanized and industrialized. From the Middle Ages until the 19th century, folk music probably had been distributed evenly throughout Europe and the Americas. After 1950, folk music was found most readily in areas that were not heavily industrialized, such as the isolated mountainous regions of North America or of Italy and in the countries of eastern and southern Europe. In the Americas, folk music of European origin became mixed with elements of non-Western music, especially African and (in Latin America) American Indian.

Much folk music can be said to be "functional" in that it is not primarily entertainment or of aesthetic interest but an accompaniment to other activities, particularly ritual, work, and dance. In a traditional folk society, music is a necessity in almost all rituals and festivals. The words of folk song can serve as chronicle, newspaper, and agent of enculturation. In modern industrial nations, folk music is perpetuated by ethnic, occupational, or religious minorities, among whom it is thought to promote self-esteem, self-preservation, and social solidarity. Such functions of folk music have been used by organizations advocating social change, such as the U.S. civil rights and trade unionism movements.

Transmission. Folk music is usually transmitted by word of mouth, or oral tradition. This means that a folk song can change as a result of the creativity of those who perform it or of their particular musical style or of their faulty memory. As it is handed down from generation to generation a folk song develops additional forms, called *variants in folk music* variants, which may differ markedly from each other. For example, a song with four musical lines (*e.g.,* *ABCD*) may lose two of these lines and take on the form *ABAB*. In turn, two new lines may be substituted for the initial two, giving it a form *EFAB*. Folk tunes also change when they cross ethnic or cultural boundaries. A German variant, for example, may exhibit characteristics of German folk music, while its variant in Czechoslovakia, although recognizably related, will assume the stylistic traits of Czech folk music. The degree to which songs change varies from culture to culture. In some, presumably those that value consistency and object to change, such as western Europe, songs change little and

slowly. In others, such as Afro-American cultures, the opposite tendency is found.

In spite of its dependence on oral tradition, folk music tends to be closely related to music in written tradition. Many folk songs originate in written form. For many centuries, popular and classical composers have adapted folk music, and in turn, influenced the oral tradition. A modern analogue of written tradition, recording, substantially influenced the oral tradition, as folk singers could hear various arrangements of folk music in private and commercial recordings. Thus, the transmission of folk music has not been an isolated process but one intertwined with other kinds of musical transmission.

Composition. The composition of folk music differs little from that of popular and classical music, except that most folk songs are composed without notation. The relationships among the sections of folk songs and their scales and rhythms are also found in the other music of the same culture. Systematic improvisation as a method of composition is found only occasionally, as in the epic songs of eastern Europe. It is often difficult to ascertain whether the same composer created both words and music in a folk song, but, in many, they are known to come from different sources.

Among the most important genres of folk music are ballads, generally short narrative songs with repeated lines, epics (longer narratives in heroic style), work songs, love and other lyrical songs, songs of a ceremonial nature accompanying the life cycle of man or the annual agricultural cycle, songs accompanying games, and lullabies. These genres are distinguished usually in their texts, but in some cultures, also in their music. Instrumental folk music is most frequently an accompaniment to dance.

Relationship to other music. The relationship of folk music to art music became a topic of interest in the late 18th century when Western intellectuals began to glorify folk and peasant life. Folk music came to be venerated as a spontaneous creation of peoples unencumbered by artistic self-consciousness and aesthetic theories and as an embodiment of the common experience of inhabitants of the locale. These traits make folk music a fructifying source for art music, particularly when it is intended to express a particular nation or ethnic group. Another theory is that folk music is not created by the folk but is popular music and art music that has "trickled down" to the folk and undergone various transformations (usually debasements) through oral tradition.

A viewpoint intermediate between these two positions has been widely held since 1950. Folk music is seen neither as merely debased art music nor as an essential component of art music. Rather, it is seen to have a symbiotic relationship to other music in the larger society of which the folk community forms a part. In Europe and the Americas the give-and-take between folk music and art music is well documented. Many folk songs collected in oral tradition have been traced to literary sources, often of considerable antiquity. Folk music has been consciously incorporated into European art music compositions throughout history, especially during periods of "renewal" such as the Renaissance, the late 18th century, and throughout the 19th and early 20th centuries.

Folk music is closely related to popular music in several ways. Societies possessing popular music also have a *Relation to popular music* folk music tradition—or remnants thereof. The partial duplication of repertories and style indicates such cross-fertilization that a given song may sometimes be called either "folk" or "popular." With reference to music, the terms folk and popular are two points on a musical continuum, rather than discrete bodies of music. From a sociological viewpoint, however, folk and popular music have less in common. Unlike folk music, popular music is primarily produced by professionals for consumption by an urban, nonparticipating mass audience. The vital criteria of folk music (*i.e.,* oral tradition, communal recreation, etc.,) are not operative.

Folk and popular music tended to merge in the 20th

century. As folk societies came increasingly within the purview of modern urban society, oral tradition was supplemented or supplanted by the radio and phonograph record. Some folk music thus transmitted maintains stylistic authenticity, but some assumes the characteristics of popular music. Much of what is called folk music in English-speaking countries is a subcategory within popular music. It is the product of urban professionals who appropriate authentic folk music styles for concert and recorded performances.

Relation to jazz and rock music

There has been some interaction between folk music and rock music, as the generic designation "folk-rock" indicates. Folk-rock arose in North America in the 1960s. In its texts, it is modern urban folk song, with topical subject matter, often on social and moral issues. Musically, however, it has the characteristics of rock in its electrified string band and percussion accompaniment. Other current music that mixes folk and popular elements includes: African high life, American jazz, rhythm and blues, country-western music, and many Latin American forms, such as the tango and bossa nova.

Relationships between church music and folk music must also be noted. Some church music derives from the application of religious texts to secular folk tunes. This practice may be seen, for example, in the hymns of the Protestant Reformation and in the revival hymns of 19th century American camp meetings, which were called "folk hymns" because of their origins and associations with folk-like groups.

There are many types of folk dance, some widespread throughout Europe, others peculiar to nations and regions, each with its typical musical style. Certain musical forms appear most typically in the folk dance music of various parts of Europe. Most prominent is a form type in which each line is repeated once, with a minor variation, usually at the end—e.g., $A^1A^2B^1B^2C^1C^2$. Vocal dance music also exists, and in northern Europe even narrative ballads were used for dancing.

Melodic form. The typical melodic form of European folk music is strophic, that is, a stanza consisting of from two to eight lines (but most typically, four lines) is repeated several times in the song between successive stanzas of the text. The relationship among the lines of the repeated stanzas varies. For example, in English folk music, four lines with different content are common (*ABCD*), but forms whose endings revert to materials presented at the beginning are also common (*e.g., ABBA, AABA, ABCA, ABAB*). Similar forms are found in eastern Europe, where the use of a melodic line at successively higher or lower levels is also important. Thus, in Hungarian folk music, the form AA^5A^5A or AAA_4A_4 (the numbers indicating intervals of transposition) is common. In Czech folk music, AA^5BA is a common form. Despite the variety of arrangement of the musical lines of a song, the textual and musical lines nearly always coincide. In western European folk music, these lines are almost always of equal length; eastern European folk music frequently departs from this principle.

Exceptions to the strophic form

Among the exceptions to the strophic form are children's songs and ditties and epic songs. The former tend to be simple: they use limited scales and rhythms and small melodic range, and they may consist of only one musical line repeated many times. They appear to form an archaic stratum of European music and tend to be similar in musical content throughout the continent.

Epic folk singing is limited to a small number of folk traditions: Balkan, Finnish, and Russian, as well as non-European cultures. The tendency to repeat and vary a musical line many times is also found in epic singing, which is to some extent improvised.

The influence of popular music on folk music, which became very strong in the 19th and 20th centuries, has tended to limit and to standardize forms. The variety of melodic forms is greater, for example, in older English, Anglo-American, German, and Czech folk music than in later music.

Most folk music is monophonic (that is, with only one melodic line), but polyphonic folk music, with several melodic lines, is found in some parts of the world. The accompaniment of melody by instruments is widespread as well, though all cultures have many songs that may be sung without it. The accompaniment of folk music in western Europe appears to have changed over the last thousand years. Originally, very simple, perhaps dronelike material was performed by string instruments such as harps, zithers, and psalteries. Later, simple harmonic sequences developed that were closely related to the practices of 18th century classical music and involved a larger variety of instruments, including especially guitars, banjos, and string ensembles. The popular folk music of the modern cities embodies still more complex harmonic idioms.

Monophonic and polyphonic forms

Polyphonic vocal folk music is far more common in eastern and southern Europe than in western Europe. Styles vary from the simple two-voiced structures using dronelike techniques and parallel singing of the same tune at different pitch levels in Italy and the Balkans to the more sophisticated choral songs in three or four voices, found in Russia, the Caucasus, and the Ukraine. Rounds are found throughout Europe. Heterophony—the simultaneous performance of variations of the same tune by two singers or by a singer and his accompanying instruments—is important among the southern Slavic peoples. Parallel singing is perhaps the most common type of folk polyphony: parallel thirds, that is, singing the same tune at an interval of a third, are found in Spain, Germany, Austria, Czechoslovakia, and farther east; parallel fourths and fifths are sung in the Slavic countries.

Instrumental polyphony

Instrumental folk polyphony is geographically more widespread than vocal. Bagpipes, for example, which use the drone principle, are ubiquitous in Europe. Scandinavian vocal music is largely monophonic, but complex styles of instrumental polyphony were developed in the repertories of various types of fiddles, such as the Norwegian Hardanger fiddle.

It must be borne in mind that certain cultures, such as the British, the Hungarian, and the Cheremis, or Mari people of Russia, while having very little polyphonic folk music, have developed highly complex repertories of monophonic folk song. Polyphony should not be considered an indication of an advanced state of art.

Rhythm and metre. In folk music, rhythm and metre largely depend on the metre of the poetry. Thus, in western Europe, where poetry is organized in metric feet, there is a tendency toward even isometric structure based on one type of metre—typically, $\frac{4}{4}$, $\frac{3}{4}$, or $\frac{6}{8}$, although $\frac{5}{4}$ also appears. In eastern Europe, generally, the number of syllables per line is the main organizing factor, regardless of the number of stressed syllables. Accordingly, the number of notes but not the number of measures is important, and repeated but complex metric units (*e.g.,* $\frac{7}{8}$, $\frac{11}{8}$, $\frac{13}{8}$, etc.) appear, particularly in Hungarian, Yugoslav, Bulgarian, and Romanian songs.

Metre and singing style

Rhythmic structure is closely related to singing style. Singers in the older, ornamented styles frequently depart from rigid metric presentation for melismata (*i.e.,* a single syllable sung to a series of notes) and other expressive effects. Generally speaking, instrumental music is more rigorously metric than vocal. Nonmetric material, some of it consisting of long, melismatic passages, is also found in vocal and instrumental music in parts of Europe influenced by Middle Eastern music, such as the Balkan and Iberian peninsulas.

Scales. Generally speaking, the scales of European folk music fit into the diatonic tone system of European art music. On the whole, the scales of folk music in Asian high cultures are closely related to those consisting of two, three, or four tones, typically using major seconds and minor thirds. These scales are normally used in single-line songs, such as children's ditties, game songs, and lullabies, and they resemble the world's simplest music, that of certain tribal cultures. Among the most important scale types in Europe is the pentatonic, usually consisting of minor thirds and major seconds; it is found throughout the continent but especially in songs and song types not strongly influenced by the art music and popular music of the cities. Diatonic modes are the third important group. The modes most frequently used are Ionian (or major), Dorian, and Mixolydian, but Aeolian, Phrygian, and Lydian are found as well. The Ionian mode is most common in western and central Europe; others are found in eastern Europe, Scandinavia, and England (as well as in English-derived music around the world).

Scales with a predominance of small intervals close to minor seconds are found in the areas once influenced by Middle Eastern music.

Instruments. The instruments of folk music vary enormously in type, design, and origin. They can be divided into roughly four classes.

Four classes of folk instruments

Among the simplest instruments are those that European folk cultures share with many tribal cultures throughout the world. Among them are the following: rattles; flutes, with and without finger holes; the bullroarer; leaf, grass, and bone whistles; and long wooden trumpets, such as the Swiss alpenhorn. These instruments tend to be associated with children's games, signalling practices and remnants of pre-Christian ritual. They evidently became distributed throughout the world many centuries ago.

A second group consists of instruments that were taken to Europe or the Americas from non-European cultures and often changed. Among them are bagpipes, the folk oboes of the Balkan countries, the banjo, the xylophone, and folk fiddles such as the Yugoslav one-stringed *gusle*.

Another group consists of the instruments developed in the European folk cultures themselves from simple materials. A characteristic example is the *Dolle*, a type of fiddle used in northwestern Germany, made from a wooden shoe. A more sophisticated one is the bowed lyre, once widespread in northern Europe but later confined mainly to Finland.

The fourth group that is of great importance comprises instruments taken from urban musical culture and from the traditions of classical and popular music and sometimes changed substantially. Prominent among these are violin, bass viol, clarinet, and guitar. In a number of cases instruments used in art music during the Middle Ages and later, but eventually abandoned, continued to be used in folk music into the 20th century. Examples include the violins with sympathetic strings found in Scandinavia (related to the viola d'amore) and the hurdygurdy, still played in France, and related to the medieval *organistrum*.

Performance styles. The manner of both vocal and instrumental performance of folk music may vary greatly. In general, they differ considerably from Western art music. The sometimes strange, harsh, and tense voice in folk song is no more or less natural—or intentional— than the vocal style of formally trained singers. The manner of singing and the tone colour of instrumental music are among the most important characteristics of a folk music. They are less subject to change over a period of time and less subject to influence than other characteristics of music such as scale, rhythm, and harmony.

Vocal quality of folk music

Speaking very broadly, European folk music is sung in one of two styles, named *parlando-rubato* and *tempo giusto* after studies of east European folk music by the eminent Hungarian composer Béla Bartók. The first style, *parlando-rubato*, is probably older. Stressing the words, it departs frequently from metric and rhythmic patterns and is often highly ornamented. The second style, *tempo giusto*, follows metric patterns more precisely and maintains an even tempo. Both styles are found in many parts of Europe and in European-derived folk music. Using other criteria, the contemporary U.S. folk specialist, Alan Lomax, found three main singing styles in Europe and the Americas. The "Eurasian," found mainly in southern Europe and in parts of Britain, is tense, ornamented, and essentially associated with solo singing. The "Old European," found in central Europe and parts of eastern Europe, is more relaxed. Produced with full voice, it is often associated with group singing

in which the voices blend well. The "modern European," found mainly in western European singing of more recent materials, is something of a compromise between the other two styles.

Before the 20th century members of a community probably tended to sing very much in the same style. In the 20th century—probably because of the influence of popular music, radio, and records—folk singers began to develop intensely personalized repertories and ways of performing, as may be seen in the work of popular folk singers.

In the Americas, the influence of African performance practices on Afro-American, as well as other folk music, has been important. Among these are the imaginative use of vocal tone colours, antiphonal and responsorial techniques, and complex rhythmic patterns.

STUDY AND EVALUATION

Knowledge of the history and development of folk music is largely conjectural. Musical notations of folk songs and descriptions of folk music culture are occasionally encountered in historical records. Such records, however, show not so much the history of folk music as the history of ideas held by the literate classes about folk music. It is assumed that throughout history literate society has possessed a musical culture different from that of their unlettered contemporaries. Their reaction to folk music frequently was one of indifference and, occasionally, derision and hostility. In medieval Europe, under the expansion of Christianity, attempts were made to suppress folk music because of its association with heathen rites and customs. Uncultivated singing styles were denigrated; Thomas Aquinas expressed a common sentiment when he likened artless singers to beasts. Some aspects of European folk music, however, became assimilated into medieval Christian liturgical music, and vice versa.

History and development of folk music

During the late 15th and 16th centuries, the literate urban classes responded more favourably to folk music than they had in the medieval period. The humanistic attitudes of the Renaissance, such as the elevation of nature and antiquity, encouraged the acceptance of folk music as a genre of rustic antique song. Some music in Renaissance manuscripts is presumed to be folk song by virtue of its musical simplicity and the rural and archaic evocations of its texts. It may, of course, have incurred stylization and change. Renaissance composers made extensive use of folk and popular music. Typical genres include polyphonic folk song settings and folk song quodlibets, or combinations of familiar songs. Folk tunes were often used as structural and motivic raw material for motets and masses, and Protestant Reformation music borrowed from folk music.

Folk music seems to have receded somewhat from the consciousness of the literate classes during the Baroque period. Folk song material in the music manuscripts and prints of the period is scarce, and there is less folk influence in cultivated music, with the notable exception of stylized dance-music forms.

During the late 18th century folk music again became important to art music, especially among the Viennese classicists. They incorporated folk tunes and the general style of folk music into their instrumental music. The growth of national historical consciousness and the idealization of the rural milieu led to the collection, preservation, and study of folk song in the late 18th and early 19th centuries. Folk song came to be considered a "national treasure" and of considerable artistic merit vis-à-vis cultivated poetry and song. National and regional folk song collections were published. Revitalization of folk music became a means of promoting nationalistic sentiment and a conservative ideology. Governmental encouragement of folk music became common after the early 19th century.

Scholarship. The search for origins and processes of development that motivated much 19th and early 20th century intellectual activity was reflected in folk music scholarship. Among the influences on research in folk music in the 19th century were anthropological concepts of cultural processes and the theory of evolution. Many scholars believed folk music to be a repository of archaisms—a legacy from which the prehistory of music, language, literature, and other cultural traits could be adduced. While later scholars concede that some traits of folk music may be centuries or even millennia old, they are less inclined to speculate on the age of archaic elements of folk music or to offer historical reconstructions other than tracing variants of individual songs or types of songs.

Scholars who specialize in folk music usually have training in ethnomusicology, a discipline concerned with elucidating music in a cross-cultural perspective. Research in the words of folk song remains the province primarily of folklorists and students of language and literature. Folk music theories are concerned mainly with how folk genres and styles and individual folk songs originated, and how, if, and why they change when diffused. Theories of folk music have been beclouded by the difficulties in recognizing, isolating, and defining a phenomenon as elusive and complex as folk music.

Contemporary scholarship

Since the last decade of the 19th century, folk music has been collected and preserved by mechanical recordings. The application of print and recording technology to folk music has made possible the revival of folk music where traditional folk life and folklore are moribund. Folk songs are frequently a part of public school music curricula; various clubs, organizations, and societies focussing in one way or another on folk music, often in conjunction with folk dance, have arisen; festivals of folk music and dance are an annual event in many communities throughout the world; conservatories of music have been established for the training of folk musicians, particularly in the Socialist nations; radio stations devote substantial portions of their programming time to the broadcasting of folk or folklike music—again, particularly in Socialist nations.

The literature on folk music is sparse in theoretical works, in historical studies, and in materials integrating and comparing the various styles of folk music in Western culture. There is a great deal of literature showing the relationship between folk music and cultivated music. Most plentiful, however, are collections of music and texts, particularly of individual countries or regions, and even of individual singers. These collections are useful for scholarly comparisons of melodies; they give an imperfect picture of performance practice, however, because Western notation cannot give a detailed description of all aspects of music. After World War II, the availability of commercial records did much to fill this gap, and archives of field recordings were developed at many institutions throughout the world. In the U.S., those of the Library of Congress and Indiana University are most important; national archives exist in most European countries, and particularly in Hungary, Czechoslovakia, Germany, and Scandinavia. Such archives provide ample research material for an enormous diversity of projects. Research has usually dealt with "authentic" (i.e., older) material not heavily influenced by urban popular music and the mass media. Popular folk music has not been studied widely. Several organizations for the study of folk music exist, particularly the International Folk Music Council and the Society for Ethnomusicology.

BIBLIOGRAPHY. Among the scholarly periodicals devoted primarily to folk music, the most important are the *International Folk Music Council Yearbook* (1969–   ), formerly the *International Folk Music Council Journal; Ethnomusicology* (1953–   ); and the *Journal of American Folklore* (1888–   ). General works on folk music of Europe and the Americas are BRUNO NETTL, *Folk and Traditional Music of the Western Continents* (1965); WERNER DANCKERT, *Das europäische Volkslied* (1939); the lengthy and subdivided article on the folk music of many countries in *Grove's Dictionary of Music and Musicians*, 5th ed. (1955); and GEORGE HERZOG, "Song," in *Funk and Wagnalls Standard Dictionary of Folklore, Mythology and Legend* (1950). An important survey of the world's folk music in its relationship to certain characteristics of cultures is ALAN LOMAX, *Folk Song Style and Culture* (1968). WALTER WIORA, *Europäischer Volksgesang*

(1952), provides an anthology of formal and melodic types in folk music; *Europäische Volksmusik und abendländische Tonkunst* (1957) explores the relationships between folk and classical music throughout European history. BELA BARTOK, *Hungarian Folk Music* (1931), is a classic study of one folk music style. A.B. LORD, *The Singer of Tales* (1960), deals with the epic traditions of eastern Europe. C.J. SHARP (comp.), *English Folk Songs from the Southern Appalachians*, 2 vol. (1932), is the pioneer collection of Anglo-American song; the total tune repertory of the most important traditional ballads in England and North America is published in B.H. BRONSON, *The Traditional Tunes of the Child Ballads*, 4 vol. (1959–70). The best general survey of Anglo-American folk song is R.D. ABRAHAMS and G. FOSS, *Anglo-American Folksong Style* (1968). The history of folk music research is treated in D.K. WILGUS, *Anglo-American Folksong Scholarship Since 1898* (1959). The modern urban folk song movement has given rise to a series of popular folk music periodicals, most of them ephemeral; notable American examples include *Broadside* (1962–   ), and *Sing Out!* (1950–   ).

(B.N.)

Folk Visual Arts

In the broadest sense, folk art refers to the art of the people, as distinguished from the sophisticated, elite, or professional product that constitutes the mainstream of art in highly developed societies. The term in this comprehensive context combines some quite disparate categories of art; therefore, as a workable field of art-historical study, folk art is generally treated separately from certain other kinds of unsophisticated arts, notably the primitive (defined as the work of prehistorical and preliterate peoples). Historically, the terms folk and popular have been used interchangeably in the art field, the former being specific in English and German (*Volkskunst*), the latter in the Romance languages (*populaire, popolare*); the term folk, however, has increasingly been adopted in the various languages, both Western and Oriental, to designate the category under discussion here. Currently, the term popular art is widely used to denote items commercially or mass produced to meet popular taste, a process distinguished from the manner of the folk artist, who typically creates by hand (or with limited mechanical facilities) objects designed for use by himself or his own circumscribed group. The distinction between folk and popular art is not absolute, however: some widely collected folk art, such as the chalkwares (painted plaster ornamental figures) common in America and the popular prints turned out for wide distribution, may be seen as the genesis of popular art; and the products and motifs long established in folk art have provided a natural source for the popular field.

Although the definition of folk art is not yet firm, it may be considered as the art created among groups that exist within the framework of a developed society but, for geographical or cultural reasons, are largely separated from the sophisticated artistic developments of their time and that produce distinctive styles and objects for local needs and tastes. The output of such art represents a unique complex of primitive impulses and traditional survivals subjected both to sophisticated influences and to highly local developments; aside from aesthetic considerations, the study of folk art is particularly revealing in regard to the relationship between art and culture.

Definition of folk art

As industry, commerce, and transportation begin to offer all people free access to the latest ideas and products, a true folk art tends to disappear; the integrity and tradition that formed its inherent character decline, and the heritage of home-produced products is undervalued for the very qualities that made it distinctive. Subsequent revivals, extensively sponsored by organizations, craft groups, governments, or commercial enterprises, are no longer the same thing.

The recognition of folk art as a special category came about during the late 19th century and was at first limited to the so-called peasant art of Europe, the "art of the land." The new intellectual climate of the time, with a romantic value attached to the simple life and the "folk soul," and the increasing spread of democratic or nationalistic ideas brought the art of the common people into focus; and it was recognized that their simple tools, utensils, and crafts had aesthetic aspects. Prior to industrialization, such folk art was widespread throughout Europe, exhibiting almost everywhere local styles created by people who had no access to the products of the wealthy and who were engaged largely in agricultural, pastoral, or maritime pursuits. As sophistication advanced, localism began to break down along major routes, but the folk arts continued on the periphery, particularly in geographically isolated regions, where they had an opportunity not only to survive but also to elaborate.

Having only limited contact with the outside world, the inhabitants preserved their traditions, art forms, and methods of workmanship over a long period and, at the same time, had to rely on their own invention to create new styles and products at need. These outstanding regional arts provide a well-defined core of material in the field of folk art.

As the early colonists emigrated to undeveloped parts of the world, they, too, were isolated from the cultural developments of the homeland and forced to rely on their own skills for most of their products. The arts they took with them were transformed, and new arts emerged under the stimulus of a different environment and through contact with native cultures; the notable folk arts of the Americas were one result.

In time it was recognized that the great Oriental civilizations offered a distinction between the sophisticated and the folk parallel to that in Europe, and the rise of Oriental folk-art scholarship established the subject on a worldwide basis.

While it is generally agreed that a folk type of art has occurred at some time in many parts of the world (and may yet appear in newly developing countries), there are various areas in which such art has so far been ignored or has not been studied as a separate category. For instance, with the notable exception of Roman folk art, the folk distinction is not usually applied to the art of ancient civilizations nor to Islāmic or Western medieval art. A summary at the present time is, therefore, necessarily concentrated on the more studied areas: European folk art of the 17th–19th centuries, colonial and postcolonial folk arts, and the folk art of certain major Eastern countries. In addition to the major folk regions, this article will deal with the categories, styles, content, and motifs of folk art.

GENERAL CONSIDERATIONS

Patterns of development

The extensive studies of European and American folk art over the past century have revealed certain patterns of folk-art development. Though these patterns are subject to revision as the field expands or is refined, they provide a basis on which cultural variations and less widespread or random occurrences may be considered.

The utilitarian aspect of folk art. Typically, the people who created the art were immediately concerned with producing the necessities of life; as a result, the art is often described as predominantly functional or utilitarian, in spite of the fact that there are important categories that are definitely not utilitarian, such as the widespread miniatures created simply for pleasure. It is true, however, that much artistic effort was absorbed in meeting everyday requirements. In the folk group, in which occupations were often seasonal or dependent on weather and where people had to provide their own amusements, the creation of useful objects became also a leisure-time activity on which creativity was lavished; a shuttle might be transformed with carving or a chest with painted designs, and even the corset stay came to be an art form. For this reason, folk art is best studied (as is primitive art) with the entire handmade product included and attention devoted to its cultural as well as its aesthetic significance. It differs from the study of sophisticated art, in which there is a long-standing distinction between fine and applied arts and a tendency to exclude, or at least segregate, the utilitarian from more strictly aesthetic forms.

Folk art was not created for museums. Certainly, some was designed to endure, such as documents, family portraits, and gravestones; occasional types were made purely for display, such as the "show towel" of the Pennsylvania Germans and the sampler (a piece of needlework with letters or verses embroidered on it as an example of skill); and certain household treasures were preserved for generations. In general, however, there was an indifference to permanence, so long as the function was served; and much of the art was expected to be either consumed or discarded after a celebrative appearance. There is a substantial percentage of intentionally ephemeral folk art—the marriage bowl broken after the ceremony, paper objects burned at funerals, festival breads, carnival figures, graffiti, snowmen; temporary symbolic designs were drawn on the threshold on feast days in India, for example, and were formed of flower petals for religious processions in Italy. Folk-art collections, thus dependent at least in part upon the accidents of survival, must be supplemented by photographic and written documentation in order for a representative view of the whole art to be obtained.

Art to be destroyed

The role of continuous tradition. The element of retention (prolonged survivals of tradition) is considered fundamental in folk art, as it is in folklore. In an isolated situation, the sophisticated ideas that penetrate are generally belated and simplified, and there is a natural trend toward conservatism. Both local and ancient traditions maintain a strong hold. Serviceable forms and familiar motifs are likely to persist, and changes are gradual in comparison to the sudden innovations possible in sophisticated art.

Yet a constant individuality and ingenuity affect the familiar mode, and an art uninhibited by arbitrary aesthetic rules takes many fresh directions. Thus, the fluctuating combination of retained and inventive elements is of significant interest.

Characteristic materials and techniques. The most easily distinguished characteristics of folk art as a whole relate to materials and techniques. Most commonly used were the natural substances that came readily to hand; thus, various materials that have little or no place in sophisticated art, such as straw, may figure importantly in folk art. Sophisticated media, such as oil painting, might be adopted if they could be manipulated, and manufactured products—notably paper, which was cheap and versatile—might be used where available. The unique forms evolved in these sophisticated media illustrate the way in which folk art draws upon the general culture in a limited way, while developing along original lines of its own.

Tools were usually few and often multipurpose: delicate Polish cut-paper designs were often executed with clumsy sheep shears; and in woodwork, chip carving (with ax or hatchet) and notch carving (V-shaped cuts with a knife) were widely used.

Some arts were well within the compass of folk technology; textiles often rival the sophisticated hand-made product in workmanship (differences being a matter of styles and themes). In many crafts, however, the folk artists evolved simpler methods of their own. Cut tin, in silhouette shapes or decorated by hand painting or pricking (marking out a design with small punctures), for example, is a common folk medium, whereas full-round bronze sculpture was not likely to be attempted. Again, the French Canadians used wood for "cathedrals" that were carpentered adaptations of their European stone prototypes.

Large-scale figures often reveal special devices that were invented to overcome technical deficiencies; some are crudely assembled from parts; many maintain a simple overall shape with details merely incised; feet might be represented by pegs inserted into bored holes. In pictorial representation, the difficulties of three-dimensional modelling, while readily solved by some groups, frequently resulted in a preference for outline and flat shapes; for the easier, profile view; and for the evolution of such forms as the silhouette and the shadow picture, made by outlining and filling in the shadow of a head

Devices used to overcome technical deficiencies

cast onto the wall or paper. The limitations forced a mutation in forms.

Folk art in the urban environment. Folk art is by no means restricted to characteristic regional groups or rural arts. It occurs, for example, among minority groups bent on preserving their ethnic or religious traditions and their typical products. There are various folk manifestations within an urban environment, particularly in connection with the celebrative arts, which have a strong traditional hold; for example, at Christmastime in Warsaw, the people carry about the city models they have made of their cathedral. Covered with salvaged coloured foil, the models incorporate a Nativity scene and are lighted by candles or, more recently, by small bulbs and batteries.

Collective versus individual art. While many folk artists are known by name and many specialized in a particular art form, the skills were mainly available to all (with a distinction between the crafts of men and women), and most of the people were productive. The originality that delights the collector was not emphasized by the people themselves, who were concerned with producing the best examples they could of the desired object decorated with the appropriate and traditional image. Without consideration of the group involved and of the circumstances of folk culture in general, the art can scarcely be interpreted.

Categories of folk art. Only a part of folk art falls into the recognized sophisticated categories of visual art, and even that part has its own adaptations.

Architecture. In architecture the focus is naturally on the basic dwelling and on a simple public or religious building. One of the oldest and most remarkable dwelling forms survives in the *trullo* of Puglia, in Italy. A circular dry-stone structure with a tall conical roof, it is often decorated with symbolic designs splashed in white; for multiple rooms, the basic construction is simply repeated.

Myron Goldfinger, New York

Street on the Island of Mykonos, Greece; Greek island folk architecture.

peated. The whitewashed stone architecture of the Greek

islands, combining basic cubic forms with a variety of free shapes and inventive projections of balconies, overhangs, and exterior stairways, has been extensively studied and acclaimed by modern architects—as have the wooden churches of eastern Europe, with their delicate, needlelike wooden spires, and the wooden-stave churches of Scandinavia. Other unique forms are the Alpine house, with its steep, wide-eaved roof designed for snow; the cave dwellings of Spain, some with several rooms and a constructed exterior front; the adobe house; and the log cabin. A characteristic design may evolve for such outbuildings as the granary (notably the *hórreos* of Galicia), the dovecote, the straw shepherd's hut, or the barn. In community building, the walled agricultural villages with radial pathways to surrounding fields, the fishing villages which are oriented to a harbour, and the American stockade cluster as well as the village common exemplify the close relationship of folk design to folk activities.

Painting. The idea of a picture to be hung on the wall is by no means universal in folk art. It occurs in Europe, notably as the ex-voto, or votive offering, hung in churches and chapels, and in America, where portraits and local scenes were executed in oil, pastel, or watercolour. More typically, the painted depictions that occur in folk art are incorporated into other objects; for example, the American clock faces bearing local landscapes. A feature of some folk art is the "picture" displayed like a painted one but executed in such nonpaint media as fern, cork, shells, or embroidery. Oil paints and prepared canvasses are sophisticated materials and, though sometimes available, were often replaced by house paint or chalk and by silk, linen, or cotton fabric. Painting on velvet and underglass painting emerged as specific folk types. The amount of decorative painting on a particular object is often very extensive; among German and German-American groups, for example, every inch of a chest, bed, or chair surface might be covered. Walls or beams were commonly decorated with geometric and floral motifs and occasionally with scenes, though the available space did not encourage anything approximating the sophisticated mural. Painting on exterior walls was a feature in some areas, including parts of North Africa and India as well as Europe. Stencil painting, widely used for furniture and walls, illustrates the folk capacity for achieving varied effects within technical limitations.

In America the technique was applied to "theorem painting" (painting on velvet through a stencil, usually done with a dauber or pad and with some attempt at shading).

Sculpture. Some form of figural sculpture and a quantity of incised or relief decoration applied to a variety of objects appear to be almost universal. Work in wood was particularly widespread, though stone, a more difficult material, was also used, especially for gravestones and religious sculpture. Papier-mâché, with its quick and bold effects, was widely adopted both in the East and West for carnival and votive figures and for a multitude of toys. The folk artist was often at his best in making small things, delighting in toys, small-scale representations of daily activities, and such oddities as ships carved inside bottles. Miniature sculptures were often skillfully executed in elaborate groups; in Russia, for example, an entire herd of cattle was mounted on a jointed trellis designed to provide a scissorlike movement to the whole. Some figural types were created to be set up in groups, as were the European crèche figures (making up the Nativity or manger scene), toy soldiers, and Chinese miniature wedding processions. The creation of useful objects in an overall sculptured shape, both in pottery and wood, is also typical. In southern Europe or in Mexico, a bottle, flask, or candlestick might take human, fish, or other forms; a Moravian beehive, for example, might be a sculptured head.

The folk print. The wood block (also used for stamping textiles) was the natural folk medium for making prints. Usually simply cut and sometimes crudely coloured or stencilled, they served to illustrate popular

The "picture" in folk art

Miniatures

subjects, with more interest often in the idea than in the depiction itself. Small prints of various saints were widely produced in Europe. Comic themes were popular, such as the "topsy-turvy world" and "man reversed" (*e.g.*, "the fish catches the man") and stock characters. Block printing was also used to produce games, announcements for travelling shows, and forms for certificates. The English broadsheets and the Mexican *calaveras* (literally "skulls," a category of prints, sometimes made from lead cuts) offer outstanding examples of the cheap printed sheets that combined a verbal message (verses, proverbs, polemics, pious themes) with illustration. The 19th-century trade cards (notice for a shop or service) are sometimes included in folk art, but doubtfully so; they were often machine printed. In fact, it is difficult to segregate the print of truly folk character from the voluminous field of either "popular" or commercial printing.

Other arts. In the folk field, the minor arts can hardly be called minor, for such universal necessities as pottery, textiles, costume, and furniture and more unusual forms such as weather vanes and scarecrows provided the most frequent opportunities for creative expression and often absorbed the aesthetic impetus that, in the sophisticated world, was associated more with the fine arts.

Both pottery and textiles range from the everyday to elaborately decorated forms that are often symbolic or highly pictorial; even common examples are typically ornamented with design in a simple slip (a mixture of clay and water) or a woven band.

Folk costume is justly included in many general works on costume, but it differs significantly from the sophisticated in several respects: in a localism so extreme that even a particular town or valley may have its own prized style and every region is distinctive; in the complete differentiation of the festival costume from ordinary cloth-

From the Scrimshaw collections at
Mystic Seaport, Mystic, Connecticut

Scrimshaw, whale tooth inscribed with sea chart by John Rause, 1790. In the White Collection, Mystic Seaport, Connecticut. Height 15.5 cm.

ing; and in a prolongation of style that is little affected either by changes of fashion or by individual taste. The motifs which are typical of festival costumes, such as the twin, cone-shaped buttons symbolizing fertility in Sardinia, are too deep-rooted in the tradition of the area to be discarded.

Furniture tends toward basic, repeated shapes, which may be left purely functional but are often extensively carved or painted. The Alsatian chair, for instance, has an upright-board back, carved with a pierced, silhouetted, bilateral design; some hundreds of variations of this simple design have been recorded within the area. Certain occupational forms emerged, according to need, such as the milking stool, the cobbler's bench, and the rocking bench, or "mammy settle."

In metalwork, the materials used to produce tools and other essentials were also turned by the craftsmen into such art forms as toleware (painted tin or tinned iron), incised copper or silver, pewter toys, and lead figurines. European wrought-iron grave crosses and shop signs are distinguished by intricate scrollwork and inventive linear depictions. Delicate bone carving is very widespread, appearing on such objects as implements, game pieces (such as chessmen), figures (notably crucifixes), and ornaments. An art peculiar to North America is the whalebone carving (scrimshaw) made by sailors while at sea.

The theatrical arts are spectacularly represented by puppetry, ranging from toy theatres, finger puppets, and the ubiquitous Punch and Judy shows to the famous puppet theatres of Sicily and Indonesia. Among the appurtenances of travelling shows and miracle plays, dating from the earlier phase of European folk art, was the hobbyhorse, which had a counterpart in festival performances in India. Musical instruments offer a profusion of types, often preserving ancient features of construction, principles of sound, and decoration: the heavy ratchets and rattles of the Alpine festivals; the shaggy bagpipes of the Abruzzi mountains; fiddles such as the rudimentary *gusle* of Yugoslavia, with its typical horsehead or horseman scroll, and the more complicated Norwegian *Hardangerfele*, with underlying sympathetic strings; and innumerable ornamented flutes, harps, horns, and dulcimers. The simple, painted clay whistle or flute is widespread, often in mimetic bird shape. | **Theatrical arts**

Specific folk categories. Any attempt to analyze folk art in terms of the established, sophisticated categories, though revealing in comparison, fails to take into account a substantial bulk of the art. Many characteristic products not subject to sophisticated aesthetic treatment have become specific fields of study and collection because of the ingenuity expended upon them—mangles (laundry beaters), molds, decorated eggs, weather vanes, decoys, powder horns, trade signs, scarecrows, and figureheads, to name a few. There are also significant objects categorized according to function; for example, animal gear represented by the woven harness of donkeys in Spain, carved and painted ox yokes and sheep collars, brass-studded and tasselled headpieces, and ornaments supposedly endowed with protective powers. Other widespread types are decorated vehicles such as gypsy and circus wagons, boats bearing symbolic motifs, and toys and miniatures in countless media.

Freedom of media. While some of the art is executed in a recognized sophisticated medium like wood carving, many other materials, such as hide, horn, straw, bamboo, and palm leaf, are characteristic in certain regions or for certain objects. In fact, there is scarcely an available material that is not utilized somewhere in folk art, from the hickory-nut doll to the commemorative picture made of human hair, and materials are often combined. This free-wheeling employment of any sort of material rivals the fertile adaptations of "found objects" in 20th-century sophisticated art—as many other modern "innovations" have a long-standing precedent in the spontaneous art of the folk. Collage, and assemblage are an old story in this field; embroidered pictures had faces painted in watercolour, and festival figures were made of anything that came to hand. Weather charms in southern Germany were often collages of—among other things —saints' pictures, amulets, and seeds. There is also a great deal of kinetic art: manipulated masks; jointed dolls, figures, and toys; whirligigs (spinning toys); pinwheels spun by wind or candle heat; and balance figures set in motion by a touch. Folk festivals, with their impromptu processions, costumed personages, antics, and props, offer almost a prototype of the 20th-century "happening." | **Kinetic art**

Style. Although the folk artist had his own criteria of function and craftsmanship, design in the theoretical sense was not a part of his training; rather, it was the natural result either of his continued use of established patterns or of instinctive methods of organization. In special instances there was deliberate imitation of well-known works of art, as in the American portraits of

George Washington and folk versions of famous Virgins and Buddhas.

Any particular folk art will necessarily share the style of its general cultural area; Chinese folk art is Chinese as well as folk. Thus, analysis of the style and recognition of its folk origin is dependent upon knowledge of the "high art" with which it interacts, as well as of the folk situation that sets it apart. When a folk piece is compared with an adjacent sophisticated one produced at the same time, the differences become apparent, whether in the nature of the object as a whole or in its material, execution, content, or style. Stylistically, the time lag is significant; for example, the Baroque curve survived in simple country churches, and elaborate floral ornament in furniture decoration, long after sophisticated European art had become neoclassical.

Commonly accepted notions of folk style

One of the commonly accepted notions of folk style is that it is naïve; it is thought to be childlike and fresh, despite the fact that some of its 19th-century critics condemned its "meaningless repetitions" and its "degenerate" forms. Repetitiveness is to be expected in the production of objects needed by all; but the artists saw only a few neighbouring examples, and to the practiced eye their art reveals many variations. Folk art is often associated with bright colour and an appealing charm, qualities sufficiently present to account for a wide popularity but counterbalanced by the sombreness and seriousness of many pieces, notably in religious art. In fact, few commonly accepted notions of folk style apply to the entire field. Execution may be free or meticulous. Representations of figures may be highly literal (even to the inclusion of actual hair and clothing), almost abstractly simplified, or monstrously exaggerated and distorted, as in, for example, the boldly painted papier-mâché carnival figures of Europe or the fantastic animal figures of the Far East.

The focus on utilitarian production leaves its mark in two opposite ways: often there is a strong decorative orientation, with a wealth of surface ornament lavished on objects that maintain a prescribed shape; on the other hand, certain categories of folk production, such as simple tools, and the work of certain groups are characterized by a functionalism so complete as to seem in tune with modern sophisticated design. Technical limitations and the demand for a quantity of certain necessary objects are conducive to simplification; the reverse may be true of such an object as the bridal bedspread, for which custom dictates extreme elaboration.

The particularly long retention of traditional forms and patterns generally results in increasingly stylized versions of themes; in crewel embroidery, for example, the representation of landscape elements is commonly reduced to a tree and hills, the hills typically shown as three simple, rounded humps; in American portrait painting, the bust or figure is conventionalized in a simple frontal form, repeated over and over again and sometimes painted in advance of a sitting, leaving only the features to be filled in. More important, perhaps, is the fact that the adoption of materials not used in sophisticated art, the forcing of a limited technology toward artistic expression, and the adaptation of rather remotely perceived sophisticated ideas to the folk artists' concept of the realities of life result in some highly original stylistic solutions.

Content and motifs. Whereas sophisticated art often reaches out for the esoteric and the unusual, the content of folk art is closely related to immediate human concerns. The major events of life were universally celebrated on the folk level in ways that demanded of art special costumes, implements, vessels, and auspicious gifts. For the newborn there might be amulets and decorated birth certificates. The period of courtship occasioned a love token, often a beautifully carved feminine implement such as a shuttle or needle case; traditional in England was a double spoon symbolizing union and plenty, whereas in Czechoslovakia it was often a painted egg or carved stick. In many regions elaborate wedding chests were carved or painted for the bride. The bridal bedspread or bed curtain, like the wedding costume, was

ornate and highly symbolic, with such motifs as Adam and Eve, the tree of life, and mating birds considered appropriate. Both weddings and funerals required processional equipment, standards, and special vehicles. In some places there were gifts for the dead, which in China took the form of paper models burned at funerals. There were memorials such as grave sculpture, pictures, and documents.

Specific memorial motifs crystallized in two American forms: the "mourning picture," executed in embroidery or watercolour, often depicting grieving figures draped around a tombstone under weeping willows, and the gravestone carved with a winged death's-head or, later, with the urn-and-willow motif.

Religious art. The prevailing religion puts its stamp on every group, providing common elements in areas that share the same religion, even though the groups are not in contact. Catholicism in the West (and, similarly, Buddhism in the East) provided rich visual conceptions that spilled over into folk art. Crucifixes, Virgins, and saints were required as images for village churches and wayside shrines; they were set up over gateways and tombs, in arches, and in homes and were used as motifs on countless objects, where they were often freely combined with secular decoration. Religious observance demanded many objects decorated with Christian symbols—baptismal scoops, altar cloths, pilgrimage bottles, lavabos (holy-water vessels). There is even a special category of "nuns' work," including small devotional objects, many in collage, as well as vestments and church textiles. A particular German sculptural type is the *Palmesel*, a half-size figure of Christ on the donkey, which is drawn through the streets on its wheeled base on Palm Sunday.

Influence of Catholicism

An outstanding category of Catholic folk art is the crèche, made up of figurines displayed at Christmas in homes or churches to re-enact the birth of Christ. The main characters of the event (holy family, Magi, shepherds, and angels) were supplemented by hundreds of lively figures drawn from peasant or village life and shown pursuing their daily activities or bearing gifts to the Christ child similar to those enumerated in folk carols.

The Protestant and Jewish faiths made fewer demands on the visual arts, but the popularity of Biblical themes

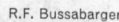
R.F. Bussabarger

Festival votive figures of Durgā, pith and tinsel, 1961, West Bengal, India. Height 5.2 m.

is apparent. A favorite motif for the American weather vane was the angel Gabriel blowing his trumpet, often executed in a style that survives from the puffing zephyrs of classical art. The noteworthy Jewish folk art of Poland was largely lost during World War II, though records of the unique folk synagogues have been preserved by the Institute of Polish Architecture. The Jewish folk-art collection in the Musée Alsacien, Strasbourg, France, includes such specific religious objects as pointers (carved sticks used to guide the reading of sacred texts) and candelabra.

Since antiquity, some form of votive art has occurred in connection with religion. In India, outdoor shrines may be surrounded by a veritable crowd of paper-mâché figures set on the ground as offerings. Catholic churches and chapels throughout the world are hung with countless small ex-votos, usually cutouts of stamped tin or silver in the shape of an afflicted part of the body—an arm, a leg, or an eye—or of the heart or other symbol. In Canadian Jesuit missions, ex-votos were even made of wampum. In Seville small ivory carvings of religious figures were left in the cathedral by soldiers going to war. Clay plaques made from molds, common in the Mediterranean area, show an inheritance from Greek times, when small clay molds of the head of Athena were stamped out in quantity as votive objects. The most significant art, however, occurs in the painted ex-voto, which provides a major type and some of the best examples of folk painting. In sophisticated art, paintings of standard religious themes were often donated to churches in fulfillment of a vow. In folk art, this votive urge found expression in small narrative paintings (only occasionally large, as in Mexico) depicting an accident, illness, or other disaster from which the victim was saved by the intervention of a saint or the Madonna.

The recognized religion, however, is only a part of folk belief, which is impregnated with concepts from earlier times. The decorated Easter egg, for example, is an evo-

Painted Easter egg from Czechoslovakia, 20th century.

lution of the egg as an ancient symbol of renewed life, and the fat, laughing figure of the Japanese Hotei (god of luck) is both a deity and a ubiquitous folk charm. There are many survivals from local pagan cults, particularly of motifs associated with life, fertility, and protection; in Calabria an animal stake may be carved with the head of the blank-eyed mother-goddess, expected to protect the tethered beast, and similar elemental forms were preserved in Czechoslovakia. Lying at the root of human experience, such themes were never completely abandoned by the folk and may appear in curious juxtaposition with Christian themes or secular uses: a Sardinian clay bowl, for example, contains a modelled wedding group with the priest standing before an altar on which a small, nude hermaphroditic deity is seated, and the Christian loaves of bread appear along with pagan phallic and fertility symbols.

Festival art. A major folk category is festival art, which owes its genesis and much of its content to ancient seasonal celebrations. Since antiquity, the solar manifestations of the summer and winter solstices and the vernal and autumnal equinoxes have been bound up with the idea of sowing and reaping, death and rebirth, year's end and year's opening; at such times it was traditionally believed that supernatural forces were in control and should be propitiated. Re-enactment of the roles of malign spirits called for the production of grotesque masks and demonic costumes and also of clamorous noisemakers (bells, horns, rattles, and the like) to drive them away. Harvest figures invoked or celebrated a good crop yield. Special foods in symbolic shapes were prepared and consumed. Varying according to the culture, many other appurtenances were created—decorated trees and poles, lanterns, banners, processional vehicles, sculptured figures and dolls, household and shrine adornments—all bearing their motifs of life symbolism.

While the magical significance of the primordial festivals may have been largely forgotten and the events reduced to horseplay and merrymaking, the customs and the art objects associated with them persisted. In Europe, masqueraders continued to impersonate such "characters" as death, the devil, the goat, the old man, and the mischief-maker; their masks were often makeshift and ephemeral, but many carved of wood and decorated with other materials are preserved and highly prized. Such personifications were also painted on banners or created by assemblage and carried about, as were the Mexican skeletal death figures.

Oriental festivals often featured plant and animal motifs. In China the dragon of the New Year was a great paper creation made to undulate by the dancing steps of the bearers underneath. In the Japanese boys' festival, painted paper carp were flown from poles as symbols of strength and virility. In Indonesia, towering decorative constructions of vegetables and fruits were borne about to celebrate the harvest.

The assimilation of ancient seasonal celebrations—the winter solstice and the Roman Saturnalia with Christmas, for example—has been extensively studied in European folklore. In folk art, it occasioned an intermingling of pagan and Christian elements, enriched by many inventions created in an exuberant festival atmosphere and readily incorporating local and current themes. The celebrative instinct found expression also in many purely local festivals commemorating a local saint, historical event, or an episode in folk life, such as the setting out of the fishing boats or the onset of rains. In Japan alone, there were hundreds of such festivals.

Other sources of folk motifs. The traditional survivals that play so significant a part in folk art stem from other sources as well. Certain motifs diffused from the earliest cultures provided a repertory of stylized symbols to meet decorative demands; for example, the rosette (a disk divided variously into petallike segments), the rayed disk and the swastika (both associated with sun symbolism), the tree of life, the chimera and other fantastic beasts, and such human-animal combinations as the siren or mermaid. The extent to which such motifs retain their meaning or may become simply an appropriate decoration for a certain type of object (as the mermaid is for boats) is problematical, but there is undoubtedly a high symbolic content in the art.

Some aspects of classical mythology fed into folk art, partly by way of later European sophisticated art, and many medieval themes remained popular; the Saracen of the Crusades is a figure that still appears as a Sicilian puppet and as a revolving target in tilting games. Early Renaissance conceptions of paradise and landscapes with stylized trees and towered towns oddly recur in 19th-century folk painting, sometimes imparting an esoteric flavour to a local scene. In fact, the body of tradition retained in folk art may be seen as growing or shifting from one century or one place to another. A folk version of the horse-and-rider motif, in typical profile view, served with only a slight change of uniform for both the Napoleonic and the American Revolutionary soldier.

Ancient pagan seasonal celebrations

Use of medieval and Renaissance themes

Although themes may fall into disuse, they do not become obsolete so readily as in sophisticated art. Yet, folk art is not merely a repository for tradition; new themes constantly evolve from old ones or out of new circumstances. In the wine-producing area around Alsace, Bacchus astride a barrel became the common motif for carved bungs (the stopper of a cask), thus utilizing the classical Bacchus for a specific local commodity. In America, the Indian was widely adopted for weather vanes, trade figures, and other objects. Similar use was made of the personification of Liberty and the emblematic eagle.

Sheet-iron weather vane, unknown artist, c. 1810. In the Shelburne Museum, Inc., Vermont. Height 1.3 m.

Geometric and plant and animal motifs

All decorative design draws heavily on geometric and plant and animal motifs. In the folk use of this material there is often such concentration on one or two motifs that they become strongly identified with the regional style, as the tulip is in Pennsylvania German art; there is also a tendency to attach a particular motif to a particular object, for which it is used repeatedly. The prevalence of animal themes reflects the importance of animals in folk life.

Aside from their frequent appearance as realistic depictions, miniatures, and design elements, some animals also have strong symbolic aspects: the snake, the horse, and the cock, for example, occur with varying significance in many parts of the world.

Representational and narrative art other than the religious is often devoted to local subjects: the family portrait, the individual farm or church, or a typical activity. In Switzerland a favourite theme was the *Alpengang*, depicting the transferral of the cattle to high pastures in the spring. Folk artists also drew upon legend, popular romance, history, and the more famous literary and visual art themes that reached them from the sophisticated world. In Sicily the deeds of Roland (Orlando), derived from the poetic accounts by Torquato Tasso and Ludovico Ariosto, were repeatedly painted and enacted in puppet shows. From history, the patriot Giuseppe Garibaldi was as popular in Italian folk art as George Washington was in American; and the Prince of Wales was a favourite figure for pub signs in England.

Account must also be taken of the folk capacity for satire. The anticlerical humour of Italy has a folk mani-

festation in caricatures of impious monks and nuns. The Russians evolved stock figurines of the snobbish officer, the vain woman, the greedy merchant, the pretty girl riding on a rooster. The early prints of London and Paris had their lampoons, and Mexico had its effigies of personages who did not meet popular approval. Out of the slow exolutions typical of a strongly traditional art, there emerges an astute view of the human situation.

MAJOR FOLK REGIONS

The major recognized folk regions in most cases have been prolific in such crafts as textiles, pottery, and carving and in the production of implements and utensils; they also often have localized costumes. This common art output forms a broad basis underlying the more distinctive arts peculiar to particular areas. The material is so voluminous that most attempts at general survey are admittedly samplings.

General summaries are commonly organized by nation, a convenient expedient, because major collections are centred in great national museums and because folk art is often studied and promoted as part of the national heritage. However, the national summary divides some groups that are homogeneous, such as the Basque region in Spain and France; and it combines, under Italy, for example, such diverse arts as the Alpine and Sicilian.

Any effort to group regions for comparative study will most logically be based on such factors as the traditional retained sources, the prevailing religion, the nature of the related sophisticated culture, and the environmental conditions that affect materials and activities.

Western. *Mediterranean.* Viewed in terms of these four factors, the European folk arts of the Mediterranean area obviously have much in common. First, there was a direct transmission from ancient Near Eastern and Greek civilization, accentuated by Greek colonization in the West and followed by Roman domination. These sources, plus the local cults that occurred everywhere, may be traced even in recent art in the continuance of a rich pottery tradition from Greek times onward and in the preservation of many motifs. Second, the religion, chiefly Roman Catholic or Greek Orthodox, demanded extensive imagery. Third, in the sophisticated cultures throughout the historical period, art of all kinds was a major activity, developing high skills that penetrated to some extent even to the more isolated folk. Finally, contact was facilitated by active trade along an extensive coastline, and varied materials were available; yet the area industrialized very slowly, so that the folk arts could continue to thrive in some localities even to the present.

Thus, it is not surprising that the arts of this region are outstanding in quantity and variety. The level of skill is apparent, sometimes in bold and facile styles, sometimes in meticulous craftsmanship. Many folk artists were capable of expert full-round sculpture, realistic painting, fine metalwork, and other difficult techniques. The motifs are varied and freely intermingled.

Among the long-surviving regional arts are those of Epirus in Greece, where an important folk centre has been established at Metsovon; the islands—the Aegean with its stone architecture, Sicily with its spectacular carved and painted carts, puppets, and pottery, and Sardinia, noted for gold ornaments, textiles, and costumes still in use; and Puglia, Calabria, and the Abruzzi region in Italy, the latter having fine lace, silver filigree (openwork), and weaving.

Southern France is affiliated with this area, as is evidenced by the style of the fine ex-votos and Nativity figures of Provence. So is the Iberian Peninsula, though in that region there are also special factors. The Moorish influence was felt particularly in Andalusia—as in the use of ivory as a material and in the arabesque tracery (ornate, interlaced openwork) of the ironwork—and the Atlantic coastline provided other connections. The Portuguese use of cork was distinctive. Galicia and the Basque region, each with a population of distinct linguistic background, developed in prolonged isolation, the results of which are clearly visible in their exceptional

Outstanding quantity and variety of Mediterranean arts

arts: the architecture presents unique features, and the Basques are unusual in their lack of pottery, though they developed remarkable dance costumes. The difficulty of communications preserved a strong folk character not only in Galicia and the Basque region but throughout the peninsula. The painted and glazed tiles (*azulejos*), the textiles (notable in Salamanca), and carved furniture are among the products notably Iberian in character. Traditional survivals were strong in the northeast, with much religious art, including prints, centred in Catalonia.

Slavic area. Another possible grouping is the Slavic area in eastern Europe and Russia. There the influences from the ancient Near East and Greece penetrated less far in early times but were transmitted (and transmuted) by the way of the Byzantine Empire and the Eastern Church. Much folk art in the area was strongly affected by the Byzantine style.

Among the transmitted elements were the themes and styles associated with icons, which were commonly hung —at wells, for example—until the mid-18th century, when their production was discouraged in Russia and thus dwindled. Two centuries of Mongol rule introduced other traditions stemming from the East and marked by the so-called animal style. Finally, in modern times, these countries have mostly had Communist governments, whose policy includes promotion of the folk arts, organization of artists into cooperatives, and even the introduction of crafts from one area into another. Although this has been a stimulus to the study of folk art, it tends to blur the distinction between the strictly folk and the revived or commercialized product. Even earlier, Russian folk art was subject to extraneous influences in a way not typical elsewhere: in the 17th century, craftsmen were requisitioned from many parts of Russia to supply products for the national economy or to work on palaces, and they were also assembled around monasteries for prescribed output.

The Russian products probably best known elsewhere are toys—intricate constructions of wood or vivid earthenware miniatures. Some of the Vyatka toys are thought to be survivals of idols made for homes, representing the innumerable local deities that preceded Christianity. Other notable arts include ceramic tiles, wooden and ceramic figurines, and bone carving in the Siberian tradition.

Carved walrus-bone comb from northern Russia, 17th century. In the Walters Art Gallery, Baltimore. 7 × 13 cm.

Eastern European woodwork

In eastern Europe, where national boundaries have been particularly confused and the population comprises various minorities, studies of the art may follow ethnic lines. The geography provides a number of distinct regions, which are as varied as coastal Dalmatia, Transdanubia, and the isolated Tatras mountains. With a heavily forested landscape, the work in wood was outstanding. It appeared in church architecture, architectural sculpture, vessels and implements, and in such special forms as the sculptured grave-post; even a corn bin might be covered with rosettes. The area was rich in festival arts, with a strong retention from pre-Christian traditions and magic rites. In Czechoslovakia there were special wedding effigies and candlesticks. Among many ancient motifs, such as vase-and-tree, sun, and heart, the cock appeared as a protective symbol that might be set on roof ridges or carved on cheese molds. Some of the art is strikingly primitive.

One of the complications arising in the study of eastern European arts is the fact that the countries involved are culturally borderline, having an affinity with Catholic Europe in the West (exemplified by the ex-votos in the brilliant Czechoslovakian glass painting) and with the Byzantine Empire in the East. The arts bracketed as Polish, including some of the finest decorative art in paper, once extended far to the east and yet are northern European.

"Justitia," Gudbrandsdal tapestry, probably late 17th century. In the Norsk Folkemuseum, Oslo. 145 × 178 cm.

Northern Europe. The situation in northern Europe was very different from that in the south, and not merely in climate. The tradition involved a different mythology, and the society lacked the sophisticated centres that had crystallized early in Greece and Italy. The Roman influences that reached northern Europe had far to travel; consequently, the transmitted motifs were fewer, and emphasis might be placed on technical execution rather than on variety. This can be seen in the prevalent and superb use of two motifs, the acanthus and the vine-and-tendril. It can also be seen in the animal style from the East, which penetrated and persisted, for example, in some fine architectural carving, with the tendency typical of this style toward flat and pierced rather than full-round rendering. Finally, although religious art was by no means lacking, the Reformation, which in itself was a popular movement, curbed the use of extensive Catholic imagery as well as the demand for religious objects.

The festival arts drew heavily on northern pagan themes, and the impulse that gave rise to pre-Lenten carnivals of the south was likely to find expression rather in municipal and occupational processions with comic giant figures drawn through the streets.

Some parts of the far north demonstrate that density of population is a factor in folk art; where farms are many miles apart and isolated; the art forms may tend to be few or even nonexistent. Even so, there may be one or two special crafts, such as the bone and horn carving of Lapland. Also, where materials are scarce, as in Iceland, variety of product depends on imports likely to be allocated to the sophisticated, not the folk. In more densely populated France, Germany, and The Netherlands, on the other hand, it is clear that peasant arts existed everywhere in the earlier periods but that the early establishment of trade routes and urban centres pushed the folk arts into special categories or into the peripheral areas.

Among the Scandinavian regions, Norway is noted for the rose painting of Hallingdal and Telemark Fylke, the needlework of Hardanger, and the pictorial weaving of Gudbrandsdalen. Sweden, among varied arts, had a unique type of built-in furniture and wall hangings that were either painted or woven with biblical and Icelandic motifs. Finland had a specific linear ornament called "dark drawing," made by bending a strip of wood until the ends meet, and metal ornaments of prehistoric origin in Karelia. Distinctive folk-art regions in Denmark include the Hedebo (now Hedeboryde) area, with its linen embroidery; the Fyn archipelago, with its colourful floral painting; and Jutland and Slesvig, with notable cabinetmaking. In the Baltic area there were many survivals of ancient motifs (swastikas, rayed disks, snakes, horse heads) used on varied products, including the remarkable crosses and roofed poles, often with symbolic wrought-iron finials (crowning ornaments).

Central Europe. In the heart of Europe, two areas demonstrate two factors involved in the formation of folk culture: the Rhineland, where wine production provided a number of special objects and motifs; and the Alpine regions, which, though extending into several countries, share a pattern of living dictated by the mountain territory. The latter region, which includes several well-defined areas—such as the Appenzell in Switzerland, the Tirol in Austria, and the Alto Adige in the south Tirol, now a part of Italy—is rich in festival arts, ceremonial foods, and implements associated with dairying (even musical cowbells).

In France, The Netherlands, and Germany, the proximity of folk groups to sophisticated culture made its mark in the variety of products, high skills, and lavish decoration of such objects as furniture. Invention was devoted to new figural types, such as the hod carrier common to lower Germany and Austria; and events such as the Napoleonic Wars made a rather quick impact, as with the soldier motif and the appearance of handwritten and ornamented documents relating to military service. The mechanical genius that made the Germanic peoples leaders in the field of sophisticated automata found folk expression in innumerable animated toys, clocks, chimes, figures, and other gadgets. While the folk art associated with Paris itself is not to be ignored, the more easily analyzed French groups are outlying, as in Brittany, with its many-figured outdoor calvaries (representations of the crucifixion) and other enduring forms.

Britain and Ireland. The tendency to separate British from other European folk arts is an oversimplification, for a number of forms are shared with northern Europe; for example, the famous horse brasses (circular harness ornaments often retaining ancient protective motifs), giant processional figures such as the Salisbury dragon, and the May tree, a celebrative decoration in pole form. England is a small country that industrialized rapidly, a factor that tends to shorten the folk-art period. Some arts that required expanding technical skills, however, could develop as folk forms: for example, the printed arts (such as the broadside, or sheet printed on one or on both sides and folded) and the hand-propelled roundabout (later the mechanized carousel), which became increasingly elaborate. Tunbridge woodwork, of glued coloured strips, is merely one example of local invention. Among the well-known categories of folk art are the inn signs (both hanging and "effigy" signs), wrought-iron work, and tombstones. Hebridean textiles and Highland plaids and sporrans (the pouch worn in front of the kilt) are also familiar products. Both Scotland and Ireland have interesting grave crosses bearing ancient symbols. Ireland, however, serves as a reminder that the creative urge of a folk group may not focus primarily on the visual arts; Irish folk art does not compare with the contribution to oral lore in that area. (The same may be said of the Negro folk minority in the United States, whose musical contribution was spectacular but whose visual art traditions were largely cut off.)

North America. The colonization of the Americas in the 17th and 18th centuries, stemming largely from Europe at a time when European folk art was flourishing, resulted in a second general area of major folk-art development. This art can be divided into that of the United States (loosely called American folk art); Canadian folk art, which has much in common with that of the United States, with its scrimshaw, ship carving, and western pioneer art, but which also has products of its own (for example, French-Canadian wood carving in Quebec); and Latin-American folk art, which has quite a different character.

For the first century and a half, the art of the eastern seaboard of the United States may be described as predominantly folk. Although there were European imports and works produced by sophisticated American artists, they were generally a pallid reflection of the art then developing in Europe, and they made little impact on a people bent on making a home in a new world. The so-called Yankee ingenuity produced a wealth of material, sometimes reminiscent of European prototypes but often new. There were, for example, dozens of handmade lighting devices and many specialized contrivances such as the trammel, for raising and lowering pots in the fireplace, and the corn planter. Fresh decorative styles,

"The Crucifixion," Fraktur by unknown artist, watercolour on paper, 1847. In the Abby Aldrich Rockefeller Folk Art Collection, Williamsburg, Virginia. 28 × 37 cm.

special forms, and new motifs contributed to an art that, either in evolution or invention, was typically American.

American folk painting is outstanding. Although there was once a tendency to view as sophisticated the artists who closely followed European styles and as folk those who worked in the rapidly emerging American manner, many of the latter have become individually known creators of a valuable body of work and have taken their place in the history of American art, some no longer viewed as belonging in the folk category. The more typical folk product comprised thousands of portraits and scenes by anonymous or local craftsman-artists or itinerant painters, who provided a vivid, if often crude, extensive record of America's ancestors and their surroundings.

As America advanced, a pattern of regional differentiation appeared, just as in Europe. In general, geographical

Margin notes:

Arts of the Alpine region

American folk painting

isolation was overcome rather quickly, one exception being the sparse settlements of the Appalachian Mountains, where Scots-Irish descendants maintained a handicraft tradition. People of varying origins, however, had brought to the "melting pot" of America their different art traditions. While they were often content with preserving a few objects and customs, some groups chose to maintain a separate identity, set apart by religion or national origin, and among them some fresh regional arts developed. The strict religious beliefs of the Shakers in New England and New York state, with their emphasis on simplicity, gave rise to clean, functional lines in furniture and architecture and to some psychologically interesting "spirit drawings" executed under the influence of religious visions. The Pennsylvania Germans (popularly called Dutch) not only had a distinctive religion but clung tenaciously to the language and traditions of their native Pfalz (Palatinate, now in the state of Rhineland-Pfalz and in Bavaria), which in art included such crafts as fine painted furniture and such motifs as the tulip, heart, and vine. Thriving in the flourishing countryside of their new home, they produced a notable body of art: Fraktur (embellished documents), painted wedding chests, decorated ceramics (including elaborate pieces created for special occasions), unique barns with exterior painted symbols ("hex signs"), pictorial embroidery, weaving, and other forms.

Arts of the American west

The American settlers who moved westward were again thrust into a folk situation comparable to that of their forebears, and a pioneer art developed. Saddlery was one of its important crafts; the covered wagon was its distinctive vehicle; and the board structures of mining towns and the sod houses of the plains were solutions to the problem of immediate housing. The flatboat and keel-

By courtesy of the Girard Foundation, Santa Fe, New Mexico

All Souls' Day toys from Oaxaca, Mexico, pottery and paper, c. 1960. In the collection of the Girard Foundation, Santa Fe, New Mexico. Height of largest figure 26.5 cm.

boat of the Mississippi River arose from specific navigational requirements.

The southwest, including part of California, is an area apart, producing art distinct from what is often called "western Americana." There the architecture was influenced by the Spanish mission and adobe styles, and a Catholic religious art was encouraged among the natives, resulting in the carved or painted imagery of saints (bultos and santos) with a strong native flavour overlying the Spanish derivation. These arts are more allied with the Latin American (as may be seen in the Museum of International Folk Art in Santa Fe).

Latin America. The different character of Latin-American folk art may be ascribed in part to the modification of a primitive culture resulting from contact with an advanced one. The settlers on the eastern seaboard of North America moved in on a primitive Indian population whose arts were relatively limited and who were rapidly pushed back or disoriented; the folk art of that area was thus essentially the product of the white settlers.

In Latin America, however, where there were some highly developed pre-Columbian cultures as well as tribal arts, intermingling was freer; this was partly because the missionary program—which included the teaching of crafts and Catholic symbols to the native population and the use of native craftsmen for church construction and for the production of religious objects—accepted an infusion of native techniques and styles. Thus, Indian crafts and motifs had a better chance of survival, and a greater degree of syncretism could occur. Furthermore, the colonizers, predominantly Spanish and Portuguese, brought with them the wealth of Mediterranean tradition and the varied imagery and forms of their home regions.

Under circumstances as favourable as these, a virtual explosion of folk art can occur, as it did, notably, in Mexico. Because Mexico seems to have a peculiar receptivity to art impulses regardless of source, the area is distinguished by a folk imagination that can create a towering, multifigured, ceramic candlestick, elaborate figures and models of straw, and fantastic fireworks. Craft motifs are handled with great spontaneity, and the festival arts are remarkable, with such original creations as the Judas figures, the skeletal musicians associated with the Day of the Dead (*día de los difuntos*), and the skulls (*calaveras*) that appear both as confections and as a theme in popular prints. The religious arts are also outstanding, with many ex-voto paintings (*retablos*) and Nativity figures in varied materials. Art that combines features of the Mediterranean and native Indian traditions occurs also in other Latin-American countries, as in the Portuguese-oriented areas of Brazil and in Argentina, which developed some arts related to the life of the cowboy of the pampas (gaucho). In some regions of Latin America, however, the indigenous Indian culture long remained unaffected and little influenced by the European colonies.

Explosion of folk art in Mexico

In the Caribbean and coastal areas there is evidence of African–Indian–European interaction: saints are painted with African physiognomy, and African decorative motifs appear on crosses, votive sculptures (the *milagre* of northeastern Brazil, for example), and such objects as laundry beaters and peanut pounders in Surinam.

Other regions. During the 16th–19th centuries, European exploration, trade, and culture expanded into many parts of the world. Colonization elsewhere, however, was not so conducive to folk evolution as in the Americas, where many settlers emigrated early, bearing folk traditions with them and expecting to make a life with their own skills. Because in many places the Europeans maintained a sophisticated enclave closely tied to the homeland, the native arts were preserved intact, inhibited, or exploited. This was fairly typical in Africa and the primitive Pacific areas, where settled colonization took hold only in the late 19th century. In South Africa, where it occurred earlier, only the Dutch (who built farmhouses of Dutch character) tended even to take their families with them.

Non-Western. In many parts of the world there have been tribal arts, some of which have nonprimitive aspects. These are sometimes bracketed with the primitive in a general category of ethnic art and are sometimes considered as folk art. But although they may have folk-like crafts and links with the outside world, they differ from true folk cultures in that they constitute homogeneous societies with traditions that are specifically ethnic rather than shared with a broad area of sophisticated culture. Such tribal folk art occurs in the Saharan Berber and Siberian areas, among the Ainu people of Japan, and in various parts of Asia.

The Eastern art recognized as truly folk has been studied, as in the West, chiefly in the areas where it exists as the unsophisticated art within a great culture. The Oriental traditions were often relatively uninterrupted, and effects from industrialization were late; while all folk dating is problematical and much of the art has perished, it is likely that some folk art in the East has a history extending back to ancient times. In Japan, however, it is usually understood as beginning in

"Cock and Hen," Ōtsu watercolour on paper, middle Edo period (1603–1867). In the Folkcraft Art Museum, Tokyo. 32.5 × 22.5 cm.
By courtesy of the Folkcraft Art Museum, Tokyo

the Edo period (17th century). Interest in folk art is particularly strong in India and Japan, where there are art scholars familiar with the Western folk concept but dedicated to the preservation of their Eastern traditions. Indian folk art was discovered in an emotional climate reminiscent of the European discovery of the folk soul; Ananda Coomaraswamy, a leader in the movement, called folk art the "main road," as distinguished from the sophisticated "bypaths." Both in India and Japan, there were sophisticated artists who deliberately identified themselves as "folk."

India and Pakistan. In India, where all of the crafts are distinguished by variety, skill, and a strong com-

By courtesy of the Museum of Childhood, Edinburgh

Balinese votive doll, dried palm leaves, *c.* 1880. In the Museum of Childhood, Edinburgh. Height 38 cm.

ponent of strictly Indian tradition, the folk distinction is not always clear-cut. It is most apparent in such objects as toys (for example, the mother-and-child figure probably related to fertility concepts), masks, works in papiermâché (votive and animal figures, for example, and dancing dolls balanced on wire), the symbolic motifs painted on the houses of the poor, and other works of art related to local custom or primitive belief. Particularly in southern India, small religious and other sculptures were created in quantity in an unmistakably folk manner; there are also some distinctive tribal arts, notably those of Assam. Pakistan has some highly regional arts: for example, the fine house carving and the ceremonial fans of Swāt, the silver ornaments of Gilgit, and the tombstones and matrimonial objects produced in the arid regions of Baluchistan.

Pakistani regional arts

Japan. Pottery and toys are probably the most widespread kinds of Japanese folk art; but there are also innumerable typical objects—lanterns, fans, umbrellas, nested boxes, and kites—exhibiting skillful use of bamboo and paper, as well as wood, lacquer, and other materials. There are thousands of wayside images, as well as sculptures for shrines and graves, in a folk style characterized by shallow carving on a simple, coarse-stone shape. An outstanding type of folk painting flourished in the Ōtsu region from the 17th to the 19th century. Clearly distinct from the sophisticated ukiyo-e painting, it was executed by farmers and artisans and depicted folk as well as Buddhist deities, popular animal motifs such as the cock-and-hen, and popular characters and genre scenes, often satirical. There are also votive pictures, some portraying the horse and traceable to the ancient horse offering. One of the late-surviving folk regions in modern Japan is on Sado island, where small cylindrical stone images were thrown into the sea to invoke pregnancy.

China. Chinese folk art must have been as extensive as any in the world, as evidenced by the descriptions of Western travellers and the souvenirs they collected and by various cultural and craft studies; but the problem of collating and analyzing the material as a folk category is forbidding. Every Chinese region has its own styles, and the entire art output is enormous. The art associated with weddings, funerals, and festivals is extravagant, even among the poor. In the country where paper was invented in antiquity, papermaking is a common skill, and the art of paper cutting is learned from childhood. Paper is used for the banner-like shop signs that give a special character to Chinese streets and for many complicated models and festival objects.

Indonesia. In its effect on folk culture, the spread of Buddhism in the Far East has some parallels with the spread of Christianity in the West. In Indonesia, for example, where Buddhism penetrated an area whose local traditions were strong enough to survive and intermingle with the new concepts, there is much temple art of a folk character. Among the abundant ephemeral folk art of Bali are the vegetal offerings and the beautifully stylized symbolic objects woven of palm leaf. Indonesian puppets and printed textiles are world famous.

BIBLIOGRAPHY. H.T. BOSSERT, *Ornamente der Volkskunst* (1949; Eng. trans., *Folk Art of Europe*, trans. by SYBIL MOHOLY NAGY, 1953, reprinted 1964), selection by the author from his *Volkskunst im Europr* (1926), a major compilation of folk designs, largely from textiles; D.P. BRANCH, *Folk Architecture of the East Mediterranean* (1966), includes Greek islands, central and southern Italy, with photos and diagrams; R.F. BUSSABARGER and B.D. ROBINS, *The Everyday Art of India* (1968), with glossary; ALFONSO CASO and D.F. RUBIN *et al.*, *Arte popular de México* (1963), a special issue of *Artes de México*, authoritative for crafts; E.O. CHRISTENSEN, *The Index of American Design* (1950), selections from a Federal Art Project study covering pre-1700–*c.* 1900; H.J. HANSEN (ed.), *Europas Volkskunst und die europäisch beeinflusste Volkskunst Amerikas* (1967; Eng. trans., *European Folk Art in Europe and the Americas*, 1968), country by country, chiefly European, with over 600 illustrations; M. HARMON *et al.*, "Folk Art," *Encyclopedia of World Art*, vol. 5, col. 451–506 (1961), a wordwide sampling of the arts, with extensive bibliography to *c.* 1960; STELLA KRAMRISCH, *Unknown India* (1968), an exhibition catalog of ritual and tribal folk art; FRANCES LICH-TEN, *Folk Art of Rural Pennsylvania* (1946), German-American motifs and products; JEAN LIPMAN, *American Primitive Painting* (1942), pioneering study of folk painters; P.S. LORD and D.J. FOLEY, *The Folk Arts and Crafts of New England* (1965), over 500 illustrations of crafts; HUGO MUNSTERBERG, *The Folk Arts of Japan* (1958), includes the modern folk-art movement and living folk arts; BERNARD RUDOFSKY, *Architecture Without Architects* (1969), on primitive and vernacular styles all over the world; R.T. WILCOX, *Folk and Festival Costume of the World* (1965), over 150 regions, 111 plates, and bibliography.

(Ma.Ha.)

Food, New Sources and Products

Since prehistory man has survived on a diet consisting of a relatively few species of plants and animals that he domesticated so long ago that their origins are forgotten. Three cereals—wheat, rice, and corn—supply the bulk of human energy, protein, and vitamin requirements. Since about the 1940s, however, the unprecedented rate of population growth, the development of new technology, and a variety of economic factors have changed traditional concepts of food supply and led to the discovery of new sources of food, especially protein, and new ways in which these materials can be marketed.

The demand for increased food supplies is related both to population increase and income. At very low levels of per capita income, small increases go primarily for purchasing food. In regions where population growth is highest and income lowest, the demand for food promises to increase very rapidly through the 1970s and 1980s and at a much faster rate than in more developed and stable regions.

Part of the new demand will be met by an agricultural revolution, under way in the 1970s, based upon new varieties of plants, intensive fertilization, and irrigation; but the diets of some of the world's population, especially young children and nursing mothers, must be supplemented by additional protein even if traditional agricultural foods such as cereals supply sufficient calories. Further, some of the rapidly rising demand for such traditional foods as milk, cheese, meat, and seafood will exceed potential sources and will therefore need to be met by synthesized substitutes similar in appearance, taste, and texture.

Food cultural habits

Cultural habits and traditions universally create food preferences and inhibitions, complicating the introduction of new sources of food. In Western countries, rice, which has about the same nutritive value and table use as wheat products, remains less preferred, a situation reflected in prices of the two foods. In Southeast Asia, seafood products are preferred with a strong fish flavour, but in Western countries the same flavour is considered objectionable.

Current food research has been largely stimulated by the rapidly growing world demand, but technological advances in other areas also have contributed. The fibre-spinning processes developed for synthetic fabrics and the U.S. and Soviet space programs have had impact. Similarly competition among food producers has provided impetus for research.

NEW SOURCES OF FOOD PROTEIN

The most significant aspect of the search for new food sources is probably the need for adequate protein, especially in regions where meat and fish are available in limited quantities.

Oilseeds. Potentially, 80,000,000 tons of oilseed protein are available per year for human feeding. The current rate of production, however, is far below this. The world production of major oilseed crops (in millions of metric tons) is: soybeans, 46.5; peanuts, 18.1; cottonseed, 22.1; and copra, 3.4. The primary purpose of cultivation of various oilseeds is to obtain edible oil for the table or for use by industry in the manufacture of margarine or shortening.

The basic process for extracting the oil is essentially the same for all oilseeds and involves either pressing or sol-

vent extraction or a combination of the two. The material remaining after removal of the oil contains primarily fibre, carbohydrate, and protein. The protein can comprise up to 50 percent of this residue, depending upon the particular oilseed. This material is either discarded, used as fertilizer (actually it is a poor source because it decomposes too slowly), or used as a source of protein in animal feeds. Currently only a small percentage is recovered in a form suitable for use in human foods. Food applications of these materials are limited because of the overly strenuous conditions under which many of them are handled to remove the oil and because of their market image as fertilizers or animal feed. Each of the oilseeds has specific problems of processing as well. The oilseed proteins are the least expensive of all of the potential new proteins in their simplest edible state, but additional refining doubles or trebles the price.

It should be noted that there is no certain method for comparing the nutritive values of various proteins; their actual worth depends upon a variety of external environmental factors, such as the other components of the diet. An approximate comparison of proteins tested in laboratory research gave the following relative nutrient values: egg, 100; casein, 60–70; soy, 40–50; yeast, 40–60; and fish protein concentrate (FPC), 70–80.

Soybeans. Soybeans are the most important of the oilseeds. Soybean oil is recovered primarily by solvent extraction, and the residue is approximately 50 percent protein. The defatted soy contains a number of undesirable constituents that must be removed or inactivated, particularly a number of physiologically active proteins. One that inhibits the important digestive enzyme trypsin must be inactivated by heat. This process must be carried out with great care, because the desirable proteins also are affected by heat in a manner that reduces their solubility and nutritive value. Other factors limiting the usefulness of soy protein are a bitter, beany off-flavour and the presence of two soluble carbohydrates (raffinose and stachyose) that lead to distension of the human gut and flatulence. Each of these factors may be ameliorated by processes that purify the protein and yield products of higher protein content. These processes will be described briefly.

Three forms of soybean

Traditionally, Oriental peoples use three forms of soybean: soy milk, a watery extract produced by cooking the beans at high temperature; tofu, a protein curd that is precipitated from the soy milk; and miso, shoyu, and other food products that are manufactured by fermentation processes.

The simplest method of purification used in Western countries involves immobilization of the protein and removal of extraneous materials. This is accomplished either by extraction with aqueous alcohol or by extraction with water at the isoelectric point; that is, the point at which the acid–alkaline factor in the substance makes it electrically neutral. The minimum solubility of soy proteins, on the pH scale of acidity–alkalinity, is at pH 4 to 5, moderately acid. Either process removes most of the undesirable soluble carbohydrates and some of the off-flavour, giving a product approximately 70 percent protein, called soy protein concentrate, a valuable food additive.

An even more refined product is created by carrying out a process the reverse of the above; the protein is made soluble by extraction at an alkaline pH and separated from the insoluble residue. The protein is then precipitated by readjustment of the pH back to the region of minimum solubility. The cycle can be repeated a number of times to increase the purity of the protein. Products of this type, called soy protein isolates (SPI), are 90 to 99 percent protein.

Almost all of the objectionable characteristics have been removed from the SPI, and the material can be incorporated in a large variety of food products. This material can be texturized by spinning into edible fibres (more fully described later).

Completely different products, full-fat soy flours, are made from dehulled beans by heating at high temperatures for short periods in an extrusion apparatus. The heating denatures the proteins and provides a greatly expanded surface that absorbs the oil to such an extent that a dry free-flowing powder can be obtained. These products are much less expensive than soy protein concentrate and are of particular interest in countries where oil is in surplus.

Cottonseed. Another potentially important source of protein, cottonseed, has very little current use in food supply. The protein of this plant is a tertiary by-product of cotton fibre and oil production, and the seed is rarely handled under conditions that would allow ultimate human consumption. Cottonseed has very small glands (a few thousandths of an inch) containing a pigment called gossypol, which is toxic to nonruminant animals. This pigment also can react with the protein to inactivate the nutritionally important amino acid lysine, reducing its nutritive value. The processing of the protein therefore must remove the gossypol without extensive damage to the protein.

These criteria for recovery of the oil can be met by a combination of prepressing and solvent extraction. In the pressing, sufficient heat is generated to inactivate the gossypol but not destroy the protein, and the last traces of oil are removed by extraction. The resulting product contains 50 to 55 percent protein, and the nutritional value can be improved greatly by addition of lysine. This protein is the basis for a vegetable protein mixture called Incaparina, which has been used in parts of Central and South America for a number of years to prevent protein malnutrition.

A newly developed glandless form of cotton without gossypol may significantly affect the future use of cottonseed protein if the yield and quality of the cotton linters can be adequately accounted for. Another development, a centrifugal process for separation of a high-protein (70 percent), low-gossypol fraction from the meal, produced by a straight solvent-extraction process, may find application if the costs involved in such a process can be lowered.

Other oilseeds. The peanut, coconut, rapeseed, and sunflower are potentially significant oilseeds. The peanut finds considerable use as a whole food because it has no toxic or indigestible components. It is important as an

Extraction processes

Radiation-Induced Plant Mutations

crop	variety name	place of release	date of release	improved features	crop	variety name	place of release	date of release	improved features
White mustard	Primex	Sweden	1950	greater seed yield and oil content	Barley	Hellas	Sweden	1967	resistant to lodging and straw breakage; increased yield, especially with heavy fertilization; resists sprouting at harvest time
Summer oil rape	Regina II	Sweden	1953	seed yield and oil content					
Pea	Weibull Stral-ärt	Sweden	1953	5–10% higher yield	Barley	Kristina	Sweden	1969	resistant to lodging and straw breakage; very high yield; outstanding malting quality
Winter barley	Jutta	Germany, East	1953	winter hardiness; yield of grain; lodging resistance					
Pea bean	Sanilac	Michigan	1956	bush type; disease resistance	Rice	SH 30–21	Rep. of China	1957	higher yield; short growing period
Spring barley	Pallas	Sweden	1958	tolerance to heavy nitrogen fertilization	Rice	KT 20–74	Rep. of China	1957	higher yield; short growing period
Peanut	N.C. 4-X	North Carolina	1959	tougher hull (better for shipping); high yield	Rice	YH 1	Rep. of China	1963	higher yield; short growing period
Oats	Florad	Florida	1960	resistant to stem rust; superior grain quality and straw stiffness	Rice	Reimei	Japan	1966	short straw; lodging resistance, especially with heavy fertilizer; less variation with location and year; tolerates lower temperatures, especially during germination and seedling stages
Pea bean	Seaway	Michigan	1960	bush type; virus resistance					
Spring barley	Mari	Sweden	1960	early maturity (8 days); stiffer straw					
Oats	Alamo-X	Texas	1961	disease resistance					
White mustard	Seco	Sweden	1961	seed yield; crude early maturity; stiff stalk	Soybean	Tainung No. 1 (R)	Rep. of China	1962	vigorous, dropping-resistant variety with the characteristics of long branches and higher yield
Bread wheat	NP 836	India	1961	awned to resist bird damage; higher yield without irrigation	Soybean	Tainung No. 2 (R)	Rep. of China	1962	vigorous, dropping-resistant variety with short internode, large seed, and adapted to acid or alkaline soil
Spring barley	VRz	Czecho-slovakia	1962	higher yield of grain; stiff straw					
Pea bean	Gratiot	Michigan	1963	better seed type					
Barley	Pennrad	Pennsylvania	1963	improved winter hardiness	Soybean	Raiden	Japan (Tokyo district)	1966	earlier maturity; shorter stem (resists lodging); maintains high yield and nematode resistance of original variety*
Bread wheat	Sharbati Sonora	India	1967	amber grain colour (preferred in India); short straw; early maturity; high protein and high lysine to protein ratio					
Bread wheat	Lewis	U.S.	1964	lodging resistance; early maturity; high yield	Soybean	Raiko	Japan (Tōhoku district)	1969	earlier maturity; shorter stem; resists lodging; higher yield; maintains nematode resistance of the original variety*
Bread wheat	Stadler	U.S.	1964	early maturity; strong straw; good yield; excellent soft quality grain; good disease resistance and winter hardiness	Pea bean	Seafarer	U.S.	1967	very early maturity; bush type; resistant to alpha, beta, and gamma races of anthracnose and bean commonmosaic races 1, 15, and 123
Bread wheat	Sinvalocho Gama	Argentina	1962	more resistance to black stem rust and leaf rust					
Bread wheat	Zenkouzi-komugi	Japan	1969	earlier maturity; shorter culm; higher yield (10–15%)	Haricot bean	Saparke 75	U.S.S.R.	1967	surpasses the initial variety on average by 55 dt/ha in green pod yield and 5.2 dt/ha in seed yield; green pods are devoid of fibre and fixed on the stem at least 5 cm higher, making mechanical harvesting possible; improved resistance to bacterial diseases
Bread wheat	Novosibir-skaia 67	U.S.S.R.	1969–70	lodging resistance; baking quality					
Durum wheat	Castel del Monte	Italy	1969	lodging resistance; high yield					
Barley	Vienna	Austria	1959	high yield; high 1,000-kernel weight; mildew resistance; lodging resistance	String bean	Universal	Germany, West	1950	early maturity, higher yield; good resistance to anthracnose
Barley	Milns Golden Promise	U.K.	1966	shorter and stiffer straw with good grain yield and malting properties, but mildew susceptible	String bean	Unima	Germany, West	1957	immune against anthracnose; resistant to *Pseudomonas phaseolicola*
Barley	Midas	U.K.	1970	short, stiff straw; erectoides habit; mildew resistance	Spring oil rape	Regina várraps elite F	Sweden	1962	higher seed yield and percent oil
Barley	Luther	U.S.	1967	shorter straw; increased grain yield and lodging resistance, especially with heavy fertilization	Castor bean	Aruna	India	1969	very early (120 days versus 270 days for mother variety); yield slightly higher
Barley	Diamant	Czecho-slovakia	1965	very high yield; short stem; very good grain and malting quality; lodging resistance	Peach	Magnif 135	Argentina	1968	bigger fruits with deeper red skin colour; 7 days earlier maturity

*Raiden, Raiko and their original variety form a set of varieties of different maturities but of similar grain quality.
Source: IAEA Bulletin II (5): 16–27 (1969); Isotope Information Center, Oak Ridge National Laboratory, Oak Ridge, Tennessee.

oilseed in India, and the protein could be very significant to that country.

A problem, not necessarily peculiar to peanut meal, is the production of highly toxic mold metabolites during unfavourable storage conditions. One toxin, aflatoxin, is a dangerous carcinogen. It has been excluded from such food supply by industrial screening. Peanut meal is approximately 50 percent protein and is poorer nutritionally than soy protein.

Coconut usually is processed by sun drying to copra, which is not an effective starting material for a protein concentrate; the protein content of the oil-free residue is only 20 percent.

Sunflower is becoming significant in European oil markets, as is rapeseed in Canada and northern Europe. Little is presently known about the value of these proteins for human consumption.

Radiation-induced plant mutations. Some mutant varieties of crops have shown increased protein content, higher yields, and resistance to plant disease. Radiation-induced mutant varieties of durum wheat, for example, have shown superior performance, and the Food and Agriculture Organization of the United Nations has recommended that some countries use them to replace their entire wheat acreage. Castor beans formerly took 270 days to mature in India and were therefore at the mercy of changes in the rainy season. A new variety, evolved from radiation-induced mutations (see RADIOISOTOPES, APPLICATIONS OF), matures in 120 days; now farmers can be assured of a good crop each year and can use the 150 days' time saved to grow other crops. Similarly, an increase in yield of maize has been achieved by a radiation-induced mutation, the first on an open-pollinated rather than self-pollinated crop.

The table lists some of the successful radiation-induced plant mutations that provide additional food crops.

Leaves, grasses, and waterweeds. There is an enormous untapped source of food in leaves, grasses, and waterweeds, which is currently utilized only by conversion to animal feeds. Some of the proteins present in the dry matter of these materials are potentially of high nutritive value.

Leaf protein concentrate

The preparation of protein from leaves and similar materials, called leaf protein concentrate (LPC), is relatively simple. The vegetable material is pulped with an excess of water, the juice pressed from the insoluble residue, and the protein precipitated by heating with or without acidification. The resulting press cake is dark green because of its high chlorophyll content and includes 40 percent dry matter, which is 60 to 70 percent protein. Improvement of the colour and flavour of the cake requires extraction of the chlorophyll and lipid with an organic solvent.

If this process were to be carried out on a large program, so that economies of scale could be reached, the cost of collection and transport to a central location would be considerable. If, on the other hand, the material is produced in small, rural village units in tropical countries, other problems arise. Such areas usually suffer from shortages of potable water and lack of cheap electricity or fuel, commodities readily available in industrial areas and essential to LPC production. There also appear to be unresolved questions concerning the digestibility of some LPC's by animals and human infants.

Marine sources. The sea is an exceedingly large resource for food and protein. Predictions of the total sustainable annual harvest that could be attained vary from 200,000,000 to 2,000,000,000 tons. This would yield between 32,000,000 and 320,000,000 tons of high-quality protein. (These figures exclude fish farming or aquaculture.) The lower figure is based on the use of present fishing techniques and is undoubtedly conservative. Most of the sea's protein is in forms that are not commonly accepted as food fish and have little present commercial value. They are either "trash" fish, such as hake or menhaden, or fish that are too small or contain too much oil for conventional processing. Going further down the food chain, the use of plankton as a source of food

is faced with technological and biological barriers, among which are collection costs, possible toxic species, and high mineral content.

A solution to the problem of how to use trash and fatty fish may be to utilize whole fish and remove the fat and water to obtain a product that can be economically stored and transported without spoilage or off-flavour. Fish protein concentrate (FPC) is such a product and is defined as any inexpensive, stable, wholesome product of high nutritive quality, hygienically prepared from fish, in which the protein and other nutrient materials are more concentrated than they were in the original raw material. Two solvent processes have been developed, and work is being done on biologically based processes using enzymes or micro-organisms.

Fish protein concentrate

The major advantage of FPC is the high nutritive value of the protein, which approximates that of animal proteins. The problems include high cost and poor performance of the material in food products. The technological problems probably can be solved, but the process can be economical only where fish is plentiful and inexpensive and probably where an FPC process can be integrated directly into an existing fishing industry.

Single-cell protein sources. Single-cell protein, or SCP, refers to any crude or refined source of protein from unicellular or simple multicellular organisms, such as bacteria, yeast, fungi, algae, and perhaps protozoa. The production of SCP is more complex than that of FPC and is shown schematically in Figure 1. Some or all of the steps

Drawing by D. Meighan

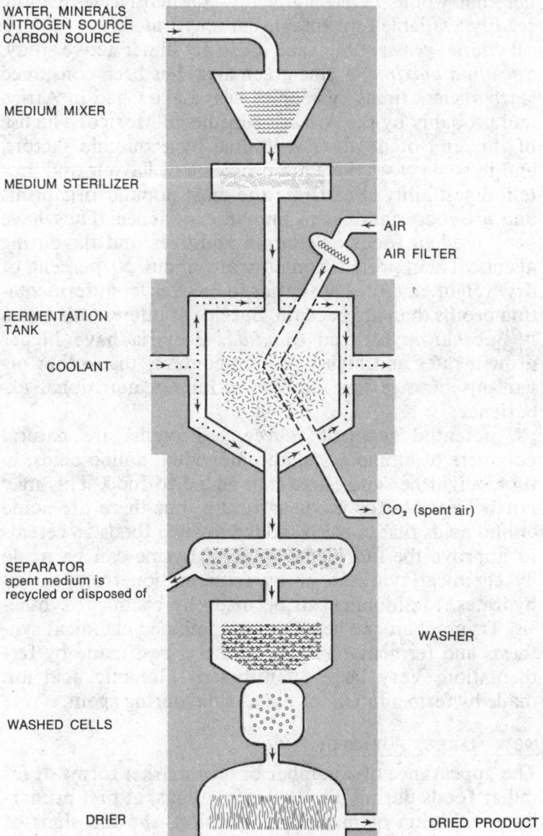

Figure 1: Manufacturing processes in the production of single-cell protein.

indicated would be required in an individual process. Most SCP processes are similar except for the type of organism and type of carbon substrate. A major attraction of SCP is that it can be produced without an agricultural base. SCP probably will be most economical in very large processing plants producing hundreds of thousands of tons of material annually. The use of SCP is relatively old in terms of human history, but the use of large quantities in food was made possible by developments in fermentation technology during and after World War II. Potentially, SCP can approach soy in cost. SCP is lower in nutritive value than FPC.

Most of the world's interest is in processes that utilize hydrocarbons or derivatives as the sole energy source for growth of the SCP micro-organism. These include petroleum products, molasses, starch, sulfite waste liquor from paper manufacture, cheese whey, and cellulose. The choice of raw material depends on the region. Natural gas or methane is abundant in the Middle East and the North Sea. Methane is very cheap and leaves no residue in the final product, but it has disadvantages: it requires a sophisticated fermentation system to prevent formation of hazardous gas mixtures; it is limited to growth of bacteria; it requires large quantities of oxygen and produces more heat; and a culture of suitable commercial performance has not yet been found.

Petroleum sources

Petroleum gas oil has been used extensively in Europe for animal-feed products, but it is doubtful that such a product would be permitted in human food because of potentially harmful residues. Most work has been on highly purified paraffinic hydrocarbons that, in themselves, would be safe in food.

Sulfite liquor and whey are of interest in locales where they are waste products, and they may be used along with starch and molasses to produce cells by conventional fermentation technology.

Another carbohydrate, cellulose, is ubiquitous in nature and of potential future interest. The main problem is the conversion of cellulose to metabolizable sugar in a manner that would be economically competitive with more readily available fermentable carbohydrates.

Bacteria, yeasts, fungi, and algae are under active study. *Spirulina maxima*, a blue-green alga, has been consumed since ancient times by peoples near Lake Chad in Africa and probably by the Aztecs of medieval Mexico. The use of this and other algae is limited by economic factors, and in some cases there are problems of flavour and protein digestibility. Yeasts are the most popular organisms and are more familiar to human experience. They have been used in foods as vitamin additives and flavouring agents. Their protein contents are about 50 percent of dry weight, and they are easier to recover from fermentation broths than are bacteria. Species of interest are mainly *Saccharomyces* and *Candida*. Bacteria have higher growth rates and higher protein contents than other organisms but are less familiar in human nutritional experience.

A potential synthetic source. Proteins are natural polymers of amino acids, and individual amino acids, in turn, might be synthesized and added to food. This may not be feasible for the near future, but there are some amino acids that could be added to such foods as cereals to improve the nutritional quality. Lysine can be made by chemical synthesis or by fermentation from carbohydrates. Methionine can be made by chemical synthesis. Tryptophan can be made by combined chemical synthesis and fermentation. Threonine is best made by fermentation. Very large quantities of glutamic acid are made by fermentation for use as a flavouring agent.

NEW MARKET FORMS OF FOOD

The appearance of a number of new market forms of familiar foods during the 1950s and 1960s, at first primarily a reflection of market competition, showed signs of considerably broader significance. Formerly technological control extended only over external forces applied to food; now alterations can be made in food composition, wholly new forms can be fabricated, and substitutes for established forms can be made acceptable. Advances in formulations, in packaging, and in preservation techniques are continuing in the 1970s.

Advances in packaging and processing. One of the most striking developments in this area was the packaging of complex dishes for preparation with minimum time and effort. The package itself often serves as a cooking utensil, an innovation that required development of materials such as foil-plastic laminates and high-speed sealing equipment. Convenience packaging brought with it some unforeseen disadvantages, it is true, when certain types of containers created a solid-waste disposal problem.

Processing and packaging have been combined in the food-service industry to deliver specific products that by now may be considered traditional, such as turkey loaves and simulated meat. Foods can be prepared commercially by such methods as microwave cooking—which is too expensive for ordinary home use—to eliminate the dangers of overcooking and undercooking, and microbiological health hazards can be minimized.

Food service industry.

The food-service industry in many countries is growing in importance in schools, hospitals, military institutions, restaurant chains with centralized food preparation or portion control, and in vending operations.

Special-purpose and dietetic foods. These are foods of novel composition or substitutes for ordinary foods or foods in which some component has been modified or replaced. Snack items have been developed with novel flavour, texture, and improved nutritive value as a result of development of such ingredients as protein concentrates and modified starches. Special equipment designed for extrusion, puffing, and cooking has yielded a variety of new shapes and forms of such familiar foods as potato chips and popcorn.

Synthetic milks and coffee whiteners have been formulated using protein concentrates and new types of fats formed through conversion of natural fats and fatty acids. The melting range of the fat must be close to human body temperature. Such foods promise not only to be economical sources of proteins and fats but to overcome religious and cultural food problems in many parts of the world. The nutrient value of these products may be subjected to control by law because of their importance to nutrition of children.

New and recently developed dietetic foods include low-calorie substitutes for weight reduction, low-sodium foods for persons with certain types of heart or circulatory problems, and low-sugar foods for persons with diabetes. Low-calorie foods may make use of nonnutritive bulking agents, such as cellulose derivatives, and may vary in form from cookies to soups to beverages. Low-sugar foods usually are formulated with synthetic sweeteners.

Texturized food products. Unique new foods have been developed from protein concentrates that texturally simulate meat, fish, and shellfish. The potential benefits of these products include low cost, controlled nutrient composition, and the possibility of restructuring and improving poorer cuts of meats.

The simplest approach to texturization is the fabrication of chewy granules that simulate ground meat. The basis is isolated gluten at concentrations high enough to produce stiff doughs. These doughs, containing suitable flavour and colour, are extruded, sliced, and dried. When rehydrated they may be used directly, for example, in casseroles.

Another approach to texturization employs thermal denaturation of dissolved protein to form chewy gels. This process can be made more or less continuous by employing cooker-extruders such as are used in the fabrication of snack products or in the preparation of full-fat soy flours.

The products are based mainly on soy proteins, and preparations containing as low as 70 percent protein can be utilized. The texture of the final products can be varied over a wide range, from tough to tender. They are intended mainly for use in stews and casseroles.

Oriented protein fibres

The most sophisticated texturization process, and the most expensive, utilizes oriented protein fibres (see Figure 2). The fibres are made primarily from soy preparations of over 70 percent (usually 90 percent or more) protein and 95 percent solubility at alkaline pH. The protein is dissolved in alkali at pH 12 at a concentration of 12 to 14 percent to give a viscous dope. This is then extruded through spinnerets into a coagulating bath of acid and salt to set the fibres. Approximately 16,000 fine fibres form a tow of ropelike consistency. The tow is taken up from the bath onto a series of reels that stretch the fibres while excess salt and acid are washed away. The final products are made by blending the fibres with fat, flavours, colouring, supplemental nutrients, stabilizers, and protein binders. The protein binder is usually egg albumen, which is used because of its thermosetting properties. This ingredient adds significantly to the cost of the product. The blended fibres then are placed in a

Figure 2: Production of edible protein fibre. Rapidly moving tow emerging from a spinning bath of food grade acid is pulled apart to show continuous monofilament structure (16,000 fibrils of 0.0015 inch diameter).

blender cooker and finally are fabricated into slices, cubes, bits, or granules. The entire process, from extraction of soy protein to final fabrication, can be carried out on a continuous basis. The composition of these products is approximately 40 percent soy fibre, with the remainder made up of variable quantities of the other ingredients. The optional ingredients may include low-cost cuts of meat that contribute flavour and colour.

FOODS DEVELOPED FOR SPACE EXPLORATIONS

The extraordinary constraints imposed by space-flight conditions on food-system design have stimulated research that may have wider application. A basic question from the beginning of manned space flight has been whether to rely on having adequate storage facilities for the total food requirements of flights, including very long flights, or to develop a regeneration system to fill part or all of the requirements. In the early 1970s such a system still promised only a low level of reliability, but work continued in the anticipation of manned interplanetary exploration and manned orbiting space stations. Regenerative, or recycle, systems under study are usually SCP generators or chemical synthesizers.

Space foods developed in the 1960s were designed to meet both engineering constraints, in the form of limited payloads, zero gravity, and acceleration pressures, and biological constraints deriving from the cramped space and remote distance from external assistance. Foods for space explorers must meet highly demanding standards for protection against microbiological contamination and must be readily and completely digested. One direction of space-food development was toward reduction of payload by providing partially or completely dehydrated items, since water has been available as a by-product of the hydrogen- and oxygen-powered fuel cells that have provided spacecraft with electrical power.

Dehydrated foods At present there are three categories of dehydrated foods: rehydratable solids, rehydratable powders, and bite-size foods consumed without rehydration. The rehydratable solid foods are formulated, cooked when necessary, molded into single-portion sizes, freeze dried, and vacuum packaged in a flexible, clear plastic package. This package is fitted at one end with a spring valve designed to receive the nozzle of a water-dispensing gun by

which the food is rehydrated. The other end of the package is fitted with a feeding tube.

The bite-size foods do not need to be rehydrated and are placed directly in the mouth. They are slightly different from the rehydratable items in that some moisture is left in the pieces to give them a softer texture. These soft-moist items usually contain added plasticizing agents, such as glycerol. The reduced moisture content and the added glycerol reduce water activity in the food, preventing the growth of almost all micro-organisms. Sorbic acid is added in small amounts to prevent mold growth and an antioxidant to inhibit rancidity.

Probably the direction of space-food research that offers the best prospect of application to world food problems is the search for food energy that, like SCP, can be manufactured without resort to any agricultural base. Such products may be uneconomical for ordinary use for the immediate future, but technological advances may make them practicable eventually. The most likely compounds are the polyols, which even today can be made at reasonably low cost (though not as low as sugar). Particularly important is the compound 1,3-butanediol and its fatty-acid esters. This material mixes with water and becomes liquid at room temperature. It has been used extensively in the plastics industry, is completely synthetic, and is available in large quantities. It is a high-energy compound containing approximately 50 percent more energy per pound than carbohydrate, the dietary component it would replace. **Non-agricultural foods**

Another high-energy compound is a special fatty acid that is metabolized in the body like a carbohydrate. A prototypical example is 2,4-dimethylheptanoic acid. These compounds should be compared to carbohydrate with respect to energy density because of the way they are metabolized; they provide approximately 100 percent more energy per pound.

Another method of food synthesis involves simulation of prebiotic conditions; that is, conditions associated with development of life. Basic industrial chemicals such as ammonia and methane, together with water, subjected to irradiation, electric discharge, or a variety of other effects, produce amino acids and sugars. In some cases, surface-active catalysts like clays accelerate these reactions. An example is the synthesis of the formose sugars from formaldehyde. A very complex mixture of such compounds can be prepared at low cost, but not all of them can be metabolized—that is, made to yield nutrient value. If suitable methods for separation of the useful components can be found, these materials could be of tremendous future significance.

Finally, techniques of submerged culture or of tissue culture can be used to produce plant foods without an agricultural base. These products would not have the traditional fresh form but might provide the familiar nutrient content and texture. Even the flavour can be wholly synthetic.

BIBLIOGRAPHY. A.M. ALTSCHUL (ed.), *Processed Plant Protein Foodstuffs* (1958), a classical exposition of the composition, chemistry, and technology of a wide variety of potential new proteins, and *World Protein Resources* (1966), a symposium report; R.I. MATELES and S.R. TANNENBAUM (eds.), *Single-Cell Protein* (1968), a summary of biological and technological aspects of single-cell protein production on hydrocarbons and other carbon sources, with a useful discussion of economic and technological factors in the use of new proteins; GRADUATE STUDENTS AT HARVARD BUSINESS SCHOOL, *The Protein Paradox: Malnutrition, Protein-Rich Foods, and the Role of Business* (1964), the best treatment of marketing aspects of new protein foods, including a history of marketing trials to 1964; PRESIDENT'S SCIENCE ADVISORY COMMITTEE, *The World Food Problem* (1968), a comprehensive survey of approaches to solve the world food problem; FOOD AND AGRICULTURE ORGANIZATION OF THE UNITED NATIONS, *The State of Food and Agriculture* (annual), the most useful source of statistics on world food production, with a detailed examination of new developments in food technology or supply; *Food Technology* (monthly), a periodical containing news and technical details of developments in new food sources and products.

(S.R.T.)

Food, Quality Control of

Every food has a number of attributes, or qualities, which may be desirable, undesirable, or even harmful. Food quality is the sum of all of these attributes, both obvious and hidden. The consumer judges a product by such obvious qualities as flavour, texture, and appearance. Composition is a hidden quality, requiring more technical evaluation, and includes nutritional value, presence or absence of various substances, and microbiological levels. Keeping quality, or shelf life, is another hidden factor.

FOOD QUALITY AND ITS EVALUATION

Quality
audit

Quality audit is the evaluation of the overall quality of the finished product. Information gained through the audit determines whether or not finished products meet predetermined standards and may bring attention to the need for correction of faulty production procedures.

Quality control includes all of the activities influencing the overall quality. Its objectives are the creation of the most favourable conditions for production of foods of a consistent quality and the minimization of the possibility of faulty production.

The application of scientific principles to food manufacture began in France in 1810, when Nicolas Appert published a work describing his method of food preservation by heat sterilization. As industrialization of food production increased, maintenance of uniform quality became essential; and with the development of food science, scientific quality-control methods were introduced.

Development of food quality control. Quality control began with the single operator or craftsman, who still performs the control function in such small-scale operations as making hand-dipped chocolates. As manufacturing operations grew larger, a foreman quality-control system developed, still used in the manufacture of many highly specialized products. But for modern, large-scale food processing, separation of quality control from production became clearly desirable. Adequate sampling of raw materials and finished products was not possible; therefore statistical methods were adopted for both sampling procedures and for interpretation of data obtained by chemical analysis. Personnel entirely divorced from production—either employed by the manufacturer, supplied by the industry, or imposed by the government—did the sampling and analyzing.

Finally, the concept of total quality control was introduced in the 1960s; in this concept quality development, quality maintenance, and quality improvement efforts of the various groups within an organization are coordinated with the goal of producing the most economical fully satisfactory food at maximum production efficiency.

Quality-
control
depart-
ments

Quality standards. Quality can be evaluated only in relation to a standard. The quality-control department within a food-manufacturing company defines and formalizes standards and is responsible for keeping deviations from these standards within predetermined limits. It provides other departments with the technical advice and information needed to achieve and maintain desired quality standards. It must also assure that the final product meets all specifications, complies with relevant laws and regulations, and reaches the consumer in satisfactory condition. Control of microbiological quality is especially important for prevention of food-borne disease and to retard microbial spoilage. Yet quality control cannot be the exclusive responsibility of the quality-control department because it must be exercised not only in the manufacturing process but earlier: in the selection of raw materials and, subsequently, in the packaging, storage, and distribution.

Most governments set food-product standards, defining chemical composition, specifying essential ingredients, stating maximum or minimum concentrations of certain ingredients, regulating food additive use, and setting tolerance limits for such contaminants as toxic metal and pesticide residue. Such government standards, enforced by a system of inspection, guarantee the consumer a satisfactory product.

Most food quality control, however, is exercised within the manufacturing organization; the following description, though generalized, applies principally to such enterprise control.

Specifications. Specifications are issued by the quality-control department after consultation with relevant production departments. Specifications are necessary for raw materials, intermediate products, finished products, and packaging materials.

Buying specifications. Buying specifications describe the material, including its source; give its analytical composition with agreed tolerances; state limits on the degree of chemical and bacterial contamination; indicate packing methods; and list satisfactory conditions of delivery, such as suitable temperature. An agreed sampling and analytical procedure is often included. When objective definition of an essential characteristic such as flavour is not possible, it is customary to stipulate that deliveries should correspond to an agreed and retained sample. The specification also usually states that the purchased material must satisfy all relevant legal requirements.

Processing specifications. Specifications for processing and for intermediate products describe processing methods and stipulate all controllable aspects of intermediate condition and composition.

Finished-product specifications. Finished-product specifications provide detailed packaging and storage instructions and advice on sampling and testing procedures.

SENSORY EVALUATION

The main objective of quality control is to keep to a minimum deviation from agreed standards. Ideally, accurate and objective chemical and physical methods should be used; but despite progress in this area, the human senses are still frequently more efficient than instrumentation in evaluating flavour and texture, and they provide a more rapid response. The reliability of information obtained through human senses can be heightened by selection and training, providing suitable environment, and using appropriate testing procedures.

Sensory
assessment
methods

The three basic sensory assessment methods are difference testing, product rating, and acceptability appraisal. Difference testing, perhaps the most frequently employed, involves assessment of the difference between the sample examined and a standard, which may exist solely in the memory of the examiner.

Testing is not limited to formal testing panels. Raw materials are usually tasted by an experienced worker before acceptance of deliveries, and food products are ordinarily tasted at various stages of the manufacturing process to allow avoidance or immediate correction of production faults.

Taste panels. Prospective taste panel members are tested for sensitivity to the primary tastes (salt, sweet, sour, bitter), for reactions to the type of foodstuff concerned, and for their ability to detect small differences in relevant characteristics. Because sensory evaluations are influenced by the environment, good ventilation and lighting are essential, and distractions minimized. Tasters are isolated in booths provided with a hatch for introduction of samples and facilities for mouth rinsing and disposal of materials. Tasters do not necessarily swallow test samples. Isolation of each panel member precludes any mutual influence, although subsequent discussion of the results between members may be valuable in maintaining interest and improving reliability.

Testing procedures. Tasting panels usually judge complete food products but, especially in the examination of raw materials, may judge specific ingredients, such as spices and flavourings, or other food additives. Sweet flavourings are tasted in the form of sugar syrups; spices are added to flour suspensions in water. Such procedures, however, are suitable only for rough sorting-out tests; final judgment must be based on tasting the ingredients as constituents of the actual products.

Difference tests. Difference testing is applied in a number of test designs, including pair comparison, duo-trio, and triangle tests. In pair comparison the judges are asked to indicate whether or not they find a difference between two coded samples, and they may also be asked to state the nature of the difference for a specific attribute. In the duo-trio test, one sample is used as a standard, and the tasters are asked which of two remaining coded samples is identical with the standard. Since the probability of a correct answer being given by chance is one in two, the triangle test, reducing the chance to one in three, is preferable. Of the three samples submitted, two are duplicates; the judges are asked to select the odd sample.

Ranking tests. In ranking tests, used for a small number of samples, the judges place a number of coded samples in order of merit based on one specified attribute. Scoring tests, suitable for the comparison of a number of test samples with a standard, require expert judges having identical understandings of the descriptive terms used. Values may be distributed with zero representing the lowest level and ten indicating the highest degree of excellence. Hedonic scaling, in which numerical values are attached to degrees of acceptability, does not require extensive training of the judges and provides suitable results for statistical examination. As in scoring tests, the choice of wording is important. To determine the lowest detectable concentrations of substances, dilution or extinction tests are used, in which amounts of the test substance are gradually reduced to zero.

Flavour profile The flavour-profile method of descriptive sensory evaluation requires sophisticated judging. Judges must recognize the four basic tastes at appropriate dilutions; be able to recognize odours; have the ability to express associations—for example, acetic acid and vinegar; and must be able to characterize and describe flavours. A closed session, in which each judge evaluates the samples separately, is followed by open discussion of the recorded results. Discrepancies in evaluation are resolved by repetition of the procedure until unanimous judgment is reached. Although the flavour-profile method offers a high degree of reproducibility, the required training time for judges and the operation itself are expensive, and results are not suitable for statistical treatment.

Consumer acceptance tests. Consumer acceptance and preference test results influence quality control, although they usually are not part of the activities of a quality-control department. Consumer preference and consumer acceptance practices do not necessarily evolve from each other. Food acceptance depends upon various social, economic, and cultural factors; preference implies the possibility of choice.

In surveying sensory quality factors that may determine preference, other factors that may influence judgment are removed from the test situation. Public attitude toward a product is usually ascertained by the use of questionnaires and interviews; the validity of the result is affected by the care used in wording the questionnaire and the objectivity of the interviewer.

OBJECTIVE EVALUATION METHODS

Chemical composition is a hidden food quality governing nutritional value. Food-product specifications state both chemical composition and tolerance limits for deviations from the specified formula.

Chemical analysis. Chemical food analysis methods are recommended and constantly revised by various organizations, among them the Association of Official Analytical Chemists (U.S.), the British Standards Institution, the Society for Analytical Chemistry (U.K.), the International Standards Institution, the International Union of Pure and Applied Chemistry, and the International Dairy Federation. Analytical methods to be used for specific determinations are sometimes prescribed by government legislation.

Subjective testing methods are used for reference; objective methods, frequently more rapid but less precise, are often applied in routine quality control. Automatic methods may be applied when large numbers of similar analyses are required.

Measurement of physical properties. Instruments used for food-product examination may be general types, often giving results in absolute physical units, such as

viscosimeters, which measure resistance of liquids to flow, and spectrophotometers, which measure the amount of light absorbed; or they may be devised for use by specific industries and calibrated in arbitrary units, such as the Brabender Farinograph, which measures the physical properties of dough.

Viscosimeters Viscosimeters use various devices to measure product viscosity. The Ostwald viscosimeter is based on rate of flow through a capillary tube; some viscosimeters measure the time in which a given volume will flow through an orifice of a specified size; others measure time required for a weight to fall through a column of the liquid; rotary viscosimeters include the Brookfield or Ferranti instruments, which measure the resistance of the liquid to the rotation of a spindle, and the MacMichael viscosimeter, which measures the influence of a rotating liquid on a suspended plunger.

The Brabender Farinograph and the Simon "Research" Extensometer are used in the baking industry to determine physical characteristics of dough, such as time required to attain standard consistency during mixing and length of time this consistency can be maintained. Gel firmness may be determined by the Bloom Gelometer; gelatin is graded on the basis of "Bloom strength," the amount of pressure required to produce a specified depression.

Instruments have been devised to measure such texture-related characteristics as resistance to shearing forces and compressibility. The vegetable industry uses such devices as the tenderometer, an instrument that determines the maturity of peas by measuring the amount of force required to produce shearing; the meat industry uses the Bostwick Consistometer to determine consistency by measuring the time required for a viscous food to flow down an inclined plane; and an instrument has been developed for making compressibility and shear tests on baking-industry products.

The spectrophotometer is used to measure colour of clear liquids. The Munsell colour-measurement system uses three or four spinning colour discs adjusted to match visually the appearance of the test object. The edible-oils industry uses the Lovibond Tintometer, or its American equivalent developed by Wesson, to compare the colour of the oil with that of standard glasses.

Microbiological evaluation. Microbiological quality control is concerned with ensuring absence of pathogenic, or disease-causing, organisms and with ascertaining levels of contamination by those micro-organisms that cause spoilage. Normal micro-organism counts in foodstuffs vary according to composition and processing methods. Some canned products are expected to be sterile; others, such as canned hams, contain some bacteria. Cheeses, fermented milk products, and raw cured meat products may have counts of harmless organisms ranging into the millions. Specifications for those processed foods Bacteria counts not expected to be sterile state the maximum acceptable organism level as determined by a total viable count, usually at temperatures between 30° and 37° C (86° and 100° F) and by a count of coliform bacteria. For some foods, counts may also be made of lipolytic organisms, anaerobic bacteria, yeasts, and molds. When the presence of pathogenic organisms is suspected, tests are made for such harmful bacteria as *Salmonella, Staphylococcus aureus, Clostridium welchii,* and *Clostridium botulinum.* In testing canned products, sample cans are first incubated, then examined for signs of deterioration.

CONTROL AND REGULATION OF FOOD QUALITY

Raw-material evaluation. No food product can be better than the raw materials in its production. Quality control requires acceptance procedures for raw materials that ensure that quality satisfies specification requirements. Daily sampling and examination of all of the raw materials are impossible, and priority is given to testing the dominant raw materials, especially for those attributes affecting the quality of the final product. Economic considerations may dictate special attention to the more expensive ingredients, such as vanilla beans, or to ingredients that may be paid for on a quality basis, such as milk. Although raw materials are ordinarily tested upon acceptance from suppliers, they may be stored for some time before use. When there is a possibility of deterioration during storage, periodic resampling and testing procedures are established and recorded in the raw-materials specification.

Additives. In addition to the main nutrients, food products contain additives. There is at present no internationally accepted definition of this term. The Food and Agriculture Organization of the United Nations (FAO) defines an additive as a nonnutritive substance intentionally added to food, generally in small quantities, to improve appearance, flavour, texture, or storage properties.

Most governments issue lists of permitted additives, stating the highest acceptable concentration, defining food products in which they may be used, and sometimes recommending the maximum daily consumption. Such legislation is revised periodically, and products may be added to or deleted from permitted lists because of additional scientific knowledge and experience in their use.

Nutrients. The most important group of food additives includes vitamins, amino acids, and minerals, which are nutrients added to foodstuffs to compensate for losses occurring during processing or to provide additional sources in diets that might otherwise be deficient in such nutrients. Examples of their use include fortification of margarine with additional vitamin A and the addition of thiamine, riboflavin, and niacinamide to flour or bread. Salt, a nutritionally indispensable additive, often has a small amount of iodide added to it to avoid a diet deficiency that can cause goitre development.

Colourings. Appearance is an important factor in food appeal, and legislation in most countries permits the addition of both natural and synthetic colouring matter. Although there are at least 46 separate dyes prepared specifically for use in food, only six of these are common to the permitted lists of most countries. In the 1960s a joint committee of the Food and Agriculture Organization and the World Health Organization was working to develop greater coordination on colouring standards.

Flavourings. Flavouring materials are added to basic foodstuffs to provide a characteristic product flavour or to supplement or modify the original flavour. Most flavouring materials are still of natural origin, but progress in organic chemistry has made it possible to analyze flavouring materials and to synthesize products identical with those found in nature. Although some countries permit use of synthetic equivalents on the same basis as their natural counterparts, other countries require extensive biological testing before such substances may be used. Testing methods may differ in various countries, and in the 1960s an FAO/WHO committee was attempting to bring about standardization.

Flavour enhancers. Flavours can also be influenced by the addition of a flavour enhancer such as monosodium glutamate, which intensifies perception of flavour.

Antimicrobial preservatives. The food industry generally relies on such physical factors as heat, cold, and low moisture for product preservation, but the use of antimicrobial preservatives is growing. Most countries control their use by legislation stating the maximum permissible concentration for each preservative for specified foods.

Plant and process control. The production of food products of consistently uniform quality is complicated by the biological variability of raw materials. In addition to the definition and maintenance of relevant processing conditions, effective quality control requires a system that will allow for rapid changes in processing conditions to compensate for seasonal or other changes in raw materials. Because raw materials may vary between deliveries, sampling and examination of each delivery is necessary to allow for appropriate modification of processing procedures.

Industrial hygiene. The keeping quality of foodstuffs, determined by microbiological factors, depends not only on the quality of the raw materials but also on cleanliness of premises used for manufacture, design and layout of plant and equipment, efficiency of cleaning and steriliz-

ing procedures, and the standard of personal hygiene observed by operators. In order to avoid hygiene hazards, quality-control experts are usually consulted before construction of new buildings, installation of new machinery, or development of new manufacturing processes. The quality-control organization is then responsible for enforcing cleaning and sterilizing procedures and meeting required product microbiological standards.

Automatic processing. Various automatic devices are used in modern food processing. Ingredient mixing is carried out automatically, either by weight or by volume. Processing time and temperature are recorded by instruments. Such factors as acidity–alkalinity, viscosity, pressures, and flow rates can be continuously recorded, and there are facilities for continuous sampling from pipelines. Detectors can monitor foods packed in nonmetal containers for contamination by ferrous metals. Reliable automatic methods are not yet available to detect the presence of other foreign bodies in prepacked food; the manufacturer has to rely on washing, screening, visual inspection of the raw materials, filtration, and general plant hygiene to minimize this hazard.

Labels on prepacked foods state the quantity present in the container, either by volume or by weight. Some machines dispense weighed amounts of foodstuffs for packaging, but most products are dispensed by volume, although the quantity declared on the packet is expressed by weight. Frequent checking is required to assure that the machine is actually dispensing required amounts. If weight is stated but a volume is dispensed, it is essential to avoid variations in product density, especially in such aerated products as ice cream. Modern machinery continuously weighs the packets moving along a belt, rejecting overweight or underweight items. A similar method can sort a batch of products, such as eggs, into several graded sizes.

Packaging. The quality of foodstuffs at the time they reach the consumer usually depends on the efficiency of the packaging operation. Most foods deteriorate eventually, but efficient packaging delays such deterioration. Loss of quality may be due to mechanical damage, moisture content changes, oxygen absorption, flavour loss, or absorption of harmful substances or foreign odours either from the packaging material itself or through the packaging materials. Quality control of packaging must ensure that all packaging materials delivered to the factory conform to previously determined specifications that cover all relevant chemical and physical characteristics of the packaging materials; dimensions and acceptable tolerances of the made-up containers; and a reference to the type of packaging machine on which the materials will be used. Quality control also requires monitoring of factory packaging operations, including checking efficiency of closures and the accuracy of date codings.

Statistical evaluation. Statistical methods are applied at various stages of food manufacture. It is sometimes possible to submit raw materials to 100 percent inspection, as in veterinary inspection of carcasses, but examination is usually limited to samples of deliveries or of finished products. The information acquired from such samples is an indication of the average quality of the consignment and the probable number of items in the consignment falling below a defined standard. The sampling rate is determined by previous experience with the product, the cost of sampling, and the cost of testing, which may involve destruction of the samples. New products, or materials known to show considerable variability, require sufficient sampling to determine mean values for important attributes and also standard deviations and the probability of a proportion of the products falling outside the acceptance limits for some attribute. Appropriate statistical methods allow prediction for a given sampling rate of the danger of not detecting faulty items in a consignment.

Control charts are widely used in the food industry, mainly as an aid to process control. Charts indicate the need for corrective action when a point falls beyond the outer limits, and their study may also give advance warning of undesirable trends. Similar charts can be used for

Control charts

Data on Individual Weights for Construction of Average and Range Charts for Samples of 5													
sample no.	1	2	3	4	5	6	7	8	9	10	11	12	13
Individual weights	4·1	4·0	4·1	4·0	4·0	3·5	3·9	4·0	4·2	4·0	4·2	4·1	4·1
	4·0	3·8	3·9	4·1	4·1	3·7	4·0	4·1	4·2	4·1	4·1	4·2	4·3
	4·0	3·9	4·1	4·1	4·0	4·0	4·3	4·0	4·2	4·1	4·1	4·0	4·2
	4·1	4·0	4·1	4·0	3·4	3·8	4·2	3·9	4·1	4·0	4·0	3·6	4·3
	4·3	4·2	3·9	4·0	4·2	3·6	4·1	4·3	4·2	3·8	4·3	4·1	4·1
Average	4·10	3·98	4·02	4·04	3·94	3·72	4·10	4·06	4·18	4·00	4·14	4·00	4·20
range	0·3	0·4	0·2	0·1	0·8	0·5	0·4	0·4	0·1	0·3	0·3	0·6	0·2

deliveries or on production lines to record compliance with specifications.

Storage and distribution. Unsuitable storage and distribution conditions may cause rapid spoilage. Factors affecting keeping quality are temperature, humidity, exposure to light, mechanical damage, and stock rotation. For a full discussion of methods of protecting against spoilage, see FOOD PRESERVATION.

FOOD REGULATION

National legislation. The earliest rules affecting food choice resulted from religious or health considerations. Later regulations were aimed at prevention of adulteration of individual foodstuffs. The first general legislation concerned with food quality was introduced in 1860 in the U.K. under the title An Act for preventing the Adulteration of Articles of Food or Drink. This narrow approach was characteristic of the earlier era; the Food and Drugs Act of 1955 greatly widened the scope of government activity by regulating food hygiene, foodstuff composition, food additive use, and processing conditions. Further consumer protection was provided by the Weights and Measures Act 1963 and by the Trade Description Act 1968.

Similarly in the U.S., where both the federal and state governments are responsible for food legislation, the earlier approach, used in the Federal Food, Drug and Cosmetic Act of 1938, was narrow; the turning point came in the Food Additives Amendment of 1958. As in the U.K., primary concern with prevention of adulteration was replaced by the desire to protect consumer health from any hazards in food processing.

The 1958 amendment divided added food chemicals into three groups: (1) Those generally recognized as safe (GRAS), (2) those with prior sanction, and (3) food additives. Food additives have to be proved harmless by means of appropriate tests before sanction can be obtained for their use in specified foodstuffs or beverages. The manufacturer is responsible for the cost of such tests. Substances included in the GRAS list are considered to be normal constituents of foodstuffs, and their use is not limited to specified products. The GRAS concept exists only in the U.S. food law system and has no equivalent in European food laws. The U.S. government has an exceptionally large number of departments concerned with food quality control. The Public Health Service has issued standards applying to drinking water and dairy products and has made recommendations regulating catering and drinking establishments and the vending of foods and beverages. Most other food regulation, such as meat and poultry inspection, is under the Department of Agriculture. Standards for the grading of fish have been published by the Department of the Interior's Bureau of Commercial Fisheries. The Department of Defense regulates the quality of food purchased for the armed forces and may establish required standards. The Treasury Department is responsible for standards applied to alcoholic beverages. Still other standards are promulgated by the Department of Commerce, the Federal Trade Commission, the Veterans Administration, and the General Services Administration.

In Canada, the principal food law is the Food and Drugs Act 1953, concerned with protection of consumer health and enforcement of honest trading. Food standards are essentially treated by separate legislation (*e.g.*, the Canada Agricultural Products Standards Act 1955).

On the continent of Europe, the six European Economic Community (EEC) countries (France, Federal Republic of Germany, Italy, Belgium, The Netherlands, and Luxembourg) had separate food legislation in the early 1970s, but the EEC Commission was seeking to bring about uniformity of such legislation, and directives on antioxidants and colourings had already been issued.

International quality control. The most important development in international food quality control has been the setting up under joint FAO/WHO auspices of the Codex Alimentarius Commission. The Commission draws up voluntary international standards that on adoption by a member country become national, statutory, or legal minimum standards with all the necessary powers of enforcement. Some countries may wish to have more restrictive internal standards but, on acceptance of the Codex standards, must permit the importation of foods satisfying the Codex standards, although suitable differentiations may be made in the labelling.

The Codex Alimentarius is a collection of internationally adopted food standards presented in a uniform manner and aimed at protecting consumer health and ensuring fair food-trade practices. Codex standards specify: (1) the product designation, definition, and composition; (2) its hygiene requirements; (3) weight and measure requirements; (4) labelling requirements; and (5) sampling, testing, and analytical methods. Publication of standards is intended to guide and promote the elaboration and establishment of definitions and requirements for foods, to assist in their harmonization, and to facilitate international trade.

Codex Alimentarius

The Codex Alimentarius will eventually include standards for all principal foods distributed to consumers, whether processed, semiprocessed, or raw. Materials used for further processing into food will be included to the extent necessary to achieve the defined purposes of the Codex Alimentarius. It will also include provisions for food hygiene, food additives, pesticide residues, contaminants, labelling and presentation, and analysis and sampling methods.

BIBLIOGRAPHY. S.M. HERSCHDOERFER (ed.), *Quality Control in the Food Industry*, 3 vol. (1967–72), is concerned with those factors influencing the quality of a finished food product. The first volume treats the general aspects of quality control in the food industry; the second and third deal with quality control in specific branches. A. KRAMER and B.A. TWIGG, *Quality Control for the Food Industry*, 3rd ed. (1970), is an extension of material used in the quality-control training program at the University of Maryland. M.A. AMERINE, R.M. PANGBORN, and E.B. ROESSLER, *Principles of Sensory Evaluation of Food* (1965), is an authoritative monograph including many references. T.A. FURIA (ed.), *Handbook of Food Additives* (1968), a detailed and well-documented treatment of direct food additives, emphasizes U.S. food and drug legislation in its discussion of the legal aspects of food-additive use. F.L. GUNDERSON, H.W. GUNDERSON, and E.R. FERGUSON, JR., *Food Standards and Definitions in the United States* (1963), provides detailed information on U.S. standards and definitions.

(S.M.H.)

Food Preservation

Techniques for preserving food from natural deterioration, following harvest or slaughter, date to prehistoric times. Among the oldest methods are drying, refrigeration, and fermentation. Such dried foods as pemmican were widely known to ancient hunters and gatherers, who also used caves and other cool places for storage. Fermentation was known by the third millenium BC in Mesopotamia and Egypt; pickling was also developed in the ancient world. Modern methods of preservation include canning, invented early in the 19th century; freezing, developed early in the 20th century; and the addition of chemicals. Packaging has played an increasingly important role in modern food preservation.

The principal causes of food spoilage are growth of micro-organisms, enzyme action, oxidation, and dehydration. The form of spoilage to which a food is susceptible depends on its composition, structure, specific micro-organisms, and storage conditions. Micro-organisms themselves are affected by temperature, moisture, oxygen concentration, available nutrients, degree of contamination with spoilage organisms, and the presence or absence of growth inhibitors. Control of one or more of these factors usually suffices to inhibit microbial spoilage.

METHODS OF PRESERVATION

Low-temperature preservation. Storage at low temperatures prolongs food life by decreasing the respiration rate of fruits and vegetables and by retarding the growth of most spoilage micro-organisms. Recommended cold-storage temperatures for selected foods are listed in Table 1. A temperature at the freezing point of water ($32°$ F,

Table 1: Recommended Cold-Storage Temperatures for Selected Foods	
food	temperature (°F)
Butter*	34
Cheese (cream)	30–36
Cheese (soft)	32–36
Condensed milk (bulk)	35–40
Cream (fresh)	32–35
Margarine	32–35
Milk (fresh)	32–35
Milk (evaporated)	36–40
Fresh fish	32
Fish (dried)	35–40
Oysters	32–34
Beer	32–40
Chocolate	38–42
Cider	32–36
Honey	40–45
Maple syrup	40–45
Molasses	40–45
Olive oil	35–40
Sauerkraut	34–38
Wine	40–45

*If butter is to be stored for longer than two or three weeks, it should be held at 0 to $-10°$ F.

$0°$ C) reduces the rate of oxygen consumption and carbon dioxide production (respiration) and, consequently, inhibits micro-organism growth. There are two principal low-temperature techniques: cooling (refrigeration) and freezing.

Refrigeration. The life of many foods may be increased by storage at temperatures below $40°$ F ($4°$ C). Cold storage is less successful with fruits and vegetables having high water content, such as melons, tomatoes, cucumbers, bananas, and pineapple. Meats profit tremendously from such refrigeration, a fact discovered early in food history. In early times ice was employed as a refrigerant principally to preserve meat.

Fruits, vegetables, eggs, dairy products, and meats are often harvested, gathered, or slaughtered some time before being refrigerated, thus allowing deterioration to begin. Refrigeration cannot improve the quality of decayed foods; it can only retard deterioration. It does, however, afford substantial protection against carbohydrate loss, the major nutrient change occurring during the respiration of fruits and vegetables. One problem of modern mechanical refrigeration—that of dehydration of foodstuffs due to moisture condensation—has been overcome through humidity control within the storage chamber and by appropriate packaging techniques.

Freezing. Meat and fish have long been frozen for preservation by Eskimos and other northern peoples. Modern mechanical freezing is applied also to a variety of other foods, and has proven highly effective because of its severely inhibiting effect on micro-organisms. Most microbial forms cannot grow at temperatures below $32°$ F and may be seriously damaged by slow freezing.

Just as the freezing point of a solution is lower than that of a pure solvent, the freezing point of food is lower than that of pure water. Thus, solid freezing usually occurs at temperatures between $32°$ F and $25°$ F ($0°$ C and $-4°$ C). The temperature of the food undergoing freezing remains relatively constant until the food is almost completely frozen, then the temperature rapidly approaches that of the freezing medium. In the quick freezing process, the temperature of the food passes through the zone of maximum ice-crystal formation ($32°$ to $25°$ F) in 30 minutes or less. The basic principle of any rapid-freeze method is speedy removal of heat from food. These methods may employ cold air blasts, direct immersion in a cooling medium, contact with refrigerated plates in a freezing chamber, or freezing with liquid air, nitrogen, or carbon dioxide. Freezing in still air is the poorest method; circulating cold air greatly accelerates freezing. **Freezing techniques**

Different foods freeze over a wide range of temperatures, and their specific freezing points are identifiable. Evaluation of the freezing curve for a food under controlled conditions reveals the phenomenon of supercooling, which is cooling below the freezing point without solidification or crystallization. Observation of a thin section of food tissue demonstrates that, following supercooling, the temperature of the cooled section then rises to the actual freezing point as solidification proceeds. If refrigeration is continued, this change in phase continues until all the free water turns to ice.

Under normal conditions, water temperature must fall below $32°$ F before ice crystals form. When an ice water slurry is forming, its temperature returns to $32°$ F.

Slow freezing forms large, needlelike ice crystals; rapid freezing results in smaller crystals, producing a finer texture. If partial melting and refreezing are repeated several times, larger and larger crystals are formed, and hence a rougher texture.

Homemade ice cream, when prepared by freezing a mixture in a freezer or refrigerator-freezer compartment, develops large ice crystals, resulting in coarse texture; the rapid freezing employed in commercial ice cream production creates a velvet-smooth consistency, because of the smaller ice crystals. Strawberries frozen by the home method lose their characteristic texture when thawed because the large, needlelike crystals formed by this slow method puncture the tissue cells. Upon thawing, the pierced cells lose their juices, leaving the berry flabby and poorly formed.

The cells of meat, poultry, fish, shellfish, fruits, and vegetables contain a jellylike protoplasm. To fix this jellylike mass, the rate of freezing must be sufficiently rapid to promote formation of minute, uniform crystals throughout the tissues. When the quick-frozen tissue is thawed, it reabsorbs the water as the ice crystals melt. If the product is refrozen slowly, or if fluctuating storage temperature encourages formation of larger crystals, the resulting punctured cells cannot reabsorb all of the fluid; it remains as free liquid, and the thawed tissues cannot return to their original jellylike state.

In addition to the effect of ice-crystal growth on frozen food quality, freezing may irreversibly change colloidal structure, fusing suspended particles as in protein coagulation in thawed milk, or curdling in thawed sauces, and causing separation.

The phenomenon of milk in an unprotected bottle or carton expanding as it freezes is well known. Such expansion on freezing occurs with many foods and must be allowed for in freeze-packaging. Not all food products increase in volume; pure water increases about 10 percent, but when large amounts of sugar are added, expansion is greatly reduced and volume may actually decrease. The sugary solution in strawberry jam occupies the same, or possibly less, space in the container in frozen form as unfrozen. **Problems of frozen-food packaging**

Frozen-food packaging must provide protection from dehydration resulting from sublimation (a change directly from solid to vapour state) and other conditions of frozen storage. Adequate packaging inhibits freezer burn, an irreversible change in the colour, texture, flavour, and nutritive value of frozen foods. Freezer burn typically gives roast beef the appearance of light brown paper.

The most complicated packaging problems involve processing and distribution of individual-serving packages (*i.e.*, frozen dinners), which often contain several different types of food in a single unit.

Low temperatures promote retention of nutrients in stored foods; freezing does not destroy nutrients, but some oxidation and destruction of vitamins may occur during the processing that precedes freezing.

Effect of freezing on nutrients and enzymes

Freezing produces little change in the nutritive value of protein, although such conditions as repeated freezing and thawing may alter food appearance and quality by reducing solubility and promoting coagulation of proteinaceous materials, eventually leading to irreversible changes such as curdling.

Fat and oil deteriorations are usually temperature dependent, and freezing is the most efficient preservation method for many fatty foods. Nevertheless, oxidative deterioration of fats and oils may occur even in frozen foods. Plant tissues are least susceptible. Fats in frozen fish tissue tend to become rancid faster than the fats in frozen animal tissues. Animal tissue reaction varies. Pork fat may become rancid after six months' storage at 0° F (−18° C); beef fat may retain good quality after two years of storage at that temperature. Rancid fats tend to have lower nutritive values than fresh, sweet fats. Rancidity development in frozen fatty tissues is greatly reduced at −30° F (−34° C). Oil and water emulsions may become destabilized by freezing, causing serious defects in precooked frozen foods and food products.

Enzyme activity is slowed by low temperature, although some enzyme activity continues at temperatures as low as −100° F (−73° C). For this reason, enzyme destruction with a short heat treatment, or blanching, before freezing and storage is the most efficient control method.

Freezing destroys certain parasites in foods. For example, *Trichinella spiralis*, the worm that causes the disease trichinosis in man, may be destroyed at all stages of development by reducing the temperature of infected food to 0° F or lower. As frozen foods are not suitable for parasite growth, freezing prevents insect infestations.

Although the complex physical, chemical, and biological changes that occur during food freezing and subsequent thawing are not completely understood, the design of a successful food-freezing process requires consideration of these changes. The basic refrigeration capacity of any unit must be adequate to lower the temperature of the food to its freezing point, freeze the food at that temperature, and lower the temperature of the frozen food to the temperature of the storage chamber. It must allow for heat produced by lighting, electrical equipment, and the entrance of air when the chamber is opened for the addition or removal of stored items. When the refrigeration requirement for a particular installation is determined, an additional 10 percent is usually allowed as a safety margin. Since refreezing a thawed mass of food may produce quality changes, storage temperatures must be maintained at a constant level—no higher than 0°·F (−18° C), preferably at −10° F (−23° C), with best results at −30° F (−34° C). Animal tissues appear less subject to damage sustained in thawing than are fruit and vegetable tissues; fruits are particularly sensitive.

Essentials of adequate frozen food storage

Preservation by drying. The terms evaporation and desiccation both refer to drying, and the term dehydration indicates an artificial drying process.

The drying of foods by fire was an ancient practice in both the New and Old worlds. Hot-air dehydration was developed in France in 1795; the device was a **vegetable dehydrator** employing a flow of hot air (105° F; 41° C) over thin slices of vegetables.

Cereal grains are preserved by drying, and the natural process is usually so efficient that no additional treatment is required. When climatic factors interfere with **proper** drying in the fields, heat must be applied artificially to avoid decomposition.

Legumes, nuts, and some fruits also mature on the plants and are dried by warm winds. Drying, in fact, is the preservation process most frequently applied to fruits. Natural sun-drying yields a highly concentrated quality product, but is not always efficient because of the unpredictability of weather.

Foodstuffs may be dried in air, superheated steam, vacuum, inert gas, or by direct application of heat. Air is the most generally used drying medium, because it is plentiful and convenient, and permits gradual drying, allowing sufficient control to avoid overheating that might result in scorching and discoloration. Air may be used both to transport heat to the food being dried and to carry away liberated moisture vapour. The use of other gases requires special moisture recovery systems.

Dehydration is an effective means of inhibiting microorganism growth. Most molds can grow on foods with as little as 16 percent moisture content; a few can grow in foods with less than 5 percent. Bacteria and yeasts usually require moisture levels greater than 30 percent. Grains, which are dried to about 12 percent moisture, receive added protection from their high solids content. Fruits, usually dried to 16 to 25 percent moisture, will still mold if exposed to both high humidity and air.

Pathogenic (toxin-producing) bacteria occasionally withstand the unfavourable environment of dried foods, causing food poisoning when the product is rehydrated and eaten. Control of bacterial contaminants in dried foods requires high quality raw materials having low contamination, adequate sanitation in the processing plant, pasteurization before drying, and storage conditions that protect from infection by dust, insects, and rodents or other animals.

Some parasites also can survive the drying process, and organisms such as *Trichinella spiralis*, a parasite found in pork muscle, must be destroyed by heat treatment before drying.

Effect of drying on nutrients

Loss of moisture content produced by drying results in increased concentration of nutrients in the remaining food mass. The proteins, fats, and carbohydrates in dried foods are present in larger amounts per unit weight than in their fresh counterparts, and the nutrient value of most reconstituted or rehydrated foods is comparable to that of fresh items. The biological value of dried protein is dependent, however, on the method of drying. Prolonged exposure to high temperatures can render the protein less useful in the diet. Low temperature treatment, on the other hand, may increase the digestibility of protein.

In vitamin content, dried meat is usually less satisfactory than fresh meat. Most of its vitamin C is lost. Thiamine is reduced, with the greatest loss occurring at high drying temperatures; small losses of riboflavin and niacin also occur.

Dried eggs, meat, milk, and vegetables are ordinarily packaged in tin or aluminum containers. Fiberboard or other types of material may be employed, but are less satisfactory than metal, which offers protection against insects and moisture loss or gain and which permits packaging with an inert gas.

In-package desiccants (drying agents) improve storage stability of dehydrated white potatoes, sweet potatoes, cabbage, carrots, beets, and onions, and give substantial protection against browning. Retention of ascorbic acid (vitamin C) is markedly improved by packaging at temperatures up to 120° F (49° C); the packaging gas may be either nitrogen or air.

Dehydration has long been practiced commercially in the production of spaghetti and other starch products. As a result of advances made during World War II, the technique was applied to a growing list of food products, including dried skim milk, potato flakes, soup mixes, instant coffee, and prepared baby foods. The reduction in weight and volume offered important economic benefits in distribution.

Freeze-dehydration process

A related technique, freeze-dehydration, employs high vacuum conditions, permitting establishment of specific temperature and pressure conditions to maintain the solid material, or substrate, at the best level for successful dehydration, encouraging satisfactory rehydration. In this process, the solid material remains frozen while the liquid portion escapes as vapour.

Exact temperature control is essential in freeze-dehydration of flesh products because of the possibility of muscle protein deterioration, but is less critical in the processing of fruit and vegetable tissue.

Adequate control of processing conditions contributes to satisfactory rehydration, with substantial retention of nutrient, colour, flavour, and texture characteristics. The first significant application of freeze-drying was in the production of an improved type of instant coffee; later experiments involved the development of shelf-storage prepared meals. Increased application of the technique is likely.

High temperature preservation: canning. In commercial canning, carefully prepared raw food is placed in a sealed container, subjected to definite elevated temperatures for the proper period of time, and finally cooled. Heating the contents of the can destroys spoilage organisms that may be present, and reinfection through exposure to air is prevented by the can's permanent seal.

Nicolas Appert, a Parisian confectioner, first succeeded in preserving certain foods in glass bottles that had been kept in boiling water for varying lengths of time. In 1810 his work was published in a treatise entitled *L'art de conserver, pendant plusieurs années, toutes les substances animales et végétales.* Appert could give no logical explanations for the effects of canning, but believed that the application of heat to a sealed container, together with the exclusion of air, combined to retard or eliminate the process of decomposition. Chemistry was in its infancy and bacteriology unknown, and a half century passed before the true causes of food spoilage came to be understood.

Invention of the tin can

Peter Durand, an Englishman, conceived and patented the idea of using tin cans instead of bottles, and by 1839, tin-coated steel containers were widely used.

The modern tin can, composed of 98.5 percent sheet steel with a thin coating of tin and manufactured on high-speed, automatic machinery, is the cheapest and most serviceable container for mass production. The sanitary or open-top can, developed about 1905–08, eliminated the use of solder in sealing the can, and a perfect closure was guaranteed by the double seamed top and bottom. Differentially coated electrolytic tin plate was used, beginning in 1951, to save tin and improve resistance to interior corrosion and exterior rusting. By 1960 containers of aluminum and of plastic material had been found commercially feasible for a restricted number of products, and improved glass jars and bottles were also in use. Enamel coatings had also been developed to replace tin as the interior lining of the can for certain foods.

An early obstacle to volume production was the time necessary for processing the filled cans of food in boiling water. In 1861 it was discovered that calcium chloride added to boiling water raised the temperature of processing from 212° F (100° C) to 240° F (116° C) or higher, and the time necessary to ensure safety in the process was reduced from 4–5 hours to 25–40 minutes. The average production in a first-class cannery was increased from 2,500 cans to about 20,000 cans per day. In 1874 the introduction of the closed steam-pressure retort further shortened the time necessary for processing, and reduced accidents and spoilage.

Products available for canning include almost every fruit, vegetable, meat, and marine product. Many specialty products are packed in small quantities. The relationship between grower and canner is often close, and the growing of crops for canning has become a highly specialized branch of agriculture.

Hand labour in the cannery has largely been supplanted by automatic machinery. Machines include washers, graders, peelers, corn huskers and cutters, bean snippers, and filling machines. Electronic devices often are used for regulating and controlling operations.

Operations commonly included for fruits, vegetables, milk, fish, meat, and specialty products include cleaning, preparatory operations, blanching, filling and exhausting, can sealing, thermal processing, cooling, labelling, casing, and storage.

Raw materials used in canning must be thoroughly cleaned. Cleaning is usually effected by automatic passage of the raw-food material through tanks of water or under high-pressure water sprays. Washing machinery of special design is used for certain products (*e.g.,* flotation washers for whole kernel corn and peas), and only potable water may be used. Some products (peas, spinach) are cleaned by air blasts or shaking to remove inedible or extraneous materials before water washing.

Cleaning and preparatory operations in canning

Preparatory operations are varied, but all aim at the removal of inedible or undesirable portions of the food and conversion of the food into the desired or necessary form for subsequent operations. Such preliminaries include sorting, trimming, vining (peas); husking, cutting, silking (corn); size or maturity grading (peas); sectioning (citrus fruits); slicing, dicing, peeling, and coring (fruits); pitting (cherries); soaking (dry beans, cherries); evaporation (milk); and many others. Many of these operations are performed by special machinery; in other instances hand operations are required.

Some products (beets, carrots, spinach, peas) require a blanching by immersion in hot water or steam to shrink or wilt the product in order to obtain desired or legal weight in the final container, and also to inactivate enzymes and thereby improve the colour and flavour of the product. Blanching must sometimes precede such operations as peeling, slicing, and dicing. Occasionally, the necessary shrinkage must be obtained by precooking rather than by blanching, as with certain meat products. In addition to its other functions, blanching in some products serves as an additional cleansing operation, removing objectionable flavouring materials acquired by the raw foods from inedible portions of plants (*e.g.,* the vine flavour of peas).

Automatic filling machines, adaptable to specific products or types of products (solid, semisolid, or liquid) and capable of high-speed operation, are employed to place the prepared food in the can. The washed, open cans are mechanically conveyed to and from the filling machines. With some foods (certain fruits, tomatoes) hand-filling methods are used.

Filling, exhausting, and sealing the cans

After being filled, the open cans containing the food, especially that of nonhomogeneous type, are usually thermally exhausted by passing automatically through a hot-water or steam bath in an exhaust box. Thermal exhausting heats and expands the food and releases gases (carbon dioxide and oxygen) from the cells. Air is also excluded by expansion of the food; after sealing, heat sterilizing, and cooling the can, the contraction of the contents produces a partial vacuum in the container. Thermal exhausting may also be effected by heating the food before it is put into the cans (as with cream-style corn). Certain products are packed chiefly by the vacuum-pack method, in which the cans are mechanically exhausted by sealing machines that withdraw air and other gases and seal the cans while they are still under vacuum.

Special automatic sealing (closing or double seaming) machines capable of operating at various speeds (from 10 to 250 cans per minute, depending upon the can size and the nature of the product) are used to seal or close the covers on the sanitary type of can. The cans are usually mechanically conveyed to and from the sealing machine, where the covers are placed automatically on the cans and the sealing operation completed. The curl on the can cover and the flange on the can body are first rolled into position and then flattened together. The thin layer of gasket material or compound originally present in the rim of the cover is dispersed between the layers of metal to ensure a hermetic (air-tight) seal on the container. Some vacuum-closing machines mechanically exhaust the can just before the double seam is formed; other types of closing machines seal cans in an atmosphere of an inert gas such as nitrogen, carbon dioxide, or helium. The vent-hole types of cans (evaporated milk, certain meat products) are sealed on special tipping machines that close the vent hole with a small drop of solder.

Heat sterilization, or thermal processing, essentially consists of subjecting the food (usually contained in the

Table 2: Classification of Canned Foods on the Basis of Processing Requirements

acidity classification	pH value	food item	food groups	spoilage agents	heat and processing requirements
	7.0	lye hominy	meat	mesophilic spore-forming anaerobic bacteria	high-temperature processing (240°–250° F)
		ripe olives, crabmeat, eggs, oysters, milk corn, duck, chicken, codfish, beef, sardines	fish milk poultry		
Low acid				thermophiles	
	6.0	corned beef, lima beans, peas, carrots, beets, asparagus, potatoes	vegetables	naturally occurring enzymes in certain processes	
	5.0	figs, tomato soup	soup		
Medium acid	4.5	ravioli, pimentos	manufactured foods	lower limit for growth of *Cl. botulinum*	
Acid		potato salad		non-spore-forming aciduric bacteria	boiling-water processing (212° F)
		tomatoes, pears, apricots, peaches, oranges	fruits		
				acidic spore-forming bacteria	
	3.7	sauerkraut, pineapple, apple, strawberry, grapefruit	berries	naturally occurring enzymes	
High acid	3.0	pickles	high acid foods (pickles)	yeasts	
		relish	high acid–high solids	molds	
		cranberry juice	foods (jam-jelly)		
		lemon juice			
		lime juice			
	2.0		very acid foods		

Heat sterilizing the cans

sealed can) to a known temperature long enough to destroy spoilage and pathogenic organisms that might be present in or on the raw-food material. Canners follow time and temperature processing schedules established by laboratories associated with the canning industry. The heat treatments necessary to preserve canned foods are determined by a number of factors; important among these is the acidity of the food or food product. Acid foods may be adequately processed by subjecting them to the temperature of boiling water. Nonacid foods must be processed at high temperatures. Processing requirements for canned foods in various acidity classifications are listed in Table 2. Most commercial processing temperatures for such foods fall in the range of 240° F (116° C) to 265° F. This temperature is attained by use of steam under pressure in a closed chest, or canner's retort.

Thermal processing equipment is of two general types: still retorts for batch operation and continuous cookers. Both types operate either at 212° F for the acid foods or under steam pressure for the nonacid products; in either case, the time of processing or cooking is regulated in order to subject the cans to the processing temperature for the proper time. Later processing installations include automatic retort controllers that regulate and record the process.

Following thermal processing, the sealed cans are cooled in cold water or in air. In water cooling, the hot cans are conveyed directly from thermal processing through tanks of cold water or through cold-water sprays; cans of large diameter must be pressure-cooled by water under pressure. Pressure cooling prevents outward straining or buckling of the can ends during the time when the internal pressure of the can is being reduced through loss of the heat of sterilization. Water cooling is continued until the can contents have an average temperature of about 100° F (38° C). At this temperature the food usually contains sufficient heat to dry the cans and prevent external rusting of the tin containers.

In air cooling, the cans are stacked in rows to permit free air circulation. Many foods cannot be cooled suitably in air.

Cans are labelled by special machines and may be placed in fibre or wood cases by hand or by machine. Cans are frequently stored without labelling, and the labelling operation is performed just before shipment. Canned foods are stored in cool, dry warehouses that are free of wide variations in temperature or humidity.

Normal vacuum cans of food are slightly concave on the ends. Bulged ends may be caused by microbial, chemical, or physical actions. Such cans may progress through various stages of swelling and finally explode.

Considerable investigation has been devoted to the effects of commercial canning on foods. Canning procedures have no practical effect on proteins, carbohydrates, and fats. When syrups or brines containing sugars are added in canning, the natural carbohydrate content of the foods is enhanced. Research has established the effect of canning on the known vitamins. In general, vitamin A and carotene (provitamin A), if protected from atmospheric oxygen, are not materially affected by the heat treatments given canned foods; vitamin D and riboflavin also appear to be unaffected. The stability of vitamin B_1 is dependent not only upon the heat treatment accorded it but also upon the acidity of the food in which it is contained. For the more acid foods there is practically no loss of this vitamin during canning; in the less acid foods, which require longer processing times at higher temperatures, the degree of retention is not great. Vitamin C is especially subject to destruction at elevated temperatures under conditions that permit free access to atmospheric oxygen. But in canning, the food is protected to a large degree from contact with oxygen; consequently, vitamin C is substantially retained.

Effect of canning on nutrients and vitamins

Fermentation and pickling. Although micro-organisms are usually thought of as causing spoilage, they are capable under certain conditions of producing desirable effects, including oxidative and alcoholic fermentation. The micro-organisms that grow in a food product, and the changes they produce, are determined by acidity, available carbohydrates, oxygen, and temperature. Untreated meat, for example, molds and putrefies; the addition of brine or salt causes different organisms to grow.

An important food preservation method combines salting to control micro-organisms selectively and fermentation to stabilize the treated tissues. The process for cucumbers is called pickling and is applied also to many other food commodities.

Pickled fruits and vegetables. Fresh fruits and vegetables soften after 24 hours in a watery solution and begin a slow, mixed fermentation-putrefaction. The addition of salt suppresses undesirable microbial activity, creating a favourable environment for the desired fermentation. Most green vegetables and fruit may be preserved by pickling.

When the pickling process is applied to a cucumber, its fermentable carbohydrate reserve is turned into acid, its colour changes from bright green to olive or yellow-green, and its tissue becomes translucent. The salt concentration is maintained at 8 to 10 percent during the first week, and is increased 1 percent a week thereafter until the solution reaches 16 percent. Under properly controlled conditions the salted, fermented cucumber, called salt stock, may be held for several years.

Salt stock is not a consumer commodity. It must be freshened and prepared into consumer items. In cucumbers this is accomplished by leaching the salt from the cured cucumber with warm water (110° to 130° F; 43 to 54° C) for 10 to 14 hours. This process is repeated at least twice, and in the final wash, alum may be added to firm the tissue, and turmeric to improve the colour.

Salt stock: basic stage in pickling

Freshened salt stock is used in the preparation of many types of pickles and relishes. Sour pickles are prepared by reprocessing freshened salt stock with weak vinegar. Sweet pickles are prepared by adding a sweet spice and vinegar solution to freshened salt stock. Processed dill pickles require the addition of dill herb and spices to the acidified brine.

Natural dill pickles are prepared from fresh cucumbers rather than from salt stock. The fresh cucumbers are packed into barrels with a mixture of brine, dill, and other spices; the acid develops naturally. These dill pickles are rarely packaged in vinegar. They are perishable unless repackaged and pasteurized.

Sauerkraut is made by bacterial fermentation of cabbage controlled by the use of salt; the acid that develops during fermentation acts as a preservative and develops the flavour.

Green olives are harvested when they have reached their full size, but are not yet fully ripe. They contain a bitter alkaloid, oleuropein, which is largely removed by a 2 percent sodium hydroxide solution. The lye is permitted to penetrate nearly two-thirds through the fruit, but not completely to the pit; a small amount of bitterness remains, imparting a characteristic flavour. The treated olives are washed to remove the lye.

Pickled meat. Meat may be preserved by dry curing or with a pickling solution. The ingredients used in curing and pickling are sodium nitrate, sodium nitrite, sodium chloride, sugar, and citric acid or vinegar.

Various methods are used: the meat may be mixed with dry ingredients; it may be soaked in pickling solution; pickling solution may be pumped or injected into the flesh; or a combination of these methods may be used.

Curing and smoking of meats

Curing may be combined with smoking. Smoke acts as a dehydrating agent and coats the meat surfaces with various chemicals, including small amounts of formaldehyde.

Deterioration of fermented and pickled products. Fermented foods and pickled products require protection against molds, which metabolize the acid developed and allow the advance of other micro-organisms. Fermented and pickled food products placed in cool storage can be expected to remain stable for several months. Longer storage periods demand more complete protection, such as canning.

Nutrient retention in fermented and pickled products is about equal to retention for products preserved by other methods. Carbohydrates usually undergo conversion to acid or to alcohol, but these are also of nutritive value. In some instances, nutrient levels are increased because of the presence of yeasts.

Concentrated moist foods: preserves and candied fruits. Foods with substantial acidity, when concentrated to 65 percent or more soluble solids, may be preserved by mild heat treatments. High acid content is not a requirement for preserving foods concentrated to over 70 percent solids.

Fruit-jelly and fruit-preserve manufacture, an important fruit by-product industry, is based upon the high-solids–high-acid principle, with its moderate heat-treatment requirements. Fruits that possess excellent qualities but are visually unattractive may be preserved and utilized in the form of concentrates, which have a pleasing taste and substantial nutritive value.

Jellies and other fruit preserves are prepared from fruit, with added sugar, concentrated by evaporation to a point where microbial spoilage cannot occur. The prepared product can be stored without hermetic sealing, although such protection is useful to control mold growth, moisture loss, and oxidation. In modern practice, vacuum sealing has replaced the use of a paraffin cover.

The jelly-forming characteristics of fruits and their extracts are due to pectin, a substance present in varying amounts in all fruits. The essential ingredients in a fruit gel are pectin, acid, sugar, and water. Flavouring and colouring agents may be added, and additional pectin and acid may be added to overcome any deficiencies in the fruit itself.

Jam is similar to jelly, but in the former the whole fruit is used, including pulp, rather than the fruit juice only. Fruit butter is a smooth, semisolid food prepared from at least five parts by weight of mashed or sieved fruit pulp to each two parts of sugar, sometimes with spices. Marmalade, usually made from citrus fruit, is the jellylike concentrate of prepared juice and sliced peel combined with sugar. Other fruit preserves are made in much the same manner, except that fruit pulp and fruits are often used. Fruit pastes are concentrated from fruit purees; they have a high solids content and usually no gel structure.

Varieties of fruit preserves

Candied and glacéed fruits are made by slow impregnation of the fruit with syrup until the concentration of sugar in the tissue is sufficiently high to prevent growth of spoilage micro-organisms. The candying process is conducted by treating fruits with syrups of progressively increasing sugar concentrations, so that the fruit does not soften into jam or become tough and leathery. After sugar impregnation, the fruit is washed and dried. The resulting candied fruit may be packaged and marketed in this condition, or may be dipped into syrup, becoming coated with a thin glazing of sugar (glacéed) and again dried.

Chemical preservation. Chemical food preservatives are substances which, under certain conditions, either delay the growth of micro-organisms without necessarily destroying them, or prevent deterioration of quality during manufacture and distribution. The former group includes some natural food constituents which, when added to foods, retard or prevent the growth of micro-organisms. Sugar is used partly for this purpose in making jams, jellies, and marmalades, and in candying fruit. The use of vinegar and salt in pickling, and of alcohol in brandying, also falls in this category. Some chemicals foreign to foods are added to prevent the growth of micro-organisms. The latter group includes some natural food constituents such as ascorbic acid (vitamin C), which is added to frozen peaches to prevent browning, and a long list of chemical compounds foreign to foods and classified as antioxidants, bleaching agents, acidulants, neutralizers, stabilizers, firming agents, and humectants.

Uses of chemical substances

Organic chemical preservatives. Sodium benzoate and other benzoates are among the principal chemical preservatives. The use of benzoates in certain products in prescribed quantity (usually not exceeding 0.1 percent) is permitted in most countries, some of which require a declaration of its use on the label of the food container. Since free benzoic acid actually is the active agent, benzoates must be used in an acid medium in order to be effective. The ability of cranberries to resist rapid deterioration is attributed to their high benzoic acid content. Benzoic acid is more effective against yeasts than against molds and bacteria.

Other organic compounds used as preservatives include vanillic acid esters, monochloroacetic acid, propionates, dehydroacetic acid, and glycols.

Inorganic chemical preservatives. Sulfur dioxide and sulfites are perhaps the most important inorganic chemical preservatives. Sulfites are more effective against molds than against yeasts and are widely used in the preservation of fruits and vegetables. Sulfur compounds are extensively used in wine making and, as in most other instances when this preservative is used, much care has to be exercized to keep the concentrations low in order to avoid undesirable effects on flavour.

Oxidizing agents such as nitrates and nitrites are commonly used in the curing of meats.

Antibiotics. Some European food-preserving agents containing antibiotics appeared on the market in the late 1940s. The use of antibiotics has since spread, though limited in most countries by government regulation pending better understanding of their operation.

Government regulation. Most governments attempt to control the addition of foreign substances to foods and the occurrence of toxic residues in foods. Regulations concerning the use of food additives, including chemical preservatives such as boric acid and hydrogen peroxide, change frequently as new compounds become available

Irradiation:
sterilization at low
temperatures

or as the desirable or undesirable properties of agents in use become better understood.

Irradiation (ionizing radiation). Radiation sterilization allows preservation of foods without marked change in their natural character. Radiation processing of foods may eliminate refrigeration requirements; limited radiation may prolong the storage life of cut meats, fresh fish, and fresh fruits and vegetables. Parasites, food-poisoning organisms, and insects in various life-cycle stages may be destroyed. Sprouting may be inhibited in potatoes and onions. Irradiation may be used in preparation of sterile enzyme solutions, tenderization of meat, coffee-bean roasting, and aging of wines.

Sterilization of foods by irradiation requires only one-fiftieth of the energy needed for thermal sterilization. It permits sterilization of substances with a temperature rise of only about 5° F (3° C).

Despite the negligible temperature rise, ionizing radiations produce widespread chemical changes in irradiated materials and under ordinary conditions can oxidize any oxidizable substance and reduce any reducible material. Enzymes are more resistant to irradiation than microorganisms, and it may be desirable to inactivate enzymes by other means, in complement to the irradiation action. Nutrients are somewhat reduced in irradiation processing, and development of protective methods requires further study. In the early 1970s, the safety of foods treated by irradiation was still the subject of testing and evaluation.

Semimoist preservation. The availability of wholesome, inexpensive antimycotics (mold inhibitors) that are effective at low levels of addition permits the development of a new category of semimoist, or intermediate-moisture food products. Semimoist technology was still being developed in the early 1970s.

In the preservation of canned bread, increased storage stability has been obtained by lowering the moisture content to 35 percent, heating, and then hermetically sealing the still-hot product to prevent reinoculation by microorganisms.

Polyunsaturated fatty acids are effective antimycotic-fungistatic agents. They have been used to prevent molding of meat, cheese, and many other refrigerated, packaged foods.

One of the problems involved in the development of semimoist foods was the need for control of enzyme activity by a nonheating process.

FOOD STORAGE AND PACKAGING

Storage. Since most foods can be stored for many years under appropriate conditions, it is important to establish the conditions and storage periods that afford the optimum balance between the cost of storage and the changes in quality of stored products. Further study is needed concerning changes in colour, odour, flavour, texture, nutrients, moisture content, staling, and rancidity. Information is also needed on the characteristics of rigid and flexible packages filled with various foods, and their interaction under various storage conditions. Experimentation has already provided important information regarding changes resulting from storage conditions.

A wide range of natural temperature and humidity conditions exist in warehouses, dugouts, shelters, and natural caves used for food storage. These can be highly satisfactory if conditions are sufficiently constant to allow prediction of storage life of the foods.

The temperatures maintained in above-ground natural-storage houses vary with site and geographical location, from below freezing to above 100° F (38° C) at relative humidities from almost 100 to 20 percent or lower.

Temperatures in caves or deeper excavations may fluctuate less than 10° F (6° C) annually. Utilization of these or similar sources of natural cool storage can yield advantages over above-ground storage in more uniform quality and increased life, or can reduce the cost of holding under refrigerated storage.

Packaging. Because it is possible to preserve food-stuffs by altering their immediate environment, packaging has become an important element in preservation.

Satisfactory packaging requires consideration of protection, economy, convenience, and appearance. Factors affecting the choice of packaging materials include product properties, storage conditions, and properties of economically available materials.

Packaging-material specifications for tensile strength, tearing resistance, heat-sealing ability, and other factors are determined by the properties of the food product to be contained and by the storage time and conditions.

Packaging is affected by the tendency of food to gain or lose moisture, its free oil or fat content, its particle size, its tendency to sift, and its susceptibility to spoilage by light, oxygen, and organisms.

Internal and external failures of both rigid and flexible containers frequently reduce quality or storage life of products. Resistance to moisture, corrosion, leakage, and package fatigue are needed to withstand high temperatures or humidities, or the corrosive action of certain products high in salt, fats, natural acids, or sulfur compounds.

Damage to containers by moisture, drying, heat, and other unfavourable conditions is cumulative. Selection of suitable containers can be as important as formulation of foods for long-term storage.

Effect of storage and packaging. Colour stability varies widely among different products and storage temperatures. The only significant change at 0° to −20° F (−18° C to −29° C) is a slightly lighter appearance, and there is no significant change in any product at 32° F (0° C). Temperatures of 47° F (8° C) result in significant changes, particularly in the less stable items.

At temperatures from 70° to 100° F (21° C to 38° C) products tend to darken, brown, fade, and lose flavour or become stale.

Extremes of temperature have adverse effects on texture. Freezing causes sufficient damage to such items as tomatoes and beans to reduce them to substandard grades. Most sauces and gravies separate with freezing; and noodles, spaghetti, and other starches tend to soften or slough. Less serious freezing damage occurs in the softening of cheeses and most vegetables. Beef and pork exhibit an increased tendency to break apart, and salmon to fragment. Frozen and thawed ham and bacon are more easily separated into strings or fibres.

At 70° F to 100° F there is softening of some meat products, drying out of certain bakery and confectionery products and syruping of others, and leakage of fats or oils from such items as cereal bars, meat bars, chocolates, and peanut butter. The storage life of various food products at 70° F is listed in Table 3. Softening or drying is

Effects of
storage
temperature
extremes

Table 3: Useful Storage Life of Plant and Animal Tissues

food product	generalized storage life (days), 70° F
Animal flesh	1–2
Fish	1–2
Poultry	1–2
Dried, salted, smoked meat and fish	360 and more
Fruits	1–7
Dried fruits	360 and more
Leafy vegetables	1–2
Root crops	7–20
Dried seeds	360 and more

seldom as serious as changes in colour or flavour in such products, but leaking of syrups or fats results in damage to wrappers and enamel linings of cans and tends to increase development of stale or rancid flavours. Insect and rodent infestation is encouraged when such products are packaged in nonrigid containers.

Loss of vitamins and nutritive values may be a more serious deterrent to long storage than loss of sensory appeal, particularly at temperatures in the 70° to 32° F range.

Two vitamins, thiamine and ascorbic acid, decrease faster in storage than either colour or palatability. Losses of 30 to 50 percent of these vitamins have been found in some samples where sensory quality remained satisfactory. It is apparent that vitamin retention, rather than sensory quality, should be the criterion in determining temperature and length of storage for foods that are important sources of thiamine or ascorbic acid. As noted above, there are no significant changes in β-carotene; and changes in niacin and riboflavin are relatively minor.

BIBLIOGRAPHY. N.W. DESROSIER, *The Technology of Food Preservation*, 3rd ed. (1970), is a comprehensive text on food preservation. L.B. JENSEN, *Man's Foods* (1953), provides a historical perspective. Food and health are treated in G.M. DACK, *Food Poisoning*, 3rd ed. rev. (1956); F.W. TANNER, *The Microbiology of Foods*, 2nd ed. (1944); and *Food-Borne Infections and Intoxications*, 2nd ed. (1953). The UNITED STATES DEPARTMENT OF AGRICULTURE, *Composition of Foods* (Handbook No. 67), provides the composition of various preserved foods; the AMERICAN SOCIETY OF HEATING, REFRIGERATING AND AIR-CONDITIONING ENGINEERS, *Refrigeration Handbook* (1969), gives detailed information on the refrigerated storage of specific commodities. Basic documents covering market diseases of fresh fruits and vegetables are in the U.S.D.A. Handbook No. 66. D.K. TRESSLER (ed.), *The Freezing Preservation of Foods*, 4th ed. (1968), is an authoritative and useful presentation of all aspects of the frozen-food industry; canning and pickling of foods is treated in W.V. CRUESS, *Commercial Fruit and Vegetable Products*, 4th ed. (1958); and in C.H. CAMPBELL, *Campbell's Book: A Manual on Canning, Preserving and Pickling* (1954). W.B. VAN ARSDEL and M.J. COPLEY (eds.), *Food Dehydration*, 2 vol. (1963–64), is a detailed treatment of the ancient practice of food drying. The CHEMICAL PUBLISHING CO., *Handbook of Food Additives* (1968), discusses the use of chemicals in foods.

(N.W.D.)

Food Service Systems

Food service systems are designed for the purpose of planning, preparing, and serving food outside the home and in large volume; in addition to commercial outlets (see RESTAURANT), the industry includes such institutional food services as those operated by schools, hospitals, industrial plants, and military services. In the U.S., where 25 percent of the retail value of food consumed is prepared and served outside the home, food service is the country's fourth largest industry. It is achieving comparable status in Europe and Japan.

Historical development. Although technological advances in food processing methods and distribution equipment have revolutionized preparation and delivery systems since World War I, quantity food service operations date much further back. Quantity food production and service, for example, characterized the monasteries, abbeys, princely households, and colleges of the Middle Ages. Then as now the principal factors affecting the organization of food service systems were the type of institution and the availability of food and labour.

Industrial food service. Provision of food for labour forces has been a necessity since earliest times when labour was either forced or hired to work in the fields, construct monuments, man ships in commercial navigation, and enlist in armies. Long before the Industrial Revolution brought the mass production factory, employers provided board and lodging for apprentices and journeymen. In 1815, Robert Owen, a mill operator in Scotland, concerned with the exploitation of children in the textile industry, established a large kitchen and eating room where meals were served at a nominal price to employees and their families. In Europe it became customary for employers to provide areas where food from home could be reheated and supplemented by beverages or other items sold at cost. In the United States the policy of subsidizing meals has been characteristic of employee food systems from early times, and by the 1890s many factories, banks, department stores, and telephone exchanges were providing food services for employees.

World Wars I and II fostered advances in mass-feeding technology; World War I saw the introduction of cafeteria service to replace less efficient table service and World War II the spread of vending machines and other quick-service equipment. The wars also stimulated the

Robert Owen's employee kitchen

development of fabricated, prepackaged food, a trend that was stimulated by the need to meet such peacetime logistics problems as those associated with mining, exploring, and other remote-location activities. Several innovative techniques for packaging and controlling food quality for extended periods of time resulted, notably as a product of space exploration.

Commercial food service. The establishment of inns and taverns as public eating places for travellers was the earliest forerunner of present-day commercial food service. The beginning of the concept of the restaurant, a public eating place exclusive of provisions for sleeping, is attributed to the cookshops of France in the 18th century, which were licensed to prepare ragouts to be eaten on the premises or taken to inns for consumption. From these beginnings commercial food services grew into the 20th century's range, which includes conventional restaurants, quick-service and self-service shops, in-flight meals aboard commercial aircraft, and others.

School and college food service. The gradual restriction of child labour was an influential factor in the development of the school lunch movement. In some European countries, public concern for education resulted in the provision of low-cost lunches to encourage school attendance. Canteens for school children were established in France as early as 1849. Victor Hugo is credited with initiating school feeding in England in 1865 by providing warm lunches in his home on the island of Guernsey for children in the local school.

Organized school feeding in the U.S. dates to the mid-19th century, when to persuade slum children to go to school, the Children's Aid Society of New York City opened an industrial school in 1853 and offered to feed all students. Federal legislation in the 1930s provided loans and surplus commodities for local programs; in 1943 schools were allocated cash assistance, and in 1946 the National School Lunch Act authorized federal grants-in-aid. Legislation enacted in 1970 amended and improved the national school lunch program. The law authorized funds for nutrition education for children and placed a positive mandate on each state to provide a free or reduced-price lunch to all needy children.

Food service in colleges is as old as the university itself; the first endowed student hostel of the Middle Ages appeared at the University of Paris in 1180. Students were responsible for the management; some later endowed houses were under the direction of the university. The question of management remained characteristic of student food services, but the principle of endowed programs remained in force into the 20th century.

Student hostels of the Middle Ages

In both school and college food service, the trend in the early 1970s was toward centralized food purchasing and preparation through a commissary operation. Prepared food items were transported either as individual servings on plates or in bulk to satellite areas for finishing, assembly, and service.

Hospital food service. Although the first hospitals of medieval Europe provided food for patients, the idea of therapeutic diets for patients developed in 19th-century military hospitals, notably the British army hospital at Scutari, Turkey, in the Crimean War (1853–56), in which Florence Nightingale organized a diet kitchen. Alexis Soyer, a London chef, contributed his services as manager to the barrack's hospital kitchen. The idea was soon copied by civil as well as military hospitals. As the nutritional and therapeutic significance of food gained recognition, so did the need for a dietitian. The functions of the hospital dietary department grew to comprise the organization and management of the total hospital food service, including the education of patients and nurses in nutrition and often extending to the preparation of food for elderly or incapacitated persons who are not hospitalized. Trends in hospital food systems of the early 1970s included automated meal-delivery systems, centralized or off-premise food preparation, preprepared and preportioned foods, and computer-assisted management procedures.

Characteristics of a food service system. To provide effective and efficient meal preparation and delivery, a food service system integrates a number of interdependent resources. These may be grouped in four categories: (1) human: direct and indirect labour; (2) material: food and supplies; (3) facility: equipment and space; and (4) operational: time and capital. Menu planning, procurement of foodstuffs, food preparation, and meal assembly and delivery comprise the basic functions of the system. To implement these functions, subsystems are designed to forecast required quantities, allocate and schedule resources, process information, handle materials, and control cost and quality.

Food service systems are obviously comparable in many ways to conventional manufacturing industries. Both acquire foodstuffs in various states of processing, convert the individual items into a product, and sell and deliver the product at a cost compatible with the objectives of the institution.

The basic end product of the food system is the meal or the individual menu items that form the meal. The menu and its associated recipes constitute the product-design specifications. Standardized recipes dictate the specific kind and type of food ingredients required, the production quantity relative to demand, and the amount and type of labour and equipment necessary to produce the menu within a prescribed time interval.

The general objectives of any food service system are to provide nutritional, safe, and palatable meals. The achievement of these objectives is dependent on the organizational structure, the application of scientific food-preparation techniques and management principles, and the effectiveness of the personnel.

The food service director plans, implements, and controls operational procedures to insure the production of quality food and service. Food-preparation techniques influence nutrient retention, acceptance, and bacteriological safety of the food. The conditions of preparation best suited to the retention of colour, flavour, aroma, and texture tend also to preserve the nutritive value. Minimum standards for sanitation and safety in food services are widely established and enforced by national and local legislation.

Current trends in food service systems. The 1960s and 1970s witnessed rapid developments in food service, especially in new market forms of food, such as frozen and dehydrated, and more automated preparation and delivery equipment. These changes have brought about new concepts in meal assembly and distribution, facility layout, labour use, and operational analysis.

Production and distribution techniques. The trend toward centralization of food preparation either on the premises or at a commissary apart from the point of service is accelerating. Many food service systems utilize centralized materials-handling methods to facilitate the movement of raw materials from storeroom to preparation area. This technique facilitates the control of product quality and cost as well as the use of unskilled personnel for supporting tasks such as weighing, assembling, and transporting ingredients. Operations with a large volume of production have implemented central purchasing, warehousing, and commissary production with distribution to satellite service units.

Assembly-line food

The centralization of production and the development of continuous batch-processing equipment have resulted in the use of the food factory concept by which products are produced in assembly-line fashion. Individual menu items are produced either for immediate service or warehouse storage depending on perishability. This technique smooths production scheduling, provides for more effective use of equipment and space, and allows menu items to be withdrawn from storage on demand.

The availability of pre-prepared and convenience menu items through commercial production or institution-operated commissaries has placed increased emphasis on meal reconstitution and delivery techniques, as illustrated by heat-and-serve or frozen preportioned meals available on mobile pallets that can be moved directly into heating equipment at the point of assembly or service. Cold food items, such as salads, may be purchased preportioned on disposable ware, in bulk form ready for por-

tioning, or may be produced on premises. When a complete ready-to-serve meal is distributed to numerous satellite units, cold and hot foods are assembled on a continuous belt and transported by automatically dispatched horizontal or vertical delivery systems.

Preparation and delivery equipment. West Germany, France, Switzerland, and Sweden are the leading designers and manufacturers of large-scale food production and meal-delivery equipment. Innovations include a vertical cutter and mixer, forced-air oven, tilting frying pan, continuous grill, automatic food-supply devices, and monorail and automatic-car meal-transport systems.

Reprinted, with permission, from *Hospitals, Journal of the American Hospital Association*, vol. 44, no. 6, p. 110 (March 16, 1970)

Continuous cooking and distribution system.

A German meal preparation and assembly system in use in several hospitals in Europe (see illustration) incorporates automatic food preparation with continuous processing equipment. The tray-assembly system is equipped with an electronically controlled guidance mechanism that indicates individual food orders at each assembly station. The system uses auxiliary electronic data-processing equipment and provides assembly control and rapid distribution of meals.

A system of supplying food via pneumatic tube at the point of patient-tray assembly was developed for hospitals in Sweden. Singly portioned, packaged, sealed, and frozen items are ordered from storage by remote control. Fresh food items are released from storage and carried on a conveyor belt directly into the automatic dispatcher of a pneumatic tube. Items to be eaten hot are brought to serving temperature in a conveyorized microwave oven before delivery via the pneumatic tube. The items are released onto a collecting belt where they are assembled according to the patients' selection.

A system designed for the University of Cologne, West Germany, can feed 2,500 patients and 4,000 employees and students in 125 locations, in 17 buildings scattered over nine city blocks. The food is processed in containers that convey food through heat zones set at predetermined temperature and cooking mediums. In the assembly section, food is portioned into plates on conveyor belts. This part of the meal is blast-frozen (a quick-freezing method) and loaded into containers to be stored according to a computer-assisted allocation and inventory system. At the time of service, fresh meal components are coordinated with frozen items. Completed trays are filed in a transfer unit to be hoisted onto a monorail for delivery. When the tray reaches the point of service, the frozen portion is heated in a microwave oven.

A meal distribution and delivery technique developed in the U.S. and used by both hospitals and airlines is based on the principle of loading hot foods over hot foods and cold foods over cold foods in thermal insulated trays, creating thermal columns for temperature retention. Hot foods for flight are precooked, frozen, and taken aboard under refrigeration. Before serving they are heated to proper temperature.

Application of scientific management. In order to achieve an optimum balance between food-production costs, product quality, and consumer satisfaction, food service administrators must know how much people are to eat, how many people are eating, and, in free-choice situations, what they will want to eat, in order to make the decisions required of them. Operational procedures are planned, kept current, and evaluated through the use of systems analysis, work measurement, and other program evaluation and review techniques.

Operations-research techniques are used to develop methods of forecasting demands for service on the food system and allocating and scheduling the utilization of system resources. Computer-assisted menu planning employing linear programming techniques (see OPERATIONS RESEARCH) has been developed to determine the optimum combination of menu items that satisfies predetermined nutrient and cost constraints. Computer simulation techniques have been used to schedule food preparation, determine optimum inventory levels, and study the effect of various patterns of customer traffic flow on the efficiency of cafeteria systems.

Computer-assisted procedures in support of managerial and operational functions have been implemented in numerous food service systems. Current applications include menu planning, production-demand forecasting, recipe sizing, purchasing, ingredient issue, inventory control, and cost accounting. The advent of the computer has provided food service directors with the opportunity to develop a management system that provides a means of common control over a number of complex and interrelated food-system functions.

BIBLIOGRAPHY. B.B. WEST, L. WOOD, and V.F. HARGER, *Food Service in Institutions*, 4th ed. (1966), a basic text presenting a comprehensive coverage of the organization and management of food service systems, quantity food production, and food-system layout and equipment; *Electronic Data Processing in Support of Hospital Dietary Services* (1969), a series of articles, reprinted from *Hospitals* magazine, describing the design and implementation of computer-assisted procedures in support of hospital dietary functions.

Principal periodicals in the field of food administration are: *Food Technology* (monthly), *Journal of the American Dietetic Association* (monthly), and *Proceedings of the Society for the Advancement of Food Service Research* (semi-annual).

(G.L.O.)

Food Supply of the World

Throughout history, the food supply of mankind, worldwide, has oscillated between scarcity and plenty. To the fertile valleys of the Tigris–Euphrates and the Nile came drought or flood and the seven lean years that toppled dynasties. When the population of Rome exceeded its food supply, foreign conquest provided grain supplies from Africa and Thrace.

When, in the mid-19th century, Europe's population suddenly began to multiply and starvation threatened, its emigrants opened up temperate lands in other continents to provide the needed grain, meat, and dairy products. Since World War II, another population explosion has started, this time in the developing countries and much more rapid than anything previously seen, and will, some say, result in widespread famine. The successes of scientists and the many possibilities of applying agricultural technology in the developing countries, however, offer hope that with appropriate effort sufficient food can be produced for all people. The United Nations has projected that world population may stabilize at some 12,-000,000,000 to 15,000,000,000 around the middle of the 21st century. Technically—in terms of the world's resources of soil and water and knowledge of agricultural

techniques—it would be possible to feed this many people; whether it will be possible in practice remains to be seen.

In primitive societies each family was self-sufficient. Nonagricultural occupations gradually emerged—those of the carriers, the priests, the artisans, who gave their services or products in exchange for food. Thus came into existence the market economy, which grew in volume and geographical extent as villages and towns increased in size. As early as Roman times it was possible to speak of a "world market" for certain foodstuffs. Portions of the market collapsed with the empire and did not reemerge until innovations in transportation and other inventions beginning in the mid-19th century created a new "world market," this time extending beyond Eurasia and Africa and covering the entire planet. Market economy

Nevertheless, a large part of mankind remains only partially linked to markets, as may be deduced from statistics that show the proportion of farm output retained on farms—that is, subsistence production. The figure, barely 1 percent in the United Kingdom and 3 percent in the United States, exceeds 50 percent in southern Asia and 80 percent in many parts of Africa. In the developing countries, with the expansion of cities and the spread of industrialization, subsistence production can be expected to decline rapidly in favour of market production.

Just as family self-sufficiency in food denoted security, so, also for reasons of security, national self-sufficiency has been a preoccupation of many governments. Most countries today are more than 90 percent self-sufficient in food, though they may have to depend on imports for exotic products such as coffee or cocoa. Significant exceptions are the United Kingdom, which produces only 60 percent of its food, and countries with poor agricultural resources such as Norway and Switzerland, which produce an even smaller proportion. Because food output in many advanced countries is increasing faster than the demand for food, their degree of self-sufficiency has tended to increase since about 1955. But because of population growth and a tendency to neglect agricultural development in favour of industry, the opposite has happened in several developing countries.

THE FOOD SHORTAGE IN DEVELOPING COUNTRIES

Trends in population and food production. In 1975 the population of the world reached 4,000,000,000, sharply divided in terms of social and economic welfare between 3,000,000,000 in the developing countries and 1,000,-000,000 in the developed countries. (As used in this article, "developed countries" include Europe, the Soviet Union, North America, Australia, New Zealand, and, for the postwar years, South Africa, Japan, and Israel; "developing countries" include, unless otherwise indicated, all other countries.) The trends in food production in each group are shown in Table 1, as of August 1977. World population, 1975

Table 1: Trends in Food Production* (1961–65 average = 100)			
item	1948–52	1956–60	1971–76
Total			
Developed countries†	68	89	130
Developing countries			
Excluding China	66	87	133
Including China	...	...	133
Per person			
Developed countries†	81	94	115
Developing countries			
Excluding China	89	98	102
Including China	...	...	104

*Excluding fish.
†Including eastern Europe and the Soviet Union.
Source: Food and Agriculture Organization, Rome.

Contrary to popular belief, total food output in the developing countries has expanded as rapidly as in the developed. It is in relation to population that the picture becomes quite different. Taking the average of the years

1961–65 as 100, production per person in the developed countries rose from 81 in 1948–52 (that is, just after World War II) to 94 in 1956–60 and 115 in 1971–76. In developing countries production per person rose fairly steadily after the war till about 1958. Thereafter it was almost stagnant. Population increase each year, about 2.3 percent, absorbed most of the increase in production.

The disquieting paradox persists: the already well-fed peoples are able to expand their food production faster than their requirements grow—despite the fact that in some of the rich countries, notably the United States, governments have deliberately restrained production—whereas for poorly fed peoples the reverse is the case. At the very end of the 1960s, as a result of the "green revolution," there were some signs of an upsurge in food production in certain developing countries, notably in Asia. During the 1970s, however, the surge was not maintained.

Since 1972 the world has been close to crisis in its food supply. In that year, poor crops were harvested in most of the major cereal-producing areas, particularly in the Soviet Union, India, and North America. World stocks were almost depleted. Stocks of cereals (outside China and the Soviet Union), which had been 26 percent of total consumption in 1970, had already fallen to 19 percent in 1972. In 1973, as a result of the poor harvests in 1972, they had been drawn down to 14 percent, and in succeeding years they went even lower.

Beginning with the 1973 season, the crop situation was complicated by both shortages and very high prices of fertilizers. Partly but not wholly because of the dramatic rise in petroleum prices, prices of fertilizers rose four- to fivefold. The rise in food and fertilizer prices hit particularly those developing countries, such as India, that did not have oil or some other product that benefitted from the price boom. At the end of the 1960s there was a worldwide surplus of fertilizers, prices were very low, little new capacity was installed, and some plants were closed down. But with world demand increasing rapidly (about 13 percent a year in developing countries), production capacity fell below worldwide demand.

As a consequence of the earlier trends, the developed countries exported larger and larger quantities of food to the developing countries. Beginning in the mid-1950s, this trade doubled, while the agricultural exports of the developing group recorded only a modest increase. At the same time the imports of food into developing countries increased more rapidly than food imports into developed countries. Using 1961–65 as 100, the ratio of exports to imports in 1973 had risen to a favourable 125 for developed countries, while that of developing countries had deteriorated to 78. This imbalance was a major cause of the worsening balance of payments experienced by the developing countries, even though an important proportion of their food imports was obtained on noncommercial terms.

The Food and Agriculture Organization (FAO) of the United Nations has calculated that, if these trends in population and food production continue, the net cereal deficit of the developing market economies would have to rise from 16,000,000 tons in 1969–71 to almost 85,-000,000 tons by 1985 in order to meet the projected increase in demand. Since it is entirely unlikely that the poor countries could finance imports of this magnitude or that rich donor countries would give so much away, ways and means will have to be found to enable the developing countries to feed themselves.

The nature of the problem. The food supply problems of the two groups of countries are therefore radically different. In the advanced countries, where food production increases at 2.7 percent per year, population at 1 percent, and per capita food consumption hardly at all, the central problem has been one of supply management. This is dwarfed by the much vaster and more urgent food supply problems of the developing countries, in which large segments of the population are malnourished or actually hungry. By 1985, simply to cover expected increases in population and modest increases in pur-

chasing power, the food supply of the developing countries will have to expand at an average rate of 3.6 percent a year.

To this challenge, no single or simple solution exists. Progress has to be organized in several directions concurrently; for instance, by making better use of existing food supplies, by increasing agricultural inputs, by strengthening research, agricultural services, and rural institutions, by pursuing appropriate national economic and population policies, and by a concerted expansion of international trade and foreign aid. Objectives in most of these fields were proposed by the FAO in its *Provisional Indicative World Plan for Agricultural Development,* published in 1969, and were subsequently updated in the proposals presented to and broadly agreed on by the United Nations World Food Conference, held in Rome in November 1974.

MAJOR PROBLEMS OF FOOD SUPPLIES

Crop production. Since World War II, food production has expanded more rapidly than during any comparable period in history. Had it not been for the equally rapid rise in population in developing countries, the problem of hunger and malnutrition would have been nearly solved. In the developed countries, almost all the increased output came from higher yields per acre, cereal acreages showing little change except in the Soviet Union, where virgin lands in the east and southeast were brought into cultivation. Wheat yields in Europe, for example, rose from 14.7 quintals per hectare (1,310 pounds per acre) in 1948–52 to 30.2 (2,690) in 1975, an annual increment of 3.1 percent. In the U.S. the average yield of corn (maize) was 24.9 quintals (2,220 pounds) in 1948–52 and 54.1 (4,830) in 1975, an annual increase of 3.5 percent. In the developing countries during the 1960s, expansion of area was responsible for about 40 percent of increased production, higher yields for the remainder.

Some of the increased cereal output in developed countries has been exported (especially from North America to developing countries that faced shortages), but the greater part has gone to livestock feeding. In the years ahead, most of the developed countries will require more feed grain but less wheat, whereas the developing countries need more cereals for both food and feed. To meet this need, intensified use of existing farmland appears generally more economic than expansion of area. Indeed, in Asia and the Near East many countries have little choice. In Africa and Latin America, although large areas remain uncultivated, the cost of opening them up and in particular of building up the means of transport needed to make them accessible would be extremely high. Bringing new land into cultivation would help to provide additional employment, however.

To increase yields per acre requires a judicious combination of physical techniques and supporting services. Plant breeding, including increasing the supplies of the much-publicized high-yielding varieties of wheat and rice, should play a major role. In the Far East the Mexican wheat and the Philippine rice seed, together with vastly improved varieties from other sources, already account for 54 percent of the wheat area and 20 percent of the rice area. Elsewhere may be found significant "islands" of progress; *e.g.*, hybrid maize in Kenya, wheat in Turkey, improved rice in Madagascar and Brazil, and wheat throughout Mexico. The area of wheat planted to high-yielding varieties in the Far East rose from 9,000 hectares (22,000 acres) in the 1965–66 season to approximately 15,000,000 hectares (37,000,000 acres) in 1973–74. Over the same period, areas under high-yielding varieties of rice rose from 49,000 hectares (121,000 acres) to approximately 17,000,000 (42,000,000).

In order to succeed, the new varieties require ample balanced fertilizer—as much as 120 kilograms of nitrogen per hectare (about 107 pounds per acre) plus appropriate quantities of phosphate and potash, for example. Fertilizer consumption between 1949–51 and 1972–73 rose in developed countries from 22 to 102 kilograms of plant nutrient per arable hectare (from about 20 to 91 pounds per acre) and in developing coun-

Exports and imports of food

Food scarcity in developing countries

Plant breeding for high yield

tries from 1.4 to 1.7 kilograms (from 1.25 to 1.50 pounds). The FAO's *Indicative World Plan* calculated that in these latter countries fertilizer consumption should increase from 2,600,000 tons (1962) to more than 31,000,000 tons (1985).

A second essential element is water. Around 1962 irrigation was used on some 72,000,000 hectares (178,000,000 acres), or 19 percent of the harvested crop area, in the countries studied by the FAO in the *Indicative World Plan*. The plan proposed to double this area by 1985, with greater emphasis than previously on groundwater, at a cost of some $36,000,000,000 plus another $11,000,000,000 for drainage, flood control, and related works.

Other necessary elements include crop protection with pesticides to combat loss of potential production, a loss estimated at more than $50,000,000,000 in the developing countries in 1965. Also, mechanization is expected to increase yields and reduce harvesting losses by more timely sowing and reaping; in suitable environments it makes multiple cropping possible. But the economics of applying mechanical power require careful study where, as in the majority of the developing countries, the farm labour supply is already excessive and destined to become more so.

Better cultivation practices can contribute much; *e.g.,* terracing, contour plowing, planting of shelter belts, growing of grass or legumes in rotation with grain or tilled crops, mulching, and growing legumes in rotation. There is no set formula. Measures must vary according to the environment and are very different, for example, in low rainfall areas of more or less level terrain from those in mountainous terrain. In the former, the chief aim would be to prevent wind erosion and to improve penetration and retention of moisture by such practices as chisel plowing, construction of small embankments or ridges, strip cropping, and stubble mulching. In the uplands, the aim would be to prevent excessive runoff and water erosion by plowing against the slope or, on steeper slopes, by building terraces. In some areas, planting of shrubbery as windbreaks serves to protect the soil and crops.

Where annual winter rainfall exceeds 400 millimetres (16 inches) in the Near East, northwest Africa, and the northern Indo-Gangetic plain, it probably would be profitable to replace the cereal–fallow rotation by alternate rain-fed cropping of cereals and fodder legumes, such as clovers and lucerne (alfalfa), with the possibility of more comprehensive rotations—including grain legumes, such as lentils and chick-peas (gram), oilseeds, or other cash crops—in areas of higher rainfall.

One of the best formulas for providing more employment and at the same time increasing incomes undoubtedly is multiple cropping. In Hong Kong, for instance, 80 percent of the vegetable farmers plant more than four crops a year and 45 percent plant seven to nine crops. While these examples cannot be imitated everywhere, there are many regions of dense population, suitable climate, and good water supply in which multiple cropping could be, but is not, practiced.

Livestock and fish. To the world's protein supply, livestock products contribute 35 percent and fish 6 percent. Formerly the production of both was concentrated in a few favoured areas. More than half of the world's milk and nearly half of its meat is produced in Europe and North America. Most of the food fish comes from waters adjacent to Europe, North America, and Japan.

Between the immediate postwar period (1948–52) and 1976, numbers of cattle increased by 34 percent in Europe (excluding the Soviet Union), 60 percent in North America, as much as 68 percent in Africa, and 63 percent in Latin America. As shown in Table 2, world meat production more than doubled during that period, both in developed countries (including the Soviet Union) and in developing countries (including China).

Fish production between 1950 and 1975 increased only modestly in North America and by 100 percent in western Europe; in the Soviet Union, however, it rose 507 percent, in East and Southeast Asia (including Japan) 205 percent, and in Africa 266 percent. Especially noteworthy was the Latin-American expansion from 640,000 tons to 15,000,000 tons (1970), mainly accounted for by the anchoveta (a small anchovy), processed in Peruvian fish-meal plants for export to industrial countries. Thereafter the catch of anchovetas declined—probably temporarily—because of changes in ocean currents. During the 1960s exports of fish meal from the Soviet Union and Latin America increased 30–40 percent, while those from Africa increased 60 percent.

It is in consumption of livestock products that the greatest difference between rich and poor peoples is observed. Thus, meat consumption approaches 230 grams (8.1 ounces) per person per day in the United States and is even higher in Argentina, Australia, and New Zealand; by contrast, it reaches only 58 grams (2.03 ounces) in Mexico, 19 grams (0.7 ounce) in Nigeria, and four grams (0.14 ounce) in India. Similarly, the consumption of milk products, which exceeds 700 grams (25 ounces) per person per day (in terms of fresh milk equivalent) in Scandinavia and 670 grams (23.6 ounces) in the United States, reaches only 75 grams (2.6 ounces) in Tanzania and 13 grams (0.46 ounce) in Thailand.

Since World War II the application of mass-production methods in the poultry industry, notably in North America and Europe, has greatly reduced the price of poultry relative to other meats and has stimulated consumption. Some further increase in beef consumption can be expected, especially in Europe, but it takes time to increase cattle numbers. Beef prices, moreover, have not become sufficiently attractive to farmers; in potential supplying regions such as Latin America and parts of Africa, disease problems inhibit the expansion of beef exports to North America and Europe. A measure of the inferiority of the cattle of developing countries is shown in Table 3. In western Europe the combined output of meat and milk per head of cattle is about 25 times that of Asia and five times that of Latin America.

Table 3: Relative Productivity of Cattle by Region, 1976

region	cattle (000,000)	production meat (000,000 tons)	production milk (000,000 tons)	total*	ratio of production to numbers of cattle
Western Europe	101	8.0	125	205	2.03
United States and Canada	142	13.4	62	196	1.38
Soviet Union	111	6.2	89	151	1.36
Australia and New Zealand	43	1.8	13	31	0.72
Latin America	266	7.9	31	110	0.41
Near East	46	0.8	7	15	0.33
Africa	130	1.7	5	22	0.17
Far East	254	0.9	11	20	0.08

*In milk equivalent, one ton of meat being taken as equal in production to 10 tons of milk.
Source: Food and Agriculture Organization, Rome.

Many lines of attack can be pursued simultaneously. Some of the major grassland areas of the developing countries are understocked, and others are hopelessly overgrazed. The introduction of range management would in time greatly augment the carrying capacity of these lands. Fodder crops can be much more widely grown, especially on irrigated land, once the national supply of food crops has become adequate. By-products, often wasted, can be turned into feed concentrates; an

Table 2: Meat Production in Developed and Developing Countries

item	1948–52 (000,000 metric tons)	1976 (000,000 metric tons)	index (1948–52) = 100	growth rate compound (percent per year)
Developed countries	32.3	81.9	254	4.0
Developing countries	16.5	39.7	241	3.7
World	48.8	121.6	249	3.9

Source: Food and Agriculture Organization, Rome.

example is the successful use of molasses combined with urea for fattening beef cattle. In some regions—*e.g.,* in many parts of Africa—customary forms of land tenure and the hoarding of animals as investment capital impede the introduction of modern cattle raising, as do religious beliefs in parts of southern Asia. Eradication of the tsetse fly from Central Africa would make available 7,000,000 square kilometres (2,700,000 square miles) for cattle raising. The Dairy Development Scheme of the FAO would link the dried milk surpluses of exporting countries to the building of dairy industries in developing countries. These programs will take time. Much more rapid expansion of meat supplies can be achieved by first developing large-scale poultry production and, where acceptable, pig production, though this, as well as beef and dairy expansion, requires the introduction of modern market structures—cold storage, transport, inspection services—and stronger price incentives. A precondition for commercial poultry and pig production is availability of grain supplies beyond human needs.

Expanding fisheries

Fisheries could also expand, since the demand for food fish and fish meal is expected approximately to double between 1965 and 1985. Necessary measures include the introduction of powered vessels and modern gear where these are yet unknown, investment in port facilities, the training of fishermen, and the creation of facilities for cooling the product during storage and distribution. In oceans intensively fished, governments will need to agree upon management and conservation measures, while areas such as the Indian Ocean, the South Pacific, and the Antarctic could be more fully utilized. The culture of fish, especially mollusks, is generally profitable in shallow coastal waters, as is the growing of carp in fresh-water ponds. Possibly within the next two decades the limit of the supply potential of currently used species will have been reached, but there remain many unexploited species to which consumer taste could adapt, such as lantern fish and Antarctic krill, the latter capable of supplying perhaps 50,000,000 tons a year when economic harvesting methods have been devised.

Better use of existing supplies of food. Another approach to increasing food supplies is to cut down the wastage that occurs at all stages. At the very start of the production process, the land itself in many regions is abused by shifting cultivation, overgrazing, lack of terracing or of tree cover, or poor drainage. The water supply is misused, with wastage of up to 50 percent through faulty design of irrigation systems, overpumping that turns groundwater brackish, or pollution that renders water unusable for either agriculture or fish culture. Animal manures in many countries are used for fuel or simply wasted, and the nutrient value of chemical fertilizers may be partially lost through incorrect application. Investment in extension services to advise farmers about correcting these malpractices would produce important and immediate benefits.

Preventing wastage

In crop husbandry, weeds, pests, and diseases can each cause losses of up to 30 percent. Birds and locusts take a heavy toll, as do primitive harvesting and winnowing methods; even in the United States, with all its modern equipment, studies show grain losses of 5 to 10 percent in the field. In developing countries the percentage is far higher.

In the animal husbandry of the developing countries, high rates of infertility and prenatal mortality are caused by reproductive disorders; poor nutrition results in gastrointestinal parasitism; endemic diseases such as inflammation of the udder reduce milk yields; and other diseases, such as foot-and-mouth disease in Latin America, impede the development of what could be a valuable export business.

Storage losses are notorious. The United States reports 3 to 7 percent grain losses in storage, but in Africa, for example, up to one-third of stored maize may be lost. Yet plastic sheets for drying grain can be had cheaply, and the construction of rat-proof bins and the fumigation of stored grains are not prohibitively expensive.

In the case of perishables, losses are even more serious and the remedies more costly. Thus, in parts of Africa,

up to 40 percent of the fruit, vegetables, and eggs sent to urban markets may be lost as a result of faulty packing, infrequent transport, and lack of cold or other suitable storage. In some Near Eastern countries, half the sheep's milk goes bad because of the lack of coolers. In the tropics, fish becomes inedible within 24 hours after removal from the water, which restricts boats without refrigeration to a narrow fishing range. The installation of cold-storage facilities becomes profitable when a sizable urban market has developed and when regular supplies can be counted on. To aid in distribution, governments are beginning to encourage the creation of marketing cooperatives and other producer organizations and to provide inspection services and market intelligence reports.

Another approach to better utilization of food is through nutritional education. The governments of certain developing countries have equipped mobile kitchens from which home economists teach housewives improved methods of cooking and of food preservation. Through school garden programs, as in Turkey, villagers are taught the nutritional value of vegetables and fruit and how to grow them. Such programs involve the modification of traditional eating habits; change comes gradually.

Nutritional education

Agricultural policies. In addition to the technical and scientific progress involved in improving the world's food supply, the social and economic aspects count for as much. In these fields governments have a major responsibility, whether in price and tax policies, in agrarian reform, in creating institutions and services, or in promoting foreign trade.

Prices and taxation. It is not enough for governments to announce a guaranteed price for a product; they must ensure that producers receive that price rather than only half or two-thirds of it. Farmers in developing countries sell their produce at unfavourable moments either because they have insufficient storage, are short of cash, or have been misinformed. In Colombia, for instance, the price of potatoes after harvest falls to one-third of the preharvest level. Remedies include the creation of a sufficient number of local buying points at which official prices are posted and inspectors are present; the construction of more storage space to permit orderly crop disposal; and the provision of credit facilities to relieve farmers from the need to make forced sales.

Taxation policy toward agriculture continues to be of much interest in developing countries. Governments cannot afford to exempt from taxation the farm people who constitute 50 to 80 percent of the total population, and yet they must ensure that taxes as well as price policies encourage rather than discourage maximum food production.

Agrarian reform. In many regions, traditional modes of land tenure interfere with expansion of food production either in direct ways or through the perpetuation of a nonprogressive social structure. Where feudal-type estates still exist, for example, the policy of subdividing them must compromise between the need to satisfy land hunger and the desirability of creating farms large enough to be profitable; and, simultaneously with subdivision, new organizations must be established for the marketing, credit, and other services formerly provided, though imperfectly, by the landlords. In several regions of Africa, customary tenures that impede rational land use are being gradually converted to individual or group ownership. In nomadic pastoral economies, where the settlement of nomads may be neither practicable nor desirable, reforms concentrate not on tenure aspects but rather on more rational stocking and range management, on the creation of more water points, and on the provision of veterinary services and supplementary feed supplies. Finally, in districts facing the problem of an excess of very small or badly fragmented farms, costly investments are involved in the consolidation of holdings. Wherever unsatisfactory tenure systems still prevail, nevertheless, bold measures of agrarian reform, although expensive and often politically difficult, are a prerequisite to the creation of the social climate in which a farming community can modernize.

Institutional support. The rapid increases in food output in advanced countries must be attributed in large part to the research and other agricultural services that were built up during previous decades. These services are still embryonic in many developing countries.

For instance, until the mid-20th century almost all of the world's agricultural research (except in regard to certain plantation crops) was conducted in temperate countries and was concerned with the problems of temperate farming. Yet much of the developing countries' agricultural land is located in the tropics. Funds are being made available by private foundations, by the World Bank, and by governments and other institutions to establish or extend in the developing countries research centres that focus not solely on the scientific problems of crops and animal husbandry but also on the social and economic aspects, which are in many cases equally influential.

Agricultural extension services

Some national governments, sometimes with outside assistance, are building up their agricultural extension services, deliberately linking them to farm credit and marketing facilities, and encouraging the creation of farmers' organizations. To provide recruits for these services and to give farmers some basic agricultural education, training programs at all levels are being established. In some countries, the doubling or even tripling of trained personnel seems to be required.

These and many other programs involve large investments that the governments of most developing countries can ill afford. A question of priorities is involved. Starting in the mid-1960s, a number of governments—the Soviet Union and India are prominent examples—in their investment programs greatly augmented the share allocated to agriculture, recognizing that farming is a basic factor in general economic development; other governments were contemplating similar action. The Food and Agriculture Organization has estimated that research and development expenditures in developing countries ought to be increased from around $360,000,000 in 1970 to about $1,250,000,000 in 1985; of the latter sum, about $350,000,000 would be provided by advanced countries and international agencies.

Agricultural trade. Although less than 10 percent of the world's food crosses national frontiers, and only a few countries, notably in western Europe, import as much as half their supplies, a number of countries, including most of the developing countries, rely on agricultural exports to furnish more than half of their foreign currency earnings. Table 4 illustrates the contrast, with respect to trade in agricultural products.

Table 4: Value of Total Agricultural Trade, 1976*

item	exports	imports
	(000,000,000 $ U.S. at current prices)	
Developed market economies	79.6	95.4
Soviet Union and eastern Europe	6.6	16.8
Total developed countries	86.2	112.2
Developing market economies	40.2	27.0
Asian centrally planned economies	2.5	3.0
Total developing countries	42.7	30.0
World total	128.9	142.2

*The definition of agricultural trade follows that of the FAO *Trade Yearbook.* Agricultural trade excludes forestry and fishery products, with the exception of fish meal and marine oils. Re-exports are normally included.
Source: Food and Agriculture Organization, Rome.

Exports

Paradoxically, the well-fed countries are net importers and the poorly fed net exporters of food. The developed countries' major agricultural exports are composed chiefly of cereals and rice (43 percent); oilseeds, vegetable oils, and sugar (27 percent); and nonfood agricultural products (13 percent). Those of the developing countries include beverages (30 percent); nonfood agricultural products (26 percent); sugar, oilseeds, and vegetable oils (23 percent).

During the decade 1963–73, the volume of the developed countries' agricultural exports rose 73 percent, but that of the developing countries rose only 21 percent

(Latin America, 25 percent; Far East, 21; Near East, 35; Africa, 7). Over the 1960s the developed countries benefitted from an increase of some 10 percent in the unit values of their exports, whereas those of developing countries suffered a more than 10 percent decline. Trade in fishery products doubled during the decade, mainly among developed countries, with some export to the developed countries from developing countries (especially fish meal from Latin America). Developing countries themselves do not import much fish.

Many developed countries have maintained tariff and nontariff barriers that shield their farmers from the competition of cheap food imports. Many meetings related to the General Agreement on Tariffs and Trade (GATT) have been devoted to a search for ways of liberalizing trade in farm products, but with little success. Major countries continue to make use of the "waiver" under which they absolve themselves from applying to agriculture the general trading rules of GATT.

Price stabilization

Strong fluctuations in world market prices have always been a particular hazard for countries that are heavily dependent on agricultural exports. Although the most dramatic instances occurred during the Great Depression of the 1930s, price fluctuations persisted during the 1950s and '60s and were particularly marked during the early 1970s. Interested governments have attempted to negotiate international commodity agreements containing price stabilization provisions. Because of economic and political complexities, few such agreements have been concluded, and even in these cases (for example, in wheat) it has often proved to be impossible to hold the price within the prescribed limits. More modest, but often more successful, has been the work of commodity study groups, in which the principal exporters and importers of a product meet regularly to review developments and on occasion to conclude informal trade arrangements. (See also COMMODITY TRADE, INTERNATIONAL.)

PROSPECTS

In assessing food-supply prospects, an attempt must be made to determine the expected increase in demand and to see how fully this demand could be met by carrying through the technical and economic programs described above.

Demand for food. What economists call "effective demand for food" is the amount that people want to buy given the money that they have. Future effective demand depends mainly on two factors: growth of population and growth of income.

Population. The biggest challenge facing the world's food supply is the population explosion in the developing countries. During the 1950s, population in these countries (excluding China and other areas of Asia having central planning) grew at 2.4 percent per year (compared with 1.2 percent in developed countries); during the 1960s the rate rose to 2.7 percent in the developing countries (and dropped to 1 percent in developed countries). The rate of growth has been increasing in the developing group but decreasing in the developed.

As shown in Table 5, the developing countries are expected to increase their populations, in the 20-year period from 1965 to 1985, by 72 percent. During this same period China and other centrally planned countries of Asia

Table 5: Prospective Population of the Developing Group

region	1965 (000,000)	1985 (000,000)	percent increase
Asia and Far East*	916	1,553	69
Near East and northwest Africa	138	244	76
Africa south of the Sahara	216	368	70
Latin America	247	426	72

*Excludes China and other centrally planned countries of Asia, for which data are lacking.
Source: Based on UN "medium" population assumption as assessed in 1973; *World Population Prospects as Assessed in 1973,* New York.

may increase from 800,000,000 to 1,200,000,000. The developed group, numbering about 1,000,000,000 in 1965, is expected to increase by less than 19 percent. About 86 of every 100 persons added between 1965 and 1985 will be born in developing countries. Although the governments of a number of developing countries are currently adopting policies regarding population, it would be unrealistic, bearing in mind the profound changes required in social attitudes, to expect a significant slowing down in population growth in the near future.

Income. Estimates based on accepted hypotheses as to the likely rate of growth of national income in the developing countries indicate that between 1969–71 and 1985 per capita demand for food will increase by about 9 percent. Combining this with the expected population growth gives an estimated increase of 66 percent in total food demand. Of the two growth factors, population and income, population will be by far the more influential, accounting for seven-tenths of the estimated increase. The increase in demand will not apply to all foods equally. Urbanization and gradually rising incomes in the developing countries will affect the composition of people's diets, bringing a modest increase in cereals and starchy foods and a large increase in livestock products, vegetables, and fruit.

Requirements for food. In the developed countries dietary energy supplies exceed estimated requirements by about 23 percent, while in developing countries they fall short by 5 percent; but 5 percent is an average, and many individuals' diets fall far below the average.

Protein
needs

The protein problem is more complex. The advanced countries have an average of 96 grams (3.4 ounces) of protein per person per day, of which more than half is animal protein; this exceeds requirements. The people of the developing countries have an average intake of only 57 grams (2 ounces) of protein per day, much of which is diverted from its true protein functions in an attempt to meet energy deficits. Among developing countries wide differences occur, largely because of ecological and cultural conditions. In moving from the diets of developed countries, which have animal products as the main source of protein, through diets based on wheat, maize, sorghum, or rice, and on to root and tuber diets, the protein intake diminishes, the quality of dietary protein declines because of imbalances in the amino acid content, the protein–energy balance deteriorates, and the gap between intake and recommended allowances widens.

Because good-quality proteins occur mainly in more expensive foodstuffs, the maldistribution of protein between income groups is more serious than that of energy supplies; and because expectant and nursing mothers and young children have special protein requirements, the deficiencies particularly affect these groups. (See also NUTRITION AND DIET, HUMAN.)

Prospective supply. In the developed countries, apart from a few poorer regions of Europe, no change in dietary energy supplies is anticipated in the near future; but in the developing countries—to eliminate the present shortage, cover the population and income increase, and provide a 10 percent safety margin—energy supplies will have to be almost doubled between 1969–71 and 1985. This lies within the capacity of most, though not all, of the developing countries, provided that they pursue vigorous policies of agricultural investment and modernization. Some will lack the physical resources for so large an expansion of food production, and perhaps some will fail to mobilize available resources sufficiently. Such countries will have recourse to larger food imports, or, if they cannot afford these, their more disadvantaged population groups will continue to experience deficiencies in energy supply.

In developed countries, no overall supply problem exists for protein. What is expected to occur is a rearrangement of the sources of protein; namely, an increase in the proportion represented by animal protein. Public assistance to supplement the incomes of specially disadvantaged groups may remain necessary, since protein foods will still be relatively expensive items in the diet.

In developing countries, it is improvement in the quality of protein and its availability to poorer people that requires attention. Part of the problem is to change traditional dietary habits through nutrition education in order to diversify the diet and obtain a better use of the available food supply. Part lies in asking the plant breeder to develop species of, for example, rice and wheat, with nutritionally more satisfactory amino acid content, as is being attempted with maize. Pulses and high-protein oilseeds can become significant supplements to cereal and starchy root diets. Much can be accomplished and relatively quickly in expanding the production of pigs, poultry, and fish. Further, the fortification of certain staple foods with amino acids, minerals, and vitamins, though costly, might be justified in particular circumstances in which specific nutrient deficiencies have been identified. Formulated protein-rich foods of this kind (*e.g.,* "superamine" in Algeria) are being developed for the feeding of the vulnerable population groups.

More unconventional sources of protein are already being developed in advanced countries: "artificial meat" from soya meal; fish protein concentrate, an odourless flour for mixing into other foods; food yeast from the byproducts of pulp and paper manufacture. Certain seaweeds are eaten in Japan and, to a lesser extent, in other Far Eastern countries. Interest has focussed on *Chlorella,* an alga that multiplies itself at fantastic speed and that, if it could be made acceptable for human consumption, would constitute an almost unlimited source of protein. Not least important is the work on single-cell protein; several factories already transform petroleum waxes into protein intended for animal feeds, and there is potential for human use as well. (See also FOOD, NEW SOURCES AND PRODUCTS.)

New foods

The relevance of these experiments to the protein deficiencies in developing countries will depend on whether the new products can be made sufficiently acceptable and sufficiently cheap. For some years to come, at least, principal reliance will continue to be placed on conventional foodstuffs.

INTERNATIONAL AID

The task of feeding the huge populations of the 1980s and feeding them at least somewhat better than today presents a challenge to scientists, educators, economists, administrators, and farmers. The greatest efforts are needed in the countries least equipped to carry out the needed programs. The rich nations already have the necessary knowledge and skills; the poor have first to attain them. Indubitably the main impetus must come from the peoples of the developing countries themselves; they and their governments must mobilize the investments and train the manpower. Yet a role remains for assistance and aid from the rich countries. Those who have plenty in terms of capital, skills, and commodities can do much to help the less fortunate nations win their battle against poverty.

Food aid. In the 1950s the United States began a large program for transferring much of its surplus food on concessional terms to needy countries. Other advanced countries also initiated such transfers on a more modest scale. Finally, in 1962, the FAO World Food Program was established to undertake multilateral food aid. Its activities include emergency feeding after such disasters as earthquakes or floods and economic and social development projects such as maternal and child feeding, animal production and dairy development, land development and improvement, land settlement, and forestry. Care is exercised that food transferred under these programs jeopardizes neither the market for the output of farmers in recipient countries nor the market for normal commercial exporters. Of course food aid, bilateral and multilateral, cannot be contemplated as a permanent element in the food supply of the poorer countries, which ultimately must become economically independent; but it does provide valuable assistance during the transitional period in which they are modernizing their agriculture. The World Food Conference agreed on a minimum target of 10,000,000 tons of food aid a year.

The FAO
World
Food
Program

Technical and financial aid. The net flow of financial resources to developing countries for all purposes, according to calculations by the Organization for Economic Co-operation and Development (OECD), rose from $9,200,000,000 in 1961 to about $40,000,000,000 in 1975. Of this, $16,000,000,000 was official assistance and $22,000,000,000 private capital flow; but official development assistance, in terms of the gross national product of donor countries, fell from 0.52 percent to 0.36 percent. A more positive element has been the increasing attention given to agriculture. Total OECD assistance to the agricultural sector was $2,633,000,000 in 1975. In 1968 the World Bank announced its intention of quadrupling its assistance to agriculture over the following five years; already in fiscal 1971–72 World Bank and International Development Association loans and credits to this sector totalled $436,000,000. By 1975 it was $1,858,000,000, but in fiscal 1976 the total dropped to $1,628,000,000. Technical assistance has expanded more rapidly than financial aid, indeed by more than 10 percent a year. Of expenditure through the UN system, agricultural projects during 1964–74 accounted for about one-third. Aid in the form of fertilizers and other production requisites has also expanded and will become increasingly crucial if the "green revolution" is to continue without too great a drain on the scarce foreign exchange resources of the developing countries.

International Fund for Agricultural Development

The World Food Conference of November 1974 called for the establishment of an International Fund for Agricultural Development, in order to obtain the necessary great increase in external financial assistance for the agriculture of the developing countries. It also agreed on a wide range of other measures, particularly concerning the acceleration of the increase in food production in the developing countries, and a coordinated system of national stock policies embodied in an International Undertaking on World Food Security. If the follow-up to the World Food Conference lives up to professions of intent, a beginning will have been made in the establishment of a world food policy.

BIBLIOGRAPHY. Current statistical and other information may be found in the following Food and Agriculture Organization (FAO) publications: *Trade Yearbook; Production Yearbook; FAO Yearbook of Fisheries Statistics; The State of Food and Agriculture; Monthly Bulletin of Agricultural Economics and Statistics.* See also *Provisional Indicative World Plan for Agricultural Development* (1969); UNITED NATIONS WORLD FOOD CONFERENCE, *Assessment of the World Food Situation, Present and Future* (1974); *The World Food Problem: Proposals for National and International Action* (1974); *Report of the World Food Conference* (1975).

(A.H.B.)

Football, American and Canadian

Football is a game with a variety of forms played between two teams that try to advance an inflated ball by carrying, kicking, or throwing it, until it has been forced into, across, or over goal markers to effect a score.

There are three main varieties of football, each with distinctive rules, regulations, and procedures. In the order of their invention they are: association football (soccer); rugby football; and football, as it evolved in the United States and, with minor differences, in Canada. Soccer, which is played the world over, is fundamentally a game of the foot. Running with the ball and passing it by hand are violations. Rugby and United States football have much more in common. Both permit carrying and throwing the ball, as well as kicking it, though in rugby the ball may never be thrown forward, as it is in the American game. Also, the principle of possession of the ball—the most fundamental departure in the evolution of the United States game—is lacking in rugby (and soccer), in which the ball may and most often does change hands in a matter of seconds; and there is less opportunity to develop a planned scheme of attack.

This article will be devoted primarily to United States football, as played in the colleges and universities, and to its principal variations. It is divided into the following sections:

I. History
  Early history
  Genesis of American football
  Emergence of the modern game
II. Play of the game
  The field and equipment
  Principles of play
III. Other principal games
  U.S. professional football
  Canadian football

The article is intended for the general reader who may have no knowledge of the sports described and is designed at most to help a spectator understand a game he may be watching. For information on specific rules or on how to play, the reader should consult works listed in the bibliography. For U.S. and Canadian football records, see SPORTING RECORD in the *Ready Reference and Index.* For information on other major varieties of football, see the text articles ASSOCIATION FOOTBALL (SOCCER); and RUGBY.

I. History

EARLY HISTORY

The beginnings of games or contests in which two teams, or sides, vied with each other in attempting to push, kick, or otherwise move a ball, or ball-like object, in opposite directions have been traced to ancient Egyptian fertility rites, as have other athletic pastimes. An ancient Chinese writer wrote that a football game was played in China as early as 300 BC, and by AD 500 round footballs stuffed with hair were in use. In ancient Greece a game with elements of football was called *harpaston.* It was much the same game that, as *harpastum*, became popular with Romans after they conquered Greece in the 2nd century BC. Play began with a ball being thrown into the air between two bands of players, each of which endeavoured to advance it beyond what would today be called the opponent's goal line. It was marked by much pushing backward and forward. In all likelihood, Roman legions introduced *harpastum* to the natives of Britain during their occupation, although one historian reports that the Irish had been kicking a stuffed ball in play 50 years earlier.

Whether or not the Romans introduced the game to the British, there were *mêlées*, or mellays, in ancient and medieval Britain in which a ball, usually an inflated animal bladder, was advanced by kicking, punching, or carrying. Royal edicts were issued against the pastime as interfering with the practice of military skills such as archery, but it flourished. In William Fitzstephen's *Description of the City of London*, published late in the 12th century, there is a reference to a football game played on Shrove Tuesday. In later years Shrove Tuesday was to become a great football day in England, a holiday on which business was suspended and the citizenry gathered for a game that officially began with the mayor making the kickoff.

Chester, a town founded by the Romans, was famed for its Shrove Tuesday football game. It was said that the game had been played for centuries in commemoration of the great day in AD 217 when a mighty flying wedge was organized to drive the Roman legions out of Chester. Elsewhere, town played town or parish opposed parish in Shrove Tuesday festival games, often involving several hundred men who played for hours until the ball had been kicked into the domain of one side or the other. These medieval mellays took place also at Derby, Corfe Castle, Alnwick, and Bromford in England and at the Cross of Scone and Midlothian in Scotland.

Football was also associated with the holiday of Candlemas Day. King Edward III prohibited the playing of football in 1365 for military reasons; and similar edicts were also issued by Richard II, Henry IV, Henry VIII, and Elizabeth I, but they had no effect. The festival matches increased in popularity. Joseph Strutt, historian of English sport, in 1801 wrote the following description:

... an equal number of competitors take the field and stand between two goals placed at a distance of 80 or 100 yards the one from the other. The goal is usually made with two sticks driven into the ground about two or three feet apart. The ball, which is commonly made of a blown bladder and cased

An early British match

with leather, is delivered in the midst of the ground, and the object of each party is to drive it through the goal of their antagonists, which being achieved the game is won. . . . When the exercise becomes exceedingly violent the players kick each others' shins without the least ceremony and some of them are overthrown at the hazard of their limbs.

Football was taken up in a less violent form in the 17th century. Youths from wealthy and aristocratic families played the game in British secondary schools, though the authorities regarded it as too rowdy for young gentlemen. Rules differed at the various schools, but all in common allowed no running with the ball or passing it forward by hand.

It was not until early in the 19th century that the restriction against running with the ball was disregarded. According to legend, this came in 1823 at Rugby School, Rugby, Warwickshire, when a schoolboy caught a kicked ball and, instead of heeling the ball or taking a free kick, tucked it under his arm and, to the amazement and consternation of the other players and onlookers, sped on to the opponents' goal. This gross violation was at first severely censured. In time, however, the idea of running with the ball won favour, and today a tablet placed in a wall at Rugby School reads:

> This stone commemorates the exploit of William Webb Ellis, who, with a fine disregard for the rules of football, as played in his time, first took the ball in his arms and ran with it, thus originating the distinctive feature of the rugby game. AD 1823.

Running with the ball was at first permitted only if the player received it by fair catch. Later, it was also allowed if the ball was caught on the first bound. Finally, all restrictions were removed. In time, other schools also accepted the new procedure.

There were no unified rules for rugby or soccer until finally, in 1863, the London Football Association was formed by clubs playing the kicking game. Rules were drafted, and carrying the ball was forbidden. Then, in 1871, rugby players from 17 clubs and three schools organized the Rugby Football Union and appointed a committee to draw up a code based on that in use at Rugby School. A year later Oxford and Cambridge met at rugby for the first time.

Both of these football games were taken up in America. Soccer was the one known in the United States before rugby was introduced in the 1870s with the cooperation of McGill University of Montreal, Canada, and immediately replaced the kicking game in favour at colleges and universities. It was rugby from which the United States style of football evolved.

GENESIS OF AMERICAN FOOTBALL

Football in its crudest form was known in America virtually from the time British colonists established their first settlements. There is evidence that as early as 1609 teams or groups of men were kicking around an air-filled bladder, as they had in their mother country. More than two centuries were to pass, however, before the game took root in the colleges.

The first college games. Students at Princeton University in 1820 played a game known as "ballown," in which a ball was batted with the fist. By 1840 an organization had been formed to schedule games and choose sides. At Harvard University a football game was played between the freshman and sophomore classes in 1827 and became an established custom, scheduled annually for the first Monday of the new college year. Because the play was so rough, the day became known as "Bloody Monday," and the faculty put an end to it in 1860. The same kind of roughhouse play was also going on at Yale University. By 1840 it was organized and known as the annual rush, and in 1851 the freshmen and sophomores started an annual contest. In 1858 the New Haven authorities halted play by denying students the use of the city green. Amherst College in Massachusetts and Brown University in Providence, Rhode Island, were other schools where the game was being played.

There were no established rules at any of the colleges, and sides might be of any number agreed upon. Follow-

Rough-house play

ing the introduction of a round, rubber ball in the 1850s, considerable skill was developed in kicking the ball a long distance and in dribbling it with the toe in short advances and sending it on to a teammate, eluding an interceptor. These were the skills of modern association football (soccer).

The Civil War (1861–65) put an end to, or severely curtailed, sports activity on college campuses; but football was played in secondary schools in New England during the hiatus. Starting in 1860, nine years before the first intercollegiate game was played between Princeton and Rutgers, secondary schools in the Boston area were meeting each other on the Common. The first formal football organization in the United States was established in 1862 by Gerritt Smith Miller, a 17-year-old student. He organized a group of Boston players into the Oneida Football Club of Boston some months prior to the formation of the London Football Association and was its president and team captain. From 1862 to 1865 the Oneida Club played all comers and never was beaten or scored upon. On November 21, 1925, the seven surviving members from the original group of 17 unveiled a marble monument in commemoration of the club at the entrance to the Common.

Following the end of the Civil War in 1865, football activity was renewed on the college campuses. In 1866 Beadle and Company of New York City published a book on cricket and football, in which Henry Chadwick, a sports authority, enumerated the rules for both varieties of football—the kicking game of soccer, or association football, and the carrying style of rugby, which was virtually unknown at the time in the United States. In 1867 so-called Princeton Rules were drawn up for the soccer style of football. They called for 25 players to a side, and a team of that number played an intramural game with the Princeton Theological Seminary. Late in the year one H.A. Alden of Matteawan, New York, patented the first football covering, a canvas layer protecting a rubber bladder. Rutgers College, New Brunswick, New Jersey, not far north of Princeton, also drew up rules in 1867, and in November 1869 the two met in the first intercollegiate game of football in the United States at New Brunswick. Some exception has been taken to so labelling the game because the game played was the soccer style of football. The distinction has also been bestowed on the first Harvard–Yale game in 1875, which was part rugby and part soccer, or on a second game between them (1876), which was rugby.

The rules drawn up for the first game between Princeton and Rutgers by the team captains were largely Rutgers' rules, since Princeton's were to be in force for a second game at Princeton a week later. These were a modification of those of the London Football Association. There was a maximum of 25 players to a side. The team first scoring six goals was the winner. The grounds were 360 feet (110 metres) long and 225 feet (70 metres) wide and the goals 24 feet (seven metres) wide. The round, inflated rubber ball that was used could be kicked or batted with the hand or fist, although no running with it or throwing it was allowed, nor any tripping or holding of a player. Rutgers won the game, 6 goals to 4. The second game, at Princeton, was won by Princeton, 8 goals to 0. A third game had been scheduled but was barred by the faculties of the two colleges.

Columbia, Cornell University of Ithaca, New York, and Yale were among the schools that took up football in the early 1870s, all adopting the kicking game. Harvard, where football had been banned, revived the game in 1871 and played what was known as the "Boston Game," essentially a kicking game with elements of rugby. The ball could be picked up, and the holder, if pursued, could run with it. This difference was of historic importance. Harvard formed its football association in 1872 with competition limited to games between the classes.

Representatives from Princeton, Yale, Columbia, and Rutgers met in New York City in 1873 and formulated the first intercollegiate rules in the United States with the code of the London Football Association as their model. The number of players on a side was set at 20. The field

Soccer—Princeton versus Rutgers, 1869

First intercollegiate rules

dimensions were 400 feet by 250 feet (120 by 75 metres). The distance between the goal posts was 25 feet (eight metres). Six goals were necessary to win, and to score a goal the ball had to pass between the goal posts. No player could throw or carry the ball.

In 1873 Yale lost to Princeton, 3 goals to 0, in the inaugural meeting of what is today intercollegiate football's oldest, continuous rivalry. Yale then met a team from England known as the Eton Players in the first international match in the United States and won, 2 goals to 1. It has been said that rugby football was played in this game, but evidence indicates that it was soccer. The Eton Players, not all of whom had gone to the famous English school, were accustomed to using only 11 men on a side, and Yale was persuaded to limit its team in this game. Yale was won over to 11-man football and thereafter fought for the principle until it was adopted generally in 1880.

Harvard, because it played a different game, had declined to participate in the 1873 rules convention and looked elsewhere for competition. It found a rival in the football club of McGill University in Montreal, Quebec. The teams met twice in the spring of 1874 at Cambridge, Massachusetts. McGill played football under the code of the Rugby Football Union of England. Harvard's football was largely soccer, but a player could run with the ball if pursued, as noted above. The first of the two games was played under Harvard's rules, with goals the only scoring medium, and Harvard won, 3 goals to 0. The next day the teams met under McGill's rules, using an egg-shaped ball, in the first intercollegiate rugby match in the United States. Canadian rugby differed from the English game in allowing tries (*i.e.*, running with the ball across the goal line, called touchdowns in the U.S.) as well as goals (kicking the ball between the goal posts) to count in the scoring. They played for an hour and a half in three periods and neither side scored. A third game was played on McGill's grounds in Montreal, again under English rules, and Harvard won by 3 tries to 0.

Harvard was won over completely to rugby as a result of its matches with McGill. Then came an event that contributed greatly to the shape of the game as it developed in the United States. Harvard challenged Yale to a game under "Concessionary Rules" and thus inaugurated one of the most celebrated of all U.S. football rivalries. The game was played in November 1875 at New Haven and was part rugby and part soccer. According to the account of the game in the Harvard *Crimson*, neither side fully understood the "Concessionary Rules." Yale men said that they differed more from their own rules than from Harvard's. They played with 15 men on a side instead of 11 as Yale would have preferred, and Harvard won by 4 goals and 4 tries, or touchdowns, to none. Despite its decisive defeat, Yale was so taken with rugby that it became a convert and adopted the rules. Observers from Princeton who saw the game also were won over to rugby, and in 1876 representatives of Princeton, Harvard, Yale, and Columbia organized the Intercollegiate Football Association. They adopted the code of the Rugby Football Union with a change in the scoring rule—instead of a match being decided by a majority of goals alone, it was decided by a majority of touchdowns. A goal was equal to four touchdowns, but in the case of a tie, a goal kicked from a touchdown took precedence over four touchdowns. The size of the field was set at 140 yards by 70 yards (130 by 60 metres), the number of players at 15 to a side, and the time of a game at two 45-minute halves. The egg-shaped leather ball replaced the round rubber ball of soccer. Yale attached such importance to limiting the teams to 11 men that it declined to become a member of the new Intercollegiate Football Association, though it was represented unofficially at its meetings and played against the other members.

Rugby thus became the American college football game just as other schools were entering the intercollegiate lists. Stevens Institute in New Jersey had played against Columbia in 1872 and Wesleyan University, Middletown, Connecticut, against Yale in 1875. Pennsylvania began,

Rugby— Harvard versus Yale, 1875

in 1876, against Princeton. The first game in the South was played between club teams from Virginia Military Institute and Washington and Lee, both in Lexington, Virginia, on the grounds of VMI in 1873. All of these newcomers played the soccer game with varying numbers of players until the switch to rugby began in 1876.

At the United States Naval Academy in Annapolis, Maryland, midshipmen were playing football in 1882, but it was not until 1888 that they began to play a representative schedule. In 1890 they challenged the United States Military Academy at West Point, and the famous service rivalry started.

The first game in the Middle West was played in 1879 between the University of Michigan, Ann Arbor, and Racine College of Wisconsin. Though Michigan had organized a team as early as 1873, it had been unable to find an opponent until the Racine game. In 1881 Michigan inaugurated intersectional competition by sending its team east to play Yale, Harvard, and Princeton, losing to all three in the space of five days. In 1887 the University of Notre Dame from South Bend, Indiana, made its bow against Michigan and lost 8–0 at South Bend. Also taking up the game in the 1880s were the University of Minnesota, Minneapolis; Northwestern University, Evanston, Illinois; Indiana University, Bloomington; Purdue University, Lafayette, Indiana; the University of Iowa, Iowa City; and Michigan State University, East Lansing; all of which, with Michigan and several others, were to form the Western Conference (Big Ten).

Inter-sectional competi-tion

On the Pacific coast, football was being played between classes at the University of California, Berkeley, as early as 1881, but it was not until the 1890s that football took hold seriously.

Seven years after VMI and Washington and Lee met in 1873, football matches began to be played elsewhere in the South. Centre College, in Danville, Kentucky, whose team would later make a kind of history by defeating Harvard, played a scoreless tie in 1880 with the University of Kentucky in Lexington. It was another eight years before the game caught on in earnest at Trinity College, Durham, North Carolina (later Duke University); at the University of North Carolina, Chapel Hill, in 1888; and at Wake Forest University, Winston-Salem, North Carolina, in 1889. Vanderbilt University, Nashville, Tennessee, played its first game in 1890; the University of Tennessee, Knoxville, and West Virginia University, Morgantown, started in 1891; and Alabama University, University, Alabama; Auburn University, Auburn, Alabama; Georgia Institute of Technology, Atlanta; the University of Georgia, Athens; and the University of Kentucky, Lexington, started in 1892. A year later Louisiana State University and Agricultural and Mechanical College, Baton Rouge; Tulane University of Louisiana, New Orleans; and the University of Mississippi, University, Mississippi, joined in, and the Southern Intercollegiate Association was organized. All of these schools with the exception of West Virginia were to be members of the powerful Southeastern Conference.

The Southwest was a late starter, but in no part of the country did the game become more of a craze. The University of Texas, Austin, was the first to organize, in 1893. Texas Agriculture and Mines (Texas A. & M.), College Station, and the University of Arkansas, Fayetteville, followed in 1894, and Texas Christian University, Fort Worth, in 1897. Baylor University of Waco, Texas, was next, in 1901, followed by Rice University of Houston, Texas, in 1912, and Southern Methodist University, Dallas, in 1915. At the start of the 1970s, all of these teams were competing in the Southwest Conference.

Evolution of American football. In its early years, the American game was purely a test of brawn, with dull pileups and entanglements of bodies in marked contrast with rugby's speed and wide-open action over the breadth and length of the field. The man who conceived and designed most of the basic changes and departures from rugby and brought about their acceptance in the conventions and rules committee meetings was Walter Camp, now rightly known as the "Father of American Football."

Walter Camp, "Father of American Football"

In 1880 Camp effected the first of the changes in the evolution of the American game. This was the substitution of scrimmage for the scrummage, or scrum, of rugby. In scrummage the ball was put between two opposing interlocked packs of rushers, or forwards, who endeavoured to heel the ball backward to their own backs. In the new scrimmage, the ball was given into the orderly possession of one team, which then put it in play without interference until the ball was "snapped." Camp defined the scrimmage procedure as follows:

A scrimmage takes place when the holder of the ball, being in the field of play, puts it down on the ground in front of him and puts it in play while on side, first, by kicking the ball; second by snapping it back with his foot. The man who first receives the ball from the snap-back shall be called the quarter-back, and shall not then rush forward with the ball under penalty of foul.

Thus Camp also initiated the role of the quarterback, which was to become the most glamorous position in football. In the same year, he finally succeeded in his efforts to have the number of players reduced from the 15 of rugby to the 11 of modern U.S. football. Camp, too, was the one who came up with the standard alignment for 11 men—seven forwards in the line, a quarterback, two halfbacks, and a fullback.

Downs and yards to gain

In 1882 Camp's next far-reaching change was the introduction of a system of downs and yardage to be gained. This followed as a result of the tactics used at the time to keep indefinite possession of the ball. Rules makers had assumed that a team given possession of the ball would inevitably surrender it in the then customary procedure of kicking the ball almost every other play. No means had been devised for forcing surrender of the ball, and a team that was unable to score but chose not to let its opponent have the chance to score was able to maintain possession indefinitely. There was no penalty for a safety (tackling a ball carrier behind his own goal line), and a team could touch the ball down behind its goal, bring it out to the 25-yard line, and do this over and over. Princeton and Yale played their 1880 game in this way, Princeton having the ball for the first half and Yale for the second, without a score and with 17 safeties being registered. There was great public dissatisfaction with such tactics, which were repeated in their 1881 game.

Camp recommended that

If on three consecutive fairs [attempts to move the ball forward] and downs a team shall not have advanced the ball five yards or lost ten, they must give up the ball to the other side at the spot where the fourth down was made.

The rule was adopted and started the practice of marking the field with horizontal lines five yards apart, giving it the appearance of a gridiron. The requirement was changed to ten yards in 1906, and in 1912 a fourth down was allowed. The rule was the heart of American football. It encouraged development of a planned running attack and abandonment of kicking as the predominant element in offensive play.

The following year Camp introduced a scoring system to end disputes over the outcome of games. Point values were given to the various scoring methods—safety, 1 point (against team in possession of the ball); touchdown, 2 points; goal after touchdown, 4; and field goal, 5. Over the years the point values changed several times; and at the start of the 1970s the safety was 2 points, the field goal 3, the touchdown 6, and the conversion after touchdown was 1 point if kicked and 2 points if the ball was run across the goal line or brought into the end zone by a completed pass.

In 1888 came another change that was to transform the pattern of the game. Tackling up to this time had been permitted only from the waist up—the rule of rugby. An 1888 rule now permitted tackling as low as the knees, and along with this there came a prohibition against linemen blocking with extended arms, requiring them to keep their arms at their sides. The forward line of players, which had been extended across the field, was therefore forced to contract. The players in the backfield behind the forward line, who also had spread wide for the lateral passing of the ball, as in rugby, also moved

close together behind their forwards for protection. In the positions in which they were now stationed, the backs formed the close-order alignment of the T—which became the original, standard arrangement of American football.

It was in the momentous 1906 football rules committee meeting that the last fundamental change in football was made—the introduction of the forward pass. Camp was far from being solely responsible for it, but his leadership in bringing together diverse groups helped bring about the legalization of the pass and the adoption of other steps taken to eliminate the brutality of football.

Mass formations. In 1890 the first of many mass formations that were to make the game so hazardous had been unveiled. The man who originated it was Amos Alonzo Stagg, famous as a player at Yale from 1885 to 1889 and far more renowned for his 63 years of coaching college teams, 41 of them at the University of Chicago. Stagg devised the "ends back" formation in his first year of coaching at the International YMCA Training School in Springfield, Massachusetts. He moved the ends from their regular positions at each end of the line to positions behind the line, where, along with the backs, they became interferers, pushers, and pullers, helping the ball carrier to advance. The resulting impact on the defense was much more forceful than anything previously known.

Earlier teams had given assistance to the ball carrier by stationing a player on each side of him to fend off tacklers. If the players convoying the ball carrier preceded him, it was a violation of the so-called off-side rule. In 1884 Princeton boldly sent its blockers in advance of the carrier—a violation—but there was no resulting penalty, and the practice became general by sufferance before any change in the rule.

Stagg's ends-back formation provided interference of a more formidable character in that the linemen were stationed in the backfield and were able to pick up more speed before contact with the opponents. In 1891 Stagg presented a second mass formation known as the "turtleback," a massing of the team into a solid oval directed against the opposing tackle. Harvard used this in 1893 and was credited by some with being the originator.

In 1892 the most devastating of the mass plays was introduced—the "flying wedge," a kickoff tactic invented at Harvard. The flying wedge was an extension of the so-called V trick, credited to both Princeton and Lehigh University, Bethlehem, Pennsylvania, in which the kicker, instead of kicking off to start the half, nudged the ball with his toe and then picked it up and ran with it as his teammates formed a V-shaped mass around him. The V was taken up by other teams and became the accepted procedure for the kickoff. In 1892 Harvard added momentum to the mass by starting the wedge in motion before the ball was put in play. This flying wedge was used against Yale at the start of the second half of their 1892 game, after Yale had employed the standard V to open the game. Instead of the customary standing start in the middle of the field (the 55-yard line), Harvard deployed its men in two files of five, 15 to 25 yards behind the captain, who stood on the 55-yard line with the ball. The two files, slanting inward from the sidelines, converged at the signal on their captain. As the flying mass reached him at top speed, he put the ball in play, flipped it to a player in the wedge, and joined in as an interferer. The ball carrier went to Yale's 25-yard line before he was stopped. So sensational was the device that it was taken up immediately and in 1893 it was in general use. It added greatly to the roughness of the game and by the end of the season, football was under heavy attack for its violence. The army and navy departments cancelled the game between the service academies in 1894, and the Intercollegiate Football Association began to break up. Only Yale and Princeton remained as members.

In 1894 the University Athletic Club of New York invited Yale, Princeton, Harvard, and Pennsylvania to send representatives to a meeting to form a new rules committee. In a dramatic revision of the rules by this group, the V trick and the flying wedge were banned by a re-

Flying wedge

quirement that the kickoff travel at least ten yards to be in play unless touched by a member of the receiving side. It was also prohibited for more than three men to group more than five yards in back of the line of scrimmage to project a mass play. Also, a player was prohibited from laying hands on an opponent unless he had the ball. A linesman was added as a third official (in addition to the referee and umpire), and playing time was cut from 90 to 70 minutes, divided into halves of 35 minutes.

But the violence of mass plays continued. In 1894 Stagg, then at the University of Chicago, introduced a "tackles back" formation and at Pennsylvania, the coach, George Woodruff, originated a "guards back" arrangement that was widely imitated. Pennsylvania, which was challenging the Big Three (Yale, Princeton, and Harvard) for supremacy as it went through a perfect season in 1894, was unwilling to abandon its guards-back formation, and Harvard declined to give up its flying wedge. Yale and Harvard broke relations after a rough 1894 game. In 1895 Yale and Princeton adopted a separate code, inviting Navy to come in with them. To curb mass play they ruled that the team on offense must have seven men on the line of scrimmage and that only one back might be in forward motion before the snap of the ball. The groups differed not only on the use of mass plays but also on permitting graduate students to play. Harvard and Pennsylvania, with large numbers of graduate students, refused to disqualify them.

Also in 1895, colleges in the Middle West, dissatisfied with the divided leadership of the East, asserted their independence. The presidents of Chicago, Illinois, Michigan, Minnesota, Northwestern, Purdue, and Wisconsin universities met and took steps toward organizing what was to become the Western Conference (Big Ten). At a second meeting in 1896 they adopted a rule barring freshmen from varsity teams and set a limit of three years on varsity eligibility. Later, they were to establish faculty control of all athletics.

The Big Ten

In the summer of 1896 the two groups in the East met in an effort to resolve their differences. They set up a permanent rules committee and put a curb on momentum in mass plays by ruling that "no player on the side in possession of the ball shall take more than one step toward his opponent's goal before the ball is in play without coming to a full stop." The matter of "coming to a full stop" was to be argued for years before momentum was to be eliminated entirely. In 1910 the rules committee required seven men on the line, to put an end to mass plays.

EMERGENCE OF THE MODERN GAME

The season of 1905 was one of the ugliest, if not the most critical, football has gone through in the United States. According to tabulations of the *Chicago Tribune*, there were 18 deaths and 159 other injuries of consequence resulting from college games. There was a mounting uproar of protest as the season progressed. Pres. Theodore Roosevelt summoned representatives of Harvard, Yale, and Princeton to the White House and requested them to take steps to save the game, observing, "Brutality and foul play should receive the same summary punishment given to a man who cheats at cards."

At a meeting in New York City late in 1905, representatives of about 60 colleges and universities appointed a football rules committee of seven members and organized the Intercollegiate Athletic Association of the United States with Capt. Palmer E. Pierce of West Point as its first president. In 1910 the association changed its name to the National Collegiate Athletic Association (NCAA) and later became the governing body of intercollegiate athletics in the United States. Under the leadership of Captain Pierce and Walter Camp of the American Football Rules Committee, the two groups met in joint session in 1906 in New York City and adopted changes that were to save the game. A member of the rules committee reported that the fundamental objectives of the 1906 meeting were

(1) to make the game both safe and more interesting for the player, (2) to make the game a distinctly more open game, (3) to remove the premium on mere weight and to develop greater opportunity for speed, agility and brains, (4) to produce a game affording broader strategic possibilities, thereby giving the lighter teams and the teams of the smaller colleges a real chance and preventing the probable outcome of so many games from being a foregone conclusion, (5) to improve the standards of sportsmanship of the game and, by developing better officiating, to remove the continual temptation to violate the rules.

One of the committee's changes was the legalization of the forward pass.

The forward pass. One of the men most instrumental in the introduction of the forward pass was John Heisman, for whom college football's most prized individual trophy was later named. In 1895 he had seen a pass thrown in a game between North Carolina and Georgia, 11 years before it was legal to throw the ball forward. The North Carolina player who caught it ran 70 yards for a touchdown. The Georgia coach protested the pass as illegal, but the referee stated that he had not seen it and allowed the touchdown.

In 1903, when football was under heavy attack for its brutality, it occurred to Heisman that the pass he had seen thrown eight years before could be the salvation of the game, loosening up the strangling mass play. He wrote to Camp suggesting that the forward pass be incorporated into the game, and in 1904 he did so again. Others joined as advocates of the pass, and it was finally approved in 1906.

In addition to legalizing the forward pass, rules changes put through in 1906 were: (1) reduction of the length of the game from 70 to 60 minutes, divided into 30-minute halves; (2) establishment of a neutral zone, separating the forward line of teams by the length of the ball; (3) increasing the distance required to be gained in three downs from five to ten yards; (4) banning of hurdling (jumping over opposing players); (5) prohibiting centres, guards, and tackles from dropping behind the line of scrimmage on offense unless they fell back five yards; (6) stipulation that punts striking the ground put all members of the kicking team on side (behind the ball) except the kicker; (7) marking of the field with lengthwise stripes five yards apart, changing it from a gridiron to a checkerboard; (8) addition of a second umpire; (9) requirement that substitutes report to the referee. A central board of officials, which Camp had advocated in 1905, was established.

Rules changes— the 1906 meeting

Despite these changes, football remained a dangerously rough game. Interlocked interference was still used, with only six men required on the offensive line. Defensive halfbacks, who formerly had supported the tackles against the running game, had to fall back to guard against the new forward pass, and the tackles took brutal punishment. In 1906 six men suffered fatal injuries.

In 1910 the rules committee acted and took the final step to end mass plays. Seven men of the offensive team were required on the forward line, and interlocked interference and aiding the runner by pushing or pulling were outlawed. The effect of these changes was so pronounced that the balance of power switched from the offense to the defense. There was a falling off in scoring, and numerous games ended in scoreless ties. To correct the imbalance, the rules committee in 1912 increased the number of downs from three to four. The length of the playing field was reduced from 110 to 100 yards (90 metres) and end zones ten yards (nine metres) deep were established behind the goal lines, within which forward passes could be completed for touchdowns. The kickoff, formerly made from the centre of the field, was moved back to the kicking side's 40-yard line.

Gradually, early restrictions on the forward pass, which discouraged its use, were removed. Following the ending of a 15-yard penalty for an incomplete pass in 1907, a requirement that the pass cross the line five yards to either side of where the ball had been put in play was done away with in 1910. This made it no longer necessary to put chalk lines down the length of the field. In 1912 the limitation of 20 yards on the distance the ball could be thrown beyond the line of scrimmage was removed. The restrictions remaining were that the pass had to be thrown from five yards behind the line and only one pass could be thrown on each scrimmage. The first of these was also eventually discarded.

The awakening to the immense possibilities of the forward pass came primarily as a result of a sensational exhibition by Notre Dame in defeating Army in the inaugural game of their rivalry in 1913 at West Point. Arranged to fill a vacant spot in Army's schedule, the game was looked upon as an easy, pleasant afternoon of sport for the home team. Notre Dame's name in football meant nothing to the East at the time. With quarterback Gus Dorais throwing to end Knute Rockne (later the most famous coach in football history) and to back Joe Pliska, Notre Dame caught Army completely unprepared and scored an astonishing 35–13 victory over the cadets and their old-style, battering-ram running game. Later that same season Army used the forward pass against Navy and won 22–9.

Actually, Notre Dame was not the trailblazer its performance made it appear to be. Numerous teams had used the pass since its inception in 1906. Probably the most successful of all in that year was a St. Louis University (Missouri) team that won every game in its season and used the pass from the very first. Stagg said that in 1906 he had 64 pass patterns. Illinois, Michigan, and Carlisle Indian School, Pennsylvania, were also experimenting, and as early as 1908 the pass was introduced in the Southwest. In 1913, the same year that Notre Dame beat Army, Texas defeated the University of Oklahoma, Norman, with the pass, and in 1915 Oklahoma averaged 30 to 35 passes a game and won all of its ten contests.

Impetus was given to the forward pass, too, in other regions of the country in the 1920s. In 1925 it carried Alabama to California's prestigious Rose Bowl game. Andrew ("Swede") Oberlander's passes carried Dartmouth College, Hanover, New Hampshire, to its first national championship. At Michigan, Benny Friedman, one of football's most famous quarterbacks, was pitching aerial strikes to Bennie Oosterbaan, equally renowned end, on the 1925 Michigan team.

Spread of the game. Whatever the style of football played in the early years, Yale almost invariably had the best team. From 1876 to 1879 it lost only one game (to Princeton) and was tied in only four. From 1880 it lost one game, to Princeton in 1885 by 6–5, and was tied four times (by Princeton) through 1887. In 1888, when the pattern of the game changed, as tackling below the waist was permitted and the offensive team took the close-order formation of the T, Yale continued supreme and that year had the most famous of its teams to the turn of the century. With Camp serving as Yale's first coach, the team scored 698 points to none for its 13 opponents. Yale continued to overwhelm its opponents to the end of the century, with infrequent defeat, usually by Princeton or Harvard, which, with Yale, formed the Big Three of early football.

In the 1890s, teams in other regions began to establish themselves as football powers. Purdue won all of its eight games in 1892, and Minnesota; Oberlin College, Oberlin, Ohio; Butler University, Indianapolis, Indiana; Centre College; Trinity (Duke); the University of Kansas, Lawrence; Colgate University, Hamilton, New York; and Johns Hopkins University, Baltimore, also had strong teams. Oberlin won all of its seven games under Heisman, who was starting an illustrious 36-year coaching career. Cornell defeated ten opponents, including Michigan, and lost only to Harvard. In 1893 Princeton had one of the strongest teams in its history. Princeton beat Yale 6–0 in what was called "the greatest sports spectacle New York or America has ever witnessed." Yale had won 37 games in a row. Stanford University, Stanford, California; Minnesota; Colgate; Grinnell College, Grinnell, Iowa; and Pennsylvania had good seasons in 1893, and the Stanford–California classic of the West Coast started.

Pennsylvania challenged the Big Three in 1894 as it set out on a four-year rampage that was to establish it as one of the new Big Four. In 1891 John Adams of Pennsylvania had been the first player from a team other than one of the Big Three to be named an All-American.

When Pennsylvania introduced its "guards back" formation in 1894, it won every game. The formation was to be irresistible for 34 successive games in 1894, 1895, and 1896, until Pennsylvania lost 6–4 to Lafayette College of Easton, Pennsylvania, in 1896. It then swept through 31 more games before losing to Harvard in 1898, after which it added Carlisle and Cornell to its victims. In the five years it scored 1,957 points and gave up only 120. One of its most outstanding players, a guard, Truxton Hare, was four times an All-America selection.

The Southern Intercollegiate Association, the first formal athletic conference, was formed in 1894 "for the development, regulation and purification of college athletics in the South." Vanderbilt's William L. Dudley was the leader. Georgia, Alabama, Georgia Tech, Sewanee (The University of the South at Sewanee, Tennessee), and North Carolina were charter members with Vanderbilt. The next year saw the organization of the Western Intercollegiate League, which was to become the Western Conference, or Big Ten, traditionally one of the strongest football conferences in the nation.

Lafayette challenged Penn for top honours in 1896, ending Penn's winning streak and beating every opponent, except for a scoreless tie with Princeton. It was the first small college to beat one of the Big Four.

The Sewanee team of 1899 was the first in the South to win wide renown. Coached by Herman Suter of Princeton, it won all of its 12 games, from North Carolina to Texas, holding 11 opponents scoreless. Five of the games were played in the space of six days on a 3,000-mile trip. Sewanee began its spectacular rise in 1898, when it won its four games with the loss of only four points. Also in 1898, Carlisle went to the West Coast to play California in the start of East–Far West competition.

The year 1901 was particularly notable. Fielding Yost began his long career as coach at the University of Michigan and his "point-a-minute" teams of 1901 to 1905 achieved one of the most remarkable records in history. In five years they scored 2,821 points to 42 for their opponents, winning 55 games, losing one and tying one. Two of their players, Willie Heston and Adolph Schulz, are ranked among the greatest of all time. At the end of the 1901 season Yost took his team west to play Stanford. On January 1, 1902, in the first Rose Bowl game at Pasadena, California, Michigan won 49–0.

In 1905 Michigan finally met defeat for the first time in 57 games, losing to the University of Chicago, coached by Stagg. The score was 2–0, on a safety, the only points Michigan gave up all season. Walter Eckersall, three times All-America and ranked for years as the best quarterback of all time as well as one of the best dropkickers in history, piloted the winning team to the national championship. Chicago was then to go on to compile a record comparable to that of the point-a-minute teams in losing only two games from 1905 to 1909.

In 1905 Yale repeated its perfect record of 1900, giving up only four points, to Princeton. The legendary Tom Shelvin was captain and All-America for the third time. Tad Jones, a Yale idol as both player and coach, was quarterback, and his brother, Howard, later one of football's most successful coaches, was also on the team. They played, too, on the 1906 and 1907 teams, which also were unbeaten, though tied by Princeton in 1906 and by Army in 1907. Tad was an All-America quarterback in 1906 and 1907.

The rise of the Carlisle Indian School to fame began in the 1907 season. Football had been introduced at Carlisle in 1894. In 1899 the Indians, whose teams never had averaged over 170 pounds, quickly mastered the game, some of them becoming remarkable kickers in both punting and dropkicking. Deception and trick plays were their forte. One of these was a so-called hunchback play, in which the ball was placed under the back of a Carlisle player's jersey, completely confounding Harvard for a touchdown in 1903.

In 1907, 1911, and 1912 Carlisle was one of the strongest teams in the country and gave the football

The
Carlisle
Indians
and Jim
Thorpe

world the player who is often ranked as the greatest of all time—Jim Thorpe. In 1907, with Thorpe making his first appearance as a substitute, the team defeated Pennsylvania, Harvard, Minnesota, and Chicago, suffering only one setback—against Princeton. This was the second year of the forward pass and the Indians took to it quickly with their skill of hand and lightness and speed of foot.

In 1911 and 1912, with Thorpe, the Indians were nearly, but not entirely, invincible. In 1911, with Thorpe kicking four field goals, one of 48 yards, they defeated a powerful Harvard team. The Indians also beat the University of Pittsburgh, Lafayette, and all others, only to lose to Syracuse University, Syracuse, New York. In 1912 they crushed Syracuse 33–0, routed Pitt 45–8, and beat the University of Toronto, Lehigh, Army, and Brown—all by wide margins—only to succumb to Pennsylvania 34–26. During the 1912 season Thorpe scored the remarkable total of 25 touchdowns and 198 points.

Jim Thorpe, a Sac and Fox Indian, was picked by Camp for his All-America teams in 1911 and 1912. In 1950 he was chosen as the greatest athlete of the 20th century, and the greatest football player of all time in polls of sportswriters and sportscasters.

Two of football's most famous coaching dynasties were started in 1908—by Percy Haughton at Harvard and Gilmour Dobie at the University of Washington, Seattle. Under Haughton, an aristocrat and an iron disciplinarian who was a master of strategy and attached far more importance than the vast majority of coaches to kicking, Harvard enjoyed its "golden age." Never before nor since has it known such success as it did from 1908 to 1915. It went through 33 games in a row without defeat in 1911–15. In the eight years Harvard won 64 games, lost four, and tied five. Gilmour Dobie established an intercollegiate record of 39 successive victories at Washington from 1908 to 1914. It was not broken until 1957. Not once in his nine years at Washington did Dobie's teams lose, while winning 58 games and tying three.

New strategies. Until 1913 football had remained a relatively dull game and the coach had received little recognition or remuneration for his services. The game was in a transitional stage from the mass brutality outlawed by the rules changes of 1906, 1910, and 1912, but it had remained almost exclusively a running and kicking game for most teams. The removal of restrictions on the forward pass and the creation of end zones, in which the pass might be caught for a touchdown, provided the impetus to make more use of the new weapon.

With the opening up of the game, the coach became more important, as a deviser of plays, pass patterns, and defensive arrangements. Only a few coaches had achieved renown.

Knute
Rockne
and Notre
Dame

Knute Rockne of Notre Dame achieved a celebrity that surpassed that of any other coach in history, with the possible exception of Stagg. Rockne created little, but he was the most magnetic of all coaches, one of the smartest and wittiest. Becoming head coach at Notre Dame in 1918, he saw his team (which included George Gipp, who Rockne later said was the greatest back Notre Dame ever had) win every game in 1919 and again in 1920. His fame became nationwide when his team of 1924 won the national championship. Sportswriter Grantland Rice began his account of that year's Notre Dame–Army game with these words:

> Outlined against the blue-gray October sky, the Four Horsemen rode again. In dramatic lore they were known as famine, pestilence, destruction and death. These are only aliases. Their real names are Stuhldreher, Miller, Crowley and Layden.

Rice's phrase became imperishable, as did the fame of the team and its coach. Harry Stuhldreher was quarterback, Elmer Layden, fullback, and Don Miller and Jim Crowley, halfbacks. The men in the line became known as the "Seven Mules." The team played north, south, east, and west and won every game, including a Rose Bowl victory over Stanford. Rockne had undefeated and untied teams also in 1929 and 1930. No one knew better than Rockne how to make the most of all the devices,

Ball carrier for Notre Dame plunges through the Stanford line during the Rose Bowl game, January 1, 1925.
Brown Brothers

including the shift (see below), with which he was so successful that football legislators finally required players in motion to come to a definite one-second stop before the snap of the ball.

The shift. Rockne credited Stagg as the originator of the shift installed at Notre Dame in 1914, in which the backs moved just before the snap of the ball from their T formation into a box alignment behind the left or right side of the line. A year later the ends also shifted out from the line. Stagg said that at the beginning of the century he started shifting linemen quickly from one side to another in the first deviation away from a balanced line and the start of the shift. In 1904 he used a backfield shift synchronously, and in 1910, a backfield shift in which the ball was snapped instantly without delay.

In addition to the Stagg-Notre Dame shift, also famous were the Minnesota (the "greatest shift ever invented"), created by Harry Williams, and the Heisman shifts. The Minnesota began with tackles back, shifting both of them to either side of an unbalanced line while simultaneously rearranging the backfield. Minnesota first used the shift about 1903 or 1904. Coach John Heisman unveiled his complex shift at Georgia Tech in 1910. It involved moving most of the line as well as the backfield just prior to the snap of the ball. In 1917 he achieved his greatest success with it when Georgia Tech defeated every opponent, crushing a strong Pennsylvania team 41–0.

The Notre Dame shift lost its effectiveness with successive decrees of the rules committee to eliminate its momentum. In 1924 it was ruled that the team must come to an absolute stop and remain stationary "momentarily." In 1927 a pause of one second was imposed. In 1931 the pause had to be "at least one second." The vogue of the shift had been waning, and after Rockne's death in 1931 it lost most of its remaining followers.

Wingback formations. Contributing to the decline of the Notre Dame system was the rise in popularity of the wingback formations originated by Glenn (Pop) Warner. One of the most creative minds in football and one of the most successful of all coaches in 44 years at Georgia, Cornell, Carlisle, Pittsburgh, Stanford, and Temple University (Philadelphia), Warner devised first a single wingback formation and then a double wingback (see Figure 2). In the single wing, the backs were in Z alignment, a halfback to the flank and just to the rear of his end on the strong side of an unbalanced line, in which the tackles were side by side. In the double wing, the other halfback moved up from his single-wing station, five yards behind centre, to the flank of his short-side end. The fullback was positioned four yards behind centre and the quarterback was a yard behind the right guard. Power, deception, and speed were emphasized in Warner single- and double-wing football. Big, hard-running quarterbacks and fullbacks were required. Warner invented the single wing in 1912, and his Carlisle team used it against Army. The double-wing formation in all probability was worked out and perfected while he was at Pittsburgh, but it was not until 1928 that it won nationwide acclaim when his Stan-

Pop
Warner

ford team overwhelmed Army in New York City. Both formations eventually lost favour because their complex, delayed manoeuvres required such precise timing as well as a quarterback of a type not commonly available. The double wing became almost extinct and the single wing a rarity after the modern T formation won favour in the 1940s.

T formation. The modern T—employing principles that Stagg had worked out over the years, including the stand-up position of the quarterback behind centre (1894), quarterback fakes and "keeper" plays in which the quarterback pretends to hand the ball to one back and then gives it to another or keeps it himself (1905), and the man in motion (1927)—was the creation in the 1930s of George Halas and his Chicago Bears coaching staff of the professional National Football League and Clark Shaughnessy, University of Chicago coach. The Bears' 73–0 defeat of the Washington Redskins in the NFL championship game of 1940 and the overwhelming success of Stanford University with it the same year started the trend toward reviving the formation. The addition of men-in-motion, flanking backs, wide receivers, and brush-blocking (the blocker only bumps his opponent to interrupt his rush and then runs on as a potential pass receiver or downfield blocker) techniques produced a fast-hitting, quick-opening attack and put a tremendous burden upon the defense. When coach Frank Leahy used the T in developing what was regarded as the greatest of Notre Dame teams in 1943, and Earl ("Red") Blaik produced three unbeaten Army teams with it in 1944, 1945, and 1946, the Rockne and Warner styles of football went into discard.

The T has not been displaced since then, although many variations have been introduced. In 1941 Don Faurot at the University of Missouri revealed the split T, with wider line spacing (splits) and a sliding, ball-carrying quarterback rather than a spinning ball feeder, with options of keeping, pitching out, and passing. Others to use the split T included Charles ("Bud") Wilkinson, whose Oklahoma teams won the national championship in 1950, 1955, and 1956, and Jim Tatum, whose Maryland teams won the championship in 1953 and beat every opponent in 1951 and 1955.

Another variation was a so-called wing T, a combination of the T and the single wing. Among its exponents was coach Lou Little of Columbia, who had devised a particularly clever single-wing attack, putting his fullback and tailback on a line to spin and fake to one another, as well as to the wingback circling around. It was this formation that produced Columbia's winning touchdown against Stanford in the 1934 Rose Bowl game. The double wing T worked out by Clarence ("Biggie") Munn at Michigan State was another variation, and there have also been the slot, double slot, highly publicized "lonely end" T of Blaik's at Army, and, in more recent years, I and wishbone T varieties and formations with split ends, wide receivers, flankers, double flankers, and other types of spreads, popular with professional teams.

Coaches, teams, and players. Football had become a national mania and large-scale business enterprise in the United States by the 1920s. Highly publicized football heroes such as the Four Horsemen of Notre Dame and Harold ("Red") Grange of Illinois won new football followers the country over. Attendance mounted: Notre Dame played to 500,000 spectators a season, Army and Navy drew 110,000 to their 1926 game in Chicago; and crowds of 90,000 in California, 80,000 in the Middle West, and 75,000 in the East became commonplace. New and larger stadiums went up across the land. The most famous coaches drew salaries of $15,000 to $20,000, far in excess of what they had been paid before World War I. The rewards of success were such that more and more colleges sought to share in them by building an arena, hiring a winning coach, and recruiting players for him to develop into an attraction that would fill the arena. As money poured in and more and more colleges assumed heavy obligations in expanding their athletic plants, the need for success became greater and greater. Winning teams were needed to attract customers and so provide

the income necessary to meet mounting budgets as football was burdened with supporting the entire structure of intercollegiate athletics.

The scramble to obtain the best high-school and preparatory-school talent led to unscrupulous recruiting practices. Financial inducements were offered to players by college coaches or athletic-department officials or by alumni, in violation of amateur regulations and ethical standards. Educational requirements were let down or waived to get good players into college and keep them there for four years. A variety of dishonest recruiting practices became widespread. Athletic scholarships were given wholesale, and large pools of funds were subscribed by alumni to bring prize athletes to their alma mater.

The college football world was rocked in 1929 when a *Carnegie Foundation Bulletin* exposed the extent of unethical practices and named some of the most prestigious universities. Respectable colleges took corrective measures, and for a while the reaction was so strong that it seemed football might be limited to intramural competition. But the intercollegiate game had too strong a hold on the public and was too strong a bond between alumni and alma mater to be downgraded more than temporarily. Also, many colleges had extensive commitments that depended upon receipts from football for their continuance.

The rising calibre of the football played in all areas of the country immediately following World War I was evidenced by Walter Camp's praise of his 1919 All-America selections as representing "the most powerful aggregation of players that has been on the gridiron for a long time." Two of Camp's first-team choices were from little Centre College in Danville, Kentucky, which came to prominence when it beat all opponents, including West Virginia, which had itself crushed powerful Princeton. Two years later Centre College scored one of the notable victories of all time in inflicting Harvard's first defeat in three years, 6–0.

The South was beginning to establish itself as a football force. In 1917 Georgia Tech, under John Heisman, had a strong claim to the national championship, and both Vanderbilt, under coach Dan McGugin, and Centre College teams won acclaim across the nation. In 1923 Wallace Wade was installed as coach at the University of Alabama and there, and later at Duke, he was to establish himself as one of the most successful coaches in history. Alabama in 1925 won every game and defeated Washington in the Rose Bowl in the first appearance there of a team from the deep South.

Bob Neyland went to Tennessee in 1926 and began one of football's great coaching dynasties. In his second year his team was unbeaten, after losing only one game in 1926. In nine years they won 76 games, lost six and were tied five times. After a year's leave of absence in 1935, Neyland returned to Tennessee, and in 1938, 1939, and 1940 his teams won every game, a total of 30, and, in 1939, shut out every opponent. Neyland's teams used the single-wing formation with a balanced line and displayed exceptional defensive strength. They won 173 games in all, lost 31, and were tied 12 times. Very few coaches have had a winning percentage equal to this.

In 1928 Georgia Tech, under coach William Alexander, defeated every opponent and then beat California in the Rose Bowl after one of the most bizarre happenings in all the history of football, in which Roy Riegels, the California centre, grabbed a ball that dropped from the hands of a Georgia back and, losing his bearings, reversed his field and sped almost 60 yards toward his own goal before a teammate overhauled him at the three-yard line. At that instant the Georgia pursuers also caught up with him and as he turned to head back, he was tackled on the one-yard line. An attempted kick out of the end zone was blocked and resulted in a safety that provided the margin of Georgia's 8–7 victory.

Bernie Bierman was another coach who contributed to the rising prestige of Southern football, although his name is most usually associated with Minnesota, where he played and later developed a succession of national champions. His earlier 1929 and 1931 Tulane teams won

Unethical recruiting practices

"Wrong way" Riegels

every game, and the 1930 eleven lost only to Northwestern.

Football on the Pacific coast was also on the rise in the 1920s because of an influx of coaching talent. Glenn Warner went to Stanford in 1924 after great success at Pittsburgh, Carlisle, and Cornell. In 1925 Howard Jones, who had turned out champion teams at Yale and Iowa, was appointed at Southern California. By 1928 Jones was challenging the supremacy Warner had taken from California, and his teams were recognized as national champions.

The six leading colleges in the Missouri Valley Conference withdrew in 1928 and organized the Missouri Valley Intercollegiate Athletic Association, known as the Big **The Big** Six: Nebraska, Missouri, Oklahoma, Kansas, Kansas **Eight** State, and Iowa State. Colorado joined in 1948 to make it the Big Seven, and in 1957 it became the Big Eight with the entry of Oklahoma State. Remaining in the Missouri Valley Conference were Tulsa, Cincinnati, Louisville, North Texas State, Wichita State, and Memphis State.

In the Rocky Mountain area few intersectional games were scheduled and little recognition was given to the teams. Colorado University at Boulder; Colorado State (known then as Colorado A. & M.) at Fort Collins; the University of Denver; the University of Utah, at Salt Lake City; Utah State at Logan; the University of Wyoming, Laramie; and Brigham Young University, Provo, Utah, withdrew from the Rocky Mountain Conference in 1938 and formed the Mountain States (Skyline) Conference.

Matty Bell started a long coaching tenure at Southern Methodist University in 1935 and in his inaugural year brought the Southwest its first national championship. Stanford invited his team to play in the Rose Bowl, marking the first appearance there of a team from the Southwest. Homer Norton, who went to Texas A. & M. when Bell left for SMU, had a national champion in 1939. The year before, Leo ("Dutch") Meyer had piloted Texas Christian to the championship.

The 1930s were ushered in not only by Notre Dame's championship team, Rockne's last, but by another of the best of all time—Wallace Wade's last Alabama eleven, which defeated Washington State in the Rose Bowl 24–0. In all, Wade took five Alabama and Duke teams to the Rose Bowl. His record for 24 years included 171 victories, 49 losses, and ten ties.

Notre Dame continued strong after Rockne's death, and other powerful teams were Michigan, Colgate, and Princeton.

Minnesota was one of the strongest teams of the 1930s, going through three years of success in 1934, 1935, and 1936, losing only one game—to Northwestern in 1936. The 1934 team, which has been rated as the best of Bierman's regime and among the greatest in football history, beat Michigan 34–0. Wisconsin was beaten by the same score. Bierman's teams were recognized as national champions in 1934, 1936, 1940, and 1941.

Along with Minnesota, the 1934 season brought forth another team now ranked among the great—Alabama. Under Frank Thomas, successor to Wade and the first to carry the Notre Dame style of football to the South, Alabama defeated every opponent, including Stanford in the Rose Bowl. In 1935 the first award of the Heisman Trophy to the outstanding college player of the year was made to Jay Berwanger of the University of Chicago.

A new style. The 1940s saw a new style of football. As the youth of the country went off to World War II and many coaches entered the armed forces, it seemed at first that intercollegiate football might have to be abandoned. Numerous colleges dropped out in 1943—among them, Stanford, Alabama, Fordham, Syracuse, Tennessee, Florida, Mississippi, Mississippi State, Oregon, Oregon State, Santa Clara, and Washington State. Others carried on only informally—as Harvard, Boston College, and Vanderbilt. But the game was kept going at most schools. Navy flying-cadet trainees in various colleges were permitted to participate in varsity sports. Freshmen also **Wartime** were made eligible. War restrictions, including dimout **restrictions** regulations, rationing of gasoline and rubber, and cur-

tailment of travel, had their effect. The Rose Bowl game of New Year's Day, 1942, was transferred east from Pasadena to the campus of Duke University in Durham because of the possibility of an enemy attack on the West Coast. Though the quality of football fell off sharply and the immediate future of the game seemed uncertain, the public attended games in increasing numbers.

In 1945 the picture changed. With the end of the war in Europe, former college stars and coaches returned to campus and veterans' benefit programs enabled many servicemen to get a higher education. The influx of veterans reached a crest in 1946—football's most prosperous season to that time, when there were so many players on campus that numerous former varsity-letter winners were unable to regain their places on their teams.

It was a changing game to which the players and coaches came back. The change to T-formation football had begun before most of them had gone to war in 1942 and 1943. This was the modern T, with man in motion, flanking backs, and other features experimented with in the distant past and developed in professional football in the 1930s. This formation, striking swiftly and deceptively through quick openings in the line, with the ball handed quickly to a darting back by a quarterback, and blockers merely brushing opponents off balance and continuing on for secondary targets, was to replace both the old wingback system of Glenn Warner, with its emphasis on power, deception, and complex manoeuvres, and the shift attack employed so successfully by Knute Rockne's Notre Dame teams and much imitated.

Among the outstanding teams of the decade was coach Clark Shaughnessy's Stanford University team of 1940, which achieved a perfect record and gave the T formation a spectacular send-off. This was in Shaughnessy's first year at Stanford, which had not won a single conference game in 1939. He was voted the coach of the year.

Army dominated the scene in 1944 and 1945 and then was challenged by Notre Dame in 1946. Coach Earl ("Red") Blaik had the finest pair of running backs in Army history at his command for the three years—Felix ("Doc") Blanchard and Glenn Davis. In 1944 Army, for the first time since 1931, defeated Notre Dame 59–0 and scored 504 points for the season, an academy record. In 1946 a game between Army and coach Frank Leahy's Notre Dame team resulted in a 0–0 stalemate, and in the most dramatic game of the season Army beat Navy 21–18, to complete a three-year record of 27 victories and one tie.

On the same day Notre Dame beat Southern California, to complete a record that, like Army's, showed all victories except for their scoreless tie. In the final ranking poll, it finished on top, and Army dropped to second place. Blaik was voted the coach of the year, in reward, partly, for the three years of 1944, 1945, and 1946—the greatest in West Point history. Glenn Davis received the Heisman Trophy, which had gone to Blanchard in 1945 and would go to Notre Dame's quarterback John Lujack in 1947.

In 1945 coach Fritz Crisler at Michigan originated what was to become famous as platoon football. Because of the shortcomings of wartime players, he formed separate units for offense and defense. At first only his line specialized while backs played both offense and defense. In **Platoon** 1947, however, Crisler began to substitute entire teams **football** drilled in offense or defense. In 1953 platoon football was temporarily abandoned following a change in the substitution rule.

Another of the strongest postwar teams was, again, Notre Dame, which, under Leahy, won 36 games and tied two from 1946 thru 1949, with no losses, and ranked first in the nation in 1946, 1947, and 1949. In 1953 the team was again undefeated, although tied once, and ranked second to Maryland. That was the last year of Leahy's successful regime. He collapsed in the dressing room during the intermission in the Georgia Tech game, and on his doctor's advice resigned as Notre Dame's coach early in 1954. In his 11 years at Notre Dame, Leahy's teams won 87 games, lost 11, and tied nine. His earlier Boston College teams in 1939 and 1940 had won 20 and lost two.

One of the most remarkable coaching records football has known began in 1948 when coach Charles ("Bud") Wilkinson started Oklahoma on a record that was to win him a place among the most successful coaches of all time. Beginning with the second game, Oklahoma, using a split T formation, won 31 games in a row before losing to Kentucky in a 1951 postseason game. From 1953 to 1957 Oklahoma compiled the longest winning streak in the history of intercollegiate football, defeating 47 opponents in succession before they lost 7–0 in the eighth game of 1957 to Notre Dame. In 1949, 1950, 1954, 1955, and 1956 Oklahoma won every game of the season. It was the national champion in 1950, 1955, and 1956, and champion of its conference from 1948 to 1959. The 1955 team created a sensation with its speed, particularly in a 20–6 victory in the Orange Bowl over a Maryland team that had been unbeaten and untied and had the most powerful defense against rushing in the country. In his 17 years at Oklahoma—from 1947 through 1963—Wilkinson had compiled a remarkable record of 145 games won, 29 lost, and four tied when he resigned to run for Congress. He was voted coach of the year in 1949. In 1958, when the substitution rule was liberalized so that it again became possible to use platoons, Coach Paul Dietzel of Louisiana State University devised a format calling for a team that played both offense and defense and separate offensive and defensive units; LSU finished an undefeated season ranked as first in the country, and Dietzel was coach of the year.

Oklahoma —the longest winning streak

In his last year before retiring as Army coach, Earl Blaik in 1958 trained a team that was unbeaten for the first time in nine years and was ranked third. Blaik originated what became known as the "lonely end" formation, in which an end was stationed 18 to 20 yards to the side of the line. He did not join his teammates in the huddle, and it was a mystery as to how he got the signal for each play. It was not until the season was over that Blaik explained that the position of the quarterback's feet furnished the cue. Army passed from this formation more than did any other Blaik team.

The year 1958 was notable for the fact that there was a scoring change for the first time since 1912. For the score after a touchdown, 2 points were awarded if it was made on a run or forward pass into the end zone; 1 point if it was made on a placement or drop kick over the crossbar between the goal posts. The ball was put on the three-yard line, instead of the two-yard line, for the conversion. The distance between the goal posts was widened the next year from 18 feet six inches, to 23 feet four inches (7.1 metres), and from then on far more field goals were to be attempted and far more were to be successful.

College football attendance increased in the 1950s, and during the decade from 1959 to 1969 it rose roughly 35 percent, from about 20,000,000 to more than 27,000,000. In 1970, attendance had the biggest rise ever in a single year—over 1,800,000—for a total of about 29,500,000. Permitting colleges to schedule an extra game accounted in part for the increase.

In the 1940s the Middle West had dominated football except for the three years Army was invincible—1944, 1945, and 1946. Notre Dame, with four national champions, Minnesota, Ohio State, and Michigan were the great powers. In the 1950s Oklahoma had gone to the top, and the deep South had great teams in Tennessee, Auburn, and LSU. The East, in Syracuse and Maryland, had its first national champions since the 1930s, other than Army. In the 1960s, however, there was a wide distribution of strength, with every section represented except the northeast. Southern California, under coach John McKay, brought the West Coast back into the mainstream for the first time since the early 1930s, with the University of California at Los Angeles (UCLA) a challenger. The University of Texas returned to a football prominence it had not had since the 1930s, and the University of Arkansas furnished the chief conference competition. Alabama returned to the height, and Ohio State, Michigan State, and Minnesota kept the Big Ten in the

The 1960s— distribution of strength

fore. Notre Dame consistently produced some of the best teams in the nation from 1964 on, and Nebraska started its climb to the very top, which they attained in 1970 and 1971.

Michigan State blockers delay onrushing linemen, as quarterback Steve Juday (23) passes to halfback Clinton Jones (26) on a rollout pattern from the T-formation against Illinois, 1965.

In 1964 the substitution rule was liberalized to permit any number of players to be sent in whenever the clock was stopped and two players when it was running. This opened the way for a partial return to platoon football. Also in 1964, Oregon and Oregon State rejoined California, Stanford, Southern California, the University of California at Los Angeles, Washington, and Washington State, in this way forming an eight-team Pacific Conference.

Few football games have generated as much interest all over the country as the Notre Dame–Michigan State game of 1966. Both unbeaten and untied, with some of the most publicized players of the season, they met before a record 80,000 in Michigan State's stadium and a television audience estimated at 33,000,000. The game ended in a 10–10 tie, as Notre Dame cautiously ran out the clock in the final minute without risking a pass in its own territory. Notre Dame was ranked first for the year and Michigan State second.

Other highlights of the decade included the performances of Southern California's halfback O.J. Simpson in 1967–68 and of the Ohio State teams of 1968–70. Simpson, a transfer student from a junior college, won All-America honours and nearly won the Heisman Trophy in his first season of major college football. With great balance, speed, and durability, he executed breakaway touchdown runs and often carried the ball 30 or 40 times to gain more than 100 yards in a single game. He led the nation in rushing in 1967 and 1968 and won the Heisman Trophy in 1968. Ohio State, with a team comprised mostly of sophomores, was national champion that year, undefeated and winner over Southern California and Simpson in the Rose Bowl. Ohio was also considered the best team in the nation through most of the 1969 and 1970 seasons but lost crucial games at the end of both years. In 1969 Ohio was bested by Michigan 24–12 in the last game of the regular season. The next year it was upset 27–17 in the Rose Bowl by Stanford.

Texas was sensational in 1969, defeating Arkansas and then Notre Dame in the Cotton Bowl, to be crowned national champion. They remained invincible through 1970 until their 30-game winning streak was ended by Notre Dame in their repeat Cotton Bowl meeting, January 1, 1971.

Speed and defense. Speed has been a key ingredient of football increasingly since the modern T formation and its variations became the major vehicle of attack. Athletes are faster, particularly the running backs and pass receivers, and so must be the pass defenders. With the

Higher
scores

use of specialists in platoons, passers and receivers are more skilled and more rested than in the days when they played both offense and defense.

Higher scores The number of points scored in a game averaged more than 42 in 1969, and the number of plays a game that year increased by 17 over 1967. This was attributable in part to the fact that the playing time had been lengthened by the change in starting the clock on the snap of the ball instead of when it is ready for play. The widening of the distance between the goal posts in 1959 also contributed to higher scoring. Whereas there were 163 field goals kicked that year, the number had risen to 555 a decade later. But the high scoring may be explained most of all by the increasing burden placed on the defense by the speed and variety of the T-formation attack.

Defense in football is far more complex than it was in the early years. Before the introduction of the forward pass, the problems of the defense were simple, though the punishment was brutal. The concentration was entirely on stopping a running attack. Linesmen stood erect or crouched and used their fists in fighting to get at the ball carrier. Backs played in close behind what amounted to a nine-man line, with the fullback just behind the line and the safety farther back. When the forward pass was adopted, the defensive halfbacks, who had been supporting their tackles, were forced to drop back to guard against the new weapon, and a roughly diamond-shaped (7–1–2–1) defense came into being. The practice of dropping the centre out of the line led to a 6–2–2–1 defense, with the centre supporting the fullback in backing up the line.

The introduction of the pass led to continually changing defenses to cope with it over the years, particularly after the modern T formation came into vogue with a never-ending variation of formations. The six-man defensive line became a five-man line in a 5–4–2 arrangement in the 1930s. Various line adaptations were used to confuse the blocking assignments. A four-man line has been a development of recent years, particularly favoured by the professionals (see Figure 2).

All-America teams. In 1889 an all-star college football team was picked, and it has been an annual custom since. Walter Camp's All-America teams appeared annually in *Collier's Weekly* for many years, but researches have established that it was Caspar Whitney who picked the first team, probably in consultation with Camp.

The first team of 1889 was published under Whitney's by-line in his periodical, *The Week's Sport*, as was the team of 1890. In 1891 Whitney became associated with *Harper's Weekly*, and in the issue of December 12 he printed his selections of 1889 and 1890 and picked his 1891 team. His selections were published in *Harper's* through 1899, except for 1897, when he was on a world tour, and from 1901 through 1907 in *Outing Magazine*, of which he had become editor.

The first All-America team that Camp picked was in 1897. He selected first, second, and third teams and his findings were published in *Harper's Weekly* of December 11. Camp's selections for 1898 were published in *Collier's* of January 7, 1899. Thereafter Camp's teams appeared annually in *Collier's*, except for 1917 through 1924. Camp died in 1925, and from that year through 1947 Grantland Rice, one of the country's most prominent sportswriters, picked the teams for *Collier's*. An article by Camp in *Collier's* in 1899 credited Whitney as the team selector from 1889 to 1896. In all likelihood, Whitney consulted with Camp in picking teams that appeared under Camp's name in the *Spalding Football Guide* from 1891 to 1896.

As football spread around the country and more and more teams took up the game, the task of picking an All-America team became more difficult. In 1948 a board from the American Football Coaches Association was set up by *Collier's*, with Rice as chairman until his death in 1954. In 1924 a rival All-America Board of football coaches had been established by the Christy Walsh syndicate to pick a team. The next year the Associated Press started selecting a team, and the other two big news-gathering agencies, the United Press and the International

News Service (which merged in 1958), came out with teams. The Football Writers Association of America annually picked a team for *Look* magazine until 1970. *Time* magazine, in 1958, started selecting a team based on the reports of scouts for the professional teams. Other magazines and newspapers have printed their own selections over the years. None has been looked upon as official to the degree that Camp's and Rice's were.

Postseason games. The postseason or "bowl game" idea was launched at Pasadena, California, on January 1, 1902, when the Tournament of Roses Committee of that city arranged the first Rose Bowl tournament game between Michigan's "point-a-minute" team, whose record gave it a strong claim to the national championship, and Stanford. Michigan won 49–0. The next game was not played until New Year's Day, 1916, when Washington State defeated Brown University 14–0. Since then, the game has been played annually between college teams, except that the 1918 and 1919 contestants were World War I service elevens. The 1942 wartime game was transferred from Pasadena to the campus of Duke University in Durham, North Carolina.

The Rose Bowl

In 1925 the East–West Shrine games for charity were started at San Francisco. This was the first of several all-star games, in which outstanding players from all over the country were invited to compete. Other post-season contests between outstanding college teams include the Orange Bowl, inaugurated in 1933 at Miami; the Sugar Bowl at New Orleans in 1935; the Sun Bowl at El Paso, Texas, in 1936; the Cotton Bowl at Dallas, Texas, in 1937; and the Gator Bowl at Jacksonville, Florida, in 1946. New Year's Day is the date of most of the major bowl contests.

II. Play of the game

THE FIELD AND EQUIPMENT

U.S. football is played on a field of grass (natural or synthetic), measuring 100 yards (91 metres) in length from goal line to goal line, with an end zone ten yards (nine metres) in depth behind each goal line, and 160 feet (49 metres) in width (Figure 1). Goal posts 23 feet four inches (7.1 metres) apart are erected on each end line, the limit of the end zone. Parallel lines the width of the field are marked five yards (4.5 metres) apart between goal lines. An inbounds line the length of the field is marked 53 feet four inches (16.25 meters) inside each side line.

By courtesy of the National Collegiate Athletic Association

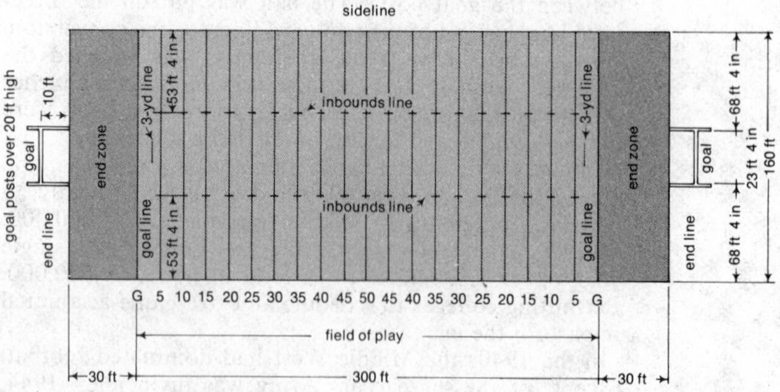

Figure 1: U.S. college football field.

The ball is oval in shape. A leather case covers a rubber bladder inflated to the pressure of 12½ to 13½ pounds (5.5 to six kilograms). Its long axis measures 11 to 11¼ inches (28 to 28.5 centimetres); its short axis measures 6.73 to 6.85 inches (17.09 to 17.40 centimetres) and its weight is from 14 to 15 ounces (400 to 425 grams). A rubber-covered ball may be used by mutual agreement.

Teams are composed of 11 players. Their uniforms consist of jerseys, snugly fitting pants to the knee, protective pads and underequipment, helmets with face masks, fitted mouth protectors, cleated shoes, and stockings.

Of the 11 members of the team, four are backs and seven are linemen. The backs are known as quarterback, left and right halfback, and fullback. They may also be called tailback, wingback, or flanker in certain offensive formations and cornerback or safety in some defensive alignments. The linemen are left end, left tackle, left guard, centre, right guard, right tackle, and right end. Since platoon football was introduced, there have actually been 22 members to a team, 11 on offense and 11 on defense, though only 11 may be on the field at a time. The players are required to wear numbers—tackles, guards, and centres being numbered from 50 to 79, ends from 80 through 99, and backs from 1 through 49.

PRINCIPLES OF PLAY
Players line up in various formations for offense and defense. When a scrimmage begins (with the snap of the ball) players must be "on side" (*i.e.*, on the proper side of the ball) and the team in possession of the ball (on offense) must have at least seven men on the line of scrimmage. One player of the offensive side may be in motion, laterally or backward. Movement of defensive players is not restricted, as long as they remain on side.

Objective and procedures. Each team's objective is to score more points than its opponent; the team having the more points at the end of the game being the winner. Points are usually scored by moving the ball by running or passing or both across the opponent's goal line for a touchdown (six points); or by kicking the ball from scrimmage by placement kick or dropkick above the crossbar and between the uprights of the goal for a field goal (three points). With each touchdown goes the privilege of trying for extra points on the conversion. The ball is put in play on the opponent's three-yard line with a scrimmage. If it is carried across the goal line by a run or a pass, two points are scored. If a conversion is kicked by placement kick or dropkick, one point is scored. Points are also scored on a safety, which is made when a play ends with the defenders of a goal in possession of the ball behind their own goal line, the impetus that caused the ball to cross the goal line having been given by the defenders themselves. The safety is scored as two points for the opponents. A touchdown may also be scored by recovering a free ball in the opponent's end zone. A forfeited game is scored as 1–0.

The playing time of a game is 60 minutes, divided into quarters of 15 minutes each. After the second quarter there is an intermission of 15 minutes (half time). Time out may be taken for various reasons during the game and the elapsed time for a game may be over two hours. After the first and third quarters there is a one-minute interval when the teams exchange goals and the ball is relocated.

Before the start of the game the referee tosses a coin in the presence of the opposing captains and asks one to call. The winner of the toss has the choice of goals or of kicking or receiving the first kickoff. The loser of the toss gets the same choice at the start of the second half.

Each half starts with a kickoff—a place-kick or dropkick from the kicking team's 40-yard line, with the receiving team behind a line ten yards distant. A member of the receiving side attempts to catch the ball or pick it up if it is rolling and run it back toward the kicking team's goal as far as possible before he is tackled or brought to a halt; except that if the kickoff carries beyond the goal line, the receiving team may let it go without touching it, and play will begin on the 20-yard line. A tackle is made by grasping the runner's body with the arms and throwing him to the ground, knocking him down with a body block, pushing him out of bounds, or by stopping his forward progress.

Following the kickoff and runback, the team in possession of the ball gets a series of four scrimmage downs during which it must either advance the ball a minimum of ten yards or forfeit possession to the defenders. Each down starts with the ball resting on the ground and with the teams separated by a neutral zone the width of the ball's length. The centre snaps or passes the ball back between his legs to a back who may run with it himself or hand it or pass it to a teammate who runs with it. Opponents try to stop any advance toward their goal by tackling the runner or by batting down or intercepting passes in flight. Each down ends when the ball becomes dead—

as when the ball carrier is stopped or tackled, when a forward pass is missed or dropped, or when the ball is thrown or carried out of bounds. At the end of any down, if the attacking team has advanced the ball ten yards from where the series started it gets a new series of four downs with a new line to gain. At the end of the fourth down, if the attacking team has not advanced the ball beyond its line to gain, the ball is given to the defenders and they become the attacking team. Scrimmage downs, in successive series for one team or the other, continue until a series ends in a score. Then comes another free kick and the same pattern (free kick–runback–scrimmage–score) is repeated until playing time for the current half expires. After a touchdown (and the try for extra points), or after a field goal, the former defenders receive an ensuing kickoff. After a safety, the defenders make a free kick from their own 20-yard line.

During any scrimmage down, usually the fourth and last, the attacking team may surrender the ball to the defenders by kicking it (punting). When that is done the kicking team may not interfere with a defender's opportunity to catch the ball. A defender may gain added protection by signalling (arm aloft) for a fair catch. If he does so, he must stand fast after a catch and the kicking team is prohibited from tackling him. The traditional privilege of making a free kick after a fair catch was abolished in 1950.

Three methods of kicking the ball are permitted: a dropkick, now rarely used, made by dropping the ball from the hands and kicking it as it touches or is rising from the ground; a place-kick, made by kicking the ball while it is resting on the ground or a tee—the ball may be steadied by another member of the team; and a punt, made by dropping the ball from the hands and kicking it before it strikes the ground.

Systems of play. In the T formation (Figure 2), three of the backs (the left halfback, the fullback, and the right halfback) line up from four to five yards behind the centre and parallel to the line, just as they did in the early days of the game. The quarterback, now as then, plays close to and directly behind the centre. In the older game, the quarterback was required by rule to handle the ball before it could be touched by any other back except on a punt. In the modern T, he always handles it so as to prevent defenders from knowing just which back has received it, a deception less likely to succeed on a direct pass.

Rockne's Notre Dame system, which enjoyed a vogue in the 1920s and 1930s but was employed by few teams after World War II, also operated behind a balanced line (Figure 2), but the backs were deployed differently, and the ball was always passed to them by direct pass from centre. The backs in the Notre Dame system first lined up in a T and then, at a given signal, jumped into a box formation to the right (see Figure 2) or left side. The two forward backs were slightly more than one yard behind the line; the two rear backs were about four and one-half yards behind it.

Warner, or single- or double-wing football, both used less often after World War II, calls for an unbalanced line (see Figure 2) and a widely deployed backfield. The line usually is unbalanced by shifting a tackle, but some coaches choose to shift a guard instead. In the single wing the forward halfback (wingback) stands one yard behind the line and up to one yard outside the end. The quarterback (blocking back) is placed about one-half yard to the rear of the wingback and about two yards inside the wingback position. The fullback (plunging back) is one and one-half yards behind and one yard inside the quarterback. The left halfback (carrying back, or tailback) is one and one-half yards to the rear and one yard inside the fullback. In single wing, teams may shift to the left as well as to the right, depending on the needs of the moment or the position on the field.

In the double wing (Figure 2), each of the halfbacks (wingbacks) stands one yard behind the line and one yard outside his end. The quarterback (blocking back) stands about two yards behind the strong side guard. The fullback (plunging back) is from three and one-half to four

Scoring

Scrimmage

Single- and double-wing formations

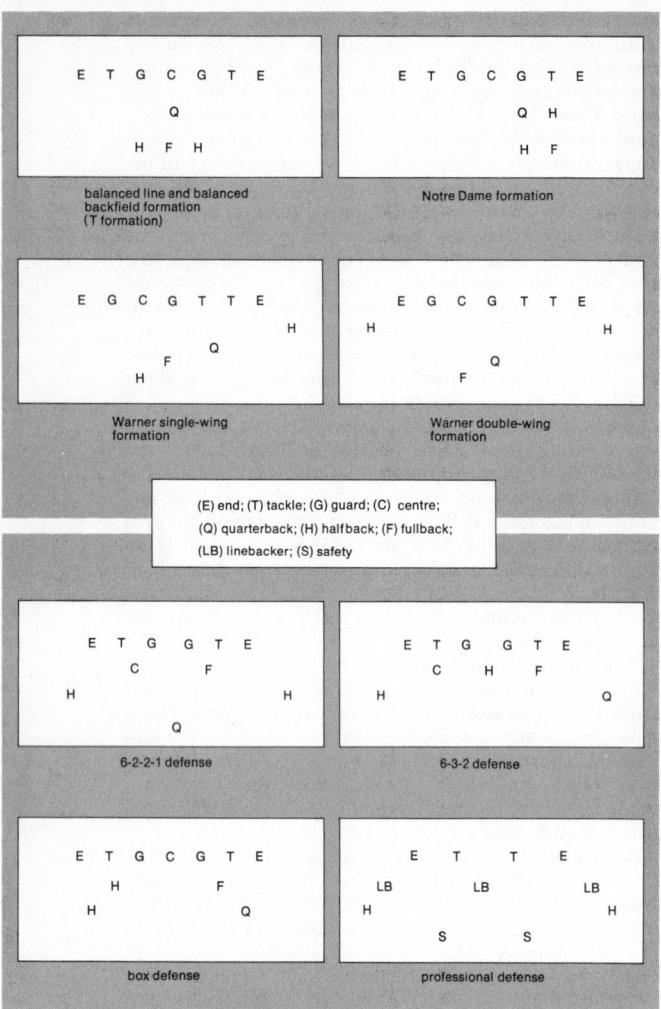

Figure 2: Offensive and defensive formations.

and one-half yards behind the centre, depending on what play has been called. The fullback is more than a plunger in the double wing. He handles the ball first on most of the plays and is a key man in starting the delicately measured reverses.

Defense. Defensive formations vary with the coaching systems and with the position of the ball on the field. A defense naturally must be much tighter when the attacking team has the ball near the defensive team's goal line than it would be near midfield.

The objectives of the defense are (1) to recover the ball if an opponent fumbles it; (2) to throw the runner for a loss or limit him to as short a gain as possible; (3) to bat down or intercept any forward pass; (4) to block and try to recover any punt; or (5) to catch a punt and run it back toward the opposing goal line.

To accomplish these ends, coaches employ various defenses. The commonest all-purpose defense is the 6–2–2–1 or 6–3–2 alignment (Figure 2). The offense must have, as noted, seven men on the line of scrimmage. The defense is free to get along with as few as it dares to leave there. In all defenses where only six men are left on the defensive scrimmage line, the centre, invariably a sturdy player, is the man withdrawn. Defenses calling for fewer than six men on the scrimmage line are used less often, but five- and even four-man lines still are commonplace.

The line on defense is spread more widely than it is on attack and is shifted to meet offensive shifts. The players who protect the zone immediately back of the line, called "linebackers," stand about one yard back of the line, usually behind the defensive tackles.

From four to ten yards behind the linebackers are the defensive halfbacks. Their lateral spacing varies with different coaches. If they are too widely spaced, a forward

pass may easily be completed between them. If they are too close together, offensive backs may more easily run outside them or passes may be completed in the "flat zones," just forward and to the right or left of the line. On an average, the defensive halfbacks stand no more than one yard outside their own ends. Back of the four forward defenders in this secondary defense stand the safety men. They are about 20 yards behind the scrimmage line on ordinary plays, but, if the attacking team is likely to kick, they may stand from 30 to 40 yards back. In the 6–3–2 alignment there is no safety man, but there are three linebackers.

The box defense (Figure 2) calls for a seven-man line, two linebackers and two men in the secondary defense. The diamond defense, now used only rarely, also calls for a seven-man line with one backer up, two defensive halfbacks, and a safety man.

Defenses calling for the five-man line are used in part to confuse the offensive players on their blocking assignments. An offensive blocker cannot block a man who is not there to be blocked. The five-man defense invariably calls for three linebackers—each a potential line defender if he is agile enough to plunge one yard forward to the threatened area of the forward wall. **The five-man line**

To stop modern attacks, coaches deploy their forces in ever-changing patterns. The rules favour the defense in that it is not required to have any set number of men on the line of scrimmage, nor do the players on defense have to come to a pause in their forward movement before the ball is put in play.

The old standard defenses had difficulty in adjusting to the split T line spacing, creating gaps. It became necessary to put more men close to the line of scrimmage. Five-man lines are now commonplace and four-man lines have ceased to be a novelty. The 4–5, 4–4, tight 5, angling 5, and the Oklahoma 5 or corner defense (which does away with the old type of end play by bringing the ends in so close that they are no longer a force for containment) are among the arrangements used. They amount to eight- or nine-man lines, leaving two or three players in the secondary. The goal is to create chaos by getting more men into the offensive backfield. Five- and four-man lines may also be used to put more men in the backfield to defend against the forward pass (Figure 2). Defensive backs may alternate methods of coverage from zone (each back defends a certain area of the field) to man-to-man (each back defends against a certain opponent). Sometimes two or three defensive backs will cover a single potential pass receiver.

Officials. The playing of a game is supervised by a referee, an umpire, a linesman, a field judge, and sometimes a back judge. The referee positions the ball, orders play started and stopped according to rule, inflicts all penalties, declares all scores, and is in overall charge. The umpire inspects and rules on equipment and the conduct of players. The linesman locates the line to gain and keeps count of the downs for each series, notes whether players are on side when each play starts, and marks the distance gained or lost by each play. The field judge keeps time, using a stopwatch or a scoreboard clock operated by an assistant, and supervises downfield play that has passed his fellow officials. The back judge assists the field judge in supervising downfield play.

Fouls and penalties. In addition to their primary duties, all officials have a joint responsibility for calling fouls; *i.e.*, infractions of the rules. Each one carries a marker, which he tosses or drops when he calls a foul. At the end of the play he reports his ruling to the referee, who inflicts the prescribed penalty. Loss of yardage and loss of a down are the penalties frequently inflicted. No team, however, may be penalized more than half the distance between the enforcement spot and its own goal line. **Common penalties** The most common fouls, with the penalty for each, are: off side (prematurely charging across a restraining line), five yards; illegal use of hand or arm (holding an opponent), 15 yards; ineligible pass receiver (in legal formation, any offensive lineman between the ends when a scrimmage starts) first touching a forward pass beyond the neutral zone, 15 yards plus loss of a down; unsportsmanlike conduct (sideline coaching, invalid fair-catch signal, illegal return of disqualified player to the game, rule violation during intermission), 15 yards; illegal position or procedure (less than seven men on the offensive scrimmage line at the snap, wingback less than one yard behind the scrimmage line at the snap, false start, illegal substitution), five yards; illegal motion (by back or lineman at the snap), five yards; delay of the game (taking more than 25 seconds to put the ball into play, excessive time-out), five yards (15 yards for delaying the start of a half); personal foul (piling on, hurdling, tripping, kicking an opponent, late tackling, etc.), 15 yards, possible ejection of the offender from the game; clipping (blocking from behind), 15 yards; roughing the kicker or place-kick holder, 15 yards; intentional grounding of a forward pass (throwing a pass into the ground to avoid a loss), five yards, loss of a down; interference with pass receiver, pass declared completed and offended team given first down on the spot of the foul; interference with pass defender, 15 yards, loss of a down; batting or kicking a free ball or illegally touching a free kick, offended team's ball at the spot of the foul. Although an incompleted forward pass does not call for a penalty as such, it does result in the loss of a down.

Any penalty may be declined by the offended team, but a player who is declared ineligible because of a personal foul must leave the game. A team will decline a penalty if the play, as completed, has given it a greater advantage than would accrue to it by accepting the penalty. An example would be a team's declining a penalty on a play that ended in its scoring a touchdown.

On the same play, fouls by both teams offset each other and the resultant penalties cancel each other.

If, on a single play, a team commits two fouls, the offended team may accept either penalty or decline both.

III. Other principal games

U.S. PROFESSIONAL FOOTBALL

Early history, 1895–1920. The first professional football game to be officially recognized as such was played in the township of Latrobe, Pennsylvania, on August 31, 1895, when a team from Latrobe beat one from Jeannette, ten miles away, by the score of 12–0. For the next ten years, Latrobe fielded a powerful team that played whenever and wherever it could for whatever returns it could earn.

One John Brallier, who later became a dentist in Latrobe, was recorded as the first "confessed" professional after he left the University of West Virginia team to play for Latrobe. Other college athletes, however, were earning expenses in scattered games of the time. Fielding Yost, later to become an outspoken opponent of professional football, played with the Greensburg, Pennsylvania, team. Walter Okeson of Lehigh, Walter Howard of Cornell, and Thomas Trenchard of Princeton were heroes of many off-the-record contests. In 1897 the entire backfield of Lafayette College in Easton, Pennsylvania, also played for Greensburg.

During the next few years other professional teams appeared. In Pittsburgh, Pennsylvania, the Allegheny Athletic Club was created, and its rosters bore the names of the most famous college players of the day. Upper New York state followed Pennsylvania into professional football soon after the start at Latrobe. There were teams in Buffalo, Syracuse, Watertown, Auburn, Corinth, Clayton, Oswego, Alexandria Bay, and Ogdensburg. On December 28, 1902, Syracuse, with Glenn ("Pop") Warner and his brother in the lineup, along with other college stars, defeated the Philadelphia Nationals, 6–0, in the first indoor football game at Madison Square Garden, New York City. Thirty years later the Chicago Bears beat the Portsmouth Spartans, 9–0, in the Chicago Stadium. These two contests were the only major-league games held indoors until the advent of domed stadiums in the 1960s.

In 1902, Connie Mack of baseball fame organized a football team that he named the Philadelphia Athletics. In the lineup was George ("Rube") Waddell, the famous pitcher of Mack's baseball team. Mack claimed the "championship of the world" after his club vanquished a squad representing Pittsburgh, which had Christy Mathewson, another great baseball pitcher, as its fullback. Mathewson had been a star during his college days at Bucknell. Bemus and Hawley Pierce, brothers and itinerant professionals from the Carlisle Indian School, played for Philadelphia.

College stars of the time did not enter the professional game as eagerly as they did in the more prosperous years after World War II, but early squads included such players as Willie Heston of Michigan, D.O. ("Tuss") McLaughry of Dartmouth, Charles Brickley of Harvard, Herbert ("Fido") Kempton of Yale, Fritz Pollard of Brown, John ("Jock") Sutherland, Earle ("Greasy") Neale, Lou Little of Pennsylvania, Arnold and Ralph Horween of Harvard, and many others.

One of the most unusual teams of history represented Columbus, Ohio, in 1906 and for several years thereafter. Sponsored by the Pennsylvania Railroad and calling itself the Panhandles, this team had six brothers, John, Ted, Frank, Phil, Fred, and Al Nesser, who were railroad workers, in its lineup. These rugged men practiced in their leisure hours after full days of railroad work. All were besieged with contracts from colleges and other professional teams, but they preferred to stay on the job at home and play the bruising game "just for fun." Only Al accepted outside offers, playing with teams in Akron and Cleveland and with the New York Giants championship team of 1927. He completed 25 years of professional football in 1931.

The combination of World War I, a chance remark by Robert Zuppke, veteran coach of the University of Illinois, and the enthusiasm of George Halas in Chicago for football combined in 1918 to spark the beginning of the modern major league game.

Zuppke, at the postseason banquet of his 1917 Illinois team (on which Halas had been an outstanding end), said that it was unfortunate that football players at the time when they were just beginning to learn something about the game were graduated from college and played it no more. A few weeks later, reporting for training at Great Lakes Naval Training Station in Illinois, Halas found several former college stars eager to continue playing. On New Year's Day in 1919, a Rose Bowl championship match was held, in which Great Lakes upset a powerful Mare Island Marines team.

Knute Rockne, who became one of the immortals of football as a coach at Notre Dame, was one of the busiest and hardest-to-trace professional players of the 1914–20 period. He played as often as he could for whatever team was offering the best salary. One team claimed he played against them in six successive games in six different uniforms. He was one of the trickiest and hardest ends to stop.

Wide World Photos

Green Bay Packers' quarterback Bart Starr being tackled as he throws a pass against the Detroit Lions, 1965.

The growing years, 1920–45. As the early days ended with the organization of the American Professional Football Association in 1920, hundreds of unrecorded warriors of the gridiron faded from the scene. Scant records had been kept and the bruising battles of pickup games were lost forever. Even the glory of the individual stars dimmed, leaving only Jim Thorpe to live a few more years in sports pages. Unpadded, often unpaid, the pioneers played a vicious and smashing game of football, often for the full 60 minutes of each encounter unless crippled beyond the possibility of completing the game. A "big" squad of those days might have contained 15 players; the modern teams of 40 players, specialists, and platoons were unknown.

Jim Thorpe was a superlative back, but his approach to the game was lighthearted and erratic. Despite contempt for ordinary training rules, however, Thorpe could run in the open, crash the line, and shatter the attack of his opponents. He ran like a later star, Harold ("Red") Grange, with swiveling hips, change of pace, and extreme confidence. Defensively, he broke up opponents with a lethal and illegal special shoulder pad with an outer covering of sheet metal, which he was ordered not to wear when the league was formed. It was said by those who had played with and against Jim Thorpe that he was one of the greatest football players of all time. Thorpe, who died in 1953, also excelled in other sports. In his honour, the towns of Mauch Chunk and East Mauch Chunk, Pennsylvania, were joined and renamed Jim Thorpe in 1954.

First professional leagues
Eleven league franchises at $100 each were sold when the American Professional Football Association was officially formed on September 17, 1920. Jim Thorpe was elected president and George Halas purchased a franchise for the Staley Starch Company of Decatur, Illinois, which had recently made him athletic director. The first 11 teams in the league were the Canton Bulldogs (Thorpe's team); Cleveland Indians; Dayton Triangles; Akron Professionals; Massillon Tigers; Rochester, New York; Rock Island, Illinois; Muncie, Indiana; Hammond, Indiana; the Chicago Cardinals; and the Decatur (Illinois) Staleys, who became the Chicago Bears in 1922.

The league had a perilous beginning that fall. Few games were played, and there seemed little chance that the league would survive. However, in April 1921 the league elected Joe Carr, an experienced promoter, as its new president. Carr created an immediate realignment of teams. Massillon, Muncie, and Hammond dropped out; Green Bay, Wisconsin; Buffalo, New York; Detroit; Columbus; and Cincinnati came in, and a full schedule was completed with the Chicago Bears winning more games than any other team. The name was changed to National Football League in 1922, with Carr continuing as president until his death in 1939. In 1933 the NFL played in two divisions, with an annual championship game. For more than a decade the National Football League survived with little support from the fans and even less from newspapers. Some franchises moved to other cities; new teams joined; some dropped out. More than 45 cities were at various times the homes of NFL teams.

The first trend toward prosperity began in 1925 when Harold "Red" Grange left the University of Illinois to play with the Chicago Bears. Grange was the biggest name in the sports world at that time, and he was the spark that professional football needed. His debut against the Chicago Cardinals drew an audience of 36,000. Seven days later 68,000 jammed New York's Polo Grounds to see him play against the Giants. Grange and the Bears then went on a coast-to-coast tour that sowed the seeds of interest in the sport. Grange established himself as one of the all-time stars of the NFL before he retired from the game in 1935.

The modern era. In 1945 a rival league, the All America Football Conference, was formed and began play in 1946 with eight clubs representing Brooklyn, Buffalo, Chicago, Cleveland, Los Angeles, Miami, New York City, and San Francisco. Dan Topping, owner of the former Brooklyn NFL team, transferred his entire squad to the AAFC. In 1947 Miami forfeited its franchise and was

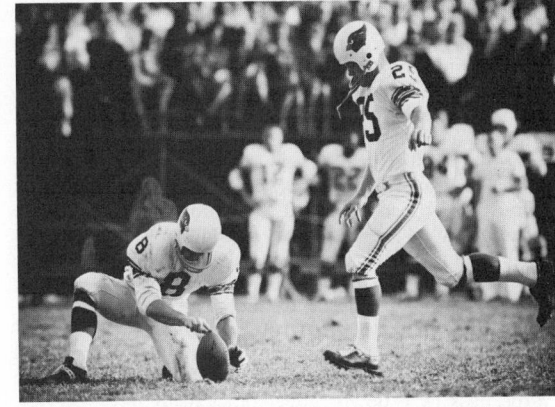

Jim Bakken (right) of the St. Louis Cardinals attempts a place-kick with Larry Wilson holding, 1964.
Jack Zehrt—FPG

replaced by Baltimore. There was considerable opposition among the NFL owners against the new league, and four years of competition for support followed. When it ended before the 1950 season, professional football in general had come of age, and the fans from coast to coast were aware of its existence. Under an agreement between the leagues, Baltimore, San Francisco, and Cleveland moved their teams into the NFL, and the balance of the AAFC players were pooled and drafted by the 13 clubs in the NFL. After one season the NFL was reorganized into 12 clubs: the New York Yanks, Chicago Bears, Chicago Cardinals, Cleveland Browns, Detroit Lions, Green Bay Packers, Los Angeles Rams, New York Giants, Philadelphia Eagles, Pittsburgh Steelers, San Francisco 49ers, and Washington Redskins. In 1952 the Yanks franchise moved to Dallas for one year, after which the Baltimore Colts, whose franchise was dropped in 1951, were allowed to pick it up and transfer it to Baltimore.

Expansion and reorganization

Attendance records started to climb rapidly as the new era opened. Bert Bell, veteran player, coach, and owner, was commissioner of the league from 1946 until his death in 1959. Pete Rozelle, general manager of the Los Angeles Rams, was named as Bell's successor in 1960. In 1960 the Cardinals moved to St. Louis, and a new team, the Dallas Cowboys, was added to the league. The Minnesota Vikings (Minneapolis-St. Paul) were added to the league in 1961, the Atlanta Falcons in 1966, and the New Orleans Saints in 1967.

In 1959 another rival, the American Football League, was organized with Texas millionaire Lamar Hunt the first president and Joe Foss, World War II air hero and former governor of South Dakota, serving as its first commissioner. Initially, in 1960, the teams were the Boston Patriots, Buffalo Bills, Denver Broncos, Houston Oilers, New York Jets, Oakland Raiders, Dallas, and Los Angeles; the Los Angeles franchise was transferred to the San Diego Chargers in 1961 and the Dallas franchise to the Kansas City Chiefs in 1963. The Miami Dolphins were added to the league in 1966.

A merger of the two leagues was announced in 1966, effective in 1970. By the start of the 1968 season, the two leagues had begun interleague play and a total of 26 cities from coast to coast was represented. In January 1970 the new National Football League began and consisted of two conferences—the National Conference and the American Conference, each with three divisions. Rozelle remained as commissioner.

The teams were aligned as follows:

National Conference, Eastern Division: Dallas, New York Giants, Philadelphia, St. Louis, Washington. *Central Division:* Chicago, Detroit, Green Bay, Minnesota. *Western Division:* Atlanta, Los Angeles, New Orleans, San Francisco.

American Conference, Eastern Division: Baltimore, Boston (changed to New England), Buffalo, Miami, New York Jets. *Central Division:* Cincinnati, Cleveland, Houston, Pittsburgh. *Western Division:* Oakland, Kansas City, San Diego, Denver.

The boom period. Interest in the new, merged leagues became apparent almost immediately. The first meeting between the champions of each of the leagues, named the Super Bowl, brought together the Green Bay Packers, NFL champions, and the Kansas City Chiefs, AFL champions.

The Packers won easily, 35–10, in Los Angeles in January 1967 before 63,036 fans. Each of the players on the winning team received $15,000 and the losers, $7,500—a far cry from the $210.34 and $140.22 the players received in the first professional play-off in 1933 between the Chicago Bears and the New York Giants. Television networks paid $2,000,000 for the telecast.

There was a new play-off system when the merger of the two leagues was completely effected in 1970. The Dallas Cowboys and the Baltimore Colts emerged as champions in their respective National and American Conferences. The Cowboys, playing in a title game for the fifth year in a row, had defeated the San Francisco 49ers 17–10 and so finally qualified for the Super Bowl. Baltimore, in the American Conference, defeated the Oakland Raiders 27–17. In the world championship game in Miami, Baltimore defeated Dallas 16–13 after trailing for more than three periods, Jim O'Brien kicking a 32-yard field goal with five seconds left.

Football became America's no. 1 professional sports attraction despite the claim of professional baseball that baseball was the "national game."

As money poured into the treasuries of the owners, there were demands from the players for a share. While the NFL and the AFL were in competition for players—before they agreed on a common draft in 1967—the bidding reached new heights. The New York Jets of the AFL were reported to have signed Joe Namath, University of Alabama quarterback, for $400,000, presumably for four years. The merger brought more conservative bidding for players. Before the 1968 season the NFL faced the serious possibility of a player strike, but an agreement increased pension benefits, insurance, and other fringe benefits, and established a $12,000 annual minimum salary for second-year players and $13,000 for players of three or more years. In 1970, in another dispute over pension benefits, veteran players boycotted the training camps. It was not until five days before the start of the exhibition season that a settlement was agreed upon.

Rules. The rules for professional football permit a more wide-open, high-scoring game than that played by the colleges, despite the fact that in the NFL only one point can be scored after touchdown, on a kick. Because the professional goals are on the goal line (the posts may be offset six feet) rather than at the back of the ten-yard end zone as in the college game, the professionals attempt and make more field goals than college teams.

In professional ball a member of the defensive team can run with a recovered fumble; the colleges call the ball dead at recovery. A professional ball carrier can rise and run if he falls to the ground unless he has gone down as the result of contact with an opponent; the collegian is down even if he simply slips and falls. The professionals have added a sixth official, the line judge, to the five who are standard in the college game. Substitutions are unrestricted.

In professional football, divisional play-offs or championship games cannot end in a tie. If the score is tied after the regulation 60 minutes, additional periods of 15 minutes each are played. The first team to score a touchdown, field goal, or safety is declared the winner, and the game ends immediately. This "sudden death" system allowed Baltimore to win the NFL championship 23–17 over New York in 1958.   (A.D.)

CANADIAN FOOTBALL

History. Football in the form of rugby was brought to Canada by British immigrants not long after William Webb Ellis' historic run with a soccer ball in 1823 on the playing fields of Rugby School. By 1862 British regiments were playing the game on an informal basis, and the formation of the Montreal Football Club in 1868 gave the sport an official Canadian birthdate.

In the United States at that time the schools were still playing according to the Princeton Rules, a game that more closely resembled soccer. Soccer might even have become the great American game if Harvard had not broken away and started playing rugby under Boston Rules, for which offense they were ostracized by their Ivy League brethren at Yale, Columbia, Princeton, and Rutgers. Harvard's search for opponents brought them into competition with Montreal's McGill University.

The schools first met in Cambridge, Massachusetts, on May 14 and 15, 1874, for two games that had a profound effect on the development of football on both sides of the border. Because McGill only brought 11 of their usual 15 players, Harvard players decided that they preferred this innovation, and 11 eventually became the standard number of a U.S. football team. The Canadians, however, returned home and reverted to the English-style game with 15 players on a side. Today, a Canadian team has 12 men on a side, a move suggested as early as 1900 by captain Thrift Burnside at the University of Toronto but not widely used until 1912.

The colleges did not set the early pace in Canadian football as they did in the United States. Instead it was the clubs, such as the Toronto Argonaut Rowing Club, the Hamilton Amateur Athletic Association, and other groups in Guelph, Stratford, London, and Port Hope, that banded together to form the first league. The colleges continued to play under the English Rugby Union rules and scorned the brawling "city" teams and their roughhouse style of play.

Inevitably, however, as Canadian schools continued to play exhibitions with college teams in the U.S., the games drew closer and closer together. Since play was relatively informal in those days, changes were readily adopted. The scrum form of scrimmage soon gave way to the set backfield, although the first centres still kicked the ball back to their backfielders with their heels.

In 1882 the Ontario Rugby Football Union was formed, immediately followed by the Quebec Rugby Football Union. These groups and others combined in a loose confederation under the name of the Canadian Rugby Football Union, later shortened to Canadian Rugby Union. The colleges formed the Intercollegiate Rugby Football Union in 1898. In its formative years Canadian football was a player's game with no stadiums, admission charges, or other forms of commercialization. By 1900 railroads were opening the west and the game was played over most of Canada's 3,000-mile expanse. Still, when Governor General Lord Earl Grey offered a cup for the amateur football championship of Canada in 1909, Ontario and Quebec were playing the best football by far, with teams in other regions more or less overlooked.

Competition for the Grey Cup, as Lord Grey's trophy came to be known, was intended to be open to every association in the country on a challenge basis. Lord Grey's advisers thought that this would help unify the country. As recently as 1954, the amateur Ontario Rugby Football Union issued a challenge and forced an additional play-off game, but in 1956 the professionals finally took full command of the cup competition and discontinued the challenge procedure. The Grey Cup game was not a prominent sports event for many years, as it seemed only to provide an endless stream of eastern champions with an opportunity to humiliate an undermanned western challenger.

As with many Canadian institutions, the game of football felt a strong U.S. influence. One of the earliest and most prominent came in the person of Frank ("Shag") Shaughnessy, a former Notre Dame player and coach who in 1912 took over as football coach at McGill. Shaughnessy was a superb athlete, a magnificent coach, and one of the great sports innovators of all time. He brought motion into the backfield, created the idea of a secondary on defense, and generally kept one step ahead of those who copied his moves. Within ten years he had completely transformed the Canadian game. Shaughnessy also had some success with other sports: although he knew nothing about hockey, he once became a coaching adviser to the Ottawa Senators and helped them to a

Stanley Cup; later he turned to baseball and became a czar of the minor leagues.

In the 1930s several U.S. college stars came north in search of jobs in cities like Winnipeg, Regina, Calgary, and Edmonton. Among them was Fritz Hanson, a running back from North Dakota State University, who in 1935 teamed with seven other Americans to lead Winnipeg through an undefeated season in the west. Winnipeg fans contributed a then unheard-of $7,500 to send the club east, where they beat a powerful Hamilton team 18–12 and brought the west its first Grey Cup. The eastern teams responded with a rule that only Americans living in town on January 1 could play during that year. When the Regina (now Saskatchewan) Roughriders won the western championship in 1936 without adhering to the rule, they were ruled ineligible for Grey Cup play. Sarnia beat Ottawa 26–20 for the cup that year amid howls of western protest. This was only one of many disputes over the years between the various unions and associations that made up the CRU.

Rise of professionals

After the 1936 controversy, the colleges withdrew from Grey Cup competition altogether. By the 1950s it was obvious that the days of amateur–professional play were numbered, as the professional teams of the Eastern Big Four (Toronto, Hamilton, Ottawa, Montreal) and the Western Interprovincial Football Union (Winnipeg, Saskatchewan, Calgary, Edmonton, Vancouver) dominated competition. In 1956 the two groups joined the Canadian Football Council (later the Canadian Football League) and the amateurs were ruled out of Grey Cup play.

A major impetus in the turn to professionalism was the 1948 Calgary team, a powerhouse built around coach Les Lear, quarterback Keith Spaith, and receivers Woody Strode and Sugarfoot Anderson, all from the U.S. After the team won in the west, a large proportion of the population of the city packed its Calgary Stampede paraphernalia aboard special trains for Toronto, where the fans staged a wild, two-day celebration and the team won the Grey Cup, beating Ottawa 12–7. After this, every city in the country felt it had to put on a better show than Calgary and hire American players to compete on the football field. The league limit on Americans per team was gradually increased from six to the present level of 15 Americans and 17 Canadians.

Canadian teams found themselves competing with U.S. professional teams for top U.S. college players. At one point, in 1953 and 1954, Harry Sonshine of the Toronto Argonauts decided to try raiding the U.S. National Football League rosters as well, regardless of contracts.

In the early 1950s outstanding U.S. players such as Heisman Trophy winner Billy Vessels, Sam Etcheverry, Tobin Rote, Indian Jack Jacobs, Bud Grant, Glenn Dobbs, Alex Webster, Tex Coulter, Frank Filchock, and dozens more came to play in the Canadian league, which at the time offered higher salaries than the NFL. With the new players came a mercurial rise in status for the Grey Cup competition, which became a week-long festival and the premier sporting event in the country.

The 1960s were sobering years, as rivalry between the National Football League and the American Football League priced the Canadians out of the top talent market. Merger of the two U.S. leagues in 1970 restored a degree of normalcy, but the Canadians continued to worry over the threat of NFL franchises moving into Toronto, Montreal, and Vancouver.

Play of the game. Although Canadian football stems from English rugby, modern rules changes have brought it closer and closer to United States football. The playing field is larger, being 110 yards (100 metres) long and 65 yards (60 metres) wide. The end zones are 25 yards (23 metres) deep. The wide field encourages lateral passing and the deep end zones, forward passing for touchdowns. There are 12 men on a team. The extra man is invariably used in the backfield or as a wide receiver on offense and as a back on defense. The other positions are the same as those in United States football and have the same names. Formerly they were different, but the many players imported from the U.S. after World War II influenced a shift to U.S. nomenclature.

There are only three downs in the Canadian game. Teams must try for the big gain, which makes the play more open than in United States football. To offset the lack of a down, defensive linemen must be one yard away from the ball when they take their stance. Also, all offensive backs may be in motion before the ball is snapped. Blocking is unlimited on rushing plays, but only eligible receivers can block downfield on passing plays after a forward pass has been completed. Blocking is not allowed on punt returns, and the punt return man may not signal for a fair catch; tacklers, however, cannot come within five yards of the safety back fielding the punt until he has touched the ball. A single point is scored if the team in possession kicks the ball over the defending team's dead line, 25 yards beyond the goal line, or if the defending team's safety back is tackled or run out of bounds in his own end zone after receiving a kick.

Other scoring is exactly the same as that of the U.S. professional game. Offensive and defensive formations are also similar to those in U.S. football. (D.Gi.)

BIBLIOGRAPHY. Accounts of the origin and early years of American football by some of its legendary names include WALTER CAMP, *American Football* (1891); AMOS ALONZO STAGG, *Touchdown!* (1927); and WALTER W. (PUDGE) HEFFELFINGER, *This Was Football* (1954). Other authoritative treatments of the early game are PARKE H. DAVIS, *Football: The American Intercollegiate Game* (1911); and A.M. WEYAND, *American Football: Its History and Development* (1926). More recent histories include ALLISON DANZIG, *The History of American Football* (1956) and *Oh, How They Played the Game* (1971); MORRIS A. BEALLE, *The History of Football at Harvard, 1874–1948* (1948); TIM COHANE, *The Yale Football Story* (1951); and HOWARD ROBERTS, *The Big Nine: The Story of Football in the Western Conference* (1948).

Reference: FRANK G. MENKE, *The Encyclopedia of Sports*, 4th rev. ed. (1969); CHRISTY WALSH, *Intercollegiate Football: A Complete Pictorial and Statistical Review from 1869 to 1934* (1934); H. CLAASSEN and S. BODA, *Ronald Encyclopedia of Football*, 3rd ed. (1963); JACK NEWCOMBE, *Fireside Book of Football* (1964), classic accounts of football games and heroes; and EDWIN POPE, *Football's Greatest Coaches* (1955), which explores the records and personalities of outstanding coaches.

Professional football: HAROLD CLAASSEN, *The History of Professional Football* (1963); HOWARD ROBERTS, *The Story of Pro Football* (1953); ROGER L. TREAT, *The Official Encyclopedia of Football*, rev. 7th ed. (1969).

Canadian football: GORDON CURRIE, *100 Years of Canadian Football* (1968); JACK SULLIVAN, *The Grey Cup Story* (1970).

Annual record and rules books: NATIONAL COLLEGIATE ATHLETIC ASSOCIATION, *Football Handbook;* NATIONAL FOOTBALL LEAGUE, *Record and Rules Manual;* NATIONAL FEDERATION OF STATE HIGH SCHOOL ATHLETIC ASSOCIATIONS, *Football Rules* and *Six-Man Football Rules and Handbook.*

(A.D./D.Gi.)

Ford, Henry

Automobile manufacturer Henry Ford revolutionized United States industry with his assembly line method of production, first employed in 1913 with his Model T automobile. The savings in time and money realized by mass production techniques enabled him to sell the vehicle at a price the public could afford, thus popularizing the automobile as a means of transportation for the average American.

Henry Ford was born on a farm in Wayne County, (near Dearborn), Michigan, on July 30, 1863, the son of Mary and William Ford, who had emigrated from Ireland in 1847. Henry attended rural schools only to the age of 15, when he found employment as a machinist's apprentice in Detroit. In his spare time he repaired watches and clocks to improve his knowledge of mechanical things, an interest that never waned. Even after he had become the master of an industrial empire, he delighted in disassembling the watches of his friends or joining the mechanics in his plant in a greasy repair job.

Intermittently during his youth, he returned to his father's farm where he built a small machine shop and sawmill. In 1888 he married Clara J. Bryant of Greenfield, Michigan; their only child was Edsel Bryant. Ford was

Ford, 1933.
By courtesy of the Ford Archives,
Henry Ford Museum, Dearborn, Michigan

then chief engineer of the Edison Company in Detroit, a position that he left in 1899 to organize with a number of associates the Detroit Automobile Company, a firm that built custom cars. He later left the company in order to build racing cars; his cars not only set records but brought Ford enough publicity to attract partners who joined in launching the Ford Motor Company in 1903. By 1908 his famous Model T had appeared; by 1913, mass production enabled Ford to sell it for $500.

The Ford Motor Company Ford's industrial philosophy was simple: reduce the price of the product, increase the volume of sales, improve production efficiency, increase output to sell at still lower prices, and so repeat the cycle indefinitely. His contemporaries, viewing the automobile as a luxury item or rich man's plaything to be custom-produced for a restricted market, regarded Ford's policies as heretical. Thus in the company's formative years, his ideas were pushed into practice against the resistance of his associates and stockholders, but the workability of those ideas was demonstrated vividly by the phenomenal growth of the Ford Motor Company. From a firm nominally capitalized at $100,000 in 1903, it became an industrial giant with a surplus balance alone of nearly $700,000,000 in 1927, when the last of the more than 15,000,000 Model T's built from 1908 to 1927 rolled off the assembly line.

During the 40-odd years that Ford ran the company, other technical advances and new ways of planning, organizing, and controlling production were developed that came to bear the "Ford label," and these advances could be attributed as much to the man as to the firm. Willingness to depart from previous practice—as by standardizing processes and products, integrating supplying industries, building assembly plants at dispersed locations, and organizing manufacturing around continuous line-to-line flow of product components—was a significant factor in the company's success.

There was a curious mixture of 19th and 20th century in Henry Ford, and his was a strong and contradictory personality. Though he rejected many of the doctrines of the business and economics of his day, on some subjects he clung to anachronistic ideas. In 1914, when workers in United States manufacturing industries were making about $11 a week on the average, he announced that every Ford worker would start receiving a minimum wage of $5 a day, a sum about 15 percent higher than salaries paid elsewhere for the same types of work. Ford

Minimum wage and profit sharing workers would also participate in a profit-sharing plan. The impact of the move, both damned and praised in the press, earned for Ford his reputation as a trailblazer. Yet at the same time, Ford tightened his paternalistic labour policy, establishing sobriety and thrift on the part of the workers as conditions for sharing in the distribution of profits.

Ford always displayed concern for the welfare of workers and believed firmly in the dignity of work. But

he resisted unionization for his employees, apparently thinking that unionism would pass away or that agitators were misleading his men. The company police in his plants for years waged a repressive campaign against union membership, and the company remained nonunion for several years after his competitors had concluded agreements with unions. After he had lost a union-recognition election conducted by the National Labor Relations Board in 1941, however, he signed the first union shop and dues checkoff contract in the automotive industry with the United Auto Workers.

Ford was a prophet of the new industrial order, yet he was reluctant to use new devices to achieve it. He had a profound distrust of bankers and of Wall Street; he preferred to finance expansion from earnings rather than by selling stock and borrowed only when it was unavoidable. In 1917 stockholders filed suit against the Ford Motor Company in order to force a distribution of most of the company's accumulated surplus, to compel future distribution of earnings, and to enjoin the company from expanding its plant. The outcome was that a special dividend had to be paid, but the right of the company to use its capital for expansion remained unimpaired. As he was able, Ford bought out the other stockholders and eventually attained complete control. He thereafter operated to suit himself, and his company ultimately became the only one of comparable size that was individually owned —a personal empire worth billions.

Assessment Though Henry Ford showed great vision and "put America on wheels" with the Model T, the first car designed for a mass market, he later failed to appreciate the dynamic character of that market. Against the advice of his management, he held out for the planetary transmission against the conventional gearshift; the mechanical against the hydraulic brake; the four cylinder against the six- or eight-cylinder engine; and a single colour, black, against the colour variety offered by other manufacturers. When, however, he was finally convinced in 1927 that the Model T had seen its day, he completely retooled and produced an entirely new car in the Model A. (Ford had produced a different Model A in 1903.) In 1932 he brought the V-8 engine on the market. Nonetheless, his adjustment to consumer demand for comfort, style, and convenience was too tardy to prevent losing first position in the industry to General Motors.

Diet faddist, foot racer, folk-dance enthusiast, collector of early Americana, philanthropist, practical joker— Ford was all of these. Consistency meant little to him. He endowed a modern hospital but subsidized a newspaper that specialized in anti-Jewish articles. During World War I he chartered a ship and sailed with an oddly as-

The winning Ford Model T entry on the road during the 1909 transcontinental race, New York City to Seattle, Washington.

sorted list of pacifist passengers to appeal to heads of state to "get the boys out of the trenches by Christmas," but during both World Wars I and II his company was a major producer of war materials. He ran for the Senate and lost but thought about running for president. He ruthlessly played his executives off against each other but banned smoking in his plants. Most important, he was a man who could make an auto in his barn with his own hands but could also make the principles of mass production work on a scale unparalleled before his time. He died on April 7, 1947, at Dearborn.

BIBLIOGRAPHY. No definitive biography exists. Much information may be found in *My Life and Work* (1922) and *Today and Tomorrow* (1926), written by HENRY FORD in collaboration with SAMUEL CROWTHER; SAMUEL S. MARQUIS, *Henry Ford: An Interpretation* (1923); WILLIAM A. SIMONDS, *Henry Ford: His Life, His Work, His Genius* (1943); WILLIAM C. RICHARDS, *The Last Billionaire: Henry Ford* (1948); KEITH SWARD, *The Legend of Henry Ford* (1948; with new preface, 1968); HARRY H. BENNETT, *We Never Called Him Henry* (1951); ALLAN NEVINS and F.E. HILL, *Ford*, 3 vol. (1954–63); B. HERSHEY, *Odyssey of Henry Ford and the Great Peace Ship* (1967); and BOOTON HERNDON, *Ford: An Unconventional Biography of the Men and Their Times* (1969).

(J.D.Ro.)

Foreign Aid Programs

Foreign aid consists of international transfers of capital, goods, or services for the benefit of other nations and their citizens. This article does not discuss two ancient and enduring forms of foreign aid: tribute paid by the weak to the strong and indemnity paid by those responsible for another nation's losses. For example, modern-day reparations payments, such as those paid by Germany after World Wars I and II, are indemnity from the victors' viewpoint and tribute from the losers'.

Two other forms of capital transfers from rich to poor countries are largely excluded from the scope of this article: the normal flow of private capital investment and the assistance offered by private voluntary organizations and individuals. When government policies are designed to subsidize or encourage these flows, through such devices as tax credits or guarantee of investment risks, such policies are an aspect of foreign aid policy and are discussed as such below.

Kinds of aid. Official foreign aid is offered in two major forms: (1) capital transfers, in cash or kind, either as grants or loans, and (2) technical assistance and training, usually as grants in the form of men and technical equipment. Technical assistance is most important at early stages of economic development, when industry and agriculture, technology, public administration, education, public health, and transportation are at a fairly primitive level. As the knowledge of modern techniques increases, the nation will be increasingly able to absorb large amounts of foreign capital. Development assistance in the form of loans or grants of capital then assume the dominant role. In countries that are very poor with little industrial development, this assistance commonly takes the form of grants or low-interest-bearing loans (as in U.S. aid to Laos or French aid to African states). As the country's income, trade, and debt-servicing capacity grow, aid may be extended largely in the form of regular loans. The rationale of economic aid assumes that when a country reaches a stage of sustained economic growth foreign aid can be reduced and cut off. The United States has stopped providing economic aid to several countries on such a premise, including Iran, Greece, and Taiwan.

Military assistance—in the form of either equipment or training advisers—has been an extremely important part of aid, both East and West. Sometimes such aid is supplemented by grants of funds for "budgetary support" to poor countries where the donor country has substantial military and political interests (as the United States has had in Taiwan, South Korea, and South Vietnam). Disaster relief is another form of foreign aid; for the United States it has become a method of reducing agricultural surpluses by distributing them to famine-stricken countries such as India.

The principal beneficiaries. The distribution of aid among recipient countries reflects varying interests and priorities. The principal beneficiaries of U.S. aid during the 1960s were India, Pakistan, South Korea, Vietnam, Turkey, Chile, Colombia, Taiwan, Brazil, U.A.R., and Israel—reflecting U.S. interests in Asia, Latin America, and the Middle East. French and British aid in that period was heavily concentrated in former colonies (particularly Algeria, overseas territories, Morocco, Senegal, and Tunisia for France; and India, Pakistan, Nigeria, Kenya, Tanzania, and Malaysia for the United Kingdom). Japanese aid focused on Asian countries—India, Indonesia, Pakistan, South Korea, the Philippines, and Taiwan—while West Germany, without any tradition in this respect, gave aid to the larger developing countries such as India, Pakistan, Brazil, Turkey, and Indonesia, and also to countries of special political or economic interest, such as Greece, the U.A.R., Israel, Chile, and Liberia. The aid of Communist countries was directed mainly to Communist-developing countries, but the Soviet Union also offered substantial aid to India, Afghanistan, Indonesia, Pakistan, the U.A.R., Syria, Iran, and African countries, notably Ghana and Algeria.

The distribution of aid among recipients was consequently the result of many different priorities. Countries near China and the Soviet Union received priority, particularly in times of armed conflict. Countries undergoing sharp political change also received substantial aid (Cuba, Ghana, Guinea, Indonesia). Although large countries—India, Indonesia, Pakistan, Brazil—received correspondingly large quantities of aid, small countries tended to receive more in relation to their population: the leading recipients of aid per capita for the period 1966–68 were Malta, Liberia, Israel, Senegal, South Vietnam, Gabon, and Jordan—all but two with populations of less than 3,000,000.

Table 1 shows how Western countries belonging to the Organization for Economic Co-operation and Development (18 European countries, the United States, and Canada) have distributed economic aid among major recipients—that is, among those receiving upward of $100,-000,000 annually.

Table 1: Flow of Economic Aid to Major Recipients from OECD Countries and Multilateral Agencies, 1960–64 and 1966–68

recipient	aid receipts ($000,000)		percent of total aid receipts 1966–68	per capita aid 1966–68 ($)
	1960–64 average	1966–68 average		
India	812	1191	16.8	2.30
Pakistan	389	480	6.8	4.00
Vietnam	206	467	6.6	27.50
South Korea	230	253	3.6	8.50
Indonesia	108	207	2.9	1.90
Brazil	186	205	2.9	2.40
Turkey	184	204	2.9	6.20
Chile	112	145	2.1	16.30
French territories in America	72	144	2.0	204.50
Colombia	68	126	1.8	6.60
Mexico	53	117	1.7	2.60
Spain	40	107	1.5	3.30
Algeria	350	105	1.5	8.40
French territories in Africa	42	99	1.4	133.90
Nigeria	35	98	1.4	2.30

Source: Organisation for Economic Co-operation and Development, *Development Assistance 1969 Review*.

HISTORY OF CHANGING CONCEPTIONS OF FOREIGN AID

Foreign aid as an instrument of national policy goes back to the 18th century, when Frederick the Great subsidized certain allies in order to assure their military support and effectiveness. This practice continued intermittently in Europe during the 19th century.

In World War I the United States made substantial loans to its European allies that became, in effect, grants when the allies defaulted on their repayments at the out-

Aid as an instrument of national policy

set of the Great Depression. Because of this experience, U.S. aid during World War II, amounting to $47,000,000,000, was offered in the form of "lend-lease": the United States provided its allies with essential equipment and supplies, and in return the allies equipped and supplied United States troops stationed abroad. After the war, outstanding lend-lease balances were settled largely as gifts.

The establishment of the United Nations Relief and Rehabilitation Administration (UNRRA), which operated from 1943 to 1946, marked an important, although largely unwitting, transition from the older conception of aid as a subsidy to a new conception of foreign aid as an institutional element of policy. UNRRA demonstrated that rich nations, notably the United States, which supplied most of the funds, were coming to view official international aid as an essential element of postwar reconstruction.

After World War II. In 1946 the United Nations set up the International Bank for Reconstruction and Development (IBRD) to make long-term loans at market rates of interest, financing its operations largely by borrowing in private capital markets. A sister agency, the International Monetary Fund, was designed to smooth out international payments difficulties. These devices, however, proved insufficient for the times. By early 1947 it was clear that a far broader and more vigorous reconstruction effort was needed for Europe. The economic and humanitarian motives for promoting large-scale reconstruction were catalyzed by political considerations—the West's fear of Soviet expansion into western Europe. The first foreign-aid response was Pres. Harry Truman's decision in March 1947 to provide military and economic aid to Greece and Turkey, which were faced by military aggression from Communist forces based in Yugoslavia. In June 1947 U.S. Secretary of State George Marshall proposed a European Recovery Program of aid to western Europe with a much heavier emphasis on economic reconstruction. The program was approved by Congress in 1948; a planning agency, the Organization for European Economic Cooperation (OEEC), was created with its seat in Paris; and, during the four-year life of the "Marshall Plan," western Europe was provided with more than $17,000,000,000 in U.S. government aid. The Marshall Plan is generally considered to have achieved its twin goals of promoting European reconstruction and preventing the westward spread of Soviet power.

In the Marshall Plan a major power had for the first time explicitly linked aid for economic reconstruction to the promotion of its political and military interests. During the period of the late 1940s and early 1950s, security motives indeed shaped the flow of aid in both the West and the Communist world directing it increasingly to underdeveloped countries. From 1950 on, for instance, the successful revolution in China and the outbreak of the Korean conflict led the United States to offer major aid to Taiwan and South Korea. During the same period, Soviet aid went exclusively to developing Communist countries—North Korea, Mongolia, China. France and the United Kingdom were still too crippled by the after-effects of war to offer much aid; their modest aid in the first post-war decade was directed toward maintaining economic and political interests in selected colonies. Other nations offered virtually no aid before 1956.

Aid for development. During the 1950s it became apparent in both the United States and the Soviet Union that direct conflict between the two powers was unlikely and that there would be a struggle for the allegiance of underdeveloped countries of the "Third World." At the same time, the emergence of China as an independent world power and the de facto withdrawal of Great Britain and Japan from major military influence in Asia led to a heavy focus of Soviet and U.S. interest in Asia. As early as January 1949 President Truman had listed as Point IV of his inaugural address a plan to make assistance available from the United States to underdeveloped countries. The Point Four program initially focused on technical assistance, largely in the fields of agriculture, public

health, and education. Some technical assistance was furnished through specialized UN agencies, including the World Health Organization (WHO), the Food and Agriculture Organization (FAO), and the United Nations Educational, Scientific, and Cultural Organization (UNESCO). Most, however, was provided initially mainly by the United States and on a bilateral basis. Private capital, domestic and foreign, was expected to provide the resources needed for industrial growth.

It soon became clear that the formula of technical assistance plus private investment was inadequate to meet the goals for Asia. During the 1950s, in consequence, the U.S. steadily increased its official grants and loans for development purposes, mainly to India, Pakistan, Taiwan, and South Korea.

Although initially both military and economic aid to underdeveloped countries were heavily concentrated on supporting U.S. security objectives in Asia, security-oriented aid was not enough to meet all the objectives of U.S. foreign policy. India, Pakistan, Brazil, Indonesia, and other developing countries were considered important to the United States but did not face external military pressures or organized insurrection. The scope of U.S. economic aid accordingly was broadened. The conception that emerged during the 1950s rejected the direct security approach, and its rationale could be expressed in the form of a syllogism: (1) economic development promotes societies that are economically strong, politically stable and able to resist Communist political and military subversion, thereby favouring U.S. national interests; (2) economic aid stimulates economic development; (3) therefore, the United States should offer aid to developing countries.

Other rich nations began to extend aid on a substantial scale in the late 1950s. The major donors were France, Germany, the United Kingdom, Japan, and Italy. Other industrialized nations that were members of the Development Assistance Committee (DAC) of the Organization for Economic Co-operation and Development (OECD) gave aid in lesser amounts. For these nations, security motives play a lesser role in their conception of aid than for the United States. For the former colonial powers— France, the United Kingdom, and Belgium—the maintenance of prior political commitments was more prominent. Japan and Germany sought to rebuild links with those underdeveloped countries that could be of political or economic importance to them. For all these countries, aid also represented an investment in trade and economic expansion. For some of the smaller donors—the Netherlands, the Scandinavian countries, Canada—the main motives have been charitable; much of their aid has been channelled through multilateral agencies such as the United Nations.

The Soviet Union, various eastern European countries, and China have also offered aid to poor nations. Their aid was not, as a rule, in the form of grants but consisted of low-interest-bearing loans or credits in barter deals. Soviet loans presented a dilemma for the Western powers. Theoretically, if a recipient country's economic needs were being met by the Soviet Union, its assistance from the West could be reduced. But this was considered politically undesirable. And the competition for favours was on. The receipt of Soviet aid usually enabled a country to get more, not less, aid from the West.

THE DONORS OF AID

U.S. aid. The United States has been by far the largest aid donor. From July 1945 to December 1970 it gave military and economic aid totalling nearly $125,000,000,000. The economic component of U.S. aid rose during the late 1950s and early 1960s, stabilizing at an annual level of about $3,500,000,000. Military aid to underdeveloped countries declined steadily from 1953 on and averaged less than a billion annually by the late 1960s. By 1970 both military and economic aid were losing favour with Congress and the public. In its appropriations for 1970–71, Congress voted less than $2,000,000,000 for aid programs. By 1968 the category of grants consisted

The widening concept of assistance

largely of technical assistance, including funds for the Peace Corps, contributions of food for relief purposes, and aid to Vietnam. Balance-of-payments considerations contributed to the decline of local-currency repayment provisions, both for loans in cash and for transfer of agricultural products. By 1970 all but a tiny fraction of U.S. lending was repayable in dollars. U.S. contributions to multilateral agencies rose steadily during the period and by 1970 reached an annual rate of more than $400,-000,000. As official bilateral aid declined, the government increased its efforts to encourage private investment through various investment guarantee and insurance schemes. In 1970 a new government organization, the Overseas Private Investment Corporation, was established to take over and expand the private investment incentive program. U.S. net private investment in poor countries rose from an average of $1,000,000,000 annually in the early 1960s to $2,000,000,000 annually at the end of the decade.

Other Western donors. The increasing part played by other countries in the extension of foreign aid is shown in Table 2, which gives data for 1956, 1962, and 1968 for the major Western countries and Japan and compares each donor's 1968 aid effort with its gross national product. By this latter criterion the U.S. ranked ninth in the relative magnitude of its foreign aid burden, behind such major donors as France, Japan, Germany, and the United Kingdom, as well as smaller nations.

Table 2: Net Annual Flow of Official Aid by Donor Country, 1956–68

($000,000)

country	1956	1962	1968	aid in 1968 as percent of Gross National Product
Australia	34	74	157	0.56
Austria	—	14	28	0.24
Belgium	20	80	93	0.45
Canada	30	54	214	0.34
Denmark	3	7	29	0.23
France	647	977	855	0.68
Germany	142	468	595	0.45
Italy	43	110	150	0.20
Japan	96	88	809	0.57
Netherlands	48	91	134	0.53
Norway	8	7	23	0.26
Portugal	3	41	35	0.68
Sweden	3	18	71	0.28
Switzerland	1	5	19	0.11
United Kingdom	205	421	428	0.42
United States	2,006	3,536	3,605	0.41
Total OECD	3,289	5,990	7,245	0.43

Sources: Organisation for Economic Co-operation and Development, *The Flow of Financial Resources To Less-Developed Countries*, 1967; OECD, *Development Assistance 1969 Review*, 1969.

The varieties of aid

The former colonial powers—France, United Kingdom, Belgium, Netherlands—not only advance relatively large amounts of aid but also offer it on generous terms, as grants or low-interest, long-term loans. In recent years Germany and Japan have substantially increased their aid levels and somewhat eased the terms of aid.

Among the smaller donors, Portugal ranked high because of its aid to its African colonies. Several small donors, including Australia, Canada, and the Scandinavian nations give much of their aid in grants, both bilateral and multilateral. France, Switzerland, Germany, and Japan give relatively little through multilateral channels. Italy, beset by poverty in underdeveloped areas at home, offers most of its modest aid in the form of loans at relatively high rates of interest. Austria, Germany, Japan, and Portugal also stress loans rather than grants and lend at somewhat higher than average interest rates, which nevertheless remain substantially below commercial terms and conditions.

By 1970 the accumulation of repayment obligations on loans extended by the donor countries had begun to create major debt service problems for the recipients: in 1970 their annual debt service payments exceeded $5,-

000,000,000. This was accentuated by the increase in private investment directed to underdeveloped countries, since the payment of dividends and interest adds to the foreign exchange burden. This meant that if foreign aid was to continue on a large scale, more of it would have to take the form of grants.

Communist aid donors. The Soviet Union, eastern Europe, and China offer substantial amounts of aid. Much of it consists of aid to other Communist countries—*e.g.*, from the Soviet Union to Bulgaria or from China to Albania. It is difficult to separate aid elements from trade flows in economic relations between Communist countries, hence estimates of aid magnitudes are highly uncertain. In 1968 the level of aid flows from the Soviet Union, eastern Europe, and China to Communist underdeveloped countries (Cuba, North Vietnam, North Korea and Mongolia) was estimated at $1,200,000,000 and the cumulative total in the period 1947–1968 at $10,000,-000,000, of which about 70 percent was provided by the Soviet Union. Most of this aid is given in the form of loans repayable at 2 or 3 percent interest or in locally produced goods. As in the case of Western aid, the donor normally requires the recipient to buy the donor's products. This "tied" aid creates special problems for recipients because the prices of donors' goods may be higher than world market prices; in effect, this imposes hidden interest charges on the borrower.

Communist countries also offer aid to non-Communist countries, particularly in strategic areas such as the Middle East. It has been estimated that from the inception of such aid in 1954 through the year 1968, the total amount offered was $10,000,000,000; only about $3,500,000,000, however, or one-third of the commitment, had actually been disbursed. In 1968, the aid offered by Communist countries to non-Communist countries totalled about $725,000,000: Soviet Union, $307,000,000; eastern Europe, $361,000,000; and China, $56,000,000.

Multilateral aid. Multilateral programs have grown steadily. The major agency is the International Bank for Reconstruction and Development, often called the World Bank, which began operations in 1946 as an independent specialized agency of the United Nations. The World Bank has two financing affiliates: the International Development Association (IDA), founded in 1960, which makes virtually interest-free long-term loans financed by members' contributions and by a subsidy from the World Bank, and the International Finance Corporation (IFC), founded in 1956, which promotes private investment in underdeveloped countries.

There are also three regional development banks, each lending funds to underdeveloped countries in its region. The oldest and largest is the Inter-American Development Bank, founded in 1959, which lends to Latin American countries partly at market rates of interest and partly at subsidized rates based on a combination of market financing and U.S. government subsidy. The African Development Bank, founded in 1964, has had little success in attracting capital. The Asian Development Bank, founded in 1965, has been more successful. It has obtained both market financing and government subscriptions, notably from the United States and Japan, and is now lending at market rates of interest to a number of Asian nations.

European countries have established two institutions for multilateral aid—the Economic Development Fund and the European Investment Bank. Both are organs of the European Economic Community (Common Market), which through them extends loans and grants to overseas countries associated with the Common Market as well as to Greece and Turkey.

The United Nations finances through grants a number of economic aid programs, both directly—through the United Nations technical assistance programs and the U.N. Special Fund—and through specialized agencies, notably UNESCO, the World Health Organization, and the Food and Agriculture Organization.

Table 3 shows the rapid growth of multilateral aid during the 1960s. The table distinguishes between commitments (formal offers of funds) and disbursements (actual expenditures). Total commitments in 1968 exceeded $2,000,000,000 annually, of which about two-fifths on the average was provided by the World Bank. Most of the aid took the form of loans for agreed projects, which accounts for the characteristic lag between commitments and disbursements. Despite the steady growth of multilateral aid, net multilateral disbursements at the end of the 1960s represented only about one-eighth of OECD members' total economic aid and only about one-tenth of the aid given by all donors including the Communist countries.

Table 3: Commitments and Disbursements by Multilateral Agencies to Less Developed Countries, 1960–68
($000,000)

	1960	1962	1964	1966	1968
New commitments	739	1,198	1,565	1,976	2,146
Gross disbursements	483	725	1,112	1,421	1,500

Source: Organisation for Economic Co-operation and Development, *Development Assistance 1968 Review.*

PROBLEMS OF FOREIGN AID

Early misconceptions. The success of some programs such as the Marshall Plan led to overoptimistic notions of what could be achieved when the aid was extended to underdeveloped countries. These misconceptions applied not only to economic aid but to military aid as well.

The aid programs of the years 1945–55 had been directed toward the rebuilding of a pre-existing economic structure (in the case of Europe) or at strengthening an existing military capability (as with the aid given by the U.S. to Greece and Turkey). Military aid, when applied to the underdeveloped countries of Asia, Africa, and Latin America, proved to be of little value to the donor countries except in time of outright warfare (Korea, Malaya, Vietnam). The work of economic development was discovered to be far more difficult than the rebuilding of Europe because it required the transformation of entire societies and not simply their reconstruction. This task, it is now recognized, will be the work of generations; it will require massive commitments of resources and major efforts at mutual understanding and cooperation.

From the standpoint of the donor countries, foreign aid has often been politically unrewarding. The governments of new nations, with their colonial heritage, are naturally suspicious of the motives of industrial nations and concerned with demonstrating their independence. Even when the donor has the full support of the government receiving aid, as the U.S. had with Taiwan and the Soviet Union with Cuba, the political results are likely to be mixed: the donor government may find itself tied to the fortunes of its client, often at considerable financial, military, and political cost. Aid-receiving nations naturally attempt to pursue what they perceive to be their own interests, which may conflict with the interests of the donor countries. Some have accepted aid from capitalist and Communist countries alike while forswearing allegiance to either; in the cases of India, Algeria, and the U.A.R., the fact that there were competing donors has sometimes enabled the recipient country to get more aid than it might otherwise have. But since foreign aid is an element of foreign policy, governments will naturally be reluctant to spend funds for no tangible political gain.

The failure of foreign aid to stimulate rapid economic development in poor countries led to considerable skepticism in parliaments and among the populations of the donor countries as to the economic merits of foreign aid. Economic aid is manifestly only one element in the complex of factors required to bring about economic development. There is no way short of absolute tyranny to bring about rapid modernization in countries where the social and political institutions are based on traditional agriculture and where political power is effectively in the hands of landowners and small, moneyed commercial-

Indifferent results of bilateral government aid

industrial groups whose interests are well served by existing social and economic structures. Economic aid has been most successful in promoting the development of countries that were at least partially modernized (Spain, Israel, Greece, Yugoslavia) or where the aid has been massive and sustained (South Korea, Taiwan, Jordan) or where modernization has proceeded under draconian measures of nationalization, forced investment, and restricted consumption (China, North Korea, North Vietnam). Rapid growth in underdeveloped countries also has been closely associated with government policies that encourage exports, even where foreign aid levels are modest (Thailand, Mexico, Pakistan, Central American countries), while slow growth has often been associated with government policies that encourage inflation and high-cost industrialization (Argentina, Uruguay, Indonesia, Chile, Algeria).

Alternatives. Most Western governments, wishing to reduce aid costs, have turned increasingly to the encouragement of private investment through guarantee schemes and tax concessions. During the period 1965–68, while government aid remained stable, donor countries' private investment rose from $4,000,000,000 to $5,800,000,000. Policies to encourage private investment offer both advantages and disadvantages. Private investment results in a transfer of capital that puts no pressure on government budgets. It is usually accompanied by managerial skills and by access to an international marketing organization and may include technical assistance. Private investors naturally require higher rates of return than official lenders. New nations, furthermore, are sensitive to the threat of foreign domination; consequently private investment may create tensions between rich and poor countries, particularly if rich countries feel obligated to intercede when foreign governments take actions that affect the interests of their nationals.

Private investment is only one of several alternatives to government foreign aid that have been suggested. The others include (1) revising the tariffs of developed countries to give preference to the manufactured exports of underdeveloped countries; (2) guaranteeing bond issues of underdeveloped countries in the international capital markets; (3) devoting some share of the proceeds from exploiting ocean resources to economic development; (4) establishing international machinery to support the prices of commodities exported by underdeveloped countries; and (5) using Special Drawing Rights (the "new money" created by the International Monetary Fund in 1969 to supplement members' international reserves of gold and foreign currency) as a source of development finance for poor nations. These alternatives to foreign aid have been taken up by spokesmen for the poor nations, who have used the United Nations Conference on Trade and Development as a platform for their views.

As the political disadvantages of country to country aid became increasingly apparent to donors, and the dimensions of the economic task more evident, interest grew in the use of multilateral channels as a vehicle for foreign aid, particularly after 1965.

The advantages of multilateral aid

The growth of the regional development banks, the expansion of World Bank lending, the refinancing of IDA (the "soft loan" affiliate of the World Bank), and the expansion of United Nations programs were elements in the new approach.

Multilateral agencies offer several advantages as agents of economic development. They are less likely to be instruments of purely national policy and at the same time less likely to fund unpromising programs under political pressure. Several of them, notably the World Bank, have earned high reputations for the effectiveness of their programs and their ability to exert benign influence on their borrowers' economic policies. Regional development banks offer their member countries a chance to plan together. To the extent that multilateral agencies finance their operations by borrowing on the financial markets, they are less subject to the pressures of national budget processes.

On the other hand, certain multilateral agencies, notably

the United Nations and the African Development Bank, have been criticized as being controlled by the aid recipients. Not all multilateral agencies have equalled the World Bank's reputation for efficiency. As multilateral agencies become increasingly important, moreover, the political pressures on them are likely to increase.

There is obviously no easy solution to the problems of designing effective foreign aid programs. The programs will continue, however, as long as poverty remains an international concern.

BIBLIOGRAPHY. Current statistics for aid given by Western countries may be found in the ORGANIZATION FOR ECONOMIC CO-OPERATION AND DEVELOPMENT, *Development Assistance* (annual reviews). For general treatments of foreign aid, see the COMMISSION ON INTERNATIONAL DEVELOPMENT, *Partners In Development* (1969); I.M.D. LITTLE and J.M. CLIFFORD, *International Aid* (1965); R.F. MIKESELL, *The Economics of Foreign Aid* (1968); and G. OHLIN, *Foreign Aid Policies Reconsidered* (1966). On the relation of foreign aid to trade and development, see H.G. JOHNSON, *Economic Policies Toward Less Developed Countries* (1967); and J. PINCUS, *Trade, Aid and Development: The Rich and Poor Nations* (1967). Proposals for restructuring U.S. aid policy may be found in R.E. ASHER, *Development Assistance in the Seventies* (1970); and in the 1970 Report of President Nixon's Task Force on International Development, *U.S. Foreign Assistance in the Seventies: A New Approach.* Specialized material on multilateral aid is contained in R.N. GARDNER and M.F. MILLIKAN (eds.), *The Global Partnership: International Agencies and Economic Development* (1968). The annual reports and publications of the INTERNATIONAL BANK FOR RECONSTRUCTION AND DEVELOPMENT and the INTERNATIONAL MONETARY FUND, as well as the proceedings of the UN CONFERENCE ON TRADE AND DEVELOPMENT, are valuable references. Political elements of foreign aid have been analyzed by G. LISKA, *The New Statecraft* (1960); J.J. KAPLAN, *The Challenge of Foreign Aid* (1967); R.A. GOLDWIN (ed.), *Why Foreign Aid?* (1963); and T. GEIGER, *The Conflicted Relationship: The West and the Transformation of Asia, Africa and Latin America* (1967). On technical assistance, see S.C. SUFRIN, *Technical Assistance: Theory and Guidelines* (1966); and OECD, *Technical Assistance and the Needs of Developing Countries* (1968). The Marshall Plan and other early U.S. technical aid programs are discussed in W.A. BROWN, JR., and R. OPIE, *American Foreign Assistance* (1953); P.M. GLICK, *The Administration of Technical Assistance* (1957); and R.E. ASHER, *Grants, Loans, and Local Currencies: Their Role in Foreign Aid* (1961).

(J.Pi.)

Forestry

Forestry is the science of managing woodlands, along with associated wastelands and waters, for the benefit of mankind. Its chief object is usually the raising and harvesting of successive crops of timber, but professional foresters increasingly have become involved in activities related to the conservation of soil, water, and wildlife resources, and in recreation.

History. Early communities of hunters and fishermen regarded the natural forests in which they lived as a form of property, either private or communal, and were ready to fight intruders to defend their assumed rights. As civilization and agriculture developed, private ownership of tracts of woodland became established in most countries, often taking the form of communal and feudal systems of forest exploitation. The typical pattern of forest management in medieval Europe, for example, was the ownership of large tracts of woodland by kings and barons. But many forests were subject to the rights of the peasants, in well-organized communes, to gather fuel, timber, and litter for use on their own properties, and to pasture defined numbers of sheep, goats, and cattle on the forest wastes. Hunting rights were vested solely in the feudal lord, who also held the sole right to fell and export timber, often to distant cities. Regulations, or forest laws, were essential to the orderly working of this system, and these were first aimed at protecting game and defining rights and responsibilities. Penalties for infringements were severe, and peasants who slew deer illegally faced the death sentence. Laws of this kind were introduced to England by William the Conqueror after 1066 and were bitterly resented by the Anglo-Saxons for generations thereafter.

Timber gradually assumed economic importance as commerce developed and forests diminished through overfelling, overgrazing by livestock, and clearance for agriculture. In England, King Edward IV promulgated a law for ensuring the regeneration of cutover woodland by the exclusion of cattle as early as 1482. But systematic management really began in the German states during the 16th century. It was prompted by the need of the landowners to maintain a steady personal income from timber exports, while ensuring the provision of firewood and timber for local use by their feudal tenants. The classic solution was the working plan, under which each forest property was divided into sections for timber felling and regeneration, so as to sustain a steady annual yield of produce—and therefore a regular annual income—for all foreseeable time. This called for accurate maps and assessments of the timber volume of standing timber crops, together with their expected rates of growth. Professional foresters had to be knowledgeable in geology, soil science, and meteorology, as well as in botany, economics, and technical aspects of timber marketing, and their calling attracted able men with university training. *The working plan*

During the 19th century the reputation of German foresters stood so high that they were employed in most continental European countries, and also by the British in their vast Indian and colonial forests. Early American foresters, including the great conservation pioneer Gifford Pinchot, gained their training at European centres. But the doctrine of responsible control had to fight a hard battle against timber merchants who sought quick profits in the exploitation of natural forests without regard to their renewal. The 20th century has seen the steady growth of national forest laws and policies designed to protect woodlands as enduring assets. The character of these reflect national political philosophies. In Communist countries all forests are owned by the state. In the U.S. both the federal and the state governments have deemed it prudent to hold substantial areas of natural forest, while allowing commercial companies and private individuals to own other areas outright. Similar patterns of ownership are found over most of Asia, western Europe, and in the British Commonwealth. In Japan the extensive forests are largely state owned. Tribal ownership is found in many African countries and proves a serious obstacle to effective modern management. Private owners are nowhere wholly free from government control, which operates in various ways, including taxation of profits, licensing permits for timber fellings, and requirements to restock cutover land. The value of timber as an industrial raw material, and of the forests themselves for soil and water conservation, makes some form of centralized control imperative. Every developed country has therefore established a forestry department, research stations, and training centres for professional foresters. International cooperation is effected by the Forestry and Forest Products Division of the United Nations' Food and Agriculture Organization, with headquarters in Rome.

Trees have been raised from seed or cuttings since Biblical times, but the earliest record of a planned forest nursery is that of William Blair, cellarer to the Abbey of Coupar Angus in Scotland, who raised trees to grow in the Highland Forest of Ferter as early as 1460. After the dissolution of the monasteries, many newly rich landowners in Scotland and England found a profitable long-term investment in artificial plantations established on poor land. John Evelyn, a courtier in the reign of Charles II, published his classic textbook *Sylva* in 1664, exhorting them to do so, and today virtually the whole of Britain's 4,500,000 acres of woodland consists of artificial plantations. Other countries had husbanded their natural forests better and had little need, until recent times, to afforest bare land. The 20th century, however, has seen a tremendous expansion of artificial plantations in all the continents, planned to meet the ever-growing needs for wood and paper as essential materials in modern civilization. *The first forest nursery*

PURPOSES OF FOREST MANAGEMENT

Multiple-use concept. Multiple-use land management has become the guiding principle for enlightened forest authorities today. It contrasts with the single-use concepts of the past, which, if continued, could only lead to growing conflicts among the interests concerned. No country has an unlimited extent of forest land, and the reservation of any considerable area for one exclusive purpose creates economic and social stresses. Multiple-use calls for exceptional skill by forest managers who must operate under imaginative forest laws attuned to local circumstances.

Forest products. The raising of lumber and other marketable forest products usually takes the lead as the first object of management, producing the highest economic returns. Timber stands must be felled (Figure 1) and re-

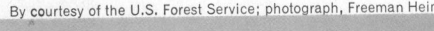
By courtesy of the U.S. Forest Service; photograph, Freeman Heim

Figure 1: Loading tree-length logs onto a truck in New York.

generated in an orderly sequence to meet continuing industrial demands. This need has run counter to some public preferences. Lovers of wilderness conditions would prefer to see all trees age and die naturally. The harvesting of timber by huge modern machinery causes a major, though infrequent, disturbance of the forest's tranquility. On the other hand, the high-grade roads that must be built to carry the heavy loads of modern trucks open up for public enjoyment woods that would otherwise remain inaccessible.

Recreation and wildlife protection. Recreation in forests assumes ever-growing importance with the development of cities whose inhabitants need a change of scene, fresh air, and freedom to wander, as a relief to the stresses of industrial and commercial life. Imaginative planning is essential to ensure that people actually find what they are seeking without damaging the forest environment or conflicting with the pleasures of others.

Hunting, shooting, and some forms of fishing require close control because the number of people seeking sport commonly exceeds the stock of animals that can provide it. Other activities, such as camping, rambling, horseback riding, and the form of cross-country footracing known as orienteering, can be enjoyed by far larger numbers of people at one time, though sites and routes must be planned to avoid disturbance of game. Popular motor roads and trails must be sited so that they do not hinder lumber working, though it is often possible to effect a separation by time, using routes for trucks during the working week, and for private cars on weekends. Facilities and supervision cost money, which can sometimes, though not always, be recouped through camping and car-parking fees.

Legislation Protection of wildlife is a further main objective. It is effected both by forest laws and by the general national and state or provincial legislation of the region concerned. Forests comprise major natural habitats and refuges for a wide range of mammals, from the elks, wolves, lynxes, and bears of northern coniferous forests to the antelopes, giraffes, elephants, lions, and tigers of tropical

savannahs and jungles. Certain birds, such as pheasants and wood grouse, have high sporting values, while others are cherished for attractive song, appearance, or rarity. Plants include rare species, such as tropical orchids, that can only exist in the humid shades of the jungles.

Forest managers have to deal with several interrelated, and sometimes directly opposed, wildlife interests, those of sportsmen, conservationists, and farmers. The needs of the forest itself require the numbers of grazing and browsing animals to be kept down to a tolerable level; otherwise renewal of tree crops becomes impossible. Reconciliation of these varying interests requires a thorough scientific understanding of each creature's life history and feeding habits, in a practical application of animal ecology. The natural annual increase of a herd of deer may be estimated, and shooting permits issued to remove the surplus stock through planned culling of the correct proportion by age and sex.

Watershed and erosion protection. In mountainous territory the value of forests for watershed and erosion protection commonly exceeds their values as sources of lumber or recreation. The classic example is found in Switzerland and the neighbouring Alpine regions where the existence of pastoral settlements in the valleys is wholly dependent on the maintenance of continuous forest cover on the foothills of the great peaks. This is combined skillfully with limited lumbering and widespread recreational use by tourists.

Every thriving forest forms a natural protective covering over the earth's soil and bedrock, effective in several ways at different levels. The impact of the large raindrops and hailstones of summer storms, which could damage bare soil, is broken by the trees' leafy canopy. Though much moisture is evaporated, and more is taken up by tree roots and later transpired (given off) by living leaves, a great deal is held by the leaf litter of the forest floor. This is slowly released through soil kept porous through the trees' root action, to feed streams, at a steady rate over a long period, with pure silt-free rainwater. By contrast, storms striking bare slopes result in rapid runoff, causing soil erosion and carrying off silt in sudden flows, leading to choked riverbeds and silted-up reservoirs downstream. Forest cover is also the ideal protection against avalanches, because winter snowfall is trapped on the forest floor, and only gradually released in the form of water during the following spring, since the forest shade delays snowmelt.

Sustained yield. Forest management originated in the desire of the large central European landowners to secure dependable income to maintain their castles and retinues of servants. Today forest management is still primarily economic in essence, because modern forest industries, mainly sawmilling and paper manufacture, can be efficient only on a continuous-operation basis.

Foresters think in long time scales, in line with the long The life of their renewable crop. Their guiding concept is rotation rotation, used in the special sense of the economic age to concept which each crop can be grown before it is succeeded by the next one. Examples of short rotation periods, both being for pulpwood in the subtropics, are 10 years for eucalyptus and 20 years for pines. Here a sustained yield could be obtained, in theory, simply by felling one-tenth or one-twentieth of the forest in turn and replanting it. Rotation periods for pulpwood in northern Europe and North America extend to 50 years. Softwood sawlogs often need 100 years to reach an economic size, while rotation periods for broadleaved trees, such as oak and beech, in central Europe, may extend to two centuries. Over so long a growing spell only part of the lumber yield is obtained by the clear cutting of a small fraction of the forest each year. The rest is secured by systematically thinning out the whole forest, each section or compartment being so treated every few years. For example, on a 100-year rotation, 1 percent of the forest would be clear cut, and a further 20 percent thinned out each year, with the whole forest completely thinned every five years. The whole forest thus contributes to the sustained yield.

Over the long periods of time involved, circumstances

Figure 2: Logs floating down a Canadian stream that winds through a coniferous forest to a pulp mill at Marathon, Ont.
By courtesy of the Photographic Survey Corporation

inevitably upset original schemes. Storms may blow down woods not yet ripe for felling, fire or insect plagues may destroy plantations, or changes in end-use may call for new sizes of logs. Management for sustained yield must therefore be flexible, with plans revised at intervals.

Sustained yield principles are likewise applied to minor forest produce. Turpentine and pitch, also known as naval stores, are obtained by the systematic tapping of the lower trunk of subtropical pines, by making successive cuts, every few days, during a succession of summers, using a chisel-like tool. This eventually kills the trees, though their lumber can be salvaged. To ensure continued yields, crops of young pines are raised rotationally to replace those felled. A similar system is followed for Para rubber, *Hevea brasiliensis*, grown in plantations, though in this case the valuable latex exudes from the bast (phloem), not from the true wood (xylem).

Cork is stripped as outer bark from the evergreen cork oak, *Quercus suber*, found in Portugal, Spain, and North Africa. This tree grows a fresh crop over an average span of 20 years. The cork groves themselves—though they endure for centuries—must eventually be renewed to maintain supplies. Coppice or sprout crops of hazel, sweet chestnut, and similar broadleaved trees, cultivated in Europe to yield small poles, likewise repeat their rotational crops at intervals of several years; but here too the stumps or stools must eventually be replaced.

Maple syrup, obtained by tapping the wood of the sugar maple, *Acer saccharum*, in New England and eastern Canada during the spring sap flow, gives a perpetual harvest, available seasonally as long as the trees thrive. Nuts come from many species of trees as perpetual autumn crops, though yields vary from year to year. For both of these products, replacement of individual trees eventually becomes essential to keep up yields.

CLASSIFICATION OF FORESTS

Botanically, nearly all forest trees fall into three main groups, conifers, monocots, and broadleaves, one of which normally takes the lead in determining the character of any natural forest.

Conifers. The earliest in the evolutionary scale, with the simplest form of wood structure, are the conifers or coniferous trees, which are also called gymnosperms or naked-seeded trees because their seeds lie exposed on the cone scales. Because the wood of most conifers is relatively soft, they are also called softwoods; another name, needle-leaved trees, arises from the shape of their leaves. Nearly all are evergreen, the larches of the genus *Larix* being the only common exceptions.

The narrow, needle-shaped leaf and evergreen habit of the conifers helps them to thrive under difficult climates. Because they can restrict transpiration of water, and make use of sunlight over most of the year, they can grow in the short seasons of the far north and high up the mountains of temperate zones. They also tolerate semi-arid climates in the subtropics. Conifers as a group grow faster, and on poorer soils, than do broadleaved trees.

The northern coniferous forest (Figure 2), or taiga, extends across North America from the Pacific to the Atlantic, on across northern Europe through Scandinavia and the U.S.S.R., and thence across Asia through Siberia to Mongolia, northern China, and northern Japan. It has outliers along all the temperate mountain ranges, including the Rockies, the Appalachians, the Alps, the Urals, and the Himalayas. Its principal trees are spruces (of the genus *Picea*), northern Pines (*Pinus*), silver firs (*Abies*), Douglas firs (*Pseudotsuga*), hemlocks (*Tsuga*), and larches (*Larix*). Together these northern softwood forests form a world resource of tremendous importance, yielding the bulk of the lumber and pulpwood handled commercially. The relatively simple structure of coniferous lumber fits it well for everyday use in building and packaging trades, while its long fibres are ideal for papermaking. Northern conifers from many lands are extensively planted in Europe, including the British Isles.

The southern coniferous forest has a discontinuous spread through the southern part of the Northern Hemi-

The northern softwood forests

sphere, including California, the southeastern states of the U.S., the Mediterranean lands of southern Europe, North Africa, Asia Minor, parts of the Asian mainland, and southern Japan. Pines are the principal trees, along with cypresses (*Cupressus* and *Chamaecyparis*), cedars (*Cedrus*), and redwoods and mammoth trees (*Sequoia* and *Sequoiadendron*). Certain southern pines such as the Californian Monterey pine (*Pinus radiata*) grow exceptionally fast, yielding sound lumber and pulpwood, and have been widely planted in subtropical Europe, Africa, and Australasia.

In addition, small areas of coniferous forest are found in the Southern Hemisphere, notably the Chile pine, *Araucaria araucana*, in the Andes, hoop pine or bunya-bunya, *Araucaria bidwillii*, in Australia, and kauri pine, *Agathis australis*, in New Zealand.

Monocots. The second group is called the monocots, or monocotyledons, a botanical classification based on the fact that these trees have one instead of two cotyledons, or seed leaves. They include principally the palms and bamboos. Palm trees form extensive savannahs in certain tropical and subtropical zones but are more usually seen along watersides or in plantations. Their lumber has no commercial value but is used locally. Palm trees have no annual rings, being made up of spirally arranged bundles of fibres, giving a light, spongy wood. Palms are valuable, however, for their various fruits (coconuts, dates, and palm-kernel oil) and leaf products (carnauba wax, raffia, and thatching and walling materials for houses and huts in the tropics).

Bamboo
Another form of tropical monocotyledonous forest is the bamboo thicket, common in Asia, composed of giant woody grasses springing from stout rootstocks. One of the most versatile plants in the world, bamboo is valuable as a construction material, as well as for hundreds of other applications, notably in high-grade paper products. Young shoots are widely eaten as vegetables and are a valuable source of certain enzymes and other substances.

Broadleaves. Finally, a more highly evolved group of forest trees is the broadleaves, also called hardwoods because the wood of most, though not all, is harder than that of coniferous softwoods. Their wood structure is complex, and each sort of broad-leaved lumber has characteristic properties that fit it for particular uses. There are three major climatic groups, forming three characteristic types of forest.

Temperate deciduous broad-leaved forests are made up of the summer-green trees of North America, northern Europe, and the temperate regions of Asia and South America. Characteristic trees are oaks (*Quercus* species), beeches (*Fagus* and *Nothofagus*), ash trees (*Fraxinus*), birches (*Betula*), elms (*Ulmus*), alders (*Alnus*), and sweet chestnuts (*Castanea*). All alike stand leafless in winter, when the climate is too cold for active life. The typical soft leaf blade of a temperate broad-leaved tree transpires water so rapidly that if it were held on the tree in winter, when low temperatures restrict sap flow, the tree would die of drought. Therefore the temperate broadleaves expand their foliage in spring, grow rapidly in summer, and shed all their leaves each fall.

Subtropical evergreen broad-leaved forests grow largely in countries with the Mediterranean type of climate, having hot, dry summers and cool, moist winters. Their trees have characteristic thick hard-surfaced leathery-textured leaves, with waxy coatings that enable them to resist water loss during summer droughts. Their evergreen habit enables them to make use of moist winters. Typical trees are the evergreen oaks, species of *Quercus*, and the madrone or *Arbutus*, while in Australia most evergreen broadleaves are species of *Eucalyptus*. Few evergreen broadleaves have high timber value, and many are little more than scrub, highly inflammable during hot, dry summers. Their world distribution embraces California; the southeastern states of the U.S.; Mexico; parts of Chile and Argentina; the Mediterranean shores of Europe, Asia, and North Africa; South Africa; and most of Australia.

Tropical evergreen broad-leaved forests grow in the hot, humid belt of high rainfall that follows the Equator around the globe. They occur in West and Central Africa, south Asia, the northern zone of Australia, and in Central and South America. Where they extend into regions of seasonal rainfall, such as monsoon zones, they become less truly evergreen, holding many trees that stand leafless during the short dry seasons. Tropical rain forests, as they are also called, hold a great variety of tree species. A few of the timbers, such as teak, *Tectona grandis*, in India, and mahogany, *Swietenia macrophylla*, in Central America, have uniquely useful properties, or ornamental appearance, and hence a high commercial value. Balsa, *Ochroma pyramidale*, from Central America, is the lightest timber known; it is used for rafts, aircraft construction, and insulation against noise, heat, or cold. As a rule these desirable kinds grow scattered amid a far larger number of poorer timbers, which are only used locally for fuel or building. These forests carry many lianas, or climbing vines, while ferns and orchids grow on the bark of tall trees, high up and out of all contact with the ground.

Tropical evergreen broadleaved forests

TECHNIQUES OF FOREST MANAGEMENT

Silviculture. The branch of forestry concerned with tending growing tree crops is called silviculture. Its successful application demands an appreciation of the ways in which trees grow both singly and in forest communities. Growth in turn depends on local soils and climate, competition from other forms of plant life, and interrelations with animals, insect pests, and the organisms that cause disease.

Silvicultural systems are divided into those employing natural regeneration, whereby tree crops are renewed by natural seeding, or occasionally sprout regrowth, and those involving artificial regeneration, whereby trees are raised from seed or cuttings. Natural regeneration is easier but may be slow and irregular; it can only renew existing forests with the same sorts of tree that grew before. Artificial regeneration needs more effort yet can prove quicker, more even, and in the long run more economical. It permits the introduction of new sorts of trees, or better strains of the pre-existing ones. While both methods have a place in reforestation, afforestation of bare lands must be done by artificial methods.

Natural regeneration. In established forests the selective cutting of marketable timber, taking one tree at a time and leaving gaps in which replacements can grow up from natural seedlings, can prove economical and also ensure the best possible use of available soil, light, and growing space. The best examples of single-tree-selection forests are found in Switzerland, on slopes where any clear felling could lead quickly to soil erosion and avalanches.

In mixed forests, especially in the tropics, selective removal of valuable marketable species carries the risk that the gaps will be filled by worthless though fast-growing "weed" trees, having no commercial value. The whole forest will therefore deteriorate as the proportion of trees worth harvesting drops. A desirable balance can be maintained by weeding, mechanically or chemically, but this may be costly.

Alternative methods of natural regeneration deal with areas of land as units, rather than with single trees. One highly effective example is employed in the Douglas fir forests along the Pacific slope of Canada and the western U.S. Logging by powerful yarding machines, using overhead cables, creates wedge-shaped gaps of cleared ground. The surrounding forest is left standing for many years in order to provide shelter and seed. Abundant seed is carried by wind on to the cleared land and gives rise, in a few years, to a full crop of seedling firs. After these have reached seed-bearing age, the areas previously left standing may be removed in their turn.

Similar systems using a pattern of strips cut across the forest, or circular plots gradually extended until they meet and coalesce, are employed in France and Germany. All demand high skill and patience by the forester, who must be able to assess the exact degrees of light and soil conditions that favour regrowth of crop trees, rather than invasion by weeds.

Regeneration from sprouts or coppice shoots, arising from the stumps of felled broad-leaved trees, was formerly a widespread practice in Europe but is diminishing today. It yields vast numbers of small poles well suited for fuel or fencing, but the timber stems that can be grown by singling these out are of low quality.

Artificial regeneration.   Artificial regeneration for the reforestation of clearings or the afforestation of bare land usually begins with seed. A few trees, such as poplars (*Populus* species) and willows (*Salix* species) can be more effectively increased by cuttings. Each tree has its own pattern and season of seed bearing, and annual crops vary in quantity or may fail altogether. Softwoods bear small winged seeds firmly lodged in hard cones. These cones are collected, as they ripen between autumn and early spring, either from freshly felled trees or by men who climb into the crowns of selected parent trees. At the seed-extraction station the cones are heated until they expand, then tumbled in a revolving drum sieve until the seed falls free. Another machine removes the wings, and the seed is then ready for sowing. Most kinds can be safely stored, sealed from fresh air in refrigerators, at temperatures close to freezing point, for several years.

The seeds of broad-leaved trees vary widely in character, from small hard grains to large nuts, and many are set in fleshy pulp, awkward to handle. Each kind needs its own techniques for harvesting and extraction, and few can be stored for more than a few months. Seed of all kinds is usually tested in a laboratory prior to sowing.

The direct sowing of harvested seed in the forest is rare because of forest seed eaters (mice, squirrels, birds) and the problem of weed growth. Trees are therefore raised in forest nurseries, where effective protection is possible. Raised seedbeds are prepared, sometimes by hand but usually by tractor-drawn tools, on well-tilled and fertilized soil. Seed is spread, by hand or by seed drills, at carefully judged densities. It is then covered over with sand or earth to a precise depth. Selective weed killers, mainly petroleum-based, are usually applied after sowing to lessen the need and cost of hand weeding. Lath screens may be needed against hot sunshine or sudden frost, and spray irrigation is frequently applied. Early growth of most kinds of forest trees is slow, and diligent weeding is needed to safeguard them from smothering by faster growing plants. After one or two years in the seedbeds they are big enough to be transplanted (Figure 3).

By courtesy of the Japanese Forestry Agency

Figure 3: Year-old larch seedlings growing in a Japanese nursery being dug for transplanting in a reforestation area.

Direct planting of seedlings in the forest only succeeds with certain kinds in favourable circumstances. Most species need a further stage in the nursery to promote the bushy root system essential for sure and speedy early growth on forest land. Nursery transplanting can be done by hand but is much speedier when mechanized. Transplanting machines, powered by their own engines, move slowly across the prepared nursery beds carrying squads of workers who feed the seedlings, one at a time, into grips, on rotating wheels. These transfer them to grooves cut in the soil by miniature plows, which are followed by earth-restoring blades and rollers that firm the soil. Machines can only operate on easily worked soil, and during limited spells in spring when the soil has thawed but tree growth has not yet become fully active. Highly efficient, they enable each team member to transplant around 8,000 trees each working day.

Weeds are controlled during the transplant stage by chemical herbicides that inhibit seed germination, or by mechanical harrows travelling between the rows. During their year or two of growth in the transplant beds, the trees become very sturdy and develop bushy roots. These factors enable them to thrive when transplanted to the forest. During moving they are protected against loss of moisture by means such as packing in polythene bags kept in the shade. Planting is restricted to favourable seasons, usually late spring in temperate climates.

On level ground, particularly on the American prairies and the Russian steppes, planting machines, which are simply larger and sturdier versions of those used in nurseries, operate efficiently. They put in several thousand trees each day, spaced an appropriate distance apart. Elsewhere, on slopes, broken or rocky ground, or amid tree stumps, planting is done by hand. The planter uses a spade or mattock to cut a notch, or dig a pit, into which he inserts the tree's roots. Earth is then replaced and stamped firmly round the tree's base.

During the following summer, and possibly for two or three summers thereafter, weed growth that would otherwise smother the small newly planted trees must be kept in check. Usually this is done with a sharp tool such as a curved sickle, a reaping hook or a billhook. Alternatively, crushing or cutting machinery may be driven between the rows of trees. Herbicides are also effective, but risky to use unless each tree is carefully shielded from contact with the weed killing chemicals. During the crop's earliest years trees that appear stunted are replaced. In some regions the lower branches of conifers are pruned away as they die through overshading, largely to improve access. Otherwise the artificially established plantation needs, and receives, no more attention than does a naturally regenerated crop.

Until the present century foresters usually accepted the land much as they found it. Their reaction to infertile soil was to plant less exacting kinds of trees and accept lower returns. Development of modern machines and a growing understanding of plant nutrition and soil chemistry now enable them to improve sites much as a farmer does, and to increase output substantially. Mechanical draining, using tractor-drawn plows to create deep open drains and so aerate the soil, is now usual on the peaty swamps of Europe, especially in Finland. On the hard heathlands of Great Britain, 300,000 acres of new afforestation land have been broken up, during the past 30 years, with sturdy plows designed to turn over firmly compacted soil layers. Plowing facilitates penetration of air, water, and tree roots, checks weed growth, and lessens fire hazard. So far it has usually been confined to strips for each row of trees, but full plowing as done on a farm promises further advantages. Forest crops are rarely irrigated as returns are too slow for the high capital cost involved.

Fertilizer trials have been concentrated on the use of nitrogen, potassium, and phosphorus, the three elements found most beneficial in agriculture. As a rule, additions of phosphorus have given greatest benefits at least cost. Only moderate amounts, around five tons of ground mineral calcium phosphate per acre, are needed. This can be spread around individual trees as two ounces per tree at planting time, or distributed evenly over the whole area at a later stage of growth, by spraying from a helicopter or light aircraft. The phosphorus is gradually taken up by the roots and carried to the leaves, where it acts as a catalyst to promote better photosynthesis and therefore

Softwood seed recovery

Weed control

Figure 4: A forest fire being isolated by plowing around it prior to backfiring to burn combustibles in its path.
By courtesy of the U.S. Forest Service

faster growth. As the leaves fall, the phosphorus is returned to the soil and recycled. Small additions therefore give perpetual benefits to the forest land. Fertilizers also are applied to maturing timber crops on nutrient-deficient soils, to gain greater volume growth over the years preceding final felling.

In theory, the quality of timber can be greatly improved by pruning away dead side branches as each overshaded limb dies. Wood formed outside the pruned zone holds no knots and fetches higher prices as "clear" lumber for specialized uses. But high labour costs, for a long-delayed price improvement, make this trimming doubtfully economic. Most clear lumber comes from the overshaded lower trunks of giant trees in natural forests and has incurred no pruning charges.

Fire prevention and control.   Forest fires seldom occur in tropical rain forests or in the deciduous broad-leaved forests of the temperate zones. But all coniferous forests, and the evergreen broadleaves of hot, dry zones, frequently develop conditions ideally suited to the spread of fire through standing trees. For this, both the air and the fuel must be dry, and the fuel must form an open matrix through which air, smoke, and the gases arising from combustion can quickly pass. Hot, sunny days with low air humidity and steady or strong breezes favour rapid fire spread. In conifer woods the resinous needles, both living and dead, and fallen branchwood make an ideal fuel bed. The leaves of evergreen broadleaves, such as hollies, madrone, evergreen oaks, and eucalyptus trees, are coated in inflammable wax and blaze fiercely even when green. Once started, fire may travel at speeds of up to ten miles per hour downwind, spreading slowly outward in other directions, until the weather changes or the fuel runs out.

Effective fire control begins with a field survey and map to identify the areas at risk, delineate them, and define and improve the barriers or firebreaks that may limit fire spread. Natural barriers include rivers, lakes, ridge tops, and tracts of bare land. Artificial barriers can be roads, railways, canals, and power-line tracks, but usually extra firebreaks must be cut to link these and provide wider gaps that fire cannot readily jump. Belts of land from 30 to 60 feet wide are cut clear of trees or left unplanted when a new forest is formed. Sometimes the soil is left bare and cultivated only at intervals to check invasion by weeds. Usually it is sown with an even crop of low perennial grasses or clovers, kept short by mowing or grazing. This checks soil erosion, provides an evergreen fireproof surface, and allows access on foot, by car, or in an emergency by fire-fighting trucks. Surfaced roads, serving also for lumber haulage and access for recreation, are of critical importance in fire fighting. Signposts are needed to guide fire crews unfamiliar with the woods, and to mark water supplies and rendezvous points.

Fire watching is essential through seasons of high risk.

Firebreaks

Wooden or steel fire towers are set on hilltops where the fire watcher, or ranger, equipped with binoculars, maps, and a direction scale that enables him to ascertain the compass direction of smoke, is linked by telephone and radio with the fire-control base. If a fire can be seen from two or more towers its precise position is quickly pinpointed by mapping the intersection of cross bearings. An alternative method of fire watching, widely used in Canada, is to fly observers in light aircraft continuously over the forest, providing both an incomparable range of view and the ability quickly to approach outbreaks, for close inspection and first-hand radio report.

Once an outbreak of fire is sighted, the critical next step is to rush trained men to the spot to suppress it, which in effect means restricting its spread. Small brush fires—the great majority of all forest fires—are attacked by beating their edges with spades, beaters consisting of flaps of noncombustible material fixed on long handles, or simply the newly cut green branches of trees. Small amounts of water can be carried on backpacks and applied forcefully by hand pumps; to give this limited amount of water maximum effect a chemical derived from plant algae is added, which makes the water adhere to smouldering foliage. Mattocks or spades are used to scrape litter aside, forming barriers of bare earth, while other firebreaks are created by felling belts of trees with axes or power saws. Trained fire crews with such hand equipment can be carried quickly to the fire by truck, or even dropped by parachute.

Motorized fire pumps prove very effective provided they can approach the fire by hard roads and can get access to ample water supplies. The volume of water that can be carried by a fire truck rarely exceeds 2,000 gallons (about 7,600 litres), only enough to quell minor outbreaks. Bulldozers, where available, can rapidly scrape away inflammable litter and build up banks of fireproof bare earth (Figure 4). Aircraft can quickly carry in water bombs consisting of waterproof cardboard containers that burst on impact, but weights are limited and skilled pilotage is needed to land the bombs at effective spots. An alternative developed on Canadian lakes is to fill the floats of a seaplane with water, which is done automatically as it skims the lake on takeoff and to discharge this through escape valves over the fire.

In combatting large fires, an almost military strategy is required. A senior forest officer must coordinate team work, usually by short-wave radio, much as a general in battle. Acting on the basis of aerial observation, he directs operations by phone and radio to all available sources of aid, including associated forests, public fire services, and the armed forces. Big blazes may last for days; plans must be made for reliefs as well as reinforcements, and for food-and-drink supplies, overnight camps, and first aid. Under such planning and control serious casualties are infrequent.

Causes of
fires

Modern organization lessens the risk of the great holocausts of the past, when whole townships went up in smoke with high loss of life. Timber losses also have been held down to a small percentage of the crops at risk, which nevertheless represents a substantial loss. Since nearly all forest fires are man-made, the only significant exceptions being those caused by lightning strikes, a major preventive measure is the education of the public. Main sources of wildfires are smokers, picnic fires, and graziers who light fires to improve spring grazing.

Insect and disease protection and control. When protecting his crops against insect pests and fungal diseases, the forester faces a formidable task. Trees are individually so large that chemical or physical treatments, which might be practicable for smaller plants in gardens, farms, or orchards, become both technically difficult and prohibitively expensive. Trees also grow larger each year, and a treatment applied today fails to reach and save next year's fresh shoots and leaves. With life spans averaging 100 years, for long-delayed harvests of lumber, the cost of annual applications, though acceptable for fruit trees, becomes altogether too high for a crop of forest trees to carry.

Foresters therefore aim, in the long-term, to avoid serious trouble by using only trees known to resist existing insect pests in the regions where they are grown. Strict quarantine measures are applied along many international frontiers to exclude foreign pests and diseases. Typically disasters have arisen where quarantine has failed or has been imposed too late. The American chestnut, *Castanea dentata*, has been virtually wiped out by the chestnut blight fungus, *Endothia parasitica*, which does little harm to related trees in its native China. Elms have suffered severely, both in Europe and in the U.S., from the elm disease fungus, *Ceratocystis ulmi*, which was first detected in the Netherlands and is carried from tree to tree by flying beetles. Minute aphids, probably introduced on living plants from Asia, now make it impossible to raise commercial crops of two conifers once valued in Britain, namely, the white pine, *Pinus strobus*, from New England, and the European silver fir, *Abies alba*, native to Switzerland. Once a quarantine barrier has been crossed, eradication is virtually impossible in the vast, irregular structure of the forest.

Short-term measures to check a sudden plague of insects, or outbreak of fungal disease, are now technically possible through the development of aircraft and insecticidal or fungicidal sprays. They demand exacting advance studies by skilled botanists, entomologists, plant pathologists, and meteorologists to determine the precise stage in each organism's life cycle and the correct weather conditions for spraying to be effective at acceptable cost.

Control of
defoliating
cater-
pillars

Action has most frequently been taken against exceptional outbreaks of defoliating caterpillars, including those of the gypsy moth in the U.S., the nun moth in Central Europe, and the pine looper moth in England. At the time of year when feeding caterpillars are most vulnerable, light aircraft fly across the forest on carefully planned courses, distributing a strong insecticide.

A disadvantage of these blanket treatments by strong chemicals is that they also eliminate parasitic and predatory insects that serve as natural controls on the pest's numbers; they may also adversely affect bird life. It has been maintained that natural control through insectivorous organisms, combined with physical factors like cold winters, provides adequate checks. Occasional drastic interference by man may possibly prove harmful by disrupting the so-called natural balance. In practice, large-scale chemical treatments of forests are infrequent and are restricted to a small proportion of the areas at risk.

Less spectacular preventive measures are commonly taken as routine steps in practical forestry to lessen anticipated losses. Nursery stock, easily reached and handled, may be sprayed with a specific fungicide in the seedbeds, or be dipped in an insecticide prior to planting in the forest. Certain harmful beetles breed below the bark of felled trees; prompt removal of the bark makes this impossible. Alternatively, the early removal of the logs

from the forest to distant sawmills transfers emerging beetles to places where they can do no harm. Stumps of freshly felled conifers can be easily and cheaply treated by brushing on a fungicide to check the white root-rot fungus, *Fomes annosus*. This is a serious agent of decay that spreads from root to root, underground, after gaining entry to the first tree it attacks via the exposed surface of a felled stump.

Every part of a growing tree—root, trunk, bark, leaf, flowers, and seed—is potentially subject to attack by some harmful insect or fungus. Continuing research by entomologists and plant pathologists facilitates effective action in emergencies.

Watershed management. The control of tree cover to safeguard watersheds plays a growing part in forest management, as greater heed is given to the conservation of soil and pure water. Forests provide a permanent and self-perpetuating cover in depth, at low cost. A watershed from which all tree cover is removed has its soil exposed to severe climatic damage.

Single-
stem
harvesting

The guiding principle of management where erosion threatens is therefore the maintenance of continual cover. Ideally, this is achieved by single-stem harvesting. Only one tree is felled at any one point, and the small gap so created is soon closed by the outward growth of its neighbours. This is effective where desirable crop species are available to fill in the gap, by natural regrowth, but it does not permit artificial planting or a change to a more profitable kind of tree. In many protection forests therefore, clear cuttings must be made, but these are kept small and are aligned along hill contours to limit downward movement of soil.

The concept of water balance sets the factors that increase water supply in the woods against those that diminish it. Water arrives as rain, snow, hail, or condensing fog. That which is interrupted by foliage is called interception loss; the remainder is called the throughfall. To this must be added stemflow, the water that is intercepted by the tree canopy and runs down the tree trunks. Evaporation takes place from both foliage and soil and is augmented, and even exceeded, by transpiration of the sap water that roots draw from the soil to support the life of the foliage above.

Water falling on a saturated soil, or conversely on a very dry one, gives immediate runoff to feed streams, which are otherwise fed by percolation through a moist, though unsaturated, soil. Deep forest soils have a high water-storage capacity. Unless they are very porous and freely draining they have a water table or level below which the subsoil is saturated. The depth of this varies seasonally with the water balance. Roots, which need air, cannot exploit soil below the water table. The drainage of land having a high water table usually increases the productivity of the forest and its seasonal water storage capacity, though the amount of water held permanently captive in the soil becomes less.

Despite this uncertain balance of water gain and loss, forests are accepted everywhere by water-supply undertakings as desirable cover. Water release from forested land is gradual and reliable, with the deep porous soil giving storage capacity additional to that of reservoirs. More important, it carries hardly any silt, whereas water running more rapidly off bare land carries sand, clay, and gravel that can silt up reservoirs. Water from forest springs is exceptionally clear and pure, requiring minimum filtration or chemical treatment. Since few people work on the watershed, risks of pollution are low, and the dangers of contamination by agricultural residues, such as dung, chemical fertilizers, and weed killers are far lower than on farm land.

Experiments to compare the water yield of two similar watersheds, one forested and the other unforested, have proved difficult in practice. It is hard to find any two areas that receive identical rainfall, either before or during the course of the experiment, which must extend over many years to cover annual and seasonal variations. It is generally agreed, however, that unforested land sheds water swiftly, causing sudden rises in the rivers below. In contrast, the outflow from forests, though less in total, is gradual, has lower peaks, and is sustained over longer periods. Over a large river system, such as that of the Mississippi, this has definite advantages since it lessens the risk of floods. It also provides conditions more favourable to fishing and navigation than does the less regular outflow from bare land.

Local weather effects The long-standing belief that forests everywhere increase rainfall has not been substantiated by scientific enquiry. Local effects can, however, prove substantial, particularly in semiarid regions where every inch of rain counts. The air above a forest, as contrasted with grassland, remains relatively cool and humid on hot days, so showers are more frequent. Fog belts, such as those found along the Pacific seaboard of North America and around the peaks of the Canary Islands, give significant water yields through the interception of water vapour by tree foliage. The vapour condenses and falls as solid water, in a process described as fog drip.

Recreation and wildlife management. From the earliest times man has looked to the forests for recreation. An old Malayan proverb asserts: "The Almighty does not count, in the reckoning of a man's years, those days that he spends in hunting." Today, when millions of workers are tied to their factory bench or office desk for most of the year, there is great need for the spiritual refreshment and physical exercise that forests can provide.

Animal life of all kinds, from elephants, giraffes, and deer to eagles, pheasants, and birds of paradise, along with rare plants such as jungle lilies, form a main attraction of the woods and oblige the forest manager to deal firmly yet diplomatically with three competing groups of people.

Those who only seek to preserve wild life—the conservationists, biologists, and nature lovers—have grown so numerous that their visits to the haunts of the rarer creatures must sometimes be controlled, lest their sheer numbers drive away the very beast or bird they come to seek. As an extreme instance, in 1962 a special law was passed in Scotland to keep thousands of photographers at a tolerable distance from the nest of a single pair of ospreys, or fish-eating hawks, unique in that country.

A second group comprises neighbouring farmers who want the numbers of animals allowed to remain in the forest restricted to levels that result in little or no damage to their crops and livestock, and in some regions, their lives. Forest-based marauders include deer that devour grain crops, wolves that take sheep, and, in Africa, lions.

The third group consists of the hunters and sportsmen who look to the woods as the resort of game birds and animals.

Obviously the same animal can present a different aspect to each group. A Bengal tiger, for example, provides a biologist with a classic example of a carnivorous beast living in harmony with a jungle environment and restraining its main prey, deer, from undue increase in numbers. But to a village peasant it is a menace to his cows and goats, and a threat to the safety of himself and his family, while a sportsman regards it as a magnificent quarry demanding all his skill.

Protection of wildlife In virtually every country the sporting aspect of woodland wildlife management is controlled, to some degree, by general game laws, which also apply outside the forests. These prescribe licenses for firearms, and the taking of specified birds and beasts; they usually lay down closed seasons during which certain game may not be shot, and also set limits to the sportsman's bag of particularly rare species. In the U.S. a peculiar situation exists whereby the game legislation of the separate states applies unchanged over most publicly owned forests. In other countries the forest managers are in a stronger position, since local game laws are adjusted to their particular requirements.

Within the concept of multiple use, which requires that forests yield timber and water besides protecting soil and providing recreation, enlightened forest managers aim to develop maximum acceptable public usage. Conflicting forms of enjoyment can usually be separated by space, and also by time of day or time of year. Skillful siting of roads, picnic points, car parks, campgrounds, and restaurants ensures that the great majority of visitors congregate in relatively small portions of a large forest. The tourist season falls around midsummer, but the main season for shooting deer or pheasants comes in the fall.

A general practice is to estimate the numbers of people likely to use recreational facilities, both the year round and at peak periods, such as national holidays falling in summer. Such estimates allow for the probability that improvements in facilities will be followed by increased public use. Restrictions to numbers below the possible demand are sometimes inevitable, but never popular, and often both difficult and costly to enforce.

In the U.S. an effective means of controlling entry, and obtaining some revenue to meet upkeep and administration costs, has been found in road tolls and parking charges. The public has become accustomed to these on freeways and in urban surroundings and regards them as reasonable in relation to the numbers of passengers that can be carried in each car. Nevertheless, these charges presuppose a high level of highway upkeep and wages for staff to collect them. In other countries, where there are long traditions, amounting in places to legal rights, of free public access to national and communally owned forests, threaded by minor roads and rights-of-way, this method is not generally applicable. Local bylaws often facilitate control but are not easily enforced over widespread woodlands.

Forests as campsites Camping is a form of woodland recreation that increases in popularity as better equipment, carried or towed by automobiles, is developed. Forests provide ideal campsites, in which large numbers of cars, tents, and caravans can be sheltered, concealed from view, and isolated from each other. The trees and their associated lakes, streams, and hills provide opportunities for walking, fishing, swimming, and nature studies.

Organization is essential, since sites must be allocated, roads and hard standings built, water supplied, and sanitary facilities installed. Fortunately funds for these developments are readily available from camping fees levied on a "pay-as-you-stay" basis.

The interpretation of what visitors see in the forests has become a growing activity of most forest services. Town dwellers often have no immediate appreciation of forest trees, plants, birds and beasts, or of geological and scenic features. Nature trails, guidebooks, signposts, forest-centre museums, and information stations assist visitors who come to learn as well as to enjoy.

WORLDWIDE STATISTICS ON FORESTRY

Detailed statistics on the world's forest wealth are compiled every five years by the Food and Agriculture Organization of the United Nations. They relate to areas of land under forest, volumes of standing timber, annual increases in timber volume, and amounts of timber harvested for use. They also bring out the areas of forest, and the volumes of timber, relative to the number of people living in each country, which may have great significance for human economy.

Areas of forest. Out of the world land area of 13,-333,000,000 hectares, some 4,126,000,000 hectares, or 32%, are classed as forest land. (One hectare is about 2½ acres.) Details are given in Table 1.

Except for Asia and the Pacific, most regions have at least one-quarter of their land surface under forest. South America, North America, and the U.S.S.R. each have over one-third.

When forest areas are related to population, great differences become apparent. The world average of 1.1 hectares per head hides two extremes. Asia and Europe, with teeming peoples on limited land, show only one-third of a hectare per head. North America has 3.4 hectares, but this is exceeded by the U.S.S.R. with 3.8, and South America with no less than 4.9.

Timber volumes. The world as a whole possesses 238,000,000,000 cubic metres of standing timber, made

Table 1: Areas of Forest

area	land area (000,000 hectares)	forest land (000,000 hectares)	percentage of land under forest	forest area per head (hectares)
North America	1,875	750	40	3.4
Central America	272	76	28	0.87
South America	1,760	890	51	4.9
Africa	2,970	710	24	2.1
Europe	471	144	31	0.32
U.S.S.R.	2,144	910	42	3.8
Asia	2,700	550	20	0.27
Pacific Area, including Australia	842	96	11	5.2
Total	13,033	4,126	32	1.1

up of 114,000,000,000 cubic metres of conifers or soft-woods, and 124,000,000,000 cubic metres of nonconifers, mainly broad-leaved trees or hardwoods (one cubic metre is about 1.3 cubic yards).

The annual timber harvest (averaged from 1960 to 1962) comprises some 2,090,000,000 cubic metres (including bark). It therefore amounts to only 1 percent of the standing volume. No reliable world figures are available for annual overall increase in volume, but general experience suggests that it balances losses due to timber harvesting, plus an inevitable "drain" due to fires, diseases, windfalls, and insect attacks.

Details, by regions, after adjusting volumes for bark, are given in Table 2.

Table 2: Annual Timber Harvest

area	standing volume of timber (000,000 cubic metres)	annual timber harvest (000,000 cubic metres)	harvest as percentage of standing volume	harvest per head (cubic metres)
North America	44,000	434	1.00	1.90
Central America	800	47	5.20	0.65
South America	78,000	199	0.25	1.30
Africa	3,800	216	5.00	0.65
Europe	12,000	353	3.00	0.74
U.S.S.R.	79,000	395	0.50	1.60
Asia	17,000	419	2.60	0.21
Pacific area, including Australia	3,800	27	7.00	1.60
total	238,000	2,090	0.90 (average)	0.65

When annual harvests are related to standing volumes, wide regional differences appear. In Europe, where most forests are accessible and all felled timber is used, 3 percent of the growing stock is cut each year. This is made good by annual regrowth, and the forests do not diminish. In North America, South America, and the U.S.S.R., the annual cut does not exceed 1 percent of the standing volume. The remoteness from markets of great expanses of conifer forests in Canada and Siberia, and of tropical jungles in the Amazon basin, explains such low proportions. In these inaccessible forests, far more wood is still lost by fire, decay, and insect attack than is cut by man for his own use.

Despite the development of coal, oil, gas, and electric power, nearly half the wood felled in the world is used as fuel. World fuel wood consumption, mainly in the less industrialized countries, amounts to 990,000,000 cubic metres annually, while industrial uses require 1,100,000,000 cubic metres, giving a total of 2,090,000,000.

World fuel wood consumption

The harvest of timber per head of the population is highest in North America, at 1.9 cubic metres per person annually, or three times the world average. The comparable figure for the U.S.S.R. is 1.6 cubic metres, but the European average is only 0.74 cubic metre. In Asia only 0.21 cubic metre of timber is harvested each year, for each inhabitant. Though these differences are adjusted to some degree by international trade, it is true to say that the forest-rich countries maintain a higher living standard than those poor in timber resources. The systematic harvesting of well-stocked forests ensures ample fuel, sawmill timber, pulpwood for the paper and

packaging industries, and raw material for many manufacturing industries.

BIBLIOGRAPHY. Forestry textbooks usually deal with one specialized aspect of the science, often in one geographic region; tree species and their native habitats vary widely. A. REHDER, *Manual of Cultivated Trees and Shrubs, Hardy in North America*, 2nd rev. ed. (1940), is a thorough regional botanical survey treating both cultivated and wild species. W. DALLIMORE and A.B. JACKSON, *A Handbook of Coniferae and Ginkgoaceae*, 4th ed. rev. (1966), gives world-wide botanical details for these major natural orders. P.W. RICHARDS, *The Tropical Rain Forest* (1952), describes the make-up of natural tree and plant associations, comprised of many species that thrive together.

The theory and practice of raising and tending tree crops are treated in such silviculture manuals as J.W. TOUMEY and F.S. KORSTIAN, *Foundations of Silviculture*, 2nd ed. rev. (1947, reprinted 1962); and F.S. BAKER, *Principles of Silviculture* (1950), discussing temperate-zone forests. Details of handling seed and young stock are comprehensively treated in J.W. TOUMEY and F.S. KORSTIAN, *Seeding and Planting in the Practice of Forestry*, 3rd ed. (1942, reprinted 1960); and in the UNITED STATES DEPARTMENT OF AGRICULTURE, *Woody-Plant Seed Manual* (1948). The care of tree crops in tropical jungles of both hemispheres is outlined in the FOOD AND AGRICULTURE ORGANIZATION, *Tropical Silviculture* (1958). A wide range of Asiatic conditions are discussed in H.G. CHAMPION and A.L. GRIFFITH, *Manual of General Silviculture for India* rev. ed. (1948); and R.S. TROUP, *Silviculture of Indian Trees* (1921), an exceptionally thorough and well-illustrated work.

Forest protection is treated in specialized textbooks discussing specific hazards. K.P. DAVIS, *Forest Fire: Control and Use* (1959), outlines fire perils, precautions, and combat. J.S. BOYCE, *Forest Pathology*, 3rd ed. (1961); and T.R. PEACE, *Pathology of Trees and Shrubs* (1962), give specific details of fungal diseases, climatic dangers, and airborne fume and salt damage. Insect pests of North American trees are described by R.F. ANDERSON, *Forest and Shade Tree Entomology* (1960); and those native to Europe by R.N. CHRYSTAL, *Insects of the British Woodlands* (1937).

Basic principles of tree felling and timber haulage are covered in N.C. BROWN, *Logging* (1949); and A.E. WACKERMAN et al., *Harvesting Timber Crops*, 2nd ed. (1966). Methods and machines evolve so rapidly that recent issues of a trade periodical, such as *World Wood* (monthly), should be consulted for current practice and equipment.

Principles of forest management, worldwide in application, are systematically outlined by D.R. JOHNSTON, A.J. GRAYSON, and R.T. BRADLEY, *Forest Planning* (1967). The requisite basis of factual survey is detailed by S.H. SPURR, *Forest Inventory* (1952); and B. HUSCH, *Forest Mensuration and Statistics* (1963). Financial implications for a particular region are given in A.C. WORRELL, *Economics of American Forestry* (1959). The leading international source of forest area and timber output statistics is the FOOD AND AGRICULTURE ORGANIZATION, *World Forest Inventory* (1963). Fundamental studies of physical bases of forest distribution and yield include: S. HADEN-GUEST (ed.), *A World Geography of Forest Resources* (1956); and S.S. PATERSON, *The Forest Area of the World and its Potential Productivity* (1956).

(H.L.E.)

Forests

The forest is a complex ecological system dominated by trees, which form a buffer for the earth against the full impact of the sun, wind, and precipitation. Whatever the type of forest—whether evergreen or deciduous, temperate or tropical—the trees that constitute it provide special environments, which in turn affect the kinds of plants and animals that can live within the forest.

THE ENVIRONMENTAL SETTING

Climate. Forests can develop wherever there is an average temperature greater than 10° C (50° F) in the warmest months and an annual rainfall in excess of 200 millimetres (about eight inches). Above these limits there exists an infinite variety of tree species grouped into a number of stable forest types determined by the particular conditions of the environment. Boundaries between these types are difficult to determine precisely, but the major forest communities can be linked to broad latitudinal zones (see Figure 1).

Physical factors affecting forests

The forests of the high latitude subpolar regions constitute the taiga and are dominated by stands of such coni-

Figure 1: (Top left) Tropical rain forest in New Guinea, showing the discontinuous
character of the upper tree stratum. (Top right) Northern coniferous forest in Nova Scotia,
of red spruce. (Bottom left) Moist temperate coniferous forest in California, of redwood.
(Bottom right) Temperate deciduous hardwood forest in Tennessee, of tulip tree, or yellow
poplar, red and sugar maples, sycamore, and American beech.
(Top left) Eric Lindgren—Ardea Photographics, (top right) Ken Brate—Photo Researchers,
(bottom left) A.C. Shelton—Publix, (bottom right) Grant Heilman

fers as pines (*Pinus*), spruces (*Picea*), and larches (*Larix*).
Taiga forests are found only in the Northern Hemisphere, where winters are long, with six months of the
year showing an average maximum temperature of less
than 0° C (32° F), there is a growing season of one to
three months, and precipitation varies between 250 millimetres (about ten inches) and 500 millimetres (20 inches),
evenly distributed throughout the year. Broad-leaved
trees predominate in the middle latitudes, where there are
six months with an average maximum temperature above
10° C (50° F), precipitation in excess of 400 millimetres
(about 16 inches), and a growing season of between 100
and 200 days. Broad-leaved deciduous forests occupy the
cooler regions and are dominated by associations of several species including oaks (*Quercus*), beeches (*Fagus*),
birches (*Betula*), aspens (*Populus*), elms (*Ulmus*), and
maples (*Acer*).

Mixed forests form a transition between the coniferous
taiga and the deciduous broad-leaved forest. Further
south, as frost becomes infrequent, the composition again
changes, and a temperate rain forest of evergreen broad-
leaved species develops. In the Southern Hemisphere the
forest type contains conifers similar to the true pines:
Kauri pine (*Agathis*), Chile pine (*Araucaria*), and white
pine (*Podocarpus*). As rainfall becomes more seasonally
distributed a scrublike forest of stunted trees develops,
typical of the Mediterranean maquis, the Californian
chaparral, and the Australian mallee. The natural vegetation of the lowland tropical latitudes is the tropical rain
forest, dominated by a rich variety of broad-leaved evergreens adapted to hot and humid conditions. Outside the
humid tropical zone, where temperatures remain high but
rainfall becomes more seasonal, the broad-leaved forest
becomes less varied and more deciduous as it yields to
the parklike savanna and then to dry thorn forest.

Precipitation and temperature play important roles in
the determination of forest type. The combined effect
controls the amount of soil water available for tree
growth. Water is lost from the forest by evaporation from
the tree crowns and by transpiration from the leaves,
both processes in large measure controlled by air temperature. In the middle latitudes an annual precipitation
of between 200 and 500 millimetres (eight to 20 inches)
concentrated in the summer months, when the evaporation power of the air is high, supports a scrublike
drought-resistant forest formation; the same precipitation, evenly distributed throughout the year, can support
a rich broad-leaved deciduous forest.

Determi-
nation of
forest type

The principal influence of sunlight is on the air temperature. At high latitudes the sun's rays strike the earth at a larger angle and therefore give less heat than at low latitudes. More solar energy is available in the tropics, where solar rays strike the earth more directly; as a consequence, tropical forests can be expected to be more productive than temperate forests. The difference is, however, not so great as might be anticipated because of the higher rate of respiration in the tropical environment. Another influence of solar radiation is through the day length (photoperiodism), which varies according to the season and affects flowering, bud opening, and a range of other physiological activities.

Topography and soil. Topography is also an important influence on forest vegetation; an increase of 300 metres (1,000 feet) in altitude is equivalent to a movement of 480 kilometres (300 miles) closer to the pole at sea level, so that a broad correlation can be drawn between montane forests and those at higher latitudes. Exact duplication of forest type is not expected, however, since the montane environment differs in important respects from that at an equivalent lowland station; notably, it has a shorter day length, greater precipitation, and higher maximum temperatures. The altitude at which the lowland forest passes into an Alpine type depends chiefly on the length of the growing season and the frequency of frosts. The zonation of forest types with increasing altitude is seen in the sub-Alpine forest formations of the middle latitudes and the montane forests of the tropics. In the middle latitudes the sub-Alpine forest is dominated by the more tolerant conifers (pines and larches), with poorly formed deciduous broad-leaved species (beeches, birches, and willows) occupying the tree line, the upper limit. In the tropics altitudinal zonation rises from the rain forest through a transition zone to a mossy forest of reduced stature, but featuring a profuse development of air plants (epiphytes), lichens, and mosses. The final stage is the development of a broad-leaved elfin forest, so called because the trees are stunted, high on tropical mountains.

Another important physical influence on forest type is the soil. The most important feature is soil depth, because this not only determines the capacity of the tree roots to reach for water and nutrients but also determines the stability of the trees. Forest soil shows considerable variability, but common features are depth, relative infertility, an undisturbed condition, a large quantity of woody perennial roots and characteristic plant and animal life. Quick-draining, highly stratified, sandy soils (podzols) are characteristic of the taiga. Brown forest soils, which are richer in nutrients, less porous, and less stratified than podzols, are characteristic of deciduous broad-leaved forests. Tropical rain forests and savanna woodlands have deep, intensely weathered clayey soils, rich in aluminum or iron, which gives them their reddish or yellowish colour. Variation in soil type may be considerable even in small areas, as for example in regions subject to past glaciation; this variation is often reflected in species preference. In the mixed broad-leaved–conifer forests of the middle latitudes, the conifers are usually found in poorer sandy soils of low alkalinity, whereas the broad-leaved trees are found on richer clayey soils.

Wind and fire. Wind plays a primary role in the creation of the forest, by assisting in pollination and seed dispersal, but has only a secondary role in its maintenance. Air movement affects transpiration and may be a significant ecological factor in determining some forest types; *e.g.*, in West Africa the dry harmattan wind reduces humidity to a very small value for short periods and is believed thereby to affect species distribution. Violent winds destroy forests either by uprooting or breaking stems; prevailing winds affect tree growth by producing eccentric stems and deformed crowns. Prominent among the physical destructive agents in the forest is fire, which usually results from man's encroachment. Infrequent natural fires arising from lightning may be responsible for the development of stable fire forest types, such as Douglas fir (*Pseudotsuga menziesii*) stands in North America and the savannas of Africa.

THE BIOTIC COMPONENT

Forests are distinguished from each other primarily by their composition. The number and variety of species present in the forest community depends upon the age and density of the tree cover, the type of climate and soil, and the geological history of the region. The richest forests in terms of total species composition are those having older and more open stands of trees, situated in favourable climates, and on fertile soils that have been relatively undisturbed in recent geological time. Thus within a given forest community there exists a complex interaction between the vegetation and the environment, which leads to the development of micro-environments with a wide variety of physical properties.

Plant stratification and its influence on the forest environment. The forest community shows an extensive vertical stratification, from the tops of the tallest trees to the tips of the deepest roots. The effect on the stratification above ground is to moderate climatic extremes progressively downward from the treetops to the soil surface.

The pattern of vertical stratification varies with forest type (see Figure 2). The conifer-dominated forest has the

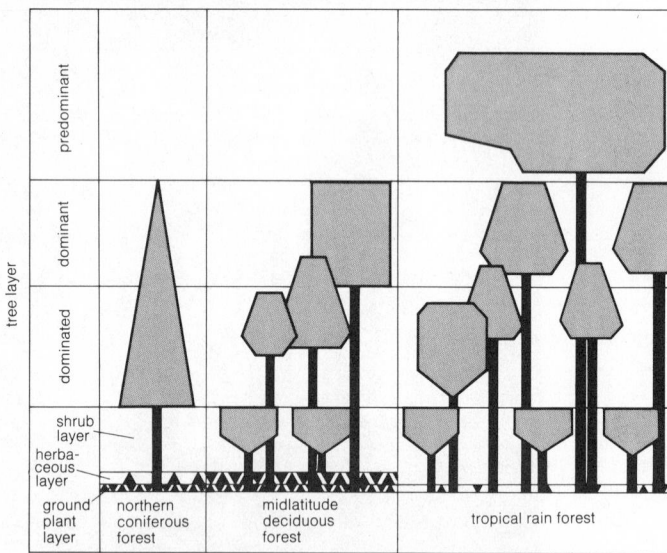

Figure 2: Vertical stratification in different forest types (tree size not to scale).

simplest structure: the tree layer is continuous up to 30 metres (98 feet) high, the shrub layer is absent or spotty, the field layer of herbaceous plants is best developed in more southerly forests, and the ground layer of liverworts, mosses, and lichens is almost uniform, particularly in the northerly forests. In the deciduous broad-leaved forests stratification becomes more complex. The continuous canopy of trees is between ten and 30 metres (33–98 feet) tall but is subdivided into distinct upper and lower stories, in addition to the shrub field and ground layers. In the tropical rain forest stratification is even more complex, with at least three canopy layers—a discontinuous uneven top layer, a level midlayer of continuous canopy (30–40 metres), and a spotty layer of shorter trees (15–20 metres) with narrow crowns. The field layer is rich in ferns that approach treelike proportions but also contains islands of herbaceous plants, which form an insignificant proportion of the total number of individuals.

Considerable lateral variability exists within each layer, or stratum, resulting from local differences in environmental conditions. Forests thus provide a great range of habitats for both other plants and animals. The most important physical factors influenced by forest structure are air temperature, precipitation, and soil characteristics; of secondary importance are sunlight and wind.

The forest environment exercises a moderating influence on air temperature, which is especially marked at the extremes of the temperature range. The forest is cooler in summer and warmer in winter, when compared with surrounding areas.

Forest soils

Richness of habitats in forests

The effect is most marked where seasonal temperature variation is greatest; *i.e.*, the further removed from the Equator the greater the effect. In the tropics, seasonal climatic variation is conditioned more by rainfall than by temperature, and, although the forest environment reduces average maximum temperatures in the wet season more than in the dry season, there is little effect on minimum temperatures.

The ameliorating effect of the forest on air temperature results from the vertical stratification of the forest vegetation. Seasonal influences are less marked as the canopy cover decreases; thus winter temperatures are little influenced in the leafless deciduous forest, although in the summer the same forest, in full leaf, shows not only differences in temperature compared with outside conditions but also a temperature gradient within the various strata of the forest. Daily fluctuations of temperature within the forest also depend upon the nature of the vertical stratification. In the single-storied temperate conifer forest, temperatures are highest nearest the tree crowns. At night, heat is radiated from the crowns and the surrounding air is cooled, increases in density, and sinks to the ground. Subcanopy temperatures are therefore lower than canopy temperatures. During the day the temperature gradient is broadened; the crowns of the tree are warmed by the sun, but at the same time shade the subcanopy region. As the canopy structure becomes more complex, more than one form of daily fluctuation in temperature can exist. In the tropics the luxuriant development of the lower tree strata may impede air movement so that at night the upper canopy may lose heat faster than the cooled night air falls. In such conditions the subcanopy at night may be warmer than the upper canopy, whereas during the day the temperature gradient is reversed. Forest vegetation also has a marked effect on soil **Forest soils** temperature. Forest soils are cooler in the day and warmer at night and show less seasonal fluctuation than similar soils outside the forest.

As precipitation falls on the forest, its movement is greatly influenced by the forest cover. The dense tree layer initially intercepts precipitation, some of which is immediately evaporated back to the atmosphere. Conifers tend to hold more water than broad-leaved trees (there is, of course, little or no interception from dormant leafless trees). Water penetrates to the soil from the canopy either through stem flow down the main trunks and thence into the soil along the root channels, or by direct absorption in the litter of the forest floor. In either case the velocity of the fall is reduced, there is little soil compaction or surface runoff and consequently a reduced risk of soil erosion. Compared with stations outside the forest, the moisture content of forest soil, particularly at the surface, tends to be high. Water is lost through surface evaporation, which is low in the forest because of the ameliorating effect of the tree cover, and by transpiration, which is high and may be a limiting factor in tree growth. The water budget for the forest will vary greatly with type and situation, but the ability of the forest cover to reduce erosion and to even out the yearly fluctuations of stream flow are recognized advantages to water catchment areas. Although there is no evidence that forest conditions affect the amount of precipitation, the forest atmosphere is always more humid than surrounding areas.

The forest floor consists of a layer of organic matter **Types of** overlying mineral soil. In the temperate regions two ma- **organic** jor types of organic matter predominate, the mull and the **matter** mor. The mull is associated with broad-leaved deciduous forests, especially those growing on relatively rich soils. It is less acid than the mor type, of a granular structure, and contains a considerable admixture of mineral soil. There is an indistinct boundary with the upper horizons, due to the activity of earthworms moving freely between the decomposed layer of litter and the mineral soil. Mor humus, on the other hand, is strongly acidic and of a matted structure (attributed to the network of fine roots). There is a distinct boundary between mor humus and mineral soil, with little evidence of the activity of mixing agents. The earthworm population is smaller, although fungal activity may be greater, than in mull. Mor is char-

acteristic of the northern coniferous zone and is especially evident under pines growing on mineral-poor soil, although some broad-leaved species, especially oaks (*Quercus*) and beeches (*Fagus*) produce a mor humus when growing on similar soils. The differences between mull and mor are generally attributed to differences in the chemical composition of the plant material from which they are derived and the nature of the mineral soil, rather than to the rate of decomposition. Tropical soils, however, are affected by the rate of decomposition. Persistently high temperatures and humid conditions accelerate decomposition of organic matter, releasing minerals rapidly. Occasionally in swampy conditions where acidic groundwater percolates laterally, and in conditions of heavy, regular rainfall, a thick peat, made up almost entirely of woody plant debris, may build up.

The forest structure produces less spectacular, though equally important changes in wind speed and solar radiation. Dense multistoried forests are most effective in reducing overall wind velocity in the subcanopy layers. The filtering of the various tree strata also affects solar radiation. A tropical rain forest typically allows not more than 1 percent of visible light to reach the forest floor, a conifer forest 10 percent, and a deciduous forest about 5 percent when in leaf but between 50 and 90 percent when leafless. Forests in full canopy approach the maximum possible efficiency in their utilization of solar energy: 60–90 percent is absorbed, and the remainder is reradiated and used up by evaporation and transpiration. In qualita- **Quality of** tive terms the light values within the forest vary since the **light** canopy vegetation absorbs more red than blue light. Blue **absorbed** light is, however, utilized at subcanopy and low-canopy levels and is said to reduce the tendency toward side branching, a possible explanation for the observation that understory trees are generally pyramidal but adopt a rounded crown when they achieve upper story height. In their youth some trees, such as oak and pine, require much sunlight, whereas others, spruce, firs, beech, and many tropical hardwoods, almost demand shade.

As indicated earlier, stratification within the forest supplies a wide variety of habitats for both plants and animals and provides the opportunity for considerable interaction between organisms.

The role of decomposer organisms. The fungi of the litter and mineral soil layers play an important role in the chain of litter decomposition and the release of nutrients in the soil. Some species live in a mutually beneficial partnership (mycorrhiza) with active tree roots, thus improving the efficiency of nutrient uptake by the trees. On the other hand, some species are parasitic and may cause devastation; *e.g.*, the chestnut blight, which has decimated the population of native chestnut in North America, and the blister rust, which is a serious pest of white pine (*Pinus strobus*). The fungus *Fomes annosus* attacks a number of conifer species; it is transmitted from tree to tree not only by spore infection via cut wood surfaces but also by root contact. Some higher plants are also parasitic; *e.g.*, the European mistletoe, and its North American counterpart, cause stem and crown deformation. Among the animals, the insects are the most mobile in the forest. They are also the most numerous and the most highly adapted as to feeding habits. Insects are an important link in the food chain between vegetation and higher animals, particularly birds. Many tree species have flowers adapted to insect pollination, the range is wide from simple nectar-rich flowers to highly structured pollination mechanisms. Insects are often highly specialized in their feeding habits; of 20 species known to occur on white pine, five are leaf feeders, three are bud feeders, three are twig feeders, two are wood borers, and two are root borers. Species preference is also noticeable; of 43 species of British weevils whose larvae feed on scots pine, oaks, and birches, all except one attacks only one species of tree. Insect damage to forests reaches disaster proportions **Serious** only when populations break through the natural control **insect** barriers; *e.g.*, the periodic defoliation of balsam fir by the **damage** spruce budworm is triggered by several summers of clear, dry weather, which favours a rapid increase in the insect population. Insects also are known carriers of the viral, bacterial, and fungal diseases of trees. As a proportion of the total insect population, however, the serious forest pests are small in number and localized in their influence.

Forest animals and their adaptations. Larger forest animals are likewise especially adapted to their environment. Sharpness of sight and smell are apparently not as useful as a sense of hearing in the forest habitat, and most gregarious animals, including birds and monkeys, are noisy in contrast to the animals of open country. The value of flying and running is also reduced, and true forest birds are poor flyers but good climbers. Movement on the ground is restricted; but elephants and the larger swines, massive in proportion to their height, can push their way through vegetation; and deer and antelope, slender and lithe, can thread their way through the forest. Specialist adaptations include those that enable the animal to move through the dense canopy layers; sharp claws (as on woodpeckers, squirrels, martens); gripping feet or prehensile tails (as on South American monkeys, porcupines, anteaters, marsupials); and parachute-like skin extensions (as on flying lizards, flying squirrels and *Rhacophorus* frogs). The tree frogs of the tropics have become so adapted to the tree crown as to have abandoned ground life almost completely. Some animals, such as birds of prey, wolves, foxes, and stags, use the forest only for shelter. Although the forest is a sheltered and ameliorated environment, food is scarce and populations are relatively low.

Each forest type has its distinctive animal life. In the deciduous broad-leaved forests snails and slugs are more numerous than in the conifer forest, a reflection of the difference in the quality and quantity of the herb layer. In temperate zones forest birds distribute seeds and insects pollinate. In the tropical rain forest, fruit bats assist in both pollination and seed dispersal.

Animal damage rarely reaches catastrophic proportions in the forest, but local damage from grazing and browsing can result in bark stripping of young trees.

SEASONAL CHANGE

The forest community changes with the seasons. Superimposed on these changes are the daily rhythms of daylight and darkness; of these effects, the length of daylight, or photoperiod, is an important component of seasonal change, or aspection. The stimulus of these changes is environmental and as a consequence is most marked in regions where temperature, precipitation, and day length are seasonally variable. The responses of organisms to periodic changes in the environment have evolved over a long period of time to parallel the external environmental conditions (see PERIODICITY, BIOLOGICAL).

Aspection is also influenced by latitude, altitude, and rainfall distribution. At high latitudes the winters are prolonged, snow and frost occurring for as long as six to eight months continuously; the spring and autumn periods are very short, and the growing season may be as short as three months. (Seasonal changes in the Southern Hemisphere are the reverse of those in the Northern Hemisphere.) Longer, cooler periods are associated with increasing altitude and are reflected in the forest composition even within the tropics. The seasonal changes in forest communities at high elevation are similar to those closely related communities at lower elevation but higher latitudes. Finally, aspection is affected by moisture availability; thus at the margins of the tropical forest belt and in Mediterranean climates, the resting period for many plants, presaged by leaf fall in deciduous species, results from a seasonal lack of moisture rather than from decreasing air temperature and decreasing day length.

In the middle latitudes of the temperate zone, characterized by the deciduous broad-leaved forest belt, six phases of the seasonal cycle are recognized. In this region aspection is most strongly evident, and the phases correlate climatic conditions with the outward appearance of the tree cover. In the early spring, or prevernal period, the hardy species and the lower storied trees bud and bloom as air temperatures and day length increase. In the upper stories, bud break is delayed, but the sap rises from the roots to the crown. The late spring, or vernal period, sees

Forest rhythms (margin note)

soil temperatures rise with air temperatures and day length reach its maximum value. As the leaves expand, shoot growth accelerates; the transpiration rate becomes more rapid as the leaves mature and as moisture in the soil becomes more readily available. At this period the vegetation is most vulnerable to frost damage. The next two periods, aestival (estival) and serotinal periods, cover early summer and midsummer, when conditions for growth are optimal. Air and soil temperatures reach their maximum, the full-storied structure of the forest is operative, and the metabolic rate is at its highest. During this period, moisture availability becomes the critical, or limiting, factor to growth; high temperatures combined with extremely dry conditions may induce a lowering of the metabolism of the tree, characterized by premature aging of leaves and a slowing down of plant activity. The autumnal period is characterized by falling air temperatures, decreasing day length, and the advent of frosts. These changes induce a gradual reduction of metabolic activity and defoliation of deciduous vegetation. Finally, the winter, or hiemal period, is characterized by low daily maximum temperatures, heavy frosts, precipitation in the form of snow, and short day lengths. During this season the trees enter a dormant stage in which metabolic activity is diminished to the minimum level necessary for survival.

Seasonal change is least marked in the higher latitudes of the temperate zone, characterized by the coniferous belt of forests. Here the species mixture is limited and simple in physiognomy, and although the conifers are evergreen, water loss through transpiration is considerably reduced as water becomes less available from the freezing soil. The evergreen habit does enable the maximum use to be made of the short growing season and conifers are particularly well adapted to a wide range of rigorous environments. The understory plants, mosses, ferns, lichens, and grasses show no spectacular seasonal changes, and the trees themselves change little in appearance with the passage of the seasons, except for the deciduous species such as the larches. Even in the species-rich coniferous zones of western North America and in Asia, aspection is not well marked in the tree cover, although breaks in the canopy reveal herb and shrub layers that show the same periodic changes that are seen typically in the broad-leaved forest.

One common feature of the extratropical forest regions is the periodic activity of the tree growth. The growing tips (meristems) in the buds, which are responsible for height growth and crown development, are most active in the spring. The lateral, or cambial, meristem, which is responsible for increase in the diameter of the tree trunk, also is most active in the spring, slowing down in the autumn and ceasing activity in the winter. All temperate trees show an annual ring structure, roughly indicative of age, resulting from the episodic nature of this cambial activity.

Periodic growth (margin note)

The essential difference in periodicity between the forest of the tropics and that of other climates is the behaviour of the different species, different individuals of the same species, and, in some cases, different parts of the same plant. Periodicity often is apparently unrelated to environmental conditions and is certainly very much less synchronized; within the tropical zone, however, the more seasonal the climate, particularly the rainfall distribution, the greater becomes the synchronization with the periodicity of the climate. Where marked dry periods occur in the wet evergreen forest, there is a marked tendency to produce new foliage at the beginning of the wet season, whereas flowering tends to occur in the dry period. Elsewhere new foliage is not always produced in response to an external stimulus, and in nearly all species leaves are produced in periodic flushes so that several generations of leaves may be found on the same tree at any given time. Meristematic activity is, however, episodic, although not annual. As in the trees of other regions, growth of the shoots is accompanied by the expansion of the buds. Well-marked growth rings often occur in the timber of the tropical rain forest trees, and in the truly deciduous species they coincide with a definite

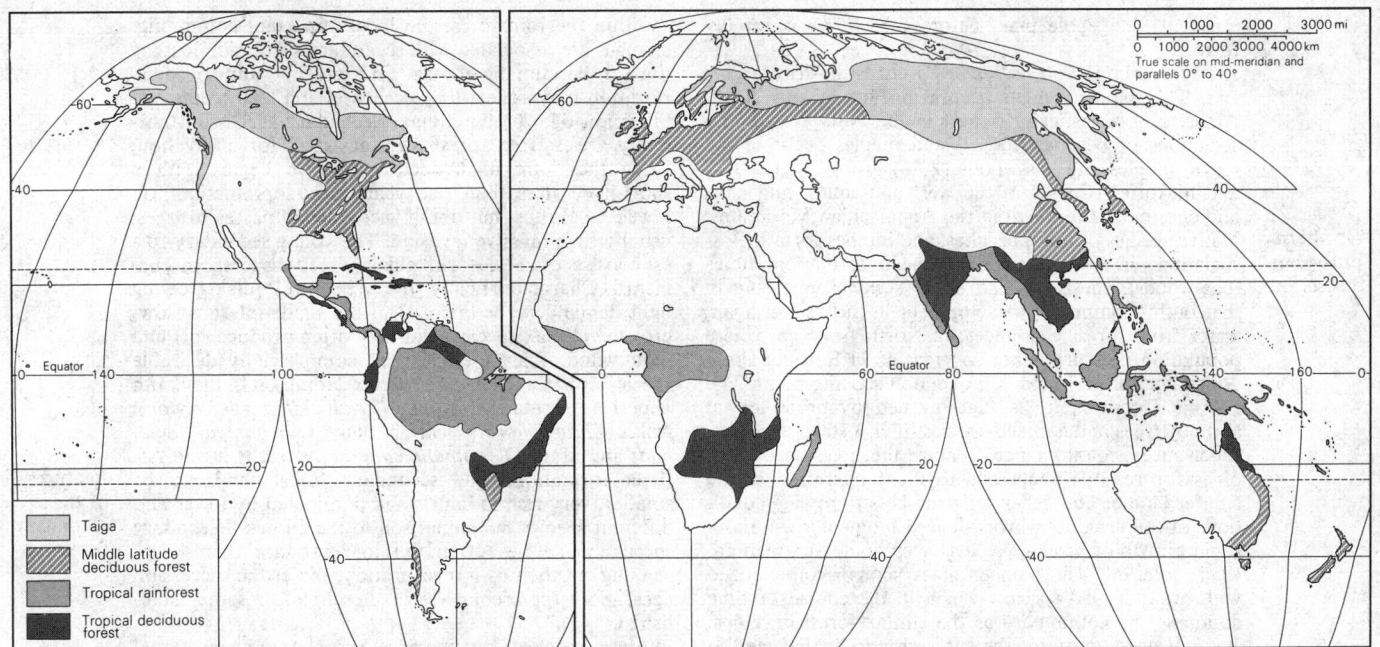

Figure 3: World distribution of major forest biomes.
Adapted from *Biological Sciences Curriculum Study Green Version High School Biology*, 2nd ed.; Chicago: Rand McNally & Co., 1968

Taiga

Middle latitude deciduous forest

Tropical rainforest

Tropical deciduous forest

Seasonal flowering

interruption of the cambial activity. As with the production of foliage, there is considerable variation both between and within species, which results in considerable diversity in the structure of the wood. Seasonal flowering is more strongly in evidence in the upper stories of the forest, probably due to the influence of slight changes in average temperature rather than in light periods. Of special interest in the tropical rain forest are those plants that cluster together and flower at the same time, the best known being species of bamboo that flower at long intervals and die after the ripening of the fruit. This habit of flowering is attributed to the necessity of particular weather conditions operating on fully developed but unopened buds.

COMMUNITY DEVELOPMENT

Forest communities represent the terminal aggregation of species in a series of associations that may have begun from primary succession—*i.e.*, colonization of bare mineral oil, exposed rock surfaces, volcanic ash, or sand dunes—or from secondary succession, in which the substrate had first been occupied by a community that, because of a catastrophic event (*e.g.*, wind devastation, fire, or man's intervention), has since been destroyed. Although successional changes may vary considerably between these two major avenues of development, the time span in each case is quite long, and the biological interactions between the various plant and animal components are rather complex. Each recognizable stage in the development of a stable, or climax, community is known as a sere. Climax forest communities, because they usually represent the terminal point of seral development, are grouped together in more or less climatically controlled geographic groupings identified as forest biomes (see Figure 3).

Coniferous forests. *Taiga.* The circumpolar high-latitude forests of the Northern Hemisphere are dominated by pines (*Pinus*), spruces (*Picea*), firs (*Abies*), and larches (*Larix*). The Eurasian and North American formations are very similar in structure, and in both the species composition changes from east to west of the formation. Important eastern formations in Europe are the native stands of Siberian pine (*Pinus sibirica*), Siberian fir (*Abies sibirica*), and Siberian and Dahurian larches (*Larix russica* and *L. gmelini*); in North America white spruce (*Picea glauca*) and balsam fir (*Abies balsamea*) are the eastern dominants. In western Europe Scots pine (*Pinus sylvestris*) and Norway spruce (*Picea abies*) ab-

solutely predominate; in western North America lodgepole pine (*Pinus contorta* var. *murrayana*) and Alpine fir (*Abies lasiocarpa*) are among the important species in the area.

The taiga forests, especially in the almost pure strands, have been exploited on a very large scale from the mid-19th century on. On cleared areas, on catastrophic burns, or whenever adequate precautions to ensure conifer regeneration are not taken, secondary succession begins. Dominated initially by herbaceous cover, the succession soon contains deciduous broad-leaved trees, especially birches (*Betula*) and aspens (*Populus*), prolific seed bearers, whose seeds are wind dispersed and of a high germination capacity. Willows (*Salix*) and alders (*Alnus*) are also early arrivals in the hardwood stage of succession. Scots pine in Europe and jack pine (*Pinus banksiana*) in North America produce the advanced succession stage. Final reversion to the climax forest is achieved after a considerable time interval through the ability of the conifer species to regenerate and grow under the shade of the canopy. In addition, conifers tend to grow taller than the broad-leaved species when in direct competition and eventually shade them out. Broad-leaved species occur in the taiga in locally induced biotic climaxes, and are common on the latitudinal and altitudinal margins of the biome.

Moist-temperate conifer forest. Forests of this distinctive type occur along the western seaboard of North America from Alaska to California and inland to the Rocky Mountains. Here conditions are very humid and a high proportion of the precipitation occurs as mist. Species domination shifts from Sitka spruce (*Picea sitchensis*) in Alaska through the western red cedar (*Thuja plicata*)–western hemlock (*Tsuga heterophylla*) association in British Columbia to Douglas fir (*Pseudotsuga menziesii*) and finally the coast redwood (*Sequoia sempervirens*). Because of the high humidity a rich understory development, especially of mosses and other moisture-loving plants, is a feature of this forest formation. The trees are massive, and they constitute the richest commercial forest in the world. As in the taiga, secondary succession features the pioneer broad-leaved species, especially the alders (*Alnus*), and in the south, maples (*Acer*). Where the humid conditions are maintained only under continuous conifer cover, oaks (*Quercus*) infiltrate late in the succession from the neighbouring transition to the Californian chaparral. Primary succession from the coast tends to be dominated by pioneer pine species,

Exploitation and recovery of the taiga

especially lodgepole pine, before the climax is rapidly formed.

Middle-latitude forests. *Deciduous broad-leaved forests.* This biome, which occurs in Europe and North America, is floristically richest in the New World. Associations of beeches (*Fagus*) and maples occur in the north, maples and basswoods (*Tilia*) in the centre, oaks and hickories (*Carya*) in the west and south, and oaks and chestnuts (*Castanea*) in the Appalachian Mountains.

Northern European forests

Native species of oaks, beeches, and birches form the associations in the northern European formation, limes (basswoods), chestnuts, and elms (*Ulmus*) appearing in the south. Community development in this region again arises from forest clearances; in North America, where population pressure is not so great as in Europe, abandoned agricultural land is a common starting point. The grassland community is first invaded by broad-leaved shrubby trees and a mixed-species thicket stage develops. Later successional changes feature the invasion of jack pines for reasons analagous to those operating in the conifer biome. The richer soils and better growing conditions of the deciduous broad-leaved biome allow a more rapid growth of broad-leaved species, some of which are shade tolerant. The pioneer pines soon become mixed with broad-leaved species, which in the course of time dominate the community as the climax forest develops. It is not uncommon for the succession to be deflected to a conifer climax by either regular burning or grazing. The pine barrens of southeastern North America, dominated by several pine species, are an example of such a climax.

Evergreen broad-leaved forests. This formation occurs both north and south of the Equator on the eastern seaboards of continental land masses. The cooler temperate formation is found in the Southern Hemisphere; in New Zealand, southern so-called false beeches (*Nothofagus*) dominate. Although evergreen, the formation has much in common with the deciduous broad-leaved forest of the north. In the warm temperate forests of the Southern Hemisphere, the beeches are joined by the southern conifers: Kauri pine (*Agathis australis*) and *Podocarpus* species in New Zealand, and *Araucaria* species in Chile. Particularly in the warmer regions secondary succession is complex and very slow. Pure strands of southern beeches develop especially on the more exposed hillsides. The southern conifers are very slow growing and are susceptible to grazing damage; once removed they are unlikely to regain their place in the community. *Nothofagus* species are very susceptible to grazing damage; recovery is difficult, and often the forest reverts to a thick grassy turf.

Tropical forest. The variety within the forest community reaches its zenith in the tropical rain forests, which occupy low-altitude areas near the Equator. Rainfall exceeds 2,000 millimetres (about 79 inches) a year and is evenly distributed with either one or two short, dry seasons of rainfall 150 millimetres (six inches) or less per month. The largest continuous rain forests occur in the Amazon and Orinoco river basins of South America. Less extensive are the rain forests on the Central American isthmus, in the Congo, Niger, and Zambezi basins of Africa, in Madagascar, and in the East Indies. The variation in temperature between winter and summer is less than that between night and day, and the suddenness and force of rain showers are unknown in other biomes. Although vegetative composition varies between geographic regions, the forest presents a remarkably uniform appearance. The trees are tall, evergreen, often shallow rooted and significantly buttressed at the base. There is a profusion of climbing plants, especially woody vines, or lianes, and air plants, or epiphytes. The profusion of vegetation within the canopy zones obscures this highly structured biome. There is perhaps a greater variety of trees in a few acres of tropical rain forest than in the entire vegetation of Europe. This richness of species is matched in the animal life as well; *e.g.*, in a six-square-mile area of the Panama Canal Zone, 20,000 insect species have been recorded. For a more complete description of this biome see JUNGLES AND RAIN FORESTS.

Largest rain forests

Within the rain forest the most important community changes are associated with secondary succession leading toward the climatic climax. Fire, grazing, and soil deterioration may deflect the succession and lead to the stabilization of a biotic climax. Secondary succession normally arises from forest clearings used for cultivation; when these are abandoned succession begins with a short-lived (less than one year) weed domination followed by shrubs, but dominance quickly passes to trees, usually by a massive invasion. The young secondary forest consists of species with efficient seed-dispersal mechanisms. Characteristically the trees are quick-growing light demanders, as opposed to the shade-tolerant slow-growing climax species, and they often produce soft and light wood. They include such commercially desirable species as balsa (*Ochroma species*), common in the South American formation; obeche (*Triplochiton scleroxylon*); iroko (*Chlorophora exsela*); okoume (*Aucoumea klaineana*) and afara (*Terminalia superba*), present in the African formation. The secondary forest tends to be smaller, very rich in lianes, and dominated by fewer and different species in comparison to the climax. Secondary succession species often fail to reproduce themselves, shading out their own regeneration, and as the succession ages, more representatives of the climax become established.

Features of the secondary forest

Forest ecotones. At the edge of forests are transitional woodland formations called forest ecotones; four types have been chosen for description. In tropical latitudes the savanna and thorn forest ecotones are intermediate formations between the rain forest and semi-arid desert. In the middle latitudes the sclerophyllous forest ecotone is a prominent formation. The final example, the mangrove swamp forest, is an ecotone between an aquatic biome and the forest.

Savannas. Savannas lie between the tropical rain forest and semidesert vegetation in a broad latitudinal zone between 5° and 20° N and S of the Equator. The dominant vegetation is an open parklike tree cover over dense, tufted and often tall grass. The climate is tropical and semihumid, with summer rain and a long dry season. Precipitation varies between 600 millimetres (about 23 inches) and 1,500 millimetres (about 59 inches); at the lower range of rainfall the savanna passes into thorn scrub, whereas at the upper limit the savanna grades into semi-evergreen or mixed deciduous forest. The savanna occurs extensively in Africa, both north and south of the Equator, covering most of the East African highlands. In South America the savannas of Venezuela and Brazil are separated by the Amazon forests. In Australia savannas are found between the forests of the wet coastal regions and the deserts of the interior. In all localities the savanna offers a unique environment for large animals, many of which, such as the zebras and giraffes of Africa, are particularly adapted to the open woodland and some, like the carnivores, to sparse woodland conditions. The environment is especially prone to fire, and it is probable that large areas of savanna are stabilized by fire. Annual burning is a common practice in Africa, and the savanna vegetation is subject to severe selection; only species resistant to periodic fires can maintain themselves. If burning is abandoned, increase in woody plant development takes place.

The dominant tree species of the savanna are typically deciduous, shedding their leaves during the dry season; they have a gnarled, Y-shaped form, branching a few feet above the ground and spreading out to an umbrella-shaped crown. In Africa, outside the influence of the savanna-closed forest margins, the *miombo* (*Brachystegia–Isoberlinia*) woodland grades into an *Acacia* formation as drought conditions increase. This formation includes also elephant grass (*Pennisetum species*) mixed with other tussock grasses of the genera *Imperata*, *Andropogan*, and *Hyparrhenia*. At their most luxuriant they are often more than 3.6 metres (12 feet) tall at the end of the growing season; their stature diminishes as conditions become drier, until, under the *Acacia* species at the border of the semi-arid desert and thorn forest, they give way to species of *Aristida*.

Savanna trees

Table 1: Gross and Net Production of Forest Communities					
forest	location	gross production (tons/ha/yr)	net production (tons/ha/yr)	respiration loss (tons/ha/yr)	respiration as a percentage of gross production
Tropical lowland	Ivory Coast	52.5	13.4	39.4	75
Tropical rain forest	South Thailand	77.4	28.5	48.9	63
Distyium racemosum	South Kyushu	73.1	21.6	52.4	72
Abies sachalinensis	East Hokkaido	47.7	21.4	26.4	55
Fagus sylvatica	Denmark	23.5	13.5	10.0	43

Source: J.R.N. Black, "The Utilisation of Solar Energy by Forests," *Physiology in Forestry, Society of Foresters of Great Britain, Rept 6th Discussion Meeting* (1966).

Thorn forests. The thorn forest is stabilized by the climate over most of its area, although occasionally it is maintained by grazing or burning. It is found on the equatorial margins of subtropical and tropical semideserts, where rainfall in a two to four month summer season rarely exceeds 700 millimetres (about 27 inches). The forest resembles the savanna woodland but is somewhat shorter in stature; the ground layer is confined to sparse arid-adapted grasses but is richer than its savanna neighbour in understory woody species. The vegetation is markedly adapted to dry conditions, the trees being deciduous or if evergreen, with leaves protected against drying; the branches often bear thorns as protection against grazing animals. Cacti and other spiney succulents appear in the ground layers and understory. The common dominant trees are native species of *Acacia*, which appear in the South American, African, and Australasian formations, in the last case displacing the *Eucalyptus species* of the savanna. In the Asian formation, *Acacia catechu* is associated with *Tectona hamiltoniana*, a deciduous nonthorny species. Like the tree species of the savanna, the thorn forest dominants are very deep rooted, competing most successfully on soils where water penetrates deeply and quickly.

Sclerophyllous woodlands. This formation, with trees rarely exceeding four metres (about 13 feet), occurs in the middle latitudes of summer drought and winter rainfall. It is typified by a warm, dry climate, as in parts of the Mediterranean, southwestern U.S., Australia, South Africa, and Chile. Characteristically the formation is

Dominance of broadleaved species

dominated by evergreen broad-leaved species; but occasionally, as in the Mediterranean formation, there is an admixture of coniferous species. Oaks are dominant in the Northern Hemisphere; in the southern counterpart, *Eucalyptus* species dominate in Australia, and elsewhere a range of uniquely characteristic genera are drawn from many families. Arid tolerant, woody, and often fire-resistant evergreen species are present in the understory. Herbaceous vegetation is normally restricted to grasses. Probably this formation is stable only where the annual rainfall is less than 300 millimetres; it is, however, maintained elsewhere in areas of higher rainfall by grazing and by burning particularly. The sclerophyllous woodlands finally fade into arid or desert conditions in all but the Mediterranean formation.

Mangrove swamp forests. Coastal mud flats throughout the tropics carry a vegetation of mangrove swamp and are particularly luxuriant in the wet tropics, where the rain forest is the stable formation. Mangroves are evergreen trees and shrubs that share similar habitat preferences and a similar appearance. Their common features include a tolerance of brackish water, the development of "breathing roots," and a marked tendency to germinate their seeds on the tree. These features enable the mangroves to pioneer the water environment and to dominate the subsequent secondary succession.

The pioneer species develops from seedlings that float out to sea and become established on shoals and sandbanks. Tiers of prop roots develop and, as groups of seedlings become established, sedimentation and the accumulation of debris builds up the soil level. A mature community develops in which the mangrove pioneer, up

to nine metres (about 30 feet) tall, is dominant. Other salt-tolerant species gradually become established, especially in associations subject to periodic flooding. The soil level continues to be raised by the accumulation of litter until it is no longer washed by water and the climax vegetation species begin to be established. In the Florida formation, *Rhizophora mangle* is the pioneer behind which develops an association in which *Avicennia nitida* is dominant. Next, the *Conocarpus* transition association of semimangrove species forms, and finally the climax rain forest develops. More complex successions are found in the Malaysian succession. Other variants include the stagnation of the succession at a mature mangrove association stage, or the development of a freshwater swamp forest rather than a climax rain forest.

PRODUCTIVITY OF FORESTS

Quantitative estimates for the productivity of forest communities are scare and unreliable. Among the reasons for these conditions are the complexity of the forest community, the longevity of tree species, and the lack of historical records of routine weight data. Moreover, there are three levels of production that might be measured. Gross, or primary, productivity is the quantity of organic matter created by photosynthesis. From this value the energy used in respiration is subtracted to give the net production, which is measured as the dry matter, or dry weight of the total community. A third measure is the merchantable production, which is the dry weight of the usable tree stems only and is calculated by multiplying the stem volume by the basic density of the wood. Although volume figures are available for most of the species under regular forest management, this measure cannot be regarded as an estimate of total production; even for a single tree it represents less than 70 percent of the total dry weight, the unmerchantable stem (1–6 percent), stump (10–18 percent), green branches and foliage (10–20 percent) making up the remainder. For a complete evaluation of forest productivity, both the vegetation and the animal life need to be measured, a task that is overwhelming in magnitude. The difficulties of measuring even the dry weight of the total plant community present extreme sampling difficulties. Much of the data available are concerned with the plant biomass (net production), and often only for the tree component. The magnitude of the loss of gross production through respiration is illustrated in Table 1, although direct comparisons are dubious since the age and stand composition is not specified.

The three levels of production

Forests are the most efficient of all terrestrial communities in the production and storage of organic matter. A very high proportion of the sunlight that falls on the forest is absorbed; the canopy provides a large area of chlorophyll-bearing tissue dispersed through a considerable volume of air for the absorption of carbon dioxide, and tree roots exploit a considerable volume of soil for water and nutrients. The three essential prerequisites for efficient photosynthesis are, therefore, effectively fulfilled, and as a consequence the forest system capitalizes on the production of organic matter. Additionally, the forest community operates efficiently through time, although forests of evergreen conifers are more efficient

Table 2: Plane Biomass of Woodlands
(units over dry weight 1000 kg/ha)

	Pinus nigra	Pinus sylvestris	Betula verrucosa	Quercus borealis	Picea abies	Nothofagus truncata	Pseudotsuga menziesii	Evergreen Gallery
Location	North-east Scotland	East England	Moscow U.S.S.R.	Minnesota U.S.A.	Sweden	New Zealand	Washington State U.S.A.	Thailand
Status	Plantation	Plantation	Natural	Natural	Natural	Natural	Natural	Natural
Age of tree in years	48	55	67	57	58	110	52	...
Tree height in metres	14	16	26	17	17	21	17	29
Number of trees/ha	1,112	760	...	800	924	490	1,157	16,209
Tree leaves	5.6	7.2	2.8	3.5	9.1	2.7	12.0	19.0
Tree branches	11.2	12.3	11.3	49.5	14.3	42.0	17.9	50.0
Tree trunks	95.1	96.7	156.7	111.9	85.3	224.8	174.8	225.2
Shrubs and herbs	7.0	2.6	2.0*	0.6	1.0*	0*	0.1	0.2
Roots	34.0	34.1	43.1	15.0	60.0*	39.2	12.3	88.5
Dead branches on trees	10.0	10.0	2.0*	21.9	2.6	1.1	11.2	...
Organic matter on ground	22.0	45.0	3.0	36.7	78.0	16.7	117.3	3.0
Total	184.9	207.9	220.9	239.1	250.2	326.5	345.6	385.9

*Estimates from other similar woodlands.
Source: J.D. Ovington, *Woodlands* (1965).

than deciduous broad-leaved forests in total as well as tree biomass production. Systematic studies of the changes in the rate of organic matter production through the life of the forest are lacking, but the data available from reforestation programs indicate that the tree component increases slowly as the canopy closes, maximizing at the point of greatest competition between trees, and thereafter falling as trees are removed or die. The contribution of the ground layer is most marked at the youngest and oldest ages of the crop—*i.e.*, when the canopy is open. Complementary data on the dry weight of foliage confirms this pattern, and it is probable that the number of stems per unit area (stand density) is as important as geographical location for both the weight of foliage and the total biomass produced. Within a given geographic region there are considerable differences between tree species in their rate of organic matter accumulation. Various estimates of timber production indicate that conifer stands usually are more productive than deciduous tree stands. Despite the lack of comprehensive data, the biomass production from the forest community is impressive (Table 2).

BIBLIOGRAPHY. M. BUSGEN, *Bau und Leben unserer Waldbäume* (1897; Eng. trans., *The Structure and Life of Forest Trees*, 3rd ed. rev. and enl. by E. MUNCH, 1929), a classic work on the structure and habit of forest tree growth, especially relevant to temperate European regions; S. GUEST-HADEN, J.K. WRIGHT, and E.M. TECLAFF (eds.), *A World Geography of Forest Resources* (1956), a well-illustrated compendium of information, largely on the commercial use of forests; J. KITTREDGE, *Forest Influences* (1948), a standard reference on climatic influences and soil and water relationships, especially in America; H.J. LUTZ and R.F. CHANDLER, *Forest Soils* (1946), a standard text on forest soil formation, especially relevant to America; J.D. OVINGTON, "Quantitative Ecology and the Woodland Ecosystem Concept," *Advances in Ecological Research*, 1:103–183 (1962), an excellent literature review, covering over 200 articles relevant to woodland productivity; and *Woodlands* (1966), an elementary but authoritative treatment of world forest types, with many illustrations; A. PAVARI, "Forest Influences," *F.A.O. For. Forest Prod. Stud.*, no. 15 (1962), a useful compilation of widely dispersed information; V.N. SUKACHEV and N.V. DYLIS, *Fundamentals of Biogeocoenology* (1968; pub. orig. in Russian, 1964), a study of forest biomes, especially relevant to Russian conditions.

(G.K.E.)

Form and Function, Biological

There is a tendency in modern biology to explain the behaviour of living things directly in terms of physics and chemistry, suggesting that biological form and function can finally be understood wholly in the interaction of atoms and molecules. Living structure, however, presents peculiar problems, for even at its lowest level it is both like and unlike nonliving constructs. Although both begin with the same atomic building blocks, and many of the interchanges of atomic particles in chemical reactions are identical, the stuff of life differs fundamentally from lifeless matter. Nonliving structure is marked by regular repetition of its atomic disposition,

which is a highly probable state. Living matter is remarkable in the irregularity of arrangement of its atoms, for example, in the genetic complex, and in the repetition of this arrangement in successive generations, a highly improbable condition. Hence biostructure tends at almost the lowest level to escape the statistical structure of physics. Living structure is distinctly nonrandom, whereas nonliving structure is wholly random. It is this intriguing uniqueness of the biological device that must be examined first, before probing it with the instruments of physics. An important concept in biology is thus the endurance of order, as distinct from the universe, where entropy and reduction to randomness prevail. The overall trend of evolution has been toward an increase in this peculiar kind of orderliness. The first goal of biology, however, is to understand the living organism. In the view of life presented here, the living entity is a homeostat, a seeker of regularity, distinct from its environment but peculiarly coupled with it. The goals that this homeostatic device seeks in the environment make up its behaviour, which persistently keeps the organism hovering about the peak of the orderly state. The crux of the evolutionary process is that the living order has a way to keep building into itself unique devices that ensure ever more probable persistence of order. This view of evolution indicates, in part, the peculiar coupling noted above. Nonrandom replication of genetic structure, random mutation and recombination, and nonrandom natural selection together yield adaptation, which makes each kind of organism able to persist in a particular kind of environment. It is at the level of adaptation that the mechanics of biological form and function become most clearly meaningful.

Structure may be defined as the observable organization that is explicit in the course of a flow of energy. Structure and behaviour are but moieties of an entity, the total adaptation of the organism to its environment. Although biomechanics tends to stress the movable parts that perform overt behaviour, in higher (more orderly) organisms the inseparable structure that makes movements meaningful is the nervous system. This is the selector that decides, on the basis of instinct and remembered learning, the course by which the most effective return to the steady state can be made.

From this total adaptation the permeating influence of form–function emerges in the continuum from atom to organism. The information immanent in the structure of the gene serves evolution, which is long-term homeostasis; that of the nervous system serves the organism, which is short-term homeostasis. In its interactions with the environment, the organism must obey the laws of physics through all aspects of its structure. Biomechanics, the study of biological form from the functional viewpoint, is an examination of the principles of engineering design as implemented in living organisms.

BASIC MECHANICS

The structure of any working device must embody two mechanical features. It must, first, be able to maintain

Interpretation of data from reforestation

its own structural integrity when outside forces act upon it, and, second, it must perform its specific functional movements. The structural properties that enable it to meet these two requirements are dictated by several types of mechanical forces.

Newton's laws of motion. Because living constructs are well within the intermediate zone in size—neither atomic nor astronomic—the laws of classical mechanics are entirely applicable to their motion. Certain of these, especially the laws of motion established by Isaac Newton, are fundamental to the understanding of biomechanics. Newton's first law states that an object at rest will remain at rest, and an object in motion will maintain that motion, unless acted upon by some force. The second law states that, when a constant force is applied, the object will accelerate at a rate proportional to the force divided by the object's mass. The energy imparted by the force causes the object to accelerate in the direction of the applied force. Newton's third law, perhaps the most central to the structure of living organisms and nonliving machines, states that, when one body exerts a force upon another, it receives an equal and opposite force.

Static forces. Even a stable or nonmoving structure may be subject to forces. For the purposes of analysis, three basic types of force may be recognized in terms of their effect on a mass: compression, tension, and shearing. Each of these is really a pair of forces. A single force may be defined in terms of magnitude and direction, together called the vector of force. If the mass is stationary, the sum of force vectors acting upon it must be zero. Simple compression consists of a pair of forces, acting in opposite directions along the same line and directed toward each other, tending to squeeze or shorten the object on which they act. Tension is the opposite; the forces are directed away from the object and tend to lengthen it. Shearing forces are opposite and parallel but in different planes, tending to slide one portion of the object along the adjacent portion, tearing it.

When force is applied to a body, two phenomena may be noted: stress and strain. Stress is the resistance among the molecules of the body to the distorting effect of the outside force. If a weight is suspended by a wire, there is tension along the wire, parallel to the axis, and the tensile stress is the resistance of the molecules measured on either side of an arbitrary cross section. Strain is the change in linear dimension (*i.e.*, the distortion) of the object as the forces act on it. The tension upon the wire supporting the weight will cause the wire to elongate while under tension; the strain is the ratio between the change in length and the original length, usually expressed as a percentage. The property of elasticity causes an object to return to its original dimension when the force is removed.

Simple machines. Basic machines, which transmit and modify forces, are common to both living and nonliving systems and are usually considered to include the lever, the inclined plane, the wedge, the screw, the wheel, and the pulley. The six may be reduced to two basic devices: the lever and the inclined plane. The wheel is simply a rigidly linked, continuous set of levers pivoting around a single terminal fulcrum (the axle) and the pulley merely a modified wheel. The wedge is a double inclined plane and the screw an inclined plane wrapped around a rod.

The lever Of these devices, the most important in biological systems is the lever. The wheel, of course, is impossible, since complete rotation of a part would tear the connections with the rest of the organism, destroying its organic unity. Although the principles of the lever are well-known, its biological implications are often overlooked. Every organism attached to, resting on, or moving on a surface and every projecting part of an organism, particularly a rigid extension, such as a leg or a branch, is subject to forces that act upon it as they would upon a simple lever. In its simplest form a lever consists of a straight bar with a fixed pivot point, the fulcrum, and two forces, one of which is usually considered applied; the other is the load. The magnitudes of the two forces are inversely related to their respective distances

from the fulcrum, and their effective directions are at right angles to the lever. Because of the inequality of the two forces, the difference between them in magnitude and direction must be borne by the fulcrum. In dynamic terms, the work (force multiplied by the displacement of the point of application) of the lever system must also balance. The distances through which the applied force and load move are directly proportional to their distances from the fulcrum.

The human forearm, when bent at a right angle, provides an excellent example of a relatively simple lever system, if the weight of the arm itself is ignored and the biceps muscle (musculus biceps brachii) is considered the sole muscle bending the arm. The elbow joint is the fulcrum. The upward force of the biceps is applied about one-sixth of the way from the elbow to the palm, which bears the load. A ten-kilogram weight held in the hand thus requires six times that force, or 60 kilograms of tensile force, by the biceps. If the arm is stationary, the elbow must provide 50 kilograms of downward force to balance the upward forces applied to the forearm. The 60 kilograms of tension in the muscle and the 50 kilograms of compression in the upper arm are transmitted to the shoulder, the difference of ten kilograms (downward) being passed to the body and thence to the ground as extra weight of the individual.

As applied in living or nonliving systems, the principles of leverage are never as simple as described above. The lever must have thickness and mass (weight) and must be attached to a firm base. The thickness of the bar may be viewed as a second lever, lying at a right angle to the first and pivoting about the same point. A force applied at right angles to the bar is transmitted to this secondary lever by the molecular adhesion of the material and lies at right angles to the short lever, taking the form of tension or compression along the bar. If the bar is horizontal and cantilevered (anchored at one end to a vertical surface) and the force a downward one (assuming for simplicity that the bar is weightless) applied at the tip, the tension in the top of the bar at any point along its

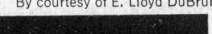
By courtesy of E. Lloyd DuBrul

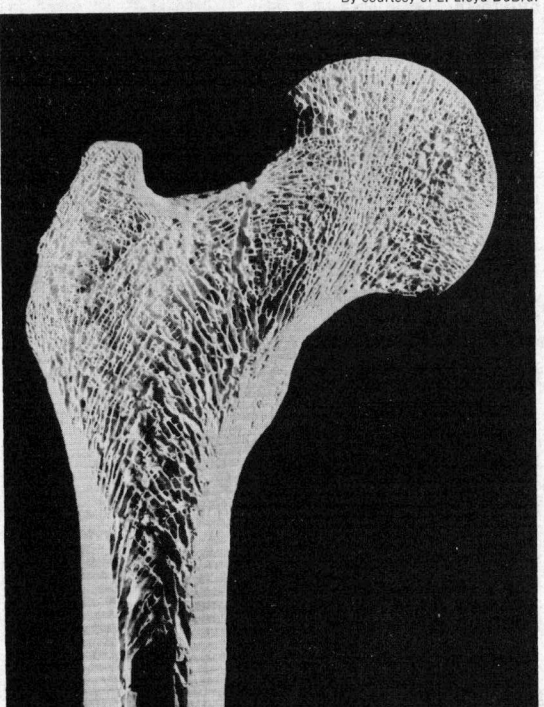

Figure 1: Internal strutting in the head of the human femur (thighbone).

length is directly proportional to the distance of the point from the tip. The lower surface of the bar will be subject to compression, in the same relationship to the applied force as the tension on the upper surface.

The application of force to the bar results in the familiar form of distortion known as bending; the bending stress is greatest at the point of attachment. Failure of a structural member usually occurs at the point where the particular force (tension, compression, or shearing) exceeds the breaking point of the material. A cantilevered bar under downward force often fails initially at the base of the upper surface, the location where the tension is greatest.

The bending limits of a bar may be increased by strengthening the region under greatest stress, by adding structural material, or by using material with greater tensile strength. This is usually achieved by lightening the centre of the beam, where the stress is less. In the pelican and the New World vulture the upper and lower walls of tubular wing bones are thicker than the lateral walls, and internal compressive stresses are borne by a series of struts, like those of many man-made girders. Human leg bones (Figure 1) also have internal struts.

The tree trunk as a lever The trunks of trees, particularly tall, straight ones, demonstrate several aspects of lever dynamics. The wind resistance of the leaves and small branches provides an enormous horizontal force, applied at a distance from the effective fulcrum, the base of the root system. Each cross section of the trunk must transmit downward the bending forces applied above it; the forces increase progressively toward the ground. The thicker base of the tapering trunk provides additional strength where needed, resulting in controlled bending. The bending of the trunk and deflection of the leaves result in reducing the applied force of the wind. The roots, extending downward and outward from the base of the trunk, provide moment arms that distribute the force to the soil. The weakest point in the system—*i.e.*, the junction of stem and roots—is sometimes strengthened by high, thin buttresses that provide both tension and compression braces (Figure 2).

Bipedal organisms, such as man and birds, must use the toes as levers to maintain stability on level surfaces. Without adhesion to the surface, toes can transmit only compressive forces and provide no resistance to a force tipping the animal backward. In both cases, stability is improved by rearward extensions—the hind toes of birds and the heel of man.

An important adaptation to bending forces is the evolution of tubular rather than solid structures in circumstances in which economy of material or lightness is of greater importance than compactness. Because the stress-bearing material is located further from the axis of the lever, a tube is substantially stronger than a rod of the same weight. A possible disadvantage is that the tube must always be of greater diameter than a rod of the same strength, but this disadvantage is often outweighed by the advantages of the tube as a conductor of liquids (*e.g.*, in vascular plants) or as a form of armour to protect vulnerable soft parts (as in arthropods, such as insects and crustaceans). The advantages have led to the evolution of tubular limb bones in terrestrial mammals and, especially, in birds.

LIMITS ON BODY SIZE

The upper limit. A structural system works dependably only within a limited range of size. The upper and lower limits of body size are often imposed by requirements determined by the ratio of body mass to area. If the proportions and composition of the organism remain constant, the mass (essentially, the weight), which is governed by the volume, varies with the cube of linear dimension. A twofold increase in linear size results in an eightfold increase in volume; a threefold increase in linear dimension results in a 27-fold increase in volume. The surface and cross-sectional areas of the organism, however, vary with the square of the linear dimension. Stresses are usually expressed in terms of force per unit of area, but the force itself is expressed in units of mass (*i.e.*, weight). The strength of a structural material is expressed in terms of the force required for breaking under tension, compression, or shearing, expressed in terms of force per unit area.

The ratio of surface (or cross section) to volume has a profound effect upon the supportive structures of plants

Figure 2: (Top) The silk-cotton tree (*Ceiba pentandra*), the expansive buttress roots of which function as lateral supports for its massive canopy. (Bottom) Close-up of the roots.
Walter H. Hodge

and animals. A sphere hanging by a wire exerts a tension on the wire that may be given as the mass of the sphere (in grams or pounds) divided by the cross-sectional area of the wire (in square millimetres or square inches). If the linear dimensions of sphere and wire are increased by the same multiples, the volume of the sphere, growing with the cube of linear change, will soon outstrip the cross section of the wire and exceed its breaking point. Thus, as the diameter of the sphere increases, that of the wire must increase at a proportionately greater rate to give effective support.

The evolutionary response to the area–volume problem is never quite as simple as a mere increase in the diameter of the supporting member, for the latter is subject to more complex forces than simple tension and compression, and the body dimensions seldom have evolved through simple proportional increases. There are, however, groups of animals, exhibiting the same basic body plan but differing sizes, in which the effects of the area–volume ratio may be seen. The legs of mammals, for example, are subject to compression stresses; those of a small antelope are extremely slender, those of a horse proportionately thicker, and those of a rhinoceros or an elephant enormously thicker. If the size of the animal were increased further, the supporting pillars (especially the long bones of the legs) would have to become so broad that they would ultimately touch, and the animal would be immobilized. In fact, practical immobility would be reached long before that point because of the limitations imposed by other factors, such as the need for increased muscle volumes, heat dissipation, and nutrition. Clearly, the modern elephants approach the upper limits for land size. Whales, supported by buoyancy, which distributes the compressive force over a broad area, attain considerably larger size, but the huge extinct reptiles, such as the dinosaurs *Brontosaurus* and *Diplodocus*, relied on the increased area of support provided by their massive tails.

Size limitations of flying animals

The problem of surface-to-volume ratios also imposes an upper limit on the size of flying animals. In such forms, as in fixed-wing aircraft, a critical factor in merely remaining aloft is wing loading, the ratio of total weight to wing area, usually expressed in terms of grams per square centimetre (gm/cm²; one gram per square centimetre equals 2.05 pounds per square foot). The allowable wing loading is dependent upon airfoil shape, wing shape, and airspeed, but the body plan of birds is limited by their genetic heritage. In general, large birds have sacrificed the propulsive power of the wing to attain airfoils and wing shapes capable of higher loadings. Despite appearances, the ruby-throated hummingbird (*Archilochus colubris*), with relatively short, narrow wings, has a much lower wing loading (0.15 gram per square centimetre) than the golden eagle (*Aquila chrysaetos*) whose long, broad wings are able to provide it with a loading no lower than about 0.9 gram per square centimetre. To be able to obtain functional wing loadings at all, birds have had to undergo great evolutionary changes from the ancestral reptile. The total skeleton has been altered, especially by the fusion of parts, and lightened through the use of an elaborate series of air sacs, extensions of those in the body. The bones are mostly thin-walled tubes, sometimes delicately strutted within. The pectoral and pelvic girdles, providing structural bases for the wings and legs, respectively, are arranged to provide maximum strength with economy of bone. The air sacs of the body allow it to be relatively large, so that the massive flight muscles can be long enough to operate at an efficient percentage of contraction. The feathers, which provide a light covering for the body and strong supportive surfaces for the wings, are hollow structures composed of the protein keratin.

In the lower range of size, the efficiency of the wing is less critical, some organisms managing to fly passively on updrafts of air without any real organs of flight. Newly hatched spiders can travel notable distances in wind, supported by wisps of web spun for that purpose.

Numerous plants achieve wind-borne dispersal merely by slowing the descent of their seeds to the ground, thus providing time for the wind to carry them considerable distances. The seeds may be provided with numerous fine hairs that catch the wind (for example, the seeds of thistles, *Cirsium*, and milkweeds, *Asclepias*), or they may have wings. Among the most striking of the latter type are the seeds of maples (*Acer*), which may be called airscrew flyers. The seed is carried in a streamlined spheroidal capsule that extends laterally into a single, eccentric wing in the form of a wide blade with a blunt leading edge, thinning to a fine trailing edge. Rigidity is achieved by a series of closely packed struts that lie parallel and close to the leading edge and turn toward the trailing edge at regular intervals, providing reinforcement in two directions. In falling from the tree, the seed rotates around the centre of the capsule because of the eccentricity of the vane, and the rotation provides lift, slowing the fall. This device does not carry as far as the downy seeds of the thistles, but it carries a larger seed.

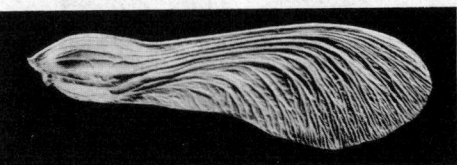

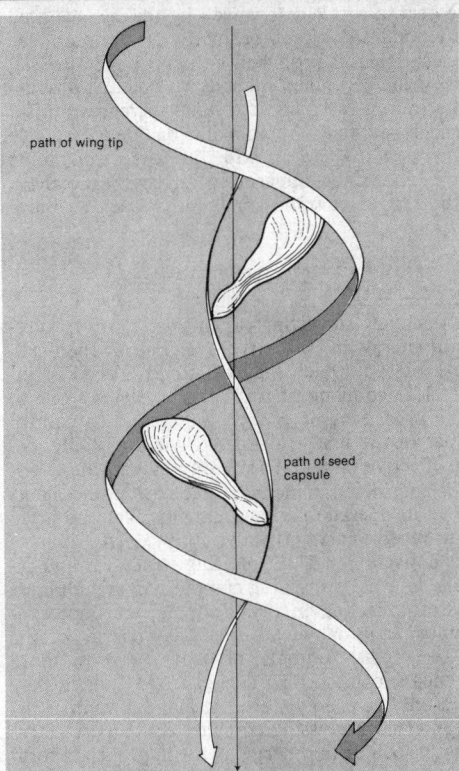

Figure 3: *Adaptation of maple seed for flight.*
(Top) Maple seed (*Acer*). (Bottom) Paths of seed pod and wing tip in descending seed.
By courtesy of (top) W. Winn; (bottom) from *Structure, Form and Movement* by Heinrich Hertel © 1966 by Litton Educational Publishing Inc. Reprinted by permission of Van Nostrand Reinhold Company

Aeronautical engineers have determined experimentally that, considering the weight, vane area, and speed of fall, this form of airscrew functions about 1.2 times as efficiently as the best designed windmill.

The lower limit. The lower limit of effective size of organisms can never approach the realm of atomic sizes. An analogy may be made to a torsion balance, which measures minute forces. The essential parts of this balance consist of two spheres attached to the ends of a slim, horizontal rod, which is suspended at its centre by a fine wire. A horizontal force, applied to either sphere, causes the rod to rotate around the axis of the wire, twisting the wire slightly. The magnitude of movement provides a measurement of the applied force. In order to measure progressively smaller forces, the size of the instrument must be decreased. At a certain point, however, the spheres and wire begin to move in the absence of any outside forces; the machine's components have become so small that the random movements of their own molecules have emerged. At this point the system has become too small to operate with mechanical reliability.

Like the torsion balance, the retina of the eye is an instrument that measures minute forces, in this case the energies of certain light waves. The retina is composed of small receptor cells, called rods and cones, that transduce (convert to neural signals), then transmit the information contained in light energy. The smallest object that can be seen with the best light microscope contains millions of molecules, indicating that the photoreceptor cells seen microscopically are comparatively large, containing countless clumps of atoms. This quantity is so great that the random movements of the individual atoms cancel one another, thereby yielding a smooth

The lower limit for light receptors

mean neural signal. If this were not so, and the photo-receptor cells were small enough to record signals of individual atoms, the brain would be forever filled with flashes and the person would see nothing.

Surface-to-volume ratios may also impose a lower limit of size for some organisms or limit the distribution of small organisms. Warm-blooded animals (mammals and birds) lose heat at a rate determined by the surface area of the body, modified, of course, by the insulation of the body covering. Heat is produced largely by metabolism, the amount being dependent on body volume. As size decreases, the ratio of surface to volume increases until a point is reached at which the animal is unable to produce heat fast enough to keep up with the loss through the skin. This phenomenon apparently imposes a northern limit on the ranges of some small birds, such as hummingbirds.

THE INCORPORATION OF SIMPLE MECHANISMS INTO COMPLEX SYSTEMS

Complex machines and living organisms transform certain types of energy into other types (*e.g.*, heat, chemical, or kinetic), some of which may be stored. To do so involves the close coupling of two major systems—one to manage the processing of energy, the second to control the activities of the first—in order to yield a stable, coordinated, effective output. The energy-management system may be considered to include three basic components which reflect its operational requirements. First, an input device must receive energy from various external sources by various collecting and transporting structures and direct it to the internal processing complex. In green plants the means of collecting energy is simple; the photosynthetic pigment chlorophyll absorbs solar energy of the needed wavelengths. Animals, of course, possess more elaborate means of absorbing energy (food), which they can take in only as energy stored in plant or animal tissues. The internal processing complex contains selective devices that distribute the energy, in the appropriate form and amount, to each of various output devices. Both plants and animals handle energy internally in the form of chemical energy in organic molecules. These are physically transported within the organism by some form of directed vascular system. The various output devices utilize the energy provided them for the performance of their individual functions. In plants the output functions include primary tissue growth (of the type appropriate to the part of the plant and to the season), some movements, and reproduction. The output functions of animals include all forms of observable behaviour, tissue growth and repair, physiological activity, and reproduction. In both groups of organisms, some output functions serve to ensure energy input; others serve to channel residues or waste to the exterior of the organism.

The control of energy-management systems

The control system serves to monitor continuously the operation of the energy-management system. Cybernetics is the science of control systems. Its principles are as valid in the behaviour of man himself as in that of his machines. It is based on two major propositions: energy changes contain information, and this information is continually recycled within the system. These cycles or reflected loops introduce the concept of feedback, which is the central feature of control. Two kinds of feedback are possible, negative or positive. Negative feedback counteracts deviation in output. Hence, for a device to perform a predetermined pattern of motion, any difference between pattern and performance is fed back as a new input of corrective information to bring the movement toward coincidence with the pattern. The value of positive feedback is less obvious. It is the reverse of the previous process; that is, it is deviation-reinforcing rather than homeokinetic. It is seen in the "fight or flight" behaviour of an animal faced with a serious survival situation. Positive feedback is also involved in evolutionary processes and apparently has been operating strongly in the later phases of human evolution, thus speeding up the process.

The feeding mechanism of woodpeckers provides a good example of the close relationship between the control system and output devices. The typical woodpecker

feeds by flaking off bark and drilling in dead wood to expose insect tunnels, from which the bird removes insects with its tongue. The tongue is a slender, spearlike organ supported within by a shaft of bone (the urohyal) in front and driven from behind by force transmitted through a pair of slender bones, the hyoid horns, which extend under the skull and around to the top of the head. The horns slide in muscular tubes which, on contraction, extend the tongue a distance greater than the length of the beak. The tip of the tongue, a hard spearhead with bristles pointing rearward, is attached to the urohyal by tiny fibres of the protein collagen. As the tongue probes a tunnel or crevice, the impact of the spearhead on any object jams the head back along the shaft. Proprioceptive nerve endings are precisely located in the fluid-filled spaces between the collagen fibres. They provide the brain with information about the type of material contacted; thus, the bird knows whether it has impaled an insect or hit the hard wood of a tree.

Control of feeding in the woodpecker

EVOLUTIONARY CHANGE IN FORM AND FUNCTION

Preadaptation. The continuity of evolution, coupled with the close dependence of the development of the organism upon its genetic endowment, means that each life-form can contain only adaptations of structures present in its ancestors. Structure and function, however, may change with evolution; a structure that evolves from one function to another is often considered to have been "preadapted" for the second function. The term preadaptation is rejected by many modern biologists as tainted with Aristotelian teleology—the implication that the earlier form of the structure was somehow determined by its ultimate function. The term does indicate, however, the potential of a structure to serve the organism in a role for which the structure was not originally evolved.

An example of the adaptive potential of feeding structures is found in the skulls of many swift predatory fishes. Such fishes are faced with the problem of seizing and swallowing prey while swimming in a dense, resistant medium. A large mouth, opening like a scoop, would slow the predator drastically, and the prey would escape. In a number of unrelated fishes, the skull has been modified from a rigid to a kinetic one through the loosening and elongation of the multiple bones that make up the mouth. The result is that, instead of having a simple hinged jaw like that of many fishes, these predators have a complex apparatus that shoots the whole mouth for-

From W.K. Gregory, *Fish Skulls; Transactions of the American Philosophical Society*

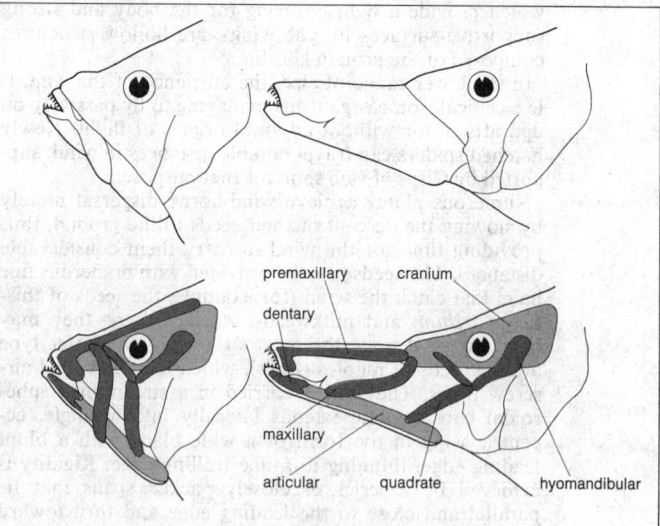

premaxillary   cranium
dentary
maxillary
articular   quadrate   hyomandibular

Figure 4: Protrusion of the jaw in the wrasse *Epibulus*.

ward at the last moment (using the mass of the body to absorb recoil energy) and envelops the prey like a sleeve. At the same time, the pharyngeal region is spread, causing a negative pressure that sucks the prey into the mouth.

An excellent example of the opportunities open to preadapted structures is found in the evolution of the mammalian auditory ossicles, a chain of three tiny bones that transmit sound through the middle ear. One ossicle, the stapes, was present (as the columella) in the reptilian ancestors of the mammals; the other two, the malleus and incus, were derived from the articular and quadrate bones, respectively, which formed the hinge joint between the jaw and the skull in reptiles. Among the many innovations that are identified with mammals is a change in jaw articulation. The dentary bone, one of many in the reptile jaw, expanded at the expense of the other bones and formed a new articulation with the braincase, in front of and outside the quadrate-articular joint. The quadrate and articular became less functional and much reduced in size, were incorporated into the ear, the quadrate becoming the incus; the articular, the malleus. Another bone of the reptilian jaw, the angular, evolved into the curved mammalian tympanic bone, which now forms the rim of the eardrum.

By virtue of their fortuitous position close to the eardrum, the quadrate and articular were ideally preadapted to serve in sound conduction. Many paleontologists believe that these bones were already aiding in sound conduction while still part of the jaw assembly. As the contribution of the bones to jaw articulation became less important, their function in sound conduction became more so, and they gradually became incorporated into the ear.

Levels of orderliness and complexity. Many of the broad concepts of biomechanics are most easily demonstrated in large or at least visible organisms. A large organism, however, is an integrated complex of substructures, some of which may be called organ systems, others merely tissues. These in turn are made up of interacting cells, each of which has certain functioning organelles. The latter are made up of molecules. Each of these levels in a large organism has parallels that exist as independent life forms. A virus, the smallest unit of matter that may be called living, is a relatively simple structure; some of the smaller viruses contain only nucleic acids and proteins. A single-celled organism, such as a protozoan or an alga, has a far more complex self-regulating apparatus, visible, in part, in the structure and variety of its components. The evolution of higher organisms may be viewed as increasing specialization, in part to balance the advantages of larger size. With specialization comes a greater necessity for effective interaction between the parts of the organism and for a master control system to coordinate the substructures and keep the organism in tune with the environment.

The process of natural selection acts on every aspect of the organism that has been genetically determined, from cell components to the configuration of the whole organism. The biomechanical principles that determine the form and function of a given component will vary, depending in part on its level in the hierarchy of complexity and in part on its role in the total system. These principles both limit and shape the ways in which the organism adapts to its environment.

BIBLIOGRAPHY. W. ROSS ASHBY, *An Introduction to Cybernetics* (1956), a college-level textbook on the basic design of control systems; E.J.W. BARRINGTON, *Invertebrate Structure and Function* (1967), a review of the adaptive morphology of the broad range of lower animals; D.A. BELL, *Intelligent Machines* (1962); D. BOOTZIN and H.C. MUFFLEY (eds.), *Biomechanics* (1969); E.L. DU BRUL, *Biomechanics of the Body* (1965), three general surveys of the functional basis for structure. K. ESAU, *Plant Anatomy*, 2nd ed. (1965), a college textbook presenting a thorough treatment of the structure of plants; SIR JAMES GRAY, *Animal Locomotion* (1968), a technical dissertation on the structural and neurological bases for locomotion; H. HERTEL, *Struktur, Form, Bewegung* (1963; Eng. trans., *Structure, Form, Movement*, 1963), emphasizes, through superb photographs, the parallels between man-made and natural structures; E. SCHRODINGER, *What Is Life?* (1944); HOMER W. SMITH, *From Fish to Philosopher* (1953); D. and K. STANLEY-JONES, *The Kybernetics of the Natural Systems* (1960); D'ARCY W. THOMPSON, *On Growth and Form*, new

ed. (1942), a highly readable explanation of the how and why of natural structures; J.Z. YOUNG, *The Life of Vertebrates*, 2nd ed. (1962), a broad discussion of the natural history, anatomy, and evolution of vertebrates, with many line drawings.

(E.L.Du B.)

Forster, E.M.

Well-known initially as a novelist, E.M. Forster was also widely read in English-speaking countries during his later years as a critic of social, political, and moral attitudes. His lack of a systematic philosophy was deliberate, harmonizing with a liberal humanist attitude that sought especially to stress the importance of the particular human being and of personal relationships.

Radio Times Hulton Picture Library

Forster.

Edward Morgan Forster was born in London on January 1, 1879. His father, an architect, died when he was a baby, and he was brought up by his mother and paternal aunts. The difference between the two families, his father's being strongly evangelical with a high sense of moral responsibility, his mother's more feckless and generous-minded, gave him an enduring insight into the nature of domestic tensions, while his education as a day-boy (day student) at Tonbridge School, Kent, was responsible for many of his later criticisms of the English public school (private) system. At King's College, Cambridge, he enjoyed a sense of liberation. For the first time he was free to follow his own intellectual inclinations; and he gained a sense of the uniqueness of the individual, of the healthiness of moderate skepticism, and of the importance of Mediterranean civilization as a counterbalance to the more straitlaced attitudes of north European countries.

On leaving Cambridge, Forster decided to devote his life to writing. His first novels and short stories were redolent of an age that was shaking off the shackles of Victorianism. While adopting certain themes (the importance of women in their own right, for example) from earlier English novelists such as George Meredith, he broke with the elaborations and intricacies favoured in the late 19th century and wrote in a freer, more colloquial style. From the first his novels included a strong strain of social comment, based on acute observation of middle class life. There was also a deeper concern, however, a belief, associated with Forster's interest in Mediterranean "paganism," that, if men and women were to achieve a satisfactory life, they needed to keep contact with the earth and to cultivate their imaginations. In an early novel, *The Longest Journey* (1907), he suggested that cultivation of either in isolation is not enough, reliance on the earth alone leading to a genial brutishness and exaggerated development of imagination undermining the individual's sense of reality.

The same theme runs through *Howards End* (1910), a more ambitious novel that brought Forster his first major success. The novel is conceived in terms of an alliance between the Schlegel sisters, Margaret and Helen, who embody the liberal imagination at its best, and Mrs. Ruth

First major success

Wilcox, the owner of the house Howards End, which has remained close to the earth for generations; spiritually they recognize a kinship against the values of Henry Wilcox and his children, who conceive life mainly in terms of commerce. In a symbolic ending, Margaret Schlegel marries Henry Wilcox and brings him back, a broken man, to Howards End, re-establishing there a link (however heavily threatened by the forces of progress around it) between the imagination and the earth.

The resolution is a precarious one, and World War I was to undermine it still further. Forster spent three wartime years in Alexandria, Egypt, doing civilian war work, and visited India twice, in 1912–13 and 1921. When he returned to former themes in his postwar novel *A Passage to India* (1924), they presented themselves in a negative form: against the vaster scale of India, in which the earth itself seems alien, a resolution between it and the imagination could appear as almost impossible to achieve. Only Adela Quested, the young girl who is most open to experience, can glimpse their possible concord, and then only momentarily, in the courtroom during the trial at which she is the central witness. Much of the novel is devoted to less spectacular values: those of seriousness and truthfulness (represented here by the administrator Fielding) and of an outgoing and benevolent sensibility (embodied in the English visitor Mrs. Moore). Neither Fielding nor Mrs. Moore is totally successful; neither totally fails. The novel ends in an uneasy equilibrium. Immediate reconciliation between Indians and British is ruled out, but the further possibilities inherent in Adela's experience, along with the surrounding uncertainties, are echoed in the ritual birth of the God of Love amid scenes of confusion at a Hindu festival.

Later thinking and attitudes

The values of truthfulness and kindness dominate Forster's later thinking. A reconciliation of humanity to the earth and its own imagination may be the ultimate ideal, but Forster sees it receding in a civilization devoting itself more and more to technological progress. The values of common sense, goodwill, and regard for the individual, on the other hand, can still be cultivated, and these underlie Forster's later pleas for more liberal attitudes. During World War II he acquired a position of particular respect as a man who had never been seduced by totalitarianisms of any kind and whose belief in personal relationships and the simple decencies seemed to embody some of the common values behind the fight against Nazism and Fascism. In 1946, his old college gave him an honorary fellowship, which enabled him to make his home in Cambridge and to keep in communication with both old and young, until his death at Coventry, England, on June 7, 1970.

Although the later Forster is an important figure in mid-20th-century culture, his emphasis on a kindly, uncommitted, and understated morality being congenial to many of his contemporaries, it is by his novels that he is more likely to be remembered, and these are best seen in the context of the preceding Romantic tradition. The novels sustain the cult of the heart's affections that was central to that tradition, but they also share with the first Romantics a concern for the status of man in nature and for his imaginative life, a concern that remains important to an age that has turned against other aspects of Romanticism.

In addition to essays, short stories, and novels, Forster wrote a biography of his great-aunt, *Marianne Thornton* (1956); a documentary account of his Indian experiences, *The Hill of Devi* (1953); and *Alexandria: A History and a Guide* (1922; new ed., 1961). *Maurice*, a novel with a homosexual theme, was published posthumously in 1971 but written many years earlier; some short stories remain in manuscript.

MAJOR WORKS

NOVELS: *Where Angels Fear to Tread* (1905); *The Longest Journey* (1907); *A Room with a View* (1908); *Howards End* (1910); *A Passage to India* (1924); and *Maurice* (posthumously, 1971).

OTHER WORKS: *Aspects of the Novel* (1927), criticism; *The Collected Tales of E.M. Forster* (1947), *Abinger Harvest* (1936), and *Two Cheers for Democracy* (1951), essays; and

Billy Budd (1951), libretto collaboration with E. Crozier for an opera by Benjamin Britten.

BIBLIOGRAPHY. B.J. KIRKPATRICK, *A Bibliography of E.M. Forster*, 2nd ed. (1968), is a recent listing of additional source material. Most manuscripts and papers are held by the Library of King's College, Cambridge; others are in the University of Texas Library. The authorized biography is being written by P.N. FURBANK. Critical works include: ROSE MACAULAY, *The Writings of E.M. Forster* (1968), a view of Forster by a late Edwardian; LIONEL TRILLING, *E.M. Forster: A Study*, 2nd rev. ed. (1965), an account of Forster as liberal humanist; F.C. CREWS, *E.M. Forster: The Perils of Humanism* (1962), a further contribution to this discussion; J.B. BEER, *The Achievement of E.M. Forster* (1962), dwelling on Forster's visionary and pagan themes; and WILFRED STONE, *The Cave and the Mountain* (1966), the most complete discussion to date of Forster's work.

(J.B.B.)

Fortifications

Fortifications are military positions that have been strengthened against attack. Fortification is the military art or science of strengthening such positions. Permanent fortifications include elaborate forts and troop shelters; they are usually constructed of masonry and are most often erected in times of peace or upon threat of war. Field fortifications are constructed when in contact with an enemy or when contact is imminent. They consist of entrenched positions for personnel and crew-served weapons; cleared fields of fire; and obstacles such as explosive mines, barbed-wire entanglements, felled trees, and antitank ditches. Both field and permanent fortifications often take advantage of natural obstacles, such as canals and rivers, and they are usually camouflaged or otherwise concealed.

Both field and permanent fortifications assist the defender to obtain the greatest advantage from his own strength and weapons while preventing the enemy from using his resources to best advantage. When supported by covering fire, for example, fortifications may force the enemy to deploy prematurely into open and less controllable formations. Fortifications may also be used to deny easier invasion routes and channel enemy operations into less advantageous paths.

Before the advent of the most modern weapons, almost all important cities and trade centres were defended by permanent fortifications, either a high wall encircling the city, a series of forts on the periphery, a walled and moated citadel within the heart of the city, or a combination or variations of the three. Fortifications also might be established at strategic points along likely routes of invasion. Throughout history coastal fortifications have been constructed to guard seaports against naval attack or to counter amphibious assault.

Some fortifications may be considered semipermanent, such as the extensive trench systems employed in World War I or the forts and base camps used in more recent times in Southeast Asia, Korea, and the Middle East. These were usually entrenched fighting positions and troop shelters reinforced by log or timber revetments and earth-filled burlap or plastic bags.

Neither fortifications nor the obstacles contributing to them are of optimum value unless actively defended by troops and guns. Antitank obstacles, for example, may be covered over by bulldozers or destroyed by demolition charges. Since no fortifications, however stoutly constructed, can be considered impregnable, an integral part of the defense is the sally or sortie, whereby troops rush out from the fortifications to engage the enemy in close combat, or the counterattack, whereby reserve forces seek to destroy or eject any troops who may have penetrated the defenses.

Importance of adequate defense

Before the invention of gunpowder led to the creation of artillery firing powerful explosive projectiles, permanent fortifications might hold up an attacker for months and even years. Sometimes starvation or the threat of starvation was all that finally induced defenders to surrender.

The effect of even fairly primitive artillery was dramatically demonstrated at Constantinople in AD 1453 when a besieging Turkish force in 55 days breached defenses that had earlier withstood sieges as long as five years. Improvements in design and construction retained considerable advantage for fortifications through ensuing years, despite improved artillery. In the two world wars, some permanent fortifications held up well against the most powerful bombardment.

Yet, in no case have fortifications proven impervious to modern weapons, and against atomic weapons permanent fortifications as known throughout history may well be a thing of the past. Although all types of fortifications have continued even in recent years to be of some value, certainly in part because nuclear weapons have not been employed, most fortifications designed to counteract the vast new explosive power of the nuclear age are constructed deep underground, not as conventional fighting positions but as protection for headquarters staffs, command and control systems, and antiballistic missiles.

Early forms

ANCIENT FORTIFICATIONS

Both field and permanent fortifications played an important role in warfare in the ancient world, but permanent fortifications were particularly effective against the limited power of ancient offensive weapons. Even the lengthy siege aimed at starving the defenders was not always effective, for the defenders were often able to supply themselves better than the besieging army could live off a hostile land. Sometimes a ruse or subterfuge, as in the legend of the Trojan Horse, was more effective than any weapon.

Early civilized tribes of Africa fought from behind a parapet filled with alternate layers of stone, earth, and logs. Sometime later came walls made of mud, sun-dried brick, or masonry and towers constructed at intervals along the wall to serve as sentry posts or as defensive bastions from which archers could cover the approaches between towers.

The first fortresses. As early as 7000 BC the city of Jericho was protected by a wall 21 feet high encompassing an area of ten acres and by an outer moat 15 feet wide and nine feet deep (7 × 5 × 3 metres) hewn through solid rock. In ancient Egypt and Assyria walls as thick as 30 feet (nine metres) and as high as 120 feet (37 metres) were constructed, frequently with a ditch in front to keep attackers at a distance. To counter such defenses, attacking forces developed devices such as scaling ladders, battering rams, torsion-activated catapults for throwing heavy missiles, tension-activated ballistae for shooting large spears, and movable towers from which to overlook the walls and rain incendiary arrows into the fortress. The defenders reinforced their bastions with similar engines of war, firing them from atop or behind the walls. The attackers sometimes resorted to mining, digging tunnels beneath the defenses, then setting fire to the timber that shored up the tunnels, causing the earth above to collapse.

One of the most renowned of the ancient fortresses was the city of Tyre, built on an island half a mile from shore. Only after a seven-month siege did one of history's great captains, Alexander the Great, succeed in breaching the defenses. The Tyrians defeated Alexander's first efforts to build a mole 200 feet wide from the mainland to the walls, but after gaining mastery of the sea around the fortress, Alexander built a fleet of barges armed with war engines and anchored them at strategic points along the defensive works. From the barges he mounted his successful assault.

Siege of Rhodes

Another famous siege was the unsuccessful Macedonian attack on the city of Rhodes, undertaken some years after Alexander's death. So large was one of the towers used in the attack that 3,400 men were required to move it up to the walls. Another 1,000 men were needed to wield a battering ram 180 feet long. Despite such impressive efforts by the attackers, Rhodes held out for six years until finally relieved by allied forces that drove off the Macedonians.

The fortresses and towers and assault devices of early Greece and Rome remain a wonder to modern engineers accustomed to steam-, hydraulic-, and diesel-operated machinery. The Romans, for example, constructed huge siege towers, one of which Caesar mentions as being 150 feet (46 metres) high. The lower stories housed the battering ram, which had either a pointed head for breaching or a ramlike head for battering. Archers in the upper stories shot arrows to drive the defenders from their ramparts. From the top of the tower, a hinged bridge might be lowered to serve a storming party. To guard the attackers against enemy missiles, the Romans used mantelets, which were great wicker or wooden shields, sometimes mounted on wheels. In some cases the attackers might approach the fortress under the protection of wooden galleries.

Protective walls. Massive, elongated walls were also a feature of early permanent fortifications. The Great Wall of China, built by the emperor Shih Huang Ti in the 3rd century BC to discourage incursions by nomadic tribes, was 1,600 miles (2575 kilometres) long, generally 25 feet (eight metres) wide at the base and 17 feet (five metres) at the top, with an average height of more than 20 feet (six metres). When the frontiers of the Roman Empire rested in northwestern Europe and Africa, the Romans built a number of continuous walls, including the Limes Germanicus, some 250 to 300 miles long (402 to 483 kilometres) from the Rhine near Neuwied to the Danube near Ratisbon, and Hadrian's Wall in Britain, 73 miles long (117 kilometres) from the Solway Firth to a point on the North Sea coast just north of Newcastle-on-Tyne. The Limes was for half its length an earthen mound with a ditch and for the other half a rough stone wall four feet (1.2 metres) thick. Hadrian's Wall was originally built of earth but later strengthened by a masonry wall eight feet (2.4 metres) thick and 16 feet (4.8 metres) high. None of the walls was defended along its entire length. Sentry posts, watchtowers, or roving patrols gave notice of enemy incursions, whereupon reserves operating from camps spaced at intervals either along the wall or several miles behind it moved to eliminate them. Remarkably preserved vestiges of these walls, including the Great Wall of China, remain to this day.

Early field fortifications. The main purpose of early field fortifications, particularly among the Greeks, was to secure an advantage by standing on higher ground so that the enemy was forced to attack uphill. The solid mass formation of the Macedonian phalanx was particularly effective on the defense when supplemented by natural or man-made obstacles. The Romans were especially adept at field fortifications, preparing fortified camps at the close of each day's march. Roman camps normally were square or rectangular, though they could vary with the details of terrain. The troops usually required three to four hours to dig a ditch around the periphery, erect a rampart of palisade from timbers carried by each man, lay out streets, and pitch tents. In hostile territory as much as half of each legion might mount guard or engage the enemy while the remainder worked. During extended campaigns the Romans strengthened the camps with towers and outlying redoubts, or small forts, and used the camps as a base for offensive forays into the surrounding territory.

Roman fortified camps

In the campaign in Gaul against the insurgent Arverni chieftain, Vercingetorix, the Romans under Julius Caesar performed a formidable engineering feat in surrounding a large number of Gauls in the fortified town of Alesia near the present French city of Dijon. With about 55,000 men, Caesar built two separate walls of "contravallation"—facing the town—and "circumvallation"—facing outward, the latter 14 miles (23 kilometres) in circumference. While holding Vercingetorix at bay with these fortifications, Caesar defeated three attempts by a Gallic relief army to break through to the besieged force. Facing starvation, Vercingetorix at last surrendered.

Among the Teutonic barbarians, the Goths developed their own version of the fortified camp. When travelling, the Goths moved in a large convoy of wagons, which they assembled at night in a circle, or laager, providing an effective fort both for defense and as a base for forage and plunder. The methods later used by the wagon trains of American pioneers against the Indians of the western plains were similar, as were procedures adopted by armoured divisions in World War II.

THE MIDDLE AGES

With the decline of the Roman Empire and the rise of feudalism, the importance of field fortifications diminished. The mounted knight depended for protection in the field on his heavy armour, while the art of permanent fortifications centred on the medieval castle. The castle built of heavy stone on high ground came early to the mainland of Europe (11th century) but was slower to develop in Britain, where simple ditches and wooden palisades continued longer. William the Conqueror used wooden forts to consolidate his conquest of England.

The medieval castle. The continental castles were typi-
Motte-and-
bailey
castles
fied by the Normans' motte-and-bailey castles. The motte was a mound surrounded by a ditch and surmounted by a wall and a single large tower, the keep or donjon. The bailey was a forecourt protected by another ditch and wall, its purpose originally being to protect the domestic animals. Entrance to the castle was by way of a retractable drawbridge. The concept of the castle was one of almost totally passive defense, for however difficult it was for the attacker to reach and assault the defenses, located as they were on virtually inaccessible terrain, it was almost as difficult for the defender to debouch rapidly to harass the attacker. Although a new weapon was introduced, the trebuchet, or mangonel, a missile-hurling machine propelled by counterweight rather than tension or torsion, starvation continued to constitute the principal offensive weapon in sieges.

As a result of the Crusades (AD 1095–1291), fortifications in western Europe underwent something of a revolution. The crusaders' encounter with powerful walled Byzantine cities and fortresses with double or triple concentric lines of turreted walls led to a strengthening of castle and city defense. The most impressive single example was the Chateau Gaillard, built by Richard the Lionhearted in Normandy, which actually improved on the eastern prototypes, although the castle's siege and capture by Philip II (1203–04) proved that an attacker willing to devote sufficient resources and time to the effort might overcome even the most powerful defenses. Yet long campaigns in this era were the exception, since feudal levies could be called to service for only a few weeks each year and mercenary armies were too expensive to maintain indefinitely.

Castles continued to be built well into the 14th century and, growing increasingly elaborate, constituted some of the most efficient fortifications of any age. The later versions were protected by a series of concentric powerful curtain walls fronted by a moat, often a lake. Gate houses were three or four stories tall, surmounted by twin towers. Machicolations (overhanging parapets), portcullises, and loopholes strengthened the defenses. Sometimes the central bailey was large enough to include a town. An example of the later castles is the Bastille in Paris (1370–83).

Mongol field fortifications. Both the art of siegecraft and that of field fortifications were rejuvenated by the Asian Mongols in both their eastern and western conquests (1190–1400). The Mongols employed mammoth siege trains with missile engines and other equipment carried on wagons and pack animals. The main body of Mongol warriors often went on to further conquest while leaving reduction of the fortress to a subordinate force. In field operations the Mongols consistently followed a tactic of defending their centre by entrenchment, employing the troops thus released for strengthening flank operations on the wings of the defended position.

THE AGE OF FIREARMS

Although gunpowder weapons appeared at least as early as the mid-14th century, they were at first inaccurate and generally ineffective cannon consisting of small metal pots or tubes. Only after the opening of the 15th century did most European armies and the Turks possess artillery weapons that posed a genuine threat to the existing medieval fortifications. When Henry V's cannon in 1415 began the second half of the Hundred Years' War by battering down the walls of Harfleur, the era of impregnable fortifications can be said to have passed.

Siege warfare. The early gunpowder weapons, tubes of cast or wrought iron, were used almost exclusively for siege operations. Known as bombards, they were moved about on ox-drawn sledges and had to be emplaced on mounds of earth or log platforms. Projectiles were either iron or stone and had no explosive content. They were nevertheless effective, as in the siege of Constantinople in 1453 when Turkish bombards battered down walls that had stood for centuries. The Turkish cannon included 70 heavy pieces, one a 19-ton behemoth firing stone balls up to 1,500 pounds in weight for a distance in excess of a mile.

By the mid-15th century so effective was the artillery of Charles VII of France—the best on the Continent—that
Effect of
artillery
the French were able to reduce all of the castles of Normandy in one year. Partly because artillery was not yet adaptable to emplacement atop or within fortifications to provide counterbattery fire, but mainly because of the increased power of the cannon, artillery by the close of the century had rendered medieval fortifications obsolete. The use of gunpowder in mining further increased the vulnerability of the castles.

Not until the closing decade of the 15th century, when the French introduced a relatively light cast-bronze cannon on two-wheeled carriages pulled by horses, was artillery to figure prominently in field operations and thus to become an important element in field fortifications. Nevertheless, as early as the Hussite Wars (1419–36) in Bohemia, the Hussite leader, John Ziska, in creating a defense called the *wagenburg*, an adaptation of the laager tactic of the Goths, effectively employed bombards in the intervals between his wagons.

Yet despite these developments, field fortifications were seldom used during the early years of the age of gunpowder. Since cannons were still relatively inaccurate and firearms cumbersome and of short range, most armies in the field relied on the strength of men in masse to repel attack. Important in the defense were bodies of disciplined, heavily armoured pikemen who stood in a variety of close formations, their pikes planted firmly on the ground and slanted toward the attacker. Pikemen of the Swiss army gained a reputation for solid defense unequalled since the days of the Macedonian phalanx.

The strengthening of permanent fortifications. By the 16th century the revolution in permanent fortifications occasioned by gunpowder was in full swing, as even the most massive medieval fortifications had become vulnerable to heavy siege guns. Some of the greatest figures of the Renaissance contributed to new developments in

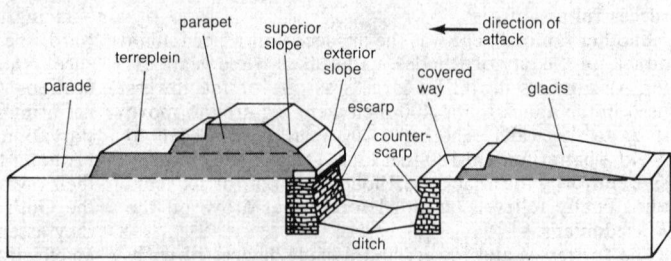

Figure 1: Cross-section of the main wall of a fortress.

permanent defenses: Leonardo da Vinci, Michelangelo, and Niccolo Machiavelli, among others. The German artist, Albrecht Dürer, wrote extensively on the theory of fortification.

As new fortifications were constructed, the walls tended to be broad and low, sometimes even sunk below ground level, in order to keep the portion exposed to artillery fire to a minimum. Triangular bastions extended outward from the walls so that defending artillery might sweep all approaches. The usual fort had five or six bastions, leading to the name of star fortress. The main wall was known as the enceinte; the top of it, the parapet; the area behind the parapet, the terreplein. An escarp or forward face of the wall led down to a wide ditch, beyond which stood the counterscarp, a low outwork defended by light artillery and small arms. Earth excavated from the ditch was spread in front of the counterscarp to create a gradually sloping terrace, or glacis, which added to the strength of the counterscarp and absorbed many of the projectiles fired from artillery pieces of limited range and elevation (see Figure 1).

As military engineers continued to search for increased defensive strength, the star fortress was replaced by the tenaille trace (see Figure 2A) in which the flanks of the bastions were placed back-to-back between the faces. Yet a certain amount of the ditch still could not be reached by fire from the bastions. This led to development of the bastioned trace (see Figure 2B), its flanks directly opposite each other and linked by curtain walls. In succeeding decades, fortifications employed varied geometric patterns with a wealth of gates, sally ports, redans, coverings and other refinements. Each part of the fortification

Improved fortress designs

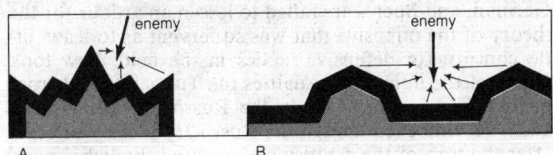

Figure 2: (A) Tenaille trace and (B) bastioned trace.

became a separate fort that could be self-sustaining with its own garrison while providing mutual support to the remainder of the units in the system.

These fortresses were constructed either as outposts or citadels in the defense of cities or as barriers along strategic routes. Border towns such as Metz and Verdun in France and Liège, Namur, and Charleroi in Belgium became critically important. Nations sought to control the approaches to their territory while retaining a base or springboard from which to counterattack or to launch a retaliatory invasion. Since the more powerful cannon now became a part of naval armament, port cities had to be protected with fortifications guarding against assault from the sea.

Modification of siege operations. The new methods of fortification having outstripped gunnery developments, long, difficult sieges again ensued. Such old devices as mantelets, galleries, and siege towers were of no use in the face of gunpowder, and even mining was of limited use because the range of artillery dictated that tunnels had to be so long that fresh air could not reach the diggers. The besiegers resorted to digging approach entrenchments. Covered by artillery fire, troops dug trenches in the direction of the fortification's outer works, then threw up earthen walls as protection for their own artillery. The guns were brought up under cover of darkness, and the process was repeated until the attackers were close enough to overwhelm the counterscarp defenders. The process again had to be repeated against the main walls.

Sieges grew longer and more costly. In 1522 the Ottoman Turks besieged Rhodes, the eastern Mediterranean stronghold of the Knights Hospitalers of St. John (a military order formed during the Crusades). Rhodes was one of the earliest of the new bastion fortresses. Although the defenders were greatly outnumbered and cut off from resupply and although the Turks at one point penetrated into the city, so appalled was the Turkish commander at

his losses that he withdrew and offered honourable terms for a treaty.

The difficulty of siege operations against the new permanent fortifications and the increased effectiveness of small arms rejuvenated the art of field fortifications. The first to combine the new power of small arms with field works was Gonzalo de Córdoba of Spain. He discerned that a few arquebusiers might utilize entrenchments to cover extensive frontages, thus enabling smaller forces to contain and then outmanoeuvre larger forces. Alexander of Parma (16th-century Spanish commander in the Low Countries) fought on several occasions against Henry IV of France from field fortifications that his veterans erected overnight. The Spaniards subsequently met their engineering match in Maurice of Nassau, commanding Dutch forces, who made skillful use of natural obstacles to swiftly construct field fortifications capable of resisting any assault.

Modern fortifications

THE ADVENT OF MODERN WARFARE

With the beginning of modern warfare in the 17th century, field fortifications continued to exercise an important influence, particularly as practiced by Gustavus Adolphus, the father of modern tactics and army organization. Gustavus and his Swedish troops constructed outposts defended by redoubts and protected their forts with palisades and entanglements. In the manner of the Romans, the Swedes dug in each night and built a wall around their camp. On the banks of the Elbe, Gustavus' troops, fighting from field fortifications backed by cannons firing at point-blank range, twice repulsed assaults by the army of the Holy Roman Empire under Johann Tserclaes, Graf von Tilly. On the other hand, field fortifications of his enemy led to one of Gustavus' more serious defeats: at Nuremberg Gustavus grew impatient for battle and ordered his forces from their entrenchments to attack the imperial army, now commanded by Count Albrecht von Wallenstein; the Swedes suffered a sharp repulse.

The influence of Vauban. Late in the 17th century, the art of permanent fortifications, already highly developed, became an even more critical element of warfare as the result of the genius of a French engineer, Sébastien de Vauban. Vauban retained the traditional plan for a fortress—inner enclosure, rampart, moat, and outer rampart—but he extended the outworks as far as possible in order to compel the enemy to begin his siege operations at a distance. He also insured that every defensive face was flanked and supported by the works behind and beside it, in the process creating a vast polygon replete with great bastions at every angle interspersed with smaller ones in between, each of which was close enough to the next to provide supporting small-arms fire.

Vauban also was a master of siegecraft. Before his time, the usual method was to approach the walls with zigzag trenches, then, with artillery brought forward, to assault from the head of the trench. Since the defenders could concentrate their fire against the head of the trench, this was a costly process. Vauban instead instituted a system of parallel trenches (see Figure 3). Some 600 yards from the fortress—the approximate maximum range of contemporary artillery—his engineers dug a trench parallel to the periphery of the fortress to serve as protection for the infantry while a preliminary artillery duel raged. Thereupon the engineers dug a series of zigzag trenches (called saps), culminating in a second parallel about halfway to the wall and within musket range; this served as forward cover for infantry and artillery. The engineers—who gradually acquired the name sappers after the name of the trenches—then dug slowly ahead under cover of wheeled shields called gabions. They dug a final third parallel near the glacis. From that point, with breaching batteries brought forward, the infantry could assault at a number of points simultaneously. Vauban's methods of fortification and siege remained standard until the later 19th century, although such 18th-century commanders as the Duke of Marlborough and Frederick the Great of Prussia came to deplore siege warfare and to circumvent

Vauban's new siege technique

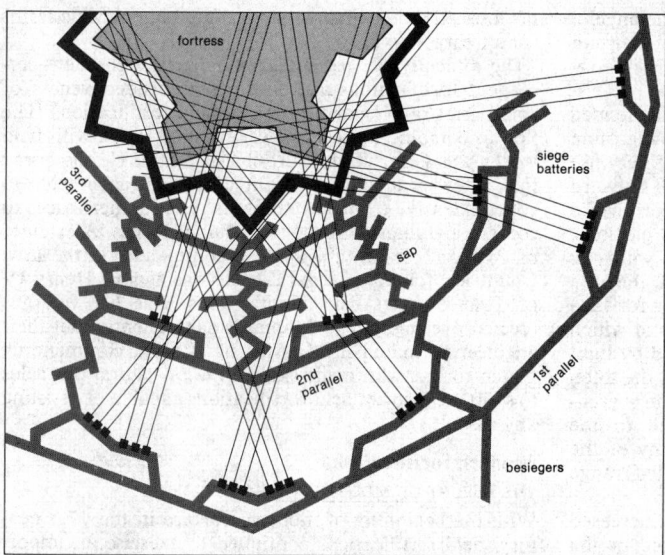

Figure 3: Attack upon a fortress using the Vauban system.

it by disciplined marches designed to manoeuvre the enemy away from the permanent forts and by expert battle-field tactics.

In North America, in the meantime, the frontier fort surrounded by a log palisade had been an integral part of warfare as Europeans pushed their settlements westward. In North America, too, in the Revolutionary War, American soldiers demonstrated again the value of field fortifications: the hasty entrenchment, the waist-high parapet, the cover of a tree or stone hedge. Within a generation American troops under Andrew Jackson at the Battle of New Orleans made effective use of cotton bales to defend their position against advancing British troops.

In the Napoleonic period the outstanding example of field fortifications was the Torres Vedras line, erected by the Duke of Wellington 25 miles north of Lisbon (1810): three lines of mutually supporting batteries and redoubts running for 30 miles through a range of low hills between the Tagus River and the sea. The rapid movements of the Napoleonic Wars generally discouraged elaborate defensive works, though Russian field fortifications played a central role in the bitterly fought battle of Borodino (1812).

Increased use of entrenchment. In the American Civil War, field fortifications emerged as an essential of warfare with both armies employing entrenchments to an extent never before seen. Troops learned to fortify newly won positions immediately, employing spades and axes carried in their packs, first digging rifle pits, then expanding them into trenches. Early in the war, Gen. Robert E. Lee adopted the frontier rifleman's breastwork composed of two logs on the parapet of the entrenchment, and many of Lee's victories were the result of his ability to use hasty entrenchments as a base for aggressive employment of fire and manoeuvre. In two notable sieges, that of Vicksburg, Miss., in the west, and Petersburg, Va., in the east, trench warfare was the accepted method of siege. In the Vicksburg siege, which lasted for almost a year, Union troops tunnelled under the defenses and placed a powder charge timed to explode after they had pulled back. In the Cold Harbor, Va., campaign, when Gen. Ulysses S. Grant sent his troops against Confederate earthworks, he lost 14,000 men in 13 days. Field mines and booby traps were used extensively, and trench mortars were developed to lob shells into opposing trenches.

At the start of the war, the United States had few permanent fortifications except on the coast, such as Fort Sumter in Charleston harbour where the first shot was fired, but the Confederate threat to Washington prompted early construction of a defense system around the capital. It included 68 separate forts, a number of blockhouses, and 20 miles of connecting trenches. Although never put to a test, the fortifications had a considerable indirect influence on the campaigns in nearby

The defense of Washington

Virginia; in the summer of 1864 they contained Confederate General Jubal Early's threat to Washington.

WORLD WAR I (1914–18)

The lesson learned in the American Civil War was for a time lost on European commanders. Even the bitter experiences of appalling losses in the Crimean, Franco-German, and Boer wars failed to lessen an ardour for the theory of the offensive that was so fervent as to leave little concern for defensive tactics in the field. Few took notice of the immense casualties the Turks inflicted from behind field fortifications in the Russo-Turkish War of 1877–78, and even though the Russo-Japanese War soon after the turn of the century underscored the lethal power of the machine gun and breech-loading rifled artillery, most European commanders saw the increased firepower as more a boon to the offensive than to the defensive.

The permanent fort. Most defensive thinking was reserved for the permanent fort, which was designed to canalize enemy advance and to afford time for national mobilization. The leading fortification engineer of the time was Henri Brialmont, who was considered a Belgian Vauban. He placed his forts, built of concrete, at an average distance of four miles from a city, as with 12 forts at Liège, and at intervals of approximately 2½ miles. At Antwerp his defense system was even more dense. He protected the big guns of his forts with turrets of steel and developed disappearing cupolas. Some forts were pentagonal, others triangular, with much of the construction underground. In building defenses along the frontier facing Germany, French engineers emulated Brialmont, with particularly strong clusters of fortresses at Verdun and Belfort. So monstrous were the forts of the time that they were known as "land battleships."

By marching through Belgium with a strong right wing (the Schlieffen plan), the Germans circumvented the powerful French fortresses. Passing between the forts at Liège, which Brialmont had intended to be connected with trenches, they took Liège in only three days, then systematically reduced the forts. Namur, also heavily fortified, resisted the powerful German guns for only four days. The concrete of the Belgian fortifications crumbled under the pounding, but the French forts at Verdun, of more recent and sturdier construction, later absorbed tremendous punishment and served as focal points for some of the war's bloodiest fighting.

The trench systems. Despite German success against the Belgian forts, the fallacy of the belief that the new firepower favoured the offensive was soon convincingly demonstrated. Once the French had checked the German right wing at the Marne River, the fighting degenerated into what was in effect a massive siege. For 600 miles, from Switzerland to the North Sea, the landscape was soon scarred with opposing systems of zigzag, timber-revetted, sandbag-reinforced trenches, fronted by tangles of barbed wire sometimes more than 150 feet deep and featured here and there by covered dugouts providing shelter for troops and horses and by observation posts in log bunkers or concrete turrets. The trench systems consisted of several lines in depth, so that if the first line was penetrated, the assailants were little better off. Rail and motor transport could rush fresh reserves forward to seal off a gap faster than the attackers could continue forward. Out beyond the trenches and the barbed wire was a muddy, virtually impassable desert called no-man's-land, where artillery fire soon eliminated habitation and vegetation alike. The fighting involved masses of men, masses of artillery, and masses of casualties. Toxic gases —asphyxiating, lachrymatory and vesicant—were introduced in a vain effort to break the dominance of the defense, which was so overpowering that for more than two years the opposing lines varied less than ten miles in either direction.

The Hindenburg Line During the winter of 1916–17, the Germans prepared a reserve trench system, the Hindenburg Line, containing deep dugouts where the men could take cover against artillery fire and machine guns emplaced in concrete shelters called pillboxes. Approximately two miles behind the forward line was a second position, almost as strong. The Hindenburg Line resisted all allied assaults in 1917, including a vast British mining operation under the Messines Ridge in Belgium that literally blew up the ridge, inflicting 17,000 casualties at one blow; the advance failed to carry beyond the ridge.

In northern Italy the fighting assumed much the same complexion. Only on the eastern front did the vast distances dictate a more open form of warfare but one equally expensive in casualties.

WORLD WAR II (1939–45)

Permanent fortifications. *The Maginot Line and the West Wall.* In the interval between world wars, several European countries built elaborate permanent fortifications. The largest was the French Maginot Line, named after a minister of defense, a system of mammoth, self-contained forts stretching from Switzerland to the vicinity of the Belgian frontier near Montmédy. The reinforced concrete of the forts was thicker than any heretofore used, the disappearing guns bigger and more heavily armoured. Ditches, embedded steel beams, and minefields guarded against tank attack. A large part of the works were completely underground. Outposts were connected to the main forts by concrete tunnels. But since French and British military leaders were convinced that if war came again with Germany, the Allies would fight in Belgium, the French failed to extend the line to the sea, relying instead on an outmoded system of unconnected fortresses left over from before World War I. It was this weakness that the Germans subsequently exploited in executing a modified version of the Schlieffen plan, cutting in behind the permanent defenses and defeating France without having to come to grips with the Maginot Line.

The Germans confronted that portion of the Maginot Line facing the Saar River with fortifications of their own, the West Wall. Later extended northward to the Dutch frontier and southward along the Rhine to Switzerland, the West Wall was not a thin line of big forts but a deep band, a mile to five miles thick, of more than 3,000 small, mutually supporting pillboxes, observation posts, and troop shelters. For passive antitank defense the line depended upon natural obstacles, such as rivers and lakes, and upon "dragon's teeth," five rows of pyramid-shaped reinforced concrete projections.

The Germans did not rely on the West Wall to halt an attack but merely to delay it until counterattacks by mobile reserves could eliminate any penetration. The value of their concept remains undetermined; the line was not attacked until late 1944, after the German armies had incurred severe defeats and lacked adequate reserves. The West Wall nevertheless forced Allied troops into costly attacks to eliminate it.

Other fort series. Elsewhere in World War II many fortifications similar to these two basic types were built.

The Italians constructed a series of new fortifications and modernized existing World War I defenses along the country's mountainous northern and northeastern frontiers; the Finns maintained a World War I defense facing the Soviet Union: the Mannerheim Line (named after a Finnish marshal and statesman); the Soviets built the Stalin Line facing Poland; the Czechoslovaks constructed what became known as the Little Maginot Line to oppose Germany; the Greeks built the Metaxas Line facing Bulgaria; and the Belgians erected a series of elaborate forts along the Albert Canal. German capture of the most elaborate and allegedly impregnable of the Belgian forts, Eben Emael, in a matter of hours in the first two days of The capture of Eben Emael the campaign against France and the Low Countries in 1940 startled the world. Arriving silently by night in gliders, troops landed atop the fort and began systematically to destroy turrets and casemates. Soon after daylight they were joined by 300 men arriving by parachute. Around noon of May 11 the 1,000-man garrison surrendered.

Despite at least comparable surprise and the same so-called blitzkrieg methods, the Germans required more time to penetrate the more dispersed forts of the Stalin Line in the U.S.S.R. The delay gained two months of invaluable time for the Soviet troops, without which they might well have been unable to stop the Germans at the gates of Moscow.

The other notable Soviet use of permanent fortifications was at Leningrad, where, with a combination of old Baltic forts, field fortifications, water barriers, and ruined buildings, they held out for 900 days—from September 1941 until January 1944—when they finally were relieved. The ordeal of Leningrad constituted one of history's more notable sieges, a defense sustained by incredible fortitude and such exigent methods as a seasonal supply line across the frozen surface of Lake Ladoga. In the historic defense of another city, Stalingrad, the Soviet army made notable use of a new material for field fortifications: rubble of a city's buildings.

In Asia and the Pacific, the most renowned permanent defenses, those of the British at Singapore, revealed an unexpected weakness. Singapore's guns faced the sea, while the Japanese approached the city from the landward side, crossed the narrow channel separating Singapore island from the mainland, and forced a British capitulation. Another famed Far East fortification, the American bastion of Corregidor in Manila Bay, held out for less than a month.

German channel defenses. The Germans employed Fritz Todt, the engineer who had designed the West Wall, and thousands of impressed labourers to construct permanent fortifications along the Belgian and French coasts facing the English Channel: the Atlantic Wall. The line consisted primarily of pillboxes and gun emplacements embedded in cliffsides or placed on the waterfronts of seaside resorts and ports. Included were massive blockhouses with disappearing guns, newsreels of which the Germans sent out through neutral sources in an effort to awe their adversaries, but the numbers of big blockhouses actually were few. Behind the line, in likely landing spots for gliders and parachutists, the Germans emplaced slanted poles, which the troops called *Rommelsspargel* (Rommel's asparagus), after their commander Field Marshal Erwin Rommel. Embedded in the sand of the beaches below the high-tide mark were numerous obstacles, varying in shape and depth, some topped with mines. Barbed wire and antitank and antipersonnel mines interlaced the whole. On the French southwestern and southern coasts similar, through less formidable, defenses were erected.

The Allies first tested the German fortifications in August of 1942 at the resort town of Dieppe in a raid by a 6,100-man force, primarily Canadians. The result was nearly catastrophic: all but 1,650 of the 5,000 who got ashore were lost.

Despite the example of Dieppe, when the Allies landed in force on the Cotentin Peninsula of Normandy on D-Day—June 6, 1944—they found the defenses far less formidable than they had anticipated. This was attributable

Beach defenses in Normandy

to a number of reasons. The Germans had constructed the strongest defenses in the Pas-de-Calais region facing the narrowest part of the English Channel and had stationed their most battleworthy troops there; demands of other fighting fronts had siphoned many of the best German troops from France; the Germans lacked air and naval support; Allied airpower was so strong that movement of German reserves was seriously impeded; landings of Allied airborne troops behind the beaches spread confusion in German ranks; and the Germans were deluded into believing the invasion was a diversion, that a second and larger invasion was to follow in the Pas-de-Calais. Only at one of the two American beaches, given the code name Omaha, was the success of the landing ever in doubt, partly because of rough seas, partly because of the chance presence of an elite German division, and partly because of the presence of high bluffs. Paradoxically, the Allies had less difficulty with the highly publicized beach defenses than they had later with field fortifications based on the Norman hedgerows, earthen embankments several feet thick and five feet high that local farmers through the centuries have erected around thousands of irregularly shaped little fields to fence their cattle and protect their crops from strong ocean winds.

Field fortifications. Field fortifications were even more extensively employed in World War II than in either the American Civil War or World War I, but they were in general less of the semipermanent trench type than of the individual or two-man position, called a slit trench, rifle pit, or foxhole. There were exceptions: great masses of humanity poured from the threatened cities of the Soviet Union, such as Leningrad, Moscow, and Stalingrad, to dig miles of zig-zag trenches not unlike those on the western front in World War I. In beleaguered footholds, such as the Bataan Peninsula and the Allied beachhead at Anzio in Italy, foxholes and other positions often were connected by communications trenches. The German Todt organization built a series of formidable field positions in the craggy mountainous terrain of Italy, oftentimes hewing them with explosives from solid rock. From the Gustav Line (so named from the symbol for *G* in the German military's phonetic alphabet) behind the Garigliano and Rapido rivers, anchored on the forbidding slopes of Monte Cassino, the Germans held the Allies at bay throughout the entire winter of 1943–44. Some of the defensive positions consisted of prefabricated steel turrets or cupolas placed over excavations. Through the winter of 1944–45 the Germans in northern Italy held a similar position called the Gothic Line, located in the precipitous northern Apennines below Florence.

Japanese defenses in the Pacific. On the Pacific islands the Japanese proved to be pertinacious masters of defense from field fortifications. Rapidly growing jungle foliage afforded ideal concealment for natural caves and log emplacements, so that Allied troops often incurred severe losses even in locating the Japanese positions. Artillery, mortars, and naval gunfire were helpful in reducing them, but more often than not final reduction was the province of little groups of infantrymen fighting with individual weapons and portable flame throwers. When the Japanese elected to defend the invasion beaches, as on Tarawa, casualties among both attackers and defenders were enormous; indeed, Tarawa was one of the bloodiest division-sized actions of the war. Even when the Japanese chose to forego beach defense, as on Okinawa, they subsequently employed field fortifications and natural obstacles with tremendous skill to prolong the campaign. The final battle, and one of the largest of the war in the Pacific, the conquest of Okinawa, required almost three months of intensive fighting. The last defenders resisted from caves on a coral promontory at the southern end of the island, their defense culminating in a mass suicide that included the commanders. More than 100,000 Japanese died on Okinawa. Another of the more tenacious Japanese defenses was conducted amid the volcanic ash and coral caves of the tiny island of Iwo Jima, later used as a way station for big American planes bombing the Japanese home islands.

The defense of Okinawa

North African and European theatres. As caves were readily adaptable by the Japanese for defense on Pacific Islands, so towns and cities of masonry construction in North Africa and Europe in many cases provided steadfast fighting positions. If cities were defended, the fighting almost always was slow and costly, as in Stalingrad on the eastern front and Aachen in the west. Even when bombing and shelling demolished many of the buildings, the defenders often fought even more tenaciously from the rubble. When some Allied commanders proposed bombing the historic Benedictine abbey atop Monte Cassino in Italy on the theory that the Germans were using it for observation and for troop shelter, others objected not only for cultural considerations but in the belief that the Germans could fight better from rubble than from the intact edifice. It was an anomaly that some earlier permanent fortifications, such as the forts around Metz dating from the mid-19th century and the medieval citadel of Juelich on the Roer River required prolonged and costly attacks to subdue them, for all the power of 20th-century weapons.

Except where sturdy buildings were available—or following a breakthrough resulting in pursuit operations in which enemy riposte was unlikely—combat troops of any army seldom paused for even brief periods without digging hasty field fortifications, either slit trenches or foxholes; and if the possibility of aerial bombardment existed, even troops performing rear-echelon duties had to have some form of protection at hand. In a hasty defensive position, a line of outposts or listening posts was usually established several hundred yards forward of the main line of resistance, while telephone or radio provided ready support from mortars and artillery to the rear. For more prolonged pauses, mines, booby traps, and trip flares were emplaced; barbed wire was strung; foxholes were covered with logs; and trees were felled to blockade roads. In forests, such as the jungles of the Pacific and Southeast Asia or the evergreen forests of northwestern Europe, overhead cover for foxholes was essential to guard against tree bursts of artillery shells, which rained deadly fragments upon the forest floor. A convenient, readily emplaced form of barbed wire was the "concertina," a coil of wire three feet in diameter, which could be stretched out in the manner of a concertina to create an effective delaying obstacle.

The foxhole. The foxhole, or variation thereof, constituted the basic field fortification of World War II. It was dug usually with an entrenching tool carried by the individual soldier and was two to five feet in diameter, depending upon whether it was to be occupied by one man, two, or three, and at least four feet deep. Sometimes it had a firing step and a drainage pit. If concealment was vital, the earth taken from the hole was carted away or dispersed beneath foliage; otherwise it might be used to create a small parapet. Holes for crew-served weapons, such as machine guns and mortars, were appreciably larger. In severe winter weather the troops might use small explosive charges to break through the frozen top crust of earth and enable them to dig. The foxhole—particularly if covered—afforded effective protection against almost any shelling except a direct hit and if dug in firm ground, was effective against the grinding action of tank treads.

THE NUCLEAR AGE

At the close of World War II most military theorists considered that permanent fortifications of the type previously employed were economically impracticable in view of their vulnerability to the incredible power of nuclear explosives and the methods, such as vertical envelopment from the air, that might be employed to reduce them. Field fortifications were another matter, since these are less costly and impose at least some delay on an enemy advance. The foxhole was expected to continue to be the mainstay of field fortifications but with even greater dispersion, both laterally and in depth, than in World War II.

As events developed through and past mid-century, neither strategic nor tactical nuclear weapons were employed, although the threat of their use was often present. Consequently, field fortifications not unlike those of World War II, but with local adjustments, were used.

The Korean War. Fought with weapons and methods little changed from World War II, the Korean War (1950–53) produced little new in fortifications. There were few permanent fortifications on the Korean peninsula, and the foxhole, barbed wire, mines, and other familiar devices comprised the field fortifications. The Chinese Communists often elected to defend the reverse slope of a hill or mountain, keeping only outposts on the forward slope and thus achieving a measure of protection for the bulk of the defenders from direct fire. In later stages of the war, as the fighting sometimes evolved into position warfare in some ways similar to that of World War I, both sides constructed extensive field fortifications across the entire breadth of the peninsula. Aside from sandbag-reinforced and covered foxholes, these included squad huts or bunkers made of heavy timber and covered with earth or sandbags, timber-revetted firing positions for crew-served weapons, and extensive communications trenches. During the long period of truce negotiations, the lines were constantly improved, and in the years of uneasy truce following the armistice, they took on many of the characteristics of permanent fortifications. A special feature was a tall wire fence across the peninsula running through the so-called demilitarized zone and protected by minefields. Constant roving patrols of each side watched for infiltrators.

The **The war in Vietnam.** In the guerrilla warfare waged in
agroville Southeast Asia during the French Indochina War (1945–54) and the Vietnam War, a number of unusual types of field fortifications were employed, yet their origins could be traced to other eras. The *agroville*, for example, a consolidated and fortified hamlet designed to protect the population from guerrilla incursions, in many ways resembled the fortified towns of ancient or medieval times. Similar methods were used by the British in defeating an insurgency in Malaya and by the Filipinos in countering the Huk rebellion in the Philippines. Triangular-shaped forts with walls of dried mud, usually occupied by local militia, and camps in remote regions manned by tribesmen with the help of U.S. Army Special Forces advisers looked much like the primitive forts of ancient times. Both U.S. and South Vietnamese forces constructed fortified base camps with exterior walls of earth topped by occasional sentry towers, in some ways resembling the semipermanent camps set up by Roman legions. The French defensive position at Dien Bien Phu, capture of which precipitated the end of the French Indochina War, had many of the characteristics of field fortifications in other eras: sandbagged and timber-revetted bunkers and firing positions, communications trenches, triangular-shaped bastions, outposts, and redoubts.

Both U.S. and South Vietnamese forces made extensive use of fire support bases, which were semipermanent entrenchments and bunkers protecting artillery batteries. Along the demilitarized zone separating North and South Vietnam, some bases had concrete emplacements and bunkers. Some of the bases served both for defense against enemy attack and as bases for patrols. The North Vietnamese and the Viet Cong insurgents established base camps in remote areas protected by log bunkers covered with earth and cleverly camouflaged. A good number of the facilities were housed in labyrinthian underground tunnels or in natural caves. The Viet Cong laced the countryside with countless booby traps of various types.

To provide a measure of protection for helicopters and other aircraft from random mortar and rocket attacks, the Americans built earth or concrete revetments several feet thick and four to five feet high on aircraft parking aprons alongside runways. Chemical defoliants were used to clear fields of fire around bases, destroy food crops in Viet Cong controlled areas, and eliminate concealed ambush positions along roads and waterways. To prevent the enemy from reoccupying base camps in jungle areas, special bulldozers called "Rome plows" levelled hundreds of acres of forest.

Other modern fortifications. Meanwhile, in the Arab-Israeli confrontations, semipermanent forts similar to the French position at Dien Bien Phu were built along the frontiers. Often Israeli farms and settlements had to be protected with field fortifications against incursions by Palestinian guerrillas.

An unusual fortification was the Berlin Wall con- *The Berlin*
structed by the Communist East German government *Wall*
through the heart of Berlin, not to keep intruders out but to prevent citizens from fleeing to West Germany. Long lines of barbed wire protected by minefields and sentry posts ran along the western boundaries of East Germany, Czechoslovakia, and Hungary for the same purpose.

No nation has in recent years constructed permanent linear fortifications such as those used in World War II. The pillboxes of the West Wall have been demolished or abandoned, and though most of the elaborate forts of the Maginot Line still exist, their utility in future conflicts is problematical, though they might provide some protection to troops and supplies against nuclear explosions.

Most permanent fortifications of the nuclear age have been designed as headquarters sites or command and control installations or are in some way related to anti-aircraft and antimissile defense. A joint U.S.-Canadian project, the North American Air Defense Command (Norad), includes a series of radar posts across northern Canada and Alaska to provide early warning of the approach of hostile bombers or missiles. The system and the aircraft and missiles supporting it are controlled from a vast underground complex embedded in rock of Cheyenne Mountain near Colorado Springs, Colo. Giant Spartan and Minuteman missiles are housed underground in "silos" with thick concrete walls. Soviet SS-9 ballistic missiles presumably are similarly protected.

BIBLIOGRAPHY. R.E. and T.N. DUPUY, *The Encyclopedia of Military History: From 3500 B.C. to the Present* (1970), is the most recent work to provide considerable material on the subject, and is amply indexed. Other works by distinguished historians on fortifications from ancient times to the present include: MONTGOMERY, VISCOUNT OF ALAMEIN, *A History of Warfare* (1968); C.B. FALLS, *The Art of War: From the Age of Napoleon to the Present Day* (1961); LYNN MONTROSS, *War Through the Ages*, 3rd rev. and enl. ed. (1960); THEODORE ROPP, *War in the Modern World* (1959); and J.F.C. FULLER, *A Military History of the Western World*, 3 vol. (1954–56). Less recent but nevertheless commendable works also covering fortifications are: U.S. MILITARY ACADEMY, DEPT. OF MILITARY ART AND ENGINEERING, *Notes on Permanent Land Fortifications* (1944); QUINCY WRIGHT, *A Study of War*, 2 vol. (1942); O.L. SPAULDING, H. NICKERSON, and J.W. WRIGHT, *Warfare: A Study of Military Methods from the Earliest Times* (1925); W.A. MITCHELL, *Outlines of the World's Military History* (1931); B.H. LIDDELL HART, *The Decisive Wars of History* (1929); R.G. ALBION, *Introduction to Military History* (1929); and E.M. LLOYD, *Review of the History of Infantry* (1908). Another work particularly helpful for the period covered is C.B. FALLS, *A Hundred Years of War, 1850–1950* (1962). Greater detail on fortifications in World War II may be found in the official history series, U.S. DEPT OF THE ARMY, OFFICE OF MILITARY HISTORY, *United States Army in World War II* (1947–); *Australia in the War of 1939–1945* (1952–); and most notably in the campaign volumes of J.R.M. BUTLER (ed.), *United Kingdom Military Series* (1952–) in *History of the Second World War* (1949–). For a treatment of Korean fortifications, see R.E. APPLEMAN, *South to the Naktong, North to the Yalu* (1961). Literature on the French Indochina War and the American experience in Vietnam is extensive; but see in particular, B.B. FALL, *Hell in a Very Small Place: The Siege of Dien Bien Phu* (1966). For the Israeli experience, see S.L.A. MARSHALL et al., *Swift Sword: The Historical Record of Israel's Victory, June 1967* (1967).

(W.H.B./C.B.MacD.)

Fossil Record

Fossils are the remains or imprints of organisms in rocks that document the history of life. Traces of various activities of organisms, such as trails, tracks, and borings, also are considered as fossils. The study of fossil animals and plants has permitted some reconstruction of the life forms and environments in remote times.

It has been estimated that the weight of all organisms that have lived on the earth since the Cambrian Period (*q.v.*) would equal the total mass of the earth. Most of the organic material ultimately is transmitted from the dead organisms to the living ones (see BIOSPHERE), but even so only an exceedingly small fraction of ancient organisms are preserved as fossils. Only organisms that have a solid and resistant skeleton can readily be preserved. Most major groups of invertebrate animals have a calcareous skeleton or shell (e.g., corals, mollusks, brachiopods, bryozoans). Other forms have shells of calcium phosphate, which also occurs in vertebrate bones, or silicon dioxide. Arthropod skeletons are composed of a hard substance termed "chitin," which may be impregnated by mineral salts (see ELEMENTS, PHYSIOLOGICAL CONCENTRATION OF).

The hard parts of organisms that do become buried in sediment are subject to changes during the conversion of that sediment to solid rock. Solutions may fill the pores of the shell or bone with mineral salts and thus fossilize the remains. The structures preserved, however, may be partly destroyed by later recrystallization. In other cases, circulating acid solutions may dissolve the original shell and leave an open cavity that corresponds to the original shell. In the formation of shales (q.v.), such open cavities may be compressed, leaving only a fossil impression. Circulating calcareous or siliceous solutions may deposit a new matrix in the cavities, however, and by this pseudomorphosis a "new" shell is formed.

Soft parts of animals or plants are very rarely preserved. Famous cases are the Cambrian Burgess Shale fossils (Canada) and the Tertiary lignite fossils of Geiselthal (Germany). The embedding of insects in amber is another example of extraordinary fossil preservation.

The great majority of fossils are preserved in a water environment because land remains are more easily destroyed. Anaerobic conditions at the bottom are favourable for preserving fine details; no bottom faunas are present (except anaerobic bacteria) to destroy the remains. Study of fossil preservation assists in reconstruction of fossil communities, providing the basis for paleoecology, paleogeography (q.v.), and evidence of climatic change (q.v.).

Study of fossils
Fossils were known in antiquity, but their meaning was not understood. Herodotus thought that the large foraminiferans preserved in the limestone of the Egyptian Pyramids were petrified lentils that served as a food supply for the pyramid workers. During the Middle Ages, fossils were looked upon as vis plastica, half-made material left over from the trial and error of creation, or merely as lusus naturae, a play of nature. Leonardo da Vinci was one of the first to understand the true nature of fossils, but it was not until the beginning of the 19th century that paleontology, the study of fossils, became one of the well-established earth sciences (q.v.). Today more than 200,000 fossil animals have been described; however, this is but a mere fraction of the millions of animals and plants that lived at various times on the earth during at least 3,000,000,000 years.

The study of fossils is primarily a biological study because knowledge of the morphology and anatomy of extinct animals and plants is fundamental to a general understanding of the living forms (see CLASSIFICATION, BIOLOGICAL; PHYLOGENY). Through fossils, it is possible to study changes of life over long time periods. Evolution (q.v.) may be interpreted from field and laboratory studies, but fossils provide another dimension, one that permits a following of the trends in evolution and the branching off of new groups through time.

Fossils have an important use in dating events in earth history (see DATING, RELATIVE AND ABSOLUTE). Each period of the geological time scale (q.v.) has its characteristic faunas and floras. Similar assemblages of fossils that occur in widely separated deposits may therefore be correlated in time and determine stratigraphic boundaries (q.v.). In addition to the utility of fossils in deciphering the geological history of the earth in general, fossils are useful in the exploration for minerals and mineral fuels. They serve to determine the stratigraphic position of coal seams, and in recent years the subsurface stratigraphy of petroleum (q.v.) and gas deposits have been studied by

means of microfossils that occur in cores of deep borings. Micropaleontology and stratigraphic paleontology have become important branches of the geological sciences (q.v.). This article is divided into the following sections:

I. The Precambrian fossil record

The apparent lack or scarcity of fossils in the Precambrian record has been a puzzle to scientists for a long time. Stromatolites occur in Precambrian sediments, particularly limestone and dolomites, and these laminated dome- or finger-shaped structures are widely distributed. The earliest ones are more than 2,000,000,000 years old, and it is probable that the thin laminae were deposited by blue-green algae.

In recent years, knowledge of Precambrian life has been greatly extended, not only because of new finds of well-preserved organisms but by the study of organic compounds that represent degradation products of dead organisms. These are termed chemicofossils, and among the more important are isoprenoid alkanes, which have been interpreted as breakdown products of chlorophyll. Samples from the Soudan Iron Formation, Minnesota, have a minimum age of 2,800,000,000 years. These isoprenoids may also be formed by inorganic processes however, though the scarcity of such carbon isotopes as carbon-18 and carbon-17 suggests degradation rather than synthesis. Isoprenoid compounds also have been traced in meteorites.

The oldest fossils
The Gunflint Chert of Ontario, Canada, contains the oldest undoubted fossils of the Precambrian. These microfossils, discovered by S.A. Tyler and E.S. Barghoorn in 1954, occur in a dark chert partly coating stromatolites in the Gunflint Iron Formation. The age of the beds is 1,900,000,000 years. The well-preserved fossils are interpreted as lower thallophytes, thread bacteria, and blue-green algae.

Silicified stromatolites from Queensland, Australia, that are 1,600,000,000 years in age contain fossil micro-organisms with a characteristic pattern resembling closely living myxophycean algae. This is a primitive group on the borderline between the plant and animal kingdoms.

The 1,200,000,000–1,400,000,000-year-old Beck Spring Dolomite from California has yielded blue-green and green algae, which evidently means that cells with a nucleus had evolved by that time. And nuclei are clearly demonstrated in cells from the Bitter Springs Formation of central Australia, which is 1,000,000,000 years old. These microfossils, even better preserved than those in the Gunflint Chert, also occur within chert stromatolites. More than 30 species, representing bacteria, blue-green algae, green algae, and fungus-like organisms, have been described.

Less certain fossil remains have been found in the South African Fig Tree series and Onverwacht formations, which are 3,100,000,000 and 3,200,000,000 years old, respectively. The presumed fossils appear as small spheroid and rod-shaped, bacteria-like bodies. Carbon isotope studies of the Fig Tree series chert suggests that the spheroids may be algae.

The Ediacaran fauna from the Pound Quartzite of South Australia was discovered in 1947 and has been studied in detail in recent years. The age of the beds is either very late Precambrian or very early Cambrian. Most important, however, is the Precambrian character of the fauna. The fossils, which occur as imprints on the surface of the flaggy quartzite beds, are well preserved and represent groups of Metazoa different from those of the Lower Cambrian above and elsewhere. The fossils have been interpreted as hydrozoans (*Ediacaria*), sea pens (*Rangea*), segmented worms, or primitive arthropods (*Spriggina*); others have been difficult to place in known groups. That more or less identical "sea pens" (*Charnia* and *Rangea*) occur in Precambrian beds in England and Siberia confirms the Precambrian aspect of the Ediacaran fauna.

Atmospheric implications The Precambrian fossils so far known agree with the theory of a primarily anoxybiotic atmosphere that became gradually oxygenic toward Paleozoic time. In the beginning, a synthesis of organic compounds was followed by the development of primitive organisms. About 3,000,000,000 years ago some of these attained the ability of photosynthesis. Because of the strong, shortwave ultraviolet radiation, the early organisms had to live in protected places, either in the water or in porous, unconsolidated sediments. Certain organisms like the stromatolites may have been protected by the calcareous mats or laminae produced during their growth.

Bacteria and blue-green algae evidently flourished during the Middle Precambrian (from 1,500,000,000 to 2,500,000,000 years ago, approximately). Cells with nuclei, possibly appearing at the end of this time, heralded a new time in biological evolution and prepared the path for the creation of higher plants and animals. At this time the atmosphere probably contained not much more than 1 percent of O_2. At the end of the Precambrian still less than 5 percent of O_2 was probably present. It has been generally assumed that because of the relatively rich and diverse life known to have existed in Cambrian time, many-celled animals, or metazoans, originated early in the Precambrian. But the fossil record and probable low content of O_2 in the atmosphere may indicate that the more advanced metazoans, needing sufficient oxygen for their respiration, developed late in the Precambrian, perhaps less than 1,000,000,000 years ago (see ATMOSPHERE, DEVELOPMENT OF; PRECAMBRIAN TIME; LIFE).

II. The Phanerozoic fossil record

THE PROTISTA

In recent years, various groups of protists including microfossils of minute planktonic forms (nanoplankton), have been subjected to comprehensive studies utilizing electron microscopy. Because of their distinct vertical and regional distribution, these forms have proved very valuable in the search for petroleum and other mineral deposits. Fossil remains are limited to the hard parts, and it often is difficult to determine taxonomic identities or even to decide whether they are plants or animals. Definitely known unicellular plants are described later. Among protozoans (*q.v.*), only the Sarcodina are of particular fossil importance. Many members of this group have skeletons or tests composed of tectin, calcite, aragonite, or silica or were formed by the agglutination of foreign particles.

Radiolaria and Foraminiferida The Radiolaria, a subclass of the Sarcodina, are well known from the radiolarian ooze of modern marine sediments. These exclusively marine forms, which are 0.05 to a few millimetres in diameter, have a silicified skeleton consisting of an intricate latticework with or without spines. Members of the group appeared in the Middle Ordovician or possibly in the Cambrian, flourished in the Carboniferous and Tertiary, and continued into Recent time. The Foraminiferida, another Sarcodina group, abound in strata from Cambrian to Recent age. Nearly 30,000 species are known, of which almost 90 percent are fossil forms.

Form and structure of the foraminifera. The foraminiferans, or "forams," are mostly marine forms of both benthonic and planktonic types. The size varies from a fraction of a millimetre to several centimetres. The animal usually secretes a support or test that may form a single chamber (primitive forms) with one or more apertures. In most species, however, new chambers are successively added to the primary one (the proloculus) with the apertures (*foramina*, hence the name) maintained through the separating walls, or septa. The chambers are arranged in characteristic patterns, either in a single row, alternating rows, in spirals where the whorls may be visible (evolute), or hidden by later whorls (involute). Their reproduction involves an alternation of asexual and sexual generations with two corresponding types of individuals. The shell wall varies considerably in structure; it may be perforate or imperforate and may be composed of organic material (freshwater forms), calcite or aragonite, or built up by agglutinated material. The calcareous shells, which may be lamellar, are either microgranular, porcellaneous imperforate, or hyaline perforate. The major taxonomic divisions are based on these shell structures. Studies of recent forms suggest that right coiling (dextral) in trochospirally coiled shells (those chambers arranged along a spiral line that does not lie in a plane) indicate populations from warm water, whereas left-

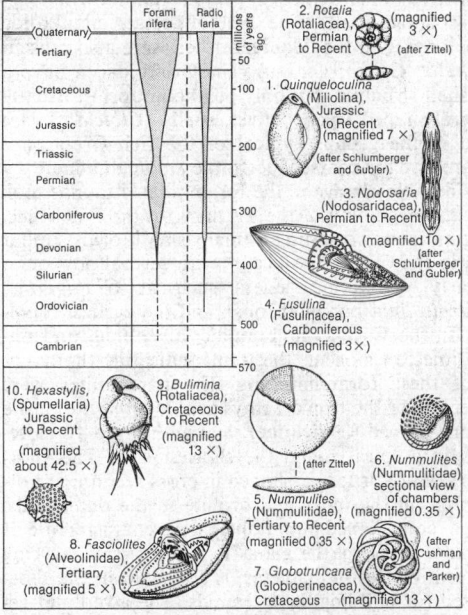

Figure 1: *Representative protists and their geological range.*
(Left) Occurrence of Foraminifera and Radiolaria in the geological record. Width of the stippled zone indicates relative abundance. (1–9) Foraminifera, (10) Radiolaria.
From (1,3,4,7) H. Wienberg Rasmussen, *Paleontologi, Fossile invertebrater*; (6) V. Porkorny, *Grundzuge der zoologischen Mikropalaontologie*; (8,10) Termier and Termier, *Paleontologie Stratigraphique*, copyright 1960, Masson & Cie, Paris; (9) L. Stormer, *Jordens og livets historie*

coiled (sinistral) ones characterize residents of colder waters.

The earliest representatives of the Foraminiferida occur in Cambrian and Ordovician rocks. They are simple forms with a single chamber and a pseudochitinous (suborder Allogromiina) or agglutinated (suborder Textulariina) shells. In the Silurian, the first enrolled tubular textularians appeared. Microgranular calcareous genera also appear in the Silurian and become very abundant in the Upper Paleozoic. Particularly important are members of the suborder Fusulinina, including, among others, the small Endothyracea and the large Fusulinacea. The Endothyridae with their mainly planispiral shells (those with chambers arranged in a spiral fashion but within the same plane) dominated the Lower Carboniferous (Mississipian) and were partly rock building. Characteristic of the Upper Carboniferous (Pennsylvanian) are the larger (up to several centimetres long) members of the Fusulinacea. They are good index fossils, and about 72 genera and more than 1,000 species have been described. *Fusulina* has a spindle-shaped shell with a lamellar outer wall.

The low chambers are coiled around the longest axis, each coil totally covering the earlier ones (involute). *Schwagerina* with fusiform to spheroid shells were mainly characteristic of the Permian.

The Triassic–Jurassic foraminiferid faunas of the Mesozoic Era (*q.v.*) were dominated by members of the suborder Nodosaridacea with hyaline perforate and lamellar shells of calcite or aragonite. *Nodosaria* has several chambers in a single row. Suborder Miliolina is also characteristic of the Mesozoic. These have porcellaneous (imperforate) shells of calcite, and the few chambers are coiled in a spiral round the longest axis. Only the distal parts of the earlier chambers are covered by the later ones (*Quinqueloculina*, *Triloculina*).

Cretaceous and Tertiary evolutionary trends. Foraminiferans were very abundant in the Cretaceous, and some limestone formations have been named for them. Among imperforate calcareous forms, representatives of the Miliolina were characteristic in the earliest Cretaceous, whereas Alveolinidae appeared in the Late Cretaceous. A great expansion of coiled hyaline calcareous foraminiferans took place in the last part of the Mesozoic (*Buliminella*, *Bolivina*), and the first Rotaliacea with shells of calcite with radial structures appeared (*Rotalia* with lens-shaped trochoid shell). The first important planktonic forms belonging to the Globigerinacea were also present (*Heterohelix*, *Globotruncana*). The Orbitoidacea have a similar shell structure, but only benthonic forms, usually with spiral-shaped, planoconvex shells (*Cibicides*), are included in the group. Typical of the rich Cretaceous faunas are also the coarsely perforate Anomalinidae.

Paleocene transition fauna A considerable change in the foraminiferid faunas took place at the beginning of the Tertiary. In the Paleocene, a transition fauna consisting of many small forms similar to those in the Cretaceous occurs with several new ones, particularly planktonic genera such as *Globigerina*, larger *Orbitolina* (porcellaneous), and the earliest *Nummulites*. In the Eocene, nummulitic, alveolinid, and miliolinid limestones occur, the terms indicating the abundance of these foraminiferans. The nummulites were characteristic of the tropic Tethys Sea. *Nummulites* has a flat to lens-shaped (lenticuline) shell with up to 40 close-set coils in a spiral round the shortest axis. The short chambers, more or less V-shaped in cross section, are often involute in the inner and evolute in the outer coils. The large, coin-shaped nummulites were characteristic of the Eocene. In Egypt the giant *N. gizehensis*, measuring several centimetres in diameter, is abundant in the limestone used for building the Pyramids. The alveolinid genus *Fasciolites* was also characteristic of this time. The large Alveolinidae resemble the fusulinids with respect to the general shape of the shell, but the latter had a micrograndular calcite shell, whereas the former has a porcellaneous imperforate shell. There are no genetic relationships between the two groups; the Alveolinidae are to some extent related to the Miliolidae. The numerous chambers in the shell of the alveolinids are divided by secondary septula into tubular chamberlets. Large foraminiferans characteristic of the Middle Tertiary (transition Paleogene–Neogene) belong to the family Miogypsinidae, a group related to the Nummulitidae. Numerous smaller foraminiferans remain and appear during Tertiary and Pleistocene times. The ecology of the later planktonic forms is known through a comparison with living species. A few genera serve as important paleotemperature indicators. The fossil record of the Foraminiferida has shown that this group has played and continues to play an important part in aquatic ecosystems (*q.v.*).

THE SPONGES

Fossil sponges have been recorded from Lower Cambrian to Recent time. Certain remains from the Precambrian have been interpreted as belonging to the Porifera (*q.v.*), but neither the structure nor the age of the fossils are sufficiently well known to warrant a determination. Among the more than 10,000 Recent species of sponges, only a limited number have hard parts capable of being preserved. Assuming similar conditions in the past, the com-

prehensive material of fossil sponges gives but a faint picture of the development of the whole group.

Structures and fossil remains. The Recent Porifera The Recent Porifera are mainly sessile, marine forms that inhabit shallow waters, but they also occur at depth in the oceans. The shapes of the sponges vary from thin covering to free bodies of very different shape. Anatomically they form a primitive group with a zoological position somewhere between unicellular flagellate protozoans and the multicellular metazoans. Characteristic of the body is a system of pores and channels through which passes a water current produced by whiplike collared flagellate cells; an interior wall faces a central cavity. Spicules, which are composed of calcite or silica, form the hard parts of sponges, and these are preserved as fossils. The spicules may be slender rods (monaxon), may form a unit of three to four axes (triaxon, tetraxon), or may be composed of rays (polyaxon). The spicules arranged with distinct angles between the axes may unite, forming solid skeleton.

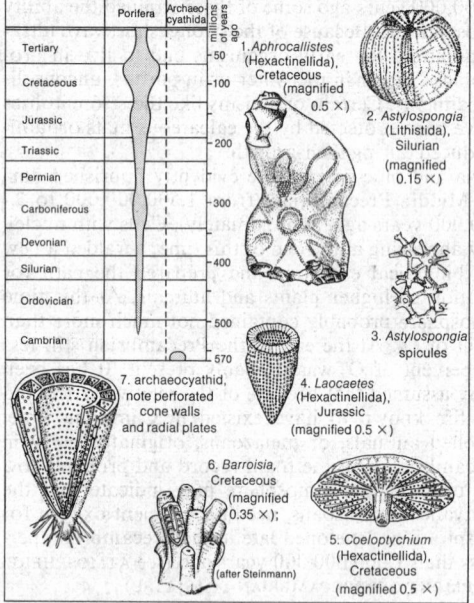

Figure 2: *Representative Porifera and Archaeocyathida and their geological range.*
(Left) Occurrence of Porifera and Archaeocyathida in the geological record. Width of stippled zone indicates relative abundance. (1–6) Porifera, (7) Archaeocyathida.
From (1,3,5,7) H. Wienberg Rasmussen, *Paleontologi, Fossile invertebrater;* (4) Termier and Termier, *Paleontologie Stratigraphique,* copyright 1960, Mason & Cie, Paris

The first fossil remains of the Porifera date from the Lower Cambrian. In the Upper Cambrian, simple monaxon desmosponges (skeleton composed of horny fibres or siliceous spicules) appear; and at the beginning of the Ordovician, lithistid forms (with solid skeleton) develop. These desmosponges form, together with bryozoans, corals, and stromatoporids, distinct reefs in the Middle Ordovician. The heteractinids are fairly evenly distributed throughout the Paleozoic, the last representatives recorded from the Permian. In the Paleozoic, the hexactinellids dominate the Late Devonian and Early Carboniferous faunas.

At the end of the Paleozoic several important groups became extinct, among others the class Heteractinida, and certain hexactinellids and lithistids of the demospongids. Most of the groups that dominated the Mesozoic faunas, however, appeared in the Carboniferous and Permian. This was the case with the Calcarea, of which the first known representatives occur in the Carboniferous. Representatives of this group became prominent in the Permian and Triassic and were reef builders at the time when the Paleozoic corals declined and the later scleractinous corals (stony corals) were ready to start their strong development. The Calcarea became extinct at the end of the Cretaceous.

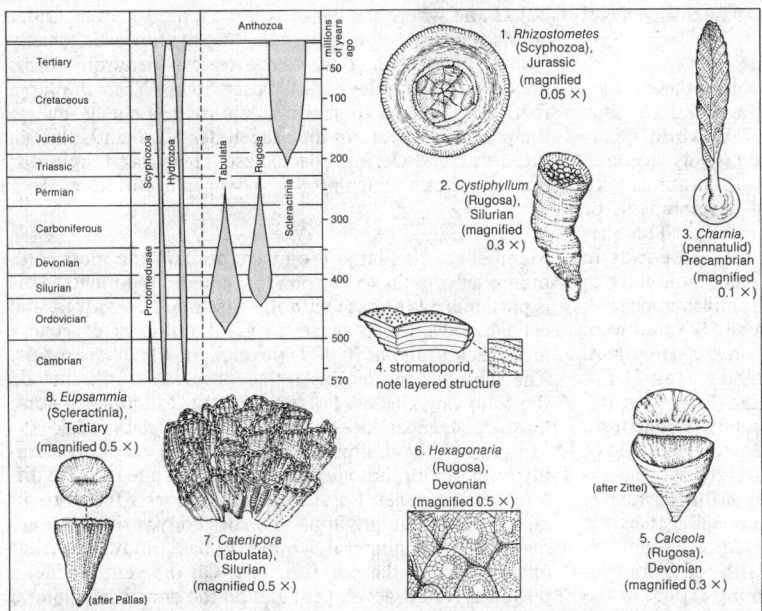

Figure 3: *Representative Coelenterata (Cnidaria) and their geological range.*
(Left) Occurrence of the classes Protomedusae, Scyphozoa, Hydrozoa, and Anthozoa in
the geological record. Anthozoa are shown in terms of the subclasses Tabulata, Rugosa,
and Scleractinia. Width of stippled zone indicates relative abundance. (1–8) Fossil
coelenterates as designated.

From (1,2,5,7) H. Wienberg Rasmussen, *Paleontologi, Fossile invertebrater;* (3) *Proceedings of the Yorkshire
Geological Society* (1958); L. Stormer, *Jordens og livets historie;* (6) Hill, *Treatise on Invertebrate Paleontology,*
courtesy of The Geological Society of America and The University of Kansas Press; (8) Termier and Termier,
Paleontologie Stratigraphique, copyright 1960, Masson & Cie, Paris

The Porifera had a strong development in the Cretaceous. A great number of genera have been described from different countries. The flint of the chalk beds may have received its silica from hexactinellid sponges. During the Cenozoic, the Porifera apparently played about the same role in the marine faunas as they do today.

Relation of sponges and archaeocyathids. The Archaeocyathida are an ancient and apparently short-lived group, once considered to be among the Porifera. More recent studies, however, have shown that they represent a separate phylum with no close affinities to the sponges or other known groups, except that certain authors have suggested that Carboniferous sponges of the Calcarea may have evolved from the archaeocyathids.

The Archaeocyathida had fragile calcite skeletons. A three- to ten-centimetre-high cup was attached to the hard bottom by rootlike extensions. The cup consists of two cones, one within the other, held apart by radial plates reaching from the inner wall of the outer cone to the outer wall of the inner. Both cones are perforated by many pores; these are very fine in the outer cone and coarser in the inner. Pores also are on the radial plates.

The archaeocyathids had a strong development in the Lower Cambrian but probably became extinct in the earlier part of the Middle Cambrian. Several classes and orders and 92 genera have been established for members of this phylum, which had a worldwide distribution. The reefs or "gardens" of archaeocyathids along ancient Cambrian shores in Australia are quite famous.

THE COELENTERATA

The Coelenterata (Cnidaria) are characterized by the presence of stinging capsules or nematocysts, and the phylum includes the hydras, siphonophores, jellyfish, sea anemones, and corals, comprising about 9,000 species, almost all of them marine (see CNIDARIA; CORAL ISLANDS, CORAL REEFS, and ATOLLS).

The fossil record of the coelenterates is chiefly based on specimens with a calcareous skeleton. Impressions of softer parts, such as the outer surface of jellyfishes and the sedimentary filling of their gastrovascular cavities, provide important information on their structure, however. The fossil coelenterates belong to the classes Protomedusae, Scyphozoa, Hydrozoa, and Anthozoa.

The class Protomedusae is represented by jellyfish-like

molds and impressions from the Precambrian and Early Ordovician, particularly in North America and Europe. The precise classification of these forms is uncertain; *Brooksella* had a subellipsoidal body with 4 to 15 radial lobes and four oral arms. A fourfold symmetry, characteristic of scyphozoans, is most abundant, but five or seven lobes are also common. *Hallidaya* and *Skinneria* from the transitional Precambrian–Cambrian in Australia show a threefold radial symmetry, possibly an offshoot of the general trend of development.

Representatives of the class Scyphozoa have been recorded from all systems, from Late Precambrian upwards to Recent time. It is difficult to be sure that the jellyfish-like imprints are scyphozoans and not medusae of hydrozoans. Paleozoic forms have been included in the Recent order Coronatida, while the well-preserved *Rhizostometes* from the Jurassic of Solnhofen in Germany has been referred to a separate order, Lithorhizostomatida.

Among the class Hydrozoa, the Recent orders Trachylinida, Hydroida, Milleporina, Stylasterina, and Siphonophorida have been recorded as fossils as well as the extinct Stromatoporidea. Trachylinids occur in the Jurassic, and possibly *Ediacaria* from the Late Precambrian belongs to the order. Middle Cambrian and Upper Carboniferous medusae are known, and a few Ordovician–Devonian impressions of pneumatophores and velae have been referred to as siphonophores. The Milleporina and Stylasterina (often united as the order Hydrocorallina) are known from Early Tertiary to Recent time. More important geologically were the Stromatoporidea, which are known from the Cambrian to the Lower Tertiary. The colonial stromatoporids secreted a calcareous skeleton, usually forming irregular rounded masses up to one metre thick. The stromatoporids were common in the Ordovician–Devonian when they formed reefs of considerable thickness.

Occurrence and evolution of corals. The class Anthozoa, or corals, comprises five subclasses, the Alcyonaria (or Octocoralla), Tabulata, Rugosa, Heterocorallia, and Scleractinia (the three last often included in subclass Zoantharia). The colonial Octocoralla have eight pinnate tentacles and a calcareous spicular or horny skeleton with no septa. Scattered fossil representatives are known from the Mesozoic onward. The Pennatulacea, or sea pens, have been recorded (with doubt) from the Silurian, and

Archae-
ocyathids

Hydro-
zoans

the Precambrian *Rangea* and *Charnia* show a superficial resemblance to the pennatulids.

The subclass Tabulata, or tetracorals, played an important part in the Paleozoic faunas. During their range, from the Cambrian to the close of the Permian, they formed important reefs in many parts of the world. Characteristic of the tabulates are the exclusively colonial mode of growth and the slender tubes or corallites with distinct partitions or tabulae and faint development, or absence, of longitudinal partitions or septa. The first representatives of the group were certain auloporids in the Middle Cambrian. A great development took place in the Middle Ordovician, when 14 new families appeared. Characteristic genera of the Ordovician and Silurian were *Favosites* (with perforate walls), *Halysites, Syringopora* (with connecting tubules between corallites), and *Heliolites* (with coenenchyme). The Ordovician *Tetradium* is a guide fossil for American Arctic faunas. Favositidae were common in the Devonian, Auloporidae and Chaetidae in the Carboniferous. The Tabulata apparently became extinct abruptly (seven families) at the end of the Permian.

Rugose corals

The subclass Rugosa, with more than 600 genera, is another important group of Paleozoic corals. Members of the group were contemporaneous with the Tabulata, appearing in the Ordovician and becoming extinct at the end of the Permian. The fairly large rugose corals were either solitary or had a colonial manner of growth. The solitary types were cone shaped or curved (horn corals) and might be attached to the substrate by rootlike appendages. Numerous minute transverse ribs and furrows on the surface of the cups probably indicate daily and seasonal growth and have been used to determine the length of the year in ancient times (see DATING, RELATIVE AND ABSOLUTE). The colonial forms were dendroid or densely packed, forming massive colonies with prismatic corallites. Characteristic of the Rugosa are the prominent and numerous septa sometimes meeting centrally to form a columella. The septa are radially arranged, but a four-part symmetry is also present (in Tetracoralla). Of the three orders of rugose corals, two (Streptelasmatida and Columnariida) and possibly a third (Ceptiphyllida) appeared in the Middle Ordovician. A rapid and strong development with reef building took place in the Middle Silurian and Lower Devonian, and later in the Devonian a great wealth of new forms appeared. A new evolution took place in the Carboniferous, and, in the Permian, members of the Cyathaxonicae might have given rise to the Scleractinia, which replaced the Rugosa in the Mesozoic. During the Paleozoic, rugose corals without dissepiments, supporting structures of horizontal plates (*Lambeophyllum* and *Columnaria*), were characteristic of the Ordovician. Dissepiments developed in early Silurian Streptelasmatina and Columnarina and particularly in the Cystiphyllida. In the Devonian, the Digonophyllidae and the Goniophyllidae (with an operculum) were common; and in the Carboniferous, forms with axial structures, such as the Lithostrotionidae and Lonsdaleiidae, prevailed. In the Carboniferous, a small group that has been distinguished as a separate subclass (Heterocoralla), characterized mainly by the unique manner of insertion of the septa in the corallite, occurs.

Reef-building corals. The subclass Scleractinia, or hexacorals, includes practically all solitary and colonial modern corals. Characteristic of the group is the essentially radial symmetry (no bilateral symmetry, such as in the Rugosa), and the ontogeny of the septa is also different. The Scleractinia are related to sea anemones, which, however, have no hard parts. The possible derivation of the Scleractinia from the Rugosa is uncertain. The oldest known representatives are from the Middle Triassic (five families); the first ones did not form reefs, but in Late Triassic time, reefs became common. Great evolution and expansion of the group occurred in the Middle Jurassic and Lower Cretaceous, with worldwide reef building.

Depth of coral reefs

The reefs have been subject to comprehensive studies, largely because they have proved to be important pockets of oil. Most recent reefs occur in tropical areas where the temperature of the water varies largely between 23°–29° C and where the depth is less than 50 metres. Other corals may be found at greater depth, however, chiefly from 20 to 500 metres, where certain dendroid forms may form comprehensive "copsewood." When the large reefs are confined to shallow depths, it is chiefly due to the presence of certain dinoflagellates (Zooxanthellae) in the coral endoderm cells. These algae need light for photosynthesis, which produces oxygen useful to corals.

THE MOLLUSCA

Members of this large group are perhaps the most common macrofossils to be found in aquatic sediments. This is particularly the case with the gastropods, bivalves, and cephalopods, which occur in great numbers of genera and species (about 70,000) throughout the Phanerozoic. The shell-bearing mollusks that occur as fossils include the following classes: Polyplacophora, Monoplacophora, Gastropoda, Scaphopoda, and Bivalvia (Pelecypoda).

In general, the mollusks (see MOLLUSCA) vary considerably both in morphology and size, but in spite of these differences the general plan of construction is the same in all groups of the phylum. The soft body, primarily segmented with a bilateral symmetry, has a mouth in front and an anus in the posterior end. On the ventral side, a powerful foot is developed; and on the dorsal side, lateral outgrowths from the mantle cover the mantle cavity with gills. This general pattern may be strongly modified by a considerable twisting or torsion of the body in gastropods and a strong bending of the body in cephalopods. The fossil remains of the mollusks are usually limited to the calcium carbonate shells secreted by the mantle; muscle scars and other impressions of soft parts occassionally provide additional information.

The class Polyplacophora, or Amphineura, are represented today by the chitons. With their simple bilateral symmetry and a segmentation indicated by a single row of dorsal plates, these forms are primitive representatives of the Mollusca. They are known from the Upper Cambrian to Recent time.

Of particular interest is the class Monoplacophora, which until quite recently was known only from shells from the Lower Paleozoic. In 1952 the Danish Galathea Expedition discovered a living species in the Pacific, essentially an unexpected living fossil; *Neopilina* has a cap-like shell that covers a bilateral body with five pairs of gills. These primitive structures indicate that the monoplacophorans developed from annelid worms. Fossil representatives are known from the Lower Cambrian to the Upper Silurian (possibly Devonian).

Snails in the fossil record

Gastropods and scaphopods. The class Gastropoda (*q.v.*), or snails, includes about 85,000 species, of which one-third are fossil species. They are recorded from the Lower Cambrian onward and were more common in the Mesozoic and Cenozoic than in the Paleozoic. Most species are marine, but freshwater and terrestrial forms also occur, evidently derived from marine ancestors.

The earliest gastropods known are the Helcionellacea, which appeared in the Lower Cambrian and apparently became extinct by Upper Cambrian time. Members of the group had a worldwide distribution, but because only the shells are known, their gastropod nature is not definitely established. By Cambrian–Ordovician time, most of the major orders of gastropods were present, a fact that demonstrates the considerable age of the group. Silurian specimens of *Bellerophon* have imprints on the shell that indicate the presence of two identical gills, a feature that must be interpreted as primitive. During the Paleozoic and the Mesozoic, the gastropods flourished and displayed a great variation in shell morphology. In the Cretaceous, forms with a well-developed siphon appeared, and this group became very common in the Tertiary. The *Pteropoda*, pelagic forms in which the mantle is modified into "fins," appeared in the Carboniferous. Small tubelike forms from the Lower Cambrian also have been referred to this group, but they may belong to the worms. The terrestrial Pulmonata (*Helix, Planorbis*) are known from the Upper Jurassic onward.

The class Scaphopoda forms a small group of mollusks

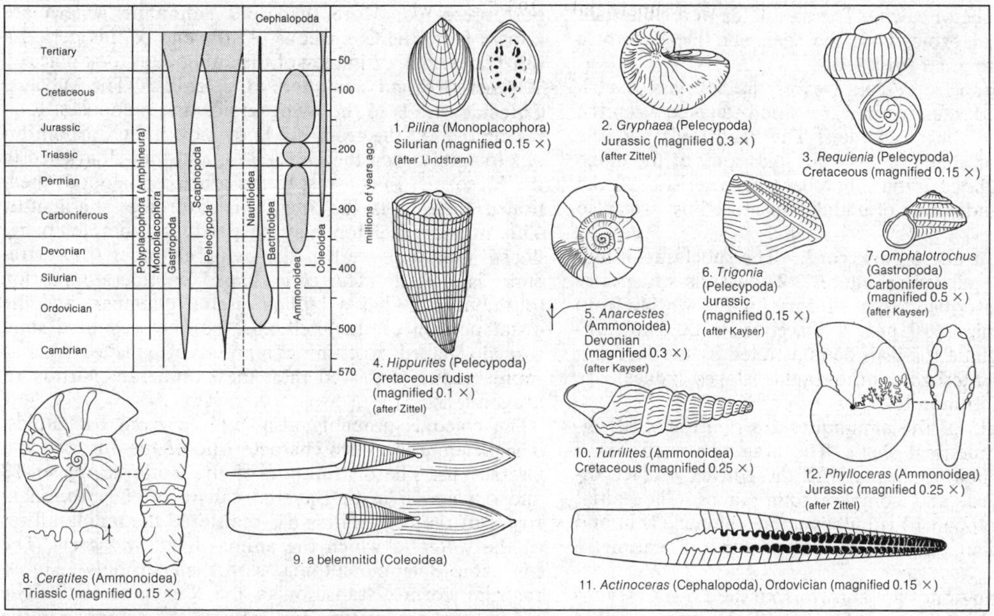

Figure 4: *Representative mollusks and their geological range.*
(Left) Occurrence of the classes Polyplacophora, Monoplacophora, Gastropoda,
Scaphopoda, Pelecypoda, and Cephalopoda in the geological record. Cephalopoda are
shown in terms of the subclasses Nautiloidea, Bactritoidea, Ammonoidea, and Coleoidea.
Width of stippled zone indicates relative abundance. (1–12) Fossil mollusks as designated.
From (1,9,11) W. Rasmussen, *Paleontologi, Fossile invertebrater;* and (8,10) *Treatise on Invertebrate
Paleontology,* courtesy of The Geological Society of America and the University of Kansas Press

Bivalves

with slender cone-shaped, bilateral shells. Adapted to a burrowing habitat, the head is reduced to a conic projection. They show affinities to the bivalves because of their bilateral symmetry and resemble the gastropods in having a radula. Scaphopods are known with certainty from Devonian and later geological systems to recent time.

Structure and evolution of pelecypods. The class Bivalvia (Pelecypoda or Lamellibranchia of other authors; see BIVALVIA) occurs in abundance throughout the Phanerozoic. The soft body is laterally compressed between two shells, a right and left shell, each of which is a mirror image of the other except when a secondary modification has taken place. No head is present, and the two rows of gill blades in the mantle cavity serve as filters for catching micro-organisms. The mantle is fused along the margins of both sides and may be prolonged into a single or doubled siphon with channels for inflowing and outgoing water currents. The two protecting shells of aragonite or calcite are held together by muscles and open and close along with a hinge plate provided with teeth and sockets. These structures and the development of the muscle scars are of major importance to the taxonomy.

The first bivalves are known from the Middle Cambrian (order Actonodontoidea). The Ribeiroida from the Lower Cambrian have been referred by some authors to the Bivalvia, but their taxonomic position is doubtful. Some of the earliest bivalves have muscle scars (of six to eight pairs of pedal retractor muscles) directly comparable to those of *Neopilina*, a feature that indicates that both groups had common ancestors. By Ordovician time, a number of more advanced and still living orders (Nuculoida, Pteroida, Arcoida, Veneroida, Lucinoida, and Praecardioida) are represented. The bivalves were subject to considerable adaptive radiation in the Ordovician, but as faunal elements they became more important in the upper part of the Paleozoic. They flourished through the Mesozoic and Cenozoic; thin-shelled forms were characteristic of soft bottoms, and thick-shelled forms were characteristic of hard bottoms, particularly reefs subject to wave action. The reef forms display a strong specialization to this habit of life. Members of the Hippuritoidea, ranging from the Jurassic to the Cretaceous, were large thick-shelled forms in which the two shells were very differently developed. *Requienia* had the left shell whorled almost like a gastropod shell, whereas the right shell formed a small operculum only. In the peculiar rudists,

so characteristic of the tropical reef faunas of the Tethys, the right shell forms a large ribbed cone covered by a disklike left shell.

Structure of cephalopods. The class Cephalopoda (*q.v.*), which is represented in the present seas by the octopus, the squid, and nautilus, is of particular interest to the paleontologist. The fossil remains of cephalopods provide valuable information of the evolution and adaptive radiations of this peculiar group. Characteristic of the cephalopod body are the well-developed head surrounded by arms or tentacles, the ventrally situated mantle cavity with one or two pairs of gills, and the presence of a funnel formed by the fused lateral portions of the mantle. In the above mentioned groups of mollusks, the soft body was generally enclosed in a solid shell; in cephalopods this was true only of the nautiloids (represented today by *Nautilus*) and the ammonites (now extinct); in the coleoids, on the other hand, the shell became covered by the mantle and reduced, and in some it was even lost. The generally elongate cone-shaped or coiled shells were divided by transverse septa into numerous gas-filled compartments; a large one at the open end served as the living chamber for the animal. A fleshy stalk or siphuncle, often enclosed in septal necks, runs from the living chamber backward to the initial compartment. The line marking the junction between the septa and the inner wall of the shell is known as the suture line, a structure of considerable taxonomic importance. Calcite may have been deposited in the gas chambers to adjust the weight and the horizontal position of the body in the water.

The cephalopods are represented today by some 150 genera, but they had a far greater development in ancient times. In the Mesozoic in particular they were the champions of the seas and have served as some of the very best guide fossils.

The first true cephalopods, the Ellesmeroceratida, appeared rather suddenly in the Upper Cambrian (certain Lower Cambrian forms, *Salterella* and *Volborthella*, have been regarded as cephalopods but probably belong to other groups). The widespread ellesmeroceratids, characteristic of the Lower Ordovician, evidently formed a central group from which both the nautiloids and the bactritoids evolved. Related to the ellesmoceratids were the Ordovician endoceratids that attained a length of nearly nine metres and had a large siphuncle partly filled

Ancestors of the octopus and squid

by an inner tube of calcite. The nautiloids were abundant during the Paleozoic; both the shell and the siphuncle were subject to great variation.

In the Silurian, representatives of the subclass Bactritoida appeared; these form a transition stage between the nautiloids and the ammonites. The bactritoids had the simple slender shells of the nautiloids and, at the same time, the bulbous initial chamber characteristic of the ammonites. Indication of undulated suture lines was also present.

Ammonites in the fossil record. The subclass Ammonoidea is of particular interest. Thousands of species have been described from all parts of the world, from Lower Devonian to Upper Cretaceous strata. Their importance as guide fossils is demonstrated by the fact that most of the Mesozoic stratigraphic stages (zones) are named after ammonites.

Coiling characteristics of ammonites

Characteristic of the ammonites are tightly coiled, bilaterally symmetrical shells. The aragonite shell has a long living chamber, septa with the convex surface directed forward, and complex suture lines. The initial chamber (protoconch) is bulbous, the siphuncle thin and mostly marginal, and the size ranges from one centimetre to 2.5 metres.

The first ammonites are known from the Lower Devonian. They evidently evolved from nautiloids, very possibly through the bactritoids, in three periods: the Upper Paleozoic, characterized by goniatites; the Triassic, characterized by ceratites; and the Jurassic–Cretaceous, characterized by the true ammonites. The earliest goniatites had one simple lobe in the suture line, and septa directed backward as in nautiloids; later representatives had several lobes and ammonoid septa. The earliest ceratids appeared in the Permian and had an "explosive" radiation in the Triassic. About 400 genera and subgenera are known. These are divided into 30 ammonite stages or zones, each of which lasted a little more than 1,000,000 years. The ceratites had simple lobes, but the saddles were serrate. In later Triassic forms (*Ptychites*), however, the suture lines became considerably more complex, almost of ammonite type.

For some unknown reason, practically all the ammonites died out at the end of the Permian. Only two families survived, and one (Otoceratacea) gave rise to the great number of ceratids in the Triassic. A second major extinction of ammonites took place at the close of the Triassic. In this case, all the ceratites left the scene, only one member of one family (Octocertacea) of the suborder Phylloceratina crossing the boundary to the Jurassic to give rise to still another explosive radiation in the Jurassic–Cretaceous. The phylloceratids, with their characteristic phylloid saddle endings, became a very stable group, remaining little changed from Triassic to Cretaceous time. From the Phylloceratina evolved the Lytoceratina (characterized by strongly divided lobes with mosslike endings), which were the main ancestors to the Ammonitina.

Aberrant ammonite forms

Of particular interest is the unusual development of the shell in some lytoceratid families. Uncoiled forms occur in the Jurassic, and in the Cretaceous various "aberrant" shell types became abundant and significant. Loosely coiled shells (*Critoceratites*), partly uncoiled shells (*Macroscaphites*), and straight ones (*Baculites*) occur together with helical forms (*Turrilites*) and forms forming an irregular tangle (*Nipponites*). These irregular ammonites have been looked upon as degenerate forms predicting the final extinction of the ammonites. It may be true to some extent for this particular group; however, "normal" ammonites lived side by side with the "aberrant" ones for 60,000,000–70,000,000 years. In the Upper Cretaceous ammonites with simple ceratites-like suture lines occur (*Tissotia*).

The suborder Ammonitina includes a great number of usually thick-shelled and strongly ornamented forms ranging from the Lower Jurassic to the Upper Cretaceous. Narrow disklike forms were probably good swimmers. Often the cover of the shell opening, the so-called aptychus composed of calcite (not aragonite), is the only

part preserved. More than 500 ammonite genera are known from the Cretaceous. At the end of this period a third, and final, extinction of the ammonites took place.

Occurrence and evolution of coleoids. The subclass Coleoidea leads to the living squids and octopuses. Representatives of the group are known from the Carboniferous (possibly even the Devonian), and they flourished in the Mesozoic. In contrast to the other cephalopods mentioned, the shell of the coleoids is covered by the mantle. This interior skeleton may be partly or completely reduced. Only one wall of the living chamber (pro-ostracum) is present. The cone-shaped cammerate portion (phragmocone) has a bulbous initial chamber, and the distal portion of the shell may be enclosed in a solid torpedo-shaped rostrum composed of calcite. This is more readily preserved than the cammerate portion of aragonite.

The coleoids probably also evolved from bactritoids. The Belemnitina were characteristic of the Jurassic and Cretaceous. The distribution of the isotopes oxygen-18 and oxygen-16 in the layered calcite of the prominent rostra of the belemnitids has registered the temperatures of the water in which the animal lived and grew. The Mesozoic Belemnoteuthina, with their strongly reduced rostrum, form a transition to the Recent teuthids. The sepiids appeared in the Tertiary and the octopods in the Upper Cretaceous.

THE CONODONTA

These enigmatic microfossils ranging from the Ordovician to the Upper Triassic, possibly Cretaceous, form another group of important index fossils. To the stratigraphers, particularly those dealing with subsurface cores, these microfossils play about the same role in the Paleozoic as do the foraminiferans in the Mesozoic and the Cenozoic. Thousands of species, or form species, rather, have been described. See the article CONODONTS for information on the occurrence and evolution of this group.

THE BRYOZOA

The calcareous skeletons of these small colonial invertebrates are common fossils in Paleozoic and younger formations. Living species are, with a few exceptions, marine; they prefer clear, not turbid, water.

Marine bryozoans (*q.v.*) belong to the class Gymnolaemata. The class has been divided into five or six orders (a last order, Cystiporata, was recently established by G.G. Astrova in 1964). The different orders are characterized mainly by the shape of the colony (zoaria) and the individuals that comprise it. Of the six orders, three are confined to the Paleozoic: the Trepostomata, the Cystoporata, and the Cryptostomata. The three remaining orders, of which the Cyclostomata and the Ctenostomata start in the Ordovician and the Cheilostomata in the Cretaceous, all live on to Recent time.

Uncertain remains from the Upper Cambrian have been interpreted as possible bryozoans. The first true bryozoans are recorded from the Lower Ordovician, and a strong development of the group took place in Middle Ordovician time, when five orders and 20 families were represented. This marked unfolding of the bryozoans coincides with a similar rapid evolution of other large groups with well-developed calcareous shells: the corals, brachiopods, and crinoids. Characteristic of the Ordovician is the semisphaeric *Diplotrypa*, while *Hallopora*, among others, is common in the Silurian. Some families did not continue into the Devonian. Bryozoans also were common throughout the Upper Paleozoic, but at the end of the Permian several families became extinct. The Fennestellidae, the "lace bryozoans," are particularly characteristic of the Carboniferous and Permian. In the Mesozoic and Cenozoic, especially in the Cretaceous and Tertiary, the cheilostoms are the most common. They appear as thin crusts on stones and shells. A common genus is *Membranipora*. As guide fossils the bryozoans have become increasingly important because of their abundance and worldwide distribution.

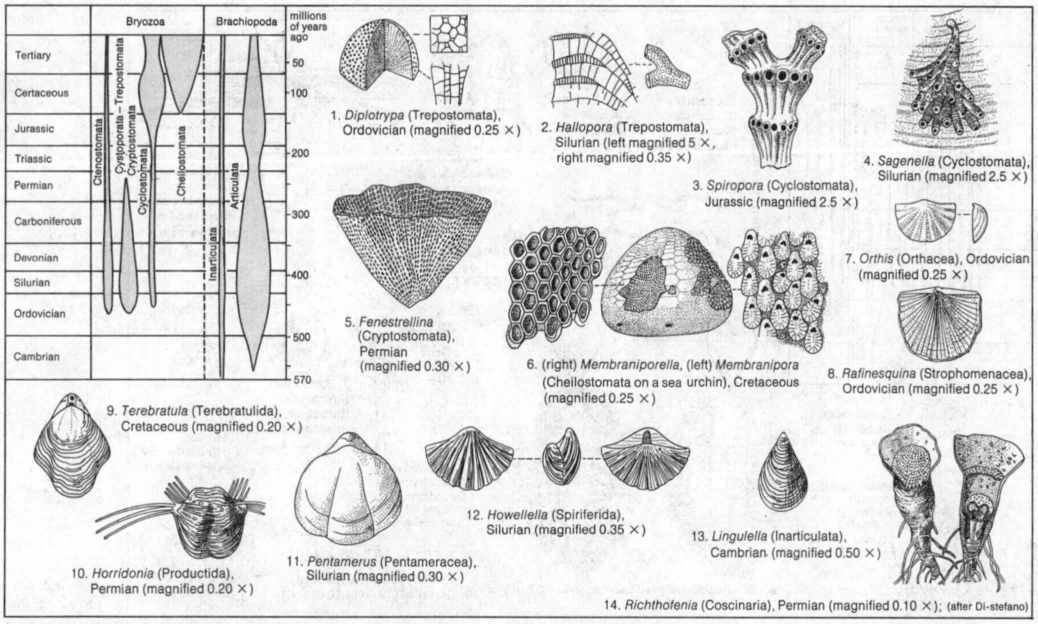

Figure 5: *Representative bryozoans and brachiopods and their geological range.*
(Left) Occurrence of orders of Bryozoa and classes of Brachiopoda in the geological
record. Width of stippled zone indicates relative abundance. (1–6) Fossil bryozoans,
(7–14) fossil brachiopods.
From (1,2,7,13) L. Stormer, *Jordens og livets historie;* (3,6,14) H. Wienberg Rasmussen, *Paleontologi,*
Fossile invertedrater

THE BRACHIOPODA

Brachio-
pod
structures

The about 260 living species of brachiopods (*q.v.*) constitute only a fraction of the approximate 30,000 fossil
species known. In the Paleozoic particularly, these "lamp
shells" flourished and to a large extent dominated the
shelly marine faunas.

Characteristic of the brachiopods are the lophophore,
an appendage around the mouth (similar to that of the
bryozoans), and the two bilaterally symmetrical shells or
valves that are secreted by the mantle. The fossil remains
left to the paleontologist are largely limited to the hard
parts comprising the valves and the skeleton supporting
the lophophore (if such a structure is present) and the
various markings on the inside of the valves. The markings on the inner shell surface are mainly muscle scars
and pallial markings made by a branched system of circulatory canals in the mantle. The muscles are placed behind the mantle cavity. In primitive brachiopods belonging to the class Inarticulata, the two valves are held together by two pairs of adductor muscles. In the class
Articulata, the two valves articulate along a posterior
hinge line, a structure that needs both adductor and di-
ductor muscles.

The shell of most inarticulate brachiopods is composed
of calcium phosphate and chitinous organic matter; some
inarticulates and all articulates have shells of calcium
carbonate. These shells are either impunctate (compact),
punctate, or pseudopunctate. The punctate shells have
fine pores, whereas the pseudopunctate ones have rodlike
calcareous bodies that, when subject to weathering, may
look like puncta.

Most brachiopods prefer a hard bottom, but soft bottom
forms occur too. In the latter case the pedicle may be
reduced to form a thin thread by which the animal was
tied to the bottom. In some species the pedicle is lost, but
in burrowing forms (*Lingula*) it is large and strong.

The taxonomy of the brachiopods is based on various
characters such as the shell structure, the pedicle opening, and the development of the cardinalia (hinge structures). Of the 11 brachiopod orders, only four, the Lingu-
lida, Acrotretida, Rhynchonellida, and Terebratulida, are
still extant. The Inarticulata are confined chiefly to the
Cambrian and Ordovician; the Articulata were common
from the Ordovician onward.

In Lower Cambrian strata seven inarticulate families
are found to appear, together with a few articulates belonging to the order Orthida. A great burst in the de-

velopment of the articulates took place at the beginning
of the Middle Ordovician. This was particularly the case
with the three superfamilies Orthacea, Plectambonitacea,
and Strophomenacea. The Pentameracea were characteristic of the Silurian, together with the Rhynchonellida
and the Atrypida, and the latter also were typical of
Devonian strata. The large, and stratigraphically important, order Spiriferida had a strong development in the
Upper Silurian, flourished throughout the Paleozoic, and
then became extinct in the Jurassic. The Productacea, a
superfamily of the Strophomenida, dominated the Carboniferous and Permian faunas (in the Lower Carboniferous 45 percent of the 142 known brachiopod genera
were Productacea). Related to productids were the highly
specialized Richthofeniacea, in which the ventral valve
was long and cone shaped while the dorsal valve formed
a small operculum within the cone. These forms were
attached to the bottom by rootlike spines and lived on
exposed coral reefs like the similar rugose corals and
rudist bivalves. The Terebratulida occur in Mesozoic
and Cenozoic deposits.

Brachio-
pods in
the fossil
record

THE ARTHROPODA

Today the arthropods have an unique position among the
animals inhabiting the earth. Because of the insects in
particular, arthropods (*q.v.*) form about 75–80 percent
of all species described, and no other metazoans have
been able to adapt themselves to so many different environments. In ancient times, the arthropods were of primary import and were rather easily preserved as fossils
because of their usually solid exoskeleton. Because of
molting, one individual could actually be preserved many
times, each molt providing a separate fossil. The arthropods have proved to be very important index fossils.
Their geological appearance from the dawn of the Cambrian until today has shed light on the complex relationships and phylogeny of the phylum's members.

This large and heterogenous phylum may have had a
polyphylitic origin. A natural systematic division of the
arthropods has proved difficult, in large part because of
the many cases of adaptions leading to parallel development in less related forms. Obviously complex organs
such as compound eyes, mandibles, and trachea have developed independently in remote groups. Six major
groups (subphyla or superclasses) of arthropods may be
separated: Onychophora, Trilobitomorpha, Chelicerata,
Crustacea, Myriapoda, and Insecta. The second and third

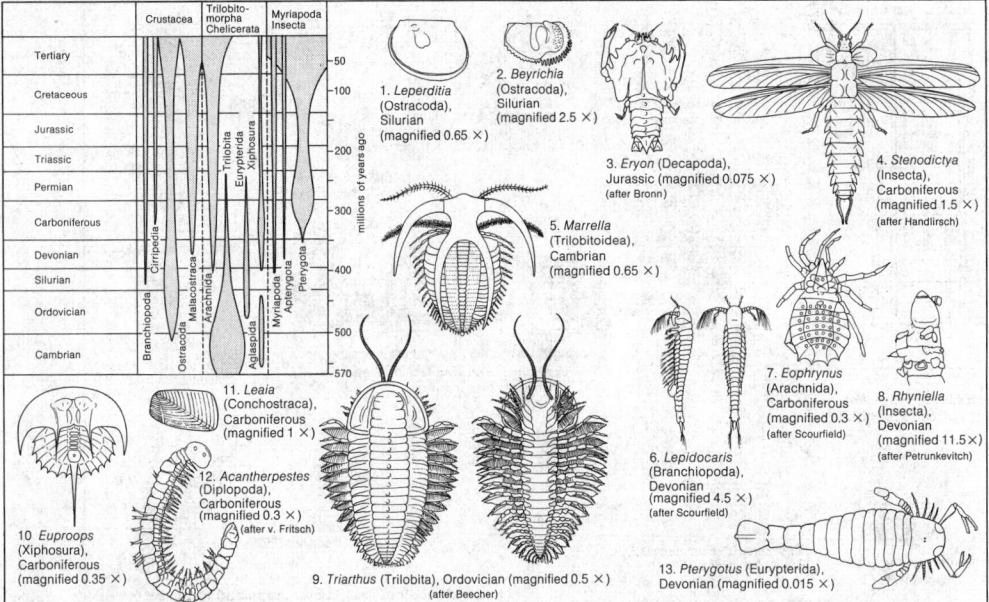

Figure 6: *Representative arthropods and their geological range.*
(Left) Occurrence of the Crustacea, Trilobitomorpha, Chelicerata, and Myriapoda and
Insecta groups in the geological record. Width of stippled zone indicates relative
abundance. (1–13) Fossil arthropods as designated.
From (1,4,6,7,9,12) H. Wienberg Rasmussen, *Paleontologi, Fossile invertebrater*; (2) Benson, *Treatise on
Invertebrate Paleontology*, courtesy of the Geological Society of America and The University of Kansas Press;
(3,11) Termier and Termier, *Paleontologie Stratigraphique*, copyright 1960, Masson & Cie, Paris; (8,10,13)
L. Stormer, *Jordens og livets historie*

groups probably belong to one stock, and the same is true
of the Myriapoda and Insecta.

Structure of trilobites. In the Cambrian about 60
percent of the fossils described are trilobites. Fifteen
hundred genera and about 10,000 species are known from
the earliest Cambrian to the end of the Permian. The
numerous trilobites vary considerably in shape and size
(from 0.5 millimetre to 700 millimetres), but it is interesting that, in spite of this diversity, the definite plan of construction seems to have remained unchanged.

The trilobite had a solid exoskeleton composed of calcite or calcium phosphate with a smooth, granulated, or
spiny surface, the shell pierced by fine canals. The dorsal
armour shows a double tripartition; a pair of longitudinal
furrows separate a median axis from the lateral pleurae,
and transverse joint lines separate the thorax from the
head shield, or cephalon, and from the tail shield, or
pygidium.

The head shield has a median axis (glabella) with transverse lobes indicating a metamer segmentation and a pair
of lateral compound eyes that might have had several
thousands facets. Lines of weakness in the shell ran
across the cheeks along the eyes. They opened during the
molting and facilitated the process. These so-called facial
sutures divide the head shield into a median portion
(cranidium) and lateral portions that represented the free
cheeks (librigenae), often provided with horns or spines.
The thorax is composed of 2–40 transverses, free segments articulated to each other and to the head shield and
tail shield. The tail shield forms a solid plate composed
of a variable number of segments.

On the ventral side of the flat trilobite body only the in-
flected marginal parts (doublure) and a large upper lip
(hypostoma) ventral to the mouth were covered by an
exoskeleton capable of being preserved under normal
conditions. The rest of the ventral surface was covered by
a thin chitinous integument. The axial portion contained
the vital portion of the body; here the appendages were
attached.

The delicate appendages are known in a limited but representative number of species ranging from the Cambrian to the Devonian. Of particular interest is the uniform development of the appendages. In front a pair of
flexible antennae occurs, and beyond these all appendages
are practically identical (with the exception of an anten-

na-like posterior appendage in one species). This primitive condition is unique among arthropods and is indicative of annelid ancestors. Four pairs of appendages behind the antennae belong to the head shield. Each appendage is biramous with a median walking leg (telopo-
dite) and a lateral comblike appendage attached to the
base, not the end of the strong coxa, as in crustaceans.
The teeth of the "comb" on the lateral branch may have
served as gills such as in the living horseshoe crabs. Because no jaws are developed and the upper lip completely
covers the front of the mouth, the trilobites probably
were mud eaters, the mud probably carried forward by
water currents and filtered through the comblike structures. A satisfactory taxonomy has not yet been established. No single character (*e.g.*, the cephalic sutures)
has proved adequate for a major classification.

Occurrence and evolution of trilobites. In the Lower
Cambrian, 21 trilobite families were present, among
them the primitive Olenellina and Redlichina, which
have a distinctly segmented axis in the cephalon, a thorax
of many segments, and a very small pygidium. More advanced forms with a larger pygidium also appeared in the
Lower Cambrian. During the Upper Cambrian, members
of the Olenida were practically the only fossils present in
the black-mud seas of Europe. The olenids probably had
large gill combs and were able to endure the stagnant
waters of these shallow seas.

The adaptive radiation of the trilobites increased until
the end of the Cambrian, and from then on a gradual decrease took place, slowly during the Ordovician and then
more rapidly through the Silurian. Several new superfamilies appeared in the Lower Ordovician, among them
the Trinucleina, Calymenina, Phacopina, and Lichida,
which gradually replaced the Lower Ordovician asaphid
faunas. The phacopina also were common in the Devonian, and the Proetacea lasted through the Carboniferous
and Permian. The class Trilobitoidea comprises a small
group chiefly confined to a number of excellently preserved arthropods from the Middle Cambrian Burgess
Shale in British Columbia. The trilobitoids are mostly
small arthropods with appendage of the characteristic trilobite type. Compared with the trilobites, the contemporaneous trilobitoids show a surprising degree of diversity,
both in the development of the body and of the appendages. The trilobitoids were able to break the strong

*Trilobite
append-
ages*

*Trilobites
and
trilobito-
morphs*

frames of construction that prevented a further development and radiation of the trilobites, yet they were not successful in their further development.

Merostomatans and arachnids. Whereas the trilobitomorphs evidently were marine forms only, members of the subphylum Chelicerata lived in saltwater and freshwater (merostomes) and adapted to both a terrestrial and parasitic mode of life (arachnids). The class Merostomata includes the Aglaspida, Xiphosura, and Eurypterida. The aglaspids, ranging from the Lower Cambrian to the Middle Ordovician, had an elongate body with a head shield, lateral eyes, a trunk or abdomen composed of 11 free segments, and a styliform terminal segment (telson). As far as is known, the appendages were simple.

The Xiphosura, including the living horseshoe crab (*Limulus*), have a long, interesting geological history. The earliest representatives in the Silurian had free segments in the abdomen. Most Silurian and Devonian forms had these free abdominal segments, but gradually they fused into a continuous abdominal shield, as is present in Recent members of the group. In the Triassic, some 200,000,000 years ago, the main traits of the present horseshoe crab were well established. More than most living archaic forms, the horseshoe crabs deserve to be called "living fossils."

The *Eurypterida*, or sea scorpions, have become famous both because of the excellently preserved specimens known and the giant size of certain species. The Devonian *Pterygotus* grew to more than 180 centimetres, longer than any other known arthropod. Most preserved chitinous exoskeletons may be shed exuviae from moltings.

The elongate body has a more or less semicircular head shield or prosoma, a 12-segmented abdomen, and a spinelike or finlike telson. Six pairs of appendages correspond to those in the Xiphosura, and the legs may be modified into swimming paddles. As in the xiphosurans, the abdomen had plate-shaped ventral appendages protecting the gills. The eurypterids appeared in the Ordovician and were common in nonmarine faunas in the Silurian and Devonian. Like the trilobites, the group became extinct at the end of the Permian.

The class Arachnida (*q.v.*) includes mostly terrestrial forms, but their ancestors probably were aquatic. In the arachnids, air-breathing structures replace gills.

Occurrence of scorpions

The earliest scorpions (see SCORPIONIDA) occur in Silurian strata. They differ from Recent forms by their coarse legs and lack of slits or spiracles leading into the book lungs. The structures indicate that the early scorpions were aquatic. True terrestrial scorpions (with spiracles) have been recorded from the Carboniferous. Yet a few Devonian occurrences have shown that certain terrestrial arachnids existed in the Lower Devonian. Aquatic arachnids may have invaded the land at the end of the Silurian, a time when the first land plants began to flourish.

Crustaceans in the fossil record. Most crustaceans (*q.v.*) are marine, a few live in freshwater, some are parasitic, and some have become adapted to a terrestrial mode of life. The chitinous, mostly calcified exoskeleton of the crustaceans provides good opportunities for fossilization. Of the many existing groups, Branchiopoda, Ostracoda, Phyllocarida, and Decapoda are important as fossils.

Characteristic of the Crustacea are the appendages of the head, the two pairs of antennae, the mandibles, and the maxillae. The Branchiopoda (*q.v.*) are known from the Silurian (possibly Ordovician) onward. In the Conchostraca the carapace is folded round the laterally compressed body giving the impression of pelecypod valves. Such carapaces of chonchostracs (" *Estheria*" and *Leaia*) are characteristic of freshwater and brackish water and possibly of the saline environments in the Late Paleozoic and Mesozoic. The branchiopods apparently form a stagnant group, the living tadpole shrimp (*Triopsapus*) being practically identical with a form found in the Triassic.

The Ostracoda, the mussel or seed shrimps, are the most common fossil crustaceans. About 900 genera are known, ranging from Cambrian to Recent time. The importance of these microfossils (from 0.2 millimetre to 5 millimetres in length) as index fossils is steadily increasing.

The ostracods have a body enclosed in two separate valves connected along a dorsal hinge line. In the Lower Cambrian, valves interpreted as ostracods have been found. A strong development of the group took place at the beginning of the Ordovician, and from then on new families gradually appeared. The order Palaeocopida were common throughout the Paleozoic, whereas the Podocopida dominated the Mesozoic and Cenozoic.

The Malacostraca, including the Phyllocarida, Decapoda (*q.v.*), and several other groups, have a more or less constant number of segments in the body. While the phyllocarids, with their large folded carapace, were rather common in the Silurian, the decapods flourished in Mesozoic and later times. The decapods appeared at the end of the Permian and had their first evolution in the Triassic. A major expansion took place in the Lower Jurassic and another in Middle Jurassic time. Crabs developed at the beginning of the Tertiary.

Insects in the fossil record. With few exceptions, insects are terrestrial forms. For this reason the fossil occurrences are relatively few, but despite this, about 12,000 species of fossil insects have been described. A related group, the Myriapoda, are little known as fossils. It is interesting to note, however, that fossil remains resembling diplopods have been described from the Upper Silurian and Lower Devonian. If these forms turn out to be true terrestrial centipedes then they are the first known land arthropods.

The class Insecta, with its more than 700,000 living species, has a unique position in the animal world (see INSECTA). Its enormous expansion may partly be due to the fact that the insects are the only arthropods that became fully adapted to a life in the air. Although the whole body is covered by chitinous integument, the wings have proved to be the most resistant parts, the part generally preserved as fossils.

Primitive wings

The fossil record does not give any information on the origin of insects, but it indicates the succession of the major groups. In the Rhynie Chert, Scotland, probably of Lower Devonian age, the first insects appear. They are typical collemboles, showing that this wingless apterygote group was well established by that time. A pair of jaws have been interpreted as possibly belonging to a pterygote insect, but their nature is uncertain. The most ancient and at the same time most primitive insect wing has been found in the Upper Devonian (U.S.S.R.). The great burst in insect development occurred in the Upper Carboniferous. In the lower part (Namurien) appear members of the primitive hemimetabol Orthoptera—cockroaches, grasshoppers, and mantids are living relatives.

Slightly higher in the geological sequence there was an almost explosive radiation comprising about 15 new families of winged insects. Most characteristic are the primitive Palaeoptera, related to dragonflies and mayflies. They had wings that could be moved up and down but not backward into a resting position. Of interest are the lateral integumental folds on the first thoracic segment, structures that have been interpreted as primitive undeveloped wings. Among the Palaeoptera were giant forms with a wingspan of nearly 70 centimetres. Insects with wings that could be turned backward covering each other became more common through the Carboniferous. Cockroaches also were characteristic of the Permian. In the dry Permian climates the insects generally were smaller than in the humid Carboniferous environments. In the Permian the first insects with a complete (holometabol) metamorphosis occur, among them beetles with leathery forewings. From the Triassic onward, all the fossil forms belong to orders also present today.

THE ECHINODERMATA

This well-defined and at the same time highly diversified phylum of marine invertebrates (see ECHINODERMATA) includes the living starfishes (asteroids), brittle stars (ophiuroids), sea urchins (echinoids), sea cucumbers (holothuroids), and sea lilies (crinoids). The echinoderms, with strong calcite skeletons, occur in all Phanerozoic systems.

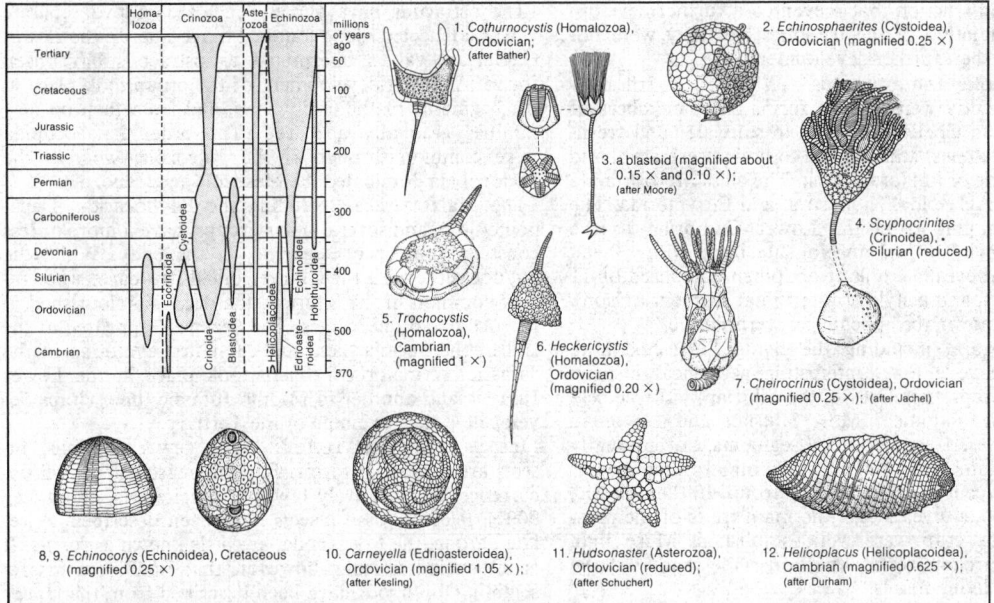

Figure 7: *Representative echinoderms and their geological range.*
(Left) Occurrence of the Homalozoa, Crinozoa, Asterozoa, and Echinozoa groups in the geological record. Width of stippled zone indicates relative abundance. (1–12) Fossil echinoderms as designated.
From (2,5,7,10–12) W. Rasmussen, *Paleontologi, Fossile invertebrater;* (3,8,9) L. Stormer, *Jordens og livets historie;* and (6) *Treatise on Invertebrate Paleontology,* courtesy of The Geological Society of America and The University of Kansas

sometimes in such abundance that thick rock formations are completely composed of their remains.

Symmetry and structures. Echinoderms are marine invertebrates with a marked radial fivefold symmetry (although a bilateral symmetry probably was primary). Characteristic is the skeleton, which is of mesodermal origin and not formed by the ectoderm as in other invertebrates. In the skeleton, crystalline calcite forms single crystals, and the plates are therefore easy to identify among fossil remains. Another characteristic feature of the echinoderms is the development of the water-circulation system present in most forms. The radial furrows, or ambulacra, form central elements in the echinoderm skeletons. The mouth and anus are interradial, and their positions vary in different groups.

The phylum has been divided into more than 15 classes, some of which have but few fossil representatives. Forms that live attached to the bottom with the mouth region directed upward are often referred to as Pelmatozoa; those that are free living with the mouth region downward or forward have been termed Eleutherozoa. This division, however, is based more on function and morphology than on genetic affinities. More appropriate seems to be a division into four subphyla, the Homalozoa, Crinozoa, Asterozoa, and Echinozoa.

The subphylum Homalozoa includes the peculiar echinoderms usually known as carpoids. They are known from the Middle Cambrian to the Lower Devonian. The depressed body covered by plates may be completely asymmetric with a stalklike appendage, yet they were probably free-living forms. No radial symmetry is present and only one ambulacrum. The shell structure and water-circulation system show that the carpoids are echinoderms; a relationship to primitive vertebrates is hardly probable in spite of certain similarities. The Homalozoa comprise three mutually very different classes that may represent very ancient, preradial radiations of the Echinodermata.

Cystoids, blastoids, and crinoids. The subphylum Crinozoa includes nine classes, of which the Cystoidea, Blastoidea, and Crinoidea are the most common fossils. Members of these groups have a radial symmetry and a sacklike spheroid or cuplike body borne on a stem attached to the ground.

In the cystoids the body may be less symmetrical, with numerous, mostly irregularly arranged plates pierced by characteristic pore structures. Free food-gathering appendages called brachioles extend from the ambulacra. The cystoids appeared at the beginning of the Ordovician and had a great development in the Middle Ordovician just like several other calcite-shelled forms. The group became extinct in the Devonian.

The blastoids also were Paleozoic but ranged from the Silurian to the Permian and were most abundant in the Lower Carboniferous. The budlike cup, the so-called theca or calyx, has a marked radial symmetry, a uniform arrangement of plates, and numerous thin brachioles forming simple external processes of the theca.

Most important are the crinoids, of which more than 5,000 species are known from Lower Ordovician to Recent time. Crinoids are rock building in some formations and may be good index fossils. The sea lilies had a length as great as 18 metres. Characteristic of the group are the strongly developed and diversified arms that carry the food—grooves extending from the mouth at the summit of the body. The theca, enclosing most of the soft parts, has the plates arranged in several horizontal cycles. {Crinoids as index fossils}

True crinoids appeared in the Ordovician, particularly in the Middle Ordovician, and they had a strong and rapid radiation. It is interesting to note that these forms had all the essential features of later representatives. Of the four major groups of crinoids, two became extinct in the Permian and one in the Triassic; the remaining group (Articulata) originated in the Triassic and has been present since then.

The origin of the Crinozoa is unknown. A heterogenous group, the Eocrinoidea, occurs in the Lower Cambrian, but the relation between this and the other members of the Crinozoa is remote.

Echinoids, holothuroids, and edrioasteroids. The echinoids, ranging from Ordovician to Recent time, have a globose to discoid body composed of a great number of plates that are radially arranged. A secondary, bilateral symmetry is demonstrated in more advanced forms, however. Characteristic of the echinoid shell is the presence of movable spines. Regular echinoids have a pronounced radial symmetry, the mouth has a ventral and central position, and the anus is at the summit of the body. The irregular echinoids have a secondary bilateral symmetry, the anus has moved backward to the posterior interradius, and the mouth, correspondingly, has moved forward.

The regular echinoids had their main development in Early Jurassic, when a number of new families appeared. The Cidarida, with large, often club-shaped, spines, are known from the Devonian and are common in the Mesozoic. Irregular echinoids, some of them adapted to a burrowing habit, are known before the Jurassic.

The holothuroids have skeletal elements consisting mostly of microscopic ossicles of calcite or iron phosphate; the skin contains numerous spicules. The holothuroids are rare as fossils, and the earliest representatives are known from the Devonian.

The discovery of a new class of echinoderms in the Lower Cambrian of California was reported in 1963. Its members, the Helicoplacoidea, had a fusiform, probably flexible body covered by spirally arranged plates. From one pole, probably from the mouth, extended a generally single ambulacrum, a structure reminiscent of the Homalozoa (carpoids). This early and peculiar group of Echinozoa, confined to the Lower Cambrian, had little in common with the other classes of echinoderms.

The Edrioasteroids were sessile, but this form may have been a secondary adaptation. They differed, however, from the Crinozoa by having a meridional pattern of symmetry. They lacked arms or brachioles, and the ambulacra probably had tube feet like those of the asteroids. For these reasons, these Lower Cambrian to Lower Carboniferous forms may be included in the Echinozoa. The usually circular edrioasteroids had a dorsal, centrally situated mouth and five curved ambulacra.

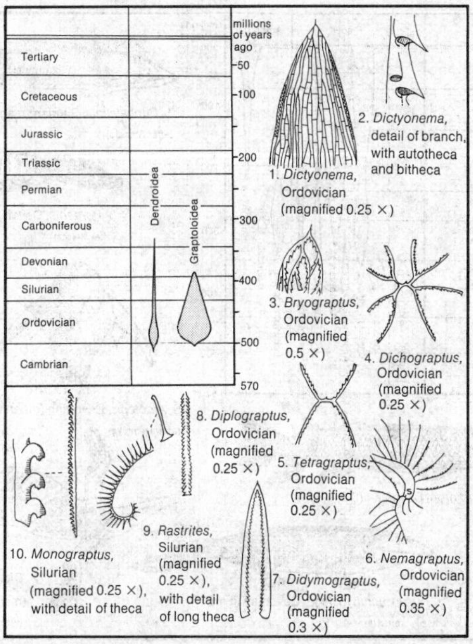

THE GRAPTOLITHINA

Like the ammonites, these Paleozoic marine invertebrates are excellent index, or zone, fossils. The Ordovician and Silurian chronozones are largely based on graptolite species that had a worldwide distribution and were restricted to distinct intervals in geological time.

Structure and growth of graptolites. Knowledge of the extinct graptolites is limited to the empty chitinous skeletons, which offer little information of the zoological position of the soft animals that inhabited the protecting covering case. More recent studies of the periderm of the skeleton, however, have demonstrated the presence of two layers, a thin external cortical layer and an internal fusellar layer with growth bands, and in a few cases a stolon has been observed below the cortical layer. These structures are closely similar to those present in certain pterobranchs belonging to the hemichordates. For this reason the graptolites are now generally looked upon as belonging to the phylum Chordata, rather than to the Hydrozoa, as previously assumed.

The skeleton of the graptolite colony (rhabdosome) has the tubiform "living chambers" or thecae arranged in single or double rows along the branches or stipes of the colony. The outer theca may be of two types, the autotheca and the bitheca, the latter mostly reduced. The thecae are connected by the so-called stolothecae, which form a continuous closed chain along the dorsal side of the stipe. The growth of the graptolite starts with a small, tubiform, initial theca, the sicula, which develops a thread (nema) and a lateral bud, from which the whole rhabdosome gradually develops. During the great radiation of the graptolites throughout the Ordovician and Silurian, the morphology of the rhabdosome, particularly the stipes and thecae, was subject to great variation. Characteristic trends of evolution were repeated in groups not closely related, complicating the taxonomy.

Evolutionary trends. The Middle and Upper Cambrian graptolites belong to the Dendrograptidae, which have been referred to a separate order Dendrograptoidea. They have mostly cone-shaped or dendroid rhabdosomes with both autothecae and bithecae arranged in one row on the stipes. Members of the order Graptoloidea appear in the Lower Ordovician. Typical species had few stipes and only autothecae; however, some of the early branched species of the group had bithecae, a fact that shows that there is not a distinct boundary between the two orders. Dendrograptids evidently gave rise to the Lower Ordovician graptolitoids that display gradual reduction of the stipes throughout the Lower Ordovician (dichograptid) fauna. This fauna was replaced in the Middle Ordovician by two-branched, mostly reclined (leptograptid)

Graptolites in the fossil record

Figure 8: *Representative graptolites and their geological range.*
(Left) Occurrence of the Dendroidea and Graptoloidea in the geological record. Width of stippled zone indicates relative abundance. (1–3) Dendroidea, (4–10) Graptoloidea.
From L. Stormer, *Jordens og livets historie*

forms and by one-branched, biserial (with two rows of thecae on the stipe) forms (diplograptid fauna). The latter lasted into the Lower Silurian, when it was replaced by one-branched, uniserial forms with specialized thecae (monograptid fauna). The Silurian graptolite faunas were dominated by the family Monograptidae, which became extinct in the Lower Devonian. While the Graptolitoidea lasted to the Upper Silurian, some of the Dendroidea existed up to Middle Carboniferous time.

The worldwide distribution of many graptolites is evidently due to a planktonic mode of life; alternatively, the individuals may have been attached to floating bodies (epiplanktonic). Most graptolites occur in black shales (graptolite facies) and other fossils usually are not present. The black mud of the shale probably was deposited slowly under anaerobic conditions. No bottom fauna was present to destroy the graptolites, which sank from better ventilated water levels above. Graptolites also occur in limestone, from which excellently preserved specimens have been etched out by acids.

THE FISHES

Most vertebrates have a solid skeleton, either external or internal, which offers good opportunities for preservation. Fossil vertebrates are known from the Ordovician and all later systems. Fossils, however, give no information concerning the origin of the vertebrates. The Ordovician forms are well organized; the stratigraphic appearance of the various groups clearly demonstrates the gradual progressive development of the vertebrates through geological time. The speed of development varied considerably between groups and from one time interval to another: within one interval, one group might display rapid development and considerable radiation while related groups might remain practically unchanged.

The fishes (see FISH) form the central group of the vertebrates. The main step in the evolution of the vertebrates is the "invention" of the jaws, a device that completely changed the life of the early vertebrates; from being mud feeders they developed into omnivorous and carnivorous forms able to feed on larger plants and animals. For this reason the vertebrates might naturally be divided into two major groups: the Agnatha (*q.v.*), or jawless forms, and the Gnathostomata, or jawed forms.

Agnatha: jawless fishes. The class Agnatha includes the living cyclostomes, the hagfishes and lampreys, which

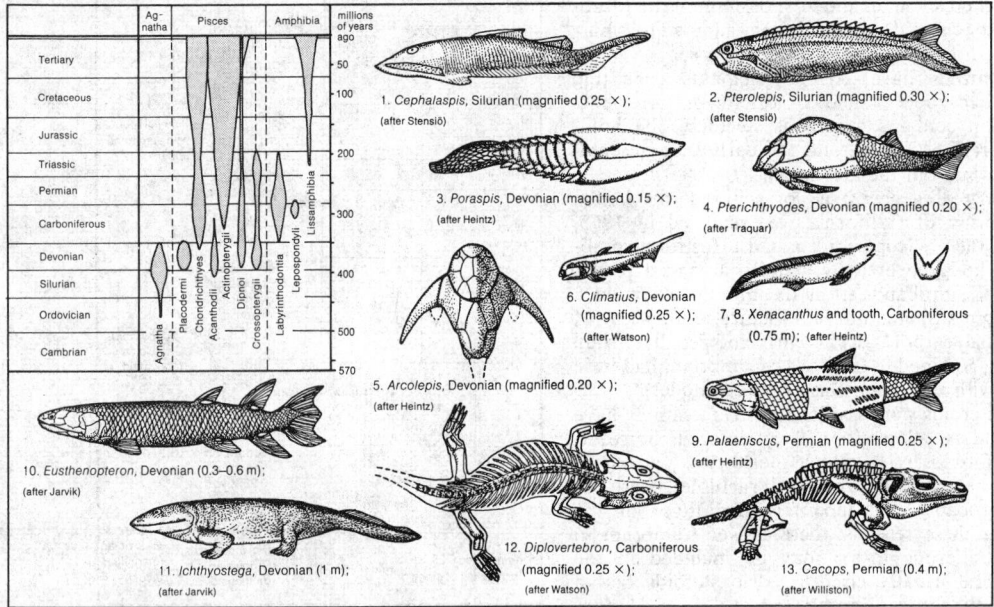

Figure 9: *Representative fishes and amphibians and their geological range.*
(Left) Occurrence of the Agnatha, Pisces, and Amphibia in the geological record. Width of
stippled zone indicates relative abundance. (1–3) Agnatha, (4,5) Placodermi,
(7,8) Chondrichthyes, (6?,9,10) Osteichthyes, (11–13) Amphibia.
From (1–3) L. Stormer, *Jordens og livets historie;* and (4–13) A.S. Romer, *Invertebrate
Paleontology* (© 1966), The University of Chicago Press, all rights reserved

Armoured fish: the ostracoderms

are but faint reflections of the rich agnath faunas of the Late Silurian and Lower Devonian. In contrast to the soft-bodied Recent forms, the ancient ostracoderms were heavily armoured, and in addition to this exoskeleton some of them had internal ossifications with distinct impressions of internal structures such as brain and nerves. The internal structures show that the ostracoderms are closely related to the living agnaths. Both in extant and extinct forms, two separate groups may be distinguished: the Diplorhina, with two nasal pockets, and the Monorhina, with a single nasal pocket. The hagfishes (*Myxine* and *Bdellostoma*) and the fossil Heterostraci (pteraspids and thelodontids) belong to the first group, the lamprey (*Petromytzon*) and the fossil Osteostraci (cephalaspids and anaspids) to the other.

The tadpole-shaped pteraspids had the anterior portion of the body covered by a solid dorsal and ventral shield. In more advanced forms these shields were split into smaller plates. A further development is found in the thelodontids (coelolepids) where the body was covered by small scales, almost like shark scales. The cephalaspids had a rather flat head shield and centrally placed eyes and pineal and nasal openings. Plate-covered lateral and median areas are interpreted as parts of sensory organs. On the ventral side, the jawless mouth is placed near the frontal margin, and farther back a number of gill openings are arranged in a circle. The anaspids had a narrow body and a fanlike tail and were probably nektonic (swimming) forms.

The earliest ostracoderms are known from the Ordovician, but these forms (*Astraspis*) are already well organized, indicating a long time of evolution of the ostracoderms before the Ordovician. The mostly nonmarine ostracoderms lived together with euryterids and, like members of this group, flourished in the Late Silurian and Devonian.

Jawed fishes. The class Acanthodii, or "spiny sharks," are fishes with jaws. The jaws were formed by a modification of an anterior pair of gill bars. The acanthodians occur in the Silurian, perhaps in the lower part, and remain in the fossil record until the Lower Permian. The acanthodians were small sharklike fishes with a considerable number of paired fins. The body was covered by small, close-set, diamond-shaped scales with a microscopic structure similar to that of the ganoid scales of bony fishes.

The class Placodermi (*q.v.*) comprises the most charac-

teristic and most spectacular fishes of the Devonian. In contrast to the other groups, they are confined to this period, with the exception of a small group (the ptyctodonts) that just reached into the earliest Carboniferous. Like the ostracoderms, the placoderms were armoured, but the thick exoskeleton was limited to the head and trunk. An internal skeleton was developed to some extent. Pectoral and pelvic fins were present.

The placoderms are commonly divided into two separate groups: the Arthrodira and Antiarchi. In both groups the shape of the head and trunk, as well as the size, display a considerable variation throughout the Devonian. The largest forms known had a length of more than 8 metres (30 feet). Characteristic of placoderms is the presence of an articulation between the head shield and trunk shield. As a general rule the armour became gradually reduced throughout the Devonian. The Middle and Upper Devonian Antiarchi had a small head with more centrally placed eyes, and the pectoral fins were covered by bony plates and articulated to the trunk shield. These weird looking fishes apparently lived in freshwater.

Sharks, skates, and rays

The sharks (see SELACHII) and chimaeras, evidently related to the placoderms, are usually united in one group—the Condrichthyes, or cartilagenous fishes. The shark-like fishes lack true bone, the denticles probably remnants of a more continuous exoskeleton in ancient forms. Because cartilage is rarely preserved, the fossil remains are generally confined to teeth and denticles only. The oldest sharks are known from the Middle Devonian, and Late Devonian forms (*Cladoselache*) have primitive, flaplike pectoral fins. Most of the ancient sharks became extinct at the end of the Paleozoic. Characteristic freshwater sharks (pleurochantids) were abundant in the Carboniferous and Early Permian. The more advanced sharks characteristic of the present seas developed through the Mesozoic, and giant Tertiary forms may have had a jaw gap of six or seven feet. Skates and rays and also the chimaeras (ratfishes) appeared in the Jurassic.

Higher bony fishes. The class Osteichthyes or higher bony fishes appeared in the Devonian. Characteristic of the group is the operculum covering the gills, a structure also present in the acanthodians. The osteichthyes are divisible into two major groups: the Actinopterygii, or ray-finned fishes, and the Sarcopterygii (Choanichthyes), or fleshy-finned fishes. The former includes the great majority of extinct and extant fishes; the latter attained a maximum in the Paleozoic and today is represented by a few lungfishes and the famous *Latimeria*, or bluefish. In the actinopterygians, the paired fins consist chiefly of rays supporting a web of skin. In the sarcopterygians, on the other hand, the well-developed paired fins are composed of flesh with an internal skeleton.

The actinpterygian first appear in the Middle Devonian. The Paleozoic–Triassic forms and certain living relics (*Polypterus* and sturgeons) constitute a separate group, the Chondrostei (*q.v.*), which have a powerful external skeleton of solid ganoid scales and a less developed (or rather reduced) internal skeleton. The tail fin is heterocercal (sharklike). In the chiefly Mesozoic Holostei (*q.v.*) the internal skeleton is more ossified and ganoid scales may be absent. The Teleostei (see TELEOSTEI, and the many separate groups of the fishes) have a well-developed internal skeleton forming a strong and elastic backbone. The thin cycloid scales form a light exoskeleton that does not impede swift movements in the water. The teleosts appear in the Jurassic and had a great adaptive radiation at the beginning of the Tertiary.

Lungfish and crosso- pterygians

The Sarcopterygii deserve particular interest because they include the ancestors of the tetrapods. The two separate groups, the Dipnoi (*q.v.*) and the Crossopterygii (*q.v.*), have many structures in common and probably had common ancestors in pre-Devonian times. In addition to the lobe fins, both groups have characteristic cosmoid scales, and lungs are usually present. Lungs, originating as sacklike extensions from the gut, are evidently an ancient structure. They probably developed in freshwater fishes (like most known fishes in the Devonian) to protect them in the dry seasons. In all actinopterygians except *Polypterus* (which live like the Devonian forms), the lungs are reduced or modified into an air bladder. In the lungfishes and one group of the crossopterygians, the rhipidistians, the nostrils have internal openings (choana) that allow the air to be inhaled without opening the mouth, a structure that also is characteristic of the tetrapods.

The lungfishes, or Dipnoi, arose in the Middle Devonian and linger on to the present time. During this long time a reduction in ossification is noticeable, but otherwise this conservative group, a blind alley in vertebrate evolution, was subject to little change.

The crossopterygians differ from the dipnois in the pattern of the skull plates and in the dentition. The group appeared in the Lower Devonian and flourished throughout this system, and the important rhipidistians became extinct in the Permian. Another group, the coelacanthids, was common in the Triassic and is represented today by *Latimeria*.

THE AMPHIBIA

The class Amphibia (*q.v.*), which is represented today by the frogs (see ANURA), the salamanders and newts (see URODELA), and the rare gymnophions, played a great role in Carboniferous to Triassic times. The amphibians were the dominating larger animals of the coal swamps, and a considerable radiation took place during the development of the group from Late Devonian to the end of the Triassic. Only a smaller group, including the extant forms, lingered on to present time. Fossil amphibians are of particular interest because they throw light on the origin of the tetrapods from fishes and at the same time demonstrate how certain primitive vertebrates were able to adapt themselves to a terrestrial mode of life.

Amphi- bians as a link between fishes and tetrapods

The Late Devonian amphibian *Ichthyostega* from Greenland clearly demonstrates its close relationships to certain crossopterygian rhipidistian fishes. In both groups the pattern of bone elements in the skull is essentially the same, and the primitive amphibians even have fishlike rays in their tails. The bones of the limbs have a distinct basic pattern in all tetrapods, and it is possible to derive this from the arrangement of the bones of the fleshy-fins of the crossopterygians.

In the early amphibians, the roof of the rather flat skull was completely covered by dermal bones; the only openings were for the eyes and nostrils, and posterior notches mark the position of the ears. The vertebral column was more ossified than in recent forms. The development of the bone elements of each vertebra vary in different forms, and this distinction is used as a basis for a classification of the amphibians. The extant forms and their immediate fossil relatives are commonly placed in one group, *Lissamphibia*, characterized by a strong reduction of the bone, particularly in the braincase and skull. The Paleozoic and Triassic forms are divided into two main groups, the Labyrinthodontia (Aspidosopondyli), with "arch-vertebra," and the Lepospondyli, with "husk-" or "ring-vertebrae."

The labyrinthodonts, also called stegocephalians because of their completely roofed skulls, have the characteristic labyrinthodont teeth present also in the crossopterygians. The body of the early forms had a nearly cylindrical cross section with laterally placed limbs. Only some of the later labyrinthodonts were better adapted to a terrestrial gait, but at this time several forms had already returned permanently to aquatic life, and the hegemony was taken over by the reptiles. Small labyrinthodonts had the size of common salamanders, but the larger ones reached a length of more than 4 metres (15 feet). The group flourished throughout the Carboniferous and Permian and became extinct at the end of the Triassic. Among the labyrinthodonts, the anthracosaurians are of great importance because they evidently include the ancestors of the reptiles and hence of all advanced vertebrates. *Seymouria*, from the Permian of Texas, is more or less a "missing link" between amphibians and reptiles. The skeleton demonstrates characters of both groups. The lepospondyls were restricted to the Carboniferous and Permian; some of them were eellike with reduced limbs.

THE REPTILIA

The class Reptilia (*q.v.*) represents the next and decisive step in the conquest of land by the vertebrates. The fossil record demonstrates the enormous radiation of the group throughout the Mesozoic, "the Age of Reptiles," a time span amounting to more than 200,000,000 years if the time of the Late Paleozoic forms is included. Of this great display of reptiles only the turtles (Chelonia), lizards and snakes (Squamata), rhynchocephalians (*q.v.*), and the crocodiles and alligators (Crocodilia) survived the Mesozoic and are present today. Characteristic of the reptiles are the large shell-covered eggs laid on land, in contrast to the small and soft water-laid eggs of the amphibians. Whereas the amphibians were dependent on an aquatic environment for their young, reptiles, so to speak, carried this environment with them on land, well protected within the egg. Compared with the amphibians, the skull of the reptiles is higher and more narrow, and the completely heavy roofed skulls are gradually replaced by lighter forms with lateral openings. The number and position of these openings are used in the classification of the reptiles, a classification that to a large extent may be artificial.

The "Age of Reptiles"

Characteristics of early reptiles. The earliest reptiles form more or less a stem group, the Cotylosauria, from which the others radiated. They flourished in the Permian and had much in common with the amphibians. As already mentioned, the genus *Seymouria* stands almost exactly on the dividing line between amphibians and reptiles.

One of the first groups to branch off from the stem reptiles was, surprisingly enough, the group leading to the mammals. These reptiles occur in the Carboniferous. They are characterized by an opening in the lower part of the cheek region of the skull (synapsid type). In the Lower Permian, the bizarre looking dimetrodons appear. They have a dorsal "sail" supported by greatly prolonged neural spines and well-differentiated teeth adapted for their carnivorous habit of life. From such early forms developed the therapsids, which are regarded as the ancestors of the Mammalia. They were rather lightly built, with the limbs placed underneath the body, not outward

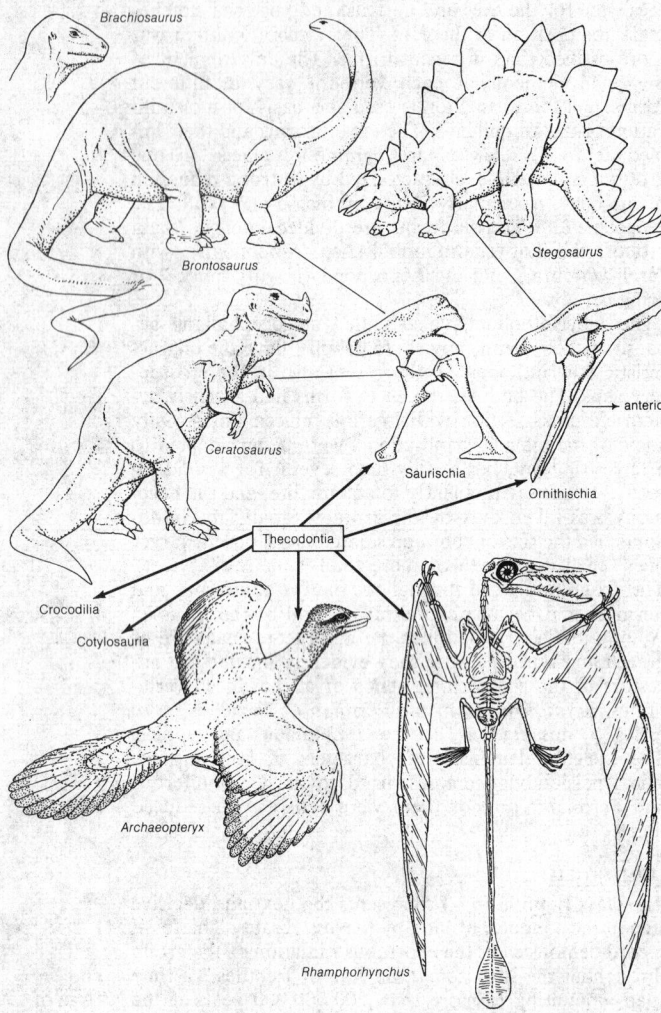

Figure 10: Evolution of reptiles and birds from the ancestral thecodonts.

as in the primitive, less active forms. Through the Late Permian and the Triassic, a trend of increasing size is noticeable, and gradually the therapsids became more and more mammal-like. The structures of the latest forms, particularly the differentiation of the teeth into incisors, canines, and molars, fill the gap between the Triassic therapsids and the first mammals appearing in the mid-Jurassic.

The main radiation of the reptiles took place at the end of the Permian. Several of the Triassic reptiles were marine. This is not necessarily a secondary adaptation. It is not unlikely that early amphibious forms remained aquatic, although they preferred to lay their eggs on land.

Ichthyo-saurs and plesiosaurs The specialized and mostly aquatic turtles have remained little changed up to Recent times. Sea turtles up to 4 metres (12 feet) in length occurred in the Cretaceous.

The Ichthyosauria, or "fish reptiles," were highly adapted to an aquatic mode of life. The fusiform body had a dorsal fin (unsupported by bones) and a well-developed tail fin, the limbs reduced to short steering paddles. The strongly modified head had large eyes and a long beak with the nares at the base. The young ichthyosaurians probably were born alive. The group became extinct at the end of the Cretaceous.

The Plesiosauria and the allied nothosaurs form a separate group, the Sauropterygia, which is characterized by skulls with the cheek opening at the top of the skull (euryapsid type). The marine plesiosaurs appeared at the end of the Triassic and were abundant during the rest of the Mesozoic. These fish-eating creatures usually have a long neck and a short trunk and tail. The strongly modified

limbs were used as "rowing" paddles rather than steering organs. Cretaceous plesiosaurians measured up to 12 metres (50 feet) in length.

The nothosaurians of the Triassic were small forms with limbs serving both as fins and feet. The amphibious forms were probably related to the ancestors of the plesiosaurians. The placodonts were also related; they had large flat teeth that were well adapted for crushing mollusks.

The lizards and snakes and their extinct relatives form a separate group, the Lepidosauria. Recent finds have shown that lizard-like forms occur in the Triassic. Like the "ruling reptiles," the lepidosaurians have two openings in the cheek region of the skull (diapsid type). The earliest representatives of the group (the eosuchians) appear in the Early Permian. The living *Sphenodon* is the only representative of the similar rhynchocephalians of the Triassic.

Spectacular representatives of the lepidosaurians were the marine fish-eating mosasaurs of the Cretaceous. They had a large head and a short neck, and with their long, slim body they looked like "sea serpents." The snakes did not appear until the Cretaceous.

Dominant terrestrial forms. The Archosauria, or "ruling reptiles," dominated the terrestrial faunas throughout the Mesozoic. The group includes the crocodiles, dinosaurs, flying reptiles, and related primitive forms. Like the lepidosaurs, the archosaurs have two temporal openings (diapsid type), but otherwise the two groups have few characters in common.

The Thecodontia form a central group of the Archosauria, a group from which all the ruling reptiles and the birds evolved. As expressed in the name, the teeth of the thecodonts and their descendents were firmly set in deep sockets. The early thecodonts were small bipedal forms (proterosuchians) with moderately reduced front legs. The group became extinct at the end of the Triassic, but before that they had given rise to the below-mentioned groups.

The Crocodilia are known from the Middle Triassic onward. The early forms were small, heavily armoured, and lizard-like. Later representatives resemble the recent ones and probably had a similar mode of life.

The Dinosauria, the most spectacular vertebrates of all time, had a worldwide distribution and lived and flourished from the Late Triassic to the end of the Cretaceous, a time span of some 150,000,000 years. During this long time interval the dinosaurs were subject to a great radiation both in shape and size; the smallest were the size of a cock, and the largest attained a length of almost 30 metres (90 feet) and a weight of up to 36–50 metric tons. **The dino-saurs**

The term dinosaur is actually an artificial term that includes two distinctly different orders of the archosaurs, two orders that evidently are not more closely related than are the crocodiles, pterosaurs, and birds. The two groups of dinosaurs, the order Saurischia and the order Ornithischia, are distinguished mainly by their different pelvic structures; the former had a triradiate and the latter a tetraradiate pelvis.

Saurischians. Members of the Saurischia were common in the Triassic. These early forms were bipedal with a well-developed tail, useful as a supporter or "balancer." The suborder Theropoda includes all the small and giant carnivorous bipeds of the Jurassic and Cretaceous. Typical of the small ones were the small head, long neck, and moderately reduced front limbs. The ostrichlike *Ornithomimus* from the Cretaceous was probably an egg robber. Both the small and large theropods have birdlike feet (fossil tracks were originally interpreted as due to large birds). The large theropods, very common in the Jurassic, have, in contrast to the small ones, a large head with a short neck; and the front limbs were strongly reduced, so much so that in the latest forms they may have been practically useless, not even able to reach the mouth. Toward the end of the Cretaceous the largest carnivores appeared. The giant flesh-eating *Tyrannosaurus* measured about 15 metres (47 feet) in length with a height of 6 metres (19 feet) in bipedal pose.

The suborder Sauropoda comprises Jurassic and Creta-

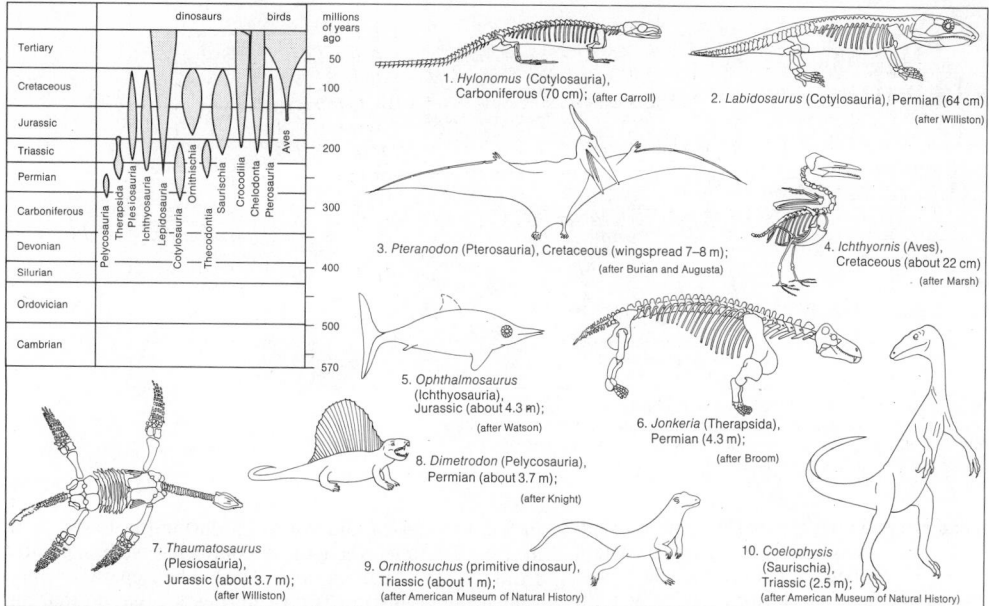

Figure 11: *Representative reptiles and birds and their geological range.*
(Left) Occurrence of dinosaurs and birds in the geological record. Width of stippled zone indicates relative abundance. (1–10) Fossil reptiles and birds as designated.
From (1,2,4) Romer, *Invertebrate Paleontology*, copyright 1966, University of Chicago; (3, 6–10) L. Stormer, *Jordens og livets historie;* (5) Termier and Termier, *Paleontologie Stratigraphique*, copyright 1960, Masson & Cie, Paris

ceous saurischians, which were herbivorous and had acquired a quadrupedal gait. In this group, the largest four-footed animals that ever lived (*Diplodocus, Brontosaurus,* and *Brachiosaurus*) are found. Characteristic of these reptiles are a small head, a long neck, a short and stout trunk borne on strong "elephantine" legs, and a long tail. The skull has an exceptionally small brain. In certain forms, the nares are placed on the top of the skull, a position suggesting that the long neck served as a "snorkel" when the large sauropod walked in deeper water. *Diplodocus* had a very long tail with a length of 26.7 metres (87.5 feet), and the more short-tailed *Brachiosaurus* measured about 25 metres (80 feet) but was larger, with an estimated weight of 50 tons.

Ornithischians. The order Ornithischia was largely confined to the Jurassic and Cretaceous. These birdlike, herbivorous dinosaurs display an extraordinary radiation during their development. In addition to a tetraradiate pelvis, they usually had a horny beak with a corresponding reduction of teeth in the frontal portion of the mouth. Four main groups have been distinguished: the bipedal ornithopods, the quadruped stegosaurs, the heavily armoured ankylosaurs, and the horned ceratopsids.

The bipedal forms include the well-known *Iguanodon*, with its spikelike "thumb" serving as a weapon. Tracks referred to this genus occur as far north as Spitsbergen. Duckbill dinosaurs (trachodons) also were common in the Cretaceous. These were probably amphibious forms; they had hundreds of leaflike teeth adapted for grinding tough plant material. Other ornithopods (hadrosaurs) had peculiar hollow crests on the head, possibly for air storage during diving.

The Jurassic stegosaurs, quadrupedal ornithischians, were peculiar looking, with a double row of large, vertically arranged plates along the back. The brain was very small and the hind legs much longer than the front ones.

The Cretaceous quadruped ankylosaurs, or "reptilian tanks," were strongly armoured, a necessary protection against the contemporaneous carnivorous theropods (they could not escape into the water as could the other amphibious dinosaurs).

The Upper Cretaceous horned ornithischians also include quadrupedal forms with a large head (making up to one-third of the total length of the body), which in *Triceratops* ranged from 5 to 6 metres (16 to 20 feet). Characteristic of the group were the prominent horns and the great frill of bones extending back over the neck, form-

ing a good protection for this vulnerable part of the body. Eggs and young individuals of the ceratopsids are known from Mongolia.

No dinosaurs survived the Cretaceous. Most groups disappeared rather suddenly at the end of this system. Many hypotheses have been put forth to explain this extinction, including climatic and environmental change and the rise of the mammals, among others. None seems wholly satisfactory, and their rather sudden extinction remains one of the great mysteries of natural history.

Sudden extinction of dinosaurs

Flying reptiles. The order Pterosauria, or flying reptiles, are known from the Jurassic and Cretaceous. Both the pterosaurs and the birds developed from the thecodonts. Both represent the reptilian conquest of the air. The pterosaurs, however, were the less successful of the two and became extinct before the end of the Cretaceous. The skeleton of the flying reptiles was light with air-filled bones. The elongate wings were composed of a membrane of skin attached to and supported by the arm and a strongly prolonged single finger of the hand. The wing was probably highly vulnerable to rupture, much more so than the wings of bats and birds. The more primitive Jurassic forms (*Rhamphorhynchus*) had a long reptilian tail, which in late Cretaceous forms was reduced to a stub. At the same time a reduction of the teeth is noticeable. Among the latest pterosaurs were very large forms (pterodonts) with a wingspread of 7 metres (25 feet) and a long crest extending backward from the head.

THE BIRDS

Representatives of the class Aves (see BIRD) occupy a unique position among the vertebrates because of the feathers that cover their warm-blooded bodies and form the essential parts of the wings. In all other basic characters, the birds are reptilian; their feathers are, in spite of their complex structures, comparable to the scales of reptiles. The structural correspondence between birds and reptiles is so far reaching that inclusion of the Aves in the Archosauria has been seriously considered.

Because of their mode of life, birds are rarely preserved as fossils; seabirds are the more common because they might be preserved in marine sediments. The lack of other fossil birds may give an erroneous impression of their appearance in the fossil record.

The classical finds of three specimens of *Archaeopteryx* in the Late Jurassic of Solnhofen in Germany demonstrate the primitive, really reptilian bird. In contrast to

The primitive, reptilian bird

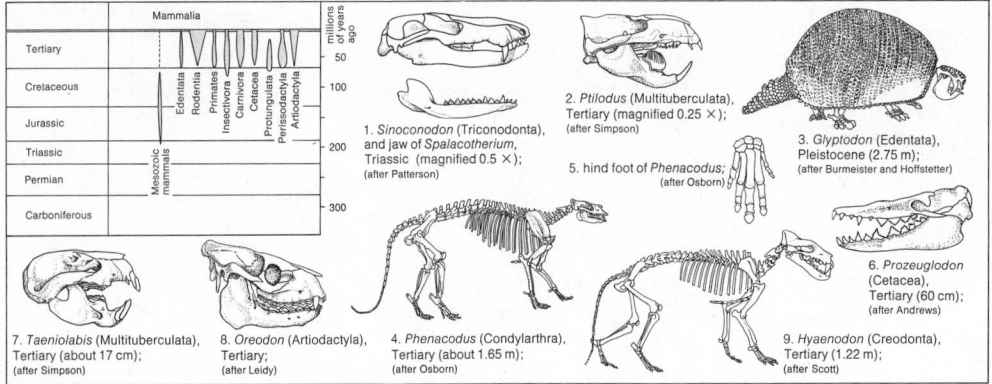

Figure 12: *Representative mammals and their geological range.*
(Left) Occurrence of principal mammalian groups in the geological record. Width of
stippled zone indicates relative abundance. (1–9) Fossil mammals as designated.
From (6) L. Størmer, *Jordens og livets historie;* and (1–5, 7–9) A.S. Romer, *Invertebrate
Paleontology* (© 1966), The University of Chicago Press, all rights reserved

later forms, it had nonpneumatic bones, a reptilian skeleton of the wings and pelvis, and a long reptilian tail.
Teeth were present in the jaws, a feature that, however,
also was maintained in Cretaceous birds. Practically nothing is known of the evolution of birds in the Lower and
Middle Cretaceous. Late Cretaceous forms, evidently seabirds (*Hesperornis*), were advanced in many characters
but still possessed teeth in their beaks.

About 20,000 species of living birds are known. Although the number of fossil forms is small, the group
evidently developed and radiated greatly during the Tertiary. Of particular interest is the development of large
flightless forms like the present ostriches. Such forms had
possibilities for development, particularly in places where
carnivores were absent and where flight was not necessary as a means of escape. This was true in Madagascar
and New Zealand, where the giant "elephant birds"
(*Aepyornis*) and moas (*Dinornis*) lived up to historical
times when they evidently were exterminated by man.

THE MAMMALS

The living, warm-blooded mammals, members of the
class Mammalia, are usually divided into three groups:
the egg-laying mammals, or Monotremata; the live-bearing pouched mammals, or Marsupialia; and the placental
mammals, or Placentalia (see MAMMALIA; MONO-
TREMATA; and MARSUPIALIA); but with present comprehensive knowledge of the many extinct mammal groups,
this classification has proved too narrow. The mono-
tremes are placed in the subclass Prototheria, some
Mesozoic forms in the subclass Allotheria, and the marsupials and placentals in the subclass Theria, the latter
divided into the Mesozoic Trituberculata, the Metatheria
(Marsupialia), and the Eutheria (Placentalia).

Characteristics and early types. Characteristic of the
mammalian skeleton and teeth (only parts generally preserved) are a thorough ossification with a reduction of
certain bones in the skull, a swelling of the braincase,
and changes in the auditory region involving an inclusion
of bones from the lower jaw.

The oldest mammals are known from the Late Triassic
of China. Throughout the Mesozoic they played a modest
role, the mice- to rat-sized forms unable to compete with
the prominent carnivorous reptiles of the time. The
Mesozoic material is scarce, and the single jaws and
teeth are difficult to place zoologically. Characteristic
were the triconodonts with three-cusped teeth and the
Multituberculata with large flat teeth and several rows of
cusps, probably herbivorous forms. Both groups differ
from the therians by lacking the angular process of the
lower jaw. The Multituberculata was the only successful
group of the Allotheria, lingering on to the Eocene.

The Pantotheria, with three-cusped molars and with
an angular jaw process, also occur in the Jurassic. This
group may have been ancestral to both Metatheria (marsupials) and Eutheria (placentals), the latter appearing in
the Cretaceous. Oppossum-like marsupials were common

in South America and Australia during the Early Tertiary, at the time when these continents were separated
from North America and Asia. The separation prevented the carnivores from entering, a situation that has
lasted until the present time in Australia.

Among the Eutheria, or placentals, the less specialized
Insectivora had a central position. The radiation of this
and other placental groups evidently started in the Cretaceous (see INSECTIVORA; CHIROPTERA).

Primates. Like the mammalian reptiles, the Primates
(*q.v.*) branched off early from the main stem of their
class. Because the early Primates apparently were tree
dwellers and lived in tropical regions, fossil material is
rare. For climbing trees the hallux had become opposa-
ble. A bipedal gait was attained later when Primates became adapted to the life in open savannas. Characteristic
of the Primates are the small, specialized extremities and
teeth; the relatively large brain size; and stereoscopic
sight (not present in the most primitive forms).

The Primates are divided into Prosimii, including lemurs; the Anthropoidea, comprising monkeys, apes and
man; and Tarsioidea. Early lemurs had a rather long
snout and a lateral position of the eyes in the Eocene.
Stereoscopic sight was introduced by Eocene tarsids,
which may have been more closely related to the ancestors of higher Primates or Anthropoidea. This group appeared in the Oligocene or late Eocene. The monkeys
(ceboids and cercopithecoids), characterized by a well-
developed tail, are known from the Oligocene onward.

The Hominoidea, including apes and man, have a more
strongly developed brain and a reduced tail. Certain remains from the Eocene of Egypt and Burma may represent generalized ancestors of apes. Among Miocene–Pliocene apes the *Proconsul*, possibly belonging to a common
genus *Dryopithecus*, stood near the ancestors of both
apes and men. This would mean that man and apes
parted in their evolution some 30,000,000 years ago.

Characteristic of early man is the making of tools from
stone. Such implements are known from the earliest Pleistocene. Human remains are very rare and scattered and
the evolution of the group is difficult to ascertain. But
four different stages, evidently not directly derived from
each other, may be distinguished (see PRIMATES).

Carnivores. The carnivores (*q.v.*) are primarily characterized by their specialized cheek teeth called the car-
nassials. The dentition, however, was more unspecialized
among the early representatives of the group. The Early
Tertiary forms have generally been placed in a separate
group, the Creodonta. Recent research indicates, however, that only two families (the Oxyaenidae and Hya-
enodontidae) of this archaic order are to be regarded as
true carnivores; the rest are probably related to primitive
ungulates. The carnivorous creodonts flourished during
the Eocene, and a few (hyenodonts) lingered on to Late
Tertiary time.

A marked radiation of the more advanced carnivores,
those belonging to order Carnivora, took place in late

Lemurs,
monkeys,
apes, and
man

Eocene and early Oligocene time. These forms developed chiefly from the insectivores through the Eocene Miacidae, small forms with carnassial teeth and relatively larger brain than the contemporaneous creodonts. Advanced carnivores comprise the mustellids and dogs appearing in the Oligocene, the bears in Miocene, the catlike aeluroids in the Eocene, and true cats in the Oligocene. Highly specialized were the sabre-toothed cats with their enormous canines, a group that persisted into the Pleistocene. The aquatic pinnipeds, with uniform teeth, are known from the Miocene onward.

The highly specialized whales, Cetacea (see WHALE), represent a separate order, although the Early Tertiary forms, like the 17-metre (55-foot) long *Basilosaurus*, evidently were fish-eating carnivores.

Hoofed mammals. The ungulates, or hoofed mammals, comprise many different types of large, herbivorous, Cenozoic mammals. Adaptions are characteristic of these herbivores. The teeth, adapted for food grinding, become high crowned and long. In order to facilitate locomotion, the gait changed from plantigrade, in which the entire foot makes contact with the ground, to digitigrade, which involves lifting the foot so that only the tips of the digits (hoofs) touched the ground.

The living "Ungulata," a rather artificial group, chiefly comprise the Artiodactyla (*q.v.*), which are the even-toed ungulates; the Perissodactyla (*q.v.*), which are the odd-toed ungulates; and the "Subungulata," of which the Proboscidea is the more prominent group. Fossil materials have added a great number of extinct forms, which demonstrate the strong radiation of the group, particularly in the Early Tertiary; at the same time these materials complicate the classification that was based on the relatively few living forms.

The earliest ungulate representatives were rather unspecialized and might be considered to be stem groups from which the later forms evolved. Archaic ungulates with a small brain and little specialized dentition have been placed in a separate group, the "Protungulata," of which the Condylarthra form the central and most unspecialized group. *Phenacodus* from the Eocene is characteristic, but even more unspecialized are certain Paleocene forms (*Tetraclaenoden*), which might have been ancestral to at least several of the later and more advanced ungulates. Among the early off shoots of the ungulate stem might be mentioned the queer-looking, heavy-bodied amblypods (pantopods); *Uintatherium* attained the size of a present-day rhinoceros. These early forms did not survive the Eocene.

Fossil
elephants The Proboscidea (*q.v.*), including elephants and related forms, comprise another group that branched off from the primitive ungulates. The highly specialized trunk and teeth of living forms were indicated by the Eocene *Moeritherium*. Through the Tertiary it is possible to follow the gradual development of the second incisor into the great tusks and also the strong reduction in the number of premolars and molars. Some Miocene forms had tusks in both jaws (*Trilophodon*) or only the lower jaw (*Deinotherium*). The mastodons appeared in the Oligocene; the large forms in the Pleistocene had large tusks but still less specialized cheek teeth.

The imposing evolution of the order Perissodactyla, particularly in the Lower Tertiary, is well documented by fossil finds, chiefly from North America. It has been possible to demonstrate the evolution of horses from lower Eocene to Recent time. From *Hyracotherium* (or *Eohippus*), which was the size of a fox terrier with few specialized cheek teeth and four toes on the front legs, a number of equoids that generally mark a continuous trend toward *Equus*, the recent horse, developed successively. Evolutionary stages are marked by *Mesohippus* (lower Oligocene), with three toes; *Parahippus* (Miocene), with more advanced teeth, indicating a change from forest-browsing to grass-feeding habits; and *Hipparion* (Pliocene), which was the size of a pony with one toe and rudiments of the lateral ones.

The spectacular tithanotheres, limited in time to the Eocene and Oligocene, developed from primitive horse-

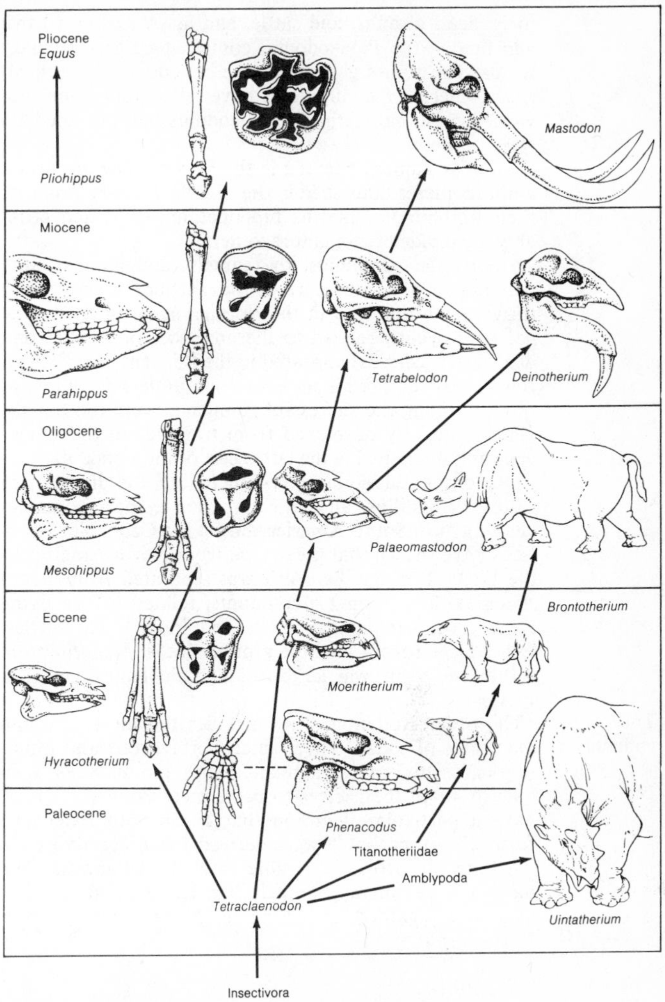

Figure 13: *Evolution of certain mammalian groups.*
The horses (Equidae) and the elephants (Proboscidea), as well as the Amblypoda and Titanotheriidae (which became extinct in the Lower Tertiary), developed from primitive forms like *Tetraclaenoden* in the earliest Tertiary.
From (hoofs, Titanotheriidae, Uintatherium) L. Stormer, *Jordens og livets historie;* and (others) A.S. Romer, *Vertebrate Paleontology* (©1966), The University of Chicago Press, all rights reserved

like forms. The late *Brontotherium* was a huge animal with hornlike processes in front of the skull.

Rhinoceroses were common during the Tertiary. Evidently derived from early tapirids, they developed parallel to the horses, showing, however, a much stronger radiation. The earliest (Eocene) forms were adapted for running, whereas the later ones became more bulky and large. Some had horns, which are composed of fused, hairlike material, not bone. The hornless *Baluchitherium* from the Oligocene of Mongolia is the largest land animal known; it attained a shoulder height of about 5.5 metres (18 feet).

Artiodactyls The order Artiodactyla includes a great number of the larger living mammals. In the Eocene, the group developed rapidly; and, particularly in the later part of the Cenozoic, it became the dominating group, considerably more so than the perissodactyls, which had their acme of development in the earlier part of the Tertiary.

Characteristic of the group is the axis of the foot, which runs between the third and fourth toe instead of the middle (third) toes as in the perissodactyls. The double pulleyed astragalus bone is also diagnostic of the group. This type of bone has been found in certain early Eocene forms resembling primitive carnivores, a fact suggesting that the ancestors of the artiodactyls were primitive condylarths.

The artiodactyls may largely be divided into three major groups: the Suina, including pigs, peccaries, hippopotamuses, anthracotheres, and others; the Ruminantia (cud chewers), including most other forms, such as camels, deer, giraffes, and cattle, and many extinct forms; and finally, the Palaeodonta, comprising Early Tertiary forms. The suines generally have bunodont (low-cusped) teeth, whereas the ruminants have selenodont (more advanced grinding) teeth. The paleodonts had intermediate types of teeth.

Primitive suines appeared in the Eocene. The important anthracotheres flourished in the Middle Tertiary, some of them amphibious like the hippopotamuses, which probably are divided from anthracotheres.

Among the ruminants, the camels (and llamas) were common in the later part of the Tertiary. Early forms (traguloids) appeared in the Eocene, some of them (the palaeomerycids) related to the ancestors of giraffes and deer. Deer (cervids) appeared in the Pliocene; the Pleistocene "Irish elk" with its enormous antlers is quite famous. Among the successful ruminants were the bovids, which evidently developed from tragulids in the Oligocene and flourished in the latter part of the Cenozoic.

The order Edentata (*q.v.*), including the living tree sloths, armadillos, and anteaters, had a spectacular development in South America during the Cenozoic. Fossil finds have shown that they came from North America in the Early Tertiary, before it was separated from South America. The extinct glyptodonts, related to the living armadillos, had stout armour and looked like turtles. Other large forms were the ground sloths; *Megatherium*, a Pliocene form, was larger than an elephant (length six metres).

The rodents   The order Rodentia (*q.v.*) includes the most common mammals of today. These small herbivorous and omnivorous forms, more than any other group, have been able to adapt themselves to present environments. They have a particular dentition that began with Paleocene forms. They probably were derived from insectivores in the Late Mesozoic. Mice date from the Oligocene. The hares and rabbits appeared in late Eocene and are now generally regarded as belonging to the separate order Lagomorpha.

THE PLANTS

The study of fossil plants, paleobotany, shows in a convincing way the gradual appearance of the various plant groups through geologic time. The general development of higher plants has been demonstrated, although the transition between several major groups is still unknown. The main types of plant fossils are (1) impressions and casts, which may show very distinctly the external morphology of the plant; (2) compressions, in which carbonaceous remains of the plant body are preserved and resistant parts like the cuticle may be present and show fine details; (3) petrifications of the plant body, which before decaying has been impregnated with silica (or other chemical substances), preserving the cell walls and other anatomical details.

Bacteria and algae.   The oldest remains of what probably have been living organisms have been found in South Africa and Rhodesia, in Precambrian rocks estimated to be about 3,000,000,000 years old.

Bacteria-like structures have been recorded both in Precambrian and younger sediments; in certain cases they are present in plant and animal tissues. Common types such as coccoid, bacilloid, filamental, or spirillar forms have been recorded. Many species have been described from the Carboniferous, mostly classified in the genus *Micrococcus*. The physiological activity of fossil bacteria cannot be traced, but there are reasons to believe that iron and sulfur bacteria took part in the formation of such deposits.

Blue-green algae (Cyanophyceae) have been identified in Precambrian deposits. They are quite common in younger deposits. Laminated calcareous structures, stromatolites, are generally interpreted as deposited by blue-green algae. The shapes vary from simple domes to complicated columns.

Unicellular planktonic algae evidently played an important role in ancient seas. Except for the coccolithophorids, diatoms, and dinoflagellates, little is known of these nanofossils, which have increasing stratigraphic importance. The Coccolithinae are flagellates with a complicated calcareous skeleton. First recorded from the Triassic (possibly also from the Early Paleozoic), they were very important in the Cretaceous when they were largely responsible for the formation of chalk deposits. In present seas they occur in great quantities. Diatoms occur in Jurassic and later systems. The dinoflagellates probably also include the little known hystrichospherids, which were common in the Early Paleozoic.

Lime-secreting green algae of the families Codiaceae and Dasycladaceae are known from the Ordovician to Recent times. The Dasycladaceae were particularly numerous in the Triassic–Jurassic, whereas today there are only a few genera and species in warm seas. Calcareous red algae (*Lithothamnion* and relatives) are widespread today and play an important role in coral reefs. They were common reef builders in the Tertiary and range from the Early Paleozoic.

The Fungi and Bryophyta are little known as fossils. Hyphae and spores of fungi occur in the Carboniferous. Among the bryophytes, members of the liverworts (Hepaticopsida) are known from the Devonian and mosses (Bryopsida) from the Permian.

Development of land plants.   The evolution of land plants started at the end of the Silurian (*Cooksonia* from Bohemia). Four main stages may be distinguished in the development of the land plants: (1) the "psilophyte flora" of the Lower and Middle Devonian, (2) the Upper Devonian–Lower Permian "Carboniferous flora," (3) the Mesozoic "gymnosperm flora," and (4) the Upper Cretaceous–Recent "angiosperm flora."

Primitive plant characteristics   At the close of the Silurian, members of the class Psilopsida (*q.v.*) appeared in the nonmarine sediments. The group includes primitive plants lacking roots and true leaves. The aerial stems were dichotomous (or pseudomonopodial), naked, or with thorns, covered by a cuticle and provided with simple stomata and an internal strand with tracheids. The isosporous sporangia were either terminal on the shoots (Rhyniaceae) or attached by short side branches to the smooth portions of the main stems (Zosterophyllaceae). The plants, which may have grown to a height of about 0.5 metre, inhabited the coastal swamps. A few species like *Taeniocrada* (Lower Devonian, Germany) were possibly aquatic. The famous Rhynie Chert of Scotland, which has yielded excellently preserved specimens of *Rhynia*, *Horneophyton*, and *Asteroxylon*, was previously regarded as Middle Devonian but is now assumed to be Lower Devonian (Emsian). In *Asteroxylon* the aerial stem was densely covered by small leaves, about five millimetres long, and had a lobed protostele. The genus shows affinities to the lycopsids (*q.v.*).

Baragwanathia from the Lower Devonian of Australia represents the oldest known member of the lycopsids. The dichotomous shoots up to 28 centimetres long have threadlike leaves, at the base of which are placed the sporangia. *Drepanophycus* and *Protolepidodendron* resemble the recent club moss *Lycopodium*.

The sphenopsids (*q.v.*) have been cited as present in Lower and Middle Devonian. The Middle Devonian *Hyenia* and the somewhat older *Protohyenia*, formerly regarded as primitive sphenopsids, are no longer so considered.

The pteropsids, or ferns (*q.v.*), probably had precursors in the Lower and Middle Devonian. *Dawsonites* and *Trimerophyton*, generally grouped with psilopsids, had structures in common with later ferns. The Upper Devonian *Archaeopteris* was long regarded as a kind of fern; however, the organization of the large leaves has been shown to differ from that of true ferns. Leaves were borne on stems with wood resembling that of conifers (*Callixylon*). At least some species were heterosporous. *Archaeopteris* is therefore now referred to a separate class, Progymnospermopsida, which points forward to the gymnosperms.

The Devonian floras thus contain the main pteridophyte, or seed-bearing, groups, and with the exception of the sphenopsids, all made their first appearance in the early

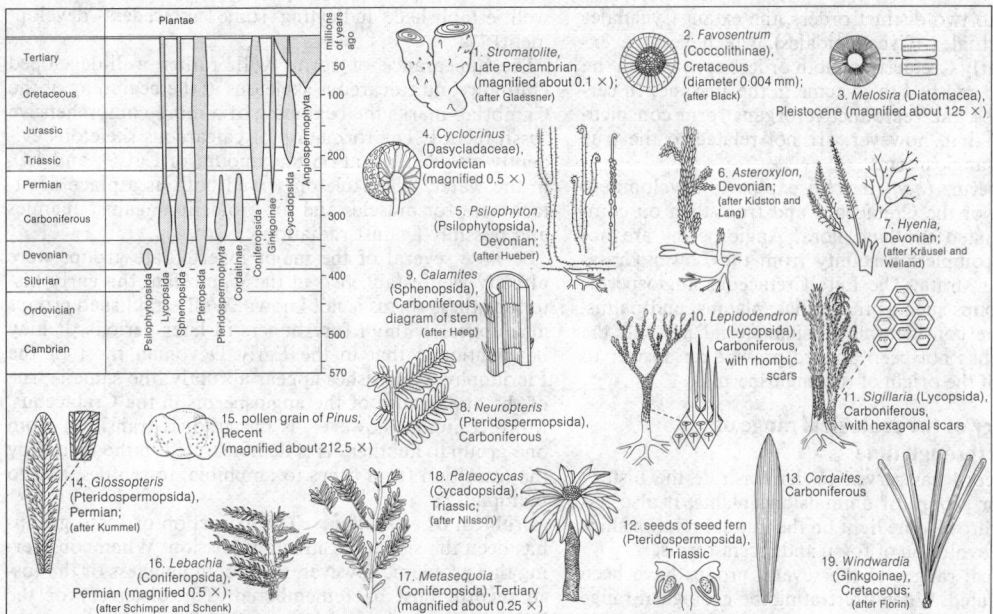

Figure 14: *Representative plants and their geological range.*
(Left) Occurrence of principal groups of plants in the geological record. Width of stippled
zone indicates relative abundance. (1–9) Fossil plants as designated.
From (1,2,4–7,18) L. Stormer, *Jordens og livets historie;* (3,15) Magnusson, *Sveriges Geologi;* (8) Termier and
Termier, *Paleontologie stratigraphique* (1960), Masson & Cie, Paris; (17) after Palaeontographica, Abteilung B,
in Schloemer-Jaeger, *Palaeontographica,* vol. 104

The Car-
boniferous
flora:
Lepido-
dendron,
Sigillaria,
Calamites,
and the
ferns

part of that period. The psilopsids were decidedly the
most primitive and were probably similar to the starting
members of the other groups. Beyond that, little is known
of the phylogeny of the various classes. In the Middle
Devonian arborescent types formed the first forests.

The Carboniferous floras were dominated by the Pteridophyta, particularly the lycopsids, sphenopsids, and the
pteropsids. Gymnosperms (*q.v.*), particularly conifer-like
members, were an important part of the flora. Most of
the coals (*q.v.*) of the Carboniferous formed from the
giant *Lepidodendron* and *Sigillaria* trees, which inhabited
widely distributed coastal (paralic) swamps, of a type
similar to the Everglades of Florida and the mangrove
swamps bordering tropical seas. *Lepidodendron* reached
a height of up to 30 metres with a maximum stem diameter of one metre. The stems had an underground part
with rootlike appendages (*Stigmaria*), and at the top of
the long stem, a crown formed by dichotomous branching. The narrow leaves present only in the upper part of
the tree were of variable length. The stem had characteristic diamond-shaped, spirally arranged scars, which actually were cushions where the leaves were attached.
Conelike strobili from a few centimetres to ¾ metre in
length contained a very large number of macrospores
and microspores. *Sigillaria* resembled *Lepidodendron* but
had a more pillar-shaped stem with a crown of grasslike
leaves and leaf bases in vertical rows. After the Permian,
the lycopsids became less important. Arborescent types
apparently did not survive the Paleozoic.

The sphenopsids had characteristic articulated stems and
leaf whorls and were also important members of the Carboniferous flora. The Upper Devonian and Lower Carboniferous Asterocalamitaceae had woody stems, and
large *Calamites* attained heights of 15–20 metres, even up
to 30 metres. Like the giant lycopsids, the sphenopsids
practically vanished at the end of the Paleozoic.

Ferns (*q.v.*) and fernlike plants were very common in
the Carboniferous and were well represented in later periods. Members of this group had true roots, stems, and
leaves, the latter showing a great variation in the development of the fronds and pinnae. Unfortunately, most fossil imprints of leaves do not show the sporangia, which
are necessary for taxonomic determinations. Most fernlike leaves have proved to belong to a separate group of
seed ferns (Pteridospermae) of the division called gymnosperms (*q.v.*). Carboniferous true ferns belong to different orders continuing into later periods.

The seed ferns differ fundamentally from the true ferns.
The fossil material does not show any distinct connection
between the vascular cryptogams and the gymnosperms
(the seedlike structures in *Lepidocarpon* do not form a
bridge). The seed ferns, ranging from the Lower Carboniferous to the Jurassic, generally had large fernlike leaves.
The seeds were enclosed in cupulas, which were attached
to leaves or to modified leaf structures. The microspo-
rangia were in sori on the lower sides of leaves or in differently arranged synangia. *Glossopteris* and *Ganga-
mopteris,* so characteristic of the Upper Carboniferous–
Permian Gondwanaland of the Southern Hemisphere,
probably belong to the pteridosperms. They had tongue-
shaped, elongate leaves and reproductive organs that have
been variously interpreted by paleobotanists.

Conifers and the occurrence of forests. The conifers
may be traced back with some certainty to the Devonian.
From Carboniferous time onward they form a major part
of the forests. The late Paleozoic *Cordaites* were large
trees, up to 30 metres in height, with a slender stem and
strongly branched crown with long (up to one metre),
strap-shaped leaves. Typical conifers such as *Lebachia*
(*Walchia*), occurring in the Upper Carboniferous and
Lower Permian, have a habitual resemblance to the extant *Araucaria* (Norfolk pine). The ovule-bearing cones
show similarities to *Cordaites.* The living Araucariaceae,
Taxodiaceae, and Pinaceae date back to the Triassic,
Jurassic, and Cretaceous, respectively. The taxodian
genera *Sequoia* and *Metasequoia* had a wide distribution
in Cretaceous and Tertiary times. *Sequoia* now is restricted to North America. *Metasequoia,* thought to be
extinct until a species was discovered in China, has been
revived in the United States as an ornamental nursery
stock. The order Ginkgoales, with the extant *Ginkgo*
(maiden hair tree), represents a relict order of gymno-
spermous plants. Their distinctive fanlike leaves are significant fossils in Mesozoic and Tertiary floras.

Most characteristic of the Mesozoic floras were the cycads, represented today by small palmlike, subtropical
ornamentals. True cycads are known from Early Triassic
time, and morphological characters of these early representatives indicate that they developed from seed ferns.
The erect, sometimes branched stems were covered by
leaf scars and bore a terminal crown of large leaves
either pennate or entire (like banana leaves). The foliage
had two distinct types of stomatal apparatus. This character and the structure of the reproductive organs divide

The
Mesozoic
flora:
cycads

the cycads into two distinct orders, the extant Cycadales and the Benettiales (Cycadeoidales), which became extinct in the Early Cretaceous. Both orders appeared in the Early Triassic and had their acme in the Jurassic. In certain bennettites, the reproductive organs form conspicuous "flowers" that, however, are not related to the true flowers of the angiosperms.

The angiosperms (q.v.) had an explosive development in the middle of the Cretaceous and from then on completely dominated the land flora. Angiosperms are not known with complete certainty from the Lower Cretaceous or older strata. The Late Cretaceous angiosperms are extant groups such as magnolias, platans, and palms. In spite of the considerable fossil material present, the fossil record has not been able to provide an answer to the problem of the origin of the angiosperms.

III. Summary of the geological range of fossil groups through time

The fossil record has served to demonstrate the history of most major groups of animals and plants. It also has been able to throw some light on the mutual relationships and trends of evolution of fossil and recent forms.

The geological ranges of the several groups have been previously treated. When illustrating the geological range and abundance of major groups it should be borne in mind that each group actually is composed of a number of separate groups, each of which has a separate development, abundance, and range. The composite curves thus do not show the actual evolutionary trends within the major groups, and the abundance of taxa in fossil groups at different times is influenced to a large extent by the variation in the completeness of the record. Fossiliferous sediments may be less common in certain periods and more common in others, for example, and abundance does not necessarily illustrate the importance of a group. The recent fauna *Homo sapiens*, for example, is hardly negligible, but this single taxon would not show up in the curve.

Development of a group. The development of a group may follow different patterns. In any of the curves an "onion-shaped" outline is common; this indicates a rapid increase in taxa shortly after the first appearance of the group. After the maximum is reached, a slow decline and a possible extinction follow. The trilobites, amphibians, and reptiles belong more or less to this group. In other cases, such as the mammals, the first step in the development of the group is insignificant and modest.

In cases of rapid unfolding, this may be due to the origin of a new successful type (a favourable plan of construction) or the conquest of a new, unoccupied biological niche. In cases of slow development, the new group may have had to compete for a considerable time with powerful existing groups before conditions for full development were present (in the case of the mammals, the reason may also have been that the successful placentals did not arrive until just before the great radiation of the mammals).

Signifi-
cance
of first
appear-
ance

The first appearance of a group in the fossil record virtually means the first appearance of members that were capable of being preserved in the sediments. Little is known of Precambrian many-celled animals and plants; however, the metazoans may not have developed very long before Cambrian time. The very long delay may chiefly be due to the slow increase in atmospheric oxygen, which was necessary for active metazoans.

The apparently sudden appearance of shell-bearing metazoans just before, and at the beginning of, the Cambrian has been a problem to geologists for a long time. The find of the ediacaran fauna, however, and more details of the Early Cambrian faunas have shown that the appearance of the metazoans in the record was not as sudden as previously believed.

The various groups appeared at different times during the 30,000,000-year interval representing the Lower Cambrian. The first to appear were the enigmatic archaeocyatids, with their fragile calcareous shell. The trilobites and other groups came a little later (but were then already

well established, indicating some antecedent development).

The appearance of forms with rather well-developed chitinous and calcareous skeletons at the beginning of the Cambrian marks the beginning of a more comprehensive fossil record. The formation of calcareous skeletons evidently was dependent on the amount of $CaCO_3$ and CO_2 in the water. The skeleton served both as a place of attachment for muscles and for protection against enemies and possibly against radiation.

Because several of the major invertebrate groups were already well established in the Cambrian, the early history of these forms is not known. Well-established groups also appear without forerunners in later periods. It may be mentioned that in the Early Devonian most of the Pteridophyta and fishes appear abruptly; the same is true of the appearance of the angiosperms in the Cretaceous. More common, however, is the gradual transition from one group to another, as is demonstrated in the record by the transition from fishes to amphibia, to reptiles, and to mammals.

Problem of extinction. The extinction of fossil groups has been the subject of much discussion. When considering this problem, however, the incompleteness of the fossil record must be remembered. The discovery of the living coelacanth *Latimeria* and the monoplacophoran *Neopilina* confirms this. It cannot be denied, however, that the record indicates the occurrence of fairly sudden extinctions of certain groups at certain times. The rate of extinction may have been greater at certain times, at the end of the Permian and at the end of the Cretaceous, for example, but the difference appears to be quantitative rather than qualitative. A more drastic example of extinction is provided by the dinosaurs. All the major groups except the primitive palaeopods and the stegosaurs became extinct, more or less simultaneously, at the end of the Cretaceous. Only two of the many ammonites survived the Paleozoic, and after a radiation in the Triassic, a new extinction took place, with only one family surviving into the Jurassic. The final extinction occurred at the end of the Cretaceous. This last extinction is, however, foreshadowed by a gradual decrease in the number of families through the Upper Cretaceous (from 22 to 11). Within certain of the dying families, an increase in size and the presence of bizarre-looking forms may be noted. This is a common accompaniment of extinctions of many groups.

The causes of extinction have been much discussed, but no single cause has been suggested that can truly explain this phenomena. Factors that influence extinctions include the following: (1) extraterrestrial, (2) geological–climatical, and (3) biological. Extinctions related to increased radiation are not well supported by the facts. Although most of the ammonite families died out at certain times, for example, the related nautiloids were little affected at the same times. A certain increase of mutations might create new competing forms, but this seems to have been of minor importance. It is possible that surface plankton to some extent might have been influenced by radiation.

Among geological factors, orogenic movements can result in major changes in the environments. The drying up of rivers and swamps might have been fatal to amphibious dinosaurs and also to the carnivorous dinosaurs that fed on them; however, such changes could have less influence on marine faunas unless accompanied by a large regression of the sea, which would alter the shallow marine environments.

Climatic changes evidently affected the land plants and animals, although migration might have saved most groups from extinction. A glacial climate could have favoured extinction in two ways. The decrease in temperature might have been too much for some groups. Glaciation also involves accumulation of ice on land and a corresponding lowering of the sea level. A general drying up of epicontinental seas and continental shelves would have had strong influence on the benthonic, shallow water faunas in particular.

Geological
and
climatic
factors

Possible biological causes include the strong competition for existing biological niches. This "struggle for life" might result in extinction. A "racial senescence" has also been advocated as a reason for extinction. Although such a cause is difficult to prove, racial senescence might have been present in certain groups, such as the trilobites and eurypterids.

Thus the causes of extinction remain unclear, but several factors probably were acting at the same time.

BIBLIOGRAPHY. H.N. ANDREWS, JR., *Studies in Paleobotany* (1961), an introductory, comprehensive treatment of paleobotany; E.S. BARGHOORN and S.A. TYLER, "Microorganisms from the Gunflint Chert," *Science*, 147:563–577 (1965), descriptions and illustrations of 1900 million-year-old organisms, with an insight into very early life forms; E. BOUREAU (ed.), *Traité de Paléobotanique* (1964, 1967), a definitive paleobotanical work; W.B. HARLAND *et al.* (eds.), *The Fossil Record* (1967), a series of technical papers dealing with various aspects of the fossil record; R.C. MOORE (ed.), *Treatise on Invertebrate Paleontology* (1954–), a multivolume, definitive work on invertebrate paleontology discussing in detail, and in a systematic manner, all fossil invertebrates; A.S. ROMER, *Vertebrate Paleontology*, 3rd ed. (1966), a readable, authoritative account.

(L.St.)

Fourier, Jean-Baptiste-Joseph, Baron

The French mathematician Joseph Fourier, known also as an Egyptologist and administrator, exerted strong influence on mathematical physics through his pioneer work, *Théorie analytique de la chaleur* (1822; Eng. trans., *The Analytical Theory of Heat*, 1878). He showed how the conduction of heat in solid bodies may be analyzed in terms of infinite mathematical series now called by his name, the Fourier series. Far transcending the particular subject of heat conduction, his work stimulated research in mathematical physics, which has since been often identified with the solution of boundary-value problems, encompassing many natural occurrences such as sunspots, tides, and the weather.

His work had a great influence on the theory of functions of a real variable, one of the main branches of modern mathematics. Moreover, he contributed substantially to the compilation and publication of the influential *Description de l'Égypte* (1808–25), summarizing in 21 volumes the cultural and scientific results of Napoleon's invasion of Egypt. The work drew attention to the ancient Egyptian civilization and marked Egyptology as a new and separate discipline.

Joseph Fourier, lithograph by Jules Boilly, 1823. In the Académie des Sciences, Paris.
Giraudon

Fourier, born March 21, 1768, in Auxerre, the son of a tailor, first attended the local military school conducted by Benedictine monks. He showed such proficiency in mathematics in his early years that he later became a teacher in mathematics at the same school. The ideals of the French Revolution then swept him into politics, and more than once his life was in danger. When the École Normale was founded in 1794 in Paris, he was among its first students, and, in 1795, he became a teacher there. The same year, after the École Polytechnique was opened, he joined its faculty and became a colleague of Gaspard Monge and other mathematicians.

In 1798, with Monge and others, Fourier accompanied Napoleon on his expedition to Egypt. Until 1801 he engaged in extensive research on Egyptian antiquities, gave advice on engineering and diplomatic undertakings, and served for three years as the secretary of the Institut d'Égypte, which Napoleon established in Cairo in 1798.

After his return to France, Fourier was charged with the publication of the enormous mass of Egyptian materials. This became the *Description de l'Égypte*, to which he also wrote a lengthy historical preface on the ancient civilization of Egypt. He was also appointed prefect (administrator for the national government and *département*) of the Isère *département*, a position he held from 1802 to 1814, with his headquarters at Grenoble. He showed great administrative ability, as in directing the drainage of swamps, while continuing his Egyptological and mathematical work. In 1809 Napoleon made him a baron. Following Napoleon's fall from power in 1815, Fourier was appointed director of the Statistical Bureau of the Seine, allowing him a period of quiet academic life in Paris. In 1817 he was elected to the Académie des Sciences, of which, in 1822, he became perpetual secretary. Because of his work in Egyptology he was elected in 1826 to the Académie Française and the Académie de Médecine.

> Egyptology

Fourier began his work on the *Théorie analytique de la chaleur* in Grenoble in 1807 and completed it in Paris in 1822. His work enabled him to express the conduction of heat in two-dimensional objects (*i.e.*, very thin sheets of material) in terms of the differential equation

$$\frac{\partial u}{\partial t} = k \left[\frac{\partial^2 u}{\partial x^2} + \frac{\partial^2 u}{\partial y^2} \right],$$

in which u is the temperature at any time t at a point (x, y) of the plane and k is a constant of proportionality called the diffusivity of the material. The problem is to find the temperature, for example, in a conducting plate, if at time $t = 0$, the temperature is given at the boundary and at the points of the plane. For the solution of such problems in one dimension, Fourier introduced series with sines and cosines as terms:

> Theory of heat

$$y = \tfrac{1}{2}a_0 + (a_1 \cos x + b_1 \sin x) + (a_2 \cos 2x + b_2 \sin 2x) + \cdots.$$

Such Fourier series, already occasionally used by Leonhard Euler and other 18th-century mathematicians, but somewhat distrusted, received through Fourier their important position in modern mathematics. He also extended this concept into the so-called Fourier integral. Doubts of the validity of the Fourier series, which led later mathematicians to a fundamental renewal of the concept of real function, were resolved by P.G.L. Dirichlet, Bernhard Riemann, Henri Lebesgue, and others.

Fourier worked on the theory almost his entire life. He was also interested in the determination of roots of algebraic equations (the so-called theorem of Fourier). He died in Paris on May 16, 1830.

BIBLIOGRAPHY

Works: Oeuvres de Fourier, 2 vol. (1888–90); *Analyse des équations déterminées* (1831); *Théorie analytique de la chaleur* (1822; Eng. trans., *The Analytical Theory of Heat*, 1878, reprinted 1955); *Description de l'Égypte*, 21 vol. (1808–25), by Fourier and others.

Biography: I. GRATTAN-GUINNESS, *Joseph Fourier, 1768–1830* (1972), is a magnificent study dealing with Fourier's mathematical physics and includes an exhaustive bibliography. See also F. ARAGO, "Joseph Fourier," in *Oeuvres complètes*, vol. 1, pp. 259–369 (1854; Eng. trans. in the *Annual Report* of the Smithsonian Institution, 1871), an elegant biography; J.R. RAVETZ, "Preliminary Notes on the Study of J.B.J. Fourier," *Arch. int. Hist. Sci.*, 13:247–251 (1960), preliminary to a critical study of Fourier's work; and RUDOLPH E. LANGER, "Fourier Series: The Genesis and Evolution of a Theory," *Am. Math. Mon.*, 54:1–86 (1947), an elementary account, the first part historical.

(D.J.S.)

Fox, Charles James

In late 18th-century British politics, Charles James Fox was a famous champion of liberty, a colossus whose career, on the face of it, was nevertheless one of almost unrelieved failure. He conducted against King George III a long and brilliant vendetta, sometimes wrongheaded but constitutionally significant; for this reason he was almost always in political opposition and, in fact, held high office for less than a year altogether. His leadership of the parliamentary opposition was marked by incredible blunders. He achieved only two important reforms, steering through Parliament a resolution pledging it to abolish the slave trade speedily, and, in the 1792 Libel Act, restoring to juries their right to decide not merely whether an allegedly libellous article had, in fact, been published but also what constituted libel in any given case and whether or not a defendant was guilty of it.

Charles James Fox, detail of an oil painting attributed to John Zoffany (c. 1734–1810). In the Henry E. Huntington Library and Art Gallery, San Marino, California.

Early life. Fox was born in London on January 24, 1749, the third son of Henry Fox, afterward 1st Baron Holland, by his wife, Lady Caroline Lennox, daughter of the 2nd duke of Richmond. Through his mother he was descended from Charles II of England and Henry IV of France. He was educated at Eton and at Hertford College, Oxford, where he acquired an extensive knowledge of the classics, to which he remained devoted for the rest of his life. His father brought him up without the least regard for morality and encouraged him, while still a schoolboy, to acquire extravagant and dissolute habits. He lost vast sums at gambling, and in 1774 his father, just before his death, paid the young man's gambling debts to the amount of £140,000. Almost 20 years later political friends not only freed him from debt but settled on him a comfortable income. He then showed his gratitude by abandoning forever both racing and gambling.

Entry into politics. Fox was procured a seat in Parliament by his father in 1768. Two years later he was appointed a junior lord of the Admiralty but gave up his office in February 1772 in order that he might be free to oppose a bill (eventually the Royal Marriage Act) designed to prevent marriages of members of the royal family unless authorized by the king or ratified by the Privy Council. He re-entered the government the following December as a junior lord of the Treasury, but the King, who already disliked him for his recent opposition, accused him of insubordination and dismissed him in February 1774.

Already a friend of Edmund Burke, he naturally gravitated into the Whig group and before long was their accepted leader in the Commons. He went into opposition just when the controversy with the American colonies was becoming acute. Believing that the colonial policy of the prime minister Lord North was unjust and oppressive, he opposed it with unrestrained violence, but he later admitted that the American war was popular in England. The series of disasters sustained by the British troops in America, culminating in the capitulation of the army led by Lord Cornwallis at Yorktown (October 1781), eventually brought down North's government (March 1782). The King had to call in a Whig ministry, of which Lord Rockingham became prime minister, and Lord Shelburne (later marquess of Lansdowne) colonial secretary; Fox became the first foreign secretary in English history.

Fox believed, erroneously, that the negotiations for peace with the Americans came within the province of the foreign secretary, and he wished to recognize the independence of the former colonies immediately and unconditionally. Shelburne wanted to withhold this recognition until the peace treaties with the European countries with which Britain had also been at war were ready for signature; and he maintained that since the independence of America had not yet been formally recognized, he, as colonial secretary, had the right to conduct the negotiations. Fox, therefore, notified his intention to resign (June 30), but before he could implement it, Rockingham died (July 1).

When the King offered the premiership to Shelburne, Fox and his friends maintained that it was for them, not for the King, to choose Rockingham's successor. This was unconstitutional; the King had the undoubted right to choose the minister. Fox and some of his friends at once resigned, but others remained to support Shelburne. The historian Sir George Otto Trevelyan described Fox's refusal to serve under Shelburne as the fatal and irreparable mistake of his life. Though his suspicions of Shelburne were far from groundless, they were exaggerated; moreover, Shelburne was in some respects the most enlightened statesman of his time.

The Fox–North coalition (1783). Fox always had a liking for coalitions; on February 14, 1783, he joined with his old enemy North to eject the new government and accomplished his object ten days later. Defending an action that was undoubtedly unpopular and damaging to his reputation, Fox maintained that it was wise and candid to end the hostility between North and himself now that its sole cause, the American war, was over.

After trying desperately for five weeks to withstand "the most unprincipled coalition the annals of this or any other nation can equal," the King had to grant it office (April 2). The Duke of Portland, a nonentity, became the nominal prime minister; Fox and North, the two secretaries of state. Although the King withheld from the ministers various customary marks of royal confidence, they had no difficulty in retaining the vote of the independent country gentlemen in the House of Commons. The new ministers did not improve their position at court by proposing to give the Prince of Wales (later George IV) an income of £100,000 a year. By remaining the intimate friend of this dissolute young man, who was detested by his father and who ostentatiously supported the coalition, Fox further outraged the King's feelings.

The coalition fell because of its India bill. Fox and North had no wish to evade their responsibility for ending a system of misgovernment in India that had alarmed and disquieted English statesmen of all parties. Their bill proposed to change the whole constitution of the East India Company, which effectively controlled British India, by transferring control of the company's territories, revenues, and commerce to seven commissioners who were to be nominated by the British government and removable only upon a vote of either house of Parliament. But vested interests took alarm, and the House

First foreign secretary

Increasing unpopularity

of Lords rejected the bill on December 17 after the King had made it known that he would consider as an enemy anyone who voted for it. The coalition was dismissed next day, and the young politician William Pitt (the Younger) accepted an invitation to form a government.

Fox increased his unpopularity by attacking the sovereign's right to choose his ministers and to appeal to the electorate to confirm his choice. Fox's opponents could now plausibly maintain that he would not even submit his case to the judgment of the nation. Many of the coalition's supporters changed sides, and the dissolution of Parliament (March 1784) completed the discomfiture of the opposition, which found itself with only about 145 members in the new House of Commons. Fox himself, however, was re-elected for the great popular constituency of Westminster, defeating the ministerial candidate.

Opposition to Pitt and Addington. Had he been even a little accommodating, Fox could have joined William Pitt's government on honourable terms in 1784, to the great advantage of the cause of reform. But his attacks on Pitt's proposed commercial concessions to Ireland in 1785 and on a commercial treaty made with France in 1787 damaged his reputation. He blundered again in 1788–89, when the King was temporarily insane, by supporting the claim of the Prince of Wales to the regency as a right—whereas Pitt maintained that Parliament alone had the right and competence to appoint a regent. Party interests, of course, were deeply involved in the constitutional dispute; the Prince's first act of power would have been to dismiss Pitt and bring in the Whigs.

Fox welcomed the outbreak of the French Revolution in 1789. War with Revolutionary France broke out in 1793, and a large part of the opposition, headed by Portland, went over to the government in 1794. The minority (50–60) adhering to Fox became one of the weakest oppositions ever known in England, and in about 1797 many opposition members even ceased to attend Parliament. Fox was dismissed from the Privy Council in 1798 for reaffirming in a public speech the doctrine of the sovereignty of the people; yet eight years later the King had to reinstate him without exacting any retraction of principle.

In 1795 Fox had secretly married Mrs. Elizabeth Armitstead, with whom he had been living for many years and to whom he always remained devoted; the marriage was revealed only in 1802. In their country house, St. Anne's Hill, near Chertsey in Surrey, he indulged his tastes for classical literature and a rural existence and found there ample compensation for all the disappointments and stresses of public life. Mrs. Fox, who bore him no children, died on July 8, 1842.

Fox approved of the peace negotiations that resulted in the treaty signed at Amiens (1802) but spoke of the "shameful surrender of all our conquests" to Napoleon. He was critical of the ministry (1801–04) of Henry Addington (afterward Viscount Sidmouth) for its failure either to preserve the peace or to put the country into an adequate state of defense to meet Napoleon's invasion threat, which followed the renewal of war in 1803. Though his motion, virtually one of censure (April 23, 1804), was defeated by 256 votes to 204, Addington's government resigned a few days later.

Pitt now wished to form a coalition government on a broad base but failed to persuade George III to waive his objections to Fox as a minister (he would have been foreign secretary), though the King was prepared to give him a foreign mission. Fox, with his usual generosity, acquiesced in this proscription, said that he was too old (at 55) to care about office, and advised his friends to join the coalition; but both they and the followers of Lord Grenville (with whom they had recently collaborated) rejected the suggestion and went into opposition.

Last years. When Grenville became prime minister after Pitt's death on January 23, 1806, the King's veto on Fox's appointment to office as foreign secretary disappeared without protest. During the earlier phase of the war against France, Fox had believed that the various European despots were fighting to destroy the newly won liberties of the French, and he had underestimated the bellicose spirit of France and the danger to England of French conquests. But by 1806 he had come to realize that France, under Napoleon, threatened the independence of Great Britain and the whole Continent.

By this time Fox's health was breaking down. Suggestions were made that he should take some less laborious office, or even that he should take a peerage to save him from the more exacting task of leading the House of Commons. Fox made his last speech in Parliament on June 19, and he died on September 13, 1806, in the Duke of Devonshire's house at Chiswick. He was buried in Westminster Abbey by the side of Pitt.

Assessment. Fox had a genius for friendship, and the secret of his political influence was the uncalculating generosity of his mind. His charm could overcome the hostility of even the most inveterate of his foes. As a statesman he had great and manifest failings. He was often governed by prejudice, and he was not a profound political thinker. Above all, he hated anything that savoured of oppression, and his attitude on various colonial issues showed his passionate determination that the peoples of the empire were no longer to be exploited. His approval of the French Revolution shattered his friendship with the statesman and political writer Edmund Burke; although privately Fox showed himself far from insensible to the horrors perpetrated by the French Republicans, he gave these feelings no adequate public expression and opposed the war with republican France as a crusade against freedom in the interests of despotism. At home the excessive power of the crown was, in his view, the great source of all the country's ills, and to the destruction of that overweening power he dedicated his life. He put forward the view, afterward accepted, that the crown must choose the prime minister from the party that commanded a majority in the House of Commons, irrespective of the sovereign's personal inclinations. Yet he was no democrat, despising public opinion if he considered it prejudiced and intolerant. He would never have countenanced the notion that property, the security of which was one of the prime preoccupations of both Whig and Tory parties, would be safe in a democratic society in which the propertyless voters would obviously be in a majority. In his view property was the true foundation of aristocracy, and a country best prospered whose government was in such hands.

Fox had a strong European sense and a deep feeling for the responsibilities of his own country as a member of a greater society with mutual obligations. It was because he held these large and generous views that his influence endured after his death, inspiring such measures as the Parliamentary Reform Act of 1832.

BIBLIOGRAPHY. For the general reader the best modern survey of the period covered by Fox's political career is JOHN STEVEN WATSON, *The Reign of George III, 1760–1815* (1960). IAN CHRISTIE, *The End of North's Ministry, 1780–82* (1958), is most useful, as also are RICHARD PARES, *King George III and the Politicians* (1953); and D.G. BARNES, *George III and William Pitt, 1783–1806* (1939, reprinted 1965). Older books that can still be read with profit are SIR GEORGE OTTO TREVELYAN, *The Early History of Charles James Fox*, new ed. (1908); and his *American Revolution*, new ed., 6 vol. (1905–16, reprinted 1964); LLOYD SANDERS, *The Holland House Circle* (1908); and G.S.H. FOX-STRANGWAYS, *The Home of the Hollands, 1605–1820* (1937). *The Memoirs of the Whig Party During My Time*, by Fox's nephew LORD HOLLAND, 2 vol. (1852–54), was almost a contemporary record. Students who wish to consult the manuscript sources for Fox's career should turn first to the *Memorials and Correspondence of Charles James Fox*, ed. (though not very accurately) by LORD JOHN RUSSELL, 2 vol. (1853). The new edition, by various editors, of Burke's correspondence, of which vol. 1 appeared in 1958, is in progress. A great deal of new correspondence and material bearing on Fox's career is in *The Later Correspondence of George III*, 5 vol. (1962–70), and *The Correspondence of George, Prince of Wales, 1770–1812*, 8 vol. (1963–71), both series edited by ARTHUR ASPINALL.

(A.As.)

Fox, George

George Fox, the founder of the Society of Friends, also known as the Quakers, initiated a movement that has

[margin notes]
Regency crisis

Hatred of oppression

Early life and activities

exerted a significant influence in the area of religious and political toleration for nearly 300 years.

He was born in July, 1624, the son of a weaver in the English village of Fenny Drayton (then Drayton-in-the-Clay), Leicestershire. Probably apprenticed for a while to a cobbler, he may also have tended sheep, but there is little evidence of any adult business occupation or of much formal education. He always seemed to have a modest amount of money. He read extensively and wrote legibly. At the age of 18 he left home in search of satisfying religious counsel or experience and later reported in his *Journal* various personal religious experiences or direct revelations, which he called "openings," that corrected, in his estimation, the traditional concepts of faith and practice in English religious life.

His religious background was apparently Puritan rather than strict Anglican, but he himself reacted even further than the Puritans from the formalism and traditionalism of the established church. He placed the God-given inward light (inspiration) above creeds and scripture and regarded personal experience as the true source of authority. In his *Journal* he wrote,

These things I did not see by the help of man, nor by the letter, though they are written in the letter, but I saw them in the light of the Lord Jesus Christ, and by his immediate Spirit and powers, as did the holy men of God, by whom the Holy Scriptures were written.

His negative attitude to ecclesiastical customs was matched by a similar attitude toward some political and economic conventions (*e.g.*, oaths, titles, and military service).

He began preaching to individuals or groups as he travelled on foot, first in the Midland counties of England, then in the northern counties, where groups of Seekers (a 17th-century Puritan sect) welcomed him and his message. Local congregations were established, gathered both by Fox and by many other itinerant men and women preachers, who were called Publishers of Truth. Thus came into being in the last years of the British Commonwealth (1649–60) the Society of Friends, as it was much later called, though its members were early nicknamed "Quakers."

Fox had most success in winning adherents and fellow workers in the Lake District counties of Westmorland and Lancashire and later in Yorkshire, London, and other areas. He and his associates suffered public hostility and official constraint. They offended religious leaders both religiously and politically by their contradiction of the ministers in the churches (based on Fox's view that ministers "bred at Oxford or Cambridge" were not qualified to be spiritual leaders in the churches) and by their refusal to honour officials, to take oaths, or to pay tithes. Fox and his associates were often arrested and imprisoned. Fox, in fact, suffered eight imprisonments between 1649 and 1673.

The restoration of the monarchy in 1660 led to special legislation against the Quakers and a widespread action against them. To meet this and other needs, George Fox encouraged local Quaker groups to organize into regular monthly and quarterly business meetings, which, with some central national meetings, became a permanent pattern of their church government. The continuing pressure was only intermittently relieved until the Toleration Act of 1689, shortly before Fox's death, gave relief to the Quakers.

Missionary work in England and other countries

In 1669 Fox made a missionary visit to Ireland, and on his return he married one of his early converts, Margaret Fell, the widow of Judge Thomas Fell of Swarthmore Hall, Ulverston, Lancashire, where Fox spent parts of the following years. In the years 1671 to 1673 he paid an important visit to the British colonies in the Caribbean and the North American mainland, strengthening and organizing the existing Quaker communities, especially in Maryland and Rhode Island. Shorter journeys in 1677 and 1684 took him to Holland (The Netherlands) and a few other parts of northern Europe. About 1675 he dictated a running summary of his life that, with supplementary material, was posthumously edited and published as his *Journal*. For most of the last 15 years of his life he lived as a boarder or visitor among friends in or about London, attending consultations and committees on practical questions, preaching at meetings for worship, and engaging in a wide correspondence with individual Friends or with congregations to whom he was known.

Throughout his life, Fox shared the contemporary practice of writing controversial pamphlets, scores of which were published. They dealt with social as well as theological questions but lacked stylistic attraction. Although he was quite familiar with the English Bible, he sometimes displayed a taste for subjects like history and grammar, in which he had little competence. He borrowed information occasionally from his learned friends.

He evidently was, as Thomas Carlyle (1795–1881) says, a man of enormous self-confidence, one who attracted rather than repelled. A magnetic personality, he was widely respected and admired by such men as William Penn, a man of culture and knowledge of the world, who left in writing an appreciation of Fox that is still the best summary of his character. His own *Journal* is naturally not entirely objective, but with its many details it forms the fullest account of the rise of Quakerism, as well as of Fox himself. It is partly due to Fox's own sense of the historic importance of the Quaker movement that much other early written material was recorded and preserved. He died January 13, 1691, in London and was buried in the Friends' burial ground near Bunhill Fields.

BIBLIOGRAPHY. *The Journal . . . of George Fox*, ed. by THOMAS ELLWOOD, with an illuminating and comprehensive introduction by WILLIAM PENN (1694), is the fundamental source. The most useful edition of the *Journal* is that ed. by JOHN L. NICKALLS (1952). It reduces the bulk of the many inserted papers and uses the manuscripts behind Ellwood's editing. Two other folio collections of his writings were issued after his death, *The Epistles of George Fox* (1698), and his doctrinal writings, *Gospel-Truth Demonstrated* (1706). All these were included in the *Works of George Fox*, 8 vol. (1831).

Modern biographies, useful because they include references to the historical setting, are VERNON NOBLE, *The Man in Leather Breeches* (1953), and HARRY EMERSON WILDES, *The Voice of the Lord* (1965). See also RUFUS M. JONES, *George Fox, Seeker and Friend* (1930), and A.N. BRAYSHAW, *The Personality of George Fox* (1933).

(H.J.C.)

Fragonard, Jean-Honoré

Jean-Honoré Fragonard has been bracketed with Watteau as one of the two great poetic painters of the unpoetical 18th century in France. A prodigiously active artist, he produced over 550 paintings, several thousand drawings (although many hundreds are known to be lost), and 35 etchings. His style, based primarily on that of Rubens, was rapid, vigorous, and fluent, never tight or fussy like that of so many of his contemporaries. Although the greater part of his active life was passed during the Neoclassical period, he continued to paint in a Rococo idiom until shortly before the French Revolution. Only five paintings by Fragonard are dated, but the chronology of the rest can be fairly accurately established from engravings, documents, etc.

Fragonard was born at Grasse on April 5, 1732, the son of a haberdasher's assistant. The family moved to Paris around 1738, and in 1747 the boy was apprenticed to a lawyer, who, noticing his appetite for drawing, suggested that he be taught painting. Fragonard's mother first approached François Boucher, the most successful contemporary French painter, who refused to take an untrained youth into his studio but recommended him to Jean-Baptiste-Siméon Chardin, under whom he was soundly grounded in the technique of painting. Boucher thereupon accepted him as a pupil (*c.* 1748) and, in 1752, his elementary training completed, recommended that he compete for a Prix de Rome scholarship, which meant that he must first study for five years under the court painter to Louis XV, Carle Van Loo, at the École Royale des Élèves Protégés in Paris. On September 17, 1756, Fragonard set off with other scholarship winners for the French Academy at Rome, but not before enjoying suffi-

Early training with Chardin and Boucher

"The Swing," oil on canvas by Jean-Honoré Fragonard,
c. 1766. In the Wallace Collection, London. 83 cm x 66 cm.

Parisian
success

cient success to receive a handsome commission from his native town for a religious painting and a municipal grant toward his travelling expenses.

At the academy, Fragonard copied many paintings, chiefly by Roman Baroque artists, and, with his friend the French painter Hubert Robert, made numerous sketches of the Roman countryside. When his scholarship ended in July 1759, he was allowed to remain in residence until, in late November, he met a wealthy amateur artist, the Abbé de Saint-Non, who was to become one of his chief patrons. Early in 1760 Saint-Non took Fragonard and Robert on a prolonged tour of Italy, where the two artists studied Italian paintings and antiquities and made hundreds of sketches of local scenery. Some of these later developed into paintings, and others were used as backgrounds for *fêtes galantes* (aristocratic gatherings in a rural setting), while Saint-Non had still others engraved and published in his *Voyage Pittoresque . . . de Naples et de Sicile* (1781–86).

Four years after returning to Paris in 1761, Fragonard exhibited a few landscape paintings and the large "Coresus Sacrifices Himself to Save Callirhoe" at the salon where it was purchased for the King. Consequently, the artist was commissioned to paint a pendant, or companion piece, granted a studio in the Louvre Palace, and accepted as an Academician. Nevertheless, after 1767 he almost ceased to exhibit at the salons, concentrating on landscapes, often in the manner of the 17th-century Dutch painter Jacob van Ruisdael ("Return of the Herd," Worcester), portraits, and decorative, semi-erotic *fêtes galantes* in the style of Boucher ("The Swing") but more fluently painted. His admiration for Rembrandt, Rubens, Hals, and a Venetian contemporary, G.B. Tiepolo, emerges in a large series of loosely and vigorously executed heads of old men, painted c. 1760–67 ("Head of an Old Man"), followed by a series of portraits (c. 1765–72) in a similar style and in which the sitters were real persons, but their fantastic costumes were emphasized rather than facial expressions ("Abbé de Saint-Non in Spanish Costume").

In 1769 he married Marie-Anne Gérard from Grasse and shortly afterward received the accolade of fashion, when in 1770 he was commissioned by Mme du Barry to decorate her newly built Pavillon de Louveciennes, with four large paintings ("Progress of Love," Frick Collection), and in 1772 received a somewhat similar commission from the notorious actress Mlle Guimard. Neither was a success, the Louveciennes paintings probably being rejected as too Rococo for a totally Neoclassical setting.

A journey to the Low Countries perhaps in 1772–73 increased his admiration for Rembrandt and Hals and was reflected in his later portraits. A second visit to Italy followed in 1773–74. As before, he concentrated on drawing picturesque Italian landscape subjects rather than on painting. The return journey was taken through Vienna, Prague, and Germany.

On his return to Paris, the family was joined by his wife's 14-year-old sister, Marguerite, with whom Fragonard fell passionately in love. This turned his interests toward a new type of subject matter: domestic scenes inspired by Rousseau's moral philosophy or romantic novels ("The Happy Family") or scenes concerned with children's upbringing, in which his son Évariste (born 1780) frequently figures ("The Schoolmistress").

In the last years preceding the French Revolution, Fragonard turned finally to Neoclassical subject matter and developed a less fluent Neoclassical style of painting ("The Fountain of Love"). This becomes increasingly evident in his latest works, the genre scenes executed in collaboration with Marguerite Gérard ("The Beloved Child").

Neo-
classical
period

Fragonard's art was too closely associated with the pre-Revolutionary period to make him acceptable during the Revolution, which also deprived him of private patrons. At first he retired to Grasse but returned to Paris in 1791, where the protection of the leading Neoclassical painter Jacques-Louis David obtained for him a post with the Museum Commission, but he was deprived of this in 1797. The rest of his life was spent in obscurity, painting little. Fragonard's death on August 22, 1806, passed almost unnoticed, and his work remained unfashionable until well after 1850, but he has since been increasingly esteemed.

MAJOR WORKS

"The Education of the Virgin" (c. 1748–52; California Palace of the Legion of Honor, San Francisco); "Girl with a Marmot" (c. 1748–52; Fogg Art Museum, Cambridge, Massachusetts); "Blind-Man's-Buff" (c. 1748–52; Toledo Museum of Art, Ohio); "The See-Saw" (c. 1750; Thyssen-Bornemisza Collection, Castagnola, Switzerland); "Winter," part of "The Seasons," overdoors for the Hôtel Matignon (c. 1751–61; Los Angeles County Museum of Art); "Landscape with Cowherd" (c. 1760–65; Detroit Institute of Arts); "Landscape and Greensward" (c. 1760–65; Musée National du Palais de Compiègne, France); "Head of an Old Man" (1760–67; Musée Jacquemart-André, Paris); "The Washerwoman" (c. 1761–65; Musée de Picardie, Amiens); "The Storm" (c. 1761–65; Louvre, Paris); "The Gardens of the Villa d'Este" (c. 1761–65; Wallace Collection, London); "The Lost Forfeit" or "Stolen Kiss" (c. 1761–65; Metropolitan Museum of Art, New York); "Landscape with Peasants and Animals" (c. 1761–65; Worcester Art Museum, Massachusetts); "The Dream of Love" (c. 1761–65; Louvre, Paris); "Coresus Sacrifices Himself to Save Callirhoe" (c. 1761–65; Louvre, Paris); "The Stable" (c. 1761; private collection); "Portrait of a Man" (c. 1763–65; André Meyer Collection, New York); "Rinaldo in the Gardens of Armida" (c. 1765; private collection, Paris); "Rinaldo in the Enchanted Forest" (c. 1765; private collection, Paris); "The Parents' Absence Turned to Account" (c. 1765; Hermitage, Leningrad); "The Stolen Shift" (c. 1765; Louvre, Paris); "All in a Blaze" (c. 1765; Louvre, Paris); "Women Bathing" (c. 1765; Louvre, Paris); "The Useless Resistance" (c. 1765–72; National Museum, Stockholm); "Abbé de Saint-Non in Spanish Costume" (c. 1765–72; Museo de Arte Moderno, Barcelona); "The Swing" (c. 1766; Wallace Collection, London); "Inspiration" (c. 1766; Louvre, Paris); "Music" (c. 1769; Louvre, Paris); "The Music Lesson" (c. 1770; Louvre, Paris); "Portrait of a Lady with a Dog" (c. 1770; Metropolitan Museum of Art, New York); "The Sleeping Bacchante" (c. 1770; Louvre, Paris); "The New Model" (c. 1770; Musée Jacquemart-André, Paris); "The Three Graces" (c. 1770; Louvre, Paris); "The Loves of Shepherds" or "The Ages of Life" (four paintings, c. 1771; Frick Collection, New York); "Love As Folly" and "Love As Conqueror" (c. 1771; National Gallery of Art, Washington, D.C.); "View of an Italian Villa" or "The Cascade" (c. 1773; Metropolitan Museum of Art, New York); "The Happy Family" (c. 1773–76; Metropolitan Museum of Art, New York, and National Gallery of Art,

Washington, D.C.); "Study Portrait of a Girl" (Wallace Collection, London); "The Washerwomen" (*c.* 1774; City Art Museum, St. Louis); "A Young Girl Reading" (*c.* 1775; National Gallery of Art, Washington, D.C.); "The Swing" (*c.* 1775; National Gallery of Art, Washington, D.C.); "Blind-Man's-Buff" (*c.* 1775; National Gallery of Art, Washington, D.C.); "The Fete at Saint-Cloud" (*c.* 1775; Banque de France); "Marie-Catherine Colombe As Victorious Venus" (*c.* 1775–76; Los Angeles County Museum of Art); "The Schoolmistress" (*c.* 1777–78; Wallace Collection, London); "The Fountain of Love" (*c.* 1780–81; private collection); "Portrait of Mme. Bergeret de Norinval" (*c.* 1785; Musée Cognacq-Jay, Paris); "The Stolen Kiss" (*c.* 1788; Hermitage, Leningrad); "Evariste Fragonard As Pierrot" (*c.* 1789–90; Wallace Collection, London); "The Beloved Child," painted with Marguerite Gérard (*c.* 1792; private collection, New York).

BIBLIOGRAPHY. The best work on Fragonard as a painter that supersedes all earlier publications and includes a catalogue raisonné is G. WILDENSTEIN, *The Paintings of Fragonard: Complete Edition* (1960). It includes a concise critical bibliography of the essential manuscript and printed sources. This is the only work of any significance in English apart from the essay of 1865 on the artist by the brothers JULES and EDMOND DE GONCOURT later reprinted in their *L'Art du dix-huitième siècle*, translated, together with certain other essays, by R. IRONSIDE in *French Eighteenth Century Painters* (1948), from the third and best edition (1881) of the Goncourts' work. The essay is important not only for its poetical interpretation of Fragonard's art but because the authors wrote just in time to interview the last surviving contacts of the artist himself. A catalogue raisonné of the drawings is being prepared by M. ALEXANDRE ANANOFF. Three volumes (out of four) covering 2,000 drawings, have so far been published (1961–68). It suffers, however, from faults of organization. The etchings have been exhaustively treated by G. WILDENSTEIN in *Fragonard aquafortiste* (1956).

(F.J.B.W.)

France

One of the oldest and historically and culturally most important nations of Europe and indeed of the whole Western world, France lies near the western end of the great Eurasian landmass, between latitudes 42° and 51° N, and covers a total area of 212,742 square miles (551,000 square kilometres). Hexagonal in outline, its territory is bordered on the north by Belgium, Luxembourg, and La Manche (the English Channel); on the west by the Atlantic Ocean and the Bay of Biscay; on the south by Spain and the Mediterranean Sea; and on the east by West Germany, Switzerland, and Italy. Its two mountain chains, the lofty Alps in the east and the Pyrenees in the southwest, form additional natural frontiers and thus leave only the northeast boundary—across which most of the great invasions afflicting the nation have been launched—open to any great extent. This geopolitical situation may well explain why the Rhine has sometimes been claimed as the natural boundary of the hexagon's sixth side, and it certainly helps to account for the relatively early achievement of national unity by the French people—a process initiated from Paris and the surrounding country, aptly named the Île de France. The climate is generally moderate, combining Atlantic, Mediterranean, and the more extreme continental influences. As a result of the strong recovery in the birth rate after World War II, the repatriation of more than 1,000,000 French citizens from its former colonies in North Africa, and the influx of foreign labour, the national territory thus circumscribed was the home of over 51,000,000 persons by the early 1970s.

Paris is both the head and the heart of France and, because of a constantly accelerating process of centralization, contains in its metropolitan area fully one-sixth of the total population, which is distributed in a very unequal manner between 38,000 *communes*, the smallest administrative units in the nation.

France has had 11 constitutions since 1791, when a constitutional monarchy was adopted. The constitution of the Third Republic, which took effect from 1875 and lasted until 1940, was in many ways the simplest and least formal of all. The present constitution, proclaimed on September 28, 1958, by Charles de Gaulle, consider-

The geo-political framework of the nation

ably strengthened the powers of the head of state. With de Gaulle's election to the presidency following the referendum of 1962, which was held on the issue of the election of the president by universal suffrage and not by a college of notables, the semipresidential character of the government appeared to be confirmed. De Gaulle was president of the Fifth Republic until 1969, and he envisaged, in a new pattern of government, not only the increase of his own "superstructural" presidential powers but also those of the infra-structure, or local authority, in matters that were not directly political, at the expense of the central government. One of his chief aims, therefore, was to decentralize the administration of France. When his bold plan to achieve this goal was rejected by the nation in a referendum held in April 1969, he immediately resigned from office. Regional reform remained a major problem of the 1970s. Decisions taken in Paris, the capital city, frequently frustrate local initiative.

Interregional commerce is also hindered by the preeminence of Paris among French cities and by matters such as the convergence of the railroads and major highways on Paris, by the insufficient number of navigable waterways, and by the natural obstacle of the Massif Central, an upland mass that hinders transverse communications between cities to the east, such as the ancient city of Lyon or the equally ancient Mediterranean port of Marseille, and those of the west, such as Bordeaux or Nantes. Finally, most of the great industrial concentrations lie east of a line running from Le Havre, in the north, to Marseille, in the south, while the western regions, which have remained more agricultural, are, generally less developed.

On the international scene, France launched, in 1950, the Communauté Européenne du Charbon et de l'Acier (European Coal and Steel Community, or ECSC)—the embryo, perhaps, of a future federation of European states—on the initiative of the statesman Jean Monnet and of the then prime minister, Robert Schuman. Although France rejected the Communauté Européenne de Défense (European Defense Community, or EDC) in 1954, it remains an active member of the Communauté Économique Européenne (European Economic Community [EEC], or Common Market), formed in 1957. The nation continues to participate in the Atlantic alliance, but it withdrew in 1966 from the pact's military organization (NATO) and thus regained full control over its own air, ground, and naval forces. As a permanent member of the United Nations Security Council—together with the United States, the Soviet Union, the United Kingdom, and the People's Republic of China—France enjoys the right to veto decisions presented before the council, a process reflecting the nation's continued international stature.

In the cultural world France has always held a high place. The dukedoms and provinces that came to be called France gave rise to Gothic architecture in the Middle Ages and to a broad Humanism in the Renaissance and the Enlightenment. The sciences have been expanded by French discoveries, and, in the arts, France has contributed richly, producing world figures in drama, poetry, the novel, and in music. In the 19th and early 20th centuries France unleashed a burst of creative energy in painting unequalled since the Italian Renaissance.

This article covers the physical and human geography of France and aspects of its contemporary economic, political, and cultural life. For related information see the articles FRANCE, HISTORY OF; FRENCH REVOLUTIONARY AND NAPOLEONIC WARS; PARIS; LYON; MARSEILLE; RHONE RIVER; LOIRE RIVER; SEINE RIVER; ALPS MOUNTAIN RANGES; PYRENEES RANGE; EUROPE.

This article is divided into the following sections:

(H.B.-M.)

I. The land

TOPOGRAPHY

The the three geological regions

The French landscape is typical of the diverse nature of continental Europe. Three main geological regions are distinguishable: the skeletal remains of ancient mountains that make up the principal massifs; the northern and western plains; and the narrow plains between the rugged younger mountains of the south and southeast.

The ancient mountains. The physical structure of France is dominated by a group of ancient mountains in the shape of a gigantic V, the sides of which form the two branches of Hercynian folding that took place between 345,000,000 and 225,000,000 years ago. The eastern branch is comprised of the Ardennes, the Vosges, and the eastern part of the Massif Central, while the Hercynian massifs to the west comprise the western part of the Massif Central and the hills of the Massif Armoricain.

The eastern branch. The Ardennes stretch into a large part of Belgium and extend into West Germany as the crystalline rocks of the Rhenish massif. Only its western extremity is located in France. An old mountain chain made of folded sedimentary rock, the Ardennes are cut by a wooded eroded plain and gashed by the deep and narrow gorges of the valleys of the Sambre and the Meuse rivers. Altogether, it is a dark and wooded area. The Vosges mountains separate the Paris Basin from the Rheinland to the east. A small asymmetric mountain chain rising gradually from the west, the Vosges fall rapidly to the east in a faulted escarpment that dominates the plain of Alsace. In the north it is completely covered by a shell of Triassic sandstone and a magnificent forest, which acts as a windshield on its slopes and summits. The southern part of the chain, which is higher, culminates in the rounded peak of crystalline rock of Ballon de Guebwiller (Mt. Guebwiller), 4,672 feet (1,424 metres) high. Although eroded by time, this small mountain is a distinctive landmark in eastern France.

The western branch. The largest geographical region in France, the plateau of the Massif Central, covers about 35,000 square miles (90,000 square kilometres), or one-sixth of the area of the country. It is an asymmetrical mountain region, sharp and high in the southeast but gradually merging with the plains of the Paris Basin and the Loire lowlands in the north and northwest. As with the Vosges, this asymmetry resulted from the Alpine folding of newer mountains upon the stumps of the old ones, which had been previously formed and severely eroded.

The Massif Central complex

The Massif Central complex is traditionally divided into four parts. In the northwest the province of Limousin is characterized by a series of stepped plateaus bounded in the east by a mountain approaching 3,300 feet (1,000 metres). A halo of peripheral plateaus about 1,100 to 1,300 feet (350 to 400 metres) high lies beneath a number of plateaus about 2,000 feet (600 metres) high. The plateaus are cut by many gorges, characterized by geological uplifting and fracturing, developments that occurred at the time of the rejuvenation due to the Alpine foldings. For the most part, the plateaus are composed of crystalline rocks, and these same rocks of the Limousin extend

into the central part of the massif, forming the high plateaus that reach 4,000 to 5,000 feet (1,200 to 1,500 metres) and that were greatly changed in the Tertiary Period (about 65,000,000 to 7,000,000 years ago). At that time gigantic faults fractured the massif, cutting both the long depressions of the Limagne plain where the Allier River flows, as well as the plains of the Loire and the Velay, the Forez, and the Roannes (Roanne) basins.

In the same epoch the great volcanic massifs of Cantal and Monts Dore rose in the central part of the region, the latter containing Puy de Sancy, which at 6,184 feet (1,885 metres) is the highest summit of the Massif Central. The Puy range dominates the western border of Limagne, and its best-known peak is Puy de Dôme (4,803 feet [1,464 metres]). Of these peaks—which are extinct volcanoes and are a dominant feature of the landscape—the most recent date back only about 10,000 years.

To the south lies the large limestone plateau known as the Causses. In a vast faulted depression, the seas of the secondary geological era deposited a 2,600-foot-thick layer of sediment on the underlying limestone. This region is marked by its aridity and its few rivers, which have cut deep canyons, the best known of which is the Tarn canyon. It is a generally dark and wooded area made up of the crystalline and volcanic rock that constitutes the rest of the massif.

The eastern border of the Massif Central snakes southward from Morvan, a small wooded massif in the north, to Montagnes Noires, a large, dark, and wooded plateau that dominates the gate of Carcassonne, a lowland area that provides a valley route between the Pyrenees and the Massif Central to the Atlantic Ocean and the Mediterranean. Between these two points lie a series of granite massifs, with pastures and forests on their western slopes and vineyards on their eastern sides, including the mountain slopes of Beaujolais, Lyonnais, Vivarais, and Cévennes. Between these massifs lie the northeast–southwest depressions of sedimentary rock, with coal deposits at Montceau-les-Mines and Saint-Étienne.

This enormous mountainous mass, which almost forms a complete barrier between the plains of the Saône and the Rhône, is an obstacle to communications in central France and has remained very isolated for a long time. It has also suffered from serious depopulation in recent times. It is the source of many rivers, which descend to the English Channel in the north, to the Atlantic in the west, and to the Mediterranean in the east, feeding numerous dams valuable for their hydroelectric power.

The Massif Armoricain

The Massif Armoricain, made of crystalline rocks and formed at the time of the Hercynian folding, extends in hilly ridges from the northwest, in Bretagne (Brittany), to the hills of Normandie (Normandy) in the east and on to the wooded upland country (known as *bo cage*) in the Vendée, to the southeast. It contains the highest point in the western plains of France, the Mont des Avaloirs (1,350 feet [417 metres] high) in the Collines des Perche (Perche Hills).

The plains and the coasts. *The northern plains.* To the east of these worn-down mountains, the plains form four different groups. The northern plain extends to the Ardennes in the southeast and to the Artois (a Hercynian ridge 682 feet [208 metres] high) in the northwest. It descends toward the North Sea and Belgium.

The Paris Basin. The Paris Basin contains the largest group of these plains. It consists of a number of plateaus and hills that slope down toward the central basin and the low-lying Paris–Orléans region. The surrounding hills are the Artois, the Ardennes, the Vosges, the Bourgogne (Burgundy) plateaus, the Morvan Massif, and the Collines de Normandie (Hills of Normandy). The Paris Basin is an accumulation of sedimentary beds of which the most recent belong to the Tertiary Period and in the central area are nearly horizontal. They make up the plateaus of Beauce, Brie, the Île de France, Vallois, and the Soissonnais, which are covered with the fertile windborne dust known as *limon*, or "loess," which dates from the glacial period. Toward the edge of the basin, the beds are older and dip down at an increasing angle. In the eastern and southeastern parts of the basin, the alterna-

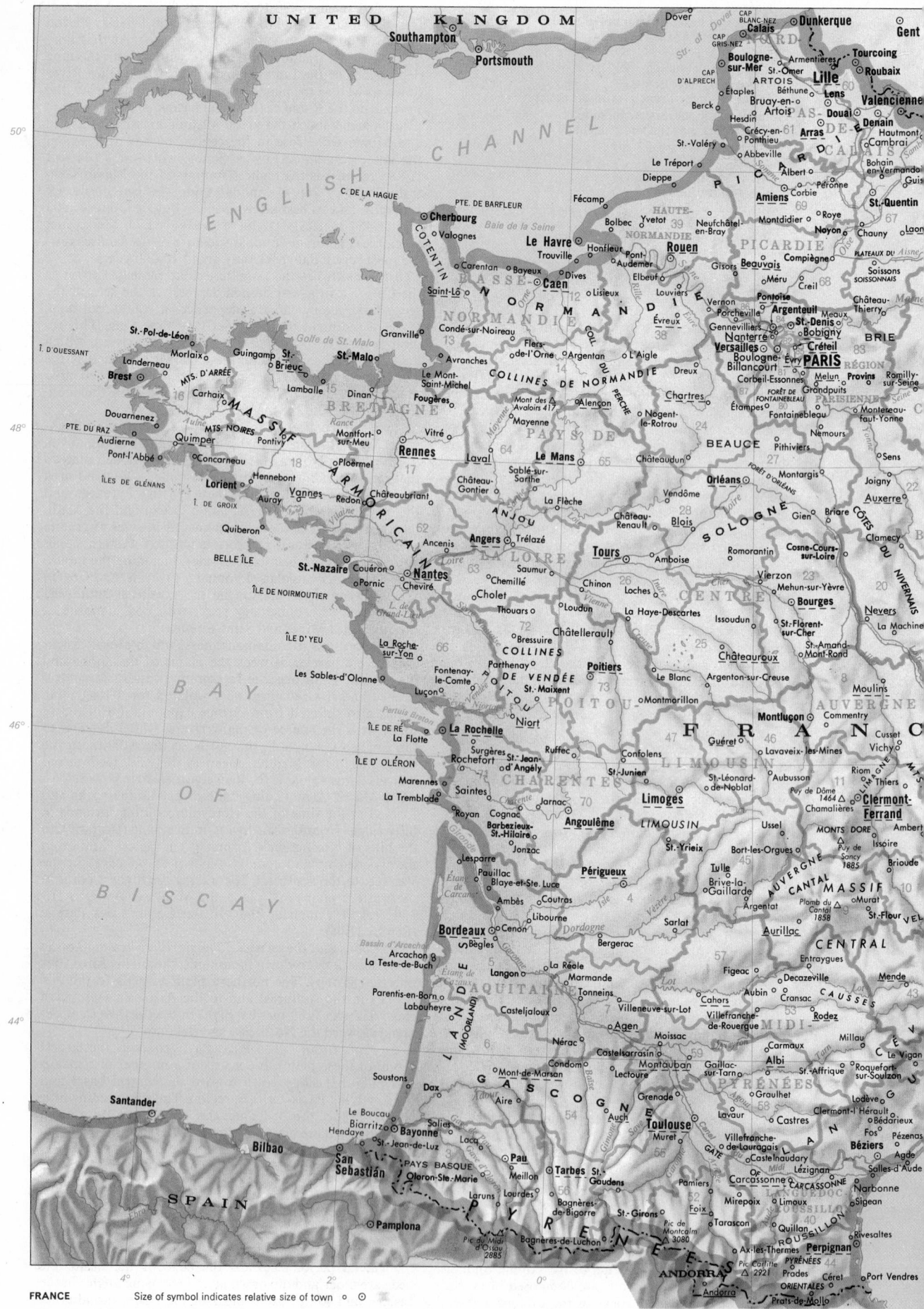

FRANCE   Size of symbol indicates relative size of town   ○ ⊙ ⊡

Elevations in metres

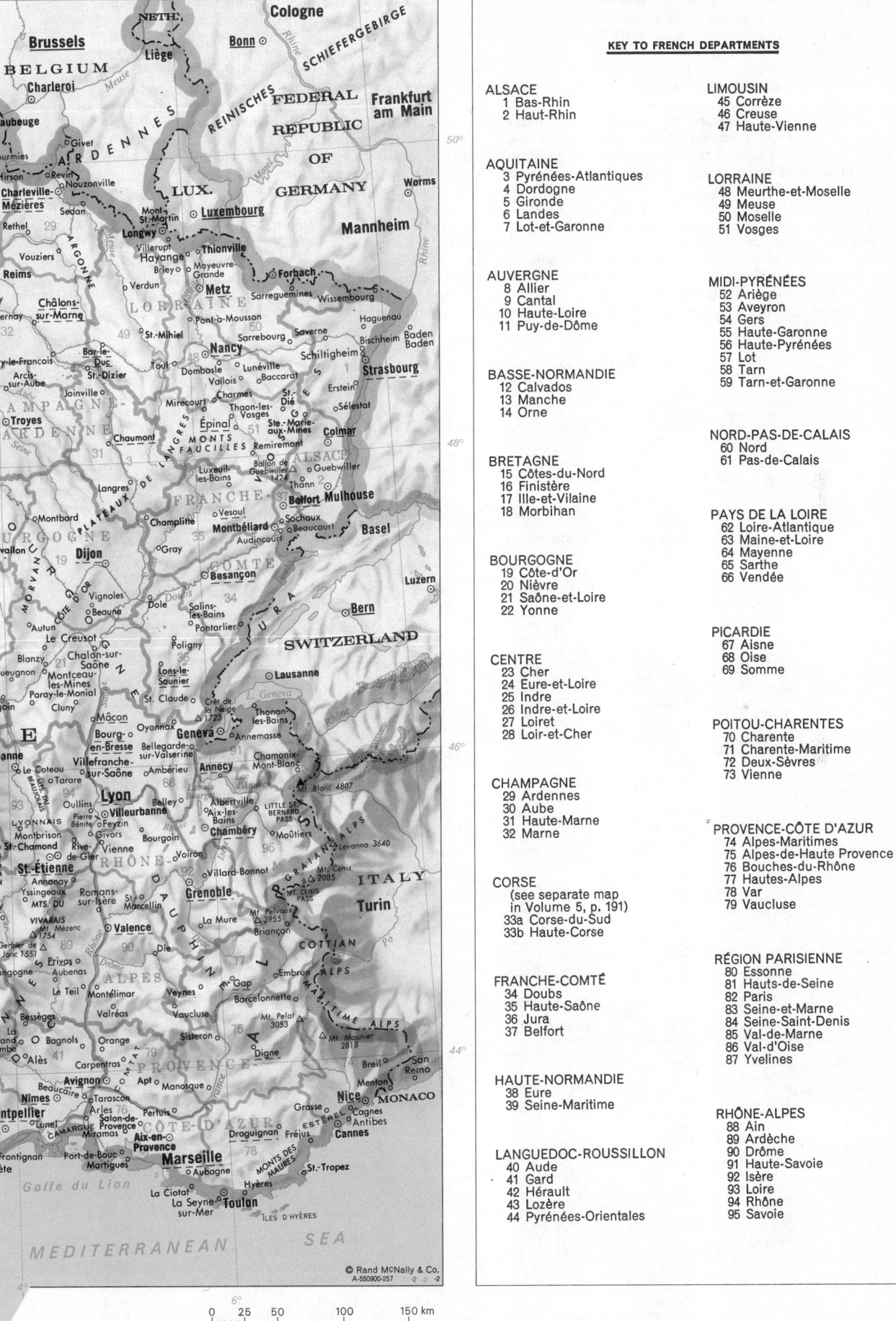

KEY TO FRENCH DEPARTMENTS

ALSACE
1 Bas-Rhin
2 Haut-Rhin

AQUITAINE
3 Pyrénées-Atlantiques
4 Dordogne
5 Gironde
6 Landes
7 Lot-et-Garonne

AUVERGNE
8 Allier
9 Cantal
10 Haute-Loire
11 Puy-de-Dôme

BASSE-NORMANDIE
12 Calvados
13 Manche
14 Orne

BRETAGNE
15 Côtes-du-Nord
16 Finistère
17 Ille-et-Vilaine
18 Morbihan

BOURGOGNE
19 Côte-d'Or
20 Nièvre
21 Saône-et-Loire
22 Yonne

CENTRE
23 Cher
24 Eure-et-Loire
25 Indre
26 Indre-et-Loire
27 Loiret
28 Loir-et-Cher

CHAMPAGNE
29 Ardennes
30 Aube
31 Haute-Marne
32 Marne

CORSE
(see separate map
in Volume 5, p. 191)
33a Corse-du-Sud
33b Haute-Corse

FRANCHE-COMTÉ
34 Doubs
35 Haute-Saône
36 Jura
37 Belfort

HAUTE-NORMANDIE
38 Eure
39 Seine-Maritime

LANGUEDOC-ROUSSILLON
40 Aude
41 Gard
42 Hérault
43 Lozère
44 Pyrénées-Orientales

LIMOUSIN
45 Corrèze
46 Creuse
47 Haute-Vienne

LORRAINE
48 Meurthe-et-Moselle
49 Meuse
50 Moselle
51 Vosges

MIDI-PYRÉNÉES
52 Ariège
53 Aveyron
54 Gers
55 Haute-Garonne
56 Haute-Pyrénées
57 Lot
58 Tarn
59 Tarn-et-Garonne

NORD-PAS-DE-CALAIS
60 Nord
61 Pas-de-Calais

PAYS DE LA LOIRE
62 Loire-Atlantique
63 Maine-et-Loire
64 Mayenne
65 Sarthe
66 Vendée

PICARDIE
67 Aisne
68 Oise
69 Somme

POITOU-CHARENTES
70 Charente
71 Charente-Maritime
72 Deux-Sèvres
73 Vienne

PROVENCE-CÔTE D'AZUR
74 Alpes-Maritimes
75 Alpes-de-Haute Provence
76 Bouches-du-Rhône
77 Hautes-Alpes
78 Var
79 Vaucluse

RÉGION PARISIENNE
80 Essonne
81 Hauts-de-Seine
82 Paris
83 Seine-et-Marne
84 Seine-Saint-Denis
85 Val-de-Marne
86 Val-d'Oise
87 Yvelines

RHÔNE-ALPES
88 Ain
89 Ardèche
90 Drôme
91 Haute-Savoie
92 Isère
93 Loire
94 Rhône
95 Savoie

tion of the hard and soft beds sloping toward the centre produces a distinctive kind of relief (known as "cuestas" in the southeast) that has been reflected in the great historical divisions of France. In the north the great chalk plains form eastern Normandie (Normandy), which is cut by the Seine Valley, and Picardie (Picardy), broken by the chalky ridge of Artois to the north. In western Normandie the Paris Basin joins the Massif Armorican.

The Loire plains. Toward the southwest the basin opens on the third group of plains, which follow the Loire Valley. The hills of this region, such as the limestone plateaus of Touraine and the crystalline plateaus of Anjou and Vendée, are cut by the broad valleys of the Loire and its tributaries. The valley, which varies in width from one to four miles, is famous for its peaceful atmosphere and for its beauty and fertility.

The Aquitaine Basin. The Loire countryside adjoins the Aquitaine Basin through the gap known as the Gate of Poitou. The Aquitaine Basin is much smaller than the Paris Basin, and, while it is bounded in the south by the Pyrenees, in the northeast it runs into the low foothills of the Massif Central. The slopes decline toward the central valley of the Garonne River. In the north there are limestone plateaus crossed by fertile valleys. In the centre, pointed hills were cut in the soft terrain during the Tertiary Period, while in the south, at the foot of the Pyrenees, there is a large sloping bank of hills composed of clastic rocks that has been cut into the shape of a fan by the rivers flowing down from the mountains. Finally, along the Atlantic coast, the Landes is a wasteland of sand dunes and marshes, much of which was reclaimed in the 19th century and transformed into pine forest.

The coasts. The coasts of the northern and western regions are as diverse as the countryside. The northern plain slopes down to the North Sea in great sandy dunes, while the hills of Artois near Belgium form the headlands of Cap Gris-Nez, Blanc-Nez, and Alprech. The chalky plateaus of Picardie and eastern Normandie face the English Channel with beautiful cliffs of white chalk that are bordered on the south by the deep estuary

Relation between topography and coastal scenery

of the Seine. West of the sandy beaches of central Normandie, the peninsulas of Cotentin and Bretagne, carved in the very hard and heterogeneous rocks of the Massif Armoricain, are bounded by variegated and picturesque coasts that are cut by capes and reefs and penetrated by deep rias (drowned river valleys). In the south, the Loire Estuary penetrates about 40 miles inland. A deep and wide arm of the sea makes up the Gironde Estuary, farther south, and a sandy coast is bordered by islands with many rock promontories. To the south of the Gironde is the smooth unbroken coastline of the Landes.

The younger mountains and adjacent plains. *Pyrenees, Jura, and Alps.* The Pyrenees, the foothills of which shelter the picturesque Basque countryside, constitute the most ancient of the more recently formed mountains in France. They stretch for more than 280 miles (450 kilometres), making a natural barrier between France and Spain. Their formation, which began in the Mesozoic Era, continued in the Tertiary and perhaps even in the beginning of the Quaternary, about 2,500,000 years ago.

The central part is the highest, composed of a series of parallel chains with passes that are few and difficult to reach, falling sharply at each end (see PYRENEES RANGE). The Jura Mountains (*q.v.*), near Switzerland, are composed of folded limestone. Their ridges extend parallel from the north-northeast to the south. The highest point is the Crêt-de-la-Neige, at 5,653 feet (1,723 metres).

The French Alps (see ALPS MOUNTAIN RANGES) are only a part of the great chain that extends throughout Europe, but they include the highest point, Mont Blanc (15,771 feet [4,807 metres] high). These majestic mountains were formed in a series of foldings that lasted from the beginning of the Tertiary to the Quaternary Period. They include the two greatest regions of permanent snow and glaciers in Europe, surmounted by the peaks of Mont Blanc and Mont Pelvoux, the latter exceeding 13,000 feet. The northern Alps, which are formed by four parallel segments (the folded chain of the Pre-Alps, the wide depression of the sub-Alpine hollow, the high central crystalline massifs, and the chains and peaks of the intra-

Divisions of the French Alps

Alpine zone), are easier to cross thanks to the great valleys created by the movement of glaciers. The relief of the southern Alps is much less orderly, and the valleys, which were not affected by glaciation, form narrow and winding gorges. Like the Pyrenees, the Alps form a natural barrier, dropping sharply down to the Po Plain in Italy.

The southern plains. Between these young mountains and the ancient Massif Central is a series of plains, including those of the Saône and the Rhône, which fan out to the Mediterranean in the great triangular delta of the Rhône and of Languedoc. In the south the Pyrenean foothills cut the basins and rocky coast of Roussillon. In the southeast the Alpine foothills adjoin the massifs of the Maures, the Estérel, and the Corsican mountains to form the coves, capes, and harbours that help to make the Mediterranean coast one of France's most beautiful.

CLIMATE AND VEGETATION

The location of France at the edge of the European continent makes it a crossroads subjected to three kinds of climatic influences: oceanic, continental, and Mediterranean. It is largely exposed to winds from the Atlantic, which in temperate latitudes blow from the west to the east. About three-quarters of France is, for most of the year, under the influence of the great cyclonic depressions that come from the Atlantic. Their exact path is determined by the variations in the relative location of the polar and tropical masses of air. In winter, moreover, areas of high pressure frequently move over the eastern part of France, notably in the Alsatian plains and the Saône region. This, added to the proximity of the Mediterranean in the south, gives France an extremely varied but generally temperate climate, as well as sufficient rainfall.

The oceanic region. The pure oceanic climate prevails in the northwest, especially in Bretagne. It is characterized by its regularity (the average yearly temperature is 52° F [11° C] at Brest); by its extreme humidity (35 inches [900 millimetres] of rain falling in 200 days of the year, as well as cloudiness, haze, and high humidity);

by the frequency and sometimes the violence of the west winds that blow nearly constantly; and by large variations in the weather which can change several times a day. This climate is very favourable to the natural plains where grass grows the year round and to hills of broom, heather, and gorse moorlands, while, on sheltered slopes, forests of oak are abundant. This oceanic climate is modified toward the north, where the winters are cooler, and toward the south, where in the Aquitaine Basin, the winters are colder and the summers warmer. There is also less rainfall, although at Toulouse great summer storms caused by continental climatic conditions are quite frequent.

The French climate is generally very favourable for natural vegetation and cultivation. Snow lies permanently only above 9,000 feet in the Alps and 9,500 feet in the Pyrenees; and only in the drier areas of France, irrigation is sometimes necessary, as in the plains of the Lower Rhône and Languedoc.

Special features of the Paris Basin

The climate of the Paris Basin is somewhere between the oceanic and the continental. The average yearly temperature is 53° F (12° C) in Paris. In addition, the relatively light annual rainfall (24 inches [619 millimetres]) follows a pattern of moderately heavy rain in spring and especially autumn, as in the oceanic countries, but the maximum amount of rain occurs in summer, with storms of the continental type. Such a climate is very favourable to the cultivation of grain crops and especially to the growth of the great forests, which once covered the centre of the Paris Basin and still exist over wide areas, even close to Paris. This same type of climate is found on the western slopes of mountains, including those of the Ardennes, Vosges, Massif Central, and western Pyrenees. In the mountains the contrast between summer and winter becomes more marked and frost and snow last for several weeks in winter; the level of rainfall usually increases and can exceed 40 or even 80 inches (1,000 or 2,000 millimetres) on the primary slopes of the western Pyrenees, one of the most humid regions in France.

The continental region. The sheltered plains of the east are particularly affected by a continental climate. The city of Strasbourg has the greatest temperature range in France, with 33° F (.6° C) in January and 66° F (19° C) in July. Winter is cold, with an average of 83 days of frost and with snow lying for several weeks, but the weather is often sunny. In the summer, storms cause maximum precipitation in June and July, although total rainfall is comparatively light. These regions are particularly suited for grain crops on the plains, vineyards on the favourably situated slopes, and beech forests on the highest slopes.

The Mediterranean region. In the southeast the Mediterranean climate extends over the plains to the coast and penetrates those of the Lower Rhône River as far as the Montélimar area. Its effects are felt in the southern Alps and in the Massif Central upon the southeast slopes of the Cévennes and the Montagne Noire and also on the eastern Pyrenees. The latitude and the proximity of the warm Mediterranean Sea means mild winters, with an average temperature of 47° F (8° C) in January at Nice and with only 3 days of frost. Precipitation is heavy (34 inches [862 millimetres] at Nice) and tends to fall in sudden downpours, especially in the autumn and spring, while summer is nearly completely dry for three to five months. The clear skies and the regularity of fine weather make it a unique area, where vegetation adapted to dryness abounds, including olive trees, box trees, thyme, rosemary, green-oak forests, cork trees, and thorny plants. In the mountainous zones there are two characteristic plant formations: the scrub formed of thorny plants and the moorland. These are found especially on the limestone soils. This region is the principal domain of the vineyard; but orange and lemon trees are also cultivated around Nice and Menton, and rice has been grown for 30 years in the Rhône Delta. Unfortunately, this area is also subject to the violent winds of the mistral, which blows from the north. The winds are caused by high-pressure areas from central France that move toward the low-pressure areas of the Gulf of Gen-

The distinctive ecology of the south

oa. Cypress hedges have been planted to protect cultivation from these winds in the Lower Rhône region. Other winds, such as the tramontana, which blows from the northeast from the Alps toward the coast, and the *marin*, which blows from the sea, also affect this area.

THE RIVER SYSTEMS

Flowing toward four seas, the English Channel, the Atlantic Ocean, the Mediterranean, and the North Sea, five great river systems drain the principle areas of France.

The Rhine system. In the east the Rhine, the second most important river in Europe after the Danube, barely touches French territory along the Alsace–Baden frontier for about 125 miles (200 kilometres). Its two great tributaries, however, the Moselle (German Mosel) and the Meuse, drain the eastern part of the Paris Basin, while the northern rivers, beyond the hills of Artois, flow into the North Sea through the Escaut (Flemish Schelde).

The Seine system. The Seine, the main river of the Paris Basin, is 485 miles (780 kilometres) long and has an outflow of 16,000 cubic feet (450 cubic metres) per second at its mouth. It flows slowly and regularly and is naturally navigable. It is the main axis of a river network that includes the Aube, the Marne, and the Oise, which flow from the eastern part of the basin, and also of short, left-bank tributaries, such as the Yonne, which has its source to the north of the Massif Central. The whole Seine network is very useful for navigation.

The Loire system. The Loire, the longest French river, flows for 634 miles (1,020 kilometres) and drains the widest area (44,400 square miles [115,000 square kilometres]). It is an extremely irregular river, with an outflow eight times greater in December and January than in August and September. Rising in the Massif Central on Mont Gerbier de Jonc, it flows for a long way over impervious terrain with steep slopes and has a system of irregular tributaries. Near its mouth it is joined by the calm waters of the Maine, a river formed by the confluence of the Mayenne, the Sarthe, and the Loir. Navigation is very limited, being confined to the Lower Loire and Maine.

The Garonne system. The Garonne, in the southwest, flows through the centre of the Aquitaine Basin. It is the shortest of the main French rivers (357 miles [575 kilometres] long), and it drains only 22,000 square miles (56,000 square kilometres). Its outflow is irregular, with high waters in winter (due to the oceanic rainfall) and in spring, when the snow melts, but with meagre flows in summer and autumn. Its source is in the centre of the Pyrenees in the valley of Aran ·(French Joyeuse), in Spain, and its main tributaries, the Tarn, the Lot, and the Dordogne, originate in the Massif Central. With the exception of the Gironde Estuary, which is formed by the confluence of the Garonne and the Dordogne and is fully penetrated by the sea, the whole network is useless for navigation and is filled with powerful, rapid, and dangerous currents.

The Rhône system. The Rhône, flowing from Lake Geneva to the Mediterranean, is the largest river in the southeast, but of its course of 500 miles (800 kilometres) only 324 are in France. It has the greatest flow and is the most industrially exploited river in France, discharging 777,000,000 cubic feet of water (22,000,000 cubic metres) per year into the delta. Its system is very different from that of the rivers of the west. It is fed by natural rainwater; by the Saône, which joins it at Lyon; and by the water from melted snow and glaciers, which is brought down from the mountains by the Isère, Drôme, and Durance rivers. The Rhône's flow, which is continuously ample, reaches a peak in spring and summer. It permits navigation, although it is often difficult travelling upstream, but large man-made projects have been completed to improve these conditions.

Coastal rivers, lakes, and lagoons. Besides these principal river systems, there are a certain number of coastal rivers, with sources near the sea, that flow directly into it. Among the most important are the calm oceanic rivers, such as the Somme, which crosses Picardie; the small

Glacial
lakes and
mountain
lakes

rivers of Normandie; the Charente; and the streams, such as the Adour, which descend from mountains.

The French hydrographical system also includes a certain number of natural lakes of different origin. There are the lakes in depressions carved out by glaciation at the periphery of mountains, such as the lakes of Annecy and Bourget. Others occur at the centre of ancient massifs and include the lakes of the Vosges. There are the circular lakes in the mountains, such as those of the Pyrenees, and the lakes caused by structural faults and lodged in narrow valleys, such as the Jura lakes. There are also a certain number of lakes of volcanic origin, such as those in the Massif Central (the crater lakes and the barrier lakes), and regions scattered with lagoons or ponds, either created by coastal phenomena, as on the Landes and Languedoc coasts, or caused by impervious terrain and poor local drainage.

THE HUMAN IMPRINT

The natural environment and man. Men have found the natural conditions of France, with its varied physical landscape, to be exceptionally favourable. From the dawn of prehistory, the vast expanse of plains, the temperate climate with sufficient rainfall everywhere, and the existence of surface soils generally favourable to agriculture have attracted and stimulated human settlement. Further, a large labour force has made possible widespread and very dense cultivation of the land. Indeed, all of the cultivable land in France has been exploited by man, even if there is now a decline in the population of the most rugged mountain regions.

The rural landscape. There are four major kinds of human activity in rural France. In the northwest is the *bocage* ("woodland") country, dominated by fields surrounded with hedges and divided by groves of trees and forests. People there are scattered on farms or in hamlets, and stock breeding is the most widely practiced occupation. In the old massifs, such as central Bretagne, or in the Massif Central, hedges have often been replaced by small stone walls. On the other hand, the plains and the plateaus of the centre and the east of the Paris Basin are characterized by open fields without boundaries between the fields that are cultivated. There are few trees, except along the rivers and the roads, and the houses in the villages are pressed tightly against one another. The greatest part of this land is under cultivation. Explanations of this famous fundamental division between "open" and "closed" patterns of settlement have been sought in the nature of the soils, in the different climates, in the ethnic diversity of the first occupants, and in the differences between the times and types of settlement.

In the Mediterranean areas there is a different kind of countryside. Small, square fields bordered by stone walls occupy the plains, while slopes are terraced, allowing for cultivation without a disastrous erosion of the soil. Traditional villages are built high up for both defensive and sanitary reasons, while the modern population has settled widely in the plains and in the valleys. Finally, in the high mountains and especially in the Alps, there is the contrast between the *adrets*, the sunny and cultivated valley slopes, and the *ubacs*, cold and humid slopes covered with forests. The variety of vegetation on the great slopes is remarkable. Cultivated fields and grasslands are found in the depths of the valleys, orchards on the first sunny embankments, then forests, Alpine vegetation, bare rocks, and finally permanent snow. The coastal plains, however, often present the classical polder landscape that is associated with reclaimed land, such as the coastal plain of Vendée. Coastal land is also used for specialized cultivations, such as the ricefields of Camargue.

The urban landscape. The urban areas obviously occupy much less space than the rural regions. The most densely populated area in France is metropolitan Paris, which covers only 0.3 percent of French territory. The other great urban agglomerations are concentrated around Lyon, Marseille, the Lower Seine Valley, northern France, and, in a more dispersed manner, Alsace, the Lower Loire, and Gironde. Altogether, only 70 percent

Over-
crowding
in the great
urban
agglomera-
tions

of the French population lives in towns, but this proportion has increased considerably and regularly in recent times. The outlying areas are generally not very developed, but cities are frequently—and unhappily—extremely crowded.

The major divisions of France. This brief review of the most characteristic elements of the French landscape has delineated its most perceptible differences, but there are divisions of a different kind.

The great natural regions of the French landscape coincide with the various regions of climate and vegetation: the Nord (North), the Paris Basin, the Nord-Ouest (Northwest), the Loire country, the Massif Central, the Aquitaine Basin, the Pyrenees, the eastern plains, the Jura, the Alps, and the Mediterranean areas. Within these natural regions, history imposed divisions that were generally founded upon the power of a local family: the duchy of Burgundy, the earldom of Picardy, the duchy of Brittany, the earldom of Toulouse, the earldom of Provence, and others. In the course of the centuries, these historical divisions were absorbed little by little by the central power of the monarchy, but the provinces have nevertheless survived and retained a certain distinctiveness, as with Normandie, Bretagne, Champagne, and Auvergne, for example. At the time of the French Revolution, a uniformity of administrative divisions was brought about by the formation of *départements*. These divisions, however, have often not succeeded in erasing the persistent influences of the ancient provincial boundaries. In the last half century it has become obvious that the *départements* were units poorly adapted to the modern economy, and, in 1955, economic regions were created as heterogeneous in size as in population, though with little effective actual powers.

In the early 1970s, France was preparing to implement a policy of "regionalization," which would give a certain degree of autonomy to different regions in France, agreed jointly with the central government. Without giving the regions powers that were strictly political, the projected reform provided for the setting up of regional councils composed of both elected members and representatives of local bodies, as well as for a consultative assembly bringing together the principal branches of activity. With its own financial resources and credits granted to it by the state, each region would find itself in a position to launch and finance a plan covering several years for industry and development. The details of the proposed plan, however, remained to be worked out.

The policy
of "region-
alization"

II. The people

THE DEVELOPMENT OF THE POPULATION

Racial origins. The French are, paradoxically, strongly conscious of belonging to a single race and a single nation, but they hardly constitute a unified racial group by any scientific gauge. Before the official discovery of the Americas at the end of the 15th century, France, located on the western extremity of the Old World, was regarded for centuries as the edge of the known world. Generations of different migrants travelling by way of the Mediterranean from the Middle East and Africa and through Europe from Central Asia and the Nordic lands settled permanently in France, forming a variegated grouping almost like a series of geological strata, since they were unable to migrate any farther. The oldest and most typical piece of evidence of these migrations is furnished by the Basque people, who inhabit the area to the west of the Pyrenees, both in Spain and France. Their language, which has been the subject of numerous studies, is also spoken by a group of people who are found in the Caucasus in the southern Soviet Union. In addition to these many migrations, France was, over the centuries, the field of numerous battles and of prolonged occupations before becoming, in the 19th and especially in the 20th century, the prime recipient of foreign immigration into Europe. This situation has given birth to a unique people who, lacking even the pretensions of being a unified racial group, are less racially prejudiced than most of their neighbours. There are, nevertheless, predominant racial types, such as the French of the north and east or those of Normandie, who are tall, blond, blue-eyed, and dolichocephalic (longheaded), bearing little resemblance to the inhabitants of Bretagne and of the Massif Central, who are mainly short, dark, dark-eyed, and brachycephalic (broad headed), or to the people of the Atlantic and Mediterranean areas, who are tall, dark, and dolichocephalic. But this is only a generalization, and a crowd of Frenchmen is as diverse in type as the French countryside is varied.

Language. French is the national language, spoken and taught everywhere. Brogues and dialects are widespread in rural areas, however, and many people tend to conserve their regional linguistic customs either through tradition or through a voluntary and deliberate return to a specific regional dialect, particularly among some young people. This tendency is strongest in the frontier areas of France. In the eastern and northern part of the country, Flemish and Alsatian are related to the Germanic languages; in the south, Provençal, Corse, and Catalan show the influence of Latin. But both Breton, a Celtic language similar to languages spoken in some western parts of the British Isles (notably Wales), and Basque are distinctly original languages. There have been increasing demands that these languages be studied in schools and universities and that they be given equal status with French, especially since some of them, such as Provençal and Breton, have to this day maintained a literary tradition.

Regional linguistic survivals

Religion. The majority of the French people belong to the Roman Catholic Church, and 90 percent have been baptized; but that is no indication of deep conviction or diligent practice. Only one adult in five regularly participates in religious worship. The northeast (Bretagne–Vendée), the east (Lorraine, Vosges, Alsace, Jura, Lyonnais, and the northern Alps), the north (Flandre), the Basque country, and the region south of the Massif Central have a higher percentage of practicing Catholics than the rest of the country. Practice is greatest among the middle classes. The areas northwest of the Massif Central and southeast of the Paris Basin, however, have become so reprobate that they have been characterized as "mission territory." Recruitment of priests is also becoming more and more difficult, even though the church is very progressive and ecumenical. Protestants, who number around 725,000, belong to several different sects. They are numerous in Alsace, in the northern Jura, in the southeastern Massif Central, and in the central Atlantic region. There are more than 500,000 adherents of Judaism, of which half are in the Parisian area, one-quarter in Marseille, and sizable numbers in Alsace and in the large eastern towns. The presence of numerous workers from North Africa is reflected by the large number of Muslims. Finally, there are several societies of freethinkers, of which the most famous is the French Masonry, with about 30,000 adherents. Large numbers, however, especially among the working classes and young people, are simply atheists and profess no religious belief.

Population growth. *Changes in total population.* The population of France was 28,000,000 in 1801, 41,194,000 in 1936, and 40,125,000 in 1946. The 1968 census showed a population of 50,000,000, which means that France ranked 13th among the countries of the world in that year and that it included slightly less than 1.5 percent of the world's population in an area that covers 0.4 percent of the Earth's surface. The population in 1972 was estimated to be over 51,000,000.

In 1801, France was the most populated state in Europe; it included one-sixth of the European population. By 1936 it had fallen to fifth, with 1/13th of the European population. Although the increase between these two dates had been 50 percent, the number of people in Italy and Germany had nearly trebled and, in the United Kingdom and The Netherlands, the number had nearly quadrupled.

The birth rate. These changes in the French population were due to an early lowering of the birth rate, linked to birth control, which began in France at the end of the 18th century—much earlier than in other countries of the world. The birth rate fell from around

Population by *département*. Numbers of *départements* are keyed to the Area and Population table.

30 per 1,000 at the beginning of the 19th century to about 15 per 1,000 in 1934–38.

Explanations for this phenomenon have been sought in the consequences of the great economic and social movements introduced by the French Revolution of 1789; the blow to the solidarity of the family by the emancipation of the individual and by the introduction of divorce; the modification of the laws of inheritance; the erosion of class barriers; the uncertain triumphs of the power of bourgeois society; and the diminution of religious sentiment. But probably more important were the effects of a series of cruel wars: the wars of the Revolution; the wars of the First Empire; the Franco-Prussian War (1870–71); and World War I (1914–18). The last alone cost France more than 1,500,000 deaths and a consequential lowering of the birth rate. Finally, the mortality rate in France has fallen less rapidly than in similarly developed neighbouring countries. It was still 15.3 per 1,000 on the eve of World War II, reflecting both the aging of the population and the effects of such social scourges as alcoholism, which produced a high mortality rate among male adults. The population of France thus increased by only 14,000,000 in 135 years, even taking into account the high immigration rate from other countries and the increase in the average life expectancy from 30 years at the beginning of the 19th century to more than 60 years at the eve of World War II. The situation in France in 1938 was dramatic, because there had been some 30,000 more deaths than births in preceding years. World War II (1939–45), following upon these conditions, could have dealt France a mortal blow. In fact, the population decreased by 1,400,000 during the war, with 700,000 dead and the exodus of some 700,000 foreigners who were forced to flee the country.

Causes of the falling birth rate

The legislative factor. New legislation was passed in 1938, however, aimed at helping the French family and thus promoting population growth, and this has been continually improved and developed since. These laws, the *politique de la famille*, have been firmly applied and reinforced, and the first positive effects began to show in 1943–44. As a result, between 1946 and 1968 France gained nearly 10,000,000 inhabitants in 22 years, a major change in birth patterns. This was due to three factors:

The politique de la famille and its effects

the return of more than 1,000,000 French who were forced to come back by the events in Morocco, Tunisia, Algeria, and Indochina; the resumption of foreign immigration; and, finally, the natural growth resulting from the excess of births over deaths.

The birth rate began to rise immediately after World War II, and it reached a maximum of 21.3 per 1,000 in 1947, owing to the increase of births in the postwar period. It then dropped slowly, however, staying at a little more than 18 per 1,000 until 1965. The rise was due to the social legislation, *la politique familiale*, which brought better health care, financial aid to families, and psychological persuasion to have more children. The assessment of the birth rate at that time showed that northern and eastern France had a birth rate five points higher than the southern and central regions of the country. With this had come the lowering, by two years, of the average age of marriage, an increase in the number of births in the early years of marriage, and a higher birth rate among middle and upper class urban dwellers. The introduction of oral contraceptives in France corresponds with a lowering of the birth rate, which became noticeable in the mid-1960s, and explains the levelling off from the high birth rate of the postwar years. In 1969 the birth rate was only 16.7 per 1,000, but it increased again slightly to around 17 per 1,000 in 1970 and 1971. Because of improved health conditions, notably through the widespread use of social security, the death rate is, nevertheless, significantly lower and did not reach more than 10.8 per 1,000 in 1971. The result is a natural increase that has maintained itself at a little more than an average of six births per 1,000 since the end of the war, although there was an excess of 358,000 births at the high point in 1948 and of 261,000 births at the low point in 1956. By 1971 the figure was nearly 330,000.

Altogether, the population of France rose by 7,100,000 between 1946 and 1968 solely by the excess of births over deaths. It was the regions of the north and of the northeast that had the most dynamic growth: the natural increase was more than 10 births per 1,000 a year in northern Lorraine and in the *département* of Doubs in 1962, compared with the national average of only 6.2 per 1,000. But there has been a negative rate of growth in the regions northwest of the Massif Central and a very low rate in the south of France, with the exception of the regions of Lyon and Grenoble.

CONTEMPORARY DEMOGRAPHY

Composition of the population. The consequences of this demographic evolution are reflected in the composition of the population. There are 1,047 women for every 1,000 men. This inequality in sexual distribution is due to two factors: the wars, which caused the death of a large number of men, and the natural inequality of life expectancy for men and women. A French woman at her birth has a life expectancy of 75.5 years, the fourth highest in the world, while a man can hope to live an average of only 68.0 years. The distribution of the population by age groups demonstrates most graphically the vicissitudes of this evolution. For each 1,000 inhabitants, France has 328 people below the age of 20, 503 aged from 20 to 60, and 170 over the age of 60. In other words, France, with The Netherlands, has the highest proportion of young people in Europe and is also among the four countries of the world having the greatest proportion of the aged. The proportion of the middle aged is abnormally low in comparison with other countries in Europe. Around 1851 only one person in ten was more than 60 years old, but by 1971 almost one person in six had passed that age. People under 40 years old, a category that comprised 50 percent of the French electorate in 1851, represented no more than 40 percent a century later, a fact that tended to favour political and social conservatism. This high proportion of the aged has created difficulties, and pension payments are a heavy burden on the national budget and on large organizations, such as the French railroads (SNCF), which listed 350,000 active employees and 410,000 retirees in 1962. There is one person over 60 years old for almost every three active men between 20 and 60, and the situa-

tion will become more acute in the future, especially if the age of retirement is lowered as demanded by the unions. Finally, there is the problem of housing and caring for the elderly, which is the responsibility of public authorities.

The paradox of contemporary France is that, while there are these problems arising from the large number of elderly, there are equal problems arising from the young. More than one in three of the French population are under 20 years old, reflecting the postwar resurgence of the birth rate. This has resulted in an emphasis on youth characterized by the growth of new commercial markets for future mothers and their children and the development of a typically Western "pop" culture, or (perhaps more accurately) counterculture, the music, fashions, and way of life aimed primarily at the teenager. Young people thus represent a distinctive group in society, rejecting in varying degrees the values of the older generation and asserting their desire to have responsibility and control over their own futures. They demand the right to vote at 18 and feel they are denied their rightful place in the nation. In addition, the problem of providing education has been an increasing one since 1950. It was necessary to hastily construct primary schools, then secondary schools, and finally universities for all of the young who were born after 1944 and who, because of a higher standard of living, pursue their studies for increasing periods of time. There are, at present, more than 10,000,000 French people of all ages in one kind of school or another (including part-time study). This figure represents about one-fifth of the population.

Immigration and emigration. *Outward movements.* Emigration has been of little significance. Through the centuries, small groups left to settle at first in North America, notably in eastern Canada (Quebec) and in Louisiana in the United States, in certain parts of Latin America that are to this day *départements* of France (Martinique, Guadeloupe, and French Guiana), and later in various countries of Africa and Asia that were part of France's colonial domain. Since decolonialization, whether forced or voluntary, many have returned to France, but others have remained overseas, either in business or in programs of technical and cultural cooperation in most of the former French territories and notably in the republics of black Africa. Currently, small numbers of French, especially from Bretagne and Normandie, make their way to Canada; a number of Basques go to Argentina, and several thousand others go to seek their fortunes in the United States or in new countries, such as Australia.

Traditional inward movements. On the other hand, France has traditionally had a very high level of immigration and an open-door policy toward immigrants. This was due to a combination of liberal tradition and economic need. Political refugees of all persuasions entered France, from the White Russians, who arrived after the 1917 Revolution in the Soviet Union, to the Spanish republicans at the end of the Spanish Civil War in 1938. Between 1850 and 1914 about 4,300,000 foreigners entered France, and between World Wars I and II nearly 3,000,000 immigrants, or 6 percent of the population, came into the country. Up to the end of World War I, immigration was free and spontaneous; most of the immigrants came from neighbouring countries, such as Italy, Spain, Belgium, and Switzerland, and they were quite quickly assimilated into the national population. The slaughter of young men and the devastations of World War I stimulated the government to draw widely from the reservoirs of foreign manpower. The Italians came in greatest numbers (35 percent), followed by the Poles (20 percent), the Spanish (15 percent), the Belgians (10 percent), and a smaller number of people from central or eastern European countries, such as the Soviet Union, Czechoslovakia, and Yugoslavia. Some of these people came in small groups and were assimilated, but, as the result of international agreements, the Poles and some of the Italians settled in well-organized communities, bringing their teachers and their priests with them, conserving their languages, and living in close-knit

The low proportion of the middle aged

Liberal traditions and economic need

groups. The Poles, for example, settled in the coal-bed regions to the north of Pas-de-Calais and the Italians in the villages of the valley of the Middle Garonne. Their provincialism created a certain number of difficulties, especially in the course of World War II when large numbers returned to their former homes or left to go elsewhere.

Recent inward movements. Soon after the war, France, disillusioned by its recent experience, reorganized its immigration policy completely, partly through the agency of a national bureau. But the bureau controlled barely one-third of those entering, because many came into the country secretly, making it very difficult to know their exact numbers. But, from an estimated 3,000,000, there were about 700,000 Italians, 600,000 Spaniards, 550,000 Portuguese, and some Belgians and Germans. In addition, a large number came from North Africa, notably Algeria (about 600,000), Morocco, and Tunisia. Black Africans are currently becoming increasingly numerous, and the French government has signed agreements with Turkey and Yugoslavia that involve their sending some of their nationals to work in France.

The working class immigrant

These working class foreigners generally come on temporary contracts, but a certain number become naturalized. Composed for the most part of adults, this population is primarily male; 38 percent work in construction and in public works, 2 percent in metallurgy, 15 percent in mechanical and electrical industry, 8 percent in agriculture, less than 1 percent in mining, and another 36 percent in domestic and other occupations. The region surrounding Paris is the greatest employer of foreign manpower, followed by the large mining and industrial regions in the north and in Lorraine, and then by the large conurbations of Marseille and Lyon. This labour force has its advantages in its mobility and its youth, but it also has its drawbacks. The larger part of the workers are unskilled and without professional qualifications. They live in France on a very small part of what they earn and send the rest to the country of their origin. In addition, they tend to live in poor and unsanitary housing, and their morale is often low. Their coming is, however, very important for the development of the French economy, and they do not compete with the local labour force since they are generally employed in the trades that young Frenchmen do not wish to follow.

Internal movements and urbanization. France is also subject to large internal migrations. There is a continual drift away from the mountains to the plains, from the countryside to the small towns, and from the small towns to the cities. Hence, the urban population has increased both relatively and absolutely. In 1861, 29 percent, or 10,790,000, of the total population were urban dwellers. By 1971 this proportion exceeded two-thirds, or 35,000,000 people, and it is estimated that it will reach three-quarters of the population by the end of the century. There were 44 cities with more than 100,000 inhabitants in 1962 and 49 in 1968. This vast movement toward the cities has not been regular but it went through two periods of acceleration. The first was immediately following World War I; the second is still going on. Since 1938 the two cities that have led the country in population growth are Toulouse, with a population in 1968 of 440,000, a gain of 20 percent between 1962 and 1968, and Grenoble, with a population in 1968 of 332,500, which represents a gain of 27 percent over 1962. Montpellier experienced significant increase with the return of refugees from Algeria (37.7 percent between 1962 and 1968).

The growth of Paris

But it is Paris and its metropolitan area that has had the greatest power of attraction for immigrants for the last 150 years. It contained less than 500,000 inhabitants in 1801 and only 4.5 percent of the national population in 1848; but by 1968 this figure had reached 18.6 percent. Of the population of Paris and its surrounding area, 44 percent were born outside its boundaries, and 10 percent of these were foreigners. The largest numbers come from Bretagne, the Massif Central, and the region of the Nord. Among the cities with populations of over 100,000, some, such as Nice and Grenoble, attract an equally diverse population because of their exceptional climate and economic conditions. On the other hand, towns such as Le Mans and the Lille–Roubaix–Tourcoing complex recruit their workers entirely from a radius of about 30 miles (50 kilometres). These migrations toward the large cities have had and will continue to have an effect on the distribution of the population as well as upon housing (thousands of abandoned homes fall to ruin in the countryside, while a grave housing shortage exists in the cities), equipment, and employment.

Most of the larger French towns have workers who commute daily from the immediate surrounding area. Once again, metropolitan Paris is the foremost example. The number of people from the Paris region who commute exceeded 100,000 at the beginning of the century and is now nearly 1,300,000. This places a heavy burden on public transport, which carries half the commuters, and it also places a burden on the roads. The Nord also has a complex pattern of daily travel around Lille (involving 37.3 percent of the active working force of the area) and in the coal-mining region; one-third of the towns in the Nord are affected by this sort of displacement.

The reasons for commuting differ greatly according to the town involved: the daily commuters number only 3 percent of the workers of Reims, 12 percent for Besançon, 18 percent for Rouen, 41 percent for Saint-Nazaire, 66 percent for Dunkerque, and 78 percent for the large Peugeot factories at Sochaux. The distances travelled also vary considerably: in the region surrounding Paris, the average commuting time is 1.5 hours per person per day. The Peugeot factories seek their manpower from as far away as 40 miles (65 kilometres). Berliet, at Lyon, transports its workers up to 50 miles (80 kilometres) by bus. Men commute more than women, and blue-collar workers more than white collar. Nevertheless, most employers favour bringing lodgings and the place of work closer together in order to cut down on the fatigue, expense, and discontent caused by such lengthy daily travel.

Commuters and *frontaliers*

In certain cases, the commuting area crosses the French border, the commuters from neighbouring countries being called *frontaliers*. This situation exists especially along the northern frontier of France, where the textile factories of Roubaix and Tourcoing and the metallurgical factories of the Sambre Valley attract Belgian workers. In addition, there are a small number of *frontaliers* in industrial northern Lorraine, which attracts a few German labourers. But the reverse situation also exists, and a number of Frenchmen, mainly from Lorraine and Alsace, commute to Germany. Certain jobs, especially in agriculture, do not require a permanent working force and thus appeal to seasonal workers. This is the case in the Mediterranean wine-growing districts, where Spaniards come to pick the grapes in autumn as they have done for years. The recent introduction of grape-picking machinery, however, is probably going to diminish this seasonal migration, which, in the early 1970s, still involved more than 100,000 people (one-half Spaniards, one-third Italians, and some Belgians and Algerians).

More than 21,000,000 people take annual vacations, and the number of people travelling during their holidays is much higher in the larger cities: 58 percent of the population vacate towns of 20 to 100,000 people; 64.3 percent leave towns of over 200,000, and 85.7 percent of Parisians leave Paris for their annual holiday. This involves the movement of considerable crowds of people during the peak seasons, such as school vacations and the large number of paid holidays that fall in August, and saturates transport facilities and popular vacation spots, especially the coastal areas and mountains. More than 15 percent of the holiday takers go abroad, 44 percent to the Iberian Peninsula, and 15 percent to Italy. Conversely, a large number of foreigners visit France; but, in the early 1970s, the economic assets of tourism were almost cancelled out by the expenditure of the French abroad. In order to cater for the needs of the tourist industry, a temporary labour force is necessary, particularly for the hotels, restaurants, and specialized

Tourism

businesses. The more affluent are not, moreover, content with one or two holidays a year, many of them having second residences where they spend their weekends. A survey in 1967 showed that one French household in five possessed a second home of this type.

Distribution of the population. The average population density in France is 245 per square mile (95 per square kilometre). This is high compared to the average density in the world (70 per square mile, [27 per square kilometre]) but relatively low compared to France's neighbouring countries (Germany 620 [240], Belgium 823 [318], The Netherlands 826 [319], Italy 470 [182]).

This average density is, however, very unequally distributed. One sparsely populated zone runs south from the outskirts of the Paris Basin to the Massif Central, and there are three regions of very low population: the French–Italian border in the southeast, the French–Spanish frontier in the southwest, and the area skirting

France, Area and Population

	key no.*	area†		population‡			key no.*	area†		population‡	
		sq mi	sq km	1968 census	1972 estimate			sq mi	sq km	1968 census	1972 estimate
Circonscriptions d'action régionale						Limousin					
Alsace						*Départements*					
Départements						Corrèze	45	2,263	5,860	238,000	238,000
Bas-Rhin	1	1,848	4,787	827,000	862,000	Creuse	46	2,146	5,559	157,000	153,000
Haut-Rhin	2	1,360	3,523	585,000	607,000	Haute-Vienne	47	2,128	5,512	342,000	349,000
Aquitaine						Lorraine					
Départements						*Départements*					
Pyrénées-Atlantiques	3	2,946	7,629	509,000	524,000	Meurthe-et-Moselle	48	2,021	5,235	705,000	729,000
Dordogne	4	3,546	9,184	374,000	368,000	Meuse	49	2,402	6,220	210,000	205,000
Gironde	5	3,861	10,000	1,009,000	1,037,000	Moselle	50	2,399	6,214	971,000	1,009,000
Landes	6	3,566	9,237	277,000	282,000	Vosges	51	2,267	5,871	388,000	397,000
Lot-et-Garonne	7	2,069	5,358	291,000	292,000	Midi-Pyrénées					
Auvergne						*Départements*					
Départements						Ariège	52	1,888	4,890	138,000	136,000
Allier	8	2,829	7,327	387,000	387,000	Aveyron	53	3,371	8,735	282,000	272,000
Cantal	9	2,217	5,741	169,000	167,000	Gers	54	2,415	6,254	182,000	178,000
Haute-Loire	10	1,917	4,965	208,000	207,000	Haute-Garonne	55	2,433	6,301	691,000	730,000
Puy-de-Dôme	11	3,071	7,955	548,000	573,000	Hautes-Pyrénées	56	1,740	4,507	226,000	230,000
Basse-Normandie (Lower-Normandy)						Lot	57	2,019	5,228	152,000	150,000
Départements						Tarn	58	2,220	5,751	332,000	334,000
Calvados	12	2,137	5,536	520,000	545,000	Tarn-et-Garonne	59	1,435	3,716	184,000	183,000
Manche	13	2,296	5,947	452,000	455,000	Nord					
Orne	14	2,355	6,100	289,000	294,000	*Départements*					
Bretagne (Britanny)						Nord	60	2,215	5,738	2,418,000	2,484,000
Départements						Pas-de-Calais	61	2,563	6,639	1,397,000	1,401,000
Côtes-du-Nord	15	2,655	6,878	506,000	509,000	Pays de la Loire					
Finistère	16	2,620	6,785	769,000	782,000	*Départements*					
Ille-et-Vilaine	17	2,609	6,758	653,000	679,000	Loire-Atlantique	62	2,661	6,893	861,000	897,000
Morbihan	18	2,611	6,763	540,000	547,000	Maine-et-Loire	63	2,753	7,131	585,000	604,000
Bourgogne, (Burgundy)						Mayenne	64	1,997	5,171	253,000	256,000
Départements						Sarthe	65	2,398	6,210	462,000	474,000
Côte-d' Or	19	3,384	8,765	421,000	444,000	Vendée	66	2,595	6,721	421,000	428,000
Nièvre	20	2,640	6,837	248,000	248,000	Picardie (Picardy)					
Saône-et-Loire	21	3,307	8,565	550,000	560,000	*Départements*					
Yonne	22	2,867	7,425	283,000	292,000	Aisne	67	2,849	7,378	526,000	532,000
Centre						Oise	68	2,261	5,857	541,000	579,000
Départements						Somme	69	2,384	6,175	512,000	526,000
Cher	23	2,791	7,228	305,000	310,000	Poitou-Charentes					
Eure-et-Loir	24	2,269	5,876	302,000	320,000	*Départements*					
Indre	25	2,617	6,778	247,000	243,000	Charente	70	2,298	5,953	331,000	332,000
Indre-et-Loire	26	2,364	6,124	438,000	466,000	Charente-Maritime	71	2,644	6,848	484,000	492,000
Loiret	27	2,603	6,742	431,000	459,000	Deux-Sèvres	72	2,318	6,004	326,000	330,000
Loir-et-Cher	28	2,438	6,314	268,000	279,000	Vienne	73	2,697	6,985	340,000	346,000
Champagne						Provence-Côte d'Azur					
Départements						*Départements*					
Ardennes	29	2,015	5,219	309,000	314,000	Alpes-Maritimes	74	1,658	4,294	722,000	756,000
Aube	30	2,317	6,002	270,000	281,000	Alpes-de-Haute Provence	75	2,681	6,944	105,000	107,000
Haute-Marne	31	2,400	6,216	214,000	217,000	Bouches-du-Rhône	76	1,974	5,112	1,470,000	1,539,000
Marne	32	3,152	8,163	485,000	519,000	Hautes-Alpes	77	2,131	5,520	92,000	91,000
Corse (Corsica)						Var	78	2,316	5,999	556,000	588,000
Département						Vaucluse	79	1,377	3,566	354,000	371,000
Corsica	33	3,352	8,681	270,000	219,000	Région Parisienne					
Franche-Comté						*Départements*					
Départements						Essonne	80	699	1,811	674,000	817,000
Doubs	34	2,019	5,228	426,000	457,000	Hauts-de-Seine	81	68	175	1,462,000	1,510,000
Haute-Saône	35	2,063	5,343	214,000	217,000	Paris	82	41	105	2,591,000	2,461,000
Jura	36	1,934	5,008	234,000	238,000	Seine-et-Marne	83	2,285	5,917	604,000	660,000
Territoire						Seine-Saint-Denis	84	91	236	1,252,000	1,350,000
Belfort	37	236	610	118,000	124,000	Val-de-Marne	85	94	244	1,121,000	1,224,000
Haute-Normandie (Upper-Normandy)						Val-d'Oise	86	482	1,249	693,000	788,000
Départements						Yvelines	87	877	2,271	853,000	965,000
Eure	38	2,318	6,004	383,000	397,000	Rhône-Alpes					
Seine-Maritime	39	2,415	6,254	1,114,000	1,167,000	*Départements*					
Languedoc						Ain	88	2,222	5,756	339,000	354,000
Départements						Ardèche	89	2,132	5,523	257,000	261,000
Aude	40	2,406	6,232	278,000	275,000	Drôme	90	2,519	6,525	343,000	366,000
Gard	41	2,258	5,848	479,000	493,000	Haute-Savoie	91	1,696	4,391	379,000	411,000
Hérault	42	2,360	6,113	591,000	620,000	Isère	92	2,886	7,474	768,000	812,000
Lozére	43	1,995	5,168	77,000	71,000	Loire	93	1,843	4,774	722,000	733,000
Pyrénées-Orientales	44	1,578	4,086	282,000	287,000	Rhône	94	1,241	3,215	1,326,000	1,421,000
						Savoie	95	2,331	6,036	289,000	302,000
						Total France		210,039§	543,998§	49,779,000§	51,487,000§

*For location of *départements* see population map.   †Land area excludes 2,703 sq mi (7,002 sq km) comprising surface areas of lakes, glaciers, and river estuaries. Total area equals 212,742 sq mi (551,000 sq km).   ‡De jure.   §Figures do not add to total given because of rounding.

the Atlantic Ocean between Gironde and Adour. In these zones, there is a density of less than 26 per square mile (10 per square kilometre), with a few exceptions. In general, eastern France, with 44 percent of the total area and 63 percent of the population, is more highly populated than western France; it contains 10 of the 12 largest French cities, with 14,300,000 inhabitants within only 2.6 percent of the total area of France. The more lightly populated regions coincide with mountainous areas; regions with poor soil such as Landes and Sologne; isolated rural regions, such as the countryside at the centre of the Aquitaine Basin and east and southeast of the Paris Basin; and, paradoxically, certain very fertile regions, such as Beauce, southwest of Paris, with its vast estates and mechanized farming, yet with a population density of less than 65 per square mile (25 per square kilometre).

Location of highly populated regions

On the other hand, the most highly populated zones correspond closely to the large urban centres. Paris has the highest population, with 8,500,000 inhabitants, followed by Lyon (1,083,000), Marseille (965,000), the Lille–Roubaix–Tourcoing conurbation (990,000), Bordeaux (550,000), Toulouse (440,000), Nantes and Saint-Nazaire (394,000), Nice (393,000), Rouen (370,000), and Toulon (340,000). The coastal areas and valleys are also areas of heavy population, as are the fertile regions, such as Alsace or Limagne, with their small or medium-size estates, or even the verdant cultivated marshes on the northern coast of Bretagne. But the present situation is only one of transition. Since the beginning of the 20th century, the mountainous regions of France have lost about one-half of their population, and, although certain regions, such as the Alps in the north, are being repopulated because of industrialization in the valleys and the construction of winter-sports resorts on the mountainsides, the southern Alps, the Massif Central, and the Pyrenees are becoming more and more depopulated. The countryside has also become subject to some depopulation, but this trend is less obvious since many non-agricultural residents live there, constituting about half of its current population of 16,000,000. In fact, about 100,000 young people leave agriculture annually, and agricultural activity now employs 16 percent of the masculine working population, compared to 35 percent before World War II.

But this movement has been very uneven. For example, less than 10 percent of the rural population remains in Bouches-du-Rhône or in Seine-Saint-Denis, but more than 75 percent still resides on the Côtes-du-Nord, in Cantal, or in Creuse. Thus, there seems to be a regrouping of the rural population: the smaller the township, the more depopulated it has become, villages of less than 100 inhabitants losing 13.4 percent of their population between 1954 and 1962. Townships with more than 1,500 inhabitants, however, have been developing rapidly and the ministry of agriculture foresees the possibility of a regrouping of rural centres with about 5,000 inhabitants, thus preventing a complete desertion of certain regions. Because of the trend toward urbanization, the smaller towns have profited from the abandonment of the mountains and the countryside; and their population, in turn, have overflowed into the spreading suburbs of the large cities.

Demographic trends and future prospects. The French population contains, at present, a large number of young people, and, despite the recent perceptible diminution of the birth rate since 1965, it is likely that there will be an increase in the number of births in years to come. In 1970, 848,000 births were registered, but the number exceeded 875,000 in 1971 and was expected to pass 1,000,000 by 1977. In 1970 the number of marriages passed 400,000 for the first time, an increase of 50,000 over preceding years. Since the mortality rate remains at present around 550,000 per year and is likely to remain relatively stable, given present medical and social conditions, there is only a small possibility of a natural growth in the population.

It is hoped that there will be a reduction in the infant mortality rate, even though it is already at 15.1 per

1,000, one of the lowest in the world. The social legislation adopted in 1969 tended to favour a family of four children, which indicated the desire on the part of the political leaders at that time to make every effort to maintain a positive rate of population growth.

Besides its growth, it is likely that the French population will undergo two major changes in the years to come. First, the movement away from the country toward the city and, second, the extension of the suburbs will continue. It is estimated that by the end of the century—of a population of around 75,000,000—60,000,000 people will be urban dwellers. On the other hand, the surplus of young people joining the job market now, in comparison with the number who joined it in the 1950s, is forcing the French economy to undergo transformation and rapid growth. The necessity to create an average of 200,000–250,000 new jobs each year will provide a definite stimulus. The size of the labour force, which was 19,500,000 at the beginning of the century but only 19,000,000 in 1950, grew by only 100,000 between 1954 and 1962, but it increased by 1,400,000 between 1962 and 1970. This growth of the labour force is expected to continue in the years to come, bringing with it grave economic and social difficulties. Since agriculture is rapidly diminishing as a large employer, it will be up to industry and especially to the service sector of the economy to provide the majority of the needed additional jobs.

Although many aspects of French demography are shared by other European countries, such as the low birth rate, the large proportion of the elderly, the relatively high population density, and the importance of the industrial and service sectors among the labour force, other aspects are especially relevant to France. This is particularly true of the high growth in the birth rate at the end of World War II, the high proportion of young people, the depopulation of whole areas of the countryside, and the necessity to create jobs rapidly for the growing labour force. (J.B.-G.)

III. The national economy
FRANCE IN THE WORLD CONTEXT

France's chief claim to fame in the economic field in recent years is the high rate of growth achieved in the 1960s despite various structural and political difficulties. In the 1950s the French economy was one of the most cushioned in Europe; it was protected from outside competition by high tariffs and bolstered internally by heavy government subsidies. In the meantime, French industry has been widely modernized and restructured so that it can now compete on a world basis with other leading industrial nations. Between 1961 and 1971 the gross national product (GNP) grew at an annual average rate of 5.8 percent, a rate of increase bettered only by Japan and equalled only by Italy, among developed non-Communist nations. In the same period West Germany and the United Kingdom grew at the average annual rate of only 4.8 percent and 2.7 percent, respectively. Between 1970 and 1980, France is expected to maintain its position as the fastest growing industrial country in the non-Communist world after Japan. In the same group of countries, France ranks third as a producer of primary aluminum, second as a producer of pig iron, and third as a producer of crude steel. France's industrial base is still narrow, however, compared with those of West Germany and the United Kingdom, and it has fewer really big companies. Agriculture, despite a movement from the land, still plays a disproportionately important role in French economy. After the Soviet Union, France is the largest agricultural nation in Europe and one of the world's leading producers of dairy produce and wheat. With Italy, France is the world's largest wine producer. Since the European Economic Community (EEC), or Common Market, came into existence, in January 1958, France has increased its trade within it more than any other member country. It is the EEC's leading agricultural producer but second to West Germany in terms of industry. France is much less dependent on external trade, however, than the other member countries; its exports

The disproportionate role of agriculture

accounted for only 13 percent of its GNP in 1971, compared with a figure of over 30 percent for the EEC as a whole and 23 percent for the United Kingdom, which in 1973 became a member of EEC. The Common Market countries' share of French trade has grown from some 22 percent of all imports and exports to almost 48 percent in 1970, and this is a trend that shows every sign of continuing throughout the 1970s.

NATURAL RESOURCES

Biological resources. France is the largest country in Europe after the Soviet Union, with a total surface area of 136,000,000 acres (55,000,000 hectares). It contains extensive tracts of fertile soil and is characterized by a temperate maritime climate. Conditions, however, vary widely within the territory, and a wide range of climatic conditions are to be found there. The total agricultural surface area takes up 90 percent of the whole. Arable land and land under permanent crops (47,700,000 acres [19,300,000 hectares]), together with permanent meadows and pasture (34,600,000 acres), account for over 60 percent of this. Forests (34,600,000 acres) take up a further 25 percent. The amount of unused but potentially productive land is estimated at 7,400,000 acres, the highest figure in Europe. Conurbations and towns, which are widely scattered, cover a relatively small proportion of the country. Although in 1971 about 40 percent of France was still under the plow, the area under direct cultivation was dropping steadily. Livestock, notably beef and milk cattle, account for 56 percent of agricultural receipts and products of a vegetable origin for only 44 percent, almost an exact reversal of the situation before World War II.

Agricultural produce. France is the largest agricultural producer in Europe, a net exporter of agricultural products, and, apart from a deficiency in tropical produce, such as coffee and certain fruits, it is basically self-sufficient. Wheat, which is grown widely, is the main cereal crop, followed by barley and oats. Rice is grown in the easily irrigated alluvial plains of the Rhône Delta, and its cultivation has spread to neighbouring *départements*. Corn (maize), formerly confined to the southwest, is now grown all over France right up to the northern regions.

Wine production

Annual French wine production varies between 1,600,000 and 1,700,000 gallons (60,000,000 and 65,000,000 hectolitres). The vine is grown south of a line from Nantes, in the northwest, to Reims, in the northeast, but the major producing regions are in the Mediterranean south. Half the total production, which is mainly for everyday consumption, comes from six *départements* in the south and southeast; Aude, Bouches-du-Rhône, Gard, Hérault, Pyrénées Orientales, and Var. The Bordeaux region produces the greatest amount of quality (*appelation controlée*) wine, followed by the southeast and the Bourgogne (Burgundy) area. Other important producing areas include Champagne, the Loire Valley, Alsace, and Charente. Fruits and vegetables are increasingly important crops, which, although widely dispersed, have been grown mainly in Comtat Venaissin (Vaucluse and Bouches-du-Rhône), Roussillon, the Saint-Pol-de-Léon region in Bretagne, Nantes, and the Paris region. These five areas account for one-half the total fruit and vegetable production, which includes a wide variety of produce, the most important being tomatoes, onions, carrots, cabbage, cauliflower, peas, French beans, artichokes, melons, apples and pears, desert grapes, cherries, apricots, peaches, and plums. Root crops, notably sugar beets, potatoes, fodder beets, and fodder turnips, are also grown. About 50,000 metric tons of tobacco are produced in the southwest and in Alsace and meet 70 percent of the country's requirements. France is a leading producer of perfume; special plants are grown for this purpose, notably in the Grasse region, near the Mediterranean, and in the Alpes-Maritimes, which produces essences from bitter-orange trees, roses, jasmine, and violets. Spike and lavender are grown in the Haute-Provence, Drôme, and Lot regions. Medicinal plants are also grown.

Livestock. In most areas of France stock breeding takes precedence over crop production. Cattle (about 22,000,000 head) account for over half of all livestock, followed by sheep and pigs, both of which represent around one-fifth of the total. Apart from the Mediterranean area, where their population is scant, cattle are distributed all over the country. Dairy breeds are raised principally in the north and west and, to a lesser extent, the major fattening breeds (beef cattle) in the Massif Central. The Normandy is the most important breed in France (4,500,000 head) and supplies both fatty and high-quality meat. Other notable breeds include the French Friesian (dairy produce), the Charollais, the Limousin, and the sandy Aquitaine (all meat producing). In 1971, 1,600,000 metric tons of cattle and calf meat were produced, while dairy herds yielded 33,000,000 metric tons of milk. Butter production is in surplus, and France is the second world producer of cheese. Sheep (over 10,000,000 head) are mainly concentrated in the mountainous regions of central and southern France (Causses, the southern Alps, and Corsica). They are bred primarily for meat, producing about 120,000 metric tons annually, and they also supply some 10 percent of the French woollen industry's needs. About 13,000,000 gallons (48,000,000 litres) of ewe's milk are produced annually in the Roquefort area, Provence, and in Corsica for the manufacture of cheese. Goats (about 924,000 head) are reared chiefly in western central and southeast France, where their milk is used exclusively to manufacture cheese.

The major cattle breeds

Forestry. About one-quarter of France is covered with forests, the principal forests being the Ardennes, Compiègne, Fontainebleau, and Orléans. Where the Atlantic (maritime) climate prevails, oaks predominate, along with beeches and poplars. Much of this area, however, has been reforested with pines and other softwoods that are more suitable for commercial and industrial use. There are valuable coniferous forests, in the mountains of the Alps, Jura, Vosges, and Pyrenees. The Landes region, with its maritime pine, is particularly important for resin and timber for the pit props used to support the roofs of underground passages in coal mines, railway ties, and telegraph poles. Deciduous trees (half of them oak) account for 66 percent of the total and conifers 34 percent (about two-thirds pine). The productive capacity of the French forests in timber and industrial wood is around 1,000,000,000 cubic feet (30,000,000 cubic metres) annually. This figure is currently being raised by continued reafforestation under the guidance of the Fonds National Forestier (National Forest Fund).

Mineral resources. With the exception of extensive deposits of coal, iron ore, and bauxite, France is not particularly rich in mineral resources. Scattered deposits of zinc, lead, copper, tin, and gold do occur in the crystalline rocks of the highlands and mountains, but they are generally small and hence supply an insignificant proportion of the country's needs. Coal is mined principally in the north alongside the Belgian frontier in the Pas-de-Calais and Nord regions (42 percent of total production) and in Lorraine to the east, in the Moselle region (32 percent of total production). Much of this coal is deeply buried, and mining tends to be both difficult and costly. Pits in Lorraine, however, have achieved the highest level of output per man in Europe. French coal reserves are estimated to be 10,000,000,000 metric tons and home production satisfies approximately 70 percent of the country's needs. In 1971 monthly average production was at the rate of 2,980,000 metric tons. France is seriously short of the coking coal necessary for smelting in the iron-and-steel industry, and, in the main, this category has to be imported. The minor coal-producing areas are in the Loire, Cévennes, Blanzy, Aquitaine, Provence, Auvergne, and Dauphiné regions. As elsewhere in Europe, coal output in France is being cut back in line with the rapid development of alternative sources of power.

Coal reserves

France ranks third in the world as a producer of iron ore after the Soviet Union and the United States. Lorraine is the main producing area, followed by Normandie, the Anjou Basin, and the Pyrenees. Reserves are estimated at 8,017,000,000 metric tons, of which Lorraine has 6,000,000,000 metric tons, Normandie 500,000,000 metric tons, and deposits in the centre and

Iron production

Pyrenees 17,000,000 metric tons. French iron ore is low grade—only 30 to 35 percent iron compared with ore of 50 to 70 percent iron content mined in other leading producer countries. It is generally easy to extract, partly because the beds are not generally disturbed by faults; hence, large-scale techniques for mechanical extraction are employed. Iron-ore production reached a peak of 66,600,000 tons in 1961 but has dropped steadily since. In 1971 total production of iron ore was 55,882,000 metric tons, sufficient to supply 90 percent of the French iron-and-steel industry's needs and to allow for sizable exports to West Germany, Belgium, and Luxembourg. As more steelworks are established on the coast, such as the plant at Dunkerque, and are thus readily accessible to high-grade imported ores, home-produced ore is bound to decrease in importance. France is one of the leading producers of bauxite, which takes its name from the small village of Les Baux, near Arles, where it was first mined in 1882. The chief workings in the early 1970s were east of there in Var, especially around Vignoles, and also in Languedoc. Total French production of bauxite was 2,997,000 metric tons in 1971, which accounted for most of the country's needs. Production of other nonferrous metals, such as zinc, lead, tin, antimony, tungsten, and vanadium, accounts for only a small proportion of the country's needs. As a gold producer, France ranks about third in Europe (48,000 troy ounces in 1969) after the Soviet Union and Yugoslavia.

Bauxite and other nonferrous reserves

A certain amount of uranium ore is mined in the Massif Central and the Vendée; a total of 800,000 metric tons was mined in 1970. Large deposits of salt are found in the Triassic rocks (about 190,000,000 years old) of Lorraine and also along the edge of the Jura Mountains, in Franche-Comté. Sea salt is also produced along the Mediterranean coast by the traditional solar-evaporation method, and there are important deposits of potash in the plain of Alsace north of Mulhouse. Total French potash production in 1971 was 13,922,000 metric tons. Potassium production in the early 1970s stood at around 1,800,000 metric tons annually, about 20 percent of total world production. France produces more than 1,800,000 metric tons of sulfur annually, mostly from natural gas.

Almost all French petroleum has to be imported, although the Parentis wells in the Landes area, on the Atlantic coast, produce a maximum of 3,000,000 metric tons of oil annually, and efforts are being made to increase home production of petroleum with prospecting in the southwest, both on land and offshore and in the North Sea area. Despite France's lack of currently producing wells, the country has an important oil-refining industry that utilizes imported crude oil. Its total annual capacity in 1971 was 116,000,000 metric tons. The principal plants are in the Nord, Basse, Seine, Atlantic, Mediterranean, and Alsace areas. And, as a result of an oil strike at Lacq at the foot of the Pyrenees in southeastern France, an extremely large field of natural gas was discovered. Worked since 1957, it supplies 180,600,000,000 cubic feet (5,000,000,000 cubic metres) annually to the grid that runs from Lacq to Paris. Gas supplies at Lacq are sufficient to last until 1980. Another field discovered more recently at Meillon is thought to be half the size of Lacq but will add considerably to the country's natural-gas production, which is rapidly replacing manufactured gas. In the north and northeast, where gas requirements are currently met by gas fed into the grid by Lorraine steelmakers as a byproduct of their coking process, natural gas from the Netherlands Groningen field was expected to replace manufactured gas by 1975. Natural gas is also imported from Algeria in liquefied form and is used in the Paris area.

Natural gas and petroleum

Hydroelectric resources. Because of its climate and geography, France enjoys considerable water resources, and, since World War II, there has been a rapid development of hydroelectric power. Major rivers include the Seine, Rhône, Saône, Garonne, and Loire, and there are 6,200 miles (10,000 kilometres) of navigable rivers, with an additional 3,300 miles (5,300 kilometres) of canals. Further, mountainous terrain in the Massif Central, in south and south central France, in the Pyrenees to the southwest, and in the Alps to the east and southeast provides ample hydroelectric potential. In 1969 there were 1,640 hydroelectric stations, including the Rance tidal power station in Bretagne, which has a total rated power of 13,000,000 kilowatts.

Hydroelectric-power production is linked to climatic conditions and thus fluctuates annually, but, at the beginning of the 1970s, it stood at 57,000,000,000 kilowatt-hours, and currently it accounts for a little over 40 percent of total electricity production.

SOURCES OF NATIONAL INCOME

Agriculture, forestry, and fishing. Agriculture and forestry accounted for 6.6 percent of the gross national product (GNP) in 1970. Although agriculture's share of total production showed a steady drop during the 1960s, it was still higher than in many other industrial nations. As the leading agricultural nation in Europe, France is virtually self-sufficient as a producer, and it exports a considerable amount of produce, especially to other Common Market countries. Yet, French agriculture is the weakest sector of the economy. In general, French farms are too small; the farmers are too numerous; and the introduction of modern methods of cultivation and husbandry has been slow.

Farming. About half the farms are less than 30 acres (12 hectares), and, although the total number of farms is diminishing by about 2 percent annually, there are still almost 1,600,000 individual holdings. In 1968 the total agricultural population, including dependents, was over 6,000,000, including over 3,000,000 who actually worked on the land, or 15 percent of the country's total working population. This proportion again has been falling steadily, for more than 150,000 farmers have been leaving the land annually in recent years. Output per worker is still much lower than in other branches of the economy, and agricultural wages are about 30 percent below those of industrial workers.

Government policy in the early 1970s was geared to restructuring the farming industry into larger units, and, through various retraining schemes, it was encouraging subsistence farmers to leave the land. Elderly farmers who left were given a small pension. As a result of these and other factors, individual farms are gradually getting larger and more efficient, particularly in the northern half of the country, and there has been a marked growth in farming cooperatives, in which equipment is pooled or farms have been actually merged together. There were 1,448 cooperatives in 1969, compared to 363 in 1967.

While productivity per acre has doubled in France since 1949, this improved performance has been marred by overproduction in some sectors, notably of fruit, dairy products, and cheap wines. To counteract this, the government is encouraging farmers to switch to meat production and to develop the canning industry to absorb seasonal fruit surpluses. Much progress has been made to raise the overall quality of wine production (high-quality wine accounts for only 14 percent of the total), and the poorest wines are now banned from the market altogether, which has somewhat mitigated the problem of overproduction. Agricultural marketing facilities have also been improved since the government establishment of a number of regional markets outside Paris. These have helped to cut transport costs and reduce price fluctuations. The farmers themselves, with government backing, have also formed marketing groups of their own.

In general, French agriculture has benefitted from the establishment of the Common Market. Increased agricultural production by the other member countries, however, has reduced sales opportunities for French products among EEC nations. This applies particularly to cereals, France's chief agricultural export, despite the hard-fought 1967 Common Market agreement on grain prices. This minimum guaranteed price has chiefly benefitted the big French wheat growers in the north at the expense of other growers, especially in the southwest, who are relatively distant from consumer centres. France gains

The chief agricultural export

over 100,000,000 francs annually from the Common Fund (the tax on food imports from outside the Common Market, paid mainly by West Germany and Italy). This helps to reduce the cost of the French government's wheat subsidy that guarantees the price of wheat. The other sectors that have benefitted most are beet sugar, wine, dairy products, and cheese.

Forestry. French forests are a vital part of the economy. Roundwood production is among the highest in Europe and is topped by only Finland and Sweden. In the 1960s total production reached a high point of 58,-700,000 cubic yards (44,900,000 cubic metres) annually, compared with a high point for the other two leading producers of some 69,000,000 cubic yards (53,000,000 cubic metres).

State- and community-owned forests account for 35 percent of the total forest area. Considerable replanting has been undertaken both by the National Department of Forests, established in 1964, which manages most of the controlled forests, and by the Fonds National Forestier (National Forest Fund), the basic instrument of French reafforestation policy, which, since its formation in 1946, has been responsible for the reafforestation of over 2,-500,000 acres (1,000,000 hectares). These operations are expected to raise the productive capacity of forests in timber and industrial wood by 5,900,000 cubic yards (4,500,000 cubic metres) annually.

Fishing. French fish catches, at 762,000 metric tons in 1970, were the fourth highest in Europe, and the industry is of considerable domestic importance. Half the fishermen live in the coastal zone of Bretagne, where they are engaged in seasonal fishing, and five ports—Boulogne-sur-Mer, Concarneau, Lorient, Douarnenez, and La Rochelle—account for over half the total French catch, which mainly consists of cod, herring, halibut, sardine, mackerel, and tunny. There is also considerable oyster cultivation in the silted estuaries and lagoons of the Biscay coast.

Mining and quarrying. Just under 1 percent of the GNP is accounted for by mining and quarrying, which is a drop of 0.8 percent of the GNP in 1960. In 1967 and 1968 monthly production indexes (1962 = 100) fell below the 1966 level of 109. A recovery in 1969 pushed the index up to 116, where it remained in 1970. Other key sectors registered a marked increase in production during the 1966–70 period.

The running down of the chief extractive industries

The poor performance of mining and quarrying is accounted for by the running down of the chief extractive industries: coal and iron ore. The coal industry, which was nationalized after World War II, has suffered from the competition of oil and other sources of energy. Production has been cut back from 60,000,000 metric tons in 1958 to an annual target of 46,500,000–49,500,000 metric tons in the early 1970s. The number of miners was reduced from 127,000 in 1960 to 91,000 in 1967, and some pits have been closed. In the early 1970s the industry received extensive annual government subsidies despite the often unfavourable structure of the coalfields, and many pits have been modernized and productivity raised. The output per man in the Lorraine coalfields of 7,500 pounds (3,400 kilograms) per man-day in 1971 is the highest in Europe. In recent years the industry has increased its chemical activities. This trend, together with further rationalization, or reorganization, of existing pits, will help to cushion the industry from the effects of falling production.

Iron-ore production has dropped from a peak of 67,-000,000 metric tons in 1960 to 55,882,000 metric tons in 1971, because French exports have suffered at the expense of much higher grade foreign ores. Moreover, as the iron-and-steel industry shifts westward to the sea from its traditional centres on the northern coalfield and in the Lorraine Basin, imported ore will be used increasingly in France itself. The modern Dunkerque steelworks, for example, already use ore from Mauritania.

The quarrying of construction materials is carried out at a wide variety of sites all over the country, and about half the production of the main categories is exported. These categories include limestone construction blocks

(about 330,000 cubic yards [250,000 cubic metres] produced annually); granite slabs (about 160,000 cubic yards annually); sawn marble slabs (2,900,000 cubic yards annually); roof slates (120,000 metric tons annually); concrete blocks (8,000,000 metric tons annually); asbestos-cement products (900,000 metric tons annually); and ready-to-use concrete (about 5,200,000 cubic yards annually).

Manufacturing. France is fourth in the league of industrial nations in the non-Communist world, ranking after West Germany. Manufacturing accounted for 37.8 percent of GNP in 1970, and the overall GNP grew by 5.7 percent annually between 1965–71, a record bettered only by Japan. Despite this, however, overall industrial performance was rather variable during the period: growth was by no means steady, and some sectors fared far better than others. Between 1966 and 1970 the monthly industrial production index rose by 22 points, and the index for manufacturing industries (excluding machinery and mechanical products) rose by 29 points. The largest increase was registered by chemicals, which rose 62 points over the period. Appropriately, France is the fourth largest exporter of chemical products in the world. The index for textiles, clothing, and footwear rose by only six points. In 1967 and in 1968, the year of a general strike, relatively poor performances were registered in all sectors. In that year, car production dropped below the level of the previous year, but real output recovered in 1969 and 1970 and, over the period of the Sixième Plan (Sixth Plan [1971–75]), was expected to grow at the rate of 6 percent annually.

Industrial problems

Although French industry has become much more competitive and exposed to international influences since the establishment of the Common Market, certain sectors lag woefully behind its main competitors. Hence, there is still considerable room for restructuring and rationalization. A major difficulty is the fact that France has fewer large firms than most other major western European countries. Of the 10 largest French production companies, moreover, three are state owned and another two are French subsidiaries of international oil concerns. Thus, the role of private French capital is relatively small. Out of a total of 689,877 firms in French industry in 1966, 614,119 employed under 10 people, and only 638 employed more than 1,000. Large- and medium-size firms, however, are as modern as any in western Europe.

The government actively encourages mergers, and industry has become much more concentrated as a result, both in the old-established industries and the newer, dynamic industries, such as chemicals and computers. In 1970, for example, Pechiney and Ugine-Kuhlmann decided to merge, thus giving France a firm of world stature in the nonferrous-metal industry and the fifth largest firm in Europe. In the steel industry two large groups, Usinor-Lorraine-Escaut and Wendel-Sidelor, account for 70 percent of the country's production; and in the period 1966–68 there were over a dozen merger and association agreements signed. In the motor industry Renault and Peugeot are working together, and the linking up of the Italian auto concern of Fiat with Citroën gives France a stake in what is now Europe's leading motor-manufacturing company (ahead of the German Volkswagen Company). These mergers appear to be intensifying in the 1970s.

France in the 1960s was able to achieve a good growth rate with a relatively low rate of investment in relation to its GNP. But a higher rate of investment, which is advocated by the government, was seen to be necessary if this progress was to be maintained. In 1970 this advocacy produced results: productive investment was 28.1 percent of the GNP, compared with West Germany's 27.3 percent. In previous years France had lagged substantially relative to West Germany and the result of this previous shortfall in investment was a lag in scientific research. Only 1.5 percent of the GNP is spent on research, compared with over 3 percent in the Soviet Union and the United States, 2.3 percent in the United Kingdom, and 1.8 percent in West Germany. The greater part of government research expenditure finances military and nuclear projects and university research. Few French firms have research facilities adequate to compete in their fields on a world scale.

Energy. France's energy requirements have risen rapidly and this rise is expected to continue. The period 1966–70 showed a rise in primary-energy consumption of approximately 30,000,000 metric tons coal equivalent, from 168,000,000 metric tons in 1965 to 226,000,000 metric tons in 1970. Coal and oil between them account for nearly 85 percent of primary-energy consumption, but since 1965, when almost equal amounts of each were used, oil has been increasing its share in total consumption at the expense of coal. In 1971 France imported 100,100,000 metric tons of oil (mainly from North Africa and the Middle East), compared with only 29,200,000 metric tons in 1959. Home oil production, which varies between 2,500,000 and 3,000,000 metric tons annually, accounts for a fairly insignificant proportion of requirements. Coal production, which supplies 80 percent of the country's needs, fell from well over 58,000,000 metric tons in 1960 to 40,100,000 metric tons in 1970.

There has been a spectacular increase in the production of natural gas, which is rapidly replacing manufactured gas both in industry and the home. In 1970, 2,650,000 metric tons of liquefied gas were produced with imports (from The Netherlands and Algeria) of 181,000 metric tons, compared with a home production of 864,000 metric tons and imports of 30,000 metric tons of liquefied gas in 1959. In 1965 gas accounted for 5 percent of primary-energy consumption; by 1975 this proportion is expected to rise to 10 percent.

Electric power

Although in the mid-1960s, hydraulic electricity accounted for over one-fifth of primary-energy production (18,800,000 metric tons of coal equivalent), its share of total electricity production (140,700,000,000 kilowatt-hours in 1970) had fallen because the output of thermal electricity has increased. About 30 percent of the country's hydroelectric potential remains untapped; yet, the best sites have already been utilized and the need to absorb home coal production and the relative cheapness of this fuel have favoured thermal stations.

In 1971 monthly average output of thermal electricity was 8,209,000 kilowatt-hours (4,500,000,000 in 1966), while monthly average output of hydraulic electricity was 3,969,000 kilowatt-hours. In the past, demand for electricity has doubled every 10 years. The production and distribution of energy in France is basically in the hands of the state. It is thus subject to tighter control and benefits from more detailed planning of future requirements than the equivalent industries in many other countries.

Electricité de France, formed in 1946 after the nationalization of electricity companies, accounts for over 85 percent of total electricity production. The company is France's largest single investor employing 94,400 people.

Charbonnages de France (the French coal board) controls and coordinates the management of French coal mines, which are split up into nine management areas. The industry was nationalized in 1946. The gas industry is controlled by the state company Gaz de France, which produces and distributes only about 30 percent of the country's gas consumption, partly because many industries produce their own gas or purchase it directly. The Lacq natural-gas deposit, France's main source of supplies, is worked by the Société Nationale des Pétroles d'Aquitaine, in which the state is majority shareholder.

A public concern, Entreprise de Recherches et d'Activités Pétrolières (ERAP), supplies about 40 percent of the country's crude-oil requirements; it owns various refineries in France (Ambès, Feyzin, Grandpuits, Porcheville) and abroad, competing with the international oil companies established in France (Shell, Esso, British Petroleum, and Mobil). ERAP's subsidiary company, Essences et Lubrifiants de France, handles distribution.

French refining capacity has risen steeply and stood at 116,000 metric tons in 1970. Net production from refineries in France rose from 28,000,000 metric tons in 1959 to 93,100,000 metric tons in 1970.

France ranks fourth in the world as a nuclear power and has already built five reactors of various types employing natural uranium, graphite, and carbonic gas for the generation of nuclear electricity. A sixth was due for completion in 1972. Various technical difficulties have so far held back the expected growth of nuclear electricity production, but it was expected to account for 5 percent of total production in 1972. Further, research is being pursued by France's Commissariat à l'Énergie Atomique (Atomic Energy Commissariat) on fast-breeder reactors and an experimental station of this type was opened in 1967.

Financial services. The state is the dominant influence in French banking and finance, and, although there are a large number of financial institutions in the country, the money and capital markets are less well developed than in other advanced economies. Equity capitalizations and new issues are much lower in relation to GNP than in other European countries, and the Paris Bourse (the main stock market) does not fulfill as important a role in the raising of industrial capital as in other countries. State loans supply much of the necessary capital. Savings in France have also tended toward state loans or bonds and (in times of crisis) gold rather than ordinary shares.

State influence in banking and finance

The Banque de France, the central bank, has the sole right of note issue. It was nationalized in 1946 when the state also took over the four leading commercial banks, Crédit Lyonnais, the Société Générale, Comptoir National d'Escompte de Paris, and the Banque Nationale pour le Commerce et l'Industrie. The last two later merged into the Banque Nationale de Paris. Between them, these banks account for half of all assets and liabilities among French banks. Out of a total of about 300 banks, about half are purely local. In addition to the commercial banks, there are a large number of specialized credit institutions, including national and regional agricultural credit banks, savings banks, and the Crédit Foncier de France (official loans to finance construction). Nevertheless, half of all savers' deposits go outside the banking system proper into the Caisse d'Épargne (the postal-check system) and Crédit Agricole.

The banking system has seen considerable reform as a result of administrative and legal measures taken in 1966 and 1967 to make it more up-to-date and competitive. The most important change was the abolition of the traditional legal distinction between merchant banks (*banques d'affaires*) and clearing banks, such as the commercial banks already mentioned (*banques de depôts*). This was accomplished by allowing the former to accept small depositors and the latter to play a bigger role in industrial finance. At the same time, the treasury reduced its issues of bonds direct to the public, and, for the banks themselves, a more modern system of treasury deposits was introduced, under which the banks were no longer forced to keep a minimum holding of treasury bills. As a result, there has been greater competition for depositors' money, and the role of the banks has been strengthened and brought closer in line with practices in what French observers often term the Anglo-Saxon countries. This new competitiveness has led to a spate of mergers, notably among the smaller merchant banks.

Until 1968, French governments generally favoured a cheap-money policy, but, at the end of 1970, the bank rate was 7 percent, after falling in two stages from its earlier high point that year of 8 percent.

Since the end of the 1960s, the Paris Bourse has shown a considerable increase in its activities. In 1969, for example, running transactions increased by 45 percent for the second year in succession and more than twice the 1967 volume. Yet the Bourse's growth was still impeded by various factors, such as the government's tendency to impose an exchange control that hampers dealings in foreign shares, the general "heaviness" of shares, and the low standard of disclosure in company accounts.

The Paris Bourse

Mutual funds, or unit trusts, were illegal until 1963, and they are still obliged to keep 30 percent of their portfolios in fixed-interest government bonds. But they have grown in recent years, and this has greatly increased public interest in investing in shares. There has also been some growth in insurance-linked funds that enjoy certain fiscal advantages.

Foreign trade. Although France's exports grew at 9 percent annually during the 1960s and showed a rise of 14.4 percent between 1970 and 1971, there has been a deficit in the visible balance of trade since 1963. Some improvement was shown when the franc was devalued by 11.1 percent in August 1969, and the balance moved into a small surplus in the early 1970s. Despite the rise in exports of goods and services, France is far less dependent on foreign trade than most other European countries. French exports account for only 13 percent of GNP, compared with a figure of over 30 percent for the Common Market as a whole and 23 percent for Great Britain.

Since the Common Market, or EEC, came into existence in January 1958, the pattern and direction of French trade has altered markedly. In 1958 imports from Common Market countries accounted for 22 percent of all French imports, but by 1970 this figure had risen to 48.3 percent. There was a similar movement in exports to the Common Market countries from 22.3 percent of the total in 1958 to 48.4 percent in 1970. Between 1965 and 1970 French exports to the EEC rose on average by 16 percent a year and imports from the EEC by 19 percent. France has increased her trade proportionately more within the EEC than any of the other member countries, her main customers being West Germany, Belgium, and Luxembourg. Although trade with countries of the franc zone (which includes most former French colonies) remains fairly steady, at around 12 percent of total trade, and France enjoys a favourable balance with those countries, trade has fallen considerably over the last 12 years. Trade with the franc zone accounted for 32 percent of the total in 1958. Outside the confines of the Common Market, France's main trading partners are the United States and Switzerland.

France's main trading partners

During the 1960s, there were significant changes in the relative importance of the main categories of goods traded. Most noticeably, imports of food, tobacco, and beverages dropped from 25.2 percent of imports in 1958 to 12.0 percent in 1971, whereas exports of food rose from 13.3 percent of total exports to 16.8 percent during the same period. And, in line with the other EEC countries, France has greatly increased her exports of machinery and transport equipment, from 23.4 percent of total exports in 1958 to 32.7 percent of the total in 1970. Imports of the same accounted for 25.0 percent of total imports in 1970, giving France a favourable balance in this sector. It seemed likely that this sector, together with chemicals and motor vehicles, which have also shown marked growth, would play an increasingly important role in French foreign trade in the 1970s.

MANAGEMENT OF THE ECONOMY

Private enterprise and the role of the government. In France the state plays a more dominant role in the management of the economy than in most of the other Western industrialized countries. The money market is generally closely supervised by the state, which, in any case, owns the three main commercial banks as well as the central bank (Banque de France). About 30 insurance companies with half the country's premium income are state owned, as are a number of credit institutions outside the banking system proper. Institutions such as insurance companies and pensions funds play a much less dynamic role in investment in France, and the stock market itself is a relatively limited source of finance for industry, which depends disproportionately on state loans. This means that the state can exercise a tight control over private-sector investment. Private industry itself occupies a relatively weak position in the economy. Out of the 10 largest production companies, three are state owned and two are French subsidiaries of international oil concerns. Investment by the public sector actually accounts for half the annual total of all investments. The sector includes coal, electricity, gas, the railways, Renault (France's largest motor manufacturer), and the tobacco industry—over which there is a state monopoly.

Under the French system of planning, which was instituted after World War II, targets are set for the various sectors of public and private industry and the whole operation is controlled and coordinated by the Commissariat général du Plan (planning office). Each plan now covers a period of five years and is based on estimates of the likely growth of production and demand in each major sector of the economy and the amount of investment needed to fulfill these targets. The plans have a good record of success. During the Fourth Plan (1962–65), for example, actual annual growth of the gross domestic product was at the rate of 4.8 percent, compared with a target rate of 5.5 percent. During the Fifth Plan (1966–70), the actual rate of growth slightly exceeded the target rate of 5 percent annually. One of the basic aims of these plans has been to improve the international competitiveness of French industry, and, as such, they have played an important part in the economy's growth in recent years.

The role of economic planning

Before a plan is approved by the government, there are consultations between the plan office and the government on the aims and structure of the final document, and then detailed discussions are held within the framework of the plan office with the interested parties, various experts, and civil servants. Apart from the budget, which is geared to the aims of the plan, the government can use a number of other techniques to regulate the economy. It can adjust the amount of public-sector investment, can determine the quantity of orders placed by government departments, which play a dominant role in some sectors (*e.g.*, the electronics industry), and can fix the price of certain basic products (*e.g.*, steel). Price increases, generally, are subject to strict government surveillance. More indirectly the government can encourage mergers or decentralization operations favoured by the plan, with offers of various tax concessions, and specify the conditions on which state loans are granted. In addition, specific grants may be made for scientific and technical research. By keeping the various interested parties informed of the effects of their decisions and of likely movements in the economy, the plan office has been able to achieve a fair degree of harmonization of the country's economic effort. And these plans have come to be regarded as models for free-enterprise societies. Improvement of French industry's international competitiveness was a central feature of government economic policy during the Fifth Plan (1966–70), and this move to restructure French industry has been carried on as a central feature of the Sixth Plan (1971–75).

Taxation. Balanced budgets have not been traditional in France, although, under Gen. Charles de Gaulle during his term as president of the Fifth Republic, from 1959 to 1969, deficits were kept down to reasonable proportions and there were surpluses in some years. The budget is not the major instrument of economic policy as it is in many other Western countries, since its outlines are laid down some six months before it comes into effect and it is thus generally too inflexible to control the business cycle. Company taxes are assessed at a flat rate equivalent to 50 percent of net profits, although this may be reduced in the case of certain capital gains.

Personal income tax is assessed at progressive rates and takes into account such factors as size of families and dependent relatives. Its impact varies, depending on the source and nature of income, and there are over a dozen different categories of taxation. At present there is no "pay-as-you-earn" (PAYE) system for deducting tax from wages at the source, and evasion is widespread on all incomes. In fact, fewer than half of all French households pay any direct tax at all, and, with over two-thirds of total tax revenue coming from indirect taxes, the French tax system is among the most inequitable in Europe. Reforms introduced in the early 1970s, however, were expected to reduce the burden of indirect taxation and remove the various inequities applying to the assessment of personal income tax so that eventually it will be assessed on the same scale for everyone. To a large extent the success of these reforms depends on the eradication of tax evasion.

Personal income tax

Social-security contributions are deducted at the source and are not included in statements of gross income. The system is financed almost entirely out of contributions levied on the first 11,970 francs of an employee's annual income. He pays 6 percent in annual contributions and the employer 20.25 percent. Total social security revenue was 14,280,000,000 francs in 1969. The government claims that about 98 percent of the population is covered for basic sickness payments.

Trade unions and employer associations. Strikes have been relatively infrequent in France, with the exception of the general stoppage of May 1968, which was the biggest in Europe since World War II and involved 9,000,000 people. When they do occur, strikes tend to be short-lived. Only about 20 percent of French workers are thought to belong to unions, and an even smaller proportion are fully paid-up active members. The unions tend to be divided among themselves on political and ideological grounds. In the past they have also been organized in geographical rather than industrial units, though individual sectors have grown up recently in major industries, notably chemicals, oil, gas, and electricity. The three largest unions are the Confédération Générale du Travail (CGT; Communist led and inclined), with an estimated membership of 2,400,000; the Confédération Française Démocratique du Travail (CFDT; Catholic inclined), with an estimated membership of 800,000; and the Force Ouvrière (FO; Socialist), with an estimated membership of 1,000,000. There is also a white-collar workers' union, the Confédération Générale des Cadres (CGC), with 250,000 members.

The employers' organization, the Conseil National du Patronat Français, represents 900,000 concerns employing around 8,000,000 workers. It is organized on a regional and industrial basis, with one unit for each industry in each region. At a national level these local units are then grouped into federations. There is also the Centre des Jeunes Patrons, which represents employers under the age of 45. There is no formal link between the Patronat and the unions; but discussions are held between them at a national level, and in the past they have reached a number of agreements on labour and social conditions. Collective-bargaining procedures are laid down for both the public and the private sectors of industry, although the government may enter directly into negotiations, as in June 1968; and it has been influential in bringing about a number of one-year agreements on wages and working conditions in several of the nationalized industries.

Wages in industry have tended to rise much more rapidly since the 1968 general strike than in earlier years. Average hourly rates rose by over 30 points on the wages index between 1968 and 1970, an unusually large increase. But in some sectors there is significant unemployment for the first time in many years. Like many other countries, France is now faced with the problems of trying to maintain full employment, keeping wage increases down to a reasonable rate, and maintaining her competitiveness in international markets. And, although French industry benefitted from the 1969 devaluation of the franc, inflation and the 1971 international monetary crisis threatened to remove these gains sooner than was expected.

Contemporary economic policies. After the relative successes of the Fourth and Fifth national economic plans, the Sixth Plan, which covers the period 1971–75, appears less certain in its objectives and quotes fewer hard figures. Over the years the French economy has become much more open to world pressures, such as the recurrent bouts of worldwide inflation; and, since the reduction and removal of the various tariff barriers, which had made France one of the most protected of world markets in the 1950s, the economy has become less easy to control. The Sixth Plan, nevertheless, looks for a growth in real output of just under 6 percent annually. This may be compared with the Organization for Economic Co-operation and Development (OECD) target rates for West Germany, Italy, and the United Kingdom over the 1970–80 period of 4.5 percent, 5.6 percent, and 3.1 percent, respectively. The main intention of the plan is to continue the reorganization and restructuring of industry begun in earlier plans, particularly in the produc-

The influence of world trends on economic policy

tion of electronics, chemicals, and machinery. Improvements are also planned for the telephone service, the roads, major ports, such as Le Havre and Marseille, and amenities in rural areas. In addition, priority has been given to the development of medium-size towns, as part of the government's long-standing drive for growth in the regions outside Paris. Old-age pensions and the lowest wages will be reviewed every year, and a range of improvements is expected to be made in the social services.

Problems and prospects. Many of the features of the Sixth Plan imply a rapid expansion of government spending. But public investment has often been used as an economic regulator in the past, so that, if the economy has to be slowed down, money earmarked for such projects as roads, housing, telephones, and schools may not be spent. At the same time social pressures have been building up in France since the troubles of May 1968, and the unions are pressing for shorter hours and earlier retirement dates. With a budget deficit forecast for 1972, the government will have little room to manoeuvre, especially since many of the cutbacks and various restrictions in spending applied after the 1969 devaluation are still in force, although some of these have been relaxed.

France's main problem remains that her industrial base is still smaller than that of West Germany or even of the United Kingdom. Although the annual value of output per person, calculated at 39,662 francs in 1971, is higher than elsewhere in the Common Market (31,500 francs in West Germany, for example, and 21,588 francs in the United Kingdom), too many people are still employed on the land and in small businesses. In the early 1970s, the labour force is expected to rise by about 1 percent a year, thus bringing potential increases in productivity. But unemployment, which was kept down to an average of about 1 percent of the labour force between 1965–70, has been rising steadily since then. In 1971 it was not serious compared, for example, to the situation in the United Kingdom, but it provides yet another warning light to the government, which is committed to full employment. Some economists believe that many of these problems could have been ameliorated if the government had plumped for a higher growth rate when deciding the targets of the Sixth Plan. But a more rapid rate was ruled out precisely because it would have exacerbated social problems brought by the provisions of earlier plans, such as the restructuring of industry, the movement from the land, and heavy spending on capital investment at the expense of housing, education, roads, and public transport. France's goal to repeat its economic successes of the 1960s in the 1970s will not be achieved without difficulty. (E.I.U.)

Dilemmas concerning the growth rate

IV. Transportation

THE OVERALL SYSTEM

Geographical and economic influences. French transportation has been influenced by a number of factors. First, the low population density in many parts of the country and the generally uneven spread of economic wealth and industrial development means that the centres of production and consumption are widely dispersed, leading to high transport costs and organizational problems. Second, the topography of the country has played a key role in the development of transport; the main routes have grown up usually along the line of the principal river valleys. Third, the concentration of one-fifth of the country's economic activity on Paris and its surrounding areas has led to the growth of a radial transport system with Paris at its centre. Finally, the rapidly expanding rate of industrialization means that new modes of transport have had to be developed, and there are inevitable difficulties in adapting a transport system that is based on a 19th-century network to the needs of the modern economy. The automobile industry is the most significant transport sector in the French economy. It consumes about 20 percent of the country's sheet steel, 50 percent of all rubber, and 90 percent of tempered glass. Although investment in all types of transportation remains high, it varies widely according to the type of transport. Thus, while investment in air transport almost doubled between

The three factors influencing the transport system

1967 and 1968 and grew by 10 percent in road transport, the French railways, the Société Nationale des Chemins de Fer Français (SNCF) showed a decline of more than 5 percent.

Freight transportation. The transportation of goods can be classified into three distinct categories, each of which has developed in a different way.

Heavy-goods consignments. First, heavy-goods consignments of 500 metric tons and over are carried either in trainloads or by waterways and pipelines. Such consignments represent one-third of the total volume of all goods transported. The principal products carried include iron ores, coal, and grains, which together represent two-thirds of the volume of such shipments; however, products such as refined hydrocarbons and chemicals are growing in importance. By 1985 the Paris region alone will require some 100,000,000 metric tons of construction materials annually, nearly half of which could be feasibly transported by shipping on the Seine.

While trainloads of such single products are some of the most profitable undertakings of the French railways, or SNCF, transportation by waterways has experienced certain difficulties. Bargemen and sailors have found it difficult to adapt to modern cargoes, despite a growing traffic in such products as grains and construction materials. Also, facilities remain generally inadequate and out-of-date, although a national plan for inland waterways has somewhat mitigated the problem with a program of conversion and modernization.

"Truckload shipment." The second category of goods transportation is the "truckload shipment," comprising consignments of up to several hundred tons. Such goods are transported in lots of three tons by road or five tons by rail, and this form of transport is the greatest in terms of ton-miles. The transport market in this category is divided between some 33,000 trucking firms and the SNCF, the latter showing a large deficit in this field, for it has been unable to increase its share of the traffic.

Retail shipments and packages. The third category is the transport of retail shipments and packages. This involves the distribution of manufactured products to retail centres; they are dispatched in consignments of low tonnage, which means a larger number of handling operations are necessary. The scattered geographical locations of the consignees and shippers of such freight has led to organizations based on the principle of group freight. Small consignments of between 66 and 330 pounds (30 to 150 kilograms) are subject to this method of handling.

The principal carriers for retail consignments are the SNCF, the railway freight agencies, the motor-freight agencies, and private trucks and delivery vans carrying their own goods. The SNCF has taken a number of measures to improve its share of the traffic in this field, and a specialized agency, the Service National des Messageries (National Carrier Service) was set up in 1970 to secure this traffic. Despite such measures, however, the carriage of retail goods by rail has continued to decline, dropping by 1970 to less than half the 3,200,000 metric tons carried in 1964. In the meantime, railroad-freight agencies have grown appreciably and now handle double the amount carried by the SNCF. These freight agencies organize the collection and local delivery of retail goods and packages, group them into larger consignments, and use the SNCF as the hauler. Competition comes mainly from the motor-freight agencies and carriers and the private trucking concerns. At least 5,000,000 metric tons annually are carried by public motor carrier transport over distances of more than 100 miles (160 kilometres).

Combined freight transport. There is, inevitably, cooperation between the different modes of transportation, despite the keen competition that is the general rule. By far the most significant is the combination of road and rail transport, and this is most marked by the development and growth of general container and transcontainer traffic. Transcontainers are containers designed specifically for one type of product. Although they still represent only a very small proportion of total traffic, the use of transcontainers is growing at the fastest rate. Rail traffic in transcontainers is fairly recent but has almost doubled

(margin note left) Container and transcontainer traffic

annually. About two-thirds of this traffic is originally ship borne and comes from the main maritime ports, the French–English trade being the most important. Containerization has given the SNCF a new opportunity to re-establish its competitiveness. A "container-express" system was established, and a Paris–Cologne connection was opened at the end of 1970. Six connections are in service, linking Paris with Metz, Strasbourg, Lyon, Marseille, Toulouse, and Bordeaux; and four connections link Bordeaux and Marseille, Toulouse and Marseille, Bordeaux and Toulouse, and Strasbourg and Marseille. About 33 inland and coastal ports are equipped for the handling of transcontainers, the ports of Le Havre, Dunkerque, and Marseille–Fos being the most important. The ports of Nantes–Saint-Nazaire, Nantes–Cheviré, and Bordeaux are also due for modernization under the Sixth Plan. Some inland ports are also being developed for container transport, notably Lille. Inland shipping has been adapted for container transport, especially by the modernization of docks at Strasbourg and Gennevilliers, which are now equipped with container cranes.

Passenger transportation. In France, as elsewhere, the automobile predominates as the most popular and widespread form of passenger transport. In 1971 the private automobile accounted for 250,000,000,000 passenger-miles (400,000,000,000 passenger-kilometres), compared to 25,500,000,000 for rail, 15,000,000,000 for public transport (buses and taxis), and 1,000,000,000 for domestic air transport. The late 1960s saw a remarkable rise in domestic air traffic, with an annual growth rate of about 22 percent. Automobile traffic grew by about 9 percent; but increase in rail traffic was negligible, and public motor transport declined.

THE COMPONENT SECTORS

Road transport. *The road network.* France, with Belgium, has the most dense highway network in Europe, with 9.5 miles (15 kilometres) of road per 10,000 inhabitants. The total length of roads is over 490,000 miles (789,000 kilometres) and represents 45 percent of the highway network in the European Economic Community (EEC). These figures may appear deceptive, however, since a large part of this highly developed network is only an inheritance from the 19th and early 20th centuries; but the French system is, nevertheless, distinguished from its neighbours by a considerable length of high-quality secondary roads. Only about 9 percent of the main roads, or *routes nationales*, carry more than 6,000 vehicles a day, and 85 percent of all road traffic is carried by only 15 percent of the network. Roads with three or more lanes account for only 7 percent of the main roads.

Passenger services. The total number of private and commercial auto vehicles in 1970 stood at 12,400,000, or one vehicle for every four people. The rural nature of France meant, however, that there were still relatively few people who travelled to work by car on a national scale. Passenger coach and bus services cover about 273,-000 miles (440,000 kilometres) regularly, connecting some 36,900 towns and villages. This form of transport is in decline, however, although it is partially offset by a growth in school and factory transport, which comprises about 15 percent of the total, and seasonal tourist transport, which accounts for a further 20 percent.

Goods services. The transport of goods by road has grown significantly in the last 25 years, taking a larger and larger share of the total. In fact, public road carriers and haulers account for 24 percent of total tonnage. Its growth has been the result of several factors, not the least of which is that it is certainly the cheapest form of long-distance transportation. Other factors include the dispersal of the units of production of major industries throughout the country, the relatively slow rate of urbanization in France, and the increasing tendency of manufacturers to order smaller quantities of goods but at a greater frequency. An annual expansion of 6 percent is forecast for this sector during the Sixth Plan.

Rail transport. The French railroad network is characterized by a strong geographical centralization inherited from the 19th century and the fact that it was created in a predominantly agricultural France. It is centred on Paris, the country's only main rail intersection, and cross-country connections still present difficulties, with the exception of recently developed routes, such as Lyon–Nantes, Bordeaux–Lyon–Geneva (Switzerland), and Calais–Basel (Switzerland).

The role of the SNCF

The SNCF (see above) was created on January 1, 1938, as the one company managing the French railroads. It is a nationalized concern, with an administrative council composed of both government representatives and administrators representing the interests of the old French railroad companies. France was the first European government to intervene directly in the management of the railroads; it did so mainly because of the lack of capital of the first railroad companies, the unprofitable nature of a large part of the rail network, and some political and strategic considerations. The state has a 51 percent control in the SNCF.

Productivity. Manpower on the railroads has decreased from 515,000 in 1938 to only 300,000 at the end of 1970. At the same time, the working week was reduced from 48 hours in 1960 to 43 hours in 1970. Yet, there has been a substantial increase in productivity, a total of 63 percent between 1960 and 1970. There has also been an improvement in the efficiency of rolling stock and locomotives, the number of unit-miles of traffic per locomotive in service increasing by 6.5 percent in 1970. The same year also registered an 8.4 percent increase in the efficiency ratio of vehicles to passengers.

Rolling stock. In 1963, 42 percent of all locomotives were still steam powered, but this figure had dropped to only 3 percent by the end of 1970, and passenger coaches are being progressively replaced and overhauled as high-speed trains are introduced. The Sixth Plan predicted that by 1975 about 80 percent of locomotives would be electric powered and the remainder would be diesel fuelled.

The rail network. The rail network is composed of 23,000 miles (about 37,000 kilometres) of track, of which 17,000 are open to passenger transport. About 5,800 miles (9,300 kilometres) are electrified, about one-quarter of the total working length. The SNCF is concentrating on developing maximum speeds on the main routes. By the end of 1970, 2,360 miles of line could accommodate speeds of 100 miles per hour and, on some sections, trains could travel more than 120 miles per hour. Finally, the construction of a new line between Paris and Lyon was being considered in the early 1970s, designed to carry gas turbine locomotives (turbo-trains) that would reduce the journey between the two cities to less than two hours.

Waterways. Inland waterways have a long history in France, and, even before the French Revolution, about 600 miles of canal were in use besides navigable rivers. The network was greatly expanded in the 19th century to serve the industrial areas, and the common pattern of centralization on Paris is also reflected in the construction of the canals.

The three major segments of the waterways network

The modern network is mainly decaying and unsuitable for current water transportation, and it is unevenly distributed throughout the country. It is not continuous, and there are significant gaps, for example on the North Sea–Mediterranean axis. The three principal parts of the network are those of Basse-Seine, the north, and the east. These regional networks are cut off by bottlenecks—for example, the present waterways linking the Rhine to the Seine or the Rhône are limited to boats with a capacity of less than 380 tons. The network is made up of 6,430 miles of waterway, of which 2,947 miles are canals and 3,480 miles are rivers. It represents about 40 percent of the European waterway network. But only about 6 percent of this system can service barges with more than 1,500 metric tons capacity. For purposes of comparison, over 25 percent of the canals in both The Netherlands and West Germany can take barges with loads of 1,500 metric tons. The French network is essentially a narrow system concentrated primarily in the north and east. Between 1920 and 1940 improvements were undertaken on the Rhine and the Rhône, and since 1945 navigation on the Rhône has been substantially improved by the construction of the Pierre Bénite barrage, which facilitated

the Saône–Rhône connection. The canalization of the Moselle was completed in 1964, and facilities in the Seine Basin have also been improved.

Air transport. The airplane still occupies only a small place in internal French transportation. Its traffic is comparable to first-class rail traffic on connections such as Paris–Nice, Paris–Marseille, or Paris–Lyon; but it is increasing at an annual rate of about 25 percent. Traffic carried by Air-Inter (the domestic airline) reached 807,800,000 passenger-miles (1,300,000,000 passenger kilometres) in 1970. About 80 percent of the air travellers are businessmen, and fares are relatively high, deterring the casual traveller.

In 1970, Orly and Le Bourget airports, at Paris, recorded a total of 12,532,000 passengers, an increase of 15 percent over 1969. About one-quarter of the traffic originated from France, one-half from another European country, about 10 percent from North or South America, and another 16 percent from other continents. Paris also handled about 229,000 metric tons of air freight. Although about 71 French cities have an airport nearby, more than 70 percent of the traffic with Paris is concentrated on 8 connections. The most important cross-country connections link Lyon to Nice, Mulhouse, Marseille, and Nantes.

THE OUTLOOK FOR FRENCH TRANSPORT POLICY

Since 1934, transport policy has been characterized by strong controls over the coordination of the various modes of transportation. Such controls have impeded the adaptation of transport to the rapid developments that have occurred since 1949 and are also contrary to the general transport policies of the EEC. The main objective of transport policy in the early 1970s was the organization of a competitive market with administrative freedom for the various sectors of transport. The first step in this direction has been achieved through the reforms noted above affecting the SNCF. Overall, these reforms aim to restore freedom of administration to the SNCF, especially in the commercial sector, and to abolish state subsidies. When this has been achieved, the government intends to reduce its constraints on other sectors, especially motor freight and the waterways.   (Mi.B.)

V. Administration and social conditions

THE STRUCTURE OF THE GOVERNMENT

The constitutional framework. *The genesis of the 1958 constitution.* Following the insurrection of May 13, 1958, in Algeria, then still a French colony, Gen. Charles de Gaulle formed a government and succeeded in passing the constitutional law of June 3, 1958, which granted him responsibility for the drafting of a new constitution. The drafting and promulgation of the new constitution differed in three main ways from the former constitutions of 1875 and 1946: first, parliament did not participate in its drafting, which was done by a government working party aided by a constitutional advisory committee and the council of state; second, French overseas territories participated in the referendum that ratified it on September 28, 1958; and, third, initial acceptance was quite widespread, since in metropolitan France 85 percent of the electorate voted, 79 percent in favour and 20 percent against, and among the overseas territories only Guinea rejected the new constitution and consequently withdrew from the French Community.

Earlier constitutions

Electoral basis. The constitution of the Fifth Republic of France came into effect on October 4, 1958, and is based on the principles of Western democracy, the will of the people being registered at elections and referenda. (Universal suffrage at the age of 21 has existed since 1848 for men and 1944 for women). The electorate in 1972 was about 30,000,000. The people elect both the members of the two national legislative assemblies, the National Assembly and the Senate, and the local assemblies. Since the constitutional revision in 1962, the people also elect the president of the republic, who was chosen in 1958 by an electoral college of 80,000 notables.

The role of referenda. The people may also be asked to ratify, by a constituent referendum (Article 89), an amendment that has already been passed by the two legislative assemblies. The constitution also made provision for legislative referenda, by which the president of the republic may submit a proposed bill to the people concerning the general organization of government (Article 11).

This procedure was used twice in settling the Algerian problem, first on January 8, 1961, approving self-determination in Algeria (when 75 percent voted in favour), and on April 8, 1962, approving the Evian Agreement, which gave Algeria its independence from France (when 91 percent voted in favour). The use of this latter procedure to amend the constitution without going through the preliminary phase of obtaining parliament's approval is perhaps constitutionally questionable, but it led to a positive result, on October 28, 1962, when the election of the president of the republic by universal suffrage was approved by 62.25 percent of those voting. On April 27, 1969, however, in a referendum concerning the transformation of the Senate into a simple economic council and the reform of the regions of France, only 47.5 percent voted in favour, bringing about De Gaulle's resignation. Finally, on April 23, 1972, the enlargement of the Common Market by the addition of Great Britain, Denmark, Iceland, and Norway was ratified by 68 percent of those who had voted, but since there had been many abstentions, this represented only 36 percent of those who were eligible to vote.

Parliamentary composition and functions. The 1958 constitution retained the parliamentary system, but it reinforced the power of the president. Under the constitution, parliament is composed of two houses, the National Assembly and the Senate. The National Assembly is made up of 485 deputies who are directly elected for a term of five years by a simple majority vote in single member constituencies, but with two ballots, only the leading candidates standing the second time. A second ballot is not necessary if any one candidate wins an absolute majority in the first ballot. The Senate is made up of 283 senators indirectly elected for nine years by a *collège électoral* consisting mainly of municipal councillors in each *département*, one of the administrative units into which France is divided. Parliament retains its dual function of legislation and control over the executive but to a lesser extent than in the past. The domain of law (Article 34) is limited to determining the regulations and fundamental principles concerning such matters as civil law, fiscal law, penal law, electoral law, civil liberties, labour laws, amnesty, and the budget. In these different matters the Parliament is sovereign, and the government cannot interfere except only in order to draw up the details for the application of laws. On the other hand the government is responsible for all other matters and the Assemblies can in no way interfere. These other matters fall within the executive power of the government under Article 37, and a Constitutional Council is responsible for seeing that these legal limits are respected. Parliament can temporarily delegate part of its legislative power to the government, which then legislates by ordinances. This procedure was used eight times between 1958 and 1970 on matters concerning Algeria, social security, and the European Common Market.

The right to initiate legislation is shared by the government and parliament. The texts of bills and proposals are studied by parliamentary commissions, but putting them on the agenda remains essentially at the discretion of the government, which can, during debate, call for a single vote on the whole of the text. Parliamentary control over the government is exercised, as in the British system, by questioning members of the government in parliament about the specifics of their performance; by questions, by committees of enquiry; and especially by challenging the legitimacy of the government, a characteristic that is an integral part of the parliamentary system. Only the National Assembly can defeat the government by passing a motion of censure by an absolute majority, as on October 5, 1962, when the government of Georges Pompidou was toppled. The government can ask for a vote of confidence in its general policy or on a

single bill. In the latter case, a bill is considered adopted unless a motion of censure obtains an absolute majority.

The strong position of the president of the republic is the predominant feature of the present regime but at the same time this creates an ambiguous situation—that is, the regime has many of the characteristics of a parliamentary system: the sharing of executive power between a non-accountable head of state and a head of government responsible to parliament, and the powers of dissolution of that government by the parliament and of parliament by the government. But, at the same time, there are other features, such as the subservience of the government to the president and since 1962 his direct election by universal suffrage, which made the system very similar to a purely presidential one. This was particularly so under the strong individual control wielded first by de Gaulle (1958–69) and then by Pompidou.

The role of the president. The president of the republic appoints the Prime Minister and his ministers; he presides over the Council of Ministers, signs the more important decrees, appoints high civil servants and judges, and has the right to dissolve the National Assembly (which de Gaulle did twice, in October 1962 and May 1968); he can hold referenda and negotiate and ratify treaties; he is commander in chief of the armed forces. Under exceptional circumstances, Article 16 allows him to concentrate all the powers of the state in his hands. This article, enforced from April to September 1961 during the Algerian crisis, has given rise to very sharp criticism because of its undemocratic nature.

De Gaulle's great influence and the pressures of unstable political conditions tended to reinforce the authority of the presidency at the expense of the rest of the government. Whereas the constitution (Article 20) charges the government to "determine and direct" the policy of the nation, de Gaulle, in fact, arrogated to himself the right to take the more important decisions, particularly concerning foreign, military, and institutional policies. The prime minister, however, is still responsible for defending governmental action before parliament. He has certain powers of control, and the administration is at his disposal.

In practice, the transfer of governmental power to the detriment of the prime minister and to the advantage of the president of the republic is highly accentuated. All major decisions are henceforth taken at the Elycée Palace (the president's headquarters) including the dismissal of the head of government, who thus finds himself, in addition to being continuously responsible to the National Assembly, responsible by unwritten law to the head of state.

The role of the Councils. The Constitutional Council, which is composed of nine members appointed for nine years by the president, the National Assembly, and the Senate, supervises the conduct of parliamentary and presidential elections. It examines the constitutionality of organic laws (those fundamentally affecting the government) and rules of parliamentary procedure, but it may be consulted on the constitutionality of other legislation, international agreements, or disputes between government and parliament. There is also an Economic and Social Council, which is made up of 200 representatives from the economic and social world. It must be consulted on laws concerning long-term programs and on development plans and may be consulted on any bills concerning economic or social matters.

Regional and local government. The main units of local government are the *départements*, the *communes*, and the overseas territories.

The départements. The *départements*, created in 1790, now number 98, including Guadeloupe, Martinique, French Guiana, and Réunion, which gained *département* status in 1946, and the new *départements* in the Région Parisienne (Paris Region), which were created in 1964. The principal governing body of each *département* is the General Council, which is elected for six years with one councillor per canton. There are between 11 and 70 cantons per *département*. The General Council is responsible for all the main departmental services: welfare, health,

Relations
between
parliament
and the
executive

The
National
Assembly
and the
Senate

Internal
Structure
of the
départements

administration, and departmental employment. It also has responsibility for local regulations, manages public and private property, and votes on the local budget. The prefect (*préfet*), whose creation dates back to 1800, represents the government in Paris within the *département*, and is the executive agent of the General Council. He directs all state administration, decides on the use of state funds, and exercises tutelary power over the deliberations of the General Council, particularly where the budget is concerned. He is assisted by a subprefect (*sous-préfet*) within each one of the 322 *arrondissements* in France, the subdivision of the *département*.

The communes. The *commune*, the smallest unit of democracy in France, dates back to the parishes of the "*ancien régime*" in the years before the Revolution. In 1970 there were 37,700.

The *commune* is organized according to a law of 1884 and has a municipal council with a minimum of nine members, who are elected for six years. The municipal council is responsible for running most of the municipal services, some of which are compulsory, such as the registry office, fire service, and funerals. It administers both public and private land, manages the public establishments of the commune, most important of which are the hospitals and the schools, employs a large number of personnel, and votes on its own budget. The council elects a mayor and his deputies. The mayor is both the chief executive of the municipal council and the representative of the Paris government in the *commune*. He is also in charge of the municipal police and through them ensures public order, security, and health and guarantees the supervision of public places to prevent such things as fires, floods, and epidemics. He directs municipal employees, implements the budget, is responsible for the registry office, and performs the duties of judicial police officer. The authorities of the *commune* are subject, particularly in financial matters, to the control of the minister of the interior, although this was relaxed somewhat in December 1970. The mayor is one of the main figures in the political and economic life of France, insofar as his functions are frequently closely linked with parliamentary or governmental mandates.

More than 24,000 *communes* have less than 500 inhabitants, and in view of their small size they have been regrouped into *commune* unions. A federal type of organization has been applied to the larger towns and cities, and urban districts were established by an ordinance in 1959 and urban communities in Bordeaux, Lille, Lyon, and Strasbourg in 1966.

The particular situation of the Parisian conurbation required a special form of organization. The capital itself, covering more than 40 square miles, has a population of nearly 2,600,000 but the conurbation includes nearly 10,000,000 people living in an area of over 4,600 square miles, which adds up to 20 percent of the population in a 2 percent area. The unity of the region is marked by the existence of an urban district created in 1961, and there is a prefect for the Région Parisienne as a whole. Local government in Paris has always been distinct. There is no elected mayor but instead 20 mayors who are appointed by the government. Since 1964 there has been only one elected assembly, the Council of Paris, with 90 members. There are two prefects, one for the Paris Region (*préfet de la Région Parisienne*), who performs the functions normally devolved on a mayor, and the prefect of police (*préfet de police*).

In the country as a whole, an attempt has been made to create some coordination at the regional level. There are 21 regional divisions with regional prefects and a Commission for Regional Economic Development (CODER).

The overseas territories. The overseas territories—the vestiges of the French empire—are scattered over four continents: in America, the islands of St. Pierre and Miquelon; in Africa, the Comoro Islands and the territory of the Afars and Issas; in the Pacific, French Polynesia, Wallis and Futuna, New Caledonia, and the Anglo-French Condominium of the New Hebrides. They enjoy a great deal of autonomy in matters reserved for metropolitan France, such as diplomacy and defense.

They govern through an assembly elected by universal suffrage and a government council, but they are subject to the tutelage of a representative of the French Republic.

Political parties. Political parties played a particularly important role under the Third and Fourth republics; but the Gaullists constantly blamed the instability of former regimes on the French party system, and political parties have lost a great deal of their influence since 1958. In the early 1970s the French political situation was characterized by the existence of a majority party (the Gaullist party) and by a divided opposition.

The Gaullists. The Gaullist party was created in 1947 by Gen. Charles de Gaulle under the name of Rassemblement du Peuple Français (RPF). Its consistent opposition to governments formed by coalitions of the other parties greatly contributed to political and governmental instability under the Fourth Republic. In the legislative elections of November 1958, the party, under the new name of Union pour la Nouvelle République (UNR), won 212 of the 485 seats in the National Assembly. In the November 1962 elections this number increased to 284 seats, including Valéry Giscard d'Estaing's independents. After a setback in the 1967 elections, when the Gaullists secured only 244 seats, the Union des Démocrates pour la République (UDR), as the party was then called, reinforced by some members from the centre Progrès et Démocratie Moderne (PDM), won a clear victory in the June 1968 elections that followed the student disorders and the May strikes. After the March 1973 elections, the Gaullists controlled 275 seats in the National Assembly aided by 55 D'Estaing's independents and 30 Centrists. The Gaullists have also held the presidency of the republic since 1958. De Gaulle was elected in December 1958, re-elected in December 1965 on the second ballot with 55 percent of the votes, and Georges Pompidou followed him from June 15, 1969, when he was elected on the second ballot with 57.5 percent of the votes. Various Gaullists had also held the presidency of the National Assembly, the premiership, and the presidencies of all the committees of the National Assembly. Paradoxically, however, Gaullist representation in the Senate had always been in the minority (for example, 30 seats out of 274 in 1970). Likewise, the Gaullists never really succeeded in getting a foothold in the municipalities, and the number of active members was quite low. As of 1973 they and their allies held 60 percent of the seats in the National Assembly, though they represented a little less than half of the electorate.

This was the case because the 1958 constitution did away with proportional representation—which had given minority parties substantial representation under the Fourth Republic—and set up the single member majority electoral system, which favours the party that controls the largest bloc of followers, in this case the Gaulists.

There are three main opposition groups.

The Communists. The chief one is the Parti Communiste Français (French Communist Party), which claims 450,000 members and regularly secures between 20 and 25 percent of the vote. At a disadvantage because of the voting systems, it has only 73 deputies and about 10 senators and controls no big city. It supported the candidacy of François Mitterrand in the 1965 presidential elections but in the 1969 elections it presented its own candidate, Jacques Duclos, long the leader of the French Communists, who obtained 21.5 percent of the votes (about 4,700,000) in the first ballot.

The non-Communist left. The non-Communist left, which, with the centre "Christian Democrat" Mouvement Républicain Populaire (MRP), dominated the Fourth Republic, has suffered from divisions since 1958. It includes the Parti Socialiste (Socialist Party, which absorbed the Convention des Institutions Républicaines in 1970, the Radical Party, and the Parti Socialiste Unifié [PSU; United Socialist Party]). The Socialist Party—with about 100,000 members, representatives in local government and the Senate and strong organization—remains, despite a drop in electoral support, one of the main French parties. In 1965 it joined with the Radical Party and the Convention of François Mitterrand to support his candi-

The importance of the mayor

Opposition parties

dacy in the presidential elections. This alliance later became the Federation of the Democratic and Socialist Left (FGDS). Mitterrand obtained 45 percent of the votes in 1965 and the FGDS 24 percent of the votes and 116 seats in the 1967 legislative elections. The Federation disbanded following its defeat in 1968, when it secured only 57 seats. The unification of the non-Communist left is thwarted by the complexity of its relations, on the right, with the Radical Party, and, on the left, with the small revolutionary Parti Socialiste Unifié (PSU). The Socialist Party concluded, in June 1972, an electoral agreement with the Communist Party. That agreement split the Radical Party, a wing of which led by Robert Fabre, rejoined that new coalition though the majority of the 20,000 members of the Radical Party, animated by its charismatic secretary general, Jean-Jacques Servan-Schreiber, a journalist and author, refused any agreement with the Communists and turned to the centre. In 1973 the non-Communist left got 23 per cent of the votes and 103 seats.

Minor groups of the centre. Finally, in the centre, a few personalities perpetuate the liberal European and parliamentary ideal of the former Mouvement Républicain Populaire (MRP) led by Robert Schuman. Although it has only a few representatives in the National Assembly, it did significantly well in the 1965 presidential elections, when Jean Lecanuet obtained 16 percent of the votes, and especially in 1969, when Alain Poher, president of the Senate and the interim president of the republic after de Gaulle's departure, obtained 42.25 percent of the votes in the second ballot. In 1973 the "Reformateurs" of Lecanuet and Servan–Schreiber won 13 per cent of the votes and 30 seats.

Justice. In France there are two types of jurisdiction: the judiciary that judges trials between private persons and punishes infringements of the penal law and an administrative judicial system responsible for settling lawsuits between public bodies, such as the state, local bodies, and public establishments, and private individuals.

The two basic types of jurisdiction

The judiciary. For civil cases, the judiciary consists of 172 higher (*grande instance*) courts and 455 lower courts, which replaced justices of the peace in 1958. For criminal cases there are *tribunaux correctionnels* ("courts of correction") and *tribunaux de police*, or "police courts," which try minor offenses. The decisions of these courts can be referred to one of the 28 courts of appeal. Felonies are brought before the assize courts established in each *département*, consisting of three judges and nine jurors.

All of these courts are subject to the control of the Cour de Cassation (Court of Cassation), as are the specialized professional courts, such as courts for industrial conciliation, courts martial, and the Cour de Sûreté de l'État (Court of State Security), founded in 1963 to try felonies and misdemeanours against national security. The supreme court interprets the law and does not judge cases but can refer a case back to a lower court.

There are some 5,000 judges recruited by competitive examinations held by what was originally the Centre National d'Études Judiciaires, created in 1958, which became the École Nationale de la Magistrature in 1970. Within this elite, a traditional distinction is made between the *magistrats du siège*, who try cases, and the *magistrats de parquet* (public prosecutors), who prosecute. Only the former enjoy the constitutional guarantee of irremovability, which forbids removal of a magistrate without his consent. The Conseil Supérieur de la Magistrature (High Council of the Judiciary) is made up of nine members appointed by the head of state from among the judiciary and makes proposals and gives its opinion on the nomination of the *magistrats du siège*. It also acts as a disciplinary council. The public prosecutor's department (Parquet) is responsible for demanding before the courts that the law be applied. It is a hierarchical body subject to the authority of the minister of justice. Judges can successively serve as members of the Siège (Bench) and the Parquet. In cases of high treason only a high court of justice made up of deputies and senators is allowed to try the president of the republic and ministers. They can also be tried in this manner if they have committed felonies or misdemeanours during their term of office.

Administrative justice. The existence of a system of administrative justice, which dates back to the year VIII of the Revolutionary period (1799), is unique to the French system though later similar institutions were set up in Italy, Belgium, Luxembourg, Greece, and Egypt. Administrative courts are first-instance courts under the control of the Conseil d'État (Council of State), so far as appeals are concerned. The Council of State plays an important role since it exercises control over the government and the administration from a jurisdictional point of view and ensures that they conform with the law. It is, moreover, empowered by the constitution to give its opinion on proposed bills and on certain decrees.

The armed forces. The overall responsibility for national defense rests with the president of the republic, who is the constitutional chief of the armed services and presides over the higher councils and committees on national defense. He is also the person who, since a decree in 1964, can give the order to bring the air and strategic forces into action. The prime minister, assisted by the secretary general for national defense and the minister of the armed forces, coordinates military policy.

Organization. The organization of the military administration was for a long time based on the division of the military into the army, navy, and air force. Since 1958, this distinction has become progressively blurred and replaced by an organization based on various functions. Thus, there are strategic nuclear forces, territorial-defense forces, mobile forces, and task forces. France has had the atomic bomb since 1960 and the hydrogen bomb since 1968. It carries out nuclear testing in the Pacific, has a strategic nuclear force, and a basic delivery system.

The role of nuclear weapons

In 1970 there were 36 Mirage IV bombers armed with a 100-kiloton atomic bomb, ground-to-ground ballistic missiles, and sea-to-ground ballistic missiles. The "Redoutable," France's first nuclear submarine, was launched in 1967, and three other nuclear submarines were planned to be brought into service before 1975. Even so, French nuclear strength is, it is claimed, 15,000 times less than that of the Soviet Union. Defense on the ground is mainly the responsibility of the land army and the gendarmerie in collaboration with civilian authorities. The coordination of defense services is ensured by the division of the country into seven military regions. The mobile forces include five mechanized divisions equipped with Patton- and AMX-type tanks, supported by tactical air commands made up in particular of Mirage III-type planes. Finally, a land-army unit is responsible for non-European missions, in particular in such African territories as Gabon and Chad, which are linked to France by defense agreements. The French Navy totals 380,000 tons, divided into two flotillas based on three maritime regions (Cherbourg, Brest, and Toulon). It includes two aircraft carriers, two cruisers, 29 frigates, 35 escort vessels, 19 submarines, and 91 minesweepers. The air force includes about 2,000 aircraft, in particular Nord 2501, Transall, and Mirage planes scattered over about 30 bases.

The military budget varies according to different estimates from 3.5 percent to 5.3 percent of the gross national product and is about 18 percent of the national budget. France withdrew from the integrated command of the North Atlantic Treaty Organization (NATO) in 1966, but remains a Western European Union (WEU) member.

The military budget

Manpower. Every Frenchman is subject to compulsory military service, except in cases of medical exemptions and some categories of conscientious objection. The annual contingent is 420,000 men, of which 70 percent are drafted into the active army or the technical-cooperation corps. Technical cooperation personnel are put at the service of the Ministry of Foreign Affairs. They do not have a general statute, and their situation varies according to the agreements reached with each country. The number of such personnel is particularly high in North Africa, West Africa, and the Malagasy Republic. The law of July 1970 set the draft age at 19, reduced the length of service to one year, and made deferments exceptional after the age of 21, except for medical students. The total active military strength is 500,600 career personnel in addition to the draftees.

THE SOCIAL SERVICES

Administration and the civil service. There are about 2,000,000 civil servants in France, including 1,300,000 civilian employees, 220,000 military employees, and 550,000 local-government employees. The largest single groups of employees are those in national education (500,000) and the post office (280,000). French administration has been strongly marked by a very strict hierarchy since the time of Napoleon. Civil servants are grouped into different corps and different ranks and are classified according to their recruitment level into four different categories. Recruitment is based on the principle of equality of opportunity, and entry is by a competitive examination. At the highest level, category A civil servants are recruited through a national school of administration, created in 1945, which gives access to the *grands corps de l'état*, which includes such bodies as the Council of State, the Court of Accounts, the Inspection of Finance, the prefectural corps, the diplomatic service, and the civil administrators' corps. The duties and rights of civil servants are defined by a general statute of 1946, which was modified by an ordinance in February 1959. Their career guarantees and their disciplinary code are extensive and are under the vigilant control of the Council of State. In return, they are duty-bound to be discreet in expressing any personal opinions, and the right to strike, which is recognized by the constitution for all Frenchmen, is more severely limited for civil servants, although this varies according to the corps. Most civil servants belong to labour unions.

Police services. The police are primarily responsible for maintaining public law and order. There are about 90,000 policemen in France, and they are responsible to the prefects in the *départements*, and to the prefects of police in Paris and the suburban *communes*. The police force is divided into public security forces and specialized police forces, such as the vice squad. The security police include the Compagnies Républicaines de Sécurité (CRS), responsible for public order; the judicial police, who carry out criminal investigations and hunt down suspects; and the complex internal intelligence and anti-espionage units. The municipal police forces are responsible to the mayor.

The organization of national education

Educational services. The organization of national education is highly centralized. Since 1968, however, following violent student riots, a movement toward decentralization has been in progress in higher education. The students had protested the lack of contact with their teachers and their denial of any voice in university administration—for instance, in determining syllabi and the courses of study. Further, they ultimately demanded that a continuous detailed check of their work should replace the generalized system of examinations.

In France there is both public and private education. All public education is free, and the expenditure on education stands at about 20 percent of the national budget, or a little less than 5 percent of the gross national product. Public education is administered by the Ministry of National Education, which draws up the curricula, employs the staff, and exercises its authority through rectors placed at the heads of the 23 academies.

Primary and secondary education. Education is compulsory between the ages of six and 16. Before the age of six, children can go to *écoles maternelles* (nursery schools) or *classes enfantines* (kindergartens), and they receive their elementary education between the ages of six and 11 in primary schools. Secondary education is first given in the *lycées*, the *collèges d'enseignement général* (CEG), and the *collèges d'enseignement téchnique* (CET) from the ages of 11 to 15.

Further secondary education is given in classical, modern, and technical *lycées*, leading to the national *baccalauréat* examination. Courses of study lasting from one to three years can lead to professional certificates or diplomas. Experiments in educational methods have been numerous since 1960. For example, there are the "snow classes" whereby an entire class is sent to the mountains with their teacher for two weeks or a month with just a small sum being paid by their parents. Since 1968 teachers, parents, and pupils themselves have been represented on the boards of directors of secondary schools.

Higher education. The law of November 12, 1968, changed higher education profoundly. Previously, universities had been divided into faculties or colleges according to the subjects taught. From 1968 on, the faculties were replaced by teaching and research units regrouped into autonomous, multidisciplinary universities co-managed by representatives elected from among the teaching staff, students, and administration. These establishments determine their own research programs, teaching methods, and means of assessment.

The state grants funds to the universities, which they divide among their departments. The degrees given are *licences* (roughly comparable to the British–American bachelor's degree), *maîtrises* (master's degree), and *agrégations* (a teaching qualification, and one of the most rigorous degrees in the world to obtain). Besides the universities there are the various *grandes écoles*, including the polytechnic and specialized colleges, and institutes such as the Institut d'Études Politiques (Institute of Political Studies).

The staff for the first degree is made up of teachers (68,000 men and 16,400 women), and for the other degrees there are professors with *licence* or *agrégation* diplomas (158,000 in secondary schools and 26,000 in higher education).

Other features. Private education is mostly Roman Catholic. Although the constitution proclaims that the state is secular, the "Debré law" of 1959 allows private establishments to sign contracts with the state that procure them financial support in exchange for a certain control.

The importance of Roman Catholic constitutions

School attendance in primary education in 1969 was 7,410,000, of which 6,370,000 attended public schools. In secondary education attendance was 4,200,000, and in higher education, which is almost exclusively public, there were 605,000 students (of which 280,000 were girls) attending about 60 universities. The number of foreign students totalled 30,000. The teachers are highly unionized. The Fédération de l'Éducation Nationale (FEN) and the Syndicat National des Instituteurs have 285,000 members. Other left-wing unions have nearly 100,000 members. The main student unions are the Union National des Étudiants de France (UNEF), the UNEF Renouveau, which is Communist, and the Fédération Nationale des Étudiants de France (FNEF).

SOCIAL CONDITIONS

Housing. France has had a continuous housing crisis since 1945. The Fourth Republic successfully carried out reconstruction after World War II, but urbanization, population growth, the repatriation of 1,000,000 Frenchmen from Algeria, immigration, and the old age of buildings continue to create growing needs. In 1970, 456,000 dwellings were built, and a rate of 500,000 per annum is forecast for the 1970s. There are 16,000,000 permanent dwellings in France, of which approximately one-third are over 100 years old and two-thirds are over 50 years old. The government itself does not build but encourages construction through premiums, loans, particularly for low-rent housing, and tax incentives. The procedure concerning the achieving of building permits was greatly simplified in 1970. City planning has become more organized with the establishment of *zones à urbaniser par priorité* (ZUP; land for immediate development) and *zones d'aménagement différé* (ZAD; land reserved for future use).

Wages and the cost of living. France has been living in an inflationary situation since 1914. The wage and price index, which was 100 in 1963, was 147 for prices in July 1972, and it was 218 for wages, which were thus increasing faster than prices. The rate of inflation in 1972 was about 7 percent. The increase in purchasing power, which was considerable in 1969 as a result of the increases granted after the widespread strikes in 1968, was 3 percent between 1965 and again in 1970–71. The low wage earner benefits from a minimum wage with a built-in cost-of-living increase, which is called the *salaire minimum interprofessionnel de croissance* (SMIC) and which was established in 1970. Its level is set annually, and all employers must respect it. As of July 1970, 750,000 wage earners were being paid according to this scale, which is at an hourly rate of 3.50 francs.

In 1969, 30 percent of all wage earners earned less than 750 francs a month; 24 percent from 750 to 1,000 francs; 32 percent from 1,000 to 1,666 francs; and 14 percent more than 1,666 francs. Men earn on average 30 percent more than women and up to 60 percent more in executive positions. A workman earns 80 percent more in Paris than in the poor *départements* of central France. Blue-collar workers are increasingly being paid salaries rather than weekly wages.

Social security and health. Almost everyone is covered by the social-security system. Social insurance was introduced in 1930 and family allowances in 1932, but the comprehensive rules for social security were not set down until the end of World War II. A network of elected social-security and family-allowance *caisses primaires* ("primary boards"), headed at the top by national *caisses*, manages a considerable budget of 75,000,000,000 francs. With the exception of the family-allowance system, the social-security system shows a deficit that is made up by the state. Receipts come from compulsory deductions from wages and from an employer's contribution. Expenditure is on retirement benefits (old-age pensions), family benefits paid for dependent children, and reimbursement of 75 percent of all medical, pharmaceutical, and hospital expenses.

French medicine complies with the principles of liberal medicine, with a free choice of doctors for the patient, freedom to decide on treatment, and a free discussion of fees. Since 1960, however, agreements have been signed at a regional level between the *caisses* and the professional medical associations. They set the level of fees, and, although doctors need not necessarily adhere to them, reimbursements from social security are very low if they do not.

Hospital reforms

The hospital reform of 1958 set up a link between hospitals and medical schools through the creation of hospital and university centres and by the introduction of common national competitive examinations giving access to both a hospital and a university career. Hospital doctors must, however, carry out full-time duties at the hospital. Private hospitals and clinics exist alongside public hospitals, and the cost of treatment in them is also partially reimbursed from social security. There are generally inadequate facilities and few hospitals and this is especially true in the case of nursing homes for the aged. In 1970 there were 68,000 doctors (one per 747 inhabitants), 20,000 dentists (one per 2,505), and more than 17,000 pharmacists.

Social groups. Of the total population of over 51,000,000, the working population numbers 20,500,000. Agriculture still employs 13 percent of the population, but people are constantly leaving the countryside. The *secteur tertiaire*, which includes the liberal professions, crafts, and administration, has grown rapidly from 30 percent in 1954 to nearly 44 percent in 1970. The industrial and transport sectors have varied little, employing about 40 percent of the working population. The standard of living of rural inhabitants remains low, and agricultural depression has become an almost permanent feature. As in most industrialized countries, the working class is losing its homogeneity and becoming socially and politically diversified, but social and professional mobility is still restricted. Although unemployment is under control, between 400,000 and 500,000 were unemployed in 1973.

(F.B.)

VI. Cultural life and institutions

THE CULTURAL MILIEU

France has an ancient civilization in which the original Celtic culture has blended with Greco-Roman and Germanic elements to form a harmonious whole.

Its rich medieval culture, fostered by scholars in monasteries and in universities, has given rise, since the end of the 15th century, to a strong tradition of Humanism.

which has always responded to the call of scientific and technical progress. Before World War II this culture was the prerogative of a still flourishing nobility, of a middle class that was ever more involved in commerce, and of an elite—often of modest means and humble background—which consisted of priests, university and scholarship students, workers, self-taught craftsmen, and members of technical societies.

Although the French had become completely literate by the end of World War I and although the general cultural level had been raised by the dissemination of information through the press and the other communications media—especially those of the cinema and of the radio—it was not until the end of World War II that a great cultural leap forward was made. Then, important governmental and parliamentary measures to provide free secondary education, to increase the number of scholarships, and to make education mandatory up to the age of 16 contributed to the social advancement of the lower classes and of the least rich members of society. In consequence, newspaper circulation rose and the setting up of permanent and mobile libraries increased the number of books in circulation—as did the publication in cheap pocket editions of outstanding works of literature, whether French or foreign. (Nowadays, a worker can—and often does—read unabridged editions of the works of Victor Hugo, Emile Zola, Shakespeare, and Pushkin.)

Changes after World War II

Nor should the effect of television, that other yet more persuasive, more attractive cultural instrument, be overlooked. Since World War II countless French families have gathered around their television sets to watch plays, films, reenactments of historical events, and art programs, as well as all kinds of educational courses and discussions of major current problems. Often a televised film or play prompts the viewer to read those works he has seen on TV or perhaps to seek out other works by the same author. On the other hand, in France as elsewhere, pictures are often substituted for text.

This modern culture reacts to life and events. The French are no longer shut in on themselves or within their own country. They feel involved in world events pictures of which they see and by which they are impressed: United Nations sessions, scenes from the wars in the Far East or in Africa, famines, earthquakes, international sports events, and space exploits. Furthermore, the French now travel, not just within France but also abroad. Thanks to aircraft and to the car, they may, even with modest means, get to know Europe and other continents. If, however, this transitory vogue for "a richer" and more varied culture in which science and technology play a large part advances at the expense of traditional culture—particularly that of Greco-Roman Humanism—nonetheless, improved health and living conditions, greater leisure, and longer vacations have all made the Frenchman of today undeniably better informed, better educated, and more cultivated than his compatriot of 50 years ago. It is, moreover, this more varied culture that he plans to exchange with people of other countries.

The diminution of Greco-Roman Humanism

THE STATE OF THE ARTS

Literature. In literature, one of the most important elements of contemporary French cultural life, the famous intellectual and Humanistic heritage of the past has not been lost. The great tradition of the 16th to the 19th century continues and the world-acknowledged figures—Michel de Montaigne, creator of the essay; the 17th-century dramatists Pierre Corneille, Molière, Jean Racine; Jean de La Fontaine, the poet of the fables, the great Voltaire and Denis Diderot, Victor Hugo, Charles Baudelaire, and Flaubert, creator of Madame Bovary; and many others—still influence modern writers. After World War II the illustrious names of such poets as Paul Valéry, Paul Claudel, and Saint-John Perse, the novelists Colette, André Gide, François Mauriac, and Henry de Monterlant continued to shine. And the year 1971 was the centenary of the birth of Marcel Proust, one of the great masters of the modern novel.

The theatre is always a living art in France, thanks to

contemporary playwrights such as Jean Anouilh, Eugène Ionesco, Jean Giraudoux, and Samuel Beckett, a bilingual writer who made Paris his home, not to speak of Fernando Arrabal, Jean Genet, Arthur Adamov, or Armand Salacrou. Major contemporary poets include Pierre Emmanuel, Louis Aragon, Patrice de La Tour du Pin, and René Char and Yves Bonnefoy.

Philosophy counts among its thinkers the Thomists Étienne Gilson and Jacques Maritain, the Christian Existentialist Gabriel Marcel, the Catholic moralist Jean Guitton, and of course, the Existentialist and Marxist Jean-Paul Sartre.

The novelists Françoise Sagan, Simone de Beauvoir, and Françoise Mallet-Joris appeared on the literary horizon after World War II and have remained there. Sartre, as well as Gide, is always read. But André Malraux, Georges Bernanos, the "new novel" of Alain Robbe-Grillet, Nathalie Sarraute, Claude Simon, and Michel Butor—born of the *Molloy* of Beckett—are the writers and works that attract the younger generation. This generation also admires the "new criticism" of Roland Barthes, the art criticism of René Huyghe, the ethnological studies of Claude Lévi-Strauss, author of *Tristes Tropiques*. André Malraux, who awakens interest as a man and as a writer, claims the place of honour.

In the field of historical study, the loss of André Maurois has been made good by the work of Pierre Gaxotte, Antoine de Lévis-Mirepoix, and even by the *Mémoires* of Gen. Charles de Gaulle, who revealed himself as a great writer.

The fine arts. The fine arts—painting, sculpture, engraving, architecture, and music—are still in favour and flourishing. The state provides for the training of artists at the École des Beaux Arts in Paris and at similar schools in the provinces. At the École des Arts Décoratifs, and at institutions such as the École Boule, training in fine cabinetwork is provided. In painters' and sculptors' studios and in the offices of architects, masters and students are brought together.

In Paris, painters and sculptors tend to congregate in Montparnasse, the Latin Quarter, and Montmartre. Both figurative art and abstract art still have their champions. Periodicals such as *Gazette des Beaux Arts* and *L'Oeil*, newspapers such as *Le Monde*, the art critic of which is André Chastel, and *Figaro*, whose music critic, "Clarendon" (Bernard Gavoty), is well thought of, educate the public and encourage artistic vocations—as do radio and television broadcasts, which are often excellent. The Conservatoire National Supérieur de Musique, the École Normale de Musique in Paris, and the Schola Cantorum have all fostered recitals by great masters or by promising young musicians. Paul Paray, Charles Munch, and Herbert von Karajan, who directed the orchestra of the Paris Opéra, revived classical masterpieces and introduced contemporary works to the Opéra and to the Opéra Comique, and the competition started by Marguerite Long helps to discover the best young musicians. Concert halls such as the Salle Gaveau and the Salle Pleyel in Paris and similar provincial halls provide a setting for musical events sponsored by young people's musical associations and by religious or secular choirs. Records and paperback books enjoy a phenomenal distribution, and it is rare nowadays for young people not to be interested in music and not to combine an interest in Bach, Mozart, and Vivaldi with their interest in pop music or Charles Trenet's and Georges Brassens' songs. Older people cannot forget Maurice Chevalier.

The cinema. The cinema has been developed into an art form by such great French directors as Julien Duvivier, Jean Renoir, Jean Delanoy, and Claude Lelouch; by such great actors as Fernandel, Michel Simon, Pierre Fresnay, and Jean Gabin; and by actresses such as Brigitte Bardot, Jeanne Moreau, and Simon Signoret. Above all, brilliant young directors appeared in recent years who are not unworthy of the older masters. A leader, with François Truffaut, of the so-called *nouvelle vague* ("new wave") of film makers that appeared in the 1950s, Jean-Luc Godard made the remarkable futuristic *Alphaville*, in which he tackled contemporary problems, as he did al-

The influence of the "new wave" films

so in *Week End* and *La Chinoise*. Truffaut, too, displayed great creative film talent in *La Mariée était en noir* (*The Bride Wore Black*), in which Jeanne Moreau starred. Jacques Demy must also be noted with his successes *Les Parapluies de Cherbourg* (*The Umbrellas of Cherbourg*) and *Les Demoiselles de Rochefort* (*The Young Girls of Rochefort*): in them, thanks to Françoise Dorléac and, above all, Catherine Deneuve, musical comedy was rediscovered. Louis Malle won attention with *Le Voleur* ("The Thief"), and Claude Chabrol made his mark with *Les Cousins*, *Le Scandale*, and *Les Biches* (*The Does*). Michel Deville's *Benjamin* succeeded with its lively freshness and daring—in the Gallic tradition. Earlier, the writer Jean Cocteau showed his great talents to be perfectly at home in creative cinema in *Les Enfants terribles* (*The Strange Ones*), *Orphée*, and other films.

Museums and monuments. The general public has benefitted from the preferential treatment given to the fine arts. The great national museums of the Louvre, Versailles, and of the Trocadéro have been enriched and remodelled, and, in such provincial museums as those at Lyon, Strasbourg, and Bordeaux, the same kind of improvements have been made. Museums such as the Musée Marmottan or the Musée Cognacq-Jay—both in Paris—have made marvellous private collections available to the public. Temporary, permanent, and travelling exhibitions are also constantly being organized.

A remarkable campaign has also been pursued on behalf of architecture. Renovations and restorations have been carried out on beautiful groups of buildings and on such historical monuments as the great houses—originally private residences—of the Marais and of the Ile Saint-Louis in Paris and also of the Grand Trianon and the opera house designed by Jacques Gabriel, both at Versailles. Throughout France, *Son et Lumière* (Sound and Light) spectacles have illuminated ancient towns as well as the ramparts at Dinan, the Place des Vosges in Paris, Le Mont-Saint-Michel, the châteaus along the Loire, and other historical buildings. A new national inventory of France's artistic heritage is being compiled with special reference to architecture. Local historical and archaeological societies, such as that in the Saint-Malo region of Bretagne, have, for example, been entrusted with compiling a preliminary regional list that will become part of a national inventory. As a result, some important archaeological finds, such as the discovery in the early 1950s of treasure (in the tomb of a Celtic princess of *c.* 500 BC) at the village of Vix, have been made. Historical monuments, public collections, and even private collections are open to the public, and owners of historical houses may obtain financial assistance to restore their property from the Services des Monuments Historiques, on condition that it is open to the public. Another great undertaking, initiated by André Malraux, former minister for cultural affairs, is the cleaning throughout France of historical monuments.

Traditions are being revived in the provinces—in Bretagne, Provence, Alsace, and the Basque country, among other regions—and a Fédération Régionaliste has been created, which bears witness to an interest in the regions and provinces quite different from that aroused by the desire for political autonomy. There is even, in Paris, a new museum of popular arts and traditions that provides a panorama of provincial folklore and local events. Together with the craze for regional costumes and religious festivals—particularly in Bretagne—it enables each Frenchman to come to know not only his country as a whole but also his own province.

The revival of provincial traditions

In the larger cities there are also museums—among which the museums at Strasbourg, at Rouen, and at the Château de la Duchesse Anne, at Dinan, should be mentioned—devoted to the arts and crafts of the provinces, their usages and customs. The clearing and restoration of old monuments is often undertaken by young amateurs of memorial history who may also organize regional spectacles of a high standard. Among the folk-dance groups, those of Bretagne, Provence, Auvergne, and Alsace are particularly interesting.

In the provinces popular education takes place at all

levels. It would be unusual, even in the smallest communities, not to find that lectures, exhibitions, concerts, libraries, and trips to other regions, even abroad, were being organized. Sometimes the initiative for such events is political or religious, but there is an increasing awareness of the various forms that art may take and of history and popular traditions. Finally, French cuisine, with its many regional specialities, is not a negligible art form.

CULTURAL INSTITUTIONS

France's cultural institutions, which stimulate activity in the fine arts, literature, science, and technology, are ultimately responsible to the Ministry of National Education, to the Ministry of State for Cultural Affairs, to the Directorate of Cultural and Technical Affairs (Direction des Affaires Culturelles et Téchniques) at the Ministry of Foreign Affairs, or to the State Secretariat for Cooperation Abroad (Secrétariat d'État à la Coopération pour l'Extérieur).

The whole nation may also continue its education with the help of educational radio broadcasts and by the lectures broadcast by universities and by public lecture courses—particularly at the Sorbonne and at the Collège de France. Furthermore, there are cultural centres in every important city, at which, with musical conservatories in the *départements*, plays, concerts, and recitals are produced. France has established the State Secretariat for Cooperation Abroad, which is responsible for sending teachers and technicians to help its former colonies and also for sending others to the advanced countries of Europe and America. Young Frenchmen may even spend time working for the secretariat instead of doing military service. The Ministry of Foreign Affairs, in conjunction with the Ministry of National Education and the Alliance Française (which does the same work as the British Council), maintains both cultural counsellors and attachés at its embassies and French *lycées* in important foreign cities. French institutes and

centres for French studies are also maintained, at which books, magazines, newspapers, records of French plays and music, and French films are provided, as are lectures and courses given by the staffs. The various international Associations of French Studies (Associations d'Études Françaises), the United Nations Educational, Scientific and Cultural Organization (UNESCO), which is headquartered in Paris, the International Association of French Teachers (Association Internationale des Professeurs de Français), and the association of French-speaking universities conclude this survey of cultural institutions that are all of help to each other.

PRESS AND BROADCASTING

French cultural life is, in fact, based on daily newspapers, periodicals, radio, and television. Beginning with Théophraste Renaudot's *La Gazette* (started in 1631 and later known as *La Gazette de France* and published until 1917) and the *Mercure de France* (which first appeared in 1890), the number of newspapers and periodicals has continued to multiply. When France was liberated at the end of World War II, a number of newspapers and periodicals that had appeared during the occupation and had supported the Vichy government were suppressed. But some of them—in fact, quite a good number —reappeared after changing their names. Among the great periodicals, one might mention the *Revue des Deux Mondes*, the *Nouvelle Revue Française*, and *Réalités;* weekly magazines include *Paris-Match, Jours de France*, and *Point de Vue-Images du Monde. Les Lettres Françaises* and *Les Nouvelles Littéraires* are literary weeklies.

The *Figaro Littéraire* ceased publication in 1970 and is now incorporated into the Saturday *Figaro*. The *Figaro* has the highest circulation and best reputation among the morning newspapers. It is moderate and right-wing, further to the right than other daily newspapers, such as *Le Parisien Libéré, L'Aurore, Combat*, the Roman Catholic *La Croix*, or the Protestant *Réforme.* Its opposite is the Communist paper *L'Humanité*. The most important of the evening papers is *Le Monde*, an informed

paper with full coverage that nevertheless reveals a curious duality in its columns, tending to lean, in the opinion of some observers, both to the right and to the left. Paris-Jour and *Paris-Soir* are more popular daily newspapers.

In addition to the Paris newspapers, there are the great provincial newspapers of which the most important, *Ouest-France*, is published at Rennes and covers Bretagne, Vendée, Normandie, and Maine provinces in detail. The *Sud-Ouest* of Bordeaux should also be mentioned, as should the *Dernières Nouvelles d'Alsace* of Strasbourg, the *Républicain Lorrain* of Lorraine, the *Nice-Matin* of Nice, and many others. All these newspapers cover political events and have special daily and periodical columns covering entertainment, the stock market, science, literature, and sports. Women's periodicals, such as *Marie-Claire, Elle*, and the *Écho de la Mode*, have a wide circulation and a high reputation. Periodicals that specialize in the arts, literature, and science are *L'Oeil, La Gazette des Beaux-Arts, Revue d'Histoire Littéraire de la France, Revue de Littérature Comparée, Science et Vie*, and *Cahiers du Cinéma*, which was associated with the new-wave cinema.

Besides the written press the oral press of radio and television should also be taken into account. The Office de Radiodiffusion et de Télévision Française (ORTF, with television broadcasts in black and white and in colour) has its headquarters in Paris on the boulevard Kennedy and operates regional centres that also provide local news and broadcasts. The television reception area has increased tenfold with the use of the satellite Telstar relays. Both radio listeners and television viewers are offered programs ranging from political, literary, artistic, and scientific news broadcasts to reports of major events and news of celebrities, films, plays, and variety shows. The French government has centralized the oral press at the Office de Radiodiffusion et de Télévision Française, which has three channels. Television is state controlled but not unduly censored, and radio and television broadcasts range from entertainment to practical and educational programs.   (C.De.)

VII. Problems and prospects

Two events of the presidency of Charles de Gaulle (1959–69) profoundly modified the conditions that shaped the immediate future of France. The first was the conclusion of the war in Algeria, which brought to an end a vast and difficult venture in decolonization, and the second was the widening of presidential powers. France had headed the second greatest colonial empire of the world, from which it had certainly gained important advantages but which had also placed heavy burdens upon the nation. While still maintaining privileged relations with most of the countries formerly under its administration, France is free from the majority of those responsibilities, which clearly encumbered her policies. Since General de Gaulle's succession was secured without the disturbances feared by many, the unpredictable element in future domestic politics centres chiefly on the difficulty of resolving possible conflicts between the powerful office of the president and the National Assembly, as well as on the Communist Party's ambition to form, with other left-wing parties, an opposition force capable of gaining a government majority.

Economically speaking, though considerable progress has been made, future successes appear to rest on the development of the interior regions and on the growth of the Common Market. Provincial urban complexes that have stable populations and the satellite towns have been called upon to limit and, if possible, to absorb the population that has spilled over from the capital. The strengthening and expansion of the Common Market should make it possible for France simultaneously to continue modernizing its agriculture and to expand its export industries.

Whether or not Europe unites to form an economic and political buffer between the United States and the Soviet Union, France has realized that it is as impossible for her as it is for any of her European neighbours to stand alone. Through intellectual traditions, abundant resources, and the extent of the French territory, which has as yet escaped the problems of overindustrialization, France should be able to distinguish itself in the quest that becomes each day more pressing for the advanced nations of the world—that is, to reconcile the requirements of scientific and technical advance with the essential needs of man, to affirm the willingness "to be" rather than "to have" and thereby to keep or rediscover an elevated "quality of life" in a new society.

(H.B.-M.)

BIBLIOGRAPHY

The landscape and the people: HILDA R. ORMSBY, *France: A Regional and Economic Geography*, 2nd ed. (1950); PHILIPPE PINCHEMEL, *Géographie de la France*, 2nd ed. (1966; Eng. trans., *France: A Geographical Survey*, 1969), includes a very complete bibliography; FRANCIS J. MONKHOUSE, *A Regional Geography of Western Europe* (1959), contains a very good presentation of the different regions of France; GEORGES CHABOT, *Géographie régionale de la France*, 2nd ed. (1969); MAURICE LE LANNOU, *Les Régions géographiques de la France*, 2 vol. (1964); *Atlas de France*, 2nd ed. (1958); *Grand Atlas de la France* (1970), excellent documentation; *Atlas économique et social pour l'aménagement du territoire*, 5 fasc. (1968–); JACQUELINE BEAUJEU-GARNIER, *La Population française*, 3rd ed. (1972) and *Le Relief de la France* (1972).

The economy: A brief general introduction to the contemporary French economy is CHARLES P. KINDLEBERGER, "The Postwar Resurgence of the French Economy," in STANLEY HOFFMANN et al., *In Search of France* (1963); see also the same author's *Economic Growth in France and Great Britain, 1851–1950* (1964). For a comparison of French economic performance with that of other Western industrial countries, see ANGUS MADDISON, *Economic Growth in the West* (1964). Various aspects of the economy are treated in ANDRE BISSON, *Institutions financières et économiques en France* (1960); DAVID GRANICK, *The European Executive* (1962); ANDRE MARCHAL, *La Pensée économique en France depuis 1945* (1953); and JOHN SHEEHAN, *Promotion and Control of Industry in Postwar France* (1963). Much has been written about the French attempt at central economic planning. Books representing different points of view include: PIERRE BAUCHET, *La Planification française*, 2nd ed. (1962; Eng. trans., *Economic Planning: The French Experience*, 1964); WARREN C. BAUM, *The French Economy and the State* (1958); STEPHEN S. COHEN, *Modern Capitalist Planning: The French Model* (1969); JOHN and ANNE-MARIE HACKETT, *Economic Planning in France* (1963); V.C. LUTZ, *French Planning* (1965); GEOFFREY DENTON, MURRAY FORSYTH, and MALCOLM MACLENNAN, *Economic Planning and Policies in Britain, France and Germany* (1968); ANDREW SHONFIELD, *Modern Capitalism* (1965). For information on current economic developments, see the annual surveys published by the Organization for Economic Cooperation and Development, *Economic Surveys: France.*

Transportation: The two principal statistical sources relative to transport (both issued annually) are the *Annuaire statistique des transports* and the *Mémento de statistiques de la S.N.C.F.*

Administrative and social conditions: (*Constitutional framework*): MARCEL PRELOT, *Précis de droit constitutionnel*, 2nd ed. (1953), a good historical and judicial synthesis of French constitutions, with emphasis on the Fifth Republic; PIERRE AVRIL, *Le Régime politique de la Vᵉ République*, 2nd ed. (1966), very good political analysis of the regime; ANDRE CHANDERNAGOR, *Un Parlement pour quoi faire?* (1967), the constitutional regime seen by a member of Parliament; FRANCOIS MITTERAND, *Le Coup d'état permanent* (1965), the Gaullist regime as seen by an opponent. (*Local structures*): BRIAN CHAPMAN, *Introduction to French Local Government* (1953); HERVE DETTON and JEAN HOURTICQ, *L'Administration régionale et locale de la France*, 5th ed. (1968). (*Parties and political life*): STANLEY HOFFMANN et al., *In Search of France* (1963); ALEXANDER WERTH, *France: 1940–1955*, 2nd ed. (1966); DOROTHY M. PICKLES, *The Fifth French Republic*, 3rd ed. (1966); HENRY W. EHRMANN, *Politics in France*, 2nd ed. (1971); PHILIP M. WILLIAMS and MARTIN HARRISON, *De Gaulle's Republic* (1960); JACQUES CHAPSAL, *La Vie politique en France depuis 1940*, 2nd ed. (1969), an excellent work that puts events in their proper places; JEAN-PAUL CHARNAY, *Le Suffrage politique en France* (1965), on presidential and legislative elections and referendums; JEAN CHARLOT, *Le Phénomène gaulliste* (1970), discusses whether the Gaullist party is similar to other parties; EMERIC DEUTSCH, DENIS LINDON, and PIERRE WEILL, *Les Familles politiques aujourd'hui en France* (1966), a useful table of French political complexity. (*Justice*): ROGER AUBENAS et al., *La Justice* (1961); RAYMOND CHARLES, *La Justice en France*, 3rd ed. (1964). (*Army*): PAUL MARIE DE LA GORCE, *La République et son armée* (1963; Eng. trans., *The French Army*, 1963); RAOUL GIRARDET, PAUL M. BOUJU, and JEAN-PIERRE H. THOMAS, *La Crise militaire française, 1945–1962* (1964), a complete, serious, and critical account of French military policy. (*Public offices*): ANDRE DE LAUBADERE, *Manuel de droit administratif*, 9th ed. (1969), a remarkable work tool; ROGER GREGOIRE, *La Fonction publique* (1954), a historical and descriptive synthesis; LOUIS FOUGERE, *La Fonction publique* (1966); BERNARD GOURNAY, JEAN-FRANCOIS KESLER, and JEANNE SIWEK-POUYDESSEAU, *L'Administration publique* (1967); GERARD BELORGEY, *Le Gouvernement et l'administration de la France* (1967), descriptive; ANTOINE PROST, *Histoire de l'enseignement en France, 1800–1967* (1968), a very well-documented, predominantly sociological study. (*Police*): *La police en France*, special issue of the journal *La Nef* (1963), several juxtaposed analyses that give an overall glimpse. (*Education*): GERALD ANTOINE, *Réforme ou renaissance de l'université* in his and JEAN-CLAUDE PASSERONS, *La Réforme de l'université* (1966); FELIX PONTEIL, *Histoire de l'enseignement en France* (1966); BERNARD MEGRINE, *La Question scolaire en France* (1960), tells about the quarrel between Catholic and lay education. (*Housing*): GILLES EBRIK and PIERRE BARJAC, *Le Logement, dossier noir de la France* (1970), condemning report; CLAUDE ALPHANDERY, *Pour une politique du logement* (1965); ERIC G. HOWES, *Housing in Britain, France and Western Germany* (1965); GILBERT MATHIEU, *Peut-on loger les français?* (1965). (*Standard of living*): GERARD LYON-CAEN, *Les Salaires* (1967), a precise and complete account; JACQUES LECAILLON and JEAN MARCHAL, "Wage-Structure and the Theory of the Distribution of Income: The French Pattern," in EDWARD MAURICE HUGH-JONES (ed.), *Wage–Structure in Theory and Practice* (1966); ARMAND CAPOCCI, *La Hiérarchie des salaires* (1964). (*Social security and public health*): PIERRE LAROQUE (ed.), *Succès et faiblesse de l'effort social français* (1961), an overall study carried out by the creator of Social Security; and (ed.), *Les Institutions sociales de la France* (1963), a complete and well-documented report on French social, hospital, and health structures; GUY DELAMOTTE, *La Santé des Français* (1962), a discussion of serious diseases and health facilities; DELORS LEVY, *Réflexions sur l'avenir du système de santé: contribution à l'élaboration d'un politique sanitaire* (1970), an official point of view. (*Social classes*): PIERRE LAROQUE, *Les Classes sociales*, 4th ed. (1968), a good résumé.

Cultural life and institutions: DOMINIQUE and MICHELE FREMY, *Quid? Tout pour tous* (annual); PAUL GINESTIER and ANDRE MAILLET, *Culture et civilisation françaises* (1962); volumes on *Métiers* and *Loisirs* in the encyclopaedia *Clartés*, vol. 7–9 (1949); *Revue de l'Enseignement Supérieur* (quarterly); *Culture Française* (4/year); *France* in *Les Guides Bleus* series.

(H.B.-M./J.B.-G./Mi.B./F.B./C.De.)

France, History of

This article traces the history of France from the breakup of the Carolingian Empire to the present. For the history of France before the mid-9th century, see MEROVINGIAN AND CAROLINGIAN EMPIRE.

The article is divided into the following sections:

I. The emergence of France

The development of France as a nation was a long process, the first stage of which can be placed in the period between the division of the Carolingian Empire in the mid-9th century and the emergence of a powerful French monarchy at the end of the 12th century.

This period, which began with the separation of the West Frankish kingdom (approximately the area of present France) from the Frankish domains in what is now Germany, was marked by a fragmentation of political power and the development of feudalism. It was a time of violence but also one of renewal, during which the culture of the High Middle Ages was formed. These trends were reflected in the country's population: stagnant and perhaps even declining during the Viking invasions of the 9th and 10th centuries, it showed a slow increase after the mid-11th century and a rapid one in the 12th century. This returning vitality was accompanied by an increase in activity, political and otherwise.

FRENCH SOCIETY IN THE EARLY MIDDLE AGES

Religion and cultural life. In the second half of the 9th century the only unifying factor in France was the Christian religion. It was a Christianity generously admixed with ancient pagan beliefs, and its gospel of peace had little effect in the chaotic atmosphere caused by repeated invasions of the country by the Vikings from the north and by Muslim raiders from the Mediterranean. During the last years of the century, a reaction began to occur against the decadence into which the Carolingian Church had fallen. Under the leadership of a few gifted individuals, new life was instilled into the monastic movement, and the church hierarchy began to take responsibility for maintaining order and justice.

The monastic revival became centred at the Abbey of Cluny in Burgundy (founded in 910). The Cluny community restored observance of monastic discipline under the Benedictine rule and, with its daughter houses, inspired a religious reform movement that came to exert a profound influence on the whole Western Church in the 11th century. In France, where in the 12th century the Cistercian movement continued the work of the Cluniacs, the reformed monasteries helped to create an atmosphere of solidarity on all levels of society.

At the same time, the French Church, in the absence of any strong leadership from the declining Carolingian monarchy, took the lead in attempting to discourage warfare between the powerful feudal magnates who governed the country. Ecclesiastical legislation, such as the Peace of God and the Truce of God, which forbade fighting on certain days or during certain seasons of the year, was designed to limit violence and disorder and encourage a return to more stable conditions.

The religious revival and the limitation of warfare made possible, in the 11th century, a new flourishing of the arts, exemplified by the profusion of new churches in the Romanesque style. Much of this was not peculiarly French; similar developments were occurring contemporaneously in Germany and other parts of western Europe, where the monastic-centred cultural movement of the 10th and 11th centuries spread out in the 12th century to other sectors of society, manifesting itself in the revival of Roman law, the development of Scholastic thought, and the founding of new educational institutions. France did, however, play a unique part in this movement because of the fame of its monastic centres and, later, of its schools (*e.g.*, Chartres, Orléans, and especially Paris, the intellectual home of such great 12th-century masters as Peter Abelard and Peter Lombard).

In this period the various French dialects that had developed from the "vulgar Latin" language of the late Roman Empire began to assume a literary form and were used in poetry. These dialects belonged to two main groups: the Langue d'Oïl in the region north of the Loire River and the Langue d'Oc to the south. This division is an indication of the substantial cultural differences between the two regions. The Langue d'Oïl, which was the ancestor of modern French, developed a rather extensive literature in the 11th century (in such forms as the warlike poems called chansons de gestes) that gives a valuable picture of contemporary society.

Langue d'Oïl and Langue d'Oc

Economic life. As in most preindustrial societies, the main activity of the people was agriculture. Technical backwardness and the unsettled conditions of the early feudal regime tended to make each locality into a self-sustaining unit. Trade was limited to essential items such as salt. The pattern of landholding that emerged in northern France was, in the main, one of large estates or domains, each with a single proprietor (the lord). The typical domain was divided into the lord's portion and a number of smaller plots worked by hereditary tenants. The lord, in addition to the produce of his own portion (worked by the tenants), was entitled to a share of each tenant's own crop. Because he was the landowner, he exercised various rights over the people on his domain (free and slave) and had judicial, police, and military powers. This gave the great landowners, as a class, enormous influence and imposed upon society a hierarchy in which the lord played the dominant role. The feudal system in its classic form was really confined to the area north of the Loire. In southern France smaller landholdings survived, and urban life and the Roman law tradition never completely died out.

The feudal system of economy was not one that precluded change and development. As the population increased, new land was cleared, new villages were founded, and different forms of land tenure were introduced. In the 12th century, the feudal system began to change as the European economy revived and communications improved. Increased trade brought new forms of power that the feudal magnates could not always control. The monarchy made use of changed conditions to increase its own power at the expense of the nobles.

Feudal polity. Feudalism, in addition to being an economic system, was also, and perhaps primarily, a political system that developed out of the one that preceded it. Although it exhibited a certain amount of diversity in different areas, there was enough similarity to create a recognizable pattern throughout the country.

As early as the mid-9th century it was clear that the West Frankish monarchy would have difficulty in exercising any centralized control over the territory allotted to it at the partition of the Carolingian Empire, the partition itself having resulted from a breakdown of central authority. Added to the problems posed by slow communications were the disrupting effects of Viking raids, which reached as far inland as Paris in 845. Establishing themselves on an island at the mouth of the Loire, the Northmen attacked Bordeaux, Toulouse, Orléans, and Angers between 863 and 873. From a base in the Somme estuary, they pillaged Amiens, Cambrai, Reims, and Soissons. But the Seine was the main attraction. In 856–860 they laid waste to the country around its lower reaches and frequently attacked Paris in subsequent years. Sometimes they were turned back by effective defenses but more often by payment of tribute. After 896 the invaders began to settle permanently in the Lower Seine Valley, where they eventually formed the Duchy of Normandy. At the same time, the Mediterranean coast was plagued by Muslim attacks and occasionally by Vikings, though the threat there was less serious.

The inability of the monarchy to protect its territory soon led to the establishment of local defense systems. Before 900 the kings were already delegating authority to regional commanders for this purpose. These commanders were often great landowners in the districts where they were given control. They thus acquired great power; they were enabled to make their positions hereditary and to treat the areas under their control as their own possessions, using their delegated authority to advance their own interests. In the early 10th century these magnates built castles to defend their lands and exercised all the functions of government. Their domains formed the basic unit of the feudal polity, establishing a pattern of fragmented authority at the expense of the central power.

Feudalism did establish a kind of solidarity based on Feudal family ties and self-interest. Its internal structure was loyalties based on vassalage (the obligation owed by a lesser lord to a greater one in return for the right to a fief). As the rights conferred by possession of a fief nearly always consisted of control over landed property, the possessor sought to make it hereditary, thus stabilizing the relationship between lord and vassal from one generation to the next. The great lords were bound, at least nominally, to the king by ties similar to those which bound their vassals, thus completing a network of mutual loyalties.

The process of fragmentation continued until the middle and in some areas until the end of the 11th century, giving the political map of France the appearance of a complex mosaic. By the beginning of the 12th century, however, the trend was reversing itself; the great lords were able to assert greater control over their vassals,

whose economic difficulties cost them a certain loss of independence. The society as a whole felt the need for a more orderly kind of existence. Thus, the great fiefs once again resumed the unified appearance they had lost in the 10th century. The king, too, was able to begin re-establishing his authority.

Adapted from Ch. Petit-Dutaillis, *The Feudal Monarchy in France and England from the Tenth to the Thirteenth Century*; Barnes & Noble, Inc., and Routledge & Kegan Paul Ltd.

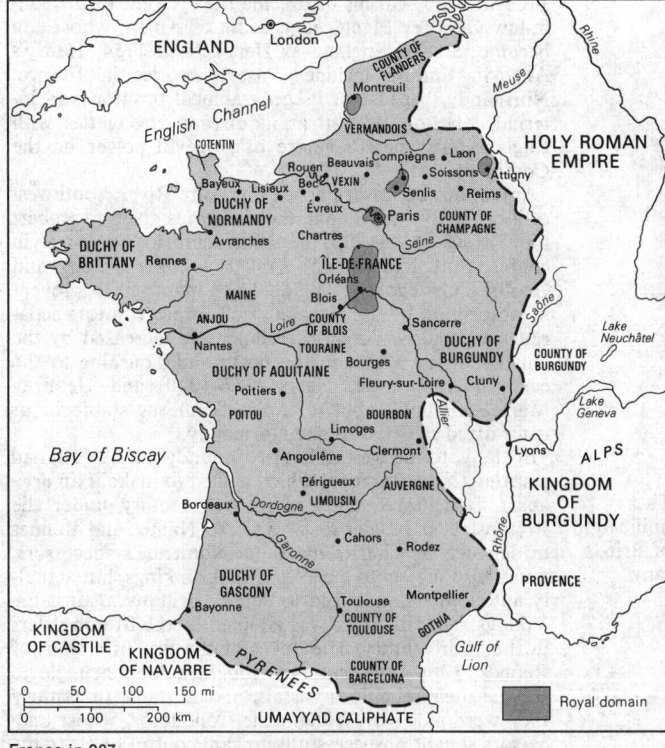

France in 987.

THE POLITICAL HISTORY OF FRANCE (C. 850–1180)

The principalities north of the Loire. Outside of the royal domain (centred around Paris), the principal territories of northern France in this period were Flanders, Normandy, Anjou, Brittany, Blois-Champagne, and Burgundy.

The northernmost of these was Flanders, where the   Flanders Carolingian king Charles the Bald installed his brother- and in-law, Baldwin Iron Arm, as count in 862. Under Bald- Normandy win's successors, Baldwin II (879–918), Arnulf (918–963), Arnulf II (965–988), Baldwin IV (988–1035), Baldwin V (1036–67), and Baldwin VI (1067–70), the county, which included part of what is now Belgium, was gradually extended eastward. By 1070 it was a powerful state with centralized institutions. Under Count Robert le Frison (1071–93), towns began to develop, and the woollen industry—the basis of Flanders' economy for the remainder of the medieval period—first became important. The direct line of Baldwin I became extinct in 1119, and there was a succession dispute following the death of Count Charles the Good (1127). Stability was restored by Thierry of Alsace (1128–68) and his son Philip (1169–91). At the end of the period, Flanders remained a major power in northern France.

The Duchy of Normandy was created in 911, when King Charles the Simple granted the area of the dioceses of Rouen, Lisieux, and Évreux to the Viking chieftain Rollo. In the following years, Rollo's successors, the Norman dukes, accepted Christianity and gradually extended their authority over the other lords of the region. Because the Carolingian king Lothair refused to recognize the Norman rule over Bayeux, Avranches, and the Cotentin, Duke Richard I (942–996) allied himself with Hugh Capet, who displaced the Carolingians and founded the Capetian dynasty in 987. Duke Richard II (996–1026) continued the Norman–Capetian alliance. Under Robert the Devil (duke 1027–35) Normandy expanded to the west, and under William the Conqueror (1035–87) it became the strongest and best governed fief in France. William's conquest of England (1066) made him a formidable rival to the French king. At the same time, Norman power was even further increased by the establishment of Norman states in Italy.

Divided between 1080 and 1106, Normandy and England were reunited under the Conqueror's grandson Henry I of England, who was duke of Normandy from 1106 to 1135. On his death, the duchy went to his son-in-law Geoffrey Plantagenet, count of Anjou, whose son became king of England as Henry II in 1154. Henry's Angevin Empire included vast territories in France. Normandy, because of its geographical position and internal cohesion, as well as its already strong ties with England, became the centre of Angevin power on the Continent.

Anjou, on the lower part of the Loire River, southwest of Normandy, was among the territories given to Robert the Strong in 866. In the 10th century, the Angevin counts, Fulk I (died 942), Fulk II (c. 942–c. 960), and Geoffrey Grisegonelle (c. 960–987), managed to prevent its absorption by the Normans and forged it into a separate principality. Anjou's territory was increased by the annexation of Maine to the north and Touraine to the east under Fulk III Nerra (987–1040) and Geoffrey Martel (1040–60), but it never became as stable or as centralized as Flanders and Normandy.

The
unification
of Brittany

Brittany, to the west of both Normandy and Anjou, had a strong Celtic tradition, which tended to make it an area apart. It achieved unity in the 9th century under the Breton leader Nomenoë, who seized Nantes and Rennes in defiance of Charles the Bald. Nomenoë's successors, nominally subject to the West Frankish kings, but actually autonomous, managed to defend Brittany against the Vikings. The title duke was adopted by the Breton rulers in the 10th century. The dukes of the line of Conan of Rennes (10th–12th centuries) fought a long struggle to subdue their rebellious vassals, and in the 11th century they were aided by William the Conqueror, whose successors sought unsuccessfully to gain control of Brittany. Duke Conan IV (1137–71) gave his daughter in marriage to Geoffrey, son of Henry II of England; Geoffrey succeeded Conan as duke in 1166; nevertheless, Brittany remained an independent entity until the end of the period.

The area around Blois, to the east of Touraine, was also entrusted to Robert the Strong and remained in the possession of his descendants until c. 940, when Thibaut the Old seized control of it and founded the line of the counts of Blois. His successors, Thibaut II, Eudes I, and Eudes II, annexed the counties of Sancerre (1015) and Champagne (1019–23), creating the House of Blois-Champagne. This aggregation achieved its greatest strength under Count Thibaut IV (II of Champagne, 1125–52); a formidable opponent of Kings Louis VI and Louis VII, Thibaut was one of the most powerful lords in France. This threat to the monarchy ended when Blois and Champagne were divided under Thibaut's sons.

French Burgundy, to the south of Champagne, was detached from the kingdom of Burgundy-Provence c. 880. Comprising the area between the Saône, the Loire, and the Upper Seine rivers, it came into the possession of the Capet family in the 10th century and remained under their control until 1361.

Thus, by the latter part of the 12th century, France north of the Loire was divided into a few large principalities (some of them associated with the English crown) coexisting with each other and with the French king, who lived in their midst.

The principalities of the south. The main territorial divisions that either existed or came into being south of the Loire in this period were Provence, Auvergne, Toulouse, and Aquitaine.

Provence, in what is now the southeasternmost part of France, was not part of the West Frankish domains; in 843 it was given to Lothair, brother of Charles the Bald. From 879 it formed the kingdom of Burgundy-Provence, whose crown was held by the rulers of Jurane Burgundy

in the 10th century and by the Holy Roman emperors in the 11th. Real power was in the hands of the local counts, who defended Provence against Muslim attacks. In the 12th century, the territory was divided between the counts of Toulouse and the counts of Barcelona.

Auvergne, centred around Clermont, though constituted as a county, remained a divided land throughout the period.

The County of Toulouse dated from 849; at that time, under Counts Frédelon (849–852) and Raymond I (852–c. 862), it included the areas around Toulouse and Rodez, some territory in the Pyrenees, and Limousin. The county became disunited after Raymond's death and remained so until the 11th century, when Counts William III Taillefer (died 1037) and Pons (1037–61) reunited it, extending their rule over much of central southern France. In the later 11th and the 12th century, Raymond IV (died 1105) and his successors gained the Crusader countship of Tripoli in Syria, but they were weakened at home by conflicts with the counts of Barcelona and the dukes of Aquitaine.

Aquitaine, which included most of western France south of the Loire, was a kingdom in the 9th century but became fragmented during the Viking invasions. In c. 950 Count William I of Poitiers assumed the title duke of Aquitaine. His successors extended their suzerainty over much of the region but failed to establish a centralized administration. Eleanor, daughter of Duke William X (died 1137), married Henry of Anjou, who became Henry II of England in 1154, and the duchy was controlled by the English crown after 1154.

English
control of
Aquitaine

None of the southern principalities had achieved much unity or cohesion by the late 12th century. This and the growing prevalence in southern France of the Cathar, or Albigensian, religious sect, condemned by the official church, made them vulnerable to the expanding Capetian monarchy in the succeeding period.

The monarchy. In 843 the three sons of the Carolingian emperor Louis I the Pious divided his empire among them. The western part of the Frankish realm (Francia Occidentalis) went to Charles the Bald.

Charles had to deal with opposition from his restless magnates, as well as the threat posed by Viking raids and the aggression of his brother Louis the German. He repelled an invasion by Louis in 858, but his assumption of the imperial crown in 878 distracted his attention from the west. It was in the subsequent period that he entrusted the defense of his kingdom to the magnates, demarcating great zones of military command that prefigured the feudal divisions of France. He sought alliances with those whom he was no longer able to crush; for example, with the Robertians, descendants of Robert the Strong and ancestors of the Capetian dynasty.

Before setting out on an expedition to Italy, Charles issued the capitulary of Quierzy-sur-Oise (877), in which he promised the magnates that during his absence no one would do anything to prejudice their position. This temporary provision, extremely favourable to them, was transformed into an inviolable principle by the magnates after Charles' death (October 877).

By force of circumstances feudalism had been established in the kingdom. Charles the Bald had had enough personal authority to withstand any unjust encroachments, and, moreover, he could rely on support of the church in so doing; but his successors were to prove incapable of following his example with success. The balance was again tilted in favour of the magnates, who now had military strength and vassals of their own.

The last Carolingians and the Robertian interventions (877–987). Charles the Bald's son and successor, Louis II le Bègue, or the Stammerer, died in 879, leaving the kingdom jointly to his sons Louis III (died 882) and Carloman; but when Carloman died (884) his half brother Charles III the Simple was an infant, and the West Frankish crown was taken by the East Frankish king and emperor, Charles III the Fat, only surviving son of Louis the German. Deposed by the East Franks in Germany in 887, Charles the Fat died in 888, whereupon the West Frankish magnates elected as king Eudes, son of Robert the Strong and the first of the Robertians to take the crown away from the Carolingian dynasty. In 893, however, Charles the Simple, with the support of some of the magnates, was crowned at Reims, and, thenceforward, he and Eudes were rivals until the latter's death in 898. It was Charles the Simple who had to allow the Northmen to settle permanently in northern France. A new revolt of the magnates led to the election of another Robertian, the brother of Eudes, to the kingship as Robert I in 922. After Robert I had been killed in battle against Charles in 923, his son-in-law Rudolph (Raoul) was elected in his place; and Charles the Simple was taken prisoner (to die in captivity in 929). Yet when Rudolph died in 936, the Robertian candidate for the crown, Hugh the Great, son of Robert I, stood aside for a Carolingian restoration in the person of Charles the Simple's son Louis IV, called d'Outremer ("from Overseas") because he had been a refugee in England since his father's deposition. Louis IV achieved much to revive the prestige of his dynasty and left the crown undisputed at his death to his son Lothair in 954. On Lothair's death in 986, the crown passed to his son Louis V le Fainéant, but, already, the Robertian Hugh Capet, son of Hugh the Great, was entertaining designs on the monarchy. Louis V's early death (987) was followed by the election of Hugh Capet as king, to the exclusion of the Carolingian pretender Charles, duke of Lower Lorraine, a younger son of Louis IV. The Carolingian dynasty in France was now definitively superseded by the Capetian heirs of the Robertian kings.

The election of Hugh Capet

Whatever their personal merits might sometimes have been, the Carolingians after 877 were at grips with a social evolution beyond their control. Occasionally, the prestige of the dynasty, strengthened by the support of the papacy, enabled the kings to prevail against their rivals, as Louis IV and his son Lothair did; but the royal house was impoverished and no longer had any property to distribute as the price for loyalty. The kings were merely tolerated or brought to power according to the interests of the great territorial princes in their quarrels with one another; for example, the dukes of Burgundy or of Normandy and the counts of Flanders.

Even so, the Carolingian dynasty had too much past glory to be left at the head of a kingdom now thoroughly feudalized. The transfer of the royal title to Hugh Capet in 987 was made largely because, despite the great extent of his inherited domain, he was the weakest of the territorial princes and could be expected to trouble no one.

The Capetians. The Capetian kings from 987 until 1180 were Hugh Capet (987–996), Robert II (996–1031), Henry I (1031–60), Philip I (1060–1108), Louis VI (1108–37), and Louis VII (1137–80). They succeeded to a thoroughly feudalized realm. To make themselves strong, the kings first needed to possess a wide domain and manifold rights allowing them to act in all parts of the kingdom. The royal domain was extended persistently, either by the king's fighting of rebellious lords openly or by his deft use of the rights permitted him as a sovereign such as confiscating fiefs and intervening in the rights of succession.

At the end of the 10th century the Capetians had only a diminutive domain, much smaller and weaker than that of many a great vassal. The essential nucleus of their lands was in the region of Paris, Orléans, Beauvais, Soissons, and Compiègne, though they also had various lands scattered all over the kingdom as well as numerous rights, the most important being that which the king exercised over episcopal churches and monasteries. The aim of the first Capetians was to control the regions within which there were royal lands; to achieve peace by reducing the plundering lords and petty vassals to obedience; and, in some circumstances, to increase their own possessions by confiscating the lands of factious vassals.

In their rise to power, the Capetians were supported by the dukes of Normandy and the counts of Anjou; but, once they had secured the crown, Hugh Capet and his successors found these and the other northern magnates to be dangerous rivals. Initially, they came into conflict with the counts of Blois; after the mid-11th century, their

chief opponents were the Normans and later the Angevins. Between 1154 and 1180, the English-based Angevin Empire, including a large, compact block of territory in France, was the principal check to the expansion of French monarchy. Philip I, Louis VI, and Louis VII did what they could to exploit rivalries among the magnates to their own advantage, but, although they were able to hold their own, they were not conspicuously successful in increasing the territorial possessions of the crown.

At the end of the 10th century, three elements of the rather weak royal administration existed side-by-side: the king and his household (his family and servants); the great officers of the realm; and the Curia Regis, a feudal court that theoretically brought together all the vassals to advise the king. For most of the 11th century, the influence of these institutions remained very limited, but after 1080 they began to evolve, partly in imitation of the bureaucratic structures that were emerging in the great fiefs.

Capetian institutions

In the traditional feudal sphere, the kings tried to improve the central administration and make better use of the court. The royal household was run by members of the royal family. The principal offices of the royal household (the constable, cupbearer, chamberlain, etc.) were, for the most part, reliable vassals from the Île-de-France. The most important exception was the seneschal (steward of the household), who was customarily a member of the count of Champagne's family. Because the king could not depend upon the seneschal's loyalty, Philip Augustus allowed the office to die out in 1191. The most important change involved the office of chancellor. Originally in charge of the royal chapel, the chancellor came to have the duty of recording and authenticating royal decrees. From the time of Louis VI, this officer was given important administrative responsibilities and became the head of a clerical staff on which the king placed great reliance. The 12th-century kings chose their chancellors with great care and saw to it that the office did not become hereditary.

Even more important than developing traditional institutions was the monarchs' skill in making use of gifted people in their service, people who might become influential without holding any particular office. An example of this was the position of Suger, abbot of Saint-Denis under Louis VI.

Outside the royal domain, the kings of this period had no administrative apparatus other than what belonged to them as feudal suzerains. The royal domain itself was administered by provosts (*prévôts*), who saw that its revenues reached the royal treasury and handled legal matters. The office of provost was hereditary in the 11th century, but Louis VII created new *prévôtés* (areas administered by provosts), thus increasing royal control and preparing the way for the later creation of the appointive office of bailiff.   (M.Pa.)

II. France, 1180 to c. 1490

FRANCE FROM 1180 TO 1328

The kings and the royal government. The French monarchy was greatly strengthened by Louis VII's successor, Philip II Augustus (ruled 1180–1223), who could claim descent from Charlemagne through his mother. Philip proved to be the ablest Capetian yet to reign. He was practical and clear-sighted in his political objectives; the extension of territorial power and the improvement of mechanisms with which to govern an expanded realm were his consistent policies. Perhaps it was not accidental that royal documents began to refer to the king of France (*rex Franciae*) instead of using the customary formula king of the Franks (*rex Francorum*) within a year or two of Philip's accession.

Philip Augustus. Philip's outstanding achievement was to wrest control from the Plantagenets of most of the domains they held in France. Intervening in struggles between Henry II of England and his sons, Philip won preliminary concessions in 1187 and 1189. He acquired strategic lands on the Norman borders following wars with Henry's sons, King Richard and King John (1196 and 1200). And when, in 1202, John failed to answer a

Territorial expansion

summons to the vassalic court of his lord, Philip Augustus confiscated his fiefs. Normandy, invaded in 1204, submitted to the Capetian in 1208. Maine, Anjou, and Touraine fell rapidly (1204–06), leaving only Aquitaine and a few peripheral domains in the contested possession of England. By the Truce of Chinon (September 18, 1214), John recognized the conquests of Philip Augustus and renounced the suzerainty of Brittany, although the complete submission of Poitou and Saintonge was to take another generation.

Philip's other acquisitions of territory, if less spectacular, were no less important for consolidating the realm. In the north he pressed the royal authority to the border of Flanders. Artois, which came under his control as a dowry with his first wife, was fully secured in 1212. Vermandois and Valois (1213) and the counties of Beaumont-sur-Oise and Clermont-en-Beauvaisis were annexed during his last years. On the southern limits of the Île-de-France Philip rounded out prior possessions in Gâtinais and Berry. Much of Auvergne, whose suzerainty had been ceded by Henry II in 1189, passed to royal control in 1214; while in the more distant south, Philip extended his influence by gaining lordship over Tournon, Cahors, Gourdon, and Montlaur in Vivarais. As the reign ended, only Brittany, Flanders, Champagne, Burgundy, and Toulouse, among great fiefs, lay outside the royal domain.

Because the territorial expansion was accomplished through traditional means—dynastic, feudal, and military—the curial administration was, outwardly, little changed. Household officers such as the butler and the constable continued to function as in the past. But Philip Augustus was even more suspicious of the seneschalship and chancellorship than his father had been; he allowed both offices to fall vacant early in his reign, entrusting their operations to lesser nobles or to clerics of the entourage. Although their activity is obscure, some of these men were beginning to specialize in justice or finance. The curia as such, however, remained undifferentiated; characteristically, the committee of regents, appointed in 1190 to hold three courts yearly while the King was absent on crusade, was expected to function both in justice and administrative review on those occasions. Prelates and nobles of the curia also served as counsellors; and enlarged councils convened, at the King's summons, on festivals or when major political or military issues were contemplated.

Innovations in royal administration
There were two considerable innovations in royal administration. First, the chancery began to keep better records of the King's activity. Documents were copied into registers before being sent out, and lists of churches, vassals, and towns were drawn up to inform the King of his military and fiscal rights. Clerks were recording the King's receipts and expenditures before (probably long before) 1202, the year for which the first written account survives.

Second, Philip acted early in his reign to secure better control of the domains he governed directly. He appointed members of his court to hold periodic local sessions, to collect extraordinary revenues, to lead military contingents, and to supervise the provosts. The new officers, called bailiffs (baillis), at first had no determined districts in which to serve (they resembled the circuit commissioners of Angevin government, whose office may have been the model for the Capetian institution). From the outset the bailiffs were paid salaries; they were more reliable than the provosts, who, by the later 12th century, generally farmed the revenues. In the newly acquired lands of the west and south, Philip and his successors instituted seneschals—functionaries similar to the bailiffs, but with recognized territorial jurisdiction from the outset.

Philip Augustus' policy toward his conquered domains was shrewd. He retained the deep-rooted customs and administrative institutions of such flourishing provinces as Anjou and Normandy; indeed, the superior fiscal procedures of Normandy soon exercised perceptible influence on Capetian accounting elsewhere. On the other hand, to secure the loyal operation of provincial insti-

tutions, Philip appointed men of his own court, typically the natives of the Île-de-France. It was a compromise that was to work well for generations to come.

Philip's relations with his subjects
The character of Philip's rule may likewise be deduced from his relations with the main classes of the population. A devoted son of the church, if not unswervingly faithful, he favoured the higher clergy in many of their interests. He opposed the infidels, heretics, and blasphemers; he supported the bishops of Laon, Beauvais, Sens, and Le Puy (among others) in their disputes with townspeople; and he granted and confirmed charters to monasteries and churches. Yet he was more insistent on his rights over the clergy than his predecessors had been. He required professions of fidelity and military service from bishops and abbots, cited prelates to his court, and sought to limit the jurisdiction of ecclesiastical courts. He supported papal policies or submitted to papal directives only to the extent that these were consistent with his temporal interests.

Toward the lay aristocracy, Philip Augustus acted energetically as suzerain and protector. Indeed, no Capetian was more fully the "feudal monarch." His war with John resulted from a breach of feudal law and was fought with feudal levies. As with ecclesiastical vassals, Philip insisted upon the service due from fiefs; he exploited the feudal incidents, notably relief and wardship; and he required his vassals to reserve their fealty for himself alone. He extended his influence by entering into treaties (*pariages*) with minor lords, often distant ones; and by confirming the acts of nobles, in numbers unprecedented, he recovered the force of the royal guarantee.

His policy toward the lesser rural and urban populations was to increase their loyalty and contribution to the crown without significantly reducing their dependence on the King and other lords. Philip offered his protection to exploited villages, and, especially during his early years, he confirmed existing "new towns," extended their privileges to other villages and otherwise favoured peasant communities. Townsmen, notably those in semiautonomous communes, gained confirmation of their charters; and the King created some new communes. Most of the latter were located in strategic proximity to the northern frontiers of the expanded royal domain (this fact, together with the obligations of service and payment specified in the charters, suggests that military motives were paramount in these foundations). More generally evident in these charters, as in others, was the desire to gain the political fidelity of a prospering class. At Paris Philip Augustus acted as did no other local lord to promote the civic interest: improving sanitation, paving streets, and building a new wall. Parisian burghers financed and administered these projects; they were associated in the fiscal supervision of the realm when the King went on crusade, but they were not favoured with a communal charter.

Civic improvements

Louis VIII. The reign of Louis VIII (ruled 1223–26) had an importance out of proportion to its brevity. It was he (husband of the formidable Blanche of Castile and father of famous sons) who first brought Languedoc under the crown of France and who inaugurated the appanages—grants of property to members of the royal family or royal favourites—through which the expanded France of later generations was to be governed. The conquest of Languedoc, following the Albigensian Crusade (against heretics in southern France) that was only tepidly supported by Philip Augustus, was not complete until the 1240s, but the royal seneschalsies of Beaucaire and Carcassonne were already functioning when Louis VIII died. And it was in keeping with that ruler's will of 1225 that the great appanages passed to his younger sons as they came of age—Artois to Robert in 1237; Poitou, Saintonge, and Auvergne to Alphonse in 1241; and Anjou and Maine to Charles in 1246.

Louis IX. The real successor to Philip Augustus, however, was his grandson, Louis IX (ruled 1226–70), in whose reign were fulfilled some of the grand tendencies of prior Capetian history.

Louis IX, who was canonized in 1297, is the best known Capetian ruler. He impressed all who came in touch with him, and the records of his reign—anecdotal and historical as well as official—leave no doubt that he commanded affection and respect in a combination and to an extent that were unique. He regarded himself as a Christian ruler, duty bound to lead his people to salvation. He led by example, precept, and correction. He earned a reputation for fairness and wisdom that enabled him to rule as absolutely as he wished; only with the crusade, perhaps, did his judgment falter. His reign was marked by consolidation, maturation, and reform rather than by innovation.

Louis IX's territorial acquisitions

In his early years baronial revolts, supported by Henry III of England, were put down by the regency, headed by the Queen Mother, with singular firmness and skill. Poitou and Saintonge remained restive largely because of the stubborn machinations of Isabella of Angoulême (King John's widow); and it was only in 1243, after a revolt planned to coincide with an uprising in Languedoc, that the feudal adjudication of 1202 was fulfilled in Aquitaine. The revolt of Raymond Trencavel, dispossessed heir to the viscounty of Béziers, halfheartedly supported by Raymond VII of Toulouse, was no more successful; its failure resulted in the vindictive destruction of the petty nobility of Languedoc, and many fiefs thereupon passed to the crown.

Such were the principal territorial acquisitions of Louis IX; but the balance of his work was to be affected further by three characteristic events. First, despite his victory of 1243, Louis remained disposed to compromise with Henry III; and in the Treaty of Paris (December 1259) Henry regained feudal title to lands and reversionary rights in Guyenne in exchange for renouncing all claims to Normandy, Anjou, Maine, Touraine, and Poitou. Similarly, by the Treaty of Corbeil (May 1258) Louis himself had abandoned ancient claims to Catalonia and Roussillon in exchange for the renunciation of Aragonese rights in Gévaudan and Rouergue. Meanwhile, upon the death of Raymond VII in 1249 the county of Toulouse had passed to Raymond's son-in-law, Alphonse of Poitiers, who proceeded to govern it as effectively as his appanage lands; and when he and his wife died without issue in 1271, their enormous inheritance reverted to the royal domain.

The ancient household administration died out in the 13th century. Offices such as the chancery and treasury became more specialized and bureaucratic, while the greater advisory personnel formed a fluctuating corps of reliable favourites: bishops, abbots, and minor nobles of the old Capetian homelands. The counsellors, meeting in diverse political and ceremonial capacities, continued to assemble with other prelates and barons during festivals or ad hoc. But the fiscal and judicial activities of the court were growing in volume and technicality. Ordinary revenues expanded apace with the royal domains; taxes ceased to be exceptional. Toward 1250, judgments of the curia began to be recorded centrally; and the judicial sessions, now often called Parlements, derived an ever-expanding jurisdiction from the King's repute.

Meanwhile, a real local administration evolved as the bailiffs and seneschals became well established in territorial circumscriptions. Complaints arose when these men, and more particularly their subordinate officers, abused their powers for personal profit or the King's. Commissions of investigation, first appointed in 1247, provided means for redress; and these investigators continued to function after Louis returned from his first crusade in 1254.

Domestic policies of Louis IX

Although previous rulers had legislated on occasion, Louis IX was the first to express his will regularly in statutory form. A great ordinance for administrative reform in 1254 resulted from the remedial inquiries. In other enactments, characteristically moral and authoritarian, Louis sought to curb private warfare (about 1258) and to promote the use of royal money while limiting that of baronial (1263–65).

Toward the clergy Louis IX manifested a sympathy born of conservatism and exceptional piety, but he was nonetheless a firm master. He opposed efforts to expand clerical jurisdictions. During his later years he supported papal taxes on the clergy for the Crusade, although in the 1240s he had joined his clergy in opposing papal preferments and impositions for a war against the Holy Roman emperor Frederick II. The lay nobles found Louis IX a frustrating ruler. Sharing few of their values, his consistent policy was to limit their ability to cause disorder. He allowed royal officials to encroach on baronial jurisdiction in many cases, and he welcomed appeals from baronial judgments. On the other hand he respected such rights as were sanctioned by provincial custom and was less forceful in exploiting feudal relationships than his grandfather had been.

The royal interest in order and justice was especially beneficial to townsmen and peasants, who had most suffered from overzealous administrators and private war. Louis IX confirmed municipal charters; but he also taxed the towns heavily, and when oligarchical urban governors mismanaged finance to the disadvantage of the lower classes as well as the King, he moved energetically (1259–62) to place the fiscal administration of 35 communes directly under the crown. A peasant crusade known as the Pastoureaux (1251) was inspired by loyalty to the King, then in trouble in the Holy Land; when its impulse was dissipated in agitation against the propertied classes, the regent had it suppressed.

Later Capetians. Louis IX was succeeded by his son, Philip III (ruled 1270–85); his grandson, Philip IV the Fair (ruled 1285–1314); and three great-grandsons, Louis X (ruled 1314–16), Philip V (ruled 1316–22), and Charles IV (ruled 1322–28). The greatest of these last Capetian reigns was that of Philip IV. Worldly and ambitious, yet pious and intelligent, he was less accommodating than his forebears, more devoted to his power than to his reputation. He brought the monarchy to a degree of coordinated strength it was not again to have in the Middle Ages. But in so doing, he strained the resources and patience of his subjects. His sons had to give in to the demands of a tired country but did so without abandoning their father's objectives. When Charles IV died without male heir in 1328, as his brothers had done before him, the royal succession was claimed by a collateral Capetian family.

These reigns were marked by further territorial consolidation. Marrying his son to the heiress of Champagne and Navarre in 1284, Philip III prepared the way for a reversion no less important than that of Toulouse (1271). Philip the Fair secured the heiress to the county of Burgundy for his son Philip in 1295 and annexed southern Flanders and Lyons in 1312. Smaller acquisitions, cumulatively of great importance, resulted from purchase: the counties of Guînes (1281), Chartres (1286), La Marche and Saintonge (1308); the viscounties of Lomagne and Auvillars (1302) and La Soule (1306); and a number of untitled lordships.

Further territorial consolidation

Through treaties, Philip the Fair extended his jurisdiction into the ecclesiastical principalities of Viviers, Cahors, Mende, and Le Puy. With his greatly expanded domain, the King could assert unprecedented authority everywhere in France. Yet it does not appear that territorial policy as such had changed. Appanages were still to be granted and to be recovered by the later Capetians. The monarchs continued to do without Brittany, Burgundy, and many lesser lordships, which did not prevent them from legislating for these lands along with the rest.

Government became more engrossing, specialized, and efficient. Although the royal curia continued to exist as an aggregate of favourites, magnates, prelates, and advisers, its ministerial element—comprising salaried officers serving at the king's pleasure—functioned increasingly in departments. The small council acquired definition from an oath first mentioned in 1269. Parlement, its sessions lengthening under a growing burden of cases, was divided into chambers of pleas, requests, and investigations (1278), and its composition and jurisdiction were regulated. Older provincial tribunals, such as the Norman Exchequer and the Jours of Troyes, became commissions of Parlement. While the direction of finance was left with the council, the Chambre des Comptes, apart from the treasury, was organized to audit accounts.

Council and chamber as well as Parlement developed appropriate jurisdiction, and all three bodies kept archives. The chancery, serving all departments, remained in the hands of lesser functionaries until 1315, when Louis X revived the title of honour.

Local administration was marked by the proliferation of officers subordinate to the bailiffs and seneschals. The chief judge (*juge-mage*) assumed the seneschal's judicial functions in the south; receivers of revenues, first appearing in Languedoc, were instituted in the bailiwicks at the end of the 13th century. Commissions of investigation continued to traverse the provinces under the later Capetians, but all too often they now functioned as fiscal agents rather than as reformers.

Many of the officers who served Philip the Fair were laymen, and many were lawyers. Impressed with the power they wielded, they promoted loyalty to the crown and a conception of the royal authority approaching that of sovereignty. Without claiming absolute power for the King, they thought in terms of his "superiority" over all men within national boundaries now (for the first time) strictly determined; and they did not hesitate to argue from Roman law that when the "state of the kingdom" was endangered, the monarch had an overriding right to the aid of all his subjects in its defense. While this doctrine, in a notorious case, was made a justification for imposing on the clergy, the later Capetians did not lose the religious mystique they had inherited from their predecessors' efforts in Christian causes. Even as political loyalties were being engrossed by the lay state, the "religion of monarchy" derived impetus from the fervent utterance of those who saw in Philip the Fair a type of Christ or the ruler of a chosen and favoured people.

It was in the requirements of war and finance that the claims of the monarchy found most concrete expression. In the 1270s, for his campaigns in the south, Philip III requested military aid from men hitherto exempt from such service. Philip the Fair, renewing these demands for his wars in Gascony and Flanders, went so far as to claim the military obligation of all free men as the basis for taxing personal property. The most persistent and lucrative taxation after 1285 was that imposed on the clergy, generally in the form of tenths and annates; sales taxes, customs, tallages on Jews and foreign businessmen, and forced loans likewise supplemented older revenues of the domain to support increased administrative expenses as well as costs of war. The most unpopular fiscal expedients were the revaluations of coinage after 1295, by which the King several times increased the profits of his mints to the confusion of merchants and bankers. The imbalance between ordinary resources and the needs of an expanding government became chronic at the end of the 13th century; yet in spite of the statist arguments of their lawyers, none of the later Capetians was moved to regard taxation as an established and justified requirement of a national government.

That is one reason why, with momentary lapses, the strongest of the later Capetians was not regarded as an arbitrary ruler. Philip the Fair revered St. Louis (Louis IX) as much as did his people; like Louis he took counsel from a relatively few unrepresentative persons. But when Philip's own policies broke with the past, he resorted to great councils and assemblies, not so much to commit the nation as to justify his course. Whether a tax was sanctioned by custom or not, even if approved by assembled magnates or townsmen, he had it negotiated —re-explained and collected—in the provinces and localities. Large central assemblies in 1302, 1303, 1308, and 1312 met to enable the King and his ministers to arouse political support for his measures against the Pope or the Knights Templars (see below). Among these were the earliest national assemblies to include representatives of towns and villages, a fact that has caused historians to classify them with the Estates-General. Under Philip the Fair and his sons, however, these convocations were not yet understood to be representative of the estates of society; only when Philip V began to summon northern and southern men separately to deliberate on fiscal matters were the estates (which made up the

Estates-General) in any way anticipated. Almost simultaneously the provincial estates were foreshadowed in the petitions of magnates and towns in several regions for relief from administrative violations of traditional privilege; but the resulting charters of 1314–15 were poorly coordinated and reactionary, and they did little to limit royal power, although the fiscal rights later claimed by the estates of Normandy could be traced to the Norman Charter of 1315.

If the policies of Philip the Fair evoked the complaint of all classes of people, it was because he had favoured none in particular; in fact, except in war and finance, the later Capetians may be said to have maintained a traditional politics toward both the nobles and towns. With the church, however, it was otherwise. Philip the Fair's insistence on taxing the clergy for defense led immediately to his conflict with Pope Boniface VIII. The latter, in the bull *Clericis laicos* (1296), issued on the protest of French and English prelates, forbade the payment of taxes by clergymen to lay rulers without papal consent; but Philip's anger and his political arguments divided the clergy, and the Pope soon found it necessary to abandon his position.

The quarrel was renewed in 1301, when the King and the magnates accused the Bishop of Pamiers of treason and heresy. Boniface rebuked Philip for seizing clerical property and debasing the coinage, among other things, and he summoned French prelates to Rome to proceed with a reform of the kingdom. Once again the clergy was split; many bishops and abbots attended an assembly at Paris in 1302 where they joined men of the other estates in addressing a remonstrance to the Pope. A year later the King adopted rougher tactics: in June 1303 many prelates acquiesced in a scheme to try the Pope before a general council, and in September the King's envoy Guillaume de Nogaret and his accomplices seized Boniface at Anagni. When the aged pope died a month later, his audacious policy collapsed entirely. The Gascon Pope Clement V (reigned 1305–14) moved the Holy See to Avignon, and a mass of his compatriots were appointed cardinals. With this pliant pontiff, the way was cleared for the strangest act of violence of the reign— the destruction of the Templars, founded during the Crusades. The Templars were aged men whose privileges seemed poorly justified after the fall of the Holy Land. But Philip's case was pressed relentlessly beyond the evidence brought forth; the King had to resort to propaganda in a vast assembly held at Tours in 1308, and it was only in 1312 that the Pope, his scruples overcome by expediency, dissolved the order. The Templars' possessions were given to the Hospitallers, and their last dignitaries were imprisoned or executed.

Foreign relations. France assumed a more active role in the politics of Christian Europe from the end of the 12th century. Philip Augustus led French contingents on the most fully international of the great Crusades (1190–91), although having once demonstrated his energy in that work of piety he could not afterward be persuaded to renew his vow. He preferred, through dynastic schemes and opportunism, to exploit his rivalry with the Plantagenets. His ambition seems to have embraced England as early as 1193, when he married Ingeborg, whose brother, the King of Denmark, had an old claim to the throne of England. When Philip repudiated Ingeborg, she and her brother appealed to the Pope; and her case, punctuated by reconciliations with Philip dictated more by policy than by sentiment, dragged on through the pontificate of Innocent III.

Meanwhile, in 1200 Philip's son Louis married Blanche of Castile, granddaughter of Henry II, through whom another claim to England was heralded. Louis's career as prince was marked by aggressive designs against King John. Innocent III was prepared to recognize Louis as king of England in 1213; and the policy was dropped only after Louis's abortive invasion of 1216–17.

It was in the play of rival coalitions that Philip Augustus had his greatest diplomatic anxiety and success. To John's alliance with Otto of Brunswick, his nephew and claimant to the empire, Philip countered by supporting a

Royal
authority
of Philip
the Fair

Destruction
of the
Templars

second claimant, Philip of Swabia. When Otto became emperor in 1209 and the counts of Flanders and Boulogne were alienated from their Capetian suzerain, Philip found himself seriously threatened in his northern heartlands. John's drive to avenge the loss of his French fiefs matured in 1214; he himself led a force from the west, and his major allies marched on Paris from the north. Philip Augustus met the allied forces at Bouvines in July 1214 and won a decisive victory. As John retreated and his coalition collapsed, there could be no doubt that Capetian France had achieved hegemony in Christian Europe.

Diplomacy of Louis IX
Louis IX acted astutely, though in ways unlike his grandfather's, to preserve the prestige of France. His treaties with Aragon and England, designed to extend and secure his domains, resulted from a cordiality better appreciated abroad than by the royal counsellors. From Navarre and Lorraine as well as from within the realm were brought disputes for his judgment; and in the Mise of Amiens (1264) Louis responded to the appeal of Henry III and the English barons to pronounce on the validity of the Provisions of Oxford (a written agreement between the King and magnates in England to reform the state of the realm). But the more absorbing issues of Louis's diplomacy lay in the east. He resisted papal urgings to take sides against Frederick II, believing in the equal legitimacy of empire and papacy. On the other hand, he allowed his brother Charles of Anjou to accept the crown of Sicily from the Pope; and for this enterprise, as for his own crusades, he allowed the papacy to tax the French clergy. His paramount foreign interest was to recover the Holy Places for Christ (a traditional ambition characteristically associated in his mind with the hope of converting the infidel: the Mongols or the Emir of Tunis).

Louis IX first took the cross in 1244, upon learning that a Turkish–Egyptian coalition had driven the Christians of the Levant back to precarious coastal positions. His expedition, well planned and well financed, set out in 1248, only to founder in Egypt within a few months. Louis himself was captured; upon his release, he spent four years in Syria in support of the Christian cause. He renewed his crusader's vow in 1267, in circumstances clouded by Angevin–Sicilian politics. Persuaded in secret by Charles, whose inordinate Mediterranean ambitions had little in common with the traditional crusade, the new expedition was diverted to Tunis. It broke up there with the King's death in 1270.

The prestige of France in Christendom lost little from these failures of Louis IX. Nor was it generally foreseen that Aquitaine and Sicily would become battlegrounds in the future. The apparent strength of his father's diplomacy precluded Philip III from changing it, even though circumstances had changed. When the misrule of Charles of Anjou caused the Sicilians to revolt in favour of Peter III of Aragon (1282), a test of the Angevin policy could no longer be deferred. Charles's friend Pope Martin IV (reigned 1281–85) excommunicated the King of Aragon and offered the vacant throne to Philip for one of his sons. Because at this juncture the crown of Navarre was destined for Philip the Fair, the whole Spanish March seemed ripe for recovery by the French. Yet the crusade against Aragon, blatantly political and impractical, came to a catastrophic end: the King himself died as his battered forces staggered out of Catalonia (October 1285). Charles of Anjou and Martin IV also died in 1285. Understandably, Philip the Fair, who had foreseen the folly of the ill-conceived attack on Aragon, ceased to permit his Mediterranean concerns to dominate his foreign policy. The issue over Sicily dragged on, but minor Capetian interests in the Pyrenees and in Castile were allowed to lapse.

Extension of French influence to the north and east
The extension of French influence and domain toward the north and east resulted from resourceful diplomacy at the expense of the empire. Philip's interest in that direction was emphasized when his sister married the son of Albert I of Germany and when he proposed first his brother and later his son as candidates for the imperial title. But it was against the English holdings in France that Philip exercised his most aggressive and portentous diplomacy.

Questions over spheres of administrative rights in Aquitaine had been creating tensions for many years. By the Treaty of Amiens (1279) the Agenais, whose status had been left in doubt when Alphonse of Poitiers died, passed to Edward I of England, who also had unsettled claims in Quercy. Serious conflict was precipitated in 1293, when clashes between French and English seamen caused Philip the Fair to summon his vassal to Parlement. When Gascon castles occupied by the French as part of the settlement were not returned to the English on schedule, Edward renounced his homage and prepared to fight for Aquitaine. The war that ensued (1294–1303) went in favour of Philip the Fair, whose armies thrust deep into Gascony. Edward retaliated by allying with Flanders and other northern princes. His dangerous campaign, concerted with the Count of Flanders in 1297, met defeat from a French force led by Robert of Artois, and during a truce from 1297 to 1303 the rival monarchs re-established the status quo ante. Edward married Philip's sister, and a marriage was projected between the prince Edward and Philip's daughter.

The heated residue of this first war was to be the chronic insubordination of Flanders. The Count having submitted and been imprisoned, it was left to the Flemish burghers to revolt against the French garrisons, and the French knights suffered a terrible defeat at Courtrai in July 1302. Thereafter, the tide turned, but only in 1305 could a settlement satisfactory to the King be reached; even then it proved impossible to win full ratification from the Flemish townsmen, whose resistance remained an invariable factor in the latent hostility between France and England.

In 1320 Philip V obtained Edward II's personal homage, but friction was increasing in Gascony again. When Edward refused to do homage to Charles IV, an old issue relating to French rights in Saint-Sardos (in Agenais) flamed into a war that once again went in favour of the French. By the Treaty of Paris (March 1327) France recovered Agenais and Bazadais and imposed a heavy indemnity on England; but a number of issues were left unresolved. Meanwhile, having married the emperor Henry VII's daughter, Charles was tempted to negotiate for the vacant imperial title in 1324; but nothing came of this. The last Capetians, troubled at home, retained their international standing among neighbouring states no less troubled.

Economy, society, and culture in the 13th century.
The primary social fact of this period is the continued growth of population. All indicators suggest growth—e.g., expansion of old towns, founding of new villages, the rising price of land—but no exact measurements are possible. A register of hearths dating from 1328 has been estimated variously to point to a total population of 15,-000,000 to 22,000,000; the total was probably slightly reduced after a crest toward the end of the 13th century. By the 1280s large portions of France had enjoyed many years of relative security and prosperity, even though private warfare had not disappeared, despite royal prohibitions. Brigandage seems actually to have worsened in the south earlier, around 1200, and the ravages and massacres of the Albigensian Crusade made Languedoc an insecure frontier for another generation (though it does not appear that the Inquisition seriously disrupted urban or rural prosperity after 1230 or so).

Population growth

The broad tendencies of social change were in keeping with political and institutional progress. The conjugal family became better recognized: Roman and especially canon law favoured its authority over the wider solidarities of clan or kin (extended family); rulers made the hearth a basis of fiscal responsibility. While mercantile practice discouraged customary restrictions on transactions, the right of repurchase by some member of the extended family (*retrait lignager*) held out in most areas of France. Meanwhile, a new territorial solidarity of great potential significance was developing: that of the legal estate or class. This was associated with the growth of towns and fostered by the consolidation of provincial

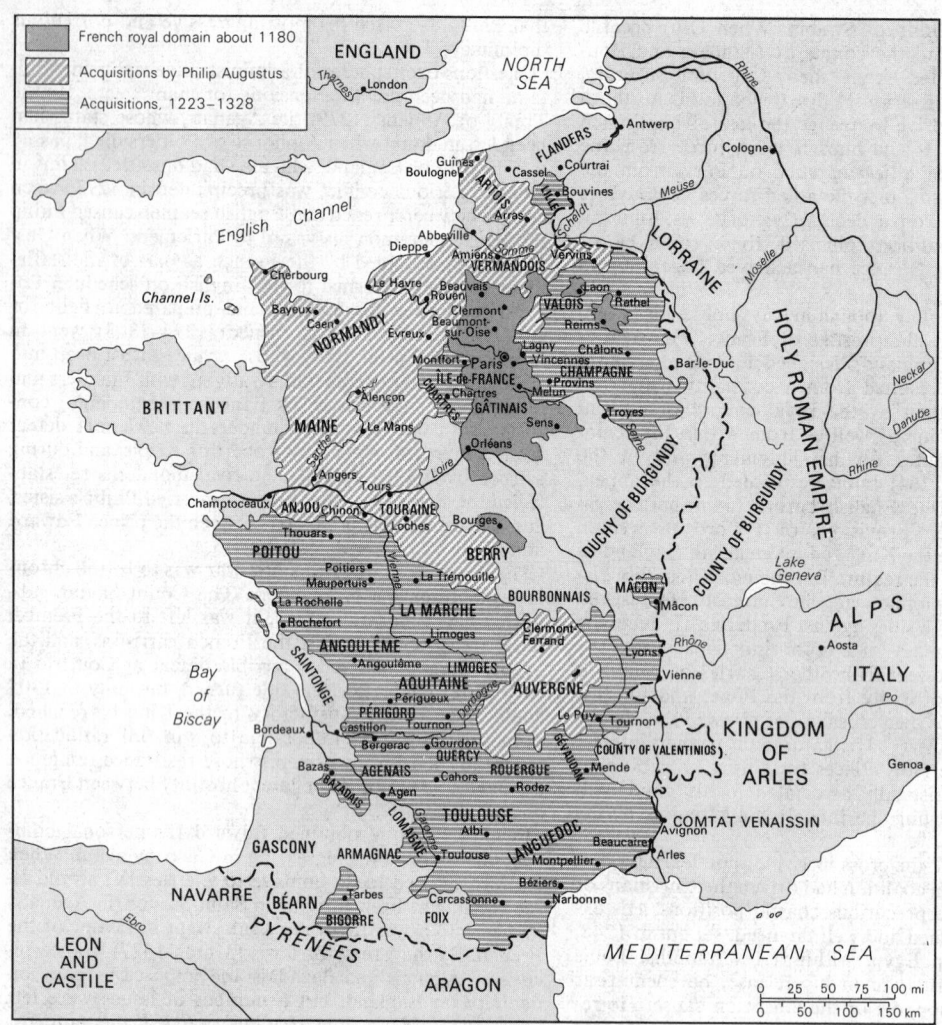

The growth of the French royal domain, 1180–1328.

custom and the fiscal impositions of count, bishop, or king. Already in 12th-century Flanders, knights (or towns) of the countryside were acting politically; and the convocation of men from these incipient estates of society occurred elsewhere in France and more often during the 13th century. Social mobility remained considerable in spite of tendencies to restrict the ranks of urban patrician or rural noble.

Urban prosperity. Town life continued to flourish. A few places, favoured by political and ecclesiastical as well as by economic circumstances, grew far larger than the rest. Paris could probably count more than 100,000 inhabitants by the late 13th century, possibly many more than that; some great provincial centres—e.g., Toulouse, Bordeaux, Arras, Rouen—may have surpassed 25,000, but most of the older cities grew more modestly. Jewish communities, which existed almost everywhere, were especially important in the towns of Champagne and Languedoc. Immigration from the countrysides probably increased as peasants sought better opportunities and independence; yet the towns remained somewhat indistinct in appearance and activity from their rural surroundings. Many urban properties had agrarian attachments, often within the walls; Paris itself was, to a surprising extent, an aggregation of expanded villages. Nevertheless, the progress of commerce, together with an important ancillary development of industry, chiefly accounts for urban prosperity in the 13th century.

The trades not only grew in volume but also became more diversified and specialized. New markets, often regional ones, arose to supplement the older centres that had developed on the basis of the long-distance exchange of relatively high-priced imperishables. Regional markets featured such agrarian staples as grains and wines as well as animals, cloth, weapons, and tools, and they facilitated the currency of foreign produce, such as glassware or spices. An increasing reliance on coinage or on monetary values may be connected with these provincial trades; sensitivity to the intrinsic values of the many French coinages was increasing everywhere toward 1200, even in the hinterlands away from main trading routes. In the late 13th century the need for money in denominations larger than the age-old penny (denarius)—primarily for use in the great commercial centres—caused Louis IX to issue the *gros tournois* (worth 12 pennies) and the gold coin (which, however, had little importance before the 14th century). A gradual long-term inflation tended to favour commercial activity.

The towns of northern France, notably in Artois, Burgundy, the Île-de-France, and especially in Champagne, prospered not only from regional exchange but also from the great overland trades connecting Normandy, England, the Baltic, and the Low Countries with the cities of Italy. The fairs of Champagne, becoming the leading entrepôt of European merchants, reached their apogee in the 13th century. Favoured by the count's privilege, the traders operated at Lagny or at Bar, or—in greater numbers—at Provins and at the "warm fair" of Troyes in June; the "cold fair" of Troyes ended the yearly cycle in October. The fairs were designated as occasions for payment and repayment, contributing significantly to the progress of banking and business accounting.

Enlarged and more diversified demand encouraged urban growth and prosperity. Townsmen were eating better: in the north, at least, the per capita consumption of meat, butter, and cheese, as well as of spices, seems to

Commerce and industry

have increased in the 13th century; as for wine, not only was more being drunk but the taste for *vins de qualité* became more acute, and the great regional vintages, notably that of Gascony, were established. Townspeople furnished their houses more amply than in the past (lamps, wooden chests, and draperies came into common use), and they produced more articles themselves.

The progress of industry, in fact, was a remarkable feature of the 13th century. Crafts in metal, wood, leather, and glass expanded in such large towns as Paris; clothwork—weaving, dyeing, fulling—prospered in regional centres such as Toulouse, with specialities in fine cloths concentrated in Artois and Flanders. In most places, however, the crafts remained in the shadow of commercial enterprise, in which the greater fortunes continued to be made. Artisanal associations proliferated everywhere; often termed brotherhood (*confratria, confraternitas*), they fostered new urban and suburban solidarities for charitable and ceremonial purposes as well as promoting economic interests.

Urban society became more competitive and more stratified. At Lyons, Bordeaux, and elsewhere, some fortunes were well enough established, usually from commerce, to enable their possessors to live as landlords, build stone houses, buy rural property, and aspire to titles of nobility. This patriciate, despite occasional setbacks at the hands of "new men," dominated municipal governments, acting as mayors and magistrates (*échevins*) in the north or as consuls in the south. While not altogether self-serving—they supported civic projects such as the building or decorating of churches—they were disinclined to share power or fiscal responsibility. Below them, often as their tenants or debtors, were small entrepreneurs, middlemen in trade (or between local industry and regional trade), master craftsmen, and bankers; and below all—and increasingly restive—was a swelling class of impoverished artisans, servants, vagabonds, and beggars.

Rural life. Rural life changed more gradually. The expanding markets favoured well-endowed or efficient lords or peasants who could produce a surplus of goods for sale. Such conditions were less common in the south than in the north, although they could be found in most wine-producing areas. But while rising prices benefitted producers, they contributed to certain difficulties in the countryside. Fixed revenues in coin proved an unsatisfactory alternative to payments in kind, which landlords specified when new land was put under cultivation. Moreover, needs and tastes became more expensive and tended to exceed aristocratic resources; lavish generosity continued to be an admired and practiced virtue, and costly crusades—occasionally lapsing into speculative adventures—continued to be launched. Larger lordships began to employ salaried estate managers, while in the south the division of landed fortunes among numerous heirs resulted in a multiplied and impoverished petty nobility. Many rural landlords fell into debt in the 13th century. And as wealth and nobility became less correlated, some nobles, especially those hard pressed, sought to close ranks against the intrusion of new men or creditors. They insisted on noble birth as a condition for knighthood, while reserving the designation of "squire" (or *donzel*, in the south) for those of noble birth awaiting or postponing the expensive dubbing (*adoubement*). At the upper extreme a noble elite, the barons, achieved recognition in administration and law.

Peasant societies also became stratified. Men unable to set aside a surplus against times of famine and those who had to borrow or rent their tools or teams found it difficult to avoid dependence on other men. In some areas serfdom was renewed, or confirmed, as jurists interpreted the more stringent types of peasant obligation in the light of the revived Roman law of slavery. But here again economic and legal status did not necessarily coincide. Rich peasants who employed other men to drive their teams could be found in any village; such people as the mayor, the lord's provost, and the peasant creditor established themselves as a rural elite, whose resources insured them against calamity and opened up diverse opportunities in prospering regional economies. Where enfranchisement

occurred, the lord usually received a good payment; even when servility persisted, there was a tendency to commute the arbitrary tallage into fixed common sums. New villages continued to be established, especially in the south, where many existent communities of peasants also received charters of elementary liberties—typically including the commuted tallage—in the 13th and early 14th centuries. In many cases, notably in Gascony, security, or defense, seems to have been the chief motive behind these foundations.

These conditions notwithstanding, the manor, or *seigneurie*, resisted fragmentation. The favourable market for grain and the psychological attachment of lords to their fathers' possessions preserved demesne land as the chief source of seigneurial income through the 13th century. Nor were labour services given up, although the discrepancy increased between work owed and work needed. Accordingly, lords resorted to paid seasonal labour, so that the margin between profit and loss became a more critical calculation than in the past. A new alternative was to lease the demesne to paid managers or sharecroppers, but this practice spread more slowly in France than in neighbouring countries. Whether lords had demesnes and servile tenants or not, the association between landlordship and power remained close. Tenancies or properties smaller than the old *mansus* appeared everywhere, but especially in the north, where horsepower and three-field crop rotations were making possible a more productive agriculture. The burgeoning viticultures of Burgundy and Gascony proved incompatible with traditional demesne lordship and encouraged sharecropping and peasant initiative. Innovation was less common in the uplands of the centre and south, where the manse tended to retain its identity and fiscal utility.

Religion. Whether in countryside or town, the lay person's touch with Christ became more personal, more direct. It was a widely shared conviction of Jewish guilt and Muslim (and Byzantine) schism that kept the crusade alive in France; the 13th was the last medieval century in which French Jews could live securely with their Christian neighbours, and their position became progressively more difficult. The regular clergy could no longer be relied upon to set standards in piety and penitence; their observance was either too relaxed or too severe to suit the new conditions, while the whole tendency of the canonical movement of the later 12th century had been to accentuate the distinctiveness of the secular priesthood and the power of holy orders. Even as it continued to expand, the Cistercian order was incapable of sustaining its ascetic impulse completely; its houses, as well as those of the older Benedictines, found their prestige and solvency alike in decline. Nor was the higher secular clergy much better situated to fulfill pastoral obligations. The bishop was by now remote from his flock, acting usually as diocesan supervisor, judge, or lord; his subordinates—the archdeacon and cathedral canons—likewise functioned primarily as administrators. Archbishops were required by the fourth Lateran Council (1215) to hold annual synods of provincial clergy, a ruling that—although imperfectly observed—probably contributed to some strengthening of discipline.

The critical reform was that of the parish ministry. When emphatic measures to improve the education and supervision of priests were adopted in the fourth Lateran Council, it was already too late in France. For more than a generation, anticlericalism and doctrinal heresy had been spreading, especially in the towns and villages of the east and south. There was a suspicion that sinning priests could not be trusted to mediate God's grace effectively, while many felt attracted to the virtue of poverty as an antidote to the worldly cupidity of a prospering society. The merchant Peter Valdes, giving up his property and family (1175–?76), took it upon himself to preach in the vernacular to his fellow townsfolk of Lyons. His followers—the "Poor Men"—going sometimes so far as to administer sacraments, contrary to the canons, failed to win papal recognition. Nevertheless, the Waldensian mission, grimly tolerated by the authorities, spread to southern towns; and Valdes himself became active in the

(margin notes)
Urban society

Peasant stratification

The clergy

campaign against the Cathar sects of southern France. Flourishing in the hill towns and villages between Toulouse and Béziers, the Cathars held alarmingly unorthodox religious beliefs; they rejected the church as the devil's work, organizing their own ministry.

For this challenge the secular clergy of Languedoc was no match. To establish an effective counterministry of learned and respectable men, the Pope deputed Cistercians to Languedoc; they were soon succeeded by St. Dominic of Calaruega, who spent a decade as mendicant preacher in Languedoc. In 1217, his order of preachers recognized by the Bishop of Toulouse and confirmed by the Pope, Dominic set out with his fellow friars to work in the wider world " by word and example."

Crusade of
Innocent
III in
Languedoc

Meanwhile, the murder of the legate Pierre de Castelnau (1208) had stirred Innocent III to promote a crusade against the heretics of Languedoc. Led by Simon de Montfort, northern barons attacked towns in the viscounty of Béziers and later in the county of Toulouse with singular fury. Despite massacres and apostasy, the failure of the enterprise as a holy war was underscored by the establishment of a papal inquisition (1233), which stiffened and institutionalized the Dominican measures of dissuasion. The procedure, which became known in many parts of France, was usually entrusted to Dominicans; it relied on the active pursuit of suspects, secret testimony, and—in case of conviction and obstinacy— delivery of the heretic to the "secular arm" for capital punishment. Taking the war and the Inquisition together, it can be said that French heresy was largely destroyed by the end of the Capetian period.

The Franciscans as well as the Dominicans had a spectacular success. Highly organized, with provincial and international administrative institutions, both orders had houses in Paris by 1220, and their members were soon working everywhere in France. Becoming preachers and confessors, they also secured chaplaincies, inspectorships, and professorships as their initiatives in piety, probity, and learning were recognized. Conflict with the secular priesthood naturally resulted; the seculars attempted unsuccessfully to exclude the mendicants from the ministry of sacraments and inveighed against conventual endowments that seemed to contradict the friars' professions of poverty. New religious orders were soon established. The friars stimulated a more active piety among lay people, favouring charitable works and foundations, private devotions, and penitential reading.

Culture and learning. Literacy and elementary learning became more widespread. The courtly tastes of the 12th century, while not obliterated, were overtaken by a more flexible and ironic sensibility evident in vernacular ballads, fables, satires, and moralizing literature, most popular in the northern towns. The burgher or knight began to take a keen interest in the tangible world about him. The taste for clarity, proportion, and articulation, coming to mature expression in the Gothic of Amiens, Paris (Notre-Dame), and Reims, achieved dazzling finesse in the church known as the Sainte-Chapelle, built at Paris by Louis IX in 1245–48 to house the crown of thorns. And the taste for order is illustrated by the reorganization of masters, students, and studies as *studia generalia* (or universities); Montpellier became a leading centre of medical learning; Orléans and Toulouse, the latter founded in 1229 to prepare clerks to combat heresy, were noted for law. Paris remained pre-eminent among the early universities; its famous schools became associated as the faculties of arts, canon law, medicine, and theology, gaining jurisdictional independence under papal protection by 1231.

During the same years, philosophical doctrines in conflict with Christian orthodoxy began to trouble the theologians, as translations of the metaphysical and scientific works of Aristotle and his commentators reached Paris. For a time the teaching of Aristotle was prohibited there; but by midcentury, when some of the "artists" who had been most attracted to the new philosophy were advancing to the theological degrees, efforts were made to incorporate Aristotelian learning in enlarged summaries of Christian knowledge. The *Summa theologica* (1266–72)

by the Italian Thomas Aquinas was the greatest synthesis of this type. Its serene power breathes no hint of the controversies in which its author was involved. St. Thomas had taken his theological degree, together with St. Bonaventure, in 1257, when the secular masters were bitterly disputing the friars' privileges within the university. In the end the Dominicans and Franciscans each retained a chair on condition of submitting to university regulations. Thomas' work, however, was less fortunate. As the arts faculty seemed increasingly disposed to take a naturalistic view of all reality, a reaction set in; and the bishop's condemnations of "error" in 1270 and 1277 were so sweeping as to render even Thomas suspect. His audacious brand of synthesis was to have no immediate imitators. Nevertheless, the social consequences of this newly organized learning were profound; it created new estates of professional men—lawyers, notaries, trained clerks, physicians, many of them laymen—whose rational and legalist outlook became firmly rooted in French culture.

The
bishop's
condemnations of
"error"

The dogmatic condemnations of the 1270s were symptomatic. Prosperity and confidence were shaken in many ways in the late 13th century. The papacy, hitherto a support for progressive causes, found itself discredited after its fiasco in the crusade against Aragon; and while the removal of the papal court to Avignon in the time of Clement V created a new centre of patronage for arts and letters, it did little to arrest the waning prestige of the church. The burdens of renewed warfare increased social tensions in the towns and depressed civic enterprise; the Jews had their assets confiscated before being expelled in 1306, and the Lombard bankers suffered like treatment in 1311. Economic indicators—while few and difficult to interpret—are generally held to suggest retardation, at least in many parts of France. The fairs of Champagne were doing a contracting business by 1300, if not before, while records of Normandy reveal declining agrarian revenues in the half century after 1260. Some regions were "saturated" with people: their existent economic technology could no longer sustain growth. Probably the population was already levelling off, if not yet decreasing, when, in 1315–17, crop failures and famine caused serious disruption and a reversion, in some places, to subsistence farming.

THE PERIOD OF THE HUNDRED YEARS' WAR

The kings and the war, 1328–1429. At the accession of the House of Valois in 1328, France was the most powerful kingdom in Europe. Its ruler could muster larger armies than his rivals elsewhere; he could tap enormous fiscal resources, including taxes authorized by sympathetic popes of French extraction; there remained only four great fiefs—the duchies of Aquitaine, Brittany, and Burgundy and the County of Flanders—outside the direct royal domain; and the king's courts continued to press a jurisdictional supremacy that was felt everywhere in the realm. It did not follow, however, that France's superior armies would fight better than its foes or that its resources would not sometimes be dissipated or withheld. France remained a collection of traditional provinces the peoples of which believed that a king should "live of his own," while military success continued to depend on the personal leadership of dynastic rulers whose qualifications as strategists had been less refined by experience and institutional progress than their judicial or administrative attributes. The history of France in the 14th century is dominated by efforts of its kings to maintain their suzerainty over the Plantagenets in Aquitaine, efforts that, despite French advantages, were long frustrated.

Philip VI. Philip VI of Valois (ruled 1328–50), grandson of Philip III, was of mature age when he became regent of France in 1328. Upon the birth of a daughter to the widow of his cousin Charles IV, the familiar issue of the succession was posed anew. It was the regent's experience, together with the circumstance that Edward III of England, grandson of Philip the Fair, was under the influence of his disreputable mother, Isabella of France, that probably disposed the council at Vincennes to recognize Philip as king (April 1328).

Philip's reign began well. Within months he crushed a revolt of the Flemish cloth towns (Cassel, August 1328), thereby recovering the effective suzerainty over Flanders that had eluded his predecessors for a generation. And in 1329 he obtained Edward III's personal homage for the duchy of Aquitaine—an act that not only secured Philip's leadership but nullified Edward's claim to the crown of France.

This initial success was soon undone. Jurisdictional questions in Gascony remained unsettled. In 1336 Philip VI appeared to be preparing massive support for David Bruce, the Scottish king at war with Edward; and in 1337, alleging defaults in feudal service, Philip ordered the confiscation of Aquitaine. Edward III renounced his homage and again laid claim to the crown of France, and war again was imminent. Despite the new Plantagenet pretensions, the basic causes of conflict were feudal and jurisdictional, not dynastic.

Edward proceeded deliberately and ominously. He fomented discontent among the Flemish clothworkers and then treated with the towns, so as to negate the count's fidelity to France; and he purchased the fidelity and service of many princes in the Rhineland and Low Countries. But to succeed, the English needed a prompt and massive victory on French soil, something Philip VI was able to avoid. Despite Edward's naval triumph off Sluis (Sluys, 1340), which confirmed English control of the seas, his initial advantage was lost as his resources and allies melted away. A truce in September 1340 was extended for several years, during which time Edward intervened in a disputed succession to the duchy of Brittany, while Philip's officials increased their pressure on Gascony. In 1345 English armies counterattacked French posts on the duchy's borders; their success emboldened Edward. Landing in Normandy (July 1346) with a well-disciplined army, he captured Caen, only to be overtaken in Picardy by a much larger French army as he moved to join his Flemish allies. At Crécy (August 26, 1346), despite serious disadvantages, the English forces won the first major battle of the war. Their victory, however, proved difficult to exploit; Edward moved on to capture Calais after a long siege, but he could then only return to England with more glory than accomplishment to his credit.

Nevertheless, Philip's failures were proving costly in money and political support. In 1340–41 he had been able to raise "extraordinary" revenue through taxes on sales, salt, and hearths, despite regional protests. The continuance of sales and salt taxes in 1343 could be extracted from the Estates of Paris only in return for the restoration of a stable coinage; and in the following years regional assemblies in the north proved even more obstinate. In the Estates of Paris in November 1347 the King heard ringing denunciations of his mismanagement and defeats and was fortunate to obtain new subsidies to support an invasion of England. But that prospect, like the war itself, evaporated when the Black Death struck Europe late in 1347, destroying life, fiscal resources, and resolve for several years thereafter.

Philip VI cannot be judged by his military failures alone. The royal domain was significantly enlarged by his acquisition of Dauphiné (technically an endowment for his grandson in 1343–49) and the city of Montpellier, the last (and wealthiest) Aragonese fief in Languedoc. As administrative expertise continued to progress, the services, such as Parlement and treasury, were regulated. Within the departments of the court and notably in the Chambre des Comptes, the exercise of power came increasingly into the hands of royal favourites, whose rivalries were stimulated by the courtly predilections of the King. Their influence and peculation together with the familiar injustices of local government came under attack in the Estates of 1343 and 1347, which, in their conditional grants of subsidy, asserted a more nearly constitutional authority than French assemblies had yet enjoyed; the fiscal powers of the provincial Estates likewise originated during the first Valois reign.

John the Good. John II the Good (ruled 1350–64) succeeded to a weakened authority and kingdom; he was a mediocrity whose suspicions and impetuosity were ill suited to the changed circumstances. John hoped to rally baronial loyalties to himself. But he failed to reconcile Charles the Bad, king of Navarre, whose strong dynastic claim to the throne (he was the grandson of Louis X) was matched by his ambition; Charles's conspiracy—at first appeased, then too violently put down—seriously weakened John during the years (1355–56) when the English war broke out anew. When Charles sought alliance with Edward III, French diplomats abandoned full sovereignty over Aquitaine, a reversal of policy too gratuitous to hold for long; its prompt revocation, with papal support, encouraged Edward's son, the Black Prince, to undertake destructive raids through Languedoc in 1355. That November the Estates of Languedoïl, meeting at Paris, insisted on controlling the military appropriations they voted; and when the Black Prince advanced from Bordeaux to Touraine in the summer of 1356, John hastened to prevent his union with rebellious Norman barons. The armies met near Poitiers in September. Once again the French had the advantage of numbers and position, only to suffer a disastrous defeat. King John allowed himself to be taken prisoner.

France was to experience no worse years than those of the regency of the dauphin Charles (regent 1356–61; King Charles V, 1364–80). Unpaid or poorly disciplined armies ravaged the countrysides. The dynasts, nobles, and townspeople had new reasons to resist the monarchy. The Dauphin showed no sign of adjusting to meet the crisis; and the Estates convoked in 1356 to provide for the King's ransom demanded sweeping administrative reforms, even imposing a council, representing the Estates, upon the regent. Their program proved unworkable, and Charles tried to resume power on terms already rejected by the Estates. This move radicalized Étienne Marcel, provost of the Parisian merchants and leader of the urban estate. Causing the brutal murders of two of the Dauphin's noble associates, Marcel only succeeded in creating an irreconcilable breach with the Dauphin, who fled Paris and convoked his own assembly at Compiègne. Marcel's enthusiasm mounted as his position became more precarious; he drew strength from alliance with Charles the Bad but failed to win the Flemish towns to his cause. The climactic complication was a terrible uprising of the peasants (Jacquerie), which broke out in Picardy in May 1358 and which antagonized Marcel's noble supporters, notably Charles the Bad, who helped to quell the disturbances. Marcel was increasingly isolated when loyalist sentiment mounted and administrative failures became evident. His assassination on July 31, 1358, not only secured the Dauphin's authority but ended the burgher influence that had originated in the Estates of 1355.

Intense efforts were then made to end the English war. Negotiations dragged past the term of truce set in 1356; when a first and too humiliating treaty was rejected by the Dauphin, Edward made yet another demonstration in France (1359). At Brétigny (May 8, 1360) King John's ransom was set at 3,000,000 gold crowns, while to England was assigned full sovereignty over Aquitaine (including Poitou). Two months later John arrived in Calais, where a first payment of ransom was made. In the definitive Treaty of Calais (October 24, 1360), for reasons not clear, the monarchs' renunciations—Edward's claim to the crown of France, John's to sovereignty over the ceded territories—were postponed. The Black Prince, however, proceeded to take control of Aquitaine, while the regent tried with little success to extract additional money for the ransom from an exhausted country. When the Estates at Amiens (October 1363) refused to ratify an irresponsible agreement between the King's replacement hostages and Edward III, John returned to captivity in London, where he died a few months later.

Charles V. Under the former dauphin, now Charles V, the fortunes of war were dramatically reversed. Charles had a high conception of royalty and a good political sense. While he shared the Valois taste for luxury and festivity, he reverted to the Capetian tradition of prudent diplomacy. He observed the Treaty of Calais,

Marginalia:

English successes under Edward III

The regency of the dauphin Charles

Efforts to end the war

which helps to explain why Edward III did not press to conclude the renunciations; but he reserved his authority in Aquitaine by inserting in his coronation oath a clause prohibiting the alienation of rights attaching to the crown.

The early years of his reign were filled with baronial politics. Charles the Bad once again revolted unsuccessfully, his dynastic claim to Burgundy running afoul of the King's; the succession to Brittany was settled by arms in favour of the Anglophile Jean de Montfort (who became John IV the Valiant). Most significant for the future, Charles V obtained the heiress to Flanders for his brother Philip the Bold, to whom Burgundy had been granted in appanage. Meanwhile, companies of mercenary soldiers, many based in strongholds of central France, were paralyzing the countrysides. Charles V commissioned the Breton captain Bertrand du Guesclin to neutralize them. Between 1365 and 1369 Bertrand employed the companies in adventurous conflicts in Spain; many of the mercenaries were killed or dispersed. The Black Prince had also intervened in Spain, and his taxes and administration in Aquitaine aroused protest. In 1369 the lords of Albret and Armagnac, having refused to permit levies of subsidy in their lands, appealed to Charles V for the judgment of his court. Although Charles hesitated, his eventual decision to accept the appeals was in keeping with the letter of the Treaty of Calais and his coronation oath.

The war with England soon broke out again. Two new
French
successes
factors worked in favour of France. First, Charles's alliance with Henry II of Trastámara, king of Castile, cost the English their naval supremacy; a Castilian fleet destroyed English reinforcements off La Rochelle in 1372, which effectively secured the success of French operations in the west. Second, Charles abandoned the defective policy of massive engagement with the enemy. Unable to command in person, he appointed Bertrand du Guesclin constable in 1370; the latter proceeded to harry the enemy and to prey on supplies with great effectiveness. Through skirmishes and sieges, the French forces soon reconquered Guyenne and Poitou, leaving only some port towns (Calais, Cherbourg, Saint-Malo, Bordeaux) in English hands. To finance these operations, Charles continued to levy the taxes on merchandise, salt (*gabelles*), and hearths that had been intended to raise John's ransom; despite serious inequities and defaults, these taxes persisted to the end of the reign. In Languedoc they were voted, assessed, and expended by the Estates; elsewhere, by transforming the deputies first chosen by the Estates in the time of John into royal officers, Charles created a fiscal administration independent of popular control. His military success owed much to the improved regulation of armed forces and defenses. Ordinances provided for the inspection and repair of fortifications, the encouragement of archery, a more dependable discipline, pay for fighting men, and even the establishment of a navy.

The last years of the reign brought disappointments. Truces were arranged; but, as there could be no more talk of ceding French sovereignty over Aquitaine, there could be no assurance of peace. More serious, the papal–French alliance collapsed. Charles V, unable to prevent Pope Gregory XI from returning to Rome in 1376, chose to support the candidacy of Robert of Geneva against the Italian Urban VI in 1378, but only Scotland and Naples followed the French lead. A schismatic pope could no longer help France much; rival popes could hardly promote peace between their political supporters. Although he had re-established the political unity of France, Charles V left an uncertain future.

Charles VI. Charles VI (ruled 1380–1422) was a minor when he succeeded his father. His uncles, each possessed of the ambition and resources to pursue independent policies, assumed control of the government. Duke Louis of Anjou soon removed himself from influence by seeking the throne of Naples; Jean, duc de Berry, received the lieutenancy of Languedoc, by then virtually an appanage; and it was left to Duke Philip the Bold of Burgundy to set the young King's policy. In Flanders,

the count of which was his father-in-law, Philip imposed his own cause upon the King. An uprising by the workers of Ghent, spreading to other towns, was met by royal force that won a crushing victory at Roosebeke in 1382. The young King returned in triumph to deal forcefully with restive populations at Paris and Rouen and in Languedoc. The provostship of the merchants was suppressed at Paris, bringing that municipality under direct royal control.

In 1388 Charles VI assumed full authority himself. He recalled his father's exiled advisers, the Marmousets, who undertook to reform the royal administration in keeping with the practice of Charles V. But the country was again wearying of taxation. The annual levies of Charles V had been discontinued in 1380 but then re-established—helping to cause the urban unrest already mentioned—and were being dissipated blatantly in royal and princely extravagance. In 1392 the King lost his sanity, a shocking event that aroused popular solicitude for the crown. His recurrent lapses into insanity, however, played into the hands of his uncles. Philip the Bold again dominated the council. Fortunately for France, England was incapable of renewing the war. The Duke of Burgundy planned an invasion of England in 1386, but it came to nothing after major preparations in Flanders. A series of truces, beginning in 1388, was followed by a reconciliation between Richard II of England and Charles VI in 1396, when the truce was extended for 28 years. Meanwhile, French nobles were reviving the Crusade, imagining a reunited West following their lead; John the Fearless' defeat at Nicopolis in 1396 was the most famous of several enterprises. To restore unity in the church, the masters of the University of Paris began to speak out vigorously; the conciliar theory that finally prevailed to end the schism owed much to them.
Insanity of
Charles VI

When conflict with England was renewed in the 15th century, circumstances had changed. Henry IV of England was committed to the recovery of English rights in France; moreover, in a civil war between Louis, duc d'Orléans, and John the Fearless (duke of Burgundy since 1404) over control of the King and the spoils thereof, both parties sought English support. And when John caused Orléans to be assassinated in Paris (November 23, 1407), the popular horror magnified the conflict. John exploited the situation by pressing for reforms; his rival's cause was taken up by Bernard VII of Armagnac, whose daughter married Orléans's sons. But John's alliance with the turbulent Parisians was no more secure than the temper of the angriest burghers; a major ordinance for administrative reform (1413) collapsed in a riot of the butchers, and in the ensuing reaction the Armagnac faction regained control of Paris. John's dangerous response was to encourage the new king of England, Henry V, to claim the French throne for himself. Henry's invasion of 1415, reminiscent of the campaign ending at Crécy, had the same result—at Agincourt the French suffered yet another major defeat, after which, characteristically, the English withdrew—but the civil war in France enabled Henry V to exploit his strength, as Edward III could not. In 1418 the Burgundian party recovered control of Paris, and the dauphin Charles embarked on a long exile in Armagnac company. But John's duplicity was limitless; while meeting with the Dauphin to betray the English, John was himself assassinated (1419). His successor, Philip the Good, renewed the alliance with Henry V. By the Treaty of Troyes (1420), the deranged Charles VI was induced to set aside the Dauphin's right of succession in favour of Henry V, who married Charles VI's daughter. The ancient dream of a dynastic union between France and England seemed to be realized; and, when Henry and Charles died within weeks of each other (1422), the infant Henry VI became king in both lands.

Charles VII. Charles VI's son Charles VII (ruled 1422–61), for his part, did not fail to claim his inheritance, though he had no proper coronation. Residing at Bourges, which his adversaries pretended was the extent of his realm, he in fact retained the fidelity of the greater part of France, including Berry, Poitou, Lyonnais, Auvergne, and Languedoc. For a time the Valois cause suffered from the ineptness of its leader and from his advisers and retainers, who prospered from the unresolved conflict. Incapable himself of military leadership, Charles put his hope in reconciliation with Philip of Burgundy—a diplomacy that thoroughly discomfited King Henry's regent, the Duke of Bedford. Nevertheless, French prestige collapsed with the abasement of the monarchy; Charles VII appears to have doubted his own legitimacy, and disorders spread again.

Joan of Arc

Then Joan of Arc appeared. Stirred by the popular memory of traditional French kingship, she found her way from her peasant home at Domrémy (on the border of Champagne and Bar) to Chinon, where she confronted Charles with her astonishing inspiration: her "voices" proclaimed a divine commission to aid the King. In April 1429 she entered Orléans, long besieged, rallying the garrison to effective sorties that soon caused the English to lift the siege. Other victories followed, in which Joan's influence was manifest, although probably exaggerated in tradition. On her insistence that only consecration at Reims could make a true king, chosen by God (a view doubtless supported by the chancellor Regnault, archbishop of Reims), it was decided to advance boldly across the Île-de-France to Reims. Charles was anointed there on July 17, 1429.

Recovery and reunification, 1429–83. The coronation of Charles VII was the last pivotal event of the Hundred Years' War. From Reims the King's army moved on triumphantly, winning capitulations from Laon, Soissons, and many lesser places and even threatening Paris before disbanding. The revived devotion to monarchy that had produced Joan was undermining English positions almost everywhere in France; the urgent necessity to discredit her explains the callous efficiency of the inquisition to which she was subjected upon being captured by the Burgundians and turned over to the English in 1430. Condemned of heresy, confessed under duress, boldly relapsed, she was burned at the stake in Rouen on May 30, 1431.

Charles and his party made no move through ecclesiastical channels to save Joan. They then proceeded deliberately to make peace with Burgundy. In the Treaty of Arras (September 21, 1435), Philip the Good bargained strongly; confirmed in the possession of domains ceded by the English, he also obtained Charles's humiliating disavowal of the murder of the Duke's father. The act, however damaging to the royal vanity, set Charles free from political obligation to the Armagnacs; the factional king now became the supreme king of France. Within a year English support collapsed in the Île-de-France, and royal soldiers entered Paris. The Truce of Tours (1444) provided for a marriage between Henry VI and the niece of Queen Mary of France; extensions of the truce gave Charles time to strengthen his military resources. War flared again in 1449, when England intervened against a duke of Brittany who had done homage to Charles VII. In 1449–50 a vigorous campaign resulted in the French conquest of Normandy, and in 1451 most of Guyenne fell to the French.

The end of the Hundred Years' War

When the English lost the minor battle of Castillon in 1453, the Hundred Years' War was over. That fact was not altogether clear to contemporaries, for no treaty was concluded and skirmishes were to recur for many years to come. But only Calais, enclosed in the Burgundian domains, remained of English possessions in France. Charles VII issued medals to commemorate his soldiers, and he ordered a review of Joan of Arc's trial, which resulted in a verdict of rehabilitation in 1456.

Governmental reforms. As hostilities were waning (1435–49), Charles VII presided over a major reorganization of government. Tested by adversity and strengthened by fortune, he had grown in political competence. The principal administrative services—chancery, Parlement, accounts—were re-established at Paris. The replacement of Burgundian sympathizers, notably in Parlement, seems to have been accomplished with moderation and tact; in local offices no purges were necessary. But it

quickly became evident that the reunited country was now too large and its officials were too numerous to get along very well with a government as centralized as Parisian bureaucrats preferred.

Remedial legislation was consistent with tendencies long apparent. Revenues from the domain were collected in the treasury, the work of which Charles VII reorganized in four regional offices. Extraordinary revenues had been administered since the 1350s in districts (*élections*), the numbers of which had vastly increased since the time of Charles V. The *élections* were now subordinated to four regional *généralités*, corresponding to the offices of treasury. The old Chambre des Comptes had lost parts of its jurisdiction to more specialized courts in 1390, of which the Cour des Aides (board of excise) had provincial divisions set up at Toulouse in 1439 and at Rouen in 1450. A provincial Parlement was definitively established at Toulouse in 1443, and there were to be others at Grenoble and Bordeaux. With all these changes the conciliar structure of government survived; policy continued to be made by the king in concert with favourites, whose numbers no reforms had delimited. The proliferation of lesser offices, many filled by lawyers, created a new stratum of gentlemen who enjoyed the king's privilege.

While the reform of offices did nothing to obliterate the older distinction between ordinary and extraordinary revenue, the work of Charles VII effectively belied the notion that the monarchy should subsist on its domain alone. That the king as lord could no longer pay his officers and soldiers was apparent to almost everyone. Early in his career Charles had resorted to the Estates to raise *aides* and *tailles* (as the old levies on sales and hearths were now called); but after convocations in the 1430s, he continued these taxes through annual ordinances no longer sanctioned by the Estates. Moreover, the preparation of annual budgets for ordinary and extraordinary revenues gave way in 1450 to a single "general statement" of finance, which, being related to demonstrable necessities, effectively institutionalized taxation in France. As the Middle Ages ended, France comprised a central core of *élections*, where local Estates, when they met at all, had little to do with fiscal matters, and a surrounding belt of "lands of Estates" (*e.g.,* Languedoc, Brittany, Normandy, and Burgundy), where custom continued to allow for consent or for the administration of taxes. Having originated in times of fiscal demands thought uncustomary and excessive, representative institutions could not generally survive once the royal impositions, from very repetition, had ceased to seem arbitrary; even where Estates persisted, their votes were more like approval than sovereign consent.

Military reforms. The fiscal reorganization facilitated equally significant military reforms. The Peace of Arras, rather than pacifying France, had only thrown the people once again to the mercies of disbanded mercenaries and brigands. In 1439 an ordinance made the recruitment of military companies the king's monopoly and provided for uniform strength in contingents, supervision, and pay. Following the Truce of Tours in 1444 no general demobilization occurred; instead the best of the larger units were reconstituted as "companies of the king's ordinance," which were standing units of cavalry well selected and well equipped; they served as local guardians of peace at local expense. With the creation of the "free archers" (1448), a militia of foot soldiers, the new standing army was complete. Making use of a newly effective artillery, its companies firmly in the king's control, supported by the people in money and spirit, France rid herself of brigands and Englishmen alike.

Regrowth of the French monarchy. Thus the monarchy recovered much of the authority it had lost during the early stages of the Hundred Years' War. Although its influence in Burgundy and Flanders, now united in a formidable dynastic association, had declined, its definitive recovery of Aquitaine consolidated a direct domain, again extensive enough to free the Valois from anxiety about landed resources. It had exploited not only a widespread distaste for the destructive self-interest of barons

Revenues

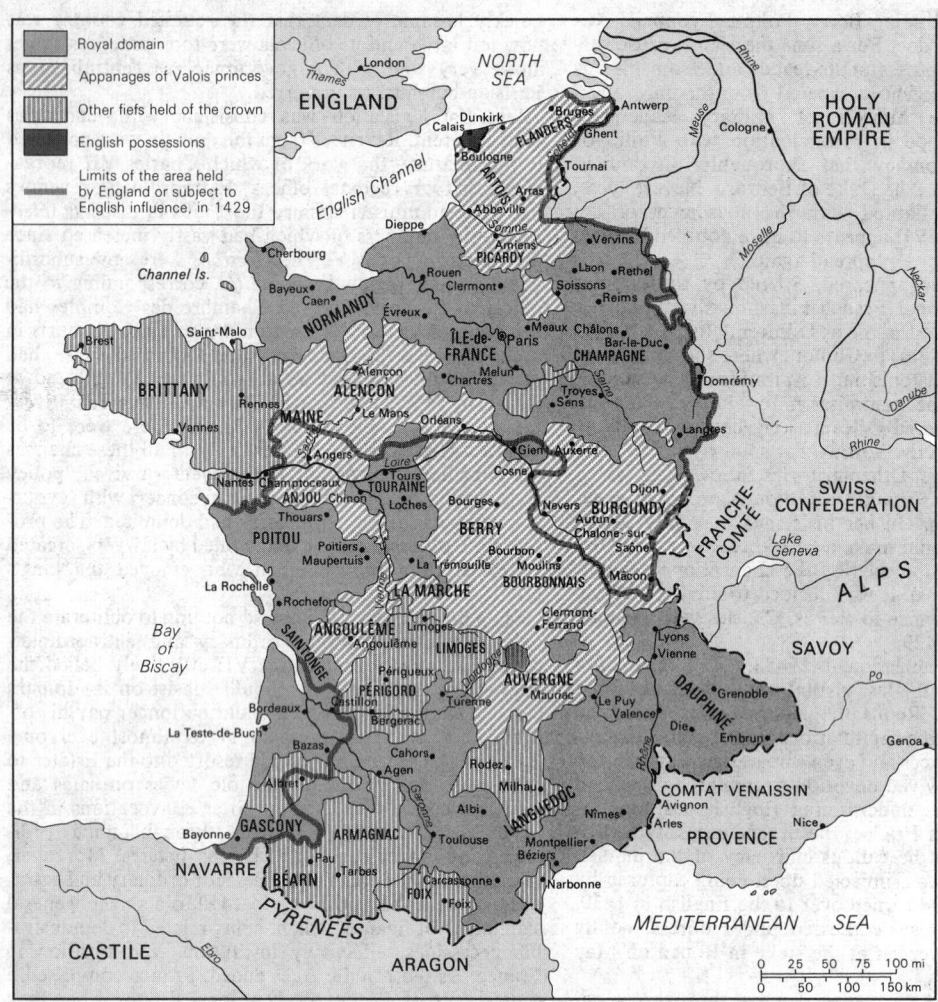

France in 1453.

From W. Shepherd, *Historical Atlas*, Harper & Row, Publishers (Barnes & Noble Books), New York; revision
Copyright © 1964 by Barnes & Noble, Inc.

and warlords but also an incipient nationalism, which, besides reviving the "religion of monarchy," put new stresses on the foreignness of Englishmen. How renewed power and Gallicanism went together was demonstrated in the Pragmatic Sanction of Bourges (1438), by which papal benefices and revenues from France were severely curtailed and the royal influence in the French church strengthened. Nevertheless, the survival of powerful dynasts and provincial interests, as a legacy of the war and the fertility of the royal house, represented a counterpoise to the crown that Philip the Fair had never known. And with the son of Charles VII, the monarchy was to be tested yet again.

Louis XI (1461–83) was shamelessly impatient for his father's death. It must be said of this strange man that he had worthy policies to pursue: the securing of the royal domain against Burgundy, Orléans, Brittany, etc., and the promotion of commerce and industry within national boundaries. His foreign policy was less consistent, ranging from the cautious in Italy to the chimerical in Spain; yet it was at the expense of Aragon that he regained title to Roussillon and Cerdagne. His methods rather than his ends were what made the reign of this ambitious, nervous, and capricious ruler so turbulent. No French king had ever imposed himself so totally and so tyrannically as Louis XI. Forgetful of past loyalties, he was betrayed as often as he himself betrayed others. Toward the clergy as toward his officials, he could be brutal and vindictive. He antagonized the nobles by revoking the Valois pensions and ceremonial and by promoting the independence of seigneurial towns. As for the royal towns, Louis respected their constitutions only so far as was consistent with royal supervision and the payment of heavy taxes; he tolerated the resurgence of urban

The tyranny of Louis XI

oligarchies. Fiscal pressures in support of the army, government, and diplomacy mounted fearfully.

Politics, under Louis XI, replaced administration as the foremost preoccupation of the realm. Arbitrary and hasty measures against the dynasts aroused the formidable League of the Public Weal, which, in 1465, appealed to the people against misgovernment and proposed a regency of the princes supported by the three estates. Louis, in turn, as on later occasions, used assemblies and proclamations to divide the princes. But the settlement of October 1465 was a grave setback for the King, whose brother Charles gained title to Normandy while Charles the Bold, soon to inherit Burgundy, acquired strategic counties and towns in Artois. To the undoing of this treaty Louis devoted great energy. Fomenting strife between Brittany and Normandy, he soon recovered the latter and isolated the former. Deaths among his rivals in Gascony enabled him to secure successions, as in Armagnac, more divided and less hostile. Increasingly, Louis's tortuous diplomacy fastened on Burgundy. The King succeeded in reconciling the Swiss cantons with Austria to form a coalition with France and the Rhenish cities; this coalition invaded Burgundy and defeated and killed Charles the Bold at Nancy (January 5, 1477). While the legal reversion of Burgundy to the crown could not be given practical effect, Louis did recover Artois. Moreover, even as he enjoyed this decisive triumph over his most dangerous rival, the entire Angevin inheritance (Anjou, Provence, and Mediterranean claims) devolved to the crown upon the death of René of Anjou in 1480. Through accident and design and the inability of the princes to collaborate effectively, Louis had succeeded in countering the threat of a princely constitution and had considerably extended the royal domain.

Economy, society, and culture in the 14th and 15th centuries. The long war, fought almost entirely in France, benefitted few but the captains and peculators; it injured almost everyone. Even the best disciplined companies lived off the land, so that French peasants and defeated townsfolk in effect paid the expenses of both sides; and undisciplined mercenary bands were a wearisome scourge in times of truce after the middle of the 14th century.

Economic distress. But the war did not alone cause economic distress. Even before it broke out, bad weather and commercial dislocations, together with overpopulation in some areas, resulted in worse famines and more frequent ones than in the past. But what most terribly damaged life and security was sickness.

The Black Death, carried on shipboard from the Levant, reached Provence in 1347, ravaged most of France in 1348, and faded out only in 1350. Bonfires to disinfect the air, collective demonstrations of penitence in northern towns, persecutions of Jews or friars—nothing worked to check the disease in populations without immunity. The mortality was staggering—the French chronicler Jean Froissart's estimate that the first wave carried off a third of the population was perhaps not far wrong; recent studies suggest that rural areas were no less afflicted than towns. And there were recurrent outbreaks of plague in later years. These afflictions and related factors were responsible for a general decline of population. Toulouse seems to have lost half of its inhabitants, falling from 40,000 to 20,000; the population of Normandy is estimated to have declined by two-thirds between 1300 and 1450. The trend was probably reversed, and perhaps strongly so, in the second quarter of the 15th century, although little is yet known about this.

The hard times affected classes and regions in different ways, degrees, and rhythms. Some places almost escaped the ravages that afflicted others repeatedly. In the countrysides, especially—save for the greatest personages—those who had most to lose suffered most. Whether for landlords or rich peasants, surpluses became harder to obtain or preserve; to many lesser lords the dangerous fortunes of war probably seemed an attractive alternative to declining yields in money or produce. Standards of living, as measured in diets or furnishings, declined. Onerous obligations and services tended to disappear as shortages of rural labour made themselves felt; the transition from servile to rental tenures was largely completed in the 15th century. Peasant uprisings, such as the Jacquerie in the relatively prosperous Île-de-France and the Tuchins in Languedoc, are too poorly documented to be well understood—both betrayed desperation born of recurrent taxation and were associated with the expression of egalitarian ideas; the Jacquerie coincided with a weakened grain market and may have been hastened by efforts of lords to enforce labour services and payments after the Black Death. The manor survived, but little remained of its human identity in the 15th century. Even minor lords lived away from their peasant tenants, protected them poorly if at all, relied on salaried managers to collect payments that, in some cases, had lost all social justification; lordship had degenerated into an unsentimental economic practice.

The cities. Urban society was also troubled. The walled town stood out ever more starkly against the countryside as siege warfare intimidated or destroyed the suburbs that had been built in a less anxious day. Royal taxation, often inequitably administered, exacerbated old tensions in the towns; fiscal policy or the regulation of wages or supplies was largely at issue in the uprisings of Flemish towns (1323–28), at Paris (1357–58, 1380–82), and at Rouen (1382). Communes continued to be revoked in the 14th century, although the kings as a rule were less interested in governing the towns than in securing their resources and fidelity. The concentration of trades and crafts in guilds became more complete and more exclusive.

Some leading commercial centres of the 13th century suffered as new trade routes developed in the empire and by sea and as textile manufactures and money markets—the latter suffering from unstable coinage—became more dispersed. The fairs of Champagne declined rapidly after 1310. Only a few capitals, such as Avignon, Bordeaux, and Paris, prospered; and even they were hard hit by plague. Nor did the French merchant or manufacturer progress competitively; his work often unspecialized, his bookkeeping old-fashioned, his tastes simple, he typically looked forward to securing his future by the purchase of land.

The church. The organized church, despite losses from war and plague, continued to be better endowed economically than morally. The popes of Avignon were less distant and—save perhaps to their French relatives, merchants, and artists—less admirable than the reformer popes of the past; and as the prestige of their schismatic successors plummeted, the higher clergy were confirmed in their incipient Gallicanism (a movement advocating administrative independence from papal control). While organized heresy had almost disappeared, reforms intended to strengthen the parish priesthood languished. Jurisdictional disputes continued to rage between mendicants and seculars and between bishops and canons or archdeacons. Christian piety even more than in the past sought encouragement in mystical or individual devotions or readings and in collective observances of the Holy Spirit or the Virgin or the patron saints of the trades that promoted elementary solidarity and charity in the towns; such confraternities were not always welcome to ecclesiastical authorities, whose deportment or jurisdiction they sometimes challenged. The popular religion of saints—more particularly of the Virgin and the Pietà—and fear of demons worked more deeply into the collective imagination, becoming very evident in the 15th century. Associated with intensified anxieties about sin and damnation, these experiences thrived in times of inscrutable and recurrent disaster.

Culture and art. Cultural circles remained strongly oriented to aristocratic values and the past. With the accession of the Valois came a high nobility, distinguished by lavish and exclusive conceits. When John II formed the Order of the Star (1351), an institution imitated by the great lords for their clientages, chivalry stood incorporated as the most distinguished of religious confraternities. The ideal of the crusade remained strong, notably among princes of the fleur-de-lis, who dominated the public life of Valois France to the point of eclipsing the monarch; beneath them many noble families disappeared while new ones emerged among the captains, lawyers, and patricians. Froissart spun out chronicles of the war at once detailed and grand, full of the frivolous ceremonial that marked the aristocratic life of his day. Tapestries created for courtly patrons idealized a life of enticing gardens, tournaments, and the hunt. Paintings as well as tapestries hung in chambers smaller and more elegant than the cavernous halls of earlier centuries. The rayonnant Gothic of the Île-de-France remained in favour through the 14th century, inspiring the chapel built by Charles V at Vincennes, while the decorative arts of furnishings and manuscripts exploited the Gothic tendencies to articulation and grace. The evocation of the classical past became less fantastic and more heroic in the humanist circles of Pierre Bersuire and Petrarch; their interests helped to attract copyists and artists to the papal court of Avignon. The *Book of Hours* (the most popular private devotional work of the later Middle Ages) might become "very rich," as in the case of a sumptuous manuscript undertaken for Jean, duc de Berry (*c.* 1410); more typically it was a pocketbook for general use by the literate, whose numbers continued to increase.

Stimulated by the commissions of Charles V, the chasm between learned and vernacular cultures narrowed: Raoul de Presles translated St. Augustine; Nicole Oresme translated Aristotle. Music resounded in old forms (ballad, virelay) even while becoming more articulate or flamboyant; Guillaume de Machaut (died 1377), the great musician-poet of the mid-14th century, composed the first polyphonic mass as well as many motets and secular lyrics. Time and space came to be better represented and measured, as evidenced by the first attempts to render perspective in art and in the erection of public clocks at Paris and Caen.

Toward 1400 Paris regained cultural leadership as a result of a new synthetic (or international) style in painting and of the initiatives of the university masters in ecclesiastical politics and theology. The efflorescence, however, was soon destroyed in the civil wars, to be succeeded later in the 15th century by more provincial activities. Universities (like Parlements) proliferated at the expense of Paris, which became the preserve of an antiquated and pedantic theology. Painters, architects, and writers regrouped under princely patrons or even under bourgeois ones, flourishing in postwar trade (Jacques Coeur's palace at Bourges exemplified the flamboyantly decorated solidity of late-medieval taste in France). A new vigour and enlarged scale in painting as in architecture contrast with the more traditional style in Burgundy, where the dukes were building on a grand and continuous past. Italianate Humanism, together with the new philology, stirred in France only in the latter third of the 15th century. (T.N.B.)

III. France, 1490–1715

FRANCE IN THE 16TH CENTURY

When Charles VIII (1483–98) led the French invasion of Italy in 1494 he initiated a series of Italian wars that were to last until the Peace of Cateau-Cambrésis in 1559. These wars were not especially successful for the French, but they corresponded to the contemporary view of the obligations of kingship. They also had their effects upon the development of the French state; in particular, they threatened to alter not only the military and administrative structure of the monarchy but even its traditional role.

Military and financial organization. The French kings of the early 16th century could look back with satisfaction at the virtual expulsion of the English from French soil in the course of the preceding century. This success offered a shining precedent for further military sallies, this time against the growing power of the Habsburgs. In 1445 the first steps had been taken to fashion a royal French army out of the ill-disciplined mercenary bands upon which French kings had traditionally relied. It was a small force—no more than 8,000 men—but it was a beginning. The role of the nobility in the army was strong, for the art of war was still considered a noble pursuit *par excellence*. The core of Charles's army that marched into Italy, the *compagnies d'ordonnance*, consisted of noble volunteers. The infantry, however, was made up of non-nobles, and by the middle of the 16th century, there were more than 30,000 infantrymen to a mere 5,000 noble horsemen. As this infantry force grew in number its organization changed. Legions, organized on a strict provincial basis (the Breton Legion, the Norman Legion, etc.), gave way to the regimental system, based on large units under a single command. This latter organization appeared during the Wars of Religion of the 16th century and survived until the time of Louis XIV. Yet such reorganization did not immediately reduce the army to a pliant tool of the crown. Not until late in the 17th century could the royal army be considered fairly under the king's control. Until then, notably during the Wars of Religion and the outbreaks of the Fronde (1648–53; see below), the loyalty of the commanders and the devotion of the troops were conspicuously inadequate. In the later part of the 17th century, the reforms of the army by Michel Le Tellier and his son the Marquis de Louvois provided Louis XIV with a formidable weapon.

The growth of a large royal army, however, was only one effect of the increased level of military activity. The financial administration of the country also underwent a drastic reorganization, which had far-reaching economic and social consequences. The king, despite his ambitions, possessed neither the resources nor the administrative machinery to maintain a large army. The medieval idea that the king should live off the revenue of his own domain persisted into the 18th century and helps to explain the formal distinction made until the reign of Francis I

The problem of royal finance

(1515–47) between ordinary and extraordinary finance; *i.e.*, between revenue emanating from the king's patrimonial rights and taxes raised throughout the kingdom. By the reign of Francis I, the king, even in times of peace, was unable to make do with his ordinary revenue from rents and seigneurial dues. In 1523 Francis established a new central treasury, the Trésor de l'Épargne, into which all his revenues, ordinary and extraordinary, were to be deposited. In 1542 he set up 16 financial and administrative divisions, the *généralités*, appointing in each a collector general with the responsibility for the collection of all royal revenues within his area. In 1551 Henry II added a treasurer general; from 1577 the *bureaux des finances*, new supervisory bodies composed of a collector general and a number of treasurers, made their appearance in each *généralité*.

Moreover, the actual collecting of taxes was increasingly handed over to tax farmers, who collected and retained a particular royal tax in place of payment to the king of an approximately equivalent sum. The more efficient methods of collection by tax farmers enabled the crown to gather a larger proportion of its revenue than previously but did not, however, solve the problem of royal finance. Even the extraordinary taxes, now added to the crown's ordinary revenue, notably the *taille*, a direct tax levied on all but the nobility and the clergy, custom duties, and the purchase tax on wine, fish, meat, and especially salt (the *gabelle*), were not adequate resources for Renaissance princes whose chief glory lay in the expensive art of war. The *taille*, the only direct tax, which weighed most heavily upon the underprivileged classes, went up from about 4,500,000 livres under Louis XI (1461–83) to 55,000,000 under Jules Cardinal Mazarin in the mid-17th century.

Successive monarchs were forced, therefore, to seek additional revenue. This was no simple matter because French kings traditionally could not tax their subjects without their consent. Indeed, there were many areas of the country where the *taille* itself could not be collected and where the king was dependent upon local agreements. The early Valois kings had negotiated with the Estates-General or with the provincial estates for their extra money; but in the middle of the 15th century, when the Hundred Years' War with England was reaching a successful conclusion, Charles VII was able to strike a bargain with the estates. In return for a reduction in overall taxation, he began to raise money to support the army without having to seek the estates' approval. In some areas of central France the provincial assemblies ceded their right to approve taxation and disappeared altogether. These provinces were known as the *pays d'élection*. But in those provinces where the provincial estates survived (the *pays d'état*), the right to vote the amount of royal taxation also survived. During the Italian wars, meetings of the estates became more frequent as the king's financial demands became more strident, and though the estates never felt themselves able to refuse to provide money, they retained the right to provide less than the monarch asked for. The king continued to rely upon the support of the provincial assemblies to provide extra revenue long after 1614, when the cumbersome Estates-General ceased to play a role in opposing financial resources for the crown.

The growth of a professional bureaucracy. But the king also found another means of filling his exchequer that had nothing to do with traditional methods: he began to sell offices on a large scale. Venality, or the sale of offices, was not novel in early 16th-century France. Traces of the practice can be found in the 13th century, but it was Francis I who opened the floodgates. The number of judges proliferated. In the Parlement of Paris alone the King created two new chambers, each containing 20 members and a further score of judges. In 1552 Henry II established a new kind of court, the *présidial*, whose jurisdiction lay between the Parlement and the bailiwick. Each of the 65 new courts had a complement of nine judges; this brought in a sizable revenue but appears to have made little difference to the efficiency of the judicial system. Nor were judicial offices the only

The sale of offices

ones put up for sale; it was also possible to purchase financial offices, such as those of treasurer general, treasurer, or the immediately inferior *élu*. It has been estimated that during the 16th century some 50,000 offices were sold by the crown.

The partial rationalization of the financial system produced an increasing number of professional advisers, who formed the embryo of a bureaucratic elite. In the course of the 16th century, as specialization grew apace, the king's council became a much more complex institution. The Conseil d'État, with its various subdivisions, formed the hub of royal government. Its members were drawn from a variety of backgrounds. The king's immediate family expected to be consulted, as did great officers of the crown, such as the chancellor, the constable, and the admiral. Also included in the council were the great territorial magnates, members of powerful aristocratic families, and the country's leading prelates. There were also masters of requests (*maîtres des requêtes*), lawyers whose expertise was invaluable when the council sat in a judicial capacity. But in the council the professional element that assumed the greatest significance in the course of the 16th and 17th centuries were the holders of the office of secretary of state. In the early years of the 14th century royal secretaries had already acquired the right to sign documents on the king's authority. From this stage, granted the stability of the crown, the development of the office from a position of subordinate but considerable importance to one of complete indispensability was predictable. Henry II gave four of his secretaries the official title of *secrétaire d'état*, and in 1561 they became full members of the royal council. Closely associated with them and destined to overshadow them in importance in the first half of the 17th century were the superintendents of finance, formally established in 1564, though exercising an already well-established function. Their responsibility was to control and safeguard royal finances and especially to prepare annual budgets containing estimates of revenue and expenditure for the following year. They also played a leading part in assessing the amount to be levied each year from the *taille* and in deciding upon the imposition of new taxes. Below the superintendents but also in the royal council in the 16th century were the intendants of finance. Originally masters of requests, they became a separate group specializing in the increasingly complex task of advising the sovereign in financial matters. In time, their role outstripped in prestige that of the other masters of requests who counselled the king.

The new administrators

There thus grew up a more specialized class of administrators, close to the crown, whose expertise rather than birth was the key to their influence; the sale of office allowed wealthy families to establish a firm base for later political and social advancement. In addition, the needy crown was perfectly prepared to sell titles of nobility as well as offices and, in return for a cash payment, to allow both nobility and office to become hereditary. Although this advancement of new men within the government might suggest a social readjustment of considerable proportions, in fact the element of continuity was more important than might at first appear. It is true that some of the ancient noble families and the king's own relatives found it increasingly difficult to fulfill their old advisory roles; yet the new men were not rejecting the established order but rather were being absorbed into it. The king's counsellors, whatever their former background, became leading noblemen by virtue of their high office: service to the crown was what mattered and that depended on the king's choice. It was not the first time that a new wave of royal servants had begun to overtake established advisers; in the 13th century the *magistri* had ousted the great barons and prelates from the Curia Regis without effecting a social revolution. What took place in the 16th and 17th centuries was another turn of the social wheel by which new men seized the opportunity to pursue those dignities and honours held by men who were themselves descendants of new men.

The Reformation. The professional class that grew up in the 16th century, however, was different in one respect from those that had gone before: it represented a predominantly secular culture—the product of Renaissance Humanism—and reflected the declining influence of the church during the Reformation. In the second half of the 16th century, the Reformation was to embroil France in a series of religious wars that were to pose a serious threat to the power of the king and his government. Lutheran works first appeared in Paris in 1519; and in 1521 Francis I, who was on the point of war with Emperor Charles V and King Henry VIII of England and who wanted to demonstrate his orthodoxy, forbade their publication. Nevertheless, interest in the new faith continued to grow, especially in the Humanist circle of Jacques Lefèvre d'Étaples. Lefèvre, who had in 1512 published an edition of the letters of St. Paul with a commentary that anticipated Martin Luther in its assertion of the doctrine of justification by faith, became the leader of a small group of moderate but orthodox reformers in the tradition of the great Dutch Humanist Desiderius Erasmus. This group included Guillaume Briçonnet, the bishop of Meaux; the mystic Gérard Roussel; and Margaret of Angoulême, the King's own sister. Although this circle was dispersed in 1525, Lutheranism had already established itself, especially in such trading centres as Lyons, where it found support among the poorer classes. The progress of the Reformation in France depended on the crown's attitude; and although Francis for political reasons had revealed initial hostility, his feelings were far from clear. He was favourably disposed toward Lefèvre and toward orthodox reform in general, though he naturally feared those extreme movements that threatened social upheaval. In addition, Francis I saw political advantages in establishing good relations with the Lutheran German princes. On the other hand, unlike them, he had no great incentive to assert his independence from Rome because the Gallican Church already enjoyed a large measure of autonomy. In 1516 the Concordat of Bologna had given the king effective control over the church in France.

In 1534, however, royal policy changed radically. Anti-Catholic placards began to appear in Paris and other major French towns, provoking a bitter Catholic reaction and a series of persecuting edicts. French Protestantism itself had changed, reinforced from the mid-1530s by the spread among the poorer classes of Languedoc and the seaboard towns of Normandy and Brittany of the ideas of John Calvin, a French exile in Geneva. Henry II (1547–59) pursued his father's harsh policies, setting up a special court (the *chambre ardente*) to deal with heresy and issuing further repressive edicts, such as that of Écouen in 1559. Yet the infusion of French Calvinism, or Huguenotism, into the French Reformation stiffened the Protestant opposition. Protestant pastors, trained in Geneva, infiltrated into the country; and by 1562 there were some 2,000 highly organized Calvinist churches in France. This spectacular spread of Calvinism persuaded the queen mother, Catherine de Médicis, who was ruling in the name of her young son, Charles IX (1560–74), to abandon the repressive religious policy of Francis I and Henry II in the name of political good sense. Guided by the moderate chancellor Michel de L'Hospital, Catherine summoned the French clergy to the Colloquy of Poissy (1561), at which an unsuccessful attempt was made to effect a religious compromise with the Huguenots; in the following year she issued the Edict of January, which allowed the Calvinists a degree of toleration. These signs of favour to the Protestants brought a violent reaction from the noble House of Guise, the champions of Catholicism in France. The first civil war began with the massacre by the partisans of François, duc de Guise, of a Huguenot congregation at Vassy (March 1562).

The influence of Calvinism

The Wars of Religion. Guise forces occupied Paris and took control of the royal family, while the Huguenots rose in the provinces and their two commanders, Louis I de Bourbon, prince de Condé, and Admiral Gaspard de Coligny, established headquarters at Orléans. The deaths of the opposing leaders—the Protestant Antoine de Bourbon, king consort of Navarre, and the Catholic marshal Jacques d'Albon, seigneur de Saint-André—and the capture of Condé caused both sides to seek peace. After the Battle of Dreux (December 1562) the war drew to a close, despite the assassination of the Duc de Guise by a Protestant fanatic. A compromise was reached at the Peace of Amboise in March 1563 whereby liberty of conscience was granted to the Huguenots but the celebration of religious services was confined to the households of the nobility and to a limited number of towns.

The second war was precipitated by Huguenot fears of an international Catholic plot. Condé and Coligny were persuaded to attempt a coup to capture Catherine and Charles IX at Meaux in September 1567 and to seek military aid from the Protestant Palatinate. In the following brief war the Catholic constable Anne de Montmorency was killed at the Battle of Saint-Denis (November 1567); the Peace of Longjumeau (March 1568) signalled another effort at compromise. This peace, however, proved little more than a truce; and a third war soon broke out in September 1568. In an attempt to restore their authority, Catherine and King Charles had dismissed L'Hospital in that month and had restored the Guise faction to favour. The edicts of pacification were rescinded; Calvinist preachers faced expulsion from France; and plans were made to seize Condé and Coligny. The former was killed at the Battle of Jarnac (1569), and the Huguenots were again defeated in that year at Moncontour. But the Catholic side failed to consolidate its successes, and yet another compromise was arranged at the Peace of Saint-Germain in August 1570.

Coligny subsequently regained the King's favour but not the Queen Mother's, and he remained an object of hatred with the Guises. In 1572 he was murdered; and at the same time some 3,000 Huguenots, gathered together in Paris to celebrate the marriage of Marguerite de Valois (later Margaret of France) to Condé's nephew, Henry III of Navarre, were massacred on the eve of the feast day of St. Bartholomew. This notorious episode was the signal for the fifth civil war, which ended in 1576 with the Peace of Monsieur, allowing the Huguenots freedom of worship outside Paris. Renewed fighting broke out in 1577 between Catholic and Protestant noblemen, who defied the King—now Henry III (1574–89)—in his attempt to assert royal authority. The Huguenots were defeated and forced by the Peace of Bergerac (1577) to accept further limitations upon their freedom. An uneasy peace followed until 1584, when, upon the death of François, duc d'Anjou, the Huguenot leader Henry of Navarre became the heir to the throne. This new situation produced the War of the Three Henrys (1585–89) during which the Guise faction—led by Henri, duc de Guise—sought to have Navarre excluded from the succession. In a welter of intrigue and murder, first the Duc de Guise and his brother Louis, cardinal de Guise (December 1588), and then Henry III himself (August 1589) were assassinated. Henry of Navarre thus assumed the throne as Henry IV (1589–1610) but had to survive five more years of civil war and embrace Catholicism before his position was secure. In its final stages, the war became a struggle against Spanish forces intervening on behalf of Isabella Clara Eugénie, the daughter of Philip II of Spain and Elizabeth of Valois, who also laid claim to the French throne. The Peace of Vervins (1598), by which Spain recognized Henry IV's title as king and the Edict of Nantes of the same year, granting substantial religious toleration to the Huguenots, ended the Wars of Religion.

The religious wars and the monarchy. This succession of civil disturbances brought the French state close to disintegration and posed a threat to the crown that would not be matched again until 1789. The chief reason for this situation lay in the nature of Calvinism, which provided a rallying point for a wide cross section of opposition and the organization necessary to make that opposition effective. Each Huguenot community created its own administrative structure to provide a tight disciplinary framework, through which the community could ensure its spiritual and material independence. The new creed attracted several elements in French society: small

artisans, shopkeepers, and the urban unemployed, who were suffering in particular from steeply rising prices; many rich townspeople and professional men who thought that material advancement would be easier to procure as Calvinists; and, after the Treaty of Cateau-Cambrésis in 1559, many nobles, especially the poorer ones who had lost with the peace their best hope of wealth and status. The adherence of large numbers of the nobility had two important effects upon the movement in France: (1) it caused many peasants to join the new creed in imitation of their noble seigneurs, thus swelling the overall number and widening its social composition; and (2) it brought a new military element into the Calvinist communities. Under the leadership of the nobility, secret religious meetings were transformed into mass public demonstrations against which the king's forces were impotent. Such demonstrations sometimes involved upward of 20,000 people. Similarly, the administrative structure that was so important in aiding the survival of the proscribed faith was transformed into a military organization. This organization was ultimately headed by Louis, prince de Condé, who assumed the title of protector general of the churches of France, thus putting all the prestige of the House of Bourbon behind the Huguenot cause. By doing so he added a new dimension to the age-old opposition of the mighty feudal subject to the crown: that opposition was now backed by a tightly knit military organization based on the Huguenot communities, by the financial contributions of wealthy bankers and businessmen, and by the dedicated religious zeal of the faithful—inspired by the example of Geneva.

At a time when the threat to the crown had never been greater, the monarchy itself presented a sorry spectacle. The struggle for political power at the centre of government after Henry II's death between the families of Guise, Bourbon, and Montmorency; the vacillating policy of Catherine de Médicis; and, most important of all, the ineptitude of three successive rulers—Francis II (1559–60), Charles IX, and Henry III—meant that local government officials were never confident of their authority in seeking to curb the growing threat of Huguenotism. Indeed, the chief opposition to Protestantism came not from the crown but from the Catholic Holy League. Because of the government's inability to control the situation, local Catholic unions or leagues began to appear in the 1560s, headed by nobles and prelates. In 1576, after the Peace of Monsieur with its concessions to the Huguenots, these local leagues were fused into a national Catholic Holy League. The league was headed by the Guise family and looked for material aid to Philip II of Spain. Its chief aims were the defeat of Protestantism in France and the restoration of ancient feudal rights and privileges. It sought, like the Protestants, to attract mass support; its clandestine organization was built around the House of Guise rather than the monarchy, from which it was increasingly alienated. In 1577 Henry III tried to nullify the league's influence, first by putting himself at its head and then by dissolving it altogether. This manoeuvre met with some success; but in 1585, when the death of Henry's brother, who had succeeded him as duc d'Anjou the previous year, made a Protestant succession to the throne much more likely, a second and far more revolutionary organization appeared. This second movement was centred in Paris among middle class professional men and members of the clergy and soon spread among the Parisian artisans, guilds, and public officials. Finally, through the intervention of the Duc de Guise, it inspired the reappearance throughout the country of the old Catholic Holy League of 1576, though now in a much more extreme and threatening form. The King himself, who was considered far too tolerant toward the Huguenots, was an object of attack. In town after town, royalist officials were replaced by members of the league. In Paris, the mob was systematically aroused; and in 1588, in the famous "Day of the Barricades," Henry III was driven from his own capital. After the murder of Guise at the end of that year, the league came out in open revolt against the crown. Towns renounced their royal allegiances and set up revolutionary governments. In

Massacre of St. Bartholomew's Day

The struggle for the central government

The Catholic Holy League in Paris

Paris, however, the league was most highly organized. There a central committee called the Sixteen was established that set up a Committee of Public Safety and conducted a reign of terror in a manner similar to the much more famous Revolution of 200 years later.

Paradoxically, this genuinely democratic and revolutionary element in the Holy League paved the way for the triumph of the Protestant leader Henry of Navarre, later Henry IV. The aristocratic members of the league took fright at the direction in which the extreme elements in the movement were proceeding. Their fears reached a climax in 1591, when the Sixteen arrested and executed three magistrates of the Parlement of Paris. The growing split in the ranks of the members of the league, combined with Henry's well-timed conversion to Catholicism, enabled him to seize the iniative and enter Paris, almost unopposed, in 1594. But the threat to the monarchy and therefore to the whole French state had been of a new and fundamental kind, and the strong position that Henry IV achieved by the time of his death is that much more remarkable. Part of his success lay in the unwillingness of his great subjects to contemplate a social and political upheaval that would displace them as well as the King from their positions of power and prestige.

Political ideology. The religious wars also engendered a luxuriant growth of political ideas that in the end provided a strong theoretical basis for the reassertion of royal authority.

A strong element in Calvin's teaching was the importance of passive obedience to secular authority—an idea that became impossible for the Huguenots to support after the Massacre of St. Bartholomew's Day. They began instead to advocate the right to attack the king if he would not guarantee them toleration. The most important Huguenot contribution in this change was the anonymous pamphlet *Vindiciae contra tyrannos* (1579), which raised fundamental questions about the prince's power and the rights of his subjects. The pamphlet advanced the idea of a twofold contract: the first contract, between God on the one hand and the ruler and his subjects on the other, recognized the belief that the king ruled under the aegis of Divine Providence; the second contract, between the king and the people, obliged the king to govern justly and the people to obey him so long as he did so. It followed from the argument in the *Vindiciae* that subjects had the right to rebel if the prince disobeyed the laws of God or refused to govern his people justly. This twofold contract was not intended to be a license for private and personal rebellion but was interpreted as justifying the corporate opposition of whole towns and provinces.

A second element in the realm of political ideas, deeply opposed to the contractual theory of the Huguenots, was *The Ultra-montanists* that of the Jesuit supporters of Ultramontanism, that is, the supporters of papal authority in France. The Ultramontanists feared that a strong national monarchy would mean the subordination of the church and the diminution of papal authority. They feared the triumph of both Huguenotism and Gallicanism in France. Their most effective controversialist was the Italian prelate Robert Bellarmine, whose *Disputationes* (3 vol., published 1586–93) and *De Potestate summi pontificis in rebus temporalibus* (1610) gave definite form to the theory of papal supremacy. By no means were all members of the league supporters of Bellarmine, though their extreme Catholicism made many of them sympathetic to his ideas. The definitive Gallican reply came in 1594 with Pierre Pithou's *Les Libertés de l'église gallicane*, which reiterated the basic tenets of Gallican doctrine: that the pope had no temporal authority in France and no more spiritual power than that bestowed on him by such conciliar decisions as the monarchy chose to recognize.

The growing support for Gallican opinion was a reflection of the emergence of the Politique Party after the Massacre of St. Bartholomew's Day. In the opinion of this moderate Catholic group, toleration should be granted to the Huguenots for the sake of peace and national unity. The Politiques were the spiritual heirs of the chancellor L'Hospital and represented an attitude of mind rather than an organized movement. Under the pressure of political events this group became convinced of the need to support a strong monarchy that could resist both Ultramontane and Huguenot excesses and the divisive influence of noble factions. They therefore increasingly identified themselves with the Gallican position. The Huguenots, too, were not slow to see the advantages for themselves of this new attitude, and the ideas of the *Vindiciae* gave way to the theory of passive obedience. The wheel had turned full circle.

With this emphasis upon passive obedience, the theory emerged of the divine right of kings. The first written *Divine-* statement of the theory in France is contained in the *right* works of Pierre de Belloy, especially his *De l'autorité theories du roi* (1588). He asserted that the monarchy was created by God and that the king was responsible to God alone. Any rebellion against the ruler, therefore, was a rebellion against the Almighty. The essential premise of the divine-right idea is that the right to command obedience cannot be bestowed by man; only God can grant such authority. God therefore chooses the king, and there can be no contractual relationship between the king and his people; to rebel even against an unjust ruler is to challenge God's choice. If the king breaks his contract with God, then he is answerable to God alone. On the wave of such ideas Henry of Navarre became king of a united France, supported by Huguenots and moderate Politique Catholics alike. The universalist doctrine of Bellarmine gave way to the national one of Pithou as the country closed ranks against Spain, the common enemy.

One other concept emerged about this time that helped to set the seal on Henry's authority: the idea of sovereignty, as expounded by Jean Bodin. In his *Six Livres de la République* (1576) Bodin argued that the political bond that made every man subject to one sovereign power overrode religious differences. Bodin provided the link divine right did not allow between the king and his people; divine right was concerned with the source of the ruler's power, sovereignty with its exercise. The needs of the political situation forced Bodin to give his sovereign virtually unlimited authority, though he insisted—as was traditionally the case in France—that the ruler should respect the sanctity of the natural law, of the fundamental laws of the kingdom, of property, and of the family. In 1614, on the occasion of the last meeting of the Estates-General before the Revolution, the Third Estate sought to have it made a fundamental law of the realm that under no pretext whatever was it permissible to disobey the king. This effort gives some indication of the extent to which the ideas of divine right and sovereignty had provided a firm theoretical base for the re-establishment of monarchical power after the dangerous years of civil war.

FRANCE IN THE EARLY 17TH CENTURY

Henry IV. The restoration of royal authority was not, of course, simply a matter of adjusting theories of kingship; there was a clear practical reason for Henry's success. The country had been torn apart for three decades, tottering on the brink of disintegration. By the time of Henry's succession, it was generally recognized that only a strong personality, independent of faction, could guarantee the unity of the state, even though that unity meant religious toleration for the Protestant minority. By the Edict of Nantes (April 13, 1598) Henry guaranteed the Huguenots freedom of conscience and the right to practice their religion publicly in certain prescribed areas of the country. As a surety against attack, the Huguenots were granted a number of fortresses, some of them, such as La Rochelle and Montpellier, extremely formidable strongholds. As individuals, Huguenots were made eligible to hold the same offices as Catholics and to attend the same schools and universities. Finally, to ensure impartial justice for them, the Edict established in the Parlement of Paris—the supreme judicial court under the king—a new chamber, the Chambre de l'Édit, containing a number of Protestant magistrates who would judge all cases involving Huguenots. Although the problem of religion was not finally settled by the Edict of Nantes, Henry did succeed in effecting an extended truce during which he could apply himself to the task of restoring the royal position.

The chief need of the monarchy was to improve the financial situation, parlous since the days of Henry II's wars and aggravated by the subsequent internecine conflict. Henry was fortunate in this connection to have the services of Maximilien de Béthune, duc de Sully, who was admitted to the King's financial council in 1596. Sully at once embarked upon a series of provincial tours, enforcing the repayment of royal debts, thereby increasing the King's revenues. He also provided the first real statements of government finances for many years; by 1598 he had become the effective head of the royal financial machine as well as a trusted member of the King's inner Cabinet. He held a variety of offices: superintendent of finances, grand master of artillery, superintendent of buildings, governor of the Bastille, and others. But it was in the field of finance that he made his greatest contribution to the welfare of the state. Sully was not an original financial thinker. He undertook no sweeping changes, contenting himself with making the existing system work. He succeeded in building up both an annual surplus and substantial reserves. The only measure he championed that might be described as novel and far-reaching was the introduction in 1604 of a new tax, the *paulette*, named after the financier Charles Paulet, which enabled officeholders to assure the heritability of their offices by paying one-sixtieth of the purchase price each year. The *paulette* was intended to increase royal revenues, though it had considerable political implications too, in effect making government offices practically hereditary. Politically, the *paulette* was to increase the independence of a wide range of royal officials, thereby limiting royal absolutism and strengthening the possibility of disinterested state service. In addition, Sully did much to reorganize fortifications and to rebuild roads and bridges after the devastation of the religious wars. In transportation his greatest work was the Briare Canal project to join the Seine and Loire rivers—the first such scheme in France—completed under Louis XIII.

Sully, however, favoured a much more cautious domestic policy overall than did his sovereign; and because Sully disliked merchants and manufacturers, he opposed many of the King's economic ventures. Henry IV believed in direct state intervention, and he took steps to fix wages and to prohibit strikes and illegal combinations of workmen. Henry's policies bore fruit especially in the textile industries, where the production of luxury silk goods and woollen and linen cloth greatly increased. Henry also took the initiative in making commercial treaties with Spain and England, thereby increasing the volume of French trade and stimulating the export of grain, cattle, and wine. Yet his efforts were not entirely successful, not least because merchants were more concerned with buying land and office (and thereby status) than with plowing back their profits into further industrial development. Though the country did assume a more prosperous air under Henry IV, that change was chiefly because of the domestic and foreign calm that followed the Peace of Vervins.

Although after Spain's agreement in 1598 to the restoration of the territorial position as it existed in 1559 Henry was not free of international complications, he was, however, able to prevent them from once more dividing his kingdom. He did have to counter a conspiracy led by one of his own marshals, Charles de Gontaut, duc de Biron, who plotted with the King of Spain and almost succeeded in raising southwest France in revolt. Henry, however, had Biron arrested and executed in 1602; this strong action against an old friend and powerful enemy had the effect of subduing the political rising and strengthening Henry's own authority. In central government Henry gave increasing power to Sully at the expense of the rest of his council; while in the provinces the use of the intendant, an official first regularly employed during the reign of Henry III, was widened to include the supervision of potentially dissident groups. The intendants also represented the crown at meetings of provin-

cial estates, enforced royal laws, and advised the king on a variety of local problems—fiscal, administrative, and military. When Henry IV was assassinated by François Ravaillac, a Catholic fanatic, in May 1610, he had gone a long way toward restoring the monarchy to a position of authority similar to that held by Francis I and Henry II and had reunified a state greatly threatened at his accession from both within and without.

Louis XIII, 1610–43. Henry's reign was followed by the regency of his widow, Marie de Médicis, who ruled on behalf of his young son Louis XIII (1610–43). Once more the security of the country was threatened as factions disputed around the throne. The work of Henry IV seemed likely to be undone. Crown and country, however, were rescued by probably the greatest minister of the whole Bourbon dynasty—the Cardinal de Richelieu (*q.v.*). Richelieu first came to the attention of the government in 1614, when he was chosen to present the final address of the clergy at the meeting of the Estates-General. His eloquence and political expertise on this occasion won him the notice of Marie de Médicis, who later appointed him her secretary. By 1616 Richelieu was secretary of state for war and foreign affairs. His career, however, received a check in the following year when he was exiled to Blois with the Queen Mother and subsequently to Avignon (1618). He began the climb back to power by negotiating the Treaty of Angoulême (1619), which reconciled Louis XIII to his mother. After the death in 1621 of Louis's favourite, Charles d'Albert, duc de Luynes, Richelieu regained effective power; he became a cardinal in 1622 and in April 1624 gained access to Louis XIII's council. On the disgrace in 1624 of the superintendent of finance, Charles de La Vieuville, he became Louis's principal minister—a position which he maintained until his death some 18 years later.

Richelieu proved an indefatigable servant of the French crown, intent on securing absolute obedience to the monarchy and on raising its international prestige. The first objective required him to crush a number of revolts of the nobles, the first of which, in 1626, involved the King's younger brother and heir, Gaston de France, duc d'Orléans. Louis acted ruthlessly, and one of the conspirators, Henri de Talleyrand, comte de Chalais, was executed. Then, in 1630, came the celebrated "Day of Dupes" when the King's life was despaired of and the Queen Mother, now allied with Gaston and the keeper of the seals, Michel de Marillac, prepared to move against Richelieu. The King, however, recovered and chose to support Richelieu against the wishes of his mother, his wife, and his confessor. Finally, at the very end of his life the Cardinal had to overcome another conspiracy headed by the young royal favourite, Henri Coiffier de Ruzé, marquis de Cinq-Mars, in which Gaston was once more implicated. Through all these crises Richelieu retained the King's support, for it was in Louis's interests, too, that such intrigues should be firmly dealt with.

In the course of strengthening royal absolutism, Richelieu also came into conflict with the Huguenots. He believed that their right under the Edict of Nantes to maintain armed fortresses weakened the King's position at home and abroad. Protestant rebellions in 1625 and 1627 persuaded the Cardinal of the need for a direct confrontation. The major Huguenot citadel of La Rochelle was attacked by royal troops in 1627 and, despite attempts by the English to assist the Protestants, fell in the following year. Another royal army marched into Languedoc, where the Huguenot forces were concentrated, and quickly overcame them. The Peace of Alais (1629) left the Huguenots free to enjoy religious and civil liberties, but they lost the military power that had made them a threat to the government. They were never to pose that sort of threat again and little more would be heard of them until Louis XIV decided to repeal Henry IV's Edict of Nantes.

Richelieu also took a great interest in economic matters. To promote economic self-sufficiency he encouraged the manufacture of tapestry, glass, silk, linen, and woollen cloth. He gave privileges to companies that established colonies in America, Africa, and the West In-

Sully's financial reforms

Henry's foreign policy

The rise of Richelieu

dies. To protect trading and colonial interests he created a navy, which by 1642 had 63 oceangoing vessels.

On the basis of these policies Richelieu was able to pursue an increasingly successful foreign policy. His first aim was the security of France by the occupation of key points on the country's frontiers lying along imperial and Spanish territories. He thus involved France in the War of the Mantuan Succession (1628–31) in northern Italy. Through diplomatic means he worked for the dismissal of Albrecht Wenzel von Wallenstein, the brilliant general fighting on the side of the emperor Ferdinand II, whose forces were threatening to destroy the Protestant princes of Germany in the Thirty Years' War. To undermine the power of the Habsburgs, he prolonged this conflict, negotiating with the United Provinces; with Gustavus II Adolphus of Sweden, with whom he concluded the subsidy Treaty of Bärwalde in 1631, agreeing to pay the Swedish king 1,000,000 livres per year to continue the war; with Gustavus' successor, Count Axel Oxenstierna; and with Bernhard, duke of Saxe-Weimar. Eventually, in 1635, Richelieu committed France to direct conflict with the Habsburgs; and before his death he had savoured the triumph of French arms in the Spanish Netherlands, Lorraine, Alsace, and Roussillon.

The career of Richelieu bears something of a contradictory aspect. He undoubtedly added to the earlier success of Henry IV and Sully in overcoming the threat of anarchy and disorder that was the legacy of the late 16th century. Indeed, his contemporary reputation was one of supreme ruthlessness and arbitrariness in the application of power. Yet he was never more than the King's creature, incapable of pursuing a course of action of which Louis disapproved, always vulnerable to the loss of royal favour and support. He was ambitious, but he recognized that his desire for power could best be satisfied within the confines of dutiful royal service. Richelieu was no innovator: he devised neither new administrative procedures nor novel methods of taxation to secure the King's authority. Indeed, the power of the great financiers grew with the government's need for additional war revenue, posing a different threat to royal absolutism. Richelieu's unique contribution lay in the single-minded devotion he gave to his objective: the increase of royal authority at home and abroad. Richelieu died in 1642, and Louis XIII died the following year. France was once again ruled by a regent, the queen mother, Anne of Austria. But the task of governing the country fell increasingly into the hands of another cardinal, Mazarin.

The Frondes. The years of Louis XIV's minority were dominated by the Frondes, a series of civil disturbances that lasted from 1648 to 1653. (The name Fronde arose from window breaking as a tactic in the resistance to Mazarin. The *fronde*, a sling for propelling stones, was a popular toy.) The government's financial difficulties were once more at the root of the trouble, and in the first few years of the regency a variety of expedients were tried to raise additional revenue for the war with Spain. There was about these expedients an air of arbitrariness and compulsion that antagonized a wide cross section of Parisian society, notably the Parlement of Paris, the animosity of which was heightened by Mazarin's use of intendants in the localities to cut across traditional legal hierarchies. Although most of the disputes were on the face of it concerned with financial exactions, below the surface an older constitutional argument was developing as Mazarin followed Richelieu in attempting to dictate from the centre in the interests of the state. The climax came when the government failed to renew the *paulette* for the members of the provincial parlements and for some of the chief legal officeholders in the capital, in the Cour des Aides, the Chambre des Comptes, and the Grand-Conseil. This decision was not a gratuitous rebuff to these magistrates but yet another attempt to gain additional revenue, this time by offering a renewal of the *paulette* in lieu of four years' salary.

At this point, the first Fronde (the Fronde of the Parlement) began with the outraged magistrates of the three courts concerned joining with the Parlement of Paris to demand redress. Their demands included the abolition of the office of intendant; a reduction in the level of the *taille;* and the restoration of normal judicial procedure in registering financial edicts in the Parlement. The regent and Mazarin at first took a conciliatory attitude, but each side gradually moved to more committed and extreme positions, and civil disturbances in Paris exacerbated an already delicate situation. The magistrates increasingly aimed their fire at Mazarin for he, like Richelieu before him, seemed to be taking over the King's authority and using it in uncharted and illegal areas. The magistrates, however, were not revolutionaries and the state of disorder in the capital frightened them. That fact, allied with fears of a Spanish invasion (for the war was still continuing with Spain despite the Peace of Westphalia in 1648), persuaded them, in 1649, to make the Peace of Rueil with the government, the terms of which were for the most part favourable to the magistrates' original demands. At this stage the second civil war broke out, the Fronde of the princes, headed by the Great Condé. The second Fronde was a pale reflection of the feudal reaction during the Wars of Religion; and although Condé succeeded in gaining control of Paris, he did not acquire the support of the Parlement except briefly and under duress. In October 1652 Condé fled to Spain, and Louis XIV re-entered his capital in triumph.

Neither Fronde posed the grievous threat to the very basis of the state that had existed in the previous century. Mazarin was the chief object of enmity and that fact itself helps to explain the less serious nature of the threat. What was at issue was not the King's authority per se but the manner in which it had been exercised since Richelieu's time, in a less personal and therefore seemingly more arbitrary fashion.

After the Frondes, Mazarin continued to play a key role in government as chief adviser to the young king, whose respect and affection he had long possessed. His career ended on a high note with a successful conclusion of the war with Spain negotiated by the Treaty of the Pyrenees (1659). According to its terms France gained Roussillon and Cerdagne in the south and Artois and a number of border towns in the north; and the Rhine became France's frontier in the east. By the treaty, too, Louis XIV was betrothed to the infanta Marie-Thérèse, the elder daughter of Philip IV of Spain. It was by any reckoning a triumphant peace, though it sowed the seeds of future European conflict over the issue of the Spanish succession (see below). When Mazarin died in 1661, Louis was confident enough to take up the reins of government without recourse to another first minister.

Before examining the most famous reign in French history, one further aspect of the previous decades requires scrutiny—the economic and social situation to which some historians have attached considerable importance, especially as an element in the so-called general European crisis of the 17th century (a series of upheavals— among them the Frondes and the English Civil War— that affected Europe in the middle of this century). A Soviet historian, Boris Porshnev, first drew particular attention to the series of local uprisings taking place in France in the first half of the 17th century. He notes that all of them contained an element of desperation as serious financial hardship brought about by exorbitant tax demands and crop failures forced the participants into action. Great fluctuations in prices and outbreaks of famine further accentuated the misery. From these observations he draws ideological conclusions that have been widely disputed. Porshnev maintains that the state was the instrument by which the dominant economic class exploited the underprivileged and that revolt was a sign of the popular resistance of the exploited masses. On the other hand, Roland Mousnier, perhaps the greatest French authority on the period, has pointed to evidence that suggests that these revolts were not always spontaneous: they were provoked in 1632 by the municipal authorities at Lyons; in 1636 by the nobility of Périgord; and in 1641 by Louis, comte de Soissons, a prince of the blood. In 1643 the conduct of bishops and magistrates in Languedoc was seen by one royal official as likely to encourage sedition there. From these examples and others like them, Mousnier concludes that the nobility was seeking to reverse the process by which the king's officials were extending the crown's authority at their expense, taxing peasants to such a degree as to limit the amount the peasants could afford to pay in seigneurial dues, insinuating the king's justice between themselves and their peasants, reducing their prestige in the local community, and trampling upon old rights and privileges. Mousnier asserts that the nobility, far from representing the oppressive state, was itself involved in a struggle against increasing state interference. The opposition provoked by the work of Richelieu and Mazarin fits well into Mousnier's view and gives it support. It remains true, however, that most popular revolts began as protests against fiscal demands that were intolerable to people already suffering grievous economic hardship and that they were often provoked by a particular incident, such as the appearance of a new tax collector or a new system of tax collection.

There was little sign of the revolutionary attitude that had characterized aspects of the 16th-century Wars of Religion. On the contrary, there were positive indications of continuing loyalty to the crown, with such rebel slogans as *"Vive le roi sans la gabelle"* or *"Vive le roi sans la taille."* Nor was the other great bastion of the establishment, the church, attacked. The substantial tax of the tenth continued to be paid to the church without complaint. During the Fronde, neither the nobles nor the magistrates represented a revolutionary political element, and even the rioters on the Parisian streets were simply desperately poor. There was no social revolution either under Henry IV, Richelieu, or Mazarin despite the appearance of increasing numbers of hereditary officeholders, aided in their dynastic ambitions by the device of the *paulette*. The elevation to noble rank of new families was a cyclical process in France that would continue through and beyond the reign of Louis XIV.

THE AGE OF LOUIS XIV

Like his predecessor Henry IV, Louis assumed plenary power at a time when few of his subjects wished to be reminded of recent civil disturbances and were content to accept his absolute authority. Throughout his long reign Louis never lost the hold over his people that he assumed at the beginning. He worked hard to project his authority in the splendid setting of Versailles, to depict it in his arrogant motto: *Nec pluribus impar* ("None his equal"), and in his sun emblem. He buttressed his authority with the divine-right doctrines elaborated by Bishop Jacques-Bénigne Bossuet and proclaimed it across Europe by force of arms. Yet he made surprisingly few institutional or administrative changes in the structure of government. Like Richelieu, Louis used the system that he had inherited and adapted it to suit his own personality and outlook. This practice may be seen first in his attitude to the machinery of central government.

The development of central government. His inner council was on the model of the royal council in Richelieu's days, a Conseil d'en Haut consisting of only three or four members and excluding the King's own relatives. Members of this council were known as ministers, but they held no formal right to the title and ceased to be minister if the King chose not to summon them. The first of these great men were Michel Le Tellier, Hugues de Lionne, and Nicolas Fouquet; but the latter was disgraced within a year, and by 1665 his place had been taken by Mazarin's former secretary, Jean-Baptiste Colbert. These three men dominated the government in the early years of Louis's personal reign, but always, as with Richelieu and Louis XIII, under the watchful and jealous eye of the King. Le Tellier had been secretary of state for military affairs under Mazarin's regime, and his greatest contribution under Louis was to reorganize the army along lines that were hardly changed until after 1789. He created a royal army, wearing the king's uniform, commanded by his officers, and ultimately responsible to the sovereign. It was a standing army of hitherto undreamed-of size, reaching 400,000 men in times of war

Louis's inner council

and requiring close regulation in matters of discipline, training, recruitment, supply, and overall organization. The success of Le Tellier and of his son Louvois, who succeeded him, goes far to explain the dominance of French arms in Europe during Louis's reign.

Lionne, the expert in foreign affairs, had been the chief French negotiator at the Peace of the Pyrenees. His effective influence with Louis is difficult to gauge; and certainly he was not the sole source of advice in foreign affairs. Lionne remains a more elusive personality than his colleagues, though there can be no doubt of his importance. It should be remembered that all important matters of state were reviewed at the Conseil d'en Haut; and the King's ministers were expected to give advice and opinions on all that was discussed, not simply on matters in the area of their particular expertise.

Colbert, however, remains the best known of these intimate counsellors. Of the 17 ministers summoned by Louis XIV to the Conseil d'en Haut during his reign, five were members of the Colbert family. In 1664, Colbert was appointed superintendent of the King's buildings, in 1665, controller general of finances, in 1669, secretary of state for the navy. His capacity for work and his grasp of detail were remarkable; but he was not an original, much less a revolutionary, thinker. Like Sully, his chief contribution to the King's finances was to make the machinery more efficient, not to substitute any new mechanisms. Colbert's first achievement was to present the King with a monthly statement of the financial situation, though his annual estimates for the following year never persuaded Louis of the need for economies if his mind was set in other directions. Yet within ten years of taking office Colbert, mainly by tightening up on the tax-collecting administration and by rationalizing the gathering of indirect taxes, did succeed in producing a surplus. He turned a large part of central and northern France into a free-trade area and gave the responsibility for collecting all indirect taxes there to a new syndicate of tax farmers called the Farmers-General. Under Colbert, the total sum levied from indirect taxation rose from 36,000,000 livres to 62,000,000.

In his industrial policy Colbert believed that France needed to produce for itself those manufactured goods that it was having to import. To achieve this mercantilist goal, derived from, among other sources, the ideas of Richelieu, Colbert was willing to invoke a variety of improvisations: direct subsidies, exemptions from the *taille*, monopoly grants, controls exercised through town guilds. Skilled foreign workmen were persuaded to settle in France and to pass on their skills to native artisans; protective tariffs were imposed. The famous tapestry works of the Gobelins family was made a state enterprise, and France became largely self-sufficient in the production of woollen cloth. Colbert also had some success in other industries, such as sugar refining, plate-glass making, and the production of silk, naval stores, and armaments. The overall results of his hard work, however, were disappointing. France underwent no industrial revolution during the reign of Louis XIV.

Much more successful were Colbert's efforts at fostering the growth of the navy. He reorganized the recruitment system on a rotary basis, seamen serving in the royal navy for six months in every three years. He refurbished the hospitals in each of the major ports; rebuilt the arsenals at Toulon and Rochefort; and increased the size of the navy from about 25 ships in 1661 to 144 in 1677. He also established schools of marine engineering, hydrography, and cartography. His interest in re-establishing French sea power was, in part, to challenge the commercial supremacy of the Dutch. He encouraged the building of the French mercantile marine and established a number of overseas trading companies, in particular the East India and Levant companies, neither of which had much success. He also attempted to protect French colonial interests in the West Indies and Canada.

Besides the Conseil d'en Haut, the King's council also met for somewhat less vital matters under a variety of different guises. The Conseil des Dépêches had particular responsibility for home affairs, including the activities

Colbert's financial reforms

French expansion, 1600–1766.

Map legend:

Acquired:
- 1601–1643
- To 1648
- To 1659
- To 1662
- Ceded to Sardinia
- To 1678
- To 1681
- 1682–1766
- Avignon to the Papacy

of the intendants; the Conseil Royal des Finances supervised important matters affecting financial aspects of the King's domain lands. These two councils, like the Conseil d'en Haut, were presided over by the King in person. But the royal council also met under three further titles to deal with judicial and administrative matters and not in the King's presence. The Conseil Privé judged disputes between individuals or bodies and dispensed the King's supreme and final judgments. The Conseil d'État et Finances expedited financial matters of secondary importance, while the Grande Direction des Finances was an administrative tribunal settling disputes between the state and individuals or corporations. Each of these subdivisions of the King's council, contained more members than the exclusive Conseil d'en Haut, made up of the secretaries of state and of financial and judicial experts.

The initial group composing the Conseil d'en Haut contributed a great deal to the basic pattern of Louis's reign, particularly in military, fiscal, naval, and commercial attitudes, partly because many of those who followed as ministers came from the same tightly knit group of royal servants. The five members of the Colbert family have been mentioned; there were also three Le Telliers; and while only one member of the Phélypeaux family, Louis II, comte de Pontchartrain, was a minister, four served as important secretaries of state. All of these counsellors reflected the attitude of the King himself: they worked extremely hard; they proffered advice but were under no illusions about the danger of arguing once Louis had made up his mind; and they favoured a protectionist, paternalist policy, whether in the organization of industry, the administration of the colonies, or the building up of the navy.

To carry out the decisions reached in his intimate and secret Conseil d'en Haut, Louis relied chiefly on his provincial intendants. Their powers were completely undifferentiated, and their commissions varied according to changes in royal policy. Like the ministers at the centre, they depended upon the King for their security of tenure. In the provinces they could exercise powers of police; raise military forces; regulate industrial, commercial, and agricultural matters; enforce censorship; administer the financial affairs of various communities; assign and collect taxes; and wield considerable judicial authority in civil and criminal affairs. Inevitably, these agents of the central government created considerable friction and hostility. These new men, with no local roots, answerable only to the King and acting almost invariably in an authoritarian context, were deeply resented by older royal officials, by municipal authorities and guilds, and by local parlements and estates—all of whom operated through well-established channels and according to traditional local privileges. The use of intendants, who held neither venal nor hereditary office, was one way in which

The intendants

the limiting effect of the sale of office on royal policies could be circumvented. The authoritarian element of Louis XIV's reign is undeniable: he was determined that no institution or social class would escape the supervision of the crown and its ministers.

In particular, the Frondes remained a painful memory from his childhood, and he never allowed the great nobles a similar opportunity for revolt. Versailles became a place of surveillance for pensioned noblemen and their families whose only serious occupation was the traditional one of arms, for the pursuit of which Louis provided ample opportunities. The second rebellious group in the Frondes, the members of the Parlement of Paris, were likewise subjected to stringent controls. In 1673 Louis produced regulations stipulating that the court's remonstrances against royal enactments sent to it could only be made in future after the laws concerned had been registered. By this device the King effectively muzzled the magistrates' criticisms of royal policy.

Louis's religious policy. Louis was also on his guard against religious dissent, and the revocation of the Edict of Nantes in 1685 was the culmination of two decades of government hostility to the Protestants in France. Louis, like most of his contemporaries, believed that toleration had no virtue and that unity in the state was extremely difficult to maintain where two or more churches were tolerated. Consequently, especially after 1678, Louis increased the degree of persecution; churches were destroyed, certain professions were put out of reach of the Huguenots, and Protestant children were taken away from their parents and brought up as Catholics. The notorious practice of dragonnades, the billeting of soldiers on Protestant families with permission to behave as brutally as they wished, was introduced. Finally, in 1685 the Edict of Nantes was revoked in order that Louis could claim that he had succeeded where Emperor Leopold I had failed—that is, in extirpating Protestantism from his realm. The revocation of the Edict of Nantes angered Protestant Europe at a time when Louis's European designs were beginning to meet serious resistance. The revocation deprived France of a number of gifted craftsmen, sailors, and soldiers. At least 600 officers, including Marshal Friedrich, Graf von Schomberg, and Henri de Massue, marquis de Ruvigny (later the earl of Galway), joined William of Orange, the leader of the Grand Alliance against Louis. Research, however, has reversed the earlier view that the decay of French industry at the end of Louis's reign was the direct result of the expulsion of Huguenot mercantile talent.

The same zeal for uniformity made Louis attack the Jansenists. The theological position of the Jansenists is difficult to define; but Louis, who was no theologian, was content with the simple fact that these zealous Catholics had taken up an unorthodox position that threatened the unity of the state. The movement had begun over the perennial issue of grace and free will as it was propounded in the *Augustinus* of Bishop Cornelius Otto Jansen, published in 1640. In 1653 Pope Innocent X condemned five propositions from Jansen's doctrine, but the movement grew in strength with notable adherents, including the cardinal de Retz and the great mathematician Blaise Pascal. In 1705 Pope Clement XI published the bull *Vineam Domini*, which further condemned the writings of Jansen; but the archbishop of Paris, Cardinal Louis-Antoine de Noailles, appeared ready to lead the Jansenist forces in opposition to the Pope. Under the influence of his confessor, Père Michel Le Tellier, Louis decided to ask the Pope for another formal condemnation of the creed. Finally, in 1713, the famous bull *Unigenitus* was promulgated, which, far from ending Jansenism, drove it in the following reign into a disruptive alliance with Gallicanism. Louis's real attitude in this situation is not entirely clear: certainly he was asserting his authoritarian insistence upon unity. He was suspicious of religious innovation; and his action is consistent with the increasingly orthodox and rigid mood of his last years. Yet in seeking the Pope's support in this matter, he was reversing years of bitter hostility toward Rome when, like many of his predecessors, including Francis I

and Henry IV, he had leaned heavily upon the support of traditional Gallican doctrine.

According to that doctrine, the French king possessed the right of temporal and spiritual regale—that is, the right to nominate new bishops and to administer and draw the revenue from bishoprics while they remained vacant. In 1673 Louis extended this right to the whole of the French kingdom, which had been enlarged in the recent War of Devolution (see below). The Pope opposed the extension over this enlarged area; and eventually, in 1682, the Gallican Articles were published as a law of the French state, asserting that the King was in no way subject to the Pope in temporal matters and that he could not be excommunicated and reaffirming the independence of the French Church from Rome. The mutual animosity of King and Pope only ended in 1693, when, following William of Orange's successful attempt to secure the English throne, Louis agreed to suspend the edict of 1682; but it was a suspension only, not a recantation. The tradition of Gallican independence remained.

Absolutism of Louis. Thus, in religious matters (except where Jansenism was concerned), in his dealings with the nobility and the Parlement, in his attitude to the economy, and in his manner of governing the country, Louis revealed a desire to exercise a paternal control of affairs that might suggest a modern dictator rather than a 17th-century king. Though such a comparison has been made, it is most misleading; neither in theoretical nor in practical terms could Louis XIV be thought of as all-powerful. First of all, the legitimacy of his position under the law—the ancient fundamental law of succession—made him the interpreter of the law and the fount of justice in the state, not a capricious autocrat. Similarly, his kingship bestowed upon him a quasi-spiritual role, symbolized by his consecration with holy oil at his coronation, which obliged him to govern justly in accordance with the laws of God and Christian morality. He was also bound by the need to take counsel; and though he always made up his own mind, he insisted on receiving advice on all important matters of state, which further restricted any arbitrary instincts. Next, there was the essentially federal nature of the country with its collection of such peripheral provinces as Brittany, Normandy, and Provence, all retaining their own estates and customs. Within both these *pays d'état* and *pays d'élection* (where the estates no longer met), there was a variety of groups and corporations, not to mention individuals, with their own legally held rights, privileges, and exemptions: the nobility, the clergy, the towns, the King's officers. To impose rigid uniformity in such a situation was both impossible and undreamed-of by contemporaries. On the contrary, one of the King's prime obligations was to uphold and respect the myriad different rights to which his subjects laid claim. Perhaps most of all the King was limited by financial stringency. Louis could and often did try to persuade the cities and provincial estates to raise their contributions and the clergy to increase the size of their *don gratuit* ("free gift"); he also created more offices and annuities. But these were mere palliatives, and the King was forced on two occasions to introduce novel measures: in 1695 he levied a capitation, or head tax, applicable to all French laymen, even to the princes of the blood; and in 1710 a *dixième* (tenth) that similarly went against the interests of the privileged classes, including the clergy, by requiring a tenth to be paid to the state from all incomes. Significantly, however, Louis made it perfectly clear on both occasions that he recognized the extraordinary and temporary nature of these impositions, made necessary by the pressures of war. It was impossible to be a despot while financial resources were so precarious. The notion persisted that the king should ordinarily live off his own *domaine*. It was also impossible while no nationwide police force existed and while the state of communications remained so poor. All these factors make it clear that a situation simply did not exist in which totalitarian government, at least by 20th-century standards, could have had any meaning.

Finally, Louis XIV remained the prisoner of France's social structure. It is sometimes alleged that the King

Revocation of the Edict of Nantes

Louis's attack on the Jansenists

Limitation of Louis's power

ruled through the bourgeoisie. It is true that a number of the most distinguished families of the reign were not of ancient nobility; but their faithful and effective service to the king was rewarded in an entirely traditional way; that is, by social elevation. Colbert's father was an unsuccessful merchant; but all his granddaughters married dukes. In other words, the opportunity to enter the highest ranks of the nobility, which had long been available in France, was simply emphasized by Louis XIV. As the greatest nobleman in France, he had no doubt that he must retain the prestige and privileges of the nobility, but he knew equally well that the nobility should not become a caste closed to ambitious and able men. His social conservatism both buttressed his authority and prevented him from exceeding it.

Foreign affairs. It is as a great European figure that Louis XIV is best known. Though from the beginning of his reign Louis pursued a vigorous foreign policy, historical opinion has tended to move away from the traditional view that Louis sought to dominate Europe, only to meet his just deserts at the end of his reign. A case can be argued for the view that Louis pursued consistent and for the most part moderate aims and pursued them successfully up to and including the Treaty of Utrecht (1713). The starting point for this interpretation is the ambiguous Peace of Münster (1648), forming part of the great European settlement of Westphalia (see THIRTY YEARS' WAR), the terms of which subsequently became a bone of contention between Bourbon and Habsburg rulers. A critical issue was the fate of the three bishoprics of Metz, Toul, and Verdun on the northeast frontier of France. These bishoprics, occupied by the French since 1552, were formally acquired in 1648 together with a number of towns in nearby Alsace. One of the main Habsburg aims in the War of the League of Augsburg, or War of the Grand Alliance (1689–97), and in the War of the Spanish Succession (1701–14) was the restoration of the three bishoprics and the province of Franche-Comté, also on the eastern frontier of France, connecting Burgundy with Alsace, which Louis had acquired at the Treaties of Nijmegen (1678–79) at the end of the Dutch War (1672–78). Louis was determined to hold on to the gains acquired, however ambiguously, in Alsace; and he hoped to add Lorraine, to the north of Franche-Comté, to further consolidate this least secure French frontier area. Lorraine was periodically occupied by French troops, notably between 1633 and 1648 and 1670 and 1697, and Louis sought through various exchange schemes to incorporate it into France. The French share of the Partition Treaties (1698, 1700) in Italy was intended as an exchange for Lorraine and not as a means of threatening English and Dutch trade with the Levant. Lorraine, however, did not become a part of France until 1766.

Louis's policy in the northeast was constant and understandable. Franche-Comté was one entry into France previously exploited by its enemies that Louis succeeded in closing in 1678. He had already closed another, the port of Dunkirk, by purchasing it from Charles II of England in 1662; a third gateway, from the southern Netherlands, was effectively barred by the military fortifications erected by his great military engineer, Sébastien Le Prestre de Vauban in the 1680s. The capture of Lorraine would have bolted yet one more dangerous entry. Of course the situation looked quite different from the Habsburg point of view, especially after Louis's seizure of the key city of Strasbourg (1681), an episode that goes to the heart of the controversial matter of his reunion policy. Following the successful Peace of Nijmegen, Louis began to employ his own judicial courts to claim sovereignty over all the dependencies of territories that he already possessed in Alsace, Franche-Comté, Metz, Toul, and Verdun. The manoeuvre enabled him to consolidate his control, especially over Alsace and Franche-Comté, though the legality of the claims to some of the alleged "dependencies" was extremely dubious. There was no legal justification whatever for Louis's greatest coup in the area—the seizure in September 1681 of the independent city of Strasbourg. To Louis this key city, the door through which imperial armies could pass

Louis's successes in the northeast

(and three times in the recently concluded war had passed) into Alsace, represented a serious threat, for Strasbourg was within easy reach of the Danube Valley and Vienna. His fears in this area may best be illustrated by his offer during the War of the League of Augsburg to waive his claim to the Spanish succession on condition that Nijmegen be respected; that Lorraine be absorbed into France (with proper compensations elsewhere); and that the Spanish and Austrian lands should not be united under one ruler. The emperor Leopold immediately rejected these proposals. When the final climactic conflict of the reign, the War of the Spanish Succession, was proceeding so badly, Louis offered to relinquish all the gains he had made from the Spanish inheritance; but he desperately hoped to hold on to Metz, Toul, Verdun, Alsace, and Franche-Comté.

Louis's attitude toward the Dutch was less moderate and more bullying. His invasion of the Spanish Netherlands in 1667 and the ensuing War of Devolution frightened the Dutch into a Triple Alliance with England and Sweden, which led to the Treaty of Aix-la-Chapelle (1668). Then, in the Dutch War that followed shortly afterward (1672–78), Louis intended to warn the Dutch that France was a serious commercial competitor and to force the Dutch to give him a free hand in the Spanish Netherlands when the issue of the Spanish succession came to the fore. He learned from that war that he could never hope to incorporate a large part of the Netherlands into France against Dutch opposition; but he also continued to fear the manner in which the Dutch might try to influence the government of the Spanish Netherlands for their own economic benefit. Here again was an example of mutual hostility and suspicion in which the interpretation of motives in Versailles and in The Hague were diametrically opposed. At the Treaty of Rijswijk (1697) the Dutch gained the right to keep a series of Dutch barrier fortresses within the southern Netherlands as a check against French aggression; it was Louis's seizure of these fortresses in 1701 that precipitated the War of the Spanish Succession.

The Dutch War

That war has usually been depicted as the most significant element in an assessment of Louis's total foreign policy: for some historians, all his relations with the rest of Europe were geared to this great issue; for others, it was the final misjudgment born of overconfidence, provoked by his own ambitious miscalculations, and destined to ruin France. It is certainly true that the approaching end of the direct ruling line in Spain had interested European rulers for many years; and the Bourbon claim to a share in that rich inheritance—deriving from Louis's marriage to Marie-Thérèse, elder daughter of King Philip IV of Spain—was accepted as a key factor in the situation: in 1668 Louis and Emperor Leopold I had gone so far as to sign a partition treaty, more than 30 years before the death of the last Spanish Habsburg, Charles II. No European statesman was surprised, therefore, at Louis's later concern when, after the signature of the Treaty of Rijswijk in 1697, he undertook negotiations with the English king William III out of which two further partition treaties emerged. The crucial moment came when Charles II's last will was published, offering the Spanish crown, in opposition to the second Partition Treaty, to Louis's grandson Philip, duc d'Anjou (later Philip V). Louis's decision to accept did not in itself provoke war. There is evidence that both William and the Dutch believed that Charles's will would name the Habsburg candidate; and they certainly had no intention, in the light of what it did contain, of trying to force the Emperor to accept the treaty, which he had always resolutely opposed. Besides, if Louis had snubbed the Spanish offer, it would have been made to Austria, and the spectre of the restoration of Charles V's empire—probably coupled with French losses on the northeastern frontiers—was intolerable. In addition, Louis had recently made peace after the War of the Grand Alliance, the hardest conflict in which he had so far been engaged; and he had no illusions about the difficulty of overcoming another coalition under William III's leadership. He did not seek war, therefore, but he did make mistakes that made war likely: his recognition of the Old Pretender as James III of England; his unexplained decision to protect his grandson's right to the French throne (he was envisaging not a single, united realm of France and Spain but two Bourbon kingdoms with the senior heir succeeding in France); his occupation of the barrier fortresses; and his seizure of the monopoly of the Spanish-American trade. When peace was signed at Utrecht in 1713, however, despite the disasters of the intervening years, Louis succeeded in holding onto the gains in Europe that he had considered vital throughout his reign, including Alsace and Strassburg. In addition, his grandson remained king of Spain, despite all of the efforts of the Grand Alliance to replace him by their candidate, the Austrian archduke Charles (as Charles III). It is true that in the darkest time of the war, during the years 1708–10, the desperate King was ready to give up these precious gains and was prevented only by the intransigence of his opponents with their impossible demand that he should himself assist in driving his grandson from the throne of Spain. Likewise, a fortuitous change of government in England in 1710, which ushered in the Tory peace ministry, and the elevation of the Archduke to the imperial title as Charles VI in 1711 weakened the unity of purpose of the Grand Alliance and enabled Louis's most effective soldier, Claude-Louis-Hector, duc de Villars, to stage a military revival. Therefore, the relatively successful conclusion of the war from France's point of view was not entirely of Louis's own fashioning, and had events forced Louis to accept a total surrender, it would have been even more tempting for historians to blame the defeat upon the excessive ambitions of an arrogant man.

Nor can it be denied that Louis was arrogant and that his arrogance aroused fear and resentment in his neighbours. Equally, he was intolerant, like most of his contemporaries, and feared by Protestant powers as the leader of a new and vengeful Counter-Reformation. Both facets of the great King need to be borne in mind when assessing his overall foreign policy, and they help to counter any tendency to overestimate the defensive nature of his strategy. That defensive element, however, is of significance and has been largely lost sight of, especially in assessments of the reign written in English. Louis frightened Europe with his quest for *la gloire*, by which he meant the favourable verdict of history on his contribution to French security and territorial integrity but which his enemies interpreted more narrowly as a preoccupation with military triumphs and vainglorious display. That contemporary interpretation, still widely accepted nearly three centuries later, does less than justice to Louis's shrewd appreciation of political realities and of France's long-term interests.

FRENCH CULTURE IN THE 17TH CENTURY

If historians are not yet agreed on the political motives of Louis XIV, they all accept, however, the cultural and artistic significance of the epoch over which he and his two 17th-century predecessors reigned. In their different ways—Henry IV's interest lay in town planning, Louis XIII's in music, and Louis XIV's in the theatre and in landscape gardening—they all actively stimulated the emergence of great talents and were aided by such royal ministers as Richelieu and Mazarin, who were considered patrons in their own right.

The rebuilding of Paris

From Henry IV's reign dates the rebuilding of Paris as a tasteful, ordered city, with the extensions to the Louvre and the building of the Pont Neuf and the Place Dauphine and, outside the capital, the renovations and extensions at Fontainebleau and Saint-Germain-en-Laye. He succeeded in making Paris what it had never been before —the centre of polite society—and he must therefore take some credit, though he was not personally interested in such matters, for the establishment of the famous salon of Catherine de Vivonne, marquise de Rambouillet, which flourished from 1617 until 1665. There, men of letters mingled with the great nobility to the mutual advantage of both. The guests at her salon included the statesmen Richelieu and the Great Condé; the epigrammatist the Duc de La Rochefoucauld; the letter writer

Marie de Rabutin-Chantal, marquise de Sévigné; the novelist Madeleine de Scudéry; the poet François de Malherbe; and the dramatist Pierre Corneille. Richelieu was a key figure in the artistic and architectural development of Paris during his years in power. He was fortunate to employ the great architect Jacques Le Mercier who built for him, close to the Louvre, the Palais-Cardinal, later the Palais-Royal, which contained two theatres and a gallery for the Cardinal's *objets d'art*. Under the same patron, Le Mercier also built the church of the Sorbonne, where Richelieu is buried. In the world of painting, the Cardinal supported Simon Vouet, who decorated the Palais-Cardinal, and Philippe de Champaigne, whose surviving portraits include famous representations of Richelieu himself. His most notable contribution, however, was in the field of letters, with the establishment, in 1634, of the Académie Française to regulate and maintain the standards of the French language. One of its first tasks was the production of a standard dictionary, a massive work published in four volumes in 1694. The Académie succeeded over the years in making the pursuit of letters socially acceptable, though still inferior to the pursuit of arms. Finally, Richelieu's great interest in the theatre persuaded him to patronize a number of dramatists, including Jean de Rotrou and Corneille. Richelieu's patronage of the arts was taken over by his great pupil Mazarin who collected some 500 paintings, which he housed in the Palais Mazarin (now the Bibliothèque Nationale), which itself was enlarged for Mazarin by the architect François Mansart. He also commissioned Louis Le Vau to rebuild part of the medieval castle of Vincennes, thus setting him off on his successful career.

Versailles

Louis XIV's patronage centred on Versailles, the great palace that also played such an important part in the political life of 17th-century France. There André Le Nôtre designed the formal gardens, which still attract a multitude of admiring visitors as they did when they were first completed. There Jules Hardouin-Mansart added the long, familiar garden facade and Charles Le Brun decorated the Gallery of Mirrors and the adjoining rooms of war and peace with unforgettable magnificence. There the composer Jean-Baptiste Lully devised and directed a number of musical entertainments with such success that Louis granted him noble status and the office of a royal secretary. There, too, the comic genius Molière was encouraged by the King's support; and after the dramatist's death Louis was directly responsible for the establishment, in 1680, of the Comédie Française. There, finally, Louis recognized the genius of Jean Racine, whose great tragedies, from *Bérénice* (1670) to *Iphigénie* (1675), earned him membership in the Académie Française and a noble office, that of *trésorier de France*, from the King.

In this burgeoning of the arts, aided though not inspired by the patronage of kings and ministers, there is a strong element of order and simplicity culminating in the classical grandeur of Racine's plays and the facade of Versailles that might seem to reflect the growth of political stability and order over which Louis XIV presided. It is, however, dangerous, of course, to tie creative achievements in the arts and sciences too closely to their political environment; and there are significant counterpoints to the theme of classical order. The philosopher René Descartes' doubting, rationalistic approach to the fundamental questions of God's existence and man's relationship to him undermined the rigid adherence to revealed truths propounded by Bishop Bossuet. The Jansenist Blaise Pascal, one of the most versatile geniuses of the century, represented and defended a minority religious movement that Louis XIV believed dangerously subversive. Toward the end of his long reign, Louis encountered the fierce social criticism of Jean de La Bruyère and the skepticism of Pierre Bayle. Yet these discordant elements are all part of the Grande Siècle, inconceivable without the regular, orthodox classicism against which they were reacting. The almost monotonous splendour of Versailles is not primarily a testimony to Louis's self-esteem any more than is the classical simplicity of Racine's tragedies: both represent a high point in creative human

Généralités or *intendances*, 1789.
From W. Shepherd, *Historical Atlas,* Harper & Row, Publishers (Barnes & Noble Books), New York; revision
Copyright © 1964 by Barnes & Noble, Inc.

achievement, and it is to his credit that the King chose to
be identified with them.   (J.H.Sh.)

IV. France, 1715–89

French society and the French government in the 100-
odd years preceding the Revolution of 1789 constituted
what is often referred to as the *ancien régime.* The use
of one term to describe this collectivity indicates that
society and the state were, at least in theory, very closely
enmeshed. Ideally, in France under the old regime, there
should have been no conflict between the bodies social
and politic, which were thought to belong together as
one organic whole. Unlike 18th-century England, the
political system of which was defined by Montesquieu
as one in which tensions were balanced and neutralized
in part through the separation of powers, the French
ancien régime in the eyes of its makers was conceived
as a system within which there should be no conflict of
any sort; hence perhaps the initial impression of concert
and order associated with the *ancien régime* as it had
evolved during the earlier decades of the reign of Louis
XIV. And indeed it has often been argued by conservative historians that, with the exception of the last decades
of the 19th century and in spite of the very strong feeling
of national cohesion that emerged so strongly before and
during the Revolution, the French have never reached
the degree of political and social cohesion that they had
achieved during the first years of the reign of Louis XV.
But the symbiosis of society and the state called the
ancien régime was not in the 18th century without defects. When, in the course of that period, French society
changed economically, intellectually, and in its patterns
of social relations, reform proved an ultimately impossible task. In order for society to change, the state would
have had to be changed as well; and every reform of the

state, within the context of the *ancien régime,* implied
some attack on vested social interest. This is not to say
that the *ancien régime* was initially a static social and
political system. It was not; but because it was cumbersome and largely irrational in its structure, political
change could be effected only slowly. The great political
problem of the *ancien régime* can therefore be described
simply as the inability or unwillingness of the state to
alter its structure so as to successfully encompass the
transformed society of 18th-century France. By waiting
too long, until the 1770s, to try to reform itself and to
alter the regulations that governed the way in which
Frenchmen related to each other and to the state, the
French monarchy lost its chance to pass from medieval-
ism to modernism; and in so doing it set the scene for a
violent revolution that it might have avoided.

THE ANCIEN REGIME

French government. The *ancien régime,* then, has to
be seen altogether as a set of governmental institutions
and a set of social institutions and as a pattern of relations between these two. Of the governmental institutions, the most important was the monarchy and the
monarchs.

The monarchy. The separation of office and office-
holder is a modern idea; to a large degree the monarchy
in 18th-century France was identified with the personality
of the monarch. Before the Revolution, a charismatic
king could still have given an aura of acceptability to
an increasingly unacceptable institutional construct.
There is no doubt that the personality of Louis XIV had
much to do with the harmonious image that Frenchmen
had, and that most historians have had since, of the
ancien régime in its earliest decades. But neither of his
successors—Louis XV and Louis XVI (reigned 1774–92)

Closeness
of society
and the
state

—was an impressive figure. The indolence of Louis XV and the incapacity of Louis XVI tarnished the image of the monarchy. Moreover, the lack of character of these two men had practical consequences as well, because the institutions of the *ancien régime* monarchy were so designed that they could not be reformed without a strong hand at the helm, such as there had been in the 17th century with Richelieu, Louis XIV, and Louis's ministers Colbert and Louvois.

Thus, the monarchy of the *ancien régime* consisted in the first place of a monarch. But it was also a set of rules that can be, and very frequently were, described as a constitution, albeit an unwritten one. Its most important characteristic was a mixture of legalism and absolutism. Louis XIV is said to have proclaimed that he was the state. In some respects he was, and both Louis XV and Louis XVI held fast to the same concept. But the absolutism of these three kings served not only the monarchical regime, but the defense of established and vested interest as well. In some respects the monarchy of the *ancien régime* was unlimited and authoritarian; in others it was most closely circumscribed. Louis XVI, for example, could, by using a *lettre de cachet* (written order), imprison any of his subjects without trial and forever; many leading intellectual figures of the day, including Voltaire and Diderot, were arrested in this way. But it is also necessary to add that neither of these two writers stayed in prison for very long and that most such letters were issued by the state to parents who sought to curb and imprison their rebellious children. Theoretically, the king ruled by divine right. Anointed at Reims, endowed with magical powers of healing, he was the fountainhead of all authority; and even Louis XVI asserted in 1787 that an act that he had promulgated was legal merely because he had wished it to be legal. The king's authority was supreme and was exercised by means of a centralized state, already bureaucratic in nature and staffed by men appointed by the king. At the top, the decisions of the state were elaborated in councils responsible only to the monarch, whose orders were enforced in the provinces by 33 intendants, who themselves gave orders to subdelegates and to a small army of some 20,000 functionaries. But it must be remembered that, although centralized and absolute in principle, the *ancien régime* monarchy in the 18th century was in fact severely limited.

The parlements. The restraints on the power of the king were largely self-imposed, but some of them were institutionalized. Though it is true that the Estates-General had not been called together since 1614, the regional medieval estates did in some places survive, notably in the Languedoc. Their formal power was not, however, a great obstacle to the monarchy, which had much reduced their role before 1700. Far more important were the judicial courts, or parlements, the authority of which rested on a very particular conception of the nature of society. The eight parlements, and especially the Parlement of Paris, were the last courts of appeals for most of the innumerable civil law suits that were a typical aspect of 18th-century French life and that figure so prominently in the literature of the times. The parlements also decided famous criminal cases and thus participated in the business of statecraft. Most importantly, their consent was required for any innovation or reform in the nature of laws or taxes. Admittedly, the king as an absolute monarch could dispense with the approval of the parlements by calling a *lit de justice* and appearing in person before the assembled courts. But the crown as the defender of tradition and of vested interest often hesitated to exercise this prerogative, and its reluctance to act meant that the parlements were allowed to become in the last four decades of the *ancien régime* a fundamental element of the political system.

Members of the parlement owned their office. Unlike the intendants and other functionaries, or *commissaires,* the *parlementaires,* or *officiers,* with very few exceptions, were not appointed by the crown. They purchased their office; and, increasingly, once the procedure had been legalized by the beginning of the 17th century, they could inherit the office on payment of a tax called the *paulette.*

This venality of public office was of fundamental importance. In the earlier decades of the *ancien régime,* it had insured social and political stability: the right to purchase these offices had enabled the possessing class to participate in the business of government in spite of the fact that the theory of French monarchic rule at that time had become increasingly absolutist. But during the 18th century, venality of office stood in the way of change because it insured that vested and complacent interest would be politically represented. Any attempt by the state to change the rules of the game after 1750 met the instant, institutionalized, and vocal opposition of the parlements. In this manner the problem of reform became increasingly insoluble: no longer could the monarch, even had he wanted to do so, reform the state through absolutist fiat. From 1715—when the regent Philippe II, duc d'Orléans, restored to the parlements some of the prerogatives they had lost under Louis XIV—until 1789, the problem of reform and the fate of the *ancien régime* would focus on the opposition of crown and parlements.

Obstacles to reform. The question of reform in the 18th century can thus be broken down in various parts: the strength of the parlements, the determination of the crown to overcome it, and the need for it to do so because of social, economic, and intellectual change. The single most important aspect of the evolution in the power of the various institutions—feudal and bureaucratic—that made up the *ancien régime* was therefore the rise in the strength of the *parlementaires* who opposed reform. The causes of this evolution were both ideological and practical. In actual fact, the *parlementaires* owed whatever representation they may have had to the fact that all Frenchmen before 1750, including the king, accepted the idea that established privilege could not be abrogated. In 18th-century France, both society and the state were based on the idea that what had been given could not be taken away. Ultimately the *parlementaires* of 1750 were able to oppose the royal will because Frenchmen—subjects and king alike—in spite of the absolutist theory of the state, accepted the privileged position of the *parlementaires* because it had a secular and proprietary basis. But the *parlementaires*—often literate, if seldom learned—also developed other abstract and theoretical justifications for their power: after 1750 they began to justify their representation in the name of fundamental natural law. Fraudulent history was also invoked by their apologists to justify the claim that the parlements derived not from the medieval parlements created as advisory bodies by the king but, rather, from the ante-Capetian and Frankish assemblies of freemen (the *judicia Francorum*).

Tradition, ideology, and history all served to increase the power of the parlements, and so did a more purely social phenomenon: the fusion of the *noblesse d'épée* (the old military aristocracy of blood) and of the *noblesse de robe* (the *parlementaires*). Ever since the beginning of the 17th century, when judicial office had become the property of the same set of established families, the owners of proprietary judicial office had drawn away from the bourgeoisie whence their lines had sprung and had moved instead toward the *noblesse d'épée.* At the hand of Louis XIV, the old aristocracy had been showered with financial and honorary favours, but it had been shorn of power. By fusing with the *parlementaires,* the older nobility regained an institutional and political focus. Intellectually more aggressive, the *parlementaires* after 1750 were also socially more assured in the opposition to the crown. Because of this, the reform of society and of the state was far more difficult to achieve after 1750 than before; vested interest was more vocal and better organized than it had been.

Even more important than the institutionalized obstacles to reform, however, was the very nature of the *ancien régime.* After 1740 the tempo of change was very rapid, and the need to reform the structure of the state was very great since society and state were so closely linked. But this very connection made progress difficult because reform in any one direction had repercussions that would be widely felt elsewhere. The fusion of the so-

ENGLAND

AUSTRIAN NETHERLANDS
• Cologne

Calais

HOLY
ROMAN
EMPIRE

• Brussels

English Channel

Lille
Arras • Douai

Channel Is.

• Amiens

Frankfurt •
• Mainz

La Havre

Rouen

• Trier

Caen

Soissons

Metz •

⊙ Paris

Nancy •
• Toul

Strasbourg

Alençon

Troyes

Colmar

Rennes ⊙

• Mayenne
• Le Mans

Orléans

Mulhouse
Basel

Angers •

Tours ⊙

Nantes •
Saumur •

Bourges

Dijon ⊙

Besançon ⊙

Nevers •

SWISS
CONFEDERATION

Poitiers •

Moulins •

Mâcon ⊙

Lake Geneva

La Rochelle •

Limoges •

Guéret •

Geneva •

Clermont-
Ferrand •

Trévoux ⊙

Saintes •

Lyons ⊙

Grenoble ⊙

KINGDOM OF
SARDINIA

• Bordeaux

COMTAT
VENAISSIN
(to the Papacy)

Bay of
Biscay

Avignon •

Montauban •

Bayonne •

Auch •

Toulouse •

Montpellier •

Aix ⊙
• Marseilles

Pau •

Narbonne •

Foix •

SPAIN

• Perpignan

Bastia •

MEDITERRANEAN
SEA

CORSICA

Barcelona •

Ajaccio •

☐ Region of the
customary (feudal) law
▨ Region of the
written (Roman) law
▬ Boundary of jurisdiction
of a *parlement* or supreme council
⊙ Seat of a *parlement*
or supreme council

0   50   100   150 mi
0   50   100 150 200 km

Laws and courts, 1789.
From W. Shepherd, *Historical Atlas,* Harper & Row, Publisher (Barnes & Noble Books), New York; revision
Copyright © 1964 by Barnes & Noble, Inc.

cial and political purposes of the *ancien régime* was at once the source of the need for change and the principal obstacle to it.

This overlap of societal and political forms had many facets. First, society and the state in the *ancien régime* were based on similar principles. Politically, the state though absolute in theory was limited in fact. Unlike the tsar or the sultan, unlike even Frederick II or Joseph II, the French kings by and large respected proprietary and vested interest, the existence of which was as fundamental a principle of social and economic organization as it was in politics. The monarchy respected the political rights of the parlements, and similarly it felt it had to respect economic monopolies and privileges—guilds had the right to protect their members by excluding outsiders from the professions; corporations had prerogatives that were not to be interfered with. France was a society not of men equal before law but of men and corporate groups, all privileged in some way but unequally privileged, with vested interests that were sanctioned by the state and could not be ignored. Any attack upon the economic and social privileges of members of the body social would have had repercussions on the body politic, and on the church as well because Catholicism was also a principle of social and political action. The king was a Christian and Catholic king, the eldest son of the church, and France was theoretically a Catholic nation (although Protestants had secured de facto toleration after 1750, they were not given civic rights until 1787). Civil records were kept by the clergy, which also dispensed education at the primary, secondary, and university level and managed public charity. Religious holidays were public holidays; and, in the theory of the *ancien régime*, the king was the Christian father of his people, and he stood to them as the father stood to his children.

In short, by the nature of its fundamental principles and by the direct effect of its interventions—social, political, religious, and economic—the state served as a very pervasive framework for social action. When the purpose of the *ancien régime* state and society overlapped, as they did in the first decades of the 18th century, the state was seen as a positive force. When a difference of purpose appeared because of economic, social, and intellectual change, the state was seen as a mere constraint. Society could only evolve if the state also evolved. But because of its very principles, the monarchy of the *ancien régime* was hard put to curb the power of the parlements, who were, in turn, hardly likely to agree to reform unless coerced, because they were far more powerful in the 1760s than they had ever been before. Thus, as the century progressed, the monarchy was increasingly condemned to immobilism in a situation in which it could not afford to remain passive. As the tempo of social and economic change swelled, together with its concomitant demands for reform, the state found itself increasingly isolated, powerless, and without a political constituency.

French society. Because of the interaction of society and politics, the evolution of French society in the 18th century is the key to the political problem of the *ancien régime* and to the coming of the Revolution. This problem, however, is a complicated one, which has to be seen in the context of the increased sophistication and number of social forms.

Until 1715, perhaps even until 1730, with the conspicuous but ultimately marginal exceptions of the freethinkers (the *libertins*) and the Protestant Huguenots, the society of *ancien régime* France had been reasonably uniform. The various provinces and *pays* (regions) of France had led separate existences; but they had been organized along the same social, economic, cultural, and

Immobi-
lism of
the
monarchy

religious lines. During the 18th century, however, besides this traditional and catholic model, which was not fundamentally affected by economic or social change, there gradually emerged a second sort of society—urban, less hierarchic, and more mobile—in which status and power depended as much on talent and wealth as on birth.

The new urban society. Numerically the urban model, even in 1789, was by far the lesser of the two. In 1715 more than 90 percent of all Frenchmen lived in the country; by 1789, although Paris had reached a population of 400,000, only 15 percent of the population was urbanized. But the urban dwellers had become far more vocal and politically aware; and it was their spokesmen who would direct the course of the Revolution in all of its various vicissitudes. Intellectual, economic, and financial change must therefore be seen in the context of a change in the internal structure of society as a whole and in the balance of power between the new urban milieu and the traditional world of the *ancien régime*, which had once included the whole of French society but which during the 18th century was being increasingly rejected by its more progressive elements.

Traditional society. All France was changing in the 18th century, but in different ways: whereas the expanding cities were affected by the new forces of trade and free thought, problems of the countryside still revolved essentially on the classic and traditional questions of good or poor harvests, size of population, and peasant–lord relations. Three phenomena were at play—a resurgence of the aristocracy, a population explosion, and a rise in prices. The merger of the *noblesse d'épée* with the legalistic *noblesse de robe* had consequences at the level of national politics, but it had an effect in the countryside as well. The newly reshaped nobility was more able to rediscover abandoned feudal rights, and it was thenceforth more able to prosecute in the courts, where it became at once judge and jury. The rules regulating the division of common lands were altered in favour of the nobility. In the 17th century the lord of a village who had wanted to divide common village property had to prove his right to do so. This procedure was reversed in 1767 and again in 1773, and some measure of enclosure of peasant lands was made possible.

The relative well-being of the nobility increased in the later decades of the *ancien régime*. The reason for this lay in the consequence for the landowners of inflation, which saw prices rise in France by more than 60 percent between 1726 and 1789. Prices rose; real wages fell by one-half; but there was no fall in the value of rents. Payments in kind and renewable leases enabled landlords to keep ahead of the price rise. The money value of their rents rose in these same years by 98 percent. Landless wage earners thus found themselves impoverished; and the beneficiaries of the rise in prices were the landowners who secured a higher price for their agricultural produce. Moreover, the plight of the poor was aggravated by demographic expansion; not only did the landless labourer earn less but he also had more mouths to feed, and he had to compete more for jobs. Because of France's great diversity in climate and fertility, conditions were widely different from place to place: Brittany, for example, reached its demographic peak in 1700, whereas the population of Quercy rose by 70 percent between 1700 and 1786. But, in France as a whole, there were 2,000,000 more peasants in 1790 than there had been in 1700. Better preventive medicine, a decline in infant mortality, and the disappearance of famines after 1709 all served to increase longevity; the yearly number of deaths per 10,000 fell from 400 in 1750, to 350 in 1775, 328 in 1790, and 298 in 1800; life expectancy rose from 21 to 27 years. Thus the number of wage earners grew ceaselessly; but the amount of arable land did not, despite government encouragement by fiscal exemption. Because emigration to cities remained low (there were as yet few factories to absorb surplus rural labour), the situation in the countryside became increasingly critical.

In his book *L'Ancien régime et la Révolution*, Alexis de Tocqueville argued that France was the European country in which peasants were most prosperous. It would be

more accurate to say that it was the country in which they were least miserable. The French peasantry was worse off in 1789 than it had been in 1730. Although a third of the land belonged to the peasants (the aristocracy owned 20 percent, the bourgeoisie 30 percent, and the church 15 percent), most of the people who lived in the country were landless labourers, whose worsening plight coincided with the greater aggressiveness of the aristocracy.

The importance of the rural conflicts was very great. The crown was already unable to rely on the nobility, which supported the parlements against the state, and now it would be unable to count on the peasants as well. This is why the *ancien régime* folded at once and almost literally disappeared overnight during the summer of 1789. The big push, it is true, came from the cities, but it was because of generalized rural unrest that the monarchy was unable to resist the attack on tradition.

THE FRENCH ECONOMY IN THE 18TH CENTURY

Tensions within the rural world made political change irresistible, but the immediate pressure for revolution came from the cities and especially from Paris. There, economic change was the most crucial and visible factor. It is hard to gauge its importance with precision: in relation to what had been taking place before 1730, it was very great; but in contrast to what was happening in England at the same time, it appears to have been more tepid. There did not, for example, take place in France as there did across the English Channel a vast reordering and commercialization of agricultural practices (the enclosure movement), and this no doubt had a profound effect on the course of French history. The English aristocracy in the 1630s had already found it feasible and even desirable to make an alliance with the commercial bourgeoisie against the monarchy, which had become their common enemy by defending medieval economic practices in both town and country. In France, however, where there was little enclosure, aristocracy and bourgeoisie followed divergent paths; the landed aristocracy, although opposed to the king for its own reason, was not the ally of the commercial interests. In France economic transformations were not strong enough to unite all the propertied interests on the new basis of capitalist wealth; they did suffice, however, to wean the urban interest away from the crown. The pattern therefore was of significant but not overwhelming economic evolution.

Industrial growth. In 1789 French agricultural techniques remained much as they had been 70 years before. But some change was registered. Total produce rose; and, although taken individually most peasants were poorer in the 1780s than they had been before, the final value of agricultural products per active person rose from a level of 850 gold francs in 1700–10 at a yearly rate of increase of 0.2 percent for the first half of the century and of nearly 1 percent in the 1780s and 1790s. And, as the value of rural produce rose, so did rural demand for urban manufactured goods and for those luxury items (textiles, porcelains, furniture, *articles de Paris*) in the production of which the French excelled before 1800. Thus in the last 50 years of the *ancien régime*, industrial production rose yearly at a rate of nearly 2 percent. Some leading sectors rose even more quickly. Coal mining, for example, had become a major industry on the eve of the Revolution. In the 1780s coal production was 5.8 percent greater than it had been in the preceding decade. Mining attracted vast amounts of capital, some of it from the aristocracy. In 1789 the Mines d'Anzin near the Belgian border already employed thousands of workers.

Nor should it be thought that France's industrial development was very far behind that of England. There is no reason to suppose that the outmoded institutional economic apparatus of the French state seriously hindered French economic growth. Although France was a generation behind England in terms of economic innovation (in France just before the Revolution, steam-driven pumps first appeared in mines and also in Paris, where they were used to pump water up from the Seine), the rate of in-

Problems of the countryside

Importance of the rural conflicts

Rise in the value of production

dustrial growth during the 18th century in France was not inferior to that of England. English industrial production in 1790 was 190 percent greater than it had been in 1700; for France, the comparative figure was no less than 260 percent. But the absolute gap between the two countries was quite great: in England coal production in 1770 reached 6,000,000 tons as against only 700,000 in France. Nonetheless, the French before 1789, in spite of their outmoded institutions, were catching up with their only rival.

Trade. France's greatest source of new economic well-being in the 18th century was trade—domestic, international, and especially colonial trade. The first colonial French empire was essentially located in America, and it was immensely lucrative. From the 17th century the French had been making sustained incursions into Canada and in India. These possessions, it is true, were both conquered by England during the Seven Years' War (1756–63); but this was not seen as a great loss by the French at the time. The Caribbean remained the most lucrative source of French colonial activity in the last 100 years of the *ancien régime*. The French shared the West Indies with Spain and England: Cuba, Puerto Rico, and the western half of Hispaniola belonged to Spain; Jamaica, to England; but Guadaloupe, Martinique, and Haiti—the richest of all nonwhite 18th-century colonies in the world—were French. There, 20,000 whites stood an uneasy watch over 160,000 black slaves, imported from Africa, where they had been purchased from black slave merchants who were paid with arms, baubles, and drink. In the islands the slaves produced sugarcane and coffee, which were refined in France at Nantes, Rochefort, and Bordeaux and often re-exported to central and northern Europe. This triangular trade grew tenfold between 1715 and 1789, and the value of international exports in the 1780s amounted to nearly one-fourth of national income. The sugar trade enriched the planters, the bankers in Paris who had acted as brokers for import and re-export, and the manufacturers of luxury goods that were shipped from France to the Caribbean; the French colonial trade was a closely watched process, governed by mercantilist protective tariffs and rules.

Growth of colonial trade

In the last two decades of the *ancien régime*, the colonial trade lost some of its appeal. Greater profits could then be had in China, India, and East Africa. Within a decade after the monopoly position of the French East India Company ended in 1769, commerce with the Far East, for example, more than doubled. But the West Indies trade remained the single most important aspect of French commercial life in the 18th century (hence, perhaps, the fact that so many of the prominent participants of the Revolutionary drama had connections with the islands). Also significant is the fact that an antislavery movement had developed in France by 1789. Montesquieu before 1750 had already criticized the institution of black slavery. In 1788 a Société des Amis des Noirs (Society of the Friends of the Blacks) was founded in Paris and counted among its members not only Lafayette, but also Jacques-Pierre Brissot, who later became the leading figure of the Girondin faction, which dominated the Revolutionary government in 1791–92. Gradually, the immoral aspects of trade in the colonies became inescapable, but its first impact was a betterment of economic conditions in France. Obviously, only a few individuals benefitted directly from the new currents of exchange; but indirectly millions of Frenchmen were affected by the invigorated tempo of economic life. The circulation of gold specie in the kingdom as a whole rose from 731,-000,000 in 1715 to some 2,000,000,000 in 1788. From America to Spain—whose trade with its colonies was under the indirect and unofficial control of French merchants—silver bullion found its way to Paris, Lyons, and from there to Geneva and central and especially southeastern Mediterranean Europe. The French national community became the basic unit of commercial life. Where, in the past, villages and even cities had lived largely closed in upon themselves or their immediate surroundings, trade became a national concept, and the awareness of the nation-state followed in its train. No

longer would Frenchmen accept as natural and harmless the multiplicity of internal tariffs and the survival of the divisive medieval administrative patterns that still coexisted with the more modern and rationalized state system, which centred on the councils and the intendants.

THE COMING OF THE REVOLUTION

Effects of the Enlightenment. Industrial and commercial change greatly affected the quality of life in urban France in the last decades of the *ancien régime*, and so did the intellectual revolution known as the Enlightenment. The effect of the Enlightenment, however, is even harder to gauge than the degree of transformation that owed to material circumstances. Today it seems hardly reasonable to suppose, as did the first historians of the Revolution and many of its contemporaries as well, that the Philosophes (the writers and thinkers of the Enlightenment) directly bore the responsibility of the Revolution. Reactionary authors throughout the 19th century were quick to blame these intellectuals whose influence was said to have imbued the French bourgeoisie with "philosophical" and abstract intellectualized visions of what was to be done. In this scheme, the protagonists of the Revolution would not have been so much the agents of some social force as the actuators of the ideas of the Enlightenment.

Not much of this narrow interpretation remains. For one, it has proved very difficult to trace precise connections between the actions of political figures and the ideas of specific philosophers. Attempts to pinpoint this relationship by enumeration and description of the books that belonged to and were presumably read by Frenchmen before the Revolution have proved largely inconclusive. What they would show is that Jean-Jacques Rousseau's political work *The Social Contract* had a very small audience indeed and that the most widely read political philosopher of the 18th century was Montesquieu, who happened to be the apologist of balanced and aristocratic government.

Literacy. A case for the impact of the Enlightenment can, however, be made in more general ways. Although books were very expensive, they were widely read. More than 30,000 titles were published between 1723 and 1789; and it has been estimated that by 1789 more than 9,000,-000 Frenchmen could at least sign their name. No illiterate soldier could rise in the French army beyond the grade of corporal. Literacy was widespread, and the impact of literature was very great. If hundreds read Rousseau's *Social Contract*, millions had read or heard of his romantic novel *La Nouvelle Héloïse*.

Impact of the Enlightenment

Education. Much greater attention too was given even before 1789 to education. The economist Anne-Robert-Jacques Turgot wrote that the basis of national unity and mores was the education of children; and in 1763 an otherwise reactionary *parlementaire* named La Chalotais even put forward a scheme for lay and national primary education. An important landmark in this respect too was the expulsion from France in 1762 of the Jesuits, who had heretofore dominated French secondary education. Increasingly, the French language was substituted for Latin in the secondary schools, or *collèges* (the forerunners of today's lycées). Rhetoric gave way to an emphasis on more "natural" manners and modes of expression. History was raised to the level of a serious discipline; with Voltaire's *Siècle de Louis XIV* (1751; "Age of Louis XIV"), modern French historiography began, and there were echoes of this new attitude in the programs of the secondary schools. Mathematics, physics, and geography were also added. Finally, the whole emphasis of education shifted—before, education had had as its primary purpose the adaptation of the young to established patterns of culture and thought; now, a greater emphasis was placed on the individual desires and propensities of children.

Principles of the Enlightenment. Thus through the impact of the printed word, through the extension of literacy, through the new emphasis and nature of secondary education, the ideas of the Enlightenment pervaded large segments of the French population. It would be difficult and even impossible to analyze French society in 1789 without making reference to the broad ideology and principles of the Enlightenment. It is difficult today to conceive of these principles as a source of revolution, so completely is modern liberal and Western society based upon them. But in the context of the *ancien régime*, based on tradition, catholicism, ruralism, hierarchy, privilege, and corporate intermediary bodies, the new ideas were revolutionary indeed.

Rationalism, nationalism, and individualism

Rationalism was the first of these, and although the Philosophes disagreed on many things, all of them, from Voltaire to Rousseau, insisted that man, privately and publicly, must build on reason. Scientism was a further aspect of this same attitude. Balloons and experimentation with electricity were by the 1780s nationwide fads and provide a testimonial to the pervasiveness of a new approach to life.

Equally important to Frenchmen of the Enlightenment were two other concepts, since then often antithetical but then perceived as compatible and even complementary: nationalism and individualism. Here again, the importance, symbolic at least, of Rousseau cannot be overrated. It was he who emphasized both the intrinsic rights of every citizen and the need for the citizen's constant involvement in collective, communal affairs. In various ways, this was a double concern that characterized the intellectual spirit of the 1780s. Though Montesquieu had defended intermediary bodies as guarantees of civic liberty, thinkers of the Enlightenment attacked them in the name of public utility and of what would later be called the rights of man. In an article written for the *Encyclopédie*, Turgot denied the sanctity of what he called foundations: "Public utility is the supreme law, and cannot be countervailed by a superstitious respect for what has been called the intents of the founders." Most foundations, he thought, had as their only purpose the satisfaction of frivolous vanity. At the other end of the social spectrum, the Protestant Rabaut Saint-Étienne, later president of the National Assembly, argued that "every time one creates a corporate body with privileges one creates a public enemy because a special interest is nothing else than this." No distinction was drawn between private interest and factional selfishness; and in 1786 the future Girondin leader Brissot was expressing what had become a platitudinous thought when he wrote that "the history of all intermediary bodies proves, in all evidence, that to bring men and to bind men together is to develop their vices and diminish their virtues."

Traditional inherited privilege, it was thought, should no longer be the guiding principle of social action. A new society should be built in which the rights of the individual would be protected by a state unfettered in its pursuit of the common good. Private benevolence for a public purpose was typical of the 1780s, and Louis XVI's finance minister, Jacques Necker, did a great deal for his reputation by endowing a hospital for sick children, which stands to this day. Public and charitable concern by 1789 had become the themes of countless didactic works of literature and painting.

Reform movement.

Sources of reformism and communality

The sources of this new feeling of reformism and communality are difficult to establish. Some of them have been mentioned: a more vigorous and comprehensive economic life, changes in the educational system, the overall impact of the Enlightenment. Others were more strictly institutional. Inevitably the centralization of government effected under Richelieu, carried out during the reign of Louis XIV, and perpetuated by his successors had emptied of their substance all the intermediary and nonnational bodies—the local estates, the municipal and regional institutions. In the system of the *ancien régime* all those groups and bodies that stood between the subject and the state no longer had any positive use. There was therefore no reason to suppose that they were necessary or that they justified the expense they entailed. By reaction, therefore, those thinking Frenchmen who wanted to enact social and political change looked to the nation and the state as their great hope. Symbolically enough, by 1780 the historical model that seemed to make sense to them was no longer England, as it had been for Montesquieu and even Voltaire, but Rome instead and, more generally, the city-state of antiquity, where the rights of the polis and of the citizen had coexisted harmoniously.

Beginnings of nationalism. So deep in fact was this transformation of opinion, which looked to equality rather than to privilege as a key to the organization of society, that it is necessary to look beyond institutional explanations in order to explain it. Nascent nationalism was also a factor. There is no doubt that for those Frenchmen whose style of life was modern, who read books, and who engaged in trade the nation became in the 18th century a far more concrete reality than it had been in the past. This can perhaps be most easily seen in the changing attitudes of French public opinion vis-à-vis the largely unchanged goals of royal diplomacy.

From 1740 onward, perhaps even from the time of the War of the Spanish Succession (1701–14), France had been too weak to try to impose its hegemony over Europe. In consequence and quite consciously, after 1740 French statesmen endeavoured to secure a double goal: in Europe, the preservation of the balance of power; and, in the world at large, the expansion of the French colonial empire and the containment of England. For the first of these reasons, during the War of the Austrian Succession (1740–48) the French sided with Prussia and against Austria because Austria was then thought to be a more dangerous power. Rather reluctantly, during the Seven Years' War (1756–63), France reversed itself and fought against Prussia, whose efforts at aggrandizement had become a threat to the status quo. In the 1770s and 1780s also, France did its best to preserve both the continental status quo and the continued independence of the smaller European states, many of which were its clients or allies —notably Poland, Sweden, the United Provinces, and Turkey. In this the French were reasonably successful; although they suffered reverses in Poland, which was partitioned, and in the United Provinces, where the Anglo-Prussian Conservative Party with Prussian military help overcame the pro-French liberal groups in 1787, the balance of power in Europe was preserved in the 1770s and 1780s.

International goals

French successes vis-à-vis England, however, were checkered. Efforts to extend French rule in India or to preserve it in Canada were more or less successful in the 1740s but were totally unsuccessful during the Seven Years' War. During that conflict France suffered grievously in spite of the entente between France and Spain, both ruled by Bourbon monarchs, and in spite of the Austrian alliance. France was unable to prevail both on the Continent and in the colonies, and for having tried too much she failed everywhere. French influence was at a very low ebb in 1763. But the endemic warfare between France and England that had begun in 1688 was not ended on that note. During the U.S. War of Independence (1775–83), the French were most careful not to be also involved in the Austro-Prussian "Potato War" (War of the Bavarian Succession) of 1778–79, and, by concentrating their efforts for the first time on maritime matters, they succeeded in holding and even reversing the advance of England.

More significant, however, than the actual diplomatic success or failure of the French crown were the reactions of the public to them. In spite of its disastrous consequence, the Seven Years' War did not lead to pronounced disaffection, because Frenchmen in the 1750s did not feel themselves involved in these matters. By the time of the U.S. War of Independence, however, matters had changed greatly. The war was very popular and was seen by the public as a justified act of legitimate revenge against the English. In a commentary on the Treaty of Paris of 1763, the French foreign minister Charles Gravier, comte de Vergennes, observed:

it is enough to read the Treaty of Paris, and particularly the negotiations which preceded it, to realize the ascendancy which England has acquired over France and to judge how much that arrogant nation savours the pleasure of having humiliated us.

Many Frenchmen shared Vergennes's opinion and rejoiced in the victories during the American war of their compatriots: Lafayette, de Grasse, Rochambeau, and Suffren. In so doing they gave indirect but forcible evidence of the development in France of a new and intransigent nationalism.

Grievances against the state and society. Thus by the 1780s the traditional concepts of the *ancien régime* state and society were being attacked from all sides. The antiquated administrative jurisdictions, the inequalities of taxation, the concept of privilege, the existence of corporations that stood between the citizen and the state, and the noninvolvement of the citizens in the national body politic had become untenable ideas. The impossibility of perpetuating the status quo was not, however, felt equally by all Frenchmen. Those who lived in the countryside disliked it for the more ordinary and classical reasons that had always driven the exploited poor to rise up at times against their more or less oppressive betters. But in the cities resentment was of a different and more implacable sort. Buoyed up by the new prosperity and by the development of industry and trade, better educated, more quickly exasperated by irrational governmental practice, more keen on asserting the oneness of the French nation and also on asserting their rights as individuals, urbanized Frenchmen of all classes found it increasingly difficult to put up with the *ancien régime.*

Social divisions. In some ways, therefore, all Frenchmen shared certain grievances. But it is important to see that they were seriously disunited in their ideas of what was to be done after the *ancien régime* had been gotten rid of. The sameness of cultural disaffection can serve to explain the unique enthusiasm and fraternity of 1789 and the unanimity of feeling on the celebration of July 14, 1790, one year after the fall of the Bastille. In that first year Lafayette, Brissot, and Robespierre largely agreed on the meaning and purpose of the Revolution. But the Revolution did not progress in a uniform and unanimous way. By 1794 the unanimity of 1790 had dissolved into sectarian terrorism and counterterrorism; and this bipolarity of political behaviour presupposes that, although united in some ways, urban and modern France on the eve of the Revolution was in other ways disunited. All Frenchmen, particularly those in the cities, were affected by the increasing reality of national markets and national cultural concern, but they were also deeply separated by lines of social class as well as by the patterns of social relations in their culture.

Roughly stated, it can be said that social divisions opposed some of the aristocracy to the upper bourgeoisie, themselves opposed to the lower middle class, to the peasants, and to the embryonic urban working class. Moreover, none of these groups was characterized by that sense of civic responsibility that makes self-government possible. Nobles and nonnobles were unable to work together for a common end; a brief experiment in aristocratic rule—Polysynodie (1715–18)—during the regency that followed the death of Louis XIV spontaneously disintegrated from the quarrelsomeness of the participants and their incapacity to work out any coherent theory or practice of government.

Sources of division

The sources of division in France were manifold, and it should not be thought that the varying groups into which the nation was divided were separated solely or principally on economic questions, as has too often been supposed. It is a misleading oversimplification to suppose that the social history of France before 1789, as well as its political history afterward, revolve merely around the opposition of the landed aristocracy to the commercial middle classes. There was indeed animosity between the poor, and more especially the rural poor, and the urbanized rich; but the "rich" in the mind of the poor included those privileged both by birth and by skill, and these included both bourgeois and aristocrats, *noblesse de robe* and *noblesse d'épée*, small-town lawyers and big-city merchants. There were no real economic differences between those people who were politically concerned, whether nobles or nonnobles. Like the aristocrats, the bourgeois, including those engaged in trade, were landowners. As landed proprietors, thousands of

bourgeois enjoyed the exercise of feudal rights; and when the bourgeoisie attacked "feudalism," it did not think so much of feudal rights, which were no burden to it because they were paid by peasants. For the bourgeoisie feudalism meant the perpetuation of privilege and irrational institutional anachronisms. In short, the differences that separated nobles and nonnobles, grands bourgeois and petits bourgeois, were more psychological and institutional than economic; this accounted for the great mobility of opinion before, during, and after the Revolution. Like the feeling of reformism, which moved the urban population as a whole, divisive social conflict often had noneconomic roots that were ideological or institutional: political alignments were therefore subject to great and sudden fluctuations. In 1787 the whole nation was united against the state. In the winter of 1788–89 the bourgeoisie and the *parlementaires* were dead set one against the other. In the summer of 1790 unanimity reigned again, but it had once again broken down by the summer of 1791. Moreover, the nation torn by civil strife in 1794 united in 1799 under the aegis of Napoleon. These waves of political unity and disunity can only be understood by referring back to the paradoxes of social unity and disunity before 1789.

Conflict between nobility and bourgeoisie

The most visible of the divisive elements that form the social background of the breakup of the revolutionary class after 1790 was the conflict that opposed the nobility to the bourgeoisie. Although, as has been seen, the transformations of the 18th century had blurred many of the social and intellectual differences that in the cities separated the bourgeoisie from the nobility, the separate and distinct existence of these two groups was still affirmed by law. Access to certain positions in the state service was limited to the aristocracy, and this was a most important consideration in a society in which there were so many bureaucrats and an official post gave much status or *considération* to its occupant. Nonnobles, or *roturiers*, did not have access to high office in the army or the church. In 1789 all the bishops and most abbots were nobles. In practice nonnobles could not become army officers, and this was a most important source of disaffection because it serves to explain why in 1789 the *ancien régime* monarchy was unable to rely on the army to suppress popular discontent. Even the upper ranks of the centralized state administration were becoming a noble preserve. Admittedly the supererogatory and honorary institutional apparatus inherited from the Middle Ages had always been an aristocratic monopoly. But whereas most of the intendants, *conseillers d'états*, and even ministers of Louis XIV had been nonnobles or recently ennobled men, their successors by 1789 were most of them securely ensconced in the aristocratic establishment. These patterns of administrative exclusion were not a lasting source of division between aristocrats and bourgeois, and, once they were abolished in 1789, the two groups found it less difficult to work together. But before 1789 institutional disqualifications weighed heavily on bourgeois perceptions of nobles and of the state.

The new bourgeois ethic

Also of importance were the theories developed by some aristocrats and accepted by many others on the racial separateness and superiority of the aristocracy. It was argued that, unlike the members of the Third Estate who were descendants of the Gauls, the nobility had sprung from the loins of the Franks, the Germanic conquerors who had swept over Gaul in the 5th and 6th centuries. Much was made of this idea, which was taken up in reverse by bourgeois theorists, who countered that if the nobles were indeed Franks, it was now time for them to return to Germany. Equally pervasive also was the diffusion in the bourgeoisie of a new personal ethic. Hard work was increasingly seen as a good value. Bourgeois permanence was contrasted to aristocratic fantasy, and a curious manifestation of this idea was the association that was made so often by the bourgeoisie between aristocracy and costly and ephemeral fetes and fireworks. It was for that reason doubly unfortunate that fireworks following the wedding of Louis XVI were marred by a riot and stampede in which dozens of people were trampled to death. More stable and harder working, the bourgeois of the 1780s also prided himself on being more moral and a better family man. One of the most pervasive and fundamental evolutions of French society in the 18th century lay in the development by the bourgeoisie of a new style of familial life, which in the next century would spread to all social classes. Unlike aristocrats, who would send their children to wet nurses, who sacrificed the interests of individual children to the perpetuation of secular family pride, and who led very public lives, the bourgeois family drew in upon itself. By 1789 birth control was already practiced in some instances to limit the number of children, all of whom it was now thought deserved their full share of attention and love. Architects began to draw up house plans that substituted for the older pattern of open rooms strung along a public corridor, designs in which rooms were clustered to give more intimacy and warmth. It is thus fair to say that by 1789 the bourgeoisie had developed a particular ethic, which even the Catholic Church recognized implicitly. Where poverty had been admirable in 1689, honesty and thrift were seen as more crucial by the clergy of 1789.

Differences of class separated bourgeois and nobles, and much the same was true of upper bourgeois and lower bourgeois, and of the bourgeoisie as a whole vis-à-vis either peasants or workers. For, although the bourgeoisie was egalitarian in some ways, it inherited from the aristocracy traditions of exclusivism and hierarchy. The average bourgeois may have envied the nobility, but he disapproved of social mobility. Moderately anticlerical, the bourgeois of 1789 nevertheless found it natural that his wife and daughters should be devout. More important still, the bourgeois was essentially authoritarian —fathers continued to exercise great control over their wives and children; and knowledge, art, literature, and politics were all seen in an authoritarian framework within which authority and standards flowed from above. Temperamentally, the bourgeois of 1789 was ill suited to participate in the debates or compromises that were already a part of politics in England or America. The parliamentarianism or libertarianism of 1688 or 1776 appealed to the bourgeois, but its social and intellectual foundations did not. Quite predictably, therefore, egalitarianism rather than self-government participationism would be the only durable conquest of the French Revolution. The tragedy of French society in 1789 was that it could not provide the basis of a viable political alternative to an institutional system it could no longer accept as valid. Tocqueville wrote that the French Revolution had been in men's minds before it began; it might be added that the broad outline of its unfolding was also predictable, given the structure of French society before 1789.

Financial crisis. The political debate of the last decades of the *ancien régime* can also be understood in this light. That the state could not go on as it was had been obvious to even its enlightened supporters for some time. Their concern was triggered by growing governmental deficits occasioned not so much by costly extravagance, as has been thought, but by war with England and by the service of the debt. In the aftermath of the Seven Years' War and at the prompting of his minister Joseph-Marie Terray, Louis XV had agreed that it would be necessary to reform and rationalize the imposition and collection of taxes, from which many nobles and many corporations were exempted and which in most of France were inefficiently collected by private tax farmers. The fiscal structure was very baroque. There were direct taxes, some of which were collected directly by the state: the *taille* (a personal tax), the capitation, and the *vingtième*, which were a form of income tax from which the nobles and officials were usually exempt. There were also indirect taxes that were paid by everyone: the salt tax, or *gabelle*, which represented nearly one-tenth of royal revenue; the *traites*, or customs duty, internal and external; and the *aides*, or excise taxes, levied on the sale of items as diverse as wine, tobacco, and iron. All the indirect taxes were extremely unpopular, and had much to do with the state's inability to rally the rural masses to its side in 1789. In the 1740s attempts had been made to amend this

The fiscal structure

system, but had foundered on the parlements' opposition to a more equitable distribution of taxation. By 1770 the swelling debt made it obvious that something should be done. Terray repudiated a part of the debt. There were forced loans and other extraordinary measures. Inevitably, these "absolutist" attacks on established privilege aroused the antagonism of vested interest. To forestall opposition, Terray's colleague, René-Nicolas de Maupeou, successfully outmanoeuvred the Paris Parlement, the members of which in the early 1770s were exiled to outlying provincial cities. The venal offices of the *parlementaires* were abolished, and new law courts were created to replace the Paris Parlement. How far th monarchy had travelled along the road to revolution was shown by the reaction of the public to the new institutions. Although the exile of the Parlement was an exercise of royal absolutism, it was also a reformist exercise carried out for the benefit of the nation and against particularist privilege. Yet it was not seen as such. Although Voltaire understood that the monarchy in this instance stood for rationalism and progress, most of enlightened opinion saw in Maupeou's action merely one more manifestation of ministerial despotism. In short, the monarchy had become so unpopular that reform at its hands was not acceptable even to those people who claimed to want reform above all things. Only the persistent support of the monarch, therefore, would have enabled Terray and Maupeou to push through these measures of enlightened despotism. Because the resistance of the privileged bodies coincided with the disenchantment of the enlightened public, the only constituency of the reformists was the royal will and the royal tradition of absolutism. But Louis XV died of smallpox in 1774. Although his death was in fact a great tragedy for the French crown and perhaps for the French nation as well, because it negated the possibility of peaceful reform pushed through from above, Louis's demise was not widely mourned.

Unpopularity of Louis XV. Genuinely popular in the earlier years of his reign, Louis XV had become thoroughly discredited by the time of his death. Although his liaison with Mme de Pompadour had borne many fruits in the form of the patronage she extended to artists as different as Voltaire and the architect Jacques-Ange Gabriel, it did nothing for the prestige of the crown. More unpopular yet was Louis XV's last mistress, Mme du Barry, a former prostitute. The King was also thought to maintain a private brothel (which was true) and to have literally starved his people by speculating on a rising price for grain (which was false).

Incompetence of Louis XVI. It is difficult to know if the unpopularity of Louis XV was due to himself or to a decline in the prestige of the monarchy. By contrast, Louis XV's grandson and successor, Louis XVI—well-meaning, obtuse, and sexually incompetent—was initially more popular; and this would seem to suggest that the crown in the 1770s could still tap the traditional sources of loyalty. But by the 1780s Louis XVI himself would also be held in contempt; and in 1789 his wife, Marie-Antoinette, was much hated. Never popular because she was by birth a member of the Austrian ruling house, which in France was traditionally disliked, she reached in 1781 a nadir of unpopularity during the prosecution of the Affair of the Diamond Necklace. (This case revolved around a cardinal, the Prince de Rohan, who had been tricked into giving a diamond necklace to a woman whom he thought to be the Queen; in this instance Marie-Antoinette was blameless, but what was remembered by public opinion was that a cardinal had thought it possible to seduce and bribe the Queen.) The discredit that befell the monarchy in consequence was immense, and Napoleon dated the beginning of the French Revolution from this very episode.

In any case, shortly after the death of Louis XV and his own accession, the new king, eager to please, recalled the Parlement, dismissed Maupeou and Terray, and recalled as his principal minister Jean-Frédéric, comte de Maurepas, a fixture from the unreformed period of the previous reign. The pressure for reform did not die out,

Decline of the monarchy

however, either in the nation at large, or among those members of the royal bureaucracy who saw that the crown could save itself only by attacking privilege and rationalizing its procedures and its fiscal system; and, in late 1774, Louis entrusted the domestic administration of the kingdom to Turgot, a reforming intendant and, by birth and connection (but by these only), a member of the ruling privileged elite, the power of which he now tried to curb. Perhaps because he thought that the success of his reforms would guarantee their acceptance, perhaps also because he thought it vain to attack the Parlement directly so soon after Maupeou's dismissal, Turgot carried through his measures without first destroying the institutional bases of privileged conservatism. He left the Parlement alone and attempted instead to reduce government expenditures and to alter the methods of tax collecting. He suggested that Protestants should be given freedom of conscience, and, in accordance with his Physiocratic laissez-faire principles, he freed the corn trade from restraint; suppressed the corvée, or forced labour service, exacted from the peasants; and abolished the guilds, which had limited both access to artisanal professions and the competition within them. In short, Turgot attempted to rationalize the state and to place the organization of society on a basis of equality before the law, arbitrarily but rationally handed down by the state.

<!-- margin note -->
Turgot's reforms

In May of 1776, however, Turgot was dismissed. Opposition to his measures had come from all sides: a poor harvest had sparked peasant disturbances, the clericalists were antagonized by Turgot's philosophical friends (his greatest and most loyal disciple was Condorcet, the future Girondin), and, when the Parlement of Paris once again refused to register the new edicts, Louis abandoned Turgot as he had dismissed Maupeou. Thenceforth, the state carried through only minor reforms, none of them on a scale commensurate to the needs that were felt by the enlightened bourgeoisie and notables of the cities and towns. The vestiges of serfdom were suppressed in 1779, and restrictions were removed from the Jews in 1784. In 1786 the salaries of the poorer country clergy were raised, and there were also improvements in the organization of the navy and the army (especially of the artillery, in which young Napoleon became a second lieutenant in 1786). Judicial procedure was also revamped: in 1780 torture was abolished, and in 1784 the king's use of lettres de cachet for purposes of arbitrary imprisonment without trial was considerably curtailed. But these were minor adjustments. Nothing was done to alter the fundamental problems of the organization of society and of the state in a manner that would be acceptable to progressive public opinion.

By the mid-1780s the state's position had in fact become truly hopeless. So great was the backlog of resentment that no concession would suffice. As a gift of the crown, no reform could be acceptable. Most remarkable was the lack of success of deliberative provincial assemblies, which had been designed to associate the political elites to the work of the intendants and of the centralized state. They would have been seen as an incredible concession 20 years before; in the 1770s and 1780s they were failures. The gap between the state and the public was so great that the state could now do nothing right.

But the problem of the state was complicated by the fact that in the 1780s most of what it did was actively and positively wrong. Having alienated conservative opinion by its attempted reforms and enlightened opinion by its failure to push them through, the crown had no constituency on which it could rely; and its only hope was to keep things as they were, in the hope that it would proceed somehow from expedient to expedient. The U.S. War of Independence, however, was a most inexpedient event. This was not due to its military denouement, for, in spite of some naval reverses in 1783, the French army and navy performed creditably during that conflict, and the position and prestige of France in Europe was greater in 1783 than it had been for 40 years. The French problem in that war was not military but financial. The cost

of the war was enormous, and it was met not by new taxation but by new borrowing, which doubled the size of the national debt. In the late 1780s, the service of the funds absorbed more than half the crown's income: by 1789 debt payments had risen to 300,000,000 livres from less than 100,000,000 before the American war. This could not go on forever, and indeed it was only because of the talent of Jacques Necker (Turgot's successor) in raising loans that the system went on as long as it did. But sooner or later, from sheer financial exhaustion, the state would have to turn to the nation, and at that point the whole set of conflicts in society—between country and city, bourgeois and noble—would have to be resolved.

<!-- margin note -->
Cost of the American war

By August of 1786 Necker's successor, Charles-Alexandre de Calonne, reached precisely that point. Although the crown had assured the moneymen that it would not default on the debt, as indeed it could not have done without alienating thousands of its natural supporters, Calonne found that he could no longer raise funds by borrowing. To resolve the ensuing impasse, in February of 1787 he summoned to Versailles the Assembly of Notables who represented the privileged orders—great nobles, bishops, parlementaires—in the hope that they would finally and of their own accord accept that transformation of the state that they had for so long resisted. But the notables refused again as the parlementaires had in 1776, this time on the grounds that Calonne's mismanagement was the only cause of the crown's problems. They argued that if Calonne were replaced by Necker, who had borrowed so successfully, all would be well. Once again, the crown yielded. Calonne was replaced by Loménie de Brienne, a cardinal, though an atheist, and a spokesman of the privileged majority of the Assembly of Notables. Almost at once, Loménie reversed himself and came to Calonne's conclusion: the state could not go on as it had; but the notables refused to be more amenable to Loménie than they had been to Calonne. Despairing of securing the consent of the privileged orders, Loménie dismissed the assembly in May of 1787, and in August the Paris Parlement was exiled to Troyes. But these were desperate measures, and already the monarchy was beginning to lose control of the political process. Indeed, for the next two years it merely floundered from one scheme to another, in the impossible hope of squaring the circle of modernistic reform, popular hostility, respect of privilege, and the preservation of royal absolutism.

<!-- margin note -->
The monarchy's loss of political control

For that reason, Loménie's exile of the Parlement in August of 1787 was not upheld. Essentially unwilling to force the privileged notables to yield their corporate rights, the crown was now unable to assert any coherent policy. The Parlement was therefore recalled in September of 1787, once again dismissed in May of 1788, and, in the face of a beginning of a breakdown of law and order and of the inability of officials to collect taxes, once more recalled to Paris by the crown in May of 1788. Paradoxically, the return of the reactionary parlementaires was saluted as a great victory by their most bitter reformist opponents. This is to be explained by the fact that the crown was now perceived by all Frenchmen as inimical: the conservative parlementaires opposed it from their reactionary point of view, and the reformists opposed it for its arbitrary repression even of the reactionaries. The crown was now essentially powerless, and on August 8, 1788, it tacitly accepted this fact by agreeing to call together the Estates-General on May 1 of the following year. At that juncture the monarchy in fact dropped out of the political debate that would now be structured by the tensions within French society. Censorship was in practice suspended, and thousands of pamphlets were circulated in Paris. The political debate of 1788–91 would thenceforth be freely conducted, and in the positions of the participants of that drama can be seen the echoes of the fundamental forces that united and divided the French nation.

In the first phase of the struggle, all those who desired a more modern, rationalized, and politically egalitarian society were opposed to the privileged order. The issue quickly polarized on the question of the composition of the estates. Should it meet in three groups, as it had in 1614, or should the members meet together (in which case the liberal minorities of the first two orders—clergy and nobility—could combine with the third and enact liberal measures)? The Parlement of Paris, which had returned in triumph on September 23, 1788, decided on September 25 that it would meet as it had before. At once the popularity of the *parlementaires* collapsed. On September 23 they were seen by the reformists as victims of royal oppression; but two days later they had become again what they in fact had always been: the defenders of the traditional social and political fabric of the *ancien régime*. In a last and fitful assertion of authority, at the behest of Necker, once again minister, the crown decided on December 27 to overrule the Parlement. The estates, it resolved, would meet separately, but the Third Estate would have as many deputies as the other two orders combined. The stage was now set for the coming Revolution.

The beginning of the Revolution. The first phase of the Revolution had opposed various groups in French society to the French state. The second phase would be characterized by a struggle between the traditionalists and the urban reformists as a whole. Subsequently, and under the pressure of events, the unity of revolutionary reformist fervour would break up, very often along those same lines of social class—economic, psychological, and moral—that had become increasingly visible after 1750. But in 1788–90 the political problem did not yet revolve around those issues. The sequence of events in those months is therefore to be seen as the assertion, against the privileged, traditionalist order and against the state, of the united power of the reformists, some of them bourgeois, some of them nobles, many of them of indeterminate social status. July 14, 1789, is only the vibrant and vivid symbol of the defeat of the *ancien régime*. By that date the revolutionary movement had been developing for more than a year. The aristocratic Fronde against the state had begun in the 1750s, and the revolution of the urban reformists against state and privilege was already a fact in late 1788.

The tasks of the reformists were much facilitated in the early months of 1789 by a gradual erosion of law and order in the countryside. The motives that drove the peasants to revolt were far different from those of the reformists. Both were interested in the problem of taxation; but, although the city dweller was concerned about efficiency and irrational expenditure, the peasants were simply interested in paying less. The peasants were keen also to destroy the feudal dues, which the reformers disliked abstractly but from which the peasants suffered concretely. Indeed, since thousands of city dwellers were also rural landlords and owners of feudal dues, there were many instances of armed conflict between urban militias and peasant bands in the late summer of 1789. After 1789, during the decade of revolution, these conflicts of material interests did at times become crucial. In the Vendée, for example, in 1793, the peasants even took sides for the aristocracy and against the reformist, urban bourgeoisie. But in the spring and summer of 1789, the great majority of Frenchmen—peasants, bourgeois, and reformists of all sorts—were able to compose their differences and to unite for a single political purpose: the destruction of the feudal, "privileged" establishment of church, state, and noble. In April and May there were numerous rural riots and attacks on convoys of grain, caused largely by an extraordinary and unusual rise in the price of bread. When the Estates-General met on May 5, the defenders of the *ancien régime* were thus in total

The united power of the reformists

From W. Shepherd, *Historical Atlas*, Harper & Row, Publishers (Barnes & Noble Books), New York; revision Copyright © 1964 by Barnes & Noble, Inc.

The *gouvernements* in 1789.

disarray. The crown was devoid of prestige, and the debris of its authority was still resented by the privileged orders, themselves unable to rely on peasant support because of the rural disorders. The victory of the reformists was therefore assured.

What followed in June and July was, if not inevitable, at least predictable. On June 17 the Third Estate declared itself to be a national assembly, and in the following days it was joined by individual reformist members of the clergy and nobility. Three days later, after having been denied admission to their usual place of meeting, the reformists met in the royal tennis court and swore an oath never to dissolve until France had secured a constitution. On June 23, in a final spasm, the crown in order to survive now sided openly with the privileged *parlementaires* and great nobles it had so recently tried to curb and made a last effort to stem the reformist tide. The King reasserted the divisions of the estates in three orders and declared null and void all the decisions taken by the Third Estate since June 17. On June 27, the crown seemed to have veered back to moderation, but in fact it persisted for some time in its attempts at resistance. Some 20,000 troops were marched in from the provinces, and it appeared that a military coup was in the offing. On July 11 the less reactionary members of the royal council were dismissed, as was Necker himself who was ordered into exile.

But this show of force was to no avail. The crown was too discredited; the army, too disloyal. Most importantly, the social forces that would traditionally have rallied to its support—traditionalist aristocrats and obtuse peasants—were too weak and indeed divided one against the other. A show of force from the side of the reformists would easily end this last-ditch effort of the *ancien régime*, and this force was provided by the Parisian crowd. Until then the political struggle had included the state, the traditionalists, and the literate reformists—some of them noble, many of them bourgeois. But now the mass of the urban population entered the political arena.

End of the *ancien régime*

In April a mob had attacked the factory of a textile manufacturer accused of starving the poor; and in early July there had been other food riots on the outskirts of Paris. By mid-July, however, the dissatisfaction of the urban poor was focussed on a more political purpose. In a show of revolutionary unity, the sans-culottes—the people of Paris who would later demand the blood of Lafayette, Brissot, Danton, and Robespierre himself—rose up to defend the liberal reformist cause, and, in so doing, brought down the *ancien régime* in ruins. On July 14 a crowd surged around the Bastille—that hated, though largely unused, symbol of absolutist oppression. Only seven people were imprisoned there, and two of them were mad. But, as a symbol, the fall of the Bastille could not be equalled. It sapped the will of the King to resist. On July 17 he recalled Necker and became in fact a constitutional monarch. The *ancien régime* was a thing of the past.

There were those who would say, with Edmund Burke, that now the glory of Europe was gone forever; and others who would herald instead the dawn of a new age of liberty, equality, and fraternity. What was certain, however, was that France and the world would never again be as they had been before.   (P.Hi.)

V. The French Revolution and Napoleon, 1789–1815

THE INITIAL REVOLUTIONARY REFORMS AND THE CONSTITUTIONAL MONARCHY

The Revolution of 1789. No sooner had the Estates-General entered into session at Versailles than the conflict between the orders declared itself: the Third Estate demanded that powers be verified in common, which implied that the estates should vote as one assembly; this would give the Third Estate an advantage, because it was the most numerous. The question was important: either the aristocracy had to yield (which meant the end of its privileges) or the Third Estate would have to acknowledge defeat (which meant the survival of the *ancien régime*). In the words of the reformist nobleman the Comte

de Mirabeau, the deputies of the Third Estate understood that they had only "to remain immovable in order to present a formidable danger to their enemies."

On June 12, 1789, the Third Estate began a roll call of all deputies on the question of the common verification of powers. The privileged bloc began to disintegrate. On June 13 only three parish priests answered to their names, on the next day, six. Foreseeing victory, the Third Estate pressed on. On June 17 it proclaimed itself the National Assembly. On June 19 the clergy decided to ally itself with the Third Estate.

Creation of the National Assembly

Encouraged by the nobility, Louis XVI decided to resist and ordered the meeting place of the estates closed. On June 20, 1789, the deputies of the Third Estate, finding the doors shut, moved to the nearby royal tennis court. There, under the presidency of the old astronomer Jean-Sylvain Bailly, the delegates swore not to adjourn until they had produced a constitution for France.

On June 23, 1789, the King held a "royal session" of the Estates-General, for the purpose of annulling the decisions of the Third Estate. He himself offered a program of reforms, one that maintained the feudal rights of the nobility. Louis threatened the deputies: "If you abandon me in this great enterprise I will work alone for the welfare of my peoples. . . . I command you to separate at once."

The King's attempt ended in failure. The commons did not budge, though the nobility and a part of the clergy withdrew. The body confirmed its earlier decrees and declared that its members were inviolable. When the royal bodyguard was ordered to disperse the deputies, the representatives of the nobility who had sided with the Third Estate objected, and the Marquis de Lafayette and others put their hands on their swords. Louis backed down.

From then on, the triumph of the Third Estate gained momentum. On June 24 the majority of the clergy sat beside it in the National Assembly. On the 27th the King, deciding to sanction what he had been unable to prevent, wrote to the minority of the clergy and the majority of the nobility, inviting them to rejoin the National Assembly. On July 9, 1789, that body proclaimed itself the National Constituent Assembly.

Thus far, the judicial revolution had been accomplished without violence. But just at the moment when the King and the aristocracy appeared ready to accept the accomplished fact, they decided, instead, to use force to bring the Third Estate back to obedience. The King clandestinely called in 17 regiments, most of them trusted Swiss or German mercenaries, ostensibly to protect property in case of mob violence in Paris, but in reality to intimidate the Constituent Assembly.

Thus, the judicial and peaceful revolution had finally miscarried. The King's appeal to the military emphasized the refusal of the aristocracy to make any concessions. But this was to leave the urban and rural masses out of account. In the summer of 1789, the storming of the Bastille in July and the so-called Great Fear that began July 20 unleashed a popular revolution and brought about the downfall of the *ancien régime*.

The economic crisis had already brought numerous mass disturbances that laid the groundwork for revolution. As early as April, a gunpowder factory and a wallpaper factory in the Faubourg Saint-Antoine in Paris had been sacked and pillaged. Earlier still, the harvest of 1788 had been a particularly bad one. Outbreaks at markets, looting of shipments of grain, and attacks on customs barriers multiplied. All this was taking place as the convocation of the Estates-General was raising immense hopes among the masses. Against this background, the action of the King and aristocrats in calling up the military and preventing a renewal of resistance logically gave rise to the notion of an "aristocratic conspiracy" and led the people to decide to act before the aristocrats could attack. Popular feeling intensified and spread, unnerving the troops and the mounted constabulary, inflaming the atmosphere of the cities. On the eve of the harvest of 1789 the crisis reached its peak. The idea of an aristocratic conspiracy and the fact of economic crisis became united in the popular mind. The people were no longer in doubt that the King meant to use force to disperse the National Assembly, in which lay all their hopes.

On the afternoon of July 12, 1789, the news of the King's dismissal of Jacques Necker, who was thought of as a reformer, became known in Paris. The theatres closed, and there were spontaneous street demonstrations. On July 13 the electors of the Third Estate ordered the creation of a "civic militia," in theory to guard the public safety but, in fact, to be a "bourgeois militia," directed against the excesses of the royal power and its regular troops on the one hand and the threat from social categories considered dangerous on the other.

On July 14, 1789, after pillaging the armory at the Invalides, a mob made its way to the Bastille, an old fortress on the east side of Paris that had come to symbolize the despotism of the *ancien régime*. Artisans and journeymen of the Faubourg Saint-Antoine, reinforced by members of the bourgeois militia and by two detachments of French guards, forced the governor, Bernard Jordan, marquis de Launay, to capitulate. He ordered the drawbridge lowered, and the people rushed in.

Interestingly, the monarchy emerged from these July days singularly disabled. The King recalled Necker and on July 17 went to Paris to sanction the appointment of Bailly as mayor and Lafayette as commandant of a bourgeois municipality and national guard. The Parisian bourgeoisie had thus taken advantage of the popular victory to assume the administration of the capital.

In the provinces, the Parisian revolution of July 14 had counterparts in various actions of the so-called municipal revolution: during the weeks of July and August 1789 the old municipal governments, in fact, disappeared; the administrators abandoned their offices; the collection of taxes was suspended; and the royal power vanished. New municipal governments were established, and local life had a rebirth. France was "municipalized."

At this point the peasants entered the scene. Famine and unemployment having vastly increased the number of vagabonds, roving bands appeared in numbers in the countryside in the spring of 1789; and the "fear of brigands" was thus added to the fear of the "aristocratic conspiracy." Local incidents brought on a series of panics—the so-called Grande Peur, or Great Fear—which, from July 20 to August 6, 1789, shook the entire country. The fear triggered a "defensive reaction," and the peasants armed themselves. Though the groundlessness of these popular terrors soon became apparent, the mechanisms of collective psychology worked so as to convert a "defensive reaction" to a "punitive will." Abandoning the pursuit of imaginary brigands, the peasants turned instead to the castles and burned the records of their manorial debts and feudal obligations. In only a few days the feudal regime had been overthrown.

The abolition of feudalism. The Constituent Assembly, during this course of events, was powerless and helpless. The majority of its members were men of property, reluctant either to sanction the peasants' actions or to widen the gulf between themselves and the peasantry and put themselves at the mercy of the King and the aristocracy.

The Assembly had no doubts at all concerning the significance of the insurrection in the countryside; breaking out at the height of the harvest season, the insurrection challenged the collection of feudal dues and the very existence of feudal rights and of tithes. Though, in principle, the bourgeoisie opposed these feudal remnants as an obstacle to the capitalistic transformation of agriculture and of the entire economy, in practice the majority of the deputies were jurists who, as such, regarded seigneurial rights as a form of legitimate individual property that could not be abolished without imperilling the social order itself. It was necessary, therefore, either to suppress the agrarian revolts or to make some immediate concessions.

The Third Estate hesitated but finally concluded an alliance with the liberal nobility. At the beginning of a memorable session on the night of August 4, 1789, Louis-Marie, vicomte de Noailles, proposed that all feudal rights should be made redeemable in money or exchanged "at the rate determined by an equitable evaluation." Armand, duc d'Aiguillon, one of the greatest landowners in the country, next insisted that "the rights in question are a form of property" and that "all property is sacred." Hence, the "proprietors of fiefs," the "lords of estates," could not be asked to accept the pure and simple renunciation of their feudal rights, unless they were granted an equitable indemnity. Having thus safeguarded their essential interests, the deputies allowed popular enthusiasm to take over: the feudal privileges of individuals and orders were abolished, together with those of the provinces and the cities.

The "abolition" of feudalism by the Constituent Assembly, however, was more apparent than real. Subsequent decrees (those of August 5–11, 1789, and March 15, 1790) passed in pursuance of the decisions taken on the night of August 4 showed how dubious the unanimity of that night of calculated enthusiasm was and how superficial the sacrifices made by the aristocracy. Feudalism, destroyed only in its institutional and legal form, lived on as an economic reality. In this regard, a distinction between "dominant" and "contractual" feudalism had come into play. The former (*i.e.*, the right to administer justice, serfdom, forced labour and *banalités*, tolls, and hunting and fishing rights) had been abolished; the latter (*i.e.*, quitrents, ground rents, and annual dues, etc.) had been declared redeemable. A further decree of May 3, 1790, set redemption at a very high rate: 20 times the annual fee for dues in money, 25 times for dues in kind —a heavy burden for the majority of the peasants, who had no reserves.

The redemption of feudal rights constituted the economic basis of the compromise with the aristocracy that a segment of the bourgeoisie had sought since 1789—a compromise that greatly favoured the feudal lord. Only the wealthier class of peasant proprietors (peasants who owned land) benefitted economically from the abolition of feudal dues. For the mass of lesser peasants, the abolition of feudalism was, in the words of Georges Lefebvre, "a bitter deception." To obtain complete enfranchisement of the soil, the peasant revolution continued in many forms until 1792 and in some regions until 1793— constituting nothing short of a masked civil war.

The reforms of the Constituent Assembly. On the night of August 4 the Constituent Assembly had made a clean sweep: henceforth all Frenchmen were equal, the territory of France was unified. The next step was one of reconstruction. But if the principles were solemnly proclaimed, they were nevertheless infringed with the same realism that had governed the working out of the compromise on feudalism.

From the beginning of August the Constituent Assembly addressed itself to the task of reconstruction. It was decided that the new constitution being prepared by the Constituent Assembly must be preceded by a declaration of rights; some wanted to supplement it by a declaration of duties, and the discussion proceeded slowly. Finally, on August 27, 1789, the Assembly adopted the Declaration of the Rights of Man and of the Citizen. The great desideratum of the constituent bourgeoisie was "freedom," in its public and political aspects. According to the Declaration, freedom is an inalienable natural right limited only by the freedom of others. Freedom is seen first of all as freedom of the person: individual freedom, protected from arbitrary accusations and arrests and safeguarded by the presumption of innocence. Masters of their person, men were to be able to speak and write, print and publish freely, on condition only that the expression of opinions not disturb the order established by law, and subject to responsibility for any abuse of the freedom. The article on freedom of worship had been debated at length prior to adoption, the clergy insisting that the Assembly should confirm the existence of a state religion and Mirabeau protesting vigorously in favour of freedom of conscience and worship. In the end, the state church was recognized; but dissident cults were to be tolerated.

With freedom the declaration closely associated equality, demanded by the bourgeoisie in opposition to the aristocracy and by the peasants in the face of the feudal lords. The declaration held that the law was to be the same for everyone, and all citizens were equal in its eyes. Dignities, offices, and employments had to be equally open to all, without distinction of birth—social distinctions were to be based only on common usefulness, on virtues and talents; taxation was to be equally distributed among all citizens, in proportion to their ability to pay.

On the political plane, the liberalism of the Constituent Assembly found expression in the Constitution of 1791, as it is called, though its principal stipulations actually had been voted as early as the end of 1789. On the basis of national sovereignty and the separation of powers, the Constitution organized a representative system characterized by the predominance of the Legislative Assembly. Political equality, however, was distorted by limiting suffrage on the basis of taxation. By the law of December 22, 1789, political rights had been reserved to a minority of property owners divided into three hierarchized categories according to the amount of taxes they paid: (1) "active" citizens grouped in primary assemblies; (2) "electors" who made up departmental electoral assemblies, and (3) citizens "eligible" for the Legislative Assembly. "Passive" citizens were excluded from the right of suffrage because they did not reach the prescribed level of taxation.

Other work of the Assembly—administrative decentralization, judicial reform, new fiscal organization, and even the reorganization of the church by the Civil Constitution of the Clergy (July 12, 1790)—was in accordance with the same preoccupation with liberalism. In the same vein, the Assembly undertook a complete administrative reorganization of the country into departments, districts, cantons, and communes, in which all administrators were elected, even bishops.

Economic freedom was not mentioned in the Declaration of Rights of 1789 or the Constitution of 1791—presumably because it was taken for granted by the members of the Constituent Assembly and also because the popular masses were profoundly attached to the old system of production and exchange, which, through regulation and taxation, to a certain extent guaranteed their conditions of life. From 1789 this attitude of laissez-faire, or "hands off," provided the foundation for the new economic and social institutions. Freedom of property followed from the abolition of feudalism. Freedom of agriculture heralded the triumph of agrarian individualism, even though a rural code of 1791 maintained—not without contradiction—the old medieval right of villagers to graze their animals on common land if the right was founded on custom. Freedom of production was generalized by the abolition of monopolies and guilds. The Allarde Law of March 2, 1791, abolished journeymen's associations, guilds, and secret societies, and privileged manufactures as well. The national market was unified by the abolition of customs dues and tolls.

Finally, there was freedom of work, indissolubly connected with freedom of enterprise: the Le Chapelier Law of June 14, 1791, though it guaranteed the right of association and of public meetings, prohibited *coalition* (collective resistance) and strikes. The free individual was also free to create and produce, to pursue profit and to employ it as he desired.

The new social and political order was reinforced by two closely connected extreme reform measures enacted to solve the financial crisis. On November 2, 1789, the property of the clergy was confiscated and put "at the disposal of the nation." On December 19, some 400,000,000 livres worth of these confiscated properties were put on sale, represented by an equal amount in assignats, 5 percent bonds constituting an obligation of the state and repayable in ecclesiastical properties. The operation failed, and on August 27, 1790, the assignat became a banknote. The depreciation of this paper currency, inflation, and the high cost of living rekindled social agitation and at the same time struck a hard blow at established wealth. Through the sale of national properties, which the assignat encouraged, the Revolution next moved

margin: Confiscation of church lands

toward a new redistribution of landed wealth, one that accentuated its social character. It is notable, however, that, like the abolition of feudal rights, the sale of national properties did not benefit the mass of the peasantry; rather, it strengthened the preponderance of the propertied classes.

The Civil Constitution of the Clergy, which was destined to raise new difficulties for the Revolution, fell within the same framework of liberalism: it followed necessarily from the confiscation of ecclesiastical properties, as well as from the reform of the state and the administration. Religious orders were abolished on February 13, 1790, and the organization of the remainder of the clergy was based on the new administrative divisions: a diocese for each department. Bishops and parish priests were elected like other officials—the latter by the electoral assembly of the district, the former by that of the *département*. The newly elected ecclesiastics were "instituted" by their ecclesiastical superiors, not by the Pope. The church of France thus became a national church; its ties to the papacy were loosened; papal briefs were subject to governmental censorship; and annates (payments to Rome) were suppressed. Though the Pope retained spiritual primacy over the French Church, all temporal jurisdiction was taken from him. The Constituent Assembly at first left it to the Pope to sanction the Civil Constitution, but he had already condemned the Declaration of the Rights of Man and of the Citizen as impious; moreover, Avignon, a papal dependency surrounded by French territory, was demanding to be annexed to France. Pius VI temporized. Tired of waiting, on November 27, 1790, the Constituent Assembly demanded that all priests swear loyalty to the Civil Constitution of the Clergy. Only seven bishops took the oath. The priests divided into two groups, more or less equal in numbers but unevenly distributed: "refractories," or "nonjurors," in the west, and "jurors," or "constitutionals," a majority in the southeast. When, on March 10 and April 13, 1791, the Pope solemnly condemned the principles of the Revolution and the Civil Constitution, the schism was complete. The country was thus cut in two. The refractory opposition strengthened the counter-revolutionary agitation, and the religious conflict came to parallel that of the civil sphere.

margin: Papal condemnation

THE RADICALIZATION OF THE REVOLUTION, 1791–93

The end of compromise. The constitutional monarchy as the bourgeoisie had sought to establish it had been based on an economic and social compromise represented by the redemption of feudal rights and on a system of suffrage based on taxation that sanctioned the rights of property and propertied classes. But this compromise finally became impossible in the face of the obstinate resistance of the mass of the lesser nobles, who for the most part lived on feudal dues, and that of the stubborn and aggressive determination of the peasants to abolish all survivals of the feudal system. Under these conditions, the social stabilization that would have allowed the constitutional monarchy to function was impossible.

From 1789 to 1791 the various bourgeois factions of the Constituent Assembly tried to arrive at a political compromise with the aristocracy. Three leaders in the Assembly are associated with these attempts: Jean-Joseph Mounier, the Marquis de Lafayette, and Antoine Barnave.

In the summer of 1789, Mounier had thought it possible that the three orders could unite in support of a limited revolution. In September 1789 he had sought the Assembly's approval for a political system that, after the pattern of the English Revolution of 1688, would have set the "notables" (the aristocracy and the upper bourgeoisie) in a dominant position over the popular masses. The "Monarchicals," or "Anglomaniacs," he led demanded an upper chamber that would have been the fortress of the aristocracy, and, for the king, an absolute veto. The Constituent Assembly refused, and the "Revolution of the Notables" failed. Mounier left Versailles after the October Days of 1789, when a Parisian mob marched there

margin: Mounier, Lafayette, and Barnave

and forced the royal family to return to Paris, where they could be watched.

Lafayette, whether from ambition or from incomprehension, revived the same policy with a different emphasis: he sought to reconcile the landed aristocracy and the commercial bourgeoisie in the framework of the constitutional monarchy. In 1790 Lafayette completely dominated political life; he triumphed at the Fête de la Fédération of July 14, 1790 (celebrating the anniversary of the fall of the Bastille), which appeared to seal the reconciliation between the monarchy and the nation. But when he showed his true position by approving the extremely harsh repression with which his cousin, François-Claude Armour, marquis de Bouillé, quelled the revolt of the garrison at Nancy in August 1790, his popularity went up in smoke.

Barnave and his friends in the Assembly, Adrien Duport and Charles, comte de Lameth—the Triumvirate—carried on the torch. No one better defined the essence of the political and social compromise that they sought than Barnave in a vehement speech before the Assembly on July 15, 1791:

Are we going to end the Revolution, are we going to begin it again? . . . One step further it cannot be made without danger; that in the line of liberty the first act that might ensue would be the annihilation of royalty; that in the line of equality the first act that might ensue would be an attack upon property.

In agreement with Lafayette, the triumvirs wanted to revise the constitution, to strengthen its emphasis on property qualifications for suffrage, and to increase the powers of the King. This policy demanded both the support of the aristocrats and the approval of Louis XVI. Its rejection by the aristocracy and the King, the appeal to the other European monarchs, and finally the outbreak of war in April 1792 (see below) once again ruined this policy of compromise.

Except for a minority of liberal nobles, the aristocracy totally rejected reform and remained stubbornly attached to its privileges, its haughty exclusivism, and its feudal mentality. As for the monarchy, its attitude proved, if proof was needed, that it was by its very nature allied to the aristocracy. The appeal to the military upon which the King had decided in the first days of July 1789 would have brought the end of the Revolution if the people had not intervened. The majority of the aristocracy accepted neither the decrees of August 5–11, 1789, nor the Declaration of Rights: not even, that is, the partial destruction of feudalism. It was the popular insurrection of October 1789 that had forced the King to accept the decrees of August. In 1790, while Louis XVI was making use of Lafayette (whom he hated), the aristocracy persisted in resisting, its hopes fed by the plots of émigrés to secure foreign intervention and the beginnings of the counter-revolution. At the same time, agrarian revolts, brought on in many regions by the need to redeem feudal rights, hardened its refusal. The King's unsuccessful attempt to leave the country in 1791, armed gatherings of émigrés on the Rhine, and finally the war that it had been the émigrés' policy to seek from 1791 proved that the monarchy and the aristocracy would betray the nation rather than yield.

For its part, the peasantry no less stubbornly refused the compromise of the redemption of feudalism. Despite the proclamation of the principle of redemption as early as August 4, 1789, those upon whom the burden of feudal dues fell could not begin to envisage their liberation until the passage of the decree of May 3, 1790, which organized the redemption in accordance with the provisions of the law of the preceding March 15. These delays exasperated even the least disaffected. The bad drafting of the decrees of August 5–11, 1789 ("The Constituent Assembly destroys the feudal régime in its entirety . . ."), increased the confusion; the peasants took the text literally and refused further payments. Their disappointment swiftly and inevitably gave way to anger, the more so because the feudal lords insisted on payment not only in the case of the rights that had been maintained, so long as they were not abolished, but also of the arrears due

for the abolished rights. Under these conditions, from 1789 to 1792 the peasants were pitted against the aristocracy in a civil war that varied in intensity in the several regions. There were serious disturbances or out-and-out peasant revolts from 1789 in the Aisne, the Norman Bocage, in Anjou, Franche-Comté, Dauphiné, Vivarais, and Roussillon. In January 1790, there were revolts in Quercy, Périgord, and Brittany; in May in the Bourbonnais. Quercy and Périgord were in insurrection again in the winter of 1791–92; in the spring it was the turn of the Gard, the Ardèche, and then of Provence. In equal measure with the popular movements in the towns, the peasant insurrections drove the Revolution forward.

The King's flight to Varennes. The King's attempt to flee the country on June 21, 1791, constituted one of the great turning points of the Revolution. At home, it proved the irreconcilable opposition between aristocratic royalty and the Revolutionary nation: it thus wrecked the experiment with constitutional monarchy. In foreign affairs, it precipitated a conflict that led to war.

About midnight on June 20, Louis XVI, disguised as a valet, left the Tuileries with his family. During the night of June 21–22 he was arrested at Varennes. The royal family was returned to Paris on the evening of June 25, amid a deathly silence, between two files of soldiers with their muskets reversed. It was the "funeral procession of the monarchy."

The Assembly maintained its composure. Creating the fiction that the King had been kidnapped, it quelled popular disturbances by using the National Guard and set about revising the Constitution, increasing its emphasis on property qualifications. The King accepted the Constitution thus revised. On September 14, 1791, he once again swore loyalty to the nation, but his attempted flight had destroyed his credibility. The split between the King and the nation was irremediable.

Meanwhile, Louis's flight and arrest had aroused an intense emotional reaction in monarchical Europe. On August 27, 1791, by the Declaration of Pillnitz, the Habsburg emperor Leopold II and King Frederick William II of Prussia threatened the Revolutionary nation with armed intervention. From that moment, war appeared inevitable.

Declaration of Pillnitz

The outbreak of war. From 1791 war had been the final recourse for the aristocracy and the monarchy. "Instead of a civil war, there will be a foreign war," Louis XVI was to write on December 14, 1791, to his agent, Louis-Auguste Le Tonnelier, baron de Breteuil, "and things will be much the better for it."

In the Legislative Assembly, which, succeeding to the Constituent Assembly, had gone into session on October 1, 1791, war was in fact sought by the left at the urging of new men later known as Girondins, then known as Brissotins, after their leader, Jacques-Pierre Brissot.

The left of the Legislative Assembly was made up of more than 130 deputies, chiefly members of the Club of the Jacobins. It was more particularly guided by two Parisian deputies, the journalist Brissot and the philosopher the Marquis de Condorcet; and it was influenced by a number of brilliant orators elected by the *département* of the Gironde—especially Pierre-Victurnien Vergniaud. Representatives of the upper mercantile bourgeoisie, the Girondins wanted to quash the counter-revolution, particularly to re-establish the value of the assignat—a prime necessity if business was to flourish. The aristocracy wanted war in order to bring about counter-revolution by a defeat; and the business bourgeoisie was not averse to war because supplying the armies constituted a traditional source of large profits. Moreover, both saw that to attack Europe's *ancien régime* would be to launch a final attack on the aristocracy, to unmask it, to bring it to unconditional surrender.

Despite opposition expressed by the future revolutionary leader Robespierre in great speeches ("Begin by turning your eyes back to our internal situation, restore order in your own house, before you carry liberty elsewhere"), on April 20, 1792, the Legislative Assembly declared war "on the king of Bohemia and Hungary," that is, on Austria alone and not on the empire. Though the war did not fulfill the expectations of either the court or the Gironde, it did help to inflame nationalistic feeling and gave the Gironde an aura of lasting prestige that even the catastrophes that followed could not dim. If the Girondins perished in the end, it was not because they had wanted a war that finally revealed the nation to itself, it was because they had not known how to conduct it.

The overthrow of the monarchy. For in fact the Girondist bourgeoisie proved incapable of conducting this war against the *ancien régime* of Europe by its own unaided efforts; its fear of the popular movement caused it to refuse the cooperation of the people. Robespierre's prophetic warning that it was necessary to destroy aristocracy within the nation before fighting it beyond the frontiers proved to be justified. Military defeats of the spring of 1792, through which the Gironde saw the need for an alliance with the people if victory was to be won, revealed its hesitations if not its duplicity: it consented to appeal to the people—as in the case of the uprising of June 20, 1792—in order to exert pressure on Louis XVI, but only insofar as the people demanded nothing more than the objectives the Girondist bourgeoisie had assigned to them.

The effects of the national crisis combined with those of the economic crisis, and together they revived the popular movement in the spring of 1792. Nationalistic surge and revolutionary thrust were inseparable: a social conflict underlay and exacerbated patriotism. The aristocrats opposed the King to the nation, which they scorned; inside the country they awaited the invader, and those who had gone into exile fought in the enemy ranks. The patriots of 1792 wished to safeguard the heritage of 1789 and carry it further. On the advice of the Girondins themselves, the "passive" (voteless) citizens donned the "cap of liberty," armed themselves with pikes, and formed more and more popular associations.

Arming of the "passive" citizens

By raising Revolutionary sentiment to fever pitch, the national crisis revived the social oppositions within the former Third Estate itself. Even more than in 1789 the bourgeoisie became uneasy. The rich were taxed to arm the volunteers, the ravages of inflation continued, and disturbances over provisions increased. The spectre of an "agrarian law" haunted the propertied bourgeoisie. Thus, the line that was soon to separate the Girondins from the more radical Montagnards began to be drawn. Already the deep reasons for what some historians later termed "the national failure" of the Girondins could be perceived: representatives of the bourgeoisie, partisans of economic freedom, they were alarmed by the popular tide that their war policy had raised.

The extremity of the danger was further testimony to both the incapacity of the Girondins and the duplicity of Louis XVI. On July 11, 1792, with the first entry of allied troops onto French soil, the Legislative Assembly declared "the fatherland in danger." But, dreading the popular movement, the Girondist leaders at the same time negotiated with the King, despite the fact that they had accused him of treating with the enemy. While the tide of popular anger swelled, the Girondins hesitated, then took fright in the face of a movement that they had nevertheless contributed to launching. Finally, a popular insurrection of August 10, 1792, which overthrew the monarchy and the Constitution of 1791, began and did its work, if not despite the Girondins, then at least without them.

The "Second Revolution"

The insurrection of August 10, 1792, was at once national and social. It was national because of the presence of battalions of *fédérés* from Marseilles and Brittany; it was social because of the participation of the "passive" citizens, who thus demolished the barriers of property qualifications. By bringing about universal suffrage and the arming of passive citizens, this "Second Revolution" integrated the lower classes into the nation and marked the advent of a degree of democracy. After abortive efforts to protest or resist, the former partisans of compromise departed. Lafayette emigrated on August 19, 1792. But, even more, the entrance of the sans-culottes (lower class artisans) onto the stage, by sanctioning the defeat of the Legislative Assembly and the constitutional

monarchy, provoked the opposition of a segment of the bourgeoisie. The radicalization of the Revolution brought on new social and political conflicts.

The defeat of the Gironde. The bourgeois Montagnards, realizing that they could not win without the support of the lower classes, allied themselves with the sans-culottes. This intrusion of the people on the political scene presented a serious threat to the interests of the upper bourgeoisie represented by the Gironde. Long months of struggle, from the summer of 1792 to the spring of 1793, were needed before the alliance between Montagnards and sans-culottes would end in the defeat of the failing Gironde.

The conflict became evident immediately after the insurrection of August 10: it crystallized in the desperate opposition between the Gironde and the radical organization that had directed the uprising. The conflict was intensified by the popular invasion of Parisian prisons and the massacre of prisoners from September 2–6, 1792: the insurrectionary leaders did not oppose these killings, and the Girondins accused them of complicity.

It was in this atmosphere of crisis that elections to the National Convention, made necessary by the suspension of the Constitution of 1791, took place. The new assembly met on September 20, 1792—the same day on which the Revolutionary army halted the invasion of the Prussian troops at Valmy, north of Paris. The German poet Johann Wolfgang von Goethe, who witnessed the battle, declared, "From this day and this place dates a new era in the history of the world."

Elections to the National Convention

On September 21, 1792, the Convention was at first unanimously in favour of abolishing the monarchy, but there soon developed a rift between the radical Montagnards and the conservative Girondins. Though this rivalry was primarily political, it had, despite their common bourgeois loyalties, an undeniable social character. The Girondins were bent upon defending property and economic freedom from the limitations demanded by the sans-culottes: regulation, taxation, requisition, enforced stabilization of the assignat. Profoundly imbued with the feeling of social hierarchies, the Girondins instinctively recoiled from the people; they reserved the monopoly of government and administration to the propertied classes, even when they declared themselves in favour of popular suffrage. Brissot inveighed against the "disorganizers," by which he meant the Montagnards, the Jacobins, the sans-culottes: "those who would level everything—properties, wealth, the price of staples, the various services owed to society."

Robespierre, leader of the Montagnards, attacked the "false patriots," who "want to set up the Republic only for themselves, who seek to govern only for the advantage of the rich." The Montagnards, and especially the Jacobins, sought to give the national reality a positive content that could rally the support of the popular masses. The Jacobin leader Louis de Saint-Just, in a speech on the food supply on November 29, 1792, emphasized the need "to relieve the people from the state of uncertainty and deprivation which corrupts them. You can, in one moment," he added, "give the French people a fatherland" by halting the ravages of inflation, by assuring the people of their subsistence, by "binding together their happiness and their freedom." Robespierre was even more outspoken on December 2, 1792, in a speech on uprisings over grain in Eure-et-Loir:

> And which is the first of these rights? That of existence. The first social law is, therefore, that which assures every member of society of the means of existence; all other laws are subordinate to it.

The necessities of the war and their national sense prompted the Montagnards to join with the sans-culottes; but they would have to be won over by a new social orientation.

The trial of Louis XVI made the conflict between Girondins and Montagnards irreconcilable by defining the new political situation.

The trial began on December 11, with the reading of an act of accusation drawn up by the Jacobin leader Robert Lindet, an account of Louis XVI's duplicity at critical

The trial of the King

periods during the Revolution. On December 26, the King's advocate read a speech for the defense, maintaining the thesis of royal inviolability as proclaimed by the Constitution of 1791.

Finally, on January 14, 1793, the Convention deliberated and passed judgment. Unanimously, Louis XVI was found guilty. An "appeal to the people," proposed by the Girondins, was rejected. The death sentence was imposed by a vote of 387 to 334, after an interminable individual roll call. On January 18 the question of reprieve was put to the vote; it was rejected by 380 to 310.

The execution of the King took place on January 21, 1793. It was a decisive blow to monarchist sentiment; it freed the idea of nation from its monarchical form. It made any compromise between the "regicides" and the "appellants" (the deputies who had voted for the appeal to the people) impossible. For the nation, identified with the Republic and founded on the strengthened solidarity between the Montagnard bourgeoisie and the sans-culotte populace, the execution of Louis XVI left no other way of salvation except victory.

The First Coalition

The crisis became general: it sealed the fate of the Gironde, which was incapable of overcoming it. On February 1, 1793, the Convention declared war on England and the United Provinces of the Netherlands, then, on March 7, on Spain. Foreign reaction against the Revolutionary nation took the form of the so-called First Coalition, the moving spirit of which was England. The republican armies met with a series of defeats in March 1793. Also in March, a counter-revolutionary rebellion against military conscription broke out in the Vendée, in western France. During these crises, the Gironde refused any concession that would have allowed the people to join in a national upsurge. Finally, a new popular insurrection, encouraged by the Montagnards and the Jacobins, overcame the Girondist resistance: the Parisian sections, in revolt from May 31 to June 2, 1793, demanded and obtained the elimination of the Girondist leaders in the Convention. The role of the Parisian populace and the setback to the upper bourgeoisie emphasize the social aspect of this movement: it opened a new phase of the Revolution.

SUCCESS AT HOME AND ABROAD: THE TERROR AND THERMIDOR, 1793–94

Establishment of the Revolutionary government. The Gironde had scarcely been eliminated before the Convention, now under the leadership of the Montagnards, found itself caught between two fires. Many of the Gironde's deputies fled to the provinces, where they fomented uprisings against the government in Paris. While the counter-revolution on the right gained fresh vigour from these federalist revolts, the popular movement, exacerbated by the high cost of living and the shortage of food, increased its pressure on the Convention from the left. At the same time, the governmental organization showed that it was incapable of controlling the situation: in the Committee of Public Safety, which was soon to become the chief organ of government, the Parisian leader Georges Danton was negotiating instead of fighting. The Montagnards, already hampered by their own contradictory position, hesitated, fearing to yield too much to the people but unable to fight the war without them. For several months the revolutionary initiative came from the popular masses, whose needs and hatreds drove them on: in the course of the summer of 1793, they imposed the major measures of public safety, from the *levée en masse* (the conscription law, August 23, 1793) to the general Maximum (price control law).

A revolutionary government then seemed all the more indispensable in order to discipline the thrust of the masses and to maintain the alliance with the bourgeoisie, which alone could furnish the necessary officials. On this twofold social base—sans-culottes of the cities and the countryside, and Montagnard and Jacobin bourgeoisie—a revolutionary government was organized piece by piece between July and December 1793: its most far-sighted architects were determined at all costs to preserve the unity of the erstwhile Third Estate—that is, the unity of

the nation. But the aspirations of the sans-culottes were only too likely to conflict with the interests of the bourgeois leaders of the Revolution. The national danger muted class antagonisms for the time being; but it was forseeable that, as victory became certain, they would reappear.

The popular thrust continued to be exerted in full vigour until the autumn of 1793. It forced the reluctant Convention and its hesitant committees to adopt severe revolutionary measures. On September 11, after great popular demonstrations, a national Maximum was adopted, fixing the price of grain. On the 17th the Law of Suspects was voted. Finally, on September 29, the general Maximum—that is, a controlled economy—was instituted. The essential elements of an emergency regime, at once political and economic, were thus fitted into place, with "coercive force," that is, the Terror, as its essential instrument of control. But what was a victory of the people also had aspects of a governmental success. The popular movement had been canalized and legality safeguarded, when legal terror won the day over direct action by the masses. The Committee of Public Safety, of which Robespierre had been a member from July 27, 1793, had had the foresight to yield in time—but on its own chosen ground: its authority emerged increased. It earlier had got rid of the extreme popular opposition represented by a faction known to moderates as the "Enragés" (madmen). On September 25, in the course of a great debate in the Convention, it silenced the opposition. The results of this governmental consolidation were sanctioned by a decree of October 10, 1793, adopted on a report made by Saint-Just: the Convention declared the government of France "revolutionary until the peace."

From then on, the Terror developed. A series of political trials began in October 1793. On October 3, 22 Girondins were made to appear before the Revolutionary Tribunal, as was Queen Marie-Antoinette, who was guillotined on October 16. When the trial of the Girondins seemed likely to drag on, the Convention decreed that the jurors could pronounce their verdict after three days of discussion; the Girondins were guillotined on October 31. During the last three months of 1793, of 395 accused persons, 117 were sentenced to death. The number of political prisoners in Paris rose from 1,500 about the end of August to 4,595 on December 1, 1793.

During this time, while the Terror was tending to be regularized under increasingly strict control by the Revolutionary government, that government itself had to face a new form of popular radicalism—de-Christianization—which posed a threat to governmental stabilization.

De-Christianization

De-Christianization first manifested itself in the *départements*, at the instigation of "representatives on mission" appointed by the Committee of Public Safety. Joseph Fouché, the representative in the Nièvre *département*, forbade all religious ceremonies outside churches, laicized funeral processions and graveyards, the entrances to which he ordered should bear the inscription: "Death is an eternal sleep." At Paris, the Commune acted prudently. The impulse came from elsewhere: de-Christianization was imposed on the Convention from outside. On November 6, 1793, at the demand of the Commune of Mennecy, near Corbeil, the Convention decreed that a commune had the right to renounce the Catholic form of worship. From then on de-Christianization gathered momentum. On November 7 the Archbishop of Paris appeared before the Convention and solemnly resigned his episcopal functions. On November 10 a festival of liberty took place in the former Cathedral of Notre-Dame, which was now consecrated to Reason. In a few days, the tide of de-Christianization carried the Parisian sections with it, and the Paris Commune closed the churches.

At the beginning of December, however, the movement was brought to a halt by Robespierre, who feared that de-Christianization might alienate neutral foreign powers. On December 6, 1793, the Convention passed a solemn decree reaffirming the principle of the freedom of worship. De-Christianization diminished but at different rates in different regions.

Despite the limited nature of its success, the Committee of Public Safety emerged the victor; it had checked the popular movement and had saved itself from being overwhelmed by the de-Christianizers. At about the same time the military situation improved. On October 16, 1793, the Austrians had been defeated at Wattignies; on December 13 and 14 the Vendéan rebels were overwhelmed in the city of Le Mans. These successes were ratified on December 4, 1793 (14 Frimaire, Year II, by the new French Revolutionary Calendar) by a constitutive decree of the Revolutionary government. The logic of events led inevitably to reconstituting administrative centralization, to strengthening the authority of the government—a necessary condition for the victory so stubbornly pursued by the Committee of Public Safety.

The Revolutionary government, 1793–94. From December 1793 to July 1794 and the so-called Thermidorian reaction, the dictatorship of the Revolutionary government was no longer contested and, indeed, enjoyed a certain stability. The theory of the Revolutionary government was developed especially by Saint-Just in a report of October 10, 1793, and by Robespierre in a report on the principles of the Revolutionary government (December 25, 1793) and one on the principles of political morality that should guide the Convention (February 5, 1794).

The Revolutionary government was a war government: "Revolution is the war waged by liberty against its enemies," wrote Robespierre. Because it is at war, "the revolutionary government requires an extraordinary activity, it must act like a thunderbolt." Hence it has at its command "coercive force," that is, the Terror. "Is force," asked Robespierre, "then made to protect crime?" But the Terror has a corrective—"virtue, the fundamental principle of democratic and popular government." Virtue, "which is to say, love of the fatherland and its laws, the magnanimous devotion which submerges all private interests in the general interest."

The Convention remained "the one centre of impulse of the government." It possessed supreme authority, and the Committees governed under its control. The Committee of Public Safety, re-elected each month, was "at the centre of execution"; the constituted bodies and the public functionaries were "under its immediate purview"; it directed diplomacy and the war, general policy, and the national economy. If certain members of the Committee specialized in certain activities, all of its members together shared in directing policy and conducting the war. As for the Committee of General Security, also re-elected each month, in accordance with the Law of Suspects of September 17, 1793, it had "under its particular purview". . ."everything relating to persons and to the general and internal police." This Committee directed the political police and Revolutionary justice—it was the minister of the Terror.

Incidence of the Terror

The Terror constituted a means of national and revolutionary defense. In the face of an ever-resurgent aristocratic conspiracy, it manifested the "defensive reaction" and the "punitive will" of the Third Estate, though henceforth disciplined by the laws and controlled by the government. Statistical studies made in 1935, by an American historian, Donald Greer, confirm this characterization. The Terror was particularly severe in those areas in which the counter-revolution reached the point of armed insurrection and overt treason. Only 15 percent of the death sentences were pronounced in Paris; 71 percent of the victims of the Terror were attributable to the two chief centres of civil war (19 percent in the southeast, 52 percent in the west). The grounds for the death sentences agree with this regional distribution; in 72 percent of the cases, they reflected armed rebellion. Like the civil war of which it was only an aspect, the Terror purged the new nation of persons considered unassimilable because they were aristocrats or had cast their lot with the aristocracy: 85 percent of them belonged to the Third Estate, 8.5 percent to the nobility, and 6.5 percent to the clergy. In another sense, the Terror contributed to the development of a feeling of national solidarity: for the moment, it muted class antagonisms

and imposed on all alike the sacrifices required by the public safety. In particular, it made it possible to impose the controlled economy necessary to the war effort and to the salvation of the nation. In this sense it was a decisive factor for victory.

Control of the economy

The controlled economy instituted by the Convention in the autumn of 1793 was less a reflection of a theoretical concept of social organization than it was a requirement of national defense. It was a matter of feeding, equipping, and arming the men of the *levée en masse*, of provisioning the populations of the cities, when external commerce was reduced to almost nothing by the blockade of France by foreign powers. Requisition fell upon all the material resources of the country, limiting freedom of enterprise. The peasant contributed his grains, his fodder, his wool, his hemp; the artisan, the product of his labour. Under certain exceptional circumstances civilians contributed arms, shoes, blankets, or sheets. All enterprises worked for the nation, under the supervision of the state, in order that production should be at the maximum. Taxation was the necessary complement to requisition. The economic controls of the general Maximum were imposed on commodities of prime necessity (the prices of 1790 increased by one-third) and on wages (the rate of 1790 increased by one-half). At the same time, ceilings were placed on profits: 5 percent for the wholesaler, 10 percent for retailers. Taxation checked speculation and restricted freedom of profit. Nationalization affected production in various degrees—especially the production of armaments and of war matériel in general, as well as foreign commerce—but essentially in proportion to military needs; the Committee of Public Safety refused to nationalize the provisioning of the civil population.

Yet the outlines of social democracy were beginning to appear. Saint-Just brilliantly defined this orientation: "There should be neither rich nor poor." It was not a question of abolishing private property but of limiting the right of inheritance and giving access to property to those who were without it. This led to the sale of national properties in small lots payable in 10 years and the free distribution of common lands in equal shares among the inhabitants of each community. Decrees of Ventôse (February 26 and March 3, 1794) provided that "indigent patriots" should be indemnified by distribution of properties confiscated from counter-revolutionaries. This social legislation was completed by a "law of national beneficence" (May 11, 1794)—nothing short of social security in embryo, for the benefit of the elderly and the sick, of mothers and widows burdened with children. "Let Europe learn that you will no longer tolerate the wretched or an oppressor on French soil," Saint-Just had declared. But to secure this social program at home it was necessary that French armies be victorious abroad.

It was to the republican armies that the Revolutionary government finally devoted all its energies. In the spring of 1794 the troop strength comprised more than 1,000,000 men divided into 12 armies. The officer corps had been purged of anti-Revolutionary elements, discipline had been re-established, and military command was closely subordinated to the civil power. Tactics and strategy had been transformed in accordance with the new political and social necessities. In the spring of 1794, the Revolutionary government had at its disposal an incomparable instrument of war. But it did not survive the victory.

Fall of the Revolutionary government. In the fall of 1793, the liquidation of the "Enragés," the halting of de-Christianization, and the veiled attacks against popular sectional organizations in Paris testified to the Revolutionary government's determination to dissociate itself from the popular movement, which, until then, it had followed rather than directed. But it thereby also put itself at the mercy of the Convention, on which it no longer had any means of exerting pressure, and left itself open to attack by its enemies both in and outside the Assembly and in public opinion. Danton, in supporting Robespierre in the matter of de-Christianization, had not been without an ulterior motive; for him, it was a means of mitigating the Terror and slowing down the Revolution. Danton's "indulgent" policy was opposed at every point to the popular program of economic controls, all-out war, and extreme terror supported by the Cordeliers. The government attack on de-Christianization and the lessening of the Terror in the *départements* from January 1794 were indications that the governmental committees, though without proscribing the extremists as the "Indulgents" demanded, were at least determined to restrict them little by little. The committees' continued attempt to undermine the popular Parisian organizations, the organ of the pro-sectional democracy, was a part of this program: in this way, they would have moderated the Terror while at the same time preserving it as an instrument. The attitude of the government finally favoured the "indulgent" offensive of the Dantonists.

At the end of the winter of 1793–94 the distinctive features that had evolved in the course of events from the establishment of the Revolutionary government hardened into a fixed pattern. While regulation, taxation, and the control of the economy—all demanded by the sans-culottes and opposed by the propertied classes—barely succeeded in ensuring the provisioning of the Parisian population, except for bread, the requirements of national defense, together with a bourgeois conception of political power, led the Revolutionary government increasingly to assure itself of the passive obedience of the popular organizations and to reduce the sans-culottist democracy to the Jacobin standard. Thus, the end of the winter saw the rise of a twofold social and political unrest that affected the Parisian populace in its material existence and its revolutionary behaviour.

The conflict between the "extremist" and the "indulgent" factions was intensified, the situation at Paris worsened, and a popular explosion appeared probable.

The moment seemed favourable to the radical patriots, led by the Cordeliers, for an act that would rid them of the Moderates and impose their own representatives on the governmental committees and on the Convention. On 24 Ventôse, Year II (March 4, 1794), the Cordeliers proclaimed the necessity for a "sacred insurrection," but the Parisian populace did not follow them. The attempt gave the Revolutionary government the occasion to end its immobility, however: it got rid of the twofold opposition. Arrested, tried, and sentenced, the Cordeliers were guillotined on March 24, 1794. They remain known to history as the Hébertists, from the name of Jacques Hébert, editor of *Le Père Duchesne*, the spokesman for the popular masses. The liquidation of the Indulgents followed: the government committees had no intention of letting themselves be overwhelmed from the right. During the night of March 29–30, the Parisian leaders Danton, Camille Desmoulins, and others were arrested and taken before the Revolutionary Tribunal; they were guillotined on April 5, 1794.

The drama of the Revolutionary calendar month of Germinal was decisive. The situation evolved at headlong speed. The condemnation of the Cordeliers made the sans-culottes lose faith in the Revolutionary government. Despite the executions of Danton and the moderate Indulgents, acts of repression against militants followed the great trials of Germinal, Year II (April 1794). Though of a limited nature, this repression developed a fear complex that paralyzed popular political life. Direct contact between the sans-culottes of the Parisian sections and the Revolutionary government had been broken off.

Freed from all opposition, the Revolutionary government embarked on a far-reaching attempt to regularize institutions and to unify political forces. In the face of the urgent national danger, it had consented to ally itself with the sans-culottes. But it had never accepted their social goals or their political methods. From Germinal to Thermidor (April to July 1794), centralization was increased and the Terror was intensified, especially by a law of 22 Prairial, Year II (June 10, 1794), known as the law of the Great Terror. The purged administrative authorities obeyed; the Convention voted without discussion. But what the Revolutionary government gained in "coercive force" it lost in support. Even the victory

won by the Revolutionary armies at Fleurus (June 26, 1794) was unable to revive popular enthusiasm. Under a factitious unity, indifference or hostility took possession of the popular mind. "The Revolution is frozen," Saint-Just wrote.

The governmental committees, by mitigating the popular movement, had delivered themselves from the fear of an insurrection; but at the same time they freed the Convention and deprived themselves of an instrument of pressure. With victory becoming more certain, there was less reason for the Convention to bear its continued rule. Between the Convention fretting under the yoke and the implacably hostile sans-culottes, the Revolutionary government was as if suspended in the void.

It was under these conditions that there arose a governmental crisis that hastened the downfall of the Revolutionary government: the government committees quarrelled and brought about their own ruin. The Committee of General Security took it ill that the Committee of Public Safety was encroaching on the duties assigned to it. In the Committee of Public Safety itself, division crept in, isolating the Robespierrist group. Robespierre resolved to lay the dispute before the Convention.

The end came quickly. On 8 Thermidor Robespierre attacked his enemies before the Convention without naming them: all felt that they were lost. They counterattacked the next day, 9 Thermidor, Year II (July 27, 1794): a coalition without principles made up of bribed deputies, predatory Terrorists, Indulgents, Moderates, a variety of extremists. Robespierre was ordered arrested. An attempted insurrection by the Paris Commune having failed, he was declared an outlaw. On 10 Thermidor, Robespierre, Saint-Just, and their partisans were guillotined without trial.

It was the end of the Revolution.

Fall of Robespierre

RETRENCHMENT AND STABILIZATION, EUROPEAN WAR, AND THE RISE OF NAPOLEON, 1795–99

The Thermidorian reaction and the rule of the Notables, 1794–95. The Thermidorian period is marked by confused rivalries, whose cross-purposes cannot hide the reality that was at stake: the "men of substance"—soon to be called the Notables—were determined to eliminate from political life the sans-culottes, the artisans, shopkeepers, and journeymen who had temporarily imposed their will upon them. As in 1793, the parliamentary struggles that pitted a radical Montagnard minority against an increasingly large conservative majority, were fundamentally paralleled by a similar conflict in society as a whole. But the popular movement, which had been an accelerating factor of the Revolution in 1793, was now disorganized and on the defensive, only able to fight in retreat.

Central to the Thermidorian policy of reaction was the abandonment of the directed economy. The Convention had accepted the Maximum only under the pressure of popular demonstrations; every sector of the bourgeoisie considered it inimical to its interests. The dislocation of the Revolutionary government and the end of the Terror necessarily brought on a slackening in controls over the economy and, finally, on December 24, 1794, the abolition of the Maximum. But the abandonment of economic restraints brought on the collapse of the assignat and the rise of severe inflation. Debtors and speculators grew rich while creditors (paid in assignats) and bourgeois of the *ancien régime* (living on fixed incomes) were ruined irretrievably. Inflation completed the social revolution. Meanwhile, the masses of the people were engulfed in despair. The winter of the Year III (1794–95) was extremely severe and only increased the wretchedness of the poor. In Paris, because of the scarcity of staples and distrust of the assignat, the price of food and fuel rose alarmingly. On the basis of 100 for 1790, the Parisian cost-of-living index rose from 580 in January 1795 to 720 in March and to 900 in April. In the spring of 1795, despair changed to rage, then to revolt.

After the defeat of a first attempt at insurrection on 12 and 13 Germinal, Year III (April 1 and 2, 1795), the people of the Parisian faubourgs (quarters) of Saint-

Abandonment of a controlled economy

Elimination of opposition

Antoine and Saint-Marcel rose on 1 Prairial, Year III (May 20, 1795), to the cry: "Bread and the Constitution of 1793." After overrunning the Convention, the rebellion quickly subsided for lack of party organization and of leaders capable of consolidating its success. Insurrection flared again the next day, 2 Prairial, with the same lack of results. On 3 Prairial (May 22, 1795) the Faubourg Saint-Antoine was surrounded by the National Guard. The insurgents had nothing to support them but their despair, and they capitulated without fighting. The popular movement was definitely broken.

In the spring of 1795 the system of the Year II was a thing of the past. The Thermidorians had undone the work of the Revolutionary government. At the same time, they reaped the benefits of its policy of national defense. After the Battle of Fleurus, the republican armies achieved a series of victories. Belgium was conquered, then the left bank of the Rhine and the United Provinces. Meanwhile, the powers of the First Coalition fell out among themselves over the division of Poland. Prussia decided to treat with the French republic. The Treaty of Basel (April 5, 1795) stipulated "peace, friendship, and good understanding between the French Republic and the King of Prussia," the latter recognizing the French possession of German territory west of the Rhine. By the Treaty of The Hague with the Dutch (May 16, 1795), France acquired the right to occupy Dutch territory south of the Rhine and a defensive and offensive alliance. By the Treaty of Basel with Spain (July 22, 1795) France agreed to evacuate previously held territory in Catalonia and the Basque country but annexed the Spanish part of Santo Domingo in the West Indies. No agreement was reached with Austria, which refused to recognize the Rhine as the frontier of France. On October 1, 1795, Belgium was annexed. By that date, the war had been resumed.

The Thermidorians' hope of a general peace grew more remote. Their policy of annexations strengthened the bonds of the Anglo-Austrian coalition, which Russia joined in September 1795. The Thermidorians passed the heavy heritage of the war on to the Directory, the regime established by the new Constitution of the Year III.

The voting of the new constitution by the Thermidorian Convention was the result of an alliance between the centre and the right, between the conservative republicans and constitutional monarchists. The declaration of rights that precedes the Constitution of the Year III marks a definite retreat from that of 1789. Article 1 of the Declaration of 1789 ("men are born and remain free and equal in rights") was abandoned. The Thermidorians, more prudent than the members of the Constituent Assembly, were careful to make it clear that only civil equality was in question: "Equality consists in the fact that the law is the same for all" (Article 3). There was no longer any question of the social rights that the Declaration of 1793 had recognized, still less of the right of insurrection. On the contrary, the right of property, which had not been defined at all in the Declaration of 1789, was now made explicit, as, indeed, it had been in the Declaration of 1793: "Property is the right to enjoy and dispose of one's possessions, one's revenues, and the fruit of one's labour and industry" (Article 5). This was to sanction economic freedom in the fullest sense. The declaration of duties that the Thermidorians added to the declaration of rights specified in its Article 8: "The maintenance of property is the foundation upon which the cultivation of the soil, all production, every means of labour and the whole social order rest." The right of suffrage was restricted, but the electoral qualification on the basis of taxation was more liberal than that of 1791: every Frenchman aged 21 who had been domiciled for a year and who paid any tax was an "active citizen."

The creators of the Directory thus sought to stabilize the Revolution on a narrow social base. The most conscious among the people were not content to be unresistingly thrust out of the nation and political life: the radical Gracchus Babeuf's unsuccessful conspiracy to overthrow the government (1796, see below) is proof of

Military victory

Constitution of the Year III

that. But social fear was a powerful instrument in the hands of the regime. The propertied classes feared above all a return to the system of the Year II, when the rich were suspected, traditional social values were subverted, and political democracy was opening the way to social levelling. Along with the lower classes, the aristocracy and a segment of the old bourgeoisie were also excluded from the political system. A law of October 25, 1795, forbade the relatives of émigrés to hold public office. The Directorial bourgeoisie, whose circumstances were moderate, distrusted the bourgeoisie of the *ancien régime*, whose higher social level was nearer to that of the aristocracy. The Thermidorians, transformed into Directorials, were determined that the republic should be bourgeois and conservative; but they rejected the support of the old bourgeoisie, fearing that it would lead them toward a restoration of the monarchy.

On so narrow a social base, the application of the Constitution of the Year III, which provided for a strict separation of powers between the executive Directory and two legislative councils—the Ancients (Conseil des Anciens) and the Five Hundred (Conseil des Cinq-Cents)—with annual elections, could only encounter insurmountable difficulties.

The first Directory, 1795–97. Confined to the narrow limits of a republic with a restricted suffrage that excluded both the popular classes and the aristocracy, the new regime remained destined to instability. Equally afraid of royalism and democracy, the Thermidorian Notables had multiplied precautions against the omnipotence of the state; the carefully constructed constitutional equilibrium of the Year III left no alternative but governmental impotence or an appeal to force. The success of the Directorial policy of stabilization depended upon finding a solution for the fundamental problems inherited from the Thermidorian period: the war abroad and the domestic economic and financial problems. As the war dragged on, the currency declined, and the economy was disrupted; a fiscal crisis was added to the monetary crisis, and the treasury was empty.

While the Directory was being established in the autumn of 1795, inflation reached its extreme limit: the value of the assignat dropped to almost nothing. On February 19, 1796, it became necessary to stop issuing —and to abandon—the assignat. A return to metallic currency seemed impossible; and a law of March 18, 1796, created a new paper currency, the mandat territorial, also valid for the purchase of national property. In six months the mandat territorial ran the same course as that which the assignat had run in five years: depreciation reached 90 percent as early as April 20, 1796. In February 1797 the mandat was fixed at 1 percent of its nominal value, officially sanctioning a bankruptcy that had long been a fact. So ended the history of the Revolutionary paper currency.

The social consequences were, as usual, catastrophic for the populace. The winter of the Year IV (1795–96) overwhelmed the earning classes by a dizzying rise in prices. The markets remained empty: the harvests of 1795 were poor; and the peasants would not accept the currency, since requisitions were no longer demanded. Opposition to the Directory grew stronger. In Paris, the former Jacobins reassembled at the Club du Panthéon and discussed re-establishing the Maximum. Revolutionary opposition took a new form when Babeuf organized his Conspiracy of the Equals.

Conspiracy of the Equals

François-Noël (Gracchus) Babeuf was the first man of the Revolution to perceive a contradiction between the demands of the right to exist and the affirmation of the right of property: going beyond utopian egalitarianism, he advocated the "community of goods and labor." Like the Jacobins and the sans-culottes, he proclaimed that the goal of society was the "general welfare," the Revolution must ensure "equality of benefits" (*l'égalité des jouissances*). But since property necessarily introduced inequality, the only way to attain real equality was to abolish private property. Each man would be bound to the skill or the industry that he had learned, and obliged to deposit the products of it in kind in a common storehouse. A simple administration of the necessities of life would distribute them with the most scrupulous equality.

The organization of the Conspiracy of the Equals during the winter of 1795–96 represented an attempt to make a fact of this "communism of equal distribution." It was well organized but seems to have had insufficient contact with the popular masses. Denounced by a police spy, Babeuf and his companion Filippo Buonarroti were arrested on May 10, 1796. After trial before the High Court of Vendôme, Babeuf (known as the Tribune of the People) was guillotined on May 27, 1797.

The Conspiracy of the Equals and Babouvism are merely an episode in the history of the Directory, but they exerted a strong influence on the revolutionaries of the 19th century.

The anti-Jacobin repression that followed the Conspiracy of the Equals made the Directory move toward the right and strengthened the power of the royalists. Meanwhile, the economic depression persisted. Contrary to all expectations, the abolition of paper currency did not revive economic activity. People hoarded their metallic currency instead of spending it. The plentiful harvest of 1796 caused agricultural prices to collapse, arousing discontent among the peasants.

Napoleon in Italy

While a powerless Directory was falling into greater and greater discredit, the prestige of victory was glorifying its conquering generals, especially the general of the Army of Italy, Napoleon Bonaparte. The days were past when the egalitarian level of the Revolutionary government and the Reign of Terror weighed on the generals: they shook off the control of the executive power and were already giving free reign to their ambitions.

The Italian campaign of 1796–97 decided the outcome of the war against Austria. His brilliant successes in 1796–97 made Bonaparte an independent force. In negotiating the Peace of Campo Formio with Austria (October 17, 1797), he completely disregarded the instructions of the Directory, organizing his conquests in accordance with his personal views. The government's policy was to establish what it regarded as France's natural frontiers, along the Rhine and the Alps. Ignoring this, Bonaparte proceeded to carve up northern Italy, ceding Venice to Austria and creating a French-dominated Cisalpine Republic in Lombardy. The Directory gave way: the domestic situation left it no alternative.

The elections of Germinal, Year V (April 1797), had indeed marked a rout of the Directorials: the monarchist right was considerably reinforced. Since the Constitution of the Year III provided no means of settling the conflict, the Directory, with Bonaparte's backing, decided to appeal to force. By the coup d'etat of 18 Fructidor, Year V (September 4, 1797), it annulled the elections, dealing a staggering blow to the liberal system: the right was decimated, the legislative arm humbled and embittered, and the political influence of the army increased. The Directory now found itself more and more the prisoner of the generals, especially of the ambitious Bonaparte.

The second Directory, 1797–99. After the coup d'etat of Fructidor and the Peace of Campo Formio, the Directory implemented an authoritarian domestic policy that in many ways foreshadowed the Napoleonic regime. But political stabilization proved impossible to realize: between the neo-Jacobin opposition and the royalists, the social base of the Directory remained narrowly Thermidorian. As long as peace prevailed on the Continent, though, the system managed to maintain itself, at the cost of new infringements of the liberal practice of the Constitution of the Year III.

After Fructidor, an emergency regime, sometimes called the Directorial Terror, was instituted; it was a pale reflection of that of the Year II; but it enabled the Directory, for a certain time, to contain the opposition of the right. The Jacobins profited by it and won the elections of Floréal, Year VI. Although the new Jacobin deputies advocated nothing that should have frightened the bourgeoisie, the Directory was determined to have a docile majority. On 22 Floréal, Year VI (May 11, 1798), the directors, claiming power to "judge" the electoral process, annulled the elections and put the governmental candidates into the councils: by this action, known as the *coup d'état de Floréal*, the Directorial party maintained its control over the legislative majority; but the regime had further discredited itself by this recourse to hypocritical violence.

Fiscal reform

Yet for a year—from the elections of Floréal, Year VI, to those of Germinal, Year VII (spring 1798–spring 1799)—the Directory regained a certain stability and power; it was able to pursue the work of financial recovery and fiscal reform begun after Fructidor. The bankruptcy of the two-thirds was sanctioned by the law of September 30, 1797; one-third of the debt was "consolidated" by being inscribed in the Great Book, or National Debt Register. This bankruptcy in some measure cleared up the financial situation. Fiscal reorganization tended to put the budget into balance again by more regular and larger receipts. In November 1797, the system of taxation was completely revised, marking a partial return to the indirect taxes abolished by the National Assembly, which weighed most heavily on the poor. The deficit nevertheless persisted. The Directory remained at the mercy of financiers, contractors, and money speculators, who became more demanding than ever: corruption increased. The evil had deep roots, and even Bonaparte's authoritarian regime proved unable to overcome it.

Economic difficulties partly cancelled out the government's laudable efforts. Deflation brought with it high credit rates and falling prices, which, in turn, retarded the economic revival. Metallic currency in circulation was scarce: by the Year IX (1801), only about 1,000,-000,000 francs were still circulating, out of 2,500,000,-000 in 1789. Credit was expensive: the habitual rate of interest was at least 10 percent and 7 percent per month for short-term loans. The banking setup remained inadequate. The fall in prices that resulted from the deflation was aggravated by abundant harvests from 1796 to 1798; agricultural prices were from one-quarter to one-third lower than those of 1790, which had also been a year of plenty. Discontent increased among the agricultural producers, large landowners, and large farmers, who were generally electors; and the popularity of the regime suffered. As usual, the agricultural crisis had repercussions in industry. Foreign commerce was paralyzed: in 1797 the seagoing merchant fleet was reduced to a tenth of its 1789 strength. Trade with the West Indies dried up; the Near East was closed after the failure of Bonaparte's Egyptian expedition (1798–99, see below).

Under these conditions, the Directory's accomplishments, which chiefly resulted from the efforts of the minister of the interior, François de Neufchâteau, could only be confined to very narrow limits. To stimulate industry in the fall of 1798 he organized the first national exposition at the Champ-de-Mars in Paris. The results were not impressive. Industrial production remained below that of 1789, technical progress was slow, and the concentration of capital remained essentially commercial. The economic weakness of the Directory goes far to account for its political difficulties. Since direction of the economy and limitation of profits were outlawed, there was nothing left but to make the regime, like the armies, live on the conquered countries. But when defeat brought the armies back home in 1799, the Directory had to increase demands on the taxpayers: its unpopularity increased proportionately. Once more the political problem moved to the centre of the stage.

After Campo Formio, only Great Britain remained in opposition to France. Instead of maintaining peace on the Continent to concentrate on this one remaining enemy, the Directory embarked on a policy of continental expansion that destroyed all possibility of stabilization abroad. France, the "great nation," surrounded itself with "sister republics," satellite states, politically submissive and economically exploited: the Batavian Republic in the Low Countries; the Helvetic Republic of Switzerland; and the Cisalpine, Roman, and the Parthenopean (Neapolitan) republics in Italy. The Directory allowed itself to be dragged into an invasion of Egypt, under Bonaparte's command, that extended the conflict to the Mediterranean. In the spring of 1799 the war became general. The Second Coalition brought together Britain, Austria, Russia, Naples, and Sweden. Soon Italy and part of Switzerland were lost, and the republic was reduced to fighting on its "natural" frontiers. The danger reawakened the energy of the nation and provoked a final Revolutionary thrust.

The Second Coalition

Even before the defeats abroad, the elections of the Year VII (1799) took place in a climate unfavourable to the Directory. The general discontent caused by the economic slump, the increase in taxation, and the reintroduction of conscription strengthened the Jacobin minority—but not to the extent that the Thermidorian bourgeoisie lost its position of power. In the crisis that began after the defeats of the spring of 1799, the Thermidorian majority had the last word. On 30 Prairial, Year VII (June 18, 1799) the councils purged the Directory, restored "pronounced" republicans to favour, and imposed measures that were in some ways reminiscent of those of the Year II: strict application of conscription, compulsory loans from wealthy citizens, law of hostages.

Now fear of the Jacobins, which had manifested itself as early as 1797, increased in scope, and the bourgeoisie determined to be done once and for all with the spectre of the Year II. It was under these conditions that the *coup d'état de 18 Brumaire*, Year VIII, took place, bringing Napoleon Bonaparte to power.

Napoleon's coup d'etat

THE CONSULATE AND THE EMPIRE, 1799–1815

The consular republic, 1799–1802. There was a great deal of continuity between the late Revolutionary period and the Napoleonic period, both in foreign and domestic affairs. The 18th Brumaire was only the last of the coups d'etat that characterized the Directory, the logical consequence of an inevitable political evolution. It did bring the republican government under the control of one man to an unprecedented degree; but the evolution of Bonaparte's personal power did not reach its final stage until 1804, when he proclaimed himself emperor. From 1792, when the Girondins had led the nation into war, an inner necessity condemned France to dictatorship, whether collective, as in the Year II, or personal, as under Bonaparte. And even personal dictatorship, no matter how great the genius and the will to power of its promoter, Bonaparte, could not impose itself on the Revolutionary nation except by maintaining the essential accomplishments of 1789.

On the day after Brumaire, Bonaparte's government was installed on the ruins of the representative system that had been established by the Constitution of the Year III.

The new constitution, that of the Year VIII, was "short and obscure" in accordance with Bonaparte's wishes. It concentrated all power in the hands of Bonaparte himself, who took the title of First Consul. Accountable to no one, he appointed ministers and public officials, initiated laws and regulated their application. The power of the legislature was virtually annihilated by dividing its authority among three assemblies: legislation was debated by the Tribunat, voted on by the Legislative Body (Corps Législatif), and its constitutionality was judged by the Senate. Popular sovereignty was theoretically proclaimed; but except for plebiscites in which the people voted "yes" or "no" on a constitutional text, the right of suffrage consisted in nominating lists of candidates that could be practically ignored. The government appointed representatives and officials as it pleased. On these foundations, the Constitution of the Year X (1802), which established the Consulate for life, and the Constitution of the Year XII (1804), which sanctioned the empire, merely increased the concentration of power in Napoleon's hands.

Constitution of the Year VIII

In reorganizing the state Bonaparte was guided more by opportunism than by any systematic scheme. Above all, it was necessary to ensure the authority of the government and the First Consul. The second Directory had in many respects laid the groundwork for this.

Financial reform was most urgently needed. The first task was to strengthen the centralized financial administration established in 1798. A law of November 24, 1799, created an administration of direct taxation to ensure a better tax base, whereas collection was restored to the state in 1800. A sinking fund was created to cover the budgetary deficits and war expenses. The need for a banking organization was also felt, particularly to facilitate discounting. On February 13, 1800, the Bank of France was created; this was a private bank formed by an association of financiers. It was not under state control, but the government did entrust it with a part of its funds. In April 1803, it was granted the exclusive privilege of issuing banknotes. The process of re-establishing a sound budget was slow, despite the revived confidence of the moneyed class. In 1802 the budget was balanced; but with the resumption of war in 1803, it was necessary to have recourse to extraordinary sources of income, and the deficit reappeared in 1804.

A monetary reform accompanied the series of financial reforms. The law of Germinal, Year XI (April 1803), fixed the monetary system on the basis of a ratio of 1 to 15½ between silver and gold, confirmed the "franc of Germinal" of 5 grams of silver $\frac{9}{10}$ths pure; it established silver as the principal monetary metal but maintained bimetallism.

These reforms were accomplished by a reinforcement of central power. A law of February 1800 took all authority from local institutions. Local elections were abolished and the General Councils of the *départements* were chosen by the First Consul from the list of departmental notabilities, the municipal councils by the prefect from the lists of communal notabilities. But these councils were purely consultative—the representatives of the central power, chiefly the departmental prefects, held all the real authority. The prefectoral corps, chosen with the utmost care, was partly inherited from the Revolution; it greatly contributed to the fame of the consular administration. The prefects, in turn, protected the interests of the Notables.

Administrative centralization

The judicial reform of March 1800 reconciled the judicial hierarchy of courts with the new principles of authority. The election of judges was abandoned; and salaries and advancement were entrusted to the state: despite the proclamation of their irremovability, judges were, in fact, made state functionaries. This reform of the state and the administration endured, and it constitutes the backbone of modern French administration.

In order definitely to consolidate his authority over the nation, Bonaparte had to win military success. He prepared the spring campaign of 1800 by keeping Prussia neutral and detaching Russia from the Coalition. Under these conditions the campaign proved to be essentially a duel between France and Austria. The victory of Marengo (June 14, 1800) and the Treaty of Lunéville (February 9, 1801) ensured peace on the Continent. Isolated, England chose to make peace at Amiens on March 27, 1802. France recovered its colonies, but England recognized neither France's "natural frontiers" nor the vassal republics. Despite this, Bonaparte had fulfilled the essential aspirations of the nation by imposing peace on Europe and preserving the frontiers established by the Revolution. But Bonaparte's ambition was already carrying him further. In the end, the pacification proved to be only a truce.

The victory and the peace increased Bonaparte's popularity. He took advantage of the opportunity to liquidate the opposition and to increase his powers.

An attempt to assassinate him in the rue Saint-Nicaise on December 24, 1800, gave him the excuse he needed to strike at the royalists and Jacobins. Joseph Fouché, his minister of police, proscribed 130 prominent republicans. Three columns were sent to attack the revived royalist insurrection in Brittany: by the end of 1801 it was liquidated. These emergency measures revived the opposition in the assemblies: the Brumairian Notables had wanted a strong government but not despotism. The political crisis of the Year IX (1801) caused a final break between them and the First Consul. Bonaparte's popular dictatorship was incompatible with the Notables' representative regime, in which the people would delegate their sovereignty without ever abdicating it, and the role of the opposition would be one of information and supervision. But these ideas, though dear to a minority, were at that time foreign to the mass of the French people.

The retrograde evolution of the consular regime was suddenly speeded up in the spring of 1802. In a few months the regime was transformed. On April 8, 1802, a new religious settlement was promulgated (see below); on the 26th amnesty was granted to the émigrés and their unsold properties restored to them; on May 1, the creation of lycées (state-supported schools) was decided; the Légion d'Honneur (an order of merit for which all citizens were eligible) was instituted on the 19th; on May 20, slavery was re-established in the colonies; finally, from May 8 to August 14, the steps were taken that established Bonaparte's power as the Consulate for life. The consular republic was being transformed into a monarchy.

To complete his domestic pacification and to consolidate his power, Bonaparte thought it expedient to deprive the counter-revolution of the weapon of religion; it was necessary to rally Roman Catholicism and the refractory clergy to the new regime and so to annul the separation of church and state. The result was the Concordat (agreement with the papacy) that had been signed on July 16, 1801, and was promulgated on April 8, 1802, accompanied by a law defining the relationship of the state to religious bodies. Roman Catholicism was recognized as the religion of the majority, but freedom of worship was guaranteed. The conclusion of peace with the church reinforced Bonaparte's personal power.

The "organization of the nation" was directed to the same end. The institution of lycées (May 1, 1802) was to aid recruitment into the "social bodies," of which the Legion d'Honneur presented the first example, while at the same time the social regulations of the system were defined by the Code Civil. The Code Civil, not promulgated until March 21, 1804, but under discussion from 1801, actually represents the keystone of the structure and, as it were, the judicial monument of the new society. To the benefit of the bourgeoisie, it reconciled the concepts of the old written, or customary, law with those of Revolutionary law. Bourgeois in inspiration, the Code Civil was above all concerned with property, defined as a natural right anterior to society. It also reflected the traditional conception of the family: it accorded great importance to the marriage contract and to problems of inheritance. The authority of the father over his wife and children, weakened by the Revolution, was reinforced. But, in the spirit of the Revolution, the Code Civil sanctioned the disappearance of the feudal aristocracy, proclaiming the principles of 1789: freedom of the person, equality of all before the law, freedom of conscience and secularity of the state, freedom of work. In the eyes of the rest of Europe it appeared as the symbol of Revolution; and wherever it was applied, it contributed to establishing the essential characteristics of contemporary society.

In 1802 the authoritarian character of the consular regime provoked a resurgence of opposition, both in the assemblies and in the army. It was promptly overcome and the ground was cleared for a reinforcement of the power of the First Consul. When the Peace of Amiens was announced to the assemblies in May 1802, the Tribunat expressed the wish that Bonaparte should be given "a signal pledge of the gratitude of the nation." Seizing the initiative, Bonaparte organized a "consultation" of the French people to decide the question of whether Napoleon Bonaparte should be "consul for life": there were 8,374 opposing votes to 3,500,000 in favour.

A senatorial law of August 4, 1802, considerably increased Bonaparte's powers, giving him the right to make peace and war, the right of pardon, the right to appoint his successor. By the end of 1802 no one could any longer doubt Napoleon's ambitions: the republic was a thing of the past. From August 15, 1802, Napoleon's birthday was celebrated as a national holiday; and in 1803, his image appeared on coins.

The Code Napoléon

The Grand Empire and Napoleonic despotism, 1802–12. The Peace of Amiens, which had allowed Bonaparte to further consolidate his dictatorial power, did not last long. Napoleon's ambition and England's desire to remain the undisputed mistress of the seas rapidly brought the resumption of hostilities.

The peace had revived the French economy, for foreign commerce especially was favoured by French domination of the Continent. This was a disappointment to the English capitalists, who realized that the economic war was continuing: they turned from a peace that was not to their profit. Bonaparte's colonial policy alarmed Britain even more. Colonial products were one of the essential objects of large-scale commerce. Bonaparte was determined to restore this source of wealth to France by recovering the Antilles. Nor did Napoleon's aggressive continental policy reassure the British, who looked on, irritated but powerless, while the French expansion continued. War was resumed in May 1803.

The first result of the war was to enable Bonaparte to re-establish a monarchy of his own. Since the initiative for the break lay with Britain, his prestige did not suffer; the British were accused of wanting to drive France back to its old frontiers. This conviction was strengthened by the support the British government gave to the royalists.

The "Anglo-royalist" conspiracy gave Bonaparte an opportunity to get rid of the opposition: Louis-Antoine-Henri de Bourbon-Condé, duc d'Enghien, a leading royalist, was seized at Ettenheim, in Baden, on the night of March 14–15, 1804, convicted of conspiracy against Napoleon by a court-martial, and shot on the morning of March 21 outside of the fortress of Vincennes. His execution or assassination sealed the rupture with the royalists and hastened the establishment of the Napoleonic empire; a new hereditary monarchy would discourage the conspirators. On April 30, 1804, a motion was made in the Tribunat "that Napoleon Bonaparte be declared Emperor and the imperial dignity be declared hereditary in his family." The Senate approved. The Constitution of the Year XII (May 18, 1804) proclaimed the establishment of the empire; in the plebescite that followed, it was approved by more than 3,500,000 voters against about 2,500.

The coronation of the Emperor by Pope Pius VII on December 2, 1804, made it clear that Napoleon was not satisfied only with the ratification by the people but that he intended to consecrate the new legitimacy by the restoration of divine right. In the last analysis, the proclamation of the empire was the final phase of an evolution, rather than a sudden mutation. The road toward monarchy had been taken long before the rupture of the peace in 1803. The concentration of powers and dictatorship to safeguard the basic achievements of 1789 and the social preponderance of the middle class had prepared the way for it. But Napoleon's ambition, fed by his personal adherents and by the passivity of the great majority, went beyond these safeguards. Instead of moderately extending France's frontiers, he extended his conquests inordinately by an endless series of wars. He broke with equality and undertook to create a new aristocracy. Yet Napoleon could not blot out the indelible mark of the Revolutionary origin of his power: in the eyes of aristocratic Europe, he remained the soldier of the Revolution.

His campaign of conquest has been variously interpreted as the defense of the ever-threatened natural frontiers, the building of a European empire, the pursuit of a mirage, or simply ambition. Georges Lefebvre, the last great historian of Napoleon, returns to "ambition" but with the qualification: "the heroic attraction of risk, the bewitching seduction of a dream, the irresistible drive of a temperament."

The Third Coalition was broken by the campaign of 1805 and by the victories of Ulm and of Austerlitz—the latter, December 2, 1805. Meanwhile, Britain retained control of the seas, having crushed the French fleet at Trafalgar (October 21, 1805). The Treaty of Pressburg left Napoleon free to organize the Confederation of the Rhine: the Germanic Holy Roman Empire disappeared. When the Fourth Coalition was organized, Napoleon de-

Renewal of the war

Defeat at Trafalgar

feated it in two campaigns. In six days two Prussian armies were annihilated in two simultaneous victories on October 14, 1806: at Auerstädt, by Louis-Nicolas Davout and, at Jena, by Napoleon himself. At Berlin, Napoleon decreed a continental blockade against British goods. After defeating the Russians at the Battle of Friedland (June 14, 1807) Napoleon made an alliance with Tsar Alexander I at Tilsit on July 7.

Spain's revolt against French rule, aided by Britain (1808), signalled the beginning of national resistances and favoured the formation of a fifth coalition. Napoleon was again the victor: defeated at Wagram (July 5–6, 1809), Austria signed the Treaty of Schönbrunn (October 14).

Napoleon was now at the apogee of his power. He was "Emperor of the French, King of Italy, Protector of the Confederation of the Rhine, Mediator of the Swiss Confederation." His brothers reigned throughout the empire: Joseph in Madrid, Louis in Holland, Jérôme in Westphalia, and his brother-in-law Joachim Murat at Naples. The Tsar was his ally. Soon the Habsburgs were to give him Archduchess Marie-Louise as his wife. In 1811 an imperial heir was born, and Napoleonic Europe enjoyed two to three years of peace: the imperial system, though still uncompleted, tended to become stabilized.

The imperial government perfected the work of the Consulate and increased administrative despotism. Public freedoms disappeared; only freedom of conscience survived, always on condition that the officially recognized cults (Christian and Jewish) should not be attacked nor atheism publicly professed. The restoration of monarchical power was accompanied by the creation of a new court, which, however, lacked the easy elegance of the court of the *ancien régime*. All the governmental machinery tended to strengthen the executive. The Tribunat disappeared in 1807; the Corps Législatif functioned in closed sessions; the Senate was quiescent. The Emperor alone governed. Administrative centralization increased. The prefects, kept well in hand by the central authority, enforced the rule of uniformity everywhere, although the government's control of the economy has been exaggerated. The Emperor was wise enough and skillful enough to reconcile divergent interests, satisfying material wants in order to silence the spirit of criticism. The press and the publishing industry were strictly supervised. Control also was exercised through the Imperial University, organized in 1807–08. Napoleon was determined to have at his disposal "a corps to regulate public morality and policy" in the manner of "the corps of 'ulamā's among the Turks." Hence, public instruction was organized as a monopoly of the state, strictly disciplined and hierarchical, with the essential function of supplying officers and civil servants. Finally, control was exercised through the churches, which were bound to the state by the Concordat and the Organic Articles.

The influence of religion and the official system of education tended to strengthen the social hierarchy that Napoleon had sought to re-establish from the period of the Consulate. The preponderance of the Notables assured him the obedience of the immense populace of the countryside, as well as urban journeymen, petty artisans, workmen, and servants.

Creation of the "nobility of the empire"

Going still further, after organizing the imperial court, from 1806 to 1808, Napoleon instituted a "nobility of the Empire" that received its statute on March 1, 1808: a nobility of office, dispensed by the master alone, hereditary, and accompanied by an income permitting the bearer of the title to maintain his rank. The authoritarian evolution of the regime, together with the Austrian marriage, accentuated this "aristocratization," and Napoleon might well have moved further in this direction if he had had time. But it was the most fragile part of Napoleon's great work. Nothing could fill the gulf created by the Revolution: despite the master's will, the imperial nobility and the old aristocracy did not fuse. The Emperor's efforts in the social area were effective only insofar as they followed the direction of historical evolution. More durable than the new nobility was the consolidation of the social preponderance of the bourgeoisie. By the role they played in the functioning of the system, the bour-geois Notables increased their influence and their prestige.

Yet the more they asserted themselves socially, the more they turned away from a regime that had stripped them of all political prerogatives. Economic distress, largely occasioned by the continental blockade, increased the disaffection of the various categories of the well-to-do, whereas the popular masses found the burden of conscription and of the *droits réunis* (indirect taxation) intolerable. The Emperor's prestige remained intact; and the nation still obeyed, but it was weary. Under these conditions Napoleon threw himself into a new adventure: the Russian Campaign.

Collapse of the Napoleonic system, 1812–15. The Grand Empire and the continental system had been constructed on the basis of the Grand Army's (Grande Armée) victories and of Napoleon's military genius: when that genius finally vacillated, the ruin of the entire system quickly followed.

Invasion of Russia

Because the very existence of the empire was founded on war, each new campaign again called it into question. The Russian Campaign, undertaken in 1812, was intended to crown the whole enterprise by doing away with the last resistance on the Continent. It ended in disaster. Napoleon entered Moscow on September 14, 1812, and ordered a retreat on October 19. In December the Grand Army no longer existed; and with it, the rampart of the empire vanished. The catastrophe was irreparable. Napoleon was not discouraged: he set about building a new army, while a sixth coalition against France was being formed. Renewed opposition by Prussia, and then Austria, brought the loss of Germany. Though the Emperor was victorious again at Lützen and Bautzen during the first campaign of 1813 and conquered again at Dresden, he was finally overwhelmed in the course of his autumn campaign at the Battle of Leipzig (October 16–19, 1813). It was the end of the Grand Empire: the French armies retreated across the Rhine.

The French Campaign (1814) was brief. It was in vain that Napoleon's genius asserted itself in a final recrudescence. Beset by a political opposition that was strengthened by his defeats, he improvised the new Army of Marie-Louise. Manoeuvring between the enemy armies, one of which was advancing through the valley of the Marne, the other through the valley of the Seine, he won a series of successes but could not prevent the allies from entering Paris on March 31, 1814. He abdicated on April 6, and after taking leave of his Old Guard in the celebrated episode of the "Farewell at Fontainebleau," he departed for his small Kingdom of Elba.

The victorious allies installed Louis XVI's brother, the Comte de Provence, as King Louis XVIII. Louis was forced to sanction the principles of 1789 and the Napoleonic reforms in a constitution known as the Charter of 1814. Reprisals taken by the returned émigrés against their enemies and the disappointment of royalists at the moderate character of the new regime hindered the functioning of the government. For Napoleon, this was the opportunity for a last adventure. Returning suddenly from Elba, he reached Paris on March 20 and took control again for the period known as the Hundred Days. War decided his fate: on June 18, 1815, the defeat at Waterloo sealed Napoleon's destiny. He abdicated for the second time on June 22; on July 15 he surrendered to the British and was exiled to the remote island of Sainte-Helena in the South Atlantic, where he died in 1821. The Emperor's exile crowned his memory with the magic of legend: a martyred victim of the kings, for the French people he became the hero of the Revolutionary nation.

Defeat at Waterloo

THE NATURE AND SIGNIFICANCE OF THE REVOLUTION

The French Revolution and its Napoleonic epilogue represent the most striking episode in the history of modern revolutions. It doubtless owes this exceptional position to the obstinacy of the aristocracy, which, clinging desperately to its feudal privileges, refused all compromise, and to the contrary relentlessness of the peasant masses. The bourgeoisie had not wanted the ruin of the aristocracy; the refusal of compromise and the counter-revolution obliged it to pursue the destruction of the old order. But it was able to do this only by allying itself with the rural and urban masses, which had to be satisfied; the Revolution became popular, the Reign of Terror made a clean sweep, feudalism was irremediably destroyed, and democracy temporarily instituted.

Destruc-
tion of
feudalism

The French Revolution swept away all the survivals of feudalism, it freed the peasants from seigneurial dues and ecclesiastical tithes, it destroyed the corporate monopolies, and it established free trade within the country. These accomplishments marked a decisive phase on the road to a new economy. The essential driving force in the Revolutionary process lay in the popular masses, rural and urban. The political instrument was the Jacobin dictatorship of the lower and middle bourgeoisie, with the support of the lower classes. The popular and peasant revolution was at the heart of the bourgeois revolution and drove it forward.

At the same time, the French Revolution shattered the structure of the state developed under the *ancien régime*, swept away the vestiges of the old autonomies, and destroyed local privileges and provincial particularisms. Further, from the Directory to the empire, it made possible the inauguration of a modern state corresponding to the interests and demands of the new society.

From this twofold point of view, the French Revolution was far from being a myth, as the English historian Alfred Cobban claimed in his *The Myth of the French Revolution* (1955). No doubt "feudalism" in the medieval sense of the word no longer corresponded to anything in 1789. But for contemporaries—the bourgeoisie and still more the peasantry—the term feudalism expressed a reality that they knew only too well (feudal rights and dues, seigneurial authority) and that was finally swept away. It is also true that the bourgeois Revolutionary assemblies were not made up of businessmen but of men from the liberal professions and public functionaries. But this provides no argument against the importance of the Revolution in the inauguration of the new economic order. The essential fact is that the old system of production and exchange was destroyed and that the French Revolution proclaimed freedom of enterprise and of profit without any restrictions, thus opening the way to the new economy. The history of the 19th century would prove that this was no myth.

A necessary phase in the general transition from the traditional European society and economy to the new, the French Revolution also has its own peculiar characteristics, which are due to the specific characteristics of French society at the end of the *ancien régime*.

In recent years, certain historians, notably the American historian R.R. Palmer and the French historian Jacques Godechot, have seen the French Revolution as part of a wider European phenomenon. According to the latter in his book *La Grande Nation* (1956), the Revolution was "only an aspect of Western—or, more precisely, Atlantic—Revolution which began in the British colonies in America shortly after 1763, and was continued by revolutionary movements in Geneva, the Netherlands, and Ireland before it reached France between 1787 and 1789; from France it returned to the Netherlands and spread to the Rhineland, Switzerland, and Italy."

But to put the French Revolution and the comparatively minor revolutions in late-18th-century Geneva, the Netherlands, and Ireland in the same class ignores the dimensions and scope of the French upheaval, as well as its dramatic character. The "Atlantic" conception of the French Revolution, by emptying it of all specific content (economic: anti-feudal and capitalistic; social: anti-aristocratic, simultaneously bourgeois and popular; national: one and indivisible), would completely deny validity to a half century of French Revolutionary historiography, from Jean Jaurès to Georges Lefebvre.   (Al.S.)

VI. France since 1815

THE RESTORATION AND CONSTITUTIONAL MONARCHY

Constitutionalism and reaction, 1815–30. *Louis XVIII, 1815–24.* King Louis XVIII's second return from exile was far from glorious. Neither the victorious powers nor Louis's French subjects viewed his restoration with much enthusiasm, yet there seemed to be no ready alternative to Bourbon rule. The allies avenged themselves for the Hundred Days by writing a new and more severe Treaty of Paris. France lost several frontier territories, notably the Saar Basin and Savoy (Savoie), that had been annexed in 1789–92; a war indemnity of 700,000,-000 francs was imposed; and, pending full payment, eastern France was to be occupied by allied troops at French expense.

Within France, political tensions were exacerbated by Napoleon's mad gamble and by the mistakes committed during the First Restoration. The problem facing the Bourbons would have been difficult enough without these tensions, namely, how to arrive at a stable compromise between those Frenchmen who saw the Revolutionary changes as irreversible and those who were determined to resurrect the *ancien régime*. The reactionary element, labelled ultra-royalists (or simply "ultras"), was now more intransigent than ever and set out to purge the country of all those who had betrayed the dynasty. A brief period of White Terror in the south claimed some 300 victims; in Paris, many high officials who had rallied to Napoleon were dismissed, and a few eminent figures, notably Marshal Michel Ney, were tried and shot. The King refused, however, to scrap the Charter of 1814, in spite of ultra pressure. When a new Chamber of Deputies was elected in August 1815, the ultras scored a sweeping victory; the surprised King, who had feared a surge of antimonarchical sentiment, greeted the legislature as *la chambre introuvable* ("the incomparable chamber"). But the political honeymoon was short-lived. Louis was shrewd enough, or cautious enough, to realize that ultra policies would divide the country and might in the end destroy the dynasty. He chose as ministers, therefore, such moderate royalists as Armand-Emmanuel du Plessis, duc de Richelieu, and Élie Decazes—men who knew the nation would not tolerate an attempt to resurrect the 18th century.

The reac-
tionaries

There followed a year of severe tension between these moderate ministers and the ultra-dominated Chamber—tension and unrest that made Europe increasingly nervous about the viability of the restored monarchy. Representatives of the occupying powers began to express their concern to the King. At last, in September 1816, his ministers persuaded him to dissolve the Chamber and order new elections, and the moderate royalists emerged with a clear majority. In spite of ultra fury, several years of relative stability ensued. Richelieu and Decazes, with solid support in the Chamber, could proceed with their attempt to pursue a moderate course. By 1818 they were able, thanks to loans from English and Dutch bankers, to pay off the war indemnity and thus to end the allied occupation; at the Congress of Aix-la-Chapelle France was welcomed back into the Concert of Europe. In domestic politics, there were some signs that France might be moving toward a British-style parliamentary monarchy, even though the Charter had carefully avoided making the King's ministers responsible to the Chamber of Deputies. In the Chamber something anticipating a party system also began to emerge: ultras on the right, independents (or liberals) on the left, constitutionalists (or moderates) in the centre. None of these factions yet possessed the real attributes of a party—disciplined organization and doctrinal coherence. The most heterogeneous of all was the independent group—an uneasy coalition of republicans, Bonapartists, and constitutional monarchists brought together by their common hostility to the Bourbons and their common determination to preserve or restore many of the Revolutionary reforms.

The era of moderate rule (1816–20) was marked by a slow but steady advance of the liberal left. Each year one-fifth of the Chamber faced re-election, and each year more independents won seats, despite the narrowly restricted suffrage. The ultras, in real or simulated panic, predicted disaster for the regime and the nation; but the King clung stubbornly to his favourite, Decazes, who by now was head of the government in all but name, and Decazes, in turn, clung to his middle way.

The
advance of
the left

The uneasy balance was wrecked in February 1820 by the assassination of the King's nephew, Charles-Ferdinand, duc de Berry. The assassin, a fanatical Bonapartist, proudly announced his purpose: to extinguish the royal line by destroying the last Bourbon still young enough to produce a male heir. In this aim he failed, for Caroline, duchesse de Berry, seven months later bore a son, whom the royalists hailed as "the miracle child." But the assassin did bring to an end the period of moderate rule and returned the ultras to power. In the wave of emotion that followed, the King dismissed Decazes and manipulated the elections in favour of the ultras, who regained control of the Chamber and dominated the new Cabinet headed by one of their leaders, Joseph, comte de Villèle.

This swing toward reaction goaded some segments of the liberal left into conspiratorial activity. A newly formed secret society called the Charbonnerie, which borrowed its name and ritual from the Italian Carbonari, laid plans for an armed insurrection, but their rising in 1822 was easily crushed. One group of conspirators—"the four sergeants of La Rochelle"—became heroic martyrs in the popular mythology of the French left. Subversion gave the government an excuse for intensified repression: the press was placed under more rigid censorship and the school system subjected to the clergy.

Meanwhile, the ultras were winning public support through a more assertive foreign policy. Spain had been in a state of quasi-civil war since 1820, when a revolt by the so-called liberal faction in the army had forced King Ferdinand VII to grant a constitution and to authorize the election of a parliament. The European powers, disturbed at the state of semi-anarchy in Spain, accepted a French offer to restore Ferdinand's authority by forcible intervention. In 1823 French troops crossed the Pyrenees and, despite predictions of disaster from the liberal left, easily took Madrid and re-established the King's untrammelled power. This successful adventure strengthened the ultra politicians and discredited their critics. In the elections of 1824 the ultras increased their grip on the Chamber and won a further victory in September 1824 when the aged Louis XVIII died, leaving the throne to a new king who was the very embodiment of the ultra spirit.

Charles X, 1824–30. Charles X, the younger brother of Louis XVIII, had spent the Revolutionary years in exile and had returned embittered rather than chastened by the experience. What France needed, in his view, was a return to the unsullied principle of divine right, buttressed by the restored authority of the established church. The new king and his Cabinet—still headed by Villèle—promptly pushed through the Chamber a series of laws of sharply partisan character. The most bitterly debated of these laws was the one that indemnified the émigrés for the loss of their property during the Revolution. The cost of the operation—almost 1,000,000,000 francs—was borne by government bondholders, whose bonds were arbitrarily converted to a lower interest rate. A severe press law hamstrung the publishers of newspapers and pamphlets; another established the death penalty for sacrilegious acts committed in churches.

Along with these signs of reaction went a vigorous campaign to reassert the authority of the Catholic Church, which had been undermined by Enlightenment skepticism and by the Revolutionary upheaval. Under the Bourbons, several new missionary orders and lay organizations were founded in an effort to revive the faith and to engage in good works. Catholic seminaries began to draw increasing numbers of students away from the state lycées. Charles X threw himself enthusiastically into the campaign for Catholic revival. The anticlericals of the liberal left were outraged, and even many moderates of Gallican sympathies were perturbed. Rumours spread that the King had secretly become a Jesuit and was planning to turn the country over to "the men in black."

King Charles and his ultra ministers might nevertheless have remained in solid control if they had been shrewd and sensitive men, aware of the rise of public discontent and flexible enough to appease it. Instead, they forged stubbornly ahead on the road to disaster. Villèle, though a talented administrator, lacked creative imagination and

charismatic appeal. As the years passed, his leadership was increasingly challenged even within his own ultra majority. A bitter personal feud between Villèle and Chateaubriand, the most colourful of the ultra politicians, undermined both the ministry and the dynasty. This internal conflict contributed to Villèle's downfall; the elections of 1827 brought a sharp resurgence of liberal and moderate strength. The King patched together a disparate ministry of moderates and ultras headed by an obscure official, Jean-Baptiste, vicomte de Martignac. But Martignac lacked Charles's confidence and failed to win the support of the more moderate leftists in the Chamber. In 1829 the King brusquely dismissed him and restored the ultras to power.

The delayed consequences of this act were to be fatal to the dynasty. The King, instead of entrusting power to an able ultra such as Villèle or a popular one such as Chateaubriand, chose a personal favourite, Jules-Auguste-Armand-Marie, prince de Polignac, a fanatical reactionary. The makeup of the Cabinet, which included several members of the most bigoted faction of "ultra-ultras," seemed to indicate the King's determination to polarize politics. That, in any case, was the immediate result. On the left, the mood turned aggressively hostile; the republicans of Paris began to organize; an Orleanist faction emerged, looking to a constitutional monarchy headed by the King's cousin, Louis-Philippe, duc d'Orléans. The liberal banker Jacques Laffitte supplied funds for a new opposition daily, *Le National*, edited by a young and vigorous team whose most notable member was Adolphe Thiers. A confrontation of some sort seemed inevitable.

Some of Polignac's ministers urged a royal coup d'etat at once, before the rejuvenated opposition could grow too strong. Instead, the King procrastinated for several months, offering no clear lead or firm policy. When the Chamber met at last in March 1830, its majority promptly voted an address to the throne denouncing the ministry. The King retaliated by dissolving the Chamber and ordering new elections in July. Both Charles and Polignac hoped that pressure on the electors, plus foreign policy successes, might shape the outcome. Such a success was won at just the opportune moment: news came that Algiers had fallen to a French expeditionary force sent to punish the Bey for assorted transgressions. But even this brilliant victory could not divert the fury of the King's critics. The opposition won 274 seats, the ministry 143. Charles's alternatives were now clear: to substitute a moderate for Polignac and to accept the role of constitutional monarch or to risk a royal coup d'etat that would leave the Charter of 1814 in tatters. Without hesitation he chose the second path. King and ministers prepared a set of decrees that dissolved the newly elected Chamber, further restricted the already narrow suffrage, and stripped away the remaining liberty of the press. These July Ordinances, made public on the 26th, completed the polarization process and ensured that the confrontation would be violent.

The Revolution of 1830. The July Revolution was a monument to the ineptitude of Charles X and his advisers. At the outset, few of the King's critics imagined it possible to overthrow the regime; they hoped merely to get rid of Polignac. As for the King, he naïvely ignored the possibility of serious trouble. No steps were taken to reinforce the army garrison in Paris; no contingency plans were prepared. Instead, Charles went off to the country to hunt, leaving the capital weakly defended. During the three days known to Frenchmen as Les Trois Glorieuses (July 27–29), protest was rapidly transmuted into insurrection; barricades went up in the streets, manned by workers, students, and petty bourgeois citizens (some of them former members of the National Guard, which Charles, in pique, had disbanded in 1827). On July 29, some army units began to fraternize with the insurgents. The King, on July 30, consented at last to dismiss Polignac and to annul the July Ordinances; but the gesture came too late. Paris was in the hands of the rebels, and plans for a new regime were crystallizing rapidly.

As the insurrection developed, two rival factions had

The polarization of politics

emerged. The republicans—mainly workers and students—gained control of the streets and took over the Hôtel de Ville, where on July 29 they set up a municipal commission. They looked to the venerable Marquis de Lafayette as their symbolic leader. The constitutional monarchists had their headquarters at the newspaper *Le National;* their candidate for the throne was Louis-Philippe, duc d'Orléans. Louis-Philippe was at first reluctant to take the risk, fearing failure and renewed exile; Adolphe Thiers undertook the task of persuading him and succeeded. On July 31 Louis-Philippe made his way through a largely hostile crowd to the Hôtel de Ville and confronted the republicans. His cause was won by Lafayette, who found a constitutional monarchy safer than the risks of Jacobin rule; Lafayette appeared on the balcony with Louis-Philippe and, wrapped in a tricolour flag, embraced the duke as the crowd cheered. Two days later Charles X abdicated at last, though on condition that the throne pass to his grandson, "the miracle child." But parliament, meeting on August 7, declared the throne vacant and on August 9 proclaimed Louis-Philippe "king of the French by the grace of God and the will of the nation."

The July monarchy.   The renovated regime (often called the July monarchy or the bourgeois monarchy) rested on an altered political theory and a broadened social base. Divine right gave way to popular sovereignty; the social centre of gravity shifted from the landowning aristocracy to the wealthy bourgeoisie. The Charter of 1814 was retained but no longer as a royal gift to the nation; it was revised by the Chamber of Deputies and in its new form imposed on the King. Censorship was abolished; the tricolour was restored as the national flag, and the National Guard was resuscitated. Catholicism was declared to be simply the religion "of the majority of Frenchmen," the voting age was lowered to 25, and the property qualification reduced to include all who paid a direct tax of 200 (formerly 300) francs. The suffrage was thus doubled, from about 90,000 to almost 200,000.

The new king seemed admirably suited to this new constitutional system. The "Citizen King" was reputed to be a liberal whose tastes and sympathies coincided with those of the upper bourgeoisie. He had spent the Revolutionary years in exile but was out of sympathy with the irreconcilable émigrés; and since his return, his house in Paris had been a gathering place for the opposition. Yet in spite of appearances, Louis-Philippe was not prepared to accept the strictly symbolic role of a monarch who (in Thiers's phrase) "reigns but does not govern." His authority, he believed, rested on heredity and not merely on the will of the Chamber; his proper function was to participate actively in decision making and not merely to appoint ministers who would govern in his name. As time went by, he was increasingly inclined to choose ministers who shared his view of the royal power. The Orleanist system thus rested on a basic ambiguity about the real locus of authority.

In the Chamber two major factions emerged, known by the rather imprecise labels right-centre and left-centre. The former group, led by the historian François Guizot, shared the King's political doctrines; it saw the revised Charter of 1814 as an adequate instrument of government that needed no further change. The left-centre, whose ablest spokesman was the kingmaker Adolphe Thiers, saw 1830 as the beginning rather than the culmination of a process of change. It favoured restricting the King's active role and broadening the suffrage to include the middle strata of the bourgeoisie. These differences of viewpoint, combined with the King's tendency to intrigue, contributed to chronic political instability during the 1830s.

The decade of the 1830s was marked also by repeated challenges to the regime by its enemies on the right and the left and by a series of attempts to assassinate the King. Both the ultras (who now came to be called legitimists) and the republicans refused to forgive "the usurper" of 1830. In 1832 the Duchesse de Berry, mother of "the miracle child," landed clandestinely in southern France in an effort to spark a general uprising; but the scheme collapsed, and most legitimists withdrew into sullen opposition. More serious was the agitation of the republicans, fed by rising labour discontent. In the most serious of these outbreaks (Lyons, 1831), 15,000 workers confronted the National Guard in the streets and suffered some 600 casualties before capitulating. Again, in 1834 there were serious disturbances in Lyons and Paris. In 1836 it was the turn of the Bonapartist pretender to challenge the regime. Since Napoleon's death in 1821, a legend had rapidly taken shape around his name. No longer detested as a ruthless autocrat who had sacrificed a generation of young Frenchmen on the battlefield, he became transmuted into the Little Corporal who had risen to the heights by his own talents and had died a victim of British jealousy. The Emperor's nephew Louis-Napoléon Bonaparte presented himself as the true heir; he crossed the frontier in 1836 and called on French troops in Strasbourg to join his cause. The venture failed ignominiously, as did also a second attempt on the Channel coast in 1840. Louis-Napoléon was condemned to prison for life but managed in 1846 to escape to England. Interspersed with these attempts at political risings were individual attacks on the King's person; the most elaborate of these plots was the one organized by a Corsican named Giuseppe Fieschi in 1835.

By 1840, however, the enemies of the regime had evidently become discouraged, and a period of remarkable stability followed. François Guizot emerged as the key figure in the ministry; he retained that role from 1840 to 1848. One of the first Protestants to attain high office in France, Guizot possessed many of the moral and intellectual qualities that marked this small but influential minority. Hard-working and intelligent, Guizot was devoted to the service of the King and to the defense of the status quo. He was convinced that the wealthy governing class was an ideal natural elite to which any Frenchman might have access through talent and effort. To those who complained of being excluded by the property qualification for voting and seeking office, Guizot's simple reply was *"enrichissez-vous!"* ("Get rich!"). Guizot was a shrewd political manipulator and kept a majority in the Chamber through judicious appointments of deputies or their friends to government posts.

Guizot shared with Louis-Philippe a strong preference for a safe-and-sane foreign policy. The King, from the beginning of his reign, had cautiously avoided risks and confrontations and had especially sought friendly relations with Britain. In 1830, when the revolution in Paris inspired the Belgians to break away from Dutch rule, Louis-Philippe avoided the temptation of seeking to annex Belgium or of placing one of his sons on the throne. Again, in 1840, when a crisis flared up in the Near East and Thiers (then head of the government) took an aggressive stance that threatened to coalesce all of Europe against France, the King had found an excuse to replace his firebrand minister. Guizot continued this cautious line through the 1840s, with the single exception of an episode in Spain. A long contest involving rival suitors for the Queen's hand finally tempted Guizot, in 1846, to try for a cheap diplomatic victory; it infuriated the British and helped to destroy the Anglo-French entente. One problem Guizot inherited from his predecessors was that of Algeria. Since 1830 the French had maintained an uneasy presence there, wavering between total withdrawal and expanded conquest. The decision to remain had been made in the mid-1830s; during the Guizot era, Gen. Thomas-Robert Bugeaud de La Piconnerie's forces broke the back of Algerian resistance, pushed the native population back into the mountains, and began the process of colonizing the rich coastal plain.

THE SECOND REPUBLIC AND SECOND EMPIRE

The Revolution of 1848.   The overthrow of the constitutional monarchy in February 1848 still seems, in retrospect, a puzzling event. The revolution has been called a result without a cause; more properly, it might be called a result out of proportion to its cause. Since 1840 the regime had settled into a kind of torpid stability; but it had provided the nation with peace abroad and relative prosperity at home. Louis-Philippe and his ministers had

The abdication of Charles X

The leadership of Guizot

Guizot's foreign policy

prided themselves on their moderation, their respect for the ideal of cautious balance embodied in the slogan *juste-milieu*. France seemed to be arriving at last at a working compromise that blended traditional ways with the reforms of the Revolutionary era.

Discontent within the July monarchy

There were, nevertheless, persistent signs of discontent. The republicans had never forgiven Louis Philippe for "confiscating" their revolution in 1830. The urban workers, moved by their misery and by the powerful social myths engendered by the Great Revolution, remained unreconciled. For a decade or more they had been increasingly drawn toward Socialism in its various utopian forms. An unprecedented flowering of Socialist thought marked the years 1840–48 in France: this was the generation of Barthélemy-Prosper Enfantin, Charles Fourier, Auguste Blanqui, Louis Blanc, Pierre-Joseph Proudhon, Étienne Cabet, and many others. Most of these system builders preached persuasion rather than violence, but they stimulated the hopes of the common man for an imminent transformation of society. Within the bourgeoisie as well, there was strong and vocal pressure for change in the form of a broadening of the political elite. Bills to extend the suffrage (and the right to hold office) to the middle bourgeoisie were repeatedly introduced in parliament but were stubbornly opposed by Guizot. Even the National Guard, that honour society of the lesser bourgeoisie, became infected with this mood of dissatisfaction.

Other factors, too, contributed to this mood. In 1846 a crop failure quickly developed into a full-scale economic crisis: food became scarce and expensive; many businesses went bankrupt; unemployment rose. Within the governing elite itself, there were signs of a moral crisis: scandals that implicated some high officials of the regime and growing dissension among the Notables. Along with this went a serious alienation of many intellectuals. Novelists such as Victor Hugo, George Sand, and Eugène Sue glorified the common man; the caricaturist Honoré Daumier exposed the foibles of the nation's leaders; historians such as Jules Michelet and Alphonse de Lamartine wrote with romantic passion about the heroic episodes of the Great Revolution.

Beginning in 1847, the leaders of the opposition set out to take advantage of this restless mood and to force the regime to grant liberal reforms. Since public political meetings were illegal, they undertook a series of political "banquets" to mobilize the forces of discontent. This campaign was to be climaxed by a mammoth banquet in Paris on February 22, 1848. But the government, fearing violence, ordered the affair cancelled. On the 22nd, crowds of protesting students and workers gathered in the streets and began to clash with the police. The King and Guizot expected no serious trouble: the weather was bad, and a large army garrison was available in case of need. But the disorders continued to spread, and the loyalty of the National Guard began to seem dubious. Toward the end of two days of rioting, Louis-Philippe faced a painful choice: to unleash the army (which would mean a bloodbath) or to appease the demonstrators. Reluctantly, he chose the second course and announced that he would replace the hated Guizot as his chief minister. But the concession came too late. That evening, an army unit guarding Guizot's official residence clashed with a mob of demonstrators, some 40 of whom died in the fusillade. By the morning of February 24, the angry crowd was threatening the royal palace. Louis-Philippe, confronted by the prospect of civil war, hesitated and then retreated once more; he announced his abdication in favour of his nine-year-old grandson and fled to England.

Abdication of Louis-Philippe

The Second Republic, 1848–52. The succession to the throne was not to be decided so easily, however. The Chamber of Deputies, invaded by a mob that demanded a republic, set up a provisional government whose members ranged from constitutional monarchists to one radical deputy, Alexandré-Auguste Ledru-Rollin. Led by the poet-deputy Alphonse de Lamartine, the members of the government proceeded to the Hôtel de Ville, where the radical republican leaders had begun to organize their own regime. After considerable palaver, the provisional government co-opted four of the radical leaders, including the Socialist theoretician Louis Blanc and a working-man who called himself Albert. Under heavy pressure from the crowd surrounding the Hôtel de Ville, the government proclaimed the republic. During the next few days, continuing pressure from the social reformers pushed the government farther than its bourgeois members really wanted to go. The government issued a right-to-work declaration, obligating the state to provide jobs for all citizens. To meet the immediate need, an emergency-relief agency called the *ateliers nationaux* (national workshops) was established. A kind of economic and social council called the Luxembourg Commission was created to study programs of social reform; Louis Blanc was named its president. The principle of universal manhood suffrage was proclaimed—an almost unprecedented experiment in that day and one that increased the electorate at a stroke from 200,000 to 9,000,000. In matters of foreign policy, on the other hand, Foreign Minister Lamartine resisted radical demands. The radicals were eager for an ideological crusade on behalf of all peoples who were thirsting for freedom: Poles, Italians, Hungarians, and Germans had launched their own revolutions and needed help. Lamartine preferred to confine himself to lip-service support, since he was aware that an armed crusade would quickly inspire an anti-French coalition of the major powers.

By April 23, when Frenchmen went to the polls to elect their constituent assembly, the initial mood of brotherhood and goodwill had been largely dissipated. Paris had become a caldron of political activism; dozens of clubs and scores of newspapers had sprung up after the revolution. Severe tension developed between moderates and radicals both within and outside the government and led to a number of violent street demonstrations that were controlled with difficulty. The *ateliers nationaux* satisfied no one: for the radicals they were a mere caricature of social reform, whereas for the moderates, they were a wasteful and dangerous experiment that attracted thousands of unemployed from every corner of France. Financial problems plagued the government, which sought a solution by imposing a special 45-centime surtax on each franc of direct property taxes; this burden weighed most heavily on the peasantry and was bitterly resented in the countryside. The radicals, fearing that universal suffrage under these conditions might produce unpleasant results, vainly urged postponement of the elections until the new voters could be "educated" as to the virtues of a social republic.

The election returns confirmed the radicals' fears: the country voted massively for moderate or conservative candidates. Radicals or socialists won only about 80 of the 880 seats; the rest were bourgeois republicans (500) or constitutional monarchists (300). Lamartine led the popularity parade, being elected in ten districts. When the Assembly convened in May, the new majority showed little patience or caution; it was determined to cut costs and end risky experiments. In spite of Lamartine's efforts to maintain broad republican unity and avert a sharp turn to the right, the Assembly abolished the Luxembourg Commission and the *ateliers nationaux* and refused to substitute a more useful program of public works to provide for the unemployed.

The June Days

The immediate consequence was a brief and bloody civil war in Paris—the so-called June Days (June 23–26, 1848). Thousands of workers suddenly cut off the state payroll were joined by sympathizers—students, artisans, employed workers—in a spontaneous protest movement. Barricades went up in many working-class sections. The Assembly turned to Gen. Louis Eugène Cavaignac as a saviour. Cavaignac had made his mark in repressing Algerian rebel tribes and was entrusted with full powers to do the same in Paris. He gave the workers time to dig themselves in, then brought up artillery against their barricades. At least 1,500 rebels were killed; 12,000 were arrested, and many were subsequently exiled to Algeria. The radical movement was decapitated; the workers withdrew into silent and bitter opposition

Social conflict now gave way to political manoeuvring and constitution making. Cavaignac was retained in office as temporary executive, while the Assembly turned to its central task. After six months of discussion, it produced a constitution that appeared to be the most democratic in Europe. The president of the republic would be chosen for a four-year term by universal male suffrage; a one-house legislative assembly would be elected for three years by the same suffrage. What remained unclear was the relationship between president and assembly and the way out of a potential deadlock between them.

This problem might not have been fatal if the right kind of president had been available in 1848. Instead, the voters chose Louis-Napoléon Bonaparte, who had returned from British exile in September, after having successfully stood for the constituent assembly in a by-election. He had made a poor initial impression; indeed, some politicians, such as Thiers, backed him for the presidency because they thought him too stupid to rule, so that he might soon be shunted aside for an Orleanist monarch. What he possessed, however, was a name—a name that Frenchmen knew and that conveyed an aura of glory, power, and public order. In December, Louis-Napoléon won by a landslide, polling 5,500,000 votes as against 2,000,000 for all other candidates combined. In May 1849 the election of the legislative assembly produced an equal surprise. The two extremes—the radical left and the monarchist right—made impressive gains, whereas the moderate republicans, who had shaped the new system, were almost wiped out. The moderates emerged with only 80 seats, the radicals with 200, the monarchists with almost 500. But the monarchist majority lacked coherence, being split into legitimist and Orleanist factions that distrusted each other and differed on political principles.

During the next two years President Bonaparte played his cards carefully, avoiding conflict with the monarchist Assembly. He pleased Catholics by restoring the Pope to his temporal throne, from which he had been driven by Roman republicans. At home, he accepted without protest a series of conservative measures adopted by the Assembly: these laws deprived one-third of all Frenchmen of the right to vote, restricted the press and public assemblage, and gave the church a firm grip on public as well as private education. Yet there was some reason to doubt that Louis-Napoléon really welcomed this trend toward conservatism. His writings of the 1840s had been marked by a kind of technocratic outlook, in the tradition of Saint-Simonian Socialism. His effort to please the Assembly probably derived from his hope that the Assembly would reciprocate: he wanted funds from the treasury to pay his personal debts and run his household and a constitutional amendment that would allow him to run for a second term.

By 1851, it was clear that the majority was not ready to give the President what he wanted. His alternatives were to step down in 1852, bereft of income and power, or to prepare a coup d'état. Some members of his entourage had long urged the latter course; Louis-Napoléon now concurred, with some reluctance.

On the early morning of December 2, 1851, some 70 leading politicians were arrested, and the outlines of a new constitution were proclaimed to the nation. It restored manhood suffrage, sharply reduced the Assembly's powers, and extended the president's term to ten years. Although the coup went off smoothly, it was followed by several days of agitation. Barricades went up in the streets; crowds clashed with troops and police in Paris and in the provinces; several hundred demonstrators were killed and 27,000 arrested. Once the resistance was broken, Louis-Napoléon proceeded with his announced plebiscite on the new constitution and was gratified to receive the approval of 92 percent of those who voted. But the authoritarian republic was only a stopgap. Officially inspired petitions for a restoration of the empire began to flow to Paris; the Senate responded to what it described as the nation's desires, and on December 2, 1852, Napoleon III was proclaimed emperor of the French. This time there was no open protest; and the voters, in a new

Louis-Napoléon's coup d'etat [margin note]

plebiscite, accorded Napoleon a handsome majority of 97 percent.

The Second Empire, 1852–70. Posterity's image of Napoleon III and his regime has not been uniform. Some historians have seen him as a shallow opportunist whose only asset was a glorious name. Others have described him as a visionary reformer and patron of progress, a man who successfully attempted to reconcile liberty and authority, national prestige and European cooperation. The Emperor's enigmatic character and the contradictions built into his regime make it possible to argue either case.

The authoritarian years. From 1852 to 1859, the empire was authoritarian in tone. Civil liberties were narrowly circumscribed; vocal opponents of the regime remained in exile or were constrained to silence; parliament's wings were clipped; elections to the Corps Législatif were spaced at six-year intervals and were "managed" by Napoleon's prefects, who sponsored official candidates. An illusion of popular control was created by the use of the plebiscite to ratify decisions already made. The Emperor and his ministers (members of his personal entourage or former Orleanist politicians) rested their authority on the peasant masses, the business class, the church, and those local notables who were willing to cooperate. Little attempt was made to install a new power elite or to create an organized Bonapartist party. Policy during the 1850s was consistently conservative; defense of the social order took precedence over reform.

The most striking achievements of these authoritarian years were in economic growth and foreign policy. France had never before experienced such vigorous economic expansion. During the Second Empire industrial production doubled, foreign trade tripled, the use of steam power increased fivefold, railway mileage sixfold. The first great investment banks were founded (*e.g.*, the Péreire brothers' Crédit Mobilier) and the first department store (the Bon Marché in Paris). The surge of French enterprise transcended frontiers: French capital and engineers built bridges, railways, docks, and sewerage systems throughout much of continental Europe.

Economic growth during the Second Empire [margin note]

In part, this burst of energy had its source in favourable world conditions: the availability of more rapid steam transportation, an influx of new gold from overseas, general recovery from the slump of 1846–51. But to some degree Napoleon's government could claim credit, too—not so much by direct intervention in economic life as by creating a favourable climate for private enterprise. Many Frenchmen took advantage of the opportunities offered; they accumulated sizable fortunes and founded enterprises that still exist today. Among these entrepreneurs, however, there was a disproportionate number of "outsiders"—notably men of Protestant or Jewish origin, or former disciples of Henri de Saint-Simon. Alongside these dynamic newcomers, the older business and banking leaders continued to operate on more cautious traditional lines. From the Second Empire onward, the French economy would combine these two contrasting sectors: a dynamic modernized element superimposed upon a largely static traditional kind of enterprise.

Napoleon's foreign policy at the outset was cautious; "the empire means peace," he assured his countrymen and the nervous powers of Europe. Yet for a ruler who bore the name Napoleon, the prudent and colourless policy of a Louis-Philippe seemed hardly appropriate. Besides, the Emperor was eager to achieve recognition from the other European monarchs, who regarded him as an upstart. It was for these reasons rather than because of urgent national interest that he became involved in the Crimean War in 1854. Britain and Russia were engaged in a contest for influence in the crumbling Turkish Empire. A dispute over the holy places in Palestine gave Napoleon an excuse to offer the British his support and thus to restore the Franco-British entente. Although the Crimean campaign was on the whole a fiasco for all of the participating armies, the French forces came off less ingloriously than the others and could with some justice pose as victors. Napoleon served as host for the Paris peace conference that ended the war in 1856. Midway through the conference, the birth of a male heir to the Emperor and his empress, Eugénie, seemed to assure the permanence of the dynasty.

The liberal years. The empire thus appeared to have compiled a record of unbroken successes and to be beyond challenge by its domestic critics. Perhaps it was this stability and self-confidence that led Napoleon, beginning in 1859, to turn in the direction of liberalizing the empire. The immediate impulse for this dramatic reversal was the attempted assassination of the Emperor in January 1858 by an Italian patriot, Felice Orsini, who sought thus to draw public attention to the frustrated hopes of Italian nationalists. Napoleon, shaken by the episode and by the reminder that in his youth he, too, had fought for Italian independence, met secretly in July 1858 with Count Cavour, premier of Piedmont; the two men laid plans designed to evict Austria from northern Italy and to convert Italy into a confederation of states headed by the Pope. In return, France was promised Nice and Savoy (Savoie). The new allies provoked the Austrians into a declaration of war in April 1859, and Napoleon led his armies across the Alps. French victories at Magenta and Solferino were followed by a somewhat premature settlement in which the Austrians turned over the province of Lombardy to the Piedmontese. The campaign had aroused the passions of Italian nationalists all up and down the peninsula; revolutions broke out in some of the smaller Italian states, and in 1860 the colourful freebooter Giuseppe Garibaldi set forth from Piedmont to conquer Sicily and Naples.

These repercussions of Napoleon's new foreign policy stirred up bitter controversy in France. Conservatives were outraged and feared that the Pope would be deposed as temporal ruler of Rome by the Italian nationalists. On the other hand, the long-silent liberal and radical opposition voiced reluctant approval. It is likely that Napoleon, whose bent toward Saint-Simonian reform ideas was strong, had never been very comfortable in his alliance with the conservatives and welcomed a chance to indulge his deeper instincts. At any rate, late in 1859 he announced the first hesitant steps toward a liberal empire. Political exiles were amnestied, press controls were relaxed, and the Corps Législatif was given slightly increased authority. An even more dramatic turn toward economic liberalism soon followed; in January 1860, Napoleon negotiated a low-tariff treaty with Britain, ending the long tradition of protectionism that had insulated French producers. By this move, however, the Emperor alienated another group of constituents—the businessmen—who until now had been his strong supporters.

Some of the Emperor's advisers had sharply opposed the turn toward liberalism. Events during the next decade seemed to confirm their warnings; for the empire now ran into increasingly stormy weather. The political opposition, stifled since 1851, showed little gratitude to its benefactor and took every opportunity to harass the government. In the 1863 elections, opposition candidates polled 2,000,000 votes, and 35 of them were elected to the Corps Législatif—including such effective spokesmen as the Orleanist Thiers and the republican Jules Favre. A downward turn in the economy played into the hands of the opposition. Foreign policy errors added to the regime's embarrassment: Napoleon's ill-conceived intervention in Mexico, where he hoped to establish a client empire under Maximilian of Austria, proved costly and futile and seemed to threaten a conflict with the United States. And from the mid-1860s, a new threat began to loom up across the Rhine: the burgeoning power of Prussia, under the guidance of Otto von Bismarck.

Despite these evil portents, Napoleon clung doggedly to his liberalization venture; additional reforms were granted throughout the decade. He expressed sympathy with the workers, granted them a kind of extra-legal right to form trade unions and to strike, and helped them organize mutual-aid societies. His minister of education, Victor Duruy, carried out an enlightened program of broadened public education, including the establishment of the first secondary education for girls. In 1867 the Emperor restored quite considerable freedom of the press and of

public assembly and further broadened the powers of the Corps Législatif. Yet the response of the voters to these concessions caused some dismay; in the elections of 1869 the opposition vote rose to 3,300,000, and the number of seats held by oppositionists more than doubled.

The Emperor now faced a momentous choice: a still further dose of liberalism or a brusque return to the authoritarian empire. He chose the former alternative; in January 1870 he asked the leader of the liberal opposition, Émile Ollivier, to form a government. Ollivier supervised the drafting of a new constitution, which, though hybrid in nature, converted the empire into a quasi-parliamentary regime. The ministers were declared to be "responsible," and their powers (as well as those of the Corps Législatif) were increased. At the same time, the Emperor retained most of his existing prerogatives, so that the real locus of power in case of a conflict was unclear. Nevertheless, the voters, when consulted by referendum (May 8, 1870), gave the new system a massive vote of confidence: 7,000,000 in favour to only 1,500,000 against. Outwardly, at least, it appeared that the Emperor had broken the rising wave of opposition and had found a widely accepted solution. But war and defeat only four months later were to prevent a fair test of the liberal empire in its final form.

The Franco-German War. Napoleon, meanwhile, had become uncomfortably involved in a diplomatic poker game with Bismarck. Prussian victories over Denmark (1864) and Austria (1866) indicated a serious shift in the European balance of power. Napoleon, aware that he faced a severe challenge, set out to strengthen his armed forces; he proposed a tighter conscription law that would increase the size of the standing army but had to retreat in the face of public and parliamentary hostility. The crisis that finally erupted in July 1870 over the succession to the Spanish throne was clumsily handled by French officials. The French successfully blocked the accession of a Hohenzollern prince in Spain, then demanded further guarantees for the future; they thus provided Bismarck with an easy opportunity to arouse German opinion and to goad France into declaring war on July 19.

Few French or foreign observers anticipated the military disaster that followed. The French armies, sunk in routine and slow to mobilize, were not yet ready to fight when the Prussian forces under Helmuth von Moltke crossed into France. One French army, under Achille-François Bazaine, was bottled up in Metz; another, under Patrice Mac-Mahon, was cornered at Sedan. There, on September 1, the Prussians won a clear-cut victory; Napoleon himself was taken prisoner. The regime could not survive such a humiliation. When the news reached Paris on September 4, crowds filled the streets and converged on the Corps Législatif, demanding the proclamation of a republic. The imperial officials put up no serious resistance; the Revolution of September 4 was the most bloodless in French history.

THE THIRD REPUBLIC

A provisional government of national defense was set up and took as its first task the continuation of the war against the invaders. Composed of the deputies representing Paris and formally headed by Gen. Louis-Jules Trochu, the new government's most forceful member was Léon Gambetta, hero of the radical republicans. Gambetta, a young Parisian lawyer of provincial origin, had been elected to the Corps Législatif in 1869 and had already made his mark through his energy and eloquence. As minister of the interior and, some weeks later, minister of war as well, he threw himself into the task of improvising military resistance. His task was complicated by the advance of the Prussian forces, which, by September 23, surrounded and besieged Paris. Gambetta shortly left the city by balloon to join several members of the government at Tours. During the next four months Gambetta's makeshift armies fought a series of indecisive battles with the Prussians in the Loire Valley and eastern France. But his attempt to send a force northward to relieve Paris from siege was frustrated by Moltke. Adolphe

Margin notes:

Intervention in Italy

Further liberal reforms

The Revolution of September 4

Thiers had been sent meanwhile to tour the capitals of Europe in search of support from the powers; but he returned empty-handed. By January 1871 it was clear that further armed resistance would be futile. Over Gambetta's angry protests, an armistice was signed with the Prussians on January 28.

One provision of the armistice called for the prompt election of a national assembly with authority to negotiate a definitive treaty of peace. That election, held on February 8, produced an assembly dominated by monarchists—more than 400 of them, compared to only 200 republicans and a few Bonapartists. The decisive issue for the voters, however, had not been the nature of the future regime but simply war or peace. Most of the monarchists had campaigned for peace; the republicans had insisted on a last-ditch fight. Most Frenchmen opted for peace, though Paris and certain provinces, such as Alsace, voted heavily for republicans. When the National Assembly convened in Bordeaux on February 13, it chose the aging Orleanist Adolphe Thiers as "chief of the executive power of the French republic." Thiers had been the most outspoken critic of Napoleon's foreign policy and had repeatedly warned the country of the Prussian danger. He set out at once to negotiate a settlement with Bismarck; on March 1 the Treaty of Frankfurt was ratified by a large majority of the Assembly. The terms were severe: France was charged a war indemnity of 5,000,000,000 francs, plus the cost of maintaining a German occupation army in eastern France until the indemnity was paid. Alsace and half of Lorraine were annexed to the new German Empire. The German Army was authorized to stage a victory march through the Arc de Triomphe de l'Étoile in Paris. After the Assembly ratified the treaty, the deputies of the lost provinces (including Léon Gambetta) resigned their seats in protest.

The Paris Commune. A few days later, the Assembly transferred the seat of government from Bordeaux to Versailles. It had scarcely arrived when it was confronted by a major civil war—the rebellion of the Paris Commune. This event, complex in itself, has been made even more difficult to understand by the mythology that later grew up around it. Karl Marx, who promptly hailed the Commune as the first great uprising of the proletariat against its bourgeois oppressors, was partly responsible for creating this mythology. There was undoubtedly a class-struggle element in the episode, but this was not the central thread. Parisians, tense and irritable after the long strain of the siege, were outraged by the action of rural France in electing a monarchist Assembly committed to what they regarded as a dishonourable peace. They were further angered by the Assembly's subsequent acts, notably those that ended the wartime moratorium on debts and rents, cut off further wage payments to the National Guard (which had been resuscitated in Paris after the empire fell), and transferred the capital to Versailles rather than to Paris.

Thiers, aware that Paris was in an ugly mood, thought it prudent to disarm the National Guard, which heavily outnumbered the regular army units at the government's disposition. Before dawn on March 18, he sent troops to confiscate the National Guard cannon on the butte of Montmartre. A crowd gathered; a bloody encounter ensued; two generals were caught and lynched by the mob. As violence spread through the city, Thiers hastily withdrew all troops and government offices from Paris and went to Versailles to plan his strategy. He appealed successfully to Bismarck to release French prisoners of war in order to form a siege army that could eventually force Paris to capitulate. During the next two months, this governmental force was slowly assembled. Within Paris, meanwhile, initial chaos gradually gave way to an improvised experiment in municipal self-government. On March 26 Parisians elected a council that promptly adopted the traditional label Commune of Paris. Its membership ranged from radical republicans of the Jacobin and Blanquist variety to Socialists of several different sorts—notably disciples of Proudhon, who favoured a decentralized federation of self-governing communes throughout France. These internal divisions prevented

any vigorous or coherent experiments in social reform and also interfered with the Commune's efforts to organize an effective armed force. Communes on the Paris model were set up briefly in several other cities (Lyons, Marseilles, Toulouse) but were quickly suppressed.

By May 21 Thiers's forces were ready to strike. In the course of "Bloody Week" (May 21–28), the Communards resisted, street by street, but were pushed back steadily to the heart of Paris. In their desperation, they executed a number of hostages (including the Archbishop of Paris) and in the last days set fire to many public buildings including the Tuileries Palace and the Hôtel de Ville. A final stand was made in Père-Lachaise Cemetery, where the last resisters were shot down against the Mur des Fédérés—ever since, a place of pilgrimage for the French left. Thiers's government took a terrible vengeance. Twenty thousand Communards were killed in the fighting or executed on the spot; thousands of survivors were deported to the penal islands, while others escaped into exile.

The formative years (1871–1905). The repression of the Paris Commune left its mark on the emerging republic. The various Socialist factions and the newly organized labour movement were left leaderless and drifting; the resultant vacuum eventually opened the way to Marxian activists in the 1880s. Much of the working class became more deeply alienated than before, but to the moderate and conservative elements, Thiers gained added stature as the preserver of law and order against "the reds." His ruthless action probably hastened the conversion of many rural and small-town Frenchmen to the idea of a republic because the regime had proved its toughness in handling subversion. A large number of by-elections to the Assembly in July 1871 brought startling gains to the republicans: they won 99 of 114 vacancies. The voters were clearly willing to accept a republic so long as it was run by a man like Thiers.

Attempts at a restoration. The monarchists, however, still held a comfortable majority in the Assembly and continued to hope and plan for a restoration. Legitimists and Orleanists remained at odds, but a compromise seemed possible. The Bourbon pretender, the Comte de Chambord ("the miracle child" of 1820), was old and childless; the Orleanist pretender, Philippe, comte de Paris, was young and prolific. The natural solution was to restore Chambord, with the Comte de Paris as his successor. Chambord, however, refused to accept the throne except on his own terms, which implied a return to the principle of absolute royal authority, unchecked by constitutional limitations. The Orleanists and even some legitimists found this too much to swallow. For the time being, they, too, settled for Thiers's presidential rule.

During the next two years Thiers's position was beyond challenge; and he gave the republic vigorous and efficient leadership. He reorganized the army and worked to restore national morale; he successfully floated two bond issues that permitted the war indemnity to be paid off in 1873, thus ending the German occupation ahead of schedule. Late in 1872, however, Thiers abjured his long-held Orleanist faith and publicly announced his conversion to republicanism. The monarchists, outraged and seeing their majority in the Assembly dwindling because of by-elections, found an excuse to force Thiers's resignation as provisional president (May 1873) and hastily substituted the commander of the army, Marshal Patrice de Mac-Mahon. Behind the scenes, monarchist politicians again set out to arrange an agreement between the two pretenders. Their hopes were once more sabotaged by Chambord, who again announced that he would return only on his own terms and under the fleur-de-lis flag of the old regime. The disheartened monarchists fell back on waiting for the Bourbon line to die out. But when Chambord passed from the scene in 1883, it was too late for a restoration.

The constitution of the Third Republic. Meanwhile, the problem of writing a constitution for the republic could no longer be postponed. The Assembly began the task in 1873; and in 1875 it adopted a series of fundamental laws, which, taken collectively, came to be known

Marginal notes:

The Treaty of Frankfurt

"Bloody Week"

Republican gains

as the constitution of the Third Republic. A patchwork compromise, it established a two-house legislature (with an indirectly elected Senate as a conservative check on the Chamber of Deputies); a Council of Ministers (Cabinet), responsible to the Chamber; and a president, elected for seven years by the two houses, with powers resembling those of a constitutional monarch. The label republic was approved by a single-vote margin. Monarchists believed that this system could be easily converted to their purposes once the right monarch was available. The constitution left untouched many aspects of the French governmental structure, notably the centralized administrative system inherited from Napoleon I, the hierarchy of courts and judges, and the Concordat of 1801, governing church–state relations. At the end of 1875, the National Assembly at last dissolved itself, and the provisional phase of the Third Republic came to an end.

End of the provisional phase

The new Senate, which heavily overrepresented rural France, was safely monarchist from the outset; and the term of President Mac-Mahon, a loyal monarchist, ran until 1880. But when the first Chamber of Deputies was elected in 1876, the republicans won more than two-thirds of the seats. A period of severe friction between Mac-Mahon and the Chamber followed, and a crisis in May 1877 produced a total deadlock. Mac-Mahon dissolved the Chamber and called on the voters' support, but again they opted for the republic, by a narrower but clear-cut margin. Léon Gambetta, who had returned to political life and had led the republicans during the campaign, called on Mac-Mahon to "give in or get out." The President gave in, naming a premier acceptable to the republican majority. Two years later partial elections gave the republicans control of the Senate, and Mac-Mahon shortly found an excuse to resign. He was replaced by a colourless republican, Jules Grévy, who was believed to favour a reduced role for the president.

Republican factions. With the republican regime apparently safe from outside attack, rival factions developed among the republicans. During the 1880s the labels Radical and Opportunist began to be attached to the two wings of the republican movement. On the left, the Radicals saw themselves as heirs to the Jacobin tradition: they stood for a strong centralized regime, intransigent anticlericalism, an assertive nationalism in foreign policy, a revision of the constitution to prune out its monarchical aspects, and such social reforms as labour laws and a graduated income tax; their most colourful spokesman was Georges Clemenceau, a ferocious debater and duellist who specialized in overthrowing Cabinets. The Opportunists (so named by a satirical journalist because of their penchant for compromises and postponements) occupied the centre seats in the Chamber; their stance was more cautious, their techniques gradualist; they were content to work within the system, and they aimed to restrict governmental interference in the affairs of private citizens. Only on the issue of the church's role in politics and education were the two factions in general agreement.

Opportunist control. Between 1879 and 1899 the Opportunists, with only brief interruptions, controlled the machinery of government. Gambetta, their most dynamic leader, had begun his career as an outspoken Radical, but in time his political instincts had prevailed. The other Opportunist leaders—men such as President Grévy and Jules Ferry—disliked Gambetta's flamboyance, however, and feared his alleged dictatorial ambitions; they kept him out of the premiership save for a brief interlude in 1881–82, shortly before his death. Ferry served as premier or in other key Cabinet posts during most of the period 1880–85 and left his mark on two institutions: the public school system and the colonial empire. His school laws made primary education free, compulsory, and secular, with religious teaching in the public schools replaced by "civic education"; a strong anticlerical bias thenceforth marked French public education. Ferry's support of various colonial expeditions—sometimes behind the back of the Chamber—gave France protectorates over Tunisia and Annam and Tongking (Tonkin),

Educational reforms and colonial expansion

a large new colony in the Congo Basin, and an initial foothold in Madagascar. This expansionist policy, unpopular at the time, led later generations to call Ferry the founder of the French empire.

In the 1885 elections, the monarchists, Bonapartists, and Radicals all made significant gains, partly because of boredom with the Opportunists, Catholic resentment over the school laws, and revived agitation by Socialist organizers. The Opportunists, lacking a clear majority in the Chamber, sought Radical support to form a Cabinet; the Radicals insisted on the inclusion of Gen. Georges Boulanger as minister of war. Within a few weeks Boulanger was the most talked-about man in France. He restored the tradition of military parades and rode at their head; he instituted popular reforms in the army; and he spoke out in chauvinistic fashion against the Germans, thus reviving the memory of 1871 and the lost provinces. The unnerved Opportunist leadership dropped him from the Cabinet and sent him in 1887 to an obscure provincial command. But Boulanger's backers urged him to plunge into politics and began to enter his name in by-elections. Privately, monarchist and Bonapartist agents also made contact with Boulanger, promising financial support and hoping to use him for their cause.

By 1889 the Boulanger movement had become a major threat to the regime. The government had placed him on the retired list, but this merely freed him to run openly for office on a vague program of constitutional revision. He triumphed in a series of by-elections, but his goal was the parliamentary election of 1889, which he hoped to turn into a kind of national plebiscite. Just prior to the election, however, believing that he was about to be arrested for subversive activities, Boulanger took flight to Brussels. His movement gradually disintegrated; word leaked out of his dealings with the monarchists, and his supporters fell away. The Opportunists' hold on the republic was strengthened by the discomfiture of those on both right and left who had been taken in by this adventurer.

A new crisis soon arose for the regime: the Panama Scandal. Ferdinand, vicomte de Lesseps, the noted French engineer who had built the Suez Canal, had organized a joint-stock company to cut a canal across the Isthmus of Panama. The venture proved difficult and costly; in 1889 the company collapsed, and large numbers of shareholders were stripped of their savings. Demands for a parliamentary investigation proved ineffective until 1892, when a muckraking journalist named Édouard Drumont obtained evidence that agents of the company had bribed a large number of politicians and journalists in a desperate effort to get funds to keep the company afloat. The directors of the company and several deputies and senators were brought to trial in 1893, but the outcome was on the whole a whitewash. The regime survived the scandal, but the effects were more serious than appeared to be the case. Cynicism about the honesty of the republic's political leadership gave added strength to the rising Socialist movement; in 1893 almost 50 Socialists won seats in the Chamber. Georges Clemenceau, unjustly accused of involvement in the scandal, was defeated; and many prominent Opportunists, tainted by the affair, withdrew and were replaced by such younger men as Raymond Poincaré and Louis Barthou, who thenceforth preferred to call themselves Progressists or Moderates.

The Panama Scandal

The dramatic Socialist gains in 1893 resulted only partly from the Panama Scandal. For more than a decade Socialism had been gaining strength among the increasingly class-conscious urban workers. The movement was weakened, however, by multiple splits into antagonistic factions. The Marxian Party created by Jules Guesde in 1880 broke up two years later into Guesdists and followers of Paul Brousse—the latter group popularly called possibilists because of their gradualist temper. In 1890 a third faction broke away, headed by Jean Allemane and limited to simon-pure proletarian members. Alongside these Marxian sects there were the Blanquistes (disciples of Auguste Blanqui); the anarchists (whose terrorist campaign in the early 1890s earned them wide notoriety); and a considerable scattering of independent Socialists (mainly intellectuals, notably Jean Jaurès). By 1900 the parties had been reduced to the two led by Guesde and Jaurès, which merged in 1905 to form the Parti Socialiste, Section Française de l'Internationale Ouvrière (SFIO).

The trade union movement, however, refused to join forces with the Socialists. Trade unions were finally legalized in 1884 and joined together to form a national Confédération Générale du Travail (CGT) in 1895. CGT leaders rejected political action in favour of direct action—sabotage, boycotts, strikes, and especially the general strike, which they saw as the ultimate weapon that would transform France into a workers' state. This doctrine, known as revolutionary syndicalism, made the French trade union movement appear to be one of the most radical in Europe. The trade union rank and file, however, was less revolutionary than its leadership. It also made relations between unions and Socialists more hostile than elsewhere.

The Dreyfus affair. The 1890s also saw the Third Republic's greatest political and moral crisis—the Dreyfus affair. In 1894 Capt. Alfred Dreyfus, a career army officer of Jewish origin, was charged with selling military secrets to the Germans. He was tried and convicted by a court-martial and sentenced to life imprisonment on Devil's Island off the South American coast. Efforts by the Dreyfus family to reopen the case were frustrated by the general belief that justice had been done. But secrets continued to leak to the German embassy in Paris, and a second officer, Maj. Marie-Charles-Ferdinand Esterhazy, became suspect. The chief of army counterintelligence, Col. Georges Picquart, eventually concluded that Esterhazy and not Dreyfus had been guilty of the original offense, but his superior officers refused to reopen the case. Rumours and scraps of evidence soon began to appear in the press; and a few politicians, notably Georges Clemenceau, took up Dreyfus' cause. But the army high command refused to discuss the affair, although army officers leaked documents to the press in an effort to discredit the critics. Each leak aroused new controversy, and by 1898 the case had become a violently divisive issue. Intellectuals of the left led the fight for Dreyfus, while right-wing politicians and many Catholic periodicals defended the honour of the army. The Socialists were split: Jaurès insisted that no Socialist could remain aloof on such a moral issue, while Guesde called the conflict a bourgeois squabble.

In 1898 some of the army's most persuasive documents against Dreyfus were discovered to be forgeries. Esterhazy promptly fled to England. In a second court-martial, late in 1899, Dreyfus was again found guilty but with extenuating circumstances; he received a presidential pardon and was later (1906) vindicated by a civilian court. For a generation the affair left deep scars on French political and intellectual life. The Moderates, who had tried to avoid involvement in the affair and in the end had split into two warring factions, lost control to the Radicals.

Radical control

A coalition Cabinet headed by René Waldeck-Rousseau, a pro-Dreyfus Moderate, took office in June 1899; the Radicals dominated the coalition, and even the Socialists supported it. From then until the end of the Third Republic the Radical Party (thenceforth called Radical-Socialist) remained the fulcrum of French political life. Both the army and the church were seriously hurt by their role in the affair; republicans of the left were more convinced than ever that both institutions were anti-republican and hostile to the rights of man enunciated during the Great Revolution. The new left majority retaliated by bringing the army under more rigorous civilian control and by embarking on a new wave of anticlerical legislation. Most religious orders were dissolved and exiled; and in 1905 a new law separated church and state, thus liquidating the Concordat of 1801.

Foreign policy. Meanwhile, some important successes were being scored in the field of foreign policy. For two decades after 1871 France had remained diplomatically isolated in Europe. Bismarck, to ward off potential ideas

of revenge in France, had shrewdly encouraged French governments to embark on colonial conquest overseas and had negotiated alliances with all those European powers that the French might otherwise have courted. He thus kept Austria-Hungary, Russia, and Italy in tow, while Britain chose to remain aloof in "splendid isolation." Upon Bismarck's fall in 1890, the German emperor William II terminated the secret treaty between Germany and Russia. The Russians began to cast about for friends and looked with some distaste toward Paris. French policy makers encouraged French bankers to make loans to the Russian government and opened negotiations for an entente. In 1891 a loose agreement provided for mutual consultation in crisis; in 1894 this was broadened into a military alliance by whose terms each partner promised to aid the other in case of attack by Germany or Germany's allies.

French European alliances

For a decade the Franco-Russian Alliance had little practical effect (though French loans did continue to flow to Russia). French diplomats turned to winning the Italians away from the Triple Alliance, and a Franco-Italian secret agreement in 1902 substantially weakened that Italian commitment. Of more central importance throughout the 1890s was a recurrent tension between France and Britain, who had been at odds in various parts of the world and whose colonial competition at times seemed to threaten war. Britain's Boer War in South Africa added further ill feeling, and some British leaders began to urge an end to "splendid isolation" in favour of an entente with a continental power—most probably Germany, which was seen as part of an Anglo-Saxon racial bloc. But the German government responded coolly to overtures in this direction, thus feeding the fears of British leaders who saw Germany as a threat to British interests. The British turned to France instead and found a willing partner in the foreign minister Théophile Delcassé. A visit to Paris by King Edward VII in 1903 helped pave the way to the Anglo-French Entente Cordiale of 1904, which resolved all outstanding colonial conflicts between the two powers but stopped short of military alliance. The new entente was consolidated a year later, when French moves to take over Morocco as a protectorate were resented by the Germans, who thought they saw an opportunity to break up the new entente. Emperor William II offered Germany's support to the Sultan of Morocco; this action irritated the British and led them to promise France strong support. In the conference of powers that followed at Algeciras (1906), France had to be content with special privileges rather than a protectorate in Morocco; but the Entente Cordiale was solidified, and it was Germany that thenceforth began to complain of isolation.

The prewar years. From 1899 to 1905 a fairly coherent coalition of left-wing and centre parties (the so-called Bloc Républicain) provided France with stable government. The Cabinets headed by Waldeck-Rousseau in 1899–1902 and Émile Combes in 1902–1905 managed to liquidate the Dreyfus affair and to carry through the anticlerical reforms that culminated in the separation of church and state. The Entente Cordiale and the Russian alliance ensured France a more influential voice in European affairs. France possessed a colonial empire second only to Britain's in size. A new period of economic growth set in after the mid-1890s. Not surprisingly, later generations were to look back on the pre-1914 decade as *la belle époque* ("the good old days").

Stable government of the Bloc Républicain

Still, some sources of sharp dissatisfaction and conflict remained. Many Catholics were outraged by the triumph of the anticlericals, and they responded to the Vatican's urging to sabotage the new system. They resisted (sometimes violently) the transfer of church property to state ownership and refused to establish lay associations to govern the church. By 1907, however, resistance was clearly futile, and they began to accept the separation law as an accomplished fact. A difficult period followed for the church. The recruitment of priests fell off sharply, and many Catholic schools were closed for lack of funds. In the long run, however, the separation law reduced the intensity of conflict between Catholics and anticlericals.

There was less reason for republicans to suspect and denounce a disestablished church.

A vocal minority on the right remained unreconciled to the radical republic and rallied round the banner of the Action Française, headed by Charles Maurras. This organization had developed at the height of the Dreyfus affair as a focal point for intellectuals who opposed a new trial for Dreyfus. Maurras, an aspiring young writer from the south, quickly emerged as its theorist and leader. In his view, France had gone astray in 1789 and had since been dominated by the "four alien nations"—Jews, Freemasons, Protestants, and *métèques* ("aliens"). He preached a return to stable institutions and an organic society, in which the monarchy and the church would be essential pillars. Maurras appealed to many traditionalists, professional men, churchmen, and army officers. Action Française readily resorted to both verbal and physical violence; and its organized bands, the Camelots du Roi, anticipated the tactics of later Fascist movements. By 1914 Maurras' movement, though still relatively small, was the most coherent and influential enemy of the republic.

Equally serious was the alienation of much of the working class. The CGT remained officially committed to revolutionary syndicalism; it rejected political action as a useless diversion of the proletariat's energies and exalted the idea of the general strike as the proper weapon to destroy bourgeois society. Although the CGT attracted only about 10 percent of French workers (most workers stubbornly refused to join any union), it was aggressive enough to cause sporadic turmoil during the period 1906–10. Several major strikes were broken by forcible repression; the government either called out troops or mobilized the strikers (who were also reservists) into the army. Proposals for labour-reform legislation drew little support in a parliament dominated by representatives of the bourgeoisie and the peasantry.

Despite the CGT, most workers by now were voting for the new unified Socialist Party. But the SFIO refused to permit its deputies to participate in or support bourgeois Cabinets (a policy dictated to the French party in 1904 by the Second International, dominated by the German Socialists) and thus condemned itself to an oppositionist stance in parliament. This destroyed the left-wing coalition that had given France stable Cabinets from 1899 to 1905. Socialist strength continued to rise, and by 1914, the party was second only to the Radicals in the Chamber of Deputies. Although its doctrine remained rigorously Marxist, in deference to the instructions of the International, the party's conduct was much more flexible. Jaurès, whose "humanitarian" Socialism was in large part derived from an older French heritage of left-wing thought, guided the Socialists in parliament toward informal cooperation with the bourgeois left in an effort to achieve domestic social reforms and an internationalist, antimilitarist foreign policy. Jaurès' central concern during the pre-1914 decade was to avert the general war that he saw looming ahead in Europe.

The Socialist withdrawal from the Bloc Républicain in 1905 forced the Radicals to look to the other centre parties as coalition partners. Until 1914—and, indeed, most of the time until 1940—France was governed by heterogeneous centre coalitions in which the Radicals most often held the key posts. In 1906 the Radical Georges Clemenceau began a three-year premiership. He proposed a long list of social reforms, including the eight-hour day and an income tax, but parliament blocked virtually all of them. More surprising was Clemenceau's ruthless suppression of strikes and his vigorous, nationalist foreign policy. In 1907 his government sponsored a rapprochement between Britain and Russia that completed the triangle of understandings thenceforth called the Triple Entente. But Clemenceau refused to risk war through all-out support of his Russian ally during the Bosnian crisis of 1908. When his Cabinet fell in 1909, Clemenceau had effectively alienated his own Radical Party and seemed unlikely ever to return to high office.

Clemenceau's successors, Aristide Briand and Joseph Caillaux, undertook a policy of détente in European affairs. Briand, like Clemenceau, belied his left-wing origins by forcibly repressing a major strike in 1910; but in foreign policy he preferred a policy of co-existence with Germany. Caillaux pushed this latter experiment even further; in 1911 he had to deal with a new crisis in Morocco, where the French were again pushing toward a protectorate against German objections; when the Germans sent a gunboat to Morocco, Caillaux made an effort at appeasement, handing over to Germany a slice of the Congo as compensation. French patriots were outraged; the Caillaux Cabinet was overthrown and replaced in January 1912 by one headed by Raymond Poincaré.

There were signs of a changing intellectual mood in the country, especially among young Frenchmen. A nationalist revival affected many Frenchmen who for a decade had grown increasingly anxious about what they regarded as the puzzling and threatening attitude of Germany's post-Bismarckian leadership; they looked once more to the army as the nation's bulwark, and its prestige was on the rise. These nationalist tendencies found their embodiment in Poincaré, whose intransigent patriotism and determination to stand up to Germany were beyond doubt. As premier in 1912–13 Poincaré devoted himself to strengthening the armed forces and to reinvigorating France's alliance system. An agreement with the British provided for a new sharing of naval responsibilities: the French concentrating in the Mediterranean, the British in the North Sea. Poincaré made a state visit to Russia to revive the sagging Franco-Russian Alliance. In January 1913 he was elected to the presidency of the republic, where, he believed, he could ensure continuity of policy during his seven-year term. In 1913 the size of the standing army was increased by lengthening the conscription period from two to three years.

Poincaré found bitter opposition on the left. The Socialists were strongly antimilitarist and hoped for an eventual reconciliation with Germany via collaboration between the two Socialist parties. They clung to the belief that the working class everywhere could block war by resorting to a general strike. A large segment of the Radical Party followed the Caillaux line, favouring Franco-German collaboration through such ventures as banking consortia for joint investment abroad. Much of rural France also lacked enthusiasm for the new nationalistic mood. The combined strength of this opposition was revealed in the parliamentary elections of 1914, when the parties of the left won a narrow victory.

World War I. Before a change in policy could be imposed, however, a new crisis in the Balkans threatened a general war. The assassination of the Austrian archduke Francis Ferdinand in Sarajevo on June 28 inaugurated five weeks of feverish negotiations, in which France's role has been much debated. Some historians have accused Poincaré and his supporters of a willingness to go to the brink of war rather than seek a negotiated settlement or use restraint on the Serbs and Russians; Poincaré's state visit to St. Petersburg at the height of the crisis has been seen as an occasion for a French promise of full support to Russia. A more judicious view is that many French statesmen had long seen the possibility and even the likelihood of a general war, and they suspected that the German government desired such a war; the Poincaré group believed that under these circumstances France could not risk the loss of its allies and a return to isolation. French support of the Serbs and the Russians, according to this view, was thus inspired by a calculated judgment regarding French security.

Germany's declaration of war against France on August 3 produced a spontaneous outburst of patriotic sentiment. Trade union and Socialist leaders, some of whom had been on a governmental list of dangerous subversives to be arrested in case of war, rallied to the colours. A national union Cabinet was formed. Parliament, after voting war credits, went into an extended recess, handing over the conduct of the war to the Cabinet and the high command. During the initial months the high command made most of the crucial decisions; the Cabinet accorded almost unlimited freedom of action to the commander in chief, Gen. Joseph Joffre, assuming that the war would

---

Margin notes:

Alienation of the working class

Centre coalition governments

Nationalist revival

German declaration of war against France

last only a few weeks and that civilian interference would only prolong hostilities.

Joffre's war plans for an immediate advance across the frontier into the lost provinces of Alsace and Lorraine were suspended when German forces struck through Belgium and threatened late in August to envelop Paris. Joffre managed to blunt the German attack and force the Germans to more defensible positions. The rival armies dug into trench positions that remained largely static until 1918. Meanwhile, the French high command continued to believe that the fate of France would be decided on the Western Front. In 1916 a powerful German artillery attack on the French fortress positions surrounding Verdun lasted from February to June and cost each side some 250,000 men. For the French, the hero of Verdun was the sector commander, Gen. Philippe Pétain.

Joffre was by now under heavy criticism in Paris. Both the Cabinet and the Chamber were determined to assert greater control over the war effort, so that the high command's authority was steadily whittled away. Joffre was finally replaced in late 1916 by Gen. Robert Nivelle. All through 1917 rival factions in the Chamber debated the conduct of the war, backing different generals and threatening Cabinet crises. Worse still, morale among the troops reached a dangerous low point in 1917, culminating in serious mutinies that affected 54 French divisions. Pétain, who replaced Nivelle in May, managed to achieve stability by a judicious combination of severity and concessions.

Nevertheless, by autumn 1917 there was widespread defeatism in France and much talk of a "white peace." The Radical leader Caillaux was prepared to try for negotiations with the Germans; but his chance never came. When the Cabinet of Premier Paul Painlevé was overthrown in November 1917, President Poincaré recalled Georges Clemenceau to the premiership. Clemenceau stood for a fight to the finish. At age 76 he still had enormous energy and doggedness, and he infused a new spirit into the country. In March 1918, when the Germans launched a last major offensive in the West, Clemenceau replaced the cautious and pessimistic Pétain with a more attack-minded general, Ferdinand Foch, and persuaded the British as well to accept him as supreme commander. The German drive was checked. On November 11 an armistice was signed in Foch's railway car near Compiègne.

The victory was won at enormous cost for France. Of the 8,000,000 Frenchmen mobilized, 1,300,000 had been killed and almost 1,000,000 crippled. Large parts of northeastern France, the nation's most advanced industrial and agricultural area, were devastated. Industrial production had fallen to 60 percent of the prewar level; economic growth had been set back by a decade. The enormous cost of the war seriously undermined the franc and foreshadowed many years of currency fluctuation. Even deeper, though largely hidden, were the psychological lesions caused by the strain of protracted warfare and by the sentiment that France could not again endure such a test.

At the Paris Peace Conference in 1919, Clemenceau, as the principal French negotiator, declared that his goal was to ensure the nation's security against a renewed German aggression. He sought, therefore, to reduce Germany's power in every possible fashion and to hedge Germany about by strong barrier nations. He knew, however, that France could not dictate the peace terms and that he would have to compromise with the Americans and British, to whom he looked for aid in case of German resurgence. His stubborn defense of French demands irritated France's wartime allies; but his willingness to compromise in the end alienated many Frenchmen, who charged him with sacrificing the nation's security. The critics—who included Poincaré and Foch—were particularly outraged when Clemenceau abandoned his initial demand that Germany give up all territory west of the Rhine and that the Saar Basin be annexed to France. These and other concessions led many right-wing deputies to oppose the Treaty of Versailles when it was presented for ratification in the autumn of 1919. Joining the op-

Effects of the war

position were the Socialists, who argued that the treaty was too harsh and that democratic Germany should not be punished for the sins of the Kaiser. A majority of the Chamber, however, reluctantly ratified Versailles and vowed to assure its enforcement to the letter.

The interwar years. Frenchmen concentrated much of their energy during the early 1920s on recovering from the war. The government undertook a vast program of reconstructing the devastated areas and had largely completed that task by 1925. To compensate for manpower losses, immigration barriers were lowered, and 2,000,000 foreign workers flooded into the country. Underlying all other concerns, however, was anxiety about the nation's security and about financing the costs of war and reconstruction. The peace settlement, in the eyes of many Frenchmen, had not provided adequate guarantees; and except among Socialists and Radicals there was little confidence in the League of Nations. American and British promises to aid France in case of future attack had been written into the treaty, but they became meaningless when the United States Senate rejected Versailles.

German reparations. A clause in the treaty had ascribed war guilt to the Germans and their allies and had obligated Germany to make reparations; the total sum due was calculated in 1921 at $33,000,000,000, but the French were aware that the British hoped to see this total reduced.

The general elections of November 1919 resulted in a massive majority for the right-wing coalition called the Bloc National. The new Chamber set out to enforce Versailles to the letter; it also sought traditional security guarantees, maintaining the largest standing army in Europe and attempting to encircle Germany with a ring of military allies (Belgium and Poland in 1920–21; Czechoslovakia, Romania, and Yugoslavia in 1924–27). But the central issue was that of German reparations. By the end of 1921 the British clearly favoured a reduction of the burden in order to get Germany back on its feet; this issue caused increasing strain between the British and French governments. Premier Briand, who seemed willing to compromise, was overthrown by the Chamber and replaced by the more intransigent Poincaré. Repeated German defaults on reparations deliveries led Poincaré in January 1923 to send French troops and engineers (supported by a token force of Belgians) into the Ruhr Valley to force German compliance or, if necessary, to collect reparations by direct seizure. The German government had to comply by that September. Germany agreed in 1924 to a revised reparations settlement, the so-called Dawes plan, and the French occupation forces were withdrawn. The plan enabled the Germans to meet their obligations on schedule during the rest of the decade, though only with the help of large American loans. In 1926 France and the United States finally reached agreement on another nagging problem—the repayment of French war debts for wartime deliveries of American munitions and other supplies.

Occupation of the Ruhr Valley

Financial crisis. The aftermath of the Ruhr occupation was to cast doubt on its apparent success. The German republic was weakened by the runaway inflation of 1923, and its future clouded; the occupation had embittered Britain and the United States. Even among Frenchmen, the victory had left a sour aftertaste because the costs of the occupation forced an increase in French taxes. In the elections of 1924, Poincaré's Bloc National was beaten by a coalition of the left, the Cartel des Gauches, and the Radicals were returned to power. But their triumph was brief; they were confronted by the nation's worst financial crisis since the war. The shaky franc went into rapid decline until there seemed to be danger of complete financial collapse. Seven Cartel Cabinets in 1924–26 wrestled ineffectively with the problem; at last the Cartel gave up, and Poincaré returned. The latter's reputation for decisive character and conservative views enabled him to win the bankers' support and to embark on such measures as slashing government expenses and increasing taxes. The franc began to rise, and it finally stabilized at about one-fifth of its 1914 value. Poincaré was hailed as "saviour of the franc," and when he resigned in 1929 for reasons of health, he was acclaimed as one of the Third Republic's outstanding statesmen.

Collective security. Poincaré, in his final term of office (1926–29), retained as foreign minister Aristide Briand, who had been named to that post by the Cartel in 1925 and who was to remain there for seven years almost without interruption. Briand sensed a change in the public mood after the Ruhr episode and proclaimed himself "the apostle of peace"; he formulated a policy that he called *apaisement*. His goal was to work for collective security through the League of Nations, for disarmament, and for a reconciliation with those Germans who favoured peaceful and cooperative methods. Briand found a ready partner in Gustav Stresemann, the German foreign minister. By the Pact of Locarno (1925), the French and German governments bound themselves not to use force to alter the existing Franco-German frontier. In subsequent years, France sponsored Germany's entry into the League of Nations and made a series of concessions softening various aspects of the Treaty of Versailles. A revised reparations agreement in 1929 (the Young Plan) further eased Germany's obligations, and in 1930 the French ended their occupation of the German Rhineland five years ahead of schedule.

Internal conflict on the left. Throughout the 1920s, however, much of the working class remained alienated from a regime that showed little concern for social reform. The CGT had emerged from the war with redoubled strength and energy, its membership swelled by the workers who had poured into new war industries in the Paris region. The Clemenceau government had rewarded labour for its war effort by legislating the eight-hour day in 1919; but when the unions pushed for more reforms, a deadlock ensued. An attempted general strike in May 1920 was easily broken, and thousands of discouraged and embittered workers abandoned the CGT. Labour's strength was further dissipated by the formation of rival Catholic and Communist trade-union federations in 1919 and 1921.

Socialist splitThe political influence of the workers was further impaired by a split in the Socialist Party in 1920. During the war, Socialist opposition to the slaughter had become increasingly vocal. The Bolshevik Revolution in Russia had reinforced this trend and offered a model that attracted many French Socialists. From 1918 onward, conflict intensified among Socialists over the possibility of joining Lenin's Comintern (Third International). At the party's annual congress in Tours in December 1920, Lenin's partisans carried the day by a large majority and shortly renamed their organization the French Communist Party (SFIC). The minority, headed by Jaurès's disciple Léon Blum, walked out of the congress and retained the traditional name SFIO. Throughout the 1920s antagonisms between these two Marxist factions hampered the left and prevented workable coalitions. Neither the Socialists nor the Communists would enter bourgeois-dominated Cabinets; the Communists refused even to make electoral agreements in support of a single left-wing candidate. The trend through the 1920s was steadily favourable to the Socialists, while the Communists steadily lost influence and members; in 1928 the Socialists won 107 seats, the Communists only 11. Many French Communists resented dictation from Moscow, and the decade saw a long series of resignations and purges; by 1930 the remnant had been thoroughly "Bolshevized" on the pattern of Lenin's own party.

The Great Depression and political crises. France at the end of the 1920s had apparently recovered its prewar stability, prosperity, and self-confidence. For a time it even seemed immune to the economic crisis that spread through Europe beginning in 1929; France went serenely on behind its high-tariff barrier, a healthy island in a chaotic world. By 1931, however, France in its turn succumbed to the effects of the Depression, and the impact was no less severe than elsewhere.

In 1932 the right-wing parties lost control of the Chamber to the Radicals and Socialists. The Radical leader Édouard Herriot returned to the premiership, with Socialist support but not participation. During the next two years Herriot and a series of successors groped for a solution to the deepening crisis. French nervousness was increased by the surge of Nazi power across the Rhine, culminating in Adolf Hitler's accession to the chancellorship in January 1933. Right-wing movements in France —some openly Fascist, others advocating a more traditional authoritarianism—grew in size and activity. By 1934 the shaky coalition was at the mercy of an incident —the Stavisky scandal, a sordid affair that tarnished the reputations of several leading Radicals. Antiparliamentary groups of the far right seized the occasion to demonstrate against the regime; on February 6 a huge rally near the Chamber of Deputies degenerated into a bloody battle with armed police, during which 15 rioters were killed and 1,500 injured. Premier Édouard Daladier, confronted by a threat of civil war, resigned in favour of a national union Cabinet under former president Gaston Doumergue. The regime survived the crisis, but serious stress persisted. Right-wing agitation was countered by unity of action on the left, grouping all the left-wing parties and the CGT; even the Communists participated in this effort, which culminated in 1935 in the formation of the Popular Front.Right-wing agitation

Doumergue's government had meanwhile disintegrated when Radical ministers resigned over the Premier's increasingly authoritarian tone. Doumergue was soon replaced by Pierre Laval, a former Socialist who had migrated toward the right. Laval embarked on a vigorous but unpopular attempt to combat the Depression through traditional techniques: sharp cuts in government spending and increased taxes. These policies wrecked his Cabinet early in 1936 and became campaign issues in the elections that spring. Those elections, probably the most bitterly contested since 1877, gave the Popular Front a narrow majority of the popular vote and a large majority in the Chamber. The Socialists for the first time became the largest party; but the greatest proportional gain went to the Communists, who jumped from ten to 72 seats.

Léon Blum, the Socialist leader, became premier. Blum, an intellectual, was the first French premier of Jewish origin. His ministers were mostly Socialists and Radicals; the Communists refused his urgent invitation to participate. At the very outset, a wave of sit-down strikes spread throughout the country, expressing workers' pent-up resentment toward past governments and their determination to get what they considered to be justice. Blum persuaded industrial leaders to grant immediate wage increases, which ended the strike. Then he pushed additional reforms through Parliament: the 40-hour week, paid vacations, collective bargaining, and the semi-nationalization of the Bank of France. Many other reform bills, however, were stalled in committee or in the Senate, which remained much more conservative than the Chamber.

Blum's social reforms were costly and controversial and were not buttressed by a program of economic reforms that might have stimulated production and restored confidence. Production surged briefly, then lagged again; unemployment remained high, rising prices offset wage gains, a flight of capital set in. When Blum attempted to impose exchange controls, the Senate rebelled and overthrew his cabinet (June 1937). The Popular Front held together for another year, but the Socialists and Radicals were irretrievably divided on economic policy. In April 1938 France returned once more to the usual pattern of homogeneous centre coalitions, with the Socialists in opposition. The Radical Daladier served as premier in 1938–40; his finance minister, Paul Reynaud, suspended most of the Popular Front reforms and sought economic recovery through more orthodox policies favoured by business.

German aggressions. Meanwhile, Hitler's accession had placed French governments in an increasingly grave foreign-policy dilemma. By 1934 many French leaders believed that a return of "Poincarism" was in order, and Doumergue's foreign minister, Louis Barthou, set out to reinforce and extend France's alliance system. He reaffirmed French ties with Poland and the "Little En-

Reinforcement and extension of alliances

tente" countries and sought new understandings with both Italy and the Soviet Union. Barthou's assassination in late 1934 weakened the new alliance policy, though Pierre Laval in 1935 paid visits to both Rome and Moscow and actually signed a mutual assistance treaty with the U.S.S.R.

Mussolini's invasion of Ethiopia in late 1935 and Hitler's military reoccupation of the Rhineland in March 1936 were serious blows to French policy. After consulting the British, the French Cabinet decided not to risk a confrontation with Hitler, who thus won a major diplomatic victory. Hitler promptly fortified the Rhine frontier, so that French guarantees of military aid to eastern European allies lost much credibility. Furthermore, Hitler and Mussolini joined forces against the status quo powers. With Italy lost, Frenchmen of the centre and right grew cool toward closer ties with the Soviet Union; they had counted on Italy to counterbalance Soviet influence. France found itself dangerously isolated, dependent on the small eastern European countries and on the uncertain prospect of British military support in crisis. Not surprisingly, French policy after 1936 showed signs of weakness and drift.

The outbreak of the Spanish Civil War in July 1936 posed a severe problem of conscience for Blum's Popular Front government: whether to send aid to the Spanish republic, the only other Popular Front regime in Europe. Reluctantly, Blum remained aloof; his Radical allies strongly opposed intervention and threatened to bring down the Cabinet. A new crisis developed in March 1938, when Hitler's troops for the first time crossed a frontier —into Austria. The French and British confined themselves to formal protests. German pressure on Czechoslovakia followed. Although France was formally committed to aid Czechoslovakia in case of aggression, Premier Daladier succumbed to British pressure to appease Hitler by a compromise settlement. The Munich Agreement of September 30 provided a breathing space but caused sharp dissension and self-doubt in France. When Hitler occupied what was left of Czechoslovakia in March 1939, it appeared to be too late for successful diplomatic or military resistance to Hitler, yet a failure to resist would hand over the Continent to German domination. From April until August the French and British sought to bring the Soviet Union into a joint pact against Hitler, with the French pressing the reluctant British to take the risks involved. A Soviet pact with Hitler instead was the last in a long chain of disasters for France. On September 3, two days after Germany invaded Poland, the French and British governments reluctantly declared war on Germany.

War against Germany

French and British attempts to aid the Poles would have been ineffective even if tried. Hitler's offer of peace immediately after Poland fell was rejected by the Western Allies. The Nazi armies smashed through The Netherlands and Belgium on May 10, 1940, and soon broke the French defensive lines near Sedan. The German blitz brought chaos all along the Allied front. In Paris, Premier Paul Reynaud (who had replaced Daladier in March) pleaded for emergency aid from Britain and the United States; the British sent some additional air units but were unwilling to denude their island of all air defense; President Roosevelt offered moral encouragement but not open intervention.

On June 10, with the Germans approaching Paris, the government departed for Tours and declared Paris an open city. British Prime Minister Winston Churchill twice flew to Tours in an effort to keep France in the war. But Reynaud, who favoured continued resistance (from North Africa, if necessary) rapidly lost ground to the defeatists in his Cabinet, headed by Pétain. On June 14 the Cabinet left Tours for Bordeaux. Churchill, in a last desperate effort, proposed a pact of "indissoluble union" that would merge France and Britain as a single nation. By the time the proposal reached Bordeaux on June 16, however, the Pétain faction had gotten control of the Cabinet. Reynaud resigned that evening; Pétain was appointed in his place and asked Germany for surrender terms. On June 22 an armistice was signed with the Germans, near Compiègne, in the same railway car that had been the scene of Foch's triumph in 1918. The armistice provided for the maintenance of a quasi-sovereign French state and for the division of the country into an occupied zone (northern France plus the western coast) and an unoccupied southern zone. France was made responsible for the German Army's occupation costs. The French Army was reduced to 100,000 men, the navy disarmed in its home ports.

Surrender to Germany

Society and culture under the Third Republic. Under the Third Republic the middle and lower sectors of society came to share political and social dominance with the rich notables. Universal suffrage gave them a new political weapon; France's peculiar socio-economic structure gave them political weight.

Economy. Republican France remained a nation of small producers, traders, and consumers. The surge of industrialization that marked the era of Napoleon III had stopped short of a full-scale industrial revolution. The new dynamic sector of the economy was far outweighed by a static or slowly changing sector. The bulk of industry remained smaller and more dispersed than in other industrializing countries. As late as the decade before 1914, 90 percent of France's industrial enterprises employed fewer than five workers each; in the extensive textile and clothing trades more than half of the employees still worked at home rather than in factories. Commerce and trade followed the same pattern, with small shops and banks surviving in profusion. Similarly, rural France was dominated by small, subsistence family farms. The proportion of farmers in the total active population, which stood at 52 percent in 1870, was still about 45 percent in 1914 and 35 percent in 1930. When grouped together, the small independent producers, traders, and farmers far outnumbered any other segment of society, including the proletariat.

The reasons given for this slow pace of socio-economic change are varied: shortages of basic natural resources; a tradition of specialization in luxury items; a code of mores that emphasized prudent management rather than risky experiment and that regarded as ideal the "family firm," small enough to be financed and managed by the owners alone. In any case, French industrialization took a different form from that of England or Germany. An initial burst of growth in the 1850s was followed by several decades of much more gradual expansion, which did not threaten the existing structure of society and the underlying value system. Most segments of society were reasonably satisfied and felt no threat to their way of life (only the members of the working class, both urban and agricultural, considered themselves outsiders and victims rather than participants); thus, the stability of the system was ensured. Not until well into the 20th century, and especially after 1918, did this state of affairs begin to change.

The governments of the Third Republic were representative of the small independents and responsive to their interests. Most of the bourgeoisie and the peasantry wanted a laissez-faire policy: low taxes, hands off the affairs of private citizens. There was little popular enthusiasm for costly ventures in foreign policy or expensive social reforms; the major exception—the conquest of colonial empire—had to be accomplished somewhat secretively and with limited resources. Only in tariff policy was laissez-faire flagrantly violated by the government, with the active consent of its bourgeois supporters. When the low-tariff treaties of Napoleon III expired in 1877, the government promptly returned to protectionism. Much of French agriculture and industry was thereby protected against more efficient foreign producers and insulated against the need for modernization. The short-range interests of the small, independent producer were thus guaranteed; the prospect of harm to his longer range interests—as well as to those of the nation as a whole—was not yet clear.

Laissez-faire policy

From 1873 to the mid-1890s the French economy experienced a period of slackness. This trend reflected a condition affecting most of Europe, although in France an epidemic of phylloxera in 1875–87 destroyed one-third of the nation's vineyards. From 1896 to 1914 industrial output rose impressively, exports increased by 75 percent, prices returned to the pre-slump level; this upturn was also generally European-wide rather than peculiar to France; but some special factors, such as the opening of a vast new iron-ore field in French Lorraine, did increase the French rate of industrial expansion. By 1914 French Lorraine had become the major centre of French iron and steel production, and France had become the world's largest exporter of raw iron ore (primarily to Germany). Yet the French were being outpaced by rivals. In 1870 France had still ranked as the world's second industrial and trading nation; by 1914 it had fallen to a poor fourth. Much of the liquid capital that might have been used for business expansion at home was being siphoned off into foreign investment; by 1914 almost one-third of such available French capital had been placed abroad—one-fourth of that sum in Russia, only one-tenth in the French colonies. Yet few Frenchmen had serious doubts about the course of economic policy under the Third Republic.

Only after the war, and particularly after 1930, were such doubts widely shared. The disruptive impact of the war exceeded the understanding not only of most citizens but also of most political leaders. Efforts to return to normality were futile because the postwar world and France had changed vastly. The enormous cost of a four-year mobilization, of reconstruction, of war debts, had to
Economic effects of World War I be borne. By the time of the Depression the government had been forced to write off a large share of war costs by devaluing the franc (1928) to one-fifth of its old value, costing many Frenchmen on fixed incomes much of their savings and shaking their confidence in the future. Still, no large group of embittered déclassés was created, ripe for the appeals of a demagogue. And after 1926 there was a brief resurgence of prosperity, so that by the end of the decade the indexes of industrial production, foreign trade, and living standards had risen well above the 1914 peak. Some illusions about the future and hopes of a happy return to prewar stability could therefore be retained.

But by 1935 industrial production had fallen to 79 percent of the 1928 level and exports to 55 percent. Registered unemployment hovered at less than 500,000, but this figure concealed the fact that many urban workers were subsisting on family farms owned by relatives. Besides, the French exported much of their unemployment: thousands of immigrant workers lost their work permits and had to return home. Not until 1938–39 did a measure of recovery set in, thanks to Reynaud's business-oriented policies, plus the stimulus of rearmament. By the time war broke out again, France had barely returned to the pre-Depression level.

The workers, always outside the bourgeois consensus, were by now largely hostile to the system; most of the gains they had finally achieved in 1936 had quickly been snatched away again. But in addition, many bourgeois Frenchmen now questioned the virtues of the traditional system. The 1930s therefore brought an intense fermentation of political and social thought; dozens of study groups and movements sprang up in Paris, seeking or preaching doctrines of drastic renovation and structures of government that might carry them out.

Cultural attainments. The cultural climate of the later 19th century in France, as in the Atlantic world general-
Positivism ly, was strongly marked by the current called Positivism. The post-1848 generation looked with contempt on what it considered the excesses and the bad taste of the preceding Romantic era. A new interest in science and a new vogue of Realism in literature and the arts prevailed during the Second Empire; it was best embodied in the novels of Gustave Flaubert and the paintings of Gustave Courbet. By the 1870s this mood had formed into what its advocates regarded as a coherent philosophic system, the content and label of which they borrowed from the French thinker Auguste Comte. These self-styled Positivists placed their faith in science and reason as the path to inevitable progress, with only the remnants of superstition (surviving mainly in the church) still blocking

the hopeful future. Although the two most influential thinkers of the early Third Republic, Hippolyte Taine and Ernest Renan, rejected the Positivist label, their writings strongly reinforced the cult of reason and science. Examples of the Positivist temper included the novelist Émile Zola and the Impressionist painters; *e.g.*, Édouard Manet, Claude Monet, Edgar Degas, Pierre-Auguste Renoir. In a scientific age, Frenchmen showed great creativity in pure science and made major discoveries in a wide variety of fields. Among the most notable figures were Louis Pasteur in medicine, Pierre and Marie Curie in physics, Marcelin Berthelot in chemistry, Henri Poincaré in mathematics, and Jean-Martin Charcot in psychopathology. The social sciences attracted fewer French pioneers, though the work of Gustave Le Bon in social psychology and Émile Durkheim in sociology had a broad and enduring impact.

Although the Positivist mood prevailed at least until World War I, it was contested by a rival current of thought that from the 1890s onward began to assert itself. To some sensitive men of artistic temperament the Positivist outlook seemed arid and narrow, much too indifferent to the emotional side of man—such was the view of the school of poets, including Paul Verlaine and Stéphane Mallarmé, who called themselves symbolists. A remarkable group of composers carried this romantic mood into music: the orthodox works of Jules Massenet, Georges Bizet, and Camille Saint-Saëns were followed by the more experimental compositions of Claude Debussy and Maurice Ravel.

Of significance was the growing influence after 1890 of such writers and thinkers as Paul Bourget, Maurice Barrès, and Henri Bergson and such painters as Paul Cézanne and Paul Gauguin. Bourget's novels challenged what he called "brutal positivism"; he attacked the search for a new ethical code derived from science and asserted such traditional values as authority, the family, and the established order. Barrès preached what he called "integral nationalism"; he called for a return to "the sources of national energy," which he found in historic institutions, the soil of the fatherland, and the solidarity between the living and the dead. Bergson, the philosopher whose lectures at the Collège de France became Parisian social events, attacked scientific dogmatism and exalted man's nonrational drives—notably a creative force that he called *élan vital*, distinguishing heroic men and nations from the plodding herd.

This new spirit had its parallel in political thought and action as well: in the syndicalist doctrines of Georges Sorel, in the activism of a minority in the labour movement, and in the resurgent nationalism that strongly affected many young Frenchmen in the years just before 1914. The new mood brought a return to the church and to an intense, emotional patriotism. In the fine arts, a younger school (including Georges Braque, Pablo Picasso, Henri Matisse, and Georges Rouault) broke violently with the Impressionists and moved toward a more intense subjectivism, an attempt to express the artist's inner vision and deeper emotions. Seeking their inspiration in the work of Paul Cézanne and Paul Gauguin, they burst upon the art world in 1905 with such impact that critics took to calling them the Fauves (the wild beasts).

The terrible strain and disillusionment of World War I weighed heavily on French cultural life during the interwar era, leading to the development of the literary and artistic movement called Dadaism, the calculated nonsense of which was inspired by a deep revulsion against the insanity of war and against the Positivist view that the world had sense and meaning. Dadaism soon gave way, though, to the more durable Surrealist movement and its principal theorist, the poet André Breton. The declared goal of Surrealist writers and artists was to free man's unconscious impulses from the distorting controls of rational reflection; creativity, they said, came from deep nonrational drives.

Alongside these self-conscious literary and artistic schools, a number of France's most notable writers remained within the older humanistic tradition, yet likewise reflected the doubts and neuroses of an age of crisis. Marcel Proust, whose massive multivolume novel *À la recherche du temps perdu* (*Remembrance of Things Past*) began to appear in 1913, used the stream-of-consciousness technique to probe, in minutely introspective fashion, into the recesses of his own mind and memory. André Gide, in similarly sensitive and introspective fashion, wrestled with the psychological difficulties arising from the conflict between a bourgeois society's values and the individual's instinctive drives.

As the mood of crisis deepened in the 1930s, so did the intensity of the challenge to old values, bringing men of frankly Fascist temper, such as Robert Brasillach, and brutally nihilistic literary experimenters, such as Louis-Ferdinand Céline. But other Frenchmen continued to create works in the older tradition: the social commentary of Roger Martin du Gard, Georges Duhamel, Jules Romains, and François Mauriac; the neoromantic novels of André Malraux, preaching a modern gospel of heroic activism; the first writings of Jean-Paul Sartre; and the essays of Emmanuel Mounier, who was to inspire the new Catholic left after World War II.

FRANCE SINCE 1940

Wartime France. The German victory left Frenchmen groping for a new policy and new leadership suited to the circumstance. Some 30 prominent politicians—among them Édouard Daladier and Pierre Mendès-France—left for North Africa to set up a government-in-exile there; but Pétain blocked that enterprise by ordering their arrest on arrival in Morocco. The Undersecretary of War in the fallen Reynaud Cabinet, Gen. Charles de Gaulle, had already flown to London and in a radio appeal on June 18, 1940, summoned patriotic Frenchmen to continue the fight; but few heard or heeded his call in the first weeks. It was to Pétain, rather, that most of the nation looked for salvation.

The Vichy government. Parliament met at Vichy on July 9–10 to consider France's future. The session was dominated by Pierre Laval, Pétain's vice premier, who was already emerging as the strong man of the government. Laval, convinced that Germany had won the war and would thenceforth control the Continent, saw it as his duty to adapt France to the new authoritarian age. By skillful manipulation, he persuaded parliament to vote itself and the Third Republic out of existence. The vote (569 to 80) authorized Pétain to draft a new constitution. The draft was never completed; but Pétain and his advisers did embark on a series of piecemeal reforms, which they labelled a National Revolution. Soon the elements of a corporative state began to emerge, and steps were taken to decentralize France by reviving the old provinces. In the early stages of Vichy, Pétain's inner circle—except for Laval and a few others—was made up of right-wing traditionalists and authoritarians. The real pro-Fascists, such as Jacques Doriot and Marcel Déat, who wanted a system modelled frankly on those of Hitler and Mussolini, soon left Vichy in disgust and settled in Paris, where they accepted German subsidies and intrigued against Pétain.

In December 1940 Pétain dismissed Laval and placed him briefly under house arrest. Laval had offended Pétain and his followers by his arrogance and his obvious taste for power. His critics charged him also with attempting to bring Vichy France back into the war in alliance with the Germans. Both Laval and Pétain had accepted Hitler's invitation to a meeting at Montoire on October 24, 1940; and during the weeks that followed, the French leaders had publicly advocated Franco-German "collaboration." Whether Laval hoped for a real Franco-German alliance remains somewhat controversial. If so, it was a futile effort because Hitler had no interest in accepting France as a trusted partner; "collaboration" remained a French and not a German slogan. Hitler tolerated the temporary existence of a quasi-independent Vichy state as a useful device to help police the country and to collect the enormously inflated occupation costs levied by the armistice.

Laval was succeeded by another prewar politician,

The end of the Third Republic

Pierre-Étienne Flandin, and he, in turn, by Adm. François Darlan, who was intensely anti-British and an intriguer by nature and who followed a devious path that involved continuing efforts at active collaboration with the Germans. Hitler, meanwhile, concentrated on draining France of raw materials and foodstuffs useful for the conduct of the war.

In April 1942 Pétain restored Laval to power, partly under German pressure. Laval retained that post until the collapse of Vichy in 1944. His role was increasingly difficult because the terrible drain of the war in the Soviet Union forced the Germans to increase their exactions. The Germans were short of manpower for their factories, and Laval, under heavy pressure, agreed to the conscription of able-bodied French workers in return for the release of some French prisoners of war. He also assumed the task of repressing the French underground movement, whose activities hampered the delivery of supplies and men to Germany. After the war, Laval and his friends were to argue that he had played a "double game" of limited collaboration to protect France against a worse fate. The alternative, they contended, would have been a German gauleiter who would have liquidated all resisters and deported all able-bodied men.

Much of Vichy's remaining autonomy and authority was destroyed in November 1942, in direct consequence of the Anglo-American landings in North Africa. Vichy troops in Morocco and Algeria briefly resisted the American invasion, then capitulated when Admiral Darlan, who happened to be visiting Algiers at the time, negotiated an armistice. On November 11 Hitler ordered his troops in the occupied zone to cross the demarcation line and to take over all of France. The Vichy government survived but only on German sufferance—a shadowy regime with little power and declining prestige.

German control of all France

The Resistance. Vichy's decline was paralleled by the rise of the anti-German underground. Within weeks of the 1940 collapse, tiny groups of Frenchmen had begun to resist. Some collected military intelligence for transmission to London; some organized escape routes for British airmen who had been shot down; some circulated anti-German leaflets; some engaged in sabotage of railways and German installations. The Resistance movement received an important infusion of strength in June 1941, when Hitler's attack on the Soviet Union brought the French Communist Party into active participation in the anti-German struggle. It was further reinforced by the German decision to conscript French workers; many draftees took to the hills and joined guerrilla bands that took the name maquis. And a kind of national unity was finally achieved in May 1943, when de Gaulle's personal representative Jean Moulin succeeded in establishing a Conseil National de la Résistance (National Resistance Council) that joined all the major movements in one federation.

De Gaulle's original call for resistance had attracted only a handful of Frenchmen who happened to be in Britain at the time. But as the British continued to fight, a trickle of volunteers from France began to find its way to his headquarters in London. De Gaulle promptly established an organization called Free France and in 1941 capped it with a body called the Comité National Français (French National Committee), for which he boldly claimed the status of a legal government-in-exile. During the next three years, first in London and then (after 1943) in Algiers, he insisted on his right to speak for France and on France's right to be heard as a great power in the councils of the Allies. His demands and his manner irked Churchill and Roosevelt and caused persistent tension. The American government unsuccessfully attempted in 1942 to sidetrack him in favour of Gen. Henri Giraud, who, immediately after the Allied landings in North Africa, was brought out of France to command the French armies in liberated North Africa and to assume a political role as well. De Gaulle arrived in Algiers in May 1943 and joined Giraud as co-president of a new French Committee of National Liberation. By the end of the year he had outmanoeuvred Giraud and emerged as the unchallenged spokesman for French resisters everywhere. Even

The Free France organization

the Communists in 1943 grudgingly accepted his leadership.

Liberation. When the Allied forces landed in Normandy on June 6, 1944, the armed underground units had grown large enough to play an important role in the battles that followed—harassing the German forces and sabotaging railways and bridges. As the Germans gradually fell back, local Resistance organizations took over town halls and prefectures from Vichy incumbents. De Gaulle's provisional government immediately sent its own delegates into the liberated areas to ensure an orderly transfer of power. On August 19 Resistance forces in Paris launched an insurrection against the German occupiers, and on August 25 Free French units under Gen. Jacques Leclerc entered the city. De Gaulle himself arrived later that day, and on the next he headed a triumphal parade down the Champs-Élysées. Most high-ranking Vichy officials (including Pétain and Laval) had moved eastward with the Germans; at the castle of Sigmaringen in Germany they adopted the posture of a government-in-exile.

De Gaulle's provisional government, formally recognized at last in October 1944 by the American, British, and Soviet governments, enjoyed unchallenged authority in liberated France. But the country had been stripped of raw materials and food by the Germans; the transportation system was severely disrupted by air bombardment and sabotage; 2,500,000 French prisoners of war, conscripted workers, and deportees were still in German camps; and the task of liquidating the Vichy heritage threatened to cause grave domestic stress. An informal and spontaneous purge of Vichy officials or supporters had already begun in the summer of 1944; summary executions by Resistance bands appear to have exceeded 10,000.

Retribution against Vichy officials

A more systematic retribution followed. Special courts set up to try citizens accused of collaboration heard 125,000 cases during the next two years. Approximately 50,000 offenders were punished by "national degradation" (loss of civic rights for a period of years); almost 40,000 received prison terms; between 700 and 800 were executed.

The Fourth Republic. Shortly after his return to Paris, de Gaulle announced that the citizens of France would determine their future governmental system as soon as the absent prisoners and deportees could be repatriated. That process was largely completed by midsummer 1945, whereupon de Gaulle scheduled a combined referendum and election for October. By an overwhelming majority (96 percent of the votes cast), the nation rejected a return to the prewar regime. The mood of the liberation era was marked by a thirst for renovation and for change.

New men of the Resistance movement dominated the constituent assembly, and the centre of gravity was heavily to the left; three-fourths of the deputies were Communists, Socialists, or Christian Democrats who had adhered to the new party of the Catholic left—the Mouvement Républicain Populaire (MRP).

Constitution of the Fourth Republic. After confirming de Gaulle in his post as provisional president, the Assembly turned to the drafting of a new constitution. Almost at once it became clear that the apparent unity forged in the Resistance was superficial and that the dominant parties differed sharply over what form the new republic should take. Most of the Christian Democrats looked to Britain or the United States for their model; they held that prewar France had been hampered by a weak, unstable executive branch and that the president and the Cabinet must henceforth be strong enough to counterbalance the power of Parliament. The Communists wanted all power vested in a one-house legislature whose members would be subject to recall by the voters at any time; the executive branch, in their view, should be merely a kind of delegated committee of parliament. The Socialists wavered and sought a compromise between these two positions.

De Gaulle remained aloof from this controversy, though it seemed obvious that he preferred the strengthened-executive pattern. Indeed, the Communists alleged that the partisans of a strong presidency had designed it for an authoritarian occupant, de Gaulle himself; their warnings had some effect on the Socialists, many of whom were likewise suspicious of both de Gaulle and his Christian Democratic supporters. De Gaulle, sensing that the Socialists would join forces with the Communists, abruptly resigned the presidency in January 1946, announcing that his task had been completed; he expected that a wave of popular protest would follow, forcing his return to office on terms that would frustrate the aims of the left-wing parties. Most Frenchmen were astounded and confused by his actions, and no such protest followed. The Assembly promptly chose a Socialist politician, Félix Gouin, as provisional president, and de Gaulle bitterly withdrew to his country estate.

De Gaulle's resignation

In May 1946 the Assembly presented its draft constitution to the voters for approval; the document represented a compromise on many issues but leaned perceptibly toward legislative domination. A clear majority of the voters rejected the draft. A new constitution was quickly drafted; it was, in fact, a somewhat revised version of the first, with a number of safeguards introduced by the Christian Democrats. It provoked de Gaulle's active intervention; he denounced the draft as unworkable and potentially disastrous and sketched out publicly for the first time his own idea of the institutional structure France needed—a stronger, more independent executive and a greatly weakened parliament. Despite his opposition, the voters in October 1946 approved the draft by a narrow margin.

Political and social changes. The institutional structure of the Fourth Republic seemed remarkably like that of the Third; in actual operation it seemed even more familiar. The lower house of parliament (now renamed the National Assembly) was once more the central locus of power; shaky coalition Cabinets again succeeded one another at brief intervals, and the lack of a clear-cut majority in the country or in Parliament hampered any vigorous or coherent action. Many politicians from the prewar period turned up once again in Cabinet posts, and the revived Radical Party furnished premiers on several occasions.

Yet outside the realm of political structure and parliamentary gamesmanship, there were real and fundamental changes. The long sequence of crises that had shaken the nation since 1930 had left a deep imprint on French attitudes. There was much less public complacency; both the routines and the values of Frenchmen had been shaken up and subjected to challenge by a generation of upheaval. Many of the new men who had emerged from the Resistance movement into political life, into business posts, or into the state bureaucracy retained a strong urge toward renovation, toward a reassertion of France's lost greatness.

This altered mood helps to explain the economic growth that marked the later years of the Fourth Republic. After a painful period of slow recovery from the war, aided by massive economic aid from the United States, a burst of industrial expansion in all branches of the economy began in the mid-1950s, unmatched in any decade of French history since the 1850s. The rate of growth for a time rivalled that of Germany and exceeded that of most other European countries. The only serious flaw in the boom was a nagging inflationary trend that weakened the franc and undermined the competitiveness of French exports. Short-lived coalition Cabinets were incapable of taking the painful measures that were needed to check this trend.

Industrial expansion in the 1950s

Colonial independence movements. A less fortunate aspect of the national urge to reassert France's stature in the world was the Fourth Republic's costly effort to hold the colonial empire. France's colonies had provided de Gaulle with his first important base of support as leader of Free France; and as the war continued, they had furnished valuable resources and manpower. The colonial peoples, therefore, now felt justified in demanding a new relationship with France; and French leaders recognized the need to grant concessions. But most of these leaders, including de Gaulle, were not prepared to permit any infringement on French sovereignty, either immediately or in the foreseeable future. For a nation seeking to rebuild its self-respect, the prospect of a loss of empire seemed unacceptable; and most Frenchmen were convinced that the native peoples overseas lacked the necessary training for self-government and that a relaxation of the French grip would merely open the way to domination by another imperial power. The constitution of 1946 therefore introduced only mild reforms: the empire was renamed the French Union, within which the colonial peoples would enjoy a narrowly limited local autonomy plus some representation in the French parliament.

This cautious reform came too late to win acceptance in many parts of the empire. The situation was most serious in Indochina, where the Japanese had displaced the French during World War II. Japan's defeat in 1945 enabled the French to regain control of southern Indochina, but the northern half was promptly taken over by a Vietnamese nationalist movement headed by the Communist Ho Chi Minh. French efforts to negotiate a compromise with Ho's regime broke down in December 1946, and a bloody eight-year war followed. In the end, the financial and psychological strain proved too great for France to bear, and, after the capture of the French stronghold of Dien Bien Phu by the Vietnamese, the French sought a face-saving solution. A conference of interested powers at Geneva in 1954 ended the war by dividing Vietnam temporarily into independent northern and southern states. Two other segments of Indochina, the former protectorates of Laos and Cambodia, had earlier been converted by the French into independent monarchies to preserve some French influence there.

On the night of October 31, 1954, barely six months after the fighting in Indochina ended, Algerian nationalists **Algerian** raised the standard of rebellion. By 1958 more than a half **revolt** million French soldiers had been sent to Algeria—the largest overseas expeditionary force in French history. France's determination to hold Algeria stemmed from a number of factors: the presence of almost a million European settlers; the legal fiction that Algeria was an integral part of France; and the recent discovery of oil in the southern desert. Fears that the rebellion might spread to Tunisia and Morocco led the French to make drastic concessions there; in 1956 both of these protectorates became sovereign states.

The long and brutal struggle in Algeria gravely affected the political life of the Fourth Republic and ended by destroying it. A vocal minority of French openly favoured a negotiated settlement, though no political leader dared take so unpopular a position. Right-wing activists, outraged at what they saw as the spread of defeatism, turned to conspiracy; both in Paris and in Algiers, extremist groups began to plot the replacement of the Fourth Republic by a tougher regime, headed by army officers or perhaps by General de Gaulle.

These plans had not yet matured when a Cabinet crisis in April–May 1958 gave the conspirators a chance to strike. On May 13, when a new Cabinet was scheduled to present its program to the National Assembly, activist groups in Algiers went into the streets in an effort to influence parliament's vote. By nightfall they were in control of the city and set up an emergency government with local army support. De Gaulle on May 15 announced that he was prepared to take power if called to do so by his fellow citizens. Two weeks of negotiations followed, interspersed with threats of violent action by the Algiers rebels. Most of the Fourth Republic's political leaders reluctantly concluded that de Gaulle's return was the only alternative to an army coup that might lead to civil war. On June 1, therefore, the National Assembly voted de Gaulle full powers for six months, thus putting a *de facto* end to the Fourth Republic.

The Fifth Republic. During his years of self-imposed exile, de Gaulle had scorned and derided the Fourth Republic and its leaders. He had briefly sought to oppose the regime by organizing a Gaullist party, but he had soon abandoned this venture in disgust and had retired to the seclusion of his country estate. Back in power, he adopted a more conciliatory line; he invited a number of old politicians to join his Cabinet, but he made sure that his own ideas would shape the future by naming his disciple Michel Debré head of a commission to draft a new constitution. This draft, approved in a referendum in September by 79 percent of the valid votes cast, embodied de Gaulle's conceptions of how France should be governed. Executive power was considerably increased at the expense of the National Assembly. The president of the republic was given much broader authority; he would henceforth be chosen by an electorate of local notables rather than by parliament, and he would select the premier, who would continue to be responsible to the National Assembly but would be less subject to its whims. In the new National Assembly, elected in November, the largest block of seats was won by a newly organized Gaullist party, the Union pour la Nouvelle République (UNR); the parties of the left suffered serious losses. In December de Gaulle was elected president for a seven-year term and appointed Debré as his first premier.

De Gaulle's first presidential term.   The new president's most immediate problems were the Algerian conflict and the inflation caused by the war. He attacked the latter, with considerable success, by a program of deflation and austerity. As for Algeria, he seemed at first to share the views of those whose slogan was "Algérie française"; but as time went by, it became clear that he was seeking a compromise that would keep an autonomous Algeria loosely linked with France. The Algerian nationalist leaders, however, were not interested in compromise, while the diehard French colonists looked increasingly to the army for support against what they began to call de Gaulle's betrayal. Open sedition followed in 1961, when a group of high army officers headed by Gen. Raoul Salan formed the Organisation de l'Armée Secrète (OAS) and attempted to stage a coup in Algiers. When the insurrection failed, the OAS turned to terrorism; there were several attempts on de Gaulle's life. The President pushed ahead nevertheless with his search for a settlement with the Algerians that would combine independence with guarantees for the safety of French colonists and their property. Such a settlement was finally worked out, and in a referendum (April 1962) more than 90 percent of the **Free** war-weary French voters approved the agreement. An **Algeria** exodus of European settlers ensued; 750,000 refugees flooded into France. The burden of absorbing them was heavy, but the prosperous French economy was able to finance the process despite some psychological strains.

The Algerian crisis speeded the process of decolonization. Some concessions to local nationalist sentiment had already been made during the 1950s, and de Gaulle's new constitution had authorized increased self-rule. But the urge for independence was irresistible, and by 1961 virtually all of the French territories in Africa had demanded and achieved it. De Gaulle's government reacted shrewdly by embarking on a program of military support and economic aid to the former colonies; most of France's foreign-aid money went to them. This policy encouraged the emergence of a French-speaking bloc of nations, which gave greater resonance to France's role in world affairs.

The Algerian settlement brought France a respite after 16 years of almost unbroken colonial wars. Premier Debré resigned (1962) and was replaced by one of de Gaulle's closest aides, Georges Pompidou. The party leaders now began to talk of amending the constitution to restore the powers of the National Assembly. Faced by this prospect, de Gaulle seized the initiative by proposing his own constitutional amendment; it provided for direct popular election of the president, thus further increasing his authority. De Gaulle's critics denounced the project as unconstitutional; a vote of censure in the National Assembly forced the Pompidou Cabinet to resign (October 6). De Gaulle retaliated by dissolving the assembly and ordering a referendum on his constitutional amendment. On October 28, 62 percent of those voting gave their approval, and in the elections (November) the Gaullist UNR won a clear majority in the new National Assembly. Pompidou was reappointed premier.

De Gaulle's second term. In 1965 de Gaulle's presidential term ended, and he declared himself a candidate for re-election. Not since 1848 had a French president been chosen by direct universal suffrage. The parties of the left coalesced behind a single candidate, François Mitterrand, and forced de Gaulle into a runoff when he fell short of an absolute majority at the first ballot. His runoff victory was narrow. His leadership had clearly failed to end the old divisions among the French. Yet the achievements of Gaullist rule were hard to ignore. He had not only disengaged France from Algeria without bringing on civil war at home, but he could also point to a steady rise in the gross national product, a solid currency, a stability of government greater than any living Frenchman had known, and a marked rise in France's international stature. France had adjusted to its new role in the European Common Market with profit rather than damage to its economy. De Gaulle could now safely indulge in such luxuries as blocking Britain's entry into the Common Market, ejecting NATO forces from France, lecturing the United States on its Vietnam policy, and calling for a "free Quebec." Most French applauded his assertive foreign policy and seemed content with the order and prosperity that accompanied his paternalistic rule.

In these circumstances, the sudden crisis of May 1968 took almost everyone by surprise. Student disorders in the universities of the Paris region had been endemic for some time; they exploded on May 3, when a rally of student radicals at the Sorbonne was broken up by the police. This minor incident quickly developed into a major confrontation: barricades went up in the Latin Quarter; street fighting broke out; the Sorbonne was occupied by student rebels and converted into a huge commune. The unrest spread to other universities and then to the factories as well; a wave of strikes rolled across France, involving several million workers and virtually paralyzing the nation. Pompidou ordered the police to evacuate the Latin Quarter and embarked on round-the-clock negotiations with labour leaders, but their agreement on improved wages and working conditions collapsed when the rank-and-file in the factories refused to end the strike.

By the last week in May, various radical factions were openly seeking to convert the crisis into a true revolution that would bring down the Fifth Republic. De Gaulle seemed incapable of grappling with or even understanding the crisis. The Communists and the trade union leaders, however, provided him with a breathing space; they opposed the radical activists' schemes, evidently fearing the loss of their followers to their more extremist and anarchical rivals. In addition, many middle class French who had initially enjoyed the excitement lost their enthusiasm as they saw established institutions disintegrating before their eyes. De Gaulle, seizing the opportune moment, mysteriously departed from Paris by helicopter on May 29. Rumours at once spread that he was about to resign.

Instead, he returned the next day with a promise of support, if needed, from the commanders of the French forces in Germany. In a dramatic four-minute radio address, he appealed to the partisans of law and order, decreed the dissolution of the National Assembly, and presented himself as the only barrier to anarchy or Communist rule. Loyal Gaullists and nervous citizens rallied round him; left-wing resistance collapsed when the Communists refused to consider a resort to force. The confrontation moved from the streets to the polls; and there, on June 23 and 30, the Gaullists won their greatest landslide. In the new National Assembly the Gaullist Union des Démocrates pour la République, or UDR (formerly UNR), with its allies, could count on three-quarters of the seats.

The repercussions of the crisis were nevertheless profound. The government, shocked by the depth and extent of discontent, made a series of concessions to the protest groups. Workers were granted improved wages and working conditions; the assembly unanimously adopted a university reform bill, intended to modernize higher education and to give teachers and students a voice in running their universities. De Gaulle took the occasion to shake up his Cabinet; the most surprising victim was Pompidou, who was replaced (July) by Maurice Couve de

Murville. De Gaulle evidently sensed the emergence of Pompidou as a powerful rival, for the Premier had shown toughness and nerve during the crisis, while the President had temporarily lost his bearings. The economy also suffered from the upheaval, which threw the budget badly out of balance and undermined the franc. Austerity measures were needed to stabilize things once more.

Although France gradually returned to normal, de Gaulle remained baffled and irritated by what the French called "the events of May." Perhaps it was to reaffirm his leadership that he proposed another test at the polls: a pair of constitutional amendments to be voted on by referendum. Their content was somewhat confusing and of secondary importance; yet de Gaulle threw his prestige into the balance, announcing that he would resign if the amendments were repudiated by the voters. Every opposition faction seized upon the chance to challenge the President. On April 27, 1969, the amendments were rejected by 53 percent of the voters, and next day de Gaulle announced his departure from office. He returned to the obscurity of his country estate, where he adhered to a strict vow of silence and turned once more to the writing of his memoirs. There, just before his 80th birthday, he died of a stroke. His passing inspired an almost worldwide chorus of praise for this extraordinary statesman.

France after de Gaulle. De Gaulle's resignation raised a double question: could his party and his new governmental system survive his departure? For a time at least, the answer seemed to be affirmative. The Gaullists closed ranks around Georges Pompidou, and he was elected in June 1969 by an impressive margin over several candidates of the left or centre. Pompidou chose another Gaullist, Jacques Chaban-Delmas, as his premier. Both men kept asserting their unswerving loyalty to the Gaullist heritage, but their style of leadership contrasted with that of the quasi-monarchical de Gaulle. Pompidou adopted a milder tone in foreign policy, easing tensions with the United States and encouraging the entry of Britain into the Common Market. At home, he showed a tendency to favour classical laissez-faire doctrines, in harmony with the bias of his industrialist and banker friends. Chaban-Delmas, on the other hand, spoke of making France over into what he called a "new society," more modern, more dynamic, more socially just. These differences contributed to a cooling of relations between the President and the Premier and eventually (July 1972) to the replacement of Chaban-Delmas by Pierre Messmer, one of de Gaulle's earliest and most fervent disciples.

Pompidou's inclination toward a conservative, business-oriented policy also encouraged a revival of the left, which had been badly shattered by the events of May–June 1968. François Mitterrand, leader of a small left-wing faction, managed in 1971 to bring about a merger of several small left-wing groups with the old but hidebound Socialist Party. Mitterrand was promptly elected secretary general of the rejuvenated party and initiated discussions with the Communists and some dissident Radicals which culminated in 1972 in a "Common Program" providing for cooperation in future elections and in an eventual left-wing government. When the National Assembly's term expired in March 1973, the leftist coalition made impressive electoral gains at the expense of the Gaullist UDR, which lost almost 100 seats. Leftist hopes were buoyed by the fact that they had won a clear majority of the popular vote and had shown special strength among young voters. They now set their sights on the presidency; Pompidou's term was due to end in 1976.

Their opportunity came sooner than expected. In April 1974 Pompidou, who had been ailing for some time, died suddenly, and this time the Gaullists failed to unite in choosing a successor. Their party caucus nominated Chaban-Delmas, but a sizable minority of Gaullists then broke discipline and came out in support of Valéry Giscard d'Estaing, candidate of the businessmen's party called the Républicains Indépendants. While the right-wing forces split, the left coalition stood solidly together behind Mitterrand as their sole candidate. He led the pack at the first round of voting, while Giscard came second, clearly outdistancing Chaban-Delmas. In the

[margin notes] Crisis in 1968 · De Gaulle's resignation · Revival of the left

Election
of Giscard
d'Estaing

runoff on May 19, Giscard eked out a narrow victory, receiving 50.8 percent of the vote. The Gaullists emerged from the campaign divided and embittered; their loss of the presidency for the first time since 1958 seemed to presage their disintegration as a political force. Still, they remained the largest party in the National Assembly, and Giscard's cabinets would be dependent on their support.

Giscard's relative youth and energetic style reminded the French of John F. Kennedy, who was said to be one of his models. Despite his ties with a conservative business party, he announced his intention to transform France into what he called an "advanced liberal society." His program included such reforms as reduction of the voting age to 18, relaxed controls on the use of contraceptives and on abortion, a capital-gains tax, and measures designed to satisfy the growing environmental movement in France. Giscard chose as his premier an even younger man, Jacques Chirac, who had led the Gaullist dissidents in supporting Giscard for the presidency. But Giscard's ambitious plans for social and economic change were quickly overtaken by the worldwide recession brought on in part by the sudden increase in the price of Middle Eastern oil. For the first time in 20 years, French industrial production stagnated; in 1975 the gross national product actually declined. Unemployment emerged as a new and serious problem, one that most of the contemporary French population had never encountered. And an old and well-known problem reappeared: inflation rose to about 10 percent a year.

These grave difficulties undermined Giscard's initial popularity and played into the hands of the left-wing coalition. Opinion polls showed a steady rise of support for the left; most of the gains went to the renovated Socialist Party, which was clearly outpacing the Communists as the leading force on the left. Meanwhile Giscard's problems were intensified by increasing friction with Chirac, whose restless ambition was coming into the open. In August 1976 Giscard pressured Chirac into resigning and replaced him with a nonpolitical "technician"—the economist Raymond Barre. Chirac's response was to consolidate his personal power base, from which he could challenge Giscard for leadership of the fight to save France from what he called the menace of collectivism. He persuaded the decaying UDR to transform itself into a more disciplined and dynamic Rassemblement pour la République (RPR; Assembly for the Republic) and to make him its president (December 5, 1976). In March 1977 he announced his candidacy for the revived post of mayor of Paris and gained a triumphant victory over Giscard's hand-picked candidate. Giscard began to seem hopelessly outclassed by this energetic and ruthless rival; some observers thought that Chirac would force him to resign the presidency. But neither Chirac nor Giscard, it seemed, would be able to stem the powerful surge of the left as it prepared for victory in the National Assembly elections due in March 1978.

All of these apparent certainties collapsed, however, when the Socialist-Communist coalition fell apart in September 1977. Leaders of the two parties had been at odds over various issues ever since the agreement on a Common Program in 1972, and the conflict intensified as the prospect of taking power became imminent. Apparently the Communists, who had initially expected to be the dominant partner in the coalition and in a future left-wing government, had no desire to enter such a government run by the Socialists and preferred to scuttle the coalition rather than play second fiddle to their Socialist partners. Whatever the motives behind the split, the effect was to destroy the left's chances; voters asked themselves how the left could govern France if its elements could not even campaign together. The elections of March 19, 1978, therefore turned into a surprising triumph for Giscard and his supporters. Giscardiens and Gaullists together won 288 seats compared to 199 for the fragmented left. And within the governing majority, it was Giscard's supporters who made the greatest gains, while Chirac's RPR suffered relative losses. The President thus emerged with a new lease on life. Yet his ability to govern France remained precarious, since his premier, Raymond Barre, still needed

Elections
of 1978

RPR support in the assembly to push through legislation and even to remain in office. Chirac during the months that followed grudgingly provided such support, but his rancour toward Giscard foreshadowed an eventual crisis. Thus the crucial political question of the post-Gaullist era was out in the open: could de Gaulle's new quasi-presidential system continue to function effectively without a de Gaulle to create and bind together a loyal assembly majority? If not, an executive–legislative confrontation seemed sooner or later inevitable. And almost as important was a second open question: had the parties of the left, by missing their great opportunity to take power in 1978, condemned themselves to political sterility for the next generation? Still, for observers of the French political scene there remained one consoling thought: that the French throughout their history have often managed to come up with surprises.   (G.Wr.)

BIBLIOGRAPHY

France in the early Middle Ages—c. 850–1180: HEINRICH FICHTENAU, *Das Karolingische Imperium* (1949; Eng. trans., *The Carolingian Empire,* 1957), a standard work on the Carolingian period; JAN DHONDT, *Études sur la naissance des principautés territoriales en France, IXᵉ–Xᵉ siècle* (1948), covers the origins of the great feudal territories of France; MARC BLOCH, *Les Caractères originaux de l'histoire rurale française,* 2 vol. (1952–56; Eng. trans., *French Rural History,* 1971); and GEORGES DUBY, *L'Économie rurale et la vie des campagnes dans l'Occident médiéval,* 2 vol. (1962; Eng. trans., *Rural Economy and Country Life in the Medieval West,* 1968), two studies of rural life during the Middle Ages; ROBERT BOUTRUCHE, *Seigneurie et féodalité,* 2 vol. (1959–70), a study of the manor and the feudal system; CHARLES PETIT-DUTAILLIS, *La Monarchie féodale en France et en Angleterre, Xᵉ–XIIIᵉ siècle* (1933; Eng. trans., *The Feudal Monarchy in France and England, from the Tenth to the Thirteenth Century,* 1936, reprinted 1964); ACHILLE LUCHAIRE, *Les Premiers Capétiens, 937–1137: Louis VII, Philippe-Auguste, Louis VIII,* 2 vol. (1901); MARCEL PACAUT, *Louis VII et son royaume* (1964); and *Les Structures politiques de l'Occident médiéval* (1969), studies of the Capetian kings; LEON and ALBERT MIROT, *Manuel de géographie historique de la France,* 2nd ed., 2 vol. (1947–50), a geographic aid to the study of French history; WILLIAM M. NEWMAN, *Le Domaine royal sous les premiers Capétiens* (1937), on the early history of the French royal domain; FERDINAND LOT and ROBERT FAWTIER, *Histoire des institutions françaises au Moyen-Age,* 2 vol. (1957); SIDNEY PAINTER, *The Rise of the Feudal Monarchies* (1951) and *French Chivalry: Chivalric Ideas and Practices in Mediaeval France* (1940); DAVID KNOWLES, *The Christian Centuries,* vol. 2, *The Middle Ages* (1968) and *Christian Monasticism* (1969); see also the relevant volumes of *The Cambridge Medieval History.*

France in the later Middle Ages—1180–1490: GEORGES DUBY and ROBERT MANDROU, *Histoire de la civilisation française,* vol. 1 (1958; new ed., 1968; Eng. trans., *A History of French Civilization,* 1964), stressing social history. The volumes in the older *Histoire de France,* 9 vol., ed. by ERNEST LAVISSE (1900–11), remain useful for this period, as also, for political history, the chapters on France in *The Cambridge Medieval History,* vol. 6–8 (1929–36). The period 1180–1328 is well treated by ROBERT FAWTIER in *Les Capétiens et la France* (1942; Eng. trans., *The Capetian Kings of France,* 1960), and, as part of a more general review of recent scholarship, by LEOPOLD GENICOT, *Le XIIIᵉ Siècle européen* (1968). Two good accounts of the later period are EDOUARD PERROY, *La Guerre de cent ans* (1945; Eng. trans., *The Hundred Years War,* 1951); and PETER S. LEWIS, *Later Medieval France: The Polity* (1968). For recent work in a broader perspective, see JACQUES HEERS, *L'Occident aux XIVᵉ et XVᵉ siècles, aspects économiques et sociaux,* 2nd ed. (1966). The best studies of individual reigns are by OTTO CARTELLIERI (Philip-Augustus), in German; CHARLES PETIT-DUTAILLIS (Louis VIII), CHARLES-VICTOR LANGLOIS (Philip III), RAYMOND CAZELLES (Philip VI), and ROLAND DELACHENAL (Charles V)—all in French. JOSEPH R. STRAYER, *The Administration of Normandy Under Saint Louis* (1932), is a valuable study; for taxation and consultation under the later Capetians, see JOSEPH R. STRAYER and CHARLES H. TAYLOR, *Studies in Early French Taxation* (1939). For economy and society, see GEORGES DUBY (*op. cit.*). On social unrest, see MICHEL MOLLAT and PHILIPPE WOLFF, *Ongles bleus, Jacques et Ciompi: les révolutions populaires en Europe aux XIVᵉ et XVᵉ siècles* (1970). The standard account of the towns is CHARLES PETIT-DUTAILLIS, *Les Communes françaises . . .* (1947).

France from 1490 to 1715: DAVID BUISSERET, *Les "Économies Royales" de Sully* (1970), the best recent analysis of Sully's contribution; JEAN P. CHARMEIL, *Les Trésoriers de France à*

l'époque de la Fronde (1964); ROGER DOUCET, Les Institutions de la France au XVIe siècle, 2 vol. (1948), indispensable; and Étude sur le gouvernement de François Ier dans ses rapports avec le Parlement de Paris, 2 vol. (1921–26); R.J. KNECHT, Francis I and Absolute Monarchy (1969), a useful survey; A.D. LUBLINSKAYA, French Absolutism: The Crucial Phase, 1620–1629 (1968; orig. pub. in Russian, 1965), an influential contribution to the recent discussion on the economic crisis of the 17th century; JAMES RUSSELL MAJOR, Representative Institutions in Renaissance France, 1421–1559 (1960); DAVID MALAND, Culture and Society in Seventeenth-Century France (1970); ROBERT MANDROU, Classes et luttes de classes en France au début du XVIIe siècle (1965); ROLAND MOUSNIER, La Vénalité des offices sous Henri IV et Louis XIII (1945), a seminal work by the most distinguished French historian of the period; and (ed.), Lettres et mémoires adressées au Chancelier Séguier, 1633–1649, 2 vol. (1964), the introduction contains Mousnier's conclusions on the controversial subject of popular uprisings during this period; BORIS PORCHNEV, Les Soulèvements populaires en France de 1623 à 1648 (1963); OREST RANUM, Richelieu and the Councillors of Louis XIII (1963), important for an understanding of Richelieu's real position; J.H. SHENNAN, Government and Society in France, 1461–1661 (1969) and The Parlement of Paris (1968); N.M. SUTHERLAND, The French Secretaries of State in the Age of Catherine de Medici (1962); VICTOR L. TAPIE, La France de Louis XIII et de Richelieu (1952); GASTON ZELLER, Les Institutions de la France au XVIe siècle (1948). (The Age of Louis XIV): LOUIS ANDRE, Louis XIV et l'Europe (1950), a valuable survey; EUGENE L. ASHER, The Resistance to the Maritime Classes (1960); CHARLES W. COLE, Colbert and a Century of French Mercantilism, 2 vol. (1939); PIERRE GOUBERT, Louis XIV et vingt millions de français (1966; Eng. trans., Louis XIV and Twenty Million Frenchmen, 1970), a recent, challenging synthesis of Louis's reign; and Beauvais et le Beauvaisis de 1600 à 1730, 2 vol. (1960), a penetrating social analysis; GEORGES LIVET, L'Intendance d'Alsace sous Louis XIV, 1648–1715 (1956); HERBERT LUTHY, La Banque protestante en France de la révocation de l'Edit de Nantes à la Révolution, 2 vol. (1959–61); HUBERT METHIVIER, Le Siècle de Louis XIV, 5th ed. (1968); JEAN ORCIBAL, Saint-Cyran et le Jansénisme (1961); LIONEL ROTHKRUG, Opposition to Louis XIV (1965); JOHN C. RULE (ed.), Louis XIV and the Craft of Kingship (1969), contains stimulating essays, especially R.M. HATTON's sympathetic analysis of Louis's foreign policy aims; WARREN C. SCOVILLE, The Persecution of Huguenots and French Economic Development, 1680–1720 (1960), important in assessing the effects of the revocation of the Edict of Nantes; JOHN B. WOLF, Louis XIV (1968).

France from 1715 to 1789: HUBERT METHIVIER, L'Ancien Régime, 2nd ed. (1964), is a useful introduction, as is C.B.A. BEHRENS, The Ancien Régime (1967). A Marxist interpretation can be found in ALBERT SOBOUL, La France à la veille de la Révolution (1966); and ALEXIS DE TOCQUEVILLE, L'Ancien Régime et la Révolution (1856; Eng. trans., The Old Régime and the French Revolution, 1955), is still basic; see ALFRED COBBAN, A History of Modern France, vol. 1, Old Régime and Revolution, 1714–1799 (1957). ROBERT FORSTER, The Nobility of Toulouse in the Eighteenth Century (1960), is one of the principal sources used by BARRINGTON MOORE in his Social Origins of Dictatorship and Democracy (1966), which deals in part with the French Revolution. ELINOR BARBER, The Bourgeoisie in 18th Century France (1955); J.H. SHENNAN, The Parlement of Paris (1968); and FRANKLIN FORD, Robe and Sword (1953) are useful. GEORGES DUBY and ROBERT MANDROU (op. cit.), is a survey of economic, social, and cultural history. HENRY SEE, La France économique et sociale au XVIIIe siècle (1925; Eng. trans., Economic and Social Conditions in France During the Eighteenth Century, 1927, reprinted 1968), is less original but still useful. All economic histories make much use of the 18th-century work of ARTHUR YOUNG, Travels in France During the Years 1787, 1788, 1789.

France from 1789 to 1815: The classic 19th-century histories of the French Revolution are those by ADOLPHE THIERS, 2nd ed., 10 vol. (1828–29; Eng. trans., 5 vol., 1894); by FRANCOIS MIGNET, 2 vol. (1824; Eng. trans., 1826); by JULES MICHELET, especially for its literary qualities, 7 vol. (1847–53; new ed., 2 vol., 1961–62; Eng. trans., 1967); by LOUIS BLANC, 12 vol. (1847–62). Some works that are theoretical rather than historical should also be mentioned: THOMAS CARLYLE, The French Revolution, 3 vol. (1837, reprinted 1972); ALEXIS DE TOCQUEVILLE (op. cit.), of the utmost importance; EDGAR QUINET, La Révolution, 2 vol. (1865); and HIPPOLYTE TAINE, Les Origines de la France contemporaine, 6 vol. (1887–94; Eng. trans., The Origins of Contemporary France, 6 vol., 1931), marked by anti-Revolutionary prejudice. Dating from the end of the 19th and the beginning of the 20th century: ALPHONSE AULARD, Histoire politique de la Révolution française (1901; Eng. trans., The French Revolution: A Political History, 1789–

1804, 1910); JEAN JAURES, Histoire socialiste de la Révolution française, 12 vol. (1901–08, reprinted 1968); P. SAGNAC, La Révolution, 1789–1792, and G. PARISET, La Révolution, 1792–1799, vol. 1 and 2 of the Histoire de France contemporaine, ed. by ERNEST LAVISSE (1920–22); ALBERT MATHIEZ, La Révolution française, 3 vol. (1925–27); Eng. trans., The French Revolution, 3 vol., 1956). An outstanding study is GEORGES LEFEBVRE, La Révolution française, 3rd ed. rev. and updated by ALBERT SOBOUL (1963; Eng. trans., The French Revolution, 2 vol., 1962–64). Recent findings are included in ALBERT SOBOUL, Précis d'histoire de la Révolution française (1962). Historical works in English include CRANE BRINTON, A Decade of Revolution, 1789–1799 (1963); LEO GERSHOY, The French Revolution and Napoleon (1933, reprinted 1964) and The Era of the French Revolution, 1789–1799: Ten Years That Shook the World (1957); JAMES M. THOMPSON, The French Revolution (1943); ALFRED COBBAN (op. cit.); ROBERT R. PALMER, The Age of the Democratic Revolution: A Political History of Europe and America, 1760–1800, 2 vol. (1959–64). The best history of Napoleon and his period is still GEORGES LEFEBVRE, Napoléon, 6th ed. rev. and updated by ALBERT SOBOUL (1969; Eng. trans., 2 vol., 1969). See also EVGENII TARLE, Napoléon (1942); EMILE TERSEN, Napoléon (1959); and FELIX PONTEIL, Napoléon Ier et l'organisation autoritaire de la France, 2nd ed. (1966)—all in French. Especially from a bibliographical point of view, reference should be made to JACQUES GODECHOT, L'Europe et l'Amérique à l'époque napoléonienne (1967). In English, The Cambridge Modern History, vol. 9 (1934); and ROBERT R. PALMER, A History of the Modern World, 4th ed. (1971), are to be noted.

France since 1815: (General surveys of the period): ALFRED COBBAN, A History of Modern France, vol. 2–3 (1965), a sophisticated synthesis by a British specialist; GORDON WRIGHT, France in Modern Times, 2nd ed. (1974), an interpretive survey from an American viewpoint. (Surveys of special topics covering all or most of the period since 1815): ADRIEN DANSETTE, Histoire religieuse de la France contemporaine, 2 vol. (1948–51; Eng. trans., Religious History of Modern France, 2 vol., 1961), a lucid account of the church's role, by a Catholic moderate; RAOUL GIRARDET, La Société militaire dans la France contemporaine, 1815–1939 (1953), on the changing role and composition of the officer corps since 1815; RENE REMOND, La Droite en France, rev. ed. (1968; Eng. trans., The Right Wing in France from 1815 to de Gaulle, 2nd ed., 1969), tracing changes and continuity; PIERRE RENOUVIN, Histoire des relations internationales: Le XIXe siècle, 2 vol. (1954–55), stressing the role of France in world affairs; CHARLES P. KINDLEBERGER, Economic Growth in France and Britain, 1851–1950 (1964), weighing rival theories about France's slow industrial development; THEODORE ZELDIN, France, 1848–1945, 2 vol. (1973–77), on modern French society, stressing its complexity and continuity; EUGEN WEBER, Peasants into Frenchmen (1976), on rural France in the 19th century. (19th-century France): GUILLAUME DE BERTIER DE SAUVIGNY, La Restauration (1963; Eng. trans., The Bourbon Restoration, 1966), the standard work on this period; DAVID H. PINKNEY, The French Revolution of 1830 (1972), a probing re-examination; LOUIS GIRARD, La IIe République (1968), a fine synthesis of the period 1848–51; KARL MARX, Die Klassenkämpfe in Frankreich 1848 bis 1850 (1850; Eng. trans., The Class Struggles in France, 1848 to 1850, 1924, reprinted 1964) and The Civil War in France (1871, reprinted 1948), continue to influence the work of many historians; J.P.T. BURY, Napoleon III and the Second Empire (1964), a thoughtful and well-informed judgment; MICHAEL HOWARD, The Franco-Prussian War (1961), an outstanding study; STEWART EDWARDS, The Paris Commune, 1871 (1972), one of the best of the many centennial re-evaluations; D.W. BROGAN, France Under the Republic (1940), a classic account by a British scholar; JACQUES CHASTENET, Histoire de la troisième république, 7 vol. (1952–63), the most detailed treatment of this subject; DAVID THOMSON, Democracy in France Since 1870, 5th ed. (1969), a penetrating essay stressing political and social aspects; DOUGLAS JOHNSON, France and the Dreyfus Affair (1966), a good assessment of the great crisis. (20th-century France): EUGEN WEBER, Action Française (1962), clarifying many aspects of French politics; MARC FERRO, La Grande Guerre, 1914–1918 (1969; Eng. trans., The Great War, 1914–1918, 1973), a fine study; ROBERT O. PAXTON, Vichy France: Old Guard and New Order, 1940–1944 (1972), a fine analysis of the Pétain regime; CHARLES DE GAULLE, Mémoires de guerre, 3 vol. (1954–60; Eng. trans., War Memoirs, 5 vol., 1955–60), indispensable for an understanding of Gaullism; PHILIP WILLIAMS, Crisis and Compromise: Politics in the Fourth Republic, 3rd ed. (1964), a standard account of the political system; STANLEY HOFFMANN et al., In Search of France (1963), an analysis of postwar France; PIERRE VIANSSON-PONTE, Histoire de la République gaullienne, 2 vol. (1970–71), a noted journalist's judgment of the Fifth Republic's Gaullist phase.

(M.Pa./T.N.B./J.H.Sh./P.Hi./Al.S./G.Wr.)

Francis of Assisi, Saint

St. Francis of Assisi, known as the "seraphic saint," was the founder of the Franciscan orders of men and women and is (with Catherine of Siena) the principal patron saint of Italy. He assumed the leadership of the religious movements of the early 13th century that were attempting to reform the medieval church, morally scarred by its struggles with civil rulers. Francis' fraternal charity and total poverty, coupled with his magnetic personality, drew thousands of followers to his side during his life and have made him in each succeeding age one of the most venerated religious figures.

Alinari—Anderson

Saint Francis, detail of a fresco by Cimabue, late 13th century. In the Lower Church of the Basilica of S. Francesco, Assisi.

Early life and career   Francis was born in 1181/82 at Assisi in Umbria, the son of Pietro di Bernardone, a cloth merchant, and the lady Pica. Nothing certain is known of the family background. At Francis' birth, his father was away on a business journey to France, and his mother had him baptized Giovanni. On his return, Pietro di Bernardone changed the infant's name to Francesco; thus his full name was Francesco di Pietro di Bernardone. Francis learned to read and write Latin at the school near the church of S. Giorgo and later acquired some knowledge of the French language and literature, especially of the troubadours. He liked to speak French, although he never did so perfectly, and even attempted to sing in it. His youth does not seem to have been marked by serious moral lapses; nevertheless, an exuberant love of life and a general spirit of worldliness made him a recognized leader of the young men of the town.

In 1202 he took part in a war between Assisi and Perugia, was held prisoner for almost a year, and on his release fell seriously ill. After his recovery, he attempted to join the papal forces under Count Gentile against Frederick II in Apulia in late 1205; at Spoleto, however, he had a vision or dream that bade him return to Assisi and await a call to a new kind of knighthood. On his return, he began to give himself to solitude and prayer so that he might know the will of God for him.

Several other episodes make up what is called his conversion: a vision of Christ while he prayed in a grotto near Assisi; an experience of poverty during a pilgrimage to Rome, where, in rags, he mingled with the beggars before St. Peter's basilica and begged alms; an incident in which he not only gave alms to a leper (he had always felt a deep repugnance for lepers) but also kissed his hand. One day at the ruined chapel of S. Damiano outside the gate of Assisi, he heard the crucifix above the altar command him: "Go, Francis, and repair my house which, as you see, is well-nigh in ruins." Taking this literally, he hurried home, gathered much of the cloth in his

father's shop and rode off to the nearby town of Foligno, where he sold both cloth and horse. He then tried to give the money to the priest at S. Damiano. Angered, his father first kept him at home and later brought him before the civil authorities. When Francis refused to answer the summons, his father called him before the bishop. Before any accusations were made, Francis, "without a word peeled off his garments even down to his breeches and restored them to his father." Covered only by a hair shirt, he said: "Until now I have called you my father on earth. But henceforth I can truly say: Our Father who art in heaven." The astonished bishop gave him a cloak, and Francis went off to the woods of Mt. Subasio above the city.

Francis had renounced material goods and family ties to embrace a life of poverty. He repaired the church of S. Damiano, restored a chapel dedicated to St. Peter the Apostle and then the now-famous little chapel of St. Mary of the Angels (Santa Maria degli Angeli), the Porziuncola, on the plain below Assisi. There on the feast of St. Matthias, February 24, 1208, he listened at mass to the Gospel account of the mission of Christ to the Apostles: "Take no gold, nor silver, nor money in your belts, no bag for your journey, nor two tunics, nor sandals, nor a staff; for the labourer deserves his food. And whatever town or village you enter, find out who is worthy in it, and stay with him until you depart" (Matt. 10:9–11). Although a layman, he began to preach to the townspeople. Disciples were attracted to him, and he composed a simple rule of life for them. In 1209, when the group of friars (as the mendicant disciples were called) numbered 12, they went to Rome to seek the approval of Pope Innocent III, who, although hesitant at first, gave his verbal approbation to their rule of life. This event, which according to tradition occurred on April 16, marked the official founding of the Franciscan Order. The friars, who were actually street preachers with no possessions of any kind and with only the Porziuncola as a centre, preached and worked first in Umbria and then, as their numbers grew, in the rest of Italy.

The Franciscan rule of life

The early Franciscan rule of life, which has not survived, set as the aim of the new life, "To follow the teachings of our Lord Jesus Christ and to walk in his footsteps." Probably no one in history has ever set himself so seriously as did Francis to imitate the life of Christ and to carry out so literally Christ's work in Christ's own way. This is the key to the character and spirit of St. Francis. To neglect this point is to show an unbalanced portrait of the saint as a lover of nature, a social worker, an itinerant preacher, and a lover of poverty.

Certainly the love of poverty is part of his spirit, and his contemporaries celebrated poverty either as his "lady," in the allegorical *Sacrum Commercium* (Eng. trans., *Francis and His Lady Poverty*, 1964), or as his "bride," in the fresco of Giotto in the lower church of S. Francesco at Assisi. It was not, however, mere external poverty he sought but the total denial of self (as in Phil. 2:7).

He considered all nature as the mirror of God and as so many steps to God. He called all creatures his "brothers" and "sisters," and in his "Canticle of the Creatures" (less properly called by such names as the "Praises of Creatures" or the "Canticle of the Sun") he referred to "Brother Sun" and "Sister Moon," the wind and water, and even "Sister Death." His long and painful illnesses were nicknamed his sisters, and he begged pardon of "Brother Ass the body" for having unduly burdened him with his penances. Above all, his deep sense of brotherhood under God embraced his fellow men, for "he considered himself no friend of Christ if he did not cherish those for whom Christ died."

In 1212 Francis began a second order for women that became known as the Poor Clares. He gave a religious habit, or dress, similar to his own to a noble lady of Assisi, later known as St. Clare (Clara) of Assisi, and then lodged her and a few companions in the church of S. Damiano, where she was joined by women of Assisi. For those who could not leave their families and homes he eventually (c. 1221) formed the Third Order of Brothers and Sisters of Penance, a lay fraternity that, without withdrawing from the world or taking religious vows, would carry out the principles of Franciscan life.

As the friars became more numerous, the order extended outside Italy. Probably in the late spring of 1212 Francis had set out for the Holy Land but was shipwrecked on the east coast of the Adriatic Sea and had to return.

A year or two later, sickness forced him to abandon a journey to the Moors in Spain. In 1217 he proposed to go to France, but Cardinal Ugolino of Segni (later Pope Gregory IX) advised him that he was needed to direct the order in Italy. He did go to Egypt, where the crusaders were besieging Damietta, in 1219. He went into the camp of the Saracens and preached to the sultan, who was impressed by him and gave him permission (it is said) to visit the holy places in Palestine.

News of disturbances among the friars in Italy forced Francis to return. There were 5,000 members of the men's order, and it was continuing to grow at a faster rate than any previous religious order; yet the order had little more than Francis' example and his brief rule of life to guide its increasing numbers. To provide someone to handle the order's practical affairs, Francis appointed Peter Catanii as his vicar; after Peter's early death in 1221 he chose Elias of Cortona. Francis asked Pope Honorius III for legislation introducing a year of probation (novitiate) for new friars and set about amplifying and revising the rule. After the new rule was approved by Honorius III in final form on November 29, 1223, Francis tended to withdraw more and more from external affairs.

Francis' vision and the stigmata of the Crucified

In the summer of 1224 Francis went to the mountain retreat of La Verna (Alvernia), not far from Assisi, to celebrate the feast of the Assumption of the Blessed Virgin Mary (August 15) and to prepare for St. Michael's Day (September 29) by a 40-day fast. There he prayed that he might know how best to please God; opening the Gospels for the answer, three times he came upon references to the Passion of Christ. As he prayed one morning, about the time of the feast of the Exaltation of the Cross (September 14), suddenly he beheld a figure coming toward him from the heights of heaven. St. Bonaventure, general of the Franciscans from 1257 to 1274 and an important thinker of the 13th century, wrote:

> As it stood above him, he saw that it was a man and yet a Seraph with six wings; his arms were extended and his feet conjoined, and his body was fixed to a cross. Two wings were raised above his head, two were extended as in flight, and two covered the whole body. The face was beautiful beyond all earthly beauty, and it smiled gently upon Francis. Conflicting emotions filled his heart, for though the vision brought great joy, the sight of the suffering and crucified figure stirred him to deepest sorrow. Pondering what this vision might mean, he finally understood that by God's providence he would be made like to the crucified Christ not by a bodily martyrdom but by conformity in mind and heart. Then as the vision disappeared, it left not only a greater ardour of love in the inner man but no less marvelously marked him outwardly with the stigmata of the Crucified.

Francis took the greatest care to hide the stigmata—the same wounds in his hands, feet, and side as Jesus Christ—in his lifetime. After the death of Francis, Brother Elias announced the stigmata to the order by a circular letter. Later, Brother Leo, who was the confessor and intimate companion of the saint and who left a written testimony of the event, said that in death Francis seemed like one just taken down from the cross.

Francis lived two years longer, in constant pain and almost totally blind (he had contracted an eye disease in the East). Medical treatment at Rieti was unsuccessful, and after a stay at Siena he was brought back to Assisi, where he died at the Porziuncola on October 3, 1226. He was buried temporarily in the church of S. Giorgio, at Assisi. Francis was canonized a saint on July 16, 1228, by Gregory IX; his feast day is October 4. In 1230 his body was transferred to the lower church of the basilica that was being erected in his memory by Elias at the west end of the city.

BIBLIOGRAPHY

The writings of St. Francis: Critical editions by LEONARD LEMMENS (1901) and by H. BOEHMER (1904); English translations by PASCAL ROBINSON (1908), LEO SHERLEY-PRICE (1959). and BENEN FAHY, with introduction and notes by PLACID HERMANN (1964).

Early biographies: Thirteenth-century biographies include THOMAS OF CELANO, *First and Second Life of St. Francis, with Selections from Treatise on the Miracles of Blessed Francis,* trans. by PLACID HERMANN (1963), writings dated, respectively, 1228–30, 1247, and c. 1253—composed by a friar who knew Francis personally and had access to material furnished by his early companions; "The Legend of the Three Companions (1246)," in *St. Francis of Assisi: His Holy Life and Love of Poverty,* trans. by PLACID HERMANN (1964), likely a source for Celano's "Second Life"; ST. BONAVENTURE, *The Greater Life of St. Francis, and the Shorter Life,* trans. by BENEN FAHY, with introduction and notes by PLACID HERMANN (1965), a theologian's approach to the saint, with some new material gathered from surviving companions (1260–62). Fourteenth-century compilations abound; the following exist in English translations: *The Mirror of Perfection,* wrongly attributed to BROTHER LEO (trans. by LEO SHERLEY-PRICE, 1959; Everyman ed., 1963); The *Fioretti* or *Little Flowers of St. Francis,* ed. by RAPHAEL BROWN (1958), ed. by LEO SHERLEY-PRICE (1959), Everyman ed. (1963)—though full of legends and even falsifications, the work gives a certain insight into the Franciscan spirit of self-abnegation, love, and spiritual joy. A more complete listing and critical evaluation of the sources of the life of St. Francis, together with all important studies up to 1963, may be found in the appendixes to OMER ENGLEBERT, *Saint Francis of Assisi: A Biography,* 2nd ed. rev. by IGNATIUS BRADY and RAPHAEL BROWN (1965).

Modern biographies: JOHANNES JORGENSEN (1907; Eng. trans., 1912; 3rd ed., 1955); FATHER CUTHBERT (1912; new ed., 1956); G.K. CHESTERTON (1924, 1957); ENGLEBERT (*op. cit.*); for others, see RAPHAEL BROWN, in Englebert's *Saint Francis,* pp. 525–527. The development of the Franciscan movement within the lifetime of St. Francis is admirably treated by CAJETAN ESSER in *Origins of the Franciscan Order* (1970); and briefly, with a biographical sketch of St. Francis, in JOHN R. MOORMAN, *A History of the Franciscan Order from Its Origins to the Year 1517* (1968). The spirituality of the saint is studied by CAJETAN ESSER and ENGELBERT GRAU in *Love's Reply,* trans. by IGNATIUS BRADY (1963).

(I.C.B.)

Francis I of France

As full of contrasts as the period in which he lived, Francis I, king of France from 1515 to 1547, was in temperament a medieval knight-king, with a passion for feats of valour, for tournaments, and for adventures; but at the same time he was a stately Renaissance king, refined, open to new ideas, and a patron of the arts and Humanist scholarship. In a century in which the world and beliefs about it were changing drastically, he transformed his country's economy and society, uniting and enlarging a kingdom composed of different races, with different customs and languages.

Early years. The son of Charles de Valois-Orleáns, comte d'Angoulême, and Louise of Savoy, Francis of Angoulême was born at Cognac on September 12, 1494. On the accession of his cousin Louis XII in 1498, Francis became heir presumptive and was given the duchy of Valois. With his sister Marguerite, he was raised by his mother, who had been widowed at the age of 20 and whom he deeply revered; he knelt whenever he spoke to her. No one had as much power over him as these two women. Idolized, he grew up following his own whims, without discipline and more infatuated with chivalrous romances, songs, and violent exercise than with classical studies. He was greatly admired by the gay, young circle of his mother's cultured court for his athletic build, his gentlemanly courtesy, and the elegance of his demeanour and manners. His need for female companions stemmed from this upbringing, as did his lack of realism and his chivalrous imagination.

Louis XII, distrustful of Francis, did not allow him to dabble in affairs of state but sent him off at the age of 18 to the frontiers, which had been attacked in force. There, Francis learned more about warfare and, being of a sensuous nature, about the licentiousness of camp life than about how to govern the state or, even more, to govern

Francis I, portrait by Pierre Dumonstier (c. 1524–1604), after a
drawing by Jean Clouet. In the Bibliothèque Nationale, Paris.
By courtesy of the Bibliotheque Nationale, Paris

himself. Shortly before his death, Louis XII married him
to Claude, his 15-year-old daughter. On January 1, 1515,
at the age of 20, Francis became king of France.

His quick and shrewd mind, his amazing memory, and
his universal curiosity compensated for his inexperience.
But, because he was outgoing and trusting and incapable
of dissembling, he was always a bad politician. The pomp
of the Reims coronation, the sumptuous cortege of the
solemn entry into Paris, and the lavish feasts revealed his
love of ceremony and also pleased the people of Paris,
who had been disheartened by a long succession of
morose and sickly sovereigns.

Promise of a great reign. Louis XII had left an army
prepared to reconquer the duchy of Milan. This ill-fated
dream of recovering his great-grandmother Valentina
Visconti's heritage—which had been lost, retaken, then
lost again—fascinated Francis in his turn. Ambitious for
glory and urged on by turbulent young nobles, he made
sure of peace with his neighbours, entrusted the regency
to his mother, and galloped off to Italy.

Victory
in Italy

At the bloody Battle of Marignano, charging at the
head of his cavalry, he defeated the reportedly invincible
Swiss mercenaries of Duke Massimiliano Sforza and his
ally Pope Leo X. After the victory, by his own wish, he
was knighted by the captain who had fought most bravely: Bayard, the most famous chevalier of his time.

The Pope received his conqueror in Bologna. Surrounded by his glittering pontifical court and by his famous artists, he dazzled Francis with concerts, banquets,
and theatrical performances. The Pope offered him a
Madonna by Raphael and negotiated a concordat that
returned to the Pope the benefices of the rich church of
France, while the nomination of prelates was assigned
to the King, who was desirous of strengthening his authority over a clergy grown too acquisitive and independent.

Buoyed up by a victor's prestige, the King spoke as a
sovereign, using for the first time the formula of absolute
power: "For such is our pleasure." Prosperity permitted
him to grant a princely pension to Sforza, as well as to
Leonardo da Vinci and other artists who brought masterpieces to his court. He also signed a perpetual peace
treaty with the Swiss and bought back Tournai from
Henry VIII of England. And, as a pledge of unalterable
friendship, the first-born royal child, Princess Louise,
was affianced to the Habsburg prince Charles, heir to The
Netherlands and, at 16, the new king of Spain.

Everything forecast a great reign. Francis I formed a
brilliant and scholarly court at which poets, musicians,
and learned men mingled with rough noblemen from the
provinces whom idleness was making dangerous. He welcomed lovely ladies at court, saying, "A court without

women is a year without spring and a spring without
roses." The arts, elegance, and chivalrous gallantry
served to refine the licentious manners of the court.

The frail queen Claude, gentle and pious, bore a child
each year. Francis respected her and sought her advice.
In the meantime, he loved the dark-haired countess Françoise de Châteaubriand, without, however, foregoing gay
nocturnal escapades with his childhood companions, who
had now become his ministers and his favourites.

Francis toured France tirelessly, showing himself to
people who had never seen a king. He was constantly
travelling on horseback, winter and summer, whether
well or ill. He became familiar with everything: men,
roads, rivers, resources, and needs. During his travels,
he emptied prisons, curtailed the abuses of judicial powers by the nobles, lavished largesse on the people, and
provided games and processions for them, speaking to
them in his grand manner, warmly and openly: "My
friends, my beloved ones . . . ."

Popularity
among the
people

Popular, happy, the father of two sons, he was the most
powerful sovereign in all Christendom when, in 1519, the
German emperor Maximilian died. The election as emperor of Maximilian's grandson Charles spelled ruin for
Francis I, for Charles, who was already king of Spain,
now encircled France with his possessions.

Rivalry with Charles V. Nineteen years old, secretive,
cool-headed, and a clever politician, the Emperor had his
mind set on a universal monarchy. His chief obstacle
was the King of France. A mortal hatred emerged from
this rivalry, leading to 27 years of savage warfare, interrupted by truces that were invariably violated. In 1520,
on the Field of Cloth of Gold near Calais, where both
displayed unprecedented magnificence, Francis vainly
sought an alliance with Henry VIII.

Hostilities between Charles V and France began in 1521
in the north and in the Pyrenees, while the two brothers
of the King's mistress were losing Milan. The soldiers remained unpaid, and the army was disintegrating. The
King, unconcerned, arose late, paid little attention to his
council, and gave orders without seeing that they were
carried out. Money disappeared into thin air. A few pay-
masters were hanged, though in vain.

In 1523 the King demanded the return to the French
state, according to law, of the vast provinces that the
great feudal duke Charles de Bourbon thought he had
inherited from his wife. Incensed, Bourbon turned traitor
and joined the Emperor's service, claiming that the
French, weary of the prodigality of their sovereign,
would rise up on an appeal from him. Commanding the
imperial army, he invaded Provence, was driven back
near Marseilles, and withdrew toward Italy. Francis I
was pursuing him when he learned of the death of his
wife Claude, at the age of 24, exhausted from seven
pregnancies. The death of his second daughter followed
soon after. Meanwhile, the English and the Germans
were advancing in the north. In vain, his mother begged
him to return: "Our good angel has abandoned us. Your
horoscope forecasts disaster!" At the Battle of Pavia in
1525, defeated and wounded, he was taken prisoner.
"Madame, to inform you of the rest of my misfortune, I
have nothing left to me save my honour and my life."

Defeat
and
imprison-
ment

As the price for the King's freedom, the Emperor demanded one-third of France, the renunciation of France's
claim to Italy, and restitution to Bourbon of his fiefs,
with the addition of Provence. "I am resolved to endure
prison for as long as God wills rather than accept terms
injurious to my kingdom!" replied the King.

Imprisoned in a dismal tower in Madrid, watched over
day and night, the recluse composed melancholy poems,
songs, and letters to his subjects, heartrending in their
humility and their tender nobility. The mortifying defeat,
the dangerous situation of his country, and the confinement aggravated his habitual migraines, the consequence
of old wounds and of newly contracted syphilis. When he
was struck down by an abscess in his head, his people,
loyal in bad fortune as in good, prayed for him. The
Archbishop of Tournon said a mass at his bedside, in
the presence of his sister Marguerite, who had hastened
to Madrid.

Decline and death.   Although Francis finally recovered, he did not cease to suffer. His personality changed. Sudden reversals of mood, excesses of severity and clemency, inconsistencies in his statesmanship and in his personal behaviour marked him; his mind sometimes wandered.

The Emperor persisted in his exorbitant claims. Resigned to die in prison, the King abdicated in favour of his eldest son. France judged this abdication to be the worst possible move. The Dauphin was too young; the country was lost without its leader. No matter what the cost, he would have to return home. The French ambassadors, with only nominal cooperation by the King, concluded the harsh Treaty of Madrid. He signed it in January 1526, declaring that the word and signature of an imprisoned knight were valueless and that it was beyond his power to dismember his kingdom. Still bedridden, he was betrothed by proxy to Eleanor, widow of the King of Portugal and sister of his jailer. The wedding was to seal the reconciliation of the two rulers and was to follow execution of the treaty. As a last condition, Francis, grieving, had to deliver his two eldest sons, seven and eight years old, as hostages.

The surrendered provinces refused to divorce themselves from France. The Emperor, furious with the perjured King, held the children prisoner for four years. His army plundered Italy and captured Pope Clement VII. Francis could not openly engage in the war that was again flaring up everywhere against Charles V. Doomed to disavow his promises to his secret allies, he fled from their envoys, either going on hunting trips from forest to forest or travelling around the country, building fairy-like castles that he occupied only fleetingly and founding the free and secular Collège de France. Anne, duchesse d'Étampes, "the most beautiful of learned ladies, and the most learned of beautiful ladies," replaced Madame de Châteaubriand, more as a companion than mistress.

Their raging hatred impelled Charles and Francis to challenge each other to a duel, which was, however, prevented. During one of the King's relapses, his mother reached an agreement with Margaret of Austria, the Emperor's aunt, to stop this deadly struggle. The ensuing Treaty of Cambrai softened that of Madrid. In order to get his children back, Francis had to abandon his allies, give up Italy, and pay 2,000,000 gold crowns. His foolish expenditures had emptied the treasury, and the ransom was collected only with difficulty. Finally, however, the little princes were able to attend their father's political marriage to Eleanor in 1530.

In 1531 the King's mother succumbed to the plague. Marguerite, having married the King of Navarre, lived at some distance. The King, grown tragically old, in 1533 presided over the marriage of his second son, Henry, to Catherine de Médicis, the niece of Clement VII.

Attempts at religious conciliation

When religious strife broke out in France, the King—tolerant, an epicurean, an admirer of the Dutch Humanist Erasmus, and patron of the great satirist Rabelais, as well as a reader of Philipp Melanchthon, the Reformer—tried to moderate the growing fanaticism. Both his sister and his mistress supported the Reformation, whereas his ministers were zealous Catholics. But the Reformers were considered republicans, and the burnings at the stake began. For five years he delayed the extermination of the Waldensian sect, only signing the order without reading it when on his deathbed.

The war with Charles V was resumed in 1536. Bereavements within the family came in quick succession. The Dauphin died at the age of 18—poisoned by Charles V, it was believed. The third son, the most dearly loved, died of the plague. One of Francis' last diplomatic achievements was an alliance with the Turks against the Emperor.

Henry VIII, by turns friend or enemy, died in January 1547. Francis, younger by two years, still had time to found the port of Le Hâvre, to send Jacques Cartier to Canada, to reform the judicial system, and to decree the use of French in all legal documents.

Wasting away with fever, dying, he wandered from castle to castle, carried on a litter. Finally, on March 31,

1547, the knight-king died at Rambouillet. Notwithstanding the personal afflictions of the last 20 years of his life, Francis was to his countrymen and to the succeeding generation *le grand roi François*.

BIBLIOGRAPHY.   FRANCOIS MEZERAY, *Histoire de France . . .*, 3 vol. (1643–51), interesting and invaluable recollections by a contemporary historian; GABRIEL H. GAILLARD. *Histoire de François Premier*, 8 vol. (1769), profound scholarship; MARGUERITE DE NAVARRE, *Lettres de Marguerite d'Angoulême . . . reine de Navarre*, 2 vol. (1841–42), stories, poetry, and letters written to her brother, Francis I; LOUISE DE SAVOY, *Comptes de Louise de Savoie . . .* (1905), the journal (ending in 1822)—of the mother of Francis I most informative on their family relationship; JEAN B. HAUREAU, *François Ier et sa cour* (1853), a minutely documented study by curator of manuscripts at the Bibliothèque Nationale; FRANCOIS AUGUSTE MARIE MIGNET, *Rivalité de François Ier et de Charles V* (1875), a very precise account of the long and tragic confrontation of the two monarchs for supremacy in Europe; FRANCIS HACKETT, *Francis the First* (1934, reprinted 1968), one of the few book-length accounts in English of the life and times of Francis I.

(M.Vi.)

Francis Joseph I

The life of Francis Joseph I, emperor of Austria from 1848 to 1916 and after his coronation in 1867 as king of Hungary, is so intimately bound up with the destinies of Austria-Hungary that his biography is in many respects a history of that state. For one thing, the Emperor, more remarkable for his devotion to duty than for any great innate talents, remained throughout his reign the key figure of Austria-Hungary; for another, his private life, coloured by tragic events, was so overshadowed by his official position that it is impossible to separate the human being from the public figure.

Francis Joseph I, 1908.

Early years

Francis Joseph was born at Schönbrunn Palace near Vienna on August 18, 1830, the eldest son of Archduke Francis Charles and Sophia, daughter of King Maximilian I Joseph of Bavaria. As his uncle Ferdinand I was childless, Francis Joseph was educated as his heir-presumptive. Particular attention was given to his military training. In the spring of 1848 he served with the Austrian forces in Italy, where Lombardy-Venetia, supported by King Charles Albert of Sardinia, had rebelled against Austrian rule. When revolution spread to the capitals of the Austrian Empire, Francis Joseph was proclaimed emperor at Olmütz (Olomouc) on December 2, 1848, after the abdication of the emperor Ferdinand—the rights of his father, the archduke, to the throne having been passed over. Hopes of a revival of monarchist sentiments were raised by his radiant, youthful appearance.

Of all his mentors, the old chancellor Metternich, with his conservative interpretation of the concept of the great European powers, probably exerted the most lasting influence on Francis Joseph. A more profound influence, however, was that of his wife, who was the duchess Elizabeth of Bavaria. He married her in 1854 and remained deeply attached to her throughout a stormy marriage.

Neo-absolutism, 1848–59. During the first ten years of his reign, the era of so-called neo-absolutism, the Emperor—aided by such outstanding advisers as Felix, Fürst zu Schwarzenberg (until 1852), Leo, Graf von Thun, and Alexander, Freiherr von Bach—inaugurated a very personal regime by taking a hand both in the formulation of foreign policy and in the strategic decisions of the time. Together with Schwarzenberg, who had become prime minister and foreign minister in 1848, Francis Joseph set out to set his empire in order.

In external affairs Schwarzenberg achieved a powerful position for Austria; in particular, with the Olmütz convention of November 1850, in which Prussia acknowledged Austria's predominance in Germany. In home affairs, however, Schwarzenberg's harsh rule and the formation of an intolerant police apparatus evoked a latent mood of rebellion. This mood became more threatening after 1851, when the government withdrew the promise of a constitution, given in 1849 under the pressure of the revolutionary troubles. That retraction had long aftereffects and led to the Liberals' permanent distrust of Francis Joseph's rule. In 1853 the people's discontent made itself felt in an attempt on the Emperor's life in Vienna and in a riot in Milan.

After Schwarzenberg's death (1852), Francis Joseph decided not to replace him as prime minister and took a greater part in politics himself. Austria's mistaken policy during the Crimean War originated largely with the Emperor, who could not make up his mind between gratitude to Russia for its help in quelling a rebellion in Hungary in 1849 and the advantage the monarchy might derive from siding with Great Britain and France. The mobilization of a part of the Austrian army in Galicia on the borders of Russia, for which Francis Joseph was ultimately responsible, in retrospect turned out to have been a grave error. It gained no friends for Austria among the Western powers but lost considerable goodwill that Tsar Nicholas I had earlier harboured for Francis Joseph.

At home, neo-absolutism resulted in a civil service staffed by highly competent experts who tried to meet the Emperor's high standards but whose limitations nevertheless became increasingly obvious in 1859–60 as they attempted to deal with the empire's complex financial problems. Army expenditures had to be curtailed in 1859, when a series of ill-fated wars began that seriously shook Austria's military reputation. Moreover, the police regime proved to be impracticable in the long run. Thus the government made critical military decisions against a background of many unresolved problems in finances and home affairs. For many of these decisions the Emperor was responsible. This was especially true of the unfortunate outcome of the war of 1859 against the Kingdom of Sardinia and France. After provoking Austria into war, Count Cavour, the prime minister of Sardinia, planned to use the French Army to oust Austria from Italy. When the imperial commander in chief proved incapable, Francis Joseph himself took over the supreme command, but he could not prevent the defeat of Solferino (June 24, 1859). Dismayed by Prussia's demand that as a condition of its intervention on the Emperor's side the Austrian army be placed under Prussian command, Francis Joseph hastily concluded the Peace of Villafranca in July 1859, under which Lombardy was ceded to Piedmont.

War with Sardinia-Piedmont

Unreconciled to this settlement, Francis Joseph adopted a foreign policy that prepared the way for a passage at arms with Italy and Prussia, by which he hoped to regain for Austria its former position in Germany and Italy, as it had been established by Metternich in 1814–15.

The years of decision, 1859–70. The mood of crisis prevailing after the defeat of 1859 caused Francis Joseph to pay renewed attention to the constitutional question. A period of constitutional experiments—alternating between federalistic and centralistic charters—kept the country in a permanent state of crisis until 1867. The congress of princes at Frankfurt in 1863, for which the reigning heads of all German states assembled with the sole exception of the King of Prussia, was a high point in Francis Joseph's life. Yet the absence of the Prussian king demonstrated that Prussia no longer regarded Austria as the leading German power.

Francis Joseph had vainly tried to postpone the decision for predominance in Germany by entering into a comradeship-in-arms with Prussia in a war against Denmark in 1864. After their victory, squabbles arose between them, and war with Prussia became inevitable. The conclusion of an alliance between Italy and Prussia pointed up the dangerous possibility that both foreign-policy problems might have to be faced at the same time, yet Francis Joseph failed in his attempt to avoid an armed conflict at least with Italy. In June 1866 Austria concluded a possibly unique agreement with Napoleon III of France that stipulated that Austrian-held Venetia was to be given to the Kingdom of Sardinia regardless of the outcome of the impending war with Prussia. As the Emperor considered it incompatible with the army's honour to cede a province without fighting, war with Italy broke out despite this agreement. In later years, Francis Joseph characterized his policy of yielding territory with one hand while fighting for it with the other as very honest but very stupid, whereas the Chancellor Friedrich, Graf von Beust, called the agreement the most shocking document that he had ever seen. Although its defeat in the war with Prussia that the Prussian prime minister Otto von Bismarck had forced on the unprepared monarchy caused Austria no territorial loss in the north, it nevertheless sealed Austria's expulsion from Germany. Nor could the victories gained by the Austrian army in the south prevent the loss of Venetia, so that Austria found itself expelled from Italy as well.

War with Prussia and Italy

The appointment of the Saxon premier, Graf von Beust, as Austrian prime minister in 1867 shows that initially Francis Joseph was once again unwilling to accept the decision. Beust's cherished project of an Austrian–French–Italian alliance against Prussia did not materialize, however; and in 1870 the attitude of the Hungarian prime minister, Count Gyula Andrássy, coupled with the rapid military successes of Prussia, prevented Austria from joining in the Franco-Prussian War at the side of France. Andrássy, appointed imperial foreign minister after Beust's dismissal in 1871, inaugurated the policy of close collaboration with Germany that later became the cornerstone of Francis Joseph's foreign policy.

The Hungarian compromise and the Dual Monarchy. The failure to achieve a federalist solution satisfactory to all nationalities had exacerbated relations among them. In 1867 it had become obvious that a compromise had to be made with the restive Hungarians. The newly appointed prime minister Beust was, however, insufficiently informed about conditions in the various parts of the Austrian Empire. The result was the *kaiserliche und königliche Doppelmonarchie*, the "imperial and royal Dual Monarchy" in which an Austrian and a Hungarian half coexisted in equal partnership. The compromise, however, gave the Hungarians considerable leverage to extend their influence. The losers were the Slav peoples, for the Bohemians (Czechs) and Poles did not share in the privileged position of the German Austrians in the Austrian, or western, half of the empire, while the Croats, Slovaks, and South Slavs had none of the prerogatives enjoyed by the Hungarians in the Hungarian, or eastern, half. With this preferred treatment, which Francis Joseph recognized as such, the multinational state had violated its inner law of the basic equality of all national groups. The individual crownland's relationship to the emperor, which in each case had been the result of a long historical evolution, was now replaced by the submission of the various nationalities to German-Austrian or Hungarian overlordship. Internal restlessness thus continued unabated. A final attempt at reform by which the

Refusal to satisfy Slav aspirations

Slavic languages were to be given equal status with Hungarian and German was vetoed by Francis Joseph under pressure from the German-Austrian nationalists. But, under the influence of the Viennese sociologist Albert Schäffle, the Emperor, who on the whole had little use for party politicians and their influence on public life, seems to have followed the continuing process of democratization in his empire with some sympathy.

Relations
with
Serbia

The question of recognition and restoration of ancient Czech rights hobbled Austro-Hungarian foreign policy and poisoned domestic politics. Even more of a handicap was the problem of the South Slavs. From 1867 on, the Hungarian-ruled Croatians found themselves subjected to a continuing process of Magyarization, Hungarian domination, eventually turned Serbia, inhabited by fellow Slavs, into the Dual Monarchy's mortal enemy.

Francis Joseph, who wholeheartedly supported the Ausgleich (Hungarian Compromise) as the constitution of the dual monarchy, failed to grasp the negative aspects of that highly complex document. Interested primarily in questions of foreign policy and military leadership, he paid too little attention to domestic affairs to understand the nationalities problem in all its gravity and urgency. In particular, he failed to see the connection between Austro-Hungarian internal affairs and their effect on the monarchy's relationship with Russia and on the political situation in the Balkans.

The German treaty and the Emperor's peace policy. Although Francis Joseph always considered foreign policy his own specialty, he was in effect guided by the ablest among his foreign ministers: Count Gyula Andrássy, Count Gusztáv Kálnoky von Köröspatak, and Count Alois Aehrenthal. Andrássy not only launched the German alliance in 1879, but, by carrying out the occupation of Bosnia-Hercegovina, which Francis Joseph had advocated and the Congress of Berlin (1878) had sanctioned, he also gained the first great foreign-policy success of the empire in the Balkans. The Emperor defended the German alliance against all opposition. He was considerably more reserved toward Italy, which had joined Germany and Austria in the Triple Alliance in 1882, and Romania, with which Austria-Hungary had concluded a secret treaty in 1883; in fact, his reticence contributed to the eventual alienation of both of those allies.

The style of Francis Joseph's foreign policy was dynastic and personal. Just as he had contributed decisively to the creation of the League of the Three Emperors (Dreikaiserbund) by appearing in Berlin in 1873 by the side of Tsar Alexander II, he endeavoured also on later occasions to forestall potential conflicts with Russia through personal contacts, without realizing the fundamental nature of the antagonism between the two countries. On a visit to St. Petersburg in 1897 and again after Tsar Nicholas II's visit in 1903, he tried to delimit Austrian and Russian interests in the Balkans—a policy that was rashly jeopardized by Aehrenthal during the crisis leading to the annexation of occupied Bosnia-Hercegovina in 1908. By then, however, the days were long past when foreign policy was a matter of friendships between sovereigns; conflicts of interest, or for that matter pan-Slav propaganda, could no longer be neutralized on the dynastic level. Also, the Emperor found it increasingly difficult to get along with his fellow sovereigns, many of them relatives, of the younger generation. Yet he seems to have appreciated the energtic, dashing, and optimistic manner of William II of Germany.

In the period 1908–14 Francis Joseph held fast to his peace policy in the face of warnings by the chief of the general staff, Franz, Graf Conrad von Hötzendorf, who repeatedly advocated a preventive war against Serbia or Italy. Yet, without having fully thought out the consequences, he let himself in July 1914 be persuaded by Graf Leopold Berchtold, the foreign minister, to issue the intransigent ultimatum to Serbia that led to World War I. On November 21, 1916, Francis Joseph died at Schönbrunn Palace.

Assessment. Although he had been raised to be a soldier and wore a uniform all his life, Francis Joseph was no more a strategist than he was a statesman. He made up for this deficiency by the careful study of documents, by an extraordinarily retentive memory, and by being a shrewd judge of character. Invariably well informed and familiar with the reports of his envoys, he was to his civil servants an unequalled model of exactitude, devotion to duty, and justice. In his time Austria-Hungary was credited with having a civil administration that was as efficient as any in Europe. Having reserved for himself the control of foreign policy and of all matters bearing on the army, he stated repeatedly that this foreign policy was his own and that any criticism of it was in reality directed at himself. While loyal to his ministers, he refused to grant them any influence beyond the limits of their respective offices; once dismissed, a minister was no longer consulted on official business. This attitude, which many considered to be both ungrateful and ungracious, sprang in part from a punctiliousness that was hard to penetrate and rendered him incapable of true friendship. In the early decades of his reign, his correct but unapproachable bearing caused Francis Joseph to be respected but not really popular. Toward the end of his life, however, he became a universally revered man, a personality that for all its defects and insufficiencies held together the rotting structure of the multinational state.

Although a gentleman of irresistible charm in personal contact, Francis Joseph was greatly feared as the head of his house. His attitude toward his family was determined primarily by dynastic considerations. His own marriage had been a love match, and he remained devoted to his fanciful, glamorous, and intelligent wife even after the marriage had been wrecked by her eccentricities. Her assassination, in Geneva on September 10, 1898, saddened him profoundly. The tragedy of the heir presumptive, the archduke Rudolf, who dramatically shot himself in a suicide love pact with a 17-year-old baroness at Mayerling on January 30, 1889, was assuredly rooted in Rudolf's unstable character. Yet the Emperor had contributed to his only son Rudolf's instability by giving him an unsuitable education, forcing him to marry Princess Stephanie of Belgium, and dealing with him in an altogether cold and uncomprehending manner. He treated his daughter-in-law with unforgiving harshness after her second, morganatic marriage, believing that family members who married beneath their station had committed a crime against the dynasty. Nor did Francis Joseph ever become reconciled to the morganatic union of the next heir presumptive, Archduke Francis Ferdinand. His statements on receiving the report of the archducal couple's murder at Sarajevo, on June 28, 1914, shows that he looked upon their fate as a token of divine retribution. These tragedies, which became public knowledge, were underlined by an unending series of sometimes very heated family disputes in the course of which Francis Joseph forced the members of the House of Habsburg-Lorraine to conform to his own notion of an archduke's dignity and position. Yet this man who became ever lonelier as time went on could be a generous and amiable family father to his daughters and those members of the house who bowed to his wishes.

The only member of the immediate family with whom he had a closer relationship was his youngest brother, the archduke Louis Victor. While he was no more than correct in his attitude toward his younger brother, the restless, talented, and ambitious Archduke Maximilian, he bears no blame for the tragedy that ended Maximilian's brief interlude as emperor of Mexico.

Family
life

Having overcome the threat to its very survival in 1848–49, Austria passed through a long metamorphosis with many ups and downs in the 68 years that Francis Joseph occupied the throne. The last half century of his reign was marked by the increasing recurrence of tensions arising from the nationalities problem. Although Francis Joseph's understanding of these problems was limited, he was able to mask this defect by the conscientious fulfillment of his bureaucratic duties. These internal stresses were reflected in a rapid change of prime ministers, whose programs were sometimes radically at variance with those of their predecessors. The direction of foreign

Assess-
ment

policy, on the other hand, continued essentially unchanged. The beginning of the 20th century saw the empire's existence—considered by many to be altogether anachronistic—severely endangered at home. Francis Joseph, who would not be forced into anything against his convictions, bore a share in all the decisions of those years. Yet his many mistakes were balanced by splendid achievements. The social legislation enacted by the prime minister Eduard, Graf von Taaffe, during the 1880s, the new penal code of 1852, the trade regulations of 1859, and the commercial code of 1862 are all examples of a civil administration that was highly regarded throughout Europe. Those achievements bore the stamp of the Emperor's own silent devotion to duty.

Through the architectural style he favoured, Francis Joseph imparted a very personal touch to his capital cities of Vienna and Budapest. Although he had no artistic gifts of his own, he always gave a free hand to the artists he employed. By ennobling numerous deserving military men, civil servants, scientists, and artists, he created an aristocracy of merit that formed the so-called second society of Vienna and acted as a bond that helped hold together the empire. In the final instance, however, Austria-Hungary derived its firmest support from his own personality.

BIBLIOGRAPHY. The most important biographies of Francis Joseph are: E.C. CORTI, *Vom Kind zum Kaiser* (1950), *Mensch und Herrscher* (1952), and with H. SOKOL, *Der alte Kaiser* (1955), popularly written; and JOSEPH REDLICH, *Kaiser Franz Joseph von Österreich* (1928; Eng. trans., *Emperor Francis Joseph of Austria*, 1929), still considered the best biography. See also EDWARD CRANKSHAW, *The Fall of the House of Habsburg* (1963); O. JASZI, *The Dissolution of the Habsburg Monarchy* (1929); ROBERT A. KANN, *The Multinational Empire: Nationalism and National Reform in the Habsburg Monarchy, 1848–1918*, 2 vol. (1950, reprinted 1964), the best presentation on this subject; and A.J.P. TAYLOR, *The Habsburg Monarchy, 1809–1918*, new ed. (1948), imaginative but not always dependable.

(K.O.v.A.)

Franck, César

The work of the Belgian (later naturalized French) composer César Franck, which did not come to full fruition until the last ten years of his life (1880–90), made him the chief figure in a movement to give French music a new seriousness, an emotional engagement, and a technical solidity comparable to that of the German 19th-century composers. His *Symphony in D Minor; Variations symphoniques* for piano and orchestra; a string quartet, a piano quintet, and a violin sonata; *Prélude, choral et fugue* for piano; and a number of organ pieces mark him as the most powerful composer to appear in France during the second half of the 19th century.

C. Caroly—J.P. Ziolo

César Franck, portrait by J. Rongier (19th century). In a private collection.

César Auguste Franck was born on December 10, 1822, at Liège, in Belgium, of a Walloon father and a mother of German descent. He showed unmistakable musical gifts that enabled him to enter the Liège conservatory at the age of eight, and his progress as a pianist was so astonishing that in 1834 his father took him on a tour of towns, including Aix and Brussels, and a year later dispatched him to Paris, where he worked with the Bohemian composer Anton Reicha, then professor at the Conservatoire de Paris. In 1836 the whole family, including the younger son Joseph, who played the violin, moved to Paris, and in 1837 César Franck entered the conservatory. Within a year he had won a Grand Prix d'Honneur by a gratuitous feat of transposition in the sight-reading test, and this honour was followed by a first prize for fugue (1840) and second prize for organ (1841). Although the boy should now normally have prepared to compete for the Prix de Rome, a prize offered yearly in Paris for study in Rome, his father was determined on a virtuoso's career for him and his violinist brother, with whom he gave concerts, and therefore removed him prematurely from the conservatory.

In order to please his father and earn much-needed money, Franck gave concerts, the programs of which were largely devoted to performing his own showy fantasias and operatic potpourris, popular at that time. After 1840, when he turned his attention increasingly to the organ, his compositions become noticeably more serious, and three trios written at this time were to impress favourably the Hungarian composer Franz Liszt. A more ambitious work was the cantata *Ruth*, which had its first performance at the conservatory on January 4, 1846.

First compositions

Unwilling concert giving, a number of bad press notices, and the teaching needed to supplement his income took a physical toll of his powers. Only when he had finally asserted himself against what amounted to the unscrupulous exploitation of his gifts by his father could he achieve maturity and peace of mind. Franck fell in love with an actress with the professional name of Desmousseaux, whose real name was Félicité Saillot, but because both her parents also worked in the theatre, the family was regarded as totally unsuitable by the elder Franck, and his son was obliged to leave home some time before marrying her in 1848.

After his marriage Franck's way of life changed little for his remaining 42 years. He earned his livelihood as an organist and teacher. He led a simple, almost ascetic life. Winter and summer he rose at 5:30, beginning his long day of teaching two hours later. Most of his composing was done in this early-morning period and during the summer holidays.

In 1851 he was appointed organist to the church of Saint-Jean-Saint-François and in 1858 to that of Sainte-Clotilde, where he was already choirmaster. From the organ loft of Sainte-Clotilde came the improvisations for which he was to become famous and also their elaboration in organ and choral works. This music, which is before all else the product of Franck's official profession, is all marked by the taste of the day, which was for a facile tenderness and saccharine sweetness in ecclesiastical music. Both Franck and his friend the French composer Charles Gounod were, however, taken to task by their clerical employers, speaking on behalf of their congregations, for the austerity and difficulty of their church music.

More important to Franck's career as a composer was his appointment as organ professor at the conservatory in 1872. This came to him as a surprise, because he had indulged in none of the preliminary intrigue customary in such cases; and his openheartedness and lack of sophistication were to make him enemies among his colleagues as well as friends among his pupils. This enmity was increased by the fact that his organ classes soon became classes of composition, and his pupils not infrequently proved superior to those of the conventional composition professors.

Organ professor at the university

The nucleus of a school of disciples had already been formed by the French composers Henri Duparc and Alexis de Castillon, who studied privately with Franck in the late 1860s, but only after the founding of the Société Nationale de Musique (February 25, 1871) was a real future assured for the deeply serious, emotionally engaged, and technically well-founded music that Franck was interested in writing and communicating to his pupils. When Vincent d'Indy, a French composer, joined the group of Franck's pupils in 1872, he brought an enthusiasm, a propagandist zeal, and an exclusive personal devotion that played a large place in restoring Franck's confidence in his powers, naturally weakened by his failure as a virtuoso pianist and as a composer. With Ernst Chausson, Pierre de Bréville, Charles Bordes, and Guy Ropartz the Franck circle was complete in the early '80s, and subsequently d'Indy's very high claims (in his biography, *César Franck*, 1906) led for a time to the suspicion that Franck was "a creation of his own pupils."

Franck's music

The music that he wrote between 1880 and his death in 1890 makes it clear that this is not true. Certainly his early years as performer and composer of virtuoso music left an indelible mark on his musical taste, which can be heard unmistakably in the last movement of the *Prélude, aria et final* for piano (completed 1887) and even momentarily in the *Variations symphoniques* (1885) for piano and orchestra. On the other hand, some of his weaker music represents an almost excessive reaction against superficiality and a cultivation of emotional intensity at all costs, drawing for the purpose on the examples of Franz Liszt, Richard Wagner, and, more remotely, Beethoven.

Franck died in Paris, partly as the result of a street accident, on November 8, 1890. The new seriousness of French music in the last quarter of the 19th century derived entirely from Franck and his pupils. Much has been made of his angelic sweetness and simplicity of character, his selflessness and innocence in the ways of the world. These traits are reflected in a blandness of manner, and they proved a handicap when Franck was faced with the necessity of producing strongly contrasting musical ideas, as in the oratorio *Les Béatitudes* (written during the 1870s and performed posthumously) and the symphonic poems *Le Chasseur maudit* (1882; *The Accursed Hunter*) and *Les Djinns* (1884). On the other hand, the violin sonata (1886) and the *Variations symphoniques* (1885) remain as all but perfect monuments of a warm and noble musical nature and a strong, thorough craftsmanship that have survived all changes of taste and emotional attitudes.

MAJOR WORKS

CHORAL WORKS: *Ruth*, a biblical eclogue (1846); *Trois Motets* (1858); *Messe à troix voix* (1860); *Trois Offertoires* (1871); *Panis Angelicus*, for tenor, organ, harp, cello, and double bass (1872); *Rédemption* (1873); *Les Béatitudes*, oratorio in eight parts (1879).

ORCHESTRAL WORKS: Five symphonic poems including *Les Éolides* (1876), *Le Chasseur maudit* (*The Accursed Hunter*, 1882), *Psyché* (1888), and *Les Djinns* (1884); *Variations symphoniques* (1885); *Symphony in D Minor* (1888).

CHAMBER MUSIC: *Quintet in F Minor for Piano and Strings* (1879); *String Quartet in D Major* (1889); *Sonata in A Major for Violin and Piano* (1886).

ORGAN: *Six Pièces* (1862); *Trois Pièces* (1878); *Trois Chorals* (1890).

PIANO: *Prélude, choral et fugue* (1884); *Prélude, aria et final* (1887).

BIBLIOGRAPHY. ALFRED CORTOT, "The Piano Music of César Franck," in *La Musique française de piano* (1930; Eng. trans., *French Piano Music*, 1932); VINCENT D'INDY, *César Franck* (1906; Eng. trans., 1909, reprinted 1929 and 1965); and LEON VALLAS, *César Franck* (Eng. trans. 1951); and *La Véritable Histoire de César Franck* (1955), are the classical studies of the composer. See also the special issue of *La Revue Musicale* (December 1922), devoted to Franck.

(M.DuP.C.)

Franco, Francisco

Francisco Franco, who achieved early renown as an outstanding military leader and the youngest general in the Spanish Army, led the Nationalist forces to victory during the Spanish Civil War, and in 1936 he was made head of state. During the course of his long rule, Spain changed greatly, moving from a largely preindustrial society in the 1940s to a partially industrialized economy with one of the world's fastest growth rates during the 1960s. Its political structure changed comparatively little, however, for Franco presided over an authoritarian regime that, though pluralistic in recognizing the claims of diverse groups, such as the church, the army, and the state worker syndicates did not rest on a system of direct democratic elections.

Keystone

Franco, 1970.

Francisco Franco Bahamonde was born at the coastal city and naval centre of El Ferrol in Galicia (northwestern Spain) on December 4, 1892. His family life was not entirely happy, for Franco's father, an officer in the Spanish Naval Administrative Corps, was eccentric, wasteful, and somewhat dissolute. More disciplined and serious than other boys of his age, Franco was close to his mother, a pious and conservative upper-middle-class Catholic. Like four generations and his elder brother before him, Franco was originally destined for a career as a naval officer, but reduction of admissions to the Naval Academy forced him to choose the army. In 1907, only 14 years old, he entered the Infantry Academy at Toledo. Three years later he graduated with the rank of second lieutenant.

Early life and training

Franco volunteered for active duty in the colonial campaigns in Spanish Morocco that had begun in 1909 and was transferred there in 1912 at the age of 19. The following year he was promoted to first lieutenant in an elite regiment of native Moroccan cavalry. At a time in which many Spanish officers were characterized by sloppiness and lack of professionalism, young Franco quickly showed his ability to command troops effectively and soon won a reputation for complete professional dedication. He devoted great care to the preparation of his unit's actions and paid more attention than was common to the troops' well-being. Reputed to be scrupulously honest, introverted, and a man of comparatively few intimate friends, he was known to shun all frivolous amusements. In 1915 he became the youngest captain in the Spanish Army. In the following year he was seriously wounded by a bullet in the abdomen and was brought back to Spain to recover. In 1920 he was chosen to be second in command of the newly organized Spanish Foreign Legion, succeeding to full command in 1923. In that year he married Carmen Polo, by whom he had a daughter. During the crucial campaigns against the Moroccan rebels, the legion played a decisive role in bringing the revolt to an end. Franco became a national hero, and in 1926, at the age of 33, he was promoted to brigadier general and at the beginning of 1928 was named director of the newly organized General Military Academy in Saragossa.

After the fall of the monarchy in 1931, the leaders of the new Spanish Republic adopted a sharply antimilitary policy, and Franco's career was temporarily halted. The General Military Academy was dissolved, and Franco was placed on the inactive list. Though he was an avowed monarchist and held the honour of being a Gentleman

Birth of the republic

of the King's Chamber, Franco accepted both the new regime and his temporary demotion with perfect discipline. When conservative forces gained control of the republic in 1933, Franco was restored to active command; in 1934 he was promoted to major general. In October 1934, during the rising of Asturian miners who opposed the admission of three members of the right to the government, Franco was called in to quell the revolt. His success in this operation brought him new prominence. In May 1935 he was appointed chief of the Spanish Army's general staff, and he began the work of tightening discipline and strengthening military institutions, both seriously weakened by the republic's earlier antimilitary position.

No longer able to retain control of the country, the centre-right government was dissolved, and new elections were announced for February 1936. By this time the Spanish political parties had split into two factions: the rightist National Bloc and the leftist Popular Front. The left proved victorious in the elections, but the new government was unable to prevent the accelerating dissolution of Spain's social and economic structure. Although Franco had never been a member of a political party, the growing anarchy impelled him to appeal to the government to declare a state of emergency. His appeal was refused, and he was removed from the general staff and sent to an obscure command in the Canary Islands. For some time he refused to commit himself to a military conspiracy against the government, but as the political system disintegrated, he finally decided to join the rebels.

Franco's military rebellion.   At dawn on July 18, 1936, Franco's manifesto acclaiming the military rebellion was broadcast from the Canary Islands, and the same morning the rising began on the mainland. The following day he flew to Morocco and within 24 hours was firmly in control of the protectorate and the Spanish Army garrisoning it. After landing in Spain, Franco and his army marched toward Madrid, which was held by the government. When the Nationalist advance came to a halt on the outskirts of the city, the military leaders, in preparation of what they believed was the final assault that would deliver Madrid and the country into their hands, decided to choose a commander in chief, or generalissimo, who would also head the rebel Nationalist government in opposition to the republic. Because of his military ability and prestige, a political record unmarred by sectarian politics and conspiracies, and his proved ability to gain military assistance from Hitler's Germany and Mussolini's Italy, Franco was the obvious choice. In part because he was not a typical Spanish "political general," Franco became head of state of the new Nationalist regime on October 1, 1936. The rebel government did not, however, gain complete control of the country for more than three years.

Franco presided over a government that was basically a military dictatorship, but he realized that it needed a regular civil structure to broaden its support; this was to be derived mainly from the antileftist middle classes. On April 19, 1937, he reorganized the Falange (the Spanish Fascist Party) and made it the rebel regime's official political movement. While expanding the Falange into a more pluralistic group, Franco made it clear that it was the government that used the party and not the other way around. Thus, his regime became an institutionalized authoritarian system, differing in this respect from the Fascist party-states of the German and Italian model.

As commander in chief in the Civil War, Franco was a careful and systematic leader. He made no rash moves and suffered only a few temporary defeats as his forces advanced slowly but steadily; the only major criticism directed at him during the campaign was that his strategy was frequently unimaginative. But thanks to the relatively superior military quality of his army and to the continuation of heavy German and Italian assistance, Franco won a complete and unconditional victory on April 1, 1939.

The Civil War had been largely a sanguinary struggle of attrition, marked by atrocities on both sides. The tens of thousands of executions carried out by the Nationalist regime, which continued during the first years after the war ended, earned Franco more reproach than any other single aspect of his rule.

Franco's dictatorship.   Although Franco had visions of restoring Spanish grandeur after the Civil War, in reality he was the leader of an exhausted country still divided internally and impoverished by a long and costly war. The stability of his government was made more precarious by the outbreak of World War II only five months later. Franco was at first shocked by Hitler's unprovoked assault on Catholic Poland and carefully avoided involvement in the war. His wartime diplomacy was perhaps Franco's ablest political achievement; it was marked by cold realism and careful timing. The evidence indicates that had Hitler ever been in a position to win a quick and total victory, Franco would have been willing to enter the conflict on Germany's side. As it was, his government remained relatively sympathetic to Hitler while carefully avoiding direct diplomatic and military commitment. After his interview with Franco in 1940 at Hendaye, France, Hitler is said to have remarked that he would "as soon have three or four teeth pulled" as go through another bargaining session like that.

World War II

The most difficult period of Franco's regime began in the aftermath of World War II, when his government was ostracized by the newly formed United Nations. He was labelled by hostile foreign opinion the "last surviving Fascist dictator" and for a time appeared to be the most hated of Western heads of state; within his country, however, as many people supported him as opposed him. The period of ostracism finally came to an end with the worsening of relations between the Soviet world and the West at the height of the Cold War. Franco could now be viewed as one of the world's leading anti-Communist statesmen, and relations with other countries began to be regularized in 1948. His international rehabilitation was advanced further in 1953 when Spain signed a 10-year military assistance pact with the United States, which was later renewed in more limited form.

Franco's domestic policies became somewhat more liberal during the 1950s and '60s, and the continuity of his regime, together with its capacity for creative evolution, won him at least a limited degree of respect from some of his critics. Franco said that he did not find the burden of government particularly heavy, and, in fact, his rule was marked by absolute self-confidence and relative indifference to criticism. He showed marked political ability in gauging the psychology of the diverse elements, ranging from moderate liberals to extreme reactionaries, whose support was necessary for his regime's survival. He maintained a careful balance among them and largely left the execution of policy to his appointees, thereby placing himself as arbiter above the storm of ordinary political conflict. To a considerable degree, the opprobrium for unsuccessful or unpopular aspects of policy tended to fall on individual ministers rather than on Franco.

Liberalization

The Falange state party, downgraded in the early 1940s, in later years became known merely as the "Movement" and lost much of its original quasi-Fascist identity.

Unlike most rulers of rightist authoritarian regimes, Franco provided for the continuity of his government after his death through an official referendum in 1947 that made the Spanish state a monarchy and ratified Franco's powers as a sort of regent for life. In 1967 he opened direct elections for a small minority of deputies to the parliament and in 1969 officially designated the then 32-year-old Prince Juan Carlos, the eldest son of the nominal pretender to the Spanish throne, as his official successor upon his death. Franco resigned his position of premier in 1973 but retained his functions as head of state, commander in chief of the armed forces, and head of the "Movement."

Franco was never a popular ruler and rarely tried to mobilize mass support. But after 1947 there was little direct or organized opposition to his rule. With the liberalization of his government and relaxation of some police powers, together with the country's marked economic development during the 1960s, Franco's image changed from that of the rigorous generalissimo to a more benign civilian elder statesman. The company of his six grandchildren and frequent hunting and fishing expeditions constituted the principal diversions of his later years. Franco's health declined markedly in the late 1960s, but advanced age brought no slackening of his self-confidence. He believed it within his power to bequeath to his country a stable continuation of his regime in an atmosphere of prosperity and accelerating modernization. He died in Madrid on November 20, 1975.

BIBLIOGRAPHY. There is no definitive biography of Franco, but the best is J.W.D. TRYTHALL, *El Caudillo: A Political Biography of Franco* (1970). The two other principal biographies are BRIAN CROZIER, *Franco: A Biographical History* (1967); and GEORGE HILLS, *Franco: The Man and His Nation* (1967). The background of the Spanish military is treated in STANLEY G. PAYNE, *Politics and the Military in Modern Spain* (1967).

(S.G.P.)

Frankfurt am Main

The largest city in the *Land* of Hessen, Federal Republic of Germany, Frankfurt am Main (Frankfort on Main) is a thriving industrial and commercial centre, lying about 19 miles east of the confluence of the Main and Rhine rivers at Mainz. The city is a main centre of communications and at the start of the 1970s had a population approaching 670,000. It is one of the federal republic's principal manufacturing towns. The birthplace of the poet Goethe and the original home of the international banking empire of the Rothschilds, Frankfurt today has both cultural and commercial fame, although it was also renowned from the 9th to the 18th century as the town in which the German kings were elected. With Germany's largest airport on its doorstep, Frankfurt has become a major centre for international trade fairs. The production of high-class sausages that immortalized its name in the "frankfurter" actually takes place in the town of Neu Isenburg, some miles to the south.

Until its destruction in 1944, during World War II, the old city of Frankfurt was the largest medieval city still intact in Germany; rapid postwar reconstruction has created an international, modern metropolis of somewhat monotonous uniformity, which is now rapidly engulfing the remaining estates, villas, parks, and gardens and the

older residential areas. Landmarks of the city's past remain, such as the round tower of the Eschenheimer Tor (1426–28), 155 feet, or 47 metres, high, and the red sandstone cathedral (dedicated to St. Bartholomew in 1239), forming a strong contrast to the background of multistory office blocks.

History. There is evidence of Celtic and Germanic settlements on the cathedral hill dating from the 1st century BC, besides Roman remains from the 1st and 2nd centuries AD. The name Frankfurt (Ford [Passage, Crossing] of the Franks) probably arose about AD 500, when the Franks drove the Alemanni south, but the first written mention of Franconofurt stems from Charlemagne's biographer, Einhard, in the late 8th century. The Pfalz (imperial castle) was the residence of the East Frankish Carolingians in the 9th century, and the first imperial election in Frankfurt took place in 856, when Lothair II was elected king of the Carolingian middle kingdom of Lotharingia. Closely associated with the castle in the mid-9th century was the Salvatorkirche (Church of the Saviour), built by Louis the German in 852, which, by 1238–39, was transformed into the cathedral dedicated to St. Bartholomew.

Origin of name

In the 10th century the small settlement was fortified, and a wooden bridge was built across the Main River. Sachsenhausen, a suburb south of the Main, probably arose after the erection of a stone bridge in the 12th century. Conrad III erected a new castle for the Hohenstaufens in the 12th century, and a wall was constructed around the market town extending down to the river. (Remnants of this wall, revealed by bombings in 1944, were subsequently restored as historic sites.) A royal bailiff replaced the governor of the castle as the head of the town soon after 1200, and a council grew up composed of elder magistrates, counsellors, and members of the guilds.

In 1311 two mayors, annually elected, replaced the royal bailiff as head of the council, and in 1372 the town became a free imperial city, a privileged status that it retained until 1806, when Napoleon organized the Confederation of the Rhine.

Frankfurt then became the seat of government for the prince primate of the Confederation of the Rhine and, in 1810, capital of the Grand Duchy of Frankfurt created by Napoleon. From 1815, when Napoleon fell, it was

Edo Koenig—Black Star

Frankfurt am Main with (centre) the cathedral dedicated to St. Bartholomew.

again a free city and, from 1816 to 1866, the seat of the German Bundestag (Federal Diet) and real capital of Germany. After the war of 1866, Frankfurt was occupied by Prussian troops and forcibly incorporated into Prussia, ending its free-city status.

The notable expansion of the city after 1333 tripled its area, and its new boundaries were fortified. Toward the end of the 14th century Sachsenhausen, too, was fortified and drawn into the city proper. From the middle of the 18th century, fine villas and garden houses had been built along the roads leading out of the city, and an increase in the numbers wishing to live there after 1866 stimulated new development. While villas lined the roads, the less wealthy moved into flats (apartments) between them. The suburbs thus created were gradually incorporated into the city.

Until World War I, the growth of Frankfurt was controlled largely by private land developers, but in the 20th century the city authorities took control in order to plan more effectively. The majority of the old city was destroyed in World War II, and postwar reconstruction has had to cater to basic public and private needs. Thus, few individual buildings in the old Gothic city have been restored exactly as before.

The contemporary city. *Demography.* The population of Frankfurt proper is decreasing, having fallen, for example, from 683,000 inhabitants in 1961 to 669,000 inhabitants in 1972; the numbers do not include the large number of the United States forces asssociated with the city. The population of the surrounding suburbs and rural communities is, however, growing rapidly. By 1970 more than 93,000 of Frankfurt's inhabitants (excluding members of the U.S. forces) were foreigners: some 21 percent of them were Yugoslavs, 19 percent Italian, 16 percent Turks, 13 percent Spaniards, and eight percent Greeks.

Modern developments. In the postwar efforts to build housing, speed and monotony prevailed, but in the 1960s the largest new suburb, Nordweststadt, with 25,000 inhabitants, was developed. It houses people from all classes in buildings that range from detached dwellings to 14-story blocks of flats. Facilities include quiet spots to walk and separate roads for fast and slow traffic. At the centre of the suburb are the offices for social, cultural, and commercial affairs that care for the many people in the suburb as well as those in the older, outlying parts of the city. Beneath the centre is the terminus of the subway that links Nordweststadt with the heart of Frankfurt.

Economic life. Trade has always accounted for Frankfurt's very existence. From being a small market serving those living around the king's palace, it grew into a flourishing city by the 12th and 13th centuries and held semiannual trading fairs that were placed under the king's official protection in 1240. Since the majority of the sales at the trade fairs were on credit, the need for a better method of currency exchange increased and by 1585 the Frankfurt Exchange was founded. In the 14th century the Frankfurt trade fair achieved international importance as the centre of the textile trade from the Netherlands, for sales of herring from the North Sea, and for furs and wax from the East. With the advent of the printing press, Frankfurt also claimed a central role in European publishing. Although much of its trade was lost to Leipzig in the 16th century, Frankfurt had also been developing a notable talent for banking, which, with the influx of Dutch, French, and Italian brokers and bankers around 1600, led it to acquire the leading international role in that field. During the 18th and 19th centuries, the Rothschild brothers lent money to numerous countries, setting up banks in London, Vienna, Paris, and Naples and practically establishing a monopoly.

After World War II, Frankfurt was able to rebuild its commercial interests, though Hannover took over the capital-investment-goods fairs while Frankfurt kept the consumer-goods fairs. Among the many exhibitions are the fur exhibition, international book fair, international automobile fair, and the international textile fair.

Frankfurt's efforts to become highly industrialized were restricted until 1866, but today there are machine-construction firms, chemical and pharmaceutical industries,

printing works, leather-goods plants, and foodstuffs facilities. Numerous government offices are also located in Frankfurt.

Transportation. Frankfurt's importance as a communications centre has grown steadily since the 13th century, and the location of the city has favoured good transportation and promoted its growth in the financial and industrial world. Its location, to the north of the Oberrheinische Tiefebene (Upper Rhine Lowlands) has made the city a crossroads for land and water traffic. Regular transportation had existed on the Main and Rhine rivers since the 14th century, but it was not until the canalization of the Main in 1883–86 that freight shipping became economically important. The first of the modern inland harbours, the west harbour, was completed in 1886 but with the construction of the east harbour (1907–12) Frankfurt became a centre for inland shipping, handling nearly 7,400,000 tons in 1971.

Following the construction of Germany's second railway line in 1838–40, linking Frankfurt and Kastel, near Mainz, and the addition of lines to the south, east, and north between 1846–52, Frankfurt rapidly became the centre of west German rail communications.

Six miles southwest of Frankfurt is the point of intersection of two main *Autobahnen*, the Hamburg–Basel highway and the Cologne–Nuremburg road. Close by is Frankfurt's Rhein-Main airport, which, built in 1936, has achieved first place among European airports for its carriage of mail (63,400 tons), second place as regards freight (352,200 tons), and third place in passenger services (after London and Paris) with 10,567,000 travellers in 1971.

Cultural life and recreation. Commercial contacts established at the many fairs have led in turn to European and international cultural exchanges and development. During the Reformation, Frankfurt remained Lutheran and in 1554 became the home of many Protestant refugees from England and the Netherlands and for many from France in the 17th century. The refugees carried their crafts and a well-developed cultural life with them, and their expertise brought further wealth, prestige, and influence to Frankfurt. The Jewish community, too, grew in size after the 16th century, contributing to the commercial life of the city. The characteristically simple exteriors of the buildings of the new merchant class were in sharp contrast to the abundance of artistic expression within their homes and places of worship. From early times the merchant classes had been generous patrons of the arts, notably engaging Albrecht Dürer, Mathias Grünewald, and Hans Baldung to provide artworks in the Dominican Church (Dominikaner Kirche).

The Städelsches Kunstinstitut (Städel Art Institute), Frankfurt's finest art gallery, founded in 1816 at the bequest of the banker Städel, contains Italian, German, French, Spanish, and Dutch paintings from the 15th to the 18th centuries. The city's collection of sculpture, containing among many masterpieces the Greek "Athena," by Myron, is housed in adjoining Liebighaus. The most famous museum is the Senckenberg Museum of natural history established by the Senckenbergsche naturforschende Gesellschaft (Senckenberg Society for Nature Research). Johann Wolfgang Goethe's birthplace was burned to the ground in World War II but has been faithfully restored. Adjoining it is the Goethe Museum and Library, one of the city's chief attractions. The citizens of Frankfurt established the Johann Wolfgang Goethe University, one of the largest in Germany, in 1914, through the amalgamation of a number of existing institutions. Besides the metropolitan Opera House and two fine theatres, there are many private theatres performing comedy, experimental drama, and all classes of entertainment. Recreational facilities are provided by the Palmengarten (Palm Garden), founded in 1868, which is famous throughout Germany for its large collection of flowers. South of the city a municipal forest of 10,000 acres encloses a golf course, and the renowned zoological garden lies in the eastern part of the city.

BIBLIOGRAPHY. WALDEMAR KRAMER, *Frankfurt-Lexikon* (1970), a standard general reference work; FRIEDRICH BOTHE,

The Nordwest-stadt suburb

Role as an international banking centre

Museums and galleries

Geschichte der Stadt Frankfurt am Main (1929, reprinted 1966), the most detailed history of the city up to the year 1927; HERMANN MEINERT, *Frankfurts Geschichte* (1964); and FRANZ LERNER, *Frankfurt im Wandel der Zeiten: Umrisse einer Geschichte des Raumes von Gross-Frankfurt* (1963), two recent historical studies; GEORGE G. WYNNE, *Frankfurt Through the Centuries* (1957), a brief survey of the history of the city written by a former U.S. high commissioner; HERMANN K. ZIMMERMANN, *Das Kunstwerk einer Stadt: Frankfurt am Main als Beispiel* (1963), a chronological description of the physical evolution of the city; GERHARD BOTT *et al.*, *Frankfurt am Main und seine Kunstschätze: Ein Wegweiser durch Kunststätten und -museen* (1956), a description of Frankfurt's architectural monuments and museum collections; WOLFGANG KLOTZER and ERNST KRATZ, *Frankfurt, Stadt- und Wirtschaftschronik* (1966); and FRANZ LERNER, *Frankfurt am Main und seine Wirtschaft* (1958), economic histories of Frankfurt.

(U.Ma.)

Franklin, Benjamin

Benjamin Franklin, next to George Washington possibly the most famous 18th-century American, by 1757 had made a small fortune, established the Poor Richard of his almanacs as an oracle on how to get ahead in the world, and become widely known in European scientific circles for his reports of electrical experiments and theories. What is more, he was then just at the beginning of a long career as a politician in the course of which he would be chief spokesmen for the British colonies in their debates with the king's ministers about self-government and would have a hand in the writing of the Declaration of Independence, the securing of financial and military aid from France during the American Revolution, the negotiation of the treaty by which Great Britain recognized its former 13 colonies as a sovereign nation, and the framing of the Constitution, which, for nearly two centuries, has been the fundamental law of the United States of America.

Franklin, portrait by Joseph-Siffred Duplessis, c. 1784.
By courtesy of the New-York Historical Society

And as impressive as Franklin's public service was, it was perhaps less remarkable than his contributions to the comfort and safety of daily life. He invented a stove, still being manufactured, to give more warmth than open fireplaces; the lightning rod and bifocal eyeglasses also were his ideas. Grasping the fact that by united effort a community may have amenities that only the wealthy few can get for themselves, he helped establish institutions that one now takes for granted: a fire company, a library, an insurance company, an academy, and a hospital. In some cases these foundations were the first of their kind in North America.

One might expect universal admiration for a man of such breadth and apparent altruism. Yet Franklin was disliked by some of his contemporaries and has ever since occasionally been attacked as a materialist or a hypocrite. D.H. Lawrence, the English novelist, regarded him as the embodiment of the worst traits of the American character. Max Weber, the German sociologist, made him the exemplar of the "Protestant ethic," a state of mind that contributed much, Weber thought, to the less admirable aspects of modern capitalism. Those who admire Franklin believe that his detractors have mistakenly identified him with Poor Richard, a *persona* of his own creation, or that they have relied too largely upon the incomplete self-portrait of his posthumously published *Autobiography.*

Early life (1706–23). Franklin was born in Boston, Massachusetts, on January 17 (January 6, old style), 1706, the tenth of the 17 children of a man who was both soapmaker and candlemaker. He learned to read very early and had one year in grammar school and another under a private teacher, but his formal education ended when he was ten. At 12 he was apprenticed to his brother James, a printer. His mastery of the printer's trade, of which he was proud to the end of his life, was achieved between 1718 and 1723. In the same period he read tirelessly and taught himself to write effectively.

His first enthusiasm was for poetry, and in the first years of his apprenticeship he wrote two occasional ballads, no copies of which have survived. His father told him that "Verse-makers were always Beggars" (*Benjamin Franklin's Memoirs*, ed. Max Farrand, University of California Press, 1949, p. 32), and thereafter his interest in poetry was sporadic. Prose was another matter. *The Spectator,* Joseph Addison and Richard Steele's famous periodical of essays, had appeared in England in 1711–12 and was to be imitated for the greater part of a century but seldom with the persistence of Franklin, the printer's apprentice. He would read an essay, make a short note of the idea of each sentence, lay aside his notes for a few days, and then try to rewrite the essay. Comparison of his version with the original showed him the need to enlarge his vocabulary. Turning some *Spectator* papers into verse and some days later reconverting them into prose, helped.

In 1721 James Franklin founded a *Spectator*-like weekly newspaper, the *New-England Courant,* to which readers were invited to contribute. Benjamin, now 16, read and perhaps set in type these contributions and decided he could do as well himself. In 1722 he wrote a series of 14 essays signed "Silence Dogood." Satire of New England funeral elegies and of the lip service paid the learned languages at Harvard College foreshadowed later literary techniques to be used by Franklin.

Late in 1722 James Franklin got into trouble with the provincial authorities and was forbidden to print or publish the *Courant.* To keep the paper going, he discharged his younger brother from his original apprenticeship and made him the paper's nominal publisher. New indentures were drawn up but not made public. Some months later, after a bitter quarrel, Benjamin walked out, sure that James would not go to law and reveal the subterfuge he had devised. "It was not fair in me to take this Advantage," he wrote later, "and this I therefore reckon one of the first Errata [mistakes, in printer's lingo] of my Life" (Farrand, p. 50).

Youthful adventures (1723–26). Failing to find work in Boston or New York, Franklin proceeded to Philadelphia. One of the dramatic scenes of the *Autobiography* is the description of his arrival on a Sunday morning, tired and hungry. Finding a bakery, he asked for three pennies' worth of bread and got "three great Puffy Rolls." Carrying one under each arm and munching on the third, he walked up Market Street past the door of the Read family, where stood Deborah, his future wife. She saw him "& thought I made as I certainly did a most awkward ridiculous Appearance" (Farrand, p. 62).

A few weeks later he was rooming at the Reads and employed as a printer. By the spring of 1724 he was enjoying the companionship of other young men with a taste for reading and he was also being urged to set up in business for himself by the governor of Pennsylvania, Sir William Keith. At Keith's suggestion, Franklin returned to Boston to try to raise the necessary capital. His father thought him too young for such a venture, so Keith offered to foot the bill himself and arranged Franklin's

Youth in Boston

Arrival in Philadelphia

passage to England so that he could choose his type and make connections with London stationers and booksellers. Franklin exchanged "some promises" with Miss Read and, with a young friend, James Ralph, as companion, boarded the "London Hope" in November, expecting to find the letters of credit and introduction that Keith had promised. Not until the ship was well out at sea did he realize that the governor had not kept his promise. A fellow passenger, a Quaker merchant by the name of Thomas Denham, told him that Keith was unreliable; eventually Franklin could write charitably: "He wish'd to please every body; and, having little to give, he gave Expectations" (Farrand, p. 106).

Years in London

In London Franklin quickly found employment in his trade and was able to lend money to Ralph, who was trying to establish himself as a writer. The two young men enjoyed the theatre and the other pleasures of the city; before long Ralph found a milliner for a mistress. When Ralph was in the country, teaching school, the milliner occasionally borrowed money from Franklin. "I grew fond of her Company," he remembered, "and being at this time under no Religious Restraints, & presuming on my Importance to her, I attempted Familiarities (another Erratum) which she repuls'd with a proper Resentment, and acquainted him with my Behaviour" (Farrand, p. 112).

Still another "erratum" in retrospect was *A Dissertation on Liberty and Necessity, Pleasure and Pain* (1725), a deistical pamphlet that he was inspired to write after having set type for the third edition of William Wollaston's moral tract, "The Religion of Nature Delineated." Franklin argued therein that since man has no real freedom of choice he is not morally responsible for his actions. He may have been consoling himself for his treatment of Deborah, to whom he had written only once.

By 1726 Franklin was tiring of London. He considered becoming an itinerant teacher of swimming, an art in which he was accomplished, but when Denham offered him a clerkship in his store in Philadelphia, with a prospect of fat commissions in the West Indian trade, he decided to return home.

Achievement of security and fame (1726–52). Denham died, however, a few months after Franklin entered his store. The young man, now 20, returned to his trade and in 1728 was able to set up a partnership with a friend. Two years later he borrowed money to become sole proprietor.

His private life at the time he became his own master was extremely complicated. Deborah Read had married, but her husband had deserted her and disappeared. One matchmaking venture failed because Franklin wanted a settlement to pay off his business debt. A strong sexual drive, "that hard-to-be-govern'd Passion of Youth" (Farrand, p. 178), was sending him to "low Women" and in the winter of 1730–31 he had a son, William, whose mother has never been identified. Franklin must have known that the child was expected when, his affection for Deborah having "revived," he "took her to Wife (Farrand, p. 180) on September 1, 1730. Their common-law marriage lasted until Deborah's death in 1774. They had two children, a son who died at four and a daughter, Sarah, later Mrs. Richard Bache, who survived them both. The illegitimate William was brought up in the household.

Wife and children

Franklin and his partner's first coup was securing the printing of Pennsylvania's paper currency. Franklin helped get this business by writing *A Modest Enquiry into the Nature and Necessity of a Paper Currency* (1729). For years thereafter Franklin was public printer not only of Pennsylvania but also of New Jersey, Delaware, and Maryland. Another money-making venture was the *Pennsylvania Gazette*, published by Franklin from 1729 and generally acknowledged as among the best of the colonial newspapers. Still another was the series of the *Poor Richard's* almanacs, printed annually from 1732 to 1757. Some failures of course occurred: a German-language newspaper that lasted less than a year and a monthly magazine that expired after six issues in 1741. Franklin was nevertheless generally prosperous; he made enough

to invest capital in real estate and in partnerships or working arrangements with printers in the Carolinas, New York, and the British West Indies. In 1748 he became a silent partner in the printing firm of Franklin and Hall, realizing in the next 18 years an average profit of almost £500 annually.

The first of his projects for social improvement by collective effort was the Junto, or Leather Apron club, organized in 1727 to debate questions of morals, politics, and natural philosophy and to exchange knowledge of business affairs that might be valuable to the more enterprising members. The need of Junto members for easier access to books led in 1731 to the organization of the Library Company of Philadelphia. Through the Junto, Franklin proposed a paid city watch, or police force. A paper read to the same group resulted in the organization of a volunteer fire company. In 1743 he called for a "constant correspondence" of men with scientific interests throughout the Colonies, and in the following year the American Philosophical Society was functioning. In 1743 also he perceived Pennsylvania's need of higher education and in 1749 published *Proposals Relating to the Education of Youth in Pennsilvania;* in 1751, the Academy of Philadelphia, from which grew the University of Pennsylvania, was founded. So successful was Franklin as a promoter that anyone with a good cause in mind was likely to turn to him for help.

Projects for social and public improvements

Franklin was also early involved in politics. He was clerk of the Pennsylvania legislature from 1736 until 1751 and postmaster of Philadelphia from 1737 until 1753. Prior to 1748, though, his most important political service was his part in organizing a militia for the defense of the colony against possible invasion by the French and the Spaniards, whose privateers were operating in the Delaware River. His skill in appealing to the self-interest of the various factions in the commonwealth, among them the Quakers, is demonstrated in *Plain Truth; or, Serious Considerations on the Present State of the City of Philadelphia and Province of Pennsylvania* (1747).

In the 1740s, electricity was a novel and fashionable subject. It was introduced to Philadelphians by an electrical machine sent to the Library Company by one of Franklin's English correspondents. In the winter of 1746–47, Franklin and three of his friends began to investigate electrical phenomena. The Philadelphia weather favoured them, as did the availability of talented instrument makers. Ingenious experiments and machines were devised and described in personal letters to England, which were relayed to the Royal Society of London or the *Gentleman's Magazine*. These papers were collected in 1751 as *Experiments and Observations on Electricity*, which was printed in a French translation in 1752. Four additional English editions and two other French editions appeared before 1769; the book was also translated into German (1758) and Italian (1774).

Investigations in electrical science

Franklin's fame spread rapidly. The experiment that he suggested to prove the identity of lightning and electricity was first made in France before he is believed to have tried the simpler but dangerous expedient of flying a kite in a thunderstorm. He and his associates concluded early that the "Electrical Fire" was "an Element diffused among, and attracted by other matter, particularly by Water and Metals" (*Papers*, III, 129-30). When a body with an over-quantity approached one with an under-quantity a discharge equalized the electrical fire in the two. This "one fluid" theory accounted for more of the observable phenomena than had any previous hypothesis, and his suggestion that buildings might be protected from lightning by erecting pointed iron rods proved both practical and dramatic. Franklin may not have been as original as some of his admirers have thought, and his collaborators may not have received their full share of credit for their assistance, but he invented many of the terms still used in discussing electricity (positive, negative, battery, conductor, and so on), and he described the experiments with lucidity.

Public service (1753–85). In 1753 Franklin became deputy postmaster general, in charge of the mails in all the northern colonies. Thereafter he began to think in intercolonial terms. His "Plan of Union," adopted by the Albany Congress in 1754, would have established a general council, with representatives from the several colonies, to organize the common defense against the encroaching French and to supervise Indian relations with new settlements. Neither the colonial legislatures nor the King's advisers were ready for such union. Reason was on Franklin's side, but the power structure was against him, and this conflict has been regarded by some authorities as the key to his entire political career.

In 1755 Franklin was nearly ruined when he promised to stand good for the loss of horses and wagons supplied by Pennsylvania farmers to support General Edward Braddock's ill-fated campaign against Fort-Duquesne at the outset of the French and Indian War. For more than two months he faced the possibility of having to pay almost £20,000 out of his own pocket. The government eventually paid.

The need of funds for defense of the frontier led the Pennsylvania legislature to seek to tax the lands of the Penn family, the proprietors under the colony's charter. Either their consent or a change in the form of government was required. In the spring of 1757 Franklin was chosen to represent the legislature in this matter, which occupied him in London for most of his time until August 1762. He negotiated a compromise, under which the Penns agreed to taxation of improved lands but not those unsurveyed. During this first mission he made close friends in England and wrote *The Interest of Great Britain Considered with Regard to Her Colonies and the Acquisitions of Canada and Guadaloupe* (1760). It was designed to urge the annexation of Canada when the war was over. There were Englishmen who preferred to leave Canada to the French, as a check on the growing strength of the 13 colonies. A simpler check, Franklin wrote, would be for Parliament to pass a law requiring midwives to stifle every third or fourth child as soon as it was born.

The Treaty of Paris (1763), ending the Seven Years' War, gave Canada to Great Britain. By that time Franklin was back in Philadelphia, where the conflict between the legislature and the proprietors continued. The legislature decided that Pennsylvania ought to become a crown colony, and by the end of 1764 Franklin was back in London to negotiate in vain for a new charter.

The tribulations of Pennsylvania were submerged, however, in the flood of feeling surrounding the so-called Stamp Act crisis. Franklin opposed the Stamp Act (he had asserted in his "Plan of Union" that taxation ought to be the prerogative of the representative legislatures), but when it had been passed he made the mistake of underestimating American emotions; he ordered stamps for Franklin and Hall and nominated a friend for the post of stamp officer in Philadelphia. His fellow citizens were outraged to the verge of violence. Deborah was so fearful of her house being mobbed that she called on male relatives for armed defense. In London Franklin quickly did an about-face and threw himself into the campaign for repeal of the hated statute. He regained his prestige by a dramatic appearance before the House of Commons, where he answered 174 questions from an audience partly friendly and partly hostile. The stenographic report showed him returning again and again to the right of the Colonies to level internal taxes by their own legislation.

Although he failed to get the new charter, Franklin was kept on as London agent for Pennsylvania, and three other colonies relied on him to represent their interests— Georgia (1768), New Jersey (1769), and Massachusetts (1770). With this support and that of the British Whigs, the party of industrialists and dissenters in favour of parliamentary and philanthropic reform, he weathered the succession of crises ending with armed clashes at Lexington and Concord. He was gradually forced to the realization that there could be no reconciliation and that his dream of a British Empire of self-governing nations would not come true. He did his best to present the American case to his friends and to the British public. Between 1765 and 1775 he published 126 newspaper articles on current controversies. At the end he was bitter, in such articles as "Rules by Which a Great Empire May Be Reduced to a Small One" and "An Edict by the King of Prussia," both first printed in the *Public Advertiser* in 1773. Taken together, they are a capsule history of the long-drawn-out contest. In January 1774, because of his share in the publication of the letters of Thomas Hutchinson, governor of Massachusetts, to his British superiors, Franklin was dismissed from the post office. In March 1775, aware that there might be war, he left England. The day after his arrival in Philadelphia he was a delegate to the Second Continental Congress, for which he served on committees for the organization of a postal system and for the drafting of the Declaration of Independence and on a commission that vainly attempted to bring Canada into the war as an ally.

In September 1776, the Congress agreed to send a commission to France to seek economic and military assistance. As one of three commissioners, Franklin arrived in Paris just before Christmas and was immediately engaged in secret negotiations with Charles Gravier, comte de Vergennes, minister of foreign affairs. Spies and informers infested his house, but Franklin was soon the hero of France, personifying the unsophisticated nobility of the New World, leading his people to freedom from the feudal past. His portrait was everywhere, on *objets d'art* from snuffboxes to chamber pots, his society sought after by diplomats, scientists, Freemasons, fashionable ladies. There was in fact a Franklin cult, not without its ridiculous side. Franklin, however, with his fur hat and spectacles, rose to the occasion with wit and social grace.

The sought-for treaties were signed in February 1778 after the British general John Burgoyne and 6,000 men had surrendered at Saratoga, New York, and it was clear that Great Britain was not going to crush the rebellion easily. Substantial loans were obtained for the revolutionists, and by the time of the final victory at Yorktown in 1781 an estimated 12,000 soldiers and 32,000 sailors had left France to support Gen. George Washington in America.

Despite these strong bonds, the peace was difficult. Spain had entered the war in 1779, hoping to recover Gibraltar but, because of the conflict of interests in Florida and Louisiana, refused to recognize American independence. France had guaranteed that there would be no separate peace. Franklin worked with Vergennes until his fellow commissioners, John Adams and John Jay, overruled him on procedure, signing preliminary agreements with Great Britain late in 1781 without prior consultation with France. The formal treaty was signed September 3, 1783.

Although Franklin wanted to return home, he was kept in Paris for two more years to help make trade treaties. His popularity unabated, he occupied himself by observing the first balloon ascension and serving on a committee appointed by Louis XVI to report on "animal magnetism," or hypnotism, a new marvel that a German physician, Franz Anton Mesmer, thought would cure many, if not all, diseases.

Last years (1785–90). At 79, with a large stone in his bladder that made travel by carriage an agony, Franklin was carried to the port of Le Havre in a litter. Back in Philadelphia he lived as quietly as possible, although he continued to take some part in public life. His most important service was as a member of the Constitutional Convention of 1787. There he failed to convince his associates that an executive committee would be better than a president as head of state and that there should be a unicameral legislature. On the last day of this momentous series of meetings, a colleague read for him a plea that the objections to the new form of government, his own among them, should be forgotten and that all delegates should unanimously support the instrument that they had hammered out. Franklin's motion for adoption by unanimous consent was promptly carried.

For the last year of his life he was bedridden, escaping severe pain only by the use of opium. He died on April 17, 1790, aged 84. Philadelphia gave him the most impressive funeral that that city had ever seen, and in France, where Louis XVI was imprisoned in the Tuileries, eulogy after eulogy poured forth to the man who to the French was the symbol of enlightenment and freedom. All Europeans remembered the epigram of Turgot, the French economist: "He snatched the lightning from the skies and the sceptre from tyrants."

MAJOR WORKS

POLITICAL AND ECONOMIC: *A Modest Enquiry into the Nature and Necessity of a Paper Currency* (1729); *Plain Truth; or Serious Considerations on the Present State of the City of Philadelphia* (1747); *Proposals Relating to the Education of Youth in Pensilvania* (1749); *Observations Concerning the Increase of Mankind* (1755); *The Way to Wealth* (1757); *The Interest of Great Britain Considered with Regard to Her Colonies and the Acquisition of Canada and Guadaloupe* (1760); *Positions to be Examined Concerning National Wealth* (1769); *Journal of the Negotiations for Peace* (1782).

RELIGIOUS, PHILOSOPHICAL, AND SCIENTIFIC: *A Dissertation on Liberty and Necessity, Pleasure and Pain* (1725); *Articles of Belief and Acts of Religion* (1728); *Experiments and Observations on Electricity* (1751).

OTHER WORKS: *Poor Richard's* (1732–57), an almanac containing a number of famous maxims; Franklin's *Autobiography* (1771–88); "Information to those who would remove to America" (1784).

BIBLIOGRAPHY. *The Papers of Benjamin Franklin,* 15 vol., ed. by L.W. LABAREE *et al.* (1959–71), with 25 additional volumes expected, will be the definitive collection. *The Writings of Benjamin Franklin,* 10 vol., ed. by A.H. SMYTH (1905–07), has heretofore been the chief collection. The fullest biography is CARL VAN DOREN, *Benjamin Franklin* (1938); the best brief one is VERNER W. CRANE, *Benjamin Franklin and a Rising People* (1954). The most recent life is THOMAS FLEMING, *The Man Who Dared the Lightning: A New Look at Benjamin Franklin* (1971). An interesting specialized study is BRUCE INGHAM GRANGER, *Benjamin Franklin, An American Man of Letters* (1964).

(T.Hor.)

Fraser River

A major river of western North America, the Fraser River drains a huge, scenic region of some 92,000 square miles (238,000 square kilometres) in the central portion of the province of British Columbia. About 70 percent of the region drained is over 3,000 feet high, and human exploitation of this rather isolated area has been relatively recent and often dramatic, involving pioneer explorers and the lure of elusive gold deposits. The natural beauties of the river course (particularly its spectacular canyon section) and the surrounding countryside have nevertheless remained relatively unspoiled, although extensive timber extraction poses some threat to the forests of the region, and the potential hydroelectric power locked up in the river course may pose a threat to the passage of fish along this traditionally salmon-filled river.

The Fraser itself is 850 miles (1,368 kilometres) long, rising in the steep western slopes of the Rocky Mountains near Jasper National Park, Alberta, thrusting northwestward and then turning sharply south before emptying into the Strait of Georgia in southwestern British Columbia, south of the city of Vancouver. The river cuts across the physiographic region known as the Interior Plateau of British Columbia, and its eastern tributaries drain the Rocky, Omineca, Cariboo, and Monashee mountains, while the western tributaries drain the eastern slopes of the Coast Mountains. The major eastern tributaries are the McGregor, Bowron, Quesnel, and Thompson; their western counterparts are the Nechako, West Road, Chilcotin, Bridge, and Lillooet. (For related information see BRITISH COLUMBIA.)

Exploration. The first European known to have explored the Fraser River was the explorer and trader Simon Fraser of the North West Company, who has bequeathed the river his name. He left Fort George, a fur-trading post at the junction of the Nechako River, in late May 1808 and travelled by canoes with 21 Indian paddlers and packers. He experienced great difficulties in running, or even bypassing, the turbulent rapids in the Fraser Canyon, particularly near the aptly named Hells Gate. He reached the delta mouth of the north arm of the river in early July, but he found further exploration blocked by seemingly hostile Indians at Musqueam (now an Indian reserve on the south edge of Vancouver).

Adventures of the first Europeans

Little use was made of the river until after the discovery of alluvial gold in sandbars north of Yale in 1858. In the gold rush that followed, the central Fraser River, from Quesnel to Soda Creek, was used by flat-bottomed river steamers to transport supplies. There is, however, no present-day use of the river for water transport, except by those ocean vessels that enter the river mouth to travel for 20 miles to dock at the port of New Westminster.

The course of the Fraser. The Fraser River has its source at an altitude of 3,640 feet (1,109 metres) at Yellowhead Lake in Yellowhead Pass in the Rocky Mountains. The small but vigorous stream then drops about 1,200 feet in 50 miles before meandering slowly northward across the flat-bottomed floor of the landform division known as the Rocky Mountain Trench. Near McBride the river is a few hundred yards across, flowing between low, steep gravel banks. Occasional patches of agricultural land are cleared on the valley floor along Highway 16, which follows the upper Fraser Valley. The river bends westward out of the Rocky Mountain Trench, is joined by the McGregor River from the north, and then cuts down into the rolling upland of the Interior Plateau of British Columbia. At the city of Prince George, the river flows fast between steep, 200-foot gravel banks and has a mean discharge of 29,100 cubic feet per second. At this point, the Nechako River joins the Fraser from the west, draining a large area of some 12,200 square miles of the Interior Plateau.

South of Prince George the slightly entrenched river banks are lower, and the river swings back and forth across its shallow, forested valley. Its volume increases as it picks up the waters of the Quesnel River, which drains the areas of heavy precipitation in the Cariboo Mountains to the east, and also of the West Road River, which drains a drier area of the Interior Plateau east of the Coast Mountains. Although the average annual precipitation of the northern Fraser River Basin may be represented by the 24 inches (610 millimetres) recorded at Prince George (made up of 15 inches of rain falling from April to October and 90 inches of winter snow), higher precipitation totals of 60 to 80 inches are recorded on the western slopes of the Cariboo Mountains.

South of the town of Quesnel, the Fraser River begins to take on its canyon character. At the junction of the Chilcotin River, flowing in from the west, the Fraser River is about 1,400 feet above sea level, and it now has a mean discharge, near Marguerite, of 51,700 cubic feet per second. The Chilcotin River itself drains an area of 7,560 square miles on the eastern side of the Coast Mountains. The general surface of the Interior Plateau rises from about 2,500 feet above sea level near Prince George to about 4,000 feet near Clinton. While this plateau was being uplifted and covered with lava flows in the geologically recent (less than 20,000,000 years ago) Miocene Epoch, the Fraser River was able to downcut a deep, straight course southward. To the south, therefore, the canyon walls become higher and slope steeply. The Thompson River (drainage basin of 19,520 square miles), which joins the Fraser from the east, also flows through a narrow canyon. The Fraser and Thompson rivers were both larger at the end of the glacial age; in the last 10,000 years these rivers have cut down into the glacial deposition in the valley floor so that raised terraces and narrow benches now line certain sections of the valley floor above and below their junction. Further south these strips of level land become rare, and at Hells Gate the river rushes through a steep, rocky canyon, with two railways and a highway carved out of the valley walls.

At Yale the river leaves the Coast Mountains and the valley widens; at Hope the Fraser Delta begins. At this point the river has an average annual volume of flow of 95,500 cubic feet per second, but there is a range from an average maximum of 300,000 cubic feet per second in the flood month of June, to an average flow of only 25,000 cubic feet per second at the time of low water in March. In recent decades the average discharge has been steadily increasing, perhaps as a result of increased snow-

The canyon section

fall in the mountains, and despite the diversion of Nechako River headwaters to the Pacific Coast, at Kemano, for hydropower. The much larger Fraser River of the glacial period built out a delta 100 miles west of Hope into the Strait of Georgia, but the present river has cut down about 200 or 300 feet into this older, higher glacial delta and has also developed its own recent flood plain close to sea level. The mouth of the Fraser has at least three main distributary channels as it discharges its load of silt into the Strait of Georgia. Prior to European settlement in the mid-19th century, the Fraser River annually flooded its low banks throughout the delta, but farmers had diked the main river by the end of the century. These dikes were raised and strengthened after a disastrous flood in early June 1948, when the maximum daily discharge exceeded 500,000 cubic feet per second.

Human exploitation. The economy of the Fraser River Basin is based mainly on forestry. Coniferous forests cover most of the Interior Plateau, except in the dry, southern valleys, which are covered with narrow strips of grassland on the lower slopes. Prior to 1940 small sawmills cut a little lumber along the three railway lines that crossed the basin. After 1950, however, the northward extension of the Pacific Great Eastern Railway (subsequently called the British Columbia Railway) and the improvement of highway facilities increased the accessibility of the forests; and the merging of smaller companies, together with the introduction of pulp mills, consuming chips and small trees, heightened the utilization of forest resources. As a result the Fraser Basin became the second area of lumber production in British Columbia. Forest products are either transported to Vancouver for overseas markets or are taken eastward by rail to central Canada and the midwestern United States. The turbulent Fraser River itself is not actually used in the forestry industry, even for the transport of logs to the sawmills.

Agriculture has not developed greatly within the river basin, except for cattle ranching on the grasslands and upper level parklands in the Chilcotin Plateau, west of the Fraser River, and the Nicola Valley, south of the Thompson River. Ranching was established in the 1860s to supply the gold mining camps and then, after gold mining declined, to supply meat to the growing city of Vancouver. The level land of the Interior Plateau around Prince George had only minor agricultural use, prior to 1940, because of the lack of any large, local urban markets. As cities such as Prince George grew, farmland expanded nearby, but, as a local occupation, farming does not compete economically with forestry.

The Fraser River is the major producer of salmon in British Columbia, and its nearby tributaries and headwater lakes are the spawning grounds of several species of salmon. These salmon ascend the river in late summer to spawn and then go downstream the following year to spend the next two or three years in the ocean. Because of these migratory habits, salmon fishing takes place mainly off the Fraser River mouth, and only Indians have fishing rights in the river basin itself. The various tributaries of the Fraser produce different numbers of salmon from year to year, depending on the two- or four-year cycles of the spawning salmon.

Although the Fraser River has an enormous potential waterpower—conservatively estimated at more than 5,000,000 horsepower, excluding its tributaries—this power remained untapped in the early 1970s, because dams could curtail or destroy the fish runs. A dam at the suggested site of Moran, north of Lillooet, for example, could produce more than 2,000,000 horsepower. If new technological advances can be used to get fish successfully past dams in both directions, then such dams would have irrigation, flood control, and recreational value, as well as being a source of power for the urban markets of Vancouver. Yet by the early 1970s the only developed waterpower sites were at Bridge River, a tributary in the southwestern part of the Fraser River Basin, and in association with the westward diversion of the headwaters of the Nechako River through a tunnel in the Coast Mountains to Kemano and Kitimat on the Pacific Coast.

Forest products

Water power

BIBLIOGRAPHY. BRUCE HUTCHISON, *The Fraser* (1965), a popular account of the history and use of the river.

(J.L.Ro.)

Frederick I Barbarossa, Emperor

Frederick I Barbarossa (Redbeard), of the House of Hohenstaufen, was one of the greatest of the Holy Roman emperors of the Middle Ages. A crusader and an effective opponent of the papacy, he became a legendary German hero, a symbol of unity to the German people.

By courtesy of the Biblioteca Apostolica Vaticana

Frederick I as crusader, miniature from a manuscript. Henry of Schäftlarn (right) dedicates to him a copy of the *History of the First Crusade* by Robert of St Remy. In the Vatican Library (Vat. Lat. 2001).

Frederick was born *c.* 1123, the son of Frederick II, duke of Swabia, and Judith, daughter of Henry IX, duke of Bavaria, of the rival dynasty of the Welfs. After succeeding his father as duke of Swabia, Frederick was elected German king on March 4, 1152, in Frankfurt, succeeding his uncle, Emperor Conrad III. Frederick's contemporaries believed that because he united in himself the blood of the Welfs and the Hohenstaufen, he would solve the internal problems of the kingdom. The announcement of his election, which he sent to Pope Eugenius III, made it plain that Frederick I was not ready to recognize the pre-eminence over the emperors that the popes had won during the quarrel over the right of investiture of bishops and abbots. Frederick, moreover, filled several vacant episcopal sees, thereby violating the Concordat of Worms of 1122. Nevertheless, he was to learn that he could not prevail against the papacy as easily as the earlier emperors, Otto I and Henry III, had done because the political balance of the West had changed. Under the powerful emperor Manuel I Comnenus, the Byzantine Empire had grown to be a political factor in the Mediterranean and in Italy. Southern Italy and Sicily were united in the Norman kingdom of Roger II. The cities of the Lombards, which had been little more than a nuisance to the earlier emperors, had now become invincible.

Frederick started his struggle for the old goal of the predominance of the Empire over the European monarchies with great political skill. By not recognizing the treaty of alliance between his predecessor, Conrad III, and Manuel I Comnenus of Byzantium against Roger II of Sicily, Frederick forced Pope Eugenius III to sign the Treaty of Constance (1153) with him because the Pope was more exposed to pressure from the Norman kingdom to the south as well as from Arnold of Brescia in Rome. Frederick promised not to make peace with the

The treaty of Constance

Roman commune, headed by Arnold (whom he hanged) or with the Normans without the agreement of the Pope. He also promised not to concede any Italian land to the Byzantine Emperor and, finally, to maintain the position of the papacy (*honor papatus*). Eugene III, on his part, promised that Frederick would receive the imperial crown and that the rights of the empire would be maintained. When Manuel of Byzantium offered Frederick a Byzantine princess as wife and attempted to induce him to fight against the Norman kingdom, Frederick refused. The successor of Eugenius III, Pope Adrian IV, honoured the Treaty of Constance and crowned Frederick emperor on June 18, 1155, in Rome.

The German princes refused to give Frederick the support necessary to attack the Sicilian kingdom, which, under Roger's son William I (reigned 1154–66), was passing through a crisis. Although Manuel now formed an allegiance with the rebellious Norman barons, the city of Genoa, and the Pope, Adrian still would not accept the Byzantine offer of help against William I of Sicily. After William had brought his crisis to an end, he was able to force the Pope to sign the Concordat of Benevento in 1156 by which Adrian gave William Sicily and the Norman principalities on the mainland as far north as Naples and Capua and granted him special rights for the Sicilian church. This new treaty was in violation of the Treaty of Constance. Cardinal Roland (later Pope Alexander III) was supposed to explain the Pope's new policy to the princes and to the Emperor at the imperial Diet of Besançon 1157. A letter from the Pope, which was translated in an inflammatory manner by the imperial chancellor Rainald of Dassel, caused a critical argument between the papal delegation and the German princes over whether or not the empire was dependent upon the papacy. Adrian explained later that he meant the word *beneficium*, which had caused all the trouble, to mean benefit and not fief.

Attempt to regain imperial rights

In 1158, after Frederick had solved several decisive domestic problems (see below), he began his second campaign in Italy, seeking the complete restoration of the imperial rights. After laying siege to and conquering Milan, which had attempted to oppose him, Frederick opened the Diet of Roncaglia. The goal of this Diet was to define and guarantee the rights of the emperor, which would bring the empire an estimated 30,000 pounds of silver per year. Frederick attempted, beginning in 1158 and especially after 1162, not only to achieve the granting of these rights but also to put a systematic financial administration into effect. His goal was to reduce imperial Italy to a system of well-controlled castles, palaces, and cities, with the self-government of the cities controlled by imperial officials. What the Emperor saw as a restoration of the imperial rights, however, was considered by the cities as a curtailment of their freedom. A tax called the *fodrum* was levied on all the inhabitants of imperial Italy; in return the Italian nobles and communes were excused from service in Frederick's armies and were guaranteed his protection. A portion of the Italian money went to the German princes; this enabled Frederick to win their support without making too many political concessions to them in Germany. The ecclesiastical princes of the empire, however, still had to render full service for Italy; the archbishopric of Mainz suffered severe financial losses because Archbishop Christian was active for a long time in Italy as imperial legate. The Italian taxes allowed Frederick to enlist mercenaries (Brabantini) in order to free himself militarily, to a certain extent, from the fief holders. The money of Italy was not, however, the only motive of Frederick's Italian policy.

The Pope, as well as the cities, felt threatened by a tightly organized imperial state in Italy. In 1159 Cardinal Octavian was elected Pope Victor IV with the support of Frederick, and Cardinal Roland was elected Pope Alexander III in a tumultuous and disputed voting session. Alexander, supported by many cardinals, was also immediately recognized by William of Sicily as the true pope. At the council of 1160 in Pavia, convened by the Emperor, only Victor IV was present and was declared the rightful pope, thereby earning Alexander's hostility.

Alexander III, one of the greatest lawyers of the church, wanted to found a papacy that would be independent of the Emperor; he excommunicated Frederick in 1160. France, England, Spain, Hungary, the Lombards, and even Emperor Manuel joined Alexander's party; Alexander retired to France in 1161, where he remained until 1165. John of Salisbury asked at that time: "Who made the Germans judges of the nations?" Barbarossa's attempt to persuade King Louis VII of France to try to heal the schism when they met at Saint-Jean-de-Losne on the Saône was of no avail. Alexander attempted to bring Frederick back into the church but with no success. At Alexander's urging, the Byzantine emperor Manuel Comnenus now prepared to form an alliance with France and was ready to recognize the Pope. In 1162 Milan was destroyed by Frederick.

Hostility of Pope Alexander III

When Victor IV died in 1164, Paschal III (reigned 1164–68) was quickly elected as the new imperial pope on the urging of Rainald of Dassel, perhaps against the will of the Emperor. Because of friction between Louis VII and Henry II of England and because the latter was embroiled in an argument with Thomas Becket, Barbarossa decided to form an alliance with Henry II. At the Diet of 1165 in Würzburg, Frederick swore not to recognize Alexander III. The promises made by the English delegates that Frederick's political wishes would be recognized were denied by Henry II, who preferred to keep Alexander under pressure, thus making things more difficult for Becket.

Following the death of William I of Sicily in 1166, Frederick felt that the time had come to strike a decisive blow against Alexander III, who had returned to Rome, and against Sicily. The Lombard League was formed to defend against the Emperor's fourth expedition to Italy. Frederick's expedition ended in disaster, however, when malaria broke out in his army. Rainald of Dassel died in Rome at this time, causing a change in the imperial strategy. When Frederick negotiated peace between Louis VII and Henry II and then sent the Bishop of Bamberg in 1170 to Alexander III and envoys to Byzantium, a détente resulted that even Alexander could not escape. In his fifth Italian campaign (1174) Frederick did not defeat the Lombards militarily, but they were forced to subject themselves to him in the Armistice of Montebello. Because Duke Henry the Lion of Saxony refused to come to his aid, however, Frederick lost the Battle of Legnano against the Lombards. He was now ready to deal with the Pope, and in 1176 they signed the Treaty of Anagni. In the Peace of Venice (1177) Barbarossa acknowledged Alexander III as the true pope. In front of the Church of St. Mark's, Barbarossa received the kiss of peace from the Pope. At Venice the imperial delegates had been able to improve the Emperor's position. Above all was the fact that, although a truce had been negotiated with the Lombards, they were not included in the peace treaty. A treaty with the Lombards was finally confirmed in the year 1183.

Acknowledgement of Alexander III

Barbarossa meanwhile had also initiated sweeping changes in his empire, where Duke Henry the Lion of Saxony was the strongest prince next to him. When Barbarossa took office, Henry had laid claim to Bavaria, the domain of the margrave Henry II Jasomirgott of Austria. Barbarossa bestowed Bavaria on Henry the Lion, and as compensation he elevated the margravate to a dukedom, with special rights. The Emperor also left the dukedom of Saxony and Mecklenburg under Henry the Lion's control, and in 1154 the Duke received the privilege of investing bishops in the colonial land east of the Elbe. The year 1158 was of great importance for the empire; Barbarossa founded the imperial territory of Pleissnerland (south of Leipzig), elevated Duke Vladislav II of Bohemia to king, and granted the Archbishop of Bremen important privileges, restoring the Bishop's lost political power. Also in 1158 Frederick promised to enfeoff Waldemar I, the Great of Denmark—that is, make him his vassal with certain rights.

Meanwhile, Henry the Lion founded the cities of Munich and Lübeck (1158). The founding of Lübeck brought German merchants to the Baltic Sea. The Duke closed a contract between the Germans and the inhabitants of Gotland and sent envoys to Scandinavia and Russia. A trade agreement was closed in 1189 with Novgorod. About 1180 German merchants reached Riga; their advance was protected by Henry's conquest of Mecklenburg (1177). By 1148 Henry had the county and the town of Stade, the most important harbour on the Elbe, in his control.

At the same time German colonists had settled in Brandenburg under the margrave Albert I the Bear and in Silesia. Barbarossa had restored the dependence of the Polish dukes during two expeditions to Poland in 1157 and 1172. Henry the Lion, the most powerful prince in northern Germany, made Brunswick his residence. He had repeatedly challenged other princes in feuds, but Archbishop Wichmann of Magdeburg, Albrecht of Brandenburg, Landgrave Louis III of Thuringia, and Archbishop Rainald of Cologne offered repeated resistance. It is not completely certain that Duke Henry's refusal of aid to Frederick in 1176 was the sole cause of his downfall. Apparently his manifold breach of the peace of the land caused the Emperor to accuse him, to conquer Lübeck, and, in 1180, through a council of the princes in Gelnhausen, to depose him. Henry lost his dukedom; Westphalia was given to the Archbishop of Cologne, and Bavaria was granted to Otto of Wittelsbach. Henry, who was married to Mathilde of England, went in exile to King Henry II of England. As a result of Henry the Lion's trial, the feudal system was made a still stronger basis of the imperial constitution. Thereafter, only those princes who had received their land directly from the Emperor were admitted to the exclusive circle of imperial princes (*Reichsfürsten*). Barbarossa elevated the princes of Pomerania to dukes, and the counts of Andechs became the dukes of Merania (in the neighbourhood of Trieste). Steiermark became a dukedom. Another important measure of Barbarossa was the elevation of the Bishop of Würzburg to duke of Franconia in 1168.

Barbarossa had attempted to hold the increasing power of the princes in check. By 1152 he had found a solution for the area of Burgundy, which also belonged to the empire. He made Duke Berthold IV of Zähringen his representative for the dukedom of Burgundy as far as the Mediterranean and married Béatrix, the daughter of Count Rainald of Burgundy (1156). Barbarossa attempted to build his own imperial territory between the areas controlled by the princes. This territory was composed of castles, cities, landholdings, ministerial seats, and single rights that were more or less thickly scattered from Swabia to Thuringia. This large territory was ruled by imperial ministerials (*ministeriales imperii*). These men had great power because many of them belonged to the Emperor's circle. The most famous of them was Kuno of Münzenberg, whose castle is preserved in the Wetterau north of Frankfurt and who founded the town of Friedberg. The territorial "peace laws" belong to his efforts to keep the Emperor in power.

Chivalry gave Barbarossa's time a special stamp. He expressed his enthusiasm for knighthood as the ideal way of life at the festival of Pentecost at Mainz in 1184, where he dubbed his sons knights. This festival was surpassed by the "Diet of Jesus Christ" in 1188, when the margravate Namur was transformed into an imperial principality. More important was Barbarossa's call to the Third Crusade in the spring of 1189 to free Jerusalem from Saladin's army, which had captured it in 1187. Before his departure he returned the former possessions of the Countess Mathilde of Tuscany, a part of the papal state, to the Pope. In 1190 the Emperor drowned while trying to cross the Saleph River.

Frederick Barbarossa had attempted to continue the imperial policy of the rulers of the Saxon and Salian lines. His state was still founded upon the noble, the high noble, and above all the newly founded rank of the imperial servants. The imperial cities in Germany were governed by royal officials (*advocatis sculteti*), and the citizens had their part in the government. The cities played no role in politics. Frederick had to recognize that the church, after the quarrel of investiture, had become a firmly controlled institution, with its powers strictly defined by law. The church had joined itself to the struggle for freedom of the economically powerful states in upper Italy. Pope Alexander III was able to force the kings of Europe (especially Louis VII of France) not to enter into a political agreement with Barbarossa. Only Philip II Augustus of France signed a treaty with Barbarossa in order to free himself from the pressures created by the Anglo-Norman occupation on the mainland. There was no chance that a continuation and increase of the imperial policy in the territories controlled by the empire would have broken the power of the princes. Germany developed into a system of territorial states after Barbarossa's death, while France developed during the time of Philip II Augustus into a centralized monarchial state. Barbarossa had a strong feeling for law and imperial prestige. His steadfast opposition to the popes and to Henry the Lion made him the symbol of German unity in the romantic glorification of the 19th century. People since the 14th century believed he was sleeping in the imperial castle of Kyffhäuser and hoped for his return. A monument to him was erected there during the years 1890–96.

BIBLIOGRAPHY. The chief contemporary source of Frederick's life is *Ottonis episcopi frisingensis Gesta Friderici I*, ed. by GEORG WAITZ and B. VON SIMSON (1912; Eng. trans., *The Deeds of Frederick Barbarossa, by Otto of Freising and His Continuator, Rahewin*, 1953). WILHELM VON GIESEBRECHT, *Geschichte der deutschen Kaiserzeit*, vol. 5–6, 1880–88 (1895), treats Frederick from a 19th-century German nationalist point of view. H. SIMONSFELD, *Jahrbücher des deutschen Reiches unter Friedrich I*, vol. 1—till 1158 only (1908), documents all that is known about Barbarossa. PETER MUNZ, *Frederick Barbarossa* (1969), is a good English-language biography, although some points are subject to dispute. ALFRED HAVERKAMP, *Herrschaftsformen der Frühstaufer in Reichsitalien*, 2 vol. (1970–71). is a very important book on the constitutional and financial history of Frederick in Italy.

(H.Pa.)

Frederick II, Emperor

Holy Roman emperor, German king, and king of Sicily, last of the great Hohenstaufen rulers, Frederick II was born on December 26, 1194, in Jesi, in the March of Ancona, Italy. He was the grandson of Emperor Frederick Barbarossa and the son of Constance of Sicily and Emperor Henry VI, who, at the time of his son's birth, was about to conquer Sicily.

At the end of 1196 the German princes elected Frederick king at Frankfurt. His father, however, failed in his attempt to gain the princes' support to make Frederick's succession hereditary. Just before embarking on a cru-

Youth

Frederick II with a falcon, miniature from his treatise, *De arte venandi cum avibus*. In the Vatican Library (MS. Palat. Lat. 1071).

Deposition of Henry the Lion

sade to the Holy Land, Emperor Henry died in September 1197 after a brief illness, only 32 years old. Though the medieval Roman Empire was at the height of its strength, the Emperor's death brought it close to dissolution.

After the death of her husband, Empress Constance had young Frederick brought to Sicily, where in May 1198 he was crowned king of Sicily. Before her death later that year, Constance loosened the bonds that joined Sicily to the empire and to Germany by appointing Pope Innocent III her son's guardian as well as regent of the Kingdom of Sicily, which was already under papal suzerainty. In Germany two rival kings were elected, Frederick's uncle Philip of Swabia and Otto of Brunswick, as Otto IV.

Even the Pope, however, did not succeed in protecting Sicily from many years of anarchy. German and papal captains, local barons, and Sicilian Saracens, as well as the cities of Genoa and Pisa, fought for mastery of the country. The situation was not stabilized until the imperial chancellor conquered Palermo in November 1206 and governed in Frederick's name. In December 1208 Frederick, then 14, was declared of age.

In 1209 he married the much older Constance of Aragon, who brought him an urgently needed troop of knights with whose help he gained control of Sicily, defeated a conspiracy of the barons, and was partially successful in regaining the crown properties that had been lost during his minority. At this time his relations with the Pope began to show signs of strain.

Frederick's Sicilian efforts were seriously endangered when at the end of 1210 Otto IV invaded the realm on the mainland and in 1211 even threatened Sicily itself. Otto withdrew, however, when in September 1211 a number of German princes deposed him and elected Frederick king.

Years of triumph. Before leaving for Germany in March 1212, Frederick had his one-year-old son Henry VII crowned king of Sicily and granted various privileges to the Holy See. Having rapidly conquered south Germany, where he met almost no opposition, Frederick was elected once again king of Germany by a large majority of princes at Frankfort in December 1212, and crowned a few days later. In the same year he concluded an alliance with France against Otto, who was decisively defeated at the Battle of Bouvines in July 1214.

Consolidation of the empire In April 1220, Frederick's nine-year-old son Henry VII was elected king by the German princes, thus negating Frederick's promise to Pope Innocent that he would relinquish control of Sicily in favour of Henry, for it meant that Sicily and Germany would eventually be united under one ruler. Although Frederick sought to exonerate himself with Pope Honorius II by claiming that the election had been held without his knowledge, he had to pay for it by surrendering extensive royal prerogatives to the German ecclesiastical princes.

Crowned emperor by the Pope in St. Peter's Church, in Rome, on November 22, 1220, Frederick confirmed on the same day the legal separation of the empire from the Kingdom of Sicily while continuing the existing personal union. In addition, he granted important privileges to the Italian ecclesiastics and issued laws against heretics, and it seemed indeed that harmony had been re-established between the Emperor and the Pope for some years to come. Frederick spent the following years consolidating his rule in Sicily. He broke the resistance of the barons to revocation of certain of their privileges and defeated the rebellious Saracens (1222–24), whom he later resettled in Apulia where they became his most faithful subjects, providing him with a loyal bodyguard immune against papal influence.

In addition to erecting a chain of castles and border fortifications, he had enlarged the harbours of his kingdom and established a navy and a fleet of merchant vessels. He instituted measures designed to bring trade under state control and make the manufacture of certain products the monopoly of the state. Finally, he created a civil service for which candidates were trained at the first European state university, in Naples, which he himself founded in 1224.

In the meantime, the Pope was reminding the Emperor of the crusading vows he had taken at his coronations in 1212 and 1220. Frederick, however, was inclined to postpone such a venture until the Italian problems had been resolved. He claimed the Kingdom of Jerusalem for himself through his marriage to Isabella (Yolande) of Brienne, the heiress of the titular king of Jerusalem, who had become his wife in 1225 after Constance had died in 1222. Before embarking for the Holy Land, Frederick convened an imperial diet for Easter 1226 in Cremona, in northern Italy, in order to reinforce certain imperial rights in Italy and to prepare for the crusade. The cities of Lombardy, however, reconstituted themselves, under the leadership of Milan, as the Lombard League, and not only sabotaged the diet at Cremona but effectively opposed Frederick's reorganization of northern Italy. **Years as a crusader**

In September 1227, when Frederick was at last ready to embark from Brindisi for the Holy Land, an epidemic broke out among the crusaders. The new pope, Gregory IX, a passionate man who belonged to the intellectual world of Francis of Assisi—his personal friend whom he canonized as early as 1228—brushed aside Frederick's justification and excommunicated him for his failure to carry out the crusade.

In June 1228, ignoring the excommunication, Frederick set sail from Brindisi. In the Holy Land, following complex negotiations, he obtained Jerusalem, Bethlehem, and Nazareth from the Sultan al-Kāmil of Egypt. It was certainly the impact of Frederick's personality on the Arab world, and not armed might, that made this treaty possible. On March 18, 1229, the excommunicated Emperor crowned himself king of Jerusalem in the Church of the Holy Sepulchre. This was the high point as well as the turning point of Frederick's conception of sovereignty. Eschatological prophecies concerning his rule were now made, and the Emperor considered himself to be a messiah, a new David. His entry into Jerusalem was compared with that of Christ on Palm Sunday, and, indeed, in a manifesto the Emperor, too, compared himself to Christ.

In the meantime, however, papal troops had penetrated into the Kingdom of Sicily. Frederick returned at once and reconquered the lost areas but did not in turn attack the Papal States. His diplomacy was rewarded: after the Treaty of San Germano (July 1230) he was absolved from excommunication the following month at Ceprano.

In August 1231, at Melfi, the Emperor issued his new constitutions for the Kingdom of Sicily. Not since the reign of the Byzantine emperor Justinian in the 6th century had the administrative law of a European state been codified. Frederick's codes contained many ideas that anticipated enlightened absolutism and the centralization of the state. During the same time, however, Frederick could not prevent his son, the German king Henry VII, from making a number of important concessions to the German princes. These concessions, confirmed by Frederick in 1232 at the diet of Cividale, strengthened the rule of the princes at the expense of the central power of the empire. These and other steps set back the development of communal self-government in Germany and furthered the independence of the principalities. In the meantime, relations between Frederick and Henry VII deteriorated steadily. Henry had been ruling independently in Germany since 1228, when in December 1234 he entered into an alliance with the Lombard League. This action amounted to high treason in the eyes of the Emperor. On Frederick's arrival in Germany, his son's rebellion collapsed; he died in a prison in Calabria in 1242.

His second wife having died in 1228, Frederick in July 1235 married Isabella of England. Shortly thereafter, he issued an edict of imperial peace, which also called for the appointment of a chief justice of the imperial court in order to protect the sovereign rights of the Emperor from further erosion.

After some military successes in Lombardy against the Lombard League, the Emperor returned to Germany in the autumn of 1236 to remove the rebellious duke Frederick of Austria and Styria from rule. In February 1237

Victory at Corte-nuova

he had his nine-year-old son Conrad IV elected king of Germany in Vienna. After several more months in Germany—it was to be his last visit—he descended into northern Italy. He defeated the Lombard League at Cortenuova, but, misjudging his strength, he rejected all Milanese peace overtures and insisted on unconditional surrender. It was a moment of grave historic importance when Frederick's hatred got the better of his judgment and blocked all possibilities of a peaceful settlement.

Struggle with the papacy. Milan and five other cities held out, and in October 1238 he had to raise the siege of Brescia. In the same year the marriage of Frederick's natural son Enzio with the Sardinian princess Adelasia and the designation of Enzio as king of Sardinia, in which the papacy claimed suzerainty, led to the final break with the Pope. Gregory IX deeply distrusted Frederick both in religious and political matters: Frederick was supposed to have jested that Moses, Christ, and Muḥammad were three impostors who had themselves been hoodwinked; and in the political arena the Pope was fearful that the Papal States were about to be isolated and encircled, particularly because a pro-imperial party had been formed in Rome. Under the pretext that the Emperor intended to drive him from Rome, Gregory excommunicated Frederick for the second time on Palm Sunday, March 20, 1239. This was the beginning of the last phase of the gigantic struggle between the papacy and the empire; it ended with the death of the Emperor and the downfall of his house.

Frederick countered the excommunication with a number of important manifestos, most of them composed by Pietro della Vigna, a member of the imperial chancery, who had outstanding literary gifts. The manifesto emphasized that the cardinals were meant to participate in the leadership of the church, and Frederick even tried to evoke solidarity among the secular princes. He also, however, intensified his military activities in northern Italy. In order to finance his constantly growing need for arms, he instituted a thorough administrative reorganization of imperial Italy (among others, the formation of ten vice regencies) and of the Kingdom of Sicily. In addition, he decreed the rigorous surveillance of the population. In central Italy he took the offensive, occupying the March of Ancona and the Duchy of Spoleto, and in February 1240 his army marched into the Papal States and threatened Rome. At the last moment, however, the Pope won the support of the Romans.

Following the defeat of a Genoese fleet bringing delegates for a papal council to Rome, more than 100 high-ranking ecclesiastics—cardinals and bishops among them—were taken as Frederick's prisoners to Apulia. This military victory proved, however, to be a political disadvantage: it provided material for propaganda depicting Frederick as an oppressor of the church.

While still encamped before Rome, Frederick received the news of Pope Gregory's death and thereupon withdrew to Sicily. In the meantime, the Mongols had invaded Europe. They were temporarily halted in the extremely bloody Battle of Liegnitz in Silesia on April 9, 1241, but probably only the sudden death of their leader Genghis Khan prevented further Mongol advances at that time.

Celestine IV's brief pontificate was followed by a long interregnum. When in 1243 Innocent IV was elected, Frederick, at the urging of the German princes and of King Louis IX of France, opened negotiations with the new pope. Agreement between the Pope and the Emperor seemed close on the evacuation of the Papal States, when in June 1244 Innocent fled the city. In Lyons he convened a council for 1245, and in July of that year deposed the Emperor, the obstacle to reconciliation apparently being the status of the Lombard communes.

Negotiations with Innocent IV

The battle between the Emperor and the papacy then raged in full fury; on the papal side the Emperor was branded as the precursor of the anti-Christ; on the imperial side he was hailed as a messiah. The Emperor supported the contemporary demand that the church return to the poverty and saintliness of the early Christian community and again appealed to the princes of Europe to join in a defensive league against the power-hungry prelates. Most of the princes, however, remained neutral, and, although two successive German antikings received little support, the Emperor steadily lost ground in Germany.

In May 1247, Frederick's planned journey to Lyons in order to plead his own case before the papal council was interrupted by the revolt of the strategically placed city of Parma. In the wake of this debacle much of central Italy and the Romagna was lost. The following year the Emperor was to suffer further blows of fate; Pietro della Vigna, for many years the Emperor's confidant, was accused of treason and committed suicide in prison. In May 1249 King Enzio of Sardinia, Frederick's favourite son, was captured by the Bolognese and was kept incarcerated until his death in 1272.

The Emperor's position, both in Italy and—through the efforts of his son, Conrad IV—in Germany, was improving when he died unexpectedly on December 13, 1250, in Castel Fiorentino in Apulia. He was buried in the cathedral of Palermo near his first wife, his parents, and his Norman grandfather.

When the news of his death was published, all Europe was deeply shaken. Doubts arose that he was really dead; false Fredericks appeared everywhere; in Sicily a legend grew that he had been conveyed to the Aetna volcano; in Germany that he was encapsuled in a mountain and would return as the latter-day emperor to punish the worldly church and peacefully re-establish the Holy Roman Empire. Yet he was also thought to live on in his heirs. In fact, however, within 22 years after his death, all of them were dead: victims of the battle with the papacy that their father had begun.

Frederick's character was marked by sharp contradictions, undoubtedly the result of his insecure and emotionally barren childhood. Enchanting amiability and gaiety were paired with cruelty; harshness and rigidity existed side by side with superior intelligence and a keen sense of reality; tolerance and intolerance went hand in hand; impulsive sensuality did not stand in the way of genuine piety; imbalance and inner discord pervaded his personality and his achievements.

Assessment

Frederick cannot be considered the first modern man on the throne, nor a pioneer of the Renaissance, as some historians have maintained. Though his gifted personality heralded some of the intellectual trends of later times, he was, all in all, a man of the Middle Ages. He had indeed had the good fortune to have grown up in Sicily in a mixed culture that uniquely combined elements of antiquity, Arabic and Jewish wisdom, the Occidental spirit of the Middle Ages, and Norman realism. The intellectual life of his court reflected this heritage. A courtly "republic of scholars," it nurtured and fostered the natural sciences as well as philosophy, poetry, and mathematics, and translations as well as original writing, both in Latin and in the vernacular. The pursuit of knowledge without special respect for traditional authorities was characteristic of Frederick and his court.

Witness to the intellectual vigour and distinction of Frederick himself and those around him are the content and style of his great legal codices and manifestos, many of them serving as examples to later generations; the edifices he erected, particularly the classic style of the Castello del Monte—a fusion of poetry and mathematics in stone; and, most outstanding, his own work *De arte venandi cum avibus*, a standard work on falconry based entirely on his own experimental research.

Frederick's concept of the emperor's function was rooted in the ideology of the late Greco-Roman period and the Judeo-Christian philosophy of the Middle Ages, emphasizing the sacredness and universal character of the office. In the light of it, Frederick claimed pre-eminence for the emperor over all other secular rulers—undoubtedly an ill-timed claim in an age when separate nation-states were developing. Thus, Frederick's policies, full of intellectual and political promise, were in actuality dogged by tragedy.

BIBLIOGRAPHY. E.A. WINKELMANN, *Kaiser Friedrich II*, 2 vol. (1889–97), a biography to the year 1233; E. KANTOROwicz, *Kaiser Friedrich der Zweite*, 2 vol. (1927–31), still the most basic work; K. HAMPE, *Kaiser Friedrich II in der Auffassung der Nachwelt* (1925); R.M. KLOOS, "Literaturbericht 1950–56," *Traditio*, 2:426–456 (1956); H.M. SCHALLER, *Kaiser Friedrich II* (1964); H. NIESE, "Zur Geschichte des geistigen Lebens am Hofe Kaiser Friedrichs II," *Historische Zeitschrift*, 108:473–546 (1912); G. WOLF (ed.), *Stupor Mundi: Zur Geschichte Friedrichs II von Hohenstaufen* (1966), a collection of the most important research papers following Kantorowicz's work.

(Gu.W.)

Frederick II the Great, of Prussia

Frederick II the Great, third king of Prussia, from 1740 to 1786, played a leading part in the breakup of the Holy Roman Empire and the rise of what had been a small, provincial kingdom into a great European power that eventually headed a new, united Germany. He ranks as one of history's great captains, who modernized warfare and reintroduced the strategy of attack, preceding Napoleon in the triple role of head of state, army organizer, and active commander in chief. He was also the first monarch to uphold, at least in theory, toleration of all religions and among the first to embody consciously the principle of enlightened despotism or benevolent autocracy. An absolute ruler (although he called himself "the first servant of the state" and described a crown as "a hat that lets the rain in"), he initiated the first codified German law and enforced general education in advance of other countries.

Frederick II, portrait by Antoine Pesne (1683–1757). In the Gemäldegalerie, Berlin.

Frederick was born on January 24, 1712, when the Prussian kingdom was only 11 years old, the third and eldest surviving son of Frederick William I and Sophie Dorothea of Hanover, daughter of George I and sister of George II of England.

Apprenticeship. His childhood and youth were unhappy, not least because they were overshadowed by family conflict caused by political rivalry between the two royal houses. His father, moreover, was a fanatically practical and self-righteous man, as well as a rabid militarist wholeheartedly opposed to his son's artistic and studious leanings.

Subjected from infancy to a Spartan regimen that placed army drill and the Lutheran catechism high on the educational syllabus but excluded Latin, poetry, philosophy, and music along with every form of "frivolous" comfort, Frederick's early taste for these may have developed in typical reaction. If so, an endless chain reaction resulted, in that despair at the son's unconventional preferences goaded the father to ever more rigorous treatment of him, which, in turn, widened the gulf between them. Instead of the "brotherly" love and trust that Frederick William had hopefully envisaged, their relationship became more and more one of open antipathy on his side and devious desperation on his son's.

As he experienced similar disappointments in his relations with his subjects (the streets would empty as though by magic when the patriarchal King went for his daily stroll), with his patronizing Hanoverian in-laws, and with the Emperor (who openly manipulated him), Frederick William's choler grew to pathological dimensions. That his war machine—except for one brief expedition early in his reign—never came to operate in earnest and that he suffered increasingly from gout, did not improve his state of mind. The periodical, roaring scenes within the royal apartments sometimes caused crowds to collect in the street outside. Even in public, at troop reviews and at court functions, the King would thrash the Crown Prince and force him to kiss the father's boots: this at a time when Frederick was past adolescence and, together with his favourite sister, Wilhelmina, the object of negotiations for a double marriage with their English cousins, the Prince of Wales and the Princess Amelia.

The climax came when, these negotiations finally broken off, Frederick saw no way out of his intolerable situation but to run away to England. With the help of two friends, lieutenants Hans Hermann von Katte and Peter Karl Christoph von Keith, Frederick made an attempt at escape in the summer of 1730. Betrayed by the last-minute qualms of Keith, who then himself fled the country, Frederick and Katte were arrested as deserters from the army, stripped of rank and civil rights, imprisoned, and brought to trial by court martial.

Attempted flight

The court martial sentenced Katte to two years' fortress imprisonment and declared itself incompetent to judge the heir to the throne. But the King, having already decreed Frederick eliminated from the line of succession, overrode the verdict. He imposed the death penalty on Katte and let it be known that the same was intended for his son. By his order, Katte was beheaded within view of Frederick's cell and Frederick was forced to look on. The 18-year-old prince, who until then had conducted himself with remarkable fortitude, was thrown into such a state of abject terror that the prison chaplain was able to inform the King of Frederick's now absolute submission. The King responded with a conditional pardon. Frederick was to earn his freedom and restitution of rank and heritage by serving an indefinite term in the civil administration.

In retrospect, Frederick came to regard this period of probation as invaluable training for his future occupation, just as he subsequently saw his father's notorious parsimony and drill mania in the light of the result—the only solvent treasury in Europe and an army second to none by virtue of its strength and discipline. At the time of his working as a clerk, however, his diligence was less enthusiastic than expedient; and, at length winning full pardon and reinstatement, complete with a country residence of his own at Rheinsberg, near Berlin, he was able to nurse his cultivated pursuits out of range of the King's eye. Married in 1733, against his inclination, to Elizabeth Christine, daughter of the Duke of Brunswick-Bevern, he filled his little court with congenial company, including painters, writers, and musicians, read and wrote and played the flute to his heart's content and struck up an ardent pen-friendship with Voltaire, the uncrowned king of the progressive intellectual movement known as the Enlightenment.

Accession to the throne. On May 31, 1740, Frederick William I died. The new king, who had awaited this event with impatience, was prostrated with grief as much to his own astonishment as to that of his friends. His friends soon had additional cause to be astonished. Like his enemies, they, too, had precipitately hailed the dawn of a regime of dilettantism and laissez-faire, only to find "the young master worse than the old one." This, to be sure, was an exaggeration. While Frederick maintained the status quo as regards the civil and military establishment in general, his first acts as sovereign included the abolition of torture as a means of judicial inquiry, abolition of press censorship, abolition of religious discrimination, and abolition of Frederick William's darling "giant" grenadier guards—composed of men measuring never less than six feet in height—which the old king had avowed his "one and only vice": an expensive luxury of dubious military value. Exiled savants were recalled and foreign scientists were invited to restock the neglected Academy of Berlin, which had been founded under Frederick's grandfather on the model of the English Royal Society. Housing and employment schemes were launched; numbers of draconic laws were abrogated, and the quality of mercy, conspicuously lacking hitherto, became an express adjunct of justice.

Also, the new king hastened to make his debut in the cosmopolitan republic of letters with the publication, under Voltaire's wing, of a treatise entitled *Antimachiavel*, which, in line with enlightened principles, affirmed a princely ethic founded on virtue, justice, and responsibility. The ideas were not so new as was their being uttered by a reigning monarch, who thereby gained his ambition to qualify as a Philosophe.

But that was no longer Frederick's sole or even principal ambition. Fame was what he craved above all things —resounding, comprehensive glory. His opportunity came soon enough, with the death of the Habsburg emperor Charles VI only five months after Frederick's accession. The Emperor left no son, and his daughter Maria Theresa succeeded to the hereditary Habsburg crown lands. All Europe had been waiting for this moment, none more tensely than the Hohenzollern House of Brandenburg-Prussia.

Foreign policies. Since 1537 the margrave-electors of Brandenburg had held a legally supported claim to three Silesian duchies, which successive Habsburg rulers of the surrounding Austrian territories had persistently frustrated, though holding out repeated promises to ratify it whenever Brandenburg's political or military assistance was required. It was at once the weakness and the stimulus of Prussia's growth that many of the Brandenburg possessions were scattered, often incontiguously, in Germany, rendering consolidation an imperative need. This, along with acquiring a commensurate prestige, without which real power must remain incomplete, had long been the driving force of Hohenzollern policy. It was part and parcel of Frederick's inheritance.

In his memoirs he made no bones about his private motives for invading Silesia, which he did in the winter of 1740. "I was young, had plenty of money and a large army, and wanted to see my name in the newspapers," he wrote, characteristically unable to repress a quip however damaging to himself or embittering to others. He nonetheless believed in the fundamental legality of his aggression, as unquestioningly as he took it for granted that every major continental power would immediately make inroads on Maria Theresa's heritage.

The Emperor had sought to make provision against his decease without male heirs by means of the Pragmatic Sanction—to obtain guaranteed recognition by the European nations of his daughter's sovereignty. As a woman, Maria Theresa was excluded from candidature to the (elective) imperial office, whose security depended on the military contingents and financial subventions furnished by the autonomous states of the empire. By reason of the prolonged Habsburg tenure of the imperial throne, Austria, though technically only one among those states, had come to rely on such support by the rest. Without it, Austria would now be extremely vulnerable. All the world, therefore, took the Emperor's death as a signal for blackmail and pickings. The Austrian government itself was under no illusions as to the value of the signatures to the Pragmatic Sanction. Frederick, however, was the first off the mark and, hence, the target of international opprobrium.

Having instructed his ambassador to submit Prussian proposals to Vienna that Austria obviously could not accept—*i.e.*, an offer of military alliance plus the Brandenburg electoral vote for Maria Theresa's husband Francis of Lorraine in the forthcoming imperial election, in return for nothing less than the whole province of Silesia— Frederick marched an army of 40,000 into that province and within seven weeks made himself master of it.

The speed of his success owed something to decades of Austrian maladministration and to the oppression of

Protestantism, as well as the strategic elements of surprise and the numerical superiority of over ten Prussian soldiers to one of the Austrian garrison forces. Military resistance was slow to materialize and civil resistance nil, largely because of the liberal and orderly fashion in which the takeover was conducted. The first pitched battle of the counteroffensive, at Mollwitz on April 10, 1741, ended in victory for the Prussians.

Frederick, who had insisted on leading the campaign in person without any previous experience of war, was persuaded by the impact of a devastating Austrian cavalry charge that the day was lost, and he galloped off the field to safety. He did not see the tide turn very shortly after and did not hear the good news for another ten hours. "Let this be a lesson to young warriors, not to despair too soon," he advised the future readers of his memoirs, wherein he closely analyzed the mistakes that had been made and paid proper tribute to "the heroism and skill of those who won the day for me." Among the latter must be counted one he did not mention in the context: an old antagonist of his and bosom friend of Frederick William, Prince Leopold of Anhalt-Dessau. It was "the Old Dessauer" to whom the Prussian army owed its two unique, prime assets: the cadenced march, which had been in disuse since the days of imperial Rome, now brought to an ultimate perfection of instant, uniform mobility; and the iron ramrod, replacing the wooden, which greatly increased firing power.

As soon as his victory became known, Frederick was inundated with congratulations and overtures by virtually every European power, while Maria Theresa, on the eve of her coronation as queen of Hungary, was about to be abandoned by all, with the exception of England, where the news of Mollwitz had arrived a fortnight late. In the upshot, France and Prussia signed a secret treaty of mutual defense in June, and in October Austria and Prussia concluded an equally secret gentleman's agreement to make peace a few weeks hence: Frederick was to keep his conquests and allow the Austrian army to retire unhindered to Moravia.

For, meanwhile, the War of the Austrian Succession had broken out, in which it was the concerted objective of Bavaria, France, and Saxony to dismember the Habsburg crown lands. Their initial progress encouraged Frederick to break his unwritten pact with Austria as quickly as he had thereby violated the signed and sealed pact with the French; and there ensued behind the lines of battle such permutations of shady negotiations all around that at least one party, Frederick, privately recorded his amazement that anyone should ever bother with treaties at all.

Dissensions among the allies were aggravated by Austrian recovery. The elector of Bavaria had been elected the new emperor, but, by the time he was crowned Charles VII, the Franco-Bavarian reverses were so drastic that they made Frederick reconsider his position yet again, especially as the Prussian army in Silesia also was now in some straits. So, after another Prussian victory in May 1742—a victory, this time, under the King's own baton—Austria and Prussia, after all, honoured their secret undertaking of the preceding autumn and concluded a separate peace. In spite of Maria Theresa's particular animosity toward Frederick and Frederick's unabated need to secure his conquests by extending them, it was in the interests of neither to have the other annihilated and thus disrupt the continental balance of power. Moved by the same consideration, England acted as mediator.

The Treaty of Breslau (June 1742) left Frederick in possession of almost the whole of Silesia and his reputation finally in shreds. Even his companions in mutual admiration, the Philosophes, who had stuck by him through thick and thin, could not forgive his perfidy when it was France, the spiritual home of the Enlightenment, that he was breaking faith with, and not merely the reactionary power of the Habsburgs. Frederick was stung to self-defense in verse and prose, which led him on by logical stages to try his hand at historiography, an art that had lately come to be regarded as the finest form of literature. His *Histoire de mon temps*, covering the

Invasion of Silesia

War of the Austrian Succession

political events of his lifetime so as to explain his actions rather than proffer excuses, did credit to his truthfulness, objectivity, and style.

Apart from the urgent need to replenish Prussian resources and integrate the Silesian acquisitions, his troubles blew over as before. The storm of moral indignation died down as swiftly as it had risen; the conqueror's aureole outshone the tarnish of treachery. Before long, those who had the best of reasons to distrust the King of Prussia wooed him again. Concurrently, however, a secret coalition formed, of Austria, England, Holland, Sardinia, and Saxony, designed to wrest from Frederick not merely his recent gains but the very holdings of his forbears. Frederick learned of this and again struck first.

Invasion of Bohemia

In August 1744 his army, 80,000 strong, entered Bohemia and took Prague, ostensibly to succour the Emperor, whose troops had been routed over and over, unable even to keep his own capital of Munich for him (Frederick quipped that the commander of the Bavarian forces was like a drum: one only heard of him when he was being beaten). In fact, Frederick had concluded yet another secret agreement with the French, who likewise were hard pressed by the resurgent Austrians. The enterprise, known as the Second Silesian War, did not long continue so prosperously for Frederick as it began. On the contrary, by Frederick's assessment, the honours of the campaign lay all with the Austrian field marshal Otto Ferdinand von Traun. Traun all along the line foiled Frederick's now-recognized strategy of forcing confrontation in open positions. Exhausted, without anything to show for their efforts, the Prussians had to withdraw to Silesia and presently face a Saxon army for good measure.

In the event, Frederick could afford to judge generously. It was he who won the war. Just when his fortunes stood at low ebb, a series of three battles in Silesia, in June, September, and December 1745, gained decisive victory for Prussia and for the Prussian King all the renown he could desire. After the Treaty of Dresden, in December 1745, at the age of 33 Frederick was styled "the Great." He was regarded as a hero everywhere except in Austria (though, even there, Maria Theresa's son, the future emperor Joseph II, was to conceive a kind of hero worship for him). If he now concentrated on the works of peace, nobody could say that it was by default.

While, during the next 11 years, his first concern was to practice what he preached by service to the civil state, he also proved himself an eager patron of the arts and of science, as well as exercising to the full his own literary urges. A spate of books and articles, occasional verse, and correspondence issued from his pen, besides the infinite paper work of government, which, even as his father, he refused to delegate. "I'll not attack a cat in future," Frederick had vowed at the end of the war, adding, "unless I am forced." So, concurrently, the army was refurbished, with a view to keeping ahead of imitators. The cavalry required more than that. It had proved no match against the Austrian horse, schooled in a century of war against the Turks. With the aid of two cavalry officers of exceptional dash and brilliance, the deficiency was methodically made good.

Seven Years' War

The Seven Years' War erupted in the late summer of 1756; as usual, all parties to it claimed that it was forced on them by necessity: Austria because of its vital interest in recapturing Silesia; France and Russia because of the threat inherent in a steady accumulation of power to Prussia; England because of its increasing maritime, mercantile, and colonial collisions with France, which now strongly recommended an Anglo-Prussian alliance—all the more when intelligence leaked out of a secret pact between Austria and France, burying their traditional antagonism, in formidable combination with Russia; and Prussia because the reduction of its territory to the merest nucleus was the object of that alliance, in which Saxony and Sweden joined for a share in the spoils. As ever, Frederick did not scruple to embrace the onus of firing the first shot.

At the head of 70,000 troops he invaded Saxony, leaving smaller contingents on guard over his northern frontier against the Swedes and in Silesia. There had been no leak of his intention. The small Saxon army was unprepared; the large Austrian forces were scattered over Bohemia and Moravia. They were defeated, not without heavy losses on the Prussian side, and on October 15 Saxony capitulated.

But Frederick had miscalculated the pressures and dynamic animating the enemy coalition, which spoiled his chances of another short bout. Notwithstanding his apparent initiative, essentially he was on the defensive, when, as he himself taught, attack was the secret of success in war. The numbers and unexpected determination of the forces arrayed against him allowed them to dictate a strategy that made it virtually impossible to employ his own. The English subsidies and military assistance from Hanover, Brunswick, and Hesse-Kassel still left Prussia bearing the brunt of seven arduous campaigns all over central Europe.

In June 1757 the hitherto unbeaten Prussian army suffered a heavy defeat at Kolín at the hands of the Austrians: a disaster exacerbated by Prussian alarm upon this ominous break in Frederick's run of luck. French troops invaded Hanover, Brunswick, and Hesse. The Duke of Cumberland, the leader of the English army, concluded a pact with the French and retired from the fray, depriving Frederick of some 50,000 troops and leaving him exposed on the western front. Yet the Prussians succeeded in beating back the French, the Austrians, and the Russians the following summer and, although once more defeated by Austrian arms in October 1758, still managed to retain possession of Silesia.

Again and again Frederick recovered from what seemed unredeemable catastrophe—even after the Battle of Kunersdorf in August 1759, the bloodiest engagement of the war and for the Prussians the most crushing. Frederick was brought all but to his knees: "All is lost," he scribbled a message home, which he thought would be his last. "Be sure I shall not survive our ruin." Seeking death, two horses shot under him, he cried out against the bullets that would not hit himself and was with difficulty prevented from planting himself on foot in the path of a troop of enemy cavalry.

The ancient core of the Prussian kingdom, Brandenburg, was overrun: the Russians occupied the capital, Berlin. Nothing but the enemy's frequent tardiness in following up a victory could have saved Frederick—unless, indeed, it was the ensuing French project of an invasion of England and, not least, the ascendancy of English arms over those of France in the transatlantic colonies and at sea. With the recall of William Pitt to the English premiership, the Duke of Cumberland's covenant with the French in Germany was rescinded, the English subsidies to Prussia were renewed on a regular basis, and the struggle to eliminate French rule in America was prosecuted with the utmost energy. All this, coupled with the victory at Minden of Anglo-Hanoverian troops over a superior French army some days before Kunersdorf, helped to dissipate the French impetus and to undermine the unanimity of Frederick's foes. Without the transfusion of English money into his drained exchequer Frederick could hardly have kept up the fight, just as without his talents and tenacity the destiny of North America would have been different.

Victories of 1760 and 1761

His genius and the extraordinary confidence that Frederick's personality inspired in his men were proved afresh in 1760 against the Austrians and in 1761 against the French. Once again Europe rang with his fame. In England, where he had never set foot, he was one of the most popular personages of the day. Nevertheless, the conquest of Canada having been accomplished, with parallel successes in India, and Pitt having been expelled from office, the British government intimated that no further aid to Prussia was forthcoming. Frederick's forces had shrunk from 150,000 to 60,000, their efficiency very much diminished through constant heavy losses and the inevitably shortened training period of recruits. But all the combatants were alike debilitated; sooner or later the war must come to an end.

That it was decided in Prussia's favour was largely due to a fortuitous event. On January 5, 1762, the empress Elizabeth of Russia died, and with her died that implacable, even personal, enmity to Frederick that had maintained Russia's long, costly participation. Elizabeth's successor, Peter III, was one of Frederick's most fervent admirers. Not only did Russia cease hostilities against Prussia but 18,000 Russian soldiers were placed at Frederick's disposal. The Russian gains were handed back to him, and Sweden, having made some headway in the north, had no alternative but to make peace also. This left only Austria and France, both impoverished in revenues and manpower. Although the coup d'etat replacing Tsar Peter with his wife, Catherine II, put an end to Russian aid, the Prussians drove the French back across the Rhine, and a general peace was concluded in February 1763.

Prussia was confirmed in its acquisions of 1740–45, including the repute of invincibility, although without any further gains. Habsburg Austria had lost its grip on the Holy Roman Empire, which itself, moreover, had been exposed as a hollow anachronism, unable to enforce on Frederick the imperial ban that had been solemnly pronounced on him. In name, the empire was to linger until 1806, when it collapsed forever under the onslaught of Napoleon. In effect, the disunited states of Germany had begun to look for leadership to Prussia some 40 years earlier. France had lost the American dominion to England, the only combatant to come out of the war with vast, unchallenged gains overseas. The causes and trends leading to the French Revolution had received a powerful push forward.

Frederick did not live to see the Revolution; nor did he perceive the portents. To him, the institution of monarchy appeared unshakable. By precept and example he succeeded in at once humanizing and depersonalizing it. The state, no longer seen as a dynastic adjunct but as a supreme object in itself, had supreme call on the sovereign and the people alike.

Domestic policies. The welfare of the state was the prerequisite to its growth, and growth in the course of nature meant expansion: "For every state, from the smallest to the greatest, the principle of enlargement is the fundamental law of life," Frederick wrote. The idea that the state might exist for the welfare of the individual, though a direct development of the idea of the state's separation from the person of the monarch, never impinged on Frederick's philosophy. At all events the axiom of Louis XIV, "L'état c'est moi," was henceforward superseded by Frederick's axiom of service.

His activities for the remaining 23 years of his life were nothing if not an illustration of this axiom. With the same obstinate vigour that had weathered the war, he set himself to the task of reconstruction. He himself had emerged from the ordeal physically an old man, racked with rheumatism and other afflictions contracted over the years of stress and harsh living conditions. For he had made a point of sharing the discomforts of his soldiers as well as their perils, and ever after he cultivated a shabbiness of attire that more than verged on the slovenly. He, who in his youth had loved silks and sumptuous colours, habitually wore the Prussian uniform he had once dubbed "the shroud." Threadbare blue coat soiled with snuff, haggard and bent, accessible to a point where petitioners would corner him on his own unguarded terrace, the lighted window of his study a familiar landmark far into the night—thus the image of "Old Fritz" impressed itself upon the nation. His silver-handled walking stick and the flute on which he continued to perform until the loss of his teeth stopped him became symbols of a living legend.

Conduct of his regime

Frederick pursued the same mercantilistic internal policy as his father and governed by the same central absolutism. The King's cabinet ministers were little more than secretaries. From the highest to the lowliest in the land, everyone was directly answerable to the sovereign; but so, too, might every subject feel free to appeal directly to the sovereign. Frederick's humanity in not a few individual cases was offset by the unchanged brutalities of

army discipline that he had vehemently condemned in Frederick William's time. Conscription continued to be supplemented by the press-gang and outright abduction. The admirable impulse given to husbandry with the systematic introduction of the potato and the sugar beet and to trade and manufacture by similar practical encouragement was offset by stringent crown monopolies and an oppressive excise system which—together with a swarm of petty officials versed in it—Frederick imported from France. This, in particular, impaired his popularity at home, which altogether declined in his later years. While rarely hesitating to overtax his subjects for the greater good of the state, Frederick frowned upon royal interference in civil process. He had long since set up safeguards against this at home, in the shape of the comprehensive Codex Fridericianus and an independent law court, established soon after his accession, to render justice immune to arbitrary pressure from any quarter whatsoever. Admittedly, he was not entirely consistent in respecting this himself; yet it gave him the greatest satisfaction to hear of a subject's invoking the law against the king. Yet, while scoffing at the mystique and trappings of anointed kingship, Frederick took pains to perpetuate a rigid class structure, in which the nobles formed a military upper caste, the burghers were committed to industry and commerce, and the soil-bound peasantry furnished the rank and file of the standing army.

Criticism or lampoons directed against his person touched him not at all; affronts to his royal dignity and aspersions on the army, however, would be visited with sharp reprisals. The celebrated dicta, "In this country everyone shall go to heaven his own way," and "All religions are equal," were by no means fully born out in Frederick's attitude to the Jews, for whom he had small regard, although he availed himself of their services and discountenanced persecution. His love of music and literature did not extend to composers like Mozart or the new wave of specifically German writers among whom was the young Goethe. Mozart he described as a "caterwauler," Goethe as an imitator of "barbaric" Shakespeare. Taught from childhood by Huguenot émigrés, as were so many noble scions of the time, the language of France was to him the only civilized modern idiom. He spoke broken German and fairly massacred that language in his pithy marginal comments to official documents: all his serious writing was in French. His manifold building projects drew on French models; classical and French literature, French and Italian painting, opera, and chamber music provided the only forms he recognized as art.

Cultural interests and friendships

His friendships with the artists and writers he liked to have around him were somewhat one-sided: the vaunted freedom of speech that prevailed at Sanssouci, his favourite residence, near Potsdam, was mostly reserved for the King himself. The friendship with Voltaire, who spent some time at Frederick's court, turned sour partly from that cause, partly deteriorating from mutual disenchantment and subsequent scurrilities and chicane. As for Frederick's relations with his wife, these appear to have been purely formal, except, possibly, for a period at the beginning of their marriage. He had no children and appointed a nephew to succeed him.

To the end of his life, he commanded a high degree of respect abroad. The world having finally condoned the seizure of Silesia, the partition of Poland in 1772, by which nearly one third of that politically retarded country was divided between Russia, Austria, and Prussia, was a deferred consequence. Frederick gained at long last the missing territorial link between the eastern Prussian dominions and the lands of Brandenburg. When his kinsman, the Bavarian elector Maximilian Joseph, died in 1777, the emperor Joseph II, Maria Theresa's eldest son, showed that his admiration of Frederick did not exclude ambitions after the Frederician pattern: he promptly attempted to annex Bavaria. The heirs of the elector Palatine, who was the lawful heir of Maximilian Joseph, appealed to Prussia for intervention. Frederick reluctantly complied and marched into Bohemia. Such was the prestige of himself and his army that, without bloodshed, though not without prolonged manoeuvring, peace was restored in 1779. Austria received a small portion of the Bavarian inheritance and Prussia reimbursed itself for its trouble in the Franconian provinces.

That was the last occasion when Frederick took the field—indeed, the last time in his reign that the Prussian army marched. It was this incident, however, that directed his foreign policy henceforth, culminating the year before his death in the League of Princes, which was formed under Frederick's aegis for the purpose of defending the integrity of the sovereign German states against imperial incursions.

He died on August 17, 1786, following a chill sustained during a troop review in pouring rain. His death was largely unregretted by his subjects. His most unpopular measures—tax farming, the tobacco monopoly, and the duty on coffee, were quickly abolished by his successor. His coffin was placed in the royal vault, where Napoleon paid it a courtesy call and Hitler deposited a golden wreath.

Personal life and reputation

His precise appearance is uncertain because in maturity Frederick declined to sit for his portrait and refused every request to put up statues or other monuments to him. The famous death mask is believed to have been tampered with by the sculptor entrusted with the casting. Another thing that has been much debated is the sexual aspect of Frederick's character. His one reputed love affair, with a married lady of Küstrin (modern Kostrzyn, Poland), remains a matter for conjecture. He was charged with homosexual practices, notably in relation to Katte and to his later factotum and confidant the valet Fredersdorf. There is no conclusive evidence in any direction.

Few historic reputations have fluctuated more than that of Frederick the Great, thanks to his intimate connection with a Prussian-dominated Germany and depending on that country's fortunes and its role in world affairs.

BIBLIOGRAPHY. THOMAS CARLYLE, *The History of Friedrich II of Prussia, Called Frederick the Great*, 6 vol. (1858–65), remains the most comprehensive biography in English, though erring somewhat on the side of open hero-worship. Altogether the literature is bedevilled by bias, for and against; but a vast amount of reliable, documented information, especially rich in political detail, is furnished by LEOPOLD VON RANKE, *Friedrich II, König von Preussen* (1847–48); and also by Frederick himself: *Die Werke Friedrichs des Grossen in deutscher Übersetzung* (1913–14; originally *Oeuvres*, 1846–1857). J.D.E. PREUSS, *Friedrich der Grosse, eine Lebensgeschichte*, 4 vol. (1843), copiously fills in the personal background. REINHOLD KOSER, *Geschichte Friedrichs des Grossen*, 4 vol. (1893–1903), adds further data to the diplomatic setting. FRANZ KUGLER's book by the same title (1840), is of interest mainly because of Adolf Menzel's wonderfully convincing illustrations, based on minute research. Useful on the military side are KARL VON CLAUSEWITZ, *Strategische Beleuchtung mehrerer Feldzüge* . . . (1863); B.H. LIDDELL HART, *Great Captains Unveiled* (1927); GORDON A. CRAIG, *The Politics of the Prussian Army, 1640–1945* (1955); and an exhaustive treatment of Frederick's wars, *Die Kriege Friedrichs des Grossen*, 12 vol., issued by the PRUSSIAN GENERAL STAFF (1890–1904). F. MEINECKE, *Die Idee der Staatsraison* (1924); and F.L. CARSTEN, *The Origins of Prussia* (1954), throw light on relevant political philosophy. K. HINRICHS, *Der Kronprinzenprozess* (1936), deals with the trial of Frederick as a deserter; O. HINTZE, *Die Seidenindustrie*, 3 vol. (1892); and S. SKALWEIT, *Die Berliner Wirtschaftskrise von 1763* (1937), with his economic policy. Biographies in English include: P. GAXOTTE, *Frédéric II* (1938; Eng. trans., *Frederick the Great*, 1942); and G.P. GOOCH, *Frederick the Great: The Ruler, the Writer, the Man* (1947). LORD ACTON's essay in *Lectures on Modern History* (1906); and EDITH SIMON, *The Making of Frederick the Great* (1963), are recommended for clarity and balanced judgment; the latter also contains a concise bibliography covering every aspect of the subject.

(E.Si.)

Frederick Henry, Prince of Orange

A renowned general and skilled politician, Frederick Henry, prince of Orange, was the first of his line to assume, as leader of the United Provinces of the Netherlands (Dutch Republic), a semimonarchical status and thus to determine foreign as well as domestic policies.

Frederick Henry was born at Delft on January 29,

Frederick Henry and his wife, Amalia van Solms, painting by Gerrit van Honthorst (1590–1656). In the Mauritshuis, The Hague, The Netherlands.
By courtesy of the Mauritshuis, The Hague

1584, less than half a year before the murder of his father, William the Silent, the principal leader of the Dutch struggle for independence from Spain.

As a younger son, he was destined by his mother, a daughter of the Huguenot leader Gaspard de Coligny, for a career in her native France; but his half brother, Maurice of Nassau, who had succeeded their father as stadtholder, as well as the States General, insisted that Frederick Henry serve his country. He was accordingly educated at the University of Leiden and made a member of the council of state at the age of 17. He began to take part in most of Maurice's military expeditions and was sent on various foreign missions. During the politico-religious crisis of the years 1617–19, precipitated by a doctrinal conflict within the Reformed, or Calvinist Church, Frederick Henry, like his mother, kept cautiously to the middle of the road.

Until the age of 40, Frederick Henry was reputed to be "too fond of women to tie himself permanently to one of them" but under strong pressure from Maurice, who had no legitimate offspring, and, almost at the latter's deathbed, he married. His wife, a lady-in-waiting to the exiled queen of Bohemia, soon acquired a fair amount of political influence as well as a universal reputation for venality, but she also managed to endow The Hague in the 17th century with some semblance of Baroque court life.

At Maurice's death, in 1625, Frederick Henry became stadtholder in five of the seven United Provinces; a sixth, Groningen, was added in 1640. Even in Friesland, the eventual succession to the office of stadtholder was assigned to Frederick Henry's son, William (born 1626). Although in theory no more than the appointed "servants" of the different assemblies of the estates, provincial and general, the princes of Orange, by establishing hereditary succession to the various stadtholderships, were clearly on their way to acquiring the status of a sovereign. In view of Frederick Henry's anomalous, somewhat awkward position as a minor princeling at the helm of the government of a federation of oligarchic republics, anachronistically flourishing in a world drifting toward absolutism, his ambition was normal.

Stadtholder and captain general

As a strategist, Frederick Henry proved himself to be the foremost disciple of his brother, Maurice, and the Dutch wars against the Spanish continued to be considered a kind of military academy for young European noblemen. The prince's universally recognized strength lay in capturing fortified "places"; once he was even heard to exclaim: "God deliver us from pitched battles," and every one of his yearly campaigns had the conquest of some important town or fortress as its aim. Hence, the borderline between the modern kingdoms of Belgium and The Netherlands came to be drawn largely according to Frederick Henry's successes and failures.

By far the most spectacular of these sieges was that of Hertogenbosch, but if the capitulation of this city marked Frederick Henry's proudest moment, it also demonstrated the inherent weakness of his position. Although his contemporaries present the prince as little short of omnipotent in the Dutch Republic, his power was based on the delicate balancing of various elements. To counterbalance the oligarchy in Holland, which contributed over 58 percent to the federal budget, the prince needed the support of the six minor members of the United Provinces and that of the Puritan masses of the country, including those in Holland.

Although not irreligious, Frederick Henry was, like his father, a champion of as far-reaching a religious tolerance as circumstances allowed. In this respect he displayed, paradoxically, a much closer affinity with his political opponents, the Holland oligarchy, than he did with his traditional supporters. Yet as far as policy making was concerned, this affinity was of little avail; for the Hollanders remained stubbornly opposed to a costly warfare, which, moreover, if waged too successfully, threatened to reintegrate the port of Antwerp as a formidable rival for Amsterdam into the political body of the free Netherlands. To make his yearly campaigns politically acceptable absorbed almost more of Frederick Henry's energies than the campaigns themselves. Clever tactician that he was, he managed, however, unlike his brother, Maurice, before and his son, William II, after him, to avoid an open conflict with the assembly of Holland.

Until about 1640, Frederick Henry alone was responsible for the United Provinces' foreign policy. From the dynastic point of view, his activities were crowned by the marriage in 1641 between his heir, William II, and Charles I's eldest daughter, Mary. Consequently, during the English Civil War, the stadtholder sided unconditionally with the King, whereas the Holland oligarchy favoured Parliament.

French alliance

More important was Frederick Henry's French policy culminating (1635) in the so-called treaty of partition between the two countries and stipulating a partitioning of the southern Netherlands, if conquered by arms from the Spanish. The treaty further provided for the yearly payment of a considerable French subsidy, thus enabling the prince to continue the war in spite of the reluctance of the war-tired assembly of Holland to finance it. But the very first campaign, of the combined French and Dutch armies under Frederick Henry's command, nearly ended in disaster, and, in spite of his conquests of the cities of Breda and Hulst, the alliance never regained its momentum. The trend toward peace with Spain became more and more irresistible, and, largely through the influence of his wife, even Frederick Henry was eventually won over to the peace party. Prematurely aged after long years of suffering from gout, he did not live to see the peace officially concluded in January 1648. He died on March 14, 1647, in his palace at The Hague and was interred with great pomp in the family vault at Delft.

BIBLIOGRAPHY. P.J. BLOK, *Frederik Hendrik, Prins van Oranje* (1924), the only modern biography, sound as to the facts, but rather unexciting; A. WADDINGTON, *La République des Provinces-Unies, la France et les Pays-Bas Espagnols de 1630 à 1650*, 2 vol. (1895–97), predominantly based on French archives and, though slightly antiquated, still indispensable for the foreign policy of the period; P. GEYL, *Oranje en Stuart, 1641–1672*, 2nd ed. (1963); J.J. POELHEKKE *De Vrede van Munster* (1948), mainly based on Spanish, Portuguese, Venetian, and Vatican archives. The English speaking reader can only be referred to P. GEYL, *Geschiedenis van de Nederlandsche Stam*, rev. ed., 6 vol. (1961–62; partial Eng. trans., *The Netherlands in the Seventeenth Century*, rev. ed., 2 vol., 1961–64), the standard work.

(J.J.P.)

Frederick William IV of Prussia

Frederick William IV, king of Prussia, a fervent believer in a God-given medieval kingship, had the misfortune to become ruler of his country at a time of social unrest and increasing demands for German national unity. Yet, though Frederick William was impressionable of character, indecisive in action, and counselled by narrow and inept men, his reign was more ineffectual than calamitous. Prussia's spirit of traditional loyalty to the crown and its deep clan divisions helped to preserve the monarchy.

Frederick William IV, detail from a portrait by Franz Krüger (1797–1857). In Monbijou Palace, Berlin.
Foto Marburg

Frederick William was born in Berlin on October 15, 1795, the son of the future king Frederick William III and Louisa of Mecklenburg-Strelitz. He was educated by tutors, mainly experienced civil servants. Though he was completely unsoldierlike by nature, his experiences in the German War of Liberation (1813–15) against Napoleon left lasting traces on his political and intellectual development. He became and remained a disciple of the German Romantic movement, with its nostalgia for the Middle Ages. Romanticism appealed to his extremely sensitive dilettante artistic nature. A draftsman and interested in architecture and landscape gardening, he was a patron of Christian Daniel Rauch, a noted sculptor, and Karl Friedrich Schinkel, an architect and city planner. His marriage in 1823 to Elizabeth of Bavaria, a convert to Lutheranism, proved happy; they had no children.

As crown prince, Frederick William developed romantic-conservative convictions that led him to approach even politics as a question of ideas and problems rather than as a matter of hard reality. Conservative philosophers, men of letters, and politicians were among his friends and the men he admired. Even though barely 20, he used his influence to restrict the promised constitution of 1815 to the creation of district and provincial estates, in which the landed aristocracy had an overwhelming majority. For him liberalism meant revolution: a modern constitution was "a scrap of paper" interposed as an intolerable barrier between the patriarchal king by divine right and his people. Though he was no absolutist and had no genuine will to domination, yet, by his romanticizing mystique and his unlimited respect for the alleged "organic growth" of the medieval estates, he stood irreconcilably opposed to the political ideas of the 19th century and to the heritage of the French Revolution. Tensions were not lessened by his genuine personal piety. As for him, cultural homogeneity outweighed political unity, but he was fundamentally opposed to the movement toward a German national state; after Prussia's occupation by Napoleon, he regarded his country's close alignment with Austria as essential. He never contested the Habsburg empire's primacy, which he saw as consecrated by history; for the king of Prussia he claimed only the military dignity of an "arch-general" of the empire.

Enemy of liberalism

Frederick William quickly disappointed the great hopes

aroused by his accession in 1840, for he was by no means willing to fulfill the constitutional aspirations of the Liberals. In 1842 he permitted only "united committees" of the provincial estates; and in 1847, after long delay, he summoned not a popular representative assembly but the United Diet, comprising all the provincial estates, with the right to grant taxes and loans but without the right to meet at regular intervals. This unwieldy body remained his ideal, even though the narrow limits of his concessions immediately produced a conflict (the diet's refusal of the proposed loan for the Berlin–Königsberg railway) and even though this first assembly of all Prussia powerfully increased the people's self-confidence on the eve of the Revolution of 1848.

Revolution of 1848   Despite belated attempts to organize a common resistance by the German governments, Frederick William IV was eventually completely overwhelmed by the revolution in March 1848 that had been inspired by the revolution of the preceding month in France. He could neither prevent the street fighting in Berlin by last-minute concessions nor ride the wave; after the withdrawal of the troops to barracks, he masked his submission to the revolution by a processional ride through Berlin under the black and red and golden flag, the symbol of the united Germany, by paying homage to the bodies of the victims of the soldiery, and by his promise that "Prussia is henceforth merged in Germany." Finally he had to convene a Prussian national assembly. Under the influence of his entourage, however, he roused himself to a stubborn resistance: he appointed his uncle, the Count of Brandenburg (a son of Frederick William II's last morganatic marriage), prime minister; removed the assembly from Berlin and then dissolved it; and imposed a constitution the first moderately liberal draft of which was modelled on that of Belgium. These measures restored the leading role to the crown and its instruments, the army and the bureaucracy, firmly supported by the recently formed Conservative party.

When, on April 3, 1849, Frederick William refused the imperial crown offered by the national assembly in Frankfurt am Main—because as a true conservative he would only accept it from the German princes—he destroyed the constitution drafted by that assembly. Under Russian and English pressure, moreover, he had withdrawn Prussian support of the rising in the duchies of Schleswig and Holstein, aimed at overthrowing Danish rule there. Next, however, largely contravening his previous policy, he attempted to establish a German union under Prussian leadership (1849–50)—though this, as a "Little German" federation, should remain allied with a "wider" federation embracing Austria. When Austria challenged this union, the King shrank from war, preferring capitulation at the Punctation of Olmütz convention. Though Prussia had to return to the federal diet at Frankfurt am Main, Prussian leadership of the German customs union, which excluded Austria, remained unchallenged.

In religious affairs Frederick William, in 1841, settled the "Cologne church conflict" on terms very favourable to the Roman Catholics, with whom, largely influenced by his love for the old and picturesque, he had great sympathy; he also furthered the reconstruction of Cologne cathedral. On the other hand, he actively promoted the joint Anglican-Lutheran bishopric of Jerusalem.

Final years   The final years of his reign were a period of reaction. Frederick William, rejecting the bureaucratic absolutism of his prime minister Otto von Manteuffel, worked above all for recasting the constitution of 1848 in a conservative mold. This included the disastrous introduction of three-class suffrage according to income in 1850 instead of universal suffrage, the retention of the monarchical character of army and bureaucracy, the re-establishment of the conservative district assemblies and the provincial diets, and the conversion (1854) of the first chamber into a house of lords entirely dominated by the predominantly aristocratic landowners. He believed this house of lords to be modelled on the English upper house, but in a political testament he implored his successors to refuse to take the oath on the Prussian constitution.

In 1857 a stroke resulted in paralysis. From this time on, with the exception of brief intervals, the King's mind was clouded, and his brother William (afterwards emperor) took on the duties of government, becoming regent in 1858. Frederick William died at Sanssouci Palace in Potsdam on January 2, 1861.

BIBLIOGRAPHY.   Although there is no definitive biography, E. LEWALTER, *Friedrich Wilhelm IV* (1938), in German, is still indispensable for the study of Frederick.

(Ha.He.)

Frederick William, the Great Elector

One of the most remarkable absolute monarchs of the 17th century, Frederick William of Brandenburg, known as the Great Elector, was the first of the three great rulers of the Hohenzollern dynasty, who also included King Frederick William I and King Frederick II the Great, of Prussia. He was the founder of the state of Brandenburg–Prussia, which he built from disorganized war-ravaged territories into an integrated state with a centralized administration and an efficient army.

Foto Marburg

The Great Elector, portrait by Adriaan Hanneman (1601–71). In the castle at Dessau, East Germany

Early years   Frederick William was born on February 16, 1620, in Cölln (later united with Berlin) on the Spree, the eldest son of the elector George William and Elizabeth Charlotte of the Palatinate, a granddaughter of William the Silent, prince of Orange.

He grew up amid the chaos of the Thirty Years' War, in which Brandenburg suffered particularly heavily, and was forced to spend his childhood years far from the Berlin court in the fortress of Küstrin, where he was educated in the Calvinist faith. His stay in Holland between his 14th and 18th years, the time divided between the University of Leiden and the court of his future father-in-law, Frederick Henry of Orange, at The Hague, left him with lasting impressions. The future elector was, above all, impressed by Holland's imposing maritime and commercial power, as well as by its pioneering achievements in military technology and organization. He retained a marked preference for Dutch architecture and agriculture and a strong desire to open Brandenburg to international commerce and maritime trade.

Attempts to establish balance of power.   When Frederick William, completely inexperienced in politics, succeeded his father as elector in December 1640, he took over a ravaged land occupied by foreign troops. Under his father's powerful favourite, Graf Adam von Schwarzenberg, Brandenburg had changed sides from the Swedes to the Habsburgs and had thus been drawn into the struggle on both sides. Residing until 1643 not in Brandenburg, the heartland of his domain, but rather in Königsberg (since 1945 Kaliningrad, U.S.S.R.), the capital of the remote duchy of Prussia, the Elector at first pursued a policy of cautious neutrality in order to escape the pressure of the rival powers. He discharged the Brandenburg troops in the service of the Habsburg emperor and concluded an armistice with Sweden.

Creation of his army

He soon recognized, however, that without an army he could never become master in his own house. In 1644, at the beginning of negotiations to conclude the Thirty Years' War, he had already started to organize his own military force. Though his army was small, Brandenburg could not support it without requisitioning funds from the duchy of Cleves, in the west, and from the duchy of Prussia. For the first time Brandenburg's territories, united only by their allegiance to the person of the Elector, were drawn together for a political purpose. The standing army was the first institution used by the increasingly absolutist rulers of Brandenburg to combat the privileges of the estates of the individual territories. It was never entirely disbanded and became the core of the 18th-century Prussian army.

This army was not big enough to allow Frederick William to conduct an independent foreign policy. Moreover, his marriage in 1646 to Louise Henriette of Orange failed to bring the anticipated Dutch support. Lacking the support of friendly great powers at the peace congress of Westphalia in 1648, he did not attain his aim of acquiring all of Pomerania, with the Oder estuary and the important harbour of Stettin (since 1945 Szczecin). He had to be content with eastern Pomerania, the secularized dioceses of Minden and Halberstadt, and the promise of the archbishopric of Magdeburg, all of which were, however, important as links to his western German possessions.

After seven years of peaceful reconstruction, Frederick William saw his political and military ability put to a difficult test with the outbreak of the First Northern War (1655–60). By invading Poland, King Charles X Gustav of Sweden sought to expand the power in the Baltic that Sweden gained by the Peace of Westphalia. Frederick William, as duke of Prussia, owed fealty to the Polish king, but, when offered an alliance by Sweden in return for control over the East Prussian ports, the Elector chose armed neutrality. When Charles Gustav rapidly overran Poland and advanced against East Prussia, Frederick William had to exchange Polish for Swedish suzerainty and provide armed support to Charles X Gustav. In the three-day Battle of Warsaw in July 1656, the untried army of Brandenburg, under the Elector's command, passed its test of fire. To keep the Elector on his side, the Swedish king granted him full sovereignty over the duchy of Prussia. This did not prevent Frederick William, when Sweden's military position deteriorated, from entering into negotiations with Poland, which now renounced suzerainty over East Prussia. With his new allies, Poland and the Habsburg emperor, the Elector drove the Swedes from western Pomerania. French intervention, however, forced Frederick William once again to give up his Pomeranian conquests. Ratified in the Treaty of Oliva in 1660, this renunciation was balanced by confirmation of the Elector's full sovereignty over the duchy of Prussia.

The Elector's ability to gain his ends arose not only from the ease with which he changed sides but also from his success in forcing the provincial estates to support the standing army independently of tax appropriations by the diets. In the second half of his reign, he removed control of taxation and finances from the estates altogether, thereby laying the groundwork for the powerful bureaucracy of later Prussian absolutism, with its standing army, fixed taxes, and an officialdom dependent on the sovereign alone.

The year 1661, in which Louis XIV assumed the reins of government in France, ushered in an era of vast power struggles in Europe. In the conflict erupting between Austria and Spain, on the one side, and France and Sweden, on the other, the Elector hoped to maintain the balance of power by preventing either side from achieving predominance. He sought not a simple policy of neutrality but rather, as he recommended to his successor in his

Dutch alliance

political testament of 1667, to advance the interests of his house by always joining the weaker power against the stronger. Here lies the basis for the continual shifts in his policy of alliances: "Brandenburg's intermittent fever," which became proverbial in the 17th century.

In 1672, when Louis XIV prepared for the invasion of Holland, Frederick William, still true to his policy of supporting the weaker power, allied himself with the Dutch states-general. Their sole European ally, he concluded an aid agreement with them, fully aware of the danger from France to his territories of Cleves on the lower Rhine. But after the unexpectedly rapid collapse of the Netherlands forced him to make a separate peace with France in 1673, the Elector adopted a policy of neutrality, which he abandoned only when the Holy Roman Empire declared war against France. In July 1674 he joined the alliance of the Habsburg emperor, Spain, and the Netherlands. Frederick William's military expectations were disappointed by the slow progress of the allies on the upper Rhine. He also suffered a more serious personal loss with the death of the gifted young heir to the throne, Karl Emil.

When the Swedes invaded Brandenburg, the Elector turned northward, and under his command his army, in June 1675, scored its first independent victory. In a contemporary folk song Frederick William was for the first time called the "Great Elector." In the same year, allied with the Emperor and with Denmark, he once more began to retrieve the spoils of the Thirty Years' War from the Swedes. For the second time he gained western Pomerania by the sword, only to lose it again under French pressure. Abandoned by his allies, he had to yield the fruits of his victory in the Peace of Saint-Germain-en-Laye in 1679.

Later policies. Frederick now decided to gain in alliance with France what he could not obtain by opposing it. In 1679 he concluded a secret pact with France, committing himself, in return for large subsidies, to support French candidates in the next elections for king of Poland and for emperor. The alliance endured as long as the Elector believed that Louis XIV would help him gain possession of western Pomerania. When he realized that this hope was vain, Frederick William changed political partners, for the last time, in 1685. The Elector's disillusionment with Louis XIV coincided with the assumption by William of Orange (later King William III of Great Britain) of his historical role as founder of the Grand Alliance against Louis XIV. The Elector, impressed that William was a prince of Orange and his own nephew, concluded a defense pact with the Netherlands in 1685. He drew still closer to William's side with the issuance of the Edict of Potsdam on November 8, 1685, in which he granted asylum to all Huguenots expelled from France by Louis XIV after the revocation of the Edict of Nantes. Thus, at the end of his life, the Great Elector returned to the political ties of his early years. He did not live to witness the great shift in the European balance of power that his nephew was to effect through his landing in England and his succeeding the Catholic Stuart King James II. But he was aware of William's plans when he died in Potsdam on May 9, 1688, the year of England's Glorious Revolution.

Last political shift

Assessment. The Great Elector bequeathed to his son Frederick (after 1701, Frederick I, king of Prussia) a well-organized state, widely respected for its sound finances and efficient army. Frederick William had gone far toward integrating his inherited and acquired territories by establishing national institutions and central administrative bodies. He did, however, endanger the further integration by endowing the children of his second marriage, contracted in 1668 with Dorothea of Holstein-Glücksburg, with semi-autonomous principalities. Many of his ambitious plans were not realized. Just as he was unable to provide a pathway to the Baltic for his country, his attempt to establish a colony on the Guinea coast of Africa remained only an episode in Brandenburg–Prussian history. He was far more successful in the economic field. The systematic colonization of the sparsely populated country, the improvement of trade routes through canal construction, and the establishment and operation of factories after the mercantilist model were begun under Frederick William. In this area, too, the Elector established a tradition that was broadened by his 18th-century successors.

Frederick William adopted the so-called government in council form of monarchical rule, whereby the ruler exercised his power with the aid of his principal council and functioned almost as a president. He always listened to his advisors' opinions but made all important decisions himself.

The political views of all rulers of that period were rooted in religion. For the Great Elector royal power was a God-given duty, a common Christian viewpoint that was given a special character by the Elector's Calvinist beliefs, which bind the ruler, just as the least of his subjects, to prove himself visibly in his daily duties. Here lies the religious basis of Frederick William's ambition for political power and of his immense, yet restrained, energy, which is still evident today in Andreas Schlüter's famous equestrian statue of the Great Elector in Berlin.

BIBLIOGRAPHY. HERMAN VON PETERSDORFF, *Der Grosse Kurfürst*, new ed. (1939), the standard biography, now in need of revision; FERDINAND SCHEVILL, *The Great Elector* (1947), the best account in English; CARL HINRICHS, "Der Grosse Kurfürst: 1620–1688," in *Die Grossen Deutschen: Deutsche Biographie*, vol. 1 (1956), a new appraisal of the Elector's personality and statesmanship; FRANCIS LUDWIG CARSTEN, *The Origins of Prussia* (1954), deals with the social and economic problems of the Elector's reign; GERHARD OESTREICH, "Friedrich Wilhelm (Grosser Kürfurst)," in *Neue Deutsche Biographie*, vol. 5 (1961), contains a very complete bibliography.

(S.Sk.)

Free Churches

A "free church," in the widest use of the term, is to be distinguished from a state-supported church as being self-supporting. Examples of such free churches are the Baptists in Scotland, where the established church is Presbyterian; the Presbyterians in England, where the Anglican Church is established; the Waldensian Church in Italy, where the Roman Catholic Church is established; and the Mission Covenant Church in Sweden, where the established church is Lutheran. The attribute "free" affirms that such a church is free of governmental or external ecclesiastical control. In the narrower sense, the term free churches was first applied collectively to four nonepiscopal Protestant evangelical communions in England that convened the first Free Church Congress in 1892 and combined in 1896 to form the National Council of the Evangelical Free Churches. In taking this step the English Baptists, Congregationalists, Methodists, and Presbyterians were acknowledging an affinity that had existed for three centuries in the case of the three orthodox "dissenting denominations" and for two centuries in the case of the Methodists. First known as Puritans before 1662, then as Nonconformists, and later as Dissenters, they preferred to be known as Free Churches at the end of the 19th century. The reasons for the positive designation were several: among them were the impact of the new unitive impulse of the ecumenical movement; a fear that the high church movement then making rapid strides would threaten the Protestantism of the national church; and a growing sense of the importance of these four denominations in the English-speaking world, especially in the United States, where their numbers and influence were great. Approximately two-fifths of the denominations represented at the opening meeting of the newly inaugurated World Council of Churches at Amsterdam in 1948 belonged to the free church family. In the English-speaking countries, the voluntary principle had won its most signal triumph in the separation of church and state.

History.   The term free churches may be relatively recent, but the phenomenon is as old as the left wing of the 16th-century Reformation. The original free church is almost certainly to be found among the greatly maligned and much persecuted Anabaptists, who led a harried life in Europe until they found tolerance and a welcome in Commonwealth England after a respite in libertarian Holland.

The Anabaptists were chiefly interested in restoring the life and order of the New Testament Church, a church that grew by obedience to the power of the Holy Spirit, not through the coercion of the earthly magistrate. They protested against a merely nominal Christianity, believing that the church should consist only of converted Christians, for which reason they baptized all who had been "christened" as infants; hence they were known as "rebaptizers" or "Anabaptists." They often called themselves "disciples" or "brethren." They celebrated the Lord's Supper as a memorial to Christ's reconciling love and as a badge or token of their faith. They also inculcated brotherly humility by keeping the feet-washing ordinance. The autonomous constitution and government of their churches expressed the priesthood of all believers. They were biblical and social radicals, denying the state's right to compel belief, refusing (except in England) to take civil oaths or to take up arms, and opposing usury. Some of them practiced a temporary Christian communism. The negative aspect of religious liberty took the form of separation of church and state, first nationally affirmed in the United States in 1775 but constitutionally guaranteed much earlier through the founders of two of the original American colonies, Roger Williams in Rhode Island and William Penn in Pennsylvania. The positive ground was the "Crown Rights of Christ the Redeemer," which he and not some outsider held in his own church, and the view that compelled religion is the parent of hypocrisy.

The free church represents a third pattern of Christianity: its first predecessor was the medieval Catholicism established in a parochial pattern of uniform Christianity, with the theoretical coordination of the rule of spiritual pope and temporal emperor; the second was the territorial church established at the religious Peace of Augsburg (1555) on the basis that the prince's religion would be the people's faith (*cujus regio ejus religio*). Unorthodoxy in religion was punished by the secular arm in the territorial national churches as vigorously as in medieval international Catholicism. An uncoerced, voluntary Christianity—to be spread by conviction, not by compulsion—was the renewal of a conception that had existed in pre-Constantinian Christianity (to the opening of the 4th century).

The magisterial Reformers believed that behind the national and territorial church organizations the one holy catholic church existed, made up of the predestined saints (Calvin) or the assembly of true believers (Luther). The radical Reformers rejected the doctrine of predestination and the concept of the invisible church (of the elect known only to God) and insisted on creating fellowships of regenerate saints (the Anabaptists and Baptists) or visible saints (the Independents) on the free, voluntary principle. The 16th-century Anabaptists left no continuing congregations in Europe, while the Baptists returned to the Continent only when the Enlightenment had disintegrated Christendom rather than converted Christians to toleration. It was only when they came to England and thence to America that they found the peace and comparative security to flourish and to make their remarkable contribution to Anglo-American democratic life.

Teachings and practices.   The fundamental principles that have animated the free churches in their government are fivefold. Their primary conception of the Christian community is that it constitutes a "gathered church," consisting of those who have been called out of the world by Christ to minister in the world and who have responded by a conscious dedication of their lives to the only king and head of the church. The free churches claim that Christians are made, not born: they are made by the divine initiative in grace and the human surrender in free faith. Founded upon a covenant relationship, which is an engagement of heart and mind as well as will, these

Anabaptists

Five fundamental principles

churches are utterly opposed to any merely nominal relationship to Christ and his church. Thus they prefer to express the "obedience of faith" in covenants and testimonies rather than to give a merely intellectual assent to historical affirmations and doctrinal tenets enshrined in creeds.

Secondly, their forms of church polity conserve the right of the Holy Spirit to rule in the churches, unfettered by the dictates of ecclesiastical hierarchy or the favour or displeasure of the political ruler. Their Christocracy (rule of Christ) gives every member an equal vote in determining the policy of the church as it seeks to perform the will of Christ in the community.

Thirdly, they witness to the priesthood of all believers and the apostolate of the laity. By this principle they declare positively that each church member is a witness to the Christian faith, and negatively they dissent from a double standard of Christian life (first-class celibate and second-class noncelibate) and all sacerdotalism and triumphalism. Free churchmen claim that their view of the church is the true middle way between an Ultramontanism that claims too much for the church and an Erastianism that claims too much for the state. Their assertion of the priesthood of all believers is the secret of their contribution to democracy, by transference from the religious to the political arena, and the secret of their success in evangelism, by the employment of lay preachers.

In the fourth place, it was the 17th-century amalgam of English Calvinism—in its Presbyterian and Independent forms—and Anabaptism that produced the free church sense of the primacy of the Gospel over the church and of revelation over its institutional expressions and that has resulted in such flexibility as is rarely seen in Catholic structures of organization. As P.T. Forsyth, a Scottish Congregationalist, has written in *Faith, Freedom, and the Future:*

> Upon English soil alone were the two great movements of the Reformation age adjusted and consummated—Reformers and Anabaptists; the Evangelical and the Libertarian; the Word and the Spirit; Fixity and Freedom; Faith and Inspiration; Reformation and Renovation; and it was in Independency that the most fruitful union took place.

In the fifth place, it is significant that Independency, the assertion and expression of the autonomy of the local church, unites Congregationalists and Baptists as well as several other denominations that are their imitators. This is authentic grass-roots religion. It provides the simplest kind of organization and one that survives persecution well.

Contributions to religion and life.   Apart from their insistence upon spiritual freedom, the chief contributions of the free churches have been in the areas of worship, missions, and public life.

Worship

In worship they have pioneered by providing the "free prayers" of their ministers as an alternative to the set forms of a stated liturgy as well as by producing metrical psalmody and hymnody. The first national handbook for worship that the English Independents and the Scottish and English Presbyterians produced in conjunction during the days of the Commonwealth was the Westminster Assembly's *Directory for the Publick Worship of God . . . in the Three Kingdoms of Scotland, England, and Ireland* (1645). This handbook determined the character of the worship of the free churches for three centuries throughout the English-speaking world. No words were prescribed for prayers but only "the general Heads, the Sense and Scope of the Prayers . . . ." This brought a new freedom and flexibility in worship.

The free churches have also pioneered in the writing of hymns in the English language. The first hymnodist in England reputedly was the Baptist minister Benjamin Keach, though his Christian lyrics were rather prosaic. The great transition from the mere recasting of psalms to the composing of Christian hymns was made by the Congregational minister Isaac Watts. He and Charles Wesley, the Methodist, produced some of the greatest hymns in the English language. Their lyricism, freshness, sincerity, and, above all, their celebration of the mighty acts of

God in Christ has made them the sung confessions of faith of the free churches of England and beyond.

The members of the free churches have always held the highest opinion of preaching. Free church sermons have been characterized by biblical fidelity, by spiritual and psychological penetration, and by passionate urgency. Among the great free church preachers have been Thomas Goodwin in the 17th century; John Wesley and Jonathan Edwards in the 18th century; C.H. Spurgeon, R.W. Dale, Joseph Parker, and John Clifford in the 19th century; and Leslie Weatherhead in the 20th century.

In general, free church worship is marked by evangelical obedience, simplicity, flexibility to suit different persons and conditions, and spiritual fervour.

The spiritual fervour of the free churches, along with Pietism, promoted the modern missionary movement in Protestantism. The Baptist cobbler William Carey, whose watchword was "Expect great things from God and attempt great things for God," contributed to the founding of the Baptist Missionary Society in 1792, when Napoleon was threatening to invade England. Three years later the London Missionary Society was formed with the help of Congregationalists (in the majority), Presbyterians, Wesleyan Methodists, and some evangelical Anglicans. This pioneer ecumenical venture was founded to allow missionaries to set up whatever form of church government (episcopal, connectional, or independent) seemed most suitable to them. The most famous free church missionary was David Livingstone (1813–73) of the London Missionary Society, whose name is forever associated with Africa.

In public life, the discussion and self-rule (at the local level) of the autonomous free churches have promoted the development of democracy in the English-speaking nations. Perhaps of even greater significance has been the attempt of the free churches to mold public life according to the ethical imperatives of the Gospel, a concern that neither Erastian nor pietistic religious communities have shared to the same extent. The free churches have played a most significant role in the creation of a public opinion that demanded the extension of the franchise, the improvement of prison conditions, the provision of universal national education, and the ending of human slavery, whether that of Africans through the slave trade or that of "these young Africans of our own growth" as Charles Lamb called the child slaves exploited in the English factories. The free churches witnessed powerfully to the theocratic impulse, so powerfully that "the Nonconformist conscience" was recognized as a significant political phenomenon.

BIBLIOGRAPHY

History: F.H. LITTELL, *The Free Church* (1957), an analysis of the concept of liberty underlying the free church view and of its aim to restitute the New Testament Church, and *The Origins of Sectarian Protestantism* (1964), a useful account of the Anabaptists in Europe and their ecclesiology; G.H. WILLIAMS, *The Radical Reformation* (1962), a superb classification and account of the major forms of radical religious protest in 16th-century Europe; P.T. FORSYTH, *Faith, Freedom, and the Future* (1912), an analysis of the distinctive contribution of the Calvinists and Anabaptists to Independency in 17th-century England; E.A. PAYNE, *Free Church Tradition in the Life of England* (1944), a good brief account of its subject, although modern thought and history are more fully covered in J.W. GRANT, *Free Churchmanship in England, 1870–1940* (1955); E.K.H. JORDAN, *Free Church Unity: History of the Free Church Council Movement, 1896–1941* (1956), an account of the modern attempt of the free churches to federate and present a common witness.

Teachings and practice: Two modern accounts are H. TOWNSEND, *Claims of the Free Churches* (1949), interesting though apologetical in outlook; and E.A. PAYNE, *Free Churchmen, Unrepentant and Repentant* (1965), an evaluation of the contemporary free church witness and its roots, both sympathetically and critically; C.P. DRIVER, *A Future for the Free Churches?* (1962), an important critique by a free churchman.

Contributions: H. DAVIES, *The English Free Churches*, 2nd ed. (1963), a short history written to emphasize the positive contributions of the free churches and, *Worship of the En-*

glish Puritans (1948), the fullest account of the origins and early development of free church worship; G.P. GOOCH, *English Democratic Ideas in the Seventeenth Century*, 2nd ed. (1927); A.D. LINDSAY, *Essentials of Democracy* (1929); and R.G. COWHERD, *Politics of English Dissent* (1956), three books concerned with the contribution of the free churches to English political life, the first two with the 17th and the third with the 19th century.

(H.M.D.)

Frege, Gottlob

Friedrich Ludwig Gottlob Frege, a German mathematician and philosopher, was the founder of modern mathematical logic. Working on the borderline between philosophy and mathematics—viz., in the philosophy of mathematics and mathematical logic (in which no intellectual precedents existed)—Frege discovered, on his own, the fundamental ideas that have made possible the whole modern development of logic and thereby invented an entire discipline. Although he confined his philosophical work to the above two areas, it has proved to be of revolutionary importance for contemporary philosophy in general; for a long time, however, his ideas were transmitted principally through the works of others, such as the Italian logician Giuseppe Peano and influential philosophers such as Bertrand Russell, coauthor of the classic *Principia Mathematica* (1910–13), and Ludwig Wittgenstein, the dominant figure in the schools of logical positivism and of linguistic analysis. Recognition of Frege's importance, however, was delayed until long after his death.

By courtesy of the Universitatsbibliothek, Jena, East Germany

Gottlob Frege.

Background, education, and vocation

Early life. Frege was born on November 8, 1848, at Wismar, where his father, Alexander Frege, was principal of a girls' high school. His mother, Auguste Frege, *née* Bialloblotzky, who was perhaps of Polish origin, outlived her husband, who died in 1866. Frege entered the University of Jena in 1869, where he studied for two years, and then went to the University of Göttingen for a further two—in mathematics, physics, chemistry, and philosophy. Frege spent the whole of his working life as a teacher of mathematics at Jena: he became a *Privatdozen* in May 1871, was given an *ausserordentlicher* (special or personal) professorship in July 1879, and became statutory professor of mathematics in May 1896. He lectured in all branches of mathematics (though his mathematical publications outside the field of logic are extremely few) and also on his own logical system. A great many of his publications, however, were expressly philosophical in character: he himself once said, "Every good mathematician is at least half a philosopher, and every good philosopher at least half a mathematician." He kept aloof from his students and even more aloof from his colleagues.

Though Frege was married, his wife died during World War I, leaving him no children of his own. There was an adopted son Alfred, however, who became an engineer.

Frege was, in religion, a liberal Lutheran and, in politics, a reactionary. He had a great love for the monarchy and for the royal house of Mecklenburg, and during World War I he developed an intense hatred of socialism and of democracy, to which he came to ascribe the loss of the war and the shame of the Treaty of Versailles. A diary kept at the end of his life reveals, as well, a loathing of the French and of Catholics and an anti-Semitism extending to a belief that the Jews must be expelled from Germany.

Frege had a vivid awareness of his own genius and a belief that it would one day be recognized; but he became increasingly embittered at the failure of scholars to recognize it during his lifetime. He delighted in controversy and polemic; but the originality of his own work, the almost total independence of his own ideas from other influences, past or present, was quite exceptional and, indeed, astonishing.

In 1879 Frege published his *Begriffsschrift* ("Concept-script"), in which, for the first time, a system of mathematical logic in the modern sense was presented. No one at the time, however—philosopher or mathematician—comprehended clearly what Frege had done, and when, some decades later, the subject began to get under way, his ideas reached others mostly as filtered through the minds of other men, such as Peano; in his lifetime there were very few—one was Bertrand Russell—to give Frege the credit due to him. He was not yet too downcast by the failure of the learned world to appreciate the *Begriffsschrift*, which, after all, discourages the reader by the use of a complex and unfamiliar symbolism to express unfamiliar ideas. He resolved, however, to compose his next book without the use of any symbols at all.

There followed a period of intensive work on the philosophy of logic and of mathematics, embodied initially in his first book, *Die Grundlagen der Arithmetik* (1884; Eng. trans., *The Foundations of Arithmetic*, 2nd rev. ed., 1953). The *Grundlagen* was a work that must on any count stand as a masterpiece of philosophical writing. The only review that the book received, however, was a devastatingly hostile one by Georg Cantor, the mathematician whose ideas were the closest to Frege's, who had not bothered to understand Frege's book before subjecting it to totally unmerited scorn.

Wounded by the reception of his second book, Frege nevertheless devoted the next decade to producing a series of brilliant philosophical articles in which he elaborated his philosophy of logic. These articles contain many deep insights, although, as Frege systematized his theories, there appeared a certain hardening into a kind of scholasticism. There followed a return to the philosophy of mathematics with the first volume of *Grundgesetze der Arithmetik* (1893; partial Eng. trans., *Basic Laws of Arithmetic*, 1964), in which Frege presented, in a modified version of the symbolic system of the *Begriffsschrift*, a rigorous development of the theory of *Grundlagen*. This, too, received only a single review (by Peano). The neglect of what was to have been his *chef d'oeuvre* finally embittered Frege, who had complained, in the preface, of the apparent ignorance of his work on the part of writers working in allied fields. The resulting bitterness shows in the style of Frege's controversial writing. Seldom has criticism of previous writers been more deadly than in his *Grundlagen;* but it is expressed with a lightness of touch and is never unfair. In volume 2 of the *Grundgesetze* (1903), however, the attacks became heavy-handed and abusive—a means of getting back at the world that had ignored him.

Later life. A worse disaster than neglect, however, was in store for him. While volume 2 of the *Grundgesetze* was at the printer's, he received on June 16, 1902, a letter from one of the few contemporaries who had read and admired his works—Bertrand Russell. The latter pointed out, modestly but correctly, the possibility of deriving a contradiction in Frege's logical system—the celebrated Russell paradox. The two exchanged many letters;

First publication

Failure of critics to understand his work

and, before the book was published, Frege had devised a modification of one of his axioms intended to restore consistency to the system. This he explained in an appendix to the book. After Frege's death, it would be shown by a Polish logician, Stanisław Leśniewski, that Frege's modified axiom still leads to contradiction. Probably Frege never discovered this. Even a brief inspection, however, of the proofs of the theorems in volume 1 would have revealed that several crucial proofs would no longer go through; and this Frege must have found out.

In any case, 1903 effectively marks the end of Frege's productive life. He never published the projected third volume of the *Grundgesetze*, and he took no part in the development of the subject, mathematical logic, that he had founded, though it had progressed considerably by the time of his death. He published a few polemical pieces; but, with the exception of three essays in the philosophy of logic produced after the end of the war, he did no further creative work. In 1912 he declined, in terms expressing deep depression, an invitation by Russell to address a mathematical congress in Cambridge.

At the very end of Frege's life, he again started to work on the philosophy of mathematics, having arrived at the conclusion that one of the fundamental bases of his earlier work—the attempt to found arithmetic on logic—had been mistaken; but the work did not progress very far and was not published.

Up to an advanced age, Frege hiked every summer in Mecklenburg, his native region. He finally retired during World War I and went to live in Bad Kleinen, in Mecklenburg, where he died on July 26, 1925.

Assessment. Frege's work represents the beginning of modern logic because of his invention of the notation of quantifiers and variables. (In natural language, generality is represented by inserting an expression like "everything" or "something" in the argument-place of the predicate; in the notation used in logic since Frege, the argument-place is filled by a variable letter, say x, and the resulting expression prefixed by a quantifier, "For every x" or "For some x," said to "bind" that variable.) By means of this notation he solved the problem that had baffled the logicians of the Middle Ages and prevented the further advance of logic ever since, viz., the analysis of sentences involving multiple generality. In him there also appeared the first clear separation between the formal characterization of logical laws and their semantic justification. His philosophical work is of an importance far more general than the area to which he principally applied it, the philosophy of mathematics: he initiated a revolution, in fact, as profound as that of René Descartes in the 17th century. Whereas Descartes had made epistemology the starting point for all philosophy, however, Frege gave this place to the theory of meaning or the philosophy of language. His work has been influential because he made the restricted part of philosophy in which he worked basic to all the rest. The effect was imparted in the first place, however, through the work of others, particularly that of Wittgenstein, who visited him in 1914 and who revered him. But, since John Austin's translation of the *Grundlagen* into English in 1950, the direct influence of Frege's writing among English-speaking philosophers has been very great. No one supposes that Frege said the last word on any topic; but there is scarcely a live question in contemporary philosophy of language for whose examination Frege's views do not form at least the best starting point.

BIBLIOGRAPHY

Works: The principal English translations of Frege's works are: J.L. AUSTIN (trans.), *The Foundations of Arithmetic: A Logico-Mathematical Enquiry into the Concept of Number*, 2nd ed. rev. (1959), a two language version; PETER GEACH and MAX BLACK (eds.), *Translations from the Philosophical Writings of Gottlob Frege*, 2nd ed. (1960); MONTGOMERY FURTH (ed. and trans.), *The Basic Laws of Arithmetic* (1964); J. VAN HEIJENOORT (ed. and trans.), "Begriffsschrift," in *From Frege to Gödel* (1967); and A. and M. QUINTON (trans.), "The Thought," in PETER F. STRAWSON (ed.), *Philosophical Logic* (1967). The German texts of most of Frege's works, including the *Grundgesetze*, are now, for the most part, reprinted and are listed together with a few other English translations in the bibliographies of the following two books: H. HERMES, F. KAMBARTEL, and F. KAULBACH (eds.), *Nachgelassene Schriften* (1969), a reprint of all Frege's surviving posthumous manuscripts other than letters; and G. GABRIEL (ed.), *Schriften zur Logik und Sprachphilosophie* (1971), a selection from the manuscripts.

Critical sources: E.D. KLEMKE (ed.), *Essays on Frege* (1968), contains most of the recent critical work on Frege of serious interest. See also LUDWIG WITTGENSTEIN, *Tractatus Logico-philosophicus* (1922; Eng. trans., 1961) and *Philosophische Untersuchungen* (written 1936–49; Eng. trans., *Philosophical Investigations*, 1953); BERTRAND RUSSELL, "On Denoting," *Mind*, 14:479–493 (1905, reprinted in *Logic and Knowledge*, ed. by R.C. MARSH, 1956); MICHAEL DUMMETT, "Frege, Gottlob," *Encyclopedia of Philosophy*, vol. 3 (1967); and the essay on Frege in G.E.M. ANSCOMBE and PETER GEACH, *Three Philosophers* (1961).

(Mi.D.)

French Guiana

French Guiana (La Guyane Française) lies on the northeast coast of South America to the north of the Equator. Bounded by Surinam (Netherlands Guiana) to the west and by Brazil to the south and east, it has an area of 34,749 square miles (90,000 square kilometres) and at the 1967 census had a population of 44,392. As a French overseas *département* (administrative district), its economic and political status differs little, legally, from that of a *département* in metropolitan France. French Guiana forms an integral part of the French Republic, forms part of the European Common Market, and is represented in the French Parliament by a senator and a deputy. The capital is Cayenne (population about 20,000).

With a territory about the size of Austria, French Guiana remains underpopulated and underdeveloped. It has a population density of only about one person per square mile. Although its reputation has improved since the notorious penal colony, associated with the name of Devil's Island (Île du Diable), was closed in 1945, the territory has experienced few other changes since that time. What roads exist are found only in the coastal region, and communication with the largely uninhabited interior is by river transport. Despite a little mining, fishing, and lumbering, French Guiana still remains economically dependent upon France.

The landscape. Geologically, the rock underlying French Guiana forms part of the Guiana Highlands, which is a crystalline massif (a large elevated block of rock) to the north of the Amazon Basin dating from the Precambrian Period (from about 4,600,000,000 to about 570,000,000 years ago). French Guiana's many rivers, most of which flow generally northeastward to the sea, have greatly eroded the rocky massif, so that no mountain ranges worthy of the name remain. Along the watershed that forms the southern frontier with Brazil, some peaks rise to about 2,300 feet (700 metres), with one peak rising to about 2,600 feet (800 metres) a little to the north. Parts of the coastal plain, which is formed of alluvium deposits, reach heights of about 650 feet (200 metres). The underlying Precambrian rock nevertheless crops out on the beaches of Cayenne and also forms the Îles du Salut, consisting of the islets of Royale, Saint-Joseph, and the Île du Diable (Devil's Island), all of which lie offshore in the vicinity of Kourou. To the southeast of Cayenne, recent marine alluvial deposits have formed a swampy coastal plain, constituting a region dominated by mangroves and grasses. Similar swampy patches occur to the west of Cayenne, but most of the plain here consists of older alluvial deposits, which form a savanna (grassy parkland) region. The remainder of the territory is covered with dense tropical evergreen forest, the character of which varies according to the type of soil and the amount of water.

From east to west, the main rivers are the Oyapock (with its tributaries the Yaroupi and Camopi); the Approuague; the Orapu; the Comté; the Kourou; the Sinnamary, joined by the Courcibo; the Iracoubo; the Mana; and the Maroni, which in its lower reaches forms the border with Surinam and into which flow the Tampoc, Inini, and Abounamy, all from French Guiana territory.

Climate. French Guiana is situated between 2° and 6° N, so that the climate is characterized by high tem-

Margin notes: Significance of his work · Forest areas

peratures, with monthly averages at Cayenne varying between 77° to 80° F (25° to 26° C). Rainfall is heavy from December to July; at Cayenne the yearly average is about 150 inches and may surpass 157 inches in places a little further southeast. In the northeast, rainfall is less plentiful, amounting to 98 inches a year, but it is more evenly distributed. The northeast trade winds blow constantly inland from the sea. Storms are rare and there are no hurricanes.

Vegetation and animal life. The vegetation is primarily tropical rain forest, which covers almost 90 percent of the land surface. The trees are almost all hardwood species. Few species of the larger wild animals are to be encountered, although among them are the tapir (a hoofed animal of the rhinoceros order), the caiman (related to the alligator), and the ocelot (a spotted leopard-like cat). Among the more exotic animals are the sloth, the great anteater, and the armadillo. There are many kinds of birds, fish, snakes, rodents, and insects. Flocks of parrots and several kinds of monkeys are common.

The landscape under human settlement. Rural settlements are divided into *communes* (the smallest of French territorial divisions), the most important of which are

supplied with running water and electricity. Most houses are of wood and are usually covered with corrugated iron roofs. Each house usually has a garden attached in which cocoanut, mango, lemon, and orange trees are grown, as well as vegetables and spices, such as pimento. Poultry are also raised. Crops are usually grown by shifting methods of cultivation at some distance from the settlements; agriculturists often live near their holdings or else live temporarily in small shelters called *carbets*. Negroes live in African-style villages composed of wooden cabins, which are often artistically decorated. Indians, who are few in number, form small groups located on the upper reaches of rivers or in the northeastern coastal region; they live in *carbets* without walls, and sleep in hammocks.

In Cayenne, the capital, wooden buildings are slowly giving way to modern houses, although the past still predominates. The town is well laid out and has now spread beyond its original boundaries; new districts are being built on the outskirts. Traffic is increasing and stores carry on a thriving trade. A modern town was recently established at Kourou, northwest of Cayenne, near the proving ground at the Guianan Space Centre which was opened in 1966.

History. Vicente Yáñez Pinzón, an associate of Christopher Columbus, explored the Guianan coast in 1500. He was followed by a host of adventurers seeking the mythical El Dorado (City of Gold) that was believed to be located in the region. Financed by Henry IV of France, a French nobleman named La Touche de la Ravardière chose the site of Cayenne in 1604; the town itself was founded by a company of merchants from Rouen in 1637. The first French attempts at colonization failed. The Dutch established themselves at Cayenne but were evicted by the French in 1664. The Guiana settlement was then sacked by the English in 1667 and by the Dutch in 1676. A frontier dispute between the French and the Portuguese appeared to have been settled in 1700 when the Portuguese accepted the Amazon River as the southeastern boundary of the settlement; but in 1713, under the terms of the Treaty of Utrecht, the frontier was moved 37 miles (60 kilometres) to the north. In the 50 years that followed, French Guiana was administered by a series of governors of differing capacities and grew slowly in both population and prosperity. Upheavals occurred, however, such as the expulsion of the Jesuits in 1762, accompanied by the dispersal of 10,000 Amerinds associated with the Jesuit missions. The Kourou expedition (1763 to 1765) was an abortive attempt at colonization; due to poor planning and tropical disease, about 14,000 people, many recruited in Europe, died. Later, from 1796 to 1799, many people were deported from France to Guiana, a large number of whom died. Under governors such as Pierre Victor Malouet (governor from 1776–78), however, the colony again grew prosperous. The French Revolution had relatively little effect; after slavery was abolished in 1794, a kind of forced labour was introduced until the re-establishment of slavery once more in 1802. Throughout the period from 1794 to 1805 political deportees were sent from France to Guiana, which was nicknamed the "dry guillotine" because of the heavy death toll that ensued among the deportees. In 1809 the colony was seized by the Portuguese but was restored to France in 1817. In the years that followed, a degree of prosperity ensued, and the interior of the country was explored. From 1827 to 1846, Mother Anne-Marie Javouhey, superior of the community of Saint-Joseph de Cluny, organized a flourishing colony for freed slaves at Mana. The final abolition of slavery in 1848 brought ruin to the plantations. Several different immigrant groups were introduced to provide labour, but only the Asian Indians were at all effective. The situation worsened when gold was discovered in 1855, after which labour was lured away from agriculture to the mines, while an influx of a variegated population of adventurers also occurred. In 1852 the first of several convict settlements was established at Saint-Laurent-du-Maroni; that on Devil's Island was to become the most notorious, although it was the least important of the prisons. Although

The Kourou space centre

FRENCH GUIANA   54°   52°

the European convicts proved unable to work in the tropical climate and died quickly, the penal colonies were continued for over 90 years, thus bringing French Guiana into disrepute. The penal system was not abolished until 1945.

The inhabitants of French Guiana have had full French citizenship and the right to vote since 1848 and representation in the French Parliament since 1870. They rallied to France in the wars of 1870 and 1914, and in World War II joined the Free French cause in 1943. The territory became a French *département* in 1946.

A predominantly Creole population

Peoples and population. Out of the total population of about 44,000 at the 1967 census, about 36,000 lived in Cayenne or its vicinity. About 25 percent of the population consists of Europeans. The majority of the population is, however, Creole, although there are some Negroes, Amerinds, and immigrant minorities. The Creoles stem from the continual ethnic and social intermixture of the groups that entered the country from Europe, Asia, and Africa, as well as from other parts of South America. Following a European style of life, they speak an Antillean Creole dialect, as well as French.

The "Negroes of the Woods"

Some of the Indians and Negroes live as Europeans, but most follow their traditional patterns of living. All are French citizens with the right to vote. The "Negroes of the Woods," as they are called, who are the descendants of escaped slaves, live on both banks of the frontier rivers, particularly the Maroni River; they form a community of about 4,000, living under either French or Dutch protection. While they have preserved an African tribal mode of life, their language has absorbed English, French, Spanish, and Dutch influences.

The Amerinds, who are the original inhabitants of Guiana, number scarcely more than 1,000, as compared with 15,000 at the end of the 17th century. They are divided into the Galibi, Arawak, and Palicur (Palikour) tribes on the coast, and the Wayana, Oyampi, and Emerillon tribes in the hinterland. The coastal groups participate in the cash economy to some extent, while those in the hinterland live by hunting, fishing, and shifting agriculture; their numbers are increasing slowly.

Among other minorities, ethnically separate communities are formed by the metropolitan French (most of whom remain only a few years), the Lebanese, and the Chinese, both of whom arrived in the 19th century under Catholic auspices. There is also a small Indonesian community, which came from Surinam in 1952. Religious affiliations are varied, but Catholicism, rather than Protestantism, predominates. The Negroes and Amerinds have preserved their traditional religions, as also have the Chinese and Indonesians. The population as a whole is increasing.

French Guiana, Area and Population

	area		population	
	sq mi	sq km	1967 census	1972 estimate
Arrondissements				
Cayenne	19,112	49,500	36,270	...
Saint-Laurent-du-Maroni	15,637	40,500	8,122	...
Total French Guiana	34,749	90,000	44,392	50,400

Source: Official government figures.

Economy. French Guiana has an artificial economy, sustained by aid from France. Agriculture is far from meeting the demand for food, which has to be increasingly imported. There is little stock raising. Fisheries, however, are able not only to meet local demand but also produce enough for export. Two shrimp canning and freezing factories, supplied by 200 trawlers, supply the American market. Some shrimps are also exported to France. Forestry, which has a considerable potential, has encountered some difficulties. Some gold, obtained by panning, is exported. The quantity varies from year to year; in 1969, for example, it represented only 3 percent of the value of all exports. There are prospects for exploiting bauxite deposits at Kaw, which amount to 50,-000,000 tons. The fact that economic and social legislation requires that salaries match those paid in metropolitan France has hindered further economic development, for which prospects are not bright.

Lack of roads

Transport. A road in the coastal region links Cayenne with Saint-Laurent-du-Maroni; from Saint-Laurent-du-Maroni one may cross the Maroni River by ferry to Surinam. There are no other main roads, although one is being built to link Cayenne to the Brazilian frontier. Access to the hinterland is by river or by air. Rivers are easily navigable for the first 10 or 15 miles, after which rapids are encountered. A private air service maintains seven airports for domestic flights. From the international airport at Rochambeau, near Cayenne, regular flights leave for France (via Martinique and Guadeloupe) and for Brazil. There is a port at Cayenne and landing places at Larivot on the Cayenne River, Kourou, and Saint-Laurent-du-Maroni. A port to accommodate larger ships is under construction at Dégrad des Cannes on the Mahury estuary. Shipping arriving in French Guiana consists almost entirely of cargo vessels.

Administration and social services. As a French overseas *département*, French Guiana is administered by a prefect and has an elected council-general of 16 members. It is also represented in the French Parliament through one deputy each in the National Assembly and Senate. Education, public health, and social security services are patterned on those provided in France. A number of students travel to French institutions in the Caribbean, or to France itself, for further education; many do not return. Radio and television programs are broadcast in French and Creole; cinemas, libraries, museums, and tropical research institutes, including the Institut Pasteur, are in Cayenne. Traditional culture has been preserved by the Amerinds and Negroes. Creole cultural manifestations include carnivals, dancing, and music, but Creole culture is slowly fading.

Prospects for the future. Prospects for future development are at best uncertain. It had been hoped that with the establishment of the Guianan Space Centre proving ground, and the associated establishment of a new town at Kourou, there might be some acceleration of local economic development; there is little sign that this has occurred. It appears likely that it will be many years before French Guiana begins to develop economically, nor is it as yet possible to see what form this development will assume.

BIBLIOGRAPHY. E. ABONNENC, J. HURAULT, and R. SABAN, *Bibliographie de la Guyane Française* (1957); *Carribbeana: 1900–1965, a Topical Bibliography* (1968).

(Je.-M.B.)

French Polynesia

French Polynesia comprises about 130 islands with a total land area of some 1,500 square miles (4,000 square kilometres) scattered over an area of the south central Pacific between latitudes 7° to 27° S and longitudes 134° to 155° W. The islands form an overseas territory of France. Their population in 1971 was approaching 120,000. (H.La./J.Fa./C.R.)

History. European discovery of the islands of French Polynesia was gradual. The southern Marquesas Islands; were discovered in 1595 by Álvaro de Mendaña de Neira; his successor, Pedro de Quiros, in 1606 discovered some of the Tuamotus. The Dutch explorer Jacob Roggeveen in 1722 discovered Makatea, Bora-Bora, and Maupiti. Capt. Samuel Wallis in 1767 discovered Tahiti, Moorea, and Tubuai-Manu. The Society Islands were named after the Royal Society, which sponsored the expedition under Capt. James Cook that observed from Tahiti in 1769 the transit of the planet Venus. In that year Cook discovered the Huahine islands, Raiatea, Tahaa, and also Rurutu in the Îles Tubuai; Tubuai itself was discovered on Cook's last voyage (1777). Rapa was discovered by George Vancouver in 1791, and in the same year Capt. Joseph Ingraham of the U.S. trading vessel "Hope" traversed the Marquesas Islands and discovered their northern group. The Îles Gambier were discovered in 1797 by Capt. James Wilson of the British missionary ship "Duff."

FRENCH POLYNESIA

The history of the Society Island groups is virtually that of Tahiti, which was made a French protectorate in 1842 and a colony in 1880. French missionaries went to the Gambier group in 1834, and in 1844 a French protectorate was proclaimed, followed by annexation in 1881. The Îles Tubuai were also evangelized from Tahiti, and as late as 1888 Rimatara and Rurutu sought British protection, which was refused. They were placed under the French protectorate in 1889 and annexed in 1900. The Tuamotus were part of the kingdom of the Pomare family of Tahiti, which came originally from Fakarava. These islands were claimed as dependencies of Tahiti within the protectorate by France in 1847 and became part of the colony in 1880. In the Marquesas, Nuku Hiva was annexed to the United States in 1813 by Capt. David Porter of the frigate "Essex," but the annexation was never ratified. French occupation of the group followed the landing of forces from a French warship, requested by the chief of Tahuata (near Hiva Oa). Soon after there was a quarrel with the French; in 1842 the chiefs ceded sovereignty to France.   (F.J.W.)

The islands (administratively termed French Colony of Oceania [EFO]) were originally ruled by a naval government, which was dissolved by an organic decree of 1885. The nearest thing to a constitution that the EFO ever had, the organic decree provided for a French governor and Privy Council and for an 18-member General Council, representing the islands, that had some control over fiscal policies. The powers of the General Council, however, were cut back in 1899, and in 1903 it was replaced by an advisory council that had none of the powers of its predecessor and the function of which was purely administrative. This situation, which was unsatisfactory to the native inhabitants, continued until French Polynesia was made an overseas territory of France in 1946.   (Ed.)

The landscape. Five distinct sets of islands may be discerned, all protrusions of parallel submarine ridges trending from the northwest to the southeast.

The Society Islands. These are the most westerly of the group and the most important in terms of land area (40 percent) and population (80 percent). Except for a few small atolls, they are of the "high island" type, resulting from the emergence of underwater volcanoes.

The volcanic cones are highly eroded and cut up into high crests and deep, radiating valleys. The often lushly vegetated mountains drop abruptly to narrow coastal strips or directly into lagoons or the sea—from the direct assaults of which the islands are protected by almost completely encircling barrier reefs.

The largest and most highly populated of the Society Islands are Tahiti and its neighbour, Moorea, both situated in the eastern Îles du Vent, or Windward Group. Tahiti, formed of two ancient volcanic cones, is particularly striking, because of its dramatic silhouette, which rises 7,333 feet above sea level. The mountains are empty of all human settlement, habitation and planting being limited to the coastal strip and valley outlets. Moorea, separated from Tahiti by a 12-mile-wide channel, is also a high island and is encircled with very white coral sand beaches. It is well connected to Tahiti by boat and taxi planes—a consequence of the booming tourist industry.

Ninety miles to the west of Tahiti are the Îles sous le Vent, or Leeward Islands, made up of five high islands and four atolls. They closely resemble the Îles du Vent in appearance. Raiatea is the largest and most densely populated; it has a coastal plain with coconut groves where stock raising is carried on. Vanilla was once an important crop but is now on the decline. Its port is Uturoa, the second city of French Polynesia. To the east of Raiatea is the island of Huahine, a volcanic structure bisected by a shallow arm of the sea. It is very picturesque and will probably develop as a tourist attraction.

Finally, to the west of Raiatea, lies the beautiful little island of Bora-Bora. It is formed from a volcanic peak rising up to 2,385 feet and dropping down abruptly to the lagoon. It is one of the centres around which the tourist trade revolves in French Polynesia.

The Tuamotu Archipelago. Lying to the east of the Society Islands, this archipelago of 325 square miles and some 7,700 inhabitants consists of more than 80 islands. These are low, flat islands or atolls of coral origin, surrounding a lagoon. The size varies greatly: the largest ones, such as Rangiroa, reach 29 square miles; the smallest are made up of a few acres of land barely protruding above the surface of the sea. Lacking soil, and with no permanent streams, they have no agricul-

Tahiti and Moorea

tural potential aside from the ever-present coconut trees. The lagoons, however, are a source of fish, pearls, and mother-of-pearl shell. Only Rangiroa, with its airport, is in close contact with Tahiti. Elsewhere, living conditions are so hard that the people are only too eager to emigrate to Tahiti. In the Tuamotus are situated the French nuclear installations. Test sites are on Mururoa and Fangataufa; the military base on Hao has an airstrip that handles military jets.

The Îles Gambier. Morphologically different, the Îles Gambier lie at the southern extremity of the Tuamotu Archipelago and include four large, high islands and a few islets (14 square miles, some 600 inhabitants). The main island is Mangareva.

The Marquesas Islands. There are 14 Marquesas Islands lying 900 miles to the northeast of Tahiti. They have a land area of 255 square miles and a population of about 5,600. Some of them are high islands (over 3,000 feet), with sharp and twisting contours. Unlike the Society Islands, they are not protected from the sea by a barrier reef, with the result that they lack a coastal plain. Approaching the islands from the sea is difficult. People live exclusively in the valleys, where they engage in farming.

The Îles Tubuai. Situated 450 miles south of Tahiti, the Îles Tubuai, or Austral Islands, make up the southernmost part of the territory.

This chain of four islands, with the addition of the isolated island of Rapa in the southeast, covers 54 square miles and contains over 5,000 inhabitants. All of the islands are of volcanic origin but of little height (300 to 1,000 feet) and with unpronounced contours. Income is derived from agriculture (taro, market vegetables) and pandanus plaiting. This plait work is sold in Papeete.

Like the Marquesas and the Tuamotu-Gambiers, the Tubuai group have poor connections with Tahiti. As elsewhere, the hard living conditions provoke a rural exodus, to the benefit of Tahiti and Papeete.

Administratively part of French Polynesia is the island of Clipperton (10° 18′ N, 109° 15′ W), some 600 miles off the coast of Mexico. An atoll of about five miles in circumference, it is presently uninhabited.

Climate. The climate is tropical—warm and humid. There is a warm rainy season from November until April and a relatively cool dry season from May until October. The dispersion of the islands through 20° of latitude, however, results in local and regional climatic variation. Except in the Marquesas and the northern Tuamotus, rainfall is abundant, falling in the form of violent showers. As much as 120 inches fall on the coastal areas. There are local variations due to differing exposures; on average, the coasts exposed to the winds receive more precipitation.

Rainfall and temperature

The temperature varies but slightly throughout the year. At Papeete, the mean average annual temperature is 79.0° F (26.1° C); the high mean average is 90.7° F (32.6° C) in March and the low mean average 70.0° F (21.1° C) in August. The Îles Tubuai (Austral), further south, enjoys a cooler climate; the low mean average can go down to 64° F (18° C) in September. The relative humidity is always high—80 to 90 percent on the average. The high areas are continually enveloped in a heavy cloud formation.

The territory is in the trade-wind zone. The dominant winds thus blow from the north and northeast, but they tend toward the southeast between May and October. There are large periods of calm (April, May, June) but with occasional tropical hurricanes or cyclones. Land breezes cool the night to 13° F (7° C) below the daytime temperature.

Vegetation and animal life. Because of the recent origin and the isolation of the islands, there is little variety in terrestrial flora and fauna. Most of the plant species were introduced by the first Polynesians, others being introduced by Europeans.

The vegetation's appearance varies with the ecological conditions. On the limestone soils of the atolls, it has a pronounced xerophious (desert-plant-type) character. On the high volcanic islands it is more diversified; ferns have

French Polynesia, Area and Population

Circonscriptions	area* sq mi	area* sq km	population 1962 census	population 1971 census
Iles Australes	54	141	4,000	5,000
Iles du Vent	459	1,188	52,000	85,000
Iles Marquises	255	661	5,000	6,000
Iles sous le Vent	154	399	16,000	16,000
Iles Tuamotu et Gambier	339	877	7,000	8,000
Total French Polynesia	1,261	3,265†	85,000†	119,000†

*Inhabited islands only; total area is 1,500 sq mi (4,000 sq km).
†Figures do not add to total given because of rounding.
Source: Official government figures.

often conquered the hills and plateaus, whereas rain forests are established in the upper valley areas. On coastal plains flourish coconut, breadfruit, and various fruit trees.

The land fauna is especially limited, and most of the species have been introduced. No mammal is indigenous, but certain ones live wild: goats, pigs, horses, cattle, and, of course, rats.

The streams are inhabited mainly by a fish, *nato*, and a shrimp (prawn) highly esteemed by gourmets. The marine fauna is rich, with fish of every shape and colour.

Human geography. *Patterns of settlement.* On the high islands, homes are scattered through the coconut groves along the coastal roads. Every two or three miles occurs a village in which are grouped together the church, the government house, the school, a shop (usually run by a Chinese), the pastor's home, and a few residences. The contemporary rural house is of concrete construction in a yard shaded by fruit trees, with a separate kitchen made from traditional materials (palm, bamboo) where food is prepared and eaten. On the atolls, the population is usually grouped together in villages located close to the passes through the surrounding reefs.

Population and business activity tend to concentrate in the Papeete area. The town consists of the old colonial city (still the business centre), residential areas (often on the heights), and tin-pan alleys hidden by foliage; it extends some 20 miles along the sea front and creeps into the valleys, that are walled in by nearby mountains.

Layout of Papeete

Urban services—water supply, sewage, electricity, and public transportation—remain inadequate, especially in the areas recently occupied by immigrants pouring in from the outer islands.

This influx is connected with the development of a class of salaried workers in French Polynesia that represented 74 percent of the economically active population in 1969.

The people. Most of the people throughout the islands may be classed as Polynesian, speaking eastern Polynesian languages. Polynesians and part Polynesians (called Demis) make up 85 percent of the total. Minority groups consist of Chinese (11 percent) and Europeans and Americans (3 percent). Although relatively few in numbers, the Demis, as a result of their position between two cultures (Polynesian and European) constitute a very important economic force and even more vital political force. Over 60 percent of the population is of protestant persuasion (Evangelical Church of Polynesia); some 30 percent is Roman Catholic, the remainder belonging to various other Christian denominations.

After half a century of decline the population stabilized between 1900 and 1920 and then underwent a considerable increase; in 1968 the birth rate was 4.57 percent and the death rate .91 percent. Polynesian emigration to New Caledonia almost stopped around 1963–64, when the French nuclear testing headquarters was established but then recommenced in 1969 with the expansion of the nickel industry in New Caledonia. With a high birth rate and the death rate reduced by sanitary developments, the population of the territory is likely to double in 20 years. In 1971, one Tahitian out of two (55 percent) lived in Papeete and its suburban area.

Economy. Many resources are used for local subsistence, including fruits, products from fishing and planting, and materials for the construction of traditional types of houses and canoes. The main exports—copra, vanilla, and mother-of-pearl shell—have greatly declined. Exports in 1970, in fact, for those products (by volume) were 62, 20, and 32 percent, respectively, of levels of 1960. This, however, has been partially compensated for by an increase in income from tourists, who increased more than twelve-fold in numbers between 1960 and 1971.

The gross internal product in 1969 was 19,185,000,000 Pacific francs (CFP 100 = $1 U.S.; CFP 240 = £1 sterling, on October 15, 1971), 9 percent of which came from agriculture, 18 percent from industry and the building trade, 3 percent from tourism, 41 percent from business and various services, and 29 percent from salaries of civil service employees.

Developments in transportation

There have been considerable developments in transportation facilities since the early 1960s, including the construction of a modern port in Papeete, construction of an international airport, and development of air services with some of the outlying islands: Moorea, the Leewards, the western Tuamotus, the Marquesas, and the Tubuai. Schooner connections within the region and with other Pacific areas are still, however, very irregular, and road systems are inadequate or nonexistent.

Administration and social conditions. Represented in the French parliament by a deputy and a senator and placed under French law, the territory is administered locally by an elected assembly and a governor. The latter is head of the territory and is appointed by the French government. Since the early 1960s a large fraction of the population has been demanding a statute of internal autonomy, with enlargement of the prerogatives of the Assembly, creation of ministerial portfolios, and the formation of a cabinet responsible to the electorate.

Schooling is compulsory and conducted largely in government-aided mission schools; literacy is 95 percent. The population has average health facilities (one doctor for 1,750 inhabitants, one hospital bed for 120 inhabitants). The standard of living is relatively high, annual per capita income being U.S. $1,450, but there are wide differences of income between the various social groups.

Cultural transition and prospects. Profoundly influenced by the West, French Polynesia's cultural and artistic traditions have been reduced to a sort of folklore, a process stimulated greatly by the tourist trade. In spite of the existence of an ethnographic museum and a local learned society, a great effort is needed to preserve the territory's cultural heritage. The absence of newspapers in Polynesian, the small amount of broadcasting in the Tahitian language, and the nonrecognition of vernacular languages as official languages on a level of equality with French all constitute a real handicap to the protection of indigenous culture.

An ethnically diverse society located at a crossroad of civilizations, French Polynesia is hunting for a cultural identity. This still-confused aspiration is expressed through the medium of political struggles centred around the demand for internal autonomy. The ties of economic dependence with France however, are being reinforced to a dangerous degree, in spite of worthy efforts at all levels to ensure substitutes for activities connected with the French nuclear program.

BIBLIOGRAPHY. PATRICK O'REILLY and EDOUARD REITMAN, *Bibliographie de Tahiti et de la Polynésie française* (1967), is an exceptionally useful tool for scholars and laymen; it includes more than 10,000 entries with many accompanied by brief summaries. Little has been published in geography; see FRANCOIS DOUMENGE, *L'Homme dans le Pacifique Sud* (1966), for the best general survey. For general documentation about pre-European ethnography, one may consult the Bernice P. Bishop Museum Bulletins; No. 9 for the Marquesas, 48 and 90 for Tahiti, 157 for Mangareva, and 70 for Tubuai. PIERRE VERIN, *L'Ancienne civilisation de Rurutu (îles Australes, Polynésie française)* (1969), is a recent work in Austral island archaeology and ethnohistory; JOSE GARANGER, "Archaeology and the Society Islands," in GENEVIEVE A. HIGHLAND *et al.* (eds.), *Polynesian Culture History* (1967); and YOSIHIKO H.

SINOTO, "Position of the Marquesas Islands in East Polynesian Prehistory," in I. YAWATA and Y.H. SINOTO (eds.), *Prehistoric Culture History* (1968), give general insights into recent archaeological advances in French Polynesia. The Chinese minority is studied in GERALD COPPENRATH, *Les Chinois de Tahiti, de l'aversion à l'assimilation, 1865–1966* (1967). Contemporary social change is documented in BENGT DANIELSSON, *Work and Life on Raroia* (1956); BEN R. FINNEY, "Polynesian Peasants and Proletarians" in *Polynesian Society Reprint Series* No. 9 (1965); PAUL OTTINO, *La Pêche au grand filet ('Upe'a rahi) à Tahiti* (1965); PAUL KAY, "Aspects of Social Structure in a Tahitian Urban Neighbourhood," *Journal of the Polynesian Society*, 72:325–371 (1963); and by ALLAN F. HANSON, *Rapan Life-Ways* (1970). The only synthesis, written by an economist, a sociologist, and two geographers, about the contemporary situation and transformations induced by the implantation of a military base for atomic tests is JEAN FAGES *et al., Tahiti et Moorea: études sur la société, l'économie et l'utilisation de l'espace* (1970). On Gauguin in Tahiti and the Marquesas, the best documented study is BENGT DANIELSSON, *Gaugin in the South Seas* (1965).

(H.La./J.Fa./C.R.)

French Revolutionary and Napoleonic Wars

The wars of the period 1792 to 1815, between France and alliances of the other major European powers, were a mixture of old and new. Broadly speaking, the weapons were old. While muskets, bayonets, guns, and cavalry weapons had been slightly improved during the 18th century and continued to be improved during these wars, the slow-firing and cumbrous smooth-bored, muzzle-loaded hand and field weapons of the War of the Spanish Succession (1701–14) were still, in basic essentials, the weapons used 150 years later in the Crimean War (see also EUROPEAN DIPLOMACY AND WARS [c. 1500–1914]).

New elements in the wars

The new element in these wars was political. The aims of the French Revolution were proclaimed to be liberty and equality, an end to autocratic regimes, and government by and for the people. If men had these rights, however, they had a corresponding responsibility to defend them against attack: the corollary of the vote was the duty of military service. In practice this meant large conscript armies instead of relatively small professional ones. As the great military writer Karl von Clausewitz was to point out, while armies of the 18th-century type still existed in France at the outbreak of the Revolution, it was not long before

. . . such a force as no one had had any conception of made its appearance. War had again suddenly become an affair of the people, and that of a people numbering thirty millions, every one of whom regarded himself as a citizen of the state.

This vital change led to much larger armies and, in consequence, to important developments in strategy and tactics. After 1800 Napoleon normally fought his campaigns in command of 250,000 men and occasionally many more, in contrast to the 60,000- to 70,000-man armies of the early and middle 18th century. Moving armies of that increased size swiftly across western and central Europe required good road- and river-transport systems and created a need for supplies that could be satisfied only by some measure of local requisitioning or by living off the land, in contrast to the elaborate and restrictive depot methods of the 18th century. On the battlefield the massed infantry column became an alternative to the thin firing line, partly because the column offered an acceptable way to deploy large numbers of rapidly trained new recruits.

One other general matter must be mentioned. If the French entered these wars in 1792 as a crusade, at first to defend the Revolution in France against the invading armies of Austria and Prussia and then to spread the Revolution to less fortunate nations, that phase of the wars came to an end by 1800, if not before. Certainly from 1805 onward and in some respects during his campaigns against the Second Coalition in 1798–1802, the wars of Napoleon were aggressive, nationalist wars designed primarily to expand French influence either by direct territorial aggrandizement or by the creation of satellite states. As a result, the armies of France, which had once been welcomed by those whom they appeared to emancipate, later found themselves opposed as aggressors by men with those same patriotic sentiments that had inspired early Revolutionary governments. Spain, Austria, Prussia, and Russia all reacted in this way to some degree and their combined efforts were sufficient, in the end, to complete the overthrow both of Napoleon himself and of much of the Revolutionary legacy he had inherited.

This account of these wars is therefore divided into two main sections, fitting the overall pattern of political and military events. The first section includes the campaigns of Revolutionary governments down to and including those waged against the Second Coalition; toward the end of this period, Napoleon, as first consul, emerged as the undisputed leader of France. The second section, covering the period of France's attempted expansion, is divided into three parts. The first begins with the resumption of hostilities between Britain and France in 1803 and ends with the Treaty of Tilsit in 1807—a period that saw the high-water mark of Napoleon's success both as general and as statesman. The second part continues to 1811, during which time Napoleon attempted to establish his position as overlord of Europe on a permanent basis, only to encounter increasing patriotic opposition first from Spain and then from Austria; while, in the background, Britain increasingly waged economic warfare against France and a steadily growing military war in Spain. The third part is the period of Napoleon's defeat and overthrow, from the invasion of Russia in June 1812 to the final catastrophe at Waterloo in June 1815.

This article is divided into the following sections:

I. The French Revolutionary Wars, 1792–1802
    The new French armies
    The outbreak of war
    The war at sea and in the colonies
    The French expedition to Egypt and Syria, 1798–1802
    The continental campaigns of the Second Coalition, 1798–1801
II. The Napoleonic Wars, 1801–15
    Lunéville to Tilsit, 1801–07
    The coercion of Europe, 1807–11
    The defeat of Napoleon, 1812–15

I. The French Revolutionary Wars, 1792–1802

THE NEW FRENCH ARMIES

French military reforms

At the outbreak of the Revolution in 1789, the French Army was probably the most efficient and progressive army in Europe, thanks to a variety of reforms introduced during the previous 20 years. The number of officers had been greatly reduced and many military sinecures abolished. A better system of training for young officers, together with improved methods of regimental accounting and administration, had been introduced. Organization into divisions, certainly for training purposes, had become standard. French artillery was being steadily improved, both in equipment and in organization, in ways from which the generals of the Revolution and Napoleon himself greatly benefitted. Finally, there were other reformers—for example, the Comte de Guibert, who published his *Essai générale de tactique* in 1773 —who criticized what they considered the restricted tactical and strategic practices of 18th-century armies and who envisaged swifter, more ruthless warfare designed to achieve much greater political success.

Guibert argued that 18th-century warfare was ineffective because it was waged with relatively small armies hampered by restricted finance and led by overcautious generals. He wrote,

> But suppose that there should arise in Europe a people endowed with energy, with genius, with resources, with government; a people which combined the virtues of austerity with a national militia and which added to them a fixed plan of aggrandizement; which never lost sight of this system; which, as it would know how to make war at small cost and subsist on its victories, would not be compelled by calculations of finance to lay down its arms. We should see that people subdue its neighbours and upset our feeble constitutions as the north wind bends the slender reeds.

These may have seemed wild words to Guibert's contemporaries, but the events of the Revolution and then of Napoleon proved them true.

But, however progressive the French Army may have been in 1789, it was still the instrument of an autocratic government and of an aristocratic social system. The officer establishment numbered fewer than 10,000, of whom over two-thirds were noblemen and hardly more than 10 percent were officers of fortune. Moreover, of the 285 members of the chamber of nobles in the States General (assembly of the clergy, nobles, and commons), over 50 percent were officers. The main problem for the National Assembly at this time, therefore, was not so much to ensure the continuation of a large and efficient army for purposes of law and order as rather to make certain that a basically royalist army did not become a centre of hostility to the new Revolutionary government. To some extent the problem was solved by emigration. Officers of noble rank were angered and made apprehensive by measures designed to embody the new ideals of liberty and equality. In February 1790 a new military constitution prescribed that all citizens were theoretically eligible for every military employment and rank, and the purchase of commissions was abolished. With the coming of the Legislative Assembly in September 1791, a new military oath was introduced in place of the oath of allegiance to the king. In response to such measures, officers of noble rank emigrated in great numbers, and, by the end of 1794, well over 5,000 of them had gone. At the same time insubordination spread rapidly. In some regiments, officers were summarily cashiered by their men, and others were elected by popular vote in their place. Political associations appeared within regiments.

By the summer of 1791 the National Assembly decided that this process had gone too far. War had not yet begun, but it was becoming more likely; and the army was growing weaker. In June, therefore, the Assembly decided to raise 170 new battalions—more than 100,000 men in all —consisting of volunteers from the National Guard. Many of these volunteers, who had been in the royalist militia originally, proved to be valuable troops. In the spring of 1792, with another 75,000 men needed, the voluntary principle of enlistment was breached for the first time; each *département* was allotted a quota and instructed to enroll by ballot if volunteers proved insufficient. A year later, with a demand for a further 300,000 men, the National Convention ordered the conscription of unmarried men between the ages of 18 and 40, again to make up any shortages in voluntary enlistment. Six months later still, in August 1793, the National Convention introduced the *levée en masse* by a decree putting all Frenchmen in permanent requisition for the nation's armies until all foreign enemies had been defeated. It was decreed,

The levée en masse

> All Frenchmen, . . . are called by their country to defend liberty. . . . From this moment until that when the enemy is driven from the territory of the republic, every Frenchman is commandeered for the needs of the armies.

Thus, the "nation in arms" was announced. By the spring of 1794, France had more than 700,000 men in its armies, and Europe was treated to its first display of total war in modern times. Thus began the process whereby Napoleon was able to command 200,000 men and more in his great victories of 1805–06 and nearly three times that number when he invaded Russia in 1812; and, in response to that threat, the Allies were able to oppose him with armies of equal size and even greater size in the years 1813–15.

There were, however, limitations in the practical application of this principle of universal military service. First, many groups, such as priests and married men, were exempt from the obligation. Next, it became the custom that a man could buy himself out of his obligation by finding and paying for a substitute, a practice that clearly favoured the rich. Thirdly, Napoleon increasingly favoured an elite professional army, which he developed in the Imperial Guard—but the most suitable men for such a force were usually those with long service, and men were often retained in the army when, by the rules

Sites associated with the French Revolutionary and Napoleonic wars.

Maps © George Philip & Son, Ltd. 1970; all other material © Cambridge University Press 1970 from *The New Cambridge Modern History,* volume XIV, "Atlas," edited by H.C. Darby and Harold Fullard

of conscription, others should have taken their places. Finally, the system worked erratically. In the middle of his career, Napoleon used many foreign regiments, thus lessening the call on Frenchmen. Even in his preparations for the 1812 campaign, only about 50 percent of those eligible for military service were actually called to the colours. In the years of defeat (1813–15), however, with few foreigners to call upon, youths below the legal age for military service were called by anticipating future obligations. This practice produced a sense of hardship and bitterness in France that had not been present in the days of great victories and, in turn, led to increased evasion of a duty that the Revolution had proclaimed a privilege.

France's example in these matters did have some influence elsewhere in Europe. Armies grew in size, and liability for military service was extended. Since political revolutions did not take place inside those countries that were the major enemies of France, however, the most important factor in the development of the concept of the nation in arms was missing. In several countries— *e.g.,* Spain, Austria, and Russia—there was a strengthening of nationalist sentiment against the French invader, and that sentiment proved to be, to some extent, an effective substitute for the demagogic appeal of the *levée en masse.* In Prussia, however, the example of France was analyzed and then, in some important ways, deliberately copied; indeed, it is arguable that the rationale of the nation in arms was more carefully worked out in Prussia than in France.

The Prussian buildup

For Prussians their defeats at Jena and Auerstädt in 1806 were not only humiliating but astounding as well. The only explanation for Prussian statesmen and soldiers

of the complete overthrow of the military machine created by Frederick the Great was to argue not that the French were better professional soldiers led by a better general but that the French were inspired by something that Prussian soldiers lacked. Clausewitz called it national spirit. If Prussia was to avenge its disastrous defeat at the hands of Napoleon, it could do so only by creating a people's army that, like the armies of France, would be composed of free men fighting for themselves and for what they believed. Free men would make better citizens; better citizens, better soldiers. The old class-ridden, savagely disciplined professional army of Frederick the Great was to be replaced by

... universality of responsibility for service in war, binding upon every class of civil society. Through this it will be possible to inculcate a proud warlike national character, to wage wearying wars of distant conquest and to withstand an overwhelming enemy attack with a national war.

The Prussian reforms from 1807 onward were designed to this end, despite opposition from the King of Prussia. Civil reforms were accompanied by attempts to reform officer training while opening up the opportunity for commissions to many more men than before; *Landwehr,* or reserve service, was added to compulsory service in the regular army; a general staff was developed in a deliberate attempt to improve provision for both planning and supply. Some of these reforms, particularly the attempt to build up a large trained reserve on the basis of short periods of initial service in the regular army, were blocked by the French at least until after the Russian Campaign in 1812. Nevertheless, the basis was laid for a rapid expansion of Prussian forces in the war of national liberation from 1813, a war in which Prussian troops fought with much the same inspiration as that which had moved the French levies of 1793 and 1794.

For Clausewitz, as has already been seen, war in this period approached its total or absolute form more closely than hitherto in modern Europe because it had now become "an affair of the whole people." And he was correct in his emphasis. It was in human more than in material resources that nationalization took place. (This legacy, although temporarily laid aside after 1815, nonetheless had a profound effect on military thinking and organization and on the debate about civil–military relationships in Europe throughout the 19th century.)

THE OUTBREAK OF WAR

Early campaigns The early campaigns of the Revolutionary Wars lack the clear pattern and something of the decisive military quality of Napoleon's campaigns between 1800 and 1807. The fighting of these early years, however, was of critical importance for the future of the Revolution; only by defeating its foreign enemies could France pursue its own chosen political course.

In June 1791 Louis XVI and his family fled from Paris, hoping to take refuge with the still largely royalist army on the eastern frontier of France. Just short of their destination, they were recognized and brought back virtually as prisoners. At this point the monarchs of Austria and Prussia began to show concern about the fate of their fellow monarch in France, and in late August 1791 they issued the Declaration of Pillnitz. The declaration appealed to the other European rulers to act together with Prussia and Austria with

> the most efficacious means, relative to their forces, in order to enable the king of France to consolidate in the most perfect liberty, the basis of monarchical government equally suitable to the rights of sovereigns and the welfare of the French nation.

Though certainly not a declaration of war, this pronouncement was bound to be taken by the French as an unwanted sign of interference in their national affairs; and France's relations with Austria and Prussia steadily worsened during the winter of 1791–92.

War was at last declared by France against Austria and, in practice, against Prussia as well, on April 20, 1792. The Legislative Assembly, as seen above, thereupon called for further volunteers to add to those already recruited from the National Guard in 1791 and also introduced the first measure of conscription. The campaign developed very slowly on both sides. The French were not sure of themselves; and the Allies assumed, overoptimistically, that no haste was necessary because the French would almost certainly give way before a threat of force. On July 30 the Allied commander, the Duke of Brunswick, crossed the Rhine and slowly advanced westward. On September 20 he faced the French, commanded by François-Christophe Kellermann and Charles-François Dumouriez, at Valmy, about 40 miles (64 kilometres) west of Verdun, having manoeuvred himself into a position between the French and the road to Paris via Châlons. The Allies numbered some 35,000 men; the French, about 50,000. After preliminary skirmishing, an artillery barrage on both sides began a little after noon at a distance of about 1,300 yards (1,189 metres). The firing was intense—Dumouriez claimed that the French fired 20,000 rounds—but the casualties were few because the distance between the armies was beyond the effective range of the guns. At one stage it appeared that the French might break; but their line was reformed, and, when Brunswick began preparations for an infantry and cavalry attack in midafternoon, he realized that the French line was still virtually intact. At that point he called off the battle, reinforced in this decision when rain began to fall. Ten days later—with the threat of bad weather, his army gravely weakened by sickness, and his line of communications insecure—Brunswick withdrew beyond the east bank of the Meuse. Dumouriez then returned to his original plan to attack the Austrian Netherlands. He won a pitched battle against the Austrians at Jemappes on November 6 and entered Brussels on November 14, overrunning the whole of Belgium by the end of the month. The Scheldt (Escaut) was declared an open river, and plans were begun for an invasion of the United Provinces of the Netherlands.

Valmy had been a mixture of good luck and tough resistance on the French side and of dilatoriness and inefficiency on Brunswick's part. Although Brunswick was correct to withdraw when he did and for the reasons given, in fact he could and should have got the fighting over sooner and then, probably, with success. No one anticipated the victory of the French—a victory that, in effect, saved the Revolution.

All was not yet plain sailing, however, for the armies of the Revolution. The sheer chanciness of Valmy was illustrated by serious reverses in 1793, a year that began badly for France. In February it declared war against Great Britain and the United Provinces—the former antagonized both by the execution of Louis XVI and by the opening of the Scheldt, the latter still threatened with invasion. In March, France declared war on Spain. From then on France was faced with a hostile array—the First Coalition, consisting of Austria, Prussia, Spain, the United Provinces, and Britain. The alliance was not, however, well knit; there were deep differences between Austria and Prussia, largely over former Polish territory, while the United Provinces and Spain had individual policies that made possible separate bargaining with the French. In March, Dumouriez was defeated by the Austrians at Neerwinden, and soon afterward he defected to the Allies. In April the French were forced to evacuate the Austrian Netherlands; in July they were defeated on the Middle Rhine at Mainz and, in November, at Kaiserslautern. **The First Coalition**

At that point the Revolutionary government—the Convention—broke all traditional bonds in organizing France virtually for total war. The *levée en masse* was declared, and Lazare Carnot, an artillery officer who later became known as the "organizer of victory," was elected to the Committee of Public Safety in charge of military affairs. The results of these changes were soon apparent. In October 1793 the French general Jean-Baptiste Jourdan defeated the Austrians at Wattignies, compelling the Austrians to raise their siege of Maubeuge and removing the immediate threat to Paris from the north. In May and June 1794 the French defeated the Austrians and British in the north at Turcoing and Fleurus, forcing the British to withdraw to the United Provinces and the Austrians to the Rhine.

With the Allies in full retreat, the danger of foreign invasion of France was past. That was not, however, the end. French army forces under Charles Pichegru in the north and Jourdan on the Rhine were soon busy expanding French territory. In the winter of 1794–95, Pichegru overran Brabant and reached Amsterdam. In the east Jourdan pursued the Austrians and Prussians to and across the Rhine. In addition, Spanish attacks in the south were pushed back, and Catalonia was invaded. By the spring of 1795, France had reached its natural frontiers; it could safely pause for breath and attempt to reach terms with some of its enemies. Prussia had withdrawn from the Allied coalition in the autumn of 1794, showing far more interest in the affairs of Poland than in those of France; in April 1795 Prussia came to terms with France, signing the Treaty of Basel, and remained a friend, if not an active ally, until 1806. In May 1795, the United Provinces, too, came to terms and became the Batavian Republic. Two months later Spain made peace with France, although a treaty was not signed for another year.

Thus, by the time the Directory came into power in France, in November 1795, only Austria, Sardinia, and Britain remained to be dealt with. In June 1796 the armies of France under Jourdan and Jean-Victor Moreau advanced into the Holy Roman Empire along the lines of the rivers Main and Neckar but were forced back across the Rhine in September. In the meantime, Napoleon was undertaking the first of his remarkable campaigns, in northern Italy, against an alliance of Austria and Sardinia. By January 1796 the French Army of Italy, commanded by Barthélemy Schérer, was stretched out along **Napoleon's first campaign** the road from Nice to Genoa. Urged by the Directory to attack the enemy, Schérer complained that he needed reinforcements and supplies and then resigned his command. On March 27 Napoleon took command and immediately began to carry out an already carefully planned strategy. Basically—and this was a type of strategy he employed on the other occasions, most notably at Waterloo—he set out to strike at Allied armies where their lines of communication converged and, by attacking them separately there, to force them back on divergent lines of communication. In this case the Allies converged down the valleys leading to the Mediterranean coast west of Genoa—the Sardinian line going back northward to Turin; the Austrian, northeastward and then eastward via Acqui, Milan, or Piacenza and thence to the line of the Minzio.

Napoleon began the campaign with 40,000 men, opposed to 50,000 of his combined enemies. Moving his troops very rapidly on interior lines, he first forced the Austrians back and then switched his troops to concentrate against the Sardinians. Within three weeks he had forced the Sardinians to capitulate and to sign an armistice at Cherasco. Then, his own lines of communication safe both along the coastal road to Marseilles and over the Alps via the Mt. Cenis Pass, he turned against the Austrians. On May 15 he entered Milan, giving the people of Lombardy their first unpleasant taste of how French armies lived off the land. Dagobert Siegmund Wurmser retreated still farther along his line of communication, and by early August he had withdrawn to Mantua, where he was besieged by Napoleon throughout the winter of 1796–97.

Mantua was of vital importance. In the summer of 1796, Napoleon hoped that its eventual capture would open up the way into the Tirol and effect his junction with the Army of the Rhine. In fact, that army had been pushed back across the Rhine well before Mantua capitulated to Napoleon in February 1797. Turning back southward briefly, to deal with a minor threat from the Pope and a temporarily threatening Sardinia, Napoleon again turned northward and drove the Austrians back beyond the lines of the Piave and Isonzo. In August preliminaries of peace between France and Austria were signed at Leoben, followed by the Treaty of Campo Formio in October 1797.

Campo Formio was the first of Napoleon's great political successes and the first formal stage in the territorial expansion of France. Austria ceded the Austrian Netherlands (later Belgium and Luxembourg) and the left bank of the Rhine to France and recognized two new French satellite states in northern Italy in the Cisalpine and Ligurian republics. Austria, having given up Milan, gained Venice instead.

THE WAR AT SEA AND IN THE COLONIES

The governments of Revolutionary France had far less success in the war at sea. The French Navy fell well below the standard of the French Army in 1789 and was then equally demoralized by indiscipline, desertion, and emigration during the early months of the Revolution; moreover, it was a very much smaller navy than Britain's —an inferiority rendered all the more serious because, at least at the outset of hostilities, Britain could count on help from the navies of the United Provinces and Spain. In August 1793 conditions reached such a pitch that royalist mutineers handed over Toulon to the British Royal Navy while, almost simultaneously, a French squadron sailing out of Brest was forced to put back to port by another mutiny. At this point the French Navy found its organizer in Jeanbon Saint-André.

Saint-André was not a professional sailor, but he was a professional revolutionary who believed that France's fortunes at sea could be revived by first getting rid of all traces of the *ancien régime* and then by imbuing officers and men alike with republican fervour. Things began badly for him; in December 1793 the British burned 42 French ships of all classes when they were forced to evacuate Toulon. At Brest, however, he did better—he reorganized the arsenal there, got rid of many officers of

British naval superiority

the royalist navy who were inefficient or disloyal, and rapidly promoted others who were willing to accept the Revolution. The first big test came in June 1794 when he sent a fleet out of Brest commanded by Adm. L.T. Villaret de Joyeuse to protect a convoy coming in from America. Villaret encountered a British fleet, and a major battle took place off Ushant on June 1. Although the convoy was saved, the French battle fleet was defeated. Villaret lost a number of his ships of the line and suffered more than 5,000 casualties. As a result, the democratization of the navy was reversed, a return to professionalism and strict discipline was encouraged, and a process of reorganization was carried out during the rest of the life of the Convention and under the Directory.

Meanwhile other European navies had come under French control either directly or as a result of alliances. The United Provinces and Spain, originally Britain's allies in the First Coalition, were out of the war by 1795 and in it again, this time on the side of France, by 1796. This improved situation at sea, accompanied by French successes on land (particularly Napoleon's campaign in northern Italy), led the Directory to attempt invasions of Ireland in December 1796 and Wales in February 1797. Both attempts failed, but in the latter month a much more important action took place. The British admiral Sir John Jervis, commanding a squadron of 15 ships of the line, encountered and routed a Spanish fleet almost twice as big off Cape St. Vincent. Thus, although Britain was by now excluded from the Mediterranean, it still held Gibraltar and was in command of the Atlantic seaboard of Spain. Farther north and despite mutinies at Spithead and the Nore in April and May 1797, things went well for Britain, too. All that summer the Dutch fleet in the Texel awaited the first suitable opportunity to invade Ireland or England. In October it sailed, only to be caught off Camperdown and defeated as handsomely as the Spanish fleet had been.

By the time of the Treaty of Campo Formio, therefore, the navies of France and its allies were back in their ports blockaded by the British Royal Navy, which in three major battles had demonstrated its superiority, based largely on better training, discipline, and tactics. On land France was supreme; at sea it had so far failed.

European waters, however, were not the only scene of important naval activity in those early years; there were operations in colonial areas as well. While attempting to gain a foothold in Europe, whether in the Mediterranean, in Brittany, or in Flanders, the British planned to deprive France of its colonies, both in order to cut off its supply of colonial raw materials and to secure the colonies for Britain itself. Britain's small army—only 20,000 men were available at the outbreak of war in 1793—made it virtually impossible to conduct an effective worldwide strategy and only too easy to fritter away precious resources on too many objectives. While colonial gains could be important to the British in securing existing supplies of raw materials or in denying vantage points to the enemy, expeditions to such places could be and often were extremely costly in terms of human life and made no direct contribution to the defeat of France in Europe. Had the 40,000 British dead lost in the West Indies by 1796 and nearly the same number rendered unfit for military service been made available for the campaign to preserve the former status of the Austrian Netherlands and the United Provinces, they might have done great harm to the enemy.

In 1794 a British force in the West Indies captured Guadeloupe and St. Lucia and established itself in the French part of Haiti. The Haitian ports were of crucial importance for the control of West Indian trade, not least because they were France's only base for operation of its cruisers to the west. Taking them, however, proved also a deathtrap for the British. The black slaves, led by Toussaint-Louverture (*q.v.*), were more concerned with their own freedom than with the Franco-British colonial war being waged over their heads. Soon they and the yellow fever had inflicted far more casualties on the British than the latter had on the French. There were, however, other British gains—the Cape of Good Hope in Africa and

Colonial operations

Ceylon in the Orient were taken from the Dutch, together with such places as Trincomalee, Pondicherry (India), and Malacca. Thus—and again by the time of Campo Formio—the British could claim that they had begun to put a stranglehold on French colonial trade or, conversely, that they had acquired enemy colonial possessions that could later be used as valuable pawns in a treaty of peace. Whether they were so used remained to be seen, and whether they were worth the price paid for them in terms of the critical war in Europe is another matter (see also LATIN AMERICA AND THE CARIBBEAN, COLONIAL: *The Wars of Independence*; HAITI, HISTORY OF).

THE FRENCH EXPEDITION TO EGYPT AND SYRIA, 1798–1802

It was at that point, with only Britain still at war with France, that the Directory appointed General Bonaparte (that, strictly, was still his proper title, although this narrative will continue to call him Napoleon) to command the army that was planning to invade Great Britain. Napoleon took command in mid-February 1798. Within a few days he concluded that invasion was impossible until France had won command of the sea. He suggested, instead, an invasion of Egypt.

Napoleon was not the first Frenchman to be attracted by this idea. In his *Considérations sur la guerre actuelle des Turcs*, the intellectual Constantin Volney, just before the Revolution, had written that, through Egypt, France could reach India and make Suez, rather than the Cape of Good Hope, the main route to the East. Egypt was a long way from India, however, whether by sea or land. By land, the route was difficult to negotiate and even more difficult to keep open. By water, everything depended upon command of the sea between Toulon and Alexandria, on the one hand, and Aden and the ports of western India, on the other. An expedition might escape a controlling enemy squadron, but no sound strategic estimate could count on a safe return. The fact that Napoleon himself evaded the Royal Navy in getting to Egypt and then in returning to France does not invalidate that view; on his return he sailed alone because he could not hope to do so safely otherwise.

Such grandiose projects, however, are not the only possible motive for Napoleon's expedition. The conquest of Egypt and particularly gaining the goodwill of Turkey as a result of dealing with the insubordinate Mamlūks would present a serious threat to Britain's Middle East trade routes. That threat would be made yet more serious if some island posts on the way, such as Malta, could be brought under French control and if the Red Sea area could be controlled from the Egyptian side. Finally, the mere threat to some of Britain's routes to India might encourage action against Britain by some of its enemies there. Thus, the Directors were persuaded, and an expedition was agreed to.

Napoleon sailed from Toulon on May 19, 1798, at the head of 40,000 men and with much apparatus designed to reorganize the whole system of government and society in Egypt. On the way, he captured Malta from the Knights of the Order of St. John and, more by luck than good judgment, evaded a British squadron under Horatio Nelson (*q.v.*) and landed safely in Egypt. Once ashore his covering fleet anchored in Aboukir Bay; there, on August 1, it was surprised by Nelson's returning squadron and promptly attacked from both the landward and the seaward sides in the Battle of the Nile; 11 French ships were destroyed or taken and only two escaped, while none of Nelson's ships was irreparably damaged.

The Battle of the Nile was one of the decisive battles of history. Britain won command of the Mediterranean and retained it. Napoleon could still operate in freedom on land, but he had virtually no hope of reinforcements or rescue; and the morale of the French Navy received a shock from which it did not recover.

Apparently undaunted, Napoleon went ahead with his plans. Gen. Louis C.A. Desaix de Veygoux left Cairo in late August to undertake the conquest of Upper Egypt, while Napoleon brought the Lower Nile area under control in preparation for further expeditions. Early in 1799 Napoleon learned that the Pasha of Syria had invaded the

Motives for invading Egypt

The Battle of the Nile

Suez Desert. It was clear to Napoleon by then both that he must expect the active hostility of the Ottoman sultan, and that his own next step must be an invasion of Syria as the first move to bringing the Middle East under French control. His advance began in early February and by mid-March had reached Acre. Both Napoleon and his British opponents well understood the strategic importance of Acre, a fortress that, guarding the entry into Palestine, would either protect or deny Napoleon's further successful progress. Writing some weeks later, Napoleon forecast that, if he captured Acre, he would advance upon Damascus and Aleppo, fire the discontented masses with enthusiasm for his cause, advance on Constantinople, and overthrow the Ottoman Empire.

These predictions, however, proved to be dreams. The British had command of the sea; Sir Sidney Smith, with a small squadron lying off Acre, fed help and advice to the garrison and resisted the French siege until Napoleon was forced to accept defeat and begin his withdrawal on May 20. By mid-June Napoleon was back in Egypt; and there he stayed until, moved much more by developments in France than by any dreams of an eastern empire, he sailed in secrecy from Alexandria with a few of his closest staff and landed at Fréjus, in southeastern France, on October 9. He left the Army of Egypt behind and never, himself, set foot in the Middle East again. His threats against Britain—first from a cross-Channel invasion in 1798 and then from Egypt and Syria in 1799—had been in vain.

The story of operations in Egypt is best taken to its conclusion here, although to do so involves anticipating later developments to some extent. Throughout the rest of 1799 and 1800 the French remained in Egypt—admittedly in control of that country but not extending French influence—cut off from the mainstream of events on the European mainland. Jean-Baptiste Kléber, left in command by Napoleon, was virtually powerless in the face of Britain's control of the sea. In January 1800, therefore, he signed the Convention of al-'Arīsh (el-Arish) with the Turks, by which he agreed to evacuate Egypt on condition that he be transported with his army back to France. The British government, however, refused to be a party to the arrangement, and the French stayed on. A year later, in March 1801, a British force landed in Egypt. The French made an unexpectedly weak resistance and, within six months, were defeated and on their way back to France.

This victory proved of little value to Britain in the subsequent Treaty of Amiens signed in March 1802. Of its colonial conquests it kept only Ceylon and Trinidad, while Malta, captured from the French in 1800, was returned to the Knights of St. John. Egypt reverted to Turkey, while France evacuated Naples and the Papal States. By not protesting against them, moreover, Britain accepted the French conquests in the Batavian (formerly the United Provinces), Helvetic (Swiss Confederation), and Cisalpine (northern Italy) republics.

End of operations in Egypt

THE CONTINENTAL CAMPAIGNS OF THE SECOND COALITION, 1798–1801

Peripheral operations of the kind described above were of little concern to Britain's Allies—the continental land powers opposed to France. The Royal Navy was valuable to them if it could encourage and support operations on the European mainland. This situation became obvious during the winter of 1797–98. Negotiations between Britain and Austria, which also involved Prussia and Russia, made it clear that an Austrian condition for declaring war against France once more was the dispatch of a British fleet into the Mediterranean—a move designed to support land operations from the sea and to encourage the Mediterranean powers generally to unite against the Directory. In May 1798 a British squadron under Nelson did sail into the Mediterranean, as seen above, and virtually wiped out the French fleet at the Battle of the Nile. From then on conditions were ready for the formation of the Second Coalition against France.

Successive acts of aggression by France had aroused bitter feelings during 1798. In February the French had

Formation
of the
Second
Coalition

driven the Pope from Rome and established a republic there; in March they invaded the Swiss Confederation and then established the Helvetic Republic; in July they began their takeover of Piedmont; in January 1799 they entered Naples and proclaimed the Parthenopean Republic; and two months later they overran Tuscany. As a result the Second Coalition against France began to take shape in the winter of 1798–99, composed of Britain, Russia, the Ottoman Empire, Naples, and Portugal; by March Austria at last declared war on France and itself joined the Coalition.

From the beginning the principal Allies were at loggerheads, and they never developed a coherent and unified strategy. Broadly speaking, the British and Russians wanted a main attack across the Rhine into France; but they fell apart after an unsuccessful joint expedition to the Helder in the autumn of 1799. Austria, on the other hand, while undoubtedly anxious about French expansion to and across the Rhine, had ambitions in Italy and was unwilling to be diverted from them.

Nevertheless, 1799 began well for the Allies. The French planned a triple attack on Austria, with one wing advancing across the Rhine and along the Danube to Vienna, a second from the Helvetic Republic into the Tirol, and a third in northern Italy to drive the Austrians back across the Adige River and on to a line of retreat via the Minzio. In March the northern attack under Jourdan was stopped by the archduke Charles at Stockach, and Jourdan withdrew back across the Rhine. In April and May the French in northern Italy were defeated first by the Austrians and then by the Russians, compelling a French army in southern Italy to withdraw northward via Genoa. Further defeats followed—at Novi in August and at Genola in November. The overthrow of the Parthenopean, Roman, and Cisalpine republics followed.

As already seen, however, the Allies disagreed over the correct strategy in pursuing these victories to the final overthrow of France; moreover, they suffered several setbacks. The joint Anglo-Russian invasion of the Batavian Republic, designed to distract the French from the Middle and Lower Rhine, succeeded in capturing the Dutch fleet but had no success on land and withdrew. In the Helvetic Republic the French general André Masséna defeated the Russians and, by forcing their withdrawal from that country, also threatened the Austrian army to the north commanded by the archduke Charles, compelling him in turn to withdraw from the Rhine to the Danube. Masséna's position in the Helvetic Republic was exposed; but the Allies were by then too divided to act energetically to outflank him. Thus, when Napoleon arrived back in Paris in late 1799, the French were again in command of the Batavian and Helvetic republics, and the left bank of the Rhine; their major setback had been in Italy, where they held only Genoa.

The
French
campaign
of 1800

Meanwhile, in France the coup d'état of 18 Brumaire, year VIII (November 9, 1799) had occurred, placing Napoleon, as first consul, in charge of his own strategy. His approach to the 1800 campaign was to settle with Austria first, expecting this to destroy the Second Coalition, all the more so because he had already taken the precaution of detaching the Russian tsar Paul from the alliance with the promise of Malta. The French campaign was planned and carried out along two supporting lines. First, one French army under Moreau crossed the Rhine through the Black Forest to drive the opposing Austrians back toward Ulm and thus afford protection and, if necessary, reinforcements from the north for French operations in northern Italy.

It was in this latter theatre that Napoleon planned his second attack. Genoa held out against a besieging Austrian army, thus dividing the available Austrian forces between the plain of Lombardy and the Ligurian coastline. Napoleon planned to advance across the Alps via the Great St. Bernard Pass, capture Milan, advance southeastward to capture Piacenza, and cut off the Austrians from their main line of retreat to the Minzio. Then, controlling both banks of the Po, he planned to turn back westward to attack the Austrians in their main concentration area at Alessandria, doing so from the Austrian rear. (This outflanking move to the enemy's rear was a strategic approach used on other occasions by Napoleon, notably at Ulm, and with great success.) In late May Napoleon crossed the Alps; he entered Milan on June 2, crossed the Po at Piacenza on the 7th, and defeated the Austrians at Marengo on the 14th. In the meantime, Genoa had fallen to the Austrians on June 4, a victory that came too late to affect the outcome of the campaign.

This defeat did not quite finish Austria. A new agreement with Britain a week after Marengo promised further resistance to Napoleon. French successes in Germany and Italy in November and December, however, developed into a serious threat to Vienna, and the emperor Francis asked for terms. By the Peace of Lunéville between France and Austria (February 1801), Austria kept Venice but surrendered all its territory west of the Rhine, including the Duchy of Luxembourg and what is now Belgium, to France; it also recognized the Cisalpine, Helvetic, Ligurian (formerly Republic of Genoa), and Batavian republics and was forced to accept the line of the Adige as the boundary between its possessions and those of France in northern Italy. In effect, the Holy Roman Empire was a thing of the past, and both western and central Germany now lay at the mercy of France. In Italy, also, French influence had now supplanted that of Austria.

II. The Napoleonic Wars, 1801–15

LUNEVILLE TO TILSIT, 1801–07

Neither the Treaty of Lunéville nor that of Amiens contained the seeds of a long-term peace—the first, because Napoleon gradually broke all its terms in the interests of French aggrandizement; the second, because both parties had signed it out of temporary exhaustion and did not regard it as satisfactory.

Consolidation and
strengthening of
French
power

After Lunéville Napoleon, who became first consul for life in 1802 and emperor in 1804, lost no time in consolidating and strengthening French power, particularly in Germany and Italy. In February 1803 the Diet of Regensburg approved French plans for the reorganization of Germany, which led to the formal death of the Holy Roman Empire in 1806. This reorganization, to some extent made necessary by French expansion to the Rhine, led to the suppression of ecclesiastical states and to considerable gains by the more important lay princes. In the process, French patronage became the controlling influence in Germany. The United Provinces—now the Batavian Republic—was bound yet closer to France by late 1801. In 1802 the Cisalpine Republic became the Italian Republic, with Napoleon as its president. In 1802 Piedmont was also incorporated into France. In 1803 Napoleon mediated in a civil war in the Helvetic Republic (which then became Helvetia) and followed that action with a new constitution strengthening French influence. Later in 1803 the French entered Hanover and took it under French protection. (Small wonder that the governments of other European countries felt that there was no predictable limit to the ambitions of the first consul.)

After Amiens Britain, although nominally at peace with France, found no basis of mutual trust for the future. Apart from Napoleon's continued aggression on the Continent, he was already imposing restrictions on British trade and, in 1803, was suspected of encouraging rebellion in Ireland. Napoleon complained that the British had not surrendered Alexandria or Malta (he was correct) and that Britain was sheltering and encouraging French émigrés. It was not therefore surprising that the two powers found themselves at war again in May 1803.

The war against Britain, to Trafalgar. At this stage Britain had no allies and would have none for nearly two years. Hostilities with France on this one-to-one basis revealed more clearly than before the stalemate that could be reached in a situation in which a great land power was opposed to a great sea power with neither able seriously to oppose the other in his own element. Napoleon could assemble 100,000 men at Boulogne—a far larger and more experienced army than anything Britain could oppose him with—but had no way of getting his soldiers into action. The Royal Navy could prevent the French Army from crossing the English Channel but had no means of attempting, let alone ensuring, the defeat of that force.

The British, first with Henry Addington and then (from May 1804) with William Pitt (see PITT, WILLIAM, THE YOUNGER) as prime minister, set about sweeping up the remaining French colonial possessions. St. Lucia, Tobago, and Guiana were taken in 1803 in the Western Hemisphere; in the same year French influence in India was further weakened by the defeat of its friends there. Then, beginning in mid-1804, Pitt began his attempts to divert and thus weaken Napoleon by rebuilding a continental coalition. In June 1804 he had reached an understanding with Russia that was converted into a formal alliance in April 1805. That August Austria joined again, and the Third Coalition was in being.

The
Third
Coalition

Meanwhile the war at sea continued. Napoleon attempted to stop Britain's trade with the Continent: he seized Cuxhaven for this purpose, only to meet with a British blockade of the mouths of the Elbe and Weser, which considerably damaged Napoleon's friend Prussia. The French also continued their attacks on British seaborne trade by means of privateers. The most important aspects of this war between France and Britain, however, were French preparations for an invasion of Britain by a cross-channel attack and Britain's blockade of the ports of France and her allies.

The naval defeats of the 1790s had not persuaded Napoleon against building new fleets. Nevertheless, his resources were decidedly inferior to those of the Royal Navy in all classes of vessels, and his own admirals preferred a defensive "fleet-in-being" strategy combined with occasional brief sorties. For Napoleon himself the chief hope lay in a possible invasion; during 1803–04 troops were assembled in the Boulogne area, together with 2,000 transports. His plans for invasion varied between one employing a heavily protected force and one conducted simply in small boats, on their own, while French squadrons provided diversions elsewhere and drew away the blockading British squadrons. The right combination of successful diversion, weather, and tide was never found. Napoleon had broken camp at Boulogne and begun a long march to the Danube against Austria seven weeks before Nelson won a great victory at Trafalgar.

For Britain the basic response to invasion was the blockade, both close and distant. British squadrons were spaced off major naval ports—from the Texel along the French and Spanish coasts off Brest, Ferrol, Cádiz, and Toulon—to prevent French and Spanish squadrons from putting to sea with supporting frigates for intercommunication. Because invasion of England or Ireland was the chief danger, it was established that squadrons would fall back to a position off Ushant if one or more powerful squadrons broke the blockade and thus threatened to act as an invasion escort. (Allowing for all the differences between warfare at sea and on land, this was not dissimilar to some important aspects of Napoleon's own strategy.) A constantly successful blockade, however, was too much to expect, and both Napoleon and the Royal Navy knew that. British forces had to be split into small squadrons. Long periods at sea meant ships would sometimes be absent for refitting without adequate replacements, and the uncertainties of the weather sometimes helped the blockaded. Once the French were at sea, the Royal Navy, despite all its precautions, was almost inevitably caught in some degree of uncertainty as to where the French would go.

End of the
war at sea

On March 31, 1805, Adm. Pierre-Charles Villeneuve, commanding the French squadron in Toulon, evaded Nelson's blockade and broke out of the Mediterranean, heading for the West Indies. Meanwhile, the other major French squadron was blockaded in Brest. Nelson chased Villeneuve to the West Indies and back, while other Royal Navy squadrons swarmed in the Channel to prevent a French concentration that could be used to convey an invasion force. Villeneuve returned and took refuge in Cádiz; and Nelson, convinced that the French had plans for the Mediterranean, followed him there. On October

20 Villeneuve, who could not stay in Cádiz because he lacked supplies and facilities, left there and was caught by Nelson off Cape Trafalgar. The French had 33 ships of the line to 27 of the British; but the latter had a tactical plan, and Villeneuve lacked one. In the Battle of Trafalgar (October 21), 18 French ships were totally lost and the rest fought their last action. This was the last battle-fleet action of these wars, and the danger of an invasion of England was ended.

The campaign against Austria, 1805. As a result of its defeat in 1800–01, Austria's influence in Germany had been greatly weakened. The old Holy Roman Empire in practice no longer existed, a fact recognized by Francis II himself when he was proclaimed emperor of Austria in August 1804. During this time Britain and Russia were drawing closer together; Alexander I of Russia broke off diplomatic relations with France in the autumn of 1804 and signed a treaty of alliance with Britain in 1805 designed to drive the French from northern Germany, Holland, Switzerland, and Naples. Austria, still weakened by the effects of past defeats, hung back. But, when Napoleon had himself crowned king of Italy in 1805 and then incorporated Genoa and the Ligurian Republic into France, Austria finally entered the Third Coalition with Britain and Russia in August of that year. Napoleon gave up his plans for invading England to deal with Austria and Russia. Writing to the French statesman Talleyrand on August 13, Napoleon announced,

My course is settled. I shall raise my camps [*i.e.*, at Boulogne] . . . by 23rd September I shall be in Germany with 200,000 men, and have 23,000 men in Italy . . . I shall march on Vienna and compel Austria to sue for peace.

The campaign conformed very nearly to that forecast.

Napoleon was faced with three problems. First he had to keep the Austrian Army separated from the Russians and persuade it to fight on its own; he planned to advance from the Middle Rhine on Vienna, if possible cutting the Austrian line of communication with Vienna somewhere between Ulm and there, thus catching the Austrian Army with an attack from its rear as he had done at Marengo. The second problem was to move 200,000 men across Europe from the Channel coast to the Middle Danube in the space of about six weeks and yet retain the ability to concentrate this vast army, if necessary within a day or two, at the critical time and place; he planned to make maximum use of the army corps system, the corps having become a unit of all arms, capable both of combining with other corps in a major battle and of operating on its own, even if only in a holding or defensive capacity, against a major enemy force. The final problem was that of provisioning so many men during so rapid an advance.

The army
corps
system

Regarding provisions, each corps had its own wagon train, and magazines were sometimes established at the most important towns en route. That system, however, did not provide enough; if magazines were not available, French armies, using this blitzkrieg strategy, had to live off the land by requisitions. Each corps was allotted a requisition area strictly in relation to its prescribed line of advance. Commenting on this later, Napoleon wrote,

We have marched without magazines; circumstances have forced us to do this; but although we have been continually victorious and found vegetables in the fields, we have nevertheless suffered a great deal, and, in a season when potatoes cannot be had from the fields a lack of magazines would lead us into the greatest misfortune.

Gen. Karl Mack, commanding the Austrian Army of about 85,000 men, played into Napoleon's hands. At the beginning of September he advanced westward through Bavaria toward Ulm without waiting for his Russian allies. At Ulm he hoped to command the line of the Danube, with his front and right protected by the Black Forest. By this advance, however, he had greatly lengthened his line of communications; and, even as late as October 9, he was still separated from his Russian allies, who were at Linz, by nearly 200 miles (322 kilometres).

Meanwhile, Napoleon's advance guard crossed the Rhine on September 24, and his army advanced on the Danube from the north and west on its prescribed corps fronts. On October 6 his forces were in the area of Donauwörth-Neuberg and then crossed the Danube, leaving Gen. Michel Ney with 40,000 men to cover Austrian escape routes to the north. Napoleon then continued to envelop Mack in the south. Mack made two unsuccessful attempts to break out of the ring and then capitulated at Ulm on October 20 with 50,000 men. (If great victories consist of beating an enemy at a minimum cost in actual fighting, then Ulm was one of the greatest of Napoleon's victories.)

Austria was not yet completely defeated. On November 13, three weeks after Trafalgar, Napoleon entered Vienna; but he still faced a combination of Russians commanded by Gen. Mikhail Kutuzov and two Austrian armies from Italy and the Tirol. Moreover, Napoleon himself was now operating at the end of a long line of communications. Had the Allies waited—they were, after all, on their own ground—time would almost certainly have been on their side; but some of them, particularly Tsar Alexander, were impatient and chose to attack. On December 2 Napoleon routed them at Austerlitz, a battlefield victory even more complete than the victory at Ulm.

In the resulting Peace of Pressburg, signed at the end of 1805, Austria ceded its last Italian possession, Venice, to France, gave the Tirol to Bavaria, and recognized the rulers of Bavaria and Württemberg as independent kings. Already cut off from the Rhineland, Austria was excluded from Italy and gravely weakened in southern Germany.

The campaigns against Prussia and Russia, 1806–07. During the 1805 campaign Prussia had been tempted to join the Allies; such a move might have threatened Napoleon's left flank as he moved along the Danube Valley and perhaps even have denied him victory. Frederick William III, however, delayed acting until after Austria had been defeated, thus weakening his position when he himself was attacked.

Throughout 1806, relations between France and Prussia steadily worsened. Despite his continued gestures of friendship toward Prussia, Napoleon appeared determined to weaken Prussian influence in northern Germany, and his independent negotiations with Britain over Hanover underlined this. Furthermore, after Austerlitz Napoleon kept the bulk of his army in Germany, stretched out along the line of the Main River; by October 1806 he had about 200,000 men on a line running from Lichtenfels through Bamberg to Würzburg. The Prussians regarded this troop concentration as a threatening gesture; Russia, too, was suspicious of Napoleon's intentions. On September 26, Frederick William III of Prussia sent an ultimatum to Napoleon demanding that the French withdraw west of the Rhine and agree to the formation of a north German confederacy under Prussian leadership. Napoleon rejected the ultimatum. On October 8 Prussia, in alliance with Russia, declared war on France.

The overall strategic situation was not unlike that in 1805. With promises of help from Russia and from Sweden and Britain too, there was much to be said for the Prussians staying on the defensive on the line of the Elbe and waiting until help arrived. The Elbe formed the great natural defense of Prussia against attack from the west, and the main passages across the river were guarded by the fortresses of Magdeburg, Wittenberg, Torgau, and Dresden, which also controlled the principal routes into Berlin and East Prussia. The one advantage of advancing west of the Elbe was that Saxony and Hesse-Kassel might join with Prussia if protected in this way but probably not otherwise. Indeed, Saxony could help Napoleon directly by offering him an unopposed passage of the Elbe at Dresden.

In fact the Duke of Brunswick, in command of the Prussian army, advanced west across the Elbe, then divided his forces in two—the main part under his command concentrated in the area of Erfurt, the other part south of him, commanded by F.L. Hohenlohe-Ingelfingen and concentrated between Hof and Saalfeld in the Upper Saale Valley. These two forces were separated by the difficult terrain of the Thuringian Forest.

For Napoleon the possible routes from the Rhine into

The location of troops on October 8, 1806.
Adapted from V. Esposito and J. Elting, *A Military History and Atlas of the Napoleonic Wars* (1964); Praeger Publishers

Prussia were either from Wesel across Westphalia and Hanover, from Frankfurt via Eisenach and Weimar to Leipzig, or from Frankfurt via Bamberg to the south of the Thuringian Forest and thence either by Leipzig or Dresden. He treated the first route, the most northerly, as cover against possible enemy retaliation, leaving a corps under E.A. Mortier to link up with a force under Louis Bonaparte, whom Napoleon had made king of Holland. This tactic meant that, with a northern escape route safe, he could risk his other lines of communication. He then planned his advance along the third route, telling Louis weeks in advance that he intended to be in position to attack the Prussians on October 12. He left Mainz on October 1, used magazines at Würzburg and Kronach on the way, and crossed the frontier of Saxony on October 8. His rapid deployment took the Prussians by surprise, and Hohenlohe promptly began to retreat northeastward toward the Elbe when contact was established on October 12, as Napoleon had predicted. On October 14 Napoleon overwhelmed Hohenlohe at Jena, while Louis-Nicolas Davout, sent round the flank to block a Prussian retreat, encountered the main Prussian force at Auerstädt and defeated them also. The battle had not gone quite in detail as Napoleon planned, but in general execution he had dictated the critical time and place and had made the Prussians conform to his own movements.

Prussian retreat followed. On October 25 Napoleon entered Berlin, and ten days later the Prussian rear guard under Gebhard Leberecht von Blücher capitulated at Lübeck. Prussian resistance was at an end. Russia, however, was still in the war; in November Napoleon invaded East Prussia and then Russian-controlled Poland, occupying Warsaw a week before Christmas. Marching still farther eastward, he met the Russian Army under Leonty Leontyevich Benningsen at Eylau (February 8, 1807), fighting a bloody and indecisive battle. In mid-June, despite his long line of communications and his earlier losses, Napoleon routed Benningsen at Friedland, driving the Russians back across the Niemen while he himself entered Königsberg.

The war was over, and peace was signed at the Treaty of Tilsit on July 9. This treaty really dealt with Prussia rather than Russia. Prussia lost all its territory west of the Elbe and the part of Poland it had gained most recently. Its territory was thus halved and its army reduced to 40,000 men, one-fifth of its previous size. (Prussia lost more, at one blow, than any other of Napoleon's principal enemies.)

Russia emerged virtually unscathed from the 1806–07 campaign. Indeed, it became an ally of France, and the

Austrian defeat (margin)

Prussian advance (margin)

The Treaty of Tilsit (margin)

events of the next few years were, to some considerable extent, based upon this Franco-Russian alliance.

Napoleonic warfare. Some characteristics of Napoleon as a strategist are clear. First, he devoted infinite care to the preparation of a campaign in all its aspects. He examined the chosen theatre of operations, however far away, in all available detail beforehand and laid down a full timetable of operations; approach routes and requisition areas were prescribed. Second, he analyzed the enemy's likely plans and reactions as carefully as his own and, in many cases, in terms of the known characteristics of individual commanders. Third, he used time and distance to surprise and deceive the enemy, catching him a day or two sooner than expected; such manoeuvres gave French forces a number of options at their disposal, thus continuing to leave the enemy uncertain of French intentions until a few hours before fighting began. (It is important to remember, however, that the blitzkrieg strategy based on these principles of action demanded good road and river transport systems for rapid and alternative movements and also a fairly high level of agricultural production to provide adequate requisitions. When he operated later in Russia, Napoleon found very different conditions from those to which he had grown accustomed in western and central Europe.)

On the battlefield, at the tactical level, Napoleon was a great general though not an innovator. He made maximum use of the weapons and tactical doctrines he inherited. Above all and like Clausewitz he believed that great strategic results can normally be achieved only by great battles; therefore, it was always his object to rout the enemy, whether on the battlefield or in retreat, and he was willing to accept heavy losses among his own men in order to achieve this result. On the battlefield, broadly speaking, his objective was to punch a hole in the enemy lines and then exploit it. For this reason, while well aware of the value of great firepower inherent in infantry line formations, he also used the heavy-infantry column. Similarly, while rarely deploying more or heavier guns than his enemies, he often massed them for concentrated force; and he sometimes used concentration of cavalry on the battlefield for the same purpose as well as for subsequent exploitation. The essence of his tactical doctrine was concentration of power, just as the essence of his strategic approach was to make that concentration available where and when it suited him best.

THE COERCION OF EUROPE, 1807–11

The peak of Napoleon's power

With the signing of the Treaty of Tilsit, Napoleon found himself at the peak of his power. So long as he and Alexander I could agree and, in agreeing, coordinate their policies, Napoleon could anticipate a time when all continental Europe would lie under his control. The Continental System that he organized in detail was the most obvious expression of his power. The first signs of decline, however, coincided with the period of ostensibly greatest power. As the expansion of French power became increasingly identified with blatant imperialism, the seeds of nationalist revolt began to bear fruit—first in Spain and then in Austria—producing movements that, in the end, broke Napoleon's power. Moreover, the Continental System was too ambitious politically, administratively, and economically, and it weakened its creator as much as it strengthened him.

The Continental System. Trade war against Britain was not initiated by Napoleon. After war broke out between Britain and France in 1793, the republic did its best to exclude British goods from the areas under its control. The Directory stepped up measures against British trade and ordered the seizure of all vessels that put in at British ports and then sailed on to France. Moreover, the theoretical inspiration of this kind of warfare was similar both before and after Napoleon became first consul. A well-established mercantilist strain in French thinking on these matters held that the best way to defeat a major trading power such as Britain was to stifle or cut off its exports and thus reduce its stocks of gold; this view was itself based on the theory that gold, produced by a favourable balance of trade, was a vital indicator of na-

tional power. Napoleon based his Continental System on these theories. The difference between him and his predecessors was a practical one—his conquests and particularly his conquest of Prussia and subsequent agreement with Russia enabled him to apply such a policy on a genuinely continental scale. Although he was a radical in his approach to methods, he remained a conservative (some would say a reactionary) in his economic theories. Finally, after Trafalgar and even more so after Britain's seizure of the Danish fleet in 1807, Napoleon had no reasonable hope of resuming normal warfare at sea; and even the threat of his privateers was severely reduced in face of an increasingly effective convoy system carried out by the Royal Navy. To that extent and whatever Napoleon's original hopes of its success, the Continental System can be regarded as a method adopted for lack of something better.

The Berlin Decree

The defeat of Prussia at Jena meant that Napoleon could control a long stretch of the Baltic coast. On November 21, 1806, Napoleon issued his Berlin Decree, which placed the British Isles in a state of blockade. This action meant that trade with Britain was prohibited and that all vessels coming to ports under French control directly from Britain or its colonies would be seized. With Russia adhering to the System and with Portugal and Spain coming under French control in 1808, Napoleon could well claim that he hoped to conquer the sea by the land. The government in London retaliated with a series of Orders in Council in 1807, the object of which was essentially to bring seaborne trade with Europe as far as possible under British control by allowing such trade in neutral ships to take place only by license. This neutral trade was considerable—in 1807 about 44 percent of all trade passing through British ports was in neutral ships, and these ships were to come under British direction as well as provide a useful source of income for the treasury through the issue of licenses.

Napoleon's reply to the Orders in Council was to take his own system a stage further. By the Fontainebleau and Milan decrees of 1807, he ordered that all neutral ships conforming with the rules laid down by the Orders in Council should be treated as enemy ships and, where possible, seized. Thus, neutrals had either to risk detention by the British or confiscation by the French; and that dilemma applied particularly to U.S. vessels. A further Fontainebleau decree of October 1810 strengthened the law against contraband and also ordered the public burning of captured British manufactures. Other decrees that year were designed to tighten up Napoleon's own system of import and export licenses.

The restrictions imposed by the Continental System and by Britain's countermeasures had serious effects upon Britain and also upon France and its continental allies and satellites. During 1808 there was a considerable drop in British exports—a fall of about 10 percent from 1806. Cotton and grain imports were also affected, leading to shortages, high prices, and unemployment. The shortage of timber hit hard at both naval and merchant shipbuilding. There was an improvement from Britain's point of view in 1809, when Portugal, Spain, and Spain's colonies escaped from French control and when the Ottoman Empire signed an agreement with Britain.

But 1811 was the most critical year of all for Britain. Its Baltic trade suffered a severe blow when Sweden was included in Napoleon's System. In that year exports to northern Europe were only one-fifth of the previous year's total, and exports to the United States were down by a quarter. Overall, British exports dropped by about a third. The trade crisis was worsened by a monetary crisis in which the pound depreciated and reserves dropped dangerously low. Many Britons talked of peace at any price; had Napoleon—who had recently agreed to the export of French grain to Britain partly to placate French farmers and partly in pursuit of his mercantilist theories—chosen to deny wheat exports to Britain at this point, hunger riots might have tipped the scale in forcing the British to make peace.

While it did produce these undoubtedly serious effects, the Continental System failed in its prime objective of defeating Britain by crippling its trade and thus ruining its credit. Napoleon's unsuccessful attack on Russia in 1812 meant that the sizable cracks in the System that had already appeared in Europe became great holes. This situation helped offset some of the effects of the outbreak of war in that year between Britain and the United States, itself a result partly of disputes about the freedom of the seas. Behind these important ups and downs of fortune, however, lay one constant factor—Britain's command of the sea. As the U.S. naval historian Alfred Thayer Mahan has pointed out, Napoleon was bound to lose a trade war against a country that, because of its vast navy and mercantile marine, could offset losses in one area of the world by opening up opportunities elsewhere. And that is precisely what Britain did. Its national debt grew enormously; but basic prosperity was founded upon increasing industrial production and trade, and Britain emerged from the war much wealthier and stronger than it had entered it.

The effects of the Continental System upon France itself were more generally damaging. Napoleon faced two problems. The first was how to make his allies and satellites continue to accept restrictions that were often harmful to them; in the end resentment about the System helped to turn allies into enemies. The second problem was in France, where his situation was equally difficult. It is true that he was always willing, perhaps wisely in a political sense, to sacrifice the interests of his European allies to those of France itself. This favouritism came out quite clearly in licenses granted much more freely to French traders. This preference, however, made little difference to French trade in the long run. At first some French traders welcomed the advantage conferred by the removal of British competition; but France, like other European countries, needed markets and colonial raw materials such as cotton and sugar. Customs receipts and exports fell drastically. Gradually Napoleon lost the support of the middle class, who had gained so much from the Revolution and on whose efficiency and loyalty Napoleon himself depended. Ersatz industries were an adventurous experiment, and some came to stay. By and large, however, the Continental System undermined—or certainly was thought to undermine—prosperity, and Napoleon could not afford that.

Austria's war of liberation, 1809. Angered by the terms imposed upon Austria after Ulm and Austerlitz and offended even more by Napoleon's further aggrandizement after the defeat of Prussia, the emperor Francis of Austria and his advisers thought they saw an opportunity for revenge in 1809. The French Army was heavily committed in Spain; and there was rising discontent in Germany, as elsewhere, from the effects of the Continental System. Moreover, the Austrian government had carried out reforms in the army after 1806 and had a military-reserve system by 1808. The tide of public opinion was moving against Napoleon; and, although there was no strong German nationalism evident in Austria or elsewhere at that stage, there was much local patriotism —for example, in the Tirol.

Napoleon was aware of events in Austria and had carefully made his plans by assuring himself of Russia's neutrality. Prussia could safely be ignored for the time being. Moreover, although he spent the winter of 1808–09 in Spain, Napoleon was back in Paris before Austria declared war on France in April 1809. By calling up 150,-000 conscripts, he had 300,000 men at his command for operations in central Europe, in addition to the troops committed in Spain.

The Austrian plan was to attack the French in Italy and Dalmatia; to advance into Poland, forestalling help from Russia and the Grand Duchy of Warsaw; and to advance westward along the Danube Valley to drive back the French concentrated at Regensburg and Augsburg before Napoleon could cross the Rhine and come to their aid. The archduke Charles, in command of this last Austrian army, was much too dilatory and allowed Napoleon to join up with Davout's forward army corps. By mid-April Napoleon had concentrated his forces and advanced toward Vienna, defeating the Archduke at Eckmühl on

April 22. The Archduke was forced north of the Danube, and Napoleon entered Vienna on May 13.

The Austrians remained strong both north of the Danube and farther south in the Tirol. Napoleon concentrated his attention on the archduke Charles and his army north of the Danube. On May 20 Napoleon crossed the river by the island of Lobau, and a battle took place at Essling-Aspern on May 21–22 in which, though not completely defeated, Napoleon was mauled seriously enough to retrace his steps across the river. He then fortified his position and, in early July, was reinforced by the army of Eugène de Beauharnais, which had come up from the south. On July 5 Napoleon crossed the Danube again with an army of more than 150,000 men and the next day defeated the archduke Charles at Wagram. An armistice was signed a few days later.

By the Peace of Schönbrunn (October 1809) Austria was yet further humiliated. It lost its Illyrian provinces and ceded much of Upper Austria to Bavaria and most of western Galicia to the Grand Duchy of Warsaw. Its efforts, however, had not been in vain; French troops were withdrawn from Spain. Moreover, Napoleon's greed in taking more Austrian territory for his satellites offended his friends as well as his enemies.

The Spanish rising and the Peninsular Campaign. A more prolonged and in many ways very different campaign was meanwhile going on in Spain and Portugal. Spain had been entirely subservient to French policies since 1796; and, although there was a flicker of resistance during the campaign against Prussia, the French victory at Jena brought Spain once more to heel. By then Napoleon was intent on compelling all Europe to accept the Continental System, and Portugal, for so long the ally of England, was an obvious gap in the System. By the Treaty of Fontainebleau of 1807, the Spanish government agreed that French troops could cross Spain on their way to conquer Portugal, and in November the French entered Lisbon. These policies led to deep differences in Spain. In May 1808 the king, Charles IV, abdicated, and in June Napoleon appointed his own brother Joseph as king of Spain. There had already been a popular rising against the French at Aranjuez in March 1808, and the events of that summer spread the flames of insurrection against what was regarded as French tyranny. A national rising against France was the result.

The importance of war in Spain was twofold. Politically it was the clearest indication to date of nationalist resistance to Napoleonic domination, even though it was not a national movement inspired by liberalism. Militarily, it afforded Britain an opportunity to undertake land operations on the mainland of Europe that, at last, were significant in relation to the operations of its allies. For the first time sea power was directly related to land power. The Iberian Peninsula was easy for Britain to get to and to use, and it was difficult for Napoleon to defend. The logistic and military basis of Britain's whole operation was Portugal, which offered a first-rate entry, via the Tagus and Lisbon, and a sound defensive position.

Napoleon himself took command in Spain late in 1808 and very nearly caught a British force before it managed to escape via Coruña. Early in 1809, however, he returned to Paris. In April 1809 Sir Arthur Wellesley (later the duke of Wellington) landed at Lisbon and took command of all British and Portuguese forces there; he had come carefully prepared and had already formed some views about the best ways to fight the hitherto invincible armies of Napoleon.

At a tactical level, Wellesley believed in the value of highly disciplined firepower delivered by an infantry line protected, wherever possible, by natural features or by such man-made features as walls; and he also believed in the importance of light infantry. Secondly, Wellesley was determined to establish an efficient supply system within his army so that it became independent, as far as possible, of army requisitions and could thus move or stay in its positions as the military situation demanded. He abhorred the French system of living off the land, and he considered that it forced the French to move when often they would have served their military purposes better by staying in position. Thirdly, he developed a highly efficient staff system, all the more necessary in a campaign with frequently divided forces; and his staff gave him, among other things, an invaluable series of maps that enabled him to move in difficult country with certainty and speed.

Wellesley's
strategy

Wellesley's strategy was to use Portugal as his base, with its land frontier defended by a number of great fortresses and with a final defensive area behind the lines of Torres Vedras around Lisbon. The sea was his chief line of supply. In 1809 Wellesley (Viscount Wellington from September 1809) had some early success, driving the French from Portugal and in July defeating them at Talavera; but by the autumn he was back behind the Portuguese frontier.

In 1810, with Austria defeated at Wagram, Napoleon sent reinforcements to Spain; and the positions were reversed. By that autumn the French had captured the Portuguese frontier fortresses and then occupied all of Portugal except the area behind the lines of Torres Vedras.

From then on, Wellington was more certain of his own strength and of enemy weaknesses. In 1811 he began the process of recovering Portugal and, principally, its frontier fortresses. In May he defeated André Masséna at Fuentes d'Onoro and captured Almeida—the first in a series of defeats suffered by the French. In 1812 he captured Ciudad Rodrigo and Badajoz before the end of April, and, in July, he routed the French at Salamanca, going on to enter Madrid in August, thus compelling French forces to withdraw from southern Spain. In the autumn of 1812, however, Wellington ran into strong French resistance as he tried to capture Burgos, and once more he withdrew to winter quarters in Portugal. In 1813 he advanced again, defeated the French at Vitoria, forced them to evacuate central Spain, and began an invasion of southern France across the Pyrenees; by the end of the year he was threatening Bayonne, and in February 1814 he captured Bordeaux. The Peninsular Campaign was now complete. Wellington's advance had been fused into the general Allied attack on France that was to bring about Napoleon's first abdication.

THE DEFEAT OF NAPOLEON, 1812–15

Although the Treaty of Tilsit had been, ostensibly, a Franco-Russian alliance and although Alexander I had refrained from embarrassing Napoleon in the difficult situation of 1809, there were increasing causes of tension between Napoleon and the Tsar. Alexander was anxious to extend Russian influence southward through the Balkans, and Napoleon wanted to prevent that influence from reaching the Mediterranean. Napoleon had created the Grand Duchy of Warsaw, and Alexander was suspicious of French influence so close at hand, particularly if Napoleon had it in mind to re-establish the old Kingdom of Poland. Finally, the working of the Continental System produced as much discontent in Russia and in areas of Russian influence as it did elsewhere.

Causes of
Franco-
Russian
disagree-
ment

The Russian Campaign, 1812. These general causes of disagreement partly came to a head in 1810–11. In February 1811 Napoleon seized the Hanse towns and the lands of the Tsar's brother-in-law—the Duke of Oldenburg. That May, when a Frenchman, Jean Bernadotte, was elevated to the throne of Sweden, it seemed to Alexander a French step toward encircling him—although, in fact, Bernadotte (Charles XIV John) proved no friend to Napoleon. In January 1812 Napoleon issued a list of grievances against Russia to his German allies, and in April Alexander presented an ultimatum to Napoleon demanding French evacuation of Prussia, compensation for Oldenburg, and virtually the creation of a neutral zone between the two power blocs. In May, Russia concluded a treaty with the Ottoman Empire and thus freed itself from trouble in the Balkans. In July 1812 a treaty of alliance was signed among Sweden, Russia, and Great Britain.

Meanwhile, Napoleon had already decided that he would invade Russia in June, and he concentrated a vast army of about 600,000 men in the Grand Duchy of War-saw, drawing heavily on troops from allies and satellites. About 450,000 men actually crossed the Niemen River at the beginning of the campaign and were opposed by fewer than half that number in the Russian forces.

Napoleon had the choice of three good roads leading from west to east and toward Moscow—from Kovno via Vilna, Vitebsk, and Smolensk; from Grodno via Minsk and so to Vitebsk; and from Brest-Litovsk via Kiev to Smolensk. He decided to take the first, the most northerly route, using the Grand Duchy of Warsaw as his strategic base and with his lines of communication lying back through what he thought were friendly areas of Poland and Prussia. His strategic approach, after assembling his armies behind the line of the Vistula from Warsaw to the coast, was to use his right flank as a defense and to attack on his left flank from Kovno eastward with his largest army under his own command.

The Russian forces were deployed in two armies. The larger of the two, commanded by Mikhail Barclay de Tolly, was along the line of the Niemen north of the Pinsk Marshes (*i.e.*, on the right, or north, flank) and comprised about 135,000 men. The Russian left-flank army, commanded by Pyotr Ivanovich Bagration, was to the south of the Pinsk Marshes in Volynia and had a smaller force of about 50,000 men. From the start, the Russian commanders were well aware of the risk of separation and envelopment and were determined on a strategy of withdrawal upon converging lines. Writing to the King of Prussia months before the campaign began, the Tsar said,

The system which has made Wellington victorious in Spain, and exhausted the French armies, is what I intend to follow —avoid pitched battles and organise long lines of communication for retreat, leading to entrenched camps.

Russian
strategy

Quite apart from avoiding the risk of defeat on the battlefield, such a strategy was bound to impose a heavy strain on Napoleon's forces in their search for food and fodder and in a constantly lengthening communications system in an enemy country. (When Clausewitz wrote some years later that one of the main strategic advantages of the defensive was the ability to make use of the goodwill of the local population, he almost certainly had this particular campaign in mind.)

Two further points of general strategic importance can be made. First, the roads in areas in which Napoleon planned to operate were mostly of poor quality and distinctly inferior in standard to the road systems of western and central Europe. Second, it was normally possible to continue campaigning in western Europe until late in the year without serious inconvenience, but, in Russian winter conditions, victory consisted of survival rather than of defeating the enemy forces; and in the search for survival Napoleon's troops were at a great disadvantage.

On June 24–25 the entire French left wing crossed the Niemen at Kovno almost unopposed. Napoleon expected soon to be behind Barclay, but, when he arrived at Vilna on June 28, he found that Barclay had moved eastward and escaped the net. Moreover and despite the summer weather, logistic problems were already retarding the speed of Napoleon's movement. Although continuing his advance against Barclay, Napoleon turned his attention southward to Bagration, wrongly supposing that the latter was retreating in a northeasterly direction and planning to prevent the two Russian armies from uniting in the area east of Vilna. But Bagration had gone southeastward instead via Minsk, thus escaping in his turn. Moving again to the north, Napoleon tried to encircle Barclay both at Vitebsk in late July and at Smolensk in mid-August. On both occasions the Russians slipped out of the net again and retreated toward Moscow.

By then the French advance was running into serious supply difficulties, which robbed Napoleon of mobility and imposed on him a blunt frontal attack strategy in place of envelopment. After a bloody action at Borodino on September 7, the Russians continued their retreat; and the pursuing French at last reached Moscow in mid-September. There they found the city devastated by fire but showing no sign of capitulation. After a month in Moscow, Napoleon himself began to retreat, and, al-

The
French in
Moscow

though he was at no time defeated by the Russians, he was forced, by the fact that they followed fast on his heels and preyed on his flanks, to follow the route by which he had earlier advanced, but now substantially denuded of supplies. This fact and the severe weather conditions took their toll. Napoleon reached Smolensk on November 8 and crossed the Beresina on the 17th. On December 5, hearing rumours of a conspiracy against him in Paris, Napoleon left his army and made for home. That army was now experiencing the Russian winter; by the time it reached and crossed the Niemen in mid-December, the temperature was −30° F (−35° C), and only about 30,000 men had survived out of the 600,000 Napoleon had so hopefully assembled the previous summer. At the Niemen the Russian pursuit stopped, and the remaining French forces continued their wretched withdrawal unopposed.

Napoleon's military power was not annihilated, as the campaigns of 1813–14 were to demonstrate. But he had lost invaluable troops; his reputation was at last open to question; and his enemies had been given a morale boost that it would take many French victories to destroy. The Russian Campaign was the real turning point in Europe's wars against France.

The campaigns of 1813–14 and Napoleon's surrender.
Napoleon's prospects were not hopeless in the spring of 1813. Opinion in Prussia was still divided about the advisability of declaring war on France. Russia itself had suffered severely during the 1812 campaign, and many influential Russians argued that, their country once made safe, there was no point in fighting to save the rest of Europe. Austrian attitudes were equivocal; Metternich showed no eagerness to join a crusade against France and seems, in some ways, to have preferred the prospect of a negotiated peace placing Napoleon in power as emperor. (After all, Napoleon was by then married to an Austrian princess—the archduchess Marie-Louise.) Russia and Prussia did, however, conclude the Treaty of Kalisch in February 1813, which was a treaty of alliance against France. During March 1813 the French forces in Prussia were driven back westward, and by mid-March they were back on the line of the Elbe. Meanwhile, Sweden had joined the Allies.

Napoleon's choices, although not entirely clear, were by no means unpromising. His opponents were divided in their political aims, as they later demonstrated at the Congress of Vienna (1814–15). He might have negotiated with them separately, thus dividing them and achieving at least a compromise peace for himself; or he could have cut his losses in Spain and restricted his fighting to the area east of the Rhine. But he was unwilling to accept the limitations implicit in such choices, and he chose instead to attempt everything without negotiation.

The campaign of 1813 consisted of two parts. The first part began when Napoleon arrived on the line of the Elbe on April 28. He had by then called up the conscripts of the classes of 1813 and 1814 and had 150,000 men at his disposal in Germany. He wanted to cross the Elbe again, strike at the heart of Prussia before it was fully ready for war, and, by threatening the Russian line of communications, draw both Prussian and Russian armies away from Austria, whose neutrality might thus be maintained. One way to do this was to advance directly on Leipzig and Dresden, compelling his enemies to accept battle or withdraw beyond the Elbe. An outright victory was an essential part of this strategy and was necessary to keep Austria and the states in the Confederation of the Rhine friendly toward France; but that victory was denied to Napoleon. Two inconclusive battles took place—the first at Lützen, southeast of Leipzig, on May 2, in which the Allies were worsted but withdrew in good order; the second at Bautzen on May 20–21, with much the same result. But Napoleon had accepted heavy losses in these battles, and he was at that point much less able to accept them than were the Allies. Further, he signed an armistice with Prussia and Russia at Pläswitz on June 4, which lasted until August 20; this, too, was more helpful to his enemies than to himself—it gave time for Prussia to mobilize its reserves and for Austria to decide to join the

Allies—and, when the armistice ended, Napoleon was relatively worse off than when it had begun.

In the second part of the campaign of 1813 the Allies put three armies into the field, comprising some 600,000 men, against whom Napoleon mustered 400,000. The Allies planned to converge from Prussia and Silesia upon Dresden; as on previous occasions, Napoleon's plan was to engage and defeat them separately. A number of distinct but related battles followed. On August 26 and 27 an Austrian army was defeated at Dresden, but on August 30 and then on September 6 the French were defeated, first at Kulm and then at Dennewitz. For Napoleon these defeats were more important than the earlier victory because the Allies continued to threaten him, gaining relatively in strength all the time. During the first part of October the Allies converged on Leipzig, where the Battle of the Nations (October 16–19) took place. By then Bavaria had joined the Allied cause, and Napoleon found himself fighting with an army of 160,000 against combined enemies who could bring against him double that number. Moreover, his enemies knew the danger of accepting battle separately and the need to maintain contact with each other.

At first Napoleon held his own. But on October 18 the Saxon forces went over to the Allies and on October 19 Napoleon was forced to retreat toward France, defeating a Bavarian force at Hanau on October 30. On November 2 Napoleon's army fell back across the Rhine at Mainz with fewer than 80,000 of the men with whom he had begun the campaign. By then virtually deprived of allies, this campaign was a blow, added to the disaster of 1812, from which Napoleon could hardly hope to recover.

Yet the Allies themselves were still not set upon the overthrow of Napoleon. In November 1813 they offered him peace if France surrendered all its conquests beyond the Rhine, the Alps, and the Pyrenees. As Napoleon knew, however, there were some among the Allies who advocated harsher terms; the British, for example, were anxious to achieve the independence of French-held Dutch and Belgian regions, and that entailed further French concessions. In the end, between Allied differences of view and Napoleon's own doubts about the possibility of continuing in power on such terms, the Allies failed to provide a basis for peace, and they determined to invade France in 1814.

The campaign of 1814, like that of the previous year, was divided into two parts. The Allies planned to move into France from the north via Dutch and Belgian territory, across the Middle Rhine in the area of Mainz and from Switzerland around the Jura Mountains—an overall plan similar to the one they would adopt in 1815. Napoleon, fighting with numerically inferior forces, decided to tackle the Allied armies separately. In the first part of the campaign (late January and February 1814) Napoleon inflicted heavy defeats on the Prussian and Austrian armies advancing from the Middle and Upper Rhine. The Allies appeared to be breaking up at this stage until more determined counsels prevailed. On March 1 Prussia, Russia, Austria, and Great Britain signed a new alliance committing themselves to war and to peace terms only on conditions agreed to by them all.

The Allies were then set on attacking Paris, and the second stage of the campaign began. Napoleon hoped to draw them off by moving into Lorraine and thus threatening their line of communication, while Paris accepted siege and resisted. The Allies, however, were not diverted by this threat, despite minor local reverses. Moreover, they were by now aware of Napoleon's plan, having captured some of his dispatches; and they also knew that many in Paris were anxious for peace. On March 30 the Allied armies reached the Paris suburbs, and resistance there soon ceased. On April 6 Napoleon abdicated and was soon on his way to exile on the island of Elba, while Louis XVIII returned to Paris as king on May 3.

Meanwhile, the Allies settled down to the task of resettling Europe after the long wars; they were still arguing the details when they found themselves at war with Napoleon again.

(margin notes)
Napoleon's choices in 1813

Retreat to France

Napoleon's abdication and exile

The Waterloo Campaign. On February 26, 1815, Napoleon escaped from Elba; he landed on the mainland of France near Antibes on March 1. He set out for Paris via the Dauphiné and on March 7 entered Grenoble without any opposition. With towns and garrisons welcoming Napoleon in what proved to be a triumphal journey, Louis XVIII left Paris on March 19; Napoleon entered the capital the next day. A week before that, the representatives of the Allies at Vienna declared Napoleon an outlaw, describing him as "the enemy and disturber of the peace of the world." The three eastern monarchies—Russia, Prussia, and Austria—together with Great Britain, made a new defensive alliance against Napoleon (only a few weeks before, those same powers had been acting more like enemies than friends in their attempts to settle the affairs of Europe), and each undertook to supply 150,000 men for the armies of the alliance and to keep them in the field until Napoleon was finally defeated.

After the failure of some diplomatic manoeuvres designed to detach Britain and Austria from the alliance, Napoleon realized that there was no alternative to fighting; and he prepared himself for an offensive campaign. First, however, he had to raise armies and equip them. There were many veterans of the Prussian and Italian campaigns in France, a large number of them already committed to serving Louis XVIII, and Napoleon found no difficulty in winning them back to his cause. Conscription of new recruits was politically dangerous; and, if Napoleon planned an early offensive, new recruits could hardly be trained in time anyway. So the existing regulars were supplemented by recalling all undischarged soldiers and those who had deserted since April 1814. Thus expanded, Napoleon's army for the 1815 campaign totalled about 250,000, of whom roughly half were available for his striking force and the rest for frontier and garrison duty. In fact, Napoleon did call up the class of 1815 at the end of May, and during June about 50,000 of them were in barracks; but they played no part in the Waterloo Campaign.

The Allied Coalition
The Allied Coalition—the seventh formed against France between 1792 and 1815—planned to raise five armies. An Anglo-Dutch army of 90,000 men commanded by Wellington and a Prussian army of 120,000 commanded by Gebhard Leberecht von Blücher were to operate from the Brussels region into France; an Austrian army of 225,000 men commanded by Karl Philipp zu Schwarzenberg was to operate on the Upper and Middle Rhine; a Russian army of 170,000 men under Barclay de Tolly was to form a strategic reserve; and, finally, an Austro-Italian army of 60,000 commanded by Johann Maria Frimont was to operate from northern Italy. The Allies planned a concentric advance on Paris beginning in late June. Early in April, Wellington left Vienna on his way to Brussels; he met Blücher at Tirlemont on May 3. These two did not expect Napoleon to take the offensive against them but agreed that, if he should do so, they would concentrate on the line between Quatre-Bras and Sombreffe. Accordingly, Blücher moved his headquarters from Liège to Namur, and Wellington established his headquarters at Brussels.

Napoleon's plans, as seen above, were basically offensive. He wanted to meet and defeat some of his enemies before the others were ready and then to go on to deal with them piecemeal while they were still concentrating. The enemy armies posing the most immediate threat were those of Wellington and Blücher. Napoleon therefore decided to attack the combined Prussian and Anglo-Dutch forces himself, in command of the Army of the North, 125,000 strong. Leaving generals Jean Rapp and Louis-Gabriel Suchet on the defensive along the Rhine and opposite the approaches from Switzerland and Italy, Napoleon's approach in the theatre he was directly concerned with was in principle similar to his first great campaign in northern Italy in 1796. He faced an enemy stronger than himself but composed of two armies converging on a common line of advance into France. If those two armies could be attacked at their "hinge" (*i.e.*, where their lines of advance converged and joined) and all the more so if they could be attacked separately,

Waterloo Campaign.
Adapted from V. Esposito and J. Elting, *A Military History and Atlas of the Napoleonic Wars* (1964); Praeger Publishers

they might be prevented from combining and even be driven back upon their divergent lines of communication. Wellington's line ran back through Brussels to Antwerp; Blücher's, via Namur, Liège, and Cologne. Napoleon's aim, therefore, was to advance from Paris to Charleroi and there force himself between the two enemy armies. If they could both be defeated, he would turn back southeastward, join Rapp opposing Schwarzenberg, and then deal with the latter. This strategy was an adventurous approach because Napoleon had few of his old marshals with him, training time had been short, and many of his senior officers were strangers to the men they led.

On June 3 Napoleon ordered the Army of the North to concentrate in the area Maubeuge-Avesnes, about 25 miles (40 kilometres) southwest of Charleroi. On June 14 he moved his own headquarters to the Charleroi area, with Wellington and Blücher still unaware of what the French were doing. By nightfall on June 15, Napoleon's forces were disposed in such a way that they could manoeuvre against either enemy as circumstances dictated. Wellington, in fact, had unintentionally helped—fearing that Napoleon might outflank him on the right and so cut off his line of retreat to Antwerp and the sea, Wellington detached a corps to cover the roads leading from Mons and Ath to Brussels, thus moving his centre of gravity eastward and away from Blücher.

Instructing Michel Ney, on the left, to occupy Quatre Bras and thus block Wellington from using the Nivelles–Namur road, Napoleon attacked the Prussians at Ligny, on the Allied left or eastern flank, on June 16. The purpose of this operation was to drive Blücher back eastward and northeastward away from Wellington, and Napoleon counted on support from Ney to reinforce his own left wing to make this possible. The Battle of Ligny was indecisive: the Prussians were, indeed, driven back, but Ney failed to understand Napoleon's strategic plans and did not send the help that might have turned the Prussian retreat into a rout. The next mistake was Napoleon's. He had assumed that, once forced back, Blücher would retreat roughly northeastward via Namur and so move away from Wellington. The Prussian commander, however, was aware of the vital need to maintain contact with Wellington and chose, therefore, to retreat northward in the direction of Wavre. Emmanuel Grouchy, who had been instructed to pursue the Prussians, thus took the wrong road; and Napoleon realized too late that his assumption was incorrect.

The third mistake was also Napoleon's. The essence of

Napoleon's mistakes

his earlier strategy in such a situation was to act more quickly than his enemies and, by gaining even a few hours, to deny them time to settle down and recover. This time Napoleon's conduct of operations fell below his own best standards. The night of June 16 and the morning of June 17 were wasted. When at last Napoleon began to move toward his left at about noon on June 17 —a move designed to attack and defeat Wellington—the latter was already well aware of Napoleon's plans and had been given time to draw his army up in a strong defensive position just south of Waterloo. Moreover, Napoleon's march, already begun late, was further hampered by heavy rain. As a result, when the Battle of Waterloo was fought on June 18 all element of surprise had been lost. And by the early evening on the 17th Blücher kept his promise to Wellington and appeared on the battlefield with invaluable reinforcements, turning the scales against Napoleon at the critical time. Waterloo was Napoleon's last battle.

Up to the morning of June 16 Napoleon's preparations for the Ligny–Waterloo Campaign suggested that his military genius was unimpaired. He moved faster than his opponents, and, as far as it lay in his power, he laid the foundations of victory. It was in his conduct of operations from the evening of the 16th until midday on the 17th that he failed.

After Waterloo, Napoleon retreated southward, and on June 21 he entered Paris. The next day he abdicated. A fortnight later Wellington and Blücher also entered Paris, bringing Louis XVIII back with them; 23 years of war were ended.

Result of the wars

Conclusion. The political result of these long wars seemed, at first, to be simply a restoration of legitimate monarchs and a return to the *ancien régime*. But the political map and, even more, the political temper of Europe had changed, and nothing could put things back as they were. In warfare something of the same sort of contradiction is evident. In the century after Waterloo, war in Europe appeared to lose its total quality; the wars of the 19th century were limited wars—wars involving political change but also wars for limited areas of territory. Yet the total quality was dormant, not dead. It influenced men's arguments and theories, if not always their actions. As the 19th century progressed, the concept of "the nation in arms" was debated more and more against the background of a steady spread of the nation-state and of democratic forms of government. Finally, total war made its appearance again with the great wars of the 20th century, which, although fought with entirely new weapons, were fought also with the ideas and the emotional impulses of a century earlier.

BIBLIOGRAPHY. General military works include: D.G. CHANDLER, *The Campaigns of Napoleon* (1966), an excellent, detailed account of all Napoleon's campaigns, with a large selection of maps; J.F.C. FULLER, *The Decisive Battles of the Western World, and Their Influence upon History*, vol. 2, ch. 11–15 (1955); R.A. HALL, *Studies in Napoleonic Strategy* (1918), a lively and thoughtful study; SIR E. HAMLEY, *The Operations of War* (1922), a professional soldier's analysis; P.G. MACKESY, *War in the Mediterranean, 1803–10* (1957); A.T. MAHAN, *The Influence of Sea Power upon the French Revolution and Empire*, 2 vol. (1893, reprinted 1965), still a standard conspectus account; A.B. RODGER, *The War of the Second Coalition, 1798–1801* (1964); THEODORE ROPP, "The French Revolution and Napoleon," in *War in the Modern World* (1959), a brief account with excellent bibliographical notes; JAC WELLER, *Wellington in the Peninsula, 1808–1814* (1962), an up-to-date, one-volume account of the Peninsular war with excellent maps; SPENSER WILKINSON, *The French Army Before Napoleon* (1915), an account of the transition from the royalist to the Revolutionary army.

(N.H.G.)

Freshwater, Geochemical Properties of

The compositions of freshwaters—that is, waters that are dilute and generally potable or suitable for drinking —vary greatly in the proportions and concentrations of contained solutes (dissolved substances). Freshwater properties are the result of the phenomena that are the concern of geochemistry, which is the study of the structure and composition of the Earth in terms of the physical and chemical processes and principles that produce and modify the minerals and rocks of the Earth. In general, this article is restricted to freshwaters on and below the land surfaces and their precursors and deals with waters that have but a few hundred milligrams per litre of total solutes, although the processes discussed are capable of yielding much larger concentrations.

Water on or within the land may have more than 1,000 milligrams per litre of any number of solutes, commonly including the cations, or positive ions (an ion is an atom or group of atoms that has lost or gained one or more electrons and as a result is negatively or positively charged), sodium (Na^+), calcium (Ca^{2+}), magnesium (Mg^{2+}), potassium (K^+), and ferrous iron (Fe^{2+}) or the anions (negative ions) chloride (Cl^-), bicarbonate (HCO_3^-), carbonate (CO_3^{2-}), or sulfate (SO_4^{2-}). It is difficult to establish a satisfactory upper limit for solute concentrations to define freshwater in terms of potability, because some waters are considered nonpotable by human beings on the basis of taste, odour, or the known presence of certain solutes. Also, bacterial contamination or parasitic infestation may render freshwater nonpotable, and there may be more compelling reasons for a nonpotable classification, such as, for example, lethal concentrations of arsenic or other poisonous substances.

Difficulty of defining potability

Similar difficulties in definition are encountered if suitability to species other than man is considered. Water suitability depends not upon salt concentration alone but also upon nutrients and poisonous substances. Boron compounds, such as boric acid (H_3BO_3) and borate ion ($H_2BO_3^-$), in concentrations harmless to man can be lethal to citrus plants, toxic to stone-fruit trees, and not harmful to other vegetation. Nor does the origin of freshwater offer a useful criterion.

Most freshwater is precipitated as snow and rain, but freshwater is also formed by repeated freezing and thawing of sea ice; the salts are excluded by fractional crystallization, yielding freshwater. Freshwaters are also formed by the condensation of natural steam in geothermal fields, such as those in Yellowstone National Park in the United States, southwestern Iceland, the upper basin of the Waikato River in New Zealand, and a number of other countries.

For information on the several water environments within the hydrosphere, see PRECIPITATION; HUMIDITY, ATMOSPHERIC; RIVERS AND RIVER SYSTEMS; LAKES AND LAKE SYSTEMS; ICE SHEETS AND GLACIERS; ICEBERGS AND PACK ICE; and GROUNDWATER. The interrelations are covered in the article HYDROLOGIC CYCLE. For more detailed treatment of water chemistry, see SOLUTIONS AND SOLUBILITY; ACID–BASE REACTIONS AND EQUILIBRIA; and WATER. See also GEOCHEMICAL EQUILIBRIA AT LOW TEMPERATURES AND PRESSURES.

FRESHWATER COMPOSITION

Evaporation from the seas, the ultimate reservoir, yields water vapour and extremely small particles of salt, aerosols that may blow in over the land. The evaporation changes the water composition markedly because the water vapour cannot take with it the solids that are in solution in the water. There is a change not only in the water's chemical composition but also in its isotopic (isotopes are varieties of a chemical element that differ in atomic weight but are very much alike in chemical properties) composition. Because of difference in molecular motion, oxygen-16 (the elemental oxygen of atomic weight 16) tends to escape more rapidly than oxygen-18 (so-called heavy oxygen, the nonradioactive isotope, which has atomic weight 18). Hydrogen also has a greater tendency to escape from liquid water during evaporation than its heavier stable isotope, deuterium (D). Thus the water vapour is enriched in oxygen-16 and hydrogen and is isotopically lighter. If the water vapour were to stay in contact with the seawater, the exchange across the interface would yield predictable equilibrium ratios of oxygen-18:oxygen-16 and deuterium:hydrogen. Removal of the water vapour, which may be swept away by the wind, precludes the equilibrium, so that the ten-

Evaporation effects

dency persists for the water vapour to be lighter isotopically than the liquid water.

Upon precipitation, the heavy oxygen and the deuterium tend to condense first, and there is another isotopic separation of fractionation, the precipitation being heavier isotopically than the remaining water vapour. The remaining water vapour condenses, yielding precipitation progressively lighter with the diminishing concentrations of the oxygen and hydrogen isotopes in the water vapour. The isotopic composition of a single storm's precipitation cannot be forecast; in part, it depends upon the origin of the water vapour. Storm systems with isotopically light polar water vapour yield isotopically light precipitation; conversely, storms with isotopically heavy tropical water vapour yield isotopically heavy precipitation. In addition, the fractionation upon condensation may vary with meteorological conditions. Though the isotopic composition of precipitation along a storm track or at a given point the storm passes cannot be accurately predicted, water can be said to be generally lighter inland and toward the poles. Only a part of the precipitation remains for long near the point at which it falls. The small amounts of precipitation that penetrate to the water table (i.e., the top surface of the water-saturated layer within the soil) are homogenized by dispersion, and groundwater (the slowly percolating water below the water table) has an isotopic composition in deuterium: hydrogen and oxyen-18:oxygen-16 that is characteristic of the locality. Water quickly lost to flow in open channels soon shifts its isotopic composition by nonequilibrium evaporation.

In addition to changes in isotopic composition, changes in chemical composition occur with phase changes. The water vapour condenses on dust or aerosol particles that are more or less soluble, and, as they fall, the drops capture more particulate matter and also dissolve gases from the air. Despite such solution reactions, precipitation is the purest water commonly found in nature. Although very dilute and hence having a high potential for dissolving matter, the capacity of precipitation to dissolve is small. Precipitation is poor in reactive ions, such as the hydrogen ion; there is too little carbon dioxide in rainwater to yield much hydrogen ion by the reaction

Capacity for chemical reactions

$$H_2O + CO_2 \rightarrow H^+ + HCO_3^-.$$
$$\text{water} \quad \text{carbon} \quad \text{hydrogen} \quad \text{bicarbonate}$$
$$\text{dioxide} \quad \text{ion} \quad \text{ion}$$

In areas of heavy precipitation, much material within the soil may be leached (i.e., removed by the percolating actions of groundwater) away, but the effect will be accomplished by very dilute solutions, a large quantity of which will remove as much material as a smaller amount of more concentrated solutions.

The most dramatic change in the composition of the precipitation occurs when it reaches the solids of the Earth's surface. Rain, which usually contains only a few milligrams per litre of dissolved matter, may be abruptly changed by reactions on foliage or the ground where concentrations rise to tens of milligrams per litre. If some of the rainwater returns to the atmosphere by evaporation or transpiration of plants there may be an increase in solute concentration in the remainder. Precipitation usually penetrates the ground in its flow to stream channels. The zone of the soil in which water does not fill all available pore spaces, the unsaturated zone, transmits water in part to the water-saturated zone (at and below the water table) and laterally down to stream channels. The most rapid changes in freshwater compositions generally occur between the surface and the water table, for groundwaters, or in the channel, if the water drains from the unsaturated zone without joining the groundwater body in the saturated zone. Within the unsaturated zone the changes in freshwater compositions are caused by leaching of the minerals present and the resultant mineral changes, termed weathering, and are a factor in soil formation. Biologic agents, which include an immense number of micro-organisms—e.g., bacteria, fungi, algae, and protozoa—greatly enhance the solution reactions. Burrowing organisms—e.g.,

moles, ground squirrels, worms, slugs, lizards, snakes, and many insects—open channels, increasing water flow; many micro-organisms—e.g., fungi, actinomycetes, and most soil bacteria—also may extract nutrients from the soil and, upon decay, may leave the mineral constituents in a form more readily soluble in infiltrating water. The greatest effect on the compositons of infiltrating water is caused by plants. Plant roots respire carbon dioxide (CO_2), tending to increase the hydrogen-ion (H^+) concentration in the water present. Most of the reactions among minerals and water involve the hydrogen ion (H^+). In water under grasslands, the concentration of carbon dioxide is approximately 1,000 times that of water in equilibrium with air. Thus, the incoming rain would have only $\frac{1}{1,000}$ the carbon dioxide content of the infiltrated water in and below the roots of the grasses; hence rainwater is far less potent a solvent than the carbon dioxide-rich water resulting from plant-root respiration. Forests commonly increase the carbon dioxide content of soil and groundwater 100 times above the content of rainwater, and even the sparse vegetation of deserts adds two to ten times the CO_2 found in rain.

Values of pH and chemical reactions. *Relative ion concentrations.* The hydrogen ion (H^+), which is of great importance to geochemical reactions, is involved in most of the reactions that control the composition of freshwaters. The effective concentration of the hydrogen ion is called the activity of the hydrogen ion and is expressed by the use of the pH scale, which is a means of representing the acidity or basicity of a solution.

The activity of the hydrogen ion

Water ionizes as $H_2O \rightleftarrows H^+ + OH^-$, and, when the concentrations of the hydrogen ion (H^+) and the hydroxide ion (OH^-) are equal (each is 10^{-7}), which is expressed as pH 7, the water is called neutral. The ionic product of water is 10^{-14} at 25° C, so that an increase in the concentration of either the negative or the positive ion results in a decrease in the concentration of the other. Accordingly, when the concentration of the hydrogen ion (H^+) is increased, for example, to 10^{-4}, the solution is acid, and the hydrogen-ion concentration is expressed by a pH number of less than 7 (pH 4 in the foregoing example). Conversely, an increase in concentration of the hydroxide ion (OH^-) to 10^{-4} results in a decrease in hydrogen-ion concentration to 10^{-10}, and the pH number is 10 for the resulting alkaline or basic solution.

In this article, low pH means concentration of the hydrogen ion (H^+) greater than that of the hydroxide ion (OH^-) and an acidic solution; high pH means concentration of the hydroxide ion greater than that of the hydrogen ion and a basic, or alkaline, solution.

Buffer capacity. Although pH values give the effective concentration of hydrogen ion (H^+), they do not indicate the capacity to supply H^+ as it is used up in various reactions. The reaction yields H^+ as CO_2 reacts.

$$CO_2 + H_2O \rightarrow H^+ + HCO_3^-$$
$$\text{carbon} \quad \text{water} \quad \text{hydrogen} \quad \text{bicarbonate}$$
$$\text{dioxide} \quad \text{ion} \quad \text{ion}$$

The amount of CO_2 available is the buffer capacity of the system, which reacts to resist changes in pH when either acids or bases are added. In effect the hydrogen ion, H^+, may react with the bicarbonate ion, HCO_3^-, and be stored as carbon dioxide and water with only a small pH change. The reaction is reversible; a small change in carbon dioxide will cause a small change in hydrogen ion and bicarbonate ion. The greater the concentrations of dissolved carbon dioxide and bicarbonate ion, the larger the buffer capacity; that is, the larger the capacity for the solution to react. Solutions rich in carbon dioxide are aggressive solvents not only because of their low pH but also, and more importantly, because they have a larger buffer capacity and, by supplying more H^+, can continue to react and dissolve more minerals.

The bicarbonate ion also acts as a buffer at higher pH values as

$$HCO_3^- \rightarrow H^+ + CO_3^{2-}.$$

This reaction is also readily reversible; if H^+ is used up, HCO_3^- ionizes to yield more, and, if H^+ is added, the

CO_3^{2-} reacts to store much more of the added H^+ as HCO_3^-.

The carbon dioxide and bicarbonate-ion concentrations are equal at 25° C at pH 6.4. The bicarbonate-ion and carbonate-ion concentrations are equal at pH 10.3. The carbon dioxide, bicarbonate-ion, carbonate-ion buffers are the dominant buffers in most freshwaters, and it is unusual to find freshwaters outside the pH range of 6 to 9. The most common causes of pH values less than 6 are oxidation of sulfides or ferrous iron. Some well waters contaminated by recently used portland cement may have pH values greater than 9. Uncontaminated waters of pH greater than 11 have been ascribed to reactions with magnesium–iron silicates (olivines and pyroxenes).

Composition generalizations. Observations of compositions of freshwaters lead to some crude qualitative generalizations, meant only to serve as a guide to what is usual. More detailed and exact relations will be developed later. The generalizations apply to waters from most igneous and metamorphic silicate rocks and to some, but certainly not all, sedimentary rocks. Hydrologic conditions to be described may also give rise to exceptions to the generalizations.

Differences in rock-mineral reactions

With these qualifications, it may be said that calcium-bearing minerals seem to react most readily with infiltrating waters. Calcium-ion (Ca^{2+}) concentrations are usually higher than the concentrations of other cations. Sodium-ion- (Na^+-) bearing minerals seem less reactive, and the Na^+ concentrations are usually below those of Ca^{2+}. Minerals bearing magnesium ion (Mg^{2+}) seem even less reactive in freshwaters than those bearing the sodium ion. Potassium-ion- (K^+-) bearing minerals apparently have even lower solubilities, and usually K^+ is the least concentrated of the common cations.

The composition ranges most commonly encountered in freshwaters are, for calcium, sodium, and magnesium ions, a few to tens of milligrams per litre, in most cases, the relative concentrations will be $Ca^{2+} > Na^+ > Mg^{2+}$. Potassium-ion (K^+) concentrations usually are in the range from a few tenths to a few milligrams per litre.

Cations. Two types of reactions supply the cations to freshwater, congruent and incongruent. Congruent reactions are those that dissolve the mineral completely, as for quartz (silica, SiO_2),

$$SiO_2 + 2H_2O \rightarrow Si(OH)_4.$$
$$\text{quartz} \quad \text{water} \quad \text{dissolved silica}$$

As simple as the reaction seems, quartz rarely is the mineral that supplies the silicate found in freshwater. Observations show that at temperatures much below 200° C (about 400° F), quartz dissolves and precipitates very sluggishly. Other silica-containing minerals react more rapidly and supply the $Si(OH)_4$ found in freshwaters. Gypsum ($CaSO_4 \cdot 2H_2O$) and anhydrite ($CaSO_4$) also dissolve congruently as

$$CaSO_4 \cdot 2H_2O = Ca^{2+} + SO_4^{2-} + 2H_2O$$
$$\text{gypsum} \quad \text{calcium ion} \quad \text{sulfate ion} \quad \text{water}$$

and

$$CaSO_4 = Ca^{2+} + SO_4^{2-}$$
$$\text{anhydrite} \quad \text{calcium ion} \quad \text{sulfate ion}$$

Calcite ($CaCo_3$) and dolomite, $CaMg(CO_3)_2$, dissolve congruently as

$$H^+ + CaCO_3 \rightarrow Ca^{2+} + HCO_3^-$$
$$\text{hydrogen ion} \quad \text{calcite} \quad \text{calcium ion} \quad \text{bicarbonate ion}$$

$$2H^+ + CaMg(CO_3)_2 \rightarrow Ca^{2+}$$
$$\text{hydrogen ion} \quad \text{dolomite} \quad \text{calcium ion}$$

$$+ Mg^{2+} + 2HCO_3^-.$$
$$\text{magnesium ion} \quad \text{bicarbonate ion}$$

As salts accumulated in saline or alkaline soils dissolve, other congruent reactions may be found, but, although such reactions are of great local importance, they are not the sources of most of the cations.

The greatest source of cations are aluminosilicate minerals. In general they react incongruently (*i.e.,* only part of the mineral dissolves, or if the mineral dissolves entirely some constituents reprecipitate). For the potassium feldspars ($KAlSi_3O_8$), the solution reaction yields more potassium ion, K^+, than silica, $Si(OH)_4$, and more silica than aluminum (in its various forms) to solution. Observations on calcium, sodium, and magnesium aluminosilicates are the same. Thus for the most common and most concentrated cations the general reaction is cation aluminosilicate → cation + aluminum-richer silicate. The result is aluminum-enriched, cation-depleted materials and ultimately leads to clays in mature soils.

It is important that incongruent reactions yield cations without corresponding anions demanded by the laws of electrostatics. The pH of most dilute waters is too low for appreciable anionic silica or aluminum. The key to the leaching process is the ubiquitous carbon dioxide–bicarbonate-ion ($CO_2 \rightarrow HCO_3^-$) relation. As the attack on the silicates proceeds, hydrogen ion (H^+) is used up and is replaced by other cations such as the calcium, sodium, magnesium, and potassium ions (Ca^{2+}, Na^+, Mg^{2+}, K^+). Not only is the electrical charge balance maintained by replacing H^+ by other cations, the reaction shown below provides the balancing anion HCO_3^-:

Demands of electrostatic laws

$$H_2O + CO_2 \rightarrow H^+ + HCO_3^-.$$
$$\text{water} \quad \text{carbon dioxide} \quad \text{hydrogen ion} \quad \text{bicarbonate ion}$$

Anions. With the exception of the congruent reactions, the sources of the anions are different from the sources of the cations. The bicarbonate ion is supplied chiefly by plant-root respiration; its source is thus, indirectly, the Earth's atmosphere. Mineral sources must be sought for other anions.

Sulfate ions are the easiest anions to account for. Locally, the important sources may be gypsum or anhydrite in sedimentary rocks or in salt accumulations in some soils; more generally, the sulfates come from oxidation of sulfide minerals. Sulfide minerals commonly occur in minor amounts in igneous, metamorphic, and sedimentary rocks. Infiltrating waters may oxidize the sulfide minerals, usually in incongruent reactions. The most common sulfide mineral is pyrite (FeS_2), and, usually, if the water contains dissolved oxygen, the reaction yields sulfate ion (SO_4^{2-}) in solution and mixtures of iron oxyhydroxides that are grouped under the name limonite.

Chloride-ion sources have long been a subject of speculation. Few common minerals have much chloride in their structure and certainly yield less chloride ion (Cl^-) than sodium ion (Na^+). It is a continuing problem to account for the Cl^- found in natural freshwaters. A supply certainly must be available to account for the sodium chloride-type brines, such as those of the Great Salt Lake of Utah. Chloride-ion sources to account for the composition of freshwaters remain a problem for further investigation. Chlorides are, of course, added by such human activities as waste disposal and salting of roads either for dust abatement or ice removal.

Anions that are minor but sometimes important include fluoride (F^-), arsenates ($H_2AsO_4^-$, $HAsO_4^{2-}$), nitrate, and phosphate. Fluoride ion (F^-) substitutes freely for hydroxide ions (OH^-) and may be a minor constituent of many hydroxyaluminosilicates, such as clays and micas; F^- also substitutes for OH^- in the common mineral apatite, $Ca_5(PO_4)_3(OH,F)$. Leaching of any of the minerals containing fluoride ion may yield F^- in solution, commonly at most a few milligrams per litre, although much higher concentrations may be found. Arsenate ions generally stem from oxidation of mineral sulfides such as orpiment (As_2S_3) and realgar (AsS), minor sulfosalts, native arsenic, or the fairly common arsenopyrite, $FeAsS$. Once oxidized, the arsenic may form any of a number of fairly soluble arsenate minerals that may be further leached.

Nitrates in water are usually the result of the oxidation of nitrogenous wastes or leaching of fertilizers, although oxidation of naturally occurring ammonium ion (NH_4^+) also is observed. The nitrogen compounds are nutrients

Organisms and freshwater composition

for a large number of organisms and, where present in high concentrations, foster unusually heavy growths of aquatic organisms. Small concentrations less than one milligram per litre of the nitrate ion, NO_3^-, may be caused by natural nitrogen fixation in soils.

Phosphates are also biologically active, being essential nutrients. High concentrations in water may promote quite heavy growths of aquatic organisms. High phosphate concentrations usually result from leaching of fertilizers or from wastes. Under natural conditions, phosphate ($H_2PO_4^-$ and HPO_4^{2-}) concentrations are of the order of a few hundredths to a few tenths of a milligram per litre. The low concentrations reflect the insolubility of the most common phosphate material, apatite. Precipitation of iron phosphates in soils and removal of phosphates by organisms also helps to keep phosphate concentrations at low levels.

CHEMICAL REACTIONS

Cation exchange. The solutes in freshwater are constantly reacting. In addition to the congruent and incongruent reactions, there is a constant exchange between solutes and coexisting solids. A very important type of exchange is cation exchange. Most minerals, except for native (i.e., uncombined) elements and sulfides, may be thought of as an oxygen–cation framework. The cations that hold the structure together, such as silicon, aluminum, magnesium, iron (Si^{4+}, Al^{3+}, Mg^{2+}, Fe^{2+}, Fe^{3+}) and the like, are much smaller than the oxygen (O^{2-}) ions. As a consequence, the surfaces of most minerals are occupied by oxygen anions (O^{2-}), in part bound ionically to the cations in the interior of the mineral. Rather weak ionic bonds may hold cations onto the surface O^{2-} ions. The reactions that involve the exchange of cations between the surface of the mineral and the solution are quite rapid; the rapidity of exchange brings about an adjustment of cation proportions at the surface to approximately the cation proportions in the solution. There are, of course, exceptions. Potassium ion (K^+) is such a good physical fit in the clay mineral illite that it nearly excludes other cations. Cationic-exchange sites range widely in selectivity for the cations, depending in part on physical dimensions and in part on charge distribution.

The reactions that remove or add solvents may be thought of in terms of transport continuity. If a solute is in solution all along the part of the water path studied, the transport is continuous; if for any of a number of physical reasons the solute precipitates, the transport is discontinuous. Many of the discontinuities in transport lead to commonly observed geologic features, such as rapid changes in water properties, distribution of mineral deposits, and biological growths on the beds of water channels. The study of reactions may be made quantitative, so that the amounts or proportions of the components of a mixture are determined through the use of thermodynamics (i.e., the study of the laws of transformation of energy from any one form to another).

Energy relation and geologic developments

Thermodynamics treats the energy relations inherent in the chemical composition of matter; one of its most useful concepts is that of equilibrium, which is the state of saturation and can be accurately described. A significant part of present geochemical study is the accurate determination of reaction quotients (i.e., the relationship between solute concentrations present and those required for undersaturation, equilibrium, and supersaturation) and changes in free energy, such as result when matter is dissolved in water, to discover the conditions necessary to dissolve and precipitate geologic materials.

Continuity of transport depends fundamentally on change in free-energy relations. During water evaporation, the reaction quotient values may exceed equilibrium conditions (at which the products of a chemical reaction themselves react to reform the original substances, and the rates of formation of the products and of reformation of the reactants are equal); deposition of material then occurs. Discontinuous transport may also occur because of chemical incompatibility; for example, two water masses within the ground may be in hydraulic

continuity but, because of different flow paths through different environments, the waters may have different compositions. Even if the two water masses are in equilibrium with the same mineral, they may be incompatible. The reason for the incompatibility is that dispersion of one water into another is directly proportional to the concentrations of ions in each mass and the relative quantities of the waters mixed. The thermodynamic state is nonlinear (i.e., the relationship between reactions and solute concentrations is not directly proportional), as may be shown in the Figure. Even though waters A

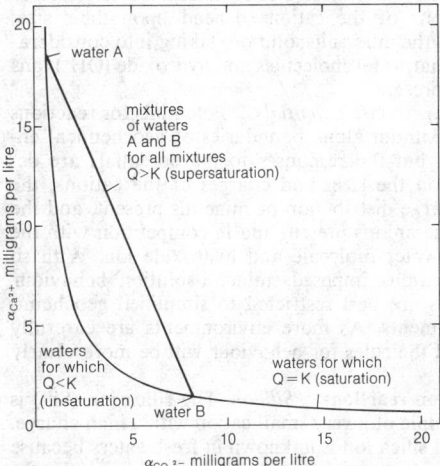

Thermodynamic concentrations of Ca^{2+} and CO_3^{2-} in two water types, A and B, which are in equilibrium with calcite. All mixtures of waters A and B are supersaturated with respect to calcite and accord with the straight line plot as shown. Q and K refer to the quantities of solvent and solute present, respectively.

and B are in equilibrium with calcite ($CaCO_3$), all mixtures are supersaturated (i.e., hold more than the maximum equilibrium quantity of dissolved matter, Ca^{2+} and CO_3^{2-} in this case, for the given temperature). Along the boundaries of such water masses, a potential exists to precipitate calcite. The boundaries may be self-perpetuating because any precipitate that forms tends to seal the boundary.

Boundary reactions. It is quite important to recognize and understand reactions—e.g., oxidation, precipitation, or dissolving of minerals—on the boundaries of environments. Observations lead to the conclusion that along boundaries of geochemical environments, the water properties change rather rapidly in time if not in space. On the boundaries, change in free-energy values for reactions may be large. Reactions in response to change in free-energy values are rapid in comparison to groundwater-flow rates, yielding reaction products over only a few centimetres to a few metres. Surface-water flow rates may be rapid enough to spread reaction products over long distances (up to several kilometres). The response to changes in free-energy values, the difference between actual and equilibrium states, is not necessarily to come to an equilibrium state. The reaction may simply reduce the available energy to a value insufficient to drive the reaction.

Along boundaries between different geochemical environments are found the highest free-energy value changes in nature. If reactions are to occur at all it will be along such boundaries. Changes in free-energy values are potentials; there can be no reaction except to reduce them. Minerals can only dissolve into unsaturated solutions; and minerals can only precipitate from supersaturated solutions. Responses to potentials are matters for observation in that they cannot be accurately predicted at present.

Observed ionic behaviour. Rough guides to reactions are available from observation or experience. The rules of behaviour depend on the cations, the anions, the ions in the water, and the water. A cation in solution is positively charged. From the laws of electrostatics, nega-

Ion associations in solution

tive charges are attracted to the cation. All anions will tend to associate with the positive ion to various degrees. The water molecules themselves will be attracted: the oxygen toward the cation, the hydrogen ions away from the cation. The smaller the cation or the higher the charge of the cation, the more water molecules and anions in solution will be attracted. As in the case of cation exchange, both physical dimensions and charge distribution are important. The smaller the cation, the fewer anions or water molecules may be in close association. The higher the charge of the cation, the greater the attraction to the water molecules or anions. Descriptions of the behaviour of the cations depend upon their size, charge, and the anions in solution, taking into consideration, also, that water molecules and hydroxide (OH$^-$) ions are always present.

Maximum response potentials. Potentials for reactions reach a maximum along boundaries of geochemical environments, but the responses to the potentials are dependent upon the sizes and charges of the cations, the size and charge distribution of minerals present, and the nature of the anions present and in competition with the ubiquitous water molecule and hydroxide ion. With so many limitations imposed, mineral-solution behaviour comparisons are best restricted to simplified geochemical environments. As more environments are carefully investigated the rules for behaviour will be more clearly defined.

Precipitation reactions. *Silicon.* The silica ion (Si^{4+}) is a good example of a very small cation with a high charge. Unhydrated silica ion is unknown in freshwaters because it will dissociate water as

$$Si^{4+} \quad + \quad 4H_2O \rightarrow Si(OH)_4 \quad + \quad 4H^+.$$

| silica ion | water | hydrated silica | hydrogen ion |

There is a competition between Si^{4+} and H$^+$ for oxygen ion (O^{2-}). Silica ion is larger than hydrogen ion but has four positive charges. At low pH values for waters, wherein the H$^+$ activity is high, the Si^{4+} competes successfully for hydroxide ion (OH$^-$). Only at high pH values, above pH 9.6 and 12, where H$^+$ activity is low, is the hydrated silica, Si(OH)$_4$, ionized to yield hydrogen ion (H$^+$) and Si(OH)$_3^-$ or Si(OH)$_2^{2-}$. In most freshwater, silica ion is tightly bound (or coordinated) to hydroxide ion. In most silicate minerals, silicon (Si^{4+}) is in tetrahedral (fourfold) coordination with oxygen (O^{2-}), as SiO$_4^{4-}$ tetrahedral groups form much of the structure. The ionic bonds of Si^{4+} with OH$^-$ and with O^{2-} are both very strong because of the high charge and small size of the silicon ion. Consequently, compounds containing Si^{4+} undergo sluggish and asymmetrical reactions. The difficulty of breaking the ionic silicon–oxygen bonds that extend throughout quartz renders the mineral very slow to dissolve. Upon dissolving, the Si promptly transforms into silicic acid, which is precipitated as amorphous, highly hydrated silica instead of quartz. Even when the hydrated silica assumes a crystalline form by taking on an orderly internal arrangement of the ions, it is rarely quartz that results. Usually, the crystalline material has the internal structure of β-cristobalite, a much more open structure than that of quartz. The compositions of freshwaters at saturation with the three forms of silica are quite different at mean annual temperatures of freshwater. Saturation with quartz yields about seven milligrams per litre SiO$_{2(aq)}$, saturation with hydrous β-cristobalite yields about 70 milligrams per litre SiO$_{2(aq)}$, and the amorphous silica hydrate yields approximately 125 milligrams per litre SiO$_{2(aq)}$ at saturation.

Aluminum precipitation. In solution aluminum also tends to associate with water and hydroxide ion. In the case of the aluminum ion, Al^{3+}, with its somewhat larger size, the coordination is sixfold, with the coordinated water molecules or ions forming an octahedral figure. More accommodating than silicon ion, which associates chiefly with the hydroxide, fluorine, and oxygen, aluminum (Al^{3+}) associates with hydroxide ion, water, sulfate ion (SO$_4^{2-}$), and other ions. As in the case of silicon, aluminum tends to coordinate with oxygen in aluminosilicates, but with octahedral (sixfold) coordination. In solution, aluminum tends to be much more hydrated than in the solid. With both a larger size and a smaller charge, aluminum behaves somewhat more regularly and rapidly than silicon; aluminum precipitates tend to crystallize much more rapidly than silicon precipitates. Crystalline aluminum precipitates that form at low pH values tend to be gibbsite [Al(OH)$_3$]; those formed at higher pH values tend to be one or more of the polymorphs the composition of which is AlO(OH). Apparently, the crystalline matter reflects in part the form of the ion in solution. At high pH values the hydrate tends to ionize, and the lower hydrogen ion (H$^+$) content of the ionized hydrate is carried into the solid. If true, then it would follow that at yet higher pH values the anhydrous mineral corundum (Al$_2$O$_3$) should form. It is little wonder that the behaviours of the most common and abundant minerals, the aluminosilicates, are so difficult to predict.

Precipitation of iron. Ferric ion, Fe^{3+}, is larger than Al^{3+} and has a precisely predictable solubility as ferric hydroxide, Fe(OH)$_3$. The precipitation prediction is far more dependable than those for either silicon or aluminum. Thus, as the size increases, behaviour becomes more regular and predictable but still does not approach a minimum state of free-energy change for the least soluble (most stable) minerals. Ferric hydroxide, Fe(OH)$_3$, is far more soluble than the least soluble (most stable) ferric iron oxide: the mineral hematite (Fe$_2$O$_3$). The solubility of Fe(OH)$_3$ is 1,000,000 times the solubility of hematite. Observations of natural environments have shown that if the potential (ΔG) exists to dissolve hematite, the rocks are free of hematite (Fe$_2$O$_3$). At just barely supersaturation, ferric hydroxide, Fe(OH)$_3$, precipitates. Thus, ferric iron (Fe^{3+}) also behaves asymmetrically; Fe(OH)$_3$ readily precipitates, Fe$_2$O$_3$ dissolves. Magnesium ion (Mg^{2+}) is of a lower charge and of about the same size as Fe^{3+}. Because of the lower charge, magnesium ion has much less tendency to form hydroxy precipitates than either Al^{3+} or Fe^{3+}. Magnesium hydroxide, Mg(OH)$_2$, forms in freshwater when the pH is 11 or greater. The potential apparently required for precipitation of Mg(OH)$_2$ is apparently equal to or possibly less than is required for the precipitation of ferric hydroxide, Fe(OH)$_3$. The study of ferrous hydroxide, Fe(OH)$_2$, is complicated by the fact that it precipitates simultaneously with magnesium hydroxide to yield a solid solution, MgFe(OH)$_2$. The waters that yield magnesium hydroxide and ferrous hydroxide in solid solution have less ferrous ion, Fe^{2+}, than magnesium ion, Mg^{2+}, in solution, presumably reflecting the lower solubility of ferrous hydroxide as compared to the solubility of magnesium hydroxide.

Geochemical limitations. If the comparison of precipitation reactions were to proceed, the rarely found mineral portlandite [Ca(OH)$_2$] would be considered. Freshwaters containing calcium ion (Ca^{2+}) and ferrous ion (Fe^{2+}) and the ubiquitous bicarbonate ion (HCO$_3^-$) much more commonly yield siderite (FeCO$_3$) and calcite (CaCO$_3$). The promising comparison of hydroxide-ion and cation relations reaches a natural limit, and a change of grounds is required for comparison of the geochemical behaviour of the cations. In spite of the larger size of Ca^{2+} compared to Fe^{2+}, siderite and calcite precipitate and dissolve with about the same change in free-energy values. Another geochemical limitation is that the freshwater must contain no dissolved oxygen if ferrous and calcium ions are to be compared. Dissolved oxygen and ferrous ion (Fe^{2+}) are incompatible, and the behaviour of ferric hydrate, Fe(OH)$_3$, may not be compared to the behaviour of calcite, CaCO$_3$, on common grounds. Although it is helpful to compare cation reactions on the base of charge–size relations, the nature of the anions must be taken into account.

In solutions free of dissolved oxygen, sulfide is often found as either dissolved hydrogen sulfide, H$_2$S, or bisulfide, HS$^-$. As an approximation, the H$_2$S–HS$^-$ distribution may be taken to be the same as the hydrogen-ion and hydroxide-ion (H$^+$–OH$^-$) distribution. Neutral pH values (near 7) yield about equal amounts of H$_2$S$_{(aq)}$ and HS$^-$. Acid solutions (pH less than 7) have

Competition between ions (margin note)

Predictability of behaviour of ferric ion (margin note)

more H_2S than HS^-, and basic solutions (pH more than 7) have more HS^- than H_2S. The behaviour of pyrite (FeS_2) has been observed on the same grounds as ferric hydroxide, $Fe(OH)_3$. For the reaction

$$Fe^{+2} \;+\; 2H_2S \;\rightarrow\; FeS_2 \;+\; 4H^+ \;+\; 2e^-,$$
ferrous   hydrogen   pyrite   hydrogen electron
ion   sulfide   ion

in which the ferrous ion is oxidized with the loss of two electrons and pyrite is precipitated, enormous supersaturations have been found, without observable precipitation of the common mineral pyrite (FeS_2). The nature of dissolved H_2S accounts for the lack of predictability. In the absence of hydrogen sulfide, the reactions between water and ferrous ion, resulting in ferrous hydroxide precipitation, and between water and pyrite, in which pyrite is dissolved, are very near to equilibrium as observations have shown. The behaviour of hydrogen sulfide is also revealed in studies of cupric sulfide (CuS) and cuprous sulfide (Cu_2S). Observations have shown that the reactions yielding cupric sulfide and cuprous sulfide are as far from equilibrium as that yielding pyrite, FeS_2.

Bacterial reduction. A common origin of hydrogen sulfide (H_2S) and bisulfide (HS^-) in freshwaters is bacterial reduction of sulfate ion, SO_4^{2-}. Organic material is commonly incorporated in sediments and may survive for geologic time. A number of reactions may occur as freshwater passes through such sediments. Oxygen is lost from solution as the organic matter oxidizes. Depending upon flow rates and the reaction rates of the organic material, the decrease in dissolved oxygen may be quite abrupt; concentrations may fall from saturation with air (approximately ten milligrams per litre) to below detection (less than 0.01 milligram per litre) within a few centimetres. As the dissolved oxygen, $O_{2(aq)}$, drops below detection, the ferric ion, Fe^{3+}, of the limonite minerals ($FeOOH$) is reduced to yield ferrous ion, Fe^{2+}. From oxidation of the organic matter, whether by dissolved oxygen, $O_{2(aq)}$, or by ferric hydroxide, $Fe(OH)_3$, carbon dioxide, CO_2, is produced. Rising carbon dioxide and ferrous-ion concentrations may cause the solubility control on Fe^{2+} to pass from ferric hydroxide, $Fe(OH)_3$, to siderite, $FeCO_3$. Sulfate may be reduced by bacteria on the surface of the organic material as in the reaction

$$2H^+ \;+\; SO_4^{2-} \;+\; 2C \;=\; H_2S \;+\; 2CO_2.$$
hydrogen sulfate carbon hydrogen carbon
ion   ion   sulfide   dioxide

There is a consumption of hydrogen ion and a tendency for a pH increase. The pH rise is in part offset by the carbon dioxide, which ionizes. Generally, freshwaters are so well buffered that large pH increases resulting from sulfate-ion reduction do not occur. The rise in hydrogen sulfide concentrations may greatly supersaturate the water with respect to metal sulfide minerals. Enormous supersaturations are needed to precipitate sulfide minerals.

Pyrite often is found as a surface-coating on the organic matter in sedimentary rocks. There is a large energy difference between sulfate ion, SO_4^{2-}, and organic matter, and bacteria utilize part of the available energy in their life processes. The bacterial wastes provide the highest sulfide concentrations along the boundary between the organic matter and the water, and the sulfides, chiefly pyrite, form there.

Changes in water character. The dissolved oxygen-free water may flow for long distances without changing its character. It may flow parallel to water containing dissolved oxygen, $O_{2(aq)}$, in which case the two waters will react along the boundary, yielding limonite cements. In the course of time, the reduced (oxyen-free) waters will discharge into an aerobic (oxygen-containing) environment, and oxidation reactions will quite rapidly change the character of the solutions. If hydrogen sulfide (H_2S) is present, organisms utilize part of the change in free energy that results from the incompatibility of $H_2S_{(aq)}$ and oxygen, $O_{2(aq)}$. In channels with rapid flow, very pale yellow growths attached to the bed are common indicators of biologic hydrogen sulfide oxidation; in more sluggish reaches or quiescent pools, jet-black organisms may dominate. In any event, the hydrogen sulfide (H_2S) is oxidized to sulfate ion (SO_4^{2-}) or to native sulfur. Ferrous ion, Fe^{2+}, is oxidized to ferric hydroxide, $Fe(OH)_3$, by organisms. A common observation in swampy areas is an iridescent "oil" film on the water surface. If the film remains broken when disturbed, it is a very thin film of $Fe(OH)_3$. Oil films rapidly coalesce after being disturbed.

The oxidation reactions may produce quite low pH values. Both hydrogen sulfide and ferrous-ion reactions yield hydrogen ion (H^+):

$$H_2S \;+\; 2O_2(aq) \;\rightarrow\; SO_4^{2-} \;+\; 2H^+$$
hydrogen oxygen   sulfate ion hydrogen
ion   ion

and

$$4Fe^{2+} \;+\; O_2(aq) \;+\; 10H_2O \;\rightarrow\; 4Fe(OH)_3 \;+\; 8H^+.$$
ferrous oxygen water   ferric   hydrogen
ion   hydroxide ion

In addition, the organisms that oxidize the Fe^{2+} live attached to the stream bed and may smother other bottom-dwelling organisms. The high H^+ concentrations may prove toxic to some aquatic organisms.

The variations in dissolved oxygen content of freshwater may interrupt the transport of sulfur, iron, oxygen, carbon dioxide, and other species. Usually, the reactions occur at the boundaries between different environments. The distance over which the reactions are spread depends on the rate of the chemical reaction and the rate of flow of the water. Generally, groundwater flows are sluggish and boundaries of geochemical environments tend to be abrupt. Surface-water flow in channels may be fast enough to spread reactions over distances as great as kilometres. It should be noted that none of the discontinuities in transport of ions has required a phase change of the water. Neither evaporation nor freezing is required to deposit any of the minerals described.

Calcite (calcium carbonate) undergoes discontinuous transport in three rather common ways. In temperate or tropical regions of low rainfall, soils may be quite dry. Permeability decreases with decreasing moisture content. Precipitation falling on such a dry soil may not penetrate to the groundwater body before being withdrawn by transpiration and evaporation. When there is evaporation, the nonvolatile solutes accumulate. Widespread accumulations of calcite in layers below the soil surface in temperate or tropical regions of low precipitation are evidence of subsurface evaporation caused by a steep temperature gradient.

A second type of calcite deposition occurs because of carbon dioxide losses. As a result of plant-root respiration, CO_2 contents of waters below the surface may be much higher than would be found at saturation with air; waters of high carbon dioxide content may be saturated (*i.e.*, may hold the maximum equilibrium quantity of dissolved matter). Upon emergence of the water onto the land surface, algal photosynthesis reduces the CO_2 content and drives the solution supersaturated, often to the extent of precipitating calcite. A third situation has been described in which water in a channel is rich in carbonate ion (CO_3^{2-}), but groundwater entering from below the bed is rich in calcium ion (Ca^{2+}). In the dispersion zone between the two waters, calcite precipitates. In all three cases, free-energy values rise to the point at which calcite, $CaCO_3$, deposits are formed.

BIBLIOGRAPHY. The important geochemical aspects of freshwaters are illustrated in the following works: JOHN D. HEM, "Study and Interpretation of the Chemical Characteristics of Natural Water," *Wat. Supply Pap., Wash. 1473* (1970); IVAN BARNES and FRANK E. CLARKE, "Chemical Properties of Ground Water and Their Corrosion and Encrustation Effects on Wells," *Prof. Pap. U.S. Geol. Surv. 498–D* (1969); ARLO W. GAMBELL and DONALD W. FISHER, "Chemical Composition of Rainfall, Eastern North Carolina and Southeastern Virginia," *Wat. Supply Pap., Wash. 1535–K* (1966);

Oxygen losses

Oxidation and water acidity

G. EVELYN HUTCHINSON, *A Treatise on Limnology*, vol. 1, *Geography, Physics and Chemistry* (1957).

(I.B.)

Freud, Sigmund

As a physician who specialized in treating the mentally ill, Sigmund Freud developed a comprehensive theory concerning the psychological structure and functioning of the human mind. He demonstrated that many illnesses with no apparent organic explanation could be treated by psychiatry or psychoanalysis. He identified and explored hidden motivations in the subconscious mind, and he perfected psychoanalytic techniques for analyzing the development and functioning of both normal and abnormal behaviour. His original and often controversial ideas have had wide applications—even beyond psychiatry—in understanding processes of artistic creation, education, and political conduct.

By courtesy of Mrs. Ernst L. Freud

Freud, 1938.

EARLY LIFE

Freud was born on May 6, 1856, in Freiberg, Moravia (now Příbor, Czechoslovakia). Ernest Jones, the English analyst who became Freud's biographer, has declared that Freud inherited "his sense of humour, his shrewd skepticism . . . his custom of pointing a moral by quoting a Jewish anecdote, his liberalism, and free thinking," from his father, who was a wool merchant. Freud claimed that he drew his "sentimentality" or "temperament" from his mother. According to Jones, Freud's intellect "was his own."

Significant childhood events. Four childhood events always stood out in Freud's memory. Before the birth of his younger brother Julius, he had had the almost exclusive love of his mother, but after the birth he admitted having had evil wishes against Julius, who suddenly died at the age of only eight months. Freud later viewed the death as a fulfillment of his evil thoughts, thereby beginning a lifelong tendency to self-reproach. Years later he wrote that he had been sexually aroused by seeing his mother naked, an event to reverberate years afterward in *Three Essays on the Theory of Sexuality*. Thus two of the problems that were to preoccupy him throughout his psychoanalytic career entered his actual experience at a time when he could not understand their true significance. First came early family conflicts between parents and children, and second, the existence of infantile sexuality.

On another occasion he recollected having deliberately urinated in his parents' bedroom at the age of seven or eight, prompting his father to remark: "That boy will never amount to anything." Beginning at an early age, allusions to this scene, accompanied by demonstrations of actual "accomplishments and successes," constantly recurred in dreams.

The fourth powerful memory destined to haunt Freud was based on his father's account of the Gentile who knocked his new fur cap into the gutter one day and shouted: "Jew—get off the pavement." When the 12-year-old boy inquired of his father how he reacted to such treatment, he replied: "I stepped into the gutter and picked up my cap." The remark permanently damaged the father's image in the boy's eyes.

Education. At nine years of age Freud entered high school (Sperl Gymnasium), quickly became head of his class, and graduated summa cum laude. Traditionally, the choice of a career for a Viennese Jew was limited to four fields—law, medicine, industry, or business—but none of these appealed to Freud, whose intense intellectual abilities had quickly become clear. Deeply impressed by Charles Darwin and his theory of natural selection, he could not at first quite reconcile his work with his own cultural and philosophic aspirations. A public reading of Goethe's *Ode to Nature* resolved his dilemma, but he became a medical student primarily to gain knowledge about human nature, not to alleviate suffering.

After he entered the University of Vienna in 1873 at the age of 17, Freud's attention was directed into correlative fields, including a seminar in philosophy. Freud later wrote:

Medical studies

> During my first three years at the University I was compelled to make the discovery that the peculiarities and limitations of my gifts denied me all success in many of the departments of science into which my youthful eagerness had plunged me.

At length he found a congenial place in the physiology laboratory of Ernst Brücke, who agreed with the view advanced by the German physicist Hermann Helmholtz that "no other forces than the common physical chemical ones are active within the organism." Freud's first excursion into psychological theorizing may have begun when he met Jean Charcot, the French neurologist, but the principles from which he later constructed his system were acquired as a medical student in the Brücke Institute. There, he did original research that clearly indicated his brilliance. According to Freud, he passed his medical examinations with excellent grades because his photographic memory enabled him to give verbatim answers directly from textbooks.

Meanwhile, the young man who seemed to thrive on work suddenly found his professional life seriously disturbed by an experience that would not surrender to the rigorous control he exercised over the other aspects of his life—he fell in love. By the summer of 1882, Martha Bernays had not only spoken of her own feelings for him but indicated that expectations of marriage were not out of place. Freud then decided to abandon science and enter the General Hospital of Vienna in order to qualify for private practice, from which he might hope to support a wife. In the course of his betrothal Freud wrote more than 900 letters to Martha, some of them warm love letters entirely at variance with the common image of him as a cold, scientific man. But poverty delayed the marriage year after year.

Freud next served for a few months in Nothnagel's division of internal medicine in Vienna. On October 12th, 1882, he joined the staff of Theodor Meynert's psychiatric clinic, where he was at once appointed *Sekundararzt* ("assistant physician"). He regarded Meynert as a brilliant anatomist of the brain and a reasonably good psychiatrist. A disorder, then known as Meynert's Amentia (hallucinatory psychosis), gave Freud the first hint of a hypothesis he later developed, the so-called wish fulfillment mechanism, which was to play an important part in his major work *The Interpretation of Dreams*.

The years from 1883 to 1885 were rich in success. He finished important research on the medulla, a region of the brain; became a *Privatdozent* ("lecturer") in Neuropathology, made discoveries on the physiological effects of the drug cocaine; and met Charcot, who dominated the world of neurology in the Salpêtrière Hospital in Paris.

Marriage. On the point of discovering the anesthetic properties of cocaine in Vienna in 1885, Freud had the opportunity to visit his fiancée, Martha Bernays, whom he had not seen for two years. He hastily wrote a brief monograph summarizing his research on cocaine and hurried to meet her. Simultaneously he wrote to an eminent German ophthalmologist, suggesting an investigation of the anesthetizing properties of cocaine for eye treatment. On returning from a brief visit to Martha, he found that decisive experiments had empirically confirmed his speculations—but that they had been done by another scientist.

Between 1882 and 1886 occurred a number of stormy scenes with Martha, the climax to which came when he asked her to denounce her brother as a scoundrel because of his alleged misuse of her funds. This unhappy event suggests the tumultuous passions that often stirred his life, in contrast to the calm, scientific person he is often supposed to have been. He married Martha in 1886, with full confidence in the future well-being of his family. Similar hopes were not at once fulfilled in his private practice, however. In 1890, as the newlyweds continued to suffer from poverty, money began to play a special role in Freud's life. By now a man of 35, he had grown into a person the power of whose presence created the illusion of height in his personality, but he was barely five feet seven inches in height. His fine moustache and intelligent eyes gave a certain flair to his appearance. Several references in his writings show his special need for either a loved friend or hated enemy. Despite his reputation as a cantankerous individual, the general trend of his moods was quite different. He could love and hate with equal passion, and, although he did not set out to charm or please, many who met him did not find him at all a difficult person.

Appear-ance and person-ality (margin)

CAREER

Development of psychoanalysis. *The role of Anna O., Josef Breuer, and Charcot.* Freud's important relationship with Breuer, the Viennese physician and physiologist, began in 1882. Breuer had treated a 21-year-old girl who had developed complex psychosomatic symptoms after the death of her father. This patient became famous in psychoanalytic history as Fraulein Anna O. After her father's death, Anna's sight and speech were seriously disturbed, her limbs frequently became paralyzed, and she recoiled from food. She could change with remarkable facility from relatively normal behaviour into the role of a recalcitrant child with alarming symptoms—a now familiar case of hysteria. Once, while the girl related to Breuer the details of one severe episode, he observed, to his astonishment, that the symptoms gradually disappeared. Breuer then supplemented his procedure by inducing hypnosis, and the results were, for a time, startlingly successful. Freud discussed the details of the case "over and over again" with Breuer. In 1885 Freud travelled to Paris for his famous encounter with Charcot, whom he tried to interest in "the talking cure," as the patient had nicknamed it, but Charcot seemed preoccupied with other matters.

The encounter proved salutary, however, for Charcot demonstrated that he could use hypnosis to induce such conditions as tremors, paralysis, anesthesia, and many other symptoms of spontaneous hysteria. In effect, Charcot's demonstrations meant that the symptoms of hysteria could be removed by thought alone and that there thus must be a powerful psychogenic factor in their origin. Later, Freud formulated the principle that "hysterical symptoms originate through the energy of the mental process being withheld from conscious influence and being diverted into bodily innervation (conversion)."

Psychoanalytic technique. In 1893 Breuer and Freud published "The Psychical Mechanism of Hysterical Phenomena" and expanded it two years later into *Studies in Hysteria.* The joint paper is the opening chapter of the book, followed by five case histories, a theoretical essay by Breuer, and a final chapter by Freud. Historically this book marked the beginning of psychoanalysis, but it was not well received in the medical world, and it was denounced in particular by the German neurologist Adolph von Strümpell, whose review so disturbed Breuer

that it permanently undermined his confidence in his own theory.

Freud had already developed the technique of free association and was gradually abandoning the old process of hypnosis. The first steps toward free association consisted in getting the patient to concentrate on a particular symptom while "attempting to recall any memories that might throw light on its origin." From a difficult, long period of refinement of hypnosis, questioning, and suggestion emerged a new technique between the years 1892 and 1895. Simultaneously, Freud's remarkable relationship with Wilhelm Fliess continued to develop. Fliess was a nose and throat specialist whose powers of bold speculation about the nature of the human psyche had already strongly attracted Freud. By 1894 they were corresponding with one another.

Jones later wrote that Freud now acted out his love–hate relationship with his father with a number of people—Fliess among them. First, he was obliged to leave his famous teacher Brücke; then, Meynert withdrew because he could not countenance Freud's growing interest in hysteria and hypnotism.

Toward the end of the 1880s, Breuer found himself unable to share Freud's growing preoccupation with sexual etiology. If Breuer and Fliess both held Helmholtz' view that the medical sciences "should aim to describe their findings in terms of physics," Fliess, unlike Breuer, did not recoil from sexuality as a basis of human behaviour. Indeed, it slowly became the core of his work. Thus, for a time, Fliess and Freud shared intellectual excitements and corresponded at length, exploring one hypothesis after another. Freud developed an exaggerated reverence for Fliess's powers and came to treat him as mentor, father figure, and passionate friend, but this relationship broke down in the end. It should be emphasized that Freud, at this stage, was a very different person from the highly independent man who dominated what came to be called the "Psychological Wednesday Circle" in Vienna with such inflexible purpose and creative power.

Early work on sexual psycho-pathology (margin)

Turning away from clinical neurology, Freud developed a deepening interest in clinical psychopathology. Patient after patient slowly convinced him that sexual etiology played a powerful role in many forms of neurosis. "With previously healthy men an anxiety neurosis is rooted in abstinence: with women it occurs mostly through coitus interruptus," he wrote. Thirteen fully analyzed cases amply substantiated what he meant: "the cause of hysteria is a passive sexual experience before puberty: *i.e.*, a traumatic seduction." Time and again patients made the remarkable statement that one parent had attempted or achieved their seduction as children. Freud then made another discovery—that these childhood seductions had in fact never occurred, but were at first fantasies, and then the reversal of a desired role.

The year 1897 was significant in many respects, not the least of which was because Freud then began to analyze himself—what many analysts today regard as an impossible feat. During most of the 1890s he himself suffered from a powerful psychoneurosis. His self-analysis not only threw him into the expected turmoil but also offered a new solution to the puzzle of childhood seduction. After observing a number of hysterical symptoms in his brother and several sisters, he concluded that even his own father might not have been free of "incestuous incrimination." Six months' further work suddenly revealed the solution: the incestuous impulse certainly arises and is sometimes fulfilled by parents, but much more widespread and representative are the wishes of children to sleep with parents of the opposite sex. The concept of the so-called Oedipal complex thus began to take form.

Self-analysis (margin)

In the same year (1897), he discussed in his correspondence the importance of dreams in psychoanalysis: they contain "the psychology of the neuroses in a nutshell."

Influence of home life and lecturing. The Bergasse, where Freud lived, opened off Vienna's historic junk market, the Tandelmarkt, and ended at the Votivkirche, the Gothic cathedral that dominates one of the most ornamental squares of Vienna. The ground floor included a butcher's shop; on one side of the entrance a name plate read "Prof. Dr. Sigm. Freud," and on the other was the plate of the butcher, whose first name was also Sigmund. Freud had been forced by his growing family to rent a second flat in the house. One of the three rooms was the patients' waiting room, a second the consulting room, and a third the study, later to become famous in

the literature. Six children were born to the Freuds in their first home, three daughters, Mathilde, Sophie, and Anna, and three sons named Jean Martin after Charcot, Oliver after Cromwell, and Ernst after Brücke. Freud remarked in a letter to Fliess that he spent a considerable amount of his life either with patients in the ground-floor flat or rushing up the stone steps that led to the mezzanine floor to visit with his family. He was devoted to his children and took an active part in their upbringing. That he had time for leisure in his very full life seems remarkable, but when he managed to relax, he played chess, patience, or the Viennese card game of Tarok. Occasionally he attended the theatre, but only the music of Mozart lured him to the opera. Still suffering from professional ostracism in many quarters, Freud joined the B'nai B'rith Society, or Jewish Club. His interest in antiquities simultaneously satisfied his fascination with the beginnings of civilization and his aesthetic sense.

By 1900 Freud was a seasoned lecturer. Fritz Wittels, a doctor-teacher-writer who belonged to the early group of Freud's followers, gave a vivid description of one occasion at the Psychiatric Clinic of the General Hospital, where Freud spoke without notes for 60 minutes to a small audience, which appeared to "hang on his words." Wittels recalled:

> His black hair, slightly grizzled, was smooth and parted on the left side. His beard was small and trimmed to a fine point. . . . His eyes were dark brown and lustrous and made a quick penetrating scrutiny of anyone who asked questions.

One other characteristic stood out in Wittels' memory—the student's stoop in his figure. Freud lectured that particular day on the shortcomings of traditional psychology as taught by Wilhelm Wundt and remarked that the old psychology had since been killed by his own new dream doctrine. According to Freud, Wundt, in continuing to follow outdated theories, was rather like the giant in Ariosto's *Orlando Furioso* who went on fighting even though his head had been cut off.

"The Interpretation of Dreams." *Preparation.* Between 1895 and 1899 Freud was deeply engrossed in researching and writing what is generally regarded as his major work, *The Interpretation of Dreams.* To Fliess on February 2, 1899, he wrote of work "to which every effort of thought has to be given . . . which gradually absorbs all other capacities . . . a sort of neoplastic substance that infiltrates into one's humanity and then replaces it." Freud, who was most at ease when he was busiest, declared that "I get on best when there is a great deal of work." He also needed a "moderate amount of misery" before he could work at full pitch. Of *The Interpretation of Dreams* he wrote, "My style in it was bad because I was feeling too well physically."

Freud worked on *The Interpretation of Dreams* while he continued his self-analysis in the years 1898 and 1899. He had many fluctuations of mood, but on March 10,

1898, in a letter to Fliess, he outlined one of the main themes of the book:

> It seems to me that the theory of wish fulfillment gives us only the psychological solution—not the biological. . . . It seems to me that biologically the dream life proceeds altogether from the relics of the prehistoric period. . . . I surmise the formula: what was seen in that prehistoric period gives rise to dreams: what was heard to phantasies: what was sexually experienced to psychoneuroses.

Bursts of writing, when the book ran smoothly, were often followed by periods of frustration and doubt. In May 1898 he commented that the book was probably "the only one of my discoveries which may survive me," but by June "the whole matter resolves itself into a platitude." There were long unhappy hours when the thought of leaving to the world such a book was a tremendous "consolation," and times when he wrote rapidly

"as if in a dream." Approaching with trepidation the last chapter, in which he was to describe the psychology of the dream processes, Freud wrote it as if the chapter were itself a dream to which he had surrendered himself.

The constancy principle. *The Interpretation of Dreams* is regarded as Freud's most original work, because in it he brilliantly analyzed the dream mechanisms of condensation, displacement, and secondary elaboration and discussed the latent content of dreams; explained the principle of wish fulfillment; described the Oedipal complex; and showed the overwhelming influence of infantile life in conditioning the human adult. Dream mechanisms condensed one subject into another, displaced one person on to another, and elaborated what sometimes turned out with cunning detail. Dreams also were seen, at this stage of his theory, as attempts to fulfill a wish. The Oedipal complex involved the emotional sexual complications between parents and children. The seventh chapter also gave Freud's fullest exposition of his theory of the mind. Between the time he wrote the "Project for a Scientific Psychology" in 1885 and *The Interpretation of Dreams,* Freud constantly refined this theory. The working principle of his model is that of "neuronic inertia," or the constancy principle, according to which the apparatus works toward the reduction of any tension that can be identified with an accumulation of "energy," variously interpreted as sexual or psychic. The primary functions are complicated by both internal and external stimulations, but the constancy-principle model describes memory formation in terms of two different classes of neurones. The secondary function of the mind is not to eliminate tensions but to maintain an optimum tension that tends toward its lowest possible level.

Six hundred copies of *The Interpretation of Dreams* were printed, and review copies were circulated. According to Jones, few scientific or general journals attempted anything resembling a serious review, although Henri S. Ellenberger, in the *Discovery of the Unconscious,* states that *The Interpretation of Dreams* had some ten reviews in learned journals within a year of publication, only one of which was unfavourable. In the first six weeks, only 123 copies were sold and another 228 in the following two years. But his work was no longer ignored.

The Psychological Wednesday Circle. The beginnings of the Vienna Psycho-Analytical Society can be traced to the year 1902, when Freud sent postcards to four comparatively unknown men, suggesting that they might organize a small group at his home once a week to discuss psychoanalytic matters. These four men were Alfred Adler, Max Kahane, Rudolf Reitler, and Wilhelm Stekel; with Freud and occasional visitors they became known as the Psychological Wednesday Circle.

Although a certain careful deliberation had entered into the conception of the Psychological Wednesday Circle, its meetings, in practice, were casual. After supper a varying number of doctors and professional men would gather around the table in Freud's waiting room to await his brisk entrance. Through the open study door it was possible to see the famous couch with the armchair, the collection of statuettes and the book-lined walls. Mrs. Freud always served cigars and black coffee before the meeting began. Freud, a heavy smoker, sometimes consumed as many as 20 cigars a day. When Freud presented a paper to the circle he would, according to Wittels, "enunciate his main contentions categorically so that they were apt to repel," but the charm of his exegesis quickly modified early resistances. Wittels stated that Freud desired "to have his own thoughts passed through the filter of other trained intelligences," and immediately qualified that statement by saying that "he wanted to look into the kaleidoscope lined with mirrors that would multiply the images he introduced into it." The Wednesday Circle slowly grew from five members in 1902 to 22 in 1908, among them Carl Jung, who was destined to become Freud's chief rival. The group developed into the Vienna Psycho-Analytical Society (1908), which in turn became The International Psycho-Analytical Association (1910). His fame rapidly spreading throughout Europe,

Freud in 1908 was invited by G. Stanley Hall, the president of Clark University, to give a course of lectures in America. The tour, which took place in 1909, was moderately successful.

Private practice. Freud returned in 1910 to Vienna, where his life was once again filled with work. Because he sometimes wrote late at night, he arose with difficulty early in the morning at 7 o'clock. After a quick breakfast and a glance at the newspaper, he was ready for his first patient at 8 o'clock. Infallibly punctual, he gave each patient exactly 55 minutes. After a five-minute interval, when he might rush into the family flat to communicate briefly with his wife, he was ready for the next patient. Lunch at 1 o'clock usually became a family affair with the children present; his frequent taciturnity and silence were the cause of embarrassment when guests were present. After lunch he felt free to walk, shop, and buy his favourite cigars until the precise hour of three, when he donned his professional frock coat. Therapeutic work then continued without a break until nine or 10 in the evening. Surprisingly, he sometimes found it difficult to keep professional confidences.

Two patients, James Strachey and his wife, had undertaken an unusual joint analysis, Mr. Strachey visiting Freud in the mornings and his wife in the afternoons. At the conscious level, Mrs. Strachey found Freud to be a simpleminded, rather gullible man, with a conventional outlook, no intellectual intolerance in his makeup, and almost too ready to respond to ideas. He made two startling statements to her: "I don't really think I'm a frightfully good analyst—I'm too impatient," and "The greatest invention some benefactor can give mankind is a form of contraception which doesn't induce neurosis."

Reacting against rumours of disturbances in Freud's family life, Jones, in his official biography, may have exaggerated the extent of family harmony. However, the suggestion is false that his sister-in-law, known as Tante Minna, replaced his wife in his emotional life, although she certainly understood Freud's work better than his wife did and must have shared his intellectual life in much greater depth. Although Jones draws an idealized picture of Freud the family man, it is certainly true that Freud allowed his children to develop freely at a time when very austere systems of upbringing were commonplace.

His writing habits varied. Instead of planning to write a certain number of words at one session, he would wait until "the spirit moved him," but a painful struggle to write even three lines might then ensue, or there might be a spontaneous flow that produced an important paper within a few weeks. Freud's writing, whenever it occurred, was not continuous but had to be fitted into his analytic work.

Writing habits

Prolonged feuds and quarrels caused successive defections from the Psycho-Analytical Society. They began as early as 1908 and throw many sidelights on the complicated characters of the men involved, including Freud. By then Freud had written several more important works, including *Psychopathology of Everyday Life* (1904); *Jokes and Their Relation with the Unconscious* (1905); and his *Three Essays on the Theory of Sexuality* (1905), which brought dismay to the medical world. He analyzed what he had learned from patients about their sexual development in earliest childhood, and he dared to suggest not only that children were subject to sexual urges but also that those urges frequently involved their parents.

Another shock for the medical world was the publication of the Dora analysis, "Fragments of an Analysis of a Case of Hysteria," which described a young girl with tendencies toward sexual perversions and was published without her permission (Dora was a cover name).

Break-up of the Wednesday Circle. By 1911 differences within the International Psycho-Analytical Association had become serious, and one founding member after another resigned or left the circle. It was as if every member, inspired by Freud, desired to match or challenge his creative outpourings. Adler, for example, developed a breakaway school, which differed in three major points from Freud's: (1) that regression was not a motivating force in neurosis; (2) that patients experienced inferiority feelings in connection with certain organs; and (3) that some patients feared the feminine role and reacted with a "masculine protest."

In her biography of Adler, Phyllis Bottome wrote that Freud, jealous of his brilliant and ambitious younger colleague, may have been responsible for setting in motion the persecution of Adler that followed. There is, of course, considerable doubt that Freud followed such a course. His friends claimed that during the long period of wrangling and resignations, he was driven by one dominating motive—to establish conditions that would preserve for the future the purity of psychoanalytic practice as he saw it. This involved the acceptance of a minimum number of basic concepts, which included the "existence of unconscious psychical processes, the theory of resistance and repression, the appreciation of the part played by sexuality and the Oedipus complex."

Adler, the first of the early circle to break away, was followed by Stekel, and finally by the man whom Freud had once nominated as the leader of the association, Carl Jung. There was much bitterness on both sides. "So we are at last rid of them," Freud wrote to another devoted member, Karl Abraham, "the brutal sanctimonious Jung and his disciples." Jung claimed that "after my break with Freud all my friends and acquaintances dropped away." As the stresses and tensions subsided, an inner council of trustworthy members of the association was formed and became known as the Committee. Freud presented to each member an antique Greek stone engraving, to be mounted in a gold ring, signifying the close harmony of their intellectual views—a somewhat mystic gesture.

Freud's view of the unconscious

Surprisingly, Freud's first systematic statement about the unconscious was not made until 1912, in response to an invitation from the London Society of Psychical Research for a contribution to its *Proceedings*. Freud stated: "We obtain our concept of the unconscious from the theory of repression." Thus when a thought was repressed out of consciousness, it remained in the mind unconsciously. In those days he freely acknowledged the source of a number of his hypotheses, and there is no doubt that the idea of an unconscious was a familiar one in the 19th century; *e.g.,* Eduard von Hartmann's book *The Philosophy of the Unconscious* (1893). Freud wrote *Totem and Taboo* in 1913 and *A General Introduction to Psychoanalysis* in 1915–16.

Freud suffered severe hardships during World War I. In 1917 he noticed a worsening of a painful swelling in the palate of his mouth, a symptom unmistakably connected with cigar smoking.

His next important book, *Beyond the Pleasure Principle* (1920), seemed to leave the limitations of biology to enter the field of transcendental metapsychology. He restated his belief in both the pleasure–unpleasure principle and homeostasis. The pleasure–unpleasure principle involved the process of adjustment from the pleasure-seeking impulses to the harsh realities of the external world. Homeostasis was the mental activity that attempted to reduce tensions to the lowest possible level. In formulating the theory of repetition compulsion—the drive to repeat fixed patterns of behaviour—he came to the conclusion that the fundamental aim of all instincts is to revert to an earlier state.

FINAL YEARS

Preservation of harmony within the Committee was very important to Freud, but by 1923 serious dissension once again brought it almost to the point of disintegration. In the same year the first serious signs of the disease that was to kill him became apparent. In a letter he wrote to Jones dated April 25, he said: "I detected two months ago a leucoplastic growth on my jaw and palate right side . . . I am still out of work and cannot swallow." Freud later consulted Marcus Hajek, a leading rhinologist, who advised a "very slight operation." Without telling his family, Freud went to Hajek's clinic, and shortly afterward he sat in the outpatient department of the clinic with blood all over his clothes, a man grimly determined not to utter a word of complaint. As Jones wrote: "The operation had not gone as expected." Only at this point did he allow his family to be informed. This was the first of 33 operations, all of which Freud bore with stoical fortitude. He made a pact with his daughter Anna that they should view his illness with cool detachment and no sentiment. Only minor concessions were made to the pact.

Notwithstanding his medical condition, he continued to publish important books. In *The Ego and the Id* (1923), he discussed further his tripartite division of the mind into id, ego, and superego. He conceived of the id as the reservoir of the instinctive impulses; the ego as a portion of the id influenced by the external world; and the superego as "the inhibitions of instinct characteristic of man." In *The Future of an Illusion*, Freud, in 1927, speculated philosophically on the nature of man, religion, and God, much to the displeasure of those who believed his undoubted erudition in psychoanalysis did not qualify him for philosophy.

Although he rejected any belief in God or an afterlife, he remained what many people called a cheerful pessimist. As his illusions slipped away in his last years, however, he gradually became a pessimistic realist. This view was confirmed by the arrival of the Nazis in Vienna in 1938. Jones had great difficulty in persuading him to leave the city, partly because he was a very sick man. Jones pointed out to him that he was not alone in the world, and that his life was very dear to many people. But Freud replied: "Alone—ah, if I were only alone I should long ago have done with life." When the Nazis actually entered his house and attempted to loot his private safe, his frail figure, white-haired and gaunt, suddenly appeared in the doorway with his eyes blazing. Even the Nazis were momentarily intimidated. At last he made the exhausting journey to England and settled into a house in London.

The cancer slowly ate its way through his cheek, and, although life became for him a long torment of pain and discomfort, he bore it with incredible stoicism. A huge prosthesis designed to shut off the mouth from the nasal cavity had become necessary, and as a result Freud's speech became thick and blurred. At last, on September 21, 1939, he said to his doctor: "My dear Schur . . . you promised me you would help me when I could no longer carry on." Schur gave him "adequate sedation," and Freud sighed with relief and fell into his last sleep just before midnight on September 23, in London.

Assessment   Freud spent most of his life refining and elaborating the brilliant theories by which he reinterpreted the nature of the human psyche. But if he had wanted his basic concepts to remain as immutable as Moses' tablets, he would be a disappointed man today. Wilhelm Reich, Karen Horney, Erich Fromm, Melanie Klein, and R.D. Laing have revised or further developed his main ideas. Moreover, serious qualifications of the sexual etiology of human behaviour have been put forward. The power of socio-economic factors in the formation of human personality and the growth of doubt about the exact relation between nature and nurture have blurred theories he once thought to be clear and distinct. Perhaps the most extreme criticisms have come from an essay entitled "What Is Wrong with Psycho-analysis?" The author, H.J. Epenck, points to the distinction German philosophers have made between *verstehende* psychology, or common-sense psychology, which tries to understand human beings, and *erklärende* psychology, which seeks a scientific description and explanation of behaviour. He states that psychoanalysis belongs to the first category—*i.e.*, it is essentially nonscientific—and, in the last analysis, is a matter of faith rather than proof. He also doubts its therapeutic value. These criticisms do not in any way diminish the stature of Freud, whose brilliant theories, therapeutic techniques, and profound insights into the submerged areas of the human psyche opened up a whole new field of psychological study. He was an original thinker who radically altered prevailing views of human nature.

MAJOR WORKS

With J. Breuer, *Studien über Hysterie* (1895; *Studies in Hysteria*, 1955); *Die Traumdeutung* (1899, dated 1900; *The Interpretation of Dreams*, 1953); *Zur Psychopathologie des Alltagslebens* (1904; *Psychopathology of Everyday Life*, 1960); *Drei Abhandlungen zur Sexualtheorie* (1905; *Three Essays on the Theory of Sexuality*, 1953); *Über Psychoanalyse* (1910; *The Origin and Development of Psycho-Analysis*, 1955); *Totem und Tabu* (1913; *Totem and Taboo*, 1955); *Zur Geschichte der psychoanalytischen Bewegung* (1914; *On the History of the Psychoanalytic Movement*, 1957); *Vorlesungen zur Einführung in die Psychoanalyse* (1917; *A General Introduction to Psychoanalysis*, 1920); *Jenseits des Lustprinzips* (1920; *Beyond the Pleasure Principle*, 1955); *Das Ich und das Es* (1923; *The Ego and the Id*, 1961); *Selbstdarstellung* (1925; *An Autobiographical Study*, 1959); *Hemmung, Symptom und Angst* (1926; *Inhibitions, Symptoms and Anxiety*, 1959); *Die Frage der Laienanalyse* (1926; *The Question of Lay-Analysis*, 1959); *Die Zukunft einer Illusion* (1927; *The Future of an Illusion*, 1961); *Das Unbehagen in der Kultur* (1930; *Civilization and Its Discontents*, 1961); *Neue Folge der Vorlesungen zur Einführung in die Psychoanalyse* (1933; *New Introductory Lectures on Psycho-Analysis*, 1964); *Der Mann Moses und die monotheistische Religion* (1939; *Moses and Monotheism*, 1960).

BIBLIOGRAPHY. ERNEST JONES, *The Life and Works of Sigmund Freud*, 3 vol. (1953–57), a thorough, accurate biography partly based on firsthand knowledge, although with an occasional hint of unnecessary esteem and an uneven style; *The Life and Works of Sigmund Freud*, ed. and abridged by LIONEL TRILLING and STEVEN MARCUS (1961), the best condensed account in one volume; MARIE BONAPARTE, ANNA FREUD, and ERNST KRIS (eds.), *Sigmund Freud, the Origins of Psychoanalysis: Letters to Wilhelm Fliess, Drafts and Notes (1887–1902)* (1954), a basic sourcebook for psychoanalytic history; SIGMUND FREUD, *Selbstdarstellung* (1925; Eng. trans., *An Autobiographical Study*, 1959), Freud's all too brief account of his own career and theories; *Letters of Sigmund Freud, 1873–1939*, selected and ed. by ERNST L. FREUD (1961); *A Psycho-Analytic Dialogue: The Letters of Sigmund Freud and Karl Abraham 1907–1926*, ed. by HILDA C. ABRAHAM and ERNST L. FREUD (1965); WILHELM FLIESS, *In eigener Sache* (1906), pamphlet (in German) about the very revealing Freud–Fliess correspondence and relationship; FRITZ WITTELS, *Sigmund Freud* (1924; Eng. trans., 1924), an anecdotal account of his personality, education, and lecturing; HANNS SACHS, *Freud: Master and Friend* (1944), a brief but sympathetic account of the author's lifelong friendship with Freud; PHYLLIS BOTTOME, *Alfred Adler*, 2nd ed. (1946), a not very satisfactory biography, biassed in favour of Adler and against Freud; THEODOR REIK, *From Thirty Years with Freud* (1940, reprinted 1963), memories and impressions of Freud chiefly as a man and scientist; HELEN W. PUNER, *Freud* (1947), his life with hints about unconventional aspects in Freud's family; WILHELM STEKEL, *Autobiography: The Life Story of a Pioneer Psychoanalyst* (1950), criticizes Freud during the period of the dissolution of the Wednesday Circle; JOSEPH WORTIS, *Fragments of an Analysis with Freud* (1954), a critical account of an analysis with Freud; CARL JUNG, *Memories, Dreams, Reflections* (1963), recollections recorded and edited by ANIELA JAFFE, throwing valuable sidelights on his relations with Freud; ERICH FROMM, *Sigmund Freud's Mission* (1959), an analysis of Freud's personality and influence; MARTHE ROBERT, *La Révolution psychoanalytique: la vie et l'oeuvre de Sigmund Freud*, 2 vol. (1964; Eng. trans., *The Psychoanalytic Revolution: Sigmund Freud's Life and Achievement*, 1966), a substantial, detailed account of Freud's life and work; HEINZ F. PETERS, *My Sister, My Spouse* (1963), first biography of Lou Andreas-Salomé, who played a part in the Wednesday Circle and the Vienna Psycho-Analytical Association; LOU ANDREAS-SALOME, *In der Schulebei Freud: Tagebuch eines Jahres 1912–1913* (1965; Eng. trans., *The Freud Journal of Lou Andreas Salomé*, 1965), day-to-day account of encounters with Freud and other members of the Wednesday Circle; C. GIOVANNI, *Sigmund Freud* (1967), a short but good biography; VINCENT BROME, *Freud and His Early Circle* (1967), a detailed account of the early personal struggles between members of the Vienna Circle, with new material not used by Jones.

Books qualifying Freud: KAREN HORNEY, *New Ways in Psycho-Analysis* (1939); WILHELM REICH, *The Discovery of the Orgone* (1942); H.J. EYSENCK, *Uses and Abuses of Psychology* (1953); M. KLEIN, P. HEIMAN and R.E. MONEY-KYRLE (eds.), *New Directions in Psycho-Analysis* (1955); HERBERT MARCUSE, *Eros and Civilisation* (1956); J.A.C. BROWN, *Freud and the Post-Freudians* (1963); PAUL ROAZEN, *Freud: Political and Social Thought* (1969).

(V.Br.)

Friends

Friends is the name of a Christian group that arose in the mid-17th century in England and the American colonies, dedicated to living in accordance with the direct inward apprehension of God, without creeds, clergy, or other ecclesiastical forms. As most powerfully expressed by George Fox (1624–91), Friends (or Quakers, as they were more often called) felt that their "experimental" discovery of God would lead to the purification of all of Christendom. It did not; but Friends founded one American colony and were dominant for a time in several others, and though their numbers in the early 1970s (about 200,000) were relatively small, they continued to make disproportionate contributions to science, industry, and especially to the Christian effort for social reform.

NATURE AND SIGNIFICANCE

The "Inward Light"

Trust in the "Inward Light" is the distinctive theme of Quakerism. The Light should not be confused with conscience or reason; it is rather "that of God in every man," which allows men an immediate sense of God's presence and his will for them. It thus informs conscience and redirects reason. The experience of hearkening to this inner Guide is mystical but corporate and practical. Meetings to worship God and await his word (always open to anyone who wishes to come) are essential to Quaker faith and practice; although the inward Seed can work in a solitary person, Friends do not meditate like monks, isolated in their cells. It is in the pregnant silence of the meeting of true waiters and worshippers that the Spirit speaks. Sometimes the meeting is too dull or worldly for any message to be heard, and sometimes there are altogether silent meetings, which are spiritually beneficial to the participants; but ideally someone has reached a new understanding that demands to be proclaimed. He or she —for Friends have always given women equality in worship—speaks or prays and thus ministers to the meeting, which weighs this "testimony" by its own experiences of God. Friends historically have rejected a formal or salaried clergy as a "hireling ministry." If God can provide his own living testimony, the Bible and the learning necessary to read it can take a subordinate place, and creeds and outward sacraments can be dispensed with altogether. But despite their emphasis on silent waiting and their distrust of "creaturely" activity, Friends are no more habituated to passive than to solitary meditation. Often the "opening" of the Inward Light is a "concern" for the sufferings of others and a mandate laid upon the conscience to take action to alleviate that suffering. Such concerns typically are laid before a meeting and thoroughly considered; any corporate action taken must be unanimous. But slow and unorganized as such action sometimes is, Friends have been led to oppose slavery, brutality in prisons and insane asylums, oppression of women, militarism, and war. Their history is thus the story of their experiences with the Inward Light and what they have had to do to be faithful to it.

HISTORY

The rise of Quakerism. There were meetings before there were Quakers. Small groups of Seekers gathered together during the Puritan Revolution in the reign of Charles I to wait upon the Lord because they despaired of spiritual help either from the Established Church or the existing Puritan bodies—Presbyterians, Congregationalists, and Baptists—through which most of them had already passed. Among these Seekers, Fox and James Nayler were perhaps the most eminent, but Edward Burrough, William Dewsbury, and Richard Farnworth also were active. The cradle of the movement was northwest England and specifically Swarthmoor Hall in northwestern Lancashire, which after 1652 became the centre of an evangelistic campaign by travelling ministers. Within a decade perhaps 20,000 to 60,000 had been converted from all social classes except the aristocracy and totally unskilled labourers. Heaviest concentrations were in the north, southwest, and in London. Travelling Friends and Cromwellian soldiers brought Quakerism to the new English settlements in Ireland; Wales and especially Scotland were less affected.

The Puritan clergy, in England and New England, greeted the rise of Quakerism with the fury that an old left often reserves for a new. Friends' religious style was impulsive and nonideological; Quakers seemed to ignore the orthodox views of the Puritans and pervert their heterodox ones. The Restoration of Charles II in 1660 was only a change of persecutors for the Quakers, with their former tormentors now sharing some of their sufferings. From the Quaker Act of 1662 until the de facto toleration of James II in 1686, when he began dispensing from taking oaths required by the Test Act (de jure toleration came in the Toleration Act of 1689), Friends were hounded by penal laws for not swearing oaths, for not going to the Church of England, for going to Quaker meetings, and for refusing tithes. Some 15,000 suffered under these laws, and almost 500 died in prison, but they continued to grow in numbers until the turn of the century.

Persecution of Quakers

At the same time they were converting and peopling America. In 1656 Quaker women preachers began work in Maryland and in the Massachusetts Bay Colony. The magistrates of Boston savagely persecuted the visitors and in 1659 and 1661 put four of them to death—the only Friends anywhere to be executed for preaching their faith. Despite this, Quakerism took root in Massachusetts and flourished in Rhode Island, where Friends for a long time were in the majority of the settlers. There were also many Friends in New Jersey, where English Quakers early secured a patent for settlement, and in North Carolina. Yearly meetings were established for New England (1661), Maryland (1672), Virginia (1673), Philadelphia (1681), New York (1695), and North Carolina (1698). The most famous Quaker colony was Pennsylvania, for which Charles II issued a charter to William Penn in 1681. Penn's "Holy Experiment" tested how far a state could be governed consistently with Friends' principles, especially pacifism and religious toleration. Toleration would allow colonists of other faiths to settle freely and perhaps become a majority; consistent pacifism would leave the colony defenseless against enemies who might have been provoked by the other settlers. Penn, entangled in English affairs, spent little time in Pennsylvania and showed consistently poor judgment in selecting his non-Quaker deputies, who were almost always at odds with the Quaker-dominated legislature. Penn also went bankrupt through mismanagement; but the Quaker influence in Pennsylvania politics remained paramount until 1756, when legislators who were Friends could no longer find a saving formula allowing them to vote support for military operations against the French and Indians fighting settlers in western Pennsylvania. Voltaire's description of Penn's agreements with the Indians as the only treaties never sworn to and never violated was slightly exaggerated; but Friends' relations with the Indians were more peaceful than those of other settlers, and had Quakers remained the only settlers, the colony might have been spared Indian wars.

William Penn's "Holy Experiment"

The age of quietism. The achievement of religious toleration in the 1690s coincided with a quietist phase in Quakerism that lasted until the 19th century. Quietism is endemic within Quakerism and emerges whenever trust in the Inward Light is stressed to the exclusion of everything else. It suits a time when little outward activity is demanded and when the peculiar traditions of a group seem particularly worth emphasizing. In the 18th century Friends had gained most of their political objectives. Their special language and dress, originally justified as a witness for honesty, simplicity, and equality, became passwords and uniforms, respectively, of a group now 75 to 90 percent composed of second- and third-generation Quakers. Strict enforcement of rules prohibiting marriage without parents' consent or to nonmembers led to the disownment, according to one estimate, of a third of the English Friends who got married in the latter half of the 18th century. More were disowned than converted, and since most members were the children of members, it is not surprising that Friends eventually came to recognize a category of "birthright" membership, which seemed to relax the expectation of conversion.

Seemingly self-absorbed in other ways, Friends in the age of quietism deepened and intensified their social concerns. English Friends were active in the campaign to end the slave trade, and American Friends, urged on by John Woolman and others, voluntarily emancipated all their own slaves between 1758 and 1800. Meetings, though slow to adopt this concern, pursued it absolutely and thoroughly; in Rhode Island Stephen Hopkins, who was governor nine times, was disowned because he would not free his one slave.

The impact of evangelicalism. Imbued with quietism and with few converts with experience of other churches, Friends might have remained in secluded religious life had it not been for the evangelical movement associated with John and Charles Wesley. Evangelical Friends were concerned with emphasizing the inerrancy and uniqueness of the Bible, the incarnation and atonement of Christ, and other characteristic Protestant doctrines which, although seldom denied by Friends, tended to be subordinated to the quietistic emphasis on the Inward Light. In the early 19th century most leading English Friends were sympathetic to evangelical ideas, although they did not lose their unity with more traditional-minded Friends.

In America unity proved more difficult. Friends had gone west—from Virginia and North Carolina because of difficulties over slavery, but also from Pennsylvania. As new yearly meetings were formed—Ohio (1812), Indiana (1821), Iowa (1863), Kansas (1872), Oregon (1893), California (1895), and Nebraska (1908), among others—ties with the London Yearly Meeting, the "mother" meeting, became weaker, and no American yearly meeting had a predominant position. Leaders of Philadelphia Yearly Meeting, mostly rich merchants with strong ties to England, were sympathetic to Evangelicalism; but many poorer country Friends left the meeting, no longer feeling a unity with the beliefs of the Philadelphia ministers and elders or with the way they exercised their authority. Elias Hicks (1748–1830), whose name was applied to these separatists, placed extreme emphasis on the Inward Light; he wrote that it might be a good thing if God withdrew the Bible, since he could inspire worshippers to write new scriptures that would probably be better than the originals. Since the various American yearly meetings corresponded with one another, the Hicksite separation spread to other yearly meetings that had to decide to which portion of Philadelphia Yearly Meeting to write. A pastoral visit to America (1837–1840) by the leading English evangelical Friend, Joseph John Gurney (one of the few systematic theologians ever produced in the Society of Friends), led to a further separation when the evangelical or "Gurneyite" New England Yearly Meeting disowned John Wilbur, an orthodox quietist Friend.

Schism is often a sign of religious vitality, and so it proved now. Whether Hicksite, Wilburite, or Gurneyite, all branches of Quakerism began to show vigour unknown in their days of torpid unity. With more vital preaching, many converts not devoted to the inherited peculiarities of Quaker tradition joined Friends; to them it seemed more important to assure a saving ministry than to preserve the traditional mode of worship. There thus grew up, especially in the Midwest and Far West, "pastoral meetings" in which a paid minister assumed the functions of delivering a sermon and exercising pastoral care of members. Such meetings often called themselves "Friends' Churches"; congregational singing was a part of the service, which might have only a few moments of silence, and baptismal and marriage ceremonies were introduced. In doctrine, worship, and polity they were not unlike Congregational churches, though they remained faithful to Friends' social testimonies. Even in England, where such innovations were not introduced, Friends, under the influence of the evangelical revival,

discontinued disownment for irregular marriages and curtailed the powers of elders and overseers, which had been a profoundly conservative force.

The 20th century. Friends in 1900 were divided into three groups. Yearly meetings of evangelical, or "orthodox," Friends were in fellowship with one another and with the London and Dublin yearly meetings. In America these Gurneyite meetings in 1902 formed the Five Years' Meeting (now the Friends United Meeting). The "conservative" American yearly meetings, in fellowship with one another, maintained traditional Quaker customs and mode of worship. The Hicksite yearly meetings, which formed the Friends General Conference in 1902, remained the most open to modern thought. During the century these divisions have been much softened. Theological distinctions have receded in importance, and the habit of cooperation in such agencies as the American Friends Service Committee has drawn Friends together. Also, "independent" meetings, often composed largely of students, have not perpetuated old divisions.

The 20th century has also seen the extension of Quakerism to Africa and continental Europe. There are now more Friends in Africa (35,531 in 1969) than in the homeland of Quakerism (20,910 members in Great Britain and 1,759 in Ireland). There are over 33,000 Friends in Kenya alone. Quakerism took root in the Netherlands in the 17th century but died out in the mid-19th, as did groups in Congéniès, France, and Bad Pyrmont, Germany. Quaker relief work in World War I and its aftermath produced new yearly meetings in Germany, The Netherlands, France, Sweden, and Switzerland, but numbers remain small: 85 in France, 126 in The Netherlands, and 151 in Switzerland in 1969, for example.

ORGANIZATION AND PUBLIC CONCERNS

Polity. Insofar as George Fox is the "founder of Quakerism," he is so chiefly because of the system of meetings for church business that he established in the years immediately after 1667, which essentially stands today. The most important meeting is the monthly meeting, which considers all applications for membership, in some localities manages Friends' properties, and acts on members' concerns. Generally, in the United States each congregation has a monthly meeting; in England and in some parts of the United States several meetings for worship combine in monthly meeting. Several monthly meetings form quarterly meetings, which are combined in yearly meetings, of which there were, in 1970, 49, ranging in membership from under 100 to over 60,000.

This array is less hierarchical than it sounds. Any Friend can attend any meeting, which tries to remain open to his concerns or the service he can perform (much in the spirit of a meeting for worship). Furthermore, all decisions must be made unanimously. The responsibility of the clerk is not to preside in a parliamentary manner but to feel for a "sense of the meeting," which draws together the thinking of the meeting to the point of action.

Though Friends have no ordination, they have always given a special place to Recorded Ministers (or Public Friends). Recorded Ministers are those whose testimony in local meetings has been officially recognized; they are free to "travel in the ministry" by visiting other meetings, should they be led to do so. Pastoral meetings maintain their Recorded Ministers, who also do much of the work of seeing to the relief of the poor, care of properties, and discipline of erring members, which elsewhere was done by elders and overseers. Ministers have usually had their own meetings together, and in most yearly meetings executive responsibility had been taken by a meeting like the Meeting for Sufferings in London (these are also called Representative meetings or committees or Permanent boards). London Meeting for Sufferings in the 17th century served as a political pressure group, lobbying Parliament for relief from persecution and using the press for public appeals; in the 19th century they extended their care to sufferings everywhere.

Corporate and personal concerns. The "public testimonies" of Friends from the very beginning included the

Evangelical Friends

Pastoral meetings

plain speech and dress and refusal of tithes, oaths, and worldly courtesies—all clearly entailed in the Quaker message. To these was added in a few years an explicit renunciation of participation in war; within the next century bankruptcy, marriage out of meeting, smuggling, and dealing in or owning slaves also became practices for which an unrepentant Friend would be disowned. These latter, especially those relating to slavery, became matters for discipline because a comparative minority of Friends persuaded the rest that they were inconsistent with Friends' principles. But not all social concerns were corporate in this sense or were enforced by sanctions.

Friends' relief work, for example, has usually arisen from an individual response to suffering, often as the result of war. From the time of the American Revolution, Quakers have been active in ministering to refugees and victims of famine—so much so that the entire Society of Friends is sometimes taken for a philanthropic organization; yet this work, recognized in 1947 by the award of the Nobel Peace Prize to the American Friends Service Committee and the (British) Friends Service Council, has mobilized many non-Quakers and thus exemplifies the interaction between the Quaker conscience and the wider world.

There have always been Friends whose concerns went well beyond what meetings were willing to adopt. Most Friends were not abolitionists before the American Civil War; they probably did not approve of the Underground Railroad nor share the early feminist views of Lucretia Mott and Susan B. Anthony. The social views of some American Friends are not unfittingly represented by the two presidents of Quaker background, Herbert Hoover and Richard M. Nixon. Often the issue has been the relationship between private witness and public policy. Some Quaker pacifists are concerned enough to make an absolute personal stand against war (for example, by refusing to register for selective service and thus forfeiting conscientious objectors' status); others are more willing to sacrifice purity for effectiveness, by working for an alleviation of international tensions even at the cost of less rigorous application of their principles.

INFLUENCE OF FRIENDS

Quaker customs and the restricted place of Friends in the social order have greatly concentrated their secular achievements. Plainness meant that painting, music, and the theatre were proscribed. For a century trust in the Inward Light inhibited the foundation of schools (though in the 19th century American Friends founded colleges like Earlham, Haverford, and Swarthmore; and individual Friends founded Bryn Mawr College, Cornell University, and Johns Hopkins University). Friends' schools put an emphasis on science; the chemist John Dalton, the geneticist Francis Galton, the anthropologist E. B. Tylor, the astronomer Arthur Eddington, and Joseph Lister, discoverer of antisepsis, were all Friends. Ruth Fry has estimated that an English Quaker has almost 50 times as great a chance as someone in the general population to be elected a Fellow of the Royal Society. In commerce Friends were trusted and got customers; they trusted one another and extended credit; thus the many successful Quaker firms and banks, of which Barclay's and Lloyd's are the best known. Friends also pioneered in inventions, developing the puddling process for iron, and the safety match, and promoting the first English railroad line.

Disdaining formal education and a clerical intelligentsia, Friends, not surprisingly, often failed theologically (that is, could not solve some of the intellectual problems of their faith). But they would agree with the 19th-century Danish religious philosopher Søren Kierkegaard that "the highest of all is not to understand the highest but to act upon it." The cause of schisms in the past—the tension between entire reliance on the Inward Light and the profession of orthodox Christian doctrines—remains unresolved. It also remains to some extent a barrier to ecumenism; the London Yearly Meeting in 1940 declined to join the World Council of Churches out of uneasiness

with its creedal basis, though some U.S. groups of Friends sent delegates to the first meeting of the council in 1948. Looked at in the context of Christendom as a whole, Friends offer a distinctive opportunity for spontaneity of worship, fellowship in mysticism, and proving mystical insight in labour for a suffering world. Many alienated from institutional Christianity have found this combination attractive; they may well feel more comfortable identifying themselves as Friends than as Christians. This may make it more difficult for Quakerism to be subsumed into a reunited Christian church; but the faith of most Friends has always been that, as Albert Schweitzer wrote in *The Quest of the Historical Jesus*, as "we do the work of Christ we shall come to know who he is."

BIBLIOGRAPHY. Good introductions to Quakerism may be found in the *Handbook of the Religious Society of Friends*, 5th ed. (1967), produced by the Friends World Committee for Consultation; and in the interpretations by D.E. TRUEBLOOD, *The People Called Quakers* (1966); and in L. BENSON, *Catholic Quakerism* (1966). The standard histories are W.C. BRAITHWAITE, *The Beginnings of Quakerism*, rev. ed. (1955), and *The Second Period of Quakerism*, rev. ed. (1961); and R.M. JONES, *The Quakers in the American Colonies* (1911), and *The Later Periods of Quakerism*, 2 vol. (1921). Many Friends' practices are codified in the London Yearly Meeting *Book of Discipline*, 2 vol. (1960); and in the Five Years' Meeting *Uniform Discipline* (1902). The masterpiece of Quaker theology is R. BARCLAY, *Theologiae verè Christianae Apologia* (1676; Eng. trans., *Apology for the True Christian Divinity*, 1678). W.C. BRAITHWAITE best explains how Friends' polity should work in *Spiritual Guidance in the Experience of the Society of Friends* (1909). See also G. WILSON, *Quaker Worship* (1952). The autobiographical work of C.E. PICKETT, *For More than Bread* (1953), an account of work with the American Friends Service Committee from 1929 to 1952, is unusually good. Quaker social thought on contemporary issues may be found in S. ALEXANDER (ed.), *Quaker Testimony Against Slavery and Racial Discrimination* (1958); and the FRIENDS HOME SERVICE COMMITTEE, *Towards a Quaker View of Sex* (1963).

(R.T.V.)

Froebel, Friedrich

Remembered mainly for his development of the kindergarten, Froebel's life and career were dominated by the conviction that all human beings have an undeniable right to self-realization through self-education.

By courtesy of the Staatliche Museen, Heidecksburg

Froebel, drawing by Friedrich Unger. In the Staatliche Museen, Heidecksburg.

Friedrich Wilhelm August Froebel was born April 21, 1782, in the town of Oberweissbach in the Thuringian Forest of Germany, the fifth child in an orthodox clergyman's family. He was only nine months old when his mother died. The trauma caused by that loss and his father's absorption in the demands of his parish, as well as his stepmother's indifference, rendered him moody, introspective, slow in learning to read, and unresponsive to intellectual interests, Denied schooling and normal contacts with children of his own age, he developed an obsessive attachment to the world of nature. He learned to observe keenly, made intuitive scientific deductions, and at a very early age formulated a profound spiritual philosophy concerning the unity of the universe.

After apprenticeship to a forester, he pursued some informal university courses at Jena until he was jailed for an unpaid debt. After brief periods as a surveyor, estate manager, and private secretary, at 23, cutting short his preparations for architecture, he impulsively took a teaching appointment in a progressive model school in Frankfurt that was run on lines advocated by the Swiss educator J.H. Pestalozzi.

Formative experiences as a private tutor

A crucial turning point came in June 1806, when he entered the household of Baron von Holtzhausen as tutor to his three sons. The Baron's failure to manifest interest in the rearing of his sons confirmed Froebel's conviction of the vital need for both father and mother to participate in the education of children. In the Baroness he saw the embodiment of ideal motherhood, and he nurtured an affinity for her, regarding her as his spiritual bride. In June 1811 he suddenly left the household to continue university study, but he kept up a secret correspondence with the Baroness for several years.

At the University of Göttingen, Froebel enunciated his "law of the sphere," his symbol of the divine forces operative in the universe, which he dreamed of applying to a comprehensive reconstruction of science and culture. He began by studying crystallography, but soon became engulfed in the Napoleonic Wars, and while a soldier developed the idea of regenerating Germany through a basic restructuring of its educational system. Returning to the University of Berlin in 1814 he became curator of its mineralogical museum, but two years later he was back in Thuringia, in the village of Griesheim, to establish his own school, which he described as the "Universal German Educational Institution." Three orphaned nephews, a brother, his sister-in-law, and her two sons comprised the household staff and student body. Froebel, despite his emphasis on the importance of the family as the true root of human life, did not marry until 1818, when he took Wilhelmine Hoffmeister, a refined and spiritually sympathetic partner, as his bride. After a year he moved the school to neighbouring Keilhau, and it soon expanded into a flourishing institution.

Froebel, unable to win government support for his project, continued to devote himself unstintingly to the school. He wrote numerous articles and in 1826 published *The Education of Man*, a philosophical presentation of principles and methods pursued at Keilhau. In 1828 the Keilhau school became suspect to the authorities as a "nest of demagogues," and, although officially absolved, Froebel was removed from direct control in 1832. After five years in Switzerland, he returned to Germany and realized only two of his ideas: the Child Nurture and Activity Institute, which by happy inspiration he renamed the Kindergarten, and a small boarding school for future teachers. Wilhelmine died a year before the official founding of the Kindergarten, in June 1840. He also started a publishing plant for play and other educational materials, including a collection of *Mother-Play and Nursery Songs*, with lengthy explanations of their meaning and use. This immensely popular book was translated into many foreign languages. He insisted that improvement of infant education was a vital preliminary to comprehensive educational and social reform. His enthusiasm was spurred on by Louise Lewin, a zealous woman 30 years his junior, whom he had helped rear at Keilhau; they were married in 1851.

The spread of the kindergarten concept

Froebel won effective worldwide support of the kindergarten movement, despite its ban as subversive by the Prussian government from 1851 until 1860. The Baroness of Marenholtz-Bülow, deeply impressed by what she had observed of Froebel's kindergarten at Marienthal in Thuringia, established kindergartens in England and throughout Europe.

Froebel died at Marienthal on June 21, 1852.

BIBLIOGRAPHY. IRENE M. LILLEY, *Friedrich Froebel: A Selection from His Writings* (1967), is the most recent documented presentation, emphasizing aspects of Froebel's life often neglected in other studies. WILLIAM H. KILPATRICK, *Froebel's Kindergarten Principles Critically Examined* (1916), is a penetrating analysis by a celebrated educator.

(S.Bl.)

Frontenac, Comte de

Louis de Buade, comte de Frontenac et Palluau, was a governor of New France and one of the architects of French expansion in North America. He was born at Saint-Germain on May 22, 1622. His father, Henri de Buade, was colonel of the Régiment de Navarre and a member of Louis XIII's entourage; his mother was Anne Phélypeaux, of the influential Pontchartrain family; Louis XIII was his godfather. He served with the French armies during the Thirty Years' War; in 1643, at the age of 21, he was colonel of the Régiment de Normandie and in 1646 was appointed a *maréchal de camp* (brigadier general). In 1648 he secretly married Anne de La Grange-Trianon, who, in consequence, was disowned by her wealthy father.

Frontenac had great personal charm and much influence at court, but he was also egoistic and unscrupulous, as well as extravagant; by 1663 his debts amounted to over 350,000 livres. In 1669 he took service as lieutenant general with the Venetian forces defending Crete against the Turks, but he had not been on the island long before he was dismissed from his post for intriguing against his superior officers.

First service in New France.   In 1672 he was appointed governor general of New France. Within a year of his arrival in the colony, he had founded a fur-trading post, Ft. Frontenac, on Lake Ontario. Shortly afterward he became associated with the Sieur de La Salle, who, with Frontenac's support, obtained royal consent to continue the explorations of Louis Jolliet down the Mississippi to its mouth. La Salle took advantage of this to found fur-trading posts at the foot of Lake Michigan and on the Illinois River, from which his men, with the connivance of Frontenac, illegally engrossed a large part of the western fur trade. This brought them into conflict with the Montreal fur traders, dividing the colony into two hostile factions. Despite repeated warnings from Louis XIV and his minister J.-B. Colbert, Frontenac also disputed violently with the officials and clergy of New France.

While these conflicts were raging within the colony, a much more serious external problem was developing. Until 1675 the Five Nations of the Iroquois Indian confederacy had remained on good terms with the French because they were under attack from the Andaste and Mohegan tribes; but in that year the Iroquois subdued the other tribes and immediately began to contest the French hold on the western fur trade, their aim being to divert it from Montreal to Albany, with themselves acting as middlemen. When they attacked the tribes allied to the French and threatened the French themselves, Frontenac tried to appease them, doing nothing to strengthen the colony's almost nonexistent defenses. This policy merely encouraged the Iroquois to press their attacks with greater vigour, until the French were in danger of being driven out of the west. During these years, too, the English Hudson's Bay Company established posts in James Bay, posing another threat to the Canadian fur trade, one that Frontenac chose to ignore. In 1682 Louis XIV recalled Frontenac because of his misgovernment. (His successor, Le Febvre de La Barre, attempted with little success to subdue the Iroquois and in 1685 was replaced by the Marquis de Denonville, who brought the Indians to terms.)

The war with England.   When England declared war on France in May 1689, Frontenac was given command of an expedition to conquer the province of New York. At the same time he was reappointed governor of New France, and Denonville was recalled for service in Europe. Frontenac's expedition was delayed by adverse weather, however, and he did not reach Quebec until October 12. The Iroquois, meanwhile, learning of Anglo-

French hostilities before the news reached New France, had launched a furious assault on the unsuspecting colony on August 5, inflicting great damage and killing or capturing about 100 Canadians. This attack, and the lateness of the season when Frontenac reached the colony, made it impossible to invade New York in force; but in January he sent three war parties to attack the English frontier settlements at Schenectady, Ft. Loyal, and Salmon Falls. All three places were destroyed with heavy loss of life for the defenders, and as a result the northern English colonies united for an assault on New France. The attacking forces, led by Sir William Phips, were repulsed at Quebec by the French under Frontenac, who distinguished himself by his prudent tactics.

The expansion of New France

During the next few years the fighting was confined to sporadic raids on the Canadian settlements by the Iroquois, but this did not prevent a rapid expansion into the west by the Canadian fur traders. Frontenac concerned himself far more with the fur trade than with pressing the war to a successful conclusion. Despite the fact that the policy of Louis XIV was to curb expansion into the interior in order to strengthen the central colony, old fur-trading posts were strengthened and new posts established by Frontenac until French influence extended beyond Lake Superior, and the flood of furs coming down to Montreal glutted the market in France. After much urging from his subordinates and the receipt of explicit orders from the minister of the marine, Frontenac finally undertook in 1696 an expedition that destroyed the villages of two of the Iroquois nations. The following year the war between England and France ended, but it was not until 1701 that a peace treaty was ratified with the Iroquois by Frontenac's successor. After a brief illness, Frontenac had died at Quebec on November 28, 1698.

Frontenac was one of the more colourful personages in North American history. His connections at the court of Louis XIV enabled him to survive failures that might have destroyed another man and won him credit for the achievements of his subordinates. It was, however, under his regime that the English and Iroquois attacks on New France were finally repulsed and the French extended their North American empire from Montreal to Lake Winnipeg and from Hudson Bay to the Gulf of Mexico.

BIBLIOGRAPHY. FRANCIS PARKMAN, *Count Frontenac and New France Under Louis XIV* (1877), a romantic account of Frontenac's career that extols his virtues and minimizes his flaws; W.J. ECCLES, *Frontenac: The Courtier Governor* (1959), a critical biography incorporating some new material.

(W.J.E.)

Frost, Robert

Robert Lee Frost used colloquial language, familiar rhythms, and symbols taken from common life to express in his poetry the quiet values of rural New England. Long denied recognition—his first book did not appear until he was nearly 40 years old—Frost himself became, toward the end of his long life, a symbol of craggy independence, laconic piety, and the courage to endure.

Life and works. Frost was born in San Francisco, California, on March 26, 1874. His father, William Prescott Frost, Jr., a New Englander and a graduate of Harvard College, was serving as headmaster of a private school in Lewistown, Pennsylvania, when he met and married a Scottish-born schoolteacher, Isabell Moodie. He took his bride to San Francisco, where he became a newspaper reporter. When Robert was 11 years old, his father died of tuberculosis. The widow and her two children (a daughter had been born in 1876) accompanied the body to Lawrence, Massachusetts, for burial; thereafter, Mrs. Frost, too poor to return to California, supported the family by teaching school in Massachusetts and New Hampshire. She exerted a strong influence on her son's personal and literary development: her Scots loyalties and her intense religious leanings may have contributed to the blend of practicality and mysticism in his poetry.

As a boy Frost was fond of baseball and football, not school books. With some difficulty, even with his mother's help, he finished grammar school in Salem, New

Frost, 1954.
Ruohomaa—Black Star

Hampshire. His attitude changed as soon as he entered high school at Lawrence, from which he was graduated in 1892 as co-valedictorian, sharing the honour with Elinor Miriam White, whom he later married. In his valedictory address he spoke warmly of the poet's responses to experience—a further indication of an interest already well established, for he had published several poems in the school paper while he was its editor.

Frost's paternal grandfather, who wanted him to become a lawyer, sent him to Dartmouth College at Hanover, New Hampshire, the following fall. But the young man, once more impatient with academic routine, stayed less than a term, departing without notice. During the next few years he lived at home in Lawrence, writing poetry and intermittently earning money as a schoolteacher, mill hand, and newspaper reporter. For two years after his marriage in 1895 he and his wife helped his mother conduct a small private school. Throughout this period he sent poems to periodicals, with little success. The first poem he sold, "My Butterfly: An Elegy," appeared in 1894 in *The Independent*, a weekly literary journal.

Academic training and school-teaching career

In the fall of 1897 Frost entered Harvard College to prepare himself for teaching Latin and Greek at the high school level. He received excellent grades in these subjects, but after less than two years he withdrew because of illness. Warned that he might be tubercular, he changed his way of life drastically, becoming a poultryman at Methuen, Massachusetts. The venture succeeded at first, and in 1900 he moved to a farm at Derry, New Hampshire, purchased for his use by his grandfather. The Frosts' first child had been born in 1896, but the boy died just before the move; their second child, a girl, was less than a year old at the time. Four other children were born to the Frosts at Derry. After Frost failed as a farmer, he turned again to teaching (1906–12).

Many of Frost's best known poems were written at Derry, but editors showed little interest. In 1911 the title to the farm passed to Frost, who had for some years been receiving a small annuity from the estate of his grandfather, who had died in 1901. Frost promptly sold the farm and took his family to England the following year, intending to give all of his time to writing. He settled at Beaconsfield in Buckinghamshire and assembled a collection of the lyric verses he had written at Derry. The manuscript was accepted by the first London publisher to whom he submitted it, and *A Boy's Will* appeared in 1913. The next year the same publisher issued Frost's collection of narrative poems, *North of Boston*. British reviewers responded so enthusiastically that overtures were soon made to him by three American publishers. In England he made the acquaintance of Ezra Pound, Edward Thomas, W.W. Gibson, T.E. Hulme, Lascelles Abercrombie, and others. Invited to a rural setting by the Georgian poets Gibson and Abercrombie, he moved to the Gloucestershire countryside in 1914. After the onset of World War I the Frosts returned to the United States, in February 1915, just when his first two books

First acclaim in England

were being published in New York. He bought a small farm at Franconia, New Hampshire; and the warm response to his poetry in the U.S. ended his obscurity.

He served as a professor of English at Amherst College (1916–20); was poet-in-residence at the University of Michigan (1921–23); returned to Amherst (1923–25) and the University of Michigan (1925–26); and thereafter taught part-time at Amherst until 1938. From 1939 to 1943 he was Ralph Waldo Emerson fellow of poetry at Harvard; from 1943 to 1949 he was Ticknor fellow in the humanities at Dartmouth College; and from 1949 to his death on January 29, 1963, in Boston, he held a sinecure as Simpson lecturer at Amherst.

Relationship between his life and his career. Any attempts to describe the characteristics and personality of Robert Frost are difficult to make because he was an extremely complicated man. Those individuals who became well enough acquainted with him to call him a friend found him a very sympathetic person, outgoing and eager to help. For example, one such friendship began with John Bartlett, a student of Frost's while he was teaching in 1909 at the Pinkerton Academy in Derry Village, New Hampshire. This friendship, which lasted as long as Bartlett lived, is recorded in Margaret Bartlett Anderson's *Robert Frost and John Bartlett: The Record of a Friendship* (1963).

There was an entirely different side to Frost's capacity for making friends. In his travels or even on the street of any of the many towns in which he lived he frequently struck up a conversation with a stranger to ask information about some point that interested him. The stranger, unaware that he was talking to a famous man, merely realized that the questions being asked him made sense and were easy to answer. Such a conversation might last for several minutes, and the stranger was almost always charmed by the simplicity and directness of Frost's manner. Under such circumstances the conversation would usually end with a natural leave-taking without any exchange of names.

Reference has already been made to the fact that, because of doctor's orders, Robert Frost became a poultry farmer and later an ordinary farmer in Derry, New Hampshire. During the years on the farm in Derry, Frost demonstrated that he was really not cut out to be a farmer. In later years, he repeatedly confessed that he failed as a farmer because he was too lazy. Some of his attempts to solve various problems that annoyed him in the life of a farmer are entertaining. For example: because he liked to sleep late and to stay up late at night either reading or writing poetry, he resented the requirement that his one cow had to be milked early in the morning. He solved this problem by easing the cow's milking schedule around until he was milking her at midnight and noon.

Interest in botany

Before he went to the Derry farm he had become an enthusiastic botanist. As a result, he devoted far more time to botanizing on his farm at Derry than he devoted to farming. As soon as his children were old enough to share his botanizing interests, he took them on many walks far beyond the limits of his farm. And, indeed, there are more poems concerned with botanizing than with farming in his first book of poems, *A Boy's Will*.

Frost's continuing interest in farming, such as his purchasing the Franconia farm immediately after his return from England, can be explained partly by his fondness of playing at farming (so long as it did not involve too much hard work) and by the fact that in his first two books he had repeatedly spoken with the voice of a farmer. In his poetry he deliberately wished to preserve the notion that he was a farmer. Within a few months after he bought the farm in Franconia, however, he accepted a teaching job at Amherst College and took up residence with his entire family in Massachusetts. For the next few years the farm in Franconia became a retreat during vacations from Amherst.

As he began to give readings further away from home, Frost still took pleasure in referring to himself not only in his poems but also in his talks as a New England farmer. When he wrote his poem entitled "New Hampshire"

(1923), he included the following witticism near the end of the poem:

I choose to be a plain New Hampshire farmer
With an income in cash of, say, a thousand
(From, say, a publisher in New York City).
. . . At present I am living in Vermont.

By the time the poet wrote these lines, he had bought another farm, at South Shaftsbury, Vermont. Although Frost made many boasts to his friends about his plan to raise large crops of apples on his new farm, with the help of his son Carol, the farm never became a financial success.

It would be a mistake to conclude that, because Frost was never a successful farmer on any of the various farms he owned, there was only a poetic significance in his repeated desire to associate himself with farms that he actually owned. These farms were much more than an important retreat from the social life that he knew as a teacher or as a reader of his poems. There was a religious significance in nature for Frost. Day after day he was content to go walking by himself across the meadows and through the woods of his own farm or beyond to property owned by a friend who would not mind his trespassing. These walks were made as happily with a companion as alone. But it was clear that he often walked alone on these rambles because it gave him time for his own thoughts and the discovery of the beginning of new poems. His motions as he walked were really those of a botanist who deeply loved what he saw on both sides of the path as he walked. His favourite time for such walks was always in the spring of the year, and the number of wild flowers that he could call by name was extraordinary.

Of particular interest to him were the wild orchids; the names of some of his favourites crop up in several of his poems: rose pogonias, ram's horn orchid, yellow lady's slipper, and the queen's head orchid. During such walks, whenever he was surprised by a plant that he had not recently seen, he frequently would exclaim aloud, "Hello!" His walks in the summer or in the fall took on an entirely different quality of botanical concern as his eyes looked for and found signs of flowers that had already gone to seed.

Although Frost was always more of a botanist than he was a farmer, he cherished ever since his Derry days the thought that sometime he might be wealthy enough to own a farm that could be run for him by one or more hired men, so that he might play at the game of farming as much or as little as he pleased. He finally did achieve a circumstance that came close to fulfilling his dream. In 1939, the year after the death of Mrs. Frost, he bought near the Bread Loaf School of English in Ripton, Vermont, a good-sized farm known as the Homer Noble farm after its previous owner. The farm spread out on a southerly slope and about one hundred yards above the farm house was a well-built cabin.

Frost's Vermont farm

At that time the head of the Bread Loaf Writer's Conference was Theodore Morrison. He was also head of a special English program at Harvard College. Frost had taken up his winter residence in an apartment on Beacon Hill in Boston, and Mrs. Morrison was serving as his secretary, helping him arrange his schedule of public readings. Frost proposed to the Morrisons that they might like to live in the Homer Noble farmhouse each summer with their two young children and that he, then, would live in the cabin up the hill and eat his meals with the Morrisons in the farm house. The plan was accepted and went into effect in the summer of 1940. Immediately thereafter, plans were made to find a married hired man who would handle the necessary farm duties throughout the year. After one unsuccessful adventure, Frost found and hired an extremely competent farmer named Stafford Dragon. Each summer before Frost and the Morrisons arrived at the Homer Noble farm, Stafford had plowed, fertilized, and planted a good-sized vegetable garden. In this way Frost did acquire a farm on which he could work as much or as little as he wished.

Appraisal. The poetry of Robert Frost appeals to an unusually wide variety of readers because it can be enjoyed in so many different ways. Eschewing the experimentation of many 20th-century poets, Frost repeatedly said he was content with "old ways to be new." From the 19th-century English Romantic poet William Wordsworth he learned that incidents and situations from common life can be described lyrically in a language close to that actually used by ordinary men and women—a point of view that made his work seem "unpoetic" by comparison with the contrived, sentimental verse in vogue before World War I. From another 19th-century English poet, Robert Browning, Frost adapted certain principles of dramatic monologue and dialogue. His study of ancient Greek and Latin authors, particularly Theocritus and Virgil, grounded him in the pastoral conventions of the eclogue, a bucolic poem usually in dialogue.

Many of Frost's readers are content to enjoy his precisely recorded observations of little-noticed details in the appearance of natural objects and the behaviour of rural characters; but his poetry offers much more. From the beginning of his literary career he endowed his rural imagery with symbolic and even metaphysical meaning. As a consequence, his best poems subtly transcend the immediate relationships of the outward individual to the interior self, to others, to nature, and to the universe in a way that illuminates the values on which his profound religious faith was built. Although his wide range of poetic mood includes fear and doubt, the affirmations predominate.

MAJOR WORKS

POEMS: *A Boy's Will* (1913), includes "Mowing," "My November Guest," "A Prayer in Spring," "Reluctance," "Storm Fear," and "The Tuft of Flowers"; *North of Boston* (1914), includes "After Apple-Picking," "Death of the Hired Man," "Home Burial," "Mending Wall," and "The Wood-Pile"; *Mountain Interval* (1916), includes "Birches," "The Impulse," "Loneliness," "An Old Man's Winter Night," " 'Out, Out—'," "The Oven Bird," "The Road Not Taken," and "The Sound of Trees"; *New Hampshire* (1923), includes "Dust of Snow," "Fire and Ice," "The Onset," "The Runaway," "Stopping by Woods on a Snowy Evening," and "To Earthward"; *West-Running Brook* (1928), includes "Acquainted with the Night," "Bereft," "Once by the Pacific," "A Soldier," and "Tree at My Window"; *A Further Range* (1936), includes "Departmental," "Desert Places," "Neither Out Far nor In Deep," "Two Tramps in Mud Time," and "A Lone Striker"; *A Witness Tree* (1942), includes "Come In," "The Gift Outright," "The Lesson for Today," "The Most of It," and "The Silken Tent"; *Steeple Bush* (1947), includes "Directive"; *In the Clearing* (1962), includes "Away!"

VERSE PLAYS: *A Masque of Reason* (1945); *A Masque of Mercy* (1947).

BIBLIOGRAPHY. *Selected Letters of Robert Frost*, ed. by LAWRENCE THOMPSON (1964), is a sampling of his correspondence. The official biography authorized by Frost is LAWRENCE THOMPSON, *Robert Frost*, vol. 1, *The Early Years, 1874–1915* (1966), vol. 2, *The Years of Triumph, 1915–1938* (1970), and vol. 3, *The Glory Years, 1938–1963* (in prep.). Earlier biographical studies include: GORHAM B. MUNSON, *Robert Frost: A Study in Sensibility and Good Sense* (1927); SIDNEY COX, *A Swinger of Birches: A Portrait of Robert Frost* (1957); and ELIZABETH S. SERGEANT, *Robert Frost: The Trial by Existence* (1960). REUBEN A. BROWER, *The Poetry of Robert Frost* (1963), is the best critical study. See also *Robert Frost: A Collection of Critical Essays*, ed. by JAMES M. COX (1962), a broad collection. W.B.S. CLYMER and CHARLES R. GREEN, *Robert Frost: A Bibliography* (1937), is now considerably out-of-date but at present the only Frost bibliography.

(L.R.T.)

Frost

Frost is a term used in two senses: (1) atmospheric water directly crystallized on the ground and on exposed objects; and (2) the occurrence of subfreezing temperatures that affect plants and crops. Frost crystals, often called hoarfrost in the aggregate, form by the passing of the invisible water vapour of the atmosphere into the ice-crystal phase without going through the intermediate liquid phase. Hoarfrost lightly covers fields and rooftops under conditions that would form dew (*q.v.*) if the temperature were above freezing at the point of formation. Sometimes the freezing temperature will be reached after dew has already formed, producing frozen dew, but this usually cannot be readily distinguished because crystals ordinarily will start forming at about the same time the freezing starts. Pertaining to plant culture, frost refers to the freezing of the aqueous solutions in the plant cells, causing these to burst and destroy the plant. Only plants containing plentiful and dilute solutions in their leaves, fruits, etc., are easily damaged. The occurrence of a killing frost without a hoarfrost deposit is sometimes popularly called a black frost.

In physiography and technology the term frost is applied to a variety of freezing processes. Thus, one speaks of the depth of frost penetration in the soil, meaning depth of frozen ground; frost action in the erosion of rocks; frost heaving of soils; frosting of surfaces by other vapours as well as that of water; frost damage to structures, newly laid cement, etc.

The most important aspect of frost in relation to plants is its determination of the length of the growing season: the period from the last killing frost in spring to the first killing frost in autumn, with reference to the tenderest crop plants. There are regions of the earth where the season reaches critically short proportions for the maturing of most usuable crops, and others where the season is so long that more than one planting of such crops as corn (maize) and alfalfa can be brought to harvest. In regions where frost is rare or absent, other factors take on more importance.

One of the most critical situations for frost is encountered in the citrus-fruit regions. There the few killing frosts likely each winter are combatted by a variety of methods, including heating the groves with special burners using oil or a petroleum-derived solid fuel, mixing the air with large fans mounted above the trees, or casting a fine water spray over and on the trees to keep the temperature at or very near the nondamaging level of 32° F (0° C).

In citrus-growing regions in the United States the government meteorological offices developed special frost-warning services with a high degree of usefulness to growers (see WEATHER FORECASTING). In the Pacific Coast fruit regions the service was extended to make it possible to prevent frost damage to deciduous fruit crops during the period of blossoming, both in the United States and in Canada. Protection of orchards was undertaken less extensively in the eastern deciduous fruit regions. Atlantic Coast and Wisconsin cranberries are protected from frost at critical times of the growth cycle by flooding the cranberry bogs with water.

The crystalline and other forms of frost deposit are a subject of aesthetic as well as scientific interest. The structures differ in some respects from those of snow (see SNOW AND SNOWFLAKES). Granular forms are called rime and are produced by the freezing of droplets of liquid water (technically called supercooled droplets), that are carried in the air at temperatures below freezing. Rime is best developed on mountaintops enveloped in supercooled clouds (*q.v.*). It is a common form of icing on aircraft. It also occurs in steam fogs around open springs, streams, lakes, or ponds in very cold weather and, in extreme conditions, around chimneys from the water vapour condensed in the flue gases.

True crystalline hoarfrost is of two classes, that which assumes columnar forms and that which assumes tabular, or platelike, forms. Generally the crystals of these two classes do not occur together on a single night; rather, one or the other will greatly predominate. Columnar or needlelike forms are found at the higher subfreezing temperatures whereas plate crystals predominate under colder conditions. In their pristine state both forms are hexagonal crystals, the columns having a hexagonal cross section and the plates appearing as flat hexagons. Because they must grow outward from some supporting object they rarely assume the perfect symmetry found in many snow crystals. Over ice-covered ponds and rivers, beautiful clusters or rosettes of fernlike or jewel-like frost collect on the surface of the ice. At very low temperatures cubical crystals are sometimes found.

Children and adults alike in cold climates have been

Types of
hoarfrost

fascinated by the beautiful and varied frost forms found on the inner surfaces of windowpanes in buildings. In most cases with heated rooms the vapour condenses as a liquid first, but if the conditions are right, as in an unheated room, the delicate, pure crystalline forms are predominant. These often resemble forests of fir trees, ferns, starry skies, castles, or submarine gardens with corals, starfish, and plants.

BIBLIOGRAPHY. U. NAKAYA, *Snow Crystals: Natural and Artificial* (1954), contains microphotographs of snow and frost crystals with explanatory text. "Frost and Prevention of Damage" is a U.S. DEPARTMENT OF AGRICULTURE pamphlet, occasionally revised, that emphasizes the protection of tree fruits.

(H.R.B.)

Frostbite

Frostbite, a literal freezing of living tissue, superficial or deep, occurs whenever heat loss from a tissue is sufficient to permit ice formation. The freezing–thawing process causes mechanical disruption from ice, intracellular and extracellular biochemical changes, tissue dehydration, local oxygen depletion, and eventually disruption of the blood corpuscles, thrombosis, or clotting, within the small blood vessels, and tissue gangrene if these conditions are not relieved.

Chilblains (an inflammatory swelling), trench foot (a painful disorder similar to frostbite), and immersion injury result after prolonged exposure to low but nonfreezing temperatures and may be recognized by changes in the character of the skin, in blood flow, and in motor and sensory responses.

To preserve vital body warmth, man, in his phylogenetic development, has evolved a private "inner climate," with a near-constant temperature of 37° C (98.6° F).

General hypothermia, or depression of the inner climate body temperature, is critical and often fatal. Below 34° C (93° F), metabolic temperature control is unstable and, if cooling persists, is lost. Coma, cardiorespiratory failure, and death may ensue, even before the level of 31° C (88° F).

Man's constant, cold-repelling temperature is maintained by a complex metabolic furnace (see METABOLISM). Ingested food is fuel for the furnace and some of the energy from its oxidation is converted into heat. This heat, transferred as needed throughout the body, principally by the blood, is contained in a skin shell that traps or dissipates warmth. Heat can be further conserved by man-made objects such as shelter and clothing.

Because tissue freezes near −5° to −6° C (23° to 21° F), the shell of the interior climate must be breached and the temperature must fall from 37° C to levels lower than −5° C before freezing occurs at a specific area. This occurs in Arctic and sub-Arctic regions, temperate zones in winter, and high altitudes throughout the world. Cold, wind, and decreasing oxygen supply encourage the condition.

Conditions conducive to frostbite. Frostbite can occur whenever the ambient temperature falls below 0° C (32° F). Without adequate food, clothing, or shelter, heat is lost successively from the interior of the body to the skin, to the layer of still, insulating air surrounding the skin, and finally to the ambient cold air. High velocity wind blowing away the insulating air cover, or the wetting of the skin, hastens the outward transfer of heat. Thus ice fishermen, hunters, trappers, campers, mountain climbers, and even the inebriate, unconscious in the alley, may all become victims of excessive heat loss.

All too impressive is the injury and death toll from cold during time of war. Armies that suffered as much from the cold as they had from the enemy include Xenophon's Greeks in Armenia (400 BC); the Swedish troops of Charles XII in the Ukraine (1708); and the army of Washington at Valley Forge (1777–78). Most classic is the saga of the Napoleonic forces fleeing Russia (1812–13). Pursued by a relentless enemy, surrounded by the hostile cold of winter, staggering onward without food, water, rest, adequate clothing or footwear, thousands of troops suffered from frostbite or froze to death. Modern armies in the Crimea, World Wars I and II, and Korea, have fared only a little better. Ancient and modern man alike, individually and in groups, and under varying conditions of peace and war, have demonstrated that unrelieved heat loss at temperatures below 0° C leads to tissue freezing, or frostbite.

Three types of individual physical and health factors can contribute to frostbite. They are (1) those conditions encouraging heat loss; (2) mechanical or physical impedance of circulation to the extremities; and (3) problems that decrease the ability of the patient to cope with the cold.

Conditions encouraging heat loss are (1) the excessive intake of alcohol, causing capillary dilation, flushing, and dissipation of heat; (2) wet clothing, permitting outward heat conduction, local cooling and freezing, often associated with hyperhidrosis, a condition in which there is an increased tendency to sweating; (3) exposed flesh; (4) fever, with radiation of heat; (5) injury, with hemorrhage, anoxia, and shock, causing general body cooling; and (6) overexercise, as in forced survival marches, draining unreplaced calories and heat.

Conditions encouraging heat loss

Factors that mechanically impede circulation to the extremities, and thus favour cooling and subsequent freezing, include (1) tight boots, gloves, or clothing; (2) blood vessel diseases that diminish the flow of blood to the extremities; (3) any injury to the blood vessel network causing local tissue oxygen depletion; (4) crushing injury or fracture, resulting in circulatory slowdown; and (5) constriction of small blood vessels as a possible result of drug action.

Conditions that decrease the ability of a person to avoid cold insult include (1) emaciation, fatigue, and inability to cope with the cold; (2) dehydration, a major problem in the cold, with subsequent blood acidity, mental derangement, coma, and death; (3) neuromuscular disease, or previous freezing or nonfreezing cold injury, with resultant sensory loss, predisposing to further cold injury; and (4) psychosis from any cause, allowing behaviour contributory to freezing, with mental disorganization, loss of thermoregulation, and resultant fall of body temperature.

Recognition and treatment. Frostbite is identified from a history of exposure to freezing temperatures in addition to clinical signs and the appearance of the affected part. Before thawing, the part is hard, cold, white, or bloodless. The skin is rigid and the depth of freezing difficult to determine. Freezing is described as either superficial, involving skin and subcutaneous tissues, or deep, involving muscle, nerve, vessels, cartilage, and bone.

In dealing with frostbite body temperature is usually restored to as near normal as possible before thawing. Rapid thawing of the hands or feet in warm water baths is a presently favoured method of therapy. Thawing time is determined by the temperature of the bath and the depth of the freezing; thawing is complete when the tip of the extremity flushes pink or red. After rapid thawing small blisters appear rapidly, spontaneously rupturing in four to ten days. A castlike scab, often black, forms after the blisters rupture. Normal tissue may have already formed below. The thawed part is usually protected to avoid both refreezing and excessive heat. Neither bandages nor dressings are used and the area is cleansed with benign soaps. Constant digital exercises are performed, to preserve joint motion. Early surgical removal of unhealthy tissue (debridement) and amputation is avoided. Whirlpool action will debride devitalized tissues.

Antibiotics are used if necessary; toxoid booster injections are a recommended precaution. After thawing, further treatment is aimed at the prevention of infection and preservation of function.

The outlook is logically best when: the frozen state is of short duration; thawing is by rapid rewarming; and blisters develop early, pink and large, and extend to the tips of the hands or toes.

The outlook is uncertain when: thawing is spontaneous, as at room temperature; the frozen state is of long duration; and the freezing is superimposed on top of a fracture or dislocation.

The outlook is poor when: thawing is delayed, as in ice and snow; thawing is by excessive heat—*e.g.*, greater than 46° C (115° F); the blisters are dark or hemorrhagic and do not extend to the distal tips; a nonfreezing cold injury is followed by freezing; and when freezing, then thawing by any means, is followed by refreezing. The last two conditions are disastrous and almost invariably necessitate amputation of the affected part.

Complica-
tions

Major complications after freezing, and following treatment, may be infection and tissue death, requiring amputation. Less tragic aftereffects are increased sweating, sensory loss, diminished subcutaneous fat pad of the toes and fingers, persistent deep pain, limitation of joint motion, and nail-bed changes. Other permanent effects include fixed scars, wasting of the small muscle, joint deformity, arthritic changes in bone, and neurovascular involvement in the extremities resulting in the inability to protect against lowered temperatures, coupled with increased sensitivity to cold.

Frostbite prevention. The prevention of frostbite is theoretically simple but occasionally impossible to accomplish. To avoid freezing, one obviously needs only to maintain the internal body temperature at the constant physiological level, to provide fuel for continued heat, and to avoid sudden or slow but continuous heat loss from the surface of the body.

Clothing in freezing weather should be dry, layered, and with warm, loose hand wear and footwear. Tight, restricting bands should not be worn. Exposed flesh should be protected from the wind—face masks, hoods, and earmuffs are helpful.

In cold, man must remain alert, avoid the excessive use of alcohol and tobacco, or drugs inhibiting his mental or physical capability.

Should freezing follow an accident, whether or not the victim is injured, intoxicated, or otherwise affected, major efforts must be made to prevent further heat loss in order to prevent death, and in any situation in which freezing has occurred, thawing should be prevented if refreezing may take place. Man survives local freezing of an extremity, even with amputation, but loss of vital temperature may result in hypothermia and death.

By any and all means, the body's internal environment must be kept at its normal temperature. Physically conditioned persons are able, better than those who are not, to withstand cold, avoid cold injury, wind chill, and mental and physical fatigue. Man in the cold must "think warm," and, most importantly, be informed regarding the effect of his geographic environment on his internal environment. To maintain body temperature is to survive the cold, no matter what the external environmental temperature.

BIBLIOGRAPHY. XENOPHON, *Anabasis*, trans. from the Greek by W.H.D. ROUSE, *The March Up Country* (1964), the classic Greek account of the effect of altitude and cold on the retreating Greeks, fleeing Persia, 400 BC; BARON D. LARREY, *Mémoires de chirurgie militaire, et campagnes de D.J. Larrey*, 4 vol. (1812–17; Eng. trans., *Surgical Memoirs of the Campaigns of Russia, Germany, and France*, 1832), a vivid account, by Napoleon's chief surgeon, of death and injury from cold in the winter retreat from Russia, and his interpretation of the disastrous effect of rapid warming (excessive campfire heat) that delayed acceptance of rapid thawing for over a century; FRANS G. BENGTSSON, *Karl XII* (1957; Eng. trans., *The Life of Charles XII, 1697–1718*, 1960), an account of cold onslaught faced by the Swedish army in Russia, Poland, and Norway; H.T. MERYMAN, "Tissue Freezing and Local Cold Injury," *Physiol Rev.*, 37:233–251 (1957), a basic physiological explanation of freezing and the effect of cold on tissues; and (ed.), *Cryobiology* (1966), a basic comprehensive text of the science of low-temperature phenomena, physical and physiological, pertaining to biological systems and organisms; "Cold, Disturbances Due to," in *Current Therapy* (annual), the current accepted methods of treatment of freezing injury; E.G. VIERECK (ed.), *Frostbite* (1964), a round-table discussion of the current concepts of basic problems of cold injury, broad in scope, by active workers in the field of low-temperature biology and medicine; W.J. MILLS, R. WHALEY, and W. FISH, "Frostbite: Experience with Rapid Rewarming and Ultrasonic Therapy," *Alaska Med.*, 2:1 (1960), 2:114 (1960), 3:28 (1961), an evaluation of the then controversial method of rapid rewarming with water; W.J. MILLS, *Frostbite: The Problems of Management and a Review of 200 Cases*, Office of Naval Research, Department of the Navy (1968), clinical results of frostbite treatment by various methods of thawing, and post-thaw care; UNITED STATES ARMY, MEDICAL DEPARTMENT, *Cold Injury, Ground Type* (1958), a report of freezing injury and its treatment in World War II, with a good historical review.

(W.J.Mi.)

Fruits and Fruit Farming

The subject of fruit and nut production deals with intensive culture of perennial plants, the fruits of which have economic significance (a nut is a fruit, botanically). It is one part of the broad subject of horticulture, which also encompasses vegetable growing and production of ornamentals and flowers. This article places further arbitrary limitations in that it does not encompass a number of very important perennial fruit crops covered elsewhere, including vanilla (see SPICES, HERBS, AND FLAVOURINGS), coffee (see COFFEE PRODUCTION), and the oil-producing tung tree and oil palm (see OILS, FATS, AND WAXES).

Botanists define a fruit in broad terms as the fleshy or dry ripened ovary of a plant surrounding the seed. A pomologist, or specialist in the science and practice of fruit growing, defines it somewhat more narrowly as the fleshy edible part of a perennial plant associated with development of the flower. A nut is any seed or fruit consisting of a kernel, usually oily, surrounded by a hard or brittle shell. Most edible nuts—*e.g.*, almond, walnut, cashew, pecan, pistachio, etc.—are well known as dessert nuts. Not all nuts are edible. Some, used as sources of oil or fat, may be regarded as oil seeds; others are used for ornament. The botanical definition of a nut, based on features of form and structure (morphology), is more restrictive: a hard, dry, one-celled, one-seeded fruit that does not split open at maturity. Among the nuts that fit both the botanical and popular conception are the acorn, chestnut, and filbert; other so-called nuts may be botanically a seed (Brazil nut), a legume (peanut), or a drupe (almond and coconut). In this article the term nut is used in its broadest sense unless otherwise indicated.

The first section of this article deals with fruit and nut growing from the standpoint of classification, economics, and geography, and the second section with basic problems and practices of fruit and nut growing, crop composition, movement, uses, and disposal.

The article is divided into the following sections and subsections:

I. Classification, economics, and geography
   Fruit and nut growing in the tropics
   Fruit growing in the subtropics
   Fruit and nut growing in the warm temperate zone
   Fruit growing in the cool temperate zone
II. Basic practices in fruit farming and marketing
   The variety: its propagation and improvement
   The site
   Planting and spacing systems
   Training and pruning
   Soil management, irrigation, and fertilization
   Pollination
   Thinning
   Pest control and preservation
   Harvesting and packing
   Postharvest physiology of fruits
   Waste materials, other uses

I. Classification, economics, and geography

Table 1 lists common and scientific names for fruits and nuts, probable original source, and important uses. Tables 2 and 3 give information on world production of some of the most important fruit and nut crops. The data are somewhat incomplete since they represent only commercial production and movement. Most fruits and nuts are used locally, in large quantity, and never pass beyond village markets. Mango, avocado, coconut, and banana, for example, are very important to diets of large populations in their areas of production. Furthermore, reasonably accurate and up-to-date production data are difficult to obtain from some countries. Based on world consumption, it is reasonably certain that the most important fruits are grape, banana, orange, apple, and mango. In second rank of importance are strawberry, olive, pear, peach, and plum, followed by pineapple, lemon, lime, grapefruit, cherry, fig, cacao, apricot, avocado, the brambles and bush fruits, and others.

Although annual yields of nuts tend to fluctuate rather widely, the filberts led as a world nut crop in the 1960s, followed closely by the pecan, English walnut, almond, and cashew. The macadamia nut, while low on the list, is likely to increase markedly in the years ahead as demand continues to exceed production.

Improvements in technology and consolidation of the fruit and nut industries in the most favoured climates have been responsible for a steady increase in yield per unit of land or per tree or plant. Thus, the total acreage or number of plants devoted to various fruit and nut crops has dropped, remained about the same, or not risen in proportion to the increase in the respective crop production.

Increased yields

FRUIT AND NUT GROWING IN THE TROPICS

Although the principal perennial fruit and nut plants of these warm regions differ in many ways, most of them are evergreen and are seriously injured or killed by freezing temperatures.

Avocado. At the time of the Spanish conquests, the avocado tree was under primitive culture in the cool tropical regions of Central and South America and on some of the Caribbean islands. In recent years intensive selection of superior varieties has formed the basis for a commercial industry on a substantial scale in the U.S., South Africa, and Mexico, and on a smaller scale in Chile, Brazil, Hawaii, and Australia. The avocado has narrow limitations in climatic adaptability. There are also inherent problems of harvesting and postharvest care. These have been largely overcome for the better shipping variety, Fuerte, whose quality, however, leaves something to be desired. Export avocados are sold mostly in luxury markets though many are purchased by former natives of tropical areas such as Puerto Rico who have emigrated to northern cities. Among the most important varieties are Fuerte, Zutano, Lula, and Booth 8.

Banana. Cultivated throughout the tropics, the banana is a highly important source of food. The ease with which this giant herb (3–6 metres high; leaves 3 metres × 650 millimetres) may be propagated from pieces of rhizome (rootstock) has made it possible for vast acreages of a few seedless varieties to be planted in widely separate regions. Important among the varieties are Gros Michel, Cavendish, and Mysore. Although the fruit (in bunches of 50–150 bananas per plant) is highly perishable, its ability to develop good eating quality after having been harvested green has permitted the efficient operation of intricately coordinated agencies of the plantation, shipping, and marketing phases that bring bananas to the temperate zone cities throughout the year. Perhaps three-quarters of the bananas for these distant markets originate in Central America, northern South America, and the islands of the Caribbean. Dried banana "figs" and other palatable products are made from bananas, but most of the fruit is sold for fresh consumption. The large green plantain type of banana is cooked and eaten in the tropics and is occasionally exported to persons who have migrated to temperate zone cities.

Pineapple. The pineapple has been distributed around the world in the humid tropics during relatively recent times. This small (about 750 millimetres) semiherbaceous perennial with drought-resistant leaves of an epiphyte, or air plant, can be cultivated successfully in somewhat drier and cooler tropical areas than the banana. Easy vegetative propagation from slips or suckers has permitted heavy concentration on a few seedless varieties, the most important of which are Smooth Cayenne, Red Spanish, and Queen. At present about half the world's commercial production originates in the Hawaiian Islands and a third in the Caribbean Islands, Central America, and northern South America. Although shipment of fresh fruit, harvested a little green, is considerable, the

canned fruit is the most important commercial product for distant markets, accounting for practically all of the Hawaiian output.

Mango. Under cultivation in the tropics for centuries, the mango is widely distributed and consumed on a local basis. In India alone, there are more than 14,000,000 acres occupied by mango trees. A small commercial industry exists in the U.S. This large evergreen tree (10–20 metres) produces best in tropical regions with a considerable dry season that coincides with the annual period of bloom. Many varieties have been selected and propagated by graftage; among the most important of these are Mulgoba, Saigon, Carabao, Haden, and Julie. In spite of its importance as a food in the regions where it is grown, there are no reliable statistics on world production. The extreme perishability of the fresh fruit and special problems of harvesting and storage have discouraged shipment to distant markets. Improved modern handling techniques may help to correct this. No appreciable volume of the fruit is processed commercially as a canned or frozen product, although considerable quantities are used for preserves and chutney.

Papaya. The papaya is a palmlike tree reaching a height of eight metres but less woody than a typical palm. The succulent fruits, resembling cantaloupes, are attached to the trunk and contain hundreds of black round seeds six millimetres in diameter attached to the inside wall of the single large cavity. This seed-propagated tree grows rapidly, bearing at the end of the first year and living for five years or more. The tree does not branch laterally and is covered by deeply lobed leaves up to 600 millimetres across and borne on hollow petioles up to 600 millimetres long. There are male, female, and hermaphroditic (plant with both female and male flowers) tree forms. Papaya is grown throughout the tropics, chiefly for local consumption. Hawaiian annual production approaches 9,000,000 kilograms, with about 1,400,000 processed. About 450,000 kilograms of papayas are harvested each from Florida and Puerto Rico. A large volume of preserved papayas are exported by Mexico, Australia, and Taiwan; fresh papayas by the Bahamas; and papaya paste and pulp by Nicaragua and Australia. Shipment overseas is largely by air; some are shipped under controlled atmosphere conditions using 2 percent oxygen with low temperature control to increase market life. At 7° C (45° F) papayas keep satisfactorily for one to three weeks and ripen at 21–26° C (70–80° F) for retail sale. A half-cup of papaya cubes contains about twice the daily vitamin C requirement for an adult and three-fifths the vitamin A, and is low in sodium and calories. Papain in papaya juice is noted for its meat-tenderizing quality.

Air shipments

Coconut. This nut is one of the most important food sources for indigenous populations of the tropics. The coconut palm reaches a height of 30 metres, is resistant to hurricane winds, has a slender, leaning trunk with annual rings and a swollen base. The top is crowned with typical palm leaves. Flower stalks push out at the base of the older leaves, bearing about 10,000 male flowers and 30 female flowers. Fifty to 100 fruits ripen in a year. The fruit is egg shaped, 300–450 millimetres in length and 150–200 millimetres in diameter. The shell is 12–18 millimetres thick with hard fibres on the outside and white meat clinging to the inside. The three "eyes" at the stem end of the fruit are the three ovarial cavities; they may be punched to withdraw the nutritious milk from the large cavity. The white meat (called copra when dried) may be grated, and has numerous culinary uses in salads, curries, candies, cake and pie toppings, etc., and as a source of coconut oil.

Cashew. This tropical bushy tree (up to 12 metres high), is grown in Central America, South America, and the West Indies, India, and East Africa. The mature tree lives 20–45 years, is widely adapted to soils, requires a minimum of attention, withstands very light frost, and produces about 30 kilograms and occasionally as high as 90 kilograms a year. The hooked beanlike nut within a shell is attached at the base of a fleshy, pear-shaped "apple" about 30 millimetres in diameter and 40 millimetres long. Though used locally in beverages, jams, and jellies, the apple is unimportant commercially. The cashew ranks high in world trade among nuts. Some 60,000 metric tons from East Africa are shipped annually to India where they are processed along with some 80,000 Indian-grown metric tons, and exported. The U.S. is the chief importer. The nut is roasted and canned, sometimes mixed with other nuts.

Brazil nut. This large picturesque tree is 30–50 metres tall, 1.2–1.5 metres in diameter, and has a smooth trunk. Branching at the top, it is tardy and light in bearing and grows mainly in the Amazon Basin of Brazil. Hardshelled at maturity, the fruit is 100–150 millimetres in diameter and contains eight to twenty-four angular seeds or nuts arranged tightly. Seeds are about 25 × 35 millimetres with white solid flesh. They are shipped and sold mostly unshelled. On arrival at destination they are stored at 1–7° C (34–45° F) and 65–70 percent relative humidity.

Macadamia. Also called the Queensland nut, the macadamia is grown commercially in Hawaii (where the trees occupy more than 3,000 acres from sea level to elevations of 800 metres) and to some extent in Australia. A small industry is developing in California. There are several species, but the "smooth-shell" *M. integrifolia* is preferred. The handsome tree begins bearing in 6–7 years, resembles an orange tree in shape and size, with long narrow prickly serrated leaves. It needs wind protection when young and judicious pruning, training, and fertilization. The macadamia tree requires 1.25–3.0 metres of rainfall, well distributed, and a good, well-drained soil, (pH 4.5–6.5) but can be grown on rocky slopes where sugar and pineapples do not thrive. The nuts are spherical, 15–20 millimetres in diameter, and contain light tan, pleasantly crisp kernels, appetizing and slightly sweet in flavour. Hawaiian improved clonal (vegetatively propagated) varieties are Kakea, Ikaiki and Keauhou. These varieties look promising in California plus the rough-shelled varieties Burdick and the Australian Elimbah. Macadamia is mainly a dessert nut and goes well at cocktail time. Demand for this nut exceeds supply; hence the price is relatively high.

Paradise nut. This nut (also called monkey pot and sapucaia nut) borne on a big forest tree in Brazil and Guiana, resembles the Brazil nut, though it has a softer shell and kernel. Nuts, 50 millimetres long, irregular-oblong and ridged, are crowded in a woody fruit 200 × 250 millimetres, which has a lid that pops off when mature, leaving the nuts hanging and dropping from vegetative (funicular) strings. Monkeys, either baited or in attempts to get the nuts, may get their heads caught in the "pot."

Oyster nut. Though long popular in its native East Africa, this "nut" (actually a gourd seed) has been marketed elsewhere as a dessert nut only since World War II. The seed is flat, from 30–50 millimetres in diameter, and covered with a fibrous layer that unfortunately prevents the use of mechanical crackers.

Swarri. This South American nut, also called the souari or butternut, from the Guianas, is sometimes imported into Europe and North America. It is about four times the size of a Brazil nut with a thick (over ten millimetres) hard shell enclosing a soft white kernel with a good flavour.

FRUIT GROWING IN THE SUBTROPICS

Perennial fruit species successful in subtropical regions possess some resistance to injury from freezing temperatures during the winter months. They also benefit from the slight seasonal periodicity of the climate. Like species of the tropics, they are usually evergreen.

Date. The majestic date palm, 20–25 metres high and crowned with pinnate leaves 3–6 metres long, is native to desert oases of the Persian Gulf. For thousands of years the fruit has been an essential part of the diet of indigenous populations living in the eastern Mediterranean basin and north Africa. Iraq leads in production,

with Algeria and Tunisia also very important. Date production has almost doubled since the 1940s. Although the palm has been distributed widely in modern times, nine-tenths of the commercial production comes from the areas of ancient culture. This may result largely from three circumstances: (1) a desert climate with no rainfall during most of the period of fruit development is essential for a marketable product, yet there must be ample soil moisture during this same period; (2) the product is stable and there is a sufficient output in the indigenous region to satisfy most of the world demand at moderate prices; (3) propagation of the superior varieties must be by offshoots from relatively young palms, and the supply is so limited as to make establishment of new date gardens in distant countries slow and expensive. In spite of this, however, a small industry based on Old World varieties, of which Deglet Noor is the most commonly planted, is flourishing in California.

Date varieties selected over the past centuries may be divided into three classes according to their physical properties and sugar content. Dry dates (sometimes called bread dates), firm and relatively low in sugars, are important locally in the Old World desert region for daily nourishment; the Thoory variety is an example. Semidry varieties soften at maturity; because they are firm enough to pack and ship well, they are the most important commercially; Deglet Noor, Dayri, and Zahidi are examples. Soft dates, used mainly as confection, are the most difficult to handle; examples of this kind are Barhee, Khadrawy, and Hayany. In Old World areas the date trunk is used for timber, leaf midribs for furniture and crates, leaflets for basketry, leaf bases and fruit stalks for fuel, and seeds for cattle feed. None of the plant is wasted.

Uses for
date trunk

Citrus. Introduced to the Western world by traders from southeastern Asia during the period from the 12th to the 18th century, the most important citrus fruits are now produced in large quantity in tropical and subtropical America, the northern and eastern Mediterranean, Australia, and South Africa. Orange, mandarin (tangerine), and grapefruit trees are most productive and develop the best quality in regions where there is some seasonal periodicity of climate. Since they are able to withstand exposure to a few degrees below freezing in midwinter, they may be intensively cultivated in regions where occasional light frosts occur as well as in the milder subtropics. Leading orange-producing countries include the U.S., Israel (Jaffa oranges), Morocco, Spain (Seville oranges), and South Africa. The mandarin orange (tangerine) is important in the U.S., Brazil, Spain, Italy, Mexico, and Japan. About 90 percent of the world's grapefruit is grown in the U.S., with Israel, Jordan, South Africa, and Brazil following. Mexico is the leader in world lime production, with Egypt second and the U.S. third. The U.S. and Italy are premier lemon producers, followed by Spain, Greece, Turkey, and Argentina. In Florida, which produces 70 percent of U.S. oranges, the four principal varieties are Parson Brown, Hamlin, Pineapple, and Valencia; the first two are sent to the early fresh-fruit market whereas perhaps half of the Pineapple and Valencia crops are sold fresh and the rest are processed into frozen concentrate. California is responsible for most of the rest of the orange crop. The main grapefruit varieties are Marsh Seedless, Foster, Ruby, and Duncan. Among tangerines, Dancy is a popular variety, much grown in Florida. There are two relatively large-fruited lime varieties: Tahiti and Bearss; the "Key" lime, once grown extensively on the Florida Keys, has almost disappeared. The main lemon varieties are Lisbon, Eureka, and Villafranca. Much of the fruit is sold fresh but increasing amounts have been processed into frozen concentrate or canned juice.

FRUIT AND NUT GROWING IN THE WARM TEMPERATE ZONE

Most perennial fruit species adapted to the warm temperate zone are deciduous, passing the winter leafless. A few (*e.g.*, the olive) are evergreen. Practically all resist temperatures below −7° C (20° F) during winter

Table 1: Scientific Names, Probable Original Source, and Uses of Fruits and Nuts

common name	scientific name of main crop	probable original source	principal uses*
Fruits			
Apple	*Malus pumila*	southeastern Europe, southwestern Asia	food, fire wood
Apricot	*Prunus armeniaca*	China	food
Avocado (alligator pear)	*Persea americana*	Mexico to Colombia	food
Banana	*Musa sapientum* (common) *M. cavendishii* (dwarf) *M. paradisiaca* (plantain)	Asia (southeastern)	food
Blackberry	*Rubus allegheniensis*		food
Blueberry	*Vaccinium corymbosum*	North America	food
Cherry	*Prunus cerasus* (tart); *P. avium* (sweet)	western Asia and eastern Europe	food, wood
Citrus			
Orange	*Citrus sinensis*	Malay archipelago	food
Grapefruit	*C. paradisi*	Jamaica (?)	food
Lemon	*C. limon*	E. Indian archipelago	food, oil
Lime	*C. aurantifolia*	E. Indian archipelago	food, oil
Cranberry	*Vaccinium macrocarpon*	North America	food
Currant	*Ribes sativum* (red) *R. nigrum* (black)	western Europe	food
Date	*Phoenix dactylifera*	southern Iraq	food
Fig	*Ficus carica*	Mediterranean area	food
Gooseberry	*Ribes hirtellum* (American) *R. uva-crispa* (European)	North America, western Europe	food
Grape	*Vitis vinifera* (European) *V. labrusca* (American)	Caspian Sea area Atlantic slope, North America	food
Guava†	*Psidium guajava* (common) *P. cattleianum* (strawberry)	tropical America	food
Mango	*Mangifera indica*	East India, Burma, Assam, Malaya	food
Mangosteen†	*Garcinia mangostana*	Southeast Asia	food
Olive	*Olea europaea*	E. Mediterranean area	food, oil
Peach	*Prunus persica*	China	food
Papaya	*Carica papaya*	Central America, Mexico	food, papain (meat tenderizer)
Passion fruit	*Passiflora edulis*	tropical America	food flavouring
Pineapple	*Ananas comosus*	West Indies	food
Plum	*Prunus domestica*	Caucasus area	food
Raspberry	*Rubus idaeus* (red) *R. occidentalis* (black) *R. neglectus* (purple)	eastern Asia	food
Strawberry	*Fragaria* sp. (8)	Americas	food
Nuts			
Almond (sweet)	*Prunus amygdalus*	W. temperate India and Persia	food
Almond (bitter)	*P. amygdalus*, var. *amara*	W. temperate India and Persia	flavouring extract
Almond, Indian	*Terminalia catappa*	W. temperate India and Persia	food
Almondette	*Buchanania lanzan*	India, Burma	food
Araucarian pine nut (piñon, pinyonie)	*Araucaria araucana*	Chile	food
Arnut (yer-nut, earth chestnut, hawk nut, lousy-nut)	*Bunium* species	W. Europe to Caucasus	food
Australian nut, *see* Macadamia			
Babassu nut	*Orbignya oleifera*	Brazil	food, fuel oil
Bambarra groundnut	*Voandzeia subterranea*	tropical Africa	food
Barbados nut (physic nut)	*Jatropha curcas*	tropical America	medicine
Baroba	*Dispoldiscus paniculatus*	Philippines	starchy seeds boiled and eaten
Beech nut, American	*Fagus grandifolia*	E. United States	
Beech nut, European	*Fagus sylvatica*	Cent. Europe, S.W. Asia	salad oil
Ben nut	*Moringa oleifera*	India, West Indies	artists' oil, lubricant
Betel nut (areca nut, pinang)	*Areca catechu*	E. tropics	masticatory
Bladder nut	*Staphylea* species	temperate North America, S. Europe, S. Asia	necklaces
Bomah nut	*Pycnocoma macrophylla*	Africa	tanning, poison
Bonduc nut	*Caesalpinia bonduc*	Tropics	medicine, beads
Brazil nut (castanea, creamnut, para nut)	*Bertholletia excelsa*	Amazon Basin, Brazil	food
Breadfruit, African	*Treculia africana*	tropical Africa	seeds ground for meal
Bread nut	*Brosimum alicastrum*	tropical America	food
Butternut (long or white walnut)	*Juglans cinerea*	E. United States, S.E. Canada	food
Butter pit, *see* Naras nut			
Candlenut	*Aleurites moluccana*	Malaysia	drying
Cashew (acajou, caja, cajou)	*Anacardium occidentale*	West Indies, Brazil	food, oil, wood, varnish, paint
Castanopsis nut (golden chinquapin, wild chestnut)	*Castanopsis* species	S.E. Asia, California	food
Chestnut	*Castanea* species	E. United States, S. Europe, N. Africa, Asia	food
Chile hazel	*Gevuina avellana*	Chile	food
Chinquapin	*Castanea* species	S.E. United States, China	food
Chufa (rush nut, earthnut, ground almond)	*Cyperus esculentus*	S. Europe	food
Cobnut, *see* Filbert			
Cobnut, Jamaican	*Omphalea diandra*	West Indies, tropical America	food, oil
Coconut	*Cocos nucifera*	Old World tropics	food, oil
Cohune nut (cahoun nut)	*Attalea cohune*	Honduras	oil
Cola nut, *see* Kola nut			
Coquilla nut	*Attalea funifera*	Brazil	turnery
Coquita nut (coker nut)	*Jubaea spectabilis*	Chile	oil, food
Coumara nut, *see* Tonka bean			
Dika nut	*Irvingia gabonensis*	W. Africa	food, oil
Doum nut (dom nut)	*Hyphaene thebaica*	N. and central Africa	turnery, vegetable ivory

Table 1: Scientific Names, Probable Original Source, and Uses of Fruits and Nuts (cont.)

common name	scientific name of main crop	probable original source	principal uses*
Filbert (hazelnut)	*Corylus* species	E. North America, S.E. Europe, Balkans, W. Asia	food
Galo nut	*Anacolosa luzoniensis*	Philippines	food
Gasso nut	*Manniophyton africanum*	W. Africa, Congo	food
Ginkgo nut	*Ginkgo biloba*	China, Japan	food
Gnetum seed	*Gnetum gnemon*	tropical Asia	food
Groundnut (wild bean)	*Apios tuberosa*	North America	tubers eaten
Grugru nut (corozo nut)	*Acrocomia aculeata*	tropical South America	beads, oil
Helicia nut	*Helicia diversifolia*	Queensland, Australia	food
Hickory nut	*Carya* species	North America, China	food
Hodgsonia seed	*Hodgsonia macrocarpa*	tropical Asia	food
Hyphaene nut, *see* Doum nut			
Indian nut, *see* Pine nut			
Inoi nut	*Poga oleosa*	W. Africa	food
Jack nut	*Artocarpus heterophyllus*	India	food
Japanese walnut (heartnut, cordate walnut)	*Juglans cordiformis ailanthifolia*	Japan	food
Java almond (Luzon or Philippine nut)	*Canarium commune*	Pacific tropics	food
Jojoba nut (goat nut, sheep nut)	*Simmondsia californica*	California, Mexico	food, hair oil
Karaka nut	*Corynocarpus laevigatus*	New Zealand	food
Kola nut	*Cola acuminata, C. nitida*	W. tropical Africa	masticatory, stimulant
Kubili nut	*Cubilia blancoi*	Philippines	food
Ling (caltrop, lingko)	*Trapa bicornis*	China	food
Litchi (lychee, Chinese nut)	*Litchi chinensis*	S. China	food
Lotus seed	*Nelumbium nelumbo*	Asia	food
Lunan nut	*Otophora fruticosa*	Pacific region	food
Macadamia (Queensland nut, Australian nut)	*Macadamia* species	Australia	food
Manketti nut	*Ricinodendron rautanenii*	S. Africa	food
Marking nut	*Semecarpus anacardium*	India	ink, varnish, food
Moreton Bay chestnut (black bean)	*Castanospermum australe*	Australia	food
Naras nut (butter pit)	*Acanthosicyos horrida*	S.W. Africa	food, oil
Nicari Palm nut	*Cocos coronata*	Brazil	food
Nitta nut (nete)	*Parkia biglobosa*	tropical Africa	food
Nutmeg	*Myristica fragrans*	East Indies	spice
Olive	*Elaeocarpus ganitrus*	India	beads, ornaments
Owusa nut	*Plukenetia conophora*	W. tropical Africa	food
Oyster nut	*Telfairia pedata*	E. Africa	food
Palm chestnut	*Guilielma gasipaes*	tropical South America	food
Palm nut	*Elaeis guineensis*	W. Africa	oil
Paradise nut (sapucaia nut)	*Lecythis zabucajo*	Brazil	food
Pascualito nut (pinonchillo)	*Garcia nutans*	Mexico to Venezuela	quick-drying oil
Peanut (groundnut)	*Arachis hypogaea*	Brazil	food
Peanut, hog	*Amphicarpa monoica*	North America	food
Pecan (Illinois nut)	*Carya illinoensis*	S. United States	food
Pili nut	*Canarium ovatum*	Pacific tropics	food
Pine nut (piñon, pignolia)	*Pinus* species	S.W. United States, Europe, Asia	food
Pistachio (pistache, green almond)	*Pistacia vera*	Mediterranean basin to Iran, S.W. Asia	food
Poison nut	*Strychnos nuxvomica*	India	medicine
Quandong nut	*Fusanus acuminatus*	Australia	food
Ravensara nut (clove nutmeg)	*Ravensara aromatica*	Madagascar	spice
Rose nut (red nut)	*Hicksbeachia pinnatifolia*	Australia	ornamental, food
Sassafras nut	*Ocotea* species	South America	aromatic
Shea butter nut	*Butyrospermum parkii*	Tropical Africa	food, soap oil
Singhara nut (water nut)	*Trapa bispinosa*	India, Kashmir	food
Snake nut	*Ophiocaryon paradoxum*	Guiana	charm for snakebite
Soap nut	*Sapindus saponaria*	S. Florida to N. South America	soap substitute
Soap nut, Indian	*Sapindus inocarpus*	India	soap substitute
Sterculia nut	*Sterculia foetida*	tropical Africa	food
Swarri nut (souari nut, sawarri nut, pekea nut, butter nut, piki)	*Caryocar* species	tropical America	food
Taccy nut	*Caryodendron orinocense*	Colombia	food
Taqua nut (ivory nut, vegetable ivory)	*Phytelephas macrocarpa*	Central America	ornaments, buttons
Tahiti chestnut (South Sea chestnut)	*Inocarpus edulis*	South Seas	food
Tallow nut (false sandalwood)	*Ximenia americana*	tropical Africa	food
Tallow nut, Chinese	*Sapium sebiferum*	China	wax for soap and candles
Tiger nut, *see* Chufa			
Tonka bean (tonqua or tonquin bean, coumara nut)	*Dipteryx odorata*	tropical South America	perfume
Torreya nut (kaya nut)	*Torreya nucifera*	China, Japan	food, oil
Tropical almond (myrobalan, tavola nut, Demerara almond)	*Terminalia catappa*	S.W. Asia	food
Tung nut (wood-oil tree)	*Aleurites* species	S. China	paint, varnish, oil
Walnut, African	*Coula edulis*	W. tropical Africa, Congo	food
Walnut, Persian	*Juglans regia*	Orient	food, wood
Walnut, Black	*J. nigra*	North America	food, wood, ground shells for blasting, polishing, etc.
Water chestnut (water caltrop)	*Trapa natans*	Europe, Asia	food
Water chestnut, Chinese (matai)	*Eleocharis tuberosa*	S. China	food
Yeheb nut	*Cordeauxia edulis*	Somalia	food

*All fruits listed are eaten fresh. Most fruits can be canned, although some freeze better such as blueberry, strawberry, raspberry, cranberry, and peach. Jellies, jams, juices, cider, and spirits are products of most fruits although some are better adapted than others, such as apple and peach. Some fruits are adapted to drying, particularly those relatively high in sugar, as prune, some peaches, fig, and some grapes. †Noncommercial.

Table 2: World Production of Major Fruits

	production (000 metric tons)*			1968 data
	average† 1948–52	1959†	1968†	1948–52 × 100
Grape	34,400	44,800	53,678	156
Orange and mandarin	12,211	16,600	27,370	224
Banana	12,121	17,900	25,448	209
Apple	13,512	14,100	20,189	149
Olive	4,900	6,390	7,411	151
Pear	3,900	4,420	7,300	187
Peach	2,400	3,800	5,791	241
Plum and prune	3,000	4,460	4,547	152
Pineapple	1,448	1,990	3,564	246
Lemon and lime	1,600	2,200	3,329	208
Grapefruit	1,700	1,800	2,715	160
Date	1,300	1,450	2,060	158
Cherry (sweet and sour)	1,200	1,360	1,776	148
Fig	1,341	1,320	1,267	94
Cacao	763	930	1,249	164
Apricot	707	1,000	1,230	174
Strawberry	400	...	952	238
Raspberry	92	...	128	139

*Metric ton is 2,204.62 lb, or 1,000 kg. †Data are for production seasons beginning in year stated.
Source: *Production Yearbook*, FAO of United Nations, Rome, volumes 15 (1961) and 23 (1969), and FAS reports, USDA, Washington.

dormancy. Most cannot be grown commercially in the subtropics or tropics because of their relatively short chilling requirement of temperatures below 7° C (45° F) for normal growth and flowering. Winter hardiness is not great. A long, warm growing season may be necessary for satisfactory productivity and fruit quality; hence, they are not well adapted to cooler regions.

Grape. The Old World grapevine (*Vitis vinifera*) is by far the most important perennial fruit in the world. It has been cultivated for thousands of years in the Mediterranean basin and southwestern Europe. In the last half of the 19th century the grape phylloxera, a plant louse carried on stock from the U.S. to France, ravaged the vineyards of central Europe until resistant rootstocks were obtained from the U.S. Although more than two-thirds of the world's grapes still come from these areas, there is now important production on all continents in the milder parts of their temperate zones, whether north or south latitude. France, Italy, and Spain are the biggest grape producers, followed by Hungary, Turkey, U.S.S.R., Algeria, Argentina, Greece, Portugal, Romania, Yugoslavia, and the U.S.

Use of grapes in wine

The fruit from this species may be consumed fresh, dried for raisins, or used for wines and alcoholic distillates. By far the largest part of the European and Mediterranean production goes into wine. Only a small portion is eaten fresh or made into raisins. The California vinifera industry, on the other hand, dries more than half its production (though this has been decreasing), ships 10 to 15 percent as table and canning stock, and uses the remaining third for wine. The important varieties differ in their versatility for these uses. Sultanina (Thompson

Table 3: World Production of Major Nut Crops

nut crop	production* (000 short tons)
Filbert	263
Pecan	220
Walnut (Persian)	170
Almond	140
Cashew	140†
Brazil nut	45‡
Chestnut	25§
Pistachio	15‖
Macadamia	5¶
Coconut	28⚲

*Figures are approximate from key areas for the 1960s. Production for local consumption not included. Short ton is 2,000 lb.
†India, East Africa. ‡Brazil. §Italy. ‖Iran, Syria, Turkey. ¶Hawaii. ⚲000,000,000 coconuts.
Source: *Production Yearbook*, FAO of United Nations, Rome, vol. 22 (1968); and FAS reports, USDA, Washington.

Seedless) and Muscat of Alexandria are grown in quantity for all three purposes; the Flame Tokay and several others are used both for fresh fruit and for specialty wines. On the other hand, Zante currant is grown only for its raisins, and a number of varieties including Zinfandel, Carignane, and Alicante Bouschet are produced exclusively for red wine.

Olive. The olive tree was under cultivation in warmer parts of the eastern Mediterranean basin some 3,000 years ago, and its spread into North Africa and southern Europe was undoubtedly completed during the Arab invasions if not before. Introduction to the New World by Spanish colonists resulted in small industries in South America and California. The world's supply of this important fruit and its oil, however, comes almost entirely from the countries bordering the Mediterranean, with Italy, Spain, Greece, and Turkey leading. Although evergreen and able to grow normally under subtropical conditions, the tree does not flower unless exposed to temperatures below 7° C (45° F) for a considerable period of time. The tree is tolerant to winter temperatures as low as −9° C (15° F), but the fruit is injured at temperatures slightly below freezing. This resistance to cold, coupled with endurance of hot summer weather and rather severe moisture deficiency, has caused the olive to be planted in many areas not suitable for other fruit crops.

Temperature requirements

The fruit is pickled in brine, canned ripe, or pressed to make olive oil. Most European production is used for olive oil, although Spain produces substantial quantities of pickled olives. Examples of important olive varieties are Manzanillo, Barouni, and Mission. Only varieties high in oil are useful for extraction; the others are processed as fruit.

Fig. Like the olive and grape, the fig tree was under cultivation in the warm temperate climate of the Mediterranean basin long before the time of Christ. Some of the varieties of that region have probably been carried down to modern times by vegetative propagation for over a thousand years. Practically all commercial production (mostly Brown Turkey variety) comes from Italy, Portugal, Spain, Turkey, Greece, and Algeria, with small production in the U.S., Mexico, Brazil, Peru, Argentina, and Australia.

The tree withstands cold to 9° C (48° F) and has a relatively short chilling requirement. Some varieties, in fact, grow and fruit satisfactorily in the tropics. Plants vary from a low bush to trees 12 metres high; leaves are wide, corrugated, and lobed to almost entire margins. The most favourable climate for growing figs is semi-arid with irrigation water available and no rain during the period of fruit maturation and drying. Such a climate facilitates sun-drying, and inhibits bacterial and fungus infection in maturing fruit. Some varieties are grown under humid conditions, however, for local sale or canning. In the U.S. the main production area is the irrigated Central Valley of California with rainfall ranging from 250 to 500 millimetres annually, and a long hot growing season. The most important varieties are Calimyrna (Lob Injir), Adriatic, Mission, and Kadota (Dottato). The first two varieties account for three-quarters of the production; practically all are dried. Mission may be dried or marketed fresh and Kadota is canned in light syrup.

Chief varieties of figs

Apricot, peach, nectarine, plum, prune, and almond. These six kinds of fruit grow on small deciduous trees of genus *Prunus* whose climatic requirements are satisfied in the warm temperate zone and whose culture extends to the milder parts of the cool temperate zone, although some plums are quite resistant to low winter temperature. All of them are cultivated widely in the climatic regions of the world to which they are adapted.

The apricot, originating in China, is somewhat more restricted climatically than the peach and plum partly because it has a shorter chilling requirement and blooms earlier, making it frost susceptible in many areas, and partly because of its great susceptibility to fungus diseases (brown and green rots), which make culture difficult in regions where summer rainfall is high. The U.S.

is the leader in apricot production, followed by Iran and Syria in Asia, and by Spain, France, Italy, and Yugoslavia in Europe. Local climatic conditions determine whether the main outlets are for fresh fruit, drying, or canning; these outlets in turn may determine the varieties and cultural practices. Thus, where an early harvest season gives the industry opportunity to exploit a premium market for fresh fruit, the main variety has been Royal (similar to Blenheim). In the regions that have midseason harvest, the drying outlet predominates and the Tilton variety has been most important. In the cooler, more northern sections, where canning and late market are the dominant outlets, Moorpark and Large Early Montgamet are important.

The peach also originated in China. Although there are varieties adapted to climates ranging from the subtropics to the milder parts of the cool temperate zone, the most important peach regions of the world have long hot growing seasons and mild winters lasting at least three months during which freezing temperatures occur frequently. The U.S. and Italy produce about half the world's crop. They are followed by France, Spain, Greece, Argentina, Japan, Turkey, Canada, South Africa, and Australia. The chilling requirement for flower buds depends on the variety; for Florida and Texas varieties it is 300–500 hours below 7° C (45° F), but up to 900 hours for some varieties grown in colder regions. Leaf buds require slightly more chilling (100–200 hours) than flower buds. As with apricots, there are three outlets for this fruit and varieties differ in accordance with them. Clingstone varieties such as Gaume, Paloro, and Halford are usually canned. Drying is also a by-product or distress outlet for other varieties like Muir and Lovell, which are especially desirable because of their relatively high-sugar and dry-matter content. The fresh-fruit market is served by a long list of delicious freestone varieties including Redhaven, Sunhigh, Triogem, Blake, Elberta and Rio-Oso-Gem.

In recent years the demand for the nectarine, essentially a fuzzless peach, has been growing. In California, the LeGrand, Late LeGrand, Sun Grand, Early Sun Grand, and Sunrise are important. In the eastern U.S., the New Jersey Nectared series is being planted.

Origin of the plum

The original plum comes from Persia. The world's plum and prune industries, however, are based mainly on two species of different origin and adaptation. The Japanese plum, *Prunus salicina*, is a small, vegetative tree with approximately the same climatic requirements as the apricot. It is most successful in semi-arid, irrigated, warm-temperature climates. Because the fruit is very high in moisture and soft, it is not useful for canning. Difficulties of handling and storage limit the opportunities for large-scale exploitation in fresh-fruit markets. The principal European species, *Prunus domestica*, is responsible for most of the commercial plum and prune production of the world. The climatic adaptability of the tree straddles the warm and cool temperate zones, and it is tolerant both to semi-arid and humid climates. European plums will withstand more soil moisture and heavier soils than peach, almond, or apricot. The most important varieties produce fruit that may be harvested in a firm condition and that has storage and shelf life of a month or more. Some varieties are very high in sugar and total solids and may be dried for prunes, as French Prune and Imperial Epineuse.

Leading countries in plum and prune production are, in order, Yugoslavia, Romania, U.S., West Germany, U.S.S.R., Bulgaria, and Hungary. World production is about 4,000,000 metric tons.

In the U.S., practically all the Japanese plums are grown in California; important varieties are Beauty, Santa Rosa, and Duarte. European plums are an important crop in Oregon, Idaho, Washington, and California. California produces all the dried prunes of the U.S.; the variety French Prune accounts for over 90 percent of the acreage. In the south of England, several varieties of the Green Gage group, Czar, Giant Prune, and Victoria are prized for their dessert qualities.

The almond tree, originating in Persia, resembles the peach but is not as hardy. It flowers earlier and may be subject to frosts in some regions. Hence, the commercial industry is confined to a climate similar to the Central Valley of California. The fruit resembles the peach, except that the outer tissues (mesocarp and exocarp) develop into a leathery hull that splits along the suture line, curls outward, and can be separated from the endocarp or shell around the kernel. There are two types of almonds, sweet and bitter, with the sweet being the well-known edible almond. Bitter almonds, which are inedible, are a source of oil (50 percent) used in flavouring extracts.

The sweet almond is cultivated in suitable regions between 28–40° north and 20–40° south of the Equator. Leading countries exporting shelled almonds in order of importance are Italy, U.S., and Spain, followed by Iran, Morocco, and Portugal. World production is approaching 150,000 short tons annually.

The Jordan variety is grown in Europe. California has developed most of its varieties from seedlings and by breeding, namely, Nonpareil, Drake, Peerless, Ne Plus Ultra, Texas or Mission, IXL, Jordanolo, and Davey. Several new varieties have been introduced recently, including Thompson, Merced, and Kapareil. The almond rootstock is commonly used, but where the water table is high, peach rootstock is used, and where oak root fungus is a problem, the Marianna plum is used. For pollination purposes, about four rows each of Ne Plus Ultra or Peerless, Nonpareil, and Mission or Drake, are alternated across the field.

Harvesting techniques

In modern harvesting, a hydraulic trunk shaker jars the nuts to the leveled ground and a rotating brush set at an angle pushes the nuts into a windrow where they are picked up by a machine that blows off the dirt, leaves, and debris, and loads the nuts into a bin pulled behind. Almonds are used extensively in candies, bakery products, and in cooking. Hulls of the soft-shelled varieties are fed to livestock with barley and alfalfa.

Filbert. The filbert grows as a shrub or a tree up to 8 metres in height; most commercial trees are about 4.5 metres tall. Leaves are rugose (veinlets sunken and the spaces between elevated), about the size of an apple leaf and roundish in shape. Male catkins and female flowers are borne separately on the same plant. Female flowers are borne in small scaly buds with the stigmas visible during flowering. Like almonds, filberts bloom early and hence may suffer from frost; flowers can withstand temperatures to −9° C (16° F). Most filberts do not fruit if pollinated by another tree of the same variety; two or more varieties must be interplanted. They are unusual among fruit trees in being wind pollinated rather than insect pollinated. The filbert shell, about 1.5 millimetres thick, is the ovary wall; the kernel is largely embryo. After pollination, several months pass before the nut begins to develop. Then the shell forms rapidly and the embryo develops. Filberts grow best in a medium loam: light sands and heavy clays are not very satisfactory. They are more tolerant of heavy clays than pecan or walnut but cannot tolerate excessive moisture. Unlike most nut trees, the filbert does not have a tap root and hence transplants easily. Commercial trees are planted in rows 6 metres apart, with similar intervals between trees in each row.

Filberts reach maximum production between 15 and 25 years of age, yielding in some years 1,400 kilograms or more per acre. Mechanical harvesting and handling is now used in the U.S. The European and giant filbert, together with some of their several hybrids, furnish the main commercial varieties in Europe and Turkey. Barcelona and DuChilly are leading varieties in the U.S., with some Brixnut. Leading filbert-producing countries in the world are Turkey, Italy, Spain, and the U.S. Yields vary widely from year to year.

Filberts are eaten fresh or roasted. Dried filberts are added to chocolates and other confectioneries; powdered nuts are mixed with wheat and rye to make bread or cake. Pickled in bay leaves and vinegar, they make a sauce. A paste of roasted and mashed filberts with sugar may be added to ice cream or cheese and dairy spreads. In Arabia filberts are used in manufacturing soaps.

Walnut. The English walnut is one of the world's five most commercially important nuts. The orchard tree reaches a height of 13–16 metres; wild specimens may reach 30 metres, with 1.5–2 metre trunk diameter. When young the tree has a whitish smooth trunk which turns to gray and is fissured with age. Most orchard trees have high trunks to permit intercropping. Leaves are compound with five to nine or more pinnate leaflets. Fruit is roundish with about a 6-millimetre green hull that breaks away at maturity. The nut shell shatters rather easily. Kernels are rich in oil, food energy, and protein.

While the trees can be grown in a cool temperate climate, warmer and longer seasons are needed for good kernel development. Leading producing countries are the U.S., France, Italy, India, Turkey, Syria, Iran, and Yugoslavia in the order listed. The U.S. produces around 90,-000 short tons annually.

Leading California varieties are Franquette, Payne, Hartley, Eureka, Placentia, Concord, Mayette.

The black walnut is distributed widely in the U.S. but is rarely grown in orchards. Most trees grow haphazardly over the landscape as seedlings, averaging 15–25 metres in height but reaching 45 metres with 2-metre-diameter trunk. The wood is particularly valuable for furniture, panelling, and gun stocks because of its colour and freedom from cracking and deterioration.

Black walnut characteristics

Leaves are pinnately compound. Nuts are borne in twos and threes and vary greatly in size among seedlings. Black walnut meat is oily, flavourful, and high in calories and energy. The nut is eaten out of the hand and is used in candy, toppings, and baked goods.

Pecan. The orchard pecan tree is 9–12 metres high, though some specimens may reach a height of 50 metres with a 2-metre-diameter trunk. Native to North America, the pecan is grown mainly in the southern U.S. and northern Mexico, with limited cultivation in Australia and South Africa. Though the pecan tolerates up to 40° C (110–120° F) it performs best around 26° C (80° F), with warm days and nights.

Leaves are compound, with nine to 17 finely toothed leaflets arranged in fern fashion. The male catkins are readily apparent in spring, while the small female flowers grow in tight clusters at the base of the shoots. At maturity, the hulls of the clustered nuts will dry, split at the four suture lines, and gradually free the nuts. The "shell out" (relative amount of meat to shell) depends on the variety; one with a high percentage of meat to shell is Success. Kernels are high in fat content, having a calorie count close to butter. Though confined mainly to the U.S. the pecan ranks highest in world nut production. Kernels are high in energy and vitamins B_1 and B_2. The oil is used in cooking and salads and has good keeping qualities. Kernels are widely used in candies, baked products, and in general cooking. Crushed shells are mixed with sand to form a good rooting medium for greenwood cuttings.

Pistachio. This nut, also called pistache, is believed to be native to Iran. It is grown in Afghanistan, India, and the Mediterranean region, with Sicily and India large exporters. It differs from all other nuts in the characteristic green colour of the kernel. A popular snack nut, it is salted, roasted, and eaten out of the shell and is used in grated form for ornamenting dishes. It has a pleasant mild flavour and good keeping qualities.

Pine Nut. Pine "nuts" (seeds), or pignolias, usually from the European stone pine (*Pinus pinea*), are relished by many people and much used in vegetarian cookery as a substitute for animal fat. As dessert they may be eaten raw, salted, and roasted, or made into sweetmeats. The seeds of many other pines also are eaten. In North America they are obtained from nut pines or piñons.

FRUIT GROWING IN THE COOL TEMPERATE ZONE

The perennial fruit species best adapted to this zone are deciduous and have relatively long chilling requirements,

are able to withstand subzero (F) temperatures when dormant, and can produce fruit of satisfactory quality in a growing season of six months or less.

Apple. The apple is distinguished from the pear by being free of grit cells. Apples are propagated by budding and grafting onto seedling stocks or clonal (vegetatively propagated) stocks depending upon the type and size tree desired. Trees may reach a height of two to three metres (compact) or six to nine metres with about equal spread, depending upon the root and/or interstock used. Leaves are simple and deciduous. Most apple varieties can be identified readily by leaf characteristics such as hairiness, serrations, shape, size, etc. Fruit is epignous (the ovary in the flower is below the floral parts); the edible fleshy part is largely receptacle. Fruits are borne terminally on spurs with some borne laterally on shoots.

In recent years there has been a world trend toward use of vegetatively propagated dwarfing stocks, closely planted, to keep the trees lower and easier to manage and harvest. Orchard trees on seedling stock may number 28 to 50 an acre, whereas those on extreme dwarfing stocks may number over 500 trees per acre planted as close as 2–3 metres in rows 3.5–4 metres apart. A trellis may be used with dwarfing or semidwarfing stocks since the roots are relatively shallow. Initial cost of orchards on dwarfing stock is considerably higher but the trees come into bearing within three to five years and pay for themselves sooner with higher yields.

Dwarfing apple stocks

The apple originated in Afghanistan where wild apple forests still exist. It is grown in the cool temperate climates and stands second to the grape in total tonnage of fruits and nuts produced throughout the world. The U.S. and France are the largest producers, with Germany, Switzerland, Italy, and the Balkan countries also important. About a fourth of the U.S. crop is Red Delicious, which is a popular variety (along with Golden Delicious) around the world; another 10 percent of the U.S. crop is McIntosh, followed in order by Golden Delicious, Rome Beauty, Jonathan, Winesap, York, and Stayman, the latter six of which are grown regionally. Delicious and Golden Delicious are showing marked increases in plantings, while McIntosh, Rome, Jonathan, York, and Stayman are showing modest increases. Cox Orange and Boskoop are popular in Europe; Bramley Seedling in the United Kingdom and Belgium; Yellow Transparent, Antonovka, McIntosh, Rhode Island Greening, and Sturmer Pippin in Russia; and Granny Smith in Australia, New Zealand, Argentina, and Chile.

The consuming public demands high-colour and quality Fancy and Extra Fancy fruit, except in eastern Europe where general-run fruit is marketed. Lower grades, with less colour and specified damage, go to processors for sauce, cider, baked apples, canning, freezing, or for pies. Fresh or frozen cider is popular the year round and is becoming more profitable to growers. In Europe, much of the apple crop goes into a carbonated sparkling cider; special varieties are grown for this purpose.

Pear. The pear is native to Afghanistan. The commercially important European pear is most successful in milder regions. The better pear varieties are susceptible to bacterial fireblight (*Erwinia amylovora*) in humid regions. Blight-resistant varieties such as Kieffer and Seckel can be grown successfully in humid areas, as can the blight-susceptible Bartlett, but special precautions must be taken with the latter. Pears are important on all continents, with Italy the leading producer, the U.S. second, and China, Japan, Turkey, Argentina, Australia, and South Africa also important.

In western Europe, Williams (Bartlett), Conference, Clapp's Favorite, Bonne Louise, and Doyenne du Comice are widely grown, with Passe Crassane important in Italy and Dr. J. Guyot in France. Leading U.S. varieties are Bartlett and Anjou. In the U.S.S.R., summer varieties are grown in the north, whereas in the south Williams, Clapp, Hardy, and Bosc are grown. Bulgaria has a favourable climate, with Bosc, Williams, Clapp, and Passe Crassane important. Many of the pear trees in Europe are grown in home gardens. In China pears have been cultivated over 2,000 years. Oriental pears are grown on trees larger than European types, but the fruit is inferior in quality with more grit cells and less aroma, but sweet and juicy. There are four groups of these Oriental pears grown in different regions.

In the U.S., Canada, and Australia, the quantity of fresh fruit used by canners amounts to about half the total commercial crop; in South Africa, canning accounts for 30 percent. In Europe, canning is unimportant. In France, about one-third the total production is made into a fermented drink called perry, in Germany half, in Switzerland about four-fifths.

Cherry. The sweet cherry and tart (sour) cherry are found in the milder apple regions of the world and succeed in a somewhat shorter growing season. Because sweet cherries may crack if exposed to rain during ripening, they are grown mostly in semi-arid climates. Tart cherries are grown mainly in a humid climate.

Cherries are widely grown in Europe, in fact, the U.S.S.R. leads in cherries (tart), producing almost double the U.S. crop. After the U.S., in order, are West Germany, Italy, France, Switzerland, Yugoslavia, and East Germany.

The commercial sweet cherry tree is held to six to eight metres, is more susceptible to damage resulting from excessive water at the roots than the tart cherry, is less winter hardy ($-26°$ C; $-15°$ F), and cannot fertilize itself. The tart cherry is four to five metres high, withstands $-32°$ C ($-25°$ F) winter temperature and can fertilize itself. Leaves are simple and medium size; the fruit is borne largely on spurs.

In the U.S., sweet cherry production is about 41 percent that of the tart cherry. The principal sweet cherry varieties are Bing, Lambert, Windsor, and Napoleon (Royal Ann); all but the last, which is used mostly for canning and artificial maraschino cherries, are sold chiefly in the fresh-fruit markets. Montmorency is the key tart cherry. The frozen and hot-pack preservation for pie stock, with increasing amounts used in maraschino cherries, tends to stabilize this crop for year-round marketing.

Cherries are grown on Mazzard or Mahaleb stocks, mostly the former, and there is yet to come a satisfactory dwarfing stock. Mechanical tree shaking of tart cherries on portable canvas catching frames and hauling in tanks of chilled water has greatly facilitated harvesting, improved profits to the grower, and delivered a better product to the processor. Sweet cherries must be loosened from the tree with a chemical growth regulator spray to facilitate mechanical harvesting since they hang tight to the tree. Trees must be pruned to adapt them to trunk shakers and catching frames.

Cherry culture in England is concentrated mostly in Kent, where the summer rainfall conditions are reasonably favourable; some trees are over 100 years old. Practically all of the fruit is consumed fresh. Important varieties include Early Rivers, Napoleon, and Noir de Guben. Tart varieties in Europe are Schattenmorelle and the newer Kelleris 16 and Rexelle. In Oceania the sweet cherry varieties include St. Margaret, Bedford Prolific, Rons, and Napoleon.

Strawberry. The cultivated strawberry, probably the most cosmopolitan of all perennial fruit plants, is grown from the cool tropics to the Arctic zone. Two factors account for its great climatic range: (1) it is evergreen and grows so close to the ground that mulch or snow can protect it from the coldest winter temperatures; (2) different varieties exhibit special adaptation to environmental conditions in this broad area.

This herbaceous plant has compound leaves with three leaflets arising from a fleshy crown that is anchored by a fibrous root system. Flowers, usually white, arise from the leaf axils. The edible portion of the fruit is largely receptacle with tiny seeds covering the outside of the berry. Runners, sent out from the "mother" crown, take root starting with the second node and form "daughter" plants that spread the planting in all directions.

While it is impossible to assert that one climate or another is the best for strawberries, the fact that annual yields of more than ten metric tons per acre are obtained from planting of the variety Lassen in some areas of California suggests that this may be one of the better climates for the species. On the other hand, strawberry growing is a sound business, yielding up to 10,000–15,000 quarts per acre in the cooler parts of the U.S., the United Kingdom, Denmark, Sweden, and Norway.

Objectives of modern strawberry breeders are to develop: (1) a series of early, midseason, and late-ripening varieties that look and taste alike, (2) a large berry that tends to have a peak ripening for mechanical harvesting and has an easy-to-remove calyx, (3) low chilling requirement for the mild climatic areas, (4) a firmer high-quality berry that withstands field rots, that ships well, and that looks appealing on the counter, and (5) varieties resistant to major pests and diseases. In the 1960s the leading North American varieties were Northwest (18 percent of total production), grown mainly in Washington and Oregon; Blakemore and Tennessee Beauty, from Arkansas to Tennessee; Tioga, Fresno, Gresno, and Shasta in California; Florida 90 in Florida and Texas; Headliner in Louisiana and Alabama; Surecrop in Illinois and Maryland; Albritton in North Carolina; Jerseybelle, Robinson and Midway in the northeast; Klondike in northern Mexico; and Redcoat in Canada. Varieties in Poland are Purpuratka, Senga Sengana, and Surprise des Halles, in Bulgaria the Madame Moutat and Senga Sengana, in Australia and New Zealand the Redgauntlet, in England the Royal Sovereign and the Cambridge numbered varieties. Strawberries are sold fresh, frozen, or preserved. The perishability of the fresh fruit and the excellence of the frozen pack has caused freezing to gain preference as the industry has perfected procedures. In addition, strawberries are preserved as jams, used in ice cream, and canned.

The U.S. leads all countries in world production followed by Poland, Yugoslavia, East Germany, and Italy. Other countries in order are Bulgaria, France, United Kingdom, Mexico, The Netherlands, Czechoslovakia, West Germany, Hungary, Australia, Canada, and others. No data are available from U.S.S.R., but it is known that plantings on some government farms may total 250 acres.

Since hand harvest is an expensive operation, several promising strawberry-harvesting machines are being tested.

Raspberry, blackberry. Commercial raspberries and blackberries, known as brambles, are of a number of species of the genus *Rubus*. They are termed biennial because the canes fruit (on leafy shoots) in their second growing season, then die. These canes may be erect or require support by trellis or stakes. The different species vary in climatic requirements, but the most important thrive in temperate regions that have neither very hot summers nor very cold winters. The blackberry withstands more summer heat and dryness than raspberries and hence is found farther south. These brambles do well in the south of England.

Some species also are cultivated in Europe as far north as Denmark, Sweden, the U.S.S.R., and in similar climates. Red raspberry varieties of importance in the United Kingdom are Lloyd George, Norfolk Giant, Malling Promise, and Malling Enterprise; in the U.S., Latham, Willamette, Ranere, Washington, and Newburgh; in the U.S.S.R., Usanka, Novost Kuzmina, and Russkaya. The blackcap and purplecap raspberries are less common; their culture is mostly confined to the eastern U.S. Plum Farmer and Cumberland are well-known blackcaps, and Sodus is a purple variety. All these fruits are marketed fresh locally or processed frozen or in jams, preserves, or in ice cream. Blackberry wine or brandy is common on store shelves. Several trailing and semitrailing blackberry species are commercially grown in the U.S. and in Europe; hybrids among them or with raspberry have produced large fruited juicy berries that taste good in preserves or canned. Among the most popular of these are the Himalaya berry, the Oregon evergreen blackberry, boysenberry, and youngberry.

Virus diseases

From the 1930s to 1960s virus diseases were so prevalent in raspberries that it was difficult to obtain profitable yields. Few berries at very high prices were seen on the fresh markets. By treating the canes with water so hot it almost kills the tissue, it is now possible to obtain virus-free propagation stocks that yield well. Hence, the future looks much brighter for this delicious fruit.

Mechanical harvesters are being used on cane fruits in the northwest U.S. for harvesting berries. The canes are machine slapped near the base with rubber fingers, jarring the ripe berries onto belts; trash is blown off, and the fruit carried to shallow crates for grading and packing. The machine, about 3.5 metres high by 3.5 metres wide, straddles the row.

Blueberry. Several species of this delicious berry are indigenous to North America. The wild fruit, now largely processed, was enjoyed by Indians and early settlers. Blueberry production in the U.S., mainly the highbush type, has increased more rapidly than any other fruit industry over the past half century. This is due to the skill and imagination of breeders and growers who began domesticating and crossing wild species of the highbush type early in the 20th century, and in recent years have improved the lowbush and rabbiteye types. The breeding and selection were mainly for flavour, larger berry, light blue colour, hardiness, and resistance to diseases and insects. This plant varies in height from 300–900 millimetres (one to three feet) for the lowbush blueberry, two to four metres for the highbush and five to six metres for the rabbiteye highbush. The highbush types are grown from Quebec and Michigan south to southern Georgia, whereas the lowbush types are found in mountainous areas from Newfoundland to Saskatchewan, south to Virginia. The rabbiteye highbush type is grown in the South from southern Georgia and northern Florida to Louisiana. Propagated from cuttings of main varieties, the nursery-grown plants are set according to ultimate size from 900 to 1,200 millimetres in rows 2.5 metres apart to 3–4.5 metres on the square for the rabbiteye type. Most blueberry soils are largely unsuitable for other types of agriculture. They are sandy loams high in organic matter and acid (pH 4.3–5.5); successful highbush plantings, however, have been fruited on upland medium loam soils neutral or slightly alkaline in humid areas.

Large mechanical harvesters that straddle the row are used on large highbush plantings mainly for harvesting blueberries for processing. Some growers pick the better first-over harvest berries by hand and then finish off the crop with harvesters for processing.

Blueberries freeze exceptionally well without any special preparation except washing. Most people can eat blueberries, which are mildly acidic, without side effects (as sometimes occur with other fruits, such as strawberries). Markets in the U.S. and throughout the world have not been fully exploited. It is probable that the blueberry industry will continue to grow in acreage and production.

Currant and gooseberry. Currants and gooseberries, closely related, are hardy deciduous bushes, well adapted to fruit growing in the cool temperate zone. Plants are of the bush type, mostly one to two metres in height, that spread and bear on leafy shoots from canes two years or older that arise from the crown area. Old, weak, bearing wood is pruned out as new wood develops. The largest U.S. red currant region extends from southern Michigan to the Hudson River Valley of New York; others lie around San Francisco, in the Willamette Valley, Oregon, and in the Puget Sound area of Washington. Gooseberries can be grown farther south than currants owing to their greater heat and drought tolerance. Black currants (most important), red currants, gooseberries, and white currants are grown in Great Britain, Germany, Poland, The Netherlands, France, Belgium, Australia, and New Zealand. Plantings in the U.S.S.R. are mostly in home gardens, with some commercial acreage near large cities.

These fruits are used primarily in preserves and jellies. Gooseberry also is an important culinary fruit in Britain and on the European continent; black currant juice has special dietary uses. Among the important red-currant varieties are Wilder and Red Lake; black currant: Mendip Gross, Seabrooks' Black, and Baldwin; gooseberry: Poorman, Careless, and Lancashire Lad.

Cranberry. The cranberry is a trailing woody plant consisting of a cover of runners and flowering and fruiting upright, forming a mat over the ground surface about one foot deep. The cranberry grows best on an acid, high-organic-matter, bog type of soil. The cranberry of North America is found wild from Newfoundland to Minnesota and south to Arkansas and the Carolinas. Commercially, it is grown on bog areas that have been levelled and ditched for drainage and for flooding during the winter season for protection against cold and frost in early spring. U.S. cranberry production totalled about 1,800,000 barrels (144 Imperial quarts per barrel) in the late 1960s. The vines are pruned by hand or a machine with comblike blades to reduce the matted condition and thin the fruiting uprights. The U.S. average yield is about 70 barrels per acre, but some bogs may exceed this figure by 25 or more barrels.

A recent harvesting development that has cut labour cost and increased the amount of berries retrieved is "water harvesting." The bog is flooded just above the uprights. A hand-guided, motor-driven, two-wheeled, bicycle-like machine with rotating wheels barred together whips the berries loose from the uprights. The berries float to the surface and are wind driven to an elevated road around the bog where they are guided into a motor-driven belt and bulk-loaded into a truck. This method has cut losses of berries by more than 20 percent. Labour costs also have been lowered markedly.

Cranberry juice is prepared from frozen berries the year around, diluted one-to-ten and sold by quarts and pints in glass jars, alone or mixed with apple juice. Many new products are being tested and sold.

Chestnut. The European or Spanish chestnut is the species comprising most of the world's commercial chestnuts exported from the Mediterranean area, mainly Italy. Large importers are the U.S., France, United Kingdom, Hungary, Switzerland, and West Germany. The other three main species of chestnut are the Japanese, common in the Japanese diet, Chinese, and the American. The Japanese chestnut tree is an abundant producer, but the nuts are poorer in texture and flavour than the European. The Chinese chestnut tree is more resistant to the blight that destroyed the European and American species in the U.S. While the Chinese chestnut is not as large as the European, it is well formed and flavourful. The American chestnut was largely destroyed by a blight in the early 1900s; it is valued both for its nuts and timber.

The important European chestnut is found in elevations up to 1,220 metres in the Mediterranean area, southern Asia, and east to the Caucasus. Trees may attain a 20-metre spread, with a 600-millimetre-diameter trunk, and be quite long-lived. Leaves are deciduous, simple, alternate, serrated, and with or without hairs. The burrlike fruits contain two to three nuts. The chinquapin, a close relative, has a similar fruit that contains only one nut. The horse-chestnut, unrelated, belongs to another genus and is not eaten.

Young trees are hard to establish, particularly during droughts, but once established they persist. Grafted scion varieties among chestnuts are not as common as with other tree fruits and nuts. A few orchards of scion varieties have been started. Selected Chinese varieties and hybrids that are being tested in the United States are Abundance, Crane, Kuling, Meiling, Nanking, Orrin, Colby, Conard, and Hemming.

Chinese varieties, hybrids

Chestnuts contain 40–45 percent carbohydrates, 5 percent oil, and about 50 percent moisture. The nuts dry rapidly if not stored under controlled humidity. They must be protected against molds. Most nuts are picked by hand, although they could be mechanically harvested. Chestnuts are served boiled, roasted, steamed, pureed, and as dressing for poultry and meats. In Korea the chestnut is almost as important an item of diet as the potato is in the U.S.

Range of the blueberry

Figure 1: *Fruit growing.*
(Left) Tractor-powered fruit tree mower pruning side and top branches; further thinning is done with pneumatic shears. (Top right) A young apple orchard in which soil management involves chemical weed control under the trees and mowed sod between the tree rows. (Bottom right) Apple trees grown on dwarf stocks to produce higher yields per ground unit.

By courtesy of (left) J & B Ltd. Yakima, Wash., (top right) Tree Fruit Research Center, Washington State University, Wenatchee, (bottom right) Michigan State University, East Lansing; photographs, (top right) R. Paul Larsen, (bottom right) R.F. Carlson

Hickory nut. Native to North America and a close relative of the pecan, the hickory has undergone relatively little domestication and improvement. The widely spread shagbark hickory probably bears the best nuts. It prefers a humid climate and is found on the upland slopes and lowlands near streams and wet places. Trees grow to 30 metres or more, upright, rectangular in form, with loose plates of bark on the trunk. Nuts are borne in twos and threes with a green hull that splits in quarters upon drying and releases the nut. Nuts are 25–40 millimetres long, oblong, pointed at one end and about 25 millimetres thick, with a relatively thin but hard shell averaging 100 seeds per pound. The kernel has aromatic properties typical only of the hickory and probably no other has as high flavour in cookery.

Scion varieties sold by nurseries include Curtis, Dover, Eliot, Hale, paper shell, and others. Nuts are permitted to fall to the ground and in competition with wildlife, mainly squirrels, they are picked up, hulled, and stored in a cool dry place throughout the winter and are edible until spring. Nuts last up to two years when stored at 0–1° C (32–34° F) and 65 percent relative humidity.

The greatest obstacles to the culture and improvement of hickories are the difficulty of successful transplanting and their delayed bearing. Other hickory nuts include shellbark, Carolina, mockernut, bitternut, many hybrids, and others. The hican is a hybrid between hickory and pecan. Hickory nuts are used in ice cream, cookies, candies, fruit cakes, and pie toppings, in addition to being eaten out of hand. The wood is valuable for tool handles.

II. Basic practices in fruit farming and marketing

Although fruit- and nut-growing enterprises cover great ranges of climates and plant materials, their technologies have many common problems and practices. The most significant of these are discussed below.

THE VARIETY: ITS PROPAGATION AND IMPROVEMENT

Selection of plants

The first step in establishing a fruit- or nut-growing industry is the selection of individual plants with high productivity and a superior product. Such an individual is a horticultural variety. If it is multiplied vegetatively from rooted cuttings, from root pieces that throw shoots, or by graftage, each plant in the group (called a clone) that results is identical with the others. Nearly all commercially important perennial fruit and nut crops are clonally propagated; *i.e.*, their varieties are multiplied vegetatively by one means or another. Some nut crops, such as the wild pecan, cashew, black walnut, hickory, and chestnut still come from trees that grow at random from seed; hence, character and quality tend to vary.

Many important varieties of fruit plants were selected generations ago. The Sultanina (Thompson Seedless) grape, the Lob Injir (Calimyrna) fig, and the Gros Michel banana have obscure origins; planted by the millions since selection, each specimen is actually a vegetative continuation of the selected individual growing on an independent root system. But regardless of the age of a fruit-growing industry, or the perfection of some of the selected varieties, a continuing search for new varieties is essential. There is always room for improvement in climatic adaptability, in insect and disease resistance, and in the solution of special horticultural or marketing problems. In fact, government experiment stations over the world now stress scientific breeding for improvement of market quality and yield of key fruit and nut crops.

Not only are varietal selection and improvement a continuing need but so also is the maintenance of existing varieties. Although an improved vegetative mutation of a variety is exceptional, the opportunities for accidental multiplication of degenerate (low quality) mutants increase in proportion to the number of specimens of the variety. As a result, care is taken to propagate a clone only from superior individuals, and in the case of citrus, where mutation is especially common, further precautions are necessary. There are, of course, occasional mutations that may greatly improve a variety and these are sought, selected, and propagated.

Vegetative propagation technique

Vegetative propagation technique varies with the individual fruit plant. Date, banana, and pineapple are multiplied by use of offshoots or suckers. Grape, fig, olive, currant, and blueberry are usually propagated from cuttings. Strawberry and black raspberry reproduce vegetatively by special organs—the former by stolons or runners, the latter by cane tip rooting or layering. Many kinds of fruit trees must be grafted or budded on especially grown rootstocks because the species to be multiplied does not root itself easily; apple, pear, peach, mango, and citrus are examples of this group. Many nut trees have a single tap root with but few branching roots, necessitating a deep hole and special care in transplanting.

Today's trend is toward a smaller tree in most fruit crops, particularly the apple and pear, and toward closer planting in hedgerow style, with carefully regulated fertilization and irrigation (Figure 1). This increases production per acre, lowers labour cost, increases early yields, and facilitates access in maintenance and harvesting. This approach, in fact, has been used for decades in Europe. Labour is the largest element of cost in fruit and nut production. Every means is exploited to reduce, facilitate, or eliminate hand labour.

With most fruit species a period of one to two years intervenes between the time a cutting is rooted and the plant is ready for setting in the field, or between graftage or budding and field planting. During this interval the plants remain in a nursery where they can be given intensive culture in rows. Pineapple and banana planting materials, however, do not require nursery care before field planting.

In choosing fruit varieties, the grower must: (1) recognize the relative adaptabilities of available varieties to the climatic and soil conditions of his farm and (2) select a group that satisfies both his management needs and the market demands from those best adapted to his conditions. For instance, an apple producer in the northeastern U.S. may raise four varieties: Milton, McIntosh Red, Red Delicious, and Rome Beauty. The main harvest seasons for these succeed each other at two-week intervals; this helps him extend the harvest period and make efficient use of his labour. The first two varieties cross-fertilize satisfactorily, as do the last two. The first of these varieties is usually marketed without storage, while the storage seasons of the others are of increasing length. This helps the grower to extend his marketing period.

THE SITE

The site of a fruit-growing enterprise is as significant in determining its success as the varieties grown. In fact, variety and site together set a ceiling on the productivity and profit that can be realized under the best management. In most developed fruit regions microclimatic conditions (climate at plant height, as influenced by slight differences in soil, soil covering, and elevation) and soil conditions are the two components of a site that determine its desirability for a fruit-growing enterprise. Sometimes (particularly with highly perishable fruits) transportation to market must also be considered.

Local conditions at a site that expose it to unusual frost hazard are as detrimental to citrus in Florida as they are to peach trees in New Zealand and apple trees in the south of England. In regions and sites where temperatures during the season may drop no more than a few degrees below freezing, artificial frost protection is sometimes used. This is accomplished by open-flame burning (petroleum bricks, logs, etc.) or heating of metal objects with oil, gas, propane, electricity, etc. (stones or stacks that radiate heat). Another technique is the spraying of water on plants, (e.g., strawberries) as long as the temperature is below freezing.

For highest productivity, most fruit trees must root extensively to a depth of one metre or more. Heavy subsoil or other conditions causing imperfect internal drainage may result in shallow, weak root systems that do not take water and nutrients efficiently from the soil. In semi-arid and arid regions, accumulation of saline soils in a subsurface layer sometimes limits rooting of fruit trees, causes abnormal foliar symptoms, and reduces yields. Tiling and surface ditching help decrease water accumulation in poorly drained subsoils and reduce wet spots in otherwise satisfactory sites. Special control of irrigation procedures and periodic leaching may alleviate the worst salt effects in saline soils. Choice of tolerant species, varieties, and rootstocks may make fruit growing economical on imperfectly drained or mildly saline sites, though plants rarely perform as well as they do on sites free from these difficulties. Coconuts, however, tolerate saline soil conditions near tropical saltwater coasts.

Climate,
soil
conditions

Once selected, a site is cleared, levelled (if needed), and cultivated. Then drainage, irrigation, and road systems are installed as required. In rolling or sloping terrain, where contour planting is needed to control erosion and conserve moisture, the locations of the plant or row positions are determined by the contour terraces and waterways established. In old lands, nematode or other pest populations make fumigation necessary before planting. In some problem California soils, giant plows and treaded tractors turn the soil to depths of one to two metres. In very infertile sites, or sites where the physical condition of the surface soil is poor, it may be helpful to grow a succession of leguminous cover crops for a year or more before planting and/or apply a fertilizer containing major fertilizer elements (nitrogen, potassium, phosphorus, calcium, sulfur) and all or certain trace elements (iron, manganese, boron, zinc, copper, molybdenum) and lime, based on a soil test.

PLANTING AND SPACING SYSTEMS

Growth, flowering habits, and light requirements on the one hand, and management problems on the other, determine the most satisfactory planting plan for a fruit- and nut-growing enterprise. There is a trend toward use of dwarfing stocks, growth control chemicals, or closer planting and training, or all of them to get the highest yields and best operation efficiency possible on a unit of ground.

Low-growing crops such as strawberry and pineapple are usually managed in beds containing several rows, or in less formal matted rows. In an acre of strawberries, 200,000 or more plants may occupy the matted rows. A pineapple plantation with two-row beds, having plants 300 millimetres (one foot) apart in rows 600 millimetres (two feet) apart totals 15,000 to 18,000 plants per acre. With such dense populations, intense competition for light, water, and nutrients causes smaller average fruit size. Nevertheless, the total yield per unit of land is usually greater than it would be with lower plant numbers.

The spacing of grapevines along a trellis row and of trees planted in hedgerows involves the same group of problems. Maximum vineyard production frequently results with vine distances of 2.4 to 2.7 metres (600 $\pm$ per acre). The trend for peach trees and spurtype apple strains is hedgerows 4.2 metres apart or closer, in rows 5.4 to 6 metres apart.

With those species and varieties that require cross-pollination by insects, the planting plan must take those special needs into account. This is a problem with apple, pear, plum, and sweet cherry orchards. At least two varieties that cross-fertilize successfully must be planted in association with each other.

TRAINING AND PRUNING

Pruning is the removal of parts of a plant to influence growth and fruitfulness. It is an important fruit-growing practice. Primary attention is given to form in the first few years after fruit trees or vines are planted. Form influences strength and longevity of the mature plant as well as efficiency of other fruit-growing practices; pruning for form is called training. As the plant approaches maximum fruitfulness and fills its allotted space, maintenance pruning for various purposes becomes increasingly important.

The grape may be trained following one of two systems: (1) spur system, cutting growth of the previous season (canes) to short spurs, (2) long-cane system, permitting canes to remain relatively long. Whether a spur or long-cane system is followed depends on the flowering habit of the variety. Relatively small trees that respond favourably to severe annual pruning (e.g., the peach and Kadota fig) are usually trained to create an open-centred tree with a scaffold of four or five main branches that originate on a short trunk and branch a number of times to provide fruiting wood. Annual renewal pruning can be reasonably efficient under these circumstances. Larger trees that do not respond favourably to heavy annual pruning are trained best to a system that encourages the main leader branch to grow erect to a height of 2.4–3.0 metres, with four or five main lateral branches at intervals on its sides forming the scaffold that carries fruiting wood up and out; this is called a modified leader system. The central leader type of tree, with one main leader up through the centre and many side branches, is common for pear and apple planted in hedgerows, and possibly for other fruits and nuts as the close-planted hedgerow system is more widely adopted.

Maintenance pruning

The principal reasons for maintenance pruning are: (1) to permit efficient spraying and harvesting operations, (2) to maintain satisfactory light exposure for most of the leaves, and (3) to create a satisfactory balance between flowering and leaf surface.

To reduce hand labour costs, larger commercial fruit growers use machine pruning (Figure 1) on many types of fruits. Peach, apple, pear, and other fruits usually planted in hedgerows are mowed across the top and sides by machine, then thinned out as needed by a follow-up crew using pneumatic clippers and hand-powered saws, operating from hydraulically manipulated scaffolds or lifts of various types.

SOIL MANAGEMENT, IRRIGATION, AND FERTILIZATION

Soil management. Two soil management practices, (1) clean cultivation and chemical weed control or both and (2) permanent sod culture, illustrate contrasting purposes and effects. In clean cultivation or chemical weed control, the surface soil is stirred periodically throughout the year or a herbicide is used to kill vegetation that competes for nutrients, water, and light. Stirring increases the decomposition rate of soil organic matter and thereby releases nitrogen and other nutrients for use by the fruit crop. It may also provide some improvement in water penetration. On the other hand, laying bare the soil surface exposes it to erosion; destruction of organic matter eventually lowers fertility and causes soil structure to change from loose and friable to tight and compacted. Though sod culture minimizes the destructive processes and may permit a modest increase in fertility, the sod itself competes with fruit plants for water and nutrients and may even compete for light. As a result, permanent sod culture is practical only with tree crops that are normally rather low in vegetation, such as apple, pear, sweet cherry, nuts, and mango. Competition from established sod may be detrimental to vigorously growing fruit plants like grape, peach, and raspberry unless adequate fertilizer and water are supplied.

Because each of these soil management systems has advantages and disadvantages, modifying or complementary practices are often used; for example, cover cropping, mulching, and chemical control of vegetation with or without strip sod in the row middles. In fact, the trend is toward mowed sod middles with strip chemical control under the trees and with overhead sprinklers during hot dry weather (Figure 1). Sprinklers not only provide water but tend to cool the plants and give fruit of better market quality without aggravating diseases. Cultivation combined with winter cover cropping has been used widely in grape, peach, cherry, bush fruit, and citrus plantings, as well as with other species. Mulching is the addition of undecomposed plant materials such as straw, hay, or processors' refuse to the soil under the plants. In orchards, mulching materials are most often applied under trees maintained in permanent sod. Strip in-row chemical control of vegetation in commercial fruit plantings has almost taken over as an economical and sound practice.

Sprinklers, cultivation, mulching

Irrigation. In semi-arid and arid regions, irrigation is necessary. Probably the maximum demand occurs in date gardens, because they expose a large leaf surface the year around under conditions of high evaporation and practically no rainfall. Irrigation in humid climates is generally being provided increasingly during extended dry periods that occur at one time or another during most growing seasons. For example, large acreages of banana are irrigated on coastal lowlands of the torrid tropics where annual rainfall exceeds 1,500 millimetres (see IRRIGATION AND DRAINAGE).

Fertilization. Needs of perennial fruit plants for fertilizers depend on the natural fertility of the soil supporting them and on their individual requirements. Of the essential elements, supplemental nitrogen is almost always needed; potassium supplements may be needed, even in some desert areas. Although strawberry, grape, peach, and a few other fruits have responded favourably to phosphorus, and although its application has been recommended, the phosphorus requirement of woody plants is low and deficiency is rather rare. Calcium deficiency may be more common than realized; lime is often desirable to reduce soil acidity and because of other indirect benefits. Inadequate magnesium in the soil has been noted by workers studying a wide range of fruit species. Of the trace elements, zinc, iron, and boron are most likely to be deficient, but copper, manganese, and molybdenum deficiencies also are being reported for some fruits in some regions. Iron deficiency is difficult to control in orchards where soils have high alkalinity. Granulated fertilizers in modern close-planted commercial orchards are usually broadcast by machine a month or two before growth starts. Additional nitrogen sometimes is applied in heavy crop years to apple, pear, and citrus.

POLLINATION

The stimulus of pollination, fertilization, and seed formation is needed to get good size, shape, and flavour of most of the fruits. (Banana, pineapple, and some citrus and fig varieties are exceptions.) Transfer of pollen from the anthers (male) to the stigmas (female) is accomplished in nature either by insects or by movement in air. It is common practice to bring beehives into the orchard during bloom. Rainy cold weather during bloom with little or no sunshine can deter activity of the honey bee (the key insect pollinator) and reduce fruit set appreciably. This is one of the main problems not fully solved by fruit researchers. Hand-pollination by daubing collected and preserved pollen onto the stigmas, (as is done with date palms) sometimes is practiced for other fruits, but this approach is not widespread.

THINNING

Removal of flowers or young fruit (thinning) is done to permit the remaining fruits to grow more rapidly and to prevent development of such a large crop that the plant is unable to flower and set a commercial crop the following year. Thinning is done by hand, mechanically, or chemically. With the date, the pistillate flower cluster is reduced in size at the time of hand-pollination. In the case of certain table grape varieties, some clusters are cut off. With Thompson seedless grape, a combination of girdling the trunk bark and judicious application of gibberellin (growth regulating) sprays at blossoming gives excellent full bunches.

Young peach fruits are thinned by striking the branches with a padded pole or by shaking the entire tree for a few seconds with a well-padded motor-driven shaker arm grasping the trunk. Hand thinning of young apple and peach fruits once was also a common practice, but because of the expense and difficulty, there has been increasing use of chemical sprays as a substitute. Two kinds of sprays are used: (1) mildly caustic sprays applied during bloom, such as Elgetol in arid regions, or (2) sprays of growth-regulating substances such as 3-CPA (2,3-chlorophenoxy propionamide) applied within a few weeks after bloom in areas with late frosts.

PEST CONTROL AND PRESERVATION

In many fruit enterprises, pest control is the most expensive and time-consuming growing practice. Where the concentration of fruit farms in an area warrants it, individual efforts are complemented by legislative measures including quarantine regulations to force removal of pest-laden, unattended orchards. Sometimes the most economical control procedure is biological in nature. There is increased research today to find and multiply parasites that kill fruit crop pests. Such biological methods are necessary as political pressures increase for ban-

Biological pest control

ning DDT and other chemicals. Selection of varieties that are immune, resistant to attack, or tolerant to specific pests, is a biological control procedure also widely used. Chemical control procedures, however, are relied on most heavily. Air-blast spray or mist-application machinery covering 70 acres of trees or more in a day is now in common use (Figure 2).

HARVESTING AND PACKING

The proper time to remove a fruit from the tree or plant varies with each fruit and is governed by whether the product will be sold and consumed within hours, or stored for weeks, months, or even a year. Most fruits are harvested as close as possible to the time they are eaten. A few, of which banana and pear are outstanding examples, may be harvested immature and still ripen satisfactorily. Orange, grapefruit, and some varieties of avocado may be "stored" on the tree for several months after

Figure 2: Air-concentrate mist blower used to spray bush fruits, grapes, and compact high-density tree fruits.

they attain good quality; this cuts costs in handling and marketing.

Many fruits, including apple, pear, orange, lemon, and grapefruit, may drop from the tree during the last part of the maturation period. Preharvest drop of these fruits can be delayed by application of dilute sprays of growth-regulating substances like naphthaleneacetic acid (NAA). The chemical spray Alar [N-(dimethylamino) succinamic acid] applied four to six weeks after bloom on apple not only reduces fruit drop at harvest but increases red colour, firmness, and return bloom the next year, in addition to other advantages.

For the fresh market, most tree and bush fruits are still harvested by hand. For processing, drying, and occasionally for fresh market, mechanical motor-driven tree and bush shakers with appropriate catching belts, bins, pallets, and electric lifts reduce harvesting and handling labour. In years to come, machinery may make it possible to machine-harvest most fruits, with no more, and possibly less, damage than with hand picking (Figure 3).

The public is becoming increasingly particular about the appearance and quality of the product it buys. Hence, store managers seek the best grades of fruits and nuts available, and growers make every effort to produce crops with attractive colour and smooth finish. Fruits are packed by government-controlled grades such as Fancy

or Extra Fancy within given size limits and are so labelled on the carton or box, together with the source. Most fruits and nuts not meeting this quality demand are processed or sent through channels using the lower grades and off sizes.

Small packages of plastic foam or wood pulp base holding four to six fruits covered and heat sealed with polyethylene plastic film are popular. These are delivered to stores in corrugated cartons holding a few dozen packages. Citrus, apples, and whole nuts or kernels also are packaged in polyethylene bags and delivered in cartons. Loose fruit may be sold in cell cartons and tray packs consisting of stacked form-fitting pulp trays in a "bushel size" box. Every effort is made to eliminate bruising.

Large truck-pulled containers with individually motor-driven refrigeration units, with or without controlled atmosphere (CO_2-O_2, to retard ripening), are loaded at the fruit source and trucked to destination or loaded on ships by derrick for overseas shipment. These sealed containers are also being used increasingly for bananas to reduce labour and handling and to deliver a better product.

Air shipment of "vine- and tree-ripe" fruit (strawberries, figs, sweet cherries, pineapples, avocados) to distances as far as from California to Europe in a day or less is becoming increasingly common with the much larger and faster cargo planes and reduced air-freight prices.

Shipment in controlled atmosphere

Table 4: Major Compositional Changes in the Edible Fraction of Several Selected Fruits

constituent	content at maturity* (percent of fresh weight)	content upon ripening† (percent of content at maturity)
Apple		
Starch	2.0	5
Soluble sugars	7.5	99
Acids (malic)	1.0	60
Protein	0.2	120
Protopectin	0.7	12
Soluble pectin	0.2	160
Avocado		
Sugars	0.4	12
Fat	20.0	105
Protein	1.8	110
Banana		
Starch	20.0	6
Sugars	0.9	2,000
Protopectin	0.5	40
Soluble pectin	0.3	150
Orange		
Sugars	10.0	105
Acids (citric)	0.9	85
Pineapple		
Sugars	15.0	103
Acid	0.8	88

* "Content at maturity" means content when the fruit is normally harvested in mature but not necessarily ripe stage. † "Content upon ripening" refers to content at edible stage.

POSTHARVEST PHYSIOLOGY OF FRUITS

Fruit ripening is a form of senescence and signifies the final stage in fruit development. A fleshy fruit is the enlarged ovary of a flower (avocado) or additional floral parts such as in apple, pear, and pineapple. Usually fertilization, and sometimes pollinaton alone, stimulate the floral parts causing a rapid cell division that leads to differentiation and the formation of the fruit structure. During this stage fruits consist of small, young cells filled with protoplasm. When the young fruit has been stimulated, presumably by plant hormones that originate from the embryonic seeds, rapid cell expansion takes place. During this stage fruits gain rapidly in size and weight. The cells develop small cavities or spaces in their tissue (become vacuolated) and begin the process of foodstuff accumulation, which lends fruits their compositional diversity. Banana, apple, and date accumulate mainly carbohydrates. Avocado and olive store fatty materials. Important constituents of most fruits are organic acids such as malic acid, found in apple and pear; citric acid, in cit-

Figure 3: *Mechanical fruit harvesting.*
(Top) Fruit harvester operating under a cherry tree. The limb shaker (at left of tree) removes the cherries which are caught on decelerator strips and carried to the bulk bin at left. (Bottom left) Cranberry harvester used on a bog to loosen and float berries. (Bottom right) Grape harvester straddling a row of Vinifera or Labrusca grapes. The berries fall on belts and are carried on escalators to the top of the harvester where they enter the arm to be deposited (at right) in a tractor-pulled bulk bin for processing.

By courtesy of (top) Agricultural Engineering Dept., New York State College of Agriculture, at Cornell University, Ithaca, N.Y., (bottom left) Rutgers University, New Brunswick, N.J., (bottom right) Chisholm Ryder Co., Inc., Niagara Falls, N.Y.

rus and pineapple; and tartaric acid, in grapes. Fruits are usually low in protein.

After cell expansion has slowed and become nominal, fruits enter the stage of maturity and undergo preparation for ripening. Some crops, such as pear and avocado, are harvested at the so-called mature-green state and allowed to ripen afterward. Most fruits are at a stage of incipient ripening before they are picked. Ripening is marked by rapid and dramatic changes that give fruits their attractive and edible character. Some of the familiar changes are softening, which results from degradation of cell wall substances; disappearance of a green background, because of chlorophyll degradation (as in pear, apple, and banana); appearance of coloured pigments such as the carotenoids—orange-yellow—and anthocyanins—red (as in orange, mango, and strawberry); a decrease in acidity and increase in the sugar content (orange, apple); and emission of the volatile substances that give many fruits their distinct aroma (as in banana, pear, and apple). In climacteric fruits (*e.g.*, banana, pear, apple), ripening is accompanied by increased respiration. In nonclimacteric fruit (*e.g.*, strawberry, cherry) this phe-

Stages of ripening

nomenon does not occur. It is thought that the transition from the mature to the ripe stage is brought about by certain "ripening" enzymes. Protein molecules act as catalysts. The activity of these enzymes leads first to various ripening reactions, and then to gradual deterioration of the fruit tissue. Table 4 lists the major compositional changes in the edible fraction of several selected fruits. Table 5 lists the composition of various fruits and nuts.

Because ripening leads to tissue breakdown, fruits are considered a highly perishable commodity. Different fruits have varying degrees of postharvest longevity. While strawberries last only a week to ten days, apples or lemons can be stored successfully for several months. Postharvest life of fruits can be extended by refrigeration with or without a modified oxygen-carbon dioxide atmosphere. Most temperate-zone fruits can be held safely at 0° to 5° C (32° to 41° F), but many subtropical and tropical fruits, including lemon, avocado, banana, and mango, show chilling injury in prolonged cold storage and consequently fail to ripen properly. Bananas do not tolerate temperatures below 12° C (about 53° F), while several avocado varieties can be stored at 7° to 8° C

Table 5: Composition of Fruits and Nuts
(100 grams, edible portion)

fruit	water (percent)	food energy (cal)	protein (g)	fat (g)	carbohydrate total (g)	carbohydrate fibre (g)	ash (g)	minerals calcium (mg)	minerals phosphorus (mg)	minerals iron (mg)	minerals sodium (mg)	minerals potassium (mg)	vitamin A (intern units)	thiamine (mg)	riboflavin (mg)	niacin (mg)	ascorbic acid (mg)
Almonds																	
Dried	4.7	598	18.6	54.2	19.5	2.6	3.0	234	504	4.7	4	773	0	0.24	0.92	3.5	Trace
Roasted and salted	0.7	627	18.6	57.7	19.5	2.6	3.5	235	504	4.7	198	773	0	0.05	0.92	3.5	0
Apples																	
Not pared	84.8	56	0.2	0.6	14.1	1.0	0.3	7	10	0.3	1	110	90	0.03	0.02	0.1	7
Pared	85.3	53	0.2	0.3	13.9	0.6	0.3	6	10	0.3	1	110	40	0.03	0.02	0.1	4
Dried, sulfured, uncooked	24.0	275	1.0	1.6	71.8	3.1	1.6	31	52	1.6	5	569	...*	0.06	0.12	0.5	10
Apricots																	
Raw	85.3	51	1.0	0.2	12.8	0.6	0.7	17	23	0.5	1	281	2,700	0.03	0.04	0.6	10
Dried, sulfured, uncooked	25.0	260	5.0	0.5	66.5	3.0	3.0	67	108	5.5	26	979	10,900	0.01	0.16	3.3	12
Avocados, raw	74.0	167	2.1	16.4	6.3	1.6	1.2	10	42	0.6	4	604	290	0.11	0.20	1.6	14
Bananas, raw	75.7	85	1.1	0.2	22.2	0.5	0.8	8	26	0.7	1	370	190	0.05	0.06	0.7	10
Blackberries, boysenberries, dewberries, loganberries and youngberries, raw	84.5	58	1.2	0.9	12.9	4.1	0.5	32	19	0.9	1	170	200	0.03	0.04	0.4	21
Blueberries, raw	83.2	62	0.7	0.5	15.3	1.5	0.3	15	13	1.0	1	81	100	(0.03)†	(0.06)	(0.5)	14
Brazil nuts	4.6	654	14.3	66.9	10.9	3.1	3.3	186	693	3.4	1	715	Trace	0.96	0.12	1.6	...
Carambola, raw	90.4	35	0.7	0.5	8.0	0.9	0.4	4	17	1.5	2	192	1,200	0.04	0.02	0.3	35
Cashew nuts	5.2	561	17.2	45.7	29.3	1.4	2.6	38	373	3.8	15	464	100	0.43	0.25	1.8	...
Cherimoya, raw	73.5	94	1.3	0.4	24.0	2.2	0.8	23	40	0.5	...	...	10	0.10	0.11	1.3	9
Cherries																	
Raw, sour	83.7	58	1.2	0.3	14.3	0.2	0.5	22	19	0.4	2	191	1,000	0.05	0.06	0.4	10
Raw, sweet	80.4	70	1.3	0.3	17.4	0.4	0.6	22	19	0.4	2	191	110	0.05	0.06	0.4	10
Chestnuts	52.5	194	2.9	1.5	42.1	1.1	1.0	27	88	1.7	6	454	...	0.22	0.22	0.6	...
Coconuts																	
Fresh meat	50.9	346	3.5	35.3	9.4	4.0	0.9	13	95	1.7	23	256	0	0.05	0.02	0.5	3
Dried, unsweetened	3.5	662	7.2	64.9	23.0	3.9	1.4	26	187	3.3	...	588	0	0.06	0.04	0.6	0
Cranberries, raw	87.9	46	0.4	0.7	10.8	1.4	0.2	14	10	0.5	2	82	40	0.03	0.02	0.1	11
Dates, raw, dry	22.5	274	2.2	0.5	72.9	2.3	1.9	59	63	3.0	1	648	50	0.09	0.10	2.2	0
Elderberries, raw	79.8	72	2.6	(0.5)	16.4	7.0	0.7	38	28	1.6	...	300	600	0.07	0.06	0.5	36
Figs																	
Raw	77.5	80	1.2	0.3	20.3	1.2	0.7	35	22	0.6	2	194	80	0.06	0.05	0.4	2
Dried, uncooked	23.0	274	4.3	1.3	69.1	5.6	2.3	126	77	3.0	34	640	80	0.10	0.10	0.7	(0)
Filberts (hazelnuts)	5.8	634	12.6	62.4	16.7	3.0	2.5	209	337	3.4	2	704	...	0.46	...	0.9	Trace
Gooseberries, raw	88.9	39	0.8	0.2	9.7	1.9	0.4	18	15	0.5	1	155	290	...	...	...	33
Grapefruit																	
Fresh, pulp	88.4	41	0.5	0.1	10.6	0.2	0.4	16	16	0.4	1	135	80	0.04	0.02	0.2	38
Fresh, juice	90.0	39	0.5	0.1	9.2	Trace	0.2	9	15	0.2	1	162	80	0.04	0.02	0.2	38
Grapes, raw																	
American (Labrusca)	81.6	69	1.3	1.0	15.7	0.6	0.4	16	12	0.4	3	158	100	0.05	0.03	0.3	4
European (Vinifera)	81.4	67	0.6	0.3	17.3	0.5	0.4	12	20	0.4	3	173	100	0.05	0.03	0.3	4
Guavas, raw	83.0	62	0.8	0.6	15.0	5.6	0.6	23	42	0.9	4	289	280	0.05	0.05	1.2	242
Lemons, raw, peeled	90.1	27	1.1	0.3	8.2	0.4	0.3	26	16	0.6	2	138	20	0.04	0.02	0.1	53
Limes, raw	89.3	28	0.7	0.2	9.5	0.5	0.3	33	18	0.6	2	102	10	0.03	0.02	0.2	37
Loquats, raw	86.5	48	0.4	0.2	12.4	0.5	0.5	20	36	0.4	...	348	670	...	...	...	1
Lychees, raw	81.9	64	0.9	0.3	16.4	0.3	0.5	8	42	0.4	3	170	...	...	0.05	...	42
Macadamia nuts	3.0	691	7.8	71.6	15.9	2.5	1.7	48	161	2.0	...	264	0	0.34	0.11	1.3	0
Mangos, raw	81.7	66	0.7	0.4	16.8	0.9	0.4	10	13	0.4	7	189	4,800	0.05	0.05	1.1	35
Nectarines, raw	81.8	64	0.6	Trace	17.1	0.4	0.5	4	24	0.5	6	294	1,650	...	...	...	13
Olives																	
Green	78.2	116	1.4	12.7	1.3	1.3	6.4	61	17	1.6	2,400	55	300	...	...	...	...
Ripe, pickled	80.0	129	1.1	13.8	2.6	1.4	2.5	84	16	1.6	813	34	60	Trace	Trace	...	...
Ripe, salted, and oiled	43.8	338	2.2	35.8	8.7	3.8	(9.5)	...	29	...	3,288	...	...	...	...	...	...
Oranges																	
Raw, peeled	86.0	49	1.0	0.2	12.2	0.5	0.6	41	20	0.4	1	200	200	0.10	0.04	0.4	(50)
Raw, juice	88.3	45	0.7	0.2	10.4	0.1	0.4	11	17	0.2	1	200	200	0.09	0.03	0.4	(50)
Papayas, raw	88.7	39	0.6	0.1	10.0	0.9	0.6	20	16	0.3	3	234	1,750	0.04	0.04	0.3	56
Passion fruit (granadilla)	75.1	90	2.2	0.7	21.2	...	0.8	13	64	1.6	28	348	700	Trace	0.13	1.5	30
Peaches																	
Raw	89.1	38	0.6	0.1	9.7	0.6	0.5	9	19	0.5	1	202	1,330	0.02	0.05	1.0	7
Dried, sulfured	25.0	262	3.1	0.7	68.3	3.1	2.9	48	117	6.0	16	950	3,900	0.01	0.19	5.3	18
Pears																	
Raw	83.2	61	0.7	0.4	15.3	1.4	0.4	8	11	0.3	2	130	20	0.02	0.04	0.1	4
Dried, sulfured	26.0	268	3.1	1.8	67.3	6.2	1.8	35	48	1.3	7	573	70	0.01	0.18	0.6	7
Pecans	3.4	687	9.2	71.2	14.6	2.3	1.6	73	289	2.4	Trace	603	130	0.86	0.13	0.9	2
Persimmons, raw																	
Kaki	78.6	77	0.7	0.4	19.7	1.6	0.6	6	26	0.3	6	174	2,710	0.03	0.02	0.1	11
Native	64.4	127	0.8	0.4	33.5	1.5	0.9	27	26	2.5	1	310	...	...	...	...	66
Pineapple, raw	85.3	52	0.4	0.2	13.7	0.4	0.4	17	8	0.5	1	146	70	0.09	0.03	0.2	17
Pine nuts																	
Pignolias	5.6	552	31.1	47.4	11.6	0.9	4.3	...	...	...	...	...	...	0.62	...	...	...
Piñons	3.1	635	13.0	60.5	20.5	1.1	2.9	12	604	5.2	...	...	30	1.28	0.23	4.5	Trace
Pistachio nuts	5.3	594	19.3	53.7	19.0	1.9	2.7	131	500	7.3	...	972	230	0.67	...	1.4	0
Plums, raw	82.1	63	0.6	0.2	16.6	0.46	0.53	14	18	0.5	1	213	275	0.05	0.03	0.5	5
Pomegranate, raw	82.3	63	0.5	0.3	16.4	0.2	0.5	3	8	0.3	3	259	Trace	0.03	0.03	0.3	4
Prunes, dried	28.0	255	2.1	0.6	67.4	1.6	1.9	51	79	3.9	8	694	1,600	0.09	0.17	1.6	3
Quinces, raw	83.8	57	0.4	0.1	15.3	1.7	0.4	11	17	0.7	4	197	40	0.02	0.03	0.2	15
Raisins	18.0	289	2.5	0.2	77.4	0.9	1.9	62	101	3.5	27	763	20	0.11	0.08	0.5	1
Raspberries, raw	82.5	65	1.3	1.0	14.5	4.0	0.5	26	22	0.9	1	185	130	0.03	0.09	0.9	21
Sapodillas, raw	76.1	89	0.5	1.1	21.8	1.4	0.5	21	12	0.8	12	193	60	Trace	0.02	0.2	14
Soursop, raw	81.7	65	1.0	0.3	16.3	1.1	0.7	14	27	0.6	14	265	10	0.07	0.05	0.9	20
Strawberries, raw	89.9	37	0.7	0.5	8.4	1.3	0.5	21	21	1.0	1	164	60	0.03	0.07	0.6	59
Tamarinds, raw	31.4	239	2.8	0.6	62.5	5.1	2.7	74	113	2.8	51	781	30	0.34	0.14	1.2	2
Tangerines, raw	88.0	44	0.6	0.2	10.5	0.3	0.3	30	16	0.3	2	150	420	0.06	0.02	0.1	31
Walnuts																	
Black	3.1	628	20.5	59.3	14.8	1.7	2.3	Trace	570	6.0	3	460	300	0.22	0.11	0.7	...
English (Persian)	3.5	651	14.8	64.0	15.8	2.1	1.9	99	380	3.1	2	450	30	0.33	0.13	0.9	2

*Leaders denote lack of reliable data, but constituent is present.   †Numbers in parentheses denote values estimated, usually from another form of the fruit or a similar fruit.
Source: Adapted by Dennis Abdalla, Rutgers University, from U.S. Department of Agriculture Handbook No. 8, ARS-USDA, Washington (1963).

(about 46° F). Fruit life can be extended further by both refrigeration and controlled atmosphere (CA) storage in which oxygen is kept at about 5 percent and carbon dioxide at 1 to 3 percent, while temperature is held at a level best suited to the particular fruit. So-called CA storage is common today for apples and pears and is being adapted to other fruits. Controlled atmosphere and refrigeration in conjunction with the removal of ethylene gas (which emanates from fruits and speeds ripening) helps slow the ripening process considerably. Golden Delicious apples and some pears are shipped in polyethylene containers in which a desirable, modified atmosphere is created by the respiring fruit.

Drying, canning, freezing

Drying is a standard practice for stabilizing the market movement of dates, figs, raisin grapes, prunes, and apricots. Canning is of paramount importance to the pineapple, peach, and pear industries, and freezing is a means of stabilizing some of the most perishable fruits, including strawberry, raspberry, and blueberry.

Nuts are susceptible to mold, souring, staleness, discoloration, and rancidity. Cured and dried nuts are kept in prolonged cold storage under controlled temperature and humidity levels. Nuts also are stored and sold in vacuum packs of carbon dioxide-enriched atmosphere.

WASTE MATERIALS, OTHER USES

Apple wood is excellent for fireplace use, and cherry and certain other fruit woods are used for the finest household furniture. The dried residue from processing apples and citrus is made into feed for conditioning livestock for market, as are waste materials from many processed fruits. Apple pumice (waste material) is spread on the orchard floor with a manure spreader to help in soil conditioning and as a source of minerals.

Nutshells have many uses. Filbert shells are made into plywood, artificial wood, and linoleum; a mixture of shells with powdered coal and lignite makes cinder blocks; shells are used in making poisonous gases and gas masks, and as fuel and mulch. Cashew shell liquid, a skin irritant, is made into resins for varnishes; kills mosquito larvae; can be impregnated in wood as a varnish to preserve against insect attack; is used in automotive brake linings and clutch facings; is used as a laminating agent for paper, cloth, and glass fibres; and is used to treat cement floors and synthetic rubber to retard deterioration. Finely ground black-walnut-shell flour is used in plastic molding powder; as a glue extender; to prevent overheating of drills; to "sand" blast jet engines; for polishing, burnishing, and deburring metal parts; for cleaning foundry molds; and to spray on tires for better traction. Pecan shells are used in place of gravel in cement walks and driveways; as fuel; as mulch and as a soil conditioner; in livestock bedding; as filler for fertilizers, feeds, etc.; in the manufacture of tanning agents, with charcoal and abrasives in hand soap; as a filler in plastic and veneer wood; and many of the same uses as black walnut shells. Some nutshells are made into beads, marbles, buttons, carving tools, ink, and ornaments. The India clearing nut is cut open and rubbed on the inside of earthenware that will contain drinking water; the juice coagulates the water impurities which sink to the bottom. The nuts of the betel palm in the Far East and of the kola tree in West Africa are chewed for their stimulatory effects.

BIBLIOGRAPHY. W.H. CHANDLER, *Deciduous Orchards*, 3rd ed. rev. (1957), detailed coverage from a chemical and physiological standpoint of all deciduous fruit crops in California and similar climates, *Evergreen Orchards*, 2nd ed. rev. (1958), cultural and handling coverage of tropical and sub-tropical fruit crops; N.F. CHILDERS, *Modern Fruit Science*, 4th ed. rev. (1969), a modern well-illustrated book on deciduous orchard and small fruit culture from planting to marketing, with extensive bibliographies, farmer tax and labour handling suggestions, and similar appendix material; J.S. SHOEMAKER, *Small-Fruit Culture* 3rd ed. (1955), in-depth culture and literature review of all important small fruits; T. WALLACE and R.G.W. BUSH (eds.), *Modern Commercial Fruit Growing* (1956), on cultural management, mainly for British and western European use; J.G. WOODROOF, *Tree Nuts: Production, Processing, Products*, 2 vol. (1967), complete books on tem-perate and tropical nuts of economic importance from planting to marketing; R.A. JAYNES (ed.), *Handbook of North American Nut Trees* (1969), a detailed discussion of mostly temperate climate nut culture, but also includes coconuts, cashew, macadamia, and pistachio.

See also *Horticultural Abstracts* (quarterly) for world coverage of technical articles on temperate and tropical fruit crops; *Journal of Horticultural Science* (quarterly); and *Journal of the American Society for Horticultural Science* (bi–monthly). The United States Department of Agriculture and State Agricultural Experiment Stations publish bulletins on the culture of fruits, on insect and disease problems, and on economic and marketing problems. Similar information is published by the British Ministry of Agriculture for fruit crops important in Great Britain.

(N.F.C.)

Fugger Family

The Fuggers were a German family who founded in the imperial city of Augsburg a textile business that grew into the biggest trading, mining, and banking concern of 15th- and 16th-century Europe. By granting huge loans to the emperors Maximilian I and Charles V, the Fuggers were able to influence the policies of these rulers.

Jakob II Fugger the Rich (right), and his chief accountant, Matthäus Schwarz, miniature, 1519. In the Herzog Anton Ulrich-Museum, Braunschweig, West Germany.

The founding fathers. Hans Fugger, a weaver born in the village of Graben in Swabia, established the family in Augsburg in 1367. By twice marrying the daughters of masters of the weavers' guild, the industrious Fugger acquired civic rights and the freedom of the company. He also became a member of the guild's committee of 12 and of the city's great council and conducted a successful textile trade. After his death in 1408, his sons Andreas and Jakob I, both of whom had learned the goldsmith's trade, jointly carried on the family business until they dissolved their partnership in 1454. Although Andreas, the more enterprising of the two, and his descendants quickly attained great wealth, they went bankrupt in 1499, as a result of an overextension of business activity and the loss of a lawsuit. These Fugger vom Reh (Fuggers of the Doe, from their coat of arms) spread over southern, central, and eastern Germany; as late as 1944, there were Fukier (descendants of the Fuggers) residing in Warsaw.

In 1441 Jakob had married the daughter of a mint master who went bankrupt three years later. Warned by this event, Jakob proceeded carefully in his business; yet by perseverance and industry he succeeded in substantially increasing his profits, and in 1463 he was made a member of the more highly respected merchants' guild. After his death in 1469, two of his seven sons,

Jakob the
Rich

Ulrich and Georg, began by profitably expanding the firm's international trade. In 1473 they were granted a coat of arms with a lily, causing this branch of the family to be called Fugger von der Lilie. With the help of their brother Markus in Rome, they handled remittances to the papal court of monies for the sale of indulgences and the procuring of church benefices. From 1508 to 1515 they leased the Roman mint. Ulrich and Georg established an agency of their own in the German merchants' building in Venice, where their youngest brother, Jakob II the Rich, who had originally been destined for an ecclesiastical career, studied modern bookkeeping from 1478 on. Taking charge of the Fugger agency in Innsbruck in 1485, he showed sound business acumen in making the firm a partner in the Tirolean mines by granting permanent loans, secured by deliveries of copper and silver, to Archduke Sigismund and King (later Emperor) Maximilian. The large profits realized from this venture encouraged the Fuggers to participate also in mining operations in Silesia. There Jakob, a shrewd and sober yet enterprising merchant, met a mining expert with whom he leased the copper mines in Neusohl (modern Banská Bystrica, Czechoslovakia) in 1495, eventually building them up into the greatest mining centre of the time.

In 1494 the Fuggers established their first public company with a capital of 54,385 guilders, a sum that was to be doubled two years later when Jakob persuaded the Prince Bishop of Brixen to join the company as a silent partner. Jakob's aim was to establish a copper monopoly by opening foundries in Hohenkirchen and Fuggerau (named for the family, in Carinthia, now Austria) and by expanding the sales organization in Europe, especially the Antwerp agency. True to his motto, "I want to gain while I can," Jakob, unhappily married since 1498 and without an heir, engaged in all manner of commerce, including the lucrative spice trade. The taciturn and hard-driving merchant had long ago assumed the direction of the firm. The death of his chief creditor, the Prince Bishop of Brixen, whose inheritance was claimed by the Pope, brought about a serious crisis that Jakob managed to solve through shrewd negotiations. Prudently, he divided the company's assets equally into cash holdings, production plants and merchandise, landed properties, and precious stones. In 1504 he thus secretly purchased from the city of Basel a portion of the captured crown jewels of Charles the Bold, duke of Burgundy. Laying the foundation for the family's widely distributed landholdings, he acquired the countships of Kirchberg and Weissenhorn from Maximilian I in 1507. In 1514, the Emperor made him a count.

Financier
of
emperors
and enemy
of Protes-
tantism

The chief financial supporter of Maximilian I's policies since 1490, Fugger was identified with these policies for better or for worse, even though he refused to support Maximilian's bid for the papacy. His greatest achievement was the financing of the election of Charles V, Maximilian's successor, as emperor. Of the total election expenses of 852,000 guilders, Jakob Fugger alone raised almost 544,000 in order to eliminate Francis I of France. By skillful negotiations he arranged to have this debt repaid out of the Maestrazgo—the lease of the revenues paid to the Spanish crown by the three great knightly orders. A part of the sum came from the mercury mines of Almadén and the silver mines of Guadalcanal. In 1516 he also made an ally of King Henry VIII of England by granting him various loans.

At the height of his power Jakob Fugger was sharply criticized by his contemporaries, especially by the German Humanist and reformer Ulrich von Hutten and by Martin Luther, for his stand on interest charges (the Fuggers were among the merchant dynasties that urged the Pope to rescind or amend the medieval prohibition on the levying of interest) and the sale of indulgences and benefices, as well as for his loan policies. The imperial fiscal and governmental authorities in Nürnberg brought action against him and other merchants to halt their monopolistic tendencies. Fugger's position was furthermore threatened by social unrest among the miners in the Tirol and at Neusohl in Hungary, by attempts of the

Hungarian nobles to nationalize his mines, and by the Peasants' Revolt. At the Augsburg headquarters he was threatened by an uprising of artisans. Fugger mastered these crises through sheer tenacity and fixity of purpose. Albrecht Dürer has immortalized the severe, taciturn countenance of the master merchant. As head of the company, Fugger, who was himself a man of few wants, created monuments to his time that have survived for centuries—in the Fugger buildings and the splendid memorial chapel and above all in the Fuggerei, the world's oldest social settlement, which he endowed as a peaceful haven for his impoverished old servants and fellow citizens. In his last years, seeing his work and his church threatened by the Reformation, he fought the new movement.

Decline of the House.   At his death in 1525, Jakob the Rich bequeathed to his nephew Anton Fugger, who had been destined for the succession since 1517, company assets totalling 2,032,652 guilders. The new chief, an ambitious and very talented businessman, guided the firm with a firm hand. In 1527 he married Anna Rehlinger, a patrician's daughter who bore him four sons. Most of Anton's time was taken up with the securing of permanent loans for the emperors Charles V and Ferdinand I, and for King Philip II of Spain. In accordance with his credo that money is the sinews of war—*pecunia nervus bellorum*—Fugger, a strict Roman Catholic, granted the Emperor credits that proved to be decisive in the struggle against the Protestants and particularly in the war against the Schmalkaldic League of Protestant princes and cities. While large sales of fustian cloth to England and loans extended to its kings proved to be profitable, the formerly rich yield of the Tirolean and Hungarian mines decreased until Anton gave up Neusohl altogether in 1547. With dogged resolution but indifferent success, he tried to make up for these losses by establishing new trade ties with Peru and Chile and by engaging in mining ventures in Sweden and Norway, as well as in the slave trade from Africa to America. He was, however, more successful in the spice trade and the importation of Hungarian cattle. National resentments in Spain forced him to renounce the Maestrazgo lease after 1542 and to give up the silver mines of Guadalcanal. Nonetheless, Anton Fugger had, by 1546, amassed 5,100,000 guilders—the highest capital in the company's history.

His health weakened in 1540, Anton Fugger reacted more acutely to the shifts in his fortunes; since his sons and nephews showed little interest in business, he even considered dissolving the firm. When that proved impossible, he stubbornly tried to carry on, although he could satisfy the demand for credit only by increased borrowing. An inventory taken after his death in 1560 showed assets of 5,600,000 and liabilities of 5,400,000 guilders (2,900,000 in Spain alone). Anton had, however, safeguarded part of his fortune through the timely purchase of Babenhausen and other landed estates. After the personal bankruptcy of his nephew Hans Jakob Fugger, who had become a partner in 1543 and who eventually became Bavarian chancellor, Anton's oldest son, Markus, carried on the business successfully, if on a reduced scale. During the period 1563–1641 the company, which was not completely dissolved until after the Thirty Years' War, earned some 50,000,000 ducats from the production of mercury at Almadén alone.

Shoring
up of the
Fugger
fortune

While Jakob and Anton Fugger had hardly made use of their title as counts, their descendants, showing little mercantile inclination, acquired a Humanistic education at European universities. Marrying within their class, they spent most of their lives on their estates, where they established valuable libraries and built magnificent residences. It is to Jakob and Anton Fugger's land purchases that the three surviving lines of the family (all dating from the mid-16th century)—the counts Fugger-Kirchberg of Oberkirchberg, the prince Fugger-Glött of Kirchheim, and the prince Fugger-Babenhausen of Babenhausen—owe the preservation of a part of the great wealth once held by the family firm.

The Fugger family may be considered a prototype of

the trading company of the early capitalistic era. In overcoming the economic concepts of the Middle Ages, they used methods that have evoked, both in their time and in the present, admiration as well as violent criticism.

BIBLIOGRAPHY. G. VON POLNITZ' comprehensive presentation *Die Fugger*, 3rd ed. (1970), offers the best survey of the Fugger family and contains an extensive bibliography. The same author's biographies *Jakob Fugger*, 2 vol. (1949–51), and *Anton Fugger*, 4 vol. (1958–71; vol. 5 in prep.), are instructive source-books based on research in major European archives. L.L. SCHICK, *Un Grand homme d'affaires au début du XVIe siècle: Jacob Fugger* (1957), is a biography written from a professional banker's viewpoint. R. EHRENBERG, *Das Zeitalter der Fugger*, 2 vol. (1896; Eng. trans., with some sections omitted, *Capital and Finance in the Age of the Renaissance: A Study of the Fuggers and Their Connections*, 1928), is a pioneering study of money and credit circulation in the 16th century. WILHELM MASSEN, *Hans Jakob Fugger (1516–1575) ein Beitrag zur Geschichte des XVI. Jahrhunderts* (1922); REINHARD HILDEBRANDT, *Die "Georg Fuggerischen Erben"* (1966); and ROBERT MANDROU, *Les Fugger, propriétaires fonciers en Souabe, 1560–1618* (1969), are all exemplary studies of the company's later development. H. KELLENBENZ, *Die Fuggersche Maestrazgopacht (1525–1542)* (1967), describes the history of the Maestrazgo lease and its development while administered by the Fuggers.

(F.Br.)

Fugue

Although the statement is debatable, it is often said that the fugue is the most complex and highly developed type of composition in Western music. The term fugue, derived from *fuga*, the Latin word for "flight," was first used about 1330 by Jacques de Liège, the author of *Speculum musicae*, an important medieval treatise. At that time it referred to a technique of musical writing based on strict imitation. Later, after its emergence as an independent musical form in the 17th century, the fugue became a composition in counterpoint based on a generating theme, in which different parts, or voices, enter successively in imitation, as if in pursuit of each other. The heir of all the compositional techniques that had developed earlier, it differs from its ancestors (the motet, the ricercar, the canzona) in having a more specifically tonal character, unity of form, and a greater economy.

DESCRIPTION OF THE FUGUE

The fugue is written in counterpoint, two or more lines that sound simultaneously. Counterpoint's laws and techniques have developed from the 10th century to the Renaissance, a period during which Western music was essentially polyphonic. One of the main problems was the harmonic aspect of the meeting of the voices, and the rules of counterpoint are always precise regarding the use of consonance and dissonance. Counterpoint deals also with movement between the parts. It includes various techniques of development, among which imitation is probably the most remarkable feature of polyphonic music. There are many kinds of imitations. The strictest is the canon, in which the melody stated by the first voice is later reproduced by the second voice. A good example is the song "Frère Jacques." Other common types of imitation include inversion of all the intervals, augmentation (in which the rhythmic values are doubled), diminution (in which they are reduced), or even retrograde imitation, in which the last note of one voice becomes the first note of the next. All these techniques are used in fugal composition, which is characterized more by its "language" than by its form.

Elements. The fugue is written for a certain number of voices, or instrumental parts. The most frequent are fugues for three or four voices, but there are also fugues for two, five, or more voices. Although the fugal form varies from composer to composer, there are certain common elements.

Subject. The subject is the theme of the fugue. It is stated alone by the first voice before being taken up by the others. In the course of the fugue, it will be stated in different keys, and it will be sometimes slightly modified or inverted. Some of its elements may be developed separately.

Answer. The second voice brings in the answer, generally stated in the key of the dominant (the fifth degree of the major or minor scale). If it reproduces the subject exactly, it is called a real answer. But in most cases, in order to preserve the tonal unity of the fugue, the answer has to undergo a "mutation" that alters some of its melodic intervals and makes the modulation to the dominant key smoother. This is called the tonal answer.

Countersubject. The countersubject accompanies the answer. If it is maintained throughout the fugue, it is called sustained or obbligato countersubject and will follow the subject like its shadow for each new statement. Subject and countersubject are the two principal "actors" of the fugue, and theoretically all the musical substance must be derived from them.

Exposition. The first part of the fugue, which includes the successive entrance of the voices, in subject–answer alternation, is called exposition. This progressive enrichment of the polyphonic web is one of the most striking traits of the fugue. In some fugues, after the exposition, the composer brings in the answer followed by the subject. This is called counterexposition.

Episode. An episode is any passage, developed or not, that links two statements of the subject. It is characteristically written in imitative style. Generally it uses a motive from the subject or the countersubject, but sometimes a new element is introduced. There is a great variety of episodes.

Stretto. When the subject overlaps the answer (or the answer the subject), it is called a stretto. This device, whereby the entries are drawn more closely together, is often used at the end of the fugue, where it achieves spectacular effects.

Plan of the fugue. Once past the exposition, the plan of the fugue depends on the will of the composer and the resources of its thematic elements. For instance, the Danish composer Dietrich Buxtehude (died 1707) often presents the subject and the answer only in the principal and in the dominant keys, in short expositions linked by small episodes. With J.S. Bach, the tonal plan becomes more elaborate and includes a journey to the principal neighbouring keys. Since the composer adapts his plan to the character and to the potential of his themes, the itinerary is always different. That is why in his hands the fugue becomes the most versatile of musical forms; each fugue of Bach brings a new solution to the problem of the relation between form and content.

The "school fugue." Theorists created an ideal plan of the fugue and gradually perfected it, in the 19th century, as fewer and fewer real fugues were being written. They devised a tripartite form consisting of the exposition, the development, and the stretto.

VARIETIES OF FUGUE

Simple fugue. This is monothematic, without a maintained countersubject (such as the *Fugue in D Major* of Bach's work *The Well-Tempered Clavier*, Book I, No. 5). More elaborate fugues use one or more countersubjects. In a counterfugue, the answer imitates the subject by inversion. There are beautiful examples of this technique in Bach's work *The Art of the Fugue*, numbers 5 to 7.

Double fugue. There are two ways of writing a double fugue; either the two subjects may be presented simultaneously, in which case the fugue is not very different from a fugue with countersubject (Bach, *Fugue in B Minor on a Theme of Corelli*, BWV 579), or else the second subject has a special exposition. The latter yields, in general, a tripartite scheme: exposition and development of the first subject, exposition and development of the second subject, and finally combination of the two elements, which are devised so that they can be superimposed. A splendid example is given by Bach's *Toccata and Fugue in F Major* for organ, BWV 540. The same principles apply to a triple or quadruple fugue.

Fughetta. This is a miniature fugue but strictly written, whereas the fugato starts like a fugue but gives up its discipline once past the exposition.

Choral fugues. The fugue plays a considerable role in works for chorus and orchestra. Generally the chorus

Types of imitation

Versatility of the fugue

sings in strict counterpoint, while the instruments play an expressive or decorative accompaniment. The composition techniques of the fugue can also be used in forms as universal as the prelude, the aria, the chorus, the overture, the concerto, and others.

LITERATURE OF THE FUGUE

Since vocal polyphony was based on a text that had to be sung by each of the parts (either simultaneously or, more frequently, in imitation), it was not very much concerned with the problem of form. That is why theorists and musicians concentrated on questions of texture.

At first the term *fuga* applied to strict imitations (which would now be called canons); the concept evolved in a more general sense when it was realized that a freer use of all kinds of imitations offered much more stimulating opportunities. Besides the purely vocal polyphony, the first independent forms of keyboard music (the ricercar, the canzona, the capriccio, the fantasia) testify to the remarkable development of what can be called the fugal style of the 16th and 17th centuries. In this evolution, the role of the Italian composer Andrea Gabrieli and of the English virginalists was preponderant. The two great precursors of the fugue proper were the Dutch composer J.P. Sweelinck (died 1621) and the Italian Girolamo Frescobaldi (died 1643). Both greatly influenced the keyboard music of the 17th century, in particular through their students Samuel Scheidt and Johann Jakob Froberger. In Germany, a generation of musicians dominated by Buxtehude gave the fugue its modern form by putting it in a tonal perspective and abandoning the fragmentary style of their predecessors. Almost all the composers of the 17th century contributed to the history of the fugue.

J.S. Bach. The genius of Bach found particular expression in the fugue, perhaps because it allies the strictest economy of language to a relative freedom of form. Each of his fugues amazes by the freshness of its inspiration, the wonders of its writing, or by its gigantic proportions, all marvellously represented in the two volumes of *The Well-Tempered Clavier* (1722–44), two sets of 24 preludes and fugues going through the cycle of the 24 major and minor keys. Some of his organ fugues tend toward development, some toward symmetry, and some toward virtuosity; others take the form of double fugues.

Bach's *Art of the Fugue*

His last work, *The Art of the Fugue*, is a collection of 14 fugues and four canons, all based on a theme in D minor and its inversion. All the resources and procedures of the fugue are demonstrated in what constitutes the most inspiring treatise on fugue, a treatise without words, in which music speaks alone. After being long slighted as a purely theoretical work, *The Art of the Fugue* has won a high place in the hearts of music lovers, who see it as Bach's musical testament. Bach's cantatas, passions, and oratorios abound in admirable fugues.

Handel and after. Handel's fugues are less erudite than those of Bach and sometimes employ looser counterpoint, but they touch the listener by their vitality and their harmonious proportions. The great fugal sections of his oratorios are more important than his keyboard fugues.

After Bach the fugue lost much of its importance. With the appearance of the sonata, the musical taste changed, and composers tended to consider counterpoint as an archaic discipline. Nonetheless, the fugue retained a place in choral works, and fugal methods were kept in the sonata form, particularly in the development section.

A great passion for Bach led Mozart (died 1791) to a more contrapuntal style. This influence is obvious in the *Fugue in C Minor*, for two pianos, K. 426, which, though pure Mozart, is nonetheless a homage to Bach. In ingenuity and mastery, Mozart rivalled the greatest contrapuntists in, for instance, the great choruses of the *Mass in C Minor*, K. 427, or in the final development of the *Jupiter Symphony*.

Beethoven. Beethoven resorted more and more to fugal technique in his last works. He confessed that he wrote his fugues with the greatest difficulty, and it is true that his counterpoint gives an impression of effort.

Most of the fugal passages integrated into his last sonatas and quartets create a dramatic tension. Far from being a scholastic technique, the fugue was for Beethoven a means to reach the expressive limits of an idea. He used this language in particular circumstances. The strange and desolate atmosphere of the opening fugue of the *String Quartet in C Sharp Minor*, Opus 131, brings to mind the 20th-century fugue in the first section of the *Music for Strings, Percussion and Celesta* of Béla Bartók. The Promethean side of Beethoven asserts itself particularly in the *Great Fugue* from the *String Quartet in B Flat Major*, Opus 130, and the noble fugal section of the *Missa Solemnis*. Unlike Mozart's classical fugues, Beethoven's are rather irrational in form but are justified by their creative power alone.

The Romantic era. Compared with the fugues of Beethoven, those of Felix Mendelssohn defer to traditional rules. Critics sense in them a nostalgia for Bach, sometimes weakened by a touch of sentimentalism. A more authentic romantic breath animates the fugues of Robert Schumann on B.A.C.H. (the German letters for the notes B♭–A–C–B♮), but the fugue is not his natural language. The genre is more suited to César Franck, as may be seen in his *Prélude, fugue et variation*, or in his *Prélude, chorale et fugue*. His harmonic sensitivity enriches a contrapuntal technique while not breaking with tradition. The fugues of Franz Liszt are entirely different: once past the exposition, he cannot renounce symphonic developments. There is an original use of the fugato before the re-exposition in his *Piano Sonata in B Minor*. The fugal style was used to varying degree by the major composers of the 19th century, including Brahms in his *German Requiem*, Richard Wagner in his opera *Die Meistersinger*, and Verdi in his *Requiem* and at the end of his last opera, *Falstaff*.

Among the post-Romantics, who cultivated their own exaggerated form of counterpoint, mention must be made of Max Reger, whose admirers took him as the heir of J.S. Bach. Though that appears to be going too far, his counterpoint does possess vitality in works such as the *Variations and Fugue on a Theme by Mozart*, for orchestra, or the fugue on the chorale melody "Wachet auf, ruft uns die Stimme," for organ.

The 20th century. As an autonomous form, the fugue played only a modest role in the first half of the 20th century. The most beautiful example is the already mentioned fugue of the *Music for Strings, Percussion and Celesta* of Béla Bartók, a born contrapuntist. This is a true model of fugal treatment in a post-tonal style. The methods of the fugue are also found in his *Sonata for Two Pianos and Percussion* and in his admirable quartets.

Bartók's use of fugue

Stravinsky, though influenced by the composers of the 17th and 18th centuries, showed no particular interest in the fugue. Although the second part of his *Symphony of Psalms* can be considered a double fugue, it does not strike the listener as such.

In his collection of interludes and fugues, called *Ludus Tonalis*, Paul Hindemith seems to have drawn his inspiration from Bach's *Well-Tempered Clavier*. Although an interesting work, it did not herald a rebirth of the fugue. A new conception of counterpoint appeared in the works of Arnold Schoenberg and Anton von Webern. The serial techniques of composers like Pierre Boulez can, to a certain extent, claim some kind of kinship with fugal language, and a work such as the *Passion According to St. Luke* of Krzysztof Penderecki testifies to the permanence of a musical form the history of which is probably unfinished.

BIBLIOGRAPHY. Major historical treatises on the study of the fugal style include: N. VINCENTINO, *L'Antica Musica ridotta alla moderna prattica* (1555); GIOSEFFO ZARLINO, *Institutioni harmoniche* (1558; Eng. trans. of pt. 3, *The Art of Counterpoint*, 1968); THOMAS MORLEY, *A Plaine and Easie Introduction to Practicall Musicke* (1597; new ed. by R.A. HARMAN, 1952); JAN PIETERSZOON SWEELINCK, *Kompositionslehre* (1670, reissued 1891); JOHANN JOSEPH FUX, *Gradus ad parnassum*, 2 vol. (1725; Eng. trans., *Steps to Parnassus*, 1943), part of this work ed. and trans. by ALFRED MANN as "The Study of Fugue," in *Musical Quarterly*, vol. 36–37 (1950–

War I as commander of a crash-boat flotilla. In recognition of his invention of special life-saving equipment, he was awarded an appointment to the U.S. Naval Academy at Annapolis. In 1917 he married Anne Hewlett, daughter of James Monroe Hewlett, a well-known architect and muralist, later a director of the American Academy in Rome. Hewlett had invented a modular construction system using a compressed fibre block; and after the war Fuller and Hewlett formed a construction company, using this material (later known as Soundex, a Celotex product), in modules, for house construction. In this operation, Fuller himself supervised the erection of several hundred houses; the experience taught him that construction with craft labour is disastrously wasteful: "The experience made me realize that craft building—in which each house is a pilot model for a design which never has any runs—is an art which belongs to the middle ages."

In 1922, soon after the founding of the construction organization, The Stockade Building System, his first daughter, Alexandra, died at the age of four. She had suffered, in succession, influenza, polio, and spinal meningitis—illnesses epidemic at the time, and whose spread Fuller blamed partially on inadequacies of the environment. He concluded that the inadequacies were unnecessary, and that the environment can be controlled; it can be "valved" to human advantage. Fuller's key to controlling the environment is comprehensive anticipatory design.

The Stockade Building System encountered financial difficulties in 1927. Fuller, a minority stockholder, was forced out. He found himself stranded in Chicago, without income, alienated, dismayed, confused.

At this point in his life, Fuller made what he called a "blind date with principle." He resolved to devote his remaining years to a nonprofit search for design patterns that could maximize the social uses of the world's energy resources and evolving industrial complex. The inventions, discoveries, and economic strategies that followed have been interim factors related to this end.

The Dymaxion house and Dymaxion automobile

In 1927, in the course of the development of his comprehensive strategy, he invented and demonstrated a factory-assembled, air-deliverable house, later called the Dymaxion house, which had its own utilities. Regarding air–land–water transportation as a necessary adjunct to his totally autonomous house, he designed in 1928, and manufactured in 1933, the first limited, land-taxiing prototype of his omnidirectional vehicle, the Dymaxion car. This automobile, the first streamlined car, could cross open fields like a jeep, accelerate to 120 miles per hour (190 kilometres per hour), make a 180° turn in its own length, carry 12 passengers, and average 28 miles per gallon of gasoline. Equipped with all-around bumpers, it provided maximum protection to its occupants in event of collision. In 1943, at the request of the industrialist Henry Kaiser, Fuller developed a new version of the Dymaxion car embodying advantages of the improved technology. The new version was planned to be powered by three separate air-cooled engines, each coupled to its own wheel by a variable fluid drive. The coupling system provided maximum torque with minimum engine size. Once starting inertia was overcome, only a single engine was required to maintain cruising speed. Thus the car could average 40 to 50 miles per gallon of gas, and could operate with a minimum of pollution. All wheels were steerable; the car consequently could move sidewise like a crab, parking in a space no greater than its own length. The projected 1943 Dymaxion, like its predecessor, was never put into commercial production, possibly because of the resistance of the automotive industry to radical innovations.

Assuming that there is in nature a vectorial, or directionally oriented, system of forces that provide maximum strength with minimum structures, as is the case in the nested tetrahedron lattices of organic compounds and of metals, Fuller developed a vectorial system of geometry that he called "Energetic-Synergetic geometry." The basic unit of this system is the tetrahedron (a pyramid shape with four sides, including the base), which, in combination with octahedrons (eight-sided shapes), forms the most economic space-filling structures. The architectural consequence of the use of this geometry by Fuller was the geodesic dome, a frame the total strength of which increases in logarithmic ratio to its size. Because geodesic domes have no limiting dimensions, they can be used, as Fuller has proposed, as "sky breaks" over entire cities, making possible comprehensive environment control, including the economic use of hostile terrain, as in the Arctic Circle or Antarctica.

The geodesic dome

Many thousands of geodesic domes have been erected in various parts of the world, the most publicized of which was the United States exhibition dome at Expo 67 in Montreal. One houses the tropical exhibit area of a St. Louis botanical garden; another, the Union Tank Car Company's dome, was built in 1958 in Baton Rouge, Louisiana. This dome, at the time of its construction the largest clear span structure in existence, is 384 feet (117 metres) in diameter and 116 feet (35 metres) in height. A geodesic dome for the shopping centre of East St. Louis, Illinois, has a planned diameter of a half mile (about 0.8 kilometre).

Other inventions and developments by Fuller include a system of cartography that presents all the land areas of the world without significant distortion; die-stamped prefabricated bathrooms; tetrahedronal, floating cities; underwater geodesic-domed farms; and expendable paper domes. But Fuller does not regard himself as an inventor or an architect. All of his developments, in his view, are accidental or interim incidents in the growth of world strategy, which aims at a radical solution of world problems by finding means to do more with less.

He once wrote:

I did not set out to design a house that hung from a pole, or to manufacture a new type of automobile, invent a new system of map projection, develop geodesic domes or Energetic-Synergetic geometry. I started with the universe—as an organization of energy systems of which all our experiences and possible experiences are only local instances. I could have ended up with a pair of flying slippers.

Comprehensive and anticipatory design initiative alone, he holds—exclusive of politics and political theory—can solve the problems of human shelter, nutrition, transportation, and pollution; and it can solve these with a fraction of the materials now inefficiently used. Moreover, energy, ever more available, directed by cumulative information stored in computers, is capable of synthesizing raw materials, of machining and packaging commodities, and of supplying the physical needs of the total global population.

Fuller has been research professor at Southern Illinois University (Carbondale) since 1959. In 1968 the board of trustees named him university professor, the second faculty member so distinguished in the university's history. On recommendation of the Royal Institute of British Architects, Queen Elizabeth II awarded Fuller the Royal Gold Medal for Architecture. He also received the 1968 Gold Medal Award of the National Institute of Arts and Letters.

BIBLIOGRAPHY

Critical appraisals of Fuller's life and work: ROBERT W. MARKS, *The Dymaxion World of Buckminster Fuller* (1960), which contains a detailed explanation of Fuller's energetic-synergetic geometry and technical descriptions of Fuller's inventions and structures prior to 1960; JOHN MCHALE, *R. Buckminster Fuller* (1962), a critical evaluation of Fuller's architectural achievements.

Basic writings of Fuller: Nine Chains to the Moon (1938, reprinted 1963), an outline of his general technological strategy for maximizing social applications of energy resources. Developments of this central theme, with additional technical data, may be found in *Education Automation: Freeing the Scholar to Return to His Studies* (1962); *Ideas and Integrities: A Spontaneous Autobiographical Disclosure* (1963); *No More Secondhand God, and Other Writings* (1962); *Utopia or Oblivion: The Prospects for Humanity* (1969); and *Operating Manual for Spaceship Earth* (1969).

(R.W.M.)

Fulton, Robert

Robert Fulton, U.S. inventor and artist who led in the development of the steamboat, employed his talents as a portrait and landscape painter to finance the building of his first models. He brought steamboating from the experimental stage to its successful commercial status by the synthesis and extension of the most practical engineering ideas of the United States and Europe.

Fulton, oil painting by Benjamin West, 1806. In the collection of the New York State Historical Association, Cooperstown.

Fulton was born on a farm in Lancaster County, Pennsylvania, on November 14, 1765. When the unproductive farm was lost by mortgage foreclosure in 1771, the family moved to Lancaster, where Fulton's father died in 1774 (not 1786 as is generally written). Having learned to read and write at home, Fulton was sent at age eight to a Quaker school; later he became an apprentice in a Philadelphia jewelry shop, where he specialized in the painting of miniature portraits on ivory for lockets and rings.

Early training

After settling his mother on a small farm in western Pennsylvania in 1786, Fulton went to Bath, Virginia, to recover from a severe cough. There the paintings of the young man—tall, graceful, and an engaging conversationalist—were admired by people who advised him to study in Europe. On returning to Philadelphia, Fulton applied himself to painting and the search for a sponsor. Local merchants, eager to raise the city's cultural level, financed his passage to London in 1787.

Although Fulton's reception in London was cordial, his paintings made little impression; they showed neither the style nor the promise required to provide him more than a precarious living. Meanwhile, he became acquainted with new inventions for propelling boats: a water jet ejected by a steam pump and a single, mechanical paddle. His own experiments led him to conclude that several revolving paddles at the stern would be most effective.

Beginning in 1794, however, having admitted defeat as a painter, Fulton turned his principal efforts toward canal engineering. His *Treatise on the Improvement of Canal Navigation*, in 1796, dealt with a complete system of inland water transportation based on small canals extending throughout the countryside. He included details on inclined planes for raising boats—he did not favour locks—aqueducts for valley crossings, boats for specialized cargo, and bridge designs featuring bowstring beams to transmit only vertical loads to the piers. A few bridges were built to his design in the British Isles, but his canal ideas were nowhere accepted.

Undaunted, he travelled in 1797 to Paris, where he proposed the idea of a submarine, the "Nautilus," to be used in France's war with Britain; it would creep under the hulls of British warships and leave a powder charge to be exploded later. The French government rejected the idea, however, as an atrocious and dishonourable way to fight. In 1800 he was able to build the "Nautilus" at his own expense; he conducted trials on the Seine and finally obtained government sanction for an attack, but wind and tide enabled two British ships to elude his slow vessel.

In 1801 Fulton met Robert R. Livingston, a member of the committee that drafted the U.S. Declaration of Independence. Before becoming minister to France, Livingston had obtained a 20-year monopoly of steamboat navigation within the state of New York. The two men decided to share the expense of building a steamboat in Paris using Fulton's design—a side paddlewheel, 66-foot- (20-metre-) long boat, with an eight-horsepower engine of French design. Although the engine broke the hull, they were encouraged by success with another hull. Fulton ordered parts for a 24-horsepower engine from Boulton and Watt for a boat on the Hudson, and Livingston obtained an extension on his monopoly of steamboat navigation.

Returning to London in 1804, Fulton advanced his ideas with the British government for submersible and low-lying craft that would carry explosives in an attack. Two raids against the French using his novel craft, however, were unsuccessful. In 1805, after Nelson's victory at Trafalgar, it was apparent that Britain was in control of the seas without the aid of Fulton's temperamental weapons. In the same year, the parts for his projected steamboat were ready for shipment to the United States, but Fulton spent a desperate year attempting to collect money he felt the British owed him.

Arriving in New York in December 1806, Fulton at once set to work supervising the construction of the steamboat that had been planned in Paris with Livingston. He also attempted to interest the United States government in a submarine, but his demonstration of it was a fiasco. By early August 1807 a 150-foot- (45-metre-) long "Steamboat," as Fulton called it, was ready for trials. Its single-cylinder condensing steam engine (24-inch bore and four-foot stroke) drove two 15-foot-diameter side paddlewheels; it consumed oak and pine fuel, which produced steam at a pressure of two to three pounds per square inch. The 150-mile (240-kilometre) trial run from New York to Albany required 32 hours (an average of almost 4.7 miles [7.6 kilometres] per hour), considerably better time than the four miles per hour required by the monopoly. The passage was epic because sailing sloops required four days for the same trip.

The "Steamboat"

After building an enginehouse, raising the bulwark, and installing berths in the cabins of the now-renamed "North River Steamboat," Fulton began commercial trips in September. He made three round trips fortnightly between New York and Albany, carrying passengers and light freight. Problems, however, still remained: the inevitable mechanical difficulties, for example, and the jealous sloopboatmen, who through "inadvertence" would ram the unprotected paddlewheels of their new rivals. During the first winter season he stiffened and widened the hull, replaced the cast-iron crankshaft with a forging, fitted guards over the wheels, and installed larger and quite lush passenger accommodations. These modifications made it essentially a different boat, which was registered in 1808 as "The New North River Steamboat of Clermont," soon reduced to "Clermont" by the press.

In 1808 Fulton married his partner's niece, Harriet Livingston, by whom he had a son and three daughters.

In 1811 the Fulton-designed, Pittsburgh-built "New Orleans" was sent south to validate the Livingston–Fulton steamboat monopoly of the New Orleans Territory. The trip was slow and perilous, river conditions being desperate because of America's first recorded, and also largest, earthquake, which had destroyed New Madrid just below the confluence of the Ohio and Mississippi rivers. Fulton's low-powered vessel remained at New Orleans, for it could go no farther upstream than Natchez. He built three boats for Western rivers that were based at New Orleans, but none could conquer the passage to Pittsburgh.

Fulton was a member of the 1812 commission that recommended building the Erie Canal. With the English blockade the same year, he insisted that a mobile floating gun platform be built—the world's first steam warship—to protect New York harbour against the British fleet. The "Demologos" incorporated new and novel ideas: two parallel hulls, with paddlewheel between; the steam engine in one hull, and boilers and stacks in the other. Launched in 1814, the heavily gunned and armoured steamship underwent successful sea trials; when peace came in December, it was transferred to the Brooklyn Navy Yard, where it was destroyed by an accidental explosion in 1829. By 1810 three of Fulton's boats served the Hudson and Raritan rivers. His steamboats also replaced the horse ferries that were used for heavily travelled river crossings in New York, Boston, and Philadelphia. He retained the typical broad double-ended hulls that needed no turning for the return passage. Manhattan's crosstown Fulton Street, named in 1816, was the principal thoroughfare connecting the two river terminals.

Commercial development

Fulton spent much of his wealth in litigations involving the pirating of patents relating to steamboats and in trying to suppress rival steamboat builders who found loopholes in the state-granted monopoly. His wealth was further depleted by his unsuccessful submarine projects, investments in paintings, and financial assistance to farmer kin and young artists. After testifying at a legal hearing in Trenton, early in 1815, he became chilled en route home to New York, where he died on February 24. His family made claims on the United States government for services rendered. A bill of $100,000 for the relief of the heirs finally passed the Congress in 1846 but was reduced to $76,300, with no interest.

A Hudson–Fulton Celebration in 1909 commemorated the success of "The North River Steamboat of Clermont" and the discovery in 1609 of the North River by the English navigator who was the first to sail upstream to Albany. A "Robert Fulton" commemorative stamp was issued in 1965, the bicentenary of his birth; and the two-story farmhouse, his birthplace, has been acquired and restored by the Pennsylvania Historical and Museum Commission.

BIBLIOGRAPHY. J.T. FLEXNER, *Steamboats Come True* (1944), a scholarly study of the principal American steamboat protagonists—Fitch, Rumsey, Livingston, Stevens, and Fulton—is a sober evaluation that presents much material untouched by earlier biographers such as Fulton's close friend, C.D. COLDEN, *The Life of Robert Fulton* (1817); an admirer, J.F. REIGART, *The Life of Robert Fulton* (1856); and his great-granddaughter A.C. SUTCLIFFE, *Robert Fulton and the "Clermont"* (1909), among others. H.W. DICKINSON, *Robert Fulton, Engineer and Artist* (1913), deals with technical matters in an exemplary way. For a phase, there is W.B. PARSONS, *Robert Fulton and the Submarine* (1922).

(R.S.H.)

Fundamentalist and Evangelical Churches

Fundamentalist and Evangelical churches comprise a mixed group of theologically conservative communions that stress the full, and often verbal, inspiration of the Bible and its complete authority over faith and practice. They preach that a felicitous eternal life is won only as the gift of God's grace through a radical conversion and commitment to Christ as Saviour.

NATURE AND SIGNIFICANCE

This group of churches arose in the United States in the 1920s out of the dissension and potential schism that existed within several Protestant denominations. They are derived from one group of dissenters who called themselves Fundamentalists and who claimed to defend the standards of orthodox Christianity. An opposing group, referred to either as Liberals or Modernists, attempted to assimilate the work of 19th-century biblical criticism and to make the church relevant to the social dilemmas of that era. Fundamentalists charged that Modernism was betraying Christianity and abandoning the Gospel in favour of the new science. Modernists claimed that there could be no hope for a church that wrapped itself in an outworn theology and ignored modern thought. During the same decade the anti-evolution

Fundamentalism and Liberalism (Modernism)

crusade broke out, and Fundamentalists became involved, especially in the famous 1925 "monkey" trial (concerning the state law prohibiting the teaching of Charles Darwin's theory of evolution in public schools) of John T. Scopes in Dayton, Tennessee.

Fifty years later, Modernism and Liberalism had practically disappeared, and the theologies that succeeded them had only a historical relationship to the thought of such Modernists as Shailer Mathews, Charles Briggs, and A.C. McGiffert, Sr. But Fundamentalism has survived and is flourishing. After World War II, due to the pejorative associations clinging to the older name, Fundamentalists began to call themselves Evangelicals. No religious census exists that reveals their numbers, and only a few denominations, such as the Conservative Baptist Association of America, or more loosely organized bodies, such as the Independent Fundamental Churches of America, can be definitely categorized as Fundamentalist. The National Association of Evangelicals, a cooperative, ecumenical agency founded largely by Fundamentalists, claimed a membership of approximately 3,000,000 in 1971. The numerical strength of these churches does not indicate the impressive influence of Fundamentalist views found in many major Protestant denominations, as demonstrated in the popular adage "Scratch a Protestant and you will find a Fundamentalist."

HISTORY

Origins. The roots of Fundamentalism are found in the history of the American millenarian movement. In the 1830s and 1840s, a great deal of excitement was generated in the United States by expectations of the Second Advent of Christ and an ensuing thousand years of peace ("the millennium"). For the most part this excitement was related to the preaching of a group of ministers who had been converted to the proclamation then being made by a New York farmer, William Miller, that the second coming might be expected in or before 1843. These adventists were effective in winning the support of 50,000 to 100,000 adherents, but the failure of the prediction virtually destroyed the movement and brought the millenarian cause into disrepute. Critics of millenarianism during the next few decades used adventism as a reproach with which to destroy the credibility of anyone maintaining the doctrine of Christ's imminent advent. In Great Britain, where the Millerites were known but not influential, the millenarian movement, beginning about 1825, made rapid progress among the evangelical party within the Church of England and contributed to the formation of new dissenting groups, such as the Catholic Apostolic Church and the Plymouth Brethren. English influence made a significant impact in America at the time of Miller's prominence and sustained interest in the Second Coming where it might otherwise have disappeared.

Millenarianism

By the 1870s millenarian interest increased in those churches associated with the Reformed tradition, particularly among American Episcopalians, Presbyterians, and Dutch Reformed. The greatest impact of these views was felt in the East and Northeast and in urban centres, such as St. Louis and Chicago, where ministers kept abreast of current theological literature.

Scattered interest in the subject of the imminent return of Christ was concentrated and built into a movement largely through the Niagara Bible Conference. Initiated by James Inglis, a New York City Baptist minister, shortly before his death in 1872, the conference continued under James H. Brookes (1830–97), a St. Louis Presbyterian minister and editor of the influential millenarian periodical *The Truth*. Other early millenarian leaders included George C. Needham, a Baptist Evangelist (1840–1902); William J. Erdman (1834–1923), a Presbyterian minister noted for his skill as a biblical expositor; and William R. Nicholson (1822–1901), who left the Episcopal Church in 1873 and became a bishop in the small Reformed Episcopal denomination. Toward the close of the century, the movement attracted leaders such as the prominent Boston Baptist minister Adoniram J.

Gordon (1836–95); and Maurice Baldwin (1836–1904), bishop of Huron in the Church of Canada. The group held annual summer conferences, which generally met at Niagara-on-the-Lake, Ontario, until 1899. The millenarians associated with the Niagara Conference also sponsored a series of public conferences in major cities beginning in 1878, such as the Bible and Prophetic Conference in New York City.

Development of Fundamentalist views. Beliefs that the condition of the church and society generally were deteriorating to the point of alarm, that nothing could save the Christian or improve the lot of this earth except the coming of Christ, and that the return of Christ was indeed promised in the Scriptures and might be expected at any moment placed them squarely within the apocalyptic tradition. Critics called them Millerites, but the millenarians pointed out that they carefully refrained from any date setting. These premillennialists (another name often applied to them) found their views opposed by progressive millennialists, or postmillennialists. Premillennialists were less optimistic than progressive millennialists. Traditionally, postmillennialists were confident that the churches were succeeding with the task of evangelism; that social, moral, and economic progress was being made in the world with God's help (especially in America); and that Christ would return at that point in the not too distant future when the world was fitted for such a king. The millenarian movement began to grow within America when confidence in America's destiny first began to wane among some Protestant leaders, faced as they were with labour unrest, social discontent, and the rising tide of Roman Catholic immigration.

The appeal of the millenarian movement was not simply due to a loss of confidence in the American dream. A serious concern with the interpretation of the Bible also won many converts to the millenarian movement. In the early 19th century, most of the Protestant churches defended the Bible as the inspired Word of God, but biblical authority meant something special to the millenarians. They believed that the Scriptures predicted an apostasy in Christendom and a degeneracy within society during the last days and that the only remedy foretold by biblical authors was the return of Christ at a time that 19th-century millenarians were convinced could be no later than their own generation.

Authority of the Bible

Millenarian theology was articulated before biblical criticism raised doubts about the meaning of the biblical text. Many American Protestants found it possible to accept the results of 19th-century biblical criticism and to support their faith upon a new understanding of the authority of the Bible, but millenarians could not.

During the late 1880s and 1890s the challenge to the prevailing assumptions about the Bible began to create a serious problem for the millenarians, but the Fundamentalist controversy did not break out then; it was instead postponed for a generation. Concerned by the progress of biblical criticism, millenarian leaders did not despair. Their apocalyptic theology taught them not to expect any improvement in the world. While much of the church seemed about to be swept into infidelity, the millenarian movement entered the period of its greatest prominence and national influence. As the century drew to a close, the Protestant evangelist Dwight L. Moody (1837–99) lent support to their movement, providing in his Northfield conferences an influential platform for millenarian expression. Millenarians supported foreign missions work and influenced the surge of missionary zeal that was eventually institutionalized as the Student Volunteer Movement. Also, they found within the Princeton Theological Seminary at Princeton, New Jersey, a group of scholars interested in defending the authority and inspiration of the Bible.

Millenarians invited the Princeton professors to their conferences and adopted their arguments in defense of the Bible. Virtually none of the Princeton faculty adopted millenarianism and some opposed it strongly, but both parties appreciated each other's support on the issue of biblical authority.

Cooperation of millenarians and defenders of biblical inerrancy

The high point of millenarian influence upon the conservative tradition within evangelical Protestantism occurred when millenarians cooperated with other defenders of the inerrant Bible in founding the American Bible League in 1902 and in writing a series of 12 pamphlets entitled *The Fundamentals.* Over 250,000 of each of these pamphlets were distributed free to ministers and laymen from 1909 to 1915 through the philanthropy of Lyman and Milton Stewart, brothers whose fortune was made in the California oil industry and whose theology was millenarian. Without rancour or hysteria, *The Fundamentals* attacked the current theories of biblical criticism and reasserted the authority of the Bible, using the arguments developed at Princeton Seminary. The series was a summary of the previous generation's attempt to defeat biblical criticism and Modernism through argument.

Almost all of the leaders who had founded the Niagara Conference had died by 1914. The new generation of leaders were not as firmly attached to their denominations as were their predecessors. And their defense of the millenarian cause was more militant and uncompromising. During the last years of the 19th century, disagreements over prophetic interpretation were expressed, but James H. Brookes held the dissident factions together. Within a few years of his death, however, the Niagara Conference was abandoned, and shortly thereafter a paper war broke out between the two leading millenarian periodicals, *Watchword and Truth* and *Our Hope,* that deeply divided the movement.

The Fundamentalist-Modernist controversy. At the end of World War I, the millenarians, alarmed by the growth of Liberalism and disturbed over more general symptoms of social degeneracy, held a number of conferences in New York City and Philadelphia, which were successful enough to encourage the formation of a larger and more comprehensive organization in 1919, the World's Christian Fundamentals Association. As a result of this conference, the millenarian movement changed its name without changing its basic character. Furthermore, the 1919 conference placed planks in a platform on which the millenarian-Fundamentalist movement would stand for the next 30 years. The leaders reiterated the creedal basis of the movement, with its characteristic biblical and millenarian articles, called for the exorcism of Modernism and all its associated demons (especially evolution), practically abandoned the universities and placed their faith in the more recently founded Bible institutes, denounced the unitive and cooperative spirit exemplified in the Federal Council of the Churches of Christ in America, and threatened schism if this type of spiritual decline persisted. In spite of vigorous leadership from men like W.B. Riley (pastor of First Baptist Church in Minneapolis), A.C. Dixon (Baptist pastor and evangelist), and R.A. Torrey (evangelist and superintendent of Moody Bible Institute), however, the association never prospered. Dozens of conferences were held in which evolution was hotly condemned and the educational institutions of the country were denounced for abandoning biblical teaching, but even these gatherings could not be sustained after 1928.

Rising tide of Liberalism

During the late 19th century, the liberal faction in the church had numbered only a few men, most of them professors in seminaries or universities. Their acceptance of higher criticism was generally viewed with apprehension by parishioners, the clergy, and officials of their denominations. Where legal machinery existed to examine the new teachings, as it did in the Presbyterian denomination, the verdict was given against the innovations of Liberals such as the biblical theologian Charles A. Briggs (1841–1913). Within a few decades, however, such protests were abandoned as the evidence for the new understanding of the Bible mounted and a new generation of seminarians joined the Liberal cause. By 1914, among the Episcopal, Methodist, Baptist, and Presbyterian denominations in the North, Liberalism had gained many adherents. The battle to prevent the reception and spread of these new views had been lost. During the 1920s it only remained to be decided whether the Liberals could be forced out of the denominations.

The decade of the '20s was marked by intemperate behaviour on the part of many Americans. The war created tensions and frustrations within America that the Armistice of 1918 did little to reduce. Fears of the menace of Communism, labour unrest, and violence appeared in sermons immediately after the war. The American rejection of the League of Nations indicated that many Americans found the new world of international politics not to their liking. The Fundamentalists of the 1920s shared these fears and a mood of intellectual isolationism.

Not every Protestant denomination was affected by controversy during the 1920s. In some, such as the Southern Baptist denomination, Modernism had not yet become prominent. In others, such as the Methodist and Episcopal churches, Modernism had gained many adherents; but the opposition did not become well enough organized and the governmental structures of the denominations did not lend themselves to the kind of campaign necessary to bring the issue to a focus. Serious controversy did erupt, however, among the Northern Baptists and the Presbyterians in the Northern states. Within the Presbyterian Church, conservatives reflecting the theological position of Princeton Seminary had, with the help of the millenarians, imposed a set of essential doctrines upon the denomination in 1910, declaring the inerrant inspiration of the Bible, the virgin birth of Christ, and the Atonement (redemptive activity), Resurrection, and miracle-working power of Christ necessary to the Christian faith. In 1922, when a New York minister, Harry Emerson Fosdick, soon to become a leading Modernist spokesman, protested the activities of millenarians in foreign mission fields in a sermon entitled "Shall the Fundamentalists Win?" the conservatives and millenarians in the denomination were able to force Fosdick, who was a Baptist, out of his position as pastor of the First Presbyterian Church of New York City.

A withdrawal of the Liberals had been the solution desired by millenarians such as James H. Brookes and conservatives such as the Princeton professor J. Gresham Machen. To avoid a schism within the Presbyterian Church in the U.S., a Commission of Fifteen was appointed to work out a compromise. The report of the commission took the position that the Presbyterian denomination had traditionally tolerated a diversity of opinion and rejected the right of the general assembly to determine which were the essential doctrines of the Christian faith. The report virtually destroyed the conservatives' position. Within the Presbyterian denomination, the Fundamentalist-Modernist controversy meant not the victory of the Modernists but the defeat of the Fundamentalists.

The focus of discord within the Northern Baptist denomination was in their annual convention, which functioned much like the convention of a political party. Beginning in 1920, a group of Baptists calling themselves the National Federation of Fundamentalists began holding annual preconvention conferences on Baptist fundamentals. Thus organized, they attempted to carry their views into the convention. When the tactics of the National Federation failed to make immediate progress, some of the more militant Baptist Fundamentalists founded the Baptist Bible Union. Among the Baptists, however, as among the Presbyterians, divisions among the Fundamentalists caused their defeat.

Displeasure with the teaching of evolution, as well as anxiety over the spread of biblical criticism, gained momentum in the 1920s. Fundamentalists, believing that the Bible could not be reconciled with the view of the origin of life taught by Charles Darwin, opposed evolution; but not every opponent of evolution was a Fundamentalist. Anti-evolution crusaders lobbied for legislation to prevent the teaching of evolution in the public schools. Tennessee passed such a statute, which was challenged in the courts in 1925 at the instigation of the American Civil Liberties Union. John T. Scopes, a science teacher in the small town of Dayton, offered to serve as the defendant

against the charge of having taught evolution. Two of the foremost public figures of that decade, William Jennings Bryan, a conservative Presbyterian Fundamentalist, and Clarence Darrow, a defense counsel in notable criminal trials, made headlines as the assistant prosecuting attorney and the defense attorney, respectively.

By the end of the 1920s the Fundamentalist controversy was nearly over, but the Fundamentalist movement was not dead. The history of Fundamentalism had begun in the 1870s with the establishment of the millenarian movement, not in the 1920s. The Fundamentalist controversy was an episode in the history of Fundamentalism that contributed little more to the movement than its new name. Although the decade of the 1920s marked the period of Fundamentalism's greatest national attention, it was not a time of strength for the cause. The years that followed were a period of rebuilding.

Institutional development. During the 1930s and 1940s, Fundamentalists gradually withdrew from conflict and from the national spotlight. During this period the institutional structure of modern Fundamentalism developed. Some Fundamentalists broke away from their denominations to form new churches, such as the Presbyterians, led by J. Gresham Machen, who in 1936 formed the Presbyterian Church in America, or the Baptists, who left the Northern Baptist Convention to establish the General Association of Regular Baptists. Some remained within congregations of the larger denominations. But most Fundamentalists joined a congregation of one of the smaller sects that had remained faithful to the creed of biblical literalism and premillennialism, such as the Christian and Missionary Alliance, the Plymouth Brethren, and the Evangelical Free Church, or one of the many independent Bible churches and tabernacles that arose during that period.

Much of the structure of modern Fundamentalism is provided by Bible institutes and Bible colleges. Many of these schools, such as the Moody Bible Institute in Chicago or the Bible Institute of Los Angeles, in addition to teaching their students, publish periodicals, broadcast from their own radio stations, hold conferences, and maintain a staff of extension speakers. They operate very much like denominational headquarters, providing a bond between otherwise isolated congregations. In the arts and sciences the strongest bastion has long been Wheaton College, a scholarly college in a suburb of Chicago. There is also a series of organizations for Fundamentalists paralleling the professional and business organizations of American society. Doctors, scientists, athletes, social workers, historians, businessmen, nurses, students, and others may join groups designed especially for their interest or vocational area. Chapters of the Inter-Varsity Christian Fellowship, or Campus Crusade for Christ, exist on hundreds of university and college campuses to provide religious support similar to that provided by organizations of the major Protestant denominations and Roman Catholics. The American Scientific Affiliation, which in 1970 numbered 1,437 practicing scientists of Evangelical belief, holds meetings and publishes a journal in which the compatibility of science with the Bible and with a Christian world view is emphasized.

Paralleling the ecumenical bodies of Protestantism are the American Council of Christian Churches founded in 1941 and the National Association of Evangelicals founded in 1942. The ACCC was (until 1969) virtually the voice of one man, Carl McIntire, who spoke against larger ecumenical bodies, such as the National Council of Churches, and against the danger of the Communist conspiracy to destroy America. The NAE operates as a coordinating body for its members but implements no programs of its own.

The most significant influences upon the Fundamentalist and Evangelical churches in America since World War II have been the prosperity of the postwar decades, the religious revival of the 1950s, and the alleged threat of Communist subversion. Evangelicals as a group should not be categorized among the socially or economically

The essentials of Fundamentalism

Anti-evolutionism

Bible institutes and colleges

disadvantaged. In an era in which a typical Evangelical might be found living in a suburban community, worshipping in a new and attractive church building, driving a late model automobile, and even travelling to Europe or Palestine for a vacation, there is little relevance to the stereotyped view that Fundamentalism is a religion of the dispossessed or economically disinherited.

Analysis of the revival of the 1950s supports this argument. Periods of religious concern have occurred with great regularity in American history since the time of Jonathan Edwards and have often reflected the dominant values of the generation that experienced them. During the 1950s an example of these values was Billy Graham, the Fundamentalist revivalist. Dressing like a junior executive, Graham utilized the new technology of television to urge upon America the need to repent of its wickedness and "make a decision for Christ." Graham's sermons made it clear that Fundamentalism had largely dropped its warfare with science, had come to terms with industrial-urban society, and willingly accepted the prosperity brought by science. Graham still warned that America would suffer judgment if it did not repent its immorality, and immorality was categorized most often as individual guilt for individual sins. The examples cited were usually drawn from areas related to domestic problems or the increasing crime rate. Graham's continued prominence and popularity among Fundamentalists reflect a transformation in the public image of the Fundamentalist in comparison to the decade of the 1920s. He has become widely accepted as a part of the mainstream of American society.

Anti-Communism and the Fundamentalists Anxiety over the threat of Communist subversion has also played an important role in modern Fundamentalist history. The threat of Communism closely resembled the traditional foes of Fundamentalism, biblical criticism and evolution: it came from abroad, seemed to spread uncontrollably and subversively, and tended to undermine Christianity. And in an era in which American Evangelicals were prospering in a burgeoning economy, it provided a good place in which to locate the Satanic activities that no believer doubted were operating in the world. Anti-Communism during the 1950s and 1960s virtually duplicated the history of the anti-evolution crusade of the 1920s.

DOCTRINES AND PRACTICES

Traditionally Fundamentalist belief has been defined in terms of five doctrines (inerrant inspiration of the Bible, and the virgin birth, Atonement, Resurrection, and miracle-working power of Christ) usually referred to as the five points of Fundamentalism. Fundamentalists often define their faith in creedal statements, but they have never adopted any particular group of five doctrines as essential. An early historian of the movement, S.G. Cole, erroneously described the 14-point creed of the Niagara Conference as a 5-point declaration. The Presbyterian Church affirmed five points as essential to orthodoxy in their denomination in 1910, 1916, and 1923, but this statement contained nothing about the Second Coming of Christ.

Most Fundamentalists would subscribe to the creed written in 1878 for the Niagara Conference by James H. Brookes, which includes the following affirmations: the verbal inspiration of the Bible, preserving it completely from error in the original manuscripts; the Trinity; the total depravity of man; the necessity of a "new birth" for salvation; substitutionary atonement; assurance of salvation to the believer; and the premillennial Second Coming of Christ. The Scofield Reference Bible, with its detailed footnotes and cross-references that encourage premillennial Bible study, has had a formative influence upon Fundamentalist thought.

Fundamentalist beliefs have not changed significantly since 1878. The greatest theological excitement in the history of modern Fundamentalism has been caused by the theology of Karl Barth. Although Barth began to achieve a reputation in Europe soon after World War I, it was not until the late 1940s that he began to influence

Fundamentalist theologians. Intrigued by Barth's emphasis upon the Bible as the Word of God, they hoped that they might find in his theology a sign of Liberalism's return to the Fundamentalists' biblical positions. A number of Fundamentalist scholars travelled to Basle (Switzerland) to study with Barth, but it became clear that, though Barth placed great stress upon biblical authority, he accepted the findings of the biblical critics and, thus, was unacceptable to Fundamentalists.

Though Fundamentalists are not notably ascetic, they do observe certain taboos. Most Fundamentalists do not smoke or drink alcoholic beverages and usually do not dance or attend movies and plays. At most Bible institutes and Fundamentalist colleges, these practices are strictly forbidden. Worship practices may vary from denomination to denomination but are usually nonliturgical and heavily influenced by revivalism. A sermon with congregational singing and prayer are common elements of Fundamentalist services.

Fundamentalism, though stereotyped in the public mind as a Southern rural phenomenon, was founded in the Northeast. The National Association of Evangelicals, the present organization of churches upholding Fundamentalist principles in varying degrees, has its headquarters in Wheaton, Illinois. *Christianity Today*, a conservative periodical published in Washington, D.C., is the major voice of Fundamentalism today.

BIBLIOGRAPHY. E.R. SANDEEN, *The Roots of Fundamentalism* (1970), is a recent attempt to define the character of the Fundamentalist movement and to describe its origins in the millenarianism of the 19th century (extensive bibliography). S.G. COLE, *The History of Fundamentalism* (1931), accurately describes the events of the 1920s. L. GASPER, *The Fundamentalist Movement* (1963), provides some description of the movement since 1930.

(E.R.S.)

Fundy, Bay of

An inlet of the Atlantic Ocean between the Canadian provinces of Nova Scotia on the south and east and New Brunswick on the north and west, the Bay of Fundy is famous for its fast-running tides that, with the aid of its peculiar coastal physiography, produce rises as great as 70 feet (21 metres), the highest in the world. Aside from the spectacular rock formations and forests of its shorelines and the fine agricultural lands created by dikes from its on-land marshes, the bay has come into prominence as a major potential source of hydroelectricity, but one that continues to present great engineering difficulties and other problems of feasibility.

Location and unique character

The bay, 32 miles (51 kilometres) across at its entrance and 94 miles (151 kilometres) long, covers some 3,600 square miles (9,300 square kilometres). Its shores are indented by numerous coves and several large deepwater harbours, the main ones at Saint John and St. Andrews in New Brunswick and Digby and Hantsport in Nova Scotia, all harbour towns that burgeoned during the great lumbering, shipping, and shipbuilding activity of the 19th and early 20th centuries. In 1948 an 80-square-mile section of shore and stream-riven hills in New Brunswick was set aside as Fundy National Park.

Steep bedrock cliffs up to 200 feet high bound the bay and channel its waters until they separate into two narrow niches, Chignecto Bay on the north and Minas Basin on the south. In these, the tide range is magnified by the narrowness and shape of the bay, a rise of 46 feet (14 metres) being common in Chignecto Bay and 53 feet (16 metres) in Minas Basin. When the tide runs out the channels become veins of red mud, reflecting the erosion of the outcrops of red sandstone and shale along the coast. The rising tide produces a "reversing falls" at the mouth of the Saint John River, and the tidal surge up the Petitcodiac River toward Moncton has a bore, or tidal wave, that is three to six feet high at its crest, with the tide rising a phenomenal eight to 11 feet (2.4 to 3.4 metres) per hour.

Passamaquoddy Bay, astride the Maine–New Brunswick border, over several decades has been the focus of investigations into the feasibility of harnessing the hydro

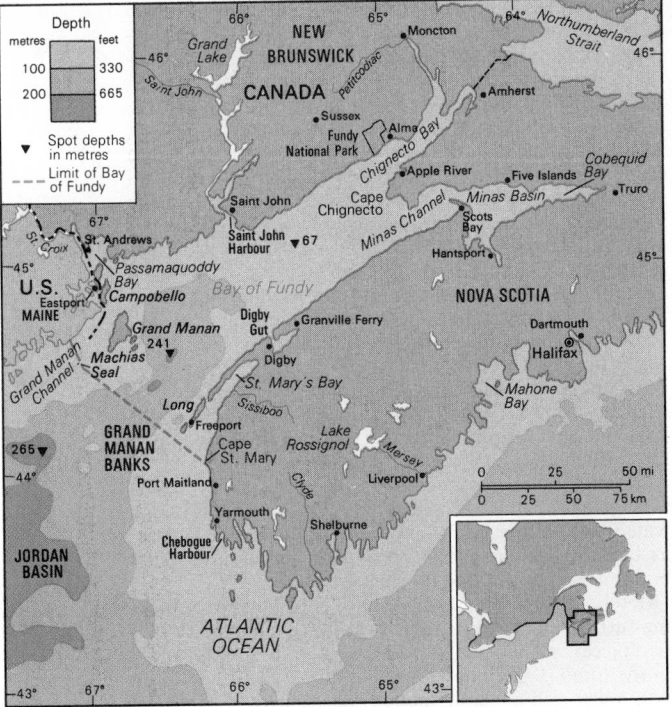

The Bay of Fundy.

Furniture and Accessory Furnishings

The word furniture comes from the French *fourniture*, which means equipment. In most other European languages, however, the corresponding word (German *Möbel*; French *meuble*; Spanish *mueble*; Italian *mobile*) is derived from the Latin adjective *mobilis*, meaning movable. The continental terms describe the intrinsic character of furniture better than the English word. To be furniture, it must be movable.

In general, furniture produced in the last 5,000 years has not undergone innovative development in any profound sense. An Egyptian folding stool dating from about 1500 BC fulfills the same functional requirements and possesses the same basic features as a modern one. Only in the mid-20th century, with entirely new, unnatural, and artificial materials such as plastic and completely new fabrication techniques such as casting have there been signs of a radical revision of the concept of furniture.

Since furniture presupposes some degree of residential permanency, it is understandable that no independent furniture types seem to have been developed among the Africans, the Melanesians, the Eskimos in Greenland, the American Indians, or the Mongolian nomads in Asia.

This article deals with the materials, processes and techniques, ornamentation, kinds of furniture, and, finally, with the history of furniture.

This article is divided into the following sections:

I. General considerations

MATERIALS

Wood. Wood is the most used and possibly the best suited material for making furniture. Although there are over a hundred different kinds that can be used for furniture, some woods have natural properties that make them superior to the others.

Advantages of wood   A relatively cheap material, wood lends itself to various kinds of treatment; for example, it can be stained, painted, gilded, and glued. It can be shaped by means of hand- or power-operated cutting and drilling tools. Heated, it can be bent to a certain extent into a predetermined shape and thereafter will retain the shape. The an-

---

Plans and problems of hydroelectric projects

potentiality. This bay's tidal flow is immense—some 70,000,000,000 cubic feet (2,000,000,000 cubic metres) entering and leaving on the twice-daily turn of the tide—more than ten times the flow of the Rance River Estuary in Bretagne (Brittany), site of the only existing tidal-power plant. The possibilities of Passamaquoddy, whose tides average an 18-foot rise and reach 25 feet during the spring, were studied first in the 1920s, and a large-scale damming project was recommended. It was, however, too ambitious for its time, and economic support collapsed during the Depression of the 1930s. A Work Projects Administration (WPA) plan was blocked by the United States Congress in 1937.

After World War II, a joint United States–Canadian commission again attacked the problem, and, in the 1960s, an engineering report reconsidered the plans that had been made and the drawbacks that had been brought to light in the previous studies. In addition to the continuing engineering difficulties and the immense costs involved, other factors impeding development include the extensive navigation on Fundy, the tidal currents running as much as 20 feet per second, the increasing concern over possible environmental damage resulting from such development, and the opposition of private power interests to a public power program.

It would appear that the Fundy project eventually will be judged against the background of the emerging energy crisis both in the U.S. and Canada and the limitations in power technology that these nations must eventually face. With developmental programs for energy tied so closely to environmental concerns, the Bay of Fundy may yet realize its potentiality not only as a natural phenomenon of interest to tourists, oceanographers, and scientists but also for the possible effective blending of long-range conservation and management policies concerning the use of national and international resources.

BIBLIOGRAPHY. Materials readily comprehensible by the layman include L.J. BURPEE, "New Brunswick Down by the Sea," *Natn. Geogr. Mag.*, 79:595–614 (1941); E.P. CLANCY, "Power from the Tides," in *The Tides* (1968); BARRY COMMONER, "Is Science Getting Out of Hand?" in *Science and Survival* (1966); E.D. KOONS, "The Origin of the Bay of Fundy and Associated Submarine Scarps," *J. Geomorph.*, 4:237–249 (1941); and P.A. ZAHL, "The Giant Tides of Fundy," *Natn. Geogr. Mag.*, 112:153–192 (1957). See also publications on geology and natural history of the Fundy National Park published by the Canadian government.

(M.M.M.)

nual rings in wood create a structure with varying character, which in itself provides a natural ornamental surface, in which patterns can be formed by means of precalculated juxtapositions. Colours range from white, yellow, green, red, brown, grey to black through countless

Carved wood chairs (1600s) and wood-panelled room (1682–85) from the *Schlössli* at Flims, Switzerland, and through the door an English carved oak bed (late 1500s) from Cumnor Palace, Berkshire. In the Metropolitan Museum of Art, New York City.

intermediary tones. By juxtaposing wood of different colours, extremely rich effects have been achieved, especially in the 17th and 18th centuries. Wood, if stored under favourable conditions, is durable, and pieces of furniture from the oldest civilizations—Egypt, for example—are still extant. Last, most wood has an aromatic scent.

Developments in the sphere of craftsmanship and mechanical techniques, during the past two hundred years or so, have made furniture production both cheaper and quicker. Using timber as a basis and applying techniques such as shredding, heating and glueing, it has been possible to evolve new materials. To an increasing extent, cabinetmakers and furniture factories are using semimanufactured wood such as veneer, carcass wood, plywood, laminated board, and hardboard (fibreboard).

Use of veneer

Veneer is a very thin layer of particularly fine wood that has been glued on to inferior wood in order to produce a smooth and beautiful surface. It would hardly be possible to achieve such a surface by using solid wood, partly because of the expense, partly because of its brittleness, and partly because the grain can never be shown off to its best advantage when the timber is cut into solid boards.

The practice of veneering furniture has been known since the time of pharaonic Egypt, but it was not fully exploited until the beginning of the 18th century. During the Rococo period, especially, great virtuosity was displayed by the craftsman in the veneering of curving, concave, and convex surfaces; for instance, as found on chests of drawers.

Veneer is made by sawing, machine-cutting, and peeling. Saw-cut veneer is best, but because of the relatively large loss of wood in the form of sawdust, it is also the most expensive. Therefore, furniture veneer, as a rule, is machine-cut.

Veneering is done on carcass wood, either in the form of a solid surface or a surface composed of several layers glued together. Old furniture is nearly always veneered on solid wood of an inferior quality to the veneer, such as beech, oak, or deal. High-quality English mahogany furniture made in the 18th century, however, was veneered with mahogany on mahogany. In the 20th century, machine-made laminated board of various thicknesses is generally used. The advantage of ready-made laminated board is that it does not shrink. Wood expands and contracts in various ways, and its strength can vary axially, radially, or tangentially; by blocking the wood—*i.e.*, glueing pieces of wood together in different directions—such differences are eliminated and equal strength is obtained both longitudinally and laterally. The characteristic feature of laminated board is that the veneer on both sides encloses a wooden board composed of narrow strips of wood glued together on edge. The board is therefore thick enough to be suitable for table tops or doors.

If laminated board consists only of single sheets of veneer glued together, it is known as plywood. Plywood is widely used in the manufacture of furniture, particularly as backing for chests and other storage pieces, for the bottoms of drawers, and for shelves.

Metal. Metals have been used since antiquity for making furniture or ornaments for furniture. Splendid Egyptian pieces, such as the thrones and stool that were found in the tomb of the youthful Tutankhamen (14th century BC), were rich in gold mounts (decorative details). In ancient Greece, bronze, iron, and silver were used for making furniture. Finds that were buried in the ashes of Pompeii and Herculaneum in Italy included tables with folding underframes and beds made partly or entirely of metal.

Throughout the Middle Ages the metal chair—for example, the 7th-century throne belonging to Dagobert I, king of the Franks—was used for special ceremonies.

Various examples of silver furniture have been preserved; not solid metal, they consist of embossed (decorated with relief) or chased (hammered) plates of silver fastened to a wooden core. Silver furniture was made for palaces in the days when monarchs amassed enormous wealth. In times of war, the silver mountings were melted down and turned into silver coins; it was thus that all the silver furniture disappeared from the royal palaces of France.

During the 18th and 19th centuries, iron furniture became a typical industrial product. Iron beds in particular became popular. Because they could be easily folded up, they were much in demand as camp beds; one used by Napoleon at St. Helena is a famous example. As ordinary beds in private homes or hotels, they could be decorated with brass ornaments such as big knobs screwed onto their posts. Iron has also been used for chairs; for instance, rocking chairs or, perhaps more frequently, garden chairs that can stand out in the rain, protected only by a coat of paint.

Popularity of iron furniture

The possibilities of steel for furniture were explored in Germany during the 1920s, notably by architects associated with the Bauhaus, where architects, designers, and artists experimented with modern materials. Experiments were made with steel springs and chromium-plated steel tubing. The genre was soon imitated, and tubular steel furniture became a symbol of functionalism. Since then, thinner tubing and plaited wire, with a resiliency similar to that found in wickerwork chairs have been used. Because of its lightness, aluminum became a furniture material.

Metal, however, is still employed primarily for locks, mounts, and hinges used on furniture or for purely ornamental purposes. In the Middle Ages, simply constructed chests demanded extensive use of iron bands to provide extra strength, and the ends of these bands were cut to form decorative shapes. Cabinets of the Renaissance and Baroque periods were decorated with mounts of pewter or bronze. Inlaid objects, decorated with material such as wood or ivory, set into the surface of the veneer furniture made at royal furniture workshops in France, especially so-called boulle furniture, were marked by an elaborate style of marquetry (patterns formed by the insertion of pieces of wood, shell, ivory, or metal into a wood veneer) influenced by Oriental traditions, in which blue-tempered steel, brass, and copper were customarily used.

In the 17th and 18th centuries, especially in England and the American colonies, a refined style for furniture mounts, keyhole escutcheons (an ornamental shield around a keyhole), hinges, and the like, all based largely on Chinese models, was developed. The design of these mounts was dictated by a clear functional purpose, in contrast to contemporary French Rococo mounts, the majority of which were ornamental, often at the expense of utility. French bronze founders displayed great skill in making purely decorative mounts for the bodies of chests of drawers and protective mounts for corners and legs. No essentially new, independent forms of furniture mounts seem to have been developed since the 18th century.

Other materials. Among other secondary materials in furniture making, glass has been used in the form of mirrorglass or as a purely decorative, illusionistic element in cabinets and writing desks. Italian craftsmen have made glass furniture; that is, wooden furniture covered with silvered glass in various colours. Ivory and other forms of bone were used as inlay material in Egyptian furniture. During the 17th and 18th centuries, ivory was widely used for inlay work in cupboard doors and table tops.

Tortoiseshell was also used, as a costly inlay on a silvered ground, in furniture made during the Renaissance and Baroque periods. Mother-of-pearl has been used, particularly as inlay material and for keyhole escutcheons. Marble and, to a certain extent, plaster of paris have been used, especially in the 18th century, for the tops of chests of drawers and console tables, and in the 19th century for the tops of washstands and dressing tables.

Papier-mâché and plastics In Victorian England, papier-mâché (a molding material made of paper pulped with glue and other additives) was used to make such items of furniture as fire screens, small tables and chairs, and clock cases. Finally, since World War II, various plastic materials have been used quite extensively in the construction of chairs with seats and backs molded in one piece and provided with a metal base.

STYLISTIC AND DECORATIVE PROCESSES AND TECHNIQUES

Constructional style and stylization. In general, furniture can be designed in two styles, one of which is constructional in that the appearance of the piece reflects the way it is put together, and the other of which is stylized in that the appearance of the piece conceals the way it is put together, the principle being to make the joints flush with adjoining members so as to give the impression that the object is made in one piece.

Examples of furniture made in a purely constructive style are forms employing wickerwork or bamboo, in which even the greatest display of imaginativeness in design and pattern serves to make the construction stronger and more resilient.

Constructional details and joints are not normally visible and are, therefore, seldom of aesthetic importance to the external appearance, but joints can be emphasized artistically. The Greek form of chair known as the klismos demonstrates its joints boldly in the form of solid junctions holding the legs, seat, and stiles together. The curvature of the legs and of the backrest suggests elasticity. Extremely delicate joinery with invisible joints can be deliberately indicated by means of inlay work, examples of which can be seen in ancient Egyptian furniture.

Stick-back and tubular steel chairs are also examples of constructional styles. The stick-back chair consists of a solid seat into which the legs, back staves, and possibly the armrests are directly mortised (joined by a tenon or projecting part of one piece of wood and mortise or groove in the other piece). Furniture of bent steel tubing, particularly tables, chairs, and stools, was manufactured

on an industrial basis in Germany in the 1920s. In this fashion a new constructional style arose, for the steel tube, which makes smaller dimensions possible, was so strong that it opened up the possibility of completely new, untraditional designs. Bent steel tubes form a resilient structure.

Stylization In contrast to the constructional style is stylization, in which there is no internal conformity between the motifs and the strength of the joints. There have been any number of examples of stylization throughout the history of furniture. In both Egyptian and Chinese furniture the joints might be deliberately concealed by painting or lacquer. Chinese furniture can also appear stylized in the sense that it gives an impression of having been put to-

Greek klismos and small footstool, marble grave Stele of Hegeso, 2nd half of the 5th century BC. In the National Archaeological Museum, Athens.

gether in a more constructive manner than is actually the case. (In other words, stylization attempts to make joints flush with adjoining members so as to give the impression of an uninterrupted, harmonious, or sensitive contour. When two pieces of wood are joined together with a modern, strong glue, the resulting joint will be so rigid that, in the event of a severe shock to the piece, the wood itself will be more likely to break than will the actual joint.)

A good example of stylization is to be found in French furniture made around the middle of the 18th century. In French Rococo commodes, only the back is straight. The serpentine front and sides meet in sharp corners, at which the joints are covered by brass mounts. The number and position of the drawers is concealed by an overall pattern of veneer and bronze ornament that disregards the edges of the drawers. (In a number of cases the bronze mounts on the front consist of fanciful handles and keyhole escutcheons, but are never emphasized the way they are in corresponding English commodes, even in the case of false drawer fronts or drawers provided with moulding that serves to protect the veneer.) The fully developed French Rococo chair with armrests has no visible joints. The back, arms, and frame form a continuous whole; the difference between supported and supporting members is concealed. There are no stretchers (horizontal rods) between the legs to strengthen the construction, which is solid enough by reason of the thick dimensions of the members that meet in the seat frame. To counteract the impression of heaviness in these essentially thick dimensions, the wood is molded to give a sensation of lightness without in any way weakening the construction. A chair of this type when painted or gilded looks as if it had been made in one piece, which is precisely the intention.

Decorative processes and techniques. Whether constructional principles are exploited as a motif or elegance of overall shape is stressed through stylization, every piece of furniture can be embellished in one way or another. A piece of furniture may be embellished by effects produced in the structural wood itself or in another kind of wood added to the first; that is, by carving and turning or by inlay work. Alternatively, the piece can be decorated by the addition of materials other than wood, such as bronze, ivory, or marble. Finally, in the case of furniture meant for sitting or lying on, there is the possibility of textile enrichment in such forms as upholstery, loose covers, and cushions.

Carving. There are examples of furniture carving in Egypt at the time of the pyramids: animal legs of cedarwood on biers, beds, and chairs; and ducks' heads terminating the legs of folding stools. A more constructionally determined type of carving resulted in the creation of elegant headrests that took the place of pillows in a hot climate.

Whereas carving does not appear to have played a significant part in Greek and Roman furniture, it was a dominant feature of European furniture of the Middle Ages. The fronts of chests bear Gothic perpendicular tracery (decorative interlacing of lines) in imitation of the decorative stonework found in ecclesiastical architecture.

Another source of inspiration for carved ornaments in bourgeois furniture was the ecclesiastical wood carving found in choir stalls and altarpieces. The art of the wood-carver also flourished in Islām during the Middle Ages, especially in kiosks (open pavilions), oriel (large bay windows projecting from the wall and supported by brackets) windows, and Qur'ān lecterns. The most original and remarkable form of medieval carved ornamentation was the linenfold, which resembled folded sheets of linen laid on the surface of the wood. Although the motif was widely known, its origins are obscure.

During the Renaissance, wood-carvers changed motifs: new ornamental riches, partly inspired by the forms of classical antiquity, began to adorn cupboards and chests. Acanthus leaf designs, strapwork (narrow bands folded, crossed, and sometimes interlaced), Moresque designs, the auricular (resembling a flowered Alpine primrose) style, bunches of fruit, and scrollwork for over a hundred years dominated the figure-carving repertoires of European cabinetmakers.

During the 17th century the fashion for carved work at first receded but came to the fore again in the console tables (tables designed to fit against the wall), mirror frames, and high-backed chairs of Court Baroque. In striking contrast to lacquer cabinets of Japan, sumptuous, gilded carved work became popular on the stands invariably made for them in Europe.

In the 18th century, wood-carvers enjoyed a final splendid period of prosperity when the Rococo style of ornamentation called for the plastic effects obtainable through carving. Whole panels of woodwork, doors, mirror frames, chairs, and settees were adorned with the finest wood carving, featuring combinations of mussel-shell patterns and naturalistic vines and plant tendrils. Even in English furniture of more sober design there were ample opportunities for carved work; for example, in the many chairback variations in the Chippendale manner.

American cabinetmakers were particularly skillful at carving block fronts (the sides curving forward and the middle receding) on the drawers of chests of drawers, and the English at framing tea tables with piecrust (scalloped) tops.

Turned work. Turning is a process by which parts of furniture, such as legs and posts, are shaped while turning on a lathe. Turned work is found on Greco-Roman furniture. It is not certain whether the technique was actually employed in Egyptian furniture, though some members look as though they might have been turned. It was particularly in the shaping of wooden chair legs that Greek joiners used the lathe; the same sharp edges and deep molding seem to be repeated in the legs of bronze furniture. It is possibly ancient turned work traditions upheld in Byzantium that are reflected in certain chairs of medieval form found, for example, in Norway; made of pinewood, the construction consists principally of turned staves (thin bars), some with appendant loose rings, some of them fluted (grooved). Similar turned chairs were made in Wales in the 16th century. In the 17th century, turned work was concentrated on pillars for cupboards and on ball feet, but is also seen on chair and table legs, on which rich variations involving twisted and intertwining forms occur. Turned work in ivory also flourished in the 17th century. Except for the Windsor chair, or stick-back, however, the craft of the turner played no significant role in English furniture of the 18th century; it is similarly alien to French Rococo furniture.

Inlay and marquetry. Inlaid woodwork, in which decorative material such as wood or ivory is set into the surface of the veneer, has accompanied the art of furniture making for thousands of years. Ivory inlay can be seen in Egyptian furniture, particularly in small, meticulously executed toilet caskets, but it is difficult to locate in Greek and Roman furniture, today known almost exclusively from pictorial representations.

In medieval Europe, inlay work gave way to wood carving and then experienced a rich period of development during the Renaissance in Italy. Italian intarsia (mosaic of wood) work found particular favour in panels over the backs of choir stalls and in the private studies and chapels, or oratories, of princes. An intarsia study of the Duke of Urbino, an Italian nobleman and patron of the arts, is still preserved in the palace of Urbino, and a corresponding room, originally at Gubbio, is now in the Metropolitan Museum of Art in New York. Together with illusionism, linear perspective (the technique of representing on a plane or curved surface the spatial relation of objects as they might appear to the eye), which had just been discovered, achieved triumphs in Italian intarsia work.

Ivory was used on both Renaissance and Baroque cupboards, sparingly to begin with, lavishly later on. Inlay work was especially used in the many splendid German and French cabinets of the period. In Holland and England an extremely rich form of marquetry (patterns formed by the insertion of pieces of wood, shell, ivory,

(margin left, upper) Islāmic wood carving

(margin right, lower) Italian intarsia work

By courtesy of the Bibliotheque de l'Arsenal, Paris; photograph, Eddy van der Veen

French Rococo chairs by Louis Delanois (1731–92). In the Bibliothèque de l'Arsenal, Paris.

or metal into the wood veneer) was developed, incorporating floral motifs in various kinds of exotic wood on walnut. English grandfather clocks made around 1700 often had richly inlaid cases. It was in France, however, during the Rococo period especially that inlay work reached unprecedented levels of quality. The serpentine sides and fronts of commodes were veneered with costly woods whose often relatively simple grain patterns formed an effective background for richly ornamented mounts of gilded bronze.

Upholstery and covers. Upholstery and covers belong to the sphere of furniture designed for sitting or lying on. From the Orient, Europeans learned the use of wickerwork, which provided a ventilated and resilient background for loose cushions. The upholstered chair is a genuinely European phenomenon that achieved its most distinguished and logical form in England during the 18th century. Poor heating systems in houses, general prosperity, and a desire for comfort were the conditions that gave rise to a number of imaginatively varied types of upholstered armchairs in which the only wood visible is in the legs, with the back closing right up against the sitter and side wings affording protection from possible drafts.

The upholstered chair created a new effect that depended almost entirely upon the craftsmanship of the upholsterer. The upholstered chair or sofa has remained a specialty of the Anglo-Saxon world; club life in particular contributed to its popularity and resulted in heavily stuffed forms including that of the so-called chesterfield.

By mid-20th century, new materials such as foam rubber and various types of plastic composition had inspired independent methods that dispensed entirely with traditional upholstery techniques. Upholstery was succeeded by molded plastic forms and by sacks filled with plastic balls that are able to conform to the changing positions of the body.

Imagery and ornamentation. Painted and plastic images, or ornamental decoration, on furniture are secondary processes compared with construction and design. Some of the best and most expressive furniture forms, such as the Greek klismos chair and the English Windsor chair, are quite independent of imagery or ornamentation. On the other hand, no period in the history of furniture is entirely devoid of these secondary processes.

Superfluousness of furniture decoration

All furniture decoration is normally concentrated where it will not be in the way; for example, on the legs, arms, and backs of chairs; on the ends and canopies of beds; on the legs and stretchers of tables; and on all vertical surfaces of cupboards and chests of drawers. The superfluous nature of furniture decoration is particularly pronounced in forms that express rank or prestige. The thrones of kings and bishops, the seats of guild masters, beds of state, the writing desks of chief executives, and the like have all lent themselves to imagery and ornamentation; and as the functional aspect of the piece has declined, it has seemed that the amount of ornamentation has increased. Purely functional milk stools and typewriting tables are devoid of ornamentation. This division can be noted with varying clarity throughout the history of furniture.

At times the ornamentation itself has, in a sense, been functional. The decoration of the earliest examples of furniture from Mesopotamia and Egypt, for example, had a symbolic or magical function. The legs of Sumerian stools are shaped like those of an ox, which was the guardian animal of the city of Ur. Egyptian furniture shows a much wider development of furniture legs based on animal models. Three-footed stools ending in dogs' paws, folding stools with legs in the shape of ducks' heads, and bed legs in the form of lions' feet are known from a thousand years of Egyptian furniture history. Tables with lions' legs can be seen on Assyrian reliefs. Similar animal symbols are known from representations of Greek furniture. Sometimes the arms as well as the legs of Greek chairs had animal shapes—terminating, for example, in the head of a lion or a

ram. It is thought likely that ceremonial seats and thrones featured animal motifs partly as a magical expression of the transference of power. This ancient tradition lived on in European furniture; for example, in thrones, where griffons, lions, and eagles played a prominent part in the decoration.

Even in the furniture of antiquity it is difficult to differentiate between the symbolic and the aesthetic in decorative features. It is clear, however, that the animal world has always been one of the primary sources of ornamental motifs in furniture. Animal legs and heads are found, for example, as terminal decorations in the French Rococo chair and imitations thereof. The animal leg played a prominent part in English furniture of the 18th century and later passed into American furniture. English cabinetmakers and chair makers devised a naturalistically carved lion's foot and a characteristic claw-and-ball foot, a motif that may stem from Chinese forms of ornamentation (not, however, on furniture) such as the dragon's claw holding a ball or a pearl. Richly carved English mahogany chairs sometimes also feature the heads of birds, lions, or dogs as terminal decorations on the arms. Although the majority of Chinese chairs and tables are supported by straight legs of rounded wood, Chinese thrones and seats for dignitaries have curved legs that, for some unknown reason, may be imitations of elephant trunks.

Animal and architectural motifs

Next to the animal world—and of more recent origin—architecture is the most important source of decorative motifs in furniture. In the late Middle Ages, the perpendicular tracery of Gothic architecture was transferred through the craft of the wood-carver to the fronts of chests. Italian chests and walnut cupboards of the same period were modelled on the marble sarcophagi of classical antiquity, which are entirely architectonic in form. During the Renaissance and Baroque periods the column was introduced as a strikingly decorative frontal feature in the form of table legs and on cupboards. The fronts of very big, heavy cupboards particularly lent themselves to architectonic composition corresponding to the portals and gables of houses. At the same time, the ornamental wealth of the Renaissance broke through in rosettes, cupids, and fruits on panelling and frames.

During the Court Baroque period under Louis XIV in France, the royal official style left its mark not only on ornate pieces of furniture but also on panels, doors, mirror frames, and, indeed, even on the facades of palaces and châteaus and the layout of formal gardens. The coherence between interior and furniture was even more pronounced during the Rococo period and under Louis XVI, culminating temporarily in the furniture and rooms of the French Empire style.

The 19th century often seems to have offered nothing more than a breathless repetition of this coherence between the ornamental design of furniture and the architecture of the interior—both revivals of the styles of the past. A new style did not arise until the close of the century. French Art Nouveau furniture, with its gliding vegetable forms, must be seen in conjunction with the houses and rooms for which it was executed. The furniture of Antonio Gaudí, a Spanish architect and designer, for example, had a profound coherence with his own buildings; and the strangely expressive and stylized furniture of a Scottish architect, Charles Rennie Mackintosh, forms an integral part of his buildings and interiors in Glasgow.

Art Nouveau furniture

The influence of architecture on furniture can also manifest itself in a lack of ornament. There is a relationship, for example, between functionalistic architecture as it was first manifested in the 1920s at the Bauhaus in Germany and steel furniture designed by the German architect Mies van der Rohe.

KINDS OF FURNITURE

Chair. Of all furniture forms, the chair may be the most interesting. While most other forms (except the bed) are intended to support objects, the chair supports man. The term chair is used here in the widest sense, from stool to throne to derivative forms such as the

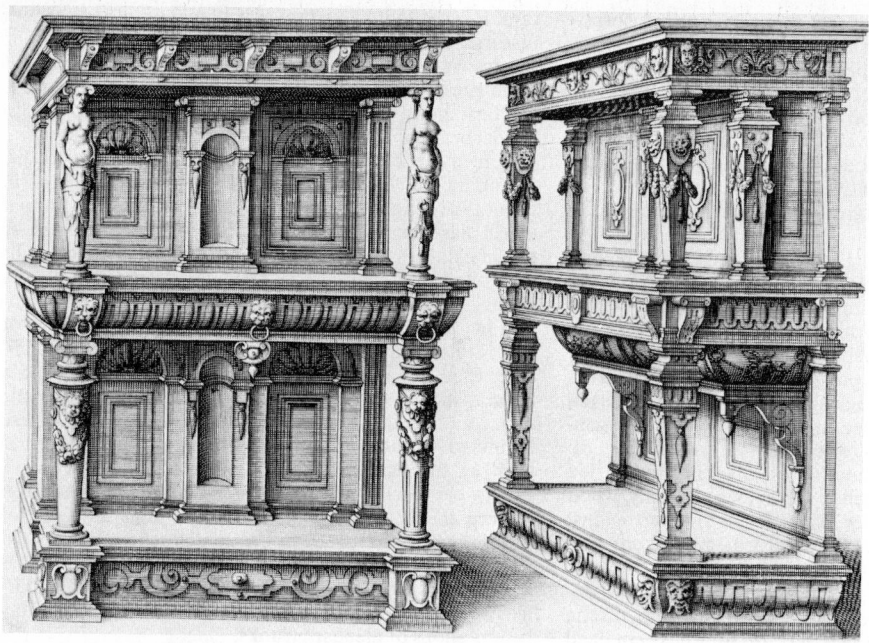

Dutch Renaissance designs for cabinet furniture with columns, by Paul Vredeman de Vries. (1567–1630?).
By courtesy of the Victoria and Albert Museum, London; photograph, John Webb

bench and sofa, which may be regarded as extended or connected chairs, and whose character (*i.e.*, whether they are intended for sitting or reclining) is not clearly defined.

The social history of the chair is as interesting as its history as an art and craft. The chair is not merely a physical support and an aesthetic object; it is also an indicator of human worthiness. One is offered a chair; one does not just sit down anywhere at all without being asked to do so. Chair forms may also involve an indication of rank. At the old royal courts there were social distinctions between sitting on a chair with arms, on a chair with a back but no arms, and having to make do with a stool. In the 20th century, the director's or manager's chair has been an indicator of superior dignity, and even in democratic parliaments the speaker sits on a raised level.

As a furniture form, the chair encompasses a wealth of variations. There are chairs designed to match man's age and physical condition (the high chair, the wheelchair) and for his position in society (the executive chair, the throne). In the olden days there were chairs to be born in (birth chairs); in the 20th century, there have been chairs to die in (the electric chair). There are chairs with one, two, three, and four legs, chairs with or without arms, and chairs with or without backs. There are chairs that can be folded up, chairs on wheels, and chairs on runners.

Modern living has developed special chairs for automobiles and aircraft. All of these chair forms have been evolved to conform to changing human needs. Because of its close association with man, the chair appears to its full advantage only when in use. Whereas it makes no difference to one's appreciation of a cupboard or a chest of drawers whether there is anything inside or not, a chair is best seen and evaluated with a person sitting on it, for chair and sitter complement one another. Thus the various parts of a chair have been given names corresponding to the parts of the human body: arms, legs, feet, back, and seat.

Because the basic function of the chair is to support man, its value is judged primarily on how well it fulfills this practical role. In the construction of a chair, the designer is bound by certain static laws and principal measurements. Within these limits, however, he has great freedom.

The history of the chair covers a period of several thousand years. There are civilizations that have created distinctive chair forms, expressive of the highest en-deavour in the spheres of technique and aesthetics. Among such cultures, special mention must be made of ancient Egypt and Greece; China; Spain and Holland in the 17th century; England in the 18th century; and France in the 18th century during the reigns of Louis XV and Louis XVI.

Egypt.   Two ancient Egyptian chair forms, both the result of careful design, are known from discoveries made in tombs. One of these is a four-legged chair with a back, the other a folding stool. The classical Egyptian chair has four legs shaped like those of an animal, a curved seat, and a sloping back supported by vertical stretchers. In this way a strong triangular construction was obtained. There was apparently no marked difference between the construction of Egyptian thrones and chairs for ordinary citizens. The main difference lies in the decorative ornamentation, in the choice of costly inlays. The Egyptian folding stool probably was developed as an easily portable seat for officers. As a camp stool the form persisted until much later times. But the stool also took on the character of a ceremonial seat, its mechanical function as a folding stool being forgotten. This can already be observed, from as early as 1366–57 BC in two stools, executed in ebony with ivory inlay work and gold mounts, from the tomb of Tutankhamen. They are in the form of folding stools but cannot be folded as the seats are of wood. The simple construction of the folding stool, consisting of two frames that turn on metal bolts and support a seat of leather or fabric fastened between them, reappears somewhat later in the Bronze Age folding chairs of Scandinavia and northern Germany. The best known of these is the folding stool, made of ashwood, found at Guldhj (National Museum in Copenhagen).

Greece and Rome.   The typical Greek chair, the klismos, is known not from any ancient specimen still extant, but from a wealth of pictorial material. The best known is the klismos depicted on the Hegeso Stele at the Dipylon burial place outside Athens (*c.* 410 BC). It is a chair with a backward-sloping, curved backboard and four curving legs, only two of which are shown. These unusual legs were presumably executed in bent wood and were therefore subjected to great pressure from the weight of the sitter. The joints fastening the legs to the frame of the seat are therefore very strong and clearly indicated.

The Romans adopted the Greek chair; a number of statues of seated Romans show several examples of a heavier and apparently somewhat more crudely con-

The classical Egyptian chair

Golden throne from the tomb of Tutankhamen at Thebes, wood overlaid with gold and inlaid with faience, glass, and calcite, Egypt, 18th dynasty, c. 1350 BC. In the Egyptian Museum.
Photo by F.L. Kenett © George Rainbird Ltd., 1963

structed klismos. Both types, the light and the heavy, were revived during the Classicist period. The klismos chair is found in French Empire furniture, in English Regency, and in special forms of considerable originality in Denmark and Sweden around 1800.

China. The ancestry of the chair in China cannot be traced as far back as in Egypt and Greece. Since the T'ang dynasty (AD 618–907) an unbroken series of drawings and paintings has been preserved showing the interiors and exteriors of Chinese houses and their furniture. Also preserved since the 16th century are a number of chairs of wood or lacquered wood that bear an astonishing resemblance to representations of older chairs.

Two major Chinese chair forms

As was the case in Egypt, there were two major chair forms in China: a chair with four legs and a folding stool. The four-legged chair is found both with and without arms but always with a square seat and straight stiles (upright side supports) to support the back. In one form, however, the stiles are slightly curved above the arms so as to conform to the rhythm of the S-shaped back splat (the central upright of a chairback). All three parts are mortised into the yoke-like top rail. While the design of the back splat exercised an influence on English chairs of the Queen Anne period, wooden members that only to a limited extent reinforce corner joints (and are loose into the bargain) represent a feature exclusive to Chinese chairs. The four legs pass through the seat frame, which closes about the rounded staves. All members are round in section or have rounded edges—it is as though one can just discern a bamboo tradition hovering in the background. The seat is uncomfortable and may have a plaited bottom. These chairs must have required the sitter to remain stiff and upright; for if too much pressure is exerted on the back, the chair has a tendency to topple over. In patriarchal Chinese homes of this period armchairs presumably were reserved for the senior members of the family, for they were held in great esteem.

The Chinese folding stool is presumed to have travelled to China from the West. It does not differ so very much

from the Egyptian or Scandinavian folding stools, but it has a variation in that the top rail is elegantly joined to the two legs of the stool by means of a curved member, which is often provided with metal mounts. From a Western viewpoint the overall effect of both these furniture forms is stylized. The constructive and decorative elements are combined in a manner that is simultaneously naïve and refined. The pieced-together appearance is a result of the fact that the individual members do not appear to have been joined together with either glue or screws, but have been mortised into one another and locked into position in the manner of a Chinese puzzle.

Spain: 17th century. The Golden Age of Spain during the 17th century also left its mark on the chair. Paintings show a type of chair with a relatively crude wooden frame; a back and seat, nailed on, consist of two layers of leather, with horsehair stuffing in between, stitched to produce a pattern of small pads. The front board and a corresponding board at the back could be folded after loosening some small iron hooks. Thus the chair was an easily portable piece of furniture for travelling which, at the same time, had the dignity of a four-legged, high-backed armchair.

Holland: 17th century. A low, square, upholstered type of chair can be seen in engravings of interiors of affluent Dutch homes by Abraham Bosse, a French artist, and in paintings by the Dutch artists Jan Vermeer and Gerard Terborch. Although this kind of chair is also found in countries where Dutch styles of interior decoration and Dutch furniture won favour, it is not certain that the form actually originated in Holland. Normally, the legs of the chair are smooth, round in section, and of slender dimensions; they are sometimes baluster-shaped (vase-shaped) or twisted. It is clearly a bourgeois piece of furniture and was made in considerable numbers, as can be seen from one of Abraham Bosse's engravings, in which a whole row of such chairs has been lined up against a wall. The form asserts itself by virtue of its harmonious proportions and fine upholstery in gilt leather or fabric bordered with fringes.

France and England: 17th and 18th centuries. The French Rococo chair in its most mature form—that is, as developed in Paris around 1750—spread over most of Europe and has been imitated or copied into the mid-20th century. The model owes its popularity to a combination of comfort and elegance. The seat conforms to the human body and permits a relaxed sitting position. The back is bow-shaped, the legs curved. Normally the seat and back are upholstered, and there are small upholstered pads on the armrests. Smooth transitions achieved between seat frame, legs, and back disguise all the joints, which are solidly constructed on craftsman-like principles despite the absence of stretchers between the legs.

French Rococo chair

French Rococo chairs and imitations thereof employ wood of fairly thick dimensions; but all members are deeply molded, all superfluous wood has been cut away, and finer examples may be further embellished with very delicate and decorative carving. The wood may be left in its natural state, painted, or gilded. Silk damask or tapestry is used for the upholstery on the seat, back, and armrests; canework is sometimes used in place of upholstery.

English chairs of the 18th century are more differentiated in design than the French. The French taste for stylistic uniformity, which spread from the most distinguished circles in Paris and Versailles over most of France and won favour in several parts of the Continent, had no parallel in England. Prior to 1740, the most commonly used wood was walnut; thereafter, and for the rest of the century, it was mahogany. Walnut, though beautiful in hue, was soft and therefore less suited to wood carving than to rounded, curving forms. Outer surfaces, such as the back and seat frame, were usually veneered. During the walnut period, highly overstuffed armchairs, covered with leather or embroidered material, were also developed. The best upholstery of this period is precisely and firmly modelled and accentuated

Low, square, upholstered chairs typical of 17th-century Dutch homes shown in "Recreation," engraving by Abraham Bosse, 1635.

by braiding or tacks. When imports of mahogany became common, no specifically new chair designs appeared, but the character of the woodwork changed. Mahogany, having a firmer, closer grain, could be cut thinner, which meant that individual parts of the chair could be more slender in shape. Mahogany also lent itself better to carving than walnut. Carving was concentrated more on the arms and back than on the legs, which as a rule were straight and smooth with chamfered (bevelled) edges and molding. There was a wealth of variety in chairback designs, featuring elegant, pierced, vase-shaped splats or two upright posts connected by horizontal slats (ladder-back).

Stick-back chair

Alongside the French Rococo chair and the best English chairs in walnut and mahogany, the more countrified stick-back chair was relatively unaffected by the stylistic changes of the day. Originally a medieval form, known, for example, from paintings by Pieter Bruegel the Elder and still found in mid-20th century in the churches and inns of southern Europe, the stick-back chair (in all of its variations) consists basically of a solid, saddle-shaped seat into which the legs, back staves, and possibly the armrests are directly mortised. This typically peasant form underwent a renewal and a process of refinement in England and America during the 18th century. Under the name Windsor chair (a term that seems to have been used for the first time in 1731) or Philadelphia chair, it became well-known and was widely distributed throughout the world. Related in form to the Windsor chair is an American chair made by members of the Shaker sect in the workshops they set up in their small, closed religious communities. Some of the best examples of these were executed around the middle of the 19th century at the Shaker headquarters in Pennsylvania.

Late 18th to 20th century. During the Neoclassical period, no basic changes took place in chair forms, but legs became straight and dimensions lighter. Backs in the shape of classical vases replaced the fanciful outlines of the Rococo period. Around 1800, freely executed imitations of Greek and Roman chairs of the klismos type, with curved legs and backrest, appeared. French chairs of the Empire period, executed in dark mahogany and embellished with ornate bronze mounts, created a ponderous effect.

In cheaper versions of inferior workmanship, bourgeois chairs of the 19th century carried on the traditions of the 17th and 18th centuries. The only real innovations were the bentwood (wood that has been bent and shaped)

chairs in beech that became popular all over the world and are still made in the 20th century. Around 1900 the continental Art Nouveau and *Jugendstil* styles (French and German styles characterized by organic foliate forms, sinuous lines, and non-geometric forms), and the Arts and Crafts movement in England (established by the English poet and decorator William Morris to reintroduce standards of medieval craftsmanship), gave rise to original chair designs by Eugène Gaillard in France, Henry van de Velde in Belgium, Josef Hoffman in Austria, Antonio Gaudí in Spain, and Charles Rennie Mackintosh in Scotland. These new furniture styles did not exercise wide, let alone decisive influence. The Art Nouveau chairs designed by the French architect Hector Guimard, for example, are collector's pieces, but his name is known to a broader public only because of his fanciful entrances to the Paris Métro.

Modern. After World War I, the Bauhaus school in Germany became a creative centre for entirely revolutionary thinking, resulting, for example, in tubular steel chairs designed by the architects Marcel Breuer, Ludwig

Bentwood rocking chair designed by Michael Thonet, Vienna, c. 1860. In the Technisches Museum für Industrie und Gewerbe, Vienna.

Twentieth-century chair design.
(Left) Chrome-plate tubular steel armchair with canvas seat back and armrests, designed by Marcel Breuer, Germany, 1925. In the Museum of Modern Art, New York. (Centre) Chrome-plated steel lounge chair (Barcelona chair) with leather cushions and supporting straps, designed by Ludwig Mies van der Rohe, Germany, 1929. In the Museum of Modern Art, New York. (Right) Molded plastic armchair reinforced with glass fibres, designed by Charles Eames, U.S., 1949.

By courtesy of (left, centre) the Museum of Modern Art, New York, (left) gift of Herbert Bayer, (centre) gift of Knoll Associates, Inc., (right) Herman Miller Furniture Co.

Mies van der Rohe, and others. During World War II, the aircraft industry accelerated the development of laminated wood and molded plastic furniture. The dominant chair forms of this period go back to designs by a Finn, Alvar Aalto, Brun Mathsson, and an American, Charles Eames. Rapid technical developments, in conjunction with a severance from all tradition, suggest that completely new chair forms will probably be evolved in the future.

Table. *Fixed and mechanical tables.* In general, tables can be divided into fixed and mechanical types. The fixed table, consisting of a square or round top supported by one or more legs, is the least complicated from the viewpoint of craftsmanship. It is a form that requires wood of thick dimensions in order to make the joints by which the top is fastened to the legs strong enough to resist lateral pressure. Old Spanish or Italian tables are

By courtesy of the Kunstindustrimuseet, Copenhagen

Walnut table with wrought-iron stretchers, Spain, early 17th century. In the Kunstindustrimuseet, Copenhagen.

often constructed with sloping stretchers to counteract this pressure. The simplest way to make a table steady without exaggerating the dimensions of the individual parts is to fasten the legs to an underframe. Fixed tabletops can also make do with a single leg; for example, the Pedestal so-called pedestal table, terminating in a tripod or quad- table ripod. Pedestal tables topple over easily, however, unless both top and pedestal are particularly heavy. Three-legged tables with a fixed top provide a more reliable support than a single-legged type but are unstable when subjected to uneven pressure from above.

The term mechanical refers to all tables whose tops can be enlarged or reduced according to need. Such tables may require pivotable or collapsible legs to augment the strength of the top. A familiar solution to the extension of a tabletop is the so-called Dutch system, known since the 17th century from Dutch engravings and paint-

ings, in which the extension leaves, when pulled, slide out on sloping runners. When the leaves have been fully extended, the top is lifted and then dropped into place. The table height remains the same. The construction demands great accuracy and skill on the part of the craftsman. There are also more complicated forms of extension tables with runners enabling the legs as well as the leaves to be drawn out; extra leaves can then be inserted.

Tables with flaps also are constructed to take up less space when folded away and can be variously made, either with flaps that are supported by brackets that swing out on hinges or on so-called gate legs. During the 18th century, England was a leader in the design of ingenious folding tables, especially card tables. In the gateleg card table, the top can be folded so as to occupy   Gateleg half the space, and when opened is supported by a leg   table that swings out like a gate. In another system, the square underframe can be extended to form a rectangular top, the two sides being divided by hinges. On modern card tables, all four legs can be folded up within the frame surrounding the top; when not in use, the tables can therefore be stored easily.

Historical forms and styles. Round stone tables on low pedestal legs are known in Egypt from the time of the pyramids (*c.* 2700 BC). Egyptian limestone reliefs also show tables of normal height. Dating from the later dynasties, crude wooden tables with architectonic molding have been preserved. No tables have survived from ancient Greece. From the Roman ruins of Pompeii and Herculaneum, however, there are examples of monumental table supports or side members made of marble decorated with relief work and metal tables, many of them of the folding type. All wooden furniture has been lost, however.

Several wooden-topped communion tables dating from the early Middle Ages still stand in churches, hidden by altar cloths or built into boxes. Usually, such tables rest either on solid masonry or on a stone socle (a projecting member beneath the base of a superstructure), but they are sometimes elegantly supported by several columns. Generally, communion tables are made of stone, and since one stands before them, they are higher than the usual table. Examples of wooden tables preserved from the late Middle Ages are, as a rule, long narrow tops fastened to side members.

The interesting feature about the tables of the Renaissance and Baroque periods is their constructive and aesthetic design. Their thick and heavy tops rest on an underframe; the legs are baluster-shaped or turned, with deeply carved bulbous decoration. In the 17th century and later, table forms were widely differentiated and made for a great variety of purposes; *i.e.*, dining tables, library tables, drawing-room tables, card tables, tea tables, small candlestick tables, sideboards, and console tables.

From the Ming dynasty and the 18th century, several interesting Chinese fixed-top table forms have been preserved, in which the constructive elements are in some cases emphasized and in others deliberately disguised. Like other Chinese furniture forms, the tables create a stylized effect, with a naïve, calculated character. Chinese tables may be completely covered with lacquer and gilt ornamentation, but sometimes the wood is left in its natural colour.

Bed. In Homer's *Odyssey* there is a description of how Odysseus made his own bed: the trunk of an olive tree was cut to the exact shape and planed smooth; after holes had been drilled in the framework, oxhide thongs, dyed crimson, were threaded back and forth to make a pliant web; finally, the wood was embellished with inlay work in gold, silver, and ivory.

As a furniture form, the bed is as old as the chair. In principle the construction of the bed is extraordinarily simple: it consists merely of a rectangular platform raised in some way or other slightly above floor level. A considerable number of bed forms cannot be classed as furniture at all. Alcoves and bunks in ships, railway carriages, and airplanes belong more to the sphere of building trade joinery than to cabinetmaking.

That a number of beautiful and original bed forms of fine artistic execution have been created since antiquity is attributable to the fact that the bed gives the furniture designer rich possibilities in terms of framing and presentation, particularly in conjunction with textiles. Apart from the actual bedclothes, which will always be of greater importance than the actual platform and the surrounding framework, imaginative experiments combining the practical and the impressive—in four-poster beds and tentlike canopies, for example—have been made for centuries.

An Egyptian bier dating from the 1st dynasty (*c.* 3100–2890 BC) shows the original form of the bed: a rectangular framework of staves, round in section and mortised into one another so as to leave the ends free lengthwise, supported on four small legs carved to represent stylized lions' feet. Amusingly, the feet face in the same direction —as if they were walking with the dead person. This is characteristic of all Egyptian beds. Made of cedarwood, the light framework is higher at the head than at the foot; and whereas the foot is always terminated by a footboard, there is no board at the head. The beds were so constructed because the Egyptians when sleeping or resting used a stool-like support for the head. Essential to the Egyptian bed, countless examples of this piece of equipment—made usually of wood but sometimes of ivory and faience—have been found in Egyptian tombs. The actual framework of the bed was often covered with plaited leather thongs.

In China, a bed in the form of a complete little house, with an anteroom in the form of a veranda, was placed in the middle of the room.

Before central heating and a knowledge of hygiene became common, the closed bed was the generally accepted form in cold climates. The simplest way to avoid drafts was to place the bed in an alcove—as was the practice in farmhouses right up to the 19th century. The most frequently encountered form of bed in European civilization, however, was the four-poster. Throughout the Middle Ages and later, the four-poster was developed in a variety of forms. Already during the Middle Ages, beds were designed for clearly ceremonial effect. The four posts supported an expanse of cloth that extended from the head like a canopy, just as the most distinguished row of choir stalls in a church was crowned by a baldachin (an ornamental structure resembling a canopy). Miniatures in illuminated manuscripts of the same period show tentlike beds entirely closed by drapery and curtains.

In the time of the absolute monarchies in the 17th and 18th centuries, pompous four-posters were developed in which the surrounding textile drapery completely concealed the wooden construction of the bed, thereby achieving a synthesis of practical and ceremonial considerations. Every palace or mansion had a chamber of

The four-poster

state among its official reception rooms. Contemporary memoirs describe the complicated ceremony that took place at Louis XIV's daily awakening. Where his royal highness spent the night was his own concern, but his awakening was an act of state, in the conduct of which princes of the blood, dukes, and distinguished courtiers all had their respective duties: one would draw aside the bed-curtain, another would have the royal dressing gown ready, another the royal slippers. It was the first audience of the day, the king's levee. A large number of 17th- and 18th-century four-poster beds are still preserved in palaces, country houses, and museums; and most of them have a clearly dramatic, almost theatrical effect. The four-poster beds of the Baroque and Rococo periods, moreover, reflect great artistic refinement, especially in the rare instances in which they can still be seen in their original interiors complete with their entire textile adornment. Such beds of state are typical of continental Europe. In England and America, particularly toward the end of the 18th century, greater interest was taken in showing off the bedposts and the upper framework connecting them. Many English four-posters have slender, finely carved mahogany posts, whereas on the Continent the corresponding parts may be entirely covered with the same silken material as that used for the curtains, canopy, and bedspread.

During the Empire period in France an entirely new form of bed was developed and won favour throughout most of Europe. The design was inspired by the Roman couch as known from reliefs and from excavations in Pompeii and Herculaneum. The frame was very high, and the bed ends consisted of volutes (spiral or scroll-shaped forms) of equal height. The bed was crowned by a tentlike superstructure, and the martial aspect was further emphasized by the use of spears to support the draperies and curtains; the whole bedroom, in fact, might well be draped like a tent. In these surroundings, the army commanders of Napoleon's time could feel like the caesars and consuls of ancient Rome. During a campaign, however, collapsible iron camp beds were more practical. Napoleon owned several and died in one on St. Helena in 1821. As a furniture form, the iron bed was a neutral framework built to support bedclothes and equipped with stanchions (upright supports) for curtains; it was light, transportable, and spartan.

Empire bed

Among plantation owners in the West Indies and the southern United States, a type of four-poster popular at the beginning of the 19th century was dominated by wood, rather than textile hangings. The posts supported very light, roughly made wooden frames, to which thin, white mosquito netting was fastened to protect the sleeper. The monumental and dignified effect was obtained by the quality of the woodwork. Of thick dimensions, the wood is solid mahogany polished to a high gloss. The four bedposts are not necessarily identical at the head and foot of the bed, but all have bulbous and turned sections, exaggerated almost to the point of crudeness. The headboards and footboards are imaginatively designed with voluted gables (triangular decoration) and galleries (ornamental railings) supported on pillars. Besides the practical function of these West Indian beds, they also served to indicate the importance of their owner; like the royal four-poster of the days of absolute monarchy, they clearly showed the difference between master and slave.

In the 20th century, the bed has belonged exclusively to one's private life; and compared with those of the past, modern beds are simple. Four-posters are still "modern," possibly because they appeal to something primitive, namely the sensation of sleeping in a tent. In general, development has been concentrated on improving the quality of bedclothes and increasing the amount of comfort by attention to springs, spring mattresses, eiderdowns, and pillows. The actual woodwork of the bed is usually restricted to joined veneered sections of laminated board, canework sometimes being used for the headboards and footboards.

Storage furniture. *Chest.* The chest, including the coffin (and sarcophagus), is an ancient primitive furniture form that has survived into the 20th century. The design

Japanned, four-poster bed with canopy in the Chinese style, probably made by the firm of William Linnell for the Chinese bedroom at Badminton House, Gloucestershire, England, *c.* 1750–54. In the Victoria and Albert Museum, London.
By courtesy of the Victoria and Albert Museum, London

of a clothes chest is optional; its size depends on changing demands. The construction of a coffin, on the other hand, is a set task. The format is determined by certain principal dimensions, and the human figure has at all times exercised an influence on the shape of the coffin; the Egyptian mummy case, which takes on the form of the swathed corpse, is an example. Traditional features of ancient Roman sarcophagi, and simplified versions of the monumental style of the Baroque and Renaissance periods continue to thrive.

Early medieval chests
The principal constructional features of early medieval chests lasted until the Renaissance. The so-called Oseberg ship, dating from the Viking era (9th century AD) and discovered in 1904 in Vestfold, Norway, included among the furniture on board a chest made of oak planks secured by iron bands. The planks are not mortised together, and the end sections stand vertical, thereby forming feet, wider at the bottom than above. The lid is formed by a single curved oak plank that has been roughhewn into shape. The bottom of the chest rests in a groove cut into the end sections. The wooden construction, a primitive form of carpentry, is held together by broad iron bands, the nails are tin-plated. In this Oseberg chest, the iron mounts essential to the construction constitute the decorative element as well. All medieval chests are developments of the same principle: a piece of carpentry with decorative iron mounts, but the principle found freer application in medieval church doors than in the chests of the period.

The chest often appears in portable form as a traveller's trunk that can also serve as a stationary piece of furniture. A number of painted, parchment-covered Florentine chests dating from the middle of the 15th century have been preserved. These were used as trunks by young girls on their way to enter a convent and later stood in their cells as pieces of storage furniture for clothes and other personal belongings. A "nun's chest" of this type is in principle quite different from the sumptuous cassoni of the Italian Renaissance that were adorned with gilded stucco work and painted panels.

"Nun's chest"

Cassoni were stationary pieces of palace furniture. Specifically designed for travelling, however, were Javanese camphorwood chests that made the long voyage round the Cape of Good Hope full of stuffs and spices and eventually came to rest in an English manor house or in a gabled Dutch mansion in Amsterdam. The plank construction with metal mounts is of primitive craftsmanship. The large, smooth expanses of reddish-brown wood, with their elaborate openwork brass mounts and big, chased bolt heads to take the brunt of rough handling, have a kind of sophisticated crudeness about them. On later camphorwood chests the brass mounts are sunk flush with the surface of the wood, just as on portable writing desks and toilet cases of the French Empire period. Veneered wood was not suitable for chests intended for travel purposes, but it was possible to cover the entire chest with leather fastened with metal nails, possibly to form a pattern. Several beautiful, leather-covered chests made in Italy and Spain in the 17th century are known, and the form persisted in the large wardrobe trunks of succeeding centuries.

When furniture-making techniques demanding the skill of the cabinetmaker evolved during the Renaissance, frames, panels, and carving appeared on chests. In southern Europe, walnut lent itself admirably to carving; in northern Europe, oak. While the Italians were inspired by the molding and decorative plant ornamentation of the stone sarcophagi of ancient Rome, in northern Europe late medieval wood carving traditions were continued. As a rule the carved woodwork was picked out (trimmed) with paint and gilded. In the 18th century, the chest was largely supplanted for storage purposes by the chest of drawers and the commode (low chest of drawers), but it never entirely disappeared. Particularly in the big country houses of England and America, chests of mahogany or walnut were used for a long time, often having drawers in the bottom and finely fashioned brass mounts that revealed Chinese influence.

Cupboard. Strictly speaking, the cupboard is a derivative form of the chest. Early Renaissance cupboards re-

Renaissance cassone, painted and gilded wood, Florence, 15th century. In the Victoria and Albert Museum, London.

By courtesy of the Victoria and Albert Museum, London; photograph, John Webb

sembled two chests placed one on top of the other, but they were opened from the front by means of doors. The design and construction of the cupboard's pronounced front have always provided ample scope for artistic composition, and it is no mere coincidence that the cupboard more than any other furniture form should have closer links with architecture. It literally invited an architectonic composition: socle, columns, cornice. This development can be traced from the close of the Middle Ages in a large number of southern German and Tirolean cupboards bearing late Gothic perpendicular tracery and smooth surfaces veneered with ashwood. Very large cupboards took on their most striking form, however, during the Renaissance in 17th-century Holland and northern Germany. In molding and composition, they have much in common with architectural facades, but their picturesque and textural effects are the result of refined craftsmanship. The use of veneer was almost essential if these large expanses of wood were to be infused with life. A carcass of wood was given a veneer of fine walnut; socle, frames, columns, and cornice were decorated with veneered black ebony. The doors were furnished with strong locks, and the keyhole was concealed behind a sliding middle column. The cornice was often decoratively crowned with a set of Dutch faience or Chinese porcelain vases. These heavy cupboards were made to appear lighter by placing them on big, turned ball feet.

Chinese cupboards

In marked contrast to the European Baroque cupboards, Chinese cupboards of the same period were simple, smooth-surfaced, and boxlike. Their construction was based on a simple system of uprights and frames, and as a rule they were made in pairs. If painted, a large decorative painting was spread across the entire surface, including the doors. Inside, Chinese cupboards are finished with great care and painted in a different colour from the outside. The mounts are of various white and yellow metal alloys, smooth, either round or square; and the locks are secured with prismatically designed padlocks. Japanese and Siamese cupboards, apart from certain independent features, follow the old Chinese traditions.

The clothes cupboard of the 19th and 20th centuries, an indispensable piece of bedroom furniture wherever there are no built-in cupboards, is based on traditional features of the 18th-century English clothespress but equipped to meet the changing fashions of modern times.

Bookcases. Bookcases or bookshelves are a less interesting form of storage furniture from the viewpoint of furniture history. Perhaps the most significant innovation appeared in 18th-century England in the bookcase with adjustable shelves and a closed-off lower section for folio files. The shelves were protected by glass doors consisting of an ingenious trelliswork of carved wood. Bookcases and shelves become interesting only when they form part of specially designed library interiors and when several shelves full of books create an intimate, compact whole.

Mixed forms. Apart from the kinds of storage furniture already mentioned, there are numerous combination forms. An ordinary table can be used as a writing desk, and the only differences between the typical French Rococo writing desk of the 18th century and other tables are the drawers in the underframe and the leather-covered top. The novelty of Louis XV's writing desk consists of a rolltop device for closing the writing flap. In England a special type of writing desk was developed which, besides drawers in the underframe, has a side cupboard fitted with additional drawers and, occasionally, sliding trays. Some have a false drawer front that can be pulled out to form a writing surface. When a writing desk has a cupboard built on the top of it and is placed on a chest of drawers, the result is a cabinet or secretary. There are also bookcases with lower sections equipped with a flap, either hinged or sliding, for writing. All of these combinations, frequently of ingenious design, were made anonymously in England during the 18th century, apparently having arisen from a desire on the part of the well-to-do middle classes to develop a sophisticated and differentiated pattern of life.

English writing desks

A special group of storage furniture embraces the various forms of corner furniture, low or high cupboards that were made in pairs (just as in the case of several other old furniture forms) particularly for small rooms, in which they became fixed components of the interior scheme.

Kitchen furniture and furnishings. Kitchen furniture and furnishings go back to antiquity. In the Middle Ages, the kitchen, because of its fireplace, was the most centrally placed room in the home. Later, closed fireplaces were constructed in the form of stoves; and cupboards, sinks, and plate racks were as a rule fixed to the wall. The kitchen in a modern home, if not combined with a dining area, is a small room filled with concentrated and complicated equipment. On the other hand, institutional kitchens have expanded enormously. Outdoor cooking equipment, such as various forms of openair grills, also forms part of the kitchen furniture of the 20th century.

Bathroom furniture and fixtures. Bathrooms in large private homes were not unknown in the 18th century, and splendidly equipped marble bathrooms are still preserved in several European palaces and mansions. It was, however, not until the 19th century that bathrooms in private homes became more commonplace. Fixtures generally include a toilet, bidet, washbasin, bath, mirror, and shelves. It was only in the 20th century that the equipping of bathrooms became a separate industry with a wide variety of special forms of bathroom furniture and fixtures. The materials used are porcelain, enamel, plastic, wood, and stainless steel.

Specialized furniture. Office furniture in the widest sense of the term has undergone rapid developments since mid-19th century. Such pieces as the high desks used by clerks in old offices and the big American rolltop desks have been replaced by carefully designed standard forms of writing desks with side cupboards, typewriting tables, filing cabinets, and office chairs with adjustable

Office furniture

backs and swivel seats. From office furniture one passes naturally to the vast sphere of institutional furniture: theatre furnishings in the form of rows of connected seats, restaurant furniture, furniture for conference rooms, laboratories, workshops, and factories. Several of these specialized furnishings reflect past traditions. The way in which the British House of Commons is furnished, for example, derives without doubt from the pattern in which choir stalls were grouped in medieval churches; whereas the semicircular, often amphitheatrically designed assembly halls of the United States Congress and the parliaments of many European countries are developed forms of academies of surgery or other university auditoriums. Similarly, museums, libraries, and archives have their special furniture in the form of showcases, desks, special tables, and socles.

There are also furnishings for movable premises, primarily railway carriages equipped for sleeping or dining, passenger ocean liners with cabins, airplanes, buses, coaches, and private cars.

Finally, there is the large, highly heterogeneous group comprising outdoor or open-air furniture; for example, furniture for gardens, balconies, terraces, and solaria.

KINDS OF ACCESSORY FURNISHINGS

Besides the aforementioned kinds of furniture and all the many special forms (which it would be almost impossible to list), there is an extensive group of accessory furnishings that is not furniture in the strict sense but, nevertheless, constitutes an important element in the furnishing of interiors. Included here are clocks and other mechanical works, mirrors, textiles, screens, stoves, and fireplaces; and a number of smaller articles made by cabinetmakers, such as boxes, caskets, sewing tables, wastepaper baskets, lighting fixtures, frames, panelling, and floor surfaces.

Clocks. Clocks are considered furnishings if the movement is enclosed within a case, which need not necessarily be of wood. Clocks can be divided into table clocks and long-case clocks. There were two creative centres for table clocks, namely England and France. In 17th- and 18th-century France, the table clock became an object of monumental design, the best examples of which are minor works of sculpture. The actual movement is framed by a marble socle, and the clockface by a sculptural frame of solid bronze incorporating freely molded figures and ornamentation. Some of France's best sculptors and bronze casters were engaged in the creation of decorative frames for clock movements. A French speciality, imitated elsewhere on the Continent, was the wall clock, or so-called cartel clock, the earliest examples of which were designed by a goldsmith and ornamentalist, Juste Meissonnier. The clockface is the centre of an ornament, or rocaille-cartouche, cast in bronze, sometimes garnished with figures of symbolic significance; for example, Time, a man with a scythe, or a crowing cock. In England, where tastes were more bourgeois, the fine movements made by skillful London clockmakers were built into wooden cases, architectonic in composition and featuring pilasters (partly recessed columns) and cornices. Simple walnut cases could be adorned with metal ornaments and brass balls. The more expensive table clocks were concealed in cases embellished with inlaid wood or tortoiseshell.

Long-case clocks were also made in France and England. French long-case clocks are monumental and richly designed. In the reign of Louis XIV there were long-case clocks of the boulle type with metal and tortoiseshell inlay work. Later, in the 18th century and especially during the Rococo period, the case that concealed the weights acquired more dramatic form: richly inlaid wooden surfaces were framed and adorned by magnificently gilded Rococo ornaments in bronze. The English long-case clock was to a greater extent a piece of furniture, and the main features of its construction remained unaltered throughout the 18th century. The long-case clock stands on a base, or socle, from which the somewhat narrower case for the weights rises up, crowned by the framework of the actual movement and

clockface. The last-named section is in reality a table clock mounted on a weight case. Each individual section of the long-case clock is thus clearly separate; each has its distinct function; and no attempt was made, as in France, to veil the independence of the individual parts. The weight case is provided with a door in which there may be a window through which the position of the weights can be observed.

During the 18th century, barometers became increasingly popular. The mechanism was provided with a decorative wooden framework intended to harmonize with the other furniture in a room.

Mirrors. The use of mirror glass in furnishings arose during the 17th century. The discoloration of the melted glass because of silvering and, not least, the prohibitive cost and difficulty of manufacturing mirror glass of considerable size restricted the possibilities of large-scale application. The mirror gallery at Versailles was thus an outstanding technical achievement for its time. When Louis XIV strode through the gallery at the head of his court, the glass walls reflected the diamonds in his crown. This effect was imitated to a greater or lesser degree in all the courts of Europe. In the 18th century the wall mirror found its way into most interiors. The popularity and wide distribution of mirror glass was stimulated by the need for an increased amount of artificial light. During the 16th and 17th centuries, this need had been satisfied by placing candles in front of highly polished concave metal plates. By using silvered mirror glass, the light effect was multiplied. From then on, large mirrors hung over console tables were a necessary and functional part of rooms illumined by artificial light.

Fabrics. The use of fabrics in furnishing rooms is closely bound up with the need for heating. In the primitively heated rooms of the Middle Ages, textiles were used to keep out cold and drafts. In 12th- and 13th-century churches, painted textile drapery can still be discerned beneath the picture friezes. In rather cold churches, just as in poorly heated homes, loosely hung textile wall coverings were of the greatest importance. They were hung loosely because of the practice of taking them down and moving them, together with the relatively few items of furniture, according to need. It was not until the end of the 17th century and during the 18th century that tapestries and other forms of textile wall hanging became fixtures; that is, fastened to the wall within frames. Wall pictures made of paper and, subsequently, patterned wallpaper became a cheaper substitute for textile wall hangings during the 19th century. Screens or room dividers were often covered with textiles, partly to afford protection against direct radiant heat and partly to create cozy corners in large rooms. Framed screens were often covered with pieces of tapestry, with other woven materials, or with gilt leather.

Fireplaces. The heating of rooms and large halls remained a major problem until the advent of modern central heating systems. The open hearth was replaced during the late Middle Ages by the fireplace, which is merely an architectonic way of framing the burning logs. During the period when it was important as a source of heat, the fireplace became the object of design work by significant artists. A Scottish architect, Robert Adam, and his brothers and an Italian architect and engraver, Giambattista Piranesi, made considerable artistic contributions to the design and construction of fireplaces.

Other accessory furnishings. Small utility objects constitute an important part of the furnishing of interiors. Several of them are the work of cabinetmakers; for example, boxes for writing paper and playing cards, caskets for letters and documents, trays for serving or presentation. Accessory furnishings include the various articles, large and small, that are employed in the course of domestic work—from small looms to lace pillows, spinning wheels, embroidery frames, and sewing tables. Women's chattels, partly in the form of equipment for domestic needs and partly in the form of items of storage furniture for such small items as pins, scissors, wool, and materials, all had their place in the home.

Finally, the structure and decoration of the walls, ceil-

Table clocks

Long-case clocks

Mirror gallery at Versailles

Portable wall hangings

ings, and floors—for example, panelling, stucco work, parquet flooring, carpets—also come under the heading of accessory furnishings. (Er.L.)

II. History

WESTERN

Egypt. Beds, stools, throne chairs, and boxes were the chief forms of furniture in ancient Egypt. Although only a few important examples of actual furniture survive, stone carvings, fresco paintings, and models made as funerary offerings present rich documentary evidence.

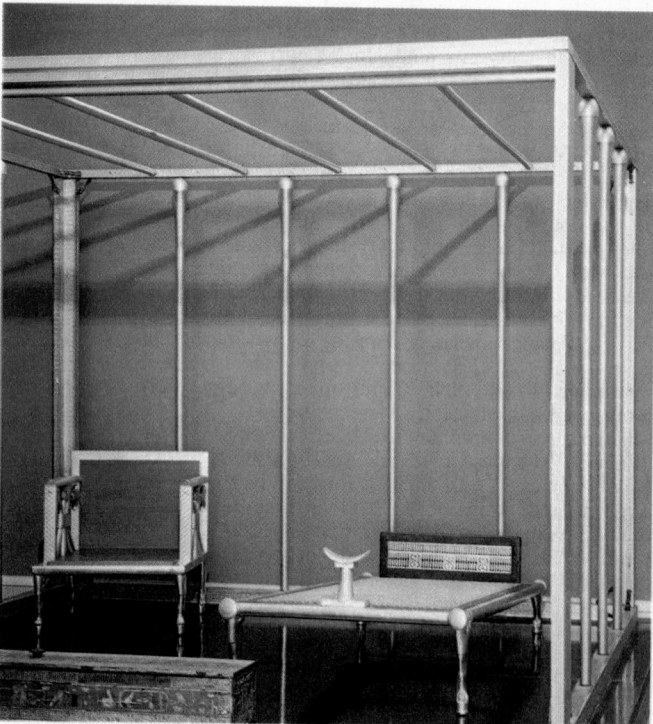

Reconstructed bed canopy with bed, chair, and curtain box from the tomb of Queen Hetepheres at Giza, wood overlaid with gold foil, Egypt, 4th dynasty, c. 2600 BC. A bed, with detachable footboard of inlaid faience and silvered headrest, and a low armchair stand beneath a canopy designed to take hangings. In the Museum of Fine Arts, Boston. Original in the Egyptian Museum.

Construction of the Egyptian bed

The bed may have been the earliest form; it was constructed of wood and consisted of a simple framework supported on four legs. A flax cord, plaited, was lashed to the sides of the framework. The cords were woven together from opposite sides of the framework to form a springy surface for the sleeper. In the 18th dynasty (c. 1567–1320 BC) beds sloped up toward the head, and a painted or carved wooden footboard prevented the sleeper from slipping down.

The great beds found in the tomb of Tutankhamen were put together with bronze hooks and staples so that they could be dismantled or folded to facilitate storage and transportation; furniture existed in small quantities and when the pharaohs toured their lands, they took their beds with them. In the same tomb was a folding wooden bed with bronze hinges.

Instead of pillows, wooden or ivory headrests were used. These were so essentially individual, being made to the measure of the owner, that they were often placed in tombs to be used by the dead man on his arrival in the land of eternity. Folding headrests were probably for the use of travellers.

Early stools for ceremonial purposes were merely squared blocks of stone. When made of wood, the stool had a flint seat (later shaped concavely) covered with a soft cushion. In time the stool developed into the chair by the addition of a back and arms. Such throne chairs were reserved for use by personages of great importance.

Footstools were of wood. The royal footstool was painted with the figures of traditional enemies of Egypt so that the pharaoh might symbolically tread his enemies under his feet. Carvings of animal feet on straight chair legs were common, as were legs shaped like those of animals. Boxes, often elaborately painted, or baskets were used for keeping clothes or other objects. Tables were almost unknown; a pottery or wooden stand supporting a flat basketwork tray held dishes for a meal, and wooden stands held great pottery jars containing water, wine, or beer.

The Egyptians used thin veneers of wood glued together for coffin cases; this gave great durability. Egyptian furniture in general was light and easily transportable; its decoration was usually derived from religious symbols, and stylistic change was very slow.

Mesopotamia. The furniture of Mesopotamia and neighbouring ancient civilizations of the Middle East had beds, stools, chairs, and boxes as principal forms. Documentary evidence is provided chiefly by relief carvings. The forms were constructed in the same manner as Egyptian furniture except that members were heavier, curves were less frequent, and joints were more abrupt. Ornament was richly applied in the form of cast-bronze and carved-bone finials (crowning ornaments, usually foliated) and studs, many of which survive in museums. Mesopotamia originated three features that were to persist in classical furniture in Greece and Italy and thus were transmitted to other western civilizations. First was the decoration of furniture legs with sharply profiled metal rings, one above another, like many bracelets on an arm; this was the origin of the turned wooden legs so frequent in later styles. Second was the use of heavy fringes on furniture covers, blending the design of frame and cushion into one effect; this was much lightened by classical taste but was revived in Neoclassicism. Third was the typical furniture grouping that survived intact into the Dark Ages of Europe: the couch on which the main personage or personages reclined for eating or conversation; the small table to hold refreshments, which could be moved up to the couch; and the chair, on which sat an entertainer—wife, hetaera (courtesan), musician, or the like—who looked after the desires of the reclining superior personages. From this old hierarchy of furniture derive the cumbersome court regulations concerning who may sit and on what, persisting in the palaces and ceremonies of 20th-century monarchs.

Mesopotamian ornamentation

Greece. Principal furniture forms were couches, chairs (with and without arms), stools, tables, chests, and boxes. From extant examples, the depiction of furniture on vases and in relief carvings, and literary descriptions, much more is known about Greek furniture than about Egyptian. At Knossos, a built-in throne of stucco, much restored, is often considered to represent pre-Hellenic furniture in the Aegean area. Primitive Aegean pottery shows rounded chair forms, perhaps indicating basketry models, and Bronze Age sculpture shows complex-membered chair frames.

In ancient Greek homes, the couch, used for reclining by day and as a bed by night, held an important place. The earliest couches probably resembled Egyptian beds in structure and possibly in style. The legs occasionally imitated those of animals with claw feet or hoofs, but usually they were either turned on the lathe and ornamented with moldings or cut from a flat slab of wood sharply silhouetted and decorated in various ways—with incised designs or with volutes, rosettes, and other patterns in high relief. From about the 6th century BC, the legs projected above the couch frame; these projections became headboards and footboards, the latter eventually made lower than the headboards. In Hellenistic times headrests and footrests were carved and decorated with bronze medallions carrying busts of children, satyrs, or heads of birds and animals in high relief. Turned legs largely replaced rectangular ones. Although a bronze bed of the 2nd century BC has been found at Priene and marble couches sometimes occur in tombs, the usual material was wood. The legs often terminated in metal feet and sometimes were encased in bronze moldings, and

The Greek couch

farthingale chairs, were introduced in the early 17th century to accommodate the wide skirts, called farthingales, that were popular at the time. Farthingale chairs had upholstered seats and a low, rectangular upholstered back raised on short supports a little above the seat. Armchairs of similar design were made. Turkey work (a type of needlework) and velvet were usually employed for upholstery.

Early in the 16th century a new style of bed design appeared; the greater part of the frame was left exposed and was enriched with carving and other decoration, making the frame itself an important part of the design. Favourite carvers' motifs for beds and other types of furniture included strapwork, grotesque masks, and caryatids (draped female figures), bulbous turned pillars and supports, arcading (decorating consisting of arches or arcades), and patterns of scrolled foliage. The heavily turned "cup and cover" motif is frequently found on bedposts in the later 16th century. The cumbersome Gothic trestle tables were replaced by "joyned tables," with tops fixed to the frames. Draw tables, which could be conveniently lengthened by pulling out the two leaves concealed under the top, were also introduced. Table legs and sides were decorated with carving and inlay, and the cup and cover motif is often found on the legs. Various types of cupboards were made, usually in two stages, or levels. In court cupboards both stages were left open. A simple form of chest of drawers was introduced about 1620.

17th century: the Baroque style. During the 17th century, the Baroque style had a marked effect upon furniture design throughout western Europe. Large wardrobes, cupboards, and cabinets had twisted columns, broken pediments, and heavy moldings. In Baroque fur-

Flamboyantly carved late Baroque chair made of boxwood by Andrea Brustolon, Venice, c. 1690. In the Ca' Rezzonico, Venice.
Foto Ferruzzi

niture the details are related to the whole; instead of a framework of unrelated surfaces, each detail contributes to the harmonious movement of the overall design. The Baroque style was adopted in the Low Countries in the 1620s and extended late into the 17th century, when Germany and England began to develop it. It owed much to the Oriental influence that swept over Europe in the 17th century, when several maritime countries, particularly Portugal, Holland, and England, established regular trading relations with India and the Far East. Lacquered furniture and domestic goods were imported from the East, where Oriental craftsmen also worked in a pseudo-European style from designs supplied by the traders. Before the end of the 17th century, Oriental decorative techniques were being widely imitated in Europe, and the roots of the "Chinese taste" were firmly entrenched. Heavy tropical woods were also brought to Europe, and from these, furniture was made that borrowed much from the prevailing taste for Oriental elaboration.

Influence of Oriental decorative techniques

Flanders and Holland. The early Flemish Baroque furniture, dating from the second quarter of the 17th century, was but a slight adaptation of the late Renaissance style. Typical are the oak cupboards with four doors and the chairs with seats and backs of velvet or leather held in place by nails.

In Holland the Baroque style did not encroach on late Renaissance furniture until nearly 1640. Dutch furniture of this period can be distinguished by its simpler design and a preference for molded panels over carved ornament. Later, marquetry decoration and walnut-veneer surfaces became the most common decorative treatments. At the end of the century lacquered furniture became popular.

Italy. Though it was in Italian architecture, painting, and sculpture that the Baroque style was evolved, Italy was not the first to apply this style to furniture. But by the mid-17th century Italy was producing flamboyantly carved, painted, and gilded furniture, decorated with such typical motifs as cupids, acanthus, shells, and boldly drawn scrolls, and was further enriching chairs and stools with fine-cut velvets and table tops with marble or *pietra dura* (a mosaic-like technique in which coloured stones are cut and shaped and inlaid in a design). Chairs and stools with exaggerated scrolled arms and legs, and

Turners (Photography) Ltd.

One of a pair of Baroque cabinets inlaid with *pietra dura* made for Louis XIV by the Italian furniture maker and sculptor, Domenico Cucci, at the Gobelins factory, France, 1681–83. In the collection of the Duke of Northumberland, Alnwick Castle, Northumberland, England.

handsome walnut and ebony cabinets and cupboards with carved decoration on the pediments, friezes, and corners and sometimes inlaid with marble or *pietra dura* set in molded panels, typify the Italian furniture of the later Baroque phase.

France. In France the Italian influence of the 16th century was gradually assimilated, and a national style of furniture was evolved that soon spread its influence into neighbouring countries. The reign of Louis XIII, covering most of the first half of the 17th century, was a time of transition. The Gobelins factory was founded by Louis XIV for the production of deluxe furniture and furnishings for the royal palaces and the national buildings. The painter Charles Le Brun was appointed the director in 1663. Furniture was veneered with tortoiseshell or foreign woods, inlaid with brass, pewter and ivory, or heavily gilded all over. At times it was even completely overlaid with repoussé (formed in relief) silver. The name of André-Charles Boulle is particularly associated with this style of decoration. His cabinets and tables were completely covered by sheets of tortoiseshell and brass cut into intricate patterns so as to fit into one another, the tortoiseshell alternately forming the pattern and the ground; hence the two types, boulle (buhl) and counterboulle. The light, fanciful designs of the architect and designer Jean Berain were much used for this work. Heavy gilt bronze mounts protected the corners and other parts from friction and rough handling, and provided further ornament.

Gobelins factory

England. After the Restoration, from 1660 onward, there was almost revolutionary progress in English cabinetmaking, as it came to be called at about this time. On its return, the exiled court introduced French and Dutch fashions, and the English craftsmen were considerably helped in supplying the tastes of the nobility by a large influx of foreign workmen. Furniture became lighter, more highly finished, and better adapted to varying needs. The general increase in technical skill of the cabinetmaker between 1660 and about 1690 is astonishing. Walnut was the favourite wood, though the use of oak continued in the country districts for many generations. New processes appeared, notably veneering wide surfaces with thin sheets of wood into which floral patterns in marquetry often were inserted. In the earlier period of the Restoration these patterns were large, but toward the end of the century they grew smaller and more intricate, leading eventually to the type of marquetry made up of numerous small scrolls and called seaweed marquetry.

The passion for colour found an outlet in lacquer decoration in England as in other European countries. The importation of works of art from the East had begun in Tudor times but was of little account until after the Restoration, when the taste became widespread. The diarist John Evelyn and others reported their friends' houses to be furnished with Indian screens or panelled in the finest "japan" (the process that imitated Oriental lacquery was called "japanning" in England).

New forms of furniture in the 17th century

New forms of furniture began to develop: the daybed, a form of couch with an adjustable end; the winged armchairs; the upholstered armchair called in the 17th century a sleeping chair; and, a little later, toward the end of the century, sofas with backs and arms carried comfort a step further. Velvet, silks, and needlework were the usual materials for upholstery. Various kinds of writing furniture were rapidly developed, including toward the end of the century, the bureau with enclosed desk and interior fittings of small drawers and pigeonholes.

Chests of drawers came into more general use. Mirrors were no longer rarities, though glass remained expensive. The frames were carved, lacquered, or decorated with marquetry. Fashions succeeded each other with great rapidity. Chairs show these changes most clearly, developing in a brief period from mere seats of Charles II, while, later, straight tapering baluster forms were used. In the grander beds of this period, the tester (canopy), back, and posts were covered with material. The beds were of enormous height with elaborately molded cornices and had ostrich plumes or vase-shaped finials at the corners of the tester. These state beds were strongly influenced by the designs of the French architect Daniel Marot, who went from France to England to work for William and Mary.

Edwin Smith

Late Stuart style dining room, Belton House (1685–89), near Grantham, Lincolnshire, England.

During the late 17th century and on into the first half of the 18th century, a certain amount of elaborately carved and gilded furniture, much influenced by the style of Louis XIV, was produced in England. Foremost among the makers of this deluxe furniture were three cabinetmakers: John Pelletier, Gerrit Jensen, and James Moore. Toward the end of the 17th century, during the reign of William and Mary, Baroque furniture tended to become simpler and the use of ornament was somewhat restrained. At the beginning of the 18th century, during the reign of Queen Anne, a new and simpler style arose, much influenced by the contemporary furniture of Holland. Carving and applied ornament were reduced to a minimum and the beauty of a piece was made to rely on carefully designed curved lines and the colour of fine walnut veneers. The cabriole leg, originally devised in classical times and based on the curve of an animal's leg, was introduced into England from the Continent about 1700. Terminating in a claw-and-ball or paw foot and soon discarding the stretcher, it was widely used on chairs and tables and for every kind of support. The stretcher had become obsolete because of improved joining and gluing. Chairs had hooped uprights, and fiddle-shaped splats curved to support the back. Tallboys, or double chests of drawers, cabinets fitted with shelves, and bureaus in two stages met the demand for greater convenience, as did a new range of dining, card, and other tables.

Queen Anne style

The American colonies. As in all colonial settlements, the furniture of the American colonies reflected the style preferences of the individual national groups. This influence, coupled with the existence of new ma-

terials and the time lag in transmitting styles and tastes from the home country, in some instances produced highly individual furniture.

Information in inventories and wills about 17th-century furniture of the English colonies indicates that it existed in its simplest forms—stools, benches, tables, cupboards, and a few chairs. This furniture, often made of oak, recalled the tradition of Elizabethan England and was turned and decorated with chip carving, often picked-out in earth colours. By the end of the century, pine, maple, and other woods were used.

The Dutch and Scandinavian settlers carried with them individual furniture forms whose influence remained local.

Awakening of fashion consciousness

By 1700 the effect of French and Dutch fashions on late Stuart furniture in England had become evident in the American colonies. Fashion consciousness appeared, though for decades to come the furniture of the average colonial home kept to the earlier tradition evolved from medieval joining. The box chest was succeeded by the chest of drawers, often placed on a stand with turned legs. Chairs began to replace stools; and the early heavy, turned, and wainscot (panelled back) types gave way to simplified versions of the high-back scrolled forms of the English Restoration fashion. The daybed appeared with its upholstered pad. Small folding tables, cabinets, and the tiered dresser to store and display tableware testify to the rapidly increasing standard of comfort among the more prosperous. Carved surface decoration was largely replaced by colour, through the use of paint, veneers, or inlays of contrasting wood.

These innovations accompanied the use of the cabriole, or reverse curve, which, about 1725, became the favoured form for legs of chairs, tables, cabinets, and stands. At first it had little or no carving and a simple paw foot, but the design was elaborated, and this cabriole leg became the principal feature of the so-called Queen Anne style that dominated colonial furniture designs until the Revolution. Walnut became the principal wood of the early 18th century.

Influence of French furniture

18th century: the Rococo style. The influence of French furniture was predominant in Europe during the 18th century. In the second half of the century England played a leading role in establishing the Neoclassical style, and for supreme craftsmanship provided an inspiration to workshops in several countries; but in the diffusion of the two styles, the Rococo and the Neoclassic, French designs were universally imitated, with varying degrees of success.

France. The transitional phase in French furniture from Baroque to Rococo is called Regence. The heavy, monumental style of the earlier part of Louis's reign was gradually replaced by a lighter and more fluent curvilinear style. The leading exponent of the Regence style was Charles Cressent, *ébéniste* ("cabinetmaker") to the regent Philippe II, duc d'Orléans. In his work the ormolu (a brass imitation of gold) mounts, so important a part of the design of French furniture in the 18th century, became equal to if not more important than, the marquetry decoration of the carcass. The curvilinear form was introduced not only to externals, such as legs and supports, but, in the bombé (rounded sides and front) commodes that first appeared during this period, to the case itself. High-quality marquetry in coloured woods replaced ebony.

Characteristics of the Rococo style

The Rococo style, a development of the Regence, affected French furniture design from about 1735 to 1765. The word is derived from rocailles, used to designate the artificial grottoes and fantastic arrangements of rocks in the garden of Versailles; the shell was one of the basic forms of Rococo ornament. The style was based on asymmetrical design, light and full of movement. The furniture of this period was designed on sinuous and complicated lines. Designs of Juste Meissonier, goldsmith to Louis XV, sculptor and architect, were instrumental in creating the Rococo. The repertory of ornament was large and included the C-scroll, scrolled foliage, floral motifs, ribbon and, on occasion, trophies formed of musical instruments or gardening implements.

The Rococo Chinese taste had conventions of its own: pagodas, exotic birds, Chinese figures, icicles, and dripping water. The graceful bombé commode, often with marble top and two or three drawers, the surface enriched with finely modelled ormolu mounts, was popular. Under Cressent's influence the mounts predominated, though later in the century the marquetry decoration gained first importance. Commodes and other pieces were decorated with marquetry of floral or geometrical patterns, or sometimes with lacquer decoration, again combined with ormolu mounts. The most celebrated makers of mounts during Louis XV's reign were Jacques Caffieri and his son Philippe. Jean-François Oeben was made *ébéniste du roi* (cabinetmaker to the king) in 1754; a pupil of Boulle, he was the most celebrated cabinetmaker of the period.

Giraudon

Rococo writing desk, the *bureau du roi*, with intricate pictorial marquetry and elaborate ormolu mounts made for Louis XV, begun by Jean-François Oeben in 1760 and completed by Jean-Henri Riesner, 1769. In Versailles.

England. About 1720, mahogany was imported into England and slowly superseded walnut as the fashionable wood for furniture. The Palladian (after the Italian Renaissance architect Andrea Palladio) interiors demanded furniture more striking and larger in scale than the walnut-veneered pieces of the early 18th century. Inspired by the interiors of French and Italian palaces, architects such as William Kent began to design furniture. The design was classical, in keeping with the traditions of Palladio and the English architect Inigo Jones; the ornament was Baroque. At Holkham Hall in Norfolk, Rousham Hall in Oxfordshire, and elsewhere, Kent's furniture may be seen in its proper environment: gilt mirrors and side tables with sets of chairs and settees covered with patterned velvets matching the grandeur of elaborate architectural Palladian interior decoration.

Despite the resistance of the Palladian classicists who deplored its asymmetrical principles, in the 1740s the Rococo style crept into English decoration and furniture design. During this decade pattern books of ornament in the full Rococo style by Matthias Lock and Henry Copeland were published in London; and in 1754 Thomas Chippendale published his *Gentleman and Cabinet Maker's Director*, which provided patterns for a wide range of English furniture in the Rococo style and its Chinese and Gothic offshoots. During the following years several similar works were published by such craftsmen and designers as William Ince and Thomas Mayhew, Thomas Johnson, and Robert Manwaring. The Rococo style was firmly established in England through-

The work of Thomas Chippendale

out the 1750s and into the 1760s. Chippendale and other cabinetmakers borrowed not only ornament from the French rocaille but designs for individual types. Chippendale's fame rests largely on his publication, though in fact it has now been more or less conclusively proved that he himself was not responsible for the designs, but employed two other designers, Lock and Copeland. There were several cabinetmakers—for example, William Vile and John Cobb—whose only memorial is a small quantity of furniture attributable to them. Though it has become the practice to speak of a Chippendale chair or a Vile commode, this does not imply that the pieces were actually made by these craftsmen but that they were made in their workshops.

By mid-18th century every act of the day that necessitated the use of furniture was catered to by some specialized piece, while the basic furniture such as chairs, cupboards, beds, and tables were designed and decorated in innumerable forms. The number of variants on the Rococo chair splat runs into several hundreds. The ingenuity of the cabinetmaker and carver knew few limitations.

The Gothic taste
An offshoot of the Rococo style, the Gothic taste was particularly well developed in England. Starting early in the century as a literary device, in the 1740s it began to take more solid shape in architecture, interior decoration, and furniture. As with furniture in the Chinese taste, Gothic furniture bore no relation to its medieval equivalents; the ornaments, such as tracery and cusped (a point formed by the intersection of two arcs or foils) arches, applied to furniture were borrowed from Gothic architecture. The Gothic taste was much publicized by the writer Horace Walpole's celebrated villa, Strawberry Hill, in Middlesex, England. Chippendale included designs for furniture in the Gothic taste in all three editions of his *Director*.

The American colonies. Shortly after 1750 the earlier cabriole style was transformed by two factors. One was the rapidly increasing popularity of mahogany. The other was the influence of the English version of free Rococo ornament, as reflected in the publication of Chippendale's book of patterns.

While the Southern planter still depended largely upon London for his fine furnishings, the merchants of Philadelphia, New York, Newport, and Boston were well rewarded by their patronage of local craftsmen. In Philadelphia a local version of the Chippendale style was brought to the highest mastery by such craftsmen as Thomas Affleck, Jonathan Gostelowe, Benjamin Randolph, and William Savery. In Newport, Rhode Island, the genius of the John Goddard and John Townsend cabinetmaking families evolved an equally distinctive style by developing a block front decorated by the patterns of the wood grains instead of carving, as used by their contemporaries in Philadelphia. In spite of the Philadelphians' evident desire to match the works of the best London shops, they actually created their own style as distinct from that of England as the innovations of their Newport colleagues. The cabinetmakers of Boston, New York, and the Connecticut valley also produced work of high quality and a definitely local flavour. Maintaining

Colonial Chippendale
its hold on popular taste until well after the Revolution, this colonial Chippendale retained more of the sturdy elegance of the earlier cabriole style than did its English equivalent. The tendency of English design to massiveness and surface decoration contrasts with the vertical and linear tendency in much colonial design.

18th century: the Neoclassical style. *France.* The Neoclassical style, sometimes called Louis Seize, or Louis XVI, began in the 1750s. Tiring of the Rococo style, craftsmen of the 18th century turned for inspiration to classical art. The movement was stimulated by archaeological discoveries, by travel in Italy, Greece, and the Near East, and by the publication, all over Europe, of works on the classical monuments. The Neoclassical style, based on straight lines and rectilinear forms and using a selection of classical ornaments, was first applied to French furniture during the 1760s. Classical motifs at first were sparingly applied to furniture of unchanged

form, but slowly the curved line of rococo was replaced by a simpler and more severe rectilinear design: chair legs became straight, tapered, and fluted; commodes and other storage furniture were no longer of bombé form. Marquetry was still widely used for decoration, and some cabinets were made of ebony inset with panels of Japanese lacquer. Boulle, which had not been employed in Louis XV's reign, returned to fashion. A greater number of pieces were signed during this period (signing had been made compulsory in Paris), and Jean-Henri Riesener, Martin Carlin, and Jean Saunier were a few of the leading cabinetmakers. Several German craftsmen migrated to France because of the royal patronage, among them Abraham and David Roentgen, Adam Weisweiler, and Guillaume Beneman. Of workers in bronze mounts, Pierre Gouthière was supreme.

These craftsmen were often directly under the patronage of the king, having their workshops in the cellars of the Louvre. Within the shop there was a division of labour, with one craftsman specializing in furniture construction, another in lacquering, and so forth. The craftsmen and the shop were licensed by the government.

England. The classical reaction, which set in shortly after 1760, reimposed a classical discipline on design, though of a lighter and more delicate touch than that of the previous classicists, the Palladians. Robert Adam, whose name is inseparably associated with this movement, had, like earlier architects, studied in Italy. There he sought inspiration in the monuments of both classical times and the Renaissance. When given a free hand, he included interior decoration and furniture in his architectural schemes, one of the best examples being his alterations and redecorations at Osterley, Middlesex, where he provided harmonious designs for even the lock plates and chimney pieces. His furniture makes restrained use of classical ornament; but paterae (disks with a design in relief or intaglio), husks (a drop ornament made of whorls of conventionalized foliage usually in a diminishing series), rams' heads, and urns are less eloquent of the change than the symmetrical structural lines. Marquetry, ormolu mounts, and painting were employed as decoration. Adam's furniture was copied and modified by contemporary cabinetmakers such as George Hepplewhite in his *Cabinet-Maker and Upholsterer's Guide* (1788).

In the last 20 years of the 18th century there was a tendency toward greater refinement, lightness, and delicacy in furniture design. Symmetry of form and excellence of proportion were retained for the most part. Heart- and shield-shaped backs on chairs and settees and tapered and fluted supports for tables and other pieces are characteristic; feathers, wheat ears, and shells are prominent in the painted or inlaid decoration. This refinement, strongly feminine in character, is represented in Thomas Sheraton's *Cabinet-Maker and Upholsterers' Drawing Book* (1791).

The work of Thomas Sheraton

The United States. The new classicism introduced into England by Robert and James Adam in the 1760s came into vogue in the new republic during the last years of the century. The shipowners and merchants of Salem, Boston, and New York equipped their mansions with the work of Samuel McIntire, John Seymour, and Duncan Phyfe, each of whom produced individual interpretations of the Hepplewhite–Sheraton mode. This early Federal style is characterized by small-scale rectangular design and by a preference for light-toned wood finishes. Surfaces are generally unbroken but decorated with bandings and inlays of contrasting woods, or in Phyfe's case with low relief carvings in the Adam manner. The most typical pieces are the sideboard (a piece of dining room furniture with compartments and shelves for dishes) and the small secretary desk, both of which developed a peculiarly American form.

19th century. The Empire style began in Paris about the time of the Revolution and quickly spread throughout Europe, each country adapting it to its own national taste. In England it is commonly called the Regency style. Two French architects, Charles Percier and Pierre Fontaine, who designed the furnishings for the state-

Neoclassical dining room from Lansdowne House, Berkeley Square, London, designed by
Robert Adam, c. 1765. In the Metropolitan Museum of Art, New York.
By courtesy of the Metropolitan Museum of Art, New York, Rogers Fund, 1932

rooms of Napoleon, contributed in great measure to the creation of the style. Their ideas were incorporated and propagated in *Recueil de décorations intérieures* (1801 and 1812; "Collection of Interior Decoration").

Characteristics of the Empire style

Basically the new style was a continuation of the Neoclassical style, with a much stronger archaeological bias, leading to direct copying of classical types of furniture; to this was added a new repertory of Egyptian ornament, stimulated by Napoleon's campaigns in Egypt. Mahogany-veneered furniture with ormolu mounts assumed the shapes of Roman, Greek, and Egyptian chairs and tables, with winged-lion supports and pilasters headed with sphinxes' busts or palm leaves; where no classical prototypes existed, contemporary designs were enlivened with classical ornament.

In England, Thomas Hope, an amateur designer with some knowledge of antiquities, was the chief exponent of the Regency style and entirely decorated his country house, Deepdene, Surrey, in it. When the fashion was taken up by cabinetmakers, the results were often woefully incongruous. Mahogany and rosewood were used with bronzed or gilt ornament, and metal inlay, a cheaper technique, replaced inlay and marquetry. Along with this style came a renewed enthusiasm for the Chinese taste, as best exemplified in the furniture and decoration of the Brighton Pavilion. Between the 1820s and 1830s, in the final stages of the Regency style, both the design and construction of furniture in England and on the Continent showed signs of heaviness and overelaboration that heralded the general decline throughout Europe in the 19th century.

The work of Duncan Phyfe

In the United States the style was widely adopted. Its chief native practitioner was the New York cabinetmaker Duncan Phyfe, who in the first decade of the century produced furniture for the wealthy of his city. His designs gave a unique interpretation to Empire ideas. French cabinetmakers, such as Charles-Honoré Lannuier, emigrated to the United States at this time and produced furniture in a stricter French style.

By the 19th century, with increases in the efficiency of transportation and communication, styles became more universal in their adoption but still maintained national and regional differences.

The Empire style, which carried over into the 19th century, began a series of styles that revived form and decoration from the past. This reinterpretation often resulted in a product removed from the principles of the original style. The introduction of the machine and of the factory method sometimes brought about a decline in quality in furniture production.

Biedermeier style

The Biedermeier style, which originated in Germany and Austria, flourished in the prosperous middle class homes of Europe from about 1815 to 1848. This style is characterized by classical simplicity. Chairs had curved legs, and sofas had rolled arms and generous upholstery. Mahogany veneers and light birch, grained ash, pear, and cherry were used. The design and much of the ornament were influenced by the Empire style, in particular the Grecian element. The style took its name from "Papa Biedermeier," a fictitious character whose column, offering opinions on taste in furniture, appeared in Austrian newspapers.

In the 1820s there was a revival of the Gothic style, which in England was partly stimulated by romantic literature such as the novels of Sir Walter Scott. Losing all the lightness and humour of the mid-18th-century Gothic revival, heavy medieval motifs were profusely and indiscriminately applied to every type of furniture.

A series of other revival styles followed the Gothic. The Rococo revival was one of the most popular; it borrowed the curvilinear elements of the French Louis XV style, especially the cabriole leg, and restated them in a heavier idiom. Entire suites of this furniture were fashioned in mahogany, rosewood, and walnut, the price being highly dependent upon the amount of carving on the frame.

During the first half of the 19th century (the exact date is unknown), metal springs were introduced into furniture construction. The spring construction made chairs and sofas much more comfortable than had the stuffing employed by cabinetmakers during the 18th century.

Another technical improvement introduced into furniture design was the use of plywood. Plywood had great strength and stability and could be more intricately curved than a natural piece of wood. One of the chief exponents of this technique in the United States was John Henry Belter, who was born in Germany in 1804 and served his cabinetmaker's apprenticeship in Württemberg. He reached a height of popularity in the 1850s. Belter's work is mainly in the Louis XV revival style.

Parlor furniture made by Duncan Phyfe for Samuel A. Foot, New York, 1837. In the Metropolitan Museum of Art, New York, 19th Century Centennial Exhibition, 1970.
By courtesy of the Metropolitan Museum of Art, New York, 1966 Purchase, L.E. Katzenbach Foundation Gift

Michael Thonet, an Austrian craftsman, experimented with bending layers of veneer in Boppard, Germany. Thonet was successful in perfecting a process for bending solid beechwood by heat into curvilinear shapes. His chairs, popular during the latter half of the 19th century, are still made.

Elizabethan and Louis XIV revival furniture was also very popular. The Baroque twisted upright was one of the chief elements employed. The straight, turned leg was also reintroduced. This elaborately upholstered furniture was produced in suites and was blocky and square in its overall form, in contrast to the Rococo revival form.

The Louis XVI style was reintroduced in suites of furniture with round tapering legs, oval backs on chairs and sofas, and elaborate upholstery. The Louis XVI leg was often used on comfortable upholstered furniture whose structure consisted primarily of a flexible metal, or "Turkish," frame. The only wood visible on this furniture was in the legs, the remainder of the frame being completely upholstered. In such furniture the art of the upholsterer reached its height through the use of elaborate tufting, tassels, and braids.

The influence of William Morris The English poet and artist William Morris has been called the father of the modern movement. Sickened by the shoddiness of the machine-produced goods of his own day, he turned for inspiration to the handcraftsmanship of the Middle Ages and, basing his own work on their designs and methods, attempted to revive a respect for fine craftsmanship and to stir the aesthetic sense of his contemporaries. His influence, though important, might have been greater if, instead of turning away from the machine, he had applied his high ideals to discovering a way in which machines might be used to the best advantage. Morris' followers in the field of cabinetmaking included such designer–craftsmen as Ernest Gimson and the Barnsley family who, working with a few assistants, produced small quantities of high-quality handmade furniture, the craftsmanship of which has never been rivalled. The example of Morris and his followers was so widely copied on the Continent that many people believe modern furniture design originated exclusively there.

During the third quarter of the century, there was a movement in England toward greater simplicity and aesthetic beauty in furniture. The straight and simple lines of Japanese design served as a source of inspiration. The result was the aesthetic, or artistic, style; its chief exponents, producing both designs and furniture, were Edward Godwin and Christopher Dresser.

Henry van de Velde, a Belgian architect and designer, followed in the footsteps of William Morris and was the conscious propagandist of the Art Nouveau style, which flourished from about 1893 to 1910. Characterized by moving, sinuous curves, the style found its inspiration in organic and natural forms and in the Japanese prints that were so popular in Europe during the third quarter of the 19th century. Van de Velde's furniture was often designed *en suite* so that it would give an effect of totality to a room. The interiors of a house in Brussels, created by another Belgian architect, Victor Horta, well illustrate the sinuous curves and natural forms employed by the Art Nouveau designers. The movement was also adopted in France where Hector Guimard was one of its chief exponents. A variant of the style is seen in furniture produced by the Scottish architect Charles Rennie Mackintosh. The Art Nouveau style in furniture design was not as popular in England or in the United States as it was on the Continent. (J.T.B.)

Art Nouveau style

Modern. After the late 19th century, furniture design in the West was divided into two main categories: revivals of past styles—only occasionally precise reproductions, more often free adaptations; and various expressions of changing modern life. The latter category absorbed the best as well as the most progressive talents of the era.

Modern furniture design after World War I was of three kinds: functionalist modern—progressive, adhering to an aesthetic of the machine and often designed by leading architects; transitional modern, which came to be called contemporary and was infused with elements from the past; and commercial modern, called "Borax" because hawkers of that cleanser used to offer premiums, and the word became associated with extra values which commercial furniture often offered by the manner in which it was advertised, or in overblown forms and gaudy veneers. All furniture design was influenced by the social and economic trends of the era: formal living de-

Indo-Dutch furniture

as clearly as the latter reflects Portuguese. There are two types of Indo-Dutch furniture. The first, which was made on the Coromandel coast, was mainly in light-coloured woods, the decoration being inlaid bone, incised and lacquered. The second is a style of carved ebony furniture which, although commonly found in India and often thought to be Indian in origin, was in fact made at Batavia (modern Djakarta) in Java, the Dutch administrative headquarters in the East. The carved relief decoration of the ebony furniture is floral in character and closely related to the flowering-tree style of contemporary Indo-Dutch embroidered bedspreads and hangings in which the tulip is prominent.

With the growth of British power in India in the 18th century, all Indo-European furniture styles came increasingly under English influence. Whole suites were made in the manner of Chippendale and Sheraton, not only for European buyers but also for Indian rulers who increasingly favoured European styles of furniture.

In the 19th century, Indian artistic standards degenerated, as is clearly reflected in the furniture of the period. The emphasis was on decorative elaboration for its own sake and, although much 19th-century Indian wood carving shows great technical skill, this rarely compensates for formlessness and stereotyped ornament.

(J.T.B.)

BIBLIOGRAPHY. OLE WANSCHER, *Møbelkunsten* (1966; Eng. trans., *The Art of Furniture*, 1967), the best chronological survey of the art of furniture (with illustrations).

Near East and classical antiquity: A. LUCAS, *Ancient Egyptian Materials and Industries*, 3rd ed. (1948), still indispensable; HOWARD CARTER and A.C. MACE, *The Tomb of Thut-Ankh-Amen*, 3 vol. (1923–27); GISELA M. RICHTER, *The Furniture of the Greeks, Etruscans and Romans* (1966), the standard reference work in this area.

Middle Ages: VIOLLET-LE-DUC, *Dictionnaire raisonné du mobilier français de l'époque carlovingienne à la Rénaissance*, 6 vol. (1858–75), still an authoritative work.

Renaissance and later: (Italy): GEORGE LELAND HUNTER, *Italian Furniture and Interiors*, 2 vol. (1918), mostly illustrations; WILLIAM M. ODOM, *A History of Italian Furniture from the 14th to the Early 19th Centuries*, 2 vol. (1918–19). (*Spain*): ARTHUR BYNE and MILDRED STAPLEY, *Spanish Interiors and Furniture* (1921), profusely illustrated with scale drawings and photographs. (*Germany*): HEINRICH KREISEL, *Die Kunst des deutschen Möbels*, 2 vol. (1968–70), the most thorough and by far the best illustrated history of German furniture. (*France*): PIERRE VERLET, *Le Mobilier royal français*, 2 vol. (1945–55); *Les Meubles français du XVIIIᵉ siècle*, 2 vol. (1956), a learned treatise on French furniture. (*England and the colonies*): PERCY MACQUOID and RALPH EDWARDS, *The Dictionary of English Furniture from the Middle Ages to the Late Georgian Period*, 2nd ed., 3 vol. (1954), the best documented survey of English and American furniture; RALPH FASTENEDGE, *English Furniture Styles from 1500 to 1830* (1962), an excellent elementary introduction to the study of English furniture; ANTHONY COLERIDGE, *Chippendale Furniture* (1968), a well-illustrated study of Chippendale and his contemporaries; CLIFFORD MUSGRAVE, *Adam and Hepplewhite and Other Neo-Classical Furniture* (1966), written by one of the best informed students of the Neoclassical English style of furniture; CHARLES F. MONTGOMERY, *American Furniture* (1966), a good survey of Federal period furniture.

19th century and modern: R.W. SYMONDS and B.B. WHINERAY, *Victorian Furniture* (1962), with many good illustrations; SERGE GRANDJEAN, *Empire Furniture, 1800 to 1825* (1966); NIKOLAUS PEVSNER, *Pioneers of Modern Design from William Morris to Walter Gropius* (1960); JEAN CASSOU, EMILE LANGUI, and NIKOLAUS PEVSNER, *Les Sources du vingtième siècle* (1961); E.D. and F. ANDREWS, *Shaker Furniture: The Craftsmanship of an American Communal Sect* (1937).

(Er.L./E.J.Wo./J.T.B.)

Furniture Industry

The modern manufacture of furniture, as distinct from its design, is a major mass-production industry in Europe, the U.S., and other advanced regions. It is very largely a 20th-century industry, its development having awaited the growth of a mass consumer market as well as the development of the mass-production technique. Earlier furniture making was a handicraft, going back to the most ancient civilizations.

History. Examples of ancient furniture are extremely rare, but there is considerable knowledge of the pieces made by craftsmen in China, India, Egypt, Mesopotamia, Greece, and Rome from pictorial representations. Beds, tables, chairs, boxes, stools, chests, and other pieces were nearly always made of natural wood, though veneering was known in Egypt, where it was used to produce coffin cases of great durability. The Romans too used veneers, though chiefly for decorative purposes. Bronze was also used in Roman tables, stools, and couch frames. Pompeian wall paintings show that plain, undecorated wooden tables and benches were standard in kitchens and workshops and that panelled cupboards were common. Chests for valuables were covered with plates or bound with iron.

The early Middle Ages were much poorer in household furnishings of every kind than the Roman world, but in the 14th and 15th century a growing affluence brought a major revival of furniture making, with many new types of cupboards, boxes with compartments, and various sorts of desks appearing. The religious houses in particular were well supplied with furniture. Framed panelling, reintroduced in the Burgundian Netherlands, quickly spread. The mortise and tenon and mitre provided greatly improved joints.

Introduction of veneering

The growing sophistication in technique brought a revolutionary change in the men who made furniture. Where previously carpenters and joiners had made furniture along with every kind of building construction in wood, several circumstances combined to create a new profession: that of cabinetmaker. The most important technical factor was the introduction, or reintroduction, of veneering, first in western Europe, then in Britain, North America, and elsewhere.

In the earlier system of framework and panel, the framing gave the required strength in both length and width, the panel being a mere filling held in grooves. Its attractive appearance was the result of highlights and shadows produced by the framing, moldings, and carving, which formed the chief means of decoration. The grain of the wood was incidental.

The introduction of veneering coincided with the use of walnut as a furniture wood. It was soon realized that the grain of such a wood could be of decorative value, especially as veneering made it possible to use such visually attractive parts of the wood as burrs, butts, and curls, unreliable if used as solid wood. It became the custom to have the grain of the veneer generally run crosswise because of its decorative appearance. Marquetry (a form of inlay in veneer) was another example of the decorative use of the grain and colour of wood in surfaces unbroken by panelling.

In addition to veneering and the new system of construction it involved, an impetus to the establishment of the trade of furniture making came from the increasing market demand provided by the growing affluence of the 17th and 18th centuries. In the new system of construction, plain, flat parts are dovetailed together and then veneered. It can be contrasted with the traditional framed method of rails and stiles put together with mortise and tenon joints, the panels fitting in grooves.

Coinciding with this change, or preceding it by a few years, was another breakaway: that of the chairmaker, who had become another specialized craftsman. At first chairmaking was closely associated with wood turning but by the 18th century turned legs were largely replaced by shaped legs of the cabriole type. Chairmaking has remained a separate branch of furniture making ever since.

This growth of cabinetmaking as a trade of its own eventually resulted in a considerable degree of standardization of methods of construction, particularly in the types of joints used and in the thicknesses of wood for the various parts. It also resulted in an increased division of labour. Turnery became a separate trade, while the cabinetmaker assembled the turned parts; veneer and marquetry cutting was not done by the cabinetmaker although he laid both; carving too called for the skill and experience and tools of a craftsman who did nothing else. Another specialist, the upholsterer, did his work after the chairmaker had made the frame; and it seems likely that finishing was seldom done by the cabinetmaker. This was certainly the case later in the 19th century when French polishing became the standard method of finishing furniture.

An important 19th-century change was the separation within the industry of those who made furniture from those who sold it. Previously the customer commissioned a cabinetmaker, perhaps after consulting a design book by Chippendale, Hepplewhite, or Sheraton. Or he might work out his requirements in consultation with the cabinetmaker or, if he were sufficiently wealthy, employ an architect or designer. After the midyears of the 19th century the showroom gained popularity. A large store often retained its own workshops where special items were made to customers' requirements, but for the greater part it became the practice to buy wholesale from furniture making firms.

MODERN FURNITURE MANUFACTURE

Materials. Modern methods of furniture construction are largely based on the availability of man-made materials such as reliable plywood, laminated board, chipboard, and hardboard as distinct from natural solid wood. It is not merely that manufacturers prefer the one to the other but rather that these substances are free from the great drawback fundamental to wood—movement. Natural wood shrinks as it dries or swells as it absorbs moisture from an atmosphere more humid than itself, and this movement must be allowed for in the method of construction. Unless this is done troubles may arise: splits along the grain or open joints on the one hand or jammed drawers or doors on the other. Over the years cabinetmakers have worked out ingenious systems to avoid these troubles in the use of solid wood, but today made-up materials may be regarded as inert if of good quality. To an extent solid wood has still to be used, notably for items that have to be turned, cut to shape, or molded, and for lippings to conceal the edges of manufactured boards; but virtually everything in the form of flat panels is made up.

Natural wood. The increase in the demand for reasonably priced furniture has placed a premium on the economical use of wood. Natural wood is extremely wasteful as a material. Hardly more than 25 percent of the natural substance of a tree actually goes into the furniture made of solid wood. When account is taken of the loss in sawdust in conversion from the tree trunk (taking off the outer slab portions and sapwood) and the further loss in bringing the lumber to usable size in the workshop (the offcuts, waste in sawing shapes, in turning, in planing, cutting joints, and final cleaning up), it becomes evident that much more wood is wasted than used.

Plywood. In making plywood, the veneers are peeled rotary fashion from the log by a long knife fitted to a lathelike machine. The resulting veneer can be of unlimited width to be cut up as required. There is no loss in sawdust, and the peeling is continued until only a polelike centre is left. Much the same applies to laminated board in which both the core material and the outer plies are peeled. In the case of chipboard the timber is merely regarded as raw material to be reduced to fine chips that are dried, compressed, and assembled into boards, with resin glue as an adhesive. Where a natural wood grain is desired, a veneer is flat sliced from a flitch (longitudinal section) selected for the beauty of its grain.

Certain materials, notably chipboard, must be machined, because trimming at the edges by hand almost always shows as a deterioration. It cannot be planed; the plane merely forms dust rather than taking shavings and, owing to the abrasive nature of the material, the edge of the cutter is quickly lost. Consequently, when a panel of a certain size is required, it needs to be machine sawed to size, no further trimming being needed. This is only practicable with a precision saw capable of fine adjustment. Furthermore it requires a saw blade having tungsten teeth to resist abrasion. The same applies to any plywood or laminated board assembled with resin glue.

Another influence on the construction of furniture is the introduction of new types of adhesives in place of the traditional animal glue. Many are highly water resistant, some waterproof. Some can be applied cold, avoiding the complication of heating joints before assembly. They can be cured by heat in a matter of minutes, leaving presses and other apparatus free for other work.

Other materials. Although wood has always been regarded as the traditional material for furniture making, several other materials are now used, either entirely replacing wood or combined with it. Plastic laminate, widely used for table and other tops, is obtainable in various colours and designs and in photographically reproduced natural wood grain. Its advantages are that it resists all liquid stains, is largely heat proof against burn marks, is mark free, and is easily wiped clean. It is laid as a form of veneer on any of the man-made materials—multiply, laminated board, or chipboard, usually with a contact adhesive. As a plastic edging is needed that must be applied before the main top is put down, an essential machine tool is the portable router with veneer-trimming unit. It trims the overlapping edges of the main plastic panel without cutting into the edging.

Metal is also used to some extent, particularly for the stands and legs of furniture. Iron is generally preferred, the parts joined by welding.

Finishes too have been revolutionized. French polish, the traditional finish of the Victorian period, and indeed up to the 1930s, has been largely replaced by gloss or eggshell lacquers, which are sprayed on and are heat and water resistant and are so hard as to be practically mark free.

Storage and transport. Two technologies important to furniture making are storage and transport. The space taken up by furniture in relation to the actual material used in its construction is disproportionately large; when furniture is mass-produced an enormous amount of storage space is required. This applies equally to its transport, especially when it has to be shipped abroad. Consequently a great deal of furniture is made of the "knock-down" type; that is, it can be taken to pieces and stacked flat. A wardrobe made in this way may occupy only a quarter of its assembled space when disassembled. Originally, parts were joined by screw fastenings, but a whole range of fittings has been devised to achieve the same result more easily and with more precision. Most such fittings require little more than recessing or the boring of holes, operations easily machined. Most work on cam, screw, or wedge action.

Woodworking machinery. The decline of the direct link between customer and maker, due to the rapid development of retail trade, was largely made possible by the invention of several woodworking machines, mostly steam powered. Much handwork remained, however, and only large manufacturers could afford major machinery installation. In the early 20th century it was still possible for a cabinetmaker in Britain or Europe to earn a living, though in most cases he installed a basic machine such as a circular saw or worked in a district in which machine shops were available. Thus in Shoreditch, London, whole streets of houses were occupied by cabinetmakers, often several in one house, who made pieces that varied from the finest individual items to the cheapest, turned out in pairs or perhaps six at a time. These men had their machining done in the trade machine shops that abounded in the district. The shops produced nothing themselves but performed any machining that was brought to them: sawing, spindle molding, fretting, turning, planing, and so on. These practices continued up to the beginning of World War I and for a time afterward, although most of the large stores also had their workshops where they made not only individual items for customers but also furniture in quantity to pattern.

But in the U.S., the development of mass-production furniture manufacture was already well advanced, with the principal manufacturing centres at Grand Rapids, Michigan; Jamestown, New York; and High Point, North Carolina. "Grand Rapids" became a byword for inexpensive furniture of reliable quality. Furniture factories have never become large in comparison with the huge production units in such industries as automobiles and steel—few today employ more than 100 persons—because of the continuing need for some hand operations. But their machines for many purposes and the volume in which they operated gave them insuperable advantages in cost over the old-fashioned craftsman. Mass-produced furniture began to have a serious impact in Britain and Europe between the wars.

The shortage of timber during and after World War II made conditions extremely difficult for the furniture maker; but in the 1950s there was a gradual return to more decorative furniture, marked by the introduction of new materials, new machines, adhesives, and finishes.

Modern commercial furniture production may be roughly divided into groups: general furniture—bookcases, wardrobes, tables, etc.; chairs and upholstered suites; and specialized items. Each of these may be further subdivided according to quality and type. In addition to this commercial furniture there are the specialized items made by a few hand craftsmen to special commission. Such goods are necessarily expensive, partly because they are individual pieces made singly to design and also because the best selected materials are used. Furthermore, hand methods are largely used that are costly because they are time-consuming. Even in this field, however, the machine has encroached to an extent. Thus a circular saw is invariably installed because its advantages are so obvious. There is no merit in laboriously ripping boards to size when a machine will do the work as well or better.

Though furniture produced by modern hand craftsmen is beautifully made from the best materials, it often requires considerable discernment to detect the difference between it and the best commercial furniture.

Period furniture. In a class by itself is the manufacture of reproduction period furniture. The best work in this field is of an extremely high standard; and, although it often has to make concession to modern materials in using veneered plywood or laminated board for parts, it usually follows traditional methods of construction, at least where visible machine work would be obvious. On the other hand, all veneers are put down in a press, moldings worked on the spindle molder, and shapes cut on the bandsaw or jigsaw.

It is in this work that wood carving is chiefly used. Because of its high cost, carving has largely disappeared from modern commercial furniture, but to the manufacturer of reproduction furniture it is an obvious necessity. From early times and certainly from the 17th century, wood carving has been a separate trade. A highly skilled calling, it demands artistic sense as well as manual dexterity. It has become divided into classes of which furniture and indoor decoration represent only one branch, with further subdivision within the branch.

In the commercial grade of furniture there is wide variation in quality, from the lowest priced goods to high-grade items in which individual hand workmanship is used for processes where the quality would suffer if the machine were used. Thus drawer dovetails are cut by hand, and sometimes even hand-cut joints are used.

Modern factory layout. Most modern factories are laid out on mass-production lines. The earlier factories often had a cabinet shop, which had its rows of benches for individual work; a cabinetmaker needing machining done carried his wood to the machinist. Today the timber is cut to usable sizes in a main conversion shop and brought to the required moisture content in a kilning section. In the kiln, air is forced through stripped stacks by fans that periodically change the direction of the air flow. In recent years radio-frequency heating has been widely used to dry both natural wood and plywood. The applied radio frequency produces molecular activity in wood and resins (such as those in plywood glue); part of the molecular energy is converted into heat that greatly reduces the time required to dry the wood thoroughly and evenly and to set the glue. The wood is placed in a press between two metal plates to which the power is applied; great thicknesses of wood can be dried evenly by this method.

From the drying section the wood proceeds to the planing and jointing shop, in which it is reduced to the required section and any tenoning, dowelling, or dovetailing carried out. There is also a veneer department, and in many respects this has become one of the most important departments. In it veneers are jointed in width where necessary, and a remarkable recent invention is a machine that sews veneers together with fine fibreglass, the stitching passing through half the thickness of the veneer only. It does this with amazing speed and accuracy. Where required, veneers are matched, giving a balanced appearance; and any small defects are repaired by placing a waste veneer beneath, cutting through both simultaneously, and interchanging the cutout pieces. Veneer pressing follows, and, although multiplate presses are still used to an extent, the tendency in large-production work is toward the progressive presser. At one end of this the resin glue is applied with a spreader, the veneers placed in position on the groundwork, and the whole passed in batches beneath the presser where it is heat cured in about a minute and ejected at the other end ready for further operations.

It is in the assembly shop that the line or conveyor-belt system begins. This is not usually in continuous movement but takes the form of a series of loose rollers over which the work can easily be pushed by one man. Special cramping jigs are set up so that, for example, a wardrobe can be glued up in one operation by power-driven rams. The jig ensures squareness, and the resin glue is cured in a matter of seconds by radio-frequency heating. In fact, by the time the operator has applied glue to the joints of one set of parts, the previous assembly has hardened and can be removed to the conveyor, leaving the jig free for another cramping operation.

From this point onward the work remains on the conveyor belt, passing to a sanding shop where joints are levelled and finally to the finishing shop where it is stained, spray polished, and fine sanded and waxed. Lastly there is a fitters' shop, where doors are hinged, handles put on, mirrors fitted, and so on.

Before passing to stock or to the packers' department every piece has to be passed by an examiner who chalks any defect or attaches a small, coloured label indicating that there is a fault in either the woodwork or the finish.

Only a constant flow of orders in large quantities justifies such a setup. Smaller firms contract their veneering to outside specialists, have their turning done outside, and also any other work for which they are not equipped. The aim is to maintain a constant flow of production, which involves a balance in personnel in the various departments to avoid a holdup in any stage.

The production process. A basic preliminary in all furniture production is the provision of working drawings. In a firm of any size there is invariably a special department where full-size drawings are prepared from small-scale drawings provided by the designer. In some cases the designer may make his own full-size, detailed drawings; but in a large firm it is more usual for a draftsman to work out the practical details, though usually in consultation with the designer, who advises on proportions and decorative details. The hand craftsman, in contrast, usually does the whole thing himself. In the small-scale drawing the general form and essential requirements are worked out; the full-size drawing shows proportions and constructional details. A sample piece is made to check the design and cutting problems. Cutting lists are prepared; the cost of materials, fittings, finish, etc. figured; and an estimate of machining and assembly time worked out. When the work is to be produced in quantity, costs are lowered considerably because only one setting of the machine and only one set of cutters are needed for the whole run of any particular part.

Selection of timber, already passed through the seasoning kiln and converted to standard thicknesses, follows. The wood passes to the machine shop, where it is sawed to size, planed, molded, grooved, or rebated as required.

Modern hand craftsmen

Sanding, finishing, and fitting

When a number of parts must be cut exactly alike, they are clamped in forms having the proper contour and are then brought in contact with high-speed rotating knives that shape the part to proper size as the form rides against a guide on hand or automatic shapers and routers. Intricately carved pieces such as legs are roughly carved on multiple-spindle carving machines. These duplicate a master leg by means of a follower point that is guided along the surface of the model and imparts the same motions to as many as 32 high-speed rotating knives as they whittle the leg blanks. After the rough carving, the pieces are machine sanded and finished by a hand carver.

If veneering is required, this is now done. Jointing follows—tenoning, dowelling, dovetailing, etc. Automatic machines often combine several operations. Exposed parts are sanded on edge belt sanders, three-drum travelling-bed sanders, or belt sanders. Rounded parts are sanded on soft pneumatic drums, and carved parts are sanded on a buffer, a machine in which shredded sandpaper is supported by brushes on a revolving wheel.

Furniture assembly
Finally the work passes to the assembly shop where door frames are put together, drawers glued up, and carcasses assembled. After the glue has set, the parts may be returned to the machine department for machining that could not be performed before assembly, such as sanding the joints and shaping the edges. Then it returns to the assembly department for final assembly; air-driven clamps are used when the design permits; otherwise the piece is pressed by hand clamps. Unless electronically cured glues are used, clamps must be applied long enough to ensure a good bond. The completed article is cleaned to remove excess glue, inspected, and hand sanded. Finally, staining and spray polishing is done and fittings added.

In individually crafted work there is always a great deal of fitting to be done—doors trimmed and drawers made to run easily without slackness. In mass-production work this problem would be serious. It is almost entirely avoided by making drawers an easy rather than snug fit and by sanding the edges of doors to templet size so that they automatically fit the carcasses, which in their turn are made to standard size.

The art of chairmaking. Chairmaking has been a separate branch of furniture making since the mid-17th century. One of the most intricate branches of woodwork, it involves odd angles, compound shapes, and awkward joints and at the same time calls for maximum strength, chairs being subjected to more strain than most other furniture. There are three main types of chairs: the Windsor chair, made largely from turned parts, with solid wood seat; the framed type of dining chair with either loose or stuff-over seat; and the upholstered chair.

In Britain the Windsor chair belongs traditionally to the High Wycombe District of Buckinghamshire where beechtrees abound. Until relatively recent times men worked in huts in the beech woods making turned parts for chairs. They felled the trees, cut the trunks and larger branches into suitable lengths, and split them into pieces of a section large enough to permit chair legs and uprights to be turned and also to provide lighter members for rails, etc. They turned the parts on a primitive pole lathe in which a cord was attached to a treadle, taken around the wood to be turned and up to a springy sapling anchored at the lower end to pegs outside the hut. The power was supplied by treadle, the cord revolving the wood; then as the foot was raised the spring of the sapling lifted the treadle and at the same time turned the work backward. The turning gouge or chisel could be used on the downward stroke of the foot only, but the economy of effort was amazing. A complete leg could be rounded, the curves and beads formed, and the ends brought to the required diameter in a matter of seconds. Of course, working in green timber enabled the turning to be done much more easily and quickly than if the wood were dry.

These bodgers, as they were called, made only the turned parts and delivered them to chairmaking firms for assembling. They had no overhead expenses, no power costs, and the only lighting they needed in winter was an oil lamp or candles. They were long able to compete with powered workshops.

The Windsor chair
The manufacture of the Windsor chair of Victorian and Edwardian times was a specialized trade. The seat, invariably of elm, was hollowed out (bottomed) with a form of adze, and the holes for the legs were bored with a brace fitted with a spoon bit held at the required angle solely by judgment. The better chairs had a hooped back of yew. Today this hand work has been replaced by boring machines that are fitted with a jig to maintain the correct angle. The hollowing of the seat is machined to an extent, but the depth is only slight, compared with the early hand work. Furthermore, traditional timbers—elm, beech, and yew—are frequently replaced by imported timbers.

The quality of framed chairs of the dining type varies widely, but perhaps the outstanding general feature of modern dining chairs is the wide use of dowelled joints rather than mortise and tenon. In the late 19th century this had already occurred to a large extent, the chairmaker's kit of tools invariably including a dowel plate with a series of holes through which the craftsman hammered roughly squared pegs to form the dowels. Today machine-made dowels are universal, with a glue-escape slot cut in. Dowelling is a far quicker and consequently cheaper process than mortising and tenoning, especially in shaped work where the curved part frequently must be joined at odd angles.

When a chair has compound curvature it becomes difficult and expensive to make. A chair back may be shaped in both front and side elevation (and often in plan as well). Taste and experience are indispensable in providing a continuous curve that will be aesthetically satisfying from every angle. Over the years, experience has been built up, especially on traditional models following period lines; a chairmaker's workshop invariably carries bundles of templets in plywood for the various parts of chairs, with the fullness provided (where necessary) for a good line.

Dining chairs may be made in sets of half-dozens or dozens, or more cheaply in batches of 50 or 100, depending upon the capacity of the factory. In some cases parts are standardized and interchangeable in different designs of chairs.

The upholstering of dining chairs is a separate trade, though carried out in the same factory, and may be of the loose seat, stuff-over, or plywood-covered type. Traditional stuffing materials such as horsehair have largely been replaced by foam rubber and synthetics.

Full upholstery furniture. The manufacture of fully upholstered pieces is often a separate branch, though large manufacturers often make both upholstered and nonupholstered types. It remains to a great extent a handicraft, for the skill of trained and experienced craftsmen is needed in turning out quality pieces. The standard upholstery foundation consists of a system of coiled steel springs resting on a webbing of burlap and tied to the furniture frame, which may be of wood, fibreglass, or plywood. The springs are embedded in a filling material, such as rubberized hair, foam rubber, palm fibre, or Spanish moss; and the spring system is topped by a thick padding of cotton or foam rubber in sheet form. Muslin is frequently employed as an inner covering for this assembly, while a durable upholstery fabric is used as an outer and finishing cover. Loose cushions are filled with special spring units in a bedding of foam rubber or down; the springs are covered with layers of cotton, and the entire assembly is encased in upholstery fabric.

Only a few mechanical aids have proved satisfactory in upholstery. Multiple layers of fabric can be cut efficiently and economically by machines in production-line operations, and staples are used instead of tacks on less expensive pieces. But the mass production of such components as the basic coiled-spring system and the mechanical handling of such materials as the bedding, or filler, have not proved efficient and economical. Some useful substitutes have been found, however, for the coiled-spring supporting unit; they include the modern nonsagging springs that may be clipped to the frame and the steel bands that are held to the frame by helical springs. Sponge rubber may be molded to constitute a complete seat that is firm and comfortable. Webbed seat frames also are used, and the natural resiliency of wood is utilized in building springy plywood supporting structures.

Future trends. Despite the developments in modern upholstery, there is still a demand for traditional methods, particularly in the reproduction trade, but even here the scarcity of traditional materials is a problem and frequently synthetics are used.

The future will doubtless see a continued decline in the use of natural wood except in veneer form. Large trees yielding finely figured woods are becoming ever scarcer and more expensive. The days when huge, 30-inch table tops, panels, cabinet ends, and other large items could be made of solid Cuban or Honduras mahogany without a joint are past. The finest figured woods are sliced into veneers. Where solid wood is essential, as in turned or shaped parts, an inferior wood stained to match is frequently used. Plastic laminates are a strong rival even to natural wood veneers, especially for such parts as table tops that are subjected to considerable wear and are likely to be used on an increasing scale.

Yet it is doubtful if wood will ever be entirely replaced. Something about the nature of wood appeals to aesthetic taste. It is likely to be used increasingly in the form of manufactured boards. Apart from the increased demand for furniture and the growing shortage of finely figured woods, such boards carry certain advantages such as freedom from movement and availability in large unjointed dimensions, advantages that outweigh the minor drawback of the necessary lipping of edges.

The use of materials made to size as needed rather than natural wood (which might in some circumstances require the adaptation of design to suit the peculiarities of the timber), plus ever-increasing mechanization, has resulted in the trend of woodwork towards engineering, a trend likely to accelerate. Yet in the 1970s both in Europe and America the most striking characteristic of the furniture industry is its continued decentralization, with great numbers of small and medium-sized producers.

BIBLIOGRAPHY. Information on the furniture industry and trade may be found in W. SKINNER *et al.*, *Manufacturing Policy in the Furniture Industry*, 3rd ed. (1968); D.E. BOND and R.J. WONNACOTT, *Trade Liberalization and the Canadian Furniture Industry* (1968); S.H. SLOM, *Profitable Furniture Retailing* (1967); and J.L. OLIVER, *The Development and Structure of the Furniture Industry* (1966). Descriptions and illustrations of types of furniture, mostly antique, are given in J.E. GLOAG, *A Short Dictionary of Furniture*, rev. and enl. ed. (1969); and ERNEST JOYCE, *The Technique of Furniture Making* (1970). Works by C.H. HAYWARD include: *English Period Furniture Designs* (1969), a history of styles from the 16th through the mid-19th centuries; *Period Furniture Designs*, rev. ed. (1968), measured drawings of period pieces and their construction; and *Antique or Fake?* (1970), on how old furniture was made. A handbook on woodworking techniques and on the design and construction of modern furniture is J. and R. HOOPER, *Modern Furniture and Fittings*, 2nd ed. rev. (1955). For descriptions and illustrations of craftsman-made furniture, see A.E. BRADSHAW, *Handmade Woodwork of the Twentieth Century* (1962); and L.J. MAYES, *History of Chair Making in High Wycombe* (1960).

(C.H.H.)

Furs

Fur, the fine, soft, hairy covering—or coat—of a mammal, usually consists of a layer of relatively short, soft, barbed hairs next to the skin, helping to maintain body temperature, and a top layer formed by longer, stiff, smooth hairs growing up through the underlying layer, serving to shed rain.

Man, in using the fur of animals for both its warmth and its attractive appearance, applies various processes that make furs wearable and enhance their attractiveness. This article provides a brief history of man's use of furs; gives characteristics of the furs of various animals; surveys the modern fur trade; and treats the processes involved in preparing fur pelts for use in the manufacture of fur garments.

HISTORY

The use of fur as an item of apparel apparently began in a prehistoric period. In the Earth's colder regions, where man required both food and warmth, it is likely that animal fur was used as a body covering soon after man began to eat animal flesh. Although fur was a necessity in the cold northern forests, almost every civilization has valued furs as an adornment. The Chinese are said to have esteemed furs 3,500 years ago; the Greek legend of Jason and the Golden Fleece may have originated in some unusually perilous but successful fur-trading voyage to the Euxine (Black Sea); and furs were among the luxuries Rome adopted from Greece. The narrowing distinction between fur as a necessity and fur as a luxury influenced subsequent development of the fur trade.

In medieval Europe, furs, mainly of northern and central European origin, were an important element in commerce. The Hanseatic League, an association of trading towns in the Baltic area, was especially active in the fur trade, importing many types of skins from Novgorod, Russia, to western Europe.

Although sumptuary regulations forbade furs to monks and to all but the highest ecclesiastics and placed restrictions on their use by the laity, they were widely popular in all parts of Europe, especially for men's attire. Ermine, sable, and marten were among the most esteemed.

The fur trade played an important role in the exploration and settlement of North America. Patents of discovery and charters to early settlements frequently mentioned "trade in furs," and much interior exploration resulted from the search for furs, especially by French trappers and traders who penetrated to the Mississippi.

North American fur trade

The English Hudson's Bay Company entered the fur trade in the latter half of the 17th century, eventually spreading its trading posts and interests from Vancouver, British Columbia, to Prince Edward Island and northward to the Arctic Ocean.

The fur trade of the 18th and early 19th centuries, involving extensive barter with Indian trappers, was a profitable business. The supply of furs appeared inexhaustible, and the demand grew steadily as the Industrial Revolution in Britain and western Europe created new wealth and a desire for more goods.

Russian fur trappers and hunters in the meantime pressed eastward; at the beginning of the 18th century they were active in the Kamchatka area in eastern Siberia. Fur trading was a Russian government monopoly under which the crown acquired all furs, including sable, ermine, and sea otter, at modest prices. Following the discovery of the breeding islands of the sea otter, these animals were almost exterminated by hunters. The northern fur seal population of the newer hunting grounds of Alaska was also greatly reduced by excessive hunting.

In the 20th century the Soviet Union, the United States, and Canada were among the world's major suppliers, and the United States was the leading consumer. The need for conservation measures, especially among endangered species, gained increasing recognition in the late 1960s and early 1970s.

PELT CHARACTERISTICS

Fur pelts are animal skins with the hair forming the body covering remaining intact. The true furs consist of a soft, dense undercoat, called ground hair, underhair, or underwool, and a longer protective covering called guard hair or top hair. The pelts of certain animals, lacking either guard or ground hair, are not true furs, although used commercially as furs. Persian lamb, for example, sold as a fur, has only underwool and no guard hairs; monkey fur has guard hairs but no underhair. Mink, with its dense ground hair and long, glossy guard hair, is an example of a true fur. The Table gives pelt characteristics for the major furs used commercially and also indicates the chief countries of origin for each.

Fur pelts

The skin is composed of a lower layer, or dermis, consisting mainly of connective tissue, toughened during processing to form the leather; and the upper layer, or epidermis, composed mainly of nonliving cells. The epidermis is removed during processing.

Effects of seasons. Furbearing animals in northern regions produce their fullest coats in response to shortening day length prior to the cold season, when they will require protection from the cold. The fur becomes denser and glossier, reaching its peak quality by the time the heavy frosts begin. The animal also stores up a layer of fat beneath the skin from earlier feeding and, as food becomes scarce, metabolizes the fat to obtain energy. In mild winters, with food supplies remaining available, the animal does not use up the fat layer. Furbearers in cold climates produce long, lustrous hair and thin, somewhat weak skin; warm climates produce shorter, coarser, less dense hair and thicker, stiffer skin.

In spring, with a full coat no longer required for warmth, the animal begins to shed its fur, and the skin toughens. By summer, with much of the ground and guard hair lost, the coat colour becomes dull, and the remaining hair coarsens. At the end of summer, with little reserve fatty tissue remaining, the skin takes on a bluish colour. Fur pelts taken at this period are described as "blue pelts." With the return of colder temperatures, the bluish colour gradually fades, and the skin becomes clear, creamy in colour, and more supple. Ground and guard hairs have the greatest amount of colour pigment in the summer and are lightest in colour during late winter and in the spring.

Pelt nomenclature. The various divisions of fur pelts, as used in the fur industry, are identified in Figure 1. The term grotzen refers to the centre back strip, usually darker than other areas, dividing the pelt into two large sec-

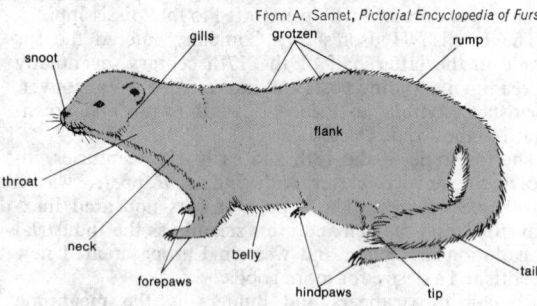

From A. Samet, *Pictorial Encyclopedia of Furs*

Figure 1: Pelt sections used in the fur industry.

tions. It is usually the coarsest portion, and when the hair is very long and coarse, it may protrude, as in the wolf.

THE FUR INDUSTRY

Furs traded commercially originate from both wild sources and fur farms (or ranches), with the greatest proportion obtained by farming. The 1970–71 world production of mink pelts, for example, accounting for about 60–70 percent of the world's fur trade, was approximately 25,492,000, with 25,062,000 from ranches and only 430,000 from wild sources. Countries producing over 1,000,000 ranch pelts included the Soviet Union (5,800,000), the United States (5,000,000), Denmark (3,900,000), Finland (2,900,000), Norway (2,400,000), Sweden (1,650,000), and Canada (1,300,000). The leading wild mink sources were the United States (250,000), Canada (100,000), and the Soviet Union (70,000).

Wild sources. Wild furs for commercial use are obtained from over 80 countries distributed on all six continents, but they come mainly from cold climates where the temperature ensures the growth of thick, luxuriant fur. North America has the greatest variety of furbearers, with 40 different indigenous types.

Endan-
gered
species

In the late 1960s and early 1970s, both individual governments and international organizations became concerned about the possible extinction of endangered species, and some countries enacted legislation restricting or

prohibiting commercial use of certain furbearing animals. Such animals included spider monkeys from Guatemala and Costa Rica and squirrel monkeys from Costa Rica; Canada's northern kit fox; the giant otter of the Amazon Basin; the southern fur seal of Peru, Argentina, and Ecuador; the Mediterranean monk seal, native to countries of the Mediterranean area; the Asiatic cheetah of the Soviet Union, Afghanistan, Iran, and Saudi Arabia; the Spanish lynx, native to Spain; India's Asiatic lion; the Sinai leopard of Sinai and Saudi Arabia; the Amur leopard of Korea and the Soviet Union; the Barbary leopard, found in Morocco, Algeria, and Tunisia; the Bali, Javan, and Sumatran tigers of Indonesia; and the Caspian tiger, native to Afghanistan and Iran.

Wild furbearing animals are usually caught with baited traps. Trapping in most of the world is licensed by, and subject to, control of state, provincial, or other governmental agencies, and, in order to preserve a reservoir of animals, the season in which animals may be trapped and the numbers that can be taken are generally restricted.

Trapping is usually practiced during the season in which the fur reaches its prime. The kind and size of trap employed depends on the animal to be taken, its habitat, and weather conditions. Traps are usually dyed and treated with orange shellac or a mixture of asphalt and varnish, making them less noticeable to the animals. The choice of lure depends upon the animal to be taken. Fox urine, for example, is a common fox lure.

The traps, concealed in areas frequented by the animal, are secured by chains attached to stakes, trees, or large stones. Muskrat and mink traps are often set underwater to drown the trapped animal quickly.

Fur farming. Fur farming, the keeping and breeding of animals for their pelts, is an ancient practice. Although livestock techniques were generally adapted, certain problems peculiar to the raising of wild species under confinement required special research.

An early research station was established by the Canadian government, in cooperation with the Canadian National Silver Fox Breeders Association, at Summerside, Prince Edward Island, in 1920, and a United States experimental station was started at Saratoga Springs, New York, in 1923, moving in 1953 to Ithaca, New York, where it functioned in cooperation with Cornell University. By 1940 the U.S. government was involved in cooperative research programs with several colleges and universities, with some stations concentrating on diseases of furbearing animals. The United States fur fibre laboratory at Beltsville, Maryland, became involved in studies on fur fibre origin, development, and growth. Several Canadian provinces have undertaken furbearing animal research. Sweden, Norway, and Denmark began similar research as the importance of fur farming in their economies increased.

Although the quality of early pelts was not as fine as that of the wild types, research eventually resulted in improved techniques of management, feeding, and breeding, producing many of the most desirable furs available. Thousands of mutations resulted from controlled matings of animals in captivity (see also ANIMAL BREEDING).

Fox farming. The silver fox, especially popular in the late 1930s and early 1940s, is a mutation of a red fox, with the reddish-orange colour replaced by black, and the white band on the guard hairs giving a silvery effect. Silver foxes obtained by trapping were nearly black, but controlled mating over a 20-year period produced the bright silver fox, with extremely wide white bands and the black portions free from the original rusty brown. Because the black colour is dependent upon a single genetic recessive factor, the mating of black or silver foxes always produces silver-black foxes. Such matings are rare in the wild state, and only a small percentage of wild foxes are of the silver type.

The breeding of silver foxes in captivity, first accomplished on Prince Edward Island in 1894, was at first carried on with much secrecy. After an especially beautiful silver fox skin brought £580 (nearly $3,000) at auction in London, and other skins commanded high prices

Silver fox

in Europe and the United States, the cost of breeding stock rose rapidly. A pair of foxes worth $3,000 in 1910 jumped to $35,000 in 1913, and extensive speculation developed even for options on newborn pups.

At first, any odd-coloured fox pups in a litter were discarded for fear that the purity of the stock would be questioned. Later, enterprising fox farmers eventually mated these pups, developing such profitable mutant colours as white, platinum, pearl, and blue.

Pair, or monogamous, mating of foxes was at first deemed necessary to obtain the desired colour, but polygamous breeding eventually became common. Foxes produce one litter per year, whelped after a gestation period of 49–55 days. An average of four young per litter is considered satisfactory. At about seven months of age the pups weigh from 10 to 15 pounds (four to seven kilograms). They are pelted in November and December of the first year, and those pups selected for the herd are bred during late winter and early spring of the following year.

Peak production of silver and other mutation fox skins was reached in 1939, with the United States, Canada, and the Scandinavian countries being the major producers. By the early 1950s production of silver fox pelts was drastically reduced as mink became more fashionable, and many fox farmers reduced their operations or changed to mink. In the early 1970s, however, there was a trend toward renewed importance of fox as a fashionable fur.

Mink ranching. Minks, raised in captivity for their fur as early as 1866, were not produced in quantity until about 1930 but have grown steadily in popularity, accounting for about 75 percent of the fur trade by the early 1960s.

Mature female minks weigh about one and one-half or two pounds, and the males weigh about four pounds. Minks can be bred when about 11 months old, and mating, commonly polygamous, is usually in March. Because there is a varying time of delayed implantation of the embryos, the gestation period varies from 40 to 76 days, with a litter average of four considered satisfactory. Pelting takes place about the last of November.

Much of the increased popularity of mink fur has resulted from the development of such mutant colours as

Major Furs in Commercial Use

	chief countries of origin	pelt characteristics		chief countries of origin	pelt characteristics
Badger	Asia, Europe, North America	long, white ground hair; coarse, white guard hair with blackish-brown or pale brown bands; good wearing qualities	Silver fox	North America, Europe, Asia	mutation of red fox; usually ranch-bred; blue-black ground hair; silvery guard hair with black base, white centre portion, and black tip
Baum Marten (see *Marten*)			Guanaco or its young, the guanaquito	southern South America	dense, soft, fawn-coloured fur
Beaver	North America	glossy tan to dark brown colour; dense, silky, medium length ground hair; guard hair is coarse and frequently removed; good wearing qualities; medium weight	Hamster, black-bellied	Europe, Asia	flat yellow-brown fur with black markings; fairly thick ground hair and longer, somewhat scant guard hair; good wearing qualities
Broadtail (see *Lamb*)			Karakul (breed name; see *Lamb*)		
Calf, young of the ox	Northern Hemisphere	short, thick, dark hair; frequently sheared and dyed to resemble such flat furs as pony or leopard; poor wearing qualities	Kid, young of the goat	Asia, Africa	short, black, gray, or white hair, usually curly or wavy; no ground hair; frequently dyed; poor wearing qualities; thin leather
Chinchilla	South America (Andes mountains); also raised on ranches in the U.S.	fine, soft, lustrous, bluish-gray fur; short to medium length; fragile, lightweight; luxury fur	Kolinsky (yellow weasel)	U.S.S.R. (Siberia), China, Korean peninsula, Japan	yellow-brown with short, fine ground hair and long, silky guard hair; frequently dyed brown; fair to good wearing qualities; lightweight
Civet cat (or civet)	Africa	short, thick, dark ground hair; silky, black guard hair with white markings; fair to good wearing qualities	Lamb, young of the sheep		woolly ground hair; no guard hair; wavy or curly
Coney (see *Rabbit*)			Broadtail	Turkistan, Afghanistan, Southwest Africa	very young or unborn karakul lamb; flat, lustrous hair with curl not yet formed; waviness produces moiré effect; thin leather; poor to fair wearing qualities
Coypu (see *Nutria*)					
Ermine	Europe, Asia, U.S.S.R. (Siberia)	white colour, some species turning tan in summer; white fur is sometimes dyed brown or bleached; poor to fair wearing qualities, lightweight, luxury fur; Soviet ermine has most dense fur and commands highest price	Broadtail processed lamb	Argentina	sheared, pressed, and dyed to resemble broadtail; fair to good wearing qualities
Fisher	North America	dark brown ground hair; long, black, lustrous guard hair; good wearing qualities	Indian lamb	India	curled and lustrous white, gray, or black hair; sometimes dyed beige or brown; pelts light in weight
Fox		soft, dense, fine ground hair; long guard hair; lower grades have coarser hair; poor to fair wearing qualities	Karakul, or caracul, lamb	U.S.S.R., China	short to long, glossy, curled or wavy hair; white, brown, or black colour; poor to fair wearing qualities
Arctic fox (blue fox, white fox)	frigid zone of North America, Greenland, Iceland, Europe, Asia	blue fox combines gray, brown, and blue or may have gray ground hair with brown guard hair; white fox is more delicate and is often dyed various shades	Mouton-dyed lamb (process)	North America, South Africa, South America	unkinked, dyed, and sheared to resemble beaver; also dyed novelty colours
Black fox	North America, Europe	mutation of red fox; bluish-black or brownish-black in colour; usually ranch-bred	Persian lamb	Turkistan, Afghanistan, Southwest Africa	fur of very young lambs; lustrous and tightly curled; gray, brown, or black colour; may be dyed for uniformity; poor to good wearing qualities
Cross fox	North America, Europe, Asia	mutation of red fox; yellowish to orange in colour with darker marking forming cross on spine and shoulders; frequently dyed	Lapin (see *Rabbit*)		
Kit fox	North America	soft, creamy yellow ground hair and white top hair; sometimes dyed grayish-blue	Leopard	Africa, Ceylon	short, flat, silky guard hair; tawny or buff colour with black or dark brown rosettes; good wearing qualities
Red fox	throughout Northern Hemisphere, North Africa, Australia	colour pale to deep red, with darker shades preferred; frequently dyed	Lynx	North America, northern Europe, Asia	soft, long, silky ground and guard hair; grayish-buff to tawny colour with darker markings; sometimes dyed pale blue, pale brown, or black

Mink
mutations

pale brown, medium brown, white, and a very dark brown sometimes described as black. The pelts of new mutations are usually the most costly, since the number of skins available is quite low until sufficient offspring can be bred to meet the demand.

Chinchilla raising. During the early 1900s many wild chinchillas were trapped for their fur, eventually leading to a scarcity. Chinchilla farming began at that time, and 50 years later more than 500,000 chinchillas were being raised in captivity in the United States, one-fourth as many in Canada, and a small number in other countries.

Until 1954, operations were largely in selling breeding stock. In June of that year, however, the first auction of a large quantity of chinchilla pelts from ranch-raised animals was held. The fur is marketed through associations of breeders such as the Empress Chinchilla Breeders of America, Inc., or through United Chinchilla Associates. Chinchilla is a luxury fur, extremely soft, fine, and silky, and blue-gray in colour, and may have varying widths of white bands on the guard hair.

Marten farming. Martens, forest fur animals closely related to the sable, weigh from one and one-half to three pounds at maturity. Many attempts to raise martens in captivity have failed because only about 15–20 percent of the females produce young.

Martens breed in July and August and, after several months of delayed implantation, whelp in April. The delay in implantation can be shortened by artificial lighting, simulating early spring conditions and causing the martens to whelp in December instead of April.

Other fur animals. Karakul sheep and somewhat similar breeds of sheep, raised in the Soviet Union and the Middle Eastern countries for hundreds of years, produce the desirable black Persian lambskins and similar types. The best pelts are obtained from newborn lambs, for at that age the curl is in its prime. Southwest Africa produces several million Persian lambskins annually. These sheep were developed after many years of selective mating of Karakul rams to progeny originating from white sheep. Selected skins from white lambs are sheared and usually dyed to be sold as mouton.

The farming of several other fur animals has been initiated but has not materialized commercially because of availability of furs from the wild supply. Among these

Major Furs in Commercial Use (continued)

	chief countries of origin	pelt characteristics		chief countries of origin	pelt characteristics
Marmot	U.S.S.R., Mongolia	brownish to black fur; frequently dyed brown with darker tips to resemble mink; poor to fair wearing qualities	Pony, young of the horse	Europe, South America	lustrous, flat guard hair; no ground hairs; may have moiré-like pattern; frequently dyed black or bleached and dyed tan; poor to fair wearing qualities
Marten		dense underfur with long, stiff, glossy guard hair			
American marten	North America	colour ranges from blue-black through various brown shades to a pale yellow that is usually dyed; medium length fur; fair wearing qualities	Rabbit	regions throughout the world	white, gray, brown, fawn, black, or mottled fur; frequently plucked and dyed to resemble other furs, or in novelty colours; poor to fair wearing qualities
Baum marten	Europe, Asia Minor, Asia	yellowish-brown colour; frequently dyed deep brown; fair wearing qualities	Raccoon	North America, South America	long fur, gray to black colour, sometimes with reddish tint; good wearing qualities; heavy weight
Stone marten	Europe, Asia Minor, Asia	grayish-white ground hair and dark brown guard hair; good wearing qualities	Sable	U.S.S.R. (Siberia)	bluish-black or brown colour; dense ground hair and long, silky, lustrous guard hair; fair wearing qualities; medium weight; luxury fur; finest type is called crown sable
Mink	North America, Europe	colour ranges from very dark brown through reddish-brown and also includes various mutant colours; dense, short, fine ground hair; lustrous guard hair; good wearing qualities; fairly lightweight; luxury fur	Seal, fur	U.S. (Alaska), South Africa, South America, Japan, U.S.S.R. (Siberia)	frequently dyed black or brown with black tips; guard hairs are coarse and usually removed
Mole	Europe	gray to black colour with fine, soft, lustrous ground and guard hairs that are of similar length; poor wearing quality; lightweight	Seal, hair	North America, Scandinavia	bluish-black colour; some types have white blotches giving a mottled effect; sometimes dyed brown; no ground hair; flat, wiry guard hair
Mouton (see *Lamb*)			Seal, harp	North Atlantic and Arctic oceans	very young animals have fluffy white fur; adults have light grayish or yellowish, flat, coarse guard hair and no ground hair
Muskrat	North America, U.S.S.R.	soft, dense, gray ground hair; long, lustrous, stiff, dark brown guard hair; fair to good wearing qualities; medium weight			
Nutria (coypu)	U.S., South America	short, dense, dark bluish-brown ground hair; stiff guard hairs are usually plucked; fair wearing qualities	Skunk	North America, South America	dense, bluish-black ground hair; long, glossy guard hair; two white stripes extend down the pelt back; frequently plucked and dyed; good wearing qualities; heavy weight
Ocelot	Mexico, Central America, South America	flat fur with short ground hair and little guard hair; black markings on tawny-yellow or gray ground; poor to fair wearing qualities	Squirrel	U.S.S.R. (Siberia)	lustrous, fluffy steel-blue fur, sometimes with red streaks; frequently dyed; long, dense ground hair and slightly longer, silky guard hair; poor to fair wearing qualities; lightweight
Opossum	North America, South America, Australasia	yellowish-brown or gray colour; medium length, coarse fur; fair to good wearing qualities; medium weight	Weasel	throughout Northern Hemisphere	pure white fur in winter, turning yellowish in spring and brown in summer; frequently dyed beige or brown; short, thick fur; fair to good wearing qualities
Otter	regions throughout the world	dense, fine, short, ground hair is gray, medium brown, or dark brown in colour; the stiff, long, silvery guard hairs have lighter tips; frequently plucked and dyed; good wearing qualities; medium weight	Wolf	throughout Northern Hemisphere	long-haired fur with dense ground hair; off-white, yellowish, brownish-gray, or black colour; frequently dyed gray, brown, or black; fair to good wearing qualities; heavy weight
Otter, sea	U.S. (Alaska), U.S.S.R. (Siberia)	light brown to black colour with sprinkling of white hairs; silky-textured ground and guard hairs	Wolverine	North America, U.S.S.R. (Siberia)	blackish or bluish-brown colour with tan stripe on sides; coarse texture; good wearing qualities
Persian lamb (see *Lamb*)					

are beaver, nutria, fisher, muskrat, fitch, raccoon, and skunk. The potential of such farming depends upon the demand created by fashion trends and the development of new and desirable colours.

Rabbit skins from animals raised in hutches primarily for their meat have been used in the fur trade from time to time. Selected skins from the older animals of Europe have proved satisfactory in the natural state or sheared and dyed, but only a small percentage of the skins from the eight-week-old "fryer" rabbits in the United States are suitable for fur garments. Very few rabbits are raised primarily for their fur.

Collection and distribution. Many fur skins are delivered or sold to collecting agents, who sell them to merchants in various fur centres. Skin merchants maintain stocks of furs, selling to manufacturers or retail furriers. Most raw fur skins, however, are shipped to auction houses, which act as marketing agents, offering the skins at public auction to skin merchants, manufacturers, and commission brokers who buy for merchants and manufacturers. The auction houses receive fees based on the prices paid at auction.

Major fur auction centres are in New York City, London, Leningrad, and Montreal. Regular auctions of secondary importance are held in Greenville, S.C., where dressed fur sealskins are sold semi-annually; Seattle, Wash.; Minneapolis, Minn.; Winnipeg, Man.; Edmonton, Alta.; Vancouver, B.C.; Regina, Sask.; Copenhagen, Den.; Oslo, Nor.; and Stockholm, Swed. Melbourne and Sydney are the main centres for rabbit skin auctions, which are also held in London. The Hudson's Bay Company is the dominant fur-collecting organization and marketing agent in the world, with auction houses in London, Montreal, and New York City. The London Public Sales holds major auctions in the spring, summer, autumn, and winter.

The major auctions in London, New York, and Montreal draw an international audience and often last a week or longer. The Leningrad sales, held in January, July, and October, are conducted by Soyushpushnina, an official Soviet agency, which buys the skins from state and collective farms and controls domestic and foreign marketing.

Fur processing. *Fur dressing.* Fur skins are dressed to make them suitable for use. The fur dresser aims at the creation of a soft, pliable leather; the removal of superfluous matter from the pelt; and the preservation and enhancement of the natural lustre of the fur. The details of

the process vary with the nature and condition of the skin treated, but there are usually at least four distinct stages in the operation. First, there is the preliminary cleaning and softening of the pelt; then fleshing (removal of fleshy matter from the skin) and stretching; then leathering, a tanning process that results in the formation of a leather on the skin (see also LEATHER AND HIDES); and then a final cleaning. Separate processes in the fur dresser's art are unhairing, or plucking (the removal of guard hairs where necessary); shaving of the leather side to decrease weight, impart suppleness, and improve draping qualities; and sometimes shearing of the ground hair of such furs as fur seal, muskrat, raccoon, and beaver to achieve a desired depth.

Though it originated in a primitive and haphazard manner, modern fur dressing is a highly developed process that requires considerable mechanical equipment. The largest fur processing centre is in New York.

Fur dyeing. Fur dyeing is an ancient art, but its modern development began in the latter part of the 19th century with the development of chemical compounds known as fur bases. Before that period fur was mainly dyed with vegetable or mineral colouring matters, but the fur bases have largely superseded the older materials because of their simplified application. The use of synthetic compounds has enabled fur dyers to produce a wider variety of colours, leading to the use of many skins that are unattractive in their natural colours but that can be dressed and dyed to make attractive furs. Furs may be bleached to eliminate yellowish colour in white pelts, to lighten colour so that pelts may be dyed light shades, or to eliminate natural colour that would interfere with a desired shade in dyeing. They may also be tipped, or top blended, a process in which the guard hairs, and sometimes the ground hairs, are lightly brushed with a dyestuff. New colours are an important selling point among fur retailers, making possible such shades as blonde, beige, charcoal and platinum gray, blue, white, and even pink and red, in addition to the traditional browns and blacks of natural furs and the various mutation colours developed in such furs as minks. Innovations made possible by the fur processor's art have produced changes in the handling of furs. For example, the long-haired, brown raccoon coat of the 1920s became a sheared, lighter weight fur available in blonde, beige, or white, as well as the natural colour. Dyers often keep their techniques secret, guarding them from competitors.

Europe's chief dyeing centres are in France, Belgium,

Auction centres

Bleaching

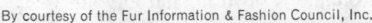
By courtesy of the Fur Information & Fashion Council, Inc.

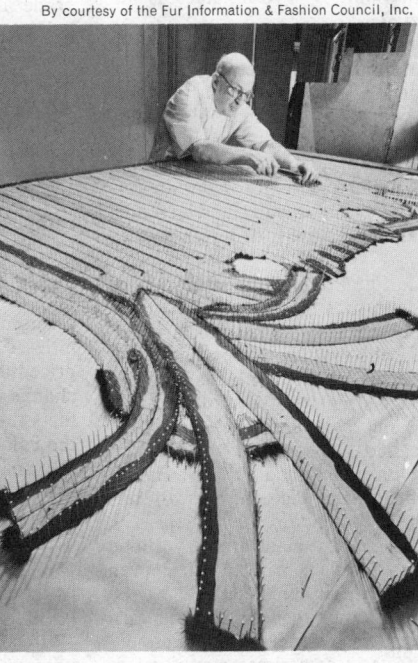

Figure 2: *Fur manufacture techniques.*
(Left) A cutter performing the first step in the letting-out technique of slicing the skin into diagonal strips. (Right) Wetted skins nailed down to dry in the exact shape required for the finished coat.

and London. Leipzig was the major centre until after World War II, when its experts relocated in Frankfurt, London, and New York.

Fur manufacturing. Furriery, the production of fur garments, has progressed from primitive methods of sewing skins together to a highly skilled and intricate process. Fashion influences both the popularity of specific furs and the design of fur garments. Designs are created by custom furriers, by stylists working for individual manufacturers, and by commercial designers who sell patterns to manufacturers and retailers. Fur manufacturing remains, essentially, a handicraft industry. The cutter, for example, matches pelts according to colour and quality in order to achieve uniformity of colour and texture in the finished garment and also cuts the skins to conform to the designer's pattern with a minimum of wastage. Sewing, performed on power-driven machines, requires much skill.

There are two main types of fur manufacture, the letting-out method and the skin-on-skin method.

Letting-out process. This technique, usually applied to mink, is employed to accentuate length, minimize width, and improve draping qualities. It involves slicing every skin into diagonal strips one-eighth to one-quarter inch in width and sewing the strips together to make a longer and narrower skin that will run the full length of the garment without seams showing on the fur side (see Figure 2, left). In recent years the letting-out process has been used with furs other than mink, such as nutria, sheared raccoon, and beaver, but with modifications to enhance the beauty of the particular fur.

Skin-on-skin process. The less costly skin-on-skin method consists of sewing one full skin adjacent to another in a uniform alignment. This method is sometimes employed to sew the leftovers of full skins, such as paws and flanks, into blanket-like "plates" that are then fashioned into garments.

Finishing operations. After the skins are prepared by the cutter, they are made up into sections that are dampened, then stretched and nailed to fit a pattern on a wooden nailing board and dried on the form (see Figure 2, right). The dried sections are then sewn together.

Glazing

In the glazing operation that follows, the fur is again dampened, and the hair is arranged in the desired direction by mechanical means. Gums and similar materials are applied to hold the hairs in position, and the fur is slowly dried. The setting materials frequently increase the lustre of the fur.

After this treatment, the lining is sewn in, and any additional sewing is completed.

Retail distribution. Fur manufacturers distribute their products by selling to retailers or to wholesalers who sell to retailers. Custom furriers design and manufacture garments for sale to the consumer and may also carry stocks of ready-to-wear furs. Apparel specialty stores and department stores often carry ready-to-wear furs as part of a general stock. Retailers usually maintain fur-servicing departments that clean, repair, and remodel garments for customers and also store furs in refrigerated vaults.

In the United States, the Fur Products Labeling Act of 1951, amended in 1961, requires that the animal name and country of origin be specified on the labels of all furs. Garments made of pelts that have been altered to resemble another fur must be labelled with the name of the actual pelt used. A garment made of Canadian muskrat that has been sheared and dyed black to resemble fur seal can no longer be called Hudson seal but must be labelled "dyed muskrat; origin: Canada." Government regulations in other countries vary but are generally less stringent than those of the United States.

Man-made synthetic furs, usually made from synthetic fibre blends, increasingly simulate natural furs, even duplicating the ground and guard hairs. Usually woven or knitted to a backing, they are either dyed in the yarn stage or printed with colour in the fabric stage. Less expensive than natural furs, and sometimes combined in garments with furs, they are not considered luxury products.

BIBLIOGRAPHY. F.G. ASHBROOK, *Furs Glamorous and Practical* (1954), discusses the history, sources, uses, design, and care of furs. MAX BACHRACH, *Fur*, 3rd ed. (1953), is an extensively illustrated work describing furbearing animals, the classification of their furs, the determination of fur pelt quality, fur dressing and dyeing methods, and the use of microscopy in the study of fur fibres. ARTHUR SAMET, *Pictorial Encyclopedia of Furs*, rev. ed. (1950), with 600 illustrations, provides a comprehensive treatment of the fur industry, including geographical origin of furs, seasonal changes in furbearers, fur manufacturing, and fur care and handling. WILLIAM E. AUSTIN, *Fur Dressing and Fur Dyeing* (1922), treats the various phases of fur dressing and the techniques of fur dyeing, including related equipment and the various fur dyes. *Fur Age Weekly* is a trade publication for the fur industry.

(O.Gi.)

Futures

Origins and development

From very early times, and in many lines of trade, buyers and sellers have found it advantageous to enter into contracts—termed futures contracts—calling for delivery of a commodity at a later date. Dutch whalers in the 16th century entered into forward sales contracts before sailing, partly to finance their voyage and partly to get a better price for their product. Potato growers in Maine in the U.S. from early times made forward sales of potatoes at planting time. The European futures markets arose out of import trade. Cotton importers in Liverpool, for example, entered forward contracts with U.S. exporters from around 1840. With the introduction of the fast transatlantic Cunard mail services, it became possible for cotton exporters in the United States to send samples to Liverpool in advance of the slow cargo ships, which carried the bulk of the cotton. Futures trading within the United States in the form of "to arrive" contracts appears to have commenced before the railroad days (1850s) in Chicago. Merchants in Chicago who bought wheat from outlying territories were not sure when they would obtain delivery or what their quality would be. Under these conditions, the introduction of "to arrive" contracts enabled the sellers to get a better price for their product and buyers to avoid serious price risk.

Futures trading of this sort in grains, coffee, cotton and oilseeds also arose in other centres such as Antwerp, Amsterdam, Bremen, Le Havre, Alexandria and Osaka between the 17th and the middle of the 19th centuries. In the process of evolution, "to arrive" contracts became standardized with respect to grade and delivery period, with allowances for grade adjustment when the delivered grade happened to be different. These developments helped to enlarge the volume of trade, encouraging more trading by merchants who dealt in the physical commodity and also the entry of speculators, who were interested not in the commodity itself but in the favourable movement of its price in order to make profits. The larger volume of trading lowered the transaction costs, and by stages the trading became impersonal. The rise of the clearing house depersonalized the buyer-seller relations completely, giving rise to the present form of futures trading.

ECONOMIC FUNCTIONS OF THE FUTURES CONTRACT

Commodity futures markets provide insurance opportunities to merchants and processors against the risk of price fluctuation. In the case of a trader, an adverse price change brought either by supply or demand change affects the total value of his commitments; and the larger the value of his inventory, the larger the risk to which he is exposed. The futures market provides a mechanism for the trader to lower the per unit inventory risk on his commitments in the cash market (where actual physical delivery of the commodity must eventually be made) through what is known as hedging. A trader is termed a hedger if his commitments in the cash market are offset by opposite commitments in the futures market. An example would be that of a grain elevator operator who buys wheat in the country and at the same time sells a futures contract for the same quantity of wheat. When his wheat is delivered later to the terminal market or to the processor in a normal market, he buys back his futures contract. Any change of price that occurred during the interval should have been cancelled out by mutually compensatory movements in his cash and futures holdings. The hedger thus hopes to protect himself against loss resulting from price changes by transferring the risk to a speculator who relies upon his skill in forecasting price movements.

For a better understanding of the process involved, the distinctive features of the cash market and the futures market should be made clear. The cash market may be either a spot market concerned with immediate physical delivery of the specified commodity or a forward market, where the delivery of the specified commodity is made at some later date. Futures markets, on the other hand, generally permit trading in a number of grades of the commodity to protect hedger sellers from being "cornered" by speculator buyers who might otherwise insist on delivery of a particular grade whose stocks are small. Since a number of alternative grades can be tendered, the futures market is not suitable for the acquisition of the physical commodity. For this reason, physical delivery of the commodities in fulfillment of the futures contract generally does not take place, and the contract is usually settled between buyers and sellers by paying the difference between the buying and selling price. Several futures contracts in a commodity are traded during a year. Thus, five wheat contracts, July, September, December, March, and May, and six soybean contracts, September, November, January, March, May and July are traded on the Board of Trade of the City of Chicago. The length of these contracts is for a period of about ten months, and a contract for "September wheat" or "September soybean" indicates the month the contract matures.

Hedging as insurance

Though hedging is a form of insurance, it seldom provides perfect protection. The insurance is based on the fact that the cash and futures prices move together and are well correlated. The price spread between the cash and futures, however, is not invariant. The hedgers, therefore, run the risk that the price spread, known as the "basis," could move against them. The possibility of such an unfavourable movement in the basis is known as basis risk. Thus hedgers, through their commitment in the futures market, substitute basis risk for the price risk they would have taken in carrying unhedged stocks. It must be emphasized, however, that risk reduction is not the final objective with merchants and processors; what they seek to do is to maximize profits.

The availability of capital for financing the holding of inventories depends on whether they are hedged or not. The bankers' willingness to finance them increases with the proportion of the inventory that is hedged. For example, the banks may advance loans to the extent of only 50 percent of the value of unhedged inventories and 90 percent if they are all hedged, a difference explained by the fact that hedging reduces the risk on which the amount of the loan and the interest rate depend. Merchants and processors can therefore derive a twofold advantage from futures trading; they can insure against price decline and they can secure larger and cheaper loans from the banks.

THE THEORY AND PRACTICE OF HEDGING

There are two rival hypotheses concerning the motives for and costs of hedging. The first of these, advanced by John Maynard Keynes and J.R. Hicks, suggests that risk reduction is the prime motive for hedging and that hedgers pay a risk premium to speculators for assuming risk. The Keynes-Hicks hypothesis states that under normal conditions in commodity markets, when demand, supply, and spot prices are expected to remain unchanged for some months to come and there is uncertainty in traders' minds regarding these expectations, the futures price, say, for one month's delivery is bound to be below the spot price that traders expect to prevail one month later. This condition exists because inventory holders would be ready to hedge themselves from the risk of price fluctuations by selling futures to speculators below the expected spot price. By selling futures below the expected spot price, according to the theory, inventory holders who hedge pay a risk premium to speculators.

The rival hypothesis of Holbrook Working maintains that hedging is done with the expectation of a profit from a favourable change in the spot-futures price relation, to simplify business decisions, and to cut costs, and not for the sake of reducing risk alone. Hedgers, according to Working, are arbitrageurs; *i.e.*, they take advantage of a temporary price difference between two markets to buy in one and sell in the other. They thus speculate on the basis and assume risk.

A compromise between these rival theories and a more balanced view regarding the need for hedging and the scope of hedging activities is that hedging is motivated by the desire to reduce risks, as suggested by the Keynes-Hicks theory, but that the levels of inventory held by merchants and processors are determined by expected hedging profits, as Working has emphasized.

The long and short hedger

There are two categories of hedgers in the futures market: they are called short and long hedgers. Short hedgers are merchants and processors who acquire inventories of the commodity in the spot market and who simultaneously sell an equivalent amount or less in the futures market. The hedgers in this case are said to be long on their spot transaction and short in the futures transaction. Wheat merchants or wheat flour mills who either have 100,000 bushels of wheat as inventory or have bought it for later delivery are said to short hedge if they sell 100,000 bushels of wheat in futures contracts. By holding inventories, both merchants and processors can make their purchases when it is most opportune and lower their transaction costs through fewer transactions. Another advantage to the processing firm in holding inventory is that it makes it possible to avoid interruption in production. It must be borne in mind that short hedgers do not normally deliver the physical commodity in fulfillment of the futures contract. They "lift the hedge" by repurchasing the futures contract at the prevailing futures price when they sell the raw material or the processed good in the spot market.

The merchants and processors do not generally hedge all their inventories for the sake of reduced risk. The decision on what part of inventories to hedge is based on their expectations relating to return from holding hedged and unhedged inventories in storage, given the cost incurred in both forms of inventory holding. The return per unit inventory to merchants and processors on their hedged inventories, when liquidated, is the change in the spot price less the change in the futures price and the storage costs. Their return on per unit unhedged inventory is the change in spot price less storage costs.

Long hedgers, in contrast, are merchants and processors who have made formal commitments to deliver a specified quantity of raw material or processed goods at a later date at a price currently agreed upon and who do not now have the stocks of the raw material necessary to fulfill their forward commitment. The parties who have made the commitment generally seek to hedge against the risk of price rise in the raw material between the time of making the forward contract and the time of acquiring the raw material stocks for fulfilling the contract. The hedging is done by buying futures contracts of the raw material equal in quantity to what is needed to fulfill the forward commitment.

The question arises under what circumstances the long hedger might prefer the purchase of futures to the alternative of immediately buying the raw material through spot or forward purchase to meet the obligations of his forward sale. He may prefer buying futures to buying in the cash market (spot or forward) if current cash prices are high because of scarcity. Generally there is an increase in the amount of long hedging when, as the season advances, spot prices rise, inventory holdings fall, and the new crop is not yet available. Long hedging is not as risk-reducing as it may appear at first sight. The long hedger processor, for example, who buys raw material futures to satisfy his forward commitment of the processed good may find that the raw material delivered to him in futures is not of suitable grade and quality to meet the obligations of the forward sale. Quite often, therefore, he may sell his futures contract and purchase raw material of the grade needed. If the spot price of the raw material moves unfavourably relative to the price of the processed good sold forward by him, the long hedger actually increases the risk by buying futures instead of buying the raw material in the cash market. Long hedging, unlike short hedging, may serve to increase risk, and the total risk on long hedging increases with the size of the commitment.

The volume of short hedging tends to be large when stocks in commercial hands are large and when the cash price is below the futures price; a reversal in this situation brings a decline. Conversely, the volume of long hedging is large when stocks are small and the cash price is above the futures price. Short hedging has a marked seasonal pattern, reaching a peak when commercial stocks are largest and the basis is favourable and then declining as the season advances. The seasonal pattern is less marked in long hedging. Generally there is an excess of short over long hedging during the bulk of the crop year.

The speculator's role
Apart from hedgers, the futures market includes speculators, and these can also be classified in two categories, namely, long and short speculators. The long speculators are those who expect the price to rise above the current level and assume risks by purchasing futures contracts. Short speculators are those who expect the price to fall. They sell futures contracts. In a futures market the total short selling position, made up of short hedgers and short speculators, and the total long buying position, made up of long hedgers and long speculators, must always be equal. Any excess of short over long hedging must be balanced by an equal excess of long over short speculation. Since short hedging exceeds long hedging for most of the crop year, hedgers are generally short and speculators, therefore, are generally long.

Futures markets have flourished and become important in commodities where sizeable inventories have to be stored and carried forward for meeting the consumption needs of the entire season. Successful futures trading requires a large volume with low transaction costs and that spot and futures prices be well correlated in order to make hedging effective.

IMPORTANT FUTURES MARKETS

Based on the number and volume of commodities in which active futures trading exists, the United States occupies first place. The Chicago Board of Trade, the largest of the world's futures markets in terms of volume and value of business, is the centre for trading in wheat, corn, oats, rye, soybeans, soybean oil, and soybean meal. About 30 commodities in all are traded on organized exchanges in the United States. The wheat market in Minneapolis, the cotton and wool markets in New York City, and the markets in frozen pork bellies and live hogs in the midwestern United States are among them. The number of commodities in which futures trading takes place are far fewer outside the United States.

There are futures markets for wool in London, Paris, and Sydney; for cotton in Liverpool and Bombay; for sugar in London and Paris; for jute goods in Calcutta; for black pepper in Cochin, India; and for turmeric in Sāngli, India. As a result of government controls on futures markets and also of international commodity agreements, the volume of futures trading in several countries has been adversely affected. The commodity markets in Europe, with few exceptions, have been dormant since the end of World War II. Many of the Indian commodity markets, such as those in gur, jute, and oilseeds, which were once active, have met the same fate. The recurrent arguments in the United States, India, and elsewhere against the futures markets are that they encourage speculation and that the participation of speculators causes price instability. These arguments have led to the demand that markets be controlled or prohibited from functioning. To refute such allegations requires a comparison between price variations in the presence and absence of speculation, which is impossible for commodities that have futures markets, since it is not meaningful to say for these markets what the price would have been in the absence of speculation.

BIBLIOGRAPHY. An extensive summary of available work on commodities and futures trading is provided by JAMES B. WOY, *Commodities Futures Trading: A Bibliographic Guide* (1976). Recent work on the specific methods and rules of the major world exchanges is included in BRIAN REIDY and JOHN EDWARDS, *Guide to World Commodity Markets*, 2nd ed. (1979). Basic works on commodity futures trading include GERALD GOLD, *Modern Commodity Futures Trading*, 4th ed., rev. (1966, © 1959); BRUCE G. GOULD, *The Dow-Jones-Irwin Guide to Commodities Trading* (1973); and RALPH M. AINSWORTH, *Basic Principles of Commodity Futures Speculation* (1979). Legal aspects of futures trading are addressed in the Corporate Law & Practice Handbook Series, *Commodities and Futures Trading, 1977* (1977). G. BLAU, "Some Aspects of the Theory of Futures Trading," *Rev. Econ. Stud.*, 12:1–30 (1944–45), a discussion of the purpose and organization of futures markets, reasons for carrying commodities over time, the relation between cash and futures prices, and the role of arbitrage; M.J. BRENNAN, "The Supply of Storage," *American Economic Review*, 48:50–72 (1958), theory of supply of storage in relation to risk premium; P.H. COOTNER, "Speculation and Hedging," *Food Res. Inst. Stud.*, suppl. to vol. 7, pp. 65–105 (1967), theory and practice of hedging and speculation; R.W. GRAY, "The Search For a Risk Premium," *J. Polit. Economy*, 69:250–260 (1961), surveys empirical tests of the Keynes-Hicks hypothesis; J.R. HICKS, *Value and Capital*, 2nd ed., pp. 135–142 (1946), theory of "normal backwardation" also known as the Keynes-Hicks hypothesis; H.S. HOUTHAKKER, "Scope and Limits of Futures Trading," in *The Allocation of Economic Resources*, pp. 134–159 (1959), discussion of the nature of uncertainty faced by individuals and groups, cash and futures markets, futures trading and hedging, and conditions of futures trading; "Can Speculators Forecast Prices?" *Rev. Econ. and Statistics*, 39:143–151 (1957), empirical study of profits and losses for large speculators, large hedgers, and small traders in the U.S.; J.M. KEYNES, *A Treatise on Money*, vol. 2 (1930), pp. 142–144, theory of "normal backwardation" formulated by Keynes; C.S. ROCKWELL, "Normal Backwardation, Forecasting and the Returns to Commodity Futures Traders," *Food Res. Inst. Stud.*, suppl. to vol. 7, pp. 107–130 (1967), empirical evidence on the returns to futures traders in large and small markets; L.G. TELSER, "Futures Trading and the Storage of Cotton and Wheat," *J. Polit. Economy*, 66:233–255 (1958), theory of storage in futures markets; "The Supply of Speculative Services in Wheat, Corn and Soybeans," *Food Res. Inst. Stud.*, suppl. to vol. 7, pp. 131–176 (1967), empirical investigation of returns to speculators and hedgers in the wheat, corn, and soybeans markets in the U.S.; H. WORKING, "Theory of the Inverse Carrying Charge in Futures Markets," *J. Farm Econ.*, 30:1–28 (1948), theory of inverse carrying charge seeking to explain futures market conditions when deferred futures are below the price of near futures, and futures price is below the spot price; "Futures Trading and Hedging," *Am. Econ. Rev.*, 43:314–343 (1953), theory that hedging is done for a variety of different reasons and not for reducing risk alone; and "New Concepts Concerning Futures Markets and Prices," *Am. Econ. Rev.*, 52:431–459 (1962), new concepts relating to futures markets that describe the role of hedging and the functions of futures markets.

(L.S.V.)

Gabon

The Gabonese Republic (République Gabonaise), on the west coast of Africa, sits astride the Equator, with a total area estimated at 103,347 square miles (267,667 square kilometres) and a population early in the 1980s estimated variously from 600,000 to 1,400,000. The republic is bordered by the Atlantic Ocean to the west, Equatorial Guinea and Cameroon to the north, and the People's Republic of the Congo to the south and east. The island state of São Tomé e Príncipe is situated off the coast. Gabon's capital has always been Libreville (or Freetown), named for the freed slaves who landed there after 1849.

Although it has been independent since 1960, Gabon—formerly one of the four colonies comprising French Equatorial Africa—has retained close economic, political, and cultural ties with France. One indication of this is that the French expatriate population has risen from about 6,000 in 1960 to more than 40,000 in 1980. France also purchases about 16 percent of Gabon's output of manganese and is sole purchaser of uranium from the country's mines. Gabon purchases more than 68 percent of its imports from France, and the former colonizing power is the republic's major source of aid. Blessed with their own rich and interesting cultures, the Gabonese nonetheless have a deep respect and affection for the language and culture of France.

Relations with neighbouring African countries are generally good, although the Gabonese have resented the presence of teachers, workers, and merchants from these states and from Benin. Gabon is a member of the Central African Economic and Customs Union, the Common Afro-Mauritian Organization, the Organization of African Unity, and other international organizations. Once a year, Gabon's president meets with the French head of state and other French-speaking African leaders in a Franco-African summit. Diplomatic relations are maintained with more than 30 countries. (For further historical aspects, see CENTRAL AFRICA, HISTORY OF.) (B.Wn.)

Modern history. Written records of the history of the Gabon region begin with the late 15th century. In about 1472 Portuguese navigators first arrived at the Gabon Estuary, which they named Gabão (Hooded Cloak) because of its shape. Soon afterward, Lopo Gonçalves rounded Cap Lopez, and in 1475 Ruy de Sequeira reached Cap St. Catherine, 100 miles to the south. Portuguese from São Tomé often visited the estuary coast to trade in hardwoods and ivory. In the 17th century the Dutch settled on Isla de Corisco, 37 miles north, from where they ravaged the Gabon Estuary. The coast also attracted the English and French, but the greater part of the region's trade remained with the Portuguese.

The slave trade, nominally abolished in the early 19th century, continued in the Gabon area until about 1880. Slaves from the interior were collected by coastal peoples and crowded into barracoons (temporary enclosures) on the coast to await the arrival of European ships. In 1839 Capt. L.-E. Bouet-Willaumez, a French naval officer in charge of antislavery patrols in the area, reached an agreement with King Denis, a local chief on the south bank of the Gabon Estuary. In 1841, Bouet-Willaumez also negotiated a treaty with King Louis that secured the north bank, where Fort-d'Aumale was built in 1843. Christian missions were established in 1842–44, and to a group of villages on the Gabon Estuary was added a small settlement of refugee slaves from the ship "Elizia"; together with the French fort, the settlement was named Libreville (Free Town) in 1849. In 1855 Paul B. du Chaillu, a U.S. citizen of French origin, was commissioned by the National Academy of Sciences in Philadelphia to explore the Gabon Estuary and its delta. His journeys, in the course of which he explored the valley of the Ogooué River, penetrated the Ngounie River to the Massif du Chaillu (Chaillu Mountains). The explorer A.M.A. Aymes in 1867 and the British trader R.B.N. Walker in 1873 attempted ascents of the Ogooué, the confluence of which with the Ivindo was reached in 1874 by Alfred Marche and L.E.H. Dupont, marquis de Compiègne. The source of the Ogooué was reached in 1877 by Pierre Savorgnan de Brazza, who in 1880 founded Franceville. A French governor was appointed to Gabon in 1886, and the area was attached to Congo Français (French Congo; 1897–1910) and then to Afrique Équatoriale Française (AEF: French Equatorial Africa). Its frontiers with Cameroon were delimited in 1885 and those with Spanish Guinea (later Equatorial Guinea) in 1900. Serious resistance to colonization by the Fang, Koto, and Mitshogo peoples lasted from 1905 until 1911.

During World War II, Free French troops took over Gabon from the Vichy government in 1940. In 1946 Gabon became an overseas territory of France with its own territorial assembly, to which elections under universal suffrage were first held in 1957. In 1958 the country became an autonomous republic within the French Community and, after concluding agreements with France, Gabon declared its independence on August 17, 1960.

The politics and government of the republic were initially dominated by Leon M'ba, who had been elected mayor of Libreville in 1956 and who was the leader of the Bloc Démocratique Gabonais (Democratic Bloc of Gabon) at the time of independence. He was elected to a seven-year

term as president in 1961, and he pursued policies of close cooperation with France and balanced economic development. M'ba's tendency toward the establishment of a one-party state gave rise to an unsuccessful coup led by the political opposition and the army in February 1964. After elections held two months later, the opposition party was outlawed.

M'ba was reelected in March 1967, but he died that November. The presidency passed to Albert-Bernard (now Omar) Bongo, who in 1968 declared Gabon to be a one-party state and created the Parti Démocratique Gabonais (PDG; Democratic Party of Gabon). Bongo was elected president in 1973 and reelected in 1979. He maintained the policies of steady economic growth and close relations with France, while expanding Gabon's diplomatic influence in Africa. (Ed.)

The landscape. *Relief and drainage.* The very narrow coastal plain—often no more than 20 miles (32 kilometres) wide in the south—is formed of sandstone and alluvium; northward it broadens to a width of 100 miles, with outcrops of chalk, limestone, and Cretaceous sandstone. North of the most westerly point, Cap Lopez, the contour of the coast is also more jagged than that in the south, since the Atlantic's northward–flowing Benguela Current, which softens the coastline by creating sandbars that cause lagoons to form at river mouths, is no longer effective here. Inland, the relief is characterized by a series of granite plateaus, ranging generally northeast to southeast and rising to heights of from 1,000 to 2,000 feet (300 to 600 metres). Further to the west and north, the Monts de Cristal (Crystal Mountains) surround the rolling hills associated with the Ivindo Basin and the Woleu and Ntem rivers. To the south, the Ogooué River drains through a sandstone saddleback before emptying into the lowlands through the granite formations of the Lambaréné region. Granite also forms the mountains of the Massif du Chaillu, Gabon's central watershed, south of the Ogooué, which rises to an elevation of approximately 3,000 feet, except where topped by the 3,215-foot (980-metre) height of Mont Iboundji.

Climate, vegetation, and animal life. Gabon is characterized by the heat and humidity typical of an equatorial region. Rainfall varies from an annual average of 120 inches (3,050 millimetres) at Libreville to 150 inches on the northwest coast, with almost the total amount falling between October and May. In the period from June to September there is virtually no rain, but humidity remains high. Temperature shows little seasonal variation, the daily average being about 81° F (about 27° C).

About 75 percent of the country is covered by a dense equatorial rain forest containing more than 3,000 species of vegetation, including the okoumé, a hardwood tree that forms the backbone of Gabon's wood industry. The dense forest vegetation makes the country an animal paradise; antelopes, monkeys, gorillas, and tropical birds, as well as several varieties of elephants, flourish in abundance. (J.v.H.)

The landscape under human settlement. Gabon's major towns—Libreville (1978 est.; 225,000), Port-Gentil (103,000), Lambaréné (26,000), Mouanda (23,000), Mouila, Oyem, Franceville, and Bitam—may contain approximately 50 percent of the total population. The remainder is scattered widely among about 4,000 rural villages, concentrated along the rivers and roads, often with a population no more than a few families. While Port-Gentil has developed mainly as an industrial town, Libreville became in the 1970s one of the most sophisticated cities in Africa: broad boulevards, modern hotels and office buildings, a new airport, discotheques, and elegant shops and restaurants frequented by Europeans and Gabonese civil servants have transformed the city. Libreville also has one of the highest costs of living in the world because of the scarcity of land for accommodations and because the underdevelopment of local agriculture necessitates the importing of a high percentage of the food consumed.

Although traditional customs are strong, the government since 1960 has made a concerted effort to equalize the social and economic opportunities of men and women.

Marginal notes:

Beginnings of colonization

Presidencies of M'ba and Bongo

Monts de Cristal

The towns

Gabon, Area and Population

Provinces	area sq mi	area sq km	population 1970 census*	population 1978 estimate
Estuaire	8,008	20,740	195,000	359,000
Haut–Ogooué	14,111	36,547	127,000	213,000
Moyen–Ogooué	7,156	18,535	52,000	49,000
Ngounié	14,575	37,750	130,000	118,000
Nyanga	8,218	21,285	67,000	98,000
Ogooué–Ivindo	17,790	46,075	60,000	53,000
Ogooué–Lolo	9,799	25,380	52,000	49,000
Ogooué–Maritime	8,838	22,890	120,000	195,000
Woleu–Ntem	14,851	38,465	148,000	166,000
Total Gabon	103,347†	267,667	950,000†	1,300,000

*De jure. †Figures do not add to totals given because of rounding.
Source: Official government figures.

Young men and women are now educated together and are trained to serve in positions including those of magistrates, teachers, nurses, and members of the armed forces.

People and population. *Linguistic, ethnic, and religious groups.* Any ethnographic map of Gabon would necessarily be extremely complicated, showing more than 40 ethnic groups with different languages. The Fang, who belong to the larger Pahouin group of Central Africa, account for more than one-third of the total population; they live north of the Ogooué River. The largest groups south of the river are the Punu, Sira, and Nzebi; their less numerous neighbours are the Teke and Kota. One of the smallest ethnic groups is the Omyènè, who, located on the Atlantic coast, played an important role in Gabonese history.

Somewhat more than 50 percent of the population, estimated at 600,000, is Christian, with about twice as many Roman Catholics as Protestants. About 3,000 people are Muslims. Others have kept their traditional African religions.

Demography. With a population estimated at about 600,000, Gabon, like its neighbours in Central Africa, has a very low population density. The annual growth rate for the region is about 2.3 percent, and for Gabon it is probably not much more than 1 percent each year. This situation is partially explained by a high instance of infertility, caused by disease and malnutrition.

The national economy. *Agriculture.* Although about half of the population is engaged solely in agriculture (primarily subsistence farming), it plays but a small part in the economy of the country as a whole. The appeal of the towns, where better educational and job opportunities are offered, is irresistible for young Gabonese. The second five-year plan of 1971–75 emphasized agriculture, but by 1980 the country continued to produce only enough food to satisfy 10 to 15 percent of its needs. Plans during the 1980s included the expansion of rice production at Ndendé in the southwest, the development of vegetable and fruit growing at Franceville, and the extension of cocoa production in the Woleu-Ntem area.

Forestry. For many years Gabon's forests, covering 75 to 85 percent of its territory, were its principal natural resource. Newly discovered and exploited mineral wealth had by the early 1970s forced raw wood and forest products into second place, and by the early 1980s, wood accounted for less than 10 percent of Gabon's exports. The principal forest districts have been at Kango, Booué, Fougamou, Ndjolé, Mitzic, and Mouila. The forest resources near the coast and rivers are practically exhausted. Exploitation of the forests of the interior began in the late 1970s with the construction of the Transgabon Railroad, the first portion of which (Owendo–Ndjolé) opened in 1979.

Mining. Manganese mined at Moanda (west of Franceville) is of high quality; reserves of possibly 200,000,000 tons make Gabon second only to the Soviet Union in manganese. In the 1970s, Gabon exported more than 2,000,000 metric tons, worth some U.S. $100,000,000 annually. Principal purchasers are the United States, France, West Germany, Norway, and Japan.

In 1956, a reserve of uranium was discovered at Mouana, also in the southeastern part of the country. Exploitation was in progress by 1961, with a processing factory constructed on the site. In the late 1970s, annual production was about 1,500 tons, with about 44,000 tons still in the ground. France purchases almost all the annual uranium production; U.S. companies have been searching for other deposits.

Petroleum represented more than 70 percent of Gabon's total exports in the late 1970s, with an estimated reserve of 63,900,000 tons. Gabon joined the Organization of Petroleum Exporting Countries (OPEC) in 1975. Of the 14

(margin: Uranium and petroleum)

companies operating in Gabon in 1980, the French-based Elf Gabon was the most important. Offshore fields are the most productive in the area of Port-Gentil, and exploration is continuing.

Iron ore of good quality (60 to 65 percent iron) has been discovered at Belinga, near Makokou in the northeast. Reserves are estimated at more than 1,000,000,000 tons. Because of the inaccessibility of the deposits, however, full-scale mining was not expected until the third stage of the Transgabon Railroad was completed. Because construction of the railroad is in the direction of the southeast rather than toward the northeast where the iron is located, it is unlikely that the line will reach Belinga much before the end of the century.

Industry, trade, and foreign aid. Light industry has been expanding and diversifying since the opening in 1967 of a petroleum refinery at Port-Gentil. The refinery and its support operations (a shipyard and metalworking facilities) overshadow other manufacturing enterprises, which include cement and cigarette factories, a sugar refinery, breweries, light electronics, palm oil and flour mills, and two textile-printing factories. In the early 1980s, planned projects included expansion of the fishing industry to include a tuna fish canning plant and a general promotion of small enterprises that would hire Gabonese. Franceville, the president's home, continued to develop.

In 1980, about 90 percent of total exports were composed of oil, manganese, uranium, and forest products—shipped primarily to France, the United States, and West Germany. Gabon also traded with Canada, Belgium, The Netherlands, Italy, and other states, and maintained a generally favourable balance of trade. Gabon has often been one of the rare African states with an annual trade surplus, but it imports essential items such as food, machinery, and chemicals from France, the United States, Belgium, West Germany, and several other countries. It also imports food from Zimbabwe and South Africa.

The government borrowed heavily from France, Germany, the European Economic Community (EEC), and many banks for the purpose of building the Transgabon Railroad, a huge presidential palace, and hotels. Creditors insisted that the government accept advice from the International Monetary Fund, and, beginning in 1978, the government initiated a plan to reduce its debts. By the early 1980s, it appeared that the debt was more manageable and that Gabon could hope for a more healthy economy.

The close ties between Paris and Libreville are seen most clearly in the fact that more than half of all monies obtained either through direct foreign aid or investment come from France. The EEC has sent millions of dollars in payments to make up for any losses in the value of wood exports. In 1978, Gabon borrowed U.S. $80,000,000 from French and U.S. banks and later another U.S. $90,000,-

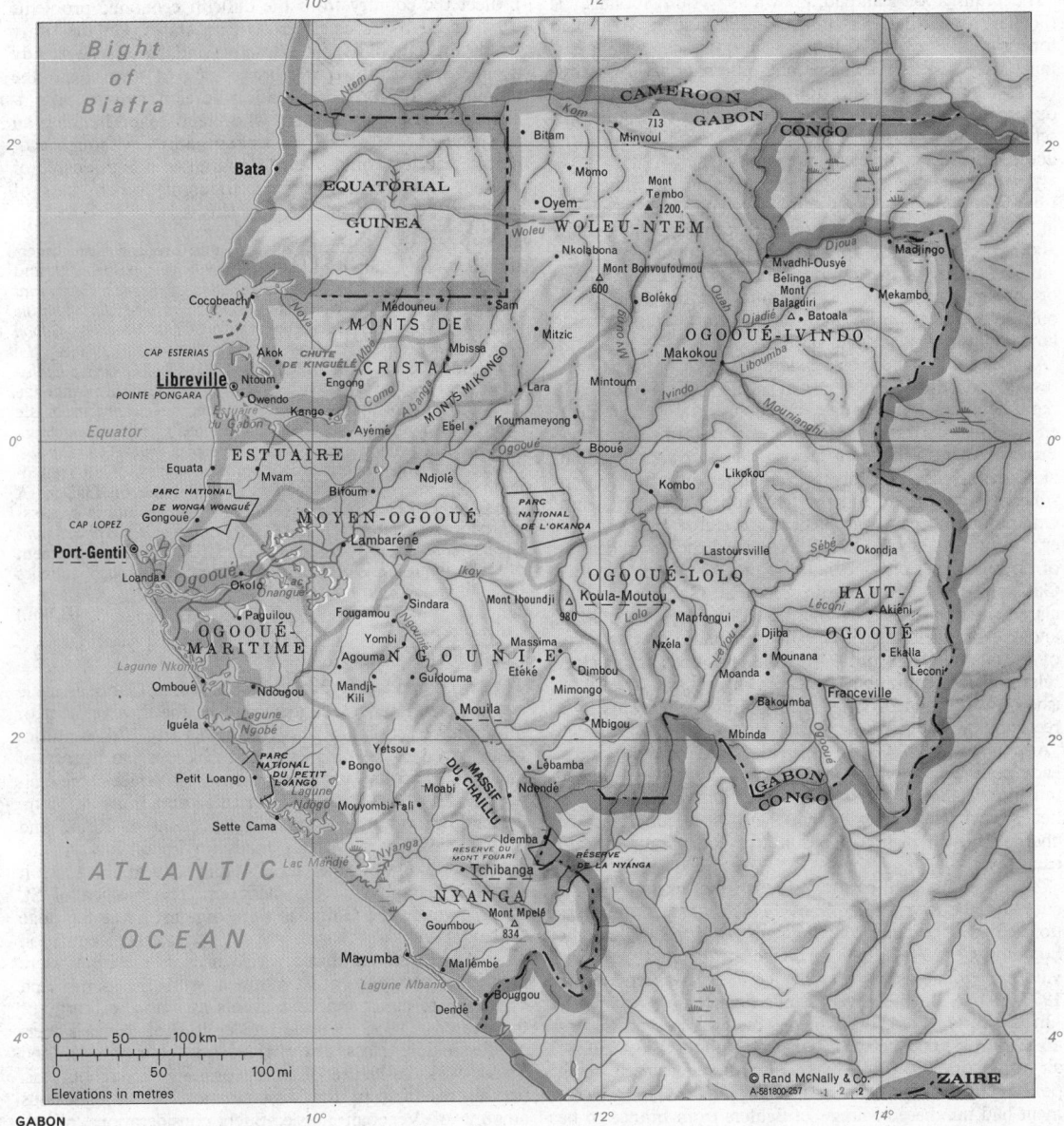

000 from French banks. The World Bank has also granted loans for road construction.

Management of the economy. Membership in the Franc Zone gives Gabon considerable stability. The CFA (Communauté Financière Africaine) franc is automatically convertible to French francs, giving trading partners confidence in Gabonese currency. The government has also encouraged foreign investors with its policy of economic liberalism, although there is governmental direction and planning. Thus, private investments totalled almost U.S. $1,000,000,000 in 1980, and Gabon had the highest per capita income in tropical Africa.

Transport. Overland transportation facilities have always been poorly developed, and government officials and entrepreneurs have depended on the airplane. This situation was one reason for the construction of the Transgabon Railroad, which was planned to cover 600 miles between the coastal port of Owendo and Franceville by 1985. The government also has promised to improve roads for vehicular traffic.

The Ogooué River is navigable upstream from its mouth on the Atlantic to Ndjolé, only about 150 miles inland. The Ogooué and other rivers such as the Abanga and the Nyanga can be used, however, to transport logs floated downstream from the interior forests. Uranium and manganese usually are exported through the neighbouring Congolese port of Pointe-Noire. A deepwater port at Owendo, nine miles from Libreville, opened in 1964, and the port at Port-Gentil was being improved in 1980.

The Transgabon Railroad, known as "Transgabonais," is the key to the nation's transportation system. It is paid for primarily by the Gabonese and French, with assistance from West Germany and international organizations. The first section, from Owendo to Ndjolé, was opened in December 1978, and the section to Booué was scheduled to open in 1982. If there are no difficulties, the line should be completed to Franceville by 1985.

Air travel connections are poor, although two lines link Libreville and Port-Gentil with Paris and cities elsewhere in Africa. Domestic air service is provided at one or another of about 30 public and more than 50 private airports (many of the latter connected with the petroleum or forestry industries). Most airports are for light planes only, but a new facility at Franceville can accommodate large military and civilian aircraft.

Administration and social conditions. According to the revised constitution of February 15, 1967, Gabon is a republic under the executive direction of a president elected by direct universal suffrage for a period of seven years. Provision is also made for a prime minister and a National Assembly of 47 members to assume legislative responsibilities and for an independent Supreme Court. Since Omar Bongo became president in December 1967, however, politics in Gabon has tended toward the centralization of power in one person. In 1968, the Parti Démocratique Gabonais (PDG; Democratic Party of Gabon) was declared the only legal party permitted to exist by the state, and the president thereafter often assumed the portfolios of various ministries or awarded key positions to his close relatives. A constitutional amendment in April 1975 abolished the position of vice president. President Bongo was reelected to another seven-year term in 1979.

Administratively, Gabon is divided into nine provinces, each consisting of many departments, which are divided into districts. A governor heads each province; a prefect heads each department; and there is a subprefect in charge of each district. Consultative councils operate at each level.

The judicial system consists of a series of customary law courts at the lowest level, above which jurisdiction moves upward to a criminal court, a court of appeals, and the Supreme Court (all three of which are located in Libreville). An audit office (cour des comptes) was created in 1977 to oversee the government's finances.

In the early 1980s, the armed forces were comprised of an army of 1,000 persons; a navy of about 100; and an air force of 200. There were also a gendarmerie, civil police, and a security force totalling 1,600. The government had purchased Mirage jet fighters from France to be stationed at a new air base in the southern part of the country.

Gabon claims that a majority of its children of primary-school age are in school, and it is true that a large percentage of the population speaks French. Education is mandatory from the ages of six to 16, and possibly a third of the population over 13 years of age is literate in French. In 1977–78, the government estimated that about 140,000 children were in primary schools, about 21,600 in secondary schools, and 1,300 in third-level institutions. Probably 1,000 Gabonese were studying outside the country, mainly in France. The Université Omar Bongo was founded in 1970.

Health facilities remained inadequate as the 1980s began, particularly outside the cities. The area of Libreville accounted for about 50 percent of all hospitals, laboratories, and related health-care institutions. The ratio of doctors to patients was about one for every 5,000.

Cultural life and institutions. Radio-Gabon at Libreville can be heard throughout Gabon, and more Gabonese listen to it than to radio stations broadcasting from Cameroon and the Congo. The country also has television facilities, including an Earth satellite station that began to broadcast in 1973. The *Gabon Matin* daily newspaper, published by the Gabonese Press Agency in Libreville; *Dialogue*, the organ of the Democratic Party; and other publications faithfully reflect the government's views, as do radio and television programs.

Prospects for the future. Gabon's natural resources protect the country from the difficult economic problems experienced by some other African states. On the other hand, the emphasis on extractive industries, the steady décline in agriculture, the burgeoning of towns, and the dominance of foreigners and a foreign culture pose a serious problem for leaders who claim to be building an independent, united, self-respecting nation. Although economic security would seem to guarantee a high degree of internal stability in the years to come, other goals of independence seem increasingly elusive.

BIBLIOGRAPHY. Historical background useful for an understanding of Gabon is provided in VIRGINIA THOMPSON and RICHARD ADLOFF, *The Emerging States of French Equatorial Africa* (1960); BRIAN WEINSTEIN, *Gabon: Nation-Building on the Ogooué* (1966); K. DAVID PATTERSON, *The Northern Gabon Coast to 1875* (1975); and PIERRE ALEXANDRE and J. BINET, *Le groupe dit Pahouin (Fang-Boulou-Beti)* (1958; *The Group Called Pahouin [Fang-Bulu-Beti]*, 1959). The best English-language annual review of political and economic developments in the country is contained in COLIN LEGUM (ed.), *Africa Contemporary Record: Annual Survey and Documents* (1968–). *Europe, France Outre-mer* publishes an annual survey of all francophone countries, with a regular special issue on Gabon. A good study of the country's economic background is CATHERINE COQUERY-VIDROVITCH, *Le Congo au temps des grandes compagnies concessionnaires, 1898–1930* (1972). The government of Gabon and the World Bank also regularly publish statistics on Gabon.

(B.Wn.)

Gabrieli Family

The two composers Andrea and Giovanni Gabrieli, uncle and nephew, made a contribution to the development of music in Venice in the late 16th and early 17th centuries that proved to be of great significance in the history of music in general. This was because of Venice's pre-eminent position as a cultural, artistic, and musical centre during the late Renaissance. Independent of Rome and the papacy, Venice was the focus for liberal ideas in the arts, but, like any other large Italian city at the time, it also had a court life of splendour. The basilica of St. Mark's, where the Gabrielis were organists, was the doge (duke) of Venice's chapel, not an ecclesiastical entity on its own, so that the music with which its musicians were involved was concerned as much with the pomp and ceremony of court and civic events as with the liturgy of the church. The civic pride and culture of Venice's mercantile middle class also helped to foster music, and Venice was the centre of music printing throughout this period, resulting in the dissemination of an enormous amount of Venetian music. Such considerations of en-

Transgabon Railroad

Education

vironment are as important as the genius of the two Gabrielis themselves in accounting for the fame they achieved in their lifetime, a fame fully appreciated in the 20th century.

Andrea Gabrieli. He was born *c.* 1520 in the Canareggio (now Cannareggio) quarter of Venice, but nothing is known about Andrea Gabrieli until 1536, when he became a singer at St. Mark's and a pupil of its music director, the great Franco-Flemish composer Adriaan Willaert. From Willaert he learned the art of writing polyphonic motets (choral settings in four or more vocal parts) and in particular that of composing for separated choirs placed in different parts of the church with consequent stereophonic effect, a new and exciting way of exploiting the acoustical properties of a large building like St. Mark's. It is possible that Andrea was a singer at Verona Cathedral around 1550. In 1558 he became organist at the church of S. Geremia in Venice but soon left for an extended period of foreign travel. He served in the Bavarian court chapel at Munich under another great Franco-Fleming, Orlando di Lasso, then visited the court of Graz in Austria, and finally was patronized by the noble Fugger family in Augsburg. This transalpine sojourn afforded a chance for Andrea to cement Venetian ties, musically, with Catholic areas to the north.

Organist at
St. Mark's

In 1564 he returned to Venice to become second organist at St. Mark's, which he remained until 1584, when he succeeded the virtuoso performer Claudio Merulo as first organist—a position he held until his death in 1586. Despite his profession, not much of his output in these years was organ music; there were several volumes of madrigals, socially enjoyable settings of Italian poetry to be sung at private houses or cultural academies, where musical life flourished. And there was the large-scale choral and instrumental music for ceremonies of church and state, for which Andrea is best known today. Some of these works were published posthumously in 1587: one of the finest is the *Magnificat* for three choirs and orchestra, doubtless intended to be performed in St. Mark's.

Giovanni Gabrieli. Born probably in 1556, Giovanni Gabrieli studied with his uncle, whom he regarded with almost filial affection. To the latter's foreign travels and connections, Giovanni owed his chance to become known abroad. Giovanni also served (1575–79) under di Lasso in Munich, during which time his early talent and fame were apparent (one of his madrigals was published in 1575 in a collection of Munich composers). In 1584 he returned to Venice and a year later succeeded his uncle as second organist of St. Mark's—the post he held for life. After Andrea's death in 1586, Giovanni quickly assumed the limelight in the field of ceremonial music, though he was never so active as a madrigalist. The publication of his uncle's music in 1587 was a mark of respect but also included some of his own church music, which demonstrated his musical debt to Andrea. Giovanni's foreign connections included Hans Leo Hassler, the German composer and former pupil of Andrea, who avidly adopted the Venetian style; and patrons, such as the Fugger family and archduke Ferdinand of Austria.

Career as
a teacher

In later years Giovanni became a famous teacher who attracted many pupils from northern Europe. His most notable student was the German Heinrich Schütz, who studied with Gabrieli from 1609 to 1612. After 1587 Giovanni's principal publications were the two immense *Sacrae symphoniae* of 1597 and 1615 (printed posthumously), both of which contained purely instrumental music for church use or massive choral and instrumental motets for the liturgy. Like his uncle, he usually conceived the music for separated choirs but showed an increasing tendency to specify which instruments were to be used and which choirs were to consist of soloists and full choir, as well as to distinguish the musical style of each, thus initiating a completely new approach to the creation of musical colour and orchestration. In the well-known *Sonata pian'e forte*, for eight instruments, directions to play loud and soft are given. Among the motets, his masterpiece is perhaps *In ecclesiis*, for four soloists, four-part choir, violin, three cornets, two trombones, and

organ, these forces pitted against one another in an endless variety of combinations.

There is no record of Giovanni's mariage, but because he often pleaded for a salary advance from the St. Mark's authorities "on account of his numerous family," he obviously had a wife and children. He died in Venice, probably on August 12, 1612.

MAJOR WORKS
Andrea Gabrieli

Madrigals for three to six voices in various collections; masses in six parts, *Primus liber missarum* (1572); *Magnificat* for three choirs; motets; various ricercari and canzoni.

Giovanni Gabrieli

Various motets, among them *In ecclesiis;* madrigals in various collections; *Canzoni e sonate* (1615); *Sacrae symphoniae*, book 1 (1597), including the *Sonata pian'e forte; Sacrae symphoniae* (1615); *Concerti di Andrea et di Giovanni Gabrieli a 6–16 voci* (1587, containing pieces by Andrea).

BIBLIOGRAPHY. E.F. KENTON, *The Life and Works of Giovanni Gabrieli* (1967), is not very reliable and tends to contradict itself. The best feature is the thematic index, though this is difficult to use. The opening chapters are a translation of those from C. VON WINTERFELD, *Johannes Gabrieli und sein Zeitalter*, 3 vol. (1834), still the definitive work on Giovanni. More recent summary information and stylistic criticism may be found in G. REESE, *Music in the Renaissance* (1954).

(J.L.A.R.)

Gainsborough, Thomas

Of all the 18th-century English painters, Thomas Gainsborough was the most versatile and original, always prepared to experiment with new ideas and techniques. He alone among the great portrait painters of the era also devoted serious attention to landscapes. Unlike his contemporary Sir Joshua Reynolds, he was no great believer in an academic tradition and laughed at the fashion for history painting; an instinctive painter, he delighted in the poetry of paint. In his racy letters Gainsborough shows a warm-hearted and generous character and an independent mind. His comments on his own work and methods, as well as on some of the old masters, are very revealing and throw considerable light on contemporary views of art.

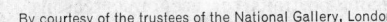

"The Morning Walk," oil on canvas by Thomas Gainsborough. In the National Gallery, London. 2.36 × 1.79 m.

Early life and Suffolk period. Gainsborough was baptized at Sudbury in Suffolk on May 14, 1727, the youngest son of John Gainsborough, a maker of woollen goods. When he was 13, he persuaded his father to send him to London to study on the strength of his promise at landscape. He worked as an assistant to Hubert Gravelot, a French painter and engraver and an important figure in London art circles at the time. From him Gainsborough learned something of the French Rococo idiom, which had a considerable influence on the development of his style. In 1746 in London he married Margaret Burr, the illegitimate daughter of the Duke of Beaufort. Soon afterward he returned to Suffolk and settled in Ipswich in 1752; his daughters Mary and Margaret were born in 1748 and 1752. In Ipswich Gainsborough met his first biographer, Philip Thicknesse. He early acquired some reputation as a portrait and landscape painter and made an adequate living.

Gainsborough declared that his first love was landscape and began to learn the language of this art from the Dutch 17th-century landscapists, who by 1740 were becoming popular with English collectors; his first landscapes were influenced by Jan Wynants. The earliest dated picture with a landscape background is a study of a bull terrier—"Bumper—A Bull Terrier" (1745; Sir Edward Bacon Collection, Raveningham, Norfolk), in which many of the details are taken straight from Wynants. But by 1748, when he painted "Cornard Wood," Jacob van Ruisdael had become the predominant influence; although it is full of naturalistic detail, Gainsborough probably never painted directly from nature. "The Charterhouse," one of his few topographical views, dates from the same year as "Cornard Wood" and in the subtle effect of light on various surfaces proclaims Dutch influence. In the background to "Mr. and Mrs. Andrews," he anticipates the realism of the great English landscapist of the next century, John Constable, but for the most part fancy held sway. In many of the early landscapes the influence of Rococo design learned from Gravelot is evident, together with a feeling for the French pastoral tradition. "The Woodcutter Courting a Milkmaid" is an Anglicized version of a French theme, which recalls compositions by Jean-Honoré Fragonard. Although Gainsborough preferred landscape, he knew he must paint portraits for economic reasons. The small heads painted in Suffolk, although sometimes rather stiff, are penetrating character studies delicately and freely pencilled, particularly the jaunty self-portrait in a cocked hat at Houghton. Gainsborough painted few full-length portraits in Suffolk. "Mr. William Woollaston," although an ambitious composition, is intimate and informal. The "Painter's Daughters Chasing a Butterfly," composed in the last years at Ipswich, is, in its easy naturalism and sympathetic understanding, one of the best English portraits of children.

As well as straight portraits, he painted in Suffolk a number of delightful spontaneous groups of small figures in landscapes closely related to conversation pieces. "Mr. and Mrs. Andrews," which has been described as the most English of English pictures, is set in a typical Suffolk landscape. "Lady and Gentleman in Landscape" is more Frenchified, with its vivacious Rococo rhythms, but "Heneage Lloyd and His Sister" is more stylized, the charming little figures being posed against a conventional background of steps and decorative urns.

Bath period. To obtain a wider public, Gainsborough moved in 1759 to Bath, where his studio was soon thronged with fashionable sitters. He moved in musical and theatrical circles, and among his friends were members of the Linley family, whose portraits he painted. At Bath he also met the actor David Garrick, for whom he had a profound admiration and whom he painted on many occasions. His passion for music and the stage continued throughout his life. In the west country he visited many of the great houses and at Wilton fell under the spell of Anthony Van Dyck, the predominating influence in his later work. In spite of the demand for portraits, he continued to paint landscapes.

In 1761 he sent a portrait of Earl Nugent to the Society of Artists, and in the following year the first notice of his work appeared in the London press. Throughout the 1760s he exhibited regularly in London and in 1768 was elected a foundation member of the Royal Academy. Characteristically he never took much part in the deliberations.

After he moved to Bath, Gainsborough had less time for landscape and worked a good deal from memory, often drawing by candlelight from little model landscapes set up in his studio. About 1760 Peter Paul Rubens supplanted the Dutch painters as Gainsborough's chief love. This is particularly noticeable in "Peasants Returning from Market," with its rich colour and beautiful creamy pastel shades. The influence of Rubens is also apparent in "The Harvest Wagon" in the fluency of the drawing and the scale of the great beech trees so different from the stubby oaks of Suffolk. The idyllic scene is a perfect blend of the real and the ideal. The group in the cart is based on Rubens' "Descent from the Cross" (1611–14) in Antwerp Cathedral, which Gainsborough copied.

In Bath, Gainsborough had to satisfy a more sophisticated clientele and adopted a more formal and elegant portrait style based largely on a study of Van Dyck at Wilton, where he made a free copy of Van Dyck's painting of the Pembroke family. By 1769, when he painted "Isabella Countess of Sefton," it is easy to see the refining influence of Van Dyck in the dignified simplicity of the design and the subtle muted colouring. One of Gainsborough's most famous pictures, "The Blue Boy," was probably painted in 1770. In painting this subject in Van Dyck dress, he was following an 18th-century fashion in painting, as well as doing homage to his hero. The influence of Van Dyck is most clearly seen in the more official portraits. "John, 4th Duke of Argyll" in his splendid robes is composed in the grand manner, and "Augustus John, Third Earl of Bristol" rivals Reynolds' portraits of the kind. Gainsborough preferred to paint his friends rather than public figures, and a group of portraits of the 1760s—Uvedale Price, Sir William St. Quinton, and Thomas Coward, all oldish men of strong character—illustrate Gainsborough's sense of humor and his individual approach to sympathetic sitters.

London period. In 1774 he moved to London and settled in part of Schomberg House in Pall Mall. Fairly soon he began to be noticed by the royal family and partly because of his informality and Tory politics was preferred by George III above the official court painter, Sir Joshua Reynolds. In 1781 he was commissioned to paint the King and Queen.

Gainsborough continued his landscape work. "The Watering Place" was described by Horace Walpole, the English man of letters, as in the style of Rubens, but it also has much of the classic calm of Claude Lorrain, whose etchings Gainsborough owned. In 1783 he made an expedition to the Lake District to see for himself the "wild" scenery extolled by the devotees of the picturesque. On his return he painted a number of mountain scenes that have analogies with the work of Gaspar Dughet, whose works were widely distributed in English country houses. Some sea pieces dating from the 1780s show a new kind of realism, harking back to the Dutch seascape tradition. During his last years Gainsborough was haunted by his nostalgia for Arcadia in the English countryside and painted a series of pictures of peasant life more ideal than real, for example, "The Cottage Door." But one of the latest landscapes, "The Market Cart," is less idealized and more true to nature and looks forward to Constable in its treatment of the light breaking through the massive foliage.

Gainsborough was the only important English portrait painter to devote much time to landscape drawing. He composed a great many drawings in a variety of mediums including chalk, pen and wash, and watercolour, some of them varnished. He was always eager to find new papers and new techniques. He produced a magic lantern to give striking lighting effects; the box is still in the Victoria and Albert Museum, together with some of the slides. In addition Gainsborough made a series of soft-ground etchings and aquatints. He never sold his drawings and, al-

Early landscapes

Influence of Van Dyck

Idealized country scenes

though many of them are closely related to pictures, they are not studies in the ordinary sense but works of art in their own right.

Gainsborough was not methodical in keeping sitter books, and comparatively few of the portraits in the early years in London are dated. In 1777 he exhibited at the Royal Academy the well-known "Mrs. Graham," "C.F. Abel," "William Henry, Duke of Gloucester," and "Maria, Duchess of Gloucester," all deliberately glamorous and painted in richly heightened colour. "Queen Charlotte" is more restrained; the painting of the flounced white dress decorated with ribbons and laces makes her look every inch a queen. It is significant that Gainsborough, unlike most of his contemporaries, did not generally use drapery painters. In 1784 he quarrelled with the Academy because they insisted on hanging the "Three Eldest Princesses" at the normal height from the floor, which Gainsborough maintained was too high to appreciate his lightness of touch and delicate pencilling. In protest he withdrew the pictures he had intended for the exhibition and never showed again at the Academy.

In some of Gainsborough's later portraits of women, he dispensed with precise finish, and, without sacrificing the likeness, he concentrated on the general effect. "Mrs. Sheridan" melts into the landscape, while "Lady Bate Dudley," a symphony in blue and green, is an insubstantial form, almost an abstract. "Mrs. Siddons," on the other hand, shows that Gainsborough could still paint a splendid objective study. Few of the later male portraits are of a pronounced character, but exceptions are two particularly good pictures of musicians, "Johann Christian Fischer" and the unfinished "Lord Abingdon" (private collection).

Later portraits

A new venture in 1783 was "The Mall in St. James' Park," a park scene described by Horace Walpole as "all a flutter like a lady's fan." "The Morning Walk," with romanticized figures strolling in a landscape, is painted in the same spirit.

The "fancy pictures" painted in the 1780s gave Gainsborough particular pleasure. They are full-sized, idealized portraits of country children and peasants painted from models—for example, "The Cottage Girl with a Bowl of Milk." The idea appeared in immature form in the little rustic Suffolk figures, and he may have been fired to exploit it further by seeing the 17th-century Spanish painter Bartolomé Murillo's "St. John," which he copied.

He died August 2, 1788, and was buried in Kew churchyard. Gainsborough was the most inventive and original of 18th-century portraitists, and yet he complained of Reynolds, "Damn him, how various he is."

MAJOR WORKS
Paintings

PORTRAITS: "Lady and Gentleman in Landscape" (1746; Louvre, Paris); "Mr. and Mrs. Andrews" (c. 1750; National Gallery, London); "Heneage Lloyd and His Sister" (c. 1750; Fitzwilliam Museum, Cambridge); "Mr. William Woollaston" (late 1750s; Christchurch Mansion Museum, Ipswich); "Painter's Daughters Chasing a Butterfly" (c. 1758; National Gallery, London); "Ann Ford, Mrs. Philip Thicknesse" (1760; Cincinnati Art Museum); "Maria, Duchess of Gloucester" (early 1760s; Los Angeles County Museum); "Gertrude, Lady Alston" (mid-1760s; Louvre); "John, 4th Duke of Argyll" (1767; Scottish National Portrait Gallery, Edinburgh); "Hon. Thomas Needham" (1768; Ascott House, Berkshire); "John, 10th Viscount Kilmorey" (c. 1768; Tate Gallery, London); "Augustus John, Third Earl of Bristol" (1768; National Trust, Ickworth); "Isabella, Countess of Sefton" (1769; Croxteth Hall, Lancashire); "The Blue Boy" (c. 1770; Henry E. Huntington Library and Art Gallery, San Marino, California); "Penelope, Viscountess Ligonier" (1771; Henry E. Huntington Library and Art Gallery); "Dr. Ralph Schomberg" (1771–72; National Gallery, London); "The Linley Sisters—Mrs. Sheridan and Mrs. Tickell" (c. 1772; Dulwich College Picture Gallery, Dulwich); "William Henry, Duke of Gloucester" (c. 1775; Chewton Manor, North Somerset, Somerset); "Mrs. Graham" (c. 1777; National Gallery of Scotland, Edinburgh); "C. F. Abel" (1777; Henry E. Huntington Library and Art Gallery); "Johann Christian Fischer" (1780; Buckingham Palace, London); "Mrs. Robinson," popularly nicknamed "Perdita," (1781; Wallace Collection, London); "Queen Charlotte" (1781; Windsor Castle); "Lord Rodney" (1783; Earl of Roseberry Collection, Dalmeny, West

Lothian); "Mrs. Siddons" (c. 1783; National Gallery, London); "Three Eldest Princesses," also called "Princess Charlotte and Her Two Sisters," (1784, painted for the Royal Academy but not exhibited; Buckingham Palace); "Mrs. Sheridan" (c. 1785; National Gallery of Art, Washington, D.C.); "Lady Bate Dudley" (1787; Lord Burton Collection, Needwood House, Derbyshire).

LANDSCAPES AND "FANCY PICTURES": "The Charterhouse" (1748; Foundling Hospital, London); "Cornard Wood," popularly nicknamed "Gainsborough's Forest" (1748; National Gallery, London); "The Woodcutter Courting a Milkmaid" (1753; Duke of Bedford Collection, Woburn Abbey, Bedfordshire); "Peasants Returning from Market" (c. 1767; Toledo Museum of Art, Ohio); "The Harvest Wagon" (c. 1770; Barber Institute, Birmingham, England); "The Watering Place" (1777; National Gallery, London); "The Cottage Door" (c. 1780; Henry E. Huntington Library and Art Gallery, San Marino, California); "The Mall in St. James' Park" (1783; Frick Collection, New York); "The Morning Walk" (1785; National Gallery, London); "The Cottage with Dog and Pitcher" (1785; Sir Alfred Beit Collection, Russborough, Co. Wicklow, Ireland); "The Cottage Girl with a Bowl of Milk" (1786; South African National Gallery, Capetown); "The Market Cart" (1786; Tate Gallery, London); "The Wood Gatherers," also known as "Cottage Children" (1787; Metropolitan Museum of Art, New York); "Boy with a Cat-Morning" (1787; Metropolitan Museum of Art, New York).

BIBLIOGRAPHY. WILLIAM T. WHITLEY, *Thomas Gainsborough* (1915), the definitive biography; ELLIS WATERHOUSE, *Gainsborough* (1958), the most complete catalog of the paintings, very fully illustrated with an important critical introductory essay; MARY WOODALL (ed.), *The Letters of Thomas Gainsborough*, rev. ed. (1963); JOHN HAYES, *The Drawings of Thomas Gainsborough*, 2 vol. (1970), the definitive work on the drawings with a catalog of 900 items, 462 illustrations, and a full up-to-date bibliography of Gainsborough literature.

(M.Wo.)

Gajah Mada

The prime minister of the Majapahit empire, which ruled Java in the 13th–16th century, Gajah Mada is believed to have united the whole of Indonesia in the 14th century. No information is available on his early life, except that he was born a commoner. He rose to power on his intelligence, courage, and loyalty to King Jayanagara (1309–28) during a rebellion led by Kuti in 1319. He served as the head of the royal bodyguard that escorted King Jayanagara to Badander, when Kuti captured the capital of Majapahit. After finding a safe place for the King, he returned to the capital and spread the rumour that the King had been killed. He discovered that many officers were upset by the King's supposed death and that Kuti was apparently unpopular among the people. Knowing, therefore, that the King still had loyal followers, Gajah Mada secretly organized a counterinsurrection, in which Kuti was killed and the King was restored. As a reward, Gajah Mada was appointed as the *patih* (minister) of Daha and, later, the *patih* of Daha and Janggala, a position that made him a member of the ruling elite. Prapanca, a court poet and historian, described Gajah Mada as "eloquent, sharp of speech, upright, and sober-minded."

Rise to power

Gajah Mada's loyalty to Jayanagara waned, however, when the King took possession of his wife. In 1328, when Jayanagara was ill, Gajah Mada instructed Tancha, the court physician, to kill the King during an operation. Upon the death of the King, Tancha was blamed and executed by Gajah Mada. Since the King had no son, his daughter Tribhuvana became ruler.

During the reign of Tribhuvana (1328–50), Gajah Mada gradually became the most powerful figure in Majapahit. In 1331 a rebellion took place in Sadeng (eastern Java). Gajah Mada immediately sent a military expedition to the area, but a minister of Majapahit named Kembar attempted to stop him from entering Sadeng. Gajah Mada broke the blockade and won the battle.

Upon his return, Gajah Mada was appointed as *mapatih*, or prime minister, of Majapahit. At the same time, he took a solemn oath before the council of ministers that he would not enjoy *palapa* (privileges of vacation or the revenue from his fief) before he conquered the whole archipelago for Majapahit. When Kembar and other ministers ridiculed this fantastic boast, Gajah Mada, with the help of the Queen, removed Kembar and his follow-ers from office. In 1343, in accordance with his plans, Gajah Mada led a military expedition that conquered Bali.

Tribhuvana abdicated in 1350 and was succeeded by her son Hayam Wuruk, perhaps the best-known king of Majapahit. During his reign, Majapahit reached the zenith of its power and controlled the whole of the Indonesian archipelago. The young king seemed content to leave the direction of affairs entirely in the hands of his prime minister.

The year after Hayam Wuruk's accession, Gajah Mada attempted to spread Majapahit influence to the western Java kingdom of Sunda. He sent a mission to Sunda ex-pressing the wish of Hayam Wuruk to marry the daughter of the King of Sunda. The King consented and brought the Princess, together with some of his noblemen, to Majapahit. They camped in Bubat, north of the capital, in a large field where the wedding was supposed to take place. A disagreement ensued between Gajah Mada and the Sundanese king. The former wanted the King to sur-render the Princess to Hayam Wuruk, but the King and his noblemen insisted that the Princess, as the queen of Majapahit, should have a status equal to that of Hayam Wuruk.

Gajah Mada brought in troops and intended to decide the issue by force. The Sundanese noblemen preferred death to dishonour; instead of a happy wedding, a bloody massacre took place. The King of Sunda was killed, as were the Princess and the Sundanese noblemen. After the massacre, Sunda seems to have acknowledged the over-lordship of Majapahit for a time but, ultimately, recov-ered its independence.

Massacre of the west Javanese

By courtesy of the Trawulan Museum, Indonesia

Terra-cotta head identified as Gajah Mada. In the Trawulan Site Museum, Indonesia.

To glorify his power, Gajah Mada built a temple on the boundary line of Singhasāri kingdom in eastern Java to equate himself with the last king of Singhasāri. It was under his patronage that Prapanca began the composi-tion of *Nāgarakertāgama*, the epic of Majapahit. A law book that had a great significance in Javanese history was also compiled under his instructions.

Gajah Mada also played a major role in the direction of internal policy. He occupied numerous positions, in-cluding that of chief officer of the palace. The range of his activities was so great that when he died, Hayam Wuruk found it necessary to appoint four ministers to take over the positions that had previously been the responsibility of Gajah Mada alone. Gajah Mada's death (1364) occurred under mysterious circumstances. Some writers claim that he was poisoned by Hayam Wuruk, who had come to fear his minister's power. The evidence, however, is inconclusive.

Gajah Mada's role in unifying the Indonesian archi-pelago caused early Indonesian nationalists to consider him a great national hero, and the first Indonesian uni-versity in Jogjakarta, established in 1946, was named after him.

BIBLIOGRAPHY.   D.G.E. HALL, *A History of Southeast Asia*, 3rd ed., pp. 65–93 (1968), a detailed and comprehensive sec-tion on the history of Java in relation to Singhasāri and Ma-japahit; THEODORE G.T. PIGEAUD (ed.), *Java in the Fourteenth Century: A Study in Cultural History*, 5 vol. (1960–63), in-cludes the complete translation of the Javanese chronicle, *Nāgarakertāgama*, together with its original text, commen-taries, and recapitulation, by a leading Dutch scholar in the field—a major source for the history of Singhasāri and Ma-japahit; B.H.M. VLEKKE, *Nusantara: A History of Indonesia*, rev. ed., pp. 69–79 (1965), a well-researched section on Gajah Mada in a standard textbook on the history of Indonesia.

(L.Sur.)

Galápagos Islands

The Galápagos archipelago (Archipiélago de Colón) in the Pacific Ocean lies athwart the Equator about 600 miles west of the coast of Ecuador. It consists of 16 islands, as well as numerous islets and rocks, with a total area amounting to 3,000 square miles (8,000 square ki-lometres), scattered over approximately 23,000 square miles (60,000 square kilometres) of ocean. The islands are formed of lava piles, dotted with volcanoes that are not all extinct.

The archipelago, the geologic origin of which remains in dispute, is renowned for its unusual animal life. It takes its name from its giant land tortoises (the old Span-ish word for which is *galápago*), which are considered among the oldest living creatures on earth. Discovered in 1535, the islands remained unsettled until 1832, when Ecuador annexed them. The islands became internation-ally famous after Charles Darwin (*q.v.*), the English nat-uralist generally credited with being the originator of the theory of evolution, visited the islands in 1835 and, from his observations of animal life there, received inspiration for many of his views on natural selection. The popula-tion of the islands numbered about 3,800 in 1971; it con-sisted mainly of Ecuadorians, who subsist on agriculture and fisheries.

The nomenclature of the islands tends to be confusing. In 1832 the group was renamed Archipiélago de Colón, but this name has not been generally used; even Ecua-dorians call the islands the Galápagos. Most of the is-lands have at least two and sometimes more names. The English names of individual islands date from the 18th-century buccaneering era. The official Spanish names from 1832 are replacing the old ones in common use, but in scientific literature the old names are still preferred.

The largest of the islands, Isabela (Albemarle), is ap-proximately 82 miles long and comprises more than half of the total land area of the archipelago. In places it reaches heights of 5,600 feet above sea level. The second largest island is Santa Cruz (Indefatigable Island), upon which the Charles Darwin biological station is located. It is sponsored by the Ecuadorian government in coop-eration with the Charles Darwin Foundation in Brussels, Belgium, and has been established to promote scientific studies and to protect the indigenous vegetation and animal life.

Geomorphology.   The archipelago is of volcanic ori-gin. The islands are located along fracture zones in the earth's crust that run north-northwest and are crossed by other fracture lines running east-northeast.

The islands themselves are mainly shield volcanoes (vol-canoes formed from lava flows, which make gently slop-ing, broadly rounded cones) and volcanic rocks that rise from 7,000 to 10,000 feet above the sea floor and up to 6,000 feet above sea level. Most of the volcanoes measure 10 to 20 miles across at the base. The calderas (a caldera is a crater, the diameter of which is many times that of the volcanic vent, that is formed either by the collapse of the central part of the volcano or by explosions of unusual violence) at the summits are large and deep; that on Fernandina Island (Narborough) is 2 by 4½ miles across, and 2,700 feet deep. The largest caldera is Volcan Sierra Negra in southeast Isabela, measuring about six to four miles across. The age of the islands is unknown, but beds of rock containing fossils on Santa Cruz and Baltra (South Seymour) islands date to the Plio-cene Epoch, which lasted from 7,000,000 to 4,500,000

Volcanoes

years ago. Potassium-argon dating, a radioactive method of determining age (see DATING, RELATIVE AND ABSOLUTE), indicates that the oldest lavas on Española (Hood Island) are 2,000,000 years old. Recent volcanic eruptions have occurred on Fernandina (1968) and on Isabela (1957 and 1963) as well as on Pinta (Abingdon), Marchena (Bindloe), and San Salvador (James).

The rocks forming the islands are predominately basalts—blackish fine-grained rocks, formed under heat and pressure—most of which contain large crystals of plagioclase, one of the commonest rock-forming minerals. A few rocks are rich in olivine, a silicate formed of magnesium and iron, after which andesites, dark-grayish volcanic rocks, are the most frequently encountered.

Older theories assuming a former land connection with South America have now been abandoned, since there is neither geological nor other evidence to support them. The submarine platform from which the islands arise is separated by a trench from the continental shelf.

The rugged appearance of the landscape is striking. The high volcanoes of the western islands are scarred by recent lava flows and marked by numerous volcanic craters. Bizarre cliffs guard the coastline. The older islands are worn down and appear less spectacular.

Climate. The climate is characterized by low rainfall, low humidity, and relatively low air and water temperatures. These peculiarities are caused by the Humboldt Current, a cold ocean current coming from the south. The cool layer of air above the current moves landward, then warms up, and desiccates the islands. Only the higher regions experience precipitation—amounting to about 50 inches a year—during most seasons, and permanent freshwater lakes and ponds are found only at these levels. Mean daily maximum temperatures along the coast range from 80° to 88° F (26° to 31° C), while minimum temperatures range from 66° to 74° F (18° to 27° C).

Effects of the trade winds

The islands lie in the path of the southeast trade winds, which, when crossing the Equator, curve to the west, so that their usual direction is nearly south. In July and August a subsidiary wind system is dominant and curves east. The prevailing currents run toward the west and northwest at an average speed of one knot (1.15 mph). The surface water is warmest (80° F or 26° C) during January to April; from July to September the temperature drops to 62° F (16° C). Low stratus clouds predominate from April to December. They break up during the day and form again at night. On the windward side they are thicker, causing fog rains, called *garúa*, in the upper regions. The heaviest drizzle occurs from June to December, called the *garúa* season. The coastal regions experience a relatively dry season at this time. From January to May the highlands have a dry season with much sunshine and only occasional showers; at the same time, however, a rainy season occurs in the arid lowlands. Average annual rainfall on the coast amounts to ten inches. February to April are the warmest months and August to October the coolest.

Vegetation. There are about 700 species of higher plants. Of these, 250 species, or 40 percent, are endemic. The plant life shows close affinities to that of South and Central America.

Due to the climatic changes at different altitudes four main vegetational zones can be distinguished. These are: (1) The arid lowlands, which are covered by an open cactus forest. (2) The transition zone, covered with a forest in which pisonia, fish fuddle, and guava trees dominate. The underbrush is dense. Cacti occur only in the lower half of this zone. (3) The moist forest region, which is dominated by a *Scalesia* forest (a relict form of vegetation) with dense underbrush. (4) The treeless upland zone, which is covered with ferns and grasses.

Animal life. The close affinities to the fauna of South and Central America demonstrate that the bulk of the island animals originated there. The difficulty of crossing the ocean accounts for the paucity of animal life. The British Isles, for example, possess over 20,000 species of insects, whereas only about 700 species have been named in the Galápagos Islands so far. The same pattern prevails for other forms of animal life. Amphibians are lacking, reptiles are poorly represented, and land mammals are represented by only seven rodents and two bats. There are only about 80 species and subspecies of birds breeding on the islands; the bulk of land birds consist of the Darwin finches, named for the English naturalist.

Galápagos animal life is nevertheless of extreme interest for several reasons, which include the following. Firstly, there is a high percentage of endemic forms; all of the reptiles, with the exception of one night lizard, and most of the resident birds are endemic. Secondly, species have developed subspecies on the different islands. Thirdly, the Darwin finches have developed a multitude of adaptive types from one common ancestor. They differ mainly in beak shape and size. Fourthly, there are many other types that have evolved by adaptation. The marine iguanas, for example, which feed on seaweed and in some places cover the coastal rocks in hundreds, are unique. Another species of interest is the flightless cormorant. Fifthly, the giant tortoises survive as a relic on the larger islands. Giant tortoises were once widespread on the continents but became extinct. (The only other giant tortoises to survive are a different species, found in the Seychelles Islands in the Indian Ocean.) Sixthly, many terrestrial vertebrates show a striking lack of fear of land predators and of man. In addition, species of Antarctic origin, such as penguins and fur seals, live on the islands side by side with tropical animals.

The Darwin finches

The endemic Galápagos animals are today endangered by numerous animals that have been introduced and run wild. Goats, for example, compete with endemic types for food, while hogs, dogs, cats, and introduced rats attack mainly the eggs and young of the reptiles and birds. Both animals and plants are protected by laws, which are enforced by the Darwin Foundation. Many of the islands have the formal status of nature reserves.

The inhabitants. The island settlers, who are mostly Ecuadorians but also include some Europeans, live in small settlements on San Cristóbal (Chatham), Santa María (Charles), Isabela, and Santa Cruz islands. Fishing and agriculture are the two main sources of income. The islands were discovered in 1535 by Bishop Tomás de Berlanga. They were first marked on a map in 1570 by the Flemish cartographer Abraham Ortelius. They were later frequented by English buccaneers, and later still by whaling ships.

Economic resources. In the past, shipping, and especially Pacific whalers, visited the islands to obtain supplies of water and giant tortoises. Today wild goats live on many of the islands; wild cattle, a source of food for the settlers, are common on Isabela, Santa Cruz, Santa María, and San Salvador.

Less than 4 percent of the land area of the islands is fit for agriculture. Parts of the moist highlands on Santa Cruz, San Cristóbal, Santa María, and southern Isabela are cultivated, producing common vegetables, tropical fruits, and field crops. Coffee is exported to the mainland. Cattle are also raised for export. The people living close to the coast subsist mainly by fishing; groupers (large fish related to the sea bass) form the most profitable export. Spiny lobsters are abundant; there is a freezing plant at Academy Bay on Santa Cruz Island. Tuna fishing in the waters around the island is practiced by United States firms. Forest resources are mainly for local use. There are few mineral resources. Salt of high quality is mined near Villamil. Efforts to mine salt on San Salvador and sulfur on Isabela proved unprofitable.

Prospects for the future. Breeds of cattle and crops could be improved, but since Ecuador produces the same types of crops, export prospects are not promising. Prospects for the development of tourism, however, seem favourable, providing that the characteristic fauna remains intact. In the early 1970s the vegetation and animal life were endangered by man. Of the main islands only Fernandina, Genovesa (Tower), Darwin (Culpepper), and Wenman (Wolf) remained virtually untouched by man.

BIBLIOGRAPHY. C.W. BEEBE, *Galápagos: World's End* (1924); I. EIBL-EIBESFELDT, *Survey on the Galápagos Islands,*

UNESCO *Mission Reports* No. 8 (1959), and *Galápagos, die Arche Noah im Pazifik* (1960; Eng. trans., *Galápagos: The Noah's Ark of the Pacific*, 1960); and B. NELSON, *Galápagos: Islands of Birds* (1968), general surveys with observations on animal behaviour (illustrated); R.I. BOWMAN, *Morphological Differentiation and Adaptation in the Galápagos Finches* (1961); and D.L. LACK, *Darwin's Finches* (1947), scientific monographs on the Darwin finches; C.M. LARREA, *El Archipiélago de Colón (Galápagos) des Cubrimiento*, 2nd ed. (1960); J. LARUELLE, "Galápagos," *Natuurwet. Tijdschr.*, 47: 3–236 (1967), Flemish with French summary; and J. DORST and J. LARUELLE, *The First Seven Years of the Charles Darwin Foundation for the Galápagos Isles, 1959–1966* (1967), notable for extensive bibliographies. Larrea writes from a historical standpoint, while Laruelle presents a scientific survey, covering geology in particular. R.I. BOWMAN (ed.), *The Galápagos: Proceedings of the Symposia of the Galápagos International Scientific Project* (1966); and K. BROWER (ed.), *Galápagos: The Flow of Wildness*, 2 vol. (1968), magnificently illustrated.

(I.E.-E.)

Galaxies, External

Galaxies are vast systems of stars that also contain gas and dust in various concentrations and are distributed in groups and clusters throughout space to the limits of astronomical observation. The thousands of stars distinguishable to the unaided eye and the millions more making up the Milky Way system belong to the same Galaxy of which Earth's solar system is a vanishingly small part. This Galaxy is often given a capital *G* in print to distinguish it from others, but it is only one of innumerable systems and no more than a typical member of its class.

Observers looking out beyond the Galaxy find the external galaxies ever fainter and more numerous as more powerful telescopes reach ever farther into space. In apparent diameter and apparent brightness they range from the Large Magellanic Cloud, readily visible to the unaided eyes of observers in the Southern Hemisphere, to specks of the 23rd magnitude, scarcely distinguishable by the largest telescopes. Each of these galaxies, sometimes called island universes, is composed of myriads of stars—probably between 10^9 and 10^{11} stars per galaxy. In many, as in the Galaxy, nebulae, star clusters, and interstellar matter can be detected.

Components of galaxies

Most, perhaps all, galaxies are arranged in groups or clusters of from a few to a few thousand members each. The nearest external galaxies, the Magellanic Clouds, lie perhaps 150,000 light-years from the Earth (a light-year is the distance traversed by light in a year of travel at a constant 300,000 kilometres [186,000 miles] per second, roughly 9.5 times 10^{12} kilometres [5.9 times 10^{12} miles]). The most distant galaxies observable are at several times 10^8 light-years' distance. Diameters of galaxies are measured generally in tens of thousands of light-years, while the distance between galaxies within a cluster averages perhaps 1,000,000 or 2,000,000 light-years, and the spaces between clusters of galaxies may be a hundred times again as great. The observable universe may contain about as many galaxies (on the order of 10^{11}) as the Galaxy in which Earth lies contains individual stars.

EARLY HISTORY OF THE STUDY OF GALAXIES

Until the 20th century the existence of external galaxies was uncertain. Lumped together in the broad class of "nebulae" were all nebulous-appearing celestial objects except comets, whose transient nature set them apart. Included were galaxies, star clusters whose individual members were rendered indistinguishable by distance, and the galactic (*i.e.*, within the Galaxy) clouds of glowing interstellar gas now called bright nebulae. The external galaxies continued to be called extragalactic nebulae well after the middle of the century, although their true nature had been effectively demonstrated in the 1920s.

Historical records of observations of luminous patches in the sky go back as far as Hipparchus (2nd century BC), who included some nebulous star clusters in the earliest known star catalog. The Andromeda Nebula (with the Magellanic Clouds, one of three external galaxies visible without optical aid) was recorded by the Arabian astronomer aṣ-Ṣūfī, in *Book of the Fixed Stars*, epoch AD 964.

Following the invention of the telescope in the first years of the 17th century, "nebulae" of all kinds began to be extensively studied and cataloged. Speculation arose, in the writings of the 18th-century philosophers Immanuel Kant from Germany, Emanuel Swedenborg from Sweden, and Thomas Wright from England, that some of these nebulous objects might be systems like the Milky Way, so distant that their individual stars could not be distinguished. Not until the early years of the 20th century, however, had enough observational data been collected to permit a scientific attack on the problem. In 1917 a U.S. astronomer, George Willis Ritchey, discovered, on a photograph of the "nebula" known by its catalog number as NGC 6946, taken at Mount Wilson Observatory (now part of the Hale Observatories), in California, what appeared to be a nova. Novae, or exploding stars, are fairly common in the Galaxy, but this one seemed unusually faint, as if it were extraordinarily distant. Looking through other Mount Wilson photographs, Ritchey found that two more novae had appeared in the Andromeda Nebula in 1909. Heber D. Curtis, at Lick Observatory, also in California, searched his photographs and found other novae had occurred in other nebulous objects. Because of the faintness of the novae, he concluded that these objects must be well outside the stellar system of the Galaxy. A U.S. astronomer, Harlow Shapley, who had made an early attempt to measure the size of the Galaxy, did not believe the starlike objects found by Ritchey and Curtis were novae and supposed all nebulae to be associated with the Galaxy. A controversy arose, culminating in 1921 in a debate between Curtis and Shapley before the United States' National Academy of Sciences. The matter was not settled until 1924, when Edwin Powell Hubble, working with the 100-inch telescope at Mount Wilson, discovered stars of a type called Cepheid variables in the Andromeda and Triangulum nebulae and in NGC 6822, and he demonstrated that these stars were the exact counterparts of similar Cepheid variables known in the Milky Way system; from their faintness he calculated the distances of the nebulae in which they occurred and proved conclusively that these nebulae were star systems far outside the Milky Way and similar to it.

Discovery of extragalactic novae

Discovery of Cepheid variables

STATISTICAL PROPERTIES OF GALAXIES

Classification. The most generally accepted scheme of classification for the galaxies is one proposed by Hubble in 1926. It is represented schematically in Figure 1. This system arranges in a single homogeneous pattern nearly 98 percent of the numerous galaxies that are sufficiently large and bright to show appreciable structure on photographs taken with telescopes of moderate power (regular galaxies); the remaining 2 or 3 percent that do not readily fall into the system are called irregular galaxies. The basic feature of the classification is, to use Hubble's words, "conspicuous evidence of rotational symmetry about dominating, central nuclei." It was formerly thought that individual galaxies evolved through the various stages of the classification sequence, but this view is no longer generally held.

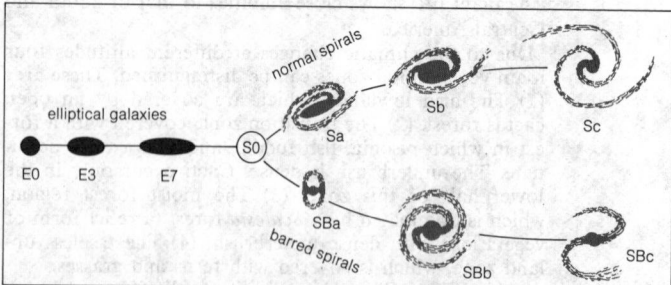

Figure 1: Hubble's system of classification for galaxies (see text).

Elliptical galaxies, denoted by E in Figure 1, have forms ranging from globular to lenticular, with the degree of ellipticity indicated by numerals from 0 to 7. Statistical analysis of the frequency of occurrence of the different forms shows that there are actually globular, or spherical, galaxies and that not all of the apparently round ones can be accounted for as flattened galaxies with polar axes in the line of sight. The analysis shows, however, that the lenticular objects are much more common and that there is a definite limiting ellipticity at a 3:1 ratio of the axes. When the flattening becomes greater, the galaxies no longer appear as smooth, unresolved objects, and, at a certain stage of the sequence, indicated by S0, they begin to show structure that in general is of spiral character. Two different spiral forms are found: normal spirals, designated by S, and barred spirals, symbolized by SB. Within these two classes spirals are designated a, b, or c, in order of the degree of resolution possible—*i.e.*, of the increasing clarity of the structure of the spiral arms; thus, a well-resolved normal spiral would be referred to as Sc, a barred one as SBc. The prefix "d" indicates a dwarf galaxy. Several dwarf elliptical (dE) galaxies are known in relatively nearby space; many others may exist, undetected, at greater distances.

Morgan's classification system

In 1958 William W. Morgan of the Yerkes Observatory, Wisconsin, devised a supplementary classification scheme aimed at describing the stellar population of galaxies having different Hubble types. By analogy with the classification of stars according to their temperatures, in which stars are designated O, B, A, F, G, K, and M in decreasing order of temperature, Morgan classified galaxies as a, af, f, fg, g, gk, and k according to the type of stars providing most of their light. There is a strong correlation between Hubble type and Morgan type, with the irregular galaxies predominantly a and af, the Sc galaxies af–fg, and the E galaxies being gk and k.

The extragalactic distance scale. Distances of galaxies are most accurately determined from studies of objects within them that may be recognized and compared with their counterparts in the Milky Way. These objects may be brightest stars, variable stars, star clusters, gaseous nebulae, or novae. When these can be identified, their apparent magnitudes, m, are measured and compared with their absolute magnitudes, M, which are assumed to be the same as those for corresponding galactic objects. By definition, M equals m at a distance of 32.6 light-years.

Once an extragalactic object's apparent magnitude is measured and its absolute magnitude assumed to be known, the distance, d, is computed from the simple **Distance formula**

$$5\log d = (m - M + 5),$$

which assumes that the apparent brightness of an object varies inversely as the square of the distance. If there is reason to believe that somewhere along the line of sight to the extragalactic object there is matter that absorbs some of the light, a correction is determined or estimated for the apparent magnitude, which, of course, is made too faint by any obscuring material. Such matter may be present in the Galaxy, in the external galaxy whose distance is sought, or possibly in intergalactic space. Correction for its effect often is difficult to make, and there may be considerable uncertainty even with the best procedure.

In practice, the use of individual objects within galaxies for distance determination is limited to a few hundred of the nearest and brightest galaxies. Vast numbers of galaxies are so far and faint that even the largest telescopes cannot single out objects within them for individual study. Thus it is necessary to use other distance criteria, which may be apparent diameter, total magnitude (entire light of a galaxy), and red shift (a shift of spectrum lines toward the red end of the spectrum, which increases with increasing distance of the source). These quantities all have to be calibrated, or evaluated, in terms of the distance criteria used for the nearer galaxies, before they can be used to obtain distances on an absolute scale of light-years.

Apparent distribution of galaxies. As a result of extensive counts of galaxies on photographs, it is now known that their distribution is nonrandom over the sky and approximately uniform in depth. This last result is of great theoretical and practical value for cosmological studies.

Counts per unit area of sky. Long before the advent of photography, it was generally known from visual observations that the "white" nebulae, now called galaxies, tended to avoid the Milky Way and that there was appreciable clustering in high galactic latitudes, especially in the constellations Coma Berenices and Virgo close to the north pole of the Galaxy. With the development of photography, more and ever more galaxies were counted. The zone of avoidance around the central plane of the Milky Way (a zone characterized by an apparent absence of galaxies) and the regions of clustering became more precisely defined. A number of counts in the early 20th century suggested the general outlines of the distribution and gave hints as to the total number of galaxies within reach of certain telescopes, but the problem of counts of galaxies was not put on a firm quantitative basis until 1934. In that year Hubble published the results of surveys in which more than 44,000 galaxies were counted in 1,300 sample regions rather evenly distributed over three-quarters of the sky. For the first time, the counts were calibrated and referred to specified limiting magnitudes. With all the data reduced to standard conditions, it became clear that the numbers of galaxies decreased in a very regular way as the Milky Way was approached. The rate of decrease, in fact, was just that to be expected from a thin obscuring layer in which the absorption is proportional to the light path in the stratum—a familiar analogy is the dimming of stars as they approach the horizon. What is called the zone of avoidance along the Milky Way is thus but the effect of looking in the plane of the stratum, where the absorption is at a maximum that approaches complete opacity; toward the poles of the Galaxy the absorption is at a minimum, with the light reduced by only 20 percent. In the more populous areas, on the other hand, there is a conspicuous tendency for the galaxies to cluster. They occur in pairs, in small to large groups of several to 100 galaxies, and in great clusters that include more than 500 members, as in the aggregations in the constellations Coma Berenices and Virgo.

Zone of avoidance

Numbers and distribution in depth. Galaxies populate space with an approximately constant density as far as telescopes can reach. This determination has been made from counts of galaxies to successively fainter limiting magnitudes. For the brightest objects, it is only necessary to total to each limiting magnitude the number of galaxies whose magnitudes have been individually determined. For the faintest objects, on the other hand, it is much simpler to count galaxies to limiting magnitudes determined by exposures of different lengths, or by telescopes of different light-gathering power. This indirect procedure is expedient because the faintest galaxies are overwhelmingly too numerous to estimate their individual brightnesses. With the numbers of galaxies established to increasingly fainter magnitudes, it is relatively easy to test the hypothesis of constant space density. This is done by noting whether the numbers of galaxies counted are proportional to the volumes of space in which they are found. More precisely, a simple calculation shows that the rate of increase is by a factor of 4 when the limiting brightness decreases by one magnitude. For galaxies fainter than about the 18th magnitude photographic magnitudes become abnormally faint, with the result that the observed number falls below that expected on the basis of a uniform distribution.

Extensive surveys have shown that clustering of galaxies is by far the rule rather than the exception. A Swiss astronomer, Fritz Zwicky, reported in 1952 that, on one plate covering about 40 square degrees in Corona Borealis, nearly 100 clusters could be identified. The existence of so many clusters suggests that they, instead of individual galaxies, may be the fundamental building blocks of the universe. If this is the case, then clusters of galaxies promise to provide significant information on the structure of the universe, in addition to having served as stepping-stones for determination of the extragalactic distance scale.

Clusters and superclusters

If only the brighter galaxies to the 12th or 13th magnitude are considered, they show a tendency, first noted in 1923, to occur in a great circle band around the sky. It is a belt with an average width of 12° that runs nearly perpendicular to the Milky Way, which it crosses in the northern constellation of Cassiopeia and again in the southern one of Circinus. The northern arc includes the Virgo cluster with its extensions to the south in Centaurus and to the north in Coma Berenices, Canes Venatici, and Ursa Major. The southern part is less populous, but there are series of groups of bright galaxies in Andromeda, Pisces, Cetus, Sculptor, and beyond into far southern skies.

The possibility that these brightest galaxies may form in space an extended "metagalactic" system or cloud, which may also include the Galaxy, has been suggested by a number of investigators. In shape it would be a flattened system of some tens of millions of light-years in diameter and one-tenth as thick. But this interpretation is uncertain. Evidence found in the early 1950s gave strong support to the concept of a "local supergalaxy" that includes the Milky Way and has the great Virgo cluster of galaxies as a dominant feature near its centre. If this is a valid assumption, then the Galaxy, in addition to being close to the principal plane of the supersystem, would be about three-fourths of the way from the centre to the edge, since the bright galaxies in the Coma Berenices–Virgo region around the north galactic pole are thought to be three times more distant than some groups of large spirals in the opposite direction toward the south galactic pole. The supersystem would be, of course, many millions of light-years in diameter.

The "local super-galaxy"

A local supercluster of bright galaxies may not be unique. The existence of similar systems has been suggested by other observers. Firm observational evidence is difficult to obtain, and some astronomers prefer the interpretation that a patchy distribution of clusters is caused by dark obscuring intergalactic material, distributed in patches. Either interpretation has profound significance for attempts to infer the structure and nature of the universe; there is no theoretical understanding of how such superclustering or such extensive dark intergalactic clouds could have come into existence. To resolve the problem on an observational basis, much time with large telescopes will be required.

The nearby galaxies. What is known as the Local Group comprises Earth's Galaxy and 18 or 20 others, occupying a volume of space perhaps 2,000,000 light-years in diameter. The Local Group is in no way remarkable among clusters of galaxies. Like other clusters, it is probably held together by the mutual gravitational attraction of its members, of which the Galaxy seems to be one of the largest. About half of the Local Group are elliptical galaxies, with the remainder spiral or irregular in shape. There may be undiscovered members of the group; one probable member, the giant elliptical Maffei I, was discovered by its infrared radiation in the late 1960s. Intervening dust clouds had prevented its visible light from reaching Earth.

PHYSICAL PROPERTIES OF GALAXIES

The stellar content of galaxies, their masses, rotations, and the ratio of mass to total luminosity are physical properties that bear on the structural forms, evolution, age, and ultimately, one may hope, on the problem of the origin of galaxies.

Stellar populations and evolution. In 1944 the U.S. astronomer Walter Baade, using the Mount Wilson 100-inch reflector to maximum advantage in a sky darkened by a wartime blackout of city lights, reported the resolution for the first time of the amorphous nuclear region of the Andromeda Nebulae into myriads of faint stars. At the same time he also resolved the several fainter elliptical companions of the large spiral. These were results of great importance, for they showed that the generally smooth and featureless light in elliptical galaxies and in nuclei of spirals comes from stars of a different kind than those forming spiral arms. In the latter the brightest stars are blue–white supergiants often enmeshed in dark and bright nebulous material, while in the nuclear regions and in elliptical galaxies the brightest stars are yellow–red giants, and in these regions there is no dust and bright gaseous matter. Since blue–white supergiant stars may be hundreds of times intrinsically more luminous than giants, it is easy to understand why elliptical galaxies were, and still are, so difficult to resolve into stars, even with the largest telescopes.

Baade's observations represented a telescopic triumph, and his interpretation of them proved to be of surpassing significance. First, he stressed the close association of blue supergiants, interstellar material, and diffuse bright and dark gaseous nebulae in spiral structure, which he termed stellar Population I. Second, he emphasized the similarities of the spherical distributions, colours, and luminosities of the galactic globular cluster stars with the elliptical galaxies and the nuclear-region red giants, which he called stellar Population II. These two populations can be distinguished in the Galaxy, because they have different dynamics (properties related to motion): type I participates primarily in the general rotation in the principal plane and has a small internal velocity dispersion; type II, on the other hand, shows little tendency toward general rotation and has a high internal velocity range. Thus type I is essentially a disk, or fundamental-plane, population, while type II is a halolike population surrounding and permeating the entire system. The distinction between the two populations, however, goes even deeper than their differences in spatial distribution and dynamics. As the result of much modern work stimulated by Baade's discoveries, it is known that the two populations represent separate stages in stellar evolution: Population II is older, perhaps by several times 10^9 years.

Stellar populations

The blue supergiants of Population I pour out radiation at so high a rate that they consume their hydrogen fuel in the astronomically short time of a few millions or tens of millions of years. Since these stars are present in the spiral arms of galaxies generally and can be identified in galaxies over a wide range of distances, their relatively brief lifetimes mean that they must be continually forming in the spiral structure; otherwise, they should not be seen over such a long range in time as inferred from their distances. Since their formation and fleeting cosmic existence require enormous quantities of hydrogen, the basic fuel, the conclusion is almost inescapable that they originate from the hydrogen-rich interstellar gas and dust. The red giants of Population II, on the other hand, have spent most of their lives as relatively faint stars, not much brighter intrinsically than the Sun, and so they have been rewarded for their economical rate of spending energy by lifetimes hundreds of times longer. The red stars in the centre of the Andromeda Nebula and in its elliptical companions are embedded in an innumerable swarm of dwarf stars, which will in turn become red giants when they have reached a certain stage in their evolution and will replace the red giants seen now when those burn out. But because there is no dust or gas in that region, new bright blue stars can no longer form there. The dwarf stars must originally have formed out of an interstellar medium, but their present properties suggest that they did so at a time far in the past and have long since diffused out of the regions where they were born. The oldest of them may have formed at a time when the entire parent system consisted largely of a primeval turbulent mass, rather than a well-defined, rotating, thin disk.

Following Baade's fundamental work, it was realized that two distinct stellar populations are not sufficient to describe the variety of stars observed (see also STAR). Five types are often distinguished: extreme Population II, intermediate Population II, disk population, intermediate Population I, and extreme Population I. Although it appears that there is a continual gradation from one type to another, consideration of the evolutionary differences among the several types, or populations, of stars sheds light on the question of how a whole galaxy may evolve. Detailed spectroscopic analysis shows that the oldest observable stars have very small abundances of the heavier elements in their makeup, compared with the young, hot, blue stars and the gaseous nebulae. By relating the ages, population types, and locations of the different kinds of stars in the Galaxy with their chemical composition,

Extension of Baade's classification

it has been possible to build up a qualitative picture of a progression from an initial turbulent, roughly spherical cloud of gas, out of which the oldest stars formed, to the building of increasing amounts of the heavier chemical elements in successive generations of stars, and the gradual shrinking of the uncondensed material to a central plane, leading to the Galaxy's present form. New stars can form only where there are gas and dust, and so they are confined to this central plane. But the details of the picture remain obscure, and it seems that the process of heavy-element synthesis in the Galaxy has been an uneven and patchy one.

For other galaxies the sort of precise photometric and spectroscopic information obtainable for stars and gas clouds in the Milky Way is much more difficult to acquire, and the necessary observations take a long time, even with the largest telescopes. Astronomers hope to be able to relate this information to the structural forms of galaxies and see whether the various kinds—irregulars, barred spirals, normal spirals, and ellipticals—can be arranged chronologically. But basic properties of galaxies, such as their masses, the amount of their rotation (their angular momenta), and quantitative values of their primeval magnetic fields and turbulent motions, may all play an important part in determining their evolution. It remains to be seen whether or not the variety of forms of galaxies indicates a great range in age.

Rotation of spiral galaxies. The most casual glance at photographs of spiral galaxies suggests rotation, which is readily revealed spectroscopically for systems tilted toward the line of sight. It was proven in 1914 that the central parts of several of the brightest spirals, including the Andromeda Nebula (M31), have a component of rotation in the line of sight. Earth's Galaxy, a spiral similar to M31, was shown in 1927 to be rotating. Because of the extreme faintness of the light from galaxies, further progress was slow, and even by 1950 only the two nearest and apparently largest spirals, M31 and M33, had been studied in any detail. In these, astronomers were able to follow the character of the rotation out to the extreme limits shown on photographs.

In succeeding decades, new spectrographic methods were used. By the mid-1960s it was clear that rotation is a very general property of galaxies of all structural forms; it is easiest to measure in spirals with plenty of interstellar gas, but it is also present in S0 galaxies and ellipticals with little or no interstellar matter. These rotations can be used to determine the masses of galaxies (see below *Masses of galaxies*).

Direction of rotation in spirals. Closely allied with the character of the rotational motion of spirals is the question of how the movement takes place with respect to the curvature of the spiral arms; in other words, whether the arms appear to be winding or unwinding. A U.S. astronomer, Vesto Melvin Slipher, pioneered in this field, and, on the basis of his rotation measures and his inferences of the true spatial orientation of the galaxies from their apparent or projected forms, he concluded that all spirals probably rotate in the same manner: the central part turns into the spiral arms like a coil spring being wound up.

The interpretation of photographs of spirals, to determine which edge is nearer the observer, is not easy, and not until the 1940s was it generally accepted that all spirals rotate in the same way: as the central part turns, the arms lag behind.

Persistence of spiral structure. Spiral galaxies have in general two arms, starting at diametrically opposite sides of the nucleus and having the form of equiangular spirals making one to one and a half complete windings. If galaxies were rotating like solid wheels, any structure, spiral or otherwise, would remain undisturbed. The spectroscopic measurements, however, clearly show that galaxies do not rotate as solid bodies but differentially, like a cup of coffee being stirred. The time for one rotation in a well-studied spiral galaxy, NGC 5055, varies from about 20,000,000 years near its centre to 200,000,000 years at its outer edges. In its total lifetime of about 10,000,000,-000 years, one would expect any spiral structure initially

possessed by the galaxy to have been wound up so many times as to be now unrecognizable. The only way to resolve this difficulty is to show that spiral structure is a transient but continually renewed property, and this was plausibly done in 1963–64 by the U.S. astronomer Chia-Chiao Lin and colleagues, at the Massachusetts Institute of Technology. They showed mathematically that a uniform, thin, infinitely large rotating disk is unstable and will form a density wave in the gaseous material, and the most likely form of this density wave is a two-armed trailing spiral. The wave will always be present but will travel slowly through the galaxy; since new, hot, massive, highly luminous stars can form only where the gas and dust tend to collect, this spiral structure will always be outlined by the successive generations of short-lived blue–white supergiant stars. In the late 1960s an alternate explanation of spiral arms was suggested, namely, that they are formed by material thrown out from the spinning galactic nuclei. Density waves

Masses of galaxies. According to Newton's law of gravitation, the centrifugal acceleration at any point in a rotating galaxy must balance the gravitational attraction of all the mass lying interior to that point. Since the centrifugal acceleration is determined by the rotational velocity and by the distance from the centre, measurement of the rotation curve can be used to calculate the distribution of mass and the total mass of any galaxy. By this means the masses of the Galaxy, of the Andromeda and Triangulum nebulae, and of about 50 other spiral galaxies have been determined. These masses range from approximately 300,000,000,000 times the mass of the Sun, for giant galaxies like the Andromeda Nebula, to values about one-hundredth of that for small galaxies. In even smaller galaxies it becomes more difficult to detect and measure rotation; therefore, most of the determinations lie in the range given above. The rotational velocities, plotted against distance from the centre, give graphs that are usually concave to the axis on which distance from the centre is plotted; mathematical analysis of such curves shows that the mass concentration is greatest in the centre and the density of matter decreases smoothly outward from the centre.

As well as being commonly distributed in groups and clusters, galaxies often occur in pairs in the same way as do stars. As with double stars, measurements of the separations and orbital velocities of double galaxies yield their masses. For elliptical galaxies the average masses, determined in this way, come out to be about ten times greater than for spirals. Since the diameters of ellipticals and spirals are about the same, this difference points to a striking difference in average density and raises the question as to whether this might be the cause of the different forms and different stellar populations in the two kinds of galaxies. A reasonable hypothesis is that star formation might be much more rapid in ellipticals, as a consequence of their greater density; virtually all the gas and dust might have been used up early in their lifetimes so that only the old, long-lived stars remain to be seen now. The difference in masses and densities between ellipticals and spirals militates against the earlier theory that galaxies might evolve through the sequence irregulars–spirals–ellipticals. Such evolution would have to be accompanied by an increase in mass and density. Pairs of galaxies

If knowledge of the masses of elliptical galaxies rested solely upon average determinations from double galaxies, the difference between spirals and ellipticals could be explained as the result of some spurious statistical effect. Although it is very difficult to determine rotations of ellipticals, since, unlike spirals, they have no interstellar gas to produce the emission that is spectroscopically easy to measure for motion in the observer's line of sight, there is another way of determining masses in stellar systems. In the centres of galaxies, the average random speeds of the stars are governed by the gravitational force acting upon them and hence by the total mass. It is possible to measure the average speeds of stars in the centres of galaxies by measuring the broadening of spectrum lines produced by the aggregate of stars. From the average speeds of these stars in the centre, the mass of the whole galaxy can be calculated. In 1968 about six individual determinations had been made in this way. These individual determinations span a very wide range, from 3×10^9 solar masses for M32, the small elliptical companion of the Andromeda Nebula, to about 10^{12} solar masses in the giant ellipticals in the nearby Virgo cluster; throughout this range the densities of the ellipticals seemed to be about ten times greater than those of the spirals.

Peculiar galaxies.   There are some galaxies so irregular in form that they are well described by the term peculiar. These are interesting because they may represent transient structural forms and hence might throw light on the evolution of galaxies. In Moscow, the Soviet astronomer B.A. Vorontsov-Velyaminov in 1959 made a photographic catalog of about 350 of such strange objects; seven years later, in 1966, at Mount Wilson and Palomar observatories (now Hale Observatories), the U.S. astronomer Halton Arp made a more detailed photographic atlas and catalog.

Compact galactic systems   Another class of peculiar galaxies is the compact systems. Some of these are so compact as to be barely distinguishable from stars on the photographs, yet, when examined with spectrographs, they are clearly seen to be galaxies of a very dense structure. In the late 1960s their relationship to normal galaxies was not understood.

Among the galaxies, some are emitting intense radio radiation (see below *Radio observations of galaxies*). These, the radio galaxies, often have peculiar structures, such as prominent clouds and lanes of dust, as in NGC 5128, or a fountain of hot gas spurting out of the central region, as in M82. These structural peculiarities, together with the spectroscopic information, suggest that those galaxies have been subjected to violent explosions in their centres (see below).

RADIO OBSERVATIONS OF GALAXIES

Radio radiation from the Milky Way was first detected in 1932, but this work was largely neglected until after World War II, when the men who had developed radar built the first radio telescopes and began systematically to do astronomy at radio wavelengths. It is convenient to divide radio observations into those dealing with spectral lines and those dealing with the continuous radiation at all radio wavelengths.

Line radiation.   The radiation of 21-centimetre wavelength emitted by clouds of hydrogen in space was first detected in an extragalactic system in 1953 by Australian radio astronomers, who observed both Magellanic Clouds and in 1954 determined the distribution of neutral hydrogen in both clouds and in the common envelope in which they appeared to be embedded. Later work has confirmed and refined these results. The neutral (not ionized) hydrogen in the Large Magellanic Cloud amounts to approximately 10 percent of its total mass; about the same total amount of hydrogen is in the Small Magellanic Cloud, whose mass, not accurately known, is probably less than that of the Large Magellanic Cloud.

As previously noted (see above *Masses of galaxies*), 21-centimetre radiation has been detected in many other spiral and irregular galaxies, where it has been used to derive the mass of neutral hydrogen and the rotation and hence the total mass of the galaxy. In cases in which both optical spectroscopic and 21-centimetre measurements have been made for the same galaxy, the red shifts have been found to be in good agreement over the long range of wavelength. The 21-centimetre radiation has not yet been detected, however, in any very distant galaxies.

Other radio line radiations that have been detected in gaseous nebulae in the Milky Way are those caused by the molecule OH, at rest frequencies of 1,612, 1,665, 1,667, and 1,721 million cycles per second (megahertz), or wavelengths of 17–19 centimetres, which have been seen in absorption and in emission, and high-order lines produced by the recombination of ionized hydrogen, which have been seen in emission at a number of wavelengths. None of these has been detected in other galaxies.

Continuum radiation.   A few years after the end of World War II, radio astronomers found that the sky contains a number of discrete sources of continuum radio radiation—*i.e.*, radiation spread continuously over a wide range of radio wavelengths (see RADIO SOURCES, ASTRONOMICAL). Australian radio astronomers in 1949 pinpointed three of the discrete sources with sufficient accuracy to make reasonably certain their correspondence with three optically known celestial objects, including the peculiar elliptical external galaxies NGC 5128 and NGC 4486 (M87).

The two strongest radio sources in the sky (not counting the Sun) were Cygnus A and Cassiopeia A, and their identification was achieved in 1954. Cygnus A was found to be a peculiar, rather distant galaxy with a double nucleus, while Cassiopeia A was discovered to be a faint galactic nebula—*i.e.*, one within the Galaxy. Optical spectrograms of these two sources showed that both contained much highly excited hot gas and that the filaments of Cassiopeia A were moving at enormous speeds, several thousand miles per second. The suggestion of I.S. Shklovsky in the U.S.S.R. that Cassiopeia A is the remnant of a supernova (violently exploding star) was generally accepted by 1958, when a detailed study of the speeds in the gas had shown that the nebula was expanding.

In the decade following 1954, astronomers in England and Australia produced catalogs of radio sources whose positions were gradually refined in accuracy, and the identification of sources continued. Until 1960 the identified extra-solar-system sources were always found to be either galactic nebulae or external galaxies. The galactic nebulae proved to be of two kinds, either arcs or expanding clouds of gas that were shown to be most probably remnants of supernovae or clouds of hot gas such as the Orion Nebula. The physical processes producing the radio radiation proved to be different in the two cases.

Physical processes that produce radio radiation   In nebulae like that in Orion the random motions of the negatively charged particles, electrons, in the vicinity of the positively charged protons, or hydrogen nuclei, produce optical radiation and radio radiation. This radiation depends upon the temperature of the gas and is called thermal radiation. Galactic nebulae that consist of hot clouds of gas, mainly hydrogen, and that are not the remains of supernova explosions emit radio radiation by this process.

The radio and optical radiation of much of the Crab Nebula and the radio radiation of the external galaxies cannot be explained in this way. A suggestion by Swedish astronomers, that radiation of the kind known in the giant laboratory synchrotrons (machines used by physicists to accelerate subatomic particles) might be astrophysically important, was developed by a group of Soviet theoreticians. This synchrotron radiation is produced by charged particles being accelerated in magnetic fields; it is highly polarized, and the way in which the intensity varies with wavelength, dependent upon the energies of the charged particles, has a characteristic form that fits well the observations of the discrete radio sources. It was discovered in 1956 that the light in the raylike blue jet extending from the centre of the strongly radio-emitting galaxy NGC 4486 (M87) is strongly polarized, which meant that it must be synchrotron radiation. By 1958 the theory of synchrotron radiation was generally accepted for the nonthermal sources.

Violent events in nuclei of galaxies.   Very large total energies are necessary to produce the synchrotron radiation. Such energies were known to be released in the supernovae (violent stellar explosions), but some even larger energy supply was required for the much more powerful radio sources in galaxies. In 1943 the U.S. astronomer C.K. Seyfert, working at the Mount Wilson Observatory, studied a small class of about a dozen spiral galaxies that have very small, intensely bright centres, or nuclei. He showed that these nuclei contain hot gas moving very violently, at speeds of several thousand miles per second. The proportion of spiral galaxies that are like this and have come to be called Seyfert galaxies is about 2 percent. The Seyfert galaxies

The galaxy M87, a powerful X-ray and radio source, was found in 1960 to have hot gas in its nucleus, with large outward motions of nearly 600 miles (1,000 kilometres) per second. Such observations suggest some violent explosive event in the centre of the galaxy.

In 1962 evidence was presented that a violent explosion occurred about 1,000,000 years ago in the nucleus of a bright irregular radio-emitting galaxy in Ursa Major, NGC 3034 (M82). This galaxy had been shown in 1960 to be rotating. Its orientation to the line of sight is close to edge-on (see Figure 2). Speeds of nearly 100 miles

By courtesy of Hale Observatories

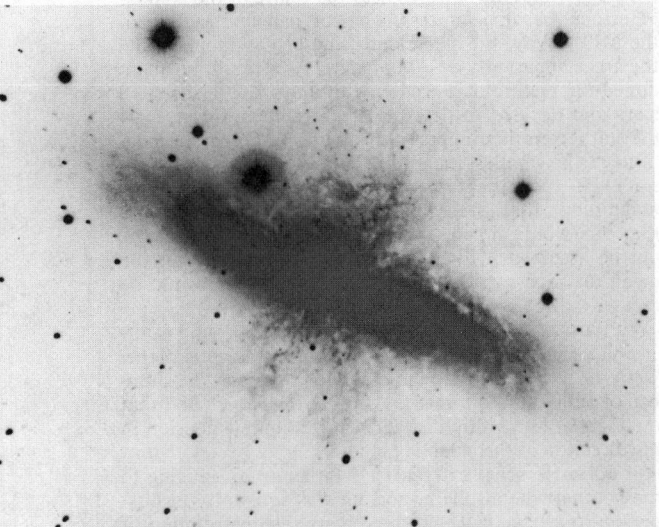

Figure 2: *Exploding galaxy M82 in Ursa Major.*
The inner-region filaments, mainly hydrogen, seem to have been ejected from the nucleus about 1,500,000 years ago in galactic time, or 11,500,000 years ago in Earth time; M82 is 10,000,000 light-years distant. The farthest filaments are more than 20,000 light-years from the nucleus, and the mass thrown out is equivalent to 5,000,000 Suns.

(160 kilometres) per second were measured in gaseous filaments along the minor axis, where there should be no effect of rotation visible, so that the only way the filaments could be moving was outward from the centre of NGC 3034. Other astronomers measured a high degree of polarization in some of these filaments, thus showing that they were shining by means of synchrotron radiation.

In 1965 it was found that a similar explosion had occurred in the centre of the peculiar spiral NGC 1275, also a strong emitter of radio radiation and the brightest member of the Perseus cluster of galaxies. This galaxy has a complicated pattern of filaments on one side of it, with a velocity of nearly 2,000 miles (3,000 kilometres) per second relative to its centre. In 1954, after the very strong radio source Cygnus A had been identified with a faint double-centred galaxy, it was suggested that all radio galaxies were the results of collisions between galaxies. Such collisions would involve enormous amounts of energy. But several of the brighter radio galaxies were obviously single. Even NGC 1275, which had been considered a prime example of a pair of colliding galaxies, proved under more detailed examination to be better explained as the result of a gigantic explosion some one or two million years ago. The detailed physics of all these violent processes in galaxies remained in doubt.

BIBLIOGRAPHY. There are sections on galaxies in many general textbooks in astronomy that are not highly technical —for example, in GEORGE O. ABELL, *Exploration of the Universe*, 2nd ed., ch. 31–32 (1969); JOHN C. BRANDT, *New Horizons in Astronomy*, ch. 13 (1972); and ALBRECHT UNSOLD, *Der neue Kosmos* (1967; Eng. trans., *The New Cosmos*, pt. 3, 1969). A classic that is highly readable, written by the founder of modern studies of galaxies, is EDWIN P. HUBBLE, *The Realm of the Nebulae* (1937). A more technical book that can still be read easily by high-school students and undergraduates in science is PAUL W. HODGE, *The Physics and Astronomy of Galaxies and Cosmology* (1966). Hodge's book does not contain much mathematics but gives more information than the chapters listed in the works above; some familiarity with astronomical nomenclature is assumed. Forms of galaxies are treated in ALLAN SANDAGE, *The Hubble Atlas of Galaxies* (1961), which gives a beautiful collection

of photographs of galaxies, together with a detailed introduction describing the classification scheme and a historical account of early work. At a much more technical level, suitable for advanced undergraduates or graduate students, there are several long chapters in the numerous volumes of the series *Annual Review of Astronomy and Astrophysics*, on various topics concerning galaxies. Attention is drawn especially to the following chapters: MORTON S. ROBERTS, "The Content of Galaxies: Stars and Gas," and IVAN R. KING, "The Dynamics of Galaxies," both in vol. 1 (1963); GEORGE O. ABELL, "Clustering of Galaxies," vol. 3 (1965); B.J. BOK, "Magellanic Clouds," and ALAN T. MOFFET, "The Structure of Radio Galaxies," both in vol. 4 (1966); G.R. BURBIDGE, "The Nuclei of Galaxies," vol. 8 (1970); and PAUL W. HODGE, "Dwarf Galaxies," vol. 9 (1971).

(E.M.B.)

Galaxy, The

The term galaxy derives from the Greek word *galaxias*, meaning "milky way," given to the luminous band of stars that crosses the celestial sphere. The term was later extended to cover the whole Milky Way system. Other such star systems, formerly called extragalactic nebulae, are now called galaxies with a lowercase initial.

The Galaxy is a lens-shaped system containing about 100,000,000,000 (10^{11}) stars and a great amount of interstellar matter made up of gas and dust. It has a central nucleus in which the star density is greater than that of the outer parts of the lens, and it is surrounded by a very tenuous halo with few stars and almost no gas and dust. The solar system is very near the galactic plane—*i.e.*, the plane of symmetry of the lens—out far from the nucleus. From the Earth, the stars and interstellar matter near the galactic plane are seen from a point almost in the plane, and the concentration of stars gives rise to the luminous band of the Milky Way. In the northern sky it stretches from the constellation Aquila through Cygnus, Cepheus, Cassiopeia, Perseus, Auriga, Taurus, and Gemini to Orion, and in the southern sky from Monoceros through Puppis, Vela, Carina, Crux, Centaurus, Circinus, Norma, and Scorpius to Sagittarius. The centre of the Galaxy lies in the direction of Sagittarius.

The Milky Way band is very irregular, and parts of it differ appreciably in brilliance. Among the most conspicuous bright areas are the star clouds in Scutum, Norma, Carina, Cygnus, and Sagittarius. Dark spots and lanes are caused by interstellar dust that is obscuring the stars behind it. Best known in the northern sky is a dark band called the Great Rift, which divides the Milky Way into two branches between Cygnus and Sagittarius. In the southern constellation of Crux, the Coalsack appears to the naked eye as a black cloud, blacker than any other part of the sky.

If the Milky Way is studied with the aid of a good pair of binoculars or with a small telescope, most of its bright clouds are resolved into thousands of faint stars; some, called nebulae, remain unresolved and are gaseous objects. Many open or galactic clusters may be seen in or near the Milky Way band; for instance, the Pleiades in the north and the Jewel Box (Kappa Crucis) in the southern constellation Crux. A rich galactic cluster may contain 3,000 stars. Some distance away from the bright band, much denser and apparently nearly spherical groups called globular clusters are found; these may contain up to 1,000,000 stars. Clusters, nebulae, stars, and gas can all give important information about galactic structure.

Distribution of the stars, gas, and dust in the galactic plane

Photographic techniques are frequently used for Milky Way research. The complexity encountered in the Milky Way is obvious from Figure 1, which shows a two square degree field in the southern Milky Way.

The idea that the Galaxy might be a spiral galaxy, now well established, arose about 1930. The spiral arms have been traced by optical and radio observations. The rotation of the system around the galactic centre is known; Earth's Sun moves with the system at a speed of about 250 kilometres per second.

The formation of the Galaxy, its evolution, and the development of the spiral structure are still not fully understood (see, however, below).

This article is divided into the following sections:

I. Investigations of the Galaxy

THE 18 TH AND 19 TH CENTURIES

At the middle of the 18th century it was generally accepted that there was a "stellar system" in which the stars were arranged in space more or less symmetrically about the Milky Way. Philosophical speculations populated the whole universe with similar stellar systems.

The first systematic observational approach to the problem of the structure of the Galaxy was made by Sir William Herschel. His method of star counts, which he called "star gauges," gave the first overall picture of the Galaxy

By courtesy of B.E. Westerlund

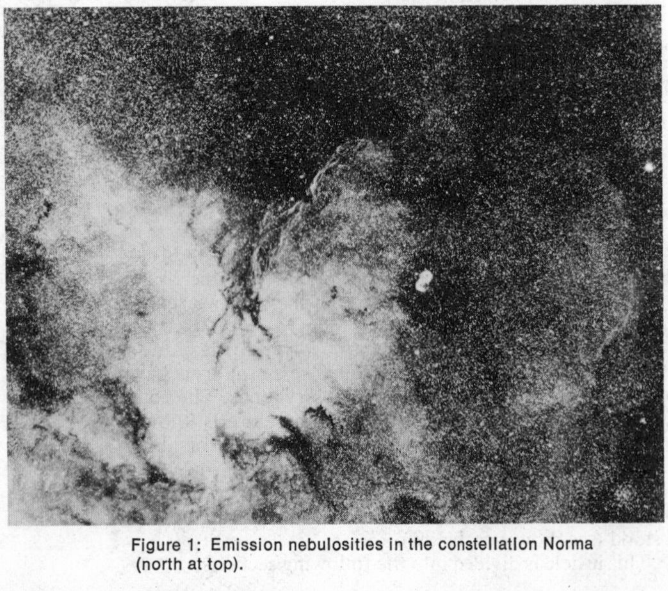

Figure 1: Emission nebulosities in the constellation Norma (north at top).

in 1785. The number of stars in a given area of the sky were counted for several thousand fields, chosen to represent the distribution of stars relative to the Milky Way.

Herschel assumed that the stars were uniformly distributed over the sky, that the system was finite, and that the penetrating power of his telescopes was sufficient to reach the borders of the system in all directions. He concluded that the Galaxy extended about five times as far in the galactic plane as it did perpendicular to the plane. According to him, the Sun was near the centre of the system.

Herschel became impressed by the patchy structure of the Milky Way, the star clouds, the bright nebulae, and the areas apparently devoid of stars. As a result, he abandoned the picture of a system with uniformly distributed stars and decided to determine the relative distances of the stars from their apparent brightnesses (apparent magnitudes, the smallest magnitude representing the brightest star). He took the same absolute luminosity (absolute magnitude), that of the Sun, for all stars. He was aware that this would not be strictly true for individual stars, but he assumed it to be statistically correct so that the mean distance of stars of the sixth magnitude would be greater than that of stars of the fifth magnitude.

With larger and larger telescopes, Herschel found fainter and fainter stars in the directions in the galactic plane, while in directions perpendicular to the plane the number of faint stars diminished rapidly. He concluded that the Galaxy was a thin disk of nearly infinite extension in the direction of the galactic plane.

Sir John Herschel extended his father's star gauging to the southern hemisphere, and he was probably the first person to notice, in 1847, the remarkable distribution of the bright stars spread out across the sky in a great circle inclined at an angle of about 20° to the galactic plane. About 30 years later an astronomer named Benjamin Gould suggested that this arrangement, now called Gould's Belt, indicated that the Sun was in a small star cluster. Its significance is still under discussion.

Sir John Herschel's extensive studies of "extragalactic nebulae," other galaxies, were also important for comparison with and understanding of the Galaxy. In 1833 he described the Whirlpool Nebula, designated M51 in the Messier catalog, as consisting of a bright round nebula surrounded at some distance by a ring that was double in one part. He pointed out that, for an observer near the central mass, the ring, if it consisted of stars, would appear much as the Milky Way does from Earth.

The coordinates of the apex (the point in the sky toward which the Sun in its peculiar motion appears to be moving in relation to the stars), found about the middle of the 19th century, confirmed the direction of the solar motion toward the constellation of Hercules, as found by Sir William Herschel nearly a century earlier. The *Bonner Durchmusterung*, a major star catalog with accompanying charts, gives positions and estimated brightnesses for nearly 400,000 stars in the sky north of 23° southern declination. It appeared between 1859 and 1886 and was followed by two southern surveys: the *Córdoba Durchmusterung*, published between 1892 and 1932, for nearly 610,000 stars south of 22° S, and the *Cape Photographic Durchmusterung*, published between 1896 and 1900, with over 450,000 stars south of 19° S. Photographs were needed to reveal the nature of the many regions devoid of stars in the Milky Way, almost always due to obscuration by dark nebulae. In 1927 a list of 349 such objects with a brief description of each was published. Dark markings that might be only vacancies among the stars were left out, implying that the remainder were considered to be nonluminous, obscuring clouds. At about the same time a method of star counts to be used to obtain the distances to the obscuring clouds was proposed. Also nearly simultaneously with the nebula catalog there appeared a list of 1,550 dark nebulae found from studies of the stellar density variations on photographic survey charts of the entire sky (see ASTRONOMICAL MAPS).

THE 20 TH CENTURY

In the last decades of the 19th century, two quite different contributions to the progress of stellar astronomy,

Kinematics of the Galaxy

analyses of star positions and of motions, gave much the same picture of the Milky Way system; this picture was generally adopted by early 20th-century astronomers.

In both, the fluctuations of density along the galactic equator were first considered to be of minor importance but were later taken into account. The system based on positions was found to be finite whereas the one based on motions faded out to zero, but the models otherwise show much similarity; in both, the Galaxy is a strongly flattened spheroid with, in the finite system, a diameter of 7,000 parsecs and a thickness of 1,850 parsecs. (One parsec = 3.26 light-years. The mean distance from the Earth to the Sun—the astronomical unit—subtends an angle of one second of arc at a distance of one parsec.) The available observational material—distances, motions, and spectra of the stars—was too scanty to allow reliable solutions. In 1906 an extensive program for observations of visual and photographic magnitudes, spectra, parallaxes, distances, proper motions, and radial velocities (speeds in the line of sight) of the stars in 206 areas was proposed as a way of revealing the characteristics of the stellar system. International cooperation in this program (Jacobus Cornelis Kapteyn's plan of Selected Areas) is still going on.

Many stars form close groupings and apparently belong together. These groupings are called open, or galactic, clusters; the Pleiades is a typical example. Sir William Herschel used them in his study of the form and extent of the Galaxy. He and his son, Sir John, also knew most of the globular clusters known today, and both had noticed the difference in distribution of stars in the two types of cluster. The globular clusters have a high central concentration of stars (in contrast to the open clusters) and, as indicated by the name, a spherical symmetry.

At the end of the 19th century, photographic research on star clusters made rapid progress. The spectra of more than 1,000 stars in galactic clusters were studied, and hundreds of variable stars, including a type called RR Lyrae variables, were detected in some globular clusters. The importance of the two types of clusters for understanding the structure of the Galaxy became clear through the work of two United States astronomers, Harlow Shapley and Robert J. Trumpler. Shapley determined the distances of 69 globular clusters from their total brightness, apparent diameters, and the magnitudes of their RR Lyrae variables and of the 25 brightest stars. He was able to show that the galactic centre was in Sagittarius at a great distance from the Sun. His work on the galactic clusters also helped to establish a picture of galactic structure. His catalog gives a total of 93 globular and 249 galactic clusters; from them he derived a value of 70,000 parsecs for the diameter of the Galaxy and a thickness of about 7,000 parsecs. These results were revolutionary, as the Galaxy's size was increased about tenfold over the model obtained from star counts; and the Sun was now assigned a highly eccentric position.

Most astronomers continued for awhile to support the star-count model. The proponents for the two models agreed on three points: (1) there is no interstellar absorption; (2) the relative distances of the globular clusters as determined by Shapley are correct; and (3) the stars in the clusters and in remote parts of the Milky Way are not peculiar but resemble those in the Sun's neighbourhood. Except for accepting point (1), Shapley was more correct in the determination of the dimensions of the Galaxy.

Discovery of interstellar absorption

Trumpler in 1930 determined the distances of 100 galactic clusters from a study of the magnitudes and spectral types of their stars; his catalogs give a total of 334 clusters. From his study of the relation between the diameter and distances of the clusters he showed that there is absorption of light in the Galaxy. This absorption occurs mainly in a thin layer in the galactic plane, but it may be observed at all galactic latitudes. The existence of a general absorption (which produces a dimming of the light of distant stars) of 0.5 magnitude per kiloparsec had been found in 1929, but definite acceptance of it came only in 1930, when Trumpler published the results of his investigations. With proper corrections for the effects of interstellar absorption, the dimensions of the Galaxy became: diameter between 25 and 30 kiloparsecs; the Sun 8.2 kiloparsecs from the centre.

II. Basic information

DISTANCE DETERMINATIONS IN THE GALAXY

Further investigations were aimed at determining the internal structure of the Galaxy. Accurate distances for individual objects, and, to this end, ways of discovering intrinsic brightness and details of the spectra of stars, were needed. The quantity that can then be deduced is the absolute magnitude of a star; that is, its brightness on a logarithmic scale.

All distance determinations depend on certain fundamental methods, which are described in PARALLAX, ASTRONOMICAL.

Trigonometric parallax. The basic quantity called trigonometric parallax is determined geometrically by direct measurement. The annual parallax, p, of a star is defined as the angle in seconds of arc ($''$) that the mean distance, r, from the Earth to the Sun subtends at the star. The relationship between the distance, d, of a star and the parallax is $p = 206,265'' \times r/d$. Corresponding units of parallax and distance are seconds of arc and parsecs. A star at a distance of one parsec (pc) will have a parallax of one second of arc; the distance, r, would subtend an angle of one second of arc at the star at this distance. The parsec is equal to 206,265 astronomical units. Thus, d (pc) $= 1/p''$. Since $r = 1.49675 \times 10^{13}$ cm, 1 pc $= 3.086 \times 10^{18}$ cm.

The nearest star has a parallax of 0.76 second of arc. The direct method is useful to a distance of 20 parsecs. Other methods must be used for greater distances.

Photometric methods. The fundamental relation between the apparent brightness, m, and the intrinsic (absolute) brightness, M, both in magnitudes (logarithm of light energy), is

$$5 \times \log d = (m - M) + 5. \qquad (1)$$

The quantity $m - M$ is called the distance modulus of the star. For the determination of distances with the aid of the relation above, m is obtained from photometric observations. M must be obtained from established and calibrated luminosity criteria. The most important are derived from analysis of the stellar spectra (see STAR).

Absolute magnitudes and the distance modulus

The stars are divided into spectral types and luminosity classes on the basis of the appearances of their spectra, the intensity ratio of certain absorption lines, and the intensities of selected lines. The currently most used classification system is the Yerkes system, with spectral types O, B, A, F, G, K, M, R, N, and S and luminosity classes I to V. The classification by spectral type is essentially a temperature classification; the O stars are the hottest, with surface temperatures up to 40,000° K. Their spectra are dominated by lines of ionized atoms. The Sun is a typical G star of about 6,000° K. The spectra of this class are dominated by lines caused by the presence of metals, as in the Sun. The cool red stars of class M have temperatures below 4,000° K; and R, N, and S stars are equally cool with spectra rich in molecular bands.

The luminosity classes group the stars according to size: class I (a and b) contains supergiants; class II, bright giants; class III, normal giants; class IV, subgiants; and class V, main sequence and dwarfs. A giant star has a much more extensive atmosphere, a much lower density, and a much brighter absolute magnitude than a dwarf has. Assignment of a spectral class and luminosity class places a star uniquely in the two-dimensional Yerkes classification system. Once the luminosity classes have been calibrated in absolute magnitudes by observations of nearby stars with well-known distances, they serve for determinations of distances for those stars for which spectra may be obtained but for which geometrical distances cannot be determined.

The absolute magnitudes of very distant stars may also be determined by multicolour photometry. The colour index of a star is defined as the difference between its apparent magnitude in two well-defined spectral regions; e.g., blue and visual (yellow). A combination of two or more colour indices (blue − visual, ultraviolet − blue, etc.) gives quantities that may be calibrated to yield the value of M. Photometric observations of selected spectral lines have been used successfully in the direct determination of M.

For certain types of variable stars (Cepheids, RR Lyrae stars), relations that exist between the period, the luminosity, and the colour permit the determination of M.

For the "exploding" stars, the novae and supernovae, the absolute magnitudes at maximum light are well defined and may be considered known. The apparent magnitude, m, at maximum light is also needed to find the distance from equation (1). It may be observed if the nova is seen at maximum, or it may be derived from the light curve.

Problems in establishing distances for very distant stars The main difficulties in determining the distances for the very distant stars are:

1. The effect of the interstellar absorption, mentioned above, and usually written A_λ. With this correction, which enters as a subtraction from $m - M$, equation (1) above becomes

$$5 \times \log d = (m - M) - A_\lambda + 5. \qquad (2)$$

The absorption is usually determined from the interstellar reddening, denoted by R, and the colour excess, denoted by E, of the star. The following relation holds:

$$A_\lambda = R \times E. \qquad (3)$$

The coefficient R may vary with the direction in space, but to what extent is not yet known. The colour excess, E, is determined as the difference between the observed colour, which is affected by distance of a star, and the intrinsic colour of its class in the Yerkes classification system.

2. The accurate calibration of spectroscopic and photometric criteria.

3. Lack of knowledge of the extent and influence of a variation in chemical composition of stars from one part of the Galaxy to another.

STELLAR VELOCITIES

Components of stellar motion. The speeds of the stars in the line of sight and across the sky are called radial velocities and proper motions. The radial velocities cause shifts of the wavelengths, $\Delta\lambda$, of the spectral lines due to the Doppler effect. If c stands for the velocity of light, and λ_0 for the laboratory position of the line in question, the wavelength, $\Delta\lambda$, is then related to the radial velocity, V km/sec, by the formula $V/c = \Delta\lambda/\lambda_0$. A red shift means that the star is moving away from the Earth. The proper motions, μ, of the stars are measured first as a change in position, a very small angle expressed in seconds of arc per year. The star positions are measured at intervals of 10 to 50 years relative to very distant stars or external galaxies with no significant motion (see STAR). To find the actual speed across the sky, called the tangential velocity, T, a scale provided by the star's distance (or parallax) is needed. Then, if p is the parallax of the star in seconds of arc,

$$T = 4.74 \, \frac{\mu}{p} \, \text{(km/sec)}.$$

The space velocity v of the star is the square root of the sum of the squares of the radial and tangential components, V and T: $v = (V^2 + T^2)^{1/2}$, and the angle between the space velocity and the line of sight is also readily determined.

For many studies of motions in the Galaxy the space motion v is divided into a set of components related to directions in the Galaxy: U, directed away from the galactic centre; V, in the direction of galactic rotation; and W, toward the north galactic pole.

The local standard of rest **The solar motion.** Radial velocities are always referred to the Sun and are normally reduced to the local standard of rest (LSR). This is a point moving at the mean speed of all stars near the Sun. The motion of the Sun relative to the LSR is referred to as the solar motion. The point on the celestial sphere toward which the Sun is moving is called the apex of the solar motion; the stars located in that direction appear on the average to be approaching,

while stars in the antapex direction appear to be receding. Star streaming is observed as a reflex of the solar motion. It is, of course, seen in the radial velocities as well as in the proper motions of the stars, and both types may be used for the determination of the direction of the solar motion. The radial velocity data will also give the velocity of the Sun relative to the LSR. If, in addition, the distances of the stars are known, their space motions may be used.

Different spectral classes of stars yield different solutions for the solar motion, largely reflecting the fact that the stars of the various classes differ appreciably in age. Table 1 gives the adopted components of the solar motion.

Table 1: Adopted Components of the Solar Motion and Velocity Dispersions

type	solar motion (km/sec)			spread in velocities (km/sec)		
	U_s	V_s	W_s	U	V	W
cO-cB5	−9.0	+13.4	+3.7	12	11	9
cF-cM	−7.9	+11.7	+6.5	13	9	7
gA	−13.4	+11.6	+10.3	22	13	9
gF	−19.7	+18.5	+9.5	28	15	9
gG	−7.2	+11.1	+6.9	26	18	15
gK0	−10.6	+18.6	+6.5	31	21	16
gK3	−9.0	+17.6	+6.4	31	21	17
gM	−4.5	+18.3	+6.2	31	23	16
Carbon stars	−10.7	+31.8	+3.5	48	23	16
Subgiants	−8.0	+28.0	+8.0	43	27	24
B0	−9.6	+14.5	+6.7	10	9	6
dA0	−7.3	+13.7	+7.2	15	9	9
dA5	−8.5	+7.8	+7.4	20	9	9
dF5	−10.1	+12.3	+6.2	27	17	17
dG0	−14.5	+21.1	+6.4	26	18	20
dG5	−8.1	+22.1	+4.3	32	17	15
dK0	−10.8	+14.9	+7.4	28	16	11
dK5	−9.5	+22.4	+5.8	35	20	16
dM0	−6.1	+14.6	+6.9	32	21	19
dM5	−9.8	+19.3	+8.6	31	23	16
White dwarfs	−6	+37	+8	50	33	25
Planetary nebulae	−8	+29	+8	45	35	20
Classical Cepheids	−8.6	+12.0	+7.6	13	9	5
Interstellar Ca II	−11.4	+14.4	+8.2	...	6	...

Frequently the standard solar motion is used. It is defined as the solar motion relative to the stars forming the majority in the general catalogs of radial velocities and proper motions. It has the values $U_s = -10.4$ km/sec, $V_s = +14.8$ km/sec, $W_s = +7.3$ km/sec, corresponding to $v_s = 19.5$ km/sec in the direction with galactic coordinates $l = 56°$, $b = +23°$.

III. Interpretations of observational data

THE STARS AND STAR CLUSTERS NEAREST THE SUN

The nearest stars. Within five parsecs from the Sun, 41 stars are known. Of these, 11 are visual binaries or multiple systems, so that the total number of known components is 55. Only four of these stars are more luminous than the Sun, viz., Sirius, Altair, Procyon, and Alpha Centauri, which are also among the 20 brightest stars seen in the sky. Five of the stars in the immediate neighbourhood of the Earth are white dwarfs; the others are main-sequence stars, preponderately dwarf stars of class M (see Figure 2). Within 20 parsecs from the Sun, about 1,100 stars (including all components in multiple systems) are known. Knowledge of these stars is incomplete; if the space density of stars for the interval from zero to four parsecs is one, it is only 0.28 for the interval 15–20 parsecs. Ninety percent of these stars are main-sequence stars of type G to M.

The nearby clusters. The stars of a galactic cluster are close together in space. If a cluster is real and stable, all its stars should share a common motion. They should move through space in parallel paths and with identical speeds. If they are sufficiently close to the Earth to show measurable proper motions, they are referred to as moving clusters. The importance of the Hyades cluster, which is the prototype of this class, is notable. The most complete study of the Hyades cluster shows it to be a flattened system with its shortest axis perpendicular to

Moving clusters

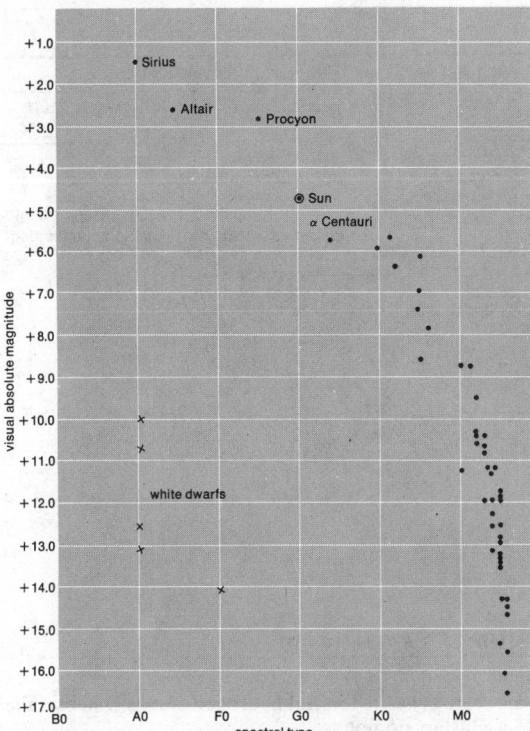

Figure 2: Hertzsprung–Russell diagram for the nearest stars (see text).
From van de Kamp in B.J. Bok and P.F. Bok, *The Milky Way*, 3rd ed. (1957); Harvard University Press

the galactic plane and about two-thirds as long as the axis in the plane. The cluster is only 40 parsecs from the Sun. The stars are concentrated somewhat irregularly toward the centre of the cluster. The bluest star is of spectral type A2, and there are a few G- and K-type giant stars. The majority of the cluster members are G- and K-type main-sequence stars. The average density of cluster stars is at least three times the average density for the region around the Sun.

The total number of moving clusters is small, since almost all galactic clusters are so far away that they do not show measurable proper motions. The Ursa Major cluster, the Alpha Persei association, and the Scorpius–Centaurus association are well-proved moving clusters. A number of moving groups have recently been identified. Among the stars studied are the bright A-type stars. Their distribution in the velocity plane (U, V) is roughly elliptical, but it shows also a high degree of clumpiness; the clumps have been identified with five groups of kinematically related stars.

THE HERTZSPRUNG–RUSSELL DIAGRAM

A graphic representation in which spectral type is plotted against absolute magnitude is called a Hertzsprung–Russell (H–R) diagram, after the two astronomers who discovered the relations between the spectral types and the absolute magnitudes of the stars (Figure 2; see also STAR; STAR CLUSTERS AND STELLAR ASSOCIATIONS).

Stars are never distributed at random in an H–R diagram but form sequences according to which the stars are classified. The reasons for the existence of sequences is that for stars of the same chemical composition there is a certain value of the intrinsic brightness, luminosity (L), and temperature (T) for each value of the mass. When groups of stars of the same mass form different sequences in the H–R diagram it is concluded that they have different chemical composition.

Stellar populations

Two stellar populations with differences in metal content, space distribution, and kinematic properties exist. A German astronomer, Walter Baade, was the first to realize this from his observations of the Andromeda galaxy, M31 (31 in the Messier catalog). Population I stars are young, metal-rich objects found in the spiral arms and associated with interstellar dust and gas. Population II stars

are old and metal-poor and much less concentrated to the galactic plane than the young stars. A sequence of intermediate populations is likely.

The spectral type is nowadays frequently replaced by the colour index, $B - V$ (blue magnitude minus visual), in the H–R diagram; it is then also called a colour–magnitude diagram. A diagram for a number of young galactic clusters belonging to Population I and similar diagrams for an old galactic cluster and for globular clusters, representing Population II, are given in the article STAR CLUSTERS AND STELLAR ASSOCIATIONS.

The galactic clusters serve the important purpose of calibrating the H–R diagram. Several of them are nearby clusters: the Hyades, the Pleiades, Praesepe, the Coma Berenices cluster, and NGC 752 (NGC stands for Johann Dreyer's *New General Catalogue of Nebulae and Clusters of Stars*). Some more remote clusters have been added for the completion of the zero-age main sequence (ZAMS); notable are NGC 2362, *h* and *chi* Persei, M67. The ZAMS is the path or locus in the colour-absolute magnitude diagram of stars that have completed their gravitational contraction but have not yet evolved further as a result of the hydrogen burning in their cores. The calibration of the diagram started with the Hyades, for which the distance is known from direct measurements. Some of its stars on the lower part of the sequence have not yet had time to evolve. To this part of the sequence the unevolved parts of the Pleiades, a well-known cluster in the constellation Coma Berenices, and others are fitted; and the ZAMS is thus extended to the younger and more luminous stars.

The composite colour-absolute magnitude diagram of the nearby young clusters gives a tool for the determination of accurate distances to remote galactic clusters; after correcting for interstellar absorption, their apparent magnitude-colour diagrams are fitted to the ZAMS and the distance modulus, $m - M$, is read directly. The diagrams also give a reliable method for estimating ages of galactic clusters; the spectral type or colour of the hottest star still on the ZAMS, at the turnoff point, gives the age of the cluster. Thus, NGC 2362 is about 10^6, the Pleiades 2×10^7, the Hyades 4×10^8, and M67 5×10^9 years old.

THE STARS AND INTERSTELLAR MATERIAL

To discover the size and shape of the Galaxy, the Sun's position in the system, and the distribution and total content of stars and interstellar material, regions at great distances must be surveyed. At the time that the program for the Selected Areas was proposed, it appeared reasonable to count the stars in successive magnitude intervals to faint limits in many parts of the sky and to determine from these counts the stellar density at various distances from the Sun. It is necessary to assume that the general luminosity function (*i.e.*, the number of stars per unit volume and interval of absolute magnitude), is the same everywhere in the galactic system and equal to the one known for the solar neighbourhood.

The general luminosity function

This approach has given valuable information out to distances of about one kiloparsec, particularly when the material has been divided according to spectral classes. At greater distances, however, it is not certain that the general luminosity function applies, and a different approach has to be used. Certain types of objects have turned out to be particularly suitable for galactic studies. A summary of typical objects representing the most well-defined population is given in Table 2. Some of the groups are considered below in more detail.

Extreme Population I. All objects in this class are important in outlining the spiral structure of the Galaxy.

The gas. The optically identifiable gas is mainly hydrogen, emitting radiation, notably at the wavelength called H-alpha in the red. The locations in which the gas is found are called H II regions. For observable emission to be produced, the combination of a hot exciting star and an interstellar density of one to 10 hydrogen atoms per cubic centimetre is necessary.

When the Andromeda galaxy, M31, was searched for H II regions in 1951, about 300 discrete emission regions were found, almost all of them clearly associated with the

Table 2: The Stellar Populations

	Population I		disk population	Population II	
	extreme Population I	older Population I		intermediate Population II	halo Population II
Members	gas	A-type stars	stars of galactic nucleus	high-velocity stars with z-velocities > 30 km/sec	subdwarfs
	young stars associated with the present spiral structure	strong-line stars	planetary nebulae		globular clusters
		Me dwarfs	novae	long-period variables with periods < 250 days and spectral types earlier than M5e	RR Lyrae stars with periods longer than 0.4 days
	supergiants		RR Lyrae stars with periods < 0.4 days		
	Cepheids		weak-line stars		
	T Tauri stars				
	galactic clusters of Trumpler's class I				
Average height over galactic plane (kiloparsecs)	120	160	400	700	2,000
Average velocity perpendicular to galactic plane, z (km/sec)	8	10	17	25	75
Axial ratio of spheroidal distribution	100	?	25?	5	2
Concentration toward centre	little	little	strong?	strong	strong
Distribution	extremely patchy, spiral arms	patchy, spiral arms	smooth?	smooth	smooth
Age (10^9 years)	0.1	0.1 to 1.5	1.5 to 5.0	6.0 to 5.0	6
Total mass (10^9_{sun})	2	5	47 (combined disk and intermediate)		16

spiral arms. Near the nucleus of this galaxy the arms are represented by dark lanes (dust lanes) only.

Similar surveys of the Sun's Galaxy began in 1952 and have since then been carried out extensively. Figure 3

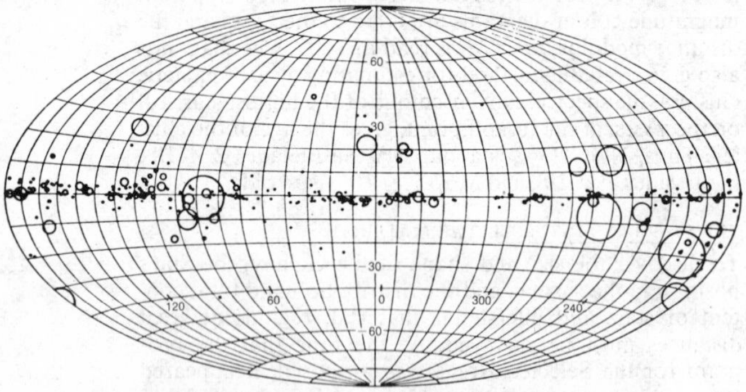

Figure 3: The distribution of emission nebulae in galactic coordinates. The sizes of the circles and dots indicate the apparent sizes of the nebulae (see text).

shows the observed distribution of about 400 H II regions (bright emission nebulae) in galactic coordinates. Most of them are probably within two kiloparsecs of the Sun, indicating that at least 10,000 H II regions may exist in the Galaxy. Figure 3 shows that the concentration of H II regions is high in the direction of the galactic centre ($l = 0°$, $b = 0°$) and that there is a pronounced gap in the interval between $l = 298°$ and $l = 333°$. Other concentrations and gaps may be seen. Their positions are related to the spiral structure of the Galaxy in a way similar to that observed in M31.

The galactic clusters. The distances to remote galactic clusters can be obtained with high accuracy by fitting their observed main sequences to the zero-age main sequences as described above. The space distributions thus obtained will give useful information about the structure of the Galaxy. In addition, because the ages of the various clusters can be relatively well determined, valuable information is obtained about the evolution of various features in the Galaxy with which the clusters are connected.

Over 500 galactic clusters are known, most of them within two kiloparsecs of the Sun. The local space density of clusters is about 700 per cubic kiloparsec, indicating a total number of between 10,000 and 100,000 in the Galaxy. The young clusters (*i.e.*, those containing O and B stars) show a strong tendency to concentrate in the

same regions as the ionized hydrogen clouds, whereas the older clusters do not.

The high-luminosity stars. The high-luminosity stars of early type, the O–B stars (O to B2), frequently form associations. An association, unlike a cluster, has a star density considerably less than that of the surrounding field and is thus likely to dissipate rather rapidly, probably in about 10^7 years. Many associations are also expanding. It appears likely that all O- and B-type stars in the Galaxy originated in O-associations, and the existence of these very young groupings indicates that star formation is still going on in the Galaxy.

Several thousand O–B stars have been found in spectral surveys using telescopes equipped with objective prisms. Most of them are within two or three kiloparsecs of the Sun. Their distribution is similar to that of H II regions and young clusters.

The distribution of 27 O–B stars within 400 parsecs from the Sun is similar to that of the nearby H II regions. They define a plane inclined about 20° to the galactic plane, coinciding well with Gould's Belt, which may be a tilted system relatively close to the Sun.

The supergiant stars of spectral types A5 and later are probably distributed rather similarly to the O–B stars. For most types the absolute magnitudes are not sufficiently well known for accurate distance determination. The M-type supergiants have been found in O-associations in the Galaxy as well as in the Large Magellanic Cloud. Best known in the Galaxy are the 13 M-type supergiants in the region of h and chi Persei, belonging to the O-association I Persei. This type of association may represent a brief period in the evolution when the most massive stars have evolved away from the main sequence but the association has not yet diffused into the field.

M supergiants are relatively easy to detect in low-dispersion spectral surveys in infrared light, in which the effect of interstellar absorption is less pronounced. They should therefore give information about the galactic structure at distances not attainable by means of the blue luminous stars.

Very important for studies of galactic structure are the so-called Wolf–Rayet stars, recognized by their strong emission features caused by helium, carbon, oxygen, nitrogen, and other atoms. They have been identified in the Galaxy up to 10 kiloparsecs from the Sun. Their connection with O-associations and H II regions has been clearly established by their distribution in the Large Magellanic Cloud, the galaxy nearest to the Earth. Unfortunately, there are only about 120 objects of this class known in the Galaxy so far.

Supergiant and Wolf–Rayet stars

The T-associations. T Tauri variables are young stars formed out of the interstellar dust and gas clouds in which they are found. They are faint dwarf stars, usually identified from their variability or their emission-line spectra. They are usually found in groups, named T-associations. One of the best known is in the Orion Nebula.

The classical Cepheids. These stars belong to a class of pulsating variables with regular luminosity variation, named after the prototype, Delta Cephei. The periods of the galactic Cepheids lie mainly between two and 40 days. Together with the luminosity variation occurs a colour change; the star becomes redder as it becomes fainter. An extremely important relation between the period and the average brightness of a Cepheid was found in 1912 through studies of the Cepheids in the Small Magellanic Cloud, one of the two nearest galaxies: the longer the period, the more luminous the Cepheid. As all the stars in the Small Magellanic Cloud are at about the same distance from the Earth, it may be concluded that this relation is due to the intrinsic qualities of the stars.

When a zero-point has been established, this relation provides a method for the determination of accurate distances of individual Cepheids. The zero-point depends strongly on observations of Cepheids in clusters with known distances.

Nowadays, the distances of the classical Cepheids are determined from the period–luminosity–colour relation. It is also possible to estimate rather accurately the age of a Cepheid from its period. The youngest Cepheids, 3×10^7 years old or younger (with periods longer than 11.25 days), have a galactic distribution similar to that of the H II regions and the youngest clusters.

Older Population I. The majority of stars identified in spectral surveys are main-sequence stars from B5 to F5 and normal giant stars from F8 to M. Knowledge of this group of common stars is limited to a rather small volume near the Sun. Occasionally, in unobscured regions, their distribution has been obtained out to two kiloparsecs; the normal limit is more like 1,000 parsecs.

Concentrations of B5 stars have been found between 500 and 1,000 parsecs from the Sun, concentrations of B8 to A0 stars within 500 parsecs from the Sun as well as at distances of one kiloparsec, and between 1.5 and two kiloparsecs in certain directions.

A conspicuous grouping of F0 to F5 stars occurs around the Sun. An average decrease in space density of 65 percent has been observed over the first 600 parsecs from it. It has been proposed that the grouping is a transient phenomenon with a maximum age of 2×10^7 years.

The G8 to K3 giant stars are uniformly distributed in the region from the Sun, and the whole group of common giants shows a remarkably constant space density from two kiloparsecs in the anticentre direction to two kiloparsecs toward the galactic centre.

Further studies of the B8 to A3 stars within 500 parsecs of the Sun indicate that they are associated with the local spiral structure, and, if the Sun is situated toward the inner edge of the local spiral arm, the A-type stars also predominate toward the inner edge of this arm.

The disk population. *Planetary nebulae.* The planetary nebulae are gaseous objects that often appear as faint, greenish disks, not unlike the images of Uranus and Neptune. Their spectra are rich in emission lines of hydrogen, helium, and forbidden lines (so called because they violate certain rules governing transition probabilities) of oxygen, neon, nitrogen, and other elements. There is also a continuous bright background that is often faint. The emission lines make these objects easy to identify at great distances, and their radial velocities can likewise be determined. With few exceptions, however, the distances of these objects are still poorly known.

The distribution of the presently known 1,000 or so planetary nebulae shows a high concentration toward the galactic centre and a pronounced concentration toward the galactic plane. The majority of the planetary nebulae seen in the galactic centre direction are actually at the centre of the Galaxy.

Novae. Information about this group of "exploding" stars is incomplete. At distances beyond 800 parsecs from the Sun most novae discovered are of high intrinsic brightness. Various expressions for the determination of their absolute magnitudes at maximum brightness have been given; the most reliable appear to be connected with the time it takes the nova to decrease three magnitudes in blue lights. The values vary between $M = -6$ and -8 magnitudes. In the H–R diagram the novae at minimum are intermediate between stars called white dwarfs and the subluminous B stars. The novae are highly concentrated toward the galactic plane but also toward the galactic centre.

The supernovae. Supernovae, exploding stars that are immensely more powerful than ordinary novae, belong to two fundamentally different types. Type I objects form a group with closely similar light curves and spectra. At maximum their mean absolute magnitudes are -19, nearly 10,000,000,000 times more brilliant than the Sun. They belong to Population II. The type II objects form a group with some similarities in light curves and spectra but also with marked individual differences. At maximum they are bluer than type I but less luminous; the mean absolute magnitude is about -17.7. They are members of Population I.

Remnants of several supernovae have been identified in the Galaxy; best known are the Crab Nebula (supernova of 1054), Tycho's star (1572), and Kepler's star (1604).

The frequency of supernovae in the Galaxy is one supernova per 26 ± 10 years. The type II supernovae have a frequency of one event per 38–60 years; this is compatible with the assumption that all stars in the mass range from four to nine solar masses eventually become first supernovae and finally pulsars (see below). Type I supernovae are tentatively identified with exploding white dwarf stars whose parent stars had masses greater than nine solar masses. During the lifetime of the Galaxy there may have been 2.6×10^9 supernovae of type II involving nearly 10 percent of the mass of the Galaxy. The corresponding estimates for type I supernovae are 5×10^8 and 4 percent of the mass (see also STAR).

Intermediate Population II. Most stars near the Sun have velocities relative to it not above 30 kilometres per second, but some, the high-velocity stars, greatly exceed this value. Stars with velocities in excess of 60 kilometres per second are generally counted in this class. Over 600 such objects have been cataloged.

The velocity vectors for the high-velocity stars within 20 parsecs of the Sun are concentrated almost entirely in one hemisphere; no high-velocity star is seen moving toward the Cygnus section of the Milky Way. Their velocity vectors are also concentrated toward the galactic plane.

The percentage of high-velocity stars for the various spectral types is given in Table 3. The H–R diagram for the high-velocity stars resembles mostly that of the cluster known as M67, which contains the old Population I.

The high-velocity stars

Table 3: High-Velocity Stars in Various Spectral Types			
stellar type	percentage with high velocities	stellar type	percentage with high velocities
O	0	G0–G9 (main sequence)	16
B0–A3 (supergiants)	0	K0–K9 (giants)	5.7
B0–B9 (main sequence)	0.4	K0–K9 (main sequence)	18
Cepheids	0	M (giants)	1.7
A0–A9 (main sequence)	0.1	M (dwarfs)	47
F0–F9 (main sequence)	3.4	RR Lyrae stars	72
G0–G9 (giants)	3.9	Globular clusters	100

Peculiarities in the spectra of the high-velocity stars are: in the range F5 to G5 they show a general weakening of the atomic lines; and in the range G6 to K4 the giants and subgiants show a deficiency in cyanogen. Thus, the high-velocity stars are metal-poor and may be found by the use of spectroscopic criteria.

Halo Population II. *The globular clusters.* About 200 globular clusters are known within the Galaxy. Their distribution in galactic longitude is remarkable; one-third of them are found in the general direction of the galactic centre and practically all are in the "galactic-centre-half" of the sky as seen from the Sun. Their distribution projected on a plane perpendicular to the galactic plane is shown in Figure 4 together with some lines of equal mass density. The globular clusters form a spherical system. Their stellar content is different from that in the solar neighbourhood and is frequently used as prototype for Population II. There are, however, important differences in chemical composition between the globular clusters in different parts of the Galaxy. It is found that the more metal-rich globular clusters are concentrated toward the galactic centre, whereas the clusters of very low metal content are found from 12 to 16 kiloparsecs from the centre.

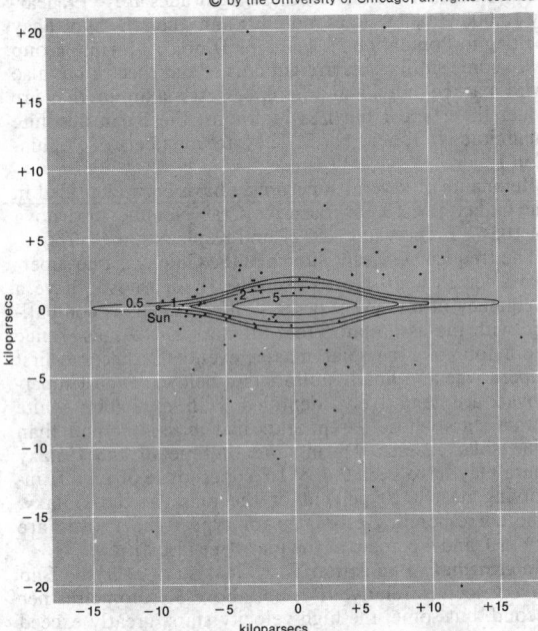

Figure 4: The distribution of globular clusters projected on a plane perpendicular to the galactic plane and passing through the galactic centre and the Sun. Lines of equal mass density are also drawn, but the high stellar density in the galactic centre is not indicated. North is at the top. Distances from the centre of the Galaxy in kiloparsecs are given below and to left of figure.

Absolute magnitudes for the stars in the globular clusters have been obtained by fitting the main sequences to a Hyades-like main sequence with low metal content; so far this has been done for four clusters. The mean absolute blue magnitude of the 25 brightest stars was thus found to be −0.8 magnitudes and that for the RR Lyrae stars to be +0.5 magnitudes.

The RR Lyrae stars. In the horizontal branch of the colour-magnitude sequence of a globular cluster is a region occupied by RR Lyrae stars in many clusters. These pulsating cluster variables identify two different types of globular clusters; those with RR Lyrae stars with periods around 0.54 day have a higher metal content than those with periods around 0.64 day.

The distribution of the RR Lyrae field stars (those not associated with any cluster) over the sky is uniform with no indication of any concentration. The average period for these stars is 0.54 day. The absolute magnitudes needed for the determination of their space distribution have been obtained from the RR Lyrae stars in the globular clusters.

Interstellar lines in stellar spectra. The first interstellar absorption line was discovered in 1904. The wavelengths of lines called H and K lines (of ionized calcium) in the spectrum of the spectroscopic binary Delta Orionis were found not to vary at all during the binary period. This showed that they were formed not in the star, but in front of it. In 1909 an interstellar origin for those features was suggested, and the existence of similar lines due to sodium was predicted. The "stationary" D-lines of sodium in

(margin note, left) Discovery of the interstellar absorption lines

Delta Orionis and other stars were discovered 10 years later.

Systematic observations of such lines in 1933 firmly established that interstellar matter takes part in galactic rotation. The galactic-rotation wavelength shift of the interstellar Ca II lines in the spectra of 314 early-type stars was found to be about one-half that of the stars in which they were observed. Initially this was taken to indicate a nearly uniform density distribution of the absorbing matter between the Earth and the stars. It was, however, soon obvious that the interstellar matter was distributed differently.

Two American astronomers, O.C. Wilson and Paul Merrill, have concluded that "the observations can be accounted for by making the hypothesis that interstellar sodium occurs in discrete aggregations or clouds, which, while participating in the general galactic rotation, have in addition considerable random motions." The known interstellar atomic and molecular lines are listed in Table 4 together with a number of diffuse lines that have not yet been identified.

Table 4: Interstellar Absorption Features

atomic lines		molecular lines		diffuse lines
atom or ion	λ (Å)	molecule	λ (Å)	λ (Å)
Na I	3302.34	CH	4300.31	4430.6
	2.94		3890.23	4760
	5889.95		86.39	5780.5
	95.92		78.77	5797.1
			3146.01	6203.0
K I	7664.91		43.15	6270.0
	98.98		37.53	6283.9
				6613.9
Ca I	4226.73	CN	3874.61	
			75.77	
Ca II	3933.66		74.00	
	68.47			
		CH+	4232.58	
Ti II	3072.97		3957.74	
	3229.19		3745.33	
	41.98			
	83.76			
Fe I	3719.94			
	3859.91			

Interstellar lines of ionized calcium and of some molecules found in the spectra of 300 bright O and B stars were studied at high dispersions in the 1940s. Multiple components occurred frequently. Generally, the multiplicity indicated a series of clouds at different distances in the line of sight. Their different velocities caused different wavelength shifts and arose from galactic rotation.

Attempts have been made to describe the system of interstellar clouds by the mean number of clouds per kiloparsec in the galactic plane. For this to be possible, the clouds must have a random distribution, but while this may possibly be true in the solar neighbourhood, it is not in the Galaxy as a whole. A typical large cloud may have a radius of about 15 parsecs and a total mass of 7,000 solar masses, and its dust would absorb one magnitude in the blue spectral region. There would be 0.7 such clouds per kiloparsec. Smaller clouds must be present here and there to explain the observations.

Interstellar dust. Interstellar dust may be observed as reflection nebulae that scatter the light from bright stars near them, as dark nebulae that absorb starlight, and by polarization effects.

Reflection nebulae. Reflection nebulae have recently been found to form groups called R-associations. Some of them coincide with O-associations, others with T-associations. Their space density in the solar neighbourhood appears higher than that of O-associations. This is due to the higher density of late B and A stars, which dominate the R-associations. Their distribution is similar to that of O-associations. Most nebulae are found within 20° of the galactic plane. Their distribution along the galactic equator is somewhat uneven. Some parts appear almost unobscured, but photometric observations establish that no absorption due to scattered dust occurs.

Distances to dark nebulae can be determined from star counts in the observed area and in a clear comparison area (see NEBULA).

The discrete-cloud picture of the interstellar gas, based on the interstellar absorption lines, originates from the studies of the interstellar dust. It has been shown that the clouds of dust and gas may be regarded as identical. Certain small dust clouds have attracted great interest.

Globules. Globules are dust clouds of high density with diameters up to about one parsec and masses up to about 30 solar masses. Similar small units of the hydroxyl radical, OH, have been found by radio astronomers. It appears likely that these units will collapse gradually into stars or clusters of stars.

Interstellar absorption and polarization of starlight. The proportion of starlight absorbed increases with decreasing wavelength, producing selective absorption or reddening. Observations now extend out to wavelengths of two to five microns, and there is some doubt about the validity of a general law of reddening.

Polarization produces a preferred plane of vibration for the light waves; it is observed only in stars that also show interstellar absorption effects. The polarization, p, is connected with the colour excess, E_{B-V}, in such a way that p is less than or equal to $0.195 \times E_{B-V}$.

The directions of the electric vectors of polarized light tend to lie parallel to the galactic plane over a long range of galactic longitude, though there are more complex regions.

Effects of interstellar dust

Both the absorption and polarization effects are caused by the interstellar dust grains. To produce polarization effects the grains have to be elongated and aligned. The observations are best explained by assuming the alignment to be caused by a magnetic field.

A suggested explanation is that the elongated dust grains are paramagnetic—that is, that they behave like tiny permanent magnets—and rotate rapidly as a result of collisions with interstellar gas atoms. The short axes of the grains will be aligned with the direction of the magnetic field. As the field is frequently parallel to the galactic plane, the particles will be aligned with their short axes parallel to the plane. Hence, the strongest radiation will be received in the plane containing the short axis and the line of sight. This is the direction of the electric vector and gives the projection of the magnetic field on the plane of the sky.

The amount of polarization in any direction depends on the number of dust particles and the degree of alignment. The longitudinal dependence of polarization makes it possible to determine the mean direction of a spiral arm, provided that the axis of the arm and the direction of the magnetic field are parallel.

Observations show that the polarization decreases toward ultraviolet as well as toward infrared light from a maximum in between. This is quite different from the wavelength dependence of the interstellar absorption, which is approximately inversely proportional to the wavelength in the visual region. Theoretical computations indicate that the dust particles may consist mainly of ice and graphite, though complete agreement with observations has not yet been obtained. Various proposed grain types are: dielectric ("dirty" ice), metallic (iron), graphite, ferrite, coated grains (core of graphite, coated with dirty ice), and large free radicals (for further details, see INTERSTELLAR MEDIUM).

Radio observations. *The radio continuum.* Following the discovery of radio radiation from the Milky Way in 1931, many large-scale surveys have been completed in the radio continuum, the first in 1944. The common result of all surveys appears to be confirmation that the regions of equal intensity of radio radiation are arranged more or less symmetrically about the galactic equator. All surveys show that the radiation with maximum intensity reaches the Earth from the direction of the Milky Way centre in Sagittarius.

The observed radio spectrum extends over a wide wavelength range, from a few millimetres to about 30 metres, with the cutoff at each end produced by the Earth's atmosphere. At long wavelengths, the radio background from the Galaxy extends over the whole sky with many superposed local sources of various sizes. There is a clear concentration toward the galactic plane. "Steps" in the longitude distribution can be seen near the plane; they correspond to spiral arms seen "end-on." A number of spurs are also noted; they extend frequently almost perpendicularly from the plane. At wavelengths less than 50 centimetres the background is detectable only in a narrow strip along the Milky Way, about four degrees wide. In this band are many stronger sources. Sources found outside the band are frequently extragalactic.

The difference in continuum distribution at different wavelengths (the spectral index) over the sky shows that more than one emission mechanism must be operating. Emission produced by exchange of energy between free electrons (called free-free emission) occurs in ionized hydrogen and is found in H II regions (some of the distant ones may be optically obscured) and in a general background concentrated to a thin layer. The synchrotron process (emission through acceleration in a magnetic field) is seen in the disk, the spurs, the radio halo, and in supernova remnants of which about 40 are known.

Polarization of radio wavelengths may be observed as:

Studies of polarization of radio wavelengths

1. Linear polarization of the galactic background radiation. Most of the areas with observable polarization lie in a band about 60° wide, containing a great circle through the galactic poles, intersecting the plane at longitudes 340° and 160°, a direction perpendicular to that of the main local field.

2. Faraday rotation (a rotation of the polarization direction during passage through a magnetic field) and depolarization of the polarized emission from the background are observed as a disappearance of the polarization for wavelengths over one metre.

3. Faraday rotation of the radiation from extragalactic sources gives information about the longitudinal component of the magnetic field through the nearby galactic disk.

Polarization studies can be used only to study the local region.

The 21-centimetre line. Produced by neutral hydrogen atoms, the 21-centimetre line is observed from galactic hydrogen all over the sky, with a major concentration along the Milky Way. No increase of intensity toward the galactic centre direction has been found. Some of the line detail is related to optically observable features.

The 21-centimetre line has a very small natural width at 1,420.406 megahertz. The broadening of the galactic profiles is essentially due to the Doppler effect, caused partly by thermal motions in the gas clouds but mainly by galactic rotation and mass motions. The main peaks of the profiles are closely related to the spiral structure of the Galaxy.

Several extensive surveys have been carried out along the Milky Way band, and an enormous amount of data is now available.

Twenty-one-centimetre absorption lines have been observed in the direction of discrete continuum sources; they can be used to estimate the distances to the sources and to investigate the excitation temperature of the hydrogen. So-called Zeeman splitting has been observed in the absorption lines.

The hydroxyl (OH) lines. The group of four lines, with wavelengths near 18 centimetres, is produced by an interaction between the spin of an unpaired electron and the molecular rotation with additional effects produced by hyperfine splitting (a separation of a spectral line into several components in a magnetic or electric field). The frequencies of the lines are 1,612, 1,665, 1,667, and 1,720 megahertz, with intensity ratios of 1:5:9:1 under local thermodynamic equilibrium. The transition probability of the main lines is 10,000 times that for the 21-centimetre line of neutral hydrogen.

The OH lines can be seen in absorption in front of many continuum sources. As the velocities are generally close to those found for H I, the OH is most likely widely distributed throughout the H I regions.

Nonthermal, very complex, OH emission has been detected from over 20 H II regions. Most of the line components are very narrow, and the line-intensity ratios are anomalous. The sources are very small in angular size (e.g., in one source, less than 0″.02 or less than 35 astronomical units). Nothing optically significant has been seen at these positions.

Some of the sources show marked time variations, and many components show strong circular or linear polarization. There is general agreement that a maser phenomenon is responsible for the nonthermal emission, but the detailed mechanism is not yet understood. Nonthermal OH emission has also been observed in a number of infrared stars. Low-level thermal OH emission has been detected from nearby dust clouds.

Recombination lines. Many of the high-level transitions in excited hydrogen atoms have been detected at radio wavelengths from H II regions. These transitions occur when an electron cascades down through a series of levels during the recombination of a hydrogen atom. A frequently observed line occurs at 5,008.9 megahertz, near six centimetres, when the principal quantum number changes from 110 to 109; this is called the H-109α transition. The recombination-line observations enable H II regions to be seen all over the Galaxy and their kinematics to be investigated.

Helium recombination lines and a possible carbon line have also been observed from many H II regions.

Interstellar molecules. A large number of molecules have now been discovered in interstellar space (see INTERSTELLAR MEDIUM). These discoveries provide new knowledge about the composition of the Galaxy. Although the molecules are trace constituents, typically less than one part per million of neutral hydrogen, the study of their excitations and abundances gives important measures of the present physical conditions in the Galaxy and of the history of the interstellar gas and dust clouds.

The processes that form these molecules are not well understood but are probably dependent on dust grains associated with the gaseous clouds. Some molecular species have been found only in specific directions in certain very dense clouds.

The interstellar clouds are frequently quite inhomogeneous and show rather large velocity spreads and temperature variations; the denser ones are probably subject to considerable instability and activity, which may include the formation of stars.

Pulsars. Pulsars can be considered as continuum emitters, since their radiation covers a very broad spectral range, and as line emitters, because the very precise pulse repetition rate corresponds to a sharp low-frequency spectral line (see PULSAR).

Studies of pulsars are often concerned with the intrinsic properties of the objects, but pulsars can also be used to study the mean electron density in the interstellar medium through measurements of the pulse dispersion effects. As more pulsars are detected, they should contribute information on galactic structure. The more than 60 known pulsars (December 1971) appear to be concentrated in the local and Sagittarius arms, and their mean height above the plane is consistent with that of known supernova remnants.

Infrared observations. The infrared spectral region includes wavelengths between one micron and one millimetre. Intensive studies using available atmospheric windows between one and 20 microns and airborne telescopes for wavelengths between 50 and 500 microns have been undertaken.

In a sky survey at 2.2 microns, between declinations −33° and +80°, about 5,600 sources brighter than 4 × 10⁻²⁵ watts per square metre per hertz have been detected. Most of these sources are identified with late-type giants of type K5 and later. The 50 reddest sources, with colour-temperatures of the order of 1,000° K, have not been identified with cataloged optical sources.

Many of the galactic infrared sources are stars with an infrared excess over the blackbody radiation of a temperature corresponding to the spectral type.

Almost all stellar infrared excesses are assumed to arise from thermal radiation in a circumstellar dust shell. The amount of energy contributed by the circumstellar com-

ponent, however, varies widely from one type of star to another.

A strong correlation has been found between the visual polarization and the infrared excess at 11 microns; this is related to the scattering and absorption of the solid particles in the circumstellar clouds.

The origin of the dust shells may be either the remnants of the dust cloud from which the star was born, or material ejected from the central star.

In some objects infrared excess is of special interest:

The infrared excess in carbon stars is a smooth function of the wavelength. This may be explained by a dust shell forming an extension of the stellar atmosphere and composed of graphite particles.

The T Tauri stars in general have large infrared excesses. The circumstellar shell may be a remnant of the protostar but may also be partly ejected material.

All observed Be (emission) and Of stars have infrared excesses at 3.5 microns. The nonstellar component is consistent with free-free emission of ionized hydrogen.

At 20 microns the brightest known celestial source outside the solar system is a famous southern object called Eta Carinae. Its cool infrared component cannot be adequately represented by blackbody radiation at a single temperature. A more detailed dust model is needed to explain the data. The Orion Nebula (M42), the Lagoon Nebula (M8), and the Omega Nebula (M17) have been studied in detail in the infrared; strong sources are associated with all three.

Their infrared radiation is due either to dust heated by the radiation from the stars and gas in the nebula, or to dust and gas associated with the process of star formation and heated by gravitational contraction.

The main components of infrared radiation from the galactic nucleus are:

1. A one-degree source, observed between 1 and 5 microns. Its maximum brightness is within 15″ of the centre of the radio source Sagittarius A and within 4′ of the dynamical centre of the Galaxy. If the source of this radiation is stellar, the density of the stars in the core of the galactic nucleus has to be at least 10⁷ times larger than that in the solar neighbourhood. The radiation from these stars is also affected by about 30 magnitudes of visual absorption. At 2.2 microns a point source is found with a luminosity 3×10^5 times the solar luminosity, as if it were at the distance of the galactic centre. It is probably a bright star like Alpha Orionis (Betelgeuse).

2. A 15″ source coincident with Sagittarius A and isolated mainly at 10 and 20 microns. Its energy distribution suggests that there may also be a concentration of dust in the central one-parsec core and that the source is thermal re-emission of absorbed starlight.

3. A 2° × 4° source found at 100 microns and rich in fine structure. It has three major constituents that are similar to the distribution at 11-centimetre wavelength. The brightest region nearly coincides with the dynamical centre of the Galaxy, a weaker one with the H II region Sagittarius B. The origin of the 100-micron source is unknown, but the similarity to the 2.2-micron distribution suggests that a significant portion of the 100-micron flux is thermal re-radiation of starlight.

X-ray and gamma radiation. *X-ray sources.* X-rays occupy the spectral region below 100 Å, the soft X-rays from 100 to 1 Å and the hard X-rays below 0.1 Å. Rockets or satellites must be used for observations of the soft X-rays from cosmic sources; the hard X-rays and gamma rays can be detected from balloons.

About 50 cosmic X-ray sources are known, at least seven of which are extragalactic. It is believed that the emission takes place in optically thin clouds of plasma by thermal or nonthermal processes.

The galactic sources show a high concentration to the galactic plane. The optical counterparts appear to be either peculiar stellar objects or supernova remnants. Best studied is the stellar object Scorpius X-1. Its optical spectrum shows lines of hydrogen, helium, and oxygen in emission on a high-temperature continuum. The continuum shows variable intensity; the "star" shows rapid oscillations as well as slower fluctuations and also short flares.

Infrared emission from the galactic nucleus

Observations of gamma radiation. Galactic high-energy gamma radiation is observed from balloons or satellites, since the Earth's atmosphere is impenetrable to it. Several point sources have been found as well as a diffuse source at the galactic centre. The flux of gamma rays appears to be about four times greater along the galactic plane near the centre than in the rest of the sky. One source appears to be variable. There are many theories for the formation of gamma rays; many of them are based on the formation of subatomic particles known as π^0 mesons (*e.g.*, by cosmic ray protons colliding with interstellar hydrogen) and their subsequent decay into gamma rays. The only model allowing for variability pictures the gamma rays as produced in stars by events similar to solar flares.

IV. Galactic structure and dynamics

THE GEOMETRY OF THE GALAXY

Galactic systems of coordinates. The position of a celestial object in the sky is usually given by its equatorial coordinates, right ascension and declination. These are analogous to longitude and latitude.

For studies of the Milky Way the galactic system is better adapted. The plane of the galactic equator is defined by the great circle that best approximates the band of the Milky Way. The points 90° away from the galactic equator are called the north and south galactic poles. The galactic latitude, *b*, is the angular distance from the galactic equator to the object, positive to the north, negative to the south; the galactic latitude of the south galactic pole is $b = -90°$. The galactic longitude, *l*, is measured in degrees along the galactic equator.

In the old system the zero point for the galactic longitude was the point at which the galactic equator intersected the celestial equator. The new system uses the direction to the galactic centre as zero point and has also a slightly different galactic plane. It corresponds to the position of the plane of neutral hydrogen in the Galaxy, whereas the plane in the old system was derived from the apparent distribution of the stars. The new system has been in general use since 1960; its north pole has the equatorial coordinates $12^h 49^m$, $+27° 24'$ (epoch 1950) and the direction to the galactic centre is at $17^h 42^m.4$, $-28° 55'$.

The dimensions of the Galaxy. The main part of the Galaxy is shaped like a flat, round disk with a diameter of about 30 kiloparsecs and a thickness of about one kiloparsec near the Sun. The objects of the halo Population II are distributed in a flattened spheroid (axes in the ratio 1:2), concentric to the centre of the disk and with a diameter of about 50 kiloparsecs.

The distance of the Sun from the galactic centre is still uncertain. Since 1963 the value 10 kiloparsecs has been used, based on the space distribution of RR Lyrae stars and globular clusters in the galactic centre. The RR Lyrae stars may not be as luminous as previously assumed; this would tend to "shrink" the distance somewhat. Prior to 1963 a value 8.2 kiloparsecs was used.

REGIONS OF THE GALAXY

The distribution of objects perpendicular to the galactic plane. The distribution of disk population stars and halo stars at various distances from the galactic plane has been studied spectroscopically and photometrically in the directions of the poles and of other high-latitude areas. Figure 5 shows the distribution of some selected types of objects.

Halo stars have been successfully separated from the disk population by means of three-colour photometry. They have been identified in the north galactic pole area at distances of 14 kiloparsecs. A comparison of their density distribution in this direction and in a field at galactic latitude +21° indicates that the halo may be flattened. In other fields there are signs of strong local variations, so that a symmetrical model may not be correct.

Almost no disk population objects are found beyond two kiloparsecs from the plane. From studies of the kinematics and the colours of bright F and G stars and of subdwarfs, now within 200 parsecs of the Sun, it has been

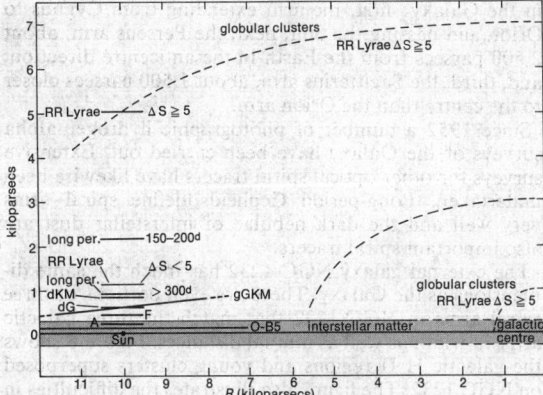

Figure 5: The space distribution of representative objects for various star populations projected on a plane perpendicular to the galactic plane and passing through the centre and the Sun. The horizontal lines indicate the distance from the galactic plane at which the density has fallen to one-tenth of that in the plane. *R* is the distance from the galactic centre. The RR Lyrae stars with high "ΔS" values have lowest metal content. The dashed lines indicate schematic (tentative) distributions (see text).

concluded that the stars with normal metal content will all remain within 800 parsecs of the plane, whereas the metal-poor halo objects will move much farther, maybe up to nine kiloparsecs, from the plane. The metal-richest stars will remain within about 400 parsecs of the plane. Even in this disk, however, about 10 percent of the dwarf F5 to K stars are halo objects.

The extreme Population II objects (globular clusters, RR Lyrae stars, subdwarfs) form a spheroidal subsystem with a radius of about 25 kiloparsecs from the centre of the Galaxy. Its concentration toward the centre is strong. The total mass is estimated to about 16×10^9 solar masses.

There has been much discussion about the existence and the definition of a radio halo (corona). A division into a physical halo and a radio halo has been proposed. The physical halo is needed to explain the gradual transition from the galactic disk, with a gas density of 10^{-24} gram per cubic centimetre and a magnetic field of 10^{-5} gauss, to the intergalactic space, with a density of 10^{-28} gram per cubic centimetre and a field of 10^{-7} to 10^{-8} gauss. It would extend to about one kiloparsec above the galactic plane and have a density higher than 10^{-28} gram per cubic metre and a magnetic field of about 10^{-6} to 10^{-7} gauss.

The radio halo can be observed at metre wavelengths. It is assumed to have a radius of 15 to 20 kiloparsecs. The observed emission may be explained if the magnetic field is about 3×10^{-6} gauss and the density of relativistic electrons (moving at near the speed of light) equal to that observed near the Earth. The interpretation of the observations of this nonthermal radiation is still open to discussion.

The galactic centre. Most of the red giant stars in the central bulge of the Galaxy show a metal content between the metal-poor globular clusters, like M3, and the old metal-rich open clusters, like NGC 188. Optical observations of the centre itself are virtually impossible because of the heavy absorption. In the general region of the centre, globular clusters, RR Lyrae stars, novae, and planetary nebulae have been observed. Most other information about the centre is received from infrared and radio observations (see below).

The spiral arms. From observations of certain kinds of objects in the spiral structure in M31, it was evident that some of them were suitable for tracing out spiral structure in the Galaxy. Such objects all belong to the extreme Population I (Table 2); they are very young and thus cannot have moved very far from the positions in which they were formed. In 1952 a search for H II regions in the Galaxy similar to that undertaken earlier for M31 was made. Many were found, and a study of their distances was carried out using the stars exciting the radiation. The search led to the detection of portions of three spiral arms in the Galaxy: first, the arm extending from Cygnus to Orion and passing the Sun; next, the Perseus arm, about 2,500 parsecs from the Earth in the anticentre direction; and, third, the Sagittarius arm, about 1,500 parsecs closer to the centre than the Orion arm.

Since 1952 a number of photographic hydrogen-alpha surveys of the Galaxy have been carried out. Extensive surveys for other optical spiral tracers have likewise been undertaken. Long-period Cepheids define spiral arms very well and the dark nebulae of interstellar dust are also important spiral tracers.

Comparisons with spiral structure in other galaxies The external galaxy NGC 1232 has much the same dimensions as the Galaxy. There are even portions of three spiral arms in NGC 1232 that match the three galactic arms in width as well as mutual distances. Figure 6 shows the galactic H II regions and young clusters superposed on NGC 1232. The figure also illustrates the difficulties in determining the structure of the Galaxy; these spiral tracers are still limited to the Earth's immediate neighbourhood.

By courtesy of W. Becker

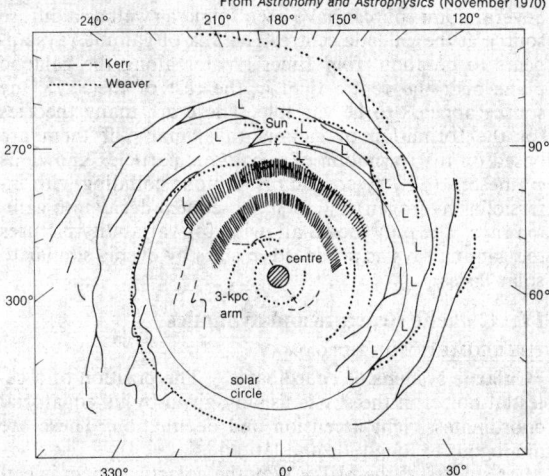

Figure 6: Space distribution of young galactic clusters and H II regions (open circles) superposed on a photograph of the spiral galaxy NGC 1232, which has the same dimensions as our Galaxy. Parts of three spiral arms outlined by the circles may be seen.

Some of the red giant stars have a distribution that is correlated with the spiral structure.

The carbon stars of class N tend to concentrate in spiral arm regions. They also tend to cluster and to form pairs.

The distribution of the R-type stars as well as their kinematics indicate that they belong to an older population with no obvious correlation to the spiral structure. The early M giant stars (M0–M2) show a concentration to the spiral arms; their space density is at least five to seven times as high in the spiral arms as in the interarm regions.

The intermediate M giant stars (M5–M6) are uniformly distributed in arm and interarm regions but show an appreciable increase in density toward the galactic centre.

The late M stars show a uniform density over the galactic disk with no increase toward the galactic centre.

The S-type stars are rather rare and apparently a mixture of two groups with different space distribution, one of which is closely related to the spiral structure. The stars in this group are frequently found embedded in nebulosity and in dust clouds.

The 21-centimetre line of neutral hydrogen has turned out to be a powerful tool for studying the spiral structure at great distances. Interpretation of the observations faces two basic difficulties:

1. The distances are kinematic; the observed Doppler velocities are converted to distances under the assumption that differential rotation is the most important motion. Usually the rotation is assumed to be circular and axisymmetric.

2. An enormous amount of fine structure is observed and may confuse the large-scale pattern. Figure 7 shows

two interpretations of the neutral hydrogen distribution in the Galaxy.

Figure 7: Two interpretations (by astronomers Frank Kerr and Harold Weaver) of the distribution of neutral hydrogen in the Galaxy. "L" marks regions deficient in H I, according to Kerr. Dashed lines and hatched areas indicate uncertain positions. The directions around the diagram are galactic longitudes (see text).

MAGNETIC FIELDS IN THE GALAXY

The existence of a magnetic field in the interstellar gas would account for: (1) the lack of a preferred direction for the arrival of the cosmic rays; (2) the Zeeman effect observed in the 21-centimetre line of atomic hydrogen; (3) the linear polarization of the light from many stars; (4) the synchrotron radiation observed as galactic background radio emission; (5) the rotation of the plane of polarization for extragalactic radio sources, called Faraday rotation. The amount of Faraday rotation is closely correlated with galactic latitude—that is, with the length of the line of sight in the disk of the Galaxy. It is the most convincing evidence that a magnetic field exists.

The intensity of the galactic interstellar magnetic field can be estimated from (2), (3), (4), and (5). The value found is about 5×10^{-6} gauss. This is very low but is of importance on a cosmic scale. The origin of the galactic magnetic field is not known.

A theoretical model of the magnetic field. Polarization measurements of 1,400 southern stars (mostly within 500 parsecs of the Sun) with northern hemisphere results (for a total of 7,000 stars) provide data for a description of the magnetic field in the solar neighbourhood. The observations are best understood if the magnetic field lines form tightly wound right-hand spiral curves (helices with pitch angle 7°), which lie on the surface of imaginary tubes having elliptical cross sections with dimensions in the ratio one to three with major axes parallel to the galactic plane. The helical pattern is inclined at 40° to the plane of the Galaxy, anticlockwise viewed from the north galactic pole. The Sun is 100 parsecs toward the galactic centre from the magnetic axis and 10 parsecs below the galactic plane. Studies of the available data indicate that the optical polarization is produced within 500 parsecs from the Sun.

The model provides a simple explanation for the spurs and ridges of continuum radio emission, which may be tracers of the field lines. Nonthermal electrons are injected into the helix from sources near the plane and spiral away along the field lines; in this way, they can appear as spurs of emission.

To provide an explanation of the Faraday rotation (see above), it may be necessary to have a large-scale field in the direction of galactic longitude $l = 90°$ and $b = 0°$; the helix is then seen as an added local phenomenon.

The Zeeman effect. In a magnetic field, many spectral lines are split into a number of components, close together and separated in wavelength according to the field strength. This is the Zeeman effect. The possibility of measuring interstellar magnetic fields by Zeeman splitting of the 21-centimetre line was proposed about 1957. Zeeman splitting has now been observed in many neutral hydrogen clouds. In all Zeeman observations made so far the directions of the fields fit the helical-plus-longitudinal field model. There are, however, large problems with the field strengths.

The strongest fields are found in the densest clouds, and the field strength is the result of amplification by contraction of the clouds. By extrapolation from the H I clouds to the average interstellar space, the mean interstellar magnetic field is found to be between one and three microgauss for mean interstellar densities of H I between 0.7 and two atoms per cubic centimetre.

Pulsar data. The rotation measures and the dispersion measures of the radiation from pulsars have been used to determine the magnetic field strength. The average value found is about 1.6 microgauss, in good agreement with the results from the Zeeman data.

Elongation of gas and dust clouds by the magnetic field. Data for eight intermediate-velocity H I clouds and for six of the high-velocity clouds show that they are elongated in the direction of the helical magnetic field. A similar study for 16 dust clouds showed that they are more closely aligned to the magnetic field than to the galactic plane.

THE STRUCTURE OF THE GALAXY AS A WHOLE

The most complete information comes from the 21-centimetre line observations.

In and near the galactic plane the profiles of the 21-centimetre line show various bumps that indicate large concentrations of neutral hydrogen moving at various speeds. These bumps appear to vary with the longitude and may represent sections of spiral arms.

If the gas moves in circular orbits around the galactic centre, a rotation curve can be derived from these observations. The velocities may then be converted into distances and a picture of the distribution of the gas throughout the galactic disk obtained (see Figure 7).

It is generally possible to follow the spiral arms of distant systems through an entire galaxy even though the arms are frequently broken up into spurs and branches. In the Galaxy this is more difficult and the effort has not yet been entirely successful.

Two rotation curves have been obtained between four and 10 kiloparsecs from the galactic centre (Figure 8). In

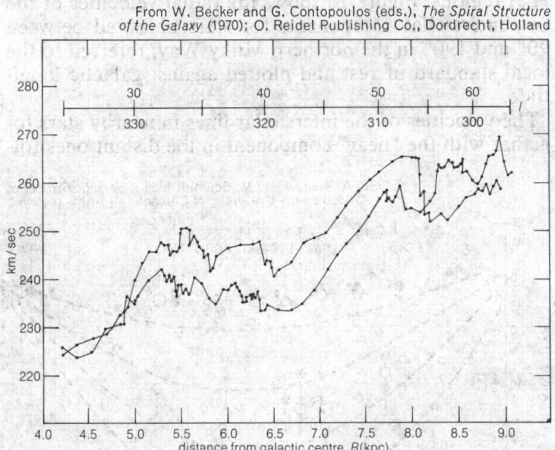

From W. Becker and G. Contopoulos (eds.), *The Spiral Structure of the Galaxy* (1970); O. Reidel Publishing Co., Dordrecht, Holland

Figure 8: Galactic rotation curves from the 21-cm hydrogen emission line observations. Top curve refers to the gas north of (above) the galactic plane, bottom curve to points south of (below) the plane. The scale is set by the Sun's distance from the centre of the Galaxy, here taken as 10 kiloparsecs. The quantities *l* indicated above the curves are galactic longitudes.

them, two bumps may be seen at about the same distance on both sides of the centre. One bump seems to be caused by a systematic streaming of gas just outside the Sagittarius arm; this gas has a higher angular velocity in the direction of the general rotation than does the gas in the arm.

In the inner part of the Galaxy the derived density max-

ima for the hydrogen distribution fall rather well into a spiral pattern.

At a distance of four kiloparsecs from the galactic centre, radical changes in the distribution and motion of the interstellar gas occur.

The gas density is apparently about three times lower within four kiloparsecs of the centre than it is in the regions farther out. The gas in the central region could possibly be in a form unobservable in the 21-centimetre line, but it is more likely that it has been pushed away from the region. A similar emptiness has been observed in the central part of the Andromeda Nebula.

The most regular feature in the inner region is the so-called three-kiloparsec arm; its gas absorbs the radiation at 21 centimetres from the strong radio source Sagittarius A in the galactic centre. In this direction, the arm has an outward velocity of 53 kilometres per second. Some of the gas is moving toward the centre, but most of it moves outward. The total mass of the quadrant of this arm that can be adequately distinguished is about 4×10^7 solar masses.

Gas is observed on the far side of the centre with still higher velocities away from the nucleus, up to 200 kilometres per second; the total amount of gas is about the same as in the three-kiloparsec arm.

If these arms were expanding continuously they would empty the inner region in 30,000,000 to 50,000,000 years. Just outside this region is an annular region in which the radiation from ionized hydrogen is exceptionally strong. This may be connected with a final stopping of the expanding gas.

Within 800 parsecs of the centre a new phenomenon occurs; very high negative velocities are observed between longitude $-5°$ and $0°$. The whole structure appears to be a rotating disk. This region in the Galaxy can be matched in the Andromeda Nebula, and the same is true for the central concentrations as seen in the infrared observations.

The total mass of the nuclear disk is estimated to be 5×10^6 solar masses. The disk must have an exceedingly sharp outer edge in the plane of the Galaxy, but there is some high-velocity gas outside the plane.

At somewhat higher latitudes near the centre, gas is seen streaming away from the centre at angles of 45° to the galactic plane. This may be gas expelled from the nucleus.

Even more complicated phenomena are found still closer to the nucleus. There is a concentration of fairly strong radio sources, mainly H II regions (see above). The radial velocities of these radio sources do not agree well with those found for the nuclear disk; velocities of $+40$ to $+60$ kilometres per second have been found, while the rotation velocity of the disk is $+200$ kilometres per second.

The most striking radio source near the centre is nonthermal. It is situated very close to the dynamical centre of the Galaxy and may well be the centre. It is intrinsically very bright; its size is about seven by three parsecs. An infrared source of 15-parsec diameter coincides precisely with the nonthermal source; as noted above, this may be a large concentration of stars. The source contains a sharp nucleus with a diameter less than five seconds of arc (0.2 parsec).

Much information on the nuclear part has come from observations of the OH-absorption lines. These lines are very much stronger 200 parsecs from the centre relative to those of neutral hydrogen (H I) than elsewhere in the Galaxy. This indicates a great abundance of molecules, probably also of H_2. The OH lines also show a flow into the Sagittarius A source. Complicated streaming occurs near the centre of the nuclear disk. At higher latitudes, high-velocity neutral hydrogen is found in some places, though always with small surface density.

All neutral hydrogen velocities higher than 100 kilometres per second and at galactic latitudes greater than $\pm 20°$ are negative relative to the local standard of rest (see above). They are also limited to a relatively small region of the sky and are not as frequent in the southern hemisphere. They occur up to very high latitudes. At these velocities the gas appears to be concentrated in fairly isolated, generally elongated clouds. Generally there is systematic streaming toward the galactic plane.

The most important problem is to find the distance to these clouds.

Intermediate-velocity neutral hydrogen has been found in the direction of stars with interstellar lines of ionized calcium. In three stars, at more than one kiloparsec from the galactic plane, the velocities of ionized calcium and neutral hydrogen agree well. For three other stars closer to the plane than 300 parsecs, no ionized calcium has been found, and it is then possible that the intermediate-velocity clouds are between 600 and 1,000 parsecs from the plane.

No data are available for the higher-velocity clouds. The properties of the intermediate-velocity and the high-velocity clouds are so similar that it is reasonable to assume that the latter are also within the Galaxy, at relatively large distances from the plane.

THE ROTATION OF THE GALAXY

Bertil Lindblad's studies

In 1926 a Swedish astronomer, Bertil Lindblad, studied the motion of the high-velocity stars, which is asymmetrical with respect to the stars of the solar neighbourhood, the low-velocity stars. He reasoned that while the high-velocity stars cannot belong to the same system as the low-velocity stars because of the asymmetry in their motions, they must be related to the rest of the Galaxy because their motions are symmetrical about the galactic plane. He showed that the effect could be explained if (1) the Sun and other low-velocity stars have high rotation velocities around a distant centre, and (2) the high-velocity stars have much smaller velocities of rotations. Thus, the stellar system may be divided into a series of subsystems with rotational symmetry around one axis but with different speeds of rotation at the same distance from this axis. These systems would then also have different degrees of flattening. The most flattened systems have a high star density but one that decreases with decreasing speed of rotation. The centre of the stellar system should lie in the galactic plane in a direction at right angles to the direction of the asymmetrical drift.

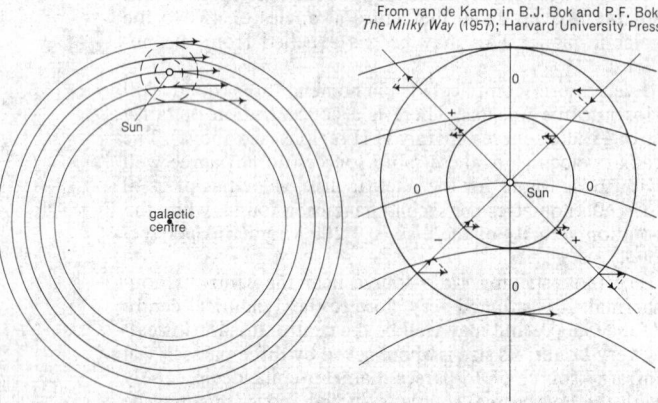

Figure 9: The effect of galactic rotation on the radial velocities (speeds in the line of sight). (Left) The arrows represent the variation of rotational velocity with the distance from the centre. (Right) The arrows represent the velocities as observed. The radial velocity components are also shown (see text).

The work of Jan Oort

Observational evidence confirming this idea was provided about a year later by the Dutch astronomer Jan Oort, who also showed that the Galaxy does not rotate as a solid body; the innermost parts rotate fastest. If most of the mass is concentrated at the centre, the velocity of rotation should be nearly proportional to $1/r^2$ (r = distance from the centre of the Galaxy), and differential effects proportional to the distance from the Sun would be observed in both the proper motions and the radial velocities (Figure 9).

The radial velocities (RV) and proper motions of the stars in the solar neighbourhood vary systematically with the galactic longitude. In the directions to the centre and

anticentre and perpendicular to them, the radial velocities are zero. In between, smooth curves are obtained, giving a double wave for the whole system. Similar results are obtained for the proper motions.

The effect of differential galactic rotation shows up as a change in average speed of about 15 kilometres per second per kiloparsec. This is known as Oort's constant, A. If μ_1 is the proper motion in the direction of galactic longitude and another rotation constant $B = -10$ kilometres per second per kiloparsec, Oort's rotation formulas are

$$RV = Ar \sin 2l$$
$$\mu_1 = Ar \cos 2l + Br.$$

The theory of galactic rotation also explains another problem that had puzzled astronomers. In 1904 more stars were found to move toward the constellations of Orion and Scutum (diametrically opposed directions) than toward any other point. The line connecting these directions lies in the plane of the Milky Way, and a connection was suspected between the motions and galactic structure. Lindblad suggested that small perturbations of the stars would result in departures from circular orbits, and these departures would be more pronounced in the directions of the centre and anticentre, nearly as observed.

Different values of the solar motion relative to stars of different spectral classes are obtained. This occurs because all stars are not of the same age, and their velocity distributions are affected by the local conditions at the time of their formation, and by encounters with other stars and interstellar matter.

Another possibly disturbing effect is the admixtures of different kinematic groups.

Table 1 shows that main-sequence stars and giants earlier than F and all supergiants show a markedly smaller velocity dispersion than main-sequence stars and giants of later types. These young stars appear to move in almost circular orbits around the galactic centre. The O and B stars with equal velocity dispersions in U and V are kinematically distinct from all other types. They still reflect the velocity distribution of the interstellar gas.

The radial velocities of interstellar lines. Studies at high spectral dispersion have shown that the calcium and sodium clouds that produce interstellar absorption lines are arranged in space essentially in the same way as the H II regions. Figure 10 shows the radial velocities of the two interstellar components for stars observed between 90° and 190° in the northern Milky Way, referred to the local standard of rest and plotted against galactic longitude.

The velocities of the interstellar lines in nearby stars together with the "near" component in the distant ones fol-

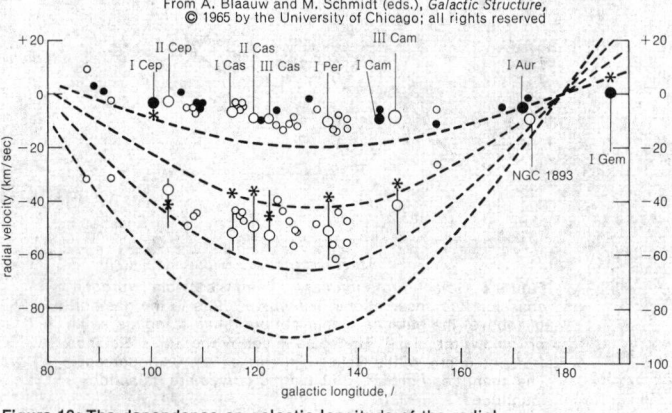

Figure 10: The dependence on galactic longitude of the radial velocities measured from interstellar lines in stellar spectra. Small black circles indicate stars in the local (Orion) arm; small open circles, stars in the Perseus arm. Larger symbols indicate mean values (stars in associations whose names are given; the actual velocities are marked as asterisks). Vertical lines show the range of velocity of the various components. Theoretical curves for the radial components of galactic rotation for points in the galactic plane at distances from the sun of $r = 1$ (top curve), 2, 3, and 4 kiloparsecs are drawn.

low the galactic rotation curve well for a distance of about 0.5 kiloparsec from the Sun. The distant components define a galactic rotation curve at a distance of between two and three kiloparsecs. The radial velocities of the distant stars are never far from those derived for the "remote" interstellar components. This indicates that these components arise very near the stars in whose spectra they are seen. It also implies that the mean density of sodium or ionized calcium is much lower between the clouds forming the two components than it is close to the Sun and other stars.

The motions of the planetary nebulae. The radial velocities of the planetary nebulae are shown in Figure 11, plotted against the galactic longitude. The distribution, except at 0° longitude, is easily understood if the planetary nebulae move in circular orbits at different speeds. The high dispersion of velocities near 0° longitude requires the presence of many objects with highly elliptical orbits. It is at present not possible to say whether all planetary nebulae form one kinematic subsystem or whether they are divided between a flattened rotating system with circular orbits and a spherical system with elliptical orbits and low rotation.

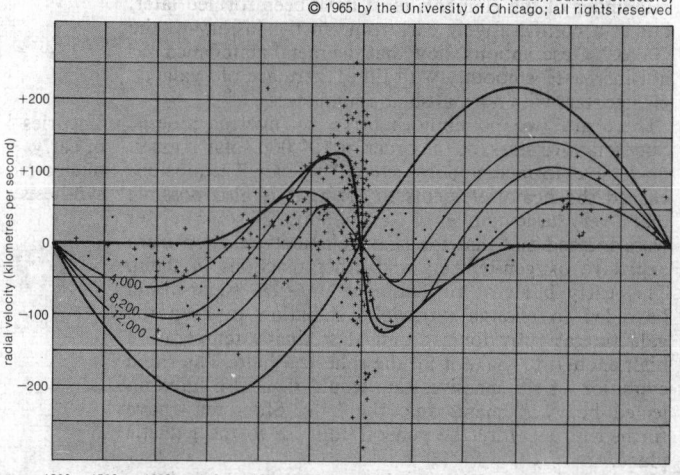

Figure 11: Radial velocities of planetary nebulae reduced to the local standard of rest. Heavy curves represent extremes between which the velocities should lie for circular orbits. Thin lines represent velocities at distances indicated (left) in parsecs from the Sun. Angles below the figure are galactic longitudes (see text).

The motions of the local standard of rest (LSR) around the centre of the Galaxy. Such motions can be determined only if there is an inertial frame in the Galaxy. Such a frame would be provided by reference objects that are not rotating or otherwise accelerating in the Galaxy. It can be assumed because of their spherical distribution that the system of globular clusters does not rotate relative to a frame of this type in the Galaxy. The tangential velocity of the LSR caused by galactic rotation may be determined from the radial velocities of individual clusters. The most recent result, from a study of 70 clusters, is a tangential velocity of 167 ± 30 kilometres per second in the direction $l = 90°$, $b = 0°$.

The galaxies in the Local Group may move at random relative to the Galaxy. If so, they can also be used to define an inertial frame. One study shows a velocity of 292 ± 32 kilometres per second in the direction $l = 106°$, $b = -6°$. From this it is concluded that the LSR has a rotational velocity of about 250 kilometres per second in the direction $l = 90°$, $b = 0°$. The globular cluster system may then rotate around the galactic centre with a group velocity of about 80 kilometres per second.

V. The origin and evolution of the Galaxy

FORMATION OF THE GALAXY

The problem of how the Galaxy was formed is intimately connected with cosmology, the study of the formation and structure of the whole universe. The classical ap-

proach to cosmology is based on the red shift–apparent magnitude relation for the fainter galaxies; the more distant a galaxy, the higher is its apparent velocity as calculated from the red shift of the spectral lines. This general recession is the basis for the so-called "big-bang" cosmology, in which the universe is taken to have originated in a superdense state nearly 10,000,000,000 years ago, and for the "steady-state" cosmology in which the universe looks exactly the same all the time (see UNIVERSE, ORIGIN AND EVOLUTION OF).

Another basic cosmological phenomenon, which may be directly tested, is the following. If the universe began with a big bang, or primeval fireball, there must be an isotropic, thermal (blackbody) radiation field, which at the present time would have a temperature of a few degrees Kelvin.

Low-energy cosmic radiation was discovered in 1965 over a wavelength range from about 20 to three centimetres. It gave a typical blackbody curve with a temperature of 3° K; this curve was extended to 2.6 millimetres from studies of the effect of radiation at this wavelength on the interstellar CN molecules. The isotropy of the radiation was also established to better than ±0.5 percent.

A definite proof of the primeval fireball phenomenon would rule out a number of cosmologies. The steady-state theory would be ruled out because its universe was never in a dense state. Any cosmology including a visible edge to the matter-filled part of space would be ruled out, because the radiation produced in the early days would long since have left the universe.

There are, however, still conflicting data. Balloon observations have shown that a large flux of radiation much greater than expected at the peak of the 3° K blackbody curve is present. If these observations are correct and this excess radiation is cosmic, it could be line or continuum radiation superposed on the blackbody radiation from the primeval fireball. The only possibility consistent with the steady-state theory would be to interpret all background radiation as coming from a large number of discrete sources.

In the big-bang theory, all galaxies would have been formed at the beginning from original density fluctuations that led to gravitational instabilities and the formation of protogalaxies. In the steady-state theory, matter is created continuously in regions of highest densities, the nuclei of galaxies; and galaxies are formed continuously.

GALACTIC EVOLUTION

In one classification scheme for galaxies—*i.e.*, involving designations elliptical (E), lens-shaped (SO), spiral (Sa, Sb, Sc), and irregular (Irr)—the Galaxy is classified Sb or Sbc. This scheme is based on form alone (the apparent ratio of central bulge to the disk, openness of spiral pattern, resolution of the arms into luminous stars), but a systematic change in stellar content follows the order of the sequence of form. Along the sequence Irr–Sc–Sb–Sa–SO–E, gas and dust amounts and young stars decrease and the mean colours are increasingly red. These effects could be explained as an evolutionary sequence. In an Sc galaxy, luminous stars are still forming, and since it is still rich in gas and dust, new generations will form by further condensation. The galaxy will eventually be depleted of prestellar material, the young stars will have evolved, and there will be no new stars or spiral arms; a galaxy similar to the present SO system will be produced. It is not likely, however, that the present SO systems have evolved from Sc galaxies; the latter appear to have sufficient gas to sustain their present rate of star formation for 10^{10} years and more. Also, all galaxies appear to have nearly the same age.

It also appears clear from studies of the intrinsic flattening of galaxies that true spirals and SO galaxies can never have evolved from or into elliptical galaxies. A Swedish astronomer named Erik Holmberg studied the mean total mass density of galaxies and found that the early-type (E) systems have the greatest values. He argued that evolution along the sequence from Sc to SO was therefore impossible (the density would have to increase

The "big-bang" and "steady-state" theories

too much) and that the only effect of aging is that a galaxy becomes redder. It is not yet clear that the difference in densities is as large as Holmberg found.

Collapse of the Galaxy from its protocloud

From a study of the motions of the very old stars in the solar neighbourhood, it has been inferred that the Galaxy collapsed from its protocloud on a time scale of about 2×10^8 years. During the collapse, some stars were formed and an enrichment in metals occurred. Much of the protocloud remained in gaseous form and settled, after energy losses, into a stable centrifugal disk. This disk in the Galaxy contains stars at least 8×10^9 years old. Similar disks may be seen in external spiral and SO systems.

The old stellar disk and spheroidal components, which contain most of the mass of spiral systems, may not have changed since their formation. The amount of gas left over after the formation of the old stellar components would have determined the present morphological type of the spiral systems.

It is not yet known how galaxies form and how they evolve. The result from a collapsing protocloud could equally well have been obtained if matter were ejected from a centre to form halo stars and spiral arms.

If the spiral arms represent the tracks of material ejected from centres of a galaxy, the mechanism for forming the arms may be found. Many galaxies have expelled pairs of plasma clouds in opposite directions. Also, luminous material has been seen, apparently ejected from nuclei of galaxies. (The "jets" in M87 show opposing ejections of luminous material.) As soon as differential rotation affects any jet or similar phenomenon in the disk of a galaxy, it will be drawn out into a spiral form much as in an ignited pinwheel. The tendency for opposite ejections will then lead to the predominant symmetrical two-arm spiral galaxies.

According to this theory, the spiral arms of the Galaxy were established at one time and will be wound up by differential rotation. The bright supergiant stars and the gas excited by them would fade in about 10^7 to 10^8 years. During this period, the shearing effect of the differential rotation would make the arms longer and thinner. Thus, galaxies with well wound-up, circular, thin arms would have gone through this evolution; those observed are of type Sa with a large nuclear bulge.

The ejection theory also explains the class of galaxies with companions on the ends of spiral arms. Such companions are most likely rather short-lived, and they and the arms will decay after a few revolutions of the Galaxy. More ejections from the nucleus are required for new arms to form. Split and bifurcated spiral arms are explained by secondary ejections in the arms. They are hard to account for by gravitation-interaction theories.

Hydromagnetic and gravitational theories of the formation of spiral structure. Undoubtedly, the magnetic field must play an important role in the equilibrium and motion of the interstellar medium. A weak, large-scale intergalactic magnetic field has been proposed; also a slightly ionized intergalactic gas may be present that would affect the protogalaxies in different ways depending upon the angle between the field and the axes of rotation. This would also explain the formation of spiral galaxies with the typical two-arm pattern and an internal helical field of about 5×10^{-6} gauss. Proponents for the gravitational models claim, however, that the magnetic field plays only a secondary role in the formation of the spiral pattern and that the necessary systematic field would have to be stronger than that observed in order to affect its development; it would then be too strong for star formation to occur.

The density wave theory

The concept of density waves as a basis for spiral structure goes back to Bertil Lindblad, who proposed leading spiral arms, whereas observational evidence suggested trailing arms. Both types of arm systems are possible. Lindblad emphasized individual stellar orbits, and this made it difficult to derive the collective behaviour of the stars that form the spiral structure. Work on the gaseous interstellar medium has shown how a rather inconspicuous density wave in the stellar distribution may produce a spiral gravitational field as a fluctuation in the smooth field. The gas, which will react strongly to even small fluctuations, will gather in these regions and act as an efficient spiral tracer. With a pattern speed of 13.5 kilometres per second per kiloparsec and the Schmidt mass model for the Galaxy, a system of two trailing arms is derived. The Schmidt model consists of a central mass point, 0.07×10^{11} solar masses; a spheroid, 0.82×10^{11} solar masses; and a shell, 0.93×10^{11} solar masses. Of the total mass of 1.8×10^{11} solar masses, one half is inside a spheroidal surface with axial ratio 0.05 drawn through the Sun.

The density wave theory accounts for the grand design of the spiral pattern over the whole disk and also for the absence of regular arms of ionized hydrogen in the inner four kiloparsecs of the Galaxy. It also stresses the coexistence of material arms and density waves and possibly of several wave patterns. Thus, of the local arms, the Sagittarius and Perseus arms belong to the primary spiral pattern, and the Orion arm is a material arm. The Carina–Cygnus feature would be an arm in a secondary spiral pattern.

Chemical evolution. Most cosmologies based on an expanding universe require that the Galaxy was originally formed almost entirely out of hydrogen and helium. The remainder of the elements must have been formed later, but at a comparatively early time in the history of the Galaxy. Observations show that the metal abundance has not increased smoothly with time; there are old galactic cluster stars with normal solar abundances.

Theories of early nucleosynthesis

There are two possibilities for early nucleosynthesis. Supermassive stars, of the order of 100,000 solar masses, may have formed and by small "big-bang" explosions caused the heavy elements to form. It is also possible that a very large number of stars of about 20 solar masses were formed and that the heavy elements resulted from explosive oxygen-burning and other reactions in them. This early burst of formation of massive stars would have led to enough ultraviolet radiation to keep the galactic gas fully ionized and at a kinetic temperature high enough to make it fill the spherical halo. The rapid evolution of the massive stars would then also have injected heavy elements into the halo. Stars may have formed in it before the general collapse to the galactic plane.

Star formation. The physical conditions of the interstellar material from which stars are formed are not yet exactly known. Apart from the general layer of neutral hydrogen, however, which in the spiral arms has a density of about one atom per cubic centimetre, there are clouds of appreciably higher densities, up to 10^3 atoms per cubic centimetre. There is some ionization in these clouds; probably the electron density is about 10^{-4} times the hydrogen density. The clouds are also in motion, with average velocities of about 15 kilometres per second, in some cases up to 100 kilometres per second.

The major uncertainty is the galactic magnetic field. Though reasons given above suggest a rather weak field of 5×10^{-6} gauss, there is some evidence for a field of up to 2×10^{-5} gauss.

The first stage in the formation of stars is the formation of an interstellar cloud. This cloud has to reach gravitational stability and then start contracting.

The second stage, the collapse of the cloud, will occur when the external pressure has reached a certain value. The critical point is represented by a certain value of the mass, above which instability sets in. If strong magnetic fields are not involved, it is relatively easy to find many clouds that are now on the verge of gravitational instability. With a strong magnetic field (2×10^{-5} gauss) present, star formation would become impossible except in extremely massive clouds, whereas the lower value of the field strength of 5×10^{-6} gauss would not be incompatible with observations.

The fragmentation of the collapsing cloud into stars would also tend to be difficult with a magnetic field present. The magnetic field would need to be separated from the gas at an early stage, or its strength sharply reduced during the later stages, to permit the fragmentation to proceed. How this could be achieved is not yet clear.

The fragmentation ceases (third stage) when the temperature of the fragment, the protostar, is so high that isothermal collapse no longer occurs. An adiabatic contraction follows with the rate of change of total energy equal to the rate of radiation from the surface. During this stage the protostar approaches the zero-age main sequence; *i.e.*, the internal temperature is reaching the values at which nuclear reaction starts.

The density wave theory for the spiral structure indicates a possible way for the formation of stars over a large region of the Galaxy more or less simultaneously.

When the gravitational potential field of spiral shape rotates within the Galaxy in the galactic plane, it produces rather dense concentrations of gas and dust that are observed as spiral arms. The density waves lead to sudden compression of the gas along a front of several kiloparsecs; this shock collects the cosmic grains into prominent dust lanes and brings the individual gas clouds into a state of gravitational collapse. Once started, the collapse will continue even after the decompression has set in. Stars will thus form simultaneously over several kiloparsecs of the central line of a spiral arm. The dust lanes are mainly seen on the inside of the arms and slightly separated from the bright young stars; the distance is due to the motion during the time necessary for star formation, and may be a few hundred parsecs.

BIBLIOGRAPHY. GEORGE O. ABELL, *Exploration of the Universe*, 2nd ed. (1969), a comprehensive introductory text to general astronomy with a wealth of information given in a number of useful appendixes; WALTER BAADE, *Evolution of Stars and Galaxies*, ed. by CECILIA PAYNE-GAPOSCHKIN (1963), a stimulating picture of an astronomer's attempt to understand the large-scale evolution of the universe, based on Baade's lectures; B.J. and P.F. BOK, *The Milky Way*, 3rd ed. (1957), an excellent introduction into galactic research with beautiful illustrations; B.T. LYNDS (ed.), *Dark Nebulae, Globules, and Protostars* (1971), a series of observational and theoretical papers on interstellar gas and dust; THORNTON and L.W. PAGE (eds.), *Stars and Clouds of the Milky Way* (1968), selected articles illustrating how astronomy has advanced our knowledge about our galaxy; ANTONIE PANNEKOEK, *De groei van ons wereldbeeld* (1951; Eng. trans., *History of Astronomy*, 1961), a review of astronomy up to the beginning of the present century; V.C. REDDISH, *The Evolution of the Galaxies* (1967), a brief account of the present knowledge about the evolution of galaxies; HARLOW SHAPLEY (ed.), *Source Book in Astronomy, 1900–1950* (1960), a collection of original contributions from various journals that illustrate the advances of astronomy made between 1900 and 1950; and OTTO STRUVE and VELTA ZEBERGS, *Astronomy of the 20th Century* (1962), a description of the working techniques of astronomers and the great advances made in this century in different branches of astronomy.

(B.E.W.)

Galen

In the history of ancient science, Galen stands as the most important physician after Hippocrates, who laid the foundations of rational medicine in the 5th century BC. Galen flourished under the Roman Empire in the 2nd century AD and achieved great renown in both East and West not only as a physician but also as a philosopher and philologist. His thinking exercised a profound influence on Byzantine and Islāmic civilizations and contributed substantially to the rise of Western science during the Renaissance.

Born in 129 in Pergamum, a city in Mysia, now Bergama, Turkey, Galen was the son of a gifted architect. The city of his birth, site of a shrine of the healing god Asclepius, significantly affected Galen's education. Many of the most distinguished personalities of the Roman Empire visited the shrine for cures, which Asclepius was thought to prescribe through revelations in the patients' dreams. A medical school was attached to the shrine, and there Galen met important men and observed the treatment of a variety of diseases. The high priest maintained a troupe of gladiators, which provided Galen with the opportunities to examine wounds and to judge the effects of medical treatment.

Since theoretical philosophy and practical medicine were closely related, Galen's father decided that he should study both subjects in his native city. His teachers represented the four principal philosophical sects: Platonism, Aristotelianism, Epicureanism, and Stoicism. This doctrinal variety helped to mold the philosophical eclecticism that characterized his entire life. He continued his studies in the educational centres of Smyrna on the west coast of Asia Minor, Corinth in Greece, and Alexandria in Egypt, where he practiced the dissection of animals and broadened his contacts with contemporary physicians. In 157 he returned to Pergamum, where, as chief physician for the gladiators, he increased his practical knowledge of anatomy and tested the best remedies for treating wounds.

In 161 the ambitious Galen, like many other successful Easterners, travelled to Rome, where he cured the ailing Aristotelian philosopher Eudemus, through whom he met many important persons in the capital city. His willingness to take on patients whom other doctors had pronounced incurable, his signal success as physician, and his immodesty concerning his conspicuous achievements aroused his colleagues' envy, which Galen arrogantly described in his books. He was soon admitted to the court of Marcus Aurelius, then co-emperor with Lucius Verus, and wrote with pride of the luminaries who attended his public lectures and dissections. These public performances greatly enhanced his prestige.

Galen abruptly ended his sojourn in the capital in 166. Although he claimed that the intolerable envy of his colleagues prompted his return to Pergamum, the plague that entered Rome with Verus' troops after a foreign war was probably a more compelling reason. In 168–169, however, he was recalled by the emperors. When Verus died of the plague, Marcus appointed Galen as physician to Commodus, his son, and the heir to the throne. The security of the appointment gave Galen the opportunity to write even more prolifically than before.

Galen based his descriptive anatomy on the dissection of lower animals, particularly the African monkey, often called the Barbary ape. Because this animal is a primate and shares certain characteristics with man, Galen made inferences concerning human anatomy. There is no doubt that he was an accurate observer, particularly of the muscles and bones. He distinguished seven pairs of cranial nerves, described the valves of the heart, and observed the structural differences between veins and arteries. Notable also were his vivisection experiments, such as tying off the recurrent laryngeal nerve to show that the brain controls the voice, performing a series of transections of the spinal cord to study muscle control, and tying off the ureters to demonstrate kidney and bladder functions. One of his most important demonstrations was that the arteries carry blood, not air, as had been taught for 400 years.

Although Galen did not discover that the blood circulates, he did achieve a valid and rational interpretation of the observed facts. According to his view, the most important organ in the vascular system was the liver, where blood was formed and the veins originated; blood vessels carried the blood out to the periphery of the body, where, according to him, it was transformed into flesh. He accounted for the large amount of blood in the aorta —the largest blood vessel leaving the heart—by suggesting a passage from the right ventricle to the left ventricle of the heart through minute pores in the wall that separates the two and by suggesting that a small amount of blood seeps through the lungs between the pulmonary artery and pulmonary veins, and so from the right to the left ventricle.

Galen believed that human health required an equilibrium between the four humours—phlegm, black bile, yellow bile, and the blood—and that, furthermore, the pneuma (thought to be a material but very subtle component carried by the blood) was responsible for guiding many body processes. As a continuation of the earlier Hippocratic conception of the unity of the organism, Galenic physiology became a powerful influence in medicine for the next 1,400 years.

Although Galen's work was primarily in medicine, he believed that a good physician must also be a philosopher

Medical training

The Galenic system

and wrote an extant essay on that subject. He was fully aware of, and critical of, the impact of Judaism and Christianity on Roman life. In particular, he accused the Jews of what he called unreasoned assertions. And he cited Christians to illustrate his view that even nonphilosophers could by good behaviour approximate the philosophic ideal. Even though he believed that nature expressed a divine purpose, he was not a monotheist in the sense of believing in one transcendent deity. Rather, in line with his eclecticism, he drew on diverse sources for his philosophical interpretations. He fully accepted Aristotle's view that "Nature does nothing in vain" and sought to show that all organic structures, such as the muscles and bones of the hand, serve the functions for which they were designed, which he attributed sometimes to a creator and sometimes to a beneficent nature.

Galen's influence

Greek manuscripts were collected and translated by enlightened Arabs during the 9th century. Ḥunayn ibn Isḥāq, an Arab physician and philologist, prepared an annotated list of 129 works of Galen that he translated from Greek or Syriac versions. During the late 11th century, copies of Ḥunayn's translations and commentaries on them by Arab physicians were translated into Latin. These Latin versions helped to enlighten European scholars as to the achievements of Greek antiquity. When medical humanists of the 15th and 16th centuries saw the need to prepare new Latin versions of Galen directly from the Greek, it was inevitable that physicians should wish to repeat the experiments and observations that Galen had recorded. This renewal of the Galenic tradition during the Renaissance was an important element in the rise of modern science. Many of Galen's writings have been lost, especially those on philosophical and literary subjects; others survive only in Arabic copies, and only a few have been translated into English. Little is known of Galen's final years. He probably never returned to Pergamum and died in about 199.

BIBLIOGRAPHY. The only full account of Galen in English is G. SARTON, Galen of Pergamon (1954), written in a popular style and not always reliable. The classic and invaluable study of Galen's career and medical practice is J. ILBERG, "Aus Galens Praxis," Neue Jahrbücher für das Klassische Altertum, Geschichte und deutsche Litteratur und für Pädagogik, 15:276–312 (1905). See also R. WALZER, Galen on Jews and Christians (1949), a scholarly study of the relevant Galenic texts. For an examination of Galen in the social context of his time, see G.W. BOWERSOCK, "The Prestige of Galen," in Greek Sophists in the Roman Empire, ch. 5 (1969). Still the best introduction to the Arabic transmission of Galen's works is G. BERGSTRASSER, "Ḥunain ibn Isḥāq: Über die syrischen und arabischen Galen-Übersetzungen," Abhandlungen für die Kunde des Morgenlandes, vol. 17, no. 2 (1925). Ḥunain's list of the books of Galen he translated is a source of valuable information on Galen's total work; how it was transmitted to the West is discussed by M. MEYERHOF in "New Light on Ḥunain Ibn Isḥāq and His Period," Isis, 8:685–724 (1926). R.E. SIEGEL, Galen's System of Physiology and Medicine (1968), is a comprehensive survey of Galenic medical thought. See also R. WALZER, "New Light on Galen's Moral Philosophy," in his Greek into Arabic, pp. 142–163 (1962). English translations with commentaries of Galen's major work in anatomy and physiology are: A.J. BROCK, On the Natural Faculties (1942 and 1963); C. SINGER, On Anatomical Procedures (1956); W.L.H. DUCKWORTH, On Anatomical Procedures, the Later Books (1962); and M.T. MAY, Galen on the Usefulness of the Parts of the Body, 2 vol. (1968). There is a partial list of the new discoveries of Galen's works in Arabic translation in Sarton (op. cit.), pp. 99–100.

English translations of Galen's works down to 1954 are also listed in Sarton, pp. 101–107. English translations after 1954 are listed in J. SCARBOROUGH, Roman Medicine, pp. 165–166 (1969).

(G.W.Bo.)

Galilee, Sea of

The Sea of Galilee (Lake Tiberias), a lake through which the Jordan River flows, is located in Israeli territory, although from 1948 to 1967 it was bordered immediately to the northeast by the cease-fire line with Syria. It is famous for its biblical associations. Located 686 feet below the level of the Mediterranean, it has a surface area of 64 square miles (166 square kilometres). The sea's maximum depth, which occurs in the northeast, is 157 feet. Measuring 13 miles from north to south and 7 miles from east to west, it is pear-shaped. Its Old Testament name was Sea of Kinneret (Kinerot), but after the exile of the Jews to Babylon in the 6th century BC it was called the Lake of Gennesaret. In the New Testament it is called the Sea of Galilee and sometimes the Sea of Tiberias. In Arabic it is called the Buḥayrat Ṭabarīyā, and in Hebrew, Yam Kinneret. (For an associated physical feature, see JORDAN RIVER.)

Historical and religious associations. Because of a pleasant climate, level topography, fertile soil, and relatively abundant water, the rivers flowing into the lake and the adjacent plains have throughout history been the source of livelihood for various peoples. At El-ʿUbeidīya, two miles south of the lake, lacustrine formations dating from about 400,000 to 500,000 years ago have revealed prehistoric tools and two human fragments, which are among the oldest in the Middle East. Canaanite (ancient Palestinian) structures have been uncovered that date back to between 1000 and 2000 BC. In the 1st century AD the region was rich and populated; the Jewish historian Flavius Josephus wrote of nine cities on the shores of the lake in ancient times, but of these only Tiberias has survived. Tiberias, on the western shore, was one of the four Jewish holy cities, and Kefar Naḥum (Capernaum), near the northwestern shore, has preserved one of the most beautiful synagogues of the Galilee region, dating from the 2nd and 3rd centuries AD. A sanctuary for the Druzes (an independent sect founded in the 11th century that followed a creed containing elements of Islām, Judaism, and Christianity) is located near Kefar Ḥittim near the western shore. The Sea of Galilee is especially well known to Christians because it was the scene of many episodes in the life of Christ. The region was also the site of the first Jewish kibbutz, Deganya, established in 1909.

Archaeological remains

Relief and environment. The Sea of Galilee is located in the great depression of the Jordan. The Plain of Gennesaret extends in a circular arc from the north to the northwest, and the Plain of Bet Ẓayda (Buteiha) in Syria extends to the northeast. To the west and the southwest the hills of Lower Galilee fall abruptly to the lake's edge. In the mid-eastern sections, the cliffs of the Plateau of Golan overlook the lake; the plateau reappears again in the southeast, becoming larger as it approaches the valley of the Yarmuk River, a tributary that has its confluence with the Jordan a few miles to the south of the lake. Also to the south, the Plain of al-Ghawr begins, but the Sea of Galilee is separated from it by a narrow ridge through which the Jordan River flows. The greatest part of the region is covered by basalts that have been formed since the Miocene Epoch began about 26,000,000 years ago and that are part of the vast area of Jebel Druze and Hauran, both located in Syria. Since the Miocene Epoch began, lacustrine limestones and marls (calcareous clays) have been deposited. The Great Eastern Rift, which forms the Jordan Trench, passes to the east of the lake; smaller and less important faults occur to the west. The depression was hollowed out at the end of the Pliocene Epoch (from 7,000,000 to 2,500,000 years ago) and was partially filled in again by lacustrine and fluvial sediments. During the humid periods of the Quaternary Period (within the last 2,500,000 years) the Dead Sea (q.v.) extended up to this point. During the mid-Pleistocene Epoch (about 1,250,000 years ago) structural movements of the earth's crust occurred, while flows of molten basalt reached the lower end of the depression through the Valley of Yarmuk. In the course of the last pluvial period, which occurred about 20,000 years ago, a great lake, called the Lake of Lisan, covered the region, with the result that formations of marls were deposited. Since then, the waters have receded; the present lake was conserved following the damming of the Jordan waters by basalt deposits.

Climate. Because of its sheltered location, low altitude, and the influence of the lake itself, the winters are mild, with temperatures averaging 57° F (14° C) in January. The absence of freezing temperatures has facilitated the cultivation of bananas, dates, citrus fruit, and vegetables. The summers are hot, with temperatures averaging 88° F (31° C), and the precipitation—almost 15 inches at Deganya—falls, in the course of a winter of less than 50 days, in the form of brief but violent showers. The winds generally alternate daily, especially in the summer, blowing onshore in the morning and offshore at night. During the winter violent winds occasionally rush into the Jordan depression, creating storms on the lake.

Hydrology. The Sea of Galilee is fed primarily by the Jordan River; the lake governs the river's flow, and strains its waters. Among streams and wadis flowing into the lake from the hills of Galilee are two small permanent streams, the Naḥal ʿAmmud and the Zalmon, and one wadi (seasonal watercourse), the Naḥal Arbel, all of which flow from the northwest; and four moderate-sized streams that flow down from the Golan Heights. In the rivers associated with the lake and at the bottom of the lake itself are many mineral deposits. Because of these deposits and because of the strong evaporation, the waters of the lake are relatively salty; seasonal variations, however, result in maximum salinity occurring in summer and fall. Annual variations also occur.

Salinity

Animal life. The lake's fish life has an affinity with that of the East African lakes. Fish species to be found include damselfish, scaleless blennies, caṭfish, mouth-breeders, and barbels. Apart from its permanent fish population, the lake is also visited by migratory fish.

The agricultural development of the region has resulted in a modification of its animal life. Wild boars, for example, abundant during earlier periods, have greatly decreased in numbers.

Resource development. For the past few centuries the Plains of Gennesaret, to the northwest, and the area around Deganya, to the south, have been systematically developed through irrigation and intensive agricultural techniques. Fishing has also been developed, notably from Tiberias and Gennesaret and at En Gev, on the eastern shore. About 1,000 tons of fish are netted annually from motorboats and trawlers; sardines are mainly caught in winter, although, together with larger fish, they are also caught at other seasons. Thermal springs have enabled modern health resorts to be created, and the baths at Tiberias are among Israel's most important winter resort attractions. Similar baths are to be found at Tabigha, or ʿEn Shevaʿ (the seven springs of Bathsheba) on the northwest shore.

The "National Water Carrier" canal

In the 1960s, the Sea of Galilee became the starting point of the "National Water Carrier," a large canal that conveys water from the Jordan River to the coastal region, as well as south to the Negev Desert. The level of the lake has been raised slightly by a dam constructed downstream; the water, flowing into the lower reaches of the Jordan River, is used as a source of hydroelectric power. Some of the water, however, is pumped by pipe to the northwest to a height almost 800 feet above the lake's level, from where it is siphoned across the gorges of Naḥal ʿAmmud and Zalmon to irrigate the country's western sector.

Transport. The small market towns on the shores of the lake rely for transport of goods and passengers to a great extent on a regular motorboat service that is maintained between them.

Prospects for the future. Before 1967, when the cease-fire line with Syria bordered the lake to the northeast, political tensions hindered the development of normal navigation and fishing activities on the lake. The future development of such activities depends upon the maintenance of political stability in the area.

The excessive salinity of the water has created problems which it is hoped will be solved by the diverting of thermal springs that now flow into the lake and by sealing apertures on the lake floor, which are now sources of salinity. (P.Sa.)

Galileo

Galileo Galilei, Italian mathematician, astronomer, and physicist, made several significant contributions to modern scientific thought. As the first man to use the tele-scope to study the skies, he amassed evidence that proved the Earth revolves around the Sun and is not the centre of the universe, as had been believed. His position represented such a radical departure from accepted thought that he was tried by the Inquisition in Rome, ordered to recant, and forced to spend the last eight years of his life under house arrest. He informally stated the principles later embodied in Newton's first two laws of motion. Because of his pioneer work in gravitation and motion and in combining mathematical analysis with experimentation, Galileo often is referred to as the founder of modern mechanics and experimental physics. Perhaps the most far-reaching of his achievements was his re-establishment of mathematical rationalism against Aristotle's logico-verbal approach and his insistence that the "Book of Nature is written in mathematical characters." From this base, he was able to found the modern experimental method (see RATIONALISM: *Religious Rationalism*).

Alinari

Galileo, oil painting by J. Sustermans, 1686. In the Uffizi, Florence.

Early years. Galileo was born at Pisa on February 15, 1564, the son of Vincenzo Galilei, a musician. He received his early education at the monastery of Vallombrosa near Florence, where his family had moved in 1574. In 1581 he entered the University of Pisa to study medicine. While in the Pisa cathedral during his first year at the university, Galileo supposedly observed a lamp swinging and found that the lamp always required the same amount of time to complete an oscillation, no matter how large the range of the swing. Later in life Galileo verified this observation experimentally and suggested that the principle of the pendulum might be applied to the regulation of clocks.

The legend of the lamp

Until he supposedly observed the swinging lamp in the cathedral, Galileo had received no instruction in mathematics. Then a geometry lesson he overheard by chance awakened his interest, and he began to study mathematics and science with Ostilio Ricci, a teacher in the Tuscan court. But in 1585, before he had received a degree, he was withdrawn from the university because of lack of funds. Returning to Florence, he lectured at the Florentine academy and in 1586 published an essay describing the hydrostatic balance, the invention of which made his name known throughout Italy. In 1589 a treatise on the centre of gravity in solids won for Galileo the honourable, but not lucrative, post of mathematics lecturer at the University of Pisa.

Galileo then began his research into the theory of motion, first disproving the Aristotelian contention that bodies of different weights fall at different speeds. Because of financial difficulties, Galileo, in 1592, applied for and was awarded the chair of mathematics at Padua, where he was to remain for 18 years and perform the bulk of his most outstanding work. At Padua he continued his research on motion and proved theoretically (about 1604) that falling bodies obey what came to be known as the law of uniformly accelerated motion (in such motion a body speeds up or slows down uniformly with time). He also gave the law of parabolic fall (*e.g.,* a ball thrown into the air follows a parabolic path). A legend that he dropped weights from the leaning tower of Pisa apparently has no basis in fact.

Research with the telescope. Galileo became convinced early in life of the truth of the Copernican theory (*i.e.,* that the planets revolve about the Sun) but was deterred from avowing his opinions—as shown in his letter of April 4, 1597, to Kepler—because of fear of ridicule. While in Venice in the spring of 1609, Galileo learned of the recent invention of the telescope. After returning to Padua he built a telescope of threefold magnifying power and quickly improved it to a power of 32. Because of the method Galileo devised for checking the curvature of the lenses, his telescopes were the first that could be used for astronomical observation and soon were in demand in all parts of Europe.

Early astronomical discoveries

As the first person to apply the telescope to a study of the skies, Galileo in late 1609 and early 1610 announced a series of astronomical discoveries. He found that the surface of the Moon was irregular and not smooth, as had been supposed; he observed that the Milky Way system was composed of a collection of stars; he discovered the satellites of Jupiter and named them Sidera Medicea (Medicean Stars) in honour of his former pupil and future employer, Cosimo II, grand duke of Tuscany. He also observed spots on the Sun, the phases of Venus, and the rings of Saturn. His first decisive astronomical observations were published in 1610 in *Sidereus Nuncius* ("The Starry Messenger"; see TELESCOPE: *Early History*).

Although the Venetian senate had granted Galileo a lifetime appointment as professor at Padua because of his findings with the telescope, he left in the summer of 1610 to become "first philosopher and mathematician" to the grand duke of Tuscany, an appointment that enabled him to devote more time to research.

Conflict with Rome. In 1611 Galileo visited Rome and demonstrated his telescope to the most eminent personages at the pontifical court. Encouraged by the flattering reception accorded to him, he ventured, in three letters on the sunspots printed at Rome in 1613 under the title *Istoria e dimostrazioni intorno alle macchie solari e loro accidenti . . .,* to take up a more definite position on the Copernican theory. Movement of the spots across the face of the Sun, Galileo maintained, proved Copernicus was right and Ptolemy wrong.

His great expository gifts and his choice of Italian, in which he was an acknowledged master of style, made his thoughts popular beyond the confines of the universities and created a powerful movement of opinion. The Aristotelian professors, seeing their vested interests threatened, united against him. They strove to cast suspicion upon him in the eyes of ecclesiastical authorities because of contradictions between the Copernican theory and the Scriptures. They obtained the cooperation of the Dominican preachers, who fulminated from the pulpit against the new impiety of "mathematicians" and secretly denounced Galileo to the Inquisition for blasphemous utterances, which, they said, he had freely invented. Gravely alarmed, Galileo agreed with one of his pupils, B. Castelli, a Benedictine monk, that something should be done to forestall a crisis. He accordingly wrote letters meant for the Grand Duke and for the Roman authorities (letters to Castelli, to the Grand Duchess Dowager, to Monsignor Dini) in which he pointed out the danger, reminding the church of its standing practice of interpreting Scripture allegorically whenever it came into conflict with scientific truth, quoting patristic authorities and warning that it would be "a terrible detriment for the souls if people found themselves convinced by proof of something that it was made then a sin to believe." He even went to Rome in person to beg the authorities to leave the way open for a change. A number of ecclesiastical experts were on his side. Unfortunately, Cardinal Robert Bellarmine, the chief theologian of the church, was un-

able to appreciate the importance of the new theories and clung to the time-honoured belief that mathematical hypotheses have nothing to do with physical reality. He only saw the danger of a scandal, which might undermine Catholicity in its fight with Protestantism. He accordingly decided that the best thing would be to check the whole issue by having Copernicanism declared "false and erroneous" and the book of Copernicus suspended by the congregation of the Index. The decree came out on March 5, 1616. On the previous February 26, however, as an act of personal consideration, Cardinal Bellarmine had granted an audience to Galileo and informed him of the forthcoming decree, warning him that he must henceforth neither "hold nor defend" the doctrine, although it could still be discussed as a mere "mathematical supposition."

The suppression of Copernicanism

For the next seven years Galileo led a life of studious retirement in his house in Bellosguardo near Florence. At the end of that time (1623), he replied to a pamphlet by Orazio Grassi about the nature of comets; the pamphlet clearly had been aimed at Galileo. His reply, titled *Saggiatore . . .* ("Assayer . . ."), was a brilliant polemic on physical reality and an exposition of the new scientific method. In it he distinguished between the primary (*i.e.,* measurable) properties of matter and the others (*e.g.,* odour) and wrote his famous pronouncement that the "Book of Nature is . . . written in mathematical characters." The book was dedicated to the new pope, Urban VIII, who as Maffeo Barberini had been a longtime friend and protector of Galileo. Pope Urban received the dedication enthusiastically.

In 1624 Galileo again went to Rome, hoping to obtain a revocation of the decree of 1616. This he did not get, but he obtained permission from the pope to write about "the systems of the world," both Ptolemaic and Copernican, as long as he discussed them noncommittally and came to the conclusion dictated to him in advance by the pontiff—that is, that man cannot presume to know how the world is really made because God could have brought about the same effects in ways unimagined by him, and he must not restrict God's omnipotence. These instructions were confirmed in writing by the head censor, Monsignor Niccolò Riccardi.

Galileo returned to Florence and spent the next several years working on his great book *Dialogo sopra i due massimi sistemi del mondo, tolemaico e copernicano* (*Dialogue Concerning the Two Chief World Systems—Ptolemaic and Copernican*, 1953).

As soon as it came out, in the year 1632, with the full and complete imprimatur of the censors, it was greeted with a tumult of applause and cries of praise from every part of the European continent as a literary and philosophical masterpiece.

On the crisis that followed there remain now only inferences. It was pointed out to the Pope that despite its noncommittal title, the work was a compelling and unabashed plea for the Copernican system. The strength of the argument made the prescribed conclusion at the end look anticlimactic and pointless. The Jesuits insisted that it could have worse consequences on the established system of teaching "than Luther and Calvin put together." The Pope, in anger, ordered a prosecution. The author being covered by license, the only legal measures would be to disavow the licensers and prohibit the book. But at that point a document was "discovered" in the file, to the effect that during his audience with Bellarmine on February 26, 1616, Galileo had been specifically enjoined from "teaching or discussing Copernicanism in any way," under the penalties of the Holy Office. His license, it was concluded, had therefore been "extorted" under false pretenses. (The consensus of historians, based on evidence made available when the file was published in 1877, has been that the document had been planted and that Galileo was never so enjoined.) The church authorities, on the strength of the "new" document, were able to prosecute him for "vehement suspicion of heresy." Notwithstanding his pleas of illness and old age, Galileo was compelled to journey to Rome in February 1633 and stand trial. He was treated with special in-

Galileo's trial

dulgence and not jailed. In a rigorous interrogation on April 12, he steadfastly denied any memory of the 1616 injunction. The commissary general of the Inquisition, obviously sympathizing with him, discreetly outlined for the authorities a way in which he might be let off with a reprimand, but on June 16 the congregation decreed that he must be sentenced. The sentence was read to him on June 21: he was guilty of having "held and taught" the Copernican doctrine and was ordered to recant. Galileo recited a formula in which he "abjured, cursed and detested" his past errors. The sentence carried imprisonment, but this portion of the penalty was immediately commuted by the Pope into house arrest and seclusion on his little estate at Arcetri near Florence, where he returned in December 1633. The sentence of house arrest remained in effect throughout the last eight years of his life.

Although confined to his estate, Galileo's prodigious mental activity continued undiminished to the last. In 1634 he completed *Discorsi e dimostrazioni mathematiche intorno a due nuove scienze attenenti alla meccanica* (*Dialogue Concerning Two New Sciences . . .*, 1914), in which he recapitulated the results of his early experiments and his mature meditations on the principles of mechanics. This, in many respects his most valuable work, was printed by Louis Elzevirs at Leiden in 1638. His last telescopic discovery—that of the Moon's diurnal and monthly librations (wobbling from side to side)—was made in 1637, only a few months before he became blind. But the fire of his genius was not even yet extinct. He continued his scientific correspondence with unbroken interest and undiminished acumen; he thought out the application of the pendulum to the regulation of clockwork, which the Dutch scientist Christiaan Huygens put into practice in 1656; he was engaged in dictating to his disciples, Vincenzo Viviani and Evangelista Torricelli, his latest ideas on the theory of impact when he was seized with the slow fever that resulted in his death at Arcetri on January 8, 1642.

Value of his work. The direct services of permanent value that Galileo rendered to astronomy are virtually summed up in his telescopic discoveries. His name is justly associated with a vast extension of the bounds of the visible universe, and his telescopic observations are a standing monument of his ability. Within two years after their discovery, he had constructed approximately accurate tables of the revolutions of Jupiter's satellites and proposed their frequent eclipses as a means of determining longitudes on land and at sea. The idea, though ingenious, has been found of little use at sea. His observations on sunspots are noteworthy for their accuracy and for the deductions he drew from them with regard to the rotation of the Sun and the revolution of the Earth.

A puzzling circumstance is Galileo's neglect of Kepler's laws, which were discovered during his lifetime. But then he believed strongly that orbits should be circular (not elliptical, as Kepler discovered) in order to keep the fabric of the cosmos in its perfect order. This preconception prevented him from giving a full formulation of the inertial law, which he himself discovered, although it usually is attributed to the French mathematician René Descartes. Galileo believed that the inertial path of a body around the Earth must be circular. Lacking the idea of Newtonian gravitation, he hoped this would allow him to explain the path of the planets as circular inertial orbits around the Sun.

The idea of a universal force of gravitation seems to have hovered on the borders of this great man's mind, but he refused to entertain it because, like Descartes, he considered it an "occult" quality. More valid instances of the anticipation of modern discoveries may be found in his prevision that a small annual parallax would eventually be found for some of the fixed stars and that extra-Saturnian planets would at some future time be ascertained to exist and in his conviction that light travels with a measurable although extremely great velocity. Although Galileo discovered, in 1610, a means of adapting his telescope to the examination of minute objects, he did not become acquainted with the compound microscope until 1624, when he saw one in Rome and, with characteristic ingenuity, immediately introduced several improvements into its construction.

A most substantial part of his work consisted undoubtedly of his contributions toward the establishment of mechanics as a science. Some valuable but isolated facts and theorems had previously been discovered and proved, but it was Galileo who first clearly grasped the idea of force as a mechanical agent. Although he did not formulate the interdependence of motion and force into laws, his writings on dynamics are everywhere suggestive of those laws, and his solutions of dynamical problems involve their recognition. In this branch of science he paved the way for the English physicist and mathematician Isaac Newton later in the century. The extraordinary advances made by him were due to his application of mathematical analysis to physical problems.

Galileo was the first man who perceived that mathematics and physics, previously kept in separate compartments, were going to join forces. He was thus able to unify celestial and terrestrial phenomena into one theory, destroying the traditional division between the world above and the world below the Moon. The method that was peculiarly his consisted in the combination of experiment with calculation—in the transformation of the concrete into the abstract and the assiduous comparison of results. He created the modern idea of experiment, which he called *cimento* ("ordeal"). This method was applied to check theoretical deductions in the investigation of the laws of falling bodies, of equilibrium and motion on an inclined plane, and of the motion of a projectile. The latter, together with his definition of momentum and other parts of his work, implied a knowledge of the laws of motion as later stated by Newton. In his *Discorso intorno alle cose che stanno in su l'acqua* ("Discourse on Things That Float"), published in 1612, he used the principle of virtual velocities to demonstrate the more elementary theorems of hydrostatics, deducing the equilibrium of fluid in a siphon, and worked out the conditions for the flotation of solid bodies in a liquid. He also constructed, in 1607, an elementary form of air thermometer.

Work in mechanics

BIBLIOGRAPHY. The first complete edition of Galileo's works was that of EUGENIO ALBERI, 16 vol. (1842–56). It is now superseded by the final *Edizione nazionale delle opere di Galileo Galilei*, 20 vol., by the Galileo scholar ANTONIO FAVARO (1890–1909, reprinted 1929–39). It contains every obtainable document and scrap of correspondence. The documents of the trial are in vol. 19.

The original documents from the archives of the Inquisition, relating to the events of 1616 and 1633, were first published in their entirety by HENRI DE L'EPINOIS, *Les Pièces du procès de Galilée* (1877). The earliest authoritative discussions are by KARL VON GEBLER, *Galileo Galilei und die römische Curie*, 2 vol. (1876–77, reprinted 1968); and EMIL WOHLWILL, *Galilei*, 2 vol. (1875–1907). More recent is GIORGIO DE SANTILLANA, *The Crime of Galileo* (1955). On the Roman Catholic side are F.R. WEGG-PROSSER, *Galileo and His Judges* (1889); ADOLF MULLER, *Galilei und die Katholische Kirche* (1910); and FILIPPO SOCCORSI, *Il Processo di Galileo* (1947).

The most important collection of monographs and scholarly sources are ANTONIO FAVARO, *Galileo Galilei e lo studio di Padova*, 2 vol. (1883, reprinted 1966), and *Scampoli Galileiani* (1886); STILLMAN DRAKE, "Galileo Gleanings," *Isis*, 6 pt., 48: 393–397, 49:26–33, 155–165, 409–413, 50:245–254 (1957–59); and *Osiris*, 13:262–290 (1958). The *Bibliografia Galileiana*, 1568–1895, by ALARICO CARLI and ANTONIO FAVARO (1896), lists more than 2,000 publications; its continuation by GIUSEPPE BOFFITO (1943) lists another 2,000.

The first English translation of Galileo's writings was THOMAS SALUSBURY, *Mathematical Collections and Translations*, 5 vol. (1661–62). Other English translations include *Dialogues Concerning Two New Sciences*, trans. by HENRY CREWE and ANTONIO DE SALVIO (1914, reprinted 1954); *Dialogue Concerning the Two Chief World Systems—Ptolemaic and Copernican*, trans. by STILLMAN DRAKE, 2nd ed. (1967); *Dialogue on the Great World Systems*, in the Salusbury Translation, ed. by GIORGIO DE SANTILLANA (1953); *Letters on Sunspots, . . .*, abridged in STILLMAN DRAKE, *Discoveries and Opinions of Galileo* (1957); and *On Motion, and On Mechanics*, trans. by I.E. DRABKIN and STILLMAN DRAKE (1960).

(G.de S.)

Galliformes

The bird order Galliformes, or gallinaceous (*i.e.*, fowllike or chicken-like) birds, includes about 240 species, of which the best known are the turkeys (family Meleagrididae); chickens, quail, partridge, pheasant and peacock (Phasianidae); guinea fowl (Numididae); and grouse (Tetraonidae). Lesser known members of the order are the megapodes (Megapodiidae); chachalacas, guans, and curassows (Cracidae); and the hoatzin (Opisthocomidae). The last is so aberrant that many authorities place it in a separate order, Opisthocomiformes.

GENERAL FEATURES

Size range and diversity of structure. Most galliforms are medium-sized birds, from the size of a pigeon to that of a domestic chicken, 40 to 60 centimetres (16 to 24 inches) long and 500 to 2,500 grams (one to five pounds) in weight. The smallest members of the order are the sparrow-sized painted quail (*Excalfactoria*), about 13 centimetres (five inches) long and about 45 grams (1½ ounces) in weight. The heaviest galliform is the common, or wild, turkey (*Meleagris gallopavo*), wild specimens of which may weigh up to 11 kilograms (about 24 pounds); the longest is the argus pheasant (*Argusianus argus*), the male of which reaches two metres (79 inches) in breeding plumage, including wing and tail feathers, whose length exceeds one metre.

The majority of gallinaceous birds are heavy bodied, with short, rounded wings and strong, four-toed feet, adapted for life on the ground; a few, such as cracids and the hoatzin, live mainly in trees. The bill is short and slightly downcurved. The flight is fast but rarely sustained for long distances, most being sedentary, nonmigratory birds.

Distribution. Some members of the order are found in virtually every habitat in sub-Arctic, temperate, and tropical regions of the larger landmasses, and a few species (ptarmigan, *Lagopus*) live within the Arctic Circle. The phasianids, the 178 species of which comprise by far the largest family, have nearly the distribution of the order. The cracids, with about 34 species, are restricted to tropical woodlands of Central and South America. The 18 species of grouse are found in northern temperate and Arctic regions of both hemispheres. The remaining groups are more restricted in distribution. The ten species of megapodes inhabit forests from the East Indies east to the Fiji Islands and south to central Australia. Guinea fowl are restricted to Africa south of the Sahara but have been widely introduced on other continents. The two turkeys are native to North and Central America; the common, or wild, turkey in temperate woodlands of eastern United States and Mexico; and the ocellated turkey (*Agriocharis ocellata*) in Guatemala, British Honduras, and the Yucatán Peninsula of Mexico. The hoatzin (*Opisthocomus hoazin*) inhabits wooded river edges in northern and eastern South America.

IMPORTANCE TO MAN

Gallinaceous birds are unquestionably the most important avian group from the human standpoint. The chicken (*Gallus domesticus*) was domesticated in southern Asia at least 4,000 years ago from a parental stock of one or more species of jungle fowl (principally *G. gallus*). Selective breeding has produced well over 100 varieties, most of which are specialized for the production of either eggs or meat. In North America and to a lesser extent in northern Europe, the turkey is raised in numbers second only to those of the chicken. Domestic breeding of the turkey has been primarily for rapid growth and high market weight, the birds being raised solely for meat. Mature toms (males) may reach 23 kilograms (about 51 pounds). In many parts of the world, guinea fowl are an important barnyard species and are valued for the readiness with which they give alarm at the approach of a predator. (For a complete account of domestic gallinaceous birds, see LIVESTOCK AND POULTRY FARMING.)

Galliform birds constitute the large majority of land game birds, in number both of species and of individuals. Populations in North America and in western Europe are often carefully managed through habitat manipulation, supplemental feeding, and artificial rearing to ensure maximum hunting yields. The common pheasant (*Phasianus colchicus*, called the ring-necked pheasant in the United States) was introduced in North America late in the 19th century and has become widely established. Several species of quail (especially those of the genera *Coturnix* and *Colinus*) and partridge (*Perdix* and *Alectoris*)

Origin of the domestic chicken

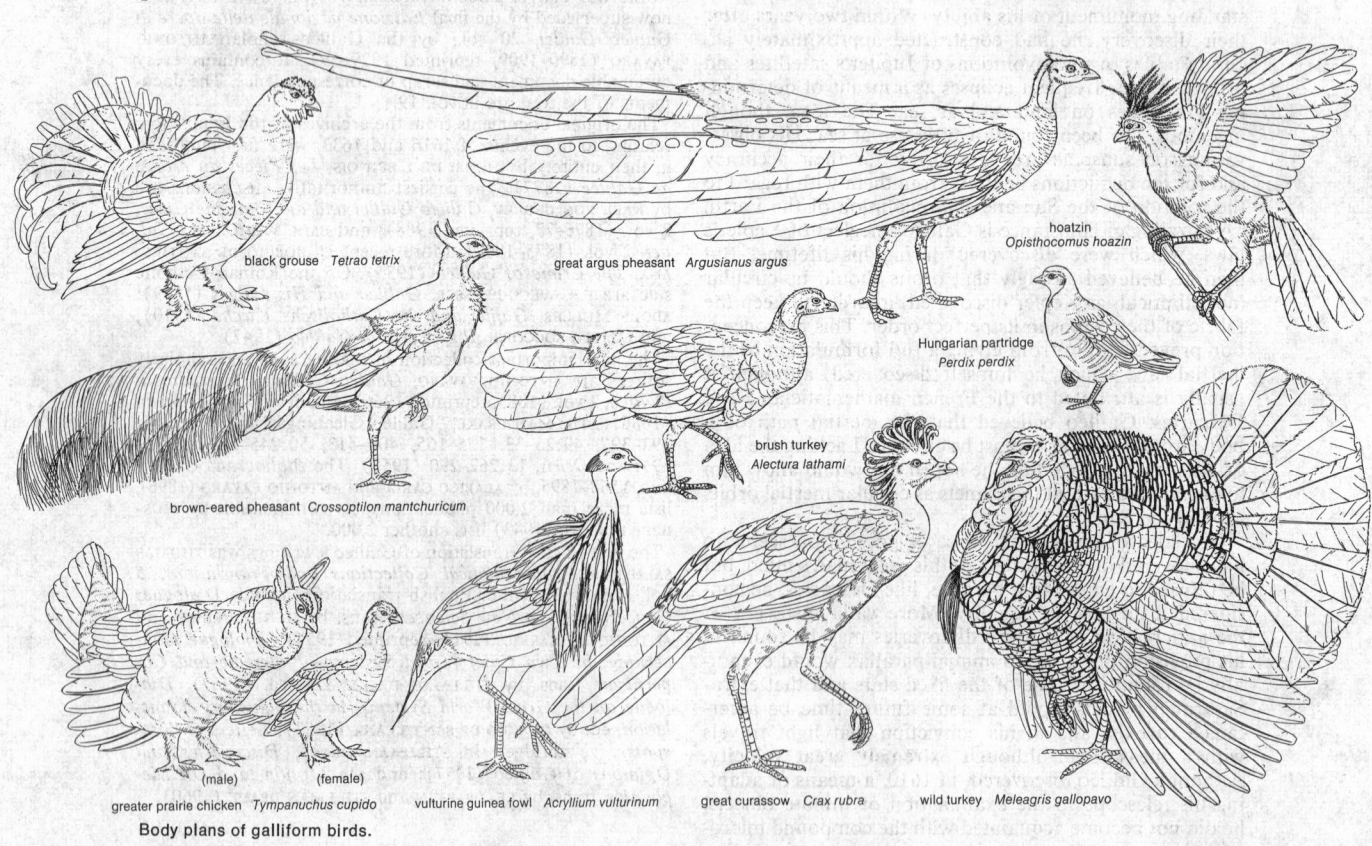

black grouse *Tetrao tetrix*

great argus pheasant *Argusianus argus*

hoatzin
Opisthocomus hoazin

Hungarian partridge
Perdix perdix

brush turkey
Alectura lathami

brown-eared pheasant *Crossoptilon mantchuricum*

(male)   (female)

greater prairie chicken *Tympanuchus cupido*   vulturine guinea fowl *Acryllium vulturinum*   great curassow *Crax rubra*   wild turkey *Meleagris gallopavo*

Body plans of galliform birds.

provide much sport hunting. A widespread tendency in game-bird management has been the introduction of species to areas where they have not been found previously.

The North American wild turkey, once nearly exterminated by overhunting, has responded to careful management and is now taken in fair numbers in the hardwood forests of the eastern United States. Grouse (including ptarmigan) are hunted throughout their range. (For further information on game birds, see HUNTING, SPORT.)

NATURAL HISTORY

Habitat selection and food habits. As an order, the galliforms inhabit a wide variety of vegetational types, including dense and open forest, open grasslands, scrub and second-growth forest, and flooded riparian (river) forests. Megapodes live in dense jungle, some appearing in the open only to lay eggs on sandy beaches. The mallee fowl (*Leipoa ocellata*) is an exception, inhabiting the eucalyptus thickets that characterize the arid interior of Australia. The majority of galliforms roost on elevated perches at night, even those species that spend the daylight hours foraging on the ground. Virtually the only ones that live in treeless regions are certain of the grouse, such as the tundra-inhabiting ptarmigan, the prairie chickens (*Tympanuchus cupido* and *T. pallidicinctus*), the sage grouse (*Centrocercus urophasianus*), and the sharp-tailed grouse (*Pedioecetes phasianellus*). The Eurasian black grouse (*Tetrao tetrix*) occurs in open country and in forested regions. Most of the true pheasant, including the peafowl, are residents of open forest with clearings. Guinea fowl of the genera *Guttera* and *Agelastes* and quail of the New World genus *Odontophorus* inhabit dense tropical forest. The hoatzin is closely associated with water and is almost never found far from it.

The food of galliforms is varied, most species being basically vegetarian, but they also take large numbers of insects, worms, and other invertebrates. Many use their feet to uncover food in leaf litter. The hoatzin feeds on leaves and fruit, especially those of arums (Araceae), rarely descending to the ground but occasionally entering the water to take small crabs or fish.

Courtship and mating. Gallinaceous birds vary considerably in reproductive behaviour, some exhibiting monogamous pair formation with a pair bond lasting through the breeding season, others showing varying types of polygamy, usually with members of both sexes being more or less promiscuous. Many, if not most, quail and partridge are monogamous, as are ptarmigan, guinea fowl, the hoatzin, some pheasant, and those megapodes and cracids that have been studied. Polygamy is known to occur in many grouse, including the North American grassland species, and in peafowl (*Pavo*) and some other phasianids. In the social displays of grouse, a number of males assemble in a special assembly area, called a court, dancing ground, arena, or lek. The dancing ground lies outside of all nesting territories, and the same ground is used year after year. Each of the males, which may number up to several dozen, has his own area within the dancing ground. There he struts and postures, producing strange calls (some of which are produced in special esophageal air sacs) to attract the females, who visit the dancing ground to select a male and copulate. Dominant males occupy central positions in the arena group and may copulate with several females. Some species, such as the black grouse and the capercaille (*Tetrao urogallus*), are variable in the degree to which males gather for display purposes, populations in more open areas tending more toward social displays. Males of the North American ruffed grouse (*Bonasa umbellus*) and those of some phasianids, the peacock pheasant (*Polyplectron*) and argus pheasant being examples, live in isolation, displaying to and copulating with any receptive female.

Nesting. The large majority of gallinaceous birds nest on the ground, the nest being only a shallow scrape, lined with soft grass or leaves. Cracids, the hoatzin, and the horned pheasant (*Tragopan*) build nests in trees, those of the cracids being relatively small for the size of the birds.

The nesting of megapodes is unique among birds. The eggs of all species are placed in sand or soil, the heat for

Polyga-mous and monoga-mous types

Male sage grouse (*Centrocercus urophasianus*) in courtship display, revealing the bare air sacs in the sides of its neck.
Harry Engels—National Audubon Society

incubation coming from solar radiation, fermentation of plant matter, or even volcanic steam. Young megapodes, extremely precocious at hatching, dig their way to the surface and forage for themselves. They are fully feathered when hatched and can fly when 24 hours old. The simplest form of nesting, found in the maleo (*Macrocephalon maleo*), Wallace's megapode (*Eulipoa wallacei*), and some individuals of Freycinet's megapode (*Megapodius freycinet*, called jungle fowl in Australia), consists of placing each egg in a hole dug in sand to a depth of up to one metre (about one yard) in a site chosen for receiving the appropriate amount of solar radiation. Once laid and buried, the egg receives no further attention from the parents.

Some members of the genus *Megapodius* (including jungle-dwelling members of *M. freycinet*) build mounds of decaying vegetation, up to ten metres (35 feet) long and five metres high. Mounds built by the brush turkeys (*Alectura, Aepypodius*, and *Talegalla*) are smaller, up to about four metres in diameter and a metre high. The mallee fowl, the most studied of the megapodes, uses a combination of solar radiation and fermentation to maintain the incubation temperature.

In the mound-building species of megapodes, the male maintains the mound for much of the year. Prior to and during the incubation period, he opens the mound once or twice a day to control the generation, absorption, and radiation of heat. It is generally believed that the bird measures the temperature of the egg chamber when opening the mound. The temperature sensing organ is not known, but the most likely organ is the tongue. By instrumentation of mallee-fowl mounds, an Australian biologist, H.J. Frith, has found that the mound is maintained within a degree or two of 33° C (91° F) throughout the period of several months that there are eggs in it. Observations of one species of brush turkey, *Alectura lathami*, indicate that the frequent opening of the mound may be as important for ventilation as for temperature control.

The eggs of most gallinaceous birds are solidly coloured in white, buff, or olive, but those of species nesting in open areas are usually protectively coloured with blotches of brown or black. There is great variation in the number of eggs laid. Most members of the order are indeterminate layers, the female producing eggs until a certain number has accumulated in the nest. This characteristic has allowed man to exploit galliforms (especially the domestic hen, of course) for egg production. If the domestic hen were a determinate layer, as are members of many other bird orders, each individual would produce her clutch of about a dozen eggs and, regardless of whether

Construction of "incubators" by megapodes

Determinate versus indeterminate layers

or not the eggs were removed, would discontinue laying for at least two months.

The clutch size varies from two to about two dozen, the largest number occurring in megapodes. Partridge, quail, and the smaller pheasant lay from 12 to more than 20 eggs, but the larger pheasant, such as the crested argus (*Rheinardia ocellata*) and the great argus, normally lay only two eggs. The hoatzin and the cracids lay two or three eggs, three being the rule in the smaller cracids, such as chachalacas. Guinea fowl lay seven to 20 eggs, and turkeys eight to 18.

Incubation is usually performed by the female alone. Males of some New World quail, including the Montezuma quail (*Cyrtonyx montezumae*), the bobwhite (*Colinus virginianus*), and other members of the genus *Colinus*, incubate for short periods. The female of the southern European red partridge (*Alectoris rufa*) has been reported to lay two clutches, one incubated by the male, the other concurrently by herself. This behaviour, unique among birds, is in need of further investigation.

It is uncertain whether or not the male hoatzin incubates the eggs. Both sexes have been observed in nest building and taking care of the young, so it is possible that the male also assists in incubation.

Care of the young. Young gallinaceous birds (except those of the hoatzin) are extremely precocious, walking and feeding within a few hours of hatching. Parental behaviour parallels mating behaviour: males of species in which a pair bond is formed usually assist in shepherding the young. Although clad in a protective coat of down and usually camouflaged with spots and streaks, the chicks suffer high mortality from predators and adverse weather. Mortality rates of 50 percent or more are reported to occur in the period of a few months between hatching and independence of the young. Partridge, quail, and grouse maintain family groups (coveys) of a dozen or more birds that remain together until the next breeding season.

The hoatzin, unusual in many ways, also differs from other galliforms in that its nestlings are hatched practically naked and are fed by the parents in the nest. The young are fed regurgitated food from the crops of their parents. Although they have a long fledging period, young hoatzins scramble about in the branches around the nest, holding on with the clawed first and second digits of the wings and, in the manner of parrots, with their bills. The fact that the second digit of the wing (now considered to be digit III, in the evolutionary sense) is free and bears a functional claw was once thought (erroneously) to indicate affinities with the reptilian forebears of birds. Most authorities now believe that the free digits are a secondary adaptation that allows the young hoatzin great mobility during its flightless period and allows it to climb out of the water, into which it may deliberately drop when danger threatens.

Most gallinaceous birds reach sexual maturity at the age of at least one year. Some species, however, may be physiologically capable of reproduction at a much earlier age. The common quail (*Coturnix coturnix*), wild individuals of which normally breed at one year of age, matures to breeding condition in seven weeks in captivity. It is uncertain whether wild birds, hatched in the spring, actually do breed during the summer; environmental control factors, especially decreasing daylength, probably prevent the attainment of breeding condition by two-month-old birds in natural situations. Even the Congo peacock (*Afropavo congensis*), a relatively large species, is able to reproduce at one year of age when reared in captivity.

Vocalizations. Like many other birds that inhabit dense cover, forest galliformes are endowed with strong voices, ranging from musical whistles to harsh screams. The repertoire of most species includes alarm notes, food calls, "crowing" by males to advertise territories, and notes used to maintain social groups. Many species are especially vocal at daybreak; a few are reported to call at night. Megapodes give clucking and cackling calls during the day and mewing calls at night. Cracids produce loud calls that have immense carrying power. Males of some species have elongated, looped tracheae (wind-

pipes), which are believed to add to the carrying power of the calls. Members of the social groups often cackle noisily together. Male peafowl utter a long mournful scream that sounds quite like a child in distress.

FORM AND FUNCTION

With the exception of the hoatzin, all galliforms have the same general body plan, being adapted for a primarily terrestrial existence. The feet and claws are large in all families, particularly so in the megapodes, reflecting their use for scratching and digging. The hind toe is larger and more functional in groups, such as the cracids, that spend much time in trees; it is smaller in the more terrestrial groups, but in none has it been lost, as it has in terrestrial birds of some other orders.

The short, rounded wings, powered by strong breast muscles (the white meat of the chicken), are indicative of the need for short, rapid bursts of flight, such as the escape from predators. Although no galliform is flightless, none is capable of long flights. The tail varies from extremely short (*e.g.*, in painted quail) to strikingly long; in many male pheasant the tail may be more than two-thirds of the bird's total length. The tails of some pheasant and of most megapodes are vaulted, having an inverted V-shape in cross section.

Male ornamental plumage is often remarkable in shape and coloration, combining spots or bars of silver, green, or purple irridescence with areas of brilliant orange, yellow, or white. Sculptured, fleshy wattles on the faces of male pheasant and grouse are often coloured a bright blue or red. In some male pheasant, such as the firebacks (*Lophura*), impeyans (*Lophophorus*), and peafowl, the head is ornamented with a small tuft of modified plumes, forming a tiny fan. Many cracids have patches of bare skin on the face or throat, usually red, yellow, or blue. Males of many curassows and guans possess head ornaments in the form of a brightly coloured fleshy knob or a bony casque (helmet) on the top of the head.

Ornamental plumage of the male

CLASSIFICATION

Distinguishing taxonomic features. The limits and interrelationships of galliform families have been determined on the basis of general body proportions, muscle and bone configurations, plumage, clutch size and egg characteristics, the appearance of the young, and some aspects of behaviour. Recent studies have utilized the biochemistry of egg white and blood proteins to indicate relationships.

Annotated classification. The classification presented below was established by the American ornithologist Alexander Wetmore, based on studies by many earlier workers.

ORDER GALLIFORMES
Suborder Galli
Family Megapodiidae (megapodes or mound builders)
  All use heat other than body heat to incubate their eggs. Large feet, small heads. Tail often vaulted. Medium to large birds, 25–65 cm (10–25 in.); sexes alike. One fossil, *Chosornis praeteritus*, from the upper Pleistocene; 7 Recent genera, 12 species; Australia and East Indies to central Polynesia.

Family Cracidae (chachalacas, guans, and curassows)
  Tail moderately long and broad. Plumage black or brown, duller in female. Most species with bare skin between eyes and beak (lores), some with fleshy wattles or other ornaments on face or crown. Medium to large; length 52–99 cm (20–39 in.); lower Eocene to present; 11 fossil and 11 Recent genera, 34 Recent species; New World tropics and subtropics, from southern Texas to Paraguay.

Family Tetraonidae (grouse)
  Distinguished by having lower leg (tarsus) and sometimes feet at least partially feathered; nostrils also feathered. Tail strong; ornamental in some species. Many with brightly coloured bare skin over eye. Medium to large; 30–90 cm (12–36 in.). Lower Miocene to present; 3 fossil and 9 Recent genera, 17 Recent species; North America and northern Eurasia.

Family Phasianidae (pheasant, quail, partridge, and relatives)
  Nostrils, feet, and (usually) tarsus unfeathered; esophageal air sacs lacking. Many species with spurs on the back of the tarsus. Plumage, especially of males, bright in many species, often with ornamental feathers; sexes usually different. Small

Chick mortality

to large; length 13–200 cm (5–80 in.); lower Miocene to present; 11 fossil and about 40 Recent genera, about 178 Recent species; virtually worldwide, except southern third of South America, northern Eurasia, and some oceanic islands.

Family Numididae (guinea fowl)

Distinguished by presence of small whitish spots on dark bluish or slate body feathers; head and neck bare or slightly feathered, often brightly coloured. Legs and feet large; spurs present only in *Phasidus* and *Agelastes*. Medium to large; length 43–75 cm (17–30 in.). No fossil species; 5 genera, 7 species; Africa south of the Sahara and Madagascar.

Family Meleagrididae (turkeys)

Distinguished by metallic sheen on feathers, bare head with red and blue skin and wattles or caruncles. Tarsal spurs of male long, of female short. Size large, length 84–110 cm (33–43 in.). Upper Pliocene to present; 1 fossil genus (Pleistocene) and 2 Recent genera, each with 1 Recent species; eastern and southern United States, Mexico, northern Guatemala, British Honduras.

Suborder Opisthocomi

Family Opisthocomidae (hoatzin)

Rather long neck and small head, with prominent crest of long feathers; beak short, stout, laterally flattened. Wings large and rounded; tail long and broad. Brown above, marked with white and russet; buff below. Nestling with 2 free, clawed digits on each wing. Adult size large, length about 61 cm (24 in.). One fossil genus (*Hoazinoides*, middle Miocene); 1 Recent genus with 1 species; river systems of northern South America.

Critical appraisal. Although the classification presented here has broad acceptance, modern authorities disagree on the numbers of species and, especially, genera in many groups. Forms once regarded as distinct are now often considered to be geographical races of larger species. The problem is particularly acute where island populations are involved, for the usual biological criterion of free interbreeding cannot be applied, and the taxonomist must infer from external appearance whether or not two forms belong to the same species. The genus *Megapodius*, for example, was considered by the American ornithologist James L. Peters, in his 1934 volume of the classic *Check-list of Birds of the World*, to comprise nine species with 25 subspecies. Another authority, Dean Amadon, in a study published in 1952, recognized only three species, with 15 subspecies.

At the generic level, taxonomy is more subjective than at the species level, the boundaries of the genus being subject only to the general views of the taxonomist as to what constitutes a genus. Recent years have seen a drift toward "lumping," with the result that what were once regarded as discrete genera are now frequently merged (lumped), a family often having fewer genera but about the same number of species. Details of the anatomy, behaviour, and distribution of many galliform species remain unknown. As more information accumulates, further changes in the lower levels of classification may be expected.

BIBLIOGRAPHY. The following works are arranged by families.

Megapodiidae: H.J. FRITH, *The Mallee-Fowl: The Bird That Builds An Incubator* (1962), is an extensive study of the breeding habits of *Leipoa ocellata*.

Cracidae: A.F. SKUTCH, "Habits of the Chestnut-winged Chachalaca," *Wilson Bull.*, 75:262–269 (1963), presents information on the breeding habits of *Ortalis garrula*. C. VAURIE, "Taxonomy of the Cracidae (Aves)," *Bull. Am. Mus. Nat. Hist.*, 138:133–259 (1968); and F. VUILLEUMIER, "Relationships and Evolution Within the Cracidae (Aves, Galliformes)," *Bull. Mus. Comp. Zool. Harv.*, 134:1–27 (1965), are two analyses of the taxonomic relationships within this family.

Tetraonidae: A.W. BOBACK, *Das Auerhuhn* (1952), is a short monograph on the capercaillie; and A.W. BOBACK and D.W. MULLER-SCHWARZE, *Das Birkhuhn* (1968), is a study of the black grouse. G.L. GIRARD, "Life History, Habits, and Food of the Sage Grouse, *Centrocercus urophasianus* Bonaparte," *Univ. Wyo. Publs.*, 3:1–56 (1937), provides insight into the natural history of this grassland species. G. BUMP et al., *The Ruffed Grouse: Life History, Propagation, Management* (1947), is a classic study of this woodland grouse.

Phasianidae: C.W. BEEBE, *A Monograph of the Pheasants*, 4 vol. (1918–22), is a classic work on the pheasants, magnificently illustrated with colour plates. A revised, less technical edition was published in two volumes under the title *Pheasants: Their Lives and Homes* (1926) and later in one volume (1936). J.T. DELACOUR, *The Pheasants of the World* (1951), is a fully illustrated treatment of the group, leaning heavily toward aviculture. H.L. STODDARD, *The Bobwhite Quail: Its Habits, Preservation and Increase* (1931), is an important book on this game species. P. WAYRE, *A Guide to the Pheasants of the World* (1969), is an extensively illustrated work with emphasis on conservation and on breeding in captivity.

Numididae: A.R. LEE, "The Guineafowl," *Fmrs' Bull. U.S. Dep. Agric. 1391* (1924), presents information on the guinea fowl, from an avicultural standpoint.

Meleagrididae: H.S. MOSBY and C.O. HANDLEY, *The Wild Turkey in Virginia* (1943), is a broad study of the natural history of *Meleagris gallopavo*. A.W. SCHORGER, *The Wild Turkey: Its History and Domestication* (1966), is primarily a historical treatise

Opisthocomidae: C.W. BEEBE, "A Contribution to the Ecology of the Adult Hoatzin," *Zoologica*, 1:45-66 (1909); and *Tropical Wildlife in British Guiana*, pp. 155–182 (1917), present information from the author's field observations of the hoatzin.

(F.H.)

Galois, Évariste

Before his tragic death in a duel at age 20, the French mathematician Évariste Galois had proposed structural and unifying concepts that were to perpetuate his memory in "Galois field," "Galois group," and "Galois theory," all among the most important topics studied in modern algebra. Although he was embittered by political oppression and frustrated by lack of educational opportunity, his work constitutes one of the finest achievements of 19th-century mathematics.

Galois, detail of an engraving by an unknown artist, 1848, after a drawing by Alfred Galois.

Galois was born October 25, 1811, in the Paris suburb of Bourg-la-Reine, where his father, Nicolas-Gabriel Galois, was an important citizen. In 1815, during the Hundred Days regime that followed Napoleon's escape from Elba Island, his father was elected mayor. Galois's mother, Adelaïde-Marie Demante, was of a distinguished family of jurists. She gave Galois an excellent education at home until 1823, when he entered the Collège Royal de Louis-le-Grand. There his education languished at the hands of mediocre and uninspiring teachers. But his mathematical ability suddenly appeared when he was able to master quickly the works of Adrien-Marie Legendre on geometry and Joseph-Louis Lagrange on algebra.

Under the guidance of Louis Richard, one of his teachers at Louis-le-Grand, Galois's further study of algebra soon led him to take up a major challenge. Mathematicians for a long time had used explicit formulas, involving only rational operations and extractions of roots, for the solution of equations up to degree four. (For example, $3x^2 + 5 = 17$ is an equation of the second degree,

Birth and early life

since it contains the exponent 2; solving an equation of this type is called a solution by radicals, because it involves extracting the square root of an expression composed of one or more terms whose coefficients appear in the equation.) The solution of quadratic, or second degree, equations goes back to ancient times. Formulas for the cubic and quartic were published in 1545 by Gerolamo Cardano, Italian mathematician and physician, after their discovery a few years earlier by the mathematicians Niccolo Tartaglia and Ludovico Ferrari. The equation of the fifth degree then defeated mathematicians until Paolo Ruffini in 1796 attempted to prove the impossibility of solving the general quintic equation by radicals. Ruffini's effort was not wholly successful, but the Norwegian mathematician Niels Abel (*q.v.*) in 1824 gave an essentially correct proof (see MATHEMATICS, HISTORY OF).

The Galois theory

Galois was unaware of Abel's work in the first stages of his investigation although he did learn of it later. This was perhaps fortunate because Galois actually had launched himself on a much more ambitious study; while yet a student, at about age 16, he sought, by what is now called the "Galois theory," a deeper understanding of the essential conditions that an equation must satisfy in order for it to be solvable by radicals (see ALGEBRAIC STRUCTURES). His method was to analyze the "admissible" permutations (a change in an ordered arrangement) of the roots of the equation. That is, in today's terminology, he formed the "group" of automorphisms (a particular kind of transformation) of the "field," obtained by adjoining the roots of the equation. His key discovery, brilliant and highly imaginative, was that solvability by radicals is possible if and only if the group of automorphisms is solvable, which means essentially that the group can be broken down into prime-order constituents (prime numbers are positive numbers greater than 1 divisible only by themselves and 1) that always have an easily understood structure. The term solvable is used because of this connection with solvability by radicals. Thus Galois perceived that solving equations of the quintic and beyond required a wholly different kind of treatment than that required for the quadratic, cubic, and quartic.

While still at Louis-le-Grand he published several minor papers. Soon disappointments and tragedy filled his life with bitterness. Three memoirs that he submitted to the Academy of Sciences were lost or rejected by the academicians, who as mathematicians were authorized to act as editors. The first was lost in 1829 by Augustin-Louis Cauchy. In each of two attempts (1827 and 1829) to enter the École Polytechnique, the leading school of French mathematics, he had a disastrous encounter with an oral examiner and failed. Then his father, after bitter clashes with conservative elements in his home town, committed suicide in 1829. The same year, realizing that his career possibilities as a professional mathematician had ended, Galois enrolled as a teacher candidate in the less prestigious École Normale Superíeure and turned to political activism. But he continued his research.

A second memoir, on algebraic functions, which he submitted in 1830 to the Academy of Sciences, was lost by Jean-Baptiste Fourier (*q.v.*). The revolution of 1830 sent the last Bourbon monarch Charles X into exile. But republicans were deeply disappointed when yet another king, Louis Philippe, ascended the throne—even though he was a citizen king who wore the tricolour of the revolution. When Galois wrote a vigorous article expressing these views, he was promptly expelled from the École Normale Superíeure. Subsequently he was arrested twice for republican activities; he was acquitted the first time but spent six months in prison on the second charge. His third memoir in 1831 was returned by Siméon-Denis Poisson with a note that it was virtually incomprehensible and should be expanded and clarified.

Untimely death

The circumstances that led to his death on May 31, 1832, in a duel in Paris have never been fully explained. It has been variously suggested that it resulted from a quarrel over a girl, that he was challenged by royalists who detested his republican views, or that an *agent provocateur* of the police was involved. Alexandre Dumas,

in his autobiography *Mes Mémoirs* (1863–65), implicated Pécheux d'Herbinville as the man who shot Galois. In any case, anticipating his death in the coming duel, Galois in feverish haste wrote a scientific last testament to his friend and former schoolmate Auguste Chevalier. In his distracted notes, there are hints that Galois had begun to develop the theory of algebraic functions, the full development of which was achieved 40 years later by the German mathematician Bernhard Riemann.

Galois's manuscripts, with annotations by Joseph Liouville, were published in 1846 in the *Journal de Mathématiques Pures et Appliquées*. In 1870 the French mathematician Camille Jordan published the full-length treatment of Galois's theory, *Traité des Substitutions*. These works rendered his discoveries fully accessible and his place secure in the history of mathematics. On June 13, 1909, a plaque was placed on Galois's modest birthplace at Bourg-la-Reine, and the mathematician Jules Tannery made an eloquent speech of dedication, which was published the same year in the *Bulletin des Sciences Mathématiques*.

BIBLIOGRAPHY. LEOPOLD INFELD, *Whom the Gods Love* (1948), is a full-length biography, in part fictional, based on a thorough examination of all available materials, with an extensive bibliography of earlier works. PAUL DUPUY, *La Vie d'Évariste Galois*, published in the *Annales Scientifiques de l'École Normale Supérieure*, 3rd Series, vol. 13, pp. 197–266 (1896), is the basic biographical work. See also ERIC TEMPLE BELL, *Men of Mathematics*, ch. 20 (1937, reprinted 1961), for a highly readable biographical sketch, featuring strong opinions of the Establishment's disastrous mistreatment of Galois. The *Écrits et mémoires mathématiques*, ed. by ROBERT BOURGNE and J.-P. AZRA with a preface by J. DIEUDONNE (1962), contains all the available writings of Galois, with a running commentary, and reproduces photographically many pages of his original manuscripts. In "Évariste Galois," *Osiris*, 3:241–259 (1937), GEORGE SARTON presents a brief critical biography. GARRETT BIRKOFF, "Galois and Group Theory," *ibid.*, pp. 260–268, is a nontechnical account of the development of Galois's ideas and their subsequent impact on group theory. Another historic survey is B. MELVIN KIERNAN, "The Development of Galois Theory from Lagrange to Artin," *Arch. Hist. Exact Sci.*, 8:40–154 (1971). Accounts of Galois theory are found in nearly every treatise on modern algebra. Brief, elegant, and self-contained is EMIL ARTIN, *Galois Theory*, 2nd ed. (1944).

(I.K.)

Galton, Sir Francis

English scientist, explorer, and anthropologist, Francis Galton, a cousin of Charles Darwin, was among the first to recognize the implications for mankind of Darwin's theory of evolution. He saw that it invalidated much of contemporary theology and that it also opened possibilities for planned human betterment. Galton coined the word eugenics to denote scientific endeavours to increase the proportion of persons with better than average genetic endowment through selective mating of marriage partners.

Francis Galton was born of Quaker ancestry on February 16, 1822, near Sparkbrook, Birmingham. His family life was happy, and he gratefully acknowledged that he owed much to his father and mother. But he had little use for the conventional classical and religious teaching he received in school and church. Indeed, he later confessed in a letter to Charles Darwin that the traditional biblical arguments had made him "wretched."

His parents had planned that he should study medicine, and a tour of medical institutions on the Continent in his teens—an unusual experience for a student of his age—was followed by training in hospitals in Birmingham and London. But at this time, in Galton's words, "a passion for travel seized me as if I had been a migratory bird." A visit to the University of Giessen, Germany, to attend lectures on chemistry was broken off in favour of travel in southeastern Europe. From Vienna he made his way through Constanza, Constantinople, Smyrna, and Athens, and he brought back from the caves of Adelsberg, in present-day Yugoslavia, specimens of a blind amphibian named *Proteus*—the first to reach England. On his return Galton went to Trinity College, Cambridge, where, as a result of overwork, he broke down in his third

Galton, oil painting by G. Graef, 1882. In the National Portrait Gallery, London.
By courtesy of the National Portrait Gallery, London

year. But he recovered quickly on changing his mode of life, as he did from similar attacks later.

After leaving Cambridge without taking a degree, Galton continued his medical studies in London. But before they were completed, his father died, leaving him "a sufficient fortune to make me independent of the medical profession." Galton was then free to indulge his craving for travel. Leisurely expeditions in 1845–46 up the Nile with friends and into the Holy Land alone were preliminaries to a carefully organized penetration into unexplored parts of southwest Africa. After consulting the Royal Geographical Society, Galton decided to investigate a possible opening from the south and west to Lake Ngami, which lies north of the Kalahari desert some 550 miles east of Walvis Bay. The expedition, which included two journeys, one northward, the other eastward, from the same base, proved to be difficult and not without danger. Though the explorers did not reach Lake Ngami, they gained valuable information. As a result, at the age of only 31, Galton was in 1853 elected a fellow of the Royal Geographical Society and, three years later, of the Royal Society. In 1853, too, Galton married. There were no children of the marriage. Galton wrote nine books and some 200 papers. They deal with many diverse subjects, including the use of fingerprints for personal identification, the correlational calculus (a branch of applied statistics)—in both of which Galton was a pioneer—twins, blood transfusions, criminality, the art of travel in undeveloped countries, and meteorology. Most of Galton's publications disclose his predilection for quantifying; an early paper, for example, dealt with a statistical test of the efficacy of prayer. Moreover, over a period of 34 years, he concerned himself with improving standards of measurement.

Although he made contributions to many fields of knowledge, eugenics remained Galton's fundamental interest, and he devoted the latter part of his life chiefly to propagating the idea of improving the physical and mental makeup of the human species by selective parenthood. In his *Hereditary Genius* (1869), in which he used the word genius to denote "an ability that was exceptionally high and at the same time inborn," his main argument was that mental and physical features are equally inherited—a proposition that was not accepted at the time. It is surprising that when Charles Darwin first read this book, he wrote to the author: "You have made a convert of an opponent in one sense for I have always maintained that, excepting fools, men did not differ much in intellect, only in zeal and hard work." This book doubtless helped Darwin to extend his evolution theory to man. Galton, unmentioned in *Origin of Species* (1859), is several times quoted in Darwin's *Descent of Man* (1871). Galton's conviction that mental traits are no less inherited than are physical characteristics was strong enough to shape his

personal religious philosophy. "We cannot doubt," he wrote, "the existence of a great power ready to hand and capable of being directed with vast benefit as soon as we have learned to understand and apply it."

Galton's *Inquiries into Human Faculty* (1883) consists of some 40 articles varying in length from 2 to 30 pages, which are mostly based on scientific papers written between 1869 and 1883. The book can in a sense be regarded as a summary of the author's views on the faculties of man. On all his topics, Galton has something original and interesting to say, and he says it with clarity, brevity, distinction, and modesty. Under the terms of his will, a eugenics chair was established at the University of London. He was knighted in 1909 and died near London on January 17, 1911.

In the 20th century Galton's name has been mainly associated with eugenics. Insofar as eugenics takes primary account of *inborn* differences between human beings, it has come under the suspicion of those who hold that cultural (social and educational) factors heavily outweigh inborn, or biological, factors in their contribution to human differences. Eugenics is accordingly often treated as an expression of class prejudice, and Galton as a reactionary. Yet to some extent this view misrepresents his thought, for his aim was not the creation of an aristocratic elite but of a population consisting entirely of superior men and women. Galton's ideas, like those of Charles Darwin, were sharply limited by his lack of an adequate theory of inheritance; the rediscovery of the work of Mendel (*q.v.*) came too late to affect Galton's contribution in any significant way.

BIBLIOGRAPHY. The most important work on Galton is KARL PEARSON, *The Life, Letters and Labours of Francis Galton*, 4 vol. (1914–30). The last volume contains letters and a comprehensive index of Galton's publications.

Galvani, Luigi

The use of electricity as a powerful form of energy developed from studies in the 18th century in northern Italy by Luigi Galvani. His discoveries led to the invention of the voltaic pile, a kind of battery that makes possible a constant source of current electricity. Galvani also performed the experiments that made possible a recognition of electrical phenomena in living things.

Galvani was born on September 9, 1737, in Bologna, Italy. He followed his father's preference for medicine by attending the University of Bologna, graduating in 1759. On obtaining the doctor of medicine degree, with a thesis (1762) *De ossibus* on the formation and development of bones, he was appointed lecturer in anatomy at the University of Bologna and professor of obstetrics at the separate Institute of Arts and Sciences. In 1762, also, he married Lucia, the only daughter of Professor Galeazzi of the Bologna Academy of Science, of which Galvani became president in 1772.

Beginning with his doctoral thesis, his early research was in comparative anatomy—such as the structure of renal tubules, nasal mucosa, and the middle ear—with a tendency toward physiology, a direction appropriate to the later work for which he is noted. Galvani's developing interest was indicated by his lectures on the anatomy of the frog in 1773 and in electrophysiology in the late 1770s, when, following the acquisition of an electrostatic machine (a large device for making sparks) and a Leyden jar (a device used to store static electricity), he began to experiment with muscular stimulation by electrical means. His notebooks indicate that, from the early 1780s, animal electricity remained his major field of investigation. Numerous ingenious observations and experiments have been credited to him; in 1786, for example, he obtained muscular contraction in a frog by touching its nerves with a pair of scissors during an electrical storm. Again, a visitor to his laboratory caused the legs of a skinned frog to kick when a scalpel touched a lumbar nerve of the animal while an electrical machine was activated. Galvani assured himself by further experiments that the twitching was, in fact, related to the electrical action. He also elicited twitching

Travels and exploration

Reputation

Studies of muscle contraction

Galvani, engraving by A. Marchi after a
drawing by F. Spagnoli.
By courtesy of the Museum National d'Histoire
Naturelle, Paris

without the aid of the electrostatic machine by pressing a copper hook into a frog's spinal cord and hanging the hook on an iron railing. Although twitching could occur during a lightning storm or with the aid of an electrostatic machine, it also occurred with only a metallic contact between leg muscles and nerves leading to them. A metallic arc connecting the two tissues could therefore be a substitute for the electrostatic machine.

Galvani delayed the announcement of his findings until 1791, when he published his essay *De Viribus Electricitatis in Motu Musculari Commentarius* (*Commentary on the Effect of Electricity on Muscular Motion*, 1953). He concluded that animal tissue contained a heretofore neglected innate, vital force, which he termed "animal electricity," which activated nerve and muscle when spanned by metal probes. He believed that this new force was a form of electricity in addition to the "natural" form that is produced by lightning or by the electric eel and torpedo ray and to the "artificial" form that is produced by friction (*i.e.*, static electricity). He considered the brain to be the most important organ for the secretion of this "electric fluid" and the nerves to be conductors of the fluid to the nerve and muscle, the tissues of which act as did the outer and inner surfaces of the Leyden jar. The flow of this electric fluid provided a stimulus for the irritable muscle fibres, according to his explanation.

Electrical nature of nerve impulse Galvani's scientific colleagues generally accepted his views, but Alessandro Volta, the outstanding professor of physics at the University of Pavia, was not convinced by the analogy between the muscle and the Leyden jar. Deciding that the frog's legs served only as an indicating electroscope, he held that the contact of dissimilar metals was the true source of stimulation; he referred to the electricity so generated as "metallic electricity" and decided that the muscle, by contracting when touched by metal, resembled the action of an electroscope. Furthermore, Volta said that if two dissimilar metals in contact both touched a muscle, agitation would also occur and increase with the dissimilarity of the metals. Galvani refuted this by obtaining muscular action with two pieces of the same material. Thus Volta rejected the idea of an "animal electric fluid," replying that the frog's legs responded to differences in metal temper, composition, and bulk. But the ensuing controversy was without personal animosity; Galvani's gentle nature and Volta's high principles precluded any harshness between them. Volta, who coined the term galvanism, said of Galvani's work that "it contains one of the most beautiful and most surprising discoveries." Nevertheless, partisan groups rallied to both sides. Giovanni Aldini, Galvani's nephew, wrote many answers to Volta's challenges.

In retrospect, Galvani and Volta are both seen to have been partly right and partly wrong. Galvani was correct in attributing muscular contractions to an electrical stimulus but wrong in identifying it as an "animal electricity." Volta correctly denied the existence of an "animal electricity" but was wrong in implying that every electrophysiological effect requires two different metals as sources of current. Galvani, shrinking from the controversy over his discovery, continued his work as teacher, obstetrician, and surgeon, treating both wealthy and needy without regard to fee. In 1794 he offered a defense of his position in an anonymous book, *Dell'Uso e dell'Attività dell'Arco Conduttore nella Contrazione dei Muscoli*, the supplement of which described muscular contraction without the need of any metal. He caused a muscle to contract by touching the exposed muscle of one frog with a nerve of another and thus established for the first time that bioelectric forces exist within living tissue.

On June 30, 1790, Galvani's devoted wife and companion died, childless, at the age of 47. In the last years of his life, Galvani refused to swear allegiance to the new Cisalpine Republic established by Napoleon. Thereupon he was dropped from the faculty rolls, and his salary was terminated. Rejecting help and much saddened, he moved into the old Galvani home in which his brother was living. Soon, however, the politicians recanted, and the professorship was again offered to Galvani without the requirement of an oath. But this welcome step was short-lived because the affront had cut short his days.

Galvani provided the major stimulus for Volta to discover a source of constant current electricity; this was the voltaic pile, or a battery, with its principles of operation combined from chemistry and physics. This discovery led to the subsequent age of electric power. Moreover, Galvani opened the way to new research in the physiology of muscle and nerve, and the entire subject of electrophysiology. Galvani died in the house of his birth on December 4, 1798, at age 61, at a time when the world was on the threshold of the great electrical revolution.

BIBLIOGRAPHY. LUIGI GALVANI, *Opere edite ed inedite del professore Luigi Galvani* (1841) and *Aggiunta*, ed. by SILVESTRO GHERARDI (1842), comprise a prime reference; *Memorie ed esperimenti inediti di Luigi Galvani* (1937), Galvani's laboratory notes; *Commentary on the Effect of Electricity on Muscular Motion* (1953), an English translation of Galvani's *De Viribus Electricitatis in Motu Musculari Commentarius* (1791), with facsimile of the Latin text, an introduction by I. BERNARD COHEN, and an extensive bibliography; C. MESINI, *Luigi Galvani* (1958), a clear and scholarly modern study (in Italian).

(B.Di.)

Gama, Vasco da

Vasco da Gama, a Portuguese navigator of the late 15th and early 16th centuries, led the Portuguese expedition of 1497–99 that opened the sea route between Europe and India by way of the Cape of Good Hope.

Early life The third son of Estêvão da Gama, a nobleman who was commander of the fortress of Sines on the coast of Alentejo province in southwest Portugal, Vasco was born in about 1460. Little is known of his early life; he may have studied at the inland town of Évora—somewhere he learned mathematics and navigation. In 1492 King John II of Portugal sent him to the port of Setúbal, south of Lisbon, and to the Algarve, Portugal's southernmost province, to seize French ships in retaliation for French peacetime depredations against Portuguese shipping— a task that Vasco rapidly and effectively performed.

In accordance with the policy of Prince Henry the Navigator, King John was planning to send a Portuguese fleet to India to open the sea route to Asia and to outflank the Muslims, who had hitherto enjoyed a monopoly of trade with India and other eastern states. Estêvão da Gama was chosen to lead the expedition, but after his death Vasco took his place. Accounts of his appointment differ; whether he was chosen by King John and this choice confirmed by King Manuel, who ascended the throne in 1495, or whether it was King Manuel who first chose him, remains unclear. According to one version, the appointment was first offered to his eldest brother Paulo, who declined because of ill health.

"Knight of the Order of Christ," identified as Vasco da Gama, portrait by an unknown artist, first half of the 16th century. In the Museu Nacional de Arte Antiga, Lisbon.
By courtesy of the Museu Nacional de Arte Antiga, Lisbon

The first voyage. Da Gama sailed from Lisbon on July 8, 1497, with a fleet of four vessels—two *naos* (medium-sized three-masted sailing ships), each of about 120 tons, named the "São Gabriel" and the "São Rafael"; a 50-ton caravel, named the "Berrio"; and a 200-ton storeship. They were accompanied to the Cape Verde Islands by another ship commanded by Bartolomeu Dias, the Portuguese navigator who had discovered the Cape of Good Hope a few years earlier and who was en route to the West African castle of São Jorge da Mina on the Gold Coast (now Ghana). With da Gama's fleet went three interpreters—two Arabic speakers and one who spoke several Bantu dialects. The fleet also carried *padroes* (stone pillars) to set up as marks of discovery and overlordship.

Passing the Canary Islands on July 15, the fleet reached the São Tiago in the Cape Verde Islands on the 26th, remaining there until August 3. Then, to avoid the currents of the Gulf of Guinea, da Gama took a circular course through the South Atlantic to the Cape of Good Hope, reaching Santa Helena Bay (in modern South Africa) on November 7. The expedition departed on November 16, but unfavourable winds delayed their rounding of the Cape of Good Hope until November 22. Three days later da Gama anchored in Mossel Bay, erected a *padrão* on an island, and ordered the storeship to be broken up. Sailing again on December 8, the fleet reached the coast of Natal on Christmas Day. On January 11, 1498, it anchored for five days near the mouth of a small river between Natal and Mozambique, which they called the Rio do Cobre (Copper River). On January 25, in what is now Mozambique, they reached the Quelimane River, which they called the Rio dos Bons Sinais (the River of Good Omens), and erected another *padrão*. By this time many of the crews were sick with scurvy; the expedition rested a month while the ships were repaired.

On March 2 the fleet reached the island of Mozambique, the inhabitants of which believed the Portuguese to be Muslims like themselves. Da Gama learned that they traded with Arab merchants and that four Arab vessels laden with gold, jewels, silver, and spices were then in port; he was also told that Prester John, the long-sought Christian ruler, lived in the interior but held many coastal cities. The Sultan of Mozambique supplied da Gama with two pilots, one of whom deserted when he discovered that the Portuguese were Christians.

The expedition reached Mombasa (now in Kenya) on April 7 and dropped anchor at Malindi (also now in Kenya) on April 14, where a pilot who knew the route to Calicut, on the southwest coast of India, was taken aboard. After a 23-day run across the Indian Ocean, the Ghāts mountains of India were sighted, and Calicut was reached on May 20. There da Gama erected a *padrão* to prove he had reached India. Welcomed by the Zamorin, the Hindu ruler, of Calicut (then the most important trading centre of southern India), he failed, however, to conclude a treaty—partly because of the hostility of Muslim merchants and partly because the trumpery presents and cheap trade goods that he had brought, while suited to the West African trade, were hardly in demand in India.

Arrival in Calicut

After tension between da Gama's expedition and the Zamorin of Calicut increased, da Gama left at the end of August, taking with him five or six Hindus so that King Manuel might learn about their customs. He visited Anjidiv Island (near Goa) before sailing for Malindi, which he reached on January 8, 1499. Unfavourable winds caused the expedition to take nearly three months crossing the Arabian Sea, and many of the crew died of scurvy. At Malindi, because of greatly reduced numbers, da Gama ordered the "São Rafael" to be burned; there he also erected a *padrão*. Mozambique, where he set up his last *padrão*, was reached on February 1. On March 20 the "São Gabriel" and "Berrio" rounded the Cape together but a month later were parted by a storm; the "Berrio" reached the Tagus River in Portugal on July 10. Da Gama, in the "São Gabriel," continued to Terceira Island in the Azores, whence he is said to have dispatched his flagship to Lisbon. He himself reached Lisbon on September 9 and made his triumphal entry nine days later, spending the interval mourning his brother Paulo, who had died on Terceira. Manuel I granted Vasco the title of *dom* (equivalent to the English "sir"), an annual pension of 1,000 cruzados, and estates.

The second voyage. To further da Gama's achievement, Manuel I dispatched the Portuguese navigator Pedro Álvares Cabral to Calicut with a fleet of 13 ships. Later, the Hindus, incited by the Muslims, rose in arms and massacred the Portuguese whom Cabral had left behind. To avenge this deed a new fleet was fitted out in Lisbon to be sent against Calicut and to establish Portuguese hegemony in the Indian Ocean. At first the command was to be given to Cabral, but it was later transferred to da Gama, who in January 1502 was given the rank of admiral. Da Gama himself commanded ten ships, which were in turn supported by two flotillas of five ships each; each flotilla being under the command of one of his relations. Sailing in February 1502, the fleet called at the Cape Verdes, reaching the port of Sofala in East Africa on June 14. After calling briefly at Mozambique, the Portuguese expedition sailed to Kilwa, in what is now Tanzania. The ruler of Kilwa, the emir Ibrāhīm, had been unfriendly to Cabral; da Gama threatened to burn Kilwa if the Emir did not submit to the Portuguese and swear loyalty to King Manuel, which he then did.

Coasting southern Arabia, da Gama then called at Goa (later the focus of Portuguese power in India) before proceeding to Cannanore, a port in southwest India to the north of Calicut, where he lay in wait for Arab shipping. After several days an Arab ship arrived with merchandise and between 200 and 400 passengers, including women and children. After seizing the cargo, da Gama shut up the passengers aboard the captured ship and set it afire, killing all on board, the cruelest act of his career.

After da Gama formed an alliance with the ruler of Cannanore, an enemy of the Zamorin, the fleet sailed to Calicut. The Zamorin offered friendship, but da Gama rejected the offer and presented an ultimatum that the Muslims be banished from the port. To show that he meant what he threatened, da Gama bombarded the port and seized and massacred 38 Hindu fishermen who had sailed out to his ships to sell their wares; their bodies were then thrown overboard, to be washed ashore. The Portuguese then sailed south to the port of Cochin, with whose ruler (an enemy of the Zamorin) they formed an alliance. After an invitation to da Gama from the Zamorin had proved to be an attempt to entrap him, the Portuguese had a brief fight with Arab ships off Calicut but put them to full flight. On February 20, 1503, the fleet left Cannanore for Mozambique on the first stage of their return voyage, reaching the Tagus on October 11.

The third voyage.   Obscurity surrounds the reception of da Gama on his return by King Manuel. Da Gama seemingly felt himself inadequately recompensed for his pains. Controversy broke out between the Admiral and the Order (*i.e.*, religious association) of São Tiago over the ownership of the town of Sines, which the Admiral had been promised but which the order refused to yield. Da Gama had married a lady of good family, Caterina de Ataíde—perhaps in 1500 after his return from his first voyage—and he then appears to have retired to the town of Évora. He was later granted additional privileges and revenues, and his wife bore him six sons. Until 1505 he continued to advise the King on Indian matters, and he was created count of Vidigueira in 1519. Not until after King Manuel died, was he again sent overseas; King John III nominated him in 1524 as Portuguese viceroy in India.

Arriving in Goa in September, da Gama immediately set himself to correct the many administrative abuses that had crept in under his predecessors. Whether from overwork or other causes, he soon fell ill and died in Cochin on December 24, 1524. In 1538 his body was taken back to Portugal. Vasco da Gama's fame rests primarily upon his opening of the sea route from western Europe to the East, thus ushering in a new era in world history. He also helped to make Portugal a world power.

BIBLIOGRAPHY.   There is no autobiography of Vasco da Gama. Portuguese chroniclers wrote at length about his voyage of 1497–99, and some of them must have had access to secret documents since destroyed. The only one translated into English is that of GASPAR CORREA (*c.* 1490–1565) from his *Lendas da India;* see *The Three Voyages of Vasco da Gama, and His Viceroyalty,* ed. by LORD STANLEY OF ALDERLEY (1869, reprinted 1963). The only firsthand account of the first voyage has also been printed in English in E.G. RAVENSTEIN (ed.), *A Journal [by an Unknown Writer] of the First Voyage of Vasco da Gama, 1497–1499* (1898, reprinted 1963). A later and more definitive edition has been printed in Portuguese in ABEL FONTOURA DA COSTA (ed.), *Roteiro da Primeira Viagem de Vasco da Gama, 1497–1499 por Alvaro Velho,* 3rd ed. (1969). The story of the voyage of 1497–99 is breezily told in HENRY H. HART, *Sea Road to the Indies* (1950). An outstanding synthesis of the background of Vasco da Gama's achievements is found in JOHN H. PARRY, *The Age of Reconnaissance: Discovery, Exploration and Settlement, 1450–1650,* 2nd ed. (1966). For brief accounts together with English translations of extracts from early documents, see JOHN H. PARRY (ed.), *The European Reconnaissance: Selected Documents* (1968). The unique manuscript copy of the three *Roteiros* (sailing directions) of Vasco da Gama's Arab pilot, Aḥmad ibn Mādjid, has not been fully translated and printed in English, but see A.G.R. TIBBETTS, *Arab Navigation in the Indian Ocean Before the Coming of the Portuguese* (1971). For the definitive Portuguese translation of the Arab text, see T.A. CHUMOVSKY (ed.), *Três Roteiros desconhecidos de Aḥmad ibn Mādjid* (1960).

(E.M.J.C.)

Gambetta, Léon

A leading 19th-century French republican statesman, Léon Gambetta played a prominent part in directing the defense of France during the Franco-Prussian war of 1870–71. In helping to found the Third Republic, he made three essential contributions: first, by his speeches and articles, he converted many Frenchmen to the ideals of moderate democratic republicanism. Second, by his political influence and personal social contacts, he gathered support for an elective democratic political party, the Republican Union. Finally, by backing Adolphe Thiers, who was elected provisional head of government by the National Assembly of 1871, against royalists and Bonapartists, he helped transform the new regime into a parliamentary republic.

Gambetta was born at Cahors, in the southwest of France, on April 2, 1838. His mother was from Gascony; his father was an Italian who had emigrated to Cahors and had opened a grocery store there. A successful pupil at the local high school, ambitious and naturally eloquent, young Gambetta refused to stay in a provincial town with no other prospect than to work in his father's

Gambetta, photograph by Étienne Carjat. In the Bibliothéque Nationale, Paris.
By courtesy of the Bibliotheque Nationale, Paris

store. Against his father's will, he went to Paris to study law.

Gambetta professed very strongly republican opinions, and his exuberant and generous nature soon made him highly popular among the Paris students. In 1859 he was called to the bar, but he was unsuccessful as a lawyer until 1868, when a political case known as the Affaire Baudin made him suddenly famous. Jean-Baptiste Baudin, a deputy (legislator) killed resisting Napoleon III's coup d'état of 1851, had become a republican martyr, and eight journalists were being prosecuted for attempting to have a monument erected in his memory. As counsel of one of the accused, Gambetta delivered an extremely forceful speech in which he indicted the imperial regime, its origin, and its policy.

Press reports of his speech made his political fortune, and almost overnight Gambetta became an acknowledged leader of the Republican Party. In 1869 he was elected to the Legislative Assembly. He opposed the steps that led to the outbreak of the Franco-German War in July 1870, but, once it had begun, he urged the quickest possible victory over the Germans. After the disastrous defeat of the French at Sedan, in which Napoleon III was captured on September 1, 1870, Gambetta played a principal role in proclaiming the republic and forming a provisional government of national defense. He became minister of the interior.

The most pressing problem of the provisional government was the defense of Paris, which was besieged by the enemy. Most members of the government stayed in the city, but Gambetta, as their delegate, left Paris in a balloon on October 17, 1870, floating over the German lines. Establishing himself at Tours, he began to arouse unoccupied France for the defense of the entire country. He became war minister as well, assuming virtually unlimited powers.

Of the two main French armies, one had been captured at Sedan, and the other was besieged at Metz and soon forced to surrender. Gambetta, as always enthusiastic and indefatigable, succeeded in raising new armies, which were trained and supplied with arms. These achieved some local successes but were more often defeated.

When Tours was threatened, Gambetta left for Bordeaux. Though he wished to continue fighting, the country was tired of war, and the provisional government signed an armistice on January 18, 1871.

The armistice convention provided for the election of a National Assembly, which met at Bordeaux in March 1871 to ratify the peace terms. Gambetta was elected a deputy for Strasbourg, in Alsace, but, after the ratification of the peace, which yielded most of Alsace and Lorraine to Germany, he lost his seat and retired for a short time to Spain.

In by-elections in July 1871 he was elected by the *dé-*

partement of the Seine. The assembly was to determine whether France would remain a republic or restore the monarchy. The majority of the deputies were monarchists. There were, however, two candidates to the throne, the heads, respectively, of the elder and the younger branch of the Bourbons, and they were unable to reach agreement. With supreme skill, Gambetta managed to push ratification of the republic through the weary assembly. The republican constitution of 1875 formed the basis of the republic until 1940.

Formation of the Third Republic

Parliamentary intrigue prevented Gambetta from being elected president of the republic, but he became president of the Chamber of Deputies, a position in which he exercised great power. He attempted to promote a tolerant republic, an "Athenian republic," as he described it. In spite of his corpulence, dishevelled beard, and badly groomed appearance, his natural warmth, generosity, and liberalism made him highly popular.

Jules Grévy, the president, disliked Gambetta and for a long time refused to ask him to form a government. After he at last was appointed premier, in November 1881, he pursued, in foreign affairs, a policy of establishing a closer relationship with Great Britain and, in domestic affairs, an ambitious program of domestic reform. He was overthrown in January 1882, before achieving either goal.

In 1872 he began a liaison with Léonie Léon, a pretty, well-educated woman, and, after his resignation, he settled with her outside Paris, with the intention of marrying her. While handling a revolver, he shot himself in the arm, and, as his health was very poor, the wound healed slowly. During his convalescence, he was stricken with appendicitis, but the doctors did not operate. He died on December 31, 1882, at the age of 44.

Assessment

He was honoured with a national funeral. His reputation has remained largely undiminished; there is hardly a town in France without a street bearing his name. Yet his fame rests on what he achieved in his long years of opposition and during the Franco-German War rather than during the two terms—totalling three years—in which he exercised power. He was a fervent advocate both of fully modern democracy—universal suffrage, freedom of the press, right of meeting, trial by jury for political offenses, separation of church and state—and of national unity. For the sake of the latter, he occasionally struck bargains with his political opponents, thus gaining an undeserved reputation as an opportunist. Undoubtedly, he was largely responsible for the consolidation of parliamentary democracy in France, but his compromises resulted in a fragile party system that served to weaken democratic government.

BIBLIOGRAPHY. *Discours et plaidoyers politiques de M. Gambetta*, 11 vol. (1881–82); P.B. GHEUSI, *Gambetta par Gambetta* (1909; Eng. trans., *Gambetta: Life and Letters*, 1910); D. HALEVY and E. PILLIAS, *Lettres de Gambetta, 1868–1882* (1938). For biographical information, see J. CHASTENET, *Gambetta* (1968), with unpublished letters and a bibliography. Also see: H.M. STANNARD, *Gambetta and the Foundation of the Third Republic* (1921); P.B. GHEUSI, *Le Roman de Gambetta* (1938); G. WORMSER, *Gambetta dans les tempêtes* (1964); and H. DUCOS, "Léonie Léon, ou Dix ans de la vie de Gambetta," in *Revue de Paris*, pp. 21–40 (1967).

(J.C.de C.)

Gambia, The

The Gambia, a West African republic, is a small state with a total area of 4,467 square miles (11,569 square kilometres). The country is a narrow enclave, from 15 to 30 miles (25 to 50 kilometres) wide and 295 miles (475 kilometres) long, stretching inland from the Atlantic Ocean and surrounded (except on its short coastal side) by Senegal. Essentially, The Gambia is a strip of land on either bank of the Gambia River. The unusual shape and size of the former British colony are attributable to arbitrary territorial compromises arising from 19th-century Anglo-French rivalry in West Africa. Its capital is Banjul (formerly Bathurst).

The Gambia, which had a population of about 524,000 in 1975, and which obtained independence from the United Kingdom on February 18, 1965 (retaining membership in the Commonwealth of Nations), is one of the poorest countries on the continent, economically dependent on a single crop, peanuts (groundnuts). With its river, the finest waterway in West Africa, it has the potential to develop into a flourishing corridor in the heart of the West African hinterland. Because The Gambia and Senegal remain politically and economically divided, however, development of the river basin is prevented by lack of coordination between the two states. The Gambian government, for example, fears that the building of an international bridge over the river might deprive The Gambia of ferry tolls, or that river traffic might be reduced in consequence, and is unwilling to forgo such immediate benefits for the sake of long-term advantages to be gained from the development of the river basin.

For an account of The Gambia's major physical feature, see GAMBIA RIVER; for historical aspects, see WEST AFRICA, HISTORY OF.

Geomorphology. The Gambia River is the country's dominant feature, flowing across a plateau of Tertiary sandstone, compacted sediment composed predominantly of quartz grains formed from 65,000,000 to 6,500,000 years ago. The landscape is generally flat, dissected terrain, with gentle slopes of not more than three degrees. In the east, narrow valleys are separated by broad interfluves or flattish hills. In the west, lower and smaller sand hills alternate with depressions up to three miles wide filled in with sand so that a flat plain is formed.

Climate. The climate is of the drier tropical type, characterized by a short and intense rainy season, occurring some time between June and October, and a longer dry season. Near the coast the rainy season lasts longer and the rainfall is heavier, diminishing eastward. At Yundum, in the west, the average annual rainfall is about 51 inches (1,300 millimetres) and the mean monthly temperature 77° F (25° C), while at Basse Santa Su, about 270 miles inland, the comparable figures are 43 inches (1,100 millimetres) and 82° F (28° C). The relative humidity is high, particularly from July to December, but drops from December to April, when the dry northeastern winds known as the harmattan are dominant. The vegetation cover of The Gambia is savanna (grassland) on the uplands, while various kinds of swamps cover the lowlying areas.

People and population. The river basin has in the past acted as a focal point for migrating groups of people from adjacent parts of West Africa, and The Gambia is consequently populated by diverse ethnic groups. About 42 percent of the population is Malinke (Mandingo), followed by Fulani, Wolof, Dyola (Yola), and Soninke (Seraculeh). There are also smaller groups of Senegalese, other African, and non-African peoples. The population (which is predominantly Muslim) at the 1973 census was 493,000, about 100,000 more persons than expected from estimates based on the 1963 census. A peculiar characteristic of the national population is its seasonal variation, caused by the influx of up to 20,000 Senegalese farm workers, most of them between ages 15 and 34.

Principal ethnic groups

The population density is quite high, with an average of 148 persons per square mile of dry land (57 per square kilometre), although distribution is uneven, with lower densities nearer the coast and higher densities inland. Patterns of settlement in The Gambia reflect three regions, expressed on both banks of the river, consisting of (1) the swamps adjacent to the river (and not extending above Kau-Ur); (2) the riverine flats, known as *banto faros* (from a Mandingo word meaning "beyond the swamp"); and (3) the sandstone uplands. Most rural settlement is concentrated on the uplands, which have better drained soils and are more healthful than the flooded swamps and estuarine *banto faros*. In the *banto faros* on the middle course of the river, however, where valleys are deeper and there is less danger of flooding, the number of village settlements increases. Many of the villages are built on the boundary between the uplands and the riverine flats.

THE GAMBIA

The rate of urban growth has been slow. Banjul, the capital, had a population of about 39,500 in 1973, while the area around Sara Job Kunda (conventionally called Serrekunda), the next largest urban area (comprising several smaller settlements), had a population of about 25,500. Only seven other settlements had as many as 3,000 inhabitants, only 66 had more than 1,000, and the rest were villages.

The national economy. The Gambia is primarily agricultural, with both men and women engaged in cultivation. On the *banto faros* of the river's middle course, fields are created by enclosing selected areas with embankments made of mud and reeds, which are cultivated by women, who grow rice, garden crops, and some peanuts. On the sandy uplands the men grow peanuts, sorghum, and millet and practice the rotation of crops. The average size of cultivated plots is 2½ acres for a man and 1¼ acres for a woman (about one and 0.5 hectare, respectively). In addition to the main cereal crops, the women also grow such subsistence crops as lentils, cassava, yams, eggplant, tomatoes, peppers, and okra. Fruit trees are also maintained.

Importance of peanuts in the economy

The Gambian economy, as noted above, is based primarily on the production of peanuts for export. Grown on the upland soils, peanuts have been the main cash crop for virtually all Gambian farmers and the source of the largest share of governmental revenue. Sown in June and July, the crop is harvested in October and November. Production has increased steadily with the help of seasonal migrants from Senegal and Guinea and with the wider use of fertilizers and ox-drawn equipment, as well as the introduction of better seed varieties. The annual output of peanuts in shell now totals around 140,000 tons. In an effort to diversify the economy, the production of palm kernels, a secondary export crop, has been encouraged since the mid-1960s, when a pilot scheme for the cultivation of oil palms was begun, using improved varieties of seed from Nigeria. Experimental cotton growing was encouraging enough for 100 acres (40 hectares) to be planted in the early 1970s.

Processing, rather than manufacturing, industries are important. Peanuts are sold unshelled to traders and agents of the Gambia Oilseeds Marketing Board, which fixes the season's price in advance, pays the producers in cash, and sells overseas. The agents arrange for the transportation of the peanuts to Banjul or to Kau-Ur, where the nuts are shelled before being shipped. After shelling, a large proportion of the crop is pressed at oil mills. Exports include nuts, oil, and cattle cake, the residue after the oil has been extracted.

Marine resources

The ocean off The Gambia has great potential for inshore and deep-sea fishing, but little public revenue has been derived from fisheries because of inadequate equipment to replace traditional techniques, which confine the fishermen to estuarial or coastal waters. Some development has nevertheless taken place, with the government lending money to encourage the use of motorized fishing boats and the construction of traditional types of smoke huts for processing fish, particularly bonga (shad, or West African herring), which is exported to West African countries. A potential European market for shrimp and prawns remains to be exploited.

Trade and finance. The Gambia has a large volume of trade for its small size, the total annual value in the mid-1970s amounting to about $200 U.S. (£100) per person. Exports go mainly to the United Kingdom (about 40 percent), The Netherlands, Portugal, and France. For the decade 1965–75, however, the country had an adverse balance of trade.

Transport. The navigability of the Gambia River has discouraged the development of good roadways, total mileage being only 1,155 miles (1,858 kilometres), less than 300 miles of which is hard-surfaced. There are no railways and no internal air services. The one good port is Banjul, and there is a small international airport nearby at Yundum. Banjul offers easy access to shipping and has good road and river connections. Improvements are planned for both the port and Yundum Airport. Prospects for tourism and trade in Banjul are good, but the remainder of the country suffers from a lack of services.

Administration and social conditions. The Gambia is an independent republic. The government is headed by a president, whose term of office is linked to the unicameral parliament, the House of Representatives. Elections are held every five years. The vice president and Cabinet members are appointed by the president from the 32 elected members of the house. There are also four house members elected by the chiefs in assembly, three nominated members who are without votes, and the attorney general, who is nominated and has a vote. The People's Progressive Party (PPP) holds about seven-eighths of the elected seats. Local administration in each of the 35 districts into which The Gambia is divided is the responsibility of the local chief, who is assisted by village heads and advisers. The 35 districts are also grouped into eight local government areas, seven of which are administered by councils consisting of a majority of elected members and the chiefs of the district. Banjul is administered by a city council.

The government provides such social services as it can afford from revenues primarily obtained from the tax on peanut exports. There are two large trade unions in existence, as well as some smaller specialized unions.

The Gambia, Area and Population

Division	area* sq mi	area* sq km	population 1973 census
Local government area			
Banjul	5	12	39,000
Kombo St. Mary	29	76	39,000
Lower River	625	1,618	43,000
MacCarthy Island			
Mid North Bank	566	1,467	47,000
Mid South Bank	551	1,428	53,000
North Bank	871	2,256	94,000
Upper River	799	2,070	87,000
Western	681	1,764	91,000
Total The Gambia	4,127	10,689†	493,000
	4,467	11,569	

*First total includes dry land and so-called "wet" lands; second total includes water; total dry land only is 3,325 sq mi (8,613 sq km).
†Detail does not add to total given because of rounding.
Source: Official government figures.

Defense. While The Gambia has no standing army, as a member of the Commonwealth of Nations it is tacitly understood it may expect defense cooperation from other Commonwealth countries. It has a 200-man para-military "field force," which is part of the 600-man police force and is concerned with internal security. A special agreement on defense and security has also been concluded with Senegal.

Education. Only 20 percent of the school-age population was enrolled in 1967. Education is mostly at the primary level, although there are some secondary schools and one teacher-training college. Gambian students seeking higher education usually travel to Sierra Leone, the United Kingdom, or the United States.

Health. There are two general hospitals and a number of health centres and dispensaries. Mosquito-control units are active, and there is a leprosy-control clinic.

Cultural life. The different tribal groups are the focus of cultural life. An official newspaper is published three times a week, and Radio Gambia, a government station, broadcasts each evening.

Prospects for the future. The Gambia can achieve prosperity only through coordinating its development with that of neighbouring states, such as Senegal and Mali. Such coordinated development might permit the growth of the port of Banjul and lessen The Gambia's present dependency upon the state of the world peanut market. Meanwhile port facilities at Banjul are being improved with assistance from the World Bank. Until political obstacles are overcome, however, the Gambia River must remain economically isolated from its natural hinterland, with its potentialities largely unused.

BIBLIOGRAPHY. H.A. GAILEY, JR., *A History of the Gambia* (1964), information on the land and people, traditional farming practices, and the economics of a monoculture; R.J. HARRISON CHURCH, "The Gambia: A Riverine Enclave," in *West Africa*, 6th ed. (1968), a valuable reference on the climate, major natural regions, and economic resources of The Gambia, including a brief history of European association with the territory; H.R. JARRETT, *A Geography of Sierra Leone and Gambia* (1954), a detailed geography covering the physical background and economic activity, especially farming.

(E.R.A.F.)

Gambia River

The Gambia River, 700 miles (1,120 kilometres) long, is one of the finest waterways in Africa and the only West African river easily accessible to oceangoing shipping. The river, which flows westward from the Republic of Guinea to empty into the Atlantic Ocean, constitutes a unifying factor for the independent state of Gambia, which consists of a narrow strip of land along both banks of the river. The political separation between Gambia and Senegal has, however, hindered the development of the resources of the river and its basin. (For detailed coverage of the state of Gambia, see the article GAMBIA, THE).

Geomorphology. From its source in the Fouta Djallon Highlands in the Republic of Guinea (*q.v.*), the Gambia follows a winding course to its mouth, which is a ria, or drowned estuary. The dividing and reuniting of river channels—a phenomenon known as braiding—has created several islands along the river's middle course, of which the two largest are Elephant Island and MacCarthy Island. The river is joined by numerous creeks called *bolons*, the largest of these being Bintang Bolon, which flows into it from the south.

The width of the river valley varies considerably along its course. At its mouth, Cape Saint Mary, it is about 12 miles (19.3 kilometres) wide. Immediately to the east it narrows like an hour glass, being a mere three miles (5 kilometres) wide between Banjul (formerly Bathurst), the capital of Gambia, on the left bank, and Barra on the opposite bank. South of Banjul it widens again until it is about seven miles (11 kilometres) across, thereafter narrowing gradually upstream to the source. Just east of Elephant Island, about 80 miles (129 kilometres) from Bathurst, it is only one mile (1.6 kilometres) wide.

The river valley is cut into a plateau of sandstone from the Tertiary Period (compacted sediment composed predominantly of quartz grains, formed from 65,000,000 to 7,000,000 years ago). For 80 miles (129 kilometres) inland from the mouth the river banks are low, consisting mainly of soft mud. Above Elephant Island, low cliffs of red ironstone (a clayey rock, heavily loaded with iron oxide) occur, interspersed with sections of swampland. Above MacCarthy Island, further upstream, the cliffs become higher, varying between 20 and 50 feet (6 and 15 metres) in height, and the valley becomes narrower.

Vegetation and animal life. Dense mangrove swamps fringe the lower river for 60 miles (97 kilometres) inland; after which freshwater swamps and salt flats on low-lying stretches alternate with dense clumps of small trees and shrubs that line the cliffs. On the higher slopes of the riverbank, swamps and shrubs give place to parkland and tall grass. The wild oil palm grows in small clumps in low swampy areas along the valley bottom.

Mangrove swamps

The vegetation of the river and of its creeks provides a favourable habitat for insects, animals, and birds. The swamps encourage mosquitoes and tsetse flies to breed. The river abounds in fish, and river creatures, including the hippopotamus and the crocodile. There is a great variety of bird life. Among the 400 known species that have been recorded are the kingfisher, the cuckoo, the swallow, the heron, the dove, the sunbird, the hawk, and the grass warbler.

Climate and soils. The river lies in a tropical climatic region that has a distinct rainy season from June to October and a distinct dry season from December to April. Three regions are associated with the river, extending from the river banks northward and southward, parallel to its flow. Closest to the river is the swamp region, which lies on deposits of clayey alluvium. Backing the swamps are grass-covered river flats known locally as *banto faros* (meaning "beyond the swamp" in the Mande language). The soils of these flats are clayey in the estuarine section of the river and become flooded with salt water during the rainy season. In the *banto faros* upstream, the soils are lighter loams (natural mixtures of sand and clay together with organic matter) that are also flooded during the rainy season, but with fresh water. Higher up the valley sides, beyond the *banto faros*, lies the sandstone plateau. Its soils are well drained, light, and relatively less fertile, supporting a vegetation of coarse tall grass and scattered trees such as the baobab and the locust bean tree (which bears pods in bunches).

Human settlement. The swampy region closest to the river, with its dense masses of mangrove trees, often growing more than 100 feet (30 metres) high, abounds in wild life but has been of little use for either agriculture or human settlement. The *banto faros* of the lower river are rendered useless for cultivation by the salt water which periodically inundates them, and settlements on them are few. The flats of the middle and upper river are of some agricultural value, however. Much of the grassland is regularly cleared, and the light soils are easily cultivable. The annual flooding of the fertile alluvial loams of the middle flats makes them especially suitable for intensive rice cultivation. On the light sandy and well-drained soils of the higher slopes, groundnuts (peanuts) grow particularly well. Cultivation and settlement have therefore taken place in the middle flats and on the higher slopes, with many villages being located on the borderline between the flats and the plateau, thus avoiding both the flooding of the lower slopes and the increasing aridity of the higher terrain.

Rice growing

Hydrology. In 1970 there was still little information available relating to the river's rate of flow. Flooding is more extreme upriver than it is nearer the mouth. To the east, a rise of 40 feet (12 metres) in the level of the water has been reported when the river is in flood. Nearer the estuary the wide valleys also become flooded, but due to the high degree of permeability of their sandy soils, the water drains rapidly. Apart from seasonal fluctuations in the water level, variations also occur at shorter intervals due to the tidal nature of the river.

Navigation. The Gambia is one of the most navigable of African rivers. Although there is a sandbar at the seaward end of the estuary, there are depths of 26 feet (8 metres) of water, so that it can be crossed by ships at any tide. Thus, while oceangoing shipping is subjected to restraints on other West African rivers, ships of 2,000 to 3,000 tons can sail 150 miles (240 kilometres) up the Gambia from Bathurst to Kuntaur, while smaller vessels can penetrate 176 miles (283 kilometres) to Georgetown. Until recently small steamers, sailing cutters, lighters towed by tug boats, and other craft sailed as far upstream as the eastern boundary between Gambia and Senegal, which coincides with the river's tidal limit. Beyond this point there is sufficient draft for launches only in the rainy season. The upper river channel, however, became silted in recent years, as a result of accelerating soil erosion caused by increasing clearance for cultivation of slopes on the riverbanks. By 1970 steamers, which formerly sailed to Fatoto, 288 miles (463 kilometres) upstream from Bathurst, had to stop at Basse Santa Su, 20 miles (32 kilometres) further down. The lower channel was also affected through the rapid erosion of the low lateritic cliffs (formed of red iron-bearing soil) bordering it, and silting of the channel necessitated the removal of the groundnut decorticating (husking) mills at Kuntaur to Kau-ur, 30 miles (48 kilometres) downstream as the crow flies, in order that larger vessels transporting the groundnut crop overseas could be accommodated.

Silting of the channel

Transport. The chief value of the river has been its transportation function. As the main artery of the state of Gambia, it is the principal means of transporting passengers, freight, and mail in the territory. North–south river crossings are provided by ferries such as those plying between Barra and Bathurst, Banni and Kerewan, Farafenni and Yelitenda, and Kau-ur and Jessadi. Out of the eight crossings in operation in 1968, only four were served by motorized craft.

Prospects for the future. Because of the political boundaries of the state of Gambia, inherited from the colonial era, the full development of the Gambia River has not yet been achieved. Until now the river, because of its navigability, has proved a boon to the state of Gambia. Without extensive dredging of the river bed, however, its navigability will deteriorate. The economic development of the river basin will, however, necessitate cooperation with the state of Senegal, whose territory entirely surrounds that of Gambia. The Gambian administration has, however, opposed such things as the construction of a bridge to carry trans-Gambian traffic, since this would deprive it of the revenue now obtained from the ferry service, and also because the bridge would restrict the movement of large ships to the first few miles of the estuary only. A proposed dam, while providing water for irrigation in the upper provinces, as well as for the generation of electricity, is also opposed because it would affect streamflow and navigability. Until a way is found to break such impasses, the greater potential for economic growth of the Gambia River will remain unrealized.

BIBLIOGRAPHY. R.J. HARRISON CHURCH, "The Gambia: A Riverine Enclave," in *West Africa*, 6th ed. (1968), includes a description of the Gambia River.

(E.R.A.F.)

Gambling

Gambling is the betting or staking of something of value, with consciousness of risk and hope of gain, on the outcome of a game, a contest, or an uncertain event the result of which may be determined by chance or accident or have an unexpected result by reason of the bettor's miscalculation.

Many activities involve elements of risk and hope of gain and may depend on the outcome of an uncertain event or events—business ventures, buying and selling stock, military strategies, and foreign relations, for example; and, indeed, participation in such enterprises is often referred to as gambling or taking a chance. This article, however, is intended to cover specifically those activities associated with gambling. The words gambling, gaming, and game are derived from the Anglo-Saxon *gamen, gamon* ("sport" or "play").

Gambling games may vary in complexity from betting on the outcome of the toss of a coin, in which the winner claims the coin the side of which he correctly guesses, to betting on cards dealt in a game such as Poker, in which strategy also applies. The outcomes of gambling games may be determined by chance alone, as in the purely random activity of a tossed pair of dice or of the ivory ball on a Roulette wheel, or by physical skill, training, or prowess in athletic contests or, again, by a combination of strategy and chance. The rules by which gambling games are played sometimes serve to confuse the relationship between the components of the game, which depend on skill and chance, so that some players may be able to manipulate the game to serve their own interests. Thus, knowledge of the game is useful to the Poker player or the horse-race gambler but is of very little use to the purchaser of a lottery ticket or to a slot-machine player.

A gambler may participate in the game itself while betting on its outcome (card games, Craps), or he may be prevented from any active participation in an event in which he has a stake (professional athletics, lotteries). Some games are dull or nearly meaningless without the accompanying betting activity and are rarely played unless wagering occurs (coin tossing, Poker, dice games, lotteries). In other games, betting is not intrinsically part of the game, and the association is merely conventional and not necessary to the performance of the game itself (horse racing, football pools). Commercial establishments may organize gambling when a portion of the money wagered by patrons can be easily acquired by participation as a favoured party in the game, by rental of space, or by withdrawing a portion of the betting pool. Some activities of very large scale (horse racing, lotteries) usually require commercial and professional organization to present and maintain them efficiently.

HISTORY OF GAMBLING

Archaeologists have found artifacts used in games of chance in Egypt dating from as early as 3500 BC. Figurines, paintings in tombs, and drawings on pottery provide many illustrations of people or gods tossing astragali (astragalus, a small bone in the ankle under the talus or heel bone of a sheep or dog; often called knucklebones) and using counting boards to record the totals of play. In many excavations of prehistoric sites of even earlier periods, astragali have been discovered in large numbers; perhaps as long ago as 40,000 years, people were tossing these bones in games of chance—but of course the rules and patterns of play are not fully known today. An astragalus is an uneven, four-sided (two sides are round) bone, each side of which was probably assigned a different value in games in which it was used. Greek and Roman adults and children played games using astragali and even made copies of them in stone and metal embellished with incised figures. The astragali are still used by some Arab and American Indian tribes. Other artifacts that might also have been used in games included "throwing-sticks" of wood or ivory (about three inches long, square or elliptical in cross section, and marked in various stylized ways); such sticks were found in ancient Britain, Greece, Rome, Egypt, and in America among the Mayans.

Early archaeological evidence

The six-sided die had evolved long before the birth of Christ. Some dice were carved from astragali, but more uniform cubes were manufactured of pottery and wood. The earliest dice, from Iraq and India, date from about 3000 BC. Somewhere about 1400 BC the arrangement of the points still used today (opposite sides always total seven) was developed.

It is likely that astragali, throwing-sticks, and dice may have been used either in gaming or in divination of the future by the casting of lots, or sortilege. Numerous references are found in the Bible to the casting of lots, and probably astragali were used on many of the occasions to which it refers. It is important to note that those occasions were not regarded as games; lots were cast as means of ending disputes, dividing or distributing property, or otherwise divining God's will. (For example, all four of

The casting of lots

the New Testament Gospels describe the casting of lots to determine the disposition of the clothes of the crucified Jesus.) None of the denunciations of the prophets against vices of the Israelites included references to games of chance, nor is there any evidence that the Jews gambled before they came under the influence of Greek and Roman civilizations after the 4th century BC. Significantly, the Talmudic word for gambling is *qubbiyya*, borrowed from the Greek *kybeia*, "dice playing."

Thus, it is known that dice were used in the casting of lots, but they also were used in games of chance. As an example, the Aryan invaders of India in the 2nd millennium BC loved to gamble; and dice games with *vibhīdaka* nuts were popular among all classes except the very religious. The Ṛgveda, a collection of Vedic hymns, includes a poem, the "Gamester's Lament," one stanza of which quotes the god Savitṛ: " 'Don't play with dice, but plow your furrow! Delight in your property, prize it highly! Look to your cattle and look to your wife, you gambler!' Thus noble Savitṛ tells me."

In the *Mahābhārata*, the Hindu epic probably written in the 1st century BC, gambling with dice is frequently and prominently described; the world itself is conceived of as a gambling game.

Tacitus describes the gambling of property and people among the early Germans. Tribal battles were occasionally concluded with a game of chance.

The evidence of ethnography and folklore. A U.S. anthropologist, A.L. Kroeber, tried to discover whether or not gambling was distributed among the cultures of the world in systematic patterns that might reveal a general association between gambling and other cultural traits. He found that the stricter sects of puritanical religions, like those of Protestantism, Buddhism, and Islām, might accept many types of athletics and games but reject gambling because, he thought, of an aversion to the emotional involvement that comes with playing for stakes of money or property. Apart from religious controls, however, the reasons why a people accept or reject gambling was a puzzle about which he could only speculate. His list of nongambling societies included the aboriginal Australians, who are indifferent to property, and also the Papuan Melanesians, who spend much time and effort in acquiring property. Other nongamblers were the Polynesians, Micronesians, some of the peoples of Indonesia, the more remote tribes of India, most of the Siberians, many East Africans, and South Americans, except for the natives of Peru, highland Bolivia, Chile, Argentina, and Paraguay. Kroeber suggested that the areas of gambling and nongambling peoples were both large and compact so that the distributions of favourable or hostile attitudes were the products of "consistent diffusion" or the transmission of attitudes about the desirability or undesirability of gambling among cultures having mutual contact. The mechanics and techniques of gambling are so simple that theories of diffusion could not account for their distribution. He could find no consistent association between gambling and characteristics of the economy, the system of wealth, or type of religion.

More recently anthropologist John Roberts demonstrated that a useful threefold division could be made of games (but not necessarily gambling games) played by tribes that had been investigated in sufficient detail. These were games of physical skill (which might or might not include strategy or chance), games of strategy (without physical skill but perhaps with chance), and games of chance alone. A study of 50 tribes from all parts of the world revealed that 43 played games of physical skill, 20 played games of chance, and 19, games of strategy. Games seem to be expressive of the themes and patterns of basic ideas of a culture, and they also are models of various cultural activities; thus, they may simulate combat, hunting, chasing, divining, or coercing. It was found that cultures in which games of chance were played usually had religious beliefs in gods or spirits that were benevolent and could be coerced—that games of chance were linked to the mastery of the supernatural. Games of strategy, on the other hand, were associated with the learning of social roles (socialization) or mastery of the

social system, whereas games of physical skill were associated with mastery of both the self and the environment. Although the study did not distinguish between gambling and nongambling games, it illustrated that games of the sort that had been the objects of betting were linked predictably with other aspects of culture. Social scientists are continuing the attempt to reveal these relationships.

Scores of references to gambling have been found in folktales from cultures around the world. Greek and Roman myths refer to a god of gambling, or luck; the Irish and Scots have tales about extraordinary stakes, or stakes not claimed by winners; but the most abundant supply of dramatic stories about gambling is found in the folk literature of Asia, extending into Southeast Asia, Japan, the Philippines, and India. The Asians have dozens of folk stories about men gambling—using their wives, sisters, daughters, their own bodies, or parts of bodies as stakes. Some of these folktales have an ancient heritage; some include gambling with gods, whereas others are entirely secular. North America is another continent with an abundance of folk material on gambling. Of all the world's societies whose cultures have been studied sufficiently to know, and who play games of chance, half are North American Indians.

Efforts to suppress gambling. Class distinctions in laws relating to the suppression of gambling have an early origin. Roman emperors were fond of dicing games and played them frequently, especially Augustus and Claudius, but Roman common people were forbidden to play except during certain seasons. Throughout the Middle Ages churchmen and kings continually made efforts to suppress gambling, and their failure to do so serves as testimony to the abiding strength of the gambling fervour. A list of the bishops of the church who sermonized against gambling goes from St. Cyprian of Carthage (*c.* AD 240) to St. Bernardino of Siena in 1423. In 1232 Frederick II issued an edict against dice playing, and Louis IX in 1255 made the manufacture of dice illegal. Most of the gaming during this long period must have been with knucklebones and dice; cards were not common until 1350. But these prohibitions were directed not at the games as much as at the vices that seemed to accompany them. The church was more concerned with the drinking and swearing brought on by, or manifested in, gaming, and the state was more concerned with idleness, thriftlessness, cheating, and crime—which may have been characteristic of conspicuous gambling. That games of chance were not in themselves thought to be evil is indicated by the invention in 960 of a clerical version of dice by Bishop Wibold of Cambray, whose intention was not to stamp out gaming but to convert it to good. English monarchs beginning with Edward III promulgated a series of prohibitory laws designed to protect manly sports and the military arts. Henry VIII, though he himself gambled, pronounced gaming houses to be unlawful because they distracted young men from the practice of archery and military preparation. Henry's stand against "common gaming houses" was to survive in England for about 400 years, until the 1960s.

MATHEMATICAL THEORY UNDERLYING GAMBLING GAMES

Background. With all the evidence of the popularity of dice playing by most classes of people during several thousand years before the 15th century, it is notable that no record has been found of the idea of statistical ratios and a theory of probability. A 13th-century French humanist, Richard de Fournival, is credited with having written a Latin poem that included a passage giving the first known calculation of the number of ways of throwing three dice (there are 216). Earlier, however, the game mentioned above as invented by Wibold in 960 listed 56 virtues that the player of his clerical dice game was supposed to practice according to the ways three dice can be thrown, irrespective of order (the number of such combinations of three dice is indeed 56). Neither Wibold nor Fournival, however, attempted to determine the relative probabilities of the separate combinations. An Italian mathematician-physician-astrologer, Gerolamo Cardano,

The investigations of A.L. Kroeber

Gambling in folklore

Math to
meet
gamblers'
needs

is believed to have written the first mathematical analysis of the cast of dice in 1526. He proposed by use of theoretical argument—and his own considerable familiarity with dice games—a probability theory from which he issued advice to his students on how to wager. Galileo took up the analysis of dice playing in the late 16th century, as did Pascal in 1654—both at the requests of gamesters who had been troubled by disappointing and costly experiences with dice. Galileo's calculations were exactly those that would be used by mathematicians today, and the modern science of probability was on its way at last. The greatest advance in theory came in the middle of the 17th century with a manuscript by Christiaan Huygens, *De Ratiociniis in Ludo Aleae* ("On Ratiocination in Dice Games"). The history of the science of probability, then, is adequately shown to owe its start to the lowly problems of games of chance.

Before the time of the Reformation, people generally believed that every event of any kind was determined by the will of God or, if not by God, by some other supernatural force or personalized entity. Such beliefs have persisted among many, perhaps most, people to the present day. In a time when they were practically universal, however, a mathematical theory based on a contrasting notion that certain events might be random (controlled by pure chance, undirected, nonpurposive) had great difficulty in becoming expressed and established. Mathematician M.G. Kendall has pointed out that

> It seems to have taken humanity several hundred years to accustom itself to a world wherein some events were without cause . . . or were determined by a causality so remote that they could be accurately represented by a non-causal model.

The idea of purely random activity is basic to the comprehension of the relationship between chance and probability.

Chances, probabilities, and odds. Events or outcomes that are equally probable have an equal chance of occurring in each instance. In games of pure chance, each instance is a completely independent one; that is, each play has the same probability as each of the others of producing a given outcome. Probability statements apply in practice to a long series of events but not to individual ones. The "law of large numbers" is an expression of the fact that the ratios predicted by probability statements are increasingly accurate as the number of events increases; but the absolute number of outcomes of a particular type departs from expectation with increasing frequency as the number of repetitions increases. It is the ratios that are accurately predictable, not the individual events or precise totals.

Use of
probability
to predict
ratios and
odds

The probability of a favourable outcome among all possibilities can be expressed: probability (p) equals the total number of favourable outcomes (f) divided by the total number of possibilities (t), or $p = f/t$. But this holds only in situations governed by chance alone. In a game of tossing two dice, for example, the total number of possible outcomes is 36 (each of six sides of one die combined with each of six sides of the other), and the number of "ways to make," say, a seven are six (made by throwing 1 and 6, 2 and 5, 3 and 4, 4 and 3, 5 and 2, or 6 and 1); therefore, the probability of throwing a seven is 6/36, or 1/6 (or approximately .167).

In most gambling games it is customary to express the idea of probability in terms of "odds against winning." This is simply the ratio of the unfavourable possibilities to the favourable ones. If the probability of throwing a seven is 1/6, then in every six throws, "on the average," one throw would be favourable and five would not; the odds against throwing a seven are therefore 5 to 1. The probability of getting "heads" in a toss of a coin is one-half; the odds are 1 to 1, called "even." Care must be used in interpreting the phrase "on the average." Again it applies most accurately to a large number of cases and is not useful in individual instances. A common gamblers' fallacy called "the doctrine of the maturity of the chances" (or "Monte Carlo fallacy") falsely assumes that each play in a game of chance is not independent of the others and that a series of outcomes of one sort should be balanced in the short run by the other possibilities. A

number of "systems" have been invented by gamblers based largely on this fallacy; casino operators are happy to encourage the use of such systems and to exploit any gambler's neglect of the strict rules of probability and independent plays.

In some games an advantage may go to the dealer, banker (the individual who collects and redistributes the stakes), or some other participant. Therefore, not all players have equal chances to win or equal payoffs. This inequality may be corrected by rotating the players among the positions in the game. Commercial gambling operators, however, usually make their profits by regularly occupying advantaged positions; or they may charge money for the opportunity to play or subtract a proportion of money from the bank on each play. In the dice game of Craps the casino returns to winners from ⅗ of 1 percent to 27 percent less than the correct odds, depending on the type of bet made. The house percentage in Roulette in U.S. casinos is 5⁵⁄₁₉ percent to 7¹⁷⁄₁₉ percent, and in European casinos it is 1¹³⁄₃₇ percent to 2²⁶⁄₃₇ percent. The house must always win in the long run. Some casinos also add rules that enhance their profits, especially rules that limit the amounts that may be staked under certain circumstances.

Players'
chances
and
operators'
profits

Many gambling games include elements of physical skill or strategy as well as of chance. The game of Poker, like most other card games, is a mixture of chance and strategy. Betting on horse racing or athletic contests involves the assessment of physical capacity and the use of other skills. In order to assure that chance is allowed to play a major role in determining the outcomes of such games, weights, handicaps, or other correctives may be introduced to give the contestants approximately equal opportunities to win, and adjustments may be made in the payoffs so that the probabilities of success and the magnitudes of the payoffs are put in inverse proportion to each other. Pari-mutuel pools in horse-race betting, for example, reflect the chances of various horses as anticipated by the players. The individual payoffs are large for those bettors whose winning horses are backed by relatively few people and small if the winners are backed by a relatively large proportion of the bettors; the more popular the choice, the lower the individual payoff. The same holds true for betting with bookmakers on athletic contests (illegal in most of the United States but legal in England). Bookmakers ordinarily accept bets on the outcome of what is regarded as an uneven match by requiring the side more likely to win to score more than a simple majority of points. In a game of United States or Canadian football, for example, the more highly regarded team would have to win by, say, more than ten points to yield an even payoff to its backers.

Unhappily, these procedures for maintaining the influence of chance can be interfered with; cheating is possible and reasonably easy in most gambling games. Much of the stigma attached to gambling has resulted from the dishonesty of its promoters, and a large proportion of modern gambling legislation is written to control cheating. More laws have been oriented, however, to efforts by governments to derive tax revenues from gambling than to control cheating. (Taxes can be levied against the incomes of the promoters or players, or of the turnover [bank, pool] itself.)

GAMBLING AND ITS CONTROL IN VARIOUS NATIONS

Prevalence of principal forms. The world's most enthusiastic gamblers are probably the Chinese and other Southeast Asians. In the years before the Communist revolution, in some provinces of China, Burma, and Thailand as much as one-third of the average farm family's income went to pay gambling debts. Before World War I most of Thailand's state revenue was derived from state-licensed gambling establishments.

Horse-racing gambling exists in many countries, including Canada, the United States, Argentina, Colombia, Mexico, Puerto Rico, Venezuela, Australia, Indonesia, Japan, the Philippines, Denmark, Great Britain, France, West Germany, Ireland, Italy, Norway, Sweden, Poland, and the Soviet Union.

Horse
racing,
casino
gambling,
and
lotteries

Casino gaming is forbidden in Switzerland, Spain, and Scandinavia. In 1960 there were fewer than a dozen casinos in England, but by 1968 approximately 1,000 had managed to find a loophole in the written law; this led to a new system of licensing and control, which by the early 1970s reduced the number to 120. In the rest of Europe there were about 180 casinos in the 1970s, some of them very large and famous houses (at Monte Carlo, Bad Homburg, Baden-Baden), others small and unpretentious. France had 80 percent of this total, Germany about 7 percent, and Italy less than 5 percent. A few of the Communist bloc countries have experimented with casinos, some of which are financed by foreign entrepreneurs. In most of the countries of Europe (and several other areas) that have casinos, local citizens are not permitted to gamble in them, but visitors from distant cities within the country and from foreign states are permitted, even encouraged, to do so. The purpose of this two-class system is to protect people from the temptations of over-indulgence at accessible casinos and also to prevent the outflow of currency to other nations. This system prevails in Monaco, for example, where gambling in the casino at Monte Carlo is the backbone of the tourist industry and provides an important share of the national income. In some parts of the Caribbean area, too, casinos form the basis of tourist industries that constitute a chief source of foreign exchange and revenue.

Among the games played regularly at casinos, Roulette, which is one of the principal gambling games in France, is played throughout the world. Crap shooting is the principal game at most American casinos. Chuck-a-luck, once a standard dice game at North and Central American casinos, has, since the 1940s, largely faded out of the picture. Slot machines are a mainstay of casinos in the United States and also are found in thousands of private clubs, restaurants, and other establishments; they are common in other countries, including Australia, where they are known as Poker machines, and in Great Britain, where they are called fruit machines. Among the card games played at casinos, Baccarat, in its popular form Chemin de fer, has remained a principal gambling game in Great Britain and in the continental casinos most often patronized by the English at Deauville, Biarritz, and the Riviera resorts. Faro, at one time the principal gambling game in the United States, has, since the ascendancy of Craps, become almost obsolete. Poker is offered at many establishments, but Blackjack has been the principal card game in U.S. casinos. The French card game Trente et Quarante (or Rouge et Noire) is played at Monte Carlo and other continental casinos.

State-licensed or state-operated lotteries are widely distributed about most of the world (see the article LOTTERY). Soccer-pool companies can be found in Great Britain, Sweden, Australia, and a few African nations.

In the United States, Nevada is the only state that permits almost all common forms of gambling (that state collected $41,000,000 in tax revenues from gambling in 1970). About half of the states permit horse racing. In 1939 all horse-race gambling was limited by law to pari-mutuel betting, the system under which bets are pooled by the track management and redistributed to the winners after taxes and revenues are deducted. A large but unknown amount of illegal betting with bookmakers has persisted, however, and in 1971 New York became the first state other than Nevada to legalize off-track betting on horse racing (see HORSE RACING).

Legislation and control. In countries in which gambling is legal, legislation and control usually are directed primarily toward ensuring that the state receives its full share of gambling revenue and toward preventing the gambler from cheating or being cheated. In countries in which some or all forms of gambling are illegal, legislation and control are more complex and subject to change. In the United States, for example, although Nevada is the only state to have legalized casino gambling, several states repeatedly have considered and reconsidered doing so. Illegal gaming houses and illegal numbers rackets exist and are generally held to be responsible for large incomes to organized criminal syndicates. A few states

have laws making it possible for local governments to legalize particular card games. Also, many states permit casino gaming in private clubs and charitable enterprises and for certain special occasions. Some churches and service clubs have offered Bingo sessions as a means of raising money, and raffles for a prize are a commonly exploited technique for raising money or publicizing a product or occasion. State and local ordinances are often quite inconsistent, as are law enforcement practices. In many localities certain forms of gambling and gambling devices, the operation of slot machines by private clubs, for example, although illegal, are tolerated. The federal law is quite definite about prohibiting materials concerning gambling to be transmitted in interstate commerce, but again law enforcement inconsistencies, smuggling, and changing legal definitions compromise the effectiveness of the law.

In 1951 the British Royal Commission on Betting, Lotteries, and Gaming issued a report that stands as a landmark in official thought concerning gambling legislation. The commission argued that legislation designed only to prohibit or restrict participation in particular forms of gambling would be likely to fail because it is difficult to enforce; it frequently becomes out-of-date; it leads to class distinctions; and it fails to provide for the ingenuity of those who would profit from promoting gambling. The commission recommended that there should be strict control over the provision of commercial gambling, including the licensing or registration of all promoters and operators. It also recommended that the law be made to apply fairly to all sections of the society and that the public be continually informed about the extent and character of gambling. The principle concerning fair application is often subverted by repressive gambling laws because the rich are able to afford many ways of indulging their risk-taking whims through such activities as stock-market speculation, travel to distant resort areas and casinos, placing bets with bookmakers with whom a line of credit has been established, and so on. The British Parliament, in its revisions of the Gaming Act, has been guided to some extent by the commission report, which, in general, takes the view that gambling is an activity that "citizens may properly indulge in moderation, but . . . that there are grave dangers in uncontrolled indulgence."

The British theory of legislation

This willingness to tolerate gambling in moderation is more difficult to find in the United States, where opinion surveys and political elections have indicated that both the public and its legislative representatives are strongly divided on questions relating to the legalization of gambling. Nevertheless, there appears to be a trend toward legalizing certain forms of gambling—particularly lotteries and off-track bookmaking. Among the gains that could be realized by legalization, it has been argued, are: the state could exert more control over gambling promoters so that cheating might be reduced, tax revenues obtained, and professional operators kept from unnecessarily promoting gambling among those to whom it might be addictive. If, as is sometimes claimed, the "criminalization" of gambling (defining it as illegal) produces a tendency for professional gamblers to try to bribe law enforcement officers, then the legalization of gambling might remove a need for corrupting officials. On the other hand, legalization of gambling might increase the total volume of gambling, encourage some citizens to gamble who would otherwise not do so, and display the state's indifference to certain moral traditions and styles of life of its people.

In addition to the articles referred to above, see also CARDS AND CARD GAMES; DICE AND DICE GAMES; and ROULETTE.

BIBLIOGRAPHY

General references: JOHN SCARNE, *Complete Guide to Gambling* (1961), especially useful discussions of cheating methods; ALAN WYKES, *Gambling* (1964), international and comparative in scope, with excellent illustrations.

Official documents: Gambling and Organized Crime, Hearings before the Permanent Subcommittee on Investigations of the Committee on Government Operations, U.S. Senate, 87th

Congress (1961); Royal Commission on Betting, Lotteries and Gaming 1949–1951 *Report* (1951).

Sociological and anthropological: ERVING GOFFMAN, *Interaction Ritual* (1967), includes an essay on the meaning of casino gaming; ROBERT D. HERMAN (ed.), *Gambling* (1967), surveys social and political issues; JOHAN HUIZINGA, *Homo ludens* (1938; Eng. trans., *Homo ludens: A Study of the Play-Element in Culture*, 1949); CHARLOTTE OLMSTED, *Heads I Win: Tails You Lose* (1962), psychology and symbolism of gambling games; J.M. ROBERTS, M.J. ARTH, and R.R. BUSH, "Games in Culture," *Am. Anthrop.*, 61:597–605 (1959); MARVIN B. SCOTT, *The Racing Game* (1968), principles of game theory applied to the sociological study of horse-race betting.

History of probability theory: M.G. KENDALL, "Studies in the History of Probability and Statistics: II. The Beginnings of a Probability Calculus," *Biometrika*, 43:1–14 (1956).

(R.D.H.)

Games, History of

The history of games is a part of the history of man as a social animal: his interrelations with other individuals and groups, his civilization and culture, and especially his play. The particular games that are the subject of this article are those more-or-less active games that adults in different parts of the world have enjoyed sufficiently in their early forms to develop for them uniform codes of rules and specifications, and to organize them for competitive play. The ones that are cited as examples are mostly those now played with a ball between opposing sides (*e.g.*, tennis, billiards, football, baseball, cricket). The article covers the early history of such games and their functions as physical outlets, displays of skill, entertainment for spectators, and pastimes bringing men and women together socially. Separate sections deal with the period of greatest growth of games in schools and clubs, their national and international organization, and the paradoxical decline of games at a time of their increasing world-wide promotion and coverage by press and television. Because the term games is given a limited definition here, it is notable, particularly when reasons for playing specified games are being inferred, that there are probably other recreational ways of achieving some of the same satisfactions. A few will be indicated as the opportunity occurs.

Readers, particularly American ones, desiring to know more about the wider subject of man's love and need of recreation are referred to Foster Rea Dulles' book, *A History of Recreation: America Learns to Play*, in which the author tells of the ways a young nation, brought up to believe "that all idle pursuits were a Satanic trap to lure the godly from the path of duty," nevertheless found itself incapable of observing what is now known to be an unnatural and harmful injunction. Man must play or pay a heavy penalty. The reader is also referred to other articles in *Encyclopædia Britannica*: see ATHLETIC GAMES AND CONTESTS; CHILDREN'S SPORTS AND GAMES; SPORTS, AMATEUR AND PROFESSIONAL; and to the historical sections of the separate articles on individual games.

For that category of nonactive games, which have provided both men and women with much pleasant pastime, amusement, intellectual stimulation, social intercourse, and—especially when played for stakes—excitement, see BOARD AND TILE GAMES; CARDS AND CARD GAMES; DICE GAMES; NUMBER GAMES AND MATHEMATICAL RECREATIONS; and WORD AND LETTER GAMES. See also BRIDGE; CHESS; CRIBBAGE; POKER; ROULETTE; and RUMMY GAMES.

EARLY HISTORY

The organization of games for competitive play and the codifying of each game's rules for general acceptance followed the improvement of communications in the 19th century and the growth of towns. Better roads, the railroads, the automobile, and the airplane have fostered national and international association. The towns growing progressively larger, sometimes into conurbations, denied the space for natural play to millions and substituted spectator games. But old ways died hard, particularly in European countries, and it was possible in the 1970s either to find games still being enjoyed that had no more than local significance, or codified games being played with local rules.

The metamorphosis of games from being unorganized, undisciplined amusements in villages and small towns into what they became in the second half of the 19th and in the 20th centuries—sophisticated occupations for thousands and mass amusement for millions—was relatively swift. It followed the pace set by the Industrial Revolution. Before that series of economic and social changes took place, games were simple alternatives to country pursuits. Contests, particularly on holy days, were occasionally arranged between different communities as social occasions or as excuses for violence. In the country, games generally were spontaneous affairs, indulged in on the spur of the moment for an unspecified time. Gambling, of course, was an exception; matches between cocks and even cricketers were arranged for that.

Importance of the ball. The most significant fact in the history of games was the early appearance of the ball. The observation that animals enjoy gambols with playthings as much as humans suggests that there may never have been a time in man's evolution when a ball substitute was not chased, batted, or thrown. In historical times the ball has always been present. The Egyptians, Greeks, Persians, and Romans were all familiar with it. The Romans had a special room set aside for ball play in their public baths. Mostly, however, the ancient world played forms of catch, as other people have done in every country ever since.

For centuries the manufacture of balls hardly changed. They were made of strips of leather sewn together and stuffed with hair, feathers, or cloth. Sometimes air-filled bladders were an alternative, and for kicking there was always a stone, the precursor of the tin can. Only in the history of the Aztec Indians and others in the same geographical area are there references to rubber balls before the 18th century: travellers to the New World reported seeing them there at the end of the 15th century. The rubber ball was used in Spain in *pelota vasca* (jai alai [*q.v.*]) before its introduction in other parts of Europe.

Those who most enjoyed playing with a ball soon found ways of hitting it farther and harder with bats or clubs of various kinds. The variety of clubs shown on friezes and urns has made it possible for the enthusiastic historian of an individual game to claim—with some truth—ancient lineage for his own. Certainly there were stick games played by the Persians, Greeks, and American Indians. Polo, a word of Tibetan origin, was apparently well known in some form to the Persians at the time of Darius I (reigned 522 to 486 BC). Golf, though claimed by Scotland in its modern form, had respectable antecedents in Roman times and in many European countries. The word golf comes, it is widely believed, from the Dutch *kolf*.

Playing areas. Another important factor in the early development of ball games was the nature of available playing areas. It was easy to appreciate the advantages of the flat surface of a courtyard, for example, and even the smallest boy could understand that a ball thrown against a relatively large and smooth wall could be made to bounce back to him. Because the bound of the leather ball was low, only a small space was needed. Many European church walls provided the opportunity, and by using them, handball games were invented. If the wall was supported by a buttress, an angle was provided for a more elaborate game (see HANDBALL AND FIVES).

Nobles and courtiers found the same kind of opportunity within the walls of castles. The original game of tennis, or *jeu de paume* ("palm of the hand game"), now known as court tennis in the United States and sometimes as royal or real tennis in England, was played as a recognized pastime in the courtyards of noble establishments in France as early as the 13th century. Played over a fringed or tassled string or a net, the game made use of the irregularities of the walls surrounding it. Some of these irregularities were carefully reproduced in courts built expressly for the game in later centuries: they had become an integral part of the game (see TENNIS AND ALLIED COURT GAMES).

Historically the game was important because through

Games as simple alternatives to country pursuits

The influence of available playing areas

its story could be traced the origin of several court games and to some extent the evolution of the racket. Nurtured in France, tennis spread to Holland, England, and Scotland. Because it was a gentleman's game played by courtiers and enjoyed by the ladies, who were able to watch from their rooms in the towers, it was one of the first ball games to be subject to some organization. Games of tennis are reported to have been played for the amusement of Queen Elizabeth I when on tour. The degree of organization is suggested by John Webster's metaphor:

We are merely the stars' tennis balls, struck and bandied
Which way please them.

Evolution of the tennis racket

In the earlier centuries it was played with the hand only, probably with several players on each side of the net. Later the hand was bound with thongs and cords, and finally a stick was inserted in the cords to make a primitive racket. But it is hard to write positively about the evolution of the racket. For example, a picture of a most elegantly dressed lady of the 14th century, described as playing *jeu de paume*, shows her obviously about to serve the ball with the help of an implement resembling a baseball bat. By the early 17th century, the highborn Prince James, duke of York, was portrayed in a tennis court holding what appears to be a strung table tennis racket. This short-handled bat was in general use by that date.

The game reached the peak of its popularity in the 16th and 17th centuries. Henry VIII's love for it is well documented. He was a good player and built himself a court, still used four centuries later, at Hampton Court Palace. Long before that, however, the populace of England and France were being forbidden to play many games because they supposedly wasted time and caused gambling.

The game the populace played was probably like fives or handball, a simple use of walls wherever they were to be found. They would also play the open-air game of tennis (called *la longue paume*) in which teams of two or more would oppose each other on different sides of a line stretched across the centre of a flat area with no boundary walls. The suggestion of modern lawn tennis was there.

Meanwhile, thousands of miles across the sea from Europe and long before the landing of Columbus, Indians in North America had taught themselves to string a racket-like implement and to play a game the refined modern descendant of which is lacrosse.

Social structure and games. The social structure of European society in the eight centuries before 1800 determined which recreations prospered and which did not. Tennis was a gentleman's game, the only outdoor ball game that was. It was played in the seclusion of a courtyard and later in private covered courts; it soon had recognized rules for match play. Football was a game not played by gentlemen, a rabble game, which it remained, in spite of its universality and popularity, until the 19th century when the age of the common man began. The exception to the rule might easily be golf. Something like it was played across open countryside from Roman times to the 19th century. It was played by gentlemen, as occasional references showed, and was played by others no doubt, but it was an unsatisfying game with a ball stuffed with feathers. Still, clubs flourished from the 18th century onward to be ready, as it turned out, for the revolution in popularity that followed the invention of the gutta-percha ball in 1845.

Social relationship of games

Joseph Strutt in his book *The Sports and Pastimes of the People of England*, first published in 1801, indicated clearly the social relationships of games by the arrangement of his material. He divided his work into four books and each book into several chapters: book I, "Rural Exercises Practised by Persons of Rank"; book II, "Rural Exercises Generally Practised"; book III, "Pastimes Usually Exercised in Towns and Cities or Places Adjoining to Them"; and book IV, "Domestic Amusements of Various Kinds and Pastimes Appropriate to Particular Seasons."

The rural exercises of book I were hunting, hawking, and horse racing, a chapter each to those pursuits which, until modern times, were denied to everyone except the land-owning classes. Practically all the ball games noticed in this article were to be found in book II. In book III,

however, there was one game, bowls (lawn bowling), deserving of attention because its acceptance by persons of rank meant that, like tennis, it reached a developed form earlier than the games of physical contact that were unthinkable for gentlemen.

Bowls and bowling. Sir Francis Drake found time to finish his game of bowls before sailing to meet the Spanish Armada in 1588. By Drake's time, the game had reached such sophistication that it was already played with biassed woods or bowls made to curve. In its simpler form, with ordinary balls, it had been played for centuries and enjoyed great popularity. A similar game, boccie, had long been played in the Piedmont.

The general idea of bowls, that of placing one bowl as near as possible to another stationary one, or jack, and, if necessary, of knocking one's opponents' bowls out of the way in order to do so, made the game virtually the same as the one children played with marbles or adults enjoyed on ice when curling. But the bias of the bowl and the introduction of sweeping for curling, both 16th century developments, heightened the skill and increased the competitive fascination of both games. The Dutch and the Scots were fond of both, and the Dutch made bowls a popular recreation in New Amsterdam in North America.

Bowling, or tenpins, has been regarded as a modern American game, and indeed it reached its highest organizational and technological development there. Derived from skittles, or ninepins, however, it was in essence one of the oldest forms of amusement. The Germans were the first to popularize it, but by late medieval times there were alleys everywhere in Europe. Henry VIII was again the man to give bowling final respectability in England. He added a bowling alley to one of his residences. It remained a tavern game, however, and, like shovelboard, was a recreation popular also with nobility, but rarely played together or in the same place.

Billiards. The only other ball game that found its way into gentlemen's houses in the 16th century was billiards. Quite how this came about is unknown, but billiards swiftly grew in popularity, and by the end of the 17th century it was an expected diversion in country houses. It was clearly related to a tavern game, and for a time wooden obstacles on the table were a common feature. The modern game dates from 1800. Its main features, however, were established long before that. English encyclopaedist Ephraim Chambers (1738) described it as "an ingenious kind of game played on an oblong table, covered with green cloth, . . . with little ivory or wooden balls. . . ."

THE FUNCTIONS OF GAMES

Looking backward over the centuries, it would seem that there have been three functions for games. The first was to rid the participant of animal spirits and excess emotions by playing rough, strenuous, and what are now called physical-contact games. The second was to excite admiration and to give pleasure to the individual and others by demonstrating skill. These objects were achieved in the display games. The third was to offer emotional outlets to large numbers of people by arranging spectacles—the spectator games—compensating for the lack of opportunity for taking part and also satisfying man's undoubted enjoyment in being, on occasion, one of a crowd. To these three functions there was added for a brief period a fourth, the function of bringing men and women together in a social situation. Common to all four but in varying degrees and dependent on the individual natures of the participants was the spirit of competition.

The functions did not remain static. From time to time they were modified as social pressures changed. Often the games served more than one purpose. Association football (soccer), universally the most popular game of the 19th and 20th centuries, moved into the spectator category after several hundred years of usefulness as an outlet for physical exuberance. In consequence, British players, the acknowledged masters for half a century, found themselves left behind in the 1950s by the artistry of the Hungarians, Spaniards, and Latin Americans. They were

Changing functions and growth of spectator sports

forced to alter their style, as they did successfully. Nevertheless, as late as the 1970s they could still be criticized for their overly physical performances.

Baseball, too, in the United States left the quieter environment of amateur display to become towards the end of the 19th century the national, professional spectator sport. Professionalism, except for coaching, was linked with spectator sports and emphasized the point of play that most excited a crowd.

In other parts of the world, notably Australia, India, and the West Indies, cricket, much to English surprise, followed suit. In this game, in the late 20th century, it was not so much the style of play that changed as the conditions under which a match was fought. Matches confined to a few hours were preferred by the crowds to the leisurely contests of former times spread over days. There was more excitement and more spectator interest and appeal.

Physical outlets. The chief physical games have been all forms of football, perhaps most of all American football, and such others as hockey, polo, hurling, and lacrosse, all of which involved chasing a ball vigorously with a stick. Most of them were played in the West in the early days by young men who were denied the pleasure of the hunt by the hierarchical structure of the feudal system. In violent play, the ball took on the attributes of the quarry. There were at first no written rules but possibly a few local ones. The games ranged from casual affairs arranged on the spur of the moment to traditional battles between two villages or two sides of a town. At the conclusion the contestants were battered and exhausted.

The authorities were constantly worried by these games. They counted the damage and deplored the waste of time when something more useful might be done like practising archery at the butts. However, in spite of laws prohibiting games and puritanical repression at a later date, it is hard to believe that some did not appreciate how essential violent play was for the young. As the poet Alfred Cochrane expressed the idea:

> I once admitted—to my shame—
> That football was a brutal game
> Because she hates it.

Two popular sports or games that are equally brutal and were always performed partly for display and partly as spectacles are boxing (fighting) and wrestling. They both date from earliest times, were part of the athletic games and contests of ancient Greece, and have been enthusiastically enjoyed at all periods and in all countries. Of the two wrestling had the higher reputation, gathering the crowds in towns and rural areas from Japan to Europe for thousands of years. The attraction was the skill exhibited and the display of violence. For some men and women in every age boxing and wrestling have been a compelling catharsis.

Displays of skill. Until recent times cricket was the most remarkable of the display games. Indigenous to England from the 17th century and played only in Holland on the European continent, cricket was exported by the English to all countries of the British Empire. It failed to take hold in the United States, perhaps because it was colonial or too unexciting for pioneering temperaments, but elsewhere, if there was a British colony, cricket was enjoyed.

For two centuries the enjoyment was predominantly in the display. A spectator who watched only a period of a three-day match or sat awhile in a field watching a village game was less concerned with the result or the prospect of excitement than with the skill of the batsman, bowler, or fieldsman. The players, too, were concerned chiefly with their own skills: if a batsman, how to master the bowler's pace or spin and to play the appropriate stroke; if a bowler, how to beat the bat by showing superior skill to the player holding it. If wrestling aroused, cricket soothed.

By the last third of the 20th century, only the games emphasizing individual performances were left to recall the once-admired virtues of display. Sometimes the artistry of a footballer or a cricketer could arouse admiration of a crowd, but generally that was regarded as a

bonus, and team games were by then assumed primarily to provide excitement. It was the diver in lonely concentration on the top board, the gymnast, the figure skater or pair, the skier, or the athlete preparing to make his jump or throw whose skillful performance mattered more than any points advantage to be gained. There was a physical or technical beauty to be achieved in display that, at the moment of performance, transcended all other aims.

Spectator entertainment. The growth of urban living promoted the advance of spectator games. Proportionately fewer and fewer people had the opportunity satisfactorily to organize their own leisure. The country way of life, which intermingled sport and work, had little in common with an industrialized society whose recreational needs were starved and needed, as it turned out, a new industry to satisfy them.

In the ancient world the usual spectator games were athletic, to which were added chariot races, wrestling, boxing, and gladiatorial contests. There was also theatre. The medieval citizen got his occasional spectator fun from fairs, jousts, and dramatic performances. He was very fond of the drama, often associated with religion, as in the mystery plays, and his audience participation was accepted and expected.

The puritanical attitudes of the 17th century reduced the amount of fun in Europe and America, and by the time their influence had waned, the shadows of the Industrial Revolution were beginning to close in. In the United States the shooting matches and the tavern games were supplemented by dances and visits to the theatre. Real freedom to enjoy oneself as one wished was a long time coming, and when it did games did not at first play much part.

It was a different story in the 19th century. Along with Barnum's American Museum and his travelling exhibitions, horse races, regattas, and athletics drew the crowds. By mid-century in the United States, baseball had begun to grip the public's imagination. For the first time in history a ball game was on its way to becoming a major spectator sport. Elsewhere it was association football, the only game ever known to attract week after week, in one part of the world or another, millions of watchers.

The attraction and worth of spectator games to an urban community too poor to be mobile were obvious. They provided excitement, interest, and romance. Cynically the games could be described as Karl Marx described religion, as "the opium of the people"; charitably they could be regarded as a logical development of man's enthusiasm for games when precluded from taking part himself. Mostly, at the beginning, the impetus came from private enthusiasm, although it proved by no means easy to turn large stadiums into successful business enterprises.

Social games. The fourth function of games—social—was at its peak short-lived. Four games at least and one other form of exercise, bicycling, owed their immense popularity between 1870 and 1914 to the opportunities they gave to men and women for sunlit dalliance and more serious flirtation. After World War I they remained enjoyable but no longer necessary, for the age of chaperones was past. The games were archery, croquet, lawn tennis, and roller skating. Men and women played them together, and it was part of the emancipation of women from Victorian bonds that they were allowed to do so. In places where the climate made it possible, ice skating performed the same function.

After World War I only lawn tennis continued as a popular mixed game, and it survived as such for another 20 years. Although its function as a social game declined, it continued to be enjoyed as a club game, as did badminton and squash rackets in the winter; and, with the rise of professional tennis in the 1960s and 1970s and the construction of numerous indoor courts, tennis achieved a strong position as both a participant and a spectator sport.

Although the social games were short-lived, the elderly in the 1970s looked back on them with nostalgia. For a section of society they symbolized an era of domestic stability and charm unknown before and unlikely to be

The appeal of violent play

Recreational needs in an industrialized society

Games for dalliance and flirtation

repeated. When the majority had automobiles, the world changed.

THE GREAT BALL-PLAYING ERA

The great ball-game-playing period began around 1850 and continued until 1939. It began in the United States and England and spread rapidly throughout the world. For some undiscoverable reason the Anglo-Saxons had a penchant for games. Some regarded it as a virtue; others, as a fault. On the continent of Europe only the Dutch shared the Anglo-Saxon passion for games, and their contribution was to encourage ice sports.

Growth in schools and clubs. In England in the 19th century the stimulus for playing ball games came from the reformed public (private) boarding schools. Except for a few poor scholars, these schools in that century were strictly for the children of the ruling and landed classes. The laxity of morals and the wildness of behaviour among the leaders of society at the end of the 18th century and the beginning of the 19th had been reflected in these schools. They had become barbaric. When the pupils were not being flogged by often incompetent teachers, they were committing the most outrageous pranks or sins. For Victorian England these schools were a scandal, and few, if any, in a much more serious society doubted the need for reform.

One of the obvious areas of reform was the use of leisure time. So lax was the discipline in most of these schools that boys, except when actually in their classrooms, were left to their own devices. They were punished for their evil ways, but little or nothing was done to provide alternative employment. Games, organized games, were a solution. They were adopted with speed. *Mens sana in corpore sano* ("a healthy mind in a healthy body") became the watchwords. Long before the end of the century the schools had become production plants for Christian gentlemen, and their training came as much from the playing field as from the classroom. Some, including the popular author Rudyard Kipling, thought it went too far.

> Then ye returned to your trinkets; then ye contented your souls,
> With the flannelled fools at the wicket or the muddied oafs at the goals.

Although cricket, rugby, association football, and rowing were the chief recreations encouraged, other games found a seasonal place: swimming in the summer, rackets and fives in the newly built courts in the winter. Matches were soon being played against nearby clubs and other schools. Although transport was still slow, unless two schools were on the same railroad, quite long distances were covered. Soon, it appeared, it was more important for a boy to win his school colours at a major game or to get a "blue" at Oxford or Cambridge than it was to win a classical or literary prize or get a first class degree in his final examination.

It was not, however, only a time for school reform; it was a time of social reform. Many were sickened by the existences led by the industrial poor; many longed to make the lives of children healthier and happier. Games for them seemed an equally good idea, particularly to those social workers brought up in the public (private) schools. Football and cricket teams were formed everywhere—out of Sunday schools, out of boys' clubs, out of factories, villages, and towns. Toward the end of the century, local authorities provided playing spaces in public parks and recreation grounds. Playing leagues at all levels were formed: the great playing era had begun.

This period was the beginning of the age of professionalism, which was to reach its peak much later. Cricket had long had a few professionals: wagering matches had been played between them as early as the 18th century. Soon very few spectator games could hold out against the tide of professionalism as old-fashioned people wanted, although the amateur tradition died hard.

In the United States the rise of organized games on the East Coast came about the same time as it did in England. The fashions for lawn tennis, croquet, roller skating, and athletics swept the area. This was all the more surprising because before the 1860s, hardly anyone had been interested in playing organized outside games. The concern for health, an American preoccupation ever since, was a contributory factor, but primarily it was the result of the United States being one of the first to be caught up in a world-wide convention.

Cricket, even in the United States, had been an exception to the absence of organized games before 1850, but baseball was also starting on its road of popularity before that date through the formation of the Knickerbocker Baseball Club in the 1840s. Baseball soon ousted cricket from popular esteem, and after the Civil War the organization of the game with professional players began in earnest.

National and international organizations. As the playing of games spread throughout the world, national organization was followed by international. Soon the automobile, the ship, and finally the airplane were carrying teams everywhere. The Imperial Cricket Conference was founded in 1909, although the first international match between England and Australia had been played as early as 1877. The international organizing body for association football, the Fédération Internationale de Football Association, began in 1904 with headquarters in Switzerland. The International Lawn Tennis Federation was founded in 1912. Some national games such as the immensely popular baseball and American football, however, remained curiously isolated from international competition.

Gambling and betting. Games have been associated throughout their history with gambling and betting. Playing ball games for money stakes has been very limited and is associated chiefly with pioneering days and in Europe with the wild behaviour of the 18th century. Once games were organized they were remarkably free from influence likely to have a bad effect on the games themselves.

The money that is made out of betting on the results of games, however, is a different matter. In Great Britain, association football (soccer) pools have come to resemble national lotteries in terms of the numbers of bettors and the amounts bet. Instead of buying a number, however, the bettor selects winning or other teams. There is much betting on the outcomes of baseball, football, and basketball games in the United States, including both professional and college football and basketball pools—all of it illegal. The popularity of the games has decreed that they should be used in this way.

DECLINE OF GAMES

In spite of the great boost given by the airplane to international and professional spectator and exhibition play, there was a steady decline in game playing and watching after World War II. Even the women who had played many games enthusiastically between the wars no longer found in a new generation the same compulsions that had seemed so strong in the 1920s and 30s. The facts of the situation were concealed by the enormous coverage given by the press and television to the best teams and the most important matches. It was possible therefore, to have an intimate knowledge of the performances of celebrated players and clubs without ever participating as a player or a spectator. There was still an immense following for games, but largely they had become gladiatorial contests viewed on television screens in the afternoons and evenings.

Large clubs vs. small. So the very large clubs prospered, supported by television rights and the great number of people who will always go to see the best. In Europe there was no end to this kind of entertainment in the association football season. If there was no international match to be watched, there were plenty of international meetings between clubs of different countries playing one another in one of the many competitions started since World War II. Soon armchair spectators knew almost as much of players in other countries as they did of their own.

Meanwhile, the smaller clubs lost members and could hardly recall the days when they played before a sizable

Role of the English public schools

Beginnings of professionalism

Focus on best teams and most important matches

crowd. Many were in serious financial trouble and were struggling to continue in the leagues. It was not hard to discover where the players and spectators had gone. Masses of them were watching star-class players and teams. In addition, relative affluence and the automobile meant for millions of others a new interest in going places. The richer half of the world was on wheels for the day or for the weekend. And if they were not on wheels, they were in the skies visiting foreign countries as a matter of course. London, Paris, Athens, Rome, New York, San Francisco, and Tokyo were available to more people than the available hotels and campsites could accommodate. Youth, too, was mobile as never before; they had something better to do, they thought, than to play games.

The game-conscious world. Nevertheless, several games enjoyed greater popularity in the second half of the 20th century than ever before. Chief among these was golf. Aided by the television cameras to promote interest in the game, the new wealth, the social side in the club house, the individual as well as the team spirit, the fact that the handicapping system made it practically never too late to learn or a player too old to continue, the possibility of a wife and husband belonging to the same club and having something to do in early retirement—all these in aggregate made it possible for golf to meet the needs of a large number of people. Moreover, the professionals, when they were followed on the course, were watched by the most experienced and most willing-to-learn crowd in history.

And for many there was still the winter and what to do with the long hours of darkness. Basketball and bowling gained players and spectators. Skiing and other winter sports attracted new millions. Badminton, squash rackets, and table tennis continued to appeal to millions for keeping fit, making social contacts, and defeating boredom. Just as association football had swept Latin-American countries as well as all Europe, so the games of table tennis and badminton appealed strongly to millions in China, Malaysia, Indonesia, and Japan. All the world was games conscious in the last quarter of the 20th century, but all the world was not playing so enthusiastically as 50 years before.

BIBLIOGRAPHY. No books deal specifically with the area covered in the above article; see the bibliographies of individual games for up-to-date historical surveys. F.R. DULLES, *America Learns to Play* (1959), is a unique account of one nation's recreational history. Similarly, J. STRUTT, *Sports and Pastimes of the People of England . . .* (1801 and later editions), provides the most comprehensive description of games played in England before 1800. For background including pictorial reference, G.M. TREVELYAN, *Illustrated English Social History*, 4 vol. (1949), should be consulted. *C.B. Fry's Magazine of Sports and Outdoor Life* (1904–17), recaptures at its height the enthusiasm for games at the beginning of the 20th century. Of the many distinguished books on the histories of individual games, M.D. WHITMAN, *Tennis Origins and Mysteries* (1932), packs a good deal of information into a small compass.

(J.Ar.)

Gandhi, Mahatma

Mohandas Karamchand Gandhi, the preeminent leader of Indian nationalism and the prophet of nonviolence in the 20th century, was born, the youngest child of his father's fourth wife, on October 2, 1869, at Porbandar, the capital of a small principality in Gujarāt in western India under British suzerainty. His father, Karamchand Gandhi, who was the dewan (chief minister) of Porbandar, did not have much in the way of a formal education but was an able administrator who knew how to steer his way between the capricious princes, their long suffering subjects, and the headstrong British political officers in power.

Gandhi's mother, Putlibai, was completely absorbed in religion, did not care much for finery and jewelry, divided her time between her home and the temple, fasted frequently, and wore herself out in days and nights of nursing whenever there was sickness in the family. Mohandas grew up in a home steeped in Vaiṣṇavism—worship of the Hindu god Viṣṇu (Vishnu)—with a strong tinge of Jainism, a morally rigorous Indian religion, whose chief tenets are nonviolence and the belief that everything in the universe is eternal. Thus he took for granted *ahiṃsā* (noninjury to all living beings), vegetarianism, fasting for self-purification, and mutual tolerance between adherents of various creeds and sects.

Margaret Bourke-White, LIFE MAGAZINE © TIME INC·

Gandhi, 1946.

Youth. The educational facilities at Porbandar were rudimentary; in the primary school that Mohandas attended the children wrote the alphabet in the dust with their fingers. Luckily for him, his father became dewan of Rājkot, another princely state. Though he occasionally won prizes and scholarships at the local schools, his record was on the whole mediocre. One of the terminal reports rated him as "good at English, fair in Arithmetic and weak in Geography; conduct very good, bad handwriting." A diffident child, he was married at the age of 13 and thus lost a year at school. He shone neither in the classroom nor on the playing field. He loved to go out on long solitary walks when he was not nursing his by now ailing father or helping his mother with her household chores.

He had learned, in his words, "to carry out the orders of the elders, not to scan them." With such extreme passivity, it is not surprising that he should have gone through a phase of adolescent rebellion, marked by secret atheism, petty thefts, furtive smoking—and most shocking of all for a boy born in a Vaiṣṇava family—meat eating. His adolescence was probably no stormier than that of most children of his age and class. What was extraordinary was the way his youthful transgressions ended.

"Never again," was his promise to himself after each escapade. And he kept his promise. Beneath an unprepossessing exterior he concealed a burning passion for self-improvement that led him to take even the heroes of Hindu mythology, such as Prahlāda and Hariścandra—legendary embodiments of truthfulness and sacrifice—as living models.

In 1887 Mohandas scraped through the matriculation examination of the University of Bombay and joined Samaldas College in Bhavnagar (Bhaunagar). As he had suddenly to switch from his native language—Gujarati—to English, he found it rather difficult to follow the lectures.

Meanwhile, his family was debating his future. Left to himself, he would have liked to be a doctor. But besides the Vaiṣṇava prejudice against vivisection, it was clear that if he was to keep up the family tradition of holding high office in one of the states in Gujarāt, he would have to qualify as a barrister. This meant a visit to England, and Mohandas, who was not too happy at Samaldas College, jumped at the proposal. His youthful imagination

Education

conceived England as "a land of philosophers and poets, the very centre of civilization." But there were several hurdles to be crossed before the visit to England could be realized. His father had left very little property; moreover, his mother was reluctant to expose her youngest child to unknown temptations and dangers in a distant land. But Mohandas was determined to visit England. One of his brothers succeeded in raising the necessary money, and his mother's doubts were allayed when he took a vow that while away from home, he would not touch wine, women, or meat. Mohandas disregarded the last obstacle, the decree of the leaders of the Medh Bania caste, to which the Gandhis belonged, who forbade his trip to England as a violation of the Hindu religion, and sailed in September 1888. Ten days after his arrival he joined the Inner Temple, one of the four London law colleges.

Law studies

England. Gandhi took his studies seriously and tried to brush up on his English and Latin by taking the London University matriculation examination. But during the three years he spent in England, his main preoccupation was with personal and moral issues rather than with academic ambitions. The transition from the half-rural atmosphere of Rājkot to the cosmopolitan life of London was not easy for him. As he struggled painfully to adapt himself to Western food, dress, and etiquette, he felt awkward. His vegetarianism became a continual source of embarrassment to him; his friends warned him that it would wreck his studies as well as his health. Fortunately for him he came across a vegetarian restaurant as well as a book providing a reasoned defense of vegetarianism, which henceforth became a matter of conviction for him, not merely a legacy of his Vaiṣṇava background. The missionary zeal he developed for vegetarianism helped to draw the pitifully shy youth out of his shell and gave him a new poise. He became a member of the executive committee of the London Vegetarian Society, attending its conferences and contributing articles to its journal.

In the vegetarian restaurants and boarding houses of England, Gandhi met not only food faddists but some earnest men and women to whom he owed his introduction to the Bible, and the *Bhagavadgītā*, the most popular expression of Hinduism in the form of a philosophical poem, which he read for the first time in its English translation by Sir Edwin Arnold. The English vegetarians were a motley crowd. They included socialists and humanitarians like Edward Carpenter, "the British Thoreau"; Fabians like George Bernard Shaw; and Theosophists like Annie Besant. Most of them were idealists, quite a few were rebels who rejected the prevailing values of the late Victorian Establishment, denounced the evils of the capitalist and industrial society, preached the cult of the simple life, and stressed the superiority of moral over material values and of cooperation over conflict. These ideas were to contribute substantially to the shaping of Gandhi's personality and, eventually, to his politics.

Return to India

Painful surprises were in store for Gandhi when he returned to India in July 1891. His mother had died in his absence, and he discovered to his dismay that the barrister's degree was not an open sesame to a lucrative career. The legal profession was already beginning to be overcrowded, and Gandhi was much too diffident to elbow his way into it. In the very first brief he argued in a Bombay court, he cut a sorry figure. Turned down even for the part-time job of a teacher in a Bombay high school, he returned to Rājkot to make a modest living by drafting petitions for litigants. Even this employment was closed to him when he incurred the displeasure of a local British officer. It was, therefore, with some relief that he accepted the none-too-attractive offer of a year's contract from an Indian firm in Natal, South Africa.

South Africa. Africa was to present to Gandhi challenges and opportunities that he could hardly have conceived. In a Durban court, he was asked by the European magistrate to take off his turban; he refused, and left the courtroom. A few days later, while travelling to Pretoria, he was unceremoniously thrown out of a first-class railway compartment and left shivering and brooding at Pietermaritzburg Station; in the further course of the journey he was beaten up by the white driver of a stagecoach because he would not travel on the footboard to make room for a European passenger; and finally he was barred from hotels reserved "for Europeans only." These humiliations were the daily lot of Indian traders and labourers in Natal who had learned to pocket them with the same resignation with which they pocketed their meagre earnings. What was new was not Gandhi's experience, but his reaction. He had so far not been conspicuous for self-assertion or aggressiveness. But something happened to him as he smarted under the insults heaped upon him. In retrospect the journey from Durban to Pretoria struck him as one of the most creative experiences of his life; it was his moment of truth. Henceforth he would not accept injustice as part of the natural or unnatural order in South Africa; he would defend his dignity as an Indian and as a man.

Reaction to segregation

While in Pretoria, Gandhi studied the conditions in which his countrymen lived and tried to educate them on their rights and duties, but he had no intention of staying on in South Africa. Indeed, in June 1894, as his year's contract drew to a close, he was back in Durban, ready to sail for India. At a farewell party given in his honour he happened to glance through the *Natal Mercury* and learned that the Natal Legislative Assembly was considering a bill to deprive Indians of the right to vote. "This is the first nail in our coffin," Gandhi told his hosts. They professed their inability to oppose the bill, and indeed their ignorance of the politics of the colony, and begged him to take up the fight on their behalf.

Until the age of 18, Gandhi had hardly ever read a newspaper. Neither as a student in England nor as a budding barrister in India had he evinced much interest in politics. Indeed, he was overcome by a terrifying stage fright whenever he stood up to read a speech at a social gathering or to defend a client in court. Nevertheless, in July 1894, when he was barely 25, he blossomed almost overnight into a proficient political campaigner. He drafted petitions to the Natal legislature and the British government and had them signed by hundreds of his compatriots. He could not prevent the passage of the bill but succeeded in drawing the attention of the public and the press in Natal, India, and England to the Natal Indians' grievances. He was persuaded to settle down in Durban to practice law and to organize the Indian community. In 1894, he founded the Natal Indian Congress of which he himself became the indefatigable secretary. Through this common political organization, he infused a spirit of solidarity in the heterogeneous Indian community. He flooded the government, the legislature, and the press with closely reasoned statements of Indian grievances. Finally, he exposed to the view of the outside world the skeleton in the imperial cupboard, the discrimination practiced against the Indian subjects of Queen Victoria in one of her own colonies in Africa. It was a measure of his success as a publicist that such important newspapers as *The Times* of London and the *Statesman* and *Englishman* of Calcutta editorially commented on the Natal Indians' grievances.

In 1896 Gandhi went to India to fetch his wife Kasturbai and their children and to canvass support for the Indians overseas. He met prominent leaders and persuaded them to address public meetings in the country's principal cities. Unfortunately for him, garbled versions of his activities and utterances reached Natal and inflamed its European population. On landing at Durban in January 1897, he was assaulted and nearly lynched by a white mob. Joseph Chamberlain, the colonial secretary in the British Cabinet, cabled the government of Natal to bring the guilty men to book, but Gandhi refused to prosecute his assailants. It was, he said, a principle with him not to seek redress of a personal wrong in a court of law.

Role in the Boer War

Gandhi was not the man to nurse a grudge. On the outbreak of the Boer War in 1899, he argued that the Indians, who claimed the full rights of citizenship in the British crown colony of Natal, were in duty bound to defend it. He raised an ambulance corps of 1,100 volunteers, out of whom 300 were free Indians and the rest indentured labourers. It was a motley crowd: barristers and accountants, artisans and labourers. It was Gandhi's task to instill in them a spirit of service to those whom they regarded as their oppressors. The editor of the *Pretoria News* has left a fascinating pen portrait of Gandhi in the battle zone:

> After a night's work which had shattered men with much bigger frames, I came across Gandhi in the early morning sitting by the roadside eating a regulation army biscuit. Every man in (General) Buller's force was dull and depressed, and damnation was heartily invoked on everything. But Gandhi was stoical in his bearing, cheerful and confident in his conversation and had a kindly eye.

The British victory in the Boer War brought little relief to the Indians in South Africa. The new regime in South Africa was to blossom into a partnership, but only between Boers and Britons. Gandhi saw that, with the exception of a few Christian missionaries and youthful idealists, he had been unable to make a perceptible impression upon the South African Europeans. In 1906 the Transvaal government published a particularly humiliating ordinance for the registration of its Indian population. The Indians held a mass protest meeting at Johannesburg in September 1906 and, under Gandhi's leadership, took a pledge to defy the ordinance if it became law in the teeth of their opposition, and to suffer all the penalties resulting from their defiance. Thus was born Satyagraha ("firmness in truth"), a new technique for redressing wrongs through inviting, rather than inflicting, suffering, for resisting the adversary without rancour and fighting him without violence.

The Satyagraha struggle in South Africa lasted for more than seven years. It had its ups and downs, but under Gandhi's leadership, the small Indian minority kept up its resistance against heavy odds. Hundreds of Indians chose to sacrifice their livelihood and liberty rather than submit to laws repugnant to their conscience and self-respect. In the final phase of the movement in 1913, hundreds of Indians, including women, went to jail, and thousands of Indian workers who had struck work in the mines bravely faced imprisonment, flogging, and even shooting. It was a terrible ordeal for the Indians, but it was also the worst possible advertisement for the South African government, which, under pressure from the governments of Britain and India, accepted a compromise negotiated by Gandhi on the one hand and the South African statesman General Jan Christiaan Smuts on the other.

"The saint has left our shores," Smuts wrote to a friend on Gandhi's departure from South Africa for India, in July 1914, "I hope for ever." Twenty-five years later, he wrote that it had been his "fate to be the antagonist of a man for whom even then I had the highest respect." Once, during his not infrequent stays in jail, Gandhi had prepared a pair of sandals for Smuts, who recalled that there was no hatred and personal ill-feeling between them, and when the fight was over, "there was the atmosphere in which a decent peace could be concluded."

As later events were to show, Gandhi's work did not provide an enduring solution for the Indian problem in South Africa. What he did to South Africa was indeed less important than what South Africa did to him. It had not treated him kindly, but by drawing him into the vortex of its racial problem, it had provided him with the ideal setting in which his peculiar talents could unfold themselves.

The religious quest. Gandhi's religious quest dated back to his childhood, the influence of his mother and of his home at Porbandar and Rājkot, but it received a great impetus after his arrival in South Africa. His Quaker friends in Pretoria failed to convert him to Christianity, but they quickened his appetite for religious studies. He was fascinated by Tolstoy's writings on Christianity, read the Qu'rān in translation, and delved into Hindu scriptures and philosophy. The study of comparative religion, talks with scholars, and his own reading of theological works brought him to the conclusion that all religions were true and yet every one of them was imperfect because they were "interpreted with poor intellects, sometimes with poor hearts, and more often misinterpreted."

Rajchandra, a brilliant young philosopher who became Gandhi's spiritual mentor, convinced him of "the subtlety and profundity" of Hinduism, the religion of his birth. And it was the *Bhagavadgītā*, which Gandhi had first read in London, that became his "spiritual dictionary" and exercised probably the greatest single influence on his life. Two Sanskrit words in the *Gita* particularly fascinated him. One was *aparigraha* (nonpossession), which implied that man had to jettison the material goods that cramped the life of the spirit and to shake off the bonds of money and property. The other was *samabhava* (equability), which enjoined him to remain unruffled by pain or pleasure, victory or defeat, and work without hope of success or fear of failure.

Return to Hinduism

These were not merely counsels of perfection. In the civil case that had brought him to South Africa in 1893, he had persuaded the antagonists to settle their differences out of court. The true function of a lawyer seemed to him "to unite parties riven asunder." He soon regarded his clients not as purchasers of his services but as friends; they consulted him not only on legal issues, but on such matters as the best way of weaning a baby or balancing the family budget. When an associate protested that clients came even on Sundays, Gandhi replied: "A man in distress cannot have Sunday rest."

Gandhi's legal earnings reached a peak figure of £5,-000 a year, but he had little interest in money making and his savings were often sunk in his public activities. In Durban, and later in Johannesburg, he kept an open table; his house was a virtual hostel for younger colleagues and political co-workers. This was something of an ordeal for his wife, without whose extraordinary patience, endurance, and self-effacement, Gandhi could hardly have devoted himself to public causes. As he broke through the conventional bonds of family and property, their life tended to shade into a community life.

Gandhi felt an irresistible attraction to a life of simplicity, manual labour, and austerity. In 1904, after reading John Ruskin's *Unto This Last*, a critique of capitalism, he set up a farm at Phoenix near Durban where he and his friends could literally live by the sweat of their brow. Six years later another colony grew up under Gandhi's fostering care near Johannesburg; it was named Tolstoy Farm after the Russian writer and moralist, whom Gandhi admired and corresponded with. Those two settlements were the precursors of the more famous *āśramas* in India, at Sābarmati near Ahmadābād (Ahmadābād), and at Sevagram near Wardha.

South Africa had not only prompted Gandhi to evolve a novel technique for political action but also transformed him into a leader of men by freeing him from bonds that make cowards of most men. "Persons in power," Professor Gilbert Murray prophetically wrote about Gandhi in the *Hibbert Journal* in 1918, "should be very careful how they deal with a man who cares nothing for sensual pleasure, nothing for riches, nothing for comfort or praise, or promotion, but is simply determined to do what he believes to be right. He is a dangerous and uncomfortable enemy, because his body which you can always conquer gives you so little purchase upon his soul."

Emergence as leader of nationalist India. From 1915 to 1918, Gandhi seemed to hover uncertainly on the periphery of Indian politics, declining to join any political agitation, supporting the British war-effort in World War I, and even recruiting soldiers for the British Indian Army. At the same time, he did not flinch from criticizing the British officials for any acts of high-handedness or from taking up the grievances of the long-suffering peasantry in Bihār and Gujarāt. Not until February 1919, provoked by the British insistence on pushing through the Rowlatt Bills, which empowered the authorities to imprison without trial those suspected of sedition, in the teeth of Indian opposition, did Gandhi reveal a sense of estrangement from the British Raj. He announced a Satyagraha struggle. The result was a virtual political earthquake that shook the subcontinent in the spring of

1919. The violent outbreaks that followed—leading, among other incidents, to the killing by British soldiers of nearly 400 Indians attending a meeting at Amritsar in the Punjab (Pañjāb) and the enactment of martial law—prompted him to stay his hand. But within a year he was again in a militant mood, having in the meantime been irrevocably alienated by British insensitiveness to Indian feeling on the Punjab tragedy and Muslim resentment on the peace terms offered to Turkey following World War I.

By the autumn of 1920, Gandhi was the dominant figure on the political stage, commanding an influence never attained by any political leader in India or perhaps in any other country. He refashioned the 35-year-old Indian National Congress into an effective political instrument of Indian nationalism: from a three-day Christmas week picnic of the upper middle-class in one of the principal cities of India, it became a mass organization with its roots in small towns and villages. Gandhi's message was simple; it was not British guns but imperfections of Indians themselves that kept their country in bondage. His program of nonviolent noncooperation with the British government included boycott not only of British manufactures but of institutions operated or aided by the British in India: legislatures, courts, offices, schools. This program electrified the country, broke the spell of fear of foreign rule, and led to arrests of thousands of Satyagrahis, who defied laws and cheerfully lined up for prison. In February 1922, the movement seemed to be on the crest of a rising wave, but alarmed by a violent outbreak in Chauri Chaura, a remote village in eastern India, Gandhi decided to call off mass civil disobedience. This was a blow to many of his followers who feared that his self-imposed restraints and scruples would reduce the nationalist struggle to pious futility. Gandhi himself was arrested on March 10, 1922, tried for sedition, and sentenced to six years' imprisonment. He was released in February 1924, after an operation for appendicitis. The political landscape had changed in his absence. The Congress party had split into two factions, one under Chitta Ranjan Das and Motilal Nehru (the father of Jawaharlal Nehru, India's first prime minister) favouring the entry of the party into legislatures, and the other, under C. Rajagopalachari and Vallabhbhai Jhaverbhai Patel, opposing it. Worst of all, the unity between Hindus and Muslims of the heyday of the noncooperation movement of 1920–22 had dissolved. Gandhi tried to draw the warring communities out of their suspicion and fanaticism by reasoning and persuasion. And finally, after a serious communal outbreak, he undertook a three weeks' fast in the autumn of 1924 to arouse the people into following the path of nonviolence.

During the mid-'twenties Gandhi took little interest in active politics and was considered a spent force. But in 1927, the British government appointed a constitutional reform commission under Sir John Simon, a prominent English lawyer and politician, that did not contain a single Indian. When the Congress and other parties boycotted the commission, the political tempo rose. After the Calcutta Congress in December 1928, where Gandhi moved the crucial resolution demanding dominion status from the British government within a year under threat of a nation-wide nonviolent campaign for complete independence, Gandhi was back at the helm of the Congress Party. In March 1930, he launched the Satyagraha against the tax on salt, which affected the poorest section of the community. One of the most spectacular and successful campaigns in Gandhi's nonviolent war against the British Raj, it resulted in the imprisonment of more than 60,000 persons. A year later, after talks with Lord Irwin, Gandhi accepted a truce, called off civil disobedience, and agreed to attend the Round Table Conference in London as the sole representative of the Indian National Congress. The conference, which concentrated on the problem of the Indian minorities rather than on the transfer of power from the British, was a great disappointment to the Indian nationalists. Moreover, when Gandhi returned to India in December 1931 he found his party facing an all-out offensive from Lord Irwin's successor, Lord Willingdon, who unleashed the sternest repression in the his-

tory of the nationalist movement against it. Gandhi was once more imprisoned, and the government tried to insulate him from the outside world and to destroy his influence. This was not an easy task. Gandhi soon regained the initiative; in September 1932, while still a prisoner, he embarked on a fast to protest against the British government's decision to segregate the untouchables (the depressed classes) by allotting them separate electorates in the new constitution. The fast produced an emotional upheaval in the country; an alternative electoral arrangement was jointly and speedily devised by the leaders of the Hindu community and the untouchables and endorsed by the British government. The fast became the starting point of a vigorous campaign for the removal of the disabilities of the untouchables whom Gandhi renamed Harijans, "the children of God."

In 1934 Gandhi resigned not only as the leader but also as a member of the Congress Party. He had come to believe that its leading members had adopted nonviolence as a political expedient and not as the fundamental creed it was for him. In place of political activity he now concentrated on his "constructive programme" of building the nation "from the bottom up"—educating rural India, which accounted for 85 percent of the population; continuing his fight against untouchability; promoting handspinning, weaving, and other cottage industries to supplement the earnings of the underemployed peasantry; and evolving a system of education best suited to the needs of the people. Gandhi himself went to live at Sevagram, a village in central India, which became the centre of his program of social and economic uplift.

The last phase. With the outbreak of World War II, the nationalist struggle in India entered its last crucial phase. Gandhi hated fascism and all it stood for, but he also hated war. The Indian National Congress, on the other hand, was not committed to pacifism and was prepared to support the British war effort if Indian self-government was assured. Once more Gandhi became politically active. The failure of the mission of Sir Stafford Cripps, a British cabinet minister, who came to India in March 1942 with an offer that Gandhi found unacceptable, the British equivocation on the transfer of power to Indian hands, and the encouragement given by high British officials to conservative and communal forces promoting discord between Muslims and Hindus impelled him to demand in the summer of 1942 an immediate British withdrawal from India. The war against the Axis, particularly Japan, was in a critical phase; the British reacted sharply by imprisoning the entire Congress leadership and set out to crush the party once for all. The popular reaction was one of shock and indignation; there were violent outbreaks that were sternly suppressed; the gulf between Britain and India became wider than ever.

A new chapter in Indo-British relations opened with the victory of the Labour Party in 1945. During the next two years, there were prolonged triangular negotiations between leaders of the Congress and the Muslim League under M.A. Jinnah and the British government culminating in the Mountbatten Plan of June 3, 1947, and the formation of the two new dominions of India and Pakistan in mid-August 1947.

It was one of the greatest disappointments of Gandhi's life that Indian freedom was realized without Indian unity. Muslim separatism had received a great boost while Gandhi and his colleagues were in jail, and in 1946–47, as the final constitutional arrangements were being negotiated, the outbreak of communal riots between Hindus and Muslims unhappily created a climate in which Gandhi's appeals to reason and justice, tolerance and trust had little chance. When partition of the subcontinent was accepted—against his advice—he threw himself heart and soul into the task of healing the scars of the communal conflict, toured the riot-torn areas in Bengal and Bihār, admonished the bigots, consoled the victims, and tried to rehabilitate the refugees. In the atmosphere of that period, surcharged with suspicion and hatred, this was a difficult and heart-breaking task. Gandhi was blamed by partisans of both the communities.

Massacre at Amritsar

Return to party leadership

Partition of British India

When persuasion failed, he went on a fast. He won at least two spectacular triumphs; in September 1947 his fasting stopped the rioting in Calcutta, and in January 1948, he shamed the city of Delhi into a communal truce. A few days later, on January 30, while he was on his way to his evening prayer meeting in Delhi, he was shot down by a young Hindu fanatic.

Place in history. The British attitude to Gandhi was one of mingled admiration, amusement, bewilderment, suspicion, and resentment. Except for a tiny minority of Christian missionaries and radical socialists, the British tended to see in him at best a utopian visionary, at worst a cunning hypocrite, whose professions of friendship for the British race were a mask for subversion of the British Raj. Gandhi was conscious of the existence of this wall of prejudice, and it was part of the strategy of Satyagraha to penetrate it.

His three major campaigns in 1920–22, 1930–34, and 1940–42 were well designed to engender that process of self-doubt and questioning that was to undermine the moral defences of his adversaries, and to contribute, together with the objective realities of the post-war world, to produce the grant of dominion status in 1947. The British abdication in India was the first step in the liquidation of the British Empire on the continents of Asia and Africa. Gandhi's image as an archrebel died hard but, as it had done to the memory of Washington, Britain, in 1969, the centenary year of Gandhi's birth, erected a statue to his memory.

Gandhi had critics in his own country, and indeed in his own party. The liberal leaders protested that he was going too fast; the young radicals complained that he was not going fast enough; left-wing politicians alleged that he was not serious about evicting the British or liquidating such vested Indian interests as princes and landlords; the leaders of the untouchables doubted his good faith as a social reformer; and Muslim leaders accused him of partiality to his own community.

Recent research has established Gandhi's role as a great mediator and reconciler. His talents in this direction were applied to conflicts between the older moderate politicians and the young radicals, the political terrorists and the parliamentarians, the urban intelligentsia and the rural masses, the traditionalists and the modernists, the caste Hindus and the untouchables, the Hindus and the Muslims, and the Indians and the British.

Primacy of religion

It was inevitable that Gandhi's role as a political leader should loom larger in public imagination, but the mainsprings of his life lay in religion, not in politics. And religion for him did not mean formalism, dogma, ritual, or sectarianism. "What I have been striving and pining to achieve these thirty years," he wrote in his autobiography, "is to see God face to face." His deepest strivings were spiritual, but unlike many of his countrymen with such aspirations, he did not retire to a cave in the Himalayas to meditate on the Absolute; he carried his cave, as he once said, within him. For him truth was not something to be discovered in the privacy of one's personal life; it had to be upheld in the challenging contexts of social and political life.

In the eyes of millions of his countrymen, he was the Mahatma (the great soul). The unthinking adoration of the huge crowds that gathered to see him all along his route made his tours a severe ordeal; he could hardly work during the day or rest at night. "The woes of the Mahatmas," he wrote, "are known only to the Mahatmas."

Gandhi won the affection and loyalty of gifted men and women, old and young, with vastly dissimilar talents and temperaments; of Europeans of every religious persuasion; and of Indians of almost every political line. Few of his political colleagues went all the way with him and accepted nonviolence as a creed; fewer still shared his food fads, his interest in mudpacks and nature cure, or his prescription of *brahmacarya*, complete renunciation of the pleasures of the flesh.

Gandhi's ideas on sex may sound quaint and unscientific. His early marriage at the age of 13 seems to have complicated his attitude to sex and charged it with feelings of guilt, but it is important to remember that total sublimation, according to the best tradition of Hindu thought, is indispensable for those who seek self-realization, and *brahmacarya* was for Gandhi part of a larger discipline in food, sleep, thought, prayer, and daily activity designed to equip himself for service of the causes to which he was totally committed. What he failed to see was that his own unique experience was no guide for the common run of mankind.

It is probably too early to judge Gandhi's place in history. He was the catalyst if not the initiator of three of the major revolutions of the 20th century: the revolutions against colonialism, racism, and violence. He wrote copiously; the collected edition of his writings may run to 80 volumes.

Much of what he wrote was in response to the needs of his co-workers and disciples and the exigencies of the political situation, but on fundamentals, he maintained a remarkable consistency, as is evident from the *Hind Swaraj* ("Indian Home Rule") published in South Africa in 1909. The strictures on Western materialism and colonialism, the reservations about industrialism and urbanization, the distrust of the modern state, and the total rejection of violence that was expressed in this book seemed romantic, if not reactionary, to the pre-World War I generation in India and the West, which had not known the shocks of two global wars, experienced the phenomenon of Hitler, and the trauma of the atom bomb. Prime Minister Jawaharlal Nehru's objective of promoting a just and egalitarian order at home, and nonalignment with military blocs abroad doubtless owed much to Gandhi, but neither he nor his colleagues in the Indian nationalist movement wholly accepted the Gandhian models in politics and economics.

In recent years Gandhi's name has been invoked by the organizers of numerous demonstrations and movements, but with a few outstanding exceptions—such as those of his disciple the land reformer Vinoba Bhave in India and the black civil rights leader Martin Luther King, Jr., in the United States—these movements have been a travesty of the ideas of Gandhi.

Yet Gandhi will probably never lack champions. Erik H. Erikson, a distinguished American psychoanalyst, in his recent work on Gandhi senses "an affinity between Gandhi's truth and the insights of modern psychology." One of the greatest admirers of Gandhi was Albert Einstein, who saw in Gandhi's nonviolence a possible antidote to the massive violence unleashed by the fission of the atom. And Gunnar Myrdal, the Swedish economist, after his survey of the socio-economic problems of the underdeveloped world, has pronounced Gandhi "in practically all fields an enlightened liberal." In a time of deepening crisis in the underdeveloped world, of social malaise in the affluent societies, of the shadow of unbridled technology and the precarious peace of nuclear terror, it seems likely that Gandhi's ideas and techniques will become increasingly relevant.

BIBLIOGRAPHY. Gandhi's autobiography, *The Story of My Experiments with Truth*, 2 vol. (1927–29), tells the story of his life up to 1921; "Satyagraha in South Africa," a pamphlet issued by the Ministry of Information and Broadcasting of India (1928), illuminates the formative two decades he spent in South Africa. The *Collected Works of Mahatma Gandhi*, 40 vol. (1958–), covers the period up to May 1929, and will eventually include all his writings, speeches, and letters.

A biography by PYARELAL, Gandhi's former Secretary, *Mahatma Gandhi*, 2nd ed., 2 vol. (1965–66), provides a richly documented chronicle of Gandhi's early and last years. D.G. TENDULKAR, *Mahatma*, rev. ed., 8 vol. (1960–63), tells the story of Gandhi's life mostly in Gandhi's own words extracted from his published writings. LOUIS FISCHER, *The Life of Mahatma Gandhi* (1950), is based largely on printed sources but includes the author's vivid personal impressions of Gandhi and India in the 1940s; B.R. NANDA, *Mahatma Gandhi: A Biography* (1958), a story of Gandhi's life as well as a critique of his thought, makes use of unpublished government records and correspondence of Gandhi. H.S.L. POLAK, H.M. BRAILSFORD, and LORD PETHICK-LAWRENCE, *Mahatma Gandhi* (1949), is a good introduction for western readers. HORACE ALEXANDER, *Gandhi Through Western Eyes* (1969);

and GEOFFREY ASHE, *Gandhi: A Study in Revolution* (1968), are sympathetic and analytical studies. ROBERT PAYNE, *The Life and Death of Mahatma Gandhi* (1969), is a readable account, with emphasis on the personal rather than political aspect.

CHANDRAN D.S. DEVANESON, *The Making of the Mahatma* (1969), covers Gandhi's childhood and youth in detail. A vivid glimpse of Gandhi in his late thirties may be found in J.J. DOKE, *M.K. Gandhi: An Indian Patriot in South Africa* (1909, reprinted 1967). E.H. ERIKSON, *Gandhi's Truth: On the Origins of Militant Nonviolence* (1969), illuminates Gandhi's life and technique by bringing to bear on them the insights of psychoanalysis.

Among the books containing reminiscences of Gandhi, the more important are: M.G. POLAK, *Mr. Gandhi: The Man* (1931); JAWAHARLAL NEHRU, *An Autobiography* (1936); S. RADHAKRISHNAN (ed.), *Mahatma Gandhi: Esays and Reflections of his Life and Work*, 2nd ed. (1949); CHANDRASHANKER SHUKLA (ed.), *Incidents of Gandhiji's Life* (1949); NIRMAL KUMAR BOSE, *My Days with Gandhi* (1953); E.S. JONES, *Mahatma Gandhi: An Interpretation* (1948); and VINCENT SHEEAN, *Lead, Kindly Light* (1949).

Among the books highly critical of Gandhi may be mentioned: B.R. AMBEDKAR, *What Congress and Gandhi Have Done to the Untouchables* (1945); SIR SANKARAN NAIR, *Gandhi and Anarchy* (1922); and I. YAJNIK, *Gandhi As I Know Him*, rev. ed. (1943).

There are numerous anthologies of Gandhi's writings. *Selected Writings of Mahatma Gandhi* (1951), by RONALD DUNCAN; and *All Men Are Brothers* (1959), published by UNESCO, are judicious selections for the general reader.

(B.R.N.)

Ganges River

The great river of the North Indian plains is officially as well as popularly called the Ganga, both in Hindi and in other Indian languages. Internationally, however, it is known by its anglicized name, the Ganges. From time immemorial it has been the holy river of the Hindus. For most of its course it is a wide and sluggish stream, flowing through one of the most fertile and densely populated tracts of territory in the world. Despite its importance, its length of 1,557 miles (2,506 kilometres) makes it only the 15th longest river in Asia, and the 39th longest river in the world.

Rising in the Himalayas and emptying into the Bay of Bengal, it drains a quarter of the territory of India, while its basin supports a concentration of about 300,000,000 people, a population larger than that of any state on earth with the exceptions of China and India. The Gangetic Plain, across which it flows, is the heartland of the region known as Hindustān and has been the cradle of successive civilizations from the Kingdom of Aśoka in the 3rd century BC, down to the Mughul Empire, founded in the 16th century.

For most of its course the Ganges flows through Indian territory, although its large delta in the Bengal area, lies mostly in Bangladesh. The general direction of the river's flow is from north-northwest to southeast. At its delta, the flow is generally southward.

Physiography. The Ganges rises in the southern Himalayas on the Indian side of the Tibet border. Its five headstreams—the Bhāgirathi, the Alaknanda, the Mandakini, the Dhauli Ganga, and the Pindar—all rise in the Uttarkhand division of the state of Uttar Pradesh. Of these, the two main headstreams are the Alaknanda (the longer of the two), which rises about 30 miles north of the Himalayan peak of Nanda Devi, and the Bhāgirathi, which originates about 10,000 feet above sea level in an ice cave at the foot of the Himalayan glacier known as Gangotri. Gangotri itself is a sacred place for Hindu pilgrimage. The true source of the Ganges, however, is considered to be at Gaumukh, about 13 miles south of Gangotri.

After the Alaknanda and Bhāgirathi unite at Devaprayāg, they form a main stream known as the Ganga, which cuts through the outer (southern) Himalayas to emerge from the mountains at Rishikesh. It then flows onto the plain at Hardwār, a place that is held sacred by the Hindus.

Although there is a seasonal variation in the river's flow, its volume increases markedly as it receives more tributaries and enters a region of heavier rainfall. From April to June the melting Himalayan snows feed the river, while in the rainy season from July to September the rain-bearing monsoon winds cause floods. Within the state of Uttar Pradesh, the principal right bank tributaries are the Jumna (Yamuna) River that flows past Delhi, the capital of India, to join the Ganges near Allahābād and the Tons that descends from the Vindhya Range in the state of Madhya Pradesh and joins it soon after. The left bank tributaries in Uttar Pradesh are the Rāmganga, the Gomati, and the Ghāghara.

The Ganges next enters the state of Bihar, where its main tributaries from the Himalayan region to the north are the Gandak, the Burhi Gandak, the Ghugri, and the Kosi and its most important southern tributary is the Son. In West Bengal, the last Indian state that the Ganges enters, the Mahānanda joins it from the north. (Throughout West Bengal in India, as well as in Bangladesh, the Ganges is locally called the Padma). The river then skirts the Rājmahāl Hills to the south, and flows southeast to Farakka, at the apex of the delta. The westernmost distributary of the delta is the Hooghly, on the east bank of which stands the city of Calcutta. The Hooghly itself is joined by two tributaries flowing in from the west, the Dāmodar and the Rupnarayan. In Bangladesh, the Ganges is joined by the mighty Brahmaputra (which for about 150 miles before the junction is called Yamuna) near Goalundo Ghāt. The combined stream, now called the Padma, joins with the Meghna River above Chandpur. The waters then flow to the Bay of Bengal through innumerable channels, the largest of which is known as the Meghna Estuary.

Dacca, the principal city of Bangladesh, stands on the Burhi Ganga, a tributary of the Dhaleswari. Apart from the Hooghly and the Meghna, the other distributary streams which form the Ganges Delta are: in West Bengal, the Jalangi; and in Bangladesh, the Matabhanga, the Bhairab, the Kobadak, the Gorai (Madhumati), and the Ariāl Khān.

The lengths of the major tributaries of the Ganges, in miles, are as follows: the Jumna (860), the Rāmganga (428), the Ghāghara (600), the Son (487), the Gandak (263), the Burhi Gandak (378), the Kosi (450), the Mahānanda (180), the Dāmodar (368), and the Brahmaputra (1,800).

The delta. The Ganges, as well as its tributaries and distributaries, is constantly vulnerable to changes in its course in the delta region. Such changes have occurred in comparatively recent times, especially since 1750. In 1785, the Brahmaputra flowed past the city of Mymensingh; it now flows more than 40 miles west of it before joining the Ganges.

The delta, the seaward prolongation of silt deposits from the Ganges and Brahmaputra river valleys, covers an area of about 22,000 square miles and is composed of repeated alternations of clays, sands, and marls, with recurring layers of peat, lignite, and beds of what were once forests. The new deposits of the delta, known in Hindi and Urdu as the *khadar*, naturally occur in the vicinity of the present channels.

The southern surface of the Ganges Delta has been formed by the rapid and comparatively recent deposition of enormous loads of silt. To the east, the seaward side of the delta is being changed at a rapid rate by the formation of new lands, known as *chārs*, and new islands. So much silt is deposited here that the 100 fathom line lies much farther out to sea than it does, for example, off the mouth of the Indus in the Arabian Sea. The western coastline of the delta has, however, remained practically unchanged since the 18th century.

The rivers in the West Bengal area, being sluggish, have been described as dead or dying; little water passes down them to the sea. In the Bangladesh delta region, the rivers are broad and active, carrying plentiful water; they are connected by innumerable creeks. During the rains, from June to October, the greater part of the region is flooded to a depth of several feet, leaving the villages and homesteads, which are built on artificially raised land, isolated above the flood waters. Communication between

The Himalayan headstreams

Silt deposits in the delta

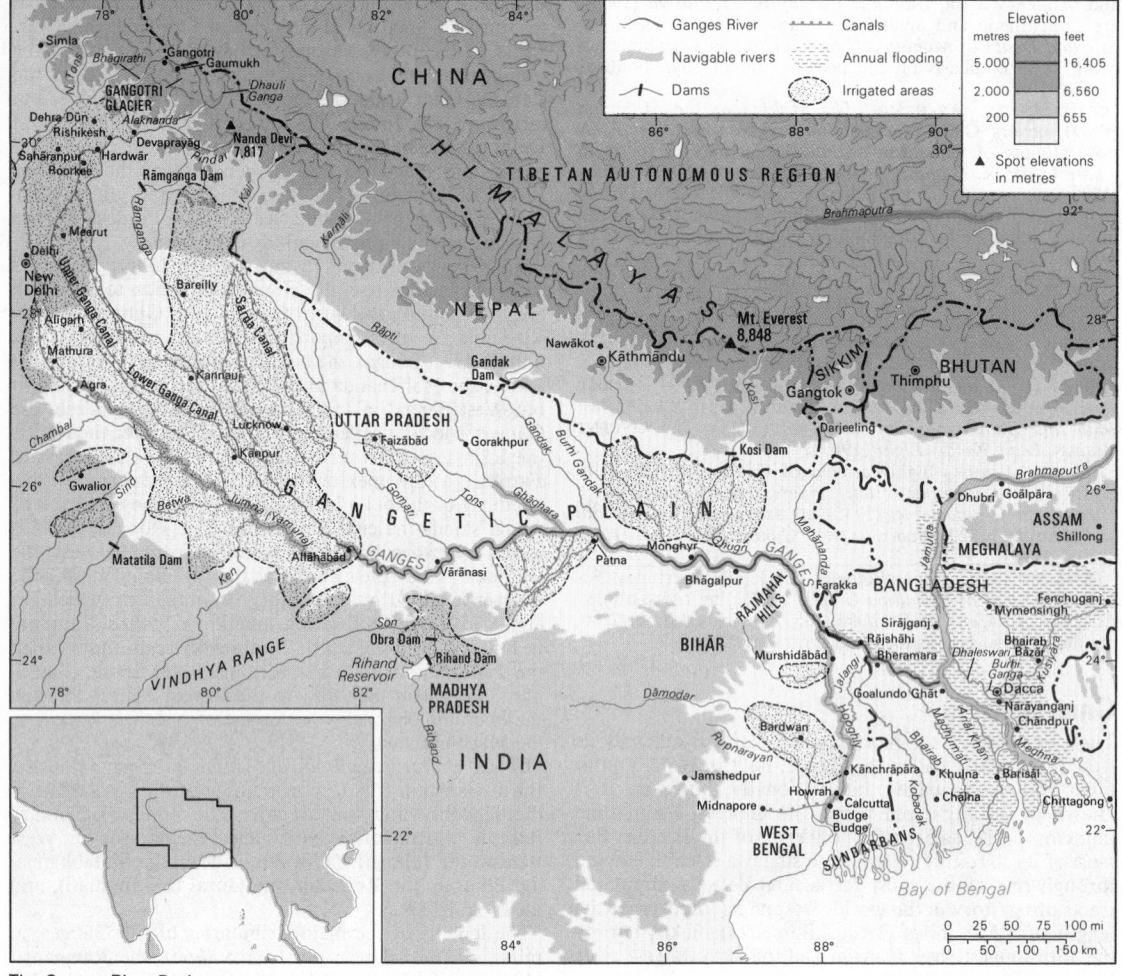

The Ganges River Basin.
Irrigation data from L. Cantor, *A World Geography of Irrigation;* Edinburgh, Oliver and Boyd, 1967; flooding data
from R. Rawson, *The Monsoon Lands of Asia*

settlements during this season can be accomplished only
by boat.

To the seaward side of the delta as a whole there is a
vast stretch of tidal forests and swampland. The forests,
which are called Sundarbans (Sanskrit meaning "beautiful forest"), are protected by India and Bangladesh. For
conservation purposes, no permanent settlement is permitted in them.

In certain parts of the delta, there occur layers of peat,
composed of forest vegetation and rice plants. In many
natural depressions, known as *bil*, peat, still in the process
of formation, is used as a fertilizer by local farmers. In
recent years, it also has been dried and used as a domestic
and industrial fuel.

Climate and hydrography. The Ganges Basin contains
the largest river system on the subcontinent. The water
supply is dependent partly on the rains brought by the
monsoon winds from July to October, as well as on the
flow from melting Himalayan snows, in the hot season
from April to June. Precipitation in the river basin accompanies the southwest monsoon winds, but is also related to cyclones that originate in the Bay of Bengal between June and October. Only a small amount of rainfall
occurs in December and January. The average annual
rainfall varies from 30 inches at the western end of the
basin to over 90 inches at the eastern end. (In the Upper
Gangetic Plain in Uttar Pradesh rainfall averages about
30 to 40 inches, in the Middle Plain of Bihār from 40 to
60 inches, and in the delta region between 60 and 100
inches.) The delta region experiences strong cyclonic
storms both before the commencement of the monsoon
season, from March to May, and at the end of it, from
September to October. Some of these storms result in
much loss of life and destruction of homes, crops, and
livestock. One such storm, which occurred in November

1970, was of catastrophic proportions, resulting in deaths
of at least 200,000 people.

Since there is little variation in relief over the entire surface of the Gangetic Plain, the river's rate of flow is slow.
Between the Jumna River at Delhi and the Bay of Bengal, a distance of nearly 1,000 miles, the elevation drops
nearly 700 feet. Altogether the Ganges-Brahmaputra
plains extend over an area of 300,000 square miles. The
alluvial mantle of the plain, which in some places is
more than 6,000 feet thick, is possibly not more than
10,000 years old.

Vegetation, animals, and birds. The Ganges-Jamuna
area was once densely forested; historical writings indicate that in the 16th and 17th centuries wild elephants,
buffalo, bison, rhinoceroses, lions, and tigers were hunted
there. Most of the original natural vegetation has disappeared from the Gangetic Basin as a whole, and the land
is now intensely cultivated to meet the needs of an evergrowing population. Wild animals are few, except for
deer, boars, and wildcats, and some wolves, jackals, and
foxes. Only in the Sundarban area of the delta are some
Bengal tigers, crocodiles, and marsh deer still found. Fish
abound in all the rivers; especially in the delta area where
they form an important item of diet. Many varieties of
birds are found, such as mynah birds, parrots, crows,
kites, partridges, and fowls. In winter, duck and snipe migrate south across the high Himalayas, settling in large
numbers in water-covered areas. In the Bengal area common fish include featherbacks (Notopteridae), barbs
(Cyprinidae), walking catfish, gouramis (Anabantidae),
and milkfish (Chanidae).

The people of the Gangetic Plain. Ethnically, the people of the Ganges Basin are of mixed origin. In the
west and centre of the basin they were originally descended from Aryan ancestors. Later, Turks, Mongols,

Disappearance of
original
vegetation

Afghans, Persians, and Arabs came from the west and intermingled with them. To the east and south, largely in the Bengal area, an admixture of Tibetan, Burmese, and miscellaneous hill people has also occurred. The Europeans, arriving still later, did not settle or intermarry to any extent.

Historically the Gangetic Plain has constituted the heartland of Hindustān and has cradled its successive civilizations. The centre of the pre-Christian empire of Aśoka was Patna (Pāṭaliputra), standing on the banks of the Ganges in Bihār. The centres of the great Mughal Empire were at Delhi and Āgra, on the western peripheries of the Gangetic Basin. Kannauj on the Ganges, north of Kānpur, was the centre of the feudatory Empire of Harṣa, which covered most of North India in the middle of the 7th century. During the Muslim era, which began in the 12th century, Muslim rule extended not only over the plain, but over all of Bengal as well. Dacca and Murshidābād in the delta region were centres of Muslim power.

The British, having founded Calcutta on the banks of the Hooghly in the late 17th century, gradually advanced up the valley of the Ganges, reaching Delhi in the mid-19th century.

A great number of cities have been built on the Gangetic Plain. Among the most notable are Roorkee, Sahāranpur, Meerut, Āgra (the city of the famous Tāj Mahal mausoleum), Mathura (esteemed as the birthplace of the Hindu god Kṛṣṇa), Alīgarh, Kānpur, Bareilly, Lucknow, Allahābād, Vārānasi (Benares; the holy city of the Hindus), Patna, Bhāgalpur, Rājshāhi, Murshidābād, Bardwan, Calcutta, Howrah, Dacca, Khulna, and Barisāl.

In the delta, the area down the Bhāgirathi-Hooghly Channel was urbanized even before the arrival of the British; subsequent growth of commerce and industry resulted in further urbanization. The aggregate population of Calcutta and its 37 satellite towns, known as the Calcutta Metropolitan District, exceeds 7,000,000. Stretching along both banks of the Hooghly for about 50 miles, the urban-industrial conglomeration extends from Kānchrāpāra-Kalyāni in the north to Budge Budge in the south.

The holy river

The religious importance of the Ganges may exceed that of any other river in the world. It has been revered from the earliest times, and today is regarded as the holiest of rivers by about 350,000,000 Hindus. While places of Hindu pilgrimage, called *tirath*, are located throughout the subcontinent, those that are situated on the Ganges have particular significance. Among these are the confluence of the Ganges and the Jumna at Allahābād, where a bathing festival, or *melā*, is held in January and February, during which about 400,000 persons immerse themselves in the river. Other holy places for immersion are at Vārānasi (Benares), or Kāśī, and at Hardwār.

The Hooghly River at Calcutta is also regarded as holy. The places of pilgrimage on the Ganges also include Gangotri and the junction of the Alaknanda and Bhāgirathi headstreams. The Hindus cast their dead upon the river, believing that they will thus go straight to heaven, and cremation ghats (temples at the summit of riverside steps) for burning the dead have been built in many places on the banks of the Ganges.

Irrigation. Use of the Ganges water for irrigation, either when the river is in flood, or by means of gravity canals, has been common since early times. Such irrigation is described in scriptures and mythological books written long before the Christian era. Megasthenes, a Greek ambassador who was in India, recorded the use of irrigation in the 4th century BC. Irrigation was highly developed during the period of Muslim rule from the 12th century onward, and the Mughal kings later constructed several canals. The canal system was further extended by the British.

The cultivated area of the Ganges Valley in Uttar Pradesh and Bihār benefits from a system of irrigation canals which have increased the production of such cash crops as sugarcane, cotton, and oilseeds. The older canals are mainly in the Ganges-Jumna Doab, a word which

means "land between two rivers." The Upper Ganga Canal (which with its distributaries is 5,950 miles long), which begins at Hardwār, was opened in 1856; the Lower Ganga Canal (5,120 miles with distributaries), opened in 1880, begins at Naraura. The Sarda Canal irrigates about 1,000,000 acres of land in Oudh, in Uttar Pradesh. The land north of the Ganges, being higher, is difficult to irrigate by canal, and water in the subsoil must be pumped to the surface by electricity. The expansion of irrigation into this area has, therefore, depended on the availability of power in the northern part of Uttar Pradesh. Large areas in Uttar Pradesh and in Bihār are also irrigated by channels running from hand-dug wells.

The Ganges-Kobadak scheme in Bangladesh, largely an irrigation plan, covers parts of the districts of Khulna, Jessore, and Kushtia, lying within the moribund part of the delta where the rivers are choked with silt and vegetational overgrowth.

The Ganges-Kobadak scheme

Total annual rainfall in this region is generally below 60 inches, and winters are comparatively dry. The system of irrigation is based on both gravity canals and lifting devices. Power is provided by a thermal plant situated at Bheramara, on the Ganges in the Kushtia District. The first part of the scheme, already in operation, diverts the Ganges water through a 60-mile canal into the moribund Kobadak River, a distributary of the Ganges, in order to irrigate 100,000 acres. A large-scale dredging of the Kobadak in the Khulna District is planned as the next stage.

Navigation. In ancient times the Ganges and some of its tributaries, especially in the east, were navigable. According to the Greek Megasthenes, navigation took place on the Ganges and its main tributaries in the 4th century BC. In the 14th century, inland river navigation in the Ganges Basin was still flourishing. In the 19th century, irrigation-cum-navigation canals formed the main arteries of the water-transport system. The advent of paddle-steamers revolutionized inland transport, stimulating the growth of the indigo industry in Bihār and Bengal. Regular steamer services ran from Calcutta up the Ganges to Allahābād and far beyond, as well as to Āgra on the Jumna, and up the Brahmaputra River. Altogether, these services covered about 5,000 miles of waterways; they are still continued today under governmental auspices in both India and Pakistan. Much of the inland water traffic is carried on by various types of rural river-craft.

The decline of large-scale water transport began with the construction of railways during the mid-19th century. The increasing withdrawal of water for irrigation has also affected navigation. Today, the river traffic is insignificant beyond the middle Ganges Basin around Allahābād.

West Bengal and Bangladesh, however, continue to rely on the waterways to transport jute, tea, grain, and other agricultural and rural products. Principal river ports are Chālna, Khulna, Barisāl, Chāndpur, Nārāyanganj, Goalundo Ghāt, Sirājganj, Bhairab Bāzār, and Fenchuganj, in Bangladesh; and in India, Calcutta, Goālpāra, Dhubri, and Dibrugarh. The partition of India and Pakistan in 1947 produced far-reaching changes, virtually halting the large trade in tea and jute formerly carried to Calcutta from Assam by inland waterway.

In Bangladesh, inland water transport is the responsibility of the Inland Water Transport Authority (IWTA). In India, the comparable authority is the Ganga Brahmaputra Water Transport Board.

The construction of the Farakka Barrage at the head of the delta, just inside Indian territory in West Bengal, was a bone of contention between India and Pakistan (Bangladesh was, before 1971, the province of East Pakistan).

The dispute over the Ganges waters

According to the Indian view, the port of Calcutta was deteriorating due to the deposit of silt and the intrusion of saline seawater. In order to ameliorate the condition of Calcutta by flushing away the seawater and raising the water level, it was proposed that quantities of freshwater be diverted from the Ganges at the site of the Farakka Barrage which was partially opened in 1972.

Major Hydroelectric Projects on the Ganges and Its Tributaries

name	location	completion data	purpose	height		length		reservoir capacity (acre feet)	installed power capacity (000 kw)
				feet	metres	feet	metres		
Jumna Hydel Scheme I	Jumna River, Uttar Pradesh	under construction	hydroelectric	...	...	...	...	...	85
Jumna Hydel Scheme II	Tons River, Uttar Pradesh	under construction	irrigation hydroelectric	...	...	360	110	2,500	260
Rihand (Govind Ballabhpant Sagar)	Rihand River, Uttar Pradesh	1962	hydroelectric	264	80	3,065	934	8,600,000	300
Rāmganga	Rāmganga River, Uttar Pradesh	under construction	irrigation hydroelectric	357	109	1,830	558	1,920,000	180
Subarnarekha	Subarnarekha River, Bihār	under construction		...	...	...	...	...	130
Obra	Rihand River, Uttar Pradesh	under construction	hydroelectric	92	28	1,588	484	103,000	100
Matatila	Betwa River, Uttar Pradesh	1963	irrigation hydroelectric	80	25	20,720	6,315	918,000	30
Kosi	Kosi River, Bihār	under construction	hydroelectric	...	...	...	...	...	20
Gandak	Gandak River, Bihār	under construction	irrigation hydroelectric	...	...	...	...	...	15
Jaldhāka	Jaldhāka River, West Bengal	1967	hydroelectric irrigation	...	...	...	...	...	9

Source: Government of India, Publication Division, *India 1969* (1969); Central Board of Irrigation and Power, *A Handbook of Irrigation and Power Data* (1962); *The Times of India Directory and Yearbook* (1968); M.R. Chandhuri, *Power Resources in India* (1970); International Commission on Large Dams, *World Register of Dams* (1965).

The water is carried by means of a large canal into the Bhāgirathi River, which joins the Hooghly River, on the banks of which stands Calcutta.

According to Pakistan, all riparian countries should exercise joint control over the waters of international rivers for the sake of mutual prosperity. The Ganges waters are also vital to irrigation, to navigation, and to the prevention of saline incursions in Bangladesh. Pakistan maintained that the Farakka Barrage would deprive East Pakistan (now Bangladesh) of a valuable source of water upon which its prosperity depends. Agreement on the Ganges waters dispute was reached between India and Bangladesh after the creation of the latter as an independent state in 1971.

Hydroelectric power. The largest number of streams in the Ganges Basin originate in the Himalayas. Power generation from these rivers depends upon the extent to which, by using water storage, the river flows can be regulated.

The hydroelectric potential of the Ganges Basin has been estimated at about 4,800,000 kilowatts, representing an annual output of 25,400,000,000 kilowatt hours.

Future prospects. The Ganges Basin is one of the world's most populous areas. It is predominantly agricultural and produces a wide range of food and cash crops including wheat, sugarcane, oilseeds, cotton, and millet in the upper basin; rice, sugarcane, and tobacco in the middle basin; and jute, sugarcane, and tobacco in the lower basin.

In recent years, modern industry has also been established in many places, based on local raw materials and on the availability of power. A network of roads and railways serves the entire basin. Future prospects, however, depend upon the improvement and modernization of agriculture, as well as on the growth of large and medium-sized industry based on the availability of cheap energy. The expansion of irrigation and an increase in the generation of cheap hydroelectric power therefore hold the key to meeting the challenge of an increasing population and to future prosperity.

BIBLIOGRAPHY. W.H. ARDEN WOOD, "Rivers and Man in the Indus-Ganges Alluvial Plain," *Scottish Geographical Magazine*, 40:1–16 (1924); INDIA (REPUBLIC), MINISTRY OF TRANSPORT AND COMMUNICATIONS, *Inland Water Transport* (1963); INDIA (REPUBLIC), CENTRAL BOARD OF IRRIGATION AND POWER, *Development of Irrigation in India* (1965); SATISA-CHANDRA MAJUMDAR, *Rivers of the Bengal Delta* (1942); NAFIS AHMAD, *An Economic Geography of East Pakistan*, 2nd ed. (1968); 21ST INTERNATIONAL GEOGRAPHICAL CONGRESS, DELHI, *Mountains and Rivers of India* (1968); ERIC NEWBY, *Slowly Down the Ganges* (1966).

(N.A.)

García Lorca, Federico

Poet and dramatist alike, Federico García Lorca is the most celebrated of 20th-century Spanish writers. He was the outstanding member of a group of writers who might have brought about a new Golden Age for Spanish literature had it not been for the Civil War, during which many died and others were scattered into exile. Lorca's work is at once both intensely Spanish and universal, traditional and innovative. His plays and much of his poetry are deeply rooted in Andalusia—its cities, Córdoba, Granada, Seville; its landscapes, its gypsies and peasants, its Civil Guard, its saints, its ancient code of honour. Yet he also wrote about the Negroes of Harlem and about Walt Whitman.

No matter how localized the subject of his work, the recurrent themes that appear in them are universal: love and lust, death, motherhood, a brotherly compassion for the poor and humble, and, above all, cruelty, violence, and death resulting when primordial passions are frustrated by convention. The elemental passion in Lorca's poetry is expressed largely through concrete, voluptuous, sulfurous, vibrating, sometimes surrealistically juxtaposed images and symbols. He is a poet who, as he says, has "fire in my hands."

Federico García Lorca was born on June 5, 1898, at Fuente Vaqueros, a village in the province of Granada. His father was a farmer, his mother a schoolteacher. Struck by his musical gifts, his mother became his first piano teacher.

Archivo Mas

García Lorca, oil painting by Serrano, 1935.

Early life
When the family moved to the city of Granada, Lorca attended a Jesuit school there. At his father's urging, he then read law at the University of Granada but soon abandoned law to study literature, painting, and music. A precocious composer and excellent performer, he was "the musician" to his friends. To their surprise, in 1918 he published *Impresiones y paisajes* ("Impressions and Landscapes"), a book of prose inspired by a trip he had taken into Castile. The book suggested that Lorca soon might become known as "the writer."

In 1919 he entered the *residencia de estudiantes* (residence of scholars) at the University of Madrid, a large university that had become the cultural centre of the Spanish capital. There he became friends with artists and writers of his own generation, including the painter Salvador Dalí, the film maker Luis Buñuel, and the poet Rafael Alberti; there he also met well-known older figures such as the poet Juan Ramón Jiménez.

During his first two years at the *residencia*, Lorca's poetry became known in literary circles throughout the whole of Spain. Yet he had published hardly any of his work. "Verse is made to be recited," he said, "in a book it is dead." And so, at the *residencia* and elsewhere in Madrid, like a medieval troubador, he read his poetry and plays. Thus, throughout his career, his works were often composed and passed on by word of mouth long before they were published.

At the same time that he was composing the experimental poems that would later be published as *Libro de poemas* (1921; "Book of Poems"); *Primeras canciones* (1936; "First Songs"); and *Canciones* (1927; "Songs"). He was also writing his first play, *El maleficio de la mariposa* (*Butterfly's Evil Spell*), which opened in 1920 at the Eslava Theater in Madrid. A disastrous failure, it closed after the first night.

Lorca found the true bent of his genius when he collaborated with the distinguished composer Manuel de Falla on the folk music festival Fiesta de cante Jondo at Granada in 1922. In the traditions of folk and gypsy music, Lorca seemed to find a resolution of his musical, poetical, and spiritual impulses. *Poema del cante jondo* (written 1922, published 1931; "Poem of the Cante Jondo") and *Romancero gitano* (written 1924–27, published 1928; *The Gypsy Ballads*) were to be the lyrical expression of this resolution.

Gypsy Ballads
In the 18 poems of *Gypsy Ballads* Lorca combined the ancient magic of a traditional literary form—the Spanish ballad (*romance*)—with startling new images. The description, for example, in "The Ballad of the Spanish Civil Guard," of the Guard riding ominously toward a gypsy village:

> Los caballos negros son.
> Las herraduras son negras.
> Sobre las capas relucen
> manchas de tinta y de cera.
> Tienen, por eso no lloran,
> de plomo las calaveras.
> Con el alma de charol
> vienen por la carretera.
>
> Black are the horses.
> The horseshoes are black.
> On the dark capes glisten
> stains of ink and of wax.
> Their skulls are leaden,
> which is why they don't weep.
> With their patent-leather souls
> they come down the street.
>
> (Federico García Lorca, *Selected Poems*, translated by A.L. Lloyd. Copyright 1955 by New Directions Publishing Corporation. Reprinted by permission of New Directions Publishing Corporation.)

While Lorca was writing *Gypsy Ballads*, he was also writing plays. His first dramatic success came in 1927 with the Barcelona production of *Mariana Pineda*, a poetic and romantic verse drama, with scenery by Salvador Dalí. The same year and the same city also saw the first public exhibition of Lorca's drawings.

The publication of *Gypsy Ballads* in 1928 brought Lorca sudden international fame but little happiness. Displeased about the creation of what he called "the myth of my gypsy-hood" and tormented by an emotional crisis that he described as "one of the most painful states I have had in my life," he sought relief and a new source of inspiration in the United States and Cuba in 1929–1930.

The trip inspired *Poeta en Nueva York* (*Poet in New York*), published posthumously in 1940. In this work, Lorca's horror at what he saw as the death in life of a mechanized civilization is conveyed by the surrealistic juxtaposition of brutal, tortured images:

> Con una cuchara
> arrancaba los ojos a los cocodrilos
> y golpeaba el trasero de los monos.
> Con una cuchara.
>
> With a spoon
> he gouged out the crocodile's eyes
> and thumped on the monkey-rumps,
> with a spoon.
>
> ("The King of Harlem," in Federico García Lorca, *Poet in New York*, translated by Ben Belitt. Copyright 1955 by Ben Belitt. Reprinted by permission of New Directions Publishing Corporation.)

By 1931 Lorca was back in Spain where he began the poems to be published as *Diván del Tamarit* (1936; "Divan of Tamarit") and again wrote for the theatre. Expressing the passionate enthusiasm for marionettes that he had had since childhood, he wrote two puppet plays: *Los títeres de cachiporra* (*The Billy Club Puppets*) and *Retablillo de Don Cristóbal* (*The Puppet Play of Don Cristóbal*). Even these puppet farces were clouded by melancholy.

Bringing classical theatre to the uneducated
The advent of the Republic in Spain made it possible for Lorca to plunge fully into the theatre. The Ministry of National Education subsidized La Barraca, a troupe of students who, from 1932 to 1935, brought masterpieces of the classical theatre to uneducated workers and peasants. Founder, driving spirit, director, and musician for La Barraca, Lorca staged Lope de Vega, Calderón de la Barca, and Cervantes, thereby acquiring immense theatrical experience.

The result was the first of a trilogy of folk dramas, *Bodas de sangre* (*Blood Wedding*), staged in 1933. The theme was inspired by a news item: a bride had fled on her wedding day with the man whom she secretly loved, and the rivals had killed each other. In Lorca's play the characters become pawns in a tragedy of fate. They are trapped in a conflict between primitive passions and civilization's unyielding code of honour—a conflict that ends in death.

In 1934 the goring and subsequent death of a bullfighter who had been Lorca's friend inspired "Llanto por Ignacio Sánchez Mejías" (published 1935; "Lament for Ignacio Mejías"). Lorca's greatest poem, the finest elegy in modern Spanish literature and one of the finest in all literature, it beats with the hollow, haunting, dirgelike refrain, repeated over and over again: "A las cinco de la tarde" ("At five in the afternoon"):

> A las cinco de la tarde.
> Eran las cinco en punto de la tarde.
> Un niño trajo la blanca sábana
> *a las cinco de la tarde.*
> Una espuerta de cal ya prevenida.
> *a las cinco de la tarde.*
> Lo demás era muerte y sólo muerte
> *a las cinco de la tarde.*
>
> At five in the afternoon.
> It was exactly five in the afternoon.
> A boy brought the white sheet
> *at five in the afternoon.*
> A frail of lime ready prepared
> *at five in the afternoon.*
> The rest was death, and death alone
> *at five in the afternoon.*

Later in 1934, *Yerma*—the second of Lorca's folk drama trilogy and, along with *Blood Wedding*, one of the few successful poetic tragedies of the 20th century—was produced. The play—"a tragic poem"—is about the torment of a woman who, despairing over her childless state, kills her sterile husband. On an evening in June 1936, at the home of friends, Lorca read the final play of the trilogy, *La casa de Bernarda Alba* (*The House of Bernarda Alba*). Almost entirely in prose, the play is about four daughters who, shut up by their tyrannical mother in a house of mourning, burn with hatred and lust.

In July, alarmed by the outbreak of the Civil War, Lorca left Madrid for Granada. But his fate fulfilled the premonition of violent death that haunts his works. In Granada, Lorca, one of the century's great poets, was shot without trial by the Nationalists in the night of August 19–20, 1936. Lo demás era muerte y sólo muerte ("The rest was death, and death alone").

MAJOR WORKS

POETRY: *Canciones* (1927); *Romancero gitano* (1928; *The Gypsy Ballads*, 1953); *Poema del cante jondo* (1931); *Poeta en Nueva York* (posthumously published 1940; *The Poet in New York*, 1940); "Llanto por Ignacio Sánchez Mejías" (1935; trans. in *Lament for the Death of a Bullfighter, and Other Poems*, 1937).

PLAYS: *Bodas de sangre* (1933: *Blood Wedding*, 1939); *Yerma* (1934; Eng. trans., 1941); *La casa de Bernarda Alba* (1936; *The House of Bernarda Alba*). These three plays were all translated in *Three Tragedies of Federico García Lorca* (1947). Also, *Doña Rosita la soltera* (1935; *Doña Rosita, the Spinster*, 1941).

BIBLIOGRAPHY. MARCELLE AUCLAIR, *Enfances et mort de Garcia Lorca* (1968), the only complete study of Lorca published to date; ARTURO BAREA, *Lorca: The Poet and His People* (1944), an analysis of the poet and his work by a Spaniard of Lorca's generation; ROBERT LIMA, *The Theatre of Garcia Lorca* (1963), the plays viewed historically, critically, and biographically, with an extensive bibliography of Lorca's theatre that includes adaptations of texts for operas and ballets; JOHN B. TREND, *Lorca and the Spanish Poetic Tradition* (1956), contains an informative chapter on Lorca by an English hispanist who knew him at the start of his poetic career; HOWARD T. YOUNG, *The Victorious Expression: A Study of Four Contemporary Spanish Poets* (1964), has an intelligent study of the poet that includes an annotated list of English translations of his work; JOSE A. BALBONTIN, *Tres poetas de España* (1957; Eng. trans., *Three Spanish Poets*, 1961), traces Lorca's development and includes a number of his poems in translation; MANUEL DURAN (ed.), *Lorca: A Collection of Critical Essays* (1962), articles on both Lorca's poetry and theatre by a heterogeneous group of scholars, poets, and critics; three works that are interesting but present variously one-sided views of Lorca are: CARL W. COBB, *Federico García Lorca* (1967); EDWIN HONIG, *García Lorca*, rev. ed. (1968); and ROY CAMPBELL, *Lorca: An Appreciation of His Poetry* (1952), which also contains translations by Campbell that make Lorca's poetry sound unduly English.

(M.A.)

Garden and Landscape Design

Garden and landscape design are a substantial part but by no means all of the work of the profession of landscape architecture. Defined as "the art of arranging land and the objects upon it for human use and enjoyment," landscape architecture includes also site planning, land planning, master planning, urban design, and environmental planning. Site planning involves plans for specific developments in which precise arrangements of buildings, roadways, utilities, landscape elements, topography, water features, and vegetation are shown. Land planning is for larger scale developments involving subdivision into several or many parcels, including analyses of land and landscape, feasibility studies for economic, social, political, technical, and ecological constraints, and detailed site plans as needed. Master planning is for land use, conservation, and development at still larger scales, involving comprehensive areas or units of landscape topography or comprehensive systems such as open space, park-recreation, water and drainage, transportation, or utilities. Urban design is the planning and design of the open-space components of urbanized areas; it involves working with architects on the building patterns, engineers on the traffic and utility patterns, graphic and industrial designers on street furniture, signs, and lighting, planners on overall land use and circulation, economists on economic feasibility, and sociologists on social feasi-

Components of landscape architecture

bility, needs, and desires. Environmental planning is for natural or urbanized regions or substantial areas within them, in which the impact of development upon land and natural systems, their capacity to carry and sustain development, or their needs for preservation and conservation are analyzed exhaustively and developed as constraints upon urban design, master, land, and site planning. Within this framework of comprehensive survey, study, analysis, planning, and design of the continuous natural and humanized environment, garden and landscape design represent the final, detailed, precise, intensive refinement and implementation of all previous plans.

Ideally all of these planning and design phases follow one another closely in a continuous sequential process, but this rarely happens. Various levels of planning and design are performed by different people at different times; often the more comprehensive phases are not performed at all or in an over-simplified manner. The wise gardener, therefore, always begins with a careful analysis of conditions surrounding his project.

Garden and landscape design deals with the treatment of land areas not covered by buildings, when those areas are considered important to visual experience, with or without utilitarian function. Typically, these land areas are of four types: those closely related to single buildings, such as front yards, side yards, and backyards, or more extensive grounds; those around and between groups of buildings, such as campuses, civic and cultural centres, commercial and industrial complexes; those bordering and paralleling transportation and utility corridors, such as parkways, freeways, waterways, power easements; and park-recreation open-space areas and systems. These areas may be of any size, from small urban courtyards and suburban gardens to many thousands of acres of regional, state, or national parks. Although usually conceived as vegetated green spaces on natural ground, they can include also playgrounds, urban plazas, covered malls, roof gardens, and decks, which may be almost entirely formed by construction and paving.

Function of garden and landscape design

Garden and landscape design, therefore, works with a wide range of natural and processed materials capable of holding up well in the specific local climatic conditions of the site. These materials include earth, rock, water, and plants, either existing on the site or brought in; and construction materials such as concrete, stone, brick, wood, tile, metal, and glass.

Garden and landscape design is uniquely concerned with direct relations among art, science, and nature. It operates exactly at the frontier between man and nature, developing transitional connecting zones between the outside limits of buildings and engineering structures and the natural forms and processes that surround them. This is true for large houses and gardens in the country, for regional parks at the edges of cities, for urban and suburban gardens, for urban plazas and roof decks; it is true wherever soil exists to be treated, wherever it may be brought in to fill containers, wherever open spaces are exposed to the weather.

If garden and landscape design is concerned with the relations between man and nature, it is also largely determined by one or the other of the conflicting philosophies about how man does or should relate to nature. Man knows that biologically and physiologically he is the product of natural evolution, that his organic system is similar to that of the animals. Yet man's great technological accomplishments lead him to feel that he is above, beyond, or outside nature, that he has conquered and dominated the wilderness and has it now within his power to remake the world into complete synthetic environments. Every work of garden and landscape design reflects one or the other of these conflicting attitudes. The Japanese garden, for example, is inspired by the notion of man as a part of nature; the Renaissance garden, by the idea that man is nature's master. Garden and landscape design thus reveals much about a culture and a period.

Garden and landscape design is an art insofar as it creates for people experiences that uplift their spirits, expand their vision, and invigorate their lives. It is a science insofar as it develops precise knowledge of its processes and materials. And it is directly related to and expressive of nature insofar as it incorporates natural materials and scenes without major change in their character. When the preservation of natural landscape is primary, as in a regional park, art and science appear in the skill and sensitivity with which necessary facilities and changes are related to the natural landscape. At the other extreme, in an urban plaza, trees in boxes or openings in the paving may be the only natural elements; art and science then appear in the design and construction of the total plaza, including its display of trees as symbols of nature, as pleasing forms, and as sources of shade.

Art, science, and nature become most intimately interlocked in certain aspects of horticulture expressed in designed gardens and landscapes: in improved varieties of herbaceous and woody plants; in the cultural practices that stimulate their maximum contributions to the scene; and in the techniques and skills for directing and reshaping the forms of plants—in a range from trimmed hedges and topiary (careful sculptural cutting), through espaliered (trained to grow flat against a wall or trellis) and pollarded (cut back to the trunk to promote a dense head of foliage) trees, to ultimate refinements such as the Japanese practice of removing individual needles from pine trees.

No doubt much art recognizes, expresses, or symbolizes nature in some way. Only the arts of garden and landscape, however, produce works in which nature participates directly in varying degrees of integration with more processed forms and materials.

Functional and technical aspects

As in most other arts, garden and landscape design must solve not only aesthetic but also technical and functional problems. Gardens are for horticulture as well as for viewing, parks are for active recreation as well as for passive relaxation. The surface of the earth must be covered to prevent erosion, dust in summer, and mud in winter. Water persists in running downhill, and even light garden structures must have adequate footings.

This does not mean, however, that there is an inherent or inevitable conflict between utility and beauty. Such conflicts usually develop either because the designer tries to carry out an aesthetic concept that ignores the technical and functional requirements of the problem or because the program is so demanding technically, functionally, or economically that it eliminates aesthetic considerations from the design process. In most garden and landscape design situations it is necessary first to evaluate the technical conditions and functional demands and then to derive from them design concepts that resolve them.

The vegetated landscape that covered most of the earth's continents before man began to build still surrounds and penetrates even his largest metropolises. All of man's efforts to design gardens and to preserve and develop green open space in and around his cities are efforts to maintain contact with this original pastoral, rural landscape. Designed gardens and landscapes, by filling the open areas in cities, create a kind of continuity in space between man's structural urban landscapes and the open rural landscapes beyond.

Designed gardens and landscapes have a special kind of continuity in time. Buildings, paintings, and sculpture may survive longer than specific plants, but the constant cyclical growth and change in plants provide a continuous time dimension that static structures and sculpture can never achieve. From the annual flower to the redwood that began, so the story goes, when Christ was crucified, planting has a regular continuity and annual seasonal expression that measure for men the stages and generations of their lives.

This article will discuss the aesthetic and physical components of design, the various kinds of private and public design, and the role and development of gardening in the history of man. It is divided into the following sections:

I. Design components

AESTHETIC COMPONENTS

Elements. The traditional elements of design are space, mass, line, or outline; colour, tone, light, and shade; texture; scent; and time, as related to climate, natural light, season, and growth factors.

Space. Space is air or atmospheric volume defined by physical elements and man's visual imagination. Space has floors: earth, rock, grass, low planting, concrete, asphalt, stone, brick, wood, carpet, tile, linoleum. It has sides or walls: topography, rock, vegetation, vertical structures. And it has ceilings: treetops, structural coverage, or the sky. The most easily understood spaces are the rooms, terraces, patios, and gardens of private residences. A room is defined precisely and unavoidably by floor, walls, and ceiling, particularly with doors closed and windows draped. Beyond these rooms there are the streets, squares, plazas, parks, and public buildings of the city. An urban plaza surrounded by major buildings likewise has positive floors and walls, with sky for ceiling. The fields, meadows, orchards, groves, forests, plains, lakes, river and stream valleys, hills, and mountains of the wider landscape have less precise and regular enclosures. Patios may have fences and walls, gardens hedges and trellises, but in parks there are loose spaces of many soft sizes and forms, defined by trees, ground forms, and shrubbery masses. And in the open landscape there are many different apparent space scales, from the intimate, small farming scenes of New England, Portugal, or Japan to the almost limitless panoramas of the Great Plains, Southwest deserts, or Rocky Mountains. In all of these, space is defined by ground or floor surfaces below, obstacles that block vision horizontally or terminate it at the horizon, and sky overhead. Man's sense of space in all of them results partly from what he actually sees and partly from his imaginative extension, interpretation, and structuring of what he actually sees. Thus, a sand dune, a rock, and a cactus may become a "room" in the desert, while the entire Yosemite Valley is a great room housing thousands of people.

Mass. Mass is the opposite of space. They define each other and depend upon each other for visual existence. Mass may be topographical earth forms, rock outcrops and boulders, trees and shrub groups, buildings, and water forms—streams, lakes, or waterfalls. These are masses in the larger landscape, even though they also incorporate spaces within themselves. Trees, shrubs, and buildings have multiple spaces within them, even though they read as masses from outside. Water forms contain spaces for divers and aquatic life, but of a different density.

Line. Line in the landscape may be the sharp edge of paving, structure, or rock; the boundary between two different surface materials, as grass and ivy; the edge of a shadow; or the silhouette outline of any three-dimensional form, such as a rock, plant, or building. Whatever its source, a line in the landscape plays an important role in the way man sees, interprets, and relates to the scene. A line may lead the eye into the distance, around a corner and out of the scene, or around the scene and back again, holding the viewer within it. It is similar to the role of lines in a painting, holding the viewer within

Lines in
painting
and
landscape
compared

or leading him out of the composition. In a landscape, however, the function of lines is vastly more complicated and difficult to predict. The pattern—that is, the form created by lines—is three-dimensional in any given scene that is viewed. It is four-dimensional in that a spectator continues to move through the landscape over periods of time. The pattern changes throughout each day because of the changing light and shade patterns produced by the movement of the earth around the sun. And the pattern is never exactly the same on one day as on any previous day, because of changes in the weather, the seasons, and the elements of the landscape. Buildings, topography, and rocks may be maintained almost the same for substantial periods of time; but vegetation changes constantly, with both seasonal adjustments and annual growth. That is one reason why landscapes without vegetation seem static, lifeless, and monotonous.

Colour. Colour gives physical landscapes that final dimension of real life, definition, and interest. Spring blossoms and fresh green leaves, after the cold barrenness of winter, herald a new season of vitality and fun. After the deep and stable green of summer, fall colours mark a last resurgence of liveliness before the winter barrenness sets in again. The apparent sizes and forms of landscape spaces change with each such seasonal change: bright colours advance, dull colours recede, changing apparent distances.

Structural colours, too, affect the apparent sizes and forms of landscape spaces. Most obvious is the negative effect of bright billboards upon quiet landscapes. To most people billboards seem destructive and arbitrary intrusions; they do not grow out of the scene but are forced onto it. Yet man-made forms—even billboards—can be made to appear to be a part of nature to the extent that they are designed to harmonize with the existing scene.

The aim of the garden and landscape designer is to combine the strong, artificial colours of paint and structure with the softer and more subdued grays, greens, browns, and blues of nature as well as with seasonal outbursts of the purest and truest colours in the world.

Colour
variations

Colour varies by hue, the actual colours from the colour wheel; by value, the strength of the colours, bright or pale; the tone or grayness, how pure they are or how grayed by admixture with other colours; by the way that light and shade play on them; and by the texture, smooth or rough, of the surface they are on. All of these factors are taken into account by the garden and landscape designer.

Light and shade. Because the sun—and, to a lesser extent, the moon, stars, fire, and artificial lighting—has the property of casting shadows, landscape design, in placing trees, structures, and other elements on the land, must always take into consideration the light and shade resulting from such placement.

Light and shade are not the same in all parts of a country or the world. Light is welcome in cool, gray, northern climates, shade in hot, bright, desert or tropical regions. In the clear air of unspoiled deserts, man sees so far that he loses all sense of size, scale, and distance; in the foggy humidity of the western coasts of Europe and North America distances seen and objects perceived change from day to day, sometimes from hour to hour, so that one lives with a continuing sense of mystery and variety. Landscape design must, ideally, remain sensitive to and work carefully with the light and shade relations that are most desirable in each different region or subregion.

Texture. Texture—the smoothness or roughness of surfaces—is another element of landscape design. It is perceived primarily by feeling, although through vision one approximates the textures of different surfaces and imagines how they would feel. The surface texture of the earth may vary from fine sand or silt to coarse clods, gravel, or boulders. The texture of plant coverage may vary from fine bent grasses through coarser meadow grasses to brush, ivy, or cactus. Wall surfaces range from the smoothness of glass and plaster to the roughness of brick, stone, or rough-sawn lumber.

Felt textures must be intimate to be experienced. Visual textures may be experienced at any distance. Farther away, larger elements participate in texture effects; at medium distances the foliage of trees and the size of rocks create textural qualities; from an airplane or hilltop the size and arrangement of buildings, topographic forms, masses of vegetation, or water create textural effects.

Scent. Scent is a delicate and subtle element in landscape experience, often lost to 20th-century man because of widespread pollution of the air with foul-smelling exhaust and waste gases. The fragrance of flower and fruit is one of the traditional delights of garden and park, still attainable through sensitive selection and arrangement of plants.

Time, climate, and season. Unlike the static continuity of architectural and urban monuments, garden and landscape spaces are dependent on maintenance, which determines whether the form envisioned by the original designers will endure or change over decades or centuries. The Saihō-ji garden and many others in Japan continue today in much the same form as they began because of continuing maintenance. On the other hand, the inadequate maintenance of the Renaissance gardens—designed as geometric architectural abstractions, to which

Maintenance of
gardens

Flower garden at Mount Vernon, Virginia, showing the traditional elements of garden and landscape design.

plant forms were made to conform by clipping and trimming—has allowed many of the larger plants to resume their natural forms. The results, however pleasant, are not what the designers envisioned. Instead of hundreds of years, the typical suburban garden in the United States has a predictable life of about five years. Ownership or tenancy tends to change in that cycle, with unpredictable results in the garden.

Time and climate are closely interrelated in their effects on garden and landscape spaces. Because relations between temperature and moisture, light and shade, change daily throughout the year, every region and locality on earth—in fact, every building site—has its own climate, unlike any other. Therefore, garden and landscape design for every region, locality, and site may be expected to be different. Nevertheless, climates can be generalized in certain broad categories that are similar, though not identical, over large areas of the earth.

Climatic factors having major impact on garden and landscape design are temperature range (hot to cold), precipitation range (high to low, rain to snow), their combinations (hot, wet summers; hot, dry summers; cold, wet winters; cold, dry winters; and so on), growing season (year around in the tropics, a few weeks in the Arctic), atmospheric humidity (clear air or clouds, fog, mist) and its effects on visibility and light–shade patterns, air movement (winds, breezes) and its effect on the other factors (cooling in hot weather, chilling in cold, moving clouds and fog).

The combination of all of these factors affects how one sees the landscape (bright, clear desert distances; soft, mysterious, changeable foggy landscapes), what one expects from design (shade from the sun, protection from the wind, shelter from rain and snow), and how one designs gardens and landscapes. The patios, cloisters, and oases of Mediterranean and Middle East regions, the romantic naturalistic parks of Europe, China, and eastern North America, the esoteric garden abstractions of Japan—all of these different approaches to design were inspired partly by the particular qualities of the landscape climate in which they developed.

Time and natural light are, of course, intimately interlocked in the daily cycle of night and day, in the seasonal cycles (light is different in summer and winter because of differences in temperature and humidity), and in the annual cycles (long days in summer, short days in winter).

Time, climate, light, and season are all reflected in garden and landscape in the growth and change of plants. In the tropics, growth is constant, taken for granted, a problem of control. As growing seasons become shorter in the north and south or at higher elevations, they become more precious. In far northern and southern latitudes the short summer is a period of rejoicing and outdoor activity. A tree that will mature in five to ten years in Southern California or Florida will require 30 to 40 years in the North Central states. Spring blossoms, fall colour, the change from summer green to winter's exposed branch structures, all of these mark the seasonal changes clearly and strongly in the Eastern United States, in Europe, and in other temperate areas.

Principles. The traditional principles of design deal with the arrangement or organization of the elements, as expressed in specific materials, on a specific site. The site —a piece of land, with surface form and internal content —may in itself require reshaping. On it will be placed— or may already exist—buildings, roads, minor structures, trees, shrubs, ground-cover planting, water elements, rocks.

The elements of design are contained in these individual components and in specific relations that may develop among them on a particular site. The principles of design—which deal with overall relations—are unity and variety, rhythm and balance, accent and contrast, scale and proportion, and composite three-dimensional spatial form.

Unity and variety. Unity and variety are derived from the number of elements, or kinds of material, within a given visual area and from the way they are combined. A brick building or a rose garden is unified by concentration on one material. The difficulty of achieving a sense of unity increases as the number of elements, or kinds of material, increase. A building of six materials or a garden of 30 kinds of plants, for example, will have more variety but unity can be achieved only by careful organization and arrangement. At a certain point, which varies with the situation and the skill of the designer, it becomes impossible to establish unity. Variety then dominates.

Rhythm and balance. Rhythm and balance result from the three-dimensional arrangement of elements and materials on the site. Rhythm is a sequence or repetition of similar elements—as a double row of trees. It tends to emphasize direction and movement, as along an allée toward a viewpoint or terminus. Balance is the sense one

Grand east–west axis of the gardens at Versailles, France, showing the traditional principles of garden and landscape design. Designed by André Le Nôtre (1613–1700).

gets, looking in any direction, that the elements to one's left balance those to one's right and the feeling one has that the views one has just experienced are in equilibrium with what one sees now. The most obvious examples of balance are the symmetrical axial Renaissance gardens of Europe, but these are not the only or even the most interesting ways to achieve balance.

Accent and contrast. Accent and contrast enliven arrangements that may be so balanced, orderly, and harmonious as to be dull. An accent is an element that differs from everything around it, as silver-gray foliage against dark-green conifers, but is limited in quantity in relation to surrounding elements. Contrast is stronger: two different elements may be juxtaposed in almost equal quantity to emphasize the special qualities of each. Well-known examples are the formal palace in the informal park, the green park in the densely built-up city. Accent and contrast are more difficult to handle successfully than straightforward, simple, harmonious design. An example of the failure to handle it successfully is the common practice of lining a street with alternate specimens of two quite different trees, as pines and cherries, which merely cancel each other out.

Scale and proportion. Scale refers to the apparent (not the actual) size of a landscape space or of the elements within it. Proportion is the determined relations among the sizes of all the parts within an element and of all the elements within a space. Thus, the proportionate sizes of the legs, arms, and back of a garden bench, for example, determine the scale of the seat. And the overall size of the seat, in proportionate relation to walk width, arbor height, lawn area, tree size, and so on, helps to determine the scale of the garden.

Composite three-dimensional spatial form. Composite three-dimensional spatial form results from the delineation of a block of air by physical elements, which enclose and enframe the space and establish its relations with neighbouring spaces, distant views, and so on. A patio with paved floor and walled enclosure (with perhaps a grilled outlook) and sheltered by trees or pergola structures (arbor or trellis) is an obvious example of this form.

The design process. The design process has been called in the past modes of composition and style or period selection. In the first quarter of the 20th century, the arts, including architectural, garden, and landscape design, were dominated by traditional, eclectic, preconceived systems of form and approach called the Beaux Arts system, after the famous school in Paris. In essence, these systems told designers what to design and where. Their only choice and their only skill lay in how to adapt preconceived systems—such as formal and informal gardens—to the particular problem at hand. Innovation consisted of timid new relationships among traditional elements.

In the first quarter of the century there also occurred what is called the modern revolt. Beginning in painting and sculpture, it soon swept through architecture and reached garden and landscape design toward the end of the quarter in Europe, reaching the United States in about 1935.

The essence of the modern revolt was the rejection of preconceived or traditional styles, periods, rules, regulations, or systems governing design. In place of these, systems and processes developed for analyzing problems and situations in their own terms and in terms of the modern resources available for solving them. Basic to the new theories was the idea that designed forms should arise from and express each specific situation and the contemporary, industrial culture around it. By the 1970s all fields of design seemed to be dominated by these theories; but, although submerged, traditional Beaux Arts design continues to surface regularly in strange new combinations with modern forms. A form of this eclecticism emerged in the early 1970s, when architects once again designed symmetrical monumental buildings with little functional or structural expression, and traditional formal–informal concepts in garden and landscape design began to reappear.

PHYSICAL COMPONENTS

Natural components. Natural components of garden and landscape design include earth, rock, water, and plants.

Earth. As a base for design, earth is the floor of landscape spaces, the root medium in which half of every plant lives, the foundation for structures, the vehicle for surface and subsurface drainage of excess water, and a sculptural material in its own right.

As a floor, earth can be seen as an abstract surface. If apparently level, with just enough slope for drainage, it is ready to be covered with paving, grass, ground cover, or other planting, which is necessary to avoid dust in dry weather and mud in wet weather; if sloping or irregular, earthwork may be necessary to conform to new construction or to the design plan, to provide adequate drainage, or in order to relate properly to neighbouring topography and views.

As a root medium for plants, earth must be understood as soil. One must know the type and depth of soil before planning a garden or landscape. Soil occurs in layers: topsoil, in which there is a high percentage of organic humus and micro-organisms; subsoil, which is more sterile as it gets deeper; and bedrock, which is not yet broken up. There are many variations in these layers. In the mountains there may be only a few inches of soil over rock; in old valleys the soil may be hundreds of feet deep. Most plants require one to six feet of topsoil, with good drainage, but there are plants that will grow in rock, sand, sterile soil, boggy land, shallow water, or plain water. If the soil is not adequate for the planting desired or if the form of the earth is to be changed, then new soil conditions adequate for planting must be created.

As a foundation for structures, earth must be dry and firm. Although structures can be built in almost any soil conditions, they become more and more expensive as the earth becomes less dry and firm. Desirable foundation conditions, the exact opposite of the loose, moist soil that is best for most plants, create many technical problems in the relations between structures and plant areas.

As a drainage vehicle, earth absorbs a high percentage of the water that falls on its surface. This absorbed water may be stored below ground, or it may move horizontally through sloping soil patterns. Surface water that is not absorbed, either because the soil is saturated or because the slope of the ground makes it run off too fast, must drain away on the surface. This creates many technical problems, especially if the surface is not covered to prevent erosion or if a great deal of land is covered by roofed structures or paved surfaces, which increase the amount of water running off because none is absorbed.

As a sculptural material, earth can be contoured to conform with functional and maintenance demands. Rolling natural hills and golf-course earth forms demonstrate the potential. Slopes must not be too steep for planting to hold, unless they are structurally retained.

Rock. Rock is a major factor in some regions, minor in others, nonexistent in some. It varies in size from sand through pebbles, cobbles, boulders, and fixed outcrops to solid-rock mountains. It varies in form from square or jagged, newly cut or broken to rounded forms produced by the action of water. It varies also in colour and in texture. It can be used as a ground cover, dry or in cement; in vertical structures with various degrees of cutting and finishing; to simulate natural rock formations; and in sculptural groupings that emphasize the natural form of the rocks, as the Japanese do so well.

Water. Water is essential to all gardens and landscapes, even in the desert, although amounts vary considerably. As a design element, water contributes coolness, moisture, sparkle, lightness, depth, serenity, the possibility of aquatic plants and animals, and recreation. It may run through natural stream and river channels and collect in natural ponds, lakes, and seas, or it may be kept in structural channels and pools, recirculated to avoid waste. In some soil conditions it may be necessary to seal the bottoms of natural-appearing streams and

Marginal notes:

Difference between accent and contrast

The modern revolt in design

Understanding earth as soil

Aesthetic qualities of water

The natural components of garden and landscape design.
(Left) Rocks and raked sand; Garden of the Ryōan-ji, 15th century, Kyōto, Japan. (Centre)
Water and plants; Gardens of the Generálife, Granada, Spain. (Right) Earth and plants;
Bluebell Wood, Winkworth Arboretum, Surrey, England.
By courtesy of (left) the International Society for Educational Information, Tokyo, (right) the National Trust;
photographs, (centre) Ewing Galloway, (right) Andy Williams

ponds to hold the water. Under natural conditions water runs downhill through naturally formed channels and collects in low spots or bowls of firm form. Water also may be pumped uphill or thrown into the air in jets and fountains. Water is used increasingly throughout countries with technically complex artificial irrigation systems, which become distinctive landscape elements.

Plants. Plants are considered the primary material of gardens and landscapes, by contrast with the concentration of structures in cities. They may be grouped and organized for design purposes in several ways: by size (trees, shrubs, low plants, grass); by form (vertical, horizontal, round, irregular); by texture (size, shape, and arrangement of foliage and structure); by colour (flowers, fruit, foliage, structure); by rate of growth (fast, medium, slow); by seasonal effect (spring, summer, fall, winter); by fragrance (flowers, fruit, foliage); by environmental requirements (soil, drainage, sun–shade, temperature range, pests and diseases, pruning needs). All of these properties affect the selection, arrangement, and maintenance of plants in designed landscapes.

Animals are also important in designed landscapes, particularly, of course, in zoos and agricultural scenes. The incompatibility of dogs and well-maintained gardens, however, is well-known.

Finally, people are prime elements in garden and landscape design, not only as clients and users but also as a visual component that brings life to landscape spaces and validates the success or failure of the design.

Structural components. Structural components of garden and landscape include structures closely related to the earth, enclosure structures, shelter structures, engineering structures, and special buildings.

Earth-related structures. Earth-related structures include paving (walks, roads, terraces, patios) and change-of-level structures (retaining walls, steps, ramps, bridges), which must be made of materials that will resist decay, such as brick, stone, concrete, asphalt. These structures provide the connections for movement and circulation and the areas for intensive gathering, social use, or active recreation. They embody a substantial and complex technology.

Enclosure structures. Enclosure structures, such as walls and fences, are designed to control vision or movement or both. They may be of various heights, three to ten feet (one to three metres) or more, and of many materials: brick, stone, or concrete masonry; wood; metal; sheet materials such as glass, plastic, asbestos, pressed boards. Because they are at eye level and extend and connect buildings, they are very important in intimate visual design.

Shelter structures. Shelter structures, designed to protect from sun, rain, or wind, may incorporate enclosure elements at the sides with overhead elements, which may be open framework pergolas or arbors carrying vines or solid opaque or translucent roofs. Among such structures are gazebos, pavilions, garden temples, summer houses, hermit huts, follies, ruins, and grottoes.

Engineering structures. Engineering structures tend to appear unexpectedly, because incongruously, in gardens and landscapes. They are usually mechanical or electrical transformers, vents, valves, siphons, drains, culverts, headwalls, dams, and many other nameless and mysterious forms. In a good landscape design, these structures are integrated into the overall plan.

Special buildings. Special buildings include many that are nearly as complete as the fully enclosed buildings that are the province of the architect: greenhouses, conservatories, orangeries, tool sheds, dovecotes and pigeon houses, icehouses, root houses, bathhouses, playhouses, and many more. These are usually auxiliary in scale and detail in relation to the main house or other buildings but relate to them in character and detail.

Shelter structures, engineering structures, and special buildings are important in garden and landscape because they introduce precise geometric forms intermediate in scale between main buildings and landscape. If scattered or designed indiscriminately, they can destroy a pleasant landscape; carefully designed, they can be so grouped or arranged as to create rhythmic connections and patterns within the overall architectural-landscape design concept.

Importance of structures and buildings in design

Sculptural components and outdoor furnishings. Sculptural components of garden and landscape have traditionally been predictable forms and types: figurative sculpture, decorative urns and plaques, fountains, sundials, birdbaths, cisterns, and wells. All of these continue to appear as elements of the persistent underground Beaux Arts vocabulary. In contemporary design, however, they are eliminated or take on new forms derived from modern sculpture. The possibility now exists for the production of gardens and landscapes so completely sculptured that one cannot tell where design stops and sculpture begins.

Outdoor furnishings and equipment include all of those fixed and movable elements that tend to appear in garden or landscape after the plans are done and installed and therefore without benefit of design control. In the garden they are seats, tables, barbecues, umbrellas, plant containers, supports, and guards, as well as lights and light systems. In the public landscape they include these garden elements and many more: signs, trash containers, alarm boxes, mailboxes, newsstands, kiosks, service elements, telephone stands. If all of these elements are not predicted insofar as possible in the original design plans, incorporated in them, and carefully controlled thereafter, they can destroy carefully planned landscapes. One red oil drum for trash can dominate the visual experience of a large, pastoral picnic area.

Garden of the Kinkaku-ji (Golden Pavilion), showing the pavilion as a structural component of garden and landscape design, 15th century, Kyōto, Japan.
By courtesy cf the Consulate General of Japan, Chicago

II. Kinds of design

The landscape is everything one sees from wherever one is, still or moving. The landscape as a work of individual art is any garden or estate space designed, developed, and maintained for the private experience of an individual or family, a space not accessible to others either physically or visually. The landscape as a work of collective art is everything beyond this private range: everything seen beyond the confines of private gardens or estates, all borrowed landscapes, all streetscapes, all city, metropolitan, and regional landscapes, and their accumulation in national, continental, hemispheric, and world landscapes. This collective art may be good or bad depending on whether it results from the accidental accumulation of individual and conflicting efforts or from controlled and planned efforts.

PRIVATE OR RESIDENTIAL DESIGN

The history of landscape design is largely the history of landscape as a work of private, individual art. Plazas (structural public open spaces, not dominated by foliage), throughout classical, medieval, and Renaissance history, were the concessions of the ruling class to the need for public meeting places; but it was not until Central Park was developed in New York City in the mid-19th century that this need reached the level of designed public green spaces. During most of its history, landscape design was of three kinds: private utilitarian farms and gardens; private gardens in which the enhancement of the quality of living was paramount; and private gardens designed to express the power and benevolence of the ruling or upper classes. The expansion in scale of private gardens beyond the needs of private living led inexorably, first, to the dedication of such spaces to public use and then to the development of public gardens and parks designed for public use.

The private garden, however, has remained the centre for private fantasy and a means of escape from the grinding and difficult world of reality. The most important aspect of the private garden is its privacy: from the physical world, by means of distance and enclosure; from the social world, by separation and exclusion. Space and greenery are also important. The space may be very small, perhaps a tiny courtyard, and greenery limited to one or two plants, but these make possible that private world of fantasy that may make the difference between sanity and lunacy. The 20th-century mass migration to the suburbs is the latest expression of this need.

Generally, the private garden occupies a space some-

Kinds of private gardens

where between 20 feet square and one quarter of an acre (100 feet square). The forms of private gardens range from the formalism of pure geometry or the artistic representation of natural processes through the variations of standard gardening techniques and the informalism of letting nature take its course to various manifestations of literary, poetic, historic, and subjective concepts.

When housing moves from single-family, detached buildings on private lots to higher density variations—duplexes, semidetached villas, town houses, clusters, condominiums, low- and high-rise apartments—new relationships between private and public design develop. As population density increases, private design shrinks, and public design increases. Somewhere between the extremes of the single-family dwelling with minimum public space and the high-rise apartment with minimum private space there is an optimum relationship in which the real needs for both private and public space and facilities can be expressed. Perhaps the best potential lies in town-house, cluster-house, and condominium developments, in which there is a flexible relationship between public and private space and facilities.

PUBLIC DESIGN

Because of fixation on the notion that the original resource of land and landscape, continuous from sea to shining sea, is best organized for private or public use by gridiron subdivision into innumerable separate parcels, public landscape design begins at the level of single buildings on single lots, with frontyards and backyards. The buildings may be government offices, quasi-public companies, or private corporations, but all tend to be designed in terms of public and private spaces, as though they were private residences for the groups involved.

Campus design begins when publicly accessible buildings grow into complexes of two or more, for religious, commercial, industrial, governmental, or educational use. Instead of or in addition to simple frontyard and backyard design, there are more complex systems of spaces between buildings, which vary from courtyards and quadrangles of varying forms and dimensions to passageways connecting them in varying widths and degrees of overhead coverage. The open spaces range in character from paved architectural courtyards and cloisters to open playing fields and parklike spaces. Campus design makes possible the richest, most complex and rewarding range of relationships between architectural and landscape design. Perhaps the best examples of campus design, in which the sequential experience of

Campus design

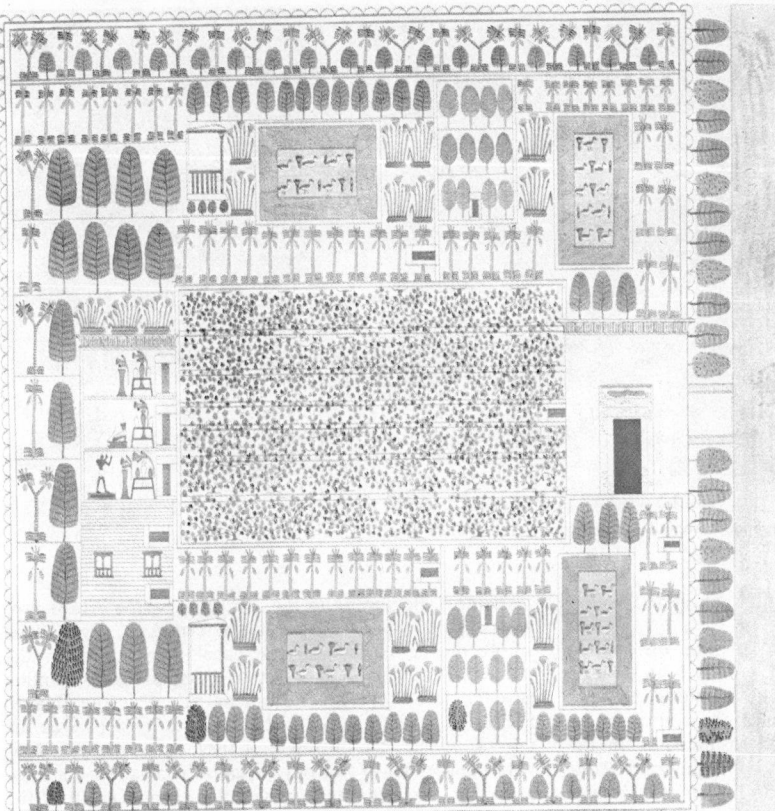

Earliest surviving detailed garden plan, the estate of an Egyptian official, *c.* 1400 BC.
From Ippolito Rosellini, *I monumenti dell' Egitto e della Nubia.* In the New York
Public Library.
By courtesy of the New York Public Library, Oriental Division, Astor, Lenox and Tilden Foundations

Urban
design

indoor and outdoor space approaches the maximum, are
the religious, educational, and civic complexes of Europe,
developed before the idea of gridiron subdivision fragmented environmental design. There are also many fine
examples in the United States of similar institutions that
have transcended or resisted subdivision.

In the broader area of urban design, which deals with
whole communities or sectors of urban areas, landscape
architecture deals with such open-space components as
public gardens, parks and playgrounds, plazas, squares,
and malls. In these urban spaces, the designer attempts
to meet the need for community, for play and recreation,
for refreshment and relaxation, for individual withdrawal
in a gregarious atmosphere. While in quantity they may
be inadequate in comparison, say, to Europe, qualita-
tively the United States has many fine examples of public
open spaces.

Towns, cities, and metropolitan areas may be said to
have three basic components: buildings, designed by
architects or builders; open spaces, designed by landscape architects or technicians; and circulation-utility
corridors—the street, highway, railway, and rapid-transit
systems—which are usually planned and designed by
engineers.

The basic structure of urban areas consists of the open
spaces together with corridors comprising a total open-
space system, defined by and connecting the buildings.
The corridors have usually been considered merely a
utilitarian framework, connecting and servicing buildings and quality open spaces, channelling traffic and
utilities throughout urban areas, and connecting them
with the open country around. Modern urban thinking
has begun to go beyond this concept, to see the total
open-space-corridor system as the major qualitative
structure of the city, which, when viewed in conjunction
with overall building design, is seen to establish the city's
basic character.

From this point of view the role of landscape architecture, once limited to tasteful planting of corridors designed by engineers, begins to expand. Some urban plan-

ners would expand it even further, believing that open-
space corridors should be designed throughout primarily
as social spaces for people and only secondarily as utilitarian passages for vehicles.

Commemorative sites—cemeteries, historic spots, bat-
tlefields—are important to man because they memorial-
ize and symbolize important events in personal, local,
national, or world history. Wherever they occur—in
urban, rural, or primeval areas—these sites or areas are
marked with stone or bronze memorials and often drama-
tized with more elaborately designed developments. The
designs tend to follow traditional and conservative precedents, often impressive but seldom imaginative. It is
still difficult to equal Asplund's Forest Crematorium
(1940) in Stockholm or the Fosse Ardeatine memorial in
Rome. (G.Ec.)

III. Historical development

WESTERN

Antiquity. *Egyptian.* The earliest surviving detailed
garden plan, dating from about 1400 BC, is of a garden
belonging to an Egyptian high court official at Thebes.
The main entrance is aligned on a pergola (trellis-
bordered) walk of vines leading directly to the dwelling.
The rest of the garden is laid out with tree-lined avenues,
four rectangular ponds containing waterfowl, and two
garden pavilions. Although rigidly symmetrical, the garden is divided into self-contained, walled enclosures,
so that the symmetry of the whole could not have been
apparent to the viewer. Such a highly developed pattern
argues a considerable incubation period, and it is likely
that similar enclosed pleasure gardens had been designed
as early as 2800 BC.

Assyrian, Babylonian, and Persian. The gardens of
Assyria, Babylon, and Persia were of three kinds: large,
enclosed game reserves such as the garden of Eden described by the Hebrews in the Old Testament; pleasure
gardens, which were essentially places where shade and
cool water could be privately enjoyed; and sacred enclosures rising in man-made terraces, planted with trees

The
earliest
surviving
garden
plan

Frescoed wall of fruit trees, palms, and oleanders from the garden room, Villa of Livia, Rome, *c.* 50 BC. In the Museo Nazionale Romano, Rome.
SCALA, New York

and shrubs, forming an artificial hill such as the Hanging Garden of Babylon.

Greek and Hellenistic. The urban life of ancient Greece led to the development of houses built around central, private courtyards. Lined with colonnades that gave access to the rooms of the house, the courtyard, or peristyle, was open to the sky and insulated from the street. In the peristyle was a garden consisting of a water supply and potted plants. Much of life, however, was lived in public. The sports grounds, where exercise was taken, became popular gathering places and developed into the original academy and lyceum, which included the exercise ground, seats for spectators, porticoes for bad weather, statues of honored athletes, and groves of shade trees. These public recreation grounds (academies and lyceums) set the type for the later classical Roman villa garden and the 19th-century European public park. A third type of garden familiar to the Greeks was the sacred landscape, such as the Vale of Tempe or the mountain sanctuary of Delphi.

The relatively austere Greek taste was transformed in the Hellenistic Age (*c.* 323 BC–30 BC) by the influence of the East. Luxurious pleasure grounds were made, especially at colonies such as Alexandria and Syracuse. These gardens were conspicuously luxurious in their display of precious materials, and artificial in their use of hydraulic automata.

Roman. Roman gardens derived from the Greek, those in the seaside resorts of Pompeii and Herculaneum (1st century BC) following the Hellenistic pattern. These small, enclosed town gardens were visually extended by landscapes painted on the walls. Throughout the imperial period, the more ambitious villa gardens flourished in many forms on sites carefully chosen for climate and aspect.

The most elaborate was that of Nero's Golden House, which covered over 300 acres (120 hectares) in the middle of Rome and included an artificial lake (where the Colosseum now stands) and a theatrically pastoral landscape of plowland, vineyard, pasture, and wood. More influential in later times was the vast garden complex of Hadrian's Villa, of which extensive ruins can still be found near Tivoli.

Middle Ages. The barbarian invasions of the 4th and 5th centuries AD destroyed Roman civilization and with it the gardens of western Europe. The Eastern Empire, centred on Constantinople, retained its hold on Greece and much of Asia Minor for another millennium; and Byzantine gardens persisted in the Hellenistic tradition, laying more emphasis on wonder-provoking apparatus than on aesthetic values. A recurrent feature of these gardens was a tree of gold or silver equipped with birds that flapped their wings and sang and branches that sprayed wine or perfume.

Islāmic. Beginning in the 7th century, the Arabs progressively captured much of western Asia, Egypt, the whole of the North African coast, and Spain; in the process, they spread features of Persian and Byzantine gardens across the Mediterranean as far as the Iberian Peninsula. Most characteristic of these gardens was the use of water—the ultimate luxury to desert dwellers, who appreciated it not only because it allowed plants to grow but also because it cooled the air and gratified the ear with the sound of its movement. It was commonly used in regularly shaped, often rectangular, pools. The

Shallow tiled pool and water channels characteristic of the Islāmic garden. "Sultan of Syria Holding an Audience in His Garden," Persian miniature from the manuscript (1522–23) of the *Būstān* by Saʿdī. In the Metropolitan Museum of Art, New York.

Byzantine gardens

water was kept moving by simply designed fountains and fed by narrow canals resembling agricultural irrigation channels. Because water was rarely abundant, the pools were shallow but increased in apparent depth by a blue tile lining.

These pools of water graced Islāmic gardens—such as those of the Alhambra in Granada—that resembled the Hellenistic colonnaded courtyard. The gardens provided shade, excluded hot winds, and created the sense of being in a jewelled private world, insulated from normal pressures. Expanses of water mirroring the sky gave an impression of spaciousness and introduced lightness, brightness, and an air of unreality to the enclosed space. In the Moorish Caliphate of Cordoba in Spain, in the valley of the Guadalquiver, there were said to have been 50,000 villas, all of which probably had such garden courts.

The greatest period of garden making in the Islāmic world was the 14th century. In the vicinity of the conqueror Timur Lenk's capital of Samarkand, the names of 11 royal gardens are recorded, and there were probably others belonging to his nobles. Whereas gardens of the Alhambra type were architecturally conceived within the total plan of a building, some of the more extensive Timurid gardens and their derivatives, the Mughal gardens of India, were pleasances of water, meadow, trees, and flowers, in which buildings took a subordinate place. Although these garden buildings were permanent, their subordinate role and the lightness and luxuriating frivolity of their design mark them as heirs of the casually positioned tents seasonally erected in hunting parks. There were also gardens of strictly architectural design— huge walled enclosures with corner towers, a central palace, regularly disposed avenues, and tanks of water. Deer and pheasants were kept in these gardens, which combined the quality of hunting park and of *hortus conclusus*, or closed garden. Trees were planted sometimes in regular quincuncial patterns (one in the middle and one at each corner of a square or rectangle) but more often freely. In all types of Islāmic gardens, flowers were lavishly used. Their presence was even simulated in garden carpets and in the woven hangings that were used as temporary screens.

Influential on later Western practice were the parks made by the Saracen emirs of Sicily. The Normans who conquered the Saracens in the 11th century adopted the manner of life of those they had overthrown, and thus the emirs' gardens survived their makers. A large area of the Conca d'Oro, the great natural amphitheatre behind Palermo, was taken up with pleasure grounds—walled enclosures large enough to contain woods and hills, canals, artificial lakes, groves of oranges and lemons, fountains, water stairways, and wild creatures running free. Parks made by the Saracen emirs of Sicily

Western European. In Europe, beyond the limits of the Islāmic conquest, the destruction of civilized society by the barbarian tribes had been nearly complete; but the physical remains of the past shaped the reviving future: the peristyle gardens of Roman villas became the cloisters of Christian basilicas. Security and leisure existed only in the monastic system, which also preserved some of the traditional skills of cultivation. For some time the only type of garden was the cloister, with its well, herbs, pot plants, and shaded walk. Then secular gardens began to appear, but they were usually of limited extent, confined within the fortifications of a castle and often raised well above ground level on a battlemented turret. These Gothic gardens were rectangular, with the traditional division into four parts by paths, the quarters again subdivided according to the amount of ground available and the convenience of cultivation. At the point of principle intersection was a well, which, when elaborated, became the vertical feature of the garden. Seats—often of turf— were constructed in the walls. Many flowers were grown, but their season was short; after June and often earlier, the beds were flowerless. More extensive and elaborate gardens were rare.

In 13th-century Italy, through the influence of the Holy Roman emperor Frederick II, who had spent much of his youth in Sicily, the example of the Saracen emirs was felt in Apulia and Naples. The *Triumph of Death*, painted by the Florentine artist Andrea Orcagna (Pisa, Campo Santo), shows a garden of considerably greater Italian gardens of the Middle Ages

Medieval walled garden combining a grassy and shaded pleasure area with an herb garden. *Roman de la Rose*, miniature from a 15th-century French manuscript. In the British Museum.

extent than the cloister or battlement type. Gardens like this existed also in Lombardy, where the court of Gian Galeazzo Visconti, the founder of the great walled park of Pavia, cultivated the arts of civilized life. In describing the Royal Gardens at Naples, the writer and poet Giovanni Boccaccio speaks of statues disposed regularly around a lawn, interspersed with marble seats. Such a garden suggests that Frederick II's classicizing influence extended into the mid-14th century. Also significant was the garden of Hesdin in Picardy, which became famous throughout France for its automata and water tricks. It was made by a crusader who, having returned to France by way of Palermo in 1270, no doubt incorporated in his garden what he had seen of Saracenic gardens there and in Syria. In northern Europe, Hesdin was an exotic creation without parallel for several centuries.

Renaissance to modern: 15th to 20th centuries.   *Italian.* The increasing prosperity of western Europe and man's increasing confidence in himself and in his capacity to impose order on the external world was reflected in the gardens of Italy by the mid-15th century. The change began near Florence, where the old medieval enclosures began to open up. The rectangles, which had been dissociated, were now sited one behind the other, thus prolonging the main axis, which was now aligned on the centre of the dwelling. This change inevitably introduced the idea that house and garden were a coherent, complementary whole. And, because villas were increasingly sited for amenity rather than defense, gardens became less enclosed, more susceptible first to visual, then to actual extension.

The unity of house and garden, together with the need for physical adjustment to the sloping sites favoured by classical precedent, threw the planning of the new Renaissance garden into the hands of architects. Most influential was the garden courtyard designed by Donato Bramante at the Vatican to link the Papal palace with the Villa Belvedere; the uneven site and the disparity in bulk of the two buildings was overcome with terraces and stairways. It remained an enclosed garden but one far removed from the earlier cloistral courtyards. The garden of the Belvedere combined the function of an open-air room with that of an outdoor sculpture gallery.

The ingredients of the Renaissance garden thus separately established were united in varying proportions. The typical evolved garden of the period was characterized by some openness of aspect, axial development, a tendency to prolongation, unity of concept between house and garden emphasized by a considerable "built"

element of stone, lavish employment of statuary (often in the form of fountains), and the proliferation of such classical accents as grottoes, nymphaea (Roman buildings with a fountain, plants, and sculpture), urns, and inscriptions. There is no adequate evidence that this type of garden had an exact equivalent in the classical period, although there is evidence that each of its elements existed.

The variation in style among Italian gardens is considerable and is due not only to the date they were made, the exigencies of the site, and regional variation but also to their social function. The scale of the garden compartments at the back of the Villa Gamberaia at Settignano (1610), for example, is small in contrast with the extensive view over Florence from the front and thus suggests intimate use by members of a small household. The more extensive parterre garden (an ornamental garden with paths between the beds) of the Villa Lante at Bagnaia (begun 1564) is designed neither for solitary enjoyment nor for a crowd but for a select, discerning company—as is the garden of the far more splendid Villa Farnese at Caprarola (completed 1587). The most remarkable mid-16th-century garden, that of the Villa d'Este at Tivoli (1550), is situated on a steep slope of the Sabine hills. The river that plunges down this slope is harnessed to an astonishing variety of fountains, including a "water organ." Although the garden is designed around a central axis, the stream is not used centrally but is led about the garden in order to take maximum advantage of its force. Unlike the less copious stream of the Villa Lante garden, which quietly emphasizes the central axis, the Tivoli stream is ostentatious. The Villa d'Este is, in fact, a spectacular permanent theatrical performance meant to astonish and impress the multitude. A different impression is given by the Boboli Gardens of the Pitti Palace at Florence (1550). Though, like the Villa d'Este gardens, they were designed for a crowd—specifically, for state functions—they are not dramatic in themselves. Unless used ceremonially, they are lifeless and arid. The ruined garden associated with, though detached from, the Orsini Castle at Bomarzo is a remarkable aberration. Its original layout probably consisted of a grove in which were concealed the stone giants and strange monsters that now astonish visitors. The garden reflects the strained individualism of the mid-16th-century style termed Mannerist.

Flowers were extensively used in most Italian gardens, but because of the shortness of their season they could not be the principle feature. Beds were divided into decorative geometric compartments by trimmed herbs, rosemary, lavender, or box. In general, more emphasis was

The typical Italian Renaissance garden

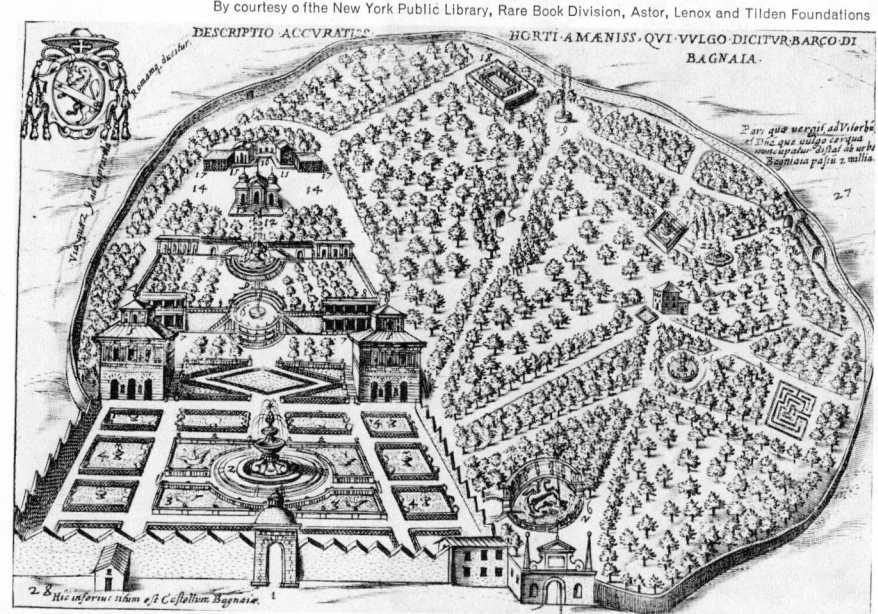

Plan of the Villa Lante at Bagnaia, Italy, showing the parterre gardens and enclosed park. From Giacomo Lauro, *Antiquae Urbis Splendor*, 1612. In the New York Public Library.

Elaborate hillside fountain in the gardens of the Villa d'Este at Tivoli, Italy, mid-16th century.
G. Tomish—Photo Researchers

given to evergreens; ilex, cypress, laurel, and ivy gave shade and were an enduring contrast to stonework.

17th- and 18th-century French. The French invasions of Italy in the last quarter of the 16th and first quarter of the 17th centuries introduced to France the idioms of the Italian garden. The first garden coordinated with dwelling appeared at the Château of Anet (1547–56) and was designed by the architect Philibert Delorme; but, despite its evident sophistication, it remained an inward-looking, essentially medieval garden. The first sign of prolongation and calculated extension of vision beyond the garden proper appeared in the grounds of Dampierre. Here the moat that formerly surrounded French castles became an ornamental body of water on one side and a decorative canal on the other. Both aspects of the new garden design —coordination with the dwelling and extension along a central axis—were united at the château of Richelieu (1631) and later at Vaux-le-Vicomte (completed 1661),

the château of Nicolas Fouquet, the minister of finance. On Fouquet's fall in the mid-17th century, his team of artists—which included the landscape designer André Le Nôtre—was taken over by the young Louis XIV, and the gardens of Versailles were begun.

The French version of the Italian garden was created in the plain of north France, which largely conditioned the manner of its development. The array of steep terraces linked by stairways, which characterized the Villa d'Este and many others, was predominant in France only at St. Germain-en-Laye, where the steep site permitted it. Elsewhere, grandeur on the scale that competitive pride demanded was achieved by extraordinary extension: an axial development suggesting a domain coextensive with the world. The French 17th-century garden, a manifestation of Baroque taste, required variety as well as unlimited vista and achieved it with fountains, parterres, and lesser gardens disposed within the boscages (wooded enclosures) that flanked the central axis. These hidden gardens were the successors of the *giardini segreti* of the Italians but had a different function; they were not retreats for private contemplation or intimate conversation but the setting for ingenious theatrical entr'actes. Distinctively French was the unified and elaborate treatment of the compartmentalized garden beds, which the Italians had made in a variety of forms. These *compartiments de broderie* were arabesques, sometimes of box edging and flowers but more often of coloured stones and sand. The Persians had copied their flower gardens on carpets and taken them indoors; the French laid out their grounds in the form of carpets. The French garden was marked by a ruthlessly logical extension of practices that had been empirically evolved in Italy.

French cultural dominance of Europe in the early 18th century led to an almost universal adoption of Versailles as the model for palatial gardens. Even at Naples, where the gardens of Poggio Reale had astonished the invading French in the late 15th century, a vast layout inspired by the axial extent of Versailles was developed at Caserta; and, as far away as Peter the Great's Peterhof in Russia, a pseudo-Versailles was laid out by the French gardener Alexandre-Jean-Baptiste Le Blond. Impressive exercises in the same manner were carried out in Germany and Austria. In Holland, also, the example of the French garden was irresistible, although local conditions as well as

Alain Perceval, Paris

Parterre de broderie composed of box, brick dust, earth, and sand at the château of Vaux-le-Vicomte, France, a late-19th-century re-creation by Henri Duchêne based upon late-17th-century designs by André Le Nôtre.

"Garden at Utrecht," by Issac de Moucheron (1667–1744) showing the Dutch preference for high, trimmed hedges and alleyways. In the City of Birmingham Museum and Art Gallery, Birmingham, England.
By courtesy of the City of Birmingham Museum and Art Gallery, Birmingham, England; photograph, Reilly and Constantine

national temperament led to regional variation. Because Dutch canals were busy highways, they generally flanked gardens rather than constituted the main axis. No luxury in Holland, water was less extravagantly used than in drier, hotter climates. Moreover, fountains were less common because the absence of high ground required that they be power driven. Finally, because stone was scarce, terraces were usually held by turf banks rather than by retaining walls, and sculpture was often of lead. Another kind of sculpture typical of the Dutch garden was topiary: trees and shrubs were trained, cut, and trimmed into sculptural, ornamental shapes. Social conditions made the apparent extension of a geometric garden scheme easy, for a man-made landscape already existed in the intensively cultivated Netherlands. In Spain, aridity as well as Islāmic tradition perpetuated the patio garden, a room of air and shade in the tradition of the Greek peristyle. Although a famous layout in the French style was made on high ground at La Granja, where the cooler air and an ample head of water made it acceptable, the classical extension garden remained basically alien to the Iberian Peninsula.

17th- and 18th-century English. The Italian pronouncement "things planted should reflect the shape of things built" had ensured that gardens were essentially open-air buildings and the making of them the province of architects. Before the 18th century, geometric regularity had been applied in great details of design and in small. England was committed to a version of the French geometric extension garden but with an emphasis on characteristic English grass lawns and gravel walks. Whereas the typical French vista was along the main axis, with subordinate vistas at right angles to it, in the two most influential gardens in England, St. James's and Hampton Court, the vistas sprang like the rays of the sun from a semi-circle. With the accession of William and Mary (1689–1702), Dutch influence led to widespread use of topiaried yew and box.

In 18th-century England, man became increasingly aware of the natural world of which he was a part. Rather than imposing his man-made geometric order on the natural world, he began to consider adjusting his own life to it. Literary men, notably Alexander Pope and Joseph Addison, began to question the propriety of trees being carved into artificial shapes as substitutes for masonry and to advocate the restoration of free forms.

The man who led the revolt against the "artificial," symmetrical garden style was the painter and architect William Kent, the factotum of the Earl of Burlington. Together Burlington and Kent created at Chiswick House (1734) a garden with a meandering stream and an "irregular" path. As the writer Horatio Walpole put it, Kent's "principle was that nature abhors a straight line." The process of relaxing the garden's architectural discipline advanced with speed. At Stowe, Buckinghamshire, the original enclosed, geometrical garden was amended over the years until a totally different, "irregular" formality was achieved. Trees, for example, were allowed to assume their natural forms, and a large expanse of water was redesigned into two irregularly shaped lakes.

The use of the ha-ha, or sunken fence, to create and at the same time conceal the physical division between garden and contiguous park grounds (a division needed to keep grazing animals out of the garden) was a major step in the creation of the new, "natural" garden. Walpole explains the purpose of the visual unification:

> The contiguous ground of the park without the sunk fence was to be harmonized with the lawn within; and the garden in its turn was to be set free from its prime regularity, that it might assort with the wilder country without.

The face of the "country without" was altered by the rage that afflicted the English nobility for planting vast areas of trees. Much of England was covered with new parks, traversed by rides and avenues that primarily were conceived as visual extensions of the garden paths. The

Revolt against the "artificial" symmetrical garden

Noel Habgood, Eastborne

Idealized natural landscape, gardens at Stourhead, Wiltshire, designed by the owner, Henry Hoare, 18th century.

Reconstruction of the 16th-century gardens at Villandry, in the Loire Valley, France.
Edwin Smith

The "natural" English gardens of the 18th century

unification of park and garden was virtually completed by Lancelot "Capability" Brown (1715–83) by the simple expedient of making the garden into a park. "Capability" (so-called because he always spoke of a place as having "capabilities of improvement") developed the current aesthetic that an undulating line was "natural" and that it was the "line of beauty" by using little statuary and few buildings and concentrating on designing landscapes according to nature's harmonies and gradients. His landscapes consist of expanses of grass, irregularly shaped bodies of water, and trees placed singly and in clumps.

Although the adherents of the new English school of garden design were in agreement in their abhorrence of the straight, classical line and the geometrically ordered garden, they did not agree on what the natural garden should be. Unlike Brown, for example, the taste for the romantic and the literary led many to seek inspiration in the dramatic and the bizarre, in the remote past, and in remote, exotic places. The Brownian style was strongly challenged, for example, by the "Picturesque" school, led by Sir Uvedale Price and the artist-parson William Gilpin, who argued, quite correctly, that the "naturalism" of the Brownians was no less unnatural than the geometric regularity of Le Nôtre's Versailles and that sudden declivities, rocky chasms, and rotting tree trunks (all deliberately designed) were more proper for the natural garden than were enormous, undulating meadows accented with tight clumps of thickly planted trees. Another school of opinion created what might be called the English garden of poetic bric-a-brac. The aim in this garden was to create an air of accident and surprise and to arouse varied sensations (solemnity, sublimity, terror) in the viewer—sensations evoked by associations with the remote in time and space. Wandering through the grounds one came upon classical statues, urns, and temples; Gothic ruins, ivy-covered and inhabited by owls; or Chinese pagodas and bridges. After Horatio Walpole recorded the first appearance of chinoiserie at Wroxton in 1753 (a garden no doubt laid out some years before), "Chinese" and Gothic details were featured, together with classic temples, in most fashionable grounds.

By 1760 the enthusiasm for this style had diminished in England; but in Europe the poetic bric-a-brac garden (*le jardin anglo-chinois*, or *le jardin anglais*, as the French called it) was almost as widely emulated as Versailles had been. In Italy, for example, Renaissance gardens were destroyed to make way for the new fashion, as at the Villa Mansi near Lucca. In France, the sculpted group of "Apollo Attended by the Nymphs" was removed from the classical "Grotto of Thetis" on the terrace of Versailles to a secluded boscage garden, where it was housed under ornamental "Turkish" tents; eventually it was moved from there to a simulated rocky cavern in the *jardin anglais* of the Petit Trianon. The *jardin anglais* was to be found even at Queluz in Portugal and in the Potsdam garden of Frederick the Great of Prussia.

English influence on European gardens

19th century. Increasing world trade and travel brought to late-18th-century Europe a flood of exotic plants whose period of flowering greatly extended the potential season of the flower garden. Although the emphasis in Italian Renaissance gardens, in the classical Baroque gardens of France, in the lawns and gravelled walks of 17th-century England, and in the Brownian park garden was upon design, they had rarely been totally without flowers. In most gardens flowers were grown, sometimes in great numbers and variety; but flower gardens in the modern sense were limited to cottages, to small town gardens, and to relatively small enclosures within larger gardens. The accessibility of new plants, together with avidity for new experience and a high-minded concern with natural science, not only gave renewed life to the flower garden but was the first step toward the evolution of the garden from work of art to museum of plants. A compromise between the new flower garden and the Brownian park was effected by Humphry Repton. He was largely responsible for popularizing the open terrace overlooking the park, which frankly admitted the different functions of park and garden and also emphasized their stylistic disharmony. The plant collectors' garden, or "gardenesque" style, was most strongly advanced by J.C. Loudon in the mid-19th century. Loudon urged that garden making be taken out of the hands of the architect, the painter, and the cultivated dilettante and left to the professional plantsman.

The undiscerning use of the new palette that importation and plant breeding had made available was so patently an aesthetic disaster that by the end of the 19th century attempts were made to break its hold. The architect Sir Reginald Blomfield advocated a return to the formal garden, but to this, insofar as it required dressed stonework, there were economic objections. More successful and more in tune with the escapist needs of the increasing number of urban dwellers were the teaching and practice of William Robinson, who attacked both the old ceremonial garden and the collectors' garden with equal vigour and preached that botany was a science, but gardening was an art. Under his leadership a more critical awareness was brought to the planning and planting of gardens. His own garden at Gravetye Manor demonstrated that plants look best where they grow best and that they should be allowed to develop their natural forms. Adapting Robinson's principles, Gertrude Jekyll applied the cult of free forms over a substructure of concealed architectural regularity, bringing the art of the flower garden to its highest point.

Early gardens in the United States

In North America, where for a long time most men were preoccupied with making a world, not a garden, ornamental gardens were slow to take hold. In the gardens that did exist, the rectilinear style popular in late-17th- and early-18th-century Europe persisted well into the 18th century—perhaps because it met man's psychological need to feel he could master a world that was still largely untamed. The town gardens of Williamsburg (begun in 1698) were typical of the Anglo-Dutch urban gardens that were being attacked everywhere in 18th-century Europe except Holland. And Belmont, in Pennsylvania, was laid out as late as the 1870s with mazes, topiary, and statues, in a style that would have been popular in England about two centuries before.

Although garden improvers set up in business in the United States, there is no evidence that they prospered until the 19th century, when one hears of André Parmentier, a Frenchman, who worked on Hosack's estate at Hyde Park and then of A.J. Downing, a successful protagonist of the gardenesque, who was succeeded by Calvert Vaux and Frederick Law Olmstead (the latter the originator of the title and profession of landscape architect), the planners of Central Park in New York (begun 1857) and of public parks throughout the country.

The eclecticism of the 19th century was universal in the Western world. Besides the gardens that were fundamentally Reptonian—that is, an attempted compromise between the Brownian park garden and the Loudonian flower garden—gardens of almost every conceivable style were copied; designing teams such as Sir Charles Barry, the architect, and William Eden Nesfield, the painter, in England, for example, produced Italianate parterres as well as winding paths through thickets.

Modern. A sense of history still plays a part in 20th-century gardening. The desire to maintain and reproduce old gardens, such as the reconstruction of the 16th-century gardens of Villandry in France and the colonial gardens of Williamsburg in the United States, is not peculiarly modern (similar things were done in the 19th century); but, as man increasingly needs the reassurance of the past, it is likely to be, within limits, an accelerating process. Attempts to create a distinctive modern idiom are rare. Gardens large by modern standards are still made, in styles that vary from a version of the grand early-18th-century manner at Anglesey Abbey in Cambridgeshire to an inflated Jekyllism crossed with gardenesque at Bodnant near Conway. An air either of controlled wilderness or of slightly run-to-seed orderliness is preferred. Modern public gardens, which have evolved from the large private gardens of the past, seek instant popular applause for the quantity and brightness of their flowers. In Brazil Roberto Burle Marx uses tropical materials to give an air of contemporaneity to traditional modes of design. Gardens frequently reflect Japanese influence, particularly in America.

Most characteristic of the 20th century is functional planning, in which landscape architects concentrate upon the arrangement of open spaces surrounding factories, offices, communal dwellings, and arterial roads. The aim of such planning has been to provide, at best, a satisfactory setting for the practical aspects of living. It is gardening only in the negative, "tidying up" sense, with little concern for the traditional garden purpose of awakening delight. So starved has the spirit of those living in heavily populated regions become, however, that demands grow more and more insistent for gardening in the positive sense—for environmental planning with a chief goal not of facilitating man's economic activities but of refreshing his spirit.

Functional planning

NON-WESTERN

Chinese. Western gardens for many centuries were architectural, functioning as open-air rooms and demonstrating Western man's insistence on physical control of his environment. Because of a different philosophical approach, Oriental gardens are of a totally different type.

China—which is to Eastern civilization what Egypt, Greece, and Rome are to Western—practiced at the beginning of its history an animist form of religion. The

Parque del Este, Caracas, designed by Roberto Burle Marx, 1959.

sky, mountains, seas, rivers, and rocks were thought to be the materialization of spirits whom men regarded as their fellow inhabitants in a crowded world. Such a belief emphasized the importance of good manners toward the world of nature as well as toward the world of men. Against this background the Chinese philosopher Lao-tzu taught the quietist philosophy of Taoism, which held that one should integrate oneself with the rhythms of life; Confucius preached moderation as a means of attaining spiritual calm; and the teaching of Buddha elevated the attainment of calm to a mystical plane.

Such a history of thought led the Chinese to take keen pleasure in the calm landscape of the remote countryside. Because of the physical difficulty of frequent visits to the sources of such delight, the Chinese recorded them in landscape paintings and made three-dimensional imitations of them near at hand. Their gardens were therefore representational, sometimes direct but more often by substitution, making use of similar means to recreate the emotions that choice natural landscapes evoked. The kind of landscape that appealed was generally of a balanced sort; for the Chinese had discovered the principle of complementary forms, of male and female, of upright and recumbent, rough and smooth, mountain and plain, rocks and water, from which the classic harmonies were created. The principle of scroll painting, whereby the landscape is exposed not in one but in a continual succession of views, was applied also in gardens; and grounds were arranged so that one passed pleasantly from viewpoint to viewpoint, each calculated to give a different pleasure appropriate to its situation. A refined and expectant aestheticism, which their philosophy had inculcated, taught the Chinese to ignore nothing that would prepare the mind for the reception of such experiences, and every turn of path and slope of ground was carefully calculated to induce the suitable attitude. As the garden was in effect a complex of linked, related, but distinct sensations, seats and shelters were situated at chosen spots so that the pleasures that had been meticulously prepared for could be quietly savoured. Kiosks and pavilions were built at places where the dawn could best be watched or where the moonlight shone on the water or where autumn foliage was seen to advantage or where the wind made music in the bamboos. Such gardens were intended not for displays of wealth and magnificence to impress the multitude but for the delectation of the owner, who felt his own character enhanced by his capacity for refined sensation and sensitive perception and who chose friends

The typical Chinese garden

to share these pleasures with the same discernment as he planned his garden.

Based on natural scenery, Chinese gardens avoided symmetry. Rather than dominating the landscape, the many buildings in the garden "grew up" as the land dictated. A fanciful variety of design, curving roof lines, and absence of walls on one or on all sides brought these structures into harmony with the trees around them. Sometimes they were given the rustic representational character of a fisherman's hut or hermit's retreat. Bridges were often copied from the most primitive rough timber or stone-slab raised pathways. Rocks gathered from great distances became a universal decorative feature, and a high connoisseurship developed in connection with their colour, shape, and placement.

Although the troubled 20th century has largely destroyed the old gardens, paintings and detailed descriptions of them dating from the Sung dynasty (AD 960–1279) reveal a remarkable historical consistency. Nearly all the characteristic features of the classic Chinese garden—man-made hills, carefully chosen and placed rocks, meanders and cascades of water, the island and the bridge—were present from the earliest times.

Chinese gardens were made known to the West by Marco Polo, who described the palace grounds of the last Sung emperors, during whose reign the arts were at their most refined. Other accounts reached Europe from time to time but had little immediate effect except at Bomarzo, the Mannerist Italian garden that had no successors. In the 17th century, the English diplomat and essayist Sir William Temple, sufficiently familiar with travellers' tales to describe the Chinese principle of irregularity and hidden symmetry, helped prepare the English mind for the revolution in garden design of the second quarter of the 18th century. Chinese example was not the sole or the most important source of the new English garden; but the account of Father Attiret, a Jesuit at the Manchu court, published in France in 1747 and in England five years later, promoted the use of Chinese ornament in such gardens as Kew and Wroxton and hastened the "irregularizing" of grounds. The famous *Dissertation on Oriental Gardening* by the English architect Sir William Chambers (1772) was a fanciful account intended to further the current revolt in England against the almost universal Brownian park garden. Influence of the West on Chinese gardens was slight. Elaborate fountain works, Baroque garden pavilions, and mazes—all of which the Jesuits made for the imperial garden at Yüan Ming

Influence of Chinese gardens on the West

Harmony and intimacy of the Chinese garden. "Enjoyment of the Chrysanthemum Flowers," ink and colours on paper by Hua Yen, 1753. In the St. Louis Art Museum.

Yüan—took no root in Chinese culture. Not until the 20th century did European regularity occasionally become evident near the Chinese dwelling; at the same time, improved Western hybrids of plant species that had originated in the East appeared in China.

Japanese. Chinese culture permeated the Far East and, by way of Korea, infiltrated Japan. By the year AD 1000 Japan was already developing a distinctive national art best described as a stylized, ritualistic version of the Chinese. The typical early Japanese garden lay to the south of the dwelling and consisted of a narrow pond or lake orientated through its longer axis and containing an

William G. Froelich, Jr.

Pond and moss-covered bridge, Katsura Imperial Gardens, Kyōto, Japan.

island. At the north end of the pond was an artificial hill from which a secondary stream descended in a cascade. These stereotyped gardens of the Heian period (AD 794–1185) show by their careful reproduction of magical detail that they derive from a single prototype—certainly Chinese. Variation entered only through the compulsion of the site and the detailed handling of stones and trees.

Creativity began to replace imitation in the Kamakura period (1192–1333). Although there were many subsidiary styles, gardens were broadly classified, according to terrain, as either hill or flat. The hill garden, consisting of hills and ponds, came to be associated with Mt. Fuji, the mountain of ideal form. The flat garden represented a surface of water—lake or sea—with its adjacent shores and islands. Since the scale was so small—a heap of earth 30 feet (nine metres) high representing a mountain and a half-acre (0.2-hectare) pond, an arm of the sea—the intention was to reproduce the spirit rather than the features of the chosen landscape. Association and symbolism thus played a major role in the creation and appreciation of these gardens.

The scaling down of landscapes to garden size was logically continued to the point where miniature gardens were made in trays as small as a foot square containing lakes, streams, islands, hills, bridges, garden houses, and real trees painstakingly cultivated to an appropriate scale. These small, portable gardens reflected the extreme of the picturesque tradition of Oriental gardening.

Two characteristic Japanese styles are the abstract garden and the tea garden. The most famous example of the

Types of Japanese gardens

former is the garden of the Ryōan-ji in Kyōto, where an area about the size of a tennis court is covered with raked sand and set with 15 stones divided into five groups. If anything is represented here, it is some rocky islets in a sea, but the appeal of the garden lies essentially in the charm of its relationships. The Japanese tea garden grew out of an esoteric ritual originated in China and connected with the taking of tea. The tea cult, which flourished from the 14th to the end of the 16th centuries, was calculated to instill humility, restraint, sensibility, and other cognate virtues. The gardens through which the guests approached the teahouse were governed by severe rules of design intended to create an appropriate spiritual atmosphere, such as the "lonely precincts of a secluded mountain shrine" or "a landscape in clouded moonlight, with a half-gloom between the trees" or any mood "in harmony with the spirit of tea." Even the precise number and arrangement of nails in the teahouse door were specified.

The Japanese fondness for systematization led them to classify garden treatment as well as subject. Three standard treatments were recognized: the elaborate, the moderate, and the modest. Once the degree of finish was determined, certain rules were followed to preserve consistency. The Taoist doctrine of complementary forms was at the root of much Japanese design, but the cult of stones is also central to Japanese gardening. The nine stones, five standing and four recumbent, used in Buddhist gardens were symbols of the nine spirits of the Buddhist pantheon; the shapes and postures chosen were presumed to have a relationship with the character and history of the persons represented. Sacred associations played a part in profane gardens as well. It was regarded as inauspicious, for example, if three stones, the "Guardian Stone," the "Stone of Adoration," and the "Stone of the Two Deities" (or the "Stone of Completeness"), were not present. In addition to the sacred symbols, a whole armoury of poetic associations and symbols grew up, and stones, according to their shape and use, acquired such names as "Torrentbreaking Stone," "Recumbent Ox Stone," "Propitious Cloud Stone," and "Seagull-resting Stone." Beyond what they represented, stones were part of an aesthetic design and had to be placed so that their positions appeared natural and their relationships harmonious. The concentration of the interest on such detail as the shape of a rock or the moss on a stone lantern led at times to an overemphatic picturesqueness and an accumulation of minor features that, to Occidental eyes accustomed to a more general survey, may seem cluttered and restless. Nevertheless, Japanese gardening has had and continues to have an influence on the gardens of the West, particularly in the United States. The influence appears not so much in direct imitation of Japanese themes as in the selection and presentation of detail.

The use of stones

Indian. The influence of Chinese culture throughout the East was such that other indigenous cultures usually succumbed to it; but India was an exception. Western garden styles were introduced into northern India first through contact with Iranian culture, then by the invasion of Alexander the Great and the subsequent Hellenistic influence, and, finally, by the invading Mughals, who introduced the Islāmic garden. In southern India and in Ceylon elaborate gardens existed before the birth of the Buddha (563? BC). In such a garden—containing baths, lotus-covered pools, trees, and beds of flowers—the Buddha himself was born beneath a tree. Anciently worshipped by the Hindus, trees thus acquired an additional sanctity. Buddhist temples were associated with gardens whose purpose was to promote contemplation and whose preferred sites were therefore away from cities.

African, Oceanic, and pre-Columbian. The African cultures beyond European and Asiatic influence did not evolve pleasure gardens, although in their more settled societies a beginning had perhaps been made. Nor is more than a love of flowers and a casual cultivation of decorative plants recorded of the Oceanic peoples; but of the Aztecs of Mexico and the Incas of Peru the conquistadors reported elaborate gardens with terraced hills, groves, fountains, and ornamental ponds that were es-

Architecturally planned park landscape for an Imperial residence, containing an artificially meandering river and pavilions. An example of the ideal landscapes of Mughal India. Miniature from a 17th- or 18th-century album. In the Staatliche Museen zu Berlin.
By courtesy of the Staatliche Museen zu Berlin

sentially royal pleasure grounds, reflecting a need for private solace and public display not unlike contemporary gardens in the West.   (D.P.Cl.)

BIBLIOGRAPHY. The 19th and 20th centuries have seen a spate of gardening literature, both of the how-to-do-it variety and of specialized studies of national types. General works include DEREK CLIFFORD, *A History of Garden Design,* 2nd ed. (1966), an attempt to relate garden design to cultural history; and MARIE LUISE GOTHEIN, *A History of Garden Art,* 2 vol., trans. from the German by MRS. ARCHER-HIND (1928), the most valuable detailed general history.

National Studies: (*America*): WILLIAM COBBETT, *The American Gardener* (1821); A.J. DOWNING, *A Treatise on the Theory and Practice of Landscape Gardening* (1841); C.L. OLMSTEAD, *Forty Years of Landscape Architecture,* 2 vol. (1922–28; reprinted in 1 vol., 1970), (*Brazil*): P.M. BARDI, *The Tropical Gardens of Burle Marx* (1964). (*China*): OSVALD SIREN, *Gardens of China* (1949). (*Great Britain*): ALICIA AMHERST, *A History of Gardening in England,* 3rd ed. (1910); SIR REGINALD BLOMFIELD and F. INIGO THOMAS, *The Formal Garden in England,* 3rd ed. (1901, reprinted 1936); M. HADFIELD, *Gardening in Britain* (1960); CHRISTOPHER HUSSEY, *English Gardens and Landscapes, 1700–1750* (1967); EDWARD S. HYAMS, *The English Garden* (1964), a well informed guide book. (*India*): C.M. VILLIERS-STUART, *Gardens of the Great Mughals* (1913). (*Italy*): J.C. SHEPHERD and GEOFFREY JELLICOE, *Italian Gardens of the Renaissance,* 3rd ed. (1966), the best book; GEORGINA MASSON, *Italian Gardens,* new ed. (1966), a well informed but not always accurate guide book that lacks historical coherence; INIGO TRIGG, *The Art of Garden Design in Italy* (1906), the source of many 20th-century reproductions of Italian gardens; EDITH WHARTON, *Italian Villas and Their Gardens* (1904), still worth attention. (*Japan*): LORRAINE E. KUCK, *The World of the Japanese Garden* (1968), the best book; J. CONDOR, *Landscape Gardening in Japan* (1893); J. HARADA, *The Gardens of Japan* (1928). (*Persia*): DONALD N. WILBER, *Persian Gardens and Garden Pavilions* (1962). (*Spain*): C.M. VILLIERS-STUART, *Spanish Gardens: Their History, Types and Features,* (1929).

Modern Works: PETER F. SHEPHEARD, *Modern Gardens* (1953); THOMAS D. CHURCH, *Gardens Are for People* (1955); JAMES C. ROSE, *Creative Gardens* (1958); GARRETT ECKBO, *The Art of Home Landscaping* (1956); *The Landscape We See* (1969); PETER COATS, *Great Gardens of the Western World* (1963); ELIZABETH B. KASSLER, *Modern Gardens and the Landscape* (1964); SUSAN and GEOFFREY JELLICOE, *Modern Private Gardens* (1968); GEOFFREY JELLICOE, *Studies in Landscape Design* (1960); LAWRENCE HALPRIN, *Cities* (1963); EDMUND N. BACON, *Design of Cities* (1967); IAN L. MCHARG, *Design with Nature* (1969).

(D.P.Cl./G.Ec.)

Gardening

Gardening belongs both to art and to science: to art in that it deals with the grouping of plants in harmonious or pleasing arrangements in the landscape; to science in that it is concerned with the techniques of cultivating plants and producing satisfactory growth.

The personal value of, and interest in, gardening obviously derives as much from the relaxation that the practice provides as from the appreciation of the garden itself. The home garden—like the Roman atrium or the Spanish patio—can be a place of repose and seclusion: it can offer a protected corner from the winds of nature as well as from the winds of everyday concern. The therapeutic effect of gardening has been expounded by many; it has a salutory value not only because it requires physical work but also because it fosters a hopeful and anticipatory mood conducive to contentment.

GENERAL FEATURES

Definitions. Horticulture includes the growing of flowers, fruits, and vegetables as crops for profit, as in market gardening, or truck farming; the growing of plants for sale, as in nursery gardening; and the cultivation of a plot of ground for the growing of flowers, fruits, and vegetables for private enjoyment or consumption. In this last sense, only is horticulture equivalent to gardening in its popular and unqualified meaning.

Nursery gardening is a business of considerable current investment. Plant nurseries and seedsmen provide an expanding list of cultivated and improved varieties of garden plants, and an annually increasing volume of plant material is shipped and sold throughout the world to satisfy the demand now put upon such businesses by the growing number of home gardeners. Other horticultural enterprises include the raising of flowers for the cut-flower market and landscape architecture and design (see the articles HORTICULTURE; and GARDEN AND

The business of gardening

LANDSCAPE DESIGN). Since plants in gardens often are grown in conditions very different from their natural environment, and often have been highly selected or bred through many generations to develop larger flowers or fruits than are found in the wild plants, it is necessary to protect them from competition with other more-vigorous plants by weeding and by other garden operations and to apply to their cultivation principles derived from plant physiology, chemistry, and botany, often modified by the experience of the planter. Although the basic principles involved in growing plants are the same in all parts of the world, the practice naturally needs much adaptation to local conditions.

Historical background. *Early history.* Of the earliest recorded garden, the garden of Eden, there are no details. It has sometimes been placed in Mesopotamia (now Iraq). The hanging gardens of Babylon may have been terraces arranged around a steep hill. Some of the early Egyptian wall paintings show boats gliding through pools of water lilies and lotuses, some of which may have been cultivated; and a picture in one of the tombs in the Valley of the Kings shows a gardener tying vines to a trellis. Minoan frescoes taken from the Palace of Knossos in Crete, probably of one of the Middle Minoan periods (c. 2200–1600 BC), show lilies, irises, rockroses, and possibly saffron crocus. The garden of Alcinous, which was probably in Corfu, and the enclosed gardens, vineyards, and fruit trees at Ithaca described nostalgically by Odysseus in the *Odyssey* probably date from about 1250 BC.

In the earliest times, as today in the Middle East, shade was the first requisite of any garden, and so the garden of Cyrus II the Great was a garden of trees and orchards. In classical Rome, the record shows fully and clearly that the Romans enjoyed their gardens, which were mainly enclosed courts with some emphasis on herbal plants. The rose was then one of the favourites, and topiary art was practiced with box shrubs.

In China plant knowledge and gardening developed very early. The first Chinese work about plants may have been the classical herbal of Shen Nung, said to have reigned about 2800 BC, but it was not put into writing until the 1st century AD, and most of it is now lost except for a few excerpts in later works.

Medieval gardening revolved largely around the monasteries. There may have been many other gardens as well, but probably the scribes at the monasteries kept better records. The garden was still essentially a small enclosed area, and the plants grown were mainly herbs for medicinal purposes, vegetables for food, vines, and fruit.

The Renaissance garden

Gardens, however, were reborn all over Europe during the Renaissance, with most activity in the south, especially in Italy. Such flowers as lilies, roses, carnations (gillyflowers), and many others, appear in the backgrounds of many pictures and tapestries. The garden remained an enclosed area, the proverbial haven of quiet and peace in a troubled world. The earliest Renaissance herbals show knowledge of a great variety of plants, and the information given was in most cases derived from original observations of the living plants rather than from tradition and hearsay, but copying from other works was also fairly common, and the same wood blocks were passed on for illustrations from book to book.

The earliest specifically English book devoted to gardening is probably one by a Mayster (Master) Ian Gardener, *The Feate of Gardening*, a practical little work said to be a copy made about 1440 of a work originally written about 40 years earlier.

17th and 18th century. The range of garden plants growing at the end of the 16th and early in the 17th centuries in the Netherlands is well shown by the delightful engravings in the various herbals of the time.

The earliest botanic garden was that of Pisa (1543), closely followed by Padua (1545). The first English botanic garden, that of Oxford, was founded in 1621, followed by the great one at Edinburgh in 1667. Kew was founded almost a century later, in 1759. These botanic

gardens contributed substantially to the art and science of horticulture and still do, as demonstrations of diverse plants and as diffusers of plants to other gardens and of knowledge (see also BOTANICAL GARDEN).

In the 17th century both the range of plants available and interest in gardens increased considerably. It was during this time that the royal gardens and estate gardens were prominent. In the mid-17th century began the extensive development of majestic park gardens in France. These were laid out on an immense scale with elaborate waterworks and borders of pleached trees, but one of their principles was that the main feature of the layout should be clear and easily seen from one central point, generally the terrace of the château.

The influence of French gardens spread to England in the 18th century, where it found expression in gentle, parklike landscape gardens. Again, these were not gardens of flowers but parks for the delectation of the owner and his household retinue and friends. The English gardens relied for their effect on clever adaptations of the landscape with lakes, gentle slopes, and clumps of trees as well as most carefully placed temples in the Roman style. Sometimes, a romantic but sham ruin was created as a focal point for the eye, and artificial grottoes were constructed. Literally, small armies of labourers must have been used in shifting the soil.

The rise of the small home garden

Gardens in North America were smaller, trimmer, and neater, with box edgings and pleached trees, like those of Williamsburg in Virginia, so lovingly and carefully reconstructed in the 20th century. In the late 18th and early 19th centuries, a more intensive interest in the individual plant and its beauty was exemplified by the great flower books of the period, illustrated by well-known artists of the time, and by the *Botanical Magazine* (founded in 1787 and published in the mid-20th century as *Curtis's Botanical Magazine*) with its fine-coloured plates. Gardening became an international art, and such books were circulated over Europe as were also the prized plants that they portrayed. In addition to large parks, smaller gardens were just beginning to be developed.

From the 19th century. Smaller gardens became widespread in the 19th century; a floral retreat was no longer the sole property of the rich. Many good gardening features were undoubtedly swept away in the making of the great landscape gardens of the 18th century, with their emphasis on naturalism and curves and their abhorrence of a straight line. Much that was good in those landscape gardens unfortunately was later elaborated and filled in with intricate bedding schemes and fussy detail in the 19th century. It was a complete contrast from earlier styles. The craft of gardening, rather than the art, was in the ascendant; but it was a more widely spread craft, extending from the manor down to the small suburban garden. In this century began the rise of societies of horticulture and botany, which played a great part in the encouragement of horticulture thereafter.

A passion for masses of brightly coloured flowers, in place of the softer greens of the grass and trees of the landscape garden, became the ruling theme, but with this change came interest also in the individual plant, in the making of large collections of different plants, and in the superb cultivation of outstanding specimens for competition and exhibition. It was the beginning of the age of specialization in plants. It was also the beginning of the age of the great plant collectors, of plant introduction, selection of plants, and plant breeding (see PLANT BREEDING).

Indoor gardening

In the winter, gardening was entirely an indoor enjoyment in the elaborate conservatories and supporting greenhouses, except for a few enlightened estate owners who began to plant arboretums, based especially on the North American conifers that were then just introduced. Expeditions of many botanist-explorers returned with a wealth of exotic plant material. The flood of plants was so large that it could not be contained in the trim Victorian or Edwardian gardens, nor did such introductions as rhododendrons, lilies, and other plants fit well into such ordered schemes. But they did fit well into the woodlands, which were then thinned, cleaned up, and opened out to become part of the garden.

New plants brought new gardening habits, which continued into the second half of the 20th century and were exemplified by the great woodland gardens of the first half of the 20th century. It was an exciting time in gardens when so much new was flowering. The system of awards given to plants by the horticultural societies increased enthusiasm for new plants and also for better varieties of old plants, and the demand for these stimulated the nurserymen to grow and supply them.

While the shortage and high cost of labour in mid-20th century limited the size and content of privately as opposed to publicly maintained gardens, the enthusiasm for horticulture was greater and more widespread than ever before over all the temperate and tropical world, and the number of gardens increased. Labour-saving tools, more natural as opposed to more formal methods of growing plants, and the great discoveries of plant physiology and pest control made possible the spread of horticulture, both as a profession and as a hobby and relaxation from other work. Combined with this, a specialist interest by certain gardeners in one particular genus or group of plants rather than a diffused interest in a large range of plants brought with it a great upsurge of plant breeding in the 1920s, which enriched gardens with an increasing supply of floral novelties.

THE HOME GARDEN

Common aspects of gardens. To apartment dwellers, as well as to homeowners, the hobby of gardening can be a source of much pleasure. An outdoor space—no matter how small—can be a garden, an area tended for a spot of beauty or for food. Even a window box, or pots on a window sill, can support a succession of blossoms and some easily grown herbs or vegetables.

The grounds about a house are an extension of the home itself and can add greatly to its attractiveness. Portions may be set aside for privacy, for recreation, for utility, and for an aesthetic setting for the house. Such home gardens have certain features in common: (1) A boundary or visual limit, within which the garden is framed, usually a hedge, shrub border, fence, wall, or other screen as background. (2) Provision for enjoying and utilizing the garden by way of paths, vistas, seating, and separation of areas. (3) Focal points, including unusual or favoured plants, sculpture, or some other dramatic feature such as a pool, waterfall, entryway, etc. (4) A pattern, or major theme—as formal or informal, traditional or contemporary, natural or exotic, subdued or stimulating, etc.

These features are the basic elements of a home-garden plan and can help in creating a unified, overall garden scheme that will provide seasonal development of a planting in relation to the house and other existing features of more or less permanent nature, such as large trees and topographical features.

Styles in gardens

Styles in gardens vary from formal and ordered—in which symmetrical balance and a rather regular grouping of plants is evident—to informal and natural, in which the design is basically that found in nature and only subtly modified, if at all. The distinction admittedly is difficult to maintain, for each of these features may be blended in a garden. Traditional gardens, classic in the arrangement of borders and beds, are often contrasted with contemporary gardens, in which design elements are usually conspicuous and exhibit clearly the influence of man. Eastern gardens, especially the Japanese gardens, are classic and quite traditional in their own countries but are strikingly different elsewhere; in Western countries, therefore, such gardens are often considered contemporary and novel. Gardens, of course, can be anything the gardener wants: wild or ordered, utilitarian (a vegetable patch or cut-flower plot) or aesthetic —geometrical or free form. (An account of the styles popular historically, with description of famous gardens, is given in the article GARDEN AND LANDSCAPE DESIGN.)

Permanent elements. The more or less permanent plants considered in the garden plan are the lawn and turf areas, ground covers, shrubs and vines, and trees. More transitory and therefore requiring continued concern are the herbaceous plants, such as the short-lived annual (one season) and biennials (two season), and the perennials and bulbous plants, which resume growth each year.

Lawns and ground covers. Areas of turf, or lawn, provide the green expanse that links all other garden plantings together. They usually consist of grasses— thousands to the square metre—kept shorn close to the ground to provide a green carpet. But grasses are not the only plants suitable for such cover. Lawns can be of almost any low-growing plant that spreads rapidly to clothe the ground. Such nongrass covers are called ground covers and include a variety of creeping plants.

The main grasses used in cool areas for fine-textured lawns are fescues (*Festuca* species), bluegrasses (*Poa* species), and bents (*Agrostis* species), often in mixtures. A rougher lawn mixture may contain ryegrass (*Lolium* species). In drier tropical and subtropical regions, Bermuda grass (*Cynodon dactylon*) is frequently used, but it does not make nearly so fine a lawn as those seen in temperate regions of higher rainfall.

Lawn grasses

Ground covers are perennial plants used as grass substitutes in regions where grasses do poorly or are sometimes combined with grassy areas to produce a desired design. The deep greens, bronzes, and other colours that ground-cover plants can provide offer pleasing contrasts to the green of a turf. Ground covers, however, are not so durable as lawns and do not sustain themselves as well under foot traffic and other activities, Among the better known plants used as ground covers are Japanese spurge (*Pachysandra terminalis*), common periwinkle (*Vinca minor*), lily of the valley (*Convallaria majalis*), ajuga or bugleweed (*Ajuga reptans*), bishop's weed or goutweed (*Aegopodium podagraria*), many stonecrops (*Sedum* species), dichondra (*Dichondra repens*), and many ivies (*Hedera* species).

Shrubs and vines. Smaller woody plants, such as shrubs and bushes, have several stems arising from the base. These plants attain heights up to about six metres (about 20 feet). They often form the largest part of modern gardens since their cultivation requires less labour than that of herbaceous plants, and some flowering shrubs have extended blooming periods. Among the popular garden shrubs are lilac (*Syringa vulgaris*), privet (*Ligustrum* species), spirea (*Spiraea* species), honeysuckle (*Lonicera* species), forsythia (*Forsythia* species), mock orange (*Philadelphus* species), and hydrangea (*Hydrangea* species).

Bushlike azaleas (*Azalea* species) and rhododendrons (*Rhododendron* species) provide colourful blossoms in shady spots where other shrubs find it difficult to grow.

Vines are often useful in softening the sharp lines of buildings, fences, and other structures. They can provide shade as an awning or cover on an arbour or garden house. Some species are also useful as ground covers on steep slopes and terraces. Among the many woody perennial vines for the garden are the ivies, trumpet vine (*Bignonia*, or *Campsis, radicans*), clematis (*Clematis* species), wisteria (*Wisteria chinensis*), climbing roses, annual herbaceous vines such as morning glory (*Ipomoea* species) and ornamental gourds, the last of which can provide rapid but temporary coverage of unsightly objects.

Trees. Trees are the most permanent features of a garden plan. Since they form the structural foundation of the home garden, care should be taken to choose trees that, when mature, fit the site where they were planted. The range of tree sizes, shapes, and colours is vast enough to suit almost any gardening scheme, from shrubby dwarf trees to giant shade trees, from slow to rapid growers, from all shades of green to bronzes, reds, yellows, and purples. A balance between evergreen trees, such as pines and spruces, and deciduous trees, such as oaks, maples, and beeches, can provide protection and visual interest year around (see TREE).

Transitory elements. *Herbaceous plants.* Herbaceous plants, which die down annually and have no woody stem above ground, are readily divided into three categories, as mentioned earlier: (1) Annuals, plants that complete their life cycle in one year, are usually grown from seed sown in the spring either in the place they are to flower or in separate containers, from which they are subsequently moved into their final position. Annuals flower in summer and die down in winter after setting seed. Many brilliantly coloured ornamental plants as well as many weeds belong in this category. (2) Biennials are plants sown from seed one year, generally during the summer. They flower the second season and then die. (3) Herbaceous perennials are those that die down to the ground each year but whose roots remain alive and send up new top growth each year. They are an important group in horticulture, whether grown as individual plants or in the assembly of the herbaceous border.

Bulbous plants. For horticultural purposes, bulbous plants are defined to include those plants that have true bulbs, corms, and a few with tubers or rhizomes. A bulb is defined as a modified shoot with a disklike basal plate and above it a number of fleshy scales that take the place of leaves and contain foods such as starch, sugar, and some proteins. Each year a new stem arises from the centre. A corm consists of the swollen base of a stem, generally rounded or flattened at the top and covered with a membranous tunic in which reserve food materials are stored. A tuber or rhizome is not the base of the stem but rather a swollen part of an underground stem; it is often knobbly.

All such plants have evolved in places where they can survive in a semidormant state over a long unfavourable season, either cold, mountain winters or long, summer droughts.

KINDS OF GARDENS

Flower gardens. Though flower gardens may vary in different countries in the different plants that are grown, the basic planning and principles are nearly the same, whether the gardens are formal or informal. Trees and shrubs are the mainstay of a well-designed flower garden. In designing a garden, these permanent features are usually considered first, and the spaces for herbaceous plants, annuals, and bulbs are arranged around them. The range of flowering trees and shrubs is enormous. It is important, however, that such plants be appropriate to the areas they will occupy when mature. Thus it is little use planting a forest tree that will grow to 100 feet high and 50 feet across in a small suburban front garden 30 feet square, but a narrow flowering cherry or redbud tree would be quite suitable. Bare-rooted trees and shrubs are best set in the garden while they are dormant. Plants rooted in a ball of soil or in a container, however, can be planted at any time.

Blending and contrast of colour as well as of forms are important aspects to consider in planning a garden.

The old-fashioned garden The older type of herbaceous border was designed to give a maximum display of colour in summer, but many gardeners now prefer arranging for some flowers during the early spring as well, at the expense of some bare patches later. This is often done by planting early-flowering bulbs in groups toward the front. Mixed borders of flowering shrubs combined with herbaceous plants are also popular and do not require quite so much maintenance as the completely herbaceous border. Borders of annuals are brilliant with colour during the summer, but sowing, thinning, supporting, and planting out half-hardy plants requires extensive labour if the border is large.

Groups of half-hardy annuals may be planted at the end of spring to fill gaps left by the spring-flowering bulbs. The perpetual-flowering roses and some of the larger shrub roses look well toward the back of such a border, but the hybrid tea roses and the floribunda and polyantha roses are usually grown in separate rose beds or in a rose garden by themselves.

Woodland gardens. The informal woodland garden is the natural descendant of the shrubby "wilderness" of

earlier times. The essence of the woodland garden is informality and naturalness. Paths curve rather than run straight and are of mulch or grass rather than pavement. A miniature "wilderness" Trees are thinned to allow enough light, particularly in the glades, but irregular groups may be left, and any mature tree of character can be a focal point. Plants are chosen largely from those that are woodlanders in their native countries: rhododendron, magnolia, pieris, and maple among the trees and shrubs; lily, daffodil, and snowdrops among the bulbs; primrose, hellebore, Saint-John's-wort, epimedium, and many others among the herbs.

A woodland garden is a labour-saving way of gardening; it need not be kept very neat and tidy.

Rock gardens. Rock gardens are designed to look as if they are a natural part of a rocky hillside or slope. If rocks are added, they are generally laid on their larger edges, as in natural strata. A few large boulders usually look better than a number of small rocks. In a well-designed rock garden, rocks are arranged so that there are various exposures for sun-tolerant plants such as rock-roses and for shade-tolerant plants such as primulas, which often do better in a cool, north-facing aspect. Many smaller perennial plants are available for filling plants in vertical cracks among the rock faces.

The main rocks from which rock gardens are constructed are sandstone and limestone. Sandstone, less irregular and pitted generally, looks more restful and natural, but there are certain plants, notably most of the dianthus, which do best in limestone. Granite is generally regarded as too hard and unsuitable for the rock garden since it weathers very slowly.

Water gardens. The water garden represents one of the oldest forms of gardening. There are records and pictures of water lilies made by the Egyptians as far back as 2000 BC. The Japanese have also made water gardens to their own particular and beautiful patterns for many centuries. In the centre is often a Japanese lantern of stone and perhaps a flat trellis roof of wisteria extending out over the water. In Europe and North America, water gardens range from formal pools with rectangular or circular outline, sometimes with fountains in the centre and often without plants or with just one or two water lilies (*Nymphaea*), to informal pools of irregular outline planted with water lilies and other water plants and surrounded by boggy or damp parts where moisture-tolerant plants can be grown. Unless the pool contains suitable oxygenating plants, the water will not keep clear nor will any introduced fish live. Most water plants, including even the large water lilies, do well in still water ¾ to 1½ metres deep (2–5 feet). Water lilies may be planted in baskets let down to the bottom or directly in the mud of the bottom. In the case of new plantings, water is added gradually as the plants grow until full depth is achieved. Temperate water lilies are all-day bloomers, but many of the tropical and subtropical ones open their flowers only in the evenings.

In temperate countries, water gardens can also be made under glass and the pools kept heated. In such cases, more tropical plants, such as the great *Victoria amazonica* (*V. regia*) or the lotus (*Nelumbo nucifera*), may be grown together with papyrus reeds at the edge. The range of moisture-loving plants for damp places at the edge of the pool is very great and includes many very beautiful plants such as the candelabra primulas, calthas, irises, and osmunda ferns.

Herb and vegetable gardens. Most of the medieval gardens and the first botanic gardens were largely herb gardens containing plants used for medicinal purposes or herbs such as thyme, parsley, rosemary, fennel, marjoram and dill for savouring foods. A small herb garden planted near the kitchen door can be both decorative and useful, or a group of herbs can be planted together in a convenient place. The term herb garden is usually used now to denote a garden of herbs used for cooking, and the medicinal aspect is rarely considered. A herb garden needs a sunny position since the majority of the plants grown are native to warm, dry regions.

The planting of vegetables is a part of many gardens,

although as gardens get smaller and labour for gardens more expensive, this is the part of the garden on which many tend to economize.

The vegetable garden requires an open and sunny location. Good cultivation and preparation of the ground is important for successful vegetable growing, and it is also desirable to practice a rotation of crops as in farming. The usual period of rotation for vegetables is three years; this also helps to prevent the carry-over from season to season of certain pests and diseases.

The old French *potager*, the prized vegetable garden, was grown to be decorative as well as useful; the short rows with little hedges around and the high standard of cultivation represent a model of the art of vegetable growing. The elaborate parterre vegetable garden at the Château de Villandry is perhaps the finest example in Europe of a decorative vegetable garden.

Growing vegetables for exhibition is a separate craft that requires techniques more thorough than the usual vegetable gardener will manage, but the increase in size that can be obtained is considerable.

Specialty gardens. *Roof gardens.* The modern tendency in architecture for flat roofs has made possible the development of attractive roof gardens in urban areas above private houses and commercial buildings such as big department stores. These gardens follow the same principles as others except that the depth of soil is less because of the weight and therefore limits the size of plants to be used. The plants are generally set in tubs or other containers, but elaborate roof gardens have been made with small pools and beds. Beds of flowering plants are suitable, among which may be stood tubs of specimen plants to produce a desired effect.

Indoor plants and window boxes. The growing of houseplants is a very popular feature of horticulture. It has been found that many plants of tropical forests, such as the aroids and some of the figs—particularly *Ficus elastica*—and herbs such as African violets (*Saintpaulia*) grow well in centrally heated houses provided with adequate moisture; they do not require high intensity of light. The modern picture window, however, with its wide expanse of undivided glass, combines particularly well with large houseplants, and specimens up to six feet or more may be grown if space permits; alternatively, the plants may be kept to a modest size by constant pruning, but correct choice of plants is important. The range of houseplants is very large, and large specialist nurseries supply them.

Scented gardens. Scent is one of the characters that many people appreciate highly in flowers. Gardens in which scent from both leaves and flowers is the main criterion for inclusion of a plant have been established for the benefit of blind people in some parks and can give much pleasure. Many plants with highly scented flowers or leaves do not have very decorative or brilliantly coloured flowers, but this is of no consequence to a blind person. For such a garden, the plants must be made easy to touch, and thus they are usually grown in raised beds. Many of these scented plants must be bruised or rubbed to yield their fragrance; others become strongly scented in full sun.

THE PRINCIPLES OF GARDENING

Soil requirements. Soil is obviously the basic factor in the cultivation of all plants, although in a few specialized instances soilless cultivation in water, gravel, or sand enriched with suitable chemicals (hydroponics) has been quite successful.

Soil consists of particles, mainly mineral, derived from the breakdown of rocks and other substances but also including organic matter. In the pore spaces between the particles, both soil water containing dissolved salts and air circulate. This air contains more carbon dioxide and less oxygen than the atmosphere. It and the soil water also contain immense quantities of minute living organisms, many so small that they cannot be seen even with a microscope. For plant roots, this pore space into which they must penetrate and from which they obtain much of their nourishment is very important, as are the prop-

erties of the surfaces of the soil particles, which vary in different kinds of soils.

Soils can be roughly divided into three main types on the basis of their usefulness horticulturally, but many areas contain a mixture.

Clays. Clays, in which the particles are very fine, are called in horticulture heavy soils, since it is hard work to turn them over with a spade. They can be very fertile but tend to be lacking in good drainage, holding their water closely adhered to the soil particles; therefore, they cannot be worked when wet, and under pressure they tend to compact down tightly, driving out the air. During drought they tend to become hard and even to develop large cracks so that they cannot be worked satisfactorily. Clay soils can be lightened with as much humus as can be dug into them.

Sands and gravels. Sands and gravels are opposite in properties to clay. The soil particles are large, and the soils are called light because they are easy to work and turn in nearly all weather. Since their water-holding capacity is very low, however, they tend to dry out quickly. They are "hungry" soils requiring great quantities of manures, humus, and fertilizers to keep them prolific.

Peats and heaths. Peats and heaths are usually very acid and ill drained. They result where conditions have prevented the complete breakdown of old vegetable matter into humus, generally because of poor aeration and surplus acid bog water. Much peat is derived from the decaying roots of sphagnum moss, useful for mulching in the garden. A heath soil is generally less fertile, consisting of a large mixture of sand with the peat and tending to be very low in mineral content and in water-retaining capacity.

The ideal garden soil is a medium loam consisting of a mixture of clay and sand, fairly rich in humus and easily worked, and not forming large clods when dry. The consistency of the soil is important, for a porous, properly tilled soil provides a medium through which roots can penetrate readily and rapidly. Another factor of importance in soils is the acidity or alkalinity, which is generally expressed chemically as a "pH number" that can be ascertained by a simple test with litmus paper. The neutral point is pH 7; numbers below this are acid and above it alkaline. Soil alkalinity is usually derived from free calcium carbonate or a similar alkaline salt.

Feeding: fertilizing and watering. Maximum return can be obtained only from soil that contains an ample supply of the elements necessary for plant growth, combined with sufficient moisture to enable them to be dissolved and then absorbed through the plant hairs. The three main elements required for plant growth are nitrogen, potassium, and phosphorus, which are taken up by the plant in the form of salts; but a number of trace elements—magnesium, sulfur, iron, manganese, copper, zinc, boron, molybdenum, chlorine, and sodium—are also required in much smaller amounts.

Manuring with farmyard manure or garden compost can supply the majority of these requirements. These manures, however, are scarce and expensive in many areas, and so it is often necessary to use mineral fertilizers as well as organic ones. The soil, however, is such a complex substance with so many interrelated factors contributing to its fertility that all fertilizers must be applied both in moderation and in balance with each other according to the deficiencies of the soil and the requirements of the particular crop. Different crops have very different fertilizer requirements. Compost, decayed organic matter from vegetable wastes such as kitchen scraps, grass clippings, and leaves, is of benefit in providing nutrients and humus to soils.

Manures are generally best dug into the ground in autumn in most temperate countries, but they may also be used as mulches in the spring to control weeds. The mulches are then dug into the ground in the autumn.

Watering of newly placed plants and of all plants during periods of drought is an essential gardening chore. Proper (*i.e.*, deep and thorough) watering—not simply sprinkling the soil surface—can result in greatly improved growth. Water is essential in itself, but it also

The French *potager*

Manures and composts

makes minerals available to plants in solution, the only form usable by plants. All plants benefit from watering during drought. About 2½ centimetres (one inch) of water applied weekly to the soil surface will percolate down about 15 centimetres (about six inches); this is a minimal subsistence amount for many herbaceous garden plants, and small trees and shrubs require more. Thorough and deep watering once a week is beneficial to plants by encouraging deep penetration of roots, which in turn enables plants to survive dry surface conditions.

Protection. Practically all plants have a definite figure of tolerance to cold, below which temperature they are killed. Many plants from tropical or subtropical regions cannot survive frost and are killed by temperatures below 32° F (0° C). Others, called half-hardy, can withstand a few degrees of frost. Fortunately, many of the best garden plants are completely hardy and will withstand any low temperatures that are likely to be reached in the temperate regions. Tolerance of cold depends considerably on the state of the plant at the time of exposure. A dormant plant, for example, can withstand much lower temperatures than one in active growth in which the vessels of the stem are full of sap. A plant in dry soil can usually withstand lower temperatures than one in moist soil. Many plants have an adaptation for enduring winter conditions: annuals by seeding; bulbous plants by dying back to an underground storage organ; herbaceous perennials by dying back to ground level.

The simplest form of protection for a plant is a wrapping to keep warmer air around it—a mulch (leaves, soil, ashes, etc.) placed in winter over the crown of a slightly tender plant, or sacking placed around it. This last method is particularly useful for plants that lose their leaves and become dormant seasonally; it is not, therefore, so suitable for evergreens, which utilize their leaves year round.

"Forcing" flowers

Glass structures such as greenhouses or outdoor frames can provide additional protection for tender plants. Such structures can be heated and the temperature regulated by a thermostat to any required degree. Thus in temperate regions, orchids and other tropical plants can be grown so that they flower throughout the winter, many "forced" to flower earlier than their normal season by the higher temperature. Greenhouses are roughly divided by gardeners into four categories: (1) The cold house, in which there is no supplementary heating and which is only suitable for plants that will not be killed by a few degrees of frost, such as alpines, or bulbous plants, such as daffodils in pots. The exclusion of wind and the heat from the sun will keep such a house appreciably warmer than the temperature outside. (2) The coolhouse, in which the minimum temperature is kept at 45° F (7° C). Most amateurs' greenhouses fall into this class and a very large range of plants can be grown in them. (3) The intermediate house, in which the minimum temperature is kept at 55° or 60° F (13° or 16° C) is suitable for a wide range of orchids. (4) The stove house, or hothouse, in which the minimum temperature is kept above 60° F (16° C) and in which tropical plants such as anthuriums and cattleyas can be grown.

Pruning. Pruning, which consists of restricting plants to a desired shape, is one of the most important of horticultural arts. Where trees and shrubs are left to grow naturally, they often become much too large for their space in the garden. Also they may grow lanky and misshapen and have much dead growth. Where a branch or shoot is cut, it will often be induced to make a number of young shoots from below the cut, and these are likely to flower more freely than the older branches. Fruit trees in particular when pruned annually often give fruit of finer quality, larger in size, freer of disease, and of better colour. Many shrubs benefit from the cutting out of all weak or dead wood and the shortening of strong shoots each winter. Hard pruning, or "heading back," cutting to within a few inches of the base of the shoot, is often used to rejuvenate shrubs that have become too large or that flower poorly. Pruning, started when the plant is young, obviates the need of drastic and risky remedial pruning later of a large, old, or misshapen bush or tree.

Pruning implements must be kept sharp for making clean cuts that lessen infection. The removal of a heavy branch often is done in stages to avoid tearing the bark below the final cut. Large cuts are generally painted over with a preservative.

Propagation. The production, or propagation, of new individuals is either from seed, in which case there is likely to be some variation in the progeny, or vegetatively, by division, cuttings, grafting, budding, or layering. In all these latter cases, the progeny are literally parts of the parent plant and so do not vary from it. A group of such plants is known as a clone. Often, as with cereals and flower seeds of annuals, seedsmen have been able, by continual breeding and weeding out, to introduce pure strains that breed true and without perceptible variation. They still, however, may carry genetic variation.

Seeds are usually sown in the spring either in the open ground, as in the case of most vegetables and hardy annuals, or in containers indoors as in the case of half-hardy annuals. A few seeds, however, especially those of alpines and other cold-adapted plants, require a period of freezing before they will germinate, as indeed happens in their own environment.

Propagation by cuttings is used for many shrubs. This is done generally toward midsummer in most cases, but the exact season will vary in accordance with the state of ripening of the wood. Young shoots of the current season are usually the most successful for rooting. Roses are usually propagated by budding, in which a bud from the rose desired is inserted in rootstock just above ground level. Fruit trees are usually propagated by grafting, in which a young shoot is inserted in the stock. Layering is a method by which a young shoot is pegged down in the ground with the end twisted upward almost at right angles; the lower side of the wood just before the twist is wounded so as to induce rooting. When this takes place, the layer is severed from the parent.

Control of weeds. This is a basic, and probably the most arduous, factor of cultivation and has been carried on from the time the earliest nomads settled down to an agricultural life. It has always been necessary to free the chosen crops of competition from other plants. For smaller weeds hoeing is practicable. The weeds are cut off by the action of the hoe and left to wither on the surface. Hand weeding, by pulling out individual weeds, is often necessary in gardens, particularly in the rock garden, in seed boxes, and often in the herbaceous border or among annuals. Chemical and biological control of weeds developed greatly after World War II, and has made much mechanical cultivation unnecessary (see WEED CONTROL).

Control of pests and diseases. Damage to plants is most often caused by pests such as insects, mites, eelworms, and other small creatures but may also be caused by mammals and rodents such as deer, rabbits, and mice. Damage by disease is that caused by fungi, bacteria, and viruses.

Pest control through vigilance

Prevention is generally better than cure, and constant vigilance is necessary to prevent a pest infestation or a disease outbreak. Control can be obtained by the use of chemical sprays, dusts, and fumigants, but some of these are so potent that they should be used only by the experienced operator. Considerable evidence is available regarding the possible harmful long-term effects on the biological chain of excessive use of some of these noxious chemicals, particularly the hydrocarbons (see CONSERVATION OF NATURAL RESOURCES). Some control can be obtained through good garden practices: clearing up all dead and diseased material and burning it; pruning and thinning so that a reasonable circulation of air is obtained through the plants; and crop rotation. Some control may also be obtained through the natural biological predators, but even allowing for all these factors, the absence of chemical control would diminish food crops by a considerable percentage. The breeding of plants immune to certain pests and diseases is also a valuable means of control (see PEST CONTROL; DISEASES OF PLANTS).

Mechanical aids. Mechanical devices to aid the gardener include tillers, lawn mowers, hedge cutters, sprinklers, and a variety of more esoteric equipment that has made gardening an easier pursuit. Such machines are not a substitute for good judgment and technique in the garden, however, nor will they give anyone a completely labour-free garden. They will enable a considerably larger area to be cultivated and maintained than if all labour had to be by hand.

HORTICULTURAL REGIONS

Temperate zones. These zones for horticulture cannot be defined exactly by lines of latitude or longitude but are usually regarded as including those areas where frost in winter occurs, even though this may be rare. Thus most parts of Europe, North America, and north Asia are included, though some parts of the United States, such as southern California and Florida, are considered subtropical. A few parts of the north coast of the Mediterranean and the Mediterranean islands are also subtropical. In the Southern Hemisphere, practically all of New Zealand, a few parts of Australia, and the southern part of South America have temperate climates. For horticultural purposes altitude is also a factor: the lower slopes of great mountain ranges such as the Himalayas and the Andes, for example, are included. Thus the temperate zones are very wide and the range of plants which can be grown there is enormous, probably greater than in either the subtropical or tropical zone. In the temperate zone are the great coniferous and deciduous forests: pine, spruce, fir, most of the cypresses, the deciduous oaks (but excluding many of the evergreen ones), ash birch, and lime (linden).

The temperate zones are also the areas of the grasses—the finest lawns particularly are in the regions of moderate or high rainfall—and of the great cereal crops. Rice is excluded as being tropical, but wheat, barley, corn (maize), and rye grow well in the temperate zones.

The winter rest

A great asset for plants in the temperate zones is the winter resting season, which clearly differentiates them from tropical plants, which tend to grow continuously. Thus bulbs, annuals, herbaceous perennials, and the deciduous habit in trees are means by which temperate-zone plants pass the resting season undamaged. Another influence is the varying length of darkness and light throughout the year, so that many, such as chrysanthemums, have a strong photoperiodism. The chrysanthemum flowers only in short daylight periods, although artificial simulation can produce flowers the year round.

Most of the great gardens of the world have been developed in temperate zones. Particular features such as rose gardens, herbaceous borders, annual borders, woodland gardens, and rock gardens are also those of temperate-zone gardens. Nearly all depend for their success on the winter resting period.

Tropical zones. There is no sharp line of demarcation between the tropics and the subtropics. Just as many tropical plants may be cultivated in the subtropics, so also many subtropical and even temperate plants may be grown satisfactorily in the tropics, especially at high elevations. As an example, the scarlet runner bean, a common plant in temperate regions, grows, flowers, and develops pods normally on the high slopes of Mt. Meru in Africa near the Equator; it will not, however, set pods in Hong Kong, a subtropical situation a little south of the Tropic of Cancer but at a low elevation. In addition to elevation, another determinant is the annual distribution of rainfall. Plants that will grow and flower in the monsoon areas, as in India, will not succeed where the climate is uniformly wet, as in Bougainville in the Solomon Islands. Another factor is the length of day, the number of hours the sun is above the horizon; some plants will only flower if the day is long, others make their growth during the long days and flower when the day is short. Certain cosmos strains are so sensitive that, where the day is always about 12 hours, as near the Equator, they will flower when only a few inches high; whereas if grown near the Tropics of Cancer or Capricon, they will attain a height of several feet, if the seeds are sown in the spring, before flowering in the short days of autumn and winter. Poinsettia is a short-day plant that may be seen in flower in Singapore on any day of the year, while in Trinidad it is a blaze of glory only at Christmas.

In the tropics of Asia and parts of Central and South America, where more exotic plants have been established and distributed, the dominant features of the gardens are flowering trees, shrubs, and climbers. Herbaceous plants are relatively few, but many kinds of orchids can be grown.

Vegetable crops vary in kind and quality with the presence or absence of periodic dry seasons. In the uniformly wet tropics, the choice is limited to certain root crops and still fewer greens. Sweet potatoes will grow and bear good crops where the average monthly rainfall, throughout the year, exceeds ten inches; they grow even better where there is a dry season. The same can be said of taro, yams, and cassava. Tropical greens from Malaya are not as good as those grown in South China, the Hawaiian Islands, or Puerto Rico. They include several spinaches, of which Chinese spinach or amaranth is the best; several cabbages; Chinese onions and chives; several gourds, cucumbers, and, where there is a dry season, watermelons. Brinjals or eggplants, peppers, and okra are widely cultivated. Many kinds of bean can be grown successfully, including the French bean from the American subtropics, the many varieties of the African cowpea, and yard-long bean. The yam bean, a native of tropical America, is grown for its edible tuber. In the drier areas the pigeon pea, the soybean, the peanut, and the Tientsin green bean are important crops. Miscellaneous crops include watercress, ginger, lotus, and bamboo.

BIBLIOGRAPHY. Practically all governments now support agencies that conduct horticultural research and publish bulletins relating to the cultivation of fruits, vegetables, and ornamental plants. Similarly, many academic institutions and horticultural organizations provide courses of study and publish gardening information. The references that follow are only a sample of the numerous books available on all aspects of gardening. Many of them have additional references for further reading on particular topics in gardening.

History: The history of gardening may be found in many of the large works on gardening and particularly in the historical section in *Curtis's Botanical Magazine Index* (1956); E. HYAMS, *Of Gardens and Gardeners* (1969); J. VON MIKLOS and E. FIORE, *The History, the Beauty, the Riches of the Gardener's World* (1969).

General: J.U. CROCKETT, *The Time-Life Encyclopedia of Gardening* (1971–), a series of several volumes, highly readable and lavishly illustrated; D.M. REID, *Botany for the Gardener* (1967), a presentation of the principles underlying the practice of gardening; R. PAGE, *The Education of a Gardener* (1962), a work helpful in planning a garden; KAREL CAPEK, *Gardener's Year* (Eng. trans. 1931, reprinted 1963), a delightful record of an annual cycle by this famous Romanian playwright; T.H. EVERETT, *Gardening Handbook* (1970); D.J. EDWARDS, *Gardening Explained* (1969); CARLTON B. LEES, *Gardens, Plants, and Man* (1970), a popular account of the significance of gardens. The following works are substantial and detailed books of a more difficult level: G.H. PRESTON (ed.), *The Complete Book of Gardening*, rev. ed. (1954); ROYAL HORTICULTURAL SOCIETY, *Dictionary of Gardening*, 2nd ed., 4 vol. (1951) and *Supplement* (1969); R. HAY and P.M. SYNGE, *The Dictionary of Garden Plants in Colour* (1969); L.H. BAILEY, *Manual of Cultivated Plants Most Commonly Grown in the Continental United States and Canada*, rev. ed. (1949); *Hortus Second* (1951); J.W. STEPHENSON, *Gardener's Directory* (1960); N. TAYLOR (ed.), *Encyclopedia of Gardening*, 4th ed. (1961); M.B. CRANE and W.J.C. LAWRENCE, *The Genetics of Garden Plants*, 4th ed. (1952); *Practical Plant Breeding*, rev. 3rd ed. (1952).

Cultivation of plants: G.W. ADRIANCE and F.R. BRISON, *Propagation of Horticultural Plants,* 2nd ed. (1955); E.P. CHRISTOPHER, *Introductory Horticulture* (1958); J.P. MAHLSTEDE and E.S. HABER, *Plant Propagation* (1957); M. FREE, *Plant Propagation in Pictures* (1957).

Ornamental trees and shrubs: S.A. PEARCE, *Ornamental Trees for Garden and Roadside Planting* (1961); A. REHDER, *Manual of Cultivated Trees and Shrubs Hardy in North America, Exclusive of the Subtropical and Warmer Temperate Regions*, 2nd ed. rev. (1940); W.J. BEAN, *Trees and Shrubs Hardy in the British Isles*, 8th ed., vol. 1 (1970); E.H.M. and P.A. COX, *Modern Shrubs* (1958); A.D.C. LE SUEUR, *The Care and Repair of Ornamental Trees*, rev. ed. (1949); P.P. PIRONE, *Tree Maintenance*, 3rd ed. (1959).

Flowers and lawns: A. BLOOM, *Hardy Perennials* (1957); C. LLOYD, *The Mixed Border* (1957); F. PERRY, *Guide to Border Plants: Hardy Herbaceous Perennials* (1957); *Water Gardening*, 3rd rev. ed. (1961); P.M. SYNGE, *Collins Guide to Bulbs* (1961); E.B. ANDERSON, *Dwarf Bulbs for the Rock Garden* (1959); SIR F.C. STERN, *A Chalk Garden* (1960); C. KELWAY, *Seaside Gardening* (1964); R.B. DAWSON, *Practical Lawn Craft and Management of Sports Turf*, 5th ed. rev. (1959).

Fruits and vegetables: ROYAL HORTICULTURAL SOCIETY, *The Fruit Garden Displayed*, rev. ed. (1965); *The Vegetable Garden Displayed*, rev. ed. (1961); N.B. BAGENAL, *The Fruit Grower's Handbook* (1949); R. BUSH, *Tree Fruit Growing*, rev. ed. (1962); R.J. GARNER, *The Grafter's Handbook*, 3rd ed. rev. (1967); S.M. GAULT, *Vegetables for Garden and Exhibition* (1956).

Horticultural regions (subtropical and tropical zones): J.W. PURSEGLOVE, *Tropical Crops: Dicotyledons*, 2 vol. (1968); H.F. MACMILLAN, *Tropical Planting and Gardening, with special Reference to Ceylon*, 5th ed. (1943), still by far the best single volume for the tropics; A.J. JEX-BLAKE (ed.), *Gardening in East Africa*, 4th ed. (1957); E. BLATTER and W.S. MILLARD, *Some Beautiful Indian Trees*, 2nd ed. rev. (1954), not confined to trees native to India; T.M. GREENSILL, *Tropical Gardening* (1966).

Garden types: J.A. and C.L. GRANT, *Garden Design Illustrated* (1954; paperback edition, 1967); P.E. TRUEX, *The City Gardener* (1964); L. ROPER, *Successful Town Gardening* (1957); J.M. BERRISFORD, *The Wild Garden* (1966); X. FIELD, *Town and Roof Gardens* (1967); V.W. STEVENSON, *Patio, Rooftop and Balcony Gardening* (1967).

Pests and diseases: D.E. GREEN, *Diseases of Vegetables* (1943); B.O. DODGE and H.W. RICKETT, *Diseases and Pests of Ornamental Plants*, 3rd ed. (1960); K.M. SMITH, *A Textbook of Plant Virus Diseases*, 2nd ed. (1957); G. FOX WILSON, *Horticultural Pests: Detection and Control*, 3rd ed. (1960).

(G.A.C.H./P.M.Sy./Ed.)

Garibaldi, Giuseppe

Giuseppe Garibaldi, the most distinguished soldier of the Risorgimento, the movement that united Italy, was known in his day as a great revolutionary, a patron of protest movements all over Europe and the Americas, and was one of the most skillful guerrilla generals of all time. First widely known for his military exploits in South America, his name became a household word in 1849 with his unsuccessful defense of Rome against the French and Austrians. Of all his successes, the most remarkable was an expedition of "the Thousand" in 1860, when an invading force under his command landed in Sicily, defeated the larger army of the King of Naples, and ended by conquering half of Italy, and playing a key role in the country's unification.

Garibaldi, 1866.
Deutsche Fotothek, Dresden

Garibaldi was born on July 4, 1807, in the French town of Nice, which was largely settled by people of Italian stock. His family was one of fishermen and coastal traders, and for over ten years he himself was a sailor on the Mediterranean and the Black Sea. In 1832 he acquired a master's certificate as a merchant captain. By 1833–34, when he served in the navy of the kingdom of Piedmont-Sardinia, he had come under the influence of Giuseppe Mazzini, the great prophet of Italian nationalism, and the French Socialist thinker, the Comte de Saint-Simon. Under Mazzini's inspiration, Garibaldi, in 1834, took part in a mutiny intended to provoke a republican revolution in Piedmont, but the plot failed; he himself escaped to France and in his absence was condemned to death by a Genoese court.

Exile in South America. From 1836 to 1848 Garibaldi lived in South America as an exile, and these years of turmoil and revolution in that continent strongly influenced his career. He volunteered to serve the Rio Grande do Sul republic as a naval captain in the unsuccessful attempt by that small state to break free from the Brazilian empire. Actually, he did little more than prey on Brazilian shipping. In the course of often harrowing adventures on land and sea, he managed to elope with Anna Maria Ribeiro da Silva (known as Anita), a married woman, who remained his companion in arms until her death. After a succession of victories by the Brazilians in 1839–40, he finally decided to leave the service of Rio Grande. Driving a herd of cattle, he made the long trek to Montevideo with Anita and their son. There he tried his hand as commercial traveller and teacher but could not accustom himself to civilian life. In 1842 he was put in charge of the tiny Uruguayan navy in another liberation war—this time against Juan Manuel de Rosas, the dictator of Argentina. The following year, again in the service of Uruguay, he took command of a newly formed Italian Legion at Montevideo; these men formed the first of the "Redshirts," with whom his name henceforth became associated. After he won a small but heroic engagement at the Battle of Sant'Antonio in 1846, his fame reached even to Europe, and in Italy a sword of honour, paid for by subscriptions, was donated to him. For a short time in 1847 he was in charge of the defense of Montevideo. On this occasion he first came to the attention of Alexandre Dumas *père*, who later did much to foster his reputation. He also greatly impressed other foreign observers as an honest and able man. His South American experiences gave him invaluable training in the techniques of guerrilla warfare that he was later to use with great effect against French and Austrian armies, which had not been taught how to counter them. And these first exploits in the cause of freedom cast him in the mold of a professional rebel, an indomitable individualist who all his life continued to wear the gaucho costume of the pampas and to act as if life were a perpetual battle for liberty.

War of liberation. In April 1848 Garibaldi led 60 members of his Italian Legion back to Italy to fight for the Risorgimento, or resurrection, of Italy in the war of independence against the Austrians. He first offered to fight for Pope Pius IX, and—when his offer was refused—for Charles Albert, the king of Piedmont-Sardinia. The King, too, rebuffed him, for Garibaldi's conviction as a rebel in 1834 was still remembered; moreover, the regular army despised this self-taught guerrilla leader. Garibaldi went, therefore, to the aid of the city of Milan, where Mazzini had already arrived and had given the war of liberation a more republican and radical turn. Charles Albert, after his defeat at the hands of the Austrians at Custoza, agreed to an armistice, but Garibaldi continued in the name of Milan what had become his private war, and emerged creditably from two engagements with the Austrians at Luino and Morazzone. But at the end of August, heavily outnumbered, he had to retreat across the frontier to Switzerland.

For a time Garibaldi settled down at Nice with Anita (whom he had married in 1842) and their three children, but his resolve to help free Italy from foreign rule was now stronger than ever. He was confirmed in his purpose by his belief—which he and only a handful of others shared with Mazzini—that the many Italian states, though often engaged in internecine warfare, could nonetheless be unified into a single state. When Pius IX, threatened by liberal forces within the papal states, fled

Marginal notes: First marriage · Champion of Milan

letters, in 1907 and 1930; and R.C. ALEXANDER in 1928, the long missing Paris 1751 *Diary of David Garrick.*

(C.O.)

Garrison, William Lloyd

The figure of William Lloyd Garrison, if not his program for abolishing slavery in the United States, dominated the 30-year Abolitionist crusade that ended successfully in 1865 with the adoption of the 13th Amendment to the Constitution of the United States. Neither an effective organizer nor a political strategist, Garrison first achieved notoriety and, finally, acclaim as the editorial voice of the antislavery conscience, denouncing slavery as a national sin and demanding immediate and unconditional emancipation. "On this subject," he promised in the first issue of his Abolitionist newspaper, *The Liberator,* in 1831, "I do not wish to think, or speak, or write, with moderation. . . . I am in earnest—I will not equivocate—I will not excuse—I will not retreat a single inch—AND I WILL BE HEARD." When he stopped publishing *The Liberator* in 1865, he had come to personify for millions of Americans the moral fervour and tenacity that had sustained the Abolitionist cause.

Garrison.

Early life Born on December 12 (or 10), 1805, in Newburyport, Massachusetts, the son of an itinerant seaman who subsequently deserted his family, Garrison grew up in an atmosphere of declining New England Federalism and lively Christian benevolence—twin sources of the Abolitionist movement, which he joined at the age of 25. As editor of the *National Philanthropist* (Boston) in 1828 and the *Journal of the Times* (Bennington, Vermont) in 1828–29, he served his apprenticeship in the moral reform cause. In 1829, with a pioneer Abolitionist, Benjamin Lundy, in Baltimore, he became coeditor of the *Genius of Universal Emancipation;* he also served a short term in jail for libelling a Newburyport merchant who was engaged in the coastal slave trade. Released in June 1830, Garrison returned to Boston and, a year later, established *The Liberator,* which became known as the most uncompromising of American antislavery journals.

Like most of the Abolitionists he recruited, Garrison was a convert from the American Colonization Society, which advocated the return of free blacks to Africa, to the principle of "immediate emancipation," borrowed from English Abolitionists. "Immediatism," however variously it was interpreted by American reformers, condemned slavery as a national sin, called for emancipation at the earliest possible moment, and proposed schemes for incorporating the freedmen into American **Recogni-** society. Through *The Liberator,* which circulated widely **tion as the** both in England and the United States, Garrison soon **most** achieved recognition as the most radical of American an- **radical** tislavery advocates. In 1832 he founded the New En- **Abolition-** gland Anti-Slavery Society, the first immediatist society **ist** in the country, and in 1833 he helped organize the Amer-

ican Anti-Slavery Society, writing its Declaration of Sentiments and serving as its first corresponding secretary. It was primarily as an editorialist, however, excoriating slaveowners and their moderate opponents alike, that he became known and feared. "If those who deserve the lash feel it and wince at it," he wrote in explaining his refusal to alter his harsh tone, "I shall be assured that I am striking the right persons in the right place."

In 1837, in the wake of financial panic and the failure of Abolitionist campaigns to gain support in the North, Garrison renounced church and state and embraced doctrines of Christian "perfectionism," which combined abolition, women's rights, and nonresistance, in the biblical injunction to "come out" from a corrupt society by refusing to obey its laws and support its institutions. From this blend of pacificism and anarchism came the Garrisonian principle of "No Union With Slaveholders," formulated in 1844 as a demand for peaceful Northern secession from a slaveholding South.

By 1840 Garrison's increasingly personal definition of the slavery problem had precipitated a crisis within the American Anti-Slavery Society, a majority of whose members disapproved of both the participation of women and Garrison's no-government theories. Dissension reached a climax in 1840, when the Garrisonians voted a series of resolutions admitting women and thus forced their conservative opponents to secede and form the rival American and Foreign Anti-Slavery Society. Later that year a group of politically minded Abolitionists also deserted Garrison's standard and founded the Liberty Party. Thus, 1840 witnessed the disruption of the national organization and left Garrison in control of a relative handful of followers loyal to his "come-outer" doctrine but deprived of the support of new antislavery converts and of the Northern reform community at large.

In the two decades between the schism of 1840 and the Civil War, Garrison's influence waned as his radicalism increased. The decade before the war saw his opposition to slavery and to the federal government reach its peak: *The Liberator* denounced the Compromise of 1850, condemned the Kansas-Nebraska Act, damned the Dred Scott decision, and hailed John Brown's Raid as "God's method of dealing retribution upon the head of the tyrant." In 1854 Garrison publicly burned a copy of the Constitution at an Abolitionist rally in Framingham, Massachusetts. Three years later he held an abortive secessionist convention in Worcester, Massachusetts.

The Civil War forced Garrison to choose between his pacifist beliefs and emancipation. Placing freedom for the slave foremost, he supported Abraham Lincoln faithfully and in 1863 welcomed the Emancipation Proclamation as the fulfillment of all his hopes. Emancipation **Latent** brought to the surface the latent conservatism in his pro- **conserva-** gram for the freedmen, whose political rights he was not **tism** prepared to guarantee immediately. In 1865 he attempted without success to dissolve the American Anti-Slavery Society and then resigned. In December 1865 he published the last issue of *The Liberator* and announced that "my vocation as an abolitionist is ended." He spent his last 14 years in retirement from public affairs, regularly supporting the Republican Party and continuing to champion temperance, women's rights, pacifism, and free trade. "It is enough for me," he explained in justifying his refusal to participate in radical equalitarian politics, "that every yoke is broken, and every bondman set free." He died in New York City on May 24, 1879.

BIBLIOGRAPHY. The standard biography is WENDELL P. and FRANCIS J. GARRISON, *William Lloyd Garrison, 1805–1879: The Story of His Life Told by His Children,* 4 vol. (1885–89). Still useful are two contemporary accounts: OLIVER JOHNSON, *William Lloyd Garrison and His Times* (1879); and SAMUEL J. MAY, *Some Recollections of Our Antislavery Conflict* (1869); as well as the sympathetic neo-abolitionist essay by JOHN JAY CHAPMAN, *William Lloyd Garrison* (1913). For more recent estimates, see RUSSELL B. NYE, *William Lloyd Garrison and the Humanitarian Reformers* (1955); WALTER M. MERRILL, *Against Wind and Tide: A Biography of William Lloyd Garrison* (1963); and JOHN L. THOMAS, *The Liberator, William Lloyd Garrison* (1963).

(J.L.T.)

Gaseous State

A gas is one of the three major states, or phases, of matter, the others being liquid and solid; less clearly definable, but also referred to as states of matter, are plasma, colloids, and amorphous conditions, such as glass. Each state of matter has properties that distinguish it from the others and that are, therefore, independent of the particular substance being studied. Thus, the gaseous state has properties simply as a gas, and if any substance in a gaseous state is condensed to the liquid state, the identical substance will have the distinctly different properties of a liquid. The most familiar example is water, whose properties as ice, liquid, and vapour (gas) are dramatically different within the temperature and pressure ranges of everyday experience.

GENERAL PROPERTIES

All matter consists of atoms or molecules or mixtures of these in constant motion, whether it is through space, called translational motion, or motion in one place, called vibrational motion. In the gaseous state, each particle moves about in three dimensions almost independently of the influence of nearby particles, whereas in liquids and solids the motion of the same atoms and molecules is subordinated to the forces exerted on them by their neighbours. The freely moving atoms and molecules of a gas are constantly colliding with one another and rebounding to produce a pressure that is transmitted throughout the bulk of the gas and against the walls of the container; thus, one of the most obvious properties of the gaseous state is that a gas fills completely whatever container it is put in. The earth's atmosphere, consisting of a mixture of gases, reveals many of the properties of the gaseous state to simple observation. For example, a gas can be compressed, as with a bicycle pump. When a gas is heated, it expands and rises, as over a hot radiator; if a gas is cooled enough, it condenses to a liquid, as with breath on a cold window. The earth's weather is largely the result of changes in the gaseous properties of air, the most important change being that of temperature, which leads, among other things, to pressure changes and to the amount of water vapour the mixture can absorb; all clouds, precipitation, storms, winds, and clear skies are phenomena that can be explained in terms of the properties of gases. The compressibility and expansion properties of the gaseous state are utilized in all sorts of ways in industry and in everyday life. For example, whatever fuel is used, the internal-combustion engine, steam engine, jet engine, rocket, and guns are all designed to utilize the properties of the gaseous state. This is also true of the arts of cooking, welding steel, and deep-sea diving, of the performance of aircraft, the operation of windmills, and so on. It is the gaseous properties of oxygen that have determined the evolution of lungs, organs that can handle only gases, not liquids or solids.

It would seem, therefore, that a great deal must have been learned about gases long ago, even by primitive man, but this is not the case. Although gases have been studied experimentally and theoretically since antiquity, any systematic discussion of gases is based upon experimental data collected during the last two centuries and upon theories that began to develop only during the 19th century and that are still evolving. The fact is that it is exceedingly difficult and often impossible to explain the behaviour of gases in terms that allow precise predictions to be made concerning gaseous behaviour under various known conditions.

There are two distinct ways of discussing the gaseous state. First, there is the laboratory description of the behaviour of a bulk volume of gas trapped in a container. This is a macroscopic view, independent of the atomic theory of matter, since it deals with properties, easy to measure, of a vast number of particles, such as the pressure they exert all together on the walls of their container or their temperature as measured by a thermometer. Description in terms of bulk measurable properties is called (phenomenological) thermodynamics and trans-

port theory. Second, there is the particle description of a gas; this is a microscopic view that deals with the individual properties of the particles and how these properties collectively give rise to the observed behaviour of a gas when studied in the laboratory. Description in these terms is called statistical thermodynamics and kinetic theory. During the last 150 years, increasingly successful attempts have been made to develop a complete theory that will coordinate these two distinct descriptions.

THERMODYNAMIC APPROACH TO GASES

Gases range from simple gases, whose particles are single atoms (monatomic), such as neon or helium, to the complex multi-atom (polyatomic) gases, such as the hydrocarbons, obtained in the petroleum industry. The cost of determining all the physical and chemical properties of every gas is prohibitive in terms of time and money, and any procedure that allows predictions to be made of some properties in lieu of actual measurements is of great value. The science of thermodynamics provides general rules that relate some of the behaviour of all gases on the basis of limited data. Of particular importance is the relationship among the pressure, volume, and temperature of a gas, since these are the three properties usually easiest to measure. For example, low pressures are measured by balancing the pressure of the contained gas through a tube against a vertical column of mercury (the height of the column gives an accurate measure of the pressure the mercury exerts on the gas), while for gases at high pressure a free-piston gauge is used, the pressure of the gas being balanced by applying an external force, such as weights of known value, to the piston. Temperature can be measured by a variety of devices, including gas or liquid thermometers, resistance thermometers, and thermocouples. The relationship among pressure, volume, and temperature is called the thermal equation of state. The relationship may be expressed as a precise mathematical equation or as a collection of graphs or tables. The thermodynamics of gases is concerned with the twofold problem of determining the thermal equation of state (see below *Thermal equation of state*) of just a few gases and attempting to predict values for all other gases using the equation; thereafter, the prediction of all of the other properties of a gas can be made in terms of its pressure, volume, and temperature.

The simple gas laws. The relationships between the volume of a gas and its temperature and pressure embody easily measured, basic properties of all gases. These relationships have been deduced and put in the form of equations called the gas laws. The first gas law, discovered by the English physicist Robert Boyle and named after him (in France the law is named after Edme Mariotte), states that the volume of a given quantity of gas varies inversely with the pressure exerted on it. That is, if a gas is compressed to half its volume, the pressure it will exert on its container will be twice as much, or, if the pressure on a gas is doubled, the volume will be reduced by one-half; a limiting factor is that the temperature must not change, for, if it does, the pressure-volume relationship will not hold. In symbols, Boyle's law is written: V varies as (or $\propto$) $1/P$, V being the volume and P the pressure. This can be stated as an equation by introducing a constant (depending on the units of volume and pressure used and on the amount of gas) that has been found experimentally: $V = k_1 \, 1/P$; that is, the volume equals the product of the constant and the reciprocal of the pressure. The second gas law was worked out (1787) by the French physicist Jacques-Alexandre-César Charles and named after him and also after Joseph-Louis Gay-Lussac, a French chemist who repeated Charles' experiments and published his results in 1802. It states that the volume of gas varies directly as its absolute temperature (see below *Thermal equation of state*), if the pressure is kept constant. That is to say, if the temperature of a gas is increased the volume will increase proportionately, as long as the pressure within the gas does not change. In symbols, V varies as (or $\propto$) T, T being the absolute temperature. In equation form, the relationship is $V = k_2 \, T$, k_2 being a constant determined through experiment. In

Familiar properties

Macroscopic and microscopic descriptions

Boyle's law

words, then, the volume of a specified amount of any gas expands whether with a rise in temperature or with a reduction in pressure, and the gas contracts if it is cooled or if the pressure is increased, and the changes can be calculated by using one or the other of the two gas laws.

Thermal equation of state. If both pressure and temperature are changed at the same time, both equations must be used to calculate the change in volume, pressure, or temperature that is obtained when the other factors are changed. A single equation can be derived from Boyle's and Charles' laws: the product of the pressure and the volume equals the product of the temperature and a constant, R, called the universal gas constant. In symbols the equation is written: $P\overline{V} = RT$, P being the pressure, T the absolute temperature, and $\overline{V}$ the volume of one mole of gas. A mole is a quantity of substance such that its weight in grams is numerically the same as the molecular weight of the substance; *e.g.*, the molecular weight of oxygen (O_2) is 32; therefore, one mole of oxygen is that quantity that weighs 32 grams. The universal gas constant, R, is 1.987 calories per mole degree, a figure found by experiment. The absolute-temperature scale was devised (1848) by the English physicist William Thomson, later Lord Kelvin, on the basis of his work with heat. Charles had already found that all gases shrank $\frac{1}{273}$ of their volume when they were cooled 1° C, and Kelvin reasoned that if a gas could be cooled 273° below 0° C, the energy of its molecules would become zero. This hypothetical temperature was given the name absolute zero, and the scale of temperatures built on absolute zero, in which each degree was equivalent to a degree on the Celsius thermometer, was called the absolute scale of temperature. Recently, this has been changed to the Kelvin scale and is written ° K, but 0° K, which is equal by definition to −273.15° C, is still called absolute zero.

The equation is called the thermal equation of state, and it is the most important of the mathematical descriptions worked out for gases, since by simply measuring any two of the unknowns, the third can be calculated. It is applicable to a large variety of gaseous conditions in industry and science, including astronomy.

General shortcomings. The thermal equation of state, however, is not applicable to all gases under all conditions. It is an approximation, however, that is certainly accurate for most gases at pressures of less than a few atmospheres and at temperatures between room temperature and several hundred degrees higher.

Ideal gas. Because of this common behaviour pattern, a hypothetical gas, called the ideal, or perfect, gas, has been proposed that obeys the equation exactly under all conditions. The importance of the concept is twofold. First, it provides a criterion of behaviour that most real (as opposed to ideal) gases approach; and, second, there is an exact particle theory for such a gas. The difference between the ideal gas and any real gas is due to several factors, the most obvious being that every molecule has a real volume, and the total volume of the molecules in a container is, therefore, a significant figure when the space occupied by the gas (the $\overline{V}$ in the equation) becomes relatively small; the physical volume of the gas molecules is not taken into account in the equation. Much more important factors that also are excluded concern forces of interaction among atoms and molecules that come into play under various conditions, especially near condensation; at condensation the phenomenon of latent heat (see below *Discrepancies between observed behaviour and the equation of state*) is not taken into account; and, of course, the fact that molecules have different shapes and that their collisions would be affected by these distinct shapes is also not part of the calculations that can be made using $P\overline{V} = RT$. Still another factor enters when the temperature is raised sufficiently to ionize the molecules and then decompose them and, finally, to strip atoms of all their electrons. Such a gas, consisting only of positively charged nuclei and electrons, is called plasma, and its properties, since each particle has an electric charge, differ altogether from those of a normal gas, whose particles are electrically neutral. In passing from normal gaseous state to plasma, therefore,

Absolute zero

the changes cannot be predicted by the thermal equation of state. The simple gas laws would be absolutely correct for a gas if each molecule were simply a mathematical point in space.

In addition to pressure, volume, and temperature, another important thermodynamic property of a gas is its energy. The change in energy with changing volume of any gas that is kept at a constant temperature can be calculated from thermodynamic theory, using the same thermal equation of state. The dependence of the energy on temperature is known as the heat capacity of a gas, and this must be determined experimentally when the gas is held at constant volume or pressure. A knowledge of the thermal equation of state and the heat capacity allows all of the other thermodynamic properties of many gases to be deduced without further measurement.

It took centuries for these principles to be discovered. Historical highlights were the speculations of Francis Bacon (1620) that heat was not an indestructible fluid called caloric, which everyone believed could enter or leave a gas, but rather that heat was some form of motion of particles. Boyle and Charles developed the concept of the thermal equation of state, while Joseph Black, an English chemist, established (1770) the idea of a heat capacity and energy of a gas in his studies of gas calorimetry. The American Benjamin Thompson, later Count von Rumford (1798), and the Englishman James Prescott Joule (1845) finally disproved the caloric theory of heat. The laws of thermodynamics, which interrelate these properties, were discovered and formulated during the 19th century.

Discrepancies between observed behaviour and the equation of state. If a graph is plotted of the mutual changes in pressure, volume, and temperature of a gas, then a three-dimensional surface is obtained. Such a graph for any laboratory gas being manipulated in a container shows that, for a certain pressure and temperature, the gas will change its phase; *i.e.*, the substance can appear as a gas or a liquid or a solid. It is not easy to picture a three-dimensional surface, and it is usual to make two-dimensional projections of this surface onto a piece of paper. There are three such projections, and the most important one is the graph of pressure against volume. This will be a family of curves such that each member of the family will be a graph of pressure versus volume for a gas kept at constant temperature. Historically, laboratory experiments showed that for some gases, like oxygen and nitrogen, if the temperature were kept at room temperature, then no matter how much the gas pressure was increased (and the volume thereby decreased), the gas never condensed into a liquid; *i.e.*, the pressure-versus-volume curve was a smooth one, with no sharp jumps or kinks in it. On the other hand, for many gases kept at room temperature, as the pressure was increased, a discontinuity in behaviour occurred, and the gas started to condense into a liquid. During condensation, the pressure and the temperature remained constant, while the volume of the mixture of gas and liquid decreased until all of the gas had turned to liquid. Thereafter, a further increase in pressure (still maintaining a constant temperature) resulted in a slight decrease in the volume of the liquid. In addition, as the gas condensed, it released energy, even though its temperature remained constant. This is the phenomenon called the latent heat of condensation, which was discovered by Black (1757) and studied systematically by Black and a colleague (1764), in the case of water vapour condensing into liquid water.

In spite of these early studies of condensation, prior to the work of the Irish physical chemist Thomas Andrews (1869), the conditions necessary to liquefy a gas by compressing it at constant temperature were not clear. Andrews established the existence of a critical-temperature curve, the significance of which was that if the actual temperature of the gas being compressed were greater than this critical temperature, then no amount of compression would liquefy the gas. If, however, the gas were compressed at a constant temperature below the critical temperature, condensation would always occur. If the temperature of the gas is kept just below the critical

Early speculations

temperature as the gas is compressed, then the volume change during condensation is small, while, if the gas being compressed is kept at just the critical temperature, then the gas passes directly into the liquid without any change in volume at all. The name critical point is given to that point on the constant critical-temperature curve that represents the termination of any observable distinction between the gaseous and liquid phases. Neither vaporization nor liquefaction, in the sense of boiling or droplet condensation, occur in substances having a temperature greater than the critical temperature.

An important problem that arises as a gas is compressed at constant temperature is whether the gas obeys the thermally perfect equation of state. In general, this equation is found to hold to within 1 percent as the gas density (which is the mass of gas contained in a fixed volume or, more importantly, the actual number of gas particles in a fixed volume) rises from the density of the gas at room temperature and pressure up to about 100 times this value. Thereafter, deviations from the predictions of the thermally perfect gas equation of state appear, until eventually the equation becomes completely wrong when the gas starts to condense, since during condensation the pressure and temperature remain constant, and the volume decreases.

Empirical equations for specific gases. The problem of determining the thermal equations of state of a real gas (as opposed to the hypothetical thermally perfect gas) is an old one. The first serious attempt was made by the Dutch physicist Johannes Diederik van der Waals (1873), who formulated a thermal equation of state containing two adjustable parameters (arbitrary constants that characterize certain variable factors in a system) that could be found by comparing experimental values of pressure, volume, and temperature measured in the laboratory with theoretical values containing the adjustable parameters predicted by his equation of state. There are now well over 100 empirical thermal equations of state available for a whole range of gases. Of the two best known, one contains five adjustable parameters, and the other contains eight adjustable parameters. These complicated equations can reproduce the complete range of observed pressure, volume, and temperature behaviour from the gas phase through condensation into liquid phase for a very wide range of gases. They are very useful for interpolation—*i.e.*, predicting values intermediate between measured values—but they suffer, as do all other empirical thermal equations of state, in that the adjustable parameters are not related directly to any aspect of the particle behaviour of the gas.

Virial equation of state. The particles of any real gas are surrounded by fields of force, so that the particles interact with each other, even when separated in the gaseous phase. These interparticle forces (called intermolecular forces) are the whole essence of real-gas behaviour, and any thermal equation of state must allow for these forces. Intermolecular forces do not include gravitational force, because, for the small masses of gas that occur in containers of laboratory or industrial size, gravitational force between particles is negligible. Gravitational effects in gases are important only when discussing the structure of the earth's atmosphere or of interstellar events.

There is only one way of writing the thermal equation of state of a real gas that will both fit laboratory data and also show the effect of intermolecular forces. This is called the virial equation of state, and it is derived from the thermal equation of state for an ideal gas by taking into account the attraction or repulsion between the molecules. It is written as a mathematical series with a very large number of terms:

$$\frac{P\overline{V}}{RT} = 1 + \frac{B(T)}{\overline{V}} + \frac{C(T)}{\overline{V}^2} + \frac{D(T)}{\overline{V}^3} + \dots.$$

The quantities $B(T)$, $C(T)$, $D(T)$, etc., are called the second, third, and fourth virial coefficients, the first virial coefficient being unity. They are all independent of the gas pressure and density and depend only on the temperature. Viewed as a purely empirical thermal equation

of state, the virial equation is not particularly convenient, because, at moderately high gas densities, many terms must be added up, and, at very high densities, such as those that occur when the gas is condensing into a liquid, the equation may actually diverge and, therefore, be useless. In spite of this, the virial equation is of the utmost importance, because it forms a link between purely macroscopic (*i.e.*, bulk) properties, such as pressure, volume, and temperature, and microscopic properties, such as the intermolecular forces between the particles.

Because of difficulties associated with the virial equation of state for the case of dense gases during condensation, empirical thermal equations of state are still used today. Of particular value is the principle of corresponding states or phases, a law stating that all substances obey the same thermal equation of state, provided the equation is written in reduced variables; *i.e.*,

$$\frac{P\overline{V}}{RT} = \text{Function}\left(\frac{P}{P_{\text{crit}}}, \frac{T}{T_{\text{crit}}}\right).$$

This means that the product of pressure and volume, divided by the product of the universal gas constant and the absolute temperature, equals not unity, as would be the case with an ideal gas, but some mathematical function that should be the same for all substances. The reason why the actual pressure and temperature of the gas (on the right-hand side, which corrects the discrepancy between ideal and real gas) are divided by the critical pressure (P_{crit}) and critical temperature (T_{crit}) is that, as already noted, the critical-point values are unique for every substance, and, therefore, they represent a reference point closely related to the condensation of a gas.

THE PARTICLE-DESCRIPTION APPROACH TO GASES

Although thermodynamics provides a very general and very powerful discipline for determining the interrelationships among the many physical and chemical properties of gases, it is quite unable to predict the actual numerical value of these properties. It can predict, for example, the relationship between the constant-pressure heat capacity and constant-volume heat capacity of all gases in terms of the thermal equation of state, but it cannot predict the numerical value of either heat capacity of any gas. Calculations of the numerical values of the properties of gases require a microscopic theory based on the fact that all gases are composed of particles that may be single (monatomic) atoms or complicated polyatomic molecules. For the normal range of temperatures encountered in industrial applications (but not aerospace applications), all atoms may be regarded as particles possessing no internal structure; *i.e.*, they are considered to be solid particles. When atoms are bound together into polyatomic molecules, however, these molecules do possess internal structure; for example, the simplest polyatomic molecules consist of only two atoms bound together. Such a structure can rotate end over end and, therefore, possesses an internal mode of motion called molecular rotation. In addition, the two atoms may vibrate as if connected by a spring, so that the molecule also possesses another internal mode of motion, called molecular vibration. More complicated molecules can possess more complicated rotations and vibrations.

The use of any laboratory container of gas involves many billions (10^9) of particles; for example, one cubic metre of air at standard conditions contains more than 10^{24} particles. Every one of these particles is moving throughout the container in random fashion, and this is called the external mode of motion, or the random thermal translational motion of the particle. It is called thermal because the intensity of this motion bears a direct relationship to the temperature: the greater the thermal energy of the particle the faster it moves through space. In addition, if the particle is polyatomic, it also possesses internal modes of motion, such as rotational and vibrational motion. In principle, all of these motions, both internal and external, are governed by the laws of quantum mechanics. In practice, however, the translational motion can often be accurately described by the

Margin notes:

Critical point

Intermolecular forces

The vast numbers of gas particles

much simpler laws of Newtonian mechanics. Such a simplification does not usually hold for the internal motions, but in some cases it is valid for the rotational motion. Consequently, a discussion of the quantum internal motions may be expected to be more involved than the Newtonian external motion of translation. For gases at densities near atmospheric density, all of the particles spend most of their time moving with a constant speed, called the thermal speed, just as if they alone occupied the container; *i.e.*, any particle behaves as if it were alone in its container, notwithstanding the enormous number of other particles also present. At any instant of time, however, about 1 particle in 100,000 will be colliding with another particle or the container walls, and, in a time interval of one second, each particle of the gas will experience about 1,000,000,000 collisions. A collision between two particles is called a binary collision, and in such a collision both particles may change their speeds and the directions in which they were moving.

Distribution functions. The microscopic picture of a gas, then, is one of billions of particles in incessant thermal motion (a manifestation of its thermal energy), each particle now and again suffering a collision as it wanders randomly throughout its container. Clearly, it would not be sensible to try to follow the behaviour of each particle, even if these could be seen, which they cannot. In fact, if the position in space and the speed of each of a million particles could be written down every second, it would still take the age of the universe to write down the same information for all of the particles in a normal-sized room, and this information would be true only for an instant of time. Actually, this is no loss, because the behaviour of individual particles is not interesting. All that is really of importance is their macroscopic behaviour; *i.e.*, their behaviour averaged out over the vast number of particles in the container. Mathematical statistics is able to handle large numbers, and the procedure for dealing with the problem is to examine the behaviour of groups of particles, where each group consists of a very large number of particles that all possess some common properties. The common properties used are the positions in space and the speeds of particles, and this leads to the concept of what is called a distribution function. The distribution function is a mathematical equation that indicates what fraction of all the vast number of particles in the container have spatial positions lying within some arbitrarily chosen, exceedingly small region of the container and whose thermal speeds lie within an exceedingly small spread of speeds about some arbitrarily chosen speed.

More precisely, the distribution function is the probable number of such particles, the word probable being a reminder that it is impossible to say exactly how many particles even an exceedingly small region of the container actually contains at a given instant; the reason is that the number continually varies about its most probable value as a result of the random arrival and departure of individual particles, so that there is a higher or lower particle density in the minute region than the average density, which can be calculated with great precision by dividing the total number of particles by the total volume of the container. These variations, or fluctuations, in density arise as an inevitable consequence of the particulate nature of a gas and lead to observable effects in the laboratory.

Forces affecting distribution function. A knowledge of the distribution function is essential for any microscopic theory of a gas; however, its determination involves postulating some mathematical description of a gas particle and how a gas-particle collision actually occurs. In any real gas, even a binary collision—one between two particles only—is a complicated process, because each particle is surrounded by a force field that varies in space. This force field is such that it attracts another particle when that other particle is relatively far away but repels it when the other particle comes relatively close. That these intermolecular forces exist is evident from the fact that gases do condense into liquids, a phenomenon that cannot be explained except as a consequence of attrac-

Binary collisions (margin)

tive forces at work between the particles. In addition, liquids strongly resist being compressed, which must be evidence of the repulsive forces. The long-range attractive forces, called van der Waals forces, arise from electrostatic interactions between the whole particles. Short-range forces arise when the electron clouds that surround the nuclei of atoms in a molecule overlap. These short-range forces are called valence forces, and they become stronger than the van der Waals forces when the two particles come sufficiently close together in a binary collision.

Van der Waals forces (margin)

Multiparticle collisions. So far, the discussion has been concerned with gases at pressures near atmospheric pressure and density near that of normal atmosphere, a condition in which binary collisions alone are significant. As the density of the gas is increased, there is the possibility of three particles coming together at the same place and colliding in what is called a ternary collision. Perhaps even four particles and, in dense gases, an even higher number of particles may come together in a collision. To include ternary and higher order collisions in the discussion, the nature of the intermolecular forces among the various colliding particles must be known. It is just this specification of the forces among collision partners that gives rise to the various mathematical theories of a gas. It has been shown that the most complete and satisfactory theory is the one designed for a dilute gas, in which ternary and higher order collisions can be completely ignored. The dilute gas is not the same as the thermally perfect gas, a distinction that will be discussed later. If ternary and higher order collisions must be allowed for, then a dense gas is under consideration, and the theories for it are still incomplete.

Theory of binary collisions in dilute gas. It has been stated that every particle spends most of its time moving freely with a constant speed between collisions throughout its container. Of course, any such collision may, and usually does, change the speed of each particle; each retains this new speed undiminished until the next collision. Consequently, only the single-particle distribution function is important, since the laboratory properties of the gas will not depend upon the relative spatial positions and speeds of clusters of two or more particles but only upon the spatial position and speed of particles taken one at a time. Although collisions between particles in a dilute gas are infrequent as far as any particle is concerned, they must be allowed for. If the gas consists of monatomic, structureless particles, then, in a binary collision, the mass, momentum, and thermal kinetic energy (energy due to random motion) of the collison partners remain constant. This is known as an elastic binary collision. If the particles are polyatomic molecules possessing internal structure and internal motions, then, in a binary collision, although mass and momentum remain constant, it is possible that some of the thermal kinetic energy of the collision pair may be transformed into internal energy of the molecules by increasing the amount of energy already involved in the internal motions of rotation and vibration. This is called an inelastic binary collision.

BOLTZMANN TRANSPORT EQUATION

It is not difficult to derive the mathematical equation, called the Boltzmann transport equation, that describes the way the single-particle distribution function changes with time due to both types of binary collision, but it is a difficult equation to solve. Although the Boltzmann equation lies at the very heart of transport theory, it cannot be solved in general terms but only under special conditions, which, fortunately, are not too restricted. This article is concerned with two solutions of the Boltzmann equation, the equilibrium solution and the near-equilibrium solution.

Equilibrium solution for Boltzmann equation. The equilibrium solution is considered first. Mathematical analysis shows that if no external forces act on the gas, then the distribution function tends toward a value that is independent of spatial position and time, a value called the Maxwellian translational distribution function of thermal speeds. The existence of this value means that the gas reaches a uniform steady state known as a state of thermodynamic equilibrium. In this equilibrium state, all of the laboratory properties of the gas—pressure, density, temperature, energy, heat capacity, and entropy—are constant, and, in addition, the pressure, temperature, and density have the same values throughout the entire volume of the gas. Entropy is a measure of the disorganization of a gas. In any gas there is always some of the energy that can be converted into work (which is usually what an engineer wants); the amount that can be converted is determined by the entropy of the gas (see THERMODYNAMICS, PRINCIPLES OF). The equilibrium state is achieved because there is an overall balance in the collision processes suffered by the particles; *i.e.*, the number of particles with any particular spread, or range, of thermal speeds remains the same anywhere in the container because of a balance between the numbers of particles gaining and losing a given change of thermal speed due to binary collisions. In addition, further analysis (known as Boltzmann's H-theorem) shows that there is a detailed balance in the binary collisions, so that the number of particles in a particular thermal-speed spread, which are changed by binary collisions of a specified type, is exactly balanced by the same number of inverse collisions; if, for example, a collision is speed depleting for one of the particles, then the inverse collision is speed replenishing for the same particle. An inverse collision is distinguished from a reverse collision, in which the two particles merely reverse their original paths in space. The existence of the Maxwellian translational distribution function of speeds has been confirmed by direct measurement using a molecular beam. (Such a beam is produced by allowing gas particles to escape from a minuscule hole in the walls of a heated tube into a space kept at very low pressure by vacuum pumps; the individual particles fall in the earth's gravitational field and are separated out according to their thermal speeds.)

Maxwellian speed distribution function. The Maxwellian speed distribution for a dilute gas is, in fact, a general result and holds for dense gases as well. Once the translational distribution function (Maxwellian) of a gas has been obtained, it is a simple procedure to calculate the many equilibrium properties of the gas, such as the number of particles colliding with the container walls every second, by allowing for particles coming from all directions and with all thermal speeds. The result can be used to calculate the average force that the particles exert on the walls as they rebound from it, and that force is a measure of the pressure of the gas, since the collisions are sufficiently numerous to be thought of as a continuous force on the walls. Intermolecular forces affect the calculated pressure, because the attractive van der Waals forces exerted by the particles within the body of the gas restrain particles that are just about to collide with the wall. In addition, the mean free path of a particle can be calculated as the average distance travelled by a particle between binary collisions. A particle interpretation of the temperature of a gas can also be obtained in terms of the average kinetic energy of the particles as they move randomly throughout their container.

Equilibrium distribution function for internal energies. The Maxwellian distribution function refers to the external motions of the particles but does not refer to their internal motions of rotation and vibration. It might be expected that just as there is an equilibrium distribution function for the translational random kinetic energy, so there would be an equilibrium distribution function for the internal energies as well. In an evaluation of this equilibrium internal energy distribution function, a mathematical term arises that is called the internal partition function of the gas. The partition function, which is a mathematical series, has no immediate direct physical meaning but is intimately related to the manner in which the total energy of the gas particles, due to their structure together with the energy involved in the effects of intermolecular forces, is divided up (partitioned) among the particles. It is here that kinetic molecular theory merges into statistical thermodynamics, because the basic problem of the latter is to decide just how the total

Entropy

energy of the gas in equilibrium is to be divided up among the various energy modes of the particles. The analysis of the partitioning of energy examines the infinite number of ways the energy can be distributed and seeks to find if there is a preferred, or most probable, partitioning that is overwhelmingly likely to occur. The results of the analysis are expressed in terms of the partition functions of the various energy modes of the gas particles, which, as has been said, are very closely related to the equilibrium distribution functions of kinetic theory. The evaluation of the internal partition functions for thermally perfect gases is relatively easy, and it is possible to calculate all of the thermodynamic properties (*e.g.*, energy, heat capacity, entropy, etc.) of a thermally perfect dilute gas of particles possessing internal structure. If, however, the gas is one of interacting particles, then the evaluation of the internal partition function can be difficult, especially if the gas is dense, requiring an evaluation of the effect of ternary and higher order collisions.

The link between thermodynamic and microscopic properties. The partition function provides a direct link between the microscopic properties of the particles—their quantum energy states, their moments of inertia, their intermolecular potentials, etc.—and the laboratory properties of the gas—the thermal equation of state, the thermodynamic energy, heat capacity, and entropy. If the thermal equation of state of a gas of interacting particles is evaluated from the partition functions, then it turns out to be the virial (average kinetic energy) equation of state already introduced above. Each virial coefficient involves a mathematical quantity called the cluster integral. The second virial coefficient involves that cluster integral relating to the binary collision, while the third virial coefficient involves the cluster integral relating to ternary collisions, etc. Consequently, to evaluate the cluster integral, the dynamics of the collision must be calculated for a known intermolecular potential. For a dilute gas, where binary collisions alone are involved, the second virial coefficient can be evaluated for a variety of intermolecular potentials (see below *Mathematical models: virial coefficients*). To calculate the higher order cluster integrals, it is customary, because of ignorance of the true behaviour of three or more mutually interacting particles (called the many-body problem), to make the assumption of pairwise additivity: this states that the intermolecular forces involved in a many-particle collision are made up of the sum of two particle forces; for example, if three or more particles are interacting, then their interaction energy is the sum of their energies obtained by taking them in pairs. Although the assumption must be made in order to evaluate the cluster integrals, it is only approximate. Consequently, the third virial coefficient can be evaluated only approximately, which is the case for higher virial coefficients as well.

The ideal gas versus real gas. The relationship between the hypothetical thermally perfect gas, discussed earlier, and a real gas is that the former is a special type of the latter. The thermally perfect gas has particles that are not surrounded by attractive intermolecular force fields, so that its particles do not interact when separated. They can be thought of as rigid particles that interact with other particles only at the instant of collision, when, on touching, they repel each other with infinite force. Any gas of rigid particles will show thermally perfect behaviour provided its density is sufficiently low so that the second and higher virial coefficients are all extremely small; if the particles are "point" particles of vanishingly small volume, then all of the virial coefficients are zero, and the gas is thermally perfect at all densities. It is for this reason that the internal-partition functions for thermally perfect gases can readily be evaluated.

Origins of particle theory of gases. The particle description of gases grew from ideas in the 17th and 18th centuries concerning special aspects of the collective behaviour of structureless gas particles that were supposed to have no surrounding force fields. The pressure exerted by such a gas on the walls of its containers was calculated, and the idea developed that temperature was re-

The many-body problem

lated to particle motion. In the 19th century, the heat capacity of a gas kept at constant volume was calculated and found not to agree with experimentally measured values. When the heat capacity at constant pressure was calculated for the same gas, agreement was obtained with experimental values. The ratio of the two heat capacities was also calculated, and the idea was introduced that gas particles that possessed internal structure also had internal energy modes, such as molecular rotation and vibration. The idea of mean free path and the concept of binary collision were introduced. The first formal mathematical attempt to calculate the single-particle distribution function of a dilute gas was made by Maxwell in 1859 and refined by Boltzmann in 1868. The work of Maxwell and Boltzmann led directly to the classical (Newtonian) statistical thermodynamic theory of dilute gases of structureless particles in thermodynamic equilibrium in terms of the external, or translational, partition function. The idea of imperfect gases, real gases whose particles are surrounded by force fields, goes back to Newton. The first attempt to analyze them correctly was made in the 18th century, but it was van der Waals (1873) who first deduced the thermal equation of state of a real gas. The German physicist Rudolf Clausius developed (1875) a general theorem that gives the relationship between the intermolecular forces and the thermal equation of state, but it was not until 1902 that the virial equation of state and the virial coefficients were introduced. The statistical thermodynamic theory of imperfect gases was formulated in general terms by the American physicist J. Willard Gibbs (1901) using classical Newtonian mechanics. The previous year, the German scientist Max Planck discovered energy quantization, but it was not until later that the quantum statistical thermodynamics of real gases was developed by Satyendra Nath Bose and, independently, by Albert Einstein in 1924 and Enrico Fermi and Paul A.M. Dirac in 1926.

Mathematical models: virial coefficients. Various mathematical models have been suggested for the intermolecular force between two particles. The commonest assumption is one that is made for the sake of mathematical simplicity, and it assumes that the particles are both essentially spherical, so that the force between them does not depend upon their orientation in space (the intermolecular force has no angular dependence and is spherically symmetrical) but only upon their distance apart. Intermolecular forces are more often discussed in terms of the intermolecular potential energy between the particles. The simplest spherically symmetrical intermolecular potential is the rigid-sphere potential, which states that the particle is a solid sphere of prescribed size but not surrounded by an attractive force field. Such an intermolecular potential belongs to the thermally perfect gas. Among the many spherically symmetrical intermolecular potentials that have been proposed, the commonest and most useful is called the Lennard-Jones potential, which accurately describes the attractive van der Waals forces and, in addition, includes a term that gives the repulsive valence force, chosen for mathematical convenience and also because it is in good agreement with experiment. Virial coefficients have been calculated for many such intermolecular potentials, and it is found that they are more sensitive to the attractive force than to the repulsive one, so that any comparison between measured and calculated virial coefficients should yield information on the attractive van der Waals forces. The results of all of these calculations show that all virial coefficients should be negative at low temperatures, becoming zero at some intermediate temperature and rising to a positive maximum value at high temperature. Consequently, a determination of the pressure, volume, and temperature behaviour of a gas over a wide range of values of these properties should yield experimental data that can be interpreted in terms of the values of the virial coefficients. Experimentally, only the second and third virial coefficients can be measured, since the others are too small. In addition, the intermolecular potential cannot be determined uniquely merely by making laboratory measurements on pressure, volume, and temperature. An in-

direct procedure must be used, by assuming a mathematical equation for the intermolecular potential that contains unspecified constants, then calculating the virial coefficients and their dependence on temperature and then comparing experimental and theoretical results in order to determine the unspecified constants. Thereafter, the intermolecular potential, now with known constants, can be used to calculate other measurable gas properties that also depend upon the virial coefficients, such as the Joule-Thomson coefficient, the heat of sublimation of crystals, and the transport coefficients (see below *Transport coefficients*). The ability of the intermolecular potential to predict the experimentally observed values of these properties is a good test of its accuracy. Unfortunately, the largest virial coefficient (the second) is not very sensitive to the precise form of the attractive intermolecular force, while the third virial coefficient suffers from uncertainties about the effects of assuming pairwise additivity and also the effects of experimental error, since it is so small. Because of these limitations, any comparison of theoretically calculated and experimentally observed virial coefficients seldom eliminates an assumed form of intermolecular potential; rather, it gives the best form from a group of assumed forms on the basis that the best form fits the widest range of properties.

Virial equation of state and dense gas. It had been hoped that the virial equation of state would be applicable to dense gases and even to condensing gases, provided that a sufficient number of virial coefficients were taken into consideration. Several difficulties have arisen, however. For example, for ternary and higher order collisions, the intermolecular potential must be guessed on the basis of pairwise additivity, and this means that the cluster integrals for many-particle collisions are only very approximately known and may be seriously in error. Also, during condensation, when an enormously large number of particles are mutually interacting, the cluster integrals become dependent on the volume of the gas as the clusters get bigger and bigger. This is a branch of statistical thermodynamics that is not well understood and is still under active investigation. It seems clear that a virial expansion up to the fifth virial coefficient is mathematically convergent for densities as high as the density of the saturated vapour, that portion of the gas still uncondensed; however, the virial expansion is mathematically divergent and, therefore, useless for the density of the liquid. Consequently, the virial expansion cannot give a theory that goes right through the condensation transition from entire gas to entire liquid. There is no complete theory of condensation available at the present time. Ultimately, the virial expansion must fail altogether at very high densities, when the concept of the existence of individual interacting particles loses its meaning. This has led to another approach to the thermal equation of state of extremely dense gases and of liquids where a structure is assumed and where the question of how this structure arose is ignored.

Latent-heat theory. Another phenomenon that a theory of condensation should predict is the latent heat; namely, the release of energy from a gas that is condensing as its temperature remains constant. There is no theory for the latent heat, because it is intimately related to the condensation process, and, at the present time, knowledge of latent heats is dependent on thermodynamics. An equation called the Clausius-Clapeyron equation enables the latent heat of condensation to be deduced from knowledge of the rate of change of vapour pressure with temperature, together with knowledge of the densities of the liquid and vapour in the mixture. The latent heat depends upon the pressure and temperature at which condensation occurs, and it becomes zero at the critical point. The Clausius-Clapeyron equation, being a thermodynamic equation, is independent of the particle theory of matter.

Historically, specific forms for the intermolecular potential were studied by Maxwell (1866) and others, but it was not until 1924 that the effects of both attractive and repulsive forces were considered. The physical explanation of why repulsive forces arise was given in 1927, and in 1930 the van der Waals attractive forces were explained. A virial-equation approach to the problem of the condensation of a gas into a liquid was pioneered in 1927 and considerably extended in 1937.

Nonequilibrium solution for the equation. Turning aside from the equilibrium solution of the Boltzmann transport equation, which describes the state of thermodynamic equilibrium of any gas, be it dilute or dense, the case can now be considered where the gas is in a nonuniform state. If there are variations (*i.e.*, gradients) of density, gas velocity, or temperature in the gas, then transport processes arise. This means that some physical property of the gas flows through the gas down the gradients. If the property transported is mass, then the transport process is called diffusion, and it arises because of a gradient in the density of particles between any two regions of the gas. If the property transported is momentum, then it is viscosity that arises from gradients of gas velocity in the gas, such as will occur if the gas is in motion along a wall. If the property transported is thermal energy, then the transport process is called thermal conduction, and it arises if there are regions of different temperature in the gas. The three transport processes are characterized by three transport coefficients.

For a dilute gas in which only binary collisions need be considered, the governing equation is the Boltzmann transport equation; it gives the space and time behaviour of the single-particle distribution function. The entire equation can be mathematically manipulated to give certain mathematical relationships called the flux vectors, which contain the transport coefficients. To evaluate the flux vectors and, therefore, the transport coefficients, two things must be known; namely, the single-particle distribution function of the nonuniform gas and, because the transport processes are related to binary collisions between particles, details of the dynamics of a binary collision, which, as has been pointed out, require a knowledge of the intermolecular potential.

Transport coefficients. It has been remarked that the Boltzmann transport equation for binary collisions can be solved only under special conditions: the effective diameters of the particles must be much less than their mean free path, and the changes in density, gas velocity, and temperature over a mean free path must be extremely small. Under these conditions, the Boltzmann equation can be solved (the Chapman-Enskog solution) by using the method of successive approximations; it yields a solution for the nonequilibrium distribution function in the form of a mathematical series. Each term in the series represents an increasing departure from the Maxwellian equilibrium distribution function, so that the nonequilibrium distribution function is expressed in terms of the localized density, gas velocity, and temperature values, all of which vary throughout the volume of the gas and also vary with time. The first approximation to the solution is one that is valid for small spatial gradients and gives a measure of the number of particles transferred, or the flux vectors, that depend on these gradients, so that the transport coefficients can be calculated after the intermolecular potential has been specified. In this respect, the calculation of the three transport coefficients is completely analogous to a calculation of the virial coefficients of the equilibrium gas; that is, the intermolecular potential is specified; the collision integral, a mathematical quantity relating the angle of deflection of one particle with respect to the other involved in the binary collision, is calculated; and, thereafter, the flux vectors are calculated, and the transport coefficients are obtained in terms of the assumed intermolecular potential.

Transport coefficients have been calculated for a variety of spherically symmetrical and other types of intermolecular potentials. Such calculations show that, although the transport coefficients are more sensitive to the repulsive than to the attractive part of the force between two particles (whereas the virial coefficient is just the converse), they depend essentially upon the fact that there is a repulsive force and not much on the precise form of the force. As with the virial coefficients, the form of the intermolecular potential that agrees with laboratory measurements of the transport coefficients cannot be deduced.

Transport coefficient for dilute, polyatomic gas. The Chapman-Enskog solution of the Boltzmann equation was originally framed to deal with dilute, monatomic gases of structureless particles where all binary collisions are elastic. For the commoner case of polyatomic molecules, allowance must be made for inelastic collisions between nonspherical particles, when random kinetic energy is converted into internal energy of rotation and vibration. A Chapman-Enskog type of solution has been given to the Boltzmann equation for a dilute, polyatomic gas, but it involves details of the intermolecular potential in an inelastic binary collision that are still unknown. A simplified version of this theory, in which the inelastic collisions are dealt with in terms of rotational and vibrational relaxation times, (see below *Thermal relaxation stage*) has been given, and studies show that inelastic binary collisions do not appreciably affect the diffusion and viscosity coefficients but do significantly affect the thermal-conduction coefficient. Such a result would be expected, since the thermal-conduction coefficient deals with energy transfer through the gas, and inelastic collisions are concerned with energy-transfer processes between particles. The problem of calculating the transport coefficients of dilute, polyatomic gases is still under investigation, and much remains to be done.

Transport coefficient for nonchaotic gas. When the gas density is more than about 100 times atmospheric density, ternary and higher order collisions must be considered in addition to binary collisions, and this consideration affects the transport coefficients profoundly. The Boltzmann transport equation and its Chapman-Enskog solution are not applicable to the dense gas, because what may be called molecular chaos may not exist. Molecular chaos, which must hold if the Boltzmann equation is to be applicable, requires at all times that the spatial positions and speeds of the particles involved in collisions be in no way related to each other (they are not correlated), so that there is no effect of previous collisions on any collision occurring, which means that the results of a collision must depend upon the immediate state of the particles during the collision and not on their previous history. Molecular chaos is readily achieved in a dilute gas, because particle correlation is negligible, since a recollision between the same two particles is extremely unlikely. In a dense gas, a substantial proportion of all particles are suffering collisions at any instant, and such collisions may be recollisions, because the mean free path becomes comparable with the particle diameter (in a dilute gas, the mean free path is very large compared with the particle diameter, and most of the time particles in a dilute gas are travelling freely). In such a recollision, spatial positions and speeds may be correlated, and, thus, molecular chaos—and, therefore, the Boltzmann equation—no longer holds. What is required is a multiparticle distribution function that allows for particle correlation (*i.e.*, the relative spatial positions and speeds of clusters of two or more particles), recognizing the fact that any one particle can affect the spatial positions and speeds of all of the other particles in its vicinity.

Distribution function for N particles. It is possible to write down the equation (the Liouville equation) that gives the changes in space and time of the N-particle distribution function, N being the total number of gas particles in the container, a total that is, as has been discussed, an enormous number. From the equation it is possible to derive, by mathematical methods, a chain of equations in which each equation in the chain involves the changes in space and time of two consecutive lower order (*i.e.*, fewer particles) distribution functions.

At the end of the chain, there will be an equation that gives the single-particle distribution function used in the Boltzmann equation, in terms of the two-particle distribution function. The chain of equations is called the BBGKY hierarchy of equations. For purposes of calculation, the chain of equations must be broken, since it is

[margin: Properties transported]

[margin: Recollisions]

impossible to handle a vast number of equations at the same time, by making some assumption about the dependence of some higher-order distribution function on the lower-order distribution functions and then dealing with a finite, as opposed to an effectively infinite, set of chain equations.

Time scales. One method of doing this is based on a realization that if a gas achieves a state of thermodynamic equilibrium, or a nonequilibrium steady state with unchanging gradients of properties, solely by collisions between particles—be they collisions of second or of higher order, elastic or inelastic—then the process of achieving that state will require a finite time because such collisions do not occur infinitely fast. The problem of calculating the uniform state of thermodynamic equilibrium or nonuniform steady state of a gas is still unsolved and represents a great challenge to present-day research workers. Any progress that has been made has been based on the recognition that, during this approach to a final state, several quite different time scales are involved. The first time scale is that appropriate to the initial stage. This time scale is the duration of a collision; that is, the quotient of the effective range of the intermolecular force field between two colliding particles and their average random thermal relative speed; it has a value of about 10^{-13} second. Analysis of the initial stage is a dynamic problem dealing with the detailed motions of individual particles, and the gas cannot be described in terms of its laboratory properties, such as density, gas velocity, and temperature. The next characteristic time interval is that between collisions, about 10^{-11} second. In between the two times, the gas is being brought into a state where a statistical description is possible in terms of distribution functions but where a laboratory description is still not yet possible in terms of density, gas velocity, and temperature. This may be called the kinetic stage, and the gas must be described by its multiparticle distribution function. After a time equal to the duration of a collision—*i.e.,* after the initial stage—all the multiparticle distribution functions have changed so rapidly that they can all be described in terms of the single-particle distribution function, which effectively has not changed at all. Assuming such a simplification has enabled researchers to solve the BBGKY chain of equations that describe the kinetic stage and that allow, in principle, for multiparticle collisions before molecular chaos is established. Unfortunately, the solution is a mathematical series that diverges and, therefore, is useless when four-particle and higher-order collisions are considered. It would appear that the method (named Bogolyubov) is valid for gases having densities such that binary and ternary, but no higher-order, collisions occur.

This is as far as the kinetic theory of dense gases has been developed; a completely different approach may be required, one that does not treat a dense gas as a gas in which multiparticle collisions occur in terms of the binary, ternary, and higher-order collisions.

SPECIAL CONDITIONS

Hydrodynamic properties of a gas. The initial and kinetic stages in the process by which a gas approaches an equilibrium state or a steady nonuniform state take place so rapidly that they are, to all intents and purposes, beyond laboratory measurement. In view of the great difficulties involved in developing a theory of these stages, the discussion will revert to a consideration of the behaviour of a gas after they are complete. The next stage in the approach of the gas to its final state, one that does lie within the capabilities of laboratory techniques, is that describable by the Boltzmann equation, involving the single-particle distribution function and its solutions. This is called the hydrodynamic stage, because it can be described by mathematical equations that involve properties such as density, gas velocity, and temperature, rather than the statistical concept of a distribution function. The equations are called the Navier-Stokes and the Burnett equations of hydrodynamics. If the gas is polyatomic, there is another stage, which is the final approach to thermodynamic equilibrium or to a steady nonuniform

state; this is the thermal-relaxation stage and involves energy exchanges between the external (translational) energy mode and the internal energy modes of the polyatomic molecules.

Hydrodynamic stage. Rather than continue the discussion in general terms, it is easier to consider an important application of the hydrodynamic and thermal-relaxation stages: the passage of a plane sound wave through a gas. Such a sound wave causes any randomly chosen, small volume of gas to be alternately compressed and expanded, so that the density, gas velocity, and temperature of the small volume will vary cyclically with time as the sound wave continues to pass through the gas. The compressions heat the gas, and the expansions, called rarefactions, cool it. Transport processes, especially the transfer of heat and of momentum, occur between the regions of compression and rarefaction, and in each cycle some of the forward-directed energy of the sound wave is converted into random thermal energy of the gas. The energy of the sound wave suffers classical (*i.e.,* Newtonian) absorption and also classical dispersion, and the speed of passage of the wave through the gas depends upon the frequency of the alternations of compression and expansion. The frequencies for which significant soundwave absorption and dispersion occur are usually higher than the frequencies of sound waves audible to the human ear, and the waves are called ultrasonic. Such waves disturb the state of thermodynamic equilibrium of the gas, and the rate of return to a state of thermodynamic equilibrium can be measured in the laboratory. This is the hydrodynamic stage governed by the macroscopic equations of Navier and Stokes and of Burnett.

Classical absorption and dispersion (the type just described) is the only type of energy-loss process occurring when a sound wave passes through a monatomic gas, whose particles possess no internal structure. If, however, the gas is composed of polyatomic molecules, much larger absorption and dispersion result from thermalrelaxation processes. Thermal relaxation is a consequence of the fact that the internal energy modes of polyatomic molecules cannot change their energies as quickly as the external (translational) energy mode.

The physical picture is one in which, before passage of the sound wave, the gas is in a state of thermodynamic equilibrium with the total energy partitioned out, in accordance with the partition functions already referred to, between the various energy modes. The sound wave comes along and disturbs this equilibrium, because the compressions increase the total energy of the gas, while the rarefactions decrease the total energy. The change in energy must be distributed between the various energy modes (external and internal) of the particles to allow a new state of equilibrium to be achieved. The redistribution (or repartitioning) requires inelastic collisions to transfer the energy from the external translational mode into the internal energy modes, and such inelastic collisions take a finite time to occur. Evidence obtained from experimental studies of the absorption and dispersion of ultrasonic waves by polyatomic gases suggests that the energy is transferred between the various energy modes by binary inelastic collisions, even for exceptionally dense gases having densities approaching those of liquids. It is found that the translational energy relaxation time (the time taken for the translational energy distribution function to change to its new equilibrium value) is about equal to the time between binary collisions. In addition, the rotational energy relaxation time for all polyatomic molecules (except such simple diatomic molecules as oxygen, nitrogen, and hydrogen) is only slightly longer. The vibrational energy relaxation time, however, may lie between 10^{-8} and 10^{-5} second, depending on the molecule concerned. Consequently, the vibrational energy changes in polyatomic molecules cannot keep in step, or in equilibrium, with the very rapid translational and rotational energy changes that occur as the sound wave passes through the gas. To calculate the amount of absorption and dispersion that occurs requires a calculation of the number of binary inelastic collisions occurring in the polyatomic gas every second and knowledge of how

Sound waves

Time scales

this number depends upon the density and temperature of the gas. It is a problem in quantum mechanics involving two polyatomic molecules, not necessarily possessing spherical symmetry, interacting with some complex intermolecular potential that depends upon the spatial orientation of the two molecules, as well as on their separation distance. Such a complicated collision problem can be solved only in rather approximate terms; it is a much more difficult calculation than that needed to evaluate the virial and transport coefficients of monatomic gases. The relative simplicity of the treatment of monatomic gases derives from the applicability of Newtonian mechanics to elastic collisions uncomplicated by the participation of internal energy modes and thermal-relaxation effects.

Thermal relaxation stage. Approximate calculations of inelastic collisions show that at any given temperature the relaxation time depends, roughly speaking, on the amount of energy to be exchanged between the translational energy mode and the internal energy mode under discussion. It does not take much energy to set molecular rotations into motion, and many of the binary collisions that occur in a room-temperature polyatomic gas are, in fact, sufficiently energetic to cause molecular rotation (they are inelastic collisions), and this is why rotational relaxation times are not much greater than the time between binary elastic collisions. It usually requires, however, a considerably larger amount of energy to start off molecular vibrations, and exceedingly few of the binary collisions in a room-temperature polyatomic gas are sufficiently energetic to pass translational energy into the vibrational energy modes of the molecules; hence, the vibrational relaxation time is long.

High temperatures. Since internal energy-relaxation-time measurements are capable of yielding valuable information on intermolecular forces, considerable effort is being given to studies of the temperature dependence of relaxation times. Ultrasonic absorption studies are limited to gases at room temperature and a few hundred degrees above it, so that another technique must be found to study high-temperature gas relaxation behaviour that is becoming so important in modern aerospace technology, as in the flow of a hot gas through a rocket nozzle. Such a technique is the shock-wave method, in which relaxation processes can be studied up to temperatures as high as 1,000,000°. The shock-wave method has been used for studying not only rotational and vibrational relaxation processes in polyatomic gases but also dissociation relaxation processes, in which the molecular vibrations have become so energetic that the atoms of the molecule fly apart and the molecule breaks up. In addition, at higher temperatures, the individual atoms, which previously had behaved as structureless particles, show that they are formed from electrons and nuclei, because electronic excitation of the electrons occurs, eventually resulting, perhaps, in ionization of the atoms, whereby they lose one or more of their electrons.

Chemical reactions in gases. Dissociation and ionization processes are more commonly thought of as chemical reactions. Polyatomic gases are capable of undergoing a vast number of different chemical reactions where the chemical bonds that bind atoms into molecules and electrons into atoms are broken and the molecules or atoms thereby change their chemical nature. Among the striking features of chemical reactions is the strong dependence of their velocities on density and temperature, indicating that reactions proceed because of inelastic collisions between molecules. Chemical-reaction-rate theory is a branch of kinetic theory, and a quantum kinetic theory of chemical reactions exists that is very similar in description to the kinetic theory of the transport processes in dilute, polyatomic gases and which suffers from all the limitations of that theory.

Summary. In conclusion, it can be stated that laboratory experiments on gases can provide a vast amount of data relating to the physical and chemical behaviour of gases as their pressure, density, temperature, and gas velocities are changed. It is the task of statistical thermodynamics and kinetic theory to provide procedures for calculating the various equilibrium and nonequilibrium

properties of gases. The equilibrium properties can be determined in terms of the virial coefficients and partition functions. The nonequilibrium properties must be determined in terms of the effective sizes of the particles (their collision cross sections) as they mutually interact because of the intermolecular forces that exist among them. Quantum mechanics is capable of solving these problems in principle but is far from doing so in practice. What has been achieved is a satisfactorily complete particle description of the thermodynamic equilibrium and transport properties of dilute, monatomic gases in terms of some assumed form of intermolecular potential. In addition, there is an equally satisfactory particle description of the thermodynamic equilibrium properties of dilute, polyatomic gases, but there is no comparable quantitative theory for their transport properties. The theory of the thermodynamic equilibrium and transport properties of dense gases is still incomplete and will remain so until a great deal more is known about both the many-body problem (the mutual interaction of three or more particles) and how to calculate exact inelastic collision cross sections.

BIBLIOGRAPHY. The full theory of the equilibrium properties of gases is given in J.O. HIRSCHFELDER, C.F. CURTISS, and R.B. BIRD, *The Molecular Theory of Gases and Liquids*, corrected printing (1965); the full theory of the transport processes of gases in S. CHAPMAN and T.G. COWLING, *The Mathematical Theory of Non-Uniform Gases*, 3rd ed. (1970); and the full theory of thermal-relaxation processes in gases in J.F. CLARKE and M. MCCHESNEY, *The Dynamics of Real Gases* (1964). A good but rather dated compilation of experimental values of equilibrium and transport properties of gases and liquids is R.C. REID and T.K. SHERWOOD, *The Properties of Liquids and Gases* (1958).

(M.McC.)

Gases, Industrial and Domestic

Industrial and domestic gases include a variety of gases, some occurring naturally in the earth or atmosphere, some manufactured, which are used for heating or in certain manufacturing processes. The leading domestic gas throughout the world is natural gas, or methane, employed for space heating and cooling, for heating water, and for cooking. Gas manufactured from coal and oil is still burned in many countries but is being rapidly supplanted in industrialized areas by less expensive and more convenient natural gas, as reserves are discovered and long-distance pipelines constructed.

Industrial gases have a much broader range of chemical composition than domestic gas. This article includes not only manufactured gases consumed by industry for heat and power and as a chemical raw material but also other gases used extensively in industrial processing. Gases can be conveniently divided into two groups: those that are or can be recovered by the liquefaction of air, including oxygen, nitrogen, carbon dioxide, and the noble gases (helium, argon, krypton, xenon, and radon); and those that are manufactured and used in large quantities as intermediates in the production of another product, and in smaller quantities directly. They include hydrogen, carbon monoxide, acetylene, chlorine, ammonia, sulfur dioxide, and mixtures of hydrogen and carbon monoxide; other gases, such as fluorine, hydrogen chloride, hydrogen cyanide, and hydrogen sulfide, which are used commercially in relatively small quantities, are not covered. For each gas, its history, reserves, methods of production, transportation, prices, and uses are discussed.

RESIDENTIAL AND INDUSTRIAL HEATING GASES

Manufactured gas. Manufactured gas, first produced in the late 18th century by heating coal in the absence of air, soon replaced the candle and oil lamp as a principal source of illumination. The charter for the first gas company was granted in London in 1812, with other cities of the world soon following. Gas was used first for street lighting and public buildings and later for private residences. When electricity, which provides a better, safer light, displaced gaslight in the late 19th century, the gas industry sought applications of its product in heating.

Coal gas, produced by the distillation of coal, has a

Coal gas

heating value ranging from about 475 to 560 British thermal units per cubic foot (about 30 litres), depending on the temperature to which the coal is heated and the nature of the coal used. A British thermal unit (BTU) is the quantity of heat required to raise the temperature of one pound (454 grams) of water 1° F (0.56° C). Coke-oven gas, given off when coal is carbonized to make coke, the fuel for the blast-furnace production of pig iron, has a composition similar to coal gas and, in the past, was used extensively to supplement coal-gas supplies. Coke-oven gas, on leaving the oven, is treated to remove tar, ammonia, light oil, and other chemical substances before it is distributed to consumers. The coke ovens may be fueled by part of the coke-oven gas unless industry demand for it is high; if so, the ovens can be heated with a lower quality gas made in other ways from coal.

Another type of manufactured gas, called water gas, is made by a cyclic process in which steam is blown over a bed of burning coke. Water gas has a heating value of about 300 British thermal units per cubic foot, which can be increased to 500 or more, however, by carbureting it with petroleum fractions—a process in which the heat contained in the water gas raises the temperature of the oil high enough to convert it into hydrocarbon gases with high heating values. The heating value of water gas is increased to these levels to make it suitable for distribution to consumers.

Producer gas, which is easier and less costly to manufacture than either coal or water gas, has a much lower heating value (about 130 British thermal units per cubic foot) because it is produced in a continuous, air-using process that dilutes it with nitrogen. The largest use for producer gas is in industrial plants and for heating coke ovens when industry demand for coke-oven gas is high. When the gas is burned where it is produced, it is more valuable because it still contains the heat of its manufacturing process. When producer gas must be transported long distances, it cools and loses this heat.

Other manufactured gases are produced from various petroleum fractions or from natural gas. Originally, such gases were added to enrich gases of lower heating value made from coal to achieve a uniform-quality product. Production processes include (1) reforming of natural gas (and other higher molecular weight hydrocarbon gases) at high temperatures to break up the molecule; (2) cracking (breaking down into smaller molecules) of natural gas or other lightweight hydrocarbons over a catalyst; and (3) cracking oil into lightweight gases (oil gas) with a high heating value. A large number of processes, employing a wide variety of different types of equipment, have been developed for each of these raw materials. At any given location the particular manufacturing method depends on many engineering and economic factors.

Manufactured and natural gases have frequently been mixed to obtain the desired heating value and other physical and chemical properties. The amount of mixed gas supplied in any given area generally depends on the relative costs of manufactured and natural gas.

Generally speaking, the production and consumption of manufactured gas has declined steadily as new reserves of natural gas have been discovered and as long-distance pipelines have been built. The two largest sources of manufactured gas have been carbureted water gas and coke-oven gas. Bituminous coal has been the principal raw material, with lesser quantities of coke, anthracite, oil, and tar providing the balance.

Natural gas. Proved natural-gas reserves of the world, excluding the Soviet Union, are estimated at approximately 10^{15} cubic feet. The United States has the largest share, about 25 percent, and Algeria the next largest. Important quantities are also found in Iran, The Netherlands, Saudi Arabia, Canada, Kuwait, and in the North Sea off the United Kingdom. The deposits found in The Netherlands and the North Sea have created a rapidly expanding market for natural gas in western Europe. Eastern Europe is supplied by the Soviet Union, which has recently increased its estimate of reserves; if the estimate proves accurate, the Soviet Union reserve will be the largest in the world.

World reserves of natural gas

Natural gas occurs in reservoirs beneath the surface of the earth; its existence must be proved by drilling. With the large discoveries under the North Sea and the Gulf of Mexico, drilling interest has shifted from onshore to offshore locations, resulting in development of new technology for drilling wells at ever-increasing depths (see also PETROLEUM AND GAS EXTRACTION). Though offshore drilling costs are much higher than those onshore, the potential for finding new gas reservoirs is thought to be much higher.

Distribution and storage. Natural gas usually undergoes processing of some kind before it is transported to the consumer, the amount and type of processing depending on the chemical characteristics of the gas as it comes from the well. If it is present, hydrogen sulfide must be removed (by-product sulfur is recovered and sold). Other nonhydrocarbon gases may also be removed to meet standards prescribed for pipeline gas. Valuable higher hydrocarbons (natural-gas liquids) are normally recovered before the natural gas is transported to markets.

Production and marketing arrangements vary in different parts of the world. In some nations, such as Mexico and the Soviet Union, the industry is completely nationalized. In Britain, Japan, Italy, and France exploration and development are carried out by either private firms or the government, but transportation and distribution are a government monopoly. In the United States, exploration, production, and transportation are handled by private firms, regulated by federal, state, and local commissions.

Storage facilities for natural gas have grown substantially. In the United States, for example, where demand is usually maximum during the winter months, it is not economically feasible to construct pipelines large enough to meet peak demands. Thus, natural-gas storage, mainly in depleted gas or oil reservoirs located near the large-volume consumers, has grown rapidly. Where natural storage facilities are not available, the product is stored in liquid form.

Underground gas storage

Consumption. Consumption patterns for natural gas vary. In western Europe, natural gas has not been available in most countries until very recently; therefore, it supplies only about 30 percent of gas demand, with liquefied petroleum gas supplying another 9 percent. In homes, it is used for cooking and water heating but is not as widely applied in space heating as it is in the United States. As natural gas becomes more widely available, however, its consumption is expected to increase. In western Europe, natural gas provides the same advantages to industrial users as it does in homes and thus is expected to continue making significant inroads into this market at the expense of coal and, to a lesser extent, oil. In the early 1970s, however, the cost of European natural gas was still much higher than U.S. gas.

By far the major use of natural gas is as fuel, though increasing amounts are being taken by the chemical industry for raw material. Among industries consuming large volumes are food, paper, chemicals, petroleum refining, and primary metals. In the United States, a large amount fuels household heating plants; in the Soviet Union, a considerable volume goes for electric-power generation.

In the chemical industry, natural gas supplies an ideal feedstock (raw-material source) for the manufacture of ammonia, methanol, acetylene, and hydrogen. Its advantages over other raw materials include longer life and lower capital requirements for plant facilities, generally lower operating costs, and less air pollution. Worldwide, natural gas supplies about 20 percent of total energy demand, with the United States consuming about 60 percent of the marketed production in 1970. Estimates made by the Economic Commission for Europe predict that the increases for natural-gas demand between 1967 and 1980 will be about 308 percent for western Europe, 286 percent for eastern Europe, 283 percent for the Soviet Union, but only 29 percent for the United States. Despite the rapid growth in natural-gas usage, there are still some countries where lack of marketing capabilities prevents utilization of all the gas produced.

Future world gas consumption

In South America, gas production exceeds 3×10^{12} cubic feet per year, of which about one-third is unsold and must be flared (burned at the well). Projections of future gas demand forecast large new world requirements, if the gas can be supplied. Incentives to increase exploration and drilling are expected to lead to additional supplies of natural gas, since large, yet-to-be-discovered deposits are believed to exist.

Ultimate recoverable (with present technology and economics) world reserves are estimated at 13.3×10^{15} cubic feet. The value of these reserves depends upon the ability of producers to transport the product to market. In this respect, an advantage of natural gas over oil is that a gas pipeline in a cold climate does not need to be kept heated as does an oil pipeline. In a region such as the North Slope of Alaska, this consideration raises ecological problems. Of course, possible damage done to land during construction of a pipeline is a concern with either gas or oil.

Some very large reserves of natural gas have been discovered but are uneconomic to tap. Gas and petroleum are held underground, as in a sponge, between grains of sand or in the spaces inside porous rocks, rather than in a simple pool. Sometimes the gas is so tightly held that it will not flow out easily, and extraction is uneconomic. Experiments using nuclear explosives to break up these tight formations and thus to increase gas flow to economic levels have been performed in the United States (SEE PETROLEUM AND GAS EXTRACTION).

Another potential method for augmenting natural gas supplies is by the gasification of coal. When coal reacts with oxygen and steam under controlled conditions, it is converted to a mixture containing hydrogen, methane, oxides of carbon, and impurities. After the impurities are removed, the gas can be upgraded to a product that is essentially methane, a gas with a much higher heating value than that previously manufactured from coal. A number of different upgrading processes have been studied on a pilot-plant scale, and many appear to be technically feasible, but the economics of producing a synthetic gas from coal had not yet been demonstrated in the early 1970s.

Other petroleum-based gases. These include liquefied petroleum gas and ethane.

Liquefied petroleum gas (LPG). Composed of propane, butane, or propane–butane mixtures, liquefied petroleum gas is part of the natural-gas liquid obtained at natural-gasoline plants, recycling plants, and petroleum fractionators after separating out the natural gas. Though founded early in the 20th century, the liquefied-petroleum-gas industry did not experience rapid growth until after World War II.

Reserves of liquefied petroleum gas and ethane (see below) are linked to natural gas and petroleum reserves. Estimates in 1968 put reserves of all natural-gas liquids (only part of which are liquefied petroleum gas) at 8,000,-000,000 barrels. One barrel equals 42 U.S. gallons or 159 litres. At an average ratio of liquefied petroleum gas and ethane to total natural-gas liquids of about 3:5 this would represent ten years' supply at 1970 consumption rates. Strong demand and improved processing methods have encouraged production of maximum yields of liquefied petroleum gas and ethane from natural gas.

Transported and stored in liquid form under moderate pressure, either in steel cylinders for home use or in railroad tank cars, tanker trucks, barges, or pipelines, liquefied petroleum gas changes to gaseous form when the pressure is released and then can be used like natural gas. The product is stored in pressurized containers above ground and, more recently, in underground storage caverns.

About 40 percent of annual production goes for residential and commercial purposes, while another 40 percent is used as a raw material in the chemical industry. Important domestic users are farmers, who receive the product in steel cylinders and use it for cooking, water heating, powering trucks and tractors, burning weeds, drying crops, and curing tobacco. Liquefied petroleum gas also finds use in synthetic-rubber manufacture; in in-

Transportation and storage of liquefied petroleum gas

ternal-combustion engines of taxis, trucks, and buses; in oil refineries; and in electrical utilities, where it has begun to supplant other fossil fuels, which cause objectionable amounts of pollution.

Ethane. Ethane is also recovered from natural-gas liquids or can be produced by cracking light petroleum fractions. Shipped as a liquid under moderate pressure, ethane is used both as a fuel and in a number of chemical processes. Relatively large amounts are consumed in the production of acetylene, the raw material for the manufacture of ethylene oxide, polyethylene plastics, styrene plastics, and ethyl alcohol.

GASES PRODUCED BY LIQUEFACTION OF AIR

Oxygen. The most abundant of the chemical elements, oxygen comprises about 21 percent by volume of the earth's atmosphere and is the most important of the industrial gases. Usually produced by cooling air until it liquefies (see illustration), then separating out its com-

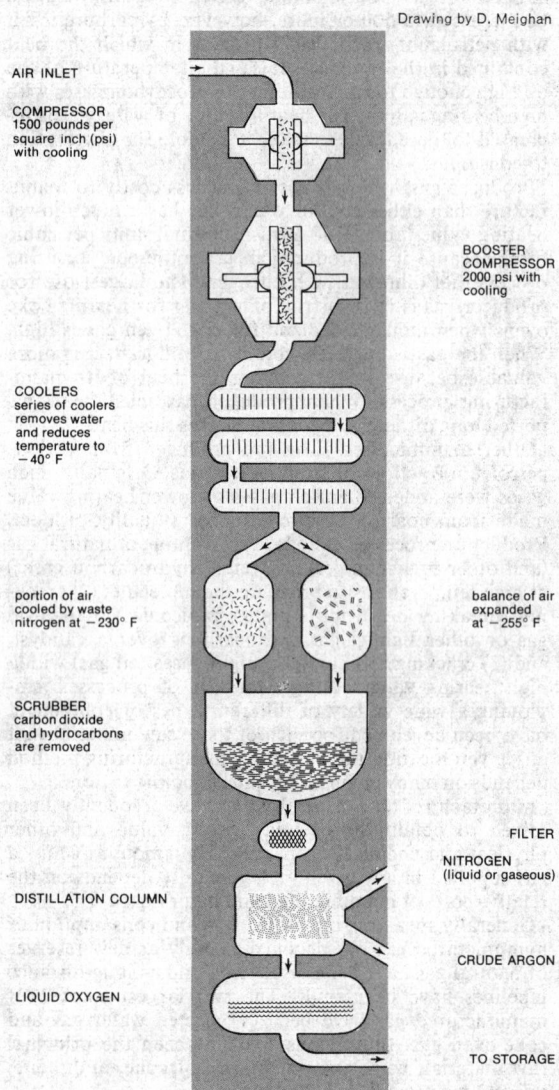

Drawing by D. Meighan

AIR INLET

COMPRESSOR
1500 pounds per square inch (psi) with cooling

BOOSTER COMPRESSOR
2000 psi with cooling

COOLERS
series of coolers removes water and reduces temperature to −40° F

portion of air cooled by waste nitrogen at −230° F

balance of air expanded at −255° F

SCRUBBER
carbon dioxide and hydrocarbons are removed

FILTER

NITROGEN
(liquid or gaseous)

DISTILLATION COLUMN

CRUDE ARGON

LIQUID OXYGEN

TO STORAGE

Steps involved in the liquefaction of air.

ponent gases, oxygen may also be obtained as a by-product of the electrolysis of water in the production of hydrogen. Electrolysis involves passing an electric current through water, separating it into hydrogen and oxygen. Electrolysis, however, is economically feasible only if small quantities are required and low-cost electric power is available.

Of the total world production of oxygen in 1969, the United States produced about 30 percent, or about 12,800,000 tons. Japan produced 9,700,000 tons, or about 22 percent, while the Soviet Union and West Germany each accounted for about 11 percent of the total. During the 1960s world production increased more than fourfold.

Demands for large amounts of oxygen have resulted from the introduction of the basic oxygen process in the steel industry. Large oxygen plants sometimes serve a single consumer; frequently, however, a single plant provides for a number of consumers through a pipeline distribution system. Oxygen is marketed in eight different grades, according to the percentage of oxygen in the gas and to the type and quantity of impurities that are permitted.

Oxygen transport methods

Gaseous oxygen is transported at high pressures in steel cylinders, tank cars, and tube trailers. Liquid oxygen is shipped in insulated cylinders, tank trucks, and tank cars. In small quantities, liquid oxygen is shipped in insulated containers similar to those used for liquid nitrogen and liquid air. For large volumes, oxygen is often pipelined (the cheapest method of transportation). Oxygen prices have steadily declined, owing to improvements in production technology and economies of scale made possible by the large-volume demands of the steel industry. Plants with capacities as large as 1,400 tons per day have come into operation. The cost of power is the principal item of direct operating expense, so that site location generally is a compromise between nearness to markets and cost of electricity.

Most industrial oxygen is consumed in primary metal processing, with the steel industry taking the lion's share. The second-largest outlet for oxygen is in the manufacture of industrial chemicals, with acetylene manufacture comprising nearly half of this market. Ethylene oxide, methanol, and titanium dioxide production also require large amounts of oxygen. The gas is also used in a wide variety of other applications: in waste-water treatment; in liquid-oxygen explosives; in such aerospace applications as oxidizing liquid propellants and supplying life-support systems; in hospitals for the artificial atmosphere in oxygen tents and incubators and in the gaseous mixture in anesthetics; in torches for cutting and welding metals; and in a low-cost method of drilling certain types of hard rock formations in preparation for blasting.

Nitrogen. Because nitrogen—a colourless, odourless, tasteless gas—comprises about 78 percent of the earth's atmosphere, it is only natural that its large-volume preparation is by air liquefaction. The gas also occurs in a combined state in proteins, in other organic materials, in ammonium salts, and in large natural deposits as potassium and sodium nitrates. Reserves are virtually unlimited. During the 1960s, world nitrogen production increased sharply from about 2,700,000 tons in 1960 to 18,100,000 tons in 1969.

Producing nitrogen from the liquefaction of air

In the production of nitrogen by the liquefaction of air, the air is separated into its two major components, oxygen and nitrogen, by fractional distillation at extremely low temperatures. Nitrogen, with the higher boiling point, evaporates out, leaving oxygen in the liquid form. Costs of manufacturing elemental nitrogen depend mainly on the scale of operations, on the cost of electricity, and on purity requirements. Small volumes of nitrogen can be prepared on site by passing ammonia over a catalyst that causes it to dissociate into nitrogen and hydrogen. The hydrogen can be burned away, leaving only nitrogen. If purity is not important, a nitrogen-rich gas can be made simply by burning fuels in an inert-gas generator that consumes the oxygen and keeps the nitrogen.

Nitrogen is shipped in small quantities at high pressures in steel cylinders, in highway tube trailers, and in railroad tank cars that consist of several tubular containers mounted on a railcar. Liquid nitrogen is shipped in small, portable, heavily insulated containers holding up to 25 gallons (100 litres) and in special insulated tank cars.

The principal use of nitrogen in chemical processing is in the manufacture of ammonia, although the nitrogen is furnished as a mixture with hydrogen. About 35 percent of the relatively pure elemental nitrogen produced goes into a variety of other chemical processes that re-

quire an inert gas as a blanketing agent to prevent oxidation, fire, or explosion; or for drying or purging equipment of an undesired substance; for pressuring; or as a diluent. Metal processing provides another major market for elemental nitrogen (about 27 percent of the total). Nitrogen serves to control the atmosphere in annealing and heat-treating furnaces; to prepare metals such as rare earths; and, as a liquid, to harden steel and shrink metal. Other demands for nitrogen are divided among electronic products, aerospace applications, food processing, and miscellaneous uses. Nitrogen gas is used by the petroleum industry to regenerate spent reforming catalysts, to make petroleum wax, and to provide a blanket against the oxidation of gasoline while it is in storage.

In the electric and electronic industries, nitrogen competes with argon and helium, as it does in chemical processing. It purges and fills electronic devices and high-voltage compression cables (which it also tests); and, in liquid form, it acts as a coolant for electronic equipment. In aerospace applications, nitrogen is mostly used in liquid form. In the food industry, liquid nitrogen finds applications in processing, transportation, and storage of frozen food to prevent deterioration.

The miscellaneous category includes the use of nitrogen as a gas or liquid in the manufacture of float glass (plate glass formed on top of molten metal), for preservation of biologicals, for pulverizing plastics, and for refrigeration-shielding of hydrogen, helium, and neon.

Carbon dioxide. Exhaled by all animals and an important product in the decay of organic materials, carbon dioxide was one of the earliest gases to be identified and has been widely used for more than 70 years. Reserves can be considered limitless, since the gas can be extracted from the atmosphere and the earth and manufactured in several different ways.

Making carbon dioxide

Carbon dioxide can be produced in commercial quantities at any location by burning coke or other fuels that yield a gas low in dust and sulfur oxides. The carbon dioxide–nitrogen mixture produced by this process is bubbled through an absorbing solution; the nitrogen is discharged to the atmosphere, and the carbon dioxide is recovered from the absorbing solution, which is reused. Dry Ice, or frozen carbon dioxide, is produced by evaporating liquid carbon dioxide rapidly. When the vapours arising from the liquid are pumped away, the remaining liquid carbon dioxide cools until it freezes.

Carbon dioxide may be transported under high pressure in liquid form in steel cylinders; as a low-pressure liquid in insulated portable tanks, in tank trucks, and in railroad tank cars; or as a solid in large blocks wrapped in heavy paper or in insulated bags. The wrappings are used to minimize losses caused by the large temperature difference between the Dry Ice and the surrounding air. Demand for carbon dioxide in liquid form has rapidly increased, because it is more convenient to ship, store, and use than Dry Ice.

The largest quantities of gaseous carbon dioxide go into the carbonation of beverages, which require a gas of a high degree of purity so that their taste or odour will not be affected. Carbon dioxide also is important in gas welding, hardening molds in foundries, purging and filling industrial equipment with inert gas, preparing carbonates, and in a large number of other industrial chemical processes.

Liquid carbon dioxide finds employment as a blasting agent in coal mining, in fire extinguishers, and in fracturing of oil wells. Solid carbon dioxide is widely used as a refrigerant for ice cream, meat products, and frozen foods, especially during their transport, and, in smaller quantities, as a convenient, quick refrigerant.

The noble gases. The rare, or noble, gases, helium, neon, argon, krypton, xenon, and radon, are all found in the atmosphere. Argon is by far the most abundant, comprising nearly 1 percent of dry air by weight, against a total for the other gases of only 0.002 percent. All of the rare gases are colourless, odourless, and tasteless and are generally considered chemically inert, although some chemical compounds have been prepared from them.

Argon, krypton, neon, and xenon are produced as by-products of the liquefaction of air. Commercial quantities of helium are extracted from natural gas. The small quantities of radon used generally are prepared from the decay products of radioactive radium.

Helium. Lightest of the noble gases, helium was isolated in 1895 but was not produced in volume until after World War I. Between the two world wars, helium was used almost exclusively for lighter-than-air craft, with only small quantities for weather balloons and for creating synthetic atmospheres for diving operations and medical treatment.

Helium in World War II

In World War II large quantities were taken for submarine-searching blimps and as an inert gas in shielded-arc welding. After the war, consumption continued to increase steadily until 1966, when it began to decline. Leading world production in 1970 was the United States with 647,000,000 cubic feet (other than helium stored for conservation purposes); followed by the Soviet Union, with a reported 70,000,000 cubic feet; Canada, with 35,000,000 cubic feet; and France, which had a 1969 plant capacity of 7,000,000 cubic feet.

Although helium can be separated from the air, all commercial production is from natural gas, containing helium in relatively high percentages. Helium is extracted by cooling natural gas to the point at which it condenses to a liquid, leaving behind an uncondensed mixture of helium and nitrogen. Known as crude helium, this mixture is separated from the liquid natural gas and then further cooled until the nitrogen condenses. The liquid nitrogen is removed, and the helium gas remaining is purified to a concentration of 99.995 percent by passing it through a bed of activated charcoal at liquid-nitrogen temperatures.

Helium is transported as a gas, compressed to high pressure in gas cylinders. Larger volumes are shipped in specially designed railroad tank cars or in highway tube trailers. As larger volumes are marketed, an increasingly large share is transported as a liquid, to lower costs. Liquid helium is shipped in containers ranging in size from a few to more than 10,000 gallons.

Helium has the lowest boiling point of any element, $-268.6°$ C $(-452°$ F), or only $4.5°$ C above absolute zero. Helium has a wide variety of applications in which its properties of inertness, low weight, and low temperature are of value. These include purging and pressurizing liquid rocket propellants (oxygen and hydrogen), creating the controlled atmospheres needed in growing germanium and silicon crystals, and shielded-arc welding of various metals and alloys. Other smaller volume uses are for leak detection on production lines for products that require a leakproof system; as a lifting gas for the chromatographic analysis of mixtures of gaseous compounds; and in synthetic breathing mixtures. Because of its unique low-temperature properties, it finds many diverse applications where the lowest possible temperatures are required.

Argon. Argon was discovered in 1894, but large-scale production did not begin until 1914, when 8,000 cubic feet was made, by chemical methods, to fill light bulbs. In 1915 argon was first produced commercially by the liquefaction of air, also for use in filling light bulbs.

Reserves of argon

Resources of argon can be considered unlimited, since the argon extracted from the atmosphere is returned unchanged. In 1970 the world productive capacity for argon extraction was greater than demand. If demand for argon should increase greatly, however, the simple addition of the necessary facilities at oxygen-producing plants could easily provide all foreseeable projected requirements.

Argon's boiling point is intermediate between those of oxygen and nitrogen; thus, an argon-rich mixture is extracted from the centre of the liquid-air-distillation column, as oxygen and nitrogen are being produced. This argon-rich mixture can be further redistilled to yield a high-purity product.

World argon production has been increasing rapidly since the end of World War II. In 1950 only 50,000,000 cubic feet of argon was used but, by 1969, this had increased to 2,800,000,000 cubic feet, a nearly 60-fold increase in 20 years. The United States leads world production with about 40 percent of the total. With improved technology, argon prices have fallen steadily since 1950, and, because argon is less expensive than helium, it has been displacing helium in markets where the two gases are essentially interchangeable.

Argon is transported in steel cylinders at high pressures when used in small quantities. Large deliveries of liquid argon are made in railroad tank cars or tank trucks.

Argon is very stable and does not readily react chemically with other materials. This property accounts for most of its demand, as in shielded-arc welding of such metals as stainless steel, aluminum, magnesium, titanium, and copper and nickel alloys in which the welds must be protected from atmospheric oxygen while being formed. Argon also provides the inert atmosphere in which silicon and germanium crystals are grown for use in transistors. Except for a small number of specialty units, all modern incandescent and fluorescent electric-light sources contain argon, as do many electron tubes. Argon provides an inert atmosphere, preventing oxidation during the refining of metals. Other miscellaneous outlets include electric-arc cutting of nonferrous metal sheet and plate and in producing, melting, and rolling titanium. In 1968 the steel industry found that bubbling argon through molten steel drives unwanted oxides to the surface, where they then can be removed.

Neon, krypton, and xenon. The three gases neon, krypton, and xenon were all discovered in 1898. Neon was first produced commercially as a by-product of air liquefaction in 1907. Krypton and xenon were produced in commercial quantities at a later date, when it was discovered that, with careful treatment, these gases could be produced from impure liquid oxygen in which they concentrate when air is liquefied.

Virtually unlimited quantities of these gases can be produced, if needed, by liquefaction of air. Neon, the most abundant of the three, occurs in air in concentrations of 18.18 parts per million (ppm); krypton, in concentrations of 1.14 ppm; and xenon, .086 ppm.

In producing the three gases, air is first liquefied, leaving an uncondensed fraction containing neon and the other two gases. The neon is then separated by adsorption on activated charcoal, the krypton and xenon remaining with the crude oxygen after the separation of the air into oxygen and nitrogen streams. Distillation of the crude oxygen concentrates the krypton and xenon, after which they are absorbed on silica gel and further treated to increase their purity. When large quantities are needed, the gases are distributed in standard steel cylinders under pressure. Small amounts are shipped in glass containers at atmospheric pressure.

Neon's role in subatomic research

Neon provides the atmosphere in cloud chambers for the detection of subatomic particles, its largest use, followed by its application in liquid form as a coolant for electronic infrared and radar detection devices. The familiar neon signs still take small amounts of neon, which, under low pressure, emit a red light when an electric current passes through it. As it becomes less expensive, krypton is being more widely used in incandescent bulbs, since it imparts longer life and more light efficiency than argon or other gases. Xenon is used in high-intensity lights, in ultraviolet sources, and in flash lamps.

Radon. Discovered in 1900, radon is the only radioactive noble gas. It is one of the products of the radioactive decay of radium, its only useful source. It is prepared from aqueous solutions of radium salts by pumping off and purifying the gases that form when radium decays.

Because of its short half-life of less than four days, radon's applications are quite limited. In the past it was employed in medicine for studies of the biological effects of ionizing radiation, as a source of gamma radiation in clinical research, and in metallurgy for the detection of flaws in welds and gauging of metal thicknesses. Longer lived radioisotopes and high-voltage X-ray machines have largely supplanted radon, however, for those purposes.

GASES DERIVED FROM OTHER SOURCES

Hydrogen. Colourless, odourless, and tasteless, hydrogen is the lightest element in nature and an industrial gas with one of the fastest growing demands in the world. Large-scale production of hydrogen to produce synthetic ammonia began between 1910 and 1920; in the following years large quantities went into the production of methanol and the hydrogenation of fats and oils and in high-temperature, hydrogen–oxygen flames for cutting and welding metals.

Supplies of hydrogen are virtually limitless, since it can be produced from water, natural gas, coal, crude oil, and many other substances. Thus, production cost determines the choice of raw material at any location. Electrolysis of water could produce hydrogen in any quantity required, but electric-power cost is relatively high.

Until natural gas became generally available, hydrogen was produced primarily by the reaction of coke with steam to yield water gas, a mixture of hydrogen and carbon monoxide. The carbon monoxide in water gas was reacted with steam over a catalyst to form more hydrogen and carbon dioxide. The carbon dioxide was removed by absorption along with other impurities, leaving hydrogen as the product. With the widespread introduction of natural gas into commercial markets, hydrogen manufacturers shifted from coke to natural gas, from which hydrogen can be made by two different methods. In the first, the steam-reforming process, natural gas is reacted with steam over a catalyst at high temperatures to produce a mixture of hydrogen and carbon oxides. In the second, the partial-oxidation process, the natural gas is reacted with oxygen under pressure, forming a mixture of hydrogen and carbon monoxide along with small quantities of other impurities. Other hydrocarbons, even heavy petroleum fractions, can be substituted for natural gas; a disadvantage is the high cost of oxygen.

Catalytic steam process

The catalytic steam process, which yields a very pure hydrogen at high pressures, requires a sulfur-free hydrocarbon feedstock with few or no unsaturated hydrocarbons. In the early 1960s a new process was developed that permitted steam reforming of naphtha, thus extending the scope of the process to higher molecular weight petroleum fractions. In all processes, some further purification of the primary gas produced is necessary for high-quality hydrogen.

The cost of making hydrogen in large volumes is generally lowest for steam reforming, followed by partial oxidation of hydrocarbons, production by reaction of steam and coke, and electrolysis, the latter two practical only in small-scale operations. Production from coke is declining rapidly worldwide as the availability of natural gas increases. As demand for natural gas grows, however, it is anticipated that supplies will be supplemented by synthesis gas produced from coal.

In small quantities, hydrogen is marketed at high pressures in steel cylinders. Large-volume consumers generally manufacture their own hydrogen on the site and thus require few extensive storage or distribution facilities. Hydrogen is generally stored at low pressure in gasholders of either the dry or the wet type. Wet gasholders use water as a sealant to contain the gas while dry gasholders have flexible connectors that permit movement as gas is inserted or removed from the holder. Commercially available hydrogen is sold as a gas or highly purified liquid. As consumption of hydrogen for fuel and propellant in space flight has grown, large, insulated liquid-storage tanks have been constructed. Liquid hydrogen is transported in truck trailers and railroad cars with specially designed insulation.

As the scale of operations has grown, the price of hydrogen has declined steadily, resulting in a continual improvement in overall efficiency, better heat recovery, higher operating pressures, better use of raw materials, improved catalysts, and increased automation. World hydrogen production in 1969 was 5.3×10^{12} cubic feet, with the United States the largest producer (2.1×10^{12} cubic feet).

The production of synthetic ammonia and petroleum refining take the greatest quantities of hydrogen. The two major hydrogen-consuming refinery operations are hydrotreating and hydrocracking. Hydrotreating includes removing undesirable sulfur compounds from petroleum feedstocks, hydrogenation of olefin compounds, and treatment of lubricating oils and jet fuels. Hydrocracking involves simultaneous catalytic cracking (breaking apart long molecules) and hydrogenation (see PETROLEUM REFINING). The hydrocracking process has been growing faster than that of hydrotreating; the need to remove sulfur from fuel feedstocks to meet air-pollution standards, however, may reverse that trend. In the United States, refineries must produce supplemental hydrogen to supply the demands of the two processes. European refineries do not use hydrotreating or hydrocracking as extensively as in the U.S. Consequently the hydrogen produced in other refining steps is in excess of process requirements and is used as fuel. The remainder of the hydrogen goes into the manufacture of methanol, oxoalcohols, and other organic chemicals and into the hydrogenation of vegetable and animal fats and oils. Other smaller but important uses are for the production of pharmaceuticals, for cooling in the electronics and electrical-machinery industry, for welding, and as rocket fuel.

Hydrocracking and hydrotreating

Carbon monoxide. Carbon monoxide, a colourless, odourless, and tasteless compound of carbon and oxygen, is a constituent of synthesis gas (a mixture of hydrogen and carbon monoxide; see below *Synthesis gas*) and is produced by a variety of methods. Large volumes of carbon monoxide are generated in blast furnaces during pig-iron manufacture, but it is so diluted with nitrogen that it is used almost exclusively for heating at steel mills.

Pure, or enriched, carbon monoxide can be obtained by its absorption in solutions of various copper compounds or by its low-temperature separation from other gases with which it is associated. The low-temperature separation method, with or without fractionation, is more common with gases produced from hydrocarbon feedstocks; and, since they are much more widely used than other feedstocks, most carbon monoxide is separated by low-temperature condensation.

Carbon monoxide is largely consumed in mixtures with hydrogen (synthesis gas) and, consequently, is not normally transported. When shipped, whether by rail, highway or boat, carbon monoxide is carried only in steel cylinders. The gas is sold in several different grades of purity.

Carbon monoxide is important in the production of phosgene gas, made by reacting carbon monoxide with chlorine over activated charcoal at elevated temperatures. Phosgene is used largely in the production of chemicals that serve as raw materials for plastics and adhesives. Carbon monoxide is also reacted with acetylene and water to form acrylic acid and with ethylene and ethyl alcohol to form ethyl acrylate. In a newly developed process, large volumes of carbon monoxide are reacted with methyl alcohol along with a rhodium catalyst to make acetic acid.

Products from carbon monoxide

Synthesis gas. Synthesis gas, a mixture of hydrogen and carbon monoxide, usually serves as an intermediate in the manufacture of some other chemical product. In a direct chemical reaction, it may be necessary first to adjust the ratio of hydrogen to carbon monoxide, either by additional processing of the original synthesis gas or, when it is made from petroleum fractions, by modifying the feed streams during the primary production of the gas. For example, if additional carbon dioxide is injected with the steam and methane, a synthesis gas with a higher percentage of carbon monoxide is produced.

Mixtures of hydrogen and carbon monoxide, when passed over different catalysts at various temperatures and pressures, produce a wide variety of hydrocarbons. In all the processes, mixtures of hydrocarbons are formed; in making methane and methanol, however, a nearly pure single product results. The largest commercial consumption of synthesis gas is in producing methanol, which is made by passing synthesis gas over a catalyst at very high pressure and elevated temperature.

Relatively large quantities of synthesis gas also go into the production of aldehydes from olefins (a type of unsaturated hydrocarbon) under the oxo reaction process. Synthesis gas and olefins are brought together in the presence of a cobalt catalyst in the liquid phase at elevated temperatures and pressures. The resulting aldehydes are usually intermediate products and are subjected to further reactions with hydrogen to form alcohols.

Very large volumes of synthesis gas may be needed in the future, if synthetic liquid or gaseous fuels are produced from coal. The only commercial synthetic liquid-fuel plant in operation is in South Africa. A small plant by petroleum-industry standards, it produces only 5,000 to 6,000 barrels per day along with some petrochemicals. The synthesis gas is produced from coal at high pressure and temperature, using a mixture of oxygen and steam. The purified gas is then reacted over a catalyst under two different processes: one for synthetic liquid fuels, the other for petrochemicals. Even this single small plant requires an enormous quantity of purified synthesis gas per day. A large synthetic-fuels industry would bring a demand for synthesis gas dwarfing present requirements.

Ammonia. Ammonia gas was first produced from ammonium chloride late in the 18th century, but it was not until the 1870s that it became available in commercial quantities as a by-product of the carbonization of coal. Large volumes were not produced, however, until the development (1913) of the so-called Haber process, in which atmospheric nitrogen is combined with hydrogen to make ammonia. Because ammonia can be made by combining nitrogen from air with hydrogen, which can be produced from water, there is no limit to the amount that can be produced.

Haber process of making ammonia

The Haber process and its modern modifications convert a mixture of three parts of hydrogen and one part of nitrogen into ammonia gas by reacting the mixture at high pressure and high temperatures over any of several catalysts. The two raw materials, hydrogen and nitrogen, are taken from the most economical source at any given location.

Anhydrous (dry) ammonia is transported as a liquefied gas in cylinders, in tanks, and in tank cars. Refrigerated barges are the least costly transportation method. Large volumes of ammonia are generally stored in insulated and refrigerated containers. Two long-distance pipelines have been constructed in the United States to carry anhydrous ammonia from large plants located near low-cost raw materials. The anhydrous ammonia is applied directly as a fertilizer and is transported in vehicles designed to carry it into the fields.

For many years ammonia plants were relatively small and located near markets to minimize high transportation costs. As improved transport methods were developed and as larger volumes supplanted solid salts such as ammonium nitrate as fertilizers, transportation costs were further reduced. As a result, ammonia plants could become larger and achieve further economies from large-scale production.

While there are more than 2,500 different uses for industrial ammonia, most is taken by agriculture, largely in the form of liquid ammonia or ammoniacal solutions. Ammonium nitrate, sulfate, phosphate, and urea provide the balance of ammonium compounds for agriculture. Another major market for ammonia is in the production of nitric acid, from which, in turn, ammonium nitrate, explosives, propellants, and urethane plastic foam are made. Other smaller quantities are taken for the production of hydrogen cyanide and amines.

World production of ammonia is growing rapidly to meet the greatly increased demand for fertilizer.

Acetylene. Commercial production of acetylene began in 1892 with the discovery of a method for manufacturing calcium carbide from coke and lime. Acetylene is formed when calcium carbide is brought in contact with water. The earliest use of acetylene was for illumination, since, on burning, it gives a pure white light similar to sunlight. Other early uses were in cutting and welding metals. In recent years it has been consumed in large volumes by the chemical industry.

Though acetylene can be manufactured under a variety of processes, a large portion is still made from calcium carbide and water. Several variations of the original process have been developed to avoid the high temperatures and pressures that can result from the rapid generation of heat as the reaction proceeds. More recently, increasing amounts of acetylene have been produced from hydrocarbons. Energy to convert the hydrocarbons to acetylene can be supplied by an electrical discharge, in regenerative furnaces, and by combustion in either one or two stages. In all hydrocarbon processes, the primary product must be further treated to remove impurities from the crude acetylene gas, the degree of purification depending on the final use of the acetylene. For example, a very pure product is needed in catalytic chemical reactions to avoid damaging the catalyst. The relative economics of producing acetylene from calcium carbide and from hydrocarbons depends on the cost of the raw materials at any given location and on the value of the other products formed.

Explosion danger of acetylene

Acetylene can decompose explosively even in the absence of oxygen. The strength of the detonation depends on such factors as the initial pressure and the presence or absence of oxygen. Gaseous acetylene is not handled at pressures of more than 15 pounds per square inch (one kilogram per square centimetre) above atmospheric pressure (a total of two atmospheres) except in specialized equipment. Because of its explosive tendency, acetylene is stored and shipped in special steel tanks that contain porous filler whose minute cellular spaces are saturated with acetone. Under these conditions acetylene can be contained at moderate pressures without danger of explosion. Because of the special handling required for acetylene, the lowest cost form in which it can be transported is as calcium carbide, from which acetylene is easily made.

The chemical industry consumes most acetylene output to make such products as vinyl chloride, acetaldehyde, acrylonitrile, vinyl acetate, and vinyl ethers. These in turn go into the production of a diverse group of plastics, synthetic rubber, dyestuffs, and pharmaceuticals. The remainder is used for oxyacetylene welding and cutting; small amounts are still employed for special-purpose lighting.

Sulfur dioxide. Though a large number of different oxides of sulfur have been identified, sulfur dioxide is the one of major commercial importance. It occurs in nature and has served various purposes for thousands of years. The combustion of fuels containing sulfur produces sulfur oxides, a major source of air pollution. A large number of processes aimed at reducing sulfur oxide emissions into the atmosphere are under study. These processes either remove the sulfur from the fuel before combustion or scrub the sulfur oxides from the flue gases before they are emitted into the air.

Reserves of sulfur-bearing materials from which sulfur oxide could be produced are very large. Reserves of native sulfur and other sulfur compounds of commercial importance are also abundant. A large, new source of sulfur dioxide may develop as a by-product from one of the anti-air-pollution processes being studied. Should a synthetic-fuels industry develop to meet the increased demands for gaseous and liquid fuels, another large potential source of sulfur oxides could emerge, since at some point in the process some sulfur compounds must be removed from the gases resulting from the gasification of coal.

Sulfur dioxide is commercially produced by the combustion of native sulfur or pyrites (iron disulfide) in burners of a variety of designs. After cooling, the sulfur dioxide is separated from the nitrogen (left after the combustion of sulfur with air) by absorption, either with water or alkaline solutions or slurries (watery mixtures). Some sulfur oxides are removed from the waste gases at smelters and marketed commercially. Other, small-scale sources are from the combustion of hydrogen sulfide recovered at oil refineries and coke-oven plants.

Sulfur dioxide is stored and transported as a liquid under pressure. Smaller quantities are shipped in steel cylinders, large quantities in tank cars.

Sulfur dioxide is an intermediate product in the manufacture of sulfuric acid but is not isolated for this purpose. Pulping and bleaching wood and paper manufacture take the greatest amounts of sulfur dioxide. Although it is normally manufactured at the pulp mill, large quantities of liquid sulfur dioxide must also be purchased. Soybean-protein preservation and oil and metal refining are among other markets for the gas.

Chlorine. Though first identified as a chemical element in 1774, chlorine was not used extensively until World War I. During the 1920s nearly one-half of the chlorine made went into the manufacture of paper and pulp, but, as new markets were found, the share going to the paper industry declined. Reserves of chlorine must be viewed as limitless, since it can be produced from the electrolysis of seawater and from salt solutions.

Chlorine has been produced commercially for nearly 70 years by the electrolysis of salt solutions, which produces chlorine, sodium hydroxide, and hydrogen. As it is necessary to keep the sodium hydroxide and chlorine separate during production, two basically different methods have been developed: the mercury process and the diaphragm process. In the mercury process, the salt solution floats on a flowing stream of mercury, and, when the electric current is applied, the chlorine collects at the anode (positive electrode) and sodium amalgam at the cathode (negative electrode). Water is added to sodium amalgam to produce hydrogen, sodium hydroxide, and mercury, which can then be recycled.

In the diaphragm process, the chlorine is separated from the hydrogen and sodium hydroxide by an asbestos diaphragm when the electric current is applied to the salt solution. Because chlorine plants require large amounts of salt solution and electricity, most are located where these are abundant and low in cost.

Whenever possible, chlorine is shipped in either liquid or gaseous form by pipeline. The next preferred shipping method is in bulk quantities in barges. Railroad tank cars, however, are by far the most common method of shipping chlorine. Smaller quantities are shipped in cylinders and in tank trucks.

The largest share of chlorine output goes into the production of other chemicals, especially chlorinated hydrocarbons and vinyl plastics. Two of the most important chlorinated hydrocarbons are methyl chloride, used as a refrigerant, as a solvent, in plastics, and as a food additive; and fluorocarbon-12, a refrigerant. Polyvinyl chloride, another chlorine product, is an important plastic.

Chlorine is still used as a gas for bleaching paper and in water purification, both uses depending on the high level of chemical reactivity of chlorine. Smaller quantities of chlorine are taken for the production of insecticides and herbicides, for the manufacture of gasoline additives, and for the production of such metals as magnesium, titanium, and zirconium.

BIBLIOGRAPHY. AMERICAN GAS ASSOCIATION, *Historical Statistics of the Gas Industry* (1956), complete historical record of statistics relating to energy reserves, gas production, transmission and distribution, underground storage, customers, sales, revenues, utilization, finances, labour, and prices for U.S. and Canada; ORGANIZATION FOR ECONOMIC COOPERATION AND DEVELOPMENT, *Impact of Natural Gas on the Consumption of Energy in the OECD European Member Countries* (1969), describes natural gas in the energy economy of the Western European countries, its availability, the policies of the countries in the field of natural gas, competition of natural gas with other fuels, and the future role of natural gas in energy supply and its impact in practice; EMIL R. RIEGEL (ed.), *Industrial Chemistry*, (1962), an authoritative textbook on industrial processes covering the methods of manufacture of most industrial gases, the raw materials used, properties and uses of the products, and methods of storage and distribution; A.L. WADDAMS, *Chemicals from Petroleum*, 2nd ed. (1968), describes methods of producing synthesis gas from coke, petroleum, and natural gas by the numerous processes being commercially used and also the furthur utilization of these gases for the production of ammonia, methyl alcohol, oxo process, and phosgene; GERHARD A. COOK (ed.), *Argon, Helium, and the Rare Gases*, 2 vol. (1961), a very comprehensive and authoritative text on the rare gases covering their history, nuclear structure and reactions, atomic structure, chemical properties, gas-phase properties, thermodynamic properties,

liquid- and solid-state properties, phase equilibria, production, cryogenic and nuclear applications, inert atmospheres in metallurgy, inert gas shielded arc welding, and utilization in light sources and in medical applications; THE CHLORINE INSTITUTE, N.Y., *Chlorine Facts* (1968), a booklet that describes methods of chlorine manufacture, methods of shipping, safety precautions, the spectrum of uses, and gives statistical information on production.

(H.Pe.)

Gasoline Engine

The gasoline engine is a specialized form of internal-combustion engine in which power is obtained by burning a mixture of gasoline vapour and air. The mixture is ignited electrically by a spark plug. Most gasoline engines are of the so-called reciprocating piston type, but recent developments suggest that superior performance in some respects may be obtained from either rotary piston (see below) or turbine types. Engines closely related to the gasoline engine include the diesel and the jet; for descriptions of these, see DIESEL ENGINE; JET ENGINE.

The gasoline engine is the most widely used of all internal-combustion engines. Size and power range from small engines of less than one horsepower, used in certain portable applications, to aircraft engines that may produce as much as 35,000 horsepower. Though more gasoline engines are used in automobiles than in any other single application, such engines represent less than half the total number in use throughout the world.

History

While attempts to devise heat engines were made in ancient times, the steam engine of the 18th century was the first successful type. The internal-combustion engine, which followed in the 19th century as an improvement over the steam engine for many applications, cannot be attributed to any single inventor. The piston, thought to date as far back as 150 BC, was used by metal workers in pumps for blowing air. The piston and cylinder were basic to the steam engine, which brought the component to a high state of efficiency. But the steam engine suffered from low thermal efficiency, great weight and bulk, and inconvenience of operation, all of which were primarily traceable to the necessity of burning the fuel in a furnace separate from the engine. It became evident that a self-contained power unit was desirable.

As early as the 17th century several experimenters first tried to use hot gaseous products to operate pumps. By 1820 an engine was built in England in which hydrogen-air mixtures were exploded in a chamber. The chamber was then cooled to create a vacuum acting on a piston. The sale of such gas engines began in 1823. They were heavy and crude but contained many essential elements of later, more successful devices. In 1824, a French physicist, Sadi Carnot, published his now classic pamphlet, "Reflections on the Motive Power of Heat," which outlined fundamental internal-combustion theory. In the next several years engines using pressure resulting from combustion of fuels rather than vacuum and engines in which the fuel was compressed before burning were built, but none proved satisfactory, until in 1860 Étienne Lenoir of France marketed an engine that operated on illuminating gas and gave reasonably satisfactory service. The Lenoir engine was essentially a converted double-acting steam engine with slide valves to admit gas and air and to discharge exhaust products. Although it developed little power and utilized only about 4 percent of the energy in the gas, several hundred were sold over a period of years.

A major theoretical advance took place with the publication in Paris in 1862 of a description of the ideal operating cycle of an internal-combustion engine. The author, Alphonse Beau de Rochas, laid down the following conditions as necessary for optimum efficiency: (1) maximum cylinder volume with minimum cooling surface; (2) maximum rapidity of expansion; (3) maximum ratio of expansion; and (4) maximum pressure of the ignited charge. He described the sequence of operations necessary as (1) suction during an entire outstroke of the piston; (2) compression during the following instroke; (3)

Electrolysis of salt solutions (margin note)

The ideal operating cycle (margin note)

ignition of the charge at dead centre and expansion during the next outstroke (the power stroke); and (4) forcing out the burned gases during the next instroke.

The engine Beau de Rochas described thus had a four-stroke cycle, in contrast to the two-stroke cycle (intake-ignition and power-exhaust) of the Lenoir engine. Beau de Rochas never built an engine, and no four-stroke engine appeared for 14 years. When it did it was the product of a German engineer, Nikolaus Otto, whose firm, Otto and Langen, of Deutz, earlier produced and marketed an improved two-stroke engine employing a vertical cylinder, open at the top and fitted with a heavy piston, below which was the combustion chamber. Gas and air were drawn into the cylinder during the first half of the upstroke, the charge was ignited electrically, and the piston lifted by the explosion. Although the piston tended to continue upward after the pressure on its underside had been reduced to a partial vacuum, atmospheric pressure acting on the top of the piston, together with the piston's weight, caused it to descend immediately. The motion was transmitted to a shaft and heavy flywheel by a toothed rack extending downward and meshing with a gear on the shaft. This gear turned freely on the shaft during the upward stroke, but a free-wheeling clutch engaged on the downward stroke and applied torque to the shaft. The engine was very noisy, of small power capacity, and the rack-and-pinion mechanism was mechanically unsound, but it consumed less than half as much fuel per unit of power as did the Lenoir engine and thus succeeded commercially.

In 1876 the firm applied the Beau de Rochas four-stroke cycle in the design of a new engine. It was an immediate success. In spite of its great weight and poor economy, nearly 50,000 engines with a combined capacity of about 200,000 horsepower were sold in 17 years, to be followed by the rapid development of a wide variety of engines of the same type. Manufacture of the Otto engine in the United States began in 1878, following the grant to Otto of a U.S. patent in 1877.

Basic principles

Combustion processes

In all internal-combustion engines the products of combustion act directly on piston or rotor surfaces, whereas the external-combustion engine employs a secondary working fluid that is interposed between the combustion chamber and the power-producing elements. Fundamentally, the steam engine operates with a high-pressure working medium produced by utilizing the expansion accompanying the vaporization of a liquid; by contrast, the internal-combustion engine utilizes the large volume of high-temperature combustion products that, when confined, become a high-pressure gaseous medium.

GENERAL CONSIDERATIONS

Classification. The many types of internal-combustion engines can be grouped in a number of different ways on the basis of similarities among them. Important methods of classification include application, type of fuel and method of injection, ignition, reciprocating piston or rotary, cylinder arrangement, strokes per cycle, cooling system, and valve type and location. These various classifications will be discussed further as the various engine types are described.

Valve type and arrangement. Valves for controlling intake and exhaust may be located overhead, on one side, side and overhead, or on opposite sides of the cylinder. These are all the so-called poppet or mushroom valves consisting of a stem with one end enlarged to form a head that permits flow through a passage surrounding the stem when raised from its seat and prevents flow when the head is moved down to contact the valve seat formed in the cylinder block.

Another group of engines uses sliding valves that are usually of the sleeve type surrounding the cylinder bore.

Pressure application. Some power plants use the same combustion principle but apply the pressure resulting from combustion to different mechanical elements. There are, for example, gas turbines in which the products of combustion are directed through nozzles against the blades of a turbine rotor to cause it to rotate. In the jet engine, the products of combustion simply flow through a nozzle and the reaction force tends to move the nozzle in the opposite direction.

Rotary engines

The Wankel and Tri-Dyne engines (see below) burn the fuel within the engine; they are rotary and do not have conventional cylinders fitted with reciprocating pistons. Instead, the gas pressure acts upon surfaces formed by the configuration of a rotor. Both the gas-turbine and the jet engine have combustion furnaces separate from the power-producing units. The power is produced by the action of the products of combustion on the blades of the turbine or the interior wall of the jet nozzle.

Comparison with other engines. The so-called Stirling hot-air engine that was widely used early in the nineteenth century burned the fuel in an external chamber. A heat exchanger was employed to heat a secondary fluid (air) that was in contact with the piston faces in the cylinders. The products of combustion thus did not do the work of driving the pistons. This engine is not an internal-combustion engine, but because of the superior continuous combustion process used, it is of interest as a possible low-pollution engine.

The gasoline engine may now be defined as an engine designed to burn a volatile liquid fuel with ignition initiated by an electrical spark. When such an engine is compared with other types, certain similarities and differences are evident as well as some advantages and disadvantages. The diesel engine and the gas engine (an engine utilizing a gas such as propane as the fuel) have a good deal in common with the gasoline engine, since they are all cylinder-and-piston engines burning fuel-air mixtures in contact with moving components (piston, turbine blades). The important differences that distinguish the diesel engine are that it has a fuel-injection system (see below) and no spark-ignition system. The diesel is heavier and more expensive per horsepower of output, but it has a longer life and operates at less cost per horsepower-hour because it burns less fuel, and diesel fuel in general is less expensive than gasoline.

Because it does not have the quiet, smooth-running characteristic or the flexibility of the gasoline engine, the diesel engine has had little application in passenger automobiles. It has, however, taken over from the gasoline engine almost all of the heavy-duty vehicle field. Trucks, tractors, and buses, except for the smallest sizes, are diesel-powered.

The gas engine

The gas engine has much in common with the gasoline engine; in fact, in some instances their differences are very slight at best. Structurally, the difference lies primarily in the substitution of a gas-mixing valve for a carburetor. The cylinder and piston configurations are the same. In general, gases have better antiknock qualities than gasoline (see below), permitting slightly higher compression ratios without knock or other combustion difficulties.

From the standpoint of application, the gas engine burning natural gas, manufactured gas, or industrial by-product gas is limited primarily to stationary power plant use because it must remain connected to the gas pipe line. If, however, the fuel is liquefied petroleum gas, sometimes called bottled gas, the containers of gas can be carried in a vehicle, leading to much flexibility in applications. The present obstacle is that facilities are not readily available for replenishing the gas supply. Dual carburetors have been produced experimentally that make it possible to operate an engine on either liquefied petroleum gas or gasoline; thus dual gas-gasoline engines are a distinct possibility.

ENGINE TYPES

Of the different techniques for recovering the power from the combustion process the most important so far has been the four-stroke cycle, a conception now over 100 years old.

Four-stroke cycle. The four-stroke cycle is illustrated in Figure 1. With the inlet valve open, the piston first descends on the intake stroke. An explosive mixture of gasoline vapour and air is drawn into the cylinder by the

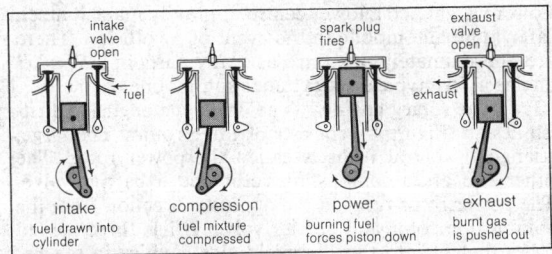

Figure 1: Strokes of the four-stroke cycle.

partial vacuum thus created. The mixture is compressed as the piston ascends on the compression stroke with both valves closed. As the end of the stroke is approached, the charge is ignited by an electric spark. The power stroke follows, with both valves still closed and the gas pressure, due to the expansion of the burned gas, pressing on the piston crown. During the exhaust stroke, the ascending piston forces the spent products of combustion through the open exhaust valve. The cycle then repeats itself. Each cycle thus requires four strokes of the piston—intake, compression, power, and exhaust—and two revolutions of the crankshaft.

A disadvantage of the four-stroke cycle is that only half as many power strokes are completed as in the two-stroke cycle (see below) and only half as much power can be expected from an engine of a given size at a given operating speed. The four-stroke cycle, however, provides more positive clearing out of exhaust gases (scavenging) and reloading of the cylinders, reducing the amount of loss of fresh charge to the exhaust.

Two-stroke cycle. The two-stroke cycle was developed in 1878. In it the compression and power stroke of the four-stroke cycle are carried out without the inlet and exhaust strokes, thus requiring only one revolution of the crankshaft to complete the cycle.

Figure 2 illustrates the two-stroke-cycle engine of a so-

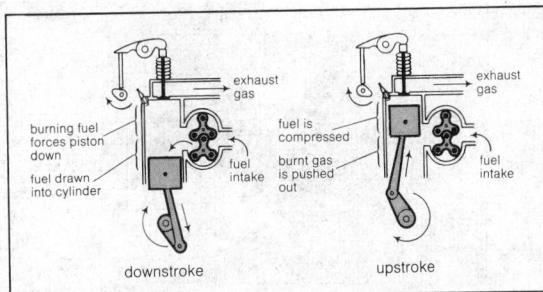

Figure 2: Blower-scavenged, two-stroke-cycle engine with uniflow scavenging.

called uniflow type in which the fresh fuel mixture is forced into the cylinder through circumferential ports by a rotary blower. The exhaust gases pass through poppet valves in the cylinder head that are opened and closed by a cam-follower mechanism. The valves are timed to start to open toward the end of the power stroke after the cylinder pressure has dropped appreciably. The inlet ports in the cylinder wall start to uncover after the exhaust opening has decreased the cylinder pressure to the inlet pressure produced by the blower. The exhaust valves are allowed to remain open for a few degrees of crank rotation after the inlet ports have been covered by the rising piston on the compression stroke, thus allowing the persistency of flow more thoroughly to scavenge the cylinder. The compression and power strokes are similar to those of the four-stroke engine.

In 1891 a simplified version of the two-stroke-cycle engine was introduced, using crankcase compression to pump the fresh charge into the cylinder. Instead of intake ports extending entirely around the lower cylinder wall, this engine has intake ports only half way around; a second set of ports starts a little higher in the cylinder wall in the other half of the cylinder bore. These larger ports lead to the exhaust system. The inlet ports connect to a transfer passage leading to the fully enclosed crank-

Crankcase compression

case. A spring-loaded inlet valve admits air into the crankcase on the upward or compression stroke of the piston. Air trapped in the crankcase is compressed by the descent of the piston on its power stroke. The piston thus uncovers the exhaust ports near the end of the power stroke and slightly later it uncovers the inlet or transfer port on the opposite side of the cylinder to admit the compressed fresh mixture from the crankcase. The top face of the piston is designed to provide a deflector or baffle that directs the fresh load upward on the inlet side of the cylinder and then downward on the exhaust side, thus pushing the spent gases of the previous cycle out through the exhaust port on that side. This outflow continues after the inlet ports are covered by the rising piston on the compression stroke until the exhaust ports are covered and compression of the fresh load begins. This loading process, called loop scavenging, is the simplest known method of replacing the exhaust products with a fresh mixture and completing the cycle with only compression and power strokes. The system is used in many small gasoline engines such as small outboard motors and for gasoline-powered appliances. A disadvantage is that the return flow of the gases causes a slight loss of fresh charge through the exhaust ports. Because of this loss, carburetor engines operating on the two-stroke cycle lack the fuel economy of four-stroke engines. The loss can be avoided by equipping them with fuel-injection systems (see below) instead of carburetors and injecting the fuel directly into the cylinders after scavenging. Such an arrangement is attractive as a means of attaining high power output from a relatively small engine, and development of the turbocharger (see below *Supercharger*) for this application may hold promise of further improvement.

Opposed-piston engine. The opposed-piston engine also provides uniflow scavenging. This engine (Figure 3A) has two pistons moving in opposite directions in the same cylinder. Two sets of ports extending entirely around the cylinder bore are so located that one set is covered and uncovered by one piston and the other set is controlled by the second piston. A second crankshaft, to which the upper pistons are attached, is located at the top of the engine and the two shafts are connected by gears.

The opposed-piston design has two major advantages: reciprocating masses move in opposite directions, providing excellent balance; and the poppet valves necessary in other uniflow-scavenged two-stroke-cycle engines are eliminated.

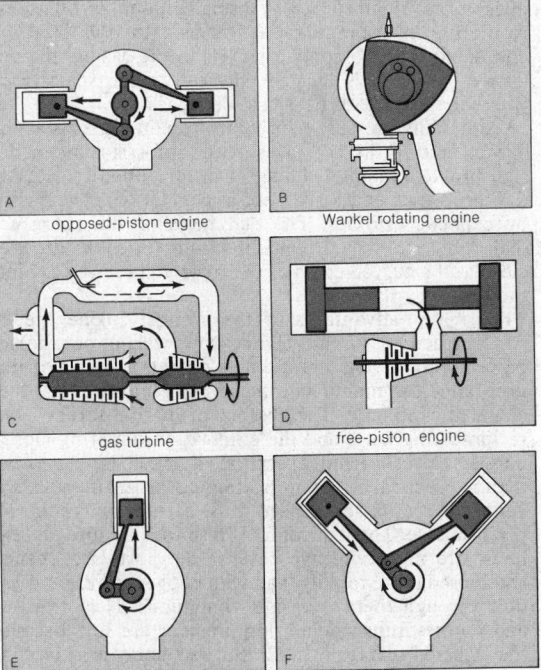

opposed-piston engine

Wankel rotating engine

gas turbine

free-piston engine

in-line engine

V-8 engine

Figure 3: Internal-combustion engines.

Wankel rotary engine. A rotary-piston internal-combustion engine developed in Germany is radically different in structure from conventional reciprocating-piston engines. The engine was conceived by Felix Wankel, a specialist in the design of sealing devices, and experimental engines were built and tested by a German firm beginning in 1956. Instead of pistons that move up and down in cylinders, the Wankel engine has an equilateral triangular orbiting rotor (see Figure 3B). The rotor turns in a closed chamber and the three apexes of the rotor maintain a continuous sliding contact with the curved inner surface of the casing. The curve-sided rotor forms three crescent-shaped chambers between its sides and the curved wall of the casing. The volumes of the chambers vary with the rotor motion. Maximum volume is attained in each chamber when the side of the rotor forming it is parallel with the minor diameter of the casing, and the volume is reduced to a minimum when the rotor side is parallel with the major diameter. Shallow pockets recessed in the flank of the rotor control the shape of the combustion chambers and establish the compression ratio of the engine.

Action of the rotor

In turning about its central axis the rotor must follow a circular orbit about the geometric centre of the casing. The necessary orbiting rotation is attained by means of a central bore in the rotor in which an internal gear is fitted to mesh with a stationary pinion fixed immovably to the centre of the casing. The rotor is guided by fitting its central bore to an eccentric formed on the output shaft that passes through the centre of the stationary pinion. This eccentric also harnesses the rotor to the shaft so that torque is applied when gas pressure is exerted against the rotor flanks as the fuel and air charges burn. A 3-to-1 gear ratio causes the output shaft to turn three times as fast as the rotor turns about the eccentric. Each quarter turn of the rotor completes an expansion or a compression, permitting intake, compression, expansion, and exhaust to be accomplished during one turn of the rotor. The only moving parts are the rotor and the output shaft.

The fuel mixture is supplied by a carburetor and enters the combustion chambers through an intake port in one of the end plates of the casing. An exhaust port is formed in one of the flattened sides of the casing wall and a spark plug is located in a pocket communicating with the chambers through a small throat in the opposite side of the casing wall.

The rotor and its gears and bearings are lubricated and cooled by oil circulating through the hollow rotor. The apex vanes are lubricated by a small amount of oil added to the fuel in proportions as low as 1 to 200. Water is circulated through cooling jackets in the casing, the entrance to which is located adjacent to the spark plug where the temperature tends to be highest.

Maintaining pressure-tight joints by suitable seals at the apexes and on the end faces of the rotor is a major design problem. Radial sliding vanes are fitted in slots at the three apex edges and kept in contact with the casing by expander springs. The end faces of the rotor are sealed by arc-shaped segmental rings fitted in grooves close to the curved edges of the rotor and pressed against the casing by flat springs.

Advantages of the Wankel engine

The major advantages of the Wankel engine are its small space requirements and low weight per horsepower, smooth and vibrationless operation, quiet operation, and low manufacturing costs resulting from mechanical simplicity. The absence of inertial forces from reciprocating parts and the elimination of spring-closed poppet valves permit operation at much higher speed than is practical for reciprocating-piston engines, an advantage because shaft speed must be high for optimum performance. The induction of fresh fuel mixture and exhaust are more effective because the ports are opened and closed more rapidly than with poppet valves, and gas flow through them is almost continuous. Heat transfer and the resulting cooling requirement are low because the jacketed surface is small. Fuel economy is at least as good as that of conventional engines, providing knock-free combustion with a wider range of permissible fuels.

Lower weight and a lower centre of gravity make it much safer in an automobile in the event of a collision. There are approximately one third as many parts in a Wankel engine as in a typical six-cylinder automobile engine.

Tri-Dyne rotary engine. The Tri-Dyne engine, a British design (Figure 4), consists of three rotors. The large, triangular central rotor is called the power rotor. The other two are a combustion rotor and a barrier valve. The power rotor turns in the opposite direction from the combustion rotor and barrier valve. It has three curved lobes that fit into three semicircular cavities in the periphery of each of the two smaller rotors. The three are geared together by spur-shaped gears on the end of each rotor; all turn at the same speed. The motion is entirely rotary and there is no eccentricity. The three cavities in the combustion rotor form the combustion chambers and the profiles of all three rotors are such that, while not actually touching each other, they interact to connect these cavities alternately with the inlet and exhaust pipes

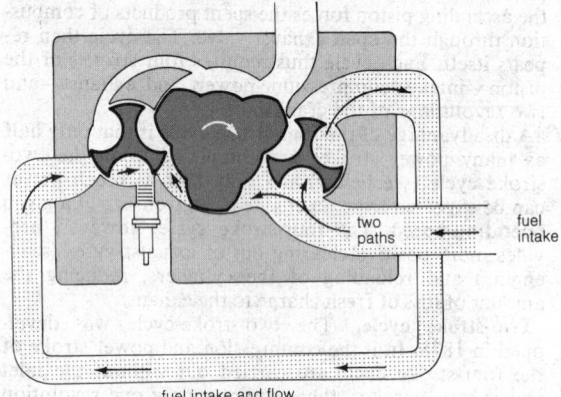

fuel intake and flow

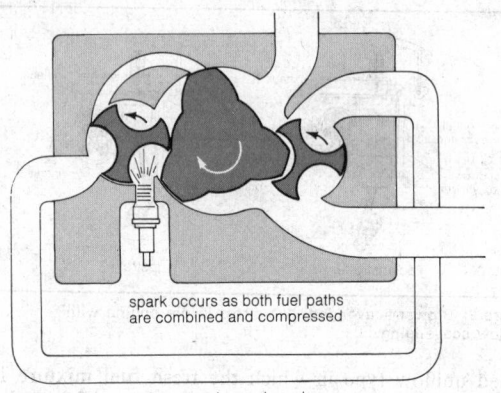

spark occurs as both fuel paths are combined and compressed

compression and spark

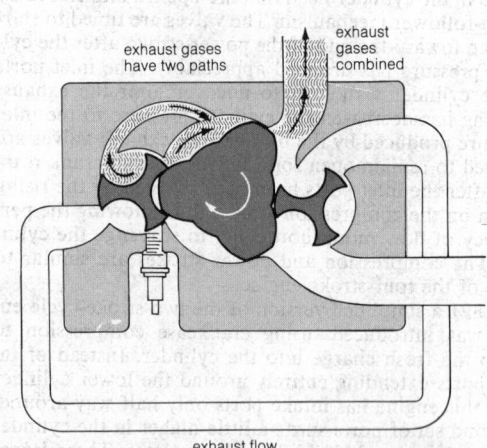

exhaust flow

Figure 4: Simplified sketches showing operating principles of the Tri-Dyne engine.

and isolate them during the combustion process. It is not necessary that the cavities be positively sealed because of the high speed of operation. Clearance of 0.004 inch (0.01 millimetre) is provided between the interacting surfaces. Two spark plugs are installed in the casing at a point where they communicate with the combustion rotor cavities as they pass at the instant of firing. The advantage of this engine over the Wankel engine lies in the elimination of the seals that the latter requires at the apexes of its triangular rotor that limit the speed at which it can operate and are difficult to lubricate.

The gas turbine. Many of the imperfections of the reciprocating-piston engine are traceable to the noncontinuous motion and the cyclic interruption of combustion. The fundamental principle of the gas turbine was known before that of any other type of heat engine; historians have recorded that a toy turbine was built by Hero of Alexandria about the time of Christ. Nevertheless, practical development of the gas turbine did not take place until the 20th century.

The gas turbine is a simple power plant (Figure 3C). A compressor supplies air at about three to six times atmospheric pressure to a combustion chamber into which fuel (gasoline) is sprayed, thus maintaining continuous combustion. The resulting large volume of high-temperature gaseous products then expands through the turbine unit to atmospheric pressure. The compressor and turbine rotors may be on the same shaft. The excess of power developed in the turbine unit over that required to turn the compressor rotor is the power delivered by the engine (see also TURBINE; JET ENGINE).

The free-piston engine. In a free-piston engine (Figure 3D) the pistons are not connected to a crankshaft, as in a conventional engine; the exhaust gases transmit their power to a turbine instead. Originally built as an air compressor, the engine was first used extensively by the Germans for launching torpedoes in World War II. It is not strictly a gasoline engine in the true sense, because the fuel charge is ignited by the heat of compression rather than by a spark plug. Thus it falls into the diesel engine class (see DIESEL ENGINE).

Engine construction and operation

A gasoline engine is made up of a large number of components that must be carefully engineered to work together. The major components are described below.

OVERALL STRUCTURE

The overall structure of a gasoline engine depends almost entirely upon the intended application. Many components require only slight modification. Apart from the type of cycle (two- or four-stroke) the provision for mounting is the main structural difference among automotive, marine, stationary, and aviation engines. When a clutch and transmission are used, as in automobiles, the engine is commonly of the so-called unit-power-plant type with a bell-shaped housing surrounding the flywheel and attached to the rear flange of the cylinder block integral with, or attached to, the transmission gear case. The clutch is incorporated in the flywheel of the engine. Three-point suspension is used in such engines; that is, projections on each side of the bell housing fit into the vehicle side frame members and a central tubular extension at the centre of the front end of the cylinder block attaches to the front cross member of the frame. This construction permits some flexing of the vehicle frame without stressing the basic structure of the engine.

The following description of general engine construction indicates the essential components of an engine and introduces the nomenclature of the various parts. The four-stroke cycle automobile engine is used as the basic type. Figure 5 shows a cross section of a typical automobile engine with the important parts indicated.

Cylinder block. The main structural member of all automotive engines is a cylinder block that usually extends upward from the centre line of the main support for the crankshaft to the junction with the cylinder head. The block serves as the structural framework of the engine and carries the mounting pad by which the engine

Engine suspension

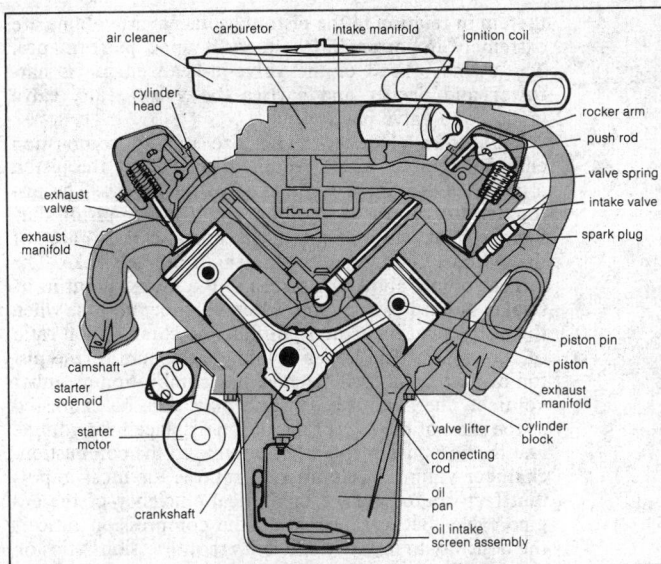

Figure 5: Cross section of an overhead valve V-8 engine.
By courtesy of Cadillac Motor Car Division

is supported in the chassis. Large, stationary power-plant engines and marine engines are built up from a foundation or bedplate and have upper and lower crankcases that are separate from the cylinder assemblies. The cylinder block of an automobile engine is a casting with appropriate machined surfaces and threaded holes for attaching the cylinder head, main bearings, oil pan, and other units. The crankcase is formed by the portion of the cylinder block below the cylinder bores and the stamped metal oil pan that forms the lower enclosure of the engine and also serves as a lubricating oil reservoir or sump.

The cylinders are openings of circular cross section that extend through the upper portion of the block with interior walls bored and polished to form smooth, accurate bearing surfaces. The cylinders of heavy-duty engines are usually fitted with removable liners made of metal more wear-resistant than that used in the block casting.

There are two arrangements of cylinders in common automotive use—the vertical or in-line type (Figure 3E) and the V type (Figure 3F). The in-line engine has a single row of cylinders extending vertically upward from the crankcase and aligned with the crankshaft main bearings. The V type has two rows of cylinders, usually forming an angle of 60 degrees or 90 degrees between the two banks. V-8 engines (eight cylinders) are usually of the 90-degree type. Some small 6-cylinder aviation engines have horizontally opposed cylinders.

A passage bored lengthwise in the block houses the camshaft that operates the valves. A gear or chain compartment for the camshaft drive from the crankshaft is formed between the front or rear end of the block and a cover plate. The bell housing is formed at the rear of the cylinder block to enclose the flywheel and provide for attachment of a transmission housing. Water jackets are formed around the cylinders with suitable cored connecting passages for circulation of the coolant.

The design of the cylinder block is affected by the location of the valves of the four-stroke-cycle engine and by the provision of cylinder ports in the two-stroke type. An overhead-valve engine, which has largely replaced the L-head type, has its valves entirely in the cylinder head. The cylinder block of the L-head engine is extended to one side of the cylinder bores, with the valve seats and passages for inlet and exhaust, together with the valve guides, formed in this extension of the block. The cylinder head then becomes merely a water-jacketed cover, providing threaded locations for the spark plugs and with its underside so profiled that a combustion chamber of desired size and shape is formed above each cylinder bore. The shape of the space forming the combustion chamber when the piston is at its closest approach to the cylinder head and volume contained

Block design

therein in relation to the piston displacement volume are extremely important in their effect upon performance. The cylinder head of the valve-in-head engine is narrower and deeper and carries the valve seats, valve guides, and valve ports.

Combustion chamber. The size of the combustion chamber relative to the volume displaced by the piston establishes the compression ratio of the engine. The piston displacement is the volume swept by the piston during one stroke and is equal to the cross-sectional area of the cylinder multiplied by the length of the stroke. The larger volume above the piston at the lowest point in its stroke, divided by the combustion-chamber volume when the piston is at its highest point, is the compression ratio of the engine. The larger volume is the sum of the piston-displacement volume and the combustion-chamber volume. The compression ratio may thus be expressed as the ratio of the sum of the piston displacement volume and the combustion-chamber volume to the combustion-chamber volume. Compression ratio is the most important factor affecting the theoretical efficiency of the engine cycle. Because increasing the compression ratio is the best way to improve efficiency, compression ratios on automobile engines have tended to increase. This requires stronger, more durable materials.

Pistons. The pistons are cup-shaped cylindrical castings of steel or aluminum alloy. The upper, closed end, called the crown, forms the lower surface of the combustion chamber and receives the force applied by the combustion gases. The outer surface is machined to fit the cylinder bore closely and is grooved to receive piston rings that seal the gap between the piston and the cylinder wall. In the upper piston grooves there are plain compression rings that prevent the combustion gases from blowing past the piston. The lower rings are vented to distribute and limit the amount of lubricant on the cylinder wall. Piston pin supports (bosses) are cast in opposite sides of the piston and hardened steel pins fitted into these bosses pass through the upper end of the connecting rod.

Connecting rod and crankshaft. A forged steel connecting rod connects the piston to a throw (offset portion) of the crankshaft and converts the reciprocating motion of the piston to the rotating motion of the crank. The lower, larger end of the rod is bored to take a precision bearing insert lined with Babbit or other bearing metal and closely fitted to the crank pin. V-type engines usually have opposite cylinders staggered sufficiently to permit the two connecting rods that operate on each crank throw to be side by side. Some larger engines employ fork-and-blade rods with the rods in the same plane and cylinders exactly opposite each other.

V-type engines

Each connecting rod in an in-line engine or each pair of rods in a V-type engine is attached to a throw of the crankshaft. Each throw consists of a crankpin with a bearing surface, on which the connecting rod bearing insert is fitted, and two radial cheeks that connect it to the portions of the crankshaft that turn in the main bearings, supported by the cylinder block. Sufficient throws are provided to serve all the cylinders, and the angles between them equal the angular firing intervals between the cylinders. The throws of a six-cylinder, four-stroke-cycle crankshaft are spaced 120 degrees apart so that the six cylinders fire at equal intervals in two full rotations of the shaft. Those of an eight-cylinder engine are 90 degrees apart. The position of each throw along the shaft depends upon the firing order of the cylinders. Firing sequence is chosen to distribute the power impulses along the length of the engine to minimize vibration. Consideration is also given to the fluid flow pattern in the intake and exhaust manifolds. The standard firing order for a six-cylinder engine is 1-5-3-6-2-4, which illustrates the practice of alternating successive impulses between the front and rear valves of the engine whenever possible. Balance is further improved by adding counterweights to the crankshaft to offset the eccentric masses of metal in the crank throws.

The crankshaft design also establishes the length of the piston stroke because the radial offset of each throw is equal to half the stroke imparted to the piston. The ratio of the piston stroke to the cylinder bore diameter is an important design consideration. In the early years of engine development no logical basis for the establishment of this ratio existed and a range from unity to one and one-half was used by different manufacturers. As engine speeds increased, however, and it became apparent that friction horsepower increased with piston speed rather than with crankshaft rotating speed, there began a trend toward short-stroke engines. Strokes were shortened to as much as 20 percent less than the bores.

From the requirement for the two-cylinder engine a general rule for the layout of the throws of four-stroke-cycle multicylinder crankshafts can be expressed. Regardless of the number of cylinders, two pistons must arrive at top dead centre in unison so that a second cylinder is ready to fire exactly 360 degrees after each cylinder fires. Half of the cylinders then will fire during each turn of the crankshaft. To follow this rule, there must be an even number of cylinders in order that there may be pairs of cylinders whose pistons move in unison.

Crank throw layout

An eight-cylinder engine fires each time its crankshaft makes a quarter turn if the intervals between impulses are equal. The crankshaft for an eight-cylinder, in-line engine is designed with each of its eight throws a quarter turn away from another throw.

For best lengthwise balance, the cylinders whose pistons are in phase are the first and last cylinders of an in-line engine, the second and next to the last, continuing in that order with crank throws that are in alignment equidistant from the centre of the engine.

Valves, pushrods, and rocker arms. The valve-in-head engine has push rods that extend upward from the cam followers to rocker arms mounted on the cylinder head that contact the valve stems and transmit the motion produced by the cam profile to the valves. Clearance (usually termed tappet clearance) must be maintained between the ends of the valve stems and the lifter mechanism to assure proper closing of the valves when the engine temperature changes. This is done by providing push-rod length adjustment or by the use of hydraulic lifters.

Noisy and erratic valve operation can be eliminated with entirely mechanical valve lifter linkage only if the tappet clearance between the rocker arms and the valve stems is closely maintained at the specified value for the engine as measured with a thickness gauge. Hydraulic valve lifters, now commonly used on automobile engines, eliminate the need for periodic adjustment of clearance.

The hydraulic lifter comprises a cam follower that is moved up and down by contact with the cam profile, and an inner bore into which the valve lifter is closely fitted and retained by a spring clip. The valve lifter, in turn, is a cup closed at the top by a freely moving cylindrical plug that has a socket at the top to fit the lower end of the push rod. This plug is pushed upward by a light spring that is merely capable of taking up the clearance between the valve stem and the rocker arm. A small hole is drilled in the bottom of the valve-lifter cup to admit lubricating oil that enters the cam follower from the engine lubricating system through a passage in the cylinder block. A small steel ball serves as a check valve to admit the oil into the valve-fitter cup but prevent its escape. When the clearance in the entire linkage between the cam profile and the valve stem is being taken up by the spring in the valve lifter, oil flows into the lifter chamber past the ball check and is trapped there to maintain this no-clearance condition as the engine operates. Expansion or contraction of the valve linkage is compensated by oil seepage from the lifter to correct for expansion of parts and oil flow into the chamber if clearance tends to be produced between the push rod and the lifter. Complete closure of valve is then assured at all times without tappet noise.

The intake valve must be open while the piston is descending on the intake stroke of the piston and the exhaust valve must be open while the piston is rising on the exhaust stroke. It would seem, therefore, that the opening and closing of the two valves would occur at the appropriate top and bottom dead centre points of the crankshaft. The time required for the valves to open and close, however, and the effects of high speed upon the starting and stopping of the flow of the gases requires that for optimum performance the opening events occur before the crankshaft dead centre positions and that the closing events be delayed until after dead centre.

Valve timing

All four valve events, inlet opening, inlet closing, exhaust opening, and exhaust closing are accordingly displaced appreciably from the top and bottom dead centres. Opening events are earlier and closing events are later to permit ramps to be incorporated in the cam profiles to allow gradual initial opening and final closing to avoid slamming of the valves. Ramps are provided to start the lift gradually and to slow the valve down before it contacts its seat. Early opening and late closure are also for the purpose of using the inertia or persistence of flow of the gases to assist in filling and emptying the cylinder.

Camshaft. The camshaft, which opens and closes the valves, is driven from the crankshaft by a chain drive or gears on the front end of the engine. Because one turn of the camshaft completes the valve operation for an entire cycle of the engine and the four-stroke cycle engine makes two crankshaft revolutions to complete one cycle, the camshaft turns half as fast as the crankshaft. It is located above and to one side of the crankshaft, which places it directly under the valves of the L-head engine or the push rods that extend down from the rocker arms of the valve-in-head engine. Because of the long push rods and the rocker arms, the speed of the valve-in-head engine is limited to that at which the cam followers can remain in contact with the cams when the valves are closing. Above that limiting speed the valves are said to float and their motion becomes erratic. For this reason, the overhead-camshaft engine is increasing in popularity. Located immediately above the valves, this type of camshaft is driven either by a vertical shaft and bevel gears or by a cog belt. Although new in automobiles, this arrangement was used as early as World War I in some aircraft engines.

Flywheel. The cycle of the internal-combustion engine is such that torque (turning force) is applied only intermittently as each cylinder fires. Between these power impulses the pistons rising on compression and the opposition to rotation caused by the load carried by the engine apply negative torque. The alternating acceleration caused by the power impulse and deceleration caused by compression results in nonuniform rotation. To counter this tendency to slow down and speed up is the function of the flywheel, attached to one end of the crankshaft. The flywheel consists of a heavy circular cast iron disc with a hub for attachment to the engine. Its heavy rotating mass has sufficient momentum to oppose all changes in its rotational speed, and to force the crankshaft to turn steadily at this speed. The engine thus runs smoothly with no evidence of rotational pulsations. The outer rim of the flywheel usually carries gear teeth cut on it to mesh with the starter motor. The driving component of a clutch or fluid coupling for the transmission may be incorporated in the flywheel.

Bearings. The crankshaft has bearing surfaces on each crank throw and three or more main bearings. These are heavily loaded because of the reciprocating forces at each cylinder applied to the crankshaft and the weight of the crankshaft and flywheel. All but the smallest engines use split shell bearings, usually made of bronze with Babbitt-metal linings. The surface material is sufficiently soft to minimize the possibility of scoring the crankshaft in the event of inadequate lubrication. The smallest engines usually have cast Babbitt bearings. A small amount of bearing clearance is necessary to permit an oil film to separate the surfaces (see also MACHINES AND MACHINE COMPONENTS).

Ignition. Electric ignition systems may be classified as magneto and battery-and-coil systems. Though these are similar in basic principle, the magneto is self-contained and requires only the spark plugs and connecting wires to complete the system, whereas the battery-and-coil system involves several separate components. The circuit consists of a battery, one terminal of which is grounded

while the other leads through a switch to the primary winding of the coil, and then to a circuit breaker where it is again grounded. Rotation of the circuit-breaker cam opens and closes the primary circuit. The secondary circuit, consisting of several thousand turns of fine wire, leads to the rotor of the distributor, which acts as a rotary switch, selecting the spark plug to be placed in the circuit. Each plug is connected to one of the outer terminals of the distributor to receive an electrical impulse in proper sequence. When the primary circuit is broken, a high potential (up to 20,000 volts) is developed in the secondary winding and conducted to the appropriate spark plug.

The spark plug is an important component of the ignition system and is the one that must operate under the most severe conditions. Because it is exposed to combustion-chamber temperatures and pressures and contaminating products of combustion, it requires more service attention and is usually the shortest-lived component of the gasoline engine. It consists of a steel shell threaded to fit a standard 14-millimetre hole in the cylinder head. A copper gasket insures a gas-tight fit between cylinder head and plug. A fused ceramic insulating element is molded into the plug body and the steel centre electrode passes through the insulator up to the connector to which the high-voltage lead from the distributor is attached. The other electrode is welded to the metal body of the plug, which is grounded to the cylinder head.

It is essential that the spark gap be as specified for the particular engine. Gauges are available to aid in making this adjustment by bending the ground electrode as required. Manufacturers specify gaps ranging from 0.020 inch to 0.040 inch (0.508 to 1.016 millimetre) between the centre electrode and the ground electrode. If the plug gap is too large, the possibility of misfiring increases. If the gap is too small, the spark will not be sufficiently intense. Gap growth from erosion of the electrodes may be corrected. The high voltage for the spark plug may also be produced by a capacitor discharge ignition system, which consists of a source of 250 to 300 volts direct-current power applied to a storage capacitor, a device for storing an electrical charge. A lead from the capacitor goes to one side of the spark coil primary through cam-actuated breaker points or an electronic switching device. At the instant this switching device establishes a contact, the capacitor discharges through the primary of the spark coil and an instantaneous high voltage is delivered to the distributor and thence to the spark plug.

Capacitor ignition system

The capacitor discharge system stem provides a more intense spark, thus improving starting a cold or flooded engine. It continues to fire the plugs when they are fouled by carbon or other deposits or when the spark gap has widened because of erosion of the points. Other advantages include increased spark plug life, improved firing over wider speed range, and better moisture tolerance.

The capacitor discharge ignition system is now being introduced for engines such as the Wankel; it has been used on research engines for many years.

A magneto is a fixed-magnet, alternating-current generator designed to generate sufficient voltage to fire the spark plugs. A high-tension magneto is entirely self-contained and requires only spark plugs, wires, and switches to do what is required in meeting ignition requirements. Everything else is built in.

Carburetor. The gasoline carburetor is a device that introduces fuel into the air stream as it flows into the engine. A simple carburetor is shown diagrammatically in Figure 6. Gasoline is maintained in the float chamber by the float-actuated valve at a level slightly below the outlet of the jet. Air flows downward through the throat, past the throttle valve, and into the intake manifold. A throat is formed by the reduced diameter and acceleration of the air through this smaller passage causes a decrease in pressure proportional to the amount of air flowing. This decrease in throat pressure results in fuel flow from the jet into the air stream. Any increase in air flow caused by change in engine speed or throttle position increases the pressure differential acting on the fuel and causes more fuel to flow.

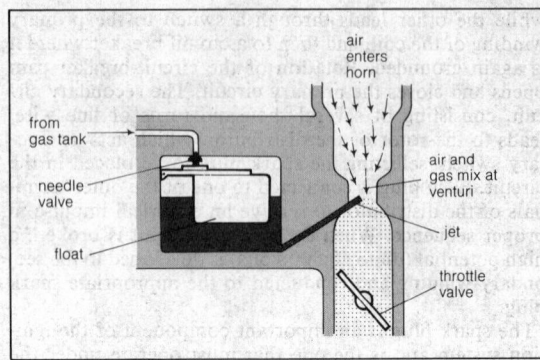

Figure 6: A simple carburetor.

The volume ratio of air to fuel established by the throat and fuel jet sizes will be maintained with increased flow, but the weight of fuel per pound of air increases because the air expands to a lower density as the throat pressure decreases. This enriching tendency necessitates the inclusion of a compensating device in a practical carburetor. Carburetor design is further complicated by the need for an enriching device to provide a maximum-power ratio at full throttle, a choke to facilitate starting a cold engine, an idling system to provide the special needs of light-load operation and an accelerating device to supply additional fuel while the throttle is being opened.

Fuel injection. Gasoline-injection systems in which the fuel is forcefully injected into the cylinder by a pump were available for airplane engines before World War II and were extensively used then in aircraft. The performance of engines with this equipment was excellent, but the much greater cost of fuel injection systems compared with that of carburetors limited their application. Efforts to simplify and lower the cost of fuel-injection equipment without impairing performance yielded multicylinder

Pumps
versus
carburetors

pumps that could compete in cost with four-barrel carburetors. Gasoline injection equipment may consist of distributor systems employing a single pump for all of the cylinders, or multipumps.

The principal advantages of gasoline injection over the carburetor are: improved fuel economy because of more accurate fuel and air proportioning; greater power because of the elimination of fuel heating; elimination of inlet icing; and more uniform and direct delivery of fuel load to the cylinders.

Supercharger. The efficiency of the charging process in an automotive engine usually rises to a peak of slightly more than 80 percent at about half the rated speed of the engine and then decreases considerably at higher speed. This change in air charge per cycle with engine speed is reflected in proportionate changes in the torque or turning effort applied to the crankshaft and causes the power the engine can deliver at full throttle to reach a maximum as engine speed increases. At speeds above this peaking speed the air charge introduced per cycle falls off so rapidly that less power is developed than at lower speeds. The inability of the engine to draw in a full charge of fresh air at high speeds limits the power output of the engine.

Supercharging overcomes this disadvantage by the use of a pump or blower to raise the pressure of the air supplied to the cylinders, increasing the weight of charge. The loss in power suffered by unsupercharged engines at high altitudes can be largely restored; it is also possible to more than double the power of an engine by supercharging. Increased charge density and temperature, resulting from supercharging, increase the tendency for combustion knock or roughness in the spark-ignition engine and thus necessitates an undesirable decrease in compression ratio or the use of an antiknock fuel.

The supercharging blower may be geared to the crankshaft, in which case the power consumed in driving it is added to the friction loss of the engine. The turbocharger employs a gas turbine operated by the exhaust gases to drive a centrifugal blower. The turbocharged engine not only gains increased power capacity but also operates at

improved fuel economy. Airplane engines are usually supercharged both by geared blowers and by turbochargers to provide the large pumping capacity needed at high altitude.

Cooling system. The cylinders of all internal-combustion engines require cooling because of the inability of the engine to convert all of the energy released by combustion into useful work. Liquid cooling is employed in most gasoline engines, whether the engines are for use in automobiles or elsewhere. The liquid is circulated around the cylinders to pick up heat, and then through a radiator to dissipate the heat. Usually a thermostat is located in the circulating system to maintain the design jacket temperature, 160° to 180° F (71° to 82° C). The cooling system is usually pressurized to raise the boiling point of the coolant so that a higher outlet temperature can be maintained to improve thermal efficiency and increase the heat transfer capacity of the radiator. A pressure cap on the radiator maintains this pressure by valves that open outwardly at the design pressure and inwardly to prevent a vacuum as the system cools.

Some engines, particularly aviation engines and small units for mowers, chain saws, and other appliances, are air cooled. Air cooling is accomplished by forming thin metal fins on the exterior surfaces of the cylinders to increase the rate of heat transfer by exposing more metal surface to the cooling air. Air is forced to flow rapidly through the spaces between the fins by fans or blowers. Airplane engines are especially well adapted to air cooling because the propeller air stream provides ample cooling air without any power consumption.

Air cooling

Lubrication system. Lubrication is employed to reduce friction by interposing a film between rubbing parts. The lubrication system must continuously replace the films.

The lubricants commonly employed are refined from crude oil after the fuels have been removed. Their viscosities must be appropriate for each engine and the oil must be suitable for the severity of the operating conditions. Oils are improved with additives that reduce oxidation, inhibit corrosion, and act as detergents to disperse deposit-forming gums and solid contaminants. Various systems of numbers are used to designate oil viscosity; the lower the number, the lighter the body of the oil. Certain oils contain additives that oppose their change in viscosity between the winter and summer.

Oil filters, if regularly serviced, can remove solid contaminants from crankcase oil, but chemical reactions may form liquids that are corrosive and damaging. Depletion of the additives also limits the useful life of lubricating oils.

The lubrication system is fed by the oil sump that forms the lower enclosure of the engine. Oil is taken from the sump by a pump, usually of the gear type, and delivered under pressure to a system of passages or channels drilled through the engine. In some instances a so-called full-flow filter runs the length of the engine between the pump and the main oil passage. In other engines bypass filters continuously bleed off a small quantity of oil and return the filtered oil to the sump.

Oil is supplied under pressure to crankshaft and camshaft main bearings. Adjacent crank throws are drilled to enable the oil to flow from the supply at the main bearings to the crankpins. Leaking oil from all of the crankshaft bearings is sprayed on the cylinder walls, cams, and up into the pistons to lubricate the piston pins. Additional passages intersect the cam-follower openings and supply oil to hydraulic valve lifters when used. A spring-loaded pressure-relief valve maintains the pressure at the proper level.

Exhaust system. Exhaust gases from an internal-combustion engine are passed through a muffler to suppress audible vibrations. The pressure in the engine when the exhaust valve opens causes an initial gas outflow at explosive velocity. Successive discharges from the cylinders set up pressure pulsations that produce a sharp barking sound. The muffler damps out or absorbs these pulsations so that the gases leave the outlet as a relatively smooth, quiet stream.

Mufflers of early design contained sets of baffles that reversed the flow of the gases or otherwise caused them to follow devious paths so that interference between the pressure waves reduced the pulsations. The mufflers most commonly used in modern motor vehicles employ resonating chambers communicating with the passages through which the gases flow. Gas vibrations are set up in each of these chambers at the fundamental frequency determined by its dimensions. These vibrations cancel or absorb those present in the exhaust stream of about the same frequency. Several such chambers, each tuned to one of the predominant frequencies present in the exhaust stream, effectively reduce noise.

Emission control

Emission control devices to reduce air pollution are frequently added to the exhaust system. Beds of a suitable catalyst (a material for promoting desirable reactions) are placed in the muffler to reduce unburned hydrocarbons and carbon monoxide in the exhaust output. These catalysts are adversely affected by tetraethyl lead in gasoline.

The reactor system for controlling emission is composed of a belt-driven air compressor connected to small nozzles installed in the exhaust manifold facing the outlet from each exhaust valve. A small jet of air is thus directed toward the red-hot outflowing combustion products to provide oxygen to consume the hydrocarbons and carbon-monoxide.

FUELS

Gasoline was originally considered dangerous and was discarded and destroyed at the early refineries, which were manufacturing kerosene for lamps. As the gasoline engine developed, gasoline and the engine were harmonized to attain the best possible matching of characteristics. The most important properties of gasoline are its volatility and antiknock quality. Volatility is a measure of the ease of vaporization of gasoline in the carburetor. The volatility is made higher for winter use to make engines start more readily and lower in summer to avoid vapour lock (blockage of gasoline feedline by excessive gasoline vapour) and excessive evaporation loss.

To suit the needs of a modern engine a gasoline must have the volatility for which the fuel system of the engine was designed, and antiknock quality sufficient to avoid knock under normal operation. Though other specifications must also be met, volatility and knock rating are the most important. The size and structural arrangement of the molecules principally determine the knocking tendency of a gasoline as well as its volatility. (For a detailed description of antiknock gasoline blending techniques, SEE PETROLEUM REFINING.)

Tetraethyl lead, added to gasolines for many years to improve antiknock fuelling, has been found to contaminate the exhaust gases with poisonous lead oxides, and the practice is ending. Lower compression ratios and improved combustion-chamber designs are eliminating the need for extremely high antiknock gasolines.

Lubricating oil is added to gasoline used in crankcase-compression two-stroke cycle engines.

PERFORMANCE

The performance of an engine is expressed in terms of power, speed, and fuel economy. The three quantities are evaluated with a dynamometer, a laboratory device that applies a controllable load in the form of resistance to the turning of the crankshaft and also measures the torque exerted at the shaft coupling. The resistance imposed by a dynamometer may be so adjusted that the desired engine speed is established at any throttle position. It is thus possible to run the engine at various speeds throughout its operating range, to maintain these operating conditions continuously, and to measure the precise load and speed at which each run is made. Additional test equipment permits measurement of the exact quantity of fuel consumed as well as the duration of the runs. From these data the power-speed-economy relationships can be calculated, and performance plotted.

The power produced by an engine is expressed in horsepower, a unit established by James Watt, who tested several horses to determine the rate at which they could work and decided that 33,000 foot-pounds per minute was a liberal unit. A foot-pound is equivalent to lifting a weight of one pound a distance of one foot.

Power measurements

When the power developed is measured by means of a dynamometer or similar braking device, it is called brake horsepower. This is the power actually delivered by the engine and is therefore the capacity of the engine. The power developed in the combustion chambers of the engine is greater than the delivered power because of friction and other mechanical losses. This power loss, called the friction horsepower, can be evaluated by "motoring" the engine (driving it in a forward direction) with a suitable dynamometer when no fuel is being burned. The power developed in the cylinder can then be found by adding the friction horsepower to the brake horsepower. This quantity is the indicated horsepower of the engine, so called from an instrument known as the engine indicator, which is used to measure the pressure on the piston and thus calculate the power developed in the cylinder.

Mechanical efficiency is defined as brake horsepower in percent of indicated horsepower and is usually between 70 percent and 90 percent within the normal operating speed range.

A quantity called brake mean effective pressure is obtained by multiplying the mean effective pressure of an engine by its mechanical efficiency. This is a commonly used index expressing the ability of the engine, per unit of cylinder bore, to develop useful pressure in the cylinders and delivery power. If the power delivered is increased by any change other than an increase in speed or cylinder dimensions, its brake mean effective pressure increases proportionately.

APPLICATIONS

Gasoline engines can be built to meet the requirements of practically any conceivable power-plant application. In some instances, however, other kinds of engines or electric motors have certain advantages. The important applications for which the gasoline engine is most likely to be chosen in preference to other types are in the areas of passenger automobiles, small trucks and buses, aircraft, outboard and small inboard marine units, moderate-sized stationary pumping, lighting plant, machine tool and similar installations, and power tools.

Automobile engines range from small four-cylinder engines of less than 100 horsepower to 500 cubic inch piston displacement engines developing well over 400 horsepower. These engines meet the needs of motor-car propulsion so well that in the early 1970s they had practically no competition in that field.

BIBLIOGRAPHY. L.C. LICHTY, *Combustion Engine Processes,* rev. 6th ed. (1967), a specialized discussion of selected important aspects; H.L. SOLBERG, O.C. CROMER, and A.R. SPALDING, *Thermal Engineering* (1960), a textbook on the engineering applications of heat; H.F. BLANCHARD and R. RITCHEN, *Auto Engines and Electrical Systems,* 4th ed. (1967), a well-illustrated discussion of maintenance and repair information; E.F. OBERT, *Internal Combustion Engines,* 3rd ed. (1968), a general textbook. See also the following journals: SAE *Journal* (monthly), complete engineering activity reports; *Automobile Engineer* (monthly), reports on European developments and progress; and the *Engineer* (bi-monthly), a report on British automobile industry progress.

(O.C.C.)

Gasterosteiformes

Gasterosteiformes is an order of fishes characterized generally by soft fin rays, pelvic fins located on the abdomen, an air bladder without a duct to the gut, and a primitive kidney. Gill structures are somewhat degenerate. Most species have bony rings around the body or ganoid (*i.e.,* thick, bony, enamelled, and diamond-shaped) plates rather than scales. Families within the order are Gasterosteidae (sticklebacks), Aulorhynchidae (tube snout), Indostomidae (indostomid), Aulostomidae (trumpet fishes), Fistulariidae (cornetfishes), Centriscidae (shrimpfishes), Macrorhamphosidae (snipefishes), Solenostomidae (ghost pipefishes), and Syngnathidae (pipefishes and sea horses).

shrimpfish
Centriscus scutatus

sea dragon
Phycodurus eques

sea horse
Hippocampus erectus

cornetfish
Fistularia tabacaria

northern pipefish
Syngnathus fuscus

trumpet fish
Aulostomus chinensis

bellows fish
Macrorhamphosus elevatus

threespine stickleback
Gasterosteus aculeatus

Representative gasterosteiform fishes.
Drawing by J. Helmer based on (G,F) G. Whitley and J. Allan, *The Sea-Horse and Its Relatives;* (D,E,H) A.H. Leim and W.B. Scott, *Fishes of the Atlantic Coast of Canada* (1966), Fisheries Research Board of Canada, reproduced by permission of Information Canada

Natural history. *Distribution, size, and importance.* Gasterosteiform fishes occur in both salt water and freshwater and are widely distributed. The smallest species are about three centimetres (1.2 inches) long, the largest about 200 centimetres (about 80 inches). They are of limited economic importance, but many forms are popular aquarium fishes. Two families, Indostomidae and Aulorhynchidae, are represented by only one species each.

Reproduction and life cycle. Except for sticklebacks, pipefishes, and sea horses, little is known of the life cycles of Gasterosteiformes. The male stickleback builds nests of plant materials cemented together with mucus secretions. The usually drab body hues of the male change, reflecting red, which is sexually attractive to the female. Male pipefishes and sea horses brood the eggs, deposited by the female within the male's brooding pouch. The brooding organ of the male sea dragon is a specialized area of soft skin beneath the tail. In some ghost pipefishes, eggs are fastened to the female on filaments of skin in pouches formed by specialized fins on the ventral, or lower, side. The dwarf sea horse, *Hippocampus zosterae*, breeds nine months of the year; eggs hatch after ten days into miniatures of the adult. They mature in two or three months and live less than a year. Tube snouts deposit eggs in cavities of ascidia (primitive colonial chordates) or in masses of algae bound with threads secreted in a manner similar to that of sticklebacks. Egg clusters, often multiple, are cared for by the

male. Snipefish eggs are enveloped in a mucilaginous substance from which the larvae are freed as development proceeds. Cornetfishes lay free pelagic (*i.e.*, drifting) eggs; thus, they do not receive parental care. The reproductive habits of shrimpfishes and trumpet fishes are unknown.

Ecology and behaviour. For defense, most gasterosteiforms assume a vertical position among grasses, gorgonians (*i.e.*, sea fans, a type of coral), and sea urchins. Such a posture serves to camouflage them; it also tends to present body spines or shields to predators normally oriented to the horizontal plane.

In most families, locomotion is by means of the caudal, or tail, fin. Snipefishes swim forward or backward with equal ease on the vertical plane and do not seek shelter among marine growths. The caudal fin is absent in sea horses. The coiled tail of the sea horse is used for gripping seaweed and other plants or objects. Propulsion is by means of the dorsal fin (*i.e.*, the large fin arising from the midline of the back). Tiny pectoral fins are used for steering. Vertical movement is by swimming. All fishes with an air bladder use it to some degree for vertical motion. With little effort the sea horse rises or settles to another depth by changing the air volume within the bladder.

With the exception of the snipefishes, most gasterosteiforms live among a wide variety of aquatic growths where they find food and safety and reproduce. Certain pipefishes and sticklebacks, in particular, are able to tolerate a wide range of salinity.

Form and function. Sticklebacks are the most varied in form. The number of spines and bony plates is greatest in individuals living in the ocean. Each heavily armoured marine species is represented by half-mailed or naked (plateless) varieties in brackish or fresh waters. They are small scaleless fishes that grow to about 15 centimetres (six inches) in length. The short jaws are well armed with sharp teeth. The body is more nearly fusiform (*i.e.*, tapered at both ends) than are those of other members of the order. Body plates may be absent or may vary in number. The soft dorsal fin is preceded by from two to 11 free spines, each connected to the dorsal surface by its own triangular membrane. Pelvic fins are thoracic (*i.e.*, near the midsection) in position, each with a well-developed spine and one or two soft rays. The anal fin is preceded by a spine. The caudal fin is truncate (*i.e.*, abbreviated).

The body of the tube snout is elongated, slender, and cylindrical. It is tipped by a prolonged snout, the small, toothed mouth of which has a hinged upper jaw. The scaleless body is armoured with series of embedded bony plates. The first dorsal fin is represented by about 25 free spines; the rayed dorsal fin is far back on the body above the anal fin. Pectoral fins are broad and the caudal fin furcate (forked).

In the indostomids the elongated body is covered with bony rings as in pipefishes and sea horses. The small mouth is at the tip of the snout. The teeth are minute, the gills rather lobe shaped, and the eyes large. The anterior (*i.e.*, forward) dorsal fin consists of five isolated spines. Ventral fins (*i.e.*, paired fins arising from the sides of the belly) bear no spine, have four rays each, and are located not far behind the pectorals. The anal fin is below the soft dorsal fin, and the rounded caudal fin has a short peduncle, or stem.

Trumpet fishes, which seldom grow to more than 30 centimetres (one foot) in length, have an elongated, compressed, scaled body; the snout is prolonged into a rigid tubelike beak. The short, weak jaws have minute teeth. There are numerous dorsal spines. The ventral fins are abdominal; the caudal fin is truncate.

Cornetfishes, which grow to more than 180 centimetres (six feet) in length, are similar in structure to trumpet fishes; however, there are no scales. Instead, bony plates are embedded in the skin. Dorsal spines are absent, and the ventral fins are located in the abdominal region; each has a spine and four rays. Four anterior vertebrae are elongated. The backbone extends through the forked caudal fin as a long central filament.

Brooding
organ
of the
male

Stickle-
backs

Shrimpfishes, also known as razor fishes, are small, with toothless jaws at the end of a long snout. Scales are absent; the back is covered by transparent plates, forming the cuirass. Anteriorly the cuirass is affixed to the ribs; posteriorly it extends beyond the displaced dorsal, caudal, and anal fins. The body is compressed to a sharp edge ventrally; hence the name razor fish.

In snipefishes the tubular snout has short jaws. The body form is variable, but all snipefishes tend to be short and deep and partly covered with the bony-plated cuirass, which is strengthened by its union with parts of the vertebrae. Areas lacking plates sometimes have scales. In addition to having several shorter spines, the dorsal fin has a very long, strong, serrated spine reaching nearly to the tip of the caudal fin. Each ventral fin has one spine and five rays. A long snout, and two posterior "handles" of spine and tail lends an appearance that is the basis for another common name, bellows fish.

Ghost pipefishes have a tubular snout tipped with a small mouth; the short body has spinous dorsal and ventral fins. Gills are reduced to lobe-shaped tufts attached to rudimentary gill arches. Bony plates unite to form rings. This supporting external framework has reduced the need for well-developed musculature. Ventral fins and a pointed caudal fin are large in proportion to the body size.

Pipefishes

Pipefishes are long and slender. The axis of the head is in line with that of the body, and the long snout is tipped with a small mouth. Bony rings replace scales. The dorsal and pectoral fins are spineless, and ventral fins are absent. Generally, the caudal fin is rounded and reduced, but it is effective in moving the fish rapidly through the water. The slender posterior body portion, though not truly prehensile (*i.e.*, capable of coiling and grasping), can be somewhat used in that manner. Sea horses are similar to pipefishes but differ in several important respects. The head is at an angle to the body proper. This, in addition to the shape of the head, creates a somewhat horselike appearance. The tail is prehensile and lacks a caudal fin.

Evolution and classification. *Paleontology*. Gasterosteiformes appears to represent an early but highly specialized branch of the Acanthopterygii. Its evolution has been traced through limited paleontological data. Fossil sticklebacks occur in Miocene (7,000,000 to 26,000,000 years ago) strata and are moderately abundant in Tertiary (2,500,000 to 65,000,000 years ago) strata. Most of the order occurs in fossil remains in Eocene (38,000,000 to 54,000,000 years ago) and Oligocene (26,000,000 to 38,000,000 years ago) strata in the area of Monte Bolca near Verona, Italy. Deposits there (and in Sumatra) include an extinct family, Protosyngnathidae, related to the tube snouts. Trumpet-fish species, a closely related extinct scaleless family, Urosphenidae, and a small species of cornetfish have also been found there. Shrimpfishes, too, are within these strata, as well as in Oligocene deposits in various parts of Europe. Snipefishes are represented by an extinct genus, as are ghost pipefishes. Pipefishes are in Miocene deposits in Sicily. Tertiary rocks contain *Syngnathus* and *Calamostoma*, pipefish forms with a close relationship to true sea horses. Fossil sea horses are unknown.

Distinguishing taxonomic features. The Gasterosteiformes are classified mainly on the basis of general body form, the structure and distribution of scales or body plates, fin form and position, and the structure of the skeleton and its individual parts.

Annotated classification. The classification here is essentially that of P.H. Greenwood *et al.* (Bulletin of the American Museum of Natural History, no. 131, 1966).

ORDER GASTEROSTEIFORMES
Eocene to Recent. Frequently with strong spines in dorsal and pelvic fins, spines absent in some; snout often elongated; body often with dermal plates; 9 families, marine and freshwater, widely distributed. Length about 3–200 cm.

Suborder Gasterosteidei
Family Gasterosteidae (sticklebacks)
Jaws short, armed with sharp teeth; body quite fusiform (tapered at both ends); body plates may be absent or may vary in number; body length to about 15 cm; 11 species, fresh, brackish, and marine waters of Northern Hemisphere.

Family Aulorhynchidae (tube snout)
Body elongated, slender, and cylindrical; snout long, upper jaw hinged. One species, occurs in northeastern Pacific Ocean.

Family Indostomidae (indostomid)
Body elongated, covered with bony rings; teeth minute, gills lobe-shaped, eyes large. One species, *Indostomus paradoxus*, found in Lake Indawgyi in northern Burma.

Suborder Aulostomoidei
Family Aulostomidae (trumpet fishes)
Body elongated and compressed sideways; jaws short and weak, teeth minute; dorsal spines numerous; length to about 30 cm; about 4 species, tropical seas.

Family Fistulariidae (cornetfishes)
Similar in appearance to Aulostomidae; no scales, bony plates imbedded in skin; dorsal spines absent; backbone extends through caudal fin as a central filament. Grow to more than 180 cm; about 4 species, tropical seas.

Family Centriscidae (shrimpfishes)
Body small, jaws toothless, scales absent, back covered by transparent plates; 4 species, shallow waters of Indian and Pacific Oceans.

Suborder Syngnathoidei
Family Macrorhamphosidae (snipefishes)
Snout tubular, jaws short, body rather short and deep; in profile shaped like bellows; 11 species, temperate and tropical seas.

Family Solenostomidae (ghost pipefishes)
Snout tubular, mouth small; body short, with spiny dorsal and ventral fins; bony plates united to form body rings; about 5 species, tropical Indo-Pacific waters.

Family Syngnathidae (pipefishes and sea horses)
Pipefishes long and slender, snout tipped with small mouth; dorsal and pectoral fins spineless, ventral fins absent. Sea horses with head bent downward in horselike relation to body; tail prehensile; bony rings instead of scales; about 24 species of sea horses, widely distributed, marine; about 150 species of pipefishes widely distributed in shallow tropical seas.

Critical appraisal. The American Fisheries Society (Special Publication No. 6, 1970) arranges the Gasterosteiformes as in Greenwood *et. al.*, above, with the following exceptions: suborders are not used; family Gasterosteidae is expanded to include Aulorhynchidae; family Centriscidae is expanded to include Macrorhamphosidae.

Of the several families considered in this article, the Indostomidae are the least known. They appear to be intermediate between Gasterosteidae and Aulostomidae.

A tenth family, Pegasidae, is tentatively placed between Gasterosteidae and Syngnathidae. Some authorities list them separately as Pegasiformes. These small fishes are the so-called sea moths, found in Asiatic seas. The toothless mouth is not terminal but lies under the head and is overhung by a snout, or rostrum, often adorned with spines. The body is protected by knobby armoured plates, with the posterior portion rather elongated, square to rectangular in cross section and bearing a small dorsal fin. Spines along either side of this region may be absent or developed to varying degrees. Pectoral fins form expansive fans on either side. Ventral fins are reduced to a few fingerlike rays used for crawling on the bottom. The pegasids have no air bladder. Swimming ability for more than short distances is poor. Fossils of Pegasidae are unknown.

BIBLIOGRAPHY. AMERICAN FISHERIES SOCIETY, *A List of Common and Scientific Names of Fishes from the United States and Canada*, 3rd ed. (1970); LEO BERG, *Classification of Fishes Both Recent and Fossil* (1947), English and Russian; W.A. CLEMENS and G.V. WILBY, *Fishes of the Pacific Coast of Canada*, 2nd ed. (1961), limited in breadth and depth due to few order representatives in that range; EARL S. HERALD, *Living Fishes of the World* (1961); DAVID STARR JORDAN, *Fishes*, rev. ed. (1925), an excellent systematic work, although the nomenclature requires revision (college level); A.H. LEIM and W.B. SCOTT, *Fishes of the Atlantic Coast of Canada* (1966), a work broader in scope than Clemens-Wilby (above); N. TINBERGEN, "The Curious Behavior of the Stickleback," *Scient. Am.*, 187:22–26 (1952), a popularized segment of the author's 1951 *Study of Instinct*; GILBERT WHITLEY and JOYCE ALLAN, *The Sea-Horse and Its Relatives* (1958), a brief, supposedly popularized account of order members in Australian waters—of amazing scope, interest, and depth.

(W.Z.)

Gastronomy

Gastronomy is the art of selecting, preparing, serving, and enjoying fine food. Brillat-Savarin, the celebrated French aphorist and gastronomic authority of the 18th century, called gastronomy "the intelligent knowledge of whatever concerns man's nourishment."

Through the ages gastronomy has proved to be a stronger cultural force among the peoples of the world than linguistic or other influences. Today, the world may be divided into definite gastronomic regions, areas where distinctive cuisines prevail and common culinary methods are practiced. Most of Asia, for example, is in the region of the rice and coconut cuisine. Rice is the staple there, enjoyed by millions who speak a broad variety of languages and have little in common except their dietary habits. India and Indonesia are the lands of the spices, the distinctive feature of the cooking of those lands being the generous and imaginative use of spices to lend an added zest to foods. Olive oil is the common denominator of the Mediterranean cuisines. In Spain, south Italy, Portugal, Greece, and the Middle Eastern lands rimming the Mediterranean, it is the basic cooking fat. Northern Europe and North America use a variety of cooking fats: butter, cream, lard, goose and chicken fats, but the common gastronomic denominator throughout most of these lands is wheat, the basic crop. Latin America is the land of corn (maize) in every form.

The gastronomic regions of the world

This article covers the history of gastronomy from ancient civilizations through Greece and Rome, the Middle Ages, and the Italian Renaissance; the development of the great cuisines of France and of China; and the leading regional and national cuisines of the world.

HISTORY

The first significant step toward the development of gastronomy was the use of fire by primitive man to cook his food, which gave rise to the first meals as families gathered around the fire to share the foods they had cooked. Prehistoric cave paintings such as those in Les Trois-Frères in Ariège, in southern France, depict these early gastronomic events.

In the ancient civilizations of Assyria, Babylonia, Persia, and Egypt, the selection, preparation, service, and enjoyment of food was practiced on an elaborate scale. In the Book of Daniel the Bible tells how Belshazzar, the king of the Chaldeans, "made a great feast to a thousand of his lords, and drank wine before the thousand." He then commanded gold and silver vessels to be brought, and he and his wives, princes, and concubines drank wine and praised gods of gold, silver, brass, iron, wood, and stone.

Greece and Rome. In ancient Greece, the Athenians believed that mealtime afforded an opportunity to nourish the spirit as well as the body. They reclined on couches while eating and accompanied their repasts with music, poetry, and dancing. The Greeks provided a philosophical basis for good living, Epicureanism. It held that pleasure was the main purpose of life; but pleasure was not intended to imply the self-indulgence that it connotes today. The Epicureans believed that pleasure could best be achieved by practicing self-restraint and indulging as few desires as possible. Today the epicure is defined as one who is "endowed with sensitive and discriminating tastes in food and wine."

Epicurean restraint and Roman excesses

The ancient Greeks practiced moderation in all things, but the Romans were known for their excesses. Ordinary citizens subsisted on barley or wheat porridge, fish, and ground pine nuts (edible pine seeds), but the Roman emperors and wealthy aristocrats gorged themselves on a staggering variety of foods. They staged lavish banquets where as many as 100 different kinds of fish were served, as well as mountainous quantities of beef, pork, veal, lamb, wild boar, venison, ostrich, duck, and peacock. They ordered ice and snow hauled down from the Alps

to refrigerate their perishable foods, and they dispatched emissaries to the outposts of the Roman Empire in search of exotic delicacies. Mushrooms were gathered in France, and Juvenal describes a dinner at his patron's house where mullet from Corsica and lampreys from Sicily were served.

Yet whereas the Romans placed great value on exotic delicacies, they were not gastronomes in the true sense of the word. The term implies a sensitivity and discrimination that they lacked. The unbridled appetites of the Roman emperors and nobles often carried them to wild extremes. The emperor Caligula drank pearls dissolved in vinegar. Maximus reportedly consumed 60 pounds of meat in a day, and Albinus was alleged to have eaten 300 figs, 100 peaches, ten melons, and vast quantities of other foods at a single sitting. Lucullus was an immensely wealthy man who entertained so lavishly that his name became a symbol for extravagance and culinary excellence.

The vulgarity and ostentation of Roman banquets were satirized by Petronius in the *Satyricon*. A former slave named Trimalchio entertains at a gargantuan feast at which the guests are treated to one outlandish spectacle after the other. A donkey is brought in on a tray, encircled with silver dishes bearing dormice that have been dipped in honey. A huge sow is carved and live thrushes fly up from the platter. A chef cuts open the belly of a roast pig, and out pour blood sausages and blood puddings.

The Middle Ages. Through most of the Middle Ages banquets and feasts were characterized by their crudity and extravagance. In more affluent households in Gaul, for example, huge quarters of beef, mutton, and pork were served. Wild game was frequently served, including wild boar, hedgehog, roebuck, crane, heron, and peacock. Meats and other foods were cooked on spits and in caldrons positioned close by the tables. Diners seated themselves on bundles of straw and gobbled huge quantities of food, sometimes drawing knives from sheaths in their sword scabbards to saw off huge chunks of meat.

The Frankish emperor Charlemagne introduced a touch of refinement. He decorated the walls of his banquet halls with ivy. Floors were strewn with flowers. Tables were laid with silver and gold utensils, but food was coarse, and menus offered little variety. The subtle seasonings and sauces that later were to characterize French cooking were still unknown. An insight into the relative crudeness of the French culinary art during the Middle Ages is provided by *Le Viander* (c. 1375), the first French cookbook of importance. It was written by Guillame Tirel, more familiarly known as Taillevent, who served as chef to King Charles VI. Like the Romans, he used bread as the thickener for his sauces, instead of flour (which has been used for the past two centuries). He relied heavily on spices—such as ginger, cinnamon, cloves, and nutmeg (a Moorish influence via Spain and Italy). His menus consisted mostly of soups, meats, and poultry, which were so heavily seasoned that the taste of the food was largely obscured. French cooking ultimately would be distinguished by the subtlety of its seasonings and sauces and by the imaginative blend of textures and flavours. But in Taillevent's day the principal object of cooking was to disguise the flavour of the unrefrigerated food rather than to complement it.

The first French cookbook of importance

The Italian Renaissance. The turning point in the development of gastronomic excellence was the Italian Renaissance. By the beginning of the 15th century wealthy merchants in Italy were dining in elegant style. In place of the crude slabs of meat served elsewhere, they savoured such delicacies as mushrooms, garlic, truffles, tournedos (thick slices of beef fillets), lasagne, or ravioli. In wealthier households such delicacies were served in sumptuous style. When Vincenzo I, the duke of Mantua, celebrated his wedding feast in 1581, a guest reported that there were

100 ladies beautiful beyond measure and most richly garbed . . . on a handsome sideboard, was visible a perspective of divers cups, carafes and goblets, and such beautiful vessels of Venetian glass as I think would defy description . . .

The duke's wedding feast lasted three hours. Tables were laid with delicately embroidered cloths. The guest reported that

the first service from the sideboard was large salads decked out with various fantasies such as animals made of citron, castles of turnips, high walls of lemons; and variegated with slices of ham, mullet roes, herrings, tunny, anchovies, capers, olives, caviar, together with candied flowers and other preserves.

The duke's guest also reported that the tables were tastefully and imaginatively decorated.

There were three large statues in marzipan. One was the horse of Campidoglio come to life, the second Hercules with the lion, and the third a unicorn with its horn in the dragon's mouth.

The bounty of these tables was almost beyond belief.

The table was filled with many other things—jellies, blancmanges in half relief, spiced hard-bake, royal wafers, Milanese biscuits, pine kernels, minced meat, salami, cakes of pistachio nuts, sweet almond twists, flaky pastries . . . Indian turkey hens stuffed and roasted on the spit, marinated pullets, fresh grapes, strawberries strewn with sugar, wild cherries, and asparagus cooked in butter in various ways.

DEVELOPMENT OF FRENCH GRANDE CUISINE

The Italian influence on France. Italy has been called the mother of the Western cuisines, and perhaps its greatest contribution was its influence on France. The crucial event was the arrival of Catherine de Médicis in France in the 16th century. The great granddaughter of Lorenzo the Magnificent, Catherine married the young man who later was to become Henry II of France. She brought with her a retinue of Florentine cooks who were schooled in the subtleties of Renaissance cooking—in preparing such elegant dishes as aspics, sweetbreads, artichoke hearts, truffles, liver crépinettes, quennelles of poultry, macaroons, iced cream, and zabagliones. Catherine also introduced a new elegance and refinement to the French table. Although during Charlemagne's reign, ladies were admitted to the royal table on special occasions it was during her regime that this became the rule and not the exception. Tables were decorated with silver objects fashioned by Benvenuto Cellini. Guests sipped wine from fine Venetian crystal and ate off beautiful glazed dishes. An observer reported that

the Court of Catherine de' Médici was a veritable earthly paradise and a school for all the chivalry and flower of France. Ladies shone there like stars in the sky on a fine night.

Catherine de Médicis' Florentine cooks

Catherine's cousin, Marie de Médicis, who married Henry IV of France, also advanced the culinary arts. An important new cookbook appeared in her time. It was called *Le Cuisinier françois* (1652) and was written by La Varenne, an outstanding chef, who is believed to have learned to cook in Marie de Médicis' kitchens. La Varenne's cookbook reflected the great progress since the time of Taillevent. He was the first to present recipes in alphabetical order, and his book included the first instructions for vegetable cooking. By now spices were no longer used to disguise the taste of food. Truffles and mushrooms provided subtle accents for meats, and roasts were served in their own juices to retain their essential flavours. A basic point of French gastronomy was established; the purpose of cooking and of seasoning and spices was to bring out the natural flavours of foods—to enhance rather than disguise their flavour. In keeping with this principle, La Varenne cooked fish in a fumet, or stock made with the cooked fish trimmings (head, tail, and bones). The heavy sauces using bread as a thickener were discarded in favour of the roux, which is made of flour and butter or another animal fat.

The French view of cooking

Contributions of the Sun King. La Varenne's cookbook was a gastronomic landmark, but a long time was to pass before the French cuisine would achieve its modern forms. In pre-Revolutionary France extravagance and ostentation were the hallmarks of gastronomy. Perhaps the most extravagant Frenchman of the time was the Sun King, Louis XIV, who wined and dined in unparalleled splendour at his palace at Versailles. There the kitchens were some distance from the king's quarters; the food was prepared by a staff of more than 300 people, and was carried to the royal quarters by a procession headed by two archers, the lord steward, and other notables. As the cry "the King's meat," proclaimed their progress, an assemblage laden with baskets of knives, forks, spoons, toothpicks, seasonings, and spices, solemnly made their way to the king's quarters. Before the king dined tasters sampled the food to make certain it had not been poisoned. The king himself was such a prodigious eater that members of the court and other dignitaries considered it a privilege merely to stand by and watch him devour his food. His sister-in-law reported that at one meal he ate

four plates of different soups, an entire pheasant, a partridge, a large plateful of salad, mutton cut up in its juice with garlic, two good pieces of ham, a plateful of cakes, and fruits and jams.

Louis XIV is remembered principally for his extravagance, but he was genuinely interested in the culinary arts. He established a new protocol for the table; dishes were served in a definite order instead of being piled there in a jumble. The fork came to be widely used in France during his reign, and the manufacture of fine porcelain (Sèvres) was begun. The king himself hired a lawyer-agronomist, La Quintinie, to supervise the gardens at Versailles, and was intensely interested in the fruits and vegetables—strawberries, asparagus, peas, and melons—that were grown there. He paid special honour to members of his kitchen staff, conferring the title of officer on his cooks.

Table protocol and use of the fork

New order and logic. During the reigns of Louis XV and Louis XVI, culinary methods were refined and a new order and logic were introduced into the French cuisine. Brillat-Savarin noted that in the reign of Louis XV

there was generally established more orderliness of meals, more cleanliness and elegance, and those refinements of service, which having increased steadily to our own time . . .

By the time of the Revolution the interest in the culinary arts had intensified to the point where Brillat-Savarin could report:

The ranks of every profession concerned with the sale or preparation of food, including cooks, caterers, confectioners, pastry cooks, provision merchants and the like, have multiplied in ever-increasing proportions . . . New Professions have arisen; that, for example, of the pastry cook—in his domain are biscuits, macaroons, fancy cakes, meringues . . . The art of preserving has also become a profession in itself, whereby we are enabled to enjoy, at all times of the year, things naturally peculiar to one or other season . . . French cookery has annexed dishes of foreign extraction . . . A wide variety of vessels, utensils and accessories of every sort has been invented, so that foreigners coming to Paris find many objects on the table the very names of which they know not, nor dare to ask their use.

The Revolution changed almost every aspect of French life: political, economic, social, and gastronomic as well. In pre-Revolutionary days the country's leading chefs performed their art in wealthy aristocratic households. When the Revolution was over those who had survived the guillotine and remained in the country found employment in restaurants. The restaurant became the principal arena for the development of the French cuisine, and henceforth French gastronomy was to be carried forward by a succession of talented chefs, men whose culinary genius has not been matched in any other land. From the long roll of great French chefs, a select company have made a lasting contribution to gastronomy.

The Revolution and the rise of the restaurant

The great French chefs. The first, and in many ways the most important of all French chefs, was Marie-Antoine Carême, who has been called the Architect of the French Cuisine. As the French novelist and gastronome Alexandre Dumas *père* related the story, when Carême, born shortly before the Revolution, the 16th child of an impoverished stonemason, was only 11, his father took him to the gates of Paris one evening, fed him supper at a tavern, and abandoned him in the street. Fortunately for gastronomy, Carême found his way to an eating house, where he was put to work in the kitchen. Later he moved to a fine pastry shop where he learned to cook, read, and draw.

Carême was an architect at heart. He liked to stroll about Paris, admiring the great classic buildings, and he fell into the habit of visiting the Bibliothèque Royale, where he spent long hours studying prints and engravings of the great architectural masterpieces of Greece, Rome, and Egypt. He designed massive, elaborate table decorations called *pièces montées* (mounted pieces) as an outlet for his passionate interest in architecture. In an age of Neoclassicism his tables were embellished with replicas of classic temples, rotundas, and bridges constructed with spun sugar, glue, wax, and pastry dough. Each of these objects was fashioned with an architect's precision, for Carême considered confectionery to be "architecture's main branch," and he spent many months executing these designs, rendering every detail with great exactness.

Carême was employed by the French foreign minister, Charles-Maurice de Talleyrand, who was not only a clever diplomat but a gastronome of distinction. Talleyrand believed that a fine table was the best setting for diplomatic manoeuvring. Following his service with Talleyrand, Carême practiced his art for a succession of kings and nobles. He catered a series of feasts for Czar Alexander of Russia, was *chef de cuisine* to England's Prince Regent (who later became George IV), and finally was employed by the Baroness Rothschild in Paris.

Today Carême's monumental table displays seem ostentatious almost beyond belief, but he lived in an opulent age that was obsessed with classical architecture and literature. To appreciate him fully, it is necessary to put him in the context of his time. Before Carême, the French cuisine was largely a jumble of dishes; little concern was given to textures and flavours. Carême brought a new logic to the cuisine. "I want order and taste," he said. "A well displayed meal is enhanced one hundred per cent in my eyes." Every detail of his meals was planned and executed with the greatest of care. Colours were carefully matched, and textures and flavours carefully balanced. Even the table displays, mammoth as they were, were designed and carried out with an architect's precision.

Carême's voluminous cookbooks, *L'Art de la cuisine au dix-neuvième siècle* (1833) and *Le Pâtissier royal Parisien* (1815), included hundreds of recipes, menus for every day in the year, a history of French cooking, sketches for Carême's monumental *pièces montées*, instructions for garnishes, decorations, and tips on marketing and organizing the kitchen.

After Carême, the two men who probably had the greatest impact on French gastronomy and that of the world at large were Prosper Montagné and Georges-Auguste Escoffier. Montagné was one of the great French chefs of all time, and he achieved a secure place in gastronomic history by creating *Larousse Gastronomique* (1938), the basic encyclopaedia of French gastronomy. As a young man, while serving as an assistant chef at the Grand Hotel in Monte Carlo, he came to the conclusion that all *pièces montées*, superfluous garnitures and decorations, should be discarded. This was a drastic step, and Montagné's call might have gone unheeded had it not been brought to the attention of Escoffier. Escoffier was unimpressed at first. But his friend and literary collaborator Philéas Gilbert (also an outstanding chef) persuaded him that Montagné was right. Escoffier became a zealot for culinary reform, insisting on refining and modifying nearly every aspect of the cuisine. He simplified food decorations, greatly shortened the menus, accelerated the service, and organized teams of cooks to prepare the food more expertly and efficiently.

All of this progress was greatly facilitated by the introduction of the Russian table service around 1860. Before then, the service *à la française* was used. Under that method the meal was divided into three sections or services. All of the dishes of each service were brought in from the kitchen and arrayed on the table at once. Then, when this service was finished, all of the dishes of the next service were brought in. The first service consisted of everything from soups to roasts. The second service comprised cold roasts and vegetables, and the third was the desserts. Under the Russian table service, which was popularized by the great chef Félix Urbain-Dubois, each guest was served each course individually, while the food was still hot.

Escoffier invented scores of new dishes. One was *poularde Derby*, roast chicken with rice, truffles, and foie gras stuffing, garnished with truffles and foie gras. Other better known Escoffier inventions were *pêche Melba* and Melba toast, tributes to the Australian soprano Nellie Melba.

In naming some of his culinary creations after friends and celebrities Escoffier was following a well-established tradition. *Tournedos Rossini*, the tender slices of the heart of the fillet of beef, topped by foie gras and truffles, was named after the celebrated Italian composer. The composer Guiseppe Verdi and the actress Sarah Bernhardt were among those who were similarly honoured. Many famous dishes have taken their names from the chefs who invented them—*Sole Dugléré*, for example, was named after the chef Adolphe Dugléré, who presided at the Café Anglais in Paris in the middle of the 19th century. French dishes have also been named after their dominant colours, such as *carmen* or *cardinale*, which refers to a pinkish-reddish hue. Great events have also given dishes their names: chicken Marengo, for example, was named after the battle in 1800 in which Napoleon defeated the Austrians.

Escoffier created a cold dish called chicken Jeannette. It was named after a ship that was crushed by icebergs. Escoffier's creation was stuffed breast of chicken, and, in honour of the ill-fated ship, he served it on top of a ship carved out of ice.

The Grande Cuisine of France is the only structured and organized system of gastronomy in the world. Many dishes are interrelated, and their names contain clues as to their ingredients. For example, soups are broken down into "consommés" (clear soups), "potages" (thick soups), "crèmes" (cream soups), and "veloutés" (made with a white sauce). Within each of these categories there are sub-categories, depending upon the base used, the thickening agent, the garniture, the flavouring spice, herb, or alcohol, and other considerations.

Escoffier's fame today rests mostly on the cookbooks he wrote—*Le Livre des menus* (1924), *Ma Cuisine* (1934), and *Le Guide culinaire* (1921), written in collaboration with Gilbert—in which he codified the French cuisine in its modern form, setting down thousands of menus and clarifying the principles of French gastronomy. With the great hotel entrepreneur, César Ritz, he established a string of the world's most luxurious hostelries in Paris, Rome, Madrid, New York, Budapest (Hungary), Montreal, Philadelphia, and Pittsburgh (Pennsylvania).

Since Escoffier's day, French gastronomy has continued to evolve toward greater simplicity and order. The difference between the French cuisine of today and that of Escoffier probably is as great as that between Escoffier and Carême. Nowadays, people spend less time eating. Packaged and frozen foods have made great inroads—to the despair of the more fastidious gastronomes. Judging by the progress made in the so-called convenience foods, however, it is apparent that soon food technology will raise the eating standards of the general public in highly industrialized countries.

Use of wines and sauces. French gastronomy is distinguished not only by the genius of its chefs, but by well-established culinary practices as well. One of these practices is the use of fine wines, such as those produced in Bordeaux and Burgundy, as accompaniments to good food. The proper choice of wines—according to vintages, vineyards, shippers—is an indispensable part of French gastronomy.

In the preparation of food, the hallmark of French gastronomy is the delicate sauces that are used to enhance the flavours and textures. Sauces are prepared with stocks, or *fonds de cuisine*, "the foundations of cooking." These stocks are made by simmering meats, bones, poultry or fish trimmings, vegetables, and herbs in water to distill the essence of their flavours.

The basic sauces

There are literally hundreds of French sauces, but among the more familiar ones are the families of white sauces, brown sauces, and tomato sauces, the mayonnaise family, and the hollandaise family. White sauces, which are served with poultry, fish, veal, or vegetables, are prepared by making a white roux, a mixture of butter and flour, which is cooked and stirred to smoothness. Béchamel sauce is prepared by adding milk and seasoning to this thickening agent. Sauce velouté is made by mixing a fish, poultry, or veal stock with the roux. A broad variety of sauces is derived from these basic white sauces. Sauce mornay, the famous cheese sauce, for example, is simply sauce béchamel with grated cheese and seasonings. Sauce suprême is béchamel with cream. Sauce normande is prepared by mixing a fish velouté with tarragon and white wine or vermouth.

Brown sauces, which are served with red meats, chicken, turkey, veal, or game, are prepared by simmering a meat stock for many hours and then thickening it with a brown roux, a mixture of butter and flour cooked until it turns brown. Among the better known brown sauces are sauce ragout, which is flavoured with bone trimmings or giblets; sauce diable, which is seasoned with lots of pepper; sauce piquant, a brown sauce with pickles and capers, and sauce Robert, which is seasoned with mustard.

The hollandaise family is another important branch of French sauces. Hollandaise is closely related to mayonnaise. It is prepared by delicately flavouring warmed egg yolks with lemon juice and then carefully stirring in melted butter until the mixture achieves a creamy, yellow thickness. Sauce mousseline is made by adding whipped cream to hollandaise, while sauce bernaise also has an egg and butter base with tarragon, shallots, wine, vinegar, and pepper. Sauce vin blanc also belongs to the hollandaise family with the addition of a white-wine fish stock.

GASTRONOMY IN CHINA

Apart from the French cuisine, the highest expression of the gastronomic art is generally regarded to have been that of the Chinese. It is no accident that China and France should have had produced the world's most distinctive and respected cuisines. Both countries were naturally blessed with an abundance and rich variety of raw ingredients. In each of these countries gastronomy traditionally commanded great interest and respect. The intellectual, artistic, political, and financial leaders of China and France traditionally attached great importance to good eating. It has already been noted how this worked in the case of the Bourbon kings of France and with statesmen of such eminence as Talleyrand. In ancient China the preparation and service of food played an important part in court rituals. The first act of many emperors was to appoint a court chef, and once they were on the job these chefs strove mightily to outdo each other.

The gastronomic tradition

In ancient China, hunting and foraging supplied much of the food. Wild game, such as deer, elk, boar, muntjak (a small deer), wolf, quail, and pheasant, was eaten, along with beef, mutton, and pork. Vegetables such as royal fern, smartweed, and the leafy thistle (*Sonchus*), were picked off the land. Meats were preserved by salt-curing, pounding with spices, or fermenting in wine. To provide a contrast in flavours the meat was fried in the fat of a different animal.

As Chinese agriculture developed, a more varied fare began to emerge and tastes grew more refined. By the time of Confucius (551–479 BC) gastronomes of considerable sophistication had appeared on the scene. Confucius wrote of one of these fastidious eaters,

For him the rice could never be white enough. When it was not cooked right, he would not eat. When the food was not in season, he would not eat. When the meat was not cut correctly, he would not eat. When the food was not served with the proper sauce, he would not eat.

Emergence of a cuisine. Like all other forms of *haute cuisine*, classic Chinese cooking is the product of an af-

fluent society. By the 2nd century AD the Chinese court had achieved great splendour, and the complaint was heard that idle noblemen were lounging about all day, feasting on smoked meats and roasts.

By the 10th or 11th century a distinctive cuisine had begun to emerge, one that was to reach its zenith in the Ch' ing dynasty (1644–1912). This cuisine was a unique blend of simplicity and elegance. The object of cooking and the preparation of food was to extract from each ingredient its unique and most enjoyable quality.

As in the case of the French cuisine, the hors d'oeuvre set the tone of the meal. "The hors d'oeuvre must look neat," say the Chinese gastronomic authorities Tsuifeng Lin and her daughter Hsiang Ju Lin.

They are best served in matched dishes, each containing one item. Many people like to garnish the dishes with parsley and vegetables cut in the shape of birds, fish, bats, etc., or even to make baskets of flowers from food. These are all acceptable if kept under control, and if the rest of the meal is served in the same florid style. The worst offense would be to start with a florid display of food and then suddenly change style midway. . .

Common foods and traditions. Certain foods and culinary traditions are prevalent throughout most of the country. Rice is the staple except in the north, where wheat flour takes its place. Fish is extremely important in all regions. Pork, chicken, and duck are widely consumed, as well as large quantities of such vegetables as mushrooms, bamboo shoots, water chestnuts, and bean sprouts. The Chinese season their dishes with monosodium glutamate and soybean sauce, which takes the place of salt. Another distinctive feature of Chinese cooking is the varied and highly imaginative use of fat, which is prepared in many different ways and achieves the quality of a true delicacy in the hands of a talented Chinese cook. The Chinese take tea with their meals, whether green or fermented. Jasmine tea is served with flowers and leaves in small-handled cups.

The great Chinese schools. Traditionally, China is divided into five gastronomic regions, three of which are characterized by the great schools of Chinese cooking, Peking, Szechwan, and Chekiang-Kiangsu. The other two regions, Fukien and Kwangtung, are of lesser importance from a gastronomic point of view.

Peking. Peking is the land of fried bean curd and water chestnuts. In pre-Communist days vendors sold steamed bread and watermelon seeds in the streets. They dispensed buns called *paotse* that were stuffed with pork and pork fat, and *chiaotse*, or crescents, cylindrical rolls filled with garlic, cabbage, pork, scallions, and monosodium glutamate. Wheatcakes wrapped around a filling of scallions and garlic, and noodles with minced pork sauce are also traditional Peking specialties. But the greatest of all delicacies of this region is of course the Peking duck. This elaborate, world-renowned dish requires lengthy preparation and is served in three separate courses. In preparing it, the skin is first puffed out from the duck by introducing air between the skin and the flesh. The duck is then hung out to dry for at least 24 hours, preferably in a stiff, cold breeze. This pulls the skin away from the meat. Then the duck is roasted until the skin is crisp and brown. The skin is removed, painted with Hoisin sauce (a sweet, spicy sauce made of soybeans) and served inside the folds of a bun as the first course. The duck meat is carved from the bones and cut into slivers. Sautéed onions, ginger, and peppers are added to the duck meat and cooked with bean sprouts or bamboo slivers. This forms the second course. The third course is a soup. The duck bones are crushed and then water, ginger, and onion are added. The mixture is boiled, then drained, and the residue is cooked with cabbage and sugar until the cabbage is tender.

The preparation of Peking duck

Szechwan. The cooking of Szechwan in central China is distinguished by the use of hot peppers, which are indigenous to the region. The peppers lend an immediate sensation of fiery hotness to the food, but once this initial reaction passes, a mingled flavour of sweet, sour, salty, fragrant, and bitter flavour asserts itself. Fried pork slices, for example, are cooked with onions, ginger, red pepper, and soy sauce to achieve this aromatic hotness.

Chekiang and Kiangsu. The provinces of Chekiang and Kiangsu feature a broad variety of fish—shad, mullet, perch, and prawns. Minced chicken and bean-curd slivers are also specialties of these provinces. Foods are often arranged in pretty floral patterns before serving.

Fukien. Fukien, which lies farther south, features shredded fish, shredded pork, and *popia*, or thin bean-curd crepes filled with pork, scallions, bamboo shoots, prawns, and snow peas.

Kwangtung. To Americans perhaps, the most familiar form of Chinese cooking is that of Kwangtung, for Canton lies within this coastal province. Mushrooms, sparrows, wild ducks, snails, snakes, eels, oysters, frogs, turtles, and winkles are among the many exotic ingredients of the province. More familiar to Westerners are such Cantonese specialties as egg roll, egg foo yung, and roast pork.

CUISINES OF THE WORLD

Japanese. Nowhere has greater care and imagination been given to the presentation of food than in Japan. The delicacy and exquisiteness of Japanese table arrangements are matched only by the fragile beauty of Japanese painting.

The Japanese bride receives as many as 50 different kinds of dishes as wedding gifts and she may use a dozen at one meal. She will devote the most painstaking attention to the angle at which a sprig of green vegetable is propped against a lump of crabmeat, or the way a fish is garnished. Meals are served in many small dishes, but the total amounts offered each diner are large.

The waters around Japan abound with fish and shellfish, and Japanese seafood is regarded by many gourmets as the finest in the world. Fish is eaten raw (*sashimi*), broiled, or fried in deep fat (*tempura*), or salted and broiled (*shioyaki*). The popular *tempura* method of deep frying food was learned from Portuguese traders who came to Japan in the 16th century. Rice is the staple; it accompanies every meal. *Sushi*, or vinegared rice, is served with a variety of toppings and fillings, including mushrooms, squid, fish, shrimp, and caviar.

The Japanese like clear soups, garnished with eggs, vegetables, or seafood. The thicker "miso" soups are flavoured with fermented soybean paste. Japanese vegetables include bamboo shoots, snow peas, eggplant, mushrooms, and potatoes. The popular sukiyaki consists of beef and vegetables simmered in soy sauce. Pork or chicken may be substituted for the beef. Saké or fermented rice wine is the national drink, and tea is taken with all meals and at virtually all hours of the day.

The Japanese tea ceremony or chanoyu is a highly formalized ritual dating back to the 13th century. The tea is meticulously prepared and is accompanied by a variety of delicate seasonal dishes. Every aspect of the ceremony—the setting, the flavours and textures of foods, the colours and shapes of the containers, even the conversation—is carefully calculated to achieve the most harmonious and satisfying effect.

Indian. Spices are a distinctive feature of the cooking of India and Indonesia. In India, every good cook prepares a curry—a mixture of such fragrant powdered spices as cardamom, cinnamon, cloves, cumin, nutmeg, and turmeric. The spice blend is kept in a jar in the kitchen and is used to season all sorts of foods.

India is, of course, predominantly Hindu, and the Hindus have developed what is perhaps the world's greatest vegetarian cuisine. They use cereals, pulses (lentils, peas, and beans), and rice with great imagination to produce a widely varied but meatless cuisine. Indian cooks prepare delicious chutneys, highly seasoned vegetables and fruits used as side dishes that must be fresh to be fully appreciated. They also make such little delicacies as *idlis*, cakes of rice and lentils that are cooked by steaming; *pakoras*, vegetables fried in chickpea batter; and *jalebis*, pretzel-like tidbits made by deep-frying a batter of wheat and chickpea flour and soaked in a sweet syrup. *Raytas*, yogurt with fruits or vegetables, are another favourite.

Other specialties include *biryāni*, a family of complicated rice dishes cooked with meats or shrimp; *samosa*, a flaky, stuffed, deep-fried pastry; *korma*, lamb curry made with a thick sauce using crushed nuts and yogurt; *masala*, the dry or wet base for curry; and a great variety of breads and hot wafers, including *naan*, *pappadam*, *parāthas*, and *chapātīs*.

In southern India and especially in Andhra, the food is seasoned with fresh chili peppers and can be fiery hot. Lamb is the most important dish in northern India. It is prepared in hundreds of different ways as kabobs, curries, roasts, and in lamb and rice dishes. In pre-independence days the Mughal cuisine there ranked among the most lavish in the world. The Mughal cuisine developed during the Muslim empire of the great Mughal kingdom. It is based, mostly because of religious and geographic limitations, on lamb. The preparations are mostly roasted, barbecued dishes, also kabobs and the so-called dry curries, versus the stew-type cooking of the south.

In India festivals and holidays are marked by feasting and revelry. Among the more prominent festivals are Onam, a rice harvest celebration; Dīwālī which marks the beginning of the Hindu New Year; Dashera, which marks the triumph of the good Prince Rama over evil; and Holī, the festival of lights, which honours Lord Krishna, an incarnation of the god Vishnu. Feasting and the offering of food to gods and friends are a highlight of these festivals.

The Pacific and Southeast Asia. The cuisine of the Pacific and Southeast Asia is a fascinating melange of raw ingredients, methods, and dishes with a strong influence of the Chinese cuisine. The most important ingredients to tie together this vast area are the coconut, which is used in every one of these countries; rice, which is the basic food everywhere except in the Philippines; native spices and herbs, especially the omnipresent ginger and chili. The skillful use of condiments and relishes makes these countries gastronomically individual entities.

A Hawaiian staple is the taro bulb, which is the main ingredient for many dishes of the famous luau feasts, chopped and steamed alone, or mixed with other ingredients, often wrapped in ti leaves. Poi is also made out of the taro root, after being peeled, cooked, and mashed into a paste.

Another famous delicacy is *lomi lomi*, a fresh salmon that is hand massaged to break down its tissues and remove the salt, and then the chunks are mixed with onion and tomatoes. Besides the stone-baked pig, which is always a part of the luau, and several other local specialties, the Hawaiians adapted a number of Chinese, Japanese, Korean, and Indian dishes, together with a great many standard U.S. dishes.

Indonesia consists of several thousand islands, yet its cuisine is almost unified by the use of coconut. It is employed as a vegetable, main course, ingredient, cooking fat, relish, fruit, and even beverage in the popular *tjendol* throughout the islands. Although 300 years of Dutch occupation, a sizable Chinese population, and Portuguese merchants had a very strong influence on the islands' cooking style, Indonesia still can boast of a unique cuisine. Because rice (*nasi*) is the most important part of their meals, all other preparations are actually served to surround and enhance the rice itself. The Dutch themselves created *rijsttafel*, which formalized into an almost endless procession of beautifully arranged, carefully organized dishes, ranging from sweet to sour, from mild to very spicy, from cold to hot.

Each guest was given two plates and was served a long succession of excellent dishes. On one plate a meat or fish preparation would be served, and the other would be filled with rice. The entire meal, with all its courses, took from two to three hours. Since Indonesia gained independence, the *rijsttafel* has been replaced by the *prasmanan*, a lengthy, buffet-style meal also featuring scores of dishes.

One of the nationally popular preparations is *nasi goreng* that originates in China's fried-rice concept. In the Indonesian version, however, most of the meats, vegetables, and garnishes surround the pile of fried rice and only the diner mixes them while eating it, allowing many fascinating taste and texture combinations.

Although there are many dishes common to all areas, each region has its own specialties and style of cooking. The West Javanese cooking is rather mild and tends to be much simpler than that of Central Java, which favours very hot, rich, and sweet flavours. East Java, on the other hand, is the place where the spicing becomes very complex and subtle, and the Balinese enjoy many of the dishes forbidden to the Muslim population. For instance, the Bali Hindu religion allows the eating of pork, and *sáte babi*, the little skewers of charcoal-grilled pork bits, is one of the more interesting of their preparations.

One of the most essential elements of an Indonesian meal is the *sambals*. These are spicy-hot condiments that are served separately to be mixed with the various foods to make it as "fiery" as the individual desires. *Krupuk*, the deep-fried shrimp wafers, also originated in Indonesia before turning up in other nations' cuisines. Few Indonesian meals exist without *gado-gado*, an interesting melange of cooked and raw vegetables and bean cake with a sauce made of peanuts, coconut, and spices. Sumatra and Malaysia absorbed much of the Arab and Indian culinary influences. *Rendang*, for instance, is a beef stew that absorbs a large amount of coconut milk, using the same technique as some of the so-called dry curries of India. *Gulai* is this area's favourite version of liquid-type curry so common in India.

The Philippine food is much simpler than many of the other Pacific and Southeast Asian cuisines. Although the four centuries of Spanish domination brought considerable influence to this part of the world, it does have some specialties that can be called its own. Perhaps most typical of these is the fish paste called *bagoong* and the liquid flavouring sauce *patis*. Both are based on fermented seafood and, depending on the area or the household, their variety is almost limitless. Generally speaking, a sour-salty taste is the single most characteristic taste of the Philippines.

Perhaps the strongest Chinese influence can be detected in Vietnam, which was dominated or ruled by China throughout the 2nd millennium. The degree of influence is discernible even in the manner of eating. For instance, this is the only country in the entire area of the Pacific and Southeast Asia where the food is eaten with chopsticks. *Nuoc mam*, a flavouring sauce, is used in many dishes and, although it is related to the Philippine *patis*, it really is a specifically Vietnamese flavour, based again on fermented salted fish and spices. Almost every nation's southern inhabitants prefer their food spicier than those in the northern region and Vietnam is no exception. The tie-in perhaps between the two is the use of fish, which is the most important part of the daily diet. The recent French occupation in Vietnam mostly contributed to the level of the gastronomy of the upper classes, without influencing much of the average housewife's cooking.

One of the most complex and structured cuisines of the entire area is the one of Thailand. The fact that the Thais lived in comparative peace and political independence had beneficial influence on their gastronomy, together with the fact that, just as in China and France, the ruling classes were actively interested in gastronomy. Having basically the same ingredients to work with as Indonesia, Malaysia, or India, the categories of the Thai repertoire are not unlike those countries, but the subtleties and complexities of flavour and texture are often superior. For instance, *nam prik*, the spicy Thai condiment, has even more varieties than the *sambals* do with many more ideas employed in their combinations. *Kaeng* is a liquid stew (or perhaps soup-stew) to be mixed with rice. It is very strongly related to the liquid curries, but again the repertoire of *kaengs* is infinitely larger than almost any other food family in Southeast Asia. Within the formalized gastronomy, the Chinese and Indian influences blend in with such artistry that the emerging cuisine of Thailand is truly its own.

Middle Eastern. Eggplant, olives, and yogurt are widely eaten in all Middle Eastern countries. Chickpeas are toasted or ground up. Lamb is the staple meat throughout the region.

The Turkish influence is still dominant in the countries of the old Ottoman Empire: Turkey, Greece, Bulgaria, and part of Yugoslavia. Vine leaves stuffed with rice and meat are popular. They are called *dolma* in Turkey. *Börek*, a turnover filled with meat or cheese, is another favourite. *Şişkebabı* (shishkebab), skewered mutton or lamb, is enjoyed in all these countries, as is *kofte*, a lamb pattie. Yogurt dishes and a sweet known as halvah are commonly found. A favourite dessert is baklava, a rich pastry filled with nuts and dipped in honey or syrup. (Baklava was brought by Turkish invaders to Hungary in the 16th century where it became strudel.)

The Arab states of the Middle East and North Africa share many fine dishes. Among these is the hotly seasoned eggplant dip called *bābā qhanūj*. Other dishes common to the Arab countries include *hummus bī tahīnah*, chickpeas with a sesame paste; *tabbūlah*, a salad of onions, chopped tomatoes, radishes, parsley, and mint; and *kibbi*, a ground mixture of wheat and lamb.

African. The great indigenous dish of North Africa is couscous—steamed wheat or seminola grains—served with meats, poultry, and vegetables piled on top of and around the grain. Another is *brik*, a deep-fried pastry turnover stuffed with fish or meat and a whole egg. A sampler from this continent would include, in East Africa, peanut (groundnut) soup and beef and cassava stew, cooked with coconut, chilies, and coriander; in West Africa, fish *imojo*, a fish and seafood salad; in Ethiopia, *yetemola cheguara*, steamed stuffed whole tripe. South Africans prepare a cinnamon- and clove-flavoured stew called lamb and pumpkin *bredi*, and date and onion salad. Angola has a yellow coconut pudding in which the colour comes from the predominance of eggs among the ingredients.

Spanish and Portuguese. Spain and Portugal have much in common from a culinary point of view. Olive oil is the cooking oil of both countries. Cod is widely used. The *cocido*, a heavy stew of boiled chicken, meats, and vegetables, is Spain's national dish. In Portugal it is called the *cozido*.

But the two countries also have their own distinctive dishes, which vary greatly from one region to the next. The paella is perhaps Spain's best-known dish. It is a colourful combination of rice, chicken, pork, clams, mussels, shrimp, peppers, sausages, and peas. The home of the paella is Valencia, but the dish varies from one province to the next. Another regional specialty is the *zarzuela*, a Catalonian seafood medley, a stew of fish, lobster, shrimp, scallops, clams, ham, almonds, white wine, and saffron. Fish is popular throughout Spain, especially cod, hake, and red snapper. Many people consider the Basque-style cooking (*à la Vasca*) the best in Spain. It is a surprisingly sophisticated cuisine for one based on ancient shepherds' cooking. *Tapas* are appetizers served in Spanish bars, and often there are several dozen varieties from which to choose. *Jamón serrano*, a mountain-cured ham; chorizo sausages; gazpacho, a cold puree of vegetable soup; and empanada meat pies are some of the highlights of the quite remarkable cuisine of Spain.

The Portuguese kitchen produces somewhat spicier and richer foods, favouring hearty soups, marinated seafoods, braised meats, and such spices as cumin and coriander. The entire Iberian Peninsula is strongly influenced by the honey-almond paste, figs, and dates of the Moors.

Italian. The Italians are especially fond of pasta *asciutta* (an unending variety of dried noodles), the huge assortment of hot and cold appetizers known as antipasti; sausage and salami; *gelati e granite*, ice creams and ices; and *caffè espresso*, coffee made by forcing steam through the coffee grounds.

Italy, like France or China, has many culinary regions, but basically the north's staple is rice and butter and the south lives on pasta and cooks with olive oil. Cooking techniques are less important than the quality of the raw ingredients.

Bologna's rich cooking is perhaps the best of the

Culinary influence of the old Ottoman Empire

northern cuisine with its famed *tagliatelle*, *tortellini*, and other freshly made noodle preparations, egg pastas, sausages, and complex main courses. Piedmont supplies many of the finest chefs to the luxury restaurants around the world. Its local white truffles and Fontina cheese are the base for their *fonduta*, the famous hot melted cheese casserole eaten with bread bits.

Lombardy cooks exclusively with butter, replacing the pasta with rice and corn-flour polenta, and blends successfully the cooking style of several of the northern provinces. Genoese cooking's most characteristic flavour comes from the use of basil leaves pounded into a sauce called *pesto* together with cheese, garlic, pine nuts, and olive oil. Florence is famous for its *Chianina* beef cattle that provide the meat for its *bistecca alla Fioentina*.

Alla Romana-type cooking produces the best gnocchis, *calamaretti* (baby squid), *abbacchio* (young lamb, usually roasted with rosemary), and vegetable preparations. Naples represents the best gastronomy of southern Italy with the use of pasta, crusty white bread, robust tomato sauces, mozzarella, and other types of cheese. Generally speaking, the array of fresh herbs and some of the finest vegetables and fruits of Europe, fine seafood, and the liberal use of fresh herbs create the best moments of the Italian gastronomy.

Austro-Hungarian. The gastronomic regions of the world existing today do not conform to geographic or political divisions. A good example is the Austro-Hungarian cuisine, a culinary entity the boundaries of which have not been discernible on maps since the end of World War I. This gastronomical region comprises the old Austro-Hungarian Empire. It includes Austria and Hungary, as well as parts of Romania, Yugoslavia, and Czechoslovakia. The people of these countries live in different political, economic, and social systems and speak different languages, but their culinary heritage remains as a link between them. *Gulyás*, or goulash, occurs in varying forms in all of these countries. Wiener schnitzel (breaded veal cutlets) is eaten throughout the area. Coffeehouses are popular throughout this part of the world. In Austria a traveller will encounter *nockerl;* in Hungary, he may eat *nokedli;* in Czechoslovakia he will find a similar food under the name *noky*, in Serbia under the name *nokla*. In Hungary the *nokedli* would accompany *pörkölt*, a stew made by browning onion in lard and adding paprika, or a *paprikás*, similar to the above, but with the addition of sweet or sour cream. As dessert he would order *Rigó Jancsi*, a chocolate square glazed with chocolate and filled with chocolate mousse. Cakes, tortes, and desserts are the glory of this cuisine. Prune dumplings, strudels, the coffee ring called *gugelhupf*, and the Dobos torte, a caramel-topped cake filled with chocolate-cocoa cream, are enjoyed. And one of the greatest glories of Vienna's old empire is Sacher torte, a chocolate sponge cake with a touch of apricot jam, iced with a bittersweet chocolate.

Each section developed its own specialties. Czechoslovakia, for instance, cooks *játernice* (a sausage made with innards), bakes *kolačić* (coffee cake), and makes *povidla* (prune jam). Austria offers *Backhendl* (breaded-fried spring chicken), *Tafelspitz* (the boiled beef considered the finest, a cut near the tail of the steer), Linzer torte (a ground almond and jam lattice cake), *buchteln* (jelly buns), and *Palatschinken* (thin pancakes with various fillings). In Yugoslavia there are the *čevapčići* (charcoal-grilled meatballs), *gibanica* (cheesecake), *lonac* (a Bosnian meat and vegetable stew), and *šumadija* (a tea made with plum brandy and caramelized sugar).

Slavic. Russia is the mother country of the Slavic cuisine, another culinary entity that does not exist on the map. This cuisine comprises the Soviet Union, Armenia, Poland, Albania, and parts of Yugoslavia and Bulgaria. A Russian-speaking traveller through this region might find it difficult to make himself understood, but he could order the familiar borsch, a beet or cabbage soup, wherever he went. He might dine on blintzes (stuffed pancakes) or *zrazy* (stuffed fried fish or seafood). He could enjoy beef stroganoff, beef cooked with onions in sour cream, or sample a seafood pie called *rakov*. Wherever he went, vodka would be the most popular drink.

The Russians developed *zakusky*, their equivalent of the French hors d'oeuvres. *Potage Bagration* (cream of veal with asparagus tips) is also part of the French Grande Cuisine together with many other dishes the French chefs learned in the Russian court kitchens. Interesting specialties are the *botvinya* (green vegetable soup with a fish base), *solyanka* (cucumber soup), *pelemeni* (Siberian meat dumplings, boiled, fried, and served with sour cream), *kasha* (buckwheat porridge), *holubtsi* (Ukrainian stuffed cabbage), *bitki* (meat- or fish balls with strong spices), *packha* (cottage-cream cheesecake with candied fruits made in a pyramid shape for Easter), and *babka* (a round coffee cake).

German. The emphasis of the cuisine of Germany and its neighbours is on "hearty" foods—roast meats, dumplings, fish dishes, cream sauces, puddings, and rich desserts. The Germans eat sauerbraten, a marinated pot roast with a sweet-and-sour sauce, the earthy hasenpfeffer (rabbit stew), *Königsberger klopse* (a fancy meatball), *badischer Hecht* (a sour cream baked pike), and *Schweinebraten mit pflaumen und apfeln* (roast pork with prune and apple stuffing). They like sausages; sauerkraut (fermented cabbage); dumplings; thick soups made from potatoes, peas, or lentils; herring; and roast meats, or braten. They wash these foods down with great quantities of beer, and for dessert they prefer puddings, fruit pancakes, or dumplings, egg custards, jellies topped with whipped cream, the medieval invention marzipan (an almond paste confection), lebkuchen (a kind of gingerbread), and *Baumkuchen* (the tree-cake baked on a special horizontal spit).

Scandinavian. Fish is a mainstay of the Scandinavian diet. It is prepared in many different ways; a favourite appetizer is *gravlax*, salmon marinated in salt and dill and accompanied by a mustard sauce. Swedish pancakes are popular and are served with lingonberries or fruit preserves.

Sweden's great contribution to international eating is the smorgasbord, literally a "bread-and-butter table," but actually a sumptuous feast of three courses. The first course is herring—filleted, pickled, baked, jellied, stewed, or prepared in many other different ways. Cold meats comprise the second course, whereas the third course is made up of Swedish meatballs and other hot dishes.

Danish open sandwiches, called *smørrebrød*, became popular all over the world. There are many fine dishes in these north European countries, such as the following: *nyponsoppe* (Swedish rose-hip, almond, and whipped-cream soup), *vorshmack* (ground meat, herring, and onion cooked Finnish style), "Jansson's Temptation" (a Swedish potato and anchovy casserole), *frikadeller* (a Danish mixed ground meat hamburger, sautéed in butter), *kalakukko* (a Finnish bird-shaped pie stuffed with fish), *sandkage* (Danish sand cake), and *krumkage* (a Norwegian Christmas cookie). Aquavit, the favourite grain or potato spirit of Scandinavia, is an ideal beverage for the cold seasons.

British. The English like roast beef with the muffin or pie known as Yorkshire pudding; steak and kidney pie, and veal and ham pie are other English favourites. They eat fish—haddock, mackerel, and smoked kipper—especially fish-and-chips, or deep-fried potatoes. They are also fond of jellies, jams, marmalade, hot cross buns, crumpets, and scones.

Traditional fare in the British Isles would include beef tea (a beef extract), whitebait (miniature fish, fried and eaten as snacks), boxty (Irish potato pancakes), brawn (aspic made with pork bits), cockaleekie (Scottish hen and leek soup), bubble and squeak (chopped, fried leftover meat and vegetables), angels on horseback (grilled oysters wrapped in bacon), kedgeree (a casserole of smoked fish, rice, and eggs), shepherd's pie (ground lamb and beef with onion and topped with mashed potatoes), crumpets (hot muffins), banbury cake (a spiced flat cake made with dried fruits), fool (a fruit custard), and syllabub (a dessert made with whipped cream, lemon, wine, and sugar). The savoury, a nonsweet course served instead of or after the dessert, is an interesting custom in the British Isles. Bitter is the most popular English beer

The sumptuous bread-and-butter table

in pubs. In the winter, hard cider, a fermented apple juice in varying strengths, is often preferred.

Latin American. Corn (maize) is the culinary common denominator of Latin America. Ground into meal, it is used in Mexico to prepare the corn pancakes known as tortillas. Tortillas provide a variety of other Mexican specialties. Enchiladas are tortillas dipped in sauce, then fried and rolled up with a filling of pork or chicken. *Tostados* are tortillas fried crisp and sprinkled with onion, chili peppers, grated cheese, or meat. *Quesadillas* are tortillas folded over a filling of meat, beans, cheese, or vegetables. Another, different use of corn is for tamales, which are steamed, filled corn husks.

Chili peppers are widely used to season Latin-American dishes. Beans are another distinctive food. Brazil's national dish, the *feijoada completa*, consists of a bed of rice with black beans, sausages, beef tongue, spareribs, and dried beef, sprinkled with toasted manioc meal, and garnished with orange slices. Argentina is famous for its beef. Empanadas served there are beef-filled turnovers. A favourite dessert in all of these lands is flan, or caramel custard.

North American. The United States is a culinary, as well as racial, melting pot. European, Middle Eastern, African, and Oriental influences are evident. In New York, for example, can be found almost any kind of food on earth. Outside New York, Greek food and Cuban food are common in Florida, German food in the cities of the Middle West, Chinese food in California, Huguenot food in Charleston, South Carolina, African food in the South and most other parts of the country, Mexican and Spanish food in the Southwest, and Portuguese dishes in New England—all of it adapted and modified to suit the local tastes.

Outside the great metropolitan areas, American food used to have a distinctive regional character. New England was famous for its clam and lobster dishes, its New England boiled dinner, and its red flannel hash. The South, with its fried chicken and many forms of cornbread, was one of the country's most distinctive culinary regions. The Far West prided itself on its Dungeness crab, abalone, fish, and shellfish.

But as communications and transportation have improved, and packaged and frozen foods have come into being, people all over the country read the same recipes in newspapers or magazines. They go to cooking schools where the same principles are taught, and they watch the same cooking lessons on television. As a result, regional distinctions have tended to fade and cooking has become more uniform all the time.

North America has contributed many fine gastronomic institutions. North American cities such as New York, New Orleans, San Francisco, and Montreal have produced many excellent restaurants and hotels. The Mississippi riverboats of the 19th century were floating gourmet palaces. But the unique American contribution to gastronomy has been quick-service and convenience foods. The first cafeteria came into being in San Francisco during the Gold Rush of 1849. The first automated cafeterias were introduced in New York and Philadelphia. Coffee shops, sandwich counters, and drive-in restaurants are uniquely American institutions. Vegetables, fruits, and meats are quick-frozen, packaged, and shipped to stores thousands of miles away. Perhaps the ultimate in packaged, convenience foods is the capsuled meals provided for United States astronauts for their journeys to the moon.

BIBLIOGRAPHY. PROSPER MONTAGNE, *Larousse Gastronomique* (1938), the most authoritive contemporary encyclopaedia of food, wine, and cookery, from prehistoric stages to the modern day; J.A. BRILLAT-SAVARIN, *Physiologie du goût* (1826), classic that set the stage for thinking about dining as an experience and a form of art, and its philosophy and aphorisms became the foundation of modern gastronomy; ANDRE L. SIMON, *A Concise Encyclopaedia of Gastronomy* (1952), a most complete history relating to its subject, written by the dean of food and beverage writing; J.J. WEBER, *Universal-Lexicon der Kochkunst*, 3 vol. (1913), the German viewpoint expressed in a concise encyclopaedia; U. DUBOIS and E. BERNARD, *La Cuisine classique*, 2 vol. (1856), perhaps the only work that perhaps no one questions as the finest expression of the Golden Age of the French Grande Cuisine; ALEXIS SOYER, *The Pantaropheon* (1853), a world history of food and its preparation from the early ages with many arbitrary but important observations on gastronomy; ABRAHAM HAYWARD, *The Art of Dining* (1889), a small book containing much of the material on the 18th- and 19th-century gastronomy, chefs, and related subjects that has since been used in countless books; GEORGE H. ELLWANGER, *The Pleasures of the Table* (1902), a popular book with considerable original material on eating and drinking habits and gastronomic influences of the past; P. NORTON SHAND, *A Book of Food* (1928), a highly personal approach to gastronomy, manners, and foods throughout the world.

(G.L.)

Gastropoda

The class Gastropoda, a subgroup of the phylum Mollusca, comprises the snails. Gastropod, which means "belly-footed," refers to the broad tapered foot on which these animals glide.

The gastropods include land, freshwater, and marine forms. Land gastropods lacking shells are commonly called slugs; marine forms lacking shells are known as nudibranchs or sea slugs.

Because they occupy such a wide range of habitats and show such different ways of living, gastropods are a difficult group to describe succinctly. A few are used as food, a very few transmit animal diseases (only a fraction of these carry human diseases), and some have shells used as ornaments or in making jewelry; most, however, act as scavengers, removing dead animal and plant matter.

GENERAL FEATURES

Abundance and distribution. The gastropods constitute the largest group of mollusks in terms of species and are one of the few animal groups to inhabit successfully all three environmental systems—ocean, freshwater, and land. Of the perhaps 50,000 species, 23,000 are marine, 22,000 are terrestrial, and 5,000 are freshwater. Gastropods have been dredged from the deepest ocean trenches and from glacial lakes in the Himalayas. A few land-snail species, such as *Vitrina*, can be found crawling on snowbanks in Alpine meadows; others inhabit the driest deserts. In these hostile regions a snail survives by retreating into its shell and waiting for the short, infrequent wet conditions during which it can feed and reproduce. Often the wait is long: specimens of the Egyptian desert snail (*Eremina desertorum*) have survived four years, and some Mexican desert snails have lived for six years without food or water in museum collections. Their period of survival under natural conditions is probably even longer.

Snails and slugs are sometimes especially abundant. Millions of some brackish-water species occur on mud flats. An acre of British farmland may have 250,000 slugs; one region in Panama averaged 7,500,000 land snails per acre. Despite this, gastropods often pass unobserved. Snails are marginally terrestrial, being active in areas or periods of high humidity. They are conspicuous and abundant only on the seashore and in shallow ocean waters. Even in these habitats their shells, often covered with algae and debris, look like bits of encrusted rock.

Size and appearance. The size range of gastropods is considerable. Some marine snails (*Homalogyra*) and forest-litter snails (*Punctum*) are less than 0.04 of an inch (one millimetre) long as adults. The largest land snail, the African *Achatina achatina*, is almost eight inches long; the largest marine species, the Australian *Megalatractus aruanus*, may exceed two feet in shell length. The longest snail, however, is *Parenteroxenos doglieli*, which lives as a parasite in the body cavity of a sea cucumber: it is almost 52 inches (132 centimetres) long, though only 0.2 inch (0.5 centimetre) in diameter. Probably 90 percent of all gastropods are less than one inch long.

The basic groups of gastropods are the prosobranchs, marine and land dwellers with a protective covering (operculum) to plug the opening in the shell and with a rather simple body structure; the opisthobranchs, marine

Corn dishes, beans, and chili peppers

Quick-service and frozen foods

Survival under desert conditions

Snails as
food

species many of which show a reduction in both the shell and visceral mass; and the pulmonates, land, freshwater, and marine dwellers with a "lung," or pulmonary, cavity and more complex body structures. These groups, which separated over 350,000,000 years ago, have undergone considerable evolution. Gastropods show a great variety of structure (Figure 1) and habits and are thus an excellent group to demonstrate evolutionary principles. The snails display a wide variety of shells, from those of the colourfully decorated tree snails of the tropics to the plain drab shells of pond snails of temperate zones.

Importance to man. From earliest times, man has utilized many snails as food. Periwinkles (*Littorina*) from Europe and South Africa, queen conchs (*Strombus gigas*) in the West Indies, abalones (*Haliotis*) in California and Japan, and turban shells (*Turbo*) in the Pacific are the most frequently eaten snails. Occasionally limpets are used, and many species of whelks are caught for fish bait. Land snails of the family Helicidae have been eaten in the Middle East and Europe since prehistoric times. Today, many tons of the European edible snails *Helix aspersa* and *H. pomatia*, in addition to several species of *Otala* and *Eobania* from Morocco and Algeria, are exported to the United States as food. During World War II, the Japanese introduced the giant African snail (*Achatina fulica*) onto various Pacific Islands to serve as food for their troops.

In some places, introductions of *Achatina* and *Helix* have resulted in damage to crops and gardens by these rapidly multiplying snails. California orange groves are plagued by *Helix aspersa*, and in the eastern United States many slugs accidentally introduced from Europe are a great nuisance in gardens. Freshwater snails of the family Bythinidae sometimes become so numerous that they clog the filter systems of big city pumping stations.

Shells of certain snails are highly prized by collectors, and a few rare species may be very highly valued. The operculum of some *Turbo* species is used in making earrings; cameos are cut from the shell of the Red Sea snail *Cassis rufa*. Abalone shells are used in many cultures for decorative purposes; the shell of the golden cowrie served at one time as a badge of a chief in Fiji. Shells have been used as money: at one time the price of a bride in West Africa was 100,000 cowries.

More serious matters concern the few freshwater snails (*Pomatiopsis, Bulinus, Biomphalaria*) that serve as intermediate hosts for parasitic worms of man. More than half the deaths in Egypt, for example, are at least in part caused by the ravages of schistosomiasis, a disease caused by minute blood flukes (schistosomes) with a complicated life cycle. Both snails and flukes are most common in areas where fields are irrigated. The building of dams for paddy irrigation can increase the disease percentage from 5 percent to over 90 percent in less than four years.

Snails as
intermediate
hosts of
disease
organisms

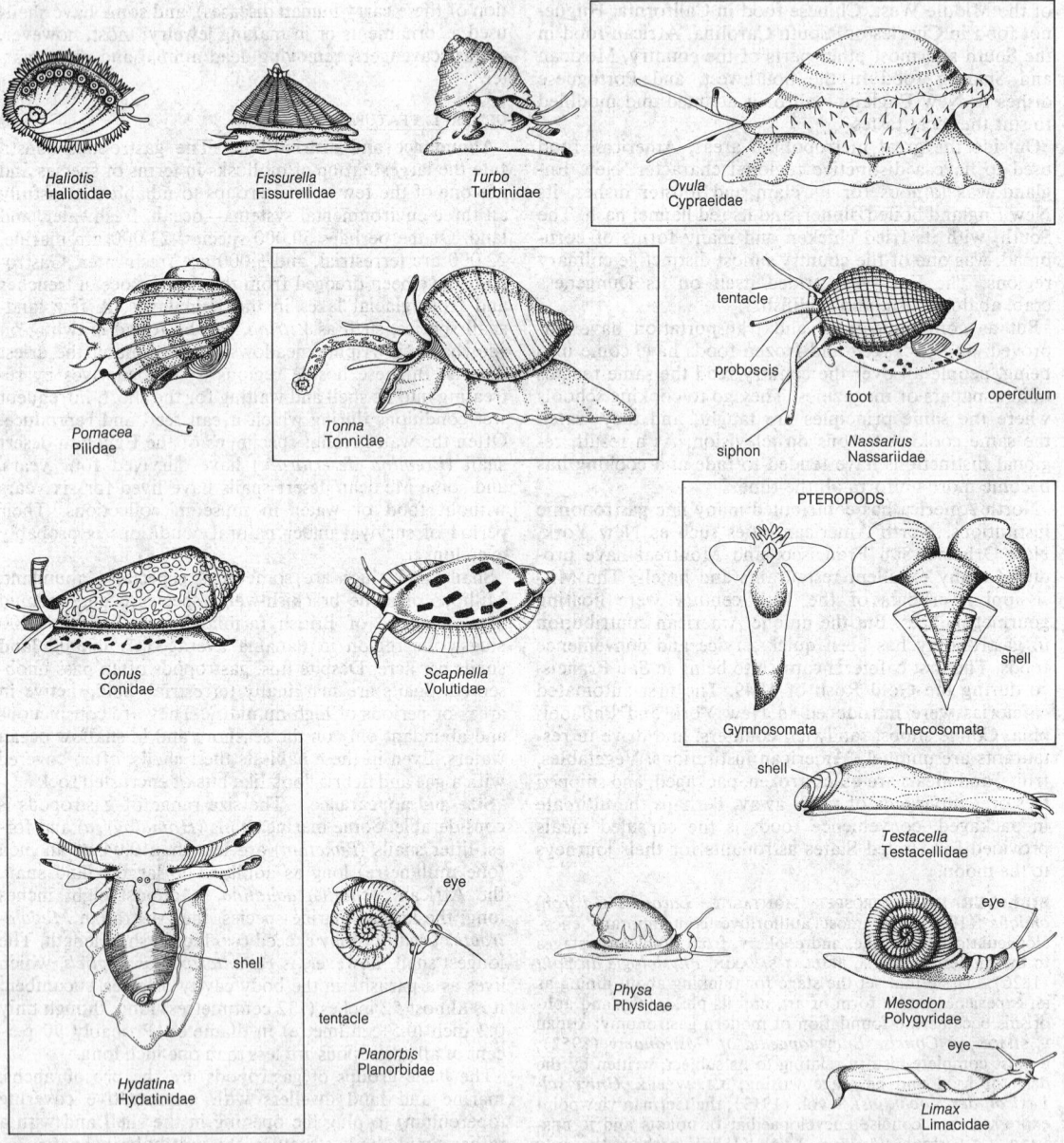

Haliotis
Haliotidae

Fissurella
Fissurellidae

Turbo
Turbinidae

Ovula
Cypraeidae

Pomacea
Pilidae

Tonna
Tonnidae

tentacle

proboscis

foot

operculum

siphon

Nassarius
Nassariidae

Conus
Conidae

Scaphella
Volutidae

PTEROPODS

shell

Gymnosomata

Thecosomata

shell

Testacella
Testacellidae

shell

eye

tentacle

Planorbis
Planorbidae

Physa
Physidae

eye

Mesodon
Polygyridae

Hydatina
Hydatinidae

eye

Limax
Limacidae

Figure 1: Diversity among gastropods.

Schistosomes also parasitize birds and mammals. Occasionally, swimmers in the United States develop a skin rash called swimmer's itch, resulting from bird schistosomes trying, only partly successfully, to penetrate human skin. They die in the upper skin layers, and their decomposition causes the local infection. Other health problems are caused by several snails and slugs (*e.g.*, *Bradybaena*, *Angustipes*, *Veronicella*) that serve as intermediate hosts for the rat lungworm. If an infected land snail or slug is accidentally chopped up in a salad and eaten, the worm can migrate to the brain and encyst, causing moderate to severe damage. Poisonous cone shells, from tropical oceans, have caused human deaths through collectors' careless handling of the living snail.

Most gastropods, however, are useful to man in that they help break down the dead bodies of plants and animals into substances that can be used by plants to manufacture new organic compounds. In both field and forest, as in ponds, rivers, and oceans, gastropods are an important part of this decomposer group.

NATURAL HISTORY

Because the gastropods occupy such a bewildering array of habitats and exist under such a wide range of environments, it is virtually impossible to present a generalized living pattern. Instead, emphasis is given in this section to the evolutionary shifts with respect to feeding mechanisms, life cycle and reproduction, and ecology.

Feeding mechanisms. As in all molluscan groups except the bivalves, gastropods have a peculiar organ called an odontophore at the anterior end of the digestive tract. Generally, this organ forms a broad ribbon (radula) covered with a few to many thousand "teeth" (denticles). The radula is used in feeding: muscles extrude the radula from the mouth, spread it out, and then pull it back into the mouth carrying particles or pieces of food and debris into the esophagus. Although attached at both ends, the radula grows continuously during the gastropod's life, with new rows of denticles being formed posteriorly to replace the worn denticles cast off at the anterior end. Both form and number of denticles vary greatly among species—the differences correlating with food and habitat changes. Radular denticles are shown in Figure 2.

Evidently, the most primitive type of gastropod feeding involved browsing and grazing of algae from rocks. Some species (archaeogastropods) still retain the basic rhipidoglossan radula, with its many slender marginal teeth in each transverse row. During use the outer, or marginal, denticles swing outward, and the radula is curled under the anterior end of the odontophore. The latter is pressed against the feeding surface, and, one row at a time, the denticles are erected and scrape across the surface, removing fine particles as the odontophore is withdrawn into the mouth. As the marginals swing inward, food particles are carried toward the midline of the radula and collected into a mucous mass. By folding the teeth inward, damage to the mouth lining is avoided and food particles are concentrated. Mucus-bound food particles are then passed through the esophagus and into the gut for sorting and digestion.

From this basic pattern, numerous specializations have developed, including docoglossan, taenioglossate, rachiglossate, and toxoglossate radulae. Many limpets, which scrape algae directly from rock surfaces, have what is called a docoglossa radula, with the marginals greatly reduced in number. *Patella*, for example, has five pairs of cartilages and greatly increased musculature. When the radula is extruded, several rows of denticles on the lower odontophoral margin are pressed against the surface. There is no elevation of single rows and no lateral movement of the few marginals. Consequently, wear against the rock surface is great, and, although the denticles are heavily impregnated with mineral salts, tooth damage and loss is extensive. In rock-grazing species, replacement and growth are relatively rapid, and the radula is very long in relation to shell size. In some European limpets, the radula is three times as long as the shell, whereas, in the Indo-Pacific gastropod *Tectarius pagoda*, it is more than seven times the shell length.

The odontophore: a rasping organ

Wear and replacement of "teeth"

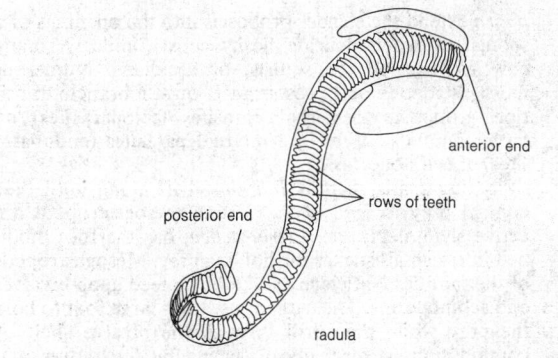

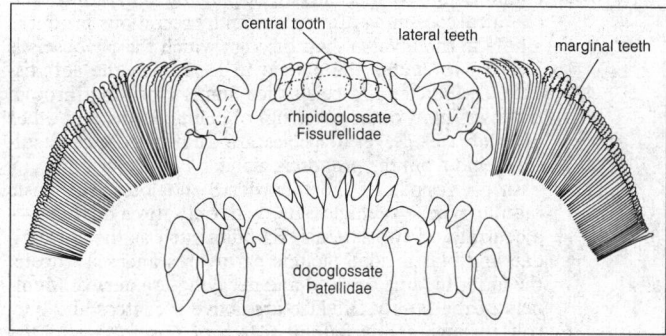

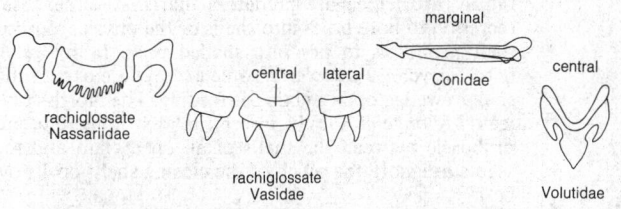

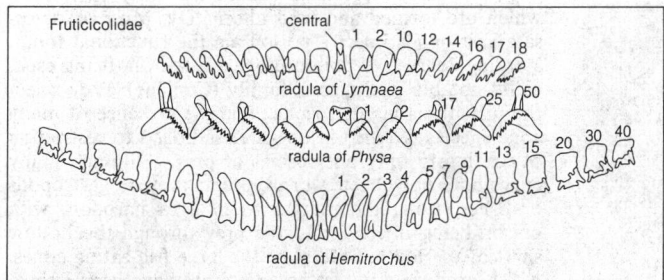

Figure 2: Gastropod radula and types of teeth.

Members of the suborder Mesogastropoda (or Taenioglossa) have a taenioglossate radula, in which a central tooth is flanked on either side by three laterals, for a total of seven denticles. This is a highly flexible pattern, which has allowed great diversity in feeding by alteration of cusp and tooth size. Many periwinkles (family Littorinidae) scrape algae from rock surfaces, as do the limpets; the small snail *Omalogyra* scrapes surface cells of algae and sucks out the cytoplasm. Larger mesogastropods, such as *Strombus*, graze upon standing algae in sand or mud flats. Often members of a genus may show striking differences. The limpet-like *Hipponyx antiquatus* attaches permanently in rock crevices or on clamshells, where organic debris can accumulate, and feeds on the accumulations, whereas *H. australis* attaches to the shell of the archaeogastropod *Turbo*, near its exhalant water current, to capture and consume fecal pellets. Other limpet-like, or burrowing, mesogastropods collect food particles off the gill and pass them into the mouth by action of hairlike projections (cilia). *Hipponyx* and *Aporrhais* grasp the trapped particles with the radular teeth, whereas in *Crepidula* a food-laden mucous cord is formed, bits of which are torn off by the radula.

Gastropods that feed on sessile (inactive) animals have evolved an extensible proboscis capable of reaching into narrow openings. Such minute sponge feeders as *Tri-*

phora extend the slender proboscis into the openings of a sponge to reach delicate fleshy cells. Similarly, many cowries feed on sea squirts, or ascidians. Numerous mesogastropods and prosobranch–opisthobranch transition groups are external parasites (ectoparasites) on larger animals. A few are internal parasites (endoparasites) of echinoderms.

Floating snails such as *Janthina* drift along until they contact prey to feed upon. Certain mesogastropods are active swimmers; one, *Pterotrachea*, has the foot modified into a small sucker for holding prey. Mesogastropods of the families Naticidae and Doliidae feed upon bivalves and echinoderms. The naticids use their large foot to hold the prey while they drill through the bivalve shell. A combination of mechanical rasping by the radula and chemical loosening of the calcium by secretions produces a hole in the bivalve shell through which the proboscis is inserted to enable the naticid to feed upon the soft tissues. Doliids tend to be surface hunters, drilling through the tests (hard outer covering) of echinoderms and other invertebrates. Several species are known to secrete sulfuric acid from the proboscis gland.

In gastropods of the suborder Stenoglossa, the basic radular type is rachiglossate, with only three denticles— a central and two laterals. Families such as the Buccinidae and Nassariidae include carnivores and scavengers, the latter feeding on dead and decaying organisms. Members of the family Olividae are active predators and burrow through sandy flats in search of prey; those of the family Muricidae are predators that may either use a secretion to bore holes into shells or the physical force of their proboscis to pry into shelled prey. Many genera (*e.g.*, *Busycon*, *Fasciolaria*, some *Murex*) use part of their shell to wedge open a clam for feeding. The North American *Melongena* simply inserts its very long muscular proboscis between the shells of an open clam and then seems to ignore the pinch of the closing shells on its own flesh.

Finally, the toxoglossate radula has only two teeth, which are formed and used alternately. Most toxoglossate gastropods inject a poison via the functional tooth. Varying degrees of poison usage are known, being especially notable in the cone family (Conidae). Prey selection usually is highly specific, and the presence of many cone species (*Conus*) in one area is linked to restriction of feeding to only one species of prey. Although many cones hunt polychaete worms, others prey on gastropods or fishes, using the radular tooth as a harpoon, with poison being injected into the prey through the hollow shaft of the tooth. Several of the large fish-eating cones, which produce a potent nerve poison, have been known to kill humans.

Opisthobranch gastropods show less clearly defined types of radular structure. Anaspideans such as *Dolabella* may have up to 460 teeth per row with a total of 25,000 denticles; sacoglossans have only one longitudinal row of teeth. In terms of feeding, opisthobranchs are extremely varied. Besides the algae-sucking sacoglossans, *Aplysia* cuts up strips of seaweed several centimetres long (about an inch) for swallowing, and a number of the more primitive species feed on algae encrusted on rocks. Perhaps the majority of opisthobranchs, including the sea slugs, are predators on sessile animals, ascidians and coelenterates being especially favoured. Pyramidellids are ectoparasites on a variety of organisms. *Calma* feeds on fish eggs. *Scaphander* and *Haminea* swallow whole mollusks, which then are crushed in the gizzard by a series of calcareous plates. Some of the pteropods are ciliary feeders on micro-organisms, whereas others, such as *Clione*, are fast-swimming predators of the pteropods.

Pulmonate gastropods are predominantly herbivores, with only a few scavenging and predatory species. Basically, on the radula there is a central tooth flanked by a few to many denticles, which may be differentiated into laterals and marginals. The central tooth may be reduced in size or lost, whereas the other teeth show modifications correlated with diet. Primitively, the pulmonate radular tooth has three raised points, or cusps (*i.e.*, is tricuspid), but modifications involving splitting of cusps or reductions to one cusp are numerous. With each successive appearance of a carnivorous type during evolution, however, the teeth have been reduced in number, each tooth usually having one long, sickle-shaped cusp. The New Caledonian *Ptychorhytida*, for example, has 11 teeth: three large laterals on either side of a middle row of five tiny sickle-shaped teeth. The American *Euglandina* has about 30 teeth in a row, with the posterior margins modified into a supporting buttress. Tree-climbing algal and lichen feeders, such as the East African *Rhachidina* and neotropical *Orthalicus,* have broad, gougelike median cusps for scraping, whereas feeders on decaying vegetation have narrow, sharp-edged cusps for slicing. Many of the latter species have extremely large numbers of denticles. A Thailand species, *Durgella libas*, has 148,000 denticles, even though the size of its shell is less than 0.5 inch (1.25 centimetres).

Unquestionably, much of the diversity achieved by the gastropods relates to the evolutionary shifts in radular structure, which have led to exploitation of a variety of food sources. Predators capable of swimming, surface crawling, and burrowing to capture prey have evolved among the prosobranchs and opisthobranchs; predators that produce chemical substances for entering the shells of their prey have evolved among the mesogastropods (Naticidae, Tonnacea), stenoglossans (Muricidae), and a nudibranch opisthobranch (*Okadaia*); and, in the pulmonates, predation and thus a carnivorous diet have evolved at least 12 times.

Life cycle and reproduction. Equally important to the success of the gastropods has been a life-history pattern capable of wide variation. Only in the most primitive prosobranchs are the sex products released into the water for fertilization to take place outside the female. The fertilized egg hatches into a free-swimming form (trochophore larva), which undergoes torsion, a 180° rotation of the fleshy organs from a posterior to an anterior position behind the head. Upon the expansion of the ciliary girdle of the trochophore larva into large, heavily ciliated swimming lobes (vela), the larva is called a veliger. Torsion is an embryological distinction of the gastropods (a diagram of its stages is shown in the article MOLLUSCA). One possible advantage of torsion to the larva is provision of a place to withdraw the vulnerable head and velar lobes. Torsion has resulted in both advantages and disadvantages that channelled the patterns of further evolution of the gastropods.

In some species the veliger stage may persist for a long period of larval life, during which dispersal of the species occurs. The veliger has a small shell into which the velar lobes and head can be withdrawn and a larval heart that seems to exist solely to provide circulation in the velar lobes. Food consists of certain organisms called diatoms and other small plankton collected by ciliary currents of the velum and channelled by the currents into the mouth. Special excretory cells located on either side of the mouth and the larval heart disappear when the veliger settles to the bottom and changes into a crawling snail. Upon settling, the snail starts a typical pattern of rapid growth until sexual maturity, at which point growth either ceases or is greatly slowed, because energy is being diverted to the production of the next generation. In opisthobranchs and many pulmonates, the life-span is about one year, although there are notable exceptions. Prosobranchs in general seem to have a much longer life-span, with some species of the freshwater *Vivipara* having lived 20 years in captivity. Desert and arid-area snails form a conspicuous exception to the generally short life-span of pulmonates. Some southwestern U.S. species have a life-span of more than 15 years. This, of course, includes the semidormant stages assumed during unfavourably dry periods. Whether the total length of active life substantially exceeds that of related pulmonates living in moist areas is unknown.

Several trends are evident in gastropod evolution from this basic pattern. First, there is a tendency toward development of internal fertilization, with pallial reproductive tubes of male and female becoming closed tubes and a male copulatory organ developing on the right side of the head for transmission of sperm to the female. Second, the trochophore and veliger stages tend to be passed within an egg capsule provided with a food supply, rather than as free-swimming periods during which the immature organisms must find their own food. At first, provision of nutriment for the young probably involved laying eggs in a mucous mass. As evolution progressed, capsules containing yolk and with a protective cover might have been laid singly or in masses. Still later forms may have provided parental care of the eggs or egg mass. Finally the egg was retained inside a brood pouch or the uterus until the young were ready to hatch (ovoviviparity). Third, there are tendencies toward sex reversal and the development of hermaphroditism—the presence of both male and female sex organs in one animal; hermaphroditism occurs in most opisthobranchs and pulmonates.

Such changes occurred more than once during gastropod evolution, and there is no clear pattern of changes that would suggest relationships. The differences correlate with habitat and frequently are seen within species of one genus. *Littorina*, on the English coasts, is a classic example: *Littorina neritoides* lives in crevices of exposed rocks above normal high water but releases floating (pelagic) egg capsules during fortnightly high tides or storms; *L. littorea*, on the lower half of the shore, also has pelagic egg capsules, which hatch six days later into veligers; *L. littoralis*, which lives on seaweeds that are rarely exposed by the tides, deposits gelatinous egg masses on the seaweeds, and the larvae pass through the veliger stage in the egg mass, emerging in two to three weeks as crawling young; and *L. saxatilis*, which extends from midtide level to several feet above the high-water mark, retains the eggs inside the female until they hatch as crawling young.

In the most primitive prosobranchs, the duct carrying eggs or sperm (gonoduct) opens into the kidney or renopericardial duct; in higher archaeogastropods it opens into the ureter. Separation of the excretory and reproductive ducts occurred later in evolution and is evident in the mesogastropods and stenoglossans. The female individuals of these latter forms have the upper portion of the oviduct specialized for secreting nutritive material around the fertilized eggs and the lower portion for encapsulating the egg and nutritive material.

Storing sperm in the female Various ways have been developed for storing sperm received from another individual and for transferring sperm. Prosobranchs such as *Cerithiopsis*, *Janthina*, and *Turritella* have extremely large sperm that carry thousands of smaller sperm from the male into the oviduct of the female; the large sperm swim the comparatively great distance between individuals. More frequently a penis is used to insert a stream of sperm into a special storage organ or the oviduct. In the opisthobranch *Limapontia*, the penis stylet injects sperms through the body wall into a storage organ (bursa) of the mate.

Internal fertilization is a necessity for land gastropods, which, accordingly, have appropriate specializations for sperm transfer. The more primitive species directly transfer a stream or gelatinous mass of sperm by insertion of the penis. One individual can act as a male and the other as a female, or copulation can be reciprocal. During evolution, loosely adherent masses of sperm gave rise to enclosed packets of sperm and then to horny or calcareous sperm bundles (spermatophores) with elaborately ornamented exteriors. In some Southeast Asian land snails (helicarionids), the long, curved, horny spermatophore has rows of three- to five-pronged spikes on either side of a shaft. Frequently, as many as 12 such spermatophores are found inside the bursa of a female. Closely related species show clear differences in the number and spacing of these spikes. Undoubtedly, this difference provides a method of species recognition among these snails. Other pulmonates depend on explicit courtship patterns (limacid slugs) or structural differences in the penis (endodontid land snails) to distinguish close relatives. The European dart-bearing helices, particularly *Cepaea* species, have elaborate rituals of courtship, in which a calcareous dart is jabbed into the flesh of the potential partner as a prelude to mating. Two closely related species, *C. hortensis* and *C. nemoralis*, which overlap in distribution, have different forms of darts, thus helping each species recognize its own kind.

Sex reversal Of general interest is the pattern of sex reversal seen in some prosobranchs. Most members of the family Calyptraeidae begin life as functional males but, after a transitional phase, spend their remaining span as females. *Crepidula* species attach to one spot when young and rarely move again. Other members of the species frequently attach to the shell surface of a settled individual, forming piles of up to 19 specimens. The younger ones on top are male, the old ones on the bottom female, and those in the middle are intermediate in sex. Isolated young function as males for only a week or two, but young males in a pile remain male for a longer period, through some unidentified influence of the larger females underneath. Some limpets also undergo sex reversal, but the circumstances are much less striking than those in *Crepidula*.

Egg production is correlated with the degree of care given the eggs or young. The extremes are the production of enormous numbers of eggs, which receive no care and hence suffer mass mortality (a fraction of 1 percent surviving), and the production of only one or two eggs, which receive intensive care. Of course, there are many gradations between the extremes. Many mesogastropods and all stenoglossans produce egg capsules that may contain from one to more than 1,000 eggs. In *Busycon*, for example, each capsule may contain up to 1,000 eggs, but extensive cannibalism occurs among the early hatched young and upon unhatched eggs in the capsule. *Strombus* can lay a tubular string of eggs 23 metres (75 feet) long, with up to 460,000 eggs. Many *Conus* cement up to 1,500,000 eggs in capsules on the undersides of rocks. Opisthobranchs weave delicate ribbons of eggs in colourful sheets—sometimes up to 50 millimetres (two inches) of ribbon per hour—that contain many millions of eggs. In these cases, the eggs hatch into swimming veligers. Freshwater snails frequently deposit eggs in capsules on plant leaves or rocks, but the number of eggs is much less than in the marine gastropods.

Parental care of eggs Direct care of the eggs is given in different ways. A small trochid, *Clanculus bertheloti*, deposits its eggs in grooves on the shell surface and covers them with a sheet of mucus to hold them in place; many *Neptunea* simply cement the egg capsules to their shell surface. Many *Crepidula* deposit a mass of 5,000 to 20,000 eggs under the shell edge just in front of the female's foot, brooding them until they hatch as veligers. Freshwater viviparids and thiarids have either uterine or neck brood pouches, in which the fertilized eggs develop to a crawling stage. The vermetid *Stephopoma* and the acmaeid *Acmaea rubella* brood their young in the mantle cavity between the fleshy body and the shell. A number of endodontid land snails on the Pacific Islands deposit their eggs in the umbilicus, an opening in the shell base. In one species, *Libera fratercula*, the young gnaw their way out through the apex of the maternal shell. One pteropod, *Hydromeles*, has an internal brood chamber that apparently ruptures, freeing the young into the body cavity of the parent; it is suspected that the escape of the young results in the parent's death.

Even without direct care of the eggs, land snails generally lay fewer than 200 eggs at a time, compared with the millions produced by many marine species. This reflects the different problems encountered on land and the lower mortality of larvae that are protected within the egg coverings. Many slugs and some snails bury egg masses in soil or under moist pieces of bark. Others, such as *Discus*, scatter their eggs singly over bark and decaying wood. One tropical genus (*Amphidromus*) rolls a leaf into a tube, seals one end with mucus, and lays its eggs in the cylinder thus formed. The South American *Strophocheilus* lays one large egg about four centimetres long (1.5 inch). Among the many ways in which land snails minimize losses from drying is the adoption of ovoviviparity, or the hatching of eggs within the parent body.

As in the case of feeding mechanisms, the basically simple pattern of reproduction shows considerable diversity in the different habitats occupied by gastropods. Both prosobranchs and pulmonates have colonized land and freshwaters and show similar alterations in reproduction.

Ecological relationships. Although all levels of the ocean are inhabited by snails, they are in greatest abundance in and just below the tidal zones, where food is most abundant. On rocky shores they are arranged in bands determined by physical factors of the environment and, to some degree, by predation. The extent of their effect on a coastline is indicated by the estimate that an average population of 860,000,000 *Littorina* on one square mile of rocky shore ingests 2,200 tons of material each year, only about 55 tons of which is organic matter. Limpets of all types are even more influential in such habitats, browsing and grazing on the algae and sessile animals. One interesting characteristic of limpets is that of homing. Numerous species have the tendency to settle on one spot and to feed on regular pathways from this home base.

Some larger prosobranchs are selective herbivores, cutting off one- to two-centimetre (0.4- to 0.8-inch) strips of seaweed for swallowing. More characteristic of the sand and mud flats are scavengers that indiscriminately take in surface debris; scavengers are found in various of the groups, including limpets, strombids, and nassariids. Carnivores include both surface hunters and burrowing forms such as the naticids. As an adaptation to sedentary life, several families have adopted a form of mucociliary feeding by collecting food particles from water currents. Sensory reception is highly developed in many carnivores, some of which employ a peculiar organ in the pallial cavity (the osphradium) to detect prey.

During the evolution of prosobranchs and opisthobranchs, floating and swimming forms have evolved several times. *Janthina* builds a float of air bubbles in mucus; the float is attached to the middle part of the foot. Heteropods swim either by undulations of the foot or by the action of fleshy fins. Pelagic opisthobranchs show almost every conceivable type of swimming mechanism and are at times extremely abundant on the ocean surface. Many opisthobranchs and most small freshwater pulmonates can glide on the underside of the surface film of the water but are not able to swim.

Diversity of mollusks in the ocean has resulted from specialization in food resources within habitats and tidal zonation. Temperature and salinity are the prime physical factors limiting range extensions, usually by preventing successful breeding rather than by preventing settlement and growth of young.

Migration of the snails into freshwater and onto land required new adaptations. Physiological and biochemical adjustments are the same in all taxonomic groups, but the snails had extra problems to solve, relating to their basic feeding and reproductive patterns. In the ocean, dispersal can take place via a veliger stage transported passively by currents and waves. In streams and rivers such a means of dispersal would result in downstream spread only. Hence, the veliger stage was suppressed; instead, many freshwater prosobranchs brood the young inside the female, and pulmonates attach egg capsules to rocks, to vegetation, or to other snail shells. This essentially restricts snail dispersal to individual movement. In prosobranchs with separate sexes, the freshwater distributions closely follow drainage systems, because, in order to colonize a new body of water, either a pregnant female or both a male and a female must be transported at about the same time. Most pulmonates in freshwater are hermaphrodites and are capable of self-fertilization as well as cross-fertilization with other individuals. As a result, any pulmonate entering a new body of water can establish a considerable population of that species in a short time. For this reason, isolated ponds often have several species of pulmonates but only rarely prosobranch gastropods. In crawling over waterweeds, the pulmonates frequently come in contact with the feet or feathers of wading birds to which they adhere accidentally by mucus secretion and are carried to a new pond.

Land snails avoid drying out in several ways. Proso-

branchs retreat into their shells, and the operculum effectively seals the opening against the exterior. In the tropics, land operculates have developed elaborate breathing tubes to allow gas exchange during dry periods and yet minimize water loss. Pulmonates lack an operculum, but many forms secrete either simple mucous coverings (epiphragms) across the shell aperture or, in some arid areas, a calcium-impregnated seal that is almost as thick as the shell itself. Most land snails, however, have adjusted to life on land primarily through behaviour patterns. They stay in areas of high moisture or retreat into damp niches during short dry spells. A few burrow into soil. *Sonorella* species survive by remaining dormant during the years between rains; many genital structures are reduced or lost to minimize use of energy in reproductive activities.

Only in the wet and warm tropics have tree snails developed. These species have brightly coloured shells that usually are much thinner than those of their terrestrial counterparts. In the humid mountain regions of the world, where a constant supply of moisture is available throughout the year, there has been a marked tendency toward reduction of the shell and the evolution of slugs. This probably results from two different selective pressures that reinforce each other. The shell, useful primarily in providing protection against drying out, is no longer needed when moisture is plentiful. Secondly, construction of the shell requires large quantities of calcium, which generally is in short supply on volcanic-mountain slopes. With the need for the shell lessened and the primary constituent in short supply, any mutation favouring shell reduction is advantageous. Although most slugs seem to have evolved in mountain areas, their spread into lowlands is greatly aided by irrigation and garden watering.

By far the majority of land snails occupy the surface litter and upper soil zone. This microhabitat is generally moist, and food is plentiful in the form of decaying animals and plants as well as fungi. Most land snails have shells that are drab in colour and inconspicuous. Frequently, the shell surface is highly sculpted. The minute species (less than three millimetres [0.1 inch] in diameter) face a problem of predation by small arthropods. The normal instinct of a snail to withdraw into its shell is of no help, since the predator simply follows the snail into its shell. Elaborate barriers that narrow the shell opening and tiny spines along the opening must provide some protection, since this construction occurs in more than 12 pulmonate families.

Most land snails feed directly on decaying plant matter, which is a simple shift in feeding behaviour from the primitive browsing of their marine ancestors. About 30 percent of land snails scrape algae from tree trunks or limbs or consume fungae hyphae (threadlike structures). The carnivorous habit probably evolved through a transition period of carrion eaters. Many slugs feed on dead animal matter as well as plants. Pursuit and capture of other snails or earthworms demand increased sensory equipment and more rapid motion. Most carnivores, such as *Euglandina*, have greatly elongated bodies for reaching further into the shells of their victims. The New Zealand *Paryphanta* smothers its earthworm prey in its broad foot before it eats the worm.

Locomotion. The foot is the organ of locomotion in land gastropods. In swimming and sessile forms, however, the foot is greatly reduced and in many groups greatly modified. The normal progression of a snail is by muscular action, with a series of contraction waves proceeding from the posterior to the anterior end of the gliding portion of the foot. This type of progression is called monotaxic locomotion. A few groups have the foot divided into right and left halves, with separate waves moving on each side, a condition termed ditaxic locomotion. Certain species move by the action of cilia of the foot on the mucous sheet secreted by the anterior part of the foot. When the foot is narrow, as in *Strombus* and *Aporrhais*, the animal moves in fits and starts, tumbling along by a digging action of the foot and the pointed operculum. Most prosobranchs are relatively slow moving, with a speed of less than eight centimetres (about three inches) per minute, although *Haliotis* has been reported to move at almost ten times that rate.

Many opisthobranchs employ monotaxic locomotion; some can glide on the underside of water-surface films through ciliary action. Swimming has been achieved in a number of ways. Body undulations propel such large snails as *Dendronotus* and *Melibe*. Pteropods, *Gastropteron*, *Akera*, and others move foot flaps (parapodia) to provide motion. The sea hare, *Aplysia*, uses an inchworm-like progression, and some nudibranchs swim by beating accessory breathing organs (cerata).

Freshwater pulmonates use ciliary action on a bed of mucus secreted by the snail. Many snails, especially *Physa*, can form a cord of mucus from the water surface to the bottom.

Land pulmonates depend on a combination of muscular action and cilia. In many of these species, the foot is divided longitudinally into three parts, with locomotor activity confined to the central section, which glides on a mucous track. An additional use of slime by slugs is in mating. A slime rope is secreted from which the mating pair suspend themselves. If irritated, slugs can secrete copious quantities of slime. This reaction is the basis for one method of controlling slugs: spreading enough ashes in slug-infested areas causes exhaustion and death of the animals through overproduction of slime.

Rate of movement in the land pulmonates varies greatly. Some small, tropical, brightly coloured sluglike species will, when disturbed, travel very rapidly with the anterior half of the foot lifted off the ground. This can continue for a distance of two or three feet at a rate of almost four feet (122 centimetres) a minute in snails less than two to three centimetres (or about one inch) in body length. Large species, such as *Achatina* or *Strophocheilus*, are much slower, and carnivores are usually relatively fast moving.

FORM AND FUNCTION

The shell. The typical snail has a calcareous shell coiled in a spiral pattern around a central axis, or columella. Generally, the later coils, or whorls, are larger than the earlier ones. At the end of the last whorl is the aperture, or opening, on the outer lip of which shell growth occurs. The shell is secreted by the fleshy part of the animal called the mantle, first by outward additions to the shell lip and then by secretion of inner thickening layers. The outer layer, or periostracum, is a mixture of proteins known as conchin. Inner layers of calcium carbonate interlace with a network of conchin and are impregnated with a variety of mineral salts. The calcium usually is in the form of calcite crystals in marine species and aragonite crystals in terrestrial species, but mixtures of crystal types do occur.

Modifications and ornamentations of the basic shell are widely variable. Frequently, the shell is altered into a nonspiral cap or a cup-shaped limpet form as an adaptation to life in swift currents (freshwater Ancylidae) or amid pounding waves on rocks (marine Acmaeidae, Patellidae, Fissurellidae, and Calyptraeidae). In many groups, such as the abalones (Haliotidae), only traces of spiral coiling are evident, because the rate of successive whorl widths is so large that the last, or body whorl, occupies more than 90 percent of the shell volume. Elaborate surface sculpture, including knobs and spines, develop as protection against predation. In a few species of the genera *Leucozonia* and *Acanthina*, a spine on the lip edge is used to wedge open clam valves so that the snail can feed. As implied earlier, land gastropods in dry regions tend to have very thick shells; on the other hand, those in very humid mountain situations have thin shells or none at all. Many carnivorous snails have the calcareous part of the shell greatly reduced. The New Zealand *Paryphanta* is perhaps the most extreme example: the calcareous layer is only a thin sheet, and the outer, organic periostracum accounts for 90 percent of the shell thickness.

The body. The gastropod body consists of four main parts: visceral hump, mantle, head, and foot. The body is attached to the shell either by one columellar muscle or by a series of muscles. Typical snails can withdraw the head and foot into the shell, but numerous species have

Shell ornamentation

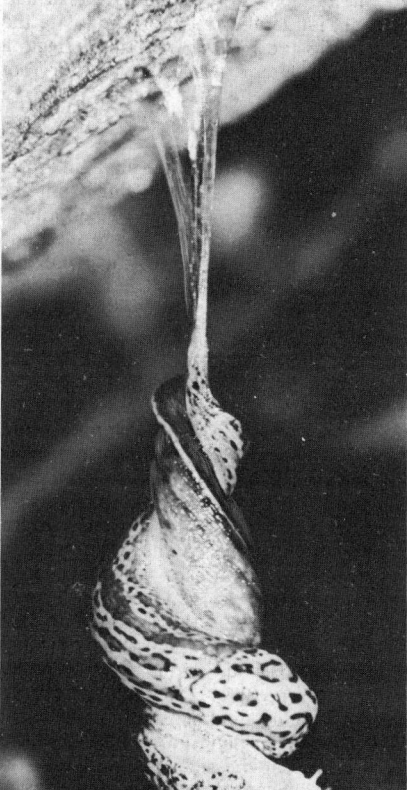

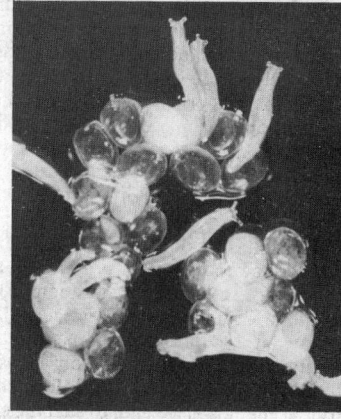

Slug life cycle.
Stages in the life cycle of the black slug (*Limax*), a hermaphroditic pulmonate. (Left) Pair of slugs, having lowered themselves from a branch by means of a mutually produced mucous string, intertwine and mate while suspended. (Top) Shiny, gelatinous eggs are laid in clusters in sheltered places. (Right) Eggs hatching and recently emerged slugs.
Lynwood M. Chase

shells so reduced in size as to be unable to contain the body; slugs, of course have either an internal shell vestige or no shell at all.

The visceral hump.   The visceral hump is always contained within the shell; it generally holds the bulk of the digestive, reproductive, excretory, and respiratory systems (Figure 3). A significant part of the visceral hump consists of the pallial cavity. In both prosobranchs and shelled opisthobranchs, this is a cavity completely open anteriorly; in pulmonates it is closed except for a narrow pore. The upper surface of the pallial cavity serves a respiratory function. In marine species, the ciliated lining of the cavity produces a water current that passes pos-

The pallial cavity *(margin note)*

From (B) *Treatise on Invertebrate Paleontology;* courtesy of the Geological Society of America and the University of Kansas Press

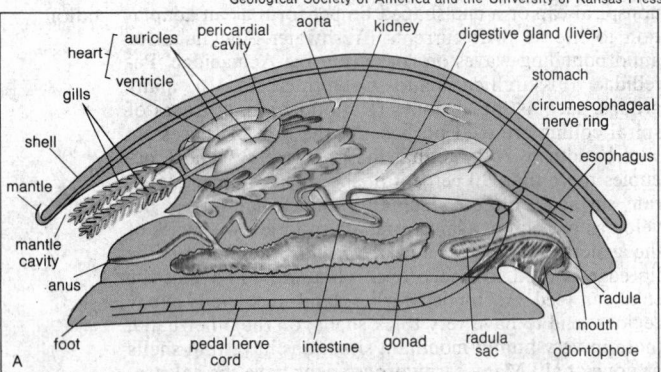

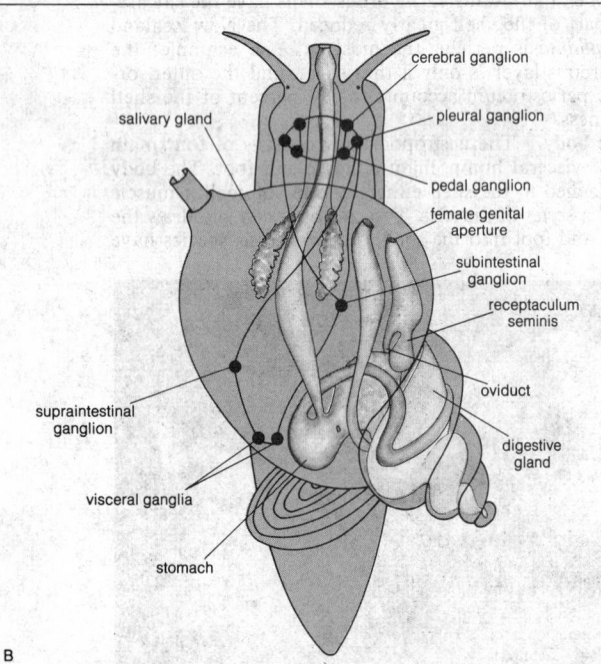

Figure 3: *Adult gastropod structure.*
(A) Primitive; (B) advanced.

teriorly across the gill, or ctenidium, and the osphradium, which is thought to be a sensory receptor of chemical changes in the environment. Both organs lie on the left anterior side of the cavity. The water current sweeps across the posterior part of the pallial cavity, where the nephridiopore, or kidney opening, lies, and then passes anteriorly along the right margin past the anus, through which undigested particles of food are eliminated, and usually past the gonopore, through which sexual products are released.

An often overlooked function of the pallial cavity is as a space for containment of the head and foot, when these organs are retracted in an attempt to avoid a predator or to avoid drying out (in land snails) during dry periods. Many land pulmonates apparently also use the pallial cavity to retain water. Prosobranchs use the operculum, the horny or calcareous disk located on the back of the foot at the posterior end, to seal the shell opening.

The mantle.   The mantle is the fleshy lining of the outer wall of the shell; it roofs the pallial cavity. At its anterior end lie glandular tissues that deposit the various shell layers. In terrestrial forms with reduced shells, various lobes and laps extend anteriorly over the neck and head or are reflected back over the shell surface. These are highly vascularized and probably serve both in respiration and in water balance of the body. Many marine forms have the mantle collar extended forward and rolled into a siphon, which functions in both food location and chemoreception.

The head.   Generally, the head is bilaterally symmetrical, bearing one or two pairs of tentacles, often with accessory palps, and the mouth in the middle of the ventral margin. Eyespots or, rarely, eyes capable of image formation are present near or on the larger pair of tentacles. In stylommatophoran land snails the upper tentacles, or ommatophores, are invaginable (capable of being rolled in), and the eyes are borne at the tips. In freshwater basommatophorans and most prosobranchs, the eyes are located at the base of the tentacles, although in such forms as *Strombus* the eyes are elevated onto an accessory stalk. Prosobranchs have contractile (not invaginable) tentacles. In carnivorous snails, the lateral lips of the mouth form lobes called labial palps, which help to locate prey. The mouth itself frequently is prolonged into a proboscis that extends well in front of the tentacles. Carnivorous species often have a proboscis capable of great extension, either invaginable or contractile.

The foot.   Although the basic form of the foot is a flat, broadly tapered, muscular organ, which is highly glandularized and usually ciliated, numerous modifications occur in various groups. Frequently, there is an anterior-posterior division into a propodium and a metapodium, with the former capable of being reflexed over the shell. In *Strombus*, the foot is greatly narrowed; in limpets and abalones, it is broadly expanded and serves as an adhesive disk. In pelagic gastropods, the foot is a swimming organ. Many prosobranchs and some opisthobranchs have lateral projections of the foot called parapodia; they are used in swimming or else are reflexed over the shell surface. An unusual feature found in several kinds of land slugs, some nudibranchs, and the stenoglossan marine family Harpidae, is the ability to self-amputate the posterior portion of the foot, which remains wriggling violently to distract a predator, while the anterior foot and visceral mass creep slowly away to safety.

Modifications of the foot *(margin note)*

EVOLUTION AND PALEONTOLOGY

The basic trends in snail evolution involve changing from a herbivorous to a carnivorous diet, shifting from the ocean to freshwater and terrestrial life, and adopting a sluglike form through reduction or loss of the shell and visceral hump. Each change has occurred independently several times in the course of gastropod evolution.

Prosobranch gastropods are the most primitive. One group, the Diotocardia, which retains two sets of pallial organs, is nearest to the generalized gastropod in structure. Gradual loss of the right set of pallial organs occurs in the Trochacea and Neritacea, thus providing a transition to the more highly developed Monotocardia, with only one set of pallial organs. Among the numerous changes in the Monotocardia are a reduction in numbers of radular teeth and a shift from grazing on algae and fungi to consumption of larger sessile organisms and predation. The two main divisions of the Monotocardia show different evolutionary patterns. Although most Taenioglossa have remained coastal marine, several families moved into freshwater. Others crossed to land directly from the tidal zone, rather than passing through a freshwater transitional period. At the peak of prosobranch evolution are the predatory Stenoglossa, all marine inhabitants, with highly modified radular teeth and often well-developed poison glands to aid in capturing prey. Reduction and loss of the right pallial organs are correlated with more efficient respiration and sensory apparatuses, in which a water current crosses over the sensory organs and gills on the left side, then out on the right side, together with excretory and fecal deposits.

Opisthobranchs probably arose from an unknown group of primitive prosobranchs and have evolved extensively into different lines showing a reduction of the visceral hump and shell. In certain forms the foot is shortened, and external cerata develop to provide a respiratory surface to replace the lost mantle-cavity surface. Such groups as the Pyramidellacea contain a mixture of prosobranch and opisthobranch characteristics.

Pulmonates show varying degrees of adjustment to freshwater and land life, with increasing union of the male and female gonoducts characterizing the more advanced groups. Similarly, the highly advanced Holopoda and Limacacea show complex accessory organs on the genitalia and a more sophisticated means of water conservation through development of a closed secondary ureter and resorption of water from the excretory products. More than a dozen different groups of pulmonates have become predators, usually upon other snails or earthworms.

The earliest gastropods

Fossil gastropods are known from Cambrian deposits (more than 500,000,000 years old). Since the shell is often very similar in unrelated families, fossil gastropods more than 350,000,000 years old are not usually placed in the classification outlined below but instead are treated separately. Most stenoglossan prosobranchs appeared near the end of the Mesozoic (about 65,000,000 years ago), and many groups of land snails are known from Eocene formations (38,000,000 to 54,000,000 years old). Snails had their adaptive radiation early in geologic history. Living genera of marine, freshwater, and land-snail families are known from Miocene to Oligocene deposits (26,000,000 to 38,000,000 years old). Unlike mammals, who have undergone great evolutionary change in the last 50,000,000 years, gastropods have shown little progressive evolution during that time.

CLASSIFICATION

Distinguishing taxonomic features. Higher category groupings of the gastropods depend on the relative importance assigned to the nervous system or to the pattern of respiration. The groupings date back to observations made in the mid-1800s. The following provide the basic data from which a classification can be derived: patterns of change in the reduction of torsion from a streptoneurous (twisted) to a euthyneurous (straight) nerve loop; progressive loss of the right part of the primitively paired pallial organs; increasing sophistication of hermaphroditism (both sexes in one animal); tendency toward reduction of the visceral hump and shell; multiple changes from a herbivorous to a carnivorous diet; habitat shifts to freshwater and land from the marine environment and, occasionally, return from the land to the ocean; and shifts in locomotor mechanics.

Euthyneury has evolved separately in the opisthobranchs and pulmonates; a few opisthobranchs, such as the Acteonidae, retain a streptoneurous nervous system.

The division into Prosobranchia, Opisthobranchia, and Pulmonata recognizes basic adaptive patterns and is utilized here, although with the recognition that, in particular, the Pulmonata probably have arisen from several discrete lineages (i.e., are polyphyletic in origin).

Annotated classification. The classification given here borrows from many sources; the general follows V. Fretter and A. Graham (1962), as does the internal classification of the Prosobranchia. Internal classification of the Opisthobranchia is basically that of C.F. Boettger (1954) except that the Onchidiacea are considered to be pulmonates. The Pulmonata is classified according to A. Solem (1974).

CLASS GASTROPODA (snails and slugs)
About 50,000 species widely distributed in marine, freshwater, and land regions; snails typically with a calcareous shell; slugs with greatly reduced shell; length ranges from about 0.04 inch to 52 inches.

Subclass Prosobranchia
Streptoneurous (twisted) gastropods with an anteriorly located mantle cavity (space lined with epidermis); operculum (protective cover) generally present; sexes separate; shell can usually hold entire animal; primarily marine, several freshwater and terrestrial groups; About 26,000 species.

Order Diotocardia (Archaeogastropoda)
Heart usually with 2 auricles; 1 or 2 internal gills; no penis, siphon (organ used in food location), or proboscis (feeding organ); nervous system not concentrated; sex cells discharged by way of the right nephridium (kidney). About 3,000 species.

Superfamily Zeugobranchia (Pleurotomariacea). Slit shells (Pleurotomariidae) in deep ocean waters; abalones (Haliotidae) in shallow waters along rocky shores of western North America, Japan, Australia, and South Africa; keyhole limpets (Fissurellidae) in intertidal rocky areas.

Superfamily Patellacea (Docoglossa). Conical-shelled limpets, without slits or holes, found in rocky shallow waters (Acmaeidae and Patellidae).

Superfamily Trochacea. Small to large spiral shells in shallow to deep ocean waters, often brightly coloured, with or without heavy shell ornamentation; Trochidae (top shells), Turbinidae (turban shells), and Phasianellidae (pheasant shells).

Superfamily Neritacea. Small, generally intertidal marine shells (Neritidae), with some freshwater dwellers, particularly in Indonesia and the Philippines (Neritidae), and 2 groups of land dwellers: one sparsely distributed in the Old World (Hydrocenidae) and one widely distributed in both Old and New World tropics (Helicinidae).

Order Monotocardia
Heart with 1 auricle; 1 gill, often modified; siphon and chemoreception osphradium (sensory receptor) progressively more complex; penis present; head frequently modified into a proboscis; nervous system progressively more concentrated. About 23,000 species.

Suborder Taenioglossa (Mesogastropoda). Radula (broad ribbonlike structure covered with teeth) taenioglossate (with 7 denticles, or teeth) or reduced; most taxa herbivorous; a few families parasites or predators.

Superfamily Cyclophoracea. Land snails, particularly abundant in the West Indies and southern Asia to the Melanesian islands.

Superfamily Viviparacea. Large, 1 to 2 inch, globular pond and river snails of the Northern Hemisphere (Viviparidae) and tropical regions (Ampullariidae); frequently used in freshwater aquariums with tropical fish.

Superfamily Littorinacea. Periwinkles, on rocky shores (Littorinidae) of all oceans; land snails of the West Indies, part of Africa, and Europe (Pomatiasidae).

Superfamily Rissoacea. About 17 families of small to minute, generally cylindrical, marine, freshwater and land snails found in most tropical and warm-temperate regions of the world.

Superfamily Cerithiacea. Minute to large, generally elaborately sculptured shells, common in mud flats and mangroves, many species sand dwellers, with 1 group of families (Thiaridae, Pleuroceridae, Melanopsidae) especially abundant and varied in the Tennessee and Alabama River systems; 13 marine families, including worm shells (Vermetidae), horn shells (Potamididae), and button shells (Modulidae).

Superfamily Strombacea. Conchs (Strombidae) of tropical oceans and the pelican's foot shells (Aporrhaidae) of near Arctic waters, have foot and operculum greatly modified and move with a lurching motion; feed on algae and plants; some species used for human food.

Superfamily Calyptraeacea. Cap shells (Capulidae) and slipper shells (Calyptraeidae) are limpets with irregularly shaped shells with a small internal cup or shelf; many species show sex reversal, becoming males early in life, then changing into females during old age; common on rocks, clamshells, and in dead large snail shells in most oceans.

Superfamily Cypraeacea. Cowrie shells (Cypraeidae) and egg shells (Ovulidae) have highly polished and brilliantly coloured shells; mantle, which may cover the shell, is a totally different colour pattern; if touched, members of group suddenly withdraw, the change in colour serving to confuse predators; common in shallow tropical oceans, some species in cooler waters.

Superfamily Naticacea. Moon shells (Naticidae) medium-sized, globular predators on burrowing bivalves, bore a hole in the clamshell using acid secretions, then insert the radula to feed; common in most oceans.

Superfamily Ptenoglossa (or Scalacea). Wentletraps (Epitoniidae) live in shallow to deep ocean waters; purple snails (Janthinidae) float on the ocean surface after building a raft of bubbles; large numbers of bubble shells occasionally blow ashore.

Superfamily Aglossa. Parasitic or predatory snails either with a reduced radula or with none, jaws often modified into a stylet-shaped structure; many occur on echinoderms; consists of several poorly known families.

Superfamily Doliacea (Tonnacea). Generally tropical predators on echinoderms; often burrow in sand; includes helmet shells (Cassidae), tun shells (Doliidae), frog shells (Bursidae), triton shells (Cymatiidae), and fig shells (Ficidae); frog and triton shells often live in rocky areas; most species large in size.

Suborder Stenoglossa (Neogastropoda). Carnivorous or scavengers with rachiglossate (with 3 denticles) or taxoglossate (with 2 denticles) radula; shell often with long siphonal canal; proboscis well developed and often extensible; shells generally large; all marine.

Superfamily Muricacea. Murex shells (Muricidae), rock shells (Purpuridae), and coral shells (Coralliophilidae) are common predators, often boring into shells of their prey; rock shells common in cooler waters; others mostly tropical.

Superfamily Buccineacea. Scavengers that have lost the mechanisms for boring; dove shells (Columbellidae), mud snails (Nassariidae), tulip shells (Fasciolariidae), whelks (Buccinidae), and crown conchs (Galeodidae) mainly cool-water species; but dove and tulip shells have many tropical representatives.

Superfamily Volutacea. Harp shells (Harpidae), olive shells (Olividae), mitre shells (Mitridae), volute shells (Volutidae), nutmeg shells (Cancellariidae), and marginellas (Marginellidae) generally have operculum reduced or lacking; most are tropical ocean dwellers, active predators or scavengers; many olive, volute, and marginella shells are highly polished and colourful.

Superfamily Toxoglossa. Auger shells (Terebridae), cone shells (Conidae) and turrid shells (Turridae) are carnivorous marine snails with poison glands attached to highly modified radular teeth; several cone shells have caused human deaths through poisoning and can catch and kill fish.

Subclass Opisthobranchia
Shell reduced or lacking, usually too small for withdrawal of animal; mantle cavity often lost, rotated to right side and facing anteriorly; hermaphroditic; marine except for 4 species; operculum generally lost; nerve ganglia (clusters) very concentrated. About 2,000 species.

Order Cephalaspidea
Shell present, often capable of containing whole body; head shield developed; Acteonidae with operculum; 14 families.

Order Pyramidellacea
Spiral shell; operculum present; gill and radula absent; long proboscis with stylet; ectoparasitic; generally minute; in warm oceanic areas.

Order Acochlidacea
Three families with visceral mass longer than foot; 4 species in freshwater; a few with sexes in separate animals; size minute.

Order Philinoglossacea
No head appendages; gill lacking; no external shell; 2 families.

Order Anaspidea
Sea hares (Aplysiidae); 1 other small family; shell reduced to flat plate; feed on large seaweed rather than microscopic algae.

Order Notaspidea
Shell and gill usually present; no parapodia (extensions of foot); sperm groove open; shell prominent, reduced, or hidden by mantle; 2 families.

Order Sacoglossa
One file of radular teeth; sperm duct a closed tube; shell reduced to bivalved (Juliidae); many feed by sucking juices out of algae; several families with uncertain limits.

Order Thecosomata
Shell present; pelagic (open-sea dwelling) ciliary feeders; no gill; 6 families.

Order Gymnosomata
Shell absent; no mantle cavity; complicated feeding mechanisms; pelagic carnivores; 7 families.

Order Nudibranchia
Sea slugs without shell, mantle cavity, osphradium, or internal gill; many, as carnivores, feed on sessile animals; few swimmers (family Tethyidae); highly colourful, often conspicuous.

Subclass Pulmonata
Mantle cavity altered into a pulmonary sac; no gills or operculum; 1 auricle of heart anterior to ventricle; hermaphroditic; shell spiral to limpet-like, often reduced to a fragment hidden by mantle; mainly terrestrial or freshwater, few marine. About 21,200 species.

Superorder Systellommatophora
Mantle cavity absent; anal and usually nephridial opening at posterior; male gonopore behind right tentacle; female gonopore middle of right side; sole of foot narrow; no shell; 2

pairs of retractile, or invaginable, tentacles. Marine (Onchidiidae), terrestrial and herbivorous (Veronicellidae), or terrestrial and carnivorous (Rathouisiidae). About 200 species.

Superorder Basommatophora
Mantle cavity present; eyes at base of 1 pair of tentacles; male and female gonopore separate, usually on right side of body; shell conical to patelliform; mostly freshwater, but a few land and marine taxa. (No agreement exists concerning suprafamilial classification of the Basommatophora. The following superfamilies, though not grouped into formal orders and suborders, are listed in order of increasing specialization.) About 1,000 species.

Superfamily Patelliformia. Brackish water or marine limpets with (Siphonariidae) gill-like structures or with a lung (Gadinidae).

Superfamily Amphibolacea. Operculum present; shell conical; with pulmonary cavity; brackish water; burrow in sand; 1 family.

Superfamily Ellobiacea. Conical shells; pulmonary chamber; tidal zone, salt flats, under rocks in spray zone, to completely terrestrial; 2 families.

Superfamily Lymnaeacea. Small to large, spiral-shelled snails of ponds, lakes, and rivers. One limpet group (Lancidae) and larger typical group (Lymnaeidae).

Superfamily Ancylacea. Limpets (Ancylidae), ramshorns (Planorbidae), and pond snails (Physidae); all restricted to freshwater habitats.

Superorder Stylommatophora
Mantle cavity a pulmonary sac; gonopores with common opening on right side or at most narrowly separated; shell conical to vestigial, heavily to weakly calcified; eyes at tips of upper (usually) tentacles; terrestrial. About 20,000 species.

Order Orthurethra
Pore of ureter opening into pallial cavity (part of the viscera) near anterior margin of lung after ureter passes forward from anterior kidney margin. About 6,000 species.

Superfamily Achatinellacea. Minute to medium-sized Pacific Island land snails with multicuspid radular denticles; many Hawaiian species highly coloured and variable.

Superfamilies Cionellacea and Pupillacea. Minute leaf-litter to arboreal snails, occasionally (Enidae) large; shells often with denticles in the aperture; 10 families.

Superfamily Partulacea. Small generally arboreal snails found on high volcanic islands of Polynesia and Micronesia, a few in Melanesia.

Order Mesurethra
Ureter represented by lateral opening of very short kidney, pore of ureter opening near or behind middle of pallial cavity. About 1,500 species.

Superfamily Clausiliacea. Elongated shells of West Indian shore salt-spray zone (Cerionidae) or Andean mountains of South America and Eurasia (Clausiliidae).

Superfamily Strophocheilacea. Large helicoidal to elongated shells of South America (Strophocheilidae) or southwest Africa (Dorcasiidae).

Order Sigmurethra
Ureter originates near anterior margin of kidney, follows backward to posterior end, then reflexes forward along hindgut to open alongside anus; position greatly altered in sluglike forms. About 12,500 species.

Suborder Holopodopes. A group of 4 superfamilies.
Superfamily Achatinacea. Besides the giant African snail, 4 families, including many species spread by commerce throughout the world.

Superfamilies Streptaxacea and Rhytidacea. Carnivorous snails and slugs (4 families) in most tropical areas, plus the herbivorous Acavidae of Australia, Ceylon, and Madagascar.

Superfamily Bulimulacea. Large, often arboreal snails of Melanesia and Neotropica (Bulimulidae); long, cylindrical snails of West Indies and Central America (Urocoptidae).

Suborder Aulacopoda. A group of 3 superfamilies.
Superfamily Succineacea. A problematic group including amber snails (Succineidae), which inhabit swamps and damp areas, and peculiar slugs from the South Pacific (Athoracophoridae).

Superfamily Arionacea. Marginal teeth of radula with squarish basal plates and 1 to several cusps; small litter or tree snails mainly in Southern Hemisphere (Endodontidae), and slugs (Arionidae and Philomycidae) of the Northern Hemisphere.

Superfamily Limacacea. Marginal teeth of radula with narrow, lengthened basal plates, usually unicuspid; zonitid snails with smooth shells and many sluglike species, common in wet, tropical areas and in temperate regions; about 12 families, including limacid and milacid slugs.

Suborder Holopoda. A group of 3 superfamilies.

Superfamily Polygyracea. Common woodland snails of eastern North America (Polygyridae), plus a Neotropical group (Thysanophoridae) and a relict group of Asia (Corillidae).

Superfamily Oleacinacea. Carnivorous (Oleaciniidae) and herbivorous (Sagdidae) snails of the Neotropical region.

Superfamily Helicacea. Land snails without (Oreohelicidae and Camaenidae) or with (Bradybaenidae, Helminthoglyptidae, and Helicidae) accessory glands on the genitalia; dominant land snails in most regions, including the edible snails of Europe (Helicidae).

BIBLIOGRAPHY. C.R. BOETTGER, "Basommatophora," in G. GRIMPE and E. WAGLER (eds.), *Die Tierwelt der Nord- und Ostsee*, vol. 35 (1944), a classic account in German of European fresh-water molluscan biology; and "Die Systematik der euthyneuren Schnecken," *Zool. Anz.*, suppl. 18, pp. 253–280 (1954), an account of opisthobranch classification; V. FRETTER and A. GRAHAM, *British Prosobranch Molluscs* (1962), an essential reference for the student; L.H. HYMAN, *The Invertebrates*, vol. 6, *Mollusca I* (1967), a comprehensive synthesis of the technical literature and the basic reference work; K.Y. JOHNSTONE, *Collecting Seashells* (1970), a popular account with emphasis on Gulf Coast species; H.A. PILSBRY, *Land Mollusca of North America (North of Mexico)*, 2 vol. (1939–48), one of the best single sources on land shell species; E.F. RICKETTS and J. CALVIN, *Between Pacific Tides*, 3rd ed. rev. by JOEL W. HEDGPETH (1962), an ecological treatment of West American mollusks; A. SOLEM, "Classification of Land Snails," in FRETTER and PEAKE, *Pulmonata* (in prep.), a revised classification of land snails and a survey of classification schemes; H. JANUS, *Unsere Schnecken und Muscheln* (1958; Eng. trans., *The Young Specialist Looks at Land and Fresh-Water Molluscs*, 1965), a popular account of nonmarine mollusks.

(G.A.So.)

Gaudí, Antonio

The work of the architect Antonio Gaudí is remarkable for its range of forms, textures, and polychromy and for the free, expressive way in which these elements of his art seem to be composed. The complex geometries of a Gaudí building so coincide with its architectural structure that the whole, including its surface, gives the appearance of being a natural object in complete conformity with nature's laws. Such a sense of total unity also informed the life of Gaudí; his personal and professional lives were one, and his collected comments about the art of building are essentially aphorisms about the art of living. He was totally dedicated to architecture, which for him was a totality of many arts.

By courtesy of Archivo Amigos de Gaudí, Barcelona; photograph, Foto Aleu

The Colonia Güell church by Antonio Gaudí, 1898–c. 1915. In Santa Coloma de Cervelló, Spain.

Antonio Gaudí y Cornet was born on June 25, 1852, in or near the provincial Catalan city of Reus, on the Mediterranean coast, in Spain. Of humble origins, he was the son of a coppersmith who was to live with him in later life, together with a niece; Gaudí never married.

Showing an early interest in architecture, he went in 1869/70 to Barcelona, which was then the political and intellectual centre of Catalonia as well as Spain's most modern city. He did not graduate until eight years later, his studies having been interrupted by military service and other intermittent activities.

Gaudí's style of architecture went through several phases. On emergence from the Escuela Provincial de Arquitectura in Barcelona in 1878, he practiced a rather florid Victorianism that had been evident in his school projects, but he quickly developed a manner of composing by means of unprecedented juxtapositions of geometric masses the surfaces of which were highly animated with patterned brick or stone, gay ceramic tiles, and floral or reptilian metalwork. The general effect, although not the details, is Moorish—or Mudéjar, as Spain's special mixture of Muslim and Christian design is called. Examples of his Mudéjar style are the Casa Vicens and "El Capricho" of 1883–85, and the Güell Estate (Finca Güell) and Palacio Güell of the later 1880s, all but "El Capricho" located in Barcelona. Next, Gaudí experimented with the dynamic possibilities of historic styles: the Gothic (at the Palacio Episcopal, Astorga, 1887–94, and Casa de los Botines, León, 1891–94) and the Baroque (Casa Calvet at Barcelona, 1898–1901). But after 1902 his designs elude conventional stylistic nomenclature.

Except for certain overt symbols of nature or religion, Gaudí's buildings became essentially representations of their structure and materials. In his Torre (villa) Bell Esguard and the Güell Park, in Barcelona, and in the Colonia Güell church, south of that city, he arrived at a type of structure that has come to be called equilibrated —that is, a structure designed to stand on its own without internal bracing, external buttressing, and the like—or, as Gaudí observed, as a tree stands. Among the primary elements of his system were piers and columns that tilt to transmit diagonal thrusts, and thin-shell, laminated tile vaults that exert very little thrust. Gaudí applied his equilibrated system to two multi-storied Barcelona apartment buildings: the Casa Batlló, a renovation that incorporated new equilibrated elements, notably the facade; and the Casa Milá, the several floors of which are structured like clusters of tile lily pads with steel beam veins. As was so often his practice, he designed the two buildings, in their shapes and surfaces, as metaphors of the mountainous and maritime character of Catalonia.

As an admired, if eccentric, architect, Gaudí was an important participant in the Catalan *Renaixensa*, an artistic revival, especially of the arts and crafts, combined with a political revival in the form of fervent anti-Castilian "Catalanism"; both movements sought to reinvigorate the way of life in Catalonia that had long been suppressed by the Castilian-dominated and Madrid-centred government in Spain. The religious symbol of the *Renaixensa* in Barcelona was the church of the Sagrada Familia, a project that was to occupy Gaudí throughout his entire career. He was commissioned to build this church as early as 1883, but he did not live to see it finished. Working on it, he became increasingly pious; after 1910 he abandoned virtually all other work and even secluded himself on its site and resided in its workshop. In his 75th year, while on his way to vespers, he was struck down by a trolley car, and he died from the injuries on June 10, 1926.

In his drawings and models for the uncompleted church of the Sagrada Familia (only one transept with one of its four towers was finished at his death), he equilibrated the cathedral-Gothic style beyond recognition into a complexly symbolic forest of helicoidal piers, hyperboloid vaults and sidewalls, and hyperbolic paraboloid roof that boggles the mind and outdoes the bizarre concrete shells built throughout the world in the 1960s by engineers and architects inspired by Gaudí. Apart from this and a similar, often uncritical, admiration for Gaudí by Surrealist and Abstract Expressionist painters and sculptors, Gaudí's influence was quite local, represented mainly by a few devotees of his equilibrated structure. He was ignored during the 1920s and '30s, when the International Style was the dominant architectural mode. By the 1960s, however, he came to be revered by professionals and laymen alike for the boundless and tenacious imagination that he used to attack each design challenge with which he was presented.

MAJOR WORKS

Most of the major works of Gaudí are in or near Barcelona.

Marginal notes:
Gaudí's styles and historic phases

His equilibrated system

Influence on his followers

Casa Vicens (1883–85); church of the Sagrada Familia (begun 1882, Gaudí in charge 1883–1926); Villa "El Capricho," Comillas, Santander (1883–85); Finca Güell (Güell Estate; *c.* 1884–87); Palacio Güell (1886–89); Palacio Episcopal, Astorga (1887–94); Colegio (school) de Sta. Teresa de Jesús (1888–91); Casa de los Botines, León (1891–94); Casa Calvet (1898–1901; some furnishings to 1904); Colonia Güell church, Santa Coloma de Cervelló (1898–*c.* 1915); Villa Bell Esguard (1900–02); Park Güell (1900–14); liturgical renovation of the cathedral of Palma, Majorca (1901–15); Casa Batlló (1904–06); Casa Milá (1906–10).

Gaudí's surviving drawings and modern measured drawings of his works are also in Barcelona, mainly at the Escuela Técnica Superior de Arquitectura, the Amigos de Gaudí, and the Sagrada Familia workshop. Small museums of Gaudí's work exist at the Park Güell and at the church of the Sagrada Familia in Barcelona.

BIBLIOGRAPHY. The most complete bibliography to date is in Ráfols' books, supplemented by Collins 1960 and Pane (all cited below). The Amigos de Gaudí of Barcelona and the Catalan Archive of Art and Architecture in New York are the primary research archives.

Biography and criticism: JUAN BERGOS, *Gaudí, l'home i l'obra* (1954); ENRIQUE CASANELLES, *Nueva vision de Gaudí* (1965; Eng. trans., *Antonio Gaudí: A Reappraisal,* 1967), critical essays; ALEJANDRO CIRICI PELLICER, *El arte modernista catalán* (1951 and 1960), comprehensive on background, with more than 500 illustrations; GEORGE R. COLLINS, *Antonio Gaudí* (1960), chronology and annotated bibliography; "Antonio Gaudí: Structure and Form," *Perspecta,* 8:63–90 (1963), a summary of Gaudí's structural procedures; "Transfer of Thin Masonry Vaulting from Spain to America," *J. Soc. Archit. Hist.,* 27:176–201 (1968), includes complete bibliography on the Catalan vaulting tradition that Gaudí inherited; "Gaudí and the Catalan Movement," *Pap. Am. Assn. Archit. Bibliographers* (in press), a listing of some 1,800 publications, based on the Catalan archive at Columbia University; and with JUAN BASSEGODA NONELL, *Portfolio of Gaudí Drawings* (in press), large size reproductions of drawings by Gaudí and architectural drawings of his buildings; and (ed.), *La Vision artistique et religieuse de Gaudí* (1969; Eng. trans., *Gaudí, the Visionary,* 1971), essays by Salvador Dalí, R. Descharnes, J. Alevedra, F. Pujols, and photos by C. Prévost—strong on anecdote and Gaudí as sculptor; CESAR MARTINELL, *Gaudí; su vida, su teoria, su obra* (1967), an encyclopaedic work summarizing the author's many publications; and *Conversaciones con Gaudí* (1969), the most complete collection of Gaudí's sayings; ROBERTO PANE, *Antoni Gaudí* (1964), the most detailed work to its date of publication (in Italian); ISIDRO PUIG BOADA, *El Templo de la Sagrada Familia* (1952), the most useful monograph on a single project; JOSE F. RAFOLS and FRANCISCO FOLGUERA, *Gaudí* (1929), the first and most basic monograph (in Spanish), with complete bibliography and chronology—originally 1928 in Catalan, later, and briefer, by Ráfols in Catalan, 1952 and 1960; JOSE L. SERT and JAMES J. SWEENEY, *Antoni Gaudí,* rev. ed. (1970), contains Sert's earlier valuable essays. The Barcelona periodicals *El Propagador de la Devoción a San José* (1867–1936, 1943–48), and its successor *Templo* (1948–   ), are dedicated to the church of the Sagrada Familia and, inevitably, to Gaudí.

(G.R.Co.)

Gauguin, Paul

Paul Gauguin, the leading French painter of the Postimpressionist period, in the late 19th century, was unique in his ability to hold a mysterious balance between idea, perception, and visual image. His pictures make their effect visually, not as a result of literary overtones. He was a great stylistic innovator, and, when he rejected the conception of a picture as a mirror image of an actual scene and turned from an empirical to a conceptual method of pictorial representation, his step was decisive for the developments in art during the first half of the 20th century.

Eugène-Henri-Paul Gauguin was born in Paris on June 7, 1848, the son of a journalist from Orléans and of a mother who was half French and half Peruvian Creole. After Napoleon III's coup d'etat, the Gauguin family moved in 1851 to Lima, and four years later Paul and his mother returned to Orléans. At the age of 17 he went to sea and for six years sailed about the world in freighters or men-of-war. In 1871 he joined the stockbroking firm of Bertin in Paris and in 1873 married a Danish girl, Mette Sophie Gad. His artistic leanings were first aroused by his guardian, Gustave Arosa, whose collection included pictures by Corot, Delacroix, and Millet,

Early years

"Self-Portrait," panel painting by Paul Gauguin, 1889. In the National Gallery of Art, Washington, D.C. 0.792 m × 0.513 m.
By courtesy of the National Gallery of Art, Washington, D.C., the Chester Dale Collection

and by a fellow stockbroker, Émile Schuffenecker, with whom he started painting. Gauguin soon started going to a studio to draw from a model and receive instruction. In 1876 his "Landscape at Viroflay" was accepted for the official annual exhibition, the Salon. He developed a taste for Impressionist painting and between 1876 and 1881 assembled an impressive group of paintings by Manet, Cézanne, Pissarro, Monet, and Jongkind.

Gauguin met Camille Pissarro in 1875–76 and began to work with him, struggling to master the techniques of drawing and painting. In 1880 he was invited to contribute to the fifth Impressionist exhibition, and this invitation was repeated in 1881 and 1882. He spent holidays painting with Pissarro and Paul Cézanne and made visible progress, though his early works are often marred by clumsiness and have drab colouring. Gauguin thus became more and more absorbed by painting and in 1883, when the Paris stock exchange crashed and he lost his job, he decided "to paint every day." This was a decision that changed the course of his whole life. He had a wife and four children, but he had no income and no one would buy his paintings. In 1884 Gauguin and his family moved to Copenhagen, where his wife's parents proved unsympathetic, and his marriage broke up. He returned to Paris in 1885, determined to sacrifice everything for his artistic vocation. From then on he lived in penury and discomfort, his health was undermined by hardship, he became an outcast from the society to which he had belonged and could never establish himself in any other, and he came to despise Europe and civilization.

In 1886 the expressive possibilities of colour were revealed to him in the pictures of Georges Seurat and Paul Signac, and he began to occupy himself with this aspect of painting at Pont-Aven, Brittany. Gauguin then had two decisive experiences: a meeting with Vincent van Gogh in Paris (1886) and a journey to Martinique (1887). The one brought him into contact with a passionate personality who had similar pictorial ideas and tried to involve him in working them out communally; this attempt came to a disastrous end after a few weeks at Arles in 1888. The other enabled Gauguin to discover for himself the brilliant colouring and sensuous delights of a tropical landscape and to experience the charm of a primitive

Break with Impressionism

community living the "natural" life. Gauguin decided to seek through painting an emotional release, in consequence of which he reacted against Impressionism. The key to his artistic attitude from 1888 on is to be found in these significant phrases:

> Primitive art proceeds from the spirit and makes use of nature. The so-called refined art proceeds from sensuality and serves nature. Nature is the servant of the former and the mistress of the latter. She demeans man's spirit by allowing him to adore her. That is the way by which we have tumbled into the abominable error of naturalism.

Gauguin therefore set out to redeem this error by "a reasoned and frank return to the beginning, that is to say to primitive art." A possible method for arriving at a new form of pictorial representation was suggested to him by Émile Bernard, a young artist well acquainted with stained glass, manuscripts, and folk art. He pointed out that in these arts reality was generally depicted in non-imitative terms and that the pictorial image was made up of areas of pure colour separated by heavy black outlines. Such was the origin of the style known as *cloisonnisme* or *synthétisme*, which attained its most expressive possibilities in such paintings by Gauguin as "The Vision After the Sermon" (1888), "Bonjour Monsieur Gauguin!" and "The Yellow Christ" (1889).

When Gauguin broke with his Impressionistic past he gave up using lines and colours to fool the eye into accepting the flat painted image as a re-creation of an actual scene and explored instead the capacity of these pictorial means to induce in a spectator a particular feeling. His forms became ideated and his colours suggestive abstractions. Maurice Denis, in *Théories* (1920), described a small painting executed by Paul Sérusier under Gauguin's direction in 1888; this landscape seemed to

> have no form as a result of being synthetically represented in violet, vermilion, Veronese green and other pure colours.... "How does that tree appear to you?" Gauguin had asked. "It's green isn't it? All right, do it in green, the finest green on your palette. And that shadow? Isn't it blue? Well then, don't be frightened of making it as blue as possible." Thus [writes Denis] was presented to us for the first time, in a paradoxical but unforgettable manner, the fertile conception of a painting as "a flat surface covered with colours arranged in a certain order."

Gauguin's primitivism

Gauguin indulged in "primitivism" because he could make a more easily intelligible image; his simple colour harmonies intensified this image; and, because he wanted his pictures to be pleasing to the eye, he aimed at a decorative effect. His purpose in all this was to express pictorially an "idea." It was as a result of this that he was acclaimed as a leading painter of the Symbolist movement. Gauguin's whole work is a protest against the soul-destroying materialism of bourgeois civilization. "Civilization that makes you suffer. Barbarism which is to me rejuvenation," he wrote (1891) to the Swedish playwright August Strindberg. So Gauguin installed himself in Brittany (Pont-Aven and Le Pouldu, 1889–90, 1894), Tahiti (1891–93, 1895–1901), and the Marquesas Islands (1901–03), where he could paint scenes of "natural" men and women.

Before 1891, Gauguin tended to flatten things deliberately, and his effect was often strained, but throughout the 1890s his primitivism became less aggressive as the influences of J.-A.-D. Ingres and Puvis de Chavannes led to increasingly rounded and modelled forms and a more sinuous line. This process can be followed in works such as "Nafea Faa Ipoipo" ("When Shall We be Married?"), "Nave Nave Mahana" ("Holiday"), and "Golden Bodies." Simultaneously, Gauguin's images became more luxuriant and more naturally poetic as he developed his marvellously orchestrated tonal harmonies. His chief Tahitian work—"Where Do We Come From? What Are We? Where Are We Going?"—is an immense canvas painted in 1897–98. This is the consummate expression of much that he had painted in the previous six years, and the aura of dreamlike, poetic inconsequence which surrounds this semi-philosophical allegory of primitive life is most powerful.

From 1899 on, Gauguin became increasingly ill and was continually in pain; he was also involved in frequent rows with the governing authorities for siding with the natives against them. Yet despite melancholy, his last pictures still have serenity and hope. He died at Atuana (Marquesas) on May 8, 1903.

Gauguin's influence

In 1889–90 a group of young followers had gathered round him at Pont-Aven, including Sérusier, Charles Filiger, and Denis, who transmitted Gauguin's ideas to Édouard Vuillard and Pierre Bonnard. The Norwegian painter Edvard Munch owed much to Gauguin, as did the painters of the Fauve group—Henri Matisse in particular—who profited from his use of colour. Gauguin's primitivism and stylistic simplifications greatly affected the young Picasso and led to the aesthetic appreciation of Negro art and hence to the evolution of Cubism. In Germany, too, Gauguin's influence was very strong.

MAJOR WORKS
FRANCE: "La Seine au Pont d'Iéna" (1875; Louvre, Paris); "Seamstress" (1880; Ny Carlsberg Glyptotek, Copenhagen); "Still Life in an Interior" (1885; private collection, U.S.); "Dance of Four Breton Women" (1886; Neue Pinakothek, Munich); "Martinique Landscape" (1887; National Gallery of Scotland, Edinburgh); "The Vision After the Sermon" (1888; National Gallery of Scotland); "The Swineherd" (1888; N. Simon Collection, Los Angeles); "Old Women of Arles" (1888; Art Institute of Chicago); "La Belle Angèle" (1889; Louvre); "Bonjour Monsieur Gauguin!" (1889; Národní Galerie, Prague); "Self-Portrait" (1889; National Gallery of Art, Washington, D.C.); "The Yellow Christ" (1889; Albright-Knox Art Gallery, Buffalo, N.Y.); "Marie Derrien" (1890; Art Institute of Chicago); "La Perte du pucelage" (1890–91; Chrysler Art Museum, Provincetown, Mass.).

TAHITI: "Femmes de Tahiti ou sur la plage" (1891; Louvre); "Street in Tahiti" (1891; Toledo Museum of Art, Ohio); "Suzanne Bambridge" (1891; Musées Royaux des Beaux-Arts, Brussels); "Reverie" (1891; William Rockhill Nelson and Atkins Museum of Fine Arts, Kansas City, Mo.); "Ia Orana Maria" (1891; Metropolitan Museum of Art, New York); "Nafea Faa Ipoipo" ("When Shall We Be Married?"; 1892; Kunstmuseum, Basel); "The Market" (1892; Kunstmuseum); "Manao Tupapau" (1892; private collection, U.S.); "Hina Tefatou" (1893; Museum of Modern Art, New York); "Poèmes Barbares" (1896; Fogg Art Museum, Cambridge, Mass.); "The Moulin David" (1896; Louvre); "Women with Mangoes" ("The King's Wife"; 1896; Pushkin Museum, Moscow); "Nave Nave Mahana" ("Holiday"; 1896; Musée des Beaux-Arts, Lyon); "Te Rerioa" (1897; Courtauld Institute Galleries, London); "Nevermore" (1897; Courtauld Institute Galleries); "Where Do We Come From? What Are We? Where Are We Going?" (1897–98; Museum of Fine Arts, Boston); "The White Horse" (1898; Louvre); "Two Tahitian Women" (1899; Metropolitan Museum of Art, New York); "Sunflowers and Pears" (1901; private collection, Paris); "Golden Bodies" (1901, Louvre); "L'Appel" (1902; Cleveland Museum of Art, Ohio); "Contes barbares" (1902; Museum Folkwang, Essen, West Germany).

BIBLIOGRAPHY. Only in recent years has an effort been made to get at the true facts of Gauguin's unhappy life and to divorce them from the legends that have grown up around his personality. Gauguin was the first to romanticize his own existence, by way of consoling himself and deceiving the world, while for reasons of their own many of his friends carried on the process. The most reliable source documents for information about Gauguin are his own letters, but unfortunately many of those to his wife and friends have still only been published in French in an incomplete and, textually as well as chronologically, inaccurate version. His personal writings are more significant for the light they throw on his character, imaginative processes, ideals, and imagery than for their factual accuracy. There is no definitive biography of Gauguin.

Biographies by friends: CHARLES MORICE, *Paul Gauguin*, new ed. (1920), in French; JEAN DE ROTONCHAMP, *Paul Gauguin, 1848–1903*, 2nd ed. (1925), in French; memoirs by his son, POLA GAUGUIN, *My Father, Paul Gauguin* (Eng. trans. 1937).

Other biographies: HENRI PERRUCHOT, *La Vie de Gauguin* (1961; Eng. trans., 1963); BENGT DANIELSSON, *Gauguins söderhavsår* (1964; Eng. trans., *Gauguin in the South Seas*, 1966); WAYNE V. ANDERSEN, *Gauguin's Paradise Lost* (1971).

Letters: *Lettres de Gauguin à sa femme et à ses amis* (1946; Eng. trans., *Gauguin's Letters to His Wife and Friends*, 1948), an unreliable translation; *Lettres de Paul Gauguin à Georges-Daniel de Monfreid* (1918; Eng. trans., 1923).

Personal writings: (Autobiographical): *The Intimate Journals of Paul Gauguin* (1923, reprinted 1952); *Racontars de*

Rapin (1951); SUZANNE DAMIRON (ed.), *Cahier pour Aline* (1963). (*South Sea mythology and sources of Imagery*): *Noa-Noa* (1924, reprinted 1961); *Ancien culte Mahorie* (1951).

Studies of special aspects of Gauguin's work: JOHN RE-WALD, *Post-Impressionism*, 2nd ed. (1962); MERETE BODEL-SEN, *Gauguin's Ceramics* (1964); *Gauguin, sa vie, son oeuvre,* special number of *Gazette des Beaux Arts,* vol. 47 (1958); WLADYSLAWA JAWORSKA, *Gauguin and the Pont-Aven School* (Eng. trans. 1972); H.R. ROOKMAAKER, *Synthetist Art Theories: Genesis and Nature of the Ideas on Art of Gauguin and His Circle* (1959); BENGT DANIELSSON and P. O'REILLY, *Gauguin journaliste à Tahiti et ses articles des "guêpes"* (1966).

(D.C.)

Gaul

Gaul (Latin Gallia) was the name given by the ancient Romans to the country inhabited by the Gauls—the Celtic peoples of present France, Belgium, western Germany, and northern Italy. These peoples began to move south and west from the Rhine Valley before 1500 BC; they reached the Mediterranean coast by the 5th century BC and by the 4th had moved into the Po Valley and down the Adriatic shore of Italy. There they were influenced by their more civilized Etruscan neighbours. Before the 7th century BC they had come into contact with the Greeks, and had frequent commercial relations with them after *c.* 600.

Cisalpine Gaul. In 350 BC the Gauls took possession of Bononia (Bologna), completing their occupation of what the Romans called Gallia Cisalpina (Gaul this side of the Alps). The Cisalpine Gauls were composed of several peoples: the Insubres (around Milan), the Cenomani (around Brescia and Verona), the Boii (between the Po and Apennine Mountains), and the Senones (between the Apennines and the Adriatic Sea), whose country was called the Ager Gallicus (the Gallic domain) by the Romans. The Gauls' capture and sack of Rome in 390 BC was a bitter experience for the Romans and was an important motive for their later conquest of Gaul.

The Gauls' sack of Rome

Between 350 and 300 there are no recorded Gallic expeditions into central Italy. A new wave of expansion, probably caused by fresh Celtic migrations from the north, began after 300, and in the 3rd century BC friction between the Romans and Gauls in Italy reached its highest point. The Gauls won victories at Clusium (Chiusi) in 295 and Arretium (Arezzo) in 284. They were stopped by the Romans at Sentinum (near present Sassoferrato) in 295 and at Lake Vadimon in 283. In the same period Rome began to found colonies in the borderland between its territory and that of the Gauls, seeking to prevent further Gallic expansion. After a period of peace (282–250) the Gauls began to push south once more. They suffered a major defeat at Cape Telamon (Talamone). The Cenomani were thereafter subjects and allies of Rome. In a series of offensives between 225 and 218 BC, the Romans inflicted defeat on the Insubres; they occupied Mediolanum (Milan) and founded colonies at Cremona and Placentia (Piacenza). The Carthaginian general Hannibal invaded the area in 218. After some initial conflicts with the Gauls he was able to make use of their help against the Romans. With the defeat of the Carthaginians, the Cisalpine Gallic peoples one by one submitted to Rome: the Cenomani in 197, the Insubres in 196, and the Boii in 191. Bononia became a Roman colony in 189 and Aquileia in 181. From this time on Cisalpine Gaul was subject to Roman rule.

Possession of this Gallic territory gave the Romans an advantage in extending their power into the rest of Gaul. It provided them with a base and a source for recruiting soldiers who knew the Gallic language and customs.

The Roman conquest of Gallia Narbonensis. Underwater explorations off the coast of southern France have shown that as early as the 2nd century BC Italian merchants controlled the greater part of sea traffic between Transalpine Gaul and the rest of the Mediterranean area. This commercial hegemony prepared the way for territorial conquest.

In 154 the Romans, at the request of the town of Massilia (Marseilles), conducted operations against the Ligurians in the area around Nicaea (Nice). Two expeditions, one in 125 and another in 124, led to the subjugation of the Vocontii, and to the defeat of the Salluvii. The Romans then made an alliance with the Aedui that gave them control over the routes between the Rhône, Saône, and Loire rivers and allowed them to intervene in the Rhône valley against the Arverni and Allobroges, enemies of the Aedui.

In 122 the Roman consul Domitius Ahenobarbus led an army through the Alps and defeated the Allobroges near the confluence of the Rhône and Sorgue rivers. Bituitus, king of the Arverni, intervened but was defeated in 121. Domitius established Roman control over the Rhône valley between 120 and 117. Narbo Martius (Narbonne) was founded as a colony in 118.

The invasion of the Rhône valley by the Germanic Cimbri and Teutones between 120 and 103 impressed on the Romans the strategic importance of their new acquisition. They were unsuccessful against the invaders until Marius defeated them at Aquae Sextiae (Aix) and Vercellae (Vercelli) in 102.

In the 1st century BC exploitation of the province of Narbonensis by governors, tax collectors, and bankers caused great discontent among the population. In 63 the Allobroges sent a delegation to Rome to protest to the Senate against these injustices, but were given only promises in reply. The result was a rebellion in 62 that had to be put down by Roman armies.

Roman expansion northward. Julius Caesar led the Roman forces that conquered the remainder of Gaul between 58 and 50 BC. The entire country was under Roman rule from then until the second half of the 5th century AD. The final phase of Roman conquest was triggered by the migration of the Helvetii into Gaul from what is now Switzerland, and the movement of Germanic peoples, notably the Suevi under Ariovistus, into northeastern Gaul. The Helvetii were halted at Bibracte (near present Autun) in 58. The Romans then turned to the Germans, who had occupied Alsace, defeating them near present Mulhouse in the same year.

Caesar's campaigns

Caesar extended Roman authority over most of Gaul with relatively little difficulty between 57 and 54, but the

Roman Gaul from the 1st to the 3rd centuries AD.
Adapted from *Westermann Grosser Atlas zur Weltgeschichte;* Georg Westermann Verlag, Braunschweig

outbreak of a general revolt in 53 necessitated a second, and far more arduous, conquest.

The revolt, led by the Gallic chieftain Vercingetorix, brought Caesar back to Gaul. A siege war followed, centred in the area between the Loire and Allier rivers. The Romans took Avaricum (modern Bourges) and prevented the southern rebels from joining forces with the Belgae in the north, finally defeating and capturing Vercingetorix at his stronghold in Alesia (near modern Alise-Sainte-Reine). This campaign demonstrated Caesar's military genius and the Gauls' fatal lack of organization. Some resistance continued after Vercingetorix's defeat, particularly by the Belgae and the peoples of the Massif Central, but by 50 Roman supremacy was re-established.

Caesar destroyed Gaul's capacity for resistance but left its cities with a large degree of autonomy. Gallic soldiers served him faithfully during his civil wars with Pompey (49–45). During those wars, in 49, Caesar's forces captured the pro-Pompeian city of Massilia after a long and difficult siege.

The colonies of Lugdunum (Lyon) and Augusta Raurica were founded in 43. Lugdunum became the administrative capital and economic centre of Roman Gaul. It was also a centre for Gallic religious assemblies surviving from pre-Roman times. In 27 BC, after the pacification of the more remote areas in the Alps and Pyrenees, the emperor Augustus divided Transalpine Gaul into four provinces: Narbonensis (present southeastern France), Aquitania (western France south of the Loire River), Celtica or Lugdunensis (between the Loire and the Seine), and Belgica (between the Seine and the Rhine, extending into present Switzerland). Germania Inferior and Germania Superior were created from parts of eastern Belgica late in the 1st century AD. Aquitania, Celtica, and Belgica were collectively known as the "Three Gauls" or Gallia Comata (long-haired Gaul). Augustus founded colonies for Roman veterans in Narbonensis, and encouraged the establishment of towns in other parts of the country. He also promoted the construction of a road system, conducted a census for taxation purposes, and established an ordinance survey. The extension of Roman control east to the Elbe River was prevented by a rising of the German tribes (AD 6) and the subsequent defeat of the Romans under Varus in AD 9.

Initially, the Gauls resisted romanization, but the suppression of a Gallic rebellion by the emperor Tiberius in AD 21 proved to be a turning point. It broke the power of the old Gallic land-owning class, which was the mainstay of Celtic civilization. This class had suffered from Roman taxation and was unable to adapt to the new regime which favoured the development of an urban class of merchants and craftsmen loyal to the emperor. Roman colonization also encouraged small-scale agriculture and raised the standard of living in rural areas.

The emperor Claudius (reigned 41–54) paved the way for the political integration of the Gallic nobles by making them eligible for membership in the Roman Senate. They were then given posts in the Roman administration. This policy furthered the assimilation of Gaul.

The Roman conquest of Britain in the last part of the 1st century opened up a new market for Gallic exports, which, with the completion of Gaul's road system and increased commerce with other parts of northern Europe, led to expansion of the Gallo-Roman economy and furthered the prosperity of the urban middle class.

Roman Gaul. By the time of Nero (reigned 54–68), Gaul had become sufficiently integrated into the Roman system to play a major role in imperial politics. The rebellion of Gaius Julius Vindex, governor of Lugdunensis (68), began the movement that ended in Nero's overthrow. In 70 a rebellion of the Batavi in the north, and the Treveri of the Moselle region, was suppressed by Vespasian.

In the political situation of the later 1st century, a division developed between the civilian and military classes in Roman Gaul. One was representative of the senatorial aristocracy and the interior provinces (Gallia Comata), and favoured permissive government, including the independence of the cities and the prerogatives of the no-

[margin: Political and economic integration]

bility. The other represented the frontier army districts and the cities dependent on them; this group favoured more authoritarian control. The opposition between these factions dominated the political life of Gaul until the end of the Roman period.

In the period of the Flavian emperors (AD 69–96), the conquest and colonization of the Agri Decumates or tithe land (present southwestern Germany) and the construction of a line of fortifications—the *limes*—connecting the middle Rhine with the upper Danube, extended the frontiers of Gaul and increased the influence of the frontier-military faction. The authoritarian government of the Flavians was popular with the army and the inhabitants of the newly annexed territories, but disliked by the civilian aristocracy. Economic expansion continued. An active industrial sector developed in northeastern Gaul, and agricultural production was stimulated by the colonization of the Agri Decumates. Under Vespasian (69–79) increasing amounts of government land came into the possession of small private owners.

In 96, when Nerva was made emperor by the Senate, his policies aroused the army, and there were disturbances along the Rhine frontier. Order was restored by Trajan in 97, and under him began a period of peace and stability that lasted until the time of Marcus Aurelius (reigned 161–80), when there was an uprising of the Sequani (in the Jura region) and the limes was crossed by German invaders. Under Commodus (reigned 180–92) an army of deserters and brigands laid waste to the southwest. The civil wars that followed Commodus' death had part of their origin in Gaul, where there was a rebellion among Rhine legions. An economic recession also began under Marcus Aurelius.

Christianity was introduced probably early in the 2nd century; over the next 200 years Gaul became an important Christian centre in the Western Empire.

[margin: The spread of Christianity]

The period of decline. In the 3rd century the country shared in the general decline of the Roman system in the West. Its towns, which often lacked a secure economic base, were hardest hit. The aristocracy was also hard pressed by increasing tax burdens, but was less hurt by the falling value of currency because its wealth was primarily in the land. The aristocracy were also given favoured treatment by some of the 3rd-century emperors. Many small farmers were ruined, though, and agricultural land tended to become concentrated in large estates. The army largely dominated politics, and the administration began to exercise increasing control over the economy in an attempt to arrest the growing inflation, mounting prices, and impoverishment of the wage-earning population. The Severan emperors (193–235) attempted to take corrective measures. The limes was restored and the Rhine frontier reoccupied; new industries—glassmaking at Colonia (Cologne) and Vienne (Vienna), weaving at Lugdunum—were introduced in an attempt to diversify the economy.

In the period 235–75, Gaul experienced a series of civil wars and invasions. The unity of the Western Empire disappeared for a time; after 260, an independent empire including Gaul, Spain, and Britain was established as a measure of self-defense in the wake of an invasion by the Germanic Franks. It was governed from Augusta Treverorum (Trier) by three successive rulers: Postumus, Victorinus, and Tetricus. In 273 the Roman emperor Aurelian reunited Gaul to the empire after defeating Tetricus near modern Chalons. The survival of locally minted coins and other artifacts from the period of the Gallic empire indicate a revival of the old Celtic tradition. The limes had been abandoned in 260, and in 275 the Agri Decumates was permanently evacuated. In 276, the country down to the borders of Spain was devastated by a new Germanic invasion. In the chaos that followed, bands of peasants and townsmen (Bagaudae) turned to brigandage. Order was restored once again by the emperors Aurelian and Probus, who fortified the principal towns to guard against future invasions.

Under Diocletian (reigned 284–305), Trier became the capital of one of the four new divisions of the empire, established to facilitate defense and administration. Gaul

[margin: Diocletian's reforms]

was governed by two "sub-emperors," Maximian (reigned 286–93) and Constantius Chlorus (reigned 293–306). Maximian established effective defenses against the Germans and suppressed the Bagaudae. Constantius put down the revolt of Marcus Aurelius Carausius in Britain and Gaul. The restoration of Gaul took 15 years, and the efforts of a numerous corps of officers and administrators. The old senatorial aristocracy was favoured once more. One of Constantius' projects was the revival of the school of rhetoric at Augustodunum (Autun).

In 306, on the death of Constantius, his son Constantine came to power. Seeking to make Trier the rival of Rome, Constantine beautified it with a circus, an amphitheatre, a forum, basilicas, and baths. In 312 he became emperor, and returned to Gaul only on short visits.

In 350 a usurper, Magnentius, tried to seize power, provoking a civil war in the course of which the Franks and Alemanni invaded northeastern Gaul. Julian (later, as emperor, called Julian the Apostate) defeated the Alemanni at Argentoratum (Strasbourg) in 357, and in the next few years expelled the Germans and reformed the administration of Gaul. The frontiers were precariously held until the great invasions of Vandals and other tribes at the end of 406. Even then Gaul remained a bastion of Roman civilization. A Roman general, Aetius, led his Gothic and Frankish allies to victory over the invading Huns in 451, and the classical literary tradition was kept alive in this last period of the empire by Ausonius, Symmachus, Sidonius Apollinaris, and other Gallic writers.

In the 5th century the Visigoths established themselves in Aquitania, the Franks occupied all of Belgica, and the Burgundians settled along the Rhine. Long before the Frankish Merovingians established control over the country in the early 6th century, Roman authority in Gaul had ceased to be a reality. (For the later history of the area, see MEROVINGIAN AND CAROLINGIAN AGE.)

BIBLIOGRAPHY

History: For material on the inhabitants, see J.J. HATT, *Celts and Gallo-Romans* (Eng. trans. 1970); and E.M. WIGHTMAN, *Roman Trier and Treveri* (1970). R. LATOUCHE, *Gaulois et Francs, de Vercingétorix à Charlemagne* (1965; Eng. trans., *Caesar to Charlemagne: The Beginning of France*, 1968), is more general. C. JULLIAN, *Histoire de la Gaule*, 8 vol. (1908–26), is still fundamental. See also O. BROGAN, *Roman Gaul* (1953); G.E.F. CHILVER, *Cisalpine Gaul: Social and Economic History from 49 B.C. to the Death of Trajan* (1941), which spans nearly two centuries in time; and A. GRENIER, *La Gaule romaine* (1937), mainly economic. T.R.E. HOLMES, *Caesar's Conquest of Gaul*, 2nd ed. (1911); and A. RAMBAUD, *Histoire de la Civilisation français*, 2 vol. (1885–87; Eng. trans., *Christian Gaul*, 1886), are still worth perusing.

Social and cultural life: Different facets are covered in D.E. EVANS, *Gaulish Personal Names: A Study of Some Continental Celtic Formations* (1967); E. ESPERANDIEU, *Recueil général des bas-reliefs, statues et bustes de la Gaule romaine*, 11 vol. (1907–38, reprinted 1966), a monumental survey of the art of the province and period; and C.B. PASCAL, *The Cults of Cisalpine Gaul* (1964). A more panoramic picture of the arts is given by M. POBE, *The Art of Roman Gaul: A Thousand Years of Celtic Art and Culture* (1961), supplemented by J.A. STANFIELD and G. SIMPSON, *Central Gaulish Potters* (1958); and N.V.L. RYBOT, *Armorican Art* (1952). For other cultural activities treated, see T.J. HAARHOFF, *Schools of Gaul: A Study of Pagan and Christian Education in the Last Century of the Western Empire*, 2nd ed. (1958); and S. DILL, *Roman Society in Gaul in the Merovingian Age* (1926, reprinted 1970). Still informative is G.T. STOKES, *Greek in Gaul down to A.D. 700* (1892).

Miscellaneous: J. WHATMOUGH, *The Dialects of Ancient Gaul: Prolegomena and Records of the Dialects* (1970), is useful on language. L.C. WEST, *Roman Gaul: The Objects of Trade* (1935), is also instructive; for a topographical account of a site, see the still relevant P.G. HAMERTON, *The Mount: Narrative of a Visit to the Site of a Gaulish City on Mount Beuvray* (1897).

(J.-J.H.)

Gaulle, Charles de

Charles de Gaulle twice saved his country from disaster and restored it to political and constitutional normality and twice retired voluntarily into private life when it became clear that he no longer had the support of the majority of his fellow citizens. A rare, if not unique, figure in political life, he combined these achievements with distinction both as a writer and as a military theoretician. Indeed, he did not emerge as a political figure until he was nearly 50 years old, though his previous career, both as soldier and writer, had already revealed some of the moral, intellectual, political, and temperamental qualities that characterized his subsequent career: first, as leader of a vanquished France and head of its first provisional postwar governments; second, as president of the Republic; and third, as autobiographer and historian of the events in which he had taken part.

Bruno Barbey—Magnum

De Gaulle, 1967.

Charles-André-Marie-Joseph de Gaulle was born on Nov. 22, 1890, in Lille. The second son of a Catholic, patriotic and nationalist, upper middle class family, he was brought up in a scholarly atmosphere. The family had produced historians and writers, and his father taught philosophy and literature. But as a boy, Charles de Gaulle already showed a passionate interest in military matters. He was trained at the Military Academy of Saint-Cyr and, in 1913, as a young second lieutenant, joined an infantry regiment commanded by Col. Philippe Pétain.

His military career showed him to be an intelligent, hard working, and zealous young soldier, a man of original mind, great self-assurance, and outstanding courage. In World War I, he fought at Verdun, was three times wounded, spent two years and eight months as a prisoner of war (during which time he made five unsuccessful attempts to escape), and was three times mentioned in dispatches. After a brief visit to Poland as member of a military mission, a year's teaching at Saint-Cyr, and a two-year course of special training in strategy and tactics at the École Supérieure de Guerre (War College), he was promoted by Marshal Pétain in 1925 to the Staff of the Conseil Supérieur de la Guerre (Supreme War Council). During 1927–29, and again during 1936–38, he served as major in the army occupying the Rhineland and was able to see for himself both the potential danger of German aggression and the inadequacy of the French defense effort. He also spent two years in the Middle East and then, having been promoted to lieutenant colonel, spent four years as a member of the secretariat of the Conseil supérieur de la Défense Nationale (National Defense Council).

His writing career began with a study of his reflections on the relation of the civil and military powers in Germany (*La Discorde chez l'ennemi*, 1924), followed by lectures on his conception of leadership, published in 1932, *Le Fil de l'epée* (English translation, *The Edge of the Sword*, 1960). A study on military theory, *Vers l'armée de métier*, in 1934 (English translation, *The Army of the Future*, 1940), defended the idea of a small professional army, highly mechanized and mobile, in

His early military career

preference to the static theories of the time, exemplified in reliance on the Maginot Line, which, running along the German and part of the Belgian frontier, was intended to protect France against German attack. He also wrote a memorandum in which he tried, even as late as January 1940, to convert politicians to his way of thinking. His views made him unpopular with his military superiors, and, in 1938, the question of his right to publish under his own signature a historical study of the French Army, *La France et son armée* (*France and Her Army*, 1945) led to a dispute with Marshal Pétain.

World War II. At the outbreak of World War II he was in command of a brigade of tanks attached to the French 5th Army. In May 1940, having been made a temporary brigadier general in the 4th Armoured Division—the rank that he retained for the rest of his life—he was twice given the opportunity to apply his theories on tank warfare, as far as that was possible with the inadequate material available at the time. As a result, he was mentioned by Gen. Maxime Weygand, the commander-in-chief, in a dispatch of June 2, as "an admirable, energetic, and courageous leader." On June 6, he entered the government of Paul Reynaud as undersecretary of state for defense and war, and undertook several missions to England to explore the possibilities of continuing the war. When the Reynaud government was replaced by that of Marshal Pétain, who intended to seek an armistice with the Germans, de Gaulle left for England. On June 18, he broadcast from London his first appeal to his compatriots to continue the war under his leadership.

Contrary to popular legend, this appeal did not include the famous phrase: "France has lost a battle; she has not lost the war." That phrase appeared on posters in England. But the emphasis was the same: the war could be won, France was not alone, General de Gaulle would lead French resistance from London. On August 2, 1940, a French military court tried him and sentenced him in absentia to death, deprivation of military rank, and confiscation of property.

De Gaulle entered on his wartime career as a political leader with tremendous liabilities. He had only a handful of haphazardly recruited political supporters and volunteers for what were to become the Free French Forces. He had no political status and was virtually unknown both in England and in France. What assets he had were wholly personal: his absolute belief in his own mission, his conviction that he possessed the qualities of leadership he had described in his writings, his total devotion to France, and the strength of character (or obstinacy, as it often appeared to the British) to fight for French interests as he saw them with all the resources at his disposal, however puny they might be. His impact on his hosts was unforgettably described by Sir Winston Churchill in *Their Finest Hour*:

> He had to be rude to the British to prove to French eyes that he was not a British puppet. He certainly carried out this policy with perseverance. He even one day explained this technique to me, and I fully comprehended the extraordinary difficulties of his problem. I have always admired his massive strength.

His liabilities in the eyes of his own countrymen were increased by the fact that, to the politicians of the left, a career officer who was a practicing Catholic was not an immediately acceptable political leader, while to those on the right he was a rebel against Philippe Pétain, a national hero and then France's only field marshal. Gradually, however, the course of the war, the broadcasts from London, the action of the Free French Forces, and the contacts of resistance groups in France either with his own organization or with those of the British secret services brought national recognition of his leadership. But full recognition by his allies came only after the liberation of Paris and the demonstration beyond all doubt of the French nation's acceptance of him.

Meanwhile, in London, de Gaulle's relations with the British government were never easy and de Gaulle often added to the strain, at times through his own misjudgment or touchiness. In 1943 he moved his headquarters to Algiers, where he became president of the French Committee of National Liberation—the central organization guiding the Free French war effort—at first jointly with Gen. Henri Giraud. De Gaulle's successful campaign to edge Giraud out gave the world proof of his skill in political manoeuvre. On Sept 9, 1944, he and his shadow government—the Committee of National Liberation—returned from Algiers to Paris. He headed two successive provisional governments but, on January 20, 1946, abruptly resigned apparently owing to irritation with the political parties forming the left-wing tripartite coalition government.

From then until 1958 he remained an opponent of what became, in November 1946, the Fourth French Republic. He campaigned against the new constitution, which he disapproved of as being likely to lead to a repetition of the political and governmental inadequacies of the Third Republic, which in part had led to France's capitulation to Germany in 1940. In April 1947, he formed the Rassemblement du Peuple Français (RPF), a mass movement that grew rapidly in strength and that to all intents and purposes became a political party in 1951, when it obtained 120 seats in the National Assembly in the elections of that year. The movement expressed de Gaulle's hostility to the constitution, to the party system, and, in particular, to the French Communists, whom he described as *les séparatistes* because of their unswerving loyalty to Moscow directives. He became dissatisfied with the parliamentary group, however, and in 1953 severed his connection with the parliamentary organization. In 1955 the RPF organization in the country was disbanded.

From 1955 to 1958, the General himself made no public appearances but retired to his home in Colombey-les-deux-Églises, where he continued to write his memoirs. Between 1954 and 1969, three volumes were published, dealing with the years from 1940 to 1946 (*L'Appel*, 1940–42; *L'Unité*, 1942–44; and *Le Salut*, 1944–46; English translations: *The Call to Honour*, 1955; *Unity*, 1959; *Salvation*, 1960). The last was completed only after his return to power in 1958, and it is possible, therefore, that the reasons there given for his retirement in 1946 owe something to hindsight. "In the prevailing state of affairs, I decided to go, because the disease was too advanced to be cured before the inevitable upheaval." At what precise point of time he began to feel that he might be called on to take up his mission again is a question on which accounts differ. The concluding words of the third volume of the memoirs describe his feelings during this period in the political wilderness but give no hint:

> An old man, worn out by all that he has gone through, remote from events, feeling the cold approach of eternity, but never tired of looking for the gleam of hope among the shadows.

Postwar return to public life. His compatriots were deeply divided on the question of his return. The reasons for their hesitations belong to the political history of the period. But, to those who know them, these reasons help to justify the view that the opportunity that presented itself in May 1958 (when the insurrection that had broken out in Algiers threatened to bring civil war to France) must have entailed for de Gaulle the most carefully balanced calculation of a life that had had its share of political gambles. He was cautious, for it was by no means certain that the French Parliament would accept his return on any conditions that he could accept. He affirmed his determination not to come to power by other than legal means, and there was never any evidence of his association with insurgent plans to bring him back. It was in any case inconsistent with his conception of leadership either to risk becoming an instrument of sedition or to risk political failure. On the other hand, his carefully worded statements (on May 15, 19, and 27) certainly helped the insurgents. On June 1, three days after President René Coty threatened to resign unless de Gaulle's return to power was accepted, he presented himself before the National Assembly as a prime minister designate and on the following day attended the session (having been duly "invested" as prime minister) and was authorized to reform the constitution and accorded the special powers that he demanded.

The man who then became head of government and, on Dec. 21, 1958, was elected president of the Republic had learned a great deal from his wartime exile and his postwar experiences, both in government and in opposition. The powers given to the president in the new constitution, which had been approved by referendum on Sept. 28, 1958, and especially those providing for the use of the referendum and for presidential rule during a state of emergency, reflected his firm conviction that a strong state required a leader with power to make decisions. His belief in his own "legitimacy"—by which he understood the essential rightness of his claim to be the leader and the incarnation of France—was now accompanied by the realization that his fellow citizens would share this view only in a crisis and that he must, therefore, take steps to retain the support of the general public and to disarm the power of "the system of parties" in Parliament, always potentially hostile to him. Since he believed firmly that power must rest on popular consent, his tactics were first to obtain consent to the personal control of government policy by the president and then to ensure its renewal in regular consultations through elections or referendums. He, therefore, undertook throughout his presidency what was virtually a continuous election campaign, in the form of provincial tours, in which he visited every *département* and during which he was able to meet ordinary citizens as well as local notabilities. He appeared on television several times a year. In order to be able to control government policy effectively, he relied as far as possible on ministers who were *compagnons*—that is, whose Gaullist loyalties went back to the wartime days—and he relied on their use of the constitutional provisions to curb the powers of the deputies to obstruct parliamentary business or harass governments. He retained the essential parliamentary function in a democracy; namely, the right to criticize governments and to withdraw confidence in them. The right of the National Assembly to dismiss governments was exercised on only one occasion, on October 5, 1962, in circumstances described below. There were frequent complaints of progovernmental bias on the radio, but these had been regularly made under pre-Gaullist regimes. Under a law of 1881, insults to the president of the Republic constitute an offense, and, though there was certainly more recourse to this law under the presidency of de Gaulle than under previous regimes, it presented no obstacle at all to political criticisms of Gaullist policies and Gaullist ministers in the press and in political parties, where criticism of the president's political actions and statements was continuous and widespread.

For the first four years of his presidency, de Gaulle's indispensability, as providing the only remaining hope of ending the Algerian war without civil disorder, protected him from serious challenge by his opponents. But the demands of the Algerian war prevented him from doing

more than prepare the way for future positive policies. He used these years to strengthen the country's economic situation, to plan the future reorganization of the army, to develop an independent nuclear deterrent, and to prevent fresh "Algerias" in the future, by providing for the constitutional transformation of the African overseas territories into 12 politically independent states, still effectively bound to France by ties of language and culture, as well as by their need of French technical, financial, and administrative aid to ensure their political survival. But from the middle of 1962 onward, with the recognition of an independent Algerian state, it became necessary to consolidate his own position by obtaining a fresh vote of confidence from the electorate, for he was no longer politically indispensable.

One lesson that he had learned from his experience as wartime leader and from the failure of the RPF was that his personal position was stronger if he remained, at least in theory, above the political and party battle, as he had tried to do during the wartime and early postwar years. In his press conference of Oct. 23, 1958, before the elections of 1958, he had therefore forbidden his supporters to use his name, "even in the form of an adjective," in the title of any group or candidate. In 1962

the issue on which he asked for the renewal of confidence in his leadership was the constitutional provision governing the election of the president. He offered the electors the choice between his resignation and acceptance of a constitutional amendment substituting election by universal suffrage for election by an electoral college consisting of some 80,000 members, mainly mayors and local notabilities. On October 28, the electors' reply was 13,-150,516 votes in favour of the amendment and 7,974,538 against. The government's defeat in the National Assembly, on a censure motion condemning the use of the referendum in order to amend the constitution, entailed a general election in November, in which the Gaullist party gained an additional 64 seats, thus obtaining, with the support of a group of some 30 conservative deputies, a majority in the National Assembly. The first real challenge to the continuance of his mission had been successfully met. From November 1962 onward, he was in a position of strength that allowed him to carry out, with public consent, the plans that he regarded as essential in order to restore France to the status in the world that he had always regarded as its permanent right—that of a great power, in no way inferior to those whom he liked to call "the Anglo-Saxons." His methods belonged essentially to the man. As a soldier, he had always seen military problems as inseparable from politics. As a statesman, he fought his political battles like a military campaign, using all the devices that he had learned to use so effectively in his dependent situation in London, in order to transform France's postwar international position of weakness into one of strength and to overcome opposition to his plans at home. These devices have been often described by his fellow citizens: "egoism, pride, aloofness, guile," according to Raymond Aron; "empiricism, intuition, flexibility of mind if not of soul . . ." according to one of the most perceptive of his biographers (Jean Lacouture, *De Gaulle*).

During the first phase of his subsequent career, from 1962 until his re-election as president in 1965, he used the European Economic Community (EEC) as an instrument in the service of French interests and especially of agricultural interests. He attempted to use it to establish a European political communuity, of which France would be the leader, but fell back on German cooperation under the Franco-German Treaty of January 1963, when it was clear that agreement on political cooperation was not obtainable from France's five partners. The rejection, in January 1963, of Great Britain's application to join the EEC was also a personal decision. France's participation in the supranational defense organizations of the North Atlantic Treaty Organization (NATO) was progessively withdrawn, because de Gaulle's policy for France was one of "national independence" and of international cooperation based, not on any supranational organization but only on agreements between nation-states. This was the main theme of his presidential campaign in 1965. On Dec. 21, 1965, he was re-elected, though only on the second ballot, and on March 7, 1966, he announced France's complete withdrawal from NATO, though not from the Atlantic Alliance.

During the three years and four months of the second term of his presidency, he turned his attention increasingly to wider fields. He had already begun the policy, described by him as that of "*détente* and cooperation" with countries behind the Iron Curtain, by encouraging trade and cultural relations with the Soviet Union and the countries of eastern Europe, and by recognizing Communist China in January 1964. For the solution of the conflict in Indochina he advocated a policy of neutrality for all nations concerned. This was to be based on a negotiated peace, of which a necessary preliminary was to be the withdrawal of all U.S. troops from Vietnam, though he never indicated at what date he thought this might become possible. These activities, together with visits to Mexico, all the countries of Latin America, Canada, and the Far East, formed part of a consistent policy aiming first at increasing the influence of France in French-speaking countries or countries in which there existed some bond derived from a common attachment to Latin culture; then in Europe, which he saw as going, sooner or later, beyond the boundaries created by membership in the European Economic Community or the division into western and eastern blocs; and finally in a world, in which he foresaw the gradual dissolution of the two great blocs. In his scheme, France could hope to play an important role, both by virtue of its independence of, and its good relations with, the Soviet Union as well as the United States and by virtue of the confidence in France that this independence could create in the uncommitted nations of sub-Saharan Africa and more especially in the countries of the Middle East and North Africa, which belonged, as he saw it, to France's natural sphere of influence.

Circumstances were against his success. First, while remaining within the Atlantic Alliance and dependent in practice on U.S. nuclear defense, he felt obliged to take up attitudes that were generally interpreted as anti-American. Anti-Americanism was popular with many of the uncommitted countries that he hoped to influence, and wartime experiences had made it popular with many of his own countrymen. But it was not popular with his partners in Europe. Second, the theory of what he called "desatellization," the progressive loosening of the Soviet hold on the countries of eastern Europe, was brutally invalidated by the Soviet invasion of Czechoslovakia in 1968. Nor was there any evidence that France carried any real weight with the countries that it hoped to influence. The Latin American tour did nothing to weaken the dominant influence of the United States. De Gaulle's policies of neutrality, whether in the Vietnamese War or in the Arab–Israeli War of 1967, did not influence the combatants nor were his *bona fides* as an "honest broker" recognized by them. In any event, as the political and economic crisis of May 1968 revealed, France had neither the internal cohesion nor the financial resources to play the role of leader in what, in his frequently repeated but never defined phrase, de Gaulle called "Europe from the Atlantic to the Urals."

It was the impact of cold facts such as these that led many of his opponents to conclude with Jean Lacouture that:

> Of all contemporary statesmen, Charles de Gaulle is the one whose political destiny will be seen to have depended most constantly on words. The soldier—brought out of obscurity by writing a book; the rebel—made into the leader of a nation by a speech; the man in opposition—who survived politically owing to a few interviews with the press; the President ruling by radio and television; and finally the lone wolf—in touch by words alone with the fickle mob. . . .

The truth is far more complex, though the last year of his presidency certainly justified the view that he could no longer count on his "words"—what it was then fashionable to call charisma but what he preferred to call "the personal equation." For this, circumstances were mainly responsible. His strength had been in his appeal for unity against a common enemy—in 1940, Germany; in 1958, subversion and civil disorder. In 1968 there was no common enemy. Once order had been restored, the students' and workers' revolt was seen for what it was, a temporary outburst of hysteria by sections of the community with real grievances but mutually incompatible aims. The solution of their problems required the patient negotiation of a government rather than leadership by a man of destiny. Moreover, the first of his broadcasts during the disturbances (on May 24), with its call for yet another referendum and its promises of "participation," proved ineffectual. The second, on May 30, was authoritative and brought a massive demonstration of support and a landslide Gaullist victory in the subsequent election, but the victory was for peace and normality rather than for the President and his policies.

There is no doubt that in the long run de Gaulle's position was weakened by the revolt of May 1968. When, in April 1969, he called once again for a referendum, it was not clear whether or not he really wanted to remain in power. If he did, he made three major errors of judgment. First, the referendum, calling for the acceptance of regional reorganization and a reform of the Senate, was presented to the electors, as other referenda had been, as a choice between acceptance of both (though the second measure was generally unpopular) or of his own resignation. Second, the diplomatic methods that had been welcomed during his first term, as assertions of France's claim to equality with, and influence among, the great powers had been creating increasing unease for the past few years. In September 1966, his advocacy in Phnom Penh of Vietnamese neutrality had been widely interpreted as an expression of personal anti-Americanism. In 1967, on his visit to Canada, he had seemed to be actively encouraging French-Canadian separatism. His declarations of neutrality in the Arab–Israeli War had seemed, to a population that was in the main pro-Israel, to show pro-Arab bias. France was not actively involved in, but had not formally withdrawn from, the Atlantic Alliance, and the so-called independent nuclear deterrent was neither independent nor within France's means, as the cost in terms of neglect of the needs of conventional forces and of basic social and economic reforms was by then revealing. And, third, the question: "After de Gaulle, who?" had been answered by the president himself, when he dismissed Georges Pompidou in 1968 after a record six years as prime minister, thus leaving him free to present himself in his own way as a credible and acceptable successor to the presidency.

On April 28, 1969, following his defeat in the referendum, de Gaulle resigned and returned to Colombey-les-deux-Églises, to permanent retirement and a resumption of the writing of his memoirs. He died there on November 9, 1970, of a heart attack. Throughout the decade of his presidency, his aims and actions had been the subject of more exegesis and speculation than those of any other French statesman.

Assessment. To some, de Gaulle was a 19th-century traditionalist or a nationalist—perhaps influenced by the ideas of Charles Maurras—who sought to recover for France a status that was no more than an outdated dream, while his picture of France was a nostalgic abstraction. To others, he was a farsighted statesman, subtle, and intelligent, who merely used popular "myths" as a means of persuading his fellow countrymen to accept his leadership, while he sought to compel them to make the economic and political adjustments required by the conditions of the 20th century. And there were some to whom de Gaulle's ideas themselves were also, in part at least, popular myths used by him as political instruments to enable him to take the maximum advantage of circumstances. These saw him as a pragmatist, an opportunist, even a gambler, doing what he could in incredibly difficult circumstances but with a fundamental fatalism, even pessimism, regarding the extent to which any political leader can change the "nature of things" or any French leader the nature of French politics. To some, he offered the only hope of obtaining the political stability that had eluded all regimes since the Revolution. But to others, he was inescapably an anachronism, because they saw him only as a man to turn to in a crisis, a man "at his best in the storm" and, as such, a passing phenomenon.

History will certainly recognize his undeniable qualities. As president, he maintained a regime of republican legality demonstrably based on popular consent and, when that ceased to be forthcoming, left the scene with dignity. He settled the problem of Algeria when no one else could, and though the cost in internal dissension and violence was high, the patience and political astuteness that he brought to what had seemed an insoluble task prevented the cost from being much higher. He achieved the peaceful "decolonization" of France's African territories in the shortest possible time, with a minimum of friction and a maximum of cooperation. These were personal achievements in the sense that he alone combined the sureness of purpose, authority, and courage to take the necessary decisions with all the political and personal risks that they often entailed—and these included several attempts to assassinate him. He also had the courage both to undertake unpalatable policies and to confront his compatriots with uncomfortable facts.

The qualities were accompanied by political and per-

Crisis of May 1968

Retirement and death

sonal liabilities, the consequences of which were bound to create problems for post-Gaullist statesmen. He was neither a team man nor a conciliator but a man alone, who disliked sharing either power or credit with ministers, Parliament, or parties, apparently refusing to recognize that these, imperfect as they may be, make up the permanent machinery of all stable democratic government. He served eternal France while distrusting Frenchmen and sometimes combined farsighted political strategy with nearsighted and even petty personal tactics. As an internationalist he understood the need for the strong to help the weak better than the need, at times, to make concessions that might be to France's short-term disadvantage in the interests of its long-term international relations.

As revealed in the memoirs, the personality of the man is deliberately submerged in that of the statesman and the leader. He appears as an artifact, the embodiment of "the leader" he describes in *Le Fil de l'épée*, and is often, indeed, referred to in the third person. That is how his contemporaries saw him. His personality is in sharp contrast with that other national hero in the same "darkest hour." While Winston Churchill was a career politician with a profound faith in Parliament and a passionate interest in defense, an expansive, warm-hearted man, with capricious, and even puckish, streaks, Charles de Gaulle was a career soldier with a passionate, indeed all-consuming, interest in politics and a profound contempt for career politicians. He was an aloof and remote man, because, in his own words, "authority requires prestige, and prestige requires remoteness." Future biographers may find, as their predecessors have done, that the "private face" of de Gaulle remains unknown and is perhaps unknowable.

BIBLIOGRAPHY. JEAN LACOUTURE, *De Gaulle* (1969; Eng. trans., 1970), the most penetrating study to date; AIDAN CRAWLEY, *De Gaulle* (1969), a critical but fair-minded study from a British point of view; EDWARD ASHCROFT, *De Gaulle* (1962), a straightforward account of his life up to 1962, sympathetic to Gaullism; DAVID THOMSON, *Two Frenchmen: Pierre Laval and Charles de Gaulle* (1951), the best short study of the prewar military career and the war years; FRANCOIS MAURIAC, *De Gaulle* (1964; Eng. trans., 1966), an adulatory biography including copious quotations from de Gaulle's speeches and press conferences; ALEXANDER WERTH, *De Gaulle* (1965), a journalistic, readable account; F.R. WILLIS (ed.), *De Gaulle: Anachronism, Realist, or Prophet?* (1966), a symposium on different aspects of de Gaulle that is somewhat superficial, but provides a useful introduction.

(D.M.P.)

Gauss, Carl Friedrich

Carl Friedrich Gauss, who, with Archimedes and Newton, ranks as one of the greatest mathematicians of all time, at an early age overturned the theories and methods of 18th-century mathematics and, following his own revolutionary theory of numbers, opened the way to a mid-19th-century rigorization of analysis. Although he contributed significantly to pure mathematics, he also made practical applications of importance for 20th-century astronomy, geodesy, and electromagnetism. His own dictum, "Mathematics, the queen of the sciences, and arithmetic, the queen of mathematics," aptly conveys his perception of the pivotal role of mathematics in science.

Born on April 30, 1777, in Brunswick, now in West Germany, Gauss was the only son of poor parents. Impressed by his ability in mathematics and languages, his teachers and his devoted mother recommended him to the Duke of Brunswick, who granted him financial assistance to continue his education in secondary school and from 1795 to 1798 to study mathematics at the University of Göttingen. In 1799 he obtained his doctorate in absentia from the university at Helmstedt. The subject of his dissertation was a proof of the fundamental theorem of algebra—which was proven only partially before Gauss—which states that every algebraic equation with complex coefficients has complex solutions; moreover, Gauss skillfully formulated and proved this theorem without the use of complex numbers.

At age 24 he published the *Disquisitiones Arithmeticae*,

Gauss, oil painting by C.A. Jensen (1792–1870). In the Archiv der Georg-August-Universität, Göttingen, West Germany.
By courtesy of the Archiv der Georg-August-Universitat, Gottingen, West Germany

one of the most brilliant achievements in the history of mathematics, in which he formulated systematic and widely influential concepts and methods of number theory—dealing with relationships and properties of integers $(-2, -1, 0, +1, +2, \cdots)$—which, for him, was of paramount importance in mathematics. He dealt extensively with the theory of congruent numbers—(*i.e.*, those numbers that have the same remainder when they are divided by another number (for example, 7 and 9 are congruent modulo the number 2 since there is a remainder of 1 when each is divided by 2); he gave the first proof of the law of quadratic reciprocity, which has to do with the quadratic residues (a is called quadratic residue with respect to b, if there is an integer x such that when a is divided by b, the remainder is the same as x^2 divided by b); and he applied this law to special cases of equations in which he was able to bring together algebraic, arithmetic, and geometric ideas. Using number theory, for example, Gauss proposed an algebraic solution to the geometric problem of constructing a regular polygon that has n sides. Euclid had shown that regular polygons, with 3, 4, 5, and 15 sides and those the sides of which result from doubling the above could be constructed geometrically with compass and ruler. No progress had been made in this subject since then. Gauss developed a criterion based on number theory by which it can be decided whether a regular polygon with any given number of corners can be geometrically constructed: these include, for example, the regular polygon with 17 sides, which he inscribed within a circle using only compass and ruler, the first such discovery since the time of Euclid.

This work on number theory contributed to the modern arithmetical theory of algebraic numbers—that is, to the solution of algebraic equations—in which Gauss introduced the first step—that is, the arithmetic of all complex numbers $a + b\sqrt{-1}$, in which a and b are integers. The complex numbers $a + b\sqrt{-1}$ had been introduced only intuitively before Gauss. In the *Disquisitiones Arithmeticae* Gauss did not hesitate to use complex numbers $a + b\sqrt{-1}$, in which a and b are real numbers. In 1831 (published 1832) he gave a detailed explanation of how an exact theory of complex numbers can be developed with the aid of representation in the x, y plane.

In 1801 Gauss had the opportunity to apply his superior computational skills in a dramatic way and, by so doing, to express gratitude to the Duke for assisting him in obtaining an education. On the first day of the year, a body, subsequently identified as an asteroid and named Ceres, was discovered as it seemed to approach the Sun. Astronomers had been unable to calculate its orbit, although they could observe it for 40 days until lost from view.

Contributions to number theory

Astronomical and geodetic research

After only three observations Gauss developed a technique for calculating its orbital components with such accuracy that several astronomers late in 1801 and early in 1802 were able to locate Ceres again without difficulty. As part of his technique, Gauss used his method of least squares, developed about 1794, a method by which the best estimated value is derived from the minimum sums of squared differences in a particular computation. This achievement in astronomy won Gauss prompt recognition. His methods, which he described in his book, in 1809, *Theoria Motus Corporum Coelestium*, are still in use today, and only a few modifications have been required to adapt his methods for modern computers. He had similar success with the asteroid Pallas, for which he refined his calculations to take into account the perturbations of its orbit by planets.

The Duke continued to finance Gauss's research so generously that in 1803 he was able to decline an offer of a professorship in St. Petersburg, where he was by then a corresponding member of the Academy of Sciences. In 1807 he became professor of astronomy and director of the new observatory at the University of Göttingen, where he remained for the rest of his life. His first wife died in 1809, after a marriage of four years and soon after the birth of their third child. From his second marriage (1810–31) were born two sons and a daughter.

About 1820 Gauss turned his attention to geodesy—the mathematical determination of the shape and size of the Earth's surface—to which he devoted much time in theoretical studies and field work. To increase the accuracy of surveying he invented the heliotrope, an instrument by which sunlight could be utilized to secure more accurate measurements. By introducing what is now known as the Gaussian error curve, he showed how probability could be represented by a bell-shaped curve, commonly called the normal curve of variation, which is basic to descriptions of statistically distributed data. He also was interested in determining the shape of the Earth by actual geodetic measurements, which led him back to pure theory. Using data from these measurements, he developed a theory of curved surfaces by which characteristics of a surface could be found solely by measuring the lengths of the curves that lie on the surface. This "intrinsic-surface theory" inspired one of his students, Bernhard Riemann, to develop a general intrinsic geometry of spaces with three or more dimensions. It was the subject of Riemann's inaugural lecture at Göttingen in 1854, and is said to have agitated Gauss. About 60 years later Riemann's ideas formed the mathematical basis for Einstein's general theory of relativity.

Contributions to non-Euclidean geometry and to physics

Gauss was one of the first to doubt that Euclidean geometry was inherent in nature and thought. Euclid was the first to build a systematic geometry. Certain basic ideas in his model are called axioms; they were the points of departure from which his entire system was constructed through pure logic. Of these, the parallel axiom played a prominent role from the beginning. According to this axiom, only one line can be drawn parallel to a given line through any point not on the given line. From this axiom soon arose the supposition that it can be deduced out of the other axioms and thus can be omitted from the system of axioms. All proofs of it however contained errors, and Gauss was one of the first to realize how there might be a geometry in which the parallel axiom does not apply. Gradually he came to the revolutionary conclusion that there is indeed such a geometry that is internally consistent and free of contradiction. Because it ran counter to contemporary views, he feared publication (see GEOMETRY, NON-EUCLIDEAN).

When a Hungarian, János Bolyai, and a Russian, Nikolay Lobachevsky, independently published a non-Euclidean geometry around 1830, Gauss announced that he had made the same conclusions approximately 30 years before. Neither did he publish his work on special complex functions, perhaps because he was unable to derive them from more general principles. Thus, this theory had to be reconstructed by other mathematicians from his calculations in work extending over several decades after his death.

Closely related to his interest in gravitation and magnetism was his published paper in 1840 on real analysis. This paper became the starting point for the modern theory of potential. It is probably the only work he did that failed to meet his own high standards. Only at the beginning of the 20th century was it possible for mathematicians to develop potential theory anew, on the basis of different principles or by finding the conditions under which Gauss's conclusions are completely correct.

Around 1830, principles of extremals (maximum and minimum quantities) began to assume a substantial role in his mathematical investigations of physical problems, such as the conditions in which a fluid remains at rest. In his treatment of capillary action, he devised mathematical formulations that took into account the mutual actions of all the particles in a fluid system, the force of gravity, and the interaction of its fluid particles and the particles of solid or fluid with which it is in contact. This work contributed to the development of the principle of the conservation of energy. Beginning in 1830, Gauss worked closely with the physicist Wilhelm Weber. As a result of their intense interest in terrestrial magnetism, they organized a worldwide system of stations for systematic observations. The most important practical result of their work in electromagnetism was the development, by other workers, of electric telegraphy. Because their finances were limited, their experiments were conducted on only a small scale; Gauss was rather frightened at the thought of worldwide communication.

Gauss was deeply religious, aristocratic in bearing, and conservative. He remained aloof from the progressive political currents of his time, asking only that his country enable him to do his creative work undisturbed. In Gauss, apparent contrasts were combined in an effective harmony. A brilliant arithmetician with a phenomenal memory for numbers, he was at once a profound theoretician and an outstanding practical mathematician. Theory and practice were mutually stimulating to him. Teaching was his only aversion, and, thus, he had only a few students. Instead, he effected the development of mathematics through his publications, about 155 titles, to which he devoted the greatest care. Three principles guided his work: "Pauca, sed matura" ("Few, but ripe"), his favourite saying; the motto "Ut nihil amplius desiderandum relictum sit" ("That nothing further remains to be done."); and his requirement of utmost rigour. It is evident from his posthumous works that there are extensive and important papers that he never published because, in his opinion, they did not satisfy one of these principles. He pursued a research topic in mathematics only when he might anticipate meaningful relationships of ideas and results that were commendable because of their elegance or generality. He was not inspired by the prospect of practical applications, for he sought truth for its own sake, finding his reward and pleasure in the success of his efforts alone.

The golden anniversary of the granting of the doctorate to Gauss was celebrated in 1849. For this event, he prepared a new edition of his earlier proofs of the fundamental theorem of algebra, which, because of his declining health, was his last publication. The honour that gave him the greatest joy, however, was the bestowal of honorary citizenship on him by the city of Göttingen. On the basis of his outstanding research in mathematics, astronomy, geodesy, and physics, he was elected as a fellow in many academies and learned societies. He declined numerous invitations of other universities to become a professor, and remained on the faculty of the University of Göttingen until his death on February 23, 1855. Soon after his death, coins were struck in his honour. The title of *mathematicorum princeps* is a fitting tribute.

Personality

BIBLIOGRAPHY. A recent study is TORD HALL, *Gauss, matematikernas konung* (1965; Eng. trans., *Carl Friedrich Gauss: A Biography*, 1970). WOLFGANG SARTORIUS VON WALTERSHAUSEN, *Gauss zum Gedächtniss* (1856), was written as a nonmathematical account of his life by a friend. See also *Carl Friedrich Gauss Werke*, 12 vol. (1863–1933), for publications, posthumous works, a part of Gauss's correspondence, and commentaries by the publishers; HANS REICHARDT (ed.), *C.F. Gauss Gedenkband anlässlich des 100 Todestages am 23, Februar 1855* (1957), which contains essays by prominent specialists on various aspects of Gauss's work, as well as facts on his life and activities; and ERIC T. BELL, "The Prince of Mathematicians," in *Men of Mathematics* (1937, reprinted 1961).

(H.Re.)

Gay-Lussac, Joseph-Louis

The French chemist and physicist Joseph-Louis Gay-Lussac was a pioneer in the study of gases, recognizing the simplicity of the laws describing the physical properties and chemical reactions of matter in the gaseous state. He also made a variety of significant contributions to all branches of chemistry and excelled in careful quantitative experimentation.

Gay-Lussac, engraving by Ambroise Tardieu (1788–1841).
By courtesy of the Bibliotheque Nationale, Paris

Gay-Lussac was born on December 6, 1778, at Saint Léonard in the *département* of Haute-Vienne. His father, a public official and judge under Louis XVI, was imprisoned for aristocratic sympathies during the Revolution. Young Gay-Lussac entered the new École Polytechnique in Paris in 1797 and was graduated in 1800. He started further engineering studies at the École des Ponts et Chaussées but withdrew in 1801 when invited to become assistant to the distinguished chemist Claude-Louis Berthollet. Much of Gay-Lussac's early research was done in the laboratory at Berthollet's country house at Arcueil, near Paris. This village was the centre of an active group of young scientists known as the Arcueil circle and guided by Berthollet and Pierre-Simon Laplace, both of whom enjoyed the patronage of Napoleon.

Early investigations

Gay-Lussac's first major investigation was a study of the thermal expansion of gases. In 1802 he showed that all gases expand by the same fraction of their volume for the same increase in temperature. The existence of this common thermal-expansion coefficient made it possible to define a new temperature scale, the profound thermodynamic significance of which was established by Sir William Thomson (later Lord Kelvin) almost half a century later. On August 24, 1804, Gay-Lussac and Jean-Baptiste Biot ascended in a hydrogen-filled balloon to a height of some 13,000 feet (about 4,000 metres) in order to study the variation of the Earth's magnetic intensity with altitude. Gay-Lussac made a second ascent alone on September 16 of the same year, reaching a height of 23,018 feet (7,016 metres), an altitude record that was unbroken for half a century. On his second flight Gay-Lussac repeated the magnetic measurements, studied the variation of pressure and temperature, and collected samples of air at an altitude of more than 20,000 feet (6,000 metres). He concluded from his observations and subsequent analyses that both the Earth's magnetic intensity and the chemical composition of the atmosphere were constant up to the altitude he had reached.

Shortly after the balloon flights, Gay-Lussac began to collaborate with Alexander von Humboldt, a Prussian nobleman, world traveller, self-taught scientist, and (later) scientific popularizer, who was then a new member of the Arcueil circle. Their experiments led in 1805 to a precise determination of the relative proportions with which hydrogen and oxygen combine to form water. Gay-Lussac emphasized that the proportion by volume rather than by weight should be studied, and the results justified his position: one volume of oxygen combines with two volumes of hydrogen in forming water.

On December 31, 1808, the year in which he was married, Gay-Lussac announced the law that now bears his name and constitutes his greatest contribution to science. By this time he had been elected a member of the Institut de France and appointed to a professorship in Paris. His chemical researches in collaboration with another French chemist, Louis-Jacques Thenard, had brought him back to the problem of the proportions in which chemical reagents combine. His own experiments, in conjunction with results already reported by others, led Gay-Lussac to the conclusion that "gases combine in very simple proportions" and that "the apparent contraction in volume which they experience on combination has also a simple relation to the volume of the gases, or at least to one of them." This relationship is known as the law of combining volumes and as Gay-Lussac's law. Among the simple proportions he cited as examples were the equal combining volumes of hydrogen chloride and ammonia and the 2:1 ratio of the combining volumes of carbon monoxide and oxygen.

Gay-Lussac's law

Gay-Lussac pointed out that the simple regularities of his law were realized only for gases, for which matter behaves in the simplest and most universal manner. It is worth noting that the English chemist John Dalton's laws of definite and multiple proportions in chemical composition (formulated in the same period) referred to combining weights and not to volumes. This basic difference in approach led each scientist to be skeptical of the other's results, and they did not reach mutual understanding. (The Italian physicist Amedeo Avogadro showed how the results of Dalton and Gay-Lussac could be reconciled.)

The collaborative work Gay-Lussac did with Thenard was prompted by Sir Humphry Davy's successful electrochemical research, and they used methods similar to Davy's to study the chemical effects of the electric current. After Davy isolated potassium and sodium, Gay-Lussac and Thenard prepared much larger quantities of the two newly discovered elements by purely chemical methods and were able to establish the properties of potassium. They anticipated Davy in discovering the element boron, which they named. Gay-Lussac and Davy independently and virtually simultaneously studied the properties of iodine (named by Gay-Lussac) in 1813.

Gay-Lussac's studies of hydrogen chloride, hydrogen iodide, and hydrogen fluoride prepared the way for a new theory of the nature of acids, although Gay-Lussac himself did not formulate it. (It had been held several years earlier by Antoine Lavoisier that oxygen is a common constituent of all acids.) In further work along this line, Gay-Lussac showed prussic acid (hydrocyanic acid, or hydrogen cyanide) to be composed only of hydrogen, carbon, and nitrogen. In 1815 he identified the gas cyanogen, $(CN)_2$, and pointed out that the combination of one carbon atom (C) and one nitrogen atom (N) acted as a compound radical—*i.e.*, a group of atoms acting as a single unit in chemical reactions.

Among Gay-Lussac's many other investigations were his early analyses of vegetable and animal substances, his studies of the solubility of salts as a function of temperature, and his important contributions to volumetric analysis. In 1832 he gave up his professorship of physics to accept the chair of chemistry at the Muséum National d'Histoire Naturelle in Paris. He also held a number of advisory positions, in which he used his technical knowledge to suggest improvements in industrial chemical processes.

He was elected to the Chamber of Deputies in 1831, 1834, and 1837 and in 1839 accepted a peerage from Louis-Philippe, after having refused one that had been offered years earlier by Charles X. Gay-Lussac died in Paris on May 9, 1850, and was buried in Père Lachaise Cemetery.

BIBLIOGRAPHY. A more detailed discussion of Gay-Lussac's work may be found in the article by MAURICE P. CROSLAND in *Dictionary of Scientific Biography*, vol. 5, pp. 317–327 (1972), that contains a bibliography of Gay-Lussac's major works and works about him. See also CROSLAND's *The Society of Arcueil: A View of French Science at the Time of Napoleon I* (1967); and EDMOND BLANC and LEON DELHOUME, *La vie émouvante et noble de Gay-Lussac* (1950).

Gemstones

The word gem derives from the Latin *gemma*, "a bud," which was once used for engraved stones such as cameo or intaglio. Subsequently it came to embrace those minerals, except the metals, that man uses for personal adornment. The term has been extended to include pearl and a few other materials of organic origin. It is still true that diamond, ruby, emerald, and sapphire come first to most minds, but less popular gems may surpass some of the above in beauty and indeed in value. In his desire for more of these beautiful objects than nature has provided, man has striven to synthesize them, and in recent time he has met with considerable success. It is still possible, however, to distinguish the synthetic from the natural, and each occupies its own role in the modern world. Some of the synthetic gems have important applications in industry and have supplanted the natural material. In the field of gems, however, the natural still holds prime place and value. By the middle of the 20th century, the terms precious and semiprecious, once applied to gems, largely had been discarded.

The use of gemstones dates to prehistory; evidence of their use turns up in graves wherever man dwelt. They were used for decoration and as amulets, and because of their value, they could be used as currency; the treasuries of many countries, particularly in the East, bulked large with gemstones. They still offer a means of condensing great value into minimum bulk for easy and hidden transportation.

For much relevant information on the mineralogy and crystallography of the gemstones, see also MINERALS; the separate articles on pertinent mineral groups (*e.g.*, OLIVINES; SILICA MINERALS); and for individual gem and mineral entries, see RELATED ENTRIES under GEMSTONES in the *Ready Reference and Index*.

GEM MINERALS

Although there are approximately 2,000 mineral species, less than 100 of these provide material usable for gems. The number is very much less if only those commonly for sale in the average jewelry store are considered. Some of these minerals supply more than one gem (*e.g.*, corundum: ruby and sapphire), and in the following discussions, the gems will be discussed under the appropriate mineral name.

Why is a gem so designated? What makes it one? The prime requisite for a gem is that it must be beautiful: if it does not attract, then it is worthless. The beauty may lie in colour or in lack of colour. In the latter case, extreme limpidity or "fire" or both may provide the attraction. Iridescence, opalescence, asterism, chatoyance, pattern, and lustre are other features that may make a material beautiful. It must also be rare and durable. The latter is necessary if the gem is to retain the polish applied to it and to withstand the wear and tear of constant handling. These features make a gemstone, but fashion also plays a part. Not all gems have these requisites in the same degree, which is, of course, the reason for variation in value of different minerals and of different gems of the same mineral.

Qualities required in a gem

Beryl. Beryl is a mineral that provides four specifically named gems of different colours: emerald, green; aquamarine, blue; morganite, pink; and heliodor, golden. In addition, some gems may be known as beryl but with the appropriate colour prefixed. The mineral is a beryllium aluminum silicate, and the several named varieties differ from each other in many small ways.

Emerald. Emerald, the green beryl, is, after ruby, the most valuable gem. It owes its colour to the presence of a trace of chromic oxide; variations in the colour of emeralds may be due to additional traces of iron and possibly vanadium. The earliest known mines for emerald were in Egypt in the Sikait-Zubara region near the Red Sea. Operated as early as 2000 BC, then lost for centuries, their locations were rediscovered only in the 19th century. It is probable that the emeralds of virtually all ancient jewelry came from these so-called Cleopatra's Mines.

Figure 1: Emerald box from the crown jewels of Iran. Size *c*. 6 × 5 × 3 cm.

The world's finest emeralds come from Colombia. Those from the Chivor Mine are blue-green and occur in pockets of crystals with albite and pyrite in fissure veins in clayey sediments of (probably) Cretaceous age. These Chivor emeralds have tiny, well-formed crystals of pyrite, which identify their locality. The emeralds found at the Muzo Mine are a rich, velvety green. They occur with quartz in calcite veins in limestones and shale. Colombian emeralds appear distinctly red when viewed through a Chelsea filter; Siberian emeralds appear pink, but most other emeralds appear green.

When the Spaniards invaded South America, they found the Incas in possession of vast quantities of fine emeralds, which they seized and transported to Europe, where they were avidly received. The French traveller and jewel trader Jean-Baptiste Tavernier, in his *Travels in India of Jean Baptiste Tavernier*, states that the Spaniards carried emeralds across the Pacific Ocean to Southeast Asia. These fine emeralds were purchased in tremendous quantity by the Moghuls and in due course fell into the hands of the Persian Nadir Shah in the sack of Delhi in 1739. Thousands of these emeralds, five over 300 carats in weight, still grace the collection of the crown jewels of Iran.

The Russians, who had long shown a liking for emeralds, in 1830 located a deposit of emeralds in mica, talc, and chlorite schists in the Ural Mountains near Ekaterinburg, now known as Sverdlovsk. These gems are lighter in colour than the Colombian stones and in general more flawed.

Emeralds have been found also in New South Wales, Western Australia, the State of Rājasthān in India, Brazil, Austria, Transvaal, and Rhodesia. Those from Rhodesia are small but of superb quality.

Because of their high value, few large, fine emeralds are included in Western museum collections, but there is a fine 48-carat, hexagonal cut emerald in the Palace da Ajuda, Lisbon. Many fine emeralds, including a step cut of 136.25 carats, are exhibited in the Armoury and Diamond Fund in the Kremlin in Moscow and in the

Topkapi Museum in Istanbul, but without doubt the largest and finest collection of this beautiful gem is in the crown jewels of Iran.

Aquamarine. Aquamarine is the sky-blue to greenish-blue variety of beryl, the most prized colour being the former. The colour is due to a trace of iron and usually is original, but it often is produced by heat treatment of greenish or even brownish crystals. Crystals usually show more complex terminations than do emeralds and may occur in large size and flawless condition, usually in pegmatite (coarse granite) dikes. Along with beryl of other colours it is found in Minas, Gerais, Brazil, near Sverdlovsk in the Urals, and in some other localities in the U.S.S.R. It is found also in the Malagasy Republic and several places in the New England states of the U.S. The Smithsonian Institution and the Geological Museum, London, have large, fine aquamarines on display.

Morganite. The pink beryl is known as morganite after the American financier John Pierpont Morgan, who was a lover of gems. Its colour is due to the presence of a trace of lithium. Like other beryls, with the exception of emerald, crystals of this gem occur in pegmatite dikes. Fine gem material comes from Minas Gerais, Brazil, the Malagasy Republic, and San Diego County, California. A fine 236-carat morganite and several other large stones are displayed in the Smithsonian Institution, Washington, D.C.

Yellow beryls and heliodor. Yellow beryls in fine quality and colour are found usually wherever aquamarines occur. Many shades of colour, from greenish yellow through pure yellow to fine golden yellow (heliodor), may be procured. The yellow colour is probably due to iron, but that of heliodor is attributed to the presence of a trace of uranium oxide. A tremendous, 2,054-carat, greenish-yellow Brazilian beryl and a 133-carat, yellow Malagasy stone are displayed in the Smithsonian Institution.

Other beryls. When the green colour of beryl is caused by iron rather than chromium, the gem is referred to as green beryl. Colourless beryl is known sometimes as goshenite, but it is seldom cut as a gem. A bright orange coloured beryl, some of which has been cut into gems, has been mined in the Governador Valadares region of Minas Gerais, along with aquamarine. A nearly clean, 1,625-carat, step-cut orange stone is displayed by the Royal Ontario Museum. No special name has been given to this colour.

The various coloured beryls are simulated by other gems, synthetic corundum and spinel, and by glass. Emerald has been synthesized hydrothermally.

Chrysoberyl. The mineral chrysoberyl provides greenish-yellow, yellow, green, and brownish gems of the same name and, in addition, two other gems, alexandrite and cat's-eye (sometimes called cymophane). Chrysoberyl is an oxide of beryllium and aluminum. Chromic oxide in small amount replacing alumina gives the green colour to alexandrite. There are no synthetic chrysoberyls, but simulations of alexandrite are common. These are either synthetic corundum or synthetic spinel, with the former more common. It appears grayish green in daylight and rather purple in incandescent tungsten light. Quartz cat's eyes may appear similar to chrysoberyl cat's eyes, but the low specific gravity and hardness are positive identification.

Chrysoberyl is a pleasingly lively gem, which is usually faceted in mixed cut; however, alexandrite and cat's-eye are the more interesting. Alexandrite has the peculiar property of appearing green in daylight and red in incandescent tungsten artificial light. The change is so startling and these gems are so rare that they command a very high price. In cat's-eye, very narrow parallel hollow tubes cause a sharp cat's-eye or chatoyant effect when the stone is cabochon cut with the base parallel to the tubes. The fineness of the tubes also produces an opalescent appearance that distinguishes it from the quartz variety of cat's-eye. These gems also are held in very high esteem, the value increasing with the richness of colour and sharpness of line. The finest alexandrites

were found in mica schist with emerald, northeast of Sverdlovsk (Ekaterinburg) in the Ural Mountains of the U.S.S.R. The gem was named after Tsar Alexander II on whose 21st birthday the discovery was made. Alexandrites also are found as pebbles in the Ceylon gem gravels, but these are less prized than the Russian gems. Their colour is less green, in artificial light there is considerable brown in the red, and the colour change is often not so marked. The Ceylonese gem gravels are the most important source of cat's-eye, and the state of Minas Gerais, Brazil, produces the best chrysoberyls. Other localities for chrysoberyl are the Malagasy Republic; Mogok, Burma; and Rhodesia.

The Hope chrysoberyl, once in the Hope collection with the more famous Hope diamond, is a flawless, yellowish-green, oval brilliant that weighs 45 carats. It is displayed in the British Museum of Natural History along with two fine Ceylon alexandrites, a 43-carat, square brilliant and a somewhat smaller one of 27.5 carats. The Smithsonian Institution has a 66-carat Ceylon alexandrite, a 121-carat chrysoberyl, and two great cat's-eyes of 172 carats and 58 carats, the latter cat's-eye known as the Maharani.

Corundum. Corundum, the oxide of aluminum (Al_2O_3), provides two gems, ruby and sapphire, which differ only in colour. The red gems are designated ruby and all other colours are sapphire. In the trade, however, sapphires other than blue in colour are called fancy sapphires. The name *padparadschah* (Sinhalese "lotus colour") is sometimes used for those sapphires of orange colour. The fine red colour of ruby is due to a trace of chromium oxide, that of blue sapphire to iron and titanium. Ruby is the most valued of gemstones, and its hardness of 9 exceeds that of any natural material save diamond.

Rubies and blue sapphires show marked dichroism (the property of presenting different colours in two different directions), and the darkest colour is presented when the stone is viewed along the hexagonal axis of the crystal. Faceted stones must be cut with the table facet at right angles to this direction in order to obtain the greatest depth of colour.

Mogok, 75 miles (120 kilometres) north of Mandalay, Burma, has produced the finest rubies from prehistoric times. Fine rubies, but of a slightly brownish hue, are produced in southeast Thailand and western Cambodia near the Thailand border. These rubies show little if any fluorescence. The red corundum of Ceylon is more correctly called pink sapphire. Ruby is also found in Tanzania, India, and a few other countries. Sapphires occur in and around Ratnapura, Sri Lanka (formerly Ceylon); Mogok, Burma; Kashmir; Thailand; Cambodia; Queensland and New South Wales, Australia; and Montana. Fine star rubies come from Mogok, whereas fine star sapphires have been found in both Mogok and Ceylonese deposits.

Rubies of large size have always been rare. Historically, any ruby found in the mines of Burma that exceeded ten carats was reserved to the ruler. It seems likely that many such stones were broken to reduce their weight and so save them from appropriation. Nevertheless, some did survive and many are displayed among the crown jewels of Iran. The finest and largest star ruby is the de Long (100 carats) in the American Museum of Natural History. The Smithsonian Institution displays 50- and 34-carat star rubies. The red gems known as the Timur ruby, Black Prince's ruby, and Catherine the Great's ruby, are all red spinels. Sapphires occur in larger size, and fine blue-faceted stones may be seen in such collections as the British and Iranian crown jewels. Large star sapphires also are known. The largest, the Star of India—a gray-blue, 563-carat stone from Ceylon—is in the American Museum of Natural History, as is the 116-carat, deep-purple Midnight Star. In the Smithsonian Institution are the blue, 330-carat Star of Asia; the blue, 316-carat Star of Artaban; and the blue, 98.6-carat Countess of Bismark. The 194-carat, blue Star of Lanka and an unnamed blue. 174.76-carat star sapphire are in

Nature and occurrence of cat's-eye

Some famous rubies of the world

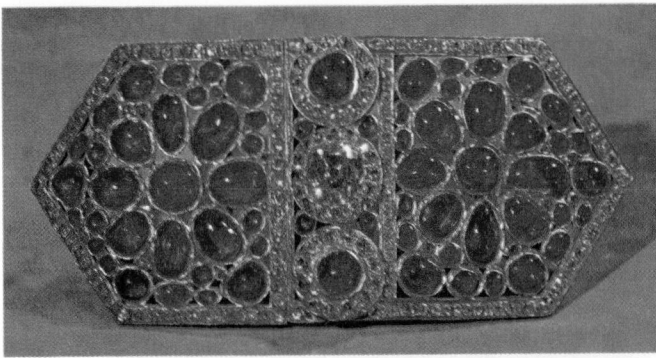

Figure 2: (Top) Ruby buckle from the crown jewels of Iran,
composed of 84 cabochon-cut Burmese rubies, a pale yellow
diamond, and smaller faceted diamonds. Length 16.7 cm.
(Bottom) Synthetic ruby crystal grown by the Czochralski
technique at Bell Laboratories, Murray Hill, N.J.
Approximately 6.98 cm.

By courtesy of (top) the Royal Ontario Museum, Toronto, (bottom) Bell Laboratories,
Murray Hill, N.J.

the Royal Ontario Museum, along with a faceted, golden-
yellow, 179.41-carat sapphire.

Diamond. Diamond is the most popular of gemstones
and is supposed to be the symbol of true love. It is the
hardest substance known and is ranked 10 on the Mohs
Scale. Sometimes there are so many natural faces on a
diamond crystal that it appears almost spherical. It has
excellent cleavage parallel to the four planes of the octahedron and therefore may be easily damaged by a blow.
Strong dispersion of light is the cause of the "fire" in this
gem. The best diamond is considered to be completely
colourless, without tinge of yellow. On rare occasions,
diamonds are found that display pure yellow, red, blue,
or green, and such stones are highly prized. The lustre of
the diamond is adamantine, a hard brilliant lustre, which
is the result of the high refractive index and the strong
dispersion (prismatic effect) of the mineral. The term is
derived from the Greek name *adamas* ("invincible") for
diamond. Composition of the stone is pure carbon, although inclusions may be small crystals of the minerals
diamond, diopside, enstatite, pyrope garnet, graphite,
iron hydroxide, magnetite, olivine, rutile, serpentine, and
chrome spinel. Diamonds with inclusions obvious to the
eye are usually used commercially for grinding and cutting. Some diamonds fluoresce in ultraviolet light, but
the colours are unpredictable, blue-white being most
common but green, peach, and apricot not infrequent.

Since the beauty of the colourless, relatively small
diamond is dependent on the fire that it displays, great
care must be taken in cutting. It was for this gem that
the brilliant cut was designed, and the angle between the
crown and pavilion facets is calculated so that the maximum of white light entering the crown will be reflected
back from the pavilion facets and be as widely separated
into its spectral colours as possible. If the diamond is
large enough, such cutting is not required, because the
white light travels far enough in traversing the stone so
that its spectrum is well developed. Such is the case with
large Indian diamonds that still retain their rather crude
pre-18th century cutting.

History of
diamond
discoveries

The world's diamonds came almost entirely from India
until the discovery of diamond in Brazil about 1725. It
is not known when they were discovered in India, but
they were reportedly known to Alexander the Great
nearly 2,000 years before Tavernier gave a written account of the diamond mines as they were at the time of
his visit in 1642. It was from the Golconda area, near
Hyderābād in south-central India, that most of the

famous historical diamonds came: the *Kūh-e Nūr,
Daryā-i Nūr,* Orlov, *Taj-e-Māh,* the Hope, and others.
Production in India waned as Brazilian production increased, and in time Brazil became the bigger producer
until in 1867 diamonds were discovered in South Africa.
In due course that country and its neighbours took over
first place, a position still held. Not until some time
after the discovery of diamonds in Africa was it known
in what rocks diamonds originated. In India and Brazil
the diamonds are found in gravel deposits or in somewhat consolidated sedimentary rocks, which are obviously not the original deposit. In South Africa they
were eventually traced to cylindrical bodies of igneous
rock, called pipes, that come from great depths in the
earth. This rock, a brecciated, ultrabasic material, is
known as kimberlite, after the original diamond mining
town of Kimberley. Because of its rather bluish-gray
colour, the miners dubbed it "blue ground." On the surface, this material weathers to a yellowish colour. In the
more than a century since the initial discovery, diamonds
have been found also in Rhodesia, South West Africa,
Congo, Angola, Ghana, Sierra Leone, Guinea, and Tanzania. It was in the latter country that a Canadian geologist, John Thoburn Williamson, found, by scientific
search, the source of the alluvial diamonds in the largest
diamond pipe yet known.

Figure 3: (Left) The Hope diamond; 44.5 carats. (Right) The
Star of Asia; 330-carat sapphire. Both in the Smithsonian
Institution, Washington, D.C.

The need for diamonds in the U.S.S.R. initiated a scientific search, and in 1955 diamonds were discovered in
pipes in far eastern Siberia, in the valley of the Vilyuysk
River, a tributary of the Lena. Diamonds are still produced in Brazil, and there is a small production from
India. Diamonds are found also in British Guiana and
Venezuela. Borneo, an early producer in a very small
way, still provides limited production of small stones.
Small diamonds, mainly of industrial grade, are found
occasionally in New South Wales and Queensland in
Australia. In North America, diamonds occur in a pipe
of peridotite (a rock similar in composition and origin
to kimberlite) at Murfreesboro, Arkansas. The largest
diamond found there was a 40.23-carat crystal. The deposit is now worked as a tourist attraction. Some fifty
diamonds have been found in the glacial gravels that lie
south of the Great Lakes. It seems likely that the source
of these stones lie in or north of the Great Lakes in
Canada, but they have not been discovered.

Feldspar. The feldspars (*q.v.*) are a group of sodium,
calcium, and potassium aluminum silicate minerals that
provide some gem and ornamental materials. Those of
interest as gems fall into two subgroups; one contains the
potash feldspars, orthoclase and microcline, and the
other consists of the plagioclase feldspars. All feldspars
have vitreous lustre and hardness of about 6, with two

excellent cleavages at about right angles. Gem material occurs in pegmatite dikes.

Potash feldspars. Orthoclase is the monoclinic potash feldspar and is found occasionally in transparent yellow crystals and lumps that are faceted into an attractive yellow stone, albeit without fire. This material comes from Itongay, Malagasy Republic.

Moonstone is colourless orthoclase that exhibits a blue opalescence or schiller from within the stone. The material is not pure orthoclase but an interlayering of very thin individuals (discrete plates) of orthoclase and the corresponding sodium feldspar, albite. The material from the gem gravels of Ceylon and Mogok, Burma, is the best. Indian moonstone is somewhat opaque and displays a variety of colours, from white through yellowish and reddish to bluish gray.

Amazonite (also called amazonstone) is the green variety of microcline, the triclinic potash feldspar. It is usually opaque, but a transparent variety has been reported recently from Baffin Island. It is not uncommon in small amounts in pegmatite dikes. The principal localities are: Virginia, Colorado, and other states in the U.S.; Ontario and Quebec, Canada; Minas Gerais, Brazil; Ural Mountains, U.S.S.R.; Malagasy Republic; and Tanzania. Because of its opacity it is cut *en cabochon*, as beads, and for ornaments. The colour varies from yellow green to blue green and from quite pale to very deep colour.

Plagioclase feldspars. All members of the plagioclase series exhibit fine, repeated, lamellar twinning (essentially plates that are side by side), which gives rise to fine parallel striae on the surface parallel to the base. Three varieties serve as gem materials.

Peristerite, a soda-rich variety, occurs in white and pastel shades of pink to gray. It shows a fine iridescence in flashes of pink and blue. Fine peristerite comes from the Canadian provinces of Ontario and Quebec, particularly the areas bordering the Ottawa River.

Sunstone, sometimes called aventurine feldspar, is an oligoclase (intermediate plagioclase) that has inclusions of tiny platelike crystals of iron oxide (goethite or hematite) arranged in parallel orientation through the host material. The reflections from the flakes give the otherwise colourless material a pleasing reddish glow. Sunstones occur on the south coast of Norway, Lake Baikal in the U.S.S.R., and in minor amounts in pegmatite dikes in many areas.

Labradorite is usually gray-coloured with brilliant iridescence, which, as in peristerite, may spread across large areas. Solid colours, as red, yellow, green, blue, and purple, or a mixture of two or more colours, may be displayed. The material may be cut *en cabochon* or slabbed. It was named for the fine deposit near Nain on the coast of Labrador, Canada. Gem quality labradorite occurs also in minor amounts in other countries.

Garnet. Garnet is a group of silicate minerals (*q.v.*), all of which are similar in crystal habit and correspond to the same general chemical formula even though the elements differ. Although spoken of as individuals, the members of the garnet group are probably only the relatively pure end members in several series of intermingled solid solutions (literally solids dissolved in other solids). Some of the physical and optical properties therefore vary considerably.

Pyrope and almandine. Pyrope always contains some iron and chromium, which are responsible for its blood-red colour. There seems to be a continuous solution series (no break or discontinuity in composition) with almandine, an iron aluminium silicate, which is a dark-red stone, often with a trace of purple. The colour of these gems is frequently quite dark, and to bring out the beauty they are often cut as hollow cabochons. Almandine occurs wherever there are metamorphic schists and gneisses. Two of the best localities of gem material are in Rājasthān, India, and in Brazil. Pyrope is found in the gem gravels of Ceylon and in Arizona. Asteriated (star-bearing) almandine has been found in India and Idaho.

Spessartine (*spessartite*). Spessartine is a manganese aluminium silicate in which some manganese commonly

is replaced by ferrous iron, and the alumina by ferric iron. The colour is usually yellowish orange but may range through brownish to orange-red. It can be confused with the similarly coloured hessonite. Spessartine is rare and is not often found in the cut form. It occurs in the Ceylon and Burmese gem gravels; Malagasy Republic; and Virginia.

Grossularite. Grossularite is a calcium aluminum silicate with a colour range from brownish yellow through brownish orange to orange, red, and green. Chrome green grossularite comes from Tanzania. Transparent material in the other colours, more usually called hessonite, comes mostly from the Ceylon gem gravels.

Andradite. Andradite is a calcium iron silicate; a variety containing a trace of chromium is termed demantoid, the most desired garnet and one of the rarest of gems. Demantoid is emerald green, has an adamantine lustre similar to that of diamond, a lower hardness, and a higher dispersion. Its "fire," however, may not be so apparent due to the deep colour of the gem. The main occurrence is in serpentine in the Ural Mountains of the U.S.S.R. in the Sissertsk district.

Uvarovite. Uvarovite is a garnet that occurs in lovely green crystals; their size, unfortunately, is too small for use as gems.

Jade. The term jade includes two massive mineral species, jadeite and nephrite, which have a certain similarity in appearance. Nephrite has been carved and revered by the Chinese for 3,000 years and is called by them *yu* (Jewel of Heaven). Jadeite was not introduced into China until the middle of the 18th century. As a result, much of the material thought of by Westerners as Chinese jade is nephrite. In addition to its use by the Chinese for beautiful carvings, jade has been used for tools, ornaments, and burial objects by Maori of New Zealand, the Indians of North and Central America, and by the Japanese in the vicinity of their small deposits at Omi and Kotaki on Honshu Island. Apparently the Spaniards who invaded Mexico saw a resemblance in the flat pebbles of jade to kidneys and called them kidney stones. Hence from *piedra de ijada* (stone of the loins) came "jade," and from *piedra de los riñónes* (kidney stones) came the Latin *lapis nephriticus* and the English word nephrite.

Nephrite. Nephrite varies in colour as a function of iron content, ranging from a deep spinach green to a near white known as mutton-fat, a jade much loved by the Chinese. It is a member of the amphiboles (*q.v.*) but is cryptocrystalline in form.

For centuries, nephrite was carried by camel train from Khotan in Sinkiang Province in far western China. There nephrite occurs as a thick layer in metamorphic schists and gneisses and as large boulders in the nearby streams. It is also found as very dark green boulders in the vicinity of Lake Baikal in southern Siberia. New Zealand jade is a dark green nephrite found *in situ* in talc and serpentine rocks at several places on the west side of South Island, where it is known as New Zealand greenstone, Maori jade, or axestone. Nephrite is found in northwestern Alaska; British Columbia; Lander, Wyoming; and in Placer County, California. Boulders from California and the Fraser River were shipped to China by Chinese gold miners and railroad labourers, respectively, and carved pieces undoubtedly have been returned as "Chinese jade." Small pieces of alluvial nephrite have been found in Mexico and Brazil. The occurrence of the stone in what is now part of Poland may be the source of the material found in the Swiss Lake dwellings.

Jadeite. Jadeite is one of the pyroxenes (*q.v.*) and always contains some calcium and magnesium. It is both harder and heavier than nephrite, not so fibrous, and is cryptocrystalline. Jadeite ranges in colour from pure white to black; it may occur in shades of red and brown, yellow, blue, mauve, and various shades of green, with which colour the name is wrongly considered synonymous. It is seldom that any of the colours occurs alone in a block of any size, and mottling is common. The most prized jadeite is the very translucent rich emerald green called "Imperial jade."

Amazonstone, sunstone, and labradorite

Uses and occurrence of jadeite and nephrite

The only important source of jadeite is in Burma, about 60 miles by jungle track northwest of Mogaung, the jade shipping point on the railroad to Rangoon. The jadeite occurs in bands in metamorphic rocks, from which it is mined. It is also obtained as alluvial boulders from the bed of the Uru River and other nearby streams. Jadeite has been found in minor amounts in a number of localities in California, and it occurs with nephrite in relatively small amounts in Japan, near Omi and Kotaki on the north side of Honshu Island. Some jadeite occurs in Central America, possibly near Costa Rica.

Jade is highly prized and there are a number of simulations. White jadeite has been dyed a fine bright green colour, but the colour is concentrated in fractures and on grain boundaries, and it is said to fade. A hard serpentine called bowenite, in light and dark green shades, is used in quantity to simulate nephrite. Much of this material comes from China, but is of worldwide occurrence. Bowenite is softer than jade, however, and a scratch test with a knife point on the base is usually sufficient to make the distinction. This material is sold as "New Jade"; it is attractive in its own right, but not as a fraud.

Lapis lazuli. The beautiful, blue, ornamental material lapis lazuli is a rock in which the principal components are the blue minerals haüynite and sodalite. Small crystals of pyrite, small amounts of white calcite, and other minor accessories commonly are included. The material is fine-grained and opaque and is usually cut as beads and plates or is carved. The darker the blue and the smaller the amount of pyrite and calcite present, the more highly it is prized. The physical properties of the material approximate those of haüynite but are modified by the presence of the pyrite and calcite.

Antiquity of lapis extraction Lapis, as it is called in the trade, occurs in thermally metamorphosed limestones. The best material comes from north of the Hindu Kush Mountains of Badakhshan in northern Afghanistan, where for 6,000 years it has been extracted by primitive methods in relatively small blocks (about ten pounds). Lapis lazuli of a lighter blue is found also in Chile, and it has been reported from a number of other localities, including Colorado and Baffin Island. During the tsarist regime of Russia, great quantities of lapis lazuli were used in the form of small plates about one inch square to veneer ornamental objects. Many of these may be seen in museums, in particular the Hermitage and St. Isaac's Cathedral in Leningrad. Because of the beauty and rarity of lapis, simulations are attempted, with particles of brass or gold sometimes included to imitate the pyrite. Such materials as glass, sintered synthetic blue spinel, plaster of Paris dyed blue, and dyed jasper have been encountered in the guise of lapis. A natural simulation, massive sodalite, has been found in mineable quantity in Ontario; in Bahia, Brazil; and in South West Africa. It is more crystalline in appearance, usually lacks pyrite and calcite inclusions, and has a lower specific gravity.

Olivine (peridot). The olivines (*q.v.*) are magnesium iron silicate minerals, and the magnesium-rich member chrysolite provides the gem peridot. The finest material is dark bottle green, but light yellowish green and brownish shades are known. Peridot is relatively soft and must be treated with care. There is little fire and so it is usually step cut, depending on its somewhat oily vitreous lustre and colour for its beauty.

The two sources of the best material are the Island of Zebirget (also known as Saint John's Island) in the Red Sea and near Mogok in Burma. The Zebirget gems often contain inclusions of brown biotite flakes, whereas those of Burma may contain crystals of magnetite. Large stones are not uncommon; there are peridots of 310 and 287 carats in the U.S. National Museum in Washington; a 146.17-carat in the Geological Museum, London; and a 193-carat in the U.S.S.R. Diamond Fund. The two gems with which peridot has been most commonly confused are emerald and chrysoberyl. The greater specific gravity and strong birefringence (transmission of light in different crystallographic directions) of peridot easily distinguish it.

Opal. Opal provides a gem that is highly prized for its iridescence. When this play of colour is not present the material is usually of little consequence. Chemically it is a hydrate of silica (SiO_2) and traditionally has been considered as an amorphous silica gel. Refinements in research techniques indicate that there is some form of crystallized silica present and that, in the case of iridescent material, the silica is present as minute spherical particles arranged in a three-dimensional lattice from which the spectral colours are produced by diffraction.

The quantity of water in opal ranges from 6 to 10 percent. It is deposited in openings of various shapes in sedimentary and igneous rocks through the action of hot water. It may replace mollusk shells, vegetable material, and even mineral crystals (see also SILICA MINERALS).

(Top) John H. Gerard—EB Inc., (bottom) John H. Gerard

Figure 4: *Opals from Australia.*
(Top) Black opal from the collection of the Department of Earth Sciences, Washington University, St. Louis, Mo. (Bottom) Cabochon-cut black opals, jelly opal (centre, right), and fire opal (upper left) from the collection of Joseph and Helen Guetterman, Belleville, Ill.

Iridescence and fire A number of gem varieties are recognized: white opal, black opal, water opal, and fire opal. In white opal, the body colour is in light pastel shades, whereas in black opal, it is dark-gray to black or blue. In both, the iridescence springs from the surface since the material is nearly opaque. Water opal has a transparent colourless body from the interior of which a spangled pattern emanates when the stone is viewed in incident light. In a rare variety of water opal, known as contra luz opal, the iridescence is seen only by transmitted light. Fire opal is transparent to translucent, orange-red to red in colour, with or without iridescence or fire, which of course may be masked by the depth of the body colour.

Opals are usually cut *en cabochon* or in slabs; faceting is reserved for fire opal. In the latter case, the table of the stone is usually buff topped, that is slightly convex. Since opal often occurs in thin seams and is opaque, it may be cut *en cabochon* but with the back often including considerable material that may be the country rock or non-iridescent opal, usually referred to as potch.

All opal until modern times came from mines near Czerwenitza, Czechoslovakia. White opal occurs in volcanic rocks in this area and has been mined there since

Figure 5: *Uncut varieties of quartz.*
(Left, top row, left to right) Rose quartz from Virginia, smoky quartz from Montana, jasper from Nevada. (Bottom row) Smoky quartz from Arkansas, citrine from Brazil, tiger's-eye from South Africa. In the collection of the Department of Earth Sciences, Washington University, St. Louis, Mo. (Right) White-tipped amethyst from Guerrero, Mexico.

(Left) John H. Gerard—EB Inc., (right) Lee Boltin

Roman times. Australia, however, is the big modern producer. The deposit at Lightning Ridge in northwestern New South Wales, discovered in the early 1900s, produces magnificent black opal from sandstones. More recent discoveries are at Coober Pedy (1915) and Andamooka (1930), both in South Australia. Opal has been found in numerous places in Mexico, but at the present time most production is centred on Queretaro, about 140 miles northwest of Mexico City. In that area, white opal, water opal, and fire opal occur as amygdules in rhyolite (fillings in cavities of volcanic rocks). In the United States the most important occurrence is in Virgin Valley, Humboldt County, Nevada, where black opal replaces wood.

Quartz. Quartz is a silica mineral species that, through variation of crystallization and colour, gives rise to a considerable number of varieties. Depending on colour, the gems are: colourless—rock crystal; lilac to purple—amethyst; shades of brown—cairngorm (with smoky tinge, smoky quartz; and when nearly black, morion); yellow—citrine.

Macrocrystalline quartz. Rock crystal is sometimes faceted. In the past, large crystals were carved into art objects and spheres, particularly by the Japanese and Chinese. Many museums display fine carved rock crystal objects dating even from Grecian times. Probably the largest sphere is the one in the U.S. National Museum, 12⅝ inches in diameter, weighing 106¾ pounds, and flawless. Large transparent crystals have come from the Malagasy Republic; Kai Province, Japan; Sakangyi, Burma; the states of Goyaz, Bahia, and Minas Gerais, Brazil. The latter is the principal source today. Rock crystal exhibiting inclusions of rutile needles is called rutilated quartz and may be used for carved objects.

The original cairngorm was found in the Cairngorm Mountains of Scotland. Faceted stones are still popular in Scotland, but most faceting cairngorm now comes from Brazil and is probably heat-treated amethyst. Fine crystals of brown quartz have come from Switzerland, from Colorado and Maine, among other localities in the U.S., and from Japan and other countries.

Citrine occurs naturally in shades from light yellow to reddish yellow. Most of the material on the market, however, is heat-treated amethyst from Brazil.

Colours of amethyst

Amethyst occurs usually in stubby crystals lining the interior walls of rock cavities. Only occasionally, as in Mexico, are the prism faces much developed. The colour, which may vary in intensity, may also vary in shade from bluish to reddish purple. Colour may be concentrated in the crystal tips, but care in cutting can cause the finished stone to appear uniformly coloured. By heating to temperatures up to 500° C, amethyst from various sources may provide a variety of colours in yellow, red, and even green. The yellow shades are most popular and are frequently, though wrongly, marketed as topaz.

Rose quartz seldom occurs as crystals but rather as coarse semitranslucent crystalline masses in pegmatite. These masses are used principally for carving.

Quartz containing closely packed fibres of asbestos in parallel orientation will provide quartz cat's-eye, some examples of which are rather similar to chrysoberyl cat's-eye. The quartz variety, however, lacks the translucency, sharpness of line, and slight opalescence of chrysoberyl. Quartz cat's-eyes may be yellow to gray-green and occur chiefly in the Ceylon gem gravels.

Quartz, pseudomorphous (false form) after blue asbestos called crocidolite, provides a massive chatoyant material which is used in carved objects and jewelry. If the material retains its blue colour, it is referred to as hawk's-eye. Usually, however, the iron content of the original material has become oxidized and the resulting golden-coloured material is known as tiger's-eye. Tiger's-eye turns red if heat treated and may be chemically bleached and then dyed. The best tiger's-eye comes from South West Africa.

Aventurine is a granular quartzite, a metamorphic rock, in which flakes of mica or other minerals may be included. A green variety used in jewelry comes mainly from Mysore, India.

Cryptocrystalline quartz. In this material, submicroscopic fibres of quartz are embedded in common opal in a mixture too fine grained to resolve except under magnification in polarized light. Some of it occurs in nature in gem quality.

Massive forms of the material are known as chalcedony, banded forms as agate. Both are produced by deposition from solution in openings, joints, or other cavities in older rocks, often basic volcanics such as basalt. The colour of chalcedony may be white, gray to blue gray, yellow to red, or green. The reddish-coloured variety is called carnelian. A "nephrite green" chalcedony, found in Rhodesia, owes its colour to the presence of chromium but the colour of most green chalcedony results from the presence of nickel. Such material, of which the apple green is most prized, is called chrysoprase. It is translucent and is usually cut as cabochons or slightly buff-topped stones with many facets around the girdle. As chrysoprase has always been scarce, simulations in glass and dyed gray chalcedony have been common.

Agate and its varieties

Most agate is banded and usually occurs in shades of gray although it may be coloured naturally. The present colour of most chalcedony and agate has been produced by dyeing in Idar-Oberstein, West Germany. Some agate contains inclusions of other minerals, in a branching or dendritic pattern. Black inclusions are manganese dioxide, green are chlorite, and red are iron oxide. Numerous varieties of agate have been given special names based on some feature such as pattern. One such material, known as moss agate, may be cut to exhibit interesting patterns that resemble trees, scenes, etc. Agates are of common occurrence, but their most important commercial source is in the Rio Grande do Sul area of Brazil and Uruguay. Thousands of tons of agates have been collected in North America in recent years.

Agate in which the bands are straight and parallel is known as onyx, and the bands are usually alternately black and white or gray. If the bands are alternately red or brown with white, the material is known as sardonyx. Much of the material marketed today is dyed, the coloured bands being separated by white bands impervious to the dyeing agent.

Jasper is an opaque form of cryptocrystalline quartz that is often strongly coloured: yellow, green, brown, red, and gray varieties are known. Dark-green jasper is also called plasma. When the latter contains red spots of iron oxide it is called bloodstone (heliotrope).

Buried organic material may be replaced by silica while retaining the cell structure. Petrified wood is a common pseudomorph of this type and is used for ornamental purposes.

Spinel. The gem spinel is an oxide of magnesium and aluminum that may contain iron, manganese, and chromium. These possibilities give rise to a wide variety of colour; carmine red, orange red, amethyst, and blue spinels are known. In the past, the red variety was thought to be ruby and was called balas ruby, probably for the source that was reported by Marco Polo to be in Badakhshan in Afghanistan on the Oxus River (Amu Darya). Although the red spinel resembles ruby, it may be distinguished by its single and lower index of refraction and its lower specific gravity. All the spinels take a fine polish but only the red one provides a gem in much demand. The two principal sources of gem spinel today are in the ruby and sapphire deposits of Mogok, Upper Burma, and in the gem gravels near Ratnapura, Sri Lanka. The deposits of Marco Polo's time in Afghanistan seem to have been worked out long ago.

Three world famous gems—the Timur ruby (361 carats) and the Black Prince's ruby (170 carats), both in the British crown jewels, and Catherine the Great's ruby (414 carats)—in the Russian Imperial crown gems are actually polished lumps of red spinel. All are matched in quality and surpassed in size by a 500-carat, polished but unfaceted red spinel in the crown jewels of Iran.

Topaz. Topaz is a gem of many colours, despite the common belief that all topaz is yellow and all yellow stones are topaz. Crystals may be colourless, blue, yellow, or brown. The most prized colour is the sherry brown. Although natural pink topaz is known, most is obtained through heat treatment of yellow material. Topaz may occur as crystals in cavities in fine-grained volcanic rocks but the origin of most gem material is as crystals in pegmatite dikes. In Minas Gerais, Brazil, where much gem topaz is found, the crystals are embedded in clays. The best localities for gem topaz are Ouro Preto, Brazil; in the Ural Mountains near Sverdlovsk, U.S.S.R.; and at Sakangyi, about 20 miles west of Mogok in Upper Burma.

Because of its transparency, topaz is usually faceted in brilliant or mixed cut, but the large gems are usually step cut. Crystals are often large and large cut stones are not rare. The 1,680-carat Braganza "diamond" of the Portuguese crown jewels is thought to be a colourless topaz. The Smithsonian Institution and the Royal Ontario Museum display large blue topazes of 3,273 and 3,000 carats, respectively. In addition, the Smithsonian displays a 7,725-carat yellow, a 1,469-carat yellow-green, and a 129-carat sherry topaz. The Royal Ontario Museum displays also a peach-coloured 364.79-carat stone from Burma and a magnificent 159.14-carat sherry-brown topaz from Brazil. The British Museum of Natural History possesses a 614-carat blue topaz and a colourless stone of 1,300 carats, while in the Geological Museum,

Large cut stones

Figure 6: (Top row, left to right) Amethyst and citrine from Brazil. (Second row) Golden or yellow beryl from Brazil, kunzite from California, aquamarine from Brazil, peridot from the Red Sea area. (Bottom row) Two of the colour varieties of topaz, both from Brazil. In the collections of Walter C. Blatt, St. Louis, Mo., and William V. Schmidt, New York.
John H. Gerard—EB Inc.

London, there are an emerald-cut blue topaz of 385.26 carats and an oval mixed-cut pink topaz of 33.46 carats.

Tourmaline. Tourmaline is a borosilicate mineral of variable composition that supplies gem material in almost kaleidoscopic colour variety: red, yellow, green, blue, brown, and variations of these. In the past some of these colours have been recognized by special names: red and pink—rubellite, blue—indicolite, colourless—achroite, and brown—dravite. Other colours were called tourmaline with the appropriate colour prefixed. This latter nomenclature is now being broadened, and the special names are being less used. Some material is chatoyant and some provide bicoloured stones, red at one end, green at the other, with possibly a colourless zone between. Tourmaline usually occurs in prismatic crystals with small dispersion and, therefore, with little fire. Its beauty depends on its colour and fine vitreous lustre.

John H. Gerard—EB Inc.

Figure 7: Tourmaline crystals from the United States (horizontal crystals in foreground) and from Brazil (other examples). In the collection of Joseph and Helen Guetterman, Belleville, Ill.

A most important feature of tourmaline is its marked dichroism, and this feature must be considered in cutting the gem. If a crystal has pleasing colour when viewed at right angles to its length it will be almost opaque when viewed along its length. It should therefore be cut with its table parallel to the long axis of the crystal. By contrast, some tourmalines may appear too light in colour if cut in this orientation and should be cut so that the table is at right angles to the long axis, thus appreciably deepening the preferred colour. The mixed cut seems to be most favoured in the faceting of tourmaline. Crystals containing large flawless areas are rare, and faceted tourmalines in excess of 100 carats are quite scarce. The Smithsonian Institution displays five tourmalines above this figure, the largest being a 173-carat champagne-coloured mixed cut from Mozambique. Fine stones below 100 carats are displayed in many museum collections.

Tourmaline commonly occurs in pegmatite dikes but also is found as rounded pebbles in gem gravels such as those of Ceylon. Fine gem tourmalines occur near Mursinka in the Ural Mountains, U.S.S.R.; Mogok in Upper Burma; northeastern Minas Gerais, Brazil; the Malagasy Republic (Island of Madagascar); South West Africa; Tanzania; and in Pala, California, and Paris, Maine.

Colours and fracturing **Turquoise.** Turquoise is an opaque mineral prized as a gem since antiquity. Except in parts of the Far East, the most prized colour is sky-blue (robin's-egg blue), the desirability decreasing with increase of green colour. Turquoise is one of the complex phosphate minerals (*q.v.*) and is found in veinlets, with the iron oxide limonite, in weathered volcanic rocks. Although tiny crystals have been found in Virginia, the actual gem material is massive. Sometimes the turquoise has been fractured and recemented by limonite. Such material is called turquoise matrix. Pure pieces larger than a walnut have always been rare. Turquoise fades on exposure to sunlight and its colour may be damaged by absorption of grease, perspiration, and coloured liquids. It is almost always cut *en cabochon* or is carved or engraved.

The finest material has always been obtained from Nīshāpūr, near Meshed in northeastern Iran. Exports from this source reached Europe through Turkey, and it is likely that the name turquoise, which is French for *Turkish*, originated in this way. The Iranian output now appears to be small and most is exported to the U.S.S.R. and India. Turquoise is found in the U.S. in New Mexico, Arizona, Nevada, and California. It was mined by the ancient Egyptians in the Sinai Peninsula.

Zircon. Zircon is a zirconium silicate with traces of iron, hafnium, uranium, and thorium. The mineral may be brown, leaf green, blue, golden, or colourless, and heat treatment can cause colour changes.

Colourless zircon, because its dispersion rivals that of diamond, has been used as a substitute for that gem. It may be distinguished readily, however, by its double refraction, much greater specific gravity, and by its relative softness. The brilliant cut brings out the maximum beauty in zircons of all colours. Most gem zircons come from Pailin, Cambodia, and near Chantaburi, Thailand, but they are also found in the gem gravels around Ratnapura, Sri Lanka.

Other gems. At the present time there are countless numbers of amateur lapidaries, many of whom rival or surpass professionals in skill. Since any mineral specimen that is beautiful, rare, and relatively durable may be cut as a gemstone, many minerals not mentioned above may appear in gem collections as collectors' items. Occasionally there may be enough of the material available and enough public demand so that the gem enters the normal retail market.

Spodumene. Spodumene is a lithium aluminum silicate whose beauty lies in its colour. It may be colourless or greenish yellow, but the two best colours are rose pink to purplish red, and emerald green. Those in the reddish shades provide the gem variety kunzite, named after the gemmologist George Frederick Kunz. Large crystals, originating in pegmatite dikes, have been found in the Malagasy Republic, in Connecticut and the Pala district of California, and in Governador Valadares, Minas Gerais, Brazil. A chrome-bearing emerald-green variety called hiddenite occurs in North Carolina, but in very small amounts.

Scapolite. Scapolite is a sodium aluminum silicate that may be colourless, pink, yellow, gray, or white. The major producers are Mogok, Upper Burma; Malagasy Republic; and the state of Espirito Santo, Brazil. Only the yellow variety is found outside Burma. The Smithsonian Institution displays a 288-carat colourless, a 30-carat colourless cat's-eye, and others. There is a yellow 76.11-carat Brazilian in the Geological Museum, London. The best scapolites in the Royal Ontario Museum are a 65.63-carat colourless mixed cut and an 18.30-carat pink cat's-eye.

Zoisite. In 1967, near Arusha in the Gerevi Hills in Tanzania, gemmy pebbles and pleochroic (differently coloured in different directions) crystals of a blue- to amethyst-coloured mineral were discovered. Eventually identified as zoisite, but never before seen in such discrete and large crystals, it is being offered by some gem dealers under the name "Tanzanite." Stones cut to exhibit the deep sapphire blue usually show flashes of purple in the outer crown facets due to the amazing pleochroism. Although most gem zoisite is amazingly free of inclusions, a cat's-eye of 18.2 carats has been obtained by the Smithsonian Institution, which also displays a very dark blue 122.7-carat faceted stone. The largest zoisite in the Royal Ontario Museum collection is a fine sapphire blue of 26.90 carats. **Tanzanite from Africa**

Sinhalite. A pale-yellow-brown to dark-brown borate mineral identified in 1952 but considered previously to be peridot is found in the Ceylon gem gravels. The name is derived from the Sanskrit name for Ceylon. Sinhalite is still a collector's item.

ORNAMENTAL MATERIALS

Although not gems in the strict sense, a number of minerals find use as ornamental materials because of their rich colour or pattern or both. Amazonite, chalcedony and agate, jade, jasper, labradorite, and lapis lazuli have been described above. Others that merit mention are: alabaster, blue-john (a massive fluorite from Derbyshire, England), malachite, rhodonite, serpentine, and sodalite (see the *Ready Reference and Index* for descriptions.)

Pearls. Pearls are organic in origin, and they have been prized since early times for the beauty of their form, colour, and lustre. They are formed in mollusks by the natural secretion of nacre, a mixture of organic conchiolin and tiny platy crystals of aragonite, around an irritant, such as a parasite or grain of sand, within the body of the animal. The pearls used in the gem trade are produced in the mollusk genus *Pinctada*. Beds of such mollusks were avidly harvested in the past in the Persian Gulf and across the Indian Ocean to northern Australia. Pearls also have been obtained off the shores of Venezuela and along the Pacific coast of Mexico.

John H. Gerard—EB Inc.

Figure 8: Natural pearls from the Persian Gulf. In the collections of Walter C. Blatt, St. Louis, Mo., and William V. Schmidt, New York.

Few new natural pearls enter today's market due to depletion of oyster beds, increase in costs of harvesting, and the high development of the Japanese cultured pearl industry. In this process, baby oysters, called spat, are collected in submerged cages and carefully tended until they are three years old. Then small beads of mother-of-pearl are inserted carefully into the mantle of each oyster and they are returned to their submerged cages for periods ranging from three to six years. During this time, the oyster secretes nacre in the usual manner around the artificially induced irritant. After harvesting, the pearls are graded for colour, size, and thickness of nacre. **Production of cultured pearls**

It is said that the natural life of pearls, unlike the inorganic gems, is probably less than 300 years. This period may be drastically shortened by exposing the pearl to hot and arid conditions, which will dry out the conchiolin, or, conversely, to very moist conditions, which may cause the conchiolin to swell and the pearl to peel. They must therefore be handled with care in order to preserve the beauty of their orient, the natural pearly lustre. Most pearls are white or silvery white but they may be pinkish, yellowish, dark gray, or black. Other colours—yellow, blue, purple, green, and bronze—occasionally are found. Pearls may be treated by bleaching or dyeing to improve colour.

Other organic gems. In addition to pearl, a number of other organic materials are considered as gems.

Amber. Amber is a fossil resin, usually yellowish brown, but on occasion deep brown to red, green, or blue. It is an amorphous hydrocarbon and may contain particles of various foreign materials, trapped insects, and air bubbles. Its lustre is greasy to resinous. The most noted occurrence of amber is along the shores of the Baltic Sea, where pieces have been washed up by wave action. Other important occurrences are along the coast of Sicily, in Romania, and in Burma near Myitkina.

Coral. Coral is the skeletal material of calcium carbonate built up by small animals that live in colonies in the sea. This material is usually branchlike and occurs in a variety of colours, of which the most sought after are rose red to red. The best coral comes from the Mediterranean Sea, particularly off the coasts of Algeria and Tunisia. A black horny coral growth, probably conchiolin, which hardens on exposure to air, has been obtained off the islands of Hawaii. Coral is carved into art objects and cut as beads, cameos, and other ornaments.

John H. Gerard—EB Inc.

Figure 9: (Top) Red coral from Italy. (Centre row, left to right) Serpentine from Burma, bloodstone or heliotrope from India, malachite from Rhodesia. (Bottom row) Tiger's-eye from Republic of South Africa, carnelian from Brazil, turquoise from Iran. In the collections of Walter C. Blatt, St. Louis, Mo., and William V. Schmidt, New York.

Ivory. The use of ivory for ornamental purposes dates to prehistory. The term should be restricted to the material derived from the tusks of certain animals, namely, the elephant, hippopotamus, warthog, walrus, sperm whale, narwhal, and the extinct mammoth (fossil ivory). The pale cream colour of new ivory darkens with age to yellow. All types are brittle and will not peel as do the plastics used to simulate them.

Jet. Jet is a dense variety of lignite formed by the submersion of driftwood in the mud of the sea floor. It has been recovered since Roman times from the shales near Whitby in northeast England. It takes a high polish and was once popular as mourning and ecclesiastical jewelry but has been superseded by black onyx, black tourmaline, and plastics. Because it is actually a variety of coal it will burn.

Birthstones. One of the earliest uses of gemstones was as talismans to bring good fortune or to ward off evil. About the middle of the 16th century, gems were assigned to each month, and a person looked on the gem of his birth month as his birthstone, hoping that its possession would bring him safety and fortune. The stones originally chosen were related to those of the Breastplate of the High Priest (biblical), but the list has varied from time to time. Although modern buyers probably seldom

credit the gems with supernatural powers, the "birthstone of the month" is still a popular feature of the jewelry trade. The current representatives are:

Birthstones of the Months	
month	stone
January	garnet
February	amethyst
March	bloodstone or aquamarine
April	diamond
May	emerald
June	pearl or moonstone
July	ruby
August	sardonyx or peridot
September	sapphire
October	opal or tourmaline
November	topaz or citrine
December	turquoise or lapis lazuli

IDENTIFICATION OF GEMSTONES

Because of the high intrinsic value of gems, testing for identification must be of a nondestructive nature. For example, under suitable conditions diamond will burn completely to carbon dioxide, leaving little or no residue. It is exceedingly good proof that the material *was* diamond. The tests carried out by gemmologists usually consist of determination of optical properties and specific gravity. Only when other tests to establish identity are unavailable is recourse made to the hardness test with its attendant risk.

Index of refraction. When light enters a mineral there is a change in its velocity and a concomitant change of direction. These changes are characteristic for a given substance or material and are measured in terms of a parameter called the index of refraction (see MINERALS). In gemmological testing, refractive indices are determined on a small instrument known as a refractometer. The stone is placed face down on the prism or hemisphere of the instrument and the index is read directly on an internal scale. By using a polarizing eyepiece or by changing the orientation of the gem or both, it may be determined whether the gem has more than one index of refraction. These simple steps go far toward identification of the gem.

Pleochroism. The gem may be placed between the crossed polarizers of a polariscope to provide further evidence of its optical character. This instrument may be used also to determine the nature of pleochroism in a coloured gem but pleochroism usually is determined with a dichroscope, in which the pleochroic colours are observed, two at a time, side by side in the eyepiece. Quite delicate differences of colour may be noted, and, by turning the gem, it may be determined if there are three colours, two, or only one.

Specific gravity. Specific gravity, or density of a gem, is a characteristic property but, like the index of refraction, it may show limited variations depending on slight changes in chemical composition and the presence or absence of inclusions. In the latter instance, the specific gravity of an emerald (G = 2.70) might be increased slightly by the presence of small crystals of pyrite (G = 5.0), or decreased by the presence of cavities containing fluid or gas. Two similar-appearing gemstones may have similar indices of refraction or similar specific gravity, but it is unlikely that they will show similarity in both respects. The combination of tests is therefore diagnostic.

Fluorescence. Further diagnostic information may be obtained by examination of the absorption lines of gemstones as observed in a spectroscope. Ultraviolet light is useful in some tests. For example, ruby and red spinel fluoresce red, but red garnet and red tourmaline do not; natural emerald does not fluoresce but most synthetic emerald fluoresces red.

The Chelsea filter is a simple device that transmits only red light and yellow green. Emerald, despite its green colour, absorbs yellow-green light and yet transmits deep red, which is masked in normal vision by the dark-green

Physical and optical tests

colour. Because the filter will not transmit the dark-green colour, the dark red is transmitted and most emeralds viewed through such a filter appear red or pink. Green glass and most other green gems appear green through the filter. Exceptions are demantoid garnet and a newly-discovered chromium-bearing tourmaline from Tanzania. Green fluorite and green zircon may exhibit a pink colour and care must be used in evaluating the results of this test since neither Indian nor South African emeralds show any colour change.

Other observations. Magnification by the microscope, the simple jeweller's loupe, or the hand lens may supply much information: uniformity, zoning, or patchiness of colour; diagnostic inclusions (*e.g.*, the horsetail-like wisps in demantoid or the curved bands of bubble inclusions in synthetic corundum); double images of back facet edges that are indicative of double refraction; "feathers" along incipient cleavages; scratches and other signs of wear on the surface indicative of a relatively soft gem; the shape of nicks in the girdle indicating the nature of cleavage or fracture or both.

THE CUTTING OF GEMS

The first gemstone was doubtless picked up because it was attractive to look at and the finder was satisfied with it. In order not to lose it, he may have placed it in a pouch, pierced it, or put a groove around it so that he could tie it with a thong to his person. In time, handling of the object may have resulted in a semblance of a polish on the surface and the realization that polishing provided an improvement in appearance. The practice of polishing a lump without increasing the symmetry was long the vogue and became even more important when, in the course of time, gems took on the importance of a form of currency. Any diminution of the size and weight of the stone would therefore be a diminution in the asset. Most gemstones, however, contain inclusions or other flaws such as cleavage feathers and cracks. It was found subsequently that such faults could be hidden, at least in part, and the value of the stone upgraded if multitudes of tiny flat surfaces or facets were applied all over the surface of the stone, the weight being decreased very little in the process. Symmetrical arrangement of facets followed and eventually angles between major facets were carefully calculated to make the most of the optical properties of a particular gem.

There are still two schools of thought with reference to beauty in a gemstone. In the Orient, it is argued that the weight of a gemstone should be retained as much as possible even at the expense of beauty of colour and symmetry. In the Western world, however, beauty of colour and symmetry are paramount. As a result, many gems cut in the East have lumpy form, particularly below the girdle, and must be recut before being offered on the Western market. Unlike native-cut Ceylon stones, however, those of Thailand are magnificently cut. Some of the principal kinds of cuts are as follows:

Cabochon. The cabochon is a symmetrical derivation of the polished lump. It usually has one flat surface that may be circular or elliptical in plan and has a shallow to steep dome. It is used for opaque gems, such as turquoise; iridescent gems such as opal; chatoyant and asteriated stones; and opalescent material such as moonstone. Occasionally it may be produced as a double cabochon, the curvature of the lower portion being seldom as steep as that of the upper.

Rose cuts. One of the earliest symmetrical faceted forms is the rose cut. Basically it is a cabochon to which facets have been added, usually in two concentric zones. The standard rose cut consists of six triangular shallow facets on top, surrounded by a steeper zone of 12 facets, also triangular. Modifications may provide rose-cut beads and drops, or pendeloques. If the latter are circular in cross section they are called rose-cut briolettes. Rose cuts in various forms have been applied to all the transparent gems known in the past and may be seen in quantity and large size (even exceeding 100 carats) in such collections as those of Topkapı and Iran.

The brilliant. It is not known when faceting of diamond had its beginning, but by Tavernier's time in the middle of the 17th century many lapidaries in India were cutting this gem. Most were fashioned as rose cuts, which undoubtedly conserved the most weight from a cleavage fragment of diamond; however, attempts were made to polish the rather commonly occurring octahedral crystals. The faces of this form are the hardest and are almost impossible to polish. By slightly altering the angle of abrasion, however, the material may be ground and polished, using diamond dust. The first result was essentially an eight-faced polished octahedron called a diamond point. Then came the grinding away of one corner until the new flat surface, called the table, was half the width of the stone at the girdle, or broadest portion. The opposite tip was blunted to form a small face, called a culet, applied to prevent accidental splitting of the stone. This ten-faced form, still essentially an octahedron, was termed the table cut. Although used principally for diamond it was also used for spinel, which exhibits the same crystallographic habit. Toward the end of the 17th century a Venetian, Vincenti Peruzzi, produced the prototype of the modern brilliant. The brilliant cut is based on the table cut with the addition of more facets. The important feature, however, is that the index of refraction of the diamond is taken into account in calculating the angles between the crown and pavilion facets. In this way, white light entering crown facets is totally reflected from the pavilion facets and returned through the crown to the eye. Because diamond has strong dispersion or "fire," the farther the white light travels before re-emerging, the more the ray of white light will be spread into its spectral colours. The standard brilliant as now cut is only slightly modified from Peruzzi's original. It is based on eight-fold symmetry with 32 facets plus the table in the crown, or upper portion, and 24 facets plus a culet in the pavilion, or lower portion. Modifications, particularly in larger stones, may increase these numbers, but the major angles remain fixed. The brilliant form is used for many gems—both colourless and coloured. In such cases, however, the angles between crown and pavilion facets are adapted to the refractive index of the particular gem.

Step cut or trap cut. This popular style of cutting is most used on coloured gems. It consists, as in the brilliant, of a crown and pavilion; however, the facets are arranged in zones parallel to the girdle. The basic shape is square or rectangular in cross section but it may have the corners truncated (a form often called the emerald cut) or, indeed, have any cross section that the lapidary may choose. Other things being equal, the angles between crown and pavilion facets should take into account the refractive index of the gem in order to return as much light as possible through the crown and prevent "bleeding" of light out through the pavilion. Bad bleeding makes a stone appear to have a big hole in the pavilion. In practice, however, the depth of the stone is often adjusted to modify the colour; if a very dark stone it may be cut shallow, and, if a pale colour, it will be cut as deep as possible to increase the colour.

Mixed cut. Another popular cut is the mixed cut. Usually such stones have a brilliant-cut crown and step-cut pavilions but the reverse is sometimes seen.

COLOUR IMPROVEMENT

Because colour or lack of it has much to do with the beauty of gemstones, many practices have been developed to assist nature. The proper cutting of a gem, as mentioned above, may markedly benefit the final colour. In some gems, as in amethyst and sapphire, colour is patchy. A good cutter can often fashion such a stone so that, when viewed through the crown, its colour appears to be dispersed evenly throughout.

Some gemstones change colour when heated, and the practice is so old and the results often so permanent that it is accepted in the gem trade. The method varies somewhat for different species but is basically one of heating the raw material in a container to a predetermined temperature under controlled conditions. Thus amethyst be-

Differing concepts of beauty in gems

Enhancing the fire of diamond

comes yellow citrine and yellowish-brown topaz from Ouro Preto, Brazil, becomes a delightful rose pink. Brown zircons heated under reducing conditions turn colourless, blue, or blue green, but in an oxidizing atmosphere turn colourless, golden yellow, and occasionally red.

Changes in the colour of some gemstones also can be produced by exposure to radium or X-rays. Unfortunately the colour is usually either of short duration or fades on exposure to sunlight. Still another method of improving the colour of a gemstone is the application of a pigment or coloured foil to the pavilion facets. This adds to the colour and, in the case of the foil, assists in reflecting light from facets not cut at the proper angle.

GEM COLLECTIONS

National gem treasures

In past centuries gems and jewels belonging to royalty have served two purposes. In wearing and displaying them, the ruler proclaimed his wealth and, by implication, his power and his right to rule. They served also as a treasury with which to purchase supplies of all kinds both in peace and war, to reward friends, and if necessary to buy off an enemy. Much of a nation's history may be connected with its crown jewels. Today, displayed statically behind glass for citizen and foreign visitor alike to see, these gems recall the country's periods of glory and provide glimpses of the tastes and characters of those who developed them. Some collections, such as those of the British and Iranians, are still drawn on periodically for coronations and to lesser degree for state occasions. The Iranian collection still acts as a national treasury in that it provides a backing for a part of the note issue. With the passing of the monarchy in such countries as the U.S.S.R. and Turkey, crown jewels have become museum collections to serve only as objects of beauty and lessons in history.

Crown jewels of Britain. The crown jewels of Britain probably have been viewed by more people than those of any other country. Before 1968, they were displayed in the Wakefield Tower of the Tower of London, but in that year a new and bigger jewel house was located elsewhere in the Tower complex in order to give visitors more opportunity to view and to study them. The collection is most noted for the regalia, which includes the historic St. Edward's crown, the orb and sceptre (all used in the coronation ceremonies), and the Imperial State crown. Some of the world's finest gems are included in this collection. Cullinan I, the world's largest cut diamond, is set in the sceptre: Cullinan II, the second largest cut diamond, is in the State crown, as are the Black Prince's ruby and the Stuart sapphire. The *Kūh-e Nūr*, the diamond with the longest recorded history and traditionally set in the crown of the queen consort, is at the present time set in the crown worn by the Queen Mother on state occasions.

Crown jewels of Iran. In 1960, the crown jewels of Iran were placed on public view in a specially constructed vault in the National Bank (Bank Melli) building in Tehrān. The bulk of the gems are the remnant of the booty acquired at the sack of Delhi by Nadir Shah in 1739. In their vast numbers, size, and quality they surpass any other collection of gems available to public view. Among the oldest objects are Nadir's gem-covered sword and buckler, but at least one gem, the *Daryā-i Nūr* diamond, seems to be traceable to 1642, when Tavernier saw it in Delhi. Most of the objects—throne, art objects, household wares, jewelry, arms, and armour—were made for the Qājār dynasty or were gifts to its members by other monarchs. With the coming of the Pahlavi dynasty in 1925, a new crown was produced and since that time a number of pieces of fine jewelry have been added. The most recent additions were the Empress' crown, jewelry, and other pieces, made for the occasion of the coronation in 1967 of Muhammad Reza Shah. The gems for all these items were drawn from older objects or from the large quantity of unset stones. Noteworthy among the gems are seven faceted diamonds of more than 100 carats each, five emeralds each in excess of 300 carats, the

world's largest and fourth largest red spinels, and a number of magnificent Burmese rubies in excess of 10 carats each. Here is displayed the greatest known aggregation of Indian diamonds, Colombian emeralds, Afghan spinels, and Burmese rubies. More gem-studded treasures, including a great bed-throne, are displayed in the Museum of the Golestān Palace, also in Tehrān.

The Diamond Fund and other collections of the U.S.S.R. The Diamond Fund of the U.S.S.R. is housed in the Kremlin in Moscow and has been available to the general public since 1967. The crowns and other regalia of the tsarist regime are displayed but of particular gemmological interest are the Orlov and the Shah diamonds, the "ruby" of Catherine the Great, blue sapphires of 258.8 and 200 carats, a 136.25-carat step-cut emerald, and many diamonds from the Siberian diamond field. Nearby, in the Armoury of the Kremlin, are other treasures: thrones, icons, arms, armour, and harness, richly set with gemstones. In the Hermitage Museum, the former winter palace of the tsars in Leningrad, other treasures and ornamental minerals remain in bountiful profusion.

Crown jewels of Turkey. The treasures of the Sultans of Turkey are now housed in four rooms of their former palace, the Topkapı Museum in Istanbul. They consist of gem-studded thrones, arms and armour, temple ornaments from Mecca, jikas and other personal jewelry, and various art objects. Noteworthy among the gemstones are an 86-carat pendeloque diamond, as well as large emeralds and red spinels.

Other collections. A number of other museums have been able to build quite substantial collections of gems and jewelry. The most notable of these are: American Museum of Natural History, New York; British Museum (Natural History), London; Field Museum of Natural History, Chicago; The Geological Museum, London; Royal Ontario Museum, Toronto; Smithsonian Institution, Washington; The Victoria and Albert Museum, London.

SYNTHETIC GEMSTONES

Growth from solution and growth from melts

Synthetic gemstones are produced in several ways that are derived from two principal methods, growth from solution and growth from a melt. In crystal growth from solution, the chemical components of the crystal are dissolved in a suitable solvent to produce a saturated solution. By allowing the temperature to lower or the solvent to evaporate, the solution becomes supersaturated and crystals of the desired substance may be produced. In actual practice in the production of synthetic gem materials, the process is usually carried out under high temperature and pressure; the hydrothermal technique or high-melting "fluxes" are used to dissolve the components.

The most widely used melt technique is the one invented by Verneuil (about 1890). In it, powder of the appropriate chemical composition is fused in an intense oxyhydrogen flame. Directed by the flame to a target, the fused matter gradually builds up a boule, a roughly cylindrical body, of sometimes several inches in length. The material of the boule has been known to crystallize as a single crystal, with the characteristic atomic structure and physical properties of the chemical substance, but because of the rapidity of growth, crystal faces are usually lacking. The production of boules requires that the chemicals and gases used be of exceptional purity. The desired colour is introduced by the addition of a small amount of foreign material. This method is used in the commercial production of synthetic corundum, spinel, rutile, and strontium titanate.

Ruby and sapphire. Ruby and sapphire may be produced by the Verneuil process, hydrothermally, and from flux. At the present time, the only economic method is the Verneuil technique. If made of pure aluminum oxide (alumina), the boule would be colourless. Suitable colours are obtained by the addition of small amounts of oxides, for example chromic oxide (about 8 percent) for ruby. Ruby and sapphire in most colours, except an acceptable blue, are produced in this way. Blue sapphire is usually simulated by a suitably coloured spinel. Asteriated boules are produced by adding a trace (0.1 to 0.3 percent) of titanium oxide to the alumina powder. After manufacture, the boule is heat treated and the titanium oxide precipitates as rutile needles, arranged in three intersecting planes.

Emerald. For more than a century, attempts have been made to synthesize the beautiful and valuable emerald, primarily by hydrothermal crystallization. The best known to date has been the process of Carroll F. Chatham of San Francisco. The process is secret but is said to be hydrothermal, which seems likely judging from groups of crystals that have appeared on the market. It is said further that crushed beryl is used as raw material and that a small crystal may be used as a "seed" in a tungsten or molybdate melt. Further reports indicate that the usable crystals take about one year to grow.

Distinc-
tions
between
synthetic
and
natural
emeralds

The Chatham synthetic emerald, grown as a crystal, does not exhibit curved growth lines as do corundum boules from the Verneuil furnace. There are, however, inclusions, which, although similar to those of natural emerald, are sufficiently different to be recognized by an expert. They are veil-like feathers either like waving curtains or in parallel bands. The feathers contain many liquid- and gas-filled inclusions. Because of the rather high content of these light inclusions, synthetic emerald has a specific gravity of about 2.65, sufficiently less than natural emerald that it will float in a liquid in which natural emerald sinks.

Spinel. Only the red natural spinel has appreciable value as a gem, and synthetic spinel of this colour apparently has been difficult to achieve. A red synthetic spinel is now marketed, but the stones are small due to the severe fracturing of the boules. Synthetic spinel finds its greatest use as simulations of other gems. Blue spinel can be prepared that comes closer to the colour of blue sapphire than does synthetic blue corundum. Most synthetic blue sapphires on the market are synthetic spinel and therefore are really simulated blue sapphire. Pale-blue spinel is also used to simulate aquamarine, for which there is no commercial synthetic. Other colours may simulate other important gems.

Rutile. Rutile is an interesting synthetic because gem material of the mineral rutile (TiO_2) is exceedingly rare. The synthetic appeared in 1948 and is a Verneuil product using purified titanium oxide powder. The usual colour is a very pale yellow, but other colours (yellow, orange, red, blue, and green) have been produced. It has very strong birefringence and cut stones exhibit marked doubling of back facet edges. The specific gravity is 4.25, heavier than corundum, and the dispersion—about six times that of diamond—is the most amazing feature of this material, providing it with phenomenal "fire." Unfortunately, it is relatively soft. As a material for personal adornment, it provides a fiery stone. As a simulation of diamond it is identified by lack of hardness, birefringence, specific gravity, and lack of the transparency that marks most of the diamonds. It has been marketed under the name Titania.

Strontium titanate. Still another synthetic is strontium titanate, a chemical as yet unknown in nature. It crystallizes in the isometric system, as does diamond, and is produced as water-clear, colourless boules. Cut stones show no doubling of back facet edges when viewed through the table, the index of refraction is 2.41, and the dispersion is four times as great as that of diamond. It is remarkably heavy, with a specific gravity of 5.13, but rather soft. Marketed under the names Fabulite and Starilian, it provides a remarkable simulation for diamond, far outdoing it in "fire." Its high specific gravity and softness provide ready identification.

Diamond. Diamond has not been synthesized in size suitable for gem use and little need be said here concerning it. Attempts at synthesis, with little or no success, have been recorded for a hundred years, but in 1955, the General Electric Company, announced successful synthesis of diamond. Since that time, other companies have

succeeded also, and gem-quality crystals as large as one-eighth of an inch have been produced. The method involves the melting of graphite with catalyst metals under high temperature ($+2,000°$ C) and tremendous pressure ($+1,000,000$ pounds per square inch). The crystals are very small but are excellent for cutting and grinding, and for some applications they are preferred to the crushed natural material.

IMITATION GEMSTONES

Glass and plastic. The first imitation gemstone was used in prehistoric times. In early Egypt, beads and other objects were made of faience, which consists of a vitreous glaze over a gritty core. Later Egyptians simulated a number of the colourful gems in glass. Indeed, glass still provides the bulk of material used to simulate gems for costume jewelry. Today there are two main types of glass used in gem simulation. The type known as bottle or window glass is used for the cheap, molded imitations. The better simulations are made from a glass containing lead oxide and sometimes salts of thallium. The lead and thallium increase the dispersion and brilliancy of the glass. The best of this type of glass is called strass, after its discoverer. The amount of polishing that these "gems" receive depends on the quality of the glass used and the market for which the simulation is prepared. In the cheapest, the table may be the only facet polished. Added brilliance may be obtained by coating the pavilion facets with a mirrorlike surface of evaporated metal. A new method of making glass (or paste) gemstones is to coat the pavilions of glass stones with a coloured pigment.

The glasses usually offer little trouble in identification. Except in the narrow range of beryl and topaz, specific gravities and refractive indices do not match those of natural gemstones. No gems in that range are isotropic as is glass. In addition, glass may show trapped bubbles and curved stria. Such identifying features are particularly present in the cheaper paste.

Plastics of various kinds may be coloured and are used for some simulations of gemstones. The low specific gravities, indices of refraction, and softness are immediate clues to their identity. Brown plastics are used to simulate amber, which is likewise organic, soft, and light.

Simulated pearls. Imitation or simulated pearls are produced in quantity by coating beads of opalescent glass (plastic beads may be used in cheaper varieties) with pearl essence. This material is made by dissolving a derivative of fish scales in nitrocellulose lacquer, an appropriate colour being added if desired. Up to ten coats of lacquer are applied in order to build up the lustre. If the beads are hollow, the specific gravity will be lower than that of natural or cultured pearls, and if solid, the specific gravity is usually higher. The surface looks like blotting paper, while the nacre of the true pearl shows tiny overlapping platelike crystals. The perforation shows the ragged edge of the coating and the glassy interior.

BIBLIOGRAPHY

Classics: JEAN-BAPTISTE TAVERNIER, *Les six voyages de J.B. Tavernier* (1676; Eng. trans. by J. PHILLIPS, 1677–78), *Travels in India of Jean Baptiste Tavernier*, 2 vol. trans from the orig. French edition of 1676 by V. BALL, 2nd ed. by W. COOKE (1925), a comprehensive account of the ancient gem industry; M.H. BAUER, *Precious Stones*, trans. from the German by L.J. SPENCER (1904, reprinted 1968), a most detailed and still valuable work on gems; G.F. KUNZ, *Gems and Precious Stones of North America* (1892, reprinted 1968), the systematic treatise of its day; and with C.H. STEVENSON, *Book of the Pearl* (1908).

General: E.H. KRAUS and C.B. SLAWSON, *Gems and Gem Materials*, 5th ed. (1947), authoritative; J. SINKANKAS, *Gemstones of North America* (1959), including an extensive bibliography; R. WEBSTER, *Gems*, 2 vol. (1962), the best comprehensive modern work.

Gem identification: B.W. ANDERSON, *Gem Testing*, 7th ed. (1964); R.T. LIDDICOAT, *Handbook of Gem Identification*, 6th ed. (1962).

Glossaries: L.L. COPELAND (ed.), *Diamond Dictionary* (1960); R.M. SHIPLEY, *Dictionary of Gems and Gemology*, 5th ed. (1951).

Popular: S.H. BALL, *Roman Book on Precious Stones* (1950), a translation of the 37th book of PLINY's *Natural History* with introduction and notes; G.F. KUNZ, *Curious Lore of Precious Stones* (1913); H.P. WHITLOCK, *Story of the Gems* (1936), popular but authoritative; and with M.L. EHRMANN, *Story of Jade* (1949); G.C. WILLIAMSON, *Book of Amber* (1932); M. WILSON, *Gems* (1967).

Gem cutting: P. GRODZINSKI, *Diamond Technology*, 2nd ed. (1953); J.H. HOWARD, *Revised Lapidary Handbook* (1946); J. SINKANKAS, *Gem Cutting* (1955).

Synthesis: K. NASSAU, *Growing Synthetic Crystals* (1964).

Notable gems and collections: L.L. COPELAND, *Diamonds, Famous, Notable and Unique* (1966); P.E. DESAUTELS, *Gems in the Smithsonian Institution* (1965); D.D. DUNCAN, *The Kremlin* (1960), description of the treasures in the Armoury; M. HOLMES, *The Crown Jewels* (1953), guidebook to the crown jewels of England; V.B. MEEN and A.D. TUSHINGHAM, *Crown Jewels of Iran* (1968); B.A. RYBAKOV (ed.), *Treasures in the Kremlin* (1963); E.F. TWINING, *A History of the Crown Jewels of Europe* (1960), a comprehensive treatment with an extensive bibliography by country.

Journals: *Australian Gemmologist* (quarterly); *Gems and Gemology* (quarterly); *The Journal of Gemmology* (quarterly); *Lapidary Journal* (monthly).

(V.B.M.)

Gene

Genes are the carriers of the genetic information passed on from generation to generation in the sex cells of all organisms, according to the principles discussed in the article HEREDITY.

The evidence is overwhelming that the basic genetic material constituting the gene is fundamentally the same in all living organisms: it consists of chainlike molecules of nucleic acids—deoxyribonucleic acid (DNA) in most organisms and ribonucleic acid (RNA) in certain viruses—and is usually associated in a linear arrangement that, in part, constitutes the chromosome.

The term gene no longer stands simply for a discrete structural unit of heredity of definite and invariable length. It is now thought of as an operational entity whose properties depend upon the mode of measurement. These refinements in definition of genetic material are explained below in the section *Nature of the gene*.

An account of the development of the gene concept precedes the discussion of gene structure and function according to the following outline:

Development of the gene theory

BLOOD HEREDITY VERSUS PARTICULATE HEREDITY

Before the time of the Austrian monk-naturalist Gregor Mendel, it was universally believed that heredity was carried by blood and that the bloods of the parents are blended in the offspring. Mendel proved that at least some traits that differentiate varieties of peas are inherited through factors that do not blend but actually segregate when the sex cells are formed. Although published in 1866, the work of Mendel was unappreciated until 1900. The British evolutionist Charles Darwin fully realized that understanding the mechanism of heredity was of basic importance for his theory of organic evolution. In 1868 Darwin published *The Variation of Animals and Plants Under Domestication*, to which he added an appendix containing his "Provisional Hypothesis of Pangenesis." In this acknowledgedly speculative venture, he surmised that all cells of the body shed into the bloodstream minute particles called gemmules (or pangenes), which assemble to form the sex cells. A gemmule was imagined to be a representative, perhaps a tiny model, of the cell that produced it. When a body cell was altered by some environmental agency, it gave rise to altered gemmules. This detail was important to Darwin because, in common with his contemporaries, he believed in the inheritance of acquired characters. While the hypothesis of pangenesis seemed to explain adequately at the same time the transmission of inherited and of acquired traits, it was experimentally disproved.

In 1889 a Dutch botanist, Hugo de Vries, advanced the theory of intracellular pangenesis. By then, most biologists no longer regarded inheritance of acquired traits as a well-founded hypothesis, and evidence was rapidly accumulating that the chromosomes of cell nuclei were the carriers of the hereditary materials. De Vries proposed that the pangenes constituted the chromosomes and passed only from the nuclei into the cell cytoplasm, where they became active. Each cell was believed to contain many different pangenes, each of which could become active in different cells (thus explaining why cells become different in the developing organism).

August Weismann, a German biologist and one of the founders of the chromosomal theory of heredity (1892)—the forerunner of the gene theory—believed that the hereditary materials were composed of determinants that specified the characteristics of different cells. The sex cells were thought to contain sets of determinants for all cells, but, during the cleavage of a fertilized egg and the cell divisions in a developing embryo, the determinants were gradually sorted out, so that finally every cell retained only the determinants needed to specify the characteristics of a certain tissue or organ. The sex cells were the exception; they had to retain a full set of the determinants, which could be passed on to the offspring. These cells carried the germ plasm, which can be considered potentially immortal, since it may be transmitted from generation to generation without end (Figure 1). In every

Darwin's notion of "pangenesis"

The continuity of the germ plasm

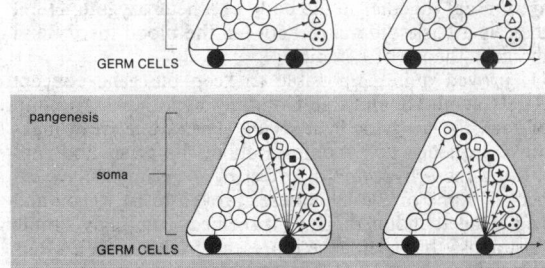

From *Life: An Introduction to Biology* by George Gaylord Simpson and William S. Beck, copyright © 1957, 1965, by Harcourt Brace Jovanovich, Inc., and reproduced with their permission

Figure 1: Weismann's concept of the continuity of the germ plasm (see text).

generation the germ plasm constructs the somatoplasm (or soma), the body that is its temporary container and vehicle. The body is mortal; it dies after it transmits its germ plasm to the progeny. In unicellular organisms, which reproduce by simple fission, the separation of the germ plasm and the body does not exist; these organisms, themselves, are potentially immortal. Weismann's hypothesis was, thus, an antithesis of Darwin's hypothesis of pangenesis. Instead of the sex cells being compounded of the gemmules shed by the body, Weismann admitted only the passage of the determinants from the germ plasma to the body. Quite consistently with this view, Weismann rejected the possibility that characters acquired by the body may be inherited.

From the vantage point of present-day knowledge, these pre-Mendelian speculations may appear naïve. Their historical importance is, however, unquestionable. They led to the abandonment of the notion that heredity is transmitted by blood and to the acceptance of the idea that the hereditary materials are particulate. The scientific climate had changed when Mendel's work was rediscovered in 1900, and his approach to the study of heredity was not so strange and unfamiliar as it was in 1866.

THE CONCEPT OF THE GENE

Gregor Mendel was by no means the first to experiment on plant heredity, but he did it in a systematic and inspired way. Mendel's data revealed to him that each parent contained pairs of factors but contributed only one member of each pair to its offspring. It was also clear that the factors retained their individuality from generation to generation, whether they asserted themselves or not, and united randomly in the offspring.

The significance of Mendel's experiments

The gametes (ovules and pollen grains in plants, egg cells and spermatozoa in animals) of course do not display differentiating characters such as colours or shapes of flowers, seeds, eyes, hair, etc. And yet Mendel's experiments demonstrated that the gametes do contain some formative elements or factors that indeed are responsible for the appearance of characters in the organism. Mendel's results were confirmed and extended in 1900 and thereafter to many species of plants and animals, including man. A Danish biologist, Wilhelm Johannsen, proposed in 1909 to call the formative elements, or factors, genes, not to be confused with the speculative pangenes, determinants, etc.

Mendel's pea varieties with, for example, purple and white flowers carried alternative forms of one gene that allowed the plants to develop flowers of these colours; such alternative states of a single gene are now termed allelomorphs (or alleles). Each "pure" variety contained two similar alleles, or a double dose of genes for each trait, and was called a homozygote. Each hybrid variety, which is derived from crossing two pure varieties, necessarily had two unlike alleles for each trait and was called a heterozygote. When the heterozygote formed sex cells, the alternative alleles segregated and passed into different and equally numerous cells. The sex cells were "pure" since they contained only one allele for a character; for example, either the allele for purple or for white flowers but not both and not a mixture of the two. These considerations led to Mendel's law of segregation, or the law of the purity of the gametes: different alleles of genes do not mix or contaminate each other while they are present together in the body of a heterozygote. Here, then, is a basic difference between the blood theory and the gene theory of heredity.

It proved quite impossible to keep the gene concept purely symbolic and free from any hypotheses. In point of fact, the progress in studying genes came from making a sequence of hypotheses about the genes and submitting these hypotheses to test by experiments. As expected, some of the hypotheses proved to be wrong and had to be abandoned. Thus, it seemed temptingly simple to suppose that each gene represents in the sex cell a certain unit character and that the organism is an aggregate, a sort of a mosaic composed of such unit characters. In the development of an organism from a fertilized egg, each gene would add its proper unit character to those produced by other genes, until the body is fully formed. In a sense, this hypothesis was a throwback to something like Weismann's determinants, except that the unit characters were no longer thought of as representing body parts or single cells but rather as representing qualities, such as colour, pattern, shape, or size.

Because of their brevity, expressions such as "the gene for blue eyes" or "the gene for blood group A" are used even now; these expressions are likely to mislead a beginner into believing that there is a one-to-one relationship between each gene and an independent unit char-

acter, or trait, for which a given gene is responsible. This is actually not so. What looks like a trait controlled by a single gene is frequently the result of interaction of several or many genes (Figure 2). The variety of coat col-

Relation of genes to traits

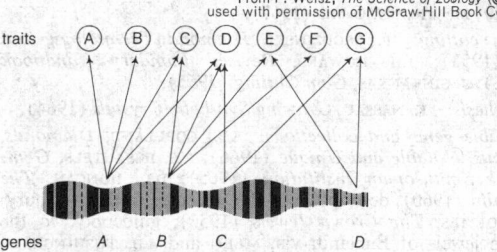

Figure 2: The relationship between genes and traits (see text).

ours found in domestic dogs, cats, rabbits, horses, cattle, and other mammals, for example, results from often very complex interactions of many genes, some of them represented by several alternative forms (multiple alleles). The difference between the skin colours of Negroes and of whites is the result of the joint action of several genes, each of which increases or decreases the skin pigmentation relatively slightly. Conversely, many genes act on constellations of seemingly unrelated traits. Such genes are called pleiotropic. In man, many hereditary diseases are caused by single gene changes that produce combinations or syndromes of traits, some structural, others physiological or psychological. Thus, phenylketonuria is inherited as a simple recessive; the afflicted homozygotes have their mental development severely retarded, and their urine contains large amounts of phenylalanine and phenylpyruvic acid. In general, the development of an individual of any species is controlled by all the genes he carries; characters of traits are merely descriptive aspects of this unitary process.

THE REALITY OF THE GENE

Although genes were originally simply symbols useful to explain the observable facts of Mendelian segregation, it soon became evident that they had physical reality as component parts of the chromosomes of cell nuclei. A group of brilliant biologists, among them Theodor Boveri, Wilhelm Roux, and August Weismann in Germany and Edmund B. Wilson in the United States, inferred that the heredity transmitted from one generation to the next must be carried in the chromosomes of the sex cells. This inference had been reached in the closing decade of the 19th century; *i.e.*, before the rediscovery of Mendel's laws. The question of whether the Mendelian genes were also carried in the chromosome logically presented itself.

The parallel between chromosomes and genes. The behaviour of the chromosomes during the processes of maturation of sex cells (meiosis) is precisely such that the Mendelian segregation of the genes carried in these chromosomes can be envisaged as a simple and necessary consequence. During meiosis the chromosomes unite in pairs, divide, exchange segments, and then disjoin and pass to different sex cells (gametes). Suppose, then, that the maternal chromosome of a given pair carries an allele of a gene different from that in the paternal member of the chromosome pair. These gene alleles will segregate, one-half of the gametes formed carrying one allele and the other half carrying the other. If female and male gametes unite at random at fertilization—*i.e.*, if there is no tendency for sex cells with similar or with different gene alleles to seek out or to avoid each other—the segregation ratios observed by Mendel necessarily follow.

The correctness of the above reasoning was demonstrated experimentally by the renowned U.S. geneticists Thomas Hunt Morgan, Calvin B. Bridges, Hermann J. Muller, and Alfred H. Sturtevant. Morgan and his colleagues made use of the then new experimental material, the vinegar fly (often called fruit fly) *Drosophila melano-*

The "fruit fly" school of genetics

gaster. This fly has four pairs of chromosomes in each of its body cells, while its sex cells carry only four chromosomes, one representative of each pair. The chromosomes of maternal and paternal origins in different pairs are distributed randomly at meiosis, and the microscopically observed random distribution of the chromosomes is paralleled by the random assortment of genes discovered by Mendel. In *Drosophila*, however, more than four, and eventually several hundred, variant genes were discovered. Clearly then, a chromosome may contain several genes. If so, can the random assortment of the genes be an invariable rule? The genes carried on the same chromosomes do exhibit some tendency to remain together in inheritance. As the chromosome is transmitted, so are all its genes transmitted. This tendency, called linkage, was shown to parallel the chromosome assortment at meiosis. The known genes in *Drosophila* belong to four linkage groups, the same number as that of the chromosome pairs. Moreover, one linkage group consists of genes that express themselves in individuals of one sex—that is, they exhibit a sex-linked inheritance; this linkage group is carried in the X chromosome, which is also responsible for the determination of sex. Of the remaining three chromosome pairs, two are large and one very small; correspondingly, there are two linkage groups with many genes and one with relatively few, as demonstrated in the progenies of crosses.

The analysis of the relationship between the genes and the chromosomes can be carried further. In the formation of sex cells, genes located in different chromosomes are assorted at random; *i.e.*, by chance they remain together in the original parental combinations in 50 percent of the sex cells and, because of crossing-over (see below), form new combinations in the remaining 50 percent. This expectation, however, is not always realized, because genes carried on the same chromosome are linked in various degrees—quite tightly, loosely, or moderately—the frequency of new gene combinations ranging from near 0 to 50 percent. The closer together the genes are in the chromosomes, the tighter the linkage and the lower the frequency of recombination; conversely, the farther apart the genes are, the looser the linkage and the higher the frequency of recombination. Consequently, the degree of linkage may be used as a measure of the distance between the genes. The members of each chromosome pair twist around each other at meiosis, establishing points of contact called chiasmata (singular, chiasma), and exchange segments. This crossing-over and exchange of chromosome segments was pointed out by Morgan as the explanation of linkage and recombination. A chiasma will be formed less often between neighbouring genes than between genes far apart in the chromosome.

The linear order of genes. Morgan's idea was expanded into a theory of the linear arrangement of the genes in the chromosomes. When the frequencies of recombination (expressed in crossover units) between genes *A* and *B* and *B* and *C* are known (Figure 3). If crossing-

From C. Villee, *Biology*, 5th ed. (1967);
W.B. Saunders Company, Philadelphia

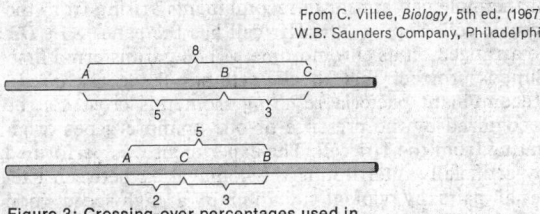

Figure 3: Crossing-over percentages used in establishing the linear order of genes in a chromosome (see text).

over between *A* and *B* occurs 5% of the time and crossing-over between *B* and *C* occurs 3% of the time, then, when the percentage of crossing-over between *A* and *C* is tested, it is either 8% (*AB* + *BC*) or 2% (*AB* − *BC*). This suggests that the genes are arranged in the chromosome in a linear file, either *ABC*, if crossing-over between *A* and *C* is 8%, or *ACB*, if crossing-over is 2%. When *AB* and *BC* are large (say, 10% or more), *AC* may be

less than *AB* + *BC*. This is explained by the occurrence in the chromosome of more than a single chiasma between the loci of remote genes. Knowing the degree of linkage of several genes in the same chromosome, it is possible to plot a genetic map of the chromosome. Genetic maps of the chromosomes of *Drosophila melanogaster* were first published in 1915 in *The Mechanism of Mendelian Heredity* by Morgan, Sturtevant, Muller, and Bridges. At present, genetic maps of various degrees of precision exist for several organisms.

The genetic, or linkage, maps of chromosomes are constructed entirely on the basis of statistical data concerning the frequencies of recombination between linked genes observed in various crossing experiments. In principle at least, such maps could as well be drawn had the actual, microscopically visible chromosomes never been discovered. A proof that the linear order of the genes shown on the genetic maps is really the same as their arrangement in the chromosomes became possible after the discoveries of various chromosomal aberrations in *Drosophila melanogaster*. Sections of chromosomes are sometimes lost (deficiency or deletion), reduplicated (duplication), transferred from one chromosome to another (translocation), or rotated by 180° in the same chromosome (inversion), as shown in Figure 4. Chromo-

From C. Villee, *Biology*, 5th ed. (1967);
W.B. Saunders Company, Philadelphia

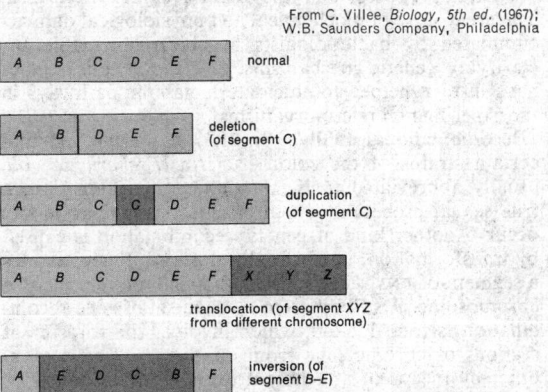

Figure 4: Types of chromosomal mutations.

somal aberrations are generally rare, but their frequencies are increased in the progenies of parents treated with high-energy radiations. Using techniques developed chiefly in *Drosophila* and in corn, the chromosomal aberrations can be studied genetically. The blocks of genes that are lost, duplicated, translocated, or inverted can be delimited in terms of the sections of the genetic maps. Some chromosomal aberrations can also be discovered under the microscope, because they make certain chromosomes longer or shorter than normal, or fragmented. Extraordinary refinement in the study of the locations of genes in chromosomes became possible after the discovery of giant chromosomes in the cells of salivary glands of many flies, including *Drosophila*. They appear to consist of alternating dark (stainable by nuclear dyes) and light bands or disks; because the total length of the salivary-gland chromosomes is a hundred or more times greater than of those in other *Drosophila* cells, it is possible to see chromosomal changes so minute that they escape detection in the normal-sized chromosomes. The first cytological maps, showing the location of certain genes of *Drosophila melanogaster*, were drawn at first for the chromosomes in the developing sex cells and nerve cells and subsequently, with far greater precision, in the giant chromosomes of the salivary glands.

The linear order of the genes as shown on the genetic maps coincides with that on cytological maps, but the relative distances are not always the same. This is explained by the more frequent occurrence of chiasmata in some parts of the chromosomes than in other parts. The salient fact, however, is that the symbolic genes finally were shown to be material particles in the chromosomes. The question inevitably arose whether the genes are absolutely discrete particles or only segments

Linkage of genes

Proof of the linear order of genes

of some kind of a continuum. A chromosome with its genes has sometimes been likened to a string of beads. Many investigators found this simile much too crude and envisaged genetic variations as generalized changes in whole chromosomes. Molecular-level analysis of the genes (see below) eventually established that the actual situation lies somewhere between these extremes, but some evidence of interdependence of neighbouring or adjacent genes was obtained through the discovery of position effects. The functioning of a gene apparently depends not only on the intrinsic properties of that gene but on those of the neighbouring genes as well.

Influence of genes on other genes

Nature of the gene

Perhaps the most impressive and spectacular advance of biology in the 20th century was the discovery of the nature of the genetic material. The way information is encoded in the genes has been clarified, and much has been learned about the mechanisms that translate this information into the developmental processes of the organism.

FUNCTIONAL ANALYSIS

Role of microbes in genetic mechanisms

While the pioneers of genetics used higher plants and animals as experimental materials, much of the work since the late 1940s has been done with micro-organisms —bacteria, viruses, and the mold *Neurospora crassa*. The great store of biochemical and physiological data accumulated by bacteriologists has been invaluable for clarifying genetic mechanisms, and the genetic studies have in turn helped to elucidate metabolic pathways in the experimental micro-organisms.

Recombinational ability. In 1947 it was proved that certain strains of the colon bacteria (*Escherichia coli*, usually abbreviated to *E. coli*) undergo conjugation, a true sexual process in which genetic recombination can occur. Another kind of genetic recombination is caused by transformation, in which a bacterial cell incorporates a segment of DNA received from the medium into its own chromosome. A still different mechanism of gene recombination is transduction, which involves the transfer of sections of chromosome from one bacterial cell to another by means of attachment to the chromosome of a bacteriophage (bacterial virus). A diagrammatic representation of these processes is shown in Figure 5.

The discovery of the sexual process (see below) was made possible by the availability of mutant strains differing in nutritional requirements. Ordinary strains of *E. coli* grow well on a minimal medium of a simple carbon source, usually the sugar glucose and several inorganic elements. Some mutants require particular carbon sources; for example, a mutant may grow well on a glucose medium but not on a medium containing the sugar galactose. Consider two strains of *E. coli*, each of which has two different mutants that change the nutritional requirements of their carriers. If the ordinary so-called wild-type *E. coli* carries the genes *ABCD*, the two mutant strains can be represented as *ABcd* and *abCD*, where the lowercase letters stand for variant gene alleles that result in the inability of their carriers to grow on the minimal medium. Thus, *ABCD* bacteria grow on the minimal medium well, while *ABcd* and *abCD* strains require mediums with certain chemical substances in addition to those in the minimal one. Cultures of *ABcd* and *abCD* bacteria were mixed together, and, after a short period of time, samples of the mixture were taken and placed on solid minimal medium in Petri dishes. Most of the bacteria failed to grow, but some colonies of cells did appear. These colonies consisted of cells carrying the genes *ABCD*, like the wild-type *E. coli*. The appearances of *ABCD* cells were far too numerous to be accounted for by simultaneous mutation. Their appearance in the mixtures must be the result of gene recombination.

Certain strains of *E. coli* manifest recombination through conjugation. Two mating types, conveniently referred to as "males" and "females," have been found. Male bacterial cells are determined by the presence of a genetic factor called F (for "fertility"), while female cells lack the F factor. Male cells are designated F⁺; female cells are designated F⁻. In males, the F factor can exist in

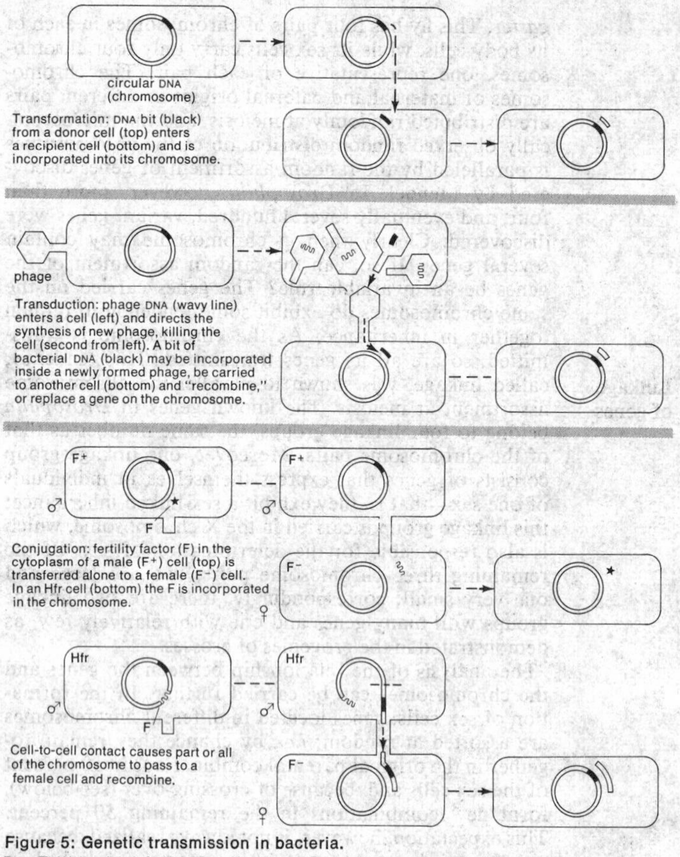

Transformation: DNA bit (black) from a donor cell (top) enters a recipient cell (bottom) and is incorporated into its chromosome.

Transduction: phage DNA (wavy line) enters a cell (left) and directs the synthesis of new phage, killing the cell (second from left). A bit of bacterial DNA (black) may be incorporated inside a newly formed phage, be carried to another cell (bottom) and "recombine," or replace a gene on the chromosome.

Conjugation: fertility factor (F) in the cytoplasm of a male (F⁺) cell (top) is transferred alone to a female (F⁻) cell. In an Hfr cell (bottom) the F is incorporated in the chromosome.

Cell-to-cell contact causes part or all of the chromosome to pass to a female cell and recombine.

Figure 5: Genetic transmission in bacteria.

From T. Watanabe, *Infectious Drug Resistance*. Copyright © 1967 by Scientific American, Inc. All rights reserved.

two states, either as an integral part of the male bacterial chromosome or as a free particle in the cytoplasm. Males with a free F factor can conjugate with an F⁻ cell, but only the F factor is transmitted to the F⁻ cell. But male cells with an integrated F factor always transfer parts of their chromosomes to the female cells. These male F⁺ cells are designated Hfr because they yield a high frequency of recombination with F⁻ cells.

A cross between F⁺ cells that are not Hfr and F⁻ cells results in conjugation, but only the previously mentioned F factor is transferred. Only F⁺ cells result from such matings. In crosses between Hfr cells and F⁻ cells, however, a portion of the bacterial chromosome is transferred; recombination occurs between the portion of the transferred chromosome and the F⁻ chromosome.

Gene transfer in bacteria

The observation that the F factor is rarely transferred in an Hfr × F⁻ cross led to the hypothesis that the F factor is the last piece of the chromosome to be transferred. Electron-microscope photographs revealed a cytoplasmic tube connecting bacteria of opposite mating types during conjugation of Hfr × F⁻ cells. The progress of chromosome transfer can be followed by recording which genes of the male cell appear in recombinants arising from the female cell. Suppose the Hfr cell has the genes *ABCDE* so arranged on its chromosome, *A* being transferred first. Suppose further that the F⁻ cell has the genes *abcde*. Recombinant bacteria resulting from this cross can be recognized by the presence of one or more genes originating from the Hfr cell. The experiment was performed by artificially interrupting the conjugation between bacterial pairs by violent agitation in a high-speed food blender (Figure 6). When conjugation was interrupted after five minutes, only a small portion of the male chromosome was transferred, and, inasmuch as the *A* gene was not located at the tip of the transferred portion of the chromosome, no recombinants were observed. When mating continued for 20 to 30 minutes, several or all genes were transferred, and recombinants were observed. Transfer of the entire male chromosome is rare, requiring about a two-hour mating. The F factor (not in diagram) was transferred last, thus confirming the hypothesis that is is located at the end of the chromosome.

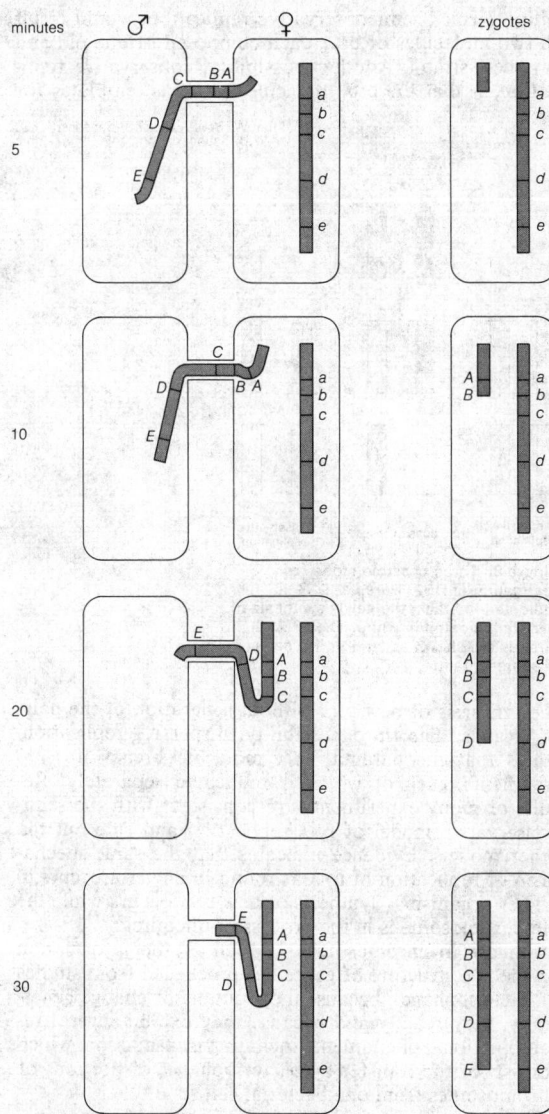

Figure 6: Diagram of the results of an interrupted mating experiment in *Escherichia coli* bacteria. The bacterial chromosomes, normally circular, are shown linearly for ease in representation (see text).

From W. Hayes, *The Genetics of Bacteria and Their Viruses* (1964); John Wiley & Sons, Inc.

Evidence for DNA as the genetic material

Data derived from the interrupted-mating experiment can be used to construct genetic maps of the bacterial chromosome. The length of time needed for a gene to be transferred is a measure of its position along the chromosome. Several Hfr strains have been found that transfer their genes in different orders. Analysis of these strains indicates that the bacterial chromosome is a circular structure. The various Hfr strains result from the integration of the F factor at different points along the circular chromosome. At the beginning of the conjugation, the chromosome breaks at the location of the F factor; the chromosome tip not containing F is transferred to the F⁻ cell first.

Information transferral. The evidence that nucleic acids, especially deoxyribonucleic acid (DNA), act as the carriers of the genetic information came convergently and within a short period of time from several sources (for the chemistry of these complex molecules, see NUCLEIC ACIDS). The amounts of DNA per nucleus vary greatly in different animals. The amphibian *Amphiuma* has 168×10^{-9} milligrams of DNA per cell, while the jellyfish *Cassiopeia* has only 1.43×10^{-9} milligrams. Man is intermediate, with about 6×10^{-9} milligrams DNA per cell. There is, however, a remarkable constancy of DNA quantity in the nuclei of cells of different tissues in each species. The only exception to this rule is that the nuclei of gametes, such as spermatozoa in animals, have, within

the limits of error of the measurements, one-half of the amount of DNA present in body cells. This is exactly what one should expect, since meiosis results in the gametes being reduced to one set of chromosomes. No other cell constituents show such constancy.

Further evidence involving DNA as the genetic material was provided by the demonstration that the "transforming principle," which induces changes in the pneumonia bacteria (pneumococci), consists of DNA. The ability of pneumococci to cause infection, the virulence, depends on the presence of a polysaccharide (composed of sugar subunits) envelope surrounding the bacterial cells. When grown on laboratory culture mediums, virulent pneumococci produce large colonies that have a smooth, glistening surface. Bacteria from such cultures produce infection in mice. After many transfers on fresh laboratory mediums, however, the bacteria tend to lose their polysaccharide envelopes and their ability to infect mice; correlated with these changes is the change to small colonies with rough outlines. The smooth and the rough variants are designated S and R, respectively. Mice inoculated with either the living R pneumococci or the heat-killed S pneumococci remain free of infection, but mice inoculated with a mixture of living R and heat-killed S bacteria become infected. Living S pneumococcal cultures can be obtained from such animals, proof that the virulent S cells were reconstituted from the mixture inoculated. Some material derived from the dead S bacteria induced the transformation of R into S strains. This material was shown by extensive chemical tests to be DNA. Thus, it is the hereditary material from the dead bacteria that determines the genetic character induced in the living ones.

Effect of the DNA of dead bacteria on living bacteria

How does the DNA of the dead cells accomplish the transformation of the living ones? It evidently must penetrate the wall of the living cell. Once a section of the transforming DNA strand is inside the recipient cell, there apparently occurs a pairing between homologous regions of the bacterial chromosome and the transforming DNA. There must follow breakage and subsequent reunion of the bacterial chromosome and the transforming DNA. Thus a portion of the transforming DNA becomes integrated into the bacterial chromosome. If this model is valid, one would expect that genes located near each other on the transforming DNA would appear together more often in a transformed cell than will genes relatively far apart in the transforming DNA. This expectation is fulfilled, and the principle has been utilized as a means of mapping the donor cell chromosome.

Further evidence that DNA serves as the physical basis of heredity was obtained in the early 1950s, using bacteriophages that attack *E. coli*. The bacteriophage (or simply phage) is an ultramicroscopic tadpole-shaped body, with a hexagonal head, a cylindrical tail, an end plate, and six tail fibres (see VIRUSES). The head contains the DNA; the outer surface and the tail consist of protein. A phage particle attacking *E. coli* attaches itself by its tail plate to the surface of the host bacterial cell. The DNA from the head then passes through the tail and into the body of the host. The metabolic machinery of the bacterial cell is subverted to make phage DNA and phage protein. When a new generation of the phage particles is ready inside the bacterium, destruction (lysis) of the latter takes place, and a hundred or more new phage particles are released into the external medium, where they can attack other bacterial cells.

STRUCTURAL ANALYSIS

The remarkable properties of the nucleic acids, which qualify these substances to serve as the carriers of the genetic information, have claimed the attention of many investigators. The groundwork was laid by pioneer biochemists who found that nucleic acids are long chainlike molecules, the backbones of which consist of repeated sequences of phosphate and sugar linkages—ribose sugar in RNA and deoxyribose sugars in DNA (see NUCLEIC ACIDS). Attached to the sugar links in the backbone are two kinds of purines, adenine (A) and guanine (G), and two kinds of pyrimidines, cytosine (C) and thymine (T) in DNA or cytosine (C) and uracil (U) in RNA. A single purine or a pyrimidine is attached to each sugar, the compound being called a nucleotide. The nucleic acids extracted from different species of animals and plants have different proportions of the four nucleotides. Some are relatively richer in adenine and thymine, while others have more guanine and cytosine; however, the ratios of A to T, and also of G to C, are equal.

Molecular structure. On the basis of results of X-ray crystallography on DNA, James Watson and Francis Crick proposed in 1953 their now-famous model, which shows DNA as composed of two spirally wound (helical) chains, in which the A's (adenines) in one chain are always linked by hydrogen bonds to T's and the G's in one chain to C's in the other. This model fulfills the basic requirements—it makes it possible to envisage how genes replicate their precise structures when their copies are synthesized. It also makes it possible to explain how a gene can carry genetic information written in some chemical code. And, finally, it helps to envisage how mutational changes in the genes are produced.

The Watson–Crick model of DNA

The Watson–Crick model of the genetic material permits an explanation of the mechanism of precise replication of genes (Figure 7). The paired complementary

From *Molecular Biology of Bacterial Viruses* by Gunther S. Stent. W.H. Freeman and Company, copyright © 1963.

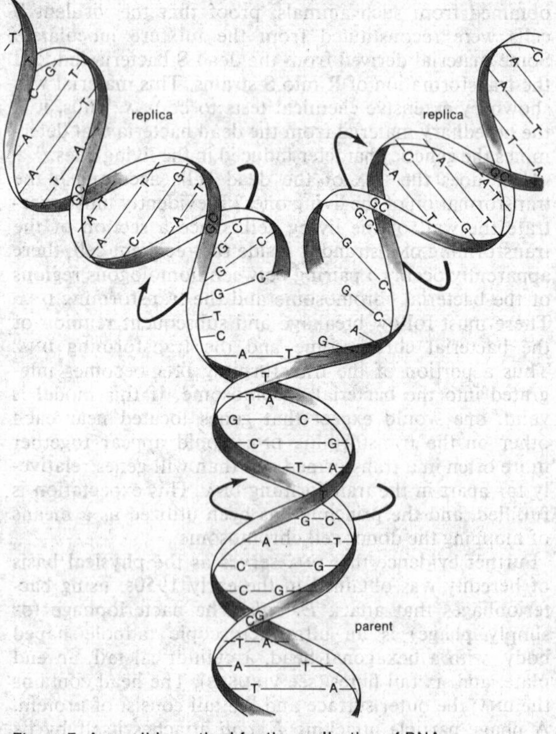

Figure 7: A possible method for the replication of DNA according to Watson and Crick. The arrows indicate the direction of rotation.

strands of the DNA molecule may separate as a result of a breakage of the hydrogen bonds between the nucleotides. If free nucleotides (base + sugar + phosphate) are present in the medium surrounding the gene, they might pair with the complementary bases on the single strands of DNA. An enzyme, DNA polymerase, functions to form the phosphate bonds between the sugars in the DNA backbone. It has been used in the synthesis of DNA in vitro, in cell-free systems. The enzyme is extracted from rapidly dividing cells of the familiar bacterium *E. coli*. A supply of the four nucleotides, A, T, G, and C, is provided, as well as a source of energy, adenosine triphosphate (ATP). To start DNA synthesis another key component is added—a trace of DNA to serve as a primer. The kind of DNA that is synthesized depends on the primer. Even though the enzyme came from *E. coli*, if the primer is DNA of some quite different organism, such as cattle, the DNA that is synthesized is not *E. coli* but cattle DNA.

There were at least three possible ways to envisage the mechanism of replication of DNA (Figure 8). One possi-

bility, termed semiconservative replication, would result in two molecules of DNA, each composed of one old and one new strand. Another possibility, conservative replication, is that the DNA molecules serve as templates for

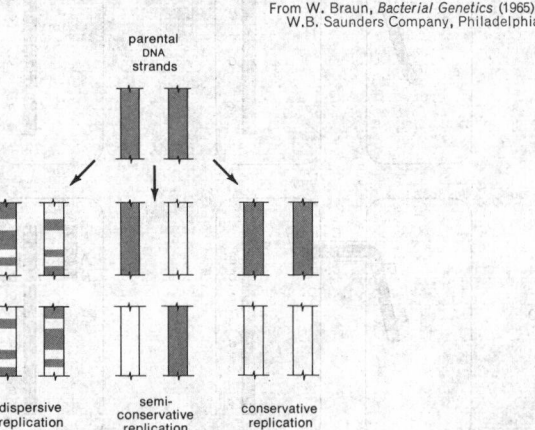

From W. Braun, *Bacterial Genetics* (1965); W.B. Saunders Company, Philadelphia

Figure 8: Three possible modes of replication of DNA. Parental DNA is indicated in black: the newly synthesized DNA is indicated in white. The DNA strands are shown as straight for ease in representation.

the synthesis of new DNA without separation of the pairs of strands. The third possibility, dispersive replication, states that the parental DNA molecule breaks up into fragments, each of which is replicated separately. Results of many experiments are consistent with the semiconservative model of DNA replication and rule out the other models. Evidence indicates that the same mechanism of replication of DNA as found in bacteria occurs in higher organisms. Synthesis of new DNA occurs while the old chromosome is in the process of uncoiling.

Changes in chromosomes. Much of the information on the fine structure of genes has proceeded from studies of bacteriophages, because they mutate, or change genetically, very readily and because they exhibit several recombinational phenomena, including transduction, which consists of the transfer by bacteriophages of portions of chromosomes from one bacterial cell to another.

Mutation. Suppose that a drop of some substance suspected of containing bacteriophages is placed on the surface of a culture medium consisting of agar covered with a layer of *E. coli* bacteria. If phages are present, they will infect the bacteria and eventually cause their death. The bacteria layer will develop holes, or plaques, as a result of the destruction of the individual bacteria by lysis. Because each plaque develops from a single phage particle, the number of such plaques formed gives an estimate of the abundance of phages in the inoculum. Each type of phage forms a plaque of characteristic appearance; thus, mutations can be detected as variations in plaque form.

Crosses between mutant phages of different types can be made if a single bacterium is simultaneously infected with two phage mutants. A proportion of the progeny phage will be recombinants for the mutants in question. If a bacterium is infected with two types of phages, one having the genes *Ab* and the other *aB*, recombination results in the appearance of some phage particles having the genes *ab* and *AB*. This method of crosses has been utilized to construct a genetic map of the bacteriophage designated T4 phage. The map is circular, indicating the physical continuity of the T4 chromosome.

Not all bacteriophages cause the destruction of their host cell by lysis. A class of phages termed temperate has the ability to enter into a symbiotic relationship with the bacterial host cell. The chromosome of the temperate phage becomes incorporated into the bacterial chromosome and is replicated only when the bacterial chromosome replicates. A bacterial cell in this state is termed lysogenic for the phage in question. If, however, the chromosome of a temperate phage becomes dissociated

Mutant phages that reveal a circular chromosome

from the bacterial chromosome, it is capable of autonomous replication, which results in the lysis of the host cell. A temperate phage can be artificially induced to enter an autonomous state through the action of such stimuli as ultraviolet light.

Transduction. The mechanism of transduction seems to be as follows. The chromosome of the phage particle is a ring-shaped structure. This chromosome pairs with a certain region of the bacterial chromosome. Both chromosomes then break, and the reunion of the broken ends results in the insertion of the phage chromosomal material into the bacterial chromosome.

Transduction has been utilized to construct a map of the bacterial chromosome. The genes that lie close together in the chromosome will usually undergo transduction together, and, if three or four genes are followed simultaneously, their order in the chromosome can be determined.

Complementation. The classical Morgan–Muller conception of the gene was defined as a unit of function (its mutants changing, for example, the eye colour, the wings, or the bristle shape in *Drosophila* flies); a unit of recombination (having a definite position on the genetic map); and a unit of mutation (similar mutational changes arising repeatedly). These three criteria of defining and delimiting the genes usually coincided and thus gave concordant results. Genetic experiments on *Drosophila* flies, however, deal with numbers of individuals generally several orders of magnitude smaller than are involved in many experiments with micro-organisms. Beginning in 1955, detailed studies on portions (the "rII region") of the chromosome of the bacteriophage T4 were responsible for a change in definition of the gene. A U.S. geneticist, Seymour Benzer, found a mutant (r) of the phage T4 that caused rapid lysis of one strain (B) of *E. coli* but could not lyse another strain (*E. coli* K12 [λ]). This latter strain, however, was lysogenic for the phage lambda (λ). This finding led to the development of complementation, or cis–trans, tests and to the detection of very small frequencies of recombination. When various combinations of rII mutants are used to infect *E. coli* K, two kinds of results are observed. In some combinations of mutants normal plaques are formed, while other combinations yield no plaques. The mutants belong to two groups called rIIA and rIIB, which have altered functionally different regions of the phage chromosome. When two mutants belong to different groups they complement each other, reciprocally compensate for each other's deficiency, and give viable phages that produce normal plaques.

According to the classical gene theory, the mutants that do not complement each other must be alleles of the same gene. But, since it can be determined by recombination mapping that all rIIA mutants do not occur at a single spot on the phage chromosome, the definition of a gene must be altered. The functional groups of mutants may be designated as cistrons (defined by cis–trans tests). All mutations that are functionally allelic are, therefore, members of a cistron.

This material also provides an extremely sensitive method for detecting recombination between mutants within a given cistron. *E. coli* B may be infected with two rIIA mutants that permit normal reproduction and crossing-over. After the cells are lysed, progeny phages are collected, and *E. coli* K and B are infected with known quantities of phage. If recombination occurs, a few small plaques representing wild-type phage appear on the K host. The number of plaques on the B host gives an estimate of the total number of phage particles used. The ratio of the number of plaques on K to the number on B hosts is an estimate of the amount of recombination between the two mutants in question. This method is sensitive enough to detect one recombination event in 100,000,000. The amount of recombination between two mutants is then used as an estimate of the distance between them in the chromosome. When many such mutants are crossed by this method, a map of the rII region of the bacteriophage chromosome emerges, on which all rIIA mutants, as determined by complementation tests,

fall into one segment, while all rIIB mutations fall in another segment.

To localize the some 3,000 mutants of the rII type on the chromosome map involves an enormous amount of time and labour, even though phage crosses can be made rapidly. The problem is more manageable with the aid of mutants that apparently result from deletions (deficiencies) of short sections of the phage chromosome. Utilizing deficiency mutants, sites at which mutation or recombination can occur are more easily mapped within the rII region of the chromosome. The names muton and recon have been proposed for the smallest units that can mutate and recombine. The rII region represents about 2 percent of the total length of the genetic map of the phage T4 chromosome, and the DNA composing this region is estimated to contain about 4,000 nucleotide pairs. The large number of mutation and recombination sites discovered in the rII region of the chromosome suggests that the mutation and recombination units may be the nucleotide pairs. The genetic units of function, recombination, and mutation thus do not coincide. The Morgan–Muller gene corresponds most closely to the modern conception of the cistron as a unit of function.

Extranuclear genetic material. Some characteristics of organisms do not show Mendelian segregation and, among higher organisms, are inherited through the maternal line only (see HEREDITY). Thus, the cells of green plants contain in their cytoplasm bodies called chloroplasts, which carry the green pigment chlorophyll. In corn (maize), variants are known whose leaves are striped green and yellow because of the absence of chlorophyll in the chloroplasts of some cells. Since no chloroplasts are present in pollen grains, the conclusion is that chloroplasts are self-replicating bodies in egg cells and in part control their own characteristics.

Similar conclusions of maternal inheritance have been drawn from studies of certain growth mutants in yeasts and in the bread mold *Neurospora crassa*. The presence of extranuclear genetic materials suggests that DNA· must be present within the cellular bodies in question.

In the early 1960s the existence of DNA within chloroplasts and mitochondria was demonstrated. The subsequent discoveries of ribosomes, transfer RNAs, and other enzymes within mitochondria and chloroplasts suggest that these cytoplasmic bodies may synthesize part if not all their own proteins.

Genes and development

GENE ACTION

The one gene–one enzyme hypothesis. The study of mutations that alter metabolic processes has shed light on the mode of action of the genes in the development of the organism. The normal expression of a genetic trait (such as eye colour in *Drosophila* flies) involves a chain of chemical reactions transforming a substance A into B, B into C, C into D, etc. Each transformation is facilitated by a specific enzyme, and each enzyme is a product of a certain gene, hence the one gene–one enzyme hypothesis. A mutation, then, may stand for the absence of an enzyme.

In the early 1940s studies of biochemical mutants in the bread mold *N. crassa* were very significant in advancing knowledge of gene action. Most strains of this mold grow well on a minimal medium containing sugar, an inorganic nitrogen source, and the vitamin biotin. Some mutant strains, however, do not grow on the minimal medium and require for growth the addition of certain substances that normal *N. crassa* can synthesize itself. Among many mutants studied in *N. crassa*, those concerned with synthesis of the amino acid tryptophan proved particularly favourable for study. Tryptophan is synthesized as follows: anthranilic acid (A) → indole (B) → tryptophan (C). Mutants were found that blocked the step A → B, others that blocked B → C. Apparently, each step is facilitated by an enzyme produced by a separate gene, and a mutational change in the gene may cause a lack of the enzyme or may make it ineffective.

The determination of protein structure and synthesis. Proteins, basic components of living organisms, are con-

Margin notes:

Revision of the definition of the gene

Cistrons

Mutons and recons

Role of genes in enzyme production

structed from nitrogen-containing compounds called amino acids. Some 20 amino acids are commonly found in naturally occurring proteins. The amino acids are linked together in the proteins by a specific chemical bond, the peptide bond, to form long chains. It is the sequence of the amino acids in a protein that is uniquely determined by the sequence of the four bases in DNA. The amino-acid sequence or primary structure of a protein usually determines the three-dimensional structure that the complete protein molecule will take. Interactions between various chemical groups on the amino-acid units of protein are responsible for the three-dimensional structure that results. Three groups of proteins can be recognized: (1) enzymes, or catalytic proteins, which participate in almost all chemical reactions that take place in cells of living bodies; (2) structural proteins, which form the building blocks of cellular components; and (3) regulatory, or control, proteins, which interact with genes or their products to control the amounts and presumably the times of production of still other protein molecules.

The amino-acid sequence of a protein such as human hemoglobin shows that these molecules are composed of several protein subunits, usually called polypeptide chains, linked together by chemical bonds. Normal hemoglobin (A) is composed of four polypeptide chains, two alphas (α) and two betas (β), whose amino-acid sequences show considerable similarity.

An example of the difficulty encountered by the one gene–one enzyme hypothesis is provided by the variants in the human hemoglobin molecule. Genetic studies of individuals having mutant hemoglobins have shown that the alpha and beta chains of hemoglobin are controlled by two genes located on two different chromosomes. This suggests that the one gene–one enzyme hypothesis should be modified to a one gene–one polypeptide chain hypothesis.

The one gene–one polypeptide chain

Further studies of mutant hemoglobins have elucidated how the gene might control the specific amino-acid sequence of a polypeptide. A hereditary disease in humans, sickle-cell anemia, was first discovered in Africa and the Mediterranean regions of Europe and Asia. Clinical manifestations of this affliction include a change in the form of the red blood cells to a sicklelike shape. Chemical study of the hemoglobins of persons with sickle-cell anemia revealed the presence of an abnormal hemoglobin designated hemoglobin S. Hemoglobin S is composed of two normal alpha chains and two altered beta chains. A study of the amino-acid sequence of the mutant beta chain revealed a single amino-acid substitution: the glutamic acid at a certain position in the normal chain had been replaced by valine in the mutant chain. Several other mutant hemoglobins were discovered, and their analyses again showed a single amino-acid substitution, compared with the hemoglobin present in "normal" persons. The mutants responsible for these variant hemoglobins evidently alter the genes so that a single amino-acid difference appears in the mutant. Table 1 lists some of these abnormal hemoglobins. Hemoglobin I, for ex-

ample, shows a substitution of aspartic acid for lysine at position 16 in the alpha chain. The beta chain of hemoglobin C has a lysine substituted for glutamic acid at position 6.

Further evidence for the genetic control of the amino-acid sequences in polypeptide chains of proteins was obtained in 1964 in studies on *E. coli.* The enzyme tryptophan synthetase in *E. coli* consists of two polypeptide chains, designated A and B. A number of mutants exist that result in inactive forms of the enzyme, the result of amino-acid substitutions in the A chain. Precise genetic mapping of these mutants reveals a collinearity, an exact linear correspondence between the mutants on the genetic map and the positions of amino-acid substitutions in the altered A-chain polypeptides. The collinearity of the genetic map and the polypeptide chains is convincing evidence that specific regions of a gene encode for the sequence of amino acids in polypeptide chains.

THE GENETIC CODE

The discovery of the ways in which the sequence of the nucleotides in the DNA of a chromosome is translated into the sequence of amino acids in a protein is one of the outstanding achievements of molecular biology. This is often called the transcription function of DNA, to distinguish it from the duplication function, in which DNA replicates itself (see above).

The "letters" of the genetic alphabet. The information contained in DNA is first transcribed into an RNA molecule, from which the information is subsequently translated into protein. The hypothesis can be represented thus: DNA → RNA → protein. Reverse transfer does not occur; *i.e.,* there is no storage of information in the protein molecules and no transcription of it back into nucleic acids. This is sometimes referred to as "the central dogma" of molecular genetics.

The central dogma of molecular genetics

Tiny particles in the cytoplasm of cells have been identified as the sites of protein synthesis. These particles, called ribosomes, consist of both RNA and protein. Besides the ribosomal RNA, another kind of RNA, called messenger RNA (mRNA), found both in the nucleus and in the cytoplasm, serves as a carrier of the genetic information from the nuclear DNA to the ribosomal RNA. The sequence of the genetic letters, A (adenine), T (thymine), C (cytosine), and G (guanine), in the DNA is first transcribed into the corresponding sequence of the letters A, U (uracil), C, and G in the messenger RNA. This occurs through the action of the enzyme RNA polymerase. This enzyme synthesizes RNA in a test tube from a mixture of the A, U, C, and G bases, but it does so only in the presence of a primer DNA. The sequence of the bases in the primer is copied in the RNA. The steps involved in this process are: (1) the DNA double helix unwinds by breaking the hydrogen bonds between the corresponding bases in the paired strands; (2) the RNA polymerase forms the bonds between the RNA bases that are complementary to the bases in the DNA; and (3) the messenger RNA thus formed passes into the cytoplasm and becomes attached to a ribosome.

The process of protein synthesis is represented diagrammatically in Figure 9. The information contained in the sequence of the bases (letters) in the messenger RNA is then translated into a sequence of amino acids in a protein. This requires the presence of still another molecule that is capable of recognizing the code for a specific amino acid and selectively making the amino acid available at the right point in the protein synthesis, a soluble RNA fraction within cells that can bind amino acids. Soluble, or transfer, RNA (sRNA, or tRNA) is a single-stranded molecule that forms about 20 percent of the total cellular RNA. If amino acids and a source of energy (usually ATP) are added to a mixture of transfer RNA's, reversible binding of the amino acids to the RNA molecules occurs. Furthermore, each amino acid is bonded to a specific transfer RNA molecule by a specific activating enzyme. There are at least 20 different transfer RNA's and activating enzymes that correspond to the 20 amino acids commonly found in proteins. The amino acid–transfer RNA complex becomes attached to the ribosome with its messenger RNA

Table 1: Amino Acid Substitutions in Abnormal Human Hemoglobins

hemoglobin type	substitution	position in chain
	in the alpha chain:	
I	aspartic acid for lysine	16
G-Honolulu	glutamine for glutamic acid	30
Norfolk	aspartic acid for glycine	57
M-Boston	tyrosine for histidine	58
G-Philadelphia	lysine for asparagine	68
	in the beta chain:	
S	valine for glutamic acid	6
C	lysine for glutamic acid	6
G-San Jose	glycine for glutamic acid	7
E	lysine for glutamic acid	26
M-Saskatoon	tyrosine for histidine	63
Zurich	arginine for histidine	63
M-Milwaukee-1	glutamic acid for valine	67
D-Punjab	glutamine for glutamic acid	121

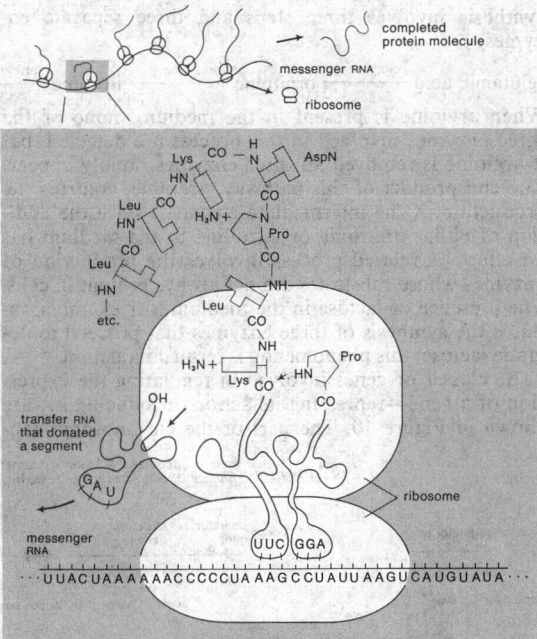

Figure 9: *Synthesis of protein.*
(Top) The messenger RNA shown with a ribosome (in stages) "reading" its message, the translation occurring from left to right, and the polypeptide chain growing as the ribosome proceeds along the messenger RNA. **(Bottom)** A highly magnified ribosome in the process of "reading" a messenger RNA molecule. The ribosome has just "read" an AAG sequence off the messenger RNA, and a specific transfer RNA molecule (UUC) moves into place carrying the amino acid lysine (Lys), which is then added to the polypeptide chain. Next in position to be read is CCU, which draws a transfer RNA molecule carrying the amino acid proline (Pro) to be transferred to the growing polypeptide chain. The ribosome moves from left to right along the messenger RNA molecule. Each ribosome has two binding sites for transfer RNA: one that holds the growing polypeptide chain and a second for positioning a new transfer RNA molecule for processing.
From T. Jukes, *Molecules and Evolution* (1966); Columbia University Press

molecule; the addition of the amino acid to the growing polypeptide chain then occurs. A sequence of bases (anti-codon) on the transfer RNA molecule pairs with a complementary sequence (codon) on the messenger RNA molecule, which is held in the correct position by the ribosome. Once the recognition has occurred, a peptide bond is formed between the amino acid bound to the transfer RNA and the growing polypeptide chain.

Reading the code. How do the four letters—A, T, C, and G—specify, or code, for 20 different amino acids? If a single letter coded for an amino acid, only four amino acids could be specified. If two bases were needed to specify an amino acid, then 16 different combinations could be constructed, again an insufficient number (20 amino acids must be accounted for). Combinations of three letters allow 64 different words to be constructed, more than the necessary minimal number. A three-letter, triplet, code could be constructed in at least three different ways: (1) with words overlapping; (2) with words not overlapping and punctuated; and (3) with words not overlapping and not punctuated. An overlapping code is composed of words that overlap each other—*i.e.*, the letters of any given word may belong to one, two, or three words. The DNA might contain, for example, the sequence A G C G T T A C G; the first word is AGC, the second CGT, and so on. This type of code is improbable, because of the restrictions it would place upon the possible sequence of amino acids in protein. As the example above shows, if the first word is AGC, the second word must begin with C, etc. Examination of amino-acid sequences in a protein such as hemoglobin indicates that any amino acid can follow any other—a possibility not allowed for by an overlapping code.

If the code is nonoverlapping, a problem of distinguishing words from each other arises. DNA contains no spaces separating the words as in written sentences; therefore,

there must be other indications of specific starting points for messenger RNA synthesis. The base sequence AGC AGC AGC ... could be punctuated by the presence of a fourth base, T, between each AGC triplet. This would reduce the number of possible triplets to 27. That a punctuated code of this type is not realized is seen from the evidence of the degeneracy in the code for some amino acids. The degeneracy means that some amino acids are coded for by more than one triplet, and a punctuated code does not allow enough words. A second objection to this type of code comes from a consideration of the effects of mutation on the coding sequence. If one of the punctuation marks mutates to another base, or a coding base mutates to a punctuation mark, the resulting sequence will be complete nonsense functionally.

The third possibility is a nonoverlapping, nonpunctuated code, in which the reading starts from a specific point. In all organisms studied in this respect this is the method of coding used. If the reading of the genetic message begins at a fixed place in a DNA strand, then the addition or the removal of a single letter will alter the message from that point on. Suppose that the DNA message read from left to right reveals the triplets GAC, TCA, and TTA (which are transcribed in the RNA code as CUG, AGU, AAU). Deletion of the first T alters the reading frame so that triplets GAC, CAT, TA ... will be read. The first triplet is unchanged, but all the remaining triplets may specify wrong amino acids. The chemical addition of a base to the sequence likewise shifts the reading frame; such a mutant will also specify wrong amino acids beyond the point of the base addition. If an original mutant resulted from the deletion of a base from the DNA, the addition of a base at a point beyond the first mutation would restore the reading frame of the DNA sequence, and would result in nearly normal function. In the bacteriophage T4, assume that the original wild-type phage DNA sequence within the rII region reads ACT GGC TAG CTG TCA TCG. ... Deletion of the C in the second triplet results in the following triplets being read: ACT, GGT, AGC, TGT, CAT, CG. ... This is an rII mutant. The subsequent addition of a base (A) between the third and fourth mutant triplets results in the following sequence: ACT GGT AGC ATG TCA TCG .... Note that the first, fifth, and sixth triplets are identical to those in the original wild-type phage. Only the second, third, and fourth triplets are altered, and the reading of the code from the fourth triplet on will be identical to that in the wild-type phage. Frequently, suppressor mutations occur in proximity to other mutations and restore the reading frame of the DNA sequence, thereby allowing a sequence of amino acids differing only slightly from the original one to be formed in the protein.

A knowledge of the base sequence in the messenger RNA and the resulting amino-acid sequence in protein reveals the code for each amino acid. The triplet UUU, for example, is the code for the amino acid phenylalanine, corresponding to the sequence AAA in the DNA. Poly-A (AAA) and poly-C (CCC) messenger RNA's code for lysine and proline, respectively.

Other triplets were tested for their coding abilities by synthesizing messenger RNA molecules with varying proportions of the two bases. If, for example, a mixture of the two bases U and C in a 5:1 proportion are synthesized into RNA, the possible triplets and their probable frequency in the synthetic messenger RNA can be easily determined. The triplet UUU will be most common and will appear with the frequency ($\frac{5}{6} \times \frac{5}{6} \times \frac{5}{6}$); the triplets UUC, UCU, and CUU will appear in the frequencies of $\frac{5}{6} \times \frac{5}{6} \times \frac{1}{6}$; the triplets UCC, CUC, and CCU will be the next most frequent and will appear with a frequency of $\frac{5}{6} \times \frac{1}{6} \times \frac{1}{6}$; while the triplet CCC should appear only $\frac{1}{216}$ of the time. A messenger RNA of this composition should result in the incorporation into protein of eight different amino acids. In fact, only four amino acids were present in the protein produced; this means that several of these triplets encode for the same amino acid and therefore that the code is degenerate.

The RNA code triplets (or codons) and the amino acids

for which they stand are shown in Table 2. Triplets have recently been discovered that encode for starting and for stopping the synthesis of protein chains in *E. coli*. Many

Table 2: The Genetic Code: Nucleotide Triplets (Codons) Specifying Different Amino Acids in Protein Chains*

DNA triplet	RNA triplet	amino acid	DNA triplet	RNA triplet	amino acid
AAA	UUU	phenylalanine	ACA	UGU	cysteine
AAG	UUC		ACG	UGC	
AAT	UUA		ACC	UGG	tryptophan
AAC	UUG		ATA	UAU	tyrosine
GAA	CUU	leucine	ATG	UAC	
GAG	CUC		ATT	UAA	
GAT	CUA		ATC	UAG	(termination: end of specification)
GAC	CUG		ACT	UGA	
AGA	UCU		GCA	CGU	
AGG	UCC		GCG	CGC	
AGT	UCA	serine	GCT	CGA	arginine
AGC	UCG		GCC	CGG	
TCA	AGU		TCT	AGA	
TCG	AGC		TCC	AGG	
GGA	CCU		GTA	CAU	histidine
GGG	CCC	proline	GTG	CAC	
GGT	CCA		GTT	CAA	glutamine (GluN)
GGC	CCG		GTC	CAG	
TAA	AUU		TTA	AAU	asparagine (AspN)
TAG	AUC	isoleucine (Ileu)	TTG	AAC	
TAT	AUA		TTT	AAA	lysine
TAC	AUG	methionine	TTC	AAG	
TGA	ACU		CCA	GGU	
TGG	ACC	threonine	CCG	GGC	glycine
TGT	ACA		CCT	GGA	
TGC	ACG		CCC	GGG	
CAA	GUU		CTA	GAU	aspartic acid
CAG	GUC	valine	CTG	GAC	
CAT	GUA		CTT	GAA	glutamic acid
CAC	GUG		CTC	GAG	
CGA	GCU				
CGG	GCC	alanine			
CGT	GCA				
CGC	GCG				

*The columns may be read: the DNA triplet is transcribed into an RNA triplet, which then directs the production of an amino acid.

proteins of *E. coli* begin with the amino acid methionine. Two different transfer RNAs for methionine are known to exist, only one of which functions to initiate protein synthesis. After synthesis of the protein, an enzyme may remove a portion of the beginning of the chain to eliminate the obligatory methionine molecule. The second transfer RNA for methionine allows this amino acid to be incorporated into the middle of a polypeptide.

Ending the code

Termination of protein synthesis appears to be effected by three different RNA triplets: UAA, UAG, UGA. These triplets were discovered as mutations that produced premature cessation of protein synthesis in many different genes. The exact mechanism of polypeptide-chain termination is not known, although the action of a special transfer RNA molecule is suspected.

REGULATION OF GENES

The operon system. The evidence accumulated in genetics makes it virtually certain that not all the genes present in a cell are active in directing the specific processes of protein synthesis. Gene action can be switched on or off, depending on the position of a cell in the body and the stage of body development, as well as on the external environment.

The control of the gene activity has been elucidated in *E. coli*. A culture of these bacteria growing on a minimal medium is able to synthesize the amino acids needed to construct the proteins from carbohydrates and a nitrogen source. The synthesis requires the presence of certain enzymes whose activities can be detected in a growing culture. If the culture of bacteria is supplied with certain amino acids, the synthesis of the enzymes that synthesize these amino acids is quickly arrested. This phenomenon is known as repression, and the enzymes affected are repressible enzymes. The pathway for the synthesis of the amino acid arginine in *E. coli* is a good example. This

synthesis involves three steps and three separate enzymes:

$$\text{glutamic acid} \xrightarrow{\text{enzyme A}} \text{ornithine} \xrightarrow{\text{enzyme B}} \text{citrulline} \xrightarrow{\text{enzyme C}} \text{arginine.}$$

When arginine is present in the medium, none of the three enzymes involved in this process are detected, but if arginine is removed all three enzymes rapidly appear. The end product of this pathway, arginine, controls the production of the intermediate enzymes, since the addition of either ornithine or citrulline to the medium has no effect. A related process involves the production of enzymes whose substrates are not always present in cells. The presence of lactose in the medium, for example, induces the synthesis of three enzymes that proceed to degrade lactose; this phenomenon is termed induction.

The classes of genes involved in regulating the expression of a gene—repressing its action or inducing it—are shown in Figure 10. The part of the chromosome con-

From F. Jacob and J. Monod, *Journal of Molecular Biology* (1961); Academic Press, Inc.

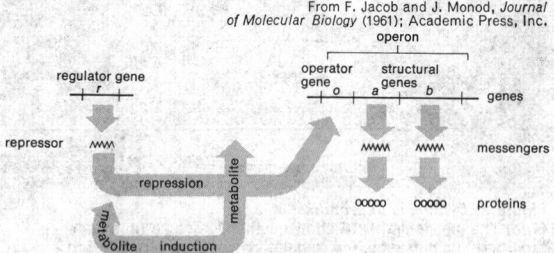

Figure 10: Model of the operon and its relation to the regulator gene.

taining the genes concerned is divided into two regions, one of which includes the operator and structural genes. This is termed an operon. The other part contains only the regulator gene. The regulator gene need not be located close to the operon. The regulator gene produces some substance, a repressor, which affects a second gene, an operator. There are several lines of evidence that suggest that the repressor substance is a protein molecule. It would be necessary for such a molecule to have at least two areas or sites that interact with the operator gene or a metabolite or both to influence structural genes (repress or induce their action, depending on given conditions).

Other influences on genes. The orderly complexity of the mechanism of cell division ensures that a dividing cell will give rise to two daughter cells with exactly similar chromosomes. Yet, as a fertilized egg cell gives rise to more and more body cells, these cells differentiate and become distinct from each other. A nerve cell, a muscle cell, a liver cell, and others are strikingly different; if each contains exactly the same chromosomes and genes, how are these differences explained? The same genes are present in all the daughter cells, but different genes become active in different types of cells.

The operon model (see above) furnishes a plausible explanation of how different genes may be active at different times in different tissues. Very suggestive evidence of such variable gene activity comes from observations of the giant chromosomes present in the cells of larval salivary glands and some other tissues of certain flies. At certain stages of the development of a larva, some of the stainable disks or bands in these chromosomes expand and at other stages contract again. The expansion is apparently caused by a localized uncoiling of the gene strings composing the giant chromosomes. The expanded portions of a chromosome are called puffs. There is good evidence that the bands in the giant chromosomes correspond to small groups of genes or even to single genes. Detailed observations on the giant chromosomes in different tissues of the larva of the midge *Chironomus* showed the banding patterns to be identical throughout but the puffing patterns to vary from tissue to tissue. A plausible conclusion is that all cells had identical complements of genes but that different genes were active in each tissue. The puffing patterns of a tissue also varied precisely with the development stage of the insect.

Variability of gene activity in different tissues

The study of the mechanisms of cellular differentiation was advanced by the discovery of nitrogen-rich proteins associated with DNA. These proteins, called histones, have the capability to affect the structure of the genetic material so as to allow or repress the gene activity. The lateral loops of the so-called lampbrush chromosomes (large, fuzzy-appearing chromosomes) in developing amphibian egg cells react to histones by contracting. The rate of RNA synthesis in lampbrush chromosomes is greatest when the lateral loops are fully expanded. The addition of histones to isolated calf-thymus nuclei inhibits various synthetic reactions, such as ATP and RNA synthesis. The removal of histones from nuclei results in enhanced RNA synthesis. Electron-microscopic examination of untreated nuclei shows that the genetic material exists in two discrete states: a compact, darkly staining mass and a diffuse, poorly staining matrix. It has been demonstrated that the overwhelming majority of RNA synthesis occurs in areas of diffuse genetic material. The addition of histones results in an increase in the amount of compact genetic material, while the removal of histones results in the dispersal of the genetic material. This work indicates that changes in the appearance of the genetic material will result in new patterns of RNA synthesis.

The mechanism of the histone effects was studied by examining chemical reactions that affect chemical groups other than the amino acids contained in histones. The attachment to histones of chemical groups called acetyl apparently causes some structural change in the genetic material that allows more genes to produce messenger RNA.

Reversible addition and subtraction of acetyl groups in histones may, then, control the gene action in development. Several problems remain to be solved. Histones may control the general gene activity, but development involves the activation and repression of specific gene systems. At present no mechanism is known that would give the needed specificity to histones. The reversible acetylation of histones controls its regulatory activity, but what controls the rate of histone acetylation? The operon model discussed above can be utilized as a first step in an approach to these problems. A combination of several operons into a complex regulatory system gives a system whose properties remotely approach those observed in differentiating cells. The inescapable conclusion is that an organism is a highly complex system, composed of many tissues, each of which interacts with the others and with the environment in a precise, predictable manner.

BIBLIOGRAPHY. E.A. CARLSON, *The Gene: A Critical History* (1966); P.E. HARTMAN and S.R. SUSKIND, *Gene Action* (1965), a short account of how genes operate; J.D. WATSON, *Molecular Biology of the Gene*, 2nd ed. (1970), a clear, concise, well-illustrated textbook covering the ultimate active units of heredity. The following articles published in the journal *Scientific American* are readable and well illustrated: S. BENZER, "The Fine Structure of the Gene," 206:70–84 (1962); J. CAIRNS, "The Bacterial Chromosome," 214:36–44 (1966); F.H.C. CRICK, "The Genetic Code," 207:66–74 (1962) and "The Genetic Code: III," 215:55–62 (1966); F. JACOB and E.L. WOLLMAN, "Viruses and Genes," 204:92–107 (1961); and M.W. NIRENBERG, "The Genetic Code: II," 208:80–95 (1963).

(Ro.R./T.D.)

Genealogy

The word genealogy comes from two Greek words—one meaning "race" or "family" and the other "to speak." Thus is derived "to trace ancestry," the science of studying family history. The term pedigree, used to describe a genealogy as set forth in chart or other written form, comes from the Latin *pes* ("foot") and *grus* ("crane") and is derived from a sign resembling a crane's foot, used to indicate lines of descent in early west European genealogies. Chart pedigrees, familiar to most people from school history books, include arrow shapes, parallel lines, a crinkled line denoting illegitimacy, and the sign = denoting marriage. Genealogy is a universal phenomenon and, in forms varying from the rudimentary to the comparatively complex, is found in all nations and periods. In this article the history of genealogy will be outlined, followed by an account of the work of modern genealogists, professional and amateur, and as organized in associations.

Development of genealogical study. The history of genealogy can be divided most easily into three stages. The first is that of oral tradition; the second, that in which certain pedigrees were committed to writing. The third stage comprises the period from approximately 1500 in western Europe and later in the English-speaking world, during which the whole basis of genealogy widened to such an extent that it is now possible for the majority of people in western Europe to trace their ancestry.

Oral tradition and biblical sources. In the early days of civilization, before written records were made, oral traditions were necessarily important. Without the art of writing, reliance must be placed on memory, aided possibly by mnemonic systems like that of knot arrangements used by the pre-Hispanic Peruvians, or beads employed by the Maori of New Zealand. The ancient Scottish sennachy, or royal bard, could recite the pedigree of the old Scots kings at the latter's inauguration, and the nobles of Peru, who boasted a common descent with the sovereign, were able to preserve their pedigrees despite the complexity resulting from the practice of polygamy. Oral transmission of genealogical information is almost always as a list of names—the lineages of the ancient Irish kings, for example. Events of outstanding importance are occasionally incorporated in such lists.

Numerous Oriental genealogies appear in the Old Testament. A cursory examination of these will reveal that they belong to the first and second stages in the history of genealogy, as described above. The systematic keeping of genealogical records, as in Europe since 1500, did not occur until very recently in Asia and Africa.

In southern India the ruling house of the maharajas of Travancore claimed to trace its descent, direct and unbroken, from the old Cēra kings of southern India (referred to as independent sovereigns in one of the edicts of Aśoka, the great Mauryan emperor of the 3rd century BC). A claim that inscriptions of the rulers of Travancore have been found from the 9th century AD comes from a statement issued by the secretariat of the maharaja of Travancore. Its reliability may be judged along with the genealogies of princes in northern India shown in Lt. Col. James Tod's monumental work, *Annals and Antiquities of Rajasthan* (1829, republished 1950). Referring to the lineages of Indian princes as being known since the early centuries BC, Tod wrote, "If, after all, these are fabricated genealogies of the ancient families of India, the fabrication is of ancient date, and they are all they know themselves upon the subject." The very long Oriental genealogies begin as oral pedigrees and were later written down, but they concern only princes or great persons.

In Africa the one instance of a claim to very long descent, that of the Emperor of Ethiopia, bears a similarity to Tod's Rājput genealogies. The Emperor is said to descend from the marriage of King Solomon with the Queen of Sheba. The tradition was written down more than 15 centuries ago; it is therefore older than the history of most European monarchies, but it cannot, of course, be substantiated by documentary proof.

Under European influence, the greater Oriental countries have adopted the practice of keeping systematic records for all citizens. In China, with its ancient system of ancestor worship, long, drawn-out pedigrees, including claims to descent from Confucius, are not unknown. The establishment of the Chinese Republic in 1911 brought with it registration of vital statistics.

In modern Japan, as might be expected from its thoroughgoing Westernization, the registration of vital statistics is regulated by law. The Family Registration Law of 1947, and later enactments, require a comprehensive registration of a Japanese national from his birth to his death. Such information, however, is kept in local registration offices, and there is no system in Japan for

Oriental genealogies

gathering together, recording, and preserving the information in one central place (although of course the results of statistics, such as the number of births, is known to the central authority). Such an exact system of registration covers only the era of modern Japan. The present-day pedigree of the Japanese emperors has a divine origin; it is mainly a string of names, easily recited and memorized, mixed with semifabulous legends and first written down in the early centuries of the Christian Era. Such pedigrees are concerned only with exalted persons, royal or noble.

Biblical genealogies
In the Old Testament there are many genealogies, the object of which is to show descent from Adam, Noah, and Abraham. By the time these genealogies had become part of the Jewish scriptures, the concept of racial purity had reinforced the keeping of family records. Genealogies of Jesus Christ in the New Testament aim at showing his descent from David, the one in St. Luke's Gospel going as far back as Adam, "who was the son of God." The idea of divine origin was reflected everywhere in a wildly polytheistic form among the Gentiles. Almost without exception, the heroes whose genealogies were recited by the bards had their paternity ascribed to the gods, or to persons such as Romulus who were regarded as having become divine. Greek fables abound in stories of great men begotten by gods and mortals.

In Roman genealogies heroes were always descended from gods. Julius Caesar, for example, was supposed to have sprung from the line of Aeneas, and thus from that of Venus. Among the Romans, traditions of descent remained vague even when written. Caesar's murderer, Brutus, was popularly supposed to be of the same family as an ancient Brutus, who had expelled the Tarquins, but no pedigree appears to have existed to substantiate the belief.

Among the northern nations that overwhelmed the western Roman Empire, belief in divine sonship was general. For Saxon rulers of the English kingdoms it was necessary to be descended from the god Woden.

Early written records. With the invention of writing, the oral became the written tradition. This occurred in Greece and Rome, where genealogies were recorded in poems and in histories. But genealogy did not at this stage become a science, because when writers dealt with it, they did so either incidentally in their narrative or because they were concerned with the family relationships of their gods.

Maximum length of genealogies
The historian Edward Gibbon's observation that "the proudest families are content to lose in the darkness of the middle ages, the tree of their pedigree" may be challenged in the light of recorded genealogies. The male line of Charlemagne has been traced to St. Arnulf, bishop of Metz, who died about 635. Several royal line descents are traceable to the 6th century, as, in England, is the tree of Louis Mountbatten, 1st Earl Mountbatten. The ancestry of Queen Elizabeth II goes to Egbert of Wessex (about 825), beyond him to Cerdic (c. 500), and, if another series of names is accepted, to Woden (an actual man later divinized by the Germans), in the 3rd century AD.

With the conversion of the barbarians to Christianity the recording of their regal traditions began. Examples occur in Ireland, Wales, and England. It was natural for the first chroniclers, who were mostly monks, to write down the oral pedigrees of the kings in whose realms they lived. Students of the Irish regal pedigrees are prepared to accept two or three generations before the time of St. Patrick (flourished 5th century AD) as genuine, and it is quite probable that name lists of the Irish kings are valid back to the 3rd century AD. Similarly, in Wales, the ancestry of the greatest Welsh families can be traced for a millennium. Among the Anglo-Saxons there were similar bardic pedigrees recorded by monastic scribes, and many of these might have survived but for the destruction of the Old English ruling class during the Norman Conquest. A regular feature of such old pedigrees recorded by monks was an attempt to link them with the genealogies of the Scriptures. In an Anglo-Saxon pedigree of great length—that of the kings of Wessex (the

ancestors of Elizabeth II)—the line is thus traced to Sceaf, "a son of Noah born in the Ark." In the process of working out the connection between scriptural and regal genealogies, the monks adopted a reverse technique to that of the 4th-century-BC Greek mythographer Euhemerus; *i.e.,* they downgraded the old gods to human status.

From roughly 1100 to 1500, the emphasis of genealogists was on pedigrees of royal and noble lines. Claims to a throne, as with the dozen or so claimants to the Scottish crown after the death of Alexander III in 1286 and of his direct heir, Margaret the Maid of Norway in 1290, frequently involved genealogical trees. The truth was sometimes bent to suit some political end, but, on the whole, medieval European records are genealogically valid. This is because they were not primarily intended to supply genealogical information but to record land transactions, taxation, and lawsuits. The facts of family history are incidental and are therefore generally reliable. Exact dates of birth, marriage, and death are rarely given. A man is said to be of age "by Michaelmas 1330."

This period also saw the emergence of pedigrees of lesser folk. Land transactions involved claims in the local courts of the lords. Serfdom gave way to villenage; the latter involved so many days of labour on the lord's demesne and also the inability to move from the estate without the lord's consent. There was strong inducement for a man to prove that he was not a villein and for the bailiff to show that he was. In several part of England, pedigrees of villeins or persons claimed as such have been worked out over periods of 100–150 years.

It was during the third period in European genealogical history that records that came to include everyone began. This period extends from 1500 to the present. As feudalism gradually gave way, new classes of citizens arose. In England the appearance of a powerful mercantile and business community was reflected in the growth of the middle classes, from which was continually recruited a new nobility and gentry. In turn, owing to the English rule of inheritance by primogeniture and the fact that unlike the continental nobility English nobility has never extended beyond the reigning peer and his wife, the middle classes themselves continually received the younger children of peers and gentry. Two other factors leading to the proliferation of records were the enormous changes caused by the Reformation and the great re-emphasis on individual religion and the desire of Renaissance monarchs to have more exact information about all their subjects.

Modern genealogy. Amateurs in the subject of genealogy are almost always actuated by the desire to trace their own family history. In the course of so doing they discover and work with general principles which apply to pedigrees other than their own, though records other than those applicable to their own case do not interest them. The professional genealogist is concerned not with one family but with many, and with the principles of genealogical research which arise from a wide study. As there are no university courses in the subject and therefore no degrees or other certificates of professional proficiency, the professional must be largely self-taught.

Qualifications of the professional genealogist
The disciplines required of a professional genealogist include a deep knowledge of the history of the country with which he is concerned and of its neighbours. National history determines the form of national genealogy, and genealogy can illuminate many aspects of national history that might otherwise remain obscure. The Wars of the Roses, for example, are hard to grasp unless genealogical trees showing relationships of the contestants are studied, and the course of the American Revolution is easier to understand when the links between George Washington and his compeers with the old English landed families who overthrew the Stuarts are comprehended. An understanding of the principles of law, especially of land law, the ability to decipher court hand or medieval script, an understanding of heraldry, and an intimate knowledge of the study of surnames and place names are also essential to the genealogist. Variations in surname spelling can be bewildering. The key is in the

sound of the name, for a medieval scribe could not ask the illiterate person before him to spell his name.

The main task undertaken by the professional genealogist is the tracing of pedigrees for clients, this being the staple of his work. Clients often consult genealogists when they wish to establish their family background, or, when having tried to trace it, they have come to a stop.

The writing of private family histories by professionals is very common. The material has usually been worked out by others who wish it to be checked and written by a professional.

The amateur genealogist, as already mentioned, is usually concerned only with his own family. The standard of amateur work varies with the individual, from the truly bad to the excellent.

Amateur genealogical work has increased greatly since 1945. In the United States there has been a long interest in the subject. The New England Historic Genealogical Society, the Augustan Society (based in California) and many state societies are of note. The Mormons (the Church of Jesus Christ of Latter-day Saints) have built up in Salt Lake City, Utah, a microfilm library of genealogical records from Britain and continental Europe, which is probably unequalled. In Canada, Australia, New Zealand, and South Africa the study of genealogy by private persons and by associations is growing rapidly. In England there is a Society of Genealogists, and there are corresponding bodies for Ireland and Scotland. In Spain there is an International Institute of Genealogy and Heraldry, which since 1955 has organized international congresses held in many European capitals at intervals of two years. In Czechoslovakia, by way of contrast, the national Genealogical Society has been dissolved, and in general it has not been feasible to obtain genealogical details from Communist countries, though it is probable that changes are now occurring in this respect. Jewish records are in a separate class. With the establishment of the state of Israel in 1948, a very great effort has been made to centralize information about the Jews of continental Europe under the care and direction of the Jewish Historical Archives in Jerusalem.

In tracing family history, the worker follows certain rules. He works backward from the present. This is an elementary caution constantly put on one side by amateurs, who tend to trace forward from a person of the same name who may well be unrelated. As there cannot in the nature of things be a gap in a pedigree, no assumptions as to relationship can be allowed without very strong reason to accept them. Good and bad features in the ancestry have to be accepted: bastardy has to be allowed for, as well as regal ancestry by legitimate lines. An ancestor's wrongdoing must also be allowed for, though with passage of time this is usually taken in a romantic sense. Registration of birth, marriage, and death first became compulsory in England in 1837. Public records in most other Western countries began at varying dates in the 19th century. Census records are of great importance. They began in the U.S. as early as 1791; in Britain in 1801 (papers kept only from 1841); and even earlier in French Canada, in 1655–66. Parish registers began in England in 1538, though they are rarely preserved from that date. In most countries they begin later, but in Spain the oldest extant is dated 1394, and there are 1,636 parishes having records prior to 1570. In England, Nonconformist records have been kept by various bodies, and many are now held officially at Somerset House, London, or the Public Record Office. In America the settlers were generally trying to get away from established church and controlling state. They were vigorous individualists who kept careful records of their lives and of the organization of their new communities. Examples of detail in New England records can be seen in many of the 1,600 pedigrees contained in *American Families with British Ancestry* (500 page suppl. to John Burke's *Landed Gentry*, 1939); in A.M. Burke's *Prominent Families of the United States of America*, and in the many volumes of family history produced in the United States.

Wills are of the utmost importance as a source of genealogical information. Ships' lists of passengers are useful in supplying dates for immigrant ancestors' departure for the New World, but since they do not indicate place of origin, but only the port of departure, the original habitat must be sought elsewhere. Without a knowledge of the ancestor's place of origin in the home land it is useless in almost all cases to attempt a search.

With the aid of the type of record mentioned above, and with help from family Bibles, tombstones, and plaques and brasses in churches, it is as a rule possible for a person of English antecedents to trace some 250–300 years of ancestry. Before the 17th century, everything depends on the social position of the ancestors. Tax records, lawsuits, and purchases and sales of land are the chief sources for tracing a family before 1600. The Pipe Rolls extend from the reign of Henry II (1154–89) to that of Queen Victoria, with an interrupted beginning also in the time of Henry I (1100–35). Monastic records are of great importance as showing grants or ownership of land. The pleas of the crown deal with suits at law and contain much detail about families. There are many Rolls besides those of the Pipe which give a great deal of incidental genealogical information. *Inquisitiones post mortem* show the position of an heir; *i.e.*, his age and other details. As the centuries are passed, the numbers of those who can prove a descent by the male line dwindles, until by the time of the Norman Conquest scarcely half a dozen pedigrees can be traced in the male line for either Saxon or Norman.

Regarding deposition of public records, two principles have been followed by archivists: that of centralization and that of diffused local holdings. The former has many obvious advantages and was adopted in Scotland and in Ireland. It has one disadvantage—destruction of the records at one stroke. This happened in Dublin on April 13, 1922, when Irish factions fighting with each other burned most of the Irish records. The second system, by which records are stored in a number of depositories, prevails to a considerable extent in England. Although the Public Record Office at Somerset House and the British Museum library are places of centralized record, the parish registers remain outside them, scattered in numerous parishes or county offices. County records contain masses of material not to be found in London.

From the 16th century there has been an increasing accumulation of written material, which deals either exclusively or incidentally with genealogy. William Camden (1551–1623), a learned English antiquary and historian, did much to raise the standards of genealogical research. He was the first English writer on surnames, and his work was not resumed for nearly 200 years. Sir William Dugdale, a younger contemporary of Camden, made a beginning with his *Antiquities of Warwickshire* to the great output of county histories written between the 17th and 19th centuries. The revolution in modern genealogy was the application to its study of canons of historical and literary criticism formulated in Europe from 1800. Their application to genealogy was fairly late, as is illustrated by the fact that the 19th-century English historian Thomas Macaulay, critically perceptive in most other spheres, accepted what amounted to family myths as true genealogy. Later writers, J.H. Round, W. Farrer, C. Lewis Loyd, C.T. Clay, and the editors of the *Complete Peerage* are of the greatest importance.

BIBLIOGRAPHY. For an outline of the sources and methods of procedure, see L.G. PINE, *Trace Your Ancestors*, 3rd ed. rev. (1964). Also useful is A.J. WILLIS, *Genealogy for Beginners* (1955). J. UNETT, *Making a Pedigree*, 2nd ed. (1961), contains information on medieval records. G. HAMILTON EDWARDS, *In Search of Ancestry* (1966), is a larger work with more detail, especially on naval and military sources. On American genealogy, see G.H. DOANE, *Searching for Your Ancestors: The How and Why of Genealogy*, 3rd ed. (1960); and J.S. SWEET, *Genealogy and Local History: An Archival and Bibliographical Guide*, 2nd rev. ed. (1959). See also L.G. PINE, *American Origins: A Handbook of Genealogical Sources Throughout Europe* (1960) and *The Genealogist's Encyclopedia* (1969).

(L.G.P.)

Main genealogical sources

Genetics

Genetics is the branch of biology concerned with heredity. Since prehistoric times, man has recognized the influence of heredity and has applied its principles to the improvement of cultivated crops and domestic animals. A Babylonian tablet more than 6,000 years old, for example, shows pedigrees of horses and indicates possible inherited characteristics; other old carvings show cross-pollination of date palm trees. Most of the mechanisms of heredity, however, remained a mystery until the 20th century, when scientifically supported information became available.

Genetics may be defined as the study of the way in which genes operate and the way in which they are transmitted from parents to offspring. Modern genetics involves study of the mechanism of gene action—the way in which the genetic material (deoxyribonucleic acid) affects physiological reactions within the cell. Although genes determine the features an individual may develop, the features that actually develop depend upon the complex interaction between genes and their environment. Normal green plants, for example, have genes containing the information necessary to synthesize the chlorophyll that gives them their green colour, and chlorophyll is synthesized in an environment containing light; i.e., the gene for chlorophyll is expressed. If the plant is placed in a dark environment, chlorophyll synthesis stops; i.e., the gene is no longer expressed.

HISTORICAL BACKGROUND

The Greek philosopher Pythagoras speculated around 500 BC that human life begins with a blend of male and female fluids, or semens, originating in body parts. Aristotle later postulated that the semens are purified blood and that blood, therefore, is the element of heredity. That this later concept persisted in the Western world is indicated by such common phrases as blue blood, blood-will-tell, blood relative, bad blood, and royal blood.

About 1651, the English physician William Harvey disproved the Greek concept; his discovery that deer embryos have the appearance of a tiny ball during early developmental stages and resemble a deer only later in development led him to conclude that the origin of the tiny ball was a small egg. Before the end of the 17th century, it had been suggested that the female structures called ovaries are the source of eggs and that sperm might carry the hereditary material of the male.

Early in the 19th century, a French scientist, Jean-Baptiste Lamarck, suggested that acquired characteristics are inherited. Around 1865 Gregor Mendel (q.v.), an Austrian monk, reported his discoveries on inheritance in garden peas. A few years later, the deoxyribonucleic acid (DNA) component of genes was isolated from pus cells, and it was discovered that salmon sperm also contain considerable amounts of DNA. Late in the 19th century, a German physician, August Weismann, showed that reproductive cells (germ plasm) are independent of other body cells (somatoplasm), thus refuting earlier hypotheses of inheritance of acquired characteristics.

20th-century discoveries

The concept of sudden changes in heredity (mutations) was introduced in the beginning of the 20th century. Discoveries concerning sex determination in insect chromosomes and gene linkage on a chromosome of sweet peas were made soon afterward in the U.S. and England. In 1908, an English mathematician and a German physician formulated the so-called Hardy-Weinberg principle, which provided the foundation for population genetics. The study of biochemical genetics was begun in 1909 in England with an effort to discover the way by which gene-induced enzyme deficiencies cause abnormalities.

Hermann J. Muller, a U.S. geneticist, induced mutations in the fruit fly with X-rays in 1927. Experiments on the mold Neurospora by two Nobel Prize-winning geneticists, George W. Beadle and Edward L. Tatum, proved that the function of most genes is to direct the synthesis of enzymes, which thus are the expression of many hereditary traits. By 1944 DNA had been proved to be the substance of heredity, and, in 1953, the Nobel Prize winners James D. Watson and F.H.C. Crick reported a structure of DNA compatible with the capability for self-duplication. Two French Nobel Prize winners, François Jacob and Jacques Monod, discovered the mechanism by which hereditary information is transferred from genes to the site of protein (enzyme) synthesis. Their work resulted in the discovery of the genetic code, by which DNA is translated into protein.

SCOPE

Nature of the science. Genetics overlaps many different branches of biology and many other sciences; e.g., chemistry, physics, mathematics, sociology, psychology, and medicine. Microbiologists who study inheritance in micro-organisms are called microbial geneticists; cytologists who study the genetics of cells are called cytogeneticists. Biochemical, or molecular, geneticists investigate the chemical nature of the gene and its methods of action. Some physicists have applied their techniques to molecular genetics, and mathematicians may specialize in population genetics. Behavioral scientists also look to genetics to solve certain problems of human and animal behaviour. Specialists in medical genetics or genetic counselling now know that many of man's afflictions are hereditary.

Topics of study. *Classical genetics.* Classical genetics, which remains a basis for all other topics in genetics, is concerned primarily with the method by which genetic traits classified as dominant (always expressed), recessive (subordinate to a dominant trait), intermediate (partially expressed), or polygenic (due to multiple genes) are transmitted in plants and animals. These traits may be sex-linked (result from the action of a gene on the sex, or X, chromosome) or autosomal (result from the action of a gene on a chromosome other than a sex chromosome). Classical genetics began with Gregor Mendel's study of inheritance in garden peas and continues with studies of inheritance in many different plants and animals.

Cytogenetics. Cytogenetics blends the skills of cytologists, who study the structure and activities of cells, with those of geneticists, who study the relationship between the mechanism of heredity and cellular activities. Cytologists discovered chromosomes and the way in which they duplicate and separate during cell division at about the same time that geneticists began to understand the behaviour of genes at the cellular level. The close correlation between the two disciplines led to their combination.

Plant and animal cytogenetics

Plant cytogenetics early became an important subdivision of cytogenetics because, as a general rule, plant chromosomes are larger than those of animals. Animal cytogenetics became important after the development of the so-called squash technique in which entire cells are pressed flat on a piece of glass and observed through a microscope; the human chromosomes have been numbered using this technique.

Microbial genetics. Micro-organisms were generally ignored by the early geneticists because they are small in size and were thought to lack variable traits and the sexual reproduction necessary for a mixing of genes from different organisms. After it was discovered that micro-organisms can have different physiological characteristics and also are able to reproduce sexually, they became objects of great interest to geneticists because they reproduce more rapidly than larger organisms; i.e., a mutation, or change, occurs in a gene about one time in 10,000,000 gene duplications, and one bacterium may produce 10,-000,000,000 offspring, among which are numerous mutants, in 48 hours.

Many discoveries in microbial genetics have been applied to other areas of genetics; for example, the way in which genes produce enzymes that function in turn to produce genetic traits has important applications to human genetics. Much of microbial genetics also applies to the study of the genetics of viruses.

Molecular genetics. Molecular genetics includes the study of the molecular nature of the gene and the method by which genes control the activities of the cell. Molecular geneticists have studied the molecular structure of a gene (e.g., that involved in the synthesis of the human blood pigment, hemoglobin) and determined the exact sequence of its components; in addition, they have created a synthetic gene by joining the components comprising a known gene in the correct sequence.

Population genetics. A study of genes in populations of animals provides information on past migrations, evolutionary relationships and extents of mixing among different varieties and species, and methods of adaptation to the environment. Statistical methods are used to analyze gene distributions and chromosomal variations in populations.

Human population geneticists have traced migration and invasion routes of man; genetic studies of present-day Europeans, for example, reveal routes of human migrations that occurred hundreds or thousands of years ago. The origin of the people inhabiting South Pacific islands and the degree of intermingling among mixed races also are studied by human population geneticists.

Behavioral genetics. Another aspect of genetics is the study of the influence of heredity on behaviour. Many characteristics once considered to be acquired behavioral patterns actually are of a hereditary nature. The role of heredity in instinctive patterns of behaviour among animals has long been recognized, but many of man's actions also have a hereditary explanation. The effect of various drugs (*e.g.*, LSD) on behavioral patterns in animals, including man, is of particular interest.

Human genetics. Some geneticists specialize in human genetics. When classical geneticists first determined the principles of heredity in plants, fruit flies, mice, and other forms of life, they tried to interpret man's heredity in a similar way but found many traits that did not fit the patterns. As techniques improved, it was found that the method of inheritance of human characteristics is the same as that for other living things.

Some human geneticists, called genetic counsellors, advise individuals concerning the probabilities for the appearance of serious hereditary defects in their children. The counsellors usually have medical training because many traits are recognizable only after special diagnostic procedures. Medical genetics is another important application of human genetics. Many medical schools devote entire departments to medical genetics, which is the study of the treatment and prevention of inherited afflictions in man.

The prospects for the future of human genetics are promising; it is possible that man may someday control his heredity; even now functional genes can be transferred from one organism to another, and certain treatments are able to cause specific kinds of mutations.

Such manipulation of genes eventually may be useful in solving many human hereditary diseases; *e.g.*, stopping the function of genes that are out of control, starting the function of nonfunctioning ones. Activation of nonfunctioning genes in some types of tissue may enable them to replace body parts that have been injured or destroyed. It is conceivable that man may someday learn to change harmful genes into normal ones.

THE STUDY OF GENETICS

Experimental breeding. When animals that differ with respect to *one* primary trait are bred, and their offspring then are bred among themselves to give a second generation, the method of inheritance of the trait can be determined; the process is known as a monohybrid cross. A dihybrid cross involves breeding individuals that differ with respect to *two* traits; the results of such crosses show whether the genes are linked on the same chromosome or are on different chromosomes. If the genes are linked, the distance between them can be determined by the number of recombinations of traits obtained, an indication of the amount of crossing over between genes. By such crosses, geneticists have established elaborate chromosome maps of many organisms showing the location of many genes on the chromosomes.

A test cross may be used to determine if animals carry recessive genes; *e.g.*, cocker spaniel dogs may be of solid colours or parti-coloured (spotted). Since the gene for parti-coloured is recessive, it may be carried (but not expressed) by some solid-coloured dogs. If a solid-coloured dog is suspected of carrying a recessive gene for parti-coloured, it is bred to a parti-coloured dog. Parti-coloured offspring indicate that the solid-coloured dog carries the recessive gene. This technique is used by animal breeders to eliminate undesirable recessive genes.

Experimental breeding is most successful in organisms with large numbers of offspring, a relatively short life cycle, and a number of variable characteristics. The fruit fly, *Drosophila*, meets these requirements and has been used extensively in breeding experiments; mice also have been used extensively.

Cytogenetic techniques. Cytogenetic techniques are closely associated with experimental breeding. Older cytogenetic techniques involve placing cells in paraffin wax, slicing thin sections, and preparing them for microscopic study. The newer and faster squash technique involves squashing entire cells and studying their chromosomes. Dyes that selectively stain various parts of the cell are used; the genes, for example, may be located by selectively staining the deoxyribonucleic acid (DNA) of which they are composed. Radioactive compounds also are valuable in determining the location of various components of the cell. Tissue-culture techniques may be used to grow cells before squashing; white blood cells can be grown from samples of human blood and studied with the squash technique.

Biochemical techniques. Biochemical techniques are used to determine the activities of genes within cells. Radioactive compounds are valuable in studies involving gene duplication and cell metabolism. Thymine is a compound found only in genes; if radioactive thymine is placed in a tissue-culture medium in which cells are growing, genes use it to duplicate themselves. When cells containing radioactive thymine are analyzed, the results show that, during duplication, genes split in half, and each half synthesizes its missing components. When radioactive uracil, a compound found only in the ribonucleic acid (RNA) component of cells, is incorporated into the RNA messengers of genes, their pathway from the chromosomes to the site of protein synthesis in the cytoplasm (ribosomes) is revealed.

Chemical tests are used to distinguish certain inherited characteristics of man; *e.g.*, urinalysis and blood analysis reveal the presence of certain inherited abnormalities—phenylketonuria, cystinuria, alkaptonuria, gout, and galactosemia. Special techniques (*e.g.*, chromatography, electrophoresis) are used to separate the components of proteins, so that inherited differences in their structures can be revealed; for example, more than 100 different kinds of human hemoglobin molecules have been identified.

Physiological techniques. Physiological techniques are used in genetic investigations. In micro-organisms, most genetic variations involve some important cell function. Some strains of one bacterium (*Escherichia coli*), for example, are able to synthesize the vitamin thiamine from simple compounds; others, which lack an enzyme necessary for this synthesis, cannot survive unless thiamine is present. The two strains can be distinguished by placing them on a thiamine-free mixture; those that grow have the gene for the enzyme, those that fail to grow do not. The technique also is applied to human cells since many inherited human abnormalities are caused by a faulty gene that fails to produce a vital enzyme; albinism, which results from an inability to produce the pigment melanin in the skin, hair, or iris of the eyes, is an example of an enzyme deficiency in man.

Immunological techniques. Many substances (*e.g.*, proteins) are antigenic; *i.e.*, when introduced into a vertebrate body, they stimulate the production of specific proteins called antibodies. Various antigens exist in red blood cells, including those that comprise the major blood groups of man (A,B,AB,O). Blood antigens of man include inherited variations, and the particular combination of antigens in an individual is almost as unique as fingerprints. Immunological techniques are used in blood-group determinations that precede blood transfusions and in determining Rh incompatibility in childbirth.

Marginal notes:

Synthetic genes

Radioactive thymine

Hybrids

Evolutionary relationships can be determined by immunological techniques. If protein from a specific fruit fly is injected into a guinea pig, and the guinea pig reacts by producing antibodies, and blood serum from the guinea pig is then mixed with proteins from the same fly, antigens and antibodies react to produce a cloudy mixture. Mixtures of guinea pig blood serum and proteins from other fruit-fly species cause various degrees of cloudiness, depending on their evolutionary relationship to the original species; *e.g.*, the closer the relationship, the greater degree of cloudiness.

Mathematical techniques. Mathematical techniques are used extensively in genetics. The laws of probability are applicable to crossbreeding and are used to predict ratios concerning the appearance of specific traits in offspring. Geneticists also use statistical methods to determine the significance of deviations from expected results. In investigations involving possible mutagenic effects of factors such as high-energy radiation and drugs, statistical tests are used to establish the validity of conclusions; statistics are used in studies of the possible effects of LSD in producing chromosome aberrations in man, for example, to show whether differences found in cells of users and nonusers of the drug are significant.

Mathematics is used by population geneticists to evaluate the distribution of genes in populations. The Hardy-Weinberg principle, for example, is important in studying animals that carry a recessive gene; when the actual number of carriers is much greater than that calculated, it is concluded that some environmental factor favours the carriers. The gene for sickle-cell anemia in Africans, for instance, is found in more people than the frequency of those who have the anemia would indicate because people who carry the gene are more resistant to malaria than noncarriers and, therefore, have a better chance of survival.

Margin note: Statistical methods

APPLICATIONS

Medicine. Genetic techniques are used in medicine to diagnose and treat inherited human disorders. Knowledge of a family history of cancer or tuberculosis may indicate a hereditary tendency to develop these afflictions. Cells from embryonic membranes reveal certain genetic abnormalities, including enzyme deficiencies, that may be present in newborn babies, and thus permit early treatment. Many countries require a blood test of newborn babies to determine the presence of an enzyme necessary to convert an amino acid, phenylalanine, into simpler products. A condition known as phenylketonuria (PKU), which results from lack of the enzyme, causes permanent brain damage, if not treated soon after birth. The presence of about 40 different types of inherited abnormalities can be detected in embryos as young as 12 weeks; the procedure, called amniocentesis, involves removal and testing of a small amount of fluid from around the embryo.

Agriculture and animal husbandry. Agriculture and animal husbandry apply genetic techniques to improve plants and animals. Plant geneticists produce new species by special treatment; *e.g.*, a hybrid grain has been produced from wheat and rye, and plants resistant to destruction by insect pests have been developed.

Margin note: Budding and grafting

Plant breeders use the techniques of budding and grafting to maintain desirable gene combinations originally obtained from crossbreeding. The use of the chemical compound colchicine, which causes chromosomes to double in number, has resulted in many new varieties of fruits, vegetables, and flowers.

Animal breeders use artificial insemination to propagate the genes of prize bulls. Prize cows can transmit their genes to hundreds of offspring by hormone treatment, which stimulates the release of many eggs that are collected, fertilized, and transplanted to foster mothers.

Industry. Various industries employ geneticists; the brewing industry, for example, may use geneticists to obtain strains of yeast that produce large quantities of alcohol. The pharmaceutical industry has developed strains of molds, bacteria, and other micro-organisms high in antibiotic yield.

SOCIETIES AND PUBLICATIONS

Many countries have one or several genetic societies, most of which publish journals. The trend is to establish more societies and journals in the fields of molecular and human genetics. Most large countries have at least three or four societies dealing directly with the field of genetics, and each has its own journal. These are in addition to many local and regional societies. Some of the better known journals in the field of genetics are: *Annales de Genetique* (France); *American Journal of Human Genetics* (U.S.); *Atti Associazione Genetica Italiana* (Italy); *Canadian Journal of Genetics and Cytology* (Canada); *Genetics* (U.S.); *International Zeitschrift für Theoretische und Angewandte Genetik* (West Germany); and *Japanese Journal of Genetics* (Japan).

BIBLIOGRAPHY. A.G. DeBUSK, *Molecular Genetics* (1968), a paperback providing concise coverage of this subject; L.C. DUNN, *A Short History of Genetics* (1965), a paperback outlining the major features of the development of genetics; I.M. LERNER, *Heredity, Evolution and Society* (1968), a discussion of the problems of society as related to genetic discoveries; J.A. PETERS (ed.), *Classic Papers in Genetics* (1959), reprints of reports of important genetic discoveries; CURT STERN, *Principles of Human Genetics*, 3rd ed. (1971), a classic work in the field, thorough coverage; M.W. STRICKBERGER, *Genetics* (1968), a college-level treatment of modern genetics; R.P. WAGNER and H.K. MITCHELL, *Genetics and Metabolism*, 2nd ed. (1964), a comprehensive account of the relationship between genes and cellular activities; A.M. WINCHESTER, *Genetics* (1971), an introductory genetics text, including all principles of the subject, but slanted toward human genetics, *Heredity: An Introduction to Genetics*, 2nd ed. (1966), a paperback providing concise coverage of the subject in terms understandable to the general reader.

(A.M.W.)

Genetics, Human

Genetics is the science of biological inheritance, the basic laws of which were discovered in the 19th century by an Austrian monk, Gregor Johann Mendel, who worked them out on pea plants grown in the garden of his Augustinian monastery. During the early part of this century, many more precise details were added during intensive study of other organisms, especially the fruit fly. Understanding of the chemical basis of genetics first began to come in the 1940s from the study of inheritance in bacteria and viruses. Since human genetics differs in no fundamental way from inheritance in other living things, the general articles HEREDITY and GENE provide relevant background material and discussions.

This article is divided into the following sections:

I. General aspects of human genetics

THE BIOLOGICAL BASIS

Egg and sperm (gametes). A human individual arises from his biological parents through the union of two cells, an egg from the mother and a sperm from the father. The human egg cell, like that of other mammals, is barely visible to the naked eye. Eggs are shed, usually one at a time, from the ovary (female sex gland) and pass down tubes (oviducts) toward the uterus. Fertilization, the process in which the sperm enters the egg, occurs in the ducts; if it does not take place, the egg disintegrates in the uterus. Fertilization represents the major event in the genetic determination of the new individual; within the fertilized egg is contained all of the hereditary material that bridges the generations. (For developments after fertilization, see EMBRYOLOGY, HUMAN.)

Chromosomes. During the early part of the present century, cellular studies with ordinary microscopes that transmit light led to the conclusion that all cells, including egg and sperm, contain material within them that at times forms into a definite number of rodlike units called chromosomes. A series of elegant microscopic studies clarified the mode of reproduction of these chromosomes when new cells are formed through the splitting (mitosis) of pre-existing cells. Chromosomes are known to be the carriers of specific hereditary factors (genes), and it has become clear that all cellular organisms (microbe, insect, cabbage, and king) inherit from pre-existing parents in the same chromosomal way.

The chemistry of genes

Methods for the chemical analysis of minute bits of biological material have been perfected to the point that the parallel study of biochemistry and genetics has proceeded most rapidly. The cell nucleus (with its chromosomal material) has been found to be made up of a chemical called deoxyribonucleic acid (DNA) in combination with protein compounds. Evidence is now overwhelming that the DNA component represents the physical basis of the hereditary material. Variations in the chemical structure of DNA molecules seem to determine differences in the mode of action of specific genes.

Proliferation, differentiation, and growth. Except in special cases, the two parents make essentially equal genetic contributions to the offspring at the time of fertilization. In humans, as in other animals, the change of the fertilized egg (zygote) into an adult individual is accomplished by processes of proliferation, differentiation, and growth. These processes are basically cellular; the zygote, a cell, proliferates by first forming two cells. These two then form four, these four, eight, and so on, until the recognizably human embryo containing billions of cells is produced. As proliferation proceeds, the cells differentiate; that is, some become specialized as muscle, some as nerve, some as liver, and so on. Prior to its division, a cell undergoes growth, manufacturing new living substance according to precise instructions from the genes (DNA) contained in the cell nucleus.

When a cell divides, the two resulting daughter cells receive materials from the mother cell. In particular, the hereditary materials of the original nucleus of the fertilized egg are duplicated during the process of mitosis. The nucleus of a normal human cell displays 46 chromosomes when it is dividing (Figure 1). One longitudinal

The genes exert their influence on cellular processes by providing chemically coded information for the production of enzymes and other proteins. The translation of gene information to new protein is accomplished in an indirect manner; sections of the DNA in a chromosome are transcribed (or copied) into molecules of a complementary chemical called ribonucleic acid (RNA), which carry the hereditary information to the places in the cell at which specific proteins are synthesized. Such hereditary influences as those referring to eye colour, blood type, stature, and disease resistance relate directly or indirectly to the action of the genes contained within the individual cells.

Meiosis. The genetic relationship of the individual to his parents can be understood by examining in detail the origin of the gametes (egg and sperm) from which he arises. Close scrutiny of the 46 chromosomes of a normal human cell shows that there are different types that vary greatly in size and shape. Among the 46, moreover, each type is normally represented twice; thus, although there are indeed 46 chromosomes present (the so-called diploid number), they can be seen to consist of 23 pairs (Figure 2).

Chromosome pairs

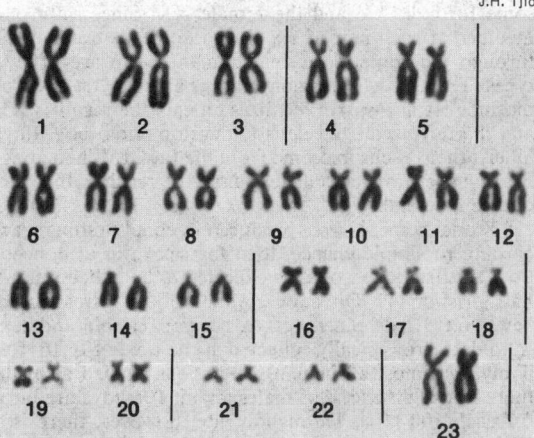

J.H. Tjio

Figure 2: Chromosome pairs. The chromosomes from Figure 1 have been arranged in pairs. The XX (23rd) pair identifies a female.

J.H. Tjio

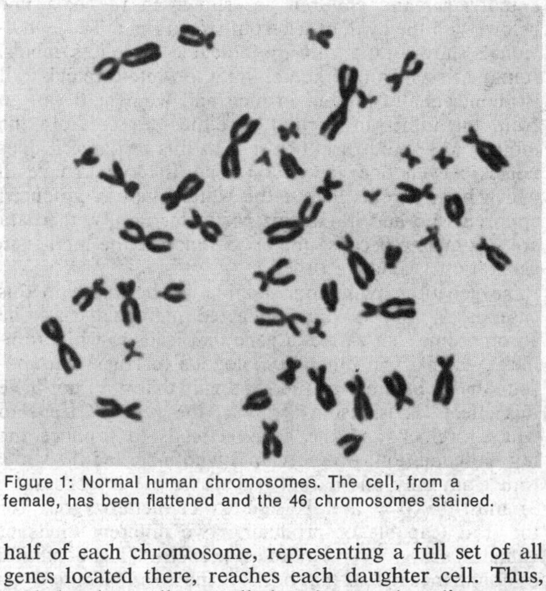

Figure 1: Normal human chromosomes. The cell, from a female, has been flattened and the 46 chromosomes stained.

half of each chromosome, representing a full set of all genes located there, reaches each daughter cell. Thus, each daughter cell normally has the same hereditary composition as that of the mother cell. In most cases, then, not only do all the cells of the body of a person have an equivalent set of genes but the genes present are duplicates of those that were present in the original fertilized egg.

Gene action. According to the principles just discussed, the hereditary material (DNA) with which each individual begins life finds its way into all his body cells.

Normally the chromosome number in the cells of a child is the same as that of his parents, egg and sperm each contributing one member of any pair and containing half the chromosome number (haploid number). Painstaking chromosome counts, for example, reveal that as each egg matures in the ovary, only one member of each of the 23 pairs of chromosomes reaches the final egg cell; a similar process occurs in the development of each sperm cell. Thus the 46 chromosomes of the normal child derive equally from the two parents. The father supplies 23 (one member of each pair) to the fertilized egg, while the other 23 come from the mother.

The cellular process that accomplishes the chromosome reduction (from the diploid to the haploid number) in the formation of gametes is called meiosis. This cycle of changes is initiated in certain diploid cells in the ovary (or testis). During meiosis the two members of each chromosome pair (homologous chromosomes) move close together in the cell. As they do this, they become greatly extended (uncoiled) and selectively exchange equivalent parts in a process called crossing-over.

Following crossing-over, two specialized cell divisions occur (the meiotic divisions). The net result of these is that one, and only one, of the strands making up the paired chromosomal unit reaches the future egg (or sperm) cell. When this occurs normally, not only is there reduction in chromosome number (46 to 23) but also the resulting single member of the chromosome pair is a new recombination (through crossing-over) of the genes present in the original diploid cell.

Recombination of genes through crossing-over and subsequent reassortment does not provide new genes. Rather, the variation already existing in the parent is placed in new combinations as his gametes are formed. Fertilization normally involves the relatively random union of two parental cells, each containing a haploid number of chromosomes that carry new, unique combinations of old genes. The number of possible hereditary combinations is hard to grasp intuitively. Even if a gross underestimate of only two differing gene pairs per chromosome were assumed, each potential human parent would be capable of producing more than 19,000,000,-000,000 genetically different kinds of sperm (or eggs). It is extremely unlikely that even one of these trillions of gene combinations would exactly duplicate that of any ancestor.

Sex determination. As a rule, the two members of each chromosome pair appear almost identical under the microscope with regard to size and shape. The single human exception to this rule is in just one pair of the 46 chromosomes normally found in the male; one of the members of one of these pairs is much shorter than the other. The comparable pair in female cells consists of two full-sized chromosomes. In view of the sexual difference, that particular pair is called the sex chromosomes. The larger chromosome is referred to as X and the smaller as Y. Thus, the normal human male has the chromosome formula XY and the female XX. Since only one member of each pair of sex chromosomes is transmitted through the gametes, normal human sperm are of two types (Y or X), whereas normal eggs all carry an X-chromosome. If a Y sperm fertilizes an egg, the result is XY and the fertilized egg begins to develop into a boy. Boys inherit their Y-chromosome from the father. When an X-bearing sperm reaches the egg first, the result is the start of a female embryo.

If X and Y sperm were produced in equal numbers, according to simple chance, then the sex ratio at conception (fertilization) would be expected to be half boys and half girls, or 1:1. Direct observation of sex ratios among newly fertilized human eggs is not yet feasible and sex-ratio data are typically collected at the time of birth. Reliably, in almost all human populations studied at birth, there is a slight excess of males; about 106 boys are born for each 100 girls. Throughout life, however, there is a slightly greater mortality of males; this slowly alters the sex ratio until, beyond the age of about 50 years, there is an excess of females. Other studies indicate that within the womb, embryo males suffer such a degree of relatively greater mortality that the sex ratio at conception might be expected to favour males even more than the 106:100 ratio observed at birth would suggest. Firm explanations for the apparent excess of male fertilizations have not been established; it is possible that Y sperm survive better than X or they may be a little more efficient in penetrating the egg. In any case, the sex differences are small, the statistical expectation for a boy (or girl) at any single birth still being close to one out of two.

SINGLE-FACTOR INHERITANCE

Genetic variation among individual people may arise from differences at one or more paired gene locations along the chromosomes. Although people tend to differ at many such points on their chromosomes, the observable effects of these gene differences are frequently so slight that it is difficult to identify the effect of each location separately. The principles of inheritance emerge more clearly when a difference at a single gene location produces conspicuous, unusual effects in the individual. Such striking departures from the norm frequently are classed as abnormalities. But it is also firmly supported that the mode of inheritance of a gene pair having a very slight effect, for example, on the height of an individual within the normal range is inherited according to the same rules as a pair causing a more drastic effect. Since the latter are easier to observe, however, examples are usually chosen for study from among them. Today the customary practice in genetics, as employed successfully by Mendel, is to simplify analysis by considering the effects of only one gene pair at a time.

Dominant inheritance. Some persons with generally dark hair show a streak of white (usually near the crown

of the head) present from their very first growth of hair. Known as white forelock (piebald trait), it is inherited in a pattern that is consistent with the notion that it involves a single gene pair (one gene for completely dark hair and another for the white-streak condition). The gene for white forelock apparently acts by interfering with pigment formation in some of the cells of the scalp, producing the white hair. Studies of families in which it occurs indicate it to be a dominant gene; that is, to dominate (or "swamp" the effect of) the gene for completely dark hair.

Figure 3 shows the inheritance of the piebald trait in

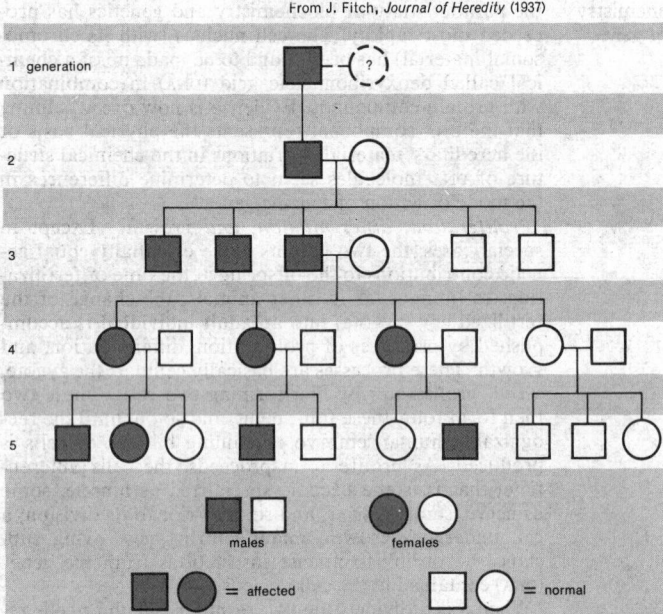

From J. Fitch, *Journal of Heredity* (1937)

Figure 3: Inheritance of white forelock through five generations of a family (see text).

a family through five generations. In pedigrees of this sort, the circles refer to females, and the squares to males; two symbols directly joined by a horizontal line represent a marriage, and children are shown in the next line below, with the birth order from left to right. Those individuals showing the trait are indicated by solid symbols. It may be seen from Figure 3 that the white-forelock trait is about equally present in men and women. It can go from the father to a child of either sex or from the mother to a child of either sex. In this pedigree it does not skip even one generation; that is, no marriage in which both parents lacked the white forelock produced children who had it. (In this particular family, the data are incomplete because the appearance of the mother in generation 1 is not recorded.)

The genetic explanation, dominant inheritance in this case, is as follows. Each affected individual has one chromosome that carries a gene that leads to white forelock, whereas the other homologous (partner) chromosome has a member of the gene pair that does not have this effect. Thus, using symbols, the gene W leads to white forelock and the gene w tends to produce the normal condition. An individual who inherited the white trait from only one parent (such as those in generation 3) must be Ww and is said to be heterozygous for the trait (capable of producing two different kinds of gametes; *e.g.*, a W sperm and a w sperm). The condition of dominance means that one W gene is sufficient to overcome the darkening effect of w. When an affected man marries a normal woman (who must be ww), half of the resulting children on the average would be expected to exhibit the trait because half of his sperm carry W and half w. Since all of the eggs of the mother are the same in the sense that they all contain the gene w (Figure 4), she is said to be homozygous (homo, "same") for the normal trait.

If an individual were to carry two dominant genes,

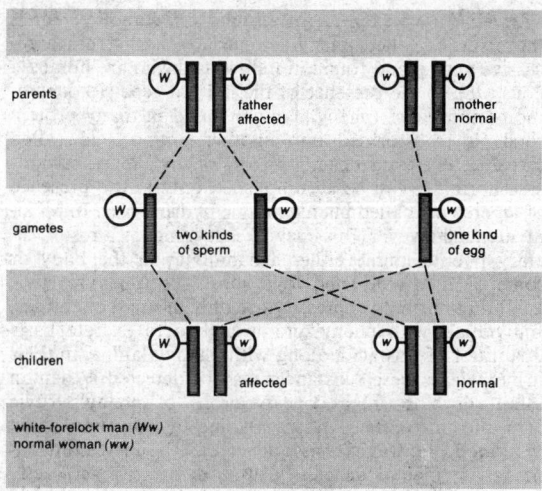

Figure 4: *Simple dominance.*
Mating of a white-forelock man (Ww) with a normal woman
(ww). The gene locations are shown on the chromosomes
(vertical bars). The W gene will occur in half the sperm of the
affected father; therefore, his children of either sex have a
50 percent chance of inheriting the trait.

Table 1: Human Characteristics Often Attributable to a Single Dominant Gene	
trait	conspicuous signs
Achondroplasia	abnormality of ossification centres in bones, resulting in dwarfism
Amyloidosis	congestive heart failure
Brachydactyly	short fingers and toes
Cataract	opacity of the lens of the eye
Cleft mentum	a bony peculiarity underlies a Y-shaped fissure in the chin
Huntington's chorea	degeneration of certain brain centres
Myotonic dystrophy	a type of muscular dystrophy with muscle wasting and loss of muscle tone
Piebald trait	white forelock of hair and other nonpigmented spots
Polydactyly	extra fingers
Ptosis	constricted or drooping eyelid
Syndactyly	"webbed" fingers or toes
Tuberous sclerosis	nodules in brain, viscera, and skin
Xeroderma pigmentosum	sensitivity to sunlight with likely development of skin cancer at an early age

having the homozygous gene formula *WW*, that person would of course show the piebald trait; a further consequence would be that none of the children would escape the white forelock, regardless of the genetic condition of the other parent.

The sight of a person with a white forelock can be attractively striking, and it is not unusual for someone with genetically normal hair colour to use bleach for cosmetic reasons. Careful examination of the hair to its very roots should help settle the matter. Furthermore, white hairs of the hereditary piebald trait are not confined to the head; a person carrying the white-forelock gene shows other spots of white hair and unpigmented skin in various parts of the body. Indeed, in conducting genetic studies it is most crucial to discover the degree to which the observable trait (called the phenotype) is attributable to the pattern of genes in the cells (the genotype) and to what extent it arises from environmental influence. The distinction between the contributions of heredity and environment is especially difficult to make in genetic studies of such traits as bodily stature, resistance to specific diseases, and level of intelligence (*e.g.*, see INTELLIGENCE, DISTRIBUTION OF). At any rate, a white patch of hair on the head may be attributed wholly to the environment (if it is the result of peroxide); to the effect of the *W* gene on pigmentation patterns (if there is no cosmetic bleaching at all); or to both factors (if a carrier of the *W* gene undertakes to increase the extent or vividness of his white forelock with chemicals).

Genotype and phenotype

Examples of simple dominant inheritance are quite frequently encountered among human characteristics. More than 300 traits may be listed that clearly show this type of inheritance; a sampling is given in Table 1. Many of these are relatively rare, abnormal, pathological conditions that may be looked upon as hereditary diseases or defects.

In the study of pedigrees, some characteristics such as the webbed-toed condition (syndactyly) show strong evidence of dominant inheritance. Occasionally, however, it is found that the characteristic skips a generation. This may be attributed to what is called lack of penetrance; that is, a person may carry the gene for syndactyly, but the effect of the gene in some cases may be so slight (of such low penetrance) as to be undetectable by ordinary means. In other words, the evidence is that an individual may carry a gene that usually elicits a dominant phenotype, but for various reasons does not show it himself. (In a roughly similar way, people can harbour germs without falling ill themselves.)

A condition called achondroplasia also appears to be transmitted by a single dominant gene that acts to impair the growth of specific cartilages in the body as the bones

are being formed. The result is a type of dwarfism in which the proportions of trunk and limbs are visibly abnormal; it is observed not only among people but in animals such as dachshunds. It must be distinguished from another type of dwarfism that produces a normally proportioned adult of very small size. The latter condition typically results from a malfunction of the pituitary gland, usually arising from injury or disease during a critical stage of the individual's early development. This may have the effect of impairing the pituitary gland's normal function of elaborating growth hormones (without which the person becomes stunted).

Single genes frequently have more than one obvious effect; a gene that causes deafness, for example, also produces abnormality of the fingernails. Called pleiotropy, such multiple effects of single genes are almost universal. Since genes operate by affecting developmental processes, a single gene change may eventually affect a number of bodily or behavioral characteristics. Thus, in achondroplasia, not only is the process of bone development altered but the consequent dwarfism affects the size, distribution, and function of the muscles and internal organs as well. It is frequently difficult to specify what effects are primary and what are secondary with regard to the action of a gene. Genetic conditions are usually named for their most easily recognized phenotypic sign (which serves as a convenient label, but by no means describes the full genotypic effect).

Multiple effects

Not only may dominance be incomplete, as in the case of syndactyly; in addition, alleles (*i.e.*, genes that may alternatively occupy the same location on a chromosome) may each produce a separate, different effect. Such a condition, called codominance, is exemplified in the human inheritance of so-called MN blood types. In this case, the blood type depends on chemical substances (antigens) in the red blood cells that are specified by a chromosome pair that can carry alternative genes (alleles) called *M* and *N*. Homozygous individuals may be *MM* or *NN*, in which cases the antigen in the blood cells is either M or N, respectively. A heterozygous *MN* person has both antigens in his red cells; that is, there is no dominance and each antigen is produced independently. At any rate, simple blood tests, using special chemicals that selectively make M cells or N cells agglutinate (stick together), can show whether a person is homozygous or heterozygous (see BLOOD GROUPS).

Recessive inheritance. More than 250 traits have been related to single genes that are recessive; that is, their effects are masked by dominant alleles and manifest themselves phenotypically only in homozygous individuals. A partial list is given in Table 2. Albinism, for example, in which the affected person lacks pigment in his skin, has white hair, and pink eyes, results only when a gene leading to albinism comes from both parents. This may result from several types of marriage. If *A* is a gene leading to normal pigmentation, and *a* is a gene leading to the albino condition, three kinds of genotypes can result:

Table 2: Human Characteristics Often Attributable to a Single Pair of Recessive Genes

trait	conspicuous signs
Acheiropody	lack of hands and feet
Albinism	lack of pigment in skin, hair, and eyes
Alkaptonuria	defect of a tissue enzyme
Amaurotic idiocy	metabolic disorder of intelligence, with blindness
Cretinism	disturbance in function of thyroid glands
Deaf-mutism	deafness from birth
Galactosemia	enzyme deficiency that results in cataracts and mental retardation
Hartnup's disease	defect of protein (amino acid) metabolism
Hyperlipidemia	abnormal fat metabolism with retarded development
Keratosis palmo-plantaris	horny skin on palms and soles
Microcephaly	abnormally small head
Phenylketonuria	enzyme disorder leading to mental retardation
Phenylthiocarbamide taste blindness	inability to taste this substance as bitter
Thalassemia	abnormal type of hemoglobin in red blood cells

AA and *Aa* exhibit normal pigmentation, and *aa* is albino. Thus, it frequently happens that both parents of an albino are phenotypically normal but are genotypically heterozygous (*Aa*), both carrying the albino gene *a*. The combinations that can occur in the children of such parents are *AA*, *Aa*, and *aa*. Only the *aa* genotype leads to albinism, and the chance of producing an albino child is one out of four. A carrier (*Aa*) married to an albino person (*aa*) will tend to have half albino children, while two albinos can produce only albino children.

Albinos

Genes that are recessive are among the most common types known in man; as methods for detecting them are perfected, it is likely that those known will come to outnumber the dominants. Unlike the case of dominant inheritance, the person showing the results of having inherited a pair of recessive genes may not only have carrier parents who escaped the phenotypic trait but even his grandparents or great-grandparents may have failed to show it. The effectiveness of the recessive gene in producing the fully developed trait, however, is not affected even by a long sojourn, hidden over many generations in heterozygous individuals.

As in the case of dominant genes, most of the recessives listed in Table 2 lead to defects, producing observable characteristics that usually are recognized as diseases. These disorders predominate in such lists since they not only are important medically but they also serve as good examples of how inheritance operates. Thus, geneticists have tended to emphasize and record extensively those genes having conspicuous effects on people who inherit them. Nevertheless, most of the so-called normal variation among persons, such as in hair, eye, and skin colour, stature, facial features, and body build, are also clearly influenced by single genes. The inheritance of these traits, however, is complicated by two major factors. First, more than one gene, and frequently many gene locations on the chromosomes, may be involved in the determination of a trait. Second, many of these characters (*e.g.*, stature) are strongly influenced by environmental conditions (*e.g.*, amount of food available during critical growth stages). The interplay of these two factors leads to a complex situation that requires methods of study that go beyond simple inference from pedigrees; these are discussed below.

In the catalog of recessive traits, many conditions derive from disturbances in cellular chemical processes and have been called inborn (hereditary) errors of metabolism. With advances in biochemistry, many of these disorders have been found to be ascribable to the malfunction or absence of one or more major enzymes in the body. It is now clear that the synthesis within the body of enzymes (which themselves are protein in nature) is under the control of specific genes. If a gene is defective, then its coding system for regulating the synthesis of the particular protein involved is likewise impaired. This may affect every cell of the body, producing a variety of effects.

Errors of metabolism

A well-known example of an inborn metabolic error is the disorder called phenylketonuria, arising from a recessive gene *p* and found in individuals who are homozygous (*pp*). In the presence of the normal gene (*P*), a common amino acid (phenylalanine) found in many protein foods is transformed into another amino acid called tyrosine. The transformation from phenylalanine to tyrosine normally can be accomplished only in the presence of an enzyme called phenylalanine hydroxylase. In *pp* individuals, however, this enzyme is lacking; as a result, dietary phenylalanine either accumulates in the body or some of it is converted to a substance (phenylpyruvic acid) that normal people produce only in small quantities. Individuals with phenylketonuria tend to excrete large quantities of this acid, along with phenylalanine, in their urine, where these substances may be detected. When an infant develops high concentrations of phenylpyruvic acid and unconverted phenylalanine that accumulate in the blood, the tragic consequence may be feeblemindedness. The mental deficiency appears to arise indirectly from an abnormal concentration of these substances in the brain. Fortunately, this very serious effect of phenylketonuria can be avoided by strict control of dietary phenylalanine, but dieting should begin as early in the infant's life as possible.

Sex-linked inheritance. The sex chromosomes (see above *Sex determination*), particularly the large X-chromosomes, carry a number of genes that are not related directly to the sexual traits of the individual. Since such genes are carried on the sex chromosomes, they are said to be sex-linked in their inheritance. More than 60 such genes have been recognized; a few of the more common are listed in Table 3. Sex-linked inheritance has special

Table 3: Human Sex-Linked Characteristics

trait	conspicuous signs
Colour blindness	red–green vision impaired
Ectodermal dysplasia	sweat glands absent or reduced
Hemophilia	hemorrhages; abnormal blood clotting
Icthyosis simplex	scaly skin
Retinitis pigmentosa	degeneration of the retina of the eye

properties that may be seen in one form of hereditary colour blindness carried only by the X-chromosome.

If the recessive gene leading to the colour blindness is called *c*, and the normal allele is *C*, then human females having a pair of X-chromosomes may have three kinds of genotype: *CC* and *Cc* girls or women commonly have normal colour vision, whereas *cc* individuals are colourblind. Typical males, on the other hand, are XY and have only a single X-chromosome and thus are either *C*Y or *c*Y genotypes. Since males receive their X-chromosomes only from their mothers, the father has no effect on the condition as found in his sons, contributing only the Y-chromosome, which carries no genes for colour vision. When a *cc* colour-blind woman marries a man who carries the *C* (colour-normal) gene on his X-chromosome, all the sons will be colour-blind and all the daughters will be phenotypically normal. In this case all the daughters will be heterozygous colour normal (*Cc*) and all the sons (*c*Y) will be colour-blind. Sex-linked inheritance is distinguished from what is called autosomal inheritance, in which the genetic factors concerned are borne on a pair of the other chromosomes (autosomes), which are not related to the determination of sex.

Colour blindness

The enzyme glucose-6-phosphate dehydrogenase (G6PD) is also under the control of a sex-linked gene location. More than 20 alleles are known to be found at this location on the X-chromosome, some of which result in an enzymatic deficiency. Deficiency in G6PD, as produced by an allele that is common among people of black African ancestry, renders the person highly sensitive to the antimalarial drug primaquine. Another variant encountered among people of Mediterranean origin results in an unusual sensitivity to the common broad bean called *Vicia fava*. This reaction, called favism, results in a sometimes fatal anemia that develops when the person eats the raw beans or even inhales the pollen of this plant.

Examination of cells from a normal human female (*e.g.*, scraped from the inside of the mouth) reveals the presence of a small, darkly staining structure (Barr body) in the nucleus of those cells that are not dividing. This body is not observed in normal males and thus provides a way of telling the sex of the person by microscopic examination. Study has revealed that the material of the Barr body in the cell comes from one of the normal female's two X-chromosomes. Condensation of the chromosome to form the Barr body appears to inactivate the genes carried by that chromosome, effectively reducing the number of functional X-chromosomes in the female cell to one. (Inactivation also occurs in the case of rare, abnormal males who have one or more surplus X-chromosomes.) Although the significance of this finding is not wholly understood, it appears that now one, now the other, of the X-chromosomes becomes inactivated during the development of the normal female.

According to one theory (the Lyon hypothesis), the tissues of some females (whose X-chromosomes are heterozygous) represent a mosaic of two kinds of cells present in approximately equal numbers because of the alternation in forming the Barr body. This appears to be borne out in studies of the cells of females who are heterozygous at the G6PD location. The two classes of cells that can be recognized actively manifest one or the other of the expected enzymatic variants. Other once-mystifying manifestations of sex-linked traits among human females also seem to be explained by mosaicism, providing additional evidence in support of the hypothesis.

Lethal genes. Some genes (*e.g.*, those affecting hair form or eye colour) are of minor importance to the health of the person and to his ability to survive physiologically. Other genes, such as those that result in the defect or absence of an important enzyme, may lead to a frail individual whose chances of survival are reduced. The spectrum of such deleterious gene effects ranges from slight to lethally severe.

A number of known genes lead to the premature death of the individual who carries them, such lethal genes generally killing the embryo very early or at least before birth. In a number of cases, a category of sublethal genes is recognized for which death may be delayed into the years of childhood. In any event, to be classified as lethal or sublethal, the gene must prevent survival of the individual to the reproductive period.

In any given case of stillbirth (or of spontaneous abortion), the action of a dominant lethal gene is difficult to distinguish from environmentally produced death during embryonic life. Nevertheless, careful study has even revealed evidence that some genes are recessive in their lethal effects. When one particular recessive gene is present in the homozygous state, for example, there is an almost complete lack of development of brain tissue in the fetus. This condition (anencephaly) invariably has a lethal effect before birth; such fetuses are commonly aborted or are stillborn. In another recessive-gene disorder known as amaurotic idiocy, fatty deposits accumulate in the brain of the fetus. The child may be born alive, but there is progressive blindness and intellectual retardation, the physiological degeneration that underlies these symptoms resulting in early death.

HUMAN BLOOD

More is known about the genetics of the blood than about any other human tissue. One reason for this is that blood samples can be easily secured and subjected to biochemical analysis without harm or major discomfort to the person being tested. Perhaps a more cogent reason is that many chemical properties of human blood display relatively simple patterns of inheritance.

Blood types. Certain chemical substances within the red blood cells (such as the MN substances noted above) may serve as antigens. When cells that contain specific antigens are introduced into the body of an experimental animal such as a rabbit, the animal responds by producing highly specific proteins (antibodies) in its own blood. In this category is perhaps the best known of the human blood groups, referred to as the ABO system. The synthesis of the two principal antigens in the ABO system is under control of genes occurring at what is apparently a single chromosome location (designated *I*). Three alleles exist at this *I* locus: one (I^A) leads to the formation of what is called antigen A, another (I^B) leads to B antigen, while the third allele (I^O) results in blood cells lacking either antigen. I^A and I^B are codominant but I^O is recessive. The various possible genotypes at this locus and the phenotypes they produce are given in Table 4. In

The ABO blood system

Table 4: The ABO Blood Groups

common designation of blood groups	genotypes	phenotypes (antigens present in blood cells)
A	$I^A I^A$ or $I^A I^O$	antigen A
B	$I^B I^B$ or $I^B I^O$	antigen B
AB	$I^A I^B$	antigen A and antigen B
O	$I^O I^O$	neither A nor B present

addition to the ABO system of the *I* locus, there are about 15 gene systems known (including MN and the well-known Rh) associated with other chromosome locations.

Rh incompatibility. The Rh antigens are of particular importance in human medicine. Curiously, however, their existence was discovered in monkeys (which resemble people in many ways). When blood from the rhesus monkey (hence the designation Rh) is injected into rabbits, the rabbits produce so-called Rh antibodies that will agglutinate not only the red blood cells of the monkey but the cells of a large proportion of human beings as well. Some people (Rh-negative individuals), however, lack the Rh antigen; the proportion of such persons varies from one human population to another. Akin to data concerning the ABO system, the evidence for Rh genes indicates that only a single chromosome locus (called *r*) is involved. At least eight Rh alleles are known for the *r* location; basically the Rh-negative condition is recessive.

A medical problem may arise when a woman who is Rh-negative carries a fetus that is Rh-positive. The first such child may have no difficulty, but later similar pregnancies may produce severely anemic newborn infants. The first Rh-positive fetus appears to immunize the Rh-negative mother; that is, she develops antibodies that may produce permanent (sometimes fatal) brain damage in any subsequent Rh-positive fetus. Damage arises from the scarcity of oxygen reaching the fetal brain because of the severe destruction of red blood cells. Measures are available for avoiding the severe effects of Rh incompatibility by transfusions to the fetus within the uterus; however, genetic counselling before marriage is especially desirable in such cases to forestall the need.

Abnormal hemoglobin. Several types of hemoglobin (the oxygen-carrying pigment in red blood cells) are known to be under the control of a single chromosome locus (called *Hb*). An especially interesting allele (Hb^S) at this locus specifies an abnormal condition called sickle-cell anemia. The disorder was named from the peculiar sicklelike shape assumed by red blood cells of affected individuals. Persons who are homozygous $Hb^S Hb^S$ are affected by a very severe anemia that is usually fatal in early life. Those who are heterozygous for Hb^S, carrying one of the alleles for a normal hemoglobin (*e.g.*, one called hemoglobin A), have no anemia; nevertheless, they may show the sickle-cell trait on microscopic examination of their blood.

The biochemical basis for sickling came to be understood when it was discovered that hemoglobin S and hemoglobin A move at different rates in an electrical field. Such means of chemical study have shown that the difference between the two hemoglobins depends on only one of nearly 600 amino acids that make up the complex protein molecule of hemoglobin. The Hb^S gene, which is held responsible for this small chemical difference, is a very good example of how a gene that changes a body protein only very slightly can have far-reaching effects

Mosaicism in women

on a person's very life. The Hb^S gene is especially common in some populations of African origin; reasons for this high incidence will be discussed below.

Abnormal blood clotting. In clotting, which serves to prevent excess loss of blood after an injury, a complex protein called fibrin is normally formed. Persons with a genetic impairment of the clotting reaction are popularly known as bleeders. A common form of this disorder (hemophilia) displays simple sex-linked inheritance. The peculiar features of this type of inheritance were described in records dating from the second century AD. Ancient Hebrew laws codified in the Talmud contain special provisions (for male infants born into families of bleeders) that authorize that the ritual of circumcision may be omitted according to a complicated set of rules governing pedigree. Study of these rules shows them to be consistent with modern understanding of the mode of sex-linked inheritance. Sex-linked hemophilia frequently has affected members of European royalty. The evidence is strong that London-born Queen Victoria, for example, was heterozygous for the trait; she bore a son who suffered from hemophilia, and the disorder appeared among the male descendants of three of her daughters.

Serum proteins. Human serum, the fluid portion of the blood that remains after clotting, contains various proteins that have been shown to be under genetic control. Study of genetic influences has flourished since the development of precise methods for separating and identifying serum proteins. These move at different rates under the impetus of an electrical field (electrophoresis), as do proteins from many other sources (*e.g.*, muscle or nerve). Since many genes act by specifying the synthesis of proteins, biochemical studies based on electrophoresis permit direct study of tissue substances that are only a metabolic step or two away from the genes themselves.

Most attention in the genetics of substances in the blood has been centred on serum proteins called haptoglobins, transferrins (which transport iron), and gamma globulins (a number of which are known to immunize against infectious diseases). Haptoglobins appear to relate to two common alleles at a single chromosome locus; the mode of inheritance of the other two seems more complicated, about 15 kinds of transferrins having been described. Like blood-cell antigen genes, serum-protein genes are distributed worldwide in the human population in a way that permits their use in tracing the origin and migration of different groups of people.

HEREDITY AND ENVIRONMENT (NATURE AND NURTURE)

It is a primary axiom in modern genetics that what is inherited from one's ancestors is a set of nucleic acid determiners (genes). To cite an example, it may be noted that blue eye colour shows recessive inheritance. The common notion that a child has "inherited" his brown eyes from his father rather than from his blue-eyed mother should be recognized for the shortcut statement that it is. Only the genes (*e.g.*, the potential for eye colour) are inherited; the actualized phenotypic trait (*e.g.*, brown eyes) is the outcome of the manner in which the pertinent gene or genes interact with the environment during the growth and development of the individual. An embryo deprived of nourishment from the environment will die before it can develop any eyes at all.

Another way of saying this is that no trait can exist or become actual without an environmental contribution. Thus, the old question of which is more important, heredity or environment, is without meaning. Both nature (heredity) and nurture (environment) are always important for every human attribute.

But this is not to say that the separate contributions of heredity and environment are equivalent for each characteristic. Dark pigmentation of the iris of the eye, for example, is under hereditary control in that one or more genes specify the synthesis and deposition in the iris of the pigment (melanin). This is one character that is relatively independent of such environmental factors as diet or climate; thus, individual differences in eye colour tend to be largely attributable to hereditary factors rather than to ordinary environmental change.

On the other hand, it is unwarranted to assume that other traits (such as height, weight, or intelligence) are as little affected by environment as in the case of eye colour. It is very easy to gather information that tall parents tend, on the average, to have tall children (and that short parents tend to produce short children), properly indicating a hereditary contribution to height. Nevertheless, it is equally manifest that growth can be stunted in the environmental absence of adequate nutrition. The dilemma arises that only the combined, final result of this nature–nurture interaction can be directly observed. There is no accurate way (in the case of a single individual) to gauge the separate contributions of heredity and environment to such a characteristic as height. An inferential way out of this dilemma is provided by studies of twins, however.

Fraternal twins. Usually a fertile human female produces a single egg about once a month. Should fertilization occur (a zygote is formed), growth of the individual child normally proceeds after the fertilized egg has become implanted in the wall of the uterus (womb). In the unusual circumstance that two unfertilized eggs are simultaneously released by the ovaries, each egg may be fertilized by a different sperm cell at about the same time, become implanted, and both grow, to result in the birth of twins.

Twins formed from separate eggs and different sperm cells can be of the same sex or of either. No matter what their sex, they are designated as fraternal twins. This terminology is used to emphasize that fraternal twins are genetically no more alike than are siblings (brothers or sisters) born years apart. Basically they differ from ordinary siblings only in having grown side by side in the womb and in having been born at approximately the same time.

Identical twins. In a major nonfraternal type of twinning, only one egg is fertilized; but during the cleavage of this single zygote into two cells, the resulting pair somehow become separated. Each of the two cells may implant in the uterus separately and grow into a complete, whole individual. In laboratory studies with the zygotes of many animal species, it has been found that in the two-celled stage (and later) a portion of the embryo, if separated under the microscope by the experimenter, may develop into a perfect, whole individual. Such splitting occurs spontaneously at the four-cell stage in some organisms (*e.g.*, the armadillo) and has been accomplished experimentally with the embryos of salamanders, among others.

The net result of splitting at an early embryonic stage may be to produce so-called identical twins. Since such twins derive from the same fertilized egg, the hereditary material from which they originate is absolutely identical in every way, down to the last gene locus. While developmental and genetic differences between one "identical" twin and another still may arise through a number of processes (*e.g.*, mutation), these twins are always found to be of the same sex. They are often breathtakingly similar in appearance, frequently down to very fine anatomic and biochemical details (although their fingerprints are differentiable).

Diagnosis of twin types. Since the initial event in the mother's body (either splitting of a single egg or two separate fertilizations) is not observed directly, inferential means are employed for diagnosing a set of twins as fraternal or identical. The birth of fraternal twins is most frequently characterized by the passage of two separate afterbirths. In many instances, identical twins are followed by only a single afterbirth, but exceptions to this phenomenon are so common that this is not a reliable method of diagnosis.

The most trustworthy method for inferring twin type is based on the determination of genetic similarity. By selecting those traits that display the least variation attributable to environmental influences (such as eye colour and blood types), it is feasible, if enough separate chromosome loci are considered, to make the diagnosis of twin type with high confidence.

Inferences from twin studies. *Metric (quantitative) traits.* By measuring the heights of a large number of or-

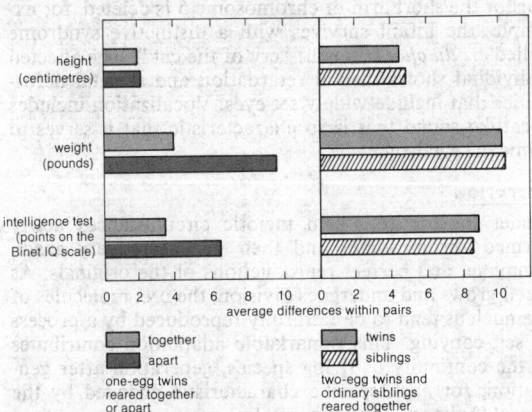

Figure 5: Measured differences between identical (one-egg) twins, between like-sexed fraternal (two-egg) twins, and between like-sexed ordinary siblings.

Adapted from H.L. Carson, *Heredity and Human Life* (1963); Columbia University Press

Twins
reared
together
and apart

dinary siblings (brothers and sisters) and of twin pairs, it may be shown that the average difference between identical twins is less than half the difference for all other siblings (see Figure 5). Any average differences between groups of identical twins are attributable with considerable confidence to the environment. Thus, since the sample of identical twins (given in Figure 5) who were reared apart (in different homes) differed little in height from identicals who were raised together, it appears that environmental–genetic influences on that trait tended to be similar for both groups.

Yet, the data for like-sexed fraternal twins reveal a much greater average difference in height (about the same as that found for ordinary siblings reared in the same home at different ages). Apparently the fraternal twins were more dissimilar than identicals (even though reared together) because the fraternals differed more among themselves in genotype. This emphasizes the great genetic similarity among identicals. Such studies can be particularly enlightening when the effects of individual genes are obscured by the influence of the environment on quantitative (measurable) traits (*e.g.*, height, weight, and intelligence).

Any trait that can be objectively measured among identical and fraternal twins can be scrutinized for the particular combination of hereditary and environmental influences that impinge upon it. The effect of environment on identical twins reared apart (Figure 5) is suggested by their relatively great average difference in body weight as compared with identical twins reared together. Weight would appear to be more strongly modified by the environment than is height.

Study of comparable characteristics among farm animals and plants suggests that such quantitative human traits as height and weight are affected by allelic differences at a number of chromosome locations: that they are not simply affected by genes at a single locus. Investigation of these gene systems with multiple locations (polygenic systems) is carried out largely through selective-breeding experiments among large groups of plants and lower animals. Human beings select their mates in a much freer fashion, and polygenic studies among people are thus severely limited.

Intelli-
gence

Intelligence is a very complex human trait; but even roughly measured as IQ, intelligence shows (Figure 5) a strong contribution from the environment. Fraternal twins, however, show relatively great dissimilarity in IQ, suggesting an important contribution from heredity as well. Twin studies involving psychological traits should be viewed with caution; for example, since identical twins tend to be singled out for special attention, their environment should not be considered equivalent even to that of other children raised in their own family.

Other traits. For traits of a more qualitative (all-or-none) nature, the twin method can also be used in efforts to assess the degree of hereditary contribution. Such investigations are based on an examination of cases in

which at least one member of the twin pair shows the trait. It is found, for example, that in about 80 percent of all identical twin pairs in which one twin shows symptoms of a psychiatric disorder called schizophrenia, the other member of the pair also shows them (that is, the two are concordant for the schizophrenic trait). In the remaining 20 percent, the twins are discordant (that is, one lacks the trait). Since identical twins often have similar environments, this information by itself does not distinguish between the effects of heredity and environment. When pairs of like-sexed fraternal twins reared together are studied, however, concordance for schizophrenia is very much lower—only about 15 percent (Figure 6).

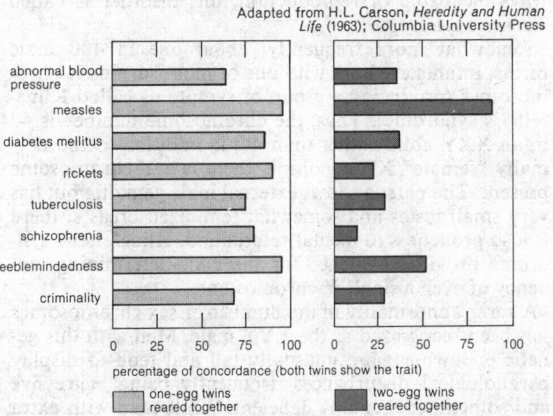

Adapted from H.L. Carson, *Heredity and Human Life* (1963); Columbia University Press

Figure 6: Concordance rates for identical (one-egg) twins and for fraternal (two-egg) twins for cases in which at least one twin shows the trait.

Schizophrenia clearly develops much more easily in some genotypes than among others; this indicates a strong hereditary predisposition to the development of the trait. The schizophrenic trait also serves as a good example of variable penetrance, in that identical twins may differ in whether they express it or not.

Studies of concordance and discordance between identical and fraternal twins have been carried out for many other human characteristics, a few of which are also summarized in Figure 6. It has, for example, been known for many years that tuberculosis is a bacterial infection of environmental origin. Yet identical twins raised in the same home show concordance for the disease far more often than do fraternal twins. This finding seems to be explained by the high degree of genetic similarity among the identical twins. While the tuberculosis germ is not inherited, one's heredity does seem to make him more (or less) susceptible to this particular infection. Thus the genes of one individual may provide the chemical basis for immunity to a disease, while the genes of another may fail to do so.

Indeed, there seem to be genetic differences among disease germs themselves that result in differences in their virulence. Thus, whether a genetically susceptible person actually develops a disease also depends in part on the heredity of the particular strain of bacteria or virus with which he must cope. Consequently, unless environmental factors such as these are adequately evaluated, the conclusions drawn from susceptibility studies can be unfortunately misleading.

Some human traits, such as susceptibility to measles, show a small (but nonetheless distinct) hereditary component. Social disorders (criminality, for example) frequently give evidence of being affected by hereditary factors. This is not to say that there is an invariably specific "criminal" gene (or gene combination) that dooms one to a career of crime. The evidence is, rather, that human personality is to some degree shaped by a number of genes, each of which may have an individually small effect. Under conditions of social pressure, genetically based personality types may turn to crime. If the pressure is absent or slight, such a person will no more fall into criminality than he will exhibit susceptibility to tuberculosis unless he happens to come in contact with a virulent germ.

Crim-
inality

CHROMOSOME VARIATIONS

Under unusual circumstances a human egg or sperm may contain an abnormal set of chromosomes; *e.g.*, too many or too few. Imbalances of this sort may be associated with abnormal appearance and behaviour.

Abnormal number of sex chromosomes. In some instances (about 1 in 3,500 female human births) a girl infant is born with only one X-chromosome instead of the usual pair (the XO condition). Such a child exhibits a total of 45 chromosomes instead of the normal 46. Development is abnormal, although the individual has female external genitalia. Nevertheless, her ovaries, uterus, and breasts fail to develop normally, and she is almost always incapable of reproduction; this disorder is called Turner's syndrome.

Somewhat more frequently, about one in 400 male births, infants are born with one or more surplus X-chromosomes (producing a group of symptoms called Klinefelter's syndrome). Thus, the chromosome number is 47 in an XXY child rather than 46; in addition to the normally "female" XX condition, there is a Y-chromosome present. The person shows external male genitalia but has very small testes and somewhat feminized breasts; there is also proneness to mental retardation. Klinefelter's syndrome provides evidence for the male-determining tendency of even a single Y-chromosome.

"Super-males" A rarer abnormality in the number of sex chromosomes has been recognized as the XYY male. Men with this genetic endowment are unusually tall and tend to display psychological disturbances, frequently being aggressive and sometimes mentally deficient. While men with extra Y-chromosomes have been found to comprise a small percentage of inmates of penal institutions surveyed, as might be expected in the case of any complex psychological trait, other XYY individuals have achieved normal social adjustment. At any rate, the practice of calling such men "supermales" seems unwarranted.

Abnormalities related to the autosomes. Occasionally a gamete is formed that contains an extra autosome (a chromosome other than X or Y). This can result in a person with three rather than the usual pair of autosomes. (In Figure 2, all pairs numbered 1 through 22 are autosomes.) If one of the larger autosomes is involved it is likely that the zygote will die before development, perhaps because there is no autosomal mechanism similar to that of X-chromosome inactivation.

One of the smallest chromosomes (from pair 21) is sometimes represented twice instead of once in the gamete (egg or sperm). After fertilization, individuals with three of these small chromosomes survive well and are recognized phenotypically as sufferers of Down's syndrome (sometimes called mongoloid idiocy). In addition to mental retardation, such individuals are short and have stubby hands and feet and abnormalities of the heart. They exhibit a peculiarity of the eyelid that gives them a superficial resemblance to Asians, hence the term mongoloid idiocy.

Down's syndrome Down's syndrome is one of the most frequently observed serious human genetic disorders, being found in about one out of 600 live births and in all racial groups. The incidence is highest when older mothers give birth, suggesting that abnormal movement of chromosome 21 may occur as the effect of maternal aging on the formation of the egg. The risk is about 100 times less among mothers in their 20s than it is for women over 45.

Some persons with typical signs of Down's syndrome even show the normal number of 46 chromosomes. Examinations indicate that, in addition to the normal pair 21, there is still a third chromosome 21 attached (translocated) to one of the larger autosomes (probably to pair 14). These cases usually involve one parent who can be shown to carry a translocation, although the parent is himself phenotypically normal. The probability for the production of a child with Down's syndrome appears to be about one out of three if the mother is the carrier, but apparently it is less if the father is the carrier.

In most cases the zygote's loss of an entire chromosome is lethal; embryonic survival is more likely when there is loss of only a small portion of one chromosome. When part of the short arm of chromosome 5 is deleted, for example, the infant survives with a distinctive syndrome called *cri du chat* (French: "cry of the cat"). The affected individual shows mental retardation and skeletal deformities that include widely set eyes. Vocalization includes a catlike sound that is so characteristic that it serves to name the syndrome.

MUTATION

Under most mitotic and meiotic circumstances newly formed chromosomes and their genes are very exact, complete, and perfect reproductions of the originals. As a cell grows and undergoes division, the DNA molecules of the nucleus tend to be faithfully reproduced by a process of self-copying. This remarkable adaptation contributes to the continuity of living species, generation after generation, for each specific characteristic encoded by the genes. Ordinary environmental changes such as gradual variation in temperature, barometric pressure, diet, or muscular activity seem to have no effect on the exactness of the process.

On occasion, however (*e.g.*, in response to environmental radioactivity), imperfect self-reproduction of chromosomal DNA molecules may occur to produce the potential for new traits; this is called mutation. Even when only a single gene in one cell is mutated, the copying process tends faithfully to reproduce the changed DNA in all the descendants of that particular cell. Indeed, mutation appears to be a basic cellular mechanism underlying the evolution (*e.g.*, descent with change) of living beings.

Somatic mutation. Mutation in any cell of the body except a germ cell (egg or sperm) is called somatic mutation. A common result of what seems to be somatic mutation is observable among blue-eyed people. Blue colour in the eyes of a person is attributable generally to a lack of pigment; possibly a single chromosome locus is involved; at any rate, the genes that produce this trait are recessive to those that generate pigment. If b represents the gene (allele) for blue eyes and B an allele coding for brown eyes, then a person with blue eyes would be represented by bb. Occasionally, however, blue-eyed persons are observed to have a small sector (or flecks) of brown (usually in one eye). This is probably the result of somatic mutation (mutation of a cell within the eye itself) of one of the b alleles to B. It is inferred that this mutation from b to B occurred in one of the embryonic cells that normally give rise to the iris of the eye, all cells descending from this one showing the brown pigment of the dominant B gene. The iris of the eye of such a person is a genetic mosaic, with most of its cells bb (blue) and a small sector of cells descended from the mutant Bb (brown). Such localized mutations do not affect the germ cells and thus are not transmitted to the next generation.

Germinal mutation. Although such mutations as the one just described cannot be inherited, if the same DNA change were to occur in an egg or sperm (germ cell), there would be a definite probability (perhaps small) that the newly mutated gene would be passed on to the next generation. In other words, it is at least theoretically possible that two bb (blue-eyed) parents could produce Bb (brown-eyed) children through germ-cell mutation. Such germinal mutations are the object of careful search by investigators, since they facilitate the study of the laws of inheritance as well as providing clues to the future direction of human evolution.

Mutation rates. Detectable results of germinal mutation among people are only very rarely encountered. Thus, the actual rate of mutation in human chromosomes defies full measurement. A major reason for this is that most mutations seem to be recessive and thus tend to be masked for generations. Efforts to measure mutation rate therefore are most conveniently directed toward selected dominant or codominant mutations for which phenotypic recognition is easier; indirect (inferential) methods of measurement are still required.

Studies of achondroplasia One dominant gene that is useful for studying human mutation rate produces the form of dwarfism called achondroplasia (Table 1). When an affected child appears in a family in which both parents are normal, the properly diagnosed condition can be ascribed to the occurrence of one new mutation. The frequency of such an event is customarily calculated on the basis of the number of gametes (egg and sperm cells) produced by the parents in one generation; for human achondroplasia, the mutation rate has been inferred to be 4.2 per 100,000 gametes. Analyses of a number of different gene loci in man and in such experimental organisms as corn (maize) and *Drosophila* (fruit fly) show that the average mutation rate among living beings is on the order of one in 100,000 gametes (10^{-5}). Nevertheless, each gene studied shows its unique mutational probability; the neurological disorder called Huntington's chorea shows only about 0.5 mutation per 100,000 gametes, whereas the figure for neurofibromatosis (a disorder with soft tumours distributed over the whole body) is from 13 to 25 per 100,000. The general average in man is about the same as for achondroplasia, roughly four per 100,000 gametes.

The word mutation may be applied to alterations in chromosome number and breakage of chromosomes (as in translocation) as well as to gene changes. The frequency of these chromosome mutations may or may not be the same as that of gene mutations. In any event, the spontaneous rate of mutation is manifestly very low by almost any criteria. Nevertheless, while the processes of heredity are conservative and generally resist change, there are environmental factors that can increase the rate of mutation.

Spontaneous and induced mutation. In all living things that have been studied, including man, there is a low level of mutation that occurs independently of the investigator's intervention and so has been generally labelled spontaneous. It is hard to ascribe any specific cause to these; spontaneous mutations are generally thought to be copying errors that are inevitable in so intricate and delicate a mechanism. Perhaps some of them may arise from relatively random events in the environment (such as cosmic rays from outer space), since it is now known that certain environmental agents will greatly increase the frequency of mutations. Paramount among these mutagens (mutation producers) are ionizing radiations of all sorts (including cosmic rays), as well as chemicals such as mustard gas and formaldehyde.

To be actively mutagenic, the agent must reach the cells themselves; for example, ultraviolet radiation (*e.g.*, the tanning rays of the sun) is mutagenic, but its low penetrating ability renders it essentially ineffective as a germinal mutagen in man. Nevertheless, sunlight seems to be a somatic mutagen; heavily tanned people are found to be prone to skin cancers, the abnormal growth presumably stemming from skin cells mutated by the sun's ultraviolet rays. By contrast, penetrating ionizing radiations such as X-rays and those that result from atomic explosions are among the most powerful germinal mutagens found; no living organism is known to have body tissues adequate to shield the germ cells from their penetration.

Radiation hazards. It was a stroke of good fortune that the damaging genetic effects of ionizing radiation were already partially known in the 1930s, a decade before the use of atomic energy burst upon the world. The obvious dangers of increasing the germinal mutation rate, already tragically high in the human species, were widely discussed during the 1950s. These genetic arguments had much to do with the suspension of atmospheric testing of atomic weapons by a number of countries.

Radioactive materials such as strontium-90 and iodine-131 are released in considerable quantities into the atmosphere by such tests. These mutagenic materials become distributed throughout the upper atmosphere and filter back to earth as radioactive fallout. Strontium-90, in particular, has created great concern because it remains active for a long time and because it readily replaces calcium in teeth and bones. This brings the mutagenic radiation close to such sensitive tissues as bone marrow, where blood cells originate. As a result, the danger of a form of blood cancer celled leukemia rises. Since most powerful mutagens are also likely to induce cancer, many investigators seek to relate this disease to a basically genetic cause. Apparently irreversible cellular changes that are

Skin cancer

associated with senescence suggest somatic mutation as a basis for the process of aging as well.

There appears to be a direct relationship between the dose of radiation received and the number of mutations induced among living cells. The more radiation (or mutagenic chemical) affecting a cell, the greater the number of expected mutations will be. At low levels of radiation, it becomes increasingly difficult to demonstrate that a proportionately small number of mutations is still being induced. Nevertheless, the adoption of an arbitrary "safe" level, below which no medical or hereditary hazard can be expected, is clearly untenable, and the safest position in this regard is that the less radiation to both germinal and somatic tissues, the better. When radiation is used for medical or dental diagnosis and treatment, the anticipated benefits should be weighed against the hazards, however small their probability.

Customarily, the risk associated with exposure to radiation is expressed as the radioactive dose (in roentgen units) that is found by experimentation to double the spontaneous germinal (hereditary) mutation rate. Among laboratory mice it has been calculated that doubling ensues at about 45 roentgen units administered as a single dose of relatively intense radiation. Such a dose given all at once apparently produces more damage than does the same dose when it accumulates over a longer period from a source of lower intensity. Thus if the source is chronic, low-level radiation (such as from dispersed fallout), the doubling dose in mice may be as high as 200 roentgen units. There is good reason to expect similar results among people; the hazards (among other objections) prohibit such experimental studies with human beings. If such studies were feasible, a radiation dose could be specified that would double the probability that the affected person will produce a child carrying a new, presumably deleterious, mutation.

General exposure to man-made radiation has not reached such high doses; present radiation levels are, nevertheless, more mutagenic than they would have been had atomic explosions never occurred. While authorities may differ as to what constitutes an "acceptable" level of man-made radiation, there is general dread that a doubling dose of radiation to the human population of the world would end in major calamity. In addition, calculations indicate that unavoidable background radiation (about 3 roentgens over 30 years) received by the average person is not sufficient to account for all the mutations that are continually arising spontaneously. There must be other, unknown factors that affect the basic rate of mutation. Until these factors are understood, the prospects for their control remain bleak.

II. Applications of human genetics

GENETIC COUNSELLING

The term genetic counselling is applied to a service, typically available in medical settings, in which prospective parents are provided with estimates of the probability that they will produce children with genetically controlled defects. Considering the great increase in understanding of human genetics, it seems likely that such counselling will be sought by an increasingly large number of persons. Genetic disorders have attracted growing attention in medical practice, especially since the urgencies of infectious disease have been reduced through such developments as antibiotic control.

Genetic counselling has been, and probably will continue to be, desired mostly by persons who seek a rational basis for deciding whether or not to limit their reproduction. Accordingly, the role of the genetic counsellor is to collect the relevant evidence by making a pedigree study of the couple concerned and then, by applying established principles of inheritance to estimate the risk, or probability, of genetic defect among their offspring. The counsellor ordinarily is in a position to estimate only the probability of trouble, leaving the final decision to the couple themselves.

That human chromosomes carry a large store ("genetic load") of recessive, potentially harmful genes is well documented; indeed, about 4 percent of live human births show defects of medical concern, at least half of which are attributable to major genetic influence. The most common situation that prompts people to seek a genetic counsellor is one in which a phenotypically normal couple produce a first child suffering from a major defect. The parents understandably want to know what the chances are that subsequent children will also be affected.

Simple inheritance. A typical example might involve an albino child born to a couple who are themselves normally pigmented. Since an albino person may face health and social problems, the parents in all likelihood will be concerned to know the probability that their next child also will be albino.

After examining the child and making sure of the diagnosis, the genetic counsellor can ascertain that albinism results in an individual who carries a pair of recessive genes for the trait; i.e., the child is homozygous for albinism. Accordingly, one albino allele must come from each parent; that is, both parents must carry the gene (must be heterozygous for it). In this case no further pedigree study is needed to give the couple the answer to their question. The probability that their next child will be albino is one out of four, one-quarter, or 25 percent; this
Parental responsibility
is readily deduced from the principles of simple recessive inheritance. What the parents do with this information is their responsibility alone; they may share a powerful desire for a second child or they may feel that an albino child still can find much reward in his life. On the other hand, they may decide (for any of a number of human reasons) that they consider the risk, even at 25 percent, as too high.

If the defect under consideration were a more threatening recessive trait (such as phenylketonuria, which poses difficulty in treatment and a serious risk of mental deficiency), a decision against taking the chance would perhaps be more likely.

Should the mother of an albino child die, the heterozygous father may plan a second marriage. He might ask the genetic counsellor to estimate the probability that this second marriage will result in another albino child. The likely case is that, in the counsellor's study of the pedigree of the prospective new wife, no history of albinism can be found in her family, since human albinism is very rare indeed. What the counsellor still needs to estimate are the maximum chances (however unlikely) that the second wife still may be heterozygous for albinism, since recessive genes may remain undetected for generations. This can be estimated from data concerning the frequency of albinism in the population (beyond the family) from which the presumed second wife is herself drawn. On a world population basis, heterozygous carriers of the recessive gene for albinism have been found to number about one in 50 persons. Accordingly, the estimate that the proposed wife might be heterozygous is the probability $\frac{1}{50}$. Since the probability is $\frac{1}{2}$ that each parent will pass on the gene if present, the probability for the production of an albino child could therefore be calculated as $\frac{1}{50} \times \frac{1}{4} = \frac{1}{200}$. This is only 0.5 percent and suggests that the chances of producing an albino child in the proposed marriage are quite remote.

The estimate made in the preceding case can be made more specific if the counsellor can find data on the particular subgroup of people from which his clients come. Genes for albinism, like many others, occur more or less frequently in different human groups. Homozygous (albino) individuals are observed only at a rate of about one in 20,000 among Europeans, one in 3,000 among black Nigerians, and one in 132 among the San Blas Indians of Panama. Clearly the frequency of carriers of albino genes is less than the world average (one out of 50) among Europeans and much higher among San Blas Indians. At any rate, the counsellor should base his estimates on the most pertinent data available.

Complex inheritance. In cases such as those just described (in which the mode of inheritance is simple), the counsellor usually can answer the questions prospective parents ask with enough confidence to cite a specific probability. This is not as readily accomplished when the genetic basis is more complicated or when the expression

(e.g., penetrance) of the gene is irregular. Congenital (present at birth) dislocation of the hip, for example, is a rare condition. It has been found that about 41 percent of identical twins are concordant for the trait but only about 3 percent of fraternal twins show concordance. This suggests a strong hereditary basis for the condition; nevertheless, since the 41-percent concordance of identical twins is by no means complete, the appearance of the trait is attributed in part to nongenetic factors. The problem is further complicated; examination of pedigrees for infants with congenital dislocation of the hip has failed to establish a simple mode of inheritance.
Congenital hip dislocation
Although lacking a firmly defined hereditary mode on which to base deductions, the counsellor still can resort to purely empirical statistics to make an estimate of risk. If, for example, a woman who exhibits dislocation wishes to marry and asks what the chances are that her children will also be affected, figures available for answer will include the fact that in one sample of 219 women known to have had the condition and who bore a total of 48 sons and 45 daughters, none of the sons showed the trait but five of the 45 daughters did. These empirical figures based on previous medical records can be used to estimate the risk even without the availability of a theoretical genetic mechanism for transmission. Medical records for a growing number of medically important human traits are constantly being augmented, and empirical risk figures are being widely used as valuable guides in genetic counselling.

Identification of carriers. Under ordinary circumstances the presence of a recessive gene is fully hidden by its normal allele, and its heterozygous carrier cannot be told by direct observation from a person who is homozygous normal for the trait. In some instances the heterozygote carrier can be recognized, and thus the counsellor's task is facilitated. Biochemical tests can sometimes help identify heterozygous carriers of the recessive phenylketonuria gene, for example.

Huntington's chorea is one disorder for which as yet no heterozygote test has been developed. This incurable nervous disease is produced by a dominant gene that usually does not manifest itself until well past the age of reproduction, the average age of the patient at the time of the first symptom being about 50 years. Accordingly, a person who has the gene rarely knows it until after his children are born. A test that could identify carriers early in their lives would help alleviate much human suffering, since such people tend to pass the offending gene on to half of their children. The gene that gives rise to Huntington's chorea apparently was introduced into North America by just three immigrant families of British origin. Nevertheless, it has been estimated that at the present time there are approximately 7,000 affected individuals among their descendants.

The genetic counsellor often is presented with a vague or diverse series of symptoms. These often may arise from one or several genes, from environmental events, or from a combination of factors. Pedigrees based on reports given by family descendants themselves are notoriously inaccurate, and frequently the genetic counsellor may be hard put to separate fancy or hearsay from fact. This problem is especially difficult to overcome in counselling clients who are concerned with such complex psychological characteristics as neurotic behaviour.

Eugenics. The term eugenics has been applied to theories and practices ostensibly designed to improve the human condition from the genetic point of view. Genetic counselling typically is a form of so-called negative eugenics, in that it tends to improve man as a species by discouraging reproduction among those deemed likely to perpetuate genes that lead to medical defects. Since so much human tragedy is attributable to such genes, there is widespread agreement that mankind would be far better off without them. Sterilization (e.g., of certain insane people) is legally required in some cases, although local laws vary greatly, even within given countries. By and large, negative eugenics is most widely acceptable when it is practiced through counselling.

On the other hand, the question of positive eugenics is

quite another matter. Such attempts are designed to identify "good" genes and thereby improve man by encouraging the reproduction of those persons who are thought to carry them. All too often, however, the desirability of particular hereditary human traits (such as skin colour or shape of nose) is as subjective and controversial a matter as is one's taste in music. Judgments clash over whether intelligence is preferable to calmness or originality to obedient tractability. Even if agreement were possible, such attributes are most unreliably measured, and finding the relative contribution of heredity and environment to each of them is most frustrating.

The difficulties appear so great that attempts to advance positive eugenics on a broad scale have been abortive. Unfortunately, efforts of governments (as in Nazi Germany) to favour the reproduction of "superior" groups of people rested on a pseudoscientific approach in which the magnitude of the role of the genes in producing desirable human attributes was grossly overstated. The Nazi slaughter of millions in the name of eugenics is a tragic chapter in history. Subtle and more disguised forms of genetic selection may be accomplished by withholding jobs, opportunities, housing, and health care from particular groups of people; such tactics may be observed in all societies. The power to isolate and deprive individuals and groups is also the power to limit their reproduction and their survival as human subspecies. Conversely, reproduction of human groups can be selectively encouraged by such measures as government subsidies for having borne children.

Failure of large-scale programs of positive eugenics

Large-scale programs of positive eugenics inevitably seem to become deeply embroiled in economic, social, and political struggle. To the extent that they are thus embroiled, their failure becomes assured. A major stumbling block is the clear evidence that enormous genetic differences exist among individuals within any large racial or ethnic group; each group exhibits genetically defective as well as genetically gifted members. The differences between groups, in contrast, are substantially smaller (if they exist at all) with regard to the genetic basis of intelligence and personality. In addition, group differences tend to be exaggerated or concealed by the considerable impact of environmental variations. Accordingly, the statement can be categorically made that there is no scientific basis on which any kind of genetic racism can be built. Thus, while lower socioeconomic classes of people traditionally have outreproduced more privileged groups, there appears to be no reason to expect genetic deterioration of the human species because of this.

Genetic engineering. Although slow in its effects, negative eugenics (based on identifying defective individuals rather than on a futile search for "inferior" groups) seems to be the most promising way in which modern human genetics can be applied for man's benefit. Indeed, fundamental discoveries in basic genetics have provided the theoretical basis upon which a science of individual genetic engineering, or intervention, can be built.

Artificial insemination is perhaps the most widely used engineering practice at the present time to circumvent male sterility in barren marriages. Sperm can be collected from fertile donors (if need be, frozen and used at a later time) to effect fertilization in a normal female whose husband cannot father children. By having his sperm stored, a man may become a father years after he has died.

Control of the embryo's sex

The theoretical possibility has existed for a long time that human X and Y spermatozoa safely could be separated by a number of possible techniques (*e.g.*, under the influence of an electrical field). Such separation, used in conjunction with artificial insemination, would result in the possibility of controlling the sex of the offspring. Despite repeated reports of success (*e.g.*, among rabbits) optimism for human sex control seems premature; a successful, acceptable technique remains to be developed for use with people.

Some geneticists have urged that positive-eugenic use be made of the presently available technique of human artificial insemination. In this view, the spermatozoa of men with presumably "outstanding" genetic endowment could

be stored in "sperm banks" for long periods and then could be used to effect fertilizations with prospective mothers who desired it. Unfortunately, fathers who have earned high social esteem for their achievements all too often produce children whom others judge mediocre or inferior. Such common disappointments are attributable to a number of factors. First, genetic recombination in the formation of the man's gametes (spermatozoa) yields a high probability that a "good" combination of genes will be broken up (if, indeed, such a combination exists in the first place). The sperm cells a man produces all can be expected to differ from the unique one his father contributed toward his existence. Then, the male parent provides only half of the child's genetic endowment, so the result is in doubt from the mother's side as well. In addition, those who achieve distinction may, like anyone else, carry genes that tend to produce undesirable effects: epilepsy, bodily malformations, blindness, or schizophrenic behaviour. Thus, the sperm-bank approach to positive eugenics seems to entail definite risk of failure; the prediction that great benefits would automatically accrue is debatable.

Optimistic predictions of the use of engineering practices in human genetics are frequently made. Although many genetic interventions are theoretically possible or have been accomplished in lower organisms, their adaptation to the special human condition has not yet been made. Perhaps the most promising of these is amniocentesis, in which cells from an embryo (or very early fetus) can be removed from within the mother (*e.g.*, hypodermically) and tested long before the birth of the child. If an abnormal chromosome, defective enzyme, or other deleterious genetic condition can be diagnosed by tests on such cells, the laws of many communities may permit abortion. Amniocentesis may become a major step toward avoiding such tragic genetic disorders as Down's syndrome (mongolian idiocy).

The human ovum has been successfully fertilized outside of the potential mother's body and, indeed, has been cultured in laboratory glassware to a many-celled stage. If desired, such an embryo can be placed in a receptive uterus and will implant. One may hope that, with the use of proper tests, implantation could be accomplished only with those embryos lacking diagnosable defects. Even this hopeful possibility should be approached with caution, however, since the number of serious human genetic diseases that can be diagnosed using cell samples is at present very small indeed.

New genes for old

Somewhat more remote, but still possible, is a technique that would replace a defective or lethal gene locus with one that is normal. This possibility is based on the discovery that engineered gene replacements are feasible in bacteria. Comparable manipulation of the genes in a mammalian cell (*e.g.*, from a dog or a person) has not been accomplished and practical use of this technique toward human betterment seems far away indeed.

Another sensational possibility is the replacement of the normal (biparental) nucleus of a fertilized egg with the nucleus of a somatic cell taken from anywhere in the body of just one person. Such replacements have been accomplished in experimental animals; in the human case, this sort of one-parent embryo might be implanted in a receptive uterus. An infant born of the implanted pregnancy would be expected to have the same genetic characteristics as the donor individual.

GENES IN POPULATIONS

Population genetics is a branch of genetic science that concerns the frequency and fate of gene differences within groups (populations) of individuals. The meaning of gene frequency can be illustrated by a system with two alleles such as those for the M and N blood types. When the homozygous individual is *MM* he shows only the M antigen in his cells; when he is *NN*, he shows only the N antigen. Heterozygous *MN* individuals show both antigens. If a village of 1,000 people is found to include 810 *MM*, 180 *MN*, and 10 *NN* individuals, it would mean that the N antigen is much rarer than the M; this may be expressed in precise terms as the gene frequency of *N*. Of a total of 2,000 alleles for this trait (each of the 1,000 people has two alleles), 200 are N: two from each of the 10 NN individuals (20) plus one more from each of the 180 MN heterozygotes. Thus the gene frequency of N is $^{200}/_{2,000}$, or 10 percent; M makes up the remainder and is therefore 90 percent.

The Hardy-Weinberg equilibrium. If the entire population of the village discussed above randomly forms couples and children are born, the same M and N gene frequency tends to appear in both generations. At reproduction, the gametes form a so-called gene pool in which 90% tend to be M and 10% N. The law of genetic equilibrium (Hardy-Weinberg law) states that, given any pair of frequencies p and q for two alleles (in this case $p = 90\%$ and $q = 10\%$), the frequencies among the zygotes of the offspring will tend to be in accordance with the ratio p^2 (for MM): $2 pq$ (for MN): q^2 (for NN). Substituting the village's values for p and q, one would expect to find (among every 1,000 children) 810 MM, 180 MN, and 10 NN, the same as in the previous generation. Such theoretical predictions are closely verified in laboratory experiments, although chance factors are likely to produce some variation from the expected gene frequencies. The Hardy-Weinberg law tends to hold experimentally regardless of the initial gene frequency: for example, when p and q are 60% and 40%. It is to be noted that p plus q always equal one (or 100%).

The law also holds for dominant–recessive gene pairs (alleles). In most cases, as pointed out earlier, the recessive a gene (for albino) is very rare compared with the dominant A (for normal pigment) in human populations.

Inferring gene frequencies

Only albino (aa) and normal phenotypes (Aa or AA) can actually be observed. If in a population of 1,000 people there are found to be 10 albino (aa) individuals ($q^2 = 1\%$, or .01), by applying the law, it may be inferred that the gene pool for these people is 10% $a(q = \sqrt{q^2})$ and that the remaining 90% is A. Once p and q have been established (in this case as 90% and 10%), one can then calculate the expected number of Aa carriers ($2pq$) and homozygous (AA) normals (p^2) as in the previous example. Even though the gene is dominant, the frequency of the normal A allele will not tend to increase when mating is random but will tend to remain at equilibrium. For purposes of genetic counselling, if a population is at Hardy-Weinberg equilibrium, one can calculate the probable frequency of the carriers of any hidden recessive gene if one knows the frequency of the double recessives (*e.g.*, albinos). In this case, it turns out that about 19% of the normals will be expected to be carriers of the a gene. As a further example, for a population in which the gene frequency for phenylketonuria is $^1/_{200}$, one may estimate the number of carriers to be about $^1/_{100}$, or 1%.

Conditions that favour the Hardy-Weinberg equilibrium. A population is most likely to remain at equilibrium if it contains a large number of individuals. If it is small, departures from random mating may result in considerable deviations from expectation. Thus, if the law is to hold, the various matings should be made according to chance; that is, they should not be selective with regard to any particular genotype. While genes such as those for the M and N blood groups show practically no evidence of affecting one's choice of a mate, it is conceivable, for example, that albinos in a population might tend to marry albinos. If such selective mating occurred, the Hardy-Weinberg equilibrium for the albino gene would be upset.

Equilibrium also is favoured by the operation of the 1:1 gametic ratio in heterozygotes expected in simple inheritance. If, for example, MN individuals were prone to produce more M gametes than N gametes, the equilibrium would be disturbed.

Unless all relevant genotypes (*e.g.*, MM, MN, and NN) have equivalent fitness to reproduce, equilibrium tends to be broken. In other words, to preserve equilibrium, the presence of N in the homozygous state should not impair or enhance in any way the ability of its carrier to reproduce relative to the other two genotypes.

Natural selection and random drift. By now it should be clear that sexual reproduction under simple (Mende-

lian) inheritance is a conservative force that tends to maintain the genetic status quo in a population. If a gene frequency is 1 percent in a population, it tends to remain at 1 percent indefinitely unless some force acts to change it. Outside of the laboratory, the most powerful force for changing gene frequencies is natural selection. In genetic terms, natural selection means that some genotypes leave more offspring than others. The capacity for the production of offspring is spoken of as Darwinian fitness or, simply, fitness. If the fitness of the three genotypes from a gene pair are all the same, then the gene frequencies will tend to remain stable in the next generation. Should the homozygous recessive genotype be lethal or produce sterile individuals (with zero fitness), then the recessive gene will tend to be underrepresented in the next generation. The result will be a change in the gene frequency.

Darwinian fitness

If such a process goes on generation after generation, the recessive gene tends slowly to be eliminated. But as the gene becomes rarer, the probability of the production of sterile (zero-fitness) individuals will also be decreased, tending to slow the rate at which that gene is removed from the population pool. The rate of decline is even slower if the homozygous genotype is not completely sterile but, as is indeed the case with albinos (aa), partially fertile. Since it is found that albino people typically produce fewer children than do normals, this contributes to natural selection against the albino a gene.

If any population is relatively small, the effects of chance may result in the total elimination of the a gene from that population, so that all members are AA. Such an event is spoken of as a fixation for gene A. Chance alone, which particularly operates through fluctuations in population size, can strikingly alter gene frequencies at intermediate levels as well. This effect is called random drift and, along with natural selection, is a powerful process of genetic change within populations. Both processes can be expressed mathematically and the rates of change of gene frequency (from generation to generation) can be calculated. Calculations also take into account evidence of definite mutation rates for given genes. Thus, if natural selection and random drift are operating to eliminate a gene such as a (albinism), the computations also should reflect the frequency with which a genes are arising as mutations. Thus, what happens to a gene in an isolated (closed) population depends on the interrelationships of natural selection, random drift, and mutation rate.

Evolution. Change in gene frequency (and thus the genetic composition of a population) is the essence of the evolutionary process. As a classic example, increase in the frequency of a gene leading to a black body colour has occurred among some populations of moths in England during the past century. The phenomenon is called industrial melanism (pigmentation), since it has been attributed to the effects of factory smoke. Moths homozygous for the "dark" gene are less conspicuous on soot-blackened surfaces such as tree trunks than are moths that carry the normal gene for light-gray mottled colour. Over the decades, the gene leading to dark colour has nearly replaced the other in heavily industrialized regions of England. Apparently, dark moths are protectively coloured and less likely to be eaten by birds. This is an example of adaptive evolution on a limited, local scale (microevolution). Human populations are also subject to microevolution, but the changes emerge more slowly since a human generation is longer than that for moths. Genes that confer increased Darwinian fitness on their carriers are expected to increase in frequency, just as those that are deleterious should tend to decrease. Even if a gene contributes only slightly to increased fitness, there will nonetheless tend to be a progressive increase in gene frequency in its favour. Although the process may be very slow, calculations over 100 to 1,000 generations indicate that even very small increases in fitness may bring about powerful changes in the composition of populations.

Micro-evolution

Genetic polymorphism. Although progressive evolutionary change may eliminate one member of a pair of alleles from a population, in some cases (known as balanced polymorphism) counteracting selective forces lead to stable gene frequencies in which both alleles are maintained. An example of balanced polymorphism is the case of the gene leading to sickle-cell anemia among some tribes of Africa. The sickling gene produces a specific type of hemoglobin (Hb^S), while normal hemoglobin is related to another allele (Hb^A). Accordingly, the possible genotypes are Hb^AHb^A, Hb^AHb^S, and Hb^SHb^S. The latter people are homozygous for the sickle-cell gene and especially prone to develop severe anemia. While the condition is not lethal before birth, such individuals rarely survive long enough to exhibit more than minimal fitness in the Darwinian sense of capacity to reproduce. On these grounds it might be concluded that natural selection eventually should drive the frequency of the Hb^S gene to complete elimination or at least down to the one in 100,-000 level of the mutation rate. One would theorize a transient polymorphism; that is, one on the way out, toward fixation of the favoured allele.

Evidence, however, seems to contradict theory since, in a number of African tribes living in their ancestral tropical lowlands where one form of malaria is widespread, the Hb^S (sickling) gene is very common indeed. On the other hand, the same gene is rare in genetically related but isolated tribes living in highlands that are free of mosquitoes that transmit this (tertian) type of malaria. This discrepancy between lowland and highland people has led to the hypothesis that the Hb^AHb^S heterozygote is more fit and capable of leaving more offspring than is the homozygous normal Hb^AHb^A in a highly malarious environment. Although the exact way in which this extra measure of protection is provided is not understood, the hypothesis seems to be borne out by the observations. Calculations indicate that when any heterozygote is favoured over both homozygotes, both alleles will tend to be retained in the population. Equilibrium gene frequencies for both Hb^A and Hb^S are expected to maintain balanced polymorphism as long as the environmental agent (malaria) remains.

Populations of African origin in malaria-free regions of the Americas, whose ancestors came from villages with high frequencies of Hb^S, exhibit much lower frequencies of the gene than do those who remain genetically balanced in the ancestral villages. Apparently there is an ongoing microevolutionary change among all such populations that are no longer subject to substantial natural selection from the effects of tertian malaria.

Genetic load. Much of the genetic polymorphism in man appears to be transient rather than balanced. In practice, it is difficult to identify all of the alleles that any given chromosome location may carry. Nevertheless, the search continues for recessive genes that produce severe effects (as homozygotes). Sometimes called the mutational load, these genes are identified as concealed mutants carried by heterozygous individuals.

Natural selection, although it may work regularly to eliminate mutations that are unfavourable for reproduction, frequently cannot consummate the elimination fast enough. The result is that these "bad" genes may accumulate in human populations. They constitute a hidden load of mutations that mankind carries as part of the price of biological existence. Almost all living organisms carry comparable genes, but among humans, for whom every defective or stillborn child may impose a poignant burden, the matter is especially serious.

More optimistically, the enormous genetic variability carried by human populations by no means consists only of deleterious recessives. Many genes individually have little effect; since they function in combination with genes at other chromosome locations, they are called polygenes. Recent estimates of polygenes that combine to affect the enzymes of human blood suggest that, as has been found in other organisms, about a third of the chromosome loci are polymorphic (as is the sickle-cell gene). Using a fairly conservative figure of genes at 10,000 chromosome locations for man, this suggests that about 3,300 locations are polymorphic in the human species.

How such great variability is maintained is a subject of active investigation and theoretical controversy. One popular theory is that much of the genetic variability is main-

The survival of "bad" genes

tained specifically because it provides superior heterozygous combinations (the balance hypothesis). Balanced polymorphism, as in the case of sickle-cell anemia, may provide increased fitness for the heterozygote, but the homozygous individual still suffers.

Consideration of the relative importance of mutational and balance loads has centred around the possibility that some genetic differences exist in which the two homozygotes and the heterozygote are neutral from the point of view of natural selection. This view is not favoured in more traditional selection theory, which holds that no two genotypes can be absolutely identical in producing reproductive fitness.

GENETICS AND THE EVOLUTION OF MAN

The origin of the human species. Human genetics, especially when considered in terms of populations, has contributed much to theories on the origin of the human species (see HOMINIDAE). Theories of man's origins are considered in detail in other articles, but suffice it to say that in many cases the evolutionary emergence of any species is associated with geographical isolation of a population. Subsequently, this population comes to represent a unique gene pool that arises when its members fail to interbreed with other contemporary groups because of the persistence of isolating mechanisms, geographical, cultural, or otherwise.

Fossil and archaeological data indicate the likelihood that man emerged as a genetic isolate from prehuman ancestors on continental Africa; limited evidence suggests the early Pleistocene age (which began more than 2,000,-000 years ago). Subsequently, the human species (*Homo sapiens*) spread to almost all habitable parts of the world. At the dawn of recorded history, the human species had already reached all continents except possibly Antarctica. From the location and character of their remains, it appears that the spread of these ancient people was accomplished by small bands, migrating groups that moved on foot (and later with the aid of horses or small, primitive rafts or boats).

Man as a genetic isolate

The human species up to recorded history was apparently made up of many semi-isolated, relatively small population groups, with only minor interconnecting migration. This ancient population in many parts of the world came to form a complex mosaic of villages or settlements, much as has been observed in more recent times among the peoples in New Guinea.

This spread was likely to have been accompanied by a combination of natural selection and random drift, which, with a high mutation rate and growing numbers of people within isolated communities, would produce and spread great genetic variability both within groups and from one isolated population to the next.

Genetic aspects of race. According to one definition, a race is a geographical subdivision of a species that differs genetically from other races (subspecies) in the frequency of one or more alleles. Some theorists, imagining the human population of the world as it might have been about 4000 BC, speculate that there were perhaps five major races, one for each inhabited major land mass.

If contemporary human groups are any indication, however, within any major racial division there were large numbers of small subdivisions. The many human population segments of today blend at the edges and frequently defy description. Systematic biological distinctions among them are difficult to make. Blood-group and other gene-frequency differences, for example, show that all Indians of the Western Hemisphere manifest major genetic similarities; nevertheless, great variability exists from one group to the next, beginning in the American Arctic and proceeding to Tierra del Fuego at the tip of South America. Only where isolation has been rigorous is an occasional group found that is genetically distinct enough to tempt specific classification (see RACES OF MANKIND).

However one chooses to distinguish the "races" of man (*e.g.*, by skin colour, hair form, stature, facial features, or whatever), it is grossly evident that they can and do mate successfully one with the other. This ready interfertility among all human subgroups heavily endorses their designation as a single animal species, *Homo sapiens.* Mating between any of the "races," no matter how superficially different, produces children who have biologically sound heredities and who are fully fertile.

The continuing genetic recombination within what is identified as a single human species provides great diversity in modern man. Many feel that this diversity provides a source of great biological strength for the future of man.

BIBLIOGRAPHY. M. BARTALOS and T.A. BARAMKI, *Medical Cytogenetics* (1967), a study of chromosome abnormalities; H.L. CARSON, *Heredity and Human Life* (1963), a general account for the nonspecialist; THEODOSIUS DOBZHANSKY, *Mankind Evolving* (1962), a classic work dealing with genetics as it relates to human variation and evolution; W. FUHRMANN and F. VOGEL, *Genetische Familienberatung* (Eng. trans., *Genetic Counseling: A Guide for the Practicing Physician*, 1969), a clear, concise, and practical introduction to the subject; P. HANDLER (ed.), *Biology and the Future of Man* (1970), a comprehensive, authoritative book; H. HARRIS, *Principles of Human Biochemical Genetics* (1970); J.C. KING, *The Biology of Race* (1971), an extremely lucid and sensible approach to this difficult subject; V.A. MCKUSICK, *Mendelian Inheritance in Man*, 2nd ed. (1968), a catalog of known hereditary factors in man; L.S. PENROSE, *The Biology of Mental Defect*, 3rd rev. ed. (1963); I.H. PORTER, *Heredity and Disease* (1968), a textbook for medical students; R.R. RACE and R. SANGER, *Blood Groups in Man* (1968); C. STERN, *Principles of Human Genetics*, 2nd ed. (1960), the major classic work on this subject; A.C. STEVENSON and B.C.C. DAVISON, *Genetic Counselling* (1970); J.S. and M.W. THOMPSON, *Genetics in Medicine* (1966).

(H.L.C.)

Geneva

One of Europe's most unusual cities, Geneva has served as a model for the so-called city-state and owes its preeminence to the triumph of human, rather than geographic, factors. It developed a cosmopolitan character from the 16th century onward, when, as the dynamic centre of the Calvinist Reformation, it became the "Protestant Rome." Its contemporary economic and cultural prestige, too, are out of proportion to its physical size (Genève canton has a total area of 109 square miles [282 square kilometres], of which 62 square miles are in the city proper) and population, nearly 174,000 by 1970 with a population of over 321,000 in the metropolitan area. Territorial isolation has, in fact, been a basic feature of this economic and political entity, which did not establish its definitive frontiers until 1815, after long historical vicissitudes. Cut off, after the Reformation, from its natural geographic surroundings in France and Savoy, Geneva was forced to establish a distant but powerful network of intellectual and economic relationships, linking it with the European continent and with emerging regions overseas.

Territorial isolation

An aristocratic republic, governed first by an elite of bankers and scholars and then, after a radical insurrection in 1846–47, by an emergent liberal bourgeoisie, Geneva has functioned primarily as a centre of commerce, in contact with both Germanic and Mediterranean countries. Badly endowed in relation to the heavy industry associated with the Industrial Revolution, Geneva became instead a centre for capital accumulation and for such specialized manufacture as watchmaking. Contemporary Geneva is, above all, a service metropolis, specializing in financial activity and housing the headquarters of many public and private international organizations.

The Geneva of the early 1970s was plagued by problems stemming from its unique traditions: there is a very high proportion of foreigners in its population; there are manpower difficulties; its limited overall area is being rapidly consumed by urban growth; the German-Swiss element in the economy is exerting increasing influence; there is poor integration with neighbouring French territories; and rail and highway facilities are inadequate. Yet the city's uniqueness remains the key to its continued prosperity. Geneva has always justified the comment of the great French statesman Talleyrand: "There are five continents, and then there is Geneva." (For further information, see SWITZERLAND; SWITZERLAND, HISTORY OF.)

HISTORY

Geneva grew up in the centre of a natural basin clearly delimited by encircling mountains. The excellent location, besides commanding the important Swiss corridor between the Alps and the Jura Mountains, is also the

By courtesy of the Swiss National Tourist Office

Geneva in its lake setting, with the International Labour Office and the Parc Villa Barton in the foreground.

focus of Alpine passes leading into Italy and, along the Saône–Rhône axis, of routes to the Mediterranean. The local climate is tempered by the presence of Lake Geneva (Lac Léman), while the Jura create a screen that diminishes rainfall.

Foundation and early growth. The original site of the city was an easily defended hill dominating the lake outlet near a convenient crossing point. Human occupation began in the Paleolithic Period and further developed in the Neolithic, which witnessed the growth of a vast lake-dwelling community built on piles. The original name of Genava (or Geneva) undoubtedly dates back to the pre-Celtic Ligurian peoples. In about 500 BC, at the time of the Roman conquest, Geneva was a fortified settlement of the Allobrogian Celts, and as early as 58 BC, Geneva served as a departure point for Caesar's campaign against the Helvetians. By 379 it was a Roman city, Christianized, and the seat of a bishop. After the Germanic invasions it became the capital of the Burgundian kingdom (443–534).

During the period of the birth of feudalism, however, Geneva—which had belonged to Lotharingia and then again to Burgundy (888–1034)—was in the centre of the lands belonging to the Genevese counts, who became hereditary after 1034. With the final extinction of the line of Genevese counts in 1401, the bishop—who was the direct vassal of the Holy Roman emperor and invested with temporal power—became pre-eminent, in spite of the ambitions of the House of Savoy, which was tightening its hold on the neighbouring territories. Geneva was now a regional centre exercising influence over a vast bishopric and, through its trade fairs, entering into the economic life of Europe. A decline began toward 1450, however, owing to competition from Lyons and to the growing power of the great national states. The fairs—which disappeared completely in the 16th century—nevertheless coincided with initial urban expansion; the town grew from its original hill site, with commercial quarters springing up along the banks of the lake and the Rhône. A foothold was also established north of the river, in the suburb of Saint-Gervais.

The Reformation. The economic diversity of this early period prepared the way for the Reformation. Religious unrest enhanced the desire of the inhabitants to escape the power of the bishop-prince (who, from the start of the 15th century, was finally bound politically to the House of Savoy) and also to expand their participation in politics, which had been inaugurated with the granting of certain franchises in 1387. In 1536 the citizens of Geneva embraced the Reformation and proclaimed a republic, supported by John Calvin between 1541 and 1564. Geneva was saved from the Duke of Savoy's counterattack by France and its Swiss allies, particularly Bern. The republic continued to defend its independence in a series of campaigns between 1589 and 1601, but, by the Treaty of Lyons (1601), Savoy ceded the Pays de Gex to France, thus severing Geneva from Switzerland. The Duke of Savoy also made an abortive attempt to take the city by surprise during the night of December 11–12, 1602, but the action of France and the Swiss cantons led to the further recognition of Geneva's independence in the Treaty of Saint-Julien (July 11, 1603).

The effect of the Reformation

The Reformation period marked a vital turning point in Genevan history, for as early as 1530 the city had razed its outlying areas and enclosed itself in a formidable system of fortifications. The inhabitants, cut off from the bishop's former territories of Jussy on the east and Peney on the west, turned to banking and to such remunerative trades as watchmaking, introduced by the French Huguenots. The influx of other refugees from Italy, Germany, and, above all, France infused the republic with new blood. They gave the "Protestant Rome" a continental dimension and brought with them a high level of culture, attested to both by the prosperity of the printing industry and by the founding of the Academy in 1559.

The modern period. The 18th century was a calm period, during which Geneva—which had benefitted from a further influx of French Protestants following the revocation of the toleration granted by the Edict of Nantes in 1685—consolidated its economic power and extended its territory through agreements with France and Sardinia. A modus vivendi was established with the House of Savoy, which continued to maintain a close watch on the city and tried, with the creation of the town of Carouge in 1772, to set up a rival commercial and religious (Catholic) bastion at the gates of the city. The oligarchic republic of Geneva was at the zenith of its prosperity, with branches of its banking houses in every country and its financial power ranging far and wide, from the court of Versailles to the new United States. Material wealth stimulated a burst of culture and artistic creativity. Although still enclosed within its walls, the city adorned itself with beautiful private mansions and public buildings, while the patricians built sumptuous country houses. Local political life was intense, featuring a seething controversy that opposed the bourgeoisie and working-class elements, the natifs, to the dominant aristocracy, a conflict that reached sufficient intensity to provoke interventions from both Paris and Turin. The birthplace of Rousseau and the sanctuary of Voltaire, Geneva was a centre of attraction for the elite of the Enlightenment and was one of the places where the new political science, derived from natural law, was developed.

In 1798, with the aid of local Jacobins, Geneva was annexed to the "Grande Nation" of the French Directory. The city was reduced to a subservient role in the Département du Léman and submitted, in 1802, to the protection of Napoleon I. The Emperor distrusted Geneva, "that city where they know English too well" (which was indeed harbouring a secret liberal and Anglophile opposition), and the French period became an era of demographic stagnation and economic recession.

The effect of the French Revolution

As early as 1813 Geneva threw in its lot with France's enemies and was thus able to claim indemnities upon the fall of the empire. The aristocratic republic was restored and undertook negotiations with the Swiss cantons to join the Helvetian Confederation and also with the Great Powers at the Congress of Vienna. On September 12, 1814, the republic was admitted to the ranks of the Swiss cantons. Through the cession of 12 Savoyard communes of the Pays de Gex in the Second Treaty of Paris (November 20, 1815), it "rounded out" its territories into a single block, linked to the rest of Switzerland. The French and Sardinian customs line was pushed back to create a free zone that constituted an economic, if not a political, hinterland.

The Restoration brought back the aristocracy, which experienced a further quarter century of glory. "Swiss Geneva" had ceased to be an autonomous political entity, and its relations with neighbouring countries were the responsibility of the federal authority. Gradually, however, the bourgeoisie and the common people began to question the aristocratic regime. They obtained concessions in 1841, but trouble broke out again in 1843. The civil war of the Sonderbund, which began in 1846 between Catholic and Protestant Swiss cantons, permitted the radicals, led by James Fazy, to go on the offensive. On October 7, 1846, the working-class suburb of Saint-Gervais revolted, and the conservative government was overthrown. The radicals, who drew up the new constitution of 1847, were thereafter masters of Geneva. James Fazy dominated the political scene until 1861. He was in many ways the founder of modern Geneva, having opened the canton to railway lines, created the Bank of Geneva, and, above all, having made widespread urban expansion possible by demolishing the fortifications.

The creation of "Swiss Geneva"

In 1860 Geneva lost its last chance for territorial growth. With the annexation of northern Savoy by France, a greater free zone was created out of the Chablais, the Faucigny, and part of Genevan territory. The city regained, and until 1914 held, its role as a regional economic capital. It also continued to assert its international influence—the Red Cross was founded in 1864, and the League of Nations was installed in 1919. In 1923, however, France suppressed the free zone in a blow that was only partially compensated by the re-establishment of the petites zones (of 1815 and 1816) in 1923. The lack of a larger free zone further accentuated Geneva's international role. In the city itself, Fazy's successors inaugurated and pursued a violently anticlerical policy, and in 1907 the separation of church and state was established by popular vote. In the late 19th century, hydroelectric power inaugurated a new industrial era, but this was hindered both by World War I and by the world financial crisis of 1929. It was not until after 1945 that the contemporary phase of demographic and economic growth got under way, signs of a prosperity that has brought problems of its own.

THE CONTEMPORARY CITY

Layout and urban structure. Geneva exhibits the classic pattern of old European cities, with a concentric arrangement of neighbourhoods in more or less continuous belts around the original nucleus. The Haute-ville, centred on the hill and marked by the Cathedral of St. Peter, is the historic heart of Geneva. The route from the rue de l'Hôtel-de-Ville to the Grand-Rue marks the crest of the Celtic settlement, and the Bourg-de-Four marks the city's first extension outside its walls. The houses here are typical of the Middle Ages and the Renaissance, and building density is high. This neighbourhood also has experienced relative depopulation in favor of such luxury businesses as antiques and interior decoration; government office buildings; and high-rise apartments and offices.

At the foot of the hill an area reclaimed from the lake and the Rhône forms a low-lying shopping district featuring big department stores and places of entertainment. On the site of the old fortifications—mostly to the south of the Rhône—suburbs, dating from the second half of the 19th century, have grown up. These are lifeless, exhibiting a uniform style, with specialized streets (one for doctors, one for banks); public buildings (museums, the Grand Théâtre, the university); and such green areas as the Promenade des Bastions. Beyond these suburbs is a new, irregular belt of working-class residential areas, close to the railway stations (Eaux-Vives, Grottes, Saint-Gervais), and industrial zones. The latter—Acacias, Jonction, Servette, Charmilles, and Secheron—exhibit little or no planning. A well-to-do residential area follows on the southern plateau (Malagnou, Champel), while the quarter housing such international agencies as the Red Cross, the International Labour Office, and the World Health Organization rises on old patrician properties north of the Rhône. The old Savoyard city of Carouge is joined to Geneva by the populous and commercial rue de Carouge. Finally, since 1945, such new satellite settlements as Onex, Meyrin, Le Ligon, and La Gradelle have sprung up in the surrounding countryside. By the 1970s the canton included 45 communes, 16 of which were united with Geneva in the city proper.

The canton's frontier has undergone a long formative process. Agreements with neighbouring states gradually brought closer together, and finally united, the scattered elements of the area's feudal mosaic. The principal mechanisms were the treaties of Paris (1749), with France, and of Turin (1754), with Sardinia, and, with these same two countries, agreements of 1815 and 1816. The current isolation of Geneva is almost complete; of the 45 roads that radiate out of Geneva, only three link the city to the rest of Switzerland. The others are intersected by the frontier. The frontier with France covers 64 miles (102 kilometres), as compared with only 3 miles shared with the neighbouring Swiss canton of Vaud.

Demography. It was not until after 1945 that the city's population began to register rapid growth, owing to the admission of other Swiss citizens and foreigners. By 1970 it reached 173,618. Natural growth was only two per thousand, compared with 20 per thousand lost through emigration. Persons over 65 years represent 18 percent of the native Genevan population, 12 percent of other Swiss residents, and only 5 percent of foreign residents. Persons under 21 years of age are approximately equally distributed. A large foreign population is one of the constants of Genevan demography. Since the 1820s the proportion of foreigners has not dropped below 16 percent, and in 1970 it stood at 34 percent. Native Genevans make up about 30 percent of the population, and the remainder are Swiss from other cantons. By the 1970s immigration to Geneva was characterized not only by the traditional contingents from Italy and France but also by a rising number from the Iberian Peninsula, the Americas, Asia, and Africa. Among the native population and in the professional classes, the Protestant element is in the majority, but, within the population as a whole, Geneva is no longer the "Protestant Rome." Roman Catholics, in fact, make up slightly more than half the population.

Economic life. Geneva has a tertiary, or service, economy; well over two thirds of the population is employed in service industries and less than 1 percent in agriculture. The latter is in decline because of the lack of land and is protected by the government. It supplies such commodities as wheat, rapeseed, dairy products, and wine.

Industry is characterized by lack of space and raw materials and by distance from vital mineral sources. Geneva has always had quality labour and internationally oriented commercial management, as well as an early start in capital accumulation. Certain older activities, such as cotton-textile manufacture, have disappeared, but watchmaking has a continuing tradition of precision and quality. Industrial production is diversified and is, above all, oriented toward export. By the 1970s the largest industry was that of precision machinery and instrument manufacture, employing approximately 16,000 workers. Principal specialties are equipment for hydraulic plants (turbines and alternators), electrical equipment, machine tools, and measuring devices. Watchmaking and jewelry making, with more than 70 firms and 4,000 employees, have lost first place in the area of mass production to those of the Jura region but are still in the forefront with respect to the creation of high-quality articles. The chemical industry, with two dozen firms and 2,500 employees, is the second largest in Switzerland, after Basel. It supplies luxury items—such as fragrances and bases for perfume—as well as medicines. The food-processing industry is well represented, with 2,000 persons employed, and Geneva also manufactures almost half of all Swiss-made cigarettes. Outside the city an industrial zone of 9,-700,000 square feet has been set up at La Praille and at the Acacias, along the railway. The manpower shortage has necessitated the influx of foreign workers. Finally, recent decades have witnessed a process of concentration through mergers and the passage to German–Swiss control of a number of large businesses in electromechanical construction, precision metallurgy, and chemicals.

Administration and services. The republic and canton of Geneva is governed by the Constitution of 1847 (as modified by later laws), which established a democracy based on universal male suffrage and extended the vote to women in 1960. Local cantonal government is exercised by an executive power, the Council of State (consisting of seven members, who are elected for four years), and by a legislature, the Great Council, which is composed of 100 deputies, who are also elected for four years by proportional ballot. Each constituent commune has its own communal assembly, administrative council, and mayor. On both communal and cantonal levels, citizens have the right of legislative initiative and of referendum. To represent it in the federal government, the canton elects two deputies to the Council of States and a number of national councillors, which varies according to population. Since 1936, power has been exercised by a coalition of national parties, excluding the Labour Party (Communist) and including the independent Christian Socialist Party (Catholic), the Liberals, Radicals, and Socialists. The rate of voter participation is one of the lowest in Switzerland and rarely attains 50 percent of those registered.

Service activities are an expression of Geneva's cosmopolitan character and its commercial and financial vocation. Commerce, banking, and insurance employ more

(margin notes) Residential areas

Industry

than 30,000 persons; hotels, 8,000; and public and private services, 26,000. The handling of capital has long been the prime mover in the city's prosperity, and banking and the stock exchange have more than 3,000 employees. Although Geneva is second to Zürich in total volume of financial transactions, it has retained a position of worldwide importance. When compared with the branches of the large Swiss banks of German-Swiss origin and with the numerous affiliates of foreign firms, the local private banks have specialized in the management of fortunes. Geneva is one of the principal sanctuaries for capital, and it has been estimated that its banks hold more than half the total amount of foreign capital in the country. Many international institutions have found a home in the city as a result of centuries-old orientation to the outside world and of the security brought by Swiss neutrality. In 1945 Geneva became the European headquarters of the United Nations and of the numerous organizations attached to it. In addition, there are more than 150 international headquarters for such private organizations as the League of Red Cross Societies, the Inter-Parliamentary Union, and the World Council of Churches. Operating on a European level and extending its activity into the industrial and technological area, CERN (the European Nuclear Research Council) appropriately juts out, territorially, onto French soil.

In the area of communications, success has been uneven. It has been said that Geneva lost the battle of the railroads in the 19th century, and the two railway stations of Cornavin and Eaux-Vives do not, in fact, link up. Geneva has been connected with Lausanne and with the Swiss highway system by a multilane expressway since 1964. The city also contributed labour and financing to the construction of the highway tunnel beneath Mt. Blanc and the Route-Blanche (White Way) to Italy. Cointrin airport, however, the second largest in Switzerland, has been more successful, and its traffic is rising continuously. Transport difficulties are aggravated by the ever increasing number of daily migrant workers who cross Geneva's borders.

Cultural life. Geneva has an ancient cultural tradition. A scholarly elite cultivated theology, philosophy, literature, and, especially since the 17th century, the exact and natural sciences. Geneva has been in the avantgarde of geology, botany, and mountaineering (both sporting and scientific). In 1872 the Academy was transformed into a university, which now has more than 8,000 students, nearly half of them foreigners. Its outstanding reputation in certain specialties (international studies, botany, the educational sciences) draws a large audience to the city. Geneva's cultural life is intense, revolving around its museums; the music conservatory and international musical performance competitions; the Orchestre de la Suisse Romande; the Théâtre; and the proceedings of international meetings held in the city.

BIBLIOGRAPHY. The collective volume, *Genève, Carrefour des Nations* (1963), provides a good introduction. *Genève, le Pays et les Hommes* (1958); PAUL GUICHONNET, *Genève: Réflexions sur un destin urbain* (1965); and CLAUDE RAFFESTIN, *Genève: Essai de géographie industrielle* (1968), covers the present-day geography and economy. Urban evolution is the subject of two significant books: LOUIS BLONDEL, *Le développement urbain de Genève à travers les siècles* (1946); and ANDRE CORBOZ, *Invention de Carouge* (1968). The historical literature is extraordinarily rich, particularly for political and religious facts and for the period previous to 1798. PAUL F. GEISENDORF, *Bibliographie raisonnée de l'histoire de Genève des origines à 1798* (1966), offers an appropriate orientation. Two general histories are P.E. MARTIN (ed.), *Histoire de Genève*, 2 vol. (1951–56); and FRANCOIS RUCHON, *Histoire politique de la République de Genève . . .* (1953). ANTHONY BABEL, *Histoire économique de Genève, des origines au début du XVIe siècle* (1963); JEAN-FRANCOIS BERGIER, *Genève et l'économie européenne de la Renaissance* (1963); and ANNE-MARIE PIUZ, *Affaires et politique: Recherches sur le commerce de Genève au XVIIe siècle* (1964), cover economic history. See also WALDEMAR DEONNA, *Les Arts à Genève des origines à la fin du XVIIIe siècle* (1942); and ALFRED BERCHTOLD, *La Suisse romande au cap du XXe siècle* (1963); *Histoire des sciences à Genève* (1955).

(P.G.)

Genghis Khan

Genghis Khan (Chingis Khan), the son of a Mongolian chieftain, was a warrior and ruler of genius who, starting from obscure and insignificant beginnings, brought all the nomadic tribes of Mongolia under the rule of himself and his family in a rigidly disciplined military state. He then turned his attention toward the settled peoples beyond the borders of his nomadic realm and began the series of campaigns of plunder and conquest that eventually carried the Mongol armies as far as the Adriatic Sea in one direction and the Pacific coast of China in the other, leading to the establishment of the great Mongol Empire.

By courtesy of the National Palace Museum, Taipei, Taiwan, Republic of China

Genghis Khan, ink and colour on silk by an unknown Chinese artist.

Historical background. With the exception of the saga-like *Secret History of the Mongols* (1240?), only non-Mongol sources provide near-contemporary information about the life of Genghis Khan. Almost all writers, even those who were in the Mongol service, have dwelt on the enormous destruction wrought by the Mongol invasions. One Arab historian openly expressed his horror at the recollection of them. Beyond the reach of the Mongols and relying on second-hand information, the 13th-century chronicler Matthew Paris called them a "detestable nation of Satan that poured out like devils from Tartarus so that they are rightly called Tartars." He was making a play on words with the classical word Tartarus (Hell) and the ancient tribal name of Tatar borne by some of the nomads, but his account catches the terror that the Mongols evoked. As the founder of the Mongol nation, the organizer of the Mongol armies, and the genius behind their campaigns, Genghis Khan must share the reputation of his people, even though his generals were frequently operating on their own, far from direct supervision. Nevertheless, it would be mistaken to see the Mongol campaigns as haphazard incursions by bands of marauding savages. Nor is it true, as some have supposed, that these campaigns were somehow brought about by a progressive desiccation of Inner Asia that compelled the nomads to look for new pastures. Nor, again, were the Mongol invasions a unique event. Genghis Khan was neither the first nor the last nomadic conqueror to burst out of the steppe and terrorize the settled periphery of Eurasia. His campaigns were merely larger in scale, more successful, and more lasting in effect than those of other leaders. They impinged more violently upon those sedentary peoples who had the habit of recording events in writing, and they affected a greater part of the Eurasian continent and a variety of different societies.

Two societies were in constant contact, two societies that were mutually hostile, if only because of their diametrically opposed ways of life, and yet these societies were interdependent. The nomads needed some of the staple products of the south and coveted its luxuries. These could be had by trade, by taxing transient caravans, or by armed raids. The settled peoples of China needed the products of the steppe to a lesser extent, but they could not ignore the presence of the nomadic barbarians and were forever preoccupied with resisting encroachment by one means or another. A strong dynasty, such as the 17th-century Manchu, could extend its military power directly over all Inner Asia. At other times the Chinese would have to play off one set of barbarians against another, transferring their support and juggling their alliances so as to prevent any one tribe from becoming too strong.

The cycle of dynastic strength and weakness in China was accompanied by another cycle, that of unity and fragmentation amongst the peoples of the steppe. At the peak of their power, a nomadic tribe under a determined leader could subjugate the other tribes to its will and, if the situation in China was one of weakness, might extend its power well beyond the steppe. In the end this extension of nomadic power over the incompatible, sedentary culture of the south brought its own nemesis. The nomads lost their traditional basis of superiority—that lightning mobility that required little in the way of supply and fodder—and were swallowed up by the Chinese they had conquered. The cycle would then be resumed; a powerful China would re-emerge, and disarray and petty squabbling among ephemeral chieftains would be the new pattern of life among the nomads. The history of the Mongol conquests illustrates this analysis perfectly, and it is against this background of political contrasts and tensions that the life of Genghis Khan must be evaluated. His campaigns were not an inexplicable natural or even God-given catastrophe but the outcome of a set of circumstances manipulated by a soldier of ambition, determination, and genius. He found his tribal world ready for unification, at a time when China and other settled states were, for one reason or another, simultaneously in decline, and he exploited the situation.

Early struggles. Various dates are given for the birth of Temüjin, as Genghis Khan was named—after a leader who was defeated by his father, Yesügei, when Temüjin was born. The chronology of Temüjin's early life is uncertain. He may have been born in 1155, in 1162 (the date favoured today in Mongolia), or in 1167. According to legend, his birth was auspicious, because he came into the world holding a clot of blood in his hand. He is also said to have been of divine origin, his first ancestor having been a gray wolf, "born with a destiny from heaven on high." Yet his early years were anything but promising. When he was nine, Yesügei, a member of the royal Borjigin clan of the Mongols, was poisoned by a band of Tatars, another nomadic people, in continuance of an old feud.

With Yesügei dead, the remainder of the clan, led by the rival Taychiut family, abandoned his widow, Höelün, and her children, considering them too weak to exercise leadership and seizing the opportunity to usurp power. For a time the small family led a life of extreme poverty, eating roots and fish instead of the normal nomad diet of mutton and mare's milk. Two anecdotes illustrate both Temüjin's straitened circumstances and, more significantly, the power he already had of attracting supporters through sheer force of personality. Once he was captured by the Taychiut, who, rather than killing him, kept him around their camps, wearing a wooden collar. One night, when they were feasting, Temüjin, noticing that he was being ineptly guarded, knocked down the sentry with a blow from his wooden collar and fled. The Taychiut searched all night for him, and he was seen by one of their people, who, impressed by the fire in his eyes, did not denounce him but helped him escape at the risk of his own life. On another occasion horse thieves came and stole eight of the nine horses that the small family owned. Temüjin pursued them. On the way he stopped to ask a young stranger, called Bo'orchu, if he had seen the horses. Bo'orchu immediately left the milking he was engaged in, gave Temüjin a fresh horse, and set out

with him to help recover the lost beasts. He refused any reward but, recognizing Temüjin's authority, attached himself irrevocably to him as a *nökör*, or free companion, abandoning his own family.

Temüjin and his family apparently preserved a considerable fund of prestige as members of the royal Borjigin clan, in spite of their rejection by it. Among other things, he was able to claim the wife to whom Yesügei had betrothed him just before his death. But the Merkit people, a tribe living in north Mongolia, bore Temüjin a grudge, because Yesügei had stolen his own wife, Höelün, from one of their men, and in their turn they ravished Temüjin's wife Börte. Temüjin felt able to appeal to Toghril, Khan of the Kereit tribe, with whom Yesügei had had the relationship of *anda*, or sworn brother, and at that time the most powerful Mongol prince, for help in recovering Börte. He had had the foresight to rekindle this friendship by presenting Toghril with a sable skin, which he himself had received as a bridal gift. He seems to have had nothing else to offer; yet, in exchange; Toghril promised to reunite Temüjin's scattered people, and he is said to have redeemed his promise by furnishing 20,000 men and persuading Jamuka, a boyhood friend of Temüjin's, to supply an army as well. The contrast between Temüjin's destitution and the huge army furnished by his allies is hard to explain, and no authority other than the narrative of the *Secret History* is available.

Rise to power. With powerful allies and a force of his own, Temüjin routed the Merkit, with the help of a strategy by which Temüjin was regularly to scotch the seeds of future rebellion. He tried never to leave an enemy in his rear; years later, before attacking China, he would first make sure that no nomad leader survived to stab him in the back. Not long after the destruction of the Merkit, he treated the nobility of the Jürkin clan in the same way. These princes, supposedly his allies, had profited by his absence on a raid against the Tatars to plunder his property. Temüjin exterminated the clan nobility and took the common people as his own soldiery and servants. When his power had grown sufficiently for him to risk a final showdown with the formidable Tatars, he first defeated them in battle and then slaughtered all those taller than the height of a cart axle. Presumably the children could be expected to grow up ignorant of their past identity and to become loyal followers of the Mongols. When the alliance with Toghril of the Kereit at last broke down and Temüjin had to dispose of this obstacle to supreme power, he dispersed the Kereit people among the Mongols as servants and troops. This ruthlessness was not mere wanton cruelty. Temüjin intended to leave alive none of the old, rival aristocrats, who might prove a focus of resistance; to provide himself with a fighting force; and, above all, to crush the sense of clan loyalties that favoured fragmentation and to unite all the nomads in personal obedience to his family. And when, in 1206, he was accepted as emperor of all the steppe people, he was to distribute thousands of families to the custody of his own relatives and companions, replacing the existing pattern of tribes and clans by something closer to a feudal structure.

At least from the time of the defeat of the Merkits, Temüjin was aiming at supremacy in the steppes for himself. The renewed friendship with Jamuka lasted only a year and a half. Then, one day while the two friends were on the march, Jamuka uttered an enigmatic remark about the choice of camping site, which provoked Temüjin's wife Börte to advise him that it was high time for the two friends to go their separate ways. What lies behind this episode is difficult to see. The story in the *Secret History* is too puzzling in its brevity and its allusive language to permit a reliable explanation. It has been suggested that Jamuka was trying to provoke a crisis in the leadership. Equally, it may be that the language is deliberately obscure to gloss over the fact that Temüjin was about to desert his comrade. In any event, Temüjin took Börte's advice. Many of Jamuka's own men also abandoned him, probably seeing in Temüjin the man they thought more likely to win in the end. The *Secret History*

Struggles between nomadic and sedentary societies

Cast out by his clan

Destruction of the Merkit

justifies their action in epic terms. One of the men tells Temüjin of a vision that had appeared to him and that could only be interpreted as meaning that Heaven and Earth had agreed that Temüjin should be lord of the empire. Looking at the situation in a more down-to-earth way, the interplay of the vacillating loyalties of the steppe may be discerned. The clansmen knew what was afoot, and some of them hastened to move over to Temüjin's side, realizing that a strong leader was in the offing and that it would be prudent to declare for him early on.

The break with Jamuka brought about a polarization within the Mongol world that was to be resolved only with the disappearance of one or the other of the rivals. Jamuka has no advocate in history. The *Secret History* has much to tell about him, not always unsympathetically, but it is essentially the chronicle of Temüjin's family; and Jamuka appears as the enemy, albeit sometimes a reluctant one. He is an enigma, a man of sufficient force of personality to lead a rival coalition of princes and to get himself elected *gur-khān*, or supreme Khan, by them. Yet he was an intriguer, a man to take the short view, ready to desert his friends, even turn on them, for the sake of a quick profit. But for Temüjin, it might have been within Jamuka's power to dominate the Mongols, but Temüjin was incomparably the greater man; and the rivalry broke Jamuka.

Gathering of the clans around Temüjin and Jamuka

Clan leaders began to group themselves around Temüjin and Jamuka, and, a few years before the turn of the century, some of them proposed to make Temüjin Khan of the Mongols. The terms in which they did so, promising him loyalty in war and the hunt, suggest that all they were looking for was a reliable general, certainly not the overlord he was to become. Indeed, later on, some of them were to desert him. Even at this time, Temüjin was only a minor chieftain, as is shown by the next important event narrated by the *Secret History*, a brawl at a feast, provoked by his nominal allies the Jürkin princes, whom he later massacred. The Chin emperor in north China, too, looked on him as of no great consequence. In one of the reversals of policy characteristic of their manipulation of the nomads, the Chin attacked their onetime allies the Tatars. Together with Toghril, Temüjin seized the opportunity of continuing the clan feud and took the Tatars in the rear. The Chin emperor rewarded Toghril with the Chinese title of *wang*, or prince, and gave Temüjin an even less exalted one. And, indeed, for the next few years the Chin had nothing to fear from Temüjin. He was fully occupied in building up his power in the steppe and posed no obvious threat to China.

Temüjin now set about systematically eliminating all rivals. Successive coalitions formed by Jamuka were defeated. The Tatars were exterminated. Toghril allowed himself to be manoeuvred by Jamuka's intrigues and by his own son's ambitions and suspicions into outright war against Temüjin, and he and his Kereit people were destroyed. Finally, in the west, the Naiman ruler, fearful of the rising power of the Mongols, tried to form yet another coalition, with the participation of Jamuka, but was utterly defeated and lost his kingdom. Jamuka, inconstant as ever, deserted the Naiman Khan at the last moment. These campaigns took place in the few years before 1206 and left Temüjin master of the steppes. In that year a great assembly was held by the River Onon, and Temüjin was proclaimed Genghis Khan: the title probably meant Universal Ruler.

Unification of the Mongol nation. The year 1206 is a turning point in the history of the Mongols and in world history: the moment when the Mongols were first ready to move out beyond the steppe. Mongolia itself took on a new shape. The petty tribal quarrels and raids were a thing of the past. Either the familiar tribe and clan names have fallen out of use or those bearing them are to be found, subsequently, scattered all over the Mongol world, testifying to the wreck of the traditional clan and tribe system. A unified Mongol nation came into existence as the personal creation of Genghis Khan and, through many vicissitudes (feudal disintegration, incipient retribalization, colonial occupation), survives to the present day. Mongol ambitions looked beyond the steppe.

Genghis Khan was ready to start on his great adventure of world conquest. The new nation was organized, above all, for war. Genghis Khan's troops were divided up on the decimal system, were rigidly disciplined, and were well equipped and supplied. The generals were his own sons or picked men, absolutely loyal to him.

Beginning of the conquest of Asia

Genghis Khan's military genius could adapt itself to rapidly changing circumstances. Initially his troops were exclusively cavalry, riding the hardy, grass-fed Mongol pony that needs no fodder. With such an army, other nomads can be defeated, but cities cannot be taken. Yet before long the Mongols were able to undertake the siege of large cities, using mangonels, catapults, ladders, burning oil, and so forth and even diverting rivers. It was only gradually, through contact with men from the more civilized states, that Genghis Khan came to realize that there were more sophisticated ways of enjoying power than simply raiding, destroying, and plundering. It was a minister of the Khan of the Naiman, the last important Mongol tribe to resist Genghis Khan, who taught him the uses of literacy and helped reduce the Mongol language to writing. The *Secret History* reports it was only after the war against the Muslim empire of Khwārezm, in the region of the Amu Darya (Oxus) and Syr Darya (Jaxartes), probably in late 1222, that Genghis Khan learned from Muslim advisers the "meaning and importance of towns." And it was another adviser, formerly in the service of the Chin emperor, who explained to him the uses of peasants and craftsmen as producers of taxable goods. He had intended to turn the cultivated fields of north China into grazing land for his horses.

The great conquests of the Mongols, which would transform them into a world power, were still to come. China was the main goal. Genghis Khan first secured his western flank by a tough campaign against the Tangut kingdom of Hsi Hsia, a northwestern border state of China, and then fell upon the Chin empire of north China in 1211. In 1214 he allowed himself to be bought off, temporarily, with a huge amount of booty, but in 1215 operations were resumed, and Peking was taken. Subsequently, the more systematic subjugation of north China was in the hands of his general Muqali. Genghis Khan himself was compelled to turn aside from China and carry out the conquest of Khwārezm. This war was provoked by the governor of the city of Otrar, who massacred a caravan of Muslim merchants who were under Genghis Khan's protection. The Khwārezmian shah refused satisfaction. War with Khwārezm would doubtless have come sooner or later, but now it could not be deferred. It was in this war that the Mongols earned their reputation for savagery and terror. City after city was stormed, the inhabitants massacred or forced to serve as advance troops for the Mongols against their own people. Fields and gardens were laid waste and irrigation works destroyed as Genghis Khan pursued his implacable vengeance against the royal house of Khwārezm. He finally withdrew in 1223 and did not lead his armies into war again until the final campaign against Hsi Hsia in 1226–27. He died on August 18, 1227.

Subjugation of China

Assessment. As far as can be judged from the disparate sources, Genghis Khan's personality was a complex one. He had great physical strength, tenacity of purpose, and an unbreakable will. He was not obstinate and would listen to advice from others, including his wives and mother. He was flexible. He could deceive but was not petty. He had a sense of the value of loyalty, unlike Toghril or Jamuka. Enemies guilty of treachery toward their lords could expect short shrift from him, but he would exploit their treachery at the same time. He was religiously minded, carried along by his sense of a divine mission, and in moments of crisis he would reverently worship the Eternal Blue Heaven, the supreme deity of the Mongols. So much is true of his early life. The picture becomes less harmonious as he moves out of his familiar sphere and comes into contact with the strange, settled world beyond the steppe. At first he could not see beyond the immediate gains to be got from massacre and rapine and, at times, was consumed by a passion for revenge. Yet all his life he could attract the loyalties of men willing to serve him, both fellow nomads and civilized men from the settled world. His fame could even persuade the aged Taoist sage Ch'ang-ch'un to journey the length of Asia to discourse upon religious matters. He was above all adaptable, a man who could learn.

Organization, discipline, mobility, and ruthlessness of purpose were the fundamental factors in his military successes. Massacres of defeated populations, with the resultant terror, were weapons he regularly used. His practice of summoning cities to surrender, and organizing the methodical slaughter of those who did not submit, has been described as psychological warfare, but his methods were crude compared with those of the 20th century; and although it was undoubtedly policy to sap resistance by fostering terror, massacre was employed for its own sake. The standard Mongol practice, especially in the war against Khwārezm, was to send agents to demoralize and divide the garrison and populace of an enemy city, mixing threats with promises. The Mongols' reputation for frightfulness often paralyzed their captives, who allowed themselves to be killed in circumstances where resistance or flight was not impossible. With fortified cities, psychological pressure was not decisive, though it saved some troublesome sieges. Many cities resisted, some for as long as six months, relying on their strength or perhaps not believing the Mongol propaganda. Indeed, the Mongols were unaccountable. Resistance brought certain destruction, but at Balkh, now in Afghanistan, the population was slaughtered in spite of a prompt surrender, for tactical reasons.

His achievements were grandiose. He united all the nomadic tribes, and with numerically inferior armies he defeated great empires, such as Khwārezm and the even more powerful Chin state. Yet he did not exhaust his people. He chose his successor, his son Ögödei, with great care, ensured that his other sons would obey him, and passed on to him an army and a state in full vigour. At the time of his death, Genghis Khan had conquered the land mass from Peking to the Caspian Sea, and his generals had raided Persia and Russia. His successors would extend their power over the whole of China, Persia, and most of Russia. They did what he did not achieve and perhaps never really intended—that is, to weld their conquests into a tightly organized empire. The destruction brought about by Genghis Khan survives in popular memory, but far more significant, these conquests were but the first stage of the Mongol Empire, greatest continental empire of medieval and modern times.

BIBLIOGRAPHY. For general reading, LEONARDO OLSCHKI, *L'Asia di Marco Polo* (1957; Eng. trans., *Marco Polo's Asia*, 1960), is recommended. The relevant pages from RENE GROUSSET, *L'Empire des steppes: Attila, Gengis-Khan, Tamerlan* (1939; Eng. trans., *The Empire of the Steppes: A History of Central Asia*, 1970), is still the best concise account of the subject, and the whole book may be read with profit. The most accessible, and perhaps the best, biography also by Grousset: *Le Conquérant du monde, Gengis-Khan* (1944; Eng. trans., *Conqueror of the World*, 1966), contains a critical bibliography. Other serious biographies are: B. VLADIMIRTSOV, *The Life of Chingis-Khan* (1930; orig. pub. in Russian, 1922); RALPH W. FOX, *Genghis Khan* (1936); and H. DESMOND MARTIN, *The Rise of Chingis Khan and His Conquest of North China* (1950.)

(C.R.B.)

Genoa

Genoa (Genova), an important port city, is the capital of Genoa (Genova) Province (*provincia*), in the Liguria Region (*regione*) of northwestern Italy; it stands at the head of a large gulf, close to the Lombard Plain and the Alpine passes leading north.

Origins and early history (to the 10th century). In ancient times, Genoa was first the site of a Ligurian fort, and in the 5th and 4th centuries BC its fine natural harbour made it a commercial emporium with Etruscan, Phoenician, and Greek contacts. From the 3rd century BC it was a major Roman station on the coastal route to Provence; another road led into Lombardy. The barbarians who overran Italy when the Roman Empire dissolved were defeated by the Byzantine general Belisarius in the mid-6th century AD, and Genoa remained under Byzantine rule until its conquest in about 643 by the Lombards, who destroyed its walls and allowed its trade to decay. Yet even in the 10th century, when Genoa was repeatedly sacked by the Saracens, a bare minimum of urban life and overseas trade still survived.

The city in the 10th–19th centuries. These Muslim raids provoked the local nobles to lead Genoa's fishermen and farmers, often in alliance with Pisa, in retaliatory attacks against the Muslims in Corsica, Sardinia, Sicily, and the Balearics. From the 11th century onward, the spoils were invested in new ventures in Naples, and Amalfi, in Sicily, Spain, and North Africa. After 1097 participation in the Crusades brought the Genoese profitable opportunities to hire out shipping and lend money, and Genoa secured trading quarters and privileges in Syrian and Byzantine ports. The Genoese extended their dominion eastward and westward along the coast, developed business activities inland, and supplemented meagre local produce by importing foodstuffs and raw materials; they became experts and innovators in shipbuilding, navigation, and cartography, in industrial and banking techniques, and in types of contracts that enabled even poor men to form partnerships and invest capital in lucrative overseas trade.

The commune of Genoa. The gradual evolution of the commune of Genoa, whose autonomy received recognition from the Holy Roman Emperor in 1162, provided a form of government that alleviated social tension and assisted the landed nobility and the flourishing bourgeoisie to collaborate in foreign enterprises. Perpetual

Genoese expansion

By courtesy of the Direzione Antichita, Belle Arti e Storia del Comune di Genova

The port of Genoa, oil painting by C. Grassi, 1597, after an original painting by an unknown artist, 1481. In the Museo Navale, Genoa, Italy.

strife among the magnates, however, led in 1191 to the appointment of a foreign podesta (chief magistrate). Despite further innovations, such as a local *capitano del popolo* ("captain of the people") in 1257, internal dissensions continued to encourage foreign intervention. In 1339 the Genoese Simone Boccanegra bécame the first of a series of local rulers, called "doges," who were chosen for life but could seldom diminish faction and disorder.

Trade rivalries. Genoa's remarkable expansion involved constant struggles with trade rivals. In 1204 the Venetians manipulated the Fourth Crusade to secure predominance in Byzantium; but the Genoese reversed the position by assisting the exiled emperor Michael Palaeologus to recapture Constantinople in 1261. In 1284 Genoa's fleet destroyed Pisan sea power at the Battle of Meloria. Corsica and Sardinia were long-established spheres of influence and colonization, but Genoese merchants were able to penetrate to distant India and England; to set up colonies in the Crimea, at Phocaea with its alum monopoly, and on Chios with its mastic; to bring back slaves and gold from North Africa; and to establish commercial communities in Cyprus and Castile.

Genoa became one of Europe's largest cities; by 1300 its population possibly approached 100,000. It had strong walls, grand patrician palaces, and churches built in black and white marble stripes. Luxurious living standards were based, in part, on imported domestic slaves.

In the 14th century, European colonial rivalries were heightened by a general economic recession and, from 1348, onward, by the disastrous visitations of the Black Death (plague). A series of bitter wars against the Aragonese, who secured control of Sardinia, and against the Venetians came to a climax in 1380, when the Genoese narrowly failed to capture Venice itself.

Genoa was as successful overseas as Venice even though the Genoese lacked the disciplined constitution and public spirit that enabled Venice to run a rigidly state-controlled colonial empire, and despite Genoa's weakness in the face of public bankruptcy and private individualism. From 1396, however, internal disorder resulted in repeated submission to foreign rule by the French and by Milan. The amalgamation in 1405 of many government creditors to form the independent Banco di San Giorgio saved the Genoese government by taking over the disastrous national debt; but the bank secured so many privileges that it came to rival the state itself. After 1453 the Genoese lost all their Black Sea and Levantine colonies except Chios to the Turks, yet they found the resilience to diversify their activities and shift them westward, discovering new commodities and markets. Genoese entrepreneurs intensified their initiatives in Aragon, Castile, and Portugal and participated in new ventures along the African coast and in the Atlantic isles. Christopher Columbus, the discoveror of America in 1492, was a Genoese.

Alliance with Spain. In 1528, in the midst of a great European struggle for supremacy, the famous Genoese admiral Andrea Doria shifted his service from France to the Holy Roman Emperor Charles V (Charles I of Spain); Genoa escaped French domination through a Spanish alliance that allowed Genoese financiers, the great specialists in exchange operations, to handle huge sums for the Spanish crown. The Genoese controlled Spanish and Neapolitan trade, and Peruvian silver poured into their banks; by about 1570 they were the principal bankers of Catholic Europe. Also in 1528 Andrea Doria introduced a new constitution giving power to the magnates, with doges elected for two-year periods. This regime provided an era of more stable though increasingly oligarchic government.

Loss of independence. Real decadence came as Genoa was increasingly excluded from the prosperous Northern and Atlantic economy. Its fortunes were dictated by the great European succession wars. The city was ruinously bombarded by the French in 1684; was occupied in 1746 by the Austrians, against whom there was a popular uprising; and lost its last Mediterranean colony, Corsica, to France in 1768. In 1796 Napoleonic troops occupied Genoa, which sustained a terrible Austrian siege

in margin: Foreign influence

in 1800. The Genoese expelled the French in 1814, but the next year's peace treaty gave Genoa to Piedmont. The resulting discontent, both republican and anti-Piedmontese, shaped Genoa-born Giuseppe Mazzini, the great prophet of the Italian Risorgimento. In 1860 Giuseppe Garibaldi sailed for Sicily from Genoa with his army of liberation.

Genoa since 1860. Genoa became the major port of the new unified Italy, rivalling Marseilles in France. Railway building, industrial development, and shipbuilding yards all inserted Genoa into the great industrial complex of northern Italy, while the Simplon and other Alpine tunnels greatly enlarged its hinterland. The city's population rose from 130,000 in 1871 to about 800,000 in the 1960s. Genoa has an important university and the other attributes of a great modern city. Its revolutionary traditions erupted in a successful insurrection against the Germans in April 1945. The heavy damage sustained during World War II was repaired, and Genoa has remained one of Italy's greatest towns.

BIBLIOGRAPHY. There is no good modern general history of Genoa, since N. LAMBOGLIA *et al.*, *Storia di Genova*, 3 vol. (1941–42), reached only to *c.* 1200. V. VITALE, *Breviario della storia di Genova*, 2 vol. (1955–56), provides an indispensable outline and a guide to the voluminous specialist literature for the period to 1815; for the subsequent period, see his "Genova," in *Enciclopedia Italiana*, vol. 16 (1932). Many useful articles and monographs appear in the *Atti della Società ligure di storia patria*, vol. 1 (1861–). See also R.S. LOPEZ, "Market Expansion: The Case of Genoa," *Journal of Economic History*, 24:445–464 (1964); E. BACH, *La cité de Gênes au XIIe siècle* (1955); and J. HEERS, *Gênes au XVe siècle: activité économique et problèmes sociaux* (1961).

(A.T.L.)

Gentianales

Gentianales is an order of flowering plants that includes more than 12,000 species in five large families and less than 150 species in six smaller ones. Although widely distributed, representatives of the order are most abundant in tropical and subtropical areas. The gentian family (Gentianaceae) is exceptional, however, in having its greatest development in the north Temperate Zone.

Economic importance. Plants noted for their economic importance are found in several families of the order. Species are important sources of food, particularly beverages; others furnish drugs, rubber, and fibres. Many plants, because of their showy flowers or peculiar structure, have gained importance as cultivated garden plants. Some are well-known because of the poisonous qualities of their seeds or vegetative portions.

Food. Coffee is the most widely used product obtained from any representative of the order Gentianales. The genus *Coffea* is a member of the family Rubiaceae, and the number of species considered in the genus varies with the interpretation given the group. One recent study places the species number at about 100; of these, only four are of commercial value. The most important species is *Coffea arabica*. Although the scientific name indicates the Arabian Peninsula as the source of coffee, some botanists now look to Ethiopia as its original home. Introduced into the Americas on the island of Martinique and French Guiana in the early part of the 18th century, it then spread to Brazil and, before the end of the century, was distributed throughout Latin America.

Drugs. Bark from trees of *Cinchona*, also of the family Rubiaceae, yield the drug quinine, which once was used throughout the world to treat malaria. The trees are native in the Andes of South America, and, although more than 40 species are known, only four are of commercial value as sources of quinine. A dwindling supply of bark, resulting from the destruction of *Cinchona* forests, led to cultivation of the species in India, Java, and Ceylon in the mid-19th century. The production of synthetic substitutes for quinine now has relieved much of the need for *Cinchona*.

Rauwolfia serpentina, a native of India in the family Apocynaceae and long used as a minor drug plant, came into prominence when it was shown to be effective in reducing high blood pressure. When demand for the roots

in margin: Coffee species

became so great that depletion of the wild plants was threatened, the government of India placed an embargo on the exportation of the roots. Research has led to the isolation of the active ingredient, an alkaloid called reserpine. An intensive survey of *Rauwolfia* species, prompted by the Indian embargo, demonstrated that reserpine is available in many of the 86 species of the genus, especially *Rauwolfia vomitoria* from tropical Africa and *Rauwolfia tetraphylla* from Central and South America.

Rubber. Rubber is one constituent of the milky juice, or latex, that is found in the well-developed system of tubes common in many species of the families Apocynaceae and Asclepiadaceae. A total of 74 genera and 258 species in the Apocynaceae and 24 genera and 90 species in the Asclepiadaceae contain measurable amounts of rubber. None approaches the importance of *Hevea*, a genus in the family Euphorbiaceae (order Euphorbiales, *q.v.*), although *Funtumia elastica* in the Apocynaceae is extensively planted for its latex throughout tropical Africa, where the climate is too dry for the successful cultivation of *Hevea*. The 20 years of growth necessary before commercial yields of latex are available, however, is an economic disadvantage of *Funtumia*. Species of many other genera in the Apocynaceae, such as *Mascarenhasia elastica*, *Landolphia owariensis*, and *Clitandra elastica* in Africa; *Hancornia speciosa* in Brazil; and *Plumeria rubra* in Mexico, have been exploited for rubber without cultivation.

In the family Asclepiadaceae, *Cryptostegia grandiflora*, originally from Africa, has been distributed to the warmer parts of the world for its rubber content. Extensive investigations of its cultivation and potential as a commercial source of rubber have been made, but difficulties encountered in collecting the latex have thus far retarded its commercial expansion.

Fibres. The fibres from plants of the milkweed genus *Asclepias* of the family Asclepiadaceae were known and utilized by the American Indians prior to the settlement of North America. The milkweeds were introduced as ornamental plants into Europe, where the fibres were rediscovered and used in Germany. No extensive exploitation of *Asclepias* fibres was made, however, because they lack the strength of other materials, such as flax and hemp.

Milkweed floss

The floss fibres on milkweed seeds have been found to contain properties comparable to kapok, the material obtained from seeds of the genus *Ceiba* in the family Bombacaceae (order Malvales, *q.v.*). The *Asclepias* floss has good insulating qualities; surface waxes and oils provide the floss with a buoyancy that could make it commercially valuable.

Ornamentals. Several members of the order Gentianales are prized as ornamentals or curiosities. Species of the genus *Gentiana* (family Gentianaceae) are frequently cultivated and highly recommended as rock garden or wildflower garden plants. The carrion flowers, species of the genus *Stapelia* in the family Asclepiadaceae, have peculiar angular and fleshy or succulent stems and are common representatives in gardens of succulents. Among the herbaceous members of the order Gentianales in cultivation are the species of *Vinca*, or the periwinkles (family Apocynaceae) and the butterfly weed (*Asclepias*) of the family Asclepiadaceae. The shrubs include the yellow Carolina jessimine (*Gelsemium*) and the butterfly bush (*Buddleja*) of the family Loganiaceae. The oleander (*Nerium*) is commonly grown in the hot, dry desert regions, along with the tropical yellow oleander (*Thevetia*); both are in the family Apocynaceae. *Bouvardia* and *Gardenia*, shrubby members of the family Rubiaceae, are cultivated in warm climates. *Allamanda* (Apocynaceae) is a tropical vine grown for its large yellow flowers. *Cryptostegia* is grown for its large, showy, lilac-coloured flowers, in addition to its value as a source of rubber.

Poisons. Poisonous chemicals are common in the family Loganiaceae. The bark of any of 12 species of *Strychnos* serves as the main or secondary ingredient used in the preparation of the arrow poison, curare. The poisonous alkaloids strychnine and brucine are obtained from the Indian species *Strychnos nux-vomica*. The alkaloids of the Saint-Ignatius'-bean of the Philippines (*Strychnos ignatii*) are valued as a remedy for cholera.

The family Apocynaceae is also noted for the poisonous qualities of many of its members. *Nerium oleander*, the oleander commonly planted as an ornamental in arid regions, is highly toxic in the fresh or dry state; poisoning results from eating parts of the plant. Several toxic chemicals have been isolated from the oleander; the glucoside (a sugar-containing substance) oleandrin is the main constituent. Likewise, *Thevetia peruviana*, the yellow oleander, is toxic if ingested, and thevetin is one of many glycosides that has been isolated as an active ingredient.

Structural diversity. Trees and shrubs predominate in the families Rubiaceae, Loganiaceae, and Apocynaceae. Herbs are the common growth form in the Gentianaceae and Menyanthaceae, and both shrubs and herbs are found in the Asclepiadaceae.

The genera *Voyria*, *Leiphaimos*, *Bartonia*, and *Obolaria* of the Gentianaceae are saprophytes, plants that do not produce their own food by photosynthesis but absorb it from dead organic matter. The genus *Dischidia* of the Asclepiadaceae is an epiphyte—a plant that lives upon the branches of trees not as parasites but only for support. To insure a source of water *Dischidia rafflesiana* has developed fleshy leaves modified into pitchers that hold rainwater and debris carried there by ants. Within these pitchers a root system develops to utilize the accumulated water.

Epiphytes also occur in the peculiar genus *Myrmecodia* of the Rubiaceae. The swollen stem of this Malaysian genus is penetrated by numerous irregular galleries that house ants. The adaptive value of this ant-to-plant relationship is not yet understood.

Symbiotic relationships between ants and plants

A similar symbiotic plant and ant relationship is found in the genera *Nauclea* and *Duroia* of the Rubiaceae. Swollen hollow internodes (stem segments) inhabited by ants occur just below the flowers in species of these genera. The position suggests that the ants protect the flowers from unwanted visitors. Species of *Duroia* and *Remijia* have flask-shaped swellings on the leaf bases that are regularly inhabited by ants.

Vines are found in the families Loganiaceae, Apocynaceae, Asclepiadaceae, and Rubiaceae. Some of the American species of *Strychnos* are vines that may attain lengths of 160 feet (50 metres) or more; the common term bushrope is applied to them. In the Apocynaceae the vines, or lianas, may be supported by the twining stem, but in the genera *Landolphia* and *Clitandra* the flower stalks become tendril-like. Both herbaceous and woody vines are common in the family Asclepiadaceae. The frequently cultivated indoor or greenhouse wax plant, *Hoya carnosa*, and *Cryptostegia grandiflora* are climbing representatives of the milkweed family.

Although the family Rubiaceae is composed for the most part of trees and shrubs, the climbing habit is represented by both herbaceous and woody twiners in the genus *Manettia*. In the same family, members of the genus *Uncaria* climb by means of branches that are converted into hooks.

The only truly aquatic representatives of the order are found in the family Menyanthaceae. *Limnanthemum* is a floating aquatic plant; *Menyanthes*, the bogbean, is a marsh plant.

Natural history. Some representatives of the family Gentianaceae depend for normal development on the presence of mycorrhizal fungi—*i.e.*, fungi that live in the roots of the plant (the host) and enter the cells to obtain nutrients by absorbing cell sap. At the same time the fungi provide some nutritive advantage for the host, which digests portions of the fungus.

Methods of pollination in most members of the order are not unusual except for the milkweed family, Asclepiadaceae, in which pollination is complex and unique. In most members of this family the pollen grains are clustered into globules, or sacs, called pollinia. Each stamen (male sexual structure) produces two pollinia, and the

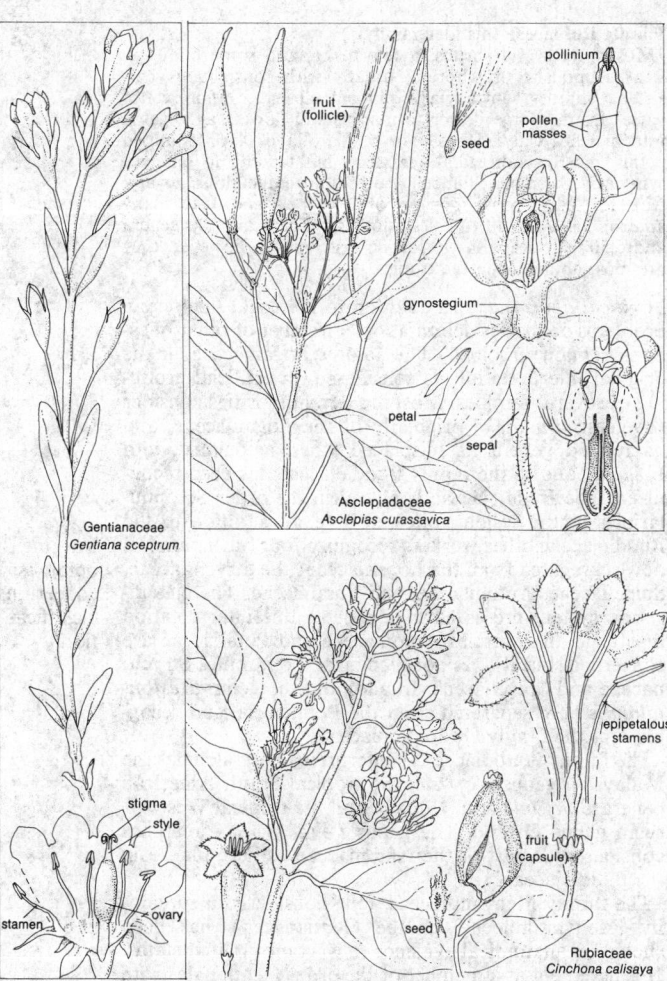

Vegetative and floral features of three of the largest families in the order Gentianales.
Drawing by M. Pahl

pollinia in adjacent anthers (pollen sacs) are connected by a structure called a translator. The translator consists of two arms and an enlarged knob, or corpusculum. The length and form of the arms vary widely and are useful in distinguishing genera.

An insect visiting the flower catches its legs in the slit between the adjacent anthers and contacts the corpusculum. As the insect leaves the flower the sticky corpusculum, arms, and pollinia adhere to the leg and are withdrawn with it, to be deposited upon the more adhesive receptive stigmatic surface (pollen-receiving region of the female structure) of the next flower.

In some members of the family Asclepiadaceae, pollination is similar to that just described, but the pollen is in clusters of four grains, or tetrads, instead of pollinia and is carried from one flower to another in open cornucopia-shaped structures.

Several genera in the Asclepiadaceae that are adapted to desert conditions have developed a fleshy or succulent form. The genus *Stapelia* from Africa and several related genera have fleshy green stems and leaves reduced to scales.

Classification. *Distinguishing taxonomic features.* With few exceptions, the families of this order form a natural group. All except the family Menyanthaceae possess simple, opposite leaves. Most species have the four or five petals of each flower united to form a gamopetalous, or fused tubular, corolla. The presence of phloem, the food-conducting cells, toward the centre of the stem (intraxylary phloem), in addition to its usual position external to the xylem, or water-conducting cells, is characteristic of all the families except the Rubiaceae, Menyanthaceae, and Dialypetalanthaceae. The ovary is superior—located above the sepals, petals, and stamens—in most families; although representatives with inferior or half-inferior ovaries can be found. In the large family Rubiaceae the ovary is normally inferior, but a few species have superior or half-inferior ovaries. The ovules have a single integument, or covering cell layer, and a single-layered nucellus, the central region of the ovule.

The five major families in the order Gentianales—Loganiaceae, Apocynaceae, Asclepiadaceae, Gentianaceae, and Rubiaceae—form a unit through the presence of opposite leaves, radially symmetrical corollas, ovaries composed of two carpels, or ovule-bearing segments, and the single integument and one-layered nucellus of the ovules. The six smaller families are mostly composed of genera that were formerly contained in the larger families; thus, for the most part, they have the same major characteristics as the large families.

Within the order the inferior position of the ovary, associated with the absence of internal phloem, is important in distinguishing the families Rubiaceae and Dialypetalanthaceae. The unusual stamen–pistil structure associated with the complex pollination mechanism separates the family Asclepiadaceae from the other families. The two separate ovaries united by a common style and stigma delimits the family Apocynaceae. The presence of a latex system points to the close association of Asclepiadaceae and Apocynaceae and separates these two families from the Gentianaceae and the Loganiaceae. The members of the Gentianaceae are primarily herbaceous, and the ovaries have parietal placentation; *i.e.*, the ovules are attached to the ovary walls. These two characters help to distinguish the Gentianaceae from the predominantly woody Loganiaceae, in which the placentation is axile—the ovules attach along the central axis of the ovary.

Annotated classification. The position of the ovary has long been considered a fundamental character suitable for placing plant families into orders. Although various authorities have discussed the affinities of the family Rubiaceae to other members of the Gentianales, the classification presented here upsets a tradition of long standing because it combines the orders Rubiales and Gentianales of most systems into the one order, Gentianales.

Three small families whose affinities are not clear also are included in the order. The Desfontainiaceae shows some relationship to the Loganiaceae, but the connection is not yet well-known enough to place the family definitely. The Menyanthaceae, long considered a part of the Gentianaceae, seems misplaced in this order. The compound leaves with alternate arrangement and absence of an internal phloem tend to set this family apart from the order Gentianales. The Dialypetalanthaceae, with its free petals, absence of internal phloem, numerous stamens, and inferior ovary, is also questionably placed in the Gentianales; further study of its single species may reveal a closer relationship to another order.

Recognition of families (margin note)

ORDER GENTIANALES
Trees, shrubs, and herbs with simple opposite leaves, except in the family Menyanthaceae. Phloem (food-conducting tissues) intraxylary—positioned toward the centre of the stem—except in the Menyanthaceae and Rubiaceae. Flowers perfect and hypogynous (with a superior ovary) except in the Rubiaceae. Corolla (collection of petals) of fused petals with 4 or 5 radially symmetrical lobes. Pistil (female structure) of 2 carpels (ovule-bearing components or segments of the pistil) with placentation—ovule attachment—to the ovary walls (parietal) or along the central axis of the ovary (axile); ovules usually numerous with 1 integument (covering) and a 1-layered nucellus (interior). Eleven families with more than 12,000 species distributed mainly in the tropics and subtropics of the world.

Family Loganiaceae
Predominantly woody plants, including lianas. Stipules (leaflike appendages at the base of leafstalks) present but variously developed. Flowers in terminal cymes (clusters that mature from the top downward). Corolla tubular, with 4 or 5 imbricated (overlapping) lobes. Ovary superior or half inferior in *Mitreola*; 2-celled with axile placentation and numerous anatropous (inverted and straight) ovules. Seeds wingless or winged, fruit a capsule. Twenty-one genera and about 500 species, distributed mostly in the tropics.

Family Antoniaceae
With the characters of Loganiaceae except with numerous overlapping scales subtending the calyx (collection of sepals);

corolla lobes valvate (not overlapping but touching edge to edge); seeds winged at each end or all around. Four genera and 8 species distributed in Malay Peninsula, tropical America, and tropical Africa.

Family Potaliaceae

With the characters of Loganiaceae except corolla contorted, of 5 to 16 lobes; fruit, a berry. Three genera and 65 species with tropical distribution.

Family Desfontainiaceae

With the characters of Loganiaceae except leaves spinose; flowers solitary or few and located terminally on stems; pistil 5-carpelled, 5-loculed (chambered). One genus and 5 species distributed in tropical South America.

Family Apocynaceae (dogbane family)

Trees, shrubs, and herbs, usually with a well-developed latex (milky-juice) system. Stipules absent. Inflorescence many-flowered, rarely of solitary flowers. Calyx lobes parted nearly to the base. Corolla salverform (trumpet-shaped) or funnel-form, the lobes contorted in the bud. Corona (a raised structure) or appendages of hairs or scales commonly found in the corolla throat or tube. Stamens attached to the petals (epipetalous) with anthers that open toward the central axis of the flower (introrse) on short filaments. Pistil of 2 carpels with free (not fused) ovaries united by a common style (the narrow upper part of the pistil) and a club-shaped stigma (pollen-receiving surface). Fruit commonly follicular (a pod that splits open) with one or both carpels maturing; rarely berrylike. Seeds numerous, comose (bearing a tuft of soft hairs) or winged. Nectar-producing glands common at base of ovary. There are 155 genera and 1,000 species distributed mainly in tropical and subtropical regions.

Family Plocospermataceae

Similar to Apocynaceae but pistil 1-loculed with 2 parietal placentae; style twice-bifid (bisected or parted into 2 branches) with 4 small clavate (club-shaped) stigmas; 2 ovules in each carpel. One genus with 3 species distributed in Mexico and Central America.

Family Asclepiadaceae (milkweed family)

Herbs or commonly herbaceous or shrubby climbers, rarely shrubs or trees; with well-developed latex system. Sepals 5 and deeply divided. Petals 5, united; lobes contorted or less commonly valvate. Stamens 5, epipetalous; filaments short and occasionally, along with corolla, bearing appendages and elaborated into complex structures. Corona single or double. Pistil 2-carpelled, with the 2 superior ovaries and styles free and the 2 stigmas united into an enlarged and flattened, conical or beaked stigmatic head. Cohering with the stigmatic head are the 5 anthers, which reduce the pollen-receiving portion of the stigma to 5 lines between the anthers. Fruit follicular with occasionally only 1 of the 2 carpels maturing. Seeds commonly comose. There are 280 genera and 2,000 species distributed mainly in the tropics.

Family Gentianaceae (gentian family)

Annual or perennial herbs, rarely shrubs, with opposite leaves that lack stipules. Sepals 4 or 5, variously divided. Petals 4 or 5 united but often deeply divided, the lobes usually contorted in the bud; hairs or scales common in corolla throat. Nectar-secreting pits with fringed margins often present near the base of the perianth segments (sepals and petals). Stamens epipetalous, anthers opening introrsely by longitudinal slits or, in *Exacum*, by terminal pores. Pistil of 2 carpels with a single style and 2-lobed stigma. Ovary with 1 locule and parietal placentae except in tribe Exacineae, which has a 2-loculed ovary and axile placentation. Ovules numerous and variously marked and winged. There are 65 genera and 1,100 species distributed mainly in the northern temperate zones of the world.

Family Menyanthaceae

Aquatic or marsh herbs with alternate, entire or trifoliolate (of 3 leaflets) leaves that have sheathing petioles (leafstalks). Intraxylary phloem absent. Sepals 5, united, valvate. Stamens 5; epipetalous near the base of the corolla tube or between the corolla lobes. Pistil of 2 carpels with a 1-loculed ovary and 2 parietal placentae; ovary superior except in *Villarsia*, which is half-inferior; style 1; stigmas 2; ovules numerous. There are 5 genera and 33 species distributed in the northern and southern temperate regions of the world.

Family Dialypetalanthaceae

Tree with opposite leaves. Intraxylary phloem absent. Flowers in bracteate (furnished with bracts—small scalelike appendages) many-flowered terminal inflorescences (clusters). Calyx of 4 sepals adnate (fused) to the ovary. Petals 4, free. Stamens numerous, ranging from 16 to 25, free from the corolla. Pistil of 2 carpels; 2 locules. Ovary inferior with axile placentation and numerous ovules. The family contains only 1 genus and 1 species (*Dialypetalanthus fuscescens*) distributed in Brazil.

Family Rubiaceae (madder family)

Mostly trees and shrubs, a few herbs, and some climbers. Leaves opposite or whorled; usually with conspicuous persistent stipules. Intraxylary phloem absent. Inflorescence varies from 1 large flower to many small flowers aggregated into a head. Calyx lobes 4 or 5. Corolla of 4 or 5 united petals, mostly with radial symmetry but tending to bilateral symmetry in some. Stamens 4 or 5 and epipetalous. Ovary, with few exceptions, inferior, of 2 carpels and 1 to many anatropous ovules. Fruit fleshy or dry. There are 500 genera and 6,500 species with worldwide distribution; however, they are most abundant in the tropics.

Critical appraisal. In addition to the usual taxonomic problems of species delimitation, a number of other questions remain unsolved. The family Loganiaceae, in its original interpretation, is considered an artificial grouping of several families. Most modern authorities consider the genus *Buddleja*, originally of the Loganiaceae, and its related genera as misplaced when associated with *Logania*, and so the family Buddlejaceae has been recognized. The Buddlejaceae is placed in the order Scrophulariales in the system followed here. In addition to the Buddlejaceae other workers recognize four other families now segregated from the Loganiaceae: the Strychnaceae, Spigeliaceae, Antoniaceae, and Potaliaceae. The classification system presented here accepts this interpretation insofar as the families Antoniaceae and Potaliaceae are concerned, but it does not recognize the families Strychnaceae and Spigeliaceae. In addition, the genus *Desfontainia* is here separated from the Potaliaceae and recognized as the family Desfontainiaceae. Varying opinions concerning classification

The family Antoniaceae as interpreted here includes the Malaysian genus *Norrisia*, the tropical South American genera *Bonyunia* and *Antonia*, and the tropical West African genus *Usteria*. The genus *Peltanthera*, sometimes considered as part of the Antoniaceae, is here placed in the Buddlejaceae.

The family Menyanthaceae, long considered a subfamily (Menyanthoideae) of the Gentianaceae, has been shown on anatomical evidence to warrant familial status. It is here kept as a member of the order Gentianales with the recognition that its relationships are not altogether clear. Some other classification systems, however, associate the Menyanthaceae with the order Polemoniales, justifying this move more on its differences from the Gentianales than its similarities to the Polemoniales.

The monotypic (containing a single genus and species) family Dialypetalanthaceae is also a family of questionable relationships. It is here kept in the Gentianales although there are few characters to warrant the association. Some workers consider it a second family, along with Rubiaceae, in the order Rubiales. Still others question its relationship but consider it best placed in the order Myrtales.

The placement of the family Rubiaceae into the order Gentianales, as is done here, represents a break from the long-standing tradition of separating families with superior ovaries from those with inferior ovaries. Although the close relationship of the Rubiaceae to the Loganiaceae is recognized by many prominent taxonomists, most continue to maintain the order Rubiales separate from the Gentianales.

To accept the Gentianales as outlined above will require a reappraisal of the generally accepted fundamental nature of the position of the ovary. The importance of intraxylary phloem, a single integument, and the thin nucellar tissue as ordinal characters all need further evaluation under this scheme of classification.

BIBLIOGRAPHY. F.J. WELLMAN, *Coffee* (1961), a popular detailed account of the history, distribution, and production of coffee; P.C. STANDLEY, "The Rubiaceae of Ecuador," *Publs. Field Mus. Nat. Hist. 285 (Bot. Series)*, 7:179–251 (1931), a taxonomic treatment of the family with a detailed history of quinine; R.E. WOODSON *et al.*, *Rauwolfia: Botany, Pharmacognosy, Chemistry, and Pharmacology* (1957), a technical study of the genus *Rauwolfia*; LOREN G. POLHAMUS, *Rubber: Botany, Production, and Utilization* (1962), a popular account of rubber; A. GERALDINE WHITING (comp.), "A Summary of the Literature on Milkweeds (*Asclepias* spp.) and Their Utilization," *Biblphical. Bull. U.S. Dep. Agric. Libr. 2* (1943), discusses in layman's terms the use of milkweed fibres; o.a. STEVENS, *Cultivation of Milkweed* (1945), discusses methods of propagation, cultivation, and yield of milkweed; A.A. LINDSEY, "Anatomical Evidence for the Menyanthaceae," *Am. J. Bot.*, 25:480–485 (1938), a technical paper comparing the anatomy of Menyanthaceae and Gentianaceae; and by the same author, "Floral Anatomy in the Gentianaceae," *Am. J. Bot.*, 27:640–651 (1940), a technical paper; B.A. KRUKOFF and J. MONACHINO, "The American Species of *Strychnos*," *Brittonia*, 4:248–322 (1943), a technical paper with a discussion of *Strychnos* and curare.

(C.T.M.,Jr.)

Gentz, Friedrich von

A passionate opponent of the French Revolution and Napoleon and a confidential adviser to the conservative Austrian statesman Clemens von Metternich, Friedrich von Gentz may also be counted among the most cogent thinkers and best stylists in the German language. His works remain a rich source for the history of Europe in the Napoleonic and post-Napoleonic era.

Gentz, portrait by Sir Thomas Lawrence (1769–1830). In Windsor Castle, Berkshire.

Gentz was born on May 2, 1764, in Breslau, then part of Prussian Silesia. His father was a Prussian civil servant; his mother came from the French Huguenot colony of Berlin, with which young Gentz liked to associate. Up to an advanced age, he wrote his diaries in French, which he wrote with the same limpid elegance that distinguished his German. Gentz studied under the great German philosopher Immanuel Kant in Königsberg. Although Gentz soon rejected the philosopher's republican idealism, radicalism, and pacifism, Kant was to have a lasting influence on his thought. Essentially self-taught, Gentz acquired his historical, juridical, and economic knowledge from books, chiefly English works.

In 1785 Gentz entered the Prussian civil service in Berlin, and in 1793 he became a secretary in the General-direktorium (War Office). Dissatisfied with his position, Gentz threw himself into the social life of the capital. For a brief period in the 1790s, Berlin—with its admixture of French émigrés, Russian, English, and Austrian aristocrats, writers, and bohemian artists from all over Germany—formed one of the intellectual centres of Europe. In this somewhat dissolute society Gentz gained a reputation as a brilliant conversationalist, ladies' man, gambler, and spendthrift. His marriage dissolved after a few years, and Gentz, who lacked the family man's temperament, did not marry again.

With the outbreak of the French Revolution, Gentz began his career as a political writer. As a pupil of Kant, he had at first hailed the Revolution as the "awakening of mankind." But he soon began to criticize the Revolution and ended by combatting it. In 1793 he published a German translation of Edmund Burke's *Reflections on the Revolution in France;* thereafter, Burke, the great

Influence of Burke

English conservative, remained for Gentz the master whose ideas most closely reflected his own and whose style he admired and imitated. In two periodicals he acquired or founded anew, *Neue deutsche Monatsschrift* and *Historisches Journal*, as well as in brochures published at irregular intervals from 1800 on, Gentz continued to analyze the great drama that unfolded in France: internal affairs and foreign policy and their correlation; the imperialism of the Jacobin extremists; and the affairs of the Directory and Napoleon. Gentz's writings of 1795–1802 are still uncannily topical. His attitude, which would now be called that of a conservative liberal, made him advocate the preservation of civic liberties against autocratic egalitarianism, the defense of the rule of law throughout Europe against illegitimate imperialism, and the maintenance of the equilibrium of powers against the encroachments of the one universal state, which, in his view, all French governments after 1793 were bound to strive for. In particular, Gentz pointed out the differences between the American and the French revolutions, seeing in the former a defense of historical rights against British usurpation, in the latter on antihistorical, aggressive, ideology-laden undertaking. This view found expression in various articles, notably in Gentz's reflections on the death of George Washington, probably the soundest European comment on that event. These political investigations were complemented by economic research, as in the great essay *Über die britische Finanzverwaltung*, which, translated into English, aroused the admiration of the British statesman William Pitt the younger.

As a politician, Gentz strove for a coalition of "Free Europe" against French despotism, a new and a better coalition after the failure of the old one. But, since Prussia observed a policy of strict neutrality during the period 1795–1806, Gentz's position in Berlin became increasingly untenable. In 1803 he accordingly moved to Vienna, the centre, as he hoped, of the Continent's resistance to Napoleon. He had visited London the year before and had been warmly welcomed as an ally by the royal family, the Cabinet, the opposition, and the press. Henceforth, he received sizable financial support from England, as he later did from many European rulers and governments. His acceptance of subsidies, however, does not necessarily imply that he was corrupt. For, while it is true that he liked to live in grand style, he accepted money only from those whose views were more or less in harmony with his own. In return, he gave his supporters the benefit, orally or in writing, of his free and independent opinion; if they wanted anything else, he broke off his connection with them.

As an independent adviser to the foreign ministry in Vienna, Gentz continued to propagandize his idea of a great European alliance that would act as one body in war or peace: "If war breaks out anywhere in Europe, you may be assured that it was I who started it." The net result of his efforts, however, was a series of disappointments: the War of the Third Coalition (1805–07) ended with the allied defeat at the Battle of Austerlitz and a rapprochement between Russia and France, and the Fourth Coalition ended with a Franco-Austrian alliance cemented by Napoleon's marriage to a Habsburg archduchess. Napoleon's decree of 1806, excluding English goods from the Continent, had the effect of jeopardizing Gentz's contacts with England, so that funds and messages from that country reached him only rarely and in insufficient measure. Gentz found himself in a state of melancholy isolation; by 1810 his advocacy of European freedom had begun to weaken.

Gentz's friendship with the new Austrian foreign minister, Metternich, helped him gain access to the Vienna state chancery, this time with the regular title of *Hofrat* (privy councillor). Metternich, whom he admired as a sceptical, worldly-wise man of affairs and a pragmatic politician, became his mentor; Gentz, in turn, became the all-powerful minister's propagandist and confidential adviser.

The War of Liberation that began with Napoleon's catastrophe in Russia and ended with his overthrow evoked

Association with Metternich

little enthusiasm in Gentz's tired spirit. He who had so long called Europe to arms against the French now wished to maintain Napoleon on his throne. He feared that Napoleon's fall would result in France in a new outbreak of radical Jacobinism and in Europe in the ascendancy of Russia—a state of affairs that he abhorred perhaps even more than French hegemony.

Gentz reached the peak of success at a time when his energies had already begun to flag. He was allowed to officiate as secretary general of the great congresses of the immediate post-Napoleonic era—those held at Vienna, Aachen (Aix-la-Chapelle), Troppau, Laibach, and Verona. It was a position that entailed many advantages by way of orders and decorations, influence, and money. As he had earlier formulated the Austrian and Prussian war manifestos against Napoleon, so he now wrote up, with the same untiring skill, the protocols of these European congresses. Yet these belated successes, unprecedented for a mere literary man, do not seem to have given him any lasting satisfaction; on the contrary, one often encounters in his diaries for this period a sense of bitterness and disillusionment, sometimes of outright cynicism. In measure as the "European System" (the post-Napoleonic alliances) weakened and finally broke down, Gentz's activities, which had at one time encompassed the Continent, were now restricted to Austria alone.

These activities were of a rigidly conservative and purely defensive nature. The idea of "European freedom" was replaced by the old order of the Continent, an idealized 18th century, which Gentz defended against the 19th. Whether it was a question of Greeks and Serbs rising up against the Turks, Spanish liberals against Bourbon absolutism, Latin Americans against Spain, German students against the German police state, or Italians fighting against the pope, the Austrians, and their own native rulers, Gentz, by lending his pen to Metternich's policy of intervention, would invariably be found on the side of the threatened old powers. He had, to be sure, demonstrated his courage in the struggle against Napoleon; but in his innermost heart he was a nervous and timid man, not without neurotic traits, who feared nothing so much as a repetition of the French Revolution. It is likely that he also felt that his own cultural background, let alone his way of life, was bound up with the old order of Europe. To his friends, he justified his attitude by arguing that, while the new—liberalism, democracy, nationalism—would surely prevail in the end, there also had to be those who did their best to retard and soften their impact. His own nature, he intimated, had predestined him for this historical service of fighting mere rearguard actions.

The last chapter in Gentz's life was a personal one: his liaison, at the age of 66, with young Fanny Elssler, a ballerina immortalized on a Vienna monument as "the smile of her century." It was his final triumph and his first complete happiness, and, when it paled, it was time for him to die (June 9, 1832). His possessions had to be auctioned off in order to satisfy the creditors. Metternich paid for the funeral.

In the eyes of a majority of his contemporaries, the mature Gentz was a shameless reactionary, a hireling of the kings, and a traitor to his own youthful convictions. The publication of his collected works and of his astoundingly extensive correspondence mitigated this verdict in the opinion of those who had a feeling for quality. Gentz's most personal documents reveal him as a man of high integrity who scorned hyperbole and demagogic falsehood and unsparingly criticized both himself and those on whose behalf he laboured. Scholars have disputed among themselves as to whether he was actually a Romantic or perhaps a Rationalist; but the question is badly put, for he was too intelligent a man to follow blindly the doctrines of any school.

BIBLIOGRAPHY. PAUL R. SWEET, *Friedrich von Gentz, Defender of the Old Order* (1941), is the definitive biography insofar as there is one. See also GOLO MANN, *Secretary of Europe: The Life of Friedrich Gentz, Enemy of Napoleon* (1946); K. MENDELSSOHN-BARTHOLDY, *Friedrich von Gentz: Ein Beitrag zur Geschichte Oesterreichs im neunzehnten Jahrhundert* (1867); and E. GUGLIA, *Friedrich von Gentz: Eine biographische Studie* (1901).

(G.Ma.)

Geochemical Equilibria at High Temperatures and Pressures

Earth scientists engaged in experimental studies are usually concerned either with geochemical reactions occurring near the surface of the Earth or with reactions occurring within the Earth. Sediments are deposited within the ocean or the hydrosphere (that is, the water portion of the Earth, as distinguished from the solid part) or beneath the atmosphere. The ocean provides a near-surface environment with a restricted range of temperature and pressure, compared with that for the formation of igneous rocks, which are produced by partial melting of material at depth, and metamorphic rocks, which are altered by high temperature and pressure after their original formation (see Figure 1). Another distinction between geochemical equilibria under these two rather disparate sets of conditions is that reactions occurring at or near the surface of the Earth are dominated by solutions. They are controlled more by changes in composition of the solutions than by changes in temperature and pressure, which are the main variables influencing deep-seated geochemical reactions.

The Earth is a chemical system that responds to changes in physical factors; that is, in the values of the physical properties that determine its characteristics and behaviour. Geochemistry, the study of the Earth's chemistry, is concerned with the distribution and migration of elements in the Earth, with the factors controlling their migrations, and with the history of the migrations. The classical geochemical approach is to study rocks now exposed at the surface and to deduce their history at or during the time they were buried within the Earth. This approach has been increasingly supplemented since 1950 by laboratory experiments. By applying appropriate pressures and temperatures to selected minerals and rocks and examining the products of this simulation of conditions believed to exist within the Earth, the reactions that can occur are determined directly. This approach provides an experimental probe through the crust of the Earth and into the upper part of the mantle. The results clarify and evaluate those from the classical approach and facilitate comparison of rival hypotheses.

The range of pressures and temperatures that occurs within the Earth's upper 100 kilometres (60 miles) can be reproduced in the laboratory with reasonable precision. Some apparatus can reproduce conditions at depths of about 600 kilometres (370 miles) but with less precision. The pressure–temperature ($P–T$) ranges of some geological and geophysical reactions are shown in Figure 1.

From P.J. Wyllie, *The Dynamic Earth: Textbook in Geosciences* (1971); John Wiley & Sons

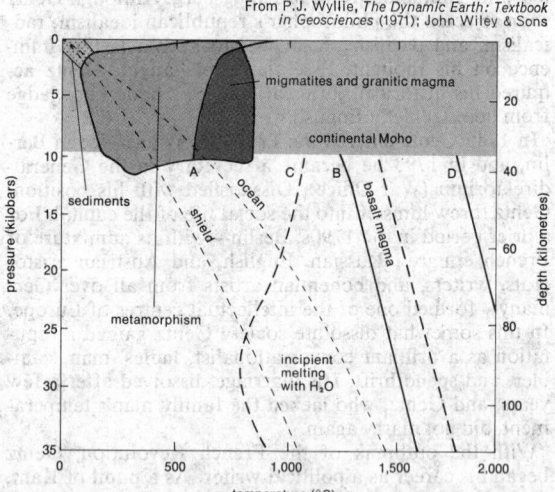

Figure 1: Ranges of pressure and temperature within which major geological processes occur. Dotted lines are estimated geotherms showing temperatures at specific depths beneath the oceans and beneath the continental shields (see text).

Metamorphism occurs up to pressures of about 10,000 atmospheres (one atmosphere is the pressure at sea level, 14.7 pounds per square inch), corresponding to the Moho depth—about 35 kilometres (22 miles) beneath the average continental crust. Line A marks the beginning of magma (*i.e.*, partially or completely melted rock materials) generation at higher temperatures. The upper mantle is believed to have a chemical composition between the plutonic rock types gabbro and peridotite. The subsolidus mineralogical changes occurring in gabbro and peridotite at pressures above 10,000 atmospheres are correlated with physical properties and boundaries within the Earth determined by geophysical methods. The zone above the line B shows conditions for the generation of basaltic magmas by partial fusion of mantle peridotite. Incipient melting can occur between the lines B and C in the mantle if traces of water are present. Geochemical reactions, like other chemical reactions, may be reversible; that is, the products of the reaction may themselves react to reform the original substances. If the rate of formation of the products and the rate of reformation of the original reactants are equal, the reaction is in equilibrium. The rate of a chemical reaction is expressed in terms of concentration, and the ratio of the two rates is embodied in what is known as the law of mass action, which is used to interpret the phenomena of geochemical equilibrium. See GEOCHEMICAL EQUILIBRIA AT LOW TEMPERATURES AND PRESSURES; HIGH-PRESSURE PHENOMENA; PHASE CHANGES AND EQUILIBRIA; THERMODYNAMICS, PRINCIPLES OF; ACID-BASE REACTIONS AND EQUILIBRIA; and EARTH, STRUCTURE AND COMPOSITION OF. For additional information on Earth materials and environments, see also MINERALS; IGNEOUS ROCKS; METAMORPHIC ROCKS; SEDIMENTARY ROCKS; ORE DEPOSITS; and ELEMENTS, GEOCHEMICAL DISTRIBUTION OF.

THERMODYNAMIC PRINCIPLES RELEVANT TO GEOLOGICAL–GEOPHYSICAL STUDIES

Systems, phases, and components. A system is any portion of the universe selected for consideration. In the thermodynamic sense, a system is an assemblage of material bodies interacting among themselves and distinguished from the surrounding medium by certain characteristics. Conditions in the Earth do not correspond precisely to those of ideal thermodynamic systems, but the latter provide concepts for the study of natural systems.

Closed and open systems

A closed system is one with walls that permit exchange of heat with the surroundings but no exchange of matter and is characterized by a fixed chemical composition. An open system can exchange heat and matter with the surrounding medium under controlled conditions. In geochemistry, the word system is usually used to describe the whole range of compositions that can be produced by mixing specified end-members (components).

The material within a system can exist in solid, liquid, or vapour state, given appropriate conditions of P and T. Each homogeneous portion of a system differing in composition or state and bounded by a surface is called a phase. Phases can theoretically be separated from each other by mechanical methods.

Components are defined as the smallest number of independently variable composition terms that are necessary and sufficient to express algebraically the compositions of all phases present in a system at equilibrium. Systems may be classified as one-component (unary), two-component (binary), etc., or multi-component, according to the number of components required to express the compositions of the phases present through the $P–T$ range under consideration.

Phase diagrams and the phase rule. When minerals are heated they may change into other polymorphic forms (*i.e.*, they may change in crystalline structure), they may dissociate into two phases, or they may melt; at high pressures, many minerals are transformed into dense polymorphs. All of these transformations are called phase changes. The most successful method yet devised for recording phase changes is the use of phase diagrams, which show the equilibrium relationships among various phases in terms of the variables T, P, and concentrations

of components (X). These are intensive parameters (*i.e.*, specific properties), the magnitudes of which do not depend on the size of the system.

For material of a given composition, such as granite or gabbro in the crust or peridotite in the mantle, the composition is defined. The phase changes can then be plotted on a $P–T$ diagram. In order to show the compositions of the phases at various points, supplemental diagrams are required. There are $(n - 1)$ independent concentration variables in an n-component system, n representing any given number. Graphical representation of phase compositions in a four-component system thus requires three dimensions, or a tetrahedron; for more complex systems, graphical representation is difficult.

The number of the variables P, T, and X, which must be arbitrarily fixed in order to define completely the state of a system at equilibrium, is called the number of degrees of freedom (f), or the variance of the system. The variance is the largest number of intensive parameters that can change independently of each other without decreasing the number of coexisting phases. A divariant ($f = 2$; that is, there are two degrees of freedom) phase assemblage occupies an area on a $P–T$ phase diagram; P and T can be changed independently of each other, and the number of phases does not change. At a given P and T, however, the compositions of the phases are fixed because there are no more degrees of freedom. A univariant ($f = 1$) phase assemblage traces a line, and an invariant ($f = 0$) phase assemblage can occur only at a single point on a $P–T$ diagram.

The variance of a system is defined for p coexistent phases, each of which contains the same c independently variable components, by the Gibbs phase rule: $f = c - p + 2$. The number 2 arises from two assumptions: (1) that the state of the system is defined by the concentration variables and only two others, namely, P and T—if other variables have to be taken into account, such as the force of gravity, electrical fields, or surface effects, then the number 2 has to be modified; (2) that the pressure is constant throughout the system, in particular across each interface. The second assumption is not true in the case of osmotic equilibrium between two liquids, and it is possible to have a system in which the pressure on the fluid phase is less than the pressure on solid phases; these conditions occur within the Earth. If there are two independent pressure variables in a system, then the "operating" phase rule becomes $f = c - p + 3$.

Systems in the Earth's crust

The mineralogical phase rule. The mineralogy of rocks suggests that a close approach to chemical equilibrium is attained during many deep-seated processes. Consider a block of the crust of uniform composition with the same assemblage of minerals throughout; this assemblage may be treated as a system. During its formation the pressure varied from the top to the bottom of the block. The geotherms (lines showing the temperatures at specific depths) in Figure 1 indicate that the temperature also would have varied, as a function of pressure. The mineral assemblage present is therefore at least divariant. For a divariant closed rock system with P and T the only intensive variables, the Gibbs phase rule becomes: $2 = c - p + 2$, or $p = c$. The variance may be greater than 2, and, for equilibrium mineral assemblages formed in finite rock masses within the Earth, the Norwegian mineralogist Victor Moritz Goldschmidt stated the mineralogical phase rule: $p \leq c$ (p is less than or equal to c), or the maximum number of minerals that can coexist in rocks in stable equilibrium is equal to the number of components.

The phase rule for open systems. When solutions and magmas migrate within the Earth, geochemical reactions and equilibria can be represented in terms of open rather than closed systems. In a thermodynamic model for an open system there are two kinds of components: inert and mobile. Inert components, c_i, remain with the system; their concentrations are defined by the initial conditions. Perfectly mobile components, c_m, can migrate in or out of the system during reactions; the chemical potentials of the mobile components are defined by conditions external to the system, regardless of what happens in the system. The state of an open system is defined in terms of P, T, x_i for the inert components and the chemical potentials of the mobile components. The phase rule for such a system is $f = c_i - p + (2 + c_m)$. A finite rock mass at equilibrium under these conditions has at least $2 + c_m$ degrees of freedom, and the mineralogical phase rule for an open system therefore becomes $p \le c_i$, or the maximum number of minerals that can coexist in rocks is equal to the number of inert components. The number of mobile components in a rock system, according to this rule, equals the difference between the total number of components ($c_m + c_i$) and the maximum number of minerals observed in the rock.

Many rock systems have been open to components such as water (H_2O) and carbon dioxide (CO_2), but it is probably rare for conditions to approach those of the model thermodynamic open system. Rocks are usually permeated by a limited amount of pore fluid (*i.e.*, a film, varying in thickness and nature, between the grains of a rock), and reaction of the fluid with the minerals changes its composition and the chemical potentials of the mobile components in the fluid. Only if large quantities of fluid flow through a rock, as in metasomatic processes (*i.e.*, replacement processes, in which new minerals of different chemical composition are produced by the introduction of material from external sources), are conditions in the thermodynamic open systems likely to be approximated. Components may be mobile but only rarely perfectly mobile.

Reaction kinetics and available time. Thermodynamics is concerned only with systems at equilibrium. Phase diagrams provide no information about the stages through which a system may pass nor anything about the rate of attainment of equilibrium. One of the major difficulties in experimental geochemistry is the attainment and recognition of stable equilibrium conditions during the short times that runs may be made in laboratory apparatus.

During the immense span of geological time, even very sluggish reactions have a good prospect of going to completion, and there is evidence that a close approach to equilibrium was achieved during the formation of many metamorphic and igneous rocks at high pressures. Equilibrium conditions are not maintained, however, as shown by the fact that rocks formed within the Earth have become exposed at the surface, with little or no change in mineralogy resulting from the large decrease in P and T. This phenomenon relates to factors such as reaction rates under conditions of decreasing T and P and the availability of fluxes such as water.

PHASE EQUILIBRIA IN MINERAL SYSTEMS

One-component, two-component, and multi-component systems. There are several approaches to the use of phase equilibria concepts that apply to petrological (*i.e.*, ore, mineral, and rock) and geochemical investigations. One approach is to study the phase relationships of a single mineral. For example, Figure 2 shows univariant phase transition boundaries for the one-component systems silicon dioxide (SiO_2), calcium carbonate ($CaCO_3$), and aluminum silicate (Al_2SiO_5). These boundaries provide limits for the conditions of formation of rocks containing the polymorphs involved. Another approach is to study a synthetic mineral assemblage or system, as a model for the more complex rock system under consideration. A third approach is to work with whole-rock multicomponent systems and to determine the conditions for the occurrence of specific reactions; the conditions can be plotted on P–T diagrams, but the compositions of phases involved have to be represented separately.

Solid–solid reactions. Several types of solid–solid mineral reactions are shown in Figure 2. There are polymorphic transitions in unary systems as mentioned above. Minerals that are stable in the Earth's crust may become unstable at high pressures, as shown by the breakdown of plagioclase feldspar (albite–anorthite solid solutions) to yield quartz and the dense minerals jadeite, kyanite, and zoisite. The stability range may be affected considerably if other minerals are involved. The reaction of anorthite with forsterite is shown at pressures much lower

The formation of rocks

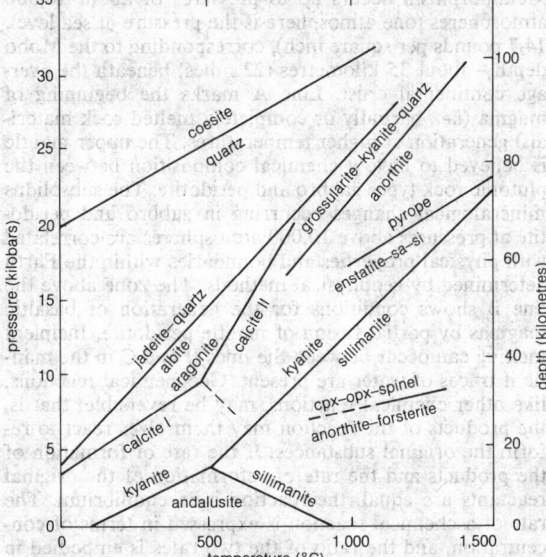

Figure 2: Solid–solid phase transitions in simple mineral systems. Abbreviations: cpx—clinopyroxene; opx—orthopyroxene; sa—sapphirine; si—sillimanite.

than the breakdown of anorthite alone. Many minerals can form stably only at high pressures, as illustrated by the formation of pyrope garnet from three other minerals. Changes of temperature or pressure may affect the compositions of coexisting minerals, and this is another important type of solid–solid reaction, one that cannot be illustrated conveniently on a P–T diagram.

The reactions in Figure 2 are all univariant. In multicomponent rock systems, many similar reactions are divariant or multi-variant, and they occur through a transition interval. One of the most significant is the transformation of gabbro, a rock which generally consists of calcic plagioclase and augite (a clinopyroxene), to eclogite, a rock with the same composition but different mineralogy. This transformation involves transitions similar to the reactions plotted in Figure 2; plagioclase and augite become unstable, and jadeitic pyroxene and pyrope are produced at their expense. Experimental determination of this complex transformation is difficult because reaction rates become extremely slow at temperatures below 900° C (1,650° F).

Dissociation reactions. Carbonates and hydrous minerals (*i.e.*, minerals with the hydroxyl group in their structure) are stable only to their dissociation temperatures. The general shape of univariant dehydration reactions is shown in Figure 3 by the curves for serpentine, muscovite, amphibole, and phlogopite; and the curve for magnesite is the sole example given of a decarbonation reaction. The dissociation temperatures of individual minerals are lowered if other minerals become involved, as shown by the curves for serpentine + brucite and muscovite + quartz.

The curves for hydrous or carbonated minerals and assemblages show the maximum temperatures for their stability under subsolidus conditions (*i.e.*, below the melting temperatures of the chemical system). Dissociation temperatures are lowered if the partial pressure of the volatile component involved, water (H_2O) or carbon dioxide (CO_2), respectively, is decreased compared to the total pressure on the solid minerals. This condition can arise in natural rock systems if the pore fluid contains additional components or if the pore fluid pressure is less than the load pressure, a condition that could occur if the vapour released migrates away from the rock. The dashed line for total pressures greater than 2,000 atmospheres shows the dissociation of muscovite + quartz if P_{H_2O} is maintained constant at 2,000 atmospheres. This line is a contour for constant P_{H_2O} on a divariant surface for the reaction in a system in which there are three independent variables, P_{total}, P_{H_2O}, and T (see discussion of open systems).

Behaviour of rock-forming minerals

The temperature of dissociation increases with pressure, and for many minerals melting temperatures may be reached. Invariant points in Figure 3 show the pressures above which phlogopite, muscovite, and muscovite + quartz dissociate to yield a liquid rather than a vapour phase. Some amphibole minerals behave the same. In the presence of a liquid phase, in contrast with the subsolidus dissociation reactions, the stability temperatures for hydrous minerals are increased if the partial pressure of water (H_2O) is decreased compared with the total pressure, shown by the curves for phlogopite in Figure 3.

With increasing pressure, the slope of the curve (dP/dT) of dissociation reactions, representing the rate of change of Pressure with Temperature, also increases toward the vertical. The slope for the dissociation curve of amphibole changes from positive to negative at pressures above about 18,000 atmospheres, in which region magnesian garnet and jadeitic pyroxene are produced; the change in slope from positive to negative is thus related to the gabbro–eclogite phase transition and the formation of dense minerals.

Geological processes include not only dissociation reactions but also hydration and carbonation reactions. The

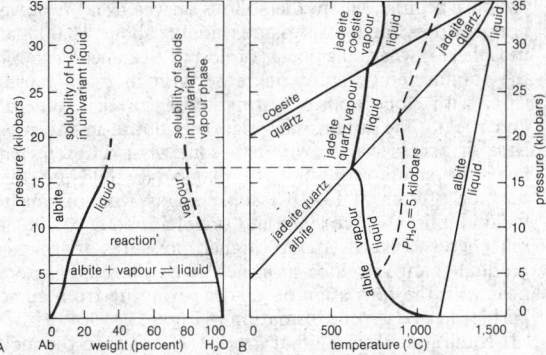

Figure 4: *Phase relationships for composition on the join albite–water.*
(A) Variations in composition of phases for the reaction albite + vapour = liquid. (B) Univariant melting curves and solid–solid transitions (see text).
From A. Boettcher and P. Wyllie, "Phase Relationships in the System NaAlSiO₄–SiO₂–H₂O to 35 Kilobars Pressure," *American Journal of Science*, Vol. 267 (1969)

Multi-component rock systems also have melting intervals. The curve for the beginning of melting of peridotite is shown in Figure 5, with a steep positive slope. The melting interval for peridotite is indicated in Figure 1 between the lines B and D. The composition of the liquid produced by partial melting of the peridotite, within a temperature interval above the solidus, corresponds in composition to basaltic magmas; the composition varies with temperature above the solidus, and with pressure.

Melting in the presence of water. Also shown in Figure 4B is the effect of water vapour under pressure on the melting temperature of albite. There is initially a marked decrease in melting temperature; this effect is reduced above a few thousand atmospheres, but the slope (dP/dT) of the univariant reaction remains negative until albite breaks down. At the invariant point generated by the formation of jadeite and quartz, the solidus curve for mixtures in the albite–water composition range changes slope, becomes ternary, and with increasing pressure the temperature of melting for jadeite and quartz in the presence of water vapour increases. Another invariant point is generated where quartz is transformed to coesite. If there is enough water to saturate the liquid (see Figure 4A), melting is completed on the univariant curve for the binary mineral-water system, but for the ternary system, the univariant solidus curve is the beginning of melting; only mixtures corresponding to the first liquid produced melt at one temperature.

This melting pattern is general for minerals in the presence of excess water. The effect of water vapour under pressure on the temperatures of beginning of melting of the major crustal rock types is shown in Figure 5. These reactions follow the same pattern; there is a low-

Effect of excess water

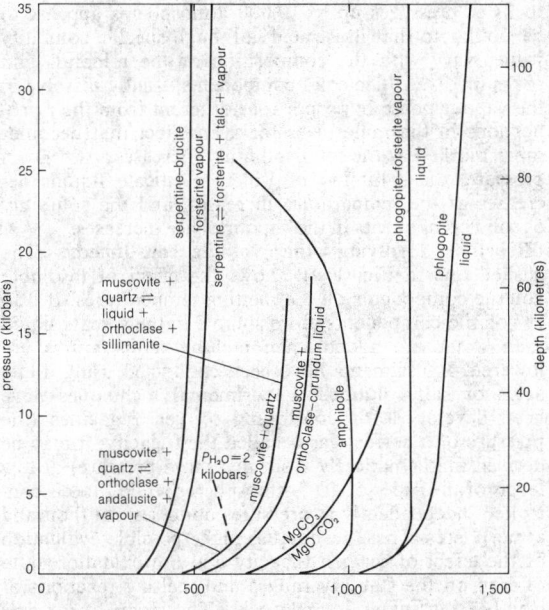

Figure 3: Dehydration and decarbonation relations in mineral systems.

univariant curves and associated divariant surfaces for open systems provide *P*, *T*, and composition limits for these reactions. The proportions of water and carbon dioxide in migrating solutions determine whether an assemblage including hydrous minerals becomes carbonated or whether an assemblage including carbonates becomes hydrated. Experimental determination of these reactions in the laboratory establishes values for equivalent reactions occurring in open systems in the Earth.

Melting reactions. In Figure 4B the univariant melting curve for a one-component system, albite, is shown. At fixed pressure albite melts completely at constant temperature. The effect of pressure is to increase the melting temperature; the slope of the melting curve (dP/dT) is steep and positive. The subsolidus curve for the breakdown of albite to form jadeite + quartz meets the albite melting curve at an invariant point; at higher pressures the system becomes binary, and the melting reaction becomes jadeite + quartz ⇌ liquid. This reaction is univariant, but for mixtures of jadeite and quartz that do not have the composition of the liquid produced (this is fixed at a given *P* and *T*, as shown by application of the phase rule), the mineral assemblage melts through a temperature interval, beginning at the univariant curve. (The reverse curvature for the albite melting curve below the invariant point is part of a complex series of changes.)

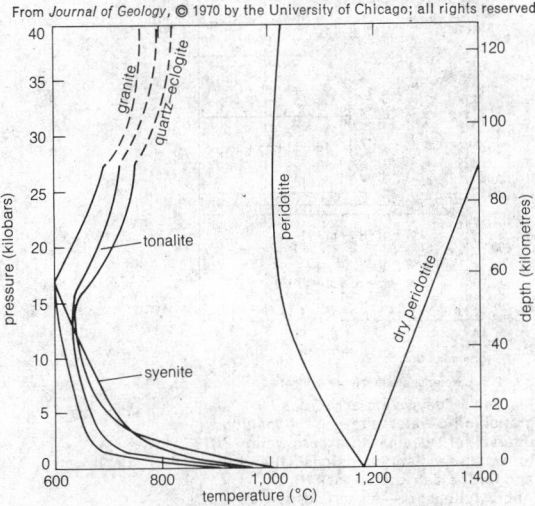

Figure 5: Melting points of major rock types in the presence of water with $H_2O = P_{total}$, compared with the solidus for dry peridotite.

pressure regime, where the solidus curves trend to lower temperatures, and at pressures above about 15,000 atmospheres, where plagioclase feldspar becomes unstable, the solidus temperatures increase with increasing pressure, with slope approximating those for dry minerals and rocks. The solidus curve for peridotite in the presence of excess water exhibits a somewhat different pattern; the small proportion of plagioclase feldspar that may be present at low pressures reacts with olivine to yield aluminous pyroxenes and spinel at about 10,000 atmospheres (Figure 2). At higher pressures there is a gradual change in slope from negative to positive, associated with the formation of garnet peridotite from spinel peridotite (see pyrope formation in Figure 2).

Effect of water deficiency If conditions are such that $P_{H_2O} < P_{total}$, then the melting temperatures are increased, as is illustrated for a simple system in Figure 4B. The dashed line for total pressures greater than 5,000 atmospheres shows the melting curve for albite (or jadeite + quartz at high pressures) in the presence of vapour with P_{H_2O} maintained constant at 5,000 atmospheres. This curve is approximately parallel with the univariant curves for dry melting, which correspond to conditions where $P_{H_2O} = 0$. This dashed curve is a contour on a divariant surface. There are as yet few experimental data on the positions of these contour lines.

The main changes in phase relationships produced if excess water is added to a dry rock are that solidus and liquidus temperatures are lowered, the melting interval between solidus and liquidus is increased, and hydrous minerals such as mica and amphibole are stabilized; these relationships become involved in reactions including a liquid (see Figure 3). For a granodiorite (a plutonic rock) with excess water at a fixed pressure of 2,000 atmospheres, Figure 6 shows the successive equilibrium assemblages, bounded by isothermal reaction lines, within the melting interval (see composition IV); the temperature interval is 270° C (490° F). For the dehydrated granodiorite composition (I), the melting interval is only 130° C (230° F), between n' and n.

Most natural conditions are water deficient, and the sequence of reactions through the melting interval of a rock is more like those illustrated for compositions II or III in Figure 6. The shaded area left of line a-b-c-d is vapour absent; there is insufficient water to saturate the liquid and hydrous minerals in the assemblages. The main changes caused by passing from the vapour-present

phase fields into the vapour-absent phase fields, with progressive decrease in water content (and in P_{H_2O}), are that the liquidus temperature increases, the temperature interval between solidus and liquidus increases, the temperature stabilities of the hydrous minerals (biotite and hornblende) increase, and the amount of liquid within a given temperature interval above the solidus decreases. In composition II, containing no vapour-phase subsolidus, the temperature of beginning of melting is about 160° C (290° F) higher than for subsolidus assemblages with vapour; melting does not begin until biotite begins to dissociate, releasing water to dissolve in the liquid.

In the $P–X$ diagram of Figure 4A are shown the compositions of the three phases, albite (Ab), liquid (L), and vapour (V), involved in the univariant melting reaction Ab + V ⇌ L, at pressures up to the invariant point at which albite breaks down. The line for the liquid composition gives the solubility of water (H_2O) in the silicate liquid as a function of pressure, and similarly the line for the vapour composition gives the solubility of the solid components in the vapour phase; the temperature varies along these curves, as shown by the corresponding reaction curve in Figure 4B. Experimental data are sparse, but the general pattern for other silicate minerals and rocks at pressures up to 10,000 atmospheres appears to be similar to that illustrated, although specific solubility values vary with the composition of the minerals and rocks involved. The solid components usually dissolve in the vapour phase in proportions different from their proportions in the mineral or rock, an effect that becomes more marked as the total solubility increases. At a given pressure, the solubility of water in silicate liquids decreases as the temperature increases, and the solubility of solid components in the vapour phase increases.

Reactions involving other volatile constituents. The dashed line in Figure 4B shows the effect of insoluble volatile components on the melting temperatures. If other volatile components more soluble in the silicate liquid than water are added, then melting temperatures are lowered. Experiments have been conducted using dilute acids or salt solutions. Experimental techniques have been developed for controlling oxygen fugacities (the pressure of a perfect gas is called the fugacity; it may be derived mathematically from measured pressure) at low levels of the order of 10^{-30} atmospheres while P_{H_2O} is controlled independently at pressures up to several thousand atmospheres. These techniques make possible evaluation of the effect of oxygen fugacity and the oxidation state of iron on the stability ranges and melting reactions of iron-bearing minerals and rocks. The study of systems containing sulfur as a component has bearing on the origin of ore deposits, and attention has been directed toward experimental determination of the solubilities of sulfides in solutions. Another type of experimental study deals with the distribution of oxygen isotopes among minerals and fluids as a function of temperature.

Silicate minerals and rocks

AREAS OF APPLICATION OF HIGH-TEMPERATURE, HIGH-PRESSURE STUDIES

Phase transitions in the Earth's interior. It has been determined experimentally that peridotite believed to approximate the upper mantle in composition undergoes a series of phase transitions with increasing pressure. At low pressures the peridotite consists dominantly of olivine, with two pyroxenes and plagioclase. With increasing pressure the plagioclase is replaced by spinel, which may dissolve in aluminous pyroxenes, and then by pyrope-rich garnet (see simple reactions in Figure 2). The garnet peridotite undergoes a major phase transformation at $P–T$ conditions corresponding to the depth interval near 400–450 kilometres, which coincides closely with the seismic discontinuity (i.e., a discontinuity within the Earth that separates materials in which Earth vibrations travel at significantly different velocities) at the beginning of the mantle transition zone. Olivine changes to a spinel-like mineral and the pyroxenes dissolve in the garnet.

The phase transformation of gabbro into eclogite is related to the univariant reactions of Figure 2 involving the breakdown of albite and anorthite and the formation of

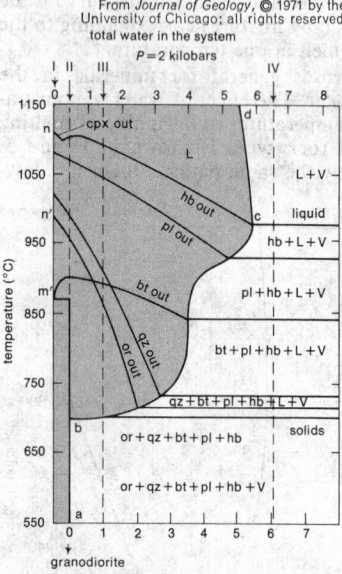

Figure 6: The system anhydrous granodiorite-water, showing the melting interval for system with excess water (IV), for water-deficient conditions (III and II), and for the dehydrated rock (I). Abbreviations: or—alkali feldspar; qz— quartz, bt—biotite; pl—plagioclase; hb— hornblende; cpx—clinopyroxene; L—liquid; V—vapour.

pyrope. There is a continuing debate about whether the gabbro–eclogite phase transformation is a cause of the Moho seismic discontinuity in some geologically active regions. Conflicting experimental results have been published and extrapolation from experiments at 1,000° C (1,800° F) to temperatures in the range 600° to 300° C (1,100° to 550° F), which approximates the natural conditions for this transition, produces conflicting interpretations of several major geophysical and petrological problems.

Metamorphic petrology: mineral reaction series and mineralogical facies. Metamorphic rocks provide a guide to temperatures and temperature gradients in the earth during the mountain-building cycle. During the burial, deformation, and metamorphism of rocks, a series of dehydration and decarbonation reactions occurs, as well as solid–solid transitions. Examples of these are plotted in Figures 2 and 3. If these two figures are superimposed, the dissociation reactions tend to cut across the solid–solid reactions, producing a grid of reaction lines bounding pigeonholes for mineral assemblages. If a rock experiences changes in P and T represented by a geotherm (see Figure 1), it will cross a series of reaction lines, and if equilibrium is maintained it undergoes a series of mineral reactions. Successive mineral assemblages are produced with progressive metamorphism. The metamorphic assemblages, or groups of metamorphic assemblages for rocks of different compositions within similar P–T intervals, are called metamorphic facies.

The concept of a petrogenetic grid, a P–T diagram traversed by experimentally determined reaction lines, was developed in 1940. Experimental studies have now turned this into an effective instrument for determining the depths and temperatures of origin of metamorphic rocks. Such calibration of observed metamorphic rocks indicates that metamorphism occurs through a wide range of conditions. It is shown in Figure 1 that some rocks are metamorphosed at moderate pressures and high temperatures, whereas others are metamorphosed at high pressures and low temperatures, possibly related to the downsinking of a cold lithosphere slab beneath an island arc or continental margin. Geotherms and geothermal gradients during mountain-building processes may thus depart significantly from the average estimates shown in Figure 1. The line A in Figure 1 for the solidus of granite–water (see Figure 5) shows that partial melting begins in high-temperature metamorphism, with the formation of migmatites (*i.e.*, altered rocks consisting of thin alternating layers of different compositions).

Igneous petrology: magma generation and crystallization. Magmas, mutual solutions of silicates with small proportions of dissolved volatile components, are generated whenever the temperature at a given depth exceeds the solidus temperature for the material present. The solidus temperature for a dry rock is much higher than for a rock in the presence of an aqueous pore fluid (Figures 1, 4B, 5, and 6, one igneous and the other metamorphic).

In the mantle, basaltic magma is derived by partial fusion of peridotite. Conditions for the melting of peridotite dry and in the presence of excess water are shown in Figure 5. For dry mantle, basaltic magma is generated in the depth–temperature range shown in Figure 1. Experimental studies have shown that the composition of the liquid produced varies as a function of the mineralogy of the peridotite, as a function of depth, and with the temperature interval above the solidus. A significant change with increasing pressure is the increased solubility of olivine in the liquid. Note that for the formation of basaltic magma at depths less than 100 kilometres (60 miles), temperatures must become considerably higher than the two estimated geotherms plotted in Figure 1. The geotherms do pass through the P–T area for incipient melting if traces of water are present, and this phenomena provides a possible interpretation for the low-velocity zone of the upper mantle identified from seismic studies. The curve C in Figure 1 differs from the solidus for peridotite-water in Figure 5, because up to pressures of about 27,000 atmospheres it is assumed that the water is stored in amphi-

bole, and melting begins only when this mineral dissociates (Figure 3, melting of Type II in Figure 6).

The crystallization sequence of magmas, once generated, can be traced on phase diagrams. Equilibrium or fractional crystallization may occur, although usually the actual conditions would be between these two extremes. Fractional crystallization may occur continuously during uprise of the magma, or it may occur at a given pressure during a temporary halt in its upwards path. The composition of the liquid eventually emplaced into the crust, or erupted as a lava, is formulated during a complex history. Experimental determination of the effect of various P–T paths on the composition of the liquid is required for explanation of the origin of basaltic magma types.

It has been experimentally established that crustal rocks with a wide range of composition, in the presence of an aqueous pore fluid, will begin to melt within a few tens of degrees of the line A in Figure 1 (compare Figures 5 and 6, composition III). Normal magma generation in the crust appears to be limited to the formation of a crystal mush containing water-undersaturated liquid of granite composition. The granite liquid may be capable of separation and independent intrusion. It is doubtful that the amount of pore fluid in a deep-seated rock would exceed 1 percent by weight, and Figure 6 shows that all of it dissolves in the granite liquid within a few degrees of the solidus. The temperature of beginning of melting is controlled by P_{H_2O}, and the amount of liquid is controlled by the proportion of granitic minerals in the rock and by the amount of water.

It is shown in Figure 6 that in order to produce liquids of intermediate composition, temperatures approaching 1,100° C (2,000° F) are required. It therefore appears that andesite and diorite liquid magmas are not produced within the crust during metamorphism unless temperatures are considerably higher than those normally considered likely. Alternative explanations involve formation by fractional crystallization of basalts with high oxygen fugacity and derivation from the mantle as primary magmas.

If slabs of lithosphere are sinking beneath island arcs and some continental margins, as required by the hypotheses of sea-floor spreading and plate tectonics (concept that the Earth's major structural features result from the collisions and general interaction of a relatively small number of large, 100-kilometre-thick lithosphere plates that form the outer layer of the Earth and move over the Earth's interior), then the study of geochemical reactions in crustal materials at pressures greater than 10,000 atmospheres is required for explanation of the evolution of island arcs and mountain chains.

Geological thermometry and barometry. The concept of a petrogenetic grid has been reviewed in the foregoing section on metamorphic petrology. A P–T phase diagram based on mineral reactions measured in the laboratory is an effective means of estimating temperatures and pressures of formation of rocks on the basis of their mineralogy. Some reactions are suitable for estimating temperatures, and others for estimating pressures; ideally, a mineral assemblage can be delineated on the petrogenetic grid in terms of both temperature and pressure.

Other aspects of geochemical reactions or equilibria provide similar information. The compositions of coexisting minerals, for example, are usually sensitive to changes in temperature and only slightly changed by pressure. Calibration of these values by experimental studies provides temperature estimates within specific mineral facies. Other mineral combinations are sensitive to pressure changes. The distribution of oxygen isotopes among coexisting minerals is a function of temperature, and this fact provides another geological thermometer that has been calibrated by high pressure geochemical experimentation.

There is always a question as to just what an estimated temperature and pressure means. Rocks have histories, and the estimated values represent simply the stage at which the P–T record became frozen in because of increasingly slow reaction rates. The petrographic study of relict and retrograde reactions occurring, respectively,

Origin of meta-morphic rocks

Production of liquid magmas

before and after the major formation process of a rock provides information about a portion of the high-P–T history of the rock. Equilibrium phase diagrams determined in the laboratory can be used to calibrate the history deduced from the nonequilibrium mineralogical relationships preserved. Slow reaction rates in the rocks and in laboratory experiments cause many interpretive problems, but, on the other hand, if reactions in response to the changing P–T conditions did not cease at some stage, there would be no historical record to examine. Eventually, with sufficient experimental, petrographical, and geological data, it may be possible to determine the complete depth–temperature–time relationships for various parts of a complex mountain range.

BIBLIOGRAPHY. B. MASON, *Principles of Geochemistry*, 3rd ed. (1966); R.C. NEWTON, "The Status and Future of High Static-Pressure Geophysical Research," in R.S. BRADLEY (ed.), *Advances in High Pressure Research*, vol. 1, pp. 195–263 (1966); P.J. WYLLIE, *The Dynamic Earth* (1971), contains chapters on high-pressure phase results applied to the mantle, crust, and crust–mantle boundary, and magma generation; J. VERHOOGEN et al., *The Earth* (1970), contains chapters on thermodynamics, igneous petrology, and metamorphic petrology; F.J. TURNER and J. VERHOOGEN, *Igneous and Metamorphic Petrology*, 2nd ed. (1960), with chapters on thermodynamics and the application of high-pressure phase diagrams to igneous and metamorphic petrology; F.J. TURNER, *Metamorphic Petrology: Mineralogical and Field Aspects* (1968), a critical appraisal of the application of high-pressure experimental data to metamorphic rocks.

(P.J.W.)

Geochemical Equilibria at Low Temperatures and Pressures

Geochemical equilibria are involved in most natural geological and hydrological processes at or near the surface of the Earth. In any geochemical system or assemblage of phases (*i.e.*, states or forms) of matter, equilibrium exists when the phases of the system do not undergo any changes of properties with the passage of time. In addition, the phases must have the same properties after any temporary disturbance of the system is followed by return to the initial conditions. Low-temperature, low-pressure studies of chemical equilibria are concerned with the processes that take place between the lowest temperature on Earth and approximately 400° C (750° F), and between near vacuum and several kilobars of pressure (one bar = 0.987 atmosphere = 14.504 pounds per square inch).

Within these limits, low-temperature, low-pressure geochemistry involves the application of the fundamentals of chemistry, especially chemical thermodynamics (*i.e.*, the mathematical treatment of the relationship of heat and work and other forms of energy to equilibrium in chemical reactions and changes of state) to the analysis and explanation of Earth processes. Such studies are useful in ecology, corrosion control, hydrology, oceanography, waste disposal, and determination of the occurrence and origin of some mineral deposits.

The ultimate goal of low-temperature, low-pressure equilibria studies is to describe the various Earth environments—*i.e.*, the combinations of such external conditions as air, light, moisture, temperature, soil, and organisms—that may influence Earth materials and water by reason of naturally or artificially imposed geochemical stresses. The parameters that have proven useful for environmental description are (1) the electromotive force or potential of reactions (Eh), (2) acidity (pH), (3) pressure, (4) temperature, (5) solubility of minerals, and (6) the chemistry of pore solutions (*i.e.*, liquids in the pores or voids and interstices) in rocks. The fundamental factors that affect these parameters are the minerals that make up the Earth's crust and the amounts of organic material and water that are present in that crust. The amount of water is controlled primarily by climate and topography. Achievement of the basic goal requires the investigation of all of the possible variations of any basic parameter and the synthesis of the results. An environment may exhibit a relatively wide range of temperatures at the Earth's surface, for example; solutions present may range

The six parameters of environmental description

from highly acidic to highly alkaline; the area may be humid, in which case the materials may be leached, or it may be arid, in which case the soluble minerals remain for long periods of time. A unified description of the Earth's environments becomes possible only when the several important parameters and their variations are examined from the viewpoint of thermodynamics. Included in this article is consideration of the principles of thermodynamics that are of special relevance to understanding geochemical equilibria at low temperatures and pressures and of geochemical diagrams that are employed to delimit environmental conditions. Additionally, there is consideration of several specific equilibria that are of significance in nature. These include carbonate, iron, and uranium systems, soil conditions, and osmotic equilibria. For further information on the earth materials involved and on the several environments, see MINERALS; CLAY MINERALS; IGNEOUS ROCKS; SEDIMENTARY ROCKS; ORE DEPOSITS; ELEMENTS, GEOCHEMICAL DISTRIBUTION OF; OCEANS AND SEAS; FRESHWATER, GEOCHEMICAL PROPERTIES OF; GROUNDWATER; WEATHERING; DURICRUSTS; and SOILS. See also THERMODYNAMICS, PRINCIPLES OF; CHEMICAL EQUILIBRIA; and GEOCHEMICAL EQUILIBRIA AT HIGH TEMPERATURES AND PRESSURES.

PRINCIPLES AND TECHNIQUES

Law of mass action and the equilibrium constant. The energy distribution within all chemical systems is such that all processes strive to achieve equilibrium. All chemical reactions are reversible; that is, the products of the reaction may themselves react to reform the original substances; at equilibrium the rate of formation of the products and the rate of reformation of the original reactants are equal. The law of mass action states that the driving force of a chemical reaction is proportional to the concentration of the reacting substances at a particular time. For a system at equilibrium, for example, the reaction of a moles (a mole is the molecular weight of a substance in grams) of A with b moles of B to form c moles of C and d moles of D is: $aA + bB \rightleftarrows cC + dD$, in which the rates to the right and left are equal. The product of the activities (concentrations, in the nonthermodynamic sense) of the reaction products C and D raised to the powers of their numerical coefficients (c, d), divided by the product of the activities of the reactants A and B raised to the powers of their numerical coefficients (a, b), is a constant at a given temperature. This is the so-called thermodynamic equilibrium constant, K_{eq}; in this case it is

$$K_{eq} = \frac{\alpha_C{}^c \alpha_D{}^d}{\alpha_A{}^a \alpha_B{}^b}$$

in which the Greek letter alpha, α, denotes thermodynamic concentration or activity, and a, b, c, d are the numbers of moles of substances A, B, C, D as before.

The relation is valid for reactions between solid, liquid, and gaseous phases or combinations of these phases. Activity is a measure of the effective or active concentration of any phase involved in a reaction. One example is a reaction involving one or more solid phases (minerals) and a solution (water) phase. In infinitely dilute solutions activity is virtually equal to chemical concentration, but as a solution becomes more concentrated (contains more dissolved solids), the dissolved components in the solution and the solvent (generally water) cease behaving ideally; their effective concentrations, or activities, do not change proportionally with their chemical concentrations. A correction for deviations from the ideal is required by the fact that as the concentration of a solution is increased, ions (atoms that have gained or lost electrons and thus are positively or negatively charged) interact with one another and with water molecules. For this reason it is necessary to change from standard units of chemical concentration to those of activity in order that ion-activity products, K_{iap}, the actual equilibrium constants, may be compared with laboratory-determined thermodynamic equilibrium constants, K_{eq}, to ascertain which minerals are in equilibrium with, and therefore presumably controlling, the chemistry of a natural water.

Most chemical analyses of waters are expressed in units of milligrams per litre (mg/l) or milliequivalents per litre (meq/l). To convert these values to activity, it is necessary to change them to units of molality. A one-molal solution is defined as one that contains a mole (an amount of a substance in grams that corresponds to the sum of the atomic weights of all the atoms in the molecule) of solute in 1,000 grams of water. Molar concentrations are not used in thermodynamic studies (molar solutions are referred to a litre volume of solution) because of the temperature dependency of the volume and, hence, the concentration of such solutions.

Standard state, activity, and activity coefficient. A standard state for a given substance is the sum of its physical and chemical properties at an arbitrarily chosen set of reference conditions; a standard state may be varied for convenience, depending on the problem being studied. In its standard state, the activity of a pure phase is defined as unity.

Problems in defining the standard state of a gaseous phase

The standard state of a pure solid phase (whether an element or compound) is generally chosen at a specified temperature and, usually, at one atmosphere total pressure. Thus, the standard state of the mineral corundum, Al_2O_3, at 308.16° K (35° C or 95° F) would be written Al_2O_3 corundum, 308.16° and would have unit activity.

The standard state of a gaseous phase is more difficult to define because only perfect gases (those that obey the ideal gas law) have unit activity at the specified temperature and one atmosphere pressure. Thus, the activity of a perfect gas is equal to the pressure: $\alpha_{gas} = P_{gas}$. Real gases generally deviate from the ideal gas law; therefore, the standard state of a real gas is defined to have unit activity at a specified temperature and at that pressure at which the gas pressure would be one atmosphere if the gas obeyed the ideal gas law. As pressure on a real gas is lowered, it approaches the behaviour of an ideal gas. But at higher pressures the activity is not equal to the pressure ($\alpha_{gas} \neq P_{gas}$), and it is necessary to add an additional term phi, ϕ, the gas-activity coefficient to equate activity to pressure, namely: $\alpha_{gas} = P\phi_{gas}$.

The standard state of a pure liquid (such as the element mercury, Hg, or the compound water, H_2O) is generally defined as its state at a specified temperature and at one atmosphere pressure. If the standard state of water is chosen as one atmosphere pressure and 323.16° K (50° C, or 122° F), for example, then it has unit activity under these conditions.

The standard state of a substance dissolved in a solvent, as an ion or as an uncharged species in water (*e.g.*, calcium ion, Ca^{2+}, and aqueous carbon dioxide, CO_{2aq}), is defined by extrapolation to unit activity from behaviour in an infinitely dilute solution, in which the dissolved species acts ideally. In dilute solutions, molality is nearly equal to activity; for more concentrated solutions, a correction factor must be used. The correction factor, which provides a connection between activity, α_i, and molality, m_i, of the individual ionic species, is given by the equation

$$\alpha_i = \gamma_i m_i, \quad \text{or} \quad \gamma_i = \frac{\alpha_i}{m_i},$$

in which the Greek letter gamma (sub-i), γ_i, is the activity coefficient of component i. The activity coefficient for various ions may be calculated from standard water analyses by use of an empirical (the Debye–Hückel) equation, which equates the logarithm of the activity coefficient to the ionic charge, ionic diameter, and ionic strength of solution, namely:

$$\log \gamma_i = \frac{-Az_i^2 \Gamma^{1/2}}{1 + a_i B \Gamma^{1/2}}$$

in which A and B are temperature-dependent constants, z_i is the charge on the ion, a_i represents the effective diameter of the ion in solution, and the Greek letter gamma, Γ, is the ionic strength of the solution. Values for A, B, and a_i are given in standard textbooks on physical chemistry or solution chemistry. The Debye–Hückel equation gives reasonable values for activity coefficients up to an ionic strength of about 0.1, which corresponds to concentrations of dissolved solids in typical natural

waters of about 5,000 to 8,000 milligrams per litre. Drinking-water supplies contain less than 2,000 milligrams per litre and usually less than 1,000 milligrams per litre, whereas ocean water contains about 35,000 milligrams per litre dissolved solids.

Free energy and equilibrium. If a system is not at equilibrium, it will tend to react spontaneously with a release of energy. The so-called Gibbs free-energy function, ΔG, provides a true measure of the driving force of a chemical reaction because free energy connotes the available work that can be done by a system. The Gibbs free energy of reaction is the sum of the free energies of formation of products less the sum of the free energies of formation of reactants; that is:

$$\Delta G_R^0 = \Sigma \Delta G^0_{f\,products} - \Sigma \Delta G^0_{f\,reactants},$$

Gibbs free energy

in which G_R^0 is the free energy of the reaction and the Greek letter sigma, Σ, represents a summation. When ΔG_R^0 is zero, there is no net chemical work obtainable; the system is at equilibrium. If ΔG_R^0 is negative, the process may proceed spontaneously; a positive value means that work (energy) must be put into the system for the reaction to proceed. The equilibrium constant can be calculated from ΔG_R^0 according to the relation

$$\Delta G_R^0 = -RT \ln K_{eq},$$

in which R is a constant, T is temperature, and $\ln K_{eq}$ is the natural logarithm of the equilibrium constant.

The standard state for the calculation of free-energy values is commonly taken as that of the pure substance at 25° C or 77° F (298.16° K) and one atmosphere total pressure. Because natural systems of interest are commonly at some temperature other than 25° C, it is necessary to extrapolate free-energy data from 25° C to the temperature of the natural system. This may be done by using an equation (Gibbs–Helmholtz), which states that at constant pressure the free energy equals the heat of reaction plus the product of temperature and the rate of change of free energy with temperature, namely:

$$\Delta G = \Delta H + \left(\frac{\partial \Delta G}{\partial T}\right)_P,$$

in which ΔH is enthalpy or heat of reaction (enthalpy is the heat change during a chemical process at constant pressure) and $\left(\frac{\partial \Delta G}{\partial T}\right)_P$ is the rate of change of free energy with temperature at constant pressure. By mathematical operations on the last two equations, the so-called van't Hoff equation relating the change in equilibrium constant with change in temperature to the enthalpy and absolute temperature is obtained:

$$\left(\frac{\partial \ln K_{eq}}{\partial T}\right)_P = \frac{\Delta H}{RT^2},$$

in which the symbols are as previously defined. This equation may be used to calculate equilibrium constants at temperatures other than 25° C. It generally provides a fair approximation only if the actual temperature is not far from 25° C. For larger variations, the assumption that ΔH is independent of temperature (which is explicit in the van't Hoff equation) is invalid.

Pressure changes also affect the rate of change of the Gibbs free-energy function. The rate of change of free energy with change of pressure at constant temperature is equal to the change in volume, namely:

$$\left(\frac{\partial \Delta G}{\partial P}\right)_T = \Delta V_R,$$

in which ΔV_R is the molal volume change of the reaction. It is calculated in a manner similar to the Gibbs free energy of reaction.

In most natural systems both temperature and pressure are subject to change. If the compositions of the phases do not change during a reaction (*e.g.*, during congruent dissolution) and if the system remains at equilibrium, then the Clausius–Clapeyron equation, which defines the rate of change of pressure with respect to temperature is useful. This can be expressed

$$\frac{dP}{dT} = \frac{\Delta H_R}{T\Delta V_R},$$

in which ΔH_R is the total enthalpy change of the reaction, T is absolute temperature, and ΔV_R is again the molal volume change.

Nernst equation and Eh-pH relation. In order to understand chemical reactions that involve an exchange of electrons, it is necessary to measure the electromotive force (emf) of the reaction. If the reaction is reversible, then the reversible emf, E^0, is related to the Gibbs free energy of reaction ΔG_R^0 by the expression

$$\Delta G_R^0 = nE^0 F,$$

in which n is the number of electrons involved in the reaction, E^0 is the calculated potential of the cell when all species are at unit activity, and F is the faraday (i.e., the quantity of electricity transferred per equivalent weight of an element or ion). The cell potential can be shown to be related to the natural logarithm of the equilibrium constant by:

$$E^0 = -(RT/nF)\ln K,$$

in which K is the equilibrium constant, T is absolute temperature, R is a constant, and n and F are as defined above. In most chemical reactions the activity of all species is generally not unity, in which case the free-energy function equals the free energy of the reaction plus the product of temperature and the logarithm of the equilibrium constant:

$$\Delta G = \Delta G_R^0 + RT\ln K,$$

in which ΔG is the free energy function, ΔG_R^0 is the free energy of the reaction, T is temperature, R is a constant, and K is the equilibrium constant.

The cell potential can be related to the equilibrium constant by:

$$\text{Eh} = E^0 + (RT/nF)\ln K,$$

in which Eh is the potential measured against the standard hydrogen–electrode reaction involving the decomposition of hydrogen to hydrogen ions plus electrons (which, by convention, has an emf equal to zero) and E^0 is again the potential when all ionic species are at unity activity. This is a form of the Nernst equation; at standard pressure (one atmosphere) and temperature ($298.16°$ K), the factor (RT/nF) can be reduced and

$$\text{Eh} = E^0 + \frac{0.05916}{n} \log K.$$

Many chemical elements are capable of existing in more than one valence state (i.e., combining capacity, the numerical expression of which represents the number of electrons an atom can gain, lose, or share in a chemical reaction). Thus, iron may exist as metallic iron with no net charge, as the ferrous ion with a net charge of plus two, or as the ferric ion with a net charge of plus three. In addition, complex ions, such as the iron hydroxide ions $Fe(OH)^{2+}$, $Fe(OH)^+_2$, and $FeO(OH)^-$, are possible under appropriate conditions of oxidation–reduction potential (redox, or Eh) and pH. The pH of a solution is defined as the negative logarithm of the hydrogen–ion activity. Thus, if the activity of the hydrogen ion is $10^{-7.3}$, then the pH of the solution is plus 7.3. Because of the large number of similarly behaving elements, many chemical reactions in geologic environments may be expressed in terms of Eh, or pH, or by a combination of Eh and pH. For this reason, Eh-pH diagrams (the plotted relations of Eh and pH) provide an excellent pictorial method for portraying such reactions. By drawing lines on these diagrams to denote the activity of each possible dissolved species, the oxidation–reduction potential of the environment can be estimated from study of the solid phases present and from determination of the activity of dissolved species in equilibrium with the solid phases.

Reaction types. One of the primary tasks of low-temperature studies is to determine which minerals are in

Use of Eh-pH diagrams to depict elements in more than one valence state

equilibrium with their physical and chemical environment. This can be done by means of simple calculations that utilize the equations cited thus far. Examples of the several types of reactions are considered below.

Solid-solid reactions. There are many reactions involving only solids that are geologically important. Any reaction for which free-energy data exist can be tested by means of the Gibbs free-energy equation. The reaction of calcite, $CaCO_3$, with magnesite, $MgCO_3$, to produce dolomite, $CaMg(CO_3)_2$, provides a common example. If the reaction occurs at 25° C and one atmosphere pressure and if the solids are pure, then they are in their standard states and have unit activity. Under these conditions, the reaction can be written

$$CaCO_3 + MgCO_3 = CaMg(CO_3)_2.$$

Applying the relation that the free energy of reaction is equal to the free energy of the products (dolomite) minus the free energy of the reactants (calcite and magnesite) yields:

$$\Delta G_R^0 = \Delta G^0_{\text{dolomite}} - (\Delta G^0_{\text{calcite}} + \Delta G^0_{\text{magnesite}});$$

and substituting the appropriate free energy values at 25° C and one atmosphere of pressure:

$$\Delta G_R^0 = (-516.56) - (-269.98 - 246.11) = -0.47 \text{ kilocalorie.}$$

Because the free energy of reaction is negative, this means that dolomite is the stable mineral at the given conditions of temperature and pressure. That is, it would require an input of $+0.47$ kilocalorie to drive the reaction in the opposite direction, converting dolomite to calcite and magnesite.

Solids and pure water. Reactions that involve only solids and pure water can be treated similarly to solid–solid reactions, because the activity of pure water is unity. An example of importance in nature is the reaction: anhydrite, $CaSO_4$, plus water, H_2O, to yield gypsum, $CaSO_4 \cdot 2H_2O$. This is written

$$CaSO_4 + 2H_2O = CaSO_4 \cdot 2H_2O.$$

Applying again the relation that the free energy of the reaction is equal to the free energy of the products minus the free energy of the reactants:

$$\Delta G_R^0 = \Delta G^0_{\text{gypsum}} - (\Delta G^0_{\text{anhydrite}} + 2\Delta G^0_{\text{water}})$$
$$\Delta G_R^0 = 429.19 - (-315.56 + 2(-56.9)).$$

In this instance, the free energy of the reaction

$$\Delta G_R^0 = -0.25 \text{ kilocalorie.}$$

Thus, this reaction also tends to go in the direction of the product (gypsum) at 25° C and one atmosphere pressure. One of the reasons that the hydration (addition of water) of anhydrite is important is that a mole of gypsum is much less dense than a mole of anhydrite. If, therefore, hydration occurs in confined space, as in the subsurface environment, the pressure may be significantly increased. Also, the reaction gives off heat and consequently changes both the pressure and the temperature of the system.

Gases and solids or solutions reactions. Reactions between gases and solids or solutions are geologically common and are readily handled thermodynamically. The reaction between a solution that contains calcium ions and CO_2 gas, that reacts to produce calcium carbonate ($CaCO_3$) and hydrogen ion (H^+), for example, can be written

$$Ca^{2+} + CO_2 + H_2O = CaCO_3 + 2H^+.$$

The equilibrium constant for this reaction is obtained by dividing the products by the reactants as before:

$$K = \frac{\alpha_{CaCO_3} \cdot (\alpha_{H^+})^2}{\alpha_{Ca^{2+}} \cdot \alpha_{H_2O} \cdot P_{CO_2}},$$

in which the Greek letter alpha (α) represents activity and P_{CO_2} represents the pressure of carbon dioxide in the solution. Because the activities of pure water and solids are unity the expression reduces to:

This equation says that equilibrium between the given

$$K = \frac{(\alpha_{H^+})^2}{\alpha_{Ca^{2+}} \cdot P_{CO_2}}.$$

solution (calcium ions and water) and a gas (such as the Earth's atmosphere) is a function of the amount of calcium ($\alpha_{Ca^{2+}}$), the square of the amount of hydrogen (expressed either as α_{H^+} or as pH), and the pressure of the gas (P_{CO_2}).

Geochemical diagrams. *Partial-pressure diagrams.* It is often convenient to portray diagrammatically the relations between mineral species in order to better understand their origin and mode of occurrence. One such diagram of broad practical value is the partial-pressure diagram. Any reaction that can be written so as to include a gas phase can be illustrated on such a diagram. As shown in Figure 1, which portrays the copper–sulfur–

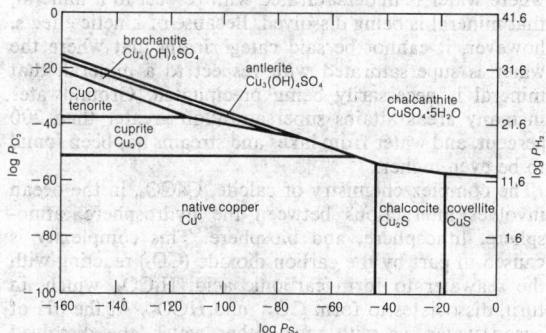

Figure 1: Partial-pressure diagram of the Cu-S-O system with water as a mobile excess compound, at 25°C and one atmosphere total pressure (see text).

oxygen system, the lines on the diagram that separate solid phases represent the equilibrium condition between the two minerals. The reaction whereby native copper, Cu, reacts with sulfur, S, to produce chalcocite, Cu_2S, for instance is expressed by:

$$2Cu + \tfrac{1}{2}S_2 = Cu_2S,$$

and the equilibrium constant (K) is

$$K = \frac{1}{\sqrt{P_{S_2}}},$$

in which P_{S_2} is the partial pressure of sulfur gas in the system. The free energy of this reaction is -30.2 kilocalories, and the equilibrium constant, K, is $10^{22.14}$; for this value of K, the partial pressure of sulfur at which the two minerals, Cu and Cu_2S, are in equilibrium is therefore $10^{-44.28}$. This is the position of the phase boundary on Figure 1. In like manner, boundaries involving oxides can also be calculated. Those reactions that involve only oxygen or sulfur in the gas phase plot as either horizontal or vertical lines on the figure. Those reactions that involve both gases plot as slanted lines. The slope depends on the relative amounts of the two gases involved. The diagram indicates that one could find Cu and Cu_2O in the same geological environment but that the pair Cu plus CuO is not geochemically stable; the two phases should always be separated by Cu_2O. The diagram also indicates that Cu_2O, CuO, and $Cu_4(OH)_6SO_4$ can coexist at a unique combination of gas pressures. The point where all three phases occur is commonly called a triple point.

Eh–pH diagrams. Another commonly used geochemical diagram is the Eh–pH plot illustrated in Figure 2. By means of the Nernst equation, which relates the potential electromotive force of a reaction to the equilibrium constant, it is possible to construct a picture of mineral relations for elements that commonly exist in several valence states. Copper provides a useful example because it can exist in nature as the element Cu^0 and in both the cuprous (Cu^+) and cupric (Cu^{2+}) states.

The upper slanted boundary on Figure 2 represents the conditions under which water decomposes to oxygen.

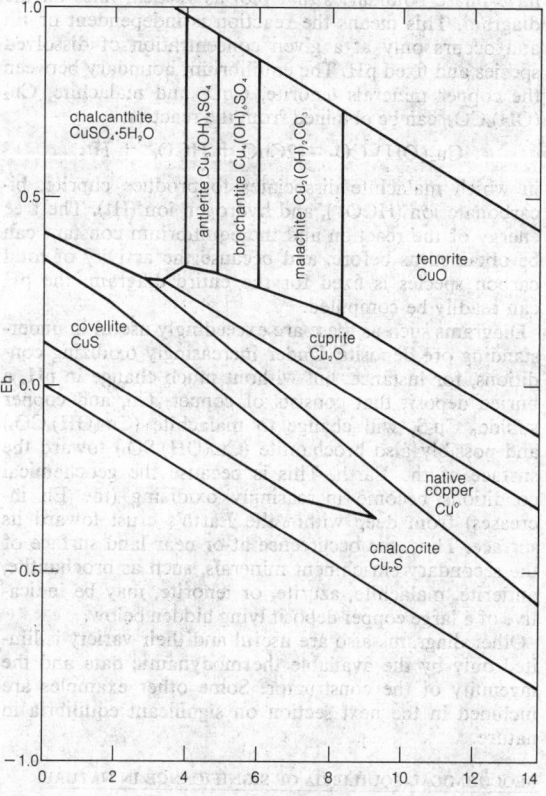

Figure 2: Eh–pH diagram of stability relations in the system Cu-S-C-H$_2$O at 25°C and one atmosphere pressure (see text).

The reaction, at one atmosphere pressure and 298.16° K (25° C, or 77° F) is

$$2H_2O = O_2 + 4H^+ + 4e^-,$$

in which the products of decomposition are four hydrogen ions (H^+) and four electrons (e^-), in addition to oxygen (O_2). The equilibrium constant in this case is simply the logarithm of the activity of the hydrogen ions (α_{H^+}) raised to the fourth power because four ions are present. Thus, the Nernst equation relating cell potential and the equilibrium constant is:

$$Eh = E^0 + \frac{0.059}{4}\log(\alpha_{H^+})^4,$$

in which Eh is the potential of the reaction measured against the hydrogen electrode half cell (emf = 0), and E^0 is the potential when all ionic species are at unit activity. Because pH is defined as the negative logarithm of the activity of the hydrogen ion ($-\log \alpha_{H^+}$):

$$Eh = E^0 - 0.059 \, pH.$$

This basic relationship defines the slope; by using the free energy relationship to cell potential previously given ($\Delta G_R^0 = nE^0F$) it is possible to solve E^0 and obtain:

$$Eh = 1.23 - 0.059 \, pH.$$

In like manner, it is possible to solve for the intercept and slope of the bottom boundary on Figure 2, which represents the conditions under which water breaks down to hydrogen gas at one atmosphere pressure.

Lines between various pairs of copper-bearing minerals on Figure 2 represent equilibrium conditions between those pairs. Considering the conditions under which native copper is oxidized to cuprite, Cu_2O, for example:

$$2Cu^0 + H_2O = Cu_2O + 2H^+ + 2e^-,$$

in which Cu^0 is native copper, reacting with water to produce cuprite, hydrogen ions, and two electrons (e^-). The slope and intercept on the diagram can be determined in the manner given above for the $H_2O:O_2$ relation.

Those reactions that do not involve a change in valence state (*i.e.*, only involve dissolved species but no electrons) have phase boundaries that plot as vertical lines on the diagram. This means the reaction is independent of Eh and occurs only at a given concentration of dissolved species and fixed pH. The equilibrium boundary between the copper minerals tenorite, CuO, and malachite, $Cu_2(OH)_2CO_3$, can be obtained from the reaction

$$Cu_2(OH)_2CO_3 = 2CuO + HCO_3^- + H^+,$$

in which malachite dissociates to produce cuprite, bicarbonate ion (HCO_3^-), and hydrogen ion (H^+). The free energy of the reaction and the equilibrium constant can be obtained as before, and because the activity of total carbon species is fixed for the entire diagram, the pH can readily be computed.

Use of geochemical diagrams with ore deposits

Diagrams such as these are exceedingly useful in understanding ore deposits. Under increasingly oxidizing conditions, for instance, but without much change in pH, a buried deposit that consists of copper, Cu, and copper sulfide, Cu_2S, will change to malachite ($Cu_2(OH)_2CO_3$) and possibly also brochantite ($Cu_4(OH)_6SO_4$) toward the surface of the Earth. This is because the geochemical conditions become increasingly oxidizing (the Eh increases) from deep within the Earth's crust toward its surface. Thus, the occurrence at or near land surface of the secondary enrichment minerals, such as brochantite, antlerite, malachite, azurite, or tenorite, may be indicative of a large copper deposit lying hidden below.

Other diagrams also are useful and their variety is limited only by the available thermodynamic data and the ingenuity of the constructor. Some other examples are included in the next section on significant equilibria in nature.

GEOCHEMICAL EQUILIBRIA OF SIGNIFICANCE IN NATURE

Carbonate equilibria in water. The principal significance of the equilibrium constant in geochemistry is that it provides a means of calculating departure from equilibrium between the aqueous phase and solid mineralogic phases. Departure is determined by comparison of the thermodynamic equilibrium constant, K_{eq}, with the ion-activity product, K_{iap}, which is calculated from chemical analysis of water. Equilibrium studies identify the minerals that control the chemistry of water and assist in predicting changes that may occur with time or as a result of stress upon hydrologic systems. Determination of whether water is in equilibrium with a particular mineral requires knowledge of the equilibrium constant, $K_{mineral}$, which is obtained from physical–chemical laboratories, and the ion activity product, K_{iap}, which is calculated from chemical analysis of water. For example, in the solution of calcite to produce calcium and carbonate ions

$$CaCO_3 = Ca^{2+} + CO_3^{2-},$$

in which $CaCO_3$ is calcite, Ca^{2+} is calcium ion, and CO_3^{2-} is carbonate ion, the equilibrium constant would be

$$K_{calcite} = \frac{\alpha_{Ca^{2+}} \cdot \alpha_{CO_3^{2-}}}{\alpha_{CaCO_3}},$$

in which the Greek letter alpha (α) again represents activity—of the calcium and carbonate ions and of calcite. The ion-activity product, as its name suggests, is equal to the product of the ions, namely:

$$K_{iap} = \alpha_{Ca^{2+}} \cdot \alpha_{CO_3^{2-}}.$$

The activities are calculated from chemical analysis of water, but because the dominant carbonate species in solution in water is bicarbonate rather than carbonate ion, the required reaction is bicarbonate dissociating to produce hydrogen ion and carbonate ion

$$HCO_3^- = H^+ + CO_3^{2-},$$

in which HCO_3^- is bicarbonate, H^+ is hydrogen ion, and CO_3^{2-} is carbonate ion. The equilibrium constant for this reaction is given by

$$K_{HCO_3^-} = \frac{\alpha_{H^+} \cdot \alpha_{CO_3^{2-}}}{\alpha_{HCO_3^-}},$$

in which $K_{HCO_3^-}$ is the equilibrium constant and the Greek letter (α) is activity of hydrogen, carbonate, and bicarbonate ions. Rearranging this equation to obtain the activity of the carbonate ion ($\alpha_{CO_3^{2-}}$):

$$\alpha_{CO_3^{2-}} = \frac{K_{HCO_3^-} \cdot \alpha_{HCO_3^-}}{\alpha_{H^+}},$$

in which $K_{HCO_3^-}$ is a thermodynamic constant at a given temperature, activity of the bicarbonate (HCO_3^-) is calculated from chemical analysis of the water, and activity of the hydrogen ion is determined from the pH of the water.

By making temperature corrections, the ion-activity product for calcite ($CaCO_3$) can be calculated from activities of calcium and carbonate ions and compared with the equilibrium constant $K_{calcite}$. Because all systems in nature tend toward equilibrium, it is well established that where water is undersaturated with respect to a mineral, that mineral is being dissolved. Because of kinetic effects, however, it cannot be said categorically that where the water is supersaturated with respect to a mineral, that mineral is necessarily being precipitated. Groundwater in many areas attains supersaturation greater than 200 percent, and water from lakes and streams has been found to be even higher.

The complex chemistry of calcite, $CaCO_3$, in the ocean involves interactions between the hydrosphere, atmosphere, lithosphere, and biosphere. This complexity is caused in part by the carbon dioxide (CO_2) reacting with the seawater to form carbonic acid, H_2CO_3, which, in turn, dissociates to form CO_3^{2-} and HCO_3^-. At the pH of ocean water, as with most other water, the dissolved carbonate is in the form of HCO_3^-. Because carbon dioxide, CO_2, is involved in photosynthesis, its partial pressure exhibits systematic diurnal and seasonal cycles, which are reflected in changes of $CaCO_3$ equilibrium. Both mineral forms of $CaCO_3$ (calcite and aragonite) are found in the sea, with calcite being the more abundant. Aragonite is precipitated primarily by organisms, is metastable (an intermediate condition) with respect to calcite, and is converted to calcite under normal marine conditions.

Calcite saturation in the Atlantic and Pacific oceans

Warm surface water of the ocean is supersaturated with respect to calcite. Values as high as 300 percent of saturation are common in the equatorial Atlantic Ocean. In the polar regions, the supersaturation is generally less than 150 percent. Studies of the waters off Bermuda indicate that only the deepest water is in equilibrium with the sediment present, in this case an ooze containing aragonite, and that the bulk of the water is supersaturated with respect to calcite. Factors such as particle size and magnesium content of the sediments seem to be important in controlling the degree of saturation. Low-magnesium calcite is the least soluble; calcite with 20 to 30 percent magnesium carbonate, $MgCO_3$, is the most soluble; and aragonite is intermediate.

In the Pacific Ocean, except for surface water, the water mass is undersaturated with respect to calcite. Pacific water with a temperature of about 14° C (57° F) tends to be saturated with respect to calcite; waters warmer than 20° C (68° F) are saturated with respect to aragonite.

Although ocean water is sometimes supersaturated with respect to a few other minerals, notably the apatites of the Pacific Ocean, it is undersaturated with respect to most minerals. A great amount of investigative work has been done, but the carbonate equilibrium of the oceans is still imperfectly understood, and fundamental questions about the rates of reactions remain.

Iron equilibria. Several geochemical principles that are involved in chemical weathering and sedimentation processes can be examined in terms of the behaviour of iron, which is typical of the elements in nature that exist in more than one valence state. The iron phases that are stable at near-surface conditions are native iron and the iron oxides hematite (Fe_2O_3) and magnetite (Fe_3O_4). One of the early fundamental tasks was determination of the activities of various dissolved ionic species involving iron, oxygen, and water [Fe^{3+}, $Fe(OH)^{2+}$, $Fe(OH)_2^{2+}$, FeO_2^-,

Fe(OH)$^+$, HFeO$_2^-$, and Fe^{2+}], and a few others (for which free-energy data are not available) that are in equilibrium with the solid oxides.

Both the number of solid phases and dissolved species are greatly increased when carbon dioxide, dissolved sulfur, and silica are added to the system. These relations have been described and explained largely by use of Eh–pH diagrams. A summary of the type of understanding gained from this approach is as follows:

During weathering, part of the iron in the minerals of igneous rocks (those derived from silicate melts at high temperatures and pressures) is oxidized to cause the familiar brown, yellow, and red discoloration to the rock surface, and part of the iron is dissolved as ferrous ion, Fe^{2+}. The ferrous ion can be transported for long distances if the solutions remain slightly acidic and reducing, and if they do not contain other ions that would cause precipitation. The most common ions are carbonate, sulfide, and silicate; the precipitation reaction for any of these is aided by an increase in alkalinity of the solution. Primary controls on the precipitation of iron compounds are: the concentration of various ions; the acidity or alkalinity of the solution; and the degree of reduction of the environment. Iron sulfide, for example, precipitates only under extreme reducing conditions or from a solution in which the concentration of sulfide is great. The precipitation of iron carbonate and iron silicate depends primarily on the relative concentrations of bicarbonate and silicate ions. Ferrous iron oxidizes to hematite most readily under alkaline conditions (*i.e.*, conditions of pH greater than 7). The metal stays in solution as long as conditions remain constant and precipitates as any one of a number of minerals when conditions change. The precipitation reactions can occur in many different geologic situations, as summarized by the American geochemist K.B. Krauskopf (*Introduction to Geochemistry*, McGraw-Hill Book Co., 1967):

> . . . by oxidation at the site of the original iron mineral, before any transportation has taken place; by oxidation in soil derived from the original rock, after only minor movement within the soil layer; by oxidation in streams, lakes, or swamps, when the water is aerated and loses its contained organic matter; in seawater, as oxide if the water is aerated, as carbonate or silicate if the water is mildly reducing, as sulfide if the redox potential is low and sulfur is abundant.

In some situations in which iron could be expected to precipitate, ferric oxide instead remains in suspension as an iron colloid and can be carried for long distances. This is the form in which iron is transported in aerated surface water. In some geologic environments, bacteria act as iron-precipitating agents by using the oxidation of iron compounds as an energy-producing reaction for their life processes.

In addition to their contribution to the understanding of the occurrence of iron-ore minerals, iron-equilibrium studies have been extremely important in groundwater chemistry. A serious problem for many water users is objectionably high concentrations of dissolved iron that make the water unusable for many purposes. Another equally serious problem is the corrosion of well casings and pumps, which causes a great deal of maintenance expense. An adequate description of the local environment based on Eh, pH, mineralogy of aquifers (water-bearing strata) and direction of groundwater movement has made it possible in many places to predict the concentration of dissolved iron and to outline methods of treatment in potential water supplies before construction of wells. Similarly, the first step in developing a corrosion-abatement program is such a description of the chemical system in order to identify the deleterious corrosion and concomitant encrustation processes.

Uranium–vanadium equilibrium. The search for radioactive materials after World War II provided a great impetus for scientists to study chemical equilibrium because of complex problems associated with the origin and occurrence of uranium ores. Principles of modern low-temperature geochemistry were largely developed during this period of exploration for radioactive ores. Before about 1950, the chief uranium ore in the United States was carnotite, a hydrated, potassium-bearing uranium, and vanadium oxide compound (K$_2$(UO$_2$)$_2$V$_2$O$_8$ • 0 to 3H$_2$O), and it was believed to be a primary mineral precipitated during deposition of the surrounding sediments. The mineral is fully oxidized; uranium has a valence of six (U^{6+}) and vanadium a valence of five (V^{5+}). In deeper deposits, however, ore was found in which the valence states U^{4+} and V^{3+} existed, indicating a lesser degree of oxidation. Further search and study ultimately proved that uraninite (UO$_2$), in which uranium has a valence of four, is the primary mineral, and carnotite is the secondary mineral resulting from oxidation processes. Before this conclusion was reached, several important questions had to be resolved in order to develop a consistent theory that led to a successful exploration program. The American geochemists R.M. Garrels and C.L. Christ have succinctly stated the problem as follows,

> . . . if an unoxidized uranium ore consists of uraninite, montroseite, and pyrite, with some sphalerite and galena, will oxidation yield the complex mineral assemblages observed? What oxidation products can coexist stably? Which minerals will oxidize first under near equilibrium conditions?

The solution was achieved by superposition of various Eh–pH diagrams constructed in the manner described in the foregoing discussion.

Details of uranium chemistry explain much of the origin and occurrence of its ore minerals. Although uranium has many valence states ($+2$, $+3$, $+4$, $+5$, and $+6$), only the $+4$ and $+6$ states are of geologic interest. Vanadium exists in the natural state in valences of $+3$, $+4$, and $+5$ and is complicated further by the great variety of complex ions. Uranium in its two lowest valence states is a sufficiently powerful reducing agent to decompose water to form hydrogen gas; in the presence of water, the $+5$ valence state is unstable with respect to $+4$ and $+6$ as follows:

$$2UO_2^+ + 4H^+ = UO_2^{+2} + U^{+4} + 2H_2O.$$
$$(U = +5) \qquad (U = +6)$$

in which UO$_2^+$ is uranium oxide containing uranium in the $+5$ state and UO$_2^{+2}$ is uranium oxide containing uranium in the $+6$ state. The transition from valence state $+4$ to $+6$ occurs in the following reaction:

$$U^{4+} + 2H_2O = UO_2^{2+} + 4H^+ + 2e^-,$$

in which uranium in the $+4$ state combines with water to produce U^{+6}-bearing uranium oxide, from hydrogen ions (H$^+$) and two electrons (e$^-$). The reaction has a potential (E$^\circ = +0.33$ volt) that is within the normal range for redox potentials in nature. By obtaining equilibrium constants from free-energy data for various reactions, as discussed in the section on principles and techniques, it is quite easy to explain why the particular minerals are stable in the selected environments in which the ores exist.

Kaolinite–gibbsite equilibria. The distribution, origin, and formation of clay minerals demonstrate another group of chemical reactions that occur in nature. Clay minerals are hydrous aluminum silicates, and many contain other metals, primarily magnesium, iron, calcium, sodium, and potassium. The chemical composition of clay does not determine its properties, such as degree of plasticity and capacity for ion exchange. The primary control on clay properties is structure of the clay minerals, which may be examined by X-ray-diffraction cameras and electron microscopes. Many intriguing and unanswered questions of geochemistry remain centred around the origin of clay minerals. It is generally believed that clay is the stable product of weathering; that is, the minerals that represent final attainment of equilibrium between the original constituents of rock-forming minerals and conditions at the Earth's surface. It has not been clearly demonstrated whether the different clay minerals represent adjustments to slightly different weathering environments, or whether some of the minerals represent metastable intermediate varieties that are formed during weathering and ultimately are converted to other clay minerals. Experimental laboratory work suggests that acid solutions (pH less than 7) favour formation of kaolinite, and that basic or alkaline solutions (pH greater than 7) favour formation of montmorillonite. This conclusion is partly corroborated by data on the geologic occurrence of the two minerals.

Kaolinite is commonly the chief clay mineral in soils that occur on well-drained slopes in humid climates, where abundant vegetation makes soil solutions acid and where cations are effectively leached away (leaching is the percolating action of groundwater). Montmorillonite is characteristic of soils in less humid climates, where soil solutions are mainly alkaline and where cations are moved less rapidly. Illite is formed in environments that contain a high concentration of potassium ion and can be formed from montmorillonite. Illite is the common clay mineral in alkaline soils of desert areas.

The formation of bauxite   Another question of long standing has been the formation of bauxite, the important aluminum ore. The essence of the problem of origin of bauxite lies in the relation between kaolinite, $H_4Al_2Si_2O_9$, and gibbsite, $Al_2O_3 \cdot 3H_2O$. In many geological areas, kaolinite is the mineral that precedes the final dissolution of solids by agents of weathering. In other areas, the persistent mineral is gibbsite.

If equilibrium between kaolinite, gibbsite, dissolved silica, and water is assumed, then the following reaction can be written:

$$H_4Al_2Si_2O_9 + 5H_2O = Al_2O_3 \cdot 3H_2O + 2H_4SiO_4.$$

kaolinite   water   gibbsite   dissolved silica

Severe leaching conditions generally are accepted as required for the formation of gibbsite, and the pore water must be reasonably pure; its activity therefore is fixed at unity. The equilibrium constant for the reaction is $K_{eq} = [H_4SiO_4]^2$, and the free energy of the reaction is $+12.7$ kilocalories. Equilibrium is attained between gibbsite and kaolinite at a fixed value of the activity ($=$ concentration) of dissolved silica of about two parts per million of dissolved silica. At any lower value of dissolved silica, kaolinite should tend to dissolve, leaving a residuum of gibbsite.

The stability of gibbsite (Al_2O_3) can be shown (Figure 3)

From Robert M. Garrels and Charles L. Christ, *Solutions, Minerals, and Equilibria*, p. 358 (1965); Harper and Row

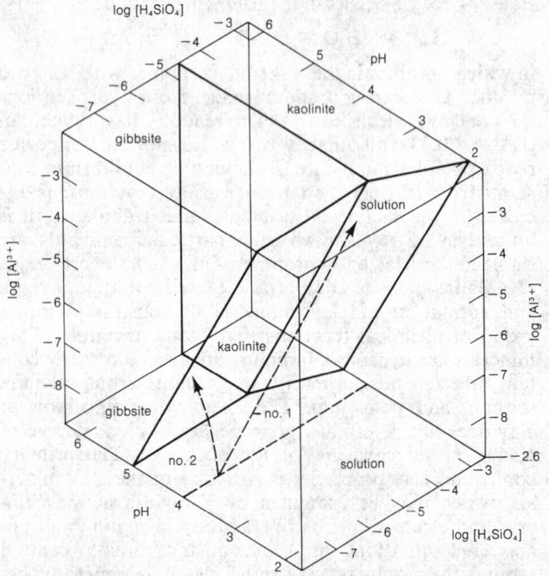

Figure 3: Gibbsite-kaolinite solution relations at 25° C and one atmosphere pressure, for acid conditions (see text).

as a volume on a diagram using pH, Al^{3+}, and dissolved silica (H_4SiO_4) as variables, even though its stability alone is independent of H_4SiO_4. The boundary between gibbsite and kaolinite is a plane representing a fixed activity of H_4SiO_4. At H_4SiO_4 activities greater than this value, kaolinite can be expected to dissolve congruently and thus leave no gibbsite residue. The prevalence of kaolinite in the upper levels of most soils formed under strong leaching conditions leads to the prediction that most soil-solution compositions are toward the rear of Figure 3.

The dashed arrows show the change in solution composition that results if kaolinite dissolves at a fixed pH. Under such conditions, the ratio of H_4SiO_4 to Al^{3+} in solution is maintained at unity. If a kaolinite soil is subjected to leaching by rainwater, with pH fixed at 4, perhaps by living plants or decomposing organic materials that release carbon dioxide, CO_2, to the soil water, the solution composition will change along the line indicated by arrow 1, and the soil field intersected is that of kaolinite. In other words, kaolinite dissolves congruently to leave a kaolinite residue. On the other hand, if there is no pH buffering (*i.e.*, stabilizing action by dissolved substances that release hydrogen ion) hydrogen ion (H^+) will be used up when kaolinite dissolves, and the solution composition will change along a path similar to that shown by arrow 2, indicating incongruent solution of kaolinite to produce a gibbsite residue.

The diagram thus leads to a hypothesis concerning some major controls on the formation of bauxite and serves to show the utility of such methods of representation as stimuli to the collection of data about relations that might not otherwise be deduced. Most soils in areas of high rainfall and concomitant high leaching rates are kaolinitic; they also tend to have low pH values. The low pH apparently results in part from a high carbon dioxide content in the soil atmosphere, an effect induced by decomposition of organic materials in the soil and in part from pH lowering at the surfaces of roots. Perhaps under exceptional conditions of high rainfall and high temperature, bacterial decomposition is so rapid that carbon dioxide resulting from organic decomposition passes directly into the atmosphere, and the soils are so heavily leached that plant ground cover is relatively sparse. If these conditions occur, rainwater descending through the soil will be relatively unbuffered, and gibbsite residue could result. Whatever the details of the explanation, it does appear that the requirement of abundant unbuffered soil water for bauxite formation is in accordance with the occurrence of low silica–high alumina soil residues.

Osmotic equilibria.   Certain earth materials, such as compacted clay minerals (shale), can act as semipermeable membranes; these materials restrict or prevent the passage of ions while allowing relatively unrestricted flow of neutral species, such as the water molecule. Among the phenomena resulting from the ion-exclusion properties of membranes are hyperfiltration and the development of osmotic pressure and of differences in electrical potential across them.

Hyperfiltration occurs when an electrolyte solution flows through a semipermeable membrane. As a result of ion exclusion, the effluent is less concentrated than the original solution.

Movement of water across a semipermeable membrane in the absence of an externally applied pressure differential may result from the existence of different salt concentrations on opposite sides of the membrane, from the existence of an electrical potential across the membrane, and also from the existence of different thermal-energy levels on either side of the membrane. Such phenomena are termed, respectively, chemical osmosis, electro-osmosis, and thermo-osmosis. Any one or a combination of these phenomena may cause pressure differentials across a membrane.

Chemical osmosis, electro-osmosis, and thermo-osmosis

The phenomenon of chemical osmosis will occur when two aqueous phases having different salt concentrations (that is, different activities of water) are separated by a semipermeable membrane. At constant temperature, a greater net transfer of water will occur from the less saline solution (in which the activity of water is higher) through the membrane into the more saline solution (lower activity of water), causing the pressure to increase in the more saline solution and to decrease in the less saline, if the two solutions are confined. The pressure that must be applied to the more saline side of the membrane to cause the passage of water in both directions to be equal is termed osmotic pressure. An equation to express the relation between osmotic pressure and solution concentration, derived from thermodynamic arguments, is

$$\pi = \frac{RT}{V^0_{H_2O}} \ln \frac{\alpha^I_{H_2O}}{\alpha^{II}_{H_2O}},$$

in which π (pi) is osmotic pressure, $V^0_{H_2O}$ is the molar volume of pure water, $\alpha^I_{H_2O}$ and $\alpha^{II}_{H_2O}$ are the activities of water in solutions I and II, respectively, R is a constant, and T is absolute temperature.

The flow of water through the membrane to establish osmotic equilibrium is accompanied by ion-exclusion effects, which will increase the salinity of the solution on the low-pressure side of the membrane. The solution that passes through the membrane is less saline than that on either side and will tend to decrease the salinity on the high-pressure side of the membrane.

Some pressure and salinity data regarding water-bearing sedimentary rocks cannot be explained by simple gravitational flow of water or by solution of minerals. Certain of such geological relations can be explained by osmotically induced cross-formational movement of water, through shale that serves as a semipermeable membrane, from an aquifer in which water has a low concentration of dissolved salts to one in which water is more concentrated. Similarly, an externally applied pressure differential on the fluid phase may cause cross-formational water flow through a semipermeable shale membrane, with resultant ion-exclusion effects commonly referred to as salt filtering or hyperfiltration.

It has been postulated that salt filtering by clay or shale membranes may account for the formation of brine, some of which has a dissolved solids concentration greatly exceeding that of seawater. These various speculations are supported by experimental laboratory investigations.

The exact mechanism by which ion-exclusion occurs is not fully understood. One widely held hypothesis involves the fact that clay minerals have a net charge deficiency. To maintain overall electrical neutrality, the clay absorbs a large number of cations and some anions. As the clay is compacted, the absorbed ions from either side of a pore or channel overlap, so that the pore becomes positively charged. This charged channel repels cations from entering, and, in order to maintain electric neutrality across the membrane, anions are also restricted from moving through the membrane pores.

BIBLIOGRAPHY. WILLIAM BACK and B.B. HANSHAW, "Chemical Geohydrology," in VEN TE CHOW (ed.), *Advances in Hydroscience*, vol. 2 (1965), a summary of the application of principles of thermodynamics and geochemistry to hydrologic systems to understand the behaviour of ions in nature and the observed chemical character of water; R.M. GARRELS and C.L. CHRIST, *Solutions, Minerals, and Equilibria* (1965), an excellent text that indicates the techniques of geochemical investigation, primarily in terms of the equilibrium of carbonates, silicates, and oxidation-reduction reactions; K.B. KRAUSKOPF, *Introduction to Geochemistry* (1967), a comprehensive, up-to-date text that emphasizes the application of theoretical geochemistry to geologic processes; R.A. HORNE, *Marine Chemistry* (1969), a modern and comprehensive description of the chemical nature of the ocean with a clear explanation of controlling chemical reactions and processes.

(B.B.H./Wi.B.)

Geography

Geography—*geō*, meaning "the earth," and *graphein*, "to write"—is the science that describes the Earth's surface. The concept of the discipline is simple, its study complex. The content is enormous and is constantly changing in both space and time. Since the features of the Earth's surface cannot be considered apart from the atmosphere above and the outer layers of the crust below, a zone of considerable vertical extent must be held in view, and all the phenomena, natural and man-made, that occur within it must be examined. This article falls into three parts. The first part is a short introduction that states in general terms the nature of geography as a discipline, outlines its interrelationship with other sciences, and notes briefly the changing role of the geographer from early times to the present day. The second part is a survey of geographical exploration that reveals how much of the world was known and therefore studied in times past. The third part presents a discussion of modern geographical concepts. There are separate articles on CLIMATE; CLIMATIC CHANGE; CONTINENTAL DRIFT; CONTINENTAL SHELF AND SLOPE; CONTINENTS, DEVELOPMENT OF; MAPS AND MAPPING; OCEAN BASINS; OCEAN CURRENTS; OCEANIC RIDGES; OCEANS AND SEAS; and OCEANS, DEVELOPMENT OF; and also on individual continents, countries, cities, states, and physical features, as well as biographical articles on individual explorers. Articles on related disciplines within the physical, biological, and social sciences may also be consulted.

The aims of geography and its relationship to other sciences. The aim of the geographer is not merely to paint a word picture, however vivid, of the surface features of the Earth nor merely to map them, however accurately. While he must do these things, his work begins, not ends, with the collection and depiction of data and with the perception of the spatial patterns they make. To understand the patterns, he must analyze the location of the elements, establish the networks that link them, and seek to identify the processes that bring them about and subsequently alter them. The patterns are studied not as separate designs but, rather, as they occur together in close interrelationship. Furthermore, areas and places cannot be studied in isolation if reality is to be preserved. The city of London, for example, must be looked at within the context of England, England within Europe, and Europe within the world. Nature has few sharp boundaries, and man—increasingly mobile, his communication lines ever more speedy, efficient, and far-flung—is realizing more and more forcibly the unity of the world. So vast a field demands from its students clarity of purpose, patient and objective investigation, and integrity of interpretation if progress in its understanding is to be made. *[margin: The interrelationship of spatial patterns]*

If the subject itself is logically indivisible, its study must be subdivided if it is to be manageable. There are two ways of doing this: either the Earth's surface may be considered part by part, the approach of regional geography; or the elements that create the spatial patterns may be grouped like with like, the approach of systematic geography.

In the first half of the 20th century, the regional approach was perhaps predominant. The examination of all the geographical elements within a chosen area, as they interacted to give the area a unique character, and thus to differentiate it from other areas, was considered the ultimate aim of the geographer. In the second half of the century, however, it was thought by some that, since the Industrial Revolution began, there has been so rapid a spread of ideals, ideas, and techniques that regional differences have become of less importance than regional similarities. Thus, there has been a trend in favour of the systematic approach that represents an endeavour to form hypotheses to explain those features of spatial patterns that many areas share in common.

Systematic geography may be conveniently subdivided into physical geography, including climatology, hydrography, and the study of landforms; biogeography, the geography of soils and of plant, animal, and human populations; and human geography, the geography of the economic, political, and social activities of man in organized communities. Historical geography is concerned primarily with the human geography of the past and is of importance because so many of the present spatial patterns owe much to earlier ones.

Each of the groups of elements that the geographer examines in their association in spatial patterns is in its own right the subject of study of another specialist. Thus, there are close links between the geographer and the meteorologist, geologist, biologist, demographer, economist, political scientist, sociologist, and historian. The geographer even has links with the psychologist, philosopher, and theologian, because ideas as well as material things often find geographical expression. The geographer also needs a knowledge of the science and art of surveying and of cartography, for the map is the record of geographical data, and its constant study is second in importance only to work on the ground itself. By the early 1970s, statistical techniques, with the help of com- *[margin: Relationship to other subjects of study]* puters and the building of models, had become fashionable aids to geographical analysis. In all these disciplines the geographer is a learner, not an investigator; he acquires from other scientists specific knowledge about each group of elements in which he is interested and, in return, gives them information about their spatial relationships with other phenomena.

It is, perhaps, the ecologist and the geographer who have the most in common. The unit of the ecologist is the ecosystem, a functional unit that includes both organisms and their nonliving environment. An ecosystem may vary in size and complexity from a pond to an ocean or from a copse to a forest. Some geographers have, indeed, defined their study as being that of human ecology, but this definition is not wholly valid: the ecologist's aim is the study of the functioning of his unit; the geographer's aim is the study of the distribution of functional units and of the spatial patterns that they form.

The evolution of the role of the geographer. The geographer has played many roles—as an explorer of the unknown world; as a map maker recording the geographical facts; as a scientist collating and arranging information to guide the search for more; and as a teacher educating his pupils the better to understand and appreciate the world of which they are a part.

In ancient Babylonia and Egypt, the geographer was most valued as a surveyor, remapping the boundaries that so often were obliterated by floods. In Greece, the geographer, then synonymous with the cosmographer, was a universal scientist since the specialist sciences, both natural and social, were as yet undifferentiated. Pythagoras and Aristotle, the Greek philosophers of the 6th century and 4th century BC, respectively, believed the Earth to be a sphere, and Pythagoras taught that it revolved around a central fire. Herodotus, the Greek historian of the 6th century BC, prefaced his history with a description of his world, speculated about the causes of volcanic eruptions and earthquakes, and discussed the courses of the major rivers and the reasons for the Nile floods. The Romans, essentially a practical people, were little interested in cosmographical hypotheses or geographical conundrums, but they needed roadbooks and road maps to guide soldiers and administrators throughout their empire: the Roman geographers were again the surveyors.

During the long years of internal dissension and external attack that followed the breakup of the Roman Empire in the West, scholars congregating in remote places looked inward, not outward; they studied the Bible, not the world, so that geographers became the henchmen of the theologians. The maps they produced were not attempts to portray reality but, in modern parlance, were "models," illustrating theological concepts. In these centuries, the Muslims, not the Christians, were the scientists; Arab geographers in the 11th and 12th centuries preserved, added to, and handed on the Greek learning that early Christendom had first ignored and then lost.

Stimulated by this fruitful contact with the Arabs, Western geographers shook themselves free from the bondage of the medieval Christian Church, only to be enthralled anew—by Greek ideas, in general, and by the concepts of Ptolemy, the 2nd-century Greek geographer and astronomer, in particular. Because these geographers were not original thinkers but mere popularizers of Greek ideas, they even discarded Arab additions and corrections. Ptolemy's maps, drawn from tables constructed in the 2nd century AD, were regarded as authoritative until the 16th century. It was, indeed, belief in Ptolemy's exaggerated representation of the west–east extent of Asia that encouraged Christopher Columbus and fellow adventurers to sail westward on their momentous voyages.

Geography in the Age of Discovery The role of the geographers in the 15th- and 16th-century Age of Discovery was twofold: to promote exploration and to record the new knowledge on new maps. Of the men who backed the voyages some were scholars: among these were the Portuguese prince Henry the Navigator and, in England, the mathematician John Dee, the translator Richard Eden (both Cambridge dons), and the

Oxford geographer Richard Hakluyt. Others—including the Englishmen Roger Barlow, Robert Thorne, and John Frampton—were merchants. The map makers were equally important; the maps of the Venetian Contarini (1506), the German Martin Waldsemüller (1507), and the Dutch cartographer Johann Ruysch (1508) show early attempts to fit the new discoveries into Ptolemy's scheme. The great Dutch cartographers—Gerardus Mercator and Abraham Ortelius in the 16th century and Jodocus Hondius and Willem Blaeu in the late 16th and early 17th centuries—supported by the interests of a still growing empire, produced up-to-date atlases that at last outmoded the Ptolemies.

In the course of the 18th century, the governments of the day and the learned societies replaced individual geographers as patrons of explorers, and the central authorities, with the aid of professional surveyors and cartographers, took their place as map makers. The function of the geographers became primarily the study of the ever-increasing knowledge of the features of the Earth's surface.

Emergence of the geographical discipline The emergence of geography as an independent discipline in the universities was presaged by the interest taken in the subject by the 18th-century philosophers. The German writer Johann Wolfgang von Goethe, the German poet Friederich Schiller, and the German philosopher Friederich Hegel, by their interest in nature, the French philosopher Baron Charles de Montesquieu, by his discussion of the effects of the environment on nations in his book *De l'esprit des lois* ("The Spirit of Law"), published in 1748, and the German philosopher Immanuel Kant, through the lectures he gave on physical geography as a "part of the theory of knowledge," all stimulated the study of geography.

Two Germans of the late 18th and early 19th centuries —Alexander von Humboldt, a natural scientist, and Carl Ritter, a historian—were the first to write and teach as academic geographers. Both attempted—Humboldt in *Kosmos* ("Cosmos"), Ritter in *Die Erdkunde* ("Geography")—to write books that would order and arrange all geographical knowledge in a systematic fashion: both died with their mammoth works unfinished, although their concepts laid the foundation of modern geography. The essential role of the geographer since their day has been that of the scholar, the scientist, and the teacher.

But the geographer has not lost his practical functions. With increasing confidence he emerges from the seclusion of the university to take his part in public life. Contemporary geographers, developing specialized studies, play a role in a society that is much concerned with planning the proper use of its environment.

A survey of geographical exploration

The world as known to the Incas of Peru in the 15th century must have had little in common with the world as known to their contemporaries the Italians. A survey of geographical exploration must therefore be made from a particular viewpoint; in this article the viewpoint is that of Europe.

The motives that spur men to examine their environment are many. Strong among them are the satisfaction of curiosity, the pursuit of trade, the conversion of the heathen, and the desire for security and political power. At different times and in different places, different motives are dominant; sometimes one motive inspires the promoters of discovery, another, the men who carry out the search.

The threads of geographical exploration are continuous and, being entwined one with another, are difficult to break or separate; three major sections may nevertheless be recognized. The first is the exploration of the Old World centred on the Mediterranean Sea; the second is the Age of Discovery, during which, in the search for sea routes to Cathay (the name by which China became known to medieval Europe), a New World was found; the third is the establishment of the geographical relationships of the New World to the Old and the elucidation of the major physical features of the continental interiors—in short, the delineation of the modern world.

A comparative study of the maps of the world illustrating this article and one in any modern atlas reveals vividly the progress that man has made in the exploration of the Earth.

THE EXPLORATION OF THE OLD WORLD

The period from the earliest recorded history to the beginning of the 15th century sees knowledge of the world widen from a river valley surrounded by mountains or desert (the views of Babylonia and Egypt) to a Mediterranean world with hinterlands extending from the Sahara to the Gobi deserts and from the Atlantic to the Indian oceans (the view of Greece and Rome), and later expand again to include the far northern lands beyond the Baltic and another and dazzling civilization in the Far East (the medieval view).

Map showing the geographical knowledge of the world derived from the writings of Hecataeus of Miletus, c. 500 BC.

The earliest known map

The earliest known surviving map, dating probably from the time of Sargon of Akkad (about 2334–2279 BC), shows canals or rivers—perhaps the Tigris and a tributary—and surrounding mountains. The rapid colonization of the shores of the Mediterranean and of the Black Sea by Phoenicia and the Greek city-states in the first millennium BC must have been accompanied by the exploration of their hinterlands by countless unknown soldiers and traders. Herodotus prefaces his *History* (written in the 5th century BC) with a geographical description of the then known world: it reveals that the coastlines of the Mediterranean and the Black Sea had by then been explored. (See the Herodotus map in the article MAPS AND MAPPING.)

Stories survive of a few men who are credited with bringing new knowledge from distant journeys. Herodotus tells of five young adventurers of the tribe of the Nasamones living on the desert edge of Cyrenaica in North Africa, who journeyed southwest for many months across the desert, reaching a great river flowing from west to east; this presumably was the Niger, although Herodotus thought it to be the Upper Nile.

Exploration of the Atlantic coastlines. Beyond the Pillars of Hercules (the Strait of Gibraltar), the Carthaginians (from the Phoenician city of Carthage in what is now Tunisia), holding both shores of the strait, early ventured out into the Atlantic. A Greek translation of a Punic (Carthaginian) inscription states that Hanno, a Carthaginian, was sent forth about 500 BC with 60 ships

and 30,000 colonists "to found cities." Even allowing for a possible great exaggeration of numbers, this expedition, if it occurred, can hardly have been the first exploratory voyage along the coast of West Africa. Some think that Hanno reached only the desert edge south of the Atlas, others identify the "deep river infested with crocodiles and hippopotamuses" with the Sénégal River, and the island where men "scampered up steep rocks and pelted us with stones" with one off the coast of Sierra Leone. There is no record that Hanno's voyage was followed up before the era of Henry the Navigator.

About the same time, Himilico, another Carthaginian, set forth on a voyage northward; he explored the coast of Spain, reached Brittany, and in his four-month cruise may have visited Britain. Two centuries later, about 300 BC, Carthaginian power at the gate of the Mediterranean temporarily slackened as a result of squabbles with the Greek city of Syracuse on the island of Sicily, so Pytheas, a Greek explorer of Massilia (Marseille), sailed through. His story is only known from fragments of the work of a contemporary historian, Timaeus (who lived in the 4th and 3rd centuries BC), as retold by the Roman savant Pliny the Elder, the Greek geographer Strabo, and the Greek historian Diodorus Siculus, all of whom were critical of its truth. It is probable that Pytheas, having coasted the shores of the Bay of Biscay, crossed from the island of Ouessant (Ushant), off the French coast of Brittany, to Cornwall in southwest England, perhaps seeking tin. He may have sailed round Britain; he describes it as a triangle and also relates that the inhabitants "harvest grain crops by cutting off the ears . . . and storing them in covered granges." Around Thule, "the northernmost of the British Isles, six days sail from Britain," there is "neither sea nor air but a mixture like sea-lung . . . binds everything together," a reference perhaps to drift ice or dense sea fog. Thule has been identified with Iceland (too far north), with Mainland island of the Shetland group (too far south), and perhaps, most plausibly, with Norway. Pytheas returned to Brittany and explored "beyond the Rhine"; he may have reached the Elbe. The voyage of Pytheas, like that of Hanno, does not seem to have been followed up. Herodotus concludes by saying "whether the sea girds Europe round on the north none can tell."

It was not Mediterranean folk but Northmen from Scandinavia, emigrating from their difficult lands centuries later, who carried exploration farther in the North Atlantic. From the 8th to the 11th century bands of Northmen, mainly Swedish, trading southeastward across the Russian plains, were active under the name of Varangians in the ports of the Black Sea. At the same time other groups, mainly Danish, raiding, trading, and settling along the coasts of the North Sea, arrived in the Mediterranean in the guise of Normans. Neither these Swedes nor Danes were exploring lands which were unknown to civilized Europeans, but doubtless they brought to these Europeans new knowledge of the distant northern lands.

The Northmen

It was the Norsemen of Norway who were the true explorers although, since little of their exploits was known to contemporaries and that little soon forgotten, they perhaps added less to the common store of Europe's knowledge than their less adventurous compatriots. About AD 890, Othere of Norway, "desirous to try how far that country extended north," sailed round the North Cape, along the coast of Lapland to the White Sea. But most Norsemen sailing in high latitudes explored not eastward but westward. Sweeping down the outer edge of Britain, settling in Orkney, Shetland, the Hebrides, and Ireland, they then voyaged on to Iceland, where in 870 they settled among Irish colonists who had preceded them by some two centuries. The Norsemen may well have arrived piloted by Irish sailors; and Irish refugees from Iceland, fleeing before the Norsemen, may have been the first discoverers of Greenland and Newfoundland, although this is mere surmise. The saga of Eric the Red (*Eiriks saga rauda;* also called *Thorfinns saga Karlsefnis*), a Norwegian, gives the story of the discovery of Greenland in 982; the west coast was explored, and at least two settlements were established on it. About AD 1000, one Bjarni Herjulfsson, on his way from Iceland to Greenland, was blown off course far to the southwest; he saw an unknown shore and returned to tell his tale. Leif, Eric's son, together with some 30 others, set out in 1001 to explore. They probably reached the coasts of Labrador and Newfoundland; some think that the farthest point south reached by the settlers, as described in the sagas, fits best with Maryland or Virginia, but others contend that the lands about the Gulf of St. Lawrence are more probably designated. The area was named Vinland, as grapes grew there, but it has been suggested that the "grapes" referred to were in fact cranberries. Attempts at colonization were unsuccessful, the Norsemen withdrew, and, although the Greenland colonies lingered on for some four centuries, little knowledge of these first discoveries came down to colour the vision of the seamen of Cádiz or Bristol; the voyages of Christopher Columbus and John Cabot had their strongest inspirations in quite other traditions.

The exploration of the coastlines of the Indian Ocean and the China Sea. Trade, across the land bridges and through the gulfs linking those parts of Asia, Africa, and Europe that lie between the Mediterranean and Arabian seas, was actively pursued from very early times. It is therefore not surprising that exploratory voyages early revealed the coastlines of the Indian Ocean. Herodotus wrote of Necho II, king of Egypt in the late 7th and early 6th centuries BC, that "when he stopped digging the canal . . . from the Nile to the Arabian Gulf . . . [he] sent forth Phoenician men in ships ordering them to sail back by the Pillars of Hercules." According to the story, this, in three years, they did. Upon their return, "they told things . . . unbelievable by me," says Herodotus, "namely that in sailing round Libya they had the sun on the right hand." Whatever he thought of the story of the sun, Herodotus was inclined to believe in the voyage: "Libya, that is Africa, shows that it has sea all round except the part that borders on Asia." Strabo records another story with the same theme: one Eudoxus, returning from a voyage to India in about 108 BC, was blown far to the south of Cape Guardafui. Where he landed he found a wooden prow with a horse carved on it, and he was told by the Africans that it came from a wrecked ship of men from the west.

About 510 BC, Darius the Great, king of Persia, sent one of his officers, Scylax of Caria, to explore the Indus. Scylax travelled overland to the Kabul River, reached the Indus, followed it to the sea, sailed westward, and, passing by the Persian Gulf (which was already well-known), explored the Red Sea, finally arriving at Arsinoë, near modern Suez. The greater part of the campaigns of the famous conqueror Alexander the Great were military exploratory journeys. The earlier expeditions through Babylonia and Persia were through regions already familiar to the Greeks, but later ones through the great tract of land from the south of the Caspian Sea to the mountains of the Hindu Kush brought the Greeks much new geographical knowledge. Alexander and his army crossed the mountains to the Indus Valley and then made a westward march from the lower Indus to Susa through the desolate country along the southern edge of the Iranian plateau; Nearchus, his admiral, in command of the naval forces of the expedition, waited for the favourable monsoon and then sailed from the mouth of the Indus to the mouth of the Euphrates, exploring the Asiatic coast of the Persian Gulf on his way.

As Roman power grew, increasing wealth brought increasing demands for Oriental luxuries; this led to great commercial activity in the eastern seas. As the coasts became well-known, the seasonal character of the monsoonal winds was skillfully used; the southwest monsoon was long known as Hippalus, named for a sailor who was credited with being the first to sail with it direct from the Gulf of Aden to the coast of the Indian peninsula. During the reign of the Roman emperor Hadrian in the 1st century BC, Western traders reached Siam (now Thailand), Cambodia, Sumatra, and Java; a few seem also to have penetrated northward to the coast of China. In AD 161,

according to Chinese records, an "embassy" came from the Roman emperor Marcus Aurelius to the emperor Huan Ti, bearing goods that Huan Ti gratefully received as "tribute." Ptolemy, however, does not know of these voyages: he sweeps his peninsula of Colmorgo (Malay) southwestward to join the eastward trend of his coast of Africa, thus creating a closed Indian Ocean (see the map of Ptolemy in the article MAPS AND MAPPING). He presumably did not believe the story of the circumnavigation of Africa. As the 2nd century AD passed, and Roman power declined, trade with the eastern seas did not cease but was gradually taken over by Ethiopians, Parthians, and Arabs. The Arabs, most successful of all, dominated eastern sea routes from the 3rd to the 15th century. In the tales of derring-do of Sindbad the Sailor (a hero of the collection of Arabian tales of unknown date and authorship called *The Thousand and One Nights*), there may be found, behind the fiction, the knowledge of these adventurous Arab sailors and traders, supplying detail to fill in the outline of the geography of the Indian Ocean.

The land routes of Central Asia. The prelude to the Age of Discovery, however, is to be found neither in the Norse explorations in the Atlantic nor in the Arab activities in the Indian Ocean but, rather, in the land journeys of Italian missionaries and merchants that linked the Mediterranean coasts to the China Sea. Cosmas Indicopleustes, an Alexandrian geographer writing in the 6th century, knew that Tzinitza (China) could be reached by sailing eastward, but he added: "one who comes by the overland route from Tzinitza to Persia makes a very short cut." Goods had certainly passed this way since Roman times, but they usually changed hands at many a mart, for disorganized and often warring tribes lived along the routes. In the 13th century the political geography changed. In 1216 a Mongol chief assumed the title of Gengis Khan and, after campaigns in China that gave him control there, turned his conquering armies westward. He and his successors built up an enormous empire until, in the late 13th century, one of them, Kublai Khan, reigned supreme from the Black Sea to the Yellow Sea. Europeans of perspicacity saw the opportunities that friendship with the Mongol power might bring. If Christian Europe could only convert the Mongols, this would at one and the same time heavily tip the scales against Muslim and in favour of Christian power and also give political protection to Christian merchants along the silk routes to the legendary sources of wealth in China. With these opportunities in mind, Pope Innocent IV sent friars to "diligently search out all things that concerned the state of the Tartars," and to exhort them "to give over their bloudie slaughter of mankinde and to receive the Christian faith." Among others, Giovanni da Pian del Carpini in 1245 and Willem van Ruysbroeck in 1253 went forth to follow these instructions. Travelling the great caravan routes from southern Russia, north of the Caspian and Aral seas and north of the Tien Shan, they eventually reached the court of the emperor at Karakorum. Carpini returned confident that the Emperor was about to become a Christian; Ruysbroeck told of the city in Cathay "having walls of silver and towers of golde"; he had not seen it but had been "crediblie informed" of it.

But the greatest of the 13th-century travellers in Asia were the Polos, wealthy merchants of Venice. In 1260 the brothers Nicolo and Maffeo Polo set out on a trading expedition to the Crimea. After two years they were ready to return to Venice, but, finding the way home blocked by war, they travelled eastward to Bukhara (now in the Uzbek Soviet Socialist Republic in the Soviet Union), where they spent another three years. They then accepted an invitation to accompany a party of Tatar envoys returning to the court of Kublai Khan at Cambaluc, near Peking. The Khan received them well, provided them with a gold tablet as a safe-conduct back to Europe, and gave them a letter begging the Pope to send "some hundred wise men, learned in the law of Christ and conversant with the seven Arts to preach to his people." The Polos arrived home, "having toiled three years on the way," to find that Pope Clement IV was dead. Two years

The campaigns of Alexander the Great

Travels of the Polos

later they set off again, without the wise men, but taking with them Nicolo's son, Marco Polo, then a youth of 17. (Marco kept detailed notes of all he saw and, late in life when a captive of the Genoese, dictated to a fellow prisoner a book containing an account of his travels.) This time the Polos took a different route: starting from the port of Ormuz on the Persian Gulf, they crossed Persia to the Pamirs and then followed a caravan route along the southern edge of the Tarim Basin and Gobi Desert to Cambaluc. Knowledge of the route is interesting, but the great contribution of Marco Polo to the geographical knowledge of the West lay in his vivid descriptions of the East. He had great opportunities of seeing China and appreciating its life, for he was taken into the service of the Khan and was sent as an administrator to great cities, busy ports, and remote provinces, with instructions to write full reports. In his book he described how, upon every main highroad, at a distance apart of 25 or 30 miles (40 to 50 kilometres), there were stations, with houses of accommodation for travellers, with 400 good horses kept in constant readiness at each station. He also reported that, along the roads, the Grand Khan caused trees to be planted, both to provide shade in summer and to mark the route in winter when the ground was covered with snow. Marco Polo lived and worked in western China, visiting the provinces of Shensi, Szechwan, and Yunnan, as well as the borders of Burma. He frequently visited "the noble and magnificent city of Quinsay [Hangchou], a name that signifies the Celestial City and which it merits from its pre-eminence to all others in the world in point of grandeur and beauty." Cipango (Japan) he did not visit but heard about it from merchants and sailors: "it is situated at a distance of 1,500 miles from the mainland . . . They have gold in the greatest abundance its sources being inexhaustible." The most detailed descriptions and the greatest superlatives were reserved for Cambaluc, capital of Cathay, whose splendours were beyond compare; to this city, he said,

> everything that is most rare and valuable in all parts of the world finds its way: . . . for not fewer than 1,000 carriages and pack-horses loaded with raw silk make their daily entry; and gold tissues and silks of various kinds are manufactured to an immense extent.

No wonder that, when Europe learned of these things, it became enthralled. After 17 years, the Venetians were permitted to depart; they returned to Europe by sea. After visiting Java they sailed through the Strait of Malacca (again proving the error of Ptolemy) and, landing at Ormuz, they travelled cross-country to Armenia, and so home to Venice, which they reached in 1295.

Other European travellers in Asia

A few travellers followed the Polos. Giovanni da Montecorvino, a Franciscan friar from Italy, became archbishop of Peking and lived in China from 1294 to 1328. Friar Oderic of Pordenone, an Italian monk, became a missionary, journeying throughout the greater part of Asia between 1316 and 1330. He reached Peking by way of India and Malaya, then travelled by sea to Canton; he returned to Europe by way of Central Asia, visiting Tibet in 1325—the first European to do so. Friar Oderic's account of his journeys had considerable influence in his day: it was from it that the spurious traveller, the English writer Sir John Mandeville, quarried most of his stories.

Ibn Baṭṭūṭah, an Arab of Tangier, journeyed farther perhaps than any other medieval traveller. In 1325 he set out to make the traditional pilgrimage to Mecca and in some 30 years he visited the greater part of the Old World, covering, it has been said, more than 75,000 miles. He was the first to explore much of Arabia; he travelled extensively in India; he reached Java and Southeast Asia. Then toward the end of his life he returned to the west where, after visiting Spain, he explored western Sudan "to the northernmost province of the Negroes." He reached the Niger, which he calls the Nile, and was astonished by the huge hippopotamuses "taking them to be elephants." When he finally returned to Fez in Morocco he "kissed the hand of the Commander of the Faithful the Sultan . . . and settled down under the wing of his bounty." He wrote a vivid and perspicacious account of his travels but his book did not become known

to Christian Europe for centuries. It was Marco Polo's book that was the most popular of all. Some 138 manuscripts of it survive: it was translated before 1500 into Latin, German, and Spanish, and the first English translation was published in 1577. For centuries Europe's maps of the Far East were based on the information provided by Marco Polo; even as late as 1533 Johannes Schöner, the German maker of globes, wrote:

> Behind the Sinae and the Ceres [legendary cities of Central Asia] . . . many countries were discovered by one Marco Polo . . . and the sea coasts of these countries have now recently again been explored by Columbus and Amerigo Vespucci in navigating the Indian Ocean.

Columbus possessed and annotated a copy of the Latin edition (1483–85) of Marco Polo's book, and in his journal he identified many of his own discoveries with places that Marco Polo describes.

Thus, with Ptolemy in one hand and Marco Polo in the other, the European explorers of the Age of Discovery set forth to try to reach Cathay and Cipango by new ways; Ptolemy promised that the way was short, Marco Polo that the reward was great.

THE AGE OF DISCOVERY

In the 100 years from the mid-15th to the mid-16th century, a combination of circumstances stimulated men to seek new routes; and it was new routes rather than new lands that filled the minds of kings and commoners, scholars and seamen. First, toward the end of the 14th century, the vast empire of the Mongols was breaking up; thus, Western merchants could no longer be ensured of safe-conduct along the land routes. Secondly, the growing power of the Ottoman Turks, who were hostile to Christians, blocked yet more firmly the outlets to the Mediterranean of the ancient sea routes from the East. Thirdly, new nations on the Atlantic shores of Europe were now ready to seek overseas trade and adventure.

The sea route east by south to Cathay. Henry the Navigator, prince of Portugal, initiated the first great enterprise of the Age of Discovery—the search for a sea route east by south to Cathay. His motives were mixed. He was curious about the world; he was interested in new navigational aids and better ship design and was anxious to test them; he was also a crusader and hoped that, by sailing south and then east along the coast of Africa, Arab power in North Africa could be attacked from the rear. The promotion of profitable trade was yet another motive; he aimed to divert the Guinea trade in gold and ivory away from its routes across the Sahara to the Moors of Barbary (North Africa) and instead channel it via the sea route to Portugal. How soon the idea of finding a new sea route to Cathay came consciously into Henry's mind is not clear; but certainly by his death in 1460 he had formulated this aim.

Henry the Navigator

Expedition after expedition was sent forth throughout the 15th century to explore the coast of Africa. In 1445, the Portuguese navigator Dinas Dias reached the mouth of the Sénégal, which "men say comes from the Nile, being one of the most glorious rivers of Earth, flowing from the Garden of Eden and the earthly paradise." Once the desert coast had been passed, the sailors pushed on: in 1455 and 1456 Alvise Ca' da mosto made voyages to Gambia and the Cape Verde Islands. All seemed promising; trade was good with the riverine peoples, and the coast was trending hopefully eastward. Then the disappointing fact was realized: the head of a great gulf had been reached, and, beyond, the coast seemed to stretch endlessly southward. Yet, when Columbus sought backing for his plan to sail westward across the Atlantic to the Indies, he was refused—"seeing that King John II [Henry's successor] ordered the coast of Africa to be explored with the intention of going by that route to India."

King John II sought to establish two routes: the first, a land and sea route through Egypt and Ethiopia to the Red Sea and the Indian Ocean and, the second, a sea route around the southern shores of Africa, the latter an act of faith, since Ptolemy's map showed a landlocked Indian Ocean. In 1487, a Portuguese emissary, Pêro da Covilhã, successfully followed the first route but, on re-

The search for routes to Asia

turning to Cairo he reported that, in order to travel to India, the Portuguese "could navigate by their coasts and the seas of Guinea." In the same year another Portuguese navigator, Bartolomeu Dias, found encouraging evidence that this was so. In 1487 he rounded the Cape of Storms in such bad weather that he did not see it, but he satisfied himself that the coast was now trending northeastward; before turning back, he reached the Great Fish River, in what is now South Africa. On the return voyage, he sighted the Cape and set up a pillar upon it to mark its discovery.

The seaway was now open, but eight years were to elapse before it was exploited. In 1492 Columbus had apparently reached the East by a much easier route. By the end of the decade, however, doubts of the validity of Columbus' claim were current. Interest was therefore renewed in establishing the sea route south by east to the known riches of India. In 1497 a Portuguese captain, Vasco da Gama, sailed in command of a fleet under instructions to reach Calicut, on India's west coast. This he did after a magnificent voyage around the Cape of Storms (which he renamed the Cape of Good Hope) and along the unknown coast of East Africa. Yet another Portuguese fleet set out in 1500, this one being under the command of Pedro Alvarez Cabral; on the advice of da Gama, Cabral steered southwestward to avoid the calms of the Guinea coast; thus, en route for Calicut, Brazil was discovered. Soon trading depots, known as factories, were built along the African coast, at the strategic entrances to the Red Sea and the Persian Gulf, and along the shores of the Indian peninsula. In 1511 the Portuguese established a base at Malacca, commanding the straits into the China Sea; in 1511 and 1512, the Moluccas, or Spice Islands, and Java were reached; in 1557 the trading port of Macau was founded at the mouth of the Canton River. Europe had arrived in the East. It was in the end the Portuguese, not the Turks, who destroyed the commercial supremacy of the Italian cities, which had been based on a monopoly of Europe's trade with the East by land. But Portugal was soon overextended; it was therefore the Dutch, the English, and the French who in the long run reaped the harvest of her enterprise.

Some idea of the knowledge that these trading explorers brought to the common store may be gained by a study of contemporary maps. The map of the German Henricus Martellus, published in 1492, shows the shores of North Africa and of the Gulf of Guinea more or less correctly and was probably taken from numerous seamen's charts. The delineation of the west coast of southern Africa from the Guinea Gulf to the Cape suggests a knowledge of the charts of the expedition of Bartolomeu Dias. The coastlines of the Indian Ocean are largely Ptolemaic with two exceptions: first, the Indian Ocean is no longer landlocked; and second, the Malay Peninsula is shown twice —once according to Ptolemy and once again, presumably, according to Marco Polo. The Contarini map of 1506 shows further advances; the shape of Africa is generally accurate, and there is new knowledge of the Indian Ocean, although it is curiously treated. Peninsular India (on which Cananor and Calicut are named) is shown; although too small, it is, however, recognizable. There is even an indication to the east of it of the Bay of Bengal, with a great river running into it. Eastward of this is Ptolemy's India, with the huge island of Taprobane—a muddled representation of the Indian peninsula and Ceylon. East again, as on the map of Henricus Martellus, the Malay Peninsula appears twice. Ptolemy's bonds were hard to break.

The sea route west to Cathay. It is not known when the idea originated of sailing westward in order to reach

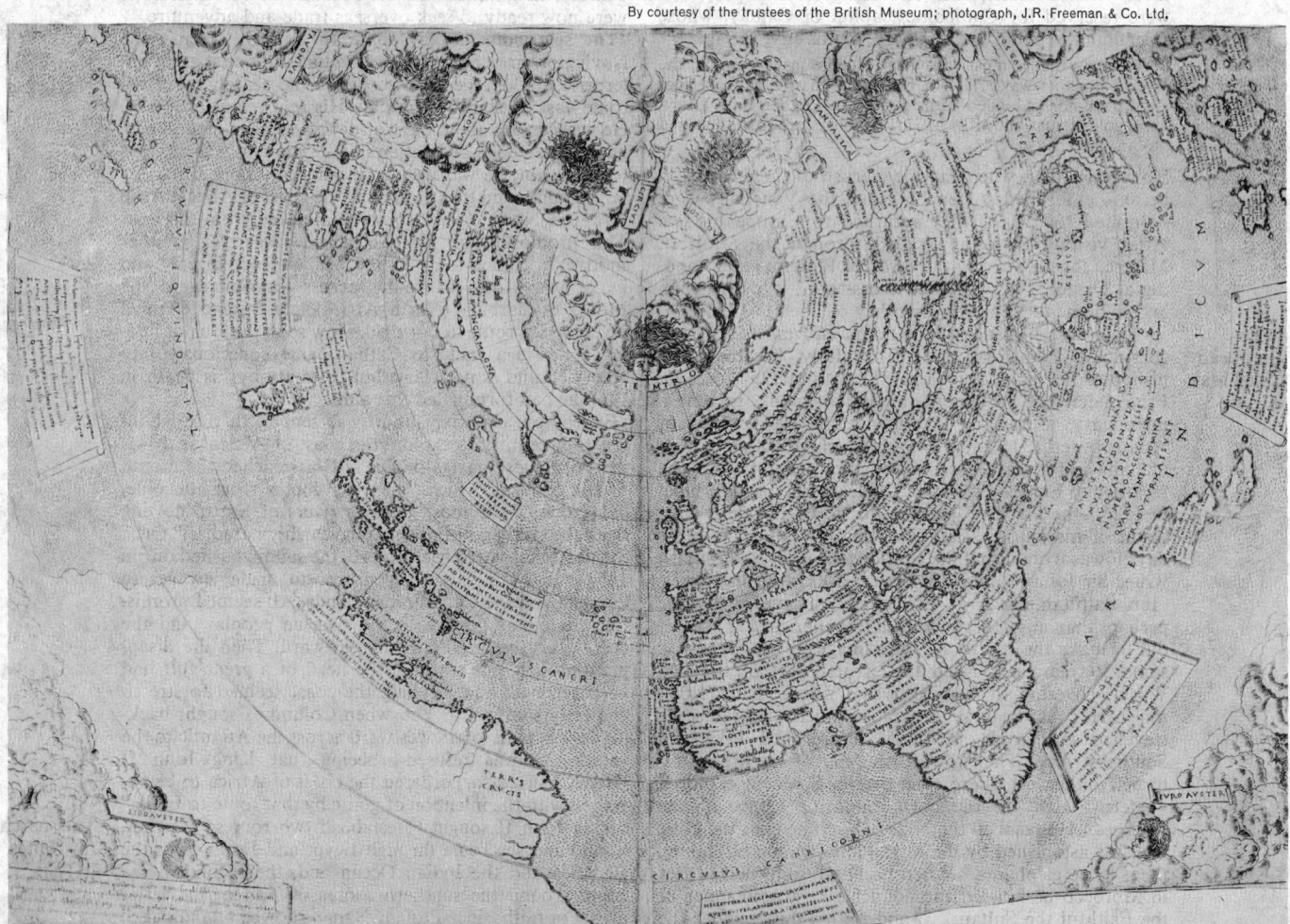

World map by J.M. Contarini, 1506, depicting the expanding horizons becoming known to European geographers in the Age of Discovery.

Cathay. Many sailors set forth searching for islands in the west; and it was a commonplace among scientists that the east could be reached by sailing west, but to believe this a practicable voyage was an entirely different matter. Christopher Columbus, a Genoese or Spaniard who had settled in Lisbon about 1477, argued that Cipango lay a mere 2,500 nautical miles west of the Canary Islands in the eastern Atlantic. He took 45 instead of 60 nautical miles as the value of a degree; he accepted Ptolemy's exaggerated west–east extent of Asia and then added to it the lands described by Marco Polo, thus reducing the true distance between the Canaries and Cipango by about one-third. He could not convince the Portuguese scientists nor the merchants of Lisbon that his idea was worth backing; but eventually he obtained the support of King Ferdinand and Queen Isabella of Spain. The sovereigns probably argued that the cost of equipping the expedition would not be very great; the loss, if it failed, could be borne; the gain, should it succeed, was incalculable—indeed, it might divert to Spain all the wealth of Asia.

The voyages of Columbus

On August 3, 1492, Columbus sailed from Palos, Spain, with three small ships manned by Spaniards. From the Canaries he sailed westward, for, on the evidence of the globes and maps in which he had faith, Japan was on the same latitude. If Japan should be missed, Columbus thought that the route adopted would land him, only a little further on, on the coast of China itself. Fair winds favoured him, the sea was calm, and, on October 12, landfall was made on an island now generally identified as Watling Island in the Bahamas. With the help of Amerindians, the ships reached Cuba and then Haiti. Although there was no sign of the wealth of the lands of Kublai Khan, Columbus nevertheless seemed convinced that he had reached China, since, according to his reckoning, he was beyond Japan. A second voyage in 1493 and 1494, searching fruitlessly for the court of Kublai Khan, further explored the islands of "the Indies." Doubts seem to have arisen among the would-be colonists as to the identity of the islands since Columbus made all take an oath that Cuba was the southeast promontory of Asia—the Golden Chersonese. On his third voyage, in 1498, Columbus sighted Trinidad, entered the Gulf of Paria, on the coast of what is now Venezuela, and annexed for Spain "a very great continent . . . until today unknown." On a fourth voyage, from 1502 to 1504, he coasted Central America from Honduras to Darien on the Isthmus of Panama, seeking a navigable passage to the west. What passage he had in mind is obscure; if he still believed he had reached Asia, perhaps he sought a way through Ptolemy's Golden Chersonese into the Indian Ocean.

The tenacity, the courage, the skill in navigation that Columbus showed makes him stand out among the very few explorers who have changed substantially men's ideas about the world. At the time, however, his efforts must have seemed ill-rewarded: he found no emperor's court rich in spices, silks, gold, or precious stones but had to contend with mutinous sailors, dissident colonists, and disappointed sovereigns. He died at Valladolid in 1506. Did he believe to the end that he had reached Cathay, or did he dimly perceive that he had found a New World?

Whatever Columbus thought, it was clear to others that there was much to be investigated, and probably much to be gained, by exploration westward. Not only in Lisbon and Cádiz but also in other Atlantic ports, groups of men congregated in hopes of joining in the search. In England, Bristol, with its western outlook and Icelandic trade, was the port best placed to nurture adventurous seamen. In the latter part of the 15th century, John Cabot, with his wife and three sons, came to Bristol from Genoa or Venice. His project to sail west gained support, and with one small ship, the "Matthew," he set out in May 1497, taking a course due west from Dursey Head, Ireland. His landfall on the other side of the ocean was probably on the northern peninsula of what is now known as Newfoundland. From here, Cabot explored southward, perhaps encouraged to do so, even if seeking a westward passage, by ice in the Strait of Belle Isle. Little is known of John Cabot's first voyage, and almost nothing of his second, in 1498, from which he did not return, but his voyages in high latitudes represented almost as great a navigational feat as those of Columbus.

The coasts between the landfalls of Columbus and of John Cabot were charted in the first quarter of the 16th century by Italian, French, Spanish, and Portuguese sailors. Sebastian Cabot, son of John, gained a great reputation as a navigator and promoter of Atlantic exploration, but whether this was based primarily on his own experience or on the achievements of his father is uncertain. In 1499 Amerigo Vespucci, an Italian merchant living in Seville, together with the Spanish explorer Alonso de Ojeda, explored the north coast of South America from Surinam to the Golfo de Venezuela. His lively and embellished description of these lands became popular, and Waldseemüller, on his map of 1507, gave the name America to the southern part of the continent.

Contarini's map

The 1506 map of Contarini represented a brave attempt to collate the mass of new information, true and false, that accrued from these western voyages. The land explored by Columbus on his third voyage and by Vespucci and de Ojeda in 1499 is shown at the bottom left of the map as a promontory of a great northern bulge of a continent extending far to the south. The northeast coast of Asia at the top left is pulled out into a great peninsula on which is shown a big river and some mountains representing Contarini's concept of Newfoundland and the lands found by the Cabots and others. In the wide sea that separates these northern lands from South America, the West Indies are shown. Halfway between the Indies and the coast of Asia, Japan is drawn. A legend placed between Japan and China reveals the state of opinion among at least some contemporary geographers; it presumably refers to the fourth voyage of Columbus in 1502 and may be an addition to the map. It runs:

Christopher Columbus, Viceroy of Spain, sailing westwards, reached the Spanish islands after many hardships and dangers. Weighing anchor thence he sailed to the province called Ciambra [a province which then adjoined Cochinchina].

Others did not agree with Contarini's interpretation. To more and more men it was becoming plain that a New World had been found, although for a long time there was little inclination to explore it but instead a great determination to find a way past it to the wealth of Asia. Yet the voyage of the Portuguese navigator Ferdinand Magellan, from 1519 to 1521, dispelled two long-cherished illusions: first, that there was an easy way through the barrier and, second, that, once the barrier was passed, Cathay was near at hand.

Magellan's voyages

Ferdinand Magellan had served in the East Indies as a young man. Familiar with the long sea route to Asia eastward from Europe via the Cape of Good Hope, he was convinced that there must be an easier sea route westward. His plan was in accord with Spanish hopes; five Spanish ships were fitted out in Seville, and in August 1519 they sailed under his command first to the Cape Verde Islands, and thence to Brazil. Standing offshore, they then sailed southward along the east coast of South America; the estuary of the Río de la Plata was explored in the vain hope that it might prove to be a strait leading to the Pacific. Magellan's ships then sailed south along the coast of Patagonia. The Gulf of St. George, and doubtless many more small embayments, raised hopes that a strait had been found, only to dash them; at last at Port Julian, at 49°15′ S, winter quarters were established. In September 1520, a southward course was set once more, until, finally, on October 21, Magellan found a strait leading westward. It proved to be an extremely difficult one: it was long, deep, torturous, and rock-walled; bedevilled by icy squalls and dense fogs, it was a miracle that three of the five ships got through its 325-mile length. After 38 days, they sailed out into the open ocean. Once away from land, the ocean seemed calm enough; Magellan consequently named it the Pacific. The Pacific, however, proved to be of vast extent, and for 14 weeks the little ships sailed on a northwesterly course without encountering land. Short of food and water, the sailors ate sawdust mixed with ship's biscuits and chewed the leather parts of their gear to keep themselves alive. At last, on March 6, 1521, exhausted and scurvy-ridden, they landed at the island of Guam. Ten days later they reached the Philippines, where Magellan was killed in a local quarrel. The survivors, in two ships, sailed on to the Moluccas; thus, sailing westward, they arrived at last in territory already known to the Portuguese sailing eastward. One ship attempted, but failed, to return across the Pacific. The remaining ship, the "Vittoria," laden with spices, under the command of the Spanish navigator Juan Sebastián del Cano, sailed alone across the Indian Ocean, rounded the Cape of Good Hope, and arrived at Seville on September 9, 1522, with only 18 survivors of the 239 men who had set sail with the expedition three years earlier. Del Cano, not having allowed for the fact that his circumnavigation had caused him to gain a day, was greatly puzzled to find that his carefully kept log was one day out; he was, however, delighted to discover that the cargo that he had brought back more than paid for the expenses of the voyage.

It is fitting to consider this first circumnavigation as marking the close of the Age of Discovery. Magellan and his men had demonstrated that Columbus had discovered a New World and not the route to China and that Columbus' "Indies"—the West Indies—were separated from the East Indies by a vast ocean.

Not all the major problems of world geography were, however, now solved. Two great questions still remained unanswered. Were there "northern passages" between the Atlantic and Pacific oceans more easily navigable than the dangerous Strait of Magellan to the south? Was there a great landmass somewhere in the vastness of the southern oceans—a Terra Australis ("southern land") that would balance the northern continents?

THE EMERGENCE OF THE MODERN WORLD

The centuries that have elapsed since the Age of Discovery have seen the end of dreams of easy routes to the East by the north, the discovery of Australasia and Antarctica in place of Terra Australis Incognita, and the identification of the major features of the continental interiors.

While, as in earlier centuries, traders and missionaries often proved themselves also to be intrepid explorers, in this most recent period of geographical discovery the seeker after knowledge for its own sake played a greater part than ever before.

The northern passages. Roger Barlow, in his *Briefe Summe of Geographie*, written in 1540–41, asserted that "the shortest route, the northern, has been reserved by Divine Providence for England."

The search for a Northeast Passage

The concept of a Northeast Passage was at first favoured by the English: it was thought that, although its entry was in high latitudes, it "turning itself, trendeth towards the southeast . . . and stretcheth directly to Cathay." It was also argued that the cold lands bordering this route would provide a much needed market for English cloth. In 1553 a trading company, later known as the Muscovy Company, was formed with Sebastian Cabot as its governor. Under its auspices numerous expeditions were sent out. In 1553 an expedition set sail under the command of Sir Hugh Willoughby; Willoughby's ship was lost, but the exploration continued under the leadership of its pilot general, Richard Chancellor. Chancellor and his men wintered in the White Sea, and next spring "after much adoe at last came to Mosco." Between 1557 and 1560, another English voyager, Anthony Jenkinson, following up this opening, travelled from the White Sea to Moscow, then to the Caspian, and so on to Bukhara, thus reaching the old east–west trade routes by a new way. Soon, attempts to find a passage to Cathay were replaced by efforts to divert the trade of the ancient silk routes from their traditional outlets on the Black Sea to new northern outlets on the White Sea.

The Dutch next took up the search for the passage. The Dutch navigator William Barents made three expeditions between 1594 and 1597 (when he died in Novaya Zemlya). The English navigator Henry Hudson, in the employ of the Dutch, discovered between 1605 and 1607 that ice blocked the way both east and west of Svalbard (Spitsbergen). Between 1725 and 1729, and from 1734 to

1743, a series of expeditions inspired by the Danish-Russian explorer Vitus Bering attempted the passage from the eastern end, but it was not until 1878–79 that Baron Erik Nordenskiöld, the Finnish-Swedish scientist and explorer, sailed through it.

The Northwest Passage, on the other hand, also had its strong supporters. In 1576 Humphrey Gilbert, the English soldier and navigator, argued that "Mangia [South China], Quinzay [Hangchow] and the Moluccas are nearer to us by the North West than by the North East," while John Dee in 1577 set out the view that the Strait of Anian, separating America from Asia, led southwest "along the backeside of Newfoundland." In 1534 Jacques Cartier, the French navigator, explored the St. Lawrence estuary. In 1576 the English explorer Sir Martin Frobisher found the bay named after him. Between 1585 and 1587, the English navigator John Davis explored Cumberland Sound and the western shore of Greenland to 73° N; although he met "a mighty block of ice," he reported that "the passage is most probable and the execution easy." In 1610 Henry Hudson sailed through Hudson Strait to Hudson Bay, confident, before he was set adrift by a mutinous crew, that success was at hand. Between 1612 and 1615, three English voyagers—Robert Bylot, Sir Thomas Button, and William Baffin—thoroughly explored the bay, returning convinced that there was no strait out of it leading westward. As in the quest for a Northeast Passage, interest turned from the search for a route leading to the riches of the East to the exploitation of local resources. Englishmen of the Hudson's Bay Company, founded in 1670 to trade in furs, explored the wide hinterlands of the St. Lawrence estuary and Hudson Bay. Further search for the passage itself did not take place until the 19th century: Sir William Parry (1819–25), Sir John Franklin (1819–45) and more than 40 expeditions sent out to search for Franklin and his party failed to find it. It was left to the Norwegian explorer Roald Amundsen to be the first to sail through the passage, which he did in 1903–05.

Eastward voyages to the Pacific. By the end of the 16th century, Portugal in the East held only the ports of Goa and Diu, in India, and Macau, in China. The English dominated the trade of India, and the Dutch that of the East Indies. It was the Dutch, trading on the fringes of the known world, who were the explorers. Victualling their ships at the Cape, they soon learned that, by sailing east for some 3,000 miles (5,000 kilometres) before turning north, they would encounter favourable winds in setting a course toward the Spice Islands (now the Moluccas). Before long, reports were received of landfalls made on an unknown coast; as early as 1618, a Dutch skipper suggested that "this land is a fit point to be made by ships . . . *in order* to get a fixed course for Java." Thereafter, the west coast of Australia was gradually charted: it was identified by some as the coast of the great southern continent shown on Mercator's map, and, by others, as the continent of Loach or Beach mentioned by Marco Polo, interpreted as lying to the south of Malacca; Polo, however, was probably describing the Malay Peninsula.

The discovery of Australia

In 1642, a farsighted governor general of the Dutch East India Company, Anthony van Diemen, sent out the Dutch navigator Abel Tasman for the immediate purpose of making an exploratory voyage, but with the ultimate aim of developing trade. Sailing first south then east from Mauritius, Tasman landed on the coast of Tasmania, after which he coasted round the island to the south and, sailing east, discovered the South Island of New Zealand; "we trust that this is the mainland coast of the unknown South land," he wrote. He sailed north without finding Cook Strait, and, making a sweeping arc on his voyage back to the Dutch port of Batavia (today Djakarta, capital of Indonesia), he discovered the Tonga and the Fiji islands. In 1644, on a second voyage, he traced the north coast of Australia from Cape York (which he thought to be a part of New Guinea) to the North West Cape.

Westward voyages to the Pacific. The earlier European explorers in the Pacific were primarily in search of trade or booty; the later ones were primarily in search of information.

The traders, for the most part Spaniards, established land portages from harbours on the Caribbean to harbours on the west coast of Central and South America; from the Pacific coast ports of the Americas, they then set a course westward to the Philippines. Many of their ships crossed and recrossed the Pacific without making a landfall; many islands were found, named, and lost, only to be found again without recognition, renamed, and perhaps lost yet again. In the days before longitude could be accurately fixed, such uncertainty was not surprising.

Some voyages—for example, those of Álvaro de Mendaña de Neira, the Spanish explorer, in 1567 and 1568; Mendaña and the Portuguese navigator Pedro Fernández de Quirós in 1595; Quirós and another Portuguese explorer, Luis de Torres, in 1606—had, among other motives, the purpose of finding the great southern continent. Quirós was sure that in Espiritu Santo in the New Hebrides he had found his goal; he "took possession of the site on which is to be founded the New Jerusalem." Torres sailed from there to New Guinea and thence to Manila, in the Philippines. In doing so, he coasted the south shore of New Guinea, sailing through Torres Strait, unaware that another continent lay on his left hand.

The English were rivals of the Spaniards in the search for wealth in unknown lands in the Pacific. Two English seamen, Sir Francis Drake and Thomas Cavendish, circumnavigated the world from west to east in 1577 to 1580 and 1586 to 1588, respectively. One of Drake's avowed objects was the search for Terra Australis. Once through Magellan's straits, however, strong winds made him turn north—perhaps not reluctantly; he then sailed along the coast of Peru with great financial profit, and continuing northward, perhaps in search of the Strait of Anian, he explored the west coast of North America to 48° N. He returned south to winter in New Albion (California); the next summer he sailed on the Spanish route to Manila, then returning home by the Cape.

Despite the fact that he participated in several buccaneering voyages, the English seaman William Dampier, who was active in the late 17th and early 18th centuries, may be regarded as the first to travel mainly to satisfy scientific curiosity. He wrote: "I was well satisfied enough knowing that, the further we went, the more knowledge and experience I should get, which was the main thing I regarded." His book *A New Voyage Round the World*, published in 1697, further popularized the idea of a great southern continent.

In the late 18th century, the final phase of Pacific exploration occurred. The French sent the explorer Louis-Antoine de Bougainville to the Pacific in 1768. He appears to have been more of a skeptic than many of his contemporaries, for, while he agreed "that it is difficult to conceive such a number of low islands and almost drowned lands without a continent near them," at the same time he maintained that "if any considerable land existed hereabouts we could not fail meeting with it." The British, for their part, commissioned John Byron in 1764 and Samuel Wallis and Phillip Carteret in 1766 "to discover unknown lands and to explore the coast of New Albion." For all the navigational skill and personal endurance shown by captains and crews, the rewards of these voyages in increasing geographical knowledge were not great. The courses sailed were in the familiar waters of the southern tropics, none was through the dangerous waters of higher latitudes.

Cook's voyages in the Pacific

Capt. James Cook, the English navigator, in three magnificent voyages at long last succeeded in demolishing the fables about Pacific geography. He was given command of an expedition to observe the transit of the planet Venus at Tahiti on June 3, 1769; with the observation completed, he carried out his instructions to search the area between 40° and 35° S "until you discover it [Terra Australis] or fall in with the eastern side of the land discovered by Tasman and now called New Zealand." He reached New Zealand, circumnavigated both islands, sailed westward, and on April 19, 1770, made landfall on the eastern coast of Australia. He then turned northward, charting carefully, being well aware of the dangers of the Great Barrier Reef. At Cape York, Cook took possession of the whole eastern coast, to which he gave the name New South Wales. He sailed through Torres Strait, recognizing as he did so that New Guinea was an island. When Cook sailed back to England by Batavia and the Cape, the coastline of the fifth continent was almost complete; only in the south did it still remain unknown. In 1798 to 1799, two British navigators, George Bass and Matthew Flinders, circumnavigated Tasmania, and in 1801–03 Flinders charted the coast of the Great Australian Bight and circumnavigated the continent, thereby proving that there was no strait from the bight to the Gulf of Carpentaria.

In a second voyage, from 1772 to 1775, which in many ways was the greatest of the three, Cook searched systematically for the elusive continent that many still believed might exist. The first summer he examined the area to the south of the Indian Ocean; in the second, he searched the ocean between New Zealand and Cape Horn; and, in the third, the ocean between Cape Horn and the Cape of Good Hope. He sailed home convinced that the great southern continent of the map makers (*i.e.*, a continent in the South Pacific east of New Zealand) was a fable.

With the exploration of the Pacific completed, interest in a Northwest Passage revived. In 1778 Cook proceeded to latitude 65° N, but he found no way through the ice barrier either to east or to west. He then sailed south to Hawaii, where he was killed in a dispute with the islanders.

Terra Australis Incognita had disappeared: there was now no unknown landmass in the southern oceans. It was Matthew Flinders who suggested that the fifth continent should be named Australia—a name that had long associations with the South Seas and that accorded well with the names of the other continents.

The continental interiors. At the opening of the 19th century, the major features of Europe, Asia, and North and South America were known; in Africa some classical misconceptions still persisted; inland Australia was still almost blank; and Antarctica was not on the map at all.

The river systems were the key to African geography. The existence of a great river in the interior of West Africa was known to the Greeks, but in which direction it flowed and whether it found an outlet in the Sénégal, the Gambia, the Congo, or even the Nile were in dispute. A young Scottish surgeon, Mungo Park, was asked to explore it by the African Association of London. In 1796 Park, who had travelled inland from the Gambia, saw "the long sought for majestic Niger flowing slowly *eastwards*." On a second expedition, attempting to follow its course to the mouth, he was drowned near Bussa, in what is now Nigeria. In 1830 an English explorer, Richard Lander, travelled from the Bight of Benin, on the West African coast, to Bussa, and he then navigated the river down to its mouth, which was revealed as being one of the delta distributaries that, because of the trade in palm oil, were known to traders as "the oil rivers" on the Gulf of Guinea.

Exploration of the Zambezi

The Zambezi, in south central Africa, was not known at all until, in the mid-19th century, the Scottish missionary-explorer David Livingstone crossed the Kalahari from the south, found Lake Ngami, and, hearing of populous areas farther north, came upon the river in midcourse. On a great exploratory journey from 1852 to 1856, the main purpose of which was to expose the slave trade, he first travelled upstream, crossed the watershed between the tributaries of the upper Zambezi and those of the lower Congo, and reached the west coast at Luanda, Angola. From there a year's march brought him back to his starting point near the falls that the Africans called "smoke does sound" but that Livingstone prosaically renamed the Victoria Falls; from here he followed the Zambezi downstream, reaching the east coast at Quelimane, in Portuguese East Africa (Mozambique). On his second journey, sent out by the British government to test the navigability of the lower Zambezi, he explored the Shire (Chire) and Rovuma rivers and reached Lake Nyasa. His last journey, from 1865 to 1871, was undertaken at the behest of the president of Britain's Royal Geographical Society (succes-

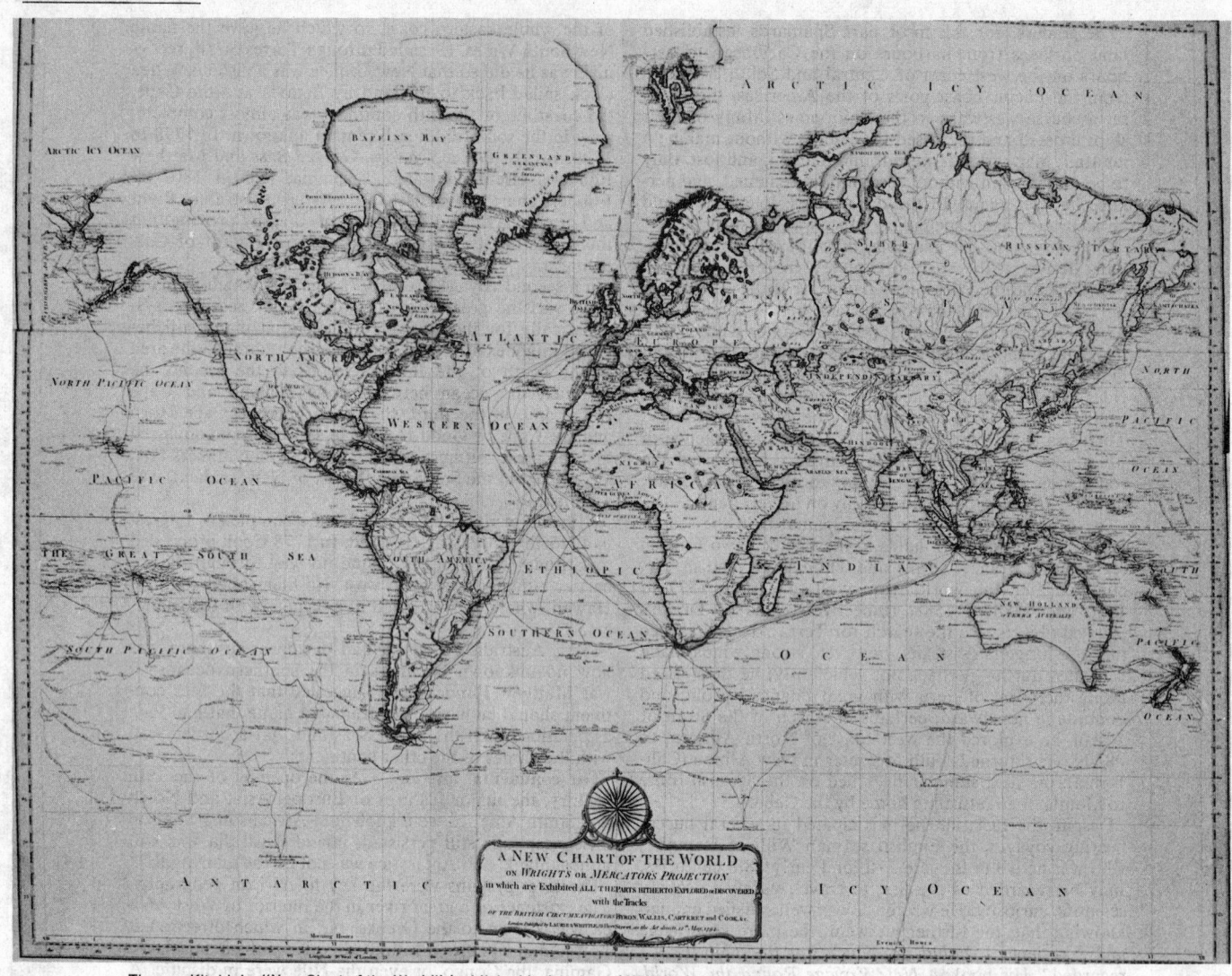

Thomas Kitchin's "New Chart of the World" (published by Laurie and Whittle, London, 1794), illustrating the state of geographical knowledge before the exploration of Antarctica and some of the continental interiors.

By courtesy of the Royal Geographical Society, London; photograph, John Webb

sor to the African Association) "to solve a question of intense geographical interest . . . namely the watershed or watersheds of southern Africa." On this journey Livingstone investigated the complex drainage system between Lake Nyasa and Lake Tanganyika and explored the headwaters of the Congo. He refused to return to England with the Welsh explorer Henry Morton Stanley, who was sent to his rescue in 1871, as he was still uncertain of the position of the watershed between the Nile and the Congo; he wondered if the Lualaba was perhaps a headstream of the Nile. He struggled back to the maze of waterways around Lake Bangweulu and died there in 1873.

The source of the Nile The whereabouts of the source of the Nile had intrigued men since the days of the pharaohs. A Scottish explorer, James Bruce, travelling in Ethiopia in 1770, visited the two fountains in Lake Tana, the source of the Blue Nile, first discovered by the Portuguese priest Paez in 1618. The English explorers Richard Burton and John Speke discovered Lake Tanganyika in 1857. Speke then travelled north alone and reached the southern creek of a lake, which he named Victoria Nyanza. Without exploring farther, he returned to England, sure that he had found the source of the Nile. He was right—but he had not seen the outlet, and Burton did not believe him. In 1862 Speke, travelling with the Scottish explorer James Grant, found the Ripon Falls, in Uganda (now submerged following the construction of a dam for Owen Falls hydroelectric station), and "saw without any doubt that Old Father Nile rises in Victoria Nyanza." Stanley completed the puzzle in 1875; he circumnavigated Vic-

toria Nyanza, crossed to the Lualaba, followed that river to the Congo, and then followed the Congo to its mouth. The pattern made by the river systems of Africa was elucidated at last.

The interior of Australia also posed a problem: was its heart an inland sea or a desert? This question did not arouse anything approaching the same degree of public interest that was taken in the geography of Africa. Exploration was slow; the early settlers on the eastern coast found that the valleys led to impassable walls at the valley heads. In 1813 the Australian explorer Gregory Blaxland successfully crossed the Blue Mountains by following a ridge instead of taking a valley route. Rivers were found beyond the mountains, but they did not behave as expected. Another explorer, the Australian John Oxley, in 1818 observed: "on every hill a spring, in every valley a rivulet, but the river itself disappears." He guessed that the great fan of rivers that drained the western slopes of the Great Dividing Range of eastern Australia fell into an inland sea. The Australian Charles Sturt resolved the problem by an imaginative journey made in 1829–30. He embarked on the Murrumbidgee River and was "hurried into a great and noble river [the Murray]." A week later he encountered another big river flowing into the Murray from the north, which he rightly concluded was the Darling, the middle course of which he had explored the year before. The voyage ended when he found that the Murray drained into Encounter Bay on the south coast. The heart of Australia was not an inland sea but a desert. Many more expeditions were needed to map the continent's major features, but two revealed its great extent. In 1840–41 the Australian Edward John Eyre travelled along the south coast from Adelaide to Albany, a distance of more than 1,300 miles (2,100 kilometres); the Australians Robert Burke and William John Wills travelled from Melbourne in the southeast to the Gulf of Carpentaria in the north.

Exploring the polar regions

The exploration of the polar regions was the work of the first half of the 20th century. Scientific curiosity mainly inspired the various enterprises, although political rivalry also played some part.

In the North Polar regions, the scientific age began with the voyaging of William Scoresby, an English whaler and scientist, who in 1806 reached 81°21′ N. In 1828 an English explorer, Sir William Parry, travelling over drift ice from Svalbard, reached 82° N. The Norwegian explorer Fridtjof Nansen in 1893 attempted to reach the Pole by allowing his ship, the "Fram," to be frozen into the ice in the East Siberian Sea in the hope that a current would carry her over the Pole to east Greenland. At 84° N 102° E, Nansen with a companion left the ship and travelled by sled to 86°13′ N: the ship eventually emerged from the pack ice north of Svalbard. In 1909 an American explorer, Robert Peary, reached the North Pole by journeying by sled with 50 Eskimos from Ellesmere Island, northwest of Greenland. Soundings of 9,000 feet (2,700 metres) were made within five miles (eight kilometres) of the Pole; it seemed, therefore, that there was no continent here. In 1958 the United States submarines "Skate" and "Nautilus" travelled across the Arctic under the ice cap.

The great southern continent, having been located within the Antarctic Circle by Captain Cook, lay there neglected for some 50 years. From 1839 to 1843, the English rear admiral James Ross, in command of the ships "Erebus" and "Terror," explored the coast of Victoria Land. In 1894 Leonard Christensen, captain of a Norwegian whaler, landed a party at Cape Adare, the first to set foot on Antarctica. In the first decade of the 20th century, various explorers, including Britons such as William Bruce, Robert Falcon Scott, and Sir Ernest Henry Shackleton, the German Erich von Drygalski, and the Frenchman Jean-Baptiste Charcot, confirmed the existence of an ice cap of continental dimensions. In 1908–09 Shackleton led a brilliant expedition, during which he examined the Great Barrier, climbed to 11,000 feet (3,400 metres), and reached 88°23′ S. Scott and his party reached the Pole on January 17, 1912, but only to find that the Norwegian explorer Roald Amundsen had already been there on December 11, 1911; Scott's party, caught in a blizzard, died on their return journey. In 1928 Sir Hubert Wilkins, the British explorer and aviator, flew over Grahamland, using Deception Island as a base. In 1957 and 1958 the British explorer Vivian Fuchs and Sir Edmund Hillary, the New Zealand mountaineer, travelled across the continent.   (J.B.Mi.)

The modern discipline of geography

As indicated in the brief survey introducing this article, academic geography is primarily concerned with areal differentiation; that is, with the distribution, or spatial variation, of phenomena on the Earth's surface and within its atmospheric envelope. The contemporary discipline —the concepts and structure of which are examined in detail in the remainder of this article—deals with the differences as well as with the similarities between places, with the distribution of the environmental features (both physical and man-made) of the Earth, and with the associations between these features. Thus, although the adjective geographic is popularly applied to relief features only, in reality it possesses a much wider connotation.

The development and distinctiveness of geography as an academic discipline stem from man's curiosity about spatial variations in his environment. The Earth is composed not of uniform areas but of an intricate series of overlapping zones of different characteristics. Geography seeks to provide a coherent and organized understanding of this subject matter, whose variations originate from the social, economic, and political processes of a varied human race and from the basic physical and biotic processes that produce differences in climate, relief, and vegetation. Animate human processes, however, are mediated through decision-making structures of various kinds, and these add still another level of complexity to any attempt at explanation, and there is an ever present danger of repeating 19th-century deterministic explanations whereby man's actions were popularly considered to be controlled by his environment. Controlled observation and experimentation are much more likely to provide the causal relationships involved in inanimate geographical processes.

Animate and inanimate geographical processes

Geography is concerned not so much with the uniqueness of spatial distributions as with their regularities. It is also accepted that the subject matter of geography is one of common concern among many disciplines, each of which approaches and structures the phenomena under study in a different way. With geography the special perspective is the spatial one, and it is this that provides the basis for the individual organizational method of the geographer and the corpus of spatial concepts and generalizations that constitutes the discipline.

Despite the enormous success of the analytical method in science, whereby subject matter has been broken down into increasingly specialized parts for academic study, scientists often feel that many problems are capable of solution only by interdisciplinary effort and by methods —notably systems analysis—that stress the connection between processes. Geography is well placed to benefit from these approaches, for the subject has an interdisciplinary perspective simply because it looks at a series of processes from one particular viewpoint. Since the early 1960s, geography has seen significant changes in its methodology, changes that have placed the discipline in the mainstream of modern scientific inquiry. These changes, together with advances resulting from the application of quantitative techniques, have enabled geographers to cope more precisely with a greater number of facts. The scope of the subject nevertheless remains enormous, and this makes the organization of the spatial approach a particularly important aspect of the training of a geographer. Yet geographers are still interested only in the regional scale, the study of the Earth as the home of man.

The limitations of the spatial approach

CHARACTERISTICS OF GEOGRAPHICAL INQUIRY

The restriction of geographical studies to a spatial perspective and a regional level of resolution has, in turn, produced an extensive overlap between geography and the everyday interests and experience of the layman, as well as with other academic fields. Geography has also frequently lost part of its academic territory because individual aspects of geographical knowledge have been subjected to specialist scrutiny and, through an ever present tendency to "fission," have crystallized out as separate sciences.

The problem of overlap. The problem of overlap has increased in recent years, notably as the result of the development of virtually instantaneous global communication and the increased social mobility in advanced nations, which have afforded an opportunity to great numbers of people to experience and describe regional environmental differences. Geographers thus no longer hold (as they did in the medieval period) a monopoly on this type of information. Most laymen nevertheless satisfy their curiosity about different places in the world by communicating individual descriptions, and only rarely does lay description bear the traditional characteristics of systematic inquiry—the careful measurement, integration, and accurate presentation of material.

The breadth of the subject matter of geography also means that there is considerable overlap between the work of geographers and other academics—an overlap that occasionally makes it difficult to distinguish the essential geographic contribution. This problem has been partially resolved by the development of specialized inquiries designed to focus upon specific clusters of phenomena or processes within geography. These specialisms —"systematics"—have close links with other academic

The role
of
"sys-
tematics"

fields; thus, political geography investigates the interrelationships between geography and political science, and biogeography applies geographical principles to biology (see below *The branches of geographical inquiry*). Geography has also studied some areas of knowledge—notably those that do not form the basis of a separate academic discipline, as in the case of the study of landforms (geomorphology) or of settlements—from a viewpoint over and above that of purely spatial interest. Geomorphology has been of marginal interest to geologists in Europe, and geographers have thus been to the fore in this field. In North America, however, the interest of geologists in contemporary landforms has been stronger, and the field is an area of genuine interdisciplinary effort. The study of human settlements has only recently become the subject of major professional inquiry; many aspects, especially of urban settlement, have thus been studied by geographers.

Conversely, many aspects of scientific study that traditionally are primarily geographic in method have been embedded in other disciplines: distributional studies of individual phenomena as diverse as plants or diseases have been undertaken by botanists or medical research workers. Other fields, as in the case of the study of international trade flows or of territorial behaviour in housing estates, have been developed, respectively, by economists and sociologists. Most geographers interested in such movement patterns have concentrated on the regional scale, studying such features as the spheres of influence of towns, the migration of people, or the definition of metropolitan regions.

In addition, other, more practical studies have hitherto been carried out by market analysts, economists, engineers, and others responsible for the location of new industries or shopping centres, despite the basically geographical nature of the problem. Geography as a distinct academic discipline is also intimately connected with four other fields: regional science, ecology, planning, and ekistics, all with a common interest in responding to spatial problems in the environment. There are, however, some differences in objective and scope: regional scientists are interested primarily in theoretical and statistical approaches to human, especially economic, distributions; ecologists study the biosphere with particular reference to the interrelationships between plants and animals and their environment; planners collect information on a spatial basis but are more interested in the applications of this knowledge; and ekistics, a recent addition to the academic ranks, seeks to provide a science of human settlements.

The problem of fission. Modern geographers regard their subject as a "following" rather than a "leading" discipline; most major breakthroughs in scientific understanding, they recognize, tend to be made in other fields. This is a reversal of the subject's role in past centuries, during which geography was often called the "mother" of the natural and social sciences, as in the case of academic disciplines as diverse as pedology (the study of soils) or social anthropology. This type of fission was also seen in more technical areas; for example, surveys of regional land use and agriculture of the kind pioneered by British geographers in the 1930s have since been adopted on a worldwide basis. The greater infusion of capital and the concentration of research effort implicit in these changes have inevitably stimulated major developments in this field of study, and the application of Earth satellite photography and mapping is likely to provide even greater breakthroughs.

Geography
as the
"mother"
of the
sciences

The classic example of such academic fission away from geography lies in the realm of geodesy and cartography. Although geographers still teach the rudiments of these subjects, they have become specialized disciplines in their own right. The beginning of this separation can be traced back to the dual heritage of the classical Greek geographers—the regional descriptions of Strabo and Ptolemy's linear representation of the Earth's features by symbols and lines. Between the Renaissance and the 19th century, the Ptolemic tradition became associated with the need for precise—and increasingly mathematical—

navigational aids and survey and map-projection techniques and also with the military sponsorships of map production. Geodesy thus moved toward applied problems and away from the main geographic consensus. Cartography specialists are found in most university geography departments, but they are now something of an anachronism.

The "new geography." For geography the decade of the 1960s was characterized by a fundamental re-examination of the subject's approach to spatial analysis. The impact of these methodological changes has been so considerable that it has given rise to the appellation "the new geography," a reference not to any basic change in the aims of geography but rather to the remarkable technical and methodological innovations that have provided geographers with a new set of descriptive and analytical procedures.

These changes are as fundamental in nature as those introduced by the German scholars Alexander von Humboldt and Carl Ritter, the founders of modern geography, in the mid-19th century. Humboldt and Ritter replaced the gazetteer descriptions and the often-quaint armchair speculation about foreign lands of their predecessors with a formalized, systematic approach. Both men emphasized the role of direct and personal observation and the general need for an empirical approach in any geographical inquiry. Although these methods were an essential component of progress in a formal 19th-century discipline, they seem to have encouraged a later generation of geographers to overemphasize direct observation through fieldwork and to underestimate the part played by speculation in the initial stages of any study. The fieldwork tradition is still an important aspect of geography, but the introduction of more rigorous methods of data collection in society as a whole (at least in the developed nations of the Northern Hemisphere) has rendered individual fieldwork unnecessary in much geographical study.

The
founders
of modern
geography

There were, however, some geographers who did not accept the empirical, inductive approaches favoured by the majority of their colleagues. Thus, in studying the central-place systems, or urban networks, of south Germany in the 1930s, Walter Christaller carefully distinguished among all the possible sources of variation that could affect the pattern of agricultural service centres, put forward a theoretical explanation, and only then tested the empirical evidence. Although Christaller's central-place theory has been found to have a number of limitations, his methodological approach ensures him a major place in any consideration of contemporary geography. During the late 1950s, recognition of the work of Christaller and of other geographers pursuing his line of thought provided the impetus for a number of methodological advances; the result was a complete overthrow of the established consensus. The assimilation of statistical techniques into geography was the most visible of these changes, which were sometimes also known as the "quantitative revolution." A less visible but perhaps more significant change was the deliberate placing of spatial associations in hypothesis-testing frameworks amenable to the application of exact statistical testing techniques. Finally, the application of advanced statistical procedures (notably multivariate analysis) and of computer technology has, together with the accumulation of data from remote sensor devices, enabled geographers to accommodate a larger number of variables in any analysis with greater speed and objectivity.

These technical changes are not unique to geography, for, since the 1950s, they have had similar impact on most of the other natural and social sciences. In the case of geography, the conceptual changes that accompanied such quantitative developments—changes that involve the application of most of the methods of modern science—have been of greater long-term relevance: geographers have begun to create a series of stringent spatial concepts in which the development of laws and theories is a major goal. Mathematical models and methods, using probabilistic concepts and advanced simulation techniques, provide a new armoury of techniques and descriptions, while the more informal layman's approach has fallen by the wayside.

All of these advances have resulted in a shift in emphasis away from the descriptive side of the discipline and toward practical applications. This is especially true of the study of animate processes, in which, as has been noted, the presence of consciousness has prompted the study of decision making in a spatial context, particularly in the economic field. In this area—obviously of major importance in the developing regions of the globe and in the centrally planned economies—the empirical tradition of the geographer has served to correct the rather abstract thinking (often expressed in models of optimal, rather than realistic, conditions) of the professional economist. Locational analysis of this kind is now in the forefront of geographical endeavour, a trend that fits in well with increasing public concern for effective control of the natural and, particularly, the man-made environment.

Practical applications of geography

THE BRANCHES OF GEOGRAPHICAL INQUIRY

Geography's major contribution to knowledge thus consists of extending and disseminating information about the spatial variation and problems of the Earth's physical and social environment. In ancient and medieval times, geography progressed from describing the characteristic features of different countries to plotting the location of such features with greater accuracy. During the 20th century, more attention has been paid to systematic studies of geographical data, while at the same time a strong tradition of field observation and of interest in the natural and human aspects of geographic phenomena have combined to make geography one of the first disciplines to fulfill a bridging function between the natural and social sciences. As a result, the branches of geographical inquiry fall into three major areas: studies associated with the regional concept, the major systematic branches of human geography, and the major systematic branches of physical geography.

The regional concept. *Regions and regional classifications.* In both social and natural sciences, there are many words used in everyday language that also have a specific professional meaning: "region" is one such word. The term derives from the subjective awareness of differences among places on the Earth's surface, and professional regional description is one of the ways geographers introduce order into their description of the spatial variations that create these differences. Although it could be argued that no two places on the Earth's surface are completely identical, there is no need to assume, conversely, that these places can therefore be described only as unique entities. All places share some features in common, and these can be identified and described. The differences can then be analyzed. Acceptance of this important generalization leads directly to a realization of the need to place it in an organizational framework. For the modern geographer, the region is just such an intellectual concept, for it provides a logical way of reducing the complexity of the real world to a smaller and more comprehensible number of elements.

Although the region represents an organization of a set of characteristics possessed by part of terrestrial space, it must be distinguished clearly from mathematical space, which has no real-world relevance. In order to comprise a region, a set of areas must have some common characteristic that differentiates it from other areas, and the areas must be contiguous. For example, a set of areas each experiencing over 50 inches of rainfall or each containing households with an average per capita income of over $1,000 (or 1,000 rupees or 1,000 yen) per year, if contiguous, provide an example of a homogeneous region (sometimes also called a uniform or a formal region), as they are defined on the basis of the homogeneity of some formal named characteristic. At this stage, it does not matter whether these areas are in excess (moderately or wildly) of the rainfall or income limits: these values are merely the operational definitions of this particular type of homogeneity. Subsequently, other, additional regions may indeed be described—perhaps com-

Homogeneous regions

prised of areas experiencing over 100 inches of rainfall or of areas where per capita income is over $1,500, and so on.

These examples deal only with one geographical feature at a time, but the basic idea has been extended to define regions characterized by two or more features; these are known professionally as multiple-feature homogeneous regions. Using the examples described above, this type of region could be found by identifying an area with over 50 inches of rainfall in which income is over $1,000 per capita. When all the distributional characteristics of areas are used to define homogeneity, the term compages has been applied. For example, an area with a distinctive combination of climate, relief, and vegetation, as well as cultural and economic patterns (such as the Mekong Delta in Viet Nam), could be described as a compages on a world scale.

Two other types of region widely known to the professional geographer are the "polarized" (or "functional") region and the "programming" region. In the former case, homogeneity is defined not by the material description of some structural geographic characteristic but by reference to the similarity of relationships or functions among the constituent parts of the area. A simple example of a functional region is the trading area of a town, which may have a core (an area that represents the heart of the organization or function, perhaps the number of customers patronizing a shopping centre) and a periphery, which is characterized by a decline in the influence of this function outward from the centre. The edges of the region (zones of transition) are represented by the points at which the functional relationships are dissipated and disappear, perhaps to be replaced by influences emanating from other centres: in the example, there would be a fringe area in which potential customers would have the choice of patronizing another shopping centre.

In the case of the programming region, an active rather than a descriptive entity, the region is designed to serve a particular objective within the designated space. The best examples are afforded by political areas or planning regions. The Tennessee Valley Authority was created in the 1930s to improve the ecological balance in an impoverished area of the United States and to raise the standard of living of people within the area. Similar projects were initiated under the first Soviet five-year plans, and since that time most countries of the world, developed and developing, have defined special development areas in which tax or other financial incentives are used alongside direct government assistance to prevent future decay or to promote future growth in the economy of the area. All such projects represent, to the geographer, examples of programming regions.

All these regions are defined on different bases, so there is no reason why they should coincide fully with any particular area; yet, programming regions are often defined on the basis of some other regional type. For example, one urgent contemporary issue of concern to the geographer stems from the multiplicity of municipalities and the conflicting jurisdictions within large urban areas; many people have proposed one simple territorial unit for the government of each of the large cities of the world. If such regions were defined on the basis of homogeneity of land use, the units would be restricted to the contiguous built-up areas of the cities, but, if they were defined on the basis of functional homogeneity, the suburbs and satellites beyond the immediate built-up areas could be included, as well as smaller towns within the metropolitan spheres of influence. A major task of urban geographers—working in a context of accelerating world urbanism—has been to resolve these problems in order to achieve an effective definition of various metropolitan areas.

Programming regions

The application of modern scientific methods to geographical problems has clarified much of the previous thinking about regions. Most contemporary geographers consider that regionalization is not an intuitive art but is a process of classification with basic similarities to other classifications. The utility of any single approach to the professional definition of a region depends on the purpose of the classification, and this, it is felt, should be stated clearly at the beginning of the exercise. Such attitudes are of comparatively recent origin and cannot be considered an absolute consensus. Older opinions still survive, in particular, the belief among more traditional geographers that there is some "natural" system of regions that represents the best classification for many purposes, and that it is the task of the profession to search for this system. Most geographers believe that these "natural" regions are as elusive as the natural classifications sought for in other disciplines, but this view must be qualified in two important respects. First of all, a sizable group of geographers accepts the multiplicity of regional classifications but believes that in any particular case there is some scale of regionalization that is more appropriate than others. The idea may be compared to the resolution level of a microscope—a variety of magnifications is possible but the understanding of the characteristics of any object may be clarified by the use of one particular resolution level. The second qualification is more important, as it rests upon a major difference of opinion between Western (mostly European and North American) and Marxist geographers. Most Soviet geographers extend their Marxist–Leninist view of society to the belief that there is one natural system of economic regions that will best integrate the social and environmental variations of society and act as a foundation for building Socialism and Communism. These regions should, they feel, be isolated and translated into programming regions. Yet, in spite of these theoretical problems, the differences on the practical side of regional classification are minimal. Indeed, much of the credit for early work on the application of quantitative methods to regional classification must go to such Polish geographers as K. Dziewonski. The ideas were extended by Brian J.L. Berry and others in the United States by the early 1960s. The 1960s, as a whole, witnessed a tremendous expansion of worldwide interest in this line of inquiry. Geographers have begun to test the utility of a whole range of statistical grouping and clustering methods for regional classification. These re-orientations have, nevertheless, only clarified the objectivity of regional analysis. They have not changed the fundamental purposes of regionalization, which is to give names to particular areas, to make it easier to transmit and store information about places, to provide inductive generalizations, and to provide data for planning purposes.

Regional geography. The formal study of regions and the creation of regional generalizations is the primary responsibility of regional geography, although the recent development of regional science has made significant theoretical contributions to the study of human distributions. The scope of regional geography is potentially enormous because it attempts to involve all the significant locational features known about any area, primarily by using multifeature homogeneous and polarized regions of the type described above. Since this information is increasing at an accelerating rate, regional studies are in constant danger of fragmentation, not least because of a factual overload. There is a danger of a return to the gazetteer approach to description, in which facts are listed by location and little attempt is made to integrate them. These problems are especially relevant to human distributions, in which the rapidity of changes means that the generalizations established are time dependent, and in constant need of updating. The result is that it is difficult for the regional geographer to construct the type of concise and immutable generalization that seems to be possible in many of the physical sciences.

Although the problem of information overload, as it is called, has increased in severity, integration of the geographical facts within the confines of one single study or even the production of a concise generalization has always been difficult. Out of the wide variety of regional studies produced by geographers, the most successful has probably been a series of monographs—known as *Géographie universelle*—emanating (1927–48) from the French school of geographers. The series was initially planned by Paul Vidal de la Blache, but most of the direction was carried out after his death by Lucien Gallois, with Emmanuel de Martonne and Albert Demangeon among the principal contributors. This series depended heavily on the identification of *pays*, a French term describing areas with a distinctively integrated assemblage of physical and human features. These monographs became classics of modern geography not only because they were prepared by scholars with rigorous, incisive minds but also because they were written in a clear, concise, literary style.

The classic French monographs

Despite the overall success of the French school of geography, a comparison of the individual regional monographs demonstrates that the interpretation of industrial areas was not as good as that of other regions, primarily because of the absence in such areas of the intimate man–land associations so characteristic of pre-industrial rural societies. The subjectivity of the regional definitions also made it hard to test the utility of the regional classifications and interpretations offered. Overall, however, the studies did lead to the emergence of a school of thought that regarded regional geography as the core of the entire discipline. Many geographers still seem to accept this view, but they are becoming a minority and are particularly vulnerable to criticism when they describe regions from a subjective standpoint.

The difficulty of encompassing all the geographical facts of an area in one regional study contributed to a variation of the *pays* approach. Instead of attempting to use all the salient facts, the "theme" approach searches for some feature or key to the understanding of the area. The development of the theme is similar to the approach used by historians who regarded the "frontier" concept as the primary motive force in U.S. history. In essence, this development takes the distribution of some key criterion (for example, language), considers its relationship to other features (*e.g.*, a distinctive cultural assemblage), and attempts to provide an explanation for the spatial variation in this distribution. Although the theme approach has been used with great effect in many areas, it suffers from the obvious defect of overdependence on one characteristic or set of characteristics. Recognition of the persistence of social and economic discrepancies between the regions of a country has nevertheless led, in many nations, to a series of developmental programs designed to eradicate these differences. Geographers have thus been employed in identifying and monitoring these trends or have produced regional studies that have drawn attention to some developing aspects of society in such a way that they become the springboard for popular concern. Two of the recent examples are a study of urbanization on the northeast seaboard of the United States by a leading French geographer, Jean Gottmann, which created public awareness of "megalopolis"; and "Paris et le désert français" by his compatriot J.F. Gravier, which was especially influential in demonstrating the extent of regional imbalance within France and the dominating position of Paris—a matter of no small concern to a series of French administrations.

The "theme" approach

Regionalism. Other scholars have also been interested in the regional concept and have applied the idea to their own disciplines. Usually the term regionalism is used in a broad descriptive way: a good example is the phenomenon known as political regionalism (or sectionalism), which refers to the localized persistence of a set of voting patterns or other manifestations of political behaviour. Although the identification of such areas is clearly another application of the regional concept of the geographer, it is usually carried out in a subjective and descriptive way. For example, the work of regional novelists and artists, who by persistently setting their stories or paintings within the framework of a particular landscape have created an artistic appreciation of the essential features of the area, has achieved great popularity. Most countries have examples of this type of description: one of the best known in the English language is contained in the writings of Thomas Hardy, who combined elements of the southern English landscape to produce a fictitious area that he referred to as Wessex. Elsewhere the classic

The role of regional novelists

descriptions of the interior of Brazil by Euclides da Cunha in *Os Sertões* brilliantly capture the feeling as well as the nature and history of the landscape.

This type of writing has heightened the overall public appreciation of the differences between places. In addition, a revival of interest in political regionalism has occurred in most countries in recent years. The reasons for this are complex but may perhaps be attributed to two basic causes. The first cause is political and economic in aspect: modern governments have become more interventionist in all aspects of society, and the growth of an administrative bureaucracy has led to the centralization of power in many areas. Structural changes in economic life have also resulted in the persistence of social and economic variations within most countries, creating an expanding metropolitan or industrial "core" area and a visibly different declining or stagnating periphery. The second cause is largely cultural in nature: most countries retain areas in which a separate culture, or subculture, is significant. Linguistic or religious differences are particularly important in such cases. When combined with a resentment of economic progress in, say, the metropolitan core of the nation state, these cultural differences may encourage a regional feeling of political inferiority, and have indeed created major problems for many contemporary states. In some cases, regionalism survives in part in distinctive voting patterns that persist through generations, as was the case of the traditional allegiance to the Democratic Party in the Southern states of the United States. Elsewhere, the feeling of distinctiveness is translated into a resurgent tribalism, as in much of Africa, or a resurgent nationalism, as in Quebec, Scotland, Wales, Brittany, or Croatia. The modern geographer—hopefully in a position to supply objective data underlying regional trends—can play an important role in such cases.

Human geography. Human geography, as a branch of the modern discipline, deals with the changing distribution and spatial organization of a variety of human characteristics, ranging from great urban centres built by man to the geographical diffusion of specific technical innovations in agriculture. By applying geographical methods and techniques of analysis to such features, the knowledge accumulated in other social studies—history, politics, economics, and sociology—may be seen in a new light and often extended considerably.

The three basic innovations in recent years

Three changes have occurred in this branch of geography in recent years: the first was the application of the new conceptual methods and quantitative techniques to human distributions, which produced greater precision in all aspects of the field. The recent adoption of model building and simulation techniques has provided human geographers with some of the benefits of experimentation, allowing them to vary the inputs, or functional relationships, used with any model to produce alternative results. For example, the effect of building a new town within the trade area of existing towns could be calculated in this way. A set of attractiveness indices based on potential sales volume could be used alongside existing travel behaviour to predict future "shopping flows" to various sizes of centres. The second change was in the explicit study of the role of perception and images in mediating between man's actions and his social and physical environment. These variables are being measured precisely and incorporated into analytical frameworks, instead of being used in a descriptive fashion. These behavioral and decision-making approaches have isolated the differences between cultural preferences for various types of environment and produced a greater appreciation of the reasons lying behind any individual use of the environment. A classic illustration of this type of approach frequently has been produced by the responses of Eskimo and American children to photographs of Arctic shorelines and mixed woodland and grass landscapes. To most Americans, the Arctic is inhospitable, to the Eskimo it is "home," an area containing a known set of potential food resources, not the unexplored and unknown environment represented by temperate woodlands. The third change is related to the organization of the individual systematic branches of human geography;

the new methods resulted in a greater cooperation between geographers working in the five major traditional areas: social and cultural geography, political geography, economic geography, urban geography, and historical geography. These subdivisions, nevertheless, remain important in their own right.

Social and cultural geography. Social and cultural geography developed out of an interest in mapping such distributions as age–sex differences in human populations, the ethnic background of rural groups, or with tracing the changing distributions of such cultural features as language and religion. These traditional interests are still important and have been improved by the application of more sophisticated cartographic and quantitative methods. Influenced by the contributions of T. Hägerstrand and other Swedish geographers, contemporary research is now often devoted to a complicated analysis of the stages and rules by which social and cultural phenomena are diffused over time and space. Less attention is paid to the individuality of a particular process or phenomena—an artifact, a cultural trait, a population movement, or a disease distribution—and more emphasis is given to formalizing the decision-making structures and patterns of territorial behaviour to which these specific distributions can be related.

Political geography. All political systems, when seen from the viewpoint of the geographer, have two basic characteristics: the process by which they function and—more significantly—the territory to which they are bound. This intimate association provides the basis for the field of political geography, which deals with the spatial analysis of political phenomena, either through the study of a political area or through the study of the impact of political decisions upon man's environment. This branch of the discipline obviously calls for a close working relationship with both political scientists and historians. During the late 19th and the early 20th centuries, this field was one of the most influential in human geography. Scholars such as Friedrich Ratzel in Germany and Sir Halford John Mackinder in England contributed substantially to theories of global strategy and to the development of what became known as geopolitics. The subsequent misapplication and distortion of these views, particularly their use as a justification for the territorial expansion of Nazi Germany in the 1930s, resulted in a marked avoidance of the field by later generations of geographers.

Geography and geopolitics

Most contemporary effort in political geography has been applied to the study of political areas, whether at the international, national, regional, city, or even very local scale. The analysis of political boundaries and their reorganization has attracted considerable interest, as has the evolution, structure, and functioning of political areas. The use of modern techniques of analysis has led to attempts to measure the efficiency and effectiveness of all types of political areas. In recent years there has been some revival of interest in the study of the geographical aspects of political and territorial behaviour and of the geographical impact of political decisions. For example, there have been studies, by political geographers, of the distribution of voting patterns and of the decision-making structures lying behind the creation of such political entities as capital cities, national parks, metropolitan areas, or even such specific territorial legislation as that concerning fishing rights or offshore limits. There is a marked emphasis on the development of conceptual models, rather than on the presentation of relevant information in the form of empirical case studies.

Economic geography. Economic geography seeks to explain the location of the production and consumption of economic commodities, services, and transactions. Most early studies were empirically orientated and concerned with the worldwide distribution of such individual types of production as wheat, cotton, gold, and power generation. Special attention was paid to the association of these enterprises with the physical environment and the delimitation of economic regions. Today, as much attention is paid to the impact of government regulation or the distributional effects of differential freight rates. The experience obtained from a series of case studies of such occurrences has been used to formulate a much more abstract approach to the field, in which the principles of economic location are developed on a theoretical basis: the early contributions of three German location theorists—Johann von Thünen in agriculture and Alfred Weber and August Lösch in industrial production—were of great significance. Modern economic trends have involved greater attention—at least in developed Western countries—to the market as the major locational factor behind the siting of many industries and also to the interaction and linkages between individual productive and consumptive units. As a result, the analysis of the urban-industrial complex has become one of the most important aspects of contemporary economic geography; it is associated closely with the formulation of regional government policy.

Urban geography. Unlike the other fields mentioned above, urban geography does not focus upon an individual set of processes but studies the geography of a particular type of area, namely, those defined as urban regions. This branch of the discipline began with the analysis of the location of towns, but most contemporary research concentrates upon four separate areas of interest. The first, the spatial study of the role of the city in society, forms an essential backcloth for all the other groups, since it deals with the growth of urbanization, the extent and problems of world urbanization, and the definition of urban and metropolitan units. The second area of interest lies in the classification of city types, the identification of the unique social and economic character of one city compared with all other cities. Closely connected with this interest is the study of the influence of cities, an approach that has been dominated by studies of trade areas and the consequences of urban sprawl into the countryside. The fourth field of interest is the study of the city as area. In many countries the European and Japanese tradition of studies of the morphology (that is, of the layout and buildings) of cities has been recently superseded by a North American tradition that pays more attention to changing spatial variations in the social, commercial, and industrial patterns of towns. Typologies of commercial structures and urban social systems, the processes seen to lie behind the formation of ghettos, and also the migration of groups and individuals within the city have been popular areas of study in this connection. Many of the new quantitative techniques that have transformed modern geography were first applied to studies in urban geography, and urban geographers have also been leaders in the application of mathematical models to geographical studies. They also have close ties with urban planning agencies, although this link is perhaps more developed in those nations that place great emphasis on central-planning systems.

Historical geography. The strong association of many European geographers with the disciplines of history and archaeology led to the early separation of historical geography as a distinct branch of the discipline. Historical geographers were concerned with either a series of reconstructions of past landscapes or the study of spatial change in one or more characteristics of an area through time, perhaps over several centuries. Most of the historical geography written in recent years has used this approach, although distinctive contemporary trends place an emphasis on the application of precise quantitative measurements to such historical changes and also on attempts to analyze rigorously the decision-making structures that are envisaged as having contributed to these changes. The reconstruction of past landscapes is easier to define and bears close analogies to regional geography, although few recent studies have been as successful as the classic monographs produced by H.C. Darby (an interpretation of the Domesday Book, the great survey of 11th-century England originally compiled at the request of William the Conqueror) or Carl Ortwin Sauer (with respect to sequential occupations of Southern California).

Other branches of human geography. A wide variety of other systematic branches can be postulated, since

there are potentially as many fields as there are clusters of human phenomena. Thus, population geography has close links with the discipline of demography and deals with the distribution of specific population characteristics. Significant modern trends in this area include the application of sophisticated mapping and analytical techniques to demographic data. There are also developing interests in concepts of optimum population density and population pressure in relation to regional land resources. Transportation geography has been developed primarily by economic geographers interested in transactions and flows across space. Much of the research has been devoted to the refinement of transportation models for the city, and geographers working in this field have a close association with transport engineers. Agricultural geography developed out of cultural and economic geography and studies the geography of agricultural systems. This focus leads to studies of the distribution of crop types, as well as the physical and economic relationships involved. Important emphasis is placed upon land-tenure systems and the effect of varying cropping practices on the management of resources.

Physical geography. Until recent years, analytical studies in physical geography progressed at a rate faster than those in human geography. This may reflect the earlier adoption by physical geographers of that accurate instrumentation that provided precise quantified data for analysis. The greater stability of most—though not all—physical processes and the fact that they were not mediated through conscious decision-making structures also provided obvious advantages in this respect.

Three major trends can be differentiated within the systematic branches of contemporary physical geography. First, more sophisticated data-collecting and technical-processing systems have been applied to physical distributions. For example, infrared photography has added another dimension to the traditional dependence on black and white air photography for studying large-scale vegetation systems and pollution hazards. Second, process-orientated approaches have tended to replace distributional studies of the pattern or form of physical features. This has generated a much greater degree of rapport between geographers and other scientists, notably geophysicists. Third, the interrelationship between human and physical processes has also been reactivated as a major area of study, and there have been attempts to measure the varying human response to changes in the physical environment, and, in particular, their effect on man's evaluation and perception of his environment. This has led to greater interest in the need for conservation of natural resources or for the designation and preservation of areas of special scientific value. Other studies include the analysis of flood hazard (especially concerning the human settlement of river floodplains); of climate modification by man, especially in urban and industrial areas; of drought or hail damage to crop systems; and even of the effect of cultural traditions upon land use.

Geomorphology. A major subbranch of physical geography, geomorphology is the science of landforms and has been jointly cultivated by geographers and geologists. It is often regarded as a separate discipline. Several individual specializations within geomorphology have become associated with the study of single processes—thus, volcanology studies volcanoes and seismology studies earthquakes.

The earliest geomorphological studies concentrated on the origin and distribution of the Earth's landforms, a process involving the description, identification, and classification of each landform according to its origin—whether the feature was an erosional or depositional product of, for example, river-system, glacial, or wind action. As many landforms were relict features, the product of some long-extinct physical process (as in the case of features resulting from Ice Age glaciation), geomorphologists tended to view the landscape in terms of chronological development. In the case of river systems, this led to an overdependence on the theory of the cycle of erosion, originally formulated by a U.S. geologist William Morris Davis but derived from the biological cycle

Marginal notes:

The four areas of urban interest

Modern techniques of data collection

of youth, maturity, and old age that was popular in the late 19th century.

These interests remain important, especially for British geomorphologists, but more emphasis is now being placed on the physical processes of change, particularly as more accurate dating techniques can now be applied. Studies of the movement of silt and pebbles in rivers, glaciers, and oceans and also of alterations in river beds or in what is termed shoreline geometry are becoming more frequent. The result is often a greater involvement with engineering principles.

Climatology. Climatology is concerned with the seasonal characteristics of weather patterns experienced over various parts of the Earth and with the processes that contribute to these features. Although the subject is dependent on the fundamentals of meteorology, which is itself closely linked to the basic laws of physics and hydrodynamics, the geographical perspective leads to an emphasis on the spatial results of these weather processes. Once the development of standardized recording equipment had produced comparable data on the basic climatic variables of temperature, rainfall, and windflow, geographers were able to formulate systems for a classification of the major climatic zones of the Earth. Today, there is less emphasis on classification and more on the processes themselves. This has encouraged research on the energy and water balance of the atmosphere and the simulation of climatic systems. Many geographers also seem to prefer to study microclimates (the climates of small regions). Since the microclimate of any area is significantly modified by the surface characteristics of the Earth, a considerable literature on the modifications of climate by surface texture and topography is developing, with emphasis upon the heat-island effects of large cities and the influence of local conditions on the distribution of air pollution.

The study of micro- climates

Biogeography. Biogeography is the study of the geographical distribution of plants and animals. Its particular approach is shared with ecologists, although they tend to focus on the environmental relationships of plants and animals rather than on trying to produce regional descriptions and explanations of variations in the biosphere. Modern biogeographers have concentrated on the study of plants, have been responsible for mapping large-scale vegetation zones, and for relating the characteristics of such zones to variations in relief, climate, and soils. Recent trends also involve the application of concepts of the ecosystem to geographical distributions in order to produce quantified descriptions of the biological input and output within any area. These methods include the study of the inflow of energy, productivity, transformation, and decomposition of matter. This approach has more than an academic value, as it enables a much more accurate measurement of the effect of man or animals on any specific regional association. Indeed, this applied aspect, especially in the field of conservation and the reconciliation of conflicting uses of land, has become a major interest of most biogeographers.

Other branches of physical geography. Physical geography, like human geography, has a number of other subbranches. Geographical studies in the science of soils (pedology) have been most closely associated with mapping the distribution of soil types and relating these characteristics to other environmental features. In particular, the impact of soil variations on crop yields, vegetation type, and the effect of cultural and agricultural cropping practices on soil erosion have been investigated. Hence, the analysis of soil characteristics in isolation has been left to the soil chemist, and geographers use the results of such specialists' work in their own studies.

Similar remarks can be made about geographical interest in the science of water and water flow (hydrology). It is not the hydraulic or chemical properties of water flow that are of major interest to the modern geographer but the effect of water distribution on the rest of the environment. Flood and drought studies, together with water-resource evaluation, bring the hydrologist in close contact with the climatologist. In addition, the impact of floods, droughts, or even normal water runoff on the hu-

man occupance of an area or the relationship of these processes to landforms or vegetation are also of geographical concern.

Medical geography spans the human and physical branches of the subject and may be traced back to the interest of Greek geographers in the influence of climate on health, death rates, and diseases. During the 19th century the relationships discovered were often expressed in a deterministic manner, thus giving undue emphasis to the effects of climate and other physical features. Today, geographers still cooperate with physicians in using modern techniques for mapping the distribution of deaths from various diseases (often an interesting indicator of the economic development of regions), and the information thus gained may also provide clues indicating some of the causal processes behind distributional variations. Given the amount of specialized medical knowledge required, work in this field is usually undertaken in medical-research institutes, although some geographers produced a series of valuable studies of the impact of climate on human physiology during World War II.

The distribution of diseases

METHODOLOGICAL PROBLEMS AND PROSPECTS

The tendency to fission and overlap so characteristic of geographical inquiry, when combined with a geographic methodology that has not created any technological mystique, has often produced predictions of the disintegration of geography as a specialized discipline. Since the 1960s, however, there has been a remarkable renewal of interest in man's social and physical environment and in the future organization of global society. As a result, greater attention has been paid to regional and distributional studies and to the interrelationship between man and his environment. Geography has contributed substantially to the discussion of these issues. This is particularly true where the subject is developed in a formal, educational way within existing high school systems, a situation that is perhaps more applicable to Europe (including the Soviet Union) than to the United States or to the countries of the developing world. Geography is not, however, the sole focus of efforts to organize coherent environmental studies: an interdisciplinary effort is required for a complete understanding in this area, and geographers can only contribute an individual set of perspectives and skills. Yet, it is still true that the impact of this specifically geographical contribution is impeded by a set of basic problems that continually re-assert themselves.

The problem of numbers. The formal contribution of geography to environmental knowledge is diminished by the limited numbers of practicing professional geographers, a situation that is exacerbated by the fact that the majority of geographers are engaged in teaching rather than in research. This ensures that geographers cannot generate their own body of data accumulated through empirical studies but are forced to use information from a wide variety of other sources. As the geographical field is shared with other people, it seems that geographers will continue to make the most of their limited resources by paying more attention to the formalization of concepts and techniques, some of which may have general application.

The problem of the analytical method. The analytical standards employed by other scientists have not always been as rigorously employed in geography, primarily because of the difficulty of isolating the problems in a controlled laboratory environment. In addition, replication (the name technically given to the series of repetitive experiments needed to verify general relationships) can rarely be employed. Temporal and spatial variations ensure that the relationships to be studied in any environment may alter at another time period and will certainly have a different value in another area. More rigorous research designs and the use of model-building and simulation techniques may mitigate these problems but are unlikely to eradicate them completely.

The lack of a controlled laboratory environment

The problem of scale. The perennial geographical problem seems to be that of scale. Generalizations and relationships established at one scale of geographical inquiry may not be useful at another scale. This makes it difficult for the contemporary geographer to present an integrated account of an area in which local generalizations fit neatly into continental size comments. Other scientists—for example, physicists—have the same problem when they are dealing with issues at the fundamental particle, electron, or atomic scale, but they rarely try to treat these relationships simultaneously. The geographer's problem is that the everyday experience of man is at a local level, and he must attempt to build up generalizations from this "particle" level, with all its distortions and individuality.

The problem of correlations. Another constant geographical issue concerns the nature of spatial correlations. Not only is it true that correlations formulated at one scale do not always apply at another, but an association between two variables in any area may be of a casual rather than a causal nature. Although this is a well-established feature of statistical analysis, it has produced confusion in the past and led to the assumption that, since the characteristics of people in one type of environment are similar to those in another, there must be a causal environmental connection or else contact between the two peoples. Parallel processes of development frequently represent a more viable alternative explanation.

The problem of individual objects. Unlike most disciplines, geography did not emerge by defining a set of discrete individual entities that could be dissected or classified academically, as in the case of the rocks of the geologist or the plants of the botanist. The result is partially a problem of "identity" and perhaps underlies the assumption of methodological uniqueness that has been associated with the philosophy of geography since it was first formulated in its modern form by the German philosopher Immanuel Kant. Although this issue has now been resolved by the realization that all disciplines define, operationally, the object of their study, it means that geographers must be constantly wary about the way in which they derive information. Thus, geographical distortions in the size of census-collection units make it difficult to produce comparable generalizations at the same scale for different sets of data. Fortunately, many planning agencies and census bureaus are investigating the possibility of adopting grid-coordinate reference systems for their geographical basis. As remote sensor devices operate on the same principle, information retrieval, integration, and processing in the future may be eased considerably.

The problem of measurement and techniques. Despite undoubted advances in geographical understanding gained by the enthusiastic use of more precise quantitative techniques, some doubts have been raised as to the appropriateness of some of the measures. Many of the standard statistical tests, such as the concept of mean and standard deviation, were not formulated with respect to spatial distributions, and they may need adjustments or even replacement when used in the study of geographical data. Perhaps of greater relevance is the growing realization that geometries other than the Euclidean may be more usefully used in geography, a factor that would have enormous methodological impact on our future understanding of man and his geographic environment. Be that as it may, the modern geographer, in spite of his vast and often bewildering array of mathematical techniques and in spite of being closeted in a laboratory-like atmosphere, still retains much of the curiosity about man and his differing ways of life on our planet that moved his Classical and medieval predecessors to push out the boundaries of the known world.   (W.K.D.D.)

Non-Euclidian concepts of geographical space

BIBLIOGRAPHY

Sources and institutions: The major English-language bibliographic sources are *Geographical Abstracts, Current Geographical Publications,* and *New Geographical Literature and Maps.* Two comprehensive dictionaries of geographical terms are L. DUDLEY STAMP (ed.), *A Glossary of Geographical Terms* (1961); and F.J. MONKHOUSE, *A Dictionary of Geography* (1965). A guide to an international list of geographical journals and series of research papers is provided by C.D. HARRIS and J.D. FELLMANN, in the *International List of Geographical Serials,* 2nd ed. rev. (1971). The International Geographical Union is the world organization of geographers and meets every four years, although representatives of commissions on various geographical topics meet with much greater frequency. It issues the *I.G.U. Bulletin.* The most comprehensive list of geographical societies, institutions, and academic geographers is contained in EMIL MEYNEN (ed.), *Orbis geographicus: World Directory of Geography* (1964); see also G.R. CRONE, *Modern Geographers: An Outline of Progress in Geography Since 1800 A.D.* (1951), a short, well-balanced survey; R.A. SKELTON, *Explorers' Maps* (1958), which deals with the role of the geographer as map-maker and contains excellent illustrations; R.E. DICKINSON and O.J.R. HOWARTH, *The Making of Geography* (1933), still a very useful summary; and R.E. DICKINSON, *The Makers of Modern Geography* (1969), a more detailed study of the German and French geographers.

General works: The basic sources for information on the contemporary methodology of geography are the NATIONAL ACADEMY OF SCIENCES, *The Science of Geography* (1965); WILLIAM BUNGE, *Theoretical Geography* (1962); DAVID HARVEY, *Explanation in Geography* (1969); and E.A. ACKERMAN, *Geography As a Fundamental Research Discipline* (1958). These approaches may be contrasted with the older consensus, represented by RICHARD HARTSHORNE, *The Nature of Geography* (1939); or his more recent statement, *Perspective on the Nature of Geography* (1959). More substantive reviews of the literature in specific fields of geography are provided by RICHARD J. CHORLEY and PETER HAGGETT (eds.), *Models in Geography* (1967), and can be compared with P.E. JAMES and C.F. JONES (eds.), *American Geography: Inventory and Prospect* (1954). Two collections of essays provide articles that chart the progress of the recent methodological and technical developments, namely, W.K.D. DAVIES (ed.), *The Conceptual Revolution in Geography* (1972); and B.J.L. BERRY and DUANE MARBLE (comps.), *Spatial Analysis* (1968). The reawakening of interest in the interrelationship between man and his environment may also be traced in W.L. THOMAS (ed.), *Man's Role in Changing the Face of the Earth* (1956); and RICHARD J. CHORLEY (ed.), *Water, Earth and Man* (1969). More specific studies include T.F. SAARINEN, *Perception of the Drought Hazard on the Great Plains* (1966); and JAN BURTON and R.W. KATES (eds.), *Readings in Resource Management and Conservation* (1965).

Human geography: Valuable summaries of the impact of modern geographical methodology on the study of human distributions are provided by PETER HAGGETT, *Locational Analysis in Human Geography* (1965); and RONALD ABLER, JOHN S. ADAMS, and PETER GOULD, *Spatial Organization: The Geographer's View of the World* (1971). More specific contributions dealing with the behavioral approach may be found in ALLAN R. PRED, *Behavior and Location,* pt. 1 (1967); and KEVIN R. COX and R.G. GOLLEDGE (eds.), *Behavioral Problems in Geography* (1969). Studies of spatial perception are still in their infancy, but a useful collection of introductory studies is provided by DAVID LOWENTHAL (ed.), *Environmental Perception and Behavior* (1967).

Social and cultural geography: Influential in the development of a quantitative and theoretical approach to movements is TORSTEN HAGERSTRAND, *Innovation Diffusion As a Spatial Process* (1967). More traditional approaches are provided by the collection of essays in P.L. WAGNER and M.W. MIKESELL, *Readings in Cultural Geography* (1962); and F.E. DOHRS and L.M. SOMMERS (comps.), *Cultural Geography: Selected Readings* (1967).

Political geography: A basic collection of essays surveying the field is contained in R.E. KASPERSON and J.V. MINGHI (eds.), *The Structure of Political Geography* (1969). HAROLD and MARGARET SPROUT, *The Ecological Perspective on Human Affairs* (1965), provides a concise overview of the relationships between human society and the geographical environment.

Economic geography: Two traditional, empirically based textbooks in the field are GUNNAR ALEXANDERSSON, *Geography of Manufacturing* (1967); and J.W. ALEXANDER, *Economic Geography* (1963), and with H.H. MCCARTY and JAMES B. LINDBERG, *A Preface to Economic Geography* (1966), providing a more rigorous introduction to concepts and principles. A basic, theoretical survey is found in AUGUST LOSCH, *Die räumliche Ordnung der Wirtschaft,* 2nd ed. (1944; Eng. trans., *The Economics of Location,* 1954). WALTER CHRISTALLER, *Die zentralen Orte in Süddeutschland* (1933; Eng. trans., *Central Places in Southern Germany,* 1966), is one of the first attempts to produce a major theoretical study in geography. The limitation of this central-place theory and more recent empirical evidence in the field is shown in B.J.L. BERRY, *Geography of Market Centers and Retail Distribution* (1967). A joint venture by economists and geographers led to the production of a multivolume survey of world agriculture, entitled *World Agricultural Atlas* (Instituto Geografico de Agostini, 1969). Two comprehensive, introductory, systematic studies of world agricultural patterns are PETER LAUT, *Agricultural Geography*, 2 vol. (1968); and HOWARD F. GREGOR, *The Geography of Agriculture* (1970).

Urban geography: A classic study of the urbanization of an area is provided by JEAN GOTTMANN, *Megalopolis: The Urbanized Northeastern Seaboard of the United States* (1961). More specific examples of the functional approach to urban geography may be found in B.J.L. BERRY and FRANK E. HORTON (eds.), *Geographic Perspectives on the Urban Systems* (1970). This may be compared with the more traditional world surveys found in JACQUELINE BEAUJEU-GARNIER and GEORGES CHABOT, *Traité de géographie urbaine* (1963; Eng. trans., *Urban Geography*, 1967); or the historical-morphological emphasis of R.E. DICKINSON, *The West European City*, 2nd ed. rev. (1962).

Historical geography: The alternative approaches to historical geography can be seen by comparing H.C. DARBY (ed.), *An Historical Geography of England Before 1800* (1936); and A.R.H. BAKER, JOHN D. HAMSHERE, and JOHN LANGTON (comps.), *Geographical Interpretations of Historical Sources* (1970); and with CLIFFORD T. SMITH, *An Historical Geography of Western Europe Before 1800* (1967).

Physical geography (Climate): Introductory works on climate are represented by R.G. BARRY and RICHARD J. CHORLEY, *Atmosphere, Weather and Climate* (1968); and J.A. DAY and G.L. STERNES, *Climate and Weather* (1970). A comprehensive bibliography on urban climates may be found in T.J. CHANDLER, *Selected Bibliography on Urban Climate* (1970). See also T.J. CHANDLER, *The Climate of London* (1965). Although an interest of physicians rather than of geographers, SIDNEY H. LICHT (ed.), *Medical Climatology* (1964), demonstrates the degree of medical specialism required in geographical studies of human physiology. *(Geomorphology):* Traditional approaches to the study of landforms are represented by W.D. THORNBURY, *Principles of Geomorphology*, 2nd ed. (1968); and ARTHUR HOLMES, *Principles of Physical Geology* (1965). More specific examples of modern trends in specific branches may be seen in MARIE MORISAWA, *Streams: Their Dynamics and Morphology* (1968); CLIFFORD EMBLETON and C.A. KING, *Glacial and Periglacial Geomorphology* (1968). A survey of world landscape morphology has been attempted by LESTER C. KING, *Morphology of the Earth*, 2nd ed. (1967). *(Biogeography):* One of the classics of the field, M.I. NEWBIGIN, *Plant and Animal Geography* (1936, reprinted 1968), has only recently been superseded by DAVID WATTS, *Principles of Biogeography* (1971), although the close relationships with ecology ensure that many geographers use standard ecological sources. Useful examples of the geographical approach are provided by S.R. EYRE, *Vegetation and Soils*, 2nd ed. (1968) and *World Vegetation Types* (1971).

Exploration: HERODOTUS, *History*, trans. by J. ENOCH POWELL, 2 vol. (1949); STRABO, *Geography*, trans. by H.L. JONES, 8 vol. (1917–32); M.P. CHARLESWORTH, *Trade-Routes and Commerce of the Roman Empire*, 2nd ed. rev. (1970); PETER G. FOOTE and DAVID M. WILSON, *The Viking Achievement* (1970); GEORGE KIMBLE, *Geography in the Middle Ages* (1938, reprinted 1968); E.G.R. TAYLOR, *Tudor Geography, 1485–1583* (1930, reprinted 1968) and *Late Tudor and Early Stuart Geography, 1583–1650* (1934, reprinted 1968); EDWARD HEAWOOD, *A History of Geographical Discovery in the Seventeenth and Eighteenth Centuries* (1912, reprinted 1965); J.N.L. BAKER, *A History of Geographical Discovery and Exploration*, rev. ed. (1937), still perhaps the best single volume on the whole field; SIR PERCY M. SYKES, *A History of Exploration from the Earliest Times to the Present Day*, 2nd ed. (1936), a very readable account. *(On the classical period):* E.H. BUNBURY, *A History of Ancient Geography Among the Greeks and Romans*, 2nd ed., 2 vol. (1883), a standard work; J.O. THOMSON, *A History of Ancient Geography* (1948), well-documented review of geographical knowledge of the period and a discussion of the geographical theories; MAX CARY and E.H. WARMINGTON, *The Ancient Explorers* (1929), a readable account of recorded exploratory journeys. *(On the medieval period):* C.R. BEAZLEY, *The Dawn of Modern Geography*, 3 vol. (1897–1906), a standard work on geographical ideas and knowledge AD 300–1420; ARTHUR P. NEWTON (ed.), *Travel and Travellers of the Middle Ages* (1926, reprinted 1968); JOHN K. WRIGHT, *Geographical Lore of the Time of the Crusades* (1925, reprinted 1965); *The Travels of Marco Polo the Venetian*—SIR HENRY YULE edited the standard edition, but the Everyman edition is the most readily available. *(On the Age of Discovery):* A.P. NEWTON (ed.), *The Great Age of Discovery* (1932, reprinted 1969); CECIL JANE (ed.), *Select Documents Illustrating the Four Voyages of Columbus*, 2 vol. (1930–33); J.A. WILLIAMSON, *The Voyages of the Cabots . . .* (1929) and *The Cabot Voyages and Bristol Discovery*

Under Henry VII (1962); F.H.H. GUILLEMARD, *Life of Ferdinand Magellan* (1890, reprinted 1971). *(On the modern period):* RICHARD HAKLUYT, *The Principall Navigations, Voiages and Discoueries of the English Nation*, 3 vol. (1598–1600)—a useful and accessible edition has been edited by JOHN MASEFIELD (1927–28); J.C. BEAGLEHOLE, *The Exploration of the Pacific*, 3rd ed. (1966); *The Journals of Captain James Cook on His Voyages of Discovery*, 3 vol. (1955–67); MARGERY PERHAM and JACK SIMMONS (eds.), *African Discovery*, 2nd ed. (1957); ERNEST SCOTT (ed.), *Australian Discovery*, 2 vol. (1929, reprinted 1966), a wide selection of passages from the journals of African and Australian explorers, with comment; CLEMENTS MARKHAM, *The Lands of Silence* (1921); ROBERT HUXLEY (ed.), *Scott's Last Expedition*, 2nd enl. ed. (1964).

(J.B.Mi./W.K.D.D.)

Geological Sciences

The geological sciences deal with the study of the Earth. Their major divisions include physical and historical geology, paleontology (the study of fossils), sedimentology (the study of sediments and their conversion to rock), geomorphology (the study of landforms and surface processes), stratigraphy (the study of strata, or layered rocks), geophysics, geodesy (the study of the form of the Earth), geochemistry, mineralogy and crystallography, petrology (the study of rocks), structural geology (the study of rock geometry and deformation), engineering geology, the various branches of economic geology, including mining geology and petroleum geology, and certain aspects of hydrology, oceanography, meteorology, and the planetary sciences. These divisions are so intimately interrelated that no sharp boundaries truly exist. Furthermore, they intergrade with physics, chemistry, biology, and some branches of engineering, including civil engineering, mining engineering, and petroleum engineering. The term geology, meaning literally the study of the Earth, is broadly inclusive and can be regarded as embracing all of the geological sciences. The purpose of this article is to treat the nature, scope, and methods of the geological sciences rather than the substantive knowledge garnered by the many divisions and aspects of the geological sciences, which is taken up in detail in other articles. For treatment of the relation of the geological sciences to the hydrologic and atmospheric sciences, and to science and technology in general, see EARTH SCIENCES.

This article is divided into the following sections:

I. Study of the composition of the Earth
    Mineralogy
    Petrology
        Igneous petrology
        Sedimentary petrology
        Metamorphic petrology
    Economic geology
    Geochemistry
        Chemistry of the Earth
        Isotopic geochemistry
II. Study of the structure of the Earth
    Geodesy and geophysics
        Figure of the Earth
        Scope and techniques of geophysics
    Structural geology
        Small-scale features
        Large-scale features
    Volcanology
III. Study of surface features and processes
    Geomorphology and glacial geology
    Engineering, environmental, and urban geology
IV. Study of Earth history
    Historical geology
    Paleontology
    Stratigraphy and sedimentology
    Astrogeology

Generally speaking, geology is concerned with the rocks that form the outer part of the solid Earth. An understanding of these rocks and of changes in their composition and arrangement that have occurred and are now going on involves principles and techniques of physics and chemistry. Geophysics and geochemistry are logical outgrowths of this overlap in interest that extends beyond the visible rocky shell to deeper zones of the Earth. Biology also plays an essential role in the study of rocks because many rocks show the effects of biologic processes and contain records of animals and plants that lived in past ages. Paleontology, the study of fossils, is an essential part of geology; the aid of organic chemistry is required for study of the interactions among rock materials and many biological substances. Nearly all geological study seeks to determine an order of events, and a main objective of the science is to work out the full history of the Earth and its animal and plant inhabitants.

The intergradational nature of the divisions of the geological sciences requires that geological scientists be versatile in their approach to problems. There has been a progressive shift, particularly notable in the past several decades, for geologists to employ a variety of disciplines and subdisciplines. Modern practice in petrology involves extensive use of chemistry and physics and, to a lesser extent, various mathematical tools, including statistics and differential equations. Paleontology also may involve at times the use of statistics, organic chemistry, physical chemistry, and many physical aspects of geology. Mathematical models and the statistical analysis of data are important facets of geomorphology, stratigraphy and sedimentology, and other divisions previously cited. Hence, an important element in the training of geologists is an appreciation of the role of other disciplines, both within the geological sciences and in disciplines outside geology. Some of the problems of geology are so strongly dependent upon allied sciences that chemists, physicists, and mathematicians have been attracted to them.

The geological sciences serve man in a variety of ways. As in all sciences, one of the strong motivating forces is man's curiosity about nature. Many of the great problems of geology, such as the origin and development of mountains and the evolution of the Earth's crust and ocean basins, are replete with unanswered questions. Yet, the excitement of geology and its essence as a science or group of sciences lie in the search for answers. The goals of geology are not solely to yield answers to problems of nature, however. Geological applications that are useful to man in a practical and commercial sense are also sought. Exploration for deposits of metallic ores, such as those of iron, copper, lead, zinc, gold, and silver, for example, are broadly guided by geology, often coupled with applied aspects of geophysics and geochemistry. The search for petroleum also is strongly influenced by those aspects of geology dealing with the deposition and deformation of sedimentary rocks and with the flow of underground fluids, including water, oil, and natural gas. Also notable is the rise in the use of engineering geology in land-use planning, particularly in urban areas, where geological considerations generally should have great influence on the location of buildings, bridges, roads, nuclear reactors, and other structures, with respect to the ability of soil and underlying rocks to provide support and with regard to avoidance of landslides and potential earthquake hazards in many parts of the world.

I. Study of the composition of the Earth
MINERALOGY
Mineralogy is the scientific study of minerals, the basic units of composition of most rocks. By generally accepted definition, a mineral is a naturally occurring solid material of more or less specific chemical composition that generally occurs in crystalline form and is usually inorganic in nature. Although oil and coal are commonly referred to as minerals (or more specifically as mineral fuels), neither oil nor coal is a mineral as defined in geology because neither is crystalline and both have an organic origin. It is difficult, however, to define the term mineral simply and precisely because there are numerous exceptions to those qualities that generally define a mineral.

Mineralogy as a discipline has had very close historical ties with geology as a whole. Minerals as basic constituents of rocks and ore deposits are quite obviously an integral aspect of geology. The problems and techniques of mineralogy, however, are distinct in many respects from those of the rest of geology, with the result that

mineralogy has grown to be a large and complex discipline in itself. Its ties to other disciplines, notably chemistry and physics, are almost as strong as its ties with geology.

Approximately 3,000 distinct mineral species are recognized, but comparatively few are important in the kinds of rocks that are abundant in the outer part of the Earth. Thus a few related minerals known as the feldspars, together with quartz and mica, are the essential ingredients in granite and its near relatives. Limestones, which are widely distributed on all continents, consist largely of only two minerals, calcite and dolomite. Many rocks have a more complex mineralogy, and in some the mineral particles are so minute that they can be identified only through highly specialized techniques. Several clay minerals important in rocks known as shales or clay stones, for example, cannot be resolved by the most powerful optical microscopes and must be studied by methods mentioned below.

Under favourable conditions mineral substances have grown into nearly perfect crystals that have distinctive external forms. Silicon dioxide forms clear crystals of quartz that are hexagonal prisms with terminations shaped as pyramids; iron sulfide forms perfect cubes of pyrite, the faces marked with parallel lines. But when a substance crystallizes in bulk, crowding of grains growing from neighbouring centres prevents formation of recognizable crystals, though each mineral is formed with its peculiar internal atomic structure. Modern laboratories have varied and highly effective devices for working out the mineral content of rock materials. Standard equipment is the petrographic microscope, constructed for viewing thin sections of rock that are ground uniformly to a thickness of about 0.025 millimetre (0.001 inch) in light that is polarized by polarizing prisms incorporated in the microscope. If the rock is crystalline, its essential minerals can be determined by their peculiar optical properties as revealed in transmitted light under magnification, provided that the individual crystal grains can be distinguished. Opaque minerals, such as those with a high content of metallic elements, require a technique employing reflected light from polished surfaces. This kind of microscopic analysis has particular application to metallic ore minerals. Another device exposes mineral grains to X-rays, which pass through a specimen and outline on photographic film a pattern that represents its atomic structure, peculiar to a given mineral species. Substances such as clay minerals are made up of particles that are submicroscopic to ordinary petrographic microscopes. Such particles become clearly visible under the electron microscope, however, which gives images with diameters tens of thousands of times. The several clay minerals also can be identified by a technique known as differential thermal analysis, which takes advantage of pronounced differences in thermal properties. The instrument used in the analysis automatically draws graphs that are recognized as peculiar to given mineral compositions.

The science of crystallography is concerned with the geometrical properties and internal structure of crystals. Because minerals are generally crystalline, crystallography is an essential aspect of mineralogy. The domain of crystallography has grown well beyond mineralogy, however, and is also closely tied with metallurgy, ceramics, and other aspects of materials science, and with physics, chemistry, and biochemistry, all of which are concerned to some degree with the properties of crystalline materials, including those of both inorganic and organic origin. The instruments of crystallography include those listed above, notably the polarizing or petrographic microscope and X-ray-diffraction equipment. In addition, an instrument known as a goniometer, which determines angles between crystal faces, is in common use.

Analytical chemistry plays a major role in the study of minerals and rocks. An exact quantitative analysis is a valuable supplement to other techniques, and for many specimens the chemical examination plays a major role. Rocks with glassy texture have no clear atomic organization and therefore are not generally responsive to mi-

Purpose of the geological sciences

Importance to man

Optical examination of minerals and crystals

Chemical analysis and mineral synthesis

croscopic study. Natural glasses are common in rocks of volcanic origin. In many such specimens, however, small mineral grains scattered through a glassy groundmass can be recognized under a microscope, giving information to supplement the chemical study; but the quantitative analysis is of first importance.

Although a major concern of mineralogy is to describe and classify the geometrical, chemical, and physical properties of minerals, it is also concerned with their origin. Physical chemistry and thermodynamics are basic scientific tools for understanding mineral origin. Some of the observational data of mineralogy consist of the behaviour of solutions in precipitating crystalline materials under controlled conditions in the laboratory. Certain minerals can be created synthetically under conditions in which temperature and concentration of solutions are carefully monitored. Other experimental methods include study of the transformation of solids at relatively high temperatures and pressures to yield specific minerals or assemblages of minerals. Experimental data obtained in the laboratory, coupled with chemical and physical theory, enable the conditions of origin of many naturally occurring minerals to be inferred. For information on the substantive aspects of mineralogy, see MINERALS; CRYSTALLOGRAPHY; the several articles on specific mineral groups, such as FELDSPARS; or CLAY MINERALS; and the article GEOCHEMICAL EQUILIBRIA AT HIGH TEMPERATURES AND PRESSURES, particularly for basic information on mineral synthesis.

PETROLOGY

Petrology is the study of rocks, and, because most rocks are composed of minerals, petrology is strongly dependent on mineralogy. In many respects mineralogy and petrology share the same problems; for example, the physical conditions that prevail (pressure, temperature, time, and presence or absence of water) when particular minerals or mineral assemblages are formed. Although petrology is in principle concerned with rocks throughout the crust, as well as those of the inner depths of the Earth, in practice the discipline is mainly concerned with those that are accessible in the outer part of the Earth's crust. Rock specimens obtained from the surface of the Moon and those that ultimately will be obtained from other planets are also proper considerations of petrology.

The rocks of the Earth's crust are exposed to view only on continents and islands, which form almost 30 percent of the earth's surface. The known rocks are divisible into three main groups: igneous rocks, which have solidified from molten silicate material called magma; sedimentary rocks, which are composed of fragments derived from pre-existing rocks, or from materials precipitated from solution, or from organic products; and metamorphic rocks, which have been derived from either igneous or sedimentary rocks under conditions that caused changes in composition, texture, and internal structure.

Igneous petrology. The igneous rocks are formed as either extrusive or intrusive masses. Extrusive rocks are products of volcanic action; they appear at the surface as molten lavas that spread in sheets and harden, or they are made up of fragments, large and small, blown from vents by violent gaseous explosions. Intrusive rocks have formed by slow cooling of molten masses below the Earth's surface; many such bodies are now exposed to view because long-continued erosion has removed the cover of older rocks. Some of these bodies may have been magma reservoirs that supplied volcanoes in the past.

The grain size or texture of igneous rocks is closely related to the mode of origin. Lavas generally are fine-grained, even glassy, because rapid loss of heat and resulting solidification allowed little or no opportunity for mineral grains to grow. But the same kind of magma, under a cover of solid rock thousands of feet thick, will lose heat very slowly; accordingly, the grains will have a much longer time period for growth, and the resultant rock will be coarse-grained. Examples are ordinary granites in which all grains of the essential minerals can be distinguished with the unaided eye. A rock with similar

chemical composition that formed in a lava flow may have a uniform appearance, with no distinguishable grains; magnification up to 50 or 100 times under a petrographic microscope may reveal a texture and mineral composition strikingly like that of the granite, however. Such a rock, known as rhyolite, is said to have aphanitic (*i.e.*, invisible) texture.

In a general way the textures of igneous rocks vary according to the depth at which the bodies were formed. Deep-seated (abyssal or plutonic) bodies are coarse-grained; intrusive bodies that cooled at shallower depths (hypabyssal masses) generally have medium to fine grains; and extrusive rocks are fine-grained to glassy. There are, however, some complexities in this general rule. Many sheets of rhyolite lava have large and well-formed crystals of feldspar and quartz isolated in an aphanitic groundmass; such rock is called rhyolite porphyry, and its crystals are called phenocrysts. Presumably these formed in a quiescent magma body underground, part of which was erupted in a volcanic outbreak, whereupon the magma enclosing the crystals cooled quickly to form rock with fine grain size. Such porphyritic texture is common also in bodies of both the shallow- and deep-zone intrusive rock types. In such rocks the groundmass has visible grains that are much smaller than the enclosed phenocrysts. The contrasting grain size in all porphyries suggests an abrupt change in physical–chemical conditions while the parent bodies were forming.

Knowledge of intrusive igneous bodies has been built up slowly by comparative studies, some in regions in which erosion has brought to light only the masses that developed at shallow depths, others in profoundly eroded belts in which what might be called the bones of extinct mountains can be seen. Beneath growing mountain chains around the Pacific Ocean, igneous intrusive action is doubtless now in progress, though beyond the range of direct observation. Study of extrusive activity and the resulting rocks is more favourable because of opportunities for direct observation. Active volcanic centres are widely distributed, and some of these are under continuous observation. The behaviour of Vesuvius and other Mediterranean volcanoes has been watched through many centuries, and well-equipped scientific stations have been in operation for some decades at a number of active centres. Study of active volcanoes is supplemented by observations made on great volumes of older volcanic products, which, because they accumulated on the Earth's surface, are much more accessible than the intrusive bodies that have come into view only through chance exposure by erosion.

Igneous petrology has several main concerns. An older, but still important aspect, is the classification of igneous rocks according to those properties that may be studied and observed more or less directly (descriptive classification) or their classification according to inferred conditions of origin (genetic classification). The principal problems of igneous petrology concern the source of materials in rock, the mode of emplacement of igneous bodies, and the physical and chemical conditions of origin. Many of these problems are approached through traditional methods that involve microscopic study of thin sections and field mapping at various levels of detail of rocks exposed at the surface. When mine workings or core holes permit underground observation, large-scale geometrical relationships may be observed and interpreted in three dimensions. Of particular note is the rise in the past two decades of experimental methods in which high pressures and elevated temperatures are obtained under simulated rock-forming conditions in the laboratory. The experimentalist can create synthetic igneous rocks, such as granites, from materials placed in small cylinders under carefully observed conditions. The small, artificially produced specimens of igneous rock may be compared with actual specimens of igneous rock, and, in turn, the range of physical conditions under which actual igneous rocks have formed can be deduced. The Geophysical Laboratory of the Carnegie Institution of Washington, D.C., established in 1904, has been a leader in experimental ig-

Textures, composition, and origin

Concerns of igneous petrology

neous petrology. For further information on the substantive aspects of igneous petrology, see IGNEOUS ROCKS; IGNEOUS ROCKS, EXTRUSIVE; IGNEOUS ROCKS, INTRUSIVE; and IGNEOUS ROCKS, PYROCLASTIC. See also VOLCANOES; and GEOCHEMICAL EQUILIBRIA AT HIGH TEMPERATURES AND PRESSURES, particularly for basic information on rock synthesis.

Sedimentary petrology. Rock materials exposed to air and moisture are subject to continual change, both physical and chemical. Bedrock is broken into pieces, large and small, which are moved by running water and other agents to lower elevations and spread in sheets over lake bottoms, floodplains, and sea floors. Dissolved matter is carried to seas and other water bodies, and some of it is precipitated either chemically or by the action of organisms. The deposited material becomes compacted, and in time much of it is cemented into firm rock. Generally, the process of deposition is not continuous but sporadic, and sheets of material representing separate episodes come to form distinct layers of rock. As a result the sedimentary rocks are stratified; the individual layers form beds or strata.

Large parts of every continental mass are covered with sedimentary rocks that represent deposits formed during many periods of the Earth's history. In part these bedded rocks are nearly horizontal, as they were originally; but in large areas, particularly in mountain belts, they show various degrees of tilting and deformation. The principal kinds of sedimentary rocks include conglomerate, sandstone, mudstone, siltstone, shale, limestone, dolomite, and gypsum.

Sedimentary petrology is concerned with the description and classification of sedimentary rocks, interpretation of the processes of transportation and deposition of the sedimentary materials forming the rocks, the environment that prevailed at the time the sediments were deposited, and the alteration (compaction, cementation, and chemical and mineralogical modification) of the sedimentary material after deposition.

There are two main branches of sedimentary petrology. One branch deals with carbonate rocks, namely limestones and dolomites, composed principally of calcium carbonate (calcite) and calcium magnesium carbonate (dolomite). A major concern of carbonate petrology is to devise classification systems that are capable of describing the large numbers of types of limestones and dolomites. Much of the complexity in classifying carbonate rocks stems partly from the fact that many limestones and dolomites have been formed, directly or indirectly, through the influence of organisms, including bacteria, lime-secreting algae, various shelled organisms including mollusks and brachiopods, and by corals. In limestones and dolomites that were deposited under marine conditions, commonly in shallow warm seas, much of the material initially forming the rock consists of skeletons or fragments of skeletons of lime-secreting organisms. In many examples, this skeletal material is preserved as fossils; alternatively, the original material may have been dissolved and recrystallized. Some of the major problems of carbonate petrology concern the physical and biological conditions of the environments in which carbonate material has been deposited, including water depth, temperature, degree of illumination by sunlight, motion by waves and currents, and the salinity and other chemical aspects of the water in which deposition occurred. The problems of carbonate petrology are strongly interdisciplinary and involve biology, physical chemistry, and biochemistry.

The other principal branch of sedimentary petrology is concerned with the sediments and sedimentary rocks that are essentially noncalcareous. These include sands and sandstones, clays and claystones or mudstones, siltstones, conglomerates, glacial till, and the varieties of sandstones, siltstones, and conglomerates; for example, the graywacke-type sandstones and siltstones. These rocks are broadly known as clastic rocks because they consist of distinct particles or clasts. Like the other branches of petrology, clastic petrology is concerned with classification, particularly with respect to the mineral composition of fragments or particles, as well as the shapes of particles (angular versus rounded), and the degree of homogeneity of particle sizes. Other main concerns of clastic petrology are the mode of transportation of sedimentary materials, including the transportation of clay, silt, and fine sand by wind, and the transportation of these and coarser materials through suspension in water, through traction by waves and currents in rivers, lakes, and seas, and sediment transport by ice.

Sedimentary petrology is also concerned with the small-scale structural features of sediments and sedimentary rocks. There is no sharp division between large-scale structural and sedimentary features, which are also the domain of structural geology and stratigraphy, and the small-scale features. Structural features that can be conveniently seen in a specimen that can be held in the hand are within the domain of sedimentary petrology. These features include the geometrical attitude of mineral grains with respect to each other, small-scale cross stratification, the shapes and interconnections of pore spaces, and the presence of fractures and veinlets that fill fractures. Collectively, small-scale structural features may be described as the fabric of the rock, although the term fabric is also commonly applied to the arrangement of mineral grains. The attribute of fabric is also an important aspect of igneous rocks and metamorphic rocks.

For further information on the substantive aspects of sedimentary petrology, see SEDIMENTARY ROCKS; CONGLOMERATES AND BRECCIAS; SANDSTONES; GRAYWACKES; SHALES; LIMESTONES AND DOLOMITES; SILICEOUS ROCKS; and EVAPORITES. See also MARINE SEDIMENTS; and GEOCHEMICAL EQUILIBRIA AT LOW TEMPERATURES AND PRESSURES, particularly for basic information on the conditions of formation of certain sedimentary mineral deposits.

Metamorphic petrology. Metamorphism means, literally, transformation in form, and logically the term might be applied to any profound change. In geology the meaning is restricted; generally it does not include the decay of rock materials exposed to the weather or the fusion of rocks by igneous processes, although both these classes of changes have been considered to be aspects of metamorphism by some geologists. Metamorphic rocks have been developed from earlier formed igneous and sedimentary rocks by heat and pressure at some depth, most effectively in mountainous regions. Resultant changes occur in the texture, mineral composition, and structural features of the rock. Survival of some characteristics of the original rock indicates that fusion has not played an essential part in the change, nor has recrystallization at temperatures below that of fusion been so extreme as to obliterate all aspects of the original rock, save its chemical composition.

Two general kinds of metamorphic effects are recognized: (1) dynamic metamorphism, resulting from strong forces and perhaps aided by an increase in temperature from friction; and (2) thermal metamorphism, which is caused by high temperature in rocks adjacent to intrusive igneous bodies. Effects are accentuated by the introduction of elements by fluids that move from a molten mass into the surrounding rock. Susceptibility of different rocks to either types of metamorphism varies greatly. In part of the Appalachian Mountain belt in Pennsylvania, for example, coal in strongly crumpled beds has been changed to anthracite, which is a type of coal from which nearly all volatile matter has been expelled; but the shale beds adjacent to this coal are unchanged except for the crumpling. By contrast, in a more strongly deformed belt in Rhode Island, coal has been changed into graphite, and, in the enclosing shale beds, shearing has developed thin cleavage planes lined with flakes of mica. Temperature alone, however, is capable of altering rocks. Near intrusive igneous masses, shale is commonly altered to hornfels, a hard metamorphic rock studded with crystals of minerals that grew as a result of temporarily elevated temperatures as the igneous body was intruded. Beds of sandstone alongside altered shale, however, are generally unchanged except for cementation of quartz grains.

Carbonate sedimentology and clastic sedimentology

Dynamic and thermal metamorphism

Extreme metamorphism in some mountain zones has resulted from combined dynamic and thermal effects. Fluids rising from deep-seated igneous bodies or plutons have combined with rock material in deformed sedimentary rocks, and the resultant product is indistinguishable from granite that has crystallized from magma. To some extent, therefore, granite rocks may be a product of metamorphic as well as igneous processes.

Many of the metamorphic rocks consist of flaky minerals, such as mica and chlorite, set in a parallel arrangement. These minerals cause the rock to split into thin sheets, and the rocks are said to be foliated. The commonest kinds of foliated metamorphic rock are slate, phyllite, schist, and gneiss. Marble and quartzite are nonfoliated metamorphic rocks.

Problems of metamorphic petrology

The problems of metamorphic petrology are similar to those of igneous petrology in that they are generally concerned with the conditions of pressure, temperature, and gross chemical environment that prevailed when particular suites of minerals formed in various types of metamorphic rocks. Other problems include the nature and attitude of the deforming forces, as manifested in the fabric of dynamically metamorphosed rocks. Evidence derived from the study of metamorphic rocks has an important bearing on many fundamental questions in geology, such as the depth to which former sedimentary rocks that have been metamorphosed were buried. The presence of minerals that form at high pressures and that occur as replacements in rocks that have been metamorphosed form one basis for estimating the former maximum depth of burial. Other metamorphic minerals that are known to form within certain temperature ranges are forms of geologic thermometers that yield evidence about the temperatures that prevailed close to the margins of igneous bodies when they were intruded. For further information on the substantive aspects of metamorphic petrology, see METAMORPHIC ROCKS; ROCK METAMORPHISM, PRINCIPLES OF; and ROCKS, PHYSICAL PROPERTIES OF.

ECONOMIC GEOLOGY

The mineral commodities on which our civilization is heavily dependent are obtained from the Earth's crust and therefore have a prominent place in the study and practice of that branch of geology termed economic geology. In turn, economic geology consists of several principal subbranches that include the study of ore deposits, petroleum geology, and the geology of nonmetallic deposits (excluding petroleum), such as coal, stone, salt, gypsum, clay and sand, and other commercially valuable materials. The study of water in the ground, or hydrogeology, may also be classed as a branch of economic geology (see further GROUNDWATER).

Branches and objectives of economic geology

None of these branches of economic geology are sharply defined subdisciplines. Instead, they involve application in some degree of most, if not all, of the other disciplines within the geological sciences. The practice of economic geology is distinguished, however, by the fact that its objectives are to aid in the exploration for and extraction of mineral resources. The objectives are, therefore, economic. In petroleum geology, for example, a common goal is to guide oil-well-drilling programs so that the most profitable prospects are drilled, and those that are likely to be of marginal economic value, or barren, are avoided. A similar philosophy influences the other branches of economic geology. In this sense, economic geology can be considered as an aspect of business that is devoted to economic decision making. Many deposits of economic interest, particularly deposits of metallic ores, are of extreme scientific interest in themselves, however, and they have warranted intensive study that has been somewhat apart from economic considerations.

The practice of economic geology provides employment for many of the world's geologists. On a world basis, probably more than two-thirds of those persons employed in the geological sciences are engaged in work that touches on the economic aspects of geology. These include geologists whose main interests lie in many fields within the geological sciences. The oil industry collectively is the largest employer of economic geologists. Geologists with principal interests that include stratigraphy, sedimentary petrology, structural geology, paleontology, and geophysics are widely employed in the petroleum industry.

Economic geology is faced with exceptional challenges at this point in time. The world's steadily expanding population, coupled with the rise in standard of living in many countries, has caused consumption of virtually all mineral commodities to rise sharply. The consumption of oil and natural gas has grown steadily, as has that of most metals, including iron, copper, lead, zinc, and silver. Even sand and gravel, which are of relatively small unit value, are in increasing demand and are in short supply in some urban areas. The task facing economic geologists is to guide the exploration for and exploitation of these commodities and, at the same time, ensure that man's environment be as little damaged as possible. These demands are in conflict; oil cannot be produced nor iron ore mined without some degradation of the natural environment.

For further information on the substantive aspects of economic geology, see ORE DEPOSITS; PETROLEUM; NATURAL GAS; COALS; OIL SHALES; and PHOSPHORITES. See also OCEANS AND SEAS: *Economic aspects of oceans and seas.*

GEOCHEMISTRY

Chemistry of the Earth. Geochemistry is broadly concerned with the application of chemistry to virtually all aspects of geology. Inasmuch as the Earth is composed of the chemical elements, all geological materials and most geological processes can be regarded from a chemical point of view. Most problems of geochemistry are so inextricably linked with other aspects of geology that it is difficult to isolate them as purely geochemical problems. Some of the major classes of problems that broadly belong to geochemistry are as follows: (1) origin and abundance of the elements in the solar system, Galaxy, and universe (cosmochemistry); (2) abundance of elements in the major divisions of the Earth, including the core, mantle, crust, hydrosphere, and atmosphere; (3) behaviour of ions in the structure of crystals; (4) chemical reactions in cooling magmas and the origin and evolution of deeply buried intrusive igneous rocks; (5) chemistry of volcanic (extrusive) igneous rocks and of phenomena closely related to volcanic activity, including hot-spring activity, emanation of volcanic gases, and origin of ore deposits formed by hot waters derived during the late stages of cooling of igneous magmas; (6) chemical reactions involved in weathering of rocks in which earlier formed minerals decay and new minerals are created; (7) the transportation of weathering products in solution by natural waters in the ground and in streams, lakes, and the sea; (8) chemical changes that accompany compaction and cementation of unconsolidated sediments to form sedimentary rocks; and (9) the progressive chemical and mineralogical changes that take place as rocks undergo metamorphism.

Kinds of geochemical problems

One of the great, general concerns of geochemistry is the continued recycling of the materials of the Earth's crust, largely through agencies of the hydrosphere (earth's waters) and atmosphere, coupled with mountain building and other forms of deformation of the Earth's crust. Questions pertaining to the locally changing balances of the Earth's chemical elements as they undergo separation and segregation during transportation and subsequent recombination in the Earth's rock or crustal cycle are central to geochemistry. The behaviour of dissolved materials in natural waters, under the relatively low temperatures that prevail at or near the surface of the Earth, is an integral aspect of the crustal cycle. Weathering processes supply dissolved material, including silica, calcium carbonate, and other salts, to streams. These materials then enter the oceans, where some remain in solution (such as sodium chloride), whereas others are progressively removed to form certain sedimentary rocks, including limestone and dolomite, and, where conditions are conducive for the origin of deposits formed

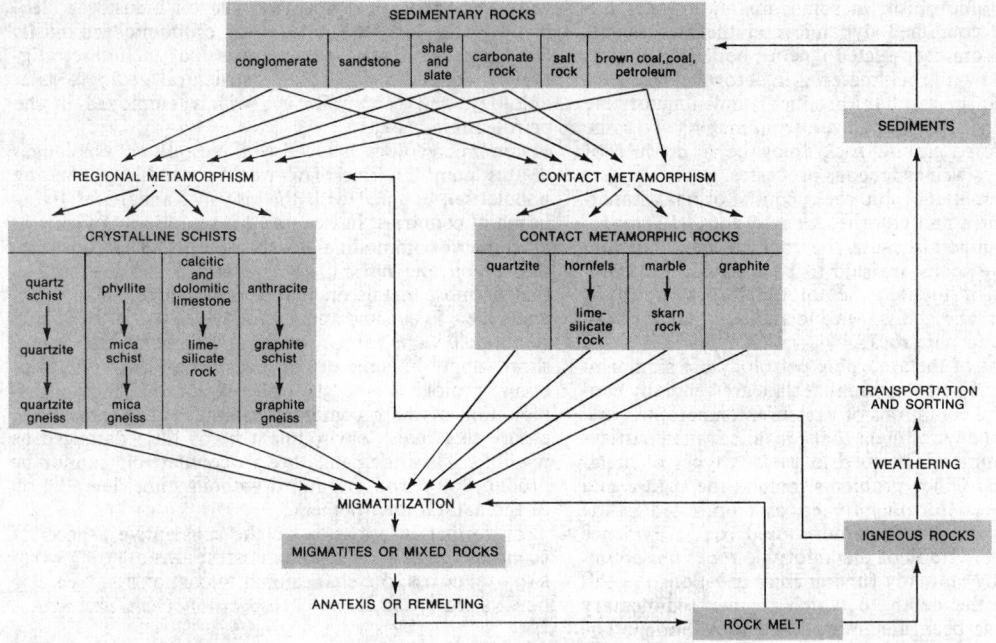

The major cycle of matter.
From K. Rankama and T.G. Sahama, *Geochemistry* (copyright 1950); University of Chicago Press

by means of evaporation, gypsum (hydrous calcium sulfate), rock salt (halite), and potash deposits may be formed.

The behaviour of biological materials and their subsequent disposition are important aspects of geochemistry, generally termed organic geochemistry or biogeochemistry. Organic geochemistry is closely allied with many aspects of biology and, of course, owes major allegiance to organic chemistry. Major problems of organic geochemistry include the question of the chemical enviroment on earth in which life originated; the modification of the hydrosphere, and particularly the atmosphere, through the effects of life; and the incorporation of organic materials in rocks, including carbonaceous material in sedimentary rocks. The origin and chemical transformations of biological material to form deposits of coal, petroleum, and natural gas are included in the last category. Organic chemical reactions influence many geochemical processes, including rock weathering and production of soil, the solution, precipitation, and secretion of such dissolved materials as calcium carbonate, and the alteration of sediments to form sedimentary rocks.

Geochemistry has applications to other subdisciplines within geology, as well as to disciplines relatively far removed from geology. At one extreme, geochemistry is linked with cosmology in a number of ways. These include the study of the chemical composition of meteorites, the relative abundance of elements in the Earth, Moon, and other planets, and the ages of meteorites and of rocks of the crust of the Earth and Moon as established by radiometric means. At another extreme, the geochemistry of traces of metals in rocks and soils and, ultimately, in the food chain has important consequences for man and for the vast body of lesser organisms on which he is dependent and with whom he coexists. Deficiencies in traces of copper and cobalt in forage plants, for example, lead to diseases in certain grazing animals and may locally influence man's health. These deficiencies are in turn related to their concentrations in rocks and the manner in which they are chemically combined within soils and rocks.

Isotopic geochemistry. One aspect of geochemistry deals with the geological role of isotopes. Some chemical elements consist of several isotopes, as do the three naturally occurring isotopes of oxygen, oxygen-16, oxygen-17, and oxygen-18. Each isotope is characterized by a particular configuration in its nucleus; all isotopes of oxygen have eight protons in their nuclei, but the number of neutrons differs. Oxygen-16 has eight neutrons

(eight neutrons plus eight protons yield a mass number of 16), oxygen-17 has nine neutrons, and oxygen-18 has ten neutrons. The mass numbers of isotopes of other elements are defined similarly, as the sum of the number of neutrons and the number of protons.

Isotopic geochemistry has several principal roles in geology. One role is concerned with the enrichment or impoverishment of various particular isotopic species that results from the influence of differences in mass of molecules that contain different isotopes. An individual water molecule that contains an oxygen-18 atom is about 11 percent heavier than a water molecule that contains an oxygen-16 atom. The difference affects the rate at which water molecules pass from one phase to another—that is, when water evaporates or passes from the liquid phase to the vapour phase or is transformed to or from the solid state. As a result, such natural processes as evaporation, condensation, and crystallization, tend to progressively fractionate or segregate isotopic species. Evaporation of water brings about a small but measurable enrichment in the proportion of oxygen-18 in the liquid phase and a corresponding impoverishment in the vapour phase. These isotopic-fractionation processes are affected by variations in temperature. As a consequence, measurements of the proportions of various isotopic species can be used as a form of geologic thermometer. The ratio of oxygen-16 to oxygen-18 in calcium carbonate secreted by various marine organisms from calcium carbonate in solution in seawater is influenced by the temperature of the seawater. Precise measurement of the proportions of oxygen-16 with respect to oxygen-18 in calcareous shells of various fossil marine organisms provides a means of estimating the temperatures of the seas in which they lived.

The varying temperatures of the oceans during and between the major advances of glaciers during the ice ages have been inferred by analyzing the isotopic composition of the skeletons of floating organisms recovered as fossils in sediment on the sea floor. Other uses of isotopic analyses that involve temperature-dependent-rate processes include the progressive removal of crystals from cooling igneous magmas.

Another major role of isotopic geochemistry that is of enormous importance in geology is radiometric age dating. The ability to quantify the geological time scale, that is, to date the events of the geological past in terms of numbers of years, is largely a result of coupling radiometric-dating techniques with older, classical methods of establishing relative geologic ages. Radiometric-dating

Oxygen isotopes and their utilization

Radio-metric dating

methods are based on the general principle that a particular radioactive isotope (radioactive parent or source material) incorporated in geological material decays at a uniform rate, producing a decay product, or daughter isotope. Some radiometric "clocks" are based on the ratio of the proportion of parent to daughter isotopes, others are based on the proportion of parent remaining, and still others are based on the proportion of daughter isotopes with respect to each other. For example, uranium-238 decays ultimately to lead-206, which is one of the four naturally occurring isotopic species of lead. Minerals that contain uranium-238 when initially formed may be dated by measuring the proportions of lead-206 and uranium-238; the older the specimen, the greater will be the proportion of lead-206 with respect to uranium-238. The decay of potassium-40 to form argon-40 (calcium-40 is also produced in this decay process) is also a widely used radiometric-dating tool, although there are several other parent-daughter pairs that are used in radiometric dating, including another isotope of uranium (uranium-235), which decays ultimately to form lead-207, and thorium-232, which decays ultimately to lead-208.

Uranium-238 and uranium-235 both decay very slowly, although uranium-235 decays more rapidly than uranium-238. The rate of decay may be expressed in several ways. One way is by the radioactive isotope's half-life, which is that interval of time in which half of any given initial amount will have decayed. The half-life of uranium-238 is about 4,510,000,000 years, whereas the half-life of uranium-235 is about 713,000,000 years. Other radioactive isotopes decay at greatly differing rates, with half-lives ranging from a small fraction of a second to quadrillions of years.

Carbon-14 is a radioactive isotope of carbon (carbon-12 and carbon-13 are stable isotopes) with a half-life of slightly more than 5,700 years. Carbon-14 is incorporated in all living material, for it is derived either directly or indirectly from its presence in atmospheric carbon dioxide. The moderately short half-life of carbon-14 makes it useful for dating biological materials that are more than a few hundred years old and less than roughly 40,000 or 50,000 years old. It has been used to provide correlation of events within this time span, particularly those of the Pleistocene Epoch involving the Earth's most recent ice ages.

For further information on the substantive aspects of geochemistry, see ELEMENTS, GEOCHEMICAL DISTRIBUTION OF; DATING, RELATIVE AND ABSOLUTE; and articles treating the geochemistry of the atmosphere and hydrosphere, namely ATMOSPHERE; FRESHWATER, GEOCHEMICAL PROPERTIES OF; and OCEANS AND SEAS. See also ICE SHEETS AND GLACIERS; CLIMATIC CHANGE, for relevant discussions involving oxygen-isotope data; and the articles GEOCHEMICAL EQUILIBRIA AT HIGH TEMPERATURES AND PRESSURES; GEOCHEMICAL EQUILIBRIA AT LOW TEMPERATURES AND PRESSURES.

II. Study of the structure of the Earth

GEODESY AND GEOPHYSICS

The purely scientific objective of geodesy is to determine the size and shape of the Earth and, in cooperation with other geological sciences, to study the internal structure of the Earth. The practical role of geodesy is to provide a network of accurately surveyed points on the Earth's surface the vertical elevations and geographic position of which are precisely known and, in turn, may be incorporated in maps. When two geographic coordinates of a control point on the Earth's surface, its latitude and longitude, are known, as well as its elevation above sea level, the location of that point is known with an accuracy within the limits of error involved in the surveying processes. In mapping large areas, such as a whole state or country, the irregularities in the curvature of the Earth must be considered. A network of precisely surveyed control points provides a skeleton to which other surveys may be tied to provide progressively finer networks of more closely spaced points. The filling-in process also belongs to the domain of geodesy. The resulting networks

Establishing latitude and longitude

of points have many uses, including anchor points or bench marks for surveys of highways and railroads and other civil features. A major use of control points is to provide reference points to which the contour lines and other features of topographic maps are tied. Most topographic maps are made through the use of photogrammetric techniques and aerial photographs.

Geophysics pertains to studies of the Earth that involve the methods and principles of physics. The scope of geophysics touches on virtually all aspects of geology, ranging from considerations of the conditions in the Earth's deep interior, where temperatures of several thousands of degrees Celsius and pressures of millions of atmospheres prevail, to the Earth's exterior, including its atmosphere and hydrosphere. In fact, geophysics properly extends to the solar system as a whole, including the other planets and the radiation that permeates space within and beyond the solar system. Thus geophysics merges with astronomy, meteorology, and physical oceanography, as well as touching upon virtually all of the geological sciences. Many of the problems of geophysics are analogous to those of astronomy because the subject studied is seldom under direct observation, and conclusions must be drawn largely on the basis of physical and mathematical interpretation of physical measurements. The study of the Earth's interior provides a good example of the geophysicist's approach to problems. Direct observation is obviously impossible. Extensive knowledge of the Earth's interior has been derived from a variety of measurements, however, including seismic waves produced by quakes that travel through the earth, measurements of the flow of heat from the earth's interior in the Earth's outer crust, and by astronomical and other geological considerations.

Figure of the Earth. The Earth's figure is that of a surface called the geoid, which over the Earth is the average sea level at each location; under the continents the geoid is an imaginary continuation of sea level. The geoid is not a uniform spheroid, however, because of the existence of irregularities in the attraction of gravity from place to place on the Earth's surface. This results from differences in the density of rocks in the Earth's crust and major variations in the thickness of the crust. These irregularities of the geoid would bring about serious errors in the surveyed location of control points if astronomical methods, which involve use of the local horizon, were used solely in determining locations. Because of these irregularities, the reference surface used in geodesy is that of a regular mathematical surface, an ellipsoid of revolution that fits the geoid as closely as possible. This reference ellipsoid is below the geoid in some places and above it in others.

Mathematically speaking, the geoid is an equipotential, or level, surface, which may be defined as a surface over which the potential function is constant, or uniform. This potential function is the result of the effect of the gravitational attraction of the Earth, coupled with the effect caused by rotation of the Earth about its axis. Over the oceans, mean sea level defines the geoid surface, but over the land areas, the geoid is an imaginary sea-level surface. If a series of canals of sufficient depth were dug over the land areas of the world and connected with the sea, the level of water in these canals would define the geoid.

Modern studies of the figure of the Earth have made use of satellite data in recent years, which have refined the established values of the earth's dimensions.

Scope and techniques of geophysics. Geophysics may be divided into a number of overlapping branches, including geodesy in many accounts, in the following way: (1) study of the variations in the Earth's gravity field; (2) seismology, the study of the Earth's crust and interior by analysis of the transmission of elastic waves that are reflected or refracted; (3) the physics of the outer parts of the atmosphere, with particular attention to the radiation bombardment from the sun and from outer space, including the influence of the Earth's magnetic field on radiation intercepted by the Earth (see further ATMOSPHERIC SCIENCES); (4) terrestrial electricity, which is the study of

The geoid and the spheroid

the storage and flow of electricity in the atmosphere and Earth; (5) geomagnetism, the study of the source, configuration, and changes in the Earth's magnetic field and the study and interpretation of the remnant magnetism in rocks induced by the Earth's magnetic field when the rocks were formed (paleomagnetism); (6) the study of the Earth's thermal properties, including the temperature distribution of the Earth's interior and the variation in the transmission of heat from the interior to the surface of the Earth; and (7) considerations relating to the deformation of the solid Earth that involve flowage of the mantle and its influence on the crust of the Earth, including broad-scale warping of the crust, mountain building, the development of large-scale rifts in the crust, and the drifting, or horizontal displacement, of continents.

Measurement of the Earth's properties
The techniques of geophysics include measurement of the Earth's gravitative field (using gravimeters and torsion balances), measurement of the magnetic field with magnetometers at the surface of the Earth or towed behind airplanes, measurement by recording seismographs of elastic waves that have been produced naturally by earthquakes or by minor movements in the Earth's crust, or artificially, through explosions, dropping of large weights on the ground, or abrupt electrical discharges. Other tools and techniques of geophysics are diverse. Some involve laboratory studies of rocks and other earth materials under high pressures and elevated temperatures. The transmission of elastic waves through the crust and interior of the Earth is strongly influenced by the behaviour of materials under the extreme conditions at depth; consequently, there is strong motive to attempt to simulate those conditions of elevated temperatures and pressures in the laboratory. At another extreme, data gathered by rockets and space satellites yield much information concerning radiation flux in space and the magnetic effects of the Earth and other planetary bodies in space, as well as providing a large improvement in precision in establishing locations in geodetic surveying, particularly over the oceans. Finally, it should be emphasized that the tools of geophysics are essentially mathematical and that most geophysical concepts are necessarily expounded mathematically.

Geophysics has major influence both as an aspect of pure science, in which the objective is pursuit of knowledge for the sake of knowledge alone, and as an applied science in which the objectives involve solution of problems of practical or commercial interest. Its principal commercial applications lie in the exploration for petroleum and, to a lesser extent, in the search for metallic ore deposits. Geophysical methods also are used in certain geological-engineering applications, as in determining the depth of alluvial fill that overlies bedrock, which is an important factor in the construction of highways and large buildings. Study of hydrology and groundwater geology also involves applied aspects of geophysics.

For further information on the substantive aspects of geodesy and geophysics, see EARTH, FIGURE OF; EARTH, STRUCTURE AND COMPOSITION OF; EARTH, GRAVITATIONAL FIELD OF; EARTH, HEAT FLOW IN; EARTH, MAGNETIC FIELD OF; EARTH, MECHANICAL PROPERTIES OF; EARTHQUAKES; and ROCKS, PHYSICAL PROPERTIES OF.

STRUCTURAL GEOLOGY

Structural geology deals with the geometrical relationships of rocks and geologic features in general. The scope of structural geology is vast, extending over a scale of sizes ranging from microscopic to the configuration of the Earth as a whole. Furthermore, most geologic features have an aspect that pertains to their geometrical or spatial relationships and therefore are properly included in the domain of structural geology.

Small-scale features. Structural features may be divided into two broad classes: the primary structures that were acquired in the genesis of a rock mass and the secondary structures that result from later deformation of the primary structures. Most layered rocks (sedimentary rocks, some lava flows, and pyroclastic deposits) were deposited initially as nearly horizontal layers. Horizontal layering is, thus, one of the aspects of rock structure.

Rocks that were initially horizontal may be deformed later by folding or by fracturing and may be displaced along fractures. If displacement has occurred and the rocks on the two sides of the fracture have moved in opposite directions from each other, the fracture is termed a fault; if displacement has not occurred (except for a minor amount of pulling apart of the rock on the two sides of the fracture), the fracture is called a joint. It is clear that faults and joints are generally secondary structures; that is, their relative age is younger than the rocks that they intersect, but their age may be only very slightly younger. Many joints in igneous rocks, for example, were produced by contraction when the rocks cooled. On the other hand, some fractures in rocks, including igneous rocks, are related to weathering processes and expansion related to removal of overlying load. These will have been produced long after the rocks were formed.

Faults, joints, and mineral orientation

Structural geology intergrades with petrology when the small-scale geometrical relationships in rocks are considered. The geometrical attitude of individual mineral grains within a rock is an aspect of that rock's structure. In sedimentary rocks, grains that are elongate commonly tend to be oriented so that their long directions are more or less parallel to the gross layering of the rock. On the other hand, in some sedimentary rocks, particularly sandstones and in some limestones composed principally of fragments, there is a lesser scale layering, termed crossbedding, or cross stratification, in which the layers are oriented at a distinct angle to the larger scale bedding or layering. These aspects of sedimentary structure are primary, having been acquired when the sediments were deposited. The attitudes of particles forming sedimentary rocks also constitute aspects of petrology, which is concerned not only with the mineral composition of rocks but also with the sizes and shapes of the mineral grains and the way in which they have been aggregated together. The geometrical relationship of mineral grains in igneous and metamorphic rocks is also an aspect common to both structural geology and to petrology. The orientation of mineral grains in some igneous rocks, for example, reflects the influence of flowage of the rock while in a molten or softened state and is, therefore, a primary structural feature. On the other hand, the orientation of grains in metamorphic rocks commonly is a result of deformation that occurred during the metamorphic processes and is, therefore, of secondary origin.

Large-scale features. Toward the other size extreme are large-scale structural features that include mountain ranges and gently warped strata that extend over large areas. They encompass the major features of the Earth itself, namely the continents, oceanic basins, mid-ocean ridges; the major faults of the crust that intersect or bound the immense plates into which the crust appears to be segmented; and the major divisions of the Earth's interior—its crust, mantle, and core.

The methods of structural geology are nearly as diverse as those of the geological sciences as a whole. Small-scale structural features may be studied either in hand specimen, or examined microscopically, using the same general techniques used in petrology, in which sections of rock mounted on glass slides are ground very thin and are then examined by transmitted light with polarizing microscopes. On larger scale, the techniques of field geology are employed. These include the preparation of geologic maps that show the areal distribution of geologic units selected for representation on the map. They also include the plotting of the orientation of such structural features as faults, joints, cleavage, small folds, and the attitude of beds with respect to three-dimensional space. A common objective is to interpret the structure at some depth below the surface. It is possible to infer with some degree of accuracy the structure beneath the surface by using information available at the surface. If geological information from drill holes or mine openings is available, however, the configuration of rocks in the subsurface commonly may be interpreted with much greater assurance as compared with interpretations involving projection to depth based largely on information obtained at the surface. Vertical graphic sections are

Field geology and the mapping of structural features

widely used to show the configuration of rocks beneath the surface. In addition, contour maps that portray the elevation of particular layers with respect to sea level or some other datum are widely used, as are contour maps that represent thickness variations. The methods of stratigraphy, the study of strata, merge with those of structural geology, particularly in dealing with sedimentary rocks.

Where large-scale features are involved, such as mountains, continents, and oceanic basins, the methods of structural geology are principally those of geophysics and include the use of seismological, magnetic, and gravitational methods. Most of the inferences concerning the depth to the base of the crust beneath chains of mountains are based on interpretation of gravitational and seismological data. It is to be emphasized, however, that a large number of aspects of geology must be brought to bear on such major questions as the depth to the roots of mountain chains. The variation in the density of rocks, which is in itself an aspect of petrology, has major influence on the ability of the Earth's crust to support chains of mountains. There is strong evidence that many major chains of mountains are literally buoyed up by roots that are of lower density than that of surrounding rocks (isostasy). These variations in density, which locally affect the gravitational field of the earth, are of major importance in geodesy and provide evidence through the form of gravity measurements that permit the configuration of the mountain roots to be interpreted. The study of the major structural features of the Earth's crust is termed tectonics or, sometimes, tectonophysics.

The processes that affect geologic structures, including those that cause deformation of rocks, rarely can be observed directly. The nature of the deforming forces and the manner in which the Earth's materials deform under stress can be studied experimentally and theoretically, however, thus providing insight into the forces of nature. One form of laboratory experimentation involves the deformation of small, cylindrical specimens of rocks under very high pressures. Other experimental methods include the use of scale models of folds and faults consisting of soft, layered materials, in which the objective is to simulate the behaviour of real strata that have undergone deformation on a larger scale over much longer time.

Theoretical studies of structural deformations employ mathematical tools derived from physics and engineering. The behaviour of layers of rock undergoing gentle folding may be likened to a series of parallel beams that undergo bending. The forces involved in the folding and bending may be represented algebraically and geometrically. Attempts to apply the tools of physical mechanics to structural geology are difficult, however, because of the irregular nature of most rock units and because of uncertainty as to the forces that cause rocks to deform, particularly over the long span of time involved in nature compared with the short-term behaviour of materials deformed experimentally in the laboratory.

For further information on the substantive aspects of structural geology, see ROCK DEFORMATION; and ROCKS, PHYSICAL PROPERTIES OF.

VOLCANOLOGY

Volcanology is the science of volcanoes and deals with their structure, petrology, and origin. It is also concerned with the contribution of volcanoes to the rock structure of the Earth's crust, with their role as contributors to the atmosphere and hydrosphere and to the balance of chemical elements in the Earth's crust, and to the relationships of volcanoes to certain forms of metallic ore deposits. In addition, the study of volcanoes is closely linked with the study of large-scale crustal phenomena, including earthquakes and mountain building.

Volcanic processes and problems

Volcanoes result from material emerging in molten form from the depths of the Earth's crust. Volcanic rocks include lavas that have solidified upon cooling after emerging in liquid form, as well as pyroclastic deposits —fragments ejected from volcanoes and spread over the slopes of volcanic mountains or blown over larger areas before deposition. The size of volcanic ejecta ranges from blocks as large as a house to fine grains of pumice and microscopic particles of volcanic ash.

Many of the problems of volcanology are closely related with those of the origin of mountains and continents. An important question concerns the origin of molten lava. Geophysical evidence indicates that the crust of the Earth behaves essentially as a rigid solid, and yet the lava emerging at the surface is liquid. It can be argued that liquefaction of lava is related to reduction of pressure as the volcanic material is transported to the surface. Understanding of the geological controls of liquefaction and the routes by which material emerges from the depths of the crust is among the major objectives of volcanology.

One of the principal motives for studying volcanoes and volcanic products is that volcanism involves processes that were important in the origin and early evolution of the Earth. Of course, virtually all present-day geologic processes have influenced the history of the earth for much of geologic time. Volcanism, however, appears to represent a class of processes that was probably much more intense in the Earth's early stages. Volcanic products include water (commonly emitted as steam or water vapour) and various gases including ammonia and carbon dioxide. The atmosphere and hydrosphere are believed to be largely derived from volcanic emanations, modified by biological processes. Much of the water present at the Earth's surface, which has aggregated mostly in the oceans but to a lesser extent in glaciers, streams, lakes, and groundwater, probably has gradually emerged from the Earth's interior by means of volcanoes, beginning very early in the earth's history. The principal components of air, nitrogen and oxygen, probably have been derived through modification of ammonia and carbon dioxide emitted by volcanoes. Emissions of vapours and gases from volcanoes are an aspect of the degassing of the Earth's interior. Although the degassing processes that affect the Earth were probably much more vigorous when it was newly formed more than 4,000,000,000 years ago, it is interesting to consider that the degassing processes are still at work; but their scale is vastly reduced compared with their former intensity.

The study of volcanoes is dependent on petrology, which involves the examination of rocks in thin section with the polarizing microscope. Volcanic rocks that are glassy contain mineral grains too small to be distinguished with the microscope. These may require chemical analysis for adequate identification and classification. Analyses of volcanic gases and of hot springs in volcanic regions provide information about the late stages of volcanic activity, which are characterized by emission of volatile materials, including sulfurous gases. Many commercially valuable deposits of ores, particularly those that consist of metallic sulfides, are believed to have formed through the influence of hot, aqueous solutions of ultimate igneous origin and are termed hydrothermal ore deposits. Although many ore deposits have been formed at substantial depths under elevated temperatures and pressures, some ore deposits, particularly those yielding sulfides of mercury and antimony, are closely related to present-day hot springs in volcanic regions.

Prediction of eruptions

Volcanoes are serious hazards to property and human life. The catastrophic destruction of Pompeii in AD 79 by the eruption of Mt. Vesuvius is, no doubt, the best-known disaster caused by volcanic eruption. Yet, there have been many other recorded volcanic disasters, including a number in the 20th century. Considering the potential for destruction wrought by renewed future activity of volcanoes that are presently dormant or only slightly active, there is large incentive to develop methods of predicting volcanic eruptions. Studies of active volcanoes in Hawaii indicate that subtle but measurable changes in the shape of volcanoes sometimes occur immediately prior to specific eruptions. On the other hand, the most important need is to predict the times of eruption of volcanoes that are now essentially dormant and that stand close to cities. Unfortunately, the intervals of quiescence and eruption of volcanoes that have been intermittently active in the past are not very useful in predicting the times of future eruptions. Obviously it would be desirable to forecast eruptions with a precision of days or weeks, but this cannot be done at present and may ultimately prove to be impossible. Nevertheless, there is continued need for research on means of predicting eruptions. The substantive aspects of volcanology are covered in the article VOLCANOES.

III. Study of surface features and processes
GEOMORPHOLOGY AND GLACIAL GEOLOGY

Geomorphology is literally the study of the form or shape of the Earth. In contrast to geodesy, however, geomorphology deals principally with the topographic features of the Earth rather than with the overall shape of the Earth. Geomorphology is concerned with the classification, description, and origin of landforms and is interdependent with many other branches of the geological sciences, particularly those dealing with processes that act on the landscape. These include glacial geology (the study of glaciers and their geological effects), hydrology (particularly fluvial processes), pedology (the study of soils), structural geology, volcanology, sedimentology, marine geology, meteorology, climatology, and aspects of biology, including plant ecology.

Processes operative on landforms
The events that influence the shape of landforms include most geologic processes, either directly or indirectly. The configuration of the Earth's surface reflects to some degree virtually all of the processes that take place at or close to the surface, as well as those that take place deep in the crust. The intricate details of the shape of a mountain range, for example, result more or less directly from the processes of erosion that are at work progressively removing material from the range. The spectrum of erosive processes includes weathering and soil-forming processes, and transportation of materials by running water, wind action, and mass movement. Glacial processes have been particularly influential in many mountainous regions. These processes are destructive in the sense that they are modifying and gradually destroying the previous form of the range. Also important in governing the external shape of the range are the constructional processes that are responsible for uplift of the mass of rock from which the range has been sculptured. A volcanic cone, for example, may be created by successive outpouring of lava, perhaps coupled with intermittent ejection of volcanic ash and tuff. If the cone has been built up rapidly, so that there has been relatively little time for erosive processes to modify its form, its shape is governed principally by the constructional processes involved in outpouring of volcanic material. But the forces of erosion begin to modify the shape of a volcanic landform almost immediately and continue indefinitely. Thus, at no time can its shape be regarded as purely constructional or purely destructional, for its shape is necessarily a consequence of the mutual interplay of these two great classes of processes.

Study of the processes that influence landforms is an important aspect of geomorphology. These include the study of activity of streams and lakes, which merges with hydrology and limnology, the transport and deposition of dust and sand by wind, the study of mass movement of material through downhill creep of soil and rock and by landslides and mudflows, and study of beach and shoreline processes that involve the mechanics and effects of waves and currents. Study of these different classes of processes forms subdisciplines that exist more or less in their own right. Yet, understanding the development of landforms and establishing a genetic classification that considers their origin are largely dependent on an understanding of processes.

The question of origin
Classification of landforms is a major aspect of geomorphology. A variety of classification systems have been devised in the past century in which a general objective has been to describe and group landforms according to the processes that shaped or influenced them. In addition, some classification systems incorporate the stage of development of landforms as an aspect of their evolutionary development through geologic time and take into consideration such influences as lithology of the rocks, the attitudes of strata and the presence of faults and joints, and factors of broad influence, including regional uplift and climatic changes.

In considering the origin of a particular landscape, for example, an intricately dissected high-plateau region such as the Grand Canyon region of the Colorado Plateau in northern Arizona, the influence of the structure of the rocks on the landscape is at once apparent. The Colorado Plateau is carved from flat-lying or gently dipping sedimentary rocks that include sandstones, limestones, and shales. The intricate steplike topography of much of the region is strongly influenced by the erosional behaviour of these rocks, particularly as a result of the alternation of resistant and relatively nonresistant rock units. If the rocks had been intricately folded instead of being only slightly deformed, the topographic configuration of the region would be vastly different. Furthermore, the climate of the region has had a large influence. The arid or semi-arid climate of the Colorado Plateau profoundly affects the vegetative cover, and this in turn influences erosion by running water. The configuration of the plateau probably would be measurably different if it had continuously evolved in a humid climate of high rainfall. Finally, the Colorado Plateau has a complex geologic history. Generally speaking, its history involves uplift of the Earth's crust over broad areas, coupled with sculpture of the land by running water, including the carving of deep canyons and their tributaries, such as the Grand Canyon, by streams. The uplift of the crust, however, did not take place as a single uniform rise but, rather, occurred intermittently, with erosion of large volumes of rock coupled with pulses of renewed uplift. The present landscape thus represents the combined effects of processes, rock materials and structures, and the region's geologic history. The scope of geomorphology embraces all these aspects.

Glacial geology can be regarded as a branch of geomorphology, although glacial geology is such a large area of research that it stands as a distinct subdiscipline within the geological sciences. Glacial geology is concerned with the properties of glaciers themselves, as well as with the effects of glaciers as agents of both erosion and deposition. Glaciers are accumulations of snow transformed into solid ice. Important questions of glacial geology concern the climatic controls that influence the occurrence of glaciers, the processes by which snow is transformed into ice, and the mechanism of the flow of ice within glaciers. Other important questions involve the manner in which glaciers serve as erosive agents, not only in mountainous regions but also over large regions where great continental glaciers now extend or once existed. Much of the topography of the northern part of North America and Eurasia, for example, has been strongly influenced by glaciers. In places, bedrock has been scoured clean of most surficial debris. Elsewhere, deposits of glacial till mantle much of the area. Other extensive deposits include unconsolidated sediments deposited in former lakes that existed temporarily as a result of dams created by glacial ice or by glacial deposits. Many presently existing lakes are of glacial origin. The Great Lakes, for example, owe their origin to the erosive effects of large lobes of glacial ice, as well as to deposits left behind by the ice sheets.

Glacial features and deposits
Other branches of the geological sciences are closely linked with glacial geology. In glaciated regions, the problems of hydrology and hydrogeology are strongly influenced by the presence of glacial deposits. Furthermore, the suitability of glacial deposits as sites for buildings, roads, and other man-made features is influenced by the mechanical properties of the deposits and by soils formed on them.

For further information on the substantive aspects of geomorphology and glacial geology, see LANDFORM EVOLUTION; GLACIATION, LANDFORMS PRODUCED BY; ICE SHEETS AND GLACIERS; and articles on the several important processes, namely WIND ACTION; FLUVIAL PROCESSES; WATER WAVES; EARTH MOVEMENTS ON SLOPES; and HILLSLOPES. See also the several articles on particular environments for coverage of their associated landforms—

i.e., COASTAL FEATURES; BEACHES; CAVES AND CAVE SYSTEMS; DESERTS; PLATEAUS AND BASINS; and others in this vein.

ENGINEERING, ENVIRONMENTAL, AND URBAN GEOLOGY

These disciplines are broadly concerned with the application of geology to construction engineering and to problems of land use. The location of a bridge, for example, involves geological considerations in selecting sites for the supporting piers. The strength of such geological materials as rock or compacted clay that occur at the sites of the piers should be adequate to support the load placed on them. Engineering geology is concerned with the engineering properties of geological materials, including their strength, permeability, and compactability, and with the influence of these properties on the selection of locations for large buildings, roads and railroads, bridges, dams and reservoirs, and other major civil features, including airfields, river and ocean piers, and harbour breakwaters. In this context, engineering geology merges with various branches of both civil engineering and soil mechanics.

Environmental geology and urban geology are closely related to engineering geology. Urban geology can be considered an aspect of environmental geology and is concerned with the application of engineering geology and other branches of geology to environmental problems in urban areas. Environmental geology is not sharply defined but is generally concerned with those aspects of geology that touch on man's environment. Broadly speaking, all aspects of geology influence man's environment, but, more specifically, environmental and urban geology deal in large measure with those aspects of geology that directly influence man's use of land. These include the stability of sites for buildings and other civil features, sources of water supply, contamination of waters by sewage and chemical pollutants, and selection of sites for burial of refuse so as to minimize pollution by seepage. Questions of geologic hazards, including earthquakes, tsunamis (water waves of seismic origin), and floods, are also broadly relevant to environmental and urban geology. The source of geological building materials, including sand, gravel, and crushed rock, is also relevant. Finally, the distribution of naturally occurring toxic or hazardous materials, such as compounds of mercury and certain radioactive materials, has an influence on man's health and therefore is properly within the sphere of environmental geology.

Pedology or soil science

Soil science, or pedology, also can be mentioned in the environmental context. It is an interdisciplinary science that owes strong allegiance to mineralogy, glacial geology, climatology, hydrology, physical chemistry, biochemistry, geochemistry, and to aspects of biology, including plant ecology, bacteriology, and mycology (the study of fungi). In agriculture, pedology is linked with agronomy and forestry. In civil engineering and in engineering geology, the physical properties of soils, including plasticity and compactability, are important considerations in the location of civil structures. The soil is the principal bridge between the inanimate physical world and the biological world. Soil is not only of both physical and biological origin but it is also a major component of the environment, affecting directly or indirectly all forms of life. Soil is not sharply distinguished from weathered rock, although a convenient definition of soil is that it is that part of the mantle of weathered material that can support rooted plants.

For information on some of the substantive aspects of the disciplines cited or alluded to here, see EARTH MOVEMENTS ON SLOPES; SOILS; WEATHERING; RIVERS AND RIVER SYSTEMS; SEDIMENT YIELD OF DRAINAGE SYSTEMS; URBAN CLIMATES; and PHYSIOGRAPHIC EFFECTS OF MAN.

IV. Study of Earth history

HISTORICAL GEOLOGY

One of the major objectives of geology is to establish the history of the Earth from its inception to the present moment in time. This is an extraordinarily difficult objective, demanding use of most of the scientific tools that the geologist has at his command. In contrast to the written records of much of human history, geological history must be inferred largely from evidence obtained from the Earth and other planets. There are many forms of evidence. The most important is provided by the geometrical relationships of rocks with respect to each other, particularly layered rocks, or strata, the relative ages of which may be determined by applying simple principles. One of the major principles of stratigraphy, the science of strata, is that within a sequence of layers of sedimentary rock, the oldest layer is necessarily at the base of a sequence of strata and that the layers are progressively younger with ascending order in the sequence. This is termed the law of superposition and is one of the great general principles of geology. There are, of course, exceptions to the law of superposition, as for example when a sequence of beds or layers has been overturned by structural deformation. These exceptions do not invalidate the law, however, for it implies that the succession of ages in a sequence of sedimentary strata is from oldest to youngest in ascending stratigraphic order. Ordinarily, beds of sedimentary rocks are deposited more or less horizontally (the law of initial horizontality). In some regions, sedimentary strata have remained more or less horizontal long after they were deposited. Some of these sedimentary rocks were deposited in shallow seas that once extended over large areas of the present continents. In many places, sedimentary rocks lie much above sea level, reflecting vertical shift of the crust relative to sea level. In regions where the rocks have been strongly deformed through folding or faulting, the original attitudes of strata may be greatly altered, and sequences of strata that were once essentially horizontal may now be steeply inclined or overturned.

Prior to the development of radiometric methods of dating rocks, the ages of rocks and other geologic features could not be expressed quantitatively or as numbers of years but instead were necessarily expressed solely in terms of relative ages, in which the age of a particular geologic feature could be expressed as relatively younger or older than other geologic features. The ages of different sequences of strata, for example, can be compared with each other in this manner, and their relative ages with respect to faults, igneous intrusions, and other features that exhibit crosscutting relationships can be established. Given such a network of relative ages, a chronology of events has been gradually established in which the relative time of origin of various geologic features is known. This is the main thread of historical geology—an ordered sequence of geological events whose occurrence and relative ages have been inferred from evidence preserved in the rocks. In turn, the development of radiometric dating methods has permitted numerical estimates of age to be incorporated in the scale of geological time.

Divisions of geological time

The geological time scale, with its geological eras, periods, and epochs, has evolved over the course of several centuries, with many of the divisions of time in present use having been initially defined in the 19th century. Although absolute-age estimates have been assigned to the divisions of geological time, it should be emphasized that the geological time scale is based on relative ages established through use of classical principles of stratigraphy and that it is not generally dependent on the presence of numerical estimates of age. The availability of quantitative methods of establishing ages has, however, added much precision to the geological time scale.

The divisions of geological time have been defined in terms of the time required for deposition of certain sequences of strata. The Cambrian Period, for example, is defined as the time during which the sedimentary rocks were deposited that form the Cambrian System of strata, as known in Wales (between 570,000,000 and 500,000,000 years ago). The definition of the Cambrian System of strata is more or less arbitrary. Strata termed Cambrian in Wales form a thick and complex sequence of strata the conditions of deposition of which are not well understood and that have been extensively structurally deformed since they were deposited. In spite of these complications and shortcomings, the Cambrian System in Wales, in effect, defines that interval of geological time that is called the Cambrian Period. Although the Cambrian Period spans a particular sequence of years, the definition of the Cambrian Period is necessarily in terms of the rocks that form the Cambrian System and is not defined in terms of a particular time span.

In spite of the seemingly precise compartmentation of geological time into the eras, periods, and epochs of the present time scale, there are many uncertainties that stem from the subjective, arbitrarily chosen boundaries between systems of strata. A major problem concerns "missing" intervals of strata that define systems. Although geological time is continuous, it cannot be assumed that the sequences of strata chosen to define intervals of geological time are necessarily continuous, and, in fact, many sequences used to define the systems of rocks are known to be incomplete. This is indicated by intervals of erosion evidenced by unconformities or breaks in continuity of deposits within the sequences.

For information on the substantive aspects of historical geology as discussed above, see GEOLOGICAL TIME SCALE; STRATIGRAPHIC BOUNDARIES; and the several articles covering the geological record—e.g., CAMBRIAN PERIOD; MESOZOIC ERA; HOLOCENE EPOCH.

PALEONTOLOGY

The geological time scale is based principally upon the relative ages of sequences of sedimentary strata. Establishing the ages of strata within a region, as well as the ages of strata in other regions and on different continents, involves stratigraphic correlation from place to place. Although correlation of strata over modest distances often can be accomplished by tracing out particular beds from place to place, correlation over long distances and over the oceans almost invariably involves comparison of fossils. With rare exceptions, fossils occur only in sedimentary strata. Paleontology, which is the science of ancient life and deals with fossils, is mutually interdependent with stratigraphy and with historical geology. Paleontology also may be considered to be a branch of biology.

Organic evolution and index fossils

Invertebrate paleontology. Organic evolution is the essential principle involved in the use of fossils for stratigraphic correlation. Organic evolution incorporates progressive irreversible changes in the succession of organisms through time. A small proportion of types of organisms has undergone little or no apparent change over long intervals of geologic time, but most organisms have progressively changed, and earlier forms have become extinct and, in turn, have been succeeded by more modern forms, ad infinitum. Organisms preserved as fossils that lived over a relatively short span of geological time and that were geographically widespread are particularly useful for stratigraphic correlation. These fossils are indices of relative geologic age and may be termed index fossils. The various subdivisions of the Cambrian System, for example, have been correlated in various parts of the world on the basis of trilobites and other invertebrate fossils preserved in Cambrian strata. Certain types of trilobites occur only in the lower part of the Cambrian System, and their presence is an indication of Early Cambrian age; this permits correlation of Lower Cambrian strata between continents. Trilobites are generally good index fossils because they were widespread occupants of shallow seas that extended over continents. The trilobites evolved steadily, and older forms progressively became extinct and were succeeded by newer forms. Trilobites as a whole, however, had an extremely long reign before their extinction at the close of the Permian Period (225,-000,000 years ago).

Fossils play another major role in geology because they serve as indicators of ancient environments. Trilobites are marine organisms and occur in association with other fossil organisms that lived in the sea. Therefore, the presence of trilobites preserved in sedimentary strata generally can be regarded as reliable evidence that the strata were deposited in the sea, and not in lakes or bogs.

The forms of fossils that are of use and interest to geology and paleontology are almost as vast as the organisms that presently populate the world. One of the major branches of paleontology is invertebrate paleontology, which is principally concerned with fossil marine invertebrate animals large enough to be seen with little or no magnification. The number of invertebrate fossil forms is large and includes brachiopods, pelecypods, cephalopods, gastropods, corals and other coelenterates (*e.g.*, jellyfish), bryozoans, sponges, various arthropods (invertebrates with limbs—*e.g.*, insects), including trilobites, echinoderms, and many other forms, some of which have no living counterparts. The invertebrates that are used as index fossils generally possess hard parts, a characteristic that has fostered their preservation as fossils. The hard parts preserved include the calcareous or chitinous shells of the brachiopods, cephalopods, pelecypods, and gastropods, the jointed exoskeletons of arthropods such as the trilobites, and the calcareous skeletons of frame-building corals and bryozoans. The vast variety of organisms lacking hard parts are poorly represented in the geological record; however, they have sometimes been found to occur as impressions or carbonized films in finely laminated sediments.

Vertebrate paleontology. Vertebrate paleontology is concerned with fossils of the vertebrates: fish, amphibians, reptiles, birds, and mammals. Although vertebrate paleontology has close ties with stratigraphy, vertebrate fossils generally have not been extensively used as index fossils for stratigraphic correlation, vertebrates generally being much larger than invertebrate fossils, and consequently more rare. Fossil mammals, however, have been widely used as index fossils for correlating certain nonmarine strata deposited during the Tertiary Period (from 65,000,000 to 2,500,000 years ago).

Micropaleontology. Micropaleontology, as its name implies, involves the study of organisms so small that they can be observed readily only under magnification. The size range of microscopic fossils, however, is immense. The term micropaleontology often connotes that aspect of paleontology devoted to the Foraminifera, which are protozoans, each consisting of a single cell and possessing a hard skeleton. Foraminifera range in size from those that are readily viewable in hand specimens, down to those that must be magnified several tens of times for easy viewing. Micropaleontology, viewed in total, however, involves successive ranges of sizes of microscopic fossils down to organisms that must be magnified hundreds of times or more for viewing. In fact, the most minute organisms under investigation in the mid-1970s were observed with electron microscopes under thousands of magnifications. The study of ultrasmall fossils is perhaps the fastest growing segment of contemporary paleontology and is dependent upon modern laboratory instruments, including electron microscopes and advanced light microscopes, as well as highly specialized methods of specimen preparation, in which the ultrasmall fossils are segregated from the rock material where they occur or where they are etched into relief, so that they may be viewed on surfaces under high magnification.

Sizes of micro-fossils

Paleobotany. Paleobotany is the study of fossil plants. The oldest widely occurring fossils are various forms of calcareous algae that apparently lived in shallow seas, although some may have lived in freshwater. Their variety is so profuse that their study forms an important branch of paleobotany. Other forms of fossil plants consist of land plants or of plants that lived in swamp forests, standing in water that was fresh or may have been brackish. The coal-forming swamps of the Pennsylvanian Period (from 325,000,000 to 280,000,000 years ago) are particularly well-known as a source of spectacularly preserved ancient plants, many of large size, although coals also have formed in swamp environments during other geological periods.

Palynology. Palynology deals with plant spores and pollen that are both ancient and modern and is a branch of paleobotany. It plays an important role in studies of ancient climates, particularly through studies of deposits formed during glacial and interglacial stages. Study of a sequence of spore- or pollen-bearing beds may reveal successive climatic changes, as indicated by changes in types of spores and pollen derived from different vegetative complexes. Spores and pollen, being minute, are borne by the wind and spread over large areas. Furthermore, spores and pollen tend to be resistant to decay and may thus be preserved in sediments under adverse conditions.

Taxonomic classification of fossils

The methods of classifying fossils have been subjected to increased scrutiny in recent years. The establishment of the taxonomic categories into which fossil organisms are classed is to a major extent a matter of individual judgment and tends to be highly subjective. Controversy reigns between the "lumpers" and "splitters," representing extremes of views among paleontologists who classify and define fossils according to species, genera, and higher taxonomic categories. At one extreme, there are those (the splitters) who tend to give relatively strong weight to small differences in form between different specimens, establishing relatively large numbers of different species and genera. At the other extreme, the lumpers tend to be conservative in the number of taxonomic categories, minimizing lesser variations by lumping specimens into a smaller number of taxonomic categories. Rigid rules for taxonomic classification are difficult or impossible to devise. Continuous evolution resulting in progressive changes in form makes compartmentation into rigid categories an artifice of convenience (see POLLEN STRATIGRAPHY).

Biometric methods. In the past decade, the methods of biometry and numerical taxonomy have risen to prominence, both in paleontology and in the classification of living organisms. The objectives of biometrical and numerical taxonomic methods include description of the shape or form of organisms statistically and the expression of taxonomic relationships quantitatively. The similarity of a given species to another species in the same genera can be expressed as a numerical coefficient. In turn, a hierarchy of relationships in a grouping of related taxonomic forms can be expressed as a matrix of coefficients. Statistical methods, particularly those of multivariate statistics, generally are needed to seek out relationships if numerical data are employed. Furthermore, the application of statistical methods has given impetus to the use of assemblages of organisms to define a taxonomic species instead of employing a single type specimen. In spite of the seeming merits of numerical taxonomy, the subject is fraught with controversy and is far from universal acceptance.

For information on the substantive aspects of paleontology, see FOSSIL RECORD, which covers invertebrate and vertebrate fossils, microfossils, and fossil plants.

STRATIGRAPHY AND SEDIMENTOLOGY

Inasmuch as stratigraphy deals principally with sedimentary rocks, it is closely allied with sedimentology, the study of sediments. Sedimentology deals with the processes of sedimentation and with the subsequent modification of sediments as they are transformed into rocks. Toward one extreme, sedimentology merges with sedimentary petrology and with mineralogy. Toward the other extreme, it merges with stratigraphy. The extremes may be viewed according to scale of size, stratigraphy dealing with the large-scale aspects, ranging from details of bedding to aspects involving variation on a regional or continental scale. Sedimentary petrology, on the other hand, deals generally with the small-scale aspects, at the hand-specimen, microscopic, and chemical levels. Sedimentology is a bridge between these extremes.

Stratigraphy, sedimentology, sedimentary petrology, and the mineralogy and geochemistry of sediments are currently the subject of intensive, coordinated research. Important questions concerned the deposition and subsequent alteration of ancient carbonate deposits (limestones and dolomites), many of which have large areal extent and which in some places pass laterally into evaporite deposits containing gypsum, anhydrite, halite, and other salts. Study of carbonate deposits now forming in modern seas is an essential aspect of this research. Other research is focussed on the deposition of alternating shales and sandstones through the influence of deltaic

and near-shore distributary systems. Comparison of modern deltas forming on continental shelves with ancient deposits of deltaic origin has sharpened insight into origin of the ancient deposits.

For information on some of the substantive aspects of stratigraphy and sedimentology, see STRATIGRAPHIC BOUNDARIES; and SEDIMENTARY ROCKS. See also RIVER DELTAS for coverage of modern work on these features.

ASTROGEOLOGY

Astrogeology is concerned with the geology of the solid bodies in the solar system, the planets and asteroids (minor planets). Questions of origin of the planets and asteroids are germane to both geology and astronomy; astrogeology is a bridge between the two groups of sciences. Except for studies of the Earth, astrogeology largely has been concerned with the geology of the Moon. Prior to the advent of manned landings on the Moon in 1969, most of the knowledge of the Moon was derived from study of photographs, made first with telescopes and later through television images telemetered to Earth from spacecraft. An intensive study of photographs has provided a basis for detailed mapping of the Moon's side that faces the Earth. By employing basic geologic principles for determining relative ages, including superposition of features and crosscutting relationships among them, it has been possible to establish a chronology of relative ages of events revealed in the surficial features of the Moon on photographs.

Some of the basic geological problems of the Moon are similar to those of the Earth. An important question concerns the age, lithologic nature, and thickness of the Moon's crust. Another is whether the Moon is internally active or is geologically dead. The Earth, of course, is active internally in both its mantle and deep crust. The craters of the Moon, which have been studied for centuries, have evoked much speculation. A key question is whether they were formed principally by impact of large meteorites, are volcanic in origin, or a combination of both. There can be little doubt, however, that meteorite impact has been of appreciable importance. Exploration of the Moon has given strong impetus to the study of impact craters on Earth. The Earth's known or suspected impact craters are geologically young, whereas most of the Moon's impact craters are undoubtedly much older, some perhaps having been formed early in the Moon's history. The lack of relatively ancient impact craters on the Earth is explained simply by the fact that early impact craters, which very probably existed in abundance, have long since been destroyed by the continuous erosional and depositional processes that occur on the Earth. On the other hand, the lack of an atmosphere and hydrosphere decrees that comparable processes have not occurred on the Moon (see further METEORITE CRATERS).

BIBLIOGRAPHY. C.R. LONGWELL, R.F. FLINT, and J.E. SANDERS, *Physical Geology* (1969), an authoritative, thorough, general coverage of the physical aspects of the geological sciences, with emphasis on the role of geologic processes as in rock cycle; J. GILLULY, A.C. WATERS, and A.O. WOODFORD, *Principles of Geology*, 4th ed. (1971), a broad treatment of physical geology; A. HOLMES, *Principles of Physical Geology* (1965), an extremely thorough, detailed coverage of physical geology; R.H. DOTT, JR., and R.L. BATTEN, *Evolution of the Earth* (1971), a readable, thorough treatment of the principles of historical geology, accompanied by a survey of the evolution of the continents; A.O. WOODFORD, *Historical Geology* (1965), a detailed treatment of the principles of interpretation of geologic history, coupled with a survey of the geologic history of North America.

(J.W.Ha.)

Geological Time Scale

The geological time scale is the calendar for events in Earth history. It is based on stratigraphy, which is the study of sedimentary rocks and their historical significance. Sedimentary rocks have accumulated through geological time in ancient marine and terrestrial environments, and they contain fossils, the remains of once-living organisms. Because living things have constantly changed by evolution through geological time, particular kinds of organisms are characteristic of particular parts of the geologic column. For this reason, the fossils that occur in sedimentary rocks provide the chief means of correlating rock units and establishing a standard geological time scale. Since the 1950s radiometric dating has provided absolute age data to supplement the relative dates obtained from the fossil record.

Types of units
There are two conceptually different kinds of units in the geological record: rock-stratigraphic units and time-stratigraphic units. Rock-stratigraphic units describe particular kinds of rocks that constitute a mappable formation. The formations in a given area generally are arranged in chronological order (younger rocks overlie older). Time-stratigraphic units, by contrast, contain rocks formed during a particular segment of geologic time without regard to the rock types involved. The boundaries of time-stratigraphic units must be inferred from fossil or other evidence. Correlation of the strata according to their age is a vital process in working out the geological history of a region.

The fundamental time-stratigraphic units are the geological systems that are defined on the basis of selected sedimentary sequences in type areas. The systems are grouped for convenience into larger units (erathems), and they are subdivided into progressively smaller units, namely, series, stages, and zones. Geological time units are simply abstractions of the time-stratigraphic units, and they are given the same names. For example, the Cambrian System, defined by a sequence of sedimentary rocks in Wales, is the basis for a pure time term, the Cambrian Period, that surely existed everywhere, although in many areas it is unrepresented or only partly represented by a rock record. Corresponding time-stratigraphic and geological time terms are as follows:

time-stratigraphic units	geologic time units
Erathem	Era
System	Period
Series	Epoch
Stage	Age
Zone	Phase

The fundamental geologic time units, the periods, are grouped into larger units called eras. From names proposed by Adam Sedgwick in 1838 and by John Phillips in 1841, the periods are placed in the Paleozoic, Mesozoic, and Cenozoic eras. These names derive from "ancient life," "middle life," and "modern life," reflecting the profound changes that occurred in living organisms at the outset of each. The eras and periods (and Cenozoic epochs) of the geological time scale are shown below.

The old rocks below the Paleozoic have always been known simply as the Precambrian. These rocks contain no diagnostic fossils and their subdivision never has been possible. Younger rocks of the Paleozoic, Mesozoic, and Cenozoic can be grouped under the complementary term Phanerozoic, which means "evident life."

Initial efforts directed toward formulating a time scale based on sedimentary rock strata were made in the late 18th century. Stratigraphers added much refinement during the 19th century, but it was not until the advent of radiometric dating in the early decades of the 20th century that they realized that the fossiliferous Phanerozoic rocks, to which their previous efforts had been almost exclusively devoted, constituted only a minor portion of geologic time. It is now known that Precambrian time represents the first 85 percent of earth history.

This article treats the historical development of the geological time scale and its calibration. On methods of dating, see DATING, RELATIVE AND ABSOLUTE; for relevant information on stratigraphy and sedimentation, see EARTH, GEOLOGICAL HISTORY OF; STRATIGRAPHIC BOUNDARIES; and SEDIMENTARY ROCKS; see also FOSSIL RECORD; PRECAMBRIAN TIME; and the several articles on the geological periods and eras (e.g., ORDOVICIAN PERIOD).

HISTORICAL DEVELOPMENT OF THE TIME SCALE

Nicolaus Steno perceived the guiding principle of superposition of strata in 1669 and was the first to express the idea that they were initially deposited in a horizontal

relative duration of eras	era	period	epoch	duration in millions of years (approx.)	millions of years ago (approx.)
Cenozoic		Quaternary	Holocene	approx. last 10,000 years	
Mesozoic			Pleistocene	2.5	2.5
Paleozoic	Cenozoic		Pliocene	4.5	7
		Tertiary	Miocene	19	26
			Oligocene	12	38
			Eocene	16	54
			Paleocene	11	65
	Mesozoic	Cretaceous		71	136
		Jurassic		54	190
		Triassic		35	225
Precambrian	Paleozoic	Permian		55	280
		Carboniferous — Pennsylvanian		45	325
		Carboniferous — Mississippian		20	345
		Devonian		50	395
		Silurian		35	430
		Ordovician		70	500
		Cambrian		70	570
		Precambrian		4,030	

formation of Earth's crust 4,600,000,000 years ago

Geological time scale.
Adapted by permission from Don L. Eicher, *Geologic Time*, Prentice-Hall (1968)

position. In 1760 Giovanni Arduino placed the rocks of the same region into three main categories: (1) Primary: crystalline rocks with metallic ores; (2) Secondary: hard stratified rocks with fossils; (3) Tertiary: weakly consolidated stratified rocks, usually with marine shells. Almost simultaneously Johann Gottlob Lehmann (1756) recognized in Thuringia a threefold grouping of rocks, which can be characterized as (1) crystalline, (2) stratified, and (3) alluvial; and within a few years similar threefold groupings of rocks were recognized elsewhere in Europe and as far away as the Urals. Recognition of threefold groupings of rocks based on the principle of superposition thus provided an early framework of thought, but rock types incorrectly were equated to geological ages. The stratified series of Lehmann, for example, generally was believed to be the result of the universal Noachian Deluge. In their search for principles of rock classification, the early workers assumed that their major rock groupings, and even the smaller rock units that composed them, each represented a discrete episode in geological time. This school of thought was codified into a rigid scheme by Abraham Gottlob Werner of Freiburg, Saxony, so that by the late 18th century, Werner's version became the reigning doctrine of the time.

Early theories

Werner thought that all rocks were deposits of a primeval ocean that once covered the entire Earth. These deposits were divided into four distinct series. The Primitive Series, deposited from the cloudy primeval ocean, included granite, gneisses, schists, and other crystalline rocks. The Transition Series included slates, graywackes, and some limestone. Both of these series consisted of "universal formations" and were considered to have enveloped the entire global surface at one time. The overlying Stratified Series, consisting of sandstone, limestone, salt, gypsum, coal, and basalt, and the Alluvial Series, consisting chiefly of sand, clay, and gravel, were deposited as the ocean water supposedly subsided below the level of the highest mountain tops.

Werner's erroneous ideas ultimately gave way to the views of James Hutton, a Scot, who in 1795 maintained that present rates of geologic processes, such as erosion of rocks and deposition of sediment, were sufficient to account for all the Earth's features provided that there had been vastly more time than the 6,000 years generally interpreted from the Scriptures. Chiefly because it required a great amount of time, Hutton's philosophy did not gain immediate favour, but it became accepted after the writings of Charles Lyell beginning in 1830.

The discoveries of Smith and Cuvier

The old idea that ages of rocks may be ascertained by their composition failed to stand up under field observations, and in the early decades of the 19th century it was replaced by the much more fruitful concept of faunal succession that was discovered by William Smith. Between the years 1793 and 1815 Smith examined rock strata throughout much of Great Britain, and he found that each sedimentary rock unit contained its own distinguishing assemblage of fossils. This was commonly the only way that different units of similar rock type could be distinguished. Smith was thus able to recognize specific rock units in areas where rock type alone was inconclusive. Utilizing his new principle, Smith produced the first geologic map of England and Wales in 1815, and this represented a landmark in the knowledge and understanding of rocks. The discovery that strata may be identified by their contained fossils made time correlation between distant localities possible.

Using Smith's methods, Georges Cuvier, a French zoologist, worked out the detailed stratigraphic sequence of vertebrates and marine invertebrates in the Tertiary strata of the Paris Basin. In 1812 he showed conclusively that many fossil invertebrates had no known counterparts living today. The reality that many once-living species had become extinct was at last clear.

The discoveries of Smith and the refinements added by Cuvier made possible the recognition of rocks of the same age in widely separated areas irrespective of rock types. It thus became feasible to define major units of sedimentary rock and, using their distinctive fossils, to distinguish their time counterparts in remote regions. Thus the stage was set for realization of a geologic time scale, and in the three decades following these discoveries most of the geologic systems in use today were defined. The geologic time scale continued to evolve slowly until the turn of the 20th century. Although it has been quite stable since then, it is still subject to future refinements. The following chronological outline traces the origin of the names currently in use.

Geological systems. *Tertiary.* Coined as a descriptive term in 1760 by Arduino, Tertiary units were traced widely. Tertiary strata were the object of Cuvier's landmark faunal studies in the Paris Basin, and following analysis of invertebrate faunas by Charles Lyell and Gérard Deshayes in the late 1820s and early 1830s, the Tertiary attained the status of a time-stratigraphic system. Today it is widely considered a system of the Cenozoic Era. Its constituent series were named in France. The Eocene, Miocene, and Pliocene were defined by Charles Lyell in 1833 on the basis of the relative proportions of living and extinct fossils in each. August von Beyrich added the Oligocene in 1854; Wilhelm Schimper the Paleocene in 1874.

Jurassic. In 1795 Alexander von Humboldt, a pioneer German geologist, recognized the strata of the Jura Mountains in northern Switzerland as a separate unit. Initially it was only a descriptive unit, but later (1839), C.L. von Buch redefined the Jurassic into a time-stratigraphic context and noted three divisions that he suggested might be further divided in accord with fossil content, a course followed by later workers.

Cretaceous. A Belgian geologist, Omalius d'Halloy, in 1822 proposed this term for strata of the Paris Basin. The term derives from the Latin word for chalk and is entirely descriptive. From the outset, the Cretaceous included more than just chalk beds, even in its type area where the lower portion consists of sandstone and shale. In 1906 T.C. Chamberlin and R.D. Salisbury proposed dividing the Cretaceous of the United States into two systems, the Comanchean below and a restricted Cretaceous above. Their proposal, however, never met with acceptance.

Carboniferous. Two British geologists, William Conybeare and William Phillips, proposed this name in 1822 for strata in central England that contained coal beds. Although the term Carboniferous is wholly descriptive, Conybeare and Phillips anticipated that their system might later be widely recognizable by its distinctive fossils.

Quaternary. In 1829 Jules Desnoyers proposed this term in the Paris Basin for a sequence of diverse sedimentary and volcanic materials that he thought to be younger than the Tertiary rocks. Today Quaternary includes the Pleistocene Series (proposed by Lyell in 1839), which constitutes deposits formed during the glacial ages, and the Holocene or Recent Series (proposed by Lyell in 1833), which dates from the last retreat of the continental glaciers from North America and Europe.

Triassic. Friedrich von Alberti, a German geologist, introduced this essentially descriptive name in 1834 to a sequence of rocks with a striking threefold division. In the type area of southern Germany, the strata are widely traceable but poorly fossiliferous. In the Alps to the south, a complete sequence of marine faunas provides the standard of reference for worldwide correlation.

The work of Sedgwick and Murchison

Cambrian and Silurian. After intensive study of the Paleozoic sequence in Wales, two British geologists, Adam Sedgwick and Roderick Impey Murchison, named the Cambrian and Silurian, respectively, for ancient Welsh tribes in 1835. Each worker attempted to recognize physical breaks in the stratigraphic record as boundaries for his system. Murchison carefully documented the abundant fossils of his Silurian strata, but Sedgwick's strata were less fossiliferous, and his breakdown of the Cambrian was essentially lithologic. Murchison had begun with the top of the Lower Paleozoic sequence in the southeast, and Sedgwick had begun at the base in the northwest and they worked toward one another. Later, when it became clear that their systems overlapped, a quarrel ensued. The controversy that followed was resolved 44 years later when Charles Lapworth named the Ordovician System for the disputed interval.

Devonian. In 1840 Murchison and Sedgwick jointly named the Devonian for the rocks of Devonshire in southern England, prior to their misunderstanding over the contact between the Cambrian and Silurian. Devonshire is a poor type area because the rocks are intensely deformed and the basal contact is not exposed. Nevertheless, the rocks are fossiliferous and can be distinguished from the Silurian below and the Carboniferous above; this led to their distinction of the Devonian. Murchison and Sedgwick showed that fossils could be used to recognize the Devonian System in the Rhineland where it is more fossiliferous and better exposed. This later came to be the worldwide standard of reference.

Permian. Murchison named his system in 1841 for the province of Perm, in Russia, where a great thickness of limestones overlies the Carboniferous. Murchison recognized that the fossils differ from those found in older and younger strata, and he ascertained that Permian strata could be identified in widespread areas by their distinctive fossils before he formally named this system.

Mississippian. Alexander Winchell introduced this term into American stratigraphic terminology in 1870 for the well-exposed Lower Carboniferous strata of the Mississippi Valley. T.C. Chamberlin and R.D. Salisbury elevated it, along with the Pennsylvanian, to system status in their influential textbook of 1906, and they justified this division largely on the basis of the supposed widespread unconformity that separated the two. The U.S. Geological Survey has recognized it officially since 1953, but it has not found use outside North America.

Ordovician. In 1879 Charles Lapworth proposed this system to include the disputed interval between the Cambrian and Silurian and to express the apparent threefold paleontological division in Early Paleozoic strata of Europe. Boundaries of Lapworth's Ordovician were solely paleontological, based chiefly on graptolites.

Pennsylvanian. In 1891 Henry Shaler Williams coined this name from the state of Pennsylvania for Upper Carboniferous strata as a counterpart to Winchell's Lower Carboniferous Mississippian strata. Chamberlin and Salisbury elevated it, with the Mississippian, to full system status in their 1906 text. Since its introduction it has been used extensively in North America, but not elsewhere. Like the Mississippian, it has been formally recognized by the U.S. Geological Survey since 1953.

Other systems. Other system names have achieved regional recognition. For example, geologists in northern Europe use Gotlandian in place of "Silurian" in its modern sense. The Eogene and Neogene are commonly used as systems of the Cenozoic Era, especially in Europe. The top of the Oligocene divides the two of them.

Stages and zones. In publications between 1840 and 1852 the French paleontologist Alcide d'Orbigny divided the Cretaceous of France into small units that he termed stages. Each stage was based on a fossil aggregate that was unique to it and that permitted its widespread recognition, unlike the much more local variations based solely on rock types. The German paleontologist Albert Oppel, in 1856–1859, refined paleontologic correlation still further. He determined the stratigraphic ranges of many species with precision in numerous localities and introduced the concept of the paleontologic zone as a subdivision of the stage. The early recognition of stages and zones based on stratigraphic ranges of fossils was strictly empirical. In 1859 the widely used practice of correlation by fossils was at last placed on a firm theoretical basis by Charles Darwin's proofs of organic evolution.

Recognition of systems in practice. The Ordovician, Devonian, and Permian systems and the epochs of the Tertiary System were proposed initially as interpretive units, on the basis of the chronologic value of their contained fossils and on their inferred significance as discrete chapters in earth history. The Cambrian, Carboniferous, Jurassic, Cretaceous, and Tertiary were proposed largely as descriptive units and were defined initially on rock type without emphasis on the potential time value of their fossils. These units, however, later yielded fossils that proved to be diagnostic of their particular position in geologic time, and these systems took their places in the time scale. Thus, regardless of just how it was conceived originally, each system has been subsequently recognized in widely separated areas entirely on the basis of distinctive fossils. The systems currently in use have proven to be remarkably convenient units, and they have been successfully discriminated in virtually all parts of the world.

Boundary problems

Many system boundaries today are problematical because they were not clearly stipulated or because type areas of adjacent systems are widely separated geographically. Those who initially defined the systems usually searched for the "natural" boundaries as interpreted from physical or biologic criteria. In many cases, however, the level of the apparently natural boundary in one area differed from that in another area. In other cases, the "natural" boundaries were in fact unconformities, namely, surfaces representing a considerable gap in geologic time between younger strata above and older rocks below. As world geologic knowledge developed, it became clear that many unconformities in type areas were represented elsewhere by continuous successions of strata that fell between defined systems. Faunas of these previously unstudied portions of the record were typically transitional between those of the overlying and underlying systems. Assignments of the problematical strata to one system or the other were somewhat arbitrary. Controversies soon arose over placement of boundaries of nearly all the systems, and many of these continue to the present day.

It appears that agreement on the placement of boundaries can be resolved only by international agreement. To this end, the International Union of Geological Sciences established an International Geological Correlation Program in 1967, which gave initial priority to the fixing of system boundaries.

RADIOMETRIC CALIBRATION OF THE TIME SCALE

Although Precambrian rocks lack useful fossils for time-stratigraphic purposes, development of the techniques of radiometric dating has provided a method for correlating

them and a potential tool for recognizing Precambrian time-stratigraphic units. In Phanerozoic rocks radiometric dates have greatly enhanced the understanding of the magnitude of geologic time and of rates of geologic processes. Although the radiometric calibration of the time scale is still in its formative stages, existing knowledge already permits the placing of a newly dated rock, whether igneous, metamorphic, or sedimentary, in the proper Phanerozoic series almost as confidently as if it contained diagnostic fossils.

Radiometric theory and methods. Radiometric dating depends on the presence in certain minerals of radioactive nuclides, which decay continuously to radiogenic daughter nuclides. Rates of radioactive decay are commonly expressed in terms of half-life, the time required for half of any given quantity of parent radioactive atoms to decay. The half-life of a radioactive nuclide is a constant and is unaffected by physical or chemical conditions or by the length of time the parent atoms have been in existence.

Most methods of radiometric dating are based on the accumulated quantity of atoms produced by radioactive decay. When a mineral containing the radioactive atoms crystallized, it contained no atoms of the decay product. With time, radioactive decay produces radiogenic daughter atoms in place of the radioactive parent atoms in the mineral's crystal lattice. At any stage of the process, the age of the mineral in years may be calculated from the ratio of daughter and parent atoms. In order for the accumulation method to yield significant results, two conditions must be satisfied: first, that the system has remained closed and there has been no addition or escape of undetected atoms during the existence of the mineral; and second, that no undetected atoms of the daughter nuclide were present in the mineral when it formed.

Dozens of radioactive nuclides occur in nature, but many are extremely rare, and others decay either too slowly or too rapidly to be of value for dating the geologic time scale. Just four nuclides (uranium-238, uranium-235, rubidium-87, and potassium-40) have provided nearly all of the radiometric ages for ancient rocks. The main methods used for age determinations of significance to the geological time scale are shown in the Table.

Chief Methods of Determining Radiometric Ages for the Geological Time Scale

parent nuclide	half-life (in 000,000 years)	daughter nuclide	minerals and rocks commonly dated
Uranium-238	4,510	lead-206	zircon uraninite pitchblende
Uranium-235	713	lead-207	zircon uraninite pitchblende
Rubidium-87	47,000	strontium-87	muscovite biotite lepidolite microcline whole metamorphic rock
Potassium-40	1,300	argon-40	muscovite biotite hornblende glauconite sanadine whole volcanic rock

Uranium-238 and uranium-235 always occur together in nature, and an advantage of the uranium–lead method is that the separate isotopes provide a cross-check in determining ages. Uranium is a rare element, and suitably datable minerals in which it occurs as a primary constituent are rare. Uranium, however, occurs in trace amounts in the common igneous mineral zircon, grains of which are isolated from their host rocks for dating. Zircons usually provide reliable radiometric dates.

The potassium–argon method is widely useful because potassium occurs abundantly in many common minerals, and laboratory techniques for measuring minute quantities of the daughter argon-40 are extremely refined. Basalts are rich in potassium-bearing minerals, but

Potassium–argon dating

individual mineral grains are so small that they cannot be isolated from the rock mass. In order to date these fine-grained rocks, a sample of the rock itself is subjected to analysis without separating mineral components, and this is termed the "whole-rock method." The whole-rock method has been applied successfully to basalts as young as 100,000 years. In addition to igneous minerals, the sedimentary mineral glauconite, which forms in certain environments, is datable by the potassium–argon method. A drawback to the potassium-argon method is that argon, being a gas, escapes easily from the host mineral grains upon heating or stress. Consequently burial to even moderate depths tends to promote argon loss and to lower the apparent age of the rock.

The rubidium–strontium method has been widely applied to igneous and metamorphic rocks, but it is especially valuable for the latter. In dating metamorphic rocks, the whole-rock method is commonly used. A weakness of the rubidium–strontium method is that the half-life of rubidium-87 is so long that it introduces a substantial measurement error in laboratory determinations, particularly in younger portions of the geologic column.

Dating sedimentary rocks. All of the methods discussed above depend very largely upon igneous and metamorphic minerals and, hence, igneous and metamorphic events can be dated with good accuracy. It has proved to be difficult, however, to tie igneous and metamorphic radiometric ages into fossil-bearing sedimentary rocks on which the geologic time scale is based. Radiometric ages have been correlated with the geologic time scale in three different ways: bracketed igneous intrusives, interbedded volcanic rocks, or authigenic minerals (those formed *in situ*) in the sedimentary strata themselves.

A dated igneous intrusive provides a minimum age for a sedimentary rock that it intrudes and a maximum age for a sedimentary rock deposited on top of it. Stratigraphic age of the intrusive may thus be bracketed between groups of strata whose geologic ages are known. Unfortunately, most intrusives are bracketed widely in time. A few, however, are bracketed within a small interval and their ages have provided key dates for the radiometric time scale.

Volcanic ash or lava flows can be introduced suddenly into sedimentary environments without interrupting sedimentation. Igneous material datable radiometrically may thus become interbedded with fossiliferous sedimentary rocks datable according to the geologic time scale. Interbedded sediments and volcanic rocks have provided some of the most valuable reference points in the radiometric time scale.

Direct radiometric dating of sedimentary rocks depends on minerals that crystallize during their deposition. The minerals cannot be detrital grains, for these simply reflect the age of the pre-existing source rock. Most direct radiometric dates of sedimentary rocks have been provided by the mineral glauconite, which sometimes crystallizes on the sea floor while marine sediments accumulate. Glauconite is a complex silicate containing potassium and hence it is datable by the potassium–argon method. Unfortunately, glauconite loses argon even if buried to moderate depths, and glauconite dates commonly err in being too young. They do, however, provide reliable minimum ages.

Radiometric calibration of the geologic time scale has only begun, but already ages of most of the important boundaries within the Phanerozoic portion of the time scale are known within fairly narrow limits, and some systems are quite well dated throughout. In some parts of the Phanerozoic scale, however, large gaps still remain for which virtually no reliable radiometric determinations have been made. Ages of the system boundaries as presently known are shown adjacent to the geologic time scale previously shown.

Subdivision of Precambrian time. Before the advent of radiometric dating, the Precambrian was never divisible into time-stratigraphic units because, unlike the Phanerozoic. Precambrian rocks contain no distinctive fos-

sils. The problem for the Precambrian, therefore, is not to determine ages of previously defined time-stratigraphic boundaries. Instead it is to establish, on the basis of the radiometric ages themselves, a usable scheme of time-stratigraphic classification.

In the Precambrian, as in the Phanerozoic, igneous and metamorphic rocks provide the vast majority of reliable dates, and orogenic episodes, which produced widespread igneous and metamorphic activity, have provided the framework for Precambrian time-stratigraphic classifications that have been attempted thus far. Many problems exist in unravelling the Precambrian radiometric record. Commonly the last orogeny that affected an area obliterates the radiometric record of all previous events. It is not clear whether or not some orogenies have been world-wide in their effect. Time-stratigraphic classifications for the Precambrian thus far have been proposed only for individual regions or continents. The Canadian Shield, for example, a region that has been extensively studied, is divisible into several large provinces that have distinctive structures and characteristic radiometric ages that cluster around 2,390, 1,640, and 880 $\times$ 10^6 years, indicating three main orogenic episodes. These provide the framework for the regional Precambrian time-stratigraphic classification. The Kenoran orogeny marks the boundary between two large time divisions, the Archaean and Proterozoic. The Hudsonian and Grenville orogenies subdivide the Proterozoic into three eras, the Aphebian, Helikian, and Hadrynian. Precambrian shields of other continents likewise contain discrete provinces in which radiometric dates cluster together, but orogenic episodes were not all synchronous with those determined for the Canadian Shield, and each region appears to have its own characteristic breakdown of Precambrian chronology. It is still highly questionable whether a single formal time-stratigraphic scheme based on radiometric methods will be found very useful for relating Precambrian rocks worldwide.

Ages of meteorites and of the Earth. Much evidence has been accumulated in recent years concerning the age of meteorites (*q.v.*), which have been studied by various radiometric dating methods. Most of them appear to have had a common time of origin at about 4,600 $\times$ 10^6 years. About 7 percent of the known meteorites consist mostly of iron, and the remainder consist chiefly of silicate minerals. Iron meteorites contain practically no uranium but considerable amounts of lead, and this lead is thought to represent primordial lead whose isotopic composition has never been altered by radiogenic additions. Assuming that the isotopic composition of primordial earth lead was the same as meteorite lead, the Earth can be treated as a closed system just like any radioactive mineral sample and dated by the uranium–lead method. First it is necessary to determine the amounts of uranium-238, uranium-235, lead-206, and lead-207 that are present in the Earth's crust today. Then, subtracting the amount of lead-206 and lead-207 inferred to have been present at the time of its origin, application of the uranium–lead method gives an age for the Earth of about 4,600 $\times$ 10^6 years. Numerous samples of Moon rocks collected by the Apollo missions likewise have ages of about 4,600 $\times$ 10^6 years, and this is now believed to be the approximate time of origin of the solar system and of formation of the Earth.

In both North America and Europe the most ancient rocks dated have indicated ages of about 3,500 $\times$ 10^6 years. The most ancient rocks known from Africa and from Australia are only slightly younger. Although the data are sparse, the similarity in ages of the oldest rocks from several continents is probably a significant coincidence. The Earth may have undergone a thermal episode at about the time that served to melt and homogenize the crust. Whether or not this speculation is valid, rocks of the Earth's crust provide no direct evidence concerning the first 1,000 $\times$ 10^6 years of earth history.

Future of the time scale. The geologic time scale is still being shaped and refined, and the potential for the greatest increase in knowledge is certainly in the Pre-

Time divisions of the Canadian Shield

cambrian. Whether or not a single worldwide framework of time-stratigraphic classification proves workable, the chronology of Precambrian events is expected to contribute significantly to the understanding of evolution of the earth's crust, atmosphere, and ocean and to the long development of life prior to the Paleozoic.

Progress in improving the Phanerozoic time scale will come about chiefly through adding of historical detail. Critical boundaries must be better defined and stabilized by international agreement in standard sections. This will require continued refinement of paleontologic zones, particularly using groups of microfossils, many of which have thus far received only cursory study. Progress in the Phanerozoic, however, like that in the Precambrian, will not be measured by the extent to which formalized classification schemes find common acceptance, but by the increase in the actual understanding and appreciation of the processes that, through geologic time, have shaped the earth.

BIBLIOGRAPHY. F.D. ADAMS, *Birth and Development of the Geological Sciences* (1938), detailed discussion of selected aspects of the history of geology; W.B.N. BERRY, *Growth of a Prehistoric Time Scale* (1968), a thorough review of the history of development of the time scale with an emphasis on the importance of organic evolution evidenced by fossils; D.L. EICHER, *Geologic Time* (1968), a modern elementary introduction to the principles of physical, biostratigraphic, and radiometric dating; H. FAUL, *Ages of Rocks, Planets and Stars* (1966), an outstanding review of the theory, methods, and materials of radiometric age determination; E.I. HAMILTON, *Applied Geochronology* (1965), a detailed summary of the application of radiometric dating to rocks, including considerable discussion of laboratory methods; W.B. HARLAND, A.G. SMITH, and B. WILCOCK (eds.), *The Phanerozoic Time-Scale* (1964), a symposium on the radiometric ages of the Phanerozoic systems, including a discussion of theory and methods, as well as the most accurate ages available for all parts of the Paleozoic, Mesozoic, and Cenozoic.

(D.L.E.)

Geometry, Algebraic

Algebraic geometry is a branch of mathematics in which the properties of a geometrical structure are described by means of algebraic expressions. Historically, the subject developed from the study of loci (collections of all points the location of which is determined by stated conditions) in projective space, again by algebraic means. A projective space of n dimensions is denoted by P_n and is a set of elements, called points, endowed with certain allowable coordinate systems. In an allowable coordinate system x each point A of P_n is determined by a set of $n+1$ numbers $(x_0, \cdots, x_n)$ that are not all zero. Two such sets, $(x_0, \cdots, x_n)$ and $(x_0', \cdots, x_n')$, determine the same point if, and only if, there is a number ρ such that $x_i = \rho x_i$ $(i = 0, \cdots, n)$. Any set $(x_0, \cdots, x_n)$ corresponding to A are the homogeneous coordinates of A in the coordinate system x. If y is any other coordinate system, the relation between the x and y coordinates $(x_0, \cdots, x_n)$, $(y_0, \cdots, y_n)$ of A is given by equations that are linear (see Box, equations 1), in which coefficients a_{ij}, b_{ij} are numbers independent of A, and ρ and σ are factors of proportionality.

BASIC CONCEPTS AND SOME PRELIMINARY REMARKS

To define an algebraic locus in P_n, an allowable coordinate system x is selected, and a set of homogeneous polynomial equations expressed through functions f_i (see 2) are derived in which the coefficients are constants. If $a_0, \cdots, a_n$ are numbers (not all zero) such that $f_i(a_0, \cdots, a_n) = 0$ $(i = 1, 2, \cdots)$, then $f_i(\rho a_0, \cdots, \rho a_n) = 0$ $(i = 1, 2, \cdots)$ for any constant ρ. The point $(a_0, \cdots, a_n)$ of P_n then satisfies the polynomial equations (see 2). The aggregate of such points form what is known as an algebraic variety U, in P_n. This definition does not depend on the coordinate system chosen. If y is another coordinate system in P_n, related to the system x by the first equations (see 1), a suitable modification of the equations (see 3) in the y coordinates define the same variety U in P_n.

To complete the definition of algebraic geometry as

the study of algebraic varieties in P_n, it is necessary to be more precise about the numbers that constitute the coordinates of points or the coefficients of equations. In classical geometry, these are taken to be complex numbers; *i.e.*, numbers involving the factor $\sqrt{-1}$. In the operations involved in algebraic geometry, only a limited number of properties of complex numbers are used.

The operations of addition and multiplication have the following properties, in which a, b, and c represent complex numbers:

A. Addition has the properties of associativity (see 4) and commutativity (see 5).

There is a unique number, 0 (zero), for which $0 + a = a$ for all a.

Corresponding to any a there is a unique number $-a$ such that $a + (-a) = 0$. This means that numbers form a commutative group under addition.

B. Multiplication has the properties that:

It is associative; *i.e.*, $a(bc) = (ab)c$.

It is commutative; *i.e.*, $ab = ba$.

There is a unique number 1 (unity) such that $a \cdot 1 = a$, for all a.

For any nonzero number, a, there is a unique number a^{-1} such that $a \cdot a^{-1} = 1$. This means that the nonzero numbers form a commutative group under multiplication.

C. $a(b + c) = ab + ac$; *i.e.*, multiplication is distributive over addition.

A set of elements (*e.g.*, a, b, and c) with two laws of composition, addition and multiplication, that obey the rules A, B, and C is called a field. Other examples of fields are the rational numbers (integers as well as all numbers obtainable as ratios of integers that are not zero, together with field properties, constituting the field Q), and the integers modulo a prime number p (the integers from 0 to $p - 1$, inclusive, together with field properties, constituting the field Z_p). Instead of taking the numbers used in the definition of algebraic geometry to be complex numbers, it is more usual to choose them from any selected field k. Projective n-space over the field k is usually denoted by $P_n(k)$. *[margin: Definition of a field]*

Given a field k_1, there may exist a subset of elements of k_1, which form a field k_2, with the same addition and multiplication; k_2 is a subfield of k_1 and k_1 an extension of k_2. If any coordinate system x is chosen in $P_n(k_1)$, those points having x coordinates that lie in k_2 form a space $P_n(k_2)$. The space $P_n(k_1)$ is then an extension of $P_n(k_2)$. An algebraic variety in $P_n(k_2)$ is defined by equations with coefficients in $k_2 \subseteq k_1$ (the symbol $\subseteq$ denotes that k_2 is identical with k_1 or is contained in k_1) and hence uniquely defines a variety of $P_n(k_1)$; but a variety of $P_n(k_1)$ need not define one in $P_n(k_2)$. If U is defined over k_2, there may be points on U, regarded as a variety in $P_n(k_1)$, that are not points of $P_n(k_2)$. The usual practice is to speak of k_2 as the field of definition of U, and points on it, when it is considered as a locus over an extension of k_2, as belonging to U in a suitable extension of k_2.

Any field k and an algebraic variety U defined over k may be considered. If α is an element of an extension of k that satisfies an algebraic equation with coefficients a_i (see 6) in which a_i is in k, α is said to be algebraic over k (rational over k if $m = 1$). There exists a field $\bar{k}$, uniquely determined to within isomorphism, such that (1) every element of $\bar{k}$ is algebraic over k; (2) every element of any extension of $\bar{k}$ that is algebraic over $\bar{k}$ belongs to k. The field $\bar{k}$ is called the algebraic closure of k. The space $P_n(k)$ can be embedded in $P_n(\bar{k})$. If U is defined over k, any point of $P_n(\bar{k})$ that lies on U is an algebraic point of U [a rational point if it lies in $P_n(k)$].

The elementary theory of systems of polynomials with coefficients in k leads to some basic properties of algebraic varieties. First, if U is defined in $P_n(k)$ by the set of polynomial equations (2), there exists a finite number r such that U is given by r equations expressed with functions f_i (see 7). Second, if $\theta(x_0, \cdots, x_n)$ is a homogeneous polynomial with coefficients in k such that $\theta(a_0, \cdots, a_n) = 0$ for every algebraic point $(a_0, \cdots, a_n)$ on U, then, for some integer s, the s power of the homogeneous polynomial is related to the r functions through equations (see 8) in which $b_i(x_0, \cdots, x_n)$ is a homogeneous polynomial of suitable degree, with coefficient in *[margin: The zero position principle]*

k. This is the *Nullstellensatz* (zero position principle) of the 19th–20th-century German mathematician David Hilbert.

If V is a second algebraic variety in $P_n(k)$, defined by s equations expressed in terms of functions g_j (see 9), then the equations (2) and (3) can be taken together to define a third algebraic variety W, which consists of all the points (in any extension of k) that lie both on U and on V. The intersection of U and V may be written $W = U \cap V$ or $V \cap U$. The union W of U and V is defined to be the variety defined by the equations composed of products of the f_i and g_i (see 10). Every point on U or on V lies on W, and every point of W not on U is such that $f_i(a_0, \cdots, a_n) \neq 0$ for some i, and it follows from (10) that the g_j are zero (see 11). Here the point lies on V, so W is the variety formed by points on U or on V (see 12). It is also noted that a distributive relation holds (see 13).

A variety W in $P_n(k)$ is said to be irreducible if the equation $W = U \cup V$, when U, V are defined over k necessarily implies $W = U$ or $W = V$. An equivalent condition is the following: W is irreducible if, and only if, it has the property that if $f(x_0, \cdots, x_n)$, $g(x_0, \cdots, x_n)$ are polynomials over k such that $f(x_0, \cdots, x_n)g(x_0, \cdots, x_n) = 0$ on W, then $f(x_1, \cdots, x_n)$ or $g(x_1, \cdots, x_n)$ vanishes at every point of W. It is to be noted that a variety W may be irreducible in $P_n(k)$, but reducible over an extension of k. If it is irreducible over every extension of k it is absolutely irreducible: if k is algebraically closed, every irreducible variety is absolutely irreducible.

Theorems derived from applications of the theory of polynomials

Further applications of the theory of polynomials lead to the following theorems: (I) Any algebraic variety W defined over k can be written in an essentially unique way as the union of a finite number of irreducible varieties; and (II) any chain $U_0 \subset U_1 \subset U_2, \cdots$ of irreducible varieties in $P_n(k)$, each of which is a proper subvariety of its successor, is of finite length. The maximum length of such a chain terminating in an irreducible variety W is $d + 1$, in which d is the dimension of W. It is to be noted that the dimension of $P_n(k)$, which is denoted dim $P_n(k)$, is equal to n. The considerations that are given above form the basis on which algebraic geometry of varieties in a projective space $P_n(k)$ is constructed. It may be noted, however, that in the case in which k is the field $\mathfrak{C}$ of complex numbers, other nonalgebraic techniques are available. This is true because of the existence in $P_n(\mathfrak{C})$ of a Hausdorff topology (named for Felix Hausdorff), namely, the complex topology. A coordinate system x in $P_n(\mathfrak{C})$ is chosen and A, B are taken to be two points of which the x-coordinates are $(a_0, \cdots, a_n)$, $(b_0, \cdots, b_n)$. The distance $d(A, B)$ between A and B is defined to be the positive square root of a certain function of the a_i, b_i and their conjugates (see 14). The sets $d(A, X)$ less than the bound ε, for all A, ε, are taken as the basic open sets, all other open sets being the unions of basic open sets; the topology of $P_n(\mathfrak{C})$ is defined by its open sets. The definition of distance in $P_n(\mathfrak{C})$ depends on the choice of the allowable coordinate system, but not the derived topology.

The complex topology in $P_n(\mathfrak{C})$ can be used to define a topology of any algebraic variety U in $P_n(\mathfrak{C})$, the open sets in U being the intersection of U with the open sets of $P_n(\mathfrak{C})$. This is of prime importance in the case in which U is irreducible, and nonsingular; that is, when every point P of U has a neighbourhood that can be put in one-to-one correspondence with the points of the complex space $(u_1, \cdots, u_d)$ by means of equations which define coordinates x_i (see 15). The space U is then a complex manifold, the study of which is a separate branch of mathematics but which can be used to develop the algebraic geometry of varieties defined over the complex field.

Another topology, the Zariski topology (after Oscar Zariski, a 20th-century Russian-born U.S. mathematician), will be introduced below into the study of varieties over any field k. Even when k is the field $\mathfrak{C}$ of complex numbers, it is quite different from the complex topology, and is not a Hausdorff topology. (That is, two different points cannot be distinguished by respective inclusion in two non-intersecting open sets.)

(1) $\qquad \rho y_i = \sum_{j=0}^{n} a_{ij} x_j, \qquad \sigma x_i = \sum_{j=0}^{n} b_{ij} y_j$

(2) $\qquad f_i(x_0, \cdots, x_n) = 0, \qquad i = 1, 2, \cdots$

(3) $\qquad f_i\left(\sum_j b_{0j} y_j, \cdots, \sum_j b_{nj} y_j\right) = 0$

(4) $\qquad a + (b + c) = (a + b) + c \quad$ (associative law)

(5) $\qquad a + b = b + a \quad$ (commutative law)

(6) $\qquad f(x) \equiv x^m + a_1 x^{m-1} + \cdots + a_m = 0$

(7) $\qquad f_i(x_0, \cdots, x_n) = 0, \qquad i = 1, 2, \cdots, r$

(8) $\qquad (\theta(x_0, \cdots, x_n))^s = \sum_{i=1}^{r} b_i(x_0, \cdots, x_n) f_i(x_0, \cdots, x_n)$

(9) $\qquad g_i(x_0, \cdots, x_n) = 0, \qquad i = 1, 2, \cdots, s$

(10) $\qquad \begin{cases} f_i(x_0, \cdots, x_n)\, g_j(x_0, \cdots, x_n) = 0, & i = 1, \cdots, r \\ j = 1, \cdots, s \end{cases}$

(11) $\qquad g_j(a_0, \cdots, a_n) = 0, \qquad j = 1, \cdots, s$

(12) $\qquad W = U \cup V = V \cup U$

(13) $\qquad V \cap (U_1 \cup U_2) = V \cap U_1 \cup V \cap U_2$

(14) $\qquad \begin{cases} 1 - \dfrac{\left(\sum_k a_k \bar{b}_k\right)\left(\sum_k \bar{a}_k b_k\right)}{\left(\sum_k a_k \bar{a}_k\right)\left(\sum_k b_k \bar{b}_k\right)} \\ \text{in which } \bar{b}_k \text{ is the complex conjugate of } b_k, \text{ and } \bar{a}_k \\ \text{is the complex conjugate of } a_k. \end{cases}$

(15) $\qquad \begin{cases} x_i = \psi_i(u_1, \cdots, u_d), \qquad i = 0, \cdots, d \\ \text{when the } \psi_i(u_1, \cdots, u_d) \text{ are analytic functions,} \\ \text{and } d \text{ is the dimension of } U. \end{cases}$

(16) $\qquad (y_1^\alpha, \cdots, y_n^\alpha) = (x_0/x_\alpha, \cdots, x_j/x_\alpha, \cdots, x_n/x_\alpha), \qquad j \neq \alpha$

PROJECTIVE AND ABSTRACT VARIETIES

Modern algebraic geometry is mainly concerned with properties of varieties that are independent of the projective spaces in which the varieties are embedded. It is therefore necessary to find a set of intrinsic properties of an algebraic variety that will lead to an abstract definition of a variety; this, in turn, leads to a generalization of the notion of a variety.

Although there are good reasons for considering algebraic varieties in a projective space $P_n(k)$, in practice there are advantages in regarding $P_n(k)$ as a union of affine spaces. The points of $P_n(k)$ that are not in the subspace such that $x_\alpha = 0$ form what is called an affine space $A_n^\alpha(k)$, with affine coordinates (see 16). If U is an algebraic variety in $P_n(k)$, the points of U in $A_n^\alpha(k)$ form an affine variety U^α. From a study of affine varieties in $A_n^\alpha(k)$, consideration can be made how to fit them together to form an algebraic variety in projective space $P_n(k)$ (briefly, a projective variety).

Affine varieties

If $A_n(k)$ is an affine space with coordinate system $(y_1, \cdots, y_n)$, the polynomials in $(y_1, \cdots, y_n)$, with coefficients in k, form a set with two laws of composition, addition and multiplication. Under addition the polynomials form a commutative group, and multiplication is associative, commutative, and distributive over addition; further, the unity 1 of k has the property that $1 \cdot f(y_1, \cdots, y_n)$

(17) $\quad \alpha, \beta \in k[y_1, \cdots, y_n], \qquad \alpha\beta = 0$

(18) $\quad \begin{cases} \text{If } f(y_1, \cdots, y_n) \text{ and } g(y_1, \cdots, y_n) \text{ vanish on } V, \text{ then} \\ f(y_1, \cdots, y_n) - g(y_1, \cdots, y_n) \text{ vanishes on } V, \text{ and} \\ a(y_1, \cdots, y_n) f(y_1, \cdots, y_n) \text{ vanish on } V \text{ for all} \\ \text{polynomials } a(y_1, \cdots, y_n) \text{ in } k[y_1, \cdots, y_n]. \end{cases}$

(19) $\quad \displaystyle\sum_{i=1}^{r} a_i(y_1, \cdots, y_n) f_i(y_1, \cdots, y_n)$

(20) $\quad \begin{cases} \text{If } \mathbf{p} \text{ is prime, it is noted that if} \\ f(\eta_1, \cdots, \eta_n) g(\eta_1, \cdots, \eta_n) = 0, \text{ then} \\ f(y_1, \cdots, y_n) \text{ lies in } \mathbf{p}, \text{ and therefore} \\ f(y_1, \cdots, y_n) \text{ or } g(y_1, \cdots, y_n) \text{ lies in } \mathbf{p}, \text{ and hence} \\ f(\eta_1, \cdots, \eta_n) = 0 \text{ or } g(\eta_1, \cdots, \eta_n) = 0 \text{ on } V; \text{ that is,} \\ k[y_1, \cdots, y_n]/\mathbf{p} \text{ is an integral domain.} \end{cases}$

(21) $\quad \begin{cases} (\alpha, \beta) + (\alpha', \beta') = (\alpha\beta' + \alpha'\beta, \beta\beta'), \\ (\alpha, \beta)(\alpha', \beta') = (\alpha\alpha', \beta\beta') \end{cases}$

(22) $\quad \begin{cases} V, \text{ and } W \subseteq W' R_{W_2}(V, k) \subseteq R_{W_2}(V, k). \text{ Two cases are of} \\ \text{special importance. (i) } W = V. \text{ In this case } R_V(V, k) \text{ is a} \\ \text{field of elements } \alpha/\beta, \text{ in which } \alpha, \beta \in R(V, k) \text{ and } \beta \\ \neq 0. \text{ It is the function field of } V. \text{ (ii) } W \text{ is defined by a} \\ \text{maximal prime of ideal } \mathbf{q} \text{ of } R(V, k); \text{ that is, } W \text{ is an} \\ \text{irreducible variety of dimension zero.} \end{cases}$

(23) $\quad R_{W^\alpha}(U^\alpha, k) \cong R_{W^\beta}(U^\beta, k)$

$= f(y_1, \cdots, y_n)$ for all polynomials $f(y_1, \cdots, y_n)$. A set with two laws of composition satisfying these properties is called a ring with unity 1. The ring of polynomials is denoted by $k[y_1, \cdots, y_n]$, and, if the product of two of its elements α and β is 0, then either α or β is 0. It is then called an integral domain.

An affine variety V is defined as the set of points satisfying a number of polynomial equations $f_i(y_1, \cdots, y_n) = 0$ $(i = 1, 2, \cdots)$. The polynomials that vanish on V have properties (see 18) that imply, in brief, that the polynomials that vanish on V form a so-called ideal $\mathbf{i}$. Given any ideal $\mathbf{i}$ in $k[y_1, \cdots, y_n]$, there exists a finite number of polynomials in $\mathbf{i}$, say $f_i(y_1, \cdots, y_n)$ $(i = 1, \cdots, r)$, such that any polynomial in $\mathbf{i}$ can be written in the form of a sum of products of f_i and a_i (see 19) for suitable polynomials $a_i(y_1, \cdots, y_n)$. The polynomials $f_i(y_1, \cdots, y_n)$ are referred to as forming a basis for $\mathbf{i}$. If V is the affine variety defined by the polynomials of $\mathbf{i}$, the set of all polynomials that vanish on V form an ideal $\mathbf{j}$; thus, $\mathbf{i} \subseteq \mathbf{j}$, and $\mathbf{j}$ is called the radical of $\mathbf{i}$.

An affine variety V is said to be irreducible if it has the property that if $f(y_1, \cdots, y_n) g(y_1, \cdots, y_n) \in \mathbf{j}$, the maximal ideal defining V necessarily implies that either $f(y_1, \cdots, y_n)$ or $g(y_1, \cdots, y_n)$ is in $\mathbf{j}$; in other words, V is irreducible if, and only if, the radical $\mathbf{j}$ is a prime ideal.

If V is an irreducible variety in $A_n(k)$, and $\mathbf{p}$ the associated prime ideal of $k[y_1, \cdots, y_n]$, then two elements α, β of $k[y_1, \cdots, y_n]$ are said to be equivalent modulo $\mathbf{p}$ if $\alpha - \beta \in \mathbf{p}$; $\mathbf{p}$ divides the elements of the ring into equivalence classes. If η_i denotes the equivalence class containing y_i, any element $f(y_1, \cdots, y_n)$ of $k[y_1, \cdots, y_n]$ belongs to an equivalence class that can be represented by $f(\eta_1, \cdots, \eta_n)$. It is clear that the equivalence classes can be added and multiplied to form a ring (with unity). This ring is denoted by $k[y_1, \cdots, y_n]/\mathbf{p}$.

This process of forming the remainder-class ring does not depend on the fact that $\mathbf{p}$ is prime. If $\mathbf{p}$ is prime, the ring is an integral domain (see 20). This integral domain is here denoted by $R(V, k)$; the intrinsic algebraic geometry on V is developed in terms of this ring, just as the geometry of varieties in $A_n(k)$ is developed in terms of $k[y, \cdots, y_n]$.

If W is any subvariety of $A_n(k)$ contained in V, and if $\mathbf{j}$ is the ideal of $k[y_1, \cdots, y_n]$ formed by all the polyno-

mials that vanish on W, because $W \subseteq V$, $\mathbf{p} \subseteq \mathbf{j}$, it is readily verified that the image of $\mathbf{j}$ in $k[y_1, \cdots, y_n]/\mathbf{p}$ is an ideal $\mathbf{j}/\mathbf{p}$ of $R(V, k)$, prime if, and only if, $\mathbf{j}$ is prime. Conversely, if $\mathbf{q}$ is an ideal of $R(V, k)$, it is the image of an ideal of $k[y_1, \cdots, y_n]$ containing $\mathbf{p}$, which is prime if, and only if, $\mathbf{q}$ is prime. Thus the varieties on V correspond to the ideals in $R(V, k)$, just as the varieties in $A_n(k)$ correspond to ideals in $k[y_1, \cdots, y_n]$. The union and intersection of varieties on V are defined as above; also the dimension of W (irreducible) on V is the maximum length (minus one) of a chain of irreducible varieties in V, $W_0 \subset W_1 \subset \cdots \subset W_r = W$, and coincides with the dimension of W as a variety of $A_n(k)$.

If W is an irreducible subvariety of V, and $\mathbf{q}$ the prime ideal of $R(V, k)$ that defines it, then the local ring of W on V can be defined and denoted by $R_W(V, k)$ as follows. All pairs (α, β) of elements of $R(V, k)$ in which $\beta \notin \mathbf{q}$ are considered. Addition and multiplication of pairs is defined in terms of addition and multiplication of components (see 21); this is allowable because $\beta \notin \mathbf{q}$, $\beta' \notin \mathbf{q}$ implies $\beta\beta' \notin \mathbf{q}$, $\mathbf{q}$ being prime. The pairs thus form a ring, with unity $(1, 1)$. The pairs of the form $(0, \beta)$ form a prime ideal of this ring, and the classes of equivalent pairs modulo this ideal form the local ring $R_W(V, k)$, which is, in fact, an integral domain. The elements of $R_W(V, k)$ are usually denoted by α/β, in which (α, β) is any pair of the equivalence class represented by the element.

It will be clear that if W, W' are irreducible varieties on V, and W is contained in W', then the same relationship holds between corresponding local rings, two cases being of special importance (see 22). When k is algebraically closed, W is a single point; more generally it consists of a finite set of points algebraically conjugate over k. An important theorem states that the intersection of the local rings of all the zero-dimensional varieties on V is the ring $R(V, k)$.

In the case of a projective algebraic variety U in $P_n(k)$, the affine varieties U^α in $A_n^\alpha(k)$ $(\alpha = 0, \cdots, n)$ have to be considered. The rings $R(U^\alpha, k)$ are all different. If W is any irreducible variety in U, however, and $W^\alpha = U^\alpha \cap W$, the local ring of W^α consists of fractions that can be represented by ratios a/b, when a and b are homogeneous polynomials in $(x^0, \cdots, x^n)$ of the same degree, each reduced modulo the equations of U. It follows that the local rings of W^α and W^β can be identified (see 23) for all α, β. In particular, the function field of U^α can be identified with that of U^β; it also defines the function field of U.

The field U can be regarded as the union of the affine varieties U^α, joined together, just as coordinate neighbourhoods are joined together to give a differentiable manifold. To be more precise, what is known as Zariski topology can be introduced into an affine variety V by defining the closed sets to be the subvarieties of V. The variety V is itself an open set. The points of U that lie in U^α and in U^β form an open set $U^{\alpha\beta}$ of U^α and an open set $U^{\beta\alpha}$ of U^β. There is a one-to-one correspondence between the points of $U^{\alpha\beta}$ and those of $U^{\beta\alpha}$, which is continuous in each direction, because open sets correspond to open sets, and the local rings of corresponding irreducible subvarieties can be identified.

This leads to the generalization of the French-born U.S. mathematician André Weil of a projective variety. If V^α $(\alpha = 1, 2, \cdots, r)$ denotes r affine algebraic varieties, consideration can be given to the case in which for each pair α, β there exist open sets $V^{\alpha\beta}$ on V^α, $V^{\beta\alpha}$ on V^β, in one-to-one continuous correspondence (continuity being defined in terms of the Zariski topology); so that the local rings of corresponding subvarieties of $V^{\alpha\beta}$ and $V^{\beta\alpha}$ are isomorphic (*i.e.*, in one-to-one correspondence with ring operations preserved). Then V^α and V^β can be joined by identifying corresponding points and corresponding local rings. The affine varieties V^α $(\alpha = 1, \cdots, r)$ can thus be joined together to give what is referred to as abstract variety V. Any point P of V lies in at least one V^α (see 24).

It may be noted that the process of constructing an abstract variety, when applied to a subset of the affine vari-

Weil's generalization of a projective variety

eties U^α that cover a projective variety U, defines an abstract variety that may form a proper open subset of U; in this case, the abstract variety is not complete. It is also possible to construct abstract varieties that cannot be embedded in a projective space.

If U or V are two abstract varieties, consideration can be given to a mapping of an open set U' of U into V that can be given locally in terms of local coordinate systems by equations (see 25). These equations (25) define the image of any algebraic point P of the domain of $(\xi_1, \cdots, \xi_n)$, provided that $Y_i(\xi_1, \cdots, \xi_n)$ is contained in the local ring of the irreducible zero-dimensional variety U_0 containing P. In this case the image of U_0 is a well-defined zero-dimensional variety V_0 of V and from the equations (25) a homomorphism (or operation preserving mapping) $R_{V_0}(V, k)$ to $R_{U_0}(U, k)$ is deduced. The equations (25) are then referred to as defining a mapping $U' \to V$ that is regular at U_0. It may be possible to use the equation to define the mapping $U \to V$ at all points of U' by giving special interpretation to the images of places on U at which the mapping is not regular. This mapping is then called a rational mapping. It is a regular mapping if it is regular at all places of U: it can be denoted by special symbolism (see 26).

Birational correspondences

Two algebraic varieties are referred to as equivalent if there is a one-to-one correspondence between them that is regular in each direction. Two varieties U and V are referred to as birationally equivalent if they contain open sets U' and V' that are in bi-regular correspondence. Much of classical algebraic geometry is devoted to the study of properties of varieties invariant under birational transformations. One of the advantages of using birational correspondences rather than bi-regular ones is that difficulties are avoided that arise as a result of the presence of singularities (multiple curves or other subvarieties). The main problem in this field is that of finding a nonsingular algebraic variety, U, that is birationally equivalent to an irreducible algebraic variety V, such that the mapping $\pi : U \to V$ is regular (but not bi-regular). The most general solution of this problem was obtained by the Japanese-born U.S. mathematician Heisuke Hironaka in 1964.

Birational correspondences can also be used to give a convenient definition of a complete variety. If U is any abstract variety and V any algebraic variety such that there is a birational correspondence between U and an open subset of V, the product $U \times V$ can be constructed with Δ denoting a set of points x, y such that x and y are corresponding points of U and V. The set of points Δ is an algebraic subvariety of $U \times V$. The abstract variety U is referred to as complete if the projection of Δ (proj Δ) on V is V, for all V. To see the significance of this definition, consideration may be given to U' being any affine open set on U; it is bi-regularly equivalent to a variety U'' in affine space $A_n(k)$. By V there may be denoted the variety in $P_n(k)$ such the U'' is an intersection of affine space and V (see 27). It readily follows that if U is not complete, proj Δ on V is an open set of V, which is a proper subset of V.

Much of the geometry on an algebraic variety U of dimension e is concerned with the subvarieties, and systems of subvarieties, on U.

The free group $G_e(U)$, generated by the irreducible subvarieties of U of dimension e, can be considered. Any element of $G_e(U)$ is of the form $\Sigma \rho_i D_i$, summation being on i, in which ρ_i is an integer (only different from zero for a finite number of i), and D_1, D_2 are irreducible varieties of U of dimension e. This element is referred to as an e-cycle. In general, two irreducible subvarieties P, Q of dimensions r, s, respectively, intersect in a variety consisting of a finite number of subvarieties of dimension $q = r + s - d$. Each of these subvarieties has a well-defined multiplicity, and with these multiplicities the intersection $P \cdot Q = Q \cdot P$ is a well-defined q-cycle. The intersection of an r-cycle and an s-cycle may possibly also be defined (see 28).

Two e-cycles D and D' on U are rationally equivalent if on the product variety $U \times L$, in which L is the straight line parameterized by (that is, described algebraically with the aid of) the elements of k, there exists an $(e + 1)$-cycle C such that C meets $U \times 0$ in $D \times 0$, and $U \times 1$ in $D' \times 1$. The e-cycles that are equivalent to zero form a subgroup $g_e(U)$ of $G_e(U)$. The remainder-class group is denoted by $A_e(U)$. If α and β belong to class rings corresponding to r- and s-cycles, respectively (see 29), then representative cycles a, b can be found in $G_r(U)$, $G_s(U)$ such that $a \cdot b$ is well defined in $G_q(U)$. If a', b' are any other representative cycles of α, β such that $a' \cdot b'$ is well defined, it readily follows that $a \cdot b$ is equivalent to $a' \cdot b'$, and hence that α, β determine a well-defined element $\alpha \cdot \beta$ of $A_q(U)$. With this definition of multiplication, the graded group (see 30) has the structure of a ring. This ring is the Chow ring of U.

The Chow ring

An important property of the Chow ring is that if f: $U \to V$ is a regular map of U on V, every irreducible subvariety on U maps to an irreducible subvariety of V, and there is a homomorphism $f_*: A(U) \to A(V)$ with $A(U)$, $A(V)$ regarded as additive groups. This homomorphism, however, does not imply a homomorphism of the rings $A(U)$, $A(V)$. On the other hand, if D is any subvariety of V, $f^{-1}D$ is a subvariety of U, and a mapping $f^*: A(V) \to A(U)$ can be deduced that is a ring homomorphism. The structure of $A(U)$ throws great light on the geometry of U. A case of special interest is that in which d, the dimension of U, is 1. The class of equivalent 0-cycles of order zero form a subgroup G of $A_0(U)$. The subgroup G can be represented by the points of a complete nonsingular projective variety of J over k, of dimension g, in which g is the genus of U (see below). The operations of the group G are represented by a regular map $J \times J \to J$. The group $A_0(U)/G$ is isomorphic to the additive group of integers.

SHEAVES AND SCHEMA

In studying algebraic varieties by means of local rings it is seldom necessary to consider individual points: the irreducible subvarieties of dimension zero are the smallest sets that must be considered. If these sets are renamed points, a variety U is then a space X consisting of points endowed with a topology (the Zariski topology) with a ring associated with each point. The set of rings is said to form a sheaf over X.

For a topological space denoted by X it is supposed that there is a ring $O(U)$ associated with each open set, U, of

(24) $\begin{cases} \text{Any point } P \text{ of } V \text{ lies in at least one } V^\alpha: \text{If } \xi_1^\alpha, \cdots, \xi_{n_\alpha}^\alpha \\ \text{generate the ring } R(V^\alpha, k) \text{ and } U' \text{ is any open set of } V^\alpha \\ \text{containing } P, U' \text{ is called an affine neighbourhood of} \\ P \text{ and } (\xi_1^\alpha, \cdots, \xi_{n_\alpha}^\alpha) \text{ are local coordinates in } U'. \end{cases}$

(25) $\begin{cases} (\xi_1, \cdots, \xi_n) \text{ and } (\eta_1, \cdots, \eta_m) \text{ on } U' \text{ and } V, \text{ by the} \\ \text{equations } \eta_i = Y_i(\xi_1, \cdots, \xi_n), i = 1, \cdots, m, \\ \text{when } Y_i(\xi_1, \cdots, \xi_n) \text{ is in the function field of } U, \\ i = 1, \cdots, m. \end{cases}$

(26) $\begin{cases} (\pi, \pi^*): \pi : U' \to V; \quad \pi^*: R_{\pi U_0}(V, k) \to R_{U_0}(U, k), \\ \text{for all zero-dimensional varieties } U_0 \text{ on } U. \end{cases}$

(27) $U'' = A_n(k) \cap V$

(28) $\begin{cases} \text{The intersection of an } r\text{-cycle } P = \Sigma \rho_j P_i \text{ and an} \\ s\text{-cycle } Q = \sum_i \sigma_i Q_i \text{ is then defined to be} \\ \Sigma \rho_i \sigma_j P_i Q_j \text{ (if it is defined at all).} \end{cases}$

(29) $\alpha \in A_r(U), \qquad \beta \in A_s(U)$

(30) $A(U) = \sum_{i=0}^{d} A_i(U)$

(31) $\begin{cases} r_{U'U}: O(U) \to O(U') \\ \text{If } U'' \subseteq U' \subseteq U, \text{ then } r_{U''U} = r_{U''U'} \circ r_{U'U} \end{cases}$

(32) $r_{PU}: O(U) \to O_P$

(33) $\begin{cases} \text{(i) There is a projection } \pi: S \to X \text{ (if } \sigma \in O_P, \pi\sigma = P); \\ \text{(ii) } \pi \text{ is locally a homeomorphism (i.e., one-to-one and} \\ \quad\ \text{continuous in both directions);} \\ \text{(iii) } \pi^{-1}P \text{ has a ring structure that is continuous.} \end{cases}$

(34) $r'_{U'U}: \Gamma(U, S) \to \Gamma(U', S);$ if $\gamma: U \to S$ is in $\Gamma(U, S)$,

then $r'_{U'U}(\gamma) = \gamma | U'$ (restriction of γ to U').

(35) $\begin{cases} \text{If } (X, O_X) \text{ is a ringed space, a pre-sheaf of modules} \\ (M(U), k_{U'U''}) \text{ can be considered, in which } M(U) \text{ is an} \\ O(U)\text{-module and } (O(U), r_{U'U}) \text{ is the canonical pre-sheaf} \\ \text{of } O_X. \text{ Suppose that the homomorphism} \\ k_{U'U}: M(U) \to M(U') \text{ is such that if } a \in M(U), \alpha \in O(U), \\ \text{then } k_{U'U}(\alpha a) = r_{U'U}\alpha \circ k_{U'U}a. \text{ The resulting sheaf of} \\ \text{modules is called an } O_X\text{-module.} \end{cases}$

(36) $\phi(U): \Gamma(U, O_Y) \to \Gamma(\theta^{-1} U, O_X)$

(37) $(\theta, \phi): (x, O_X) \to (y, O_Y)$

(38) $\to F_1 \to F_2 \to F_3 \to F_4 \to \cdots$

(39) $\{C_{\alpha_0 \cdots \alpha_p}\}$, in which $C_{\alpha_0 \cdots \alpha_p} \in \Gamma(U_{\alpha_0} \cap \cdots \cap U_{\alpha_p}, F)$.

(40) $\begin{cases} \text{The coboundary operator } \partial_p \text{ is a homomorphism} \\ \mathfrak{G}_p \to \mathfrak{G}_{p+1}, \text{ in which } \partial\{C_{\alpha_0 \cdots \alpha_p}\} = \{C_{\alpha_0 \cdots \alpha_{p+1}}\}, \\ \text{in which } C_{\alpha_0 \cdots \alpha_p} = \sum_{r=0}^{p+1} (-1)^r C'_{\alpha_0 \cdots \alpha_r \cdots \alpha_{p+1}}, C'_{\beta_0 \cdots \beta_p} \\ \text{being the restriction of } C_{\beta_0 \cdots \beta_r} \text{ to } U_{\alpha_0} \cdots U_{\alpha_{p+1}}, \\ \beta_0 \cdots \beta_p \text{ being a subset of } \alpha_0 \cdots \alpha_{p+1}. \end{cases}$

(41) $\phi_{VU}: H^p(\mathbf{U}, F) \to H^p(\mathbf{V}, F)$

X. If, further, U' is an open set contained in U, then there is a well-defined homomorphism defined in terms of a set of rings and satisfying certain conditions (see 31). Such a set of rings $O(U)$ and homomorphisms $r_{U'U}$ define a pre-sheaf over X. By considering a sequence $U_1 \supset U_2 \supset \cdots$ of open sets converging to a point P, the direct limit of the $O(U_\alpha)$ is defined, as is a ring O_P associated with P, and a homomorphism r_{PU} that maps from a set of rings to a ring (see 32). The set S of elements of O_P for all P in X may be considered; the set S can be endowed with a topology by defining open neighbourhoods of each element. If σ denotes an element of O_P, then there exists a neighbourhood U of P and an element S_U of $O(U)$ such that $r_{PU}S_U = \sigma$. If Q is any point of U, then the direct limit process defines a unique element $r_{QU}S_U$ of O_Q corresponding to S_U for every point Q of U. As Q describes U, $r_{QU}S_U$ defines a set of S (containing σ): this may define an open neighbourhood of σ. The set S is then a space with three properties (see 33); $\pi^{-1}P$ is called the stalk of S at P, and S is a sheaf of rings over X. The situation now is that X is a topological space with a privileged sheaf $O_X = S$ of rings over it. The entity (X, O_X) is called a ringed space. An algebraic variety can thus be represented as a ringed space.

A section of the sheaf S over an open set U of X is a continuous mapping $\alpha: U \to S$ such that $\pi\alpha$ maps U into itself identically. It can be verified that the section over U will have the structure of a ring, which is denoted by $\Gamma(U, S)$, and if $U' \subseteq U$ there is a homomorphism of inclusion (see 34) in terms of which a set of rings and homomorphisms can be used to form a pre-sheaf. It can be shown that the sheaf S' defined by this pre-sheaf is equal to S. The pre-sheaf $(\Gamma[U, S], r'_{U'U})$ is the canonical pre-sheaf of S.

The definition of sheaves can clearly be extended to define sheaves of groups or other sets with an algebraic structure (see 35). The resulting sheaf of modules is then called an O_X-module; its stalk at any point x is an O_x-module.

Consideration may be given to (X, O_X), (Y, O_Y) denoting two ringed spaces, with a continuous mapping $\theta : X \to Y$. If U is any open set of Y and there is a corresponding homomorphism (see 36), then if the homomorphisms $\phi(U)$ are compatible with the restriction homomorphisms on X, Y, there is obtained a homomorphism $\theta : O_Y \to O_X$ that induces a homomorphism of the stalk $O_{\theta x}$ of O_Y into O_x, for all x in X. The pair (θ, ϕ), suitably defined (see 37), is called a morphism. When (X, O_X) and (Y, O_Y) are the ringed spaces defined by algebraic varieties V_1, V_2, the morphism is just a regular mapping $V_1 \to V_2$.

To regard an algebraic variety as a ringed space and study the properties of sheaves over it has proved so powerful a method in algebraic geometry that Alexandre Grothendieck, a German-born French mathematician, has been led to a further generalization of an algebraic variety. Consideration may be given first to an affine variety. As a ringed space it is defined by an integral domain $R(V, k)$, and the points (zero-dimensional subvarieties) are defined by the maximal prime ideals of $R(V, k)$. In Grothendieck's treatment this is generalized by considering any commutative ring R. The points may no longer be defined by the maximal prime ideals of R, because if R is not a Noetherian ring (after Emmy Noether, a German mathematician) there may be no maximal ideals. Therefore all the prime ideals of R have to be considered as points. The closed sets of this aggregate are the points corresponding to prime ideals that contain an ideal $\mathbf{i}$ of R. The points, with this topology, form a space that is called an affine scheme. A pre-scheme is then defined as a ringed space that is covered by a system of open sets each of which is an affine scheme. A scheme is a pre-scheme that satisfies a further condition somewhat analogous to the completeness condition for abstract varieties. The techniques employed to study algebraic varieties by using the theory of sheaves can then be applied to schemas. Some difficulties, however, occurring in the general case, do not arise in the case when the ringed space is an algebraic variety.

In all that follows it will be assumed that (X, O_X) is the ringed space of a nonsingular irreducible projective algebraic variety X.

If F and G are taken to be two sheaves over X, then a homomorphism $\alpha : F \to G$ is a continuous mapping of F into G (when each is regarded as a topological space) that induces a homomorphism $\alpha_x : F_x \to G_x$ of the stalks at each point x. It is clear that the image F' of F in G has the structure of a sheaf, and the kernel of α; that is, the elements of F_x that map to zero in G_x for all x form a sub-sheaf of F. The quotients G_x/F_x' further form a sheaf G/F'. A sequence (see 38) of sheaves and homomorphisms is referred to as exact if the image of each homomorphism is the kernel of the following one.

For each integer p ($p \geqslant 0$) a cohomology group, $H^p(X, F)$, can be defined for any sheaf F. If $\mathbf{U} = \{U_\alpha\}$ is any covering of X by open sets, then a p-cochain of $\mathbf{U}$ is a specific system of sections (see 39). The p-cochains form a group b_p under addition. The co-boundary operator ∂_p can be defined (see 40). The elements of the kernel of ∂_p are p-cocycles and form a group γ_p; $\partial_{p-1}b_{p-1}$ is a subgroup of b_p, and because $\partial_p\partial_{p-1} = 0$, it is a subgroup β_p of γ_p. The quotient group γ_p/β_p is denoted by $H^p(\mathbf{U}, F)$. If $\mathbf{V}$ is another covering of X by open sets, $H^p(\mathbf{V}, F)$ can be defined similarly; and if $\mathbf{V}$ is a refinement of $\mathbf{U}$, so that each V_λ is contained in at least one U_α, a corresponding homomorphism can also be defined (see 41). These groups and homomorphisms define in the usual way a direct limit, denoted by $H^p(X, F)$, which is called the pth cohomology group of F. If U is any open set of X the cohomology group $H^p(U, F)$ can be defined similarly. It may be noted that if F is an O_X-module, $H^p(U, F)$ can be given the structure of an $O(U)$-module. For complete algebraic varieties over k, $\Gamma(X, 0_X) = k$, and $H^p(X, F)$ is a vector

Ringed spaces

Grothendieck's generalization

space (that is, a collection of vectors satisfying certain algebraic properties) over k.

If there is (see 42) an exact sequence of sheaves and homomorphisms, there can be defined homomorphisms

$$H^p(X, F) \xrightarrow{\alpha_p} H^p(X, G), \text{ and } H^p(X, G) \xrightarrow{\beta_p} H^p(X, H).$$

Cohomology sequences

There can also be determined $H^p(X, H) \xrightarrow{\delta_p} H^{p+1}(X, F)$, thus a sequence, called a cohomology sequence, can be obtained (see 43). For the ringed spaces (X, O_x) derived from a complete algebraic variety X, this sequence is exact. For more general ringed spaces it may not be exact. For schemes, Grothendieck defines cohomology in a different way, and the Grothendieck cohomology sequence corresponding to (42) is exact. For the spaces under consideration here the Čech cohomology (named for Eduard Čech, a Czech mathematician) coincides with the Grothendieck cohomology.

Consideration may be given to the ringed space (X, O_x) corresponding to an algebraic variety X. A coherent sheaf on it can be defined as follows: $O_x{}^n$ denotes the sheaf that is the direct sum of n copies of O_x. An O_x-module F is referred to as coherent if there can be found integers n, m and homomorphisms α, β so that a certain sequence (see 44) is exact. (On more general ringed spaces coherent sheaves have to be defined differently.) Coherent sheaves have certain properties that make them easier to deal with than more general sheaves. Their main properties are: (A) If in the exact sequence of sheaves (see 42) any two of the sheaves F, G, H are coherent, so is the third; (B) If F is a coherent sheaf, $H^p(X, F)$ is a vector space of finite dimension over k, and $H^p(X, F) = 0$ for p sufficiently large.

Consideration may be given to the free group κ generated by addition of the coherent sheaves over X. If κ' denotes the subgroup generated by elements of κ of the form $G - F - H$, for all sheaves, F, G, H, such that the sequence (42) is exact and the quotient group κ/κ' is denoted by $K(X)$, then $K(X)$ is a group having many connections with the Chow ring of the algebraic variety X that defines the ringed space (X, O_x).

Letting (X, O_x) and (Y, O_Y) be ringed spaces, assumed to be algebraic varieties, and (θ, ϕ) a morphism between them (see 45), then the effects of this morphism on sheaves on X and on Y may be considered.

A. If F is a coherent sheaf over Y, there can be defined a module $M(U)$ associated with an open set U of X by $M(U)` = \Gamma(\theta U, F)$. It is then possible to define a homomorphism (see 46) so that there is a pre-sheaf over X. The derived sheaf may be denoted by $\phi^! F$; it can be shown to be a coherent sheaf over X. Moreover, if a sequence involving F, G, H is an exact sequence of homomorphisms of coherent sheaves over Y, then a corresponding sequence of derived sheaves (see 47) is exact over X. Thus $\phi^!$ defines a homomorphism $K(Y) \to K(X)$.

B. If F is an O_x-module over X, there can be defined a pre-sheaf over Y by associating with each open set U of Y the module $\Gamma(\theta^{-1}U, F)$, and defining suitable homomorphisms between modules (see 48), in which $U' \subseteq U$. The induced sheaf over Y is denoted by $\phi_* F$. If F, G, H are O_x-modules such that the sequence (42) is exact, a sequence of homomorphisms (see 49), however, can be deduced. In general this is not exact. Thus ϕ_* does not define a homomorphism $K(X) \to K(Y)$. The image $\phi_! F$ of F in $K(Y)$ can, however, be defined as follows: If U is any open set of Y, by associating with U the $O(\theta^{-1}U)$-module $H^p(\theta^{-1}U, F)$, a pre-sheaf over Y can be defined by the usual process. Hence, a sheaf can also be defined. This is denoted by $R^p\phi_* F$. It is a coherent sheaf. The element of $K(Y)$, $\phi_! F$, is given by $\sum_{p \geq 0} (-1)^p R^p\phi_* F$, a finite sum because $H^p(\theta^{-1}U, F)$ is always zero for sufficiently large p. If the sequence (42) is an exact sequence of sheaves, the exactness of the cohomology sequence (43) leads to an equality in $K_0(Y)$ (see 50). Thus $\phi_!$ defines a homomorphism $\phi_! : K(X) \to K(Y)$.

APPLICATIONS TO ALGEBRAIC GEOMETRY

If X is a complete irreducible algebraic variety of dimension d, and (X, O_x) is the associated ringed space, then

(42) $$0 \to F \xrightarrow{\alpha} G \xrightarrow{\beta} H \to 0$$

(43) $$0 \to H^0(X, F) \xrightarrow{\alpha_0} H^0(X, G) \xrightarrow{\beta_0} H^0(X, H) \xrightarrow{\delta_0} H^1(X, F)$$
$$\to \cdots \to H^{p-1}(X, H) \xrightarrow{\delta_{p-1}} H^p(X, F) \xrightarrow{\alpha_p} \cdots$$

(44) $$O_X^n \xrightarrow{\alpha} O_X^m \xrightarrow{\beta} F \to 0$$

(45) $$\begin{cases} \theta: X \to Y \\ \phi_x: O_{\theta x} \to O_x \end{cases}$$

(46) $$h_{U'U}: M(U) \to M(U') \quad \text{for } U' \subseteq U$$

(47) $$\begin{cases} 0 \to F \to G \to H \to 0 \\ 0 \to \phi^! F \to \phi^! G \to \phi^! H \to 0 \end{cases}$$

(48) $$\Gamma(\theta^{-1}U, F) \to \Gamma(\theta^{-1}U', F)$$

(49) $$0 \to \phi_* F \to \phi_* G \to \phi_* H \to 0$$

(50) $$0 \to \phi_! F \to \phi_! G \to \phi_! H \to 0$$

(51) $$h_{UU_\alpha}: M(U_\alpha) \to M(U)$$

(52) $$F_D = H^0(x, F_D)$$

there are two groups on X: the group $K(X)$ defined above, and the Chow ring $A(X)$, regarded as an additive group. Many problems of algebraic geometry are concerned with relations between $K(X)$ and $A(X)$. Sometimes it is convenient to extend $A(X)$ so that it is the group generated by the equivalence classes of cycles with rational numbers as coefficients; the extended group is then denoted by $A(X) \times Q$, in which Q is the field of rational numbers.

If D is a divisor of X—that is, a cycle of dimension $d - 1$—there exists a covering $\mathbf{U} = (U_\alpha)$ of X so fine that in U_α there is an element ϕ_α of the function field Σ of X such that $D \cap U_\alpha = D_\alpha$ is the divisor consisting of the zero of ϕ_α minus the poles of ϕ_α, each counted with proper multiplicity. ϕ_α is determined in U_α except for a factor that has no poles or zeros in U_α. In $U_\alpha \cap U_\beta$, ϕ_α/ϕ_β has no poles or zeros. The elements Ψ of Σ such that $\Psi\phi_\alpha$ is contained in $O(U_\alpha) = \Gamma(U_\alpha, O_x)$ form a $O(U_\alpha)$-module of $M(U_\alpha)$. If $U \subseteq U_\alpha$, the $M(U)$ can be defined in the same way together with a natural homomorphism (see 51).

The modules $M(U_\alpha)$, and homomorphisms h_{UU_α} form a pre-sheaf. The sheaf obtained from it is coherent: it is denoted by F_D. Any section Ψ of F_D is an element Ψ of Σ. In the open set U_α, Ψ defines a local divisor E_α such that $F_\alpha = E_\alpha + D_\alpha$ is a positive divisor. Globally, divisors E, F of X exist such that $E = F - D$ is the divisor of the function Ψ. Hence E is rationally equivalent to zero and F is a positive divisor rationally equivalent to D. It may readily be shown that $F_D = F_D'$, in which D' is any divisor equivalent to D. Hence F_D only depends on the divisor class of D. It can be shown also that the system of all positive divisors equivalent to D is identical with the system of divisors defined by sections of F_D (see 52). $H^0(X, F_D)$ is a vector space (over k) of finite dimension whose one-dimensional vector subspaces correspond to positive divisors equivalent to D.

Thus a situation exists in which a certain class of coherent modules correspond to elements of $A(X)$. By itself, this is not very informative: what is needed is a defined homomorphism $K(X) \to A(X) \times Q$. There are two ways of special importance for establishing such a homomorphism.

Mappings using Chern classes

A. Extending an idea (the Chern classes, denoted ch, after Shiing-Shen Chern, a Chinese-born U.S. mathematician) borrowed from differential geometry, there can be defined a mapping (see 53). In a sense it generalizes the mapping of F_D to the divisor class of D given above. For F_D, ch F_D is the element of $A(X) \times Q$ defined by a sum (see 54) involving D^i, in which D^i is the equivalence class defined by the product of i divisor classes equivalent to D. The mapping ch F of any coherent sheaf is then constructed by a geometrical argument from the mappings ch F_D.

(53) $\quad ch: K(X) \to A(X) \times Q$

(54) $\quad 1 + D + \dfrac{1}{2!}D^2 + \cdots + \dfrac{1}{r!}D^r + \cdots$

(55) $\quad (\theta, \phi)(X, O_X) \to (Y, O_Y)$

(56) $\quad \begin{cases} K(X) \xrightarrow{ch} A(X) \times Q \\ \phi_! \uparrow \qquad \uparrow \phi^* \\ K(Y) \xrightarrow{ch} A(Y) \times Q \end{cases}$

(57) $\quad gr: K(X) \to A(X) \times Q$

(58) $\quad \begin{cases} (\theta, \phi): (X, O_X) \to (Y, O_Y) \text{ defines} \\ \phi_!: K(X) \to K(Y), \text{ and } \phi_*: A(X) \times Q \to A(Y) \times Q \end{cases}$

(59) $\quad \begin{cases} K(X) \xrightarrow{gr} A(X) \times Q \\ \phi! \downarrow \qquad \downarrow \phi_* \\ K(Y) \xrightarrow{gr} A(Y) \times Q \end{cases}$

(60) $\quad \phi_! F = H^0(X, F) - H^1(X, F) + H^2(X, F) - \cdots$

(61) $\quad \phi_! F = \chi(F) = \dim H^0(X, F) - \\ \qquad - \dim H^1(X, F) + \dim H^2(X, F) - \cdots$

(62) $\quad \begin{cases} 0 \to F_{-Q} \to F_D \to A_P \to 0 \\ 0 \to F_{-Q} \to O_X \to A_Q \to 0 \end{cases}$

(63) $\quad \begin{cases} \chi(F_D) = \chi(F_{-Q}) + \chi(A_P) \\ \qquad = \chi(O_x) + N \end{cases}$

(64) $\quad \begin{cases} \chi(F_D) = \dim H^0(X, F_D) - \dim H^1(X, F_D) \\ \dim H^0(X, F_D) = d \end{cases}$

(65) $\quad H^1(X, F_D) = \dim H^0(X, F_{K-D})$

(66) $\quad d = N - g + 1 + i_D$

If (θ, ϕ) denotes a regular mapping $X \to Y$ (see 55), then the mappings necessary for a specific diagram (see 56) have all been defined. A fundamental property of the homomorphism ch is that this is a commutative diagram of homomorphisms.

B. A second homomorphism (denoted gr for Grothendieck) can be defined (see 57). Corresponding to a morphism, other homomorphisms (see 58) also have been defined. Grothendieck's form of the Riemann–Roch theorem states that a certain diagram (see 59) is commutative.

All the usual forms of the Riemann–Roch theorem can be deduced from Grothendieck's formula by taking Y to be a single point: $(Y, O_y) = (P, k)$. A coherent sheaf over P is just a finite-dimensional vector space, over k, and if F is any coherent sheaf, $\phi_! F$ is then given (see 60). $A(P)$ is the group mP (m an integer) and $A(P)$ is thus

isomorphic with the additive group of integers Z. Identifying $A(P)$ with Z, a final statement can be expressed (see 61).

Consideration may be given to the case in which X is an irreducible complete curve. Any divisor D is given by $D = P - Q$, in which P and Q are positive divisors. The construction of F_{-Q}, F_D and $F_0 = O_x$ can be effected and exact sequences established (see 62) that involve A_P. Here A_P is a sheaf of which the stalk is zero except in the points of P in which it is a vector space the dimension of which is the multiplicity of the point. $\chi(A_P) = \text{ord } P$ (the number of points of P each counted with the proper multiplicity). $\chi(A_Q)$ is similarly defined. Since $\phi_!$ is a homomorphism of $K(X) \to K(P)$, a conclusion can be drawn (see 63) that involves N, in which N is the order of D; $\chi(O_x)$ is a numerical character of X, equal to $1 - g$, in which $g = \dim H^1(X, O_x)$ is the genus of X. It is possible to express (see 64) the dimension of the vector space representing the positive divisors equivalent to D; $\dim H^1(X, F_D)$ is equal to i_D, the index of speciality of D, and has the following interpretation. There is, on X, a well-defined equivalence class of divisors K, which can be defined in terms of the Chern classes of the tangent bundle of X. An equality can also be used (see 65). The combination of these results leads to a final result for d (see 66).

The same process can be applied to calculate $\chi(F_D)$ for the sheaf corresponding to any divisor class D on an irreducible variety X of dimension p in terms of characters of D, D^2, $\cdots$, D^p. The term $\dim H^0(X, F_D)$ of $\chi(D)$ gives the dimension of the linear system of positive divisors equivalent to D. The other terms $\dim H^p(X, F_D)$ are invariants of this system, which can be given interpretations in terms of classical algebraic geometry.

BIBLIOGRAPHY. BARTEL L. VAN DER WAERDEN, *Einführung in die algebraische Geometrie* (1939), contains a fuller introductory account of the geometry of varieties in projective space. The birational geometry of algebraic varieties over the field of complex numbers is dealt with in many works by Italian geometers. OSCAR ZARISKI, *Algebraic Surfaces* (1935), contains a comprehensive account of this, with a full bibliography. The notion of an abstract variety is due to ANDRE WEIL, *Foundations of Algebraic Geometry*, rev. ed. (1962); SERGE LANG, *Introduction to Algebraic Geometry* (1958), contains an elementary account. For the theory of sheaves, see ROGER GODEMONT, *Topologie algébrique et théorie des faisceaux* (1958). For information about schema, see ALEXANDRE GROTHENDIECK, *Eléments de géométrie algébrique*, 4 pt. (1960–66).

(Ed.)

Geometry, Analytic and Trigonometric

Geometry is the branch of mathematics originally thought to be concerned solely with the properties of space and objects—points, lines, angles, planes, surfaces, and solids—in space. After the work of the modern German mathematician David Hilbert, at the turn of the 20th century, the foundations of geometry were generalized and the classical concepts of space and objects in space, which derived from intuition, were replaced with abstract ideas. A step toward the generalization of classical geometry was taken when the branch of geometry known as analytical geometry was created and first used in 1637 by an outstanding French mathematician and philosopher, René Descartes. Descartes applied algebra to geometry not just in the use of algebra to manipulate the dimensions of geometric figures but also in the representation of a point by a pair of numbers and the representation of lines and curves by equations. It was a powerful general method of solving certain geometric problems and one that could be applied to certain types of curves more readily than the geometry of the Greeks that was based on axioms.

The basis of analytic geometry is the idea that a point in space can be specified by numbers giving its position. The notion that any point, for example, can be indicated by its latitude, longitude, and height above the Earth goes back to Archimedes of Syracuse and to Apollonius of Perga, who lived in the 3rd century BC. It was Descartes and another 17th-century Frenchman, Pierre de Fermat, however, who developed that notion systematically. The idea of using negative distances is due to Sir Isaac Newton in 17th-century England and the German mathematician and philosopher Gottfried Wilhelm Leibniz, in the 18th century.

An outline of the present article is as follows.

PLANE ANALYTIC GEOMETRY

Cartesian coordinates. In two dimensions the position of a point in a plane can be specified by its distance from two intersecting lines, called axes. For instance, in Figure 1 two lines at right angles to each other intersect at the point O, called the origin. One axis is the line OX, the other OY, and any point in the plane can be denoted by two numbers giving its perpendicular distances from OY and from OX.

Definition of a point in two dimensions

A general point (x, y) can be reached by travelling a distance x along OX and then a distance y along a line parallel to OY. OX is called the x-axis, OY the y-axis, and the point is said to have coordinates (x, y). In the coordinate system shown, as is indicated in the diagram, the x-coordinate is positive for points to the right of the y-axis and negative for points to the left of this axis. The y-coordinate is positive for points above the x-axis and negative for points below it. The coordinates of the origin are $(0, 0)$. All of these coordinates are called Cartesian coordinates (which are named after Descartes). If oblique axes are used, the position of a point is defined in the same way: by its distance along lines parallel to the x and y axes.

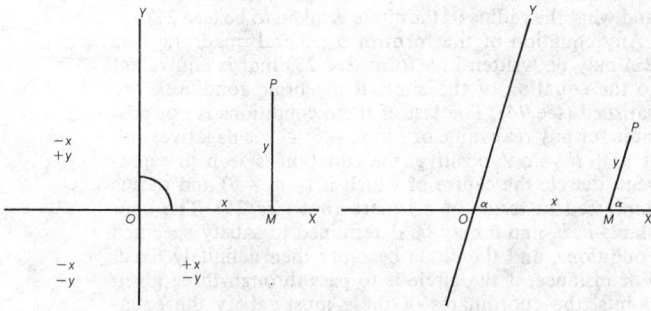

Figure 1: Cartesian coordinates, rectangular (left) and oblique (right). (See text.)

Straight lines. In a coordinate system a line can be represented by an equation. For example, all the points $(0, y)$ lie on the y-axis and have an x-coordinate that is zero. Thus the y-axis has the equation $x = 0$. Similarly, the x-axis has the equation $y = 0$. If any other line is taken through the origin, the ratio of x to y is always constant and may be expressed by the equation $y = mx$, m being a constant, or the ratio of x to y may also be expressed by an arbitrary linear combination that is restricted to equal 0 and that contains two coefficients (see Box, equation 1).

Any line can be represented by an equation obtained in

the following way. A point (x_1, y_1) is taken in the line and a new pair of axes drawn parallel to the original pair and with (x_1, y_1) as origin. If the coordinates with respect to these axes are (x', y'), the equation of the line must be of the form already given but this time containing the new variables in place of the old (see 2). Because $x' = x - x_1$ and $y' = y - y_1$, the equation of the line, in terms of the original coordinates, is a general linear expression set equal to 0 and including a constant term (see 3) in which c is a constant.

Thus every straight line has an equation of this form and every equation of this form represents a straight line. Such equations, in which the powers of x and y are unity (or one), are called linear equations.

$$(1) \quad ay + bx = 0$$

$$(2) \quad ax' + by' = 0$$

$$(3) \quad a(x - x_1) + b(y - y_1) = 0, \quad \text{or} \quad ax + by + c = 0$$

$$(4) \quad \begin{cases} ax + by + c = 0 \\ y = -\dfrac{ax}{b} - \dfrac{c}{b} \end{cases}$$

$$(5) \quad y = mx + d$$

$$(6) \quad \frac{x}{x_0} + \frac{y}{y_0} = 1$$

$$(7) \quad \frac{y - y_1}{y_2 - y_1} = \frac{x - x_1}{x_2 - x_1}$$

$$(8) \quad \begin{vmatrix} x & y & 1 \\ x_1 & y_1 & 1 \\ x_2 & y_2 & 1 \end{vmatrix} = 0$$

$$(9) \quad \begin{vmatrix} x_1 & y_1 & 1 \\ x_2 & y_2 & 1 \\ x_3 & y_3 & 1 \end{vmatrix} = 0$$

The equation with linear and constant terms a, b, c (see 4) rearranges to an expression (see 5) with y on the left and a form including slope m as coefficient of x and including y-intercept d. When Cartesian coordinates are used, m is the slope of the line and d is the intercept on the y-axis, because it is the point on the y-axis intercepted by the line. This form of the equation is particularly convenient. For instance, the line $y = x$ goes through the origin ($d = 0$) and has a gradient of 1 (see Figure 2). The line $y = -1x + 4$ intercepts the y-axis at $y = 4$ and has a gradient of -1; that is, it slopes in the opposite direction to $y = x$. If two lines have the same value of m, they are parallel; thus $y = 3x + 4$ is parallel to $y = 3x + 7$. A line with a gradient m is perpendicular to a line with a gradient $-1/m$. Thus $y = 3x + 4$ is perpendicular to $-3y = x + 6$.

Another form of the equation for a straight line is the intercept form in which the sum of the ratio of the variables to x_0 and y_0 is restricted to equal 1 (see 6). In this case, x_0 and y_0 are the intercepts on the x and y axes, respectively.

A straight line going through two points (x_1, y_1) and (x_2, y_2) has an equation that is given by a ratio of differences (see 7).

This equation is often stated in the form of a determinant, which is restricted to equal 0 (see 8). The condition for three points (x_1, y_1), (x_2, y_2), and (x_3, y_3) to be on the same line is also expressible in terms of a determinant (see 9).

Intersection of two lines. The point of intersection of two lines is found by solving their equations simultaneously. For instance, the lines with equations of specific type (see 10) may be found to meet at the point $(-2, 1)$.

Parametric equations. In some cases parametric equations are used to express a line; *i.e.*, equations giving x and y in terms of a single variable (parameter) t. For example, any line through the point (x_1, y_1) can be described by parametric equations with parameters l and n (see 11) in which l and n depend on the direction of the line. Sometimes the single parameter t is replaced by two parameters t_1 and t_2, which are related by an auxiliary equation. For example, the general point (x, y) on a line through (x_1, y_1) and (x_2, y_2) has equations that are supplemented by the condition that the sum of the two parameters should equal one (see 12).

Distances. When Cartesian coordinates are used, the distances between points can easily be found using Pythagoras' theorem. A point (x, y) at a distance from the origin $(0, 0)$ is expressed in terms of a square root (see 13). The distance between two points (x_1, y_1) and (x_2, y_2) is expressed in terms of a square root of squares of differences (see 14).

The distance from a point (x_1, y_1) to a line $ax + by + c = 0$ can also be found. The line along which the dis-

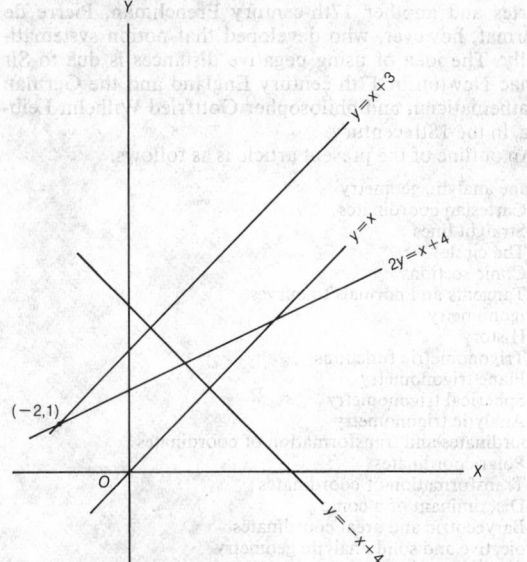

Figure 2: Straight lines (see text).

(10) $y = x + 3$ and $2y = x + 4$

(11) $x = x_1 + lt$ and $y = y_1 + nt$

(12) $x = t_1 x_1 + t_2 x_2$, $y = t_1 y_1 + t_2 y_2$,   and $t_1 + t_2 = 1$

(13) $\sqrt{(x^2 + y^2)}$

(14) $\sqrt{(x_1 - x_2)^2 + (y_1 - y_2)^2}$

(15) $\dfrac{ax_1 + by_1 + c}{\sqrt{a^2 + b^2}}$

(16) $\begin{cases} a_1 x + b_1 y + c_1 = 0 \\ a_1 x + b_1 y + c_2 = 0 \end{cases}$

(17) $\dfrac{c_1 - c_2}{\sqrt{a_1^2 + b_1^2}}$

(18) $x^2 + y^2 = r^2$

(19) $(x - h)^2 + (y - k)^2 = r^2$

(20) $x^2 + y^2 - 6x - 4y - 3 = 0$

(21) $(x - 3)^2 + (y - 2)^2 = 4^2$

(22) $x^2 + y^2 + 2ax + 2by + c = 0$

(23) $(x + a)^2 + (y + b)^2 = a^2 + b^2 - c$

(24) $h = -a$, $k = -b$,   and $r^2 = a^2 + b^2 - c$

(25) $\sqrt{(a^2 + b^2 - c)}$

(26) $x^2 + y^2 + 2ax + 2by + c = 0$

(27) $x^2 + y^2 + 2a'x + 2b'y + c' = 0$

(28) $\begin{cases} x^2 + y^2 + 2ax + 2by + c = x^2 + y^2 + 2a'x + 2b'y + c' \\ i.e.,\ 2(a - a')x + 2(b - b')y + (c - c') = 0 \end{cases}$

(29) $x^2 + y^2 + 2kx + c = 0$

tance is measured intersects $ax + by + c = 0$ at right angles, and thus its gradient is known. This, and the fact that it passes through (x_1, y_1), leads to its equation. Thus the point of intersection of this perpendicular with the original line can be found, and the distance follows (see 15). Similarly, the distance between two parallel lines (see 16) can be shown to be calculable (see 17).

The circle. A circle is a curve consisting of all those points of a plane that lie at a fixed distance from a particular point in the plane, this point being the centre. When rectangular axes are used, a point (x, y) is at a distance $(x^2 + y^2)$ from the origin, by Pythagoras' theorem. The distance between two points (x_1, y_1) and (x_2, y_2) is the square root of $(x_1 - x_2)^2 + (y_1 - y_2)^2$. If r is the radius of the circle, and it has its centre at the origin of a Cartesian coordinate system, then points on the circle have coordinates (x, y) given by the equation that again is a restricted sum of squares (see 18).

More generally, if the centre of the circle is (h, k), the equation is one that involves a sum of squares in which h and k are subtracted from the variables (see 19). For example, the equation of quadratic form with specific values of the coefficients (see 20) represents a circle of radius 4 and centre $(3, 2)$, because it can be put in the form that makes clear where the centre of the circle is and what the radius of the circle is taken to be (see 21).

Any equation of the form of a general quadratic (see 22) may be written in a form (see 23) that is equivalent to the equation of the circle if algebraic conditions are satisfied (see 24). The last of these conditions is not possible for any real value of r if $a^2 + b^2 - c$ is negative; but, if $a^2 + b^2 - c$ is positive, the equation is seen to represent a circle the centre of which is $(-a, -b)$ and radius expressed in terms of a square root (see 25). The constants a, b, and c may be determined to satisfy specified conditions, and the circle becomes then definitely fixed. For instance, if the circle is to pass through three given points, the coordinates of these must satisfy the equation, and, on substituting them for x and y, three equations are obtained giving a, b, and c.

A point (x, y) from which the tangent to the first circle expressed with parameters a, b, c (see 26) is equal to the tangent to another circle expressed with parameters that are primed (see 27) satisfies the equation that identifies two quadratic forms (see 28). This equation, if the circles have not the same centre, is of the first degree, so that the point (x, y) lies on a fixed straight line, called the radical axis of the circles. If the circles have two points in common, the radical axis is the line joining these points. The equation of a circular form and with parameter c (see 29) represents, for different values of c, different circles of which any two have the y-axis as their radical axis. These circles are said to form a coaxial system. If c is

Circles of a coaxial system

negative, all the circles pass through the same two points on the y-axis. If c is positive, none of the circles intersect. In either case one circle of the system may be found to pass through any given point that is not on the y-axis.

The equation of the tangent at a point (x_1, y_1) on a circle may be shown to be calculated from the condition that the tangent at that point has a specific slope and point of contact (see 30). If, however, (x_1, y_1) is not on but outside the circle, the equation represents the polar of (x_1, y_1); that is, the straight line joining the points of contact of tangents from (x_1, y_1).

Conic sections.   A circle is a special case of a group of curves known as conic sections, or conics. They were first studied in the 4th century BC by Menaechmus of Greece, who described them as curves obtained by the intersection of a right circular cone and a plane, hence their name. According to the angle of intersection the conic is a parabola, ellipse, circle, or hyperbola. This construction is shown in Figure 3, for a double right-circular cone. A cone can be generated by fixing a central point on a straight line segment and moving the end of the line segment around a circle. Each half of the cone thus generated is called a nappe.

An ellipse results from a section that completely cuts one nappe. A circle is a special case of an ellipse produced by a section perpendicular to the axis. A parabola is produced by a cutting plane parallel to a generating line. A section parallel to the axis cuts both nappes and produces a hyperbola.

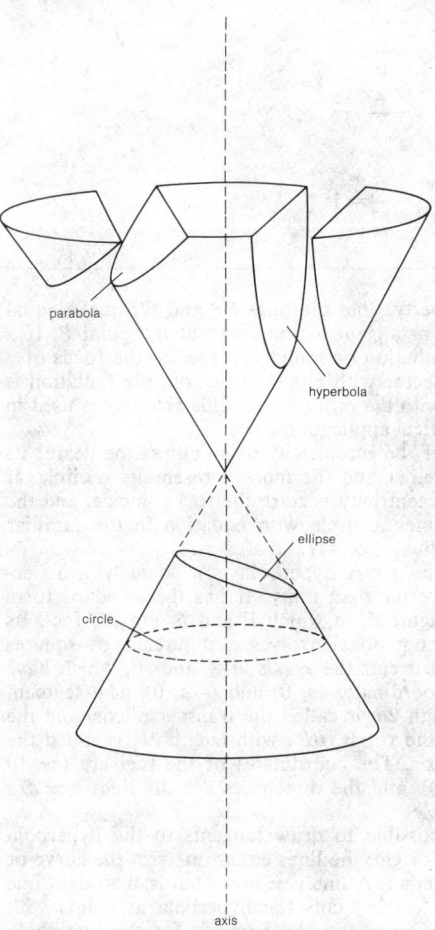

Figure 3: Conic sections (see text).

The work of the Greek mathematicians on conic sections

Menaechmus, a pupil of both the philosopher Plato and the scientist Eudoxus of Cnidus, was led to the study of conics by his efforts to solve the problem of constructing a cube twice as large by volume as a given cube, the so-called Delian problem.

The 4th-century-BC geometer Euclid wrote four books on conic sections, but his work is completely lost. Archimedes succeeded in finding the area of the ellipse and of

$$(30) \quad x_1 x + y_1 y + a(x + x_1) + b(y + y_1) + c = 0$$

$$(31) \quad ax + by + c = 0$$

$$(32) \quad \sqrt{(x_1 - p)^2 + (y_1 - q)^2}$$

$$(33) \quad \frac{ax_1 + by_1 + c}{\sqrt{a^2 + b^2}}$$

$$(34) \quad \sqrt{(x_1 - p)^2 + (y_1 - q)^2} = \frac{e(ax_1 + by_1 + c)}{\sqrt{a^2 + b^2}}$$

$$(35) \quad (a^2 + b^2)\{(x_1 - p)^2 + (y_1 - q)^2\} = e^2(ax_1 + by_1 + c)^2$$

$$(36) \quad Ax^2 + Bx^2 y + Cxy^2 + Dx + Ey + F = 0$$

$$(37) \quad \frac{x^2}{a^2} + \frac{y^2}{b^2} = 1$$

a sector of the parabola by a method closely akin to that of integral calculus, although calculus was not developed until the 17th century.

The pinnacle of Greek geometry, and perhaps of Greek mathematics in general, was reached by Apollonius of Perga in his eight books on conic sections, only the first seven of which have survived, but they contain the elementary theory of conics in a complete form. Apollonius was the first to show that all conics are sections of any circular cone, right or oblique. In studying these curves Apollonius treated them as plane curves, however, without regard to their spatial origin. The terms ellipse, hyperbola, and parabola were introduced by Apollonius.

Succeeding generations of Greek mathematicians added but little to the admirable treatise of the "Great Geometer," as Apollonius was called. An important contribution by Pappus of Alexandria in the 4th century AD, however, should be mentioned. He showed that the ratio of the distances of any point on any conic from a fixed point (the focus) and a fixed line (the directrix) is a constant. The constant ratio is called the eccentricity and is denoted by e. This is the definition used here to obtain the equation of a conic in Cartesian coordinates. The general equation of a straight line (see 31) is taken for the directrix and a fixed point (p, q) is taken for the focus. If x_1, y_1 is a point on the conic, its distance from the focus is easily obtained. It is obtained as a square root of squares of differences between the parameters involved (see 32). The perpendicular distance from (x_1, y_1) to the directrix can also be obtained (see 33). Thus, because x_1, y_1 is on a conic a condition holds that involves e (see 34), e being the eccentricity. Thus the operations of cross-multiplication and squaring are used (see 35). If the x_1 and y_1 are replaced by x and y, this gives a general equation for all points on a conic. It can be rearranged to an equation of the form of a quadratic (see 36) in which $A, B, C, D, E,$ and F are constants for a particular conic and depend on the eccentricity and the position of the focus and directrix. This general equation of a conic shows that a conic is completely determined if five points on it are known. It gives equations for an ellipse, parabola, or hyperbola depending on whether e is less than, equal to, or exceeds unity.

The ellipse.   An ellipse is a conic with an eccentricity less than unity. It is convenient to choose the focus of the ellipse on the x-axis and the directrix perpendicular to this axis. If this is done the ellipse has its centre at the origin and an equation with a sum of squares restricted to equal one (see 37). This is the standard form of the ellipse and is shown in Figure 4. It cuts the x-axis at $(a, 0)$ and $(-a, 0)$, these being the vertices. It also cuts the y-axis at $(0, b)$ and $(0, -b)$. The line AA' of length $2a$ is called the major axis, and BB', with a length $2b$, is the minor axis. The area of an ellipse is πab (the Greek

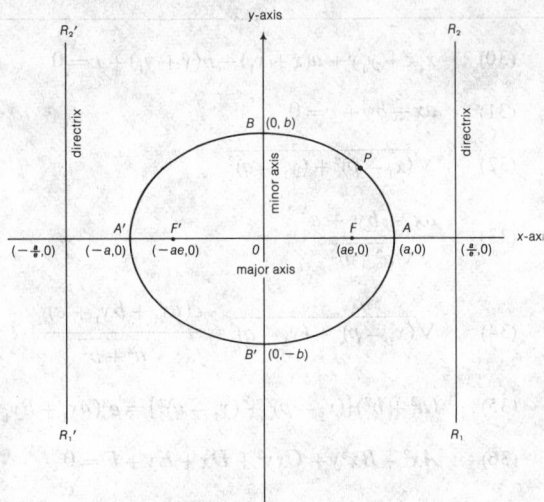

Figure 4: The standard form of the ellipse (see text).

letter pi, π, representing the ratio of the circumference to the diameter of the circle). The ellipse has in fact two foci, F and F', and two directrices, R_1R_2 and $R'_1R'_2$.

The foci are points $(ae, 0)$ and $(-ae, 0)$, and the directrices cut the x-axis at the points $(a/e, 0)$ and $(-a/e, 0)$. A circle of radius a with B as its centre cuts the x-axis at F and F'. As a consequence an algebraic expression relates e, a, and b (see 38).

If P, a point on the ellipse, has coordinates (x, y), its distance from the directrix R_1R_2 is $(a/e) - x$.

Thus from the definition the distance from the focus to the point P is determined (see 39) and the same can be calculated with respect to the focus F'. Thus the sum of these distances should add to twice the value of a (see 40). This leads to an alternative definition of the ellipse as the locus of a point that moves so that the sum of its distances from two fixed points is a constant. This property is the basis of a simple method of drawing an ellipse. Two pins are fixed at the foci and a loop of string placed over them. A pencil point is used to pull the string taut, forming a triangle, and the pencil is moved over the paper around the pins.

A circle around the ellipse with O as its centre and a radius a is called the major circle or auxiliary circle.

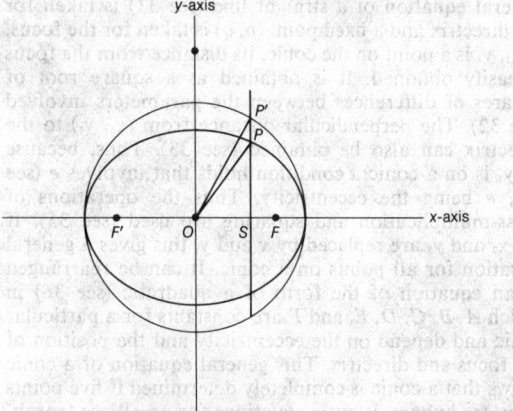

Figure 5: Ellipse and the major (or auxiliary) circle. The two foci of the ellipse are F and F'. A line that is drawn perpendicular to the x-axis at S cuts the ellipse and the circle at P and P', respectively.

Similarly, the circle with radius b and lying inside the ellipse is the minor circle. These two circles are called the eccentric circles of the ellipse.

If a line is drawn perpendicular to the x-axis from a point S, it cuts the ellipse at P and the major circle at P'. The angle SOP' is called the eccentric angle of the ellipse (Figure 5). The points P and P' are called corresponding points, and it can be shown that $P'S/PS = a/b$.

One useful property of an ellipse is known as the

$$(38) \quad ae = \sqrt{a^2 - b^2}, \quad \text{thus} \quad e^2 = 1 - \frac{b^2}{a^2}$$

$$(39) \quad \begin{cases} FP = e\left(\dfrac{a}{e} - x\right) = a - ex \\ FP' = a + ex \end{cases}$$

$$(40) \quad FP + FP' = 2a$$

$$(41) \quad x^2 + y^2 = a^2$$

$$(42) \quad \frac{x^2}{a^2} - \frac{y^2}{b^2} = 1$$

$$(43) \quad \frac{x^2}{a^2} - \frac{m^2 x^2}{b^2} = 1; \quad i.e., \quad x^2(b^2 - a^2m^2) = a^2b^2$$

$$(44) \quad x = \frac{\pm ab}{\sqrt{b^2 - a^2m^2}}$$

$$(45) \quad b^2 - a^2m^2 = 0$$

$$(46) \quad b^2 = a^2m^2 \quad \text{or} \quad m = \pm\frac{b}{a}$$

$$(47) \quad \begin{cases} y = \dfrac{b}{a}x \\ y = \dfrac{-b}{a}x \end{cases}$$

$$(48) \quad \frac{y^2}{b^2} - \frac{x^2}{a^2} = 1$$

optical property: that the lines FP and $F'P$ make equal angles with a tangent to the curve at the point P. If a source of radiation or sound is placed at the focus of a concave reflector with elliptical section, the radiation is converged onto the other focus. This property is used in certain practical applications.

The smaller the eccentricity of an ellipse the nearer its foci are together and the more it resembles a circle. If $b = a$ the eccentricity is zero, the foci coincide, and the ellipse becomes a circle with equation in the familiar form for radius a (see 41) and area πa^2.

The hyperbola. A hyperbola is a conic with an eccentricity greater than unity. It has the standard form shown in Figure 6, in which F and F' are the foci. Its equation is one that involves a difference of squares (see 42) and it cuts the x-axis at A and A', which have respective coordinates $(a, 0)$ and $(-a, 0)$. The segment AA', of length $2a$, is called the transverse axis, and the segment of the y-axis, BB', with length $2b$, is called the conjugate axis. The coordinates of the foci are $(ae, 0)$ and $(-ae, 0)$, and the directrices are the lines $x = a/e$ and $x = -a/e$.

It is not possible to draw tangents to the hyperbola through the origin; the lines either intersect the curve or miss it altogether. A line $y = mx$—that is, a straight line through the origin—cuts the hyperbola at points with x-coordinates given by the formula for the hyperbola with y replaced by mx (see 43, 44). These meeting points coincide for the value of m for which $y = mx$ is a tangent. This occurs when a simple algebraic condition is met (see 45) and x is infinity. Thus the tangent touches the curve at infinity and is called an asymptote. It has a value of m given by an algebraic solution showing two values (see 46). Thus there are two asymptotes with equations whose slopes differ by -1 (see 47).

The equation in which the roles of a and b are interchanged (see 48) is that of the conjugate hyperbola of the one above. Conjugate hyperbolas have the same asymptotes, and the conjugate axis of one is the transverse axis of the other and vice versa.

A hyperbola for which $b = a$ is called a *rectangular hyperbola* and has the equation in which the constant a^2 is equal to the difference of the variables squared (see 49). The transverse and conjugate axes are then equal, and the asymptotes have equations $y = x$ and $y = -x$. Clearly the asymptotes are perpendicular to each other and bisect the coordinate axes. If the asymptotes are used as the coordinate axes, a rectangular hyperbola has the simple equation $xy = c$, in which c is a constant. Thus the rectangular hyperbola is a graph of two inversely proportional variable quantities related by the equation $y = c/x$.

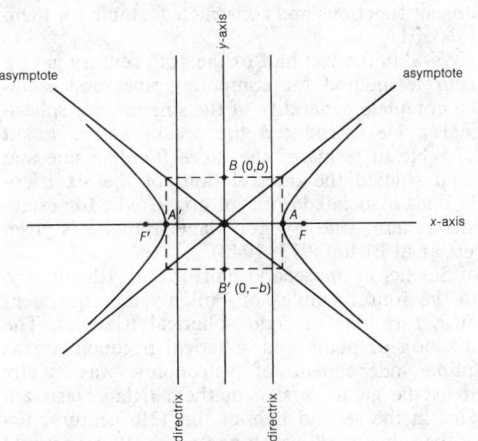

Figure 6: The hyperbola (see text).

The parabola. The parabola is a conic with an eccentricity of unity and may be thought of as a limiting case between an ellipse ($e < 1$) and a hyperbola ($e > 1$). It is the path of a point that moves in a plane so as to be equidistant from a fixed point and a fixed line. The standard form of a parabola has the equation $y^2 = 2px$ and is shown in Figure 7. The vertex is at the origin, the focus is a distance $p/2$ from the origin (its coordinates are ($p/2$, 0), and the directrix is parallel to the y-axis a distance $p/2$ on the other side of the origin (its equation is $x = -p/2$). The chord PP' through the focus perpendicular to the x-axis is called the *latus rectum* of the parabola (the *latera recta* of an ellipse and hyperbola are similarly defined).

Practical applications of the parabola

One important property of the parabola is that the angle made by a line FM from the focus to any point M with the tangent at M is equal to the angle between the tangent and a line from M parallel to the axis of symmetry. This is the basis of many practical applications because radiation or sound emitted from a source

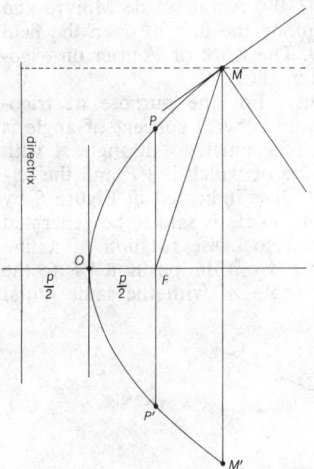

Figure 7: Parabola (see text).

(49)	$x^2 - y^2 = a^2$
(50)	$y = ax^2 + bx + c$
(51)	$\begin{cases} \dfrac{x^2}{a^2} + \dfrac{y^2}{b^2} = 1 \\ \dfrac{2x}{a^2} + \dfrac{2y}{b^2}\dfrac{dy}{dx} = 0 \end{cases}$
(52)	gradient at (x_1, y_1) is $\dfrac{-b^2 x_1}{a^2 y_1}$
(53)	$y - y_1 = m(x - x_1)$
(54)	$y - y_1 = \dfrac{-b^2 x_1}{a^2 y_1}(x - x_1)$
(55)	$\dfrac{y_1 y}{b^2} + \dfrac{x_1 x}{a^2} = \left(\dfrac{y_1^2}{b^2} + \dfrac{x_1^2}{a^2}\right)$
(56)	$\dfrac{y_1^2}{b^2} + \dfrac{x_1^2}{a^2} = 1$
(57)	$\dfrac{y y_1}{b^2} + \dfrac{x x_1}{a^2} = 1$
(58)	$\begin{cases} a^2 y_1 \\ b^2 x_1 \\ \dfrac{a^2 x}{x_1} - \dfrac{b^2 y}{y_1} = a^2 - b^2 \end{cases}$

at the focus of a reflector with a parabolic section is reflected in a parallel beam. Similarly, a parallel beam hitting the reflector is converged onto the focus. Thus parabolic reflectors are used in car headlights, searchlights, electric heaters, and many other devices.

The parabola may be thought of as an elongated ellipse with its centre and one focus and vertex all coinciding at infinity. Its optical property is thus a special case of that of an ellipse, namely the reflection of light emitted from one focus onto the other. The parabola is the trajectory of a projectile moving under the influence of gravity with no air resistance. The graph of a quadratic polynomial (see 50) is also a parabola.

Tangents and normals to curves. The equation of the tangents to a curve can be found at any point on the curve (x_1, y_1) by obtaining the gradient of the curve at that point. This is done by taking its derivative (see ANALYSIS, REAL) at the point. For example, an ellipse has an equation both sides of which can be differentiated (see 51). It follows that the gradient at the point (x_1, y_1) can be calculated (see 52) and this is the gradient m of the tangent, which, because it goes through (x_1, y_1), has an equation with m as parameter (see 53). Thus the equation of the tangent is determined (see 54). This rearranges to an equality between a linear expression and a sum of squares (see 55). Because (x_1, y_1) lies on the ellipse and involves the same sum of squares (see 56), the tangent has the equation that results by setting the linear term equal to a constant, namely the constant 1 (see 57). The normal on any point on a curve is the line perpendicular to the tangent at that point. At (x_1, y_1) it has a gradient that is easily determined, as is its equation (see 58). The tangents and normals to other curves are found in a similar way.

TRIGONOMETRY

Trigonometry is the branch of mathematics concerned with specific functions of angles and their application to calculations in geometry. For example, if a right-angled triangle contains an angle, symbolized here by the Greek letter alpha, α, the ratio of the side of the triangle opposite to α to the side opposite the right angle (the hypotenuse) is called the sine of α. The ratio of the side adjacent to α to the hypotenuse is the cosine of α. These functions are properties of the angle α, and calculated values have been tabulated for many angles. They are used in obtaining unknown angles and distances from known or measured angles in geometric figures. The subject developed from a need to compute angles and distances in such fields as astronomy, map making, surveying, and artillery range finding. Problems involving angles and distances in one plane are covered in plane trigonometry. Applications to similar problems in more than one plane of three-dimensional space are considered in spherical trigonometry.

History. Trigonometry among the early mathematicians was essentially a computational science based on geometrical theorems. What is now embodied in a formula earlier had to be described by words as a succession of computational steps, each justified by the citation of an appropriate geometrical theorem. The absence of negative numbers made necessary the discussion of many more cases in the solution of triangles. One or more steps in a solution was the passage from the length of an arc to the length of its chord (Greek) or the length of half the chord of the double arc (Hindu) or vice versa, a feat accomplished by means of a table. In the 12th century the Arabic word for the half chord of the double arc was confused with another word and translated "sinus" (sine). The difficulty of making tables with irrational entries (not expressible in ratios of integers) without decimals (first systematically introduced into arithmetic late in the 16th century) was met by selecting a circle so large that when the chords used were computed to the nearest integer the desired accuracy was attained. This unfortunately introduced into the discussions supporting the solutions the added complexity of proportionality between similar figures.

Trigonometry, uniting as it did aspects of the three disciplines of arithmetic, algebra, and geometry, progressed more slowly than did geometry. Astronomy, however, of great interest to the early Hindus and Arabs, required as a tool the solution of spherical triangles, a fact that drove them to master this art. It is, accordingly, not surprising that the development of spherical trigonometry preceded that of plane trigonometry. Not until about the 13th century did trigonometry divorce itself from astronomy and become an independent subject matter.

Early
Greek
trigo-
nometry

In the extant mathematical literature of the civilizations preceding the Greeks occur a few calculations suggestive of trigonometric calculations but no further evidence of the science. The early Greek writers appear to have advanced a step further by making calculations based on the proportionality of similar triangles. In the determination of a height by comparison of its shadow with the shadow of a known height can be seen the germ of the tangent function. Greek writers of the 4th century AD called Hipparchus, who lived in the 2nd century BC, the originator of the science of trigonometry. He was reputed to have calculated a table of chords in 12 books. To what extent he may have developed the uses of the table is unknown because the complete work is lost.

Menelaus, about the end of the 1st century, is also reputed to have produced a treatment of the trigonometry of chords in six books, but this work is also lost. An extant work contains the important theorem of Menelaus and the corresponding theorem for the sphere upon which later writers based their work on trigonometry.

The first extant work on trigonometry is contained in the *Almagest*, a work on astronomy in 13 books, produced by Ptolemy of Alexandria around the middle of the 2nd century. In one section is a table of chords at intervals of 30' (minutes), accurate to at least five places, and the method of computing the tables is explained. Another section is devoted to the solution of triangles,

particularly spherical. Theorems are verified concerning chords that involve implicitly the equivalence of the addition formulas, the half-angle formulas, and the law of sines.

No Hindu work is extant, but it is known that Hindu mathematicians made tables of sines, the half chord of the double arc, at intervals of $3° 45'$ using only the equivalent of $\sin^2 a + \cos^2 a = 1$; $\cos a = \sin (90 - a)$; and $1 - \cos 2a = 2 \sin^2 a$. These tables were used to solve right triangles, plane and spherical. This work was translated into Arabic about the last quarter of the 8th century.

In the late 9th century the Arab al-Battānī added the law of cosines for oblique spherical triangles and introduced the sine for the chord into the work of Ptolemy and also into his tables. He brought into use the tangent and cotangent functions and constructed a table for them at intervals of $1°$. Arab contributions

Abū al-Wafā' in the last half of the 10th century gave a more accurate method for computing sines and established the complete generality of the sine law for spherical triangles. He introduced the secant and cosecant (both definable in terms of the more familiar sine and cosine) and studied the interrelations of the six trigonometric lines associated with an arc. Credit for establishing the general sine law for plane triangles is given to the Persian al-Bīrūnī (973–1048).

Jabír of Seville, in the second half of the 11th century, added to the four formulas of Ptolemy the equivalent of the fifth formula for right spherical triangles. The systematization of plane and spherical trigonometry as a discipline independent of astronomy was finally achieved by the great Persian mathematician Nasir addin at-Tusi in the second half of the 13th century. Essentially, the same work was done for the Western world independently by the Prussian astronomer Johann Müller (1436–76), known as Regiomontanus, the notions of the Arabic world having filtered into Europe over several centuries, that via the East coming much later than that via Spain. The development of arithmetic and algebra allowed the successors of Regiomontanus in Europe to unify and simplify the trigonometry of the triangle by substituting the angle for arc and the ratio for the trigonometric line, and by abstracting from the cumbersome treatment of Regiomontanus the essential formulas convenient for calculations. The cosine law for plane triangles appears for the first time in the work of a 16th-century French mathematician, François Viète.

The invention of logarithms (or powers of a fixed number such that a desired numerical result is obtained as the power of the given fixed number or "base") by Napier stimulated the development of formulas suitable to their use. The law of tangents appears in the writings of Viète and the half-angle formulas in the works of an Austrian mathematician, Rhäticus, in 1568 and an English mathematician, William Oughtred, in 1657. Napier's formulas called "analogies" appeared in 1619, while the Gauss-Delambre and Mollweide relations (trigonometric in nature) came later, in 1807–09. Abraham de Moivre and Leonhard Euler were among the first to open the field of analytic trigonometry. The work of Fourier on trigonometric series appeared in 1807.

Trigonometric functions. For the purpose of trigonometry, a somewhat more general concept of angle is required than that used in geometry. An angle A with vertex at V, the initial side of which is VP and the terminal side of which is VQ, is indicated in Figure 8 by the solid circular arc. This angle is said to be generated by the continuous counterclockwise rotation of a line segment about the point V from the position VP to the position VQ. A second angle A' with the same initial

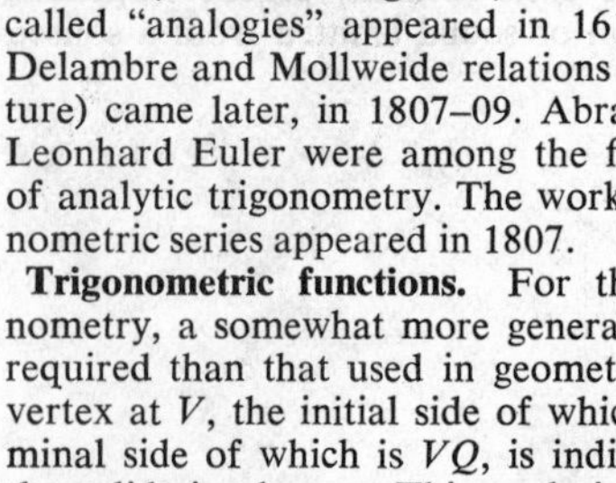

Figure 8: General angle (see text).

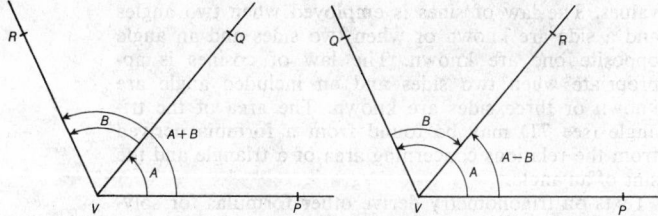

Figure 9: Addition of angles (see text).

Positive and negative angles

and terminal sides, indicated in Figure 8 by the broken circular arc, is generated by the clockwise rotation of the line segment about the point V from the position VP to the position VQ. Angles are considered positive when generated by counterclockwise rotations, negative when generated by clockwise rotations. The positive angle A and the negative angle A' in Figure 8 are generated by less than one complete rotation of the line segment about the point V. All other positive and negative angles with the same initial and terminal sides are obtained by rotating the line segment counterclockwise or clockwise, respectively, about the point V one or more complete turns before coming to rest at VQ.

Numerical values can be assigned to angles by selecting a unit of measure for angles. Besides the complete revolution and the right angle, the units commonly used are the degree and the radian. The degree is $1/90$ of a right angle. There are $60'$ (minutes) in a degree and $60''$ (seconds) in a minute. In theoretical work, the radian is the most convenient unit. It is the angle at the centre of a circle that intercepts an arc equal in length to the radius. From these definitions, it follows that 1 revolution $= 4$ right angles $= 360° = 2\pi$ radians.

Equal angles are angles with the same measure; *i.e.*, they have the same sign and the same number of degrees. Any angle $-A$ has the same number of degrees as A but is of opposite sign. Its measure, therefore, is the negative of the measure of A. If the angles A and B have the initial sides VP and VQ and the terminal sides VQ and VR, respectively, then the angle $A + B$ has the initial and terminal sides VP and VR, respectively (see Figure 9). The angle $A + B$ is called the sum of the angles A and B, and its relation to A and B when A is positive and B is positive or negative is illustrated in Figure 9. The sum $A + B$ is the angle the measure of which is the algebraic sum of the measures of A and B. The difference $A - B$ is the sum of A and $-B$. Thus all angles coterminal with angle A (*i.e.*, with the same initial and terminal sides as angle A) are given by $A \pm 360n$, in which $360n$ is an angle of n complete revolutions. The angles $(180 - A)$ and $(90 - A)$ are the supplement and complement of angle A, respectively.

Trigonometric functions of an angle. There are six functions of an angle commonly used in trigonometry. Their names and abbreviations are sine (sin), cosine (cos), tangent (tan), cotangent (cot), secant (sec), and cosecant (csc). To define these functions for any angle A, the angle is placed in position (Figure 10, left) on a rectangular coordinate system with the vertex of A at the origin and the initial side of A along the positive x-axis; r (positive) is the distance from V to any point Q on the terminal side of A, and (x, y) are the rectangular coordinates of Q. The six functions of A are then defined by six ratios (see 59). Because division by zero is not allowed, the tangent and secant are not defined for angles the terminal side of which falls on the y-axis, and the cotangent and cosecant are undefined for angles the terminal side of which falls on the x-axis. From these definitions follow three reciprocal relations for cotangent, secant, and cosecant (see 60) and the quotient identities for the tangent and cotangent (see 61). When the Pythagorean equality $x^2 + y^2 = r^2$ is divided in turn by r^2, x^2, and y^2, the three squared relations relating cosine and sine, tangent and secant, cotangent and cosecant (see 62) are obtained.

If the point Q on the terminal side of angle A in standard position has coordinates (x, y), this point will have coordinates $(x, -y)$ when on the terminal side of $-A$ in

$$(59) \quad \begin{cases} \sin A = y/r & \cot A = x/y \\ \cos A = x/r & \sec A = r/x \\ \tan A = y/x & \csc A = r/y \end{cases}$$

$$(60) \quad \begin{cases} \cot A = 1/\tan A & \sec A = 1/\cos A \\ \csc A = 1/\sin A \end{cases}$$

$$(61) \quad \tan A = \sin A/\cos A \qquad \cot A = \cos A/\sin A$$

$$(62) \quad \begin{cases} \cos^2 A + \sin^2 A = 1; & 1 + \tan^2 A = \sec^2 A \\ \cot^2 A + 1 = \csc^2 A \end{cases}$$

$$(63) \quad \begin{cases} \sin(-A) = -\sin A & \cot(-A) = -\cot A \\ \cos(-A) = \cos A & \sec(-A) = \sec A \\ \tan(-A) = -\tan A & \csc(-A) = -\csc A \end{cases}$$

$$(64) \quad \begin{cases} \sin(A \pm 90) = \pm\cos A & \cot(A \pm 90) = -\tan A \\ \cos(A \pm 90) = \mp\sin A & \sec(A \pm 90) = \mp\csc A \\ \tan(A \pm 90) = -\cot A & \csc(A \pm 90) = \pm\sec A \end{cases}$$

$$(65) \quad \begin{cases} \cos(A \pm B) = \cos A \cos B \mp \sin A \sin B \\ \sin(A \pm B) = \sin A \cos B \pm \cos A \sin B \end{cases}$$

$$(66) \quad \begin{cases} x = x' \cos B - y' \sin B \\ y = x' \sin B + y' \cos B \end{cases}$$

$$(67) \quad \begin{cases} \sin(2A) = 2 \sin A \cos A \\ \cos(2A) = \cos^2 A - \sin^2 A = 2 \cos^2 A - 1 \\ \qquad\qquad = 1 - 2 \sin^2 A \\ \sin^2(A/2) = (1 - \cos A)/2 \\ \cos^2(A/2) = (1 + \cos A)/2 \end{cases}$$

standard position. From this fact and the definitions are obtained further identities for negative angles (see 63). These relations may also be stated briefly by saying that cosine and secant are even functions, while the other four are odd functions.

It is evident that a trigonometric function has the same value for all coterminal angles. When n is an integer, therefore, $\sin(A \pm 360n) = \sin A$; there are similar relations for the other five functions. These results may be expressed by saying that the trigonometric functions are periodic and have a period of $360°$ or $180°$.

When Q on the terminal side of A in standard position has coordinates (x, y), it has coordinates $(-y, x)$ and $(y, -x)$ on the terminal side of $A + 90$ and $A - 90$ in standard position, respectively. Consequently six formulas follow (see 64). The formulas display the fact that a function of the complement of A is equal to the corresponding cofunction of A.

Of fundamental importance for the study of trigonometry are the addition formulas, or the functions of the sum or difference of two angles (see 65). These relations may be derived from formulas (see 66) for the rotation of the coordinate axes through the angle B about the origin, and these formulas are evident from Figure 10 (right), because $x = ON = OP + LM = OL \cos B + LQ \cos(B + 90)$, which is the relation already expressed (see 66). Similarly, $y = NQ = PL + MQ = OL \sin B + LQ \sin(B + 90)$, which is also an earlier expression (66). To obtain the addition formulas (65) it is only necessary to divide each equation in the given formulas (66) by $r = OQ$, and use the definitions of sine and cosine.

From the addition formulas are derived the double-angle and half-angle formulas (see 67). Numerous identities of lesser importance can be derived from the above basic identities.

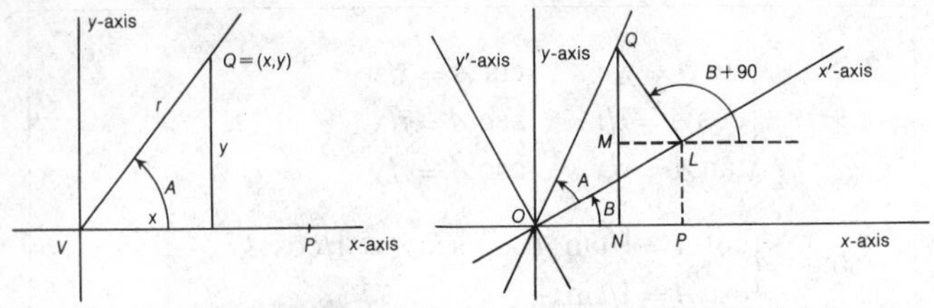

Figure 10: (Left) Angle in standard position. (Right) Rotation of axes (see text).

Tables of natural functions. To be of practical use, the values of the functions must be readily available for any given angle. The identities $\sin(A \pm 360n) = \sin A$ as well as other identities (see 64) show that the values of the functions for all angles can readily be found from the values for angles from 0° to 45°. For this reason, it is sufficient to list in a table the values of sine, cosine, tangent, and cotangent of all angles from 0° to 45° that are integral multiples of some convenient unit (commonly 1'). Such tables are called tables of natural trigonometric functions.

For angles that are not integral multiples of the unit, the values of the functions may be interpolated. Because the values of the functions are in general irrational numbers, they are entered in the table as decimals, rounded off at some convenient place. For most purposes, four or five decimal places are sufficient, and tables of this accuracy appear in most texts. Simple geometrical facts alone, however, suffice to determine the values of the trigonometric functions for the angles 0°, 30°, 45°, 60°, and 90°. These values are listed in a table, which also illustrates the arrangement used in larger tables (see 68). The names at the head of such a table are used for angles less than 45°, listed in the left-hand column; the names at the foot of the table are used for the complementary angles, larger than 45°, listed in the right-hand column. For example, from the table $\cos 30° = \frac{1}{2}\sqrt{3}$, and $\cot 60° = \frac{1}{3}\sqrt{3}$.

Plane trigonometry. In many applications of trigonometry the essential problem is the solution of triangles. If enough sides and angles are known, the remaining sides and angles as well as the area can be calculated, and the triangle is then said to be solved. Triangles can be solved by the law of sines and the law of cosines. To secure symmetry in the writing of these laws, the angles of the triangle are lettered A, B, and C and the lengths of the sides opposite the angles are lettered a, b, and c, respectively. An example of this standardization is shown in Figure 11.

The law of sines The law of sines or sine theorem is expressed as an equality involving three sine functions (see 69) while a law of cosines or cosine theorem is an identification of the cosine with an algebraic expression formed from the lengths of sides opposite the corresponding angle (see 70) with similar expressions for $\cos B$ and $\cos C$ obtained by cyclic permutation of the three letters. In Figure 11, $b \sin A = h = a \sin B$, from which the first equality follows (see 69). The second is shown by drawing a perpendicular from A to the opposite side of the triangle. Also $c = b \cos A + a \cos B$ and likewise $b = a \cos C + c \cos A$, $a = c \cos B + b \cos C$. When these three equations are multiplied by c, b, $-a$, respectively, and added, the result is $c^2 + b^2 - a^2 = 2bc \cos A$, which when divided by $2bc$ becomes an expression for $\cos A$ (see 70). To solve a triangle, all the known values are substituted into equations expressing the laws of sines and cosines (see 69, 70) and the equations are solved for the unknown

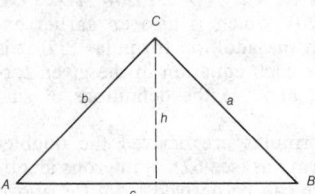

Figure 11: Standard lettering of a triangle (see text).

values. The law of sines is employed when two angles and a side are known or when two sides and an angle opposite one are known. The law of cosines is appropriate when two sides and an included angle are known or three sides are known. The area of the triangle (see 71) may be found from a formula derived from the relations concerning area of a triangle and the sine of an angle.

Texts on trigonometry derive other formulas for solving triangles and for checking the solution, especially those suited to logarithmic calculation. With the advent of calculators and electronic computers, however, computation by logarithms has lost some of its advantage, and it is no longer so necessary to adapt formulas to logarithmic computation when machines are available.

Functions of 0°, 30°, 45°, 60° and 90°

	sin	cos	tan	cot	
0	0	1	0	—	90
30	$\frac{1}{2}$	$\frac{1}{2}\sqrt{3}$	$\frac{1}{3}\sqrt{3}$	$\sqrt{3}$	60
45	$\frac{1}{2}\sqrt{2}$	$\frac{1}{2}\sqrt{2}$	1	1	45
	cos	sin	cot	tan	

(68)

(69) $$\frac{a}{\sin A} = \frac{b}{\sin B} = \frac{c}{\sin C}$$

(70) $$\cos A = \frac{b^2 + c^2 - a^2}{2bc}$$

(71) $$\text{area} = \tfrac{1}{2}bc \sin A$$

(72) $$\frac{\sin \alpha}{\sin A} = \frac{\sin \beta}{\sin B} = \frac{\sin \gamma}{\sin C}$$

(73) $$\cos \alpha = \cos \beta \cos \gamma + \sin \beta \sin \gamma \cos A$$

Spherical trigonometry. The fundamental configuration of space to which the formulas of spherical trigonometry apply is the trihedral angle formed by three rays—half lines—radiating from a point. The point is the vertex, the rays are the three edges, the planes and angles determined by the rays taken in pairs are the three faces, and the three face angles, symbolized by the Greek letters alpha, beta, and gamma, α, β, and γ, of the trihedral angle. The faces in pairs form three dihedral angles A, B, and C opposite, respectively, to the face angles. The formulas of spherical trigonometry relate the trigonometric functions of these six angles.

For the trihedral angle, there is the law of sines (see 72) that may be derived from Figure 12 (left) in which the planes PQS and PRS are perpendicular to the edges VQ and VR, respectively. The first equality is a result of the relations $\overline{PS} = \overline{QP} \sin B = \overline{VP} \sin \alpha \sin B = RP \sin A = VP \sin \beta \sin A$. The second equality may be verified in like manner.

The first law of cosines There is a first law of cosines for the trihedral (see 73) with similar expressions for $\cos \beta$ and $\cos \gamma$ obtained by cyclic permutation of the letters. In Figure 12 (right), the plane PQR is perpendicular to the edge VP. The law of cosines applied to the plane triangles PQR and VQR gives $\overline{QR^2} = \overline{PQ^2} + \overline{PR^2} - 2\,\overline{PQ}\,\overline{PR} \cos A = \overline{VQ^2} + \overline{VR^2} - 2\,\overline{VQ}\,\overline{VR} \cos \alpha$. After transposing and using the Pythagorean theorem, $2\,\overline{VQ}\,\overline{VR} \cos \alpha = 2\,\overline{VP^2} + 2\,\overline{PQ}\,\overline{PR} \cos A$. When this relationship is divided by the value $(VQ)(VR)$, it becomes the first law of cosines for the trihedral (see 73) equation using the definitions of the trigonometric functions.

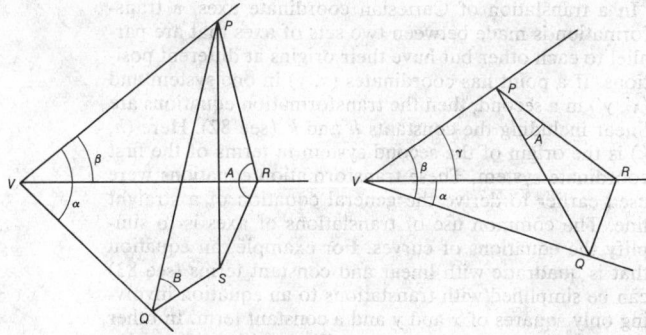

Figure 12: Trihedral angles for derivation of the laws of (left) sines and (right) cosines.

If at the vertex of a trihedral three rays are drawn perpendicular to the three inner faces of the trihedral, a second trihedral is obtained called the polar trihedral of the first. The first is also the polar of the second. The face angles α', β', and γ' of the polar trihedral are the supplements of the dihedral angles A, B, and C of the given trihedral, and hence the face angles α, β, and γ of the given trihedral are the supplements of the dihedral angles A', B', and C' of the polar trihedral.

The first law of cosines when applied to the polar trihedral and then simplified by the relations $\cos \alpha' = \cos (180 - A) = -\cos A$, and so on, yields the second law of cosines for the given trihedral (see 74) and two additional relations for $\cos B$ and $\cos C$, obtained by cyclic permutation of the letters.

When the vertices of a spherical triangle are joined to the centre of the sphere, there is formed a trihedral angle with vertex at the centre (Figure 13). The sides a, b, and c of the spherical triangle are the great circle arcs intercepted by the face angles α, β, and γ, and the angles

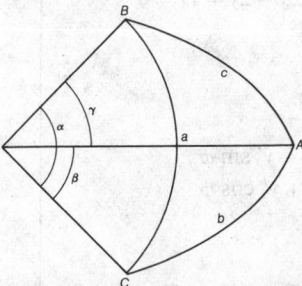

Figure 13: Spherical triangle and trihedral angle.

of the spherical triangle are the dihedral angles A, B, and C of the trihedral. The faces of the polar trihedral intersect the sphere in the polar triangle of the given spherical triangle. Because a trigonometric function of a central angle and of the intercepted arc have the same value, the law of sines (see 72) yields a law of sines for spherical triangles expressed in ratios of sine functions (see 75). Similarly, the first law of cosines (see 73) gives a law of cosines for the sides of the spherical triangle (see 76), and the second law of cosines (see 74) furnishes a law of cosines for the angles of a spherical triangle (see 77).

Solving the spherical triangle

To solve a spherical triangle, the known values are substituted in formulas, the laws of sines and cosines for the spherical triangle (see 75, 76, 77), and the resulting equations are solved for the unknowns. When three sides or two sides and the included angle are given, the law of cosines for the sides (see 76) is appropriate, and the law of cosines for the angles (see 77) is used when three angles or two angles and an included side are given. If two sides and an angle opposite one side or two angles and a side opposite one angle are given, the law of sines (see 75) is applied first, and the solution is completed by the use of a pair of equations (see 76, 77).

The area of the spherical triangle is given by the product of E and the square of r (see 78) in which r is the radius of the sphere, and E is the excess of $A + B + C$ over two

right angles measured in radians. It should also be noted that a solution of a spherical triangle yields a solution of the polar triangle.

Other relations between the sides and angles of a spherical triangle are derived in texts on spherical trigonometry. In particular, John Napier's analogies are formulas relating the half angles and half sides. Each formula contains five of the six parts and is well suited to logarithmic solutions of a spherical triangle. Other formulas of a similar character include the half-angle formulas, the half-side formulas, and the so-called analogies of Gauss-Delambre.

When angle C is 90°, the triangle is a right spherical triangle. Because $\sin C = 1$ and $\cos C = 0$, the relations in the spherical triangle (see 75, 76, 77) yield formulas (see 79) for the right spherical triangle.

Analytic trigonometry. Trigonometric functions of a real variable x are defined by means of the trigonometric functions of an angle. For example, $\sin x$ in which x is real is defined to have the value of the sine of the angle containing x radians. Similar definitions are made for the other five trigonometric functions of the real variable x. These functions satisfy the previously noted trigonometric relations (see 60–65 and 67) with A, B, 90, and 360 replaced by x, y, $\pi/2$, and 2π, respectively. The minimum period of $\tan x$ and $\cot x$ is π, and of the other four functions it is 2π.

In the calculus it is shown that $\sin x$ and $\cos x$ are sums of power series (see 80). These series may be used to compute the sine and cosine of any angle. For example, to compute the sine of 10°, it is necessary to find the value of $\sin \pi/18$ because 10° is the angle containing $\pi/18$ radians. When $\pi/18$ is substituted in the series for $\sin x$, it is found that the first two terms give 0.17365, which is correct to five decimals for the sine of 10°. By taking enough terms of the series, any number of decimal places can be correctly obtained.

Tables of the functions may be used to sketch the graphs of the functions, shown in Figure 14. The diagrams give the graph of each function for one period. To obtain the complete graph in each figure it is only necessary to extend the curve indefinitely in both directions by repetitions of the piece of graph shown in the figure.

(74)	$\cos A = -\cos B \cos C + \sin B \sin C \cos \alpha$
(75)	$\dfrac{\sin a}{\sin A} = \dfrac{\sin b}{\sin B} = \dfrac{\sin c}{\sin C}$
(76)	$\begin{cases} \cos a = \cos b \cos c + \sin b \sin c \cos A \\ \cos b = \cos c \cos a + \sin c \sin a \cos B \\ \cos c = \cos a \cos b + \sin a \sin b \cos C \end{cases}$
(77)	$\begin{cases} \cos A = -\cos B \cos C + \sin B \sin C \cos a \\ \cos B = -\cos C \cos A + \sin C \sin A \cos b \\ \cos C = -\cos A \cos B + \sin A \sin B \cos c \end{cases}$
(78)	$\text{area} = E r^2$
(79)	$\begin{cases} \sin a = \sin c \sin A = \tan b \cot B \\ \sin b = \sin c \sin B = \tan a \cot A \\ \cos c = \cos a \cos b = \operatorname{ctn} A \cot B \\ \cos A = \cos a \sin B = \tan b \cot c \\ \cos B = \cos b \sin A = \tan a \cot c \end{cases}$
(80)	$\begin{cases} \sin x = x - \dfrac{x^3}{3!} + \dfrac{x^5}{5!} - \dfrac{x^7}{7!} + \cdots \\ \cos x = 1 - \dfrac{x^2}{2!} + \dfrac{x^4}{4!} - \dfrac{x^6}{6!} + \cdots \end{cases}$

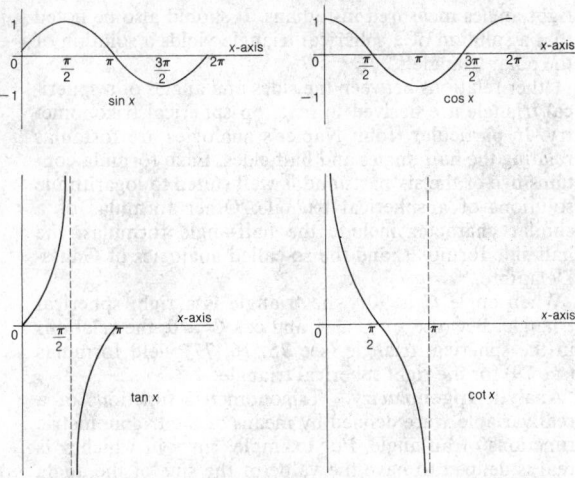

Figure 14: Graphs of some trigonometric functions.

Each of the trigonometric functions has an inverse. For instance, the inverse sine of x is the angle the sine of which is x. It is written $\sin^{-1} x$ or arc sin x. The other trigonometric functions also have inverses: arc tan x, arc cos x, etc.

COORDINATES AND TRANSFORMATION OF COORDINATES

Polar coordinates. For problems involving directions from a fixed origin (or pole) O, it is often convenient to specify a point P by its polar coordinates (r, θ), in which r is the distance OP and θ is the angle that the direction of r makes with a given initial line, which may be identified with the x-axis of rectangular Cartesian coordinates as shown in Figure 15. The point (r, θ) is the same as $(r, \theta + 2n\pi)$ for any integer n. It is sometimes desirable to allow r to be negative, so that (r, θ) is the same as $(-r, \theta + \pi)$.

Given the Cartesian equation for a curve, the polar equation for the same curve can be obtained by substituting the forms for x and y in terms of radius and angle as expressed throughout the trigonometric functions (see 81). For instance, the circle $x^2 + y^2 = a^2$ has the polar equation $(r \cos \theta)^2 + (r \sin \theta)^2 = a^2$, which reduces to $r = a$. (The positive value of r is sufficient, if θ takes all values from $-\pi$ to π or from 0 to 2π). Thus the polar equation of a circle simply expresses the fact that the curve is independent of θ and has constant radius. In a similar manner, the line $y = x \tan \alpha$ has the polar equation $\sin \theta = \cos \theta \tan \alpha$, which reduces to $\theta = \alpha$. (The other solution, $\theta = \alpha + \pi$, can be discarded if r is allowed to take negative values.) Some examples of curves in polar coordinate systems are given below in the section *Special curves*.

Transformation of coordinates. A transformation of coordinates in a plane is a change from one coordinate system to another. A point in the plane will have two sets of coordinates giving its position with respect to the two coordinate systems used. The transformation expresses the relationship between a point or locus in one system and that in another.

One type of transformation is that just discussed: the transformation between polar and Cartesian coordinates with the same origin as in Figure 16. The equations giving the transformation are $x = r \cos \phi$ and $y = r \sin \phi$. Similarly, it is possible to accomplish transformation between rectangular and oblique coordinates.

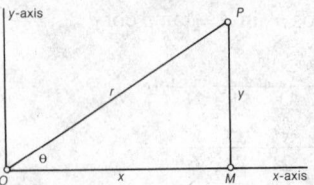

Figure 15: Cartesian and polar coordinates.

In a translation of Cartesian coordinate axes, a transformation is made between two sets of axes that are parallel to each other but have their origins at different positions. If a point has coordinates (x, y) in one system and (x', y') in a second, then the transformation equations are linear including the constants h and k (see 82). Here (h, k) is the origin of the second system in terms of the first coordinate system. These transformation equations were used earlier to derive the general equation of a straight line. The common use of translations of axes is to simplify the equations of curves. For example, an equation that is quadratic with linear and constant terms (see 83) can be simplified with translations to an equation involving only squares of x and y and a constant term. In other words, the curve represents an ellipse with its centre at the point $(3, 1)$ in the $(x–y)$ coordinate system. The equation reduces to the standard form when the coordinates are translated to this point.

A rotation of coordinate axes is one in which a pair of axes giving the coordinates of a point (x, y) are rotated through an angle ϕ to give a new pair of axes in which the point has coordinates (x', y'). This is shown in Figure 16, from which it is apparent that the transformation equations are trigonometric in form (see 84). The application of these formulas to the rectangular hyperbola involving the difference of squares (see 85), with $\phi = 45°$, leads to the equation $xy = c$, giving the form of the rectangular hyperbola when its asymptotes are used as the coordinate axes.

Rotation of coordinate axes

(81)	$x = r \cos \theta, \qquad y = r \sin \theta$
(82)	$\begin{cases} x = x' + h \\ y = y' + k \end{cases}$
(83)	$\begin{cases} 2x^2 + y^2 - 12x - 2y + 17 = 0 \\ x = x' + 3 \\ y = y' + 1 \\ x^2 + y^2/2 = 1 \end{cases}$
(84)	$\begin{cases} x = x' \cos \phi - y' \sin \phi \\ y = x' \sin \phi + y' \cos \phi \end{cases}$
(85)	$x^2 - y^2 = a^2$
(86)	$Ax^2 + Bxy + Cy^2 + Dx + Ey + F = 0$
(87)	$\Delta = \frac{1}{2} \begin{vmatrix} 2A & B & D \\ B & 2C & E \\ D & E & 2F \end{vmatrix}$
(88)	$\begin{cases} B^2 - 4AC = 0, \qquad B^2 - 4AC > 0 \\ B^2 - 4AC < 0 \end{cases}$

Discriminant of a conic. A conic is represented by a general equation of the second degree with the form that includes squared terms, cross product terms, and linear terms, as well as a constant (see 86). The discriminant is denoted by Δ (Greek delta) and is defined by a determinant in which constants of the general equation appear (see 87).

The discriminant and the expression $(B^2 - 4AC)$ are invariants for rotational and translational transformations. They are used as criteria for the form of the curve represented by the general equation.

Three cases occur that are expressed in terms of numerical values for the above expression (see 88). In the first case the curve is a parabola if Δ is not zero, and if Δ is zero the curve is two parallel or coincident straight lines or there is no (real) curve. In the second case the curve is a hyperbola if it is not the case that $\Delta = 0$ and two

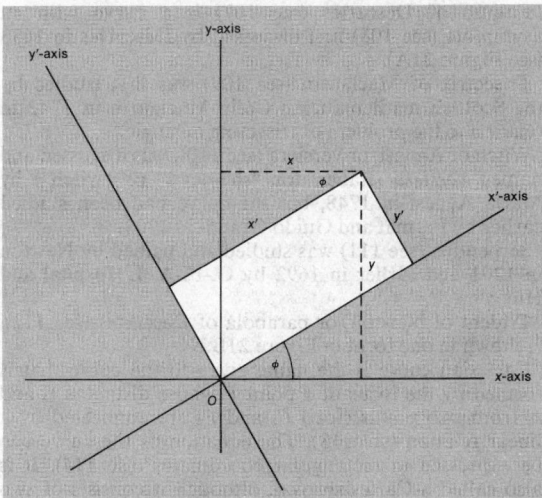

Figure 16: Rotation of axes.

intersecting lines if $\Delta = 0$. In the third case the curve is an ellipse if it is not the case that $\Delta = 0$ and becomes a single point if $\Delta = 0$.

The cases in which $\Delta = 0$ are limiting. A point is the limiting case of an ellipse in which the section of the cone is taken through its vertex. Similarly, an axial section of cones through the vertex gives two intersecting lines, a limiting case of the hyperbola. The parabola becomes a single line if the section plane is tangential to the cone and a pair of parallel lines when the vertex of the cone is at infinity (the "cone" is then a cylinder). These limiting cases are called degenerate conics. The general equation of a conic can be put in a form involving the discriminant (see 89).

Barycentric and areal coordinates. If two masses of
The centre of mass magnitude t_1 and t_2 are placed at points P_1 and P_2, their total mass appears to act at point P on the line P_1P_2. P divides the distance P_1P_2 in the ratio $t_2 : t_1$ and is known as the centroid or centre of mass. Its coordinates are rational functions of the $\{x_k\}$ and $\{t_k\}$ (see 90). For three masses in a plane at points P_1, P_2, P_3, the centroid has coordinates also rational functions of the $\{x_k\}$ and $\{t_k\}$ (see 91). Suitable values of t_1, t_2, t_3 will place the centroid P anywhere in the plane, and they are called the barycentric coordinates of the point (the centroid) with respect to the triangle of reference, $P_1P_2P_3$. They are homogeneous coordinates, because for any $k \neq 0$ masses kt_1, kt_2, and kt_3 have the same centroid as t_1, t_2, and t_3. The barycentric coordinates of P are proportional to the areas of the three triangles PP_2P_3, PP_3P_1, PP_1P_2. Accordingly, when normalized so that the sum of the $\{t_k\}$ equals 1 (see 92) they are called areal coordinates.

PROJECTIVE AND SOLID ANALYTIC GEOMETRY

Analytic projective geometry. The 16th–17th-century German astronomer Johannes Kepler conceived the idea of extending the Euclidean (or affine) plane by postulating a line at infinity the points of which lie on collections of parallel lines called "pencils." The plane so extended is called the projective plane. In terms of barycentric coordinates, the line at infinity has the equation restricting the $\{t_k\}$ to equal 0 (see 93). General projective coordinates (x_1, x_2, x_3) are derived by the substitution $t_i = k_i x_i$, in which the coefficients k_i are three constants. The line at infinity is now expressed in terms of a linear combination of coordinates (see 94) and any other homogeneous linear equation represents an ordinary line. The transition to projective geometry is completed by waiving the distinction, so that a point at infinity is treated just like any other point. This vital step was taken by another 19th-century German mathematician, Karl G.C. von Staudt. It enables the points of the projective plane to be defined as the ordered triads of numbers (x_1, x_2, x_3), not all zero, with the convention that (kx_1, kx_2, kx_3) is the same point for all nonzero values of k.

Given two points (x_1, x_2, x_3) and (y_1, y_2, y_3), or more

concisely, (x) and (y), an arbitrary point collinear with them may be expressed in the form $(x + ty)$ (see 95). In this notation, two triangles in perspective from (u) may be expressed in the concise notation (see 96). Corresponding sides of the triangles meet in three collinear points (see 97) in agreement with the two-triangle theorem of the 17th-century French mathematician Girard Desargues.

The general homogeneous linear transformation $x'_i = \Sigma c_{ij} x_j$ (summed over j), in which $\det(c_{ij}) \neq 0$, transforms collinear points into collinear points; *i.e.*, it is a collineation. For instance, the collineation that leaves unchanged the first two coordinates and modifies the third with multiplication by a constant (see 98) is a homology that leaves invariant every line through the point $(0, 0, 1)$ and every point on the line $x_3 = 0$.

Solid analytic geometry. Much of analytic geometry may be extended from two dimensions to three or more. In ordinary space a point has three Cartesian coordinates (x, y, z), a plane has a linear equation (see 99), and a line may be specified in various ways; for example, as the intersection of two planes or as the join of two points or as proceeding from a given point in a given direction.

The last aspect yields parametric equations that are linear in the parameter and in the coordinates (see 100). Polar coordinates have two spatial counterparts: cylindrical coordinates (r, θ, z), in which r and θ are related to x and y in the usual way; and spherical polar coordinates, which consist of distance from the origin, latitude (or colatitude), and longitude. Barycentric (and also other projective) coordinates are referred to a tetrahedron $P_1P_2P_3P_4$.

SPECIAL CURVES

Partly due to the study of the Greeks in pure geometry, but largely due to the influence of analytic geometry and the calculus, there have been developed a large number of special curves that have received names more or less generally accepted by mathematicians. For the purposes of the present article, it seems best to arrange the curves roughly in this order: plane algebraic curves according to degree, followed by plane transcendental curves, gen-

(89)	$Ax^2 + Bxy + Cy^2 - \dfrac{\Delta}{B^2 - 4AC} = 0$
(90)	$\dfrac{x_1 t_1 + x_2 t_2}{(t_1 + t_2)}, \quad \dfrac{y_1 t_1 + y_2 t_2}{(t_1 + t_2)}$
(91)	$\begin{cases} \dfrac{x_1 t_1 + x_2 t_2 + x_3 t_3}{t_1 + t_2 + t_3}, \quad \dfrac{y_1 t_1 + y_2 t_2 + y_3 t_3}{t_1 + t_2 + t_3} \\ \dfrac{z_1 t_1 + z_2 t_2 + z_3 t_3}{t_1 + t_2 + t_3} \end{cases}$
(92)	$t_1 + t_2 + t_3 = 1$
(93)	$t_1 + t_2 + t_3 = 0$
(94)	$k_1 x_1 + k_2 x_2 + k_3 x_3 = 0$
(95)	$(x_1 + ty_1, x_2 + ty_2, x_3 + ty_3)$
(96)	$(x)(y)(z)$ and $(x + u)(y + u)(z + u)$
(97)	$(y - z)(z - x)(x - y)$
(98)	$x'_1 = x_1 \qquad x'_2 = x_2 \qquad x'_3 = kx_3$
(99)	$ax + by + cz + d = 0$
(100)	$x = x_1 + lt \qquad y = y_1 + mt \qquad z = z_1 + nt$

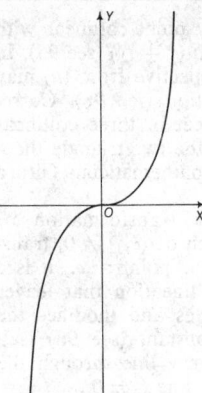

Figure 17: Cubical parabola.

eral classes of curves, and curves of double curvature. The standard equations of the curves are referred to when appropriate, and the general shapes of the most important plane curves considered are shown by accompanying figures.

Cubical parabola (see 101) is one of the canonical forms of cubics studied by Sir Isaac Newton. The special case (see 102) shown in Figure 17 was used by the German philosopher-mathematician Gottfried Wilhelm Leibniz in 1675 and (for $a = 1$) by the French mathematician Gaspard Monge in 1815.

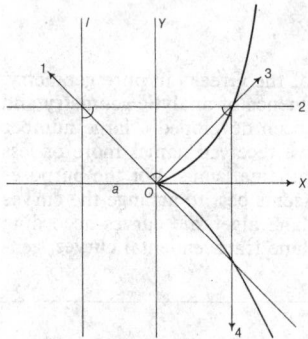

Figure 18: Semicubical parabola.

Semicubical, or Neil's, parabola (see 103) is the curve that in 1687 Leibniz proposed to find along which a particle may descend under the action of gravity so as to describe equal vertical spaces in equal times. The Dutch astronomer and physicist Christiaan Huygens found that the semicubical parabola met this requirement. The curve is called an isochronous curve (see Figure 18).

Cissoid of Diocles (see 104) is a curve invented by Diocles (c. 180 BC) in connection with the duplication of the cube (Figure 19).

Strophoid (see 105) was first considered by the English mathematician Isaac Barrow in 1670. When $\alpha = 90°$ the strophoid (see 106) is right (see Figure 20).

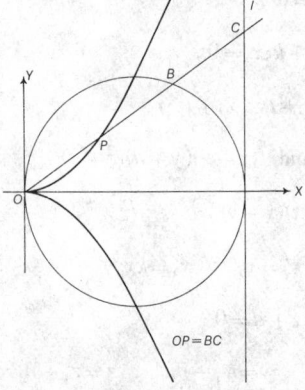

$OP = BC$

Figure 19: Cissoid of Diocles.

Folium of Descartes (see 107) is a curve with an asymptote (see 108) first discussed by Descartes in 1638 (see Figure 21A).

Trisectrix of Maclaurin (see 109) was first studied by the Scottish mathematician Colin Maclaurin in 1742 in relation to the problem of trisecting an angle.

Witch of Agnesi, or versiera (see 110), was discussed and named *versiera* (Italian for "she-devil" or "witch") by Maria Agnesi in 1748, but the curve had been studied earlier by Fermat and Guido Grandi in 1703.

Serpentine (see 111) was studied and named by Newton in 1701 and earlier in 1692 by G.-F.-A. L'Hospital and Huygens.

Trident of Newton, or parabola of Descartes (see 112), is shown in one form in Figure 21B.

Cartesian curve is the name given to the curve that is formed by the locus of a point P whose distances r_1 and r_2 from two points (foci) F_1 and F_2 are connected by a linear relation (see 113). The equation of the curve can be expressed in rectangular coordinates (see 114). It is also called a Cartesian oval, although it consists of two ovals (Figure 21C). When $m = \pm 1$ the locus is a central conic. The distance between the foci is c, and when $m = a/c$, a limaçon of Pascal results. The curve originated with Descartes in 1637 and was studied by Newton, and others.

Cassinian curve, or Cassinian ovals, or Cassinian ellipse (see 115), was first conceived by the Italian-born French astronomer Giovanni Domenico Cassini in 1680 in the study of the relative motions of the Earth and the Sun. The shape of the curve depends upon the ratio $c:a$. The curve may be defined as the locus of a point that moves so that the product of its distances from two fixed points (foci) A and B (Figure 22) is a constant, c^2. When $c > a$ the curve consists of two loops; when $c = a$ the Cassinian becomes the lemniscate of Bernoulli. The number of foci may be greater than two. By varying their number and their disposition, curves of odd shapes may be produced.

(101)	$y = ax^3 + bx^2 + cx + d$ or $y = ax^2(x - e)$
(102)	$y = ax^3$
(103)	$x^3 = ay^2$
(104)	$y^2 = x^3/(2a - x)$ or $r = 2a \tan\theta \sin\theta$
(105)	$r = a \sin(\alpha - 2\theta)/\sin(\alpha - \theta)$
(106)	$r = a \cos 2\theta/\cos\theta$ or $y^2 = x^2(a - x)/(a + x)$
(107)	$x^3 + y^3 = 3axy$
(108)	$x + y + a = 0$
(109)	$\begin{cases} x(x^2 + y^2) = a(y^2 - 3x^2) \\ \text{or } y^2 = x^2(3a + x)/(a - x) \\ \text{or } r = a \sec\theta - 4a \cos\theta = 2a \sin 3\theta/\sin 2\theta \end{cases}$
(110)	$y(x^2 + a^2) = a^3$
(111)	$x^2y + aby - a^2x = 0$ $(ab > 0)$
(112)	$xy = cx^3 + dx^2 + ex + f$
(113)	$r_1 + mr_2 = a$
(114)	$[(x^2 + y^2)(1 - m^2) + 2m^2cx + a^2 - m^2c^2]^2$ $= 4a^2(x^2 + y^2)$
(115)	$(x^2 + y^2)^2 - 2a^2(x^2 - y^2) + a^4 - c^4 = 0$

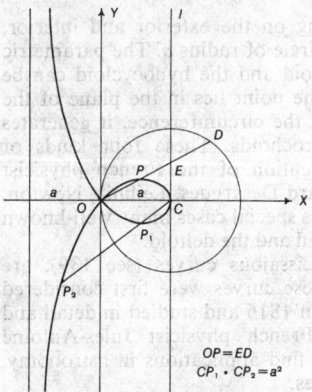

$$OP = ED$$
$$CP_1 \cdot CP_2 = a^2$$

Figure 20: Strophoid.

Lemniscate of Bernoulli (see 116) was first conceived by the Swiss mathematician Jakob Bernoulli in 1694.

Conchoid, or shell form (see 117), was devised by the Greek mathematician Nicomedes (*c.* 200 BC) in relation to the problem of the duplication of the cube. Nicomedes apparently recognized the three types of the curve shown in Figure 23.

Limaçon of Pascal (see 118) was discovered by Étienne Pascal (father of Blaise) and named by another French mathematician, Gilles-Personne Roberval, in 1650. The three forms of the curve (see 119) shown in Figure 24 correspond to various values of *b*.

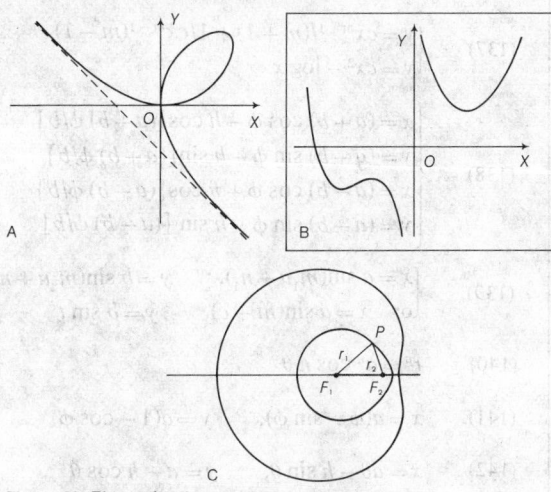

Figure 21: *Three classic curves.*
(A) Folium of Descartes. (B) Trident of Newton.
(C) Cartesian ovals.

Cardioid (see 120) is a curve (see curve 2 in Figure 24) that is the locus of a point on the circumference of a circle rolling upon the circumference of another circle of equal size.

Tricuspid, or deltoid (see 121), was first conceived by Euler (1745); see Figure 25.

Simple folium, double folium, and trifolium are curves such that

$$(x^2 + y^2)\,[y^2 + x(x + b)] = 4axy^2 \text{ or}$$
$$r = -b \cos \theta + 4a \cos \theta \sin^2 \theta.$$

The simple folium, double folium, and trifolium correspond to $b = 4a$, $b = 0$, $b = a$.

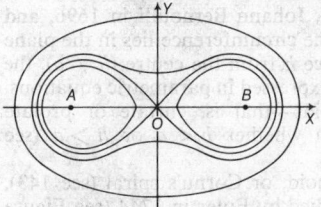

Figure 22: Cassinian ovals.

Bicorn, or cocked hat, are terms that have been applied to two different quartics (see Figure 26A). One form was named "bicorn" and discussed by the British-born U.S. mathematician James Joseph Sylvester in 1864 and by the British mathematician Arthur Cayley three years later (see 122). Another form has been referred to as a "cocked hat" (see 123).

Bullet-nose curve was discussed by P.H. Schoute in 1885. This curve and the cross curve have similar equations (see 124).

Devil's curve, or devil on two sticks (see 125), shown in Figure 26B, was first studied by the Swiss physicist Gabriel Cramer in 1750.

Eight curve (see 126) is also known as the lemniscate of Gerono.

(116)	$(x^2 + y^2)^2 = a^2(x^2 - y^2)$ or $r^2 = a^2 \cos 2\theta$
(117)	$(x - b)^2(x^2 + y^2) - a^2x^2 = 0$ or $r = a + b \sec \theta$
(118)	$(x^2 + y^2 - 2ax)^2 = b^2(x^2 + y^2)$ or $r = b + 2a \cos \theta$
(119)	$b > 2a, \qquad b = 2a, \qquad b = a$
(120)	$\begin{cases} (x^2 + y^2 - 2ax)^2 = 4a^2(x^2 + y^2) \\ r = 2a(1 + \cos \theta) \\ x = a(2 \cos \theta - \cos 2\theta), \qquad y = a(2 \sin \theta - \sin 2\theta) \end{cases}$
(121)	$\begin{cases} x = a(2 \cos \theta + \cos 2\theta), \qquad y = a(2 \sin \theta + \sin 2\theta) \\ \text{or } (x^2 + y^2 + 12ax + 9a^2)^2 - 4a(2x + 3a)^3 = 0 \end{cases}$
(122)	$2y^4 - 9y^3 - 17y^2 + 125y - xy^3 - 29xy^2 + 205xy +$ $\qquad + 72x^2y - 27x^3 - 25x^2 = 0$
(123)	$y^2(a^2 - x^2) = x^2 + a(2y - a)^2$
(124)	$\begin{cases} \dfrac{a^2}{x^2} - \dfrac{b^2}{y^2} = 1 \\ \dfrac{a^2}{x^2} + \dfrac{b^2}{y^2} = 1 \end{cases}$
(125)	$y^4 + my^2 - x^4 + nx^2 = 0$
(126)	$x^4 = a\,(x^2 - y^2)$ or $r^2 = a^2 \cos 2\theta \cos^4 \theta$
(127)	$a^2x^4 = b^4(x^2 + y^2)$ or $r = b^2/(a \cos^2 \theta)$
(128)	$y^2(x^2 + y^2) = a^2x^2$ or $r = a \cot \theta$
(129)	$b^2y^2 = x^3(a - x)$
(130)	$\begin{cases} (x^2 + y^2 - 4a^2)^3 = 108a^4y^2 \quad \text{or} \\ (r/2a)^{2/3} = (\sin \tfrac{1}{2}\theta)^{2/3} + (\cos \tfrac{1}{2}\theta)^{2/3} \end{cases}$
(131)	$(x^2 + y^2 - a^2)^3 + 27a^2x^2y^2 = 0$ or $x^{2/3} + y^{2/3} = a^{2/3}$

Kampyle of Eudoxus (see 127) was used in connection with the problem of the duplication of the cube (Figure 26C).

Kappa curve, or Gutschoven's curve (see 128), was conceived by G. van Gutschoven (*c.* 1662) and studied by Newton and Johann Bernoulli.

Pear-shaped quartic (see 129) was studied by G. de Longchamps in 1886.

Nephroid (see 130) was discovered by Huygens and Ehrenfried Walther Tschirnhausen between 1678 and 1690; it was studied by Jakob Bernoulli in 1692.

Astroid, or tetracuspid (see 131), was first discussed by Johann Bernoulli in 1691–92 (Figure 26D).

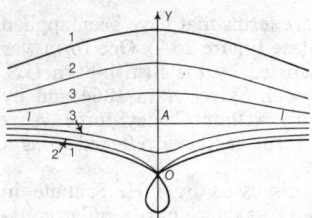

Figure 23: Conchoid.

Cayley's sextic (see 132) was discovered by Maclaurin in 1718 and studied in detail by Cayley.

Watt's curve (see 133) is the sextic curve generated by a point P of the side BC of a three-bar linkage AB, BC, CD, the points A and B remaining fixed while the others vary (see Figure 27). O is the midpoint of AD; $AO = a$, $AB = CD = b$, $BP = PC = c$; and θ varies from 0 to π.

Pearls of Sluze (see 134) was studied by Baron René Française de Sluze between 1657 and 1698 and named by Blaise Pascal.

Lamé curves (see 135) are a family of curves discussed in 1818 by the French geometer and engineer Gabriel Lamé. The curves are algebraic or transcendental depending on whether n is rational or irrational.

Rhodonea curves (see 136) were so named by the

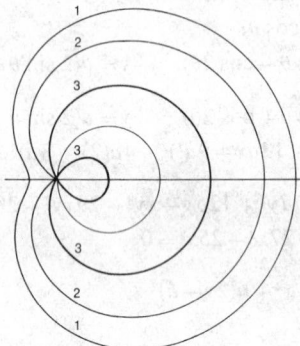

Figure 24: Limaçon of Pascal.

Italian mathematician Guido Grandi, between 1723 and 1728, because of their fancied resemblance to roses. When k is an integer there are k or $2k$ petals of the rose curves depending on whether k is odd or even, respectively. The number of petals is finite or infinite depending on whether k is rational or irrational, respectively. Several curves corresponding to particular values of k have attracted special attention.

Curve of pursuit, or pursuit curve: If a point A describes a known curve (A), the curve (P) described by a point P is a curve of pursuit if the motion of P is always directed toward A and if both A and P move with uniform velocities. The problem of the pursuit curve was first formulated and solved by the French scientist Pierre Bouguer in 1732. If (A) is a straight line, the equation of (P) has two possible forms (see 137). A study of this curve was made by Arthur Bernhart.

The epicycloid and hypocycloid are the curves traced out by points on the circumferences of circles of radius b

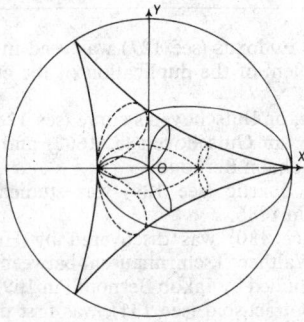

Figure 25: Tricuspid.

that roll without slipping on the exterior and interior, respectively, of a fixed circle of radius a. The parametric equations of the epicycloid and the hypocycloid can be given (see 138). When the point lies in the plane of the rolling circle but not on the circumference, it generates epitrochoids and hypotrochoids. These four kinds of curves attracted the attention of the French physicist Philippe de la Hire, Girard Desargues, Leibniz, Newton, and others. They admit as special cases many well-known curves such as the cardioid and the deltoid.

Bowditch curves, or Lissajous curves (see 139), are shown in Figure 28. These curves were first considered by Nathaniel Bowditch in 1815 and studied in detail and independently by the French physicist Jules-Antoine Lissajous in 1857. They find applications in astronomy, physics, and other sciences.

(132)	$\begin{cases} 4(x^2 + y^2 - ax)^3 = 27a^2(x^2 + y^2)^2 \quad \text{or} \\ r = 4a\cos^3(\theta/3) \end{cases}$
(133)	$r^2 = b^2 - [a\sin\theta \pm (c^2 - a^2\cos^2\theta)^{1/2}]^2$
(134)	$y^n = k(a-x)^p x^m \qquad (m, n, p \text{ are positive integers})$
(135)	$(x/a)^n + (y/b)^n = 1$
(136)	$r = a\cos k\theta \quad \text{or} \quad r = a\sin k\theta$
(137)	$\begin{cases} y = cx^{m+1}/(m+1) + 1/cx^{m-1}(m-1) \\ y = cx^2 - \log x \end{cases}$
(138)	$\begin{cases} x = (a+b)\cos\phi - h\cos[(a+b)\phi/b] \\ y = (a+b)\sin\phi - h\sin[(a+b)\phi/b] \\ x = (a-b)\cos\phi + h\cos[(a-b)\phi/b] \\ y = (a-b)\sin\phi - h\sin[(a-b)\phi/b] \end{cases}$
(139)	$\begin{cases} x = a\sin(m_1 u + n_1), \qquad y = b\sin(m_2 u + n_2) \\ \text{or} \quad x = a\sin(nt + c), \qquad y = b\sin t \end{cases}$
(140)	$r^n = a^n \cos n\theta$
(141)	$x = a(\phi - \sin\phi), \qquad y = a(1 - \cos\phi)$
(142)	$x = a\theta - h\sin\theta, \qquad y = a - h\cos\theta$
(143)	$x = \dfrac{a}{2^{1/2}} \displaystyle\int_0^v \dfrac{\sin v\, dv}{v^{1/2}}, \qquad y = \dfrac{a}{2^{1/2}} \displaystyle\int_0^v \dfrac{\cos v\, dv}{v^{1/2}}$

Sinusoidal spirals (see 140) were first studied by Maclaurin; in the general equation n is a rational number, positive or negative. For $n = -1, +1, +\frac{1}{2}, -\frac{1}{2}, -2$, and $+2$, the curve is, respectively, a line, a circle, a cardioid, a parabola, an equilateral hyperbola, and a lemniscate of Bernoulli.

Cycloid (see 141), one of the most celebrated of all special curves, is the locus of a point on the circumference of a circle of radius a that rolls without slipping along a straight line (see Figure 29). The curve was studied by Galileo (c. 1599), who gave it its name, Roberval in 1634, the English architect Sir Christopher Wren in 1658, Huygens in 1673, Johann Bernoulli in 1696, and others. If the point on the circumference lies in the plane of the circle at a distance h from the centre ($h \neq a$), the curve (see 142) may be expressed in parametric equations. The curves are trochoids—that is, curtate or prolate cycloids—depending on whether $h < a$ or $h > a$ (see Figure 29).

Euler's spiral, or clothoid, or Cornu's spiral (see 143), was discovered and studied by Euler in 1744 (see Figure 30).

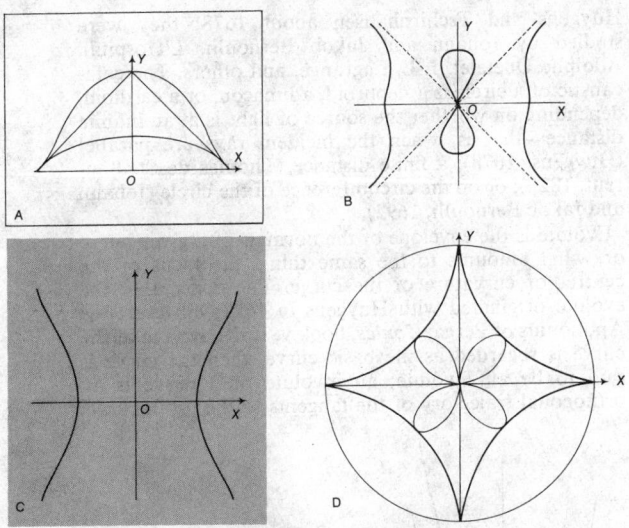

Figure 26: *Four plane algebraic curves.*
(A) Bicorn or cocked hat. (B) Devil's curve. (C) Kampyle of
Eudoxus. (D) Astroid or tetracuspid.

The family of spirals (see 144) includes four notable
curves (see 145) that result by giving a parameter m
particular values. (A) Spiral of Archimedes, obtained in
the case $m = 1$, was discussed by him about 225 BC.
(B) Fermat's spiral, obtained in the case $m = 2$, was discussed by him in 1636. (C) Hyperbolic, or reciprocal,
spiral, $m = -1$, originated with Pierre Varignon in 1704
and was studied in detail by Johann Bernoulli between
1710 and 1713 and the English mathematician Roger
Cotes in 1722. (D) Lituus, $m = -2$, originated with
Cotes in 1722. It is the locus of the point P moving in
such a manner that the area of the circular sector POP'
remains constant (see Figure 31).

Involute of a circle (see 146) is the roulette of a point on

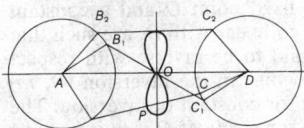

Figure 27: Watt's curve.

a straight line that rolls on a circle. It was conceived by
Huygens when he was considering clocks without pen-
dulums that might be of service to seagoing vessels.

Cochleoid is a snail-form curve with the equation
$r = a \sin \theta / \theta$ (see Figure 32). The points of contact of
parallel tangents to the cochleoid lie on a strophoid.

Figure 28: Bowditch curves.

Logarithmic, or equiangular, or logistic, spiral (see 147)
was first discussed by Descartes as the curve cutting
radius vectors from a fixed point O under a constant
angle ϕ. The form of the curve depends on c and is
independent of k (see Figure 33). The pole O is an
asymptotic point (Evangelista Torricelli, 1646). The pedal of a logarithmic spiral with respect to its pole is a
logarithmic spiral, and its evolute is an equal spiral with
the same asymptotic point (Jakob Bernoulli, 1691–93).

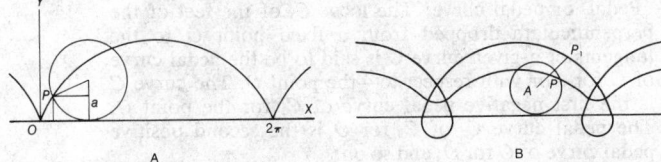

Figure 29: Cycloids.

Frequency curve, probability curve, Gaussian curve, and
normal curve of error (see 148) are the names applied to
the bell-shaped curve. This curve originated, in essence,
with the French-born mathematician Abraham de Moivre
in 1733; it has been associated more particularly with
Laplace and Gauss. The term "frequency curve" is applied to a great variety of other curves.

Logarithmic, or logistic, curve (see 149) originated
about 1640. The subtangent of the curve is equal to a,
regardless of the value of m.

Catenary, or chainette (see 150), is the form that a perfectly flexible chain assumes when suspended by its ends
and acted upon by gravity alone (see Figure 34). Its
equation was obtained by Leibniz and Huygens in 1691.
The tangents at P, P_1, and P_2 on the figure are concurrent. Euler discovered, in 1744, that a catenary revolved
about its asymptote generates a catenoid, the only minimal surface of revolution.

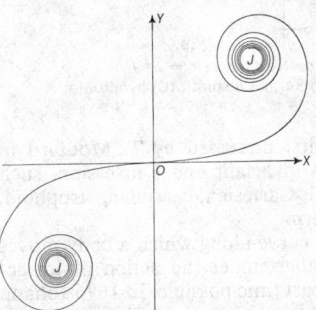

Figure 30: Euler's spiral or clothoid or
Cornu's spiral.

Tractrix, or tractory, or equitangential, curve (see 151)
was studied in detail by Huygens in 1692 and by Leibniz,
Johann Bernoulli, and others (see Figure 35). The evolute
of the tractrix is a catenary. The tractrix revolved about
its asymptote generates a pseudosphere, a surface of constant negative curvature of interest in non-Euclidean
geometry.

Quadratrix of Hippias (see 152) is a curve discovered
by Hippias of Elis (c. 430 BC) that may have been used
by him and by Dinostratus (c. 350 BC) for trisecting an
angle and for squaring the circle. The curve may be used
for dividing an angle into any number of equal parts.

$$(144) \qquad r^m = a^m \theta$$

$$(145) \quad \begin{cases} (m = 1); & r = a\theta \\ (m = 2); & r^2 = a^2\theta \\ (m = -1); & r\theta = a \\ (m = -2); & r^2\theta = a^2 \end{cases}$$

$$(146) \qquad x = a(\cos \phi + \phi \sin \phi), \qquad y = a(\sin \phi - \phi \cos \phi)$$

$$(147) \quad \begin{cases} r = ke^{c\theta} \\ c = \cot \phi \end{cases}$$

$$(148) \qquad y = (2\pi)^{-\frac{1}{2}} e^{-\frac{1}{2}x^2}$$

$$(149) \qquad x = a \log (y/m) \quad \text{or} \quad y = me^{x/a}$$

$$(150) \qquad y = \tfrac{1}{2}a(e^{x/a} + e^{-x/a}) = a \cosh(x/a)$$

$$(151) \quad \begin{cases} y^2(1 + y^2) = a^2 y^2 \\ \text{or} \quad x = a(\cos u + \log \tan [u/2]), \qquad y = a \sin u \end{cases}$$

$$(152) \qquad y = x \cot(\pi x/2a) \quad \text{or} \quad r \sin \theta = (2a/\pi)\theta$$

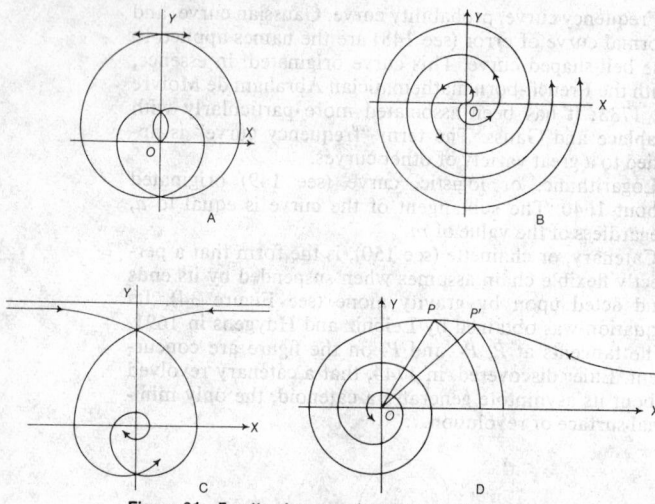

Figure 31: *Family of curves derived from* $r^m = a^m\theta$.
(A) Spiral of Archimedes; (B) Fermat's spiral; (C) hyperbola;
(D) lituus.

Anallagmatic curve, first discussed by T. Moutard in 1864, is a curve that is invariant under inversion, such as the limaçon, cardioid, Cartesian, cassinian, strophoid, and trisectrix of Maclaurin.

Brachistochrone is the curve along which a body moves from one point to another under the action of an accelerating force in the least time possible. In 1696 Johann Bernoulli proposed the question as a challenge, the accelerating force being gravity. Leibniz, Newton, Jakob Bernoulli, and L'Hospital found that the cycloid has the required property.

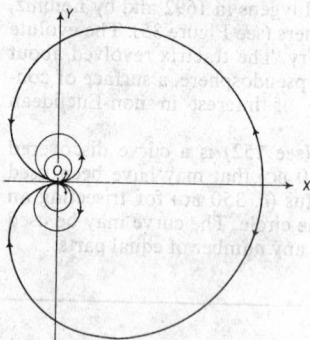

Figure 32: Cochleoid.

Caustic is an envelope of rays; more specifically, when the light rays emanating from a source are reflected by a given curve, the envelope of the reflected rays is the caustic by reflection, or catacaustic, of the given curve with respect to the source in question. When the rays from a source are refracted by a given curve, the envelope of refracted rays is called the caustic by refraction, or diacaustic, of the given curve for the source in question. Catacaustic and diacaustic surfaces may be defined in a similar way. Caustic curves originated with

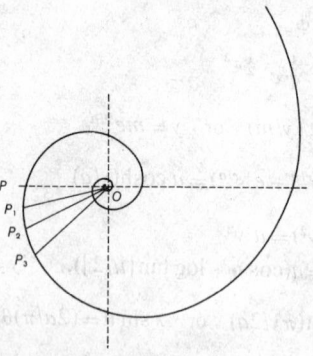

Figure 33: Logarithmic spiral.

Huygens and Tschirnhausen about 1678; they were studied by Johann and Jakob Bernoulli, L'Hospital, Adolphe Quetelet, J.-L. Lagrange, and others. The catacaustic of a circle is a nephroid, a limaçon, or a cardioid, depending on whether the source of light is at an infinite distance—that is, when the incident rays are parallel (Huygens, 1678); a finite distance (Thomas de St. Laurent, 1826); or on the circumference of the circle (Johann and Jakob Bernoulli, 1692).

Evolute is the envelope of the normals of a given curve or, what amounts to the same thing, the locus of the centres of curvature of the curve. The concept of the evolute originated with Huygens in 1673; however, see Apollonius of Perga, *Conics*, book v. If the evolute of the curve is regarded as the basic curve, then the curve is said to be an involute; an involute of a curve is an orthogonal trajectory of the tangents to the given curve.

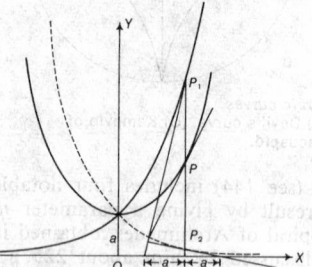

Figure 34: Catenary or chainette.

There are an infinite number of such trajectories to a given curve, and they are said to be parallel curves; that is, any two cut off equal lengths on common normals. Parallel curves may be very different in appearance; for example, Cayley's sextic and the nephroid. Leibniz was the first to consider parallel curves. Figure 36 shows two parallel curves, 3 and 4, of an astroid, 2, and also the evolute, 1, of this astroid.

Inverse curves: Given a fixed point O and a constant m, if two points P_1 and P_2, collinear with O, are such that $OP_1 \cdot OP_2 = m$, they are said to be inverse with respect to one another, or homologous, in the inversion (O, m) having O for centre and m for constant of inversion. The points P_1 and P_2 are on the same side of O if m is positive and on opposite sides if m is negative. If one of the points, say P_1, describes a curve C_1, then the curve C_2 described by P_2 is the inverse C_1 in (O, m). The relation between C_1 and C_2 is obviously reciprocal, and the two may coincide.

Isoptic curve: The locus of the points of intersection of

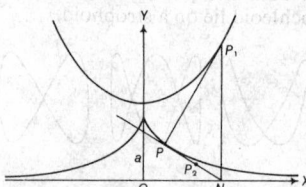

Figure 35: Tractrix or tractory or equitangential curve.

tangents to a given curve (or a pair of curves) meeting at a constant angle is an isoptic curve of the given curve or curves. When the constant angle is right, the isoptic curve is said to be the orthoptic curve. The orthoptic of a parabola is its directrix, the orthoptic of a central conic is a circle concentric with the conic (the Monge circle), and the orthoptic of a deltoid is a circle.

Pedal, or pedal curve: The locus C_1 of the feet of the perpendiculars dropped from a fixed point O to the tangents of a given curve C is said to be the pedal curve of C for—or with respect to—the point O. The curve C is the first negative pedal curve of C_1 for the point O. The pedal curve C_2 of C_1 for O is the second positive pedal curve of C for O, and so on.

Radial, or radial curve: If through a fixed point recti-

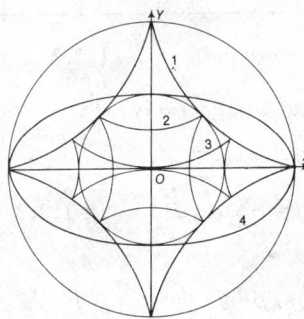

Figure 36: Evolute.

linear segments are drawn equal and parallel to the radius of curvature of a variable point of a given curve C, the locus of the end points of those segments is the radial curve, R, of C (Robert Tucker, 1864). The degree of R is equal to the degree of the evolute of C. The radial of a conic is a conic; the radial of a cycloid is a circle.

Roulette is the path of a fixed point—or the envelope of a fixed line—situated in the plane of a curve, that rolls without slipping on a fixed curve or straight line. The term is also applied to the locus of a variable point, such as the centre of curvature of the point of contact of the rolling curve. The roulette of the vertex of a parabola rolling on an equal parabola is a cissoid of Diocles. The pole of a hyperbolic spiral rolling on a straight line traces out a tractrix. A related curve is the glissette, the locus of a point or the envelope of a line fixed in the plane of a curve made to slide between given curves. For instance, the locus of a point on a rod of fixed length whose ends slide on two fixed perpendicular lines is an ellipse. The envelope (glissette) of the rod itself is an astroid.

Tautochrone is a curve down which a particle acted upon by specified forces will descend in the same amount of time from any initial point to the lowest point. When gravity is the force considered, Huygens showed in 1673 that the inverted cycloid with axis vertical has the required property. The astroid and the cardioid are tautochrones under certain conditions.

Clelies: If ϕ and θ denote the longitude and colatitude of a point P on a sphere of radius a, and if P moves so that $\theta = m\phi$ (in which m is a constant), then the locus described by P is a clelie. The locus of P was studied by Grandi in 1728, who used purely geometrical methods. Grandi also applied the term "clelies" to the curves determined by certain trigonometric equations involving the sine function (see 153).

Loxodrome, or rhumb line, or spherical helix (see 154) is usually defined as the curve cutting the meridian of a sphere at a constant angle. The curve was first conceived by Pedro Nunes in 1550. Its equations may be written in terms of β, the constant angle, and ϕ and θ, the longitude and colatitude, respectively, of a point on the loxodrome. Nunes believed that a loxodrome joining two points on a sphere was the shortest distance on the sphere between those points. But 19th-century mariners realized that great-circle sailing is preferable for shortening distances.

Helix (see 155) is the curve cutting the generators of a right circular cylinder under a constant angle, β. The helix is mentioned by Geminus (c. 70 BC); a passage in

Proclus (c. AD 460) suggests that it was known to Apollonius (c. 225 BC). It was used by Pappus of Alexandria (c. AD 300) for producing the quadratrix of Hippias of Elis. The orthogonal projection of the helix on a plane parallel to the axis of the cylinder is a sine curve. The curve that cuts the generators of a cone of revolution under a constant angle is a cylindroconical helix, or conical loxodrome (see 156), which was first discussed by Grandi in 1701.

Skew, or gauche, or space, or twisted, cubic is a space curve that may have three points in common with a plane. The skew cubic may result from the intersection of two quadratic cones, or of two ruled quadric surfaces having an element in common. It is in this form that the curve was first noticed by A.F. Möbius, a German mathematician, in 1827. The curve is the locus of the common point of three corresponding planes of three projective axial pencils of planes, or the locus of the common point of two corresponding and coplanar lines of two projective bundles. A skew cubic is determined by six points, no four of them coplanar. The cone that projects a cubic from a point in space is of third degree but reduces to second degree if the point is taken on the cubic. A line in space may be met by four tangents to a skew cubic. A line joining two points, real or conjugate imaginary, of a skew cubic is a secant of the curve, while a line having one point in common with the curve is a semisecant or transversal.

The skew cubic is also referred to as a cubical conic section. The three points of intersection of the curve with the plane at infinity may present the following four cases: (1) the three points are real and distinct; (2) one point is real and the other two are conjugate imaginary; (3) two of the points coincide; (4) all three points coincide. The corresponding curves are: (1) cubical hyperbola; (2) cubical ellipse; (3) cubical parabolic hyperbola; (4) cubical parabola.

BIBLIOGRAPHY. The reader interested in analytic geometry may wish to consult some of the following works: D.M.Y. SOMMERVILLE, *Analytical Geometry of Three Dimensions* (1934); ALAN ROBSON, *An Introduction to Analytical Geometry*, 2 vol. (1940–47); H.S.M. COXETER, *The Real Projective Plane*, 2nd ed. (1955), and *Introduction to Geometry*, 2nd ed. (1969); NIKOLAI V. EFIMOV, *An Elementary Course in Analytical Geometry*, 2 vol. (1966; orig. pub. in Russian, 1962). HENRY F. BAKER, *Principles of Geometry*, 2nd ed., vol. 2 (1929); LUTHER P. EISENHART, *Coordinate Geometry* (1939); and ROSS R. MIDDLEMISS, *Analytic Geometry*, 3rd ed. (1968), are three general references on conic sections. For the history of the conic sections, see JULIAN L. COOLIDGE, *A History of Conic Sections and Quadric Surfaces* (1945); and THOMAS L. HEATH, *A History of Greek Mathematics*, 2 vol. (1921). The following are works on various aspects of trigonometry: ERNEST W. HOBSON, *A Treatise on Plane and Advanced Trigonometry*, 7th ed. (1957); MYRA MCFADDEN, *Modern Trigonometry* (1965); SISTER MARY CLAUDIA ZELLER, *The Development of Trigonometry From Regiomontanus to Pitiscus* (1946); JOHN F. SCOTT, *A History of Mathematics from Antiquity to the Beginning of the Nineteenth Century*, 2 vol. (1958); DAVID E. SMITH, *History of Mathematics*, 2 vol. (1923–25, reprinted 1958); HERBERT E. SALZER and NORMAN LEVINE, *Table of Sines and Cosines to Ten Decimal Places at Thousandths of a Degree* (1962). For special curves, see JULIAN L. COOLIDGE, *A Treatise on Algebraic Plane Curves* (1931, reprinted 1959); HAROLD HILTON, *Plane Algebraic Curves*, 2nd ed. (1932); and ROBERT C. YATES, *A Handbook on Curves and Their Properties*, rev. ed. (1959). A considerable amount of information on special curves may be found in a variety of books and textbooks on analytic geometry, calculus, differential equations, the calculus of variations, and also mechanics.

(R.W.Bd./R.C.A./N.A.Ct./R.G.S.)

Geometry, Differential

Differential geometry has its origin in the discovery in the 17th century of the infinitesimal calculus, one part of mathematics that deals with limits. The concept of the derivative of a function is essentially identical with that of the tangent line or slope of a curve, and the integral of a function can be geometrically interpreted as the area under a curve. The geometry of curves and surfaces

(153)	$\begin{cases} a\sin\theta = b\sin m\phi \\ a\sin\theta = a - b\sin m\phi \end{cases}$
(154)	$\begin{cases} x = \sin\phi\cos\theta, \qquad y = \sin\phi\sin\theta, \qquad z = \cos\phi \\ \theta = -\tan\beta \log\tan(\phi/2) \end{cases}$
(155)	$x = a\cos\theta, \qquad y = a\sin\theta, \qquad z = a\theta\cot\beta$
(156)	$x = he^{a\theta}\cos\theta, \qquad y = he^{a\theta}\sin\theta, \qquad z = he^{a\theta}\cot\beta$

in space was studied as an application of the calculus, leading to various notions of curvature. Among the main contributors were the 18th-century mathematicians Leonhard Euler of Switzerland and Gaspard Monge of France.

In this article there follows a treatment of differential geometry topics in which, after introductory material, consideration is given to manifolds and tensor bundles, operations on tensor fields, connections, interplay between local and global properties, the Gauss-Bonnet formula, elliptic operators, and, finally, modern development in surface theory.

First and second fundamental forms

The equations of a surface S in a Euclidean space with the coordinates x_1, x_2, x_3 can be given in parametric form (see Box, equations 1). At the point (u^1, u^2) on the surface the components of a normal vector of unit length can also be given (see 2). The geometrical properties of S are then completely described by two quadratic differential forms (see 3), referred to respectively as the first and second fundamental forms of S. The 18th–19th-century German mathematician Carl Friedrich Gauss emphasized the importance of the properties of S that depend only on the first fundamental form, such as the length of a curve, the area of a domain, the geodesics (i.e., curves of shortest length), and the Gaussian curvature. Another German mathematician, Bernhard Riemann, founded in 1854 what is now known as Riemannian geometry; that is, the geometry in a space of n dimensions with the coordinates $u^\alpha, \alpha = 1, \cdots, n$, based on a quadratic differential form (see 4). This geometry is of general form and includes as special cases the non-Euclidean geometries. It serves as a model of the physical universe in Einstein's general theory of relativity (see PHYSICAL THEORIES, MATHEMATICAL ASPECTS OF: *Riemannian geometry; Relativity theory*).

Modern differential geometry stems from the basis that the objects of study are a class of spaces called manifolds equipped with additional structures. The main problems deal with the global properties of manifolds; i.e., properties that arise only when the manifolds are looked on as a whole. In global differential geometry topology is a major tool.

MANIFOLDS AND TENSOR BUNDLES

A manifold is a space that is covered by a finite or a countable number of coordinate charts with each point in a chart described by the real coordinates $x^1, \cdots, x^n$ (called local coordinates) and such that when a point belongs to two charts and has two sets of local coordinates they are related by a transformation (see 5). Here the functions f^i, with which the transformation is expressed, are dealt with on the basis of having continuous first partial derivatives with a Jacobian determinant (denoted by det), which is not equal to zero (see 6). If all such functions f^i have continuous partial derivatives of orders equal to or less than k, the manifold is said to be of class k. If all such functions have continuous partial derivatives of all orders, the manifold is said to be of class infinity. This definition is necessary because a space can rarely be described by one coordinate system. The local coordinates themselves have no geometrical meaning, and the analytical tool for the study of manifolds must be furnished by concepts that behave in a simple way under a change of local coordinates.

Tensors of covariant and contravariant order

The most important among such concepts are the tensors or tensor fields (see ANALYSIS, VECTOR AND TENSOR). A tensor of contravariant order r and covariant order s is defined by specifying its components (see 7) in each coordinate chart. Under a change of local coordinates (in which all the indices run from 1 to n) these components follow the conventional transformation rule involving first partial derivatives of the two sets of coordinates (see 8). The tensor is called contravariant if s equals zero and covariant if r equals zero. A contravariant (respectively covariant) tensor of order one—i.e., of single order—reduces to a contravariant (respectively covariant) vector. In tensor algebra, a tensor can be multiplied by a scalar quantity and two tensors of the same orders can be added. Moreover, two tensors of

$$
\begin{array}{ll}
(1) & x_i = x_i(u^1, u^2), \qquad i = 1, 2, 3 \\[2mm]
(2) & \xi_i(u^1, u^2), \qquad i = 1, 2, 3 \\[2mm]
(3) & \begin{cases} I = ds^2 = \sum_i dx_i^2 \\ II = -\sum_i dx_i\, d\xi_i, \qquad i = 1, 2, 3 \end{cases} \\[4mm]
(4) & \sum_{\alpha, \beta} g_{\alpha, \beta}(u)\, du^\alpha du^\beta, \qquad \alpha, \beta = 1, \cdots, n \\[4mm]
(5) & \begin{cases} x^i, x'^j, \qquad i, j = 1, \cdots, n \\ x'^i = f^i(x^1, \cdots, x^n) \end{cases} \\[4mm]
(6) & \dfrac{\partial(f^1, \cdots, f^n)}{\partial(x^1, \cdots, x^n)} = \det\left(\dfrac{\partial f^i}{\partial x^j}\right) \neq 0 \\[4mm]
(7) & A^{i_1 \cdots i_r}_{j_1 \cdots j_s} \\[4mm]
(8) & A'^{i_1 \cdots i_r}_{j_1 \cdots j_s} = \sum_{k, l} \dfrac{\partial x'^{i_1}}{\partial x^{k_1}} \cdots \dfrac{\partial x'^{i_r}}{\partial x^{k_r}} \dfrac{\partial x^{l_1}}{\partial x'^{j_1}} \cdots \dfrac{\partial x^{l_s}}{\partial x'^{j_s}} A^{k_1 \cdots k_r}_{l_1 \cdots l_s} \\[4mm]
(9) & C^{i_1 \cdots i_{r+p}}_{j_1 \cdots j_{s+q}} = A^{i_1 \cdots i_r}_{j_1 \cdots j_s} B^{i_{r+1} \cdots i_{r+p}}_{j_{s+1} \cdots j_{s+q}} \\[4mm]
(10) & \begin{cases} A_{ijk} \text{ is symmetric in } i, j, \text{ if } A_{ijk} = A_{jik} \\ \text{antisymmetric in } i, j, \text{ if } A_{ijk} = -A_{jik} \end{cases}
\end{array}
$$

contravariant orders r, p and covariant orders s, q, respectively, have a product that is a tensor of contravariant order $r + p$ and covariant order $s + q$ (see 9). The vanishing of a tensor (i.e., of all the components) is a condition invariant with a change of local coordinates.

A tensor is symmetric (respectively antisymmetric) in two indices if the components remain unchanged (respectively change sign) on a permutation of the indices (see 10). A covariant tensor of order s is symmetric (respectively antisymmetric) if it is symmetric (respectively antisymmetric) in every pair of indices. The symmetry or antisymmetry of a tensor is again invariant with respect to a change of local coordinates.

All the tensors of given orders at a point form a vector space and the collection of all of them forms a tensor bundle of the manifold M. In particular, all the contravariant (respectively covariant) vectors form the tangent (respectively cotangent) bundle of M. The tensor bundles are special cases of a general vector bundle over M. A vector bundle over M is a collection of vector spaces over the points of M such that it is locally a product and that the linear structures on the vector spaces (referred to as fibres) have a respective representation. Two vector bundles E and F over M can be added; their sum, $E \oplus F$, is the vector bundle the fibre of which at a point of M is the direct sum of the fibres of E and F, respectively. The set of all vector bundles over M, with this addition, is a semi-group. By the introduction of "virtual bundles" (analogous to the introduction of negative integers in elementary arithmetic), all the finite linear combinations of the vector bundles over M, real or virtual, are made into a group. Through the tensor product of vector bundles the group acquires a multiplication representation and has a ring structure. This ring is called the Grothendieck ring (after Alexandre Grothendieck, a French mathematician); or K-ring of M; it is a significant global invariant of M. For technical reasons a simpler concept is obtained by the consideration of complex vector bundles over M, although M is itself a real manifold.

The fibre need not be a vector space. An important example is when it is the space of all frames (i.e., ordered sets of n linearly independent tangent vectors) at a point P of M. The resulting fibre space, the space of all frames

Principal fibre space

at all points of M, is called the principal fibre space; its dimension is $n^2 + n$. If M is the three-dimensional Euclidean space and the vectors of the frame are supposed to form an orthonormal system, then a frame is an oriented rectangular trihedral; the corresponding fibre space plays a basic role in the method of moving trihedrals in the theory of curves and surfaces in Euclidean space and in kinematics (motion without regard to mass or force). The method of moving frames, used extensively and successfully by Élie-Joseph Cartan, a French mathematician, in differential geometry, is a forerunner of the notion of principal fibre space.

OPERATIONS ON TENSOR FIELDS; CONNECTIONS

It is important to derive new tensor fields from given ones. If f is a real-valued function (*i.e.*, a tensor field of order zero), its partial derivatives are the components of a covariant vector field called the gradient of f. If A_i is a covariant vector field, then expressions formed by taking differences of relevant partial derivatives (see 11) are the components of an antisymmetric covariant tensor field of order 2, called the curl of A_i. Generally, if there is given an antisymmetric covariant tensor field of order r, its exterior derivative is a summation of products of certain of its partial derivatives and the function sign (see 12) in which sgn is the sign of the permutation under it and the summation is over all the j's. The exterior derivative is best expressed in terms of exterior differential forms. Such a form of degree r can be represented by a linear combination involving products of differentials (see 13) in which the multiplication of the differentials is antisymmetric (see 14) and the coefficients are supposed to be antisymmetric in their indices so that they are completely determined. By the use of the transformation law of the differentials (see 15) an exterior differential form of degree r can be identified with an antisymmetric covariant tensor field of order r. The exterior derivative can then be written (see 16).

Exterior differentiation

The basic reason for the operation of exterior differentiation lies in geometry. In fact, exterior differential forms are the integrands of multiple integrals. The integral of an arbitrary quantity ω over an r-dimensional domain D includes as special cases, for $r = 1$, $n = 2$ and $r = 2$, $n = 3$, respectively, the line integral in the plane and the surface integral in space. If D is the boundary of an $(r + 1)$-dimensional domain F, then the integral of ω over domain D is equal to the integral of $d\omega$ over domain F (see 17), which is a generalization of the Gauss–Green–Stokes formulas (named after Gauss and the British mathematicians George Green and George Gabriel Stokes).

Another important operation for tensor fields is the Lie derivative, first stated by Sophus Lie, a Norwegian mathematician. If X is a contravariant vector field with the components A^k in the local coordinate system x^i, in which $i, k = 1, \cdots, n$, and f is a real-valued function, then $Xf = \Sigma A^k(\partial/\partial x^k)f$ is a new real-valued function, the directional derivative of f relative to the vector field X. In this way X can be regarded as a linear differential operator on functions. If Y is another vector field, it can be shown that the matrix $[X, Y]$, equal to $XY - YX$, is also a linear combination of $\partial/\partial x^k$ and defines a vector field. This is called the bracket operation of two vector fields. More generally, a vector field X defines an infinitesimal transformation $\delta x^i = A^i \delta t$, $i = 1, \cdots n$, and the study of the variation of a tensor field under this infinitesimal transformation leads to a new tensor field of the same type. The latter is called the Lie derivative relative to X. The Lie derivative relative to X of the tensor field $B_k{}^{ij}$ is determined by the components (see 18).

Generally a tensor field cannot be differentiated to give a new tensor field because the local coordinates have no geometrical meaning. A structure on the manifold that makes this possible is called an affine connection or simply a connection. It is given by a set of components $\Gamma_{ik}{}^j$ in each chart, which, with a change of local coordinates, follow a transformation rule (see 19). These components do not, therefore, define tensor fields. But

The affine connection

$$(11) \quad A_{ij} = \frac{1}{2}\left(\frac{\partial A_i}{\partial x^j} - \frac{\partial A_j}{\partial x^i}\right)$$

$$(12) \quad A_{i_1 \cdots i_{r+1}} = \frac{1}{(r+1)!} \sum \mathrm{sgn}\binom{j_1 \cdots j_{r+1}}{i_1 \cdots i_{r+1}} \frac{\partial A_{j_1 \cdots j_r}}{\partial x^{j_{r+1}}}$$

$$(13) \quad \omega = \frac{1}{r!} \sum_{i_1, \cdots, i_r} A_{i_1 \cdots i_r} dx^{i_1} \wedge \cdots \wedge dx^{i_r}$$

$$(14) \quad dx^i \wedge dx^j = -dx^j \wedge dx^i$$

$$(15) \quad dx'^i = \sum_j \frac{\partial x'^i}{\partial x^j} dx^j$$

$$(16) \quad d\omega = \frac{1}{r!} \sum_{i_1, \cdots, i_r} dA_{i_1 \cdots i_r} \wedge dx^{i_1} \wedge \cdots \wedge dx^{i_r}$$

$$(17) \quad \int_D \omega = \int_F d\omega$$

$$(18) \quad [L(X)B]_k^{ij} = \sum_l \left\{ A^l \frac{\partial B_k^{ij}}{\partial x^l} - B_k^{il} \frac{\partial A^j}{\partial x^l} - B_k^{lj} \frac{\partial A^i}{\partial x^l} + B_l^{ij} \frac{\partial A^l}{\partial x^k} \right\}$$

$$(19) \quad \Gamma_{ik}'^j = \sum_{l,m,r} \Gamma_{lm}^r \frac{\partial x^l}{\partial x'^i} \frac{\partial x^m}{\partial x'^k} \frac{\partial x'^j}{\partial x^r} + \sum_l \frac{\partial x'^j}{\partial x^i} \frac{\partial^2 x^l}{\partial x'^i \partial x'^k}$$

$$(20) \quad A_{j,k}^i = \frac{\partial A_j^i}{\partial x^k} + \sum_k \left(\Gamma_{lk}^i A_j^l - \Gamma_{jk}^l A_l^i \right)$$

$$(21) \quad \sum_k A_{j,k}^i \frac{dx^k}{dt} = 0$$

they can be used to derive from a tensor field of contravariant order r and covariant order s a new tensor field of contravariant order r and covariant order $s + 1$, called the covariant derivative of a tensor field. In the simple case of a tensor field $A_j{}^i$ its covariant derivative has a simply expressed form (see 20). The tensor field is called parallel along a curve $x^i = x^i(t)$ if a condition is met (see 21). In the special case of the affine space where the connection is defined by $\Gamma_{ik}{}^j = 0$, parallelism of $A_j{}^i$ means the constancy of all the components. A Riemannian manifold has a uniquely determined connection, the Levi-Civita connection (named after Tullio Levi-Civita, an Italian mathematician), which is characterized by the two properties: (A) the length of a vector remains unchanged under parallelism; and (B) $\Gamma_{ik}{}^j = \Gamma_{ki}{}^j$.

DE RHAM AND HODGE THEOREMS

The importance of exterior differential forms and their exterior derivatives lies in the fact that they help in solving problems on manifolds in which local and global properties come into interplay with a link furnished by de Rham's theorem (named after Georges de Rham, a Swiss mathematician). An exterior differential form is called closed if its exterior derivative is zero; it is called a derived form if it is the exterior derivative of another. It follows from definition that a derived form is closed. The closed forms can be divided into classes such that two forms belong to the same class if and only if their difference is a derived form. All the classes of closed forms of degree r form a real vector space H^r. This space is manageable, in the sense that contrast exists to the space of all forms of degree r or even that of all closed forms, both of which are "large" and generally infinite-dimensional. If the manifold is compact—*i.e.*, if it can be covered by a finite number of coordinate charts— de Rham's theorem says that the dimension of the space

H^r is the rth Betti number (named after Enrico Betti, a 19th-century Italian mathematician) of the manifold. The latter is an integer and is a topological invariant of the manifold that describes its connectivity properties.

The Riemannian metric

The presence of a Riemannian metric on a manifold M gives it an important structure and allows further operations. With M moreover oriented, the Riemannian metric associates with an r-vector an orthogonal $(n - r)$-vector that is coherently oriented and has the same measure. This operation extends to an operation on exterior differential forms, the so-called star operation. If ω is of degree r, then $*\omega$ is of degree $n - r$. In terms of the star operator, the codifferential of an exterior differential form of degree r is defined by δ equal to $(-1)^{nr + n + 1} * d *$; δ diminishes the degree by one. A form ω is called coclosed if $\delta\omega$ is equal to zero. Since dd is zero, then $\delta\delta$ is equal to zero and the Laplace operator Δ may be introduced (see 22), which maps a form into one of the same degree. A form ω is called harmonic if $\Delta\omega$ is equal to zero. A form that is both closed and coclosed is harmonic. On a compact manifold the converse is also true. In the special case of a real-valued function $u(x, y)$ in the Euclidean (x, y)-plane, the relation $\Delta u = -u_{xx} - u_{yy}$ applies. Thus, harmonic forms generalize the classical harmonic functions. Hodge's theorem (named after William Vallance Douglas Hodge, a British mathematician) says that on a compact orientable Riemannian manifold there is exactly one harmonic form in every class of closed forms of degree r (in the sense defined above). The theorem is a wide generalization of fundamental results on compact Riemann surfaces in complex function theory. It has important applications to algebraic geometry.

GAUSS-BONNET FORMULA AND CHARACTERISTIC CLASSES

If A^i is a contravariant vector field on a manifold with an affine connection, the second covariant derivatives $A^i{}_{,j,k}$ are in general not symmetric in j, k. The measure of their deviation from symmetry is given by the curvature tensor. More precisely, under the hypothesis that the connection is symmetric—$\Gamma_{ik}{}^j = \Gamma_{ki}{}^j$—the Ricci commutation formula applies (see 23) in which (see 24) the $R_{ljk}{}^i$ components are the components of a tensor field of contravariant order one and covariant order three. It is called the curvature tensor of the connection. From the curvature tensor the most significant invariants are built up by first introducing differential forms (see 25; referred to as the curvature forms) and then considering the coefficients of the appropriate polynomial of t (see 26). The Kronecker index $\delta_i{}^j$ is employed here, which denotes the value 1 when i is equal to j and zero when i is unequal to j. By definition $p_k(\Omega)$, $k = 1, \cdots, n$, is an exterior differential form of degree $2k$, because each $\Omega_i{}^j$ is of degree two. From the tensorial behaviour of $R_{ljk}{}^i$ there follows immediately that $p_k(\Omega)$ is independent of the choice of the local chart, thereby being forms defined over the whole manifold M. Moreover, they are closed.

The Pontryagin characteristic classes

A fundamental theorem on characteristic classes postulates that for odd k, $p_k(\Omega)$ is a derived form, whereas for even k, $p_k(\Omega)$ determines a class (in the sense of de Rham's theorem) called the Pontryagin characteristic class of M (named after the Soviet mathematician Lev Semyonovich Pontryagin). The latter class ranks among one of the first global invariants that measure the deviation of the tangent bundle of M from a product bundle. Thus the local properties of a connection, the curvature tensor, determine in their totality certain global properties, the Pontryagin characteristic classes. In particular, if M has a flat affine connection for which $R_{ljk}{}^i$ vanish identically, all the Pontryagin classes of M are zero. An example of a manifold with a nonzero Pontryagin class is the complex projective plane; i.e., the complex Euclidean plane with a line at infinity added. Therefore, this manifold, of four real dimensions, cannot be equipped with a flat affine connection. The above theorem on characteristic classes is, however, much more precise, and the following conclusion may be formulated: With M a compact oriented manifold of dimension four, and

$$(22) \qquad \Delta = (d + \delta)^2 = d\delta + \delta d$$

$$(23) \qquad A^i{}_{,j,k} - A^i{}_{,k,j} = -\sum_l R_{ljk}{}^i A^l$$

$$(24) \qquad R_{ljk}{}^i = \frac{\partial \Gamma_{lk}^i}{\partial x^j} - \frac{\partial \Gamma_{lj}^i}{\partial x^k} + \sum_m (\Gamma_{mj}^i \Gamma_{lk}^m - \Gamma_{mk}^i \Gamma_{lj}^m)$$

$$(25) \qquad \Omega_i^j = \tfrac{1}{2} \sum_{k,l} R_{ikl}^j \, dx^k \wedge dx^l$$

$$(26) \qquad \det\left(t\delta_i^j - \frac{1}{2\pi} \Omega_i^j \right) = t^n + p_1(\Omega)t^{n-1} + \cdots + p_n(\Omega)$$

$$(27) \qquad \operatorname{sign} M = \frac{1}{24\pi^2} \int_M \sum_{i,j} \Omega_i^j \wedge \Omega_j^i, \qquad i, j = 1, \cdots, 4$$

$$(28) \qquad ds^2 = \sum_{i,k} g_{ik}(x) \, dx^i \, dx^k, \qquad g_{ik} = g_{ki}$$

$$(29) \qquad \Omega_{ij} = \sum_k \Omega_i^k g_{jk}$$

$$(30) \qquad \Omega_{ij} + \Omega_{ji} = 0$$

$$(31) \qquad Pf(\Omega) = \frac{(-1)^p}{2^n \pi^p p! \sqrt{g}} \sum \epsilon_{i_1 \cdots i_n} \Omega_{i_1 i_2} \wedge \cdots \wedge \Omega_{i_{n-1} i_n}$$

$$(32) \qquad \int_M Pf(\Omega) = \chi(M)$$

for two closed forms ω, θ of degree two, the integral over M of the product of the closed forms is a real number that depends only on the classes to which the forms ω, θ belong in the space H^2 (see above *de Rham and Hodge theorems*). This defines a symmetric bilinear function on H^2; its signature—the number of its positive eigenvalues minus the number of its negative eigenvalues—is a topological invariant of M, called the signature of M. The relation between characteristic classes and curvature gives an integral formula for the signature of M (see 27). A generalization of this formula holds for any compact orientable manifold of dimension $4s$ with an affine connection according to Hirzebruch's signature theorem (named after Friedrich Ernst Peter Hirzebruch, a German mathematician).

When the affine connection is the Levi-Civita connection of a Riemannian metric given by a positive definite quadratic differential form (see 28) the curvature forms have special properties. By one such property, certain forms (see 29) are antisymmetric (see 30). In the case of manifold M of even dimension, n equal to $2p$, and oriented, an important combination of the curvature forms is given by the Pfaffian (see 31) in which a constant g is equal to $\det(g_{ij})$; the constants ϵ are equal to $+1$ or -1 according as the subscript is an even or odd permutation of $1, \cdots, n$, and is otherwise zero; and the summation is over all the i's from 1 to n. For a compact manifold M without boundary the Gauss–Bonnet formula (see 32; it is named after Gauss and Pierre-Ossian Bonnet, a 19th-century French mathematician) is one in which $\chi(M)$ is the Euler-Poincaré characteristic of M, again a topological invariant of M.

The Euler-Poincaré characteristic has also the following combinatorial interpretation: if M is subdivided into a complex of cells, of all dimensions from 0 to n, then it can be written as a sum of terms of the type $(-1)^r \alpha_r$, in which α_r is the number of r-dimensional cells in the subdivision.

A more general formula holds for the case in which M has a boundary. In the simple case that M is two-dimensional and is bounded by a sectionally smooth curve, the Gauss-Bonnet formula (see 33) is one that involves integrals and in which $\pi - \alpha_i$ are the exterior angles at the corners of the boundary curve C of M, k_g is the geodesic curvature of C, K is the Gaussian curvature, and dA is the element of area of M. In the formula, the sum of the exterior angles and integrals of the geodesic curvature and the Gaussian curvature are added to equal a constant times the Euler-Poincaré characteristic of the manifold. If K is a constant not equal to zero and M is bounded by geodesic arcs (so that $k_g = 0$), the Gauss-Bonnet formula expresses the area of a geodesic polygon in terms of its angles, a well-known result in non-Euclidean geometry. If K is zero, the Gauss-Bonnet formula contains the classical theorem that the sum of the angles of a triangle in the Euclidean plane is equal to π.

ELLIPTIC OPERATORS

Elliptic differential operators, linear or nonlinear, play an important role in differential geometry. Some of the most important global invariants of manifolds arise from the consideration of elliptic operators. If $\pi : E \to M$ be a complex vector bundle—that is, a vector bundle the fibres of which are complex vector spaces—a differentiable section $s : M \to E$ is a mapping such that the result is the identity mapping when followed by π. By ΓE is denoted the space of all differentiable sections of E. Locally s can be defined by its components $(s_1(x^i), \cdots , s_p(x^i))$, in which p is the dimension of the fibre of E. If $\phi : F \to M$ is a complex vector bundle with the same fibre dimension, a differential operator D is a mapping $D : \Gamma E \to \Gamma F$, such that Ds, as a section of the bundle F, has locally specific components (see 34, 35) in which α stands for the multi-index (see 36). The differential operator D is referred to as of order q if the absolute value of α, $|\alpha|$, is equal to or less than q. It is called elliptic in the order q if a matrix (see 37) is nonsingular whenever $(\xi_1, \cdots , \xi_n)$ is not equal to zero. A simple example of an elliptic operator is the Laplacian in (22).

If ker D (kernel of D) is the space of all sections $s \in \Gamma E$ such that Ds is zero, and if coker D (i.e., cokernel of D) is the quotient space $\Gamma F / D\Gamma E$ that is isomorphic to the kernel of the adjoint operator of D, then by a theorem in the theory of elliptic operators, if M is compact, both ker D and coker D are finite-dimensional, and the index of D can be defined (see 38) in terms of them. An index theorem conceived by the mathematicians Michael Francis Atiyah (British) and I.M. Singer (U.S.) states that the integer index D can be expressed in terms of topological invariants, depending on the bundles E, F, and the operator D. The theorem includes as special cases the Gauss-Bonnet formula, the Hirzebruch signature theorem, and the Riemann-Roch theorem for an arbitrary compact complex manifold.

ISOMETRIC IMBEDDING, SUBMANIFOLDS,
AND MODERN DEVELOPMENTS IN SURFACE THEORY

Although there is a great variety of manifolds, the Euclidean space is generally regarded as the simplest and the one with the most intuitive appeal. Whether a manifold with a certain structure is equivalent to a submanifold of a Euclidean space of sufficiently high dimension is known as the imbedding problem; the determination of the extent to which the submanifold is thus determined is the rigidity problem. When only the differentiable structure is involved, Hassler Whitney, an American mathematician, proved in 1936 that every differentiable manifold of dimension n can be imbedded in a Euclidean space of dimension $2n + 1$. That the same is true for compact real analytic manifolds was proved by another United States mathematician, Charles Bradfield Morrey, Jr., in 1958. The isometric imbedding problem deals with the imbedding of a Riemannian manifold, with whether a given Riemannian manifold is isometric to a submanifold of some Euclidean space. The local problem—the isometric imbedding of a sufficiently small piece of manifold—was solved by the French mathematicians M. Janet and Élie-Joseph Cartan in 1926, under the additional assumption of analyticity. For an n-dimensional manifold the dimension required of the ambient space is $n(n + 1)/2$, a number long conjectured

The rigidity problem (margin note)

by a Swiss mathematician, Ludwig Schläfli. Thus a two-dimensional analytic Riemannian metric is locally that of a surface in Euclidean three-space. The global isometric imbedding theorem of nonanalytic Riemannian manifolds was proved by J. Nash, Jr., in 1954–56.

A special case of the rigidity problem is concerned with the question whether two submanifolds in a Euclidean space are congruent when they are isometric as abstract Riemannian manifolds. If the dimension n of the submanifolds is greater than two, the condition of isometry is strong enough so that they are almost always congruent. A particular case occurs in the classical theory of surfaces in Euclidean three-space. A theorem that was proved in 1927 by S. Cohn-Vossen states that two closed convex surfaces (surfaces with positive Gaussian curvature everywhere) are equivalent under rigid motions if they are isometric. Easy examples show that the convexity assumption cannot be dropped. An important complement to the Cohn-Vossen theorem is a 1971 result of R. Greene and H. Wu that the conclusion remains true when the surfaces have deleted from them a finite number of their points. A related question concerns the behaviour of a continuous family of closed isometric surfaces. Liebmann proved in 1899 that with the additional hypothesis of convexity such a family must be the one obtained by the rigid motion of one of its members. It is yet an outstanding unsolved problem whether or not it is possible to omit the convexity assumption in Liebmann's theorem.

$$(33) \qquad \sum_i (\pi - \alpha_i) + \int_C k_g \, ds + \iint_M K \, dA = 2\pi \chi(M)$$

$$(34) \qquad \sum_{1 \leqslant j \leqslant p} \sum_\alpha a^j_{k,\alpha}(x^i) \, D^\alpha s_j, \qquad k = 1, \cdots , p$$

$$(35) \qquad D^\alpha = \frac{\partial^{\alpha_1}}{(\partial x^1)^{\alpha_1}} \cdots \frac{\partial^{\alpha_n}}{(\partial x^n)^{\alpha_n}}$$

$$(36) \qquad \alpha = (\alpha_1, \cdots , \alpha_n), \qquad |\alpha| = \alpha_1 + \cdots + \alpha_n$$

$$(37) \qquad \left(\sum_{|\alpha| = q} a^j_{k,\alpha} \xi^\alpha \right), \qquad \xi^\alpha = \xi_1^{\alpha_1} \cdots \xi_n^{\alpha_n}$$

$$(38) \qquad \text{ind } D = \dim \ker D - \dim \operatorname{coker} D$$

The study of submanifolds in a Euclidean (or non-Euclidean) space is an outgrowth of the classical works of Monge and Gauss and has had important developments in recent years. The new feature lies in the emphasis on global properties. The difficulty of the problems can be realized by noting that the geometrical properties are generally expressed by a system of nonlinear partial differential equations or inequalities and little is known about the behaviour of their global solutions. An important part is furnished by the global theory of surfaces in Euclidean three-space. A surface has two important scalar invariants, the mean curvature H and the Gaussian curvature K, which are defined by $H = (k_1 + k_2)/2$, $K = k_1, k_2$, in which k_1 and k_2 (referred to as the principal curvatures) are the eigenvalues of the second fundamental form relative to the first fundamental form. Surfaces with H equal to zero are called minimal surfaces, which are characterized by the local property that any small piece has the least area when compared with other surfaces with the same boundary curve. Among minimal surfaces are the catenoids and right helicoids. A famous problem of Joseph Antoine Ferdinand Plateau, a Belgian mathematician, solved by Tibor Rado and Jesse Douglas in 1930–31, is to show the existence of a minimal surface with a given boundary curve, a fact physically demonstrable by soap-bubble experiments. The solution allows minimal surfaces with singular points. In 1970 Robert Osserman, a United States mathematician,

Global properties (margin note)

proved that the solution of this classical Plateau problem must be a minimal surface that is everywhere regular. It may be readily demonstrated that there is no closed minimal surface in space.

The theory of minimal surfaces is closely related to complex function theory because minimal surfaces are characterized by the property that the spherical mapping into the unit sphere is orientation-reversing conformal. Surfaces with H equal to a constant include the spheres. Whether a closed surface of constant mean curvature is necessarily a sphere is an unanswered question. It was shown in 1955 by Aleksandr Danilovich Aleksandrov, a Soviet mathematician, that a closed surface of constant mean curvature is a sphere if it does not have self-intersections.

A surface with Gaussian curvature K equal to zero is referred to as a developable surface and generally consists of the tangent lines of a curve. It is therefore non-compact. To have meaningful results on non-compact surfaces the notion of completeness is introduced: it means that every geodesic can be indefinitely extended. Hartman and Nirenberg proved in 1959 that a complete developable surface must be a cylinder that is generated by the lines parallel to a fixed direction. A complete surface of constant positive Gaussian curvature must be closed (theorem of Myers) and must therefore be the sphere (theorem of Liebmann). David Hilbert, a German mathematician, proved that there is no complete surface of constant negative Gaussian curvature; in other words, such a surface must have a singular point. This result was extended, and it was proved in 1964 that a complete surface with Gaussian curvature $K \leqslant -c < 0$ (c is a constant) must have a singular point. More general than the surfaces of constant mean curvature or constant Gaussian curvature are the Weingarten surfaces, or W-surfaces. These surfaces satisfy a functional relation between the mean curvature and the Gaussian curvature. Some of the above results can be extended to W-surfaces.

In regard to a high-dimensional Euclidean space, many investigations have been accorded the minimal varieties of the family of submanifolds. These minimal varieties are direct generalizations of the minimal surfaces, and in respect to them a k-dimensional submanifold is minimal if a sufficiently small piece of it has the least volume compared with other k-dimensional submanifolds with the same $(k-1)$-dimensional boundary. The most important cases are k equal to 1 (geodesics) and k equal to $n-1$ (minimal hypersurfaces), in which n is the dimension of the ambient space. When n is greater than three, the solution of Plateau's problem, that of determining a minimal hypersurface with a given boundary, was only carried out by allowing the submanifold to have singularities. E. Bombieri, E. de Giorgi, and E. Giusti proved in 1969 that this is necessarily the case in high dimensions. It is a natural phenomenon in differential geometry that the study of geometrical problems calls for the introduction of objects that are not everywhere smooth. The study of the singularities and their properties according to the problems in question will likely be one of the major concerns of differential geometry in the future.

In contrast to the Plateau problem is the uniqueness problem. In 1914 S. Bernstein proved that a minimal surface in the Euclidean three-space with the coordinates x_1, x_2, x_3, which has the representation $x_3 = f(x_1, x_2)$ for all x_1, x_2, is a plane. This theorem was extended by de Giorgi, Almgren, and Simons (1965–67) to a Euclidean space of dimension equal to or less than eight. They proved that, in a Euclidean space with the coordinates $x_1, \cdots, x_n$, a minimal hypersurface that has the representation $x_n = f(x_1, \cdots, x_{n-1})$ for all values of $x_1, \cdots, x_{n-1}$ is a hyperplane. The dimension restriction is essential, for Bombieri, de Giorgi, and Giusti constructed examples in 1968 to show that the same statement is no longer true for n equal to or greater than nine.

COMPLEX MANIFOLDS

By allowing the local coordinates of a manifold to be complex numbers a class of spaces is reached that is restrictive. Such a class of spaces is of great importance in mathematics. A complex manifold is a manifold the local charts of which have coordinates represented by complex numbers such that the local coordinates of the same point in two charts, z^i and z'^k respectively, i, $k = 1, \cdots, n$, are related by a transformation expressed in terms of holomorphic functions with the Jacobian determinant not equal to zero. The integer n denotes the complex dimension, and the space, as a real manifold, is of dimension $2n$. The simplest example of a complex manifold is furnished by the Gaussian plane C, which is the space of one complex coordinate $z = x + iy$. It is the same as the plane with the two real coordinates x, y but has the additional structure that it is possible, in the Gaussian plane C, to have the notions of holomorphic (or complex analytic) functions and conformal transformations. The stereographic projection of a sphere S in the Euclidean space on C is conformal and makes S into complex manifold of dimension one. This, which is referred to as the Riemann sphere, can be regarded as the compactification of C, as a complex manifold, by the addition of a point at infinity. The compactification process is generally of great importance because it reduces the study of a non-compact space to a compact space relative to the ideal set added to the former. The same situation prevails in high dimensions. The complex projective space $P_n(C)$ of dimension n is a space whose points are described by $n+1$ homogeneous coordinates $(z_0, z_1, \cdots, z_n) \neq (0, 0, \cdots, 0)$ such that two sets of homogeneous coordinates define the same point if and only if they are proportional. The space is covered by $n+1$ charts satisfying respectively the condition z_i not equal to 0, $i = 0, 1, \cdots, n$, in which the local coordinates are z_j/z_i, $j \neq i$, $j = 0, 1, \cdots, n$. Each chart represents $P_n(C)$ with a hyperplane deleted and it itself the n-dimensional complex number space C_n. In other words, $P_n(C)$ is obtained from C_n by the addition of a hyperplane. The complex projective space is the source of an important class of complex manifolds, viz., the nonsingular algebraic varieties. They are defined by a number of homogeneous polynomial equations in the homogeneous coordinates $z_0, \cdots, z_n$.

Differential geometry plays a role in the transcendental theory of algebraic varieties because of the use made of the Hermitian metric. A Hermitian metric on a complex manifold is given in terms of the local coordinates z_i, $i = 1, \cdots, n$, by the Hermitian differential form (see 39) involving h_{ik} that are complex-valued C^∞-functions in x_j, y_j ($z_j = x_j + iy_j$, $j = 1, \cdots, n$) having the Hermitian property $\bar{h}_{ik} = h_{ki}$. In spite of its formal analogy with a Riemannian metric, the Hermitian structure has more refined properties. In particular, there is intrinsically associated with it a real-valued exterior differential form of degree two (see 40) in which the multiplication of differentials is replaced by the exterior product. The Hermitian metric is called Kählerian if Ω is closed; i.e., if $d\Omega = 0$. The Kählerian metric is said to be of restricted type if the integral of Ω over any two-dimensional integral cycle is a rational number. The previously referred to complex projective space $P_n(C)$ has a Kählerian metric of restricted type, the Fubini-Study metric, which is defined in terms of the homogeneous coordinates z (see 41). As a consequence, every nonsingular algebraic va-

The compactification process

$$(39) \quad ds^2 = \sum_{i,k} h_{ik}\, dz_i\, d\bar{z}_k, \qquad i, k = 1, \cdots, n$$

$$(40) \quad \Omega = \frac{i}{2} \sum_{i,k} h_{ik}\, dz_i \wedge d\bar{z}_k$$

$$(41) \quad ds^2 = \frac{\left(\sum_i |z_i|^2\right)\left(\sum_k dz_k\, d\bar{z}_k\right) - \left(\sum_i \bar{z}_i\, dz_i\right)\left(\sum_k z_k\, d\bar{z}_k\right)}{\left(\sum_i |z_i|^2\right)^2}$$

$$i, k = 0, 1, \cdots, n$$

Complete surfaces

riety of $P_n(C)$ inherits a Kählerian metric of restricted type. The Kodaira imbedding theorem states that the converse is true: every compact complex manifold with a Kählerian metric of restricted type can be imbedded in a complex projective space of sufficiently high dimension as an algebraic variety.

Two typical problems on complex manifolds are now presented. The first concerns the Abelian differentials, exterior differential forms (see 42), the coefficients of which are holomorphic functions. On a compact complex manifold M the maximum number of linearly independent forms of this kind of a given degree k is a finite integer h_{ko}. Their alternating sum (see 43) is referred to as the arithmetic genus of M. The relation of the arithmetic genus, which is an analytical invariant, with some of the geometrical invariants of M, the characteristic classes, is given by the Riemann-Roch-Hirzebruch theorem.

$$(42) \qquad \sum a_{i_1 \cdots i_k}(z) \, dz^{i_1} \wedge \cdots \wedge dz^{i_k}$$

$$(43) \qquad \sum_{0 \le k \le n} (-1)^k \, h_{ko}, \qquad n = \dim_C M$$

The second problem is the role played by the measures that arise from the Hermitian metric. In the simple case of a holomorphic curve $f: M \to P_1(C)$, which is the same as a meromorphic function over the Riemann surface M, the area of the image $f(M)$ leads to the Nevanlinna order function in the definition of Ahlfors-Shimizu. This and its generalizations are of fundamental importance in the study of holomorphic curves in $P_n(C)$.

LOCAL AND GLOBAL PROBLEMS

Problems in differential geometry can generally be divided into two types: local problems and global problems. The tangent space at a point and different concepts of curvature are local problems. But the validity of a certain local property throughout the manifold could impose strong restrictions on the manifold as a whole; the determination of such restrictions is a global problem. Thus, there are pieces of surfaces in Euclidean space with constant Gaussian curvature, but the spheres are the only surfaces that have constant Gaussian curvature and that are closed. Also, it is a local property for a curve on a Riemannian manifold to be a geodesic, but the index of a geodesic (*i.e.*, the number of essentially different deformations that shorten the geodesic with the end-points fixed) is a global invariant. Other problems on geodesics concern the existence or nonexistence of closed geodesics and the ergodicity of geodesic flows, both of which are global problems.

BIBLIOGRAPHY. Among the books on differential geometry the following may be recommended: SHOSHICHI KOBAYASHI and KATSUMI NOMIZU, *Foundations of Differential Geometry* (1963); JAMES J. STOKER, *Differential Geometry* (1969); FRANK W. WARNER, *Foundations of Differentiable Manifolds and Lie Groups* (1971). For topology and fibre bundles, see EDWIN H. SPANIER, *Algebraic Topology* (1966); and DALE HUSEMOLLER, *Fibre Bundles* (1966). For complex manifolds, see S. CHERN, *Complex Manifolds Without Potential Theory* (1967); and F. HIRZEBRUCH, *Neue topologische Methoden in der algebraischen Geometrie*, 2nd ed. (1962; Eng. trans., *Topological Methods in Algebraic Geometry*, 3rd ed., 1966). For K-theory and the index theorem, see MICHAEL F. ATIYAH, *K-theory* (1964); RICHARD S. PALAIS (ed.), *Seminar on the Atiyah-Singer Index Theorem* (1965); MICHAEL F. ATIYAH and I.M. SINGER, "The Index of Elliptic Operators, I–V," *Ann. Math.*, vol. 88 and 93 (1968–71). Recent papers on minimal varieties include JAMES SIMONS, "Minimal Varieties in Riemannian Manifolds," *Ann. Math.*, 88:62–105 (1968); ROBERT OSSERMAN, "A Proof of the Regularity Everywhere of the Classical Solution to Plateau's Problem," *Ann. Math.*, 91:550–569 (1970); E. BOMBIERI, E. DE GIORGI, and E. GIUSTI, "Minimal Cones and the Bernstein Problem," *Inven. Math.*, 7:243–268 (1969).

(S.S.C.)

Geometry, Euclidean

One of the outstanding achievements of the ancient Greeks was the construction of a deductive system of geometry, which, beginning with principles that they regarded as obviously true and derived from experience, culminated in quite deep theorems, some of which are still an important part of mathematics. The elementary part of the deductive system of geometry was set forth in Euclid's *Elements*, and, until the early 20th century, Euclidean geometry meant the material in that book and others written in the same spirit. Euclid reasoned on the figure drawn on the page or envisioned in the imagination, and he often assumed details and relations read from the figure that were not explicitly stated. The figure was an important constituent of the proof, although it was never made clear how far it should be used. Partly because Euclid's geometry was considered to be the only geometry, no one bothered to question or examine many of its details.

Toward the end of the 19th century another view emerged, and Euclidean geometry is now regarded as merely one example of an abstract mathematical doctrine. In any deductive theory, because each theorem is proved from preceding theorems, a beginning must be made somewhere with unproved assumptions. These assumptions are called axioms, replacing Euclid's word postulates. Whether, or in what sense, they are "true" is no concern of the theory: any set of axioms may be laid down provided that they do not yield two contradictory theorems. Likewise, as each technical term (*e.g.*, square or perpendicular) is defined by reference to earlier terms, this chain cannot lead backward indefinitely, and a beginning must be made with certain undefined terms. What these terms mean is of no concern in the abstract theory, although they may acquire meaning in some application of the theory. The undefined terms may be elements, such as point, line, or relations such as "lies on" in the statement: the point A lies on the line l. If, for example, a triangle ABC is defined as the set of points on the sides BC, CA, AB, together with the points A, B, C, then the terms "point" and "side" must either have been defined previously or be taken as undefined. The term set, however, is a concept of logic, and it is assumed that logic has already been developed. Many writers on an abstract doctrine try to reduce the number of undefined terms and of axioms to a minimum.

Deductive theory as an abstract mathematical doctrine

Until the 20th century the book of Euclid or one of its many variants was used in all schools, a use, however, that was ultimately attacked justifiably from two sides: Euclid was too abstract for beginners, yet not exact enough to satisfy modern requirements. The modern abstract treatment was initiated by mathematicians in Germany and Italy, by Moritz Pasch in 1882, Giuseppe Peano in 1889 and Mario Pieri. The most influential work was that by the well-known German mathematician David Hilbert, *Grundlagen der Geometrie* (1899; *The Foundations of Geometry*, 1902).

Euclid (*q.v.*), who lived in Alexandria in the time of the first Ptolemy (323–285/283 BC), systematized in his book the work of his predecessors, beginning with Pythagoras (died *c.* 500 BC) and his followers. It was the basis of the more advanced studies of Apollonius of Perga (3rd century BC) on conics and of Archimedes (*q.v.*; 3rd century BC) on mechanics and the areas of circles. After the collapse of European civilization the Muslim countries continued the tradition. The *Elements* was translated into Arabic during the reign of Hārūn ar-Rashīd (786–809), and the first Latin version in a complete form was made from the Arabic by the English scholastic philosopher Adelard of Bath about 1120. The book was thus known to some extent in the Middle Ages, but not until the invention of printing in the 15th century was it seriously studied at Oxford and Cambridge. The first complete English translation was that of Sir Henry Billingsley in 1570; other important editions were those of Robert Simson (Latin and English) in 1756 and Isaac Todhunter in 1862. The standard English edition is now that of Sir Thomas Little Heath, published in 1908.

The Elements

EUCLID'S WORK

Euclid's definitions and axioms. Euclid began his work with definitions, axioms, and "common notions." He describes a point as something with no part, a line (what would now be called an arc, or curve) as length without breadth, and a straight line as one that lies evenly with its points. It is clear that these cannot now be taken as definitions in the modern spirit, referring back, as they do, to notions not only undefined but obscure. His definition of a circle (the usual one), however, can be taken over into the modern abstract theory. It should be noted that straight line in modern geometry means the infinite line, whereas for Euclid it means the portion between two points, now called an interval, which can be "prolonged" in both directions.

The axioms that Euclid explicitly stated were five in number (see Box, axioms 1–5), of which the fifth, since called the parallel axiom, is the most famous. Without explicitly stating it, he assumed that the join between two points is unique.

Euclid's common notions. Euclid's common notions are also five in number (see 6–10). The first three concern "equals" or "equal things"; the fourth is interpreted now to mean that if two figures, such as intervals, angles, triangles, or circles, are such that one can be moved to coincide with the other, the figures are equal. They would now be called congruent. Two ideas run through these common notions: (1) that geometrical figures can be treated as magnitudes, and (2) that, if one figure is visibly part of another (perhaps after a motion), then the magnitude of the part is less than the magnitude of the whole.

Euclid's Book I: congruence of triangles. Euclid's Book I is in two sections, the first dealing with the congruence of triangles, without any use of parallels. It is interesting to observe that even in his first theorem, in which he constructs an equilateral triangle, Euclid assumes from the figure that two constructed circles intersect. With the aid of this construction he shows that if AB is a given interval and OX a given line, then using only the third axiom, an interval OP can be cut off OX congruent to AB. Thus his compasses can be allowed to collapse after a circle is drawn; they need not be used to transfer lengths. His fourth theorem is the first congruence of triangles. It states that if in triangles ABC, $A'B'C'$, the sides BA, BC, and the angle between them, $\angle ABC$, are respectively congruent to $B'A'$, $B'C'$, $\angle A'B'C'$, then AC is congruent to $A'C'$. (The word congruent here replaces Euclid's "equal.")

Euclid's concept of congruence   For proof he takes up triangle ABC and moves it so that B falls on B', the line BA lies along $B'A'$, and C lies on the same side of $B'A'$ as C'. He concludes that C falls on C' and hence AC on $A'C'$. Even putting aside what is meant by motion, this proof would succeed only if it were assumed that AC maintained a constant length. Since this assumption is just what the theorem is supposed to prove, the reasoning is circular. Euclid himself evidently had doubts, for he employs this "method of superposition" only once again, in the proof of the 24th theorem of the third book, although its use would have shortened many other proofs.

Euclid's Book I: other theorems. Once the first congruence has been stated, others, involving three sides, and a side and two angles, follow if it is assumed that the lengths of intervals and the sizes of angles satisfy the common notions. Euclid reads these assumptions from his figures. In the context of verifying the fifth theorem he proves that an isosceles triangle has congruent base angles. The involved proof acquired the name of *pons asinorum* ("asses' bridge," or path over which to guide the obstinate). Later, he solves the two problems, to bisect a given angle or interval and to draw a perpendicular to a line from a point not on it. The proof of theorem 16 shows that if a side of a triangle is produced, the exterior angle is greater than either of the opposite interior angles, and the proof of theorem 18 shows that if a triangle has two unequal sides, the greater side is opposite the greater angle. Following the statement of theorem 20, Euclid proves the intuitive result that the sum

of the lengths of the sides AB, BC in a triangle exceeds the length of AC, indicating that he desired to keep the number of axioms as low as possible.

Euclid's Book I: results independent of the parallel postulate. It is highly important to note that so far in Euclid's Book I no use has been made of parallel lines, defined as coplanar lines that do not meet. From theorem 16 it can be proved that if AB is any line and P a point not on it, at least one line parallel to AB can be drawn through P; and axiom 5 states in a complicated way that this parallel is the only one. The parallel axiom in its strongest form would be: given a line AB and a point P not on it, exactly one parallel can be drawn to AB through P.

The long series of attempts to prove uniqueness, using only the other postulates and axioms and the first part of Book I, resulted always in failure; but they led ultimately to a far more important success: the creation of non-Euclidean geometry, a landmark in the history of thought. With the use of the concept of parallel lines, theorem 16 can be made more precise: the exterior angle is the sum of the two opposite interior angles. *Basis for non-Euclidean geometry*

Euclid's Books I and II: equivalence of parallelograms and dissection of rectangles. The rest of Book I deals with the equivalence of parallelograms and will be analyzed later. It culminates in Pythagoras' theorem: if ACB be a right angle, the square drawn on AB is the sum of those drawn on AC and BC. This concerns the actual dissection and putting together of pieces of squares, not the formula $c^2 = a^2 + b^2$ on the numerical squares of the lengths of the sides.

In Book II, Euclid gives results on the dissection of rectangles that would now be expressed as algebraical formulas; for example, $(a + b)^2 = a^2 + 2ab + b^2$. This book concludes with the construction of a square equivalent in area to a given polygon.

Euclid's Book V: Eudoxus' treatment of incommensurables. The reason that compelled Euclid to proceed in this way must now be explained. The Pythagoreans had proved that the diagonal of a square was incommensurate with its sides; *i.e.*, no unit length exists of which both are multiples. In present-day language, $\sqrt{2}$ cannot be expressed as the quotient of two integers. Thus, the Greeks had to regard lengths as what are now called real numbers; and before such numbers could be multiplied together, a theory of real numbers was needed.

The work of Eudoxus

The Greek solution of this very difficult problem is given in Book V. It is usually ascribed to Eudoxus of Cnidus and is completely acceptable even today. Four magnitudes a, b, c, d of any kind are said to be in proportion if, using modern algebraical notation, not known to the Greeks, the following is true:

If m, n are any natural numbers, then na is less than, equal to, or greater than mb, according as nc is less than, equal to, or greater than md.

If this relation between the four terms a, b, c, d, expressed in words by the Greeks, is written $a|b \sim c|d$, then the expected consequences follow; for example, $b|a \sim d|c$, $a|c \sim b|d$, $(a+b)|b \sim (c+d)|d$. All of these are proved with complete rigour. The theory of real numbers constructed by the two great German mathematicians Karl Theodor Weierstrass and Richard Dedekind during the 19th century is a modern version of the Greek work.

Euclid's Books III, IV, VI, XI, XII, XIII. Much of the theory in books III and IV on circles is still acceptable in today's abstract treatment. Theorem 21 states that if A, B, P, Q are on a circle with P, Q on the same side of AB, then the angles APB, AQB are congruent. Theorem 31 states that if AB is a diameter and P is on the circle, the angle APB is a right angle. Theorems 35 and 36 state that if AB, CD are chords of a circle that meet in P, then the rectangle (the actual figure) the sides of which are congruent to PA, PB is equivalent to the rectangle the sides of which are congruent to PC, PD. ("Equivalent" may provisionally be regarded as meaning "of equal area.")

Theorem 11 of Book IV gives an ingenious construction for inscribing a regular pentagon in a given circle. Book VI applies the theory in V to questions of areas and proves essentially in theorem 15 that if a rectangle with sides a, b is equivalent to one with sides c, d then $a|c \sim d|b$.

Book XI, on solid geometry, uses the parallel axiom throughout, and, consequently, this book does not have the permanent value that Book I has. The work on volumes in Books XI and XII uses the method of exhaustion that is presented in theorem 1 of Book X. In modern form this would read: if a is any real number, then there is an integer n such that $|a2^{-n}|$ is less than any pre-assigned positive number. That some such device is actually needed for volumes, though not for areas of polygons, will be shown later.

The regular solids

Finally, Book XIII gives constructions for the regular solids: the tetrahedron, the four faces of which are equilateral triangles; the cube, the six faces of which are squares; the octahedron and icosahedron, the faces of which are, respectively, eight and 20 equilateral triangles; and the dodecahedron, the 12 faces of which are regular pentagons.

GEOMETRY AS AN ABSTRACT DOCTRINE

Toward the end of the 19th century the keenest thinkers in the field of geometry became increasingly concerned about the lack of true rigour in Euclid's presentation. Undoubtedly, the invention of non-Euclidean geometries did much to spur the search for a correct and complete treatment of classical geometry. The most notable work of the new type was, as has already been remarked, Hilbert's *Grundlagen der Geometrie*, published in 1899. Hilbert began by stating 21 axioms involving six primitive or undefined terms. He once made a famous comment (not actually published until 1935) to emphasize the importance of keeping the undefined terms totally abstract, that is, devoid of preconceived meaning: "One must be able to say at all times—instead of points, straight lines, and planes—tables, chairs, and beer mugs." Such a viewpoint was not widely accepted until the 20th century and, of course, had never occurred to Euclid or his followers. An Italian, Gino Fano, put it similarly even before Hilbert:

As basis for our study we assume an arbitrary collection of entities of an arbitrary nature; entities which, for brevity, we shall call points, and this quite independently of their nature.

To lay a solid foundation for Euclidean geometry, Hilbert's list of axioms or their equivalents (see 11–49) are not only sufficient but also necessary. It may be possible to manage with fewer, but even slight refinements of assumptions introduce burdensome complications. The content and style of this list are altogether different from Euclid's. A careful examination of such a list gives an idea of the nature of the problems involved when complete rigour is the goal.

The hope that Hilbert's treatment or its equivalent could be substituted for Euclid's in the schools was dashed by what the French geometer René Thom has called in the second half of the 20th century "the dreadful complexity of this work."

Points, lines, and planes

The undefined elements are called points, lines, and planes; and the set of all of them is called a space. From the last two axioms of incidence (see 17 and 18), something can be deduced about the dimension of the space. It then becomes possible for a line to be regarded as a set of points, although that is not necessary. It is equally possible for a point to be regarded as a set of lines, all the lines lying on that point (intuitively, concurrent in that point). By means of the axioms of betweenness and order (see 22–27), the abstract points of an abstract line can be shown to have all the properties associated with the intuitive notions of betweenness and order.

A plane can be defined in terms of points and lines, thereby reducing by one the number of completely undefined objects. To all the properties of the plane further properties are adjoined in order to attain three-dimensional space.

Euclid's theorem stating that two triangles are congruent if two sides and the included angle of one are equal, respectively, to two sides and the included angle of the other is replaced by the last axiom of congruence (see 35). This is rather complicated; and it is important to note that it is an axiom, not a theorem. Euclid's statement cannot be proved on the basis of the other axioms alone. That the five axioms of congruence (see 31–35) are, in fact, a sufficient basis for the theory of congruence in the plane and in space was proved by J.L. Dorroh, of the United States. Following work by Henry G. Forder of New Zealand and Pál Szász in Hungary, J.F. Rigby in England proved in the middle of the 20th century that it is possible to replace the last congruence axiom (see 35) by one that is simpler. Rigby also succeeded in weakening the first congruence axiom (see 31), and it may now be the case that the solution to the problem of finding a minimal set of axioms for congruence has finally been achieved.

With the aid of these congruence axioms, Euclid's famous parallel postulate can be restated in a simpler form (see 41).

Hilbert's division of axioms. Geometry will now be discussed, consistently with the above remarks, as an abstract doctrine with all assumptions explicit and with nothing read from the figure. Hilbert, in his *Grundlagen*, divides the axioms into five groups dealing, respectively, with incidence, order, congruence, parallels, and continuity.

The undefined elements are of three kinds: points, lines, and planes. Points will be denoted by A, B, $\cdots$, lines by a, b, $\cdots$, and planes by the Greek letters alpha, beta, $\cdots$; that is, α, β, $\cdots$. The set of all of these elements is called a space. Certain undefined relations that are considered below will hold between certain elements. The symbol $=$ between two signs will mean that the signs denote the same element. The symbol $\neq$ will mean that the elements are distinct.

Axioms of incidence. There is an undefined relation, incidence, which holds between certain points and lines or between certain points and planes. The relation is symmetric; for example, if A is incident with α, so is α with A. It will be a convenience of language to say that "A lies on a," "a goes through A," instead of "A is incident with a." Similar phrases will be used for points and planes. Conformably with this usage a line or plane may be regarded as a set of points, though this is not necessary. The axioms of incidence are expressed as eight separate statements (see 11–18). By one incidence axiom (see 17) that concerns the existence of a second point lying on the intersection of two planes, it can be deduced that space has not more than three dimensions. In fact, in four-dimensional space it is possible for two planes to meet in just one point. The last axiom (see 18) says space has not less than three dimensions. From these axioms the following statements can be deduced: if two distinct lines lie on the same plane, then either no point or just one point lies on both; given two distinct planes, either no point lies on both or just one line lies on both; if a line does not lie in a plane, then either no point or just one point lies on both.

Order and betweenness.   *Axioms of order.* In any collection of things (for example, points, numbers, men, classes), there may be a relation between certain pairs of elements, which is not symmetrical; that is, if a stands in that relation to b, then b does not stand in that relation to a. This is the case, for instance, if a, b are numbers and the relation is "less than." A general relation of this kind may be denoted by $<$, and three axioms (see 19–21) that characterize the relation $<$ may be assumed. A collection satisfying these three axioms is said to be in linear order. The set of real numbers satisfying the relation "less than" is an example.

Relation of betweenness.   In geometry there is an undefined relation connecting certain sets of three points, called betweenness.

First, if the relation between three people expressed by "A prefers B to C" is considered, then with the usual meaning of these words, it is false that A prefers C to B, but human relations might be so nicely adjusted that it always followed that C preferred B to A.

If $[ABC]$ is written for the statement "A prefers B to C," then that $[ABC]$ is true would imply that $[ACB]$ is false but $[CBA]$ is true. The undefined relation between triads of points does, in fact, have these properties.

Axioms of betweenness.   The symbol $[ABC]$ shall mean that the points A, B, C are in the relation of betweenness. Two axioms can be assumed for this relation (see 22, 23). If geometry has already been constructed, the reader may interpret $[ABC]$ to mean, say, AB, BC are perpendicular, or B is the midpoint of AC, or A, C are on a circle the centre of which is B, and consider which of these statements is true. An intuitive interpretation for which these and all the following would be true is: B is on the line AC and is between A and C.

Line defined in terms of order.   The term line was undefined in rigorous terms by Euclid. It can now be defined by means of order. If A, B are distinct points, the line AB is the set of points P such that either $[PAB]$ or $[APB]$ or $[ABP]$, together with the points A, B. When a line XY is mentioned, $X \neq Y$ is assumed. The "segment" AB is one set of points P such that $[APB]$. The interval AB is this set with A, B adjoined. The ray AB is the set of points P such that $[APB]$ or $[ABP]$.

The remaining axioms of order, based on betweenness, are expressed in four distinct statements (see 24–27). Figure 1 conveys the meaning of one axiom (see 27).

A lengthy and not very easy argument can be used to show that if there are n points on a line, they can be named $A_1, A_2, \cdots, A_n$, so that $[A_i A_j A_k]$ holds if and only if $i < j < k$ or $k < j < i$. The points of a line defined in the abstract sense now have all the properties associated with the intuitive notion of order.

Results based on order and betweenness.   *Definition of a plane.* The term plane undefined by Euclid can now be defined. If ABC is a triangle, the plane ABC is the set of all points on all lines joining any two points of the triangle. In the presence of the axioms given, this is equivalent to saying that the plane is the set of all points on the lines joining the vertices to the points on the opposite side. From either definition it can be proved that if X, Y, Z are non-collinear points on plane ABC, then ABC, XYZ coincide; *i.e.*, every point on one is on the other. Also, the so-called Pasch's axiom can be proved: if a line lies in the plane of a triangle ABC and meets the side AB, then it either goes through C or it meets side AC or side BC. A side of a triangle is taken to be a segment, not

an interval. Theorems such as these were read by Euclid from his figures, but they cannot be said to have been proved that way.

To get three dimensions, a further axiom can be assumed to the effect (see 28) that not all points are in the same plane. Then if A, B, C, D be non-coplanar points, the tetrahedron $ABCD$ can be defined as usual; and the space $ABCD$ can be defined in a way analogous to the first definition of a plane above. Finally, to restrict space to three dimensions, assume (see 29) that all points are in the same space. These last two assumptions (28, 29) will be referred to as axioms of dimension.

Theorems concerning polygons.   Theorems on the inside and outside of polygons, assumed implicitly by Euclid, can be formulated and proved from the axioms of order and betweenness. If $A_1, \cdots, A_n$ ($n > 2$) be distinct

---

THE AXIOMS OF INCIDENCE

(11)   Given distinct points A, B, there is at least one line a incident with both A, B.

(12)   There is at most one such line.

(13)   Each line has at least three points incident with it. There are at least three points not on the same line.

(14)   If A, B, C are three distinct points not on the same line, there is at least one plane incident with all three.

(15)   There is at most one such plane.

(16)   If A, B are distinct points on a line l that lies on a plane α, then all points of l lie on α. One writes "l lies on α", "α goes through l".

(17)   If a point lies on two distinct planes, at least one other point lies on both planes.

(18)   There are at least four points not on the same plane.

AXIOMS OF LINEAR ORDER

(19)   If $a \prec b$, then $a \neq b$.

(20)   If $a \prec b$ and $b \prec c$, then $a \prec c$.

(21)   If $a \neq b$, then at least one of $a \prec b$, $b \prec a$ holds.

AXIOMS OF BETWEENNESS

(22)   If $[ABC]$ is true, then A, B, C are distinct.

(23)   If $[ABC]$ is true, then $[BCA]$ is false.

AXIOMS OF ORDER

(24)   If C, D are distinct points on the line AB, then A is on the line CD.

(25)   If A, B are distinct points, there is at least one point P such that $[ABP]$.

(26)   There are (at least) three points A, B, C not on the same line.

(27)   If A, B, C are distinct points and A is not on the line BC and if $[BCD]$, $[CEA]$, then there is a point F on the line DE such that $[AFB]$.

AXIOMS OF DIMENSION

(28)   Not all points are in the same plane.

(29)   All points are in the same space.

(30)   There is a point not in S_3.

Concepts of dimension (margin)

Properties of order (margin)

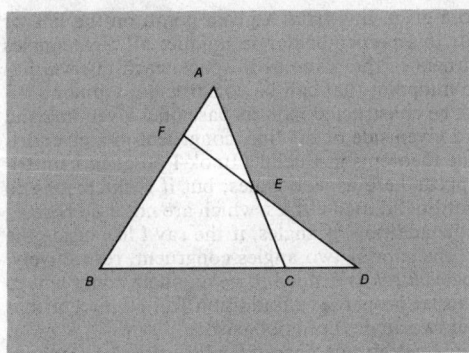

Figure 1: Illustration of an axiom of order. In the diagram, if *A*, *B*, *C* are distinct points and *A* is not on the line *BC*, and if *C* is between *B* and *D* and if *E* is between *C* and *A*, then there is a point *F* on the line *DE* such that *F* is between *A* and *B*.

points, no three consecutive points being collinear, then the set of intervals A_1A_2, A_2A_3, $\cdots A_{n-1}A_n$ form a path with vertices $A_1, \cdots, A_n$. The path is simple if no two of these intervals have a common point, not a vertex (see below), and no three of them meet in any point. If A_1, $\cdots, A_{n-1}$ are distinct, but $A_n = A_1$, the path is a polygon.

A region is a set of points, not all collinear, any two of which can be joined by a path all of whose points are in the set. If [*X*], [*Y*] are sets of points and [*S*] a set such that every path from a point of [*X*] to a point of [*Y*] meets [*S*], then [*S*] separates [*X*] from [*Y*].

The following can be proved from the axioms of order and betweenness:

If a simple polygon lies in a plane, the points of the plane not on the polygon are separated by the polygon into two regions. One of these regions, the outside, contains lines not meeting the polygon; but any line through any point of the other region, the inside, meets the polygon. Figure 2 is helpful in considering this theorem. As a preliminary, it should first be proved that a line in a plane separates the points not on it into two regions.

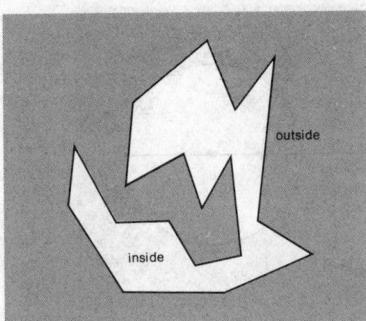

Figure 2: The points of a plane that are not on a polygon are separated by the polygon into two regions, the "inside" and the "outside."

An angle is a pair of non-collinear rays from a point *O*, the vertex. An angle in a plane separates the other points of the plane into two regions, the inside and outside, with the same properties as above. If *AOB* be an angle, the rays through *O* inside the angle can be ordered by the relation between, using the points at which they meet *AB*. Euclid read such relations from his figures.

Dissection of geometric figures. A simple polygon can be dissected into triangles with their vertices at the vertices of the polygon; that is, a set of triangles can be found, no two of which have a common inside point, and such that every point inside the polygon is inside or on one of the triangles and every point inside a triangle is inside the polygon. The corresponding theorem for space is false. An eight-faced polyhedron has been constructed, as suggested by Figure 3, which cannot be split into tetrahedra with their vertices at the vertices of the polyhedron because the join of any two vertices, unless it is an edge, lies entirely outside the polyhedron.

Abstract concept of angle

When the points on a line are ordered by the betweenness relation, intuition suggests that it should be possible to take a direction on the line so that the points could be put into linear order as discussed in the section *Axioms of order*. This can be done though the work is tedious. So also the theory of the inside and outside of polyhedra can be erected, and it can be proved that any polyhedron can be dissected into tetrahedra, though their vertices may fall inside the polyhedron.

Certain difficult theorems. These theorems follow from the axioms of order and betweenness and the first two axioms of dimension. They are not intuitively obvious and are hard to prove.

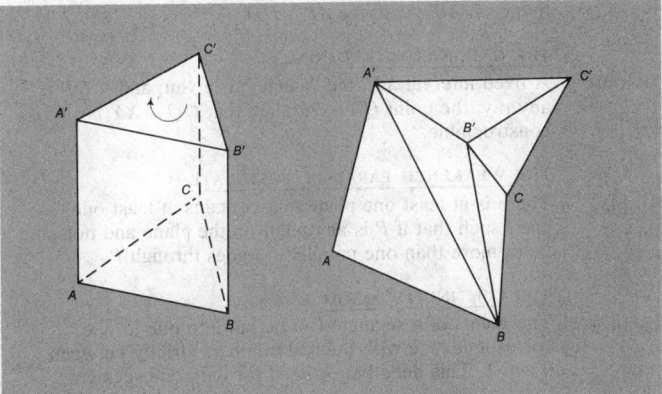

Figure 3: (Left) A prism whose base is an equilateral triangle transformed by a screw operation and a caving in of the side faces into (right) an eight-faced polyhedron. The resulting polyhedron cannot be split into tetrahedra with their vertices at the vertices of the polyhedron.

If a finite set of points in a plane is such that the line joining any two contains a third point of the set, then all the points lie on one line.

Let a convex polygon be defined as one such that the segment joining two inside points has all its points inside; then if *n* points, no three collinear, are in a plane, and all quadrilaterals formed from any four of them are convex, the points are the vertices of a convex polygon.

The convex polygon

If $l_1 \cdots l_4$ are four lines in space, no three coplanar, and the five pairs following are coplanar: l_1l_2, l_1l_3, l_1l_4, l_2l_3, l_2l_4, then l_3l_4 are coplanar.

(The Euclidean parallel axiom must not be used here.)

Congruence. *Axioms of congruence.* In his axioms of congruence, Hilbert takes as undefined the congruence of intervals and of angles. It is more fundamental to take only the congruence of point pairs as undefined, the pairs being ordered, that is (*A*, *B*) and (*B*, *A*), are regarded as distinct pairs and always $A \neq B$. The undefined relation "(*A*, *B*) is congruent to (*C*, *D*)," written $(A, B) \simeq (C, D)$, holds between certain pairs.

Five axioms (see 31–35) are assumed, and these are called the axioms of congruence. If the first four of these

---

AXIOMS OF CONGRUENCE

(31) If points *A*, *B*, *A'*, *X* are given, then there is just one point *B'* on the ray *AX* such that $(A, B) \simeq (A', B')$.

(32) If $(A, B) \simeq (C, D)$ and $(C, D) \simeq (E, F)$ then $(A, B) \simeq (E, F)$.

(33) If [*ABC*], [*A'B'C'*] and $(A, B) \simeq (A', B')$ and $(B, C) \simeq (B'C')$, then $(A, C) \simeq (A', C')$.

(34) $(A, B) \simeq (B, A)$.

(35) If *ABC*, *A'B'C'* are two triangles and if [*ABD*], [*A'B'D'*] and if (*A*, *B*), (*B*, *C*), (*C*, *A*), (*B*, *D*) are respectively congruent to (*A'*, *B'*) (*B'*, *C'*), (*C'*, *A'*), (*B'*, *D'*), then $(C, D) \simeq (C', D')$.

ELEMENTARY CONSTRUCTIONS

(36) Given two distinct points, the line on which both lie can be drawn.

(37) If two lines meet, their common point can be drawn.

(38) If A, B are distinct points,
(i). a point C can be found satisfying $[ABC]$,
(ii). a point D can be found satisfying $[ADB]$,
(iii). a point can be found not on the line AB.

(39) If CD is an interval and AB any ray, a point P can be found on AB satisfying $AP \simeq CD$.

THE GAUGE CONSTRUCTION

(40) A fixed interval XY, the "gauge", is given; and if OP is any ray, the point Q on OP such that $OQ \simeq XY$ is constructable.

THE WEAKENED PARALLEL POSTULATE

(41) There is at least one plane that contains at least one line l such that if P is any point on the plane and not on l, not more than one parallel to l goes through P.

THE CONTINUITY AXIOM

(42) The points of a segment can be put into one-to-one correspondence with the real numbers strictly between 0 and 1. This need be assumed for only one segment.

ARCHIMEDES' AXIOM

(43) If A_1, A_2, P are collinear points, then there is an integer n such that if $[A_1 A_2 \cdots A_n]$, $A_1 A_2 \simeq A_2 A_3 \simeq \cdots \simeq A_{n-1} A_n$ hold, then $[A_1 P A_n]$.

---

five axioms of congruence are assumed, then it follows that $\simeq$ is an equivalence relation in the meaning that is now current.

Two sets of points $[X]$, $[Y]$ will be called congruent if they can be put into one-to-one correspondence in such a way that if A, B in $[X]$ correspond to A', B' in $[Y]$, then $(A, B) \simeq (A', B')$. In particular, for two intervals, it can be proved that $AB \simeq CD$ if, and only if, $(A, B) \simeq (C, D)$. Since an angle is a pair of rays, then $\angle ABC \simeq \angle A'B'C'$ will hold if, when X, Y, X', Y' are, respectively, on the rays BA, BC, $B'A'$, $B'C'$ and $BX \simeq B'X'$, $BY \simeq B'Y'$, then $XY \simeq X'Y'$; and triangles ABC, $A'B'C'$ will be congruent if, and only if, the corresponding sides are congruent.

The only existence statement is in the first congruence axiom (see 31), and it makes the second axiom of order (see 25) superfluous.

Elementary constructions. There are four elementary constructions (see 36–39) corresponding to the axioms of betweenness, order, and congruence.

Geometric constructions in proofs

Theorems that can be proved. The following can be proved, roughly in the order given: three non-collinear points cannot be congruent to three collinear points; using the elementary constructions, a given angle can be bisected, the bisector is unique; a perpendicular can be

drawn to a given line from a given point, on the line or not on it; this perpendicular is unique; all right angles are congruent in the plane or in space; each interval has a unique midpoint that can be constructed; a unique triangle can be constructed with its base on a given line and lying on a given side of the line, congruent to a given triangle. The theorems in Euclid's Book I on congruent triangles appear here as side issues; but it is interesting to notice that Euclid used circles, which are not used here.

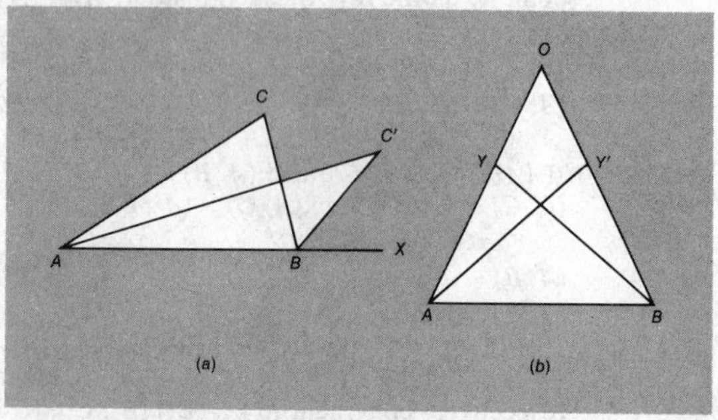

As for the addition of angles, if the ray l lies inside the angle hk, the sum of two angles congruent, respectively, to the angles hl, lk is defined to be an angle congruent to hk. The usual properties of addition follow, except that the sum of two angles need not exist.

The usual theorems on perpendicular lines and planes in space also follow from the axioms of congruence. In particular, if both planes α_1, α_2 are perpendicular to the line in which planes β, γ meet, then they meet β, γ in lines that form congruent angles. Thus, the dihedral angle between β, γ can be defined.

It also follows that if OA, OB, OC are non-coplanar rays, then the sum of the angles AOB and BOC exceeds AOC.

The work of Dorroh, Forder, Szász, and Rigby, as mentioned above, has permitted the replacement of the last congruence axiom (see 35) with the following:

If, as in Figure 4(a), $AC \simeq AC'$, $BC \simeq BC'$, and $[ABX]$, then $XC \simeq XC'$ (here C, C' may be on the same side of AB or on opposite sides, though it is proved later that the first case is impossible), provided there is adjoined the statement [see Figure 4(b)]: if $OA \simeq OB$ and Y, Y' lie on the rays OA, OB (or on the opposite rays), and $OY \simeq OY'$, then $BY \simeq AY'$.

Euclid's intersecting circles. To discuss the intersection of circles, which Euclid read from his figures, the following can be assumed (see Figure 5):

If a circle with centre A has a point X on its circumference that is inside and a point Y outside a circle with centre B that lies in the same plane, and if X, Y lie on AB then the circles have at least one common point on each side of AB.

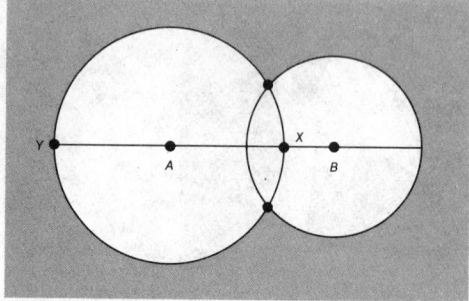

Figure 5: *Intersecting circles.*
If a circle with centre A has a point X inside, as well as a point Y outside, a second circle with centre B, and if X and Y lie on AB, then the circles have at least one common point on each side of AB.

In the presence of the congruence axioms the restriction that X, Y lie on AB can be removed; it need only be assumed that an intersection exists on one side of AB. The existence of the other and the uniqueness of both follow. From the above assumption follows the statement:

A line through a point inside a circle and in its plane meets it in just two points.

A weakening of the parallel axiom. Euclid's famous fifth axiom, the parallel axiom, can be treated as in Euclid's Book I; but in the presence of the congruence axioms it can be weakened to a simpler form (see 41).

If AB, CD are parallel, the notation $AB\|CD$ can be used.

Continuity. Hilbert assumed a very curious axiom of completeness, which is an axiom about preceding axioms. It can be replaced by an axiom (see 42) concerning continuity of a segment.

From this follows the axiom (see 43) generally attrib-

Figure 4: Two constructions [(a) and (b)] used in the theory of congruence.

PROPERTIES OF PROPORTION

(44)   If any three of s, t, s', t', are given, the fourth exists and is unique.

(45)   If $s|s' \sim t|t'$, then $t|t' \sim s|s'$

(46)   If $s|s' \sim t|t'$ and $t|t' \sim v|v'$, then $s|s \sim v|v'$.

(47)   If $s|s' \sim t|t'$, then $s'|s \sim t'|t$. Also $s|s \sim t|t$.

(48)   The statement $s|s' \sim t|t'$ implies $s|t \sim s'|t'$.

(49)   The statement $s|t \sim s'|t'$ implies $(s+t)|t \sim (s'+t')|t'$.

Archimedes' axiom

uted to Archimedes. The continuity axiom makes possible a great simplification. The continuity axiom and the axioms of betweenness and order alone can be used to prove that lines that do not meet do exist in the plane. The continuity axiom and all of the axioms of order and betweenness and dimension can be used to replace the weakened parallel postulate by the following statement: Given any line l in a plane, there is a point P, on the plane and not on the line, through which goes not more than one line not meeting l. (The point P may vary as l varies.)

Similar triangles. In this section only the axioms of betweenness, order, congruence, and parallelism will be assumed. The measure of an interval is the set of all intervals congruent to it; or, alternatively, it can be regarded as a common property of all such intervals.

Use of proportion

If $PQ \simeq AB$, $RS \simeq BC$, $[ABC]$, then the sum of the measures of PQ, RS is defined as the measure of AC. If SOS' is a right angle as in Figure 6, and T, T' lie on rays OS, OS', respectively, the measures s, s', t, t' of OS, OS', OT, OT' will be said to be in proportion, written $s|s' \simeq t|t'$, if $SS'||TT'$.

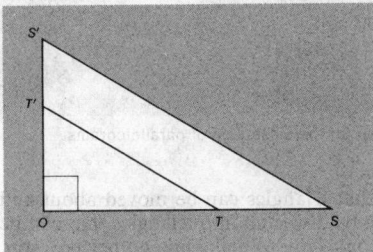

Figure 6: Construction for similar triangles (see text).

The elementary properties follow at once (see 44–47). A great part will now be played by special cases of two theorems of projective geometry, the first attributed to the Greek mathematician Pappus of Alexandria (flourished $c.$ AD 300) and the second to the 17th-century French mathematician Girard Desargues.

Theorem A (see Figure 7). If A, B, C lie on a line and A', B', C' lie on another (coplanar) line, the six points being distinct, and if $AB'||BA'$, $B'C||BC'$, then $AC'||A'C$.

Theorem B (see Figure 8). If ABC, $A'B'C'$ are two triangles, coplanar or not, the six vertices being distinct, and lines through AA', BB', CC' meet in one point and $BC||B'C'$, $CA||C'A'$, then $AB||A'B'$.

Of these theorems, B follows from Euclid's parallel postulate and the axioms of incidence, provided three dimensions are assumed but not if only two dimensions are assumed.

Although theorem A does not follow from these axioms, it follows from the axioms of betweenness and order, the axioms of congruence and parallelism, and then theorem B in the plane can be deduced from it, without using space. The work below does not use space.

From theorem A two further properties of proportion (see 48, 49) can be proved. The restriction that SOS' is a

right angle can now be removed, and the main theorem can be proved: if triangles ABC, $A'B'C'$ have corresponding angles equal, then $AB|A'B' \sim BC|B'C' \sim CA| C'A'$. When B, B' are the vertices of right angles, this theorem follows from the definition of proportion and one of the properties of proportion (48) above. The general case could be proved from this case and theorem B, and conversely theorem B follows from the general case. Hilbert avoided the use of theorem B, the proof of which is lengthy, by using the properties of a triangle and the last of the properties of proportion (see 49). When this main theorem has been proved, the rest is easy.

The algebra of intervals. If a, b, c are the measures of intervals, addition of measures has been defined and it remains to consider multiplication. If a fixed interval u is called the unit interval, then $ab = c$ means $c|b \sim a|u$. Consequently, ab is uniquely fixed by a, b; in particular $au = a$. From a property of proportion (see 48) above, $c|b \sim a|u$ implies $c|a \sim b|u$, and thus $ab = ba$. Furthermore, $ba = ca$ implies $b = c$. The following can also be deduced: $a(b + c) = ab + ac$, $(a + b)^2 = a^2 + 2ab + b^2$, $a(bc) = (ab)c$.

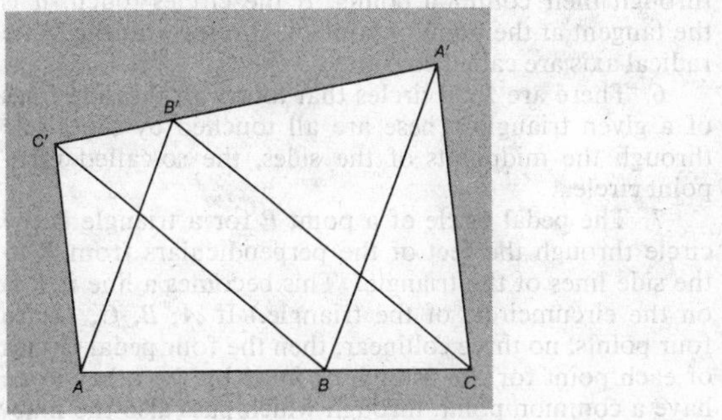

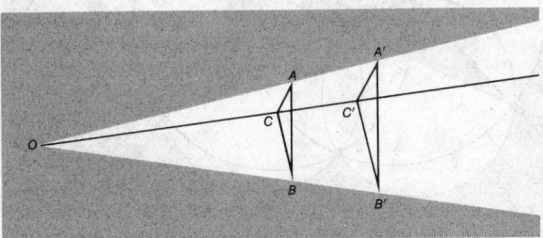

Figure 7: Construction for Pappus' theorem (see text).

From the properties of similar triangles, a well-known proof gives the theorem of Pythagoras in the form $c^2 = a^2 + b^2$. Thus the whole of Euclid's Book VI can be covered without using the theory of real numbers.

A sample of theorems. *Conclusions not based on the parallel axiom.* The first three of the following theorems can be proved on the basis of the axioms of order, betweenness, and congruence, without the parallel axiom but including the two axioms of dimension.

1. If on two lines in the same plane, or skew, points A_1, $A_2 \cdots$ are taken on one line, and B_1, $B_2 \cdots$ on the other, so that $A_1A_2 \simeq A_2A_3 \simeq \cdots \simeq B_1B_2 \sim B_2B_3 \simeq \cdots$ then the midpoints of A_1B_1, A_2B_2, $\cdots$ lie on a line. Without parallelism it is very easy to prove 2 below and very hard to prove 3:

2. The bisectors of the angles of a triangle meet in a point, the incentre.

3. The lines joining the vertices of a triangle to the midpoints of the opposite sides (the medians) meet in a point.

Conclusions dependent upon the parallel axiom. The third theorem can be much more easily proved if, to the axioms mentioned, is added the parallel axiom. With that addition, the following can also be proved.

4. If the angles of any triangle ABC are trisected as in Figure 9, then DEF is equilateral.

5. The power of a point P for a circle O, radius r, is defined as $OP^2 - r^2$. (That this number is negative when

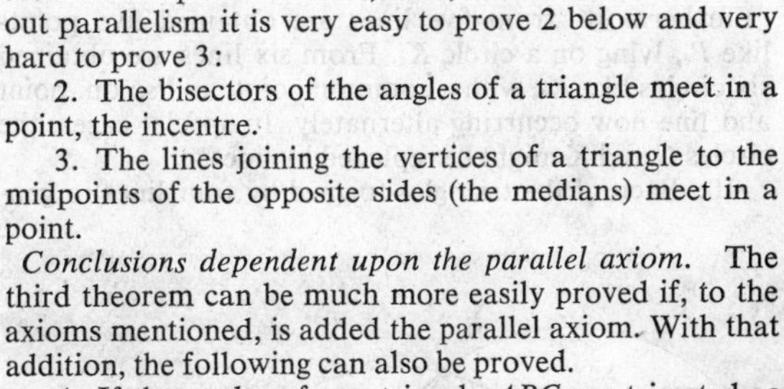

Figure 8: Construction for Desargues' theorem.

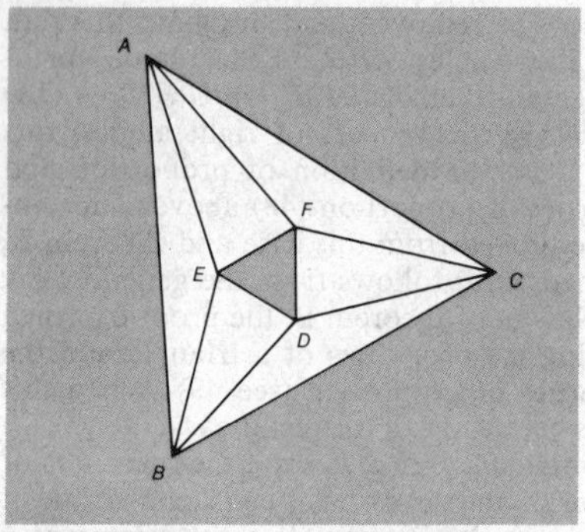

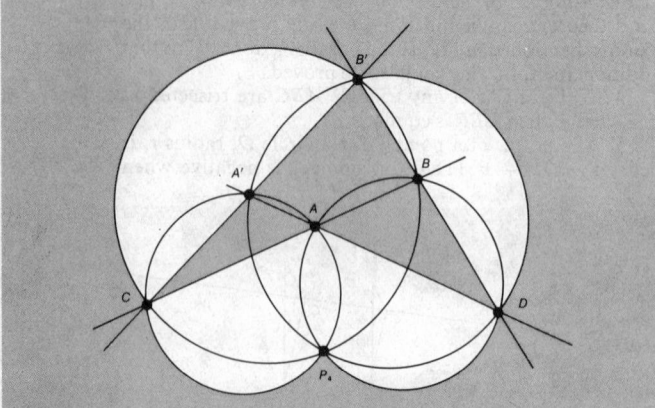

Figure 9: If the angles of triangle *ABC* (representing any triangle) are trisected, then triangle *DEF* is equilateral.

P is inside the circle is of no consequence because powers are not added.) If a point *P* moves so that it has equal powers for two circles, it describes a line called the radical axis of the two circles. If the circles intersect, it goes through their common points. If the circles touch, it is the tangent at the point of contact. Circles with the same radical axis are called coaxial.

6. There are four circles that touch all the side lines of a given triangle. These are all touched by the circle through the midpoints of the sides, the so-called nine-point circle.

7. The pedal circle of a point *P* for a triangle is the circle through the feet of the perpendiculars from *P* to the side lines of the triangle. (This becomes a line if *P* is on the circumcircle of the triangle.) If *A*, *B*, *C*, *D* are four points, no three collinear, then the four pedal circles of each point for the triangle formed by the other three have a common point, through which pass also the nine-point circles of the four triangles.

8. If a point *P* describes a line, the pedal circles of *P* for the triangle are such that there is a point that has equal powers for all the circles. If the line goes through the circumcentre of the triangle, the pedal circles have a common point.

9. A chain of theorems. All the lines of this chain are to be in general position; that is, no two are parallel, no three concur. Starting with four lines (see Figure 10), the circumcircles of the triangles formed by them meet in a point P_4 (the Miquel point) and their centres lie on a circle C_4. Five lines, taken by fours, yield five circles like C_4, passing through a point P_5, and their centres lie on a circle C_5. Six lines, taken by fives, yield six circles like C_5, passing through a point P_6, and their centres lie on a circle C_6. And so on.

Furthermore, from five lines are obtained five points like P_4, lying on a circle K_4. From six lines are obtained six circles like K_4, with a common point, and so on, point and line now occurring alternately. In special cases, the circles *C* and *K* might be replaced by lines.

10. Each of the triangles formed by four lines in gen-

The Miquel point

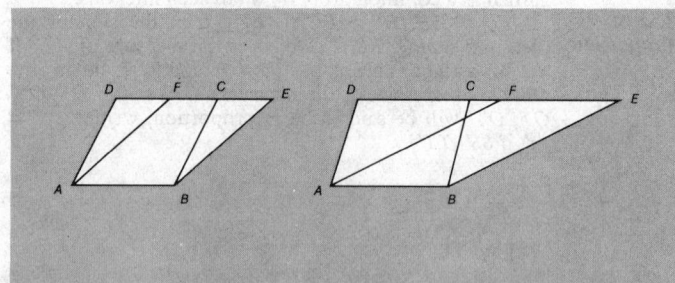

eral position has four circles touching its side lines. The centres of these 16 circles lie by fours on two orthogonal sets of four coaxial circles. The radical axes meet at the Miquel point of the four lines.

11. Two skew lines (lines that cannot both be contained in a common plane) have just one common perpendicular. If *l*, *m*, *n* are skew lines, and *l*′, *m*′, *n*′ are the common perpendiculars of the pairs (*m*, *n*), (*n*, *l*), (*l*, *m*) and l_1, m_1, n_1 are the common perpendiculars of the pairs (*l*, *l*′), (*m*, *m*′), (*n*, *n*′), then l_2, m_2, n_2 have a common perpendicular.

12. If the faces of a convex polyhedron were made of metal plates and its edges were replaced by hinges around which the faces might conceivably turn, the polyhedron would nevertheless be rigid. This so-called rigidity theorem is attributed to the 19th-century French mathematician Augustin-Louis Cauchy. It does not seem to be known, however, to what extent it applies to nonconvex polyhedra.

13. If O_1A_1, O_1B_1, O_1C_1 are any given intervals in a plane, no two on the same line, then a cube exists, the edges *OA*, *OB*, *OC* of which give these intervals by parallel projection. In general, there are two sets of such parallels but only one if the projection happens to be orthogonal.

THE MEASURE OF POLYGONS AND POLYHEDRA

Questions following from Euclid. In his treatment, Book II, of the equivalence of polygons, Euclid considered parallelograms *ABCD*, *ABEF* placed as in Figure 11. In the first case, *ABCD* can be dissected into *ABCF* and *ADF*, while *ABEF* can be dissected into *ABCF* and triangle *BEC*, which is congruent to *AFD*.

Dissection of parallelograms

Figure 11: Construction for the dissection of parallelograms (see text).

If it is assumed that triangles can be moved about and that a polygon can be dissected into triangles that can be fitted together in some way to make up another polygon, then the polygons are said to be equivalent by dissection. This is the case for the parallelograms in Figure 11, left, but it is not obviously so in Figure 11, right; nevertheless, in the latter case the parallelograms can be obtained by subtracting, respectively, the congruent triangles *BEC*, *AFD* from the complete figure. The parallelograms are then said to be equivalent by subtraction or simply equivalent.

The question arises: are two equivalent parallelograms always equivalent by dissection? Figure 12 suggests a proof that the answer is affirmative, and it can easily be made general and rigorous if it is assumed that when intervals congruent to *AX* are stepped off along the side *AD*, a point beyond *D* is eventually reached; that is, if Archimedes' axiom is assumed. It can be shown that this axiom is essential for the general proof of the theorem.

Extension from parallelograms to polygons. With reasoning similar to that of the section above and by using the axioms of betweenness and order, it can be shown that any polygon can be dissected into triangles. If Archimedes' axiom is assumed, it can be proved that equivalent polygons (subtraction being allowed) are always equivalent by dissection. For special cases this axiom is not needed.

As an example (Figure 13, left), consider the right angle *ABC* and the squares *ADEC* on *AC*, *AFGB* on *AB*, and *KGHE* on *KG*. Because the triangles *ABC*, *AFD*, *DEK*,

Figure 10: The Miquel point, P_4, the common meeting of the circles that circumscribe the triangles formed by four lines.

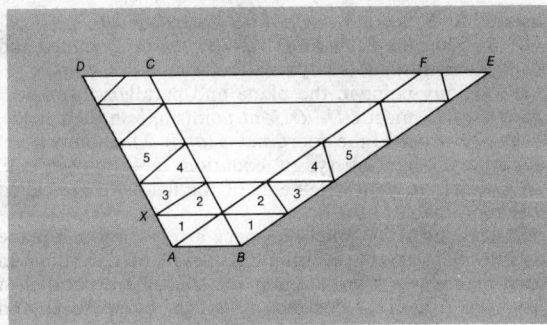

Figure 12: Construction for the proof of equivalency of parallelograms by dissection (see text).

CHE are congruent, the square on *AC* is equivalent by dissection to the figure made up of the squares on *AB*, *BC*. Here much has been read from the figure in Euclid's fashion, but all of it can be made rigorous.

Again consider a figure much used by Euclid (see Figure 13, right). *ABCD* is a parallelogram; through *E*, a point on *AC*, are drawn parallels to the sides. It follows that the parallelograms *EB*, *DE* are equivalent, because the triangles *ABC*, *CDA* are congruent, *EB* is formed from *ABC* by subtracting two triangles, and *DE* is formed from *CDA* by subtracting two triangles congruent to these.

Equivalence of measure. Using the algebra of intervals, the measure of a triangle can be defined as half the product of the measures of a side and the corresponding height. The theory of similar triangles shows that this product is independent of the side chosen. The factor ½ is introduced so that the unit *u* will be the measure of a square the side of which has measure *u*.

The measure of a polygon is defined as the sum of the measures of the triangles into which it can be dissected. This redefines the measure of a triangle; and for consistency it must be proved that the same measure is obtained for a polygon no matter how it is dissected into triangles. This is neither obvious nor easy to prove, but it can be proved using the algebra of intervals.

The theories of equivalence and of measure can now be connected. It is not hard to prove that equivalent polygons have the same measure, more difficult to prove that those with the same measure are equivalent; they are equivalent by dissection only if the Archimedian axiom is assumed. In particular, two equivalent triangles with congruent bases have congruent altitudes. In proving this, Euclid assumed one of his common notions in the form that a triangle cannot be equivalent to a subtriangle, an assumption not needed in the modern theory, in which it can be proved.

The attempt to extend this to measures of polyhedra encounters difficulties. The definitions of equivalence by dissection and of equivalence can be taken over, using tetrahedra instead of triangles. It was only in 1943 that Jean-Pierre Sydler (Swiss) proved that equivalence implied equivalence by dissection, assuming the Archimedian axiom.

The measure of a tetrahedron The measure of a tetrahedron can be defined as one-third of the product of the measures of a face and the corresponding height, and it can be proved that this is independent of the face chosen. The measure of a polyhedron, defined as the sum of the measures of the tetra-

hedra into which it can be dissected, can be proved to be independent of the dissection adopted, though the argument is involved. The real difficulty is that polyhedra of the same measure need not be equivalent. A regular tetrahedron, for example, cannot be equivalent by dissection to a cube of the same measure for the reason that it is not possible in any way to dissect the tetrahedron into subtetrahedra and fit them together to make a cube. This follows from the fact that the dihedral angle of a regular tetrahedron is not a rational multiple of a right angle. Neither does it help if equivalence by dissection is replaced by equivalence, nor does the Archimedian axiom remove the difficulty. It is for this reason that Euclid was compelled to use the theory of exhaustion in dealing with volumes.

A rounded theory can be obtained if two tetrahedra are called equivalent (T) when they have a face and corresponding altitude of the same measure, and equivalence (T) by dissection and equivalence (T) are defined only for pairs of tetrahedra of this kind. Under these suppositions, two polyhedra of the same measure are equivalent (T), although, unless the Archimedian axiom is assumed, they need not be equivalent (T) by dissection.

It can be proved that two tetrahedra equivalent (T) have the same measure if the following substitute for integration is assumed: Cavalieri's principle: If two solids, S_1 and S_2, lie between parallel planes and each plane parallel to these meet S_1 and S_2 in plane figures with the same measure, then S_1 and S_2 have the same measure. Application to the tetrahedra is simple.

TRANSFORMATION GEOMETRY

Translation and reflection in the plane. If, in a plane, *l* is a given line, *P* a point not on it, and *F* the foot of the perpendicular to *l* from *P*, and if *PF* is prolonged to *Q* so that $PF \simeq FQ$, then *Q* is called the image of *P* by reflection in *l*. If *P* describes a line, so does *Q*. If *P* describes a circle clockwise, then *Q* describes a circle anticlockwise. The transformation is called indirect because it reverses sense.

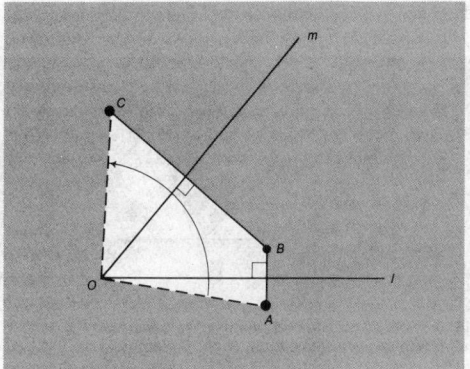

Figure 14: Reflection of a point *A* in a line *l* (to yield point *B*) followed by a reflection in line *m* (to yield point *C*). The result is a rotation through an angle twice that from *l* to *m*.

The result of a reflection in a line *l* followed by one in *m* is direct, because sense is preserved. If $l \| m$ the result is a translation taking any point *P* into a point *Q*, the distance of which from *P* is twice that between *l* and *m*. If, as in Figure 14, *l* and *m* meet in *O*, the result is a rotation around *O* through an angle twice that from *l* to *m*. Conversely, any translation or rotation can be resolved into reflections in two lines, either of which may be any line perpendicular to the direction of the translation or a line through the centre of the rotation. The other is then fixed. A displacement in a plane is a direct transformation that transforms any figure F into a congruent figure F′. If F′ is reflected in a line, the resulting transformation is an indirect displacement.

Translation producing a rotation

A direct displacement is always a translation or a rotation; an indirect displacement is the result of a translation and a reflection in a line parallel to the direction of the translation.

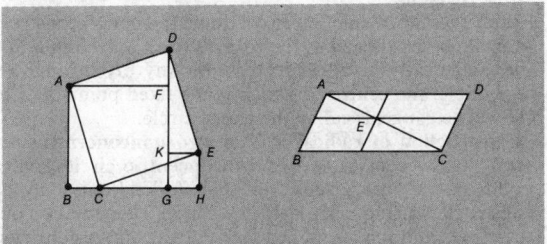

Figure 13: Constructions for the equivalence by dissection of (left) squares and (right) parallelograms (see text).

Homotheties. If O is a point in a plane, a transformation that leaves O fixed and changes any two other points A, B into A', B' on OA, OB, respectively, so that $AB \| A'B'$, is called a homothety, with centre O. A' may be on the ray OA or on the opposite ray. If C becomes C', then $AB|BC \sim A'B'|B'C'$ by similar triangles and theorem B above.

If two nonconcentric circles have centres A, B and unequal radii r, s, there are points I, E with $[AIB]$, $AI|IB \sim AE|EB \sim r|s$. In consequence, the circles are homothetic in two ways with I as the internal and E as the external centre of homothety. These points may both lie inside the circles; but, when each circle lies outside the other, I and E are points at which pairs of common tangents meet.

An example of homothety

For example: If ABC is a triangle, and D, E, F are the midpoints of the sides, the internal centre of homothety of the circles ABC, DEF is the point of concurrence of AD, BE, CF and the external centre is the point of concurrence of the altitudes of the triangle ABC. The circle DEF is the nine-point circle of triangle ABC.

The result of any sequence of homotheties and translations is a homothety or a translation.

Similitudes. If a figure $[F]$ is transformed by a homothety preceded or followed by a displacement, direct or indirect, the figure $[F']$ obtained is similar to $[F]$; that is, if A, B, C in $[F]$ correspond to A', B', C' in $[F']$, then ABC, $A'B'C'$ are similar triangles. The transformation is a similitude. This similitude is a homothety if $AB \| A'B'$ always holds. If, as in Figure 10, AB, $A'B'$ meet in C, and AA', BB' meet in D, and if the circles $AA'C$, $BB'C$ meet again in O, then the triangles OAB, $OA'B'$ are directly similar; and if the given similitude is direct, it is the result of a homothety with centre O and a rotation around O. The other two circles ABD, $A'B'D'$ also go through O, the Miquel point.

An algebra of points. The transformations can be used to construct an algebra of points. Starting with a fixed point O, the translation that takes O into A is denoted by T_A; the result of two translations T_A, T_B is denoted by T_{A+B} (see Figure 15, left). The operation $+$ has the usual properties of addition, and the addition of points can be defined: $C = A + B$ means $T_C = T_{A+B}$.

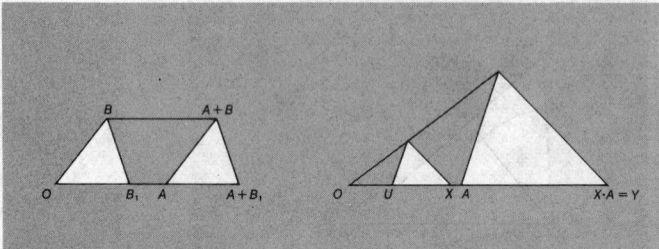

Figure 15: Effects of transformations used to construct algebras of points: (left) translation, (right) homothety.

If OU is any line through the fixed point O, and A is another point on OU, then $X \cdot A$ represents the point Y into which X is transformed by the homothety with centre O that transforms U into A (see Figure 15, right). If $X \cdot A$ is regarded as a product, then $U \cdot A = A \cdot U = A$. There is just one point X with $X \cdot A = U$; it lies on OU, and $A \cdot X = U$.

With addition and multiplication as defined above operating only on points on OU, all the formulas for a field in algebra follow from theorem B except $A \cdot B = B \cdot A$. To prove $A \cdot B = B \cdot A$, theorem A is necessary. In the resulting field, the points O and U play the parts of zero and the unit element (see Figures 7 and 8).

A coordinate geometry. It is now possible to erect a coordinate geometry in the plane (or space) using only the axioms of betweenness, order, parallelism and theorems A and B and the first two axioms of dimension, but not congruence.

Along any two distinct lines OU_1, OU_2 in a plane, the algebra of points can be constructed as above. If A on OU_1 corresponds to A' on OU_2 when $AA' \| U_1 U_2$, a one-to-one correspondence is set up such that if B corresponds to B' then $A + B$, $A \cdot B$ correspond to $A' + B'$, $A' \cdot B'$. Thus the fields on OU_1, OU_2 can be identified and their elements denoted by small letters.

If P is any point in the plane and parallels through P to OU_2, OU_1 meet OU_1, OU_2 at points a, b in their fields, P can be assigned the coordinates (a, b). The points (x, y) on a line then satisfy an equation $lx + my + n = 0$, in which l, m, n, are elements of the field and are called the coordinates of the line.

Reflections in a plane. In space a reflection in a plane is a looking-glass reflection. The result of reflections in two planes is a translation if the planes are parallel, a rotation around the common line if the planes meet, and a reflection in the common line if the planes are perpendicular. Conversely, any translation or rotation around a line can be resolved into reflections in two planes, either of which may be any plane perpendicular to the direction of the translation or any plane through the axis of rotation. The other is then fixed. If a reflector plane is interposed perpendicular to both planes, then the reflections in the planes can be replaced by reflections in two lines.

Displacements in space

A displacement in space is a transformation that takes a figure into a directly congruent figure. If it has a fixed point O, it is a rotation around a line through O. If it has no fixed point and takes A into B, it is the result of a translation along AB and a rotation around a line l through B. If the line m through B is perpendicular to both AB and l, then the translation is the result of reflections in a line m_1, parallel to m and in m itself, and the rotation is a result of reflections in m and another line through B. Thus, every displacement is the result of reflections in two lines. If these lines are skew, the displacement is the result of a translation along and a rotation around their common perpendicular line.

The result of two displacements can be found by using item 11 of the section *A sample of theorems.*

CONSTRUCTIONS

Constructions regarded as an existence theorem. Euclidean construction can be regarded as existence theorems. "To bisect a given angle," for example, can be interpreted as "every angle has a constructable bisector." Some basic constructions must be assumed.

Gauge constructions. It is convenient to assume the first three elementary constructions (36–38), but to replace the last construction (39) with the gauge construction (40). It is surprising that although the gauge construction is much weaker than the last of the elementary constructions, nevertheless, the latter can be derived from it by using the axioms of betweenness and order and the axioms of congruence even without the parallel axiom.

It is easy to show that the following constructions can be performed without the parallel axiom:

(a) Any angle can be bisected.

(b) If C is any point on OA, the point D on OB such that $OD \simeq OC$ is constructable.

(c) A perpendicular can be constructed to OA from any point on OA.

(d) Any interval can be bisected.

(e) A perpendicular can be constructed to a line through any point outside it.

(f) An angle with a given side can be constructed congruent to a given angle.

(g) If one point at which a line and a circle meet is known, the other is constructable if the centre of the circle is given.

With the aid of the parallel axiom, the gauge construction can be weakened to the form: Given a fixed point O, the gauge can be cut off from O on any ray through O. The circle, the centre of which is the fixed point O, with radius the gauge, is called the gauge circle.

Construction of radical axis of two nonconcentric circles. If the centres of two nonconcentric circles and a point on each are given, then their radical axis may be constructed using only the first three elementary constructions and the weakened form of the gauge construction, as follows:

One circle is taken as the gauge circle K, with centre O, and O' the centre of the other circle K', and N', a point on it. If N' is on OO' it is to be replaced by its reflection in a line through O'. Then $ON \| O'N'$, N chosen on K. If $NN' \| OO'$, the radical axis is the right bisector of OO'. If NN', OO' meet in S, the homothety, with centre S, which takes O into O', and N into N', may be considered as in Figure 16. Using the weakened form of the gauge construction, then P may be constructed along with another point on K, and the other point L' at which SN' meets K' and the other point Q at which SP meets K. The point Q' on K' with $OQ \| O'Q'$ corresponds to Q in the homothety. It can be proved that PN, $L'Q'$ meet on the radical axis of (K, K'); and because this is perpendicular to OO', it can be constructed. (If PN happens to be parallel to $L'Q'$, a different point P can be used.)

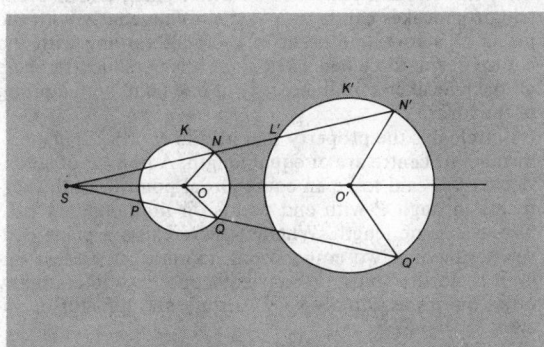

Figure 16: A construction of the radical axis of two nonconcentric circles, given the centres and a point on each.

If K', K'' are two circles, not the gauge circle K, then the radical axes of (K, K') and of (K, K'') are to be constructed. If these meet, their common point is on the radical axis of (K', K''). If they are parallel, the centres of K, K', K'' lie on a line. The circle, the centre of which is not on that line, may then be used instead of K.

Linear constructions. These are the constructions that can be performed by the first three elementary constructions and drawing parallels, assuming the axioms of betweenness and order and Euclid's parallel axiom, or assuming the first three axioms of incidence and Euclid's parallel axiom. If coordinates have been introduced and if S is a set of points, the coordinates of which are the set $a_1, a_2, \cdots, a_n$, then any point can be constructed whose coordinates are in $R = R(a_1, \cdots, a_n)$, the field obtained from $a_1, \cdots, a_2$ by additions, subtractions, multiplications, and divisions. Only points of R can be found by linear constructions from the given points because a line joining points, the coordinates of which are in R, has coordinates in R, and the point at which two nonparallel lines, the coordinates of which are in R, meet has coordinates in R.

Ruler and compass constructions. Assume now the axioms of betweenness and order, the axioms of congruence and the axiom of parallelism (in the weakened form) as well as the following:

If a coplanar line meets the gauge circle K, the points of meeting are constructable.

Now if the centre of a circle K' is given, and a point on it, then K, K' are related by a homothety or by a translation, and if a line l' goes through a point inside K', it corresponds to a line l through a point inside K. The points at which l, K meet are known, and the homothety gives those at which l', K' meet. If two circles are given, their radical axis can be found by the first three elementary constructions and the weakened form of the gauge construction, and hence their points of meeting, if they meet, can be found by the first three constructions and the assumption above. If a ruler and compass are actually used, the ruler is an unmarked straight edge, and the compasses must not be used for transferring lengths; they collapse after a circle is drawn. The axes can now be taken as ordinary rectangular Cartesian axes and the radius of K as the unit length.

With the use of the assumption above, the field obtained, from $a_1, \cdots, a_n$ by additions, subtractions, multiplications, divisions and the extraction of the square roots of positive elements already obtained, may be considered. This enlarges R to the field $\Omega_1(a_1, \cdots, a_n)$ and now all points the coordinates of which are in $\Omega_1(a_1, \cdots, a_n)$ can be constructed from points the coordinates of which are in $(a_1, \cdots, a_n)$. Because every circle has an equation of the form $(x - a)^2 + (y - b)^2 = r^2$, the algebraical counterpart of its construction is the solution of a series of linear and quadratic equations with real roots. Thus, the coordinates of the points obtained are all in $\Omega_1(a_1, \cdots, a_n)$.

An example of an element in $\Omega_1(a_1, a_2)$ is

$$\sqrt{\sqrt{a_1} + \sqrt{a_2} + \sqrt{(a_1 a_2)}}.$$

The elements obtained by changing the sign in front of any square-root sign are also in the field. If an element involves n square roots after all reductions, then, when rationalized, it satisfies an irreducible equation of degree 2^n the coefficients of which are in R. It is for this reason that two classical problems cannot be performed by ruler and compass: (1) to construct a cube the volume of which is twice that of a given cube; (2) to trisect a given angle. Both involve cube roots.

Construction of polygons

The Greek geometers knew how to construct the regular n-gon with $n = 3, 4, 5$ or 6. By inscribing these polygons in circles and repeatedly bisecting the sides, regular polygons of $n \cdot 2^m$ sides can be obtained, m being the number of bisections. Of polygons other than these, however, nothing was known up to the time of Carl Friedrich Gauss. Pierre de Fermat, who died a century before Gauss was born, had studied numbers of the form $2^{2k} + 1$, k being a positive integer. The first five Fermat numbers—3, 5, 17, 257, and 65,537—are primes. No other prime Fermat numbers have been located, and it is possible that all the rest are composite. Gauss's remarkable achievement was to show (at the age of 18) that it is possible with ruler and compass to construct a regular n-gon if n is either a prime Fermat number or a product of different prime Fermat numbers (or, of course, the same multiplied by an integral power of two). It was subsequently shown that the converse of Gauss's theorem also holds and that, therefore, these are the only regular polygons that can be so constructed.

Criterion for gauge construction. If in a ruler and gauge construction the coordinates of a desired point involve n square roots, there will always be 2^n solutions, provided all the square roots involved are real for all values of the coordinates $a_1, \cdots, a_n$ of the given points.

The problem of how to draw a circle through two points A, B touching a given line l not parallel to AB may be considered. There are two solutions if A, B are on the same side of l, but none if they are on opposite sides.

The field $\Omega_0(a_1, \cdots, a_n)$ for this problem is defined as that obtained from $R(a_1, \cdots, a_n)$ by adjoining $\sqrt{(1 + x^2)}$ in which x is already in the field. It follows that if p is a known point with coordinates in $\Omega_0(a_1, \cdots, a_n)$, there can be constructed by the first three elementary constructions and the weakened form of the gauge construction, the point $(1, p)$, and then $\sqrt{(1 + p^2, 0)}$, and, in fact, all points, the coordinates of which have the form $\sqrt{(a_1^2 + a_2^2 + \cdots + a_n^2)}$, and so all points, the coordinates of which are in $\Omega_0(a_1, \cdots, a_n)$. The proof that only such points can be drawn by the construction specified above depends on a deep theorem of algebra:

If $f(p_1, \cdots, p_n)$ is a rational function of $p_1, \cdots, p_n$ with rational coefficients and is never negative for real values of $p_1, \cdots, p_n$, then it can be expressed as the sum of squares of rational functions of $p_1, p_2, \cdots, p_n$ with rational coefficients. (A rational function is a polynomial divided by a polynomial.)

If a regular polygon can be constructed by ruler and compass, then it can be constructed by the first three elementary constructions and the weakened form of the gauge construction. For example, on a base of length 2 a regular pentagon has height $\sqrt{(5 + 2\sqrt{5})}$ and this is in $\Omega_0(1)$, because $5 + 2\sqrt{5} = (1 + \frac{1}{2}\sqrt{5})^2 + (1 + \frac{1}{2}\sqrt{5})^2 + (\frac{1}{2})^2 + (\frac{1}{2})^2$.

Constructions with compasses only. These start with given points and end with required points. If $X(Y)$ mean the circle with centre X passing through Y, three problems are: Given two pairs of points A, B and C, D:
(i) Find the point (if any) at which the lines AB and CD meet.
(ii) Find the points (if any) at which AB and $C(D)$ meet.
(iii) Find the points (if any) at which $A(B)$ and $C(D)$ meet.

Constructions (i), (ii) can be performed by (iii) if the continuity axiom is assumed. It can be concluded that any ruler and compass construction from given points to required points can be performed by compasses only.

To find a circle touching three given circles. The problem of finding a circle that touches three given circles K_1, K_2, K_3 may be considered. For simplicity the circles may be mutually external. The radical axes of each pair can be constructed by methods of the section *Construction of radical axis of two nonconcentric circles.* These axes, assumed distinct and no two parallel, all meet in a point O. The circle K orthogonal to K_1, K_2, K_3 has centre O and can be constructed. The external centres of homothety of K_1, K_2, K_3, taken in pairs, lie on a line l. If m_1 is the common chord of K and K_1, and if P_1 is the point at which it meets l, the tangents from P_1 to K_1 touch K_1 at the points of contact of one of the required circles. The other tangent circles are given by a slight modification of this construction.

GEOMETRY OF MORE THAN THREE DIMENSIONS

The axioms of betweenness and order may again be considered, but now for clarity the word space is replaced by three-dimensional space or S_3. Instead of the axiom (29) that restricts space to three dimensions, it may be assumed that there is a point not in S_3 (see 30).

If A, B, C, D are non-coplanar points, there is a point E not in the space $ABCD$. The points A, B, C, D, E are the vertices of a polytope, and the join of two of the points is an edge. The triangle, the vertices of which are three of them, is a face; the tetrahedron, the vertices of which are four of them, is a cell. A space S_4 of four dimensions is defined as the set of all points and all lines joining any two points of two cells of the polytope.

All this is completely analogous to the definitions of plane in S_3 and can be continued to $S_5, S_6, \cdots$. Finally, for some fixed n, all points are in S_n.

CONVEXITY

Convexity in Euclidean geometry. Euclidean plane and solid geometry provide a natural setting for the study of convex sets and convexity. A set S in Euclidean space is said to be convex if every straight line segment having its two end points in S lies entirely in S. In Figure 17, the

Sets in Euclidean space

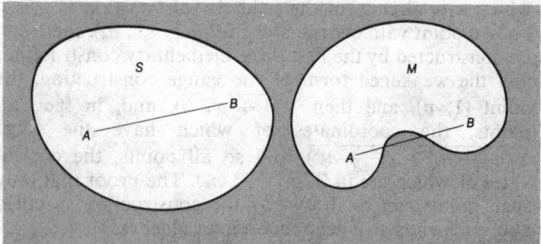

Figure 17: Examples of (left) convex and (right) nonconvex sets.

set S is convex because the line segment joining arbitrary points A and B in S always belongs completely to S. The other set M is not convex because there exist at least two points A and B in M the joining segment of which is not completely in M. The circle and the ellipse bound familiar convex sets in the plane, and in space the solid figures bounded by the sphere and the cube are common examples. It is important to note, however, that a hollow spherical shell is not convex, whereas the solid spherical ball is convex. Egg-shaped solids are convex if, and only if, the interior points are included, together with the

boundary. The isoperimetric problem of antiquity involves convexity. The solution to this problem shows that among all the simple plane regions, the bounding curves of which have the same length, the circle encloses a maximum area. A first step in proving this is to show that every nonconvex plane region is contained in a convex set with shorter boundary and with greater area. Therefore, in solving the isoperimetric problem it suffices to investigate only convex sets; the solution must be found among them.

The isoperimetric problem

The beguiling simplicity of the convexity concept has attracted both gifted novices and mature mathematicians. Euclid would have appreciated the theorem to be described later as of the Helly type, which can be paraphrased informally as follows: "If there are more than three flat circular pancakes on a flat plate, and if every trio of pancakes can be impaled simultaneously with the prong of a fork, the point of piercing varying with the choice of the three pancakes, then it is possible to impale all the pancakes simultaneously at one point with a prong of the fork."

A circle has the property that all the chords (diameters) through its centre are of equal length. A point P of a convex set S is said to be an equichordal point if all the segments through P with end points on the boundary of S have the same length. Whether there exists a plane convex set having two equichordal points is at present unknown. In the study of convexity one encounters many other questions equally easy to state and difficult to answer.

Euclidean space E itself is convex; and the points, lines, line segments, and planes are convex subsets of E. This important property more than any other has made convexity an essential part of classical Euclidean geometry. In any space in which two points determine a unique segment of the space, convexity is a natural concept. Vector spaces, with their linear operations of vector addition and scalar multiplication, have, therefore, their convex structures.

The following modern plane separation axiom has influenced geometry at the elementary level: "All the points of the plane that do not belong to a line L form two convex sets P and Q (called half-planes) such that each segment joining a point of P to a point of Q intersects L." The 19th-century axiom of Pasch states: "In the plane if a line intersects one side of a triangle and misses the three vertices, then it must intersect one of the other two sides." Both of these axioms, which involve notions of convexity, slipped by Euclid as "too obvious to mention."

Pasch's axiom

Basic concepts of convexity in the development of Euclidean point set topology. If C is a circle in the plane with centre A, then the entire set of points inside the circle is called an open circular neighbourhood of the point A, or, more briefly, a neighbourhood of A. Such a neighbourhood is convex. In Euclidean three-space, spherical neighbourhoods play the corresponding role. A point is an interior point of a set S if it has a neighbourhood entirely in S. A point P is a boundary point of S if every neighbourhood of P contains points in S and points not in S. A set is open if all of its points are interior points and closed if it contains all of its boundary points.

The set of interior points (called the interior) of a convex set S is also convex, and the set S with its boundary (called the closure) forms a convex set. Each boundary point P of a convex set in the plane E_2 is contained in a line L that supports S; intuitively, L is a tangent line, if the boundary has a tangent at P. This means that S lies in one of the closed half-planes bounded by L (see plane separation axiom above). In fact, if S is a closed set in the plane having nonempty interior, then S is convex if, and only if, through each boundary point of S there passes a line that supports S. Corresponding statements hold in Euclidean three-space E_3, so that each boundary point is contained in a plane of support to S. These results extend completely to n-dimensional Euclidean space E_n, in which the analogue of a plane is called a hyperplane. A hyperplane H separates E_n in a manner analogous to that in the plane separation axiom, yielding two closed half-spaces having H as a common boundary. It

Planes and hyperplanes

is notable that both bounded and unbounded convex sets exist, a convex set being bounded if it is contained in some sphere. A half-space, for example, is unbounded, whereas a solid cube is bounded.

A point A in the boundary of a plane convex set S having nonempty interior is an exposed point if it is contained in a line of support that intersects S in exactly one point, namely, A. A point B is an extreme point of the convex set if no segment in S contains B between its end points. A convex set is strictly convex if its boundary contains no line segments. A point B is a vertex of S if it is contained in more than one line of support to S. If S contains no vertices, it is said to be smooth. An ellipse bounds a convex set that is both strictly convex and smooth, whereas a square bounds a convex set that is neither strictly convex nor smooth. The above notions extend to E_n in a natural way.

Because the intersection of two convex sets consists of all points belonging to both, the definition of convexity implies immediately that the intersection is also convex. This is true even if the intersection is empty (null), because the empty set is convex. As a consequence of this basic property, if S is any set in Euclidean n-space there exists a smallest convex set containing S called the convex hull, or convex cover of S, which is the intersection of all convex sets that contain S. If S is convex, then S is its own convex hull. In a Euclidean space E_n every closed convex set S that is not E_n itself is the intersection of all the closed half-spaces containing S.

Among the more intriguing theorems of the 20th century is a group of geometric combinatorial theorems of so-called Helly type (see COMBINATORICS AND COMBINATORIAL GEOMETRY), an illustration of which has been given (see above *Convexity in Euclidean geometry*). The corresponding theorem for Euclidean n-space is: "If F is a family of more than n bounded closed convex sets in Euclidean n-space E_n, and if every $n + 1$ members of F have at least one point in common, then all the members of F have at least one point in common." The number $n + 1$ appearing in Helly's theorem is called the Helly number. There exists a great variety of Helly type theorems, of which two follow.

Theorems of the Helly type

1. If a family of bounded closed parallel line segments in the plane is such that every three are intersected simultaneously by at least one line, then there exists a line that simultaneously intersects all the segments in the family.

2. A picture gallery consisting of several interconnecting rooms can be imagined to have its walls completely covered with small pictures. If for each three pictures there is a point in the gallery from which all three can be seen, then there exists a point from which *all* the pictures in the gallery can be seen. (Such a region is called starshaped.) The following is one version of a separation theorem. "A valley contains a flock of (stationary) sheep and goats. If for each set of four animals a straight fence can be built that will separate the sheep from the goats, then all the sheep can be separated from all the goats by a single fence (straight line)." Here the Helly number is four. In E_n it would be $n + 2$. Helly type theorems are closely related to a fundamental theorem of Carathéodory: "Each point in the convex hull of a set S in E_n is in the convex hull of $n + 1$ or fewer points of S."

A circle in E_2 has the property that the distance between any two parallel lines of support (which in this case are also tangent lines) is constant. A convex set S with the property that the perpendicular distance between each pair of its parallel lines of support is constant is called a set of constant width. An ellipse does not bound a set of constant width: the distance between parallel lines of support at the extremities of the minor axis is less than the corresponding width for the major axis. A simple example other than the circle can be constructed as follows: If A, B, C are the vertices of an equilateral triangle, then with A as centre the (smaller) circular arc is drawn joining B and C. This construction is then repeated with B and C as centres. The union of the three arcs thus drawn bounds a convex set of constant width called the Reuleaux triangle (see Figure 18). It has vertices at the points A, B, C, whereas a circle is smooth. Nevertheless,

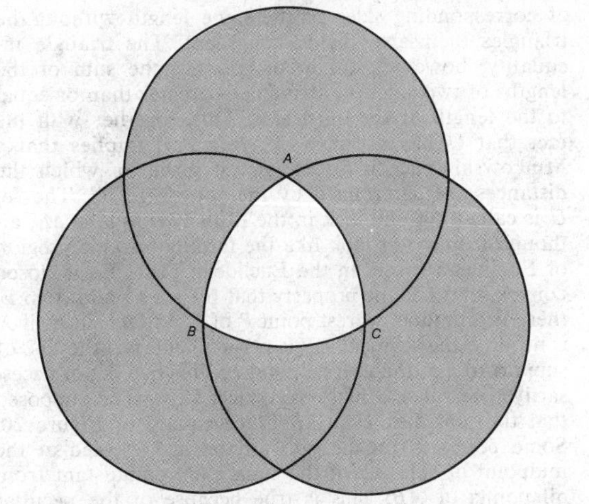

The Reuleaux triangle

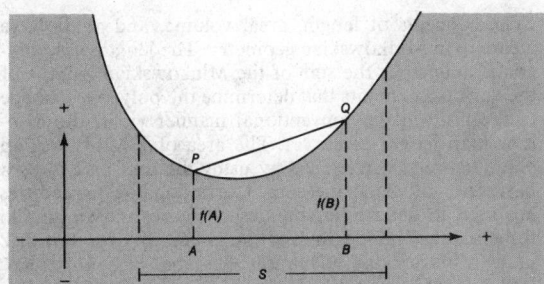

Figure 18: The Reuleaux triangle.

cylindrical rollers of cross section having the form of Figure 18 could be used to roll a heavy object, such as a crate, in a horizontal direction over level ground smoothly and without any vertical component of motion. A Reuleaux polygon can be constructed in an analogous manner, but it must always have an odd number of vertices.

Convex functions are closely related to convex sets. A graph is said to be convex if the chord joining any two points P and Q of the graph lies above that portion of the graph joining P and Q, as in Figure 19. The function $\{f(x) = x^2, x = \text{real}\}$ representing the parabola is an example of a convex function. In general, if a plane graph has the property that each of its chords PQ always lies above that portion of the graph joining P and Q, then the real-valued function that determines the graph is said to be convex. If a plane graph is convex, then the portion of the plane lying above the graph is a convex set. In higher dimensions a real-valued convex function f defined on a convex set S of E_n has a graph F in a space E_{n+1} of one higher dimension such that each vertical two-dimensional plane intersects F in a plane convex graph.

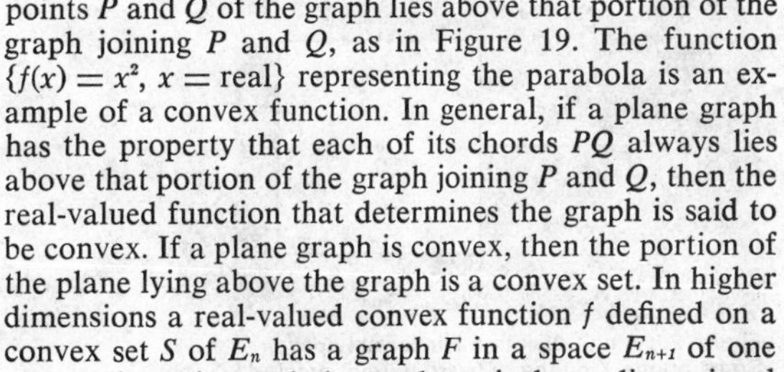

Figure 19: The graph of a convex function. Each of its chords, PQ, lies above that portion of the graph joining P and Q.

Convexity in Minkowskian geometry as compared to that in Euclidean geometry. Minkowskian geometry differs from Euclidean geometry essentially in the fact that the unit of length may vary significantly with the direction in which the measurement occurs. In order to see how the length changes with direction, U may be taken as a bounded closed convex set in the plane E_2 having an interior point O as a centre of symmetry; hence, each chord of U through O is bisected by O. As an illustration, if U is bounded by a square having O as the central point where the diagonals intersect, then (given U as fixed and choosing a point P on the boundary of U) by definition the unit of linear measure on all lines parallel to the segment OP is the Euclidean length of OP. Because the Euclidean length of OP can change as P varies on the boundary of S, it is interesting to observe that many of the theorems of classical geometry that depend upon the concept of length may be significantly altered. In Minkowskian geometry, two triangles can have all three pairs

Changes of Euclidean length

of corresponding sides of the same length without the triangles themselves being congruent. The triangle inequality, however, still holds; that is, the sum of the lengths of two sides of a triangle is greater than or equal to the length of the third side. This, together with the fact that U has a centre of symmetry, implies that a Minkowski space is also a metric space, in which the distances are determined by the convex set U. The set U is called the unit disk in the Minkowski plane M_2, although it may not look like the familiar circular region of Euclidean space. In the Euclidean plane E_2, a closed convex set S has the property that for each point X in E_2 there is a unique nearest point P of S. In fact, in E_2 if X is not in S the segment XP is perpendicular to the line of support to S at the nearest point P. This fact is not necessarily true for a Minkowski space. It may be supposed that the unit disk U in M_2 is the square of Figure 20. Some points X on the outward normal erected at the midpoint of side AB of the square are equidistant from all points of AB. This is true because of the peculiar way in which the linear measure changes with direction. By definition, in a Minkowski space, a line L_1 is perpendicular to a line L_2 if the point of intersection of L_1 and L_2 is a nearest point of L_2 relative to the points of L_1. In M_2 there may exist more than one perpendicular to a line L at a point P. A Minkowskian plane the unit disk of which is an ellipse can be shown to be Euclidean, and all others are not Euclidean. A circle is a special case of an ellipse.

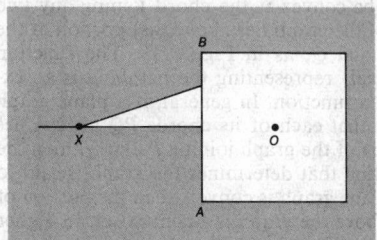

Figure 20: A unit disk in a Minkowski space. Some points X on the outward normal erected at the midpoint of a side AB are equidistant from all points of AB.

The concepts of length, area, volume, and angle have meaning in Minkowskian geometry. The length of a polygon is defined as the sum of the Minkowskian lengths of the various segments that determine the polygon. Passage to the limit in the conventional manner yields the Minkowskian length of curves. The area of a Minkowskian plane figure is determined by using the unit disk U as a basic unit of plane measure. Corresponding procedures are used to determine volumes of figures in Minkowski three-space. The length L of the boundary of a unit disk in a Minkowskian plane satisfies the inequality $3 \leqslant L/2 \leqslant 4$. (The unit disk U always has diameter 2.) If U is the square, then $L = 8$. If U is the regular hexagon, then $L = 6$. In the Euclidean plane $L = 2\pi$ and, as is well-known, $3 < \pi < 4$.

Geometric inequalities and convexity. The quantitative aspects of convexity provide a rich source for inequalities and numerical estimates. The surface area A and the volume V of a bounded convex set S in Euclidean n-space E_n are connected by the famous isoperimetric inequality, $A^n \geqslant n^n U V^{n-1}$, in which U is the volume of the unit sphere in E_n. The equality holds if, and only if, S is an n-dimensional sphere. In three space E_3, $A^3 \geqslant 36\pi V^2$. In the plane $(n = 2)$, $A^2 \geqslant 4\pi V$, in which A is the length of the boundary of S and V is the plane area of S. Among all the plane convex sets of constant width d the Reuleaux triangle contains the least area, whereas the circle contains the greatest.

The isoperimetric inequality

Packing problems are among those easiest to state and hardest to solve. A family of convex sets forms a packing if no two members of the family overlap (their interiors are disjoint). A set S is covered by a family of convex sets if each point of S belongs to some member of the family. The percentage of the space or a subset thereof

that is covered by the members of a packing determines a density of the packing. In the plane, the best packing (maximum density) for congruent circles is that in which all the circles are framed by non-overlapping plane-filling regular hexagons, so that every circle touches exactly six circles symmetrically. In three-dimensional space it is possible to bring a sphere simultaneously in contact with 12 other spheres of the same size without overlapping. It is impossible, however, to bring the central sphere into contact with 13 non-overlapping spheres of the same size; the proof is known but not easy. The best packing of congruent spheres in E_8 is still unknown; solutions exist only with certain added hypotheses.

BIBLIOGRAPHY. *The Thirteen Books of Euclid's Elements*, 3 vol. (1908; 2nd ed. rev., 1926), is the standard English translation, with extensive commentary by T.L. HEATH; DAVID HILBERT, *Grundlagen der Geometrie* (1899 and later editions; Eng. trans., *The Foundations of Geometry*, 1902), gives a logical account of Euclid's own methods and many new results. The later editions include revised reprints of very important papers of the author. The axiomatic approach now common in all branches of mathematics is due to the influence of this book and to the work of Giuseppe Peano and his school. HENRY G. FORDER, *Foundations of Euclidean Geometry* (1927), expounds in full detail the work of Hilbert, his followers, and of the American and Italian schools. H.S. MacDONALD COXETER and S.L. GREITZER, *Geometry Revisited* (1967), is a pleasant account of theorems in Euclidean geometry. For Euclidean geometry in its setting in general geometry, see HENRY G. FORDER, *Geometry* (1950); H.S. MacDONALD COXETER, *Introduction to Geometry* (1961); DANIEL PEDOE, *A Course of Geometry for Colleges and Universities* (1970); and HENRY P. MANNING, *Geometry of Four Dimensions* (1914), an excellent work. For transformation geometry, I.M. YAGLOM, *Geometric Transformations* (1962; orig. pub. in Russian, 1955), gives a good elementary introduction. Much more detailed is FRIEDRICH BACHMANN, *Aufbau der Geometrie aus dem Spiegelungsbegriff* (1959), based on papers by Hjelmslev. H.P. HUDSON, *Ruler and Compasses* (1916), is a thorough treatment of constructions. For the theory of congruence, not yet incorporated into textbooks, see J.F. RIGBY, "Axioms for Absolute Geometry," *Can. J. Math.*, 20:158–181 (1968). T. BONNESEN and W. FENCHEL, *Theorie der konvexen Körper* (1934), is excellent for the classical theory. For more recent developments the following books are representative: H.G. EGGLESTON, *Convexity* (1958); FREDERICK A. VALENTINE, *Convex Sets* (1964); and I.M. YAGLOM and V.G. BOLTYANSKY, *Convex Figures* (1961; orig. pub. in Russian, 1951). For an interesting collection of modern research papers, see the *Proceedings of the Seventh Symposium in Pure Mathematics* (1963), which includes "Helly's Theorem and Its Relatives," by L. DANZER, B. GRUNBAUM, and V. KLEE; and "Convex Curves of Constant Minkowski Breadth," by P.C. HAMMER. There exists a variety of books dealing with specialized topics in convexity. HERBERT BUSEMANN, *Convex Surfaces* (1958); and R.T. ROCKAFELLAR, *Convex Analysis* (1970), are typical. Additional references on convexity are: EDWIN F. BECKENBACH, "Convex Functions," *Bull. Am. Math. Soc.*, 54:439–460 (1948); RUSSELL V. BENSON, *Euclidean Geometry and Convexity* (1966); L. FEJES TOTH, *Lagerungen in der Ebene auf der Kugel und im Raum* (1953); B. GRUNBAUM, *Convex Polytopes* (1967); HUGO HADWIGER, *Altes und Neues über konvexe Körper* (1955); HUGO HADWIGER and HANS DEBRUNNER, *Kombinatorische Geometrie in der Ebene* (1959); Eng. trans., *Combinatorial Geometry in the Plane*, 1964); HERMANN MINKOWSKI, *Gesammelte Abhandlung* (1911); EDWIN E. MOISE, *Elementary Geometry from an Advanced Standpoint* (1963); T. MOTZKIN, *Beiträge zur Theorie der linearen Ungleichungen* (1936); and CLAUDE A. ROGERS, *Packing and Covering* (1964).

(H.G.F./F.A.V.)

Geometry, Non-Euclidean

Non-Euclidean geometry is the subject of study that results by making certain assumptions (the axioms) about points, lines, planes, and space and then drawing conclusions (the theorems) generally consistent with one's spatial intuition concerning objects of moderate size and yet rich in certain relationships that affront the intuition, particularly relationships concerning the concept of parallelism extended to large distances. For instance, similar figures (the same shape) are necessarily congruent (the same shape and size): no plan or model or map can be truly accurate. The two principal types of such a geometry are vividly distinguished by referring to the following imaginary construction. Two rays in a plane are drawn from points *A* and *B*, perpendicular to and on the same side of the line that connects *A* and *B* (Figure 1). Instead of remaining equidistant they become farther apart or closer together. In the former case, when the rays diverge, the non-Euclidean geometry is said to be hyperbolic (from the Greek *hyperballein*, "to throw beyond"). In the latter case, when the rays converge and ultimately intersect, the geometry is said to be elliptic

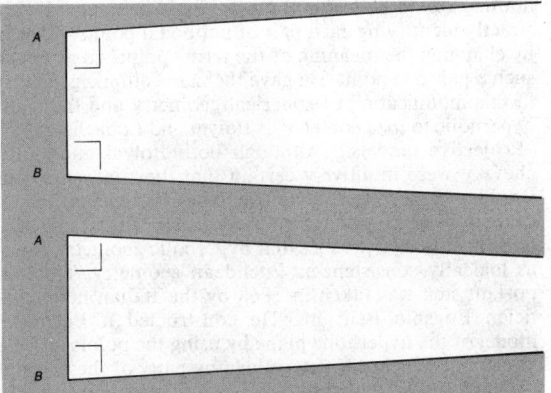

Figure 1: Rays having a common perpendicular in hyperbolic and elliptic geometries (see text).

(from *elleipein*, "to fall short"). Because it is impossible in practice to measure how far apart the rays will be when extended millions of miles, it is quite conceivable that man is living in a non-Euclidean universe. (Because intuition is developed from relatively limited observations, it is not to be trusted in this regard.) In such a world, railroad tracks can still be equidistant, but then they will not be perfectly straight.

Euclid's axioms. In the language of axiomatic mathematics, non-Euclidean geometry satisfies all of Euclid's axioms except either the fifth or the second. The axioms of Euclid are stated fully under GEOMETRY, EUCLIDEAN. (They have often been called postulates.) The second axiom states that an interval can be prolonged indefinitely. The fifth states that, if a line meets two other lines so as to make the angles *a* and *b* on one side of it together less than two right angles, the other lines, if prolonged indefinitely, will meet on this side (in Figure 2, the right side).

In hyperbolic geometry, axiom 5 is denied, because, if the ray from *A* in Figure 1 is replaced by one making a very slightly smaller angle with *AB*, the new ray from *A* and the old one from *B* may converge at first, attain a minimal distance, and then diverge (Figure 3). In elliptic geometry, axiom 5 is satisfied trivially, but axiom 2 (interpreted as giving the line an infinite length) is denied, because now the line is closed, like a circle.

History of hyperbolic geometry. It has been remarked with some justice that Euclid (4th century BC) was the first non-Euclidean geometer, because of his own evident reluctance to invoke axiom 5. At any rate, he arranged his material so that his first 28 propositions are proved without the aid of this unpleasantly complicated assumption. Such a collection of propositions, based on the first four postulates alone, has been growing ever since Euclid's time and is now known as absolute geometry. (All of these propositions are valid in hyperbolic geometry as well as Euclidean.) Until about 1800, however, all the people who thought along these lines imagined that they were operating within Euclidean geometry so that they would eventually deduce the fifth axiom as a theorem. Many believed that they had attained this goal, though in fact they had merely replaced axiom 5 by other equivalent assumptions, such as "two parallel lines are equidistant" or "three non-collinear points always lie on a circle."

A Jesuit logician named Gerolamo Saccheri of 17th- and 18th-century Italy used a more sophisticated ap-

proach: *reductio ad absurdum* (disproving a false proposition by logically deducing an absurd consequence). He tried to establish axiom 5 by denying it and seeking a consequent contradiction. In the course of his elaborate chain of deduction he discovered many of the theorems of what is now called hyperbolic geometry, although he had started with the sole purpose of demolishing them. At a certain stage he imagined he had deduced the absurdity he was seeking, and thus he narrowly missed the opportunity for a great achievement. He failed because of his pious belief that Euclid's was the only true geometry.

In 1763 the German mathematician Georg Simon Klügel listed nearly 30 attempts to prove axiom 5 and rightly concluded that the alleged proofs were all unsound. Fifty years later, a new generation of geometers, still working on the same problem, were becoming more and more frustrated. One of them, a Hungarian named Farkas Bolyai, wrote in a letter to his son János Bolyai: "I entreat you, leave the science of parallels alone · · · · . I have travelled past all reefs of this infernal Dead Sea and have always come back with a broken mast and torn sail." The son, refusing to heed this warning, continued to think about parallels until, in 1823, he saw the whole truth and declared, in his youthful enthusiasm, "I have created a new universe from nothing!" He understood that, at a certain stage, absolute geometry branches out in two directions depending on whether axiom 5 is asserted or denied. János Bolyai thus recognized two different but equally consistent geometries and published his discovery as a 24-page appendix to a textbook by his father. George Bruce Halsted called it "the most extraordinary two dozen pages in the whole history of thought." In 1832 Farkas Bolyai proudly presented a copy to his friend Carl Friedrich Gauss, then Germany's greatest mathematician, whose reply to the father had a devastating effect on János and led eventually to much criticism of Gauss. The criticism undoubtedly stemmed from the impression that a man of Gauss's stature could have afforded to acknowledge that both the concept and the confidence of its truth are essential to prior claim in any field of intellectual endeavour. The younger Bolyai had conveyed both concept and confidence by choosing the path of publication, while Gauss in his private papers had recorded only his awareness of the concept. For these reasons it seems worthwhile to quote a considerable portion of Gauss's reply (in H.S. Carslaw's translation):

I am unable to praise this work · · · · . To praise it would be to praise myself. Indeed, the whole contents of the work, the path taken by your son, the results to which he is led, coincide almost entirely with my meditations which occupied my mind partly for the last thirty or thirty-five years. So I remained quite stupefied. So far as my own work is concerned · · · my intention was not to let it be published during my lifetime · · · · . On the other hand, it was my idea to write down all this later so that at least it should not perish with me. It is therefore a pleasant surprise for me that I am spared this trouble, and I am very glad that it is just the son of my old friend who takes the precedence of me in such a remarkable manner.

It can now be seen, from his earlier correspondence, that Gauss had indeed been familiar with hyperbolic geometry, even before János was born. For instance, he wrote to the elder Bolyai in 1799: "It might well be possible that, however far apart one took the three vertices of a triangle in space, its area was always under a given limit." Again, a letter to Gauss has been preserved in which his pupil Friedrich Ludwig Wachter (1792–1817)

Figure 2: Illustration of Euclid's fifth postulate (see text).

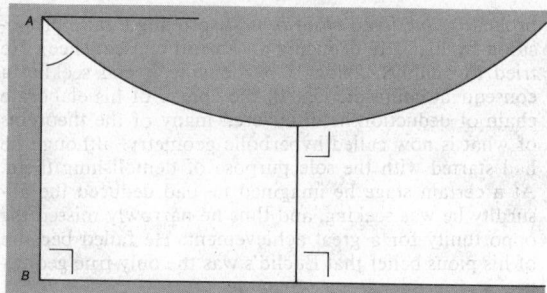

Figure 3: Ultraparallel lines (see text).

remarked a few months before his tragically early death that, if axiom 5 is denied, a sphere the radius of which tends to infinity approaches a limiting surface on which certain curves (the geodesics) behave just like the lines of the Euclidean plane. This surface, now known as the horosphere, was destined to play a vital role in the development of the subject.

Early contributors to hyperbolic and elliptical geometries

Non-Euclidean geometry and the theory of relativity have so profoundly affected today's philosophic outlook that it can hardly be imagined how shocking the denial of one of Euclid's postulates must have seemed at the beginning of the 19th century. Such considerations may help to explain why Gauss deliberately renounced his potential claim in favour of János Bolyai and his Russian contemporary Nikolay Ivanovich Lobachevsky, whose first published paper is remarkably like Bolyai's, though quite independent of it.

Lobachevsky made a deeper investigation, wrote several books, and became a professor at the University of Kazan. Gauss sent him a letter of genuine praise and arranged a corresponding membership for him in the Göttingen Academy. In marked contrast, the unhappy Bolyai received no recognition during his lifetime. In 1848 he read one of Lobachevsky's books (translated into German) and praised it warmly. Still smarting from the unkind treatment that he imagined he had received from Gauss, however, he was too timid to introduce himself to the prosperous Russian, and there is no evidence that Lobachevsky was aware of his existence. Gauss, who knew them both, was so fully occupied with his own work on other subjects that he never took the trouble to bring them together.

History of elliptic geometry. On the surface of a sphere, such as a geographical globe or the Earth itself, the shortest distance between two points is an arc of a great circle. It is natural for navigators to regard such circles as the "lines" of a special kind of two-dimensional geometry, namely spherical geometry: the geometry of figures drawn on the surface of a sphere of radius 1. It will be seen later that this is almost the same as plane elliptic geometry. Spherical geometry was studied by Menelaus of Alexandria about AD 100 and by the Arabs about 1000. Its most famous theorem (discovered by Albert Girard, a French mathematician of the early 17th century) states that the three angles of a spherical triangle (in radian measure) satisfy the inequality $A + B + C > \pi$ and that the area of a triangle is $A + B + C - \pi$. The gigantic step of extending this geometry from two dimensions to three (or more) was taken simultaneously (in the latter half of the 19th century) by Ludwig Schläfli in Switzerland and Bernhard Riemann in Germany. Schläfli regarded spherical three-dimensional space as the "surface" of the "sphere" in Euclidean four-dimensional space (that is, the hypersurface on which the four coordinates satisfy the equation $x_1^2 + x_2^2 + x_3^2 + x_4^2 = 1$). If this three-dimensional continuum represents the astronomical space in which man lives, the unit of measurement (radius of the universe) must be very large; but in terms of this unit the total length of a line is 2π. This means, as Riemann remarked, that the unboundedness of space does not necessarily imply infinitely long lines. A sufficiently powerful telescope could theoretically enable an astronomer to observe the back of his own head, apart from the fact that the light reflected from his head would require thousands of millions

of years to reach his eye. This idea, that space could be unbounded without being infinite, was adopted by Einstein in his general theory of relativity (see PHYSICAL THEORIES, MATHEMATICAL ASPECTS OF: *Relativity theory*).

Another German, Felix Klein, at the turn of the 20th century, first saw how to remedy the awkward situation in spherical geometry that two lines through any one point, being two great circles on a sphere, meet again in an antipodal point (or point on the surface of the sphere that is furthest from the first point). He realized that, because every point determines a unique antipodal point, nothing would be lost and much would be gained by abstractly identifying each pair of antipodal points—that is, by changing the meaning of the term "point" so as to call such a pair one point. He gave the name elliptic geometry to this modification of spherical geometry and the name hyperbolic to the geometry of Bolyai and Lobachevsky.

Projective models. Although both Bolyai and Lobachevsky were intuitively certain that their investigations would never lead to two contradictory statements, neither of them lived to see a rigorous demonstration of this relative consistency: the fact that hyperbolic geometry is just as logically consistent as Euclidean geometry. This important step was taken in 1868 by the Italian mathematician Eugenio Beltrami. He constructed a Euclidean model of the hyperbolic plane by using the points inside a circle and the chords determined by pairs of these points to represent the hyperbolic points and lines. Points on the circle are regarded as being infinitely far away. Thus the parallel lines of Bolyai and Lobachevsky, which "only just" fail to meet, are represented by chords having a common end, such as AN and MN in Figure 4. For any line MN of the hyperbolic plane and any point A not on this line, there are two rays from A parallel to MN, namely, AM and AN. Any line p through A inside the angle MAN intersects MN, and any line l through A in the supplement of this angle fails to intersect MN. The German mathematician Eduard Study called such a line l ultraparallel to MN. Thus, any two lines in the hyperbolic plane are either intersecting, parallel, or ultraparallel.

Beltrami's model of the hyperbolic plane

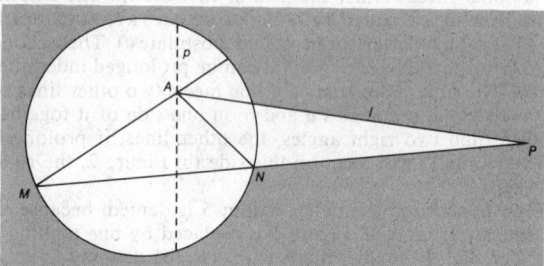

Figure 4: Rays AM and AN from A parallel to MN in the hyperbolic plane.

To be quite precise, Beltrami considered points inside the circle having the equation $x^2 + y^2 = k^2$ and defined the element ds of hyperbolic distance by a formula in which the square of this element is a quadratic function (with variable coefficients) of the differential elements dx and dy (see Box, equation 1). He observed that with this metric the geodesics are of the form $ax + by + c = 0$ (that is, Euclidean straight lines), while the Gauss curvature has the constant value $-1/k^2$. It follows, by setting $y = 0$, that a point distant r from the origin is regarded as being at hyperbolic distance $k\delta$ when δ is expressed by integrating the function $(1 - x^2)^{-1}$ from 0 to r, so that $r = \tanh \delta$ (see 2).

$$(1) \qquad ds^2 = k^2 \frac{(1 - y^2)\, dx^2 + 2xy\, dx\, dy + (1 - x^2)\, dy^2}{(1 - x^2 - y^2)^2}$$

$$(2) \qquad \delta = \int_0^r \frac{dx}{1 - x^2}$$

Meanwhile, the subject of projective geometry (see GE-OMETRY, PROJECTIVE) had been developed by the mathematicians Jean-Victor Poncelet (French) and Karl Georg Christian von Staudt (German) to the stage at which it became clear that the real projective plane admits a polarity—that is, a one-to-one correspondence between all the points A and lines a such that incidence is preserved in accordance with the principle of duality. This means that, if A is the pole of a and b is the polar of B, and if B lies on a, then b passes through A. Two lines are said to be conjugate if one passes through the pole of the other, and two points are said to be conjugate if one lies on the polar of the other (Figure 5). If no point is conjugate to itself, the polarity is said to be elliptic, and every point behaves just like every other point. The existence of one self-conjugate point, however, ensures that of many others, namely, all the points on a conic, and then the polarity is said to be hyperbolic. The polars of the self-conjugate points are the self-conjugate lines, which are the tangents of the conic. A point not on the conic is said to be inside or outside according as it lies on no tangent or on two tangents. Analogous results hold in three dimensions, with planes instead of lines and a surface instead of a curve.

Developing an idea of the English mathematician Arthur Cayley who had translated some of Schläfli's work, Klein observed that, when one polarity (the "absolute" polarity) is assumed to play a special role, real projective geometry becomes non-Euclidean, namely, elliptic or hyperbolic according to the nature of the absolute polarity. The precise connection is that conjugate lines (or planes) become perpendicular lines (or planes). In the elliptic plane, for instance, all the lines perpendicular to a given line a pass through one point A, the pole of a. (On a sphere, all the great circles perpendicular to the equator pass through the north and south poles, which Klein identified so as to form one pole.) Thus, the pole of a line AB is the point of intersection of the lines through A and B perpendicular to AB (Figure 1).

Similarly, hyperbolic geometry is determined by a hyperbolic polarity and hence by an absolute conic (or quadric). The hyperbolic plane (or space), however, is not the whole projective plane (or space) but only the region inside the absolute conic (or quadric). In other words, the lines of hyperbolic geometry are the chords of this conic (or quadric), and the two ends of such a chord are the points at infinity, or ends, of the hyperbolic line. (This projective model is thus a generalization of Beltrami's.) The condition for two lines of the hyperbolic plane (or space) to be parallel (in the sense of Bolyai and Lobachevsky) is that they have one end in common; and the set of all lines with a common end, being the set of all lines parallel to a given ray, is a pencil (or bundle) of parallels. David Hilbert, German mathematician, first used the word end in this sense so

Conjugate points and lines

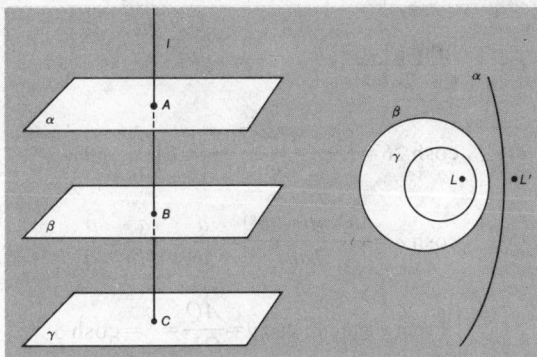

Figure 6: Three planes perpendicular to one line and their inverse models, three coaxal (non-intersecting) circles.

that each line has two ends, both infinitely far away but distinct, in contrast to the customary introduction to projective geometry, in which it is said that a line has only one point at infinity. Hilbert also gave both kinds of non-Euclidean geometry their first rigorous axiomatic treatment.

It can be seen at once from Figure 4 that any two ultraparallel lines, such as AP and MN, have a unique common perpendicular (represented by the polar of the ultrainfinite point of intersection P of the two ultraparallel lines). Hilbert gave a long and ingenious proof of this theorem, using his axioms without any appeal to the projective model.

Regarding the hyperbolic plane AMN as one plane in hyperbolic space, one can draw through each line a plane perpendicular to AMN and thus deduce properties of pairs of planes. It can be concluded that there are just three kinds of plane pairs: intersecting, so that the two planes contain a common line; parallel, having one common point at infinity, such as N; and ultraparallel, so that they have a common perpendicular. In the projective model, parallel planes intersect in a tangent line of the absolute quadric.

Inversive models. In the above-mentioned projective model of Cayley and Klein, the points and lines of hyperbolic space are represented by the interior points and chords of a quadric surface in real projective space. This quadric may be conveniently regarded as a sphere: a celestial sphere that surrounds the observer and is so large that he may be regarded as being at its centre even when he changes position. In this manner, the three-parameter family of planes in space is represented by the three-parameter family of circles on the sphere, with no distinction made between great and small circles—that is, by the three-parameter family of circles in the inversive plane. Each pair of intersecting planes is represented by a pair of intersecting circles; the line of intersection is represented by two points, arising from the two ends of the line; and the two supplementary dihedral angles (formed by the two intersecting planes) are represented by the angles of intersection of the circles. The three kinds of circle-pair—intersecting, tangent, and non-intersecting—represent three kinds of plane-pair: intersecting, parallel, and ultraparallel. Thus, the space under consideration is hyperbolic, not Euclidean.

Though this representation of hyperbolic space by the inversive plane was mentioned casually by mathematicians in England, Germany, and the United States, its first systematic development was in Germany by Heinrich Liebmann in his *Nichteuklidische Geometrie* (Leipzig, 1905, p. 54).

It is still necessary to find an appropriate meaning for the distance AB between two points A and B of the hyperbolic space. By "appropriate" it is meant that it should be properly additive so that, if A, B, C are on a line l, with B between A and C, $AB + BC = AC$. Let α, β, γ symbolize the planes through A, B, C that are perpendicular to l. Having a common perpendicular, these planes are ultraparallel in pairs and are represented by non-intersecting coaxal circles to which the same symbols α, β, γ may be assigned (Figure 6). The line l is

Inversive model of hyperbolic space; inversive distance

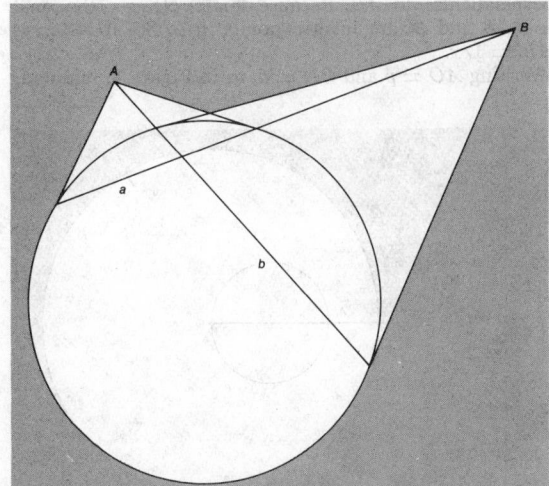

Figure 5: Conjugate lines (a and b) and conjugate points (A and B).

(3) $\left|\dfrac{a^2+b^2-c^2}{2ab}\right|$

(4) $\cosh 2\delta = \left|\dfrac{a^2+a^2-(2p)^2}{2a^2}\right| = 2\left(\dfrac{p}{a}\right)^2 - 1$

(5) $\cosh \delta = \left|\dfrac{a^2+b^2-b^2}{2ab}\right| = \dfrac{a}{2b} = \dfrac{a}{a^2/p} = \dfrac{p}{a}$

(6) $\left\{\begin{array}{l}
\text{From Figure 8: } \csc \theta = \dfrac{AQ}{ON} = \dfrac{p}{a} = \cosh \delta \\[2mm]
\hspace{2.2cm} \cot \theta = \sinh \delta \\[2mm]
\text{From trigonometry: } \tan \dfrac{1}{2}\theta = \csc \theta - \cot \theta \\[2mm]
\text{Conclusion: } \tan \dfrac{1}{2}\theta = e^{-\delta}
\end{array}\right.$

represented by the pair LL' of limiting points. (For, every plane through l is perpendicular to all three planes, and every circle through L and L' is orthogonal to all three circles.) It is therefore natural to identify the distance AB (which is the shortest distance between the planes α and β) with the inversive distance between the circles α and β.

For any two circles α and β (in the Euclidean plane) with radii a and b and distance c between their centres, an expression involving a, b, c can be found (see 3) which is an inversive invariant such that, if the circles intersect, it is the cosine of their non-obtuse angle of intersection. Further, if the circles are tangent, the same expression is equal to 1; if they are non-intersecting, it is equal to $\cosh \delta$, in which δ is their inversive distance. This is the natural logarithm of the ratio (larger to smaller) of two concentric circles into which α and β can be inverted. This kind of distance, $\delta = (\alpha\beta)$, is properly additive for coaxal circles—that is, if three circles α, β, γ occur in this order in a non-intersecting pencil, their mutual inversive distances satisfy the equation $(\alpha\beta) + (\beta\gamma) = (\alpha\gamma)$. In particular, the inversive distance between a circle and a line is half the inversive distance between two congruent circles (namely, the given circle and its image by reflection in the line). Thus, if a circle of radius a has its centre distant p from a line $(p > a)$, their inversive distance δ is given by the formula $\cosh \delta = p/a$ (see 4).

Alternatively, let O be the centre of the circle α and A the foot of the perpendicular from O to the line, as in Figure 7. After inversion in α, α remains unchanged, but the line becomes a circle having diameter $OA' = a^2/p$, that is, a circle β for which $b = c = a^2/2p$. Hence, the inversive distance δ is given by $\cosh \delta = p/a$, as before (see 5).

Let 2θ be the angle subtended by the circle α at A, the nearest point on the line (i.e., $\theta = \angle OAN$, in which AN is one of the tangents from A, as in Figure 8). Then the formula $\tan \frac{1}{2}\theta = e^{-\delta}$ can be deduced by trigonometry (see 6). This formula will be used later.

It can also be found from inversive geometry that, if three circles α, β, γ are not coaxal, they span a bundle $\alpha\beta\gamma$ (that is, the smallest set of circles that includes these three and, with any two of its members, the whole of the pencil [of coaxal circles] spanned by them). There are, in fact, three kinds of bundle, depending on whether the constant power of their radical centre is negative, zero, or positive. The circles of an elliptic bundle, like the great circles on a sphere, all intersect one fixed circle in pairs of diametrically opposite points of the fixed circle. The circles of a parabolic bundle all pass through one fixed point. If this point is the point at infinity, the bundle consists of all the lines in the Euclidean plane. Finally, the circles of a hyperbolic bundle are all orthogonal to one fixed circle, or to one fixed line (if the centres of α, β, γ happen to be all on one line).

Returning to the representation of planes in hyperbolic space by circles in the inversive plane, it is seen that the circles belonging to the three kinds of bundle—elliptic, parabolic, and hyperbolic—represent the lines in three kinds of plane—elliptic, Euclidean, and hyperbolic. In fact, the circles of an elliptic bundle, regarded as great circles on a sphere, represent planes through one point, the centre of the sphere, and such an ordinary bundle of planes behaves the same way in hyperbolic space as in Euclidean space. Second, the circles of a parabolic bundle are, in one special case, all the lines in a Euclidean plane; the corresponding planes in the hyperbolic space are all the planes parallel to one ray, and thus such planes behave like the lines in a Euclidean plane.

Elliptic, parabolic, hyperbolic bundles

Third, the circles of a hyperbolic bundle, being orthogonal to one circle, represent all the planes perpendicular to one plane ω (omega) and thus equally well represent the ω-sections of these planes, which are all the lines in this hyperbolic plane ω. This is, perhaps, the simplest way to obtain the French mathematician Henri Poincaré's representation of the lines of the hyperbolic plane by all the circles orthogonal to one circle ω (including all the diameters), or by all the circles and lines orthogonal to one line ω. Each point of the hyperbolic plane, being the intersection of two lines, is represented by two points that are images of each other by inversion in the circle ω or by reflection in the line ω. To obtain a one-to-one representation of points, Poincaré restricted attention to the inside of the circle ω or to the upper half-plane bounded by the line ω. In either form of this model, angles are still represented without distortion, while distances appear as inversive distances between suitable pairs of circles.

The angle of parallelism. In the hyperbolic plane, if BN is a ray perpendicular to AB and AN the ray from A parallel to BN (see Figure 9), then, in the notation and terminology of Lobachevsky, the angle $\Pi(\delta) = \angle BAN$ is the angle of parallelism corresponding to the distance $\delta = AB$. Using Poincaré's circle model, A can be represented by the centre of his circle ω, B by a suitable point inside ω, and BN by an arc of the circle through B orthogonal to both ω and AB. The point N, at which this arc meets ω, represents the end of the hyperbolic ray BN, and the parallel ray from A appears as the radius AN of ω, which is tangent to the arc BN at N. Comparing Figure 9 with Figure 8, it is seen that the angle of parallelism $\theta = \angle BAN$ can be expressed in terms of the hyperbolic distance δ by the formula $\tan \frac{1}{2}\Pi(\delta) = e^{-\delta}$, discovered independently by Bolyai and Lobachevsky.

Relation to hyperbolic distance

Comparison of the inversive and projective models. Figure 9 exhibits hyperbolic distances $AB = \delta$ and $AN = \infty$. It is of some interest to compare these with the corresponding Euclidean distances. For simplicity, AN may be taken to equal 1, so that ω is the unit circle with centre A in the Euclidean plane. Figure 10 shows the complete circle $MBNB'$ that represents the line MN perpendicular to AB. Because this circle is orthogonal to ω, B and B' are inverse points in ω. So, if $AB = x$, $AB' = 1/x$.

Writing $AO = p$ and $ON = a$, as in Figure 8, one finds

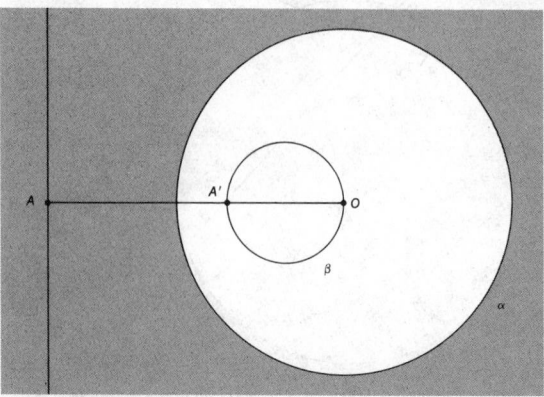

Figure 7: Circle α inverting the vertical line into circle β.

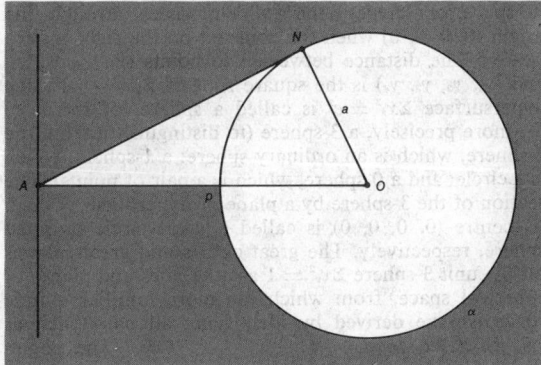

Figure 8: Circle α subtending angle 2θ at A.

that $x = \tanh \frac{1}{2}\delta$ (see 7). This is the desired relation between the Euclidean and hyperbolic distances AB when the hyperbolic line MN is represented by the arc MN orthogonal to ω.

If the same unit circle ω represents the absolute circle in Beltrami's model (with $k = 1$), it is necessary to replace this arc MN by its chord. If P be the midpoint of the chord, as in Figure 11, then the Euclidean distance $r = AP$ represents δ in this other model, and it is seen that $r = \cos\theta = \tanh\delta$. Thus, the inversive and projective models represent the hyperbolic distance δ (measured from the point represented by the centre of ω) by $\tanh\frac{1}{2}\delta$ and $\tanh\delta$, respectively.

$$(7) \quad \begin{cases} 2p = \dfrac{1}{x} + x, \qquad 2a = \dfrac{1}{x} - x, \\[2mm] \cosh\delta = \dfrac{p}{a} = \dfrac{1+x^2}{1-x^2}, \qquad x = \tanh\dfrac{\delta}{2} \end{cases}$$

Circles and spheres. The inversive plane has been used in two distinct, though related, ways. Following Poincaré, the circles (and lines) orthogonal to one circle (or line) ω represent the lines of the hyperbolic plane, and the points inside the circle (or in the upper half-plane bounded by the line) represent the points of the hyperbolic plane. Second, following Liebmann, all the circles (and lines) in the inversive plane represent the planes of hyperbolic space. In this case, lines are respresented by point-pairs, but points are not represented at all, unless it can be said that they are represented by elliptic bundles. The relation between these two representations is seen by taking Poincaré's ω to be the Liebmann representative of one particular plane in the hyperbolic space and considering the lines in this one plane, which is, of course, a hyperbolic plane.

Because either of Poincaré's models provides a point of the inversive plane for each point of the hyperbolic plane and provides a circle (or line) orthogonal to ω for each line, it is natural to ask what curve in the hyperbolic plane is represented by a circle (or line) α not orthogonal to ω. The circles (or lines) α and ω may be intersecting, tangent, or non-intersecting. If they are non-intersecting, no generality is lost by taking them to be con-

Poincaré and Liebmann representations

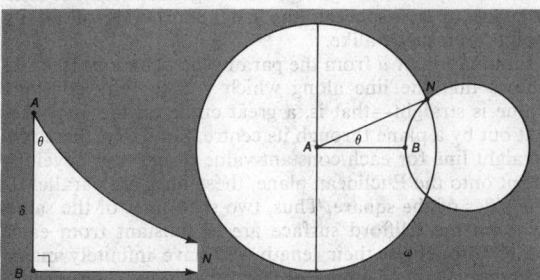

Figure 9: The angle of parallelism.

centric circles, in which case the curve is what naturally is called a circle, because it is orthogonal to its diameters, which are all the lines through its centre. More precisely, in the notation of Figure 10, a hyperbolic circle of radius δ is represented by a circle (concentric with ω) of radius $AB = x = \tanh\frac{1}{2}\delta$. Because Poincaré's circle model remains valid when transformed by inversion in any circle orthogonal to ω, it follows that any circle α inside ω represents a hyperbolic circle. The radius δ of this hyperbolic circle is determined by the inversive distance $-\log\tanh\frac{1}{2}\delta$ between α and ω. (Because $\tanh\frac{1}{2}\delta$ is less than 1, its logarithm is negative.) When α and ω are not concentric, the centre of the hyperbolic circle is represented by one of the limiting points of the coaxal pencil spanned by α and ω, not by the Euclidean centre of α.

If α and ω are tangent, no generality is lost by taking them to be two parallel lines in the Euclidean plane. Thus, in terms of the half-plane model, α is a line, in the upper half-plane, parallel to ω. The corresponding curve in the hyperbolic plane, being the limiting form of a circle when its centre moves off to infinity, is called a horocycle. Its diameters, cutting it orthogonally, are a pencil of parallels (that is, the set of all lines parallel to one ray or the set of all lines having one common end), represented by the lines perpendicular to ω, which are, of course, parallel in the Euclidean sense.

Finally, if α and ω are intersecting, no generality is lost by taking them to be intersecting lines or, more precisely, by using the half-plane model and considering two rays, from a point A on ω, making angles θ and $\pi - \theta$ with ω, as in Figure 12. These rays represent a curve having two branches, like a hyperbola, except that they are concave as seen from a point between them. It is called an equidistant curve, because it is the locus of points at a constant distance δ from a fixed axis o, represented by the line through A perpendicular to ω. To prove this constancy, it is observed that the lines along which δ is measured are the "diameters": a pencil of ultraparallels (all perpendicular to o), represented by the circles with centre A. If AN (in Figure 12) is the radius of one such circle, the distance along the corresponding diameter is the in-

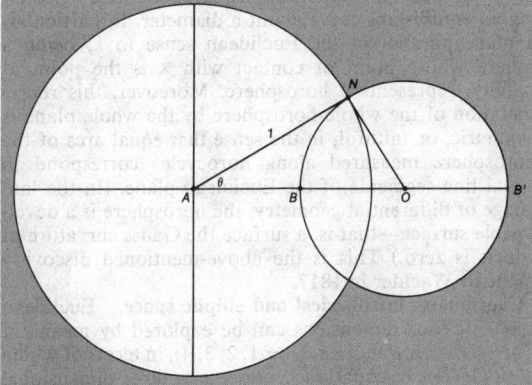

Figure 10: Poincaré's circle model.

versive distance from the line o (perpendicular to ω) to the circle that touches AN at N and has its centre on ω. Comparison with Figure 9 shows that this distance is $\delta = -\log\tan\frac{1}{2}\theta$, regardless of which circle with centre A is used. In other words, the two branches of the equidistant curve with radius δ are represented by two lines making angles $\Pi(\delta)$ and $\pi - \Pi(\delta)$ with ω. (The two branches of the curve are distant δ from its axis, one on each side.) More generally, any two circular arcs making angles $\Pi(\delta)$ and $\pi - \Pi(\delta)$ with ω at two points A and B represent such an equidistant curve.

Recalling the Euclidean theorem that any three distinct points lie either on a line or on a circle, it is seen that the hyperbolic counterpart is as follows: Any three distinct points lie either on a line or on a circle or on a horocycle or on one branch of an equidistant curve. Alternatively, if both branches are allowed: Each vertex of a triangle

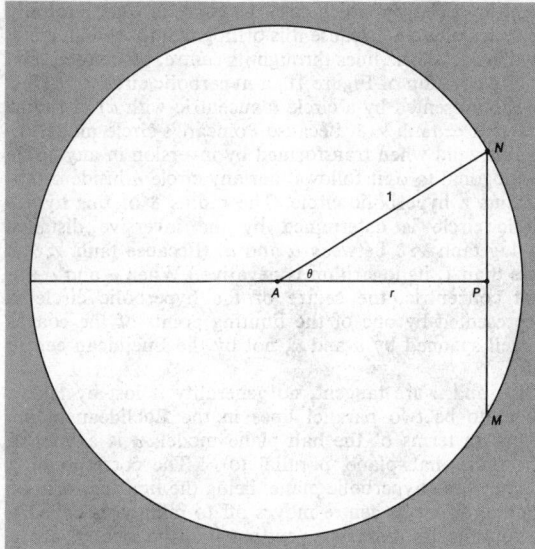

Figure 11: Beltrami's circle model.

lies on one branch of an equidistant curve such that the remaining two vertices lie on the other branch. (The axis joins the midpoints of the two sides involving the first vertex.)

For representing hyperbolic space, a useful variant of Liebmann's model is obtained by regarding each circle as the bounding equator of a hemisphere in a half-space bounded by his plane λ (lambda). The planes and lines of the hyperbolic space are then represented by spheres (or planes) and circles (or lines) orthogonal to λ, and the points are represented by the points of the half-space. It follows that a sphere not intersecting (nor touching) λ represents a sphere (obtained by rotating a circle about a diameter; a sphere tangent to λ represents a horosphere, obtained by rotating a horocycle about a diameter; and a sphere intersecting λ, or, more precisely, the lens bounded by two such spheres, images of each other by reflection in λ, represents an equidistant surface, obtained by rotating an equidistant curve about a diameter. In particular, a plane parallel in the Euclidean sense to λ, being a sphere whose point of contact with λ is the point at infinity, represents a horosphere. Moreover, this representation of the whole horosphere by the whole plane is isometric, or faithful, in the sense that equal arcs of the horosphere measured along horocycles correspond to equal line segments of the Euclidean plane. (In the language of differential geometry, the horosphere is a developable surface—that is, a surface the Gauss curvature of which is zero.) This is the above-mentioned discovery made by Wachter in 1817.

The horosphere

Coordinates in spherical and elliptic space. Euclidean space of four dimensions can be explored by means of Cartesian coordinates x_ν ($\nu = 1, 2, 3, 4$), in terms of which a single linear equation represents a three-dimensional

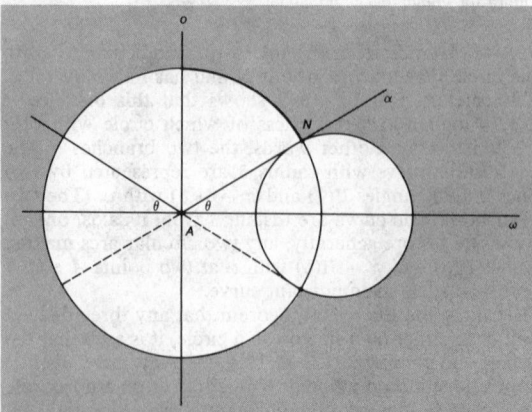

Figure 12: An equidistant curve represented by two rays.

subspace or "hyperplane" which passes through the origin (0, 0, 0, 0) when the constant on the right is zero (see 8). The distance between two points (x_1, x_2, x_3, x_4) and (y_1, y_2, y_3, y_4) is the square root of $\Sigma(x_\nu - y_\nu)^2$. The hypersurface $\Sigma x_\nu^2 = c^2$ is called a sphere (of radius c) or, more precisely, a 3-sphere (to distinguish it from the 2-sphere, which is an ordinary sphere; a 1-sphere, which is a circle; and a 0-sphere, which is a pair of points). The section of the 3-sphere by a plane or hyperplane through its centre (0, 0, 0, 0) is called a great circle or great sphere, respectively. The great circles and great spheres on the unit 3-sphere $\Sigma x_\nu^2 = 1$ are the lines and planes of spherical space, from which the more familiar elliptic space can be derived by identifying all pairs such as (x_1, x_2, x_3, x_4) and ($-x_1, -x_2, -x_3, -x_4$). The angles θ and $\pi - \theta$, in which $\cos \theta = \Sigma x_\nu y_\nu$, can be regarded either as the angles subtended by two such pairs of points at the origin or as the two distances between the points (x) and (y) of the elliptic space. Similarly, the angles ϕ and $\pi - \phi$, where $\cos \phi = \Sigma X_\nu Y_\nu$, can be regarded either as the angles between two hyperplanes $\Sigma X_\nu x_\nu = 0$ and $\Sigma Y_\nu x_\nu = 0$ of the Euclidean 4-space or as the angles between two planes [X] and [Y] of the elliptic space. The plane [X], meaning $\Sigma X_\nu x_\nu = 0$, is regarded as having coordinates [X_1, X_2, X_3, X_4] (tangential or envelope coordinates) so that the equation $\Sigma X_\nu x_\nu = 0$ expresses the fact that the plane [X] and point (x) are incident, the plane passing through the point and the point lying in the plane. It follows that the pole of the plane [X] is the point (X) that has the same coordinates.

The surface in spherical space with equation $x_1^2 + x_2^2 = x_3^2 + x_4^2 = \frac{1}{2}$ yields the rectangular Clifford surface in elliptic space (discovered by the English mathematician William Kingdon Clifford in 1873). In terms of two parameters u and v, which range independently over the

$$(8) \qquad X_1 x_1 + X_2 x_2 + X_3 x_3 + X_4 x_4 = c$$

$$(9) \quad \begin{cases} x_1 = \sqrt{\dfrac{1}{2}} \cos(u+v), & x_2 = \sqrt{\dfrac{1}{2}} \sin(u+v) \\ x_3 = \sqrt{\dfrac{1}{2}} \cos(u-v), & x_4 = \sqrt{\dfrac{1}{2}} \sin(u-v) \end{cases}$$

$$(10) \qquad dx_1^2 + dx_2^2 + dx_3^2 + dx_4^2 = du^2 + dv^2$$

$$(11) \quad \begin{cases} x_1 \cos v + x_2 \sin v = x_3 \cos v - x_4 \sin v \\ -x_1 \sin v + x_2 \cos v = x_3 \sin v + x_4 \cos v \end{cases}$$

interval from 0 to π, this surface is given by four parametric equations (see 9). It is a developable surface, like the horosphere, for u and v can be regarded as Cartesian coordinates in a Euclidean plane (see 10), and thus the surface can be developed into the region of the plane enclosed by the lines $u = 0$, $v = 0$, $u = \pi$, $v = \pi$, which form a square. The periodicity of the parameters makes each side of the square coincide with the opposite side; thus the Clifford surface, as defined above, has the topology of a torus (a doughnut-shaped surface that is generated by bending a square into a cylinder with two circular ends and then bending the cylinder until the two ends meet), even though it is a homogeneous surface (like a plane or a 2-sphere): the neighbourhoods of all its points are exactly alike.

Elimination of u from the parametric equations (see 11) shows that the line along which v takes any constant value is straight—that is, a great circle on the 3-sphere, cut out by a plane through its centre. Similarly, there is a straight line for each constant value of u. After development onto the Euclidean plane, these lines are parallel to the sides of the square. Thus, two such lines of the same type on the Clifford surface are equidistant from each other throughout their length and have infinitely many common perpendiculars of the other type. This occurrence of parallel lines in elliptic space seems paradoxical

$$(12) \quad \begin{cases} x_0 > 0; \quad x_0^2 - x_1^2 - x_2^2 = 1 \\ -X_0^2 + X_1^2 + X_2^2 = 1 \end{cases}$$

$$(13) \quad \cosh \delta = x_0 y_0 - x_1 y_1 - x_2 y_2$$

$$(14) \quad \sinh \delta = |\Sigma X_k x_k|$$

$$(15) \quad [XY] = |-X_0 Y_0 + X_1 Y_1 + X_2 Y_2|$$

$$(16) \quad (\cosh c, \sinh c \cdot \cos A, \sinh c \sin A)$$

$$(17) \quad \begin{cases} \sinh a = \sinh c \sin A \\ \cos B = \cosh b \sin A \end{cases}$$

$$(18) \quad \begin{cases} \alpha = \Pi(a), \qquad \beta = \Pi(b), \qquad \gamma = \Pi(c) \\ \cot \alpha = \cot \gamma \sin A, \qquad \cos B = \csc \beta \sin A \end{cases}$$

$$(19) \quad \alpha' = \tfrac{1}{2}\pi - \alpha, \quad A, \quad \gamma, \quad B, \quad \beta' = \tfrac{1}{2}\pi - \beta$$

$$(20) \quad \tan \alpha' \tan \gamma = \sin A = \cos \beta' \cos B$$

$$(21) \quad \tan A \tan B = \sin \gamma = \cos \alpha' \cos \beta'$$

$$(22) \quad \cot A \cot B = \cosh c = \cosh a \cosh b$$

$$(23) \quad 1 + \tfrac{1}{2}c^2 + \cdots = \left(1 + \tfrac{1}{2}a^2 + \cdots\right)\left(1 + \tfrac{1}{2}b^2 \cdots\right)$$

until it is remembered that they are skew lines, not lying in one plane. They are called Clifford parallels. More precisely, lines of one type are right parallels, of the other type left parallels, and this distinction can be maintained by continuous variation over the elliptic space. In fact, for any line l in the space, and any point A not on l (nor on the polar line of l), there are just two lines through A that are Clifford parallel to l: one right parallel and one left parallel.

Allowing A to vary, Clifford found also that all the lines right (or left) parallel to l are right (or left) parallel to one another, and among them, those that intersect an arbitrary line m do so at a constant angle, say θ, and generate a ruled quadric surface, called a Clifford surface, whose generators of the other system are left (or right) parallel to m and to one another. (The rectangular Clifford surface is the special case when θ is a right angle.) Moreover, the segments of the generators of either system intercepted between two generators of the other system all have the same length. Thus, any Clifford surface can be developed isometrically onto a Euclidean plane, the two systems of generators appearing as two systems of parallel lines (parallel in the Euclidean sense) inclined at the angle θ. Because each line has total length π, however, the whole surface is mapped onto a finite part of the Euclidean plane, namely, a rhombus of side π, the angles of which are θ and $\pi - \theta$. It follows that the general Clifford surface is topologically a torus and its total area is $\pi^2 \sin \theta$.

Coordinates in the hyperbolic plane. Klein showed that the hyperbolic plane can be explored by means of coordinates x_ν and X_ν ($\nu = 0, 1, 2$), in terms of which the absolute conic has the locus equation $x_0^2 - x_1^2 - x_2^2 = 0$ and the envelope equation $X_0^2 - X_1^2 - X_2^2 = 0$. In this notation, (x) or (x_0, x_1, x_2) is a point, $[X]$ or $[X_0, X_1, X_2]$ is a line, and these are incident (the point lying on the line) if $\Sigma X_\nu x_\nu = 0$. The polar of (x) is $[x_0, -x_1, -x_2]$, which is the same as $[-x_0, x_1, x_2]$. The line $[1, 0, 0]$ or $x_0 = 0$ has no intersection with the conic; therefore, its pole $(1, 0, 0)$ is inside the conic.

Because all the proper points of the hyperbolic plane are inside, like this one, their coordinates satisfy the inequality $x_0^2 - x_1^2 - x_2^2 > 0$.

Because all the proper lines are secants (or chords), their coordinates satisfy the inequality $X_0^2 - X_1^2 - X_2^2 < 0$. Accordingly, it is convenient to normalize the coordinates (multiplying them by suitable constants) so that they cease to be homogeneous (see 12).

In terms of such normalized coordinates, the distance δ between points (x) and (y) can be simply given (see 13), and the distance δ from the point (x) to the line $[X]$ takes a convenient form (see 14).

Two lines $[X]$ and $[Y]$ are intersecting, parallel, or ultraparallel, according as a number $[XY]$ constructed from the coordinates (see 15) is less than 1, equal to 1, or greater than 1. In the first case they are inclined at angles θ and $\pi - \theta$, where $\cos \theta = [XY]$. In the last case, when the lines are ultraparallel, the distance between them is δ, where $\cosh \delta = [XY]$.

These results about lines in the hyperbolic plane have obvious analogues for planes in hyperbolic space, obtained by inserting an extra term x_3^2 or X_3^2 or $x_3 y_3$ or $X_3 Y_3$ in the appropriate position.

Hyperbolic trigonometry. For a right-angled triangle *ABC* with *A* at $(1, 0, 0)$ and *AC* along $[0, 0, 1]$, as in Figure 13, it is seen at once that the vertex *C*, at which the right angle occurs, is $(\cosh b, \sinh b, 0)$, while the side *AB* runs along the line $[0, -\sin A, \cos A]$ and the side *BC* along $[\sinh b, -\cosh b, 0]$. Hence, the remaining vertex *B*, distant *c* from *A* along *AB*, can be expressed in terms of hyperbolic and trigonometric functions (see 16). Because the distance from *B* to *AC* is *a*, and the acute angle between *AB* and *BC* is *B*, this distance and angle can be calculated in terms of *A*, *b*, *c* (see 17). Lobachevsky preferred to avoid the use of hyperbolic functions by expressing such relations in terms of angles of parallelism (see 18). Analogy with Napier's rules for a right-angled spherical triangle prompted the German mathematician Friedrich Engel's observation that any relation between the sides and angles of a right-angled hyperbolic triangle will remain valid when the five "parts" are cyclically permuted (see 19). In this way, the above relations, in trigonometric form (see 20), yield four more pairs of relations (such as 21) that can also be expressed in terms of *a*, *b*, *c* (see 22).

This last relation expresses the hypotenuse in terms of the other two sides and is the hyperbolic counterpart of the theorem of Pythagoras. In fact, when *a*, *b*, *c* are all small (see 23) and terms of the fourth or higher degree are neglected, $c^2 = a^2 + b^2$ remains. In other words, Euclidean geometry holds in an infinitesimal neighbourhood of any point.

Transformations. According to the so-called Erlangen program of Klein, formulated in 1872, a geometry is distinguished by its group: the group of transformations under which its theorems remain true. Thus, the group for Euclidean geometry is the group of similarities, generated by all the reflections and central dilatations.

The group for hyperbolic geometry is generated by reflections alone. For instance, the product of reflections in two planes, intersecting, parallel, or ultraparallel, is a rotation, a parallel displacement, or a translation, respectively; and the most general displacement, or motion, is a twist, the product of a rotation about a line and a translation along the same line. The essence of the inversive model lies in the happy accident that this group of

The right-angled triangle

Types of transformations

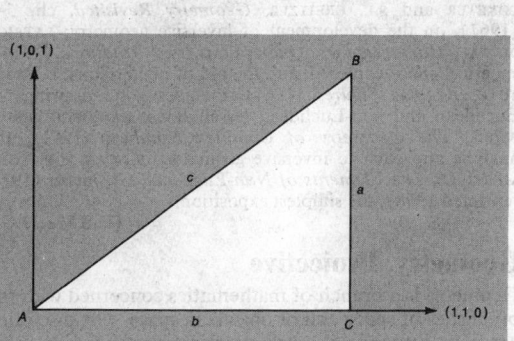

Figure 13: A right-angled triangle.

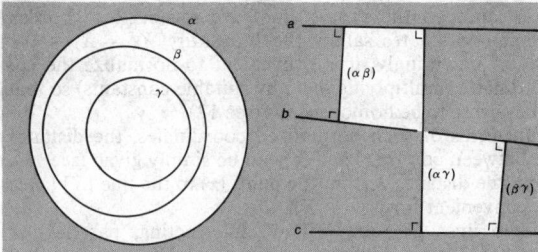

Figure 14: Three nested circles and their inverses.

hyperbolic isometries is isomorphic to the inversive group of circle-preserving transformations, which is generated by inversions in circles, including reflections in lines as a special case. The product of inversions in two circles, intersecting, tangent, or non-intersecting, is a rotary, parabolic, or dilative homography (for instance, a rotation, translation, or central dilatation); and the most general homography is the loxodromic transformation, the commutative product of a rotary homography and a dilative homography. (The most familiar instance is the dilative rotation, or spiral similarity.)

From this point of view, although the hyperbolic space and the inversive plane are isomorphic, the former may seem more familiar than the latter because of its striking analogy with Euclidean space, in which the distinction between a parallel displacement and a translation disappears. In particular, there is an interesting property of the mutual inversive distances between any three nested circles α, β, γ (such that every circle intersecting both α and γ intersects β too): they satisfy the nontriangle inequality, $(\alpha\beta) + (\beta\gamma) \leqslant (\alpha\gamma)$, with equality only when the circles are coaxal. This theorem of inversive geometry is fairly difficult to prove by either inversive or Euclidean methods, but it becomes almost obvious when expressed in terms of planes α, β, γ in hyperbolic space. Because the circles are nested, the plane β separates α and γ in the sense that every line joining a point of α to a point of γ intersects β too. Because the circles have a common orthogonal circle, it is possible to replace the planes α, β, γ by lines a, b, c, which are their sections by a plane perpendicular to all of them. In other words, the circles α, β, γ are Poincaré's model for the lines a, b, c in the hyperbolic plane. If the circles are not coaxal, the shortest distances between pairs of the lines are alternate sides of a crossed hexagon whose angles are all right angles, as in Figure 14. Because these shortest distances are equal to the inversive distances between pairs of the circles, the inequality $(\alpha\beta) + (\beta\gamma) < (\alpha\gamma)$ can be seen from the fact that the line segment marked $(\alpha\gamma)$ is the sum of two parts, one greater than $(\alpha\beta)$ and the other greater than $(\beta\gamma)$.

BIBLIOGRAPHY. ROBERTO BONOLA, *La geometría non-euclidea* (1906; Eng. trans., *Non-Euclidean Geometry: A Critical and Historical Study of Its Developments*, 1955), includes translations of the original papers by Bolyai and Lobachevsky; JULIAN L. COOLIDGE, *A Treatise on the Circle and the Sphere* (1916), an early account of inversive geometry; H.S. MACDONALD COXETER, *Non-Euclidean Geometry*, 4th ed. (1961), the projective approach, with an extensive bibliography; *Introduction to Geometry*, 2nd ed. (1969), see ch. 15–16 for absolute geometry and hyperbolic; H.S. MACDONALD COXETER and S.L. GREITZER, *Geometry Revisited*, ch. 5–6 (1967), on the development of inversive geometry; PATRICK DU VAL, *Homographies, Quaternions, and Rotations* (1964), spherical space explored with the aid of quaternions; L. FEJES TOTH, *Regular Figures* (1964), includes good drawings of Euclidean and non-Euclidean tessellations; HANS SCHWERDT-FEGER, *The Geometry of Complex Numbers* (1962), the analytic approach to inversive geometry; DUNCAN M.Y. SOMMERVILLE, *The Elements of Non-Euclidean Geometry* (1914, reprinted 1958), the simplest exposition.

(H.S.MacD.C.)

Geometry, Projective

Geometry is a branch of mathematics concerned with the properties of space and of objects in space. The discipline arose in response to such practical problems as those found in surveying. Its name is derived from Greek words

meaning earth measurement. Later, it was realized that geometry need not be limited to the classical study of flat surfaces (plane geometry) and rigid three-dimensional objects (solid geometry), but that even the most abstract thinking and imaginings of people might be represented and developed in geometric terms. Thus, various types of geometries evolved, one of which is now called projective geometry.

From the Greek period to the end of the 18th century, two momentous geometrical discoveries were made. Both concerned what was destined to be projective geometry. One was a theorem (stated in detail below) that was discovered and proved in 1639 by a French mathematician named Girard Desargues. The other was a significant broadening of a theorem (first known to Pappus of Alexandria in the 4th century) by Desargues' fellow countryman Blaise Pascal, in 1640. Yet, until the discovery of the basic postulates of projective geometry by Jean-Victor Poncelet, again of France, nearly 200 years later, Desargues's and Pascal's theorems seemed like parts of Euclidean geometry that were unlike other parts. It is significant that in their statements the only relation that mattered was that of the incidence of points and straight lines; distance, angle, congruency, or similitude played no part. (The use of the relation of incidence in the two theorems was the first indication that within the general discipline of geometry there are properties that depend on measurement—those involving distance, angle, and so forth were to be called metrical properties—and others that do not, which became the characteristics of projective geometry.) Despite the simplicity of the statements of these two basic theorems, an unusual amount of care had to be taken in proving (and even formulating) the theorems as soon as due regard was paid to what happened when two or more lines referred to in the theorems, instead of intersecting, became parallel.

The difficulties encountered in generalizing the theorems of Desargues and Pappus–Pascal were overcome; and, in effect, projective geometry was founded when Poncelet postulated points at infinity, such that every straight line is extended with a point at infinity and every plane with a line at infinity, this new point (or line) being the same point for distinct parallel lines (or planes). All infinite elements of space were supposed to lie on the infinite plane of space. The plane so defined was called the "projective plane," and, by logical extension to the next dimension, the corresponding space was called "projective space." Afterward, the distinction between original and added elements (the infinite elements) faded out. Parallelism disappeared as a relation; the only relation still left from the variety of Euclid's relations (such as betweenness, order, congruence, incidence) was that of incidence (or lying on). It is unclear why Poncelet's step was not made centuries earlier. The revival and growth of geometry in the 19th century was psychologically due to the striking simplicity of projective geometry.

After Poncelet's contribution, the major problem was to free projective geometry from its Euclidean substrate and to found it independently. This problem seemed to have been solved when Karl Georg Christian von Staudt, in Germany, started in 1847 with such incidence axioms as: two points determine one straight line; three points, not on a straight line, determine a plane; two planes intersect in a straight line, and so on. Though von Staudt's performance was admirable, he still took the relations of order (such as there being at least one point between two distinct points) in line and plane for granted without feeling the need for explicit formulations. Even worse, he in effect assumed that things proved for commensurable ratios (those expressible as rational numbers) were valid for all ratios, though centuries earlier Archimedes had provided an axiom granting the possibility of bracketing incommensurable ratios by larger and smaller commensurable ones. In 1873 a German mathematician named Felix Klein discovered the gap in von Staudt's reasoning. Though convinced of the possibility of founding projective geometry independently, Klein did not succeed in filling the gap; he did, however, make other essential contributions to the subject.

A final solution for founding projective geometry independently required the following types of postulates: the incidence axioms of the type suggested above, axioms that order the points on the projective line in such a way that the order is cyclic (or as though on a circle) and axioms that preserve this order, and, finally, some type of Archimedes axiom of the kind mentioned in the previous paragraph. This solution was possible after Georg Cantor and Richard Dedekind, German innovators in mathematics, re-examined the ancient problem of incommensurables. Their main contributions in this direction were in 1871 and 1872. About 1880 Moritz Pasch and Otto Stolz of Germany recognized the import of the Archimedean axiom. Most European geometers of the 19th century made some contributions to the study of projective geometry in general. The axioms and logical structure of the subject have been studied by many mathematicians.

PROJECTION

Perspective projection. The distinctive procedure of projective geometry is the representation or mapping of one line l or plane π onto another (l' or π') by perspective projection from any point O not lying in either (see Figures 1 and 2). This is essentially what is done when a plane object is drawn or photographed from any viewpoint. The construction whereby the image of any point P of the object π (or l) is obtained as the intersection of π' (or l') with the line OP is not limited (as in drawing a picture) to any finite portion of π (or l).

The object of projective geometry From a point of view that emphasizes basic concepts, the object of projective geometry is the study of those properties of figures that are not altered by this mapping; *i.e.*, properties that are the same for the "picture" as for the object and are not altered by any number of repetitions of the mapping. If, for instance, a plane π is mapped by projection from O_1 onto a plane π_1, this in turn from O_2 onto a plane π_2, and so on, until a mapping on a plane π' is reached, this mapping of π onto π' is called a general projective mapping, and any property of a figure that is unaltered by the first projection will be the same in π' as in π. With certain exceptions, considered below, each point of π is mapped onto an image point in π', and each line of π is mapped onto a line of π'.

Points at infinity. It is familiar that in an ordinary perspective drawing of π or π' there are certain points (and one line) in π' that correspond to nothing in π. That is, the images of a family of parallel lines in π are lines in π' all passing through one point, which is thus not the image of any point of π; and all the points of π' that thus arise from different parallel families in π lie in one line h', the so-called horizon of the picture. Similarly, there is a horizon k in π that has no image in π'; but all the lines that pass through one point of k have images in π' that are parallel.

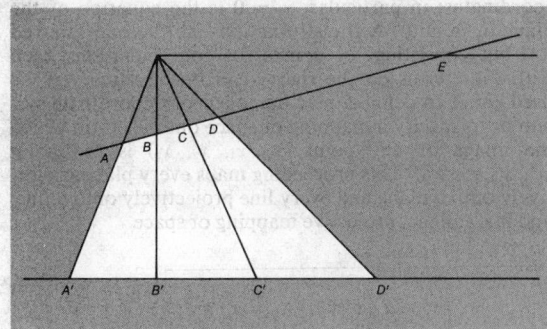

Figure 1: Central projection of one line on another (see text).

This situation causes confusion, awkward exceptions to otherwise very general theorems, and similar inconveniences. These difficulties are overcome by adding to each plane fictitious or ideal points to correspond with those of the other plane that have actually no images. It is agreed conventionally that every line contains just one ideal point—*i.e.*, a point postulated as being at infinity—which

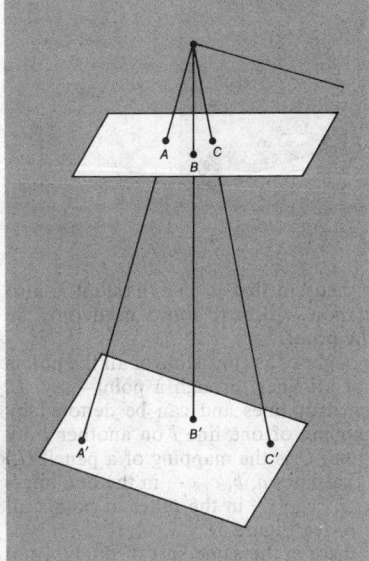

Figure 2: Central projection of one plane on another.

can be approached (though, of course, not reached) by travelling very far along the line in either direction; that all lines parallel to one another contain the same point at infinity; that all points at infinity in one plane form a line called the line at infinity; and that all planes parallel to one another contain the same line at infinity. Thus, the horizon h' is the image of the line at infinity in π, and similarly the image of the line k is the line at infinity in π'. Finally, all the points and lines at infinity in space form a single plane at infinity.

(It is not suggested, of course, that these ideal points, lines, and planes have any physical existence; but then, neither have any of the pure concepts of geometry; *e.g.*, the point that has position without magnitude or the line that has length without breadth.)

This concept of the ideal not only gives every point and line in π an image in π' and makes every point and line in π' the image of one in π but also removes troublesome exceptions from many general propositions; *e.g.*, that every two lines in the same plane intersect in a point, every two planes intersect in a line, and so on. These, with similar propositions (*e.g.*, that every two points are joined by a line and every two intersecting lines by a plane), are clearly basic to projective geometry and, when the subject is treated axiomatically, such are the axioms assumed; they are known as the projective axioms, or axioms of incidence.

Projective theorems. Theorems dealing solely with intersections of lines and of points belonging to the same line include the following, which may be cited as playing an important role in any logical development of projective geometry.

Desargues' theorem. If ABC, $A'B'C'$ are two triangles, in one plane, such that AA', BB', CC' meet in a point, the intersections of BC with $B'C'$, of CA with $C'A'$, and of AB with $A'B'$ are all in one line (see Figure 3). Basic theorems of Desargues and Pappus

Pappus' (Pascal's) theorem. If A, B, C are in one line and A', B', C' in another line in the same plane, the intersections BC' with $B'C$, of CA' with $C'A$, and of AB' with $A'B$ are all in one line (see Figure 4).

Duality. In the plane there is a kind of symmetry between points and lines called duality. In the statement of any proposition or the specification of any figure, if the words "point" and "line," "lies in" and "passes through," "intersect in" and "are joined by," etc., be interchanged throughout, a new proposition or figure is obtained, called the dual of the first. For instance, the axioms "any two points are joined by a unique line" and "any two lines intersect in a unique point" are dual to each other. It is possible to frame the axioms for a logical treatment of projective geometry in pairs dual to each other; if this is

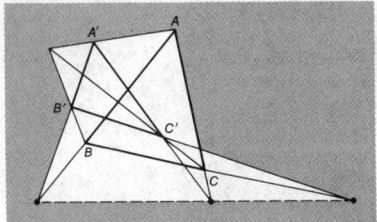

Figure 3: Desargues' theorem.

done, then for any theorem that is true, its dual is also true, for the translation indicated above need only be made all through the proof.

Dual to the line, thought of as consisting of all the points in it, is the figure of all lines through a point—say, L. This is called a pencil of lines and can be denoted by (L). Dual to the mapping of one line l on another l' by projection from a point O is the mapping of a pencil (L) on another (L'), so that lines $a, b, c, \cdots$ in the one intersect their images $a', b', c', \cdots$ in the other in points all lying in a fixed line o (see Figure 5).

In solid geometry there is the same sort of duality, not between points and lines but between points and planes, lines being dual to lines. Thus the axioms "any two points are joined by a line" and "any two planes intersect in a line" are dual to each other, as are "any two lines in one plane intersect in a point" and "any two lines through one point are joined by a plane." The dual of a plane, regarded as consisting of all the points and lines in it, is called a star and consists of all the planes and lines through a point. Geometry in a star is closely similar to that in a plane, lines and planes playing the roles of points and lines, respectively. A star can be projectively mapped on another star or on a plane; for instance, the star can be mapped on any plane π not belonging to it by taking as the image of any line or plane of the star its point or line of intersection with π. The dual of a line of points consists of all the planes through one line and is called a pencil of planes.

Projectively generated loci. Geometry, of course, contains many figures besides those consisting only of points and lines (and planes, in solid geometry); for example, the circle. If a plane π is mapped projectively on a plane π', the image of a circle is generally not a circle but a curve called a conic section (see GEOMETRY, ANALYTIC AND TRIGONOMETRIC) or, more briefly, a conic; and the image of any conic is likewise a conic. The conic can be defined in projective terms as follows:

If two pencils of lines in one plane be taken, say (O) and (O'), and the one be mapped projectively on the other, in general—i.e., unless the line OO' in (O) has itself as image in (O')—the aggregate of intersections of a line with its image consists precisely of the points of a conic; this is the definition of a conic in projective geometry.

Many other curves and surfaces can be defined similarly. For instance, if two lines l, m are skew (i.e., are not in one plane and do not intersect) and if l is mapped projectively on m, the lines joining each point of l to its image generate a surface called a ruled quadric; i.e., the points of the surface are all the points of all the lines. This family of lines, called a regulus, can also be defined as consisting of all lines that intersect not only l and m but a third line n, skew to both l and m. The important ruled quadric theorem states that any line intersecting three lines of a regulus intersects all of them. Such lines form a second regulus, generating the same surface, of which l, m, n are members.

Again, if a pencil of planes is mapped projectively on two others, the points of intersection of a plane with its two images are in general the points of a curve, called a twisted cubic; and, if a star is mapped projectively on two others, the points of intersection of a plane with its two images are the points of a cubic surface.

HOMOGENEOUS COORDINATES

Coordinates and transformations. Coordinates, or sets of numbers that specify the location of a point in a space,

are useful in projective geometry, since they allow problems to be formulated as equations and solved by algebraic methods. In an ordinary Cartesian coordinate system, however, in the plane, where the coordinates of a point are distances measured along lines parallel to two fixed perpendicular axes, the coordinates (x, y) of a point at infinity are in general both infinite but have a definite ratio to each other, x/y, depending on the direction of the parallel lines through the point. Calculations with infinite quantities of this kind are confusing, and it is convenient to represent each point not by the two numbers (x, y) but by three numbers (x_0, x_1, x_2), such that $x = x_1/x_0$, $y = x_2/x_0$. If k is any number except zero, (kx_0, kx_1, kx_2) then denote the same point as (x_0, x_1, x_2). If now $x_0 = 0$, then $x = x_1/x_0$ and $y = x_2/x_0$ are infinite but have the definite ratio $x/y = x_1/x_2$; the numbers $(0, x_1, x_2)$ thus denote a point at infinity, obviating calculation with infinite coordinates.

Such a method of representing points is called a homogeneous coordinate system, because any equation in (x, y) is equivalent to a homogeneous equation (i.e., one in which all the terms are of the same degree) in (x_0, x_1, x_2); for instance, any line has an equation of the form $a_1 x + a_2 y + a_0 = 0$, which on substituting x_1/x_0, x_2/x_0 for x, y and multiplying by x_0 becomes $a_0 x_0 + a_1 x_1 + a_2 x_2 = 0$. (The line at infinity, incidentally, has also an equation of this kind, namely $x_0 = 0$.)

As well as the homogeneous coordinate system (x_0, x_1, x_2), however, any other can equally be used, say (x'_0, x'_1, x'_2), derived from it by a linear transformation, or set of three equations that are linear in x_0, x_1, x_2, each with three coefficients (see Box, equations 1), in which the nine coefficients are sufficiently general to let these equations be solved, so as to express (x_0, x_1, x_2) in a similar form that is linear in x'_0, x'_1, x'_2 (see 2). Such a transformation leaves the equation of a line still linear and, indeed, does not alter the degree of any algebraic equation in the coordinates.

The transformation can, however, be thought of in another way. When it is a change of coordinate system (x_0, x_1, x_2) and (x'_0, x'_1, x'_2) are the coordinates of the same point in two different homogeneous coordinate systems; but they can also be taken as the coordinates of two different points, P, P', in the same system. The equations then define a mapping of the plane onto itself; the first equations define for every point P a unique image P' (see 1), and the second equations show that every point P' is the image of a unique point P (see 2). This expression is in fact the general one for a projective mapping of the plane onto itself.

In the same way, if (x, y, z) are Cartesian coordinates of a point in space, this can be denoted instead by the homogeneous coordinates (x_0, x_1, x_2, x_3), in which $x = x_1/x_0$, $y = x_2/x_0$, $z = x_3/x_0$. Every plane has an equation $a_1 x + a_2 y + a_3 z + a_0 = 0$ in the Cartesian coordinates, and hence $a_0 x_0 + a_1 x_1 + a_2 x_2 + a_3 x_3 = 0$ in the homogeneous coordinates; in particular, $x_0 = 0$ is the equation of the plane at infinity. A transformation like the one referred to—but consisting, of course, of four equations each with four terms on the right—can in the same way be used either to define a new homogeneous coordinate system or to specify a mapping of space onto itself, in which the image of any point (x_0, x_1, x_2, x_3) is the point (x'_0, x'_1, x'_2, x'_3). This proceeding maps every plane projectively onto a plane and every line projectively onto a line, and it is called a projective mapping of space.

$$(1)\quad \begin{cases} x'_0 = a_{00}x_0 + a_{01}x_1 + a_{02}x_2 \\ x'_1 = a_{10}x_0 + a_{11}x_1 + a_{12}x_2 \\ x'_2 = a_{20}x_0 + a_{21}x_1 + a_{22}x_2 \end{cases}$$

$$(2)\quad \begin{cases} x_0 = b_{00}x'_0 + b_{01}x'_1 + b_{02}x'_2 \\ x_1 = b_{10}x'_0 + b_{11}x'_1 + b_{12}x'_2 \\ x_2 = b_{20}x'_0 + b_{21}x'_1 + b_{22}x'_2 \end{cases}$$

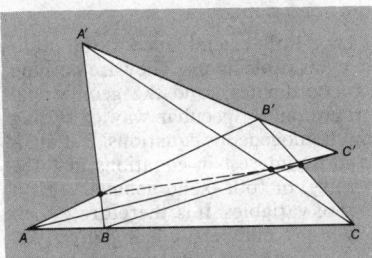

Figure 4: Pappus' (Pascal's) theory.

Duality expressed in terms of coordinates

Duality finds a very simple expression in terms of coordinates. In plane geometry, if the equation of a line l is $a_0x_0 + a_1x_1 + a_2x_2 = 0$, then (a_0, a_1, a_2) are called the homogeneous coordinates of l, and the equation is regarded as the condition for the line (a_0, a_1, a_2) to pass through the point (x_0, x_1, x_2). What is called a dual mapping of the plane onto itself can be defined by taking as the image of every point P the line with coordinates that are the same as those of P; the images of the points in a line l will then be the lines through the point L, with coordinates that are the same as those of l. This dual mapping can be defined in purely geometrical terms, but the definition in terms of coordinates is simpler.

Duality in space can be similarly treated, the homogeneous coordinates of a plane being the coefficients (a_0, a_1, a_2, a_3) in its equation $a_0x_0 + a_1x_1 + a_2x_2 + a_3x_3 = 0$.

Geometry of one dimension. Similarly, a homogeneous coordinate system (x_0x_1) can be used in a line, the position of a point in the line being determined by the ratio x_0/x_1, and a linear transformation giving either a transformation of coordinates or a projective mapping of the line on itself (see 3). Because, however, there is only one point at infinity to consider, there is no serious inconvenience in using the single coordinate $z = x_0/x_1$, in terms of which the equations expressing the transformation involve only z and its image (see 4). Such a transformation as this is known as a homographic transformation.

If $z = \alpha$, $z = \beta$, $z = \gamma$, $z = \delta$ are the coordinates of four points A, B, C, D of the line, a simple ratio constructed with these coordinates (see 5) is found to be unaltered by the homographic transformation and, thus, represents a property of the four points that is independent of the coordinate system and that is unaltered by a projective mapping. This number is called the cross ratio of the four points. If z is a Cartesian coordinate, differences such as $\alpha - \gamma$ that occur in the ratio are proportional to the segments such as AC; thus, if in any projective mapping of the line on another line or on itself the images of A, B, C, D are A', B', C', D', a ratio involving lengths of segments such as AC will be preserved under the mapping (see 6), although, of course, neither the length of a segment AC nor the ratio of two segments such as AC/AD will, in general, be equal to $A'C'$ nor to $A'C'/A'D'$, respectively.

The fundamental theorem. If A, B, C are any three points of one line and A', B', C' are any three points of either the same or another line, a projective mapping may be constructed in which the images of A, B, C are A', B', C', respectively. This construction can be made in a great variety of ways; but the fundamental theorem of projective geometry states that the actual mapping will always be the same; i.e., however the construction is made, the image of any fourth point D will be a unique point D' that is deducible from an equation that results from the previous discussion (see 6). This condition is closely re-

lated to the fact that a transformation of coordinates can be made such that any three chosen points shall have assigned values for their coordinates; in particular, if the values $z = \infty$, $z = 0$, $z = 1$ are assigned to A, B, C, the value of z at any other point D will be equal to the cross ratio of the values given for A, B, C, D.

Harmonic pairs. Especially important is the case in which the cross ratio has the value -1; i.e., when C and D divide the segment AB internally and externally in the same ratio. In this case C, D are said to separate A, B harmonically. If A, B, C are given in a line, the point D can be constructed, such that C, D separate A, B harmonically by a purely projective construction (Figure 6). Lines are drawn through A, B, C to form a triangle PQR (QR passing through A, RP through B, and PQ through C); then, if S is the intersection of AP with BQ, that of RS with ABC is the required point D.

(3)	$x_0' = ax_0 + bx_1, \qquad x_1' = cx_0 + dx_1$
(4)	$z' = \dfrac{az+b}{cz+d}, \qquad z = \dfrac{dz'-b}{-cz'+a}$
(5)	$\dfrac{(\alpha-\gamma)(\beta-\delta)}{(\alpha-\delta)(\beta-\gamma)}$
(6)	$\dfrac{A'C' \cdot B'D'}{A'D' \cdot B'C'} = \dfrac{AC \cdot BD}{AD \cdot BC}$
(7)	$cz^2 + (d-a)z - b = 0$

All these ideas and results can be transferred to the points of a conic or of a twisted cubic curve, to the lines of a pencil or a regulus, or to any other aggregate that can be mapped projectively on a line. Such a mapping is simply taken, and each member of the aggregate is given the same coordinate as its image point; four members have the same cross ratio as their image points, two pairs separate each other harmonically if their image points do so, and so forth.

COMPLEX GEOMETRY

There are many geometrical problems that, when attacked algebraically by means of coordinates, require the solution of a quadratic equation; for instance, in elementary analytic geometry, that of finding the intersections of a line with a circle or with any conic. A more important problem is that of finding the fixed points (i.e., those that are their own images) in any projective mapping of a line onto itself. If $z' = z$ in the equations that involve z and its image (see 4) a quadratic equation in z will follow (see 7), so that if and only if z satisfies this quadratic equation, the point with coordinate z will be its own image in the mapping.

Fixed points in a projective mapping

As long as operation is confined to real numbers, a quadratic equation may have two solutions, or only one, or none at all. Correspondingly, in the plane of a circle there are lines that meet it in two points (the chords), in one point (the tangents), and not at all (those completely outside the circle). In algebra, however, great simplification is obtained by enlarging the concept of number to include what are called complex numbers; i.e., numbers of the form $a + ib$, in which a and b are real numbers and i is an imaginary quantity with its square equal to -1. Every quadratic equation with coefficients that are complex numbers has two solutions that are themselves complex numbers; these may, however, be equal. In particular, if the coefficients are real, either both solutions are real or neither is.

A similar simplification is obtained in geometry by the conventional introduction of complex points, taking in fact any set of three (or, for solid geometry, four) complex numbers to be the homogeneous coordinates of a point. It can then be said, for instance, that in a plane

Introduction of complex points

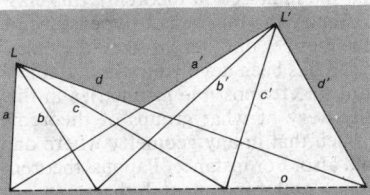

Figure 5: Mapping of a pencil of lines.

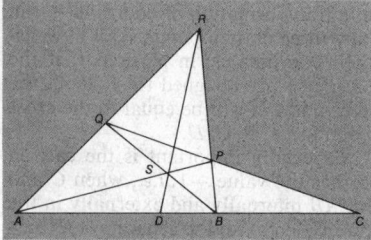

Figure 6: Projective construction of harmonic-pair division with cross ratio of −1 (see text).

every line meets every conic in two points (which may coincide, the line being then a tangent of the conic). If from the elementary point of view, and as seen in a figure, there are no common points, then the points are imaginary and the equations make it possible to write down definite imaginary values for their coordinates. In the same way, every projective mapping of a line on itself has two fixed points that may coincide.

This conventional extension of complex geometry is logically similar to the addition of points at infinity, and such an extension has similar advantages in making it possible to state results in a more general form, without the necessity of enumerating many alternative cases of each theorem.

Projective mappings. In plane geometry, a bodily rotation about a fixed centre, whereby each line through the centre is turned through the same angle, is a projective mapping of this pencil of lines on itself. The fixed lines of this mapping are imaginary and have always the same two directions; i.e., those given in any Cartesian coordinate system by the equations $y = ix$, $y = -ix$. Lines having either of these directions are called isotropic; they have the paradoxical properties that every isotropic line is perpendicular to itself and that the distance between any two points joined by an isotropic line is zero.

The points at infinity in these two directions are often called the circular points at infinity, because every circle in the plane cuts the line at infinity in these same two points. In particular, a circle of radius zero (which in Euclidean geometry consists only of its centre) in complex geometry consists of the two isotropic lines through its centre.

Group properties. The set of all projective mappings of a plane on itself forms a group; projective geometry consists of the study of those properties of figures that are unchanged by all the operations in this group. If, however, within this group is considered the smaller group (or subgroup) consisting only of those mappings in which the circular points at infinity are their own or each others' images, then every figure is the same shape as its image, though they may differ in size or scale, as well as in orientation and position. Euclidean geometry, in which the basic measurable quantities are the size of an angle and the ratio of two lengths, thus turns out to be the study of properties of figures that are unchanged by all operations of this smaller group, called the similarity group. All the ordinary properties of a figure can be expressed as its projective relations to the circular points and to the line at infinity that joins them. In particular, the angle between two lines can be expressed in terms of their cross ratio with the two isotropic lines through their intersection, and they are perpendicular if they separate the isotropic lines harmonically.

Intermediate between the similarity group and the full projective group is what is called the affine group, consisting of all mappings in which the line at infinity is its own image. Properties unchanged by these include parallelism and the ratio of parallel segments but not angles or other length ratios.

If the imaginary circular points are replaced by two real points, the similarity group then becomes that of the so-called Lorentz transformations in relativity theory; and if, instead, the mappings in which a particular conic is its own image are considered, then non-Euclidean geometry is obtained.

ABSTRACT GEOMETRIES

At this stage, points have little resemblance to the intuitive idea of a point in a drawable figure. They are nothing but sets of numbers (coordinates), and the geometrical theorems about them are only a peculiar way of stating algebraic results about homogeneous equations. But algebraically there is no more interest in equations in three variables (plane geometry) or four (solid geometry) than in those in any number of variables. It is, therefore, a convention to call a set of $n + 1$ numbers, n being any given number, $(x_0, x_1, \cdots, x_n)$ a point of n-dimensional space, always with the proviso that if k is not zero, $(x_0, x_1, \cdots, x_n)$ and $(kx_0, kx_1, \cdots, kx_n)$ are the same point. The sets that satisfy r independent linear homogeneous equations (p is a number) are those of an $(n - r)$-dimensional space lying in the whole space. All the propositions about joining spaces and intersections can be summed up in the following intersections theorem: If two spaces of p and q dimensions are joined by an r-dimensional space and intersect in an s-dimensional space, then $r + s = p + q$; if they have no intersection, the formula is satisfied by the conventional value $s = -1$.

The idea of projective geometry extended

The idea of projective geometry can be extended by choosing coordinates from a wide variety of algebraic systems. Any set of symbols that can be added, subtracted, multiplied, and divided in the usual way is called a field; for instance, the real numbers are a field and the complex numbers are another field, and the difference between the geometries obtained by using coordinates from these two fields has been shown. Many other kinds of field are possible, however. Some consist of only a finite number of elements; the simplest consists only of 0 and 1, with the relation $1 + 1 = 0$—this system being what ordinary arithmetic reduces to if all even numbers are called 0 and all odd numbers are called 1. When coordinates are chosen from this field, a geometry is obtained consisting of only seven points and seven lines (three points in each line and three lines through each point). Similarly, it is possible to construct a solid geometry of 15 points, 35 lines, and 15 planes.

Algebra also offers systems of symbols that can be added, subtracted, multiplied, and divided nearly in the usual way but in which a product ab is not necessarily equal to ba. These are called skew fields. Using such a system for coordinates, a geometry can be constructed in which the usual joining and intersecting relations are valid but in which certain theorems of ordinary geometry—notably that of the 4th-century Greek geometer Pappus of Alexandria and what have been called the fundamental and ruled quadric theorems—are no longer true.

The topic can be approached from a different point of view by saying that any (finite or infinite) aggregate of things that fall into classes satisfying relations of a certain kind can be regarded as the points of a projective geometry. For instance, if a number of men belong to a number of clubs, and if every two men belong to just one club, and every two of the clubs have just one common member, then—to give a projective plane geometry—the men can be called points, and the clubs can be called lines. Seven men—A, B, C, D, E, F, G—and seven clubs with three members each—say (ABD), (BCE), (CDF), (DEG), (EFA), (FGB), (GAC)—form a geometry that is structurally indistinguishable from that constructed from the field consisting of 0, 1 only; in fact, coordinates belonging to this field can be attached to each man so that each club is defined by a linear equation.

Similarly, if there are objects called points, grouped into classes of various sizes called lines, planes, etc., then, if these classes satisfy certain relations (of which the chief is what has been called the intersection theorem), this classification gives a geometry the number of dimensions of which depends on the number of different sizes of classes. Much modern research has been devoted to the classification of all kinds of abstractly possible geometries in this sense and to the discovery of what groups of theorems are equivalent; i.e., such that in any geometry where one holds, the others hold also. For instance, Pappus' theorem and the ruled quadric and fundamental theorems are equivalent in this sense.

There are three known main categories of projective geometry:

1. Those in which both Desargues' and the Pappus group of theorems hold. These can be of any number of dimensions and can consist of either a finite or an infinite number of points. This class includes the ordinary real and complex geometries. Every geometry of this kind is structurally equivalent to that constructed with some definite field, and its properties completely determine (and are completely determined by) those of the field.

2. Those in which Desargues' theorem holds but not Pappus' theorem nor those that go with it. These, likewise, can be of any number of dimensions and can be similarly constructed from a skew field. They always contain an infinity of points. All geometries of three or more dimensions belong to one of these two classes.

3. There can also be plane geometries, however, in which not even Desargues' theorem holds. A good many examples, both finite and infinite, have been constructed; but any general classification of these has proved to be one of the most intractable problems in modern geometry.

BIBLIOGRAPHY. Introductory general works include DIRK J. STRUIK, *Lectures on Analytic and Projective Geometry* (1953); H.S.M. COXETER, *The Real Projective Plane*, 2nd ed. (1955), a meticulous but very readable exposition of the axiomatic approach to real projective geometry of two dimensions; A. ADRIAN ALBERT and RUEBEN SANDLER, *An Introduction to Finite Projective Planes* (1968); CHARLES W. O'HARA and D.R.B. WARD, *Introduction to Projective Geometry* (1937); and GEORGE B. MATHEWS, *Projective Geometry* (1914), an easy and comparatively unsophisticated account for beginners. REINHOLD BAER, *Linear Algebra and Projective Geometry* (1952); and ABRAHAM SEIDENBERG, *Lectures in Projective Geometry* (1962), are more advanced texts. ALFRED N. WHITEHEAD, *The Axioms of Projective Geometry* (1960); and AREND HEYTING, *Axiomatic Projective Geometry* (1963), are studies from the axiomatic approach. LUIGI GREMONA, *Elementi di geometria proiettiva* (1873; Eng. trans., *Elements of Projective Geometry*, 3rd ed., 1913, reprinted 1960), is a classic in the field. OSWALD VEBLEN and JOHN W. YOUNG, *Projective Geometry*, 2 vol. (1910–18), is the classic work in English on the axiomatic approach to projective geometry in two and three dimensions. BENIAMINO SEGRE, *Lectures on Modern Geometry* (1961), combines and contrasts the axiomatic and algebraic approaches to projective geometry, with a substantial algebraic introduction, and a good deal of attention to finite, non-Pappian, and non-Desarguesian geometries.

(P.DuV.)

George III of Great Britain

King of Great Britain from 1760 to 1820, George III had one of the longest reigns in British history. During its course, Britain won an empire in the Seven Years' War but lost its American colonies. It underwent the first stages of the Industrial Revolution and fought a long and bitter struggle against revolutionary and Napoleonic France. The country emerged at the end of his reign as the leading power in Europe, but as one faced with an outmoded constitution and the threat of social revolution. On the personal side, George III's reign was a tragedy. He felt it to be his duty as king to hold an administration together, but he lacked the necessary intellectual power or emotional stability to achieve any long-term objective. Modern party politics grew out of his early efforts to form a stable ministry. He grew politically shrewder in later years, but eventually the pressures of office, dissention within his family, and recurring attacks of a hereditary nervous disorder left him bereft of his sanity,

Early years. George III, the son of Frederick Louis, prince of Wales, and Princess Augusta of Saxe-Gotha, was born on June 4, 1738 (new style). From his parents and their entourage, the young George imbibed an unreasonable dislike of his grandfather, King George II, and of all his policies. George was a child of strong feelings but of slow mental development. This unequal growth of brain and heart made him difficult to teach and too easy to command and produced in him an appearance of apathy; he could not read properly until he was

George III, painting by Peter Edward Stroehling, 1807.
By gracious permission of H.M. Queen Elizabeth II

11. His affection for his immediate family circle dominated his life.

George was 12 when his father died, leaving him heir to the throne. It is clear that, in beginning with his 18th birthday to prepare conscientiously for his future responsibilities, he tormented himself with thoughts of his inadequacy. The curious blend of obstinate determination with self-distrust, a feature of his maturity, was already evident. His method of screwing up his courage was to set himself an ideal of conduct. This ideal George thought he had found personified in John Stuart, 3rd earl of Bute, who became his inspiration, his teacher, and later his chief minister.

George was potentially a better politician than Bute, for he had tenacity and, as experience matured him, he could use guile to achieve his ends. But at his accession in 1760 in the midst of the Seven Years' War (1756–63), George did not know his own capacity nor the incapacity of his hero. As king, in 1761, he asked for a review to be made of all eligible German Protestant princesses "to save a great deal of trouble," as "marriage must sooner or later come to pass." He chose Charlotte Sophia of Mecklenburg-Strelitz and married her on September 8, 1761. Though the marriage was entered into in the spirit of public duty, thanks to the king's own need for security and his wife's strength of character, it lasted unblemished for more than 50 years. Bute's only other useful contribution to his royal pupil was to encourage his interest in botany and to implant in the court more respect for the graces of life, including patronage of the arts, than had been usual for the past half century.

Political instability, 1760–70. Politically, Bute encouraged the most disastrous of George's delusions. The government of England at the time lacked effective executive machinery, and members of Parliament were always more ready to criticize than to cooperate with it. Moreover, the ministers were, for the most part, quarrelsome and difficult to drive as a team. The King's first responsibility was to hold coalitions of great peers together. But under Bute's influence he imagined that his duty was to purify public life and to substitute duty to himself for personal intrigue. The two great men in office at the accession were the elder Pitt and Thomas Pelham-Holles, duke of Newcastle. Bute and George III disliked both. Pitt was allowed to resign (October 1761) over the question of war against Spain. Newcastle followed into retirement when his control of treasury matters seemed to be challenged. The two former ministers were each dangerous as a focal point for criticism of the new government under the touchy captaincy of Bute. The government had two principal problems: to make peace and to restore peacetime finance.

The influence of Lord Bute

The end of
the Seven
Years' War

Peace was made, but in such a way as to isolate Britain in Europe, and for almost 30 years the country suffered from the new alignments of the European powers. Nor was George III happy in his attempt to express the agreed purposes of the country that to Bute had seemed so clear. George III might "glory in the name of Briton" but his attempts to speak out for his country were ill-received. In 1765 he was being vilified by the gutter press organized by the parliamentary radical John Wilkes, while "patriotic" gentlemen, moved by Pitt or Newcastle, suspected that the peace had been botched and that the King was conspiring with Bute against their liberties. For Bute the way out was easy. He resigned (April 1763).

George realized too late that his clumsiness had destroyed one political combination and made any other difficult to assemble. He turned to George Grenville, to his uncle, William Augustus, duke of Cumberland, to Pitt, and to the 3rd duke of Grafton for help. All failed him. Grenville bullied him and offended his feelings for his mother, the princess dowager. Cumberland's nominee, Lord Rockingham, could neither combine with Pitt nor force his own cabinet to agree. Pitt (now Lord Chatham) was frustrated both in his European and his American projects and lapsed into a temporary insanity. Grafton succeeded only in involving the King in further charges of tyranny over John Wilkes. The first decade of the reign was one of such ministerial instability that little was done to solve the basic financial difficulties of the crown, made serious by the expense of the Seven Years' War. Overseas trade expanded, but the riches of the East India Company made no significant contribution to the state. The attempt to make the American colonists meet their own administrative costs only aroused them to resistance. Nor was there consistency in British colonial policy. The Stamp Act (1765) passed by Grenville was repealed by Rockingham in 1766. Indirect taxes, in the form of the Townshend Acts (1767), were imposed without calculation of their probable yield and then repealed (except for that on tea) as a manoeuvre in home politics.

George III was personally blamed for this instability. According to the Whig statesman Edmund Burke and his friends, the King could not keep a ministry because he was faithless and intrigued with friends "behind the curtain." Burke's remedy was to urge that solidity should be given to a cabinet by the building up of party loyalty: the King as a binding agent was to be replaced by the organization of groups upon agreed principles. Thus the early years of George III produced, inadvertently, the germ of modern party politics. In truth, however, the King was not guilty of causing chaos by intrigue. He had no political contact with Bute after 1766; the so-called king's friends were not his agents but rather those who looked to him for leadership such as his predecessors had given. The King's failure lay in his tactlessness and inexperience, and it was not his fault that no one group was strong enough to control the Commons.

Beginning
of the
party
system

By 1770, however, George III had learned a good deal. He was still as obstinate as ever and still felt an intense duty to guide the nation, but now he reckoned with political reality. He no longer scorned to make use of executive power for winning elections nor did he withhold his official blessing from those of whose characters he disapproved.

North's ministry, 1770–82. In 1770 the King was lucky in finding a minister, Lord North, with the power to cajole the Commons. North's policy of letting sleeping dogs lie lulled the suspicions of independent rural members who were always ready to imagine that the executive was growing too strong. As a result, 12 years of stable government followed a decade of disturbance.

George III
and the
American
colonies

Unfortunately, issues and prejudices survived from the earlier period that North could muffle but not cure. Wilkes, in spite of the King's complaints, was allowed to go unharried, but America was the greatest and the fatal issue and North could not avoid it because the English squires in Parliament agreed with their King that America must pay for its own defense and for its share of the debt remaining from the war that had given it security.

George III's personal responsibility for the loss of America lies not in any assertion of his royal prerogative. Americans, rather, were disposed to admit his personal supremacy. Their quarrel was with the assertion of the sovereignty of Parliament, and George III was eventually hated in America because he insisted upon linking himself with that Parliament. North would have had difficulty in ignoring the colonists' insults in any case; with the King and the House of Commons watching to see that he was not weak, he inevitably took the steps that led to war in 1775.

By 1779 the typical English squires in Parliament had sickened of the war, but the King remained obdurate. He argued that though the war was indefensible on economic grounds it still had to be fought, that if disobedience were seen to prosper, Ireland would follow suit. He argued also, after the French had joined the Americans in 1778, that French finances would collapse before those of Britain. So the King prolonged the war, possibly by two years, by his desperate determination and by his pressure upon Lord North. The period from 1779 to 1782 left a further black mark upon the King's reputation. By 1780 a majority in Parliament blamed North's government for the calamities that had befallen the country, yet this government remained in power. As yet there was no responsible or acceptable alternative, for the opposition was reputed to be both unpatriotic and divided, but at the time people believed that corruption alone supported an administration that was equally incapable of waging war or ending it. This supposed increase in corruption was laid directly at the King's door, for North wearily repeated his wish to resign, thus appearing to be a mere puppet of George III. When North fell at last in 1782, George III's prestige was at a low ebb. The death of Rockingham in July 1782, after four months in office, and the failure of Shelburne's ministry (1782–83) reduced George to the lowest point of all in 1783. North joined with the liberal Whig Charles James Fox to form a coalition government. North seemed to accept Fox's aim of giving a stout knock to royal control. The King was not consulted in the making up of a team of junior ministers. The intrigues of politicians in party politics were gaining importance at the expense of royal direction and George even contemplated abdication.

George and the Younger Pitt, 1783–1806. Yet within a year the King had dramatically turned the tables, carrying out amid applause the most high-handed act of royal initiative in 18th-century England. When Fox and North produced a plan to reform the East India Company, which aroused fear that they intended to perpetuate their power by controlling Eastern patronage, the King re-emerged as the guardian of the national interest. He let it be known that anyone who supported the plan in the House of Lords would be reckoned his enemy. The bill was defeated. The ministers resigned. The King was ready with a new "patriotic" leader, William Pitt, the Younger. This initiative was dangerous. Pitt's government was in a minority in the Commons and the discarded ministers were in a mood to threaten a constitutional upheaval. Everything depended on the verdict of a general election in March 1784. The country, moved by real feeling as well as by treasury influence, overwhelmingly endorsed the King's action. The King did not go on after his victory to further demonstrations of power. Though many of Pitt's ideas were unwelcome to him, he contented himself with criticism and a few grumbles. Pitt could not survive without the King and the King, if he lost Pitt, would have been at the mercy of Fox. They compromised, but the compromise left most power, with the King's willing assent, in Pitt's capable young hands. In part, this was because George had no ambitions to raise his own constitutional status but was satisfied to have a minister he could trust to act cautiously and patriotically; in part, it arose from the King's domestic preoccupations.

Pitt's appointment

George loved his children possessively and with that hysterical force that he had always shown in relations with those close to him. He was depressed by the Prince of Wales's coming of age in 1783 as it meant emancipation from the family. The King's ruefulness was soon converted into rage. The Prince associated politically with Fox's Whigs and socially with Fox's gaming friends. In contrast to George III's rather straitlaced court, the Prince's circle was gay and dissolute. As his sons escaped him, one by one, George oscillated between excitement and despair. In the crises of his reign he frequently talked of abdication; but in 1788 it was announced that it was his reason that had fled its throne.

The stresses endured by this hard-working man seemed sufficient to account for his violent breakdown. Twentieth-century medical investigation, however, has suggested that the King had an inherited defect in his metabolism known as porphyria. An excess in purple-red pigments in the blood intoxicated all parts of the nervous system, producing the agonizing pain, excited overactivity, paralysis, and delirium that the King suffered in an acute form at least four times during his reign. The porphyria diagnosis is not universally accepted by medical opinion, and whatever the reason, the King appeared mad to his ministers.

The King's incapacity produced a political storm. But while Pitt and Fox battled over the powers that the Prince of Wales should enjoy as regent, the King suddenly recovered in 1789. He was left with the fear that he might again collapse into the nightmare of madness. For the last decade of the 18th century, he was bothered more about the details than about the main lines of policy. Pitt, whose policies contented him more and more, gradually absorbed in his own following most of North's old following and even some of Fox's. After the outbreak of war with revolutionary France in 1793, all but the most radical Whigs joined the government, leaving Fox in hopeless, if eloquent, opposition.

The war with France seemed to most of the aristocracy and the upper middle class to be waged for national survival. The old King, an object of compassion in his collapse and obviously a well-meaning man, was soon a symbol of the old English order for which the country was fighting. Although his potential power in politics was greatly increased, his will to wield it was enfeebled. George enjoyed himself in encouraging farmers to grow more food; or he talked for hours (ending his sentences rhetorically and fussily with the repeated words "what, what, what?") about past conflicts, or military tactics, or even of the shortcomings of Shakespeare; or he played to himself on his harpsichord; or he regulated the lives of his daughters, who found it so much less easy to escape than did his sons. From such quiet occupations he was aroused to activity by Pitt's Irish policy at the turn of the century.

The French war had made the issue of Catholic emancipation urgent. Rebellion in Ireland, in Pitt's view, could not be cured simply by the union of the British and Irish Parliaments. Conciliation, by the political emancipation of the Roman Catholics, was a necessary concomitant of union. George III believed this proposal to be radical ruin and used all his personal prestige to have emancipation defeated. Pitt resigned (1801) and George persuaded Henry Addington (later 1st Viscount Sidmouth) to form a less adventurous cabinet. The collapse of Addington's administration in 1804, after the short Peace of Amiens (1802–03), brought Pitt back into office (1804–06), but he returned at the cost of giving up his emancipation proposals. The King was decisive in this crisis only because it was an issue upon which he felt most deeply and upon which he instinctively expressed the feelings of the majority of the backbenchers in the House of Commons, though Pitt never pushed the matter to a real trial of strength.

Last years, 1806–20. On the death of Pitt (January 1806), the King accepted Fox as foreign secretary in a coalition "ministry of all the talents" (1806–07). He even came to feel affection for Fox and sincerely to lament his death in 1806. During this short period of Whig administration, the King allowed his ministers to discuss (abortively) peace with Napoleon and to abolish the slave trade; he asserted himself and forced their resignation only when they dared to propose some amelioration of

the laws against Catholics. This second break on the Catholic issue came about in circumstances which witnessed to George's declining abilities. Still strong in body, he had become almost blind. He needed the help of a secretary in the task, which he would not reduce, of reading all the official papers. Lord Grenville thought the King had agreed to a paper which proposed the grant of higher rank in the army for papists. The King thought that his ministers were trying to trick him and that Sidmouth alone had explained to him the significance of the paper. He demanded from his ministers a promise not to bring up the subject again, for he feared he might be deceived into betraying his sworn duty to the Church of England. The perfectly proper refusal of ministers to pledge themselves for the future led to their supersession by the Tories, under Lord Portland (1807–09), Spencer Perceval (1809–12) and Lord Liverpool (1812–27), successively.

Much of the remainder of the King's lifetime was a living death. The death of his youngest child and frequent companion, Princess Amelia, in 1810, was a bitter blow; she had, in part, consoled him for his disappointment about his sons. Worse still was the return of the King's illness. In 1811 it was acknowledged that he was violently insane. The doctors continued to hope for recovery but Parliament enacted the regency of the Prince of Wales and decreed that the Queen should have the custody of her husband. He remained insane, with intervals of senile lucidity, until his death at Windsor Castle on January 29, 1820. George III's reign, on its personal side, was the tragedy of a well-intentioned man who was faced with problems too great for him to solve but from which his conscience prevented any attempt at escape.

BIBLIOGRAPHY. The best account of George III's character is JOHN BROOKE, *King George III* (1972). ROMNEY SEDGWICK's introduction to his edition of *The Letters from George III to Lord Bute, 1757–1766* (1939), vividly relates the character to the political situation. Other valuable collections of George III's letters SIR JOHN FORTESCUE, *The Correspondence of George III from 1760 to December 1783*, 6 vol. (1927–28); but see also SIR LEWIS B. NAMIER, *Additions and Corrections to Sir John Fortescue's Edition of the Correspondence of George the Third* (1937); and A. ASPINALL, *The Later Correspondence of George III*, 5 vol. (1962–70). Two quite wide surveys are RICHARD PARES, *King George III and the Politicians* (1953); and J. STEVEN WATSON, *The Reign of George III* (1960). There has been a great deal of scholarly controversy about the nature of politics in the early years of George III's reign, in which the work of SIR LEWIS B. NAMIER has been outstanding. The major works are *The Structure of Politics at the Accession of George III*, 2nd ed. (1957), and *England in the Age of the American Revolution*, 2nd ed. (1961). This approach to the political history of George III's reign has been sharply and pertinently criticized by SIR HERBERT BUTTERFIELD in *George III and the Historians* (1957). Less interest has been displayed in the latter part of George III's reign, but JOHN EHRMANN, *The Younger Pitt*, 2 vol. (1969), deals very thoroughly with the relations of George III with his most successful prime minister, William Pitt the Younger. The question of the nature of George III's illness has been raised by IDA MACALPINE and RICHARD HUNTER, *George III and the Mad Business* (1969), but their arguments for porphyria as against insanity are not fully accepted by medical opinion.

(J.S.W.)

Georgia

The largest of the American states east of the Mississippi River, Georgia was founded in 1732, at which time its boundaries were even larger—including much of the present-day states of Alabama and Mississippi. It was by many years the youngest of the 13 former English colonies whose rebellion created the United States. Its landscape presents numerous contrasts, with more soil types than any other state as it sweeps from the Appalachian Mountains in the north (on the borders of Tennessee and North Carolina) to the marshes of the Atlantic Coast on the southeast and the Okefenokee Swamp (which it shares with Florida) on the south. The Savannah and Chattahoochee rivers describe much of Georgia's eastern and western boundaries with South Carolina and Alabama, respectively.

Georgia's 58,876 square miles (152,488 square kilometres) had a population at the start of the 1970s of more than 4,500,000, of whom over 1,000,000 were black; of the total population 60 percent lived in urban areas. For most of the 19th century the state was the capital of the cotton empire of the South, but by the 1970s poultry products accounted for many times the income from cotton. Though industry has far outstripped agriculture in economic importance, 70 percent of the industrial workers remain in farm- or forestry-connected jobs.

Pre-
eminence
of Atlanta

For decades Atlanta, the capital, has been the economic and cultural focus of the Southeast. Its name evokes the largely romantic legends of the pre-Civil War South, of the traditions of Southern gentility, and of white-columned mansions along Peachtree Street, its most famous thoroughfare. The people of Georgia and the history of the state have been scarred for more than 100 years by that conflict, which was made real in Georgia by many major battles, by the Confederate prison at Andersonville in which nearly 13,000 Union prisoners died, and by the burning of Atlanta and the devastating "march to the sea" by Federal forces under Gen. William T. Sherman.

Though Atlanta by the 1970s had become very much a nationally oriented city, attracting major corporations as well as citizens from all parts of the United States, race and politics remained inextricably bound together throughout the state. Many forms of discrimination remain realities, as they do in most parts of the United States, though many Georgians in the 1970s saw their state as being in the midst of a slow but definite transition, both socially and politically. (For information on related topics, see the articles UNITED STATES; UNITED STATES, HISTORY OF THE; NORTH AMERICA; and CIVIL WAR, U.S.)

THE HISTORY OF GEORGIA

Settlement. Georgia was granted a charter as a colony by George II in 1732, well after the great English migrations of the 17th century. The prime mover in obtaining the charter was the English general and philanthropist James Edward Oglethorpe, who sought to found a colony where the poor of England could get a new start. He and other trustees encouraged the settlers to produce wines, silks, and spices, to relieve England of a dependency on foreign sources. The colony also would serve as a bulwark against the Spanish and French in the lands beyond the Carolinas.

Settlement was made at Savannah in 1733. Some colonists paid their way; the colony's trustees paid the expenses of others. Oglethorpe directed affairs in the colony, with his primary interest in military operations. Government was informal, the economy not generally successful, and military frustration was frequent; the trustees surrendered power to the royal government in 1752, a year before their charter was to expire.

Revolution and growth. With the pre-Revolutionary westward thrust of American migration, substantial settlement of Georgia began, first in a thin band along the west side of the Savannah River. Georgia's response to the revolutionary tensions of the 1770s was confused, and the war period was chaotic. After the Revolution, settlement expanded rapidly, especially westward from Augusta through the future "cotton counties" of middle Georgia. Speculations in public lands, acquisitions of more and more Indian lands, and final removal of the Creeks and Cherokees from the state paralleled the development of a largely commercial agriculture and a concomitant transportation system. The Indian removals themselves provided a poignant and traumatic chapter to the state's history. The states of Alabama and Mississippi were already settled by whites, and the Indians' move beyond the Mississippi River was a long one. It left in its wake what came to be known as the Cherokee Trail of Tears.

Civil War and aftermath. As disunion approached there was reluctance and division of feeling. Much of northern Georgia never accepted secession, and Union

sentiment was high there throughout the Civil War. The state contributed many regiments and many officers to the Confederacy, but its civil leadership was divisive and querulous. Georgia was in most respects a typical Southern state during the Reconstruction period. The Atlanta cotton expositions and the city itself rapidly became symbols of the new South that arose from the ashes of the old.

After Reconstruction, agriculture became even more commercialized. With rising cotton prices after 1900, the agricultural economy functioned at its best, though briefly. In the 1920s came the scourge of the cotton boll weevil that, with succeeding depression and war, radically altered the economic structure of the state. Since the 1920s, problems of integration have come increasingly to the forefront of Georgia's social and political life, but the state has continued to solidify its position of dominance in the regional as well as national economy and culture.

THE NATURAL AND HUMAN LANDSCAPE

The natural environment. The most southerly portions of the Blue Ridge section of the Appalachian Mountains cover northeastern and north central Georgia, whereas in the northwest a limestone valley-and-ridge country predominates above Rome and the Coosa River. The higher elevations extend southward down into the state about 75 miles, with peaks such as Kennesaw and Stone mountains near Atlanta rising starkly from the floor of the upper Piedmont. The highest point in the state, Brasstown Bald in the Blue Ridge, reaches 4,784 feet (1,458 metres) above sea level. Below the mountains the Piedmont extends to the Fall Line of the rivers—the east-to-west line of Augusta, Milledgeville, Macon, and Columbus. Along the fall region, nearly 100 miles wide, sandy hills reach in a narrow, irregular belt from Augusta to Columbus. Below these hills the rolling terrain of the coastal plain levels out to the flatlands near the coast, the "pine barrens" of the early days.

Surface
features

Soils. From the coast to the Fall Line, sands and sandy loams predominate, gray near the coast and increasingly red with higher elevations. In the Piedmont and Appalachian regions these traits continue, with an increasing amount of clay in the soils. North Georgia lands are referred to colloquially as "red land" or "gray land." In the limestone valleys and uplands in the northwest, the soils are of loams, silts, and clays and may be brown as well as gray or red.

Rivers and lakes. About half the streams of the state flow into the Atlantic Ocean and most of the rest through Alabama and Florida into the Gulf of Mexico. A few streams in north Georgia flow into the Tennessee River and thence via the Ohio and Mississippi into the Gulf. The river basins have not contributed significantly to the regional divisions, which have been defined more by elevations and soils. The inland waters of Georgia consist of 20 artificial lakes, some 70,000 small ponds created largely by the federal Soil Conservation Service, and natural lakes in the southwest near Florida. These have fostered a widespread recreational water culture.

Climate. Maritime tropical air masses dominate the climate in summer, but in other seasons continental polar air masses are not uncommon. The average January temperature in Atlanta is 39° F (4° C), in August, 79° F (26° C). Farther south, January average temperatures rise by 10° F (6° C), but in August only about 3° F (2° C). In north Georgia rain usually averages about 50 inches (1,270 millimetres) annually. The east central areas are drier, with about 44 inches. Precipitation is more evenly distributed through the seasons in north Georgia, whereas the southern and coastal areas experience more summer rains.

Vegetation and animal life. The mountains-to-the-sea topography of the southeastern states gives Georgia a natural vegetation from maple and hemlock, birch and beech near Blairsville in the north to the cyprus, tupelo, and red gum of the stream swamps below the Fall Line and to the marsh grass of the coast and islands. Through most of the Appalachians, chestnut, oak, and yellow poplar are dominant. Much of this area is now national forest. The region from Tennessee to the Fall Line is of oak-pine dominance, except for an area of pines in the west. Below the Fall Line and out of the swamps are the pines—longleaf, loblolly, and slash—exploitation of which for pulpwood is a leading economic activity. Much of the land, which had been cleared of trees for agriculture, has gone back to trees, scrub, and grasses.

Georgia's wildlife is profuse. There are alligators in the south; bear, with a hunting season in five counties near the Okefenokee Swamp; deer, with restricted hunting in most counties; grouse; opossum; quail; rabbit; raccoon; squirrel; sea turtles, with no hunting allowed; and turkey, with quite restricted hunting. In general, wildlife is in a period of transition. Deer have been seen in suburban counties and bears on golf courses in Atlanta; but solid stands of pine and unbroken pasture are not ideal for wildlife, and its future seems open. Stocking of game birds and fish is extensive. The major fish of the southern coast, except snook and bonefish, are in waters off the Georgia coast, and all major freshwater game fish of the U.S. are in Georgia's streams and lakes.

Traditional regions. Migrations and historical change have blurred the traditional regions of Georgia. In earlier times, the coastal mainland and islands were distinct, separated from middle Georgia by the pine barrens of the lower coastal plain. Rice and sea island cotton were major crops. There was a summer exodus of white families from the plantations to the southern highlands and to the North: a Savannah family might well know more people in Boston, New York, or Philadelphia than in Augusta, Macon, or Columbus. The coastal region and sea islands still support the unique culture of blacks known in South Carolina as Gullah, in Georgia as Geechee.

The early subsistence farmers known as "crackers" lived in the thinly populated pine barrens just above the coastal area. There the soil is sandy and poorly drained, and the farms and plantations existed amid near-frontier conditions through much of the 19th century.

Beyond the pine barrens to the north and west, a fabulous cotton culture flourished for more than a century. The classic period of cotton plantations and farms before the Civil War was brief in several counties. The white-columned houses generally were built in the county seats, or "courthouse towns," whereas most rural houses could be termed no more than substantial farmhomes. Mountainous northern Georgia was an area of small subsistence farms and few slaves.

Blacks were long identified with the commercial agriculture producing sea island cotton and rice on the coast and upland cotton in middle Georgia. Some modern historians use the term "black belt" as a demographic description of middle Georgia where slavery predominated, though its origin stemmed from the dark soils of Alabama.

Patterns of settlement. Plantations were cultivated by supervised group labour before the Civil War. After the war a family-plot system, called sharecropping or tenant-farming, replaced the larger labour groups and reduced immediate supervision. There were two basic arrangements in the sharecrop system with variations: in middle Georgia, the division by halves system gave the land-owner control of management and sales. The more independent north Georgian, if he did not own a small farm himself, rented by thirds and fourths and had control.

Rural Georgia was settled in a pattern of separate farms without villages or unified communities. Area names suggested such centres, but these generally were derived from the names of creeks, mountains, militia districts, and the like. Schools, churches, and stores drew people, often near neighbours, in different directions, producing a highly diffused rural community life. Urban settlements originally served political and commercial purposes as county seats and cotton markets. The Fall Line cities became railroad points, and later they and some courthouse towns in the upper Piedmont had cotton mills. Elsewhere, the country general store and small local

cotton gins declined as larger towns gradually absorbed the slight commerce and industry. Later, better roads drew people from these smaller locales to the even larger towns and cities. Today the shopping centre, neon-lighted restaurants, and service stations are scattered through both rural and urban areas in much of the state.

THE PEOPLE OF GEORGIA

Population composition. The Georgia colony languished under the trustees, and in 1752 it numbered only about 5,000 inhabitants, including English, Jews, blacks, Salzburgers from Austria at New Ebenezer and Savannah, Scottish Highlanders at Darien, and New England Congregationalists at Sunbury and Midway. Settlement was concentrated on the coast and up the Savannah River to the Augusta area. The westward movement began under the English crown, and the census of 1790 counted 82,548 persons—52,886 whites and 29,662 blacks. In each decade until the 1850s the population increased between 31 and 55 percent. During that period, the cotton counties of middle Georgia were settled. At the start of the Civil War, Georgia had nearly 1,100,000 inhabitants, about 56 percent white, 44 percent black.

Demography. Irish, German, and other massive immigrations into the United States during the 19th century affected Georgia little, and by 1910 only about 15,000 foreign-born whites resided in the state.

Churches play a significant role in the various subcultures of Georgia. The early movement for racial integration convulsed the churches even more profoundly than other institutions.

Georgia lost more people than it gained through migration in each decade from 1870 to 1960, but the total population increased steadily because of high birth rates. More whites than blacks left until 1910, generally for other Southern states to the west; since 1910 the black exodus has been greater, generally for longer distances and to the cities of the North. The first impact on the cotton economy of the boll-weevil plague of the 1920s caused massive departures of both races. The white emigration loss almost stopped in the 1950s, and in the 1960s there was a net migration gain for the first time in nearly a century. Emigration of blacks has not slowed significantly, however, and there is little prospect of change.

Mechanized and chemically controlled agriculture and abandonment of cultivated farmlands to pastures and pine forest have been major causes of migrations, as well as the black's rarely realized hopes that elsewhere he will find fewer ingrained patterns of discrimination.

In the 1930s, the first full decade that Georgia was in the national registration, Georgia's birth rate was just above 20 per 1,000 and death rates about half that. By the 1950s and 1960s the births were about two per 1,000 more than the national average and deaths were slightly less. Differences between white and nonwhite birth and death rates diminished during the 1960s. Hookworm, once an endemic infestation, was so reduced by the early 1970s that statistics were no longer kept.

THE STATE'S ECONOMY

Georgia's economy has so changed since 1940 as to cause a shift in the meaning of such words as "farm" and "industry"; and "agri-business" is a term in wide use. More people work in industry than on the farm, but a great majority of industrial jobs depend on farm or forest products. Income from poultry is regarded as farm income despite the fact that chickens are raised in factory-like structures; feed prices are quoted for 150-ton lots, and financing is by complex base-and-incentive arrangements—all indicating an extensive and highly developed "agri-business."

More conventional industries, notably automobile assembly, exploit Atlanta's nearness to southeastern markets. Three decades of prosperity have also increased commerce, and New York stores have located branches in Atlanta. Service industries are lagging, and per capita income is only about 85 percent of the national average, but overall the state's economy has become similar to that of the nation as a whole.

Exploitation of natural resources. Marble and granite quarries in northern Georgia provide one of the nation's major sources of building stone, as well as great quantities of crushed stone. The white clay known as kaolin is taken from vast pits in middle Georgia, processed, then shipped in tank cars for use in such products as ceramics and paper. Phosphate deposits in the south are largely unexploited, but this region's reserves of artesian-well water, the largest in the nation, are beginning to prove useful for agricultural irrigation.

Georgia's virgin timberlands have been cut over, but the state ranks second only to Washington state in growth of timber. Taxation of timber-growing lands has become an internal political issue, with growth rates versus tax rates a crucial argument. Lumber, plywood, and paper are major products; but Georgia is especially known for its large production of naval stores—tars and resins—from its pine forests.

Georgia lies south of the states benefitted by the dams of the Tennessee Valley Authority, but rivers contribute almost 20 percent of its electrical energy. Coastal waters provide working grounds for only a small number of fishermen, with shrimp the main catch, though there are commercial sturgeon fisheries on the Coosa and Oosanaula rivers around Rome in northwestern Georgia.

Manufacturing. Cotton textile production has occupied a major sector of Georgia's economy since the late 19th century. In the 1970s, the continuation of this specialization in textiles was evidenced by the great number of rug and carpet mills in northern Georgia, the concentration of looming and weaving skills of which make the state the major textile producer in the nation. Manufactures representing modern, sophisticated living include airplane and automobile assembly, mobile homes, chemicals, and food processing.

Agriculture. With the continuing consolidation of farms into fewer but larger units and the advent of a pervasive "agri-business," Georgia has followed nationwide trends in agriculture. Much of the poultry industry is conducted by large companies that parcel out their work to small farmers—many of whom would otherwise be unemployed—and supply them with modern poultry-raising facilities. Cattle and swine raising are important, especially in the south. Cotton is still a major crop, though far below the peak years of the early 20th century, and Georgia is the leading state in peanut production and high in tobacco. Peaches have become especially identified with Georgia, and pecans and watermelons are grown nearly everywhere in the state.

Governmental presence. The federal government affects Georgia's economy through direct purchases from industry but even more through payrolls at the several major military installations throughout the state. It produces some hydroelectric power and regulates its sale, much of it to rural electric cooperatives, and controls more than 2,000,000 acres of forests and waters.

The state government, on the other hand, functions in the economic sphere largely to promote further industrial development or financial investment in the state, which continues to rely heavily on outside money. Atlanta is the financial centre of the Southeast and headquarters of the Sixth District of the Federal Reserve Bank. Nearly three-quarters of state taxes are levied on sales, most of the rest on personal and corporate incomes. Local governments rely mainly on general property taxes.

Labour and management. Only about 15 percent of Georgia's workers are members of unions. This is below the national average. Unions are strongest in construction, the textile trades, and the steel, automotive, aircraft, and other machine industries. Racial tensions exist within union organization, but traditionally blacks have been employed in such building trades as carpentry, painting, and masonry. Unionization is hampered by a solidly entrenched "right-to-work" law prohibiting compulsory union membership in any trade or industry and by the recent rural origins of many union members that prevent them from achieving a rapid acclimatization to modern industrial procedures.

Employer groups vary from broad-based organizations striving for a good general business climate to one-industry groups with hard-line lobbies at the state and federal levels. "Agri-business" presses hard for exports to European countries, while the cotton-fabrics industry strives as determinedly against foreign imports.

Transportation. Water transportation determined the location of Georgia's earliest cities. Milledgeville was briefly the centre of an emerging road system for the settled counties in eastern Georgia and for the old military and post road running through Indian country to Alabama. Atlanta, originally called Terminus on the early railroad survey maps, had a near-optimum location for all but water transport, thus making it a hub of railroad transportation for the Southeast. With the advent of highways and then of air traffic, the city maintained its focal position.

In the 1970s, Georgia had about 5,500 miles of main and branch rail lines. Petroleum, natural gas, and butane pipelines come into the state from the Southwest. More than 500 trucking lines serve the state, and the Atlanta Airport served more than 1,000 flights daily. Twelve other cities in the state have commercial air service. Though urban transit has declined to the point of crisis, in 1971 two Atlanta-area counties voted to begin a rapid-transit service.

Navigation of 500 miles of inland waterways has been revived, and Augusta, Columbus, and Bainbridge have barge service. A state ports authority is constructing facilities at these river ports and at the harbours of Savannah and Brunswick for the distribution of numerous chemical, wood, and mineral products.

ADMINISTRATION AND SOCIAL CONDITIONS

Governmental structure. The structure of state government tends to sever governmental from political processes and thereby prevents a strong executive. Most of the activities of modern state government are controlled by elected boards, which make more than 85 percent of the state's expenditures.

The Georgia legislature was restructured in 1971 to comprise a 56-member Senate and 180-member House; districts replaced counties as units of representation. Basic units of the judiciary are a court of ordinary for probate and guardianships, and a superior, or circuit, court of general trial in each county, with auxiliary county and municipal courts. At the top of the pyramid, the Court of Appeals and the Supreme Court hear appeals from lower jurisdictions. Uniform procedures for supervision or coordination of the superior courts do not exist. Some circuits may try a case within two months, others, within 20 months. There are strong pressures for revision of administrative procedures in the courts.

Local administration. Georgia's local governments are many: in 1972 there were 159 counties, 530 municipalities, and over 350 special districts. Counties remain viable units, often performing municipal-type services. Alone and through multicounty cooperative districts, they operate forestry units, airports, hospitals, and libraries. By the early 1970s, the counties and the municipalities had organized 19 area planning and development commissions that may create corporations for housing and industrial development and that are concerned with planning for health and criminal justice.

Atlanta provides an outstanding example of the weak-mayor form of government, but an increasing number of cities have strong executives. Relations between cities and their suburbs, in which race is and will continue to be significant, remain largely unsolved.

Politics and race. A county-unit system characterized Georgia politics from 1917 to 1962. In Democratic primaries, counties were allotted two unit votes for each seat they held in the lower house of the legislature, where 121 smaller counties each held one seat, 30 middling counties held two, and the eight most populous counties held only three each. Candidates received the unit votes of counties in which they received electoral pluralities. This system extended the rural domination of the legislature to nominations in statewide Democratic primaries;

(margin note left) Quarrying and forestry

(margin note left) Worker and employer organizations

(margin note right) County, regional, and municipal government

the process was used also in congressional districts. The county-unit system tended to create alliances between candidates for governor and the "courthouse rings" of the local elite, which could carry counties, at a time when distribution of highway money among the counties played a major role in politics. Since 1962, governors have gained nomination by campaigning, with less dependence on "courthouse rings," and have also lost much of their former dominance over the legislature.

Georgia politics has been in flux since the 1950s. Voting patterns have changed, and distinctions among local, state, and national politics have increased. Republican or third-party presidential candidates carried the state after 1960. Local politics and the courthouse rings remain almost universally Democratic, and Democrats, while remaining shy of identification with the more liberal national party, continued to win all statehouse offices in the same period. Republicans, however, have won seats in Congress.

The political idiom has changed as well. Explicit racial demagoguery is no longer in evidence. Campaigns are long, and, with only occasional captive audiences, gubernatorial candidates must stump and shake hands throughout the state in a way once unnecessary.

Black voting and civil rights
Black precincts in Atlanta and Macon that were 80 to 90 percent Republican in 1956 are now Democratic by that margin or more. Whites in rural and less affluent urban areas may vote for candidates on racial issues, whereas rural elites and affluent suburbanites may vote for either party depending on the local, state, or national nature of the contest and the commitments of the candidates. Black candidacies in Atlanta have strained a long-time local coalition between blacks and the affluent. More blacks are voting in each election, but an astute black congressional candidate would want a district at least 70 percent black for a chance of winning. In the early 1970s, more than 50 blacks held elective office in Georgia.

The civil rights movement in Georgia has been characterized by legal action, many nonviolent and a few violent confrontations, selective buying campaigns, voter registration, and education. The movement has touched life in rural Georgia very little. In cities and in settings of high visibility—airports, stores, restaurants, and schools—blacks are seen in dramatically different circumstances from earlier decades. Discrimination continues, but the new head of the state patrol announced in 1971 that the mission of the patrol is to enforce the law, not custom.

Education. State-endowed county academies were created in the 1780s, but state support was not continued. Academies and numerous colleges were characteristic of the period before the Civil War, but no sustained statewide program of public education existed. Some state funds were allocated for tuition for the poor, and some counties had public schools. In 1850, 80 percent of whites were literate. The Reconstruction constitution of 1868 provided for free public education and the gradual founding of the school system from the 1870s. The public high schools have developed largely since 1912. State support of public schools is, since 1964, for nine months, and compulsory ages, since 1945, are from seven to 16 years. The racial integration of public schools increased private-school enrollments dramatically. Georgia ranks 36th among the states in expenditures per pupil and 20th in school-age children in attendance in public schools.

The public institutions of higher learning, under a unified board of regents, are headed by the University of Georgia (chartered 1785; opened 1801) in Athens and Georgia Institute of Technology (1885) and Georgia State University (1913), a downtown university, both in Atlanta. Other state colleges and new junior colleges are increasing the crisis of private colleges in the state. Rather than incorporating these colleges into the university system, the state pays Georgia students' tuition at the private colleges. The four undergraduate colleges and the graduate and professional schools of Atlanta University Center, now all on one campus, and Paine College in Augusta provide higher education primarily for blacks.

Health and welfare. There are beginnings of a new program in mental health. The old central state hospital has an increased staff and fewer patients. Another hospital has been opened on two campuses. Regional hospitals for evaluation, emergency, and short-term treatment are being established throughout the state to serve communities within a 50-mile radius. In addition, there are 60 community health-care centres for outpatient treatment, and a number of other general hospitals have been built through federal programs.

Georgia has imaginative programs in family and children's services. There are state and regional youth-development centres, and no child is committed to a jail. The state aids colleges in training welfare workers, whose activities are supplemented by a widespread volunteer program.

Housing problems, urban and rural
Housing remains inadequate, with poorer people, both rural and urban, continuing to live in flimsy structures. In the housing census of 1960, more than 40 percent of the dwellings were classified as substandard. Housing is a main concern for the area planning commissions; some of these planning commissions actively sponsor new building and renovation.

CULTURAL LIFE AND INSTITUTIONS

The arts. Atlanta rapidly is becoming the artistic centre of the Southeast. Its memorial centre, completed in 1968, brings together a major museum and a school of the visual arts with performing facilities for a major symphony orchestra and a professional resident theatre, both of which have premiered new works in music and drama. Atlanta also has cooperative galleries run by painters and sculptors and an active group of film makers.

Elsewhere in the state, there are regional ballet companies, and community theatres perform in more than 30 towns. In addition to instruction in theatre, dance, the visual arts, and music in many colleges, Georgia Institute of Technology has a school of architecture, and the University of Georgia teaches landscape architecture. Eight public museums and numerous college galleries exhibit art, and Atlanta University has a notable Afro-American collection.

Folk culture. Georgia is rich in traditional arts and crafts, especially in the mountainous north. The craft of tufted fabrics was a major factor in attracting the carpet industry that settled around Dalton. Other handcraft workers find sales opportunities through country fairs in Hiawassee and nearby Gatlinburg, Tennessee, at the Plum Nelly Clothesline in Rising Fawn-Trenton, and at many other art festivals across the state. A mountain arts cooperative has a store in Tallulah Falls, and craft shops are attached to several art galleries. A bulletin of the state Agriculture Department gives free advertising for crafts, and a quarterly publication describes many of the old craft techniques.

Traditional music is sung by authentic folk groups in the sea islands and in the mountains. Country-music conventions are held in north Georgia—with some tension between purists and users of electronic equipment. The ancient sacred harp songs of the northwest, heard in what is known as "fa-so-la" singing, have been collected, and throughout the area many prayers and sermons are delivered in singsong.

Communications. Throughout Georgia, 34 daily newspapers, five semiweeklies, and more than 200 weeklies are published. Though generally conservative, the press has tended to support the more liberal statewide candidates in recent decades. *The Atlanta Constitution* long has been recognized as among the nation's outstanding newspapers. A well-edited "underground" newspaper in Atlanta reflects many of the views of the youth culture that took over a section of Peachtree Street known as the Strip in the late 1960s. There are more than 200 radio and 15 commercial television stations in the state as well as an unusually well-directed system of educational television.

Prospects. Paradoxically, Georgia's economy continues an overall prosperity while the counties of middle

Georgia, the classic cotton country, continue to lose people and economic status to northern counties. Its location —at the heart of the Southeast—is expected to remain an asset, both economically and culturally. An end to the state's transitional political and social condition was not in sight in the mid-1970s, though black leaders with greater political orientation and sophistication were replacing the ministers who led the drives for equality in the two preceding decades.

BIBLIOGRAPHY. ELLIS MERTON COULTER, *Georgia: A Short History*, rev. ed. (1960), the best one-volume history of the state for the general reader; KENNETH COLEMAN, *The American Revolution in Georgia, 1763–1789* (1958), the definitive study of Georgia through three decades of crisis; HORACE MONTGOMERY, *Cracker Parties* (1950), a revealing study of politics in antebellum Georgia; NUMAN V. BARTLEY, *From Thurmond to Wallace: Political Tendencies in Georgia, 1948–1968* (1970), an excellent study, especially of voting; HENRY T. MALONE, *Cherokees of the Old South: A People in Transition* (1956), the definitive study of Georgia's best known Indians; T. CONN BRYAN, *Confederate Georgia* (1953), a thorough and scholarly study of Georgia during the Civil War; ALAN CONWAY, *The Reconstruction of Georgia* (1966), a study of the social and economic aspects of Reconstruction, written by a Welsh scholar; DEWEY W. GRANTHAM, *Hoke Smith and the Politics of the New South* (1958), an account of the leadership of Georgia in the New South movement; JAMES C. BONNER, *A History of Georgia Agriculture, 1732–1860* (1964), and WILLARD RANGE, *A Century of Georgia Agriculture, 1850–1950* (1954), valuable as complementary scholarly studies.

(G.He.)

Georgian Soviet Socialist Republic

Lying at the eastern end of the Black Sea just to the south of the great barrier formed by the Caucasus Mountains, the Georgian Soviet Socialist Republic, or Georgia, lies in the southernmost region of the European section of the Soviet Union, at the same latitude as Rome. Formed in 1921, it has been since 1936 one of the 15 Soviet union republics. With the notable exception of the fertile plain of Kolkhida—ancient Colchis, where the legendary Argonauts sought the Golden Fleece—the Georgian terrain is largely mountainous (85 percent of the total area) and a third is covered by forest or brushwood. There is a remarkable variety of landscape, ranging from the subtropical Black Sea shores to the ice and snow of the crest line of the Caucasus. Such contrasts are made more noteworthy by the relatively small size of the republic, which, at 26,900 square miles (69,700 square kilometres), ranks 10th among the union republics.

The roots of the Georgian people, who numbered about 4,900,000 in the mid-1970s, are deep in history. Their cultural heritage is equally ancient and rich. During the 20th century Georgia has experienced a major transformation from an economically backward outpost of the tsarist Empire to a modernized and diversified economy.

The republic is bounded to the north, at the Caucasian crests, by the Russian Soviet Federated Socialist Republic. Azerbaijan and Armenia lie to the east and southeast, and a portion of the Soviet frontier with Turkey is to the south. Georgia includes two autonomous Soviet Socialist republics, the Abkhaz (principal city Sukhumi) and the Adzhar (principal city Batumi), as well as the Yugo-Ossetian Autonomous Oblast, a unit centred on Tskhinvali. The Georgian capital is at Tbilisi (Tiflis). (For related information, see RUSSIA AND THE SOVIET UNION, HISTORY OF; SOVIET UNION; CAUCASUS MOUNTAINS; and CAUCASIAN LANGUAGES.)

Autonomous S.S.R.'s and oblast

THE LAND

Topography. The rugged Georgia terrain may be divided into three bands, all running from east to west.

The Great Caucasus Range. To the north lies the wall of the Great Caucasus, consisting of a series of parallel and transverse mountain belts, rising eastward, and often separated by deep, wild gorges. Spectacular crest line peaks include Shkhara (16,627 feet [5,068 metres]), Rustaveli (16,273 feet [4,960 metres]), Tetnults (15,918 feet [4,852 metres]), and Ushba (15,420 feet [4,700 metres]).

The cone of the extinct Kazbek (Mqinvari) volcano dominates the northernmost Bokovoy Range from a height of 16,512 feet (5,033 metres). Farther south, the central range thrusts out a number of important spurs, including those of the Lomissky (Lomisi) and Kartliysky (Kartli, Kartalinian) ranges at right angles to the general Caucasian trend. From the ice-clad flanks of these desolately beautiful high regions flow many streams and rivers.

The central trough. The southern slopes of the Great Caucasus merge into a belt of lowlands formed on a great structural depression. The Kolkhida lowlands, near the shores of the Black Sea, are covered by a thick layer of river-borne deposits, accumulated over thousands of years. Rushing down from the Great Caucasus, the major rivers of western Georgia, the Inguri, Rioni, and Kodori, flow over a broad area to the sea. The Kolkhida lowland was formerly an almost continually stagnant swamp. In a great development program, drainage canals and embankments along the rivers have been constructed and afforestation plans introduced; the region has now become of prime importance through the cultivation of subtropical and other commercial crops.

Kolkhida

To the east, the structural trough is crossed by the Meskhetsky (Meskheti) and Likhsky (Likhi) ranges, linking the Great and Little Caucasus and marking the watershed between the Black and Caspian Sea basins. Beyond, in central Georgia, between the cities of Khashuri and Mtskheta (the ancient capital), lies the inner high plateau known as the Kartalinian Plain. Surrounded by mountains on all sides and covered for the most part by deposits of the loess type, this plateau extends along the Kura (Mtkvari) River and its tributaries.

The Little Caucasus. The southern band of Georgian territory is marked by the ranges and plateaus of the Little Caucasus, which rise beyond a narrow, swampy coastal plain to reach 10,830 feet (3,301 metres) in the peak of Didi-Abuli.

Climate. *Altitude and climate.* The Caucasian barrier protects Georgia from cold air intrusions from the north, while the republic is open to the constant influence of warm, moist air from the Black Sea. Western Georgia has a humid subtropical, maritime climate, while eastern Georgia has a range of climate varying from moderately humid to a dry subtropical type.

Altitudinally, too, there are marked zones. The Kolkhida lowland, for example, has a subtropical character up to about 1,600–2,000 feet, with a zone of moist, moderately warm climate lying just above; still higher is a belt of cold, wet winters and cool summers. Above about 6,600–7,200 feet, there is an alpine climatic zone, lacking any true summer; above 11,200–11,500 feet, snow and ice reign perpetually. In eastern Georgia, farther inland, temperatures are lower than in the western portions at the same altitude.

Altitudinal zones

Western Georgia. Western Georgia has heavy year-round rainfall, totalling 40 to 80 inches (1,000 to 2,000 millimetres) and reaching a maximum in autumn and winter. Southern Kolkhida receives the most rain, and humidity decreases to the north and east. Winter in this region is mild and warm; in regions below about 2,000–2,300 feet, the mean January temperature never falls below 32° F (0° C), and warm, sunny winter weather persists in the coastal regions, where temperatures average about 41° F (5° C).

Eastern Georgia. In eastern Georgia, precipitation decreases with distance from the sea, reaching 16 to 28 inches (400 to 700 millimetres) in the plains and foothills but, nevertheless, increasing to double this amount in the mountains. The southeastern regions are the driest areas, and winter is the driest season; the rainfall maximum occurs at the end of spring. The highest lowland temperatures occur in July (about 77° F), while average January temperatures over most of the region range from 32° to 37° F.

Plant and animal life. The republic's location and its diverse terrain have given rise to a remarkable variety of landscapes. The luxuriant vegetation of the moist, subtropical Black Sea shores is relatively near to the eternal snows of the mountain peaks. Deep gorges and swift rivers give way to dry steppes, and the green of alpine meadows alternates with the darker hues of forested valleys. Soils, too, present a great variety, ranging from gray-brown and saline semi-desert types to richer red earths and podzols, with man-made improvements adding to the diversity.

Forests

About a third of the republic is covered by forests and brush. In the west, relative constancy of climate over a long period has preserved many relict and rare items, including the Pitsunda pines (*Pinus pithyusa*). The forests include oak, chestnut, beech, and alder, as well as Caucasian fir, ash, linden, and apple and pear trees. The western underbrush is dominated by evergreens (including rhododendrons and holly) and such deciduous shrubs as Caucasian bilberry and nut trees. Liana strands entwine some of the western forests. Citrus groves are found throughout the republic, and long rows of eucalyptus trees line the country roads.

Eastern Georgia has fewer forests, and the steppes are dotted with thickets of prickly underbrush, as well as a blanket of feather and beard grass. Herbaceous subalpine and alpine vegetation occurs extensively in the highest regions. Animal life is very diverse. Goats and Caucasian antelope inhabit the high mountains; rodents live in the high meadows; and a rich birdlife includes the mountain turkey, the Caucasian black grouse, and the mountain and bearded eagles. The clear rivers and mountain lakes are full of trout.

Forest regions are characterized by wild boar and roe and Caucasian deer, brown bear, lynx, wolf, fox, and jackal, and hares and squirrels. Birds range from the thrush to the black vulture and hawk. Some of these animals and birds also frequent the lowland regions, which are also the home of introduced raccoon, mink, and nutria. The lowland rivers and the Black Sea itself are also rich in fish.

THE PEOPLE

The Georgians

Composition and distribution. The likelihood is great that the Georgians (whose name for themselves is Kartveli, "Georgian" having been derived from the Persian name for them, Gorj) have always lived in this region, known to them as Sakartvelo. Georgia embraced Christianity in the 4th century. From the 6th century on, a succession of feudal states emerged there. A population of almost 5,000,000 was achieved by the 13th century, but invasions by outsiders, among whom were the Mongols, much reduced this total. More peaceful conditions followed the annexation by Russia between 1801 and 1864. By the turn of the 20th century, the population had risen to 2,000,000, and by 1975 it was estimated to be 4,923,000.

Ethnically, contemporary Georgia is not homogeneous but reflects the intermixtures and successions of the Caucasus region. Two-thirds of the people are Georgians; Armenians form nearly 10 percent, followed by Russians (about 8.5 percent), Azerbaijanis (4.6 percent), and smaller numbers of Ossetes, Greeks, Abkhaz, and a number of other minor groups.

The republic is one of the first among the union republics in terms of population density. About 90 percent of the population lives below 3,300 feet, with average density approaching 290 per square mile (112 per square kilometre) at the census of 1970. The density decreases sharply with increasing altitude.

The Georgians, a proud people with an ancient culture, have through the ages been noted as warriors as well as for their hospitality, their love of life, and their lively intelligence and sense of humour. Physically, they tend to be taller than average, with athletic, wiry bodies, complexions ranging from fair or ruddy to sallow, and generally dark hair, though fair-haired persons are seen. Their eyes are commonly hazel, with some blue and some gray. The nose shape varies, those in the east tending to be hooked, those in the west straight and thin. The standard of looks is high, and the beauty of Georgian women is legendary; many of them graced the harems of the Ottoman sultans and the shahs of Iran. The Georgians are often also remarkably long-lived.

Demographic trends. During the Soviet period the Georgian population has not only increased but has also shown a marked trend toward urbanization. From 666,000 in 1913, the urban component increased 3.6 times to some 2,398,000, or almost half the total, in 1974, while the rural component increased by only a quarter. Further, a considerable portion of the population that is defined as rural is, in fact, engaged in the urban economy of nearby cities. Enterprises for primary processing of agricultural products are being constructed in the villages, while ore-processing plants and light industry are also increasing in number. As a result, many of the slow-paced traditional villages have developed into distinctly modern communities. The number of rural inhabitants remains high because of the wide distribution of such labour-intensive branches of the economy as the tea and subtropical crop plantations.

By the mid-1970s, there were about 50 cities and a like number of towns. Tbilisi, the capital, an ancient city with many architectural monuments mingling with modern buildings, lies in eastern Georgia, partly in a scenic gorge of the Kura River. Other major centres are Kutaisi, Sukhumi, Batumi, and Tskhinvali.

THE ECONOMY

Georgia has a well-developed industry alongside a diversified and mechanized agriculture. It stands out as a region of waterpower, mineral extraction, and developing machine production. During the Eighth Five-Year Plan (1966–70) the republic's exports doubled in volume, and a hundred or more different products are now exported all over the world.

Resources. The interior of Georgia has coal deposits (notably at Tkvarcheli and Tkibuli), petroleum (at Kazeti), and a variety of other resources ranging from peat to marble. The manganese deposits of Chiatura rival those of India, Brazil, and Ghana in quantity and quality.

Its waterpower resources are considerable. The total annual river capacity has been evaluated at an average of 15,500,000 kilowatts, giving a theoretical electrical energy potential approaching 136,000,000,000 kilowatt-hours. The deepest and most powerful rivers are the Rioni and its tributaries, the Inguri, Kodori, and Bzyb. Such western rivers account for three-quarters of the total capacity, with the eastern Kura, Aragvi, Alazani, and Khrami accounting for the rest.

Water-power

Industry. *The fuel and power base.* The fuel and power foundation developed in Georgia has served as the base for industrialization. Dozens of hydroelectric stations, including the V.I. Lenin Zemo-Avchala, Rioni, and Sukhumi plants, as well as many stations powered by coal and natural gas, have been constructed. All are now combined into a single power system, an organic part of the Transcaucasian system. Under the 1966–70 Five-Year Plan, Georgia's power capacity increased 30 percent, while electric power went up 60 percent. The Inguri hydroelectric complex, under construction high in the mountains in the mid-1970s, with an 890-foot arched dam, has a planned capacity of 1,600,000 kilowatts. This station alone will produce more electric power than all the earlier stations built in Georgia.

Raw material extraction and processing. The coal industry is one of the oldest mineral extraction industries, centred on the restructured Tkibuli mines. Deposits found in Tkvarcheli and Akhaltsikhe have increased production.

Manganese and nonmetallic minerals, ranging from talc to marble, supply various industries throughout the Soviet Union.

Metallurgy and machine building. The Rustavi metallurgical plant, located near the capital, produced its first steel in 1956. Its laminated sheet iron and seamless pipe products are used throughout the Soviet Union, and by the 1970s Georgia was also producing cast and sheet iron. Zstafoni is the second major metallurgical centre.

The machine-building industry now turns out a diverse range of products, from electric railway locomotives, heavy vehicles, and earth-moving equipment to lathes and precision instruments. Specialized products include tea-gathering machines and anti-hail devices for the republic's plantations. The industry is centred in the major cities.

The chemical and building industries. The chemical industry of Georgia produces mineral fertilizers, synthetic materials and fibres, and pharmaceutical products. The building industry, using local raw materials, supplies the republic with cement, slate, and many prefabricated reinforced-concrete structures and parts.

Light industry. Commonly used manufactured goods were previously imported, in large part, from other union republics, but a ramified system of light industries set up in major consumption areas in Georgia now produces cotton, wool, and silk fabrics, as well as items of clothing.

The food industry. Products of the food industry include tea, wine, and tobacco, as well as canned foods. Georgia leads the Soviet Union in labelled table and dessert wines, producing 1,200,000 barrels (14,300,000 decalitres) annually by 1970. Cognac and champagne production is also well developed. The canning industry is developing, with the number of cans of processed foods increasing fivefold between 1950 and 1970. Other food industry activities include dairy products.

Agriculture. A distinctive feature of the Georgian economy is that agricultural land is both in short supply and difficult to work; each patch of workable land, even on steep mountain slopes, is valued highly. The relative proportion of arable land is less than that in almost any other union republic. The importance of production of labour-intensive (and highly profitable) crops, such as tea and citrus fruits, is a compensatory factor, however. The introduction of a system that now contains some 1,150 collective farms (*kolkhozy*) and 270 state farms (*sovkhozy*) has radically altered the traditional structure of landowning and working (though a considerable portion of Georgia's agricultural output still comes from private garden plots). Contemporary agriculture uses modern equipment supplied under a capital investment program, which also finances the production of mineral fertilizers and herbicides, as well as afforestation measures.

Tea, fruit, and wine. Tea plantations cover 158,000 acres (63,900 hectares), and the annual commercial tea leaf harvest accounts for around 95 percent of all Soviet production. Citrus trees occupy space equal to about a sixth of the tea area.

Georgian viticulture

The vineyards of the republic cover 274,000 acres, and the production of wine is one of the oldest and most important branches of Georgian agriculture, and perhaps the best loved. Centuries of trial and error have produced more than 500 varieties of grape.

Orchards now occupy 310,000 acres throughout the republic. Georgian fruits are varied, even slight differences in climate and soil affecting the yield, quality, and taste of the fruit.

Other commercial crops. Sugar beets and tobacco are especially significant among other commercial crops. Essential oils (geranium, rose, and jasmine) are also grown to supply the perfume industry. Grains, including wheat, are important, but quantities insufficient for the republic's needs are raised and wheat must be imported. Growing of vegetables and melons has developed in the suburbs.

Stockbreeding. Livestock raising is marked by the use of different summer and winter pastures. Sheep and goats, cattle, and pigs are raised. Poultry, bees, and silkworms are also significant.

Transportation. Georgia has a dense transportation system. More than 60,000,000 tons of freight are carried annually by rail, but in the mountainous regions road transport remains the principal means of moving both passengers and freight. The road network is about 12,900 miles (20,800 kilometres), three-quarters of which is hard-surfaced.

The seaports of Batumi and Poti are of major economic importance for the whole of Transcaucasia, and air-route links with major Soviet centres have become increasingly important.

The constitutional and political framework. The unicameral, 400-member Supreme Soviet, elected for four years from a single list of candidates, is the highest government organ; the Presidium, its working organ, consists of a chairman, two vice chairmen, a secretary, and 11 members. Local authorities are the councils of deputies in, respectively, the cities, the *raionebi* (districts), and the *aulebi* (villages).

The Supreme Court is the highest judicial organ, supported by regional and city people's courts. Criminal codes taking fuller account of the national characteristics of the republic were adopted in 1960, and their observance is supervised by a republican procurator, who serves for five years.

The Communist Party of Georgia is the only political party and, under the Communist Party of the Soviet Union, establishes policy. Georgians are dominant in the party, constituting more than three-fourths of its membership (while constituting only two-thirds of the total population).

Living conditions and social services. During the 1966–70 Five-Year Plan, average monthly wages registered a 23 percent increase, and the available consumer goods increased by half. Housing construction also had more attention. Payments from public funds (a large part of which are derived from a turnover tax on consumer goods) further provide free education, medical services, pension grants, and stipend payments and free or reduced-cost accommodation in rest homes and sanatoriums, as well as holiday pay and the maintenance of kindergartens and day nurseries.

Georgia ranks high in the level of medical services, with a ratio of 38 doctors for each 10,000 persons. The republic is famed in the Soviet Union as a health centre, a reputation stemming from the numerous therapeutic mineral springs, the sunny Black Sea coast climate, the pure air of the mountain regions, and a wide range of resorts. The Tskhaltubo baths, with warm radon water treatment for rheumatism sufferers, are especially noted.

Health facilities

Educationally, Georgia also ranks high in the Soviet Union; by some indexes it ranks higher than any other union republic. In 1971 there were 4,521 general education schools, with more than 1,000,000 enrolled. In about 70 percent of these schools Georgian is the language of instruction (1965–66 school year), in 7 percent Russian, and in 6 percent Armenian; for the Georgians, these figures are very favourable when compared with the relative proportions of these nationalities in the total population. Among students enrolled in specialized secondary schools (50,649 students in 1969–70), 81 percent were Georgians; in institutions of higher education (18 institutions, 90,121 students in 1969–70), Georgians constituted 83 percent. No fewer than 711 out of every 1,000 working people have had at least some kind of secondary or higher education. There are about 170 students at this level per 10,000 persons. Tbilisi State University was founded in 1918, during the period of the independent Georgian republic, and by the mid-1970s enrolled about 16,000 students each year. The Academy of Sciences (founded 1941) is made up of 44 separate scientific institutions, 38 of which conduct research throughout the republic. This educational system is backed up by an extensive library system of about 200 large units as well as many libraries in technical institutes and in the villages. About three-quarters of all books and brochures (2,486 titles in 1971), magazines (22), and newspapers (126) published are in the Georgian language.

Georgia is a land of ancient culture, with a written language that was developed in the early 5th century AD. Kolkhida (Colchis) early housed a school of higher rhetoric in which Greeks as well as Georgians studied. By the 12th century, academies in Ikalto and Gelati, the first medieval higher-education centres, disseminated a wide range of knowledge. The national genius was demonstrated most clearly in *Vepkhis-tqaosani* (*The Knight in the Tiger's Skin*), the epic masterpiece of the 12th-century poet Shota Rustaveli. Major figures in later Georgian literary history include a famed 18th-century writer, Sulkhan-Saba Orbeliani; the novelist and poet Ilia Chavchavadze, author of *Do You Call This a Man?*; the lyric poet Akaki Tsereteli; Alexander Qazbegi, novelist of the Caucasus; the nature poet Vazha Pshavela; Mikheil Javakhishvili, Paolo Iashvili, and Titsian Tabidze, all executed during the Stalin era; and Giorgi Leonidze and Irakli Abashidze. Important workers in other arts include the painters Niko Pirosmani (Pirosmanashvili), Irakli Toidze, Lado Gudiashvili, and Sergo Kobuladze; the composers Zakaria Paliashvili and Meliton Balanchivadze, and the founder of Georgian national ballet, Vakhtang Chabukiani. Georgian theatre, in which outstanding directors of the Soviet period are Kote Mardzhanishvili and Sandro Akhmeteli, has had a marked influence in the Soviet Union and beyond. Amateur theatre and other art forms are also very popular. There is an active Georgian film industry, and a Georgian film, *The Wedding*, directed by Mikheil Kobakhidze, won the Grand Prix for best short film at the Cannes festival in 1966.

The ancient culture of the republic is reflected in the large number of architectural monuments, including many monasteries and churches; indeed, Georgian architecture (with Armenian) played a considerable role in the development of the Byzantine style.

Maintained by preservation schemes, these buildings are attracting an increasing number of Soviet and foreign tourists.

PROBLEMS AND PROSPECTS

The 1971–75 Five-Year Plan was designed to increase industrial production by about 42 percent, with development rates highest in the nonmetallurgical and the chemical industries. Two very large industrial complexes, the Inguri Hydroelectric Station and the Madneulski (Madneuli) copper combine, were already in partial operation by the early 1970s. A noteworthy feature of current development plans is an added emphasis on further drainage and irrigation schemes. Tea production is also to be increased.

(M.L.D./Ed.)